International
Acronyms, Initialisms &
Abbreviations Dictionary

Gale's publications in the acronyms and abbreviations field include:

International Acronyms, Initialisms & Abbreviations Dictionary series:

International Acronyms, Initialisms & Abbreviations Dictionary (Volume 1). A guide to international acronyms, initialisms, abbreviations, and similar contractions, arranged alphabetically by abbreviation.

Reverse International Acronyms, Initialisms & Abbreviations Dictionary (Volume 2).A companion to Volume 1, in which terms are arranged alphabetically by meaning of the acronym, initialism, or abbreviation.

Acronyms, Initialisms & Abbreviations Dictionary series:

Acronyms, Initialisms & Abbreviations Dictionary (Volume 1). A guide to acronyms, initialisms, abbreviations, and similar contractions, arranged alphabetically by abbreviation.

Acronyms, Initialisms & Abbreviations Dictionary Supplement: (Volume 2). An interedition supplement in which terms are arranged alphabetically both by abbreviation and by meaning.

Reverse Acronyms, Initialisms & Abbreviations Dictionary (Volume 3). A companion to Volume 1 in which terms are arranged alphabetically by meaning of the acronym, initialism, or abbreviation.

Acronyms, Initialisms & Abbreviations Dictionary Subject Guide series:

Computer & Telecommunications Acronyms (Volume 1). A guide to acronyms, initialisms, abbreviations, and similar contractions, used in the field of computers and telecommunications in which terms are arranged alphabetically both by abbreviation and by meaning.

Business Acronyms (Volume 2). A guide to business-oriented acronyms, initialisms, abbreviations, and similar contractions in which terms are arranged alphabetically both by abbreviation and by meaning.

Periodical Title Abbreviations series:

Periodical Title Abbreviations: By Abbreviations (Volume 1). A guide to abbreviations commonly used for periodical titles, arranged alphabetically by abbreviation.

Periodical Title Abbreviations: By Title (Volume 2). A guide to abbreviations commonly used for periodical titles, arranged alphabetically by title.

New Periodical Title Abbreviations: (Volume 3). An interedition supplement in which terms are arranged alphabetically both by abbreviation and by title.

ISSN 0743-0523

International Acronyms, Initialisms & Abbreviations Dictionary

A Guide to over 169,000 International Acronyms, Initialisms, Abbreviations, Alphabetic Symbols, Contractions, and Similar Condensed Appellations in All Fields

Covering: Associations, Business and Trade, Communication, Correspondence, Education, Foreign and International Affairs, Government, Internet, Labor, Military Affairs, Politics, Religion, Science, Transportation, and Other Fields

FOURTH EDITION

Volume 1

Mary Rose Bonk
Regie A. Carlton
Editors

Thomas Carson
Pamela Dear
Michael Reade
Associate Editors

Phyllis Spinelli
Assistant Editor

GALE

DETROIT • NEW YORK • TORONTO • LONDON

Editors: Mary Rose Bonk,
Regie A. Carlton

Associate Editors: Thomas Carson, Pamela Dear,
Michael T. Reade

Assistant Editor: Phyllis Spinelli

Contributing Editors: Mildred Hunt, David J. Jones,
Miriam M. Steinert

Data Entry Manager: Eleanor M. Allison
Data Entry Coordinator: Gwendolyn S. Tucker
Data Entry Associates: Kenneth Benson, LySandra Davis

Production Director: Mary Beth Trimper
Production Assistant: Deborah L. Milliken

Graphic Services Manager: Barbara J. Yarrow
Desktop Publisher: C.J. Jonik

Manager, Technical Support Services: Theresa A. Rocklin
Programmer: Sheila Printup

This book is printed on acid-free paper that meets the minimum requirements of American National Standard for Information Sciences—Permanence Paper for Printed Library Materials, ANSI Z39.48-1984.

 This book is printed on recycled paper that meets the Environmental Protection Agency standards.

Library of Congress Catalog Card Number 85-642206
ISBN 0-8103-7437-4
ISSN 0743-0523

Printed in the United States of America

Contents

Highlights

169,000 Total Entries
48,000 New Terms
Comprehensive Coverage
Language or Country Identifiers
Translations
Source Citations

The fourth edition of *International Acronyms, Initialisms & Abbreviations Dictionary (IAIAD)* offers increased coverage of:

- national and multinational organizations
- research centers
- political parties
- European Community terms
- International Civil Aviation Organization location indicators

Identifiers Provided

Where possible, and if not already implied in the entry itself, a language or country designation is provided. English translations are included whenever they can be readily determined. Since terms for over 150 countries are represented in *IAIAD*, the inclusion of these identifiers can be extremely helpful.

Major Sources Cited

Codes indicate the source from which our information was obtained. This feature allows you to verify the entries and may, in some instances, lead to additional information. Complete bibliographic data about the publications cited can be found in the List of Selected Sources following the User's Guide. Terms that are obtained from miscellaneous newspapers and newsmagazines, provided by outside contributors, or discovered through independent research by the editorial staff remain uncoded.

Preface

Acronyms, initialisms, and abbreviations have become increasingly popular as a means of simplifying and speeding up both oral and written communication. Their use pervades nearly every language of the world. As political, economic, and cultural interdependence among nations grows, so also does the demand for aid in deciphering abbreviated terms.

As a companion to the *Acronyms, Initialisms, and Abbreviations Dictionary* series, *International Acronyms, Initialisms, and Abbreviations Dictionary (IAIAD)* includes abbreviations used internationally as well as tens of thousands of terms local to specific countries and not eligible for inclusion in *Acronyms, Initialisms, and Abbreviations dictionary (AIAD)*.

This fourth edition of *International Acronyms, Initialisms, and Abbreviations Dictionary* includes over 169,000 abbreviated terms. It cumulates all the entries from the previous edition and includes 48,000 terms appearing for the first time.

What Is Covered?

The editors have cast nets worldwide in order to collect entries for this series. Over 150 countries are represented. The majority of terms are of current interest, but historical entries are also included.

The major criterion for inclusion is that a term be clearly international in scope or be continental, regional, national, or local to an area. Because *AIAD* includes U.S., British, and Canadian terms, they are excluded from *IAIAD* (unless they have international significance).

The range of subjects covered is virtually unlimited and includes societies, military terms, political parties, trade and commerce terms, labor unions, government units, nuclear energy terms, research centers, and thousands of commonly abbreviated words in nearly two dozen languages.

Existing Entries Updated; Historical Entries Retained

A new edition of *IAIAD* is prepared not only by adding thousands of previously unlisted terms, but by updating many entries from the previous edition.

Extensive editorial work is done to augment the entries in *IAIAD*. Many entries are enhanced by adding categories, geographic information, and cross-references to other entries.

For *IAIAD-4*, comprehensive updating has been done on the collection of international associations and research centers. Many terms have been enhanced by the addition of English translations.

When an entry is known to have become obsolete, it is not deleted but is merely noted or cross-referenced. Entries are deleted only when known to be incorrect.

Acknowledgments

For suggestions, contributions of terms, permission to take material from personal or published sources, and for other courtesies extended during the preparation of the previous editions and the present one, the editors are indebted to the following: Mildred Hunt, David J. Jones, Miriam M. Steinert; and the embassies and/or consulate-general offices of the following nations: Austria, Columbia, Denmark, El Salvador, Finland, France, Germany, Guyana, Hungary, Italy, Nauru, the Netherlands, Poland, Sweden, and Venezuela.

Comments and Suggestions Are Welcome

Users of *IAIAD* can make unique and important contributions to supplements and future editions by notifying the staff of subject fields or languages that are not adequately covered, by suggesting sources for covering such fields or languages, and even by sending lists of terms they feel should be included.

User's Guide

The following example illustrates elements included in a typical entry:

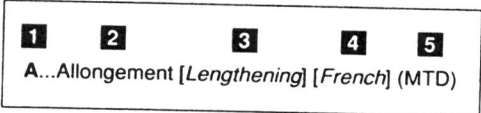

1 Acronym, Initialism, or Abbreviation

2 Word or Phrase which defines the acronym

3 English translation

4 Language or Country of origin

5 Source code (Decoded in the List of Selected Sources, following this section)

Many entries, however, do not contain all of these elements. The completeness of a listing is dependent upon both the nature of the term and the amount of information provided by the source. Some entries are without English translations, and others consist only of the English expansion of a non-English acronym. It is felt, however, that even partial information will be helpful to a user struggling through a multilingual jungle of acronyms and abbreviations. If additional information or a translation becomes available in future research, an entry will be revised.

Arrangement of Terms

Acronyms, initialisms, and abbreviations are arranged alphabetically in letter-by-letter sequence, regardless of spacing, punctuation, or capitalization. If the same abbreviation has more than one meaning, the various meanings are then subarranged alphabetically, in word-by-word sequence.

Should you wish to eliminate the guesswork from acronym formation and usage, a companion volume could help. *Reverse International Acronyms, Initialisms and Abbreviations Dictionary* contains essentially the same entries as *IAIAD,* but arranges them alphabetically by meaning, rather than by acronym or initialism.

List of Selected Sources

Each of the sources included in the following list contributed at least 50 terms. It would be impossible to cite a source for every entry because the majority of terms are sent by outside contributors, are uncovered through independent research by the editorial staff, or surface as miscellaneous broadcast or print media references .

For sources used on an ongoing basis, only the latest edition is listed. For most of the remaining sources, the edition that was used is cited. The editors will provide further information about these sources upon request.

Unless further described in an annotation, the publications listed here contain no additional information about the acronym, initialism, or abbreviation cited.

(AA)   *Abbreviations and Acronyms.* Supplement to *Directory of Scientific and Technical Societies in South Africa.* Pretoria: Council for Scientific and Industrial Research, 1990.

(ADA)   *The Australian Directory of Acronyms and Abbreviations.* 2nd ed. Comp. by David J. Jones. Leura, NSW, Australia: Second Back Row Press Pty. Ltd., 1981.

(ADPT)   *Abbreviations of Data Processing Terms.* By Wilhelm Carl and Johann J. Amkreutz. Germany: Datakontext-Verlag, 1982.

(AF)   *Reference Aid: Abbreviations in the African Press.* Arlington, Va.: Joint Publications Research Service, 1979.

(ARC)   *Agricultural Research Centres: A World Directory of Organizations and Programmes.* 2 vols. Ed. by Nigel Harvey. Harlow, Essex, England: Longman Group, 1983; distributed in US by Gale Research, Detroit.
> A world guide to official, educational, industrial, and independent research centers which support research in the fields of agriculture, veterinary medicine, horticulture, aquaculture, food science, forestry, zoology, and botany.

(ASF)   *Guide to Names and Acronyms of Organizations, Activities, and Projects.* Food and Agriculture Organization of the United Nations. Fishery Information, Data, and Statistics Services and US National Oceanic and Atmospheric Administration. Aquatic Sciences and Fisheries Information System Reference Series, Number 10, 1982.

(BARN)   *The Barnhart Abbreviations Dictionary.* Edited by Robert K. Barnhart. New York, NY: John Wiley & Sons, Inc. 1995.

(BAS)   *Benelux Abbreviations and Symbols: Law and Related Subjects.* Adolf Sprudzs. Dobbs Ferry, NY: Oceana Publications, 1971.

(BJA)   *Biblical and Judaic Acronyms.* By Lawrence Marwick. New York: Ktav Publishing House, Inc., 1979.

(BU)   *Reference Aid: Abbreviations and Acronyms Used in the Bulgarian Press.* Arlington, Va.: Joint Publications Research Service, 1978.

(CED)   *Current European Directories.* 2nd ed. Ed. by G.P. Henderson. Beckenham, Kent, England: CBD Research, 1981; distributed in US by Gale Research, Detroit.

(CL)   *Reference Aid: Abbreviations in the Cambodian and Lao Press.* Arlington, Va.: Joint Publications Research Service, 1974.

(CNC)   *American National Standard Codes for the Representation of Names of Countries, Dependencies, and Areas of Special Sovereignty for Information Interchange.* National Bureau of Standards. Washington, D.C.: U.S. Government Printing Office, 1986.
> These standard codes, approved by the International Organization for Standardization and the American National Standards Institute, are used in the international interchange of data in many fields.

(COL)   *Diccionario de Siglas y Acronismos Colombianos.* 2nd ed. By Adela Sanabria Parra. Bogota: Instituto Colombiano para el Fomento de la Educacion Superior, 1976.

(CRD)   *Computer-Readable Databases: A Directory and Data Sourcebook.* 6th ed. Edited by Kathleen Young Marcaccio. Detroit: Gale Research, 1990. [Use of source began in 1985]
> A guide to online databases, offline files available in various magnetic formats, and CD-ROM files. Entries include producer name, address, telephone number, description of coverage, vendors, and contact person.

(CZ)   *Reference Aid: Abbreviations in the Czechoslovak Press.* Arlington, Va.: Joint Publications Research Service, 1970.

(DCTA)   *Dictionary of Commercial Terms and Abbreviations.* By Alan E. Branch. London: Witherby & Co. Ltd., 1984.

(DLA)   *Bieber's Dictionary of Legal Abbreviations.* 3rd ed. By Mary Miles Prince. Buffalo, NY: William S. Hein & Co., 1988.

(DMA)   *Dictionary of Miliary Abbreviations: British, Empire, Commonwealth.* By B.K.C. Scott. Hastings, East Sussex, England: Tamarisk Books, 1982.

(DS)   *Dictionary of Shipping International Trade Terms and Abbreviations.* 3rd ed. By Alan E. Branch. London: Witherby & Co. Ltd., 1986. [Use of source began in 1976]

(DSUE)   *A Dictionary of Slang and Unconventional English.* 8th ed. By Eric Partridge. New York: Macmillan Publishing Co., 1984.

(DSCA)   *Directorio de Siglas en Ciencias Agricolas (Directory of Initials in Argricultural Science).* By Maria Jose Galrao and Orlando Arboleda-Sepulveda. 2nd ed. Turrialba, Costa Rica: IICA, 1971.

(DUND)   *Directory of United Nations Databases and Information Services.* 4th ed. Compiled by the Advisory Committee for the Coordination of Information Systems. New York: United Nations, 1990.
> A guide to computerized databases and information

systems/services. Entries include sponsoring organization, year established, type, scope, coverage, timespan, and contact information.

(EA)   *Encyclopedia of Associations.* 29th ed. Vol. 1, National Organizations of the U.S. Edited by Carol A. Schwartz and Rebecca L. Turner. Detroit: Gale Research, 1995 (and supplement 1995) [Use of source began in 1960]
> A guide to trade, professional, and other nonprofit associations that are national and international in scope and membership and that are headquartered in the United States. Entries include name and address; telephone and telex number; chief official; and a description of the purpose; activities; and structure of the organization.

(EAIO)   *Encyclopedia of Associations; International Organizations.* 29th ed. Edited by Linda Irvin. Detroit: Gale Research, 1995. [Use of source began in 1985]
> A guide to trade, professional, and other nonprofit associations that are national or international in scope and membership and that are headquartered outside the United States. Entries include name and address; principal foreign language name; telephone and telex number; chief official; and a description of the purpose, activities, and structure of the organization.

(EAS)   *Earth and Astronomical Sciences Research Centres: A World Directory of Organizations and Programmes.* 2nd ed. Harlow, Essex, England: Longman Group, 1991; distributed in US by Gale Research, Detroit.
> A directory of organizations and research establishments in geology, oceanography, and planetary disciplines. Entries include address, telephone, fax, and telex numbers, parent organization, status, senior staff, annual expenditure, activities, publications, and major clients.

(ECED)   *The European Communities Encyclopedia and Directory 1992.* London: Europa Publications Ltd., 1991; distributed in US by Gale Research, Detroit.
> A comprehensive guide to the European Communities. Entries explain widely-used acronyms and include address, telephone, telex, fax numbers and chief officers for EC-level organizations.

(ECON)   *The Economist.* London: The Economist Newspaper Ltd., 1995. [Use of source began in 1988]

(EE)   *Eastern Europe and the Commonwealth of Independent States 1992.* London: Europa Publications Ltd., 1992; distributed in US by Gale Research, Detroit.

(EECI)   *Eastern Europe and the Commonwealth of Independent States 1997.* London: Europa Publications Ltd., 1996; distributed in US by Gale Research, Detroit.

(EG)   *Reference Aid: Glossary of Special Terms, Acronyms and Abbreviations as Used in East German and Other German Publications.* Arlington, Va.: Joint Publications Research Service, 1975.

(ERC)   *Engineering Research Centres: A World Directory of Organizations and Programmes.* 2nd ed. Harlow, Essex, England: Longman Group, 1988; distributed in US by Gale Research, Detroit.
> A worldwide directory of engineering laboratories. Entries include

address, telephone, telex, and fax numbers, status, product range, parent organization, senior staff, annual expenditure, activities, publications, and major clients.

(EY) *The Europa World Year Book 1992.* London: Europa Publications Ltd., 1992; distributed in US by Gale Research, Detroit.
An annual survey containing detailed information about the political, economic, statistical, and commercial situation of the regions and countries covered.

(FAAC) *Contractions Handbook.* Changes. U.S. Department of Transportation. Federal Aviation Administration, 1993. [Use of source began in 1969]

(FEA) *The Far East and Australasia 1987.* 18th ed. London: Europa Publications Ltd., 1986; distributed in US by Gale Research, Detroit.
An annual survey containing detailed information about the political, economic, statistical, and commercial situation of the regions and countries covered.

(FLAF) *Foreign Law Abbreviations: French.* Adolf Sprudzs. Dobbs Ferry, NY: Oceana Publications Inc., 1967.

(GC) *Reference Aid: Abbreviations, Acronyms and Special Terms in the Press of Greece and Cyprus.* Arlington, Va.: Joint Publications Research Service, 1977, 1983 supplement.

(GCA) *German Chemical Abbreviations.* Gabriele E.M. Wohlauer and H.D. Gholston. New York: Special Libraries Association, 1966.

(GEA) *Government Economic Agencies of the World: An International Directory of Governmental Organizations concerned with Economic Development and Planning.* Ed. by Alan J. Day. Harlow, Essex, England: Longman Group Ltd., 1985; distributed in US by Gale Research, Detroit.
Covers over 170 countries and territories. Two introductory sections for each area cover economic data and prevailing economic and political conditions. Individual entries provide title, address, and names of chief officials of each agency. Current activities and financial structure of each agency are also detailed. An index of agency officials is provided.

(GPO) *Style Manual.* Washington, D.C.: US Government Printing Office, 1984.
Terms are included in Chapter 24, Foreign Languages.

(HU) *Reference Aid: Abbreviations, Acronyms, and Special Terms Used in the Hungarian Press.* Arlington, Va.: Joint Publications Research Service, 1978.

(ICAO) *Aircraft Type Designators.* 13th ed. International Civil Aviation Organization, August, 1981.

(ICDA) *Designators for Aircraft Operating Agencies, Aeronautical Authorities and Services.* 49th ed. International Civil Aviation Organization, June, 1982.
Document includes telephone designators and postal and telegraphic addresses of government civil aviation authorities.

(ICLI) *Location Indicators.* 51st ed. International Civil Aviation Organization, February, 1987.
Document contains addresses of flight information centers.

(IDIG)	*International Directory of Government 1995.* London: Europa Publications Ltd., 1994; distributed in US by Gale Research, Detroit.
(IID)	*Information Industry Directory.* 15th ed. Edited by Annette Novallo. Detroit: Gale Research, 1995. (and supplement, 1995).
	An international guide to computer-readable databases, database producers, and publishers, online vendors and time-sharing companies, telecommunications networks, and many other information systems and services. Entries include name and address, telephone number, chief official, and a detailed description of the purpose and function of the system or service.
(ILCA)	*Index to Legal Citations and Abbreviations.* By Donald Raistrick. Abingdon, Oxfordshire, England: Professional Books Ltd., 1981.
(IMH)	*International Marketing Handbook.* 2nd ed. Ed. by Frank E. Bair. Detroit: Gale Research, 1985.
	A guide to commercial and trade data on 142 countries of the world. Features include a list of European trade fairs and a report on growth markets in Western Europe.
(IN)	*Reference Aid: Glossary of Indonesian Abbreviations and Acronyms.* Arlington, Va.: Joint Publications Research Service, 1971.
(IRC)	*International Research Centers Directory 1992-93.* 6th ed. Ed. by Annette Piccirelli. Detroit: Gale Research, 1991.
	A world guide to government, university, independent, nonprofit, and commercial research and development centers, institutes, laboratories, bureaus, test facilities, experiment stations, and data collection and analysis centers, as well as foundations, councils, and other organizations which support research.
(LA)	*Reference Aid: Acronyms in the Latin American Press.* Arlington, Va.: Joint Publications Research Service, 1979, 1983.
(LAA)	*Latin American Initialisms and Acronyms/Lista de Siglas Latinoamericanas.* Santiago, Chile: United Nations Economic Commission for Latin America Library, 1970. Detroit: Blaine Ethridge-Books, 1974.
(LCLS)	*Symbols of American Libraries.* 14th ed. Edited by the Enhanced Cataloging Division. Washington, D.C.: Library of Congress, 1992. [Use of source began in 1980]
(MCD)	*Acronyms, Abbreviations, and Initialisms.* Compiled by Carl Lauer. St. Louis: McDonnell Douglas Corp., 1989. [Use of source began in 1969]
(ME)	*Reference Aid: Administrative Structure, Military Ranks and Organization, Police, Monetary Units, and Abbreviations Related to the Middle East Press.* Arlington, Va.: Joint Publications Research Service, 1976.
(MENA)	*The Middle East and North Africa 1987.* 33rd ed. London: Europa Publications Ltd., 1986; distributed in US by Gale Research, Detroit.
	An annual survey containing detailed information about the political, economic, statistical, and commercial situation of the regions and countries covered.

(ML)	*Reference Aid: A Glossary of Malaysian and English Abbreviations Appearing in the Press of Malaysia and Singapore.* Arlington, Va.: Joint Publications Research Service, 1972.
(MSC)	*Annotated Acronyms and Abbreviations of Marine Science Related Activities.* 3rd ed. Rev. by Charlotte M. Ashby and Alan R. Flesh. Washington, DC: US Department of Commerce. National Oceanographic and Atmospheric Administration. Environmental Data Service. National Oceanographic Data Center, 1981.
(MTD)	*A French-English Military Technical Dictionary.* By Cornelis De Witt Willcox. Washington, D.C.: US Government Printing Office, 1917.
(NATG)	*Glossary of Abbreviations Used in NATO Documents.* AAP15(B), n.p., 1979. [Use of source began in 1976]
(NAU)	*Nautical Chart Symbols and Abbreviations.* 7th ed. Washington, D.C.: Department of Defense, 1979.
(NRCH)	*A Handbook of Acronyms and Initialisms.* Nuclear Regulatory Commission. NUREG-0544. Rev. 2. Division of Technical Information and Document Control. Washington, D.C. 1985.
(OAG)	*Official Airline Guide Worldwide Edition.* Oak Brook, IL: Official Airlines Guide, Inc., 1984. [Use of source began in 1975]
(OLYM)	*"Olympic Organizations."* <http://www.com-stock.com/dave/olyorg.htm> (17 December 1996).
(OMWE)	*Opec and the World Energy Market.* By John Evans. Fully revised by Gavin Brown. 2nd ed. London: Longman Group UK Limited; distributed in US by Gale Research, Detroit.
(PD)	*Political Dissent: An International Guide to Dissident, Extra-Parliamentary, Guerrilla and Illegal Political Movements.* Comp. by Henry W. Degenhardt. Ed. by Alan J. Day. Harlow, Essex, England: Longman Group, 1983; distributed in US by Gale Research, Detroit. Includes the history and aims of approximately 1,000 organizations, with details of their leaderships
(PDAA)	*Pugh's Dictionary of Acronyms and Abbreviations: Abbreviations in Management, Technology and Information Science.* 5th ed. Eric Pugh. Chicago: American Library Association, 1987.
(POL)	*Abbreviations in the Polish Press.* Translations on Eastern Europe: Political, Sociological, and Military Affairs, no. 88. Arlington, Va.: Joint Publications Research Service, 1969.
(PPE)	*Political Parties of Europe.* 2 vols. Ed. by Vincent E. McHale. The Greenwood Historical Encyclopedia of the World's Political Parties. Westport, Conn.: Greenwood Press, 1983. One of a series of reference guides to the world's significant political parties. "Each guide provides concise histories of the political parties of a region and attempts to detail the evolution of ideology, changes in organization, membership, leadership, and each party's impact upon society."
(PWGL)	*Profiles of Worldwide Government Leaders 1996.* Bethesda, MD: World Government Directories, Inc., 1996.
(PPW)	*Political Parties of the World.* A Keesing's Reference Publication. Comp. and ed. by Alan J. Day and Henry W. Degenhardt. Harlow, Essex, England: Longman Group, 1980, 1984;

distributed in US by Gale Research, Detroit.
Covers historical development, structure, leadership, membership, policy, publications, and international affiliations. For each country, an overview of the current political situation and constitutional structure is provided.

(RO)   *Reference Aid: Abbreviations in the Romanian Press.* Arlington, Va.: Joint Publications Research Service, 1979.

(ROG) *Dictionary of Abbreviations.* By Walter T. Rogers. London: George Allen & Co. Ltd., 1913; reprinted by Gale Research, 1969.

(RU)   *Glossary of Russian Abbreviations and Acronyms.* Aerospace Technology Division, Reference Department, Library of Congress. Washington, D.C.: US Government Printing Office, 1967.

(SCAC) *South America, Central America and the Caribbean 1995.* 5th ed. London: Europa Publications Ltd., 1995; distributed in US by Gale Research, Detroit.

(SLS) *World Guide to Scientific Associations and Learned Societies/Internationales Verzeichnis wissenschaftlicher Verbande und Gesellschaften.* 4th ed. Ed. by Barbara Verrel. New York: K.G. Saur, 1984.
A directory of more than 22,000 societies and associations in all fields of science, culture, and technology. International, national, and regional organizations from 150 countries are also included.

(TCC) *Trade Contacts in China: A Directory of Import and Export Corporations.* London: Kogan Page Ltd., 1987; distributed in US by Gale Research, Detroit.
A directory of over 600 corporations in China covering a wide range of business activities. Entries include address, telephone, telex, and cable numbers, key personnel, and business activities.

(TPFD) *The Penguin French Dictionary.* Compiled by Merlin Thomas and Raymond Escoffey. London: Bloomsbury Books, 1985.

(TU)   *Reference Aid: Abbreviations, Acronyms and Special Terms in the Turkish Press of Turkey and the TFSC.* Arlington, Va.: Joint Publications Research Service, 1977.

(VNW) *Words of the Vietnam War.* Gregory R. Clark. Jefferson, NC: McFarland and Co., Inc., 1990.

(WDAA) *Webster's New World Dictionary of Acronyms and Abbreviations.* Auriel Douglas and Michael Strumpf. New York: Webster's New World, 1989.

(WED) *World Energy Directory: Organizations and Research Activities in Non-Atomic Energy.* 3rd ed. Harlow, Essex, England: Longman Group, 1988; distributed in US by Gale Research, Detroit.
Provides profiles of industrial centers, and government or university laboratories. Entries include address, telephone, telex, fax numbers, status, product range, parent organization, senior staff, annual expenditure, activities, publications, and major clients.

(WEN)	*Reference Aid: Glossary of Acronyms, Abbreviations, and Special Terms Used in Dutch, Finnish, German (Western Europe), and Scandinavian Press.* Arlington, Va.: Joint Publications Research Service, 1977.
(WER)	*Reference Aid: Glossary of Acronyms, Abbreviations, and Special Terms Used in the Western Europe Romance-Language Press.* Arlington, Va.: Joint Publications Research Service, 1977.
(WGAO)	*World Guide to Abbreviations of Organizations.* 9th ed. Revised by H.J. Heaney. London: Blackie and Son Ltd., 1991; distributed in the US by Gale Research.
(WND)	*World Nuclear Directory: Organizations and Research Activities in Atomic Energy.* 8th ed. Harlow, Essex, England: Longman Group, 1988; distributed in US by Gale Research, Detroit.
	Provides profiles of industrial centers and government or university laboratories. Entries include address, telephone, telex, fax numbers, status, product range, parent organization, senior staff, annual expenditure, activities, publications, and major clients.
(YU)	*Yugoslav Abbreviations: A Selective List.* 2nd ed. Washington, D.C.: Library of Congress, 1962.

International
Acronyms, Initialisms &
Abbreviations Dictionary

Numerics

3B .... Mauritius [*Aircraft nationality and registration mark*]   (FAAC)
3B='s .... Burn, Bash, and Bury [*The camper's code for cleanup*] [*Australia*] [*Slang*]   (DSUE)
3C .... Equatorial Guinea [*Aircraft nationality and registration mark*] (FAAC)
3D .... Swaziland [*Aircraft nationality and registration mark*]   (FAAC)
3I .... Investors in Industry International BV
3M(harom M)modszer ... Mozdulatelemzes, Munkatanulmanyozas es Munkakialakitas Modszer [*A Method Involving Time-Motion Study, Work Analysis and Formation of Work Procedures*]   (HU)
3X .... Guinea [*Aircraft nationality and registration mark*]   (FAAC)
4D's .... Drugs, Debt, Deforestation, and Democracy [*US foreign policy concerns in Latin America*]
4PM .... Persatuan Persuratan Pemuda Pemudi Melayu [*Malayan Youth Literary Association*] [*Singapore*]   (ML)
4R .... Ceylon [*Sri Lanka*] [*Aircraft nationality and registration mark*] (FAAC)
4R .... Sri Lanka [*Aircraft nationality and registration mark*]   (FAAC)
4W .... Yemen Arab Republic [*Aircraft nationality and registration mark*]   (FAAC)
4X .... Israel [*Aircraft nationality and registration mark*]   (FAAC)
5A .... Libya [*Aircraft nationality and registration mark*]
5W .... Samoa Islands [*Aircraft nationality and registration mark*]   (FAAC)
6O .... Somalia [*Aircraft nationality and registration mark*]   (FAAC)
6OS .... Somali [*Aircraft nationality and registration mark*]   (FAAC)
6V .... Senegal [*Aircraft nationality and registration mark*]   (FAAC)
6W .... Senegal [*Aircraft nationality and registration mark*]   (FAAC)
6Y .... Jamaica [*Aircraft nationality and registration mark*]   (FAAC)
7P .... Lesotho [*Aircraft nationality and registration mark*]   (FAAC)
7QY .... Malawi [*Aircraft nationality and registration mark*]   (FAAC)
7T .... Algeria [*Aircraft nationality and registration mark*]   (FAAC)
8P .... Barbados [*Aircraft nationality and registration mark*]   (FAAC)
8Q .... Maldives [*Aircraft nationality and registration mark*]   (FAAC)
8R .... Guyana [*Aircraft nationality and registration mark*]   (FAAC)
9G .... Ghana [*Aircraft nationality and registration mark*]   (FAAC)
9H .... Malta [*Aircraft nationality and registration mark*]   (FAAC)
9J .... Zambia [*Aircraft nationality and registration mark*]   (FAAC)
9L .... Sierra Leone [*Aircraft nationality and registration mark*]   (FAAC)
9M .... Malaysia [*Aircraft nationality and registration mark*]   (FAAC)
9N .... Nepal [*Aircraft nationality and registration mark*]   (FAAC)
9Q .... Congo (Leopoldville) [*Aircraft nationality and registration mark*]   (FAAC)
9Q .... Zaire [*Aircraft nationality and registration mark*]   (FAAC)
9U .... Burundi [*Aircraft nationality and registration mark*]   (FAAC)
9V .... Singapore [*Aircraft nationality and registration mark*]   (FAAC)
9XR .... Rwanda [*Aircraft nationality and registration mark*]   (FAAC)
9Y .... Trinidad and Tobago [*Aircraft nationality and registration mark*]   (FAAC)

A

A............... Aanschrijving [Benelux]   (BAS)
a............... Aari [or Aaria] [Finland]
A............... A/B Astra [Sweden] [Research code symbol]
A............... Able [Phonetic alphabet] [World War II]   (DSUE)
a............... Abra [Illustration]   (HU)
A............... Abschnitt [Section] [German]   (GCA)
A............... Absolvent [Czech]
a............... Acceleration [French]
a............... Accepte [Accepted] [French] [Banking]   (GPO)
A............... Aceite [Acceptance] [Portuguese] [Business term]
A............... Acheteur [or Acheter] [Buyer] [French] [Business term]
a............... Acier [Steel] [French]
A............... Ack [Phonetic alphabet] [Pre-World War II]   (DSUE)
A............... Acker [Acre] [German]
a............... Acte [Act] [French]
a............... Action [Share] [French] [Business term]
A............... Adjektief [Adjective] [Afrikaans]
a............... Adjektiivi [Adjective] [Finland]
A............... Advanced [Level of General Certificate of Education] [Ghana]
A............... Aerial Reconnaissance   (RU)
A............... Aether [Ether] [German]
A............... Agusta [Construzioni Aeronautiche Giovanni Agusta SpA] [Italy]
               [ICAO aircraft manufacturer identifier]   (ICAO)
a............... Agyu [Cannon, Gun]   (HU)
a............... Ajtoszam [Room Number]   (HU)
A............... Akademie [Academy] [German]   (GCA)
A............... AKTA [Level of teaching license] [Indonesia]
a............... Akzeptiert [Accepted] [German]
a............... A l'Acquitte [French]
a............... Alatt [Under, Below]   (HU)
a............... Albo [Or] [Poland]
A............... Alfa [Phonetic alphabet] [International]   (DSUE)
a............... Alias [Spanish]
A............... Alimiyah [Doctorate] [Morocco]
A............... Alkohol [Alcohol] [German]
A............... Allongement [Lengthening] [French]   (MTD)
A............... Alm [Aluminum] [German]
A............... Almhuette [Chalet] [German]
A............... Alpe [Alps] [German]
A............... Altesse [Height] [French]   (MTD)
A............... Alteza [Highness] [Spanish]
A............... Altezza [Highness] [Italian]
A............... Altitude [French]   (MTD)
a............... Am [On The] [German]   (GPO)
A............... Amatol   (RU)
A............... Ampeeri(a) [Finland]
A............... Amper [Poland]
A............... Ampere [German]   (GCA)
A............... Ampere Internacional [International Ampere] [Portuguese]
A............... Amt [Official Position] [German]
a............... An [On] [German]   (GPO)
a............... An Der [At The, On The] [German]   (GPO)
a............... Andre [Others] [Danish/Norwegian]
A............... Andritz [Commercial firm] [Austria]
A............... Angstroem [Angstrom] [German]
A............... Anna [Monetary unit] [India]
a............... Annee [Year] [French]
a............... Ano [Year] [Spanish]
A............... Anode   (RU)
A............... Antenna, Aerial   (RU)
A............... Anthracite   (RU)
A............... Apples [Phonetic alphabet] [Royal Navy World War I]   (DSUE)
A............... Aprobado [On an examination: Passed] [Spanish]
a............... Ar [Are] [A unit of area in the metric system] [German]
A............... Arab [or Arabic]   (BJA)
A............... Aramaic [Language, etc.]
a............... Are [100 square meters] [Portuguese]
a............... Are [A unit of area in the metric system] [French]

a............... Area [Spanish]
A............... Argent [Money] [French]
A............... Argonio [Argon] [Chemical element] [Portuguese]
A............... Army   (BU)
A............... Arrete [French]   (FLAF)
a............... Arroba [Thirty-two pound weight] [Portuguese]
A............... Artillerie [Artillery] [On the fleuron of a bridle] [French]   (MTD)
A............... Arzt [Doctor] [German]
A............... Asphalt   (RU)
a............... Assinado [Signed] [Portuguese] [Business term]
a............... Assure [Insured] [French]
A............... Asta Werke AG [Germany] [Research code symbol]
(A)............. Asthuette, Vorsaess-Oder Maisaesshuette [German]
a............... Asymmetrisch [Asymmetric] [German]
A............... Atagon Steel [Lus Development Corp.] [Papua New Guinea]
A............... Atlantic [Ocean]   (ABBR)
A............... Attelee [Said of a battery] [Military] [French]   (MTD)
A............... Atto [Act] [Italian]
A............... Auflage [Edition] [German]
A............... Aul [Topography]   (RU)
a............... Aus [Out] [German]
A............... Ausgabestelle [Distribution Point] [German military - World War II]
A............... Ausschnitt [Clipping] [Publishing] [German]
A............... Ausschuss [Committee]   (EG)
A............... Austral [Southern] [French]
A............... Australian
A............... Australian Capital Territory [National Union Catalogue of Australia symbol]
A............... Austria [International automobile identification tag]
A............... Automobile Gasoline   (RU)
A............... Automotrice [Diesel-propelled rail-car] [Italian]
A............... Autor [Author] [Portuguese]
A............... Autore [Author] [Italian]
A............... Avancer [Fast, as clocks] [French]
a............... Avec [With] [French]
A............... Ayer [Stream] [Malay]   (NAU)
A............... Azimuth   (RU)
A............... United Nations General Assembly Document   (ILCA)
A₂ .... Antenne₂ [French]
A2............. Botswana [Aircraft nationality and registration mark]   (FAAC)
A3............. Tonga [Aircraft nationality and registration mark]   (FAAC)
A5............. Bhutan [Aircraft nationality and registration mark]   (FAAC)
A6............. United Arab Emirates [Aircraft nationality and registration mark]   (FAAC)
A9C........... Bahrain [Aircraft nationality and registration mark]   (FAAC)
A19........... Article 19 - International Centre Against Censorship [British]   (EAIO)
A40........... Oman [Aircraft nationality and registration mark]   (FAAC)
AA............. Aatelissaaty [Estate of the Nobility] [Finland]   (WEN)
AA............. Academy of Architecture, USSR [1934-1956]   (RU)
AA............. Acetylacetone   (RU)
AA............. Acrylamide   (RU)
AA............. ActionAid [British]   (EAIO)
AA............. Active Attached Reserve [Military]
AA............. Administrative Agreement
aa............. Adoallomas [Transmitting Station, Transmitter (Radio)]   (HU)
AA............. Advance Airlines [Australia]
AA............. Advance Australia
AA............. Aerolineas Argentinas   (WGAO)
AA............. Africa
AA............. African Alliance Insurance Co. Ltd. [Nigeria]
AA............. Airship Association [British]   (EAIO)
AA............. Akademisk Arkitekforening   (WGAO)
aa............. Akademisk Avhandling [Dissertation] [Sweden]
AA............. Alcoa of Australia [Commercial firm]
AA............. Alcoholicos Anonimos [Colombia]   (COL)
AA............. Al-Fadhli and Al-Darawish [Saudi Arabia] [Commercial firm]

3

AA.............. Alkoholiste Anoniem [*Alcoholics Anonymous*] [*Afrikaans*]
A/A............. Alter Art [*Of Old Type*] [*German*]   (GCA)
AA.............. Altesses [*Highnesses*] [*French*]
AA.............. Altezas [*Highnesses*] [*Spanish*]
AA.............. Alzheimers Association [*Australia*]
AA.............. Amities Acadiennes [*France*]   (EAIO)
AA.............. Ana [*Of Each*] [*Pharmacy*]
AA.............. Anadolu Ajansi [*Anatolian (News) Agency*]   (TU)
AA.............. Anexartiti Aristera [*Independent Left*] [*Greek*]   (GC)
AA.............. Aoratoi Agonistai [*Invisible Fighters*] [*Greek*]   (GC)
AA.............. Arbeitsausschuss [*Working Committee*]   (EG)
AA.............. Architectural Association [*British*]   (EA)
AA.............. Arkhi Anadasmon [*Land Redistribution Authority*]   (GC)
AA.............. Arkhigeion Aeroporias [*Air Force Headquarters*]   (GC)
AA.............. Arma Aeronautica [*Air Force*] [*Italian*]
AA.............. Armee de l'Air [*Air Army*] [*France*]
AA.............. Army Artillery   (BU)
AA.............. Army Aviation   (RU)
AA.............. Arretes [*French*]   (FLAF)
A-A............. Arrocillo Amarillo [*Race of maize*] [*Mexico*]
AA.............. Arsenal do Alfeite [*Alfeite Arsenal*] [*Portuguese*]   (WER)
AA.............. Artilharia Anti-Aerea [*Antiaircraft Artillery*] [*Portuguese*]
                (WER)
AA.............. Asia-Africa   (ML)
AA.............. Asia Afrika [*Asia and Africa, Afro-Asian*]   (IN)
AA.............. Assistenza Automobilistica [*Organization for assisting motorists*]
                [*Italian*]
AA.............. Association of Acrobats [*Australia*]   (EA)
AA.............. Assumptionists [*Australia*]
AA.............. Astrological Association   (EAIO)
AA.............. Athletics Australia   (EAIO)
AA.............. Atomic Absorption [*Chemical analysis*]
AA.............. Auctores Antiquissimi [*Classical studies*]
aa.............. Auranala [*Finland*]
AA.............. Ausfuehrungsanweisung [*Regulatory Instructions*] [*German*]
                (DLA)
AA.............. Australian Academy of Science   (ADA)
AA.............. Australian Airlines
AA.............. Australian Archives
AA.............. Australian Army
AA.............. Auswaertiges Amt [*Foreign Ministry*] [*German*]
AA.............. Autism Association [*Australia*]
AA.............. Automatic Approval System [*Importation*] [*Japan*]   (IMH)
AA.............. Automobiel-Assosiasie [*Automobile Association*] [*Afrikaans*]
AA.............. Autores [*Authors*] [*Spanish*]
AABG........... Autores [*Authors*] [*Portuguese*]
AA.............. Autori [*Authors*] [*Italian*]
AA.............. Auxi-Atome [*French association*]
AA.............. Avisenes Arbeidsgiverforening   (WGAO)
AA.............. Congregatio Augustinianorum ab Assumptione   (WGAO)
AA.............. L'Anglais de l'Amerique [*American English*] [*Language, etc.*]
                [*French*]
AA.............. L'Arche Australia   (EAIO)
AAA............ Aboriginal Arts Australia Ltd.
AAA............ Abrasivos Americanos Asociados [*Colombia*]   (COL)
AAA............ Active Acquisition Aid
AAA............ Acupuncturists Association of Australia   (ADA)
AAA............ Advance Australia Award
AAA............ Aerosol Association of Australia
AAA............ Affirmative Action Agency [*Australia*]
AAA............ Agencia Autorizada Almacenes Murcia [*Barranquilla*]   (COL)
AAA............ Air Affairs Afrique [*Cameroon*]   (WGAO)
AAA............ Alianza Anticomunista Argentina [*Argentine Anti-Communist
                Alliance*]   (PD)
AAA............ Alianza Apostolica Anticomunista [*Anti-Communist Apostolic
                Alliance*] [*Spain*]   (PD)
AAA............ Alianza pour Accion Anticommunista [*Honduras*] [*Political
                party*]   (EY)
AAA............ Allami Allattenyesztesi Allomas [*State Stockbreeding Station*]
                (HU)
AAA............ Alleanza Armata Anti-Comunista [*Anti-Communist Armed
                Alliance*] [*Italian*]   (WER)
AAA............ Allergy Association Australia
AAA............ Ansett Airlines of Australia [*ICAO designator*]   (FAAC)
AAA............ Anti-Drug Abuse Association [*Israel*]   (EAIO)
AAA............ Apostolic Anti-Communist Alliance [*Spain*]
AAA............ Arab Airways Association Ltd.
AAA............ Arabian Auto Agency [*Saudi Arabia*]
AAA............ Arabian Auto Association [*Africa*]
AAA............ Archery Association of Australia
AAA............ Argentine Anticommunist Alliance [*Political party*]   (LAIN)
AAA............ Artillerie Anti-Aerienne [*Antiaircraft Artillery*] [*French*]
AAA............ Arts Action Australia [*An association*]
AAA............ Asia, Afrika, dan Amerika Latin [*Asia, Africa, and Latin
                America*]   (IN)
AAA............ Asociacion Apicola Argentina [*Argentina*]   (DSCA)

AAA.......... Asociacion de Amigos del Arbol [*Venezuela*]   (DSCA)
AAA.......... Association des Auditeurs et Anciens Auditeurs de l'Academie
                [*Association of Attenders and Alumni of the Hague Academy
                of International Law*]   (EAIO)
AAA.......... Association des Auditeurs et Anciens Auditeurs de l'Academie
                Internationale de Droit de la Haye
AAA.......... Association of Accountants of Australia   (ADA)
AAA.......... Assyrian Australian Association
AAA.......... Australasian Athletics Association   (ADA)
AAA.......... Australasian Authors Agency   (ADA)
AAA.......... Australia Asia Airlines [*Air carrier designation symbol*]
AAA.......... Australian Academy of Anatomy
AAA.......... Australian Academy of Art
AAA.......... Australian Aeronautical Academy
AAA.......... Australian American Association   (ADA)
AAA.......... Australian American Assurance Co. Ltd.
AAA.......... Australian Anglers' Association
AAA.......... Australian Anglo American Ltd.   (ADA)
AAA.......... Australian Antarctic Adventures
AAA.......... Australian Anthropological Association   (ADA)
AAA.......... Australian Appliance Association
AAA.......... Australian-Arab Association
AAA.......... Australian Archaeological Association   (ADA)
AAA.......... Australian Aromatherapists' Association
AAA.......... Australian Art Association   (ADA)
AAA.......... Australian Artists Association   (ADA)
AAA.......... Australian Aryan Army
AAA.......... Australian Asian Association
AAA.......... Australian Automobile Association   (ADA)
AAA.......... Auto Andes Antioquia Ltda. [*Colombia*]   (COL)
AAAA........ Accredited Advertising Agencies Australia
AAAA........ Aerial Agricultural Association of Australia
AAAA........ Antique Aeroplane Association of Australia
AAAA........ Aruba Amateur Athletic Association   (EAIO)
AAAA........ Asian Amateur Athletic Association   (WGAO)
AAAA........ Asociacion Argentina Amigos de la Astronomia [*Argentine
                Friends of Astronomy Association*] [*Buenos Aires*]   (LAA)
AAAA........ Association of Accredited Advertising Agencies [*New Zealand*]
                [*Singapore*]   (WGAO)
AAAA........ Australian Advertising Advisory Agency   (WGAO)
AAAA........ Australian Advertising Advisory Authority   (ADA)
AAAA........ Australian Association for Applied Anthropology
AAAA........ Australian Association of Advertising Agencies   (ADA)
AAAA........ Australian Automotive Aftermarket Association
AAAA........ Austrian Amateur Athletics Association   (EAIO)
AAABG..... Australian Association of Animal Breeding and Genetics
AAAC....... African Amateur Athletic Confederation   (WGAO)
AAAC....... Alliance Atlantique des Anciens Combattants   (WGAO)
AAAC....... Association of Australian Acoustical Consultants
AAAC....... Australian Aboriginal Affairs Council
AAAC....... Australian Accredited Agricultural Consultants
AAAC....... Australian Apprenticeship Advisory Committee   (ADA)
AAAC....... Australian Army Aviation Corps   (WGAO)
AAAC....... Australian Association of Agricultural Consultants
AAACE...... Alianza Apostolica y Anti-Communista de Espana   (WGAO)
AAACI...... American-Arab Association for Commerce and Industry, Inc.
AAACU..... Asian Association of Agricultural Colleges and Universities
                [*Philippines*]
AAAE....... Asian Automotive and Accessories Exhibition
AAAE....... Australian Association of Adult Education   (ADA)
AAAEENAA ... Association Amicale des Anciens Eleves de l'Ecole National
                Agronomique d'Alger   (WGAO)
AAAEINA ... Association Amicale des Anciens Eleves de l'Institut National
                Agronomique   (WGAO)
AAAF........ Arab Amateur Athletic Federation [*See also CAA*]   (EAIO)
AAAF........ Association Aeronautique et Astronautique de France
                [*Aeronautical and Astronautical Association of France*]
                (WER)
AAAH....... Australasian Association for Adolescent Health
AAAHAIL ... Association of Attenders and Alumni of The Hague Academy of
                International Law [*Netherlands*]   (EAIO)
AAAI .... Association of Australian Aerospace Industries
AAAIA....... All-India Automobile and Ancillary Industries Association
                (PDAA)
AAAID ...... Arab Authority for Agricultural Investment and Development
                [*Khartoum, Sudan*]   (EAIO)
AAAJ........ Association Afro-Asiatique des Journalistes   (WGAO)
AAAM....... Australian Anti-Apartheid Movement
AAAN....... Amateur Athletics Association of Nigeria
AAAN....... Australian Association for Armed Neutrality
AA & E..... Australian Aircraft and Engineering [*Company*]   (ADA)
AAANZ ..... Accounting Association of Australia and New Zealand
AAANZ ..... Agribusiness Association of Australia and New Zealand
AAA ofNSW ... Amateur Athletic Association of New South Wales
                [*Australia*]

AAAP .... Asian-Australian Association of Animal Production Societies (WGAO)
AAAP .... Association d'Aide et d'Assistance a la Population [*Association for Aid and Relief to the Population*] [*Cambodia*] (CL)
AAAPEA ... Australian Association Against Painful Experiments on Animals
AAAQ .... Apparel Agents' Association of Queensland [*Australia*]
AAAR .... Association des Amis d'Andre Rey
AAAR .... Association for the Advancement of Aeronautical Research [*France*]
AAAR .... Australian Archives [*National Union Catalogue of Australia symbol*]
AAAS .... Association for the Advancement of Agricultural Sciences
AAAS .... Australian Association for the Advancement of Science (ADA)
AAAS .... Austrian Association for American Studies (SLS)
AAASA ...... Apparel Agents Association of South Australia
AAASA ...... Association for the Advancement of Agricultural Sciences in Africa (EAIO)
AAASA ...... Association pour l'Avancement en Afrique des Sciences de l'Agriculture [*Association for the Advancement of Agricultural Sciences in Africa*] [*Addis Ababa, Ethiopia*]
AAASA ...... Australian and Allied All Services Association (ADA)
AAASM .... Associated African States and Madagascar (MHDB)
AAAST ...... African Association for the Advancement of Science and Technology (WGAO)
AAATP ...... Asian Alliance of Appropriate Technology Practitioners (EA)
AAAV .... Apparel Agents' Association of Victoria [*Australia*]
AAAvn .... Australian Army Aviation Corps
AAAVYT ... Asociacion Argentina de Agencias de Viajes y Turismo [*Argentine association of travel and tourism agencies*] (EY)
AAAWA .... Apparel Agents' Association of Western Australia
AAAYT ...... Associacion Agrentina de Agencias de Viajes y Turismo (WGAO)
AAB .... Abelag Aviation [*Belgium*] [*ICAO designator*] (FAAC)
AAB .... Aboriginal Arts Board [*Australia*]
AAB .... Aerial Leaflet Bomb
AAB .... Akademski Aeroklub Beograd [*Academy Aero Club of Belgrade*] [*Former Yugoslavia*] (YU)
AAB .... Alianca Anticomunista Brasileira [*Brazilian Anti-Communist Alliance*] (PD)
AAB .... Alliance Agricole Belge [*Belgium*] (EAIO)
AAB .... Allied Arab Bank
AAB .... American Australian Business
AAB .... Anti-Apartheid Bewegung
AAB .... Arab African Bank
AAB .... Arubaanse Atletiek Bond [*Aruba Amateur Athletic Association*] (EAIO)
AAB .... Asociacion Automotriz Boliviana [*Bolivian Automotive Association*] (LA)
AAB .... Asociacion de Amigos del Bosque [*Guatemala*] (DSCA)
AAB .... Asociacion de Arquitectos de Bolivia [*Association of Bolivian Architects*] [*La Paz*] (LAA)
AAB .... Associacao dos Arquivistas Brasileiros [*Brazil*] (EAIO)
AAB .... Association Atlantique Belge [*Belgian Atlantic Association*] (EAIO)
AAB .... Association of Applied Biologists [*Midlothian, Scotland*] (EA)
AAB .... Associazione Astrofili Bolognesi [*Italian*] (SLS)
AAB .... Australian Aborigines Branch (ADA)
AAB .... Australian Associated Breweries
AABA .... Associacao Atletica Brasil Acucareiro [*Brazil*] (DSCA)
AABA .... Australian Ayrshire Breeders' Association
AABAS ...... Australasian Academy of Broadcast Arts and Sciences
AABB .... Association des Archivistes et Bibliothecaires de Belgique (WGAO)
AABBC ...... Australian Alliance of Bible-Believing Christians
AABC .... Australian Army Band Corps
AABCC ...... Australian Anti-Bases Campaign Coalition
AABDFC ... Association des Archivistes Bibliothecaires Documentalistes Francophones de la Caraibe [*Association of French-speaking Archivists, Librarians and Documentalists in the Caribbean*] [*Haiti*] (PDAA)
AABE .... Asian Association for Biology Education [*Sri Lanka*] (ASF)
AABEvK .... Arbeitsgemeinschaft fur das Archiv- und Bibliothekswesen in der Evangelischen Kirche (WGAO)
AABH .... Australian Association for Better Hearing (ADA)
AABH .... Broken Hill [*Australia*] [*ICAO location identifier*] (ICLI)
AABI .... Antilles Air Boats Inc. (WGAO)
AABL .... Associated Australasian Banks in London
AABL .... Australasian [*or Australian*] Associated Banks in London (ADA)
AABL .... Australian Amateur Boxing League
AABM .... Australian Association of British Manufacturers
AABN .... Anti-Apartheid-Bewegung Netherland
AABN .... Anti-Apartheids Beweging Nederland [*Anti-Apartheid Movement*] [*South Africa*] [*Political party*] (EAIO)
AABNF ...... African Association for Biological Nitrogen-Fixation [*Egypt*] (EAIO)
AABO .... Assembly of Australian Business Organisations

AABP .... Australian Association of Business Publications (ADA)
AABR .... Australian Association of Bush Regenerators
AABSP ...... Australian Association of Business and Specialist Publishers
AABTh .... Advanced Association of Beauty Therapists [*Australia*] (ADA)
AABWA .... Association of Accountancy Bodies in West Africa [*Nigeria*] (EAIO)
AAC .... Aboriginal Advancement Council
AAC .... Aboriginal Arts and Crafts [*Australia*] (ADA)
AAC .... Aboriginal Arts Committee
AAC .... Academia Argentina de Cirugia [*Argentine Academy of Surgery*] [*Buenos Aires*] (LAA)
AAC .... Accion Anticomunista Colombiana [*Colombian Anticommunist Action*] (LA)
AAC .... Advance Australia Challenge
AAC .... Affarsarbetsgivarnas Centralforbund (WGAO)
AAC .... African Accounting Council (WGAO)
AAC .... African Association of Cartography (EA)
AAC .... African Athletics Confederation
AAC .... Agrarishe Adviescommissie (WGAO)
AAC .... Al Arish [*Egypt*] [*Airport symbol*] (OAG)
AAC .... All African Convention
AAC .... Allied Longline Agency Annual Conference [*NATO*] (NATG)
AAC .... Anglo American Corporation
AAC .... Angola Air Charter Ltd. [*ICAO designator*] (FAAC)
AAC .... Arab-African Cooperation
AAC .... Arab Air Cargo [*Iraq*]
AAC .... Arabian Automotive Company [*Saudi Arabia*] (PDAA)
AAC .... Art Advisory Committee
AAC .... Asociacion de Agricultores de Canete [*Peru*] (DSCA)
AAC .... Asociaciones de Ahorro y Credito [*Savings and Loan Associations*] [*El Salvador*] (LA)
AAC .... Association Africaine de Cartographie [*African Association of Cartography*] (EAIO)
AAC .... Association des Amidonneries de Cereales de la CEE [*EC*] (ECED)
AAC .... Association of Agricultural Centers [*Finland*] (EAIO)
AAC .... Astronomy Advisory Committee [*Australia*]
AAC .... Australian Academy of Cricket
AAC .... Australian Accommodation Council (ADA)
AAC .... Australian Aerobatic Club
AAC .... Australian Aero Club
AAC .... Australian Agricultural Company [*or Council*] (ADA)
AAC .... Australian Agricultural Council (WGAO)
AAC .... Australian Air Corps (ADA)
AAC .... Australian Aircraft Consortium (LAIN)
AAC .... Australian Aircraft Consortium Proprietary Ltd.
AAC .... Australian Alpine Club (ADA)
AAC .... Australian Asiatic Corporation Ltd. (ADA)
AAC .... Australian Association of Chiropractors (ADA)
AAC .... Australian Aviation College
AAC .... Austrian Alpine Club (WGAO)
AAC .... Awami Action Committee [*India*] [*Political party*] (PPW)
AACA .... Allied Control Commission for Austria [*World War II*]
AACA .... Asian and Australasian Congress of Anaesthesiology (WGAO)
AACA .... Association of Apex Clubs of Australia
AACA .... Australian Advisory Committee on Aeronautics (ADA)
AACART ... African-Atlantic Coast Association of Round Tables
AACB .... Allied Control Commission for Bulgaria [*World War II*]
AACB .... Association of African Central Banks [*Dakar, Senegal*]
AACB .... Australian Association of Clinical Biochemists (WGAO)
AACC .... Airport Associations Coordinating Council [*Geneva Airport, Switzerland*] (EAIO)
AACC .... All-Africa Conference of Churches [*Nairobi, Kenya*] (AF)
AACC .... Arab Air Carriers Organization (WGAO)
AACC .... Area Approach Control Centre
AACC .... Asociacion Argentina de Criadores de Caprinos (WGAO)
AACC .... Asociacion Argentina de Criadores de Cebu [*Argentina*] (LAA)
AACC .... Asociacion Argentina de Criadores de Cerdos (WGAO)
AACC .... Asociacion Argentina de Criadores de Corriedale [*Argentina*] (DSCA)
AACC .... Association des Agences-Conseils en Communication [*France*] (EAIO)
AACC .... Australian Army Catering Corps
AACC .... Australian Automobile Chamber of Commerce
AACCH ...... Asociacion Argentina Criadores de Charolais [*Argentina*] (DSCA)
AACCH ...... Australian Administrative Case Clearing House
AACCI .... Australian-Arab Chamber of Commerce and Industry
AACCPH... Australian Advisory Council for the Care of the Physically Handicapped (ADA)
AACD .... Associacao de Assistencia a Crianca Defeituosa
AACD .... Ceduna [*Australia*] [*ICAO location identifier*] (ICLI)
AACE .... African Association for Correspondence Education [*Kenya*] (SLS)
AACE .... Airborne Alternate Command Echelon [*NATO*] (NATG)

AACE .... Asociacion de Amistad Cubano-Espanol [*Cuban-Spanish Friendship Association*]   (LA)

AACE .... Association des Assureurs Cooperatifs Europeens [*Association of European Cooperative Insurers - AECI*] [*Brussels, Belgium*]   (EAIO)

AACE .... Association of European Co-operative Insurers   (WGAO)

AACE .... Australian Association for Community Education

AACF .... Australian Amateur Cycling Federation

AACF .... Australian Association for Cultural Freedom

AACG .... Allied Control Council for Germany [*World War II*]

AACH .... Allied Control Commission for Hungary [*World War II*]

AACH .... Asociacion Argentina Criadores de Hereford [*Argentina*]   (DSCA)

AACHA ..... Asociacion Argentina Criadores de Holando Argentino [*Argentina*]   (DSCA)

AACHSA ... Associate of the Australian College of Health Service Administrators

AACI .... Airports Association Council International [*Switzerland*]   (EAIO)

AACI .... Allied Control Commission for Italy [*World War II*]

AACI .... Associate of the Australian Chemical Institute   (ADA)

AACI .... Association of Americans and Canadians in Israel   (EAIO)

AACIC ...... Australian Association of Community Aid Bureaus and Information Centres

AACIO ...... Australian Association of Chief Information Officers

AACJ .... Allied Control Council for Japan [*World War II*]

AACK .... Asociacion Argentina de Criadores de Karakul [*Argentina*]   (LAA)

AACL .... Arab Association for Comparative Literature [*Algeria*]   (WGAO)

AACL .... Asociacion Argentina Criadores de Limusin [*Argentina*]   (DSCA)

AACL .... Asociacion Argentina de Criadores de Lincoln [*Argentina*]   (DSCA)

AACLAME ... Australian Advisory Council on Language and Multicultural Education

AACLS ..... Australian Association of Community Language Services

AACM .... African Anti-Colonial Movement of Kenya

AACM .... ASEAN [*Association of Southeast Asian Nations*] - Australia Consultative Meeting

AACM .... Asociacion de Amistad Cubano-Mongol [*Cuban-Mongolian Friendship Association*]   (LA)

AACM .... Associate of the Australian College of Music

AACMA .... All-Africa Church Music Association

AACMA .... Asociacion Argentina Criadores Merino Australiano [*Argentina*]   (DSCA)

AACMR .... Australian Advisory Committee on Media Research   (ADA)

AACNO ..... Australian Assembly of Captive Nations Organizations   (EAIO)

AACNP ..... Asociacion Argentina de Ciencias Naturales "Physis" [*Argentine Association of Natural Sciences "Physis"*] [*Buenos Aires*]   (LAA)

AACO .... Arab Air Carriers Organization   (EAIO)

AACO .... Australian Association of Chiropractors and Osteopaths   (ADA)

AACOBS ... Australian Advisory Committee on Bibliographical Services   (ADA)

AACP .... Association des Agences Conseils en Publicite   (WGAO)

AACP .... Association of Peruvian Authors and Composers   (EAIO)

AACP .... Australian Association of Consulting Planners

AACPA ...... Asian Association of Certified Public Accountants   (WGAO)

AACR .... Allied Control Commission for Rumania [*World War II*]

AACR .... Association for the Advancement of Civil Rights [*Gibraltar*] [*Political party*]   (PPE)

AACRDE ... Australian Advisory Committee on Research and Development in Education   (ADA)

AACREA ... Asociacion Argentina de Consorcios Regionales de Experimentacion Agricola [*Argentine Association of Regional Consortiums of Agricultural Research*]   (LA)

AACRM .... Asociacion Argentina Criadores de Romney Marsh [*Argentina*]   (DSCA)

AACS .... Asociacion Argentina Criadores de Shorthorn [*Argentina*]   (DSCA)

AACS .... Asociacion Argentina de la Ciencia del Suelo [*Argentina*]   (DSCA)

AACS .... Associate of the Australian Computer Society

AACS .... Association of Art Centres in Scotland   (WGAO)

AACS .... Australian Amateur Cine Society   (ADA)

AACS .... Australian Army Canteens Service

AACSA ...... Antique Arms Collectors Society of Australia

AACSG ...... Asociacion Argentina Criadores de Santa Gertrudis [*Argentina*]   (DSCA)

AACS(SA) ... Associate Member of the Association of Certified Secretaries [*South Africa*]   (AA)

AACT .... Adult Assessment and Coordination Team

AACT .... Autism Association of the Australian Capital Territory for Children, Adolescents, and Adults

AACTM .... Australian Association of Ceramic Tile Merchants

AACU .... Australian Catholic University [*Australian Capital Territory - Signadou Campus*] [*National Union Catalogue of Australia symbol*]

AACV .... Australian Association of Cattle Veterinarians

AACVB .... Asian Association of Convention and Visitor Bureaus   (EA)

AAD .... Afroasiatic Dialects

AAD .... Archiwum Akt Dawnych [*Archives of Old Records*]   (POL)

AAD .... Asociacion Argentina de Dermatologia [*Argentinian Association of Dermatology*]   (EAIO)

AAD .... Australian Association of Dieticians   (ADA)

AADA .... Administracion Autonoma de Almacenes Aduaneros [*Autonomous Administration of Custom Warehouses*] [*Bolivia*]   (LA)

AADA .... Antiaircraft Defense Area [*NATO*]

AADA .... Australian Action for Development Alternatives

AADA .... Australian Automobile Dealers Association

AADA .... Australian [*International*] Development Assistance [*Bureau*] [*National Union Catalogue of Australia symbol*]

AADAI ...... Arab Authority for Development and Agricultural Investment

AADC .... Australian Association for Deserted Children

AADE .... Australian Association of Dance Education

AADEC ..... Afro-Asian Organization for Economic Cooperation   (DSCA)

AADF .... Associacao dos Avicultores do Distrito Federal [*Brazil*]   (DSCA)

AADFI .... Association of African Development Finance Institutions [*Abidjan, Ivory Coast*]

AADICYT ... Asociacion Argentina de Investigadores Cientificos y Tecnologicos

AADIF .... Australian Auto Door Industry Forum

AADO .... Arab Agricultural Development Organization

AADPCII .. Association for the Advancement and Development of the Palestinian Community Inside Israel   (EAIO)

AADRII ..... Ageing and Alzheimers Diseases Research Institute, Inc. [*Australia*]

AADS .... Aboriginal Advisory and Development Services [*Northern Territory, Australia*]

AADT .... Association of Advanced Dental Technicians [*Australia*]

AAE .... Academy of Audio Engineers [*Australia*]

AAE .... Addis Ababa [*Ethiopia*] [*Seismograph station code, US Geological Survey*]

AAE .... Adult Aboriginal Education [*Australia*]

AAE .... Aeroporikon Arkhigeion Ellados [*Greek Air Force Command*]   (GC)

AAE .... Agrupacion Astronautica Espanola [*Spanish*]   (SLS)

AAE .... Amicale des Algeriens en Europe [*Association of Algerians in Europe*]   (AF)

A Ae .... Anglo-Arabe [*French*]   (MTD)

AAE .... Annaba [*Algeria*] [*Airport symbol*]   (OAG)

AAE .... Arkhigeion Aeroporikis Ekpaidevseos [*Air Force Training Headquarters*]   (GC)

AAe .... Ars Aequi; Juridisch Studentenblad [*Netherlands*]   (ILCA)

AAE .... Asia Australia Express [*Commercial firm*]   (DS)

AAE .... Asociacion Argentina de Electrotecnicos [*Argentine Association of Electrotechnicians*] [*Buenos Aires*]   (LAA)

AAE .... Asociacion Atlantica Espanola [*Spanish Atlantic Association*]   (EAIO)

AAE .... Association d'Assistance a l'Enfance [*Association for Relief to Children*] [*Cambodia*]   (CL)

AAE .... Associazione Archivistica Ecclesiastica [*Ecclesiastical Archivists Association*] [*Italy*]   (EAIO)

AAE .... Australian Antarctic Expedition [*1911-14*]

AAE .... Automatische Anrufeinrichtung [*Automatic Telephone Equipment*] [*German*]   (ADPT)

AAE .... Automatische Anschalteinrichtung [*Automatic Switching Equipment*] [*German*]   (ADPT)

AAE .... Automatische Antworteinheit [*Automatic Answering Standard*] [*German*]   (ADPT)

AAEA .... Actors and Announcers Equity Association of Australia

AAEA .... African Adult Education Association [*Later, AALAE*]   (EAIO)

AAEA .... Allied African Economic Affairs Committee [*World War II*]

AAEA .... Association Africaine de l'Education des Adultes [*African Adult Education Association*]   (AF)

AAEC .... Asociacion Argentina de Educacion Comparada [*Argentine Association of Comparative Education*]   (LA)

AAEC .... Association Africaine pour l'Enseignement par Correspondence   (WGAO)

AAEC .... Australian Aircraft and Engineering Company   (ADA)

AAEC .... Australian American Engineering Corporation Proprietary Ltd.

AAEC .... Australian Army Educational Corps   (ADA)

AAEC .... Australian Army Education Corps   (WGAO)

AAEC .... Australian Atomic Energy Commission [*Later, ANSTO*]   (ADA)

AAECE ...... Australian Association of Early Childhood Education

AAECo .... Australian Aircraft and Engineering Co.

AAEC RE .. Australian Atomic Energy Commission Research Establishment [*Sutherland, New South Wales*] [*Research center*]   (ERC)

AAED .... Asociacion Argentina para el Estudio del Dolor [*Argentine Association for the Study of Pain*]   (EAIO)

AAED .... Edinburgh [*Australia*] [*ICAO location identifier*]   (ICLI)

AAEE .... Association pour l'Accueil des Etudiants Etrangers   (WGAO)

AAEE .... Australian Association for Engineering Education

AAEE .... Australian Association for Environmental Education

AAEF......... Academie Aeronautique de France [*Aviation*]
AAEF......... Australian Air Expeditionary Force   (DMA)
AAEF......... Australian-American Educational Foundation   (ADA)
AAEMB..... Australian Aborigines Evangelical Mission Board
AAEO .... Australian Electoral Commission [*National Union Catalogue of Australia symbol*]
AAEPI....... Australian Association of Ethical Pharmaceutical Industry   (ADA)
AAER .... Association for Advancement of Educational Research [*Germany*]   (EAIO)
AAERE...... Australian Atomic Energy Research Establishment   (ADA)
AAERP...... Australian Archives Electronic Research Project
AAES......... Asociacion Azucarera de El Salvador [*Sugar Association of El Salvador*]   (LA)
AAES......... Association Africaine d'Entraide et de Solidarite [*France*]   (EAIO)
AAES......... Australian Agricultural Economics Society   (ADA)
AAES......... Australian Army Education Service   (ADA)
AAESDA... Association of Architects, Engineers, Surveyors, and Draughtsmen of Australia   (ADA)
AAESU...... Allgemeine Arabische Eisen und Stahl Union   (WGAO)
AAETA...... Asociacion Argentina Empresarios Transporte Automotor [*Transportation service*] [*Argentina*]   (EY)
AAF .... Aboriginal Affairs Foundation [*Australia*]
AAF .... Aboriginal-Australian Fellowship
AAF .... Academie d'Agriculture de France   (EAIO)
AAF .... Acceptance Advice Form
AAF .... Acetylaminofluorene   (RU)
AAF .... Advance Australia Foundation
AAF .... Agricultural Aids Foundation
AAF .... Aigle Azur [*France*] [*ICAO designator*]   (FAAC)
AAF .... American Air Filter Co.   (MHDB)
AAF .... Ancient Arts Fellowship [*Australia*]
AAF .... Asociatia Artistilor Fotografi [*Association of Photographic Artists*]   (RO)
AAF .... Asociatia Artistilor Fotografi din Republica Socialista Romania   (WGAO)
AAF .... Association des Archivistes Francais [*Association of French Archivists*]   (EAIO)
AAF .... Associazione Aziende Pubblicitarie Italiane
AAF .... Australian Air Force
AAF .... Australian Authors Fund   (ADA)
AAFA........ Australia-Albania Friendship Association   (ADA)
AAFA........ Australian Amateur Fencing Association   (ADA)
AAFAO ..... Australian Federation of AIDS Organisations [*National Union Catalogue of Australia symbol*]
AAFAWA ... Aluminium Fabricators' Association of Western Australia
AAFC........ Australian Amateur Football Council
AAFCE...... Allied Air Forces, Central Europe [*Later, AIRCENT*] [*NATO*]   (MCD)
AAFE........ Asociacion Argentina de Fomento Equino [*Argentina*]   (DSCA)
AAFEA...... Australasian Airline Flight Engineers Association   (ADA)
AAFFA...... Australian Air Freight Forwarders Association   (ADA)
AAFI........ Allied Air Forces in Italy [*World War II*]
AAFI........ Association des Anciens Fonctionnaires Internationaux [*Association of Former International Civil Servants - AFICS*] [*Geneva, Switzerland*]   (EA)
AAFI........ Australians Against Further Immigration [*An association*]
AAFIP....... Australians Against Further Immigration Party [*An association*]
AAFLI....... Asian American Free Labor Institute [*Philippines*]   (WGAO)
AAFMC..... Australian Association of Farm Management Consultants
AAFNE...... Allied Air Forces, Northern Europe [*Later, AIRNORTH*] [*NATO*]
AAFR........ Australian Armed Forces Radio
AAFRA...... Association of African Airlines
AAFSE ...... Allied Air Forces, Southern Europe [*Later, AIRSOUTH*] [*NATO*]
AAFSWPA ... Allied Air Forces, South West Pacific Area [*NATO*]   (ADA)
AAFU........ All-African Farmers' Union
AAFV........ Australian Armed Forces, Vietnam
AAFVL...... Australian Association of Film and Video Libraries
AAG.......... Aeronautical Information Service Automation Group [*ICAO*]   (DA)
AAG.......... Aerosol Generator Truck   (RU)
AAG.......... Afdeling Agrarische Geschiedenis   (WGAO)
AAG.......... Air Affaires Gabon   (WGAO)
AAG.......... Algemene Assurantie Groep [*Financial institution*] [*Netherlands*]   (EY)
AAG.......... All-Africa Games [*Begun in 1983 by the SCSA*]
AAG.......... Anthropological Association of Greece [*Research center*]   (IRC)
AAG.......... Armiska Artiljeriska Grupa [*Army Artillery Group*]   (YU)
AAG.......... Army Artillery Group   (RU)
AAG.......... Army Aviation Hospital   (RU)
AAG.......... Australian Association of Gerontology [*Sydney*]   (SLS)
AAGASE... Australian Association of Graphic Art Sales Executives
AAGD........ Australian Attorney General's Department - Lionel Murphy Library [*National Union Catalogue of Australia symbol*]

AAGF .... Australian Avocado Growers' Association
AAGG........ Asociacion Argentina de Geofisicos y Geodestas [*Argentina*]   (DSCA)
AAGH........ Asociacion de Agricultores y Ganaderos de Honduras [*Honduras*]   (DSCA)
AAGM....... Associate, Australian Guild of Music and Speech
AAGNC..... Australian Association for Geriatric Nursing Care
AAGP .... Allgemeine Aerztliche Gesellschaft fuer Psychotherapie [*Dusseldorf, German y*]   (SLS)
AAGPS...... Athletic Association of the Great Public Schools of New South Wales [*Australia*]
AAGREF ... Association Amicale de Genie Rural des Eaux et des Forets   (WGAO)
AAGS .... Association of African Geological Surveys [*See also ASGA*]   (EAIO)
AAH .... Allami Aruhaz [*State Department Store*]   (HU)
AAH .... Anyag- es Arhivatal [*Office of Materiel and Price Control*]   (HU)
AAH .... Australian Academy of the Humanities [*Canberra*]   (SLS)
AAH .... Australian Auxiliary Hospital   (ADA)
AAHA........ Asociacion de Amistad Hispano-Arabe [*Hispano-Arab Friendship Society*] [*Spain*]
AAHL....... Australian Animal Health Laboratory
AAHLIS.... Australian Association for Health Literature and Information Services
AAHO .... Afro-Asian Housing Organization [*Cairo, Egypt*]   (EAIO)
AAHPERD ... American Alliance for Health, Physical Education, Recreation and Dance   (OLYM)
AAHPM .... Association des Amis de l'Hopital Preah Monivong [*Association of Friends of Preah Monivong Hospital*] [*Cambodia*]   (CL)
AAHPSSS ... Australasian Association for the History, Philosophy, and Social Studies of Science [*Sydney, Australia*]   (SLS)
AAHQS..... Australian Agricultural Health and Quarantine Service
AAHR........ Australian Association for Humane Research
AAHS .... Australian Affiliation of Herpetological Societies
AAI .... Academie des Affaires Internationales
AAI .... Accademia Archeologica Italiana [*Rome, Italy*]   (SLS)
AAI .... Agence Africaine d'Information [*African Information Agency*] [*Zaire*]
AAI .... Alleanza Anticomunista Internazionale [*International Anticommunist Alliance*] [*Italian*]   (WER)
AAI .... Allied Armies in Italy [*Obsolete*]
AAI .... Ambon [*Indonesia*] [*Seismograph station code, US Geological Survey*]
AAI .... Assistance Automobile Internationale   (FLAF)
AAI .... Association Actuarielle Internationale [*International Actuarial Association - IAA*] [*Brussels, Belgium*]   (EAIO)
AAI .... Association of Advertisers in Ireland   (WGAO)
AAI .... Association of Art Institutions   (WGAO)
AAI .... Association of Australian Investigators
AAI .... Associazione Archivistica Ecclesiastica   (WGAO)
AAI .... Australian Air International
AAI .... Auto Alliance International [*Joint manufacturing venture of Ford Motor Co. and Mazda*]
AAI .... Pulse-Height Analyzer   (RU)
AAIA .... Alianza Anti-Imperialista Argentina [*Argentine Anti-Imperialist Alliance*]   (LA)
AAIA .... Associate of the Advertising Institute of Australia   (ADA)
AAIAS...... Associate of the Australian Institute of Aboriginal Studies
AAIATSIS ... Associate of the Australian Institute of Aboriginal and Torres Strait Islanders
AAIB......... Albaraka Algeria Islamic Bank   (EY)
AAIB......... Arab African International Bank
AAIB......... Associate of the Australian Institute of Banking
AAIB......... Associate of the Australian Institute of Building
AAIB......... Australian Association of Independent Businesses Ltd.
AAIBS...... Associate of the Australian Institute of Building Surveyors
AAIB(Snr) ... Senior Associate of the Australian Institute of Bankers
AAIC......... Africa Asia Islamic Conference
AAIC......... Agencias Associadas de Investigacao e Control de Creditos   (WGAO)
AAIC......... Air Accidents Investigation Committee [*Australia*]
AAIC......... Asian Association of Insurance Commissioners   (EAIO)
AAIC......... Australian Advertising Industry Council   (ADA)
AAIC......... Australian Artificial Intelligence Conference
AAICA...... Australian Associate of the Commonwealth Institute of Accountants
AAID .... Agence Africaine d'Information et de Documentation [*African Information and Documentation Agency*]
AAID .... Association des Artistes Independants Dakarois
AAID .... Association for Alternative Accommodation for the Intellectually Disabled
AAIE......... Associate of the Australian Institute of Export   (ADA)
AAIEx....... Associate of the Australian Institute of Export
AAIFScT ... Associate of the Australian Institute of Food Science and Technology
AAIFST..... Associate of the Australian Institute of Food Science and Technology

AAIH .... Association Amicale des Ingenieurs Horticoles et des Eleves de l'Ecole Nationale d'Horticulture de Versailles   (WGAO)
AAII .... Associate of the Australian Insurance Institute   (ADA)
AAII .... Australian Artificial Intelligence Institute
AAIIEC ..... Aeolus Automotive Industry Import & Export Corp. [*China*]
AAIIS .... Australasian Association of Institutes of Inspectors of Schools
AAILA .... Associate of the Australian Institute of Landscape Architects
AAIM .... Archives of Artillery Historical Museum   (RU)
AAIM .... Associate of the Australian Institute of Management   (ADA)
AAIMLT ... Associate of the Australian Institute of Medical Laboratory Technicians   (ADA)
AAIP .... Associate of the Australian Institute of Physics   (ADA)
AAIPD .... Accademia Artistica Internazionale "Pinocchio D'Oro" [*Italian*]   (SLS)
AAIR .... Australasian Association for Institutional Research
AAIRC ...... Australian Amateur Ice Racing Council
AAIS .... African Association of Insect Scientists [*Kenya*]   (WGAO)
AAIS .... Associate of the Australasian Institute of Secretaries   (ADA)
AAIS .... Association of African Insect Scientists
AAIS .... Australian Sports Commission - National Sport Information Centre [*National Union Catalogue of Australia symbol*]
AAISH ...... Association for the Assistance of Intellectually and Socially Handicapped People [*Australia*]
AAIT .... Associate of the Australian Institute of Travel   (ADA)
AAIT .... Australian Institute of Technology[*Reid Campus*] [*Canberra*] [*National Union Catalogue of Australia symbol*]
AAITC ...... Australian Automobile Industry Training Committee
AAIT:LS .... Australian Institute of Technology [*Reid Campus*] Library School [*Canberra*] [*National Union Catalogue of Australia Symbol*]
AAITO ...... Association of African Industrial Technology Organizations
AAIV .... Associate of the Australian Institute of Valuers
AAJ .... Arab Airways (Jerusalem) Ltd.
AAJ .... Association of African Jurists
AAJA .... Afro-Asian Journalists' Association   (NATG)
AAJD .... Asociacion Argentina de Juristas Democraticos [*Argentine Association of Democratic Lawyers*]   (LA)
AAJEPT .... Associacao de Jornalistas e Escritores Portugueses do Turismo [*Portuguese Association of Journalists and Writers on Tourism*]   (WER)
AAJWA ..... Asian Agricultural Journalists and Writers Association [*Jakarta, Indonesia*]   (EAIO)
AAK .... Acetylaspartic Acid   (RU)
AAK .... Aranuka [*Kiribati*] [*Airport symbol*]   (OAG)
AAK .... Armee de l'Air Khmere [*Cambodian Air Force*]   (CL)
AAK .... Aussenhandelsabrechnungskontor [*Foreign Trade Settlements Office*]   (EG)
AAKC .... Association d'Amitie Khmero-Chinoise [*Cambodian-Chinese Friendship Association*]   (CL)
AAL .... Aalborg [*Denmark*] [*Airport symbol*]   (OAG)
AAL .... Aboriginal Advancement League [*Australia*]
AAL .... Academia Argentina de Letras [*Argentine Academy of Letters*] [*Buenos Aires*]   (LAA)
AAL .... Adelaide Airways Ltd. [*Australia*]
AAL .... Afroasiatic Linguistics
AAL .... Architectural Aluminium Ltd. [*Fiji*]
AAL .... Argentine Academy of Letters   (EAIO)
AAL .... Asia America Line [*Commercial firm*]   (DS)
AAL .... Association of Art Libraries [*Germany*]   (EAIO)
AAL .... Association of Austrian Librarians   (EAIO)
AAL .... Australasian Association for Logic
AAL .... Australian Aborigines League
AAL .... Australian Acoustical Laboratory
AAL .... Australian Air League   (ADA)
AAL .... Australian Analytical Laboratories
AALA .... Algamiia Almasriia Lilmaktabat Almadrasiia [*Egyptian School Library Association*]   (EAIO)
AALA .... Association d'Amitie Lao-Australienne [*Lao-Australian Friendship Association*]   (CL)
AALAE ...... African Association for Literacy and Adult Education   (EA)
AALAPSO ... Afro-Asian Latin American People's Solidarity Organization
AALC .... Afro-American Labor Center   (AF)
AALC .... AGPS-AACOBS [*Australian Government Publishing Service - Australian Advisory Committee on Bibliographical Services*] Liaison Committee
AALC .... Australian Army Legal Corps   (ADA)
AALC .... Leigh Creek [*Australia*] [*ICAO location identifier*]   (ICLI)
AALCC ...... Asian-African Legal Consultative Committee [*India*]   (SLS)
AALD .... Australian Army Legal Department   (ADA)
AALDI .... Association of Agricultural Librarians and Documentalists of India   (WGAO)
AALIA .... Associate of the Australian Library and Information Association
AALNSWBG ... Australian Air League New South Wales Boys Group
AaLU .... Universidad Nacional de La Plata, La Plata, Argentina [*Library symbol*] [*Library of Congress*]   (LCLS)
AALVG ...... Australian Air League Victorian Group

AAM .... Amicale des Algeriens Musulmans
AAM .... Andidiktatorikon Agrotikon Metopon [*Antidictatorial Agrarian Front*] [*Greek*]   (GC)
AAM .... Angeborener Ausolsender Mechanismus [*Innate Release Mechanism*] [*Psychology*]
AAM .... Annual Aircraft Movements
AAM .... Anti-Apartheid Movement [*South Africa*] [*Political party*]   (EA)
AAM .... Arma Aerea de la Marina [*Naval Air Force*] [*Spanish*]   (PDAA)
AAM .... Asociacion Argentina de Marketing   (WGAO)
AAM .... Associate of the Australian Museum
AAM .... Association des Amidonneries de Mais de la CEE [*Association of the Maize Starch Industries of the European Economic Community*]
AAM .... Association des Anciens Moudjahidines [*Algeria*]
AAM .... Australian Aborigines Mission
AAM .... Australian Air Mission   (ADA)
AAM .... Australian Anti-Apartheid Movement [*An association*]
AAM .... Austrian Association for Musicology   (EAIO)
AAM .... Austrian Association of Music   (EAIO)
AAM .... Automobile Association of Malaysia   (WGAO)
AAMA .... Arab American Medical Association   (EA)
AAMA .... Australian Automotive Manufacturers' Association
AAMAM ... Associacao dos Amigos do Museu de Arte Moderna   (WGAO)
AAMBER ... Australian Antarctic Marine Biological Ecosystem Research
AAMC .... Arabian Axles Manufacturing Co. [*Saudi Arabia*]
AAMC .... Australian Army Medical Corps   (ADA)
AAME .... Australian Association for Marriage Education
AAMF .... Association Aeromedicale de France [*Aeromedical Association of France*]   (PDAA)
AAMFC ..... Australian Association of Marriage and Family Counsellors
AAMH ...... Australian Association for Maritime History   (ADA)
AAMH ...... Australian Association of Mental Health
AAMHA .... Association Africaine de Microbiologie et d'Hygiene Alimentaire [*Tunisia*]   (WGAO)
AAMI .... Associate of the Australian Marketing Institute
AAMI .... Australian Associated Motor Insurers Ltd.   (ADA)
AAMIH ..... Association des Amis du Musee International des Hussards [*Association of Friends of the International Museum of the Hussars*] [*France*]   (EAIO)
AAMIM .... Australian Association of Musical Instrument Makers
AAMMA ... Australian Agricultural Machinery Manufacturers' Association
AAMO ...... Asian Association of Management Organisations [*Kuala Lumpur, Malaysia*]
AAMO ...... Asian Association of Management Organizations
AAMPE ..... Andifasistiki Andiimperialistiki Mathitiki Parataxi Ellados [*Antifascist, Anti-Imperialist Student Faction of Greece*]   (GC)
AAMR ...... Australian Association for the Mentally Retarded
AAMRH ... International Association of Agricultural Medicine and Rural Health   (EAIO)
AAMS ...... Association of African and Malagasy States
AAMS ...... Australian Aerial Medical Services   (ADA)
AAMS ...... Australian Army Medical Service   (DMA)
AAMS ...... Azienda Autonoma dei Monopoli di Stato   (WGAO)
AAMSU ... All Assam Minority Students Union [*Indonesia*]   (WGAO)
AAMT ...... Australian Association of Mathematics Teachers   (ADA)
AAMTI ..... Association of African Maritime Training Institutes [*Egypt*]   (WGAO)
AAMUS .... Accademia Ambrosiana Medici Umanisti e Scrittori [*Italian*]   (SLS)
AAMWS .... Australian Army Medical Women's Service   (ADA)
AAMY .... Andidiktatorikon Agrotikon Metopon Ypaithrou [*Antidictatorial Agrarian Front in the Rural Areas*] [*Greek*]   (GC)
AAMZ .... Association des Amis de Maurice Zundel [*Paris, France*]   (EAIO)
AAN .... Abortion Alternative Network
AAN .... Academy of Artillery Sciences   (RU)
AAN .... Akademi Administrasi Negara [*State Administration Academy*]   (IN)
AAN .... Akademiia Artilleriiskikh Nauk   (WGAO)
AAN .... Archives of the Academy of Sciences, USSR   (RU)
AAN .... Archiwum Akt Nowych [*Archives of New Records*]   (POL)
AAN .... Arkhiv Akademii Nauk   (WGAO)
AAN .... Assemblee de l'Atlantique Nord [*North Atlantic Assembly*] [*Brussels, Belgium*]   (EAIO)
AAN .... Australian Association of Nematologists
AAN .... Australian Association of Neurologists   (ADA)
AAN .... Institute of Archives of the Bulgarian Academy of Sciences   (BU)
AAN .... Oasis International Airlines [*Spain*] [*ICAO designator*]   (FAAC)
AANA .... All Australia Netball Association
AANA .... Australian Association of National Advertisers   (ADA)
AANASS ... Abdulla Ahmed Nass [*Bahrain*] [*Commercial firm*]
AANB .... Agudat Achsaniot Noar Beisrael [*Israel Youth Hostels Association*]   (EAIO)
aand .... Aandeel [*Shape*] [*Afrikaans*]
A & A .... American and Australian Line [*Shipping*]   (ROG)

A & A .... Arbeitsschutz und Arbeitsmedizin [*Industrial Safety and Medicine*] [*German*]
A & B .... Antofagasta & Bolivia Railroad Co.   (MHDB)
A & BRC ...... Antofagasta and Bolivia Railway Co.   (MHDB)
A & E .... Access and Equity Strategy [*Australia*]
A & E .... Accident and Emergency Service [*Australia*]
A&ECA...... Anglican and Eastern Churches Association   (WGAO)
A & H .... Agricultural and Horticultural [*Australia*]
A & K .... Abercombie and Kent Egypt [*Commercial firm*]
A & M .... Aachener & Muenchener Beteiligungs [*Aachener & Muenchener, Partners*]
A & P.......... Agricultural and Pastoral [*Australia*]
A & P.......... Asia and Pacific Quality Trade Co. Ltd. [*Thailand*]
A & P.......... Attraktiv und Preiswert [*Attractive and Priced Right*] [*West German grocery products brand*]
A & R .... Angus & Robertson [*Publisher*] [*Australia*]
AANE .... Andifasistiki Andiimperialistiki Neolaia Ellados [*Antifascist, Anti-Imperialist Youth of Greece*]   (GC)
aangeb........ Aangeboden [*Offered*] [*Netherlands*]
aanget........ Aangeteken [*Registered*] [*Afrikaans*]
aangev .... Aangevuld [*Supplemented*] [*Publishing*] [*Netherlands*]
aanh .... Aanhangsel [*Appendix*] [*Afrikaans*]
AANI .... Arkticheskii i Antarkticheskii Nauchno Issledovatel'skiy Institut [*Arctic and Antarctic Scientific Research Institute*] [*Russian*]   (PDAA)
AANI .... Associate of the Australian Naval Institute
AANII....... Arkticheskiy i Antarkticheskiy Nauchno Issledovatel'skiy Institut [*Arctic and Antarctic Scientific Research Institute*] [*Russian*]   (MSC)
aank .... Aankoms [*Arrival*] [*Afrikaans*]
aanm .... Aanmerking [*Remark*] [*Afrikaans*]
AANN .... Australian Amateur News Network
AANS .... Aquaculture Association of Nova Scotia   (MSC)
AANS .... Australian Army Nursing Service   (ADA)
AANSW .... Ansett Airlines of New South Wales [*Australia*]
aant .... Aantaminen [*Pronunciation*] [*Finland*]
aant .... Aantamys [*Finland*]
aant .... Aantekening [*Note*] [*Netherlands*]   (ILCA)
aant .... Aantyy [*Finland*]
AANT .... Argentina Association of Nuclear Technology   (NUCP)
aantek .... Aantekening [*Note*] [*Publishing*] [*Netherlands*]
Aanv.......... Aanvulling [*Benelux*]   (BAS)
aanvr .... Aanvragg [*Demand*] [*Afrikaans*]
aanw .... Aanwysend [*Indicating*] [*Afrikaans*]
AAO .... Abastumani High-Mountain Astrophysical Observatory   (RU)
AAO.......... Abastumanskaya Astrofizicheskaya Observatoriya [*Abastumani Astrophysical Observatory*] [*Russian*]   (PDAA)
AAO.......... Adyge Autonomous Oblast   (RU)
AAO.......... Am Angefuehrten Orte [*At the Place Quoted*] [*German*]
AAO.......... Anaco [*Venezuela*] [*Airport symbol*]   (OAG)
aaO .... An Andern Orten [*Elsewhere*] [*German*]
aaO .... An Angegeben Orten [*In the Place Cited*] [*German*]
AAO.......... Anglo-Australian Observatory
AAO.......... Arab Advertising Organization [*Syrian Arab Republic*]   (EAIO)
AAO.......... Arbeitsgemeinschaft der Altphilologen Osterreichs   (WGAO)
AAO.......... Asian Aid Organisation [*Australia*]   (ADA)
AAO.......... Assistant Agricultural Officer
AAO.......... Australian Academy of Optometry
AAO.......... Australian Academy of Osteopathy
AAO.......... Australian Archives Office
AAO.......... Australian Archives Organization
AAO.......... Australian Army Orders
AAOB .... Associated Australian Owners and Brokers   (ADA)
AAOC....... AMOCO Algeria Oil Company
AAOC....... Australian Army Ordnance Corps   (ADA)
AAOCO..... Australian Association of Chiropractors and Osteopaths   (ADA)
AAOH .... Asian Association of Occupational Health   (EA)
AAONMS ... Ancient Arabic Order of the Nobles of the Mystic Shrine [*Freemasonry*]
AAORB ..... Association des Amis de l'Oeuvre de Richard Bellman [*Association of Friends of the Achievement of Richard Bellman*] [*France*]   (EAIO)
AAORO..... Australian Association of Registered Osteopaths   (ADA)
AAOT .... Australian Association of Occupational Therapists   (ADA)
AAP .... Advance Australia Party [*Political party*]
AAP .... Alianza Anticomunista Peruana [*Peruvian Anticommunist Alliance*]   (LA)
AAP .... Allied Administrative Publication [*NATO*]
AAP .... Arkhigeion Astynomias Poleon [*Cities Police Headquarters*] [*Greek*]   (GC)
AAP .... Arkhigos (Stolou) Aigaiou Pelagous [*Commander, Aegean Sea (Fleet)*]   (GC)
AAP .... Art Association of the Philippines   (WGAO)
AAP .... Asociaciones de Ahorro y Prestamo [*Savings and Loan Associations*] [*Chile*]   (LA)

AAP .... Associacao dos Arquitectos Portugueses [*Association of Portuguese Architects*]   (SLS)
AAP .... Association of Australasian Palaeontologists   (ADA)
AAP .... Astro Air International, Inc. [*Philippines*] [*ICAO designator*]   (FAAC)
AAP .... Australasian Association of Philosophy   (ADA)
AAP .... Australasian Association of Psychiatrists   (ADA)
AAP .... Australian Academy of Paediatrics
AAP .... Australian Assistance Plan   (ADA)
AAP .... Australian Associated Press   (ADA)
AAP .... Australian Associated Press Party Ltd.
AAP .... Australian Association of Philanthropy
AAP .... Auxiliatrices des Ames du Purgatoire [*Helpers of the Holy Souls of Purgatory*] [*France*]   (EAIO)
AAPA .... Aboriginal Affairs Planning Authority [*Western Australia*]
AAPA .... Aboriginal Areas Protection Authority [*Northern Territory, Australia*]
AAPA .... Agrupacion de Avicultura y Patologia Aviaria [*Chile*]   (DSCA)
AAPA .... Asociacion Argentina de Produccion Animal [*Argentina*]   (DSCA)
AAPA .... Asociacion Argentina de Productores Agricolas [*Argentina*]   (DSCA)
AAPA .... Association of Accredited Practitioners in Advertising [*South Africa*]   (WGAO)
AAPA .... Australian Abalone Producers' Association
AAPA .... Australian Aborigines Progressive Association
AAPA .... Australian Air Pilots Association
AAPA .... Australian Asphalt Pavement Association   (ADA)
AAPAL..... Australian Authors and Publishers Agency Limited
AAPAM ... African Association for Public Administration and Management
AAPAP...... Anglo-American Press Association of Paris [*See also APAAP*] [*France*]   (EA)
AAPAUNAM ... Asociaciones Autonomas de Personal Academico de la Universidad Nacional Autonoma de Mexico [*Autonomous Associations of Academic Personnel of the National University of Mexico*]   (LA)
AAPB........ Australian Apple and Pear Board   (ADA)
AAPBS ...... Australian Association of Permanent Building Societies   (ADA)
AAPC........ Africa Auxiliary Pioneer Corps
AAPC........ All African Peoples' Conference
AAPC........ Asociacion Argentina para el Progreso de las Ciencias [*Argentina*]   (LAA)
AAPC........ Asociacion de Amistad Portugal-Cuba [*Cuba-Portugal Friendship Association*]   (LA)
AAPC........ Australian Aluminium Production Commission   (ADA)
AAPC........ Australian Apple and Pear Corporation
AAPCHO .. Association of Asian/Pacific Community Health Organizations   (EA)
AAPCYC ... Australian Association of Police Citizens' Youth Clubs
AAPDA ... Australasian Apple Programmers and Developers Association
AAPF........ Asociacion Argentina de Proteccion Familiar   (EAIO)
AAPGA ..... Australian Apple and Pear Growers' Association
AAPH .... ASEAN [*Association of South East Asian Nations*] Association for Planning and Housing   (EAIO)
AAPI........ Associazione Aziende Pubblicitarie Italiane   (WGAO)
AAPI........ Australian Architectural Periodicals Index   (ADA)
AAPIS ...... Australian Associated Press Information Services Proprietary Ltd.
AAPJDE ... Australian Association for Peace, Justice, and Development Education
AAPL........ Association of Australian Parliamentary Librarians   (WGAO)
AAPM ...... Asian Association of Personnel Management   (WGAO)
AAPM ...... Australian Association of Practice Managers
AAPMA ... Association of Australian Port and Marine Authorities   (ADA)
AAPMBF .. Australian Air Pilots Mutual Benefit Fund
AAPO .... All African Peoples' Organization
AAPP........ Australasian Association of Psychology and Philosophy   (ADA)
AAPP........ Australian Association of Pathology Practices
AAPRA...... All-African People's Revolutionary Army
AAPRO ..... Asociacion Argentina de la Productividad [*Buenos Aires, Argentina*]   (LAA)
A-APRP..... All-African People's Revolutionary Party   (EA)
AAPS........ African Association of Political Science
AAPS........ Associate of the Australian Psychological Society
AAPS........ Australian Air Pilots' Service
AAPS........ Australian Animal Protection Society
AAPSA...... Australian Apple and Pear Shippers' Association
AAPSC...... Afro-Asian Peoples Solidarity Council   (WGAO)
AAPSO...... Afro-Asian People's Solidarity Organization [*Cairo, Egypt*]   (EAIO)
AAPSO...... Australian Association of Prisoner Support Organizations
AAPsychCorps ... Australian Army Psychology Corps
AAPT........ Asociacion Argentina de Paddle Tennis [*Argentinian Association of Paddle Tennis*]   (EAIO)
AAPT........ Australian Association for Psychological Type

AAPTS &R ... Australian Association for Predetermined Time Standards and Research
AAPW .... Australia Anzac Park West [*Department of Defence - Defense Central Library*] [*National Union Catalogue of Australia symbol*]
AAQP .... Australian Association for Quality and Participation
AAR .... Aarhus [*Denmark*] [*Airport symbol*]　(OAG)
AAR .... Active Attached Reserve [*Royal Australian Naval Reserve*]
AAR .... Anglo Australian Resources
aar .... Army Artillery　(BU)
AAR .... Asiana Airlines [*South Korea*] [*ICAO designator*]　(FAAC)
AAR .... Australian Army Reserve
AAR .... Australian Associated Resources　(ADA)
AAR .... Automatic Emergency Unloading [*Electricity*]　(RU)
AARA .... American Amateur Raquetball Association　(OLYM)
AARA .... Australian Association of Reprographic Arts　(ADA)
AARA .... Australian Awards for Research in Asia
AARASD ... Association des Amis de la Republique Arabe Sahraouie Democratique [*France*]　(EAIO)
AARC .... Asociacion de Agricultores del Rio Caulican [*Mexico*]　(LAA)
AARC .... Australian Aeronautical Research Committee　(ADA)
AARC .... Australian Amateur Rowing Council
AARC .... Australian Applied Research Centre
AARC .... Australian Automobile Racing Club　(ADA)
AARCh ...... Frequency-Controlled Emergency Unloading　(RU)
AARDC ..... Anglo-American Rhodesian Development Corporation
AARDES ... Association Algerienne pour la Recherche Demographique, Economique, et Sociale [*Algerian Association for Demographic, Economic, and Social Research*]　(AF)
aardk .... Aardkunde [*Geology*] [*Afrikaans*]
aardr .... Aardrykskunde [*Geography*] [*Afrikaans*]
AARDS ..... Australian Advertising Rate and Data Service　(WGAO)
AARE .... Australian Association for Religious Education
AARE .... Australian Association for Research in Education　(ADA)
AARF .... Australian Accounting Research Foundation　(ADA)
AARF .... Australian Advertising Research Foundation
AARF .... Australian Arthritis and Rheumatism Foundation
AARFA ...... Australian Association of Rural Fire Authorities
aarg .... Aargang [*Volume, Year*] [*Publishing Danish/Norwegian*]
aarh .... Aarhundrede [*Century*] [*Danish/Norwegian*]
AARL .... Anglo-American Research Laboratories [*Anglo-American Corp. of South Africa Ltd.*]　(EAS)
AARM .... Army Artillery Repair Shop　(RU)
AARMTO ... All Australian Register of Massage Therapists Organisation
AARN .... Association for Australian Rural Nurses
AARNet ..... Australian Academic and Research Network [*Computer science*]　(TNIG)
AARO .... Association of Americans Resident Overseas [*France*]　(EAIO)
AAROI ...... Associazione Anestesisti Rianimatori Ospedalieri Italiani [*Italian*]　(SLS)
AARP .... Asociacion Argentina de Relaciones Publicas [*Argentine Public Relations Association*]　(LA)
AARR .... Altezze Reali [*Royal Highnesses*] [*Italian*]
AARR .... Army Artillery Repair Workshop　(BU)
AARRO ..... Afro-Asian Rural Reconstruction Organization [*New Delhi, India*]
AARS .... Asian Association of Remote Sensing
AARS .... Automatic Ammonia Control Station　(RU)
AArt .... Associateship in Art [*Australia*]
AArtEd ...... Associateship in Art Education [*Australia*]
AARU .... Association of Arab Universities [*Amman, Jordan*]　(EAIO)
AAS .... Accredited Agents Scheme
AAS .... Adolph Basser Library Australian Academy of Science [*National Union Catalogue of Australia symbol*]
AAS .... Afghanistan Academy of Sciences　(EAIO)
AAS .... African Academy of Sciences
AAS .... Aircraft Arresting System
AAS .... Anotaton Agrotikon Symvoulion [*Supreme Agrarian Council*]　(GC)
AAS .... Asociacion Amigos del Suelo [*Argentina*]　(DSCA)
AAS .... Associated Asiatic Securities [*Singapore*]
AAS .... Association des Archivistes Suisses　(WGAO)
AAS .... Australian Academy of Science　(ADA)
AAS .... Australian Accounting Standard
AAS .... Australian Acoustical Society　(ADA)
AAS .... Australian Aerial Services　(ADA)
AAS .... Australian Aircraft Sales
AAS .... Australian Anthropological Society
AAS .... Australian Art Society　(ADA)
AAS .... Australian Assistance Scheme
AAS .... Australian Association of Surgeons　(ADA)
AAS .... Austrian Academy of Sciences　(EAIO)
AAS .... Austrian Air Services [*ICAO designator*]　(FAAC)
AAS .... Austrian Astronomical Society　(EAIO)
AAS .... Automobiel Assosiasie van Suid-Afrika [*Automobile Association of South Africa*]　(EAIO)

AASA .... Accademia degli Abruzzi per le Scienze e le Arti [*Italian*]　(SLS)
AASA .... Acupuncture Association of South Australia
AASA .... Ansett Airlines of South Australia
AASA .... Associacao Africana do Sul de Angola
AASA .... Associate of the Art of Speech, Australia
AASA .... Associate of the Australian Society of Accountants　(ADA)
AASA .... Association for the Advancement of Agricultural Sciences in Africa
AASA .... Association of Aerial Surveyors Australia
AASA .... Australian Association of Social Anthropologists　(WGAO)
AASAA ...... Australian Advertising Standards Advisory Authority　(ADA)
AASANA ... Administracion de Aeropuertos y Servicios Auxiliares a la Navegacion Aerea [*Administration for Airports and Auxiliary Air Navigational Services*] [*Bolivia*]　(IMH)
AASA(Snr) ... Senior Associate of the Australian Society of Accountants
AASB .... Australian Accounting Standards Board
AASC .... African-American Scholars Council, Inc.
AASC .... Allied Air Support Command [*Mediterranean*]
AASC .... Association of African Sports Confederations [*See also UCSA*] [*Yaounde, Cameroon*]　(EAIO)
AASC .... Association of Air Survey Companies [*South Africa*]　(EAIO)
AASC .... Australian Accounting Standards Committee　(ADA)
AASC .... Australian Administrative Staff College
AASC .... Australian Army Service Corps　(ADA)
AASCA ...... Australian Administrative Staff College Association
AASE .... African Association of Science Editors
AASE .... Australian Associated Stock Exchanges　(ADA)
AASE .... Australian Association of Special Education
AASF .... American-Australian Studies Foundation
AASF .... Asian Amateur Swimming Federation [*Dhaka, Bangladesh*]　(EAIO)
AASF .... Association des Architectes Sans Frontieres　(WGAO)
AASFA ...... Association d'Amitie et de Solidarite Franco-Algerienne [*Franco-Algerian Friendship and Solidarity Association*]
AASH .... Australian Association of Speech and Hearing　(ADA)
AASHFA ... Association des Amis du Service Historique Forces Armees　(WGAO)
AASI .... Association for the Advancement of Science in Israel　(EAIO)
A'ASIA ...... Australasia　(ADA)
A'ASIAN ... Australasian　(ADA)
AASLD ..... African Association for the Study of Liver Diseases　(EAIO)
AASM ...... Associated African States and Madagascar
AASM ...... Australasian Association of Secretaries and Managers
AASMB .... Australian Association of Stud Merino Breeders　(ADA)
AASMM ... Associated African States, Madagascar and Mauritius [*Later, Association of African, Caribean and Pacific States*]　(PDAA)
AASNS ...... Asian-Australasian Society of Neurological Surgeons [*Kowloon, Hong Kong*]　(EAIO)
AASoM ..... Association for the Advancement of Science of Malawi
AASP .... American Aid Society of Paris [*France*]　(EA)
AASP .... Andifasistiki Andiimperialistiki Spoudastiki Parataxi [*Antifascist, Anti-Imperialist Student Faction*] [*Greek*]　(GC)
AASP .... Argentine Association for the Study of Pain　(EAIO)
AASP .... Association Arabe de Science Politique [*Iraq*]　(WGAO)
AASP .... Association d'Agences Suisses de Publicite　(WGAO)
AASP .... Australasian Association for Suicide Prevention
AASPE ...... Andiimperialistiki Andifasistiki Spoudastiki Parataxi Ellados [*Anti-Imperialist, Antifascist Student Faction of Greece*] [*Greek*]　(GC)
AASPET .... Andiimperialistiki Andifasistiki Spoudastiki Parataxi Ergazomenon Tekhnikon [*Anti-Imperialist, Antifascist Student Faction of Working Technicians*] [*Greek*]　(GC)
AASQ .... Australian-Asian Society of Queensland
AASR .... Australian Association for the Study of Religion
AASREC ... Asian Association of Social Science Research Councils
AASS .... Association Africaine de la Science du Sol　(WGAO)
AASSC ...... Australasian Association for the Study of Socialist Countries　(ADA)
AASSR ...... Abkhaz Autonomous Soviet Socialist Republic　(RU)
AASSREC ... Association of Asian Social Science Research Councils [*New Delhi, India*]
AASTC ...... Associate in Architecture, Sydney Technical College [*Australia*]　(ADA)
AASU .... Afro-Asiatische Union
AASU .... All Africa Students Union [*See also UPE*]　(EAIO)
AASU .... Atomic Aircraft Engine, Atomic Aircraft Power Plant　(RU)
AASW .... Antarctic Surface Water [*Oceanography*]　(MSC)
AASW .... Australian Association of Scientific Workers　(ADA)
AASW .... Australian Association of Social Workers　(ADA)
AAT .... Administration et l'Assistance Technique [*des Nations Unies*] [*France*]　(FLAF)
AAT .... Agence Arabe de Travail
AAT .... Airports Authority of Thailand　(DS)
AAT .... Altay [*China*] [*Airport symbol*]　(OAG)

AAT	Anglo-Australian Telescope	
AAT	Arrete de l'Administrateur du Territoire	(FLAF)
AAT	Australian Accommodation and Tours	(ADA)
AAT	Australian Antarctic Territory	
AAT	Austrian Airtransport [*ICAO designator*]	(FAAC)
AAT	Austrian Air Transport Flugbetriebsgesellschaft mbH	(IMH)
AAT	Automobile Construction and Transportation	(RU)
AAT	United Nations Technical Assistance Administration	(BU)
AATA	Aboriginal Advancement Trust Account [*Australia*]	
AATA	African Association of Tax Administrators	(EAIO)
AATA	Arab Air Transport Association	
AATA	Association of African Tax Administrators	(WGAO)
AATA	Australian Animal Technicians' Association	(ADA)
AATAB	Agents' Association, Totalizator Agency Board, New South Wales	
AAT(ACT)	Administrative Appeals Tribunal (Australian Capital Territory)	
AATADE	Australian Association for Tertiary Art and Design Education	
AATB	Associated Air Travel Bureau	
AATC	Afro-Asian Travel Centre	
AATC	American African Trading Corporation [*Morocco*]	
AATC	Australian Academy of Tai Chi	
AATCA	Austrian Air Traffic Controllers Association	(WGAO)
AATD	Australian Association of Teachers of the Deaf	
AATDEC	Administrative Appeals Tribunal Decisions [*Database*] [*Australia*]	
AATE	Australian Association for the Teaching of English	(ADA)
AATEFL	Australian Association for the Teaching of English as a Foreign Language	(ADA)
AATEJ	Australian Association for Tertiary Education in Journalism	(ADA)
AATFS	Asian Association of Track and Field Statistics	(WGAO)
AATG	ActionAid The Gambia	
AATI	Association for the Advancement of Transplants in Israel	(EAIO)
AATI	Association of Argentine Textile Industrialists	(EAIO)
AATLH	Australian Association of Toy Libraries for the Handicapped	
AATMA	Australian Association of Taxation and Management Accountants	
AATMC	Austrian Automobile Touring and Motorcycle Club	(EAIO)
AATN	Asociacion Argentina de Tecnologia Nuclear [*Argentine Nuclear Technology Association*]	(LA)
AATNU	Administration de l'Assistance Technique des Nations Unies [*United Nations Technical Assistance Administration*]	
AATO	All Africa Teachers' Organization	(EAIO)
AATO	Australian Taxation Office - National Office [*National Union Catalogue of Australia symbol*]	
AATP	Arusha Appropriate Technology Project [*Tanzania*] [*Research center*]	(WGAO)
AATP	Asociacion de Agricultores de Te de Pastaza [*Ecuador*]	(DSCA)
AATPO	Association of African Trade Promotion Organizations [*Tangier, Morocco*]	(EAIO)
AATPS	Australian Association of Temporary Personnel Services	(ADA)
AATRAA	Association Argentina de Tecnicos de Refrigeracion y Acondicionamiento de Aire	(WGAO)
AATS	Australian Academy of Technological Sciences	(ADA)
AATSE	Australian Academy of Technological Sciences and Engineering	
AATT	Australian Army Training Team	
AATT	Australian Association for Theatre Technology	
AATTA	Arab Association of Tourism and Travel Agents	
AATTV	Australian Army Training Team, Vietnam	(VNW)
AATTVV	Australian Army Training Team, Vietnam	(VNW)
AATUF	All-African Trade Union Federation [*Later, OATUU*]	(AF)
AAT(Vic)	Administrative Appeals Tribunal (Victoria)	
AAU	Amateur Athletic Union	(OLYM)
AAU	Armenian Artistic Union	(SLS)
AAU	Association of African Universities	(EAIO)
AAU	Australia Asia Airlines Ltd. [*ICAO designator*]	(FAAC)
AAUA	Amateur Athletic Union of Australasia [*or Australia*]	(ADA)
AAUB	Antwoord as u Blief [*The Favor of an Answer Is Required*] [*Afrikaans*]	
AAUCS	Australian-Asian Universities Cooperation Scheme	(ADA)
AAUCTU	All-African Union of Christian Trade Unions	
AAUD	Australian [*National*] Audit [*Office*] [*National Union Catalogue of Australia symbol*]	
AAUN	Australian Association for the United Nations	(ADA)
AAUNE	Alumni Association of the University of New England [*Australia*]	
AAU of A	Amateur Athletic Union of Australasia [*or Australia*]	(ADA)
AAUOS	Australian-Asian Universities Cooperation Scheme	(WGAO)
AAUP	Association of Australian University Presses	
AAUP	Australian Aviation Underwriters' Pool	
AAUQ	Associate in Accountancy, University of Queensland [*Australia*]	
AAUTA	Australian Association of University Teachers of Accountancy	(WGAO)
AAUTA	Australian Association of University Teachers of Accounting	
AAV	Acupuncture Association of Victoria	
AAV	Adventist Alpine Village [*Australia*]	
AAV	Alah [*Philippines*] [*Airport symbol*]	(OAG)
AAV	Amputees' Association of Victoria [*Australia*]	
AAV	Asociacion Aurora Vivar [*Peru*]	(EAIO)
AAV	Autoalkatresz Kereskedelmi Vallalat [*Enterprise for Automobile Parts*]	(HU)
AAV	Nederlandse Vereniging van Algemene Aansprakelijkheids-Verzekeraars	(WGAO)
AAVA	Australian Automatic Vending Association	(ADA)
AAVA	Authority for Advanced Vocational Awards [*New Zealand*]	
AAVAC	Australian Association of Veterans' Athletic Clubs	
AAVC	Australian Army Veterinary Corps	(ADA)
AAVCA	Australian Affiliation of Voluntary Care Agencies	
AAVS	Aroha Adviasis Vikas Sangh [*India*]	(WGAO)
AAVTA	Australian Audio Video Tape Association	
AAVV	Autorite des Amenagements des Vallees des Voltas [*Volta Valleys Development Authority*] [*Burkina Faso*]	(GEA)
AAVYT	Asociacion Argentina de Agencias de Viajes y Turismo	(WGAO)
AAWB	Afro-Asian Writers Bureau	
AAWC	All-African Women's Conference [*or Congress*]	
AAWC	Australian Advisory War Council	(ADA)
AAWCH	Australian Association for the Welfare of Children in Hospital	
AAWE	Association of American Wives of Europeans [*France*]	(EAIO)
AAWHA	Australian Amateur Women's Hockey Association	
AAWL	Australia Asia Worker Links	
AAWM	Australian War Memorial [*National Union Catalogue of Australia symbol*]	
AAWORD	Association of African Women for Research and Development	(EAIO)
AAWPA	Australian Amateur Water Polo Association	
AAWPB	Afro-Asian Writers' Permanent Bureau	(NATG)
AAWR	Woomera [*Australia*] [*ICAO location identifier*]	(ICLI)
AAWSA	Addis Ababa Water and Sewerage Authority [*Ethiopia*]	(PDAA)
AAWU	Afro-Asian Writers Union	(WGAO)
AAWU	Australian Amateur Wrestling Union	
AAWWD	Australian Association of Welfare Workers with the Deaf	(ADA)
AAX	Araxa [*Brazil*] [*Airport symbol*]	(OAG)
AAY	Air Antares Ltd. [*Romania*] [*ICAO designator*]	(FAAC)
AAYe	Air Astronomical Almanac	(RU)
AAYSO	Afro-Asian Youth Solidarity Organization	(WGAO)
ab	Aan Boord [*On Board*] [*Afrikaans*]	
ab	Abad [*Abbot*] [*Spanish*]	
Ab	Abade [*Abbot*] [*Portuguese*]	
ab	Abandonne [*Relinquished*] [*French*]	
Ab	Abate [*Abbe*] [*Italian*]	
Ab	Abide [*Monument, Memorial*]	(TU)
ab	Abime [*Damaged, In Poor Condition*] [*French*]	
Ab	Abitanti [*Population*] [*Italian*]	
ab	Abonnement [*Subscription*] [*Publishing*] [*Netherlands*]	
AB	Aboriginal [*Australia*]	(DSUE)
ab	Absent [*Lacking, Missing*] [*French*]	
AB	Abyssinia	
Ab	Adalet Bakanligi [*Ministry of Justice*]	(TU)
Ab	Adatrechtbundel [*Benelux*]	(BAS)
AB	Address Bureau	(RU)
AB	Administratieve en Rechterlijke Beslissingen [*Benelux*]	(BAS)
AB	Advocatenblad [*Benelux*]	(BAS)
AB	Aero Talleres Boero SRL [*Argentina*] [*ICAO aircraft manufacturer identifier*]	(ICAO)
A/B	Afleweringsbrief [*Delivery of Letter*] [*Afrikaans*]	
AB	Afrikaner Broederbond [*Afrikaner Brothers League*] [*South Africa*]	(AF)
AB	Air Base	(RU)
AB	Air Berlin USA [*ICAO designator*]	(ICDA)
AB	Air Brigade	(RU)
AB	Ak Bank	(TU)
AB	Aktiebolag [*or Aktiebolaget*] [*Joint-Stock Company*] [*Sweden*]	
AB	Aktion Bildungsinformation eV	(SLS)
AB	Al Bawardi Overseas Agencies [*United Arab Emirates*] [*Commercial firm*]	
AB	Algemeen-Beskaaf(de) [*Standard Speech*] [*Afrikaans*]	
AB	Alimentos e Bebidas [*Brazil*]	(DSCA)
AB	Allami Biztosito [*State Insurance Company*]	(HU)
AB	Allan Border [*Australian cricket player*]	
AB	Alliance Balkanique [*Balkan Alliance*]	
A-B	American Film Co. - Biografia [*Former Czechoslovakia*]	
AB	Anadolu Bankasi [*Bank*] [*Turkey*]	
AB	Andesite Basalt	(RU)
AB	Angkatan Bersendjata [*Armed Forces*]	(IN)
ab+	Antibody Positive	
AB	Arbeitsbereich [*Work Report*] [*German*]	(ADPT)
AB	Arbitrale Beslissingen [*Benelux*]	(BAS)
AB	Armiska Baza [*Army Base*]	(YU)
AB	Artillery Brigade	(RU)
AB	Artium Baccalaureus [*Bachelor of Arts*]	
AB	Asfalt Betonu [*Asphalt Paved*]	(TU)

AB .... Asociacion Bancaria [*Bank Workers Association*] [*Argentina*] (LA)
AB .... Atlantik-Bruecke [*Atlantic Bridge*] [*An association*] [*Germany*] (EAIO)
AB .... Atom Bomb (RU)
aB .... Auf Bestellung [*On Order*] [*German*] (ILCA)
AB .... Augsburger Bekenntnis [*Augsburg Confession (1530)*] [*German*]
AB .... Ausfuehrungsbestimmungen [*Implementing Regulations*] [*German*] (EG)
AB .... Australian Ballet
AB .... Australian Blackfriars Priory (Canberra Catholic Library) [*National Union Catalogue of Australia symbol*]
AB .... L'Anglais Britannique [*British English*] [*Language, etc.*] [*French*]
AB .... Leaflet Bomb (RU)
AB .... Motor Transport Battalion, Truck Battalion (RU)
AB .... Nitrogen Balance (RU)
AB .... Parti des Abanyamajambere B'I [*Burundi*]
AB .... Reinforced Paper (RU)
AB .... Vereeniging der Antwerpsche Bibliophielen [*Belgium*] (WGAO)
AB .... Wet Houdende Algemene Bepalingen der Wetgeving van het Koninkrijk [*Benelux*] (BAS)
ABA .... AB Aerotransport [*Sweden*]
ABA .... African Bar Association (EAIO)
ABA .... African Builders Association [*South Africa*] (AA)
ABA .... African Business Association
ABA .... Air Book Australia (ADA)
ABA .... Aktiebolaget Aero Transport [*Swedish airline*]
ABA .... Aktiebolaget Atomenergi [*Swedish nuclear development company*]
ABA .... Alger-Bouzareah [*Algeria*] [*Seismograph station code, US Geological Survey*]
ABA .... Alien Business Act [*1979*] [*Thailand*] (IMH)
ABA .... Amateur Boxing Association of Kenya
ABA .... American, British, Australian [*Military*]
ABA .... Antiquarian Booksellers Association, International [*British*] (EAIO)
ABA .... Antoniani Benedictini Armeni [*Mechitarists*]
ABA .... Arab Bankers' Association
ABA .... Arbeitsgemeinschaft fuer Betriebliche Altersversorgung eV (SLS)
ABA .... ASEAN [*Association of South East Asian Nations*] Bankers Association [*Singapore, Singapore*] (EAIO)
ABA .... Asian Bureau of Australia (ADA)
ABA .... Asociacion Bioquimica Argentina [*Argentina*] (DSCA)
ABA .... Asociacion de Bibliotecarios Antioqueros [*Colombia*] (COL)
ABA .... Associacao Bahiana de Avicultura [*Brazil*] (DSCA)
ABA .... Associacao Brasileira de Antropologia (WGAO)
ABA .... Associated Banks Association [*Australia*]
ABA .... Association Belge des Aerosols (WGAO)
ABA .... Association Biblio-Techniques Australia [*National Union Catalogue of Australia symbol*]
ABA .... Association of Belgian Actuaries (EAIO)
ABA .... Australian Badminton Association (ADA)
ABA .... Australian Bankers' Association (ADA)
ABA .... Australian Barefoot Association
ABA .... Australian Bicentennial Authority
ABA .... Australian Biotechnology Association
ABA .... Australian Blue Asbestos
ABA .... Australian Booksellers Association (ADA)
ABA .... Australian Boomerang Association (ADA)
ABA .... Australian Borrowers' Association
ABA .... Australian Bowhunters Association (ADA)
ABA .... Australian Braille Authority
ABA .... Australian Bridge Association (ADA)
ABA .... Australian Broadcasting Authority
ABA .... Austrian Badminton Association (EAIO)
ABA .... Auxiliaire du Batiment Aveyia [*Manufacturer of plastic products*] [*Gabon*] (IMH)
a-ba--- ...... Bahrain [*MARC geographic area code*] [*Library of Congress*]
ABA .... Belgian-American Association (EAIO)
ABAA .... Australian Baldness and Alopecia Association
ABAA .... Australian Business Aircraft Association (EAIO)
ABACC ...... Alcoholic Beverages Advertising Code Council [*Australia*]
ABACO ...... Association Culturelle des Ressortiments du Bas Congo
ABACUS ... Association of Bibliographic Agencies of Britain, Australia, Canada, and the United States (ADA)
ABADCAM ... Association des Bibliothecaires, Archivistes, Documentalistes et Museographers du Cameroun (WGAO)
ABAF .... Brisbane/Archerfield [*Australia*] [*ICAO location identifier*] (ICLI)
ABAH .... Asociacion de Bibliotecarios y Archiveros de Honduras [*Honduras*] (SLS)
ABAH .... Australian Bureau of Animal Health
ABAJP ...... Association Belge des Architectes de Jardins Publics (WGAO)
ABAKO ..... Alliance des Bakongo [*Alliance of the Bakongo People*]

ABAKWA ... Alliance de Baboma-Bateke du Kwamouth [*Alliance of Baboma-Bateke People of Kwamouth*]
ABAM .... Amberley [*Australia*] [*ICAO location identifier*] (ICLI)
ABAM .... Association Belge des Assureurs Maritimes (WGAO)
ABAN .... Algemene Bond van Autorijsschoolhounders in Nederland (WGAO)
ABAN .... Amateur Badminton Association of Nigeria (EAIO)
AB & E .... Attempt Break and Enter [*Criminology*]
AB & RI ..... Animal Breeding and Research Institute [*Western Australia*]
AB &WAC ... Australian Black and White Artists' Club
ABANSW ... Amateur Beekeepers' Association of New South Wales [*Australia*]
ABANZ ..... Associated Booksellers of Australia and New Zealand (ADA)
ABAO .... Arbeitsschutz- und Brandschutzanordnung [*Ordinance Regarding Industrial Accident Prevention and Fire Protection*] (EG)
ABAP .... Associacao Brasileira de Agencias de Propaganda [*Brazilian Association of Advertising Agencies*] (LA)
ABAPE ...... Associacao Brasileira de Administracao de Pessoal (WGAO)
ABAPRA ... Asociacion de Bancos de Provincia de la Repiblica Argentina (WGAO)
ABARE ...... Australian Bureau of Agricultural and Resource Economics [*National Union Catalogue of Australia symbol*]
ABARE ...... Australian Bureau of Agricultural and Resource Economics
ABAS .... Alice Springs [*Australia*] [*ICAO location identifier*] (ICLI)
ABAS .... Ameateur Basketball Association of Scotland (WGAO)
ABAS .... Australian Buying Advisory Service Proprietary Ltd. (ADA)
Abat .... Abattoir [*Slaughterhouse*] [*Military map abbreviation World War I*] [*French*] (MTD)
ABATA ...... Able-Bodied Seaman, Air Technical Aircraft [*Navy*]
ABATC ...... Able-Bodied Seaman, Air Technical Communications [*Navy*]
ABATE ...... Alliance des Bateke [*Alliance of Bateke*]
A Batt .... A Battuta [*Music*]
ABATWL .. Able-Bodied Seaman, Air Technical Weapons Electrical [*Navy*]
ABAU .... Asociacion Bibliotecologos y Afines del Uruguay [*Uruguay*] (SLS)
ABAV .... Australian Biathlon Association Victoria
ABAVIA ... Agencias Barranquilleras de Viajes [*Barranquilla*] (COL)
ABAYA ..... Abutia-Teti Abeka Youth Association
ABAZ .... Amateur Boxing Association of Zambia
ABAZI .... Alliance des Bayanzi [*Alliance of Bayanzis*]
Abb .... Abbassamento [*Music*]
Abb .... Abbildung [*Illustration*] [*German*] (GPO)
Abb .... Abbildungen [*Illustration, figure*] [*German*] (BJA)
abb .... Abbonamento [*Subscription*] [*Italian*]
ABB .... Air Belgium [*ICAO designator*] (FAAC)
ABB .... Allgemeine Bedingungen der Volkseigenen Bauindustrie [*General Terms of the State Construction Industry*] [*German*] (EG)
ABB .... Arab-Burundi Bank SARL (EY)
ABB .... Arbeitsgemeinschaft fuer Blitzschutz und Blitzableiterbau (SLS)
ABB .... Armiska Bolnicka Baza [*Army Hospital Base*] (YU)
ABB .... Army Hospital Base (BU)
ABB .... ASEA [*Allmaenna Svenska Elektriska Aktiebolaget*]-Brown Boveri [*Swedish-Swiss manufacturing company*] [*Commercial firm*] (ECON)
ABB .... Asociacion Boliviana de Bibliotecarios (WGAO)
ABB .... Association of Belge des Banques (WGAO)
ABB .... Australian Barley Board (ADA)
ABB .... Australian Bowls Board
ABBA .... Able-Bodied Sick Bay Attendant [*Navy*]
ABBA .... Agnetha Faltskog, Bjorn Ulvaeus, Benny Andersson, Anni-Frid Lyngstad [*Swedish singing group; acronym formed from first letters of their first names*]
ABBA .... Arbejdsloshedsstatistikkens Bruger-Bank [*Danmarks Statistik*] [*Denmark*] [*Information service or system*] (CRD)
ABBA .... Asociacion de Bibliotecas Biomedicas Argentinas (WGAO)
ABBA .... Australian Bloodhorse Breeders Association
ABBA .... Australian Brahman Breeders Association (ADA)
ABBB .... Brisbane [*Australia*] [*ICAO location identifier*] (ICLI)
Abbe .... Abbaye [*Abbey*] [*Military map abbreviation World War I*] [*French*] (MTD)
ABBE .... Australian Business and Businessmen in Europe
Abbild .... Abbildung [*Illustration*] [*Publishing*] [*German*]
Abbildgn .... Abbildungen [*Illustrations*] [*Publishing*] [*German*]
ABBL .... Association des Banques et Banquiers du Luxembourg [*Benelux*] (BAS)
ABBN .... Brisbane [*Australia*] [*ICAO location identifier*] (ICLI)
abbon .... Abbonamento [*Subscription*] [*Publishing*] [*Italian*]
abbonam ..... Abbonamento [*Subscription*] [*Publishing*] [*Italian*]
abbr .... Abbreviation (TPFD)
Abbr .... Abbreviatur [*Abbreviation*] [*German*]
Abbr .... Abbreviazione [*Abbreviation*] [*Italian*]
abbr .... Abreviation [*French*] (TPFD)
ABBR .... Brisbane [*Australia*] [*ICAO location identifier*] (ICLI)
ABBS .... Antigua and Barbuda Broadcasting Service (EY)
ABBS .... Australian Bibliography and Bibliographical Services

ABBS .... Australian Bird Banding Scheme
ABBU .... Bundaberg [Australia] [ICAO location identifier]   (ICLI)
ABBX........ Brisbane [Australia] [ICAO location identifier]   (ICLI)
ABC .... ABC Aruhaz [ABC Department Store Chain]   (HU)
ABC .... ABC World Airways Guide [ICAO designator]   (FAAC)
ABC .... Abeche [Chad] [Seismograph station code, US Geological Survey] [Closed]
ABC .... Academia Brasileira de Ciencias [Brazil]   (MCD)
ABC .... Acero Beton Centrifugado [Colombia]   (COL)
ABC .... Adelaide Brighton Cement [Australia]
ABC .... Administracion de Bienestar Campesino [Farm Welfare Administration] [El Salvador]   (LAA)
ABC .... Afghan Border Crusade [Missionary association]
ABC .... Africa Bible College [Liberia]
ABC .... Africa Bibliographic Centre
ABC .... African Brotherhood Church
ABC .... Air Business Contact [France] [ICAO designator]   (FAAC)
ABC .... Alberto Betancourt & Compania, SA [Venezuela]
ABC .... Alcobaca [Brazil] [Airport symbol]   (OAG)
ABC .... Algemene Bedrijfsgroepen Centrale [General Union of Workers in Miscellaneous Industries] [Netherlands]
ABC .... Algemene Begrotings Commissie [Benelux]   (BAS)
ABC .... Alliance Biblique du Cameroun
ABC .... American Board of Commissioners for Foreign Missions
ABC .... American Business Council of Malaysia   (EAIO)
ABC .... American Business Council of Singapore   (EAIO)
ABC .... Amities Belgo-Congolaises [Belgian-Congolese Friendship Association]
ABC .... Anti-Bases Coalition [Philippines]   (EAIO)
ABC .... Anwendungs-und Bedienungsorientiertes Computersystem [A Computer System Oriented to Process and Use] [German]   (ADPT)
ABC .... Arab Banking Corporation
ABC .... Argentina, Brasil, e Chile [Argentina, Brazil, and Chile] [Portuguese]
ABC .... Argentina, Brazil, Chile
ABC .... Arme Blindee et Cavalerie [Armored Corps and Cavalry] [French]   (WER)
ABC .... Aruba, Bonaire, and Curacao [Islands]
ABC .... Asian Badminton Confederation   (WGAO)
ABC .... Asian Basketball Confederation   (EA)
ABC .... Asian Broadcasting Conference   (NTCM)
ABC .... Asociacion Bancaria de Colombia [Colombian Banking Association]   (LA)
ABC .... Associacao Brasileira de Criadores   (WGAO)
ABC .... Associacion de Bibliotecarios de Catalunya   (WGAO)
ABC .... Association Belgique-Chine [Belgian-Chinese Association]   (WER)
ABC .... Association of Black Collegians
ABC .... Audit Bureau of Circulation
ABC .... Australia Bulk Carrier [Shipping]
ABC .... Australian Band Council   (ADA)
ABC .... Australian Bank of Commerce
ABC .... Australian Baseball Council   (ADA)
ABC .... Australian Bird Count
ABC .... Australian Bowling Council   (ADA)
ABC .... Australian Boys' Choir
ABC .... Australian Breeding Center
ABC .... Australian Bridge Council   (ADA)
ABC .... Australian Broadcasting Commission   (ADA)
ABC .... Australian Broadcasting Corporation   (EY)
ABC .... Australian Bullion Company Proprietary Ltd.   (ADA)
ABC .... Caetano Do Sul [Santo] [Sao Sao Used in reference to industrial sections of these Brazilian cities]   (LA)
ABC .... Societe Antoine Bachour & Compagnie
ABCA .... America, Britain, Canada, Australia   (ADA)
ABCA .... Association Belge des Chefs d'Approvisionnement et Acheteurs   (WGAO)
ABCA .... Association des Banques Centrales Africaines [Association of African Central Banks]   (EAIO)
ABCA .... Australian Brangus Cattle Association
ABCA .... Australian Bus and Coach Association
ABCA .... Australian Bushmen's Carnival Association   (ADA)
ABCA .... Australian Business Communications Association
ABCACT ... Association of Baptist Churches of the Australian Capital Territory
ABC &PCA ... Abrasive Blast Cleaning and Protective Coating Association of New South Wales [Australia]
ABCAR...... Asociacion Brasilena de Credito y Asistensia Rural   (WGAO)
ABCAR...... Associacao Brasileira de Credito e Assistencia Rural [Brazilian Association of Credit and Rural Assistance] [Rio De Janeiro]   (LA)
ABCB........ Australian Broadcasting Control Board   (ADA)
ABCC........ Arab British Chamber of Commerce   (DCTA)
ABCC........ Australia-Brazil Chamber of Commerce
ABCC........ Australian-British Chamber of Commerce

ABCCC...... Associacao Brasileira de Criadores de Cavalos Crioulos [Brazil]   (DSCA)
ABCCC...... Associacao Brasileira dos Criadores de Cavalo Campolina [Brazil]   (DSCA)
ABCCE...... Association Belge pour le Conseil des Communes d'Europe [Belgium]   (BAS)
ABCCI....... Antigua and Barbuda Chamber of Commerce and Industry   (EAIO)
ABCCRM ... Associacao Brasileira de Criadores de Cavalos da Raca Mangalarga [Brazil]   (DSCA)
ABCCT...... Associacao Brasileira dos Criadores de Cavalo de Trote [Brazil]   (DSCA)
ABCD .... America, Britain, China, and Dutch East Indies [The ABCD Powers] [World War II]
ABCD .... Associacao Brasileira de Criadores de Devon [Brazil]   (DSCA)
ABCD .... Associacao Brasileira dos Colecionadores de Discos [Record label] [Brazil]
ABCD .... Association Belge de la Chaussure au Detail   (WGAO)
ABCD .... Australian Building Cost Database
ABCD .... Forbundet for Art, Bild, Copy och Design   (WGAO)
ABCD .... Santo Andre, Sao Bernardo Do Campos, Sao Caetano, and Diadema [Industrial cities of Greater Sao Paulo, Brazil]
ABCDEF ... Allein bei Christo die Ewige Freude [With Christ Alone Is Eternal Joy] [Motto of Albrecht Gunther, Count Schwarzburg (1582-1634)] [German]
ABCE........ Ann Baker College of English [Australia]
ABCE........ Associacao Brasileira de Consultores de Engenharia [Brazilian Association of Consulting Engineers]   (EAIO)
ABCEM..... Associacao Brasileira de Constructores de Estructuras Metalicas [Brazilian Association of Metal Structure Manufacturers]   (LA)
ABCFM..... American Board of Commissioners for Foreign Missions [Later, UCBWM]
ABCG .... Coolangatta [Australia] [ICAO location identifier]   (ICLI)
ABCHP .... Associacao Brasileira de Criadores de Hereford e Polled-Hereford [Brazil]   (DSCA)
ABCI......... Amis Belges de la Cooperation Internationale
ABCI......... Associacao Brasileira de Criadores de Ideal [Brazil]   (DSCA)
ABCI......... Australian Bureau of Criminal Intelligence
ABCK........ Able-Bodied Seaman Cook [Navy]
ABCMA .... Associacao Brasileira de Criadores de Merino Australiano [Brazil]   (DSCA)
ABCNSW ... Association of Blind Citizens of New South Wales [Australia]
ABCOOP .. Alianca Brasileira de Cooperativas [Brazil]   (DSCA)
ABCOS .... Australian Breeders Co-Operative Society Ltd.
ABCOX .... Able-bodied Seaman Coxswain [Navy]
ABCP........ Asian Buddhists Conference for Peace [Mongolia]   (EAIO)
ABCP........ Associacao Technica Brasileira de Celulose e Papel [Brazilian Technical Association for Pulp and Paper]   (PDAA)
ABCRM..... Associacao Brasileira de Criadores de Romney Marsh [Brazil]   (DSCA)
ABCS........ Associacao Brasileira de Criadores de Suinos [Brazil]   (DSCA)
ABCS........ Australian Birth Control Services
ABCS........ Automatic Broadcasting Control System [Japan]
ABCS........ Cairns [Australia] [ICAO location identifier]   (ICLI)
ABCSA ..... Australian Broadcasting Commission Staff Association   (ADA)
ABCSOA... Australian Broadcasting Corporation Senior Executives' Association
ABCSPC.... Associacao Brasileira dos Criadores de Schorthorns e Polled Schorthorn [Brazil]   (DSCA)
ABCT........ Association Belgo-Congolaise du Textile [Belgo-Congolese Textile Association] [Zaire]
ABCT........ Association Belgo-Zairoise du Textile   (WGAO)
ABCTHM ... Anton Breini Center for Tropical Health and Medicine [James Cook University] [Australia]
ABCV........ Artificial Breeding Center, Victoria [Australia]
ABCV........ Charleville [Australia] [ICAO location identifier]   (ICLI)
ABCZ........ Associacao Brasileira dos Criadores de Zebu [Brazil]   (DSCA)
ABD.......... Abadan [Iran] [Airport symbol]   (OAG)
ABD.......... Alien Business Decree [Enacted in 1972] [Thailand]   (IMH)
ABD.......... Amerika Birlesik Devletleri [United States of America]   (TU)
ABD.......... Association Belge de Documentation
ABD.......... Association Belge des Detectives   (WGAO)
ABD.......... Association Belge des Dieteticiens [Belgian Association of Dieticians]   (EAIO)
ABD.......... Association Belge du Diabete [Belgium]   (SLS)
ABD.......... Atlanta [Iceland] [ICAO designator]   (FAAC)
ABDA .... Alcohol-Related Brain Damage Association [Australia]
ABDA .... American, British, Dutch, Australian   (ADA)
ABDA .... Arbeitsgemeinschaft der Berufsvertretungen Deutscher Apotheker [Information retrieval]
ABDA .... Bundesvereinigung Deutscher Apothekerverbande [German Pharmaceutical Association Research Institute] [Information service or system]   (IID)
ABDACOM ... American-British-Dutch-Australian Supreme Command [1942]

ABDAFLOAT ... American-British-Dutch-Australian Naval Operational Command [*1942*]
ABDAIR.... American-British-Dutch-Australian Air Operational Command [*1942*]
ABDARM ... American-British-Dutch-Australian Army Operational Command [*1942*]
ABDE .... Anfang Bedenk das Ende [*At the Beginning Consider the End*] [*Motto of Bruno II, Count of Mansfeld (1545-1615)*] [*German*]
ABDE .... Association Belge pour le Droit Europeen [*Belgium*]   (BAS)
ABDEN ..... Able-Bodied Seaman Dental, NV
abdest........ Abdestillieren [*To Distill Off*] [*German*]   (GCA)
ABDI .... Asociacao Brasileira de Desenho Industrial   (WGAO)
ABDIB....... Associacao Brasileira para o Desenvolvimento das Industrias de Base [*Brazilian Association for the Development of Basic Industries*]   (LA)
ABDOSD .. Arbeitsgemeinschaft der Bibliotheken und Dokumentationsstellen der Osteuropa-, Sudosteuropa-, und DDR-Forschung   (WGAO)
ABDOSD .. Arbeitsgemeinschaft der Bibliotheken und Dokumentationsstellen der Osteuropa-, Sudosteuropa und DDR-Forschung [*Association of Libraries and Documentation Centres for the Study of Eastern Europe, South-Eastern Europe and the German Democratic Republic*]   (PDAA)
Abdr .... Abdruck [*Copy*] [*Publishing*] [*German*]
ABDR .... Association Belge de Droit Rural [*Belgium*]   (SLS)
Abd Rk....... Abderhaldensche Reaktion [*Abderhalden's Reaction*] [*German*]   (GCA)
Abds.......... Abends [*After Noon*] [*German*]
Abe............. Abade [*Abbot*] [*Portuguese*]
ABE .... Action for Better Education
ABE .... Asociacao Brasileira de Exportadores   (WGAO)
ABE .... Associacao Brasileira de Educacao [*Brazil*]   (DSCA)
ABE .... Associacao Brasileira de Exportadores [*Brazil*]   (DSCA)
ABE .... Association Belge de l'Eclairage [*Belgium*]   (SLS)
ABE .... Australian Bicentennial Exhibition
ABE .... Australian Business Economists
ABEAS ...... Associacao Brasileira de Educacao Agricola Superior [*Brazil*]   (DSCA)
ABEAS ...... Association Belge des Enterprises d'Alimentation a Succursales   (WGAO)
ABEAS ...... Association Belge des Entreprises d'Alimentation a Succursales [*Belgium*]   (EY)
ABEAS ...... Association Belge des Entreprises de Distribution [*Belgium*]   (BAS)
ABEBD...... Asociacao Brasileira de Escolas de Biblioteconomia e Documentacao   (WGAO)
ABEC........ Associacion Boliviana de Educacion Catolica   (WGAO)
ABEC........ Australian Business Education Council Ltd.
ABECAFE ... Asociacion Salvadorena de Beneficiadores y Exportadores de Cafe [*Salvadoran Association of Coffee Processors and Exporters*]   (LA)
ABECIP..... Associacao Brasileira das Empresas de Creditos Imobiliarios e Poupancas [*Brazilian Association of Building Savings and Loan Companies*]   (LA)
ABECOL... Association of Bulgarian Ecologists   (EE)
ABECOR... [*The*] Associated Banks of Europe Corp.   (IID)
ABEDA...... Arab Bank for Economic Development in Africa   (ME)
ABEDIA.... Arab Bank for Economic Development in Africa
ABEF........ Association des Bibliotheques Ecclesiastiques de France [*French*]   (SLS)
ABEF........ Brisbane [*Australia*] [*ICAO location identifier*]   (ICLI)
ABEGS...... Arab Bureau of Education for the Gulf States   (WGAO)
ABELF...... Association Belge des Editeurs de Langue Francaise   (WGAO)
ABEM .... Association Belge pour l'Etude l'Essais et l'Emploi des Materiaux [*Belgian Association for the Study, Testing and Use of Materials*]   (PDAA)
ABEO .... Altalanos Balesetelharito es Egeszsegvedo Ovorendszabaly [*General Safety Rules for Prevention of Accidents and Health Protection*]   (HU)
ABEPAS.... Association Belge des Entreprises de Produits Alimentaires Surgeles   (WGAO)
ABERT ...... Associacao Brasileira de Emissoras de Radio e Televisao   (WGAO)
ABERT ...... Associacao Brasileira de Empresas de Radio e Televisao [*Brazilian Association of Radio and Television Companies*]   (LA)
ABES .... Asociacion de Bibliotecarios de El Salvador   (WGAO)
ABES .... Associacao Brasileira de Engenharia Sanitaria e Ambiental [*Brazil*]   (SLS)
ABESH...... Antarjatik Beshamarik Sheba Sangstha [*Bangladesh*] [*An association*]   (EAIO)
abess .... Abessiivi [*Finland*]
ABETA...... Associacao Brasileira de Estudos Tecnicos de Agricultura [*Brazil*]   (DSCA)

ABETC ...... Able-Bodied Seaman Electronic Technical Communications [*Navy*]
ABETEX ... Association des Bureaux d'Etudes Travaillant a l'Exportation
ABETP ...... Able-Bodied Seaman Electrical Technical Power [*Navy*]
ABETW..... Able-Bodied Seaman Electrical Technical Weapons [*Navy*]
ABEU .... Australian Bank Employees Union   (ADA)
ABEW .... Able-Bodied Seaman Electronic Warfare [*Navy*]
ABEX .... Association Belge des Experts [*Belgium*]   (BAS)
ABF........... Abaiang [*Kiribati*] [*Airport symbol*]   (OAG)
Abf .... Abfahrt [*Departure*] [*German*]   (EG)
ABF........... Actors' Benevolent Fund [*Australia*]
ABF........... African Badminton Federation
ABF........... Arbeiter- und Bauernfakultaet [*Worker and Peasant School*]   (EG)
ABF........... Arbetarnas Bildningsforbund [*Workers' Educational Association*] [*Sweden*]   (WEN)
ABF........... Asian Baptist Federation [*Philippines*]   (EAIO)
ABF........... Association des Bibliothecaires Francais
ABF........... Australian Ballet Foundation
ABF........... Australian Baseball Federation
ABF........... Australian Basketball Federation
ABF........... Australian Bobsleigh Federation
ABF........... Australian Bowling Federation
ABF........... Australian Boxing Federation   (ADA)
ABF........... Australian Bridge Federation
ABF........... Belgian Flight Centre [*ICAO designator*]   (FAAC)
ABF........... Den Danske Antikvarboghandlerforening   (WGAO)
ABFA........ Australian Business Forms Association
ABFAB..... Absolutely Fabulous   (DSUE)
ABFAB...... Amateur Boxing Federation of Antigua-Barbuda   (EAIO)
ABFACD... Association Belge des Fabricants d'Appareils de Chauffage et de Cuisine Domestiques   (WGAO)
ABFC......... Able-Bodied Seaman Fire Control [*Navy*]
ABFCFC.... Association Belge des Filateurs de Coton et de Fibres Connexes   (WGAO)
ABFF .... Able-Bodied Seaman Firefighter [*Navy*]
ABFM....... American Board of Foreign Missions
ABFM....... Australian Baptist Foreign Mission   (ADA)
ABFMS...... American Baptist Foreign Missionary Society
ABFSU...... All-Burma Federation of Student Unions
Abfuhr........ Abfuerhrung [*Discharge*] [*German*]   (GCA)
Abg............ Abgeordnete [*or Abgeordneter*] [*Deputy*] [*German*]   (EG)
Abg............ Abgeordneter [*Member of Parliament*] [*German*]   (BARN)
ABG .... Abingdon [*Australia*] [*Airport symbol*]   (OAG)
ABG .... Alibag [*India*] [*Geomagnetic observatory code*]
ABG .... Associazione Italiana fra gli Industriali delle Acque e Bevande Gassate   (WGAO)
ABG .... Australian Bartenders' Guild
a-bg--- .... Bangladesh [*MARC geographic area code*] [*Library of Congress*]
ABGA .... Australian Blueberry Growers Association
ABGB .... Allgemeines Buergerliches Gesetzbuch [*Austrian Civil Code*]   (DLA)
ABGC .... Australian Banana Growers' Council
Abgedr .... Abgedruckt [*Printed, Reprinted*] [*German*]
abgen.......... Abgenutzt [*Worn*] [*German*]
Abges .... Abasha Hydroelectric Power Plant   (RU)
abgeschn...... Abgeschnitten [*Cut Away*] [*German*]
abgew.......... Abgewetzt [*Chafed*] [*German*]
ABGFRAL ... Associacao dos Abatedores de Gado e Frigorificos do Brasil Central [*Brazil*]   (DSCA)
Abgiz.......... Abkhaz State Publishing House   (RU)
ABGK........ Abgekuerzt [*Abbreviated*] [*German*]
ABGL........ Gladstone [*Australia*] [*ICAO location identifier*]   (ICLI)
ABGR .... American Businessmen's Group of Riyadh [*Saudi Arabia*]   (EAIO)
ABGRA ..... Asociacion de Bibliotecarios Graduados de la Republica Argentina [*Argentina*]   (SLS)
Abg z NR ... Abgeordneter zum Nationalrat [*Assembly Representative*] [*Switzerland*]
abh............. Abhaengig [*Dependent*] [*German*]
ABH........... Abhandlungen [*Transactions*] [*German*] [*Business term*]
ABH........... Alpha [*Australia*] [*Airport symbol*]   (OAG)
ABH........... Association Belge des Hopitaux   (WGAO)
ABH........... Atomsko-Biolosko-Hemisko (Oruzje, Ratovanje) [*Chemical, Biological, and Radiological (Weapons, Warfare)*]   (YU)
ABH........... Societe Air Bretagne Service [*France*] [*ICAO designator*]   (FAAC)
Abhangigk ... Abhaengigkeit [*Dependence*] [*German*]   (GCA)
ABHM....... Hamilton Island [*Australia*] [*ICAO location identifier*]   (ICLI)
ABHR .... Australian Book Heritage Resources Project
ABI .... Abidjan Industrie
ABI .... Agrobiological Institute of the Bulgarian Academy of Sciences   (BU)
ABI .... Akademickie Biuro Interwencji   (WGAO)
ABI .... Amalgamated Beverage Industries [*South Africa*]
ABI .... American-British Intelligence [*NATO*]   (NATG)

ABI .... Antigua and Barbuda Airways International Ltd. [*ICAO designator*] (FAAC)

ABI .... Arbeiter- und Bauerninspektion [*Worker and Peasant Inspectorate*] (EG)

ABI .... Arnold Bergsatraesser Institut fur Kulturwissenschaftliche Forschung (WGAO)

ABI .... Arnold-Bergstraesser-Institut fuer Kulturwissenschaftliche Forschung

ABI .... Asociacion de Bienestar Infantil [*Child Welfare Association*] [*Guatemala*] (LA)

ABI .... Associacao Brasileira de Imprensa [*Brazilian Press Association*]

ABI .... Associacao Brasileira de Imprensa (WGAO)

ABI .... Association des Bibliotheques Internationales (WGAO)

ABI .... Associazione Bancaria Italiana [*Italian Bankers' Association*] (WER)

ABI .... Associazione Bibliotecari Italiani [*Association of Italian Librarians*]

ABI .... Australian Building Industries Proprietary Ltd.

ABI .... Australian Business Incentive

ABIA .... Associacao Brasileira das Industrias da Alimentacao [*Brazil*] (DSCA)

ABIA .... Associate of the Bankers' Institute of Australasia (ADA)

ABIA .... Australian Boating Industry Association

ABIA .... Brazilian Interdisciplinary AIDS Association (EAIO)

ABIC .... Association Belge de l'Industrie du Caoutchouc (WGAO)

ABIC .... Association Belge d'Ingenieurs-Conseils et Experts (WGAO)

ABICIT ...... Association Belge dIngenieurs-Conseils diplomes Ingenieurs Techniciens (WGAO)

ABICO .... Arab-Brazilian Investment Company (LA)

ABICTIC ... Association Belge des Ingenieurs, des Chimistes et des Techniciens des Industries du Cuir (WGAO)

ABIE .... Australian Business in Europe

ABIEAS ..... Asociacion Boliviana de Instituciones de Educacion Agricola Superior [*Bolivia*] (DSCA)

ABIESI ...... Asociacion de Bibliotecarios de Instituciones de Ensenanza Superior e Investigacion [*Mexico*] (SLS)

ABIF .... Associacao Brasileira da Industria Farmaceutica [*Brazilian Pharmaceutical Industry Association*] (LA)

Abifarma .... Associacao Brasileira das Industrias Farmaceuticas (WGAO)

ABIFARMA ... Associacao Brasileira de Industria Farmaceutica [*Brazilian Association of the Pharmaceutical Industry*] (PDAA)

ABIFFA ..... Associacao Brasileira das Industrias de Fundicao de Ferro e Aco [*Brazilian Association of Iron and Steel Smelting Industries*] (LA)

ABIFT .... Arab Bank for Investment and Foreign Trade

ABIISE ...... Agrupacion de Bibliotecas para la Integracion de la Informacion Socio-Economica [*Peru*] (SLS)

ABIK .... Angkatan Belia Ibukota [*Capital City Youth Forces*] (ML)

ABIL .... Al-Baraka Investment Ltd. [*Bahrain*]

abim .... Abime [*Damaged, In Poor Condition*] [*French*]

ABIM .... Malaysian Youth Movement

ABIMAQ ... Associacao Brasileira da Industria de Maquinas [*Brazilian Association of Machine Industries*] (LA)

ABINEE .... Associacao Brasileira da Industria Electro-Electronica [*Brazilian Electro-Electronic Industry Association*] (LA)

ABIPAR .... Asociacion de Bibliotecarios del Paraguay (WGAO)

ABIPLAST ... Associacao Brasileira da Industria do Plastico [*Brazil*]

ABIQUIM ... Associacao Brasileira da Industria Quimica e de Produtos Derivados [*Brazilian Association of the Chemical and Byproducts Industry*] (LA)

ABIR .... Associacao Brasileira de Informacao Rural [*Brazil*] (DSCA)

ABIRA ...... Asociacion de Bancos del Interior de la Republica Argentina [*Association of Banks of the Interior of the Argentine Republic*] [*Buenos Aires*] (LA)

ABIS .... Anglo-Brazilian Information Service [*Information service or system*] (IID)

ABIS .... Australian Biogeographic Information System

ABIS .... Australian Biotaxonomic Information System

ABIS .... Australian Building Industry Specifications (ADA)

Abit .... Abitur [*School Exit Examination*] [*German*]

ABITA .... Association Belge des Ingenieurs et Techniciens de l'Aeronautique et de l'Astronautique [*Belgian Association of Aeronautical and Astronautical Engineers and Technicians*] (PDAA)

ABJ .... Abashiri [*Japan*] [*Seismograph station code, US Geological Survey*]

ABJ .... Abidjan [*Ivory Coast*] [*Airport symbol*] (OAG)

ABJ .... Association of Brewers of Japan (WGAO)

ABJ .... International Businessmen of Jeddah [*Saudi Arabia*] (EAIO)

ABJA .... Association Belge des Journalistes Agricoles (WGAO)

ABJD .... Association Belge des Juristes Democratiques [*Belgian Association of Democratic Lawyers*] (WER)

ABJPAA .... Association Belge des Journalistes Professionnels de l'Aeronautique et de l'Astronautique (WGAO)

ABJS .... Australian Babji Joga Sangam [*An association*]

ABK .... Abisko [*Sweden*] [*Seismograph station code, US Geological Survey*] [*Closed*]

Abk .... Abkuerzung [*Abbreviation*] [*German*] (GPO)

Abk .... Abkurzung [*Abbreviation*] [*German*] (BARN)

ABK .... Acidophilic Broth Culture (RU)

ABK .... Aerzteberatungs-Kommission [*Medical Advisory Commission*] (WEN)

ABK .... Akademie der Bildenden Kuenste

ABK .... Albatros Airline, Inc. [*Turkey*] [*ICAO designator*] (FAAC)

ABK .... Kabri Dar [*Ethiopia*] [*Airport symbol*] (OAG)

abkh .... Abkhazian (RU)

abkhaz .... Abkhazian (RU)

ABKhZ ...... Atomic, Bacteriological, and Chemical Defense (RU)

ABKO .... Societe Abou Saleh Khochen & Cie.

ABKT .... Associated Birdkeepers and Traders [*Australia*]

Abkuhl .... Abkuehlung [*Refrigeration*] [*German*] (GCA)

abl .... Ablatief [*Ablative*] [*Afrikaans*]

abl .... Ablatiivi [*Finland*]

abl .... Abril [*April*] [*Spanish*]

ABL .... Academia Brasileira de Letras [*Brazilian Academy of Letters*]

ABL .... Accra Brewery Limited

ABl .... Advocatenblad [*Benelux*] (BAS)

ABL .... Amtsblatt [*Official Gazette*] [*German*] (DLA)

ABL .... Applied Bioresearch Laboratories [*Netherlands*]

ABl .... Arbeidsblad [*Benelux*] (BAS)

ABL .... Archives of Business and Labour [*Australian National University*]

ABL .... Association Belge des Logopedes [*Belgium*] (SLS)

ABL .... Association des Banques du Liban [*Association of Banks in Lebanon*] (EAIO)

ABL .... Australian Bank Ltd.

ABL .... Australian Baseball League

ABLA .... Association Belge de Linguistique Appliquee (WGAO)

Ablager ...... Ablagerung [*Sedimentation*] [*German*] (GCA)

Ableit .... Ableitung [*Derivation*] [*German*] (GCA)

ABLFUW .. Australian Builders' Laborers Federated Union of Workers

ABLGPL ... Association Belgo-Luxembourgeoise des Gaz de Petrole Liquefies (WGAO)

ABLK .... Laverack Barracks [*Australia*] [*ICAO location identifier*] (ICLI)

ABLO .... Australian Botanical Liaison Officer

ABLR .... Longreach [*Australia*] [*ICAO location identifier*] (ICLI)

ABLS .... Australian Balloon Launching Station

ABM .... Aktiewe Burgermag [*Active Citizen Force*] [*Afrikaans*]

ABM .... American Baptist Mission

ABM .... Anti-Ballistiese Missiel [*Anti-Ballistic Missile*] [*Afrikaans*]

ABM .... Arbeitskreis fuer Betriebsfuehrung Muenchen (SLS)

ABM .... Asociacion de Banqueros de Mexico [*Mexican Association of Bankers*] (LA)

ABM .... Associacao Brasileira de Metais [*Sao Paulo, Brazil*] (LAA)

ABM .... Associacao Brasileira de Municipios [*Brazilian Association of Municipalities*] (LA)

ABM .... Associated Battery Manufacturers Ltd. [*Nigeria*]

ABM .... Association Belge du Monulinage (WGAO)

ABM .... Association of Banks in Malaysia

ABM .... Associcao de Badminton de Macau [*Macao Badminton Association*] (EAIO)

ABM .... Australian Birthright Movement [*An association*]

ABM .... Australian Board of Missions (ADA)

ABM .... Bamaga [*Australia*] [*Airport symbol*] (OAG)

ABM .... Superheavy Artillery (RU)

ABMA .... Mount Isa [*Australia*] [*ICAO location identifier*] (ICLI)

ABMAC ..... Abalone Management Advisory Committee [*Australia*]

ABMANZ .. Associated Bread Manufacturers of Australia and New Zealand

ABMC .... Maroochydore [*Australia*] [*ICAO location identifier*] (ICLI)

ABMED ..... Able-Bodied Seaman Medical [*Navy*]

ABMET .... Able-Bodied Seaman Meteorology [*Navy*]

ABMF .... Australian Barley Marketing Federation

ABMF .... Australian Bicentennial Multicultural Foundation

ABMIT ...... Association Belgo-Mediterraneenne de Lutte contra la Thalassemie (WGAO)

ABMJ .... Association of Biological Manufacturers of Japan (EAIO)

ABMK .... Mackay [*Australia*] [*ICAO location identifier*] (ICLI)

ABMP .... Association Belge des Matieres Plastiques (WGAO)

ABMS .... Associacao Brasileira de Mecanica dos Solos [*Brazil*] (SLS)

ABMS .... Australian Baptist Missionary Society (ADA)

ABMTD ... Able-Bodied Seaman Motor Transport Driver [*Navy*]

ABMTF .... Australian Bone Marrow Transplant Foundation

ABMTH ... Able-Bodied Seaman Marine Technical Hull [*Navy*]

ABMTP .... Able-Bodied Seaman Marine Technical Propulsion [*Navy*]

ABMUSN ... Able-Bodied Seaman Musician [*Navy*]

ABMW ...... Able-Bodied Seaman Mine Warfare [*Navy*]

ABMXA .... Australian Bicycle Motocross Association

ABN .... African Biosciences Network [*International Council of Scientific Unions*]

ABN .... Algemene Bank Nederland [*General Bank of the Netherlands*] (WEN)

ABN .... Algemene Nederlandse Bond van Natuursteen-bewerkende Bedrijven (WGAO)

ABN .... Allied Bank of Nigeria Ltd.

ABN .... Anti-Bolshevik Bloc of Nations [*Germany*]   (EAIO)

ABN .... Arbeitsgemeinschaft Beruflicher und Ehrenamtlicher Naturschutz [*Association of Professional and Honorary Wildlife Preservationists*]   (SLS)

a-bn--- .... Borneo Island [*MARC geographic area code*] [*Library of Congress*]

ABNEI .... Association Belge des Negociants Exportateurs et Importateurs   (WGAO)

ABNFV ...... Anorexia and Bulimia Nervosa Foundation of Victoria [*Australia*]

AbNIIK ...... Abkhaz Scientific Research Institute of Regional Studies   (RU)

ABNOC ..... Airborne Operations Center [*NATO*]   (NATG)

ABNSW ..... Agricultural Bureau of New South Wales [*Australia*]

ABNT .... Associacao Brasileira de Normas Tecnicas [*Brazilian national standards organization*]

Abnutz .... Abnutzung [*Corrosion*] [*German*]   (GCA)

ABO .... Aboriginal [*Australia*]   (DSUE)

ABO .... Absatz- und Bezugsorganisation [*Marketing and Purchasing Organization*] [*German*]   (EG)

ABO .... Aeroexpreso Bogota [*Colombia*] [*ICAO designator*]   (FAAC)

ABO .... Air Board Order

ABO .... Associacao Brasileira de Odontologia [*Brazilian Dental Association*] [*Rio De Janeiro*]   (LAA)

ABOA .... Australian Bank Officials' Association   (ADA)

ABoC .... Agricultural Bank of China

ABOCOL .. Abonos Colombianos SA [*Colombia*]   (COL)

ABOF .... Australian Bank Officials' Federation

ABOFORT ... Allami Borforgalmi Reszvenytarsasag [*State Wine Company Limited*]   (HU)

Abog .... Abogado   (SCAC)

ABOK .... Oakey [*Australia*] [*ICAO location identifier*]   (ICLI)

ABON .... Special-Purpose Air Brigade   (RU)

abond .... Abondamment [*Abundantly*] [*French*]

abonn .... Abonnement [*Subscription*] [*Publishing*] [*French*]

ABOP .... Algemene Bond van Onderwijzend Personeel [*General Association of Teaching Personnel*] [*Netherlands*]   (WEN)

Abor .... Aboriginal [*Australia*]

ABOT .... Australian [*National*] Botanic [*Gardens*] [*National Union Catalogue of Australia symbol*]

ABP .... Abra De Llog [*Philippines*] [*Seismograph station code, US Geological Survey*] [*Closed*]

ABP .... Agence Benin Presse [*Benin Press Agency*]   (AF)

ABP .... Agence Burundaise de Presse [*Burundi Press Agency*]   (AF)

ABP .... Algemene Burgerlijke Pensioenwet [*Benelux*]   (BAS)

ABP .... Arbeitgeberverband Bayerischer Papierfabriken   (WGAO)

abp .... Arcybiskup [*Archbishop*] [*Poland*]

ABP .... Artiljerisko Borbeno Pravilo [*Artillery Combat Rule*]   (YU)

ABP .... Asociacion Bancaria de Panama   (EY)

ABP .... Associacao Brasileira de Agencias de Propaganda [*Brazilian Association of Advertising Agencies*]   (LA)

ABP .... Association Belge des Paralyses   (WGAO)

abp .... Concrete Airstrip   (RU)

ABPA .... African Business Promotion Association [*Zimbabwe*]   (AF)

ABPA .... Australian Book Publishers Association   (ADA)

ABPC .... Associacao Brasileira dos Produtores de Cal [*Lime Producers Brazilian Association*]   (EAIO)

ABPC .... Association Belge de Photographie et de Cinematographie [*Belgian Photography and Cinematography Association*]   (SLS)

ABPC .... Australian Beef Promotion Committee

ABPE .... Association Belgo-Luxembourgeoise de la Presse d'Entreprise   (WGAO)

ABPH .... Able-Bodied Seaman Photography [*Navy*]

ABPM .... Associacao Brasileira de Preservacao de Madeiras [*Brazil*]   (DSCA)

ABPM .... Association of Business and Professional Men [*Australia*]

ABPN .... Anggaran Belandja dan Pendapatan Negara [*Estimate of State Income and Expenditures (National budget)*]   (IN)

ABPN .... Proserpine [*Australia*] [*ICAO location identifier*]   (ICLI)

ABPNL ...... Association Belge des Pilotes et Navigateurs de Ligne   (WGAO)

ABPPNS ... Akil Bharatiya Prakrotik Parivar Niyojan Sangh [*Natural Family Planning Association of India*]   (EAIO)

ABPR .... Asociacion de Bibliotecarios en Puerto Rica   (WGAO)

ABPSA ...... Antigua and Barbuda Public Service Association   (EY)

ABPT .... Able-Bodied Seaman Physical Training [*Navy*]

ABQ .... Associacao Brasileira de Quimica [*Brazilian Chemical Association*] [*Rio De Janeiro*]   (LAA)

ABQMG .... Able-Bodied Seaman Quartermaster Gunner [*Navy*]

ABQN .... Associacao Brasileira de Qualidade Nuclear [*Brazilian Association for Nuclear Quality*]   (LA)

abr .... Abra [*Illustration*] [*Publishing*] [*Hungary*]

Abr .... Abreuvoir [*Watering Trough*] [*Military map abbreviation World War I*] [*French*]   (MTD)

abr .... Abril [*April*] [*Portuguese*]   (GPO)

abr .... Abril [*April*] [*Spanish*]

ABR .... Afrique Benin Representation

ABR .... Air-Launched Ballistic Missile   (RU)

abr .... Artillery Brigade   (BU)

ABR .... Associacao Brasileira de Radio [*Radio Association of Brazil*]

ABR .... Ateliers Belges Reunis SA [*Belgium*]

ABR .... Contactless Automatic Pilot, Contactless Gyropilot [*Nautical term*]   (RU)

ABR .... Real-Aerovias Brasil [*Brazilian international airline*]

ABR .... Societe Ateliers Belges Reunies [*Engineering*]

ABRA .... Asociacao Brasileira de Reforma Agraria [*Brazil*]   (DSCA)

ABRA .... Asociacion de Bancos de la Republica Argentina [*Bankers' association*] [*Argentina*]   (EY)

ABRAC ...... Australian Biological Resources Advisory Committee

ABRACE .... Associacao Brasileira de Computadores Electronicos [*Brazilian Association for the Use of Electronic Computers*]   (PDAA)

ABRACO ... Associacao Brasileira de Corrosao [*Brazilian Corrosion Association*]   (PDAA)

ABRALIN ... Associacao Brasilera de Linguistica   (WGAO)

ABRAM .... Associacao Brasileira de Emprezas de Apoio Maritimo [*Brazilian Association of Marine Components Manufacturers*]   (PDAA)

ABRAMO ... Associacao Brasileira dos Mineradores de Ouro   (WGAO)

ABRANFE ... Associacao Brasileira de Metais Nao-Ferrosos [*Brazilian Nonferrous Metals Association*]   (LA)

ABRAPEC ... Associacao Brasileira de Orientacao Agro Pecuaria [*Brazil*]   (DSCA)

ABRATE ... Associacao Brasileira de Emissoras de Televisao [*Brazilian Association of Television Stations*]   (LA)

ABRATES ... Associacao Brasileira de Tradutores [*Brazilian Association of Translators*]

ABRAVA ... Associacao Brasileira de Refrigeracao, Ar Condicionado, Ventilacao, e Aquecimento [*Brazil*]

ABRD .... Australian Bicentennial Road Development

ABRDP ...... Australian Bicentennial Road Development Program

ABRE .... Associazione Bresciana di Richerche Economiche [*Italian*]   (SLS)

ABRECSA ... Association of Black Reformed Christians in South Africa   (WGAO)

Abreib .... Abreibung [*Abrasion*] [*German*]   (GCA)

ABRF .... Brisbane [*Australia*] [*ICAO location identifier*]   (ICLI)

ABRI .... Agricultural Business Research Institute [*Australia*]

ABRI .... Angkatan Bersendjata Republik Indonesia [*Armed Forces of the Republic of Indonesia*]   (IN)

ABRI .... Associatie van Belgische Raadgevende Ingenieurs en Experten   (WGAO)

ABRI .... Association Bretonne des Relais et Itineraires   (WGAO)

ABRJA ...... Associacao Brasileira de Juizes de Exposicoes de Animais [*Brazil*]   (DSCA)

ABRK .... Rockhampton [*Australia*] [*ICAO location identifier*]   (ICLI)

ABRO .... Able-Bodied Seaman Radio Operator [*Navy*]

Abrog .... Abroge [*French*]   (FLAF)

ABRP .... Able-Bodied Seaman RADAR Plotter [*Navy*]

ABRP .... Association Belge des Relations Professionnelles [*Belgium*]   (BAS)

ABRS .... Australian Biological Resources Study   (ADA)

ABS .... Abastumani [*Former USSR*] [*Seismograph station code, US Geological Survey*] [*Closed*]

Abs .... Absatz [*Paragraph*] [*German*]   (ILCA)

Abs .... Abschnitt [*Paragraph, Section*] [*German*]

Abs .... Absender [*Sender*] [*German*]   (EG)

abs .... Absent [*Lacking, Missing*] [*French*]

abs .... Absolete   (TPFD)

abs .... Absolument [*Absolutely*] [*French*]

abs .... Absolut [*Absolute*] [*German*]

abs .... Absolute   (RU)

abs .... Absolutny [*Absolute*] [*Poland*]

ABS .... Absoluut [*Absolute*] [*Afrikaans*]

ABS .... Abu Simbel [*Egypt*] [*Airport symbol*]   (OAG)

ABS .... Alliance Biblical Seminary [*Philippines*]

ABS .... Ambtenaar van de Burgerlijke Stand [*Benelux*]   (BAS)

ABS .... Asociacion Bancaria Salvadorena [*Salvadoran Banking Association*]   (LA)

ABS .... Associated Broadcasting Services [*Australia*]

ABS .... Associate of the Building Services Institute [*Australia*]

ABS .... Association des Bibliothecaires Suisses   (WGAO)

ABS .... Atomska Borbena Sredstva [*Atomic Combat Equipment*]   (YU)

ABS .... Auckland Botanical Society [*New Zealand*]   (DSCA)

ABS .... Australia Braford Society

ABS .... Australia-Britain Society

ABS .... Australian Ballet School

ABS .... Australian Ballet Society   (ADA)

ABS .... Australian Biochemical Society   (ADA)

ABS .... Australian Book Society   (ADA)

ABS .... Australian Bureau of Statistics [*Central Office*] [*National Union Catalogue of Australia symbol*]

ABs .... Autonome Brigades [*Autonomous Brigades*] [*Terrorist group*] [*French*]
ABS............ Aux Bons Soins De [*Care Of, c/o*] [*Correspondence*] [*French*]
ABSA........ Agricultural Bureau of South Australia
ABSA........ Algodonera Boliviana SA [*Bolivia*]   (DSCA)
ABSA........ Arrowsmith Bible Society in Australia [*H M Arrowsmith Library*] [*National Union Catalogue of Australia symbol*]
ABSA........ Associated Booksellers of Southern Africa   (EAIO)
ABSA........ Australian Bird Study Association
ABSA........ Australian Business Support for the Arts
ABSAC ..... Australian Building Systems Appraisal Council Ltd.   (ADA)
ABSAED ... Association Belge des Secteurs de Alimentes de L'Enfance et Dietetiques   (WGAO)
ABSBA ..... Australian Brown Swiss and Braunvieh Association
ABSC .... Applied Behavioural Studies Centre [*Australia*]
ABSC .... Australian Billiards and Snooker Council
Abscheid ... Abscheidung [*Separation*] [*German*]   (GCA)
Abschn...... Abschnitt [*Paragraph, Chapter*] [*German*]   (ILCA)
ABSE .... Able-Bodied Seaman Survival Equipment [*Navy*]
ABSEG ..... Aboriginal Secondary Grants Scheme [*Australia*]   (ADA)
abs el-magn yed ... Absolute Electromagnetic Unit   (RU)
abs el styed ... Absolute Electrostatic Unit   (RU)
ABSF .... Australian Blind Sports Federation
ABSFBN ... Air Base Squadron Fairbairn [*Royal Australian Air Force*]
Abs gen ...... Absolucion General [*Spanish*]
ABSI .... Associate of the Building Societies Institute [*Australia*]
ABSIG .... Able-Bodied Seaman Signalman [*Navy*]
abs iur ...... Absolvierter Jurist [*German*]
ABSM........ Aktiebolaget Svenska Metallverken
ABSM........ Associate of the Bendigo School of Mines [*Australia*]   (ADA)
ABSN........ Able-Bodied Seaman Stores Naval [*Navy*]
absol.......... Absolument [*Absolutely*] [*French*]
Absol......... Absolut [*Absolute*] [*German*]
Absolv .... Absolvent [*College Graduate*] [*German*]   (GCA)
Absorpt ..... Absorption [*German*]   (GCA)
Abspalt...... Abspaltung [*Cleavage*] [*German*]   (GCA)
Abspaltbark ... Abspaltbarkeit [*Cleavage Capacity*] [*German*]   (GCA)
ABSSA ...... Amateur Beekeepers' Society of South Australia
ABSSR....... Bashkir Autonomous Soviet Socialist Republic   (RU)
Abst .... Abstand [*Distance*] [*German*]   (GCA)
ABSTD...... Able-Bodied Seaman Steward [*Navy*]
ABSTD...... ABS [*Australian Bureau of Statistics*] Time-Series Database [*Information service or system*]   (CRD)
ABSTECH ... American Bureau of Shipping Worldwide Technical Services (MHDB)
abs tr .... Absolut Trocken [*Absolutely Dry*] [*German*]
abstr .... Abstrakt [*Abstract*] [*German*]   (GCA)
ABSTS ...... Australian Bureau of Statistics Time Series
ABSTVvan SA ... Angorabok Stoettelersvereniging van Suid-Afrika [*Angora Goat Stud Breeders' Society of South Africa*]   (AA)
ABSU........ Aid to Believers in the Soviet Union [*See also ACU*] [*Paris, France*]   (EAIO)
ABSU........ All Assam Bodo Students Union [*Indonesia*]   (WGAO)
ABSU........ Arab States Broadcasting Union [*Egypt*]   (WGAO)
ABSV........ Able-Bodied Seaman Stores Victualling [*Navy*]
abs v .... Absolute Weight   (RU)
abs yed ...... Absolute Unit   (RU)
ABSyM...... Association Belge des Syndicates Medicaux   (WGAO)
Absz .... Abszisse [*Abscissa*] [*German*]   (GCA)
abt .... Abonnement [*Subscription*] [*Publishing*] [*French*]
ABT .... Abteilung [*Department, Division, Section*] [*German*]
ABT .... Arabian Bank Trade [*Saudi Arabia*]
ABT .... Arabian Bulk Trade [*Saudi Arabia*] [*Commercial firm*]
ABT .... Arbeitsstelle fuer Bibliotheks Technik [*Workplace for Library Technology*] [*German*]
ABT .... Armored   (RU)
ABT .... Australian Board of Translators
ABT .... Australian Broadcasting Tribunal   (ADA)
ABT .... Automatic Bathythermograph   (RU)
a-bt--- .... Bhutan [*MARC geographic area code*] [*Library of Congress*]
ABT .... Brazilian Association of Tele-Education
ABTA........ Aboriginal Benefits Trust Account [*Australia*]
ABTA........ Australia-British Trade Association
ABTA........ Australian Baton Twirling Association
ABTA........ Australian-British Trade Association   (ADA)
ABTAC...... Australian Book Trade Advisory Committee   (ADA)
ABTC........ Australian Book Trade Committee
ABTD .... Thursday Island [*Australia*] [*ICAO location identifier*]   (ICLI)
ABTEF ...... Australian Boot Trade Employees' Federation
ABTF........ Aborigines Benefit Trust Fund [*Australia*]
ABTI......... Association Bois Tropical Ivoirien
ABTIR....... Association des Bibliotheques de Theologie et d'Information Religieuse   (WGAO)
Abtl .... Abteilung [*Section, Part (of a publication)*] [*German*]
ABTL........ Association Belge des Technologues de Laboratoire   (WGAO)
ABTL........ Townsville [*Australia*] [*ICAO location identifier*]   (ICLI)

Abtlg .... Abteilung [*Section, Part (of a publication)*] [*German*]
Abtrenn...... Abtrennung [*Separation*] [*German*]   (GCA)
ABTS .... Australian Bible Training School   (ADA)
ABTs......... Gasoline Tank Truck   (RU)
ABTsVM... Automatic High-Speed Digital Computer   (RU)
ABTT........ Townsville [*Australia*] [*ICAO location identifier*]   (ICLI)
ABTU .... Armored Troops Directorate   (RU)
ABTUC ...... All-Burma Trade Union Congress   (WGAO)
ABTV........ Armored Troops   (RU)
ABTV........ Townsville [*Australia*] [*ICAO location identifier*]   (ICLI)
ABTZ........ Armored Vehicle Spare Parts Section   (RU)
ABU .... Abuyama [*Japan*] [*Seismograph station code, US Geological Survey*]
ABU .... Aerovias Bueno Ltd. [*Colombia*] [*ICAO designator*]   (FAAC)
ABU .... African Boxing Union
ABU .... Agrupacion Bibliotecologica del Uruguay   (WGAO)
ABU .... Ahmadu Bello University [*Nigeria*]
ABU .... Alliance Biblique Universelle
ABU .... Amphibious Beach Unit [*Military*]
ABU .... Antibody Unit
ABU .... Armored Troops Directorate   (RU)
ABU .... Asia Pacific Broadcasting Union   (EAIO)
ABU .... Asociacion de Bibliotecarios del Uruguay [*Uruguay*]   (SLS)
ABU .... Association Belge-URSS [*Belgian-Soviet Association*]   (WER)
ABU .... Australian Brushmakers' Union
ABUA .... Amateur Basketball Union of Australia   (ADA)
ABUA .... Amateur Boxing Union of Australia
ABUC .... Able-Bodied Seaman Underwater Control [*Navy*]
ABUEN ..... Asociacion de Bibliotecas Universitarias y Especializadas de Nicaragua [*Nicaragua*]   (SLS)
ABU of A ... Amateur Boxing Union of Australia
ABUS........ Ausruestung fuer Bergbau und Schwerindustrie [*Equipment for Mining and Heavy Industry*] [*German*]   (EG)
ABUS........ Bibliography of Urban Studies in Australia [*A*] [*Database*] (ADA)
ABUT .... Amalgamated Bermuda Union of Teachers   (LA)
ABV .... Abschnittsbevollmaechtiger [*Section Deputy*] [*German*]
ABV .... Abschnittsbevollmaechtiger der Deutschen Volkspolizei [*Sector of the German People's Police*]   (EG)
ABV .... Abuja [*Nigeria*] [*Airport symbol*]   (OAG)
ABV .... Algemeen Belgisch Vlasverbond   (WGAO)
ABV .... Atom, Biologiai, Vegyi (Fegyverek) [*Atomic, Biological, Chemical (Weapons)*]   (HU)
ABV .... Aviation Unit for Pest Control   (RU)
ABV .... Traveling-Wave Antenna   (RU)
ABVA .... Algemene Bond van Ambtenaren [*Benelux*]   (BAS)
ABVB........ Allgemeine Bedingungen der Volkseigenen Bauindustrie [*General Terms of the State Construction Industry*]   (EG)
ABVO .... Algemene Bond van Overheidspersoneel [*General Union of Civil Servants*] [*Netherlands Antilles*]   (EY)
ABVP........ Automatic Vibrating Bunker-Feeding Device   (RU)
ABVV .... Algemeen Belgisch Vakverbond [*Belgian General Federation of Labor*]   (WEN)
ABW .... Albanian Airways [*ICAO designator*]   (FAAC)
ABW .... Algemene Bijstandswet [*Benelux*]   (BAS)
ABW .... Aruba [*ANSI three-letter standard code*]   (CNC)
ABWA .... Architects' Board of Western Australia
ABWAID... Australian Baptist World Aid and Relief Committee   (EAIO)
ABWARC ... Australian Baptist World Aid and Relief Committee   (WGAO)
Abwesenh... Abwesenheit [*Absence*] [*German*]   (GCA)
ABWP........ Weipa [*Australia*] [*ICAO location identifier*]   (ICLI)
ABWS....... Able-bodied Seaman Work Study [*Navy*]
ABWTR..... Able-Bodied Seaman Writer [*Navy*]
ABWUA .... Amateur Boxing and Wrestling Union of Australia   (ADA)
ABX .... Albury [*Australia*] [*Airport symbol*]   (OAG)
a-bx--- .... Brunei [*MARC geographic area code*] [*Library of Congress*]
Aby............ Abyssinia
ABYDAP... Asociacion de Bibliotecarios y Documentalistas Agricolas del Peru [*Peru*]   (SLS)
ABYSS....... Abyssinia
ABZ .... Ameriska Bratska Zveza [*American Fraternal Union*]   (YU)
ABZ .... Asphalt Concrete Plant   (RU)
ABZ .... Refueling Truck   (RU)
AbzG .... Abzahlungsgesetz [*Law on hire purchase agreements*] [*German*] (ILCA)
ABZT........ Association Belgo-Zairoise du Textile
Abzw .... Abzweigung [*or Strassenabzweigung*] [*Branch or Street*] [*German*]
Abzw .... Abzweigweiche [*Branch Line Switch*] [*German*]   (EG)
AC............ A Capo [*New Paragraph*] [*Italian*]
a/c .... A Cargo [*Debit Of*] [*Banking, investment*] [*Spanish*]
AC............ Accion Catolica [*Catholic Action*] [*Spanish*]   (WER)
AC............ Accion Comunista [*Communist Action*] [*Spanish*]   (WER)
AC............ Accion Cubana [*Cuban Action*] [*Venezuela*]   (LA)
Ac.............. Aceton [*Acetone*] [*German*]   (GCA)
ac.............. A Coins [*Cornerpieces*] [*French*]

ac .... Acompte [*Payment on Account*] [*French*] [*Business term*]
a/c .... A Conto [*On Account*] [*Banking, investment*] [*Italian*]   (GPO)
Ac .... Actinio [*Actinium*] [*Chemical element*] [*Portuguese*]
AC .... Actio Catholica [*Catholic Action*]   (HU)
AC .... Action Civile [*Civil Action*] [*French*]   (ILCA)
a/c .... A Cuenta [*On Account*] [*Banking, investment*] [*Spanish*]
AC .... Acuerdo de Cartagena [*Cartagena Agreement*] [*Use Andean Group*]   (LA)
AC .... Aero Club [*Australia*]
AC .... Affarsarbetsgivarnas Centralforbund   (WGAO)
AC .... Africa Committee [*Switzerland*]   (EAIO)
AC .... African Coasters [*Steamship*]   (MHDB)
AC .... Air Congo [*Zaire*]
AC .... Aircraftwoman [*Military*]
AC .... Akademikernes Centralorganisation [*Central Organization of Academians*] [*Denmark*]   (SLS)
a/c .... Al Cuidado [*Care Of*] [*Correspondence*] [*Spanish*]
AC .... Amende de Composition [*French*]   (FLAF)
AC .... Amistad Combativa [*Combat Friendship*] [*Cuban military units*]   (LA)
AC .... Ancienne Coutume [*French*]   (FLAF)
AC .... Anciens Combattants [*French*]   (FLAF)
AC .... Andina de Curtidos [*Colombia*]   (COL)
AC .... Annee Courante [*Of the Current Year*] [*French*]
AC .... Ano de Cristo [*In the Year of Our Lord*] [*Spanish*]
AC .... Antes de Cristo [*Before Christ*] [*Portuguese*]
ac .... Anul Curent [*Current Year*]   (RO)
AC .... Anwedungscode [*Application Code*] [*German*]   (ADPT)
A/C .... Ao Cuidado [*Care Of*] [*Portuguese*] [*Business term*]
ac .... Argent Comptant [*Ready Money*] [*French*] [*Business term*]
AC .... Artillerie de Corps [*Military*] [*French*]   (MTD)
AC .... Assegno Circolare [*Banker's Check*] [*Italian*] [*Business term*]
AC .... Assemblee Consultative du Conseil de l'Europe [*France*]   (FLAF)
AC .... Associacao Comercial [*Commercial Association*] [*Portuguese*]
AC .... Associacao de Caboverdeanos [*Capeverdean Association*] [*Portugal*]   (EAIO)
AC .... Atlantic Council [*Later, ACUS*] [*NATO*]   (NATG)
AC .... Atlantische Commissie [*Netherlands Atlantics Commission*]   (EAIO)
AC .... Atleticky Club [*Athletic Club*]   (CZ)
AC .... Auditor Camerae [*Auditor of the Papal Treasury*]
AC .... Ausgrabungen Carnuntum [*Carnuntum Excavations*] [*Austria*]   (EAIO)
AC .... Australia Council   (ADA)
AC .... Australian Corps   (ADA)
AC .... Australian Cruiser   (DMA)
AC .... Auto-Canon [*Military*] [*French*]   (MTD)
aC .... Avanti Cristo [*Before Christ*] [*Italian*]
ac .... Avaries Communes [*French*]
AC .... Average Cost
AC .... Avis Conforme [*Benelux*]   (BAS)
AC .... Azania Committee [*Netherlands*]   (EAIO)
AC .... Companion of the Order of Australia
AC .... Estado do Acre [*State of Acre*] [*Brazil*]
AC .... Rockwell International Corp. [*ICAO aircraft manufacturer identifier*]   (ICAO)
ACA .... Acapulco [*Mexico*] [*Airport symbol*]
ACA .... Accion Catolica Argentina [*Argentine Catholic Action*]   (LA)
ACA .... Administrative Committee on Administration [*United Nations*]
ACA .... Aged Care Australia [*An association*]
ACA .... Agence Camerounaise d'Assurances [*Cameroonian Insurance Agency*]
ACA .... Agence Centrafricaine d'Assurances
ACA .... Agence Coloniale Automobile
ACA .... Agence Congolaise d'Assurances
ACA .... Agricultural Credit Administration [*Philippines*]   (DS)
ACA .... Aircrew Association   (EAIO)
ACA .... Allied Command Atlantic   (EAIO)
ACA .... Ambtelijke Commissie Automatisering [*Netherlands*]
ACA .... American Canoe Association   (OLYM)
ACA .... American Citizens Abroad [*Switzerland*]   (EAIO)
ACA .... Anti-Corruption Agency [*Malaysia*]   (ML)
ACA .... Apex Clubs of Australia
ACA .... Argentine Automobile Club
ACA .... Armement Cotonnec Abidjan
ACA .... Art et Culture Negro-Africain
ACA .... Arts Council of Australia
ACA .... Asian Christian Association [*Taiwan*]   (EAIO)
ACA .... Asociacion Centro-americana de Anatomia   (WGAO)
ACA .... Asociacion Colombiana de Actuarios [*Colombian Actuarial Association*]   (EAIO)
ACA .... Asociacion Colombiana de Apicultores [*Colombia*]   (DSCA)
ACA .... Asociacion de Cooperativas Agrarias [*Association of Agricultural Cooperatives*]   (LA)

ACA .... Asociatia Crescatorilor de Albine [*Association of Beekeepers*]   (RO)
ACA .... Assemblee des Cardinaux et des Archeveques [*France*]
ACA .... Associacao Carioca de Avicultura [*Brazil*]   (DSCA)
ACA .... Associacao Civica Angolana [*Political party*]   (EY)
ACA .... Associacao Comercial do Amazonas [*Brazil*]   (DSCA)
ACA .... Associate of the Institute of Chartered Accountants in Australia   (ADA)
ACA .... Association des Compagnies d'Assurances Agrees au Grand-Duche de Luxembourg   (WGAO)
ACA .... Association of Consulting Architects [*New South Wales, Australia*]
ACA .... Australasian Clerical Association
ACA .... Australasian Conference Association Ltd.
ACA .... Australasian Corrosion Association   (EAIO)
ACA .... Australia Canada Association   (ADA)
ACA .... Australian Canners Association
ACA .... Australian Cardiacs' Association
ACA .... Australian Casting Association
ACA .... Australian Chinese Association   (ADA)
ACA .... Australian Chiropody Association   (ADA)
ACA .... Australian Chiropractors Association   (ADA)
ACA .... Australian Choral Association
ACA .... Australian Coal Association   (ADA)
ACA .... Australian College of Accordionists   (ADA)
ACA .... Australian College of Allergists   (ADA)
ACA .... Australian Committee on Africa
ACA .... Australian Communication Association
ACA .... Australian Consumers Association   (ADA)
ACA .... Australian Corriedale Association   (ADA)
ACA .... Australian Council for Aeronautics   (ADA)
ACA .... Australian Council of Archives
ACA .... Australian Cricket Association
ACA .... Australian Croatian Association
ACA .... Australian Croquet Association
ACA .... Australian Curling Association
ACA .... Automobil Club d'Andorra [*Automobile Club of Andorra*]   (EAIO)
ACA .... Automovil Club Argentino [*Automobile Club of Argentina*]   (EAIO)
ACAA .... Advisory Council on Australian Archives
ACAA .... Amateur Cyclists' Association of Australia   (ADA)
ACAA .... Asian Christian Art Association   (WGAO)
ACAA .... Associate of the Australasian Institute of Cost Accountants   (ADA)
ACAA .... Association of Consulting Architects Australia
ACAA .... Australian Civil Aviation Authority [*National Union Catalogue of Australia symbol*]
ACAAE ..... Australian Council on Awards in Advanced Education   (ADA)
ACAAI ...... Air Cargo Agents Association of India   (PDAA)
ACAAT ..... Australian Campaign Against Arms Trade
ACAAust ... Associate of the Institute of Chartered Accountants in Australia   (ADA)
ACABA ..... Association Chretienne Antandroy, Bara, et Antanosy [*Antandroy, Bara, and Antanosy Christian Association*] [*Malagasy*]   (AF)
ACABQ ..... Advisory Committee on Administrative and Budgetary Questions [*United Nations*]
ACABQ ..... United Nations Advisory Committee on Administrative and Budgetary Questions
ACAC .... African Civil Aviation Commission
ACAC .... Aged Care Advisory Committee [*Australia*]
ACAC .... Anti-Censorship Action Committee [*University of Witwatersrand*] [*Johannesburg, South Africa*]
ACAC .... Arab Civil Aviation Council   (WGAO)
ACAC .... Asociacion Colombiana para el Avance de la Ciencia [*Colombian Association for the Advancement of Science*]   (EAIO)
ACAC .... Australian Cinema Advertising Council
ACAC .... Australian College of Aesthetics and Cosmetology
ACAC .... Australian Conciliation and Arbitration Commission   (ADA)
ACACA ..... Australasian Conference of Assessment and Certification Agencies
ACACC ..... Asian Conference on Agricultural Credit and Cooperatives   (WGAO)
ACACED ... Asociacion Campesina de Accion Comunal Educativa y de Defensa Civil [*Colombia*]   (COL)
ACACHE .. Association of Careers Advisers in Colleges of Higher Education   (EAIO)
ACACIA .... Australia's Constitutional and Citizens Association   (ADA)
acad .... Academia [*Academy*] [*Portuguese*]
Acad .... Academician   (EECI)
Acad .... Academy   (EECI)
ACAD .... Association for Computer Aided Design Ltd. [*Australia*]   (ADA)
ACAD .... Association of Commercial Agents of Denmark   (EAIO)
ACAD .... Australian Council of Alcohol and Drugs [*National Union Catalogue of Australia symbol*]

ACADA ..... Australian Council of Alcohol and Other Drug Associations
ACADI....... Association des Cadres Dirigeants de l'Industrie [*Association of Industrial Executives*] [*France*]   (PDAA)
ACADITEC ... Academia de Dibujo Tecnico [*Colombia*]   (COL)
ACADS...... Association for Computer Aided Design
ACADS...... Australian Computer-Aided Design Systems
ACAE .... Adelaide College of Advanced Education [*Australia*]   (ADA)
ACAE .... Ateliers et Chantiers de l'Afrique Equatoriale [*Equatorial Africa Shipyards*] [*Gabon*]
ACAE .... Australian Commission [*or Committee*] on Advanced Education   (ADA)
ACAF........ Ateliers et Chantiers de l'Afrique Francaise
ACAF........ Australian Citizen Air Force   (ADA)
ACAFADE ... Central American Association of Relatives of the Detained-Disappeared [*Costa Rica*]   (EAIO)
ACAFAM ... Asociacion de Facultades de Medicina [*Honduras*]   (SLS)
ACAFOM ... Association Culturelle et Amicale des Familles d'Outre-Mer
ACAG .... Anti-Counterfeit Action Group [*Australia*]
ACAH........ Australia Calvary Hospital [*Medical Library*] [*Australian Capital Territory*] [*National Union Catalogue of Australia symbol*]
ACAHN..... Asociacion Centroamericana de Historia Natural [*Guatemala*]   (SLS)
ACAI......... Association of Ceramic Artists in Israel   (EAIO)
ACAI......... Associazione Cristiana Artigiani Italiani
ACAI......... Associazione fra i Costruttori in Acciaio Italiani [*Steel constructors association*]   (EY)
ACAI......... Australian [*Capital Territory*] Confederation of Australian Industry [*National Union Catalogue of Australia symbol*]
ACAIA...... Associate of the Customs Agents Institute of Australia
ACAIT....... Asociacion Centroamericana de Industrias Textiles [*Central American Association of Textile Industries*]   (LAA)
ACAL........ Algodoeira e Cafeeira Assai Ltd [*Brazil*]   (DSCA)
ACAL........ Australian Council for Adult Literacy   (ADA)
ACALP..... Advisory Council on Australia's Languages Policy
ACALUB... Academia de Ciencias, Artes, e Letras da Universidade do Brasil [*University of Brazil Academy of Sciences, Arts, and Letters*]   (LA)
ACAM .... Association Culturelle Afro-Mauricienne [*Afro-Mauritian Cultural Association*]   (AF)
ACAM .... Association des Compagnies d'Assurances Moyennes [*Belgium*]   (WGAO)
ACAM .... Australian Confederation of Apparel Manufacturers   (ADA)
ACAMAR ... Asociacion Centroamericana de Armadores   (WGAO)
ACAMAR ... Asociacion Centroamericana de Armadores [*Central American Association of Shipowners*] [*Guatemala*]   (EAIO)
ACAMP..... Allied Camouflage and Concealment Publication [*NATO*]   (NATG)
ACAMS..... Ashley Computer-Aided Maintenance System [*Australia*]
ACAN .... Advisory Committee on Antarctic Names   (MSC)
ACAN .... Agencia Centro Americana de Noticias [*Panama*]   (WGAO)
ACAN .... Asociacion Colombiana de Administradores de Negocios [*Colombian Business Administrators Association*]   (LA)
ACAN .... Australasian Child Abuse Network
AC &CAT ... Africa Circle and Correspondence Association for Thematicists   (EAIO)
ACANSW ... After Care Association of New South Wales [*Australia*]
ACANSW ... Australian Czech Association of New South Wales
ACANZ ..... Agricultural Council of Australia and New Zealand   (EAIO)
ACAO........ Australian Capital Territory Department of Education and the Arts [*National Union Catalogue of Australia symbol*]
ACAODA .. Australian Council of Alcohol and Other Drug Associations
ACAP........ Aboriginal Community Affairs Panel [*Australia*]
ACAP........ Acapulco [*Mexico*]   (ABBR)
ACAP........ Advisory Committee on Antarctic Programs [*Australia*]
ACAP........ Agence Camerounaise de Presse [*Cameroon Press Agency*]
ACAP........ Agence Centrafricaine de Presse [*Central African Press Agency*]
ACAP........ Annapurna Conservation Area Project [*Nepal*]
ACAP........ Asociacion Colombiana de Agencias de Publicidad [*Colombian Advertising Agencies Association*]   (LA)
ACAP........ Associacao Central da Agricultura Portuguesa [*Portuguese Central Agriculture Association*]   (EAIO)
ACAP........ Associacao do Comercio Automovel de Portugal   (WGAO)
ACAP........ Association Congolaise pour l'Amitie entre les Peuples [*Congolese Association for Friendship among Peoples*]   (AF)
ACAP........ Association for Children with Aphasic and Perceptual Difficulties [*Australia*]
ACAP........ Associazione Capi Aziende Pubblicitarie   (WGAO)
ACap........ Australian Capitol [*Record label*]
ACAP........ Australian College of Applied Psychology
ACAP........ Australian Cooperative Assessment Program
ACAPAP... South African Association for Child and Adolescent Psychiatry and Allied Professions   (AA)
ACAPESP ... Associacao das Cooperativas Agropecuarias do Estado de Sao Paulo [*Brazil*]   (DSCA)
A Capp....... A Cappella [*Unaccompanied*] [*Music*]
ACAPU ..... Agro Pecuaria [*Brazil*]   (DSCA)

ACAQ........ Advisory Committee on Air Quality [*Australia*]
ACAQ........ Autistic Children's Association of Queensland [*Australia*]
ACAR .... Asociacao de Credito e Assistencia Rural [*Brazil*]   (WGAO)
ACAR .... Asociacion Colombiana de Archivistas   (WGAO)
ACAR .... Associacao de Credito e Assistencia Rural [*Association of Credit and Rural Assistance*] [*Brazil*]
ACAR .... Australian Coal Association (Research) Ltd.   (ADA)
ACAR .... Cooperativa de Productores Agricolas de Portuguesa [*Venezuela*]   (DSCA)
ACAR-AM ... Associacao de Credito e Assistencia Rural do Estado do Amazonas [*Brazil*]   (DSCA)
ACARB...... Australian Computer Abuse Research Bureau
ACARDA .. British-Romanian Association   (EAIO)
ACAR-DF ... Associacao de Credito e Assistencia Rural do Distrito Federal [*Brazil*]   (DSCA)
ACARES ... Associacao de Credito e Assistencia Rural do Espirito Santo [*Brazil*]   (DSCA)
ACARESC ... Associacao de Credito e Assistencia Rural do Estado de Santa Catarina [*Brazil*]   (DSCA)
ACARGO .. Associacao de Credito e Assistencia Rural do Estado de Goies [*Brazil*]   (DSCA)
AC ARM.... Advanced Certificate, Australian Risk Management
ACAR-MA ... Associacao de Credito e Assistencia Rural do Estado do Maranhao [*Brazil*]   (DSCA)
ACARMAT ... Associacao de Credito e Assistencia Rural de Mato Grosso [*Brazil*]   (DSCA)
ACAR-MG ... Associacao de Credito e Assistencia Rural de Minas Gerais [*Brazil*]   (DSCA)
ACARPA ... Associacao de Credito e Assistencia Rural do Parana [*Brazil*]   (DSCA)
ACAR-PARA ... Associacao de Credito e Assistencia Rural do Estado do Para [*Brazil*]   (DSCA)
ACARPESC ... Servico de Extensao de Pesca de Santa Catarina [*Brazil*]   (ASF)
ACARPESC ... Servico de Extensao de Santa Catarina   (WGAO)
ACARRE... Australian Centre for Advanced Risk and Reliability Engineering
ACAR-RJ .. Associacao de Credito e Assistencia Rural do Estado do Rio de Janeiro [*Brazil*]   (DSCA)
ACARTSD ... African Centre for Applied Research and Training in Social Development   (EAIO)
ACARTSOD ... African Centre for Applied Research and Training in Social Development
ACAS........ Aboriginal Children's Advancement Society [*Australia*]   (ADA)
ACAS........ Aboriginal Clerical Assistants Scheme [*Australia*]
ACAS........ African Commission on Agricultural Statistics   (EA)
ACAS........ Asociacion Centroamericana de Sociologia [*Panama*]   (WGAO)
ACAS....... Association Centrale des Assistants Sociaux [*Belgium*]   (SLS)
ACAS........ Association of African Sports Confederations   (WGAO)
ACAS........ Association of Concerned African Scholars   (WGAO)
ACASA...... Autistic Children's Association of South Australia
ACASA...... Autopistas de Cataluna y Aragon, Sociedad Anonima [*Superhighways of Catalonia and Aragon, Incorporated*] [*Spanish*]   (WER)
ACASCA ... Australian Cable and Subscription Communications Association
ACASCH... Asociacion Campesina Social-Cristiana de Honduras [*Social-Christian Peasant Association of Honduras*]
ACASH ..... Association of Cooperatives and Apex Societies of Handloom [*India*]
ACASLA ... Association of Chief Architects of Scottish Local Authorities   (WGAO)
ACASP ...... Australian Commonwealth Association of Simplified Practice   (ADA)
ACASS ...... Administratia Centrala a Actiunilor Sportive Scolare [*Central Administration for School Sports Activities*]   (RO)
ACASSI..... Association of Chartered Accountants Students Societies in Ireland   (WGAO)
ACAST ...... Advisory Committee on the Application of Science and Technology to Development [*Also, ACASTD, ACST*] [*United Nations*]
ACASTD ... Advisory Committee on the Application of Science and Technology to Development [*Also, ACAST, ACST*] [*United Nations*]
ACAT .... Accio dels Cristians per l'Abolicio de la Tortura [*Action of Christians for the Abolition of Torture*] [*Spain*]   (EAIO)
ACAT .... Action de Chretiens pour la Abolition de Torture
ACAT .... Action des Chretiens pour l'Abolition de la Torture [*Action of Christians for the Abolition of Torture*] [*France*]   (EAIO)
ACAT .... Africa Cooperative Action Trust   (WGAO)
ACAT .... Australian Centre for the Arts and Technology
ACAT .... Azione dei Cristiani per l'Abolizione della Tortura [*Action of Christians for the Abolition of Torture*] [*Italy*]   (EAIO)
ACAU........ Australian Civil Affairs Unit   (VNW)
ACAV .... Agence Centrafrique de Voyage   (WGAO)
ACAV .... Asociacion Colombiana de Auxiliares de Vuelo [*Colombia*]   (COL)
ACAWA .... Amateur Canoe Association of Western Australia
ACAWU .... Aviation, Communication and Allied Workers Union   (EAIO)

ACB .... ABC [*Air Business Contact*] [*France*] [*ICAO designator*]   (FAAC)
ACB .... Aero Clube do Brasil [*Aero Club of Brazil*]
ACB .... African Continental Bank Ltd.
ACB .... Arab Central Bank   (WGAO)
ACB .... Asociacion Costarricense de Bibliotecarios   (WGAO)
ACB .... Association des Commercants Barundais [*Association of Burundi Merchants*]   (AF)
ACB .... Association of Clinical Biochemists   (WGAO)
ACB .... Ateliers et Chantiers de Bretagne [*France*] [*Nuclear energy*]   (NUCP)
ACB .... Australian Carbon Black Proprietary Ltd.
ACB .... Australian Cricket Board   (ADA)
ACB .... Australian Customs Service [*National Union Catalogue of Australia symbol*]
ACB .... Automovel Clube do Brasil [*Automobile Club of Brazil*]
ACB .... Automovil Club Boliviano [*Bolivian Automobile Club*]   (EAIO)
ACBA .... Aggregate Concrete Block Association   (WGAO)
ACBA .... Australian Council of Bursars Associations
ACBAR...... Agency Coordinating Body for Afghan Relief [*Afghanistan/ Pakistan*]   (ECON)
ACBC........ Australia-China Business Council
ACBC........ Australian Catholic Bishops' Conference
ACBC........ Australian Cricket Board of Control   (ADA)
ACBCC...... Advisory Committee to the Board and to the Committee on Commodities   (WGAO)
ACBE......... Australian Centre for Business Education
ACB-EC..... Association of Cooperative Banks of the EC [*Economy Community*] [*Belgium*]   (EAIO)
ACBF......... African Capacity Building Foundation   (ECON)
ACBI......... Agricultural Cooperatives Bank of Iran   (WGAO)
ACBIC....... Australian Centre for Brain Injured Children   (ADA)
ACBIS .... Association des Conseils en Brevets dans l'Industrie Suisse   (WGAO)
ACBTBL.... Arnold Cook Braille and Talking Book Library [*Australia*]
ACC .... Abattoir County Council [*Australia*]
ACC .... Aboriginal Coordinating Council [*Australia*]
ACC .... Academia de Ciencias de Cuba [*Academy of Sciences of Cuba*]   (LA)
Acc .... Accademia [*Academy*] [*Italian*]   (BJA)
Acc .... Accelerato [*Slow Train*] [*Italian*]
acc .... Acceptation [*Acceptance*] [*French*]
acc .... Accident [*Damage*] [*French*]
ACC .... Accion Catolica Colombiana [*Colombia*]   (COL)
ACC .... Accra [*Ghana*] [*Airport symbol*]   (OAG)
acc .... Accresciuto [*Enlarged*] [*Publishing*] [*Italian*]
ACC .... Adelaide City Council [*Australia*]
ACC .... Administrative Committee on Coordination [*of the United Nations*] [*Aviation*]
ACC .... Aeroplane Construction Committee [*Australia*]
ACC .... African Club Championships
ACC .... African Community Council
ACC .... Agricultural Credit Corporation [*Eire, Jordan*]   (WGAO)
ACC .... Allied Control Center [*NATO*]   (NATG)
ACC .... Alta Corte Costituzionale [*Supreme Constitutional Court*] [*Italian*]   (WER)
ACC .... Amazonian Cooperation Council [*Brazil*]   (EAIO)
ACC .... Anciens Combattants Coloniaux
ACC .... Anglican Consultative Council [*British*]   (EAIO)
ACC .... Antarctic Circumpolar Current [*Oceanography*]   (MSC)
ACC .... Anti-Cancer Council [*Australia*]
ACC .... Antique Collectors Club   (WGAO)
ACC .... Arab Co-Operation Council   (ECON)
ACC .... Arbitration and Conciliation Commission [*Australia*]
ACC .... Area Consultative Committee
ACC .... Asian Coconut Community [*Later, APCC*]
ACC .... Asian Cultural Council   (WGAO)
ACC .... Asmara Chamber of Commerce [*Ethiopia*]   (WGAO)
ACC .... Asociacion de Citricultores de Concordia [*Argentina*]   (DSCA)
ACC .... Associated Cement Companies [*India*]   (WGAO)
ACC .... Associated Communications Corporation   (WGAO)
ACC .... Association des Cineastes du Cambodge [*Motion Picture Association of Cambodia*]   (CL)
ACC .... Association of Computer Clubs   (WGAO)
ACC .... Association of Conservative Clubs   (WGAO)
ACC .... Association of Country Councils   (WGAO)
ACC .... Australasian Corrosion Centre, Inc.
ACC .... Australia-China Council
ACC .... Australian Chamber of Commerce   (ADA)
ACC .... Australian Chiropody Council   (ADA)
ACC .... Australian Coaching Council
ACC .... Australian Computer Conference
ACC .... Australian Copyright Council   (ADA)
ACC .... Australian Council of Churches   (ADA)
ACC .... Australian Croquet Council   (ADA)
ACC .... Automovil Club de Chile [*Automobile Club of Chile*]   (EAIO)
ACC .... Automovil Club de Colombia [*Colombia*]   (COL)

ACC .... Corrosion Prevention Centre Australasia   (EAIO)
ACCA .... Air Charter Carriers Association   (WGAO)
ACCA .... American Chamber of Commerce in Australia
ACCA .... American Chamber of Commerce in Austria   (EAIO)
ACCA .... Associated Chambers of Commerce of Australia   (WGAO)
ACCA .... Association des Caisses Communes d'Assurance   (WGAO)
ACCA .... Association of Chartered and Certified Accountants   (WGAO)
ACCA .... Association of Child Caring Agencies [*Australia*]
ACCA .... Association of Cleaning Contractors of Australia
ACCA .... Australian Centre for Contemporary Art
ACCA .... Australian Chinese Community Association   (ADA)
ACCA .... Australian Cultural Center Association
ACCA .... Auto Cycle Council of Australia
ACCAM .... Societe des Accumulateurs du Cameroun
ACC&CE ... Association of Consulting Chemists and Chemical Engineers   (WGAO)
ACCANSW ... Australian Chinese Community Association of New South Wales
ACCART ... Association des Collectionneurs de Cartes et Tarots [*Association of Playing Card and Tarot Card Collectors*] [*France*]   (EAIO)
ACCART ... Australian Council for the Care of Animals in Research and Teaching
ACCB........ American Chamber of Commerce of Bolivia   (EAIO)
ACCC........ Africa Cup of Club Champions
ACCC........ Asociacion Colombiana de Control de Calidad [*Colorado*]
ACCC........ Asociacion Colombiana de Criadores de Cebu [*Colombia*]   (DSCA)
ACCC........ Asociacion Criadores de Caballos Criollos [*Argentina*]   (DSCA)
ACCC........ Associacao dos Criadores de Cavalos Crioulos [*Brazil*]   (DSCA)
ACCC........ Associated Chinese Chamber of Commerce   (ML)
ACCC........ Association of Child Care Centres [*Australia*]
ACCC........ Australia-China Chamber of Commerce
ACCC........ Australian Competition and Consumer Commission [*Proposed*]
ACCCA...... Advisory and Coordinating Committee on Child Abuse [*Western Australia*]
ACCCI...... Australia-China Chamber of Commerce and Industry
ACCCNSW ... Association of Child Care Centers in New South Wales [*Australia*]
ACCD .... Advisory Committee on National Health Service Drugs   (WGAO)
ACCD .... Arab Council for Childhood and Development [*Egypt*]
ACCE........ Advisory Committee on Chemicals in the Environment [*Australia*]
ACCE........ African Council on Communication Education   (WGAO)
ACCE........ Asociacion de Comercio de Cereales de Espana   (EY)
ACCE........ Association of County Chief Executives   (WGAO)
ACCE........ Australian Council for Computers in Education
ACCEC...... Australian Chamber of Commerce Export Council
ACCEEAS ... Asociacion de Cooperacion Cultural y Economica Espana-Arabia Saudi [*Association of Spanish-Saudi Arabian Cultural and Economic Cooperation*] [*Spain*]
ACCEFN ... Academia Colombiana de Ciencias Exactas Fisicas y Naturales [*Colombia*]   (DSCA)
ACCEL...... Accelerando [*Quickening the Pace*] [*Music*]
ACCEPN ... Acceptation [*Acceptance*] [*French*] [*Banking*]   (ROG)
ACCESD ... Australian Council of Chairmen of Earth Science Departments
ACCESS.... Academic Consortium for Economic and Social Surveys [*Australia*]
ACCESS.... Arab Community Center for Economic and Social Services
ACCESS.... Australian Commercial Cassette Exchange and Screening Service   (ADA)
ACCESS.... Australian Contribution to the Cost of Education for Students Scheme
ACCESS.... Automated Corporate and Customer Enquiry Support [*Sydney Water Board*] [*Australia*]
ACCET ...... Asia Centre for Comparative Education   (WGAO)
ACCF........ Agence Centrafricaine des Communications Fluviales [*Central African Agency for River Communications*]   (AF)
ACCF........ American Chamber of Commerce in France   (EAIO)
ACCF........ Asia Christian Communications Fellowship [*Singapore*]   (EAIO)
ACCFA ...... Agricultural Credit and Co-operative Financing Administration [*Philippines*]   (WGAO)
ACCFA ...... Agricultural Credit Cooperative Farmers' Association [*Philippines*]
ACCFT ...... Australian Council for Children's Film and Television
ACCFTV ... Australian Council for Children's Films and Television
ACCG .... Agricultural Chemicals Consultative Group [*Australia*]
ACCG .... Associacao Catarinense de Criadores de Gado [*Brazil*]   (DSCA)
ACCGO ..... Asociacion Colombiana de Criadores de Ganado Ovino [*Colombia*]   (DSCA)
ACCHAN ... Allied Command Channel [*NATO*]
ACCI.......... Abu Dhabi Chamber of Cmmerce and Industry   (WGAO)
ACCI.......... Asociacion Centroamericana de Cooperacion Intermunicipal [*LAA*]

ACCI......... Associated Chambers of Commerce and Industry of India (IMH)
ACCI......... Association of Chambers of Commerce of Ireland (WGAO)
ACCI......... Ateliers et Chantiers de la Cote-D'Ivoire
ACCI......... Australian Computing and Communications Institute
ACCIA...... Asociacion Chilena de Comerciantes e Importadores de Automoviles [*Chilean Association of Automobile Dealers and Importers*] (LA)
accid .... Accident [*Damage*] [*French*]
ACCIM...... Associated Chambers of Commerce and Industry of Malawi (EAIO)
ACCIR...... Association Champenoise de Cooperation Inter-Regionale
ACCIS ...... Advisory Committee for the Co-Ordination of Information Systems [*Database producer*] [*Geneva, Switzerland*] [*United Nations*]
ACCIS ...... Air Command and Control Improvement System [*NATO*]
ACCKP...... Aboriginal Cultural Centre and Keeping Place [*University of New England*] [*Australia*]
ACCL......... Australian Council for Civil Liberties
ACCM ...... Advisory Council for the Church's Ministry (WGAO)
ACCMLRI ... Association des Caisses de Credit Mutuel Libres a Responsabilite Illimitee (WGAO)
ACCMM ... Associacao dos Criadores do Cavalo Mangalarga Marchador [*Brazil*] (DSCA)
ACCN .... Academia Chilena de Ciencias Naturales [*Chilean Academy of Natural Sciences*] [*Santiago*] (LAA)
ACCN .... Australian Council of Community Nursing
ACCN .... Australian Customs Clearance Statistics [*Database*]
ACCO .... Algemene Classificatie-Commissie voor de Overheidsadministratie [*Netherlands*]
ACCO .... Association of Child Care Officers (WGAO)
Accom adLib ... Accompaniment ad Libitum [*Music*]
AccomOblto ... Accompaniment Obligato [*Music*]
ACCOR ..... Associated Chambers of Commerce of Rhodesia (AF)
ACCOSCA ... African Confederation of Cooperative Savings and Credit Associations [*See also ACECA*] [*Nairobi, Kenya*] (EAIO)
ACCOZ ..... Associated Chambers of Commerce of Zimbabwe (IMH)
ACCP........ American Chamber of Commerce of the Philippines (EAIO)
ACCP .... Association of Child Psychology and Psychiatry (WGAO)
ACCRA...... Australian Chart and Code for Rural Accounting (ADA)
accresc...... Accresciuto [*Enlarged*] [*Publishing*] [*Italian*]
ACCS........ Air Command and Control System [*NATO*]
ACCS......... Antarctic Circumpolar Current System [*Oceanography*] (MSC)
ACCS......... Associazione del Commercio dei Cereali e Semi (WGAO)
ACCS........ Australian Capital Cities Secretariat (ADA)
ACCS........ Australian Carpet Classification Scheme
ACCS........ Australian Casualty Clearing Station (ADA)
ACCS........ Australian Centre for Computer Science
ACCSA ...... Allied Communications and Computer Security Agency [*NATO*] (WGAO)
ACC/SCN ... Administrative Committee on Coordination - Subcommittee on Nutrition [*United Nations*] (EAIO)
ACCT........ Agence de Cooperation Culturelle et Technique [*Agency for Cultural and Technical Cooperation*] (EAIO)
ACCT........ American Chamber of Commerce in Thailand (EAIO)
ACCTIVS ... Association of Closed Circuit Television Surveyors (WGAO)
Acc Trav..... Accidents du Travail et Invalidite de la Paix [*French*] (BAS)
ACCU .... Academisch Computer Centrum Utrecht
ACCU .... Asian Confederation of Credit Unions [*of the World Council of Credit Unions*] [*Bangkok, Thailand*] (EAIO)
ACCU .... Asian Cultural Centre for Unesco [*Japan*] (WGAO)
ACCU .... Association of Catholic Colleges and Universities (WGAO)
ACCU .... Australian Council of Cricket Unions
ACCV .... Anti-Cancer Council of Victoria [*Australia*]
ACCWW ... Association Collectionneurs et Collections Who's What [*France*] (EAIO)
ACD.......... Acandi [*Colombia*] [*Airport symbol*] (OAG)
ACD.......... Adelaide College of Divinity
ACD.......... Alliance Centriste et Democrate [*Algeria*] [*Political party*] (EY)
ACD.......... Alliance for Cultural Democracy (WGAO)
ACD.......... Association des Capacitaires en Droit [*Lawyers Association*] [*Cambodia*] (CL)
ACD.......... Australian College of Dentistry (ADA)
ACD.......... Australian College of Dermatologists (ADA)
ACD.......... Australian Convalescent Depot (ADA)
ACD.......... Automatic Call Director [*Telecommunications*]
ACD.......... Automobil-Cisterna za Dekontaminaciju [*Tank Truck for Decontamination*] [*Military*] (YU)
ACD.......... Societe des Ateliers et Chantiers Maritimes de Dakar [*Senegal*]
ACDA........ Action Concertee pour le Developpement en Afrique
ACDA .... Affiliate of the Company Directors' Association of Australia
ACDA .... Australian Club Development Association
ACDAC ..... Asociacion Colombiana de Aviadores Civiles [*Colombia*] (COL)
ACDB .... Agricultural and Co-Operative Development Bank [*Liberia*] (GEA)

ACDB .... Agriculutral and Cooperative Development Bank [*Liberia*] (WGAO)
ACDB .... Association du Catalogue Documentaire du Batiment [*Building Catalogue Association*] [*France*] (PDAA)
ACDC .... Agricultural Chemical Distribution Control System [*Australia*]
ACDC .... Assessment and Career Development Centre [*Australia*]
ACDC .... Australian Counter Disaster College
ACDE .... Advisory Committee on Dental Establishments [*Scotland*] (WGAO)
ACDE .... Asociacion Catolica de Dirigentes de Empresa [*Buenos Aires, Argentina*] (LAA)
ACDE .... Asociacion Cristiana de Dirigentes de Empresa [*Christian Association of Business Executives*] [*Argentina*] (LA)
ACDEPO... Association of Civil Defence and Emergency Planning Officers (WGAO)
ACDG .... Associazione Cristiana dei Giovani [*Young Men's Christian Association*] [*Italian*]
ACDHUM ... Asociacion Colombiana pro Derechos Humanos [*Colombian Association for Human Rights*] (EAIO)
ACDI .... Agence Canadienne de Developpement International [*Canadian International Development Agency - CIDA*]
ACDIMA... Arab Company for Drug Industries and Medical Appliances [*Kuwait*] (WGAO)
ACDM ...... Australian Culture Defence Movement (ADA)
ACDO........ Association of Civil Defence Officers (ADA)
ACDP .... Advisory Committee on Dangerous Pathogens (WGAO)
ACDP .... Agencija Cehoslovacke Drzavne Plovidbe [*Agency of the Czechoslovak State Navigation Enterprise*] [*Belgrade*] (YU)
ACDP .... Asociacion Catolica de Propagandistas [*Catholic Association of Propagandists*] [*Spanish*] (WER)
ACDP .... Australian Coalition for Disarmament and Peace
ACDP .... Australian Committee of Directors and Principals in Advanced Education Ltd.
ACDRI...... Advisory Committee on the Development of Research for Industry [*South Africa*]
ACDS........ Advisory Committee on Dangerous Substances (WGAO)
ACDS........ Anglo Continental Dental Society (WGAO)
ACDS........ Australian College of Dental Surgeons (ADA)
ACDSF ...... Aboriginal Collection District Summary Files [*Australia*]
ACDSG...... Australian Coastal Defences Study Group
ACDSNSW ... Australian Cattle Dog Society of New South Wales
ACDST ...... Agency of Cooperation for the Development through Sciences and Technology [*Belgium*] (WGAO)
ACDTPN... Association pour le Controle de la Descendance des Taureaux Pie Noirs (WGAO)
ACE .... Academia de Ciencias Economicas [*Academy of Economic Science*] [*Buenos Aires, Argentina*] (LAA)
ACE .... Accion Catolica Espanola (WGAO)
ACE .... Action by the Community Relating to the Environment [*EC*] (ECED)
ACE .... Administration de Cooperation Economique [*French*]
ACE .... African Container Express
ACE .... Agricultural Communicators in Education (WGAO)
ACE .... Alliance Cinematographique Eurafricaine
ACE .... Allied Command Europe [*NATO*]
ACE .... Allied Forces Central Europe [*NATO*] (MCD)
ACE .... Amities Chretiennes Europeennes (WGAO)
ACE .... Architects Council of Europe (DAC)
ACE .... Arquitectos Constructores Escolares [*Colombia*] (COL)
ACE .... Arrecife [*Canary Islands*] [*Airport symbol*] (OAG)
ACE .... Associated Consulting Engineers [*Lebanon*]
ACE .... Associates in Childbirth Education [*Australia*]
ACE .... Association des Compagnies Aeriennes de la CEE (WGAO)
ACE .... Association for Centrifuge Enrichment [*Made up of ten countries including Japan*]
ACE .... Association for Coal in Europe (WGAO)
ACE .... Association for Cultural Exchange (WGAO)
ACE .... Association for the Conservation of Energy (WGAO)
ACE .... Association of Circulation Executives (WGAO)
ACE .... Association of Comics Enthusiasts (WGAO)
ACE .... Association of Consulting Engineers (WGAO)
ACE .... Association of Cost Engineers (WGAO)
ACE .... Athens Center of Ekistics [*Research center*] [*Greek*] (IRC)
ACE .... Athens Centre of Ekistiks [*Greece*] (WGAO)
ACE .... Australian Capital Equity Proprietary Ltd.
ACE .... Australian Centre for Egyptology
ACE .... Australian Christian Endeavour Union (WGAO)
ACE .... Australian College of Education (ADA)
ACE .... Australian College of English
ACE .... Australian Computer Exhibition
ACE .... Australian Concert Entertainment
ACE .... Automatic Cross-Connection Equipment [*Computer science*]
ACE .... Automobile Club d'Egypte
ACE .... Avion de Combat European [*France*]
ACE .... Ayuda Cristiana Evangelica [*Santiago, Chile*] (LAA)

ACE .... NATO Allied Command Europe (WGAO)
ACE .... Race Cargo Airlines [*Ghana*] [*ICAO designator*] (FAAC)
ACEA .... Agrupamiento Cientifico de Estudos Antropologicos [*Portugal*] (DSCA)
ACEA .... Asociacion Costarricense de Economistas Agricolas [*Costa Rica*] (DSCA)
ACEA .... Associatin des Cooperatives d'Epargne et de Credit d'Afrique (WGAO)
ACEA .... Association des Constructeurs Europeens d'Automobiles [*Association of European Car Manufacturers*] [*EC*] (ECED)
ACEA .... Association des Educateurs par Correspondence d'Afrique (WGAO)
ACEA .... Association of Consulting Engineers, Australia (ADA)
ACEA .... Association of Cost and Executive Accountants [*British*] (EAIO)
ACEA .... Australian Citrus Exporters' Association
ACEA .... Australian Coal Exporters' Association (ADA)
ACEA .... Australian Council for Educational Administration
ACEAA ...... Advisory Committee on Electrical Appliances and Accessories (WGAO)
ACEAC ...... Association des Conferences Episcopales de l'Afrique Centrale (WGAO)
ACE-ACCIS ... Allied Command Europe Automated Command Control and Information System [*Proposed*] [*NATO*]
ACEACE ... Asociacion Colombiana para el Avance de la Ciencia [*Colombia*] (COL)
ACEAR ...... Atelier Central d'Etudes d'Amenagement Rural (WGAO)
ACEAV ...... Associacao Cearense de Avicultura [*Brazil*] (DSCA)
ACEB .... Advisory Council on Exhibition Birds [*Australia*]
ACEB .... Agrupamento Cientifico de Estudos Biologicos [*Portugal*] (DSCA)
ACEB .... Asociacion Colombiana de Empleados Bancarios [*Colombian Bank Employees Association*] (LA)
ACEBA ...... Aceite y Abonos del Valle Ltda. [*Colombia*] (COL)
ACEC .... Associazione Cattolica Esercenti Cinema (WGAO)
ACEC .... Ateliers de Constructions Electriques de Charleroi [*Charleroi Electrical Engineering Shops*] [*Belgium*] (WER)
ACEC .... Australian Computer Education Conference
ACECA ...... Association des Cooperatives d'Epargne et de Credit d'Afrique [*African Confederation of Cooperative Savings and Credit Associations - ACCOSCA*] [*Nairobi, Kenya*] (EAIO)
ACECCT ... Association des Conferences Episcopales du Congo, de la Republique Centrafricaine et du Tchad (WGAO)
ACECDL ... Associacao dos Comerciantes de Equipamentos Cientificos do Distrito de Lisboa (WGAO)
ACECO ..... Association pour les Compensations d'Echanges Commerciaux (WGAO)
ACEDET ... Association pour la Comparaison et l'Etude des Droits Europeens du Travail [*French*] (BAS)
ACEDI ...... American Central European Dental Institute
ACEE .... Australian Consortium on Experiential Education
ACEF .... Aboriginal Children's Education Fund [*Australia*] (ADA)
ACEF .... Asociacion Colombiana de Exportadores de Flores [*Colombian Association of Fresh Cut Flowers Exporters*] (EAIO)
ACEF .... Australian Council of Employers' Federations
ACEFH ...... Association Internationale Contre l'Exploitation du Foetus Humain (WGAO)
ACEG .... Afghan Carpet Exporters' Guild (EAIO)
ACEG .... Agrupamento Cientifico de Estudos de Geologia [*Portugal*] (DSCA)
ACEGRASAS ... Aceites y Grasas Vegetales [*Colombia*] (COL)
ACEGRAVE ... Fabrica de Aceites y Grasas Vegetales de la America Latina [*Barranquilla*] (COL)
ACEI .... Association of Consulting Engineers of Ireland (WGAO)
ACEIB .... Association des Centrales Electriques Industrielles de Belgique [*Belgium*] (BAS)
ACEID .... Asian Centre of Educational Innovation for Development [*Thailand*] (WGAO)
ACEINEM ... Asociaciones Colombianas de Educadores de Institutos de Ensenanza Media [*Colombian Secondary School Teachers Association*] (LA)
ACEJMC .. Accrediting Council on Education in Journalism and Mass Communciations (WGAO)
ACEK .... Association of Consulting Engineers of Kenya (EAIO)
Ac Eks .... Acik Eksilmesi [*Open Bidding*] (TU)
ACEL .... Association des Chefs d'Entreprises Libres (WGAO)
ACEL .... Australian Civil Engineering Library (ADA)
ACELP ...... Association for Children with Emotional and Learning Problems [*Pakistan*] (EAIO)
ACEM ...... Association of Consulting Engineers Malaysia (EAIO)
ACEM ...... Australian College of Emergency Medicine
ACEMA .... Australian Computer Equipment Manufacturers' Association
A Cemb ...... A Cembalo [*Music*]
ACEMCI ... Ateliers de Constructions Electro-Mecaniques de Cote-D'Ivoire
ACEN .... Assembly of Captive European Nations (WGAO)
ACEN .... Association of Consulting Engineers Norway (EAIO)

ACENET ... Allied Command Europe Communications Network [*NATO*] (NATG)
ACENOE .. Assistance aux Createurs d'Entreprises du Nord-Ouest Europeen [*Multinational organization*] (EAIO)
ACENTO .. Augmented Colombian El Nino Tuna Oceanography [*Project of IATTC*] (MSC)
ACENZ...... Association of Consultant Engineers of New Zealand (PDAA)
ACEO .... Association of Chief Education Officers (WGAO)
ACEP......... Advisory Committee on Export Policy (WGAO)
ACEP......... Australian Council of Egg Producers
ACEPA ..... Australian Childbirth Education and Parenting Association
ACEPA ..... Australian Commonwealth Environment Protection Agency [*National Union Catalogue of Australia symbol*]
ACEPAR ... Acero del Paraguay (EY)
ACEPE ...... Association pour le Developpement d'Actions Collectives d'Education Permanent en Europe (WGAO)
Ac Er .... Acemi Er [*Recruit*] (TU)
ACER........ Administracion de los Centros de Recria [*Venezuela*] (DSCA)
ACER........ Afro-Caribbean Educational Resource Centre [*British*]
ACER........ Associacona Costruttori Edili di Roma e Provincia (WGAO)
ACER........ Atelier Central d'Entretien et de Renovation [*Algeria*]
ACER........ Australian Council for Educational Research [*Information service or system*] (ADA)
ACERAC ... Associaton des Conferences Episcopales de la Region de l'Afrique Centrale (WGAO)
ACERM..... Associazione di Concorsie e Rassegni Musicali [*Association of Musical Competitions and Reviews*] [*Italy*]
ACERP...... Asociacion Cubana de Ejecutivos de Relaciones Publicas (WGAO)
ACERT ...... Advisory Committee for the Education of Romany and other Travellers (WGAO)
ACES........ Action Chretienne pour l'Eglise du Silence [*Belgium*]
ACES........ Advisory Council of Education for the Services [*Australia*]
ACES........ Aerolineas Centrales de Colombia [*Airline*] [*Colombia*]
ACES........ Asociacion Cafetalera de El Salvador [*Association of Salvadoran Coffee Producers*] (LA)
ACES........ Asociacion de Criadores Exportadores de Sherry [*Spain*] (EY)
ACES........ Australian Commercial Enterprise Statistics
ACES........ Australian Council for Educational Standards (ADA)
ACES........ Automovil Club de El Salvador [*Automobile Club of El Salvador*]
ACESA ..... Australian Commonwealth Engineering Standards Association (ADA)
ACESA ..... Australian Computer Equipment Suppliers' Association
ACESITA ... Central de Informacoes Companhia Acos Especiais Itabira [*Brazil*]
ACESNA ... Agence Centrafricaine pour la Securite de la Navigation Aerienne (WGAO)
ACESW ..... Association of Chief Education Social Workers (WGAO)
ACET........ Associated Consulting Engineering Team [*Saudi Arabia*]
ACET........ Association of Consultants in Education and Training (WGAO)
ACET........ Association of Consulting Engineers Tanzania (EAIO)
ACET........ Australian Council for Education through Technology (ADA)
ACETA ...... Australasian Commercial and Economics Teachers Association
ACETM..... Association Cooperative des Ecrivains du Troisieme Millenaire [*Writers of the Third Millenium's Cooperative*] [*France*] (EAIO)
ACETSW .. Australian Council for Education and Training in Social Welfare (ADA)
ACEUR ..... Allied Command Europe [*NATO*]
ACEUT...... Advisory Committee on the Educational Use of Communication Technology [*Australia*]
ACEX........ Administratia de Cercetari si Exploatari Geologice [*Geological Research and Exploitation Administration*] (RO)
ACF............ Aboriginal Cultural Foundation [*Australia*]
ACF............ Academie Canadienne Francaise [*French-Canadian Academy*] [*French*] (BARN)
ACF............ Accountants' Christian Fellowship [*Australia*]
ACF............ Active Citizens Force
ACF............ Advanced Communication Facility
ACF............ Aero Club de France [*Air Club of France*] (WER)
ACF............ Agricultural Co-operative Federation (WGAO)
ACF............ Air Cadet Force [*India*]
ACF............ Air Charter [*France*] [*ICAO designator*] (FAAC)
ACF............ Americko-Ceskoslovenska Federace [*American-Czechoslovak Federation*] (CZ)
ACF............ Amsterdam Chemie Farmacie NV [*Amsterdam Chemical Pharmacy*] [*Netherlands*]
ACF............ Arab Co-operative Federation [*Iraq*] (WGAO)
ACF............ Arap Cumhuriyetler Federasyonu [*Arab Republics Federation*] (TU)
ACF............ ASEAN Cardiologists Federation (WGAO)
ACF............ ASEAN Constructors Federation [*Indonesia*] (WGAO)
ACF............ Asian Club Federation (EAIO)
ACF............ Associacao Crista Feminina [*Association of Christian Women*] [*Portuguese*]
ACF............ Australian Calisthenics Federation
ACF............ Australian Canoe Federation (ADA)

ACF........... Australian Chess Federation   (ADA)
ACF........... Australian Children's Foundation
ACF........... Australian Chinese Forum of New South Wales
ACF........... Australian Comforts Fund   (ADA)
ACF........... Australian Commission for the Future
ACF........... Australian Conservation Foundation   (ADA)
ACF........... Australian Cooperative Foods
ACF........... Australian Corporate Finance Ltd.
ACF........... Australian Cotton Foundation
ACF........... Automobile Club de France [*Automobile Club of France*]   (WER)
ACF........... Avion de Combat Futur [*Next Generation French Combat Aircraft*] [*French*]   (WER)
ACFA........ Aero Club Federation of Australia
ACFA........ Air Charter Forwarders Association   (WGAO)
ACFA........ Army Cadet Force Association   (WGAO)
ACFA........ Association of Consulting Foresters of Australia
ACFA........ Australian Cane Farmers' Association
ACFA........ Australian Canning Fruitgrowers' Association
ACFA...... Australian Cystic Fibrosis Associations
ACFAF ...... Australian Cystic Fibrosis Associations Federation
ACFARS.... Advisory Committee on Fisheries Applications of Remote Sensing [*Australia*]
ACFAS ...... Association Canadienne Francaise pour l'Avancement des Sciences   (WGAO)
ACFB........ Associations Culturelles Franco-Bresiliennes [*Brazil*]   (WGAO)
ACFC........ Australian Canned Fruits Corporation
ACFDH .... Les Amis des Chateau-Forts et Demeures Historiques   (WGAO)
ACFF........ Australian Cranio-Facial Foundation
ACFFTU ... All Ceylon Federation of Free Trade Unions [*Sri Lanka*]
ACFHE...... Association of Colleges for Further and Higher Education   (WGAO)
ACFI......... Asociacion Chileno Francesa de Ingenieros y Tecnicos [*Santiago, Chile*]   (LAA)
ACFIMAN ... Academia de Ciencias Fisicas, Matematicas y Naturales [*Venezuela*]   (EAIO)
ACFM....... Advisory Committee on Fisheries Management   (WGAO)
ACFM....... Advisory Committee on Fishery Management [*International Council for the Exploration of the Sea*]   (MSC)
ACFM....... Association of Cereal Food Manufacturers   (WGAO)
ACFM....... Australian Council of Furniture Manufacturers
ACFMO .... Alliance de Constructeurs Francais de Machines-Outils   (WGAO)
ACFMO .... Association des Constructeurs Francais de Machines-Outils
ACFMR..... Australian Cancer Fund for Medical Research
ACFNSW .. Accountants' Fellowship of New South Wales [*Australia*]
ACFO .... Association of Car Fleet Operators   (WGAO)
ACFO .... Association of Commercial Flying Organisations of Australia   (ADA)
ACFOA...... Australian Council for Overseas Aid   (ADA)
ACFOD .... Asian Cultural Forum on Development [*Thailand*]   (PDAA)
ACFODE... Action for Development [*An association*] [*Uganda*]   (EAIO)
ACFR........ Australians for Common Sense, Freedom, and Responsibility
ACFRA ..... Assureurs Conseils Franco-Africains
ACFRS ...... Ayr Cattle Field Research Station [*Australia*]   (DSCA)
ACFS .... Australia-China Friendship Society
ACFS .... Australian Centre for Foreign Studies
ACFTU ...... All-China Federation of Trade Unions
ACFU .... Australian Commonwealth Film Unit
ACFUSA .... Anti-Cancer Foundation of the Universities of South Australia
ACFVI .... Australian Chamber of Fruit and Vegetable Industries
ACFWI-EC ... Association of the Cider and Fruit Wine Industry of the EC [*Economic Community*] [*Belgium*]   (EAIO)
ACG........... Aboriginal Consultative Group [*Australia*]
ACG........... Academie Canadienne du Genie [*Canadian Academy of Engineering*]   (EAIO)
ACG........... Aluminium Can Group [*Australia*] [*An association*]
ACG........... Anti-Counterfeiting Group   (WGAO)
ACG........... Assureurs Conseils Gabonais
ACGA .... Australian Cane Growers' Association   (ADA)
ACGA .... Australian Cashmere Growers' Association
ACGA .... Australian Citrus Growers' Association   (ADA)
ACGA .... Australian Coffee Growers Association
ACGA .... Australian Commercial Galleries Association
ACGA .... Australian Commonwealth Games Association
ACGB .... Associacao dos Criadores de Girdo Brasil [*Brazil*]   (DSCA)
ACGB .... Associacao dos Criadores de Guzera do Brasil [*Brazil*]   (DSCA)
ACGC .... Angurugu Community Government Council [*Australia*]
ACGC .... Association of Country Greyhound Clubs [*Australia*]
ACGC .... Australian Cane Growers' Council   (ADA)
ACGC .... Australian Chicken Growers' Council
ACGC .... Australian Commonwealth Grants Commission [*National Union Catalogue of Australia symbol*]
ACGF .... Australian Cherry Growers' Federation
ACGF .... Australian Citrus Growers' Federation
ACGH........ Associacao dos Criadores de Gado Holandes do Rio Grande do Sul [*Brazil*]   (DSCA)

ACGH....... Australian Coal and Gold Holdings
ACGHMG ... Associacao dos Criadores de Gado Holandes de Minas Gerais [*Brazil*]   (DSCA)
ACGIPRI... Asociacion Cooperativa del Grupo Independiete Pro Rehabilitacion Integral [*El Salvador*]   (EAIO)
ACGJ........ Associacao dos Criadores de Gado Jersey [*Brazil*]   (DSCA)
ACGJRGS ... Associacao de Criadores de Gado Jersey do Rio Grande do Sul [*Brazil*]   (DSCA)
ACGM .... Advisory Committee on Genetic Manipulation   (WGAO)
ACGN .... Australian Council of Good Nutrition
ACGP .... Australian College of General Practitioners   (ADA)
ACGPOMS ... American College of General Practitioners in Osteopathic Medicine and Surgery   (WGAO)
ACGRA ..... Australian Cotton Growers' Research Association
ACGS........ Australian Cashmere Goat Society
ACH.......... Academia Colombiana de Historia   (WGAO)
ACH.......... A. C. Hatrick Chemicals Proprietary Ltd. [*Australia*]
Ach............ Achete [*Purchase*] [*French*] [*Business term*]
ACh........... Aircraft Clock   (RU)
ACh........... Air Unit   (RU)
a-ch .... Ampere-Hour   (RU)
ACH.......... Association of Caribbean Historians [*Nassau, Bahamas*]   (EAIO)
ACH.......... Association of Community Homes   (WGAO)
ACH.......... Association of Contemporary Historians   (WGAO)
ACH.......... Australian Camp Hospital   (ADA)
ACH.......... Australian Chemical Holdings Ltd.   (ADA)
ACH.......... Australian Commonwealth Horse   (DMA)
ACh........... Digital Address   (RU)
ACHA....... Accion Chilena Anticomunista [*Chilean Anticommunist Action*] [*Political party*]   (EY)
ACHA....... Asociacion Costarricense de Hoteles y Afines [*Costa Rican Association of Hotels and Related Industries*]   (LA)
ACHA....... Asociacion Criadores de Holando Argentino [*Argentina*]   (LAA)
ACHA....... Australian Capital [*Territory*] - Health Advancement Services [*Board of Health*] [*National Union Catalogue of Australia symbol*]
AChA........ Australian Chiropody Association   (ADA)
ACHA....... Australian Community Health Association
ACHAC ..... Association des Centres pour Handicapes de l'Afrique Centrale   (WGAO)
AChAO...... Adyge (Cherkess) Autonomous Oblast   (RU)
ACHAP .... Asociacion Chilena de Agencias de Publicidad   (WGAO)
ACHAP .... Australian Computerised Human Relations Assessment Profile
ACHAPI... Asociacion Chilena de Apicultores [*Chile*]   (LAA)
ACHCA .... Australian Catholic Health Care Association
ACHCN .... Academia Chilena de Ciencias Naturales [*Chile*]   (DSCA)
AChDT ..... Automatic Timer and Rate Unit   (RU)
ACHEDO ... Association des Chercheurs de Documents [*Document Researchers Association*] [*Cambodia*]   (CL)
ACHEM .... Australian Consortium for Higher Education in Malaysia
ACHEMA ... Ausstellungs-Tegung fuer Chemisches Apparatewesen [*Triennial international chemical engineering exhibition*]
ACHESA... Asociacion Chilena de Energia Solar [*Chilean Solar Energy Association*]   (LA)
ACHET ..... Asociacion Chilena de Empresas de Turismo [*Chile*]   (EY)
ACHF .... Asociacion Colombiana de Holstein-Friesian Ltda. [*Colombia*]   (COL)
ACHIB ...... African Chamber of Hawkers and Informal Business [*South Africa*]   (ECON)
ACHIF...... Asociacion Chilena de Ingenieros Forestales [*Chile*]   (DSCA)
ACHIL...... Association des Chimistes Luxembourgeois   (WGAO)
AChIMESKh ... Azov-Black Sea Institute of Rural Mechanization and Electrification   (RU)
ACHIP....... Asociacion Chilena de Investigaciones para la Paz   (WGAO)
AChK........ Azov-Black Sea Kray   (RU)
AChK......... Pocket [*Microfilm*] Reader   (RU)
AChKh...... Amplitude-Frequency Characteristic   (RU)
ACHLIS .... Australian Clearing House for Library and Information Science [*South Australian College of Advanced Education Library*] [*Information service or system*]   (IID)
ACHM...... Asociacion Chilena Microbiologia [*Chile*]   (DSCA)
ACHM...... Asociacion de Cooperacion Hispano-Marroqui [*Association for Spanish-Moroccan Cooperation*] [*Spain*]
ACHMES ... Australian Clearing House for Middle East Studies
AChP .... Automatic Frequency Start   (RU)
ACHPER... Australian Council for Health, Physical Education, and Recreation   (ADA)
ACHPIRST ... Australian Clearing House for Publications in Recreation, Sport, and Tourism [*Information service or system*]   (IID)
AChR......... Frequency-Controlled Unloading [*Device*]   (RU)
ACHRO..... Asian Coalition of Human Rights Organisations   (WGAO)
ACHS .... Australian Catholic Historical Society   (ADA)
ACHS .... Australian Council on Healthcare Standards
ACHS .... Australian Council on Hospital Standards   (ADA)
ACHSA ..... Australian College of Health Service Administrators
ACHSE...... Australian College of Health Service Executives

ACHSIA.... Australian Health Care Services Industry Association
ACHSTS ... African Council for the Training and Promotion of Health Sciences Teachers and Specialists (WGAO)
AchsV .... Achsdruckverzeichnis [*Axle Pressure Index*] (EG)
ACHTR ...... Advisory Committee for Humid Tropics Research
AChU..... Air Reinforcement Unit (RU)
ACI .... Action Catholique Independante [*Independent Catholic Action*] [*French*] (WER)
ACI .... Actividade Nacional e Internacional de Investigacao e Informacao (WGAO)
ACI .... Aero Club Indonesia (EAIO)
ACI .... Aero Club of Israel (EAIO)
ACI .... African Cultural Institute (WGAO)
ACI .... Afrique Commerce Industrie
ACI .... Agence Congolaise d'Information [*Congolese Information Agency*] (AF)
ACI .... Agencia Central de Informacion [*Central Information Agency*] [*Dominican Republic*] (LA)
ACI .... Agrence Congolaise d'Information (WGAO)
ACI .... Air Caledonie International [*France*] [*ICAO designator*] (FAAC)
ACI .... Alderney [*Channel Islands*] [*Airport symbol*] (OAG)
ACI .... Algemene Vereniging voor de Centrale Verwarmings en luchtbehandelingsidustrie (WGAO)
ACI .... Alianza Cooperativa Internacional [*International Cooperative Alliance - ICA*] [*Spanish*] (ASF)
ACI .... Alliance Cooperative Internationale [*International Cooperative Alliance - ICA*] [*France*] (ASF)
ACI .... Anti-Communism International (EAIO)
ACI .... Approved Consumer Information
ACI .... Arbitrage Commercial International [*Benelux*] (BAS)
ACI .... Asociacion Cartografica Internacional [*International Cartographic Association - ICA*] [*Spanish*] (ASF)
ACI .... Associacao Comercial e Industrial de Novo Hamburgo [*Commercial and Industrial Association of Novo Hamburgo*] [*Brazil*] (LA)
ACI .... Association Cartographique Internationale [*International Cartographic Association - ICA*] [*French*] (ASF)
ACI .... Association for Conservation Information (WGAO)
ACI .... Association of Chambers of Commerce of Ireland (WGAO)
ACI .... Australian Consolidated Industries (ADA)
ACI .... Automation Center International [*Computer science*] (ADPT)
ACI .... Automobile Club d'Italia [*Italian Automobile Club*]
ACI .... Automobile Club of Italy (BARN)
ACI .... Awana Clubs International (EAIO)
ACI .... Azione Cattolica Italiana [*Italian Catholic Action*] (WER)
ACIA......... Asociacion Centroamericana de Informaciones Agricolas (LAA)
ACIA......... Asociacion Colombiana de Ingenieros Agronomos [*Colombia*] (COL)
ACIA......... Associate of the Catering Institute of Australia (ADA)
ACIA......... Australian Chemical Industry Council
ACIAA....... Australian Commercial and Industrial Artists' Association (ADA)
ACIAP....... Associacao Comercial, Industrial, e Agro-Pastoril de Barra-Mansa [*Brazil*] (DSCA)
ACIAR...... Australian Centre for International Agricultural Research [*National Union Catalogue of Australia symbol*]
ACIBA...... Associate of the Corporation of Insurance Brokers of Australia
ACIBS ...... Australian Council of Independent Business Schools
ACIBU...... Association des Commercants Indigenes du Burundi [*Association of Indigenous Merchants of Burundi*]
ACIC......... Accion Coordinadora de Izquierda Cristiana [*Coordinating Activity of the Christian Left*] [*Argentina*] (LA)
ACIC......... American Committee for International Conservation (WGAO)
ACIC......... Asociacion Colombiana de Ingenieros Contratistas [*Colombia*] (COL)
ACIC......... Asociacion Costarricense para Informacion y Cultura [*San Jose, Costa Rica*] (EY)
ACIC......... Asociacion de Canicultores de Imbabura y Carchi [*Ecuador*] (DSCA)
ACIC......... Associacio de Cantants i Interprets Professionals en Llengua Catalana (WGAO)
ACIC......... Australia Crime Intelligence Centre (ADA)
ACIC......... Australian Chemical Industry Council (ADA)
ACIC......... Australian Citrus Industry Council
ACICA...... Australian Centre for International Commercial Arbitration
ACICAR.... Asociacion Colombiana de Inspectores de Carreteras [*Colombia*] (COL)
ACICLISMO ... Asociacion Colombiana de Ciclismo [*Colombia*] (COL)
ACICS ...... Australian Consolidated Industries Computer Services (ADA)
ACICST..... Consortium for International Cooperation in Science and Technology (WGAO)
ACID .... Australian Communities in Danger
ACIDER.... Fabrica de Acidos Sulfurico y Derivados [*Colombia*] (COL)
ACIEAS..... Asociacion Colombiana de Instituciones de Educacion Agricola Superior [*Colombia*] (DSCA)

ACIEL ...... Accion Coordinadora de Instituciones Empresarias Libres [*Coordinating Activity for Free Enterprise Institutions*] [*Chile*] (LA)
ACIEL ...... Coordinating Action of Free Institutions of Commerce and Trade [*Argentine*] (WGAO)
ACIEM..... Asociacion Colombiana de Ingenieros Electricistas y Mecanicos [*Colombia*] (COL)
ACIEMP ... Association Catholique Internationale d'Etudes Medico-Pychologiques (WGAO)
ACIES .... Australian Comparative and International Education Society
ACIESTI ... Association Catholique Internationale des Enseignants et Chercheurs en Sciences et Techniques de l'Information [*Switzerland*] (SLS)
ACIET ...... Asociacion Colombiana de Institutos de Educacion Tecnologica [*Colombian Association of Institutes of Technology*] (COL)
ACIF .... Agricultural Construction Industry Association (WGAO)
ACIF .... Asociacion Colombiana de Ingenieros Forestales [*Colombia*] (DSCA)
ACIF .... Associacao Catolica Interamericana de Filosofia (EAIO)
ACIFA ...... L'Auxiliaire Commerciale Immobiliere Franco-Africaine
ACIJ .... African-Caribbean Institute of Jamaica [*Research center*] (IRC)
ACIJ .... Australian Centre for Independent Journalism
ACIL......... Association pour la Construction d'Immeubles Locatifs [*France*] (FLAF)
ACIL......... Australian Consolidated Industries Ltd.
ACIL......... Azevedo Campos, Irmaos Limitada
ACILECE ... Association Cooperative Intersyndicale de Librairie et d'Edition de Corps Enseignant (WGAO)
ACILOR.... Comite de Gestion Acieries Laminoirs d'Oran
ACIM .... American Committee on Italian Migration (WGAO)
ACIM .... Associate of the Chartered Institute of Managers [*Australia*] (ADA)
ACIM .... Association des Consommateurs de l'Ile Maurice [*Mauritius Consumers Association*] (AF)
ACIMA...... Australian Cellulose Insulation Manufacturers Association
ACIMALL ... Associazione Costruttori Italiani Macchine e Accessori per la Lavorazione del Legno [*Italian Woodworking Machinery and Tool Manufacturers*] (EY)
ACIMGA... Associazione Costruttori Italiani Macchine Grafiche Cartotecniche e Affini [*Italian Printing, Converting, and Paper Machinery Manufacturers Association*] (EY)
ACIMIT .... Associazione Costruttori Italiani di Macchinario per l'Industria Tessile [*Italian Textile Machinery Makers Association*] (EY)
ACIMM ..... Associazione Costruttori Italiani Macchine per Marmo e Affini
ACIMO ..... Association de Coureurs Internationaux en Multicoques Oceaniques [*Association of International Competitors on Oceanic Multihulls*] (EAIO)
ACIN .... Asociatia Cineastilor [*Association of Cinematographers*] (RO)
ACIN .... Australian Curriculum Information Network
ACINDAR ... Industria Argentina de Aceros, SA [*Argentine Steel Industries, Inc.*] (LA)
ACINDECO ... Action Internationale de Developpement Cooperatif (WGAO)
ACIO .... Australian Commerce and Industry Office
ACIP .... Agence Cooperative Interregionale de Presse (WGAO)
ACIP .... Australian Certified Investment Planners
ACIPA .... Asociacion Colombiana de Industrias Plasticas Acoplasticos (EAIO)
ACIPHIL .. Asssociation of Consultants and Independents in the Philippines (WGAO)
ACIR......... Agencias Comerciais e Industriais Reunidas
ACIR......... Arretes Coord. Relatifs aux Impots sour le Revenus [*French*] (BAS)
ACIR......... Association Culturelle Internationale: Reliance [*Leucate, France*] (EAIO)
ACIRAM... Atelierul Central de Intretinere si Reparatie a Aparatelor Medicale [*Central Workshop for the Maintenance and Repair of Medical Equipment*] (RO)
ACIRC ...... Asian Community Information Resource Centre [*Australia*]
ACIRL ...... Australian Coal Industry Research Laboratories (ADA)
ACIRRT .... Australian Centre for Industrial Relations Research and Teaching
ACIS .... Africa Church Information Service (EAIO)
ACIS .... Alto Commissariato per l'Igiene e la Sanita [*High Commissioner of Public Health*] [*Italian*] (WER)
ACIS .... Association of Contemporary Iberian Studies [*ex ISSA*] (WGAO)
ACIS .... Association pour la Cooperation Islamique [*Senegal*] (EY)
ACISCA .... Association of Christian Institutes for Social Concern in Asia [*India*] (WGAO)
ACISJF ..... Association Catholique Internationale des Services de la Jeunesse Feminine [*International Catholic Society for Girls*] [*Geneva, Switzerland*] (EAIO)
AcIT.......... Academie Internationale du Tourisme [*International Academy of Tourism*] (EAIO)
ACIT......... Association des Chimistes de l'Industrie Textile [*Association of Chemists of the Textile Industry*] (EAIO)

ACIT......... Association of Conference Interpreters of Turkey
ACITE....... Asociacion Catolica de Ingenieros, Tecnicos, y Economistas [*Spain*]   (DSCA)
ACITS....... Advisory Committee on Information Technology Standardization [*Commission of the European*]   (NITA)
ACIV......... Associate of the Commonwealth Institute of Valuers   (ADA)
ACIZ.......... Asociacion de Comerciantes e Industriales del Zulia [*Venezuela*]   (EY)
ACJ............ Alianz Mundial de Asociaciones Christianas de Jovenes   (WGAO)
ACJ............ Andean Commission of Jurists [*See also CAJ*]   (EAIO)
ACJ............ Asociacion Cristiana de Jovenes [*Young Men's Christian Association*]   (EAIO)
ACJAB...... Association Culturelle des Jeunesses Africaines du Burundi
ACJF .... Association Catholique de la Jeunesse Francaise [*France*]
ACJI.......... A Coeur Joie International [*An association*]   (EAIO)
ACJMG..... Association of Circuit Judges and Magistrates of Ghana   (EAIO)
ACJPA ...... Association Culturelle de la Jeunesse Populaire Algerienne [*Cultural Association of Algerian People's Youth*]   (AF)
ACJRB ...... Associacao dos Criadores de Jumento da Raca Brasileira [*Brazil*]   (DSCA)
ACJRP ...... Associacao dos Criadores de Jumento da Raca Pega [*Brazil*]   (DSCA)
ACJS .... Association Congolaise des Journalistes Sportifs
ACK .... Affirmative Acknowledge [*Computer Science*]   (NITA)
ACK .... Agricultural Centre Kerang Department of Agriculture of Victoria [*Australia*]   (ADA)
ACK .... Arhiv Centralnega Komiteta (KPS) [*Archives of the Central Committee (Communist Party of Slovenia)*]   (YU)
ACK .... Automobile Club du Katanga
ACKPOM ... Akademicka Centralna Komisja Porozumiewawcza Organizacji Mlodziezy [*Central Student Consultative Commission of Youth Organizations*]   (POL)
ACKSA...... All Cachar and Karingang Students Association [*Indonesia*]   (WGAO)
ACL .... Academia Carioca de Letras [*Rio De Janeiro Academy of Letters*] [*Brazil*]   (LAA)
ACL .... Academia Chilena de la Lengua [*Chilean academy*] [*Santiago*]   (LAA)
ACL .... Academia das Ciencias de Lisboa   (WGAO)
ACL .... Accion Ciudadana Liberal [*Liberal Citizens' Action*] [*Spain*] [*Political party*]   (PPE)
ACL .... Aerial Company Ltd. [*Australia*]
ACL .... Air Capitol [*Italy*] [*ICAO designator*]   (FAAC)
ACL .... Anglican Church League [*Australia*]
ACL .... Asociacion Colombiana de Locutores [*Colombian Radio and Television Announcers Association*]   (LA)
ACL .... Asociacion Costarricense de Lisiados [*Costa Rica*]   (EAIO)
ACL .... Associazione Cotoniera Liniera e delle Fibre Affini [*Italy*]   (EAIO)
ACL .... Atlantic Container Lines [*British, Swedish, French, and Dutch consortium*] [*Shipping*]
ACL .... Australasian College Libraries
ACL .... Australian Centre for Languages
ACL .... Australian Constitutional League
ACL .... Automobile Club du Grand-Duche de Luxembourg   (WGAO)
ACLA........ Africa Christian Literature Advance
ACLA........ Australasian [*or Australian*] Communications Law Association   (ADA)
ACLA........ Australian Commercial Law Association
ACLA........ Australian Criminal Lawyers' Association
ACLALS.... Association for Commonwealth Literature and Language Studies   (EAIO)
ACLANT... Allied Command Atlantic [*NATO*]
ACLANTREP ... Allied Command Atlantic Reporting System [*NATO*]   (MCD)
ACLCA...... Association of Christian Lay Training Centres in Africa [*Zambia*]   (WGAO)
ACLCP ...... Australian Community Languages and Cultural Program
ACLDB...... Australian Corporate Law Database
ACLE........ Australian Centre for Learning English
ACLEN...... Asociacion del Clero Nicaraguense   (WGAO)
ACLEN...... Asociacion Nacional del Clero [*National Association of the Clergy*] [*Nicaragua*]   (LA)
ACLF .... Advisory Committee on Live Fish [*Australia*]
ACLF .... Alliance of Central Luzon Farmers [*Philippines*]
ACLGA...... Australian Council of Local Government Associations   (ADA)
ACLGO ..... Australian Council of Local Government Officers
ACLGS ..... Australian Centre for Local Government Studies
ACLI......... Associazione Cattolica Lavoratori Italiani [*Italian*]
ACLI......... Associazioni Cristiane Lavoratori Italiani [*Christian Associations of Italian Workers*]   (WER)
ACLID...... Australian Corporate Law [*Database*]
ACLIFIM ... Asociacion Cubana de Limitados Fisicos Motores [*Cuban Association for the Physically Handicapped*]   (LA)
ACLIJ........ Asociacion Colombiana del Libro Infantil y Juvenil   (WGAO)
ACLIS ...... Australian Council of Libraries and Information Services

ACLLS...... Association for Commonwealth Literature and Languages Studies
ACLM .... Afro-Caribbean Liberation Movement [*Argentina*]   (LA)
ACLM .... Antigua Caribbean Liberation Movement [*Political party*]   (EAIO)
ACLM .... Association of Contact Lens Manufacturers   (WGAO)
ACLO .... Aboriginal Community Liaison Officer [*Australia*]
ACLOS...... Advisory Committee on the Law of the Sea   (MSC)
ACLP........ Action Committee for the Liberation of Palestine   (ME)
ACLRD..... Australian Center for Leadership Research and Development
ACLS........ Australian Christian Literature Society   (ADA)
ACLSP....... Asociacion de Criadores de Lanares del Sur del Peru [*Peru*]   (DSCA)
ACLU .... Australian Civil Liberties Union
ACLV......... Algemene Centrale der Liberale Vakbonden [*General Federation of Liberal Trade Unions*] [*Belgium*]   (WEN)
ACLVB..... Algemene Centrale der Liberale Vakbonden van Belgie   (WGAO)
ACM .... Aero Club de Monaco [*Aero Club of Monaco*]   (EAIO)
ACM .... Amsterdam Center for Mathematics and Computer Sciences
ACM .... Arab Common Market [*United Arab Republic, Iraq, Jordan, Kuwait, and Syria*]
ACM .... Asociacion de Comerciantes Mayoristas [*Wholesalers Association*] [*Nicaragua*]   (LA)
ACM .... Associacao Crista de Mocos [*Portuguese*]
ACM .... Ateliers et Chantiers du Mali
ACM .... Australian Caravan Mission   (ADA)
ACM .... Australian Carpet Manufacturers   (ADA)
ACM .... Australian Chamber of Manufactures
ACM .... Australian College of Midwives
ACM .... Australian Consolidated Minerals Ltd.   (ADA)
ACM .... Australian Consolidated Mines
ACM .... Avion de Combat Marine [*France*]
ACM .... Societe Africaine de Constructions Metalliques
ACMA .... Advisory Council on Multicultural Affairs [*Australia*]
ACMA .... Agricultural Co-operative Managers Association   (WGAO)
ACMA .... Asbestos Cement Manufacturers Association   (WGAO)
ACMA .... Asociacion Colombiana de Mecanicos de Aviacion [*Colombia*]   (COL)
ACMA .... Associated Chambers of Manufactures of Australia   (ADA)
ACMA .... Association des Classes Moyennes Angolaises [*Association of Middle-Class Angolans*]
ACMA .... Ateliers et Chantiers Maritimes d'Abidjan
ACMA .... Athletic Clothing Manufacturers Association   (WGAO)
ACMA .... Australian College of Medical Administrators   (ADA)
ACMA .... Australian Conveyor Manufacturers Association
ACMA .... Australian Council of Manufacturing Associates
ACMA .... Australian Country Music Awards
ACMA .... Australian Crane Marketers Association
ACMAF..... Association des Classes Moyennes Africaines [*African Middle Classes Association*]
ACMAP..... Australian Computerised Marriage Assessment Profile
ACMAR .... Ateliers de Construction de Materiels Routiers et de Travaux Publics   (WGAO)
ACMASC .. Associacao Crista da Mocidade - Accao Socio-Cultural [*Young Men's Christian Association - Socio-Cultural Action*] [*Portugal*]   (EAIO)
ACMB .... Association des Classes Moyennes du Burundi
ACMC .... American and Common Market Club   (EAIO)
ACMC .... Antique and Classic Motor Club [*Australia*]
ACMC .... Australian Council of Marriage Counselling
ACMCAQ ... Air Conditioning and Mechanical Contractors' Association of Queensland [*Australia*]
ACMCASA ... Air Conditioning and Mechanical Contractors' Association of South Australia
ACMCAV ... Air Conditioning and Mechanical Contractors' Association of Victoria [*Australia*]
ACMD....... Advisory Council on the Misuse of Drugs   (WGAO)
ACME .... Advisory Council on Medical Establishments [*Scotland*]   (WGAO)
ACME .... Asian Center of Missionary Education [*Philippines*]
ACME .... Association of Copper Mining Employees
ACME .... Australia Contemporary Music Ensemble   (ADA)
ACMEE...... Australian Conference on Management Education for Engineers
ACMEL..... Associated Continental Middle East Lines   (DS)
ACMET..... Advisory Council on Middle East Trade   (WGAO)
ACMF....... Australian Chicken Meat Federation
ACMF....... Australian Commonwealth Military Forces   (ADA)
ACMG .... Associacao Comercial de Minas Gerais [*Commercial Association of Minas Gerais*] [*Brazil*]   (LA)
ACM-GAMM ... Association for Computing Machinery - German Association for Applied Mathematics and Mechanics
ACMHA.... Afro-Caribbean Mental Health Association
ACMHN.... Australian Congress of Mental Health Nurses
ACMI .... Australian Contemporary Music Institute
ACML .... Anti-Common Market League   (WGAO)

ACMM...... Associate of the Conservatorium of Music, Melbourne [*Australia*]   (ADA)
ACMO....... ACE [*Allied Command Europe*] Communication Management Organization [*NATO*]   (NATG)
ACMRR .... Advisory Committee of Experts on Marine Resources Research [*ICSU*]
ACMRR .... Advisory Committee on Marine Resources Research   (WGAO)
ACMS........ African Centre for Monetary Studies
ACMS........ Agricultural Co-operation and Marketing Services   (WGAO)
ACMS........ Association Interprofessionnelle des Centres Medicaux et Sociaux de la Region Parisienne [*French*]   (SLS)
ACMS........ Australasian Conference on the Mechanics of Structures and Materials   (WGAO)
ACMS........ Australian Chamber Music Society
ACMS........ Australian Clay Minerals Society   (ADA)
ACMS........ Australian College of Metaphysical Studies
ACMT........ Ateliers de Constructions Metallurgiques Tchadiens
ACMTC..... Australian Coal Marketing and Technology Council
ACMV .... Asociacion Colombiana de Medicos Veterinarios [*Colombia*] (DSCA)
ACN........... Academia Cosmologica Nova [*International Free Academy of New Cosmology - IFANC*]   (EAIO)
ACN........... Aerolineas Centroamericanas SA [*Central American Airlines*] [*Nicaragua*] [*ICAO designator*]   (FAAC)
ACN........... Aid to the Church in Need [*Germany*]   (EAIO)
ACN........... Air Commander, Norway [*NATO*]   (NATG)
ACN........... Association of Conductors in the Netherlands   (EAIO)
ACN........... Ateliers et Chantiers de Nouakchott
ACN........... Australian Company Number
ACN........... Automobile Club National [*France*]   (EAIO)
ACNA....... Association Cinema Negro Africaine
ACNA....... Aziende Colori Nazionali Affini [*Italy*]
ACNA....... Aziende Colori Nazionali Affini Spa   (WGAO)
ACNB .... Associacao dos Criadores de Nelore do Brasil [*Brazil*]   (DSCA)
ACNB .... Australian Commonwealth Naval Board [*Obsolete*]   (ADA)
ACNC .... Advisory Committee on National Collections [*Australia*]
ACNFP...... Advisory Committee on Novel Food Processes   (WGAO)
ACNI .... Arts Council of Northern Ireland   (WGAO)
ACNL .... Algemene Conferentie der Nederlandse Letteren
ACNN........ Air Commander, North Norway [*NATO*]   (NATG)
ACNO....... Association des Comites Nationaux Olympiques [*Association of National Olympic Committees - ANOC*] [*Paris, France*] (EAIO)
ACNOA..... Association de Comites Nationaux Olympiques d'Afrique [*Association of National Olympic Committees of Africa - ANOCA*]   (EA)
ACNOA..... Association des Comites Naitionaux Olympiques d' Afrique (OLYM)
ACNOE..... Association des Comites Nationaux Olympiques d'Europe [*Association of the European National Olympic Committees - ENOC*] [*Brussels, Belgium*]   (EAIO)
ACNP .... Asociacion Catolica Nacional de Propagandistas [*National Catholic Association of Propagandists*] [*Spanish*]   (WER)
ACNS .... Advisory Committee on Nuclear Safety [*Israel*]   (PDAA)
ACNT .... Australian Council of National Trusts   (ADA)
ACNU........ Asociacion Cubana de Naciones Unidas [*Cuban United Nations Association*]   (LA)
ACNU........ Association Canadienne pour les Nations-Unies [*United Nations Association in Canada*]   (EAIO)
ACNU........ Association Congolaise pour les Nations Unies [*United Nations Association of the Congo*]   (EAIO)
ACNUR ..... Alto Comisionado de las Naciones Unidas para los Refugiados [*Office of the United Nations High Commissioner for Refugees*] [*Spanish*]   (DUND)
ACO........... Aero Sierra Eco SA de CV [*Mexico*] [*ICAO designator*]   (FAAC)
ACO........... African Curriculum Organization   (AF)
ACO........... Air Colombia [*ICAO designator*]   (FAAC)
ACO........... Arab Communist Organisation
ACO........... Asociacion Costarricense de Orquideologia Universidad de Costa Rica [*Costa Rica*]   (DSCA)
ACO.......... Association of Charity Officers   (WGAO)
ACO.......... Association of Conservation Officers   (WGAO)
ACO.......... Australian Chamber Orchestra   (ADA)
ACO.......... Australian College of Ophthalmologists   (ADA)
ACO.......... Australian College of Organists   (ADA)
ACO.......... Australian Concert Orchestra   (ADA)
ACOA .... AIDS [*Acquired Immune Deficiency Syndrome*] Council of Central Australia
ACOBE...... Asociacion Colombiana de Beisbol [*Colombia*]   (COL)
ACOBOX .. Asociacion Colombiana de Boxeo y Lucha Olimpica [*Colombia*] (COL)
ACOC .... Air Command Operations Center [*NATO*]   (NATG)
ACOC .... America's Cup Organizing Committee
ACOC .... Australian Committee on Cataloguing
ACOC .... Australian Council of Churches
ACOCERAM ... Asociacion Colombiana de Ceramistas [*Colombia*]   (COL)
ACOCS...... Australian Committee on Off-Campus Studies

ACOD....... Algemene Centrale van de Openbare Diensten [*Benelux*]   (BAS)
ACODA ..... African Community Developing Association
ACODA ..... Asociacion Colombiana de Ajedrez [*Colombia*]   (COL)
ACODAI ... Asociacion Colombiana de Administracion Industrial [*Colombia*]   (COL)
ACODAL .. Asociacion Colombiana de Acueductos y Alcantarillados [*Colombia*]   (COL)
ACODASE ... Asociacion Colombiana de Agentes de Seguros [*Colombia*] (COL)
ACODECC ... Asociacion Colombiana de Criadores de Cerdos [*Colombia*] (COL)
ACODEX .. Asociacion Colombiana de Exportadores   (WGAO)
ACOE .... Aboriginal Committee on Education [*Australia*]
ACOEP...... American College of Osteopathic Emergency Physicans (WGAO)
ACOEXA... Asociacion Colombiana de Expertos Agricolas [*Colombia*] (COL)
ACOFAL... Asociacion Colombiana de Fabricantes de Alimentos para Animales [*Colombia*]   (COL)
ACOFS...... Australian Council of Film Societies   (ADA)
ACOFT...... Australian Conference on Optical Fibre Technology
ACOG........ Atlanta Committee for the Olympic Games   (OLYM)
ACOG .... Australian College of Obstetricians and Gynaecologists
ACOGE ..... Asociacion Colombiana de Geografos   (WGAO)
ACOGE ..... Asociacion Costarricense de Gerentes y Empresarios [*Costa Rican Association of Managers and Businessmen*]   (LA)
ACOGES... Afrique Construction et Gestion
ACOGFL... Australian Council of Government Film Libraries
ACOGRAFICA ... Asociacion Colombiana de Industria Grafica [*Colombia*] (COL)
ACOGRAN ... Asociacion Colombiana de Griles, Restaurantes, y Afines [*Colombia*]   (COL)
ACOGUA ... Asociacion de Caficultores del Oriente de la Republica [*Guatemala*]   (DSCA)
ACOH .... Advisory Committee for Operational Hydrology [*WMO*]   (MSC)
ACOIN ...... Australian Core Inventory of Chemical Substances
ACOLECHE ... Asociacion Colombiana de Industrias de la Leche [*Colombia*] (COL)
ACOLFA ... Asociacion Colombiana de Fabricantes de Autopartes [*Colombian Association of Auto Parts Manufacturers*] (LA)
ACollTh..... Australian College of Theology
ACOLSURE ... Asociacion Colombiana de Suboficiales de las Fuerzas Militares en Retiro [*Colombian Association of Retired Armed Forces Noncommissioned Officers*]   (LA)
ACOLTEX ... Asociacion Colombiana de Tecnicos de Acabados Textiles (COL)
ACOM....... Advisory Committee on Objective Measurement [*Australia*]
ACOM....... Anciens Combattants Outre-Mer
ACOM....... Asociacion Colombiana de Museos, Institutos, y Casas de Cultura   (SLS)
ACOM....... Australian College of Occupational Medicine
ACOMAG ... Associazione per il Commercio delle Macchine ed Altrezzature per il Gelato   (WGAO)
ACOMDAILY ... Australian Commodities Database
ACOMEL ... Agro Comercial Exportadora Ltd [*Brazil*]   (DSCA)
ACOMEX ... Asociacion Colombiana de Comercio Exterior [*Colombia*] (DSCA)
ACOMINAS ... Aco Minas Gerais, SA [*Minas Gerais Steel Company*] [*Brazil*] (LA)
ACOMOTO ... Asociacion Colombiana de Motociclistas [*Colombia*]   (COL)
ACOMPAS ... Asociacion Colombiana de Musicos Profesionales [*Colombia*] (COL)
ACOMR .... Advisory Committee on Oceanic Meteorological Research [*WMO*]   (MSC)
ACON....... AIDS Council of New South Wales [*Australia*]
ACONC..... Australian College of Osteopathy, Naturopathy, and Chiropractic (ADA)
ACONet..... Akademisches Computer Netz [*Academic Computer Network*] [*Computer science*] [*Austria*]   (TNIG)
ACONPA .. Australian Chiropractors, Osteopaths, and Naturopathic Physicians Association   (ADA)
AConsd'Etat ... Arret du Conseil d'Etat [*French*]   (BAS)
ACOOP..... Australian Cooperative [*Bookshop Limited - Australian National University Campus*] [*National Union Catalogue of Australia symbol*]
ACOP .... Advisory Committee on Pilotage   (WGAO)
ACOP .... Analysis of Capabilities, Opportunities, and Prospects
ACOP .... Atlanta Centennial Olympic Properties   (OLYM)
ACOPAI.... Asociaciones de Cooperativas de Productos Agropecuarios Integrados [*Associations of Cooperatives of Integrated Agricultural-Livestock Products*] [*El Salvador*]   (LA)
ACOPE...... Associacao dos Comerciantes de Pescado   (WGAO)
ACOPECAFE ... Asociacion Colombiana de Pequenos Productores de Cafe [*Colombian Small Coffee Growers Association*]   (LA)
ACOPER... Asociacion de Productores y Distribuidores de Cosmeticos y Perfumes [*Colombia*]   (COL)

ACOPESCA ... Alianza Colombiana de Pesca Ltda. [*Colombia*] (COL)
ACOPI....... Asociacion Colombiana de Pequenos Industriales [*Colombia*] (COL)
ACOPI....... Asociacion Colombiana Popular de Industriales [*Colombian Small Industries Association*] (LA)
ACOPIM... Asociacion Colombiana de Personas Impedidas [*Colombian Association of Disabled People*] (EAIO)
ACOPROBAMA ... Asociacion de Comerciantes de Productos Basicos de Managua [*Association of Managua Merchants of Basic Goods*] [*Nicaragua*] (LA)
ACOPS...... Advisory Committee on Pollution of the Sea (WGAO)
ACOR........ Advisory Committee on Own Resources (WGAO)
ACORBAT ... Association for Cooperation in Banana Research in the Caribbean and Tropical America [*Guadeloupe, French West Indies*] (EAIO)
ACORD..... Advisory Council on Research and Development for Fuel and Power (WGAO)
ACORD..... Agency for Cooperation and Research in Development [*International consortium on Africa*] (ECON)
ACORD..... Agency for Cooperation in Rural Development [*Switzerland*] (WGAO)
ACORD..... Euro Action-Agency for Cooperation and Research and Development (WGAO)
ACORE ..... Asociacion Colombiana de Reservistas [*Colombian Reservists Association*] (LA)
ACORN..... Australasian Conference of Operating Room Nurses (ADA)
ACORN..... Australian Confederation of Operating Room Nurses
ACORP...... Asociacion Colombiana de Relaciones Publicas [*Colombia*] (COL)
ACORP...... Aviation Committee of Review Proposal [*Australia*]
ACOS .... Advisory Committee on Safety (WGAO)
ACOS .... Australian Chamber of Shipping
ACOS .... Australian Coordination Section of the Centre for UFO [*Unidentified Flying Object*] Studies (ADA)
ACoSA....... Aero Club of South Africa (EAIO)
ACOSA...... AIDS [*Acquired Immune Deficiency Syndrome*] Council of South Australia
ACOSA...... Aluminium Company of South Africa
ACOSA...... Australian Communications Students Association (ADA)
ACOSCA... Africa Cooperative Savings and Credit Association (AF)
ACOSH ..... Australian Council on Smoking and Health (ADA)
ACOSS ...... Australian Council of Social Service (ADA)
ACOST...... Advisory Committee on Science and Technology (WGAO)
ACOTA ..... Asociacion Colombiana de Talleres Automotores [*Colombia*] (COL)
ACOTA ..... Australian Council on the Aging (ADA)
ACOTAFE ... Australian Committee on Technical and Further Education (ADA)
ACOTANC ... Australasian Conference on Tree and Nut Crops
ACOTEL... Asociacion Colombiana de Hoteles [*Colombia*] (COL)
ACOU-SID ... Acoustic Sound Intrusion Device [*Military*] (VNW)
ACOV .... Algemeen Christelijk Onderwijzersverbond van Belgie [*Christian Teachers Union of Belgium*] (EAIO)
ACOVOL .. Agencia Coordinadora del Voluntariado de Bogota y Cundinamarca [*Colombia*] (COL)
ACP .... Accao Catolica Portuguesa [*Portuguese Catholic Action*] (WER)
ACP .... Accion Democratica Popular [*Popular Democratic Action*] [*Costa Rica*] [*Political party*]
ACP .... Action Congress Party [*Ghana*] [*Political party*] (PPW)
ACP .... Administratia Carierelor de Piatra [*Administration of Stone Quarries*] (RO)
ACP .... Advisory Committee on Pesticides (WGAO)
ACP .... Advisory Council on Prices and Incomes [*Australia*]
ACP .... African, Caribbean, and Pacific Countries [*Associated with the EEC*] (AF)
ACP .... African Comprehensive Party [*Jamaica*] [*Political party*] (EY)
ACP .... Agence Camerounaise de Presse [*Cameroonian Press Agency*]
ACP .... Agence Centrafricaine de Presse [*Central African Press Agency*]
ACP .... Agence Centrale de Publicite [*Central Advertising Agency*] [*French*] (WER)
ACP .... Agence Centrale Parisienne de Presse [*Parisian Central Press Agency*] [*French*] (AF)
ACP .... Agence Comores de Presse [*Comoran Press Agency*]
ACP .... Agence Congolaise de Presse [*Congolese Press Agency*]
ACP .... Agrupacion Comunista Proletaria [*Proletarian Communist Group*] [*Spanish*] (WER)
ACP .... Air Cape [*South Africa*] [*ICAO designator*] (FAAC)
ACP .... Albanian Communist Party [*Political party*]
ACP .... American Club of Paris [*France*]
ACP .... Arab Communist Party [*Political party*]
ACP .... Argentina Chamber of Publications (EAIO)
ACP .... Asociacion Colombiana de Periodistas [*Colombian Journalists Association*] (LA)
ACP .... Association of Cheese Processors (WGAO)
ACP .... Association of Clinical Pathologists (WGAO)

ACP .... Australia - Campbell Park [*Department of Defence*] [*Defence Central Library*] [*National Union Catalogue of Australia symbol*]
ACP .... Australia Council Press Clips [*Database*]
ACP .... Australian Centre for Photography
ACP .... Australian Christian Party [*Political party*]
ACP .... Australian City Properties
ACP .... Australian College of Paediatrics (SLS)
ACP .... Australian College of Physiotherapists
ACP .... Australian Communist Party (ADA)
ACP .... Australian Conservative Party (ADA)
ACP .... Australian Consolidated Press (ADA)
ACP .... Australian Council of Professions
ACP .... Australian Country Party [*Political party*] (BARN)
ACP .... Automovel Clube de Portugal [*Portuguese Automobile Club*] (WER)
ACP .... Etats d'Afrique, des Caraibes, et du Pacifique [*French*]
ACP .... Groupe des Sept pour la Cooperation du Secteur Prive Europeen avec l'Afrique, les Caraibes et le Pacific [*Group of Seven for European Private Sector Cooperation with Africa, the Caribbean, and the Pacific*] (EAIO)
ACPA........ Activated Carbons Producers' Association [*European Council of Chemical Manufacturers Federations*] [*Brussels, Belgium*] (EAIO)
ACPA........ American Concrete Pipe Association (WGAO)
ACPA........ ASEAN Consumer Protection Agency (WGAO)
ACPA........ Asociacion Costarricense de Productores de Algodon [*Costa Rica*] (DSCA)
ACPA........ Asociacion de Consignatarios de Productos Agricolas [*Argentina*] (DSCA)
ACPA........ Association des Chefs de Publicite d'Annonceurs de Belgique (WGAO)
ACPA........ Association of Christians in Planning and Architecture (WGAO)
ACPA........ Association of Computer Professionals, Australia (ADA)
ACPA........ Australasian Corporation of Public Accountants (ADA)
ACPA........ Australian Citrus Processors' Association
ACPA........ Australian Clay Products Association (ADA)
ACPA........ Australian Commercial Parachute Association
ACPAC...... AIDAB [*Australian International Development Assistance Bureau*] Centre for Pacific Development and Training
ACPAD..... Australian Centre for Publications Acquired for Development
ACPB........ Attack Class Patrol Boat [*Navy*]
ACPC........ Air Control Component
ACPC........ Arab Centre for Pharmaceutical and Chemical Industries [*Sahab, Jordan*] (MENA)
ACPC........ Asian Christian Peace Conference [*India*] (WGAO)
ACPC........ Australian Crime Prevention Council (ADA)
ACPCA...... Association Cinematographique Professionnelle de Conciliation et d'Arbitrage (EAIO)
ACPCAE ... Australian Conference of Principals of Colleges of Advanced Education (ADA)
ACPCP ...... Australian College of Private Consulting Psychologists
ACPD .... Association Canadienne des Professeurs de Droit (WGAO)
ACPE........ Agrupacion National Sindical de Constructores Promotores de Edificios Urbanos (WGAO)
ACPE........ Australian College of Physical Education (ADA)
ACPEA..... Australian Council on Population and Ethnic Affairs
ACPES ...... Asociacion Colombiana de Profesores de Ensenanza Secundaria [*Colombian Secondary School Teachers Association*] (LA)
ACPET...... Australian Council for Private Education and Training
ACPF........ All China Philately Federation [*China*] (EAIO)
ACPF........ Asia Crime Prevention Foundation (EAIO)
ACPF........ Asociacion del Congreso Panamericano de Ferrocarriles [*Pan American Railway Congress Association*] (EAIO)
ACPF........ Australian Cancer Patients' Federation
ACPG .... Agrupamednto Cientificos de Preparacao de Geografos para o Ultramar Portugues Instituto de Geografia, Cidade Universitaria [*Portugal*] (DSCA)
ACPG .... Association des Combattants Prisonniers de Guerre [*France*] (FLAF)
ACPG .... Australian Consolidated Press Group
ACPI......... Advisory Committee on Prices and Incomes [*Australia*]
ACPI......... Association des Conseils en Propriete Industrielle (WGAO)
ACPI......... Associazione Consulenti Pubblicitari Italiani (WGAO)
ACPM ...... Advisory Committee on Programmee Management (WGAO)
ACPM ...... Association of Corrugated Paper Makers (WGAO)
ACPMA..... Australian Clay Pipe Manufacturers' Association
ACPMED ... Department of Defence - Defence Central Library - Medical Collection [*National Union Catalogue of Australia symbol*]
ACPMME ... Association of Concentrated and Powdered Milk Manufacturers of the EEC (EAIO)
ACPN .... Ateliers et Chantiers de Pointe-Noire [*Pointe-Noire Workshops and Yards*] [*Congo*]
ACPO .... Accion Cultural Popular [*Basic education organization*] [*Colorado*]
ACPO .... Association of Chief Police Officers (WGAO)
ACPP........ Asian Center for the Progress of Peoples [*Hong Kong*] (EAIO)

ACPP......... Association for Child Psychology and Psychiatry (WGAO)
ACPP......... Australian College of Pharmacy Practice
Ac Prft....... Academisch Proefschrift [*Benelux*] (BAS)
ACPS......... Arab Company for Petroleum Services (ME)
ACPS......... Asociacion Criadores de Pardo Suizo [*Argentina*] (DSCA)
ACPSEM .. Australasian College of Physical Scientists and Engineers in Medicine
ACPSF...... Australian Cerebral Palsy Sports Federation
ACPSM ..... Association of Chartered Physiotherapists in Sports Medicine (WGAO)
ACPSM ..... Australasian College of Physical Scientists in Medicine (SLS)
ACPT........ Air Command Post [*Military*]
ACPT........ Asian Confederation of Physical Therapy (EAIO)
ACPTA...... Australian Commonwealth Post and Telegraph Association (ADA)
ACQ.......... Aero Continente [*Peru*] [*ICAO designator*] (FAAC)
ACQS......... Association of Consultant Quantity Surveyors (WGAO)
ACQSA..... Association of Consulting Quantity Surveyors, Australia
Acqt.......... Acquit [*Paid in Full*] [*French*] [*Accounting*]
acr .... Acreedor [*Creditor*] [*Spanish*] [*Business term*]
ACR .... Agencia Cubana de Radio [*Cuban Radio Agency*] (LA)
ACR .... Alien Certificate of Registration [*Immigration*] [*Philippines*] (IMH)
ACR .... Anglican Centre in Rome
ACR .... Araracuara [*Colombia*] [*Airport symbol*] (OAG)
ACR .... Arrete du Commissaire de la Republique (FLAF)
ACR .... ASA, Air Starline, AG [*Switzerland*] [*ICAO designator*] (FAAC)
ACR .... Association of Clinical Research (WGAO)
ACR .... Australian and New Zealand Conveyancing Report [*A publication*]
ACR .... Australian Catholic Relief (ADA)
ACR .... Australian Council of Recyclers
ACR .... Automobil Clubul Roman [*Romanian Automobile Club*] (RO)
ACRA .... Advisory Council on Religious Affairs [*Nigeria*]
ACRA .... Anti-Char Rapide Autopropulse [*French antitank weapon system*]
ACRA .... Association of College Registrars and Administrators (WGAO)
ACRA .... Association of Company Registration Agents (WGAO)
ACRA .... Associazione de Cooperazione Rurale in Africa
ACRA .... Atelierele Centrale de Reparatii Autovehiculare [*Central Workshops for Auto Repairs*] (RO)
ACRA .... Australian Community Recreation Association
ACRA .... Australian Computer Retailers Association
ACRA .... Central Body for Residents Associations (WGAO)
ACRB........ Australian Computer Research Board
ACRC .... Academia de Ciencias de la Republica de Cuba [*Cuba*] (DSCA)
ACRC .... Association of Coal Related Councils [*Australia*]
ACRD .... Ancient Culture Research Department [*China*] (IRC)
ACRD .... Australian Council for Rehabilitation of the Disabled [*Jean Garside Library*] [*National Union Catalogue of Australia symbol*]
ACRDP...... Australian Centennial Roads Development Program
ACRE......... Adaptive Crop Research and Extension
ACRE......... Association for Consumer Research (WGAO)
ACRE......... Australian College of Recorded Education (ADA)
ACREFI.... Associacao das Empresas de Credito, Financiamento, e Investimento [*Association of Credit, Finance, and Investment Firms*] [*Brazil*] (LA)
ACRES...... Australian Centre for Remote Sensing
ACREW..... Aircrew
ACRHSC... Aboriginal Community Recreation Health Services Centre [*Australia*]
ACRHSCSA ... Aboriginal Community Recreation Health Services Centre of South Australia
ACRI......... Applied Computer Research Institute [*La Trobe University*] [*Australia*]
ACRI......... Association for Civil Rights in Israel (EAIO)
ACrI.......... Associazione Criogenica Italiana [*Italian*] (SLS)
ACRI......... Associazione fra la Casse di Risparmio Italiano (WGAO)
ACRILIS ... Australian Centre for Research in Library and Information Science (ADA)
ACRINOR ... Acrilonitrila do Nordeste SA [*Brazil*]
ACRIP....... Australian Computer Research in Progress [*Database*]
ACRIT....... Advisory Committee for Research on Information Transfer [*Netherlands*] (NITA)
ACRL........ Association of College and Research Libraries [*ALA*] (WGAO)
ACRM .... Anti-Corruption Revolutionary Movement [*Sierra Leone*] (AF)
ACRM .... Australian College of Rehabilitation Medicine
ACRN .... Ateliers de Construction et Reparation Navales
ACRNet..... Australian Campus Radio Network (ADA)
ACROA...... Australian Council for Overseas Aid (WGAO)
ACROD..... Australian Council for Rehabilitation of the Disabled (ADA)
ACRONYM ... Anti-Cronyism Movement [*Philippines*]
ACROSS ... Africa Committee for the Rehabilitation of Southern Sudan
ACROSS ... African Committee for the Relief of Southern Sudan (WGAO)

ACROSS ... Association of Christian Resource Organizations Serving Sudan [*Kenya*] (EAIO)
ACROWE ... Association of Cooperative Retailers-Owned Wholesalers of Europe (EAIO)
ACRP......... Asian Conference on Religion and Peace [*Singapore, Singapore*] (EAIO)
ACRPH ..... Australian Council for Radio for the Print Handicapped
ACRPI .... Association for Clinical Research in the Pharmaceutical Industry (WGAO)
ACRPP ..... Association pour la Conservation et la Reproduction Photographique de la Presse (WGAO)
ACRR .... Advisory Council on Race Relations (WGAO)
ACRRSV ... Autistic Citizens' Residential and Resources Society of Victoria [*Australia*]
acrs............. Across (BARN)
ACRS........ Australian Camellia Research Society
ACRS........ Australian Coral Reef Society
ACRU .... Applied Climate Research Unit [*University of Queensland*] [*Australia*]
ACRUPTC ... Advisory Committee on Road User Performance and Traffic Codes [*Australia*]
ACRV .... Artillery Command Reconnaissance Vehicle [*Former USSR*]
ACRY .... Australian Council of Rural Youth
ACS........... Aboriginal Children's Service [*Australia*]
ACS........... Aboriginal Children's Services [*Australia*]
ACS........... Aboriginal Clerks Scheme [*Australia*]
ACS........... Additional Curates Society (WGAO)
ACS........... Aero-Club der Schweiz [*Swiss Aero Club*] (EAIO)
ACS........... African Container Service [*Nigeria*] (AF)
ACS........... Agricultural College of Sweden (DSCA)
ACS........... Air Commerce [*Yugoslavia*] [*ICAO designator*] (FAAC)
ACS........... Airfield Construction Squadron [*Australia*]
ACS........... American Carbon Society (WGAO)
ACS........... American Czechoslovak Society (EA)
ACS........... Anadolu Cam Sanayii AS [*Anatolian Glass Industry Corporation*] [*Mersin*] (TU)
ACS........... Ancillary Communications Services [*Australia*]
ACS........... Anglo-Chilean Society [*British*] (EAIO)
ACS........... Anglo-Chinese School (ML)
ACS........... Anti-Communist Society [*Belize*] (PD)
ACS........... Archives Culturelles du Senegal [*Senegal Cultural Archives*] (EAIO)
ACS........... Area Community Services [*Australia*]
acs .... Ashban Cargo Services Establishment [*Saudi Arabia*] [*Commercial firm*]
ACS........... Association of Commonwealth Students (AF)
ACS........... Association of Consulting Surveyors [*Australia*]
ACS........... Association of Cricket Statisticians (WGAO)
ACS........... Astro-Club Saturn [*France*] (EAIO)
ACS........... Attendant Care Scheme
ACS........... Australia Container Service (DS)
ACS........... Australian Cancer Society (ADA)
ACS........... Australian Card Service
ACS........... Australian Ceramic Society (ADA)
ACS........... Australian Chamber of Shipping (ADA)
ACS........... Australian Cinematographers Society (ADA)
ACS........... Australian Computer Society
ACS........... Australian Construction Services
ACS........... Australian Conversion Services Ltd. (ADA)
ACS........... Australian Customs Service
ACS........... Automobil Club der Schweiz (WGAO)
ACS........... Automobile Club of Switzerland
ACSA........ Acoustical Society of America (WGAO)
ACSA........ Aerocarga SA [*Mexico*] (WGAO)
ACSA........ Aero Club of South Australia
ACSA........ Allied Communications Security Agency [*Brussels, Belgium*] [*NATO*]
ACSA........ Association of Consulting Surveyors of Australia
ACSA........ Australian Carpetmaster Sheepbreeders' Association
ACSA........ Australian Collieries Staff Association
ACSA........ Australian Computing Service Association
ACSA........ Australian Corps of Signals Association (ADA)
ACSA........ Australian Curriculum Studies Association
ACSA........ Australian Customer Service Association
ACSA........ Austrian Company Sport Association (EAIO)
ACSA....... Ayrshire Cattle Society of Australia
ACSAA...... American Committee for South Asian Art (WGAO)
ACSAD..... Arab Center for the Study of Arid Zones and Dry Lands [*of the League of Arab States*] [*Syria*] [*Research center*] (IRC)
ACSANZ... Association for Canadian Studies in Australia and New Zealand
ACSAT...... Advisory Committee for Science and Technology
ACSB........ Australian Commonwealth Shipping Board (ADA)
ACSC........ Anglican Community Services Council [*Australia*]
ACSC........ Australian Coastal Surveillance Centre
ACSCA...... Asociacion Campesina Social Cristiana de Honduras [*Honduras*] (DSCA)

ACSCA ...... Australian Cable and Subscription Communications Association
ACSD .... Australian Confederation of Sports for the Disabled
ACSDM ..... Australian Council of Soft Drink Manufacturers (ADA)
ACSE .... Association of Consulting Structural Engineers [*Australia*] (PDAA)
AcSEC .... Accounting Standards Executive Committee [*Australia*]
ACSEDIA ... Association pour le Controle Sanitaire, l'Etude et le Developpement de l'Insemination Artificielle (WGAO)
ACSEF ...... Australian Coal and Shale Employees Federation (ADA)
ACSENSW ... Association of Consulting Structural Engineers of New South Wales [*Australia*]
ACSF .... All-China Sports Federation (EAIO)
ACSF .... Association of French Host Centers [*Paris*] [*Information service or system*] (IID)
ACSGRGS ... Associacao de Criadores de Santa Gertrudes do Rio Grande do Sul [*Brazil*] (DSCA)
ACSH .... Department of Human Services and Health [*National Union Catalogue of Australia symbol*]
ACSI .... Anya- es Csecsemovedelmi Intezet [*Institute for the Protection of Mothers and Infants*] (HU)
ACSI .... Anyagmozgatasi es Csomagolasi Intezet [*Material Handling and Packaging Institute*] (HU)
ACSI .... Association of Christian Schools International (WGAO)
ACSIL .... Admiralty Centre for Scientific Information and Liaison (WGAO)
ACSIRO .... Australia Commonwealth Scientific and Industrial Research Organization
ACSJC ...... Australian Catholic Social Justice Council
ACSM .... Assemblies, Components, Spare Parts, and Materials [*NATO*] (NATG)
ACSM .... Associateship of the Camborne School of Mines
ACSMA ..... Australian Chemical Specialities Manufacturers Association
ACSMOO ... Australian Council of Salaried Medical Officer Organisations (ADA)
ACSN .... Association for Citizens with Special Needs [*Australia*]
ACSNET ... Australian Computer Society Network
ACSNSW .. Arts and Crafts Society of New South Wales [*Australia*]
ACSO .... Australian Council of School Organisations (ADA)
ACSOC ...... Advisory Committee on State-Owned Companies [*Finland*] (EAIO)
ACSP .... Action Committee Service for Peace [*Germany*] (EAIO)
ACSP .... Aged Care Support Program [*Australia*]
ACSP .... Associacao Comercial de Sao Paulo [*Sao Paulo Commercial Association*] [*Brazil*] (LA)
ACSP .... Association of Catholic School Principals [*Australia*]
ACSPA ...... Australian Canvas and Synthetic Products Association
ACSPA ...... Australian Council of Salaried and Professional Associations (ADA)
ACSPFT ... Asian Committee for Standardization of Physical Fitness Tests [*Obu-Shi, Japan*] (EAIO)
ACSPRI ..... Australian Consortium for Social and Political Research, Incorporated (ADA)
ACSR .... Association Cinematographique Suisse Romande (WGAO)
ACSR .... Australian Centre for Security Research [*University of Western Sydney*]
ACSS .... Australian Council of Social Service
ACS-SIA ... Australian Computer Society - Software Industries Association
ACSSM ..... Association Cinematographique Suisse Romande (WGAO)
ACSSO ..... Australian Council of State School Organisations (ADA)
ACST .... Advisory Committee on the Application of Science and Technology to Development [*Also, ACAST, ACASTD*] [*United Nations*]
ACST .... Advisory Council on Science and Technology [*Australia*] (PDAA)
ACST .... Australian College of Speech Therapists (ADA)
ACSTD ...... Advisory Committee on Science and Technology for Development [*UN*] (WGAO)
ACSTT ...... Advisory Committee on Scientific and Technical Training (WGAO)
ACSTWU ... African Civil Service Technical Workers' Union
ACSV .... Arts and Crafts Society of Victoria [*Australia*]
ACSVD ...... Advisory Committee on Safety in Vehicle Design [*Australia*] (WGAO)
ACSWC ..... Australian Catholic Social Welfare Commission
ACSYS ...... Arctic Climate System Study (ECON)
ACSZ .... Agricultural and Commercial Show Society of Zambia (WGAO)
ACT .... Accident Compensation Tribunal [*Victoria, Australia*]
ACT .... Acordo Colectivo de Trabalho [*Collective Labor Agreement*] [*Portuguese*] (WER)
act .... Action [*Share*] [*French*]
ACT .... Action [*NATO*]
ACT .... Agence pour la Cooperation Technique, Industrielle, et Economique [*Technical, Industrial, and Economic Cooperation Agency*] [*French*] (WER)
ACT .... Agricultural Central Trading (WGAO)
ACT .... Aid for Children with Tracheostomies (WGAO)
ACT .... Airport Coordination Task Force [*Australia*]

ACT .... Association des Communicateurs of Techniques [*Association of Technical Communicators*] [*France*] (PDAA)
ACT .... Association of Career Teachers (WGAO)
ACT .... Association of Christian Teachers (WGAO)
ACT .... Association of Corporate Treasures (WGAO)
ACT .... Association of Cycle Traders (WGAO)
ACT .... Association of Cytogenetic Technologists (WGAO)
ACT .... Australian Capital Territory [*Government Service*] [*National Union Catalogue of Australia symbol*]
ACT .... Australian College of Theology (ADA)
ACT .... Australian Commonwealth Territory (ADA)
ACT .... Australian Community Theatre
ACT .... Northern Ireland Advisory Committee on Travellers (WGAO)
a cta .... A Cuenta [*On Account*] [*Banking, investment*] [*Spanish*]
ACTA .... Adelaide Convention and Tourism Authority [*Australia*]
ACTA .... Associated Container Transportation Australia
ACTA .... Association de Coordination Technique Agricole [*Association for the Coordination of Agricultural Techniques*] [*France*] (PDAA)
ACTA .... Association des Commissionaires de Transports Aeriens [*Switzerland*] (WGAO)
ACTA .... Association of Chart and Technical Analysts (WGAO)
ACTA .... Australasian Commercial Teachers Association
ACTA .... Australian Capital Territory Administration
ACTA .... Australian Capital Territory Athletics [*An association*]
ACTA .... Australian Catholic Theological Association
ACTA .... Australian Clay Target Association
ACTA .... Australian Council on Tertiary Awards
ACTAC ...... Association of Community Technical Aid Centres (WGAO)
ACTAC ...... Australian Children's Television Action Committee (ADA)
ACTADIE ... Australian Capital Territory Association for Drama in Education (ADA)
ACTAFL .... Australian Capital Territory Australian Football League
ACTALAC ... Asociacion Civil de Tecnicos Azucareros de la America Latina y del Caribe
ACT&UPC ... Association of Charter Trustees and Urban Parish Councils (WGAO)
ACTAOT ... Australian Capital Territory Association of Occupational Therapists (ADA)
ACTAR ...... Asian Center for Tax Administration and Research (CL)
ACTATA ... Australian Capital Territory Agriculture Teachers Association
ACTATE ... Australian Capital Territory Association for the Teaching of English
ACTAWA ... Australian Capital Territory Amateur Weightlifting Association
ACTB .... Australian Capital Territory Basketball
ACTBA ...... Australian Capital Territory Bridge Association
ACTBFC .... Australian Capital Territory Bush Fire Council
ACTBI ...... Australian Capital Territory Basketball, Inc.
ACTC .... Agency for Cultural and Technical Cooperation [*Use ACCT*] (LA)
ACTC .... Australian Ceramic Tile Council (ADA)
ACTC .... CSIRO [*Commonwealth Scientific and Industrial Research Organisation*] Activities Archive [*Database*]
ACTCA ...... Australian Capital Territory Cricket Association
ACTCAAI ... Australian Capital Territory Chinese Australian Association, Inc.
ACTCCC ... Australian Capital Territory Cross Country Club
ACTCCS .... Australian Capital Territory Council of Cultural Societies
ACTCOP .... Australian Capital Territory Council of Professions
ACTCOSS ... Australian Capital Territory Council of Social Service (ADA)
ACTCOTA ... Australian Capital Territory Council on the Ageing
ACTCPCA ... Australian Capital Territory Council of Parents and Citizens Associations
ACTCPG ... Australian Capital Territory Continence Promotion Group
ACTCTF .... Australian Capital Territory Commonwealth Teachers Federation (ADA)
ACTCUAC ... Australian Capital Territory Credit Union Association Cooperative
ACTD .... Australian Conference of TAFE [*Technical and Further Education*] Directors
ACTDC ...... Australian Capital Territory Darts Council
ACTDEC ... Supreme Court of the Australian Capital Territory Decisions [*Database*]
ACTDG ..... Advisory Committee for the Transport of Dangerous Goods [*Australia*] (PDAA)
ACTE .... Asociacion Colombiana de Tecnicos Electricistas [*Colombia*] (COL)
ACTE .... Asociacion para la Communication y Tecnologia Educativa en Puerto Rico (WGAO)
ACTE .... Australian Council for Tertiary Education
ACTEA ...... Accrediting Council for Theological Education in Africa [*of the Association of Evangelicals of Africa and Madagascar*] [*See also COHETA*] (EAIO)
ACTEIN .... Australian Capital Territory Education Information Network
ACTEW ..... Australian Capital Territory Electricity and Water
ACTF .... Activities File [*CSIRO database*] (ADA)
ACTF .... Australian Children's Television Foundation

ACTF .... CSIRO [*Commonwealth Scientific and Industrial Research Organisation*] Activities File [*Database*]
ACTFL ...... American Council on the Teaching of Foreign Languages (WGAO)
ACTFL ...... Australian Council for Teaching Foreign Languages
ACTGLS ... Australian Capital Territory German Language School
ACTGS ...... Australian Capital Territory Geographical Society
ACTGS ...... Australian Capital Territory Government Service
ACTGTA ... Australian Capital Territory Geography Teachers' Association
ACTH .... Australian College of Travel and Hospitality
ACTHA ..... Australian Capital Territory Health Authority
ACTHA ..... Australian Capital Territory Hockey Association
ACTheol .... Australian College of Theology
ACTI .... Association of Chemists of the Textile Industry [*France*] (EAIO)
ACTICE .... Authority Coordinating the Transport of Inland Continental Europe [*NATO*]
ACTIIV ..... Advisory Centre on Technology for Industry in Victoria [*Australia*]
ACTIL .... Australian Cotton Textile Industries Limited (ADA)
ACTILIS ... Australian Capital Territory Integrated Land Information System
ACTIME ... Agency for the Coordination of Transport in the Mediterranean [*NATO*] (MCD)
ACTIMED ... Agency for the Coordination of Transport in the Mediterranean [*NATO*] (NATG)
ACTIS .... Auckland Commericial and Technical Information Services [*New Zealand*] (PDAA)
ACTISPP .. Australian Capital Territory Injury Surveillance and Prevention Project
ACTISUD ... Authority for the Coordination of Inland Transport in Southern Europe [*NATO*]
ACTITFE .. Australian Capital Territory Institute of Technical and Further Education
ACTIV .... Advisory Centre on Technology for Industry in Victoria [*Australia*]
ACTIVS ..... Association Internationale pour la Lutte contre la Violence Associee au Sport (WGAO)
ACTJRU ... Australian Capital Territory Junior Rugby Union
Act Jur .... Actualite Juridique (FLAF)
Act JurDA ... Actualite Juridique "Droit Administratif" (FLAF)
Act Jur PI .. Actualite Juridique "Propriete Immobiliere" (FLAF)
Act JurTrav Publ ... Actualite Juridique "Travaux Publics" (FLAF)
ACTLAA ... Australian Capital Territory Little Athletics Association
ACTLS ...... Australian Capital Territory Law Society
ACTLS ...... Australian Capital Territory Library Service
ACTLS ...... Australian Capital Territory Lieder Society
ACTLTA ... Australian Capital Territory Lawn Tennis Association
ACTM .... Asociacion de Cafetaleros de Tingo Maria [*Peru*] (DSCA)
ACTMA .... Australian Capital Territory Marching Association
ACTMBC .. Australian Capital Territory Mini Bike Club
ACTME ..... Australian Capital Territory Miniature Enthusiasts
ACTMJA .. Australian Capital Territory Master Joiners' Association
ACTNB ...... Australian Capital Territory Nurses' Board
ACTO .... Association of Camping Tour Operators (WGAO)
ACTO .... Association of Chief Technical Officers (WGAO)
ACTOA ..... Australian Capital Territory Orienteering Association
ACTORD .. Australian Capital Territory Ordinances [*Database*]
ACTP .... Australian Accounts Preparation Manual
ACTP .... Australian Capital Territory Police
ACTPA ...... Australian Capital Territory Pistol Association
ACTPAA .... Australian Capital Territory Porcelain Artists' Association
ACTPOL .... Australian Capital Territory Police
ACTRA ...... Australian Capital Territory Reading Association
ACTRA ...... Australian Capital Territory Rogaining Association
ACTRA ...... Australian Capital Territory Rowing Association
ACTRAM ... Advisory Committee on the Safe Transport of Radioactive Materials (WGAO)
ACTRC ...... Australian Capital Territory Racing Club
ACTREG ... Australian Capital Territory Regulations [*Database*]
ACTREL ... Asociacion Colombiana de Tecnicos en Radioelectronica [*Colombia*] (COL)
ACTRRA ... Australian Capital Territory Rugby Referees' Association
ACTRTLA ... Australian Capital Territory Right to Life Association
ACTRU ...... Australian Capital Territory Rugby Union
ACTS .... African Centre for Technology Studies [*Kenya*] (EAIO)
ACTS .... Alfred C. Toepfer Schiffahrt, MB [*Commercial firm*] (DS)
ACTS .... Arab Company for Trading in Securities
ACTS .... Australian Catholic Truth Society (ADA)
ACTS .... Australian Conference on Telecommunications Software
ACTS .... Australian Convention and Travel Services
ACTS .... Australian Costume and Textile Society
ACTS .... Commonwealth Acts [*Database*]
ACTSA ...... Australian Capital Territory Softball Association
ACTSC ...... Australian Capital Territory Samoyed Club
ACTSF ...... Australian Capital Territory Soccer Federation
ACTSMS ... Australian Capital Territory Scale Modellers Society
ACTSRA ... Australian Capital Territory Squash Rackets Association

ACTSRC ... Australian Capital Territory Smallbore Rifle Club
ACTSRFC ... Australian Capital Territory Sport and Recreational Fishing Council
ACTSS .... Association of Clerical, Technical and Supervisory Staffs (WGAO)
ACTT .... Accredited Course of Teacher Training [*Victoria, Australia*]
ACTT .... African Centre for the Development, Transfer, and Adaptation of Technology
ACTT .... Approved Course of Teacher Training [*Australia*]
ACTTA ...... Australian Capital Territory Tennis Association
ACTTA ...... Australian Capital Territory Touch Association
ACTTAB ... Australian Capital Territory Totalizator Agency Board
ACTTAFE ... Australian Capital Territory Institute of Technical and Further Education
ACTTC ...... Australian Coal Trade and Technology Committee
ACTTOA ... Australian Courier and Taxi Truck Operators' Association
ACTU .... Australian Council of Trade Unions (ADA)
Actual Jur .. Actualite Juridique (FLAF)
Actual JurDr Admin ... Actualite Juridique "Droit Administratif" (FLAF)
Actual JurLoy ... Actualite Juridique "Loyers" (FLAF)
Actual JurPr Im ... Actualite Juridique "Propriete Immobiliere" (FLAF)
Actual JurURSS ... Actualite Juridique en URSS (FLAF)
ACTUC ...... All-Ceylon Trades Union Congress
ACTUP ...... AIDS Coalition to Unleash Power [*Australia*]
ACTUS ...... Action Tchadienne pour l'Unite et le Socialisme [*Chad*]
ACTV .... American Coalition for Traditional Values (WGAO)
ACTV .... Australian Capital Territory Volleyball
ACTVF ...... Australian Childrens Television Foundation
ACTWSA .. Australian Capital Territory Water Ski Association
ACU .... Achutupo [*Panama*] [*Airport symbol*] (OAG)
ACU .... Actors Church Union (WGAO)
ACU .... Administration of the Customs Union [*EEC*] (DS)
ACU .... Aerocancun [*Mexico*] [*ICAO designator*] (FAAC)
ACU .... Agrupacion Catolica Universitaria [*Catholic Group of University Students and Professionals*] (LA)
ACU .... Aide aux Croyants de l'URSS [*Aid to Believers in the Soviet Union*] [*France*] (EAIO)
ACU .... Applied Chemistry Unit [*Council for Scientific and Industrial Research*] [*South Africa*] (AA)
ACU .... Arbeitsgemeinschaft Christlicher Unternehmer (WGAO)
ACU .... Arndell Children's Unit [*Australia*]
ACU .... Asian Clearing Union (WGAO)
ACU .... Asian Currency Unit
ACU .... Asociacion Colombiana de Universidades [*Columbian Universities Association*] [*Colombia*] (COL)
ACU .... Association for Communist Unity [*Australia*]
ACU .... Association of Commonwealth Universities (WGAO)
ACU .... Association of Cricket Umpires (WGAO)
ACU .... Australian Catholic University
ACU .... Australian Cycling Union (ADA)
ACU .... Auto Cycle Union (WGAO)
ACU .... Azerbaijan Composers' Union (EAIO)
ACU .... Marine Atomic Power Plant, Shipboard Nuclear Propulsion Plant (RU)
ACUA .... Australian Computer Users' Association (ADA)
ACUABOL ... Sociedad de Acueductos y Alcantarillados de Bolivar [*Colombia*] (COL)
ACUACALDAS ... Acueductos y Alcantarillados de Caldas [*Manizales*] (COL)
ACUACAUCA ... Sociedad de Acueductos y Alcantarillados del Cauca [*Popayan*] (COL)
ACUACORDOBA ... Sociedad de Acueductos y Alcantarillados de Cordoba [*Monteria*] (COL)
ACUAMARCA ... Acueductos y Alcantarillados de Cundinamarca [*Colombia*] (COL)
ACU Aq ..... Australian Catholic University Aquinas Campus
ACUAVALLE ... Acueductos y Alcantarillados del Valle SA [*Colombia*] (COL)
ACUCA ..... Association of Christian Universities and Colleges in Asia (EA)
ACU CH .... Australian Catholic University Castle Hill Campus
ACUChrist ... Australian Catholic University Christ Campus
ACUDE ..... Asociacion de Consumidores y Usuarios de Espana (WGAO)
ACUE .... Advisory Centre for University Education [*Australia*] (ADA)
ACUERUR ... Acueductos Rurales [*Instituto Nacional de Obras Sanitarias*] [*Rural water supply division*] [*Venezuela*] (LAA)
ACUF .... Association des Combattants de la Union Francaise (WGAO)
ACUFOS ... Australian Centre for UFO [*Unidentified Flying Objects*] Studies
ACUG .... Association Culturelle de Guiberoua
ACUM .... Authors, Composers and Music Publishers Society [*Israel*] (WGAO)
ACUM .... Society of Authors, Composers, and Music Publishers in Israel (SLS)
ACUMacK ... Australian Catholic University Mackillop Campus
ACUMcA ... Australian Catholic University McAuley Campus
ACUMercy ... Australian Catholic University Mercy Campus
ACUMSM ... Australian Catholic University Mount St. Mary Campus

ACUNI ...... Asociacion de Centros de la Universidad Nacional de Ingenieria [*National Engineering University Centers Association*] [*Peru*] (LA)
ACUNOR ... Empresa Acucareira Norte [*Angola*] (EY)
ACURIL .... Association of Caribbean University, Research, and Institutional Libraries (SLS)
ACUS .... Peruvian-USSR Cultural Association (LA)
ACUSA...... Armenian Church University Student Association [*Lebanon*] (EAIO)
ACUSA...... Australian Colleges and Universities Staff Association
ACUSE...... Action Committee for a United States of Europe [*EC*] (ECED)
ACU Sign... Australian Catholic University Signadou Campus
Acust......... Acustica [*Acoustic*] [*Portuguese*]
ACV .... Advertising Club of Victoria [*Australia*]
ACV .... Algemeen Christelijk Vakverbond [*Confederation of Christian Trade Unions*] [*Belgium*] (WEN)
ACV .... Algemeen Cristelijk Vakverbond [*Belgium*] (WGAO)
ACV .... Allgemeiner Caecilien-Verband fuer die Laender der Deutschen Sprache [*International Cecilian Association for German-Speaking Countries*] [*Regensburg, Germany*] (SLS)
ACV .... Armoured Control Vehicle [*Military*]
ACV .... Army Air Cushioned Vehicle (VNW)
ACV .... Association Centrale des Veterinaires [*Central Association of Veterinarians*] [*French*]
ACV .... Associazione Calzaturifici Valenzani (WGAO)
ACV .... Stichting Afnemers Controle op Veevoeder (WGAO)
ACVAFS.... American Council of Voluntary Agencies for Foreign Service, Inc.
ACVEN ..... Advisory Committee on Vehicle Emission and Noise [*Australia*]
ACVG .... Anciens Combattants et Victimes de la Guerre
ACVII........ Australian Computerised Vocational Interest Inventory
ACVPF ...... Association des Createurs de Varietes Potageres et Florales (WGAO)
ACVS........ Australian College of Veterinary Scientists (ADA)
ACVV .... Afrikaanse Christelike Vrouevereniging [*Women's Afrikaans-Christian Association*] [*Afrikaans*]
ACVZ .... Asociacion Colombiana de Veterinarios y Zootecnistas [*Colombia*] (DSCA)
ACW .... Algemeen Christelijk Werknemersverbond [*Christian Labor Movement*] [*Belgium*] (WEN)
ACW .... Association of Catholic Women (WGAO)
ACW .... Association of Community Workers (WGAO)
ACW .... Australian Church Women
ACW .... Australian Culture Workshop
ACWA ...... Advisory Committee on Women's Affairs [*New Zealand*]
ACWA ...... Association of Children's Welfare Agencies [*Australia*]
ACWA ...... Association of Civilian Widows of Australia
ACWA ...... Australian Chinese Women's Association (ADA)
ACWB ...... Australian Council of Wool Buyers (ADA)
ACWC ...... Australian Carpet Wool Council
ACWE ...... Advisory Committee on Women's Employment (WGAO)
ACWRTUK ... American Civil War Round Table [*United Kingdom*] (WGAO)
ACWW ...... Associated Country Women of the World [*British*]
ACY .... Air City SA [*Switzerland*] [*ICAO designator*] (FAAC)
ACYC .... Association Combined Youth Clubs (WGAO)
ACYF........ Australian Council of Young Farmers (ADA)
ACYP........ Australian Coalition of Young People
ACYPE...... Atlantic Association of Young Political Leaders (WGAO)
ACZ .... Agro-Chemisches Zentrum [*Agro-Chemical Center*] (EG)
ad............... Aan De [*Benelux*] (BAS)
AD............. Abwehrdienst [*Counterintelligence Service*] [*German military - World War II*]
AD............. Accion Democratica [*Democratic Action*] [*El Salvador*] [*Political party*] (PD)
AD............. Accion Democratica [*Democratic Action*] [*Venezuela*] [*Political party*] (PPW)
AD............. Action Directe [*Direct Action*] [*Terrorist group*] [*French*] (PD)
AD............. Action for Development [*FAO*] [*United Nations*]
Ad............. Ada [*or Adasi or Adacik*] [*Island or Islet Turkish*] (NAU)
AD............. Aden Airways
Ad............. Adet [*Number*] (TU)
ad............... Adiado [*Portuguese*]
ad............... Admiral (BU)
AD............. Admission Directive [*London Stock Exchange*]
AD............. Adrenaline (RU)
ad............... Adresse [*Address*] [*French*]
AD............. Aguarda Deferimento [*Portuguese*]
AD............. Airborne (RU)
AD............. Airborne Force (RU)
AD............. Aircraft Engine (RU)
AD............. Air Division (RU)
ad............... Airdrome (BU)
AD............. Akademsko Drustvo [*Academic Society*] (YU)
AD............. Akcijska Druzba [*Joint-Stock Company*] (YU)
AD............. Akcionarsko Drustvo [*Joint-Stock Company*] (YU)

AD............. Algerian Dinar [*Monetary unit*]
AD............. Alianca Democratica [*Democratic Alliance*] [*Brazil*] [*Political party*] (EY)
AD............. Alianca Democratica [*Democratic Alliance*] [*Portugal*] [*Political party*] (PPE)
AD............. Alianza Democratica [*Democratic Alliance*] [*Chile*] [*Political party*] (PPW)
AD............. Amesos Drasis [*Immediate Action*] [*DTA, KAD, MMAD*] [*See also*] (GC)
AD............. Amis de Darl'mat [*Friends of Darl'Mat*] [*France*] (EAIO)
AD............. Amplitude Demodulator (RU)
ad............... An Der [*At The, On The*] [*German*] (GPO)
aD............... An der Donau [*On the Danube River*] [*German*] (WEN)
AD............. Andorra [*ANSI two-letter standard code*] (CNC)
AD............. Anggaran Dasar [*Statutes, Constitution (of an organization)*] (IN)
AD............. Angkatan Darat [*Army*] (IN)
AD............. Animation et Developpement [*Animation and Development*] [*An association*] [*France*] (EAIO)
AD............. Antilles Air Boats (MHDB)
AD............. Arabian Danish Paint Co. [*Saudi Arabia*]
AD............. Archaeological Society (BU)
AD............. Armadni Divadlo [*Armed Forces Theater*] [*Prague*] (CZ)
AD............. Armadni Dum [*Armed Forces Building*] (CZ)
AD............. Arterial Pressure (RU)
AD............. Artiljerija Divizije [*Artillery of a Division*] (YU)
AD............. Artillerie Divisionnaire [*Military*] [*French*] (MTD)
AD............. Artillery Battalion (RU)
AD............. Artillery Division (RU)
AD............. Atomic Engine (RU)
AD............. Ausser Dienst [*Retired*] [*German*] (GPO)
AD............. Australia Day
AD............. Australian Democrats [*Political party*] (EAIO)
AD............. Automatic Dehydrator (RU)
AD............. Avia [*Francis Lombardi eC*] [*Italy*] [*ICAO aircraft manufacturer identifier*] (ICAO)
AD............. Aviatsionnaya Diviziya [*Air Division*] [*Former USSR*]
Ad............. C. H. Boehringer Sohn, Ingelheim [*Germany*] [*Research code symbol*]
AD............. Dame of the Order of Australia (ADA)
AD............. Damped Shock Absorber (RU)
AD............. Division Artillery (RU)
AD............. Induction Motor (RU)
AD............. Joint-Stock Company (BU)
AD............. Lab. Miquel [*Spain*] [*Research code symbol*]
AD............. Mobile Shower Unit (RU)
AD............. Servantes de l'Agneu Divin [*Sisters of the Lamb of God*] [*Roman Catholic religious order*]
AD 86........ Accion Democratica 86 [*Democratic Action 1986*] [*Aruba*] [*Political party*] (EY)
ADA .... Accelerated Development Area Programme
ADA .... Action for Dysphasic Adults (WGAO)
ADA .... Adana [*Turkey*] [*Airport symbol*] (OAG)
ADA .... Advective Dynamical Analysis (of Synoptic Processes) (RU)
ADA .... Aeronautical Development Agency [*India*] (PDAA)
ADA .... Agence Dahomeenne d'Assurances
ADA .... Agricultural Development Association (WGAO)
ADA .... Agrupacion Democratica Argentina [*Argentine Democratic Group*] (LA)
ADA .... Agrupament Democratic d'Andorra [*Andorran Democratic Association*] [*Political party*] (PPW)
ADA .... Alcohol and Drug Authority [*Australia*]
ADA .... Algemene Dienstaanwijzingen [*Benelux*] (BAS)
ADA .... Allgemeine Dienstanweisung [*General Service Regulations*] (EG)
ADA .... Allgemeiner Deutscher Automobil Club [*German Automobile Association*] (PDAA)
ADA .... Alliance Democratique Africaine
ADA .... Aluminium Development Association (WGAO)
ADA .... Anotati Dioikisis Aeroporias [*Supreme Air Force Command*] (GC)
ADA .... Anti-Discrimination Act [*Australia*]
ADA .... Antique Dealers Association [*Australia*]
ADA .... Association for Downs Syndrome in Australia
ADA .... Association of Drainage Authorities (WGAO)
ADA .... Association pour le Developpement de l'Aquaculture [*French*] (ASF)
ADA .... Associazione Direttori Albergo (WGAO)
ADA .... Australia Defence Association
ADA .... Australian Civil Aviation Authority, Flying Unit [*ICAO designator*] (FAAC)
ADA .... Australian Deer Association
ADA .... Australian Dental Association (ADA)
ADA .... Australian Department of Agriculture (ADA)
ADA .... Australian Digest [*A publication*]
ADA .... Australian Diving Association

ADA........... Australian Draughts Association (ADA)
ADA........... Ayuda del Automovilista (WGAO)
ADAA....... Aboriginal Development Assistance Association [*Australia*]
ADAA....... Air Defense Action Area [*Military*]
ADAA....... Art Dealers Association of America (WGAO)
ADAA....... Australian Development Assistance Agency (ADA)
ADAB....... Association pour le Developpement de l'Assurance et de la Banque [*France*] (FLAF)
ADAB....... Australian Development Assistance Bureau (WGAO)
ADABAS... Adaptierbares Datenbanksystem
ADAC....... Allgemeiner Deutscher Automobil Club [*German Automobile Association*]
ADAC....... Associazione degli Albergatori Capresi (WGAO)
ADAC....... Australian Department of the Arts and Administrative Services - Central Library [*National Union Catalogue of Australia symbol*]
ADAC....... Avion a Decollage et Atterrissage Courts [*Short Takeoff and Landing Plane*] [*Use STOL*] (CL)
ADACA..... Aseguradora Dominicana Agropecuaria [*National company*] [*The Dominican Republic*] (EY)
ADACES... Association pour le Developpement des Activities Culturelles dans les Etablissements Scolaires (WGAO)
ADACH..... Asociacion de Algodoneros de Chinandega [*Association of Chinandega Cotton Growers*] [*Nicaragua*] (LA)
ADACI...... Associazione degli Approvvigionatori e Compratori Italiani (WGAO)
ADACS..... Australian Development Assistance Courses
ADADO.... Asociacion de Algodoneros de Oriente [*Association of Eastern Cotton Growers*] [*Nicaragua*] (LA)
ADAEE...... Autoridad para el Desarrollo del Agua y la Energia Electrica [*Pakistan*] (DSCA)
ADAEPS... Association des Anciens Eleves des Peres de Scheut
ADAF........ Arbeitskreis der Deutschen Afrika-Forschungs- und Dokumentationstellen
ADAF........ Association pour la Diffusion des Accordeonistes Francophones [*France*] (EAIO)
ADAF........ Australian Drug and Alcohol Foundation
ADAG........ Adagio [*Slow*] [*Music*]
ADAGO..... Adagio [*Slow*] [*Music*] (ROG)
ADAGP..... Association pour la Diffusion des Arts Graphiques et Plastiques (WGAO)
ADAGRO... Almacenes y Depositos Agropecuarios [*Venezuela*] (DSCA)
ADAH....... Association of Dutch Art Historians [*Netherlands*] (EAIO)
ADAI........ Associazione degli Approvvigionatori Italiani (WGAO)
ADAL........ Asociacion de Algodoneros de Leon [*Association of Leon Cotton Growers*] [*Nicaragua*] (LA)
ADAN....... Associazione degli Abergatori Napoletani (WGAO)
ADANSW... Antique Dealers Association of New South Wales [*Australia*]
ADAPC..... Associacao Democratica de Amizade Portugal-China [*Democratic Association for Portuguese-Chinese Friendship*] (WER)
adap ed...... Adapte Eden [*Which Was Adapted (From)*] (TU)
ADAPI...... Associacao dos Armadores das Pescas Industriais (WGAO)
ADAPR..... Association des Aviculteurs Producteurs Romande (WGAO)
ADAPT..... Access for Disabled People in Arts Premises Today (WGAO)
adapt.......... Adaptacao [*Adaptation*] [*Publishing*] [*Portuguese*]
adapt.......... Adaptacja [*or Adaptowal*] [*Adaptation or Adapted By*] [*Poland*]
adapt.......... Adaptation [*Adaptation*] [*Publishing*] [*French*]
adapt.......... Adapte [*Adapted*] [*Publishing*] [*French*]
ADAPT...... Association for the Development of Appropriate Philippine Technology
ADAR....... Association des Amis Republicains [*Association of Republican Friends*] [*Cambodia*] (CL)
ADARDA.. Alzheimer's Disease and Related Disorders Association of Western Australia
ADARDS... Alzheimer's Disease and Related Disorders Society [*Australia*]
ADAS........ Administratia Asigurarilor de Stat [*State Insurance Administration*] [*Bucharest*] (RO)
ADAS........ African Demonstration Centre on Sampling Agricultural Surveys
ADAS........ Agricultural Development and Advisory Service (WGAO)
ADAS........ Akaryakit Dagitim Anonim Sirkesi [*Fuel Distribution Corporation*] (TU)
ADAS........ Army Dependants Assurance Trust (WGAO)
ADAS........ Associazione Nazionale Dettaglianti Articoli Sportivi (WGAO)
ADASS...... Adult Day and Support Services [*Australia*]
ADAST...... Adamovske Strojirny [*Adamov Engineering Works*] (CZ)
ADAT........ Allied Directorate of Air Transport [*Australia*]
ADATIG.... Anglo-Dutch African Textiles Investigation Group
ADAUA..... Association pour le Developpement Naturel d'une Architecture et d'un Urbanisme Africains [*Association for the Development of Traditional African Urbanism and Architecture*] [*Mauritania, Switzerland, Upper Volta*]
ADAVIC.... Antique Dealers Association of Victoria [*Australia*]
ADB........... African Development Bank [*Also, AfDB*]
ADB........... Agricultural Development Bank [*Trinidadian and Tobagan*] (LA)
ADB........... Airborne Brigade (RU)

ADB........... Allgemeine Deutsche Binnen-Transport-Versicherungsbedingungen [*General German Inland Transportation Insurance Terms*] (EG)
ADB........... Allgemeine Deutsche Biographie [*Universal German Biography*]
ADB........... Anguilla Development Board (GEA)
ADB........... Antonov Design Bureau [*Former USSR*] [*ICAO designator*] (FAAC)
ADB........... Arbeitsgemeinschaft Deutscher Betriebsingenieure [*Cooperative of German Production Engineers*] (GCA)
ADB........... Asian Development Bank
ADBACI.... Association pour le Developpement de la Documentation, des Bibliotheques et Archives de la Cote d'Ivoire (WGAO)
ADBE........ Association of Danish Business Economists (EAIO)
ADBEX...... Antarctic Division BIOMASS Experiment [*Australia*]
ADBF........ Australian Deer Breeders' Federation
ADBI......... Agricultural Development Bank of Iran (PDAA)
ADBIENES... Administracion de Bienes y Arrendamientos [*Colombia*] (COL)
ADBN....... Agricultural Development Bank of Nepal (WGAO)
ADBP........ Agricultural Development Bank of Pakistan (GEA)
ADBPA...... Association pour le Developpement des Bibliotheques Publiques en Afrique (WGAO)
ADBR....... Association pour le Developpement des Bibliotheques de Religieuses [*French*] (SLS)
ADBR....... Association pour le Developpement des Bibliotheques des Religieuses (WGAO)
ADBS........ Association des Documentalistes et des Bibliothecaires Specialises (WGAO)
ADBS........ Association Francaise des Documentalistes et des Bibliothecaires Specialises [*French*] (SLS)
ADBU........ Amicale des Directeurs de Bibliotheques Universitaires [*French*] (SLS)
ADBU........ Association des Directeurs de Bibliotheques Universitaires (WGAO)
ADBV........ Allgemeiner Deutscher Blinden-Verband [*General German Association of the Blind*] (EG)
ADC........... Aboriginal Development Commission [*Australia*]
ADC........... Aboriginal Development Corporation
ADC........... Agricultural Development Corp. [*Jamaica*] (EY)
ADC........... Agricultural Development Corp. [*Pakistan*] (PDAA)
ADC........... Agricultural Development Corp. [*Kenya*]
ADC........... Aide-de-Camp [*Military*] [*French*]
ADC........... Airline of Adriatic [*Croatia*] [*ICAO designator*] (FAAC)
ADC........... Amsterdam Depositary Company NV [*Netherlands*]
ADC........... Andean Development Corporation (WGAO)
ADC........... Arbeitsgemeinschaft Deutscher Chorverband [*Germany*] (EAIO)
ADC........... Arsenic Development Committee [*France*] (WGAO)
ADC........... Asia Development Center (CL)
ADC........... Asociacion Democratica Colombiana [*Colombian Democratic Association*] (COL)
ADC........... Association Demografica Constarricense [*Costa Rica*] (WGAO)
ADC........... Association of District Councils (WGAO)
ADC........... Australian Dairy Corporation
ADC........... Australian Deafness Council (ADA)
ADC........... Australian Design Council
ADC........... Australian Development Corporation (ADA)
ADC........... Australian Drivers' Championship
ADCA....... Advisory Dental Council of Australia
ADCA....... Allgemeine Deutsche Credit-Anstalt [*Bank*]
ADCA....... Asociacion de Cooperativas Agrarias [*Argentina*] (DSCA)
ADCA....... Australian Department of Civil Aviation (WGAO)
ADCA....... Australian Die Casting Association
ADCB........ Abu Dhabi Commercial Bank (MENA)
ADCCQ..... ANZAC [*Australia-New Zealand Army Corps*] Day Commemoration Committee, Queensland
ADCCSA... Air Diffusion and Components Council of South Australia
ADCE........ Associacao dos Dirigentes Cristaos de Empresas (WGAO)
ADCF........ Association pour le Developpement de la Culture Fourragere [*Switzerland*] (WGAO)
ADCI........ Association of Danish Chemical Industries (EAIO)
ADCI........ Association of the Dutch Chemical Industries [*Netherlands*] (EAIO)
ADCJ........ Association of District Council Treasurers (WGAO)
ADCNET... Australian Diplomatic Communications Network Project
ADCO........ Abu Dhabi Company for Onshore Oil Operations (MENA)
ADCO........ Andean Development Co. [*Ecuador*] (DSCA)
ADCO........ Andean Development Company [*Ecuador*] (WGAO)
ADCONA... Administradores y Contadores Asociados [*Colombia*] (COL)
ADCP........ Aquaculture Development and Coordination Program
ADCS........ Australian Defence Canteens Service (ADA)
ADCSC...... Australian Dairy Corporation Selection Committee
ADCSS...... Australian Development Cooperation Scholarship Scheme
ADCT........ Association of District Council Treasurers (WGAO)
ADD........... Action on Drinking and Driving (WGAO)
add............. Addatur [*Add*] [*Pharmacy*]

ADD.......... Addis Ababa [*Ethiopia*] [*Airport symbol*]   (OAG)
Add............. Additions [*French*]   (FLAF)
ADD............ Alliance Democratique Dahomeenne
ADD.......... Arbeitsgemeinschaft Deutscher Detektive   (WGAO)
ADD.......... Arbeitskreis Dezentrale Datenverarbeitung [*Work Circle for Decentralized Data Assimulation*] [*German*]   (ADPT)
ADD.......... Asociacion Dominicana de Diarios [*Dominican Association of Daily Newspapers*] [*Dominican Republic*]   (LA)
ADD.......... Aviatsiia Dalnego Deistviia [*Long-Range Aviation*] [*Strategic bombing force of USSR*]
ADD.......... Long-Range Artillery   (RU)
ADDA........ Accion Democratica Ecuatorian   (WGAO)
ADDA........ Australian Database Development Association
ADDA........ Darwin [*Australia*] [*ICAO location identifier*]   (ICLI)
ADDCAP... Abu Dhabi Drilling Chemicals and Products Company   (MENA)
ADDD........ Darwin [*Australia*] [*ICAO location identifier*]   (ICLI)
ADDE........ Association des Depots Dentaires Europeens   (WGAO)
ADDEND ... Addendus [*To Be Added*] [*Pharmacy*]
ADDIT ...... Association for Development of Design in Tasmania [*Australia*]
ADDLIS .... Alcohol and Drug Dependence Libraries and Information Services [*Australia*]
ADDM....... Association pour le Developpement de la Documentation Medicale   (WGAO)
ADDN....... Darwin [*Australia*] [*ICAO location identifier*]   (ICLI)
ADDO .... Alokasi Devisa Daerah Otomatis [*Automatic Regional Foreign-Exchange Allocation (Percentage of export earnings returned to regions by central government)*]   (IN)
ADDU........ Alcohol and Drug Dependence Unit [*Northern Territory Health Commission*] [*Australia*]
ADDX........ Darwin [*Australia*] [*ICAO location identifier*]   (ICLI)
ADE........... Accion Democratica Ecuatoriana [*Ecuadorean Democratic Action*] [*Political party*]   (PPW)
ADE........... Adelaide [*Mount Bonython*] [*Australia*] [*Seismograph station code, US Geological Survey*]   (SEIS)
ADE........... Aden [*People's Democratic Republic of Yemen*] [*Airport symbol*]   (OAG)
ADE........... Administracion de Fomento Economico [*Puerto Rico*]   (DSCA)
ADE........... African Institute for Economic Development and Planning [*Senegal*]   (WGAO)
ADE........... Anderson Digital Equipment Proprietary Ltd. [*Australia*]
ADE........... Applications Development Environment [*Computer science*]
ADE........... Arctic Development and the Environment [*Program of the Arctic Institute of North America*]   (MSC)
ADE........... Asamblea Democratica Euzkadi [*Basque Democratic Assembly*] [*Spanish*]   (WER)
ADE........... Asociacion Democratica de Estudiantes [*Democratic Association of Students*] [*Mexico*]   (LA)
ADE........... Asociacion Distrital de Educadores [*District Teachers Association*] [*Colorado*]   (LA)
ADE........... Association Europeenne pour l'Etude de l'Alimentation et Developpement de l'Enfant [*European Association of Nutrition and Child Development*]   (EAIO)
ADE........... Australian Diamond Exploration
ADE........... Australian Driver Education   (ADA)
ADE........... Automatisation des Dossiers d'Etudes [*French*]   (ADPT)
ADEA........ Asociacion de Defensores de Animales [*Animal Protection Association*] [*Uruguay*]   (LA)
ADEA........ Association Belge pour le Developpement Pacifique de l'Energie Atomique [*Belgian Association for the Peaceful Development of Atomic Energy*]
ADEA........ Australian Diabetes Educators Association
ADEAC ..... Association d'Entrepots en Afrique Centrale   (WGAO)
ADEAC ..... Association pour le Developpement des Echanges Artistiques et Culturels
ADEARTA ... Association pour le Developpement de l'Equipement des Ateliers de Reparation des Tracteurs Agricoles   (WGAO)
ADEB .... Association des Editeurs Belges [*Association of French-language book publishers*] [*Belgium*]   (EY)
ADEB .... Association des Entrepreneurs Belges de Travaux de Genie Civil   (WGAO)
ADEB .... Association pour le Developpement de l'Exportation des Vins de Bordeaux
ADEB .... Association pour le Developpement du Bois [*France*]   (DSCA)
ADEBA...... Asociacion de Bancos Argentinos [*Argentine Bank Association*] [*Buenos Aires*]   (LA)
ADEBASQUET ... Asociacion Colombiana de Basquetbol [*Colombia*]   (COL)
ADEBCO... Association des Eglises Baptistes du Congo-Ouest [*Association of Baptist Churches of the Western Congo*]
ADEBD ..... Association des Diplomes de l'Ecole de Bilbliothecaires-Documentalistes   (WGAO)
ADEBIO.... Association pour le Developpement de la Bio-Industrie [*France*]
A de C .... Ano de Cristo [*In the Year of Our Lord*] [*Spanish*]
A de C .... Asamblea de Cataluna [*Assembly of Catalonia*] [*Spanish*]   (WER)
ADEC .... Asociacion de Exportadores de Cafe [*Guatemala*]   (DSCA)
ADEC .... Association des Entrepreneurs du Congo [*Association of Congo Entrepreneurs*]

ADEC .... Association pour le Developpement de la Cooperation Agricole   (WGAO)
ADEC .... Association pour le Developpement Educatif et Culturel
ADEC .... Australian Drug Evaluation Centre
ADEC .... Australian Drug Evaluation Committee
ADECAF ... Agence de Developpement Cafeiere [*National coffee development agency*] [*Central African Republic*]
ADECAFEH ... Asociacion de Exportadores de Cafe de Honduras [*Association of Honduran Coffee Exporters*]   (LA)
ADECELA ... Asociacion de Celadores de Antioquia [*Colombia*]   (COL)
ADECERE ... Asociacion de Empleados del Centro de Rehabilitacion [*Association of Rehabilitation Center Employees*] [*Dominican Republic*]   (LA)
ADECIF .... Associacao dos Diretores de Empresas de Credito, Investimentos, e Financiamento [*Association of Directors of Credit, Investment, and Finance Companies*] [*Brazil*]   (LA)
ADECO ..... Programa de Adiestramiento de Extensionistas en Comunicaciones, America Latina   (LAA)
ADECO ..... Programa de Adiestramiento de Extensionistas en Comunicaciones, Latinoamerica   (WGAO)
ADECOL... Asociacion de Compositores Colombianos [*Colombia*]   (COL)
ADECON .. Asociacion de Comercio Nacional Ltda. [*Colombia*]   (COL)
ADECONTA ... Asociacion de Contadores del Valle del Cauca [*Colombia*]   (COL)
ADEDY ..... Anotati Dioikousa Epitropi Dimosion Ypallilon [*Supreme Administrative Committee of Civil Servants*] [*Greek*]   (GC)
ADEE .... Association for Dental Education in Europe [*Ireland*]   (EAIO)
ADEEP...... Association d'Entraide des Eglises de Pentecote [*Pentacostal Churches Welfare Association*] [*Burundi*]   (AF)
ADEET...... Australia - Department of Employment Education and Training [*National Union Catalogue of Australia symbol*]
ADEFA...... Asociacion de Fabricantes de Automotores [*Association of Motor Vehicle Manufacturers*] [*Argentina*]   (LA)
ADEFUTBOL ... Asociacion Colombiana de Futbol [*Colombia*]   (COL)
ADEGA ..... Asociacion Colombiana de Ganaderos [*Colombia*]   (DSCA)
ADEGUI ... Asociacion Democratica Empresarial de Guipuzcoa   (WGAO)
ADEIA....... Associacao dos Docentes de Ensino Industrial e Agricola Oficial do Estado de Sao Paulo [*Brazil*]   (DSCA)
ADEIS .... Association pour le Developpement de l'Enseignement d'Image et Son   (WGAO)
a de JC ...... Antes de Jesucristo [*Before Jesus Christ*] [*Spanish*]   (GPO)
ADEKRA... Arbeitsgemeinschaft Deutscher Kraftwagen-Spediteure   (WGAO)
ADEL .... Academia de Estudios Liturgicos [*Colombia*]   (COL)
Adel............ Adelaide [*Australia*]   (ADA)
Adel............ University of Adelaide [*Australia*]   (ADA)
ADELA...... Atlantic Community Development Group for Latin America [*Joint US-European private investment company*]
ADELA...... Ayakkabi-Deri ve Lastik Sanayii AS [*Footwear, Leather, and Rubber Industry Corp.*] [*Istanbul*]   (TU)
ADELACC ... Adelaide Convention Centre [*Australia*]
ADELCA ... Administracion del Correo Aereo [*Colombia*]   (COL)
ADELE...... Automatische Datenerfassung durch Lochkarteneingabe [*Automatic Data Registration Through Use of Punch Cards*] [*German*]   (ADPT)
ADELF...... Association des Ecrivains de Langue Francaise [*Association of French-Language Writers*]   (EAIO)
ADELF...... Association des Epidemiologistes de Langue Francaise [*Association of French Language Epidemiologists*]   (EAIO)
ADELF...... Association des Epidemiologists de Langue Francaise   (WGAO)
ADEM .... Asociacion de Directores de Ensenanza Media [*Association of Mid-Level School Directors*] [*Costa Rica*]   (LA)
ADEM .... Association Democratique des Etudiants de Madagascar [*Malagasy Democratic Student Association*]   (AF)
ADEMACOL ... Asociacion de Madereros Colombianos [*Colombia*]   (COL)
ADEMA-PPLSJ ... Alliance pour la Democratie au Mali - Parti Pan-Africain pour la Liberte, la Solidarite, et la Justice [*Political party*]   (EY)
ADEMAST ... Association Nationale pour le Developpment et la Maitrise des Sciences et des Techniques [*French*]
ADENA ..... Asociacion para la Defensa de la Naturaleza [*Spanish*]   (SLS)
ADENA ..... Associacao dos Diplomados da Escola Nacional de Agronomia Universidade Rural [*Brazil*]   (DSCA)
ADENAVI ... Asociacion Nacional de Navieros [*National Shipowners Association*] [*Colorado*]   (LA)
ADEOM ..... Asociacion de Empleados y Obreros Municipales [*Association of Municipal Employees and Workers*] [*Uruguay*]   (LA)
ADEOS ..... Advanced Earth Observing Satellite [*Japan*]
ADEP .... Agence Nationale pour le Developpement de l'Education Permanente [*France*]
ADEP .... Association pour le Developpement Economique et Pastoral [*Association for Economic and Pastoral Development*] [*Algeria*]   (AF)
ADEP .... Ateliers de Decoupage et d'Emboutissage de Precision [*Algeria*]
ADEPA...... Asociacion de Entidades Periodisticas Argentinas [*Argentine Newspaper Owners Association*]   (LA)
ADEPA...... Asociacion de Productores de Algodon [*Association of Cotton Producers*] [*Bolivia*]   (LA)

ADEPA...... Association pour le Developpement de la Production Automatique (WGAO)

ADEPA...... Association pour le Developpement de la Production Automatisee [*Association for the Development of Automated Production*] [*France*] (PDAA)

ADEPAN... Asociacion Nacional de Fabricantes de Pan [*Colombia*] (COL)

ADEPHAR ... Association des Etudiants de Pharmacie [*Association of Pharmacy Students*] [*Cambodia*] (CL)

ADEPS...... Administration d'Education Physique, des Sports, et de la Vie en Plein Air [*Administration of Physical Education, Sports, and Open Air Living*] [*Belgium*]

ADEPT...... Aboriginal Distance Education Preparatory Training Program

ADEPT...... Applied Drug Education and Professional Training [*Australia*]

ADEPT...... Association d'Etudes Politiques Transeuropeennes [*Trans European Policy Studies Association - TEPSA*] (EA)

ADEPT...... Automatic Debiting and Electronic Payment for Transport [*Automotive engineering*] (ECON)

ADEQUA.. Association des Entreprises de l'Equateur

ADEQUIN ... Asociacion Quimico Industrial de Deportes [*Colombia*] (COL)

ADER .... Asociacion de Empleados de Radiodifusoras [*Association of Radiobroadcast Employees*] [*Uruguay*] (LA)

ADER .... Association des Ecrivains Reunionnais

ADERAL... Association pour le Developpement Economique et Social de la Region d'Alepe

ADERP...... Association pour le Developpement de l'Enseignement et des Recherches Scientifiques aupres des Universites de la Region Parisienne [*French*] (SLS)

A DES........ A Destra [*To the Right*] [*Italian*] (ADA)

ADES......... Alliance pour la Democratie et l'Emancipation Sociale [*Burkina Faso*] [*Political party*] (EY)

ADES......... Assemblee Departementale Economique et Sociale [*Departmental Economic and Social Assembly*] [*Algeria*]

ADES......... Association of Directors of Education in Scotland (SLS)

ADESCO... Amicale des Diplomes d'Etudes Superieures de Commerce

ADESG...... Associacao dos Diplomados da Escola Superior de Guerra [*War College Graduates Association*] [*Brazil*] (LA)

ADESKA ... Association pour le Developpement Economique et Social de Katiola

ADESPE ... Association pour le Developpement de la Science Politique Europeenne [*French*] (SLS)

adess .... Adessiivi [*Finland*]

ADET .... Asociacion de Empresas Teatrales [*Colombia*] (COL)

ADETEM ... Association Nationale pour le Developpement des Techniques de Marketing [*French*] (SLS)

ADETIC .... Asociacion de Tecnicos Industriales de Colombia [*Colombia*] (COL)

ADETIM... Association pour le Developpment des Techniques des Industries Mecaniques [*Association for the Improvement of Mechanical Engineering Techniques*] [*France*] (PDAA)

ADETOM ... Association pour le Developpement de l'Enseignement Technique d'Outre-Mer [*Association for the Development of Overseas Technical Education*] [*French*] (AF)

ADEVIDA ... Asociacion en Defensa de la Vida Humana (WGAO)

ADEX .... Asociacion de Exportadores [*Exporters Association*] [*Peru*] (LA)

ADEXA ..... Association pour le Developpement des Exportations Agricoles [*France*] (DSCA)

ADEZ .... Association des Entrepreneurs du Zaire [*Association of Zaire Entrepreneurs*] (AF)

ADEZ .... Association pour le Developpement des Etudes Zootechniques [*Belgium*] (WGAO)

ADF .... Adenosine Diphosphate (RU)

ADF .... Adenosinediphosphoric Acid (RU)

ADF .... Aerosolinteressenters Forening (WGAO)

ADF .... African Defence Federation

ADF .... African Development Foundation (EGAO)

ADF .... African Development Fund [*or Foundation*] [*African Development Bank*] (AF)

ADF .... Aktion Demokratischer Fortschritt [*Action for Democratic Progress*] [*Germany*] (PPE)

ADF .... Alcohol and Drug Foundation [*Australia*]

ADF .... Alliance pour la Democratie et la Federation [*Burkina Faso*] [*Political party*] (EY)

ADF .... Arab Deterrent Force [*Palestine*] (PD)

ADF .... Arbeitsgemeinschaft Deutscher Filztuchfabriken (WGAO)

ADF .... Asian Development Fund [*Asian Development Bank*]

ADF .... Association Dentaire Francaise [*French Dental Association*] (SLS)

ADF .... Australian Dance Foundation

ADF .... Australian Deerstalkers' Federation

ADF .... Australian Defence Force (ADA)

ADF .... Australian Diabetes Foundation

ADF .... Automotive Diesel Fuel

ADF .... Shock Absorber with Friction Damping (RU)

ADFA .... Alcohol and Drug Foundation, Australia

ADFA .... Australian Defence Force Academy

ADFA .... Australian Defence Force Academy Library [*National Union Catalogue of Australia symbol*]

ADFA .... Australian Dried Fruits Association (ADA)

ADFAB..... Australian Dairy Foods Advisory Bureau

ADFAED... Abu Dhabi Fund for Arab Economic Development (WGAO)

ADFAM .... Aid for Addicts and Families (WGAO)

ADFaS....... Australian Documentary Facsimile Society

ADFC........ Australian Dried Fruits Corporation

ADFCIV .... Association des Francophones au Centre International de Vienne (WGAO)

ADFE........ Association Democratique des Francais de l'Etranger [*Democratic Association of French Citizens Abroad*] (PPW)

ADFF........ Australian Dairy Farmers' Federation (ADA)

ADFF........ Australian Deer Farmers' Federation

ADFIAP ... Association of Development Financing Institutions in Asia and the Pacific [*Manila, Philippines*] (EA)

ADFILS..... Australian Defence Families Information and Liaison Service

ADFOA ..... Australian Duty Free Operators' Association

ADFORMS ... Australian Defense Formatted Message System [*Military*]

ADFS........ Australian Documentary Facsimile Society (ADA)

ADFV .... Alcohol and Drug Foundation of Victoria [*Australia*]

ADFVE...... Association of Dutch Fruit and Vegetable Exporters [*Netherlands*] (EAIO)

ADFWC...... Australian Defense Force Warfare Center [*Military*]

ADG.......... Action Democratique Guyanaise [*French Guiana*] [*Political party*] (EY)

ADG.......... African Development Group

ADG.......... Air Defense Guard [*Military*]

ADG.......... Antidiuretic Hormone (RU)

ADG.......... Asociacion de Disenadores Graficos de Buenos Aires [*Graphic Designers Association of Buenos Aires*] [*Argentina*] (EAIO)

ADG.......... Aviones y Servicios del Golfo SA de CV [*Mexico*] [*ICAO designator*] (FAAC)

ADG.......... Emergency Diesel Generator (RU)

ADGAS ..... Abu Dhabi Gas Liquefaction Co. [*United Arab Emirates*] (MENA)

ADGB........ Allgemeiner Deutscher Gewerkschaftsbund [*General German Labor Union Federation*] (EG)

ADGB........ Amicale de Developpement du Groupement Bangoulap

ADGE........ Air Defense Ground Environment [*NATO*] (MCD)

ADGE........ Assistant Director-General of Education [*Australia*]

ADGFAD.. Agrupacion Diseno Grafico (WGAO)

ADGIL....... Abu Dhabi Gas Industries Ltd.

ADGK........ Guards Airborne Corps (RU)

ADGLC ..... Abu Dhabi Gas Liquefaction Company (MENA)

ADGM....... Ankara Devlet Guvenlik Mahkemesi [*Ankara State Security Court*] (TU)

ADGO........ Adagio [*Slow*] [*Music*]

ADGPF...... Association pour le Developpment des Grands Ports Francais (WGAO)

ADGV........ Gove [*Australia*] [*ICAO location identifier*] (ICLI)

ADH .... Association of Dental Hospitals of the United Kingdom (WGAO)

ADH .... Societa' Adriatica [*Italy*] [*ICAO designator*] (FAAC)

Adhas........ Adhaesion [*Adhesion*] [*German*] (GCA)

ADHC........ Air Defense Hardware Committee [*NATO*] (NATG)

ADHGB...... Allgemeines Deutsches Handelsgesetzbuch von 1861 [*German commercial code*] (ILCA)

ADHIBEND ... Adhibendus [*To Be Used*] [*Pharmacy*]

ADHILAC ... Asociacion de Historiadores Latinoamericanos y del Caribe [*Mexico*] (WGAO)

ADHL-USSR ... Association for the Dissemination of the Hebrew Language in the USSR [*Israel*] (EAIO)

ADHOC .... Association of Departmental Heads of Catering (WGAO)

ADHS........ Armidale and District Historical Society [*Australia*]

ADI .... Academie Diplomatique International (WGAO)

ADI .... Academie Diplomatique Internationale [*International Diplomacy Academy*] [*French*] (SLS)

ADI .... Academy of Dentistry International (WGAO)

ADI .... Agence d'Informatique (WGAO)

ADI .... Agrupacion de Disenadores Industriales (WGAO)

AdI .... Alliance des Independants [*Independent Party*] [*Switzerland*] [*Political party*] (PPE)

ADI .... Anwenderverband Deutscher Informationsverarbeiter (WGAO)

ADI .... Anwenderverband Deutscher Informationsverarbeiter eV [*Association of the German Information Programs*] [*German*] (ADPT)

ADI .... Arab Development Institute

ADI .... Asia Dairy Industries (ADA)

ADI .... Association of the Deaf in Israel (EAIO)

ADI .... Association pour le Developpement International (WGAO)

ADI .... Associazione Detectives Italiani (WGAO)

ADI .... Associazione Dietetica Italiana [*Italian*] (SLS)

ADI .... Associazione Disegno Industriale [*Italy*]

ADI .... Associazione Italiana di Dietetica e Nutrizione Clinica [*Italian*] (SLS)

ADI .... Associazione per il Disegno Industriale (WGAO)

ADI .... Audeli Air Express [*Spain*] [*ICAO designator*]   (FAAC)

ADI .... Australian Defence Industries Proprietary Ltd.

ADI .... Automatic Smoke Annunciator   (RU)

ADI .... Avtomobilno-dorozhnyi Institut   (WGAO)

ADI .... Remote Measurement Equipment   (RU)

ADIA .... Abu Dhabi Investment Authority   (ME)

ADIA .... Academy of Diplomacy and International Affairs [*Germany*]
          (WGAO)

ADIA .... Asociacion Dominicana de Ingenieros Agronomos [*Dominican
          Association of Agronomists*] [*Dominican Republic*]   (LA)

ADIA .... Associate of the Design Institute of Australia

ADIA .... Associazione Donne Italo Australiene [*Australia*]

ADIA .... Australian Drilling Industry Association

ADIAC ...... Australian Dairy Industry Advisory Committee

ADIB .... Abu Dhabi International Bank   (WGAO)

ADIB .... Abu Dhabi International Bank, Inc.

ADIBA ...... Asociacion de Industriales de Buenos Aires [*Buenos Aires
          Manufacturers Association*] [*Argentina*]   (LA)

ADIBBEL ... Association des Diregeants des Instituts de Beaute de Belgique
          (WGAO)

ADIBOR.... Abu Dhabi Interbank Offered Rate [*Finance*]

ADIC .... Abu Dhabi Investment Company   (MENA)

ADIC .... Asociacion de Industriales de Cordoba [*Association of Cordoba
          Industrialists*] [*Argentina*]   (LA)

ADIC .... Association des Dirigeants et Cadres Chretiens [*Belgium*]
          (WGAO)

ADIC .... Australasian Display and Information Centre   (ADA)

ADIC .... Australian Dairy Industry Conference [*or Council*]   (ADA)

ADICEP .... Association des Directeurs des Centres des Matieres Plastiques
          (WGAO)

ADICEP .... Association des Directeurs des Centres Europeens des Plastiques
          [*Association of Directors of European Centres for Plastics*]
          (EAIO)

ADICIEL... Association de Diffusion de Cinema Expression Latine   (WGAO)

ADICO ...... Asociacion de Ingenieros Constructores [*Colombia*]   (COL)

ADICT....... Agricultural Development and Industrial Company of
          Tanganyika [*Tanzania*]

ADICT....... Association Internationale de Documentation Information
          Culturelle Touristique   (WGAO)

ADIDAS.... Adi Dassler [*Founder of German sporting goods company;
          acronym used as brand name of shoes manufactured by the
          firm*]

A-Dienst .... Ausrueckedienst [*Emergency Service*] [*Operational fire
          department unit on 24-hour service to handle emergencies*]
          (EG)

ADIF......... Association de Deportes, Internes et Leurs Familles [*France*]
          (FLAF)

ADIFAL .... Asociacion para el Desarrollo de la Industria de los Fertilizante
          de America Latina   (WGAO)

ADIFARCO ... Asociacion de la Industria Farmaceutica Colombiana
          [*Colombia*]   (COL)

ADIG .... Associazione per il Diabete Infantile e Giovanile [*Italian*]   (SLS)

ADIGE ...... Archivio Dati Italiani di Geologia [*Italian Geological Data
          Archive*] [*National Research Council Database*]   (IID)

ADIGE ...... Association pour le Developpment de l'Information de Gestion
          [*Association for the Development of Information
          Management*]   (ADPT)

ADIH........ Association des Industries d'Haiti   (EY)

ADIJ......... Association pour le Developpement de l'Informatique Juridique
          [*France*]   (EAIO)

Adil .... Angkatan Democratic Liberal Sabah [*Malaysia*] [*Political party*]
          (EY)

ADILINA .. Association de Diffusion de Litterature Negro-Africaine
          (WGAO)

ADILO ...... Australian Defence Intelligence Liaison Officer

ADIM .... Associacao para a Defesa dos Interesses de Macau [*Macau*]
          [*Political party*]   (FEA)

ADIMAGRO ... Asociacion de Distribuidores de Maquinaria Agricola
          [*Colombia*]   (COL)

ADIMRA... Asociacion de Industrialistas Metalurgicos de la Republica
          Argentina [*Association of Metallurgic Industrialists of the
          Argentine Republic*]   (LA)

ADIN........ Asociacion de Industrias Nauticas   (WGAO)

ADINARCO ... Asociacion de Ingenieros Arquitectos   (COL)

ADINCOL ... Sociedad Industrial y Comercial Ltda. [*Colombia*]   (COL)

ADIP......... Asociacion Dominicana de Investigaciones Pediatricas
          [*Dominican Republic*]   (EAIO)

ADIP......... Association Nationale de Defense de Elevage et du Commerce
          Rural Interprofessionnel   (WGAO)

ADIP......... Associazione Italiana dei Direttori del Personale   (WGAO)

ADIPA....... Associacao dos Distribuidores de Produtos Alimentares
          (WGAO)

ADIPA...... Association of Development, Research and Training Institutes of
          Asia and the Pacific   (WGAO)

ADIPAR.... Asociacion de Bibliotecarios del Paraguay   (WGAO)

ADIPB....... Asociacion de Damas Israelitas Pro Beneficencia [*Association of
          Israeli Women for Charity*] [*Costa Rica*]   (EAIO)

ADIPUG.... Altin Boynuz Diriltme Projesini Uygulama Grubu [*Group for the
          Execution of the Golden Horn Renovation Project*]   (TU)

ADIR .... Association des Demenageurs Internationaux Routiers [*Belgium*]
          (WGAO)

ADIR .... Australian Department of Industrial Relations [*National Union
          Catalogue of Australia symbol*]

ADIRI....... Asociatia de Drept International si Relatii Internationale
          [*Association for International Law and International
          Relations*]   (RO)

ADIS......... Agence de Diffusion Industrielle et Scientifique

ADIS......... Alcohol and Drug Information Service [*New South Wales,
          Australia*]

ADIS......... Australasian Drug Information Service Proprietary Ltd.

ADIS......... Australian Defence Information Services [*Department of
          Defence*] [*National Union Catalogue of Australia symbol*]

ADISK...... Adesmevti Dimokratiki Syndikalistiki Kinisi [*Free Democratic
          Trade Union Movement*]   (GC)

ADISOK.... Ananeotiko Dimokratiko Socialistiko Kinema [*Democratic
          Socialist Reform Movement*] [*Cyprus*] [*Political party*]
          (EY)

ADIT .... Agencija Demokraticnega Inozemskega Tiska [*Agency of the
          Democratic Foreign Press*] [*Ljubljana*]   (YU)

ADITA...... Asociacion de Industriales Textiles Argentinos [*Argentina*]

ADITC...... Australian Drilling Industry Training Committee

ADITECO ... Asociacion de Industriales Tecnicos Colombianos [*Colombia*]
          (COL)

ADITES .... Asociacion de Investigacion de la Tecnicas del Subsuelo
          [*Research Association on Subsoil Technology*] [*Spain*]
          (PDAA)

ADITIA ..... Adana Iktisadi ve Ticari Ilimler Akademisi [*Adana Academy of
          Economy and Commercial Science*] [*AITIA*] [*See also*]
          (TU)

adj .... Abbreviation   (TPFD)

adj .... Adjectif [*French*]   (TPFD)

adj .... Adjectivo [*Adjective*] [*Portuguese*]

ADJ .... Adjektief [*Adjective*] [*Afrikaans*]

adj .... Adjektiivi [*Adjective*] [*Finland*]

ADJ .... Adjudan [*Adjutant, Aide*]   (IN)

adj .... Adjunkt [*Adjunct*] [*Poland*]

adj .... Adjunktus [*Assistant Professor*]   (HU)

ADJ .... Arheolosko Drustvo Jugoslavije [*Archaeological Society of
          Yugoslavia*]   (YU)

ADJEN...... Adjudan Djenderal [*Adjutant General*]   (IN)

adjk .... Adjunk [*Adjunct*] [*Afrikaans*]

ADJP........ Asociacion Democratica de Juntas Progresistas [*Democratic
          Association of Progressive Boards*] [*Costa Rica*]   (LA)

AD(JR)...... Administrative Decisions (Judicial Review) [*Act*] [*Australia*]

adjt .... Adjudant [*Aide-de-Camp*] [*Afrikaans*]

ADK.......... Absolvent Delnickeho Kursu [*Graduate of Worker's Preparatory
          Course (for college admission)*]   (CZ)

ADK.......... Adiadochokinesis   (RU)

ADK.......... Afrikaans-Deutsche Kulturgemeinschaft [*German*]

ADK.......... Afrikaanse-Duitse Kultuurunie [*Afrikaans-German Cultural
          Association*] [*Namibia*]   (AF)

AdK.......... Akademie der Kunste [*Academy of Art*] [*German*]

ADK.......... Alliance for Democracy in Korea   (WGAO)

ADK.......... Arbeitgeberverband der Deutschen Kautschukindustrie
          (WGAO)

ADK.......... Arbeitsgemeinschaft der Deutschen Kartoffelwirtschaft
          [*Association of German Potato Science*]   (SLS)

ADK.......... Arbeitsgemeinschaft des Deutschen Kunsthandwerks   (WGAO)

ADK.......... Arbeitsgemeinschaft Deutsches Krankenhaus   (WGAO)

ADK.......... Arhiv Drzavne Komisije [*State Commission Archives*]   (YU)

ADK.......... Arkhigeion Dynameon Katadromon [*Raiding Forces Command*]
          [*Greek*]   (GC)

ADK.......... Artillery Decontamination Kit   (RU)

ADK.......... Ateliers de Kahankro

ADK.......... Aviation Development Co. Nigeria Ltd. [*ICAO designator*]
          (FAAC)

ADKh......... Anotera Dioikisis Khorofylakis [*Supreme Gendarmery
          Command*] [*Greek*]   (GC)

ADKM....... Antoko Demokraty Kristiana Malagasy [*Malagasy Christian
          Democratic Party*]   (AF)

ADL.......... Adelaide [*Australia*] [*Airport symbol*]   (OAG)

ADL.......... Adelaide [*Totalizator Agency Board code*] [*Australia*]

AdL........... A. de Lara Limited Edition Recordings [*Now Orfeo with same
          numbers*] [*Record label Great Britain*]

AdL........... Akademie der Landwirtschaftswissenschaften der Deutschen
          Demokratischen Republic [*Academy of Agricultural
          Sciences of the German Democratic Republic*] [*Research
          center*]   (ERC)

AdL........... Akademie der Landwirtschaftswissenschaften der Deutschen
          Demokratishen Republi c [*Academy of Agricultural
          Sciences of the German Democratic Republic*]   (EG)

ADL.......... Arbeitsgemeinschaft fuer Informationsverarbeitung eV
          [*Association for Information Processing*] [*German*]
          (ADPT)

ADL .... Australian Deer Ltd.
ADL .... Australian Development Ltd.
ADL .... Australian Documents Library
ADL .... Societe de Gestion de l'Aeroport de Libreville [*Airline*] [*Gabon*] (EY)
ADL .... Verband fur Informationsverarbeitung (WGAO)
ADLA .... Association Danoise de Linguistique Appliquee (WGAO)
ADLAD ..... Associazione Nazionale dei Datori di Lavoro al Personale Domestico (WGAO)
ADLAF ...... Arbeitsgemeinschaft Deutsche Lateinamerika-Forschung [*Association of German-Latin American Research*] (SLS)
ADLER ...... Genealogical and Heraldic Society [*Austria*] (EAIO)
ADLF .... Association des Dieteticiens de Langue Francaise (WGAO)
ADLIB .... Adaptive Library Management and Information System [*Computer software*] [*Australia*]
AD LIB ..... Ad Libitum [*At Pleasure, As Desired*] [*Music*]
ADLIBIT ... Ad Libitum [*At Pleasure, As Desired*] [*Music*]
ADLP .... Australian Democratic Labor Party [*Political party*] (PPW)
ADLS .... Arbeitsgemeinschaft fuer Elektronische Datenverarbeitung und Lochkartentechnik [*Association for Electronic Data Processing and Punch Card Technology*] [*German*] (ADPT)
ADLS .... Association of Dunmore Lang Students [*Australia*] (ADA)
ADLUG ..... Australian DOBIS/LIBIS Users' Group
ADLV .... Associazione Dipendenti Laici Vaticani [*Association of Vatican Lay Workers*] [*Vatican City*]
ADM .... Adder Doutchi Maggia
Adm .... Administracja [*or Administracyjny*] [*Administration or Administrative*] [*Poland*]
adm .... Administration (BU)
adm .... Administrative, Administration (RU)
adm .... Admiral [*Poland*]
ADM .... Aerolineas Dominicanas SA [*Dominican Republic*] [*ICAO designator*] (FAAC)
ADM .... Arbeitskreis Deutscher Marktforschungsinstitute eV [*Association of the German Market Research Institute*] (SLS)
ADM .... Artisans du Monde (WGAO)
ADM .... Asociacion Dental Mexicana (WGAO)
ADM .... Association of Domestic Management (WGAO)
ADM .... Association of Drum Manufacturers (WGAO)
ADM .... Association pour le Developpement du Droit Mondial (WGAO)
ADM .... Associazione Nazionale Disegno di Macchine [*Italian*] (SLS)
ADM .... Decontamination Truck (BU)
ADMA .... Abu Dhabi Marine Areas (ME)
ADMA .... American Drug Manufacturers Association (WGAO)
ADMA .... Association of Dance and Mime Artists (WGAO)
ADMA .... Australian Direct Mail Association (ADA)
ADMA .... Australian Direct Marketing Association (ADA)
ADMA .... Australian Display Manufacturers Association (ADA)
ADMAC .... Austrian Documentation Centre for Media and Communication Research [*Information service or system*] (IID)
ADMAOPCO ... Abu Dhabi Marine Operating Company (WGAO)
ADMARC ... Agricultural Development and Marketing Corporation [*Malawi*] (WGAO)
ADMB .... Agricultural Development and Marketing Board [*Northern Territory Australia*]
Adm B .... Periodieke Verzameling van Administratieve en Rechterlijke Beslissingen [*Benelux*] (BAS)
ADMBAKh .. Alkyldimethylbenzylammonium Chloride (RU)
ADMH ...... Association for Dutch Music History [*Netherlands*] (EAIO)
ADMICAL ... Association pour le Developpement du Mecenat Industriel et Commercial [*France*]
ADMIG ..... Australian Drug and Medical Information Group (ADA)
admin .... Administracja [*Administration*] (POL)
admin .... Administrasie [*or Administrateur*] [*Administration or Administrator*] [*Afrikaans*]
admin .... Administration (EECI)
Admin .... Administration (PWGL)
admin .... Administration (IDIG)
AdminApp Trib ... Administrative Appeals Tribunal [*Australia*]
ADMITRA ... Adminstration Travail (WGAO)
ADMK .... All-India Anna Dravida Munnetra Kazhagam [*Political party*] (PPW)
adml .... Admiraal [*Admiral*] [*Afrikaans*]
Adm Lex .... Administratief Lexicon [*Benelux*] (BAS)
ADMMA ... Ankara Devlet Muhendislik ve Mimarlik Akademisi [*Ankara State Academy of Engineering and Architecture*] (TU)
admon .... Administracion [*Spanish*]
admor .... Administrador [*Spanish*]
admor .... Admirador [*Admirer*] [*Portuguese*]
ADMP ...... Association de Droit Minier et Petrolier
ADMP ...... Association pour Defendre la Memoire de Petain
ADMR .... Aide a Domicile en Mileu Rural (WGAO)
admrechtspr ... Administratieve Rechtspraak [*Benelux*] (BAS)
ADMSt ...... Arbeitsgemeinschaft Deutscher Messerschmiede und Stahlwarenhandler (WGAO)

ADMT .... Association for Dance Movement Therapy (WGAO)
ADMT .... Association of Dental Manufacturers and Traders of the United Kingdom (WGAO)
adm-terr ..... Administrative and Territorial (RU)
adm ts .... Administrative Center (RU)
ADMTY .... Admiralty (NATG)
ADMV .... Allgemeiner Deutscher Motorsport-Verband [*General German Motor Sports Association*] (EG)
ADN .... Accion Democratica Nacional [*Aruba*]
ADN .... Accion Democratica Nacionalista [*Nationalist Democratic Action*] [*Bolivia*] [*Political party*] (PPW)
ADN .... Accion Democratico Nacional [*National Democratic Action*] [*Aruba*] [*Political party*] (EY)
ADN .... Acide Desoxyribonucleique [*Deoxyribonucleic Acid*] [*French*]
ADN .... Acido Desoxirribonucleico [*Deoxyribonucleic Acid*] [*Spanish*]
ADN .... Acieries du Nord
ADN .... Aerodienst GmbH [*Germany*] [*ICAO designator*] (FAAC)
ADN .... Agentia de Presa a Republicii Democrate Germane [*Press Agency of German Democratic Republic*] (RO)
ADN .... Alianza Democratica Nacionalista [*Nationalist Democratic Alliance*] [*Bolivia*] (LA)
ADN .... Allgemeiner Deutscher Nachrichtendienst [*German General News Service*] [*Germany*] (EG)
ADN .... Allgemeines Deutsches Nachrichtenburo (WGAO)
ADN .... Analyseur Differentiel Numerique [*Differential Numeric Analyser*] [*French*] (ADPT)
adn .... Artillery Battalion (RU)
ADN .... Asamblea Democratica Navarra [*Democratic Assembly of Navarra*] [*Spanish*] (WER)
ADN .... Automatic Remote Control Gun-Laying (RU)
ADNATCO ... Abu Dhabi National Tanker Company [*United Arab Emirates*] (MENA)
ADNDC ..... Abu Dhabi National Drilling Company (ME)
ADNHC .... Abu Dhabi National Hotels Company [*United Arab Emirates*]
ADNIC ...... Abu Dhabi National Insurance Company [*United Arab Emirates*] (MENA)
ADNIS ...... Acik Deniz Nakliyat Iscileri Sendikasi [*Open Sea Transport Workers' Union*] (TU)
ADNOC ..... Abu Dhabi National Oil Company (ME)
ADNOCFOD ... Abu Dhabi National Oil Company for Distribution [*United Arab Emirates*] (MENA)
ADNOE ..... Association pour la Direction Normale des Elections [*Associations for the Normal Conduct of Elections*] [*Reunion*]
ADNS .... Assistant Director of Nursing Services [*Australia*]
ADNTC .... Abu Dhabi National Tanker Company (ME)
ADO .... Agricultural Development Organization (CL)
ADO .... Airborne Detachment (RU)
ADO .... Alianza Democratica Opositora [*Panama*] (WGAO)
ADO .... Andamooka [*Australia*] [*Airport symbol*] (OAG)
adO .... An der Oder [*On the Oder River*] [*German*]
ADO .... Autodefensa Obrera [*Workers Self-Defense*] [*MAO*] [*Formerly,*] [*Colorado*] (LA)
ADO .... Avdelningen for Driftsorganisation (WGAO)
ADOC........ Abu Dhabi Oil Co. [*United Arab Emirates*] (EY)
ADOC........ Alianza Democratica de Oposicion Civilista [*Panama*] [*Political party*] (EY)
ADOCO ..... Abu Dhabi Oil Company (MENA)
ADOCO ..... Asociacion Nacional de Consumidores [*National Association of Consumers*] [*Dominican Republic*] (LA)
ADOEXPO ... Asociacion Dominicana de Exportadores [*Dominican Exporters Association*] [*Dominican Republic*] (LA)
ADOG........ Arbeitsgemeinschaft der Osterreichischen Gemeinwirtschaft (WGAO)
ADOGEN ... Asociacion de Oficiales Generales de los Institutos Armados [*General Officers Association of the Armed Forces Institutes*] [*Peru*] (LA)
ADOM .... Association pour la Documentation de l'Outre-Mer
ADOMA .... Asociacion Dominicana de Abogados [*Dominican Bar Association*] [*Dominican Republic*] (LA)
AdOR........ Anstalt des Oeffentlichen Rechts [*Institution Incorporated under Public Law*] (EG)
ADORA ..... Asociacion Dominicana de Radiodifusoras [*Dominican Association of Radio Broadcasters*] [*Dominican Republic*] (LA)
ADOSOM ... Association pour le Developpement des Oeuvres Sociales d'Outre-Mer [*Association for the Development of Social Welfare Projects Overseas*] [*French*] (AF)
ADP .... African Democratic Party [*Political party*]
ADP .... Agence Dahomeenne de Presse [*Dahomean Press Agency*]
ADP .... Agence de Distribution de Presse
ADP .... Agence Djiboutienne de Presse (EY)
ADP .... Agricultural Rural Development Pilot Programme
ADP .... Airfield Control Tower (RU)
ADP .... Alliance pour la Democratie et le Progres [*Benin*] [*Political party*] (EY)
ADP .... Anguilla Democratic Party [*Political party*] (EY)

ADP .... Asociacion Dominicana de Profesores [*Dominican Association of Teachers*] [*World Federation of Teachers Dominican Republic*] (LA)

ADP .... Asociacion Nacional de Directores de Personal [*Colombia*] (COL)

ADP .... Asociation de Disenadores Profesionales (WGAO)

ADP .... Association for Dental Prosthesis (WGAO)

ADP .... Association of Database Producers (WGAO)

ADP .... Association of Disabled Professionals (WGAO)

ADP .... Australian Democratic Party [*Political party*] (PPW)

ADP .... Automatic Long-Range Dispatcher Planning (RU)

ADP .... Azerbaijan Democratic Party [*Iran*] [*Political party*]

ADP .... Breakthrough Artillery Division (RU)

ADP .... Mobile Steam Decontamination Unit (RU)

ADPACT ... Alcohol and Drug Dependence Association of the Capital Territory [*Australia*]

ADPB .... Australian Dairy Produce Board (ADA)

ADPBA ..... Association Internationale pour le Developpement des Bibliotheques en Afrique (WGAO)

ADPC .... Abu Dhabi Petroleum Company (ME)

ADPC .... Agricultural Development Planning Center [*ASEAN*] [*Thailand*] [*Research center*] (IRC)

ADPC .... Alliance Democratique pour le Progres du Cameroun [*Political party*] (EY)

ADPC .... ASEAN Agricultural Development Plan Centre (WGAO)

ADPE .... Alliance Democratique pour le Progres et l'Emancipation [*Cameroon*] [*Political party*] (EY)

ADPEA ...... Australian Data Processing Employees Association (ADA)

ADPF .... Association pour la Diffusion de la Pensee Francaise

ADPF .... Australian Dairy Products Federation

ADPI .... Adviesdiens vir Produksie-Ingenieurswese [*Council for Scientific and Industrial Research*] [*South Africa*] (AA)

ADPI .... Asociacion Dominicana de Pequenas Industrias [*Dominican Association of Small Industry*] [*Dominican Republic*] (LA)

ADPI .... Association Internationale d'Etudes pour la Protection des Investissements (WGAO)

ADPI .... Australia Disabled Peoples' International (EAIO)

ADPIC ...... Abu Dhabi Pipeline Construction Co. (MENA)

ADPP .... Australia - Director of Public Prosecutions [*National Union Catalogue of Australia symbol*]

ADPPOC ... Abu Dhabi Petroleum Ports Operating Company (MENA)

ADPS .... Asociacion Democratica de Paz Social [*Democratic Association of Social Peace*] [*Spanish*] (WER)

ADPSO ...... Association of Data Processing Service Organizations (WGAO)

ADPSO ...... Australian Dairy Products Standards Organization

ADPSS ..... Archivio Dati e Programmi per le Scienze Sociali [*Data and Program Archive for the Social Sciences*] [*University of Milan*] [*Italy*] [*Information service or system*] (IID)

ADR .... Accord Dangereuse Routier [*European agreement on the carriage of dangerous goods by road*]

ADR .... Accord European Relative au Transport International par Route des Marchandises Dangereuses par Route [*European Agreement on the International Transport of Dangerous Goods by Road*] (PDAA)

adr .... Adres [*Address*] [*Correspondence*] [*Poland*] (POL)

adr .... Adress [*Address*] [*Correspondence*] [*Sweden*] (GPO)

adr .... Adresse [*Address*] [*Correspondence*] [*Denmark*] (GPO)

adr .... Adresse [*Address*] [*Correspondence*] [*French*]

Adr .... Adresse [*Address*] [*Correspondence*] [*German*] (GPO)

adr .... Adresse [*Address*] [*Correspondence*] [*Norway*] (GPO)

ADR .... Adria Airways [*Yugoslavia*] [*ICAO designator*] (FAAC)

ADR .... Agrement Dangereuse Routier [*Agreement on the International Carriage of Dangerous Goods by Road*] [*1968*]

ADR .... Alianza Democratica Revolucionaria [*Bolivia*] (WGAO)

ADR .... Alternative Dispute Resolution [*Australia*]

ADR .... Ammonium Dihydrogen Phosphate (RU)

ADR .... Aperture Direct Read-Out

ADR .... Applications du Roulement [*Aviation*] [*French*]

ADR .... Arbeitsgemeinschaft Deutscher Rinderzuchter (WGAO)

ADR .... Arbeitsgemeinschaft Deutscher Rubenbauerverbunde (WGAO)

ADR .... Association pour le Developpement de la Recherche [*Association for the Development of Research*] [*France*] (PDAA)

ADR .... Australian Design Rule [*Automotive technology*]

ADR .... Australian Design Rules (ADA)

ADRA .... Adressbuchausschuss der Deutschen Wirtschaft (WGAO)

ADRA .... Adventist Development and Relief Agency, International (EA)

ADRA .... Animal Diseases Research Association (WGAO)

ADRA .... Australian Dispute Resolution Association

ADRA .... Australian Drag Racing Association (ADA)

ADRAA ..... Alternative Dispute Resolution Association of Australia

ADRAF ...... Agence de Developpement Rural et d'Amenagement Foncier [*New Caledonia*] (EY)

ADRAO ..... Association pour le Developpement de la Riziculture en Afrique de l'Ouest [*West Africa Rice Development Association - WARDA*] (EAIO)

ADRC .... Archaeological Data Recording Centre [*South African Museum*] (AA)

ADRC .... Association of Drug Referral Centers [*Australia*]

ADRDI ...... Abra Diocesan Rural Development Inc. [*Philippines*] (WGAO)

ADRE .... Accion Democratica de Rescate Electoral [*Mexico*] (WGAO)

ADREF ..... Abu Dhabi National Reservoir Research Foundation [*Abu Dhabi United Arab Emirates*]

ADREPP .. Aircraft Accident Data Reporting Panel (WGAO)

ADRF .... Australian Dental Research Fund

ADRI .... Angkatan Darat Republik Indonesia [*Republic of Indonesia Army*] (IN)

ADRI .... Association pour Developpement Rural Integre [*Rwanda*] (WGAO)

ADRIPECHE ... Armement Dakarois pour le Regroupement de l'Industrie de la Peche [*Senegal*]

ADRIS ...... Association for the Development of Religious Information Systems (WGAO)

ADRM .... Darwin [*Australia*] [*ICAO location identifier*] (ICLI)

ADRRCP .. Association pour le Developpement et la Recherche en Reanimation Chirurgicale et Pediatrique (WGAO)

Adr tel ...... Adresse Telegraphique [*Telegraphic Address*] [*French*]

Adr tel ...... Adres Telegraficzny [*Telegraphic Address*] [*Poland*]

adr telegr ... Adres Telegraficzny [*Telegraphic Address*] [*Poland*]

ADRV .... Arbeitsgemeinschaft Deutscher Rechenzentrumsverbaende [*Work Group of the Associations of the German Accounting Center*] [*German*] (ADPT)

ADS .... Academie des Sciences [*Academy of Science*] [*French*]

ADS .... Accao Democrato-Social [*Social Democratic Action*] [*Mozambique*] (AF)

ADS .... Accao Democrato-Social [*Social Democratic Action*] [*Portuguese*] (WER)

ADS .... Action Democratique et Sociale

ADS .... Adult Deaf Society [*Australia*]

ADS .... Agencia de Representacoes Dias da Silva Lda. [*Portugal*] (EY)

ADS .... Aircraft Engine Construction (RU)

ADS .... Airfield Control Tower Service, Airport Control Tower Service (RU)

ADS .... Air Traffic Control Service (RU)

ADS .... Alhassan Dantata and Sons Ltd. [*Nigeria*]

ADS .... Alliance Democratique Senegalaise [*Allied Democratic Party of Senegal*] [*Political party*]

ADS .... Alzheimer's Disease Society (WGAO)

ADS .... Anotaton Dikastikon Symvoulion [*Supreme Judicial Council*] (GC)

ADS .... Arbeitsgemeinschaft Deutscher Schafzuchter (WGAO)

ADS .... Arbeitsgemeinschaft Deutscher Schweinezuchter (WGAO)

ADS .... Arbeitsgemeinschaft Deutscher Schwesternverbande (WGAO)

ADS .... Argon Arc Welding (RU)

ADS .... Arhivsko Drustvo Slovenije [*Former Yugoslavia*] (SLS)

ADS .... Armadni Delostrelecka Skupina [*Army Artillery Group*] (CZ)

ADS .... Asbestos Diseases Society

ADS .... Asociacion Demografica Salvadorena [*El Salvador*] (DSCA)

ADS .... Association of Danish Shipbuilders (EAIO)

ADS .... Association of District Secretaries (WGAO)

ADS .... Australian Driving Society

ADS .... Aviones de Sonora SA [*Mexico*] [*ICAO designator*] (FAAC)

ADS .... Azione Dynamico-Specifico [*Dynamic-Specific Action*] [*Italian*] [*Medicine*]

ADSA .... Associated Driving Schools of Australia

ADSA .... Associate of the Drama Society of Australia

ADSA .... Association of Dietitians of South(ern) Africa (AA)

ADSA .... Australian Down Syndrome Association

ADSA .... Australian Drama Studies Association

ADSADLT ... Association de Defense des Societes Agricoles Depossedees par la Loi Tunisienne du 12 Mai, 1964

ADSATIS ... Australian Defence Science and Technology Information System (ADA)

ADSB .... Allgemeine Deutsche Spediteurbedingungen [*General German Regulations for Shipping Agents*] (EG)

ADSC .... Australian Defence Studies Centre

ADSCLAT ... Associations of Distributors to the Self-Service and Coin-Operated Laundry and Allied Trades (WGAO)

ADSEN ...... Anotera Dimosia Skholi Emborikou Navtikou [*Higher Public Merchant Marine School*] (GC)

ADSF .... Australian Deaf Sports Federation

ADSF .... Australian Disabled Skiers' Federation

ADSI .... Agricultural Development Service, Inc. [*Philippines*] (WGAO)

ADSIA ...... Allied Data System Interoperability Agency [*Brussels, Belgium*] [*NATO*]

ADSKh ...... Anexartitos Dimokratikos Syndesmos Khanion [*Independent Democratic Association of Khania*] [*Greek*] (GC)

ADSL .... Association of Danish School Libraries (EAIO)

ADSL .... Australian Dental Standards Laboratory

ADSO .... Abu Dhabi Services Office [*Commercial firm*]

Adsorpt ...... Adsorption [*German*] (GCA)

ADSPSE .... Assistance for Disabled Students in Post-Secondary Education [*Australia*]

ADSRI .... Animal and Dairy Science Research Institute

ADSS........ Administracoes Distritais dos Servicos de Saude [*District Health Services Administrations*] [*Portuguese*] (WER)
ADSS........ Association of Directors of Social Services (WGAO)
ADSS........ Association of Direct Speech Suppliers (WGAO)
ADSS........ Australian Defence Scientific Service (ADA)
ADSSA...... Association pour le Developpement des Sciences Sociales Applquees (WGAO)
adsse .... Archiduchesse [*Archduchess*] [*French*] (MTD)
ADSTE...... Association of Drafting, Supervisory, and Technical Employees [*Australia*]
Adsteam..... Adelaide Steamship Co. [*Australia*]
ADSU .... Australian Disabled Students' Union
ADSW .... Association of Directors of Social Work (WGAO)
ADT .... Adresse des Donnees en Table [*Address of Data in the Table*] [*French*] (ADPT)
ADT .... Adult Diphtheria and Tetanus Virus
ADT .... Alianza del Trabajo [*Labor Alliance*] [*Spanish*] (WER)
ADT .... Aprovizionare, Desfacere, Transport [*Supply, Distribution, Transportation*] (RO)
ADT .... Australian Dance Theatre [*Adelaide*]
ADTA .... Australian Daily Travelling Allowance (ADA)
ADTA .... Australian Driver Trainers' Association
ADTA .... Societe pour le Developpement du Tabac en Afrique
ADTC .... Anglo-Dutch Trade Council (WGAO)
ADTC .... Australia Department of Transport and Communications [*Australia National Union Catalogue of Australia symbol*]
ADTC .... Tennant Creek [*Australia*] [*ICAO location identifier*] (ICLI)
ADTCB...... Association des Directeurs de Theatres Cinematographiques de Belgique (WGAO)
ADTEC..... Advanced Technology Corporation [*Australia*]
ADTF........ Australian Dairy Traders' Federation
ADTF........ Les Amis de la Terre - France [*Friends of the Earth - France*] (EAIO)
ADTI .... Amici della Terra - Italia [*Friends of the Earth - Italy*] (EAIO)
ADTI .... Association pour le Developpement du Tourisme International [*Louveciennes, France*] (EAIO)
ADTM .... Association pour le Diffusion des Techniques Menageres (WGAO)
ADTN........ Tindal [*Australia*] [*ICAO location identifier*] (ICLI)
ADTP .... Amigos da Terra - Portugal [*Friends of the Earth - Portugal*] (EAIO)
ADTRA ..... Architectural Design Teaching and Research Association
ADTsISO .. Tsentral'ni Institut Zaochnogo Obucheniia na Avtodorozhnom Transporte (WGAO)
ADTsIZO ... Central Correspondence Training Institute in Highway Transportation (RU)
ADTV .... Allgemeiner Deutscher Tanzlehrerverband (WGAO)
ADU.......... Accion Democratica Universitaria [*University Democratic Action*] [*Guatemala*] (LA)
ADU.......... Actuator Drive Unit [*Air data computer*]
ADU.......... Americans for Democracy in Ukraine (EA)
ADU.......... Analog/Digital Umsetzer [*Analog/Digital Transfer*] [*German*] (ADPT)
ADU.......... Assembleia de Delegados da Unidade [*Unit Delegate Assembly*] [*Portuguese*] (WER)
ADU.......... Automatic Dewaxing Installation (RU)
ADU.......... Automation of Dispatching Control (RU)
ADU.......... Remote-Control Equipment (RU)
Aduc.......... Archiduc [*Archduke*] [*French*] (MTD)
ADUC........ Asociacion de Universitarios de Cundinamarca [*Colombia*] (COL)
ADUSA ..... Analog/Digital Umwandlung mit Statistischer Auswertung [*Analog/Digital Conversion with Statistical Analysis*] [*German*] (ADPT)
ADUTOG ... Asociacion de Universitarios del Tolima Grande [*Ibague*] (COL)
ADV.......... Active Substance (RU)
ADV.......... Ad Valorem [*According to the Value*] [*Latin Business term*]
ADV.......... Advance Air Charters [*Canada ICAO designator*] (FAAC)
adv............ Adverbe [*French*] (TPFD)
adv............ Adverbi [*Finland*]
adv............ Adverbial [*Adverbial*] [*Portuguese*]
adv............ Adverbio [*Adverb*] [*Portuguese*]
ADV.......... Adverbium [*Adverb*] [*Afrikaans*]
adv............ Advocaat [*Barrister*] [*Netherlands*] (ILCA)
Adv............ Advocatenblad [*Benelux*] (BAS)
adv............ Advokaat [*Advocate*] [*Afrikaans*]
AdV .... Arbeitsgemeinschaft der Vermessungsverwaltungen der Laender der Bundesrepublik Deutschland [*Working Committee of the Survey Administrations of the Lander of the Federal Republik of Germany*] [*Research center*] (EAS)
ADV.......... Arbeitsgemeinschaft Deutscher Verkehrsflughafen [*German Air-Traffic Controllers Union*] (PDAA)
ADV.......... Arbeitsgemeinschaft fuer Datenverarbeitung [*Association for Data Processing*] [*Austria*] (SLS)

ADV.......... Asociacion de Dirigentes de Ventas y Mercadotecnica del Peru [*Peruvian Sales and Marketing Managers Association*] (LA)
ADV.......... Automatische Datenverarbeitung [*Automatic Data Processing*] [*German*] (ADPT)
ADV.......... Automatisierte Datenverarbeitung [*Automated Data Processing*] [*German*] (ADPT)
adv............ Averb (TPFD)
ADVB .... Associacao dos Diretores de Vendas do Brasil (WGAO)
Advbl......... Advocatenblad [*Benelux*] (BAS)
AdvCert...... Advanced Certificate
AdvCertApplMgtComm ... Advanced Certificate in Applied Management Communication
AdvCertBankFin ... Advanced Certificate in Banking and Finance
AdvCertBuildCons ... Advanced Certificate in Building Construction
AdvCertBuildInsp ... Advanced Certificate in Building Inspection
AdvCertCustomsAgProc ... Advanced Certificate in Customs Agent Procedures
AdvCertEstateAg ... Advanced Certificate in Estate Agency
AdvCertFurnProd ... Advanced Certificate in Furniture Production
AdvCertMgt ... Advanced Certificate in Management
AdvCertOffMgt ... Advanced Certificate in Office Management
AdvCertPers ... Advanced Certificate in Personnel
AdvCertSalesMgt ... Advanced Certificate in Sales Management
AdvDip....... Advanced Diploma
ADVET...... Australian Directory of Vocational Education and Training [*A publication*]
Adv-Gen..... Advocaat-Generaal bij de Hoge Raad der Nederlanden [*Benelux*] (BAS)
AdviesRvS ... Advies van de Raad van State [*Benelux*] (BAS)
ADVITEC ... Australasian Digital Video Interactive Technology
ADVO .... Apprehended Domestic Violence Order [*Australia*]
ADVS .... Automatisches Datenverarbeitungs-system [*Automatic Data Processing System*] [*German*] (ADPT)
advt .... Advertensie [*Advertisement*] [*Afrikaans*]
Adv V .... Advocatenvereniging [*Benelux*] (BAS)
Advwet .... Advocatenwet [*Benelux*] (BAS)
adw............ Adwokat [*Lawyer, Barrister*] [*Poland*]
AdW............ Akademie der Wissenschaften [*Academy of Science*] [*German*]
ADW.......... Aktion Dritte Welt
ADW.......... Arbeitsgemeinschaft der Deutschen Wertpapierbosen [*Federation of German Stock Exchanges*]
ADW.......... Arbeitsgemeinschaft der Waehlerinnen [*Association of Women Voters*] [*German*]
ADW.......... Verband Deutscher Werbeagenturen und Werbemittlungen [*German*]
Ad/y.......... Adet/Yil [*Items per Year*] [*Turkish*] [*Business term*] (TU)
Adygnatsizdat ... Adyge National Publishing House (RU)
ADYOD..... Ankara Devrimci Yuksek Ogrenim Dernegi [*Ankara Revolutionary Organization of Higher Learning*] (TU)
ADYODD ... Ankara Demokratik Yuksek Ogrenim Dayanisma Dernegi [*Ankara Higher Education Democratic Mutual Solidarity Association*] (TU)
ADZ........... San Andres Island [*Colombia*] [*Airport symbol*] (OAG)
Adzh........... Adzhar Autonomous Soviet Socialist Republic (RU)
AdzhASSR ... Adzhar Autonomous Soviet Socialist Republic (RU)
adZt........... Aus der Zeit [*Of That Time*] [*German*]
AE............. Abrechnungseinheit [*Accounting Unit*] [*German*] [*Business term*] (WEN)
AE............. Academic English
AE............. Accion Espanola [*Spanish Action*] [*Political party*] (PPE)
AE............. Acetone-Ether [*Solvent*] (RU)
AE............. Aero Flugzeugbau [*Germany*] [*ICAO aircraft manufacturer identifier*] (ICAO)
Ae............. Aether [*Ether*] [*German*]
AE............. Affaires Etrangeres [*Foreign Affairs*] [*French*] (WER)
AE............. Africa Enterprise [*Missionary association*]
AE............. Air Electrical [*NATO*] (NATG)
ae.............. Airplane (BU)
AE............. Air Squadron (RU)
AE............. Aktiebolaget Atomenergi [*Sweden*] (PDAA)
AE............. Amazon Expedition [*1976*] (MSC)
AE............. Amme Enstrumani [*Public (Legal) Instrument*] [*Cyprus*] (GC)
AE............. Angstromeinheit [*Angstrom Unit*] [*German*]
AE............. Anonymos Etaireia [*Joint Stock Company, Corporation*] [*Greek*] (GC)
AE............. Anschlusseinheit [*Line Unit, Terminal*] (EG)
AE............. Antitoxineinheit [*Antitoxin Unit*] [*German*]
AE............. Arbeitseinheit [*Work Unit*] [*German*]
ae.............. Archives Unit (BU)
AE............. Association Europeenne des Officiers Professionnels de Sapeurs-Pompiers [*European Association of Professional Fire Brigade Officers - EAPFBO*] (EAIO)
A/E .... Ausgabe/Eingabe [*Output/Input*] [*German*] (ADPT)
AE............. Auslandsentschaedigung [*Foreign Service (Hardship) Allowance, Foreign Service (Hardship) Differential*] (EG)
AE............. Austral [*or Australian*] English

AE .... Australian E Class [Submarine]
AE .... Australian Engineer
AE .... United Arab Emirates [ANSI two-letter standard code]   (CNC)
AEA .... Abemama [Kiribati] [Airport symbol]   (OAG)
AEA .... Abidjan Electric Auto-Etablissements P. Weydert & Cie.
AEA .... Aboriginal Electoral Assistant [Australia]
AEA .... Aboriginal Employment Action [Australia]
AEA .... Actors' Equity of Australia
AEA .... Agence Equatoriale d'Assurances
AEA .... Agence Europeenne d'Approvisionnement   (WGAO)
AEA .... Agricultural Education Association   (WGAO)
AEA .... Agricultural Engineers' Association   (WGAO)
AEA .... Air Europa [Spain] [ICAO designator]   (FAAC)
AEA .... Ambulance Employees Association [Australia]
AEA .... Anglican Evangelical Assembly   (WGAO)
AEA .... Applied Economic Associates [Australia]
AEA .... Art Exhibitions Australia
AEA .... Asociacion de Economistas Argentinos Instituto Superior de
                Economia [Argentina]   (DSCA)
AEA .... Asociacion de Estudiantes de Agronomia [Agronomy Students
                Association] [Panama]   (LA)
AEA .... Asociacion Espanola de Anunciantes   (WGAO)
AEA .... Associacao dos Engenheiros Agronomos do Parana [Brazil]
                (DSCA)
AEA .... Association d'Entreprises d'Affichage [Belgium]   (WGAO)
AEA .... Association Europeenne d'Athletisme [European Athletic
                Association - EAA]   (EA)
AEA .... Association Europeenne de l'Asphalte [European Mastic Asphalt
                Association - EMAA]   (EAIO)
AEA .... Association Europeenne des Audioprothesistes [European
                Association of Hearing Aid Dispensers]   (EAIO)
AEA .... Association of Estate Agents [Malta]   (WGAO)
AEA .... Association of European Airlines   (WGAO)
AEA .... Atomic Energy Authority   (WGAO)
AEA .... Attestation d'Etudes Approfondies [French]
AEA .... Australian Electronics Association   (ADA)
AEA .... Australian Esperanto Association   (ADA)
AEAA .... Asociacion de Escritores y Artistas Americanos [Association of
                American Writers and Artists] [La Habana, Cuba]   (LAA)
AEAAC...... Association Educative des Amateurs d'Astronomie du Centre
                [France]   (EAIO)
AEAC .... Agricultural Equipment Advisory Committee [Australia]
AEAC .... Asociacion Espanola de Amigos de los Castillos [Spanish]   (SLS)
AEAC .... Australian Ethnic Affairs Council
AEAF .... Australian Educational Allowance Fund
AEAFM...... Association d'Entraide des Agriculteurs Francais du Maroc
AEAI.......... Association Europeenne des Assures de l'Industrie [European
                Association of Industrial Insurers] [Brussels, Belgium]
                (EAIO)
AEAI.......... Association of Engineers and Architects in Israel   (PDAA)
AEAI.......... Association of Engineers, Architects, and Academics in the
                Technological Professions in Israel   (EAIO)
AEAIC....... European Academy of Allergology and Clinical Immunology
                (WGAO)
AEAM .... Adaptive Environmental Assessment and Management
AEAM .... Association des Evangeliques d'Afrique et Madagascar
                [Association of Evangelicals of Africa and Madagascar]
                [Kenya]
AEAM .... Association of Entertainment and Arts Management   (WGAO)
AEANC ..... Association des Eclaireurs de l'Armee Nationale Congolaise
AEAP......... Aboriginal Education Assistants Programme [University of
                Sydney] [Australia]
AEAP........ Alliance Europeenne des Agences de Presse   (WGAO)
AEAP........ Asociacion Espanola de Agencias de Publicidad   (WGAO)
AEAP........ Australian-European Awards Programme
AEAS........ Asociacion de Empresarios de Autobuses Salvadorenos
                [Association of Salvadoran Bus Owners]   (LA)
AEAS........ Asociacion Espanola de Abastecimientos de Agua Saneamiento
                [Spanish]   (ASF)
AEAS........ Association of Educational Advisers in Scotland   (WGAO)
AEASA...... Agricultural Economics Association of South Africa   (AA)
AEASA...... Automotive Exhibitors' Association of South Australia
AEAT........ Ambulance Employees' Association of Tasmania [Australia]
AEAV .... Adult Education Association of Victoria [Australia]
AEAV .... Ambulance Employees' Association of Victoria [Australia]
AEAWA..... Agricultural Educators Association of Western Australia
AEAZ .... Adult Education Association of Zambia   (SLS)
AEB .... Agrupacion Espanola de Bioingenieria   (WGAO)
AEB .... Analyses Economiques Budget [Economic Analysis Budget]
                [French]   (ADPT)
AEB .... Anthopos Ethnologische Bibliothek
AEB .... Arctic [Iceland] [ICAO designator]   (FAAC)
AEB .... Arctic Environmental Buoy [Oceanography]   (MSC)
AEB .... Asiatische Entwickeungsbank   (WGAO)
AEB .... Asociacion Ecuatoriana de Bibliotecarios [Ecuador]   (SLS)
AEB .... Asociacion Espanola de Banca [Spanish]

AEB .... Associacao dos Exportadores Brasileiros [Brazilian Exporters
                Association]   (LA)
AEB .... Association des Ecrivains Belges de Langue Francaise [Belgium]
                (SLS)
AEB .... Association des Enseignants Burundi [Association of Burundi
                Teachers]   (AF)
AEB .... Association Europeenne de la Boyauderie [European Natural
                Sausage Casings Association - ENSCA]   (EA)
AEB .... Atomic Energy Bureau [Japan]   (NUCP)
AEB .... Atomic Energy Bureau [Korea]   (NUCP)
AEB .... Australian Egg Board   (ADA)
AEBA........ Asamblea Espiritual de los Baha'is de Argentina [Spiritual
                Assembly of the Baha'is of Argentina]   (EAIO)
AEBCNSW ... Association of Ethnic Broadcasters and Coordinators of New
                South Wales [Australia]
AEBIRA .... Australian Engineering and Building Industries Research
                Association   (ADA)
AEBM .... Association des Entreprises de Montage de Belgique [Belgium]
                (BAS)
AEBPB ..... Association des Etudes Byzantines et Post-Byzantines   (WGAO)
AEBR........ Association of European Border Regions   (WGAO)
AEBTRI .... Association des Entreprises Bulgares des Transports
                Internationaux et de Routes   (WGAO)
AEBU .... Asociacion de Bancarios del Uruguay   (WGAO)
AEBU .... Asociacion de Empleados Bancarios del Uruguay [Association of
                Bank Employees of Uruguay]   (LA)
AEC .... Aboriginal Education Council [Australia]   (ADA)
AEC .... Adelaide Entertainment Centre [Australia]
AEC .... Aerocesar, Aerovias del Cesar [Colombia] [ICAO designator]
                (FAAC)
AEC .... Africa Exchange Circle [South Africa]   (EAIO)
AEC .... Agence Economique des Colonies
AEC .... Agence Europeenne de Cooperation   (WGAO)
AEC .... Agricultural Engineering Centre [Australia]
AEC .... Algemene Emigratie Centrale   (WGAO)
AEC .... All-Ewe Conference
AEC .... Arab Express Co. [Egypt]
AEC .... Arancel Externo Comun [Common External Tariff] [Andean
                pact]   (LA)
AEC .... Asociacion de Estudios del Caribe   (WGAO)
AEC .... Asociacion Espanola de la Carretera [Spanish]   (SLS)
AEC .... Asociacion Experimental Cafetalera [Guatemala]   (DSCA)
AEC .... Associacao de Educacao Catolica do Brasil [Association for
                Catholic Education in Brazil]
AEC .... Associacao Educacao Catolica [Brazil]   (WGAO)
AEC .... Association des Ecrivains Combattants [Association of Ex-
                Serviceman Writers] [French]
AEC .... Association des Enducteurs, Calandreurs et Fabricants de
                Revetements de Sols Plastiques de la CEE [Association of
                Coated Fabrics, Plastic Films and Plastic and Synthetic
                Floor Coverings of the European Economic Community]
                (PDAA)
AEC .... Association des Etudiants Congolais [Association of Congolese
                Students]   (AF)
AEC .... Association des Etudiants du Cambodge [Association of
                Cambodian Students]   (CL)
AEC .... Association Educative et Culturelle [Educational and Cultural
                Association] [Algeria]   (AF)
AEC .... Association Episcopale Catechistique [French]   (SLS)
AEC .... Association Europeenne de Ceramique [European Ceramic
                Association] [France]
AEC .... Association Europeenne des Cheminots   (WGAO)
AEC .... Association Europeenne des Conservatoires [European
                Association of Conservatories - EAC]   (EAIO)
AEC .... Association Europeenne des Contribuables [European Taxpayers
                Association - ETA]   (EA)
AEC .... Association Europeenne des Enducteurs, Calandreurs et
                Fabricants de Revetements de Sols Plastiques et
                Synthetiques   (WGAO)
AEC .... Association Europeenne pour la Cooperation [Belgium]   (DSCA)
AEC .... Associazione Europea per la Cooperazione   (WGAO)
AEC .... Atlantic Education Committee   (WGAO)
AEC .... Atomic Energy Commission of Syria [Research center]   (WND)
AEC .... Atomic Energy Corporation [South Africa]   (WGAO)
AEC .... Atomic Energy Corporation of South Africa Ltd.
AEC .... Australian Education Centre
AEC .... Australian Education Council   (ADA)
AEC .... Australian Electoral Commission
AEC .... Australian Environment Council   (ADA)
AEC .... Australian Episcopal Conference
AECA .... Asociacion de Empresarios de Combustibles de la Argentina
                [Fuel Businessmen's Association of Argentina]   (LA)
AECA .... Association Europeenne des Cadres de l'Assurance   (WGAO)
AECA .... Association Europeenne des Centres d'Audiophonologie
                [European Association of Audiophonological Centres -
                EAAC]   (EAIO)
AECA .... Australian Early Childhood Association

AECAH ..... Association Europeenne des Conservatoires, Academies de Musique, et Musikhochschulen [*European Association of Music Conservatories, Academies, and High Schools*] (EAIO)

AECAL ...... Academia Europea de Ciencias, Artes y Letras (WGAO)

AECAP ...... Association Europeenne des Centres de Lutte Contre les Poisons [*Belgium*] (SLS)

AECAP ...... Association of European Centres Against Poisons [*Belgium*] (WGAO)

AECAWA ... Association of Episcopal Conferences of Anglophone West Africa (EAIO)

AECB .... Asociacion de Estudiantes de Ciencias Basicas [*Basic Sciences Students Association*] [*Guatemala*] (LA)

AECB .... Associacao de Educacao Catolica do Brasil [*Association for Catholic Education in Brazil*] [*Rio De Janeiro*] (LAA)

AECB .... Association des Etudiants Congolais a Brazzaville [*Congolese Student Association in Brazzaville*]

AECC .... Asociacion Espanola contra el Cancer (WGAO)

AECC .... Asociacion Espanola para el Control de la Calidad [*Spanish Association for Quality Control*] (SLS)

AECC .... Association des Eclaireurs Catholiques du Congo (WGAO)

AECC .... Australian Export Commodity Classification

AECC .... Australian Export Statistics [*Database*]

AECC .... Automobile Emissions Control by Catalyst [*Belgium*] (EAIO)

AECCG ...... African Elephant Conservation Coordinating Group

AECD .... Asian Ecumenical Conference on Development (WGAO)

AECDF ...... Association des Exploitatants de Cinema et des Distributeurs de Films du Grand Duche de Luxembourg (WGAO)

AECE .... Asociacion Espanola de Comercio Exterior [*Spain*] (EY)

AECE .... Asociacion Espanola de Cooperacion Europea [*Spanish Association for European Cooperation*] (WER)

AECEA ...... Australian Early Childhood Education Association

AECEC ...... Asociacion Espanola de Comercio Exterior de Cereales y Productos Analogos (EY)

AECEF ...... Association des Ecrivains Croyants d'Expression Francaise (WGAO)

AECEWA ... Association of Episcopal Conferences of English-Speaking West Africa (WGAO)

AeCF .... Aero Club de France (WGAO)

AECG .... Aboriginal Education Consultative Group [*Australia*]

AECGV ...... Association Europeenne du Commerce en Gros des Viandes [*European Association Wholesale Trade in Meat*] [*EC*] (ECED)

AECI .... African Explosive and Chemical Industry [*Commercial firm*] (IMH)

AECI .... Association of Electrical Contractors of Ireland (WGAO)

AECI .... Association of European Conjuncture Institutes (EA)

AECI .... Association of European Cooperative Insurers [*Brussels, Belgium*] (EAIO)

AECIA ...... Australian Electronics Customer Industry Association (ADA)

AECL .... Aboriginal Enterprise Company Limited

AECL .... Asociatia Europeana a Comertului Liber [*European Free Trade Association*] (RO)

AECM ...... Association of European Candle Manufacturers (EA)

AECMA .... Association Europeenne des Constructeurs de Materiel Aerospatial [*European Association of Aerospace Manufacturers*] (EAIO)

AECMSA .. Association of Electric Cable Manufacturers of South Africa (AA)

AECNP ...... Association Europeenne des Centres Nationaux de Productivite [*European Association for National Productivity Centers - EANPC*] (EAIO)

AEC(NSW) ... Aboriginal Education Council (New South Wales) [*Australia*]

AECOPS ... Associacao de Empresas de Construcao e Obras Publicas do Sul (WGAO)

AECP .... Association de l'Entreprise a Capital Personnel [*France*] (FLAF)

AeCS .... Aero Club der Schweiz (WGAO)

AECS .... Association of European Correspondence Schools (EA)

AECS .... Australia/Europe Container Service

AED .... Academia Espanola de Dermatologia [*Spanish Academy of Dermatology*]

AED .... Arkhigeion Enoplon Dynameon [*Armed Forces Command*] [*Greek*] (GC)

AED .... Association Europeene des Decafeineurs [*European Association of Decaffeinators*] [*France*] (EAIO)

AED .... Association for Education and Development

AED .... Association of Engineering Distributors (WGAO)

AED .... Association pour l'Etude et l'Evaluation Epidemiologiques des Desastres Pays en voie de Developpement (WGAO)

AED .... Atomkernenergie-Dokumentation

AED .... Australian Ethnic Democrats [*Political party*]

AEDA .... Asociacion Espanola de Aerosoles (WGAO)

AEDA .... Asociacion Espanola de Derecho Agrario [*Spain*] (DSCA)

AEDA .... Association Europeenne des Dirigeants d'Associations (WGAO)

AEDA .... Association Europeenne pour le Droit de l'Alimentation [*Belgium*] (SLS)

AEDAP ...... Aboriginal Education Direct Assistance Program [*Australia*]

AEDBCS ... Association Europeenne des Directeurs de Bureaux de Concerts et Spectacles [*European Association of Directors of the Bureau of Concerts and Events*] [*France*] (EAIO)

AEDCL ...... Association of European Documentation Centre Libraries (WGAO)

AEDD .... Discrete Operation Aerodynamic Elements (RU)

AEDE .... Asociacion de Editores de Diarios Espanoles [*Press association*] [*Spain*] (EY)

AEDE .... Association Europeenne des Enseignants [*European Association of Teachers - EAT*] [*Switzerland*]

AEDEC ...... Association Europeenne d'Etudes Chinoises [*European Association of Chinese Studies - EACS*] (EAIO)

AEDEMO ... Asociacion Espanola de Estudios de Mercado y de Opinion Comercial (WGAO)

AEDEN ..... Asociacion de Estudios y Defensa de la Naturaleza [*Association for Studies and Protection of Nature*] [*Spanish*] (WER)

AEDEX ...... Asociacion Ecuatoriana de Exportadores [*Ecuadorean Exporters Association*] (LA)

AEDF .... Asian Economic Development Fund (WGAO)

AEDF .... Australian Executive Development Foundation (ADA)

AEDH .... Association Europeenne des Directeurs d'Hopitaux [*Later, EAHM*] (EA)

AEDI .... Accademia Europea Dentisti Implantologi [*Italian*] (SLS)

AEDIPE .... Asociacion Espanola de Direcion de Personal (WGAO)

AEDP .... Aboriginal Employment Development Policy [*Australia*]

AEDP .... Association Europeenne pour la Direction de Personnel (WGAO)

AEDST ...... Australian Eastern Daylight Saving Time (ADA)

AEDT .... Association Europeenne des Organisations Nationales des Comercants Detaillans en Textiles [*Germany*] (DSCA)

AEDT .... Australian Eastern Daylight Saving Time

AEE .... Administracion de Estabilizacion Economica [*Puerto Rico*] (DSCA)

AEE .... Aegean Aviation [*Greece*] [*ICAO designator*] (FAAC)

AEE .... Agence pour les Economies d'Energie [*France*]

AEE .... Anotati Eforevtiki Epitropi [*Supreme Supervisory Committee*] (GC)

AEE .... Asociacion Electrotecnica y Electronica Espanola [*Spanish*]

AEE .... Association of Electrical Engineers [*Finland*] (EAIO)

AEE .... Atomic Energy Establishment [*Libya*] (NUCP)

AEE .... Field Emission (RU)

AEEA .... Association Europeenne des Editeurs d'Annuaires [*European Association of Directory Publishers - EADP*] (EA)

AEEA .... Association Europeenne pour l'Enseignement de l'Architecture (WGAO)

AEEA .... European Association of Directory Publishers (WGAO)

AEEC .... Airlines Electronic Engineering Committee [*International*] (WGAO)

AEEC .... Australian Export Statistics [*Database*]

AEED .... Association Europeene des Enseignants Dentaires [*European Association of Teachers of Dentistry*] (PDAA)

AEED .... Association Europeenne pour l'Etude du Diabete [*European Association for the Study of Diabetes - EASD*] (EAIO)

AEEDO ..... Aboriginal Economic and Employment Development Officer [*Australia*]

AEEF .... Asociacion Europea de Empresas Frigoriferas [*European Association of Refrigeration Enterprises*] [*Spanish*] (ASF)

AEEF .... Association Europeene des Exploitants Frigorifiques [*European Association of Refrigeration Enterprises*] [*Belgium*] (ASF)

AEEF .... Association Europeenne de l'Ethnie Francaise (WGAO)

AEEF .... Association Europeenne des Exploitations Frigorifiques [*European Association of Refrigeration Enterprises*] [*Common Market*] [*Belgium*]

AEEFWT .. Aqua Europa - European Federation for Water Treatment [*British*] (EAIO)

AEEGS ...... American Electroencephalographic Society (WGAO)

AEEMA ...... Australian Electrical and Electronic Manufacturers Association

AEEN .... Agence Europeenne pour l'Energie Nucleaire [*France*] (NUCP)

AEEN .... Agenzia Europea per L'Energia Nucleare (NUCP)

AEEN .... Agenzia Europea per l'Energia Nucleare [*Nuclear energy*] [*Italian*] (NRCH)

AEENA ...... Anotati Epitropi Elengkhou Navtikon Atykhimaton [*Supreme Council for Control of Maritime Accidents*] [*Greek*] (GC)

AEE(NSW) ... Association for Environmental Education (New South Wales) [*Australia*]

AEEP .... Associacao das Enfermeiras e dos Enfermeiros Portugueses (WGAO)

AEEP .... Association Europeenne pour l'Etude de la Population [*European Association for Population Studies - EAPS*] (EAIO)

AEEPA ...... Association d'Etudes Europeennes de Presse Agricole [*France*] (DSCA)

AEEPJ .... Association Europeenne des Publications pour la Jeunesse (WGAO)

AEEPM ..... Association pour l'Etude des Etats Proches de la Mort [*International Association for Near-Death Studies*] (EAIO)

AEERS ...... Association d'Etude pour l'Expansion de la Recherche Scientifique

AEESA ...... Asociacion Espanola de Economia y Sociologia Agrarias [*Spain*] (DSCA)

AEESCA ... Association for Engineering Education in South and Central Asia (WGAO)

AEESEA.... Association for Engineering Education in Southeast Asia (WGAO)

AEESO ...... Association des Eleves et Etudiants de la Sous-Prefecture de Ouragahis

AEET........ Atomic Energy Establishment, [*Trombay, India*] (NUCP)

AEET........ Atomic Energy Establishment, Trombay [*India*] (PDAA)

AEEVTPLF ... Association des Etablissements d'Enseignement Veterinaire Totalement au Partiellement de la Langue Francaise (WGAO)

AEEW .... Atomic Energy Establishment Winfrith (WGAO)

AEEY........ Anonymos Elliniki Etaireia Ydaton [*Greek Water Supply Company*] (GC)

AEEZ........ Association des Entreprises de l'Est du Zaire

AEF........... Aboriginal Evangelical Fellowship

AEF........... Action Europeenne Federaliste (FLAF)

AEF........... Aero Lloyd Flugreisen GmbH [*Germany*] [*ICAO designator*] (FAAC)

AEF........... Africa Evangelical Fellowship (WGAO)

AEF........... Afrique Equatoriale Francaise [*French Equatorial Africa*] [*French*] (AF)

AEF........... Aircraft Equipment Failure

AEF........... Airfields Environment Federation (WGAO)

AEF........... Asfaltentreprenorenes Forening (WGAO)

AEF........... Asia Education Foundation

AEF........... Asociacion Espanola de Fabricantes de Caldos y Sopas [*Spanish Association of the Manufacture of Soups and Broths*] (EAIO)

AEF........... Asociacion Espanola de Financiadores (WGAO)

AEF........... Association Europeenne des Festivals [*European Association of Festivals*] [*Switzerland*] (EAIO)

AEF........... Ausschuss fuer Einheiten und Formelgroessen [*Committee for Standardization of Units and Symbols*] [*Germany*] (GCA)

AEF........... Australian Employers' Federation

AEF........... Austrian Energy Forum (EAIO)

AEF........... Background Equivalent Activity (RU)

AEFA........ Aboriginal Evangelical Fellowship of Australia

AEFA........ Association des Anciens Eleves de la Faculte d'Archeologie [*Faculty of Archeology Alumni Association*] [*Cambodia*] (CL)

AEFA........ Association Europeenne des Films Animatiques (WGAO)

AEFA........ Association of European Federations of Agro-Engineers [*EC*] (ECED)

AEFC........ Australian European Finance Corporation Group (ADA)

AEFJ .... Asociacion Espanola de Fabricantes de Juguetes (WGAO)

AEFM....... Association Europeenne des Festivals de Musique [*European Association of Music Festivals - EAMF*] (EAIO)

AEFMA..... Association Europeenne F. Matthias Alexander [*Belgium*] (WGAO)

AEFMOM ... Association des Ecrivains d'Expression Francaise de la Mer et de l'Outre-Mer

AEFOM .... Agence Economique de la France d'Outre-Mer

AEFS .... Arctic Environmental Field Station (MSC)

AEFS .... Association des Eleveurs Francaise de Southdown (WGAO)

AEFSA ..... Aboriginal Education Foundation of South Australia

AEFTOP ... Agrupacion Espanola de Fabricantes de Transmisiones Oleo-Hidraulicas y Pneumaticas (WGAO)

AEG .... Allegemeine Elektrizitats Gesellschaft [*Federal Republic of Germany*] (NUCP)

AEG .... Allgemeine Elektrizitaets-Gesellschaft [*General Electric Company*] [*German*] (EG)

AEG .... Army Evacuation Hospital (RU)

AEG .... Asociacion Espanola de Gemologia (WGAO)

AEG .... Association of Esperantist Greens [*Belgium*] (EAIO)

AEG .... Association of Exploration Geochemists [*ICSU*] (EAIO)

AEGAL...... Association Europeenne des Gaz de Petrole Liquefies (WGAO)

AEGC .... Association Europeenne de Genie Civil (WGAO)

AEGF........ Association des Etudiants Guineens en France [*Association of Guinean Students in France*] (AF)

AEGIS .... Aid for the Elderly in Government Institutions (WGAO)

AEGIS .... Australian Electronic Government Information Services

AEGIS .... Australian Environmental Geographic Information System

AEGM .... Anglican Evangelical Group Movement (WGAO)

AEGPL...... Association Europeenne des Gaz de Petrole Liquefies [*European Liquefied Petroleum Gas Association - ELPGA*] (EAIO)

AEGRAFLEX ... Association Europeenne des Graveurs et des Flexographes [*European Association of Engravers and Flexographers*] (EAIO)

AEH........... Academie Europeenne d'Histoire [*European Academy of History - EAH*] (EAIO)

AEH........... Allami Egyhazugyi Hivatal [*State Office of Church Affairs*] (HU)

AEH........... Anadolu Endustri Holding [*Anatolian Industrial Holding Co.*] [*Turkey*]

AEH........... Avia Express Ltd. [*Hungary*] [*ICAO designator*] (FAAC)

AEHA........ Australian Early Holden Association

AEHPL...... Association Europeenne pour l'Histoire de la Photographie (WGAO)

AEHW....... Aboriginal Environmental Health Worker [*Australia*]

AEI .... Abedowale Electrical Industries [*Nigeria*] [*Commercial firm*]

AEI .... Aero Espresso Italiano [*Italy*]

AEI .... Aeroexpreso Interamerican [*Colombia*] [*ICAO designator*] (FAAC)

AEI .... Agencia Europeia de Imprensa Lda. [*News agency*] [*Portugal*] (EY)

AEI .... Air Express International [*Australia*]

AEI .... Alianza Electoral Independiente [*Independent Electoral Alliance*] [*Venezuela*] (LA)

AEI .... Anotata Ekpaidevtika Idrymata [*Supreme Educational Institutions*] (GC)

AEI .... Arab Energy Institute

AEI .... Asesoria e Interventorias Ltda. [*Colombia*] (COL)

AEI .... Aspecten van de Europese Integratie [*Benelux*] (BAS)

AEI .... Associated Electrical Industries (WGAO)

AEI .... Associated Electrical Industries Export Ltda. [*Colombia*] (COL)

AEI .... Association des Ecoles Internationales (WGAO)

AEI .... Associazione Educatrice Italiana [*Italian*] (SLS)

AEI .... Associazione Elettrotecnica ed Elettronica Italiana [*Italian*] (SLS)

AEI .... Associazione Enotecnici Italiani (WGAO)

AEI .... Australian Equitable Insurance Ltd. (ADA)

AEIA........ Asociacion Escuela de Ingenieria Agronomica [*Ecuador*] (LAA)

AEIA........ Asociacion Espanola de Informatica y Automatica (WGAO)

AEIA........ Australian Electronics Industry Association

AEIAAF .... Association Europeenne de l'Industrie des Aliments pour Animaux Familiers (WGAO)

AEIAR...... Association Europeenne des Institutions d'Amenagement Rural [*European Association of Country Planning Institutions*] (EAIO)

aeib............ Fighter-Bomber Squadron (RU)

AEID .... Association Europeenne des Instituts de Recherche et de Formation en Matiere de Development (WGAO)

AEIDC....... Artic Environmental Information and Data Centre (WGAO)

AEIE......... Association of Indian Engineering Industry [*India*] (WGAO)

AEIH......... Association Europeenne des Industries de l'Habillement [*European Association of Clothing Industries*] (EA)

AEII.......... Australian Education Index [*AUSINET database*] (ADA)

AEIII .... Association of the European Independent Informatics Industry (WGAO)

AEIJA ...... Asociacion de Empleados del Instituto de Jubilaciones y Afines [*Association of Employees of the Pension Institute and Related Workers*] [*Uruguay*] (LA)

AEIOU ...... Association Europeenne pour une Interaction entre les Organismes Universitaires [*French*] (SLS)

AEIS .... Aboriginal Electoral Information Service [*Australia*]

AEIS .... Association of Electronic Industries in Singapore (PDAA)

AEISF....... Aboriginal Education Incentive Scholarship Fund [*Australia*] (ADA)

AEIT......... Asociacion Espanola de Ingenieros de Telecomunicacion (WGAO)

AEIU .... Asemblea de Estudiantes Independistas Universitarios (WGAO)

AEJ........... Air Affaires EJA France [*ICAO designator*] (FAAC)

AEK .... Aero Costa Rica [*ICAO designator*] (FAAC)

AEK .... Allami Ellenorzo Kozpont [*State Control Center*] (HU)

AEK .... Aseki [*Papua New Guinea*] [*Airport symbol*] [*Obsolete*] (OAG)

AEK .... Atomenergikommissionen [*Atomic Energy Commission*] [*Denmark*] (WEN)

AEK .... Atomik Enerjisi Komisyonu [*Atomic Energy Commission, Directorate General*] (TU)

AEK .... Avrupa Ekonomik Komisyonu [*European Economic Commission*] [*Turkish*] [*United Nations (already exists in GUS II database)*] (TU)

AEK .... Societe Anonyme des Ets. Kritikos & Cie.

AEKC........ Association des Etudiants Khmers au Cambodge [*Association of Cambodian Students in Cambodia*] (CL)

AEKGM .... Agaclandirma ve Erozyon Kontrol Genel Mudurlugu [*Forestation and Erosion Control Directorate General*] (TU)

AEKh........ Anomalous Hall Effect (RU)

AEKI........ Association of Indonesian Coffee Exporters (EY)

AEKI......... Atomenergia Kutato Intezet [*Atomic Energy Research Institute*] [*Hungary*] (WND)

AEKK .... Atomenergia Kutatasi Kozpont [*Atomic Energy Research Center*] (HU)

AEKN .... Association des Etudiants Khmers de Nancy [*Cambodian Students Association at Nancy*] [*French*] (CL)

AEKP........ Anotati Epitropi Kratikon Promitheion [*Supreme State Supplies Committee*] [*YKP*] [*See also*] (GC)

AEKS .... Association des Etudiants Khmers en Suisse [*Association of Cambodian Students in Switzerland*] (CL)

AEKS .... Automatic Electronic Logging Station (RU)

AEL .... Advanced Engineering Laboratory [*Australia*]

AEL .... Agence d'Encaissement Librevilleise
AEL .... Air Europe SpA [*Italy*] [*ICAO designator*]   (FAAC)
AEL .... Association Europeenne du Laser [*European Laser Association - ELA*]   (EA)
AEL .... Associazione Annuario Ecologico Lombardo [*Italian*]   (SLS)
AEL .... Electroplating Unit   (RU)
AELA .... Australian [*Capital Territory*] Electricity and Water Authority [*National Union Catalogue of Australia symbol*]
AELA .... Australian Equipment Lessors Association
AELC .... Agricultural Equipment Liaison Committee [*Victoria, Australia*]
AELC .... Asociacion Europea de Libre Comercio [*European Free Trade Association - EFTA*] [*Spanish*]
AELE .... Association Europeenne de Libre-Echange [*European Free Trade Association - EFTA*] [*Geneva, Switzerland*]
AELE .... Association Europeenne des Loteries d'Etat [*Switzerland*]   (WGAO)
AELF .... Association des Etudiants Lao en France [*Association of Lao Students in France*]   (CL)
AELFA ...... Asociacion Espanola de Logopedia, Foniatria y Audiologia [*Spanish*]   (SLS)
AELI .... Asociacion Europa de Libre Intercambio   (WGAO)
AELIA .... Association d'Etudes Linguistiques Interculturelles Africaines   (WGAO)
AELLA ...... Association des Entrepreneurs Luxembourgeois des Lignes d'Autobus   (WGAO)
AELP .... Advanced English Language Program [*Australia*]
AELPALALC ... Asociacion de Empresarios Latinoamericanos, Participantes en la ALALC [*Asociacion Latinoamericana de Libre Comercio*]   (LAA)
AELS .... Asociatia Europeana a Liberului Schimb [*European Free Trade Association - EFTA*]   (RO)
AELSL ...... Associacao de Estudantes dos Liceos Secundarios da Luanda [*Secondary School Students Association of Luanda*] [*Angola*]   (AF)
AELT .... Association Europeenne de Laboratoires de Teledetection [*European Association of Remote Sensing Laboratories - EARSEL*]   (EA)
AELTC ...... All England Lawn Tennis Club   (WGAO)
AEM .... Aero Madrid [*Spain*] [*ICAO designator*]   (FAAC)
AEM .... Alianza Evangelica Mundial   (WGAO)
AEM .... Allami Ellenorzes Miniszteriuma [*State Control Ministry (for Collection of Agricultural Produce)*]   (HU)
AEM .... Alto Estado Mayor [*Supreme General Staff*] [*Spanish*]   (WER)
AEM .... Andidiktatoriko Ergatiko Metopo [*Antidictatorial Labor Front*] [*Greek*]   (GC)
AEM .... Arabian Exhibition Management WLL [*Manama, Bahrain*]
AEM .... Arbeitsgemeinschaft Evangelikaler Missionen [*Switzerland*]
AEM .... Asociacion Espanola de Marketing [*Spanish*]   (SLS)
AEM .... Associacao dos Exportadores de Macau [*Macao Exporters Association*]   (EAIO)
AEM .... Association des Etudiants Malgaches [*Association of Malagasy Students*]
AEM .... Association Europeenne des Metaux [*European Association of Metals*] [*Belgium*]   (EAIO)
AEM .... Association Europeenne du Moulinage [*European Throwsters Association - ETA*]   (EA)
AEM .... European Mills Association [*EC*]   (ECED)
AEMA .... Australian Electrical Manufacturers' Association   (ADA)
AEMB .... Association Europeenne des Marches aux Bestiaux [*European Association of Livestock Markets - EALM*] [*Brussels, Belgium*]   (EAIO)
AEMC .... Atomic Energy Minerals Centre [*Pakistan*]   (IRC)
AEMC .... Australian Egg Marketing Council
AEMCH .... Asociacion de Estudiantes de Medicina y Cirugia de Honduras [*Association of Students of Medicine and Surgery of Honduras*]   (LA)
AEMD ...... Association of Electronics Manufacturers in Denmark   (EAIO)
AEMDA .... Alliance Europeenne des Associations de Myopathes   (WGAO)
AEME .... Asociacion de Empleados del Ministerio de Educacion [*Association of Education Ministry Employees*] [*El Salvador*]
AEME .... Association of Export and Marketing Executives   (WGAO)
AEME .... Association pour l'Enseignement Medical en Europe [*Association for Medical Education in Europe - AMEE*]   (EA)
AEME .... Australian Electrical and Mechanical Engineers
AEMERO ... Africa, Eastern Mediterranean, and Europe Regional Office, UNICEF
AEMF .... Association des Ecoles de Medecine d'Afrique [*Association of Medical Schools in Africa*] [*Use AMSA*]   (AF)
AEMH .... Association Europeenne des Medecins des Hopitaux [*French*]   (SLS)
AEMHSM ... Association Europeenne des Musees de l'Histoire des Sciences Medicales [*European Association of Museums of the History of Medical Sciences - EAMHMS*]   (EAIO)
AEMI .... Association Eurafricaine Miniere et Industrielle
AEMIE ...... Association Europeenne de Medecine Interne d'Ensemble [*French*]   (SLS)

AEMNA .... Association des Etudiants Musulmans Nord-Africains [*North African Muslim Students Association*]   (AF)
AEMO .... Action Educative en Milieu Ouvert   (FLAF)
AEMO .... African Elected Members Organization
AEMP .... Acetone Extract of Male Fern   (RU)
AEMP .... Association des Etudiants en Medecine et en Pharmacie [*Association of Medical and Pharmacy Students*] [*Malagasy*]   (AF)
AEMP .... Association of European Management Publishers   (WGAO)
AEMPALALC ... Asociacion de Empresarios Mexicanos, Participantes en la ALALC [*Asociacion Latinoamericana de Libre Comercio*] [*Mexico*]   (LAA)
AEMS .... American Engineering Model Society   (WGAO)
AEMSAT .. Association of European Manufacturers of Self-Adhesive Tapes   (EA)
AEMSM .... Association of European Metal Sink Manufacturers   (EAIO)
AEM/SME ... Association for Electronics Manufacturing of the Society of Manufacturing Engineers   (EAIO)
AEMT ...... Association of Electrical Machinery Trades   (WGAO)
AEMT ...... Association of Emergency Medical Technicians   (WGAO)
AEMTC ..... Association pour l'Etude de Modification et la Therapie du Comportement [*Belgian Association for the Study, Modification, and Therapy of Behavior*]   (EAIO)
AEMTM ... Association of European Machine Tool Merchants [*Berkhamsted, Hertfordshire, England*]   (EAIO)
AEMUS ..... Asociacion de Estudiantes de Musica [*Uruguay*]   (WGAO)
AEMUS ..... Association des Etudiants Malgaches en Union Sovietique [*Association of Malagasy Students in the Soviet Union*]   (AF)
AEN .... Aerial Exposure Meter   (RU)
AEN .... Affaiblissement Equivalent pour la Nettete [*Equivalent Articulation Loss*] [*French*]
AEN .... Agence de l'OCDE pour l'Energie Nucleaire [*OECD Nuclear Energy Agency - NEA*]   (EAIO)
AEN .... Agence pour l'Energie Nucleaire [*Nuclear energy*] [*French*]   (NRCH)
AEN .... Air Enterprise [*France*] [*ICAO designator*]   (FAAC)
AEN .... Alkimos Ethniki Neolaia [*Valiant National Youth*] [*Cyprus*]   (GC)
AEN .... Australian Education Network
AENA .... All England Netball Association   (WGAO)
AENA .... Association des Anciens Eleves et Eleves de l'Ecole Nationale d'Administration [*National School of Administration Alumni and Students Association*] [*Cambodia*]   (CL)
AENE .... Association Europeenne de Neuro-Endocrinologie   (WGAO)
AENF .... Association des Etudiants Nigeriens en France [*Association of Nigerian Students in France*] [*Niger*]   (AF)
AENOC ..... Association of European National Olympic Committees   (WGAO)
AENOR ..... Asociacion Espanola de Normalizacion   (WGAO)
Aenor .... Asociacion Espanola de Normalizacion y Certificacion [*Spanish*]
AENSB ...... Association de l'Ecole Nationale Superieure de Bibliothecaires [*Association of the National College of Librarians*] [*France*]   (PDAA)
AENTAMUBAN ... Association Entente et Entraide Mutuelle des Ressortissants de la Region de Bangu
AEO .... Aeroservicios Ejecutivos del Occidente SA de CV [*Mexico*] [*ICAO designator*]   (FAAC)
AEO .... Agricultural Extension Officer [*India*]
AEO .... Aioun El Atrouss [*Mauritania*] [*Airport symbol*]   (OAG)
AEO .... Air Engineering Officer [*Royal Australian Navy*]
AEO .... Anglo-Egyptian Oilfields
AeO .... Arbeitsgemeinschaft Ehemaliger Offiziere [*Working Group of Former Officers*]   (EG)
AEO .... Arbeitsgemeinschaft fur Elektronenoptik   (WGAO)
AEO .... Asociacion Espanola de Orientalistas [*Spanish*]   (SLS)
AEO .... Association of Education Officers   (WGAO)
AEO .... Association of Exhibition Organisers   (WGAO)
AEO .... Atomic Energy Organisation [*Iran*]   (NUCP)
AEO .... Atomic Energy Organization [*Iran*] [*Nuclear energy*]   (NRCH)
AEO .... Australian Electoral Office
AEO .... Australian Environmental Orchestra
AEO .... Experimental Aerodynamics Department   (RU)
AEOB .... Alkoholizmus Elleni Orszagos Bizottsag [*National Committee Against Alcohol Abuse*]   (HU)
AEOC .... Association des Entreprises de l'Ouest du Congo
AEOI .... Atomic Energy Organization of Iran   (ME)
AEOM .... Association des Etudiants d'Origine Malgache [*Association of Students of Malagasy Origin*]   (AF)
AEOM .... Association of European Open Air Museums   (WGAO)
AEOPSP ... Association Europeenne des Officers Professionnels Sapeurs-Pompiers   (WGAO)
AEOS .... Ancient Egyptian Order of Scions
AEOZ .... Association des Entreprises de l'Ouest du Zaire
AEP .... Aboriginal Education Policy [*Australia*]
AEP .... Africa Education Project
AEP .... Agence Europeenne de Productivite

AEP .... Agencia Ecuadoriana de Prensa (WGAO)

AEP .... Agencia Ecuatoriana de Prensa [*Ecuadorean Press Agency*] (LA)

AEP .... Agenzia Europea della Produttivita [*European Productivity Board*] [*Italian*] (WER)

AEP .... Airfield Clearing Station (RU)

AEP .... Airports Economic Panel [*ICAO*] (DA)

AEP .... Akathariston Engkhorion Proion [*Gross National Product*] [*Greek*] (GC)

AEP .... Amt fuer Erfindungs- und Patentwesen [*Invention and Patent Office*] (EG)

AEP .... Anelectrotonic Potential (RU)

AEP .... Anotati Epitropi Promitheion [*Supreme Supply Committee*] [*Greek*] (GC)

AEP .... Army Clearing Station (RU)

AEP .... Asociacion de Exportadores del Peru [*Association of Exports from Peru*] (EAIO)

AEP .... Association Europeenne de Podologues [*Belgium*] (WGAO)

AEP .... Association Europeenne de Psychiatrie [*Luxembourg*] (WGAO)

AEP .... Association of Educational Psychologists (WGAO)

AEP .... Association of Embroiderers and Pleaters (WGAO)

AEP .... Buenos Aires [*Argentina*] Jorge Newbery Airport [*Airport symbol*] (OAG)

AEP .... Compania Aero Transportes Panamenos SA [*Panama*] [*ICAO designator*] (FAAC)

AEPA .... All Ethiopia Peasants' Association (AF)

AEPB .... Association pour l'Emploi des Plastiques dans le Batiment (WGAO)

AEPC .... Asociacion Espanola para el Progreso de las Ciencias [*Spanish*] (SLS)

AEPE .... Asociacion Establecimientos Privados de Ensenanza [*Costa Rica*] (WGAO)

AEPE .... Asociacion Europea de Profesores del Espanol (WGAO)

AEPE .... Association pour l'Enseignement de la Pediatrie en Europe (WGAO)

AEPE .... Association pour l'Etude des Problemes de l'Europe [*Association for the Study of European Problems*]

AEPIA ...... Agrupacion Espanola de Plaguicidas (WGAO)

AEPIF ...... Association pour l'Etude et de Progres de l'Irrigation Fertilsante (WGAO)

AEPLA ..... Asociacion Espanola de Fabricantes de Agroquimicos para la Proteccion de las Plantas (WGAO)

AEPMA ..... Australian Environmental Pest Managers Association

AEPOM ..... Association pour l'Etude des Problemes d'Outre-Mer [*Association for the Study of Overseas Problems*] [*French*] (AF)

AEPP .... Southeast/East Asian English Publications in Print [*Japan Publications Guide Service*] [*Japan*] [*Information service or system*] (CRD)

AEPPA ...... Associacao de Ex-Presos Politicos Antifascistas [*Association of Former Antifascist Political Prisoners*] [*Portuguese*] (WER)

AEPPC ...... Association Europeenne des Practiciens des Procedures Collectives (WGAO)

AEPPI ...... Anonymos Etaireia Prostasias tis Pnevmatikis Idioktisias [*Company for the Protection of Intellectual Property*] [*Greek*] (GC)

AEPS .... Asociacion Espanola de Prevencion y Seguridad [*Spanish Association of Health and Safety*] (PDAA)

AEPS .... Association des Etablissements Publics de Soins [*Belgium*] (WGAO)

AEPS .... First Atomic Electric Power Plant (RU)

AEPT .... Asociacion Espanola de Prensa Tecnica (WGAO)

AEPYCC ... Asociacion de Exportadores de Pescado y Cefalopodos Congelados [*Spain*] (EY)

AEPYS ...... Anotati Epitropi Promitheion Ypourgeiou Stratiotikon [*Supreme Supply Committee of the Ministry of the Army*] [*Greek*] (GC)

Aeq .... Aequivalent [*Equivalent*] [*German*]

AEQCT ...... Asociacion Espanola de Quimicos y Coloristas Textiles [*Spanish*] (SLS)

AER .... Adler/Sochi [*Former USSR*] [*Airport symbol*] (OAG)

aer .... Aerobic (RU)

aer .... Aeronautics (TPFD)

aer .... Aeronautique [*French*] (TPFD)

AER .... Aerostat (RU)

AER .... Airfield Maintenance Company (RU)

AER .... Asociacion Ecuatoriana de Radio [*Ecuadorean Association of Radio Broadcasters*] (LA)

AER .... Asociacion Espanola de Robotica [*Spanish Association of Robotics*] (EAIO)

AER .... Assembly of European Regions [*France*] (EAIO)

AER .... Association Europeenne de Radiologie [*European Association of Radiology - EAR*] (EA)

AER .... Association Europeenne du Rhum (WGAO)

AER .... Association Europeenne pour l'Etude du Probleme des Refugies

AER .... Automatic Equipment for Optimal Power Distribution (RU)

AER .... Ejector-Type Mining Aspirator (RU)

AEr .... Motor Transport Clearing Company (BU)

AER .... Thai-American Treaty of Amity and Economic Relations (IMH)

AERA .... Association pour l'Etude et la Recherche Astronautique et Cosmique [*Association for Astronautics and Cosmic Study and Research*] [*France*] (PDAA)

AERA .... Australian Endurance Riders Association

AERAC ...... Association Auxiliaire pour l'Enseignement Superieur et la Recherche Agronomique en Cooperation (WGAO)

AERALL ... Association d'Etudes et de Recherches sur les Aeronefs Alleges (WGAO)

AERB .... Atomic Energy Regulatory Board [*India*]

AERCE ...... Asociacion Espanola de Responsables de Compras y Existencias (WGAO)

AERCF ...... Australian Earthmovers and Road Contractors Federation

AeRCs .... Aeroklub Republiky Ceskoslovenske [*Aero Club of the Czechoslovak Republic*] (CZ)

aerd .... Aerodynamics (RU)

aerd .... Airfield, Airdrome [*Topography*] (RU)

AERDC ...... Agricultural Extension and Rural Development Centre (WGAO)

AERDDP... Australian Energy Research, Development, and Demonstration Projects

AERDRI.... Agricultural Extension and Rural Development Research Institute [*Egypt*] (IRC)

AERE .... Association pour l'Etablissement des Refugies Etrangers [*France*] (FLAF)

AERE .... Atomic Energy Research Establishment (WGAO)

AEREK ..... Association des Etudiants de la Republique Khmere [*Cambodian Republic Students Association*] (CL)

AERF .... Australian Equine Research Foundation

AERG .... Alternative Education Resource Group [*Australia*]

AERI .... Agricultural Economics Research Institute (WGAO)

AERIS ...... Aerodynamic Test Station (RU)

AERL .... Arctic Environmental Research Laboratory (MSC)

AERL .... Association of Economic Representatives in London (WGAO)

AERL .... Australian Energy Research Laboratory

AERLS ..... Agricultural Extension and Research Liaison Service [*Nigeria*] (IRC)

AERLS ..... Agricultural Extension and Research Liaison Services [*Nigeria*] [*Research center*] (IRC)

AERO .... Air Education and Recreation Association (WGAO)

AEROBAL ... Association Europeenne des Fabricants de Boites en Aluminiun pour l'Aerosols (WGAO)

AEROBECO ... Becoblohm La Guaira, CA [*Venezuela*]

AEROCIVIL ... Empresa Colombiana de Aerodromos Informacion de Vuelos [*ECA*] [*Colombia*] [*Formerly,*] (COL)

AEROCOLOR ... Fotografia Aerea Forestal [*Mexico*] (DSCA)

AEROCONDOR ... Aerovias Condor de Colombia Ltda. [*Condor Airlines of Colombia Ltd.*]

AEROCOR ... Aerolineas Cordillera Ltda. [*Chile*] [*ICAO designator*] (FAAC)

AERODESA ... Aeronaves del Ecuador SA [*Ecuador*] (PDAA)

aerof .... Aerial Photometry (RU)

AEROFLOT ... Aero Flotilla [*Airline*] [*Former USSR*]

aeron .... Aeronautica [*Aeronautics*] [*Portuguese*]

AERONICA ... Aerolineas Nicaraguenses [*Nicaragua Airlines*] (EY)

AEROPERU ... Linea Aerea Peruana [*Peruvian State Airlines*]

Aeropesca .. Aerovias de Pesca y Colonizacion del Suroeste Colombiano (EY)

Aeroproyekt ... Central Office for the Surveying and Planning of Airlines and Airports (RU)

AEROSE ... Societe Aeronautique du Senegal

AEROSEA ... Servicios Especiales Aereos [*Barranquilla*] (COL)

AEROSEN ... Compagnie Aeronautique du Senegal

aerost .... Aerostatica [*Aerostatics*] [*Portuguese*]

AEROTUR ... Empresa de Turismo Aerea Cubana [*Cuban Air Travel Agency*] (LA)

AEROVENCA ... Aeronautica Venezolana CA [*Venezuela*] [*ICAO designator*] (FAAC)

AERP........ Agrupacion Espanola de Relaciones Publicas (WGAO)

aerp .... Airport [*Topography*] (RU)

AERP........ Asociacion Espanola de la Radiodifusion Privada (EY)

AERP........ Assessoria Especial de Relacoes Publicas da Presidencia da Republica [*Presidential Office Special Public Relations Staff*] [*Brazil*] (LA)

AERP........ Association Europeenne pour la Recherche sur le Pomme de Terre (WGAO)

AERPF ...... Association Europeenne pour la Reduction de la Pollution due aux Fibres (WGAO)

AERS........ Agricultural Engineering Research Station [*Kenya*] (DSCA)

AERSG ...... African Elephant and Rhino Specialist Group [*of the International Union for Conservation of Nature and Natural Resources*] (EA)

AERTA...... Association Europeenne de Radio et Television Agricole (WGAO)

AERTEL ... Association Europeenne Rubans, Tresses, Tissus Elastiques (WGAO)

AERU .... Agribusiness and Economics Research Unit [*New Zealand*] (IRC)

AERZAP ... Association pour les Etudes et Recherches de Zoologie Appliquee et de Phytopathologie [*Belgium*] (SLS)
AES............ Aalesund [*Norway*] [*Airport symbol*]
AES............ Aerolineas Centrales de Colombia [*ICAO designator*] (FAAC)
AES............ Agence Eurafricaine d'Echanges et de Services
AES............ Agregation de l'Enseignement Superieur [*French*]
AES............ Agricultural Economics Society (WGAO)
AES............ Agrupacion de Estudios Sociales [*Social Studies Association*] [*Argentina*] (LA)
aes .... Air Liaison Squadron (BU)
AES............ Amateur Entomologists Society (WGAO)
AES............ American Embassy School [*India*]
AES............ Aminoethanol Sulfate (RU)
AES............ Ankara Elektrik Sanayii ve Ticaret AS [*Ankara Electric Industry and Trade Corporation*] (TU)
AES............ Anotaton Ekpaidevtikon Symvoulion [*Supreme Educational Council*] [*Greek*] (GC)
AES............ Asian Environmental Society [*Philippines*] (WGAO)
AES............ Asociacion de Estudiantes de Secundaria [*Association of Secondary School Students*] [*El Salvador*] (LA)
AES............ Association of Ecological Societies (EAIO)
AES............ Atlantic Economic Society (WGAO)
AES............ Atomic Electric Power Plant (RU)
AES............ Atomnaia Elektrostantsiia
AES............ Australian Economic Statistics [*Database*] [*I. P. Sharp Associates*] [*Information service or system*] (CRD)
AES............ Australian Entomological Society (ADA)
AES............ Australian Equivalent Salary
AES............ Australian Exhibition Services Proprietary Ltd.
AES............ Economic Cooperation Administration [*ECA*] (RU)
AES............ Landplane Airfield (RU)
AES............ Truck-Mounted Electric Power Plant (RU)
AESA......... Aerolineas de El Salvador [*Airline*] [*El Salvador*]
AESA......... Aerolineas de El Salvador SA (WGAO)
AESA......... Agricultural Engineering Society [*Australia*] (WGAO)
AESA......... Agricultural Engineering Society (Australia) (ADA)
AESA......... Association pour l'Enseignement Social en Afrique [*Association for Social Work Education in Africa - ASWEA*] (EAIO)
AESA......... Australia to Europe Shippers' Association (ADA)
AESAL...... Academie Europeenne des Sciences, des Arts, et des Lettres [*European Academy of Arts, Sciences, and Humanities*] (EAIO)
AESAU...... Association of Eastern and Southern African Universities (WGAO)
AESC......... Architectural and Engineering Services Corporation [*Ghana*]
AESC......... Association des Anciens Etudiants en Sciences Commerciales [*Association of Former Commercial Students*] [*Cambodia*] (CL)
AESC......... Australia to Europe Shipping Conference
AESCO...... Association Europeenne des Ecoles et Colleges d'Optometre [*European Association of Schools and Colleges of Optometry - EASCO*] (EA)
AESD........ Association of Engineering and Shipbuilding Draughtsmen (WGAO)
AESDA...... Association of Architects, Engineers, Surveyors, and Draughtsmen of Australia
AESED...... Association Europeenne de Societes d'Etudes pour le Developpement (WGAO)
AESF........ Association des Ecrivans Scientifiques de France (WGAO)
AESG........ Australian Employee Survey Group
AESG........ Australian Extension Services Grant (ADA)
AESGP...... Association Europeenne des Specialites Pharmaceutiques Grand Public [*European Proprietary Association*] (EA)
AESI......... Australian Earth Sciences Information System [*Database on AUSINET*] (NITA)
AESIEAP.. Association of the Electricity Supply Industry in East Asia and the Western Pacific [*Australia*] (WGAO)
AESIMP.... Association pour l'Etude de la Sterilite et la Medicine Perinatale (WGAO)
AESIP....... Aboriginal Education Strategic Initiatives Program [*Australia*]
AESIS....... Australian Earth Sciences Information System [*Australian Mineral Foundation*] [*Information service or system*] (IID)
AESJ........ Atomic Energy Society of Japan [*Nuclear energy*] (NRCH)
AESL......... Aero Engine Service Ltd. [*Australia*]
AESLA...... Asociacion de Estudios y Solidaridad con Latinoamerica [*Association of Studies and Solidarity with Latin America*] (LA)
AESM........ All Ethiopian Socialist Movement (AF)
AESM........ All-Ethiopia Socialist Movement (WGAO)
AESNE...... Asociacion de Empleados del Servicio Nacional de Electricidad [*Association of National Electricity Service Employees*] [*Costa Rica*] (LA)
AESNW..... Art Education Society of New South Wales [*Australia*]
AESO........ Acupuncture Ethics and Standards Organisation [*Australia*]
AESOP...... Australian Executive Service Overseas Project
AESOR...... Association Europeenne de Sous-Officiers de Reserve (WGAO)

AESPA...... Assessoria de Estudos, Planejamento, Programacao, e Avaliacao [*Brazil*] (LAA)
AESPC...... Association Europeenne pour la Securite des Produits des Consummateurs (WGAO)
AESPOP... Association of European Schools of Planning (WGAO)
AESPRE.... Associatin des Ecoles de Sante Publique de la Region Europeenne (WGAO)
AESRC...... Association des Etudiants et des Sujets du Royaume du Cambodge [*Association of Students and Subjects of the Kingdom of Cambodia*] [*Used in historical material*] (CL)
AESS........ Appraisals, Evaluation, and Sectoral Study
AeSSA...... Aeronautical Society of South Africa (PDAA)
AESSCR.... Asociacion de Empleados del Seguro Social de Costa Rica [*Costa Rican Social Security Employees Association*] (LA)
AEST........ Australian Eastern Standard Time (ADA)
AEST........ Australian Eastern Summer Time (ADA)
AESTM..... Association Europeenne des Sciences et Techniques de la Mer (WGAO)
AESU........ Arabische Eisen and Stahl Union (WGAO)
AESV........ Association Europeene de Saint Vladimir (EAIO)
AET .... Aerlinte Eireann Teoranta [*Irish Air Lines*]
AET .... Aero-Palma SA [*Spain*] [*ICAO designator*] (FAAC)
AET .... Africa Educational Trust [*British*]
AET .... Allami Epitoipari Troszt [*State Trust of the Building Industry*] (HU)
AET .... Aminoethylisothiuronium (RU)
AET .... Applied Electronics Technology Proprietary Ltd. [*Australia*]
AET .... Arabian Establishment for Trade and Shipping [*Saudi Arabia*] [*Commercial firm*]
AET .... Association Europeenne de Thanatologie (WGAO)
AET .... Association Europeenne de Thermoghraphie [*French*] (SLS)
AET .... Association Europeenne de Thermographie (WGAO)
AET .... Association Europeenne Thyroide [*European Thyroid Association - ETA*] (EAIO)
AET .... Association of Auto-Electrical Technicians (WGAO)
AET .... Avrupa Ekonomik Toplulugu [*European Economic Community - EEC*] (TU)
AETA........ Adult Education Tutors' Association [*Australia*]
AETA........ Anotati Epitropi Teloneiakon Amfisvitiseon [*Supreme Committee for Customs Disputes*] [*Greek*] (GC)
AETA........ Association Europeenne Tourisme Aerien (WGAO)
AETA........ Australian East Timor Association (ADA)
AETA........ Australian Electric Traction Association (ADA)
AETA........ Australian Equestrian Trade Association
AETA........ Australian Exhibition Touring Agency
AETA........ Societe pour l'Amenagement et l'Etude du Tourisme Algerien
AETC........ Agricultural Extension Training Center
AETCF ..... Association pour l'Enseignement Technique et Commercial Francais au Maroc
AETF........ Association des Etudiants Tchadiens en France [*Association of Chadian Students in France*] [*Chad*] (AF)
AETFAT ... Association pour l'Etude Taxonomique de la Flore d'Afrique Tropicale [*Association for the Taxonomic Study of Tropical African Flora*] [*French*] (AF)
aeth .... Aetherisch [*Ethereal*] [*German*]
AETI......... Allami Epitestvedomanyi es Tervezo Intezet [*State Institute of Architecture and Design*] (HU)
AETK........ Airfield Technical Crew (RU)
AETL........ Armament and Electronics Test Laboratory [*NATO*]
A et M ...... Arts et Metiers [*Arts and Crafts*] [*French*]
AETM .... Australian Electric Transport Museum (ADA)
AETM(SA) ... Australian Electric Transport Association (South Australia)
AETOS...... Andistasiaki Ethniki Vasiliki Organosis Ellinon [*Greek National Resistance Royalist Organization*] (GC)
AETR........ Asociacion Espanola de Tecnicos de Radiologia [*Spanish*] (SLS)
AETs......... Atomic Power Plant (BU)
AETT........ Association of Education and Training Technology (WGAO)
AETT........ Australian Elizabethan Theatre Trust (ADA)
AETU........ All Ethiopia Trade Union (AF)
AETUO ..... All-Ethiopian Trade Union Organization
AETV........ Altalanos Epulettervezo Vallalat [*Architectural Design Enterprise*] (HU)
AEU .... Accident and Emergency Unit [*Australia*]
AEU .... Air Evacuation Unit [*Military*]
AEU .... Amalgamated Engineering Union [*Zimbabwe*] (AF)
AEU .... Arbeitskreis Evangelischer Unternehmer in der Bundesrepublik Deutschland (WGAO)
AEU .... Asia Electronics Union [*Japan*] (PDAA)
AEU .... Asociacion de Estudiantes Universitarios [*University Students Association*] [*Guatemala*] (LA)
AEU .... Australian Engineering Union
AEU .... Nuclear Propulsion Engine, Atomic Power Plant (RU)
AEUC .... Arab Economic Unity Council
AEUCV ..... Asociacion de Empleados de la Universidad Central de Venezuela [*Association of Employees of the Central University of Venezuela*] (LA)

AEUO....... Asociacion de Estudiantes Universitarios de Occidente [*Association of University Students of the West*] [*Guatemala*]   (LA)
AEV .... Aeroventas SA [*Mexico*] [*ICAO designator*]   (FAAC)
AEV .... Allami Epitoipari Vallalat (Veszprem) [*State Construction Enterprise (Veszprem Branch)*]   (HU)
AEV .... Arbeitsgemeinschaft Erdoelgewinnung und Verarbeitung
AEV .... Automatic Electric Switch   (RU)
AEVA .... Australian Electric Vehicle Association   (ADA)
AEVA .... Australian Equine Veterinary Association
AEVAL...... Anonymos Etaireia Viomikhanias Azotoukhon Lipasmaton [*Nitrogenous Fertilizers Corporation*]   (GC)
AEVC........ Association Europeenne de Vente par Correspondance [*European Mail Order Traders' Association*] [*Belgium*]   (EAIO)
AEVE........ Agrotiki Enosis Voreiou Ellados [*Agrarian Union of Northern Greece*]   (GC)
AEVII .... Federacion de Veterinarios Europeos de la Industria y la Investigacion   (WGAO)
AEVPC ...... Association Europeenne de Vente par Correspondance [*European Mail Order Traders' Association*] [*Belgium*]   (ECED)
AEW .... Aboriginal Education Worker [*Australia*]
AEWHA.... All England Women's Hockey   (WGAO)
AEWL .... Association of Employers of Waterside Labour [*Australia*]   (ADA)
AEWLA..... All England Women's Lacrosse Association   (WGAO)
AEWVH .... Association for the Education and Welfare of the Visually Handicapped   (WGAO)
AEWW ...... Australian Exhibition of Women's Work   (ADA)
AEXANDES ... Asociacion de Exalumnos de la Universidad de los Andes [*Colombia*]   (COL)
AEY .... Akureyri [*Iceland*] [*Airport symbol*]   (OAG)
AEYSC ...... All-European Youth and Student Cooperation   (WGAO)
AF .... AB AngpanneForeningen [*Steam Users' Association*] [*Sweden*]
AF .... Abdulla Fouad Auctioneers [*Saudi Arabia*]
AF .... Action Familiale [*Family Action*] [*Mauritius*]   (AF)
AF .... Admiral of the Fleet [*British*]
AF .... A Favor [*In Favor*] [*Spanish*]
AF .... Afghani [*Monetary unit*] [*Afghanistan*]
AF .... Afghanistan [*ANSI two-letter standard code*]   (CNC)
AF .... African Filmstrips
af .... Air Fleet   (BU)
AF .... Air France [*ICAO designator*]
af .... Air Squadron   (BU)
AF .... Akademikernes Fellesorganisasjon [*Norway*]   (SLS)
AF .... Akumulacija Fondova [*Accumulation of Funds*] [*Yugoslavian*] [*Business term*]   (YU)
AF .... Alcak Frekans [*Low Frequency*]   (TU)
AF .... Alliance Francaise
AF .... Allocations Familiales [*French*]
AF .... Alta Fidelidade [*High Fidelity*] [*Portuguese*]
AF .... Alta Frequenza [*High Frequency*] [*Use HF*] [*Italian*]   (WER)
AF .... Anbauflaeche [*Area under Cultivation*]   (EG)
AF .... Ancien Franc [*Old Franc*] [*Monetary unit*] [*French*]   (WER)
AF .... Angpanneforeningen   (WGAO)
af .... Anno Futuro [*Next Year*] [*Italian*]
AF .... Antarctic Front   (RU)
af .... Antiguo Frances [*Old French*] [*Language, etc.*] [*Spanish*]
AF .... Anwendungs-Feld [*Application Field*] [*Germany*]   (ADPT)
AF .... Arctic Front   (RU)
AF .... Arkitektforbundet [*Swedish Union of Architects, Interior Designers and Landscap e Architects*]   (EAIO)
AF .... Asthma Foundation [*Australia*]
AF .... Audio Frequencia [*Audiofrequency*] [*Portuguese*]
AF .... Audiofrequenz [*Audio Frequency*] [*German*]   (GCA)
AF .... Australia Felix   (ADA)
AF .... Australia First [*Political party*]
AF .... Auxiliary Force [*India*] [*Army*]
AF .... Avala-Film [*Establishment for the production and export of motion pictures*] [*Belgrade*]   (YU)
AF .... Flug & Fahrzeugwerke AG Altenrhein [*Switzerland*] [*ICAO aircraft manufacturer identifier*]   (ICAO)
AF .... L'Afrique [*or L'Africaine*] Francaise
AF .... Photoreconnaissance   (RU)
AFA .... Aborigines' Friends Association [*Australia*]   (ADA)
AFA .... Adelaide Festival of Arts [*Australia*]
AFA .... Advertising Federation of Australia   (ADA)
AFA .... Aerial Camera   (RU)
AFA .... Aerial Photography Equipment   (BU)
AFA .... Agribusiness Foundation of Australia
AFA .... Air Freight Association of America   (WGAO)
AFA .... Alfa Air [*Czechoslovakia*] [*ICAO designator*]   (FAAC)
AFA .... All for Australia League   (ADA)
AFA .... Amateur Fencing Association   (WGAO)
AFA .... Amatuer Football Alliance   (WGAO)

AFA .... Amicale des Femmes Algeriennes [*Algerian Woman's Association*]
AFA .... Amitie Franco-Afghane [*French Afghan Friendship Committee*]   (EAIO)
AFA .... Arbeitsgemeinschaft fur Abfallwirtschaft   (WGAO)
AFA .... Arthritis Foundation of Australia
AFA .... ASEAN Federation of Accountants   (WGAO)
AFA .... Asociacion de Fabricantes de Conservas y Productos Alimenticios [*Colombia*]   (DSCA)
AFA .... Asociacion del Futbol Aficionado [*Colombia*]   (COL)
AFA .... Asociacion Fisica Argentina [*Argentine Physical Association*] [*Cordoba*]   (LAA)
AFA .... Asociacion Folklorica Argentina   (WGAO)
AFA .... Asociacion Forestal Argentina [*Argentina*]   (DSCA)
AFA .... Assistance Forestiere Africaine [*Ivory Coast*]   (WGAO)
AFA .... Associacao Fluminense de Avicultura [*Brazil*]   (DSCA)
AFA .... Association Francaise d'Astronomie [*French*]   (SLS)
AFA .... Atheist Foundation of Australia
AfA............ Ausschuss fuer Arbeitsstudien [*Committee for Labor Studies*]   (EG)
AFA .... Australian Federation of Advertisers
AFA .... Australian Field Artillery   (ADA)
AFA .... Australian Flute Association
AFA .... Australian Folklore Association
AFA .... Australians for Animals
AFA .... Avicultural Federation of Australia
AFA .... San Rafael [*Argentina*] [*Airport symbol*]   (OAG)
AFAA .... ASEAN Federation of Advertising Associations   (WGAO)
AFAA .... ASEAN Federation of Automobile Associations   (WGAO)
AFAA .... Association of Faculties of Agriculture in Africa   (WGAO)
AFAA .... Australian Federation of Advertising Agencies   (WGAO)
AFAA .... Australian Flight Attendants' Association
AFA(ACT) ... Arthritis Foundation of Australia (Australian Capital Territory)
AFAB........ Association des Federations Africaines de Basketball [*Egypt*]   (WGAO)
AFAB........ Association Francaise d'Agriculture Biologique   (WGAO)
AFAB........ Associazone Food and Beverage   (WGAO)
AFA-B ...... Bomber Aerial Camera   (RU)
AFABA..... Association des Federations Africaines de Basketball Amateur [*African Association of Basketball Federations*] [*Egypt*]
AFABS ..... Air Force Arctic Broadcasting Squadron [*New York, NY*]   (EY)
AFABT..... Australian Federation of Aestheticians and Beauty Therapists
AFAC........ Amateur Fishermen's Advisory Council [*New South Wales, Australia*]
AFAC........ Association des Fabricants d'Aliments Controles pour le Betail [*Luxembourg*]   (WGAO)
AFAC........ Association des Fonctionnaires et Agents de la Colonie [*Association of Civil Servants and Agents of the Colony*] [*European civil servants Congo*]
AFAC........ Australian Flora Authorities Conference   (ADA)
AFACO..... Association Francaise des Amateurs Constructeurs l'Ordinateurs [*French Association of Amateur Computer Builders*]   (PDAA)
AFACPG ... Association Francaise des Amateurs de Cactees et de Plantes Grasses   (WGAO)
AFADD ..... Australian Foundation on Alcoholism and Drug Dependence   (ADA)
AFAEP ..... Association of Fashion Advertising and Editorial Photographers   (WGAO)
AFAFF...... Australian Federation of Air Freight Forwarders
AFAHA .... Association Francaise des Amateurs Horlogerie Ancienne [*France*]   (PDAA)
AFA-I........ Fighter Aerial Camera   (RU)
AFAIM..... Associate Fellow of the Australian Institute of Management   (ADA)
AFAL........ All for Australia League   (ADA)
AFAL........ Association Forestiere Africaine de Libreville
AFAL........ Association Francophone d'Amitie et de Liaison   (EA)
AFALI ...... Association Feminine pour l'Amitie Lao Internationale [*International Lao Women's Friendship Association*]   (CL)
AFAM ...... Action Familiale Africaine et Malagache   (WGAO)
AFAM ...... Australian Family Action Movement   (ADA)
AFAMI..... Associate Fellow of the Australian Marketing Institute
AFANG ..... American Friends of the Australian National Gallery
AFANT..... Amateur Fishermen's Association of the Northern Territory
AFAO .... Australian Federation of AIDS Organisations
AFAP........ Association de la Femme Africaine Progressiste   (WGAO)
AFAP........ Association des Femmes Americaines a Paris [*American Women's Group in Paris*]   (EAIO)
AFAP........ Association Francaise pour l'Accroissement de la Productivite [*French Association for Increased Productivity*]   (WER)
AFAP........ Australian Federation of Air Pilots
AFApis....... Associacao Fluminense de Apicultores [*Brazil*]   (DSCA)
AFAPTS.... Australian French Association of Professional and Technical Specialists   (ADA)
AFAQ .... Arthritis Foundation of Australia, Queensland

AFAQ .... Association Francaise pour l'Expansion des Produits Agricoles de Qualite Garantie (WGAO)

AFAQUIMA ... Asociacion de Fabricantes de Materias Quimicas [*Venezuela*] (DSCA)

AFAR .... American Friends of the Angolan Revolution

AFAR .... Asociacion Femenina de Accion Rural [*Argentina*] (LAA)

AFAR .... Azores Fixed Acoustic Range [*NATO*]

AFARB ...... Association of Friends of the Achievement of Richard Bellman [*France*] (EAIO)

AFARCO ... Afro-Arab Company for Investment and International Trade (ME)

AFARD ...... Association des Femmes Africaines pour la Recherche sur le Developpement [*Association of African Women for Research and Development - AAWORD*] (EAIO)

AFARS ...... Australian Federation of Amateur Roller Skaters

AFAS .... Anorexic Family Aid (WGAO)

AFAS .... Associatin France-Asie Sud (WGAO)

AFAS .... Association Francaise pour l'Avancement des Sciences [*French*]

AFAS .... Australian French Association of Professional and Technical Specialists (ADA)

AFASED ... African Association of Education for Development (EAIO)

AFASIC ..... Association for all Speech Impaired Children (WGAO)

AFASPA .... Association Francaise d'Amitie et de Solidarite avec les Peuples d'Afrique [*French Association for Friendship and Solidarity with the Peoples of Africa*] (AF)

AFAT .... Amateur Fencing Association of Thailand (EAIO)

AFAT .... Association Francaise de l'Assurance de Transports (WGAO)

AFAT .... Auxiliaires Feminines de l'Armee de Terre [*Women's Army Auxiliary*] [*French*] (WER)

AFAV .... Anti-Fluoridation Association of Victoria [*Australia*]

AFAX .... Australia - Faxon Company [*Australian-New Zealand Office*] [*National Union Catalogue of Australia symbol*]

afb .... Afbeelding [*Illustration*] [*Netherlands*]

AFB .... Allami Fejlesztesi Bank [*State Development Bank*] (HU)

AFB .... Allgemeinefunkspruchbuch [*General Wireless Message Book*] [*German military - World War I*]

AFB .... Arbeitsgemeinschaft Facharztlicher Berufsverbande (WGAO)

AFB .... Arbeitsstelle Friedenforschung Bonn [*Information Unit for Peace Research, Bonn*]

AfB .... Arbeitsstelle fur das Bibliothekswesen [*Library Study Centre*] [*Germany*] (PDAA)

AFB .... Asociacion Forestal Boliviana [*Bolivia*] (DSCA)

AFB .... Association Francaise du Beton (WGAO)

AFB .... Force Aerienne Belge [*Belgium*] [*ICAO designator*] (FAAC)

AFBA .... Asociacion Farmaceutica y Bioquimica Argentina [*Pharmaceutical and Biochemical Association of Argentina*] [*Buenos Aires*] (LAA)

AFBALTAP ... Allied Forces Baltic Approaches [*NATO*] (MCD)

AFBANK ... African Bank [*South Africa*]

AFBC .... Association of Football Badge Collectors (WGAO)

AFBD .... Association of Futures Brokers and Dealers (WGAO)

AFBF .... Australian Feminist Book Fortnight

AFBI .... Australian Fibre Box Industry (ADA)

afbildn .... Afbildning [*Illustration*] [*Danish/Norwegian*]

afbn .... Afbeeldingen [*Illustrations*] [*Netherlands*]

AFBPW .... Australian Federation of Business and Professional Women

AFBS .... American and Foreign Bible Society

AFBS .... Ansett Flying Boat Services [*Australia*] (ADA)

AFBW .... Algemene Federatie van Bonaireaanse Werknemers [*Netherlands Antilles*] (EY)

AFC .... Administracion de Fomento Cooperativo [*Puerto Rico*] (DSCA)

AFC .... African Farmers Committee [*See also CPA*] (EAIO)

AFC .... African Football Confederation (EAIO)

AFC .... African Forestry Commission [*UN Food and Agriculture Organization*]

AFC .... African Fruit Company

AFC .... African West Air [*Senegal*] [*ICAO designator*] (FAAC)

AFC .... Agricultural Finance Corporation [*Kenya*] (WGAO)

AFC .... Air Force College [*Australia*] (ADA)

AFC .... Alexandria Flying Club

AFC .... Asian Football Confederation (EAIO)

AFC .... Association des Femmes Cambodgiennes [*Cambodian Women's Association*] [*Use AFK*] (CL)

AFC .... Association Football Club [*Australia*]

AFC .... Association Fracaise de Cristallographie (WGAO)

AFC .... Association Francaise de Chimiurgie (WGAO)

AFC .... Association Francaise de Chirurgie (SLS)

AFC .... Association France-Containers (WGAO)

AFC .... Association of Fish Canners (WGAO)

AFC .... Australian Families for Children

AFC .... Australian Film Commission [*or Council*] (ADA)

AFC .... Australian Finance Conference (ADA)

AFC .... Australian Fisheries Council

AFC .... Australian Fluorine Chemicals

AFC .... Australian Flying Corps (ADA)

AFC .... Societe Air Froid Conditionnement

AFCA .... Association Fonciere et Commerciale Africaine [*Morocco*]

AFCA .... Association Francaise pour la Communaute Atlantique [*French Association for the Atlantic Community*] (NATG)

AFCA .... Association pour la Formation des Cadres de l'Industrie et de l'Administration

AFCA .... Association pour la Formation des Cadres de l'Industrie et de l'Administration en Langue Francaise (WGAO)

AFCA .... Association Professionelle des Fabricants de Complements pour l'Alimentation Animale (WGAO)

AFCA .... Australian Football Coaches Association

AFCAC ..... African Civil Aviation Commission [*See also CAFAC*] (EAIO)

AFCAL ...... Association Francaise de Calcul [*French computing association*] (MCD)

AFCALTI ... Association Francaise de Calcul et de Traitement de l'Information [*French Association of Calculus and the Handling of Information*] [*French*] (ADPT)

AFCAM ..... Association of Fluorocarbon Consumers and Manufacturers [*Australia*]

AFCAM ..... Ateliers Ferroviaires et Metallurgiques du Cameroun (WGAO)

AFCAN ...... Association Francaise de Calcul Numerique [*French Association of Numerical Calculus*] [*French*] (ADPT)

AFCAS ...... African Commission on Agricultural Statistics [*Ghana*] (EAIO)

AFCASOLE ... Association des Fabricants de Cafe Soluble des Pays de la CEE (WGAO)

AFCAT ...... Association Francaise de Calorimetrie et d'Analyse Thermique (WGAO)

AFCBS .... Australian Federation of Commercial Broadcasting Stations (ADA)

AFCC .... Arab Financial Consultants Company

AFCC .... Armed Forces Coordinating Committee

AFCC .... Association Francaise du Commerce des Cacaos

AFCC .... Australian Federal Cycling Council (ADA)

AFCC .... Australian Federation of Construction Contractors (ADA)

AFCCA ...... Australian Federation of Child Care Associations

AFCCRA .... Australian Financial Counselling and Credit Reform Association

AFCE .... Allied Forces Central Europe [*NATO*] (MCD)

AFCEC ...... Australian Federation of Civil Engineering Contractors (ADA)

AFCENT ... Allied Forces Central Europe [*NATO*]

AFCET ...... Association Francaise pour la Cybernetique Economique et Technique [*French Association for Economic and Technical Cybernetics*]

AFCFP .... Arab Federation of Chemical Fertilizer Producers (EA)

AFCG .... Association Folklorique Culturelle Guyanaise [*Cultural Folklore Association of French Guiana*] (LA)

AFCGC ...... Asociacion Venezolana de Criadores de Ganada Cebu (WGAO)

AFCIA .... Associate Fellow of the Catering Institute of Australia

AFCIMAT ... Asociacion de Fabricantes de Conjuntos Importantes para la Mecanizacion del Agro y el Transporte [*Argentina*] (LAA)

AFCIQ .... Association Francaise pour le Controle Industriel de Qualite [*French*] (SLS)

AFCL .... African Container Line (WGAO)

AFCM .... ASEAN [*Association of South East Asian Nations*] Federation of Cement Manufacturers [*Indonesia*] (EAIO)

AFCM .... Association of Finance Companies of Malaysia

AFCMA ..... Australian Fibreboard Container Manufacturers' Association (ADA)

AFCMO .... Association Francaise des Constructeurs de Machines Outils

AFCO .... Agricultural Finance Corporation [*Zimbabwe*] (AF)

AFCO .... Asociacion Espanola de Fabricantes de Carton Ondulado (WGAO)

AFCO .... Australian Federation of Consumer Organizations (ADA)

AFCO .... Societe Africaine de Conditionnement

AFCOA ...... Australian Council for Overseas Aid (WGAO)

AFCOD ..... Association Francaise des Conseillers de Direction (WGAO)

AFCODI .... Africaine Commerciale de Diffusion

AFCODI .... Ateliers de Freinage de la Cote-D'Ivoire

AFCOFEL ... Association Francaise Comites Economiques Agricoles de Fruits et Legumes (WGAO)

AFCOM .... Africaine de Constructions Mecaniques [*Ivory Coast*] (WGAO)

AFCONA .. African Convention on the Conservation of Nature and Natural Resources (ASF)

AFCOS ...... Association Francaise des Conseils en Organisation Scientifique (WGAO)

AFCOT ...... Association Francaise Contonniere (WGAO)

AFCS .... Association Francaise des Chasseurs de Son (WGAO)

AFCU .... Australian Federation of Credit Unions

AFCUL ...... Australian Federation of Credit Union Leagues (ADA)

AFCWU ..... African Food and Canning Workers Union [*South Africa*] (WGAO)

afd .... Afdeling [*Part*] [*Netherlands*]

afd .... Afdeling [*Part*] [*Danish/Norwegian*]

AFD .... Alliance of Free Democrats [*Hungary*] [*Political party*] (EY)

AFD .... AmtsradsForeiningen i Danmark [*Association of County Councils of Denmark*]

AFD .... Anexartiti Filelevthera Dimokratia [*Independent Liberal Democracy*] [*Greek*] (GC)

AFD .... Ankara Flarmoni Dernegi [*Ankara Philharmonic Association*] (TU)
AFD .... Associated Fashion Designers of London   (WGAO)
AFD .... Association Francaise des Diabetiques [*French Diabetes Association*]   (EAIO)
AFD .... Australian Federation for Decency
AFD .... Australian Foundation for the Disabled
AFD .... Panorama Flight Service [*ICAO designator*]   (FAAC)
AFDA .... Australian Funeral Directors Association   (ADA)
AFDAC...... Association Francaise de Documentation Automatique en Chimie
AFDAMME ... Association Francaise de Documentation Automatique en Metallurgie, Materiaux, et Electrotechnique
AfDB.......... African Development Bank [*Also, ADB*]   (EY)
AFDBP ...... Association des Fabricants et Distributeurs de Bouillons et Potages [*Association of the Manufacture of Soups and Broths*] [*Belgium*]   (EAIO)
AFDBS ...... Association Francaise des Documentaires et des Bibliothecaires Specialises [*French Association of Documentalists and Special Librarians*]   (PDAA)
AFDBS ...... Association Francaise des Documentalistes et des Bibliothecaires Specialises   (NITA)
AFDC......... Agriculture and Fishery Development Corporation [*South Korea*]   (FEA)
AFDC......... Australian Film Development Corporation
AFDC........ Australian Folkloric Dance Company [*An association*]
AFDE........ Association Francaise pour la Difusion de l'Espagnol   (WGAO)
AFDEC...... Association of Franchised Distributors of Electronic Components   (WGAO)
AFDET...... Association Francaise pour la Developpement de l'Enseignement Technique   (WGAO)
AfDF.......... African Development Fund   (WGAO)
AFDI......... Agriculteurs Francais et Developpement International   (WGAO)
AFDI......... Association Francaise des Demenageurs Internationaux   (WGAO)
AFDI......... Australian Forest Development Institute
AFDID....... Association of Furniture Designers and Interior Designers [*Iceland*]   (EAIO)
AFDIN...... African Development Information Network [*United Nations Economic Commission for Africa*] [*Ethiopia*]
AFDIN...... Association Francaise de Documentation et d'Information Nucleaires [*French Association for Nuclear Documentation and Information*]   (WER)
AFDIP ...... Association Africaine des Formateurs et Directeurs de Personnel   (WGAO)
AFDIT ...... Associazione Italiana dei Fornitori e Distributori di Informazione Telematica [*Italian Association for the Production and Distribution of Online Information*] [*Rome*] [*Information service or system*]   (IID)
AFDJ .... Administratia Fluviala a Dunarii de Jos [*Lower Danube River Administration*]   (RO)
AFE............ Administracion de Ferrocarriles del Estado [*State Railways Administration*] [*Uruguay*]   (LA)
AFE............ Administracion de Fomento Economico [*Puerto Rico*]   (DSCA)
AFE............ Airfast Service Indonesia PT [*ICAO designator*]   (FAAC)
AfE............ Amt fuer Exportkontrolle [*Office for Export Control*]   (EG)
AFE............ Asociacion de Forestales del Ecuador [*Ecuador*]   (DSCA)
AFE............ Asociacion de Futbolistas Espanoles   (WGAO)
AFE............ Association Francaise de l'Eclairage [*French*]   (SLS)
AFE............ Ateliers et Forges de l'Ebrie
AFE............ Australia-France Endowment
AFE............ Australian Federation of Employers
AFEA........ Association Francaise d'Etudes Americaines [*French*]   (SLS)
AFEAS ...... Alternative Fluorocarbon Environmental Acceptability Study [*World Meteorological Organization*]
AfeB........... Arbeitsgruppe fuer Empirische Bildungsforschung eV   (SLS)
AFEC........ Aboriginal Family Education Centre [*Australia*]
AFEC........ Association Francaise d'Etudes de la Concurrence [*France*]   (FLAF)
AFEC........ Association Francaise pour le Controle de la Qualite des Hormones Desherbantes   (WGAO)
AFEC........ Association Francaise pour l'Etude du Cancer [*French*]   (SLS)
AFEC........ Association Francophone d'Education Comparee [*French-Speaking Comparative Education Association - FSCEA*]   (EAIO)
AFECG...... Association Francaise pour l'Etude des Corps Gras [*French Oil Chemists' Association*]
AFECI .... Association des Fabricants Europeens de Chauffe-Bains et Chauffe-Eau Instantanes et de Chaudieres Murales au Gaz [*Association of European Manufacturers of Instantaneous Gas Water Heaters and Wall-Hung Boilers*]   (EA)
AFECO...... Arab-French Engine Company
AFECOGAZ ... Association de Fabricants Europeens d'Appareils de Controle pour le Gaz et l'Huile   (WGAO)
AFECOGAZ ... Association des Fabricants Europeens d'Appareils de Controle [*European Control Manufacturers Association*]   (EAIO)

AFECOR ... Association des Fabricants Europeens d'Appareils de Controle et de Regulation [*European Control Device Manufacturers' Association*] [*EC*]   (ECED)
AFECPAL ... Asociacion de Facultades y Escuelas de Contaduria Publica de America Latina   (WGAO)
AFECTI..... Association Francaise d'Experts de la Cooperation Technique Internationale [*French Association of Experts Assigned to International Technical Cooperation*]   (AF)
AFEDEF.... Association des Fabricants Europeens d'Equipements Ferroviaires [*Association of European Railway Equipment Manufacturers*]   (EAIO)
AFEDES.... Association Francaise pour l'Etude et le Developpement des Applications de l'Energie Solaire   (WGAO)
AFEDK...... Agrotiki Filelevtheri Enosis tou Dimokratikou Kendrou [*Liberal Agrarian Union of the Democratic Center*] [*Greek*]   (GC)
AFEE .... Association Francaise des Entreprises pour l'Environnement [*French Environmentalist Association*]
AFEE .... Association Francaise pour l'Etude des Eaux [*French Water Study Association*] [*Paris*] [*Information service or system*]   (IID)
AFEF .... Air Force Emergency Force
AFEF .... Australian Free Enterprise Foundation
AFEI .... Arab Federation of Engineering Industries   (WGAO)
AFEI .... Association Francaise pour l'Etiquetage d'Information   (WGAO)
AFEI .... Association of Finnish Electric Industries   (WGAO)
AFEID .... Association Francaise pour l'Etude des Irrigations et du Drainage   (WGAO)
AFEMA ..... Association des Fabricants Europeens d'Emulsifiants Alimentaires   (WGAO)
AFEMAC.. Asociacion de Fabricantes Espanoles de Maquinas de Coser y para la Confeccion   (WGAO)
AFEME ..... Asociacion de Facultades Ecuatorianas de Medicina   (WGAO)
AFEMO .... Associazione Fabbricanti Esportatori Macchine per Oreficeria [*Italy*]
AFEMS ..... European Association of Sporting Ammunition Manufacturers   (WGAO)
AFENIC .... Asociacion de Ferreteros de Nicaragua [*Association of Nicaraguan Hardware Dealers*]   (LA)
AFEO .... ASEAN Federation of Engineering Organisations [*Indonesia*]   (WGAO)
AFEO .... ASEAN [*Association of South East Asian Nations*] Federation of Engineering Organizations   (EAIO)
AFEOSz .... Altalanos Fogyasztasi Szoevetkezetek Orszagos Szoevetsege [*National Federation of Consumer Co-operatives*] [*Hungary*]   (EY)
AfEP .... Amt fuer Erfindungs- und Patentwesen [*Invention and Patent Office*]   (EG)
AFEPC ...... Australian Flour Export Promotion Committee
AFEQ........ Association Francaise pour l'Etude du Quaternaire [*French*]   (SLS)
AFERA ...... Association des Fabricants Europeens de Rubans Auto-Adhesifs [*Association of European Manufacturers of Self-Adhesive Tapes - AEMSAT*]   (EAIO)
AFERA ...... Association Francaise des Etudes et Recherches d'Afrique   (WGAO)
AFERNOD ... Association Francaise pour l'Exploitation et la Recherche des Nodules [*French*]   (MSC)
AFERO...... Asia and the Far East Regional Office [*FAO*]   (WGAO)
AFES .... Arbeitsgemeinschaft fuer Friedensforschung und Europaeische Sicherheitspolitik [*Study Group for Peace Research and European Security Policy*] [*Research center*]   (IRC)
AFES .... ASEAN Federation of Endocrine Societies [*Philippines*]   (WGAO)
AFES .... Association Francaise pour l'Etude du Sol [*French*]   (SLS)
AFES .... Australian Fellowship of Evangelical Students   (ADA)
AFESA ...... Agrupacion de Almacenistas de Ferretaria de Espana   (WGAO)
AFESD ...... Arab Fund for Economic and Social Development [*Kuwait City, Kuwait*]   (ME)
AFESGF.... Australian Fellowship of Evangelical Students, Graduates Fellowship
AFest.......... Australian Festival [*Record label*]
AFESZ....... Altalanos Fogyasztasi es Ertekesito Szovetkezetek [*General Consumer and Marketing Cooperatives*]   (HU)
AFET .... Association Francaise et Togolaise
AFETIMO ... Association Francaise pour l'Etude du Tiers Monde
AFEX........ Societe Africaine d'Expansion et d'Equipement
Aff.............. Affaire [*French*]   (FLAF)
aff.............. Affinis [*Having an Affinity with but Not Identical To*] [*Latin*]   (MAE)
AFF........... Affischeringsforetagens Forening   (WGAO)
aff............... Affluent [*Tributary*] [*French*]
AFF........... Altalanos Fuvarozasi Feltetelek [*General Transportation Manual*]   (HU)
AFF........... Anne Frank Foundation [*Netherlands*]   (EAIO)
AFF........... Anne Frank Fund [*Basel, Switzerland*]   (EAIO)
AFF........... ASEAN Football Federation   (WGAO)
AFF........... Association Francaise du Froid [*French*]   (SLS)

AFF............ Australia Farmers Federation   (WGAO)
AFF............ Australian Farmers Federation   (ADA)
AFF............ Australian Fencing Federation
AFF............ Australian Futsal Federation
AFF............ Autoridad de Fuentes Fluviales de Puerto Rico [*Puerto Rico*]
         (DSCA)
AFF............ Societe A. et F. Fourzoli
AFFA........ Actors' Feature Film Award [*Australia*]
AFFA........ Armed Forces Federation of Australia
AFFCO..... Alaska Forest Fire Council   (WGAO)
AFFCOD... Association Fracaise des Firmes de Conseillers de Direction
         (WGAO)
AFFETT.... Affettuoso [*With Expression*] [*Music*]
AFFFO...... Australian Federation of Fire Fighters Organisations
AFFGM..... Australian Federation of Friends of Galleries and Museums
AFFHC...... Australian Freedom from Hunger Campaign   (ADA)
AFFHO..... Australasian Federation of Family History Organizations   (ADA)
AFFI.......... Arab Federation for Food Industries   (EA)
AffilIWM (SA) ... Affiliate Member of the Institute of Waste Management
         (South Africa)   (AA)
AFFM........ Australian Financial Futures Market
AFFMO..... Affezionatissimo [*Very Tenderly, Pathetically*] [*Music*]   (ROG)
AFFP......... Arab Federation of Fish Producers   (WGAO)
AFFPA...... Australian Federation of Family Planning Associations   (ADA)
Affr............. Affranchi [*Paid*] [*French*] [*Business term*]
affrett........ Affrettando [*Tenderly*] [*Music*] [*Italian*] [*Music*]   (BARN)
AFFSE....... Armed Forces Food Science Establishment [*Australia*]
AFFW........ Arab Federation of Food Workers [*Trade union*]
afg.............. Afghan   (RU)
AFG........... Afghanistan [*ANSI three-letter standard code*]   (CNC)
AFG........... Ariana Afghan Airlines [*Afganistan*] [*ICAO designator*]   (FAAC)
AFG........... Association des Fabricants de Glucose de la CEE   (WGAO)
AFG........... Association Francaise de Gemmologie [*French*]   (SLS)
AFG........... Australian Factors' Guild
AFG........... Australian Fruit Growers [*An association*]
AFGE......... Photogeological Expedition   (RU)
afgek.......... Afgekondigd [*Benelux*]   (BAS)
AFGI.......... Association Fraternelle des Guineens en Cote-D'Ivoire [*Fraternal
         Association of Guineans in the Ivory Coast*]
AFGM....... Africa General Mission
AFGR........ Association Francaise de Genie Rural [*French*]   (SLS)
AFGRAD... African Graduate Fellowship Program
AFH........... Alfred Herlicq & Fils
AFH........... Australasian Film Hire   (ADA)
AFH........... Australian Federation of Haemophilia
AFH........... Australian Federation of Homeopaths
AFH........... Australian Field Hospital   (ADA)
AFH........... Australian Frontier Holidays
AFHB........ ASEAN Food Handling Bureau   (WGAO)
AFHC........ Australian Freedom from Hunger Campaign
AFHE........ Association Francaise des Historiens Economistes [*French
         Association of Economic Historians*]   (EAIO)
AFHRL...... Australian Fish Health Reference Laboratory
AFI............. Activ Foundation [*Australia*]   (EAIO)
AFI............. Aero Filipanas Ltd. [*Philippines*] [*ICAO designator*]   (FAAC)
AFI............. Agence Fonciere Industrielle [*Industrial Property Agency*]
         [*Tunisia*]   (GEA)
AFI............. Agence Francaise d'Images [*French Photo News Agency*]   (CL)
AFI............. Amplitude-Phase Measurement   (RU)
AfI............. Amt fuer Information [*Information Office*]   (EG)
AFI............. Ancient Forest International [*An association*]
AFI............. Arbeidsforskningsinstituttet [*Work Research Institute*] [*Norway*]
         (IRC)
AFI............. Armement Franco-Ivoirien
AFI............. Association des Femmes Ivoiriennes
AFI............. Association for Futures Investment   (WGAO)
AFI............. Association of Finnish Industries   (WGAO)
AFI............. Associazione dei Fonografici Italiani
AFI............. Associazione Farmaceutici dell'Industria [*Italian*]   (SLS)
AFI............. Associazione Farmacisti dell'Industria   (WGAO)
AFI............. Atlantic Financial International NV
AFI............. Australian Film Institute   (ADA)
AFI............. Australian Foundry Institute   (ADA)
AFI............. Australian Frontier Incorporated   (ADA)
AFI............. Australians against Further Immigration [*Political party*]
AFI............. Institute of Agricultural Physics   (RU)
AFI............. Institute of Astrophysics   (RU)
AFI............. Les Auxiliaires Feminines Internationales   (WGAO)
AFIA......... American Foreign Insurance Association   (EA)
AFIA......... Apparel and Fashion Industry Association of Great Britain
         (WGAO)
AFIA.......... Associate of the Federal Institute of Accountants [*Australia*]
AFIA.......... Association Francaise Interprofessionelle des Agrumes   (WGAO)
AFIAC....... Australian Film Industry Action Committee   (ADA)

AFIAS....... Association Francaise d'Intelligence Artificielle et des Systemes
         de Simulation [*French Association of Artificial Intelligence
         and Simulation Systems*]   (PDAA)
AFIC......... Andean Foreign Investment Code [*Treaty of Cartagena*]   (IMH)
AFIC......... Asian Finance/Investment Corp. [*Proposed*]   (ECON)
AFIC......... Australian Federation of Islamic Councils
AFIC......... Australian Fishing Industry Council   (ADA)
AFIC......... Australian Foundation Investment Co.
AFICAU.... Asociacion de Fomento del Intercambio Comercial Anglo-
         Uruguayo [*Montevideo, Uruguay*]   (LAA)
AFICE....... Association for International Cotton Emblem [*Brussels,
         Belgium*]   (EAIO)
AFICE....... Association Francaise des Ingenieurs et Chefs d'Entretien
         (WGAO)
AFICEP..... Association Francaise des Ingenieurs du Caoutchouc et des
         Plastiques   (WGAO)
AFICON.... Alpha Financial and Industrial Consultants [*Somalia*]
         [*Commercial firm*]
AFICS....... Association of Former International Civil Servants [*Switzerland*]
         (EAIO)
AFICTIC... Association Francaise des Ingenieurs, Chimistes, et Techniciens
         des Industries du Cuir [*French*]   (SLS)
AFID......... Agence Francaise d'Information et de Documentation [*French
         Information and Documentation Agency*]
AFID......... Australian Film Institute Distribution
AFIDA....... Asociacion de Ferias Internacionales de America [*Association of
         International Trade Fairs of America*]   (EAIO)
AFIDES..... Association Francophone Internationale des Directeurs
         d'Etablissements Scolaires [*International Association of
         French-Speaking Directors of Educational Institutions*]
         [*Anjou, PQ*]
AFIDRO.... Asociacion de Fabricantes de Productos Farmaceuticos
         [*Pharmaceutical Manufacturers Association*] [*Colorado*]
         (LA)
AFIEM...... Association Francaise pour l'Information en Economie Menagere
         (WGAO)
AFIF.......... Association Suisse des Fournisseurs de l'Industrie pour la
         Ferraille   (WGAO)
AFIGAP.... Association Francophone Internationale des Groupes
         d'Animation de la Paraplegie [*International French-
         Speaking Association of Paraplegic Therapy Groups*] [*Brie-
         Comte-Robert, France*]   (EAIO)
AFIM........ Association Francaise des Industries du Moule, Modele et
         Maquette [*French Association of Mold, Pattern and Model
         Industries*]   (EAIO)
AFIMA...... Australian Fellowship of the Israel Medical Association
AFIMAC... Association des Fabricants et Importateurs de Materiel a Air
         Comprime [*Belgium*]   (WGAO)
AFIMIN.... Association Francaise des Fabricants et Importateurs de
         Materiels et de Produitspour l'Industrie du Nettoyage
AFIN......... Alianza de Fuerzas de la Izquierda Nacional [*Alliance of the
         National Leftist Forces*] [*Bolivia*]   (LA)
AFIN......... Armed Forces Institute, Nigeria
AFIN......... Asociacion de Companias Financieras del Ecuador   (WGAO)
AFIN......... Asociacion Federada del Instituto Nacional [*Federated
         Association of the National Institute*] [*Panama*]   (LA)
AFIN......... Association Francaise des Informaticiens [*France*]
AFIN......... Australia-Wide Funeral Information [*Database*]
AFINCO.... L'Africaine Industrielle et Commerciale
AFINE....... Association Francaise pour l'Industrie Nucleaire d'Equipement
         (WGAO)
AFinLA..... Association Finlandaise de Linguistique Appliquee   (WGAO)
AFIP......... Association Francaise des Independants du Petrole   (WGAO)
AFIP......... Associazione Fotografi Italiani Professionisti   (WGAO)
AFIPMA... Associate Fellow of the Institute of Personnel Management
         (Australia)   (ADA)
AFIR......... Association Francaise des Industries de la Robinetterie   (WGAO)
AFI-RAN... Africa, India Ocean Region Air Navigation   (WGAO)
AFIRAN.... African-Indian Ocean Regional Air Navigation
AFIRD....... Association Francaise des Instituts de Recherche sur le
         Developpement [*French*]   (SLS)
AFIRE....... Australian Film Industry Research Exchange   (ADA)
AFIREC..... Association Financiere Internationale de Recherche Etude
         Cellulose   (WGAO)
AFIRO....... Association Francaise d'Informatique et de Recherche
         Operationnelle
AFIS.......... Agence Francaise d'Informations Scientifiques [*French Scientific
         Information Agency*]   (AF)
AFIS.......... Amministrazione Fiduciaria Italiana della Somalia
AFIS.......... Associazione Fabbricanti Impianti Sportivi [*Italy*]
AFIS.......... Australian Firms Information System
AFISA....... Aero Fletes Internacionales SA [*Panama*]   (PDAA)
AFIT.......... Australian Families Income Transfer [*Project*]
AFIT.......... Autofenntarto Ipari Troszt [*Industrial Trust for Auto
         Maintenance*]   (HU)

AFITAE..... Association Francaise des Ingenieurs et Techniciens de l'Aeronautique et de l'Espace [*French*]
AFIUM...... Associazione Fabbricanti Italiani di Utinsileria Meccanica (WGAO)
AFJ .... Academics for Justice [*Australia*]
AFJ .... Amt fuer Jugendfragen [*Office for Youth Affairs*] (EG)
AFJA .... Association Francaise des Journalistes Agricoles [*French*]
AFJA .... Australian Fresh Juice Association
AFJCMA... Australian Fresh Juice and Cordial Manufacturers' Association
AFJD .... Association Francaise des Juristes Democrates [*French Association of Democratic Lawyers*] (WER)
AFJET...... Association Francaise de Journalistes et Ecrivains du Tourisme (WGAO)
AFK .... Adenoidal-Pharyngeal-Conjunctival [*Virus*] (RU)
AFK .... Administration and Finance Commission (RU)
afk .... Afkorting [*Abbreviation*] [*Afrikaans*]
AFK .... Africa Air Links [*Sierra Leone*] [*ICAO designator*] (FAAC)
AfK............ Amt fuer Kirchenfragen [*Office for Church Affairs*] (EG)
AfK............ Arbeitgemeinschaft fuer Kommunikationsforschung [*Study Group for Communications Research*] [*Germany*] (PDAA)
AFK .... Arbeitsgemeinschaft fur Friedens-und Konfliktforschung (WGAO)
AFK .... Association des Femmes Khmeres [*Cambodian Women's Association*] (CL)
AFK .... Nitrogen-Phosphorus Combine (BU)
AFK .... Nitrogen-Phosphorus-Potassium Fertilizer (RU)
AFKh .... Amplitude-Phase Characteristic (RU)
AFKN .... American Forces Korea Network
AFL........... Aeroflot - Russian International Airlines [*Russian Federation*] [*ICAO designator*] (FAAC)
afl .... Afleiding [*Derivation*] [*Afrikaans*]
afl .... Aflevering [*Issue, Part*] [*Netherlands*]
afl .... Aflewering [*Delivery*] [*Afrikaans*]
AFL........... Armed Forces of Liberia (AF)
Afl .... Artillerieflieger [*Artillery Spotting Pilot*] [*German*]
AFL........... Association des Forestiers Luxembourgeois [*Association of Foresters in Luxembourg*] (EAIO)
AFL........... Association Francaise Laitiere (WGAO)
AFL........... Association Francaise pour la Lecture (WGAO)
AFL........... Australasian Federation League (ADA)
AFL........... Australasian Federation of Labour (ADA)
AFL........... Australian Fertilizers Limited (ADA)
AFL........... Australian Festival of Life
AFL........... Australian Football League
AFL........... Australian Freedom League
AFL........... Luftfahrtabteilung [*Air Force*] [*German*]
Afla .... Armeefliegerabteilung [*Army Air Force*] [*German*]
AFLA........ Asian Federation of Library Associations [*Japan*]
AFLA........ Australian Film Laboratories Association (ADA)
AFLACA ... Australian Federation of Lapidary and Allied Crafts Associations (ADA)
AFLC........ Australian Federal Libraries Committee
AFLC........ Australian Federal Libraries Council (ADA)
AFL-CIO... American Federation of Labor and Congress of Industrial Organizations (WGAO)
AFLE........ Association of French Language Epidemiologists (EAIO)
aflev........... Aflevering [*Issue, Part*] [*Netherlands*]
AFLI .... Arab Federation for Libraries and Information [*Tunisia*] (WGAO)
AFLICO .... OAU [*Organization of African Unity*] Coordinating Committee for the Liberation o f Africa [*Tanzania*] (EAIO)
AFLL .... Association of French-Language Leprologists [*Paris, France*] (EAIO)
AFLM....... Association Francaise De Lutte Contre La Mucoviscidose [*French Cystic Fibrosis Association*]
AFLNE...... Associiation Francaise pour l'Industrie Nucleaire d'Equipment [*French Association for the Nuclear Equipment Industry*] (PDAA)
AFLNS ..... Anti-Fascist League of People's Liberation (RU)
AFLO........ Associacao do Fomento a Lavoura de Oleaginosas [*Brazil*] (DSCA)
AFM .... Affretair [*Zimbabwe*] [*ICAO designator*] (FAAC)
AFM .... Allami Foldmeres [*State Geodesy Office*] (HU)
AFM .... Antifasisticna Mladina [*Anti-Fascist Youth*] (YU)
AFM .... Arbeitsgruppe fuer Menschenrechte [*Germany*]
AFM .... Asociacion Espanola de Fabricantes de Maquinas-Herramienta (WGAO)
AFM .... Association Africaine de Management
AFM .... Association Francaise contre les Myopathies (WGAO)
AFM .... Association Francaise de Musicotherapie [*France*] (EAIO)
AFM .... Aussenhandelsverband fuer Mineralol (WGAO)
AFM .... Australian Family Movement
AFM .... Australian Funds Management
AFma .... Afectisima [*Very Affectionate*] [*Feminine*] [*Spanish*]
AFMA .... Animal Feed Manufacturers' Association [*South Africa*] (AA)

AFMA .... Association of Food Marketing Agencies in Asia and the Pacific (WGAO)
AFMA .... Australian Film Making Association
AFMA .... Australian Financial Markets Association
AFMA .... Australian Fisheries Management Authority
AFMA .... Australian Folk Music Associates
AFMA .... Australian Foodservice Manufacturers' Association
AFMBE..... Australian Federation for Medical and Biological Engineering (ADA)
AFMC....... Asian Fluid Mechanics Committee [*Japan*] (EAIO)
AFMC....... Australian Fertilizer Manufacturers' Committee
AFME....... Agence Francaise pour la Maitrise de l'Energie [*French organization for alternative energy and conservation*] [*Nuclear energy*]
AFMED.... Allied Forces Mediterranean [*NATO*]
AFMLTA .. Australian Federation of Modern Language Teachers' Associations (ADA)
AFMM ..... United Kingdom Association of Fish Meal Manufactures (WGAO)
afmo .... Afectisimo [*Very Affectionate*] [*Spanish*]
AFMO ...... Association Francaise de Constructeurs de Machines-Outils (WGAO)
AFMR....... Asian Federation for Persons with Mental Handicap [*Singapore*] (WGAO)
AFMR....... Asian Federation for the Mentally Retarded [*Singapore*] (EAIO)
AFMR....... Association pour la Formation en Milieu Rural (WGAO)
AFMS .... Association of Finnish Music Schools (EAIO)
AFMS .... Australian Farm Management Society (ADA)
AFMVM... Australasian Federation of Medical and Veterinary Mycology (WGAO)
AFMW ..... Australian Federation of Medical Women (ADA)
AFN .... Aerosolforbundet Norge (WGAO)
AFN .... African International Airlines [*Lesotho*] [*ICAO designator*] (FAAC)
AFN .... Association des Femmes du Niger [*Nigerien Women's Association*] [*Niger*] (AF)
AFN .... Association of Free Newspapers (EAIO)
AFN .... Automatische Frequenznachstimmung [*German*] (ADPT)
AFNA .... Accordion Federation of North America (WGAO)
AFNE .... Allied Forces Northern Europe [*NATO*]
AFNE .... Astilleros y Fabricas Navales del Estado [*State Shipyards and Naval Factories*] [*Argentina*] (LA)
AFNIL....... Agence Francophone pour la Numerotation Internationale du Livre [*Agency for International Standard Book Numbering*] [*France*] (PDAA)
AFNMS..... Asian Federation of National Maintenance Societies (WGAO)
AFNON..... Allied Forces North Norway [*NATO*] (MCD)
AFNOR ..... Association Francaise de Normalisation [*French Association for Standardization*] [*Database producer*] (IID)
AFNOR ..... Association Francaise de Normalisation (WGAO)
AFNORTH ... Allied Forces Northern Europe [*NATO*]
AFNRJ ...... Arhiv Federativna Narodna Republika Jugoslavija [*Archives of Yugoslavia*] (YU)
AFNSW..... Arthritis Foundation of New South Wales [*Australia*]
AFNW ...... Australian Forest Nutrition Workshop
AFO .... Administration and Finance Department (RU)
AFO .... Aero Empresa Mexicana SA [*Mexico*] [*ICAO designator*] (FAAC)
afo .... Afeicoado [*Affectionate*] [*Portuguese*]
afo .... Afetuoso [*Portuguese*]
AFO .... Arab Family Organisation (WGAO)
AFO .... Arbeitsfolge [*Consequence of Work*] [*German*] (ADPT)
AFO .... Association of French Orientalists (EAIO)
AFO .... Australian Film Office
AFOA .... Aero-Feu Ouest Afrique (WGAO)
AFOA .... Antiques Fairs Organisers Association (WGAO)
AFOA .... Societe Aero-Feu Ouest Afrique
AFOCA...... Association Nationale pour la Formation Professionnelle suivant les Techniques de l'Industrie du Caoutchouc (WGAO)
AFOCEL.... Association Forets-Cellulose (EAIO)
AFOD........ Arab Federation for the Organs of the Deaf [*Damascus, Syria*] (EAIO)
AFODEP... Association pour la Formation et le Developpement en Polynesie [*Planning and Development Association of Polynesia*] (GEA)
AFODI...... Atelier de Freinage de la Cote-d'Ivoire (WGAO)
AFOEV...... Association Francaise des Observateurs d'Etoiles Variables [*French Association of Variable Star Observers*] (EAIO)
AFOF........ Australian Forces Overseas Fund (ADA)
AFOFSAG ... Australian Fellowship of Former Scouts and Guides
AfoG........... Akademie fuer Oeffentliches Gesundheitswesen in Duesseldorf [*Academy for Public Health in Dusseldorf*] (SLS)
AFOG .... Asian Federation of Obstetrics and Gynaecology (PDAA)
AFOL......... Australian Festival of Light (ADA)
AFOMJ .... Association of Fats and Oil Manufacturers of Japan (WGAO)
AFON .... Association for One Nigeria

AFOPE ...... Association Francaise d'Organisateurs Permanents dans les Enterprises   (WGAO)

AFOR .... Asvanyolajforgalmi Vallalat [*Mineral Oils Commercial Enterprise*]   (HU)

AFORCOM ... Societe Africaine de Forages et de Constructions Mecaniques   (WGAO)

AFORD ..... Alliance for Democracy [*Malawi*] [*Political party*]   (ECON)

AFOREP ... Association pour la Formation et la Recherche Psycho-Sociologiques   (WGAO)

AFORT ...... Asvanyolajforgalmi Vallalat [*Mineral Oils Commercial Enterprise*]   (HU)

AFOS .... Arab Federation of Shipping [*Iraq*]   (WGAO)

AFOSZ ...... Altalanos Fogyasztasi, Termelo es Ertekesito Szovetkezet [*General Consumers' and Producers' Marketing Cooperative Enterprise*]   (HU)

AFP .... Administradoras de Fondos de Pensione [*Chile*]   (ECON)

AFP .... Adminstradoras de Fondos Previsionales [*Chile*]

AFP .... Adventure Foundation of Pakistan   (EAIO)

AFP .... Agence France-Presse [*French Press Agency*]   (IID)

AFP .... Agency France Press   (OLYM)

AFP .... Alternative Future Project [*An association*] [*Norway*]   (EAIO)

AfP .... Amt fuer Presse [*Press Office*]   (EG)

AFP .... Armed Forces of the Philippines

AFP .... Asociacao Fiscal Portuguesa [*Portuguese Fiscal Association*]   (EAIO)

AFP .... Asociacion de Fabricantes de Papel [*Uruguay*]   (DSCA)

AFP .... Asociacion de Funcionarios Portuarios [*Association of Port Officials*] [*Uruguay*]   (LA)

AFP .... Asociacion Forestal del Peru [*Peru*]   (DSCA)

AFP .... Association Francaise de Psychiatrie   (WGAO)

AFP .... Associazione Fotoreporters Professionisti   (WGAO)

AFP .... Australian Federal Police [*National Union Catalogue of Australia symbol*]

AFP .... Portugese Air Force [*ICAO designator*]   (FAAC)

AFPA .... Advertising Film Producers Association   (WGAO)

AFPA .... Agence Nationale pour la Formation Professionelle des Adultes   (WGAO)

AFPA .... Association de Formation et Perfectionnement Agricole   (WGAO)

AFPA .... Association Francaise de la Presse de l'Automobile   (WGAO)

AFPA .... Association pour la Formation Professionnelle des Adultes [*French*]

AFPA .... Australian Film Producers' Association

AFPA .... Australian Fire Protection Association   (WGAO)

AFPBA ...... Australian Federation of Pipe Band Associations

AFPC .... Association Francaise pour la Construction [*France*]   (EAIO)

AFPE .... Association Francaise pour la Protection des Eaux [*French*]   (SLS)

AFPEP .... Association Francaise des Producteurs Exportateurs de Pommes   (WGAO)

AFPESP .... Associacao dos Funcionarios Publicos do Estado de Sao Paulo [*Sao Paulo State Civil Servants Association*] [*Brazil*]   (LA)

AFPF .... African Food and Peace Foundation [*Uganda*]   (WGAO)

AFPF .... Association Francaise pour la Production Fourragere [*France*]   (DSCA)

AFPFL .... Anti-Fascist People's Freedom League [*Myanmar*]   (FEA)

AFPIA .... Association pour la Formation Professionnelle dans les Industries de l'Ameublement [*French*]   (SLS)

AFPIC .... Association Nationale pour la Formation et la Promotion Professionnelle dans l'Industrie et le Commerce de la Chaussure et des Cuirs et Peaux [*French*]   (SLS)

AFPIC .... Association pour la Formation Professionnelle dans les Industries Cerealieres [*French*]   (SLS)

AFPL .... Alianza Federal des Pueblos Libres [*An association*]   (NTCM)

AFPMCW ... Arab Federation of Petroleum Mines and Chemical Workers   (WGAO)

AFPMH .... ASEAN Federation for Psychiatric and Mental Health   (WGAO)

AFPO .... Australian Forces Post Office   (ADA)

AFPP .... Association Francaise de Producteurs de Plantes a Proteines Legumineuses a Grosses Graines   (WGAO)

AFPPCB .... Association des Fabricants de Pates, Papiers et Cartons de Belgique [*Belgium*]   (EAIO)

AFPPI .... Association Francaise pour la Protection de la Propriete Industrielle [*France*]   (FLAF)

AFPPT .... Association pour la Formation et le Perfectionnement des Planteurs de Tabac   (WGAO)

AFPSP ...... Australian Foundation for the Peoples of the South Pacific

AFPTC .... Agricultural Farm Produce Trade Corporation [*Myanmar*]   (DS)

AfPU .... African Postal Union   (AF)

AFPU .... Association Francaise pour la Paix Universelle [*French*]   (SLS)

AFPU .... Australian Federation of Police Unions and Associations   (ADA)

AFR .... Afore [*Papua New Guinea*] [*Airport symbol*]   (OAG)

afr .... African   (BU)

Afr .... Afrikaner [*Afrikaans*]

afr .... Afrikkalainen [*African*] [*Finland*]

AFR .... Air France [*ICAO designator*]   (FAAC)

A-FR .... Algerian-Franc   (ABBR)

AfR .... Amt fuer Reparationen [*Reparations Office*]   (EG)

AFR .... Amtsradsforeningen i Danmark [*Denmark*]   (EAIO)

AFR .... Arterial Flow Rate

AFR .... Asociatia Filatelistilor [*Romania*]   (WGAO)

AFR .... Association for a Free Russia   (WGAO)

AFR .... Auktoriserade Fastighetsmaklares Riksforbund   (WGAO)

AFR .... Australian Family Reunion   (ADA)

AFR .... Australians for Reconciliation [*An association*]

AFR .... Distribution Function Analyzer, Amplitude Distribution Meter   (RU)

AFRA .... Associatin Francaise de Regulation et d'Automatisme   (WGAO)

AFRA .... Association for Rural Advancement [*South Africa*]   (EAIO)

AFRA .... Association Francaise de Regulation et d'Automatisme [*French Association of Regulation & Automatization*] [*French*]   (ADPT)

AFRA .... Average Freight Rate Assessment   (OMWE)

AFRAA ...... African Airlines Association [*Kenya*]   (AF)

AFRABI ... Societe de Presse Afrique-Abidjan

AFRACA ... African Regional Agricultural Credit Association   (EAIO)

AFRAL ...... Societe Europeenne pour l'Etude de l'Industrie de l'Aluminium en Afrique

AFRAN ...... Association Francaise pour la Recherche de l'Alimentation Normale   (WGAO)

AFRANE ... Amitie Franco-Afghane [*French Afghan Friendship Committee*]

AFRASEC ... Afro-Asian Organization for Economic Cooperation

AFRAT ...... Association pour la Formation des Ruraux aux Activites du Tourisme   (WGAO)

AFRAZES ... Afro-Asian Organization for Economic Cooperation   (RU)

AFRC .... Agriculture and Food Research Council   (WGAO)

AFRC .... Armed Forces Revolutionary Council [*Ghana*]   (PPW)

AFRC .... Armed Forces Ruling Council [*Nigeria*]

AFRDI .... Australian Furniture Research and Development Institute

AFRE .... Australian Family Reformation [*Project*]

AFREA ...... Association Francaise pour les Relations Economiques avec l'Allemagne [*France*]   (FLAF)

AFREC ...... Association Francaise pour les Recherches et les Etudes Camerounaises   (WGAO)

AFREM ..... Association Francaise de Recherches d'Essais sur les Materiaux et les Constructions [*French*]   (SLS)

AFREP ...... Association Francaise des Relations Publiques   (WGAO)

AFRESCO ... Association Francaise de Recherches et Etudes Statistiques Commerciales [*France*]   (FLAF)

AFREXIMBANK ... African Export Import Bank

AFRIC .... Agence Francaise de Representation d'Industries au Cameroun

AFRIC .... Societe Africaine Francaise de Representations Industrielles et Commerciales

AFRICA .... Association pour la Formation, la Recherche et l'Information sur le Centre de l'Afrique   (WGAO)

AFRICADIS ... Societe Africaine de Distribution

AFRICAP ... Societe Africaine de Diffusion d'Appareils Electriques

AFRICAPLAST ... Industrie Africaine des Plastiques

AFRICARE ... Societe Africaine de Reassurance [*African Reinsurance Company*]   (AF)

AFRICAUTO ... Compagnie Africaine pour l'Automobile

AFRICOL ... Africa Representacoes Industria e Comercio Limitada

AFRIDEX ... Societe Africaine d'Importation, de Distribution, et d'Exportation

AFRIFOS .. Societe Africaine du Phosphore

AFRIGA .... Armement Frigorfique Gabonais   (WGAO)

AFRIGO .... Africaine des Frigoriferes

AFRIGRAM ... Societe Africaine des Grandes Marques

AFRILAIT ... Compagnie Africaine du Lait

AFRIMA ... Afrique Materiaux

AFRIMECA ... Societe Africaine de Mecanographie

AFRIMEX ... Societe Africaine pour l'Importation et l'Exportation

AFRIMEX-CI ... Africaine Import-Export - Cote-D'Ivoire

AFRIPLAST ... Societe Africaine de Plastique

AFRISEN ... Armement Frigorifigue Senegalais   (WGAO)

AFRISEN ... Armement Frigorifique Senegalais

AFRL .... Australian Food Research Laboratories   (DSCA)

AFRO .... African Regional Organization

AFRO .... African Regional Organization of ICFTU   (WGAO)

AFRO .... Association des Fondeurs de Fromages [*Belgium*]   (WGAO)

AFRO .... Regional Office of Africa   (WGAO)

AFRom .... American Friends of Romania   (EA)

AFROSAI ... African Organization of Supreme Audit Institutions [*Lome, Togo*]   (EAIO)

AFROX ...... African Oxygen Company [*South Africa*]

AFRTLA ... Australian Federation of Right to Life Associations

AFRTS ...... American Forces Radio and Television Service [*Greenland*]   (EY)

AFS .... Aerial Photographic Service   (RU)

AFS .... Afsender [*Sender*] [*Afrikaans*]

afs .... Afsender [*Sender*] [*Denmark*]   (GPO)

AFS .... Agriculture and Forestry Secretariat

AFS............ Anne Frank Stichting [*Anne Frank Foundation*] [*Netherlands*] (EAIO)
AFS............ Antenna Feed System   (RU)
AFS............ Association for Food Self-Sufficiency   (EAIO)
AFS............ Association for Stammerers   (WGAO)
AFS............ Association of Football Statisticians   (WGAO)
AFS............ Association of Foremen and Supervisors [*Australia*]
AFS............ Australian Fabian Society
AFS............ Australian Finance and Securities Ltd.   (ADA)
AFS............ Australian Fisheries Service
AFS............ Australian Foremen's Society   (ADA)
AFS............ Australian Forestry School   (ADA)
AFS............ Australian Friesian Sahiwal [*Cattle terminology*]
AFS............ Automated Financial Services Proprietary Ltd. [*Australia*]
AFS............ Autonomous Photoregistering Recorder [*Oceanography*]   (RU)
AFS............ Auxiliary Fire Service   (WGAO)
AFS............ Azorubine-Binding Capacity   (RU)
AFS............ Combat Support Ship [*Military*]
AFS............ Water Purification Truck   (RU)
AFSA........ Arthritis Foundation of South Australia
AFSA........ Aspersoras y Fumigadoras SA [*Mexico*]   (DSCA)
AFSA........ Association des Fabricants Suisses d'Accumulateurs   (WGAO)
AFSA........ Australian Foremen Stevedores' Association   (ADA)
AFSA........ Australian Friendly Societies' Association
AFSA........ Australian National Film and Sound Archive [*National Union Catalogue of Australia symbol*]
AFSAA...... African Studies Association of Australia
AFSAAP.... African Studies Association of Australia and the Pacific
AFSAD...... Ankara Fotograf Sanatcilari Dernegi [*Ankara Photographers Society*]   (TU)
AFSAICHE ... Affiliate Member of the South African Institution of Chemical Engineers   (AA)
AFSAT ...... Systeme Africain de Telecommunications Satellite   (WGAO)
AFSAU...... Association of Faculties of Science in African Universities [*Kenya*]   (WGAO)
AFSB .... Association of Friends of Schloss Blutenburg [*Germany*]   (EAIO)
AFSB .... Australian Flying Saucer Bureau [*Defunct*]
AFSBO ...... Association des Fabricants Suisses de Bijouterie et d'Orfevreie   (WGAO)
AFSCE...... Association of Former Students of the College of Europe   (EAIO)
afschr .... Afschrift [*Copy*] [*Publishing*] [*Netherlands*]
AFSE .... Allied Forces Southern Europe [*NATO*]   (NATG)
AFSE .... Association Francaise de Science Economique [*French*]   (SLS)
AFSEL....... Afrika Selatan [*South Africa*]   (IN)
AFSG .... Anglo-French Study Group [*Group formed to consider various proposals for a tunnel beneath the English Channel*]
AFSI .... Australian Financial System Inquiry
AFSM........ Australian Fire Service Medal
AFSMAS... Association Francophone de Spectrometrie de Masse de Solides [*French-Speaking Association of Solids Mass Spectrometry*] (EAIO)
AFSMI ...... Association of Field Service Managers International   (WGAO)
AFSO........ Association of Finnish Symphony Orchestras   (EAIO)
AFSO........ Austrian Federal Sports Organization   (EAIO)
AFSOA....... Association Francaise pour la Sauvegarde de l'Orgue Ancien   (WGAO)
AFSONOR ... Allied Forces South Norway [*NATO*]   (MCD)
AFSOUTH ... Allied Forces Southern Europe [*NATO*]
AFSOUTHCOM ... Air Forces Southern Europe Command [*NATO*]
AFSP .... Association Francaise de Science Politique [*French*]   (SLS)
AFSP .... Australian Foundation for the Peoples of the South Pacific
AFSR .... Air Force Staff Requirement
AFSRS ...... Australian Flying Saucer Research Society   (ADA)
AFST .... Association of Food Scientists and Technologists [*India*]   (WGAO)
AFT............ Algemeen Fiscaal Tijdschrift [*Benelux*]   (BAS)
AFT............ Arthritis Foundation of Tasmania [*Australia*]
AFT............ Association for Family Therapy   (WGAO)
AFT............ Australian Fixed Trusts   (ADA)
AFT............ Australian Folk Trust   (ADA)
AFTA........ Arab Fund for Technical Assistance to Arab and African Countries
AFTA........ ASEAN [*Association of South East Asian Nations*] Free Trade Area   (ECON)
AFTA........ Association for Torah Advancement
AFTA........ Association of Finnish Travel Agents   (WGAO)
AFTA........ Association of French Teachers in Africa [*See also AFPA*] [*Khartoum, Sudan*]   (EAIO)
AFTA........ Atlantic Free Trade Area   (WGAO)
AFTA........ Australian Federation of Travel Agents   (BARN)
AFTA........ Australian Forum on Textile Arts
AFTAA...... Association Francaise des Techniciens de l'Alimentation Animale   (WGAO)
AFTAAAC ... Arab Fund for Technical Assistance to African and Arab Countries [*League of Arab States*] [*Tunisia*]   (MENA)

AFTAM..... Association Francaise pour l'Accueil des Travailleurs Africains et Malgaches [*French Association for the Reception of African and Malagasy Workers*]   (AF)
AFTAM..... Association pour la Formation Technique de Base des Africains et Malgaches   (WGAO)
AFTB........ Association for the Blind [*Australia*]
AFTBQ...... Association for the Blind, Queensland [*Australia*]
AFTBWA .. Association for the Blind of Western Australia
AFTC........ Assistance Forestiere, Technique, et Commerciale
AFTCC ...... Association of Film and Television in the Celtic Countries (WGAO)
AFTE........ Arab Federation for Technical Education [*Baghdad, Iraq*] (EAIO)
AFTEC ...... Association of Former Trainees of the European Communities (WGAO)
AFTERM .. Association Francaise de Terminologie   (WGAO)
AFTEX ..... Australia France Technical Exchange Program
AFTEX ..... Australia-France Technological Exchange Scheme
AFTEXTIL ... Arab Federation for Textile Industries [*Egypt*]
AFTH .... Allami Foldmeresi es Terkepeszeti Hivatal [*State Bureau of Geodetics and Cartography*]   (HU)
AFTIM ...... Association Francaise des Techniciens et Ingenieurs de Securite et des Medecins du Travail   (WGAO)
AFT-KIO... American Federation of Labor - Congress of Industrial Organizations [*AFL-CIO*]   (BU)
AFT-KPP .. American Federation of Labor - Congress of Industrial Organizations [*AFL-CIO*]   (RU)
AFTLA ...... Australian Free Trade and Liberal Association   (ADA)
AFTMA...... Australian Federation of Timber Merchants' Associations
afto .... Afecto [*Spanish*]
AFTO .... Association of Flight Training Officers   (WGAO)
AFTO .... Australian Foreign Trade Office
AFTO .... Islamic Agriculture and Food Technology Organization (WGAO)
AFTP........ Association Francaise des Techniciens du Petrole
AFTPV ...... Association Francaise des Tecniciens des Peintures, Vernis, Encres d'Imprimeria, Colles et Adhesifs [*French*]   (SLS)
AFTRI ...... Association Francaise des Transporteurs Routiers Internationaux (WGAO)
AFTRI ...... Association Francaise des Transports Routiers Internationaux [*France*]   (FLAF)
AFTRS ...... Australian Film, Television, and Radio School
AFTS .... Aeronautical Fixed Telecommunications Service   (WGAO)
AFTS .... Australian Film and Television School   (ADA)
AFTS .... Australian Flying Training School
AFTUCOT ... Societe Auxiliaire Franco-Tunisienne de Cooperation Touristique
AFTVS ...... Australian Film and Television School   (ADA)
AFTW........ Arab Federation of Transport Workers [*Libya*]   (WGAO)
AFTWUA ... Amalgamated Footwear and Textile Workers' Union of Australia
AFU .... Administration and Finance Office   (RU)
AFU .... Aerial Camera Mount   (RU)
AFU .... African Farmers' Union
AFU .... Afro Unity Airways [*Benin*] [*ICAO designator*]   (FAAC)
AFU .... Air Fighter Unit [*Tanzania*]   (AF)
AFU .... Amplitude-Phase Indicator   (RU)
AFU .... Antenna Feed   (RU)
AFU .... Arkivet for UFO-Forskning [*Archives for UFO Research*] [*Sweden*]   (EAIO)
AFU .... Association Fonciere Urbaine   (WGAO)
AFUC .... Association des Femmes Universitaires Catholiques   (WGAO)
AFUCA...... Asian Federation of Unesco Clubs and Associations   (WGAO)
AFUDE...... Asociacion de Familiares de Uruguayos Desaparecidos [*France*]
AFULE...... Australian Federated Union of Locomotive Enginemen   (ADA)
AFUMS.... Association for the Uganda Martyrs Shrines
AFUTT...... Association Francaise des Utilisateurs du Telephone et des Telecommunications [*French consumer lobby*]
AFUW ...... Australian Federation of University Women   (ADA)
AFV .... Administracion Federal de la Vivienda [*Federal Housing Administration*] [*Buenos Aires*] [*Argentina*]   (LAA)
AFV .... Archiv fuer Voelkerkunde
AFV .... Arthritis Foundation of Victoria [*Australia*]
AFV .... Australian Forces in Vietnam   (ADA)
AFV .... Australian Force, Vietnam [*Military*]
AFVN .... Vereniging van Antifascistische Oud Verzets-Strijders Nederland [*Association of Anti-Fascist Veterans in the Netherlands*] (EAIO)
AFVP........ Association Francaise des Volontaires du Progres [*French Association of Volunteers for Progress*]   (AF)
AFVPA ...... Advertising Film and Videotape Producers Association (WGAO)
AFW .... Akademie fuer Fuehrungskraefte der Wirtschaft eV [*Academy for Powerful Management of Affairs*]
AfW .... Akademie fuer Welthandel [*Academy of World Trade*]
AfW .... Arbeitskreis fuer Wehrforschung [*Association for Weapons Research*]   (SLS)
AFWA .... Arthritis Foundation of Western Australia

AFWA ...... Australian Federation for the Welfare of Animals
AFWE .... Air Forces, Western Europe [*NATO*] (NATG)
AFWFA ..... Australian Fresh Water Fishermen's Assembly
AFWIZO ... Australian Federation of the Women's International Zionist Organization
AFWV .... Association of Finnish War Veterans (EAIO)
AFZ .... Antifasisticki Front Zena [*Women's Anti-Fascist Front*] (YU)
AFZ .... Association Francaise de Zootechnie (WGAO)
AFZ .... Australian Fishing Zone
AFZA .... Australian Fishing Zone Authority
AFZC .... Australian Fishing Zone Committee
AFZh .... Women's Anti-Fascist Front (BU)
AFZJ .... Antifasisticki Front na Zenite od Jugoslavija [*Women's Anti-Fascist Front of Yugoslavia*] (YU)
AfZKW ...... Amt fuer Zoll und Kontrolle des Warenverkehrs [*Office for Customs and Control of Commodity Shipments*] (EG)
AFZM .... Antifasisticki Front na Zenite od Makedonija [*Women's Anti-Fascist Front of Macedonia*] (YU)
AG .... Action Group [*United National Independence Party Alliance of Nigeria*] [*Political party*]
AG .... Actuarieel Genootschap [*Netherlands*] (SLS)
AG .... Adjudant-Generaal [*Adjutant-General*] [*Afrikaans*]
AG .... Administration Generale [*Benelux*] (BAS)
AG .... Administrator General [*Namibia*] (AF)
AG .... Advocaat Generaal [*Benelux*] (BAS)
ag .... Agent (RU)
AG .... Agentura [*Agency*] (YU)
AG .... Agorot [*Monetary unit*] [*Israel*]
ag .... Agosto [*August*] [*Portuguese*]
ag .... Agosto [*August*] [*Spanish*]
Ag .... Agosto [*August*] [*Italian*]
Ag .... Agregacao [*Academic degree*] [*Portuguese*]
AG .... Agrigento [*Car registration plates*] [*Italian*]
AG .... Air Group (RU)
AG .... Akademicke Gymnasium [*Secondary School (with emphasis on the humanities)*] (CZ)
AG .... Aktiengesellschaft [*Corporation*] [*German*]
A/G .... Albumin-Globulin Ratio (RU)
AG .... Alcak Gerilim [*Low Tension*] (TU)
AG .... Allami Gazdasag [*State Farm*] (HU)
AG .... Amtsgericht [*Inferior Court*] [*German*]
AG .... Anatomische Gesellschaft [*Anatomical Society*] [*Germany*] (EAIO)
A-G .... Anders Gaan Leven-Geweldloos, Rechtvaardig, Open Ecologisch Netwerk [*Belgium*] [*Political party*] (ECED)
AG .... Anhydride (RU)
Ag .... Antigen (RU)
AG .... Antigua-Barbuda [*ANSI two-letter standard code*] (CNC)
AG .... Anyaggazdalkodas [*Materiel Management Department*] (HU)
AG .... Arbeitsgericht [*Labor Court*] [*German*]
AG .... Army Group (RU)
AG .... Artillery Group (RU)
AG .... Artillery Gyrocompass (RU)
AG .... Assemblee Generale
AG .... Assemblies of God in Australia
AG .... Assicurazioni Generali [*General Assurance*] [*Commercial firm*] [*Italy*]
AG .... Astronomische Gesellschaft eV [*Astronomical Society*] (SLS)
AG .... Atomgewicht [*Atomic Weight*] [*German*]
aG .... Auf Gegenseitigkeit [*Mutual*] [*German*]
ag .... Auf Grund [*By Virtue Of, On the Basis Of*] [*German*] (WEN)
AG .... Aufklaerungsgruppe [*Air Forces Reconnaissance Unit*] [*German military - World War II*]
AG .... Australian Gypsum Ltd.
AG .... Avant-Garde [*Vanguard*] [*French*] (MTD)
AG .... Aviation Personnel Settlement (RU)
AG .... Aydinlik Grubu [*Enlightenment Group*] [*Leftist students*] (TU)
AG .... Etablissements Andre Gallais
AG .... Gyro Horizon (RU)
AG .... Intelligence through Secret Agents (RU)
Ag .... Prata [*Silver*] [*Chemical element*] [*Portuguese*]
AGA .... Administracao Geral do Acucar e do Alcool [*Portugal*] (EY)
AGA .... Aeronaves del Centro [*Venezuela*] [*ICAO designator*] (FAAC)
AGA .... Agadir [*Morocco*] [*Airport symbol*] (OAG)
AGA .... Agence Gabonaise d'Assurances
AGA .... Agricola Ganadera Antelana (WGAO)
AGA .... Agricola Ganadera Antelana, SA [*Spain*] (DSCA)
AGA .... Air Group of an Army (RU)
AGA .... Architectural Granite Association (WGAO)
AGA .... Art Galleries Association (WGAO)
AGA .... Art Galleries Association of Australia (ADA)
AGA .... Artists' Guild of Australia
AGA .... Asociacion General de Agricultores [*General Association of Farmers*] [*Cuba*] (LA)
AGA .... Asociacion Geologica Argentina [*Argentina*] (DSCA)

AGA .... Asociacion Guatemalteca de Agricultores [*Guatemalan Agriculturalists' Association*]
AGA .... Associacao Gaucha de Apicultores [*Brazil*] (DSCA)
AGA .... Association des Entreprises de Gros en Alimentation Generale [*Belgium*] (WGAO)
AGA .... Association Generale Automobile [*French*] (MTD)
AGA .... Association of Arab Geologists [*ICSU*]
AGA .... Association of German Archivists (EAIO)
AGA .... Australian Garlic Association
AGA .... Australian Garrison Artillery (ADA)
AGA .... Australian Gas Association (ADA)
AGA .... Australian Gay Archives
AGA .... Australian Greek Awards
AGA .... Austrian Golf Association (EAIO)
AGAA .... Art Galleries Association of Australia
AGAAC ..... Australian Government Advertising Advisory Council (ADA)
AGAB .... Schweizerische Arbeitsgemeinschaft fuer Akademische Berufs- und Studienberatung [*Swiss Association for Academic Profession and Study Advice*] (SLS)
Agac-Is .... Turkiye Agac Sanayii Iscileri Birligi [*Turkish Wood Workers' Union*] (TU)
AGACOSTA ... Asociacion Ganadera de la Costa [*Barranquilla*] (COL)
AGAD .... Archiwum Glowne Akt Dawnych [*Main Archives of Old Records*] (POL)
AGADECO ... Asociacion de Ganaderos del Distrito Colon [*Venezuela*] (DSCA)
AGADEMA ... Ganaderos de Machiques [*Venezuela*] (DSCA)
AGADU ..... Asociacion General de Autores del Uruguay [*General Association of Uruguayan Authors*] (LA)
AGAG .... Asociacion Ganaderos del Guayabo [*Venezuela*] (DSCA)
AGAL .... Armazens Gerais Albertina Ltd [*Brazil*] (DSCA)
AGAL .... Australian Government Analytical Laboratory (ARC)
AGALEV ..... Anders Gaan Leven [*Live Differently*] [*Belgium*] [*Political party*] (PPW)
AGANAPA ... Asociacion de Ganaderos y Agricultores de la Panamericana [*Venezuela*] (DSCA)
AGANI ...... Asociacion de Ganaderos de Nisibon [*Association of Nisibon Cattlemen*] [*Dominican Republic*] (LA)
AGAO .... Asociacion de Ganaderos y Agricultores de Olancho [*Olancho Farmers and Cattlemen's Association*] [*Honduras*] (LA)
AGAPECA ... Asociacion Ganaderos de Perija [*Venezuela*] (DSCA)
AGARD ..... Advisory Group for Aerospace Research and Development [*NATO*]
AGARS ..... Association of German Agricultural Research Stations (EAIO)
AGAS .... Arbeitsgemeinschaft fuer Angewandte Sozialforschung GmbH [*Association for Practical Social Research*] (SLS)
AGAS .... Asociacion de Ganaderos y Agricultores de Sula [*Sula Farmers and Cattlemen's Association*] [*Honduras*] (LA)
AGAS .... Australian Government Advertising Service (ADA)
AGASA .... Acucar Gaucho SA [*Brazil*] (DSCA)
AGASIA ..... Asian Agriculture, Agrotechnology, and Agribusiness Exhibition and Conference
AGAV .... Asociacion Guatemalteca de Agentes de Viajes [*Guatemalan Association of Travel Agents*] (EY)
AGAVAL ... Agencias Varias Limitada [*Colombia*] (COL)
AGAWA .... Avocado Growers' Association of Western Australia
AGAZU ..... Asociacion Ganaderos del Estado Zulia [*Venezuela*] (DSCA)
agb .... Agbare [*Honorable*] [*Afrikaans*]
AGB .... Air-Service-Gabon [*ICAO designator*] (FAAC)
AGB .... Allgemeine Geschaftsbedingungen [*General Conditions of Contracts, Transactions, Etc.*] [*German*] (DLA)
AGB .... Angora Goat Breeders [*Australia*]
AGB .... Archaologische Gesellschaft zu Berlin [*Germany*] (EAIO)
AGB .... Associacao dos Geografos Brasileiros
AGB .... Association of General Banks [*South Africa*] (AA)
AGB .... Australian Guide Book Co. Ltd. (ADA)
AGB .... Bomber Gyro Horizon (RU)
AGB .... Societe d'Alimentation Generale du Benin [*General Food Company of Benin*] (AF)
AGBESA ... Empresa de Aguas del Rio Besos, Sociedad Anonima [*Spanish*] [*Business term*]
AGBGB ..... Ausfuehrungsgesetz zur Burgerlichen Gesetzbuch [*Implementing law to the civil code*] [*German*] (ILCA)
AGBU .... Animal Genetics and Breeding Unit [*Research center*] [*Australia*] (IRC)
AGC .... African Groundnut Council [*See also CAA*] [*Nigeria*]
AGC .... Agricultural Center - The Organization of the Agricultural Cooperatives in Israel (EAIO)
AGC .... Amphibious Group Command [*NATO*] (NATG)
AGC .... Ankara Gazeteciler Cemiyeti [*Ankara Journalists Society*] (TU)
AGC .... Arab Agricultural Aviation [*Egypt*] [*ICAO designator*] (FAAC)
AGC .... Asahi Blass Co. [*Japan*]
AGC .... Asamblea General de Cataluna [*General Assembly of Catalonia*] [*Spanish*] (WER)
AGC .... Ashanti Goldfields Corporation
AGC .... Australian Girls Choir
AGC .... Australian Government Centre (ADA)

AGC.......... Australian Guarantee Corporation (ADA)
AGCA........ Amicale Generale des Commercants Algeriens [*General Association of Algerian Businessmen*] [*French*] (AF)
AGCA........ Australian Greeting Card Association
AGCAF...... Association Generale des Cambodgiens de France [*General Association of Cambodians in France*] (CL)
AGCB........ Association Geologique Carpatho-Balkanique [*Carpathian Balkan Geological Association - CBGA*] (EA)
AGCC........ Australian Government Credit Card
AGCD........ Administration Generale de la Cooperation au Developpement
AGChemDok ... Arbeitsgemeinschaft Chemie-Dokumentation
AGCI......... Associazione Generale delle Cooperative Italiane [*Cooperative union*] [*Italy*] (EY)
AGCI......... Assurances Generales de Cote-D'Ivoire [*Insurance*] [*Ivory Coast*]
AGCI......... Australian Genealogical Computer Index
AGCS........ Associazione Generale delle Cooperative Somale
AGCSA....... Australian Golf Course Superintendents' Association
AGD.......... Agderfly AS [*Norway*] [*ICAO designator*] (FAAC)
AGD.......... Australian Geodetic Datum
AGD.......... Azimuth Gyro Sensor (RU)
AgD............ Intelligence Data (RU)
AGDA........ Asociacion Guatemalteca de Deportes Aereos [*Guatemala*] (EAIO)
AGDC........ Australian Gallery Directors' Council (ADA)
AGDF........ Aktionsgemeinschaft Dienst fur den Frieden [*Germany*] (EAIO)
AGDT........ Time-Delay Nose Fuze [*Aviation*] (RU)
AGDW....... Arbeitsgemeinschaft Deutscher Waldbesitzerverbande [*Germany*] (EAIO)
AGE.......... Asian Geotechnical Engineering [*Asian Institute of Technology*] [*Thailand*] (PDAA)
AGE.......... Asian Geotechnical Engineering Information Center [*Information service or system*] (IID)
AGE.......... Assemblee Generale Extraordinaire [*Extraordinary General Assembly*] (CL)
AGE.......... Association Generale des Etudiants [*General Students' Association*] [*French*] (WER)
AGE.......... Association of German Engineers (EAIO)
AGE.......... Australian General Electric (ADA)
AGE.......... Australian Government Employment
AGE.......... Garage Electrical Equipment (RU)
AGE.......... Servicios Aereos de Los Angeles SA de CV [*Mexico*] [*ICAO designator*] (FAAC)
AGE.......... Wangerooge [*Germany*] [*Airport symbol*] (OAG)
AGEA........ Association Generale des Etudiants d'Algerie
AGEA........ Australian Grain Exporters' Association
AGEAP...... Asociacion de Graduados de la Escuela Agricola Panamericana [*Association of Graduates of the Panamerican Agriculture School*] [*El Salvador*] (LA)
AGEC........ Arabian Gulf Exploration Co.
AGEC........ Arbeitsgemeinschaft Europaeischer Chorverbaende [*Federation of European Choirs*] [*Utrecht, Netherlands*] (EAIO)
AGEC........ Asociacion de Ganaderos del Estado Carabobo [*Venezuela*] (DSCA)
AGEC........ Australian Grape Exporters' Committee
AGECH...... Chilean Association of Professional Teachers
AGECO...... Agence Generale d'Echanges Commerciaux
AGECOOP ... Agence de Cooperation Culturelle et Technique [*Cultural and Technical Cooperation Agency*] (AF)
AGECOP... Agence de Cooperation Culturelle et Technique [*Cultural and Technical Cooperation Agency*] [*Use AGECOOP*] (AF)
AGED........ Association des Grandes Entreprises de Distribution de Belgique [*Trade organization*] [*Belgium*] (EY)
AGEDE...... Agencia Especial de Defesa Economica [*Brazil*] (DSCA)
AGEDI....... Agence Generale de Distribution
AGEED...... Association Generale des Eleves et Etudiants du Dahomey en France [*General Association of Dahomean Pupils and Students in France*] [*Dahomey*]
AGEF........ Armazens Gerais Ferroviarios [*Brazil*] (DSCA)
AGEF........ Association Generale des Enseignants Francais [*Algeria*]
AGEF........ Rede Federal de Armazens Gerais Ferroviarios [*Federal Network of General Railroad Warehouses*] [*Brazil*] (LA)
AGEFAN... Association Generale des Etudiants de France en Afrique Noire [*General Association of French Students in Black Africa*]
AGEG........ Association Generale des Etudiants du Gabon [*General Association of Gabonese Students*] (AF)
AGEG........ Association Generale des Etudiants Guadeloupeens [*Guadeloupe*] (PD)
A GE I....... Associazione dei Geografi Italiani [*Italian*] (SLS)
AGEK........ Association Generale des Etudiants Khmers du Cambodge [*General Association of Cambodian Students of Cambodia*] (CL)
AGEL........ Asociacion Regional de Ganaderos de Este del Lago Cabimas [*Venezuela*] (DSCA)
AGEL........ Association Generale des Etudiants du Louvanium [*General Association of Lovanium University Students*] [*Zaire*]
AGEM....... Allami Gazdasagok es Erdok Minisztere [*Minister of State Farms and Forests*] (HU)

AGEM....... Asociacion de Ganaderos del Estado Monagas [*Venezuela*] (DSCA)
AGEMICS ... Australasian Genealogical Electronic Mail International Computer Search
AGEMPP.. Association Generale des Etudiants en Medecine a Phnom Penh [*General Association of Medical Students in Phnom Penh*] [*Cambodia*] (CL)
AGENCIAUTO ... Agencia de Automoviles Ltda. [*Colombia*] (COL)
AGENEREK ... Association de la Jeunesse Nationaliste de la Republique Khmere [*Cambodian Republic Nationalist Youth Association*] [*Use AJEUNAREK*] (CL)
AGENOR.. Agence Nationale pour la Transformation et la Distribution de l'Or et Autres Metaux Precieux [*Algiers, Algeria*] (IMH)
A GENPP ... Academia Gentium "Pro Pace" [*Italian*] (SLS)
AGEP........ Association Generale de l'Enseignement Public [*General Association of Public School Teachers*] [*Algeria*] (AF)
AGEPA...... Armazens Gerais de Produtos Agricolas [*Brazil*] (DSCA)
AGEPI....... Association Guineenne des Editeurs de la Presse Independente [*Press association*] [*Guinea*] (EY)
AGEPOV... Agence Populaire de Voyage
AGEPYM ... Asociacion General de Empleados Publicos y Municipales [*General Association of Public and Municipal Employees*] [*El Salvador*] (LA)
AGER .... Association Generale des Etudiants Reunionnais [*General Association of Reunionese Students*] (AF)
AGERA...... Australian Geographical Education Research Association
AGERE...... Associazione Generale per l'Edilizia [*Italian*] (SLS)
AGERM .... Association Generale des Etudiants Reunionnais en Metropole [*General Association of Reunionese Students in France*] (AF)
AGERPRES ... Agentia Romana de Press [*Romanian Press Agency*] (RO)
A/GES....... Arkhigos/Genikou Epiteleiou Stratou [*Chief, Army General Staff*] [*Greek*] (GC)
AGES........ Asociacion de Ganaderos de El Salvador [*Association of Salvadoran Cattlemen*] (LA)
AGES........ Association Generale des Etudiants Senegalais
AGES........ Gesellschaft fur Energieplanung und Systemanalyse [*Germany*] (EAIO)
AGESCO... Asociacion Georgista Economico-Social [*Costa Rica*] (DSCA)
AGET .... Anonymos Geniki Etaireia Tsimendon [*General Cement Corporation*] [*Greek*] (GC)
AGETEX... Agence Generale des Textiles pour la Cote-d'Afrique
AGEUA..... Association Generale des Etudiants de l'Universite Abidjan [*General Association of Abidjan University Students*] [*Ivory Coast*]
AGEUNR.. Association Generale des Etudiants de l'Universite Nationale du Rwanda [*General Association of Students of the National University of Rwanda*] (AF)
AGEUS...... Asociacion General de Estudiantes Universitarios Salvadorenos [*General Association of Salvadoran University Students*] (LA)
AGEVACOOP ... Asociatia Generala a Vinzarilor Cooperatiste [*General Association of Romanian Engineers*] (RO)
AGEW .... Australian Government Engine Works (ADA)
AGF .... Agen [*France*] [*Airport symbol*] (OAG)
AGF .... Allami Gazdasagok Foigazgatosaga [*Inspectorate of State Farms*] (HU)
AGF .... Arbeitsgemeinschaft der Grossforschungs-Einrichtungen (SLS)
AGF .... Arbeitsgemeinschaft Getreideforschung eV [*Association for Grain Research*] (SLS)
AGF .... Association de Geographes Francais [*French*] (SLS)
AGF .... Association of German Foresters (EAIO)
AGF .... Assurances Generales de France [*Insurance*]
AGF .... Australian Gymnastic Federation (ADA)
Agfa........... Aktiengesellschaft fuer Anilinfabrikation [*Aniline Factory Corporation*] [*German*]
AGFA .... Amicale Generale des Femmes Algeriennes [*General Association of Algerian Women*] [*French*] (AF)
AGFIS .... Association Generale des Federations Internationales de Sports [*General Association of International Sports Federations - GAISF*] (EA)
AGFIS .... General Association of International Sports Federations (OLYM)
AGFNET... Arbeitsgemeinschaft der Grossfochungseinrichtungen [*The Association of National Research Centers of the Federal Republic of Germany*] [*Computer science*] (TNIG)
AGFU .... Gas Fractionator-Absorber (RU)
AGFW .... Arbeitsgemeinschaft Fernwaerme eV [*Study Group of Remote Heat*] (SLS)
Agg............. Aggettivo [*Adjective*] [*Italian*]
agg............. Aggiunte [*Additions*] [*Italian*]
AGG.......... Angoram [*Papua New Guinea*] [*Airport symbol*] (OAG)
AGG.......... Arbeitsgemeinschaft Gueterbefoerderungsdienst [*Working Group for Freight Transportation Service*] [*German*] (EG)
AGG.......... Arhitektonsko-Gradevinarsko-Geodetski (Fakultet) [*Faculty of Architecture, Construction, and Geodesy*] [*Zagreb*] (YU)

AGG........... Arrete du Gouverneur General [*Decree of the Governor General*] [*Used in historical material*]   (CL)

AGG........... Assurances Generales Gabonaises

AGG........... Australia - Governor-General's Office [*National Union Catalogue of Australia symbol*]

AGGD....... Association of German Graphic-Designers   (EAIO)

AGGE........ Balalae, Shortland Islands [*Solomon Islands*] [*ICAO location identifier*]   (ICLI)

AGGG....... Advisory Group on Greenhouse Gases [*Australia*]

AGGG....... Honiara [*Solomon Islands*] [*ICAO location identifier*]   (ICLI)

AGGH .... Honiara/Henderson, Guadalcanal Island [*Solomon Islands*] [*ICAO location identifier*]   (ICLI)

aggiorn .... Aggiornato [*Modernized*] [*Publishing*] [*Italian*]

AGGL........ Graciosa Bay/Luova, Santa Cruz Islands [*Solomon Islands*] [*ICAO location identifier*]   (ICLI)

AGGM....... Munda, New Georgia Islands [*Solomon Islands*] [*ICAO location identifier*]   (ICLI)

AGGN....... Gizo/Nusatupe, Gizo Island [*Solomon Islands*] [*ICAO location identifier*]   (ICLI)

AGGS .... Allgemeine Geschichtsforschende Gesellschaft der Schweiz [*International Historical Research Society of the Swiss*]   (SLS)

AGH .... Akademia Gorniczo-Hutnicza [*Academy of Mining and Metallurgy*]   (POL)

AGh .... Alpengasthaus [*Alpine Tavern*] [*German*]

AGH .... Angelholm/Helsingborg [*Sweden*] [*Airport symbol*]   (OAG)

AGH .... Australian General Hospital   (ADA)

ag h ev .... Agostai Hitvallasu Evangelikus [*Lutheran of Augsburg Confession*]   (HU)

AGHG .... Academia de Geografia e Historia de Guatemala [*Academy of Geography and History of Guatemala*]   (SLS)

AGHN .... Asociacion Guatemalteca de Historia Natural [*Natural History Association of Guatemala*]   (SLS)

AGHR....... Association Generale des Handicapes de Rwanda   (EAIO)

AGHS .... Australian Garden History Society

AGHS .... Australian Government Health Service

AGHTM.... Association Generale des Hygienistes et Techniciens Municipaux [*General Association of Municipal Health and Technical Experts*]   (EAIO)

AGI .... Agence Gabonaise d'Information [*Gabonese Information Agency*]   (AF)

AGI .... Agenzia Giornalistica Italia [*Press agency*] [*Italy*]

AGI .... Agisiyo Gatolica y'Ingo

AGI .... Agrar-Aviacion SA [*Spain*] [*ICAO designator*]   (FAAC)

AGI .... Allami Gazdasagok Igazgatosaga [*Directorate of State Farms*]   (HU)

AGI .... Alliance Graphique Internationale [*International League of Graphic Artists*] [*Zurich, Switzerland*]   (EAIO)

AGI .... Annee Geophysique Internationale [*International Geophysical Year*] [*French*]   (WER)

AGI .... Ano Geofisico Internacional [*International Geophysical Year - IGY*] [*Portuguese*]

agi.............. Anyagi [*Financial, Economic*] [*Hungarian*]   (HU)

AGI .... Arbeitsgemeinschaft Industriebau [*Association of Industrial Structures*]   (SLS)

AGI .... Association of Ghana Industries

AGI .... Associazione Genetica Italiana [*Italian*]   (SLS)

AGI .... Associazione Geofisica Italiana [*Italian*]   (SLS)

AGI .... Associazione Goliardica Italiana [*Italian Student Association*]   (WER)

AGI .... Associazione Grafologica Italiana [*Italian*]   (SLS)

AGI .... Australian Gastroenterology Institute

AGI .... Australian Grain Institute

AGI .... Autorisation Globale d'Importation [*Global Import Quotas*] [*Algeria*]

AGI .... Fighter Gyro Horizon   (RU)

AGIA .... Intelligence Gathering Vessel [*Military*]

AGIA .... Australian Geosciences Information Association   (ADA)

AGIC .... Australian Genomic Information Centre [*University of Sydney*]

AGIC .... Australian Goldmining Industry Council

AGIC .... Australian Government Insurance Commission   (ADA)

AGICO ..... Arabian General Investment Co. [*Dubai*]

AGICOA ... Association de Gestion Internationale Collective des Oeuvres Audiovisuelles [*Association for the International Collective Management of Audiovisual Works*] [*Geneva, Switzerland*]   (EAIO)

AGID .... Association of Geoscientists for International Development [*Bangkok, Thailand*]   (EAIO)

AGID .... Association of German Industrial-Designers   (EAIO)

AGIFORS ... Airline Group of International Federation of Operational Research Societies [*Denmark*]   (MCD)

AGIK .... Avrupa Guvenlik ve Isbirlik Konferansi [*European Security and Cooperation Conference*]   (TU)

AGIMA ..... Agence Immobiliere d'Afrique

AGIN .... Action Group of Immigration and Nationality

AGINCO ... Agricultura, Industria, e Comercio [*Brazil*]   (DSCA)

AGIO .... Australian Government Insurance Office   (ADA)

AGIP.......... Agence d'Illustrations pour la Presse [*Press Illustrations Agency*] [*French*]   (AF)

AGIP.......... Azienda Generale Italiana Petroli [*Italian Petroleum Enterprise*]   (AF)

Agip........... Azienda Generali Italiana Petroli   (OMWE)

AGIRC....... Association Generale des Institutions de Retraites des Cadres [*France*]   (FLAF)

AGIS .... Afrikagrupperna i Sverige

AGIS .... Agence Generale d'Information du Sud-Est Asiatique [*Southeast Asia General Information Agency*]   (CL)

AGIS .... Asociacion Guatemalteca de Instituciones de Seguros [*Insurance*]   (EY)

AGIS .... Associazione Generale Italiana dello Spettacolo [*General Italian Entertainments Association*] [*Italy*]   (EY)

agit .... Agitacio [*Agitation*]   (HU)

agit .... Agitation   (RU)

agit .... Agitational [*Propaganda*]   (BU)

Agit .... Agitato [*Agitatedly*] [*Music*]

AGITAB.... Aerial Leaflet Bomb   (RU)

agitgrupa.... Agitation Group [*Propaganda*]   (BU)

agitprop...... Agitacio es Propaganda [*Agitation and Propaganda*]   (HU)

agitprop...... Agitaciono-Propagandni [*Agitation and Propaganda*]   (YU)

AGITPROP ... Agitacni a Propagacni Oddeleni [*Agitation and Propaganda Department*]   (CZ)

agitprop...... Agitation and Propaganda Department   (BU)

agitpropchik ... Agitation and Propaganda Worker   (BU)

agitpunkt.... Propaganda Center   (BU)

AGIV .... Aktiengesellschaft fuer Industrie und Verkehrswesen [*Joint Stock Company for Industry and Traffic*]

AGJ .... Aguni [*Japan*] [*Airport symbol*]   (OAG)

AGJA......... Amicale Generale des Jeunes Algeriens [*General Association of Young Algerians*]   (AF)

AGJPB ...... Association Generale des Journalistes Professionnels de Belgique [*Belgium*]   (EAIO)

AGK.......... Adenoidal-Pharyngeal-Conjunctival [*Virus*]   (RU)

agk .... Adi Gecen Kaynak [*The Aforementioned Source*]   (TU)

AGK.......... Afrikaans Gereformeerde Kerk [*Afrikaners Reformed Church*] [*South Africa*]

AGK.......... Artiljeriska Grupa Kolona [*Artillery Column Groups*]   (YU)

AGK.......... Combination Gyro Horizon   (RU)

AGK.......... Corps Air Group   (RU)

AGKS........ Automatic Gas-Logging Station [*Pet.*]   (RU)

AGL.......... Abteilungsgewerkschaftsleitung [*Departmental Labor Union Executive Board (Enterprise)*]   (EG)

AG-L......... Aerosol Generator for Forest Pest Control   (RU)

agl .... Aglutinacao [*Agglutination*] [*Portuguese*]

AGL .... Air Angouleme [*France*] [*ICAO designator*]   (FAAC)

AGL .... Aktionsgemeinschaft Luftfahrt [*Association for Promoting Aviation*] [*Germany*]   (PDAA)

AGL .... Arbeitsgemeinschaft fuer Landschaftsentwicklung [*Association for Landscape Development*]   (SLS)

AGL .... Australian Gas Light Co.

AGL .... Wanigela [*Papua New Guinea*] [*Airport symbol*]   (OAG)

AGLA .... Australian Government Lawyers' Association

AGLA .... Australian Government Legal Aid   (ADA)

AGLAE...... Accelerateur Grand Louvre d'Analyse Elementaire [*Ion Accelerator*] [*Louvre Art Museum Paris, France*]

AGLIBS.... Attorney General's Information Service Library Subject Headings [*Database*] [*Australia*]

AGLN .... Asian Grain Legumes Network [*India*]   (EAIO)

AGLOS....... Conservational Afforestation Experimental Station   (RU)

AGLR........ Army Hospital for the Slightly Wounded   (RU)

AGLS........ Australian Government Liaison Service   (ADA)

agm............ Adi Gecen Makale [*The Aforementioned Article*]   (TU)

AGM.......... Agaclandirma ve Erozyon Kontrol Genel Mudurlugu [*Forestation and Erosion Control Directorate General*]   (TU)

AGM.......... Air Guam [*ICAO designator*]   (FAAC)

AGM.......... Allami Gazdasagok Miniszteriuma/Minisztere [*Ministry/Minister of State Farms*]   (HU)

AGM.......... Altalanos Gepipari Miniszterium/Miniszter [*Ministry/Minister of Machine Industries*]   (HU)

AGM.......... Arts Graphiques Modernes

AGM........ Australian Glass Manufacturers   (ADA)

AGM......... Societe de Developpement Americaine, Greque, et Malgache

AGMANZ ... Art Galleries and Museums Association of New Zealand   (SLS)

AGMC .... Adelaide Gem and Mineral Club [*Australia*]

AGMF .... Association Generale des Medecins de France [*General Medicine Association of France*]   (SLS)

AGMI .... Agrometeorological Institute   (RU)

AGMI .... Arkhangel'sk State Medical Institute   (RU)

AGMI....... Associazione Generale tra i Magistrati Italiani

AGMI .... Astrakhan' State Medical Institute Imeni A. V. Lunacharskiy   (RU)

AGMI .... Bureau d'Assistance Geologique et Miniere [*Tunisia*]

AGMS .... Agrometeorological Station   (RU)

AGMS .... Australian Guild of Music and Speech
Ag Mt........ Agir Makineli Tufek [*Heavy Machine Gun*]   (TU)
AGMTS..... Automatic Hydrometeorological Telemetry Station   (RU)
agn.............. Agnome [*Agnomen*] [*Portuguese*]
AGN.......... Compagnie Nationale Air Gabon [*ICAO designator*]   (FAAC)
AGNU .... Asociacion Guatemalteca Pro Naciones Unidas [*Guatemala*]
            (EAIO)
AGO.......... ACM [*Australian Consolidated Minerals*] Gold
ago............. Agosto [*August*] [*Spanish*]
AGO.......... Angola [*ANSI three-letter standard code*]   (CNC)
AGO.......... Angola Air Charter Ltd. [*ICAO designator*]   (FAAC)
AGO.......... Arbeitsgemeinschaft der Ordenshochschulen [*Association of
            Public High Schools*]   (SLS)
AGO.......... Arbeitsgerichtsordnung [*Labor Court Regulations*] [*German*]
            (EG)
AGO.......... Assemblee Generale Ordinaire [*French*]   (FLAF)
AGO.......... Automatic Geophysical Observatory   (RU)
ago............. Garage Equipment Plant   (RU)
AGO.......... Truck Detachment   (RU)
AGOFP..... Association of Greek Overseas Fishing Producers   (EAIO)
AGOG....... Australian Girls Own Gallery
AGOK....... Allami Gazdasagok Orszagos Kozpontja [*National Center for
            State Farms*]   (HU)
AGON .... Special-Purpose Air Group   (RU)
AGOP....... Australian Government Offsets Program
AGOR....... Oceanographic Research Ship
AGOS........ Aeronautical and Seaplane Experimental Construction   (RU)
AGOSI...... Allgemeine Gold und Silberscheideanstalt [*Metal smelter and
            gold dealer*] [*Germany*]
agot .... Agotado [*Out-of-Print*] [*Publishing*] [*Spanish*]
AGP.......... Administracion General de Puertos [*Argentina*]   (IMH)
AGP.......... Aerogeodetic Establishment   (RU)
AGP.......... Agence Gabonaise de Presse [*Gabonese Press Agency*]   (AF)
AGP.......... Agence Guineenne de Presse [*Guinean Press Agency*]   (AF)
AGP.......... Arbeitsgemeinschaft der Produktionsgenossenschaften [*Working
            Group of (Artisan) Producer Cooperatives*] [*German*]   (EG)
AGP.......... Asociacion de Ganaderos del Peru [*Peru*]   (DSCA)
AGP........ Asom Gana Parishad [*Assam People's Council*] [*India*] [*Political
            party*]   (FEA)
AGP.......... Assurances du Groupe de Paris [*Assurance Group of Paris*]
            [*France*]
AGP.......... Australian Grand Prix   (ADA)
AGP.......... Australian Gruen Party [*Political party*]
AGP.......... Automatic Field Damper, Automatic Field Damping   (RU)
AGP.......... Diving Gyro Horizon   (RU)
AGP.......... Malaga [*Spain*] [*Airport symbol*]   (OAG)
AGP.......... Truck-Mounted Hydraulic Crane   (RU)
AGPA .... Australian Greek Presidential Awards
AGPAEA... Association de Gestion Portuaire de l'Afrique de l'Est et de
            l'Afrique Australe [*Port Management Association of
            Eastern and Southern Africa - PMAESA*]   (EAIO)
AGPC .... Australasian Guild of Professional Cooks
AGPD .... Allgemeine Gesellschaft fur Philosophie in Deutschland
            [*Germany*]   (EAIO)
AGPI......... Ashkhabad State Pedagogical Institute Imeni M. Gor'kiy   (RU)
AGPI......... Azerbaydzhan State Pedagogical Institute Imeni V. I. Lenin
            (RU)
AGPIIYa ... Alma-Ata State Pedagogical Institute of Foreign Languages
            (RU)
AGPLAN... Arbeitsgemeinschaft fuer Planungsrechnung [*Association for
            Planning Costs*] [*German*]   (ADPT)
AGPol .... Agencja Reklamy Handlu Zagranicznego [*Advertising Agency for
            Foreign Trade*] [*Poland*]
AGPS......... Australian Government Publishing Service   (ADA)
AGPUL...... Australian Government Publications in University Libraries
AGPUND ... Arab Gulf Programme for the United Nations Development
            Organisations [*Saudi Arabia*]
AGPVO ..... Assemblee Generale, Proces-Verbal Officiel [*Nations Unies*]
            (FLAF)
AGR.......... Accounting Guidance Release [*Australia*]
agr.............. agarisch [*Benelux*]   (BAS)
AGR.......... Agences Generales Reunis
AGR.......... Agra [*India*] [*Airport symbol*]   (OAG)
Agr .... Agrar [*Agrarian*] [*German*]
agr .... Agreable [*Appealing*] [*French*]
agr .... Agricoltura [*Agriculture*] [*Italian*]
Agr .... Agricultura [*Agriculture*] [*Portuguese*]
agr .... Agricultural   (RU)
AGR.......... Agricultural Research Services, Animal Health Division
            [*Department of Agriculture*] [*ICAO designator*]   (FAAC)
agr .... Agriculture [*Agriculture*] [*French*]
Agr .... Agrikultur [*Agriculture*] [*German*]   (GCA)
Agr .... Agronom [*Albanian*]
agr .... Agronomi [*Finland*]
Agr .... Agronomic [*or Agronomist*]   (RU)
agr .... Argentine [*or Argentinean*]   (RU)

AGR.......... Auditing Guidance Release [*Australia*]
AgR............ Intelligence through Secret Agents   (RU)
AGRA .... Australian Garrison Royal Artillery   (ADA)
AGRA .... Australian Guild of Realist Artists   (ADA)
AGRACAM ... Societe des Ateliers Graphiques du Cameroun
AGRAL...... Asistencia Tecnica Agricola Ltda. [*Colombia*]   (COL)
agrar.......... Agrarian   (RU)
AGRBO ..... Australian Government Retirement Benefits Office   (ADA)
AGRECE... Agrupacion de Exportadores del Centro de Espana [*Trade
            association*] [*Spain*]   (EY)
AGREEPDDI ... General Assembly of Directors of Schools and
            Establishments Awarding the Engineering Diploma
            [*French*]
AGREGA .. Agrupaciones Regionales Ganaderas [*Nicaragua*]   (DSCA)
AGREPAL ... Agence de Repartition de Produits Alimentaires
AGREX..... Elliniki Etaireia Exagogis Georgikon Proiondon [*Greek
            Agricultural Products Export Company*]   (GC)
Agrexco...... Agricultural Export Company [*Israel*]
Agrfak........ School of Agronomy   (BU)
AGRGK ..... Air Group of the High Command Reserve   (RU)
AGRH........ Association pour la Gestion et le Developpement de Resources
            Humaines en Cote-D'Ivoire
AGRIAA.... Agricultural Information Association for Australasia
AGRICOM ... Agricultura, Industria, e Comercio [*Brazil*]   (DSCA)
AGRIDOC ... Agricultural Documentation Network [*France*]
AGRIFOR ... Societe Agricole et Forestiere du Mayumbe [*Agriculture and
            Forestry Company of Mayumbe*] [*Zaire*]
AGRILAGDO ... Societe Lagdo Agribusiness
Agrim .... Agrimensura [*Surveying*] [*Portuguese*]
AGRIMECO ... Agricultural Land Development and Mechanization
            Corporation
AGRIMER ... Banco Agricola e Mercantil [*Brazil*]   (DSCA)
AGRIMPEX ... Hungarian Foreign Trade Enterprise for Agricultural Products
AGRINDEX ... Agricultural Research Information Index [*United Nations*]
AGRINDEX ... Bibliografie van Agricultural Research Information System
AGRINTER ... Sistema Interamericana de Informacion Agricola [*Inter-
            American Agricultural Information System*]   (LA)
AGRIPOG ... Societe Agricole de Port-Gentil
AGRIS .... Agricultural Research Information System [*FAO*]
AGRIS .... International Information System for the Agricultural Sciences
            and Technology [*Food and Agriculture Organization*]
            [*United Nations Information service or system*]   (IID)
AGRISA .... Agricola Seringalista Nordeste SA [*Brazil*]   (DSCA)
agrn .... Agronomus [*Agronomist*]   (HU)
AGRO-ALFA ... Empresa Estatal de Maquinaria Agricola [*Agricultural
            equipment enterprise*] [*Mozambique*]
AGROBER ... Mezogazdasagi Tervezo es Beruhazasi Vallalat [*Agricultural
            Design and Investment Enterprise*]   (HU)
AGROCAP ... Societe Agricole du Cap Vert [*Agricultural Company of Cape
            Verde*]
AGROCOL ... Sociedad Agricola Colombiana [*Colombia*]   (COL)
agrofak....... Agricultural Division   (RU)
Agrogabon ... Societe pour le Developpement de l'Agriculture au Gabon
            [*Government agricultural development organization*]
AGROINFORM ... Information Center of the Ministry of Agriculture and
            Food [*Ministry of Agriculture and Food*] [*Information
            service or system*]   (IID)
AGROK ..... Agrotika Oikistika Kendra [*Rural Housing Centers*]   (GC)
AGROKER ... Pest, Nograd, es Komarom Megyei Mezogazdasagi Ellato
            Vallalat [*Agricultural Supply Enterprise of Pest, Nograd,
            and Komarom Megyes*]   (HU)
AGROLLANQUIHUE ... Asociacion de Agricultores de Llanquihue [*Chile*]
            (DSCA)
AGROMAPA ... Asociacion de Ganaderos de Mara y Paez [*Venezuela*]
            (DSCA)
AGROMAR ... Compania Agropecuaria Maritima [*Colombia*]   (DSCA)
AGROMAS ... A joint Hungarian-Bulgarian foreign trade enterprise for
            agricultural machinery, established in 1964   (HU)
AGROMASH ... Mezhdunarodnoe Obshchestvo po Mashinam dlja
            Ovoshchevodstva, Sadovodstva, i Vinogradstva
            [*International Association for Vine, Fruit, and Vegetable-
            Growing Mechanization*]   (EAIO)
AGROMEK ... International Exhibition for Agricultural Mechanization and
            Breeding Stock
AGROMET ... Metalurgicas Agricolas e Industriales [*Colombia*]   (DSCA)
AGROMIL ... Administradora Agro-Imobiliaria Ltd [*Brazil*]   (DSCA)
Agron .... Agronomia [*Agronomy*] [*Portuguese*]
AGROPEC ... Agropecuaria do Norte
AGROPET ... Agrupacion de Orientacion Petrolera [*Oil Policy Planning
            Group*] [*Venezuela*]   (LA)
AGROPROGRESS ... Gesellschaft fuer Planung und Beratung in der Land,
            Forst, Ernaehrungs - und Wasserwirtschaft mit
            beschraenkter haftung [*Germany*]   (DSCA)
AGRO-PROMOTION ... Societe Agbouvillaise de Promotion de l'Habitat
            Urbain et Rural
AGROPSA ... Distribuidora Agricola Pecuaria SA [*Venezuela*]   (DSCA)
AGROS ..... Agricultores Asociados [*Colombia*]   (DSCA)

AGROSEM ... Complexul pentru Valorificarea Semintelor de Legume si Materialului Saditor Pomicol [*Complex for the Utilization of Vegetable Seeds and Fruit Tree Rootings*] (RO)

AGROSERVICIO ... Instituto Agricola de Asistencia Tecnica [*Chile*] (LAA)

AGROSOL ... Agro Industrial SA [*Brazil*] (DSCA)

AGROT ..... Agrotikon Komma [*Agrarian Party*] [*Greek*] [*Political party*] (PPE)

AGROTEC ... Agricultura, Tecnica, e Comercial Ltd [*Brazil*] (DSCA)

AGROTECO ... Comercial e Tecnica Agropecuaria SA [*Brazil*] (DSCA)

AGROTERV ... Allami Gazdasagok Muszaki Tervezesi Vallalata [*Technical Planning Enterprise of the State Farms*] (HU)

AGROTERV ... Mezogazdasagi Tervezo Vallalat [*Agricultural Planning Enterprise*] (HU)

AGROTEXTIL ... Agro Textilera Venezolana [*Venezuela*] (DSCA)

AGROTROSZT ... Mezogazdasagi Ellato Troszt [*Agricultural Supply Trust*] (HU)

AGROVECO ... Agro Veterinaria Comercio Ltd [*Brazil*] (DSCA)

AGRR .... Association Generale de Retraite par Repartition [*France*] (PDAA)

AGRS .... Australian Government Rehabilitation Service

AGRT .... Association of General Retailers and Traders Union [*Malta*] (EAIO)

AGRUMAL ... Association Inter-Professionelle Algerienne des Agrumes [*Algerian Inter-Occupational Citrus Fruit Association*] (AF)

AGRUPARE ... Agrupacion Patriotica Revolucionaria [*Revolutionary Patriotic Group*] [*Dominican Republic*] (LA)

AGRUSA ... Agricultores Unidos SA [*Spain*] (DSCA)

AGS .... Agreages Grumes et Sciages

AGS .... Airborne Radioactivity Survey (RU)

AGS .... Air Gambia [*ICAO designator*] (FAAC)

AGS .... Art Gallery Society [*New South Wales, Australia*]

AGS .... Asociacion de Ganaderos de la Sierra [*Ecuador*] (DSCA)

AGS .... Assurances Generales Senegalaises [*Insurance*] (EY)

AGS .... Australian Gallery of Sport

AGS .... Australian Geomechanics Society (ADA)

AGS .... Australian Geriatrics' Society

AGS .... Australian Government Solicitor

AGS .... Weapons Announcing System [*Navy*] (RU)

AGSA .... Algodonera Guarico SA [*Venezuela*] (DSCA)

AGSA .... Anotati Geoponiki Skholi Athinon [*Supreme Agricultural School of Athens*] (GC)

AGSA .... Art Gallery of South Australia

AGSA .... Australasian Genetic Support Group Association

AGSAF ...... Australian Government Student Assistance Fund

AGSBS ofSA ... Angora Goat Stud Breeders Society of South Africa (AA)

AGSC .... Australian Guild of Screen Composers

AGSC .... Coastal Surveying Ship

AGSCH ..... Asociacion de Guias y Scouts de Chile (EAIO)

AGSh .... General Staff Academy (RU)

AGSM .... Australian Graduate School of Management (ADA)

AGSM .... Australian Graduate School of Management Corporate Data [*Information service or system*] (CRD)

AGSM .... Aviation Fuels and Lubricants (RU)

AGSO .... Australian Geological Survey Organisation [*Formerly, BMR - Bureau of Mineral Resources*]

AGSO .... Australian Government Solicitors' Office

A(G)SOA ... Anotaton (Gnomodotikon) Symvoulion Oikonomikis Anaptyxeos [*Supreme (Advisory) Council for Economic Development*] [*Greek*] (GC)

AGSOMD ... Australian Group for the Scientific Study of Mental Deficiency (ADA)

AGSSB ...... Atmospheric Geophysical and Space Sciences Branch [*Philippines*] (IRC)

AGSSOMD ... Australian Group for the Scientific Study of Mental Deficiency

AGSVT ...... Agence Generale Senegalaise de Voyage et de Tourisme

AGT .... Academy of Grain Technology [*Australia*]

AGT .... Agence Generale de Transit

AGT .... Agence Generale de Travail

AGT .... Amadeus Global Travel Distrution SA [*Spain*] [*ICAO designator*] (FAAC)

AGT .... Assemblee Generale des Travailleurs [*Algeria*]

AGT .... Assembleia Geral de Trabalhadores [*General Workers Conference*] [*Portuguese*] (WER)

AGT .... Territoriale Arbeitsgemeinschaften [*Regional Working Groups*] (EG)

AGT .... Truck Transport (RU)

AGTA .... Agence Generale de Transit en Afrique [*General Transit Agency in Afica*] [*Congo*]

AGTA .... Amicale Generale des Travailleurs Algeriens [*General Association of Algerian Workers*] [*French*] (AF)

AGTA .... Australian Geography Teachers' Association (ADA)

AGTDC ..... Accord General sur les Tarifs Douaniers et le Commerce [*General Agreement on Tariffs and Trade*] [*Switzerland*] (EAIO)

AGTF .... Administracion General de Transporte Fluvial [*Argentina*] (LAA)

AGTI .... Agence Generale de Transports Internationaux

AGTI .... Allein Gott Traue Ich [*I Trust in God Alone*] [*Motto of Dorothee, Duchess of Braunschweig-Lunebert (1546-1617)*] [*German*]

AGTI .... Altalanos Geptervezo Iroda [*General Office of Machine Design*] (HU)

AGTMM .... Association of German Textile Machinery Manufacturers (EAIO)

agto .... Agosto [*August*] [*Correspondence*] [*Spanish*]

agto .... Agosto [*August*] [*Correspondence*] [*Portuguese*] (GPO)

AGTs .... Anhydrite-Alumina Cement (RU)

AGTT .... Agence Generale de Transit et de Transports

AGTU .... Gas-Turbine Nuclear Propulsion Engine, Gas-Turbine Atomic Power Plant (RU)

AGU .... Agencia Geral do Ultramar

AGU .... Aguascalientes [*Mexico*] [*Airport symbol*] (OAG)

AGU .... Asamblea General Universitaria [*University General Assembly*] [*El Salvador*] (LA)

AGU .... Asociacion de Geografos del Uruguay [*Uruguay*] (DSCA)

AGU .... Australian Golf Union (ADA)

AGU .... Azerbaydzhan State University Imeni S. M. Kirov (RU)

AGU .... Motorized Tar Spreader (RU)

AGU .... Societe Anonyme de Transports Aeriens Air-Guadeloupe [*France*] [*ICAO designator*] (FAAC)

AGUAPA .. Asociacion Guatemalteca de Productores de Algodon [*Guatemalan Cotton Producers Association*] (LA)

AGuC .... Arbeitsgemeinschaft Mikrocomputer [*Microcomputer Association*] [*German*] (ADPT)

AGV .... Acarigua [*Venezuela*] [*Airport symbol*] (OAG)

AGV .... Agrarisch Groothandels Verbond [*Agricultural Wholesale Federation*] [*Netherlands*] (EAIO)

AGV .... Air Glaciers SA [*Switzerland*] [*ICAO designator*] (FAAC)

AGV .... Arbeitsgemeinschaft der Verbraucher eV [*Association of Consumers*] (SLS)

AGV .... As Gevolg Van [*As a Result Of*] [*Afrikaans*]

AGV .... Automatic Gas Water Heater (RU)

AGV .... Avion a Geometrie Variable [*Variable Geometry Aircraft*] [*French*]

AGV .... Avion a Grande Vitesse [*French high-speed train*]

AGV .... Mobile Hot-Air Decontamination Unit (RU)

AGVG .... Anglo-German Variable Geometry [*Aviation*] (PDAA)

AGVO .... Arbeitsgemeinschaft Vorderer Orient (MENA)

AGVPS ...... Asociatia Generala a Vinatorilor si Pescarilor Sportivi [*General Association of Sport Hunters and Fishermen*] (RO)

AGW .... Anthropologische Gesellschaft in Wien [*Anthropological Society in Vienna*] [*Austria*] (SLS)

AGWA ...... Art Gallery of Western Australia

AGWA ...... Australian Government Workers Association (ADA)

AGWAC ...... Australian Guided Weapons and Analogue Computer (ADA)

AGWAGS ... Albany Group, Western Australia Genealogical Society

AGWS .... Australian-German Welfare Society

AGWS .... Australian-Greek Welfare Society

AGWU .... Artisans and General Workers Union [*Mauritius*] (AF)

AGWU .... Australian Glass Workers' Union

AGX .... Aviogenex [*Yugoslavia*] [*ICAO designator*] (FAAC)

AGY .... Aeroguayavic [*Chile*] [*ICAO designator*] (FAAC)

AGZ .... Aggeneys [*South Africa*] [*Airport symbol*] (OAG)

AGZ .... Antiquarische Gesellschaft in Zuerich [*Antiquarian Society in Zurich*] [*Switzerland*] (SLS)

AGZ .... Arhiv Grada Zagreba [*Archives of the City of Zagreb*] (YU)

ah .... Aan Het [*Benelux*] (BAS)

AH .... Academie Internationale d'Heraldique [*Luxembourg*] (SLS)

AH .... Afrikaanse Handelsinstituut [*Afrikaans Institute of Trade*] [*South Africa*] (AF)

AH .... Akademia Handlowa [*Academy of Trade*] (POL)

AH .... Algemeen Handelsblad [*Benelux*] (BAS)

AH .... Almhuette [*Chalet*] [*German*]

AH .... Alter Herr [*Gentleman*] [*German*]

AH .... Ambassador Hotel-Amman [*Jordan*]

ah .... Ampere-Heure [*Ampere-Hour*] [*French*]

Ah .... Ampere Hora [*Ampere-Hour*] [*Portuguese*]

Ah .... Amperogodzina [*Ampere-Hour*] [*Poland*]

Ah .... Anhaenger [*Trailer*] [*German*] (GCA)

A/H .... Antwerp/Hamburg [*Range of ports between and including these two cities*] [*Shipping*] (DS)

AH .... Arhatosag [*Price Authority (of the National Planning Office)*] (HU)

AH .... Orszagos Anyag- es Arhivatal [*National Material and Price Office*] (HU)

AHA .... African Hydro-Carbon Association

AHA .... Air Alpha, AS [*Denmark*] [*ICAO designator*] (FAAC)

AHA .... Air Hostess Academy [*Australia*] (ADA)

AHA .... Akdeniz Haber Ajansi [*Mediterranean News Agency*] [*AKAJANS*] [*See also*] (TU)

AHA .... Alberta Hospital Association [*Edmonton*]

AHA .... Associate of the Australian College of Health

AHA .... Associate of the Australian Institute of Hospital Administrators (ADA)
AHA .... Association of Hungarian Artists (EAIO)
AHA .... Australian Hearing Aid
AHA .... Australian Heritage Award
AHA .... Australian Historical Association (ADA)
AHA .... Australian Hockey Association
AHA .... Australian Hospital Association (ADA)
AHA .... Australian Hotels Association (ADA)
AHA .... Australian Housewives Association (ADA)
AHA .... Australian Huntington Association
AHA .... Australian Hypnotherapists Association (ADA)
AHA .... Automotive Historians of Australia
AHAC .... Adelaide Harriers Athletic Club [Australia]
AHAC .... Asociacion de Hombres de Accion Catolica [Men's Catholic Action Association] [Argentina] (LA)
AHAK .... Aussenhandelsabrechnungskontor [Foreign Trade Settlements Office] [German] (EG)
AHAR .... Australian Heraldic Archival Record
AHASCES ... Association of Higher Academic Staff in Colleges of Education in Scotland (SLS)
AHAWA .... Australian Hungarian Association of Western Australia
AHB .... Abha [Saudi Arabia] [Airport symbol] (OAG)
AHB .... Aboriginal Heritage Branch [South Australia]
AHB .... Agudat Hametargmim Beyisrael [Israel] (EAIO)
AHB .... Area Health Board [Australia]
AHB .... Aussenhandelsbetrieb [Foreign Trade Enterprise] [German] (EG)
AHB .... Australian Honey Board
AH-Bank ... Aussenhandelsbank [Foreign Trade Bank] [German] (EG)
AHBC .... Adelaide Historical Bottle Club [Australia]
AHBS .... Army Health Benefit Society [Australia]
AHC .... Aboriginal Housing Company [Australia]
AHC .... Ad-Hoc Committee
AHC .... Animal Health Committee [Australia]
AHC .... Arrete du Haut Commissaire de France (FLAF)
AHC .... Australian Handball Council
AHC .... Australian Heritage Commission
AHC .... Australian Horticultural Corp.
AHC .... Australian Hospital Care Group
AHC .... High Court of Australia [National Union Catalogue of Australia symbol]
AHCC .... American-Hellenic Chamber of Commerce [Greece] (EAIO)
AHCEI ...... Ad Hoc Committee on Equipment Interoperability [NATO] (NATG)
AHCG .... Australasian Holy Catholic Guild (ADA)
AHCIET .... Asociacion Hispanoamericana de Centros de Investigacion y Estudios de Telecomunicaciones (EA)
AHCS .... Aboriginal Home Care Service [Australia]
AHCS .... Australian Horticultural Correspondence School
ahd .... Althochdeutsch [Old High German] [Language, etc.] [German]
AHD .... Australian Height Datum
AHD .... Czech Air Handling [Czechoslovakia] [ICAO designator] (FAAC)
AHDA ...... Australian Huntington's Disease Association
AHDC .... Aboriginal Housing Development Committee [Australia]
AHDG ...... Aboriginal Health Development Group [Australia]
AHDRC ..... Ancient History Documents Research Center [Macquarie University] [Australia]
AHDRI ...... Animal Husbandry and Dairy Research Institute
ahe............. Aan Het Einde [Benelux] (BAS)
AHE .... Australian Himalayan Expeditions
AHEA .... Australian Horticultural Exporters Association
AHEC .... Australian Health Ethics Committee
AHEC .... Australian Horticultural Export Council
AHEIA ...... Australian Higher Education Industrial Association
AHEP .... Australian Health Education Programmes (ADA)
AHEPA ..... American Hellenic Educational and Progressive Association (GC)
AHEPA ..... Australian Hellenic Education Progressive Association
AHF .... Asian Hospital Federation [Philippines] (EAIO)
AHF .... Australian Handball Federation
AHFE .... Asociacion Holstein Friesian del Ecuador [Ecuador] (DSCA)
AHFR .... Aussenhandels-Finanzierungs-Rundschreiben [Circular Letter on Financing of Foreign Trade] [German] (EG)
AHG .... Aerochago [Dominican Republic] [ICAO designator] (FAAC)
AHG .... Assembly of Heads of State and Government, OAU
AHG .... Aussenhandelsgesellschaft [Foreign Trade Company] [German] (EG)
AHGC .... Australian Horticultural Growers' Council
AHGS .... Australian Heraldry and Genealogical Society [of Canberra] [National Union Catalogue of Australia symbol]
AHHBI ...... Aguda Humanist Hilonit Beyisrael [Israel] (EAIO)
AHI .... Afrikaanse Handelsinstituut [Afrikaans Institute of Trade] [South Africa]

AHI .... Agrupacion Herrena Independiente [Spain] [Political party] (EY)
AHI .... Amahai [Indonesia] [Airport symbol] (OAG)
AHI .... Asociacion Hispano-Islamica
AHI .... Servicios Aeros de Chihuahua Aerochisa SA de CV [Mexico] [ICAO designator] (FAAC)
AHIA .... Arab Heavy Industries Ajman (ME)
AHIAA ..... Associate of the Health Institute Association of Australia (ADA)
AHIBA ..... Asociacion Hondurena de Institutos Bancarios [Honduran Association of Banking Institutes] (LA)
AHIDC ...... Australian Housing Industry Development Council
AHIE .... Australian Hospitality Industry Exhibition
AHIGSA .... Association of Heads of Independent Girls Schools of Australia
AHIR .... Allami Hirdeto [State Advertising (Enterprise)] (HU)
AHIRS ...... Australian Health Information and Research Service (ADA)
AHISA ...... Association of Heads of Independent Schools of Australia
AHITI .... Animal Health and Industries Training Institute
AHK .... Abhandlungen des Hamburgischen Kolonialinstituts [Treatise of the Hamburg Colonial Institute] [German]
AHK .... Air Hong Kong Ltd. [ICAO designator] (FAAC)
AHK .... Aktiv Hinten Kinematik [Active Rear-Axle Movement] [German]
AHKGA ..... Australian Hayward Kiwifruit Growers Association
AHKLA ..... Associate of the Hong Kong Library Association
AHL .... Aboriginal Hostels Limited [Australia]
AHL .... Additional Homestead Lease [Australia] (ADA)
AHL .... Amalgamated Holdings Limited [Australia] (ADA)
AHL .... Arabian Helicopters Ltd. [Saudi Arabia]
AHL .... Association of Hungarian Librarians (EAIO)
AHL .... Australian Home Loans Ltd.
AHM .... Altos Hornos del Mediterraneo [Spanish]
AHMAC.... Australian Health Ministers Advisory Council
AHMC...... Australian Health Ministers Conference
AHMCA.... Asociacion de Hombres de Mercadeo de Centro America [Guatemala] (DSCA)
AHMSA .... Altos Hornos de Mexico, Sociedad Anonima [Mexican Steel Mills, Incorporated] (LA)
AHN .... Air Hainaut [France] [ICAO designator] (FAAC)
ahnl .... Aehnlich [Similar] [German] (GCA)
AHO .... Aboriginal Health Organisation [Australia]
AHO .... Administrativni Hospodarske Oddeleni [Administrative Management Department] (CZ)
AHO .... Alghero [Italy] [Airport symbol] (OAG)
AHO .... Angle Horaire Origine [Hour Angle] [French]
AHO .... Aussenhandelsorganisation [Foreign Trade Organization] [German] (EG)
AHOC .... Amerada Hess Oil Corp. of Abu Dhabi [United Arab Emirates] (EY)
AHOC .... Australian Home Owners' Club
AHORROMET ... Ahorros Metropolitanos [Metropolitan Savings Corp.] [El Salvador]
AHP.......... Aerochiapas SA de CV [Mexico] [ICAO designator] (FAAC)
AHP.......... Agence Haitienne de Presse [Haitian Press Agency] (LA)
AHP.......... Allied Hydrographic Publication [NATO]
AHP.......... Associacao dos Hoteis de Portugal [Hotel Association of Portugal] (EAIO)
AHP.......... Association of Health Professionals [Australia]
AHPA .... Australian Health Professionals Association
AHPHYCO ... Association des Handicapes Physiques du Congo (EAIO)
AHPROCAFE ... Asociacion Hondurena de Productores de Cafe [Honduran Association of Coffee Producers] (LA)
AHPRT ..... Aboriginal Health Policy Review Team [Australia]
AHPS .... Australian Historical Pageantry Society (ADA)
AHPT .... Aborigines Historic Places Trust [Australia] (ADA)
AHPV .... Association of Hospital Pharmacists of Victoria [Australia]
AHQC....... Australian Hardwood Quality Council
AHR.......... Air Holland Regional (AHR) [ICAO designator] (FAAC)
AHR.......... Australasian Home Reading Union (ADA)
AHRA .... African Human Rights Research Association [Formerly, African Human Rights Study Group] (EA)
AHRC....... Australian Harness Racing Council
AHRC....... Australian Housing Research Council (ADA)
AHRC....... Australian Humanities Research Council (ADA)
AHRI .... Armauer Hansen Research Institute [Ethiopia] (IRC)
ahs............. Aan Het Slot [Benelux] (BAS)
AHS.......... Aboriginal Health Service [Australia]
AHS.......... Acute Hospital Syndrome [Used facetiously to explain the popularity of a West German soap opera]
AHS.......... Allgemeinbildende Hoehere Schule [General Education High School] [German]
AHS.......... Area Health Service [Australia]
AHS.......... Australian Health Services
AHS.......... Australian Herb Society
AHS.......... Australian Heritage Society (ADA)
AHS.......... Australian Hibiscus Society
AHS.......... Australian Hospital Ship (ADA)

AHS........... International Association of Hydrological Sciences [*See also AISH*] [*British*]
AHSA........ African Heritage Studies Association
AHSA........ American Horse Shows Association   (OLYM)
AHSA........ Arab Horse Society of Australasia   (ADA)
AHSA........ Armorial and Heraldry Society of Australasia
AHSA........ Aviation Historical Society of Australia   (ADA)
AHSC....... Australian Health Services Commission
AHSCA..... Association of Hydraulic Services Consultants Australia
AHSCP...... African Household Survey Capability Programme [*United Nations*]   (EY)
AHSLEA... Australian Hides, Skins, and Leather Exports Association
AHSPA...... Australian High School Principals Association
AHT........... Allatforgalmi es Husipari Troszt [*Livestock Trading and Meat Industry Trust*]   (HU)
AHTA....... Antigua Hotels and Tourist Association   (EY)
AHTE....... Australian Horticultural Trades Exhibition
AHTS....... Association of Head Mistresses in Technical Schools [*Australia*]
AHU.......... Al Hoceima [*Morocco*] [*Airport symbol*]   (OAG)
AHU.......... Arquivo Historico Ultramarina
AHU.......... Aussenhandelsunternehmen [*Foreign Trade Enterprise*] [*German*]   (EG)
AHV.......... Algemene Handelsvoorwaarden [*Benelux*]   (BAS)
AHV.......... Alters- und Hinterlassenen-Versicherung [*Old Age and Dependents Insurance*] [*State insurance company Liechtenstein*]   (EY)
AHV.......... Altos Hornos Vizcaya SA [*Spanish*]
AHW........ Aboriginal Health Worker [*Australia*]
ahw............. Als Het Ware [*Benelux*]   (BAS)
AHW........ Australian Hard Wheat [*Agriculture*]
AHWEP.... Aboriginal Health Worker Education Program [*Australia*]
AHWHEF ... Australian Hairdressers, Wigmakers, and Hairworkers Employees Federation
AHWTP.... Aboriginal Health Worker Training Programme [*Australia*]
AHWV...... Association for Health Without Vaccination [*France*]   (EAIO)
AHY.......... Azalavia-Azerbaijan Hava Yollari [*ICAO designator*]   (FAAC)
AHZ.......... Allami Hangversenyzenekar [*State Orchestra*]   (HU)
AHZ.......... Auto-Hrvatska, Zagreb, Trgovacko Poduzece na Veliko [*Auto-Croatia, Zagreb, Commercial Wholesale Establishment*] [*YU*]
ai .... Ad Interim   (SCAC)
AI .... Aeronautica Industrial SA [*Spain*] [*ICAO aircraft manufacturer identifier*]   (ICAO)
AI .... Aeronautica Italiana [*Italian Air Force*]   (WER)
AI .... Aerosol Inhalator   (RU)
AI .... Afrique Industrie
AI .... Agudath Israel [*Union of Israel*] [*World organization of Orthodox Jews*]
AI .... Aircraft Instruments and Aircrew Stations [*NATO*]   (NATG)
AI .... Alghanim Industries
AI .... Altesse Imperiale [*Imperial Highness*] [*French*]
AI .... Amity International   (EAIO)
AI .... Amnesty International [*London, England*]   (EAIO)
AI .... Anguilla [*ANSI two-letter standard code*]   (CNC)
AI .... Archaeological Institute   (BU)
AI .... Asbestos Institute   (EA)
AI .... Australian Independent
AI .... Aviation Institute Imeni Sergo Ordzhonikidze   (RU)
AI .... Historical Documents   (RU)
AI .... Institute of Archives   (BU)
AI .... Pulse Analyzer   (RU)
AI .... Selector [*Telephony*]   (RU)
AI-5........... Acto Institucional Numero 5 [*Institutional Act Number 5*] [*Brazil*]   (LA)
AIA .... Academie Internationale d'Astronautique [*France*]   (EAIO)
AIA .... Advertising Institute of Australia   (ADA)
AIA .... African Information Agency
AIA .... Alliance Intercontinentale d'Assurances
AIA .... Anguilla [*ANSI three-letter standard code*]   (CNC)
AIA .... Appliance Industry Association [*Australia*]
AIA .... Asbestos International Association [*British*]   (EAIO)
AIA .... Asociacion de Ingenieros Agronomos [*Uruguay*]   (LAA)
AIA .... Associacao Industrial de Angola
AIA .... Associate of the Institute of Actuaries of Australia and New Zealand   (ADA)
AIA .... Association Internationale Africaine
AIA .... Association Internationale d'Allergologie [*International Association of Allergology*]
AIA .... Association Internationale des Arbitres de Water Polo [*International Association of Water Polo Referees - IAWPR*]   (EAIO)
AIA .... Association of International Accountants [*British*]   (EAIO)
AIA .... Associazione Industrie Aerospaziali [*Aerospace Industries Association*] [*Rome, Italy*]   (WER)
AIA .... Associazione Italiana di Anglistica [*Italian*]   (SLS)

AIA .... Atelier Industriel de l'Aeronautique [*Aeronautical Industrial Workshop*] [*France*]
AIA .... Australian Incentives Association
AIA .... Australian Indonesian Association   (ADA)
AIA .... Australian Institute of Archaeology
AIA .... Australian [*National University*] - Institute of the Arts [*National Union Catalogue of Australia symbol*]
AIA .... Australian Insurance Association   (ADA)
AIA .... Australian Italian Association   (ADA)
AIA .... Automotive Industry Authority [*Australia*]
AIA .... Italian Archaeological Academy   (EAIO)
AIAA .... Agricultural Information Association for Australasia
AIAA .... Apparel Importers' Association of Australia
AIAA .... Associate of the Institute of Affiliate Accountants [*Australia*]
AIAB.......... Associate of the International Association of Book-Keepers   (DCTA)
AIAC......... Asociacion de Ingenieros Agronomos de Canete [*Peru*]   (DSCA)
AIAC......... Association Internationale des Aeroports Civils [*International Civil Airports Association - ICAA*]   (EAIO)
AIAC......... Associazione Internazionale degli Agenti di Cambio [*International Stockbrokers' Association*] [*Italian*]   (WER)
AIAC......... Associazione Internazionale di Archeologia Classica [*International Association for Classical Archaeology - IACA*]   (EAIO)
AIAC......... Australian Industry Arts Commission [*National Union Catalogue of Australia symbol*]
AIACE...... Associazione Italiana Amici del Cinema d'Essai [*Italian*]   (SLS)
AIACIUI ... Alliance Internationale des Anciens de la Cite Universitaire de Paris [*France*]   (EAIO)
AIACR....... Association Internationale des Automobile Clubs Reconnus [*International Automobile Federation*]
AIA CSA ... Australian Institute of the Arts Canberra School of Art [*National Union Catalogue of Australia symbol*]
AIA CSM .. Australian Institute of the Arts Canberra School of Music [*National Union Catalogue of Australia symbol*]
AIAD .... Associazione Internazionale degli Avvocati Democratici [*International Association of Democratic Lawyers*] [*Use IADL*] [*Italian*]   (WER)
AIAD .... Parliamentarians for Global Action   (EAIO)
AIADMK .. All-India Anna Dravida Munnetra Kazhagam [*Tamil Nadu*] [*Political party*]
AIAE......... Australian Institute of Art Education
AIA/EAC .. European Advisory Council of the Asbestos International Association [*EC*]   (ECED)
AIAF........ Associazione Italiana degli Analisti Finanziari [*Italian*]   (SLS)
AIAFD....... Association des Institutions Africaines de Financement du Developpement
AIAG .... Aluminium Industrie Aktiengesellschaft
AIAL......... Australian Institute of Administrative Law
AIAM .... Accademia Internazionale d'Arte Moderna [*Italian*]   (SLS)
AIAM .... Asociacion de Ingenieros y Arquitectos de Mexico
AIAMC..... Associazione Italiana di Analisi e Modificazione del Comportamento [*Italy*]   (EAIO)
AIAN .... Association Internationale des Approvisionneurs de Navires [*British*]   (EAIO)
AI & S ...... Australian Iron and Steel Ltd.
AIAP......... Asociatia Internationala a Artistilor Plastici [*International Association of Plastic Artists*]   (RO)
AIAP......... Associate, Institute of Australian Photography   (ADA)
AIAP......... Association Internationale des Arts Plastiques [*International Association of Art - IAA*]   (EAIO)
AIAPN...... Australian Institute of Air Pilots and Navigators
AIArbA...... Associate of the Institute of Arbitrators Australia
AIAREF .... Association Internationale des Anesthesistes - Reanimateurs d'Expression Francaise [*Belgium*]   (SLS)
AIAS......... Abeitsgemeinschaft fuer Interdisziplinaere Angewandte Sozialforschung [*Austria*]   (SLS)
AIAS......... Associazione Italiana per l'Analisi delle Sollecitazioni [*Italian*]   (SLS)
AIAS......... Australian Institute of Aboriginal Studies   (ADA)
AIAS......... Australian Institute of Aboriginal [*and Torres Strait Islander*] Studi es [*National Union Catalogue of Australia symbol*]
AIAS......... Australian Institute of Agricultural Science   (ADA)
AIAT........ Association Internationale pour le Developpement Economique et l'Aide Technique [*International Association for Economic Development and Technical Aid*] [*French*]   (AF)
AIATSIS ... Australian Institute of Aboriginal and Torres Strait Islander Studies
AIAU .... Atomic Institute of the Austrian Universities [*Research center*]   (IRC)
AIAV .... Australian Indonesian Association of Victoria [*Australia*]
AIB .... Academy of International Business   (EAIO)
AIB .... Airbus Industrie [*France*] [*ICAO designator*]   (FAAC)
AIB .... Allami Ifjusagi Bizottsag [*State Youth Committee*]   (HU)
AIB .... Allied Intelligence Bureau [*Australia*]   (ADA)
AIB .... Allied Irish Bank
AIB .... Army Engineer Battalion   (RU)

AIB .... Association Internationale de Bibliophile [*International Association of Bibliophiles - IAB*] [*Paris, France*]   (EAIO)
AIB .... Association Internationale de Bryozoologie [*International Bryozoology Association - IBA*] [*Paris, France*]   (EAIO)
AIB .... Associazione Italiana Biblioteche
AIB .... Australian Infantry Battalion   (ADA)
AIB .... Australian Institute of Bankers
AIB .... Australian Institute of Biology
AIB .... Australian Institute of Building   (ADA)
AIB .... Beirut International Airport   (ME)
AIBA......... Agricultural Inforamation Bank for Asia [*Philippines*]   (PDAA)
AIBA......... Associated Insurance Brokers of Australia
AIBA......... Associate of the Institute of Business Administration [*Australia*]
AIBA......... Association Internationale de Boxe Amateur   (OLYM)
AIBA......... International Boxing Federation   (BU)
AIBAA ...... Artists in Bark Association of Australia
AIBAN ...... Institute of Archives of the Bulgarian Academy of Sciences   (BU)
AIBBC ...... Australian Indoor Bias Bowls Council
AIBC......... Australia-Indonesia Business Council
AIBCC...... Australia-Indonesia Business Cooperation Committee
AIBD .... Asia-Pacific Institute for Broadcasting Development   (EAIO)
AIBD .... Association of International Bond Dealers [*Zurich, Switzerland*]   (EAIO)
AIBD .... International Securities Market Association [*Switzerland*]   (EAIO)
AIBDA....... Asociacion Interamericana de Bibliotecarios y Documentalistas Agricolas [*Inter-American Association of Agricultural Librarians and Documentalists*]   (EAIO)
AIBDQ ...... Association of International Bond Dealers Quotation [*Stock exchange term*]
AIBEA ...... All-India Bank Employees' Association
AIBEF ...... All-India Bank Employees' Federation
AIBGA...... All-Island Banana Growers Association [*Jamaica*]   (LA)
AIBI.......... Association Internationale de la Boulangerie Industrielle [*International Association of the Bread Industry*]   (EAIO)
AIBM .... Association Internationale des Bibliotheques, Archives, et Centres de Documentation Musicaux [*International Association of Music Libraries, Archives, and Documentation Centres - IAML*]   (EAIO)
AIBM .... Association Internationale des Bibliotheques Musicals
AIBN .... Azobis [*Isobutyronitrile*]   (RU)
AIBS .... Australian Institute of Building Surveyors   (ADA)
AIBTC ...... Association for Information Brokerage and Technological Consultancy   (EAIO)
AIC .... Academia de la Investigacion Cientifica [*Mexico*]   (DSCA)
AIC .... Academie Internationale de la Ceramique [*International Academy of Ceramics - IAC*]   (EAIO)
AIC .... Africa Information Centre [*New Zealand*]   (EAIO)
AIC .... African Independent Church
AIC .... African Inland Church
AIC .... Agricultural-Industrial Complex [*Bulgaria*]   (IMH)
AIC .... Agriculture Inputs Corporation [*Nepal*]   (GEA)
AIC .... Agrupaciones Independientes de Canarias [*Spain*] [*Political party*]   (EY)
AIC .... Air India [*ICAO designator*]   (FAAC)
AIC .... Air Infiltration Centre [*Switzerland*]
AIC .... Alternative Information Center [*Israeli news organization*]
AIC .... Arab Investment Company
AIC .... Arquitectos, Ingenieros, Constructores Ltda. [*Colombia*]   (COL)
AIC .... Artificial Insemination Centre [*Australia*]
AIC .... Asociacion Interamericana de Contabilidad [*Interamerican Accounting Association - IAA*] [*Mexico City, Mexico*]   (EAIO)
AIC .... Assistance for Isolated Children [*Scheme*] [*Australia*]
AIC .... Association des Industries des Carrieres [*Federations of Quarrying Industries*] [*Belgium*]   (EY)
AIC .... Association Internationale de Cybernetique [*International Association for Cybernetics - IAC*]   (EAIO)
AIC .... Association Internationale de la Couleur [*International Color Association*] [*Soesterberg, Netherlands*]   (EA)
AIC .... Association Internationale des Charites [*International Association of Charities - IAC*]   (EAIO)
AIC .... Association Internationale des Charites de St. Vincent De Paul [*International Association of Charities of St. Vincent De Paul*]   (EAIO)
AIC .... Association Internationale des Cordeliers [*International Songwriters' Association - ISA*]   (EAIO)
AIC .... Association Internationale du Congo
AIC .... Associations d'Interet Collectif
AIC .... Associazione Italiana di Cardiostimolazione [*Italian*]   (SLS)
AIC .... Associazione Italiana di Cartografia [*Italian*]   (SLS)
AIC .... Australian Institute of Cartographers   (ADA)
AIC .... Australian Institute of Criminology   (ADA)
AIC .... Australian Institute of Criminology [*J V Barry Library*] [*National Union Catalogue of Australia symbol*]
AIC .... Australian Intelligence Corps
AIC .... Australian Investment Conferences

AIC .... International Colour Association   (SLS)
AICA......... African Independent Churches Association [*South Africa*]   (AF)
AICA......... Agencia Informativa Catolica Argentina [*Argentine Catholic Information Agency*]   (LA)
AICA......... Asociacion pro Integracion Centroamericana   (LAA)
AICA......... Association Internationale des Critiques d'Art [*International Association of Art Critics*]   (EAIO)
AICA......... Association Internationale pour le Calcul Analogique [*International Association for Analogue Computation*] [*Later, IMACS*]
AICA......... Associazione degli Industriali delle Conserve Animali [*Meat Products Manufacturers Association*] [*Italy*]   (EY)
AICA......... Associazione Italiana Costruttori Autoattrezzature
AICA......... Associazione Italiana Culturale Aeronautica [*Italian*]   (SLS)
AICA......... Associazione Italiana per il Calcolo Automatico [*Italian Association for Automatic Data Processing*]
AICA......... Australasian Institute of Chartered Accountants
AICA......... Australasian Institute of Cost Accountants   (ADA)
AICA......... Australian Institute of Counselling in Addictions
AICAA...... Associate of the Institute of Chartered Accountants in Australia
AICB......... Association des Interets Coloniaux Belges [*Merged with AIIB into FEC*]
AICB......... Association Internationale Contre le Bruit [*International Association Against Noise*] [*ICSU*]   (EAIO)
AICC......... All-Indian Congress Committee   (PDAA)
AICC......... Association Internationale de Chimie Cerealiere [*Austria*]   (DSCA)
AICC......... Australia-India Chamber of Commerce
AICC......... Australian Import Statistics [*Database*]
AICCA...... Aboriginal and Islander Child Care Agencies [*Australia*]
AICCA...... Australian International Cabin Crew Association
AICCF ...... Association Internationale du Congres des Chemins de Fer [*International Railway Congress Association - IRCA*]   (EAIO)
AICCI ...... Australia-Israel Chamber of Commerce and Industry
AICCM..... Associated Indian Chambers of Commerce of Malaysia
AICCM..... Australian Institute for the Conservation of Cultural Materials
AICDT...... International Advisory Committee on Documentation and Terminology in Pure and Applied Science [*UNESCO*]
AICE......... Association of Innovation Centre Executives [*European Community*]
AICF......... Action Internationale Contre la Faim [*International Action Against Hunger*] [*Paris, France*]   (EAIO)
AICF......... Australian Indoor Cricket Federation
AICFO...... Asociacion Internacional para las Ciencias Fisicas del Oceano [*International Association for the Physical Sciences of the Ocean - IAPSO*] [*Spanish*]   (ASF)
AIChPYe ... Association for the Study of the European Quaternary   (RU)
AICI.......... Association Interprofessionnelle des Employeurs de la Cote-D'Ivoire
AICI.......... Associazione Architetti ed Ingegneri Consulenti Italiani [*Italy*]   (EAIO)
AICL......... Association Internationale des Critiques Litteraires [*International Association of Literary Critics*]   (EAIO)
AICL......... Australian Innovation Corporation Limited   (ADA)
AICM .... Australian Institute of Credit Management   (ADA)
AICMA..... Association Internationale des Contructeurs de Materiel Aerospatial   (PDAA)
AICMR..... Association Internationale des Constructeurs de Materiel Roulant [*International Association of Rolling Stock Builders - IARSB*]   (EAIO)
AICN .... Agence d'Information de la Chine Nouvelle [*New China News Agency*] [*Use NCNA*]   (CL)
AICN .... Asociacion de Inestigacion de la Construccion Naval [*Shipbuilding Research Association*] [*Spain*]   (PDAA)
AICO .... Asociacion Iberoamericana de Camaras de Comercio [*Ibero-American Association of Chambers of Commerce - IAACC*] [*Bogota, Colombia*]   (EAIO)
AICOBOO ... All-India Confederation of Bank Officers Organisations   (PDAA)
AICOS....... Associazione per gli Interventi di Cooperazione allo Sviluppo [*Italy*]   (EAIO)
AICP......... Asian Infrastructure Consortia Program [*Australia*]
AICP......... Associate of the International Council of Psychologists
AICP......... Association Internationale des Circuits Permanents [*Circuits International*] [*Germany*]   (EAIO)
AICPN...... Association Internationale Permanente des Congres de Navigation   (FLAF)
AICQ .... Associazione Italiana per la Qualita [*Italian Association for Quality*]   (SLS)
AIC(Q)...... Australian Institute of Cartographers (Queensland)
AICR......... Association for International Cancer Research   (EAIO)
AICR......... Association Internationale de la Croix Rouge [*International Red Cross Association*]   (CL)
AICRIP...... All-India Coordinated Rice Improvement Project
AICS .... Aboriginal Independent Community Schools [*Australia*]
AICS .... Assistance for Isolated Children Scheme [*Australia*]

AICS.......... Association Internationale du Cinema Scientifique [*French*]
(SLS)

AICS.......... Australian Inventory of Chemical Substances

AICSA...... Aero-Industrial Colombiana SA [*Colombia*]　(COL)

AICSA...... Associate of the Institute of Chartered Secretaries and
Administrators [*Australia*]

AICSA...... Australian Intervarsity Choral Societies' Association

AICT.......... Association Internationale Contre la Torture [*International
Association Against Torture*] [*Milan, Italy*]　(EAIO)

AICT.......... Association Internationale des Critiques de Theatre [*French*]
(SLS)

AICTC....... Associazione Italiana di Chimica Tessile e Coloristica [*Italian*]
(SLS)

A-ICTU..... All-India Centre of Trade Unions

AICUM..... Australian Institute of Credit Union Management

AICV.......... Accion Integral Colombo Venezolana [*Colombia*]　(COL)

AICV.......... Association des Industries des Cidres et Vins de Fruits de la CEE
[*Association of the Cider and Fruit Wine Industries of the
EEC*]　(ECED)

AICV.......... Australian Institute of Consultant Valuers

AICVF-CE ... Association des Industries de Cidre et Vins de Fruits de la CE
[*Belgium*]　(EAIO)

AICVS....... Association Internationale Contre la Violence dans le Sport
[*International Association for Non-Violent Sport - IANVS*]
[*Monte Carlo, Monaco*]　(EAIO)

AICYEE .... Association of the International Christian Youth Exchange in
Europe　(EAIO)

AID .... Agency for International Development [*State Department*] [*Also,
USAID US International Development Cooperation
Agency*]

AID .... Agricultural, Industrial, and Development [*Bank*] [*Dominica*]
(EY)

AID .... Agriculture Industrial Development [*Commercial firm*] [*Italy*]

AID .... Algemene Inspectie Dienst [*Benelux*]　(BAS)

AID .... Alliance Internationale de la Distribution par Cable
[*International Alliance for Distribution by Cable*]　(EAIO)

AID .... American Documentation Institute　(RU)

AID .... Apparatus for Artificial Respiration　(RU)

AID .... Artikkel-Indeks Database [*Norwegian Center for Informatics*]
[*Information service or system*]

AID .... Association Internationale de Documentation [*French*]　(SLS)

AID .... Association Internationale des Documentalistes

AID .... Association Internationale du Droit Commercial et du Droit des
Affaires　(FLAF)

AID .... Association Internationale pour le Developpement [*International
Development Association*] [*An affiliate of IBRD Use IDA*]
[*French*]　(CL)

AID .... Association of Industrial Designers [*Poland*]　(EAIO)

AID .... Atomics International Division

AID .... Australian Institute of Dieticians

AID .... Australian Institute of Drycleaning　(ADA)

AIDA .... Asociacion Internacional de Derecho de Aguas [*International
Association for Water Law - IAWL*] [*Spain*]　(EAIO)

AIDA .... Association Internationale de Defense des Artistes [*International
Association for the Defence of Artists*]　(EAIO)

AIDA .... Association Internationale de Droit Africain [*International
African Law Association*] [*Use IALA*]　(AF)

AIDA .... Association Internationale de Droit des Assurances
[*International Association for Insurance Law*] [*Belgium*]
(EAIO)

AIDA .... Association Internationale de la Distribution [*International
Association of Distribution*] [*Belgium*]　(EAIO)

AIDA .... Association Internationale de la Distribution des Produits
Alimentaires et des Produits de Grande Consommation
[*International Association for the Distribution of Food
Products and General Consumer Goods*]　(EAIO)

AIDA .... Associazione Italiana di Aerotecnica

AIDA .... Associazione Italiana per la Documentazione Avanzata [*Italian
Association for Advanced Documentation*] [*Information
service or system*]　(IID)

AIDA .... Australian Industries Development Association　(ADA)

AIDA .... Australian Irish Dancing Association

AIDAA ...... Associazione Italiana de Aeronautica e Astronautica

AIDAB...... Australian International Development Assistance Bureau

AIDAC...... Association Internationale de Developpement et d'Action
Communautaires [*International Association for
Community Development*] [*Marcinelle, Belgium*]　(EAIO)

AIDASA .... Association Internationale pour le Developpement en Afrique
des Sciences Humaines Appliquees [*International
Association for the Development of Applied Human Sciences
in Africa*]　(AF)

AIDB .... Agricultural and Industrial Development Bank [*Ethiopia*]　(AF)

AIDB .... Agricultural and Industrial Development Board [*Cayman
Islands*]

AIDBA....... Association Internationale pour le Developpement des
Bibliotheques en Afrique [*International Association for the
Development of Libraries in Africa*]　(AF)

AIDC .... Alliance Internationale de la Distribution par Cable
[*International Alliance for Distribution by Cable - IADC*]
(EAIO)

AIDC .... Association Internationale de Droit Constitutionnel
[*International Association of Constitutional Law - IACL*]
(EAIO)

AIDC .... Australian Industry Development Corporation　(ADA)

AIDD .... Auckland Industrial Development Division [*Department of
Scientific and Industrial Research*] [*New Zealand*]
[*Research center*]　(IRC)

AIDE .... Action Internationale pour les Droits de l'Enfant [*International
Action for the Rights of the Child - IARC*] [*Paris, France*]
(EAIO)

AIDE .... Agence Internationale pour le Developpement [*Paris, France*]
(EAIO)

AIDE .... Agencia de Informacao e Divulgacao Educacionais [*Brazil*]
(DSCA)

AIDE .... Association Internationale des Distributions d'Eau [*International
Water Supply Association - IWSA*] [*French*]　(ASF)

AIDE .... Association Internationale du Droit des Eaux [*International
Association for Water Law - IAWL*] [*French*]　(ASF)

AIDE .... Association Ivoirienne des Dirigeants d'Entreprise

AIDEC...... Association Internationale d'Expertise Chimique [*French*]　(SLS)

AIDEF .... All-India Defence Employees' Federation [*Trade union*]　(FEA)

AIDELF.... Association Internationale des Demographes de Langue
Francaise　(EAIO)

AIDEX...... Australia International Defence Equipment Exhibition

AIDF......... African Industrial Development Fund

AIDHRO ... Association Internationale pour le Developpement des
Hydrocolloides

AIDI........... Associazione Industrie Dolciarie Italiane [*Confectioners
association*] [*Italy*]　(EY)

AIDI........... Associazione Italiana di Documentazione e di Informazione
[*Italian*]　(SLS)

AIDI........... Associazione Italiana di Illuminazione [*Italian*]　(SLS)

AIDIA....... Associate of the Industrial Design Institute of Australia　(ADA)

AIDIS .... Asociacion Interamericana de Ingenieria Sanitaria [*Inter-
American Association of Sanitary Engineering*]　(LAA)

AIDLCM ... Association Internationale pour la Defense des Langues et
Cultures Menacees [*International Association for the
Defence of Threatened Languages and Cultures*]　(EAIO)

AIDN .... Association Internationale du Droit Nucleaire [*International
Nuclear Law Association - INLA*]　(EA)

AIDO .... Arab Industrial Development Organization　(EA)

AIDO .... International Association of Opera Directors [*Sweden*]　(EAIO)

AIDOAO ... Association Internationale des Diffuseurs d'Oeuvres d'Art
Originales [*International Association of Original Art
Diffusors - IAOAD*]　(EAIO)

AIDOS .... Associazione Italiana Donne per lo Sviluppo [*Italian Association
for Women in Development*]　(EAIO)

AIDP.......... Association Internationale de Droit Penal [*French*]　(SLS)

AIDR .... Asociatia Internationala pentru Dezvoltarea Rurala
[*International Association for Rural Development*]　(RO)

AIDR .... Association International de Developpement Rural
[*International Association for Rural Development*]
[*Belgium*]

AIDRF .... Australian Intellectual Disabilities Research Foundation

AIDS.......... Academy of International Dental Studies　(EAIO)

AIDS.......... Acquired Immunodeficiency Syndrome [*Medicine*]　(IDIG)

AIDS.......... Agricultural Information and Documentation Section [*Royal
Tropical Institute*] [*Netherlands*] [*Information service or
system*]　(IID)

AIDS.......... Agricultural Information Development Scheme　(EAIO)

AIDS.......... Amnesty International Danish Section　(EAIO)

AIDS.......... North Atlantic Institute for Defense Study [*NATO*]　(NATG)

AIDT .... Aboriginal Islander Dance Theatre [*Australia*]

AIDT .... Association Interparlementaire du Tourisme [*Interparliamentary
Association for Tourism*]

AIDUIM ... Association Internationale pour le Developpement des
Universites Internationales et Mondiales [*International
Association for the Development of International and World
Universities - IADIWU*] [*Aulnay-Sous-Bois, France*]
(EAIO)

AIDUM ..... Association Internationale pour le Developpement des
Universites Internationales et Mondiales [*French*]　(SLS)

AIE .... Agence Internationale de l'Energie [*International Energy Agency*]
[*Use IEA*]　(AF)

AIE .... Aiome [*Papua New Guinea*] [*Airport symbol*]　(OAG)

AIE .... Associate of the Institute of Education [*Australia*]

AIE .... Association Internationale de l'Etancheite [*International
Waterproofing Association - IWA*]　(EAIO)

AIE .... Association Internationale des Entreprises d'Equipement
Electrique [*International Association of Electrical
Contractors - IAEC*]　(EAIO)

AIE .... Associazione Internazionale degli Economisti [*International
Economists' Association*] [*Italian*]　(WER)

AIE .... Associazione Italiana Editori

AIE .... Australia Institution of Engineers [*National Union Catalogue of Australia symbol*]

AIE .... Australian Institute of Energy

AIE .... Australian Institute of Export   (ADA)

AIEA.......... Agence Internationale de l'Energie Atomique [*International Atomic Energy Agency*] [*Use IAEA*]   (AF)

AIEA.......... Agentia Internationala pentru Energia Atomica [*International Atomic Energy Agency*]   (RO)

AIEA.......... Association Internationale des Etudiants en Agriculture [*International Association of Agriculture Students - IAAS*] (EAIO)

AIEA.......... Australian Department of Immigration and Ethnic Affairs [*National Union Catalogue of Australia symbol*]

AIEA.......... Australian Institute of Educational Administration

AIEA.......... Australian Institute of Engineering Associates

AIEA.......... Australian Institute of Engineering Associates Ltd.   (ADA)

AIEAS .... Association Internationale des Etudes de l'Asie du Sud-Est [*Paris, France*]   (EAIO)

AIEB.......... Association Internationale des Etudes Byzantines [*International Association for Byzantine Studies - IABS*]   (EAIO)

AI-EC .... Amnesty International EC Representation [*Belgium*]   (EAIO)

AIECE .... Association d'Instituts Europeens de Conjoncture Economique [*Association of European Conjuncture Institutes*]   (EAIO)

AIECM...... Association Internationale d'Etude des Civilisations Mediterraneennes [*International Association of Studies on Mediterranean Civilizations*]   (EAIO)

AIEd .... Associate of the Institute of Education [*Australia*]

AIED .... Association Internationale des Etudiants Dentaires [*International Association of Dental Students - IADS*] [*British*]   (EA)

AIEE.......... Association des Instituts d'Etudes Europeennes [*Association of Institutes for European Studies*]

AIEE.......... Australian International Engineering Exhibition   (ADA)

AIEE.......... Australia's International Engineering Exhibition

AIEEA .... Association Internationale pour l'Etude de l'Economie de l'Assurance [*Switzerland*]   (EAIO)

AIEF .... Association Internationale des Etudes Francaises [*Paris, France*]   (EAIO)

AIEF .... Association Internationale pour l'Etude du Foie [*International Association for the Study of the Liver*]   (EAIO)

AIEF .... Australian International Education Foundation

AIEGA...... Association Internationale d'Eutonie Gerda Alexander [*International Association for Gerda Alexander Eutony*] [*Switzerland*]   (EAIO)

AIEGL ...... Association Internationale d'Epigraphie Grecque et Latine [*International Association for Greek and Latin Epigraphy*]   (EAIO)

AIEH .... Asociacion de Instituciones Evangelicas de Honduras

AIEH .... Australian Institute of Environmental Health

AIEI .... Association Internationale pour l'Education Integrative [*International Association for Integrative Education - IAIE*] (EAIO)

AIEI .... Association of the Indian Engineering Industry   (EY)

AIEIA .... Association Internationale des Ecoles et Instituts d'Administration [*Belgium*]   (SLS)

AIEJI........ Association Internationale des Educateurs de Jeunes Inadaptes [*International Association of Workers for Troubled Children and Youth*]   (EAIO)

AIEMA...... Association Internationale pour l'Etude de la Mosaoique Antique [*French*]   (SLS)

AIEP......... Asociacion Internacional de Escritores Policiacos [*International Association of Crime Writers*]

AIEP......... Association Internationale des Usagers d'Embranchements Particuliers [*International Association of Users of Private Branch Railway Sidings*]   (PDAA)

AIEP......... Association Internationale d'Etudes Patristiques [*International Association for Patristic Studies*]   (EAIO)

AIEPCI...... Association des Inspecteurs de l'Enseignement Primaire [*Association of Primary School Inspectors*] [*Ivory Coast*] (AF)

AIEPD....... African Institute for Economic Planning and Development

AIER......... Austrian Institute of Economic Research   (EAIO)

AIERA .... Asociacion de Importadores y Exportadores de la Republica Argentina [*Importers and Exporters Association of the Argentine Republic*]   (LA)

AIERI .... Association Internationale des Etudes et Recherches sur l'Information [*International Association of Mass Communications Research*]

AIERS ...... Association Internationale pour l'Evaluation du Rendement Scolaire [*International Association for the Valuation of Educational Achievement*]   (EAIO)

AIES .... Association Internationale pour les Etudes Sanskrites [*France*] (EAIO)

AIES .... Associazione Italiana per l'Educazione Sanitaria [*Italian*]   (SLS)

AIES .... Australian Institute of Emergency Services

AIESEC..... Association Internationale des Etudiants en Sciences Economiques et Commerciales [*International Association of Students in Economics and Commerce*] [*Brussels, Belgium*]   (EAIO)

AIESEE..... Asociatia Internationala de Studii Sud-Est Europeene [*International Association of Southeastern European Studies*]   (RO)

AIESEE..... Association Internationale d'Etudes du Sud-Est Europeen [*International Association of South-East European Studies - IASEES*]   (EAIO)

AIESEP..... Association Internationale des Ecoles Superieures d'Education Physique [*International Association for Physical Education in Higher Education*]   (EAIO)

AIESI........ Association Internationale des Ecoles des Sciences de l'Information [*International Association of Information Sciences Schools*] [*Canada*]   (EAIO)

AIESS....... Association Internationale des Ecoles de Service Social [*International Association of Schools of Social Work - IASSW*]   (EA)

AIEST ...... Association Internationale d'Experts Scientifiques du Tourisme [*International Association of Scientific Experts in Tourism*] (EAIO)

AIEU .... Australian Insurance Employees Union   (ADA)

AIF............ Agenzia Internazionale Fides [*News agency*] [*Vatican City*] (EY)

AIF............ Air Ile de France [*ICAO designator*]   (FAAC)

AIF............ Alliance Internationale des Femmes [*International Alliance of Women - IAW*] [*Valetta, Malta*]   (EAIO)

AIF............ Arbeitsgemeinschaft fuer Industrielle Forschung [*Cooperative Group for Industrial Research*] [*German*]

AIF............ Asociacion Internacional de Fomento [*International Development Association - IDA*] [*Spanish*]   (ASF)

AIF............ Association des Industriels de France Contre les Accidents du Travail [*French*]   (SLS)

AIF............ Association Internationale Futuribles [*Futuribles International*] (EAIO)

AIF............ Associazione Italiana Formatori

AIF............ Australasian Institute of Fundraising

AIF............ Australian Imperial Force   (ADA)

AIF............ Australian Imperial Forces

AIF............ Australian Infrastructure Fund

AIFA .... American International Freight Association

AIFA .... Association Internationale Francophone des Aines [*Canada*] (EAIO)

AIFAI .... Associazione Italiana Fabbricanti Apparecchi Illuminazione

AIFAN....... Association Internationale des Femmes d'Affaires Noires [*Black Business Women - International - BBWI*] [*France*]   (EAIO)

AIFC .... Australian International Finance Corporation   (ADA)

AIFE .... Association Internationale des Femmes Ecrivains [*French*] (SLS)

AIFLD ...... American Institute for Free Labor Development   (LA)

AIFLD ...... Association des Industries des Fruits et Legumes Deshydrates de la CEE [*European Organization of the Dehydrated Fruit and Vegetable Industries*] [*EC*]   (ECED)

AIFLV ...... Association de l'Industrie des Fruits et Legumes au Vinaigre, en Saumure, a l'Huile et des Produits Similaires des CE [*Association of the Industry of Fruit and Vegetables in Vinegar, Brine, Oil and Similar Products of the EC*] (ECED)

AIFM........ Association Internationale des Femmes Medecins [*Medical Women's International Association - MWIA*] [*Germany*] (EAIO)

AIFP .... Association Internationale de la Fonction Publique [*Avignon, France*]   (EAIO)

AIFRO...... Association Internationale Francophone de Recherche Odontologique [*French*]   (SLS)

AIFS .... African Improved Farming Scheme

AIFS .... Australian Institute of Family Studies

AIFS .... Australian Institute of Forensic Sciences

AIFSIA ..... Australian International Simulator Instructors' Association

AIFSPR .... Associazione Italiana di Fisica Sanitaria e di Protezione Contro le Radiazioni [*Italian*]   (SLS)

AIFST........ Australian Institute of Food Science and Technology   (ADA)

AIFUCTO ... All-India Federation of University and College Teachers' Organisations

AIFV .... Association des Ingenieurs des Villes de France [*Municipal Engineers Association of France*]   (PDAA)

AIG .... Aiguille [*Peak, Needle*] [*French*]   (ROG)

AIG .... Air Inter Gabon [*ICAO designator*]   (FAAC)

AIG .... Artiljeriske Izvidacke Grupe [*Artillery Reconnaissance Groups*] (YU)

AIG .... Association Internationale de Geodesie [*French*]   (SLS)

AIG .... Association pour l'Informatique de Gestion [*Paris, France*]

AIG .... Associazione Italiana di Galvanotecnica [*Italian*]   (SLS)

AIG .... Australian Institute of Geoscientists

AIG .... Australian Institute of Guitar

AIGA .... Asociacion Interamericana de Gastroentereologia [*Mexico*] (SLS)

AIGAM ..... Australian Institute of Graphic Arts Management (ADA)

AIGD .... Associazione Italiana Giuristi Democratici [*Italian*] (SLS)

AIGE .... Asociacion Interamericana de Gastroenterologia [*Interamerican Association of Gastroenterology*] [*Guatemala*]

Aigle .... Aiguille [*Peak, Needle*] [*Military map abbreviation World War I*] [*French*] (MTD)

AIGM .... Association Internationale de Grands Magasins [*International Association of Department Stores - IADS*] (EAIO)

AIGMF ...... All-India Glass Manufacturers Federation (PDAA)

AIGR .... Associazione Italiana di Genio Rurale [*Italian*] (SLS)

AIGS .... Australian Institute of Genealogical Studies (ADA)

AIGYPFB ... Asociacion de Ingenieros y Geologos de Yacimientos Petroliferos Fiscales Bolivianos [*Bolivia*] (SLS)

AIH .... Academie Internationale d'Heraldique [*Bridel, Luxembourg*] (EAIO)

AIH .... Asociacion Internacional de Hispanistas [*International Association of Hispanists*] [*Aalst, Belgium*] (EA)

AIH .... Association Internationale des Hydrogeologues [*International Association of Hydrogeologists*] [*French*] (SLS)

AIH .... Association Internationale d'Hotellerie [*International Hotel Association - IHA*] (EAIO)

AIH .... Australian Institute of Health [*National Union Catalogue of Australia symbol*]

AIH .... Australian Institute of Homeopathy

AIH .... Australian Institute of Horticulture (ADA)

AIH .... Australian Institute of Hospital Administrators (ADA)

AIHC .... Asociacion Internacional de Hidrologia Cientifica [*International Association of Scientific Hydrology - IASH*] [*Spanish*] (ASF)

AIHCE ...... Association Internationale d'Histoire Contemporaine de l'Europe [*International Association for Contemporary History of Europe*] [*Defunct*] (EAIO)

AIHE .... Asociacion Interamericana de Hombres de Empresa [*Inter-American Businessmen's Association*]

AIHEX ...... Asian International Hardware Exposition

AIHF .... Austrian Ice Hockey Federation (EAIO)

AIHJA ...... Association Internationale des Hautes Juridictions Administratives [*International Association of Supreme Administrative Jurisdictions*] (EAIO)

AIHK .... Avrupa Insan Haklari Komisyonu [*European Human Rights Committee*] (GC)

AIHP .... Academie Internationale d'Histoire de la Pharmacie [*International Academy of the History of Pharmacy*] (EAIO)

AIHP .... Authority for Intellectually Handicapped Persons [*Western Australia*]

AIHR .... African Institute of Human Rights (EAIO)

AIHR .... Australian Institute of Human Relations (ADA)

AIHS .... Association Internationale de Hydrologie Scientifique [*International Association of Scientific Hydrology - IASH*] [*French*] (ASF)

AIHS .... Australian Institute of Health Surveyors (ADA)

AIHS .... Australian International Hotel School

AIHV .... Association Internationale pour l'Histoire du Verre [*International Association for the History of Glass*] (EAIO)

AII .... Air India International

AII .... Associacao Interamericana de Imprensa [*Inter-American Press Association*] [*Use IAPA*] (LA)

AII .... Associazione Idrotecnica Italiana [*Italian*] (SLS)

AII .... Australian Industry Involvement

AII .... Australian InFo International

AII .... Australian Insurance Institute (ADA)

AIIA .... Atlantic Institute for International Affairs [*France*] (EA)

AIIA .... Australian Information Industry Association

AIIA .... Australian Institute of Incorporated Accountants (ADA)

AIIA .... Australian Institute of Industrial Advocates

AIIA .... Australian Institute of International Affairs (ADA)

AIIB .... Association des Interets Industriels au Congo [*Merged with AICB into FEC*]

AIIBP .... Association Internationale de l'Industrie des Bouillions et Potages [*International Association of the Manufacture of Soups and Broths*] (EAIO)

AIIC .... Arab International Insurance Company

AIIC .... Association Internationale des Interpretes de Conference [*International Association of Conference Interpreters*] (EAIO)

AIICA .... Asociacion Internacional sobre Investigaciones Relativas a la Contaminacion de las Aguas [*International Association on Water Pollution Research - IAWPR*] [*Spanish*] (ASF)

AIICO .... American International Insurance Company (Nigeria) Ltd.

AIIDAP ..... Association Internationale d'Information et de Documentation en Administration Publique [*International Association for Information and Documentation in Public Administration*] (EAIO)

AIIG .... Associazione Italiana degli Insegnanti di Geografia [*Italian*] (SLS)

AIIH .... Asociacion Internacional de Investigaciones Hydraulicas [*International Association for Hydraulic Research - IAHR*] [*Spanish*] (ASF)

AIIHPH .... All-India Institute of Hygiene and Public Health (PDAA)

AIII .... Association Internationale d'Irradiation Industrielle [*Association of International Industrial Irradiation*] (EAIO)

AIIM .... Associate of the Institution of Industrial Managers [*British*] (DCTA)

AIIM .... Association for Information and Image Management, Inc. [*Australia*]

AIIM .... Association of Independent Investment Managers (EAIO)

AIIMB .... Associazione Italiana di Ingegneria Medica e Biologica [*Italian*] (SLS)

AIIMH ...... All-India Institute of Mental Health (PDAA)

AIIMS .... All-India Institute of Medical Sciences (PDAA)

AIIMS .... Australian Inter-Service Incident Management System

AIIP .... Asociacion Internacional de Investigacion para la Paz [*International Peace Research Association*] (EAIO)

AIIP .... Australian Institute of Industrial Psychology (ADA)

AIIPA .... Associazione Italiana Industriali Prodotti Alimentari [*Food manufacturers association*] [*Italy*] (EY)

AIIPMR .... All-India Institue of Physical Medicine and Rehabilitation (PDAA)

AIIS .... Amnesty International - Icelandic Section (EAIO)

AI-IS .... Amnesty International - Israel Section (EAIO)

AIIS .... Australian International Independent School

AIISP .... Associazione Italiana per l'Igiene e la Sanita Pubblica [*Italian Association for Hygiene and Public Health*] (ASF)

AIISUP ...... Association Internationale d'Information Scolaire, Universitaire, et Professionelle [*International Association for Educational and Vocational Information - IAEVI*] (EAIO)

AIIT .... Association Internationale de l'Inspection du Travail [*French*] (SLS)

AIIU .... Australian Institute for International Understanding

AIJA .... Alliance Internationale Jeanne d'Arc [*Saint Joan's International Alliance - SJIA*] (EAIO)

AIJA .... Association Internationale des Jeunes Avocats [*Young Lawyers' International Association*] (EAIO)

AIJA .... Australian Institute of Jewish Affairs

AIJA .... Australian Institute of Judicial Administration

AIJCFA ..... All-Island Jamaica Cane Farmers Association (LA)

AIJD .... Asociacion Internacional de Juristas Democraticos [*International Association of Democratic Lawyers*] [*Use IADL*] (LA)

AIJD .... Asociatia Internationala a Juristilor Democrati [*International Association of Democratic Lawyers*] (RO)

AIJD .... Association Internationale des Juristes Democrates [*International Association of Democratic Lawyers*]

AIJE .... Association des Industries du Jute Europeennes [*France*] (DSCA)

AIJN .... Association de l'Industrie des Just et Nectars de Fruits et de Legumes de la CEE [*Association of the Industry of Juices and Nectars from Fruits and Vegetables of the EEC*] (ECED)

AIJP .... Association Italiana des Journalistes Philateliques [*International Association of Philatelic Journalists*] [*Germany*]

AIJPF .... Association Internationale des Journalistes de la Presse Feminine et Familiale [*International Association of Women and Home Page Journalists - IAWHPJ*] (EAIO)

AIK .... African Airlines International Ltd. [*Kenya*] [*ICAO designator*] (FAAC)

aik .... Aikaisemmin [*Earlier*] [*Finland*]

AIK .... Aminoimidazolecarboxamide (RU)

AIK .... Apparatus for Artificial Blood Circulation (RU)

AIK .... Arkhi Ilektrismou Kyprou [*Cyprus Electricity Authority*] (GC)

AIK .... Association des Ingenieurs Khmers [*Cambodian Engineers Association*] (CL)

AIK .... Autonomous Industrial Colony [*Kuzbass*] (RU)

AIK .... Evaporative Condenser Unit (RU)

AIK-Kuzbass ... Kuzbass Autonomous Industrial Colony (RU)

AIKM .... Ana Ikmal Merkezi [*Main Supply Center*] (TU)

AIKUP ...... Association des Intellectuels Khmers pour l'Union des Peuples [*Association of Cambodian Intellectuals for the Union of Peoples*] (CL)

AIL .... Adams International Ltd.

AIL .... Asociacion Internacional de Limnologia Teorica y Aplicada [*International Association of Theoretical and Applied Limnology - IAL*] [*Spanish*] (ASF)

AIL .... Association Internationale de Limnologie Theorique et Appliquee [*International Association of Theoretical and Applied Limnology - IAL*] [*French*] (ASF)

AIL .... Association Internationale pour la Lecture (EAIO)

AIL .... Association of International Libraries

AIL .... Australian Institute of Librarians (ADA)

AILA......... Asociacion de Industriales Latinoamericanos [*Latin American Industrialists Association - LAIA*] [*Uruguay*]
AILA......... Australian Institute of Landscape Architects   (ADA)
AILA......... Australian Institute of Loss Adjusters
AILA......... Australian Insurance Law Association
AILC......... Association Internationale de Litterature Comparee [*International Association of Comparative Literature*] [*French*]   (SLS)
AILE......... Association Internationale des Lotteries d'Etat [*International Association of State Lotteries*] [*Canada*]   (EAIO)
AILEC....... Australia Indochina Legal Co-operation
AILg.......... Association des Ingenieurs, Liege [*Association of Engineers, Liege*] [*Belgium*]
AILOT....... Allowance in Lieu of Overtime
AILR......... Australian International Law Review [*A publication*]
AILRDI..... Austrian Institute for Library Research, Documentation, and Information   (EAIO)
AIM.......... Aborigines Inland Mission of Australia   (ADA)
AIM.......... Advanced Information in Medicine
AIM.......... Africa Inland Mission   (ADA)
AIM.......... Africa Inland Mission International   (EAIO)
AIM.......... Agencia de Informacao de Mocambique [*Mozambique Information Agency*]
AIM.......... Ailuk [*Marshall Islands*] [*Airport symbol*]   (OAG)
AIM.......... Ambulancias Insulares SA [*Spain*] [*ICAO designator*]   (FAAC)
AIM.......... American Institute of Musicology   (SLS)
AIM.......... Amplitude-Impulse Modulation   (BU)
AIM.......... Amsterdam Interprofessional Market [*Amsterdam stock exchange*] [*Netherlands*]
AIM.......... APASCO [*Australian Planning and Systems Company*] Income Models
AIM.......... Arbeitsgemeinschaft Information Meeresforschung und Meerestechnik eV [*Association for Information on Ocean Research and Technology*] [*Hannover, Germany*]   (SLS)
AIM.......... Arrete Interministeriel [*French*]   (FLAF)
AIM.......... Artillery Historical Museum   (RU)
AIM.......... Asian Institute of Management [*Philippines*]   (PDAA)
AIM.......... Asociacion de Industriales Metalurgicos [*Association of Industrial Metallurgy*] [*Argentina*]   (LAA)
AIM.......... Asociacion de Industrias Metalurgicas [*Association of Industrial Metallurgy*] [*Venezuela*]   (LAA)
AIM.......... Association des Ingenieurs Electriciens sortis de l'Institut Montefiore [*Universite de Liege*] [*Belgium*]
AIM.......... Association Europeenne des Industries de Produits de Marque [*European Association of Industries of Branded Products*]   (EAIO)
AIM.......... Association Internationale de la Meunerie [*International Milling Association - IMA*]   (EAIO)
AIM.......... Association Internationale de la Mutualite [*International Association for Mutual Assistance*] [*Switzerland*]   (EAIO)
AIM.......... Association of International Marketing [*British*]   (EAIO)
AIM.......... Associazione Italiana di Metallurgia
AIM.......... Australasian Institute of Metals   (ADA)
AIM.......... Australian Independence Movement   (ADA)
AIM.......... Australian Information Media
AIM.......... Australian Inland Mission   (ADA)
AIM.......... Australian Institute of Management   (ADA)
AIM.......... Australian Institute of Metals   (PDAA)
AIM.......... Pulse-Amplitude Modulation   (RU)
AIMA....... Aborigines Inland Mission of Australia
AIMA....... All-India Management Association   (PDAA)
AIMA....... All-India Manufacturers' Association
AIMA....... Associate of the Institute of Municipal Administration [*Australia*]
AIMA....... Association Internationale des Musees d'Agriculture [*International Association of Agricultural Museums*]   (EAIO)
AIMA....... Australian Information Management Association
AIMA....... Australian Institute of Multicultural Affairs
AIMA....... Australian International Movers Association
AI Mar E ... Associate of the Institute of Marine Engineers [*British*] [*Australia*]
AIMAS...... Academie Internationale de Medecine Aeronautique et Spatiale [*International Academy of Aviation and Space Medicine IAASM*] [*Canada*]   (EA)
AIMAS...... Associazione Italiana di Medicina Aeronautica e Spaziale [*Italian Association of Aviation and Space Medicine*]   (SLS)
AIMAV ..... Association Internationale pour la Recherche et la Diffusion des Methodes Audio-Visuelles et Structuro-Globales [*International Association for Research and Diffusion of Audio-Visual and Structural-Global Methods*]   (EA)
AIMAV ..... International Association for Crosscultural Communication [*State University of Ghent*] [*Research center*] [*Belgium*]   (IRC)
AIMBE...... Association Internationale de Medecine et de Biologie de l'Environnement [*International Association of Medicine and Biology of Environment - IAMBE*] [*France*]   (EAIO)

AIMC .... Associazione Internazionale Mosaicisti Contemporanei [*International Association of Contemporary Mosaicists*]   (EAIO)
AIMCA...... Associate of the Institute of Management Consultants in Australia
AIMCS...... African International Movement of Catholic Students   (EA)
AIME .... Asociacion de Investigacion para la Mejora de la Alfalfa [*Spain*]   (DSCA)
AIME .... Australian Independent Music Exposition
AIMEA...... Association Internationale des Metiers et Enseignements d'Art [*Belgium*]   (SLS)
AIMEP...... Australian International Management Exchange Program
AIMEX...... Australia's International Mining and Exploration Exhibition   (ADA)
AIMF........ Association Internationale des Maires et Responsables des Capitales et Metropoles Partiellement ou Entierement Francophones [*International Association of Mayors Responsible for Capital Cities or Metropolises Partially or Entirely French-Speaking*]   (EA)
AIMF........ Australasian Institute of Metal Finishing   (ADA)
AIMFA...... Asociacion Internacional de Meteorologia y Fisica Atmosferica [*International Association of Meteorology and Atmospheric Physics - IAMAP*] [*Spanish*]   (ASF)
AIMG .... Amnesty International Medical Group
AIMGA ..... All India Mauritian Graduates Association   (AF)
AIMI .... Associacao Internacional de Missoes dos Israelitas [*International Board of Jewish Missions*]   (EAIO)
AIMIA....... Australian Interactive Multimedia Industry Association
AIMK .... Academy of the History of Material Culture   (RU)
AIMKTM ... Associate Member of the Institute of Marketing Management [*South Africa*]   (AA)
AIML .... All-India Moslem League
AIMLC...... Association of Island Marine Laboratories of the Caribbean   (EA)
AIMLS ..... Australian Institute of Medical Laboratory Scientists
AIMLT ..... Australasian Institute of Medical Laboratory Technology   (ADA)
AIMM .... Africa Inter-Mennonite Mission
AIMM .... Asociacion de Industriales Metalurgicos y Metalmecanicos [*Association of Industrial Metallurgists and Metalworkers*] [*Venezuela*]   (LA)
AIMM .... Associate of the Institute of Municipal Management [*Australia*]
AIMM .... Australasian Institute of Mining and Metallurgy   (ADA)
AIMM .... Australian Institute of Materials Management
AIMM .... Australian Institute of Mining and Metallurgy   (NUCP)
AIMO .... All-India Manufacturers Organisation   (PDAA)
AIMO .... Ankara Insaat Muhendisleri Odasi [*Ankara Chamber of Construction Engineers*]   (TU)
AIMO .... Associazione Italiana Manifatture Ombrelli [*Umbrella manufacturers association*] [*Italy*]   (EY)
AIMO .... Service des Affaires Indigenes et de la Main-d'Oeuvre
AIMOH..... Accademia Italiana di Medicina Omeopatica Hahnemanniana [*Italian*]   (SLS)
AIMPA...... Associate of the Institute of Personnel Management of Australia
AIMPA...... Association Internationale de Meteorologie et de Physique de l'Atmosphere [*International Association of Meteorology and Atmospheric Physics - IAMAP*] [*French*]   (ASF)
AIMPE...... Australian Institute of Marine and Power Engineers   (ADA)
AIMPES.... Associazione Italiana Manufatturieri Pelli-Cuoio e Succedanei [*Leather and Imitation Skins Association*] [*Italy*]   (EY)
AIMPLB ... All India Muslim Personal Law Board
AIMS........ Aboriginal and Islander Music School
AIMS........ Activities and Interests for Mature Students [*Australia*]
AIMS........ All-India Institute of Medial Sciences
AIMS........ Amnesty International-Mexican Section   (EAIO)
AIMS........ Asociacion Internacional de Mercadotecnia Social [*Social Marketing International Association - SMIA*] [*Defunct*] [*Mexico*]   (EAIO)
AIMS........ Association Ivoirienne de Medecine Sportive
AIMS........ Association of International Marathons and Road Races [*New Zealand*]   (EAIO)
AIMS........ Australian Industries Management Services
AIMS........ Australian Institute of Marine Science [*Research center*]   (IRC)
AIMS........ Australian Institute of Medical Scientists
AIMS........ Australian Institute of Musculo-Skeletal Research
AIMS........ Australian International Music Show
AIMT .... Association Internationale de Musees de Transports [*International Association of Transport Museums - IATM*]   (EAIO)
AIMT .... Australian Institute of Medical Technologists   (ADA)
AIN........... African International Airways [*Swaziland*] [*ICAO designator*]   (FAAC)
AIN........... Agencia de Informacion Nacional [*National News Agency*] [*Cuba*]   (LA)
AIN........... Arab Institute of Navigation [*Egypt*]   (EAIO)
AIN........... Australian and New Zealand Insurance Reporter [*A publication*]
AIN........... Australian Independent Newspapers
AIN........... Australian Institute of Navigation   (ADA)

AINA .... Arctic Institute of North America   (EAIO)
AINAI .... African Integrated Network of Administrative Information [*Proposed*]
AINBN ...... Association for the Introduction of New Biological Nomenclature [*Belgium*]   (EAIO)
AINC .... Australian Industry National Catalogue [*Department of Industry Technology and Regional Development*]
A-Ind .... Anglo-Indian   (BARN)
AIND .... Associacao da Imprensa Nao-Diaria [*Association of the Non-Dairy Press*] [*Portugal*]   (EY)
AINDT ...... Australian Institute for Non-Destructive Testing   (SLS)
AINE .... Asociacion de Ingenerios Navales de Espana [*Spanish Association of Naval Engineers*]   (PDAA)
AINEK ...... Association des Infirmiers-Infirmieres d'Etat Khmers [*Cambodian State Nurses Association*]   (CL)
AINF .... Association Interprofessionnelle de France [*Interprofessional Association of France*]   (SLS)
AINI .... Alianza InterNaciones Inca [*Peru*]   (EAIO)
AINK .... Anglo-Iranian Petroleum Company   (RU)
AI-NL .... Amnesty International - Netherlands   (EAIO)
AINLF .... Association Internationale des Navigants de Langue Francaise   (EAIO)
AINOS ...... Associazione Italiana per il Progresso dell'Anestesia in Odonto-Stomatologia [*Italian*]   (SLS)
AINP .... Association Internationale des Numismates Professionnels [*International Association of Professional Numismatists - IAPN*] [*Switzerland*]   (EAIO)
AINS .... Austpac Intelligent Network Server [*Australia*]
AINSE ...... Australian Institute of Nuclear Science and Engineering [*Research center*]   (IRC)
AINZ .... Amnesty International - New Zealand Section   (EAIO)
ainzhb .... Army Engineer Battalion   (RU)
AIO .... Academie Internationale Olympique [*International Olympic Academy*] [*Athens, Greece*]   (EAIO)
AIO .... African Insurance Organization [*Cameroon*]
AIO .... Agriculture et Industries des Oleagineux
AIO .... Arab Industries Organisation
AIO .... Arakan Independence Organization [*Myanmar*] [*Political party*]
AIO .... Australia's Independent Optometrists [*An association*]
AIOB .... Asociacion Internacional de Oceanografia Biologica [*International Association of Biological Oceanography - IABO*] [*Spanish*]   (ASF)
AIOB .... Association Internationale pour l'Oceanographie Biologique [*International Association of Biological Oceanography - IABO*]   (EAIO)
AIOC .... Anglo-Iranian Oil Company   (ME)
AIOC .... Asociacion Internacional de Quimica de los Cereales [*Austria*]   (DSCA)
AIOCC ...... Association Internationale des Organisateurs de Courses Cyclistes [*International Association of Organizers of Cycle Competitions*] [*France*]   (EAIO)
AIOE .... All-India Organization of Employers   (FEA)
AIOFM ...... Anhui Institute of Optics and Fine Mechanics [*Chinese Academy of Sciences*] [*Research center*]   (ERC)
AIOH .... Australian Institute of Occupational Hygienists
AIOM .... Associazione Italiana di Oncologia Medica [*Italian*]   (SLS)
AIOP .... Association Internationale d'Oceanographie Physique [*International Association of Physical Oceanography - IAPO*]   (MSC)
AIORMS ... Association Olympique Internationale pour la Recherche Medico-Spotive   (OLYM)
AIOSP .... Association Internationale d'Orientation Scolaire et Professionnelle [*International Association for Educational and Vocational Guidance - IAEVG*]   (EAIO)
AIOT .... Automatizalasi Informaciofeldolgozasi es Operaciokutatasi Tanacs [*Automation, Information Processing, and Operational Research Council*]   (HU)
AIP .... Aeronautical Information Publication
AIP .... Agence Internationale de Presse [*International Press Agency*] [*French*]   (AF)
AIP .... Agence Ivoirienne de Presse [*Ivory Coast*]   (AF)
AIP .... Allied Intelligence Publications [*NATO*]   (NATG)
AIP .... Alpine Aviation Inc. [*ICAO designator*]   (FAAC)
AIP .... Asociacion Interamericana de Productividad [*Inter-American Association of Productivity*]   (LAA)
AIP .... Associacao da Imprensa de Pernambuco [*Pernambuco Press Association*] [*Brazil*]   (LA)
AIP .... Associacao Industrial Portuguesa [*Industrial organization*] [*Portugal*]   (EY)
AIP .... Association Internationale de Papyrologues [*International Association of Papyrologists*]   (EAIO)
AIP .... Association Internationale de Pediatrie [*International Pediatric Association - IPA*] [*Paris, France*]   (EAIO)
AIP .... Association Internationale de Photobiologie [*International Photobiology Association*] [*Epalinges, Switzerland*]   (EA)
AIP .... Association Internationale des Ports [*International Association of Ports and Harbors - IAPH*] [*Tokyo, Japan*]   (EAIO)

AIP .... Associazione Italiana Pellicceria [*Furriers association*] [*Italy*]   (EY)
AIP .... Astronomy Institute Potsdam
AIP .... Australia in Print [*Book distributor*]
AIP .... Australian Independence Party   (ADA)
AIP .... Australian Industry Participation   (ADA)
AIP .... Australian Institute of Packaging   (ADA)
AIP .... Australian Institute of Petroleum   (ADA)
AIP .... Australian Institute of Physics   (ADA)
AIP .... Australian Intellectual Property Cases [*A publication*]
AIP .... Australia's Indigenous Peoples Party [*Political party*]
AIP .... Automatic Integrating Pulsation Meter   (RU)
AIP .... Automatic Measuring Instrument   (RU)
AIPA .... Agence d'Information Panafricaine [*Pan-African News Agency*] [*Use PAFNA*]   (AF)
AIPA .... Association Internationale de Psychologie Appliquee [*Belgium*]   (SLS)
AIPA .... Association of Importers and Producers of Admixtures [*Belgium*]   (EAIO)
AIPA .... Associazione Italiana per lo Studio della Psicologia Analitica [*Italian*]   (SLS)
AIPA .... Associazione Italiana Planificazione Aziendale [*Italy*]   (PDAA)
AIPA .... Australian Independent Publishers' Association   (ADA)
AIPA .... Australian Institute of Park Administration
AIPA .... Australian Institute of Public Administration
AIPA .... Australian Investment Planners Association
AIPAA ...... Associate of the Institute of Patent Attorneys of Australia   (ADA)
AIPADOKA ... Societe d'Articles Injectes Padoka
AIPASA ..... Aged and Invalid Pensioners' Association of South Australia
AIPC .... African Independent Pentecostal Church of Africa
AIPC .... Association Internationale des Palais des Congres [*International Association of Congress Centers*] [*Zagreb, Yugoslavia*]   (EA)
AIPC .... Association Internationale des Ponts et Charpentes [*International Association of Bridges and Construction*] [*Switzerland*]
AIPC .... Australian Institute of Pest Control   (ADA)
AIPCN ...... Asociacion Internacional Permanente de los Congresos de Navegacion [*Permanent International Association of Navigation Congresses - PIANC*] [*Spanish*]   (ASF)
AIPCN ...... Association Internationale Permanente des Congres de Navigation [*Permanent International Association of Navigation Congresses - PIANC*] [*French*]   (ASF)
AIPCR ...... Association Internationale Permanente des Congres de la Route [*Permanent International Association of Road Congresses - PIARC*]   (EAIO)
AIPDA ...... Adjun Inspektur Polisi Dua [*Assistant Police Inspector II*]   (IN)
AIPE .... Association Internationale de la Presse Echiqueenne [*International Association of Chess Press*] [*Kerteminde, Denmark*]   (EAIO)
AIPE .... Associazione Internazionale di Psicanalisi Eclettica [*Italian*]   (SLS)
AIPE .... Associazione Italiana Polistirolo Espanso
AIPEA ...... Association Internationale pour l'Etude des Argiles [*International Association for the Study of Clays*]   (EAIO)
AIPEHP .... Association Ivoirienne des Parents d'Enfants Handicapes Psychiques [*Ivorian Association of Parents of Psychologically Handicapped Children*]   (AF)
AIPELF ..... Association Internationale de Pedagogie Experimentale en Langue Francaise [*International Association of Pedagogic Experiments in the French language*] [*Belgium*]   (SLS)
AIPet .... Australian Institute of Petroleum
AIPF .... All-India Prayer Fellowship
AIPF .... Asociacion Internacional de Planificacion Familiar [*Social Marketing International Association - SMIA*]   (EAIO)
AIPFO ...... Automatic Integrating Pulsation Meter with a Fixed Interval of Averaging   (RU)
AIPG .... Amnesty International Parliamentary Group
AIPH .... Aged and Invalid Pensioners' Home
AIPH .... Association Internationale de Paleontologie Humaine   (EAIO)
AIPH .... Association Internationale des Producteurs de l'Horticulture [*International Association of Horticultural Producers*] [*Netherlands*]
AIPH .... International Association of Horticultural Producers [*The Hague, Netherlands*]   (EA)
AIPI .... Associazione delle Industrie Petrolifere Italiane
AIPI .... Associazione Internazionale dei Professori d'Italiano [*International Association of Teachers of Italian*]   (EAIO)
AIPI .... Associazione Italiana Architettura d'Interni
AIPI .... Associazione Italiana Progrettisti in Architettura d'Interni
AIPIL .... Australasians in Property in London
AIPIO .... Australian International Pilots' Industrial Organisation
AIPK .... Anglo-Iranian Petroleum Company   (BU)
AIPL .... Australian Interstate Pipe Line Co. Ltd.   (ADA)
AIPLC .... Australian Interstate Pipe Line Company Ltd.

AIPLF....... Association Internationale des Parlementaires de Langue Francaise [*International Association of French-Speaking Parliamentarians*]   (EAIO)
AIPMA...... All-India Plastics Manufacturers Associaton   (PDAA)
AIPMA...... Associate of the Institute of Personnel Management (Australia)   (ADA)
AIPND ...... Associazione Italiana Prova Non Distruttiva [*Italian Non-Destructive Testing Association*]   (PDAA)
AIPNO ...... Automatic Integrating Pulsation Pulse Meter with a Constantly Varying Interval of Averaging   (RU)
AIPO .... ASEAN [*Association of South East Asian Nations*] Inter-Parliamentary Organisation
AIPO .... Australian Intellectual Property Organisation [*National Union Catalogue of Australia symbol*]
AIPOA(SA) ... Assosiaatlede Instituut Parke en Ontspanningsadministrasie (Suid-Afrika) [*South Africa*]   (AA)
AIPP......... Australian Institute for Public Policy
AIPP......... Australian Institute of Professional Photography
AIPPh....... Association Internationale des Professeurs de Philosophie [*International Association of Teachers of Philosophy*]   (EAIO)
AIPPI .... Association Internationale pour la Protection de la Propriete Industrielle [*International Association for the Protection of Industrial Property*] [*Zurich, Switzerland*]   (EA)
AIPR......... Australian Institute of Parapsychological Research
AIPR......... Australian Institute of Parks and Recreation   (ADA)
AIPR......... Australian Institute of Psychic Research
AIPRTM ... Mansvetov Automatic Proportional Pulse Temperate Regulator   (RU)
AIPS .... Association Internationale de la Presse Sportive [*International Sport Press Association*]   (EAIO)
AIPS .... Association Internationale pour le Progres Social [*International Association for Social Progress*] [*Belgium*]   (SLS)
AIPS .... Associazione Italiana di Psicologia dello Sport [*Italian*]   (SLS)
AIPS .... Australian Institute of Political Science   (ADA)
AIP (SA).... Associate Institute of Printing (South Africa)   (AA)
AIPSA ...... Associate of the Institute of Private Secretaries (Australia)
AIP(SA)..... Australian Institute of Petroleum (South Australian Branch)
AIPSM ...... Australian Institute of Purchasing and Supply Management
aiptap .... Army Tank-Destroyer Artillery Regiment   (BU)
AIPTU ...... Adjun Inspektur Polisi Satu [*Assistant Police Inspector I*]   (IN)
AIPU .... Arab Inter-Parliamentary Union [*Syrian Arab Republic*]   (EAIO)
AIPULF..... Association Internationale des Presses Universitaires de Langue Francaise [*International Association of French Language University Presses*] [*Canada Defunct*]
AIQS......... Australian Institute of Quantity Surveyors   (ADA)
AIQSA....... Associate of the Institute of Quantity Surveyors of Australia   (ADA)
AIR .... Academic Institute of Rome [*Italy*]   (EAIO)
AIR .... Accion Independiente Revolucionaria [*Independent Revolutionary Action*] [*Venezuela*]   (LA)
AIR .... Agence Interalliee des Reparations [*France*]   (FLAF)
AIR .... Air Incident Report
AIR .... Airlift International, Inc. [*ICAO designator*]   (FAAC)
AIR .... All-India Radio
AIR .... Asociacion Interamericana de Radiodifusion [*Inter-American Association of Broadcasters - IAAB*] [*Montevideo, Uruguay*]   (EA)
AIR .... Asociacion Internacional de Radiodifusion [*International Association of Broadcasting - IAB*]   (EAIO)
AIR .... Association d'Interet Rural
AIR .... Association Internationale du Registre des Bateaux du Rhin   (FLAF)
AIR .... Australasian [*or Australian*] Institute of Radiography   (ADA)
AIR .... Australian Immigration Review [*Tribunal*] [*National Union Catalogue of Australia symbol*]
AIR .... Australian Industrial Refractories Ltd.
AIR .... Australian Industrial Registry
AIR .... Autorite Internationale de la Ruhr [*Benelux*]   (BAS)
AIR .... Evaporator Control Unit   (RU)
AIR .... Observation Battalion Operations and Procedures   (BU)
AIR .... Sound-Flash Survey, Artillery Survey   (RU)
AIRA .... Allergies and Intolerant Reactions Association [*Australian Capital Territory*]
AIRAANZ ... Association of Industrial Relations Academics of Australia and New Zealand
AIRAC...... Australian Ionising Radiation Advisory Council   (ADA)
AIRACH ... Australian Institute of Refrigeration, Air Conditioning, and Heating, Inc.   (ADA)
AIRAH ...... Australian Institute of Refrigeration, Air Conditioning, and Heating
AIRBALTAP ... Allied Air Forces, Baltic Approaches [*NATO*]   (NATG)
AIRBM...... Associazione Italiana di Radiobiologia Medica [*Italy*]   (SLS)
AIRBO...... Association Internationale pour les Recherches de Base au Haut Fourneau d'Ougree [*Belgium*]   (SLS)
AIRC......... Asociacion Interamericana de Registro Civil   (LAA)
AIRC......... Associazione Italiana per la Ricerca sul Cancro [*Italian*]   (SLS)

AIRC......... Australian Immigration Research Center
AIRC......... Australian Industrial Relations Commission
AIRCENT ... Allied Air Forces, Central Europe [*Formerly, AAFCE*] [*NATO*]
Aircom .... Air Commuter [*Airline call sign*]
AIRD .... Asian Institute for Rural Development [*India*]   (PDAA)
AIRD .... Asociacion de Industrias de la Republica Dominicana [*Association of Dominican Industries*] [*Dominican Republic*]   (LA)
AIRD .... Australian Industrial Research and Development Incentives Board
AIRDB...... Australian Industry Reports Database
AIRDEF ... Air Defense Division [*NATO*]   (NATG)
AIRDEP .... Air Deputy [*NATO*]   (NATG)
AIRDGB... Australian Industrial Research and Development Grants Board   (ADA)
AIRDI .... Australian Industrial Research and Development Incentives   (ADA)
AIRDIB .... Australian Industrial Research and Development Incentives Board   (ADA)
AIRDIS ..... Australian Industrial Research and Development Incentives Scheme   (PDAA)
AIRE .... Association Internationale des Ressources en Eau [*International Water Resources Association - IWRA*] [*French*]   (ASF)
AIRE......... Associazione Italiana per la Promozione degli Studi e delle Ricerche per l'Edilizia [*Italian*]   (SLS)
AiRE .... Automation and Radio Electronics   (RU)
AIREASTLANT ... Naval Air Forces East Atlantic Area [*NATO*]   (NATG)
AIREEA .... Associate of the Institute of Radio and Electronics Engineers, Australia   (ADA)
AIRET........ Australian Institute for Rational Emotive Therapy
AIRF......... All-India Railwaymen's Federation [*Trade union*]   (FEA)
AIRG .... Asociacion Independiente de Radiodifusoras Guatemaltecas [*Independent Association of Guatemalan Radio Broadcasting Stations*]   (LA)
AIRG .... Australian Industrial Research Group   (ADA)
AIRH........ Asociacion Internacional de Recursos Hidraulicos [*International Association for Hydraulic Research - IAHR*] [*Spanish*]   (ASF)
AIRH........ Association Internationale des Recherches Hydrauliques [*International Association for Hydraulic Research - IAHR*] [*French*]   (MSC)
AIRI.......... Associazione Industrie Risiere Italiane [*Italy*]
AIRI.......... Associazione Italiana per la Ricerca Industriale [*Italian*]   (SLS)
AIRIA........ All-India Rubber Industries Association   (PDAA)
AIRIEL...... Associazione Italiana per la Ricerca nell'Impiego degli Elastomeri [*Italian*]   (SLS)
AIRIT .... Association Internationale de Recherche en Informatique Toxicologique [*International Association of Toxicological Research and Information*] [*French*]   (SLS)
AIRMEC ... Association Internationale pour la Recherche Medicale et les Echanges Culturels [*International Association for Medical Research and Cultural Exchange*] [*Paris, France*]   (EAIO)
AIRMN ..... Associazione Italiana di Radiologia e Medicina Nucleare [*Italian Association of Radiological and Nuclear Medicine*]   (SLS)
AIRNON... Allied Air Forces, North Norway [*NATO*]   (NATG)
AIRNORTH ... Allied Air Forces, Northern Europe [*Formerly, AAFNE*] [*NATO*]
Air NZ .... Air New Zealand Ltd. [*Airline*]
AIRO .... Associazione Italiana di Ricerca Operativa [*Italian*]   (SLS)
AIRP......... Association Internationale de Relations Professionnelles [*International Industrial Relations Association - IIRA*]   (EAIO)
AIRP......... Associazione Italiana di Protezione Contro le Radiazione [*Italian*]   (SLS)
AIRP......... Associazione Italiana Relazioni Pubbliche [*Italian Public Relations Association*]
AIRPE....... Association Internationale de Recherche sur la Pollution de l'Eau [*International Association on Water Pollution Research - IAWPR*] [*French*]   (ASF)
AIRS......... African International Reservation System   (PDAA)
AIRS......... Australian Information Retrieval Services
AirSA........ Air South Australia
AIRSONOR ... Allied Air Forces, South Norway [*NATO*]   (NATG)
AIRSOUTH ... Allied Air Forces, Southern Europe [*Formerly, AAFSE*] [*NATO*]
AIRT......... Australian Institute of Radio and Television
AIRUD ...... Corps Perairan dan Udara [*Air and Water Corps (Police unit)*]   (IN)
AIS............ Accident Investigation Squad [*New South Wales Police Service*] [*Australia*]
AIS............ Aeronautical Information Section
AIS............ Air Tranport School [*Former USSR*] [*ICAO designator*]   (FAAC)
AIS............ Akademio Internacia de la Sciencoj [*International Academy of Sciences - IAS*]   (EAIO)
AIS............ Army Quartermaster Depot   (RU)
AIS............ Arorae [*Kiribati*] [*Airport symbol*]   (OAG)
AIS............ Artificial Intelligence Software [*Commercial firm*] [*Italy*]

AIS............. Association Internationale de la Savonnerie et de la Detergence [*International Association of the Soap and Detergent Industry*]   (EAIO)

AIS............. Association Internationale de la Soie [*International Silk Association - ISA*]   (EAIO)

AIS............. Association Internationale de Semiotique [*International Association for Semiotic Studies - IASS*] [*Italy*]   (SLS)

AIS............. Association Internationale de Sociologie [*International Sociological Association - ISA*]   (EAIO)

AIS............. Associazione Italiana degli Slavisti [*Italian*]   (SLS)

AIS............. Associazione Italiana di Sociologia [*Italian Association of Sociology*]   (SLS)

AIS............. Australasian Institute of Secretaries   (ADA)

AIS............. Australian Illawarra Shorthorn   (ADA)

AIS............. Australian-Indian Society

AIS............. Australian Information Service [*Promotion Australia*] [*National Union Catalogue of Australia symbol*]

AIS............. Australian Institute of Sport

AIS............. Australian Iron and Steel Ltd.   (ADA)

AIS............. Automatic Interplanetary Station [*Commonwealth of Independent States*]

AIS............. Award Information System [*Australia*]

AISA......... Africa Institute of South Africa   (EAIO)

AISA......... Association Internationale pour la Securite Aerienne [*French*]   (SLS)

AISA......... Association Internationale pour le Sport des Aveugles [*International Blind Sports Association - IBSA*] [*Farsta, Sweden*]   (EAIO)

AISA......... Association of International Schools in Africa   (EA)

AISA......... Associazione Italiana Studi Americanisti [*Italian*]   (SLS)

AISA......... Australian Institute of Systems Analysts   (ADA)

AISACT..... Association of Independent Schools of the Australian Capital Territory

AISAG....... Aeronautical Information Service Automation Group [*ICAO*]   (DA)

AISAM...... Association Internationale des Societes d'Assurance Mutuelle [*International Association of Mutual Insurance Companies*] [*Paris, France*]   (EAIO)

AISAP....... Aeronautical Information Service Automation Specialist Panel [*ICAO*]   (DA)

AISB.......... Association Internationale de Standardisation Biologique [*International Association of Biological Standardization - IABS*]   (EAIO)

AISC.......... Association Internationale des Skal Clubs [*International Association of Skal Clubs*]   (EAIO)

AISC.......... Associazione Italiana di Studi Canadesi [*Italian Association of Canadian Studies*]

AISC.......... Associazione Italiana Santa Cecilia per la Musica Sacra [*Italian*]   (SLS)

AISC.......... Australian Institute of Steel Construction   (ADA)

AISCO....... Arab Iron & Steel Co. [*Bahrain*]   (IMH)

AIS/D........ American International School/Dhaka [*Bangladesh*]

AISD.......... Associazione Italiana per lo Studio del Dolore [*Italian*]   (SLS)

AISDA....... Associazione Italiana Studi Direzione Aziendale [*Italian*]   (SLS)

AISDS....... Aboriginal and Islander Skills Development Scheme

AISDT...... Australian Institute of Surgical and Dental Technicians

AISE.......... Asociacion Internacional de Ciencias Economicas [*International Economic Association - IEA*] [*Spanish*]   (ASF)

AISE.......... Association Internationale des Sciences Economiques [*International Economic Association - IEA*] [*Paris, France*]   (EAIO)

AISE.......... Association Internationale des Statisticiens d'Enquetes [*International Association of Survey Statisticians*]   (EAIO)

AISE.......... Associazione Internazionale delle Scienze Economiche [*International Economic Association - IEA*] [*Italian*]   (WER)

AISESS..... Accademia Internazionale per le Scienze Economiche, Sociali e Sanitarie [*Italian*]   (SLS)

AISF......... Accademia Italiana di Storia della Farmacia [*Italian*]   (SLS)

AISF......... Amnesty International - French Section   (EAIO)

AISF......... Association Internationale de Solidarite Francophone

AISF......... Australian Indoor Soccer Federation

AISF......... Australian Insurance Staffs Federation   (ADA)

AISH........ Association Internationale des Sciences Hydrologiques [*International Association of Hydrological Sciences - IAHS*] [*French*]   (ASF)

AISH........ Auto-Inspektorati Shteteror [*Albanian*]

AISI.......... Associazione Italiana per lo Sviluppo Internazionale [*Italian*]   (SLS)

AISI.......... Associazione Italiana Socioanalisi Individuale [*Italian*]   (SLS)

AISJ.......... Association Internationale des Sciences Juridiques [*International Association of Legal Science - IALS*]   (EAIO)

AISL......... Associazione Italiana di Studio del Lavoro [*Italian*]   (SLS)

AISLF....... Association Internationale des Sociologues de Langue Francaise [*International Association of French Language Sociologists*]   (EAIO)

AISLLI...... Associazione Internazionale per gli Studi di Lingua e Letteratura Italiane [*International Association for the Study of the Italian Language and Literature - IASILL*]   (EAIO)

AISM......... Amnistia Internacional, Seccion Mexicana   (EAIO)

AISM......... Armenian Scientific Research Institute of Building Materials and Structures   (RU)

AISM......... Asociacion Internacional de Senalizacion Maritima [*International Association of Lighthouse Authorities - IALA*] [*Spanish*]   (ASF)

AISM......... Asociacion Internacional de Sociedades de Microbiologia [*International Association of Microbiological Societies - IAMS*] [*Spanish*]   (ASF)

AISM......... Associate, Australian Institute of Sale and Marketing Executives   (ADA)

AISM......... Association Internationale de Signalisation Maritime [*International Association of Lighthouse Authorities - IALA*] [*French*]   (ASF)

AISM......... Association Internationale des Societes de Microbiologie [*International Association of Microbiological Societies - IAMS*] [*French*]   (ASF)

AISM......... Associazione Italiana per gli Studi di Mercato [*Italian*]   (SLS)

AISM......... Associazione Italiana Scientifica di Metapsichica [*Italian*]   (SLS)

AISM......... Associazione Italiana Sclerosi Multipla [*Italian*]   (SLS)

AISM......... Australasian/International Suppliers Mart

AISME...... Australian Institute of Sales and Marketing Executives

AISNSW ... Association of Independent Schools of New South Wales [*Australia*]

AISO.......... Australian Informed Sources Limited [*National Union Catalogue of Australia symbol*]

AISP .... Association Internationale de Science Politique [*International Political Science Association - IPSA*] [*Canada*]

AISP .... Associazione Italiana di Storia Postale [*Italian*]   (SLS)

AISPIT...... Association Internationale de Seismologie et de Physique de l'Interieur de la Terre [*International Association of Seismology and Physics of the Earth's Interior - IASPEI*]   (MSC)

AISPO....... Association Internationale des Sciences Physiques de l'Ocean [*International Association for the Physical Sciences of the Ocean - IAPSO*] [*French*]   (ASF)

AISQ......... Association of Independent Schools of Queensland [*Australia*]

AISRCM ... Australian Institute of Swimming and Recreation Centre Management

AISS .... Asociacion Internacional de la Seguridad Social [*International Social Security Association - ISSA*] [*Spanish*]

AISS .... Association Internationale de la Science du Sol [*International Society of Soil Science - ISSS*]   (EAIO)

AISS .... Association Internationale de la Securite Sociale [*International Social Security Association - ISSA*] [*French*]

AISS .... Associazione Italiana di Studi Semiotici [*Italian*]   (SLS)

AISS .... Australian Innovation Sourcing Service [*Database*]

AIST .... Agency of Industrial Science and Technology [*Japan*]

AIST .... Australian Institute of Science and Technology, Inc.   (ADA)

AISU......... Arab Iron and Steel Union [*Algiers, Algeria*]   (MENA)

AISWA...... Association of Independent Schools of Western Australia

AISWG...... Advieskomitee vir Internasionale Samewerking op Wetenskaplike Gebied [*International Council of Scientific Unions*]

AISWG...... Air Interface Sub-Working Group [*NATO*]   (NATG)

AIT .... Adelaide Institute of Technology [*Australia*]

AIT .... Aitutaki [*Cook Islands*] [*Airport symbol*]   (OAG)

AIT .... Alianta Interationala de Turism [*International Touring Alliance*]   (RO)

AIT .... Alliance Internationale de Tourisme [*International Touring Alliance*]   (EAIO)

AIT .... All-in-Together Programme for Parent Education [*Australia*]

AIT .... American Institution in Thailand

AIT .... American International Airways, Inc. [*ICAO designator*]   (FAAC)

ait .... Arab International Tours Ltd. [*Jordan*]

AIT .... Asian Institute of Technology [*Bangkok, Thailand*]   (MCD)

AIT .... Asociacion de Investigacion del Transporte [*Transport Research Association*] [*Spain*]   (PDAA)

AIT .... Asociacion Internacional de Trabajadores [*International Association of Workers*] [*Spanish*]   (WER)

AIT .... Asociacion Internacional de Traductores [*Inter-American Association of Translators*]

AITA......... Annee Internationale du Tourisme Africain

AITA......... Association des Ingenieurs et Techniciens Africains

AITA......... Association Internationale des Transports Aeriens [*French*]

AITA......... Association Internationale du Theatre Amateur [*International Amateur Theatre Association - IATA*]   (EAIO)

AITA......... Association Internationale du Traite de l'Atlantique   (FLAF)

AITA......... Associazione Italiana di Tecnologia Alimentare [*Italian*]   (SLS)

AITA......... Associazione Italiana Tessili Antifiamma

AITA......... Australian Industrial Truck Association   (ADA)

AITA......... Australian Information Technology Award

AITAA....... Asian Institute of Technology Alumni Association [*Thailand*] (EAIO)

AITACI ..... Association des Ingenieurs et Techniciens Africains de Cote-D'Ivoire

AITAP .... Asociacion Interprovincial del Transporte Automotor de Pasajeros [*Argentina*]   (LAA)

AITC.......... Associate Member of the Institute of Town Clerks [*South Africa*] (AA)

AITC.......... Association for International Technical Co-Operation

AITC.......... Association Internationale des Traducteurs de Conference [*International Association of Conference Translators*] (EAIO)

AITC.......... Australian Industry and Technology Council

AITC.......... Australian Information Technology Council [*Proposed*]

AITD .... Australian Institute of Training and Development   (ADA)

AITE.......... Asociacion de Industriales Textiles del Ecuador [*Ecuadorean Textile Manufacturers Association*]   (LA)

AITE .... Australian International Technology Exhibition

AITEA .... Australian Institute of Tertiary Educational Administrators (ADA)

AITEC .... Associazione Italiana Tecnico Economica del Cemento [*Cement association*]   (EY)

AITEP .... Aboriginal and Islander Teacher Education Program [*Australia*]

AITES .... Association Internationale des Travaux en Souterrain [*International Tunneling Association*]   (SLS)

AITES-ITA ... Association Internationale des Travaux en Souterrain - International Tunneling Association [*Bron, France*]   (EA)

AITG .... Association of Israel Tour Guides   (EAIO)

AITI.......... Artikkel-Indeks Tidsskrifter [*Norwegian Center for Informatics*] [*Database*]

AITI.......... Associazione Italiana di Tecnica Idrotermale [*Italian*]   (SLS)

AITI.......... Associazione Italiana Treduttori e Interpreti [*Italian Association of Translators and Interpreters*]

AITIA .... Ankara Iktisadi ve Ticari Ilimler Akademisi [*Ankara Academy of Economy and Commercial Science*]   (TU)

AITIM .... Asociacion de Investigacion Tecnica de las Industrias de la Madera y Corcho [*Wood and Cork Industries Research Association*] [*Spanish*]   (ARC)

AITIT .... Association Internationale de la Teinture et de l'Impression Textiles [*International Association of Textile Dyers and Printers*]   (EAIO)

AITM .... Association of Irish Traditional Musicians   (SLS)

AITMA..... Australian Institute of Taxation and Management Accountants

AITME...... Association des Instituts de Theologie du Moyen-Orient [*Association of Theological Institutes in the Middle East ATIME*]   (EAIO)

AITO .... Associazione Italiana di Terapia Occupazionale [*Italian*]   (SLS)

AITO .... Australian Institute of Tourism Officers

AITP .... Associazione Italiana di Terapia Psicologiche [*Italian*]   (SLS)

AITPA .... Asociacion Industrial Textil de Proceso Algodonero [*Spain*] (EAIO)

AITPCI...... Association des Ingenieurs, Techniciens et Professionnels du Controle Industrielle [*Association of Engineers, Technicians and Training Officers of Industrial Control*]   (PDAA)

AITPM ...... Australian Institute of Traffic Planning and Management

AITS .... Amnesty International - Turkish Section [*British*]   (EAIO)

AITs.......... Automated Information Center   (RU)

AITSA .... Association of Interpreters and Translators of South Australia

AITU .... Asociacion de Industrias Textiles del Uruguay [*Association of the Textile Industry of Uruguay*]   (LAA)

AITUC....... All-India Traders Union Congress   (PDAA)

AIU .... Aboriginal Issues Unit [*Australia*]

AIU .... Asociacion Internacional de Universidades [*International Association of Universities*] [*Use IAU*] [*Spanish*]   (LA)

AIU .... Association Internationale des Universites [*International Association of Universities - IAU*]   (EAIO)

AIU .... Association Internationale des Urbanistes [*International Society of City and Regional Planners - ISOCARP*]   (EAIO)

AIU .... Association of Indian Universities   (EAIO)

AIU .... Atiu [*Cook Islands*] [*Airport symbol*]   (OAG)

AIUAS....... Australian Industrial Union of Academic Staff

AIUC .... Associazione Italiana di Urbanistica Commerciale [*French*] (SLS)

AIUFFAS ... Association Internationale des Utilsateurs de Files de Fibres Artificielles et Synthetiques [*International Association of Users of Artificial and Synthetic Yarn*] [*France*]   (PDAA)

AIUFOR.... Australian International UFO [*Unidentified Flying Object*] Research

AIUS.......... Associazione Internazionale Uomo nello Spazis [*Italian*]

AIUS.......... Australian Institute of Urban Studies [*Research center*]   (IRC)

AIUSSMRGW ... Automatisiertes Informations- und Leitungssystem Standardization und Metrologie Rat der Gegenseitigen Wirtschaftshilfe [*Automated Information and Management System - Standardization and Metrology Council for Economic Mutual Assistance*]   (EG)

AIUTA....... Association Internationale des Universites du Troisieme Age [*International Association of Universities of the Third Age*] (EAIO)

AIV .... Administratieve Informatie-Verwerking

AIV .... Australian Institute of Valuers

AIV .... Authorisation d'Importation des Vehicules [*Algeria*]

AIVA .... Association Internationale des Villes d'Avenir [*International Association of Cities of the Future*]   (EA)

AIVCIT ..... Association Internationale de Volcanologie et de Chimie de l'Interieur de la Terre [*International Association of Volcanology and Chemistry of the Earth's Interior - IAVCEI*]   (MSC)

AIVFC ...... Association Internationale des Villes Francophones des Congres [*International Association of French-Speaking Congress Towns - IAFCT*]   (EAIO)

AIVL .... Australian Intravenous League

AIVPA....... Asociacion Internacional Veterinaria de Produccion Animal [*International Veterinary Association for Animal Production*]   (SLS)

AIVPA....... Association Internationale Veterinaire de Production Animale [*International Veterinary Association for Animal Production - IVAAP*] [*Brussels, Belgium*]   (EAIO)

AIWB........ Australian Irish Welfare Bureau

AIWC .... Intelligence Watch Condition [*NATO*]   (NATG)

AIWF........ Association of the International Winter Sports Federations [*Switzerland*]   (EAIO)

AIWM(SA) ... Associate Member of the Institute of Waste Management (South Africa)   (AA)

AIWO .... Agudas Israel World Organization [*Jerusalem, Israel*]

AIWO .... Agudat Israel World Organization [*Jerusalem, Israel*]   (MENA)

AIWO .... Australian Institute of Welfare Officers   (ADA)

AIWSF ...... Association of the International Winter Sports Federations [*Berne, Switzerland*]   (EAIO)

AIYA .... Australian and International Yoga Association   (ADA)

AIYEP .... Australia-Indonesia Youth Exchange Program

AIZ .... Arkia Israel Inland Airlines [*ICAO designator*]   (FAAC)

AIZ .... Inventors' Association   (RU)

AJ .... Actualite Juridique, "Droit Administratif"   (FLAF)

aj .... A Jini [*And Others*] [*Former Czechoslovakia*]

aj .... Ajudante [*Adjutant*] [*Portuguese*]

AJ .... Al Jazirada Equipment Co. Ltd. [*Saudi Arabia*]

AJ .... Antilliaans Juristenblad [*Benelux*]   (BAS)

AJ .... Armee Juive   (BJA)

AJ .... Auberges de Jeunesse [*Youth Hostels*] [*French*]   (WER)

AJ .... Australian Jaycees

AJA............ African Jurists' Association [*Senegal*]

AJA............ Ajaccio [*Corsica*] [*Airport symbol*]   (OAG)

AJA............ Anglo-Jewish Association [*British*]   (EAIO)

AJA............ Arhiv Jugoslavenske Akademije Znanosti i Umjetnosti u Zagrebu [*Archives of the Yugoslav Academy of Sciences and Arts in Zagreb*]   (YU)

AJA............ Association des Juristes Algeriens [*Association of Algerian Jurists*]   (AF)

AJA............ Australian Jewellers' Association

AJA............ Australian Journalists' Association   (ADA)

AJAC........ Asociacion de Jovenes de Accion Catolica [*Youth Catholic Action Association*] [*Argentina*]   (LA)

AJASS...... African Jazz-Art Society and Studios

AJB............ Antilliaans Juristenblad [*Benelux*]   (BAS)

AJBA .... Association de la Jeunesse Bakoko [*Association of Bakoko Youth*]

AJBA .... Australian Jersey Breeders' Association

AJBCC ...... Australia/Japan Business Co-Operation Committee

AJBF .... Australia-Japan Business Foundation

AJC............ Academy of Japanese Culture [*Australia*]

AJC............ Asociacion Judicial de Chile [*Law Society of Chile*] [*Santiago*] (LAA)

AJC............ Association de la Jeunesse Camerounaise [*Cameroonian Youth Association*]

AJC............ Australian Jazz Convention   (ADA)

AJC............ Australian Jockey Club   (ADA)

AJC............ Avant Jesus-Christ [*Before Jesus Christ*] [*French*]

AJCC .... Adelaide Junior Chamber of Commerce [*Australia*]

AJCC .... Australian Junior Chamber of Commerce

AJCE .... Australian Joint Citrus Exporters [*An association*]

AJCL .... Australia-Japan Container Line

AJCP .... Australian Joint Copying Project   (ADA)

AJDA........ Actualite Juridique, "Droit Administratif"   (FLAF)

AJDF .... ASEAN [*Association of South East Asian Nations*] Japan Development Fund

AJE............ Alfa Jet [*Spain*] [*ICAO designator*]   (FAAC)

AJEI .... Anglo-Japanese Economic Institute [*British*]   (EAIO)

AJEI .... Australia-Japan Economic Institute   (ADA)

AJENAKO ... Association des Jeunesse Nationalistes du Kongo [*Association of Nationalist Youth of the Congo*] [*Leopoldville*]

AJES .... Association des Jeunesses Khmeres de l'Enseignement Secondaire [*Association of Cambodian Secondary Education Youth Organizations*]   (CL)

AJEUNAL ... Alliance des Jeunesse Angolaise pour la Liberte [*Alliance of Angolan Youth for Freedom*]

AJEUNAREK ... Association de la Jeunesse Nationaliste de la Republique Khmere [*Cambodian Republic Nationalist Youth Association*]   (CL)

AJF .... Australia Japan Foundation   (ADA)

AJF .... Jouf [*Saudi Arabia*] [*Airport symbol*]   (OAG)

AJFLD ...... Association des Industries des Fruits et Legumes Deshydrates de la CEE [*European Organization of the Dehydrated Fruit and Vegetable Industries*]   (EAIO)

AJGF .... Association de la Jeunesse Guineenne en France [*France-based Guinean political organization*]

AJHS .... Australian Jersey Herd Society   (ADA)

AJHS .... Australian Jewish Historical Society

AJIB .... Arab-Jordan Investment Bank   (GEA)

AJIM .... Association des Journalistes de l'Ile Maurice [*Mauritian Journalists Association*]   (AF)

AJIR .... Arhiv Jadranskog Instituta u Rijeci [*Archives of the Adriatic Institute in Rijeka*]   (YU)

AJIS .... Association de Jeunes pour l'Information sur le SIDA [*Young People's Association for Information About AIDS*] [*France*]

AJJA .... Australian Ju Jitsu Association

AJJAF ...... Association des Jeunes Juristes Africains [*France*]

AJKSKK .... Ampo Joyaku Kaitei Soshi Kokumin Kaigi [*People's Council for Preventing Revision of Security Treaty*] [*Japan*]

AJL .... Actualite Juridique, "Loyers"   (FLAF)

AJL .... Aero Jalisco SA de CV [*Mexico*] [*ICAO designator*]   (FAAC)

AJL .... Australian Journal of Linguistics [*A publication*]

AJLCA ...... All Japan Leather Costume Association   (EAIO)

AJLSA ...... All Japan Leather Scale Association   (EAIO)

AJLSPC .... Australian Joint Lamb and Sheepmeat Promotion Committee

AJM .... Air Jamaica [*ICAO designator*]   (FAAC)

AJM .... Association de la Jeunesse Mauritanienne [*Mauritanian Youth Association*]

AJMC .... Australia-Japan Ministerial Committee

AJME .... Americans for Justice in the Middle East [*Lebanon*]   (EAIO)

AJMK .... Jeunesse Madimbadienne du Secteur Kimuisi

AJ/MRDN ... AND-JEF/Mouvement Revolutionnaire pour la Democratie Nouvelle [*AND-JEF/New Democratic Revolutionary Movement*] [*Senegal*] [*Political party*]

AJMWC .... Australian Joint Maritime Warfare Centre

AJN .... Anjouan [*Comoro Islands*] [*Airport symbol*]   (OAG)

AJNOC ..... Ajman National Oil Company   (MENA)

AJO .... Aero Ejecutivo SA de CV [*Mexico*] [*ICAO designator*]   (FAAC)

AJO .... Arhiv Jugoslavenskog Odbora u Arhivu Jugoslavenske Akademije Znanosti i Umjetnosti u Zagrebu [*Archives of the Yugoslav Committee in the Archives of the Yugoslav Academy of Sciences and Arts in Zagreb*]   (YU)

AJO .... Australian Jazz Orchestra

AJOHN ..... Australian Journal of Holistic Nursing [*A publication*]

AJOM .... Association des Journalistes d'Outre-Mer

AJP .... Action pour la Justice et le Progress [*Somali*]

AJP .... Association des Journalistes Polonais [*Poland*]   (EAIO)

AJP .... Australian Journal of Pharmacy [*A publication*]

AJ-PADS .. AND JEF - Parti Africain pour la Democratie et le Socialisme [*Senegal*] [*Political party*]   (EY)

AJPC .... Association des Journalistes Professionels du Cameroun [*Association of Professional Journalists of Cameroon*]   (AF)

AJPI .... Actualite Juridique, "Propriete Immobiliere"   (FLAF)

AJR .... Asociacion de Jovenes Rebeldes [*Rebel Youth Association*] [*Cuba*]   (LA)

AJR .... Asociatia Juristilor Romani [*Association of Romanian Jurists*]   (RO)

AJRC .... Australia-Japan Research Centre [*Australian National University*]

AJRFU ...... Australian Junior Rugby Football Union

AJS .... Aeroejecutivos, Aeroservicios Ejecutivos [*Colombia*] [*ICAO designator*]   (FAAC)

AJS .... Alliance des Jeunes pour le Socialisme [*Alliance of Youth for Socialism*] [*France*] [*Political party*]   (PPE)

AJS .... Amicale des Juristes Senegalais

AJS .... Association des Jeunes de Sumbe [*Sumbe Youth Association*]

AJS .... Association des Journalistes Socialistes [*Association of Socialist Reporters*] [*Senegal*]   (AF)

AJS .... Australia-Japan Society   (ADA)

AJSMOC .. AJS [*Albert John Stevens*] and Matchless Owners Club [*Mount Sorrel, Leicestershire, England*]   (EAIO)

AJSS .... Australian Joint Staff Service

AJSSC .... Australian Joint Services Staff College [*National Union Catalogue of Australia symbol*]

AJT .... Amerijet International [*ICAO designator*]   (FAAC)

AJT .... Association des Journalistes Tunisiens [*Tunisian Journalists Association*]   (AF)

ajte .... Ajudante [*Adjutant*] [*Portuguese*]

AJTr .... Actualite Juridique, "Travaux Publics"   (FLAF)

AJU .... Aracaju [*Brazil*] [*Airport symbol*]   (OAG)

AJV .... Arab Joint Ventures

AJWE .... Australian Joint Warfare Establishment

AJWRS ..... Australian Jewish Welfare and Relief Society   (ADA)

AJWS .... Australian Jewish Welfare Society   (ADA)

AJY .... Agades [*Niger*] [*Airport symbol*]   (OAG)

AJY .... Association of Jewish Youth

AK .... Absatzkontor [*Sales Agency*]   (EG)

AK .... Adenylic Acid   (RU)

AK .... Administrative Committee [*1952-1954*]   (RU)

AK .... Administrativna Komisija (SIV) [*Administrative Commission*]   (YU)

AK .... Advokatni Komora [*Bar Association*]   (CZ)

AK .... Aero Klub [*Aero Club*]   (YU)

AK .... Afrika Komitee [*Switzerland*]   (EAIO)

AK .... Agoranomikos Kodix [*Marketing Code*] [*Greek*]   (GC)

AK .... Agrotikos Kodix [*Agricultural Code*]   (GC)

AK .... Air Corps   (RU)

AK .... Aircraft Compressor   (RU)

AK .... Aircraft Shortwave Radio   (RU)

Ak .... Akademi [*Academy*]   (TU)

AK .... Akademiai Kiado [*Publishing House of the Hungarian Academy of Sciences*]   (HU)

Ak .... Akademie [*Academy*] [*German*]   (BJA)

Ak .... Akra [*Akrotirion*] [*Cape*] [*Greek*]   (NAU)

AK .... Aktienkapital [*Share Capital*] [*German*] [*Business term*]

AK .... Aktivitaetskoeffizient [*Activity Coefficient*] [*German*]   (GCA)

AK .... Alaska   (IDIG)

AK .... Alphabetic Catalog   (RU)

AK .... Alte Kaempfer [*Old Fighters*] [*German*]

AK .... Amino Acid   (RU)

AK .... Andiproedros tis Kyverniseos [*Deputy Premier*] [*Automobile license plate designation*] [*Greek*]   (GC)

AK .... Angkatan Kepolisian [*Police Force*]   (IN)

AK .... Angola Kwanza

AK .... Antenna Switch   (RU)

ak .... Arany Korona [*Gold Crown (Hungarian currency before World War I, still used to estimate real estate values)*]   (HU)

AK .... Arbeitskraft [*Worker*] [*German*]   (EG)

AK .... Archaeographic Commission (at the Department of History of the Academy of Sciences, USSR)   (RU)

AK .... Arellenorzes Orszagos Kormanybiztosa [*National Government Commissioner of Price Control*]   (HU)

AK .... Armeekorps [*Army Corps*] [*German*]

AK .... Armee Korps [*Army Corps*] [*German*]

AK .... Armia Krajowa [*Home (Underground) Army (1942-1945)*]   (POL)

AK .... Army Corps   (RU)

AK .... 'Arse over Kettle [*Head over heels*] [*Slang*] [*British*]   (DSUE)

AK .... Artillery Compass   (RU)

AK .... Artillery Corps   (RU)

AK .... Ascorbic Acid   (RU)

AK .... Aspartic Acid   (RU)

AK .... Association of Kinoinitiatives   (EAIO)

AK .... Astikos Kodix [*Civil Code*]   (GC)

AK .... Astrocompass   (RU)

AK .... Astrocorrection   (RU)

AK .... Astronomical Almanac   (RU)

AK .... Atleticky Klub [*Athletic Club*]   (CZ)

AK .... Ausgabe Kopplung [*Output Coupling*] [*German*]   (ADPT)

AK .... Autoklub [*Automobile Club*]   (CZ)

AK .... Automatic Control   (RU)

AK .... Automatic Crane   (RU)

AK .... Automobile Club   (RU)

AK .... Aviation Club   (RU)

AK .... Avtomat Kalashnikov [*Submachine Gun*] [*Commonwealth of Independent States*]

AK .... Corps Artillery   (RU)

AK .... Emergency Button   (RU)

AK .... Instruction Address   (RU)

AK .... Kalashnikov Submachine   (RU)

AK .... Knight of the Order of Australia   (ADA)

AK .... Mechanical Pencil   (RU)

AK .... Motor Convoy   (RU)

AK .... Radioactive Well Logging   (RU)

AK .... Subscriber's Set   (RU)

AK .... Truck-Mounted Crane   (RU)

AKA .... Air Korea Co. Ltd. [*South Korea*] [*ICAO designator*]   (FAAC)

AKA .... Ankang [*China*] [*Airport symbol*]   (OAG)

AKA .... Atom Karnkraft Avfall [*Commission for Nuclear Waste Disposal*] [*Sweden*]   (WEN)

AKA .... Australian Karate Association   (ADA)

AKA .... Australian Kart Association

AKA .... Australian Kidney Association   (ADA)

AKA .... Australian Kite Association

AKA .... Australian Korfball Association

AKA .... Autonomous Finite Automaton   (RU)

AKABRI .... Akademi Angkatan Bersendjata Republik Indonesia [*Republic of Indonesia Armed Forces Academy*]   (IN)
Akad .... Akademia [*Academy*] [*Poland*]   (POL)
akad .... Akademia [*Academy*] [*Hungary*]
Akad .... Akademie [*Academy*] [*Afrikaans*]
Akad .... Akademie [*Academy*] [*German*]
akad .... Akademisch [*Academic*] [*Germany*]   (RU)
akad .... Akademisk [*Academic*] [*Sweden*]
Akademizdat ... Publishing House of the Academy of Sciences, Former USSR   (RU)
Akad K ...... Akademiai Kiado [*Publishing House of the Hungarian Academy of Sciences*]   (HU)
AKAFU ..... Swinging Aerial Camera Mount   (RU)
AKAJANS ... Ak Deniz Haber Ajansi [*Mediterranean News Agency*] [*AHA*] [*See also*]   (TU)
AKAKAT ... Association Kaonde du Katanga
AKAR .... Angkatan Keadilan Rakyat [*People's Justice Movement*] [*Malaysia*] [*Political party*]   (EY)
AKAVA ..... Akateemisammatillinen Valtuuskunta [*Academic Professional Commission*] [*Finland*]   (WEN)
AKB .... Allami Konyvesbolt [*State Book Store*]   (HU)
AKB .... Arbeitsgemeinschaft der Kunstbibliotheken [*Germany*]   (EAIO)
AKBC .... Australian Korea Business Council
AKBCC ..... Australia-Korea Business Cooperation Committee
AKBD .... Arbeitsgemeinschaft der Kirchlichen Buchereiverbande Deutschlands [*Germany*]   (EAIO)
AKBP .... Adjun Komisaris Besar Polisi [*Assistant Chief Police Commissioner*]   (IN)
AKBW ...... Algemene Kinderbijslagwet [*Benelux*]   (BAS)
AKC .... Arca Aerovias Colombians Ltda. [*Colombia*] [*ICAO designator*]   (FAAC)
AKC .... Association Khmere de Confectionneurs [*Cambodian Garment Makers Association*]   (CL)
AKCCI ...... Australia-Korea Chamber of Commerce and Industry
AKCE .... Eskisehir Iktisadi ve Ticari Ilimler Akademisi Kulturel Calismalar ve Cevre Egitimi Enstitusu [*The Cultural Activities and Environmental Training Institute of the Eskisehir Academy of Economy and Commercial Science*] [*EITIA*] [*See also*]   (TU)
AkcjaH ...... Akcja Hodowli [*Pedigree Breeding Drive*]   (POL)
AKCLIS ..... Australian Key Center in Land Information Studies
AKCNSW ... Australian Kelpie Club of New South Wales
AKD .... Agri Kultur Dernegi [*Agri/Cultural Association*]   (TU)
Ak-Der .... Akhisar Halk Kultur Dernegi [*Akhisar Peoples Cultural Organization*] [*Manisa Province*]   (TU)
AKDM .... Disisleri Bakanligi Akademisi Baskanligi [*Foreign Affairs Ministry Academy*]   (TU)
AKDOD ..... Akademicka Komisja Dzialania Organizacji Demokratycznych [*Democratic Organizations' Student Action Committee*]   (POL)
AKDS .... Truck-Mounted Oxygen Station   (RU)
AKDV .... Anstalt fuer Kommunale Datenverarbeitung [*Institution for Municipal Data Processing*] [*German*]   (ADPT)
Akdz .... Ak Deniz [*Mediterranean*]   (TU)
AKE .... Adesmeyth Kinhsh Eiphnhs [*Independent Peace Movement*] [*Greece*]   (EAIO)
AKE .... Agrotikon Komma Ellados [*Agrarian Party of Greece*] [*Political party*]
AKE .... Akieni [*Gabon*] [*Airport symbol*]   (OAG)
AKE .... Andidiktatoriko Kinima Ellados [*Antidictatorial Movement of Greece*]   (GC)
AKE .... Anexartitos Koinopolitiki Enosi [*Independent Commonwealth Union*] [*Greek*]   (GC)
AKE .... Automatic Equipment for Power-Quality Maintenance   (RU)
AKEL .... Anorthotiko Komma Ergazomenou Laou [*Progressive Party of the Working People*] [*Cyprus*] [*Political party*]   (PPW)
AKEW ...... Arbeitsgemeinschaft Kernkraftwerk der Elektrizitatswirtschaft [*Austria*]   (PDAA)
AKF .... Abdou Karim Fall
AKF .... Aga Khan Foundation [*Switzerland*]   (EAIO)
AKF .... Allami Kereskedelmi Felugyeloseg [*State Inspectorate of Trade*]   (HU)
AKF .... Amternes og Kommunernes Forskningsinstitut [*Local Government's Research Institute*] [*Denmark*]   (IRC)
AKF .... Amtskommunernes og Kommunernes Forskningsinstitut [*Regional and Local Authorities Research Institute*] [*Denmark*]   (PDAA)
AKF .... Antarctic [*or Arctic*] Whaling Flotilla   (RU)
AKF .... Australia-Korea Foundation
AKF .... Australian Karate Federation
AKF .... Australian Kendo Federation
AKF .... Australian Kidney Foundation   (ADA)
AKF .... Australian Koala Foundation
AKF .... Kufrah [*Libya*] [*Airport symbol*]   (OAG)
AKFED ...... Aga Khan Fund for Economic Development

AKFM .... Antokon'ny Kongresin'ny Fahaleovantenan'i Madagasikara [*Congress Party for Malagasy Independence*] [*Political party*]   (AF)
AKG .... Allami Kiserleti Gazdasag [*State Experimental Farm*]   (HU)
AKG .... Anguganak [*Papua New Guinea*] [*Airport symbol*]   (OAG)
AKG .... Automatic Dew-Point Hygrometer   (RU)
AKG .... Truck-Mounted Hydraulic Crane   (RU)
AKGA .... Australian Kiwifruit Growers' Association
AKh .... Academy of Arts   (RU)
AKh .... Acetylcholine   (RU)
AKh .... Aerial Chemical Bomb   (RU)
AKH .... Akhal [*Turkmenistan*] [*ICAO designator*]   (FAAC)
AKhCh ...... Administrative Unit   (RU)
AKhE .... Acetylcholinesterase   (RU)
Akh/ha ..... Arbeitskraftstunden je Hektar [*Per Hectare Man-Hours of Work*] (EG)
AKhI .... Truck for Decontaminating an Area with Chlorinated Lime   (RU)
AKhL .... Agrochemical Laboratory   (RU)
AKhM .... Absorption-Type Refrigeration Unit   (RU)
AKhM .... Architectural and Artistic Planning Workshop   (RU)
AKhO .... Administrative Department   (RU)
AKhO .... Motorized Surgical Detachment   (RU)
AKhR .... Association of Revolutionary Artists [*1928-1932*]   (RU)
AKhRR ..... Association of Artists of Revolutionary Russia [*1922-1928*]   (RU)
AKhs .... Anotaton Khimikon Symvoulion [*Supreme Chemical Council*]   (GC)
AKHSP ..... Aga Khan Health Service, Pakistan   (EAIO)
AKhTT ..... Chemistry and Solid Fuel Processing Association   (RU)
AKhU .... Administrative Office   (RU)
AKI .... Agence Khmere d'Information [*Cambodian Information Agency*]   (CL)
AKI .... Automatizalasi Kutato Intezet [*Automation Research Institute*]   (HU)
AKI .... Magyar Tudomanyos Akademia Atommag Kutato Intezete, Debrecen [*Nuclear Science Research Institute of the Hungarian Academy of Sciences, Debrecen*]   (HU)
AKII .... Azerbaydzhan "Red Banner" Industrial Institute Imeni M. Azizbekov   (RU)
AKIM .... Aguda le Kimum Mefagrim [*Israel Association for the Habilitation of the Mentally Handicapped*]   (EAIO)
AKIN .... Acoustics Institute   (RU)
AKJ .... Asahikawa [*Japan*] [*Airport symbol*]   (OAG)
AKJDOD ... Akademicka Komisja Jednosci Dzialania Organizacji Demokratycznych [*Student Commission on the Unification of Activities of Democratic Organizations*]   (POL)
AKK .... Administrative Committee on Coordination   (RU)
AKK .... Akkumulator [*Accomolator*] [*German*]   (ADPT)
akk .... Akkusatief [*Accusative*] [*Afrikaans*]
akk .... Akkusatiivi [*Accusative*] [*Finland*]
Akk .... Akkusativ [*Accusative*] [*German*]
AKK .... Antifaschistischer Kampf Kaiserslautern [*Kaiserslautern Antifascist Struggle*] [*Germany*]   (PD)
AKK .... Arufuvarozas Kezikonyve [*Handbook on Shipping of Goods*] (HU)
AKK .... Atomkraftkonsortiet [*Nuclear energy*] [*Sweden*]   (NRCH)
AKK .... Autokozlekedesi Klub [*Automobile Transportation Club*]   (HU)
AKK .... Autourheilun Kansallinen Keskusliitto [*Finnish Automobile Sport Federation*]   (EAIO)
AKK(Berlin) ... Amt fuer Kernforschung und Kerntechnik (Berlin) [*Office for Nuclear Research and Nuclear Technology*] [*Has responsibility for control, supervision, and coordination of all activities in the field of nuclear energy*] [*German*]   (EG)
AKKh .... Academy of Municipal Services Imeni K. D. Pamfilov   (RU)
AKKK .... Amicale des Khmers du Kampuchea Krom [*Association of Friends of the Khmer Krom*] [*Literally, Association of Cambodians of Lower Cambodia*]   (CL)
akkl .... Acclimatization   (RU)
Akklimatisier ... Akklimatisierung [*Acclimatization*] [*German*]   (GCA)
AKKO .... Turkish Communist Party - Marxist-Leninist [*Political party*]   (PD)
AKKP .... Anujuman-e-Kutub Khana-e-Pakistan [*Pakistan Library Association*]   (EAIO)
Akku .... Akkumulator [*Accumulator*] [*German*]
AKL .... Auckland [*New Zealand*] [*Airport symbol*]   (OAG)
AKM .... Acme [*Spain*] [*ICAO designator*]   (FAAC)
AKM .... Agazati Kapcsolatok Merlege [*Input-Output Table*]   (HU)
AKM .... Astrakhan' Regional Studies Museum   (RU)
AKM .... Chamber Music Association   (RU)
AKMC .... Azad Kashmir Muslim Conference [*Pakistan*] [*Political party*]   (FEA)
AKMED .... Arbeiderkomiteen mot EEC og Dyrtid [*Labor Committee Against the EEC and the High Cost of Living*] [*Norway*]   (WEN)
AKMIL ...... Akademi Militer Nasional [*Indonesian*]
AKMOblast ... Autonomna Kosovo-Metohiska Oblast [*Autonomous Region of Kosovo-Metohija*] [*Serbia*]   (YU)

AKMO-NRS ... Autonomna Kosovski-Metohiska Oblast - Narodna Republika Srbija [*Autonomous Region of Kosovo-Metohija, Serbia*] (YU)

AKMR ...... Autonomous Kosovo-Metohija Region   (YU)

AKN .... Cadmium-Nickel Plate Battery   (RU)

AKNI .... Azerbaydzhan "Red Banner" Petroleum Institute Imeni M. Azizbekov   (RU)

AKNo .... Aerztekammer Nordrhein   (SLS)

AKO .... Army Command   (RU)

AKO .... Kamchatka Joint-Stock Company   (RU)

AKOD .... Ankara Kibris'li Ogrenciler Dernegi [*Ankara Cypriot Students Organization*] [*Turkish Cypriot*]   (GC)

AKOKD ..... Ankara Kibrislilar Ogrenim ve Kultur Dernegi [*Ankara Cypriot (Students) Educational and Cultural Association*] [*Turkish Cypriot*]   (GC)

AKOL .... Australian Kompass Online [*Database*]

akom .... Acoustic Ohm   (RU)

AKOR .... Arbeitskreis fuer Operations-Research [*Work Circle for Operations Research*] [*German*]   (ADPT)

AKOS .... Akademi Ogrenci Stajlari Merkezi [*The Academy Student Training Center*] [*of the Eskisehir Academy of Economy and Commercial Science EITIA*] [*See also*]

AKOV .... Antifasisticka Komise Osvobozenych Veznu [*Anti-Fascist Committee of Liberated (Political) Prisoners*]   (CZ)

AKOV .... Autokozlekedesi Vallalat [*Automobile Transportation Enterprise*]   (HU)

AKP .... Adjun Komisaris Polisi [*Assistant Police Commissioner*]   (IN)

AKP .... Agence Khmere de Presse [*Cambodian Press Agency*]

AKP .... Alzhirskaia Kommunisticheskaia Partia [*Albanian Communist Party*] [*Political party*]

AKP .... American Communist Party   (BU)

AKP .... Aniline Dye Industry   (RU)

AKP .... Arbeidernes Kommunistiske Parti [*Workers' Communist Party*] [*Norway*] [*Political party*]   (PPE)

AKP .... Argentinian Communist Party [*Political party*]

AKP .... Austrian Communist Party [*Political party*]

AKP .... Automatic Brake Check Point [*Railroads*]   (RU)

akp .... Breakthrough Artillery Corps   (BU)

AKP(b) .... Azerbaydzhan Communist Party (of Bolsheviks) [*Political party*]   (RU)

AKP (M-L) ... Arbeidernes Kommunistparti (Marxist-Leninistene) [*Workers Communist Party (Marxist-Leninist)*] [*Norway*] [*Political party*]

AKPT .... Automatic Alternating-Current Compensator   (RU)

AKR .... Acetate Solvent for Leather   (RU)

AKR .... Acrylate   (RU)

AKR .... Ambtenarenreglement voor het Korps Rijkspolitie [*Benelux*]   (BAS)

AKR .... Artiljeriski Komandno-Racunarski Uredaji [*Artillery Staff Computing Equipment*]   (YU)

AKRCs ...... Autoklub Republiky Ceskoslovenske [*Automobile Club of the Czechoslovak Republic*]   (CZ)

AKRI .... Angkatan Kepolisian Republik Indonesia [*Republic of Indonesia Police Force*]   (IN)

AKRP .... Mobile Motion Picture Unit and Radio Broadcasting Station   (RU)

AKS .... Airfield Compressor Plant   (RU)

AKS .... Akateeminen Karjala Seura [*Academic Karelia Society*] [*Finland*]   (WEN)

AKS .... Akseptasie [*Acceptance*] [*Afrikaans*]

AKS .... Amatorski Klub Sportowy [*Amateur Sport Club*]   (POL)

AKS .... Augsburger Kammgarn-Spinnerei [*Augsburg Worsted Cloth Spinning Mill*]

AKS .... Auki [*Solomon Islands*] [*Airport symbol*]   (OAG)

AKS .... Automatic Logging Station   (RU)

aks .... English Cubic Sagene   (RU)

AKS .... Mobile Compressor   (RU)

AKSA .... Akrilik Kimya Sanayii AS [*Acrylic Chemical Industry Corporation*]   (TU)

AKS/L .... Laboratory of an Automatic Logging Station   (RU)

AKSM .... Anti-Fascist Committee of Soviet Youth   (RU)

AKSO .... Aksam Kiz Sanat Okulu [*Evening Trade School for Women*]   (TU)

AKSSR ...... Karelian Autonomous Soviet Socialist Republic   (RU)

akt .... Aktiivi(n) [*Finland*]

akt .... Aktiv [*Active*] [*German*]

AKT .... Amicale Khmere de Tourisme [*Cambodian Tourism Association*]   (CL)

AKT .... Association of Kindergarten Teachers [*Finland*]   (EAIO)

AKT .... Australian Trade-Union Congress

AKT .... Auto-Ja Kulietusalan Tyoentekijaeliitto [*Trade union*] [*Finland*]   (EY)

AKTG .... Adrenocorticotrophic Hormone   (RU)

AktG .... Aktiengesetz [*Law governing public companies*] [*German*]   (ILCA)

Akt-Ges ...... Aktiengesellschaft [*Corporation, Incorporated*] [*German*]

AKThB ...... Arbeitsgemeinschaft Katholisch-Theologischer Bibliotheken   (SLS)

Aktivier ...... Aktivierung [*Activation*] [*German*]   (GCA)

aktivir .... Activated   (RU)

akts .... Joint-Stock   (RU)

aktsd-vo ..... Joint-Stock Company   (BU)

akts o-vo ..... Joint-Stock Company   (RU)

AKTUR ..... Akdeniz Tarim Urunleri Konsantre Sanayii AS [*Mediterranean Agricultural Products*]   (TU)

AKTUR ..... Aksiefront vir die Behoud van Turnhalle-Beginsels [*Action Front for the Preservation of Turnhalle Principles*] [*Namibia*]   (AF)

Aktyubkhim ... Aktyubinsk Chemical Plant   (RU)

Aktyubnefterazvedka ... Aktyubinsk Petroleum Exploration Trust   (RU)

AKU .... Adiabatic Stability Constant   (RU)

AKU .... Aga Khan University [*Karachi, Pakistan*]

AKU .... Aksu [*China*] [*Airport symbol*]   (OAG)

AKU .... Automatic Monitor   (RU)

AKUKS ..... Artillery Courses for Advanced Training of Command Personnel   (RU)

AKV .... Academy of Communist Education Imeni N. K. Krupskaya   (RU)

AKV .... Air-Quantity Monitoring Unit [*Mine equipment*]   (RU)

AKV .... Allami Konyvterjeszto Vallalat [*State Book Distributing Enterprise*]   (HU)

AKV .... Automatic Capillary Viscometer   (RU)

AKV .... Automatic Humidity Regulator   (RU)

AKVF .... Amur "Red Banner" Naval Flotilla   (RU)

AKVF .... Astrakhan'-Caspian Naval Flotilla   (RU)

akvo .... Anyakonyvvezeto [*Registrar of Births, Marriages, and Deaths*]   (HU)

AKW .... Algemeen Kinderbijslagwet [*General Children's Allowance Act*] [*Netherlands*]   (WEN)

AKW .... Amberger Kaolinwerke GmbH [*Business term*]

AKW .... Amt fuer Kontrolle des Warenverkehrs [*Office for the Control of Commodity Traffic*] [*German*]   (EG)

AKW .... Arbeitsgemeinschaft fuer Kunst und Wissenschaft [*Austria*]   (SLS)

AKW .... Atomkraftwerk [*Nuclear Power Plant*] [*German*]   (EG)

AKWV .... Algemeen Katholieke Werkgevers Vereniging [*General Catholic Employers Association*] [*Netherlands*]   (WEN)

AKY .... Akyab [*Myanmar*] [*Airport symbol*]   (OAG)

AKYSDE ... Anoteron Kendron Ypiresiakou Symvouliou Dimotikis Ekpaidevseos [*Higher Center of the Public Education Service Council*] [*Greek*]   (GC)

AKZA .... Aktiekomitee Zuidelyk Afrika [*Belgium*]

AKZO .... Algemene Kunstzijde Unie [*AKU*] - Koninklijke Zout-Organon [*KZO*] [*Two companies whose merger formed AKZO*]

AKZS .... Truck-Mounted Oxygen-Charging Station   (RU)

AL .... Accion Laborista [*Laborist Action*] [*Spanish*]   (WER)

AL .... Administratief Lexicon [*Benelux*]   (BAS)

Al .... Alameda [*Tree-Shaded Walk*] [*Portuguese*]

Al .... Alan [*Field, Clearing in a Forest*]   (TU)

al .... Alanine   (TU)

AL .... Albania [*ANSI two-letter standard code*]   (CNC)

Al .... Aleja [*or Aleje*] [*Avenue*]   (POL)

al .... Alemao [*German*] [*Portuguese*]

AL .... Alessandria [*Car registration plates*] [*Italian*]

AL .... Al-Haq [*Israel*]   (EAIO)

Al .... Alinea [*Paragraph*] [*Dutch*]   (ILCA)

Al .... Alinea [*Paragraph*] [*Italian*]   (ILCA)

a/l .... A Livraison [*On Delivery of Goods*] [*French*] [*Business term*]

AL .... Alpavia [*France*] [*ICAO aircraft manufacturer identifier*]   (ICAO)

AL .... Alternative List [*Sweden*] [*Political party*]

AL .... Alternative Liste [*Alternative List*] [*Austria*] [*Political party*]

Al .... Aluminio [*Aluminum*] [*Chemical element*] [*Portuguese*]

AL .... Amigos del Libro [*Publisher*] [*Bolivia*]

a/L .... An der Lahn [*On the Lahn River*] [*German*]

AL .... Anfangsladung [*Initial Charge*] [*German*]   (GCA)

AL .... Angkatan Laut [*Navy*]   (IN)

AL .... Apres Livraison [*After Delivery of Goods*] [*French*]

A-L .... Arrete-Loi [*French*]   (BAS)

AL .... Arrete Pris par l'Autorite Locale [*French*]   (FLAF)

AL .... Artillerie Lourde [*Military*] [*French*]   (MTD)

AL .... Artillery Observer-Pilot   (RU)

AL .... Ashok Leyland [*Vehicle manufacturer*] [*India*]

aL .... Auf Lieferung [*On Delivery*] [*German*]   (GCA)

AL .... Auris Laeva [*Left Ear*] [*Medicine*]

AL .... Automatic Linguistics   (RU)

al .... Avant la Lettre [*Before Lettering*] [*Engraving*] [*French*]

AL .... Awami League [*Bangladesh*] [*Political party*]   (FEA)

AL .... Estado de Alagoas [*State of Alagoas*] [*Brazil*]

AL .... L'Air Liquide [*Commercial firm*] [*France*]

a/l .... Nuclear Powered Icebreaker, Atomic Icebreaker   (RU)

al .... Paragraph (BU)
al .... Section (BU)
AL .... Subscriber's Line (RU)
AL .... Transfer Machine (RU)
ALA .... Aboriginal Languages Association [*Australia*]
ALA .... African Literature Association
ala .... Alakulat [*Formation, Outfit*] [*Military*] (HU)
ala .... Alallomas [*Substation*] (HU)
ALA .... Alma-Ata [*Former USSR*] [*Airport symbol*] (OAG)
ALA .... Apararea Locala Anti-Aeriana [*Local Anti-Aircraft Defense*] (RO)
ALA .... Arakan Liberation Army [*Myanmar*] [*Political party*] (EY)
ALA .... Army Light Aviation [*Australia*]
ALA .... Arrocera del Litoral Argentino [*Argentina*] (DSCA)
ALA .... Artillerie Lourde de l'Armee [*Military*] [*French*] (MTD)
ALA .... Arts Law Australia [*A publication*]
ALA .... Arussi Liberation Army [*Ethiopia*] (AF)
ALA .... Asociacion Latinoamericana de Acuicultura [*Venezuela*] (ASF)
ALA .... Asociacion Latinoamericana de Archivos [*Latin American Association of Archives - LAAA*] (EAIO)
ALA .... Associacao Livre dos Agricultores [*Free Association of Farmers*] [*Portuguese*] (WER)
ALA .... Australian Labor Army (ADA)
ALA .... Australian Lebanese Association (ADA)
ALA .... Australian Legal Aid Office (ADA)
ALA .... Australian Liberal Association (ADA)
ALA .... Australian Library Association
ALA .... Australian Lifewriters' Association
ALA .... Australian Lighthouse Association
ALA .... Austral Lineas Aereas [*Airline*] [*Argentina*] (EY)
ALA .... International Association of Latin American Air Carriers [*ICAO designator*] (FAAC)
ALAA .... Applied Linguistics Association of Australia (ADA)
ALAA .... Associate of the Library Association of Australia (ADA)
ALAA .... Aviation Law Association of Australia
ALAA .... Aviation Legere de l'Armee de l'Air [*France*]
ALAB........ Alyansang Likha ng mga Anak ng Bayan [*Trade union*] [*Philippines*] (EY)
ALAC........ Adult Literacy Action Campaign [*Australia*]
ALAC........ Alcoholic Liquor Advisory Council [*New Zealand*]
ALAC........ Asociacion de Latinoamericanos en Cuba [*Association of Latin Americans in Cuba*] (LA)
ALAC........ Australian Labor Advisory Council
ALACAT ... Asociacion Latinoamericana de Agentes de Carga Aerea y Transporte [*Latin American Association of Freight and Transport Agents - LAFTA*] (EA)
ALACERG ... Asociacion Latinoamericana de Corporaciones de Educacion Agricola para Graduados (DSCA)
ALACF ...... Asociacion Latinoamericana de Ciencias Fisiologicas [*Latin American Association of Physiological Sciences*] [*ICSU*] (EAIO)
ALACODE ... Asociacion Latinoamericana de Periodistas para el Desarrollo [*Association of Latin American Journalists for Development*] (LA)
ALAD .... Arid Lands Agricultural Development [*Program*] [*Later, ICARDA Middle East*]
ALAD .... Arid Lands Agricultural Development Program [*North African*]
ALADA ..... Associacao Latino-Americana de Direito Aeronautico [*Latin American Association of Aeronautical Law*] (LA)
ALADAA... Asociacion Latinoamericana de Estudios Afroasiaticos [*Latin American Association for Afro-Asian Studies - LAAAAS*] (EAIO)
ALADI ...... Asociacion Latinoamericana de Integracion [*Latin American Integration Association*] [*Montevideo, Uruguay*] (LA)
ALADI ...... Association Latino-Americaine d'Integration [*Latin American Integration Association - LAIA*] [*French*]
ALADI ...... Latin American Integration Association [*Trade association of Argentina, Bolivia, Brazil, Chile, Colombia, Ecuador, Mexico, Paraguay, Peru, Uruguay, and Venezuela*] (BARN)
ALADIM... Asociacion Latinoamericana para el Desarrollo y la Integracion de la Mujer [*Latin American Association for the Development and Integration of Women - LAADIW*] [*Santiago, Chile*] (EAIO)
ALADIN.... Automatisering Landbouwkundige Documentatie- en Informatieverspreiding [*Netherlands*]
ALADIN.... Automatisering Landbouwkundige Dokumentatie-En Informatievespreiding in Nederland [*Automation of Agricultural Documentation and Information in the Netherlands*] [*Centre for Agricultural Publishing and Documentation*] (NITA)
ALAE........ Asociacion Latinoamericana de Entomologia [*Latin American Association of Entomology*] (LAA)
ALAEA...... Australian Licensed Aircraft Engineers Association (ADA)
ALAF........ Aluminium Africa Co. Ltd.
ALAF........ Asociacion Latinoamericana de Ferrocarriles [*Latin American Railways Association - LARA*] [*Argentina*]

ALAF........ Asociacion Latinoamericana de Fitotecnia (LAA)
ALAFAR ... Asociacion Latinoamericana de Fabricantes de Materiales Refractarios (LAA)
ALAFATA ... Asociacion Latinoamericana de Fabricantes de Tableros de Fibra, de Madera, y Similares (LAA)
ALAFEM .. Asociacion Latinoamericana de Facultades y Escuelas de Medicina de America Latina [*Latin American Association of Medical Schools and Faculties - LAAMSF*] [*Quito, Ecuador*] (EAIO)
ALAFO...... Asociacion Latinoamericana de Facultades de Odontologia [*Latin-American Association of Dental Schools*] [*Colorado*] (LAA)
ALAHUA .. Associacion Latino Americana para la Promocion de l'Habitat la Arquitectura y el Urbanismo [*Latin American Association for the Promotion of the Habitat, Architecture and Town Planning*] [*Ecuador*] (PDAA)
ALAI........ Association Litteraire et Artistique Internationale [*French*] (SLS)
ALAIC....... Asociacion Latinoamericana de Industriales del Cuero (LAA)
ALAICO.... Asociacion de Lineas Aereas Internacionales en Colombia [*Association of International Airlines in Colombia*] (LA)
ALAIH....... Asociacion Latinoamericana de Ictiologos y Herpetologos (DSCA)
ALAIN...... Australian Libraries and Information Network [*Proposed*]
ALAINEE ... Asociacion Latinoamericana de la Industria Electrica y Electronica [*Latin American Electric and Electronic Industry Association*] (LA)
ALAL........ Aluminium Algerois
ALALC....... Asociacion Latinoamericana de Libre Comercio [*Also, LAFTA*] [*Latin American Free Trade Association*]
ALALE....... Association Latino-Americaine de Libre-Echange [*Latin American Free Trade Association - LAFTA*] [*French*]
ALAMAR ... Asociacion Latinoamericana de Armadores [*Latin American Shipowners' Association*] (EAIO)
ALAMBREC ... Alambres Galvanizados Ecuatorianos, SA [*Ecuadorean Galvanized Wires, Inc.*] (LA)
ALAMOC ... Asociacion Latinoamericana de Analisis y Modificacion del Comportamiento [*Latin American Association of Behavior Analysis and Modification*] (EAIO)
ALAMSAS ... Alarko Agir Makina Sanayii Anonim Sirketi [*Alarko Heavy Machinery Industry Corporation*] (TU)
ALANAM ... Latin American Association of National Academies of Medicine (EA)
alank .... Alankomainen [*Dutch*] [*Finland*]
ALAO .... Australian Legal Aid Office (ADA)
ALAP........ Agence Litteraire et Artistique Parisienne pour les Echanges Culturels [*Parisian Literary and Artistic Agency for Cultural Exchange*] (WER)
ALAP........ Asociacion Latinoamericana de Prensa [*Latin American Press Association*] (LA)
ALAP........ Latin American Trade-Union Association (RU)
ALAPROVI ... Asociacion Latinoamericana de Productores de Vidrio [*Montevideo, Uruguay*] (LAA)
alapsz .... Alapszabaly [*or Alapszabalyok*] [*Statute or Statutes, Bylaws*] (HU)
ALAPV...... Asociacion Latinoamericana de Productores de Vidrio [*Montevideo, Uruguay*] (LAA)
ALARA...... As Low As Reasonably Achievable
ALARM.... Australian Library Annual Reports on Microfiche
ALAS........ Aboriginal Legal Aid Service [*Australia*]
ALAS........ Asociacion Latinoamericana del Suelo (DSCA)
ALAS........ Asociacion Latinoamericana de Sociologia [*Mexico*] (SLS)
ALAS........ Asociacion Latinoamericana de Sociologia [*Argentina*] (SLS)
ALASA ...... African Language Association of Southern Africa (AA)
ALASA ...... African Library Association of South Africa (SLS)
ALASEI.... Agencia Latinoamericana de Servicios Especiales de Informacion [*Latin American Special Information Service Agency*] (LA)
ALASRU ... Asociacion Latinoamericana de Sociologia Rural [*Latin American Rural Sociological Association - LARSA*] (EAIO)
ALAT........ Australian Liquid Assets Trust
ALAT........ Aviation Legere de l'Armee de Terre [*Ground Forces Tactical Air Support*] [*French*] (WER)
ALATAC ... Asociacion Latinoamericana de Transportacion Automotor por Carreteras [*Latin American Automobile Highway Transport Association*] (LA)
ALATEF.... Australian Leather and Allied Trades Employees' Federation (ADA)
ALAU .... Australian Little Athletics Union
ALAU .... Union of Latin American Universities (EA)
a la v .... A la Vista [*On View*] [*Spanish*]
ALB .... Aero Albatros [*Mexico*] [*ICAO designator*] (FAAC)
ALB .... Albania [*ANSI three-letter standard code*] (CNC)
alb .... Albanian (RU)
Alb .... Albay [*Colonel (Army) or Captain (Navy)*] (TU)
alb .... Album [*Album*] [*Publishing*] [*French*]
ALB .... Allgemeine Leistungs- und Lieferungsbedingungen [*General Delivery and Performance Terms*] [*German*] (EG)

ALB .... Antifasisticka Liga Burme [*Anti-Fascist League of Burma*] (YU)
ALB .... Arab Latin American Bank [*Peru*]
ALB .... Arbeitsgemeinschaft Landwirtschaftliches Bauwesen [*Agricultural Construction Work Group*] [*German*] (EG)
ALBA .... Aluminum Bahrain [*State enterprise*] [*Manama*] (ME)
ALBAAB ... Al-Bahrain Arab African Bank
ALBAMEX ... Alimentos Balanceados de Mexico SA de CV
Alban .... Albania
ALBART ... Allami Bauxit Aluminium Reszvenytarsasag [*State Bauxite Aluminum Company Limited*] (HU)
ALBE .... Adult Literacy and Basic Education
ALBIS .... Australian Library Based Information System (ADA)
ALBRAS .... Aluminio de Brasil, SA [*Brazilian Aluminum Corporation, Inc.*] (LA)
ALBRECO ... Groupement Algerie-Bretagne de Construction
ALBS .... Australian Limousin Breeders' Society
ALBSAC ... Adult Literacy and Basic Skills Action Coalition [*Australia*]
AlBz .... Aluminiumbronze [*Aluminum Bronze*] [*German*] (GCA)
ALC .... Aboriginal Lands Council [*Australia*]
ALC .... Aboriginal Loans Commission [*Australia*]
ALC .... African Lakes Company [*or Corporation*]
ALC .... African Liberation Committee
ALC .... Afro-American Labor Center
ALC .... A la Carte [*According to the Menu, each item ordered individually*] [*French*] (ADA)
ALC .... Alexandria Liaison Committee
ALC .... Alicante [*Spain*] [*Airport symbol*] (OAG)
ALC .... Arab League Council
ALC .... ArbeitsLivsCentrum [*Center for Working Life*]
ALC .... Asian Law Centre [*University of Melbourne*] [*Australia*]
ALC .... Associated Liquidpaperboard Converters [*Australia*]
ALC .... Australian Lacrosse Council
ALC .... Australian Leisure Club (ADA)
ALC .... Australian Lithuanian Community
ALC .... Australian Loan Council
ALCA .... Artillerie Lourde de Corps d'Armee [*Military*] [*French*] (MTD)
ALCA .... Arts Law Centre of Australia
ALCAM ..... Assemblee Legislative du Cameroun
ALCAMOR ... Assemblee Legislative du Cameroun Orientale
ALCANCALI ... Aluminio Alcan de Colombia SA [*Colombia*] (COL)
ALCASA ... Almidones de Centroamerica SA [*Honduras*] (DSCA)
ALCASA ... Aluminios del Caroni, SA [*Caroni Aluminum Company*] [*Venezuela*] (LA)
ALCATEL ... Societe Alsacienne de Constructions Atomiques de Telecommunications et d'Electronique [*France*] (PDAA)
ALCAVE ... Alambres y Cables Venezolanos, CA
ALCB .... Association Luxembourgeoise Contre le Bruit [*Luxembourg*] (SLS)
alcde .... Alcalde [*Mayor*] [*Spanish*]
ALCER ..... Asociacion para la Lucha Contra las Enfermedades Renales [*Association for the Struggle Against Kidney Diseases*] [*Spanish*] (WER)
ALCF .... Australian Law Council Foundation
ALCF .... Australian Lithuanian Catholic Federation
ALCIP ...... Societe Algerienne de Construction Industrielle et Petroliere [*Algerian Industrial and Petroleum Engineering Co.*] (AF)
ALCM ...... Association of Liquidpaperboard Carton Manufacturers
ALCMI ..... Asociacion Latinoamericana y del Caribe de Mundazas Internacionales [*Latin American and Caribbean International Moving*] [*Panama*] (EAIO)
ALCO .... Alliance des Congolais
ALCOM ..... Aluminium Company of Malaysia
ALCOMINAS ... Companhia Mineira de Aluminio [*Aluminum Company of Minas Gerais*] [*Brazil*] (LA)
ALCON ..... Alimentos Concentrados [*Honduras*] (DSCA)
ALCONH ... Alianza Campesina de Organizaciones Nacionales de Honduras [*Peasant Alliance of National Organizations of Honduras*] [*Political party*] (PD)
ALCORSS ... Australian Liaison Committee on Remote Sensing by Satellite
ALCSP .... Associacao dos Lavradores de Cafe de Sao Paulo [*Brazil*] (DSCA)
ALCVO ..... Association of Licensed Charter Vessel Owners [*Australia*]
ALCWA ..... Association of Licensed Clubs of Western Australia
ALD .... Aeronavs La Dprada SA [*Spain*] [*ICAO designator*] (FAAC)
ALD .... African Liberation Day
ALD .... Agrupacion Liberal Democratica [*Democratic Liberal Group*] [*Spanish*] (WER)
ald .... Aldaar [*In the Same Place*] [*Afrikaans*]
ALD .... Alternative Lifestyles for the Disabled [*Australia*]
ALD .... Associaiton Luxembourgeoise du Diabete [*Diabetic Association of Luxembourg*] (EAIO)
ALDA .... Australian Lead Development Association (ADA)
ALDAI ...... Associazione Lombarda Dirigenti Aziende Industriali [*Italy*]
ALDC .... Asociacion Latinoamericana de Derecho Constitucional [*Latin American Constitutional Law Association - LACLA*] (EAIO)

ALDDH ..... Argentinos por Libertades Democraticas y Derechos Humanos [*Argentines for Democratic Freedoms and Human Rights*] (LA)
ALDECA ... Aluminio de Centroamerica, SA [*Aluminum of Central America Corp.*] [*El Salvador*]
ALDEP ...... Arable Land Development Programme [*Botswana*]
ALDEV ...... African Land Development
ALDEVCO ... Aluminium Development Council [*Australia*]
ALDIM ...... Societe Algerienne des Outils Diamantes [*Algerian Diamond Tool Company*] (AF)
ALDIS .... Australian LASER Disc Information Services Proprietary Ltd.
ALDOC ..... League of Arab States Documentation and Information Center [*Information service or system*] (IID)
ALDOS ...... Automatisches Lager-Dispositions-und Optimierungssystem [*Automatic Place Disposition and Optimizing System*] [*German*] (ADPT)
ALE .... Aerolineas Especiales de Colombia [*ICAO designator*] (FAAC)
ALE .... Alliance Libre Europeenne [*European Free Alliance - EFA*] [*Political party*] [*Brussels, Belgium*] (EAIO)
ALE .... Association of Lesotho Employers (EAIO)
ALE .... Aviazione Leggera Esercito [*Army Air Corps*] [*Italy*] (PDAA)
ALEA .... Australian Livestock Exporters' Association
ALEAM ..... Association of Lao Employees of American Missions (CL)
ALEAS ...... Asociacion Latinoamericana de Educacion Agricola Superior (LAA)
alebastr ...... Alabaster Quarry [*Topography*] (RU)
ALEBCI ..... Asociacion Latino Americana de Escuelas de Bibliotecnomia y Ciencias de la Informacion
ALEC .... Arid Lands Environment Centre [*Australia*]
ALEC .... Associazione Laureati in Economia e Commercio [*Italian*] (SLS)
ALEC .... Atlas Linguistico, Etnografico de Colombia [*Colombia*] (COL)
ALEC .... Australian Legal Education Council (ADA)
ALECSO ... Arab League Educational, Cultural, and Scientific Organization [*Tunisia*]
alemp .... Alempana [*Finland*]
ALEPH ...... Automated Library Expandable Program, Hebrew University of Jerusalem [*Israel*] [*Information service or system*] (IID)
ALERB ..... Asociacion Latinoamericana de Redactores de Revistas Biologicas [*Latin American Association of Editors of Biological Journals*] (LAA)
ALERT ...... All-African Leprosy and Rehabilitation Center (AF)
ALES .... Aboriginal Languages Education Strategy [*Australia*]
ALESW ..... Australian League of Ex-Servicemen and Women
ALEXSHIP ... Alexandria Shipping & Navigation Co. [*Egypt*] (IMH)
alezds .... Alezredes [*Lieutenant Colonel*] (HU)
alezr .... Alezredes [*Lieutenant Colonel*] (HU)
ALF .... Afar Liberation Front [*Ethiopia*] (PD)
alf .... Alfabeto [*Alphabet*] [*Portuguese*]
alf .... Alferes [*Ensign*] [*Portuguese*]
ALF .... Allied Command Europe [*ICAO designator*] (FAAC)
alf .... Alphabetic (RU)
ALF .... Alta [*Norway*] [*Airport symbol*] (OAG)
ALF .... Arab Liberation Forces [*or Front*] [*Palestinian*] (ME)
ALF .... Asociacion Latinoamericana de Fitopatologia [*Colombia*] (DSCA)
ALF .... Audiologopaedisk Forening [*Denmark*] (SLS)
ALF .... Australasian [*or Australian*] Labor Federation (ADA)
ALF .... Australian Lecture Foundation
ALF .... Australian Liberation Front [*Political party*]
ALF .... Australian Library Fair
ALF .... Automated Laboratory of Photographic Methods (RU)
ALF .... Azania Liberation Front [*Sudan*]
ALF .... Azania Liberation Front [*South Africa*]
ALFA .... Aerolinea Federal Argentina [*Argentine Federal Airline*] (EY)
ALFA .... Australian Lot Feeders Association
ALFAL ...... Asociacion de Linguistica y Filologia de America Latina [*Chile*] (SLS)
ALFAL ...... Asociacion de Linguistica y Filologia de America Latina [*Venezuela*] (SLS)
ALFC .... Aboriginal Land Fund Commission [*Australia*]
ALFCE .... Allied Land Forces Central Europe [*NATO*] (NATG)
ALFE .... Asociacion Latinoamericana de Fitotecnistas de Frijol [*Colombia*] (DSCA)
ALFE .... Association Linguistique Franco-Europeenne [*French*] (SLS)
ALFEDIAM ... Association de Langue Francaise pour l'Etude du Diabete et des Maladies Metaboliques [*French*] (SLS)
ALFESA .... Almidones y Feculas SA [*Ecuador*] (DSCA)
ALFESA .... Asociacion Latinoamericana de Facultades y Escuelas Superiores de Agricultura (DSCA)
al'fol' .... Aluminum Foil (RU)
ALFOR ...... Societe Algerienne de Forage [*Algerian Drilling Company*] (AF)
ALFSE .... Allied Land Forces Southern Europe [*NATO*]
ALFSEA .... Allied Land Forces Southeast Asia [*NATO*]
ALFSEE .... Allied Land Forces Southeastern Europe [*NATO*]
ALFSH ...... Allied Land Forces Schleswig-Holstein [*NATO*] (NATG)

ALFT......... Aviation Legere de la Force Terreste [*Army Air Force*] [*Belgium*] (PDAA)
ALG........... Airlift Group [*Military*]
ALG........... Akademia Lekarska w Gdansku [*Gdansk (Danzig) Academy of Medicine*] (POL)
Alg.............. Algebra [*Portuguese*]
ALG........... Algebra [*Afrikaans*]
alg.............. Algebra, Algebraic (RU)
ALG........... Algemeen [*General*] [*Afrikaans*]
ALG........... Algiers [*Algeria*] [*Airport symbol*] (OAG)
alg.............. Algumas [*Some*] [*Portuguese*]
ALG........... Australian Lace Guild
ALG........... Australian Legal Group
ALG........... Autorite du Liptako-Gourma [*Liptako-Gourma Authority*] [*Burkina Faso*]
ALGA........ Association of Local Government Authorities [*Jamaica*] (LA)
ALGA........ Australian Local Government Association
ALGA........ Australian Lychee Growers' Association
ALGAK...... Association of Local Government Authorities in Kenya
ALGEK...... Algorithmic Language for Economics Calculations (RU)
ALGEM..... Algorithmic Language for the Description of Mathematical Economics Problems (RU)
ALGEO ..... Societe Algerienne de Geophysique [*Algerian Geophysical Company*] (AF)
ALGESA ... Aerolineas Guinea Ecuatorial Sociedad Anonima [*Equatorial Guinea*] (EY)
ALGESA ... Almacenes Generales Sociedad Anonima [*Guatemala*] (IMH)
ALGOLIMO ... Algodoeira Limoeirense [*Brazil*] (DSCA)
ALGP........ Artillerie Lourde a Grande Puissance [*Military*] [*French*] (MTD)
Alg PractRechtsverz ... Algemene Prachtische Rechtsverzameling [*Benelux*] (BAS)
ALGUSA... Algodonera Guarico [*Venezuela*] (DSCA)
alg verg....... Algemene Vergadering [*Benelux*] (BAS)
alg verord ... Algemene Verordening [*Benelux*] (BAS)
ALGWA .... Australian Local Government Women's Association (ADA)
ALH........... Albany [*Australia*] [*Airport symbol*] (OAG)
ALH........... Alfred Lawrence Holdings Ltd. [*Australia*] (ADA)
Alh .... Alhambra (BARN)
ALH........... Australian Light Horse (ADA)
ALHC........ African-Latin Help Committee
alhdgy .... Alhadnagy [*Junior Lieutenant*] [*highest rank of noncommissioned officer*] [*Formerly,*] (HU)
alhgy .... Alhadnagy [*Junior Lieutenant*] [*highest rank of noncommissioned officer*] [*Formerly,*] (HU)
ALHR........ Algerian League of Human Rights
ALI............. Air Liberia [*ICAO designator*] (FAAC)
Ali .... Angali [*Bight, Open Bay*] [*Greek*] (NAU)
ALI............. Association Lyrique Internationale [*Toulouse, France*] (EAIO)
ALI............. Associazione Legnanese dell'Industria [*Italy*]
ALI............. Australian Laser Institute
ALI............. Australian Leather Institute (ADA)
ALI............. Australian Lighting Industries
ALI............. Avio Linee Italiane
ALIA.......... Australian Library and Information Association [*National Union Catalogue of Australia symbol*]
ALIA.......... Royal Jordanian Airlines (IMH)
ALIANSA ... Alimentos de Animales, Sociedad Anonima [*Animal Food Corp.*] [*El Salvador*]
ALIATec.... Australian Library and Information Association, Library Technician
ALIAZO.... Alianca Angolana des Originarios do Zombo
ALIC.......... Australian Land Information Council
ALIC.......... Australian Libraries and Information Council
ALICA .... Associacao Latinoamericana dos Industrias de Conservas Alimenticias [*Latin American Food Canners Association*] [*Montevideo, Uruguay*] (LA)
ALICMAR ... Asociacion Latinoamericana de Investigadores en Ciencias del Mar [*Latin American Association of Marine Scientific Researchers*] [*Venezuela*] (ASF)
ALICO....... American Life Insurance Co. [*Surinam*] (EY)
ALIDE....... Asociacion Latinoamericana de Instituciones Financieras de Desarrollo [*Latin American Association of Development Financing Institutions*] [*Lima, Peru*] (EAIO)
ALIEN....... Automated Library Enquiry Network [*Murdoch University*] [*Australia*]
ALIES....... Australian Librarians in Emergency Services
ALIFAR..... Asociacion Latinoamericana de Industrias Farmaceuticas [*Latin American Association of Pharmaceutical Industries - LAAPI*] (EAIO)
alifatich...... Aliphatic (RU)
alig .... Aligazgato [*Deputy Director*] (HU)
alik .... Alikersantti [*Finland*]
ALIL.......... Asociacion Latinoamericana de Investigadores en Leguminosas [*Colombia*] (DSCA)
ALIMBA ... Productos Alimenticios da Bahia [*Brazil*] (DSCA)

ALIMPORT ... Empresa Cubana Importadora de Alimentos [*Cuban Enterprise for Import of Foodstuffs*] (LA)
ALIMUPER ... Accion para la Liberacion de la Mujer Peruana [*Peru Defunct*] (EAIO)
ALIN .... Alianza de Liberacion de la Izquierda Nacional [*National Left Liberation Alliance*] [*Bolivia*] (LA)
ALIO .... Adult Literacy Information Office [*Australia*]
ALIP.......... Australian Library and Information Professionals [*A publication*]
ALIPLAST ... Asociacion Latinoamericana de Industrias del Plastico [*Montevideo, Uruguay*] (LAA)
ALIPO....... Alianza Liberal del Pueblo [*People's Liberal Alliance*] [*Honduras*] (LA)
ALIR......... Australian Library and Information Research
ALIREC .... A corporation formed by Ito Chu with Sumitomo Metal Mining Co. Ltd., and Furukawa Co. Ltd., to continue joint uranium surveying work with AGIP of Australia
ALIS .... Automated Library Information System [*National Technological Library of Denmark*] [*Lyngby*] (IID)
ALISA ...... Australian Library and Information Science Abstracts
ALISA ...... Moscow Exchange of Building Materials [*Russian Federation*] (EY)
ALISS........ Automatisiertes Leitungs- und Informationssystem Standardwerk [*Automated Management and Information System Standard Work*] [*German*] (EG)
ALIT......... Australian Literature [*A database*] (NITA)
ALITALIA ... Aerolinee Italiane Internazionali [*Italian International Airline*] [*Facetious translation: Always Late in Takeoffs, Always Late in Arrivals*]
alitsiklich... Alicyclic (RU)
ALJ .... Aero Leasing Italiana SpA [*Italy*] [*ICAO designator*] (FAAC)
ALJ .... Alexander Bay [*South Africa*] [*Airport symbol*] (OAG)
ALJ .... Association Luxembourgeoise des Journalistes [*Luxembourg Association of Journalists*] (EAIO)
ALK .... Air Lanka [*Sri Lanka*] [*ICAO designator*] (FAAC)
Alk .... Alkalie [*Alkali*] [*German*] (GCA)
alk .... Alkalisch [*Alkaline*] [*German*]
alk .... Alkalmas [*Fit, Suitable*] (HU)
alk .... Alkalmazott [*Employee*] (HU)
alk .... Alkalmazta [*Adapted By*] [*Hungary*]
alk .... Alkerulet [*Subdistrict*] (HU)
Alk .... Alkohol [*Alcohol*] [*German*]
alk .... Alkotmany [*Constitution*] (HU)
alk .... Alkuaan [*Originally*] [*Finland*]
alkal .... Alkalisch [*Alkaline*] [*German*]
ALKD .... Association Luxembourgeoise des Kinesitherapeutes Diplomes [*Luxembourg*] (SLS)
ALKEM..... Alpha Chemie und Metallurgie, GmbH [*Nuclear energy*] (NRCH)
alkoh .... Alkoholisch [*Alcoholic*] [*German*]
alkohol....... Alkoholisch [*Alcoholic*] [*German*] (GCA)
ALKON ..... Productos Alkalinos SA [*Colombia*] (COL)
ALKOPROMET ... Pretprijatie za Promet so Alkoholni Pijaloci [*Establishment for Trade in Alcoholic Beverages*] [*Skopje*] (YU)
ALKSM..... Lenin Young Communist League of Azerbaydzhan (RU)
Alkylier...... Alkylierung [*Alkylation*] [*German*] (GCA)
ALL........... Aliserio [*Italy*] [*ICAO designator*] (FAAC)
all .... Allami [*State (adjective)*] (HU)
all .... Allando [*Permanent*] (HU)
all .... Allatiivi [*Finland*]
all .... Allegata [*Schedules, Enclosures*] [*Italian*] (ILCA)
ALL........... Australian Liberal League (ADA)
ALLA......... Allied Longline Agency [*NATO*]
ALLA......... Allied Long Lines Agency [*Brussels, Belgium*] [*NATO*] (WER)
allatt.......... Allattenyesztes [*Animal Husbandry*] (HU)
alleg........... Allegato [*Attached*] [*Publishing*] [*Italian*]
ALLEG ...... Amiral Commandant l'Escadre Legere [*Admiral, Light Squadron*] [*French*] (NATG)
all eng........ Allamilag Engedelyezett, Engedelyezve [*Licensed by the State*] (HU)
allerg......... Allergisch [*Allergic*] [*German*] (GCA)
allg .... Allgemein [*General or Generally*] [*German*] (GPO)
Allg .... Allgemeines [*General Aspects*] [*German*] (GCA)
ALLG........ Australian Law Librarians' Group (ADA)
Allgem........ Allgemein [*General*] [*Music*]
Allgett........ Allegretto [*Moderately Quick*] [*Music*]
AllgGesch Bed ... Allgemeine Geschaftsbedingungen [*General conditions of contracts, transactions, etc.*] [*German*] (ILCA)
Allgmbhoh S ... Allgemeinbildende Hoehere Schule [*General Education High School*] [*German*]
AllgVersBed ... Allgemeine Versicherungsbedingungen [*General conditions of insurance*] [*German*] (ILCA)
allg verst..... Allgemeinverstaendlich [*Popular*] [*German*]
ALLI .... Australian Legal Literature Index
ALLIAMA ... Alliance du Mayombe [*Alliance of Mayombe*] [*Angola*] (AF)
ALLIAZO ... Alleanza delle Popolazioni di Zombo

ALLIBAKAT ... Alliance des Bahemba au Katanga [*Alliance of the Bahemba in Katanga*] [*Zaire*]
All Ny .... Allami Nyomda [*State Printing Office*] (HU)
All' Ott...... All' Ottava [*At the Octave*] [*Music*]
All'Ova ...... All'Ottava [*At the Octave*] [*Music*]
ALLP .... Australian Language and Literacy Policy
Alm .... Almanca [*German*] (TU)
ALM .... Almarhum [*Deceased*] (IN)
alm .... Almindelig [*Common, Ordinary*] [*Danish/Norwegian*]
alm .... Almirante [*Admiral*] [*Portuguese*]
ALM .... American Leprosy Missions, Inc.
ALM .... Antillaanse Luchtvaart Maatschappij [*Airline*] [*Netherlands Antilles*]
ALM .... Antilliaanse Luchtvaart Maatschappij [*Netherlands*] [*ICAO designator*] (FAAC)
ALM .... Arab Liberation Movement
ALM .... Asociacion Latinoamericana de Manufactureros [*Latin American Association of Manufacturers*] (LA)
ALM .... Associated Liquor Merchants Ltd. [*Australia*]
ALM .... Australian Liquor Marketers
ALM .... Conservational Afforestation (RU)
ALMA ...... Anonima Libica Macchine Agricole
ALMA ...... Asociacion Latinoamericana de Minoristas de la Alimentacion [*Montevideo, Uruguay*] (LAA)
ALMA ...... Australijas Latviesu Maksinieku Apvieniba [*Society of Latvian Artists in Australia*]
ALMABANCO ... Almacenadora Grancolombiana SA [*Colombia*] (COL)
ALMACAFE ... Almacenes Generales de Deposito de Cafe [*Neiva*] (COL)
ALMACENAR ... Almacenes Generales de Deposito Mercantil SA [*Colombia*] (COL)
ALMACEROS ... Almacen de Aceros Ltda. [*Colombia*] (COL)
ALMADELCO ... Almacenes Generales de Deposito de Comercio SA [*Colombia*] (COL)
al'mag .... Aluminum-Magnesium Alloy (RU)
ALMAGRAN ... Almacenes Generales de Deposito Gran Colombia [*Colombia*] (COL)
ALMAGUATE ... Almacenadora Guatemalteca SA [*Guatemala*] (IMH)
ALMANGEL ... Almacenes Angel [*Colombia*] (COL)
ALMANORTE ... Almacenadora del Norte SA [*Guatemala*] (IMH)
ALMAP..... Societe Algero-Mauritanienne de Peche
ALMAVIVA ... Almacenes Generales de Deposito Sante Fe SA [*Colombia*] (DSCA)
AlMBz .... Aluminiummehrstoffbronze [*Multi-Compound Aluminum Bronze*] [*German*] (GCA)
ALMC .... Australian Lighting Manufacturing Council (ADA)
ALMERCON ... Groupe des Associations Economiques Privees de la CEE Communaute Economique Europeenne Axees sur l'Amerique Latine [*Belgium*] (DSCA)
alm-esqdra ... Almirante-de-Esquadra [*Portuguese*]
Almetzavod ... Alaverdi Metallurgical Plant (RU)
Alm NR...... Almanak voor Notariaat en Registratie [*Benelux*] (BAS)
ALMO .... African Livestock Marketing Organisation
ALMO .... Societe Mixte Algerienne de Machines-Outils [*Algerian Joint Machine Tool Co.*] (AF)
ALMP........ Aboriginal Language Maintenance Project [*Australia*]
ALN .... Acao Libertadora Nacional [*Brazilian Action for National Liberation*] [*Political party*] (LAIN)
ALN .... Alianca Libertadora Nacional [*National Liberation Alliance*] [*Brazil*] [*Political party*] (PD)
ALN .... Alianza de Liberacion Nacional [*National Liberation Alliance*] [*Argentina*] (LA)
ALN .... Armee de Liberation Nationale [*National Liberation Army*] [*Algeria*] [*Political party*] (AF)
ALN .... Armee de Liberation Nationale [*National Liberation Army*] [*Guadeloupe*] [*Political party*] (PD)
ALNA .... Armee de Liberation Nationale de l'Angola [*Angolan Army of National Liberation*]
ALND .... Australian Lawyers for Nuclear Disarmament
ALNG .... Armee de Liberation Nacionale Guineene
ALNK .... Armee de Liberation Nationale Kamerunaise [*Cameroonian Army of National Liberation*] (AF)
ALNS........ Anti-Fascist League of People's Liberation [*Burmese*] (RU)
ALO .... Alternative Liste Oesterreich [*Austrian Alternative List*] [*Political party*] (PPW)
ALO .... Arab Labour Organization
ALO .... Australian Labour Office
ALOFT...... Australian Libraries of Forestry and Timber
ALOIT....... Association of Library Officers-in-Training [*Australia*] (PDAA)
A l'OR....... A l'Orient [*At the East*] [*Freemasonry*] [*French*]
ALOR .... Australian Lubricating Oil Refinery
ALORSA... Algodonera Oriental SA [*Venezuela*] (DSCA)
aloszt........ Alosztaly [*Subunit*] [*Also used for army units*] (HU)
ALOX .... Aluminium Oxide
ALP .... Agence Lao Presse [*Lao Press Agency*] (CL)
ALP........... Agence Libyenne de Presse [*Libyan Press Agency*]
ALP........... Aleppo [*Syria*] [*Airport symbol*] (OAG)

alp .... Alperes [*Defendant*] (HU)
ALP............. Alpliner AG [*Switzerland*] [*ICAO designator*] (FAAC)
ALP........... Antigua Labour Party [*Political party*] (PPW)
ALP........... Arakan Liberation Party [*Myanmar*] [*Political party*]
ALP........... Armee de Legitimation des Pouvoirs [*Army for the Legitimation of Powers*] [*Algeria*] (AF)
ALP........... Assistance Ligne de Produit [*Assisting Line of Products*] [*French*] (ADPT)
ALP........... Astronomical Line of Position (RU)
ALP........... Australian Labour Party [*Political party*] (PPW)
ALP........... Avicultura, Lavoura, e Pecuaria Ltd [*Brazil*] (DSCA)
ALPA........ Alet ve Dayanikli Tuketim Mamulleri Pazarlama AS [*Tools and Durable Consumer Goods Marketing Corp.*] (TU)
ALPA........ Aluminio del Pacifico Ltda. [*Colombia*] (COL)
ALPA........ Amiral, Porte Avions [*Aircraft Carriers and Embarked Air Squadrons*] [*French*] (WER)
ALPA........ Asociacion Latinoamericana de Produccion Animal [*Latin American Association of Animal Production*] (LAA)
ALPA........ Asociacion Local de Productores Agricolas de El Mante [*Mexico*] (DSCA)
ALPA........ Australian Library Publishers Association
ALP(A-C).. Australian Labor Party (Anti-Communist) (ADA)
ALPAIX .... Alliance pour la Paix [*Alliance for Peace*] [*Cambodia*] (CL)
ALPAL ...... Algeria - Palma, Spain [*Submarine cable*] [*Telecommunications*]
ALPAN...... Alimentos para Animais Ltd [*Brazil*] (DSCA)
ALPANSA ... Alas Panamenas SA [*Panama*] [*ICAO designator*] (FAAC)
ALPASA.... Almacenadora del Pais Sociedad Anonima [*Guatemala*] (IMH)
ALPC........ Australian Library Promotion Council (ADA)
ALPCyT .... Asociacion Latinoamericana de Politica Cientifica y Tecnologica [*Latin American Association for Science and Technology*] [*Mexico*] (EAIO)
ALPEX ...... Alpine Experiment [*International Council of Scientific Unions*]
ALPGA ...... Australian Liquefied Petroleum Gas Association (ADA)
ALPHA ..... Australian Lobby for Physically Handicapped Adults
ALPI-CAM ... Societe Alpi Petro & Fils, Cameroun
alpk .... Alparancsnok [*Second in Command*] (HU)
ALPL......... Association of Librarians in Public Libraries [*Germany*] (EAIO)
ALPRO...... Alianza para el Progreso [*Alliance for Progress*] [*Washington, DC*]
ALPS .... Accountancy & Legal Professions Selection Ltd. [*British*] (ECON)
ALPS .... Armee de Liberation du Peuple Sahraoui [*Saharan People's Liberation Army*] (AF)
ALPS .... Asociacion Latinoamericana de Psicologia Social [*Latin American Association for Social Psychology - LAASP*] (EAIO)
ALPS .... Australian Library Publishers Society
ALPW....... Action for the Liberation of Peruvian Women (EAIO)
ALQ .... Alegrete [*Brazil*] [*Airport symbol*] [*Obsolete*] (OAG)
alq .... Alqueire [*Bushel*] [*Portuguese*]
Alq .... Alquimia [*Alchemy*] [*Portuguese*]
ALQ .... [*The*] Ancient Library of Qumran (BJA)
ALR .... Albanska Lidova Republika [*Albanian People's Republic*] (CZ)
ALR .... Alexandra [*New Zealand*] [*Airport symbol*] (OAG)
ALR .... Algarvilara Transportes Aereos Algarvios SA [*Portugal*] [*ICAO designator*] (FAAC)
ALR .... Algemeen Loodsreglement [*Benelux*] (BAS)
ALR .... Arbeitsgruppe fur Luft-und Raufahrt [*Aerospace Task Force*] [*Switzerland*] (PDAA)
ALR .... Australian League of Rights (ADA)
ALRAC...... Australian Law Reform Agencies Conference (ADA)
ALRASA ... Abortion Law Reform Association of South Australia
ALRA(WA) ... Association for the Legal Right to Abortion (Western Australia)
ALRC........ Aboriginal Land Rights Commission [*Australia*]
ALRC........ Adoption Legislation Review Committee [*Victoria, Australia*]
ALRC........ Anti-Locust Research Centre
ALRC........ Australian Law Reform Commission (ADA)
ALREG....... Societe Algerienne de Recherches et d'Etudes Geophysiques
ALRI........ Angkatan Laut Republik Indonesia [*Republic of Indonesia Navy*] (IN)
ALRM .... Aboriginal Legal Rights Movement [*Australia*] (ADA)
ALRP .... A los Reales Pies [*Spanish*]
ALS........... Aboriginal Legal Service [*Australia*] (ADA)
ALS........... Air Alsie, AS [*Denmark*] [*ICAO designator*] (FAAC)
ALS........... Australian LANDSAT [*Land Satellite*] Station
ALS........... Australian Libraries Summit
ALS........... Australian Linguistics Society (ADA)
ALS........... Australian Literature Society (ADA)
ALS........... Australian Littoral Society (ADA)
ALS........... Australian Longitudinal Survey
ALS........... Automatic Cab Signaling (RU)
ALSA........ Australasian Law Students Association
ALSAML .. Ahvenanmaan Kokoomus; Alaendsk Samling [*Aland Coalition*] [*Finland*] (PPE)
ALSATEX ... Societe Alsacienne d'Etude et d'Exploitation [*France*] (PDAA)
ALSC .... African Liberation Support Committee

ALSCA ...... Australian Leather and Suede Clothing Association
ALSD .... Amerikan Lisan ve Sanaat Dersanesi [*American Language and Trade Institute*] [*Istanbul*]   (TU)
ALSF .... Australian Liberal Students Federation   (ADA)
ALSG .... Australian Logistics Support Group
ALSM .... Association of Litigation Support Managers [*Australia*]
ALSp .... Allgemeine Leistungsbedingungen der Spedition [*General Service Terms of Shipping Agencies*]   (EG)
AlSPa .... Associazione Italiana Studi del Paranormale [*Italian*]   (SLS)
ALSPI .... Societe Alsacienne de Participations Industrielles [*French*]
AlsPS .... Associazione Italiana di Scienze Potitiche e Sociale [*Italian*]   (SLS)
ALSWA ..... Aboriginal Legal Service of Western Australia
alsz .... Alszam [*Subheading Number*]   (HU)
ALT .... Aboriginal Lands Trust [*Australia*]   (ADA)
ALT .... Albatrosz Ltd. [*Hungary*] [*ICAO designator*]   (FAAC)
alt .... Altalanos [*General, Universal, Common*] [*Hungary*]   (HU)
Alt .... Alternate   (EECI)
Alt .... Altertum [*Antiquity*] [*German*]   (GCA)
Alt .... Altesse [*Highness*] [*French*]
alt .... Altezza [*Height*] [*Italian*]
alt .... Altiszt [*Noncommissioned Officer*]   (HU)
ALT .... Assemblee Legislative du Togo
ALT .... Assistant Language Teacher
ALT .... Association d'Aide a la Lutte Contre la Trypanosomiase [*Anti-Trypanosomiasis Assistance Association*] [*Zaire*]   (AF)
ALT .... Australian Land Trusts Ltd.   (ADA)
ALTA .... Association of Local Transport Airlines [*Japan*]
ALTA .... Australasian Law Teachers Association
ALTA .... Australian Library Technicians Association   (ADA)
ALTA .... Australian Logic Teachers' Association
ALTACOR ... Alfombras, Tapetes, Cortinas [*Colombia*]   (COL)
Altaykhimles ... Altay Trust for the Production of Wood-Chemistry Raw Materials   (RU)
Altaykraypromstrom ... Altay Kray Industrial Construction and Installation Trust   (RU)
Altaysel'mash ... Altay Agricultural Machinery Plant   (RU)
altbgy .... Altabornagy [*Lieutenant General*]   (HU)
ALTD .... Australian Land Transport Development Program
ALTERSIAL ... Alternatives Technologiques et Recherches sur les Industries Agricoles et Alimentaires [*France*]
ALTG .... Association of Little Theatre Groups [*Australia*]
alti .... Altiszt [*Noncommissioned Officer*]   (HU)
ALTI .... Arkhangel'sk Forestry-Engineering Institute Imeni V. V. Kuybyshev   (RU)
altkol .... Altkoloriert [*Colored Long Ago*] [*Publishing*] [*German*]
ALTO .... Association of Leyte Teachers' Organizations [*Philippines*]   (EY)
ALTOUR... Societe Nationale Algerienne de Tourisme et d'Hotellerie [*Algiers, Algeria*]
ALTP .... Australian Land Transport Program
ALTRA ...... Entreprises Algeriennes de Grands Travaux [*Algerian Construction Works*]
ALTTC ...... Advanced Level Telecommunications Training Centre [*India*]   (PDAA)
ALTUMEC ... Societe Algerienne de Tubes et de Constructions Mecaniques
ALU .... Aboriginal Liaison Unit [*Australia*]
ALU .... Akademija za Likovnu Umetnost [*Academy of Representational Art*] [*Belgrade*]   (YU)
ALU .... Alpine Luft-Transport AB [*Switzerland*] [*ICAO designator*]   (FAAC)
ALU .... Alula [*Somalia*] [*Airport symbol*]   (OAG)
ALU .... Arab Lawyers Union [*See also UAA*] [*Cairo, Egypt*]   (EAIO)
ALU .... Associated Labor Unions [*Philippines*]   (EY)
ALUA .... Australian LIBACC [*Library Acquisition Program*] Users Association
ALUAR ..... Aluminio Argentino [*Argentine Aluminum Enterprise*]   (LA)
ALUARSAIC ... Aluminio Argentino, Sociedad Anonima Industrial, y Comercial [*Argentine Aluminum, Industrial, and Commercial Enterprise*]   (LA)
ALUCAM ... Aluminium du Cameroun [*Cameroon Aluminum*]   (AF)
ALUCI .... Aluminium de la Cote-D'Ivoire
ALUCONGO ... Societe pour la Transformation de l'Aluminium et Autres Metaux au Congo
ALUKER... Aluminium Kereskedelmi Vallalat [*Aluminum Trade Enterprise*]   (HU)
alum .... Aluminium [*Aluminum*]   (HU)
ALUPA...... Association Luxembourgeoise pour l'Utilisation Pacifique de l'Energie Atomique [*Nuclear energy*] [*French*]   (NRCH)
ALUS .... African Land Utilization and Settlement Board
ALUSAC ... Asociacion de Licenciados. Universidad Santiago de Cali   (COL)
ALUSAF ... Aluminum Corporation of South Africa
ALUSUISSE ... Schweizerische Aluminium AG [*Swiss Aluminum Joint Stock Company*]
ALUTERV ... Aluminiumipari Tervezo Intezet [*Designing Institute for the Aluminum Industry*]   (HU)
ALV .... Alsavia, Societe [*France*] [*ICAO designator*]   (FAAC)

alv .... Alvara [*Charter, Warrant*] [*Portuguese*]
alv .... Alvenaria [*Stonemasonry*] [*Portuguese*]
ALV .... Amsterdamsche Leesbibliotheekhouders Vereeniging
ALVA .... Advance Latrobe Valley Association [*Australia*]   (ADA)
ALVA .... Australian Ladies Variety Association
ALVAO ..... Association des Langues Vivantes pour l'Afrique Occidentale [*West African Modern Languages Association*] [*Nigeria*]   (PDAA)
ALVF .... Artillerie Lourde sur Voie Ferree [*Military*] [*French*]   (MTD)
Alvo .... Alvaro [*Spanish*]
ALW .... Alas Nacionales SA [*Dominican Republic*] [*ICAO designator*]   (FAAC)
ALWG .... Australian Legal Workers Group
ALWIC ...... Anti-Leprosy World Information Centre
ALWS .... Australian Lutheran World Service
ALX .... Alitaxi SRL [*Italy*] [*ICAO designator*]   (FAAC)
ALY .... Alexandria [*Egypt*] [*Airport symbol*]   (OAG)
Alyuminstroy ... Administration for the Construction of Aluminum Plants   (RU)
Alz .... Alzamento [*Raising, Lifting*] [*Music*]
ALZDA...... Australian Lead/Zinc Development Association
ALZI .... Societe Algerienne du Zinc
AM .... Abrechnungsmaschine [*Calculating Machine*] [*German*]   (ADPT)
AM .... Abschnittsmarke [*Section Mark*] [*German*]   (ADPT)
AM .... Acrylamide   (RU)
AM .... Action Monegasque [*Monegasque Action*] [*Political party*]   (PPE)
AM .... Adetto Militare [*Military Attache*] [*Italian*]   (WER)
AM .... Aeromexico [*Airline*]   (DS)
AM .... Aeronaves de Mexico SA [*Mexico*] [*ICAO designator*]   (ICDA)
A-M .... Aide-Memoire [*Memorandum*] [*French*]   (MTD)
am .... Aircraft Engine   (RU)
AM .... Akademia Medyczna [*Academy of Medicine*]   (POL)
AM .... Al-Mudayna [*Spain*]   (EAIO)
AM .... Alpes Maritimes [*French*]
am .... American   (RU)
am .... Americano [*American*] [*Italian*]
Am............. Americio [*America*] [*Portuguese*]
Am............. Amerika [*America*] [*Afrikaans*]
Am............. Amerikaans [*American*] [*Afrikaans*]
am .... Amerikanisch [*American*] [*German*]   (GCA)
Am............. Amerikanismus [*Americanism*] [*German*]
am .... Amerikkalainen [*American*] [*Finland*]
am .... Amerykanski [*American*] [*Poland*]
aM .... Am Main [*On the Main River*].[*German*]
am .... Amorph [*Amorphous*] [*German*]   (GCA)
am .... Amorphous   (RU)
am .... Amortissement [*Redemption of stock*] [*French*]
AM .... Amplitude-Modulasie [*Amplitude Modulation*] [*Afrikaans*]
AM .... Amplitude Modulation   (RU)
am .... Annyi Mint [*That Is*]   (HU)
AM .... Ansiomitali [*Finland*]
am .... Ante Meridiano [*Before Noon*] [*Spanish*]   (GPO)
am .... Antes del Mediodia [*Before Noon*] [*Spanish*]
am .... Antimeridiano [*Forenoon*] [*Italian*]   (GPO)
AM .... Apostolatus Maris [*Apostleship of the Sea - AOS*]   (EA)
AM .... Approved Market [*Business term*]
AM .... Archipelago Mundi [*An international association*]   (EA)
AM .... Arrete Ministeriel [*French*]   (FLAF)
AM .... Asamblea Majorera [*Spain*] [*Political party*]   (EY)
AM .... Asilo Mariuccia [*Italy*]   (EAIO)
AM .... Assistance Medicale
AM .... Assistant Minister [*Church of England in Australia*]
AM .... Assurance Mutuelle [*Mutual Assurance*] [*French*]
AM .... Australian Museum
AM .... Auto-Mitrailleuse [*Light Armored Car*] [*Military*] [*French*]   (MTD)
AM .... Auxiliary Minesweeper [*NATO*]
AM .... Avant Midi [*Before Noon*] [*French*]   (WER)
AM .... Ave-Maria [*Hail Mary*] [*Portuguese*]
AM .... Aviamilano [*Construzioni Aeronautiche SpA*] [*Italy*] [*ICAO aircraft manufacturer identifier*]   (ICAO)
AM .... Aviazione Militare [*Air Force*] [*Italian*]   (WER)
AM .... Avtou Makariotis [*His Beatitude*] [*Used for Patriarchs of Alexandria, Antioch, Jerusalem, Russia, Serbia, Romania, and Bulgaria; Metropolitan of Poland; and Archbishop of Cyprus*]   (GC)
AM .... Estado do Amazonas [*State of Amazonas*] [*Brazil*]
AM .... General, Public, Civil   (ML)
Am............. Magnetic Azimuth   (RU)
AM .... Member of the Order of Australia   (ADA)
AM .... Naval Air Station   (RU)
AMA .... Agricultural Manufacturers' Association [*Australia*]
AMA .... Agricultural Marketing Authority [*Zimbabwe*]   (IMH)
Ama.......... Amadeo [*Record label*] [*Austria, etc.*]
AMA .... American Missionary Association

ama............ Amiga [*Friend (Feminine)*] [*Portuguese*]
AMA.......... Art Museums Association of Australia
AMA.......... Asociacion Medica Argentina [*Argentine Medical Association*]
          [*Buenos Aires*]   (LAA)
AMA.......... Asociacion Mexicana Automovilistica [*Mexican Automobile
          Association*]   (LAA)
AMA.......... Assistance Medicale Africaine
AMA.......... Associacao dos Mulheres de Angola [*Association of Angolan
          Women*]
AMA.......... Ateliers Mecaniques de l'Atlantique
AMA.......... Australian Marching Association
AMA.......... Australian Medical Association   (ADA)
AMA.......... Australian Meteorological Association   (ADA)
AMA.......... Australian Monopoly Association
AMA.......... Auto, Moto, Avio [*Italy*]
AMA.......... Aviation Militaire Algerienne
AMA.......... Axa Midi Assurances [*Commercial firm*] [*France*]
AMAA....... Art Museums Association of Australia
AMAA....... Asociacion Mundial de Amigos del Arbol [*Mexico*]   (DSCA)
AMAA....... Associate of the Museums Association of Australia   (ADA)
AMAA....... Australian Media Accreditation Authority
AMAAN... Associate Member of the Australian Association of Neurologists
AMAC....... Asociacion de Mujeres de Accion Catolica [*Women's Catholic
          Action Association*] [*Argentina*]   (LA)
AMAC....... Assistance Medicale a l'Afrique Centrale [*Medical Assistance to
          Central Africa*] [*Belgium*]   (AF)
AMAC....... Australian Mayoral Aviation Council
AMACAM ... Assurances Mutuelles Agricoles du Cameroun
AMACG.... Association pour le Musee d'Art Contemporain a Gand
          [*Association of the Museum of Contemporary Art in Ghent*]
          [*Belgium*]   (EAIO)
AMACHICO ... Atlantic Machinery Company Ltda. [*Barranquilla*]   (COL)
AMAD....... Asociacion Magisterial de Accion Democratica [*Teachers
          Association of Democratic Action*] [*El Salvador*]   (LA)
AMAD....... Association Mondiale des Arts Divinatoires [*Divinatory Arts
          World Association - DAWA*] [*Rillieux-La-Pape, France*]
          (EAIO)
AMAD....... Auxilium Meum a Deo [*My Help Cometh from the Lord*] [(*Ps.,
          CXXI. 2) Motto of Christian, Margrave of Brandenburg-
          Baireuth (1581-1655)*]
AMADA.... Alle Macht aan de Arbeiders [*All Power to the Workers*]
          [*Belgium*] [*Political party*]   (PPW)
AMADE.... Association Mondiale des Amis de l'Enfance [*World Association
          of Children's Friends*] [*Monaco*]   (EAIO)
AMAF....... American Study in Africa
AMAFE..... Association of Manufacturers of Animal-Derived Food Enzymes
          [*EC*]   (ECED)
AMAFRAN ... Agence Maritime France-Afrique Noire
AMAG....... Austria Metal Group, AG
amaig......... Amalgamated   (EECI)
AMAIMM ... Associate Member of the Australasian Institute of Mining and
          Metallurgy   (ADA)
AMAIRAH ... Associate Member of the Australian Institute of Refrigeration,
          Air Conditioning, and Heating   (ADA)
AMAL....... Afwaj al-Muqawimah al-Lubnaniyah [*Lebanese Resistance
          Battalions*]
Amal.......... Amiral [*Admiral*] [*French*]
amalg......... Amalgamated   (SCAC)
AMALG.... Associated Multiplier Agency Liaison Group [*Australia*]
Amalgamier ... Amalgamierung [*Amalgamation*] [*German*]   (GCA)
AMAMCO ... Agence Marocaine et Mauritanienne de Cooperation
          [*Moroccan-Mauritanian Cooperation Agency*]   (AF)
AMANAL ... Amicale des Anciens Etudiants et Stagiaires d'Allemagne
AM & S...... Australian Mining and Smelting Ltd.   (ADA)
AMANGOLA ... Amigos do Manifesto Angolano
AMANIC .. Agencias Maritimas y Aduaneras de Nicaragua [*Nicaraguan
          Shipping and Customs Agencies*]   (LA)
AMANISSA ... Entreprise Nigerienne de Batiments Travaux Publics de
          Constructions
AMANO.... Association des Manianga du Nord-Luozi
AMAP....... Agence Malienne de Presse et de Publicite [*Malian Press and
          Publicity Agency*]   (AF)
AMAP....... Atelier de Modelisation de l'Architecture des Plantes [*Software
          manufacturer*] [*Paris, France*]
AMAPANAL ... Asociacion de Mutuo Auxilio de Miembros de la Policia
          Nacional [*Colombia*]   (COL)
AMAS....... Asociacion de Mujeres en Accion Social [*Association of Women
          for Social Action*] [*Uruguay*]   (LA)
AMAS....... Australian Medical Acupuncture Society
AMAT....... Associations des Musees d'Afrique Tropicale [*Museums
          Association of Tropical Africa*]   (AF)
AMATECI ... Agence Mauritanienne de Television et de Cinema
          [*Mauritanian Television and Cinema Agency*]   (AF)
AMAusIMM ... Associate Member of the Australasian Institute of Mining and
          Metallurgy   (ADA)
AM AusIMM ... Associate Member of the Australian Institute of Mining and
          Metallurgy

AMAV....... Avalon [*Australia*] [*ICAO location identifier*]   (ICLI)
AMAX....... American Metal Climax
AMAY ...... Albury [*Australia*] [*ICAO location identifier*]   (ICLI)
AMAZ....... Agence et Messageries Aeriennes Zairoises
AMB.......... Aachener & Muenchener Beteiligungs [*Aachener & Muenchener,
          Partners*]
AMB.......... Abteilung Allgemeiner Maschinenbau der Staatlichen
          Plankommission [*General Machine Building Department of
          the State Planning Commission*]   (EG)
AMB.......... Allami Mezogazdasagi Birtokok [*State Agricultural Properties*]
          (HU)
Amb........... Ambar [*Warehouse, Hold*]   (TU)
amb .... Ambasador [*Ambassador*] [*Poland*]
Amb........... Ambassadeur [*Ambassador*] [*French*]   (MTD)
AMB.......... Ambilobe [*Madagascar*] [*Airport symbol*]   (OAG)
Amb........... Ambulance [*Ambulance*] [*Military*] [*French*]   (MTD)
AMB.......... Asociacion Mexicana de Bancos [*Mexican Association of Banks*]
          (EAIO)
AMB.......... Asociacion Mexicana de Banqueros [*Mexican Bankers
          Association*]   (LA)
AMB.......... Associacao Medica Brasileira [*Brazilian Medical Association*]
AMB.......... Ateliers Metallurgiques du Batiment
AMB.......... Australian Market Basket Survey
AMB.......... Australian Meat Board   (ADA)
AMB.......... Australian Meteorology, Bureau [*Canberra Meteorological
          Office*] [*National Union Catalogue of Australia symbol*]
AMB.......... Aviation Medicine Branch [*Civil Aviation Authority*] [*Australia*]
AMB.......... Deutsche Rettungsflugwacht EV [*Germany*] [*ICAO designator*]
          (FAAC)
AMB.......... Group B Autochtonous Microflora   (RU)
amb .... Outpatient Clinic, Dispensary [*Topography*]   (RU)
amb .... Storehouse, Granary [*Topography*]   (RU)
AMBA ...... Angora Mohair Breeders of Australia
AMBA ...... Australian Merchant Bankers Association   (ADA)
AMBA ...... Australian Mohair Breeders' Association
AMBA ...... Australian Mountain Bike Association
AMBA ...... Australian Multiple Birth Association
AMBAC .... Asociacion Mexicana de Bibliotecarios, AC [*Mexican Association
          of Librarians*]   (SLS)
AMBAKHMER ... Ambassade [*or Ambassadeur*] Khmer [*Cambodian
          Embassy or Ambassador*]   (CL)
Amb C(Div) ... Ambulance de Corps (Divisionnaire) [*Military*] [*French*]
          (MTD)
AMBES ..... Aircraft Engine Designed by A. A. Mikulin and B. S. Stechkin
          (RU)
AMBI .... Automatisering en Mechanisering van de Bestuurlijke
          Informatieverwerking [*Netherlands*]
AMBIB...... Ambulantna Biblioteka [*Mobile Library*]   (YU)
AMBMO... Asociacion Mediterranea de Biologia Marina y Oceanografia
AMBP........ Anomalie Magnetique du Bassin de Paris [*French*]
Ambra........ Alhambra [*Record label*] [*Spain*]
ambtger...... Ambtenarengerecht [*Benelux*]   (BAS)
Ambtw........ Ambtenarenwet [*Benelux*]   (BAS)
AMC.......... Agricultural Marketing Corporation [*Jamaica*]   (LA)
AMC.......... Air Malta Co. Ltd. [*ICAO designator*]   (FAAC)
AMC.......... Alexander Mackie College [*Australia*]   (ADA)
AMC.......... Alma Mater Croatica [*Croatian University*] [*Zagreb*]   (YU)
AMC.......... Aparatura de Masura si Control [*Measurement and Control
          Apparatus*]   (RO)
AMC.......... Arab Mining Company
AMC.......... Associated Minerals Consolidated Ltd. [*Australia*]   (ADA)
AMC.......... Associate Members Club [*Australian Union of Students*]
AMC.......... Australasian Micrographics Congress   (ADA)
AMC.......... Australia Music Centre   (ADA)
AMC.......... Australian Manufacturing Council   (ADA)
AMC.......... Australian Maritime College
AMC.......... Australian Mathematics Competition Committee   (SLS)
AMC.......... Australian Medical Council
AMC.......... Australian Micrographics Congress   (ADA)
AMC.......... Entreprise Nationale des Appareils de Mesure et de Controle
          [*Nationalized industry*] [*Algeria*]   (EY)
AMCA ...... Academia Mexicana de Ciencia Avicola [*Mexico*]   (DSCA)
AMCA ...... Academia Mexicana de Ciencias Agricolas [*Mexico*]   (DSCA)
AMCA ...... Association pour une Meilleure Connaissance de l'Asie [*Research
          center*] [*France*]   (FEA)
AMCA ...... Australian Management College Mt. Eliza Association
AMCA ...... Australian Management Consultants Association   (ADA)
AMCA ...... Australian Migration Consultants' Association
AMCAE .... Alexander Mackie College of Advanced Education [*Australia*]
AMCAL..... Allied Master Chemists of Australia Ltd.
AMCAP..... Asociacion Mutual del Personal de la Corporacion Argentina de
          Productores de Carne [*Argentina*]   (DSCA)
AMCC .... Australia-Malaysia Chamber of Commerce
AMCC .... Australian Map Curators Circle   (ADA)
AMCCC..... Australian Maritime College Courses Committee

AMCD....... Audit and Management Consulting Division [United Nations] (ECON)
AMCEK..... Association des Membres du Corps Enseignant Khmer [Association of Members of the Cambodian Teaching Corps] (CL)
AMCH....... African Mother and Child Health Campaign
AMCHA.... National Israeli Centre for Psychosocial Support of Survivors of the Holocaust (EAIO)
AMCHAM ... American Chamber of Commerce in Australia
AMCI .... Armes et Munitions de la Cote-D'Ivoire
AMCMEA ... Australian Management College Mount Eliza Association
AMCN(NSW) ... Associate Member of the College of Nursing (New South Wales) [Australia]
AMCNSW ... Arms and Militaria Collectors' Association of New South Wales [Australia]
AMCO....... Association of Major Charitable Associations
AMCOAL ... Anglo-American Coal Corp. [South Africa]
AMCOR .... African Metals Corporation [South Africa] (AF)
AMCOS .... Australasian Mechanical Copyright Owners' Society Ltd.
AMCOVIT ... A & M Compania de Vigilancia Tecnica [Colombia] (COL)
AMCP .... Asistenta Medicala Curativo-Profilactica [Remedial-Prophylactic Medical Care] (RO)
AMCS....... Australian Manufacturing Council Secretariat
AMCU....... Australian Malaria Control Unit (ADA)
AMCV .... Armoured Mine Clearing Vehicle [Military]
AMCV .... Australia's Military Commitment to Vietnam
AMCWC ... Adelaide Medical Centre for Women and Children [Australia]
AMD......... Academia Mexicana de Dermatologia [Mexican Academy of Dermatology] (EAIO)
AMD......... Aerolineas Medellin [Colombia] [ICAO designator] (FAAC)
AMD......... Ahmedabad [India] [Airport symbol] (OAG)
AMD......... Alliance pour Une Mauritanie Democratique [Alliance for One Democratic Mauritania] (PD)
AMD......... Allied Masonic Degrees [Freemasonry]
AMD......... Askar Melayu Di-Raja [Royal Malaysian Army] (ML)
AMD......... Asociacion Medica Dominicana [Dominican Medical Association] [Santo Domingo, Dominican Republic] (LAA)
AMD......... Auto-Moto Drustvo [Automobile and Motorcycle Club] (YU)
AMD......... Avionis Marcel Dassault [France] (PDAA)
AMDA....... African Music and Drama Academy
AMDA....... Anglo-Malayan Defense Agreement (ML)
AMDA....... Asociacion Medica de Antioquia [Colombia] (COL)
AMDAC.... Assistance aux Maternites et Dispensaires d'Afrique Centrale
AMDAP .... Association of Medical Directors to the Australian Pharmaceutical Industry (ADA)
AMDB....... Arab Malaysian Development Bank
AMDB....... Australia Murray-Darling Basin [Commission] [National Union Catalogue of Australia symbol]
AMD/BA... Avions Moral Dassault/Bregnet Aviation [Later, GAMD] [French]
AMDC....... Australian Mycotoxin Data Centre
AMDE....... Association of Medical Deans in Europe (EAIO)
AMDEL..... Australian Mineral Development Laboratories [Research center] (IRC)
AMDESA ... Asociacion Mexicana de Directores de Escuelas Superiores de Agricultura [Mexico] (DSCA)
AMDET .... Administracion Municipal de Transportes [Municipal Transportation Association] [Uruguay] (LA)
AMDH ...... Academia Mexicana de Derechos Humanos [The Mexican Academy for Human Rights] (CROSS)
AMDISIS ... Associazione Medici Dentisti Italiani, Societa Italiana di Stomatologia [Italian] (SLS)
AMDL .... Australian Mineral Development Laboratories [Research center] (ADA)
AMDO....... American Merchandise Display Osaka [Department of Commerce] [Japan] (IMH)
AMDP .... Accelerated Mahaweli Diversion Programme [Sri Lanka] (FEA)
AMDP .... Advanced Management Development Program [Monash University] [Australia]
AMDP .... Agricultural Mechanization Development Program [Philippines] (IRC)
AMDP .... Arbeitsgemeinschaft fuer Methodik und Dokumentation in der Psychiatrie [Association for Methodology and Documentation in Psychiatry] [German] (ADPT)
AMDS .... Australian MARC [Machine-Readable Cataloging] Distribution Service (ADA)
AMDV....... Devonport [Australia] [ICAO location identifier] (ICLI)
AME......... Accord Monetaire Europeen [French]
AME......... Acuerdo Monetario Europeo (DSCA)
AMe......... Adenosylmethionine (RU)
AME......... African Methodist Episcopal Church
AME......... Alliance Missionnaire Evangelique [Missionary Evangelical Alliance - MEA] [Renens, Switzerland] (EAIO)
AME......... Apparent Metabolisable Energy
AME......... Asociacion Musulmana de Espana [Muslim Association of Spain]
AME......... Association for Modern Education [Australia]

AME......... Ateliers de Montage Electrique
AME......... Australian Mineral Economics Proprietary Ltd.
AME......... Fuerzas Aereas Espanolas [Spain] [ICAO designator] (FAAC)
AMEB ...... Australian Music Education Board (ADA)
AMEB ...... Australian Music Examinations Board
AMEC ...... Asociacion Mexicana de Exportadores de Cafe AC [Mexico] (DSCA)
AMEC ...... Asociacion Multisectoral de Exportadores de Cataluna [Spain] (EY)
AMEC ...... Atelier de Mecanique et Carrosserie
AMEC ...... Australian Manufacturers' Export Council
AMEC ...... Australian Marine Engineering Corp. Ltd.
AMEC ...... Australian Medical Examining Council
AMEC ...... Australian Microelectronics Centre [Griffith University]
AMEC ...... Australian Military Education Council
AMEC ...... Australian Minerals and Energy Council
AMECA .... Ateliers de Mecanique Automobile
AMECA .... Ateliers de Mecanique et d'Electricite du Centre-Afrique
AMECOBRE ... Asociacion Mexicana del Cobre [Mexico]
AMECON ... Australian Marine Engineering Consolidated Ltd.
AMEC-TB ... Association Marocaine Education Culture et Travail Benevole [Morocco] (EAIO)
AMEDCO ... American Express Middle East Development Company (ME)
AMEE ...... Agonistikon Metopon Ellinon Exoterikou [Fighting Front of Greeks Abroad] (GC)
AMEE ...... Apelevtherotikon Metopon Ellinon Exoterikou [Liberation Front of Greeks Abroad] (GC)
AMEE ...... Association for Medical Education in Europe [Scotland]
AMEEMR ... Association for Medical Education in the Eastern Mediterranean Region [United Arab Emirates] (EAIO)
AMEFC.... Australian Meat Exporters' Federal Council
AMEFO .... African Media Foundation
AMEHTS ... Adult Migrant Education Home Tutor Scheme
AMEK ...... Antifasiszta Menekulteket Ellato Kozpont [Relief Center for Anti-Fascist Refugees] (HU)
Amel.......... Ameliyat [Surgical Operation] (TU)
AMELEC .. Ateliers de Mecanique et d'Electricite [Mechanical and Electrical Workshop] [Madagascar]
AMEM ...... American Methodist Episcopal Mission
AMEN...... Asociacion Misionera Evangelica a las Naciones [Peru]
AMEN...... Melbourne/Essendon [Australia] [ICAO location identifier] (ICLI)
AMEP....... Agence Mauritanienne d'Edition et de Publicite
AMEP....... Australian Mathematics Education Program
AMEPM... Asamblea Mundial de Empresas Pequenas y Medianas [World Assembly of Small and Medium Enterprises] [AMPME India] [See also]
amer .... American (RU)
amer .... Amerikkalainen [American] [Finland]
amer .... Amerykanski [American] [Poland]
AMER ...... Associazione Micologica ed Ecologica Romana [Italian] (SLS)
AMER ...... Societe aux Menuisiers-Ebenistes Reunis
amerik........ American (RU)
amerik........ Amerikanisch [American] [German]
amer p .... American Patent (RU)
AMES....... Adult Migrant Education Service [Australia]
AMES....... Adult Migrant English Services [New South Wales, Australia]
AMES....... Asociacion de Mujeres de El Salvador [Association of Salvadoran Women] [Costa Rica] (EAIO)
AMES....... Association of Marine Engineering Schools [Liverpool, Merseyside, England] (EAIO)
AMES....... East Sale [Australia] [ICAO location identifier] (ICLI)
AMESA..... Ateliers Mecaniques et Electrotechniques SA [Switzerland] (PDAA)
AMESA..... Australasian Middle East Studies Association
AMESU.... All-Malayan Estate Staff Union (ML)
AMEU....... Association of Municipal Electricity Undertakings of South Africa
AMEX ...... Australian Metals Exchange Ltd.
AMEZ ...... African Methodist Episcopal Zion
AMF .... ACE [Allied Command Europe] Mobile Force [NATO]
AMF .... Adenosine Monophosphate (RU)
AMF .... Adenylic Acid, Adenosinemonophosphoric Acid (RU)
AMF .... Algemeen Mijnwerkersfonds [Benelux] (BAS)
AMF .... Allied Mobile Force [NATO]
AMF .... Ama [Papua New Guinea] [Airport symbol] (OAG)
Amf .... Amfion [Record label] [Mexico]
AMF .... Arab Monetary Fund
AMF .... Australian Marxist Forum
AMF .... Australian Military Forces (ADA)
AMF .... Australian Mineral Foundation (ADA)
AMF .... Militant Party for the Establishment of a Classless Society [Malagasy] (AF)
AMF(A)..... Allied Mobile Force (Air) [NATO]
AMFC....... Australian Meatworks Federal Council
AMFEP ..... Association of Microbial Food Enzyme Producers (EA)

AMFI......... Arab Marketing & Finance, Incorporated
AMF(L)..... Allied Mobile Force (Land) [*NATO*]
AMFM ...... Association Mondiale des Federalistes Mondiaux [*World Association of World Federalists - WAWF*] (EA)
AMFORT ... Association Mondiale pour la Formation Professionnelle Touristique [*French*] (SLS)
AMFPA..... Association of Mouth and Foot Painting Artists Proprietary Ltd. [*Australia*]
AMFSU ..... Amalgamated Metal, Foundry, and Shipwrights Union [*Australia*]
AMFT........ Association of Migrants from Turkey [*Australia*]
AMFWS.... Australian Medical Friends of Wine Society
AMG......... Academia Militara Generala [*General Military Academy*] (RO)
AMG......... Aide Medicale Gratuite [*Free Medical Aid*] (LA)
AMG......... Air Material AG [*Switzerland*] [*ICAO designator*] (FAAC)
AMG......... Allami Mezogazdasagi Gepallomas [*or Allami Mezogazdasagi Gepkozpont or Allami Mezogazdasagi Gepuzem*] [*State Tractor Station*] (HU)
AMG......... Alles mit Gott [*Everything with God*] [*Motto of Georg Albrecht, Margrave of Brandenburg-Baireuth (1619-66)*] [*German*]
AMG......... Amboin [*Papua New Guinea*] [*Airport symbol*] (OAG)
AMG......... Arzneimittelgesetz [*Drugs Act*] (EG)
AMG......... Assistance Medicale Gratuite [*Free Medical Assistance*] [*Algeria*]
AMG......... Ausfrech-Melcher-Grossapach [*Mercedes-Benz cars*] [*High-performance parts supplier*]
AMG......... Australian Musicians' Guild
AMGA ...... Australian Mushroom Growers Association
AMGE ...... Association Mondiale des Guides et des Eclaireuses [*World Association of Girl Guides and Girl Scouts - WAGGGS*] [*London, England*] (EAIO)
AMGECO ... African Marine General Engineering Company
AMGI .... Atelier de Mecanique Generale Ivoirien
AMGOT.... Allied Military Government in Occupied Territory
AMGP .... Asociacion Mexicana de Geologos Petroleros [*Mexico*] (DSCA)
AMGR .... Ateliers de Mecanique Generale et de Rectification
AMGS .... Australian Macadamia Growers' Society
AMH .... Australian Meat Holdings Pty. Ltd.
AMH .... Australian Military Hospital (ADA)
AMHB....... Hobart [*Australia*] [*ICAO location identifier*] (ICLI)
AMHC....... All-Mauritius Hindu Congress (AF)
AMHF .... Hobart [*Australia*] [*ICAO location identifier*] (ICLI)
AMHN ...... Aboriginal Mental Health Network [*Western Australia*]
AMHS....... Australasian Maritime Historical Society (ADA)
AMHS....... Australasian Methodist Historical Society
AMHS....... Melbourne [*Australia*] [*ICAO location identifier*] (ICLI)
AMI .... Accademia Medica Internazionale [*International Medical Academy*] [*Italian*] (SLS)
AMI .... Aeronautica Militare Italiana [*Italian Air Force*] (WER)
AMI .... Africa Music International [*Lorient, France*] (EAIO)
AMI .... Agence Maritime Internationale
AMI .... Agence Mauritienne de l'Information [*News Agency*] (EY)
AMI .... Agricultural Mechanization Institute [*South Korean*] [*Research center*] (IRC)
AMI .... Agrupamento Militar de Intervencao [*Military Intervention Group*] [*Portuguese*] (WER)
AMI .... Airline Mutual Insurance [*International Air Transport Association*]
AMI .... Air Maldives [*ICAO designator*] (FAAC)
AMI .... Air Mercury International [*Belgium*] [*ICAO designator*] (FAAC)
AMI .... Alliance for the Mentally Ill [*Australia*]
Ami .... Amiga [*Record label*] [*Germany*]
AMI .... Arbejdsmiljoinstituttet [*Institute of Occupational Health*] [*Denmark*] (IRC)
AMI .... Armement Moderne Ivoirien
AMI .... Arts, Media, and Information Policy Committee [*Australian Labor Party*] (ADA)
AMI .... Association de Murisseurs Independants [*Association of Independent Developers*] (LA)
AMI .... Association Montessori Internationale [*International Montessori Association*] [*Amsterdam, Netherlands*] (EAIO)
AMI .... Association pour la Micro-Informatique [*French*] [*Association*] (ADPT)
AMI .... Assurance Maladie-Invalidite [*National Health Insurance Program*] [*Belgium*] (WER)
AMI .... Ausonia Mineraria [*Italian*]
AMI .... Australian Marketing Institute (ADA)
AMI .... Australian Motor Industries Ltd. (ADA)
AMI .... Austria Mikrosysteme International [*Microchip producer*]
AMI .... Auxiliary Inshore Minesweeper [*NATO*]
AMI .... Azerbaydzhan State Medical Institute (RU)
AMI .... Mataram [*Indonesia*] [*Airport symbol*] (OAG)
AMIA ...... Asociacion Mexicana de la Industria Automotriz [*Mexico*] (LAA)
AMIA .... Asociacion Mutual Israelita Argentina
AMIA .... Australian Management Industrial Association
AMIA .... Australian Meat Industries Association

AMIA ...... Australian Metal Industries Association (ADA)
AMIC .... Air Movement Information Center [*NATO*] (NATG)
AMIC .... Asian Mass Communication Research and Information Centre [*Singapore*] (EAIO)
AMIC .... Australian Microcomputer Industry Clearinghouse
AMIC .... Australian Mining Industry Council
AMIC .... Australian Mortgage Insurance Corporation (ADA)
AMICAPRO ... Anciens Eleves des Missions Catholiques et Protestantes
AMICEE ... Asociacion Mexicana de Ingenieros en Communicaciones Electricas y Electronica [*Mexican Association of Electrical and Electronic Communication Engineers*] (PDAA)
AMICertMEE ... Associate Member of the Institute of Certified Mechanical and Electrical Engineers of South Africa (AA)
AMICIGIR ... Associacao Mineira de Criadores de Gir [*Brazil*] (DSCA)
AMICO ..... Arab Multinational Investment Company (MENA)
AMID ..... Arab Military Industrial Organization (ME)
AMIDA ..... Accommodation for Mildly Intellectually Disadvantaged Adults [*Australia*]
AMIDEAST ... America-Mideast Educational and Training Services, Inc. [*Research center*] [*Washington, DC*] (MENA)
AMIDEP... Asociacio Multidisciplinaria de Investigacio y Docencia en Poblacion [*Multidisciplinary Association for Research and Teaching in Demography*] [*Peru*] [*Research center*] (IRC)
AMIEA...... Associate Member of the Institution of Engineers, Australia (ADA)
AMIEAust ... Associate Member of the Institution of Engineers of Australia
AMIEU ..... Australasian Meat Industry Employees' Union (ADA)
AMIEV...... Association Medicale Internationale pour l'Etudes des Conditions de Vie et de Sante [*International Medical Association for the Study of Living Conditions and Health*] [*Sofia, Bulgaria*] (EAIO)
AMIF........ Ausonia Miniere Francaise (OMWE)
AMIF........ Societe Ausonia Miniere Francaise [*French*]
AMIG .... Associazione Mutilati e Invalidi di Guerra [*Association of Disabled Servicemen*] [*Italian*]
AMII......... Asociacion Mexicana de Ingenieros Industriales [*Mexico*]
AMIICA .... Associate Member of the Institute of Instrumentation and Control, Australia (ADA)
AMIL........ Australasian Medical Insurance Ltd.
AMIME(Aust) ... Associate Member of the Institution of Mining Engineers (Australia)
AMIMH.... Associate Member of the Institute of Materials Handling [*South Africa*] (AA)
AMIMI...... Associate Member of the Institute of the Motor Industry [*South Africa*] (AA)
A Min........ Arrete Ministeriel [*French*] (FLAF)
AMINA ..... Association Mondiale des Inventeurs [*World Association of Inventors and Researchers*] (EAIO)
Aminier ...... Aminierung [*Animation*] [*German*] (GCA)
AMINOIL ... American Independent Oil Co.
Aminoil ...... American Independent Oil Company (OMWE)
A MinRes ... Arrete du Ministre Resident [*Algeria*] (FLAF)
AMINS...... Arhiv Ministarstva Inostranih dela Srbije [*Archives of the Foreign Ministry of Serbia*] (YU)
AMInstRE(Aust) ... Associate Member of the Institution of Radio Engineers (Australia) (ADA)
AMINTER ... Agencia Maritima Internacional Ltd. [*International Maritime Agency Ltd.*] [*Portuguese*] (WER)
AMIO .... Arab Military Industries Organisation
AMIOAC .. Asociacion Mexicana de Investigacion de Operaciones y Administracion Cientifica [*Mexico*]
AMIP......... American Market for International Program [*Telecommunications*]
AMIP........ Associazione Medica Italiana di Paraplegia [*Italian*] (SLS)
AMIP........ Atmospheric Model Intercomparison Project
AMIPFAC ... Asociacion Mexicana de la Industria de Parasiticidas y Fertilizantes AC [*Mexico*] (DSCA)
AMIPRO... Amis des Missions Protestantes
AMIRA...... Australian Mineral Industries Research Association (ADA)
AMIRE..... Associate Member of the Institution of Radio and Electronics Engineers (Australia) (ADA)
AMIREE(Aust) ... Associate Member of the Institution of Radio and Electronics Engineers (Australia) (ADA)
AMIS........ Adult Migrant Information System [*Australia*]
AMIS........ Agricultural Management Information System [*European Economic Community*] (ADA)
AMIS........ Agricultural Management Information System [*Luxembourg*]
AMIS........ Australian Market Information System
AMIS........ Australian Meat Inspection Service
AMIS........ Australian Municipal Information System [*Computer Sciences of Australia Pty. Ltd.*] [*Information service or system*] (CRD)
AMISI...... Associazione Medica Italiana per lo Studio della Ipnosi [*Italian Medical Association for the Study of Hypnosis*] (SLS)
AMIST ...... Australian Meat Industry Superannuation Trust
AMIT ...... Association Marocaine des Industries Textiles

AMIT .... Intreprinderea Industriala de Stat Accesorii Mecanice pentru Industria Textila [*State Industrial Enterprise for Mechanical Accessories for the Textile Industry*] (RO)
AMITCSA ... Associate Member of the Institute of Technical Communicators of Southern Africa (AA)
AMJ .... Ahmadiyya Muslim Jama'at [*Ahmadiyya Muslim Association*] [*Nigeria*] (EAIO)
AMJ .... Almenara [*Brazil*] [*Airport symbol*] [*Obsolete*] (OAG)
AMJ .... Assemblee Mondiale de la Jeunesse [*World Assembly of Youth*] [*Use WAY*] (AF)
AMK.......... Academie Militaire Khmere [*Cambodian Military Academy*] (CL)
AMK.......... Aeromak [*Yugoslavia*] [*ICAO designator*] (FAAC)
AMK.......... Aldrig Mere Krig [*Never More War*] [*An association*] [*Denmark*] (EAIO)
AMK.......... Amino Acid (RU)
amk .... Ammoniakalisch [*Ammoniacal*] [*German*]
AMK.......... Arbeitsmittelkarten [*Machine Control Cards*] (EG)
AMK.......... Association des Medecins Khmers [*Cambodian Physicians Association*] (CL)
AMK.......... Automobile and Motorcycle Club (RU)
AMK.......... Avrupa Muttefik Komutanligi [*Allied European Command*] (TU)
AMK.......... Methacrylic Anhydride (RU)
AMKI .... King Island [*Australia*] [*ICAO location identifier*] (ICLI)
AML .... Air Malawi [*ICAO designator*] (FAAC)
AML .... Amis du Manifeste et de la Liberte [*Friends of the Manifesto of Freedom*] [*Algeria*]
AML .... Australian Military Liaison (ADA)
AML .... Auto Metralhadora Ligeira [*Light Machine Gun*] [*Portuguese*] (WER)
AML .... Automitrailleuse Legere [*Light Armored Car*] [*French*] (WER)
AML & F .... Australian Mercantile Land and Finance Co.
AMLC .... Association of Marine Laboratories of the Caribbean (EAIO)
AMLC .... Australian Meat and Livestock Corporation (ADA)
AMLG .... Australian Medical Librarians Group
AMLIPC .... Australian Meat and Livestock Industry Policy Council
AMLRDC ... Australian Meat and Livestock Research and Development Corporation
AMLT........ Launceston [*Australia*] [*ICAO location identifier*] (ICLI)
AMLV .... Laverton [*Australia*] [*ICAO location identifier*] (ICLI)
AMM........ Amman [*Jordan*] [*Airport symbol*] (OAG)
AMM........ Asia Merchant Marine [*Commercial firm*] (DS)
AMM........ Asociacion Medica Mexicana [*Mexican Medical Association*]
AMM........ Associated Metals and Minerals Corp. [*Australia*] (ADA)
AMM........ Association Medicale Mondiale [*World Medical Association - WMA*] [*Ferney-Voltaire, France*]
AMM........ Australian Medal of Merit
AMM........ Autorite Chargee des Mesures Militaires [*France*] (FLAF)
AMMA..... Australian Macadamia Manufacturers' Association
AMMA..... Australian Margarine Manufacturers Association (ADA)
AMMA..... Australian Mines and Metals Association
AMMB ..... Arab-Malaysia Merchants Bank
AMMB ..... Melbourne/Moorabbin [*Australia*] [*ICAO location identifier*] (ICLI)
AMMC...... Melbourne [*Australia*] [*ICAO location identifier*] (ICLI)
AMMD...... Ateliers de Menuiserie et de Modelage de Dakar
AMMF ...... Association Mondiale des Medecins Francophones [*Ottawa, ON*] (EAIO)
AMMG...... Mount Gambier [*Australia*] [*ICAO location identifier*] (ICLI)
AMMI .... Mildura [*Australia*] [*ICAO location identifier*] (ICLI)
AMML...... Melbourne [*Australia*] [*ICAO location identifier*] (ICLI)
AMMM..... Melbourne [*Australia*] [*ICAO location identifier*] (ICLI)
AMMP...... Aboriginal Middle Management Program [*Australia*]
AMMQ..... Macquarie Island [*Australia*] [*ICAO location identifier*] (ICLI)
AMMR...... Melbourne [*Australia*] [*ICAO location identifier*] (ICLI)
AMMRL ... Australian National Reference Laboratory in Medical Mycology
AMMTEC ... Australian Metallurgical and Mineral Testing Consultants Proprietary Ltd. (EAS)
AMMTEC Pty Ltd ... Australian Metallurgical and Mineral Testing Consultants Proprietary Ltd. (EAS)
AMMX...... Melbourne [*Australia*] [*ICAO location identifier*] (ICLI)
AMN......... Academy of Medical Sciences, USSR (RU)
AMN......... Ahli Mangku Negara [*Fifth Grade of the Most Distinguished Order of Pangkuan Negara*] [*Malaysia*] (ML)
AMN......... Air Montenegro [*Yugoslavia*] [*ICAO designator*] (FAAC)
AMN......... Ansaldo Meccanico Nucleare [*Ansaldo Nuclear Machinery*] [*Italian*] (WER)
AMN & PA ... Australian Monthly Newspapers and Periodicals Association (ADA)
AMNCL .... Alliance des Mouvements Nationalistes Congolais-Lumumba
AMNLAE ... Asociacion de Mujeres Nicaraguenses Luisa Amanda Espinoza [*Luisa Amanda Espinoza Association of Nicaraguan Women*] (LA)
AMNO ...... Arhiv Muzeja Narodne Osvoboditve [*Archives of the National Liberation Museum*] (YU)

AMNPA .... Australian Monthly Newspapers and Periodicals Association
A-MNR...... Alianza del Movimiento Nacionalista Revolucionario [*Bolivia*] (PPW)
AMNU ...... Asociacion Mexicana para las Naciones Unidas [*United Nations Association of Mexico*] (EAIO)
AMNUT.... All-Muslim National Union of Tanganyika
AMO......... Air Movement Officer [*Military*]
amo........... Amigo [*Friend (Masculine)*] [*Spanish*]
amo........... Amigo [*Friend (Masculine)*] [*Portuguese*]
AMO......... Asian Medical Organization (CL)
AMO......... Asociacion Mexicana de Orquideologia [*Mexican Orchid Association*] (EAIO)
AMO......... Electromachining, Sparkover-Initiated Discharge Machining (RU)
AMO......... Moscow Automobile Company (RU)
AMOA..... Amusement Machine Operators' Association [*Australia*]
AMOA...... Australia - National Museum of Australia [*National Union Catalogue of Australia symbol*]
AM-OB..... Single-Sideband Amplitude Modulation (RU)
AMOC...... Aston Martin Owners Club (EA)
AMOC...... Australian Mathematics Olympiad Committee
AMOCAR ... Amoniaco del Caribe [*Colombia*] (COL)
AMOISS ... Asociacion Medical-Odontologica del Instituto Salvadoreno del Seguro Social [*Medical-Dental Association of the Salvadoran Social Security Institute*] (LA)
AMOP ...... Association Musulmane pour l'Organisation du Pelerinage a la Mecque
AMOR...... Accademia Musicale Ottorino Respighi [*Italian*] (SLS)
AMOR...... Agbofi Magnans Orchestra
amort......... Amortissable [*Redeemable*] [*French*] [*Business term*]
AMOS ...... Afro-Mediterranean Orbital System [*Israel*]
AMOS ...... Agrotikai Metavatikai Oikokyriakai Skholai [*Rural Mobile Domestic Arts Schools*] (GC)
AMOS ...... Australian Meteorological and Oceanographic Society
AMOSA .... Association of Aviation Maintenance Organizations (EAIO)
AMOSA .... Aviation Maintenance Organisation of South Africa
AMOSEAS ... American Overseas Petroleum Ltd. (MENA)
Amostb...... Army Bridge Battalion (RU)
AMOSUP ... Associated Marine Officers and Seamen's Union of the Philippines [*Trade union*] (FEA)
AMP .... Aerometric Station (RU)
AMP .... Aero Transporte SA [*Peru*] [*ICAO designator*] (FAAC)
AMP .... Agence Malgache de Presse [*Malagasy Press Agency*] (AF)
AMP .... Agence Mauritanienne de Presse [*Mauritanian Press Agency*] (AF)
AMP .... Agencia del Ministerio Publico [*Public Ministry Agency*] [*Mexico*] (LA)
AMP .... Akademickie Mistrzostwa Polski [*Polish Student Sport Championship*] (POL)
AMP .... Allied Mining and Mine Countermeasures Publications [*NATO*] (NATG)
AMP .... Aminoplast (RU)
AMP .... Ampanihy [*Madagascar*] [*Airport symbol*] (OAG)
Amp .... Ampere [*German*]
amp .... Ampere [*French*]
amp .... Amperios [*Amperes*] [*Spanish*]
amp .... Ampliacao [*Enlargement*] [*Publishing*] [*Portuguese*]
amp .... Ampule (BU)
Amp .... Ampullen [*Ampoules*] (EG)
amp .... Ampuls (RU)
AMP .... Artillery Weather Post (RU)
AMP .... Asociacion de Madereros de Panama [*Panama*] (DSCA)
AMP .... Asociacion de Medios Publicitarios [*Association of Advertising Media*] [*El Salvador*] (LA)
AMP .... Association por la Mediatheque Public [*French*] (SLS)
AMP .... Australian Marijuana Party [*Political party*] (ADA)
AMP .... Australian Molasses Pool [*An association*]
AMP .... Australian Mutual Provident Society [*Insurance*]
AMP .... Mortar Artillery Regiment (RU)
AMPA ...... Asociacion Mexicana de Produccion Animal [*Mexico*] (DSCA)
AMPA ...... Australian Magazine Publishers Association (ADA)
AMPAL..... Australian Music Publishers Association Limited
AMPAM ... Australian Mutual Provident Asset Management
AMPC ...... Point Cook [*Australia*] [*ICAO location identifier*] (ICLI)
AMPCC .... Australian Manufacturing Production Commodity Classification
AMPCO .... Agricultural Marketing & Processing Company [*Jordan*]
Am Pd .... Ameryka Poludniowa [*South America*] [*Poland*]
AMPE........ Asociacion de Municipios del Peru [*Peru*] (LAA)
AMPERA ... Amanat Penderitaan Rakjat [*The Message of the People's Suffering*] (IN)
AMPERE.. Atomes et Molecules par Etudes Radio-Electriques [*Switzerland*]
AMPEREDOC ... Association Multinationale des Producteurs et Revendeurs d'Electricite-Documentation [*Multinational Association of Producers and Retailers of Electricity-Documentation*] [*Electricity Supply Board*] [*Information service or system*] (IID)

AMPFAC .. Asociacion Mexicana de Profesionistas Forestales, AC [*Mexico*] (DSCA)

Amph .... Amphion [*Record label*] [*France*]

AMPI .... Australasian Marine Photographic Index   (ADA)

AMPICH ... Asociacion de Mediana y Pequena Industria de Chile [*Chilean Medium and Light Industry Association*]   (LA)

ampl .... Ampliato [*Enlarged*] [*Publishing*] [*Italian*]

AMPLA ..... Australian Mining and Petroleum Law Association

ampli .... Amplificateur [*Amplifier*] [*French*]

AMPM ...... Asociacion Madres de Plaza de Mayo [*Mothers of the Plaza de Mayo*] [*Argentina*]   (EAIO)

AMPME .... Assemblee Mondiale des Petites et Moyennes Entreprises [*World Assembly of Small and Medium Enterprises - WASME*] [*See also AMEPM New Delhi,India*]   (EAIO)

Am Pn .... Ameryka Polnocna [*North America*] [*Poland*]

AMPOR .... Airborne Missile Proximity Optical Recorder [*Australia*]

AMPP .... Asamblea Municipal del Poder Popular [*Municipal People's Government Assembly*] [*Cuba*]   (LA)

AMPRONAC ... Asociacion Nacional de Mujeres ante la Problematica Nacional [*National Association of Women Concerned with the Nation's Problems*] [*Nicaragua*]   (LA)

AMPS .... Association Mondiale de Prospective Sociale [*World Social Prospects Study Association*] [*Geneva, Switzerland*]   (EAIO)

AMPSA ..... Association Malienne pour la Promotion Sociale des Aveugles

AMPSSA ... Australian Mutual Provident Staff Association

Amp St .... Amperestunde [*Ampere-Hour*] [*German*]   (GCA)

AMPTC ..... Arab Maritime Petroleum Transport Company [*Organization of Arab Petroleum Exporting Countries*] [*Safat, Kuwait*]   (ME)

AMPU .... Australian Modern Pentathlon Union

AMQ .... Ambon [*Indonesia*] [*Airport symbol*]   (OAG)

AMR .... Acetate Solvent for Furniture   (RU)

AMR .... Advanced Management Research [*Arab*]

AMR .... Air Specialties Corp. [*ICAO designator*]   (FAAC)

AMR .... Alliance Marxiste Revolutionnaire [*Marxist Revolutionary Alliance*] [*French*]   (WER)

AMR .... Amur Railroad   (RU)

AMR .... Arbeitskreis fuer Neue Methoden in der Regionalforschung [*Association for New Methods in Regional Research*] [*Austria*]   (SLS)

AMR .... Association de Medecine Rurale [*Association of Rural Medicine*] [*French*]   (SLS)

AMR .... Association of Mongolian Runners   (EAIO)

AMR .... Auckland Mounted Rifles [*New Zealand*]   (DMA)

AMR .... Australian Military Regulations   (ADA)

AMR .... Automatic Speed Reducer   (RU)

AMR .... Societe pour l'Amenagement du Milieu Rural

AMRA ...... Ancient Mediterranean Research Association

AMRA ...... Australian Model Railways Association   (ADA)

AMRAD .... Australian Medical Research and Development Corporation

AMRAES .. Associate Member of the Royal Aeronautical Society [*South Africa*]   (AA)

AMRC ...... Abadina Media Resource Centre [*Nigeria*]   (PDAA)

AMRC ...... Australian Meat Research Committee   (ARC)

AMRDC .... Australian Medical Research and Development Consortium

AMREF ..... African Medical and Research Foundation [*Nairobi, Kenya*] [*Research center*]   (AF)

Amrel .... Amalgamated Retail [*South African retailer*]

AMRF .... African Medical and Research Foundation [*Nairobi, Kenya*] [*Research center*]

AMRF .... Australian Mohair Research Foundation

AMRF .... Melbourne [*Australia*] [*ICAO location identifier*]   (ICLI)

AMRGS ..... Associacao Medica do Rio Grande Do Sul [*Rio Grande Do Sul Medical Association*] [*Brazil*]

AMRIP ...... Australian Marine Research in Progress

AMRJ .... Arsenal de Marinha do Rio De Janeiro [*Rio De Janeiro Navy Yard*] [*Brazil*]   (LA)

Amrl .... Amiral [*Admiral*]   (TU)

AMRO .... Amsterdam-Rotterdam Bank

Amrobank ... Amsterdam-Rotterdam Bank [*Netherlands*]

AMROCS ... Asociacion de Militares Retirados, Obreros, y Campesinos Somocistas [*Associatio of Pro-Somoza Farmers, Workers, and Retired Military Personnel*] [*Nicaragua*]   (LA)

AMRS .... Australian Machine Readable Cataloguing Record Service [*National Library of Australia*]   (NITA)

AMRS .... Australian MARC [*Machine-Readable Cataloging*] Record Service   (ADA)

AMRS .... Australian Media Research Services   (ADA)

AMS .... Aboriginal Medical Service [*Australia*]   (ADA)

AMS .... Action Medico-Sociale

AMS .... Afro-Malagasiiskii Soiuz

AMS .... Agrometeorological Station   (RU)

AMS .... Agrupacion de Militantes Socialistas [*Association of Socialist Militants*] [*Uruguay*]   (LA)

AMS .... Air Weather Service   (RU)

AMS .... Air Weather Station   (RU)

AMS .... American Missionary Society

AMS .... Amme Memurlari Sendikasi [*Public Officials' Union*] [*Cyprus*] (GC)

AMS .... Amsterdam [*Netherlands*] [*Airport symbol*]   (OAG)

AMS .... Arbetsmarknadsstyrelsen [*National Labor Market Board*] [*Sweden*]

AMS .... Army Map Service

AMS .... Army Medical Depot   (RU)

AMS .... Artillery Weather Service   (RU)

AMS .... Association des Musiciens Suisses [*Swiss Musicians' Association*] (EAIO)

AMS .... Association of Manufacturers of Souvenirs [*Netherlands*] (EAIO)

AMS .... Associazione di Medicina Sociale [*Italian*]   (SLS)

AMS .... Ateliers Mecaniques du Sahel [*Tunisia*]

AMS .... Australian Macadamia Society

AMS .... Australian Malaysian Society

AMS .... Australian Mammal Society   (ADA)

AMS .... Australian MARC [*Machine-Readable Cataloguing*] Specification

AMS .... Australian Mathematical Society   (ADA)

AMS .... Australian Medical Services   (ADA)

AMS .... Australian Merino Society

AMS .... Australian Mining and Smelting Ltd.   (ADA)

AMS .... Australian Museum Society

AMS .... Australian Museum, Sydney

AMS .... Auto-Moto Savez [*Automobile and Motorcycle Federation*] (YU)

AMS .... Auxiliary Medical Services

AMS .... Auxiliary Minesweeper [*NATO*]

AMS .... Flight Weather Report   (RU)

AMS .... Light Amplitude Meter   (RU)

AMS .... Robot Space Station   (RU)

AMS .... Swiss Museums Association   (EAIO)

AMSA ...... Anglican Men's Society in Australia

AMSA ...... Assistance Medico-Sociale en Algerie

AMSA ...... Association of Medical Schools in Africa   (AF)

AMSA ...... Australian Malaysian Singaporean Association

AMSA ...... Australian Marine Sciences Association   (ADA)

AMSA ...... Australian Maritime Safety Authority

AMSA ...... Australian Medical Students Association

AMSA ...... Australian Museum Shops Association

AMSAC .... American Society of African Culture

AMSACONSE ... Associate Member of the South African Association of Consulting Engineers   (AA)

AMSAD .... Australian Medical Society for Alcohol and Drug-Related Problems

AMSAIAA ... Associate Member of the South African Institute of Assayers and Analysts   (AA)

AMSAIMARENA ... Associate Member of the South African Institute of Marine Engineers and Naval Architects   (AA)

AMSAIMECHE ... Associate Member of the South African Institute of Mechanical Engineers   (AA)

AMSAIW ... Associate Member of the South African Institute of Welding (AA)

AMSANZ ... Aviation Medicine Society of Australia and New Zealand (ADA)

AMSAT ..... Australian Marine Science and Technology Ltd.

AMSCO .... Aircraft Manufacturing and Supply Company of Australia

AMSCREDIET ... Amsterdamse Crediet- en Handelsbank [*Bank*] [*Netherlands*]

AMSD .... Advanced Management Studies Division

AMSDEP .. Asian Manpower Skill Development Program [*United Nations*]

AMSE .... Association for Advancement of Modelling and Simulation Techniques in Enterprises [*France*]   (EAIO)

AMSE .... Association Mondiale des Sciences de l'Education [*World Association for Educational Research - WAER*]   (EAIO)

AMSEAS .. American Overseas Petroleum Ltd.

AMSF .... Australian Marathon Swimming Federation

AMSG .... Air Weather Station of the Civil Air Fleet   (RU)

AMSH .... Auto-Moto Savez Hrvatske [*Automobile and Motorcycle Federation of Croatia*]   (YU)

AMSJ .... Auto-Moto Savez Jugoslavije [*Automobile and Motorcycle Federation of Yugoslavia*]   (YU)

AMSLP ..... Association Marocaine pour le Soutien a la Lutte Palestinienne [*Moroccan Association for the Support of the Palestinian Struggle*]   (AF)

AMSME .... Association of Medical Schools in the Middle East [*Egypt*]   (SLS)

AmSoc .... American Society of Peru   (EAIO)

AMSofia .... Archaeological Museum in Sofia   (BU)

AMSS .... Auto-Moto Savez Srbije [*Automobile and Motorcycle Federation of Serbia*]   (YU)

AMSSP ..... Aeronautical Mobile Satellite Service Panel [*ICAO*]   (DA)

AMSSR ..... Moldavian Autonomous Soviet Socialist Republic   (RU)

Amst .... Amsterdam   (BARN)

AMSTAC .. Australian Marine Sciences and Technologies Advisory Committee   (ADA)
AMSTAC-FAP ... Australian Marine Sciences and Technologies Advisory Committee, Funding Advisory Panel
AMStro...... Aircraft Engine Plant   (RU)
AMSU .... Aircraft Motion Sensor Unit
AMSU .... Auto-Manual Switching Unit [Telecommunications]   (DCTA)
amsv .... Flight Weather Report   (RU)
AMSWU ... Amalgamated Metal Workers and Shipwrights' Union [Australia]
AMT .... Amalgamated Metal Trading
AMT .... Assistance Militaire Technique [Military Technical Assistance] [Niger]   (AF)
AMT .... Association of Massage Therapists [Australia]
AMTA ...... Arab Maritime Training Academy [League of Arab States]
AMTA ...... Arab Maritime Transpoprt Academy [Egypt]   (PDAA)
AMTA ...... Australian Music Therapy Association   (ADA)
AMTB .... Associacao de Missoes Transculturais Brasileiras [Missionary association] [Brazil]
AMTC .... Associate of Melbourne Technical College [Australia]   (ADA)
AMTEG .... Australian Metal Trades Export Group   (ADA)
AMTEX..... Australian Machine Tool Exhibition
AMTI .... Allami Melyepitestudomanyi Intezet [State Scientific Institute of Civil Engineering]   (HU)
AMTICP ... Asociacion Mexicana de Tecnicos de las Industrias de la Celulosa y del Palel [Mexican Technical Association of the Pulp and Paper Industries]   (PDAA)
AMTICS .... Advanced Mobile Traffic Information and Communication System [Japan]
AMTIS ...... Australian Manufacturing Technology Information System   (ADA)
amtl .... Amtlich [Official] [German]
Amtm .... Amtmann [Head, Chief] [German]
AMTOG .... Automation of Intersettlement Telephone Communications   (BU)
AMTORG ... American Trade Organization [Commonwealth of Independent States]
AMTRA .... Australian Motorcycle Trailriders' Association
AMT-RJ.... Music Therapy Association of Rio de Janeiro [Brazil]   (EAIO)
AMTS........ Automatic Long Distance Telephone Exchange   (RU)
AMTU .... Aviation Metallurgical Technical Specifications   (RU)
AMTU .... Melbourne [Australia] [ICAO location identifier]   (ICLI)
AMTV .... Australian Medical Television
AMU......... African Mathematical Union   (EA)
AMU......... African Mine Workers' Union
AMU......... Afrikanisch-Madegassische Union [African and Madagascar Union]
AMU......... Akademie Musickych Umeni [Academy of Fine Arts]   (CZ)
AMU......... Aligarh Muslim University [India]   (PDAA)
AMU......... Amadeusair GmbH [Austria] [ICAO designator]   (FAAC)
AMU......... Amanab [Papua New Guinea] [Airport symbol]   (OAG)
AMU......... Arab Maghreb Union [Morocco, Algeria, Mauritania, Tunisia, and Libya]
AMU......... Asian Monetary Unit
AMU......... Associated Metalworkers' Union [British]   (DCTA)
AMU......... Association de Medecine Urbaine [Association of Urban Medicine] [French]   (SLS)
AMUA...... Associate of Music, University of Adelaide [Australia]   (ADA)
AMUBC .... Australian Model Uniform Building Code   (ADA)
AMUDB.... African and Mauritian Union of Development Banks   (EAIO)
AMUE....... Association for the Monetary Union of Europe
AMUFOC ... Association des Etablissements Multiplicateurs de Semences Fourrageres des Communautes Europeennes [Association of Forage Seed Breeders of the European Community] [Brussels, Belgium]
AMUR....... Automatic Control and Recording Machine   (RU)
Amurknigoizdat ... Amur Book Publishing House   (RU)
Amurstal'... Amur Metallurgical Plant   (RU)
Amurverf... Amur Repair and Shipbuilding Yard   (RU)
AMUS .... Asociacion de Mujeres Universitarias Salvadorenas [Association of Salvadoran University Women]   (LA)
AMusA ...... Associate of Music, Australia   (ADA)
AMUSA .... Association of Marine Underwriters in South Africa   (AA)
AMusAGM ... Associate in Music, Australian Guild of Music and Speech
AMUT........ Arya-Mehr University of Technology [Iran]   (PDAA)
AMV......... Agencia Mocambicana de Viagens
AMV......... Aircraft Maintenance Co. [Egypt] [ICAO designator]   (FAAC)
AMV......... Artillery Weather Platoon   (RU)
AMV......... Association Mondiale Veterinaire [World Veterinary Association - WVA] [Madrid, Spain]   (EAIO)
AMV......... Atterrissage par Mauvaise Visibilite [Low-Visibility Landing] [Aviation] [French]
AMV......... Australian Merchant Vessel [Shipping]   (ADA)
AMV......... Australian Mineral Ventures
AMVA .... Amalgamated Milk Vendors Association [Australia]   (ADA)

AMVA....... Asociacion Mundial Veterinaria de Avicola [World Veterinary Poultry Association - WVPA] [Huntingdon, Cambridgeshire, England]   (EAIO)
AMVANSW ... Amalgamated Milk Vendors' Association of New South Wales [Australia]
AMvB .... Algemene Maatregel van Bestuur [Order in Council] [Netherlands]   (ILCA)
AMVC .... Archief en Museum voor het Vlaamse Cultuurleven [Netherlands]
AMVC ...... Australian Milk Vendors' Council
AMVCB.... Australian Motor Vehicle Certification Board   (ADA)
AMVES..... Asociacion de Medicos Veterinarios de El Salvador [El Salvador]   (DSCA)
AMVG .... Anciens Moudjahidine et Victimes de la Guerre [War Veterans and Victims] [Algeria]
AMVHA.... Asociacion Mundial de Veterinarios Higienistas de los Alimentos [World Association of Veterinary Food-Hygienists - WAVFH] [Berlin, Federal Republic of Germany]   (EAIO)
AMVKD .... Arcidiecesni Mirovy Vybor Katolickeho Duchovenstva [Archdiocesan Peace Committee of the Catholic Clergy] [CZ)
AMVMI .... Association Mondiale des Veterinaires Microbiologistes, Immunologistes, et Specialistes des Maladies Infectieuses [World Association of Veterinary Microbiologists, Immunologists, and Specialists in Infectious Diseases - WAVMI] [Maisons-Alfort, France]   (EAIO)
AMVPA..... Asociacion Mundial Veterinaria de Pequenos Animales [World Small Animal Veterinary Association - WSAVA] [Hatfield, Hertfordshire, England]   (EAIO)
AMvRB.... Algemene Maatregel van Rijksbestuur [Benelux]   (BAS)
AMVT .... Agence Mauritanienne de Voyage et de Transit
AMVZ .... Asociacion de Medicos Veterinarios Zootecnistas [Colombia]   (DSCA)
AMW........ Alubau und Metallverarbeitung (VEB) [Aluminum Construction and Metalworking (VEB)]   (EG)
AMW......... Ammoniakwerk Merseburg [Subsidiary of I. G. Farben] [World War II]
AMWAC ... America/West Africa Conference [Shipping]
AMW &SU ... Amalgamated Metal Workers' and Shipwrights' Union [Australia]   (ADA)
AMWC ...... Ananda Marga Women's Center [Australia]
AMWSU ... Amalgamated Metal Workers' and Shipwrights' Union [Australia]   (ADA)
AMWU...... African Mine Workers' Union
AMWU...... Amalgamated Metal Workers' Union [Australia]   (ADA)
AMWU...... Associated Mine Workers Union [Zimbabwe]   (AF)
AMWU...... Australian Manufacturing Workers' Union
AMWWA ... Association of Medical Women in Western Australia
AMWY ...... Wynyard [Australia] [ICAO location identifier]   (ICLI)
AMX......... Aerovias de Mexico SA de CV [ICAO designator]   (FAAC)
AMX......... Atelier de Construction d'Issy-Les-Moulineaux [Issy-Les-Moulineaux Construction Company] [French]   (WER)
AMX......... Ausgabematrix [Output Matrix] [German]   (ADPT)
AMY......... Ambatomainty [Madagascar] [Airport symbol]   (OAG)
AMY......... Statens Forskningssenter foer Arbeidsmedisin og Yrkeshygiene [Institute of Occupational Health] [Research center] [Norway]   (IRC)
AMYC ...... All Mauritius Youth Council   (EAIO)
AMZ.......... Air Meuse - Dat Wallonie [Belgium] [ICAO designator]   (FAAC)
AMZ.......... Alapayevsk Metallurgical Plant   (RU)
AMZ.......... Ardmore [New Zealand] [Airport symbol]   (OAG)
AMZ.......... Arheoloski Muzej, Zagreb [Archaeological Museum, Zagreb] [YU)
AMZ.......... Association des Amis de Maurice Zundel [Association of the Friends of Maurice Zundel] [France]   (EAIO)
AMZ.......... Association Mondiale de Zootechnie [World Association for Animal Production] [Use WAAP]   (AF)
AMZ.......... Australian Milking Zebu   (ADA)
AMZ.......... Lawyers for the Defense of the Rights of Man [Malagasy]   (AF)
AMZB ...... Australian Milking Zebu Breed [Agriculture]
an .... Aangehaald Nummer [Benelux]   (BAS)
AN............. Academy of Sciences   (RU)
AN............. Accion Nacional [National Action] [Spain] [Political party]   (PPE)
AN............. Acrylonitrile   (RU)
AN............. Action Nationale [National Action for People and Homeland] [Switzerland] [Political party]   (PPE)
AN............. Acuerdo Nacional [Paraguay] [Political party]   (EY)
an .... Adjutant   (BU)
AN............. Afrique Nouvelle
AN............. Agencia Nacional [National Agency] [Press agency] [Portuguese]
AN............. Agencia Nacional [National Agency] [Press agency] [Brazil]
AN............. Aircraft Carrier   (RU)
AN............. Akademia Nauk [Academy of Science] [Poland]
AN............. Akademija na Naukite [Academy of Sciences]   (YU)
AN............. Alianza Nacional [National Alliance] [Spain] [Political party]   (PPE)

A/N .... Analogique/Numerique [*Analog/Numeric*] [*French*] (ADPT)
an .... Analytic, Analytical Entry (RU)
AN.............. Anangastikos Nomos [*Compulsory Law*] [*Greek*] (GC)
an .... Ancien [*Ancient*] [*French*]
AN.............. Ancona [*Car registration plates*] [*Italian*]
AN.............. Anesthetic Apparatus (RU)
An.............. Anhang [*Appendix*] [*German*] (GCA)
An.............. Anmerkung [*Note*] [*German*]
an .... Annee [*Year*] [*Publishing*] [*French*]
An.............. Annuaire [*Yearbook*] [*French*]
An.............. Anodo [*Anode*] [*Portuguese*]
An.............. Anonyme [*Anonymous*] [*French*]
an .... Anorganisch [*Inorganic*] [*German*] (GCA)
AN.............. Antilliaanse Nieuwsbrief [*Benelux*] (BAS)
AN.............. Antonov [*Former USSR*] [*ICAO aircraft manufacturer identifier*] (ICAO)
AN.............. Assemblee Nationale [*France*] (FLAF)
AN.............. Australian National
AN.............. Automatic Equipment for Operating Reliability (RU)
AN.............. National Agreement [*Paraguay*] (PD)
AN.............. National Alliance [*Italy*] [*Political party*] (ECON)
AN.............. Netherlands Antilles [*ANSI two-letter standard code*] (CNC)
AN.............. Observation Balloon (RU)
AN.............. Pumping Unit (RU)
AN.............. Self-Contained Adjustment (RU)
ANA........... Accademia Nazionale di Agricoltura [*National Academy of Agriculture*] [*Italian*] (SLS)
ANA........... Accion Nacional Argentina [*Argentine National Action*] (LA)
ANA........... Aden News Agency [*People's Democratic Republic of Yemen*] (MENA)
ANA........... Agence Nigerienne d'Assurances
ANA........... All Nippon Airways Co. Ltd. [*Japan*] [*ICAO designator*] (FAAC)
ANA........... Anguilla National Alliance (PPW)
ana.............. Antifona [*Anthem*] [*Spanish*]
ANA........... Appropriate National Authorities [*NATO*] (NATG)
ANA........... Arab Network of America (BARN)
ANA........... Arab News Agency
ANA........... Armenian National Army [*Guerrilla force*] [*Former USSR*] (ECON)
ANA........... Article Number Association
ANA........... Asociacion Nacional de Agricultores [*National Association of Farmers*] [*El Salvador*] (LA)
ANA........... Asociacion Nacional de Armadores [*Chile*] (LAA)
ANA........... Asociacion Narinense de Apicultores [*Pasto*] (COL)
ANA........... Association of Nigerian Authors
ANA........... Association of Nordic Aeroclubs (EA)
ANA........... Associazione Nazionale Alpini [*National Association of Former Members of Alpine Regiments*] [*Italian*]
ANA........... Athenagence [*News agency*] [*Greece*] (EY)
ANA........... Australian National Airways
ANA........... Australian Natives Association (ADA)
ANA........... Australian Nuclear Association (EAIO)
ANA........... Australian Nurserymen's Association (ADA)
ANAA....... Acoustic Neuroma Association of Australasia
ANAAS ..... Australian and New Zealand Association for the Advancement of Science (PDAA)
ANAB....... Sea Marker (RU)
ANABA ..... Asociacion Nacional de Bibliotecarios, Archiveros, y Arqueologos [*National Association of Librarians, Archivists, and Archaeologists*] [*Spanish*] (SLS)
ANABAD .. Asociacion Nacional de Bibliotecarios, Archiveros, Arqueologos, y Documentalistas [*National Association of Librarians, Archivists, Archaeologists, and Documentarians*] [*Spanish*] (SLS)
ANAC....... Agence Nationale pour l'Aviation Civile [*National Agency for Civil Aviation*] [*Congo*] (AF)
anac............ Anacoreta [*Hermit*] [*Spanish*]
ANAC....... Asamblea Nacional Constituyente [*National Constituent Assembly*] [*Colorado*] (LA)
ANAC....... Asociacion Nacional Campesina [*National Association of Peasants*] [*Costa Rica*] (LA)
ANAC....... Association for New Approaches to Cancer (EAIO)
ANAC....... Associazione Nazionale Autoservizi in Concessione [*Bus service operators association*] [*Italy*] (EY)
ANAC....... Australian National Airlines Commission
ANACAFE ... Asociacion Nacional del Cafe [*National Coffee Association*] [*Guatemala*] (LA)
ANACH..... Asociacion Nacional de Campesinos Hondurenos [*National Association of Honduran Peasants*] (PD)
ANACI ...... Atelier Nationale Algerien de Confection de Drapeaux et de Travaux d'Imprimerie
ANACIMA ... Association des Anciens Combattants Indigenes du Mayombe
ANACON ... Asociacion Nacional de Confeccionistas [*Barranquilla*] (COL)
ANACR ..... Association Nationale des Anciens Combattants de la Resistance

ANACS...... Associazione Nazionale Cartellonistica Pubblicitaria Stradale [*Italy*]
ANADE ..... Asociacion de Abogados de Empresas [*Corporation Lawyers Association*] [*Mexico*] (LA)
ANADENA ... Asociacion Nacional para la Defensa de la Naturaleza [*Colombia*] (COL)
ANADIM .. Asociacion Nacional de Impresores [*Colombia*] (COL)
ANADIPP ... Association Nationale des Distributeurs de Produits Petroliers [*Haiti*] (EY)
ANADIR ... Association Nationale des Anciens Detenus et Internes Resistants [*National Association of Former Resistance Prisoners and Internees*] [*Algeria*] (AF)
ANADIS.... Australian National Animal Disease Information System (ADA)
anaer .... Anaerobic (RU)
ANAF .... Anya National Armed Forces
ANAFACT ... Analyse Factorielle [*Factoral Analysis*] (ADPT)
ANAFID.... Association Nationale de l'Amelioration Fonciere, de l'Irrigation, et du Drainage [*Morocco*]
ANAG....... Australian National Action Group
ANAGSA .. Aseguradora Nacional Agricola y Ganadera, SA [*MEX*] (DSCA)
ANAH .... Association Nationale des Agronomes Haitiens [*Haiti*] (DSCA)
ANAHL..... Australian National Animal Health Laboratory [*CSIRO*] (ADA)
ANAI .... African Network of Administrative Information [*Information service or system*] (IID)
ANAI .... Associazione Nazionale Archivistica Italiana [*National Archivists Association of Italy*] (SLS)
ANAING ... Asociacion Nacional de Auxiliares de Ingenieria [*Colombia*] (COL)
ANAIP....... Agrupacion National Autonoma de Idustriales de Plasticos [*National Approvals Board for Plastics*] [*Spain*] (PDAA)
anal .... Analityczny [*Analytic*] [*Poland*] (POL)
anal .... Analytisch [*Analytical*] [*German*]
ANALAC... Asociacion Nacional de Productores Lacteos [*National Milk Producers Association*] [*Colorado*] (LA)
ANALDEX ... Asociacion Nacional de Exportadores [*National Exporters Association*] [*Colorado*] (LA)
ANALIGE ... Accion Nacional de Liberacion de Guinea Ecuatorial
analitich ..... Analytic (RU)
ANALJA ... Asociacion Nacional de la Industria del Jabon [*Colombia*] (COL)
ANALPES ... Asociacion Nacional de Productores de Pesticidas [*Colombia*] (DSCA)
ANALTRA ... Asociacion Nacional de Transporte [*National Transportation Association*] [*Colorado*] (LA)
analyt .... Analytisch [*Analytical*] [*German*] (GCA)
ANAMACO ... Anambra Motor Manufacturing Company
ANAMH ... Australian National Association for Mental Health
ANAMINT ... Anglo-American Investment Trust [*South Africa*]
ANAMMCO ... Anambra Motor Manufacturing Company of Nigeria
ANAMMG ... Association Nationale des Anciens Moudjahidine et Mutiles de Guerre [*National Association of War Veterans and War Wounded*] [*Algeria*]
AN &MEF ... Australian Naval and Military Expeditionary Force
ANANGOLA ... Associacao dos Naturais de Angola [*Association of Angolan Natives*] (AF)
ANAO....... Australian National Audit Office
ANAP .... Anatavan Partisi [*Motherland Party*] [*Ankara, Turkey*] (MENA)
ANAP .... Asociacion Nacional de los Agricultores Pequenos [*National Association of Small Farmers*] [*Cuba*] (LA)
ANAP .... Asociacion Nicaraguense de Administracion Publica [*Nicaraguan Public Administration Association*] (LA)
ANAPAC... Association of New South Wales and Australian Capital Territory Performing Arts Centres
ANAPCI ... Association Nationale des Artistes de Cote-D'Ivoire
ANAPO ..... Alianza Nacional Popular [*National Popular Alliance*] [*Colorado*] (PD)
ANAPOR .. Alianza Nacional Popular Revolucionaria [*Revolutionary National Popular Alliance*] [*Colorado*] (LA)
ANAPPAV ... Association Nationale pour la Production, la Protection, et l'Amelioration Vegetale [*Morocco*]
ANAPRO .. Accion Nacional Progresista [*National Progressive Action*] [*Venezuela*] (LA)
ANAPROCAFE ... Asociacion Nacional de Productores de Cafe [*National Coffee Producers Association*] [*Colorado*] (LA)
ANAPROCOS ... Analisis y Pronosticos de Precios [*Price Analysis and Forecast*] [*Cuba*] (LA)
ANAPROFAR ... Asociacion Nicaraguense de Propietarios de Farmacias [*Nicaraguan Association of Pharmacy Owners*] (LA)
ANAPS...... Asociacion Nicaraguense de Amistad con los Paises Socialistas [*Nicaraguan Association of Friendship with Socialist Countries*] (LA)
ANAR........ Administracion Nacional de Avenamiento y Riego [*El Salvador*] (LAA)
ANAR........ Asociacion de Arroceros de Nicaragua [*Association of Nicaraguan Rice Growers*] (LA)
ANARE ..... Australian National Antarctic Research Expedition (ADA)
ANARE ..... Australian National Antarctic Research Expeditions [*1947-*]

ANARESAT ... Australian National Antarctic Research Satellite

ANARGA .. Associazione Nazionale Agenti Rappresentanti di Giochi, Giocattoli, e Affini [*Italy*]

ANAS .... Association Nationale des Assistants de Service Social [*National Association of Social Service Assistants*] [*French*]   (SLS)

ANAS .... Azienda Nazionale Autonoma delle Strade [*National Road Board*] [*Italian*]   (WER)

ANASAC... Agricola Nacional SAC [*National Agricultural Corporation*] [*Chile*]   (LA)

ANASIN.... Associazione Nazionale Aziende Servizi Informatica e Telematica [*Italy*]

anast.......... Anastatisch [*Anastatic*] [*Publishing*] [*German*]

ANAT .... Agence Nationale de l'Amenagement du Territoire [*National Agency for Regional Development*] [*Algeria*]   (GEA)

ANAT .... Agence Nord-Africaine des Telephones [*Morocco*]

Anat .... Anatomi [*or Anatomik*] [*Anatomy or Anatomical*]   (TU)

anat .... Anatomia [*Anatomy*] [*Finland*]

Anat .... Anatomia [*Anatomy*] [*Portuguese*]

anat .... Anatomical, Anatomy   (RU)

Anat .... Anatomie [*Anatomy*] [*German*]

anat .... Anatomique [*French*]   (TPFD)

anat .... Anatomy   (BU)

ANATO..... Asociacion Nacional de Agencias de Turismo [*Colombian Association of Tourist Agencies*]   (LA)

ANAU....... Association Nationale des Architectes et Urbanistes [*Tunisia*]

ANAU....... Nauru Island [*ICAO location identifier*]   (ICLI)

ANAV .... Academia Nacional de Agronomia y Veterinaria [*Argentina*]   (DSCA)

ANAVAR .. Analyse de Variance [*Analysis of Variants*] [*French*]   (ADPT)

ANAVE ..... Asociacion de Navieros Espanoles [*Shipping*] [*Spain*]   (EY)

ANAVI ...... Asociacion Nacional de Avicultores [*Guatemala*]   (EY)

ANAVIH... Asociacion Nacional de Avicultores de Honduras [*National Association of Honduran Poultry Raisers*]   (LA)

ANAVIT.... Asociacion Nicaraguense de Agencias de Viajes   (EY)

ANAVZA .. Association Nationale des Agences de Voyage du Zaire

ANB.......... Administracion Nacional de Bosques [*Argentina*]   (DSCA)

ANB.......... Arab National Bank [*Saudi Arabia*]

ANB.......... Asociacion de Bananeros Independientes [*National Association of Independent Banana Producers*] [*Honduras*]   (EY)

ANB.......... Asociacion Nacional Bancaria [*National Banking Association*] [*Colorado*]   (LA)

ANB.......... Associazione Nazionale Bersaglieri [*National Association of Former Members of Bersaglieri Regiments*] [*Italian*]

ANB.......... Australian National Bibliography [*AUSINET database*]

ANB.......... Austrian National Bank   (IMH)

ANBA .... Australian National Bobsleigh Association

ANBB .... Australian National Bibliography [*AUSINET database*]   (ADA)

ANBB .... Algerian Natural Body Building

ANBE .... Asociacion Nacional de Bananeros del Ecuador [*National Banana Association of Ecuador*]   (LAA)

ANBF .... Australian National Boxing Federation

ANBG........ Australian Botanic Gardens

ANBGF...... Algemene Nederlandse Bond van Groenten en Fruit Exporteurs [*Association of Dutch Fruit and Vegetable Exporters*] [*Netherlands*]   (EAIO)

ANBIBNET ... Australian National Bibliographic Network

ANB/MARC ... Australian National Bibliography in Machine-Readable Form   (ADA)

ANBPE...... Association Nationale de Bienfaisance et de Protection de l'Enfance [*Morocco*]

ANBPPI .... Association Nationale Belge pour la Protection de la Propriete Industrielle [*Belgium*]   (BAS)

ANBS........ Asian Network of Biological Sciences [*ICSU*]

ANBU .... Anlagenbuchhaltung-Programmpaket [*Program Packet for Installation Accounts*] [*German*]   (ADPT)

ANBU....... Armee Nationale du Burundi

ANBUG...... Australian Neutron Beam Users' Group

ANC.......... Academia Nacional de Ciencias [*Mexico*]   (DSCA)

ANC.......... African National Congress [*South Africa*]   (PD)

ANC.......... African National Council [*Later, UANC*] [*Zimbabwe*] [*Political party*]   (PPW)

ANC.......... African Nations' Cup [*Soccer*]

ANC.......... Air Navigation Committee [*NATO*]   (NATG)

ANC.......... Alianza Nacional Cristiana [*Costa Rica*] [*Political party*]   (EY)

ANC.......... All Nationals Congress [*Fiji*] [*Political party*]   (EY)

anc............. Ancien [*Ancient*] [*French*]

Anc............ Ancoradouro [*Roadstead*] [*Portuguese*]   (NAU)

Anc............ Ancoraggio [*Anchorage*] [*Italian*]   (NAU)

ANC.......... Area Naval Commander [*NATO*]   (NATG)

ANC.......... Asociacion Nacional Campesina Pro-Tierra [*National Peasant Association for Land*] [*Guatemala*] [*Political party*]

ANC.......... Asociacion Nacional de Caficultores [*National Coffeegrowers Association*] [*Honduras*]   (LA)

ANC.......... Assemblee Nationale Constituante [*France*]   (FLAF)

ANC.......... Associazione Nazionale Combattenti [*Ex-Soldiers Association*] [*Italian*]

ANC.......... Australian Newspaper Conference [*or Council*]

ANC.......... Australian Nursing Council

ANC.......... Australian Nutgrowers' Council

ANCA .... Allied Naval Communications Agency [*London, England*] [*NATO*]

ANCA .... Asociacion Nacional de Cultivadores de Algodon [*Venezuela*]   (LAA)

ANCA .... Australian National Council on AIDS   (EAIO)

ANCAAA .. Association for Northern and Central Australia Aboriginal Artists

ANCAHA .. Association Nationale des Collectionneurs et Amateurs d'Horlogerie Ancienne [*National Associaton of Collectors and Lovers of Antique Clocks and Watches*] [*France*]   (PDAA)

ANCAJP ... Asociacion Nacional Clubes Agricolas Juveniles Peru [*Peru*]   (DSCA)

ANCAM .... Assemblee Nationale du Cameroun

ANCAP ..... Administracion Nacional de Combustibles, Alcohol, y Portland [*National Fuels, Alcohol, and Cement Administration*] [*Uruguay*]   (LA)

ANCAR ..... Associacao Nordestina de Credito e Assistencia Rural [*Northeastern Credit and Rural Assistance Association*] [*Brazil*]   (LA)

ANCAR ..... Australian National Committee for Antarctic Research   (ADA)

ANCAR-ALAGOAS ... Associacao Nordestina de Credito e Assistencia Rural de Alagoas [*Brazil*]   (DSCA)

ANCARBA ... Associacao Nordestina de Credito e Assistencia Rural da Bahia [*Brazil*]   (DSCA)

ANCAR-CE ... Associacao Nordestina de Credito e Assistencia Rural do Ceara [*Brazil*]   (DSCA)

ANCAR-PB ... Associacao Nordestina de Credito e Assistencia Rural de Paraiba [*Brazil*]   (DSCA)

ANCARPE ... Associacao Nordestina de Credito e Assistencia Rural de Pernambuco [*Brazil*]   (DSCA)

ANCAR-PI ... Associacao Nordestina de Credito e Assistencia Rural do Piaui [*Brazil*]   (DSCA)

ANCAR-RN ... Associacao Nordestina de Credito e Assistencia Rural do Rio Grande do Norte [*Brazil*]   (DSCA)

ANCARSE ... Associacao Nordestina de Credito e Assistencia Rural de Sergipe [*Brazil*]   (DSCA)

ANCB .... Academia Nacional de Ciencias de Bolivia

ANCB .... Assocation Nationale des Comptables de Belgique [*National Association of Accountants of Belgium*]   (PDAA)

ANCB .... Australian National Council for the Blind   (ADA)

ANCBA .... Academia Nacional de Ciencias de Buenos Aires [*Argentina*]   (DSCA)

ANCC .... Academia Nacional de Ciencias de Cordoba [*Argentina*]   (DSCA)

ANCC .... Algerian National Chamber of Commerce   (EAIO)

ANCC .... Associazione Nazionale per il Controllo della Combustione [*Nuclear energy*] [*Italian*]   (NRCH)

ANCC .... Australian National Cattlemen's Council   (ADA)

ANCC .... Australian Netherlands Chamber of Commerce

ANCCAC... Australian National Committee on Computation and Automatic Control   (ADA)

ANCD....... Australian National Capital Dancers [*An association*]

ANCE .... Associazione Nazionale Commercio Estero [*Italy*]

ANCE .... Associazione Nazionale Costruttori Edile [*Builders association*] [*Italy*]   (EY)

ANCE .... Associazione Nazionale Costruttori Edile [*Industrial federation*] [*Libya*]

ANCEFN ... Academia Nacional de Ciencias Exactas, Fisicas, y Naturales [*National Academy of Exact, Physical, and Natural Sciences*] [*Buenos Aires, Argentina*] [*Research center*]   (LAA)

ANCGP ..... Asociacion Nacional de Criadores de Ganado Porcino [*Venezuela*]   (DSCA)

ANCHAR ... Asociacion Nacional de Choferes de Alquiler Revolucionarios [*National Revolutionary Taxi Drivers Association*] [*Cuba*]   (LA)

ANCI .... Adviescommissie Nationale Coordinatie Informatievoorzieningen [*Netherlands*]

ANCI .... Asociacion Nacional de Comerciantes y Industriales

ANCI .... Associazione Nazionale Calzaturifici Italiani [*Footwear manufacturers association*] [*Italy*]   (EY)

ANCI .... Associazione Nazionale Comuni Italiani [*National Association of Italian Municipalities*] [*Rome*]   (WER)

ANCI .... Ateliers Navals de Cote-D'Ivoire

ANCI .... Australian Nursing Council, Inc.

ANCIAWPRC ... Argentinian National Committee of the International Association on Water Pollution Research and Control   (EAIO)

ANCIAWPRC ... Australian National Committee of the International Association on Water Pollution Research and Control   (EAIO)

ANCIAWPRC ... Austrian National Committee of the International Association on Water Pollution Research and Control   (EAIO)

ANCIC...... Australian National Copyright Information Center
ANCIDF.... Australian National Committee of the International Dairy Federation
ANCIGY.... Australian National Committee for the International Geophysical Year   (ADA)
ANCIJE .... Asociacion Nacional de Cesantes y Jubilados de la Educacion [*National Association of Unemployed and Retired Educators*] [*Peru*]   (LA)
ANCIS...... Australian National Cartographic Information System   (ADA)
ANCISS..... Associazione Nazionale Costruttori Installatori Sistemi di Sicurezza [*Italy*]
ANCIT....... Associazione Nazionale Conservieri Ittici e delle Tonnare [*Italy*]
ANCLD ..... Australian National Committee on Large Dams   (ADA)
ANCM....... Australian Nurses Christian Movement   (ADA)
ANCMA .... Associazione Nazionale Ciclo, Motociclo Accessori [*National Cycle, Motorcycle, and Accessories Association*] [*Italy*]   (EY)
Ancn........... Ancien [*Ancient*] [*Military map abbreviation World War I*] [*French*]   (MTD)
AnCO......... An Chomhairle Oiliuna [*Industrial Training Authority*] [*Republic of Ireland*]
ANCO....... Asociacion Nacional de Criadores de Ovejas [*Ecuador*]   (LAA)
ANCODS .. Australia-Netherlands Committee on Old Dutch Shipwrecks
ANCOLD .. Australian National Committee on Large Dams   (ADA)
ANCOM.... Andean Common Market   (EAIO)
ANCOR..... American-Netherlands Club of Rotterdam
ANCOR..... Australian National Committee on Oceanic Research   (ADA)
ANCOSA .. Australian National Council of Orff Schulwerk Associations   (ADA)
ANCOSE... Associacao Nacional dos Corretores de Seguros [*Insurance representative body*] [*Portugal*]   (EY)
ANCP .... Academia Nacional de Ciencias de Panama [*Panama National Academy of Sciences*]   (EAIO)
ANCP .... Australian National Capital Planning [*Authority - Information Service*] [*National Union Catalogue of Australia symbol*]
ANCRIGAP ... Asociacion Nacional de Criadores de Ganado Porcino [*Venezuela*]   (DSCA)
ANCS .... Asociacion Nicaraguense de Comunidades Sumus [*Nicaraguan Association of Sumu Communities*]   (LA)
ANC-SA .... African National Congress of South Africa   (AF)
ANCUN..... Australian National Committee for the United Nations   (ADA)
ANCVR ..... Association Nationale des Combattants Volontaires de la Resistance
ANCWEC ... Australian National Committee, World Energy Council
ANCYL...... African National Congress Youth League [*South Africa*]   (PD)
AND........... Algerian National Movement   (RU)
AND........... Alzhirskaia Natsional'naia Dvizheniia
and .... Andere [*Other*] [*German*]
AND........... Andorra [*ANSI three-letter standard code*]   (CNC)
and .... Andre [*Others*] [*Danish/Norwegian*]
AND........... Australian National Discography
ANDA........ Administracion Nacional de Acueductos y Alcantarillados [*National Administration of Aqueducts and Sewerages*] [*El Salvador*]
ANDA........ Associacao Nacional para Difusao de Adubos [*National Association for Fertilizer Distribution*] [*Brazil*]   (LA)
ANDA........ Associacao Nordestina do Desenvolvimento Agricola [*Brazil*]   (DSCA)
ANDA........ Australian National Dance Association   (ADA)
ANDAG..... Association Nationale pour le Developpement des Antilles-Guyane [*National Association for Developing the Antilles-French Guiana*]   (LA)
ANDB........ Algemeene Nederlandsche Diamantbewerkersbond [*Netherlands*]   (BAS)
ANDC........ Australian National Dairy Committee   (ADA)
ANDCP ..... Association Nationale des Directeurs et Chefs due Personnel [*National Assocation of Personnel Manager*] [*France*]   (PDAA)
ANDCS ..... Academia Nacional de Derecho y Ciencias Sociales [*National Academy of Law and Social Sciences*] [*Buenos Aires, Argentina*]   (LAA)
ANDDI ...... Asociacion Nacional de Discapacitados [*National Association of the Disabled*] [*Chile*]   (EAIO)
ANDDOM ... Association Nationale pour le Developpement des Departements d'Outre-Mer [*National Association for Developing the Overseas Departments*]   (LA)
ANDE........ Administracion Nacional de Electricidad [*National Electric Power Administration*] [*Paraguay*]   (LA)
ANDE........ Asociacion Nacional de Educadores [*National Teachers Association*] [*Costa Rica*]   (LA)
ANDE........ Asociacion Nacional de Empresarios [*Ecuador*]   (EY)
ANDEBU .. Asociacion Nacional de Broadcasters Uruguayos [*National Association of Uruguayan Broadcasters*]   (LAA)
ANDEC ..... Acerias Nacionales del Ecuador [*Ecuador*]   (LAA)
ANDEC ..... Australian National Disease Eradication Campaign
ANDECE... Agrupacion Nacional de Derivados del Cemento [*Spain*]   (PDAA)

ANDECORP ... Asociacion Nacional de Rectores [*Colombia*]   (COL)
ANDEL ..... Asociacion Nacional de Linotipistas [*Colombia*]   (COL)
ANDEMOS ... Asociacion Nacional de Importadores de Vehiculos Automotores [*National Association of Automotive Vehicle Importers*] [*Colombia*]   (LA)
ANDEN..... Asociacion Nacional de Educadores de Nicaragua [*National Association of Nicaraguan Teachers*]   (LA)
ANDEPET ... Asociaciones Nacionales de Profesores de Ensenanza Tecnica [*National Associations of Technical School Teachers*] [*Colombia*]   (LA)
ANDEPH .. Asociacion Nacional de Empleados Publicos de Honduras [*National Association of Public Employees of Honduras*]   (EY)
Ander .... Aenderung [*Change*] [*German*]   (GCA)
ANDES...... Aerolineas Nacionales del Ecuador [*Airline*]
ANDES...... Asociacion Nacional de Educadores Salvadorenos [*National Association of Salvadoran Teachers*]   (PD)
ANDESE... Association Nationale des Docteurs es-Sciences Economiques
ANDESS ... Asociacion Nacional de Empleados del Seguro Social [*National Association of Social Security Employees*] [*Dominican Republic*]   (LA)
ANDI........ Asociacion Nacional de Industriales [*National Industrialists Association*] [*Tegucigalpa, Honduras*]   (LAA)
ANDI........ Asociacion Nacional de Industriales [*National Industrialists Association*] [*Colombia*]   (LA)
ANDIARIOS ... Asociacion de Diarios Colombianos [*Colombian Newspapers Association*]   (LA)
Andi-EFEE ... Andidiktatoriki Ethniki Foititiki Enosis Ellados [*Antidictatorial National Student Union of Greece*]   (GC)
ANDIEPH ... Asociacion Nacional de Instituciones Educativas Privadas de Honduras [*National Association of Honduran Private Education Institutes*]   (LA)
ANDIL ...... Associazione Nazionale degli Industriali del Laterizi [*Brick industry association*] [*Italy*]   (EY)
ANDIMA .. Agrupacion Nacional Sindical de Industrias de Materiales Aislantes [*Spain*]   (PDAA)
ANDIMA .. Asociacion Nacional de Industriales Madereros [*Venezuela*]   (DSCA)
ANDIN...... Associazione Nazionale di Ingegneria Nucleare [*Nuclear energy*] [*Italian*]   (NRCH)
ANDIPET ... Asociacion Nicaraguense de Distribuidores de Productos de Petroleo [*Nicaraguan Association of Petroleum Products Dealers*]   (LA)
ANDIR ...... Association Nationale des Deportees et Internes de la Resistance
ANDIS....... Associazione Nazionale di Ingegneria Sanitaria [*Italian*]   (SLS)
ANDIVA ... Asociacion Nicaraguense de Distribuidores de Vehiculos Automotrices [*Nicaraguan Association of Motor Vehicle Dealers*]   (LA)
Andizhanirmash ... Andizhan Irrigation and Reclamation Machinery Plant   (RU)
ANDL........ Australian National Defence League
ANDP........ Alliance Nationale pour la Democratie et le Progres [*Haiti*] [*Political party*]   (EY)
ANDR........ Alzhirskaia Narodnaia Demokraticheskaia Respublika
ANDRA ..... Agence Nationale pour la Gestion des Dechets Radioactifs [*National Agency for the Management of Radioctive Waste*] [*France*]   (PDAA)
ANDRE ..... Asociacion Nicaraguense Democratica Revolucionaria [*Nicaraguan Democratic Revolutionary Association*]   (LA)
ANDS .... Australian Newspaper Database System
ANDSA ..... Almacenes Nacionales de Deposito, SA [*Mexico*]   (DSCA)
ANDTSNSW ... Australian Native Dog Training Society of New South Wales [*Australia*]
ANDUD .... Asamblea Nicaraguense de Unidad Democratica [*Nicaraguan Assembly of Democratic Unity*]   (LA)
ANE........... Alkimos Neolaia EOKA [*Ethniki Organosis Kyprion Agoniston*] B [*National Organization of Cypriot Fighters B Valiant Youth*]   (GC)
ANE........... Allami Nepi Egyuttes [*State Folk Ensemble*]   (HU)
ANE........... Asociacion Numismatica Espanola [*Spanish*]   (SLS)
ANE........... Associacao Nacional dos Exportadores [*Brazil*]   (DSCA)
ANE........... Association of Nigerian Exporters
ANE........... Association of Norwegian Economists   (EAIO)
ANE........... Nora-2000 [*Bulgaria*] [*ICAO designator*]   (FAAC)
ANEA........ Asociacion Nacional de Escritores y Artistas [*National Writers and Artists Association*] [*Peru*]   (LA)
ANEA........ Associazione Nazionale Ex-Emigrati in Australia   (ADA)
ANEACh ... Asociacion Nacional de Empleados de Aduanas de Chile [*National Association of Customs Workers of Chile*]   (LA)
ANEB .... Asociacion Nacional de Empleados Bancarios [*National Bank Employees Association*] [*Colombia*]   (LA)
ANEC .... Air Navigation and Engineering Co. [*Australia*]
ANEC .... Arab National Exchange Company [*Jordan*]
ANEC .... Armenian National Education Committee   (EA)
ANEC .... Asociacion Nacional de Economistas Consultores [*National Association of Consulting Economists*] [*Mexico*]   (LA)

ANEC .... Asociacion Nacional de Economistas de Cuba [*National Association of Cuban Economists*] (LA)

ANEC .... Associacao Nacional dos Exportadores de Cereais [*Brazil*] (DSCA)

ANECIP .... Asociacion Nacional de Empleados de la Cedula de Identidad Personal [*National Association of Personal Identity Document Bureau Employees*] [*Dominican Republic*] (LA)

ANED .... Associazione Nazionale Ex-Deportati Politici nei Campi Nazisti [*National Association of Political Ex-Deportees of the Nazi Camps*] [*Italy*] [*Political party*] (EAIO)

ANEDA ..... Association Nationale d'Etudes pour la Documentation Automatique [*National Association for Studies in Automatic Documentation*] [*French*] (NITA)

ANEE .... Associacao Nacional do Escutismo Europeo [*Portugal*] (EAIO)

ANEF .... Agrupacion Nacional de Empleados Fiscales [*Trade union*] [*Chile*] (EY)

ANEF .... Asociacion Nacional de Empleados Fiscales [*National Association of Government Employees*] [*Chile*] (LA)

ANEF .... Asociacion Nacional de Entrenadores de Futbol [*National Association of Soccer Coaches*] [*Honduras*] (LA)

ANEF .... Australian Noise Exposure Forecast

ANEFHOP ... Asociacion Nacional Espanola de Fabricantes de Hormigon Preparado (EY)

ANEHOP ... Agrupacion Nacional Espanola de Fabricantes de Hormigon Preparado [*Spanish National Group of Manufacturers of Ready Mixed Concrete*] (PDAA)

ANEI .... Asociacion Nacional de Empresas Industriales [*National Association of Industrial Firms*] [*Peru*] (LA)

ANEI .... Asociacion Nacional de Estudiantes Intermedios [*National Association of Intermediate-Level Students*] [*Dominican Republic*] (LA)

ANEI .... Australian Noise Exposure Index

ANEJ .... Asociacion Nacional de Empleados Judiciales [*National Association of Judicial Employees*] [*Costa Rica*] (LA)

ANEJ .... Association Nationale des Educateurs de Jeunes Inadaptes [*French*] (SLS)

Anekd .... Anekdote [*Anecdote*] [*German*]

ANEL .... Agencias Nacionais e Estrangeiras Lda.

ANELIF .... Asamblea Nacional de Impedidos del Ecuador [*National Assembly of Disabled Peoples of Ecuador*] (EAIO)

ANEN .... African NGOs [*Nongovernmental Organizations*] Environment Network (EAIO)

ANENA ..... Association Nationale pour l'Etude de la Neige et des Avalanches [*National Association for the Study of Snow and Avalanches*] [*Research center*] [*French*] (IRC)

ANEO .... Asociacion Espanola de Extractores de Aceite de Orujo de Aceitunas (EY)

ANEP .... Agence Nationale d'Edition et de Publicite [*National Publication and Advertising Agency*] [*Algeria*] (AF)

ANEP .... Asociacion Nacional de Empleados Postales [*National Association of Postal Employees*] [*Dominican Republic*] (LA)

ANEP .... Asociacion Nacional de Empleados Publicos [*National Association of Public Employees*] [*Costa Rica*] (LA)

ANEP .... Asociacion Nacional de Empleados Publicos [*National Association of Public Employees*] [*Uruguay*] (LA)

ANEP .... Asociacion Nacional de la Empresa Privada [*National Association of Private Enterprise*] [*El Salvador*] (LA)

ANEPA ...... Asociacion Nacional de Empleados Publicos Aduanales [*National Association of Customs Employees*] [*Dominican Republic*] (LA)

ANEPA ...... Asociacion Nacional para el Estudio de Problemas Actuales [*National Association for the Study of Contemporary Problems*] [*Spanish*] (WER)

ANEPEJOS ... Anciens Eleves des Peres Josephites

ANEPI .... Associacao Nacional dos Exportadores de Produtos Industriais [*National Association of Exporters of Industrial Products*] [*Brazil*] (LA)

ANEPLA ... Associazione Nazionale Estrattori Produttori Lapidei Affini [*Polished stone slab manufacturers association*] [*Italy*] (EY)

Anera .... Asia-North America Eastbound Rate Agreement [*Shipping*]

ANERI ...... Asociacion Nacional de Empleados de Rentas Internas [*National Association of Internal Revenue Employees*] [*Dominican Republic*] (LA)

anerk .... Anerkannt [*Recognized*] [*German*]

ANES .... Asociacion de Enfermeras Graduadas [*Colombia*] (COL)

ANES .... Asociacion Nacional de Empleados Semi-Fiscales [*National Association of Semipublic Employees*] [*Chile*] (LA)

ANES .... Asociacion Nacional de Enfermeras Salvadorenas [*National Association of Salvadoran Nurses*] (LA)

ANES .... Australian National Eisteddfod Society

ANESBWA ... Association of Non-English-Speaking Background Women of Australia

ANESI .... Association Nationale des Educateurs de Jeunes Inadaptes [*France*] (FLAF)

ANET .... Asociacion Nacional de Empleados de Telecomunicaciones [*National Association of Telecommunications Employees*] [*Dominican Republic*] (LA)

ANET .... Asociacion Nacional de Empresas de Telefonos [*Colombia*] (COL)

ANET .... Associazione Nazionale Esercenti Teatri [*Italian*] (SLS)

ANEU .... Asociacion Nacional de Estudiantes Universitarios [*National Association of University Students*] [*Dominican Republic*] (LA)

ANEVEI .... Dutch Association of Egg Traders [*Netherlands*] (EAIO)

ANEXHON ... Asociacion Nacional de Exportadores de Honduras (EY)

ANEZA ..... Association Nationale des Entreprises Zairoises [*National Association of Zairian Enterprises*] (AF)

ANF .... Academia Nacional de Farmacia [*National Academy of Pharmacy*] [*Rio De Janeiro, Brazil*] (LAA)

ANF .... Aero North Icelandic, Inc. [*ICAO designator*] (FAAC)

ANF .... Agencia de Noticias Fides [*Fides News Agency*] [*Bolivia*] (LA)

ANF .... Allied Naval Forces [*NATO*]

Anf .... Anfang [*Beginning*] [*German*]

ANF .... Anti-Fascist German Popular Front (RU)

ANF .... Antofagasta [*Chile*] [*Airport symbol*] (OAG)

ANF .... Arhiva Nationala de Filme [*National Films Archive*] (RO)

ANF .... Associazione la Nostra Famiglia [*Ponte Lambro, Italy*] (EAIO)

ANF .... Atlantic Nuclear Force [*NATO*]

ANF .... Australian National Formulary

ANF .... Australian Nursing Federation (ADA)

ANF .... Australian Nutrition Foundation

ANFA .... Australian National Flag Association

ANFAC ..... Asociacion Colombiana de Fabricantes de Articulos de Caucho [*Colombia*] (COL)

ANFAC ..... Asociacion Espanola de Fabricantes de Automoviles, Camiones, Tractores y sus Motors [*Spanish Association of Vehicle Manufacturers*] (PDAA)

ANFAE ..... Asociacion Nacional de Funcionarios de Auxilio Escolar [*National Association of School Aid Officials*] [*Chile*] (LA)

Anfaerb ...... Anfarben [*Superficial Staining*] [*German*] (GCA)

ANFAL ...... Asociacion Nacional de Fabricantes de Alcoholes y Licores [*Alcohol and Liquor Producers National Association*] [*Guatemala*] (LA)

ANFANOMA ... Association National des Francais d'Afrique du Nord [*French*]

ANFAO ..... Associazione Nazionale Fabbricanti Articoli di Occhialeria [*Italy*]

ANFAS ...... Australian and New Zealand Federation of Animal Societies

ANFAVEA ... Associacao Nacional dos Fabricantes de Veiculos Automotores [*National Association of Autovehicle Manufacturers*] [*Brazil*] (LA)

ANFB .... Australian National Film Board

ANFC .... Association Nationale des Femmes Congolaises

ANFC .... Australian National Football Council

ANFCE ..... Allied Naval Forces Central Europe [*NATO*]

ANFD .... Australian National Field Days

ANFDC ..... Australian National Field Days Committee

ANFE .... Asociacion Nacional de Fomento Economico [*National Economic Development Association*] [*Costa Rica*] (LA)

ANFE .... Associazione Nazionale Famiglie degli Emigrati [*Italian*]

ANFES ...... Australian Nursing Federation Employee's Section

ANFFAS ... Associazione Nazionale Famiglie di Fanciulli e Adulti Subnormali [*Italian*] (SLS)

ANFIA .... Associazione Nazionale fra Industrie Automobilistiche [*Motor vehicle industries association*] [*Italy*] (EY)

ANFIDA ..... Associazione Nazionale fra gli Industriali degli Acquedotti [*Waterworks constructors association*] [*Italy*] (EY)

ANFIMA ... Associazione Nazionale fra i Fabbricanti di Imballaggi Metallici ed Affini [*Manufacturers of metal containers and allied articles association*] [*Italy*] (EY)

ANFOCOP ... Association Nationale pour la Formation Continue et Promotionnelle en Traitement de Surfaces [*French*] (SLS)

ANFOR ..... Association Francais Petroles de Normalisation

Anford .... Anforderung [*Demand*] [*German*] (GCA)

Anforder ..... Anforderung [*Demand*] [*German*] (GCA)

ANFP .... Asociacion Nacional de Funcionarios Publicos [*National Association of Public Employees*] [*Uruguay*] (LA)

ANFP .... Associacao dos Fabricantes de Papel [*Brazil*] (DSCA)

ANFPP ...... Agence Nationale de Formation et de Perfectionnement Professionnel [*National Training and Professional Improvement Agency*] [*Gabon*] (AF)

ANFR .... Agrupacion Nacional Femenil Revolucionaria [*National Women's Revolutionary Group*] [*Mexico*] (LA)

Anfr .... Anfrage [*Inquiry*] [*German*]

ANFRENA ... Agencia Nacional de Frete e Navegacao [*Mozambique*]

ANFRUT... Asociacion Nacional de Fruticultores [*Venezuela*] (DSCA)

ANFSA ...... Australian Nuffied Farming Scholars' Association

ANFSOC... Australian National Flower Show Organising Committee

ANFWDC ... Australian National Four Wheel Drive Council

ANG .... Academia Nacional de Geografia [*National Academy of Geography*] [*Argentina*] (EAIO)

ANG........... Agencia Noticiosa da Guine-Bissau [*Guinea-Bissau News Agency*] (AF)
ANG........... Agriculture, Food, Beverage and Tobacco Workers' Union [*Austria*] (EAIO)
ANG........... Air Niugini [*Papua New Guinea*] [*ICAO designator*] (FAAC)
ang.............. Angaende [*Concerning*] [*Denmark*] (GPO)
ang.............. Angaende [*Concerning*] [*Norway*] (GPO)
ang.............. Angaende [*Concerning*] [*Sweden*] (GPO)
Ang............. Angebot [*Offer*] [*German*]
Ang............. Angelegenheiten [*Affairs*] [*German*]
Ang............. Angestellte [*Employee*] [*German*]
ang.............. Angewandt [*Applied*] [*German*] (GCA)
ang.............. Angielski [*English*] [*Poland*] (POL)
Ang............. Angirovolion [*Anchorage*] [*Greek*] (NAU)
ANG........... Angkutan [*Transport, Transportation*] (IN)
ang.............. Angol [*English, Englishman*] (HU)
ang.............. Angolo [*Corner*] [*Publishing*] [*Italian*]
ang.............. Anhydride (RU)
ANG........... Artiljerijska Nastava Gadanja [*Artillery Target Practice*] (YU)
ANG........... Asociacion Nacional de Ganaderos [*National Cattlemen's Association*] [*Colorado*] (LA)
ANG........... Australian National Gallery [*Research Library*] [*National Union Catalogue of Australia symbol*]
ang.............. Hangar, Shed [*Topography*] (RU)
ANGA....... Australian Nashi Growers' Association
ANGA....... Australian National Gallery Association
ANGAD..... Angkutan Angkatan Darat [*Army Transport Corps*] (IN)
ANGALLOP ... Australian National Gallery Library List of Periodicals
ANGAM..... Australian National Guide to Archival Material
ANGAU..... Australia-New Guinea Administrative Unit [*World War II*]
ANGAU..... Australian New Guinea Administrative Unit (ADA)
Angeb......... Angebot [*or Angeboten*] [*Offer or Offered for Sale*] [*German*]
angeb.......... Angebunden [*Bound With*] [*Publishing*] [*German*]
angebd........ Angebunden [*Bound With*] [*Publishing*] [*German*]
ANGEE ..... Association of Non-Government Education Employees [*South Australia*]
Angekl........ Angeklagte [*Defendant*] [*German*]
Angelegenh ... Angelegenheit [*Affair*] [*German*]
anger .... Angerissen [*Slightly Torn*] [*Publishing*] [*German*]
angeschlg ... Angeschlagen [*Slightly Bruised*] [*Publishing*] [*German*]
angeschm.... Angeschmutzt [*Slightly Soiled*] [*Publishing*] [*German*]
Angest........ Angestellter [*Clerk, Employee*] [*German*]
angew .... Angewandt [*Applied*] [*German*]
ANGFA ..... Australia New Guinea Fishes Association
ANGIS...... Australian National Genomic Information Service [*University of Sydney*]
ANGKASA ... Angkatan Kerjasama [*Cooperative Movement*] (ML)
angl .... Anglikaaninen [*Anglican*] [*Finland*]
ANGL....... Anglisisme [*Anglicism*] [*Afrikaans*]
Angl .... Anglistik [*Study of English language and literature*] [*German*]
angl .... English (BU)
angl f .... English Pound (RU)
angl p .... English Patent (RU)
ANGOC.... Asian NonGovernmental Organizations Coalition for Agrarian Reform and Rural Development [*Philippines*] (EAIO)
ANGOL..... Fabrica Aga Ltda. [*Colombia*] (COL)
ANGOP..... Agencia Angola-Presse [*Angolan Press Agency*] (AF)
ANGOP..... Angolan News Agency
Angreifbark ... Angreifbarkeit [*Attackability*] [*German*] (GCA)
ANGRMS ... Australian Narrow Gauge Railway Museum Society (ADA)
ANGROGRADA ... Pretprijatie za Promet so Gradezen Material na Angro [*Building Materials Wholesale Establishment*] [*Skopje*] (YU)
ANGSOC .. Anglican Society [*Australia*]
ANGST...... Australian Non-Government Welfare Sector Tomorrow (ADA)
ANGV....... Asociacion Nacional de Ganaderos de Venezuela [*Venezuela*] (DSCA)
ANGW....... Alles nach Gottes Willen [*Everything According to the Will of God*] [*Motto for a number of members of German and Bavarian royalty during the 16th and 17th centuries*]
angw .... Angewandt [*Applied*] [*German*]
ANH .... Academia Nacional de la Historia [*National Academy of History*] [*Argentina*] (EAIO)
ANH .... Anair - Anich Airways [*Croatia*] [*ICAO designator*] (FAAC)
Anh .... Anhaenger [*Trailer*] [*German*] (GCA)
ANH .... Anhang [*Appendix*] [*German*] (EG)
Anh .... Anhydrid [*Anhydride*] [*German*] (GCA)
anh .... Anhydrisch [*Anhydrous*] [*German*] (GCA)
ANH .... Australian National Hotels Ltd. (ADA)
ANHECA.. Australian Nursing Homes and Extended Care Association
ANHG .... Academia Nacional de Historia y Geografia [*Mexico*] (DSCA)
ANHM ...... Association Nationale des Handicapes Moteurs du Senegal [*National Association of the Handicapped of Senegal*] (EAIO)
ANHSA ..... Aeronias Nacionales de Honduras Sociedad Anonima [*Airline*] [*Honduras*]

ANHUL..... Australian National Humanities Library (ADA)
anhydr........ Annydrous (BARN)
ANHYP.... Antwerpsche Hypotheekkas [*Bank*] [*Belgium*]
AN-HYP... Antwerpse Hypotheekkas [*Banking*] [*Belgium*] (EY)
ANI........... Agencia de Noticias e de Informacoes [*News and Information Agency*] [*Portuguese*] (WER)
ANI........... Agencia Nacional de Informacoes [*National Information Agency*] [*Nonexistent, see ANOP*] [*Portuguese*] (WER)
ANI........... All-Union Scientific Research Institute of Asbestos (RU)
ANI........... American Petroleum Institute [*API*] (RU)
ANI........... Arabe Non Identifie
ANI........... Association Nationale des Informatistes [*National Association of Informatists*] [*Morocco*] (EAIO)
ANI........... Association Nationale Ibobu [*Gabon*] (EAIO)
ANI........... Associazione Nazionalista Italiana [*Italian Nationalist Association*] [*Political party*] (PPE)
ANI........... Australian National Industries Ltd. (ADA)
ANI........... Australian Naval Institute
ANI........... Azerbaydzhan Petroleum Institute Imeni M. Azizbekov (RU)
ANIA .... Asociacion Nacional de Ingenieros Agronomos [*Spain*] (DSCA)
ANIA .... Asociacion Nicaraguense de Ingenieros y Arquitectos [*Nicaraguan Association of Engineers and Architects*] (LA)
ANIA .... Association Nationale des Industries Agro-Alimentaires [*Industrial organization*] [*France*] (EY)
ANIA .... Association Nationale des Invalides [*Benelux*] (BAS)
ANIA .... Associazione Nazionale fra le Imprese Assicuratrici [*National Association of Insurance Companies*] [*Italy*] (EAIO)
ANIAI....... Associazione Nazionale Ingegneri ed Architetti Italiani [*Italian*] (SLS)
ANIB .... Australian News and Information Bureau (ADA)
ANIBO ...... Associazione Nazionale Buying Office Firenze [*Italy*]
ANIC .... Agenzia Nazionale per l'Idrogenazione dei Combustibili [*National Agency for the Hydrogenation of Fuel*] [*Italian*] (WER)
ANIC .... Australian National Insect Collection
ANICA ...... Associazione Nazionale fra gli Istituti de Credito Agrario [*Bankers' organization*] [*Italy*] (EY)
ANICA ...... Associazione Nazionale Industrie Cinematografiche e Audiovisive [*Cinematograph and allied industries association*] [*Italy*] (EY)
ANICAF .... Asociacion Nacional de Industriales del Cafe [*Venezuela*] (DSCA)
ANICAM .. Associazione Nazionale dell'Industria dei Componenti Accessori e Materiali per Calzature e Pelletterie [*Footwear Components and Accessories Association*] [*Italy*] (EY)
ANICAV.... Associazione Nazionale Industriali Conserve Alimentari Vegetali [*Manufacturers of canned vegetable foods association*] [*Italy*] (EY)
ANID .... Associazione Nazionale Insegnanti di Disegno [*Italian*] (SLS)
ANIDES.... Association Nationale des Infirmiers et Infirmieres Diplomes d'Etat du Senegal
ANIDPP.... Association Nationale des Importateurs et Distributeurs de Produits Pharmaceutiques [*Haiti*] (EY)
ANIE .... Associazione Nazionale Industrie Elettrotechniche ed Elettroniche [*National Association of Electrical and Electronic Industries*] [*Milan, Italy*] (WER)
ANIEL...... Asociacion Nacional de Industrias Electronicas [*Spain*] (IMH)
ANIEL...... Asociacion Nacional de Industrias Electronicas Grupos Electronica Profesional y Telematica [*Spain*] (EAIO)
ANIERM... Asociacion Nacional de Importadores y Exportadores de la Republica Mexicana [*National Mexican Importers and Exporters Association*] (LA)
ANIEST .... Associazione Nazionale Italiana Esperti Scientifici del Turismo [*Italian*] (SLS)
ANIF .... Asociacion Nacional de Instituciones Financieras [*National Association of Financial Institutions*] [*Colorado*] (LA)
ANIFAPE ... Association Nationale pour l'Information, la Formation, et Assistance aux Parents et Educateurs [*National Association for Information, Training and Assistance to Parents and Educators*] [*Senegal*]
ANIFOP.... Association Nationale Interprofessionnelle pour la Formation Professionnelle et Technique dans l'Industrie des Plastiques [*French*] (SLS)
ANIFRMO ... Association Nationale Interprofessionnelle pour la Formation Rationelle de la Main-d'Oeuvre
ANIG .... Associazione Nazionale Importatori Giocattoli [*Italy*]
ANIG .... Associazione Nazionale Industriali Gas [*Italy*]
ANII .... Arctic Scientific Research Institute (RU)
ANII .... Artillery Scientific Research Institute (RU)
An Ik Mr.... Ana Ikmal Merkezi [*Main Supply Center*] (TU)
ANIL .... Asociacion Nacional de Industrias Licoreras [*Colombia*] (COL)
ANIM .... Agence Nationale d'Information Malienne [*Malian National Information Agency*] (AF)
ANIM .... Association Nationale Marocaine des Ingenieurs des Mines [*Moroccan National Mining Engineers Association*] (AF)
ANIM .... Associazione Nazionale Ingegneri Minerari [*Italian*] (SLS)

ANIMA ..... Associazione Nazionale Industria Meccanica Varia ed Affine [National Association of Mechanical and Allied Industries] [Milan, Italy] (WER)
ANIMI ...... Scientific Research Institute of Naval Artillery (RU)
ANIMOG ... Associazione Nazionale Italiana Medici ed Operatori Geriatrici [Italian] (SLS)
ANIPLA .... Associazione Nazionale Italiana per l'Automazione [Milan, Italy]
ANIQ .... Asociacion Nacional de Industria Quimica [National Association of the Chemical Industry] [Mexico] (LAA)
ANIR .... Asociacion Nacional de Innovadores y Racionalizadores [National Association of Innovators and Efficiency Experts] [Cuba] (LA)
ANIS .... Asociacion Nacional Indigena Salvadorena [National Association of Salvadoran Indians] (LA)
ANIS .... Associazione Nazionale dell'Industria Sammarinese [San Marino] (EAIO)
ANISA .... Anglo Navel e Industrial SA [Spain] (PDAA)
ANISC .... Association of Indigenous Nigerian Shipping Companies
ANIT .... Agence Nationale pour l'Information Touristique [National Agency for Tourist Information] [France] (PDAA)
ANIT .... Associazione Nazionale Italiana Traduttori Interpreti
ANITA ...... Associazione Nazionale Imprese Trasporti Automobilistici [Motor transport concerns association] [Italy] (EY)
ANITAF .... Associacao Nacional das Industrias Texteis Algodeiras e Fibras [Portugal] (EY)
ANITIM .... Altay Scientific Research, Planning, and Technological Institute of Machinery Manufacture (RU)
ANIVEC .... Associacao Nacional das Industrias de Vestuario e Confeccao [Portugal] (EY)
ANix .... Australian Nixa [Record label]
ANJ .... Aero-Alentejo, Servicos Aereos Lda. [Portugal] [ICAO designator] (FAAC)
ANJ .... Zanaga [Congo] [Airport symbol] (OAG)
ANJS .... Association Nationale des Journalistes Senegalais [National Association of Senegalese Reporters] (AF)
ANJV .... Algemeen Nederlands Jeugdverbond [General Netherlands Youth Federation] (WEN)
ANK .... Afrikaanse Nasionale Kultuurraad
ANK .... Afrikanskii Natsional'nyi Kongress [African National Congress]
ANK .... Air Nippon Co. Ltd. [Japan] [ICAO designator] (FAAC)
ANK .... Alban Nepkoztarsasag [Albanian People's Republic] (HU)
ANK .... Ankara [Turkey] [Airport symbol] (OAG)
Ank .... Ankunft [Arrival] [German] (EG)
ANK .... Automatic Circuit Adjustment (RU)
ANK .... Cadmium-Nickel Plate Battery (RU)
ANK .... Chinese Academy of Sciences
ANKA .... Ankara Ajansi [Ankara (News) Agency] (TU)
ANKA .... Automatic Adjustment of Circuit Amplitudes (RU)
ANKC .... Australian National Kennel Council
ANKFF ..... Australian National Kung Fu Federation
ankol .... Ankoloriert [Slightly Colored] [Publishing] [German]
ankolor ...... Ankoloriert [Slightly Colored] [Publishing] [German]
An-Kon...... Antalya Konsantre Sebze Meyve Isleme Sanayi ve Ticaret AS [Antalya Concentrated Fruit and Vegetable Processing Industry and Trade Corp.] (TU)
AnKT .... Annotated Labor Code (BU)
ANL.......... Academia Nacional de Letras [Uruguay] (SLS)
ANL.......... Accademia Nazionale dei Lincei [Lincei National Academy] [Italian] (WER)
Anl .... Anlage [Equipment] [German] (EG)
anl .... Anlatan [Explanatory] (TU)
A-NL........ Anti-NAZI League
ANL.......... Armee Nationale Laotienne [Lao National Army] (CL)
ANL.......... Associated National Life Insurance [Australia]
ANL.......... Australasian [or Australian] National League (ADA)
ANL.......... Australian National Library [National Union Catalogue of Australia symbol]
ANL.......... Australian National Line (DS)
ANL.......... Australian Native Landscapes
ANLAS...... Anlagenbrechnungssystem [Installation Accounting System] [German] (ADPT)
ANLLF ..... Association des Neurologues Liberaux de Langue Francaise [Association of French-Speaking Private Neurologists] [France] (EAIO)
ANM.......... Academia Nacional de Medicina [National Academy of Medicine] [Rio De Janeiro, Brazil] (LAA)
anm .... Anmaerkning [Note] [Denmark] (GPO)
anm .... Anmarkning [Note] [Sweden] (GPO)
Anm .... Anmeldung [Application] [German] (GCA)
Anm .... Anmerkung [Note] [German] (GPO)
ANM.......... Antalaha [Madagascar] [Airport symbol] (OAG)
ANM.......... Arab Nationalist Movement (ME)
ANM.......... Associacao dos Naturais de Mocambique [Association of Native-Born Mozambicans]
ANM......... Australian Nationalists Movement
ANM.......... Australian Newsprint Mills Ltd. (ADA)

ANM.......... New Music (Australia) [Record label]
ANMADERAS ... Asociacion Nacional de Industrias Forestales Madereras y Derivadas [Colombia] (COL)
ANMB....... Algemene Nederlandse Bedrijfsbond voor de Metaalnijverheid en de Electrotechnische Industrie [Netherlands] (BAS)
ANMB....... Australian National Music Bibliography
anme.......... Anonyme [Anonymous] [Used to indicate limited liability] [French]
ANMEF..... Australian Naval and Military Expeditionary Force (ADA)
Anmerk..... Anmerkung [Note] [German]
Anmerkg .... Anmerkung [Note] [German]
Anmerkgn.. Anmerkung [Note] [German]
ANMI .... Allied Naval Maneuvering Instructions [NATO] (NATG)
Anmkgn .... Anmerkung [Note] [German]
ANMM...... Asociacion Nacional de Mineros Medianos [National Medium Miners Association] [Bolivia] (EAIO)
ANMM...... Australian National Maritime Museum
ANMP....... Afghan National Movement Party [Political party] (EY)
ANMRC .... Australian Numerical Meteorology Research Centre (ADA)
anmrkn....... Anmerkning [Note] [Danish/Norwegian]
ANMRSA ... Association Nationale du Marketing, Recherche, Strategie, Action [National Association of Marketing, Research, Strategy, and Action] [France] (EAIO)
ANMUL.... Australian National Music Library
ANMZSSR ... Akademia Nauk Medycznych ZSSR [Academy of Medical Sciences of the USSR] (POL)
ANN .... African Newspapers of Nigeria Ltd.
ANN .... Agencia de Noticias Nueva Nicaragua [New Nicaraguan News Agency] (LA)
ANN .... Agencia Nicaraguense de Noticias [News agency] (EY)
Ann .... Annalen [Annals] [German]
ann .... Annotatie [Annotation] [Benelux] (BAS)
ann .... Annotation (RU)
ann .... Annulation [Benelux] (BAS)
annot .... Annotated (RU)
annot .... Annotazione [Annotation] [Publishing] [Italian]
annot .... Annote [or Annotation] [Annotated or Annotation Publishing] [French]
annotaz....... Annotazione [Annotation] [Publishing] [Italian]
annotir....... Annotated (RU)
Ann RechtPol Wtsch ... Annalen voor Rechtsgeleerdheid en Staatswetenschappen [Benelux] (BAS)
ANO .... Aboriginal Paraprofessional Nutrition Officer [Australia]
ANO .... Air North Ltd. [Australia] [ICAO designator] (FAAC)
AnO .... Anordnung [Direction, Instruction] [German] (ILCA)
ANO .... Armiia Natsionalnovo Osvobozhdeniia
ANO .... Navigation Lights (RU)
ANOA......... Algerian National Liberation Army (RU)
ANOBCT-EC ... Association of National Organizations in the Bakery and Confectionery Trade in the EC [European Community] [Belgium] (EAIO)
ANOC....... Asociacion Nacional de Organizaciones Campesinas [National Association of Peasant Organizations] [Chile] (LA)
ANOC....... Association of National Olympic Committees [See also ACNO] [Paris, France] (EAIO)
ANOCA..... African National Olympic Committees of Africa (OLYM)
ANOCA..... Association of National Olympic Committees of Africa (EA)
ANOF....... Algemene Nederlandse Onderwijzers Federatie [General Netherlands Teachers' Federation] (WEN)
ANOG .... Australian National Observer Group
ANOK....... Akcioni Narodnooslobodilacki Komitet [National Liberation Action Committee] (YU)
anon........... Anoniem [Anonymous] [Netherlands]
Anon.......... Anonimo [Anonymous] [Spanish]
anon.......... Anonym [Anonymous] [German]
Anon.......... Anonyme [Anonymous] [French]
anon.......... Anonymous (BU)
ANOP....... Agencia Noticiosa Portuguesa [Portuguese News Agency] (WER)
ANOP....... Australian Nationwide Opinion Polls (ADA)
Anord .... Anordnung [Arrangement] [German] (GCA)
Anordn....... Anordnung [Arrangement] [German] (GCA)
ANORG.... Anorganies(e) [Inorganic] [Afrikaans]
anorg......... Anorganisch [Inorganic] [German]
ANOS........ Australian Native Orchid Society (ADA)
anot .... Annotated (BU)
Anot .... Anotatos [Maximum, Supreme] [Greek] (GC)
ANP .... Academy of the Petroleum Industry (RU)
ANP .... Accao Nacional Popular [National Popular Action] [Angola] [Political party] (AF)
ANP.......... Administracion Nacional de Puertos [National Ports Administration] [Uruguay] (LA)
ANP.......... Agence Nigerienne de Presse [News Agency] [Niger] (EY)
ANP.......... Akademia Nauk Politycznych [Academy of Political Sciences] (POL)
ANP........... Algemeen Nederlandsch Politieweekblad [Netherlands] (BAS)

ANP .... Algemeen Nederlands Persbureau [*General Netherlands Press Agency*] (WEN)
ANP .... Alianza Nacional de Propietaristas [*Bolivia*] (LAA)
ANP .... Alianza Nacional Popular [*National Popular Alliance*] [*Colorado*] (LA)
ANP .... Allied Navigation Publications [*NATO*] (NATG)
ANP .... Apatite and Nepheline Rock (RU)
ANP .... Arbeitsgemeinschaft Nuklear Prozesswarme [*Germany*] (PDAA)
ANP .... Armee Nationale Populaire [*People's National Army*] [*Algeria*] (AF)
ANP .... Artillery Observation Post (RU)
ANP .... Asociacion Nacional de Periodistas [*National Journalists Association*] [*Peru*] (LA)
ANP .... Asociacion Nacional de Periodistas [*National Journalists Association*] [*Colorado*] (LA)
ANP .... Assemblee Nationale Populaire [*National Popular Assembly*] [*Malagasy*] (AF)
ANP .... Australian Nationalist Party (ADA)
ANP .... Australian National Party [*Political party*]
ANP .... Austrian People's Party (RU)
ANP .... Awami National Party [*Pakistan*] [*Political party*] (FEA)
ANP .... Direct Support Artillery (RU)
ANPA .... Armee Nationale Populaire Algerienne [*National Popular Algerian Army*]
ANPA .... Asociacion Nacional de Peritos Agrarios [*National Association of Agrarian Experts*] [*Dominican Republic*] (LA)
ANPA .... Asociacion Nacional de Productores de Arroz [*Peru*] (DSCA)
ANPA .... Asociacion Nacional de Profesionales Agricolas [*National Association of Agricultural Professionals*] [*Dominican Republic*] (LA)
ANPA .... Association Nationale pour la Production Animale [*Morocco*]
ANPA .... Australian National Publicity Association (ADA)
ANPA .... Australian Newspaper Proprietors Association (ADA)
ANPAE ...... Associazione Nazionale Produttori di Argille Espanse [*Italy*]
ANPAF ...... Asociacion Nacional de Padres de Familia [*National Association of Heads of Families*] [*Nicaragua*] (LA)
ANPAM .... Associazione Nazionale Produttori Armi e Munizioni [*Arms and munitions producers association*] [*Italy*] (EY)
ANPAT ...... Association Nationale pour la Prevention des Accidents du Travail [*National Association for the Prevention of Work Accidents*] [*French*] (BAS)
ANPC .... Aanvullend Nationaal Paritair Comite [*Benelux*] (BAS)
ANPC .... Australian National Playwrights' Conference (ADA)
ANPCC ...... Asociacion Nacional de Productores de Coco y Copra [*Venezuela*] (DSCA)
ANPE .... Agence Nationale pour l'Emploi [*National Employment Agency*] [*French*]
ANPE .... Anadolu Petrolleri AS [*Anatolian Petroleum Corporation*] (TU)
ANPE .... Association Nationale pour la Promotion de l'Enseignement [*National Association for the Advancement of Education*] [*Mauritius*] (AF)
ANPEC ...... Associacao Nacional de Programas de Pos-Graduacao em Economia [*National Association of Economics Graduate Programs*] [*Brazil*] (LA)
ANPEF ...... Asociacion Nacional de Profesores de Educacion Fisica [*National Association of Physical Education Teachers*] [*Peru*] (LA)
ANPEF ...... Asociacion Nacional de Profesores de Educacion Fisica [*National Association of Physical Education Teachers*] [*Colombia*] (COL)
ANPEN ..... Asociacion Nacional de Profesores de Educacion Normal [*National Association of Normal School Teachers*] [*Peru*] (LA)
ANPES ...... Asociacion Nacional de Profesores de Educacion Secundaria [*National Association of Secondary Education Teachers*] [*Peru*] (LA)
ANPES ...... Associacao Nacional de Programacao Economico-Social [*Brazil*] (DSCA)
ANPESCA ... Asociacion Nacional de Industrias Pesqueras y Derivadas [*Colombia*] (COL)
ANPET ...... Asociacion Nacional de Profesores de Educacion Tecnica [*National Association of Technical Education Teachers*] [*Peru*] (LA)
ANPEX ...... Australian National Philatelic Exhibition (ADA)
ANPG .... Asamblea Nacional Popular Galega [*People's National Assembly of Galicia*] [*Spanish*] (WER)
ANPI .... Asociacion Nacional de Pequenos Industriales [*National Association of Small Industries*] [*Honduras*] (EY)
ANPI .... Association Nationale pour la Protection Contre l'Incendie [*Belgium*] (SLS)
ANPI .... Associazione Nazionale Partigiani d'Italia [*National Association of Italian Partisans*] (WER)
ANPP .... Artillery in Direct Support of Infantry (RU)
ANPP .... Asamblea Nacional del Poder Popular [*National People's Government Assembly*] [*Cuba*] (LA)
ANPP .... Asociacion Nacional de Periodistas del Peru [*National Association of Peruvian Journalists*] (LA)

ANPP .... Asociacion Nacional de Profesionales Publicitarios [*Colombia*] (COL)
ANPROBA ... Asociacion Nacional de Productores de Banano [*National Association of Banana Producers*] [*Nicaragua*] (LA)
ANPROCOM ... Asociacion Nacional de Propietarios de Compra y Venta [*Colombia*] (COL)
ANPROS ... Asociacion Nacional de Productores de Semillas [*National Association of Seed Producers*] [*Chile*] (LA)
ANPROSE ... Asociacion Nacional de Productores de Semillas Certificadas [*Venezuela*] (DSCA)
ANPROSOR ... Asociacion Nacional de Productores de Sorgo [*National Association of Sorghum Producers*] [*Nicaragua*] (LA)
ANPS .... Asociacion Nacional de Produccion de Semillas [*Chile*] (DSCA)
ANPS .... Asociacion Nacional de Productores de Semillas [*Colombia*] (DSCA)
ANPUEU .. Association Nationale des Proprietaires et Usagers d'Embranchements Particuliers [*National Association of Owners and Users of Private Branch Railway Sidings*] [*France*] (PDAA)
ANPUR ..... Associazione Nazionale Professori Universitari di Ruolo [*Italian*] (SLS)
ANPW .... Australian National Parks and Wildlife Service [*National Union Catalogue of Australia symbol*]
ANPWS ..... Australian National Parks and Wildlife Service [*1975*] (ADA)
ANQUE ..... Associacion Nacional de Qumicos de Espana [*National Chemical Association*] [*Spain*] (PDAA)
ANR .... Aeronorte SA [*Colombia*] [*ICAO designator*] (FAAC)
ANR .... Aktion Neue Rechte [*Action New Right*] (EG)
ANR .... Antwerp [*Belgium*] [*Airport symbol*] (OAG)
ANR .... Assemblee Nationale Revolutionnaire [*National Revolutionary Assembly*] [*Benin*] (AF)
ANR .... Association of Modern Directors (RU)
ANR .... Australian National Railways (ADA)
ANR .... Australian Naval Reserve
ANRAC ..... Asociacion Nacional de Radioaficionados de Cuba [*National Association of Amateur Radio Operators of Cuba*] (LA)
ANRAC ..... Australian Nurse Registering Authorities Council
ANRADIO ... Asociacion Nacional de Radio, Television, y Cine [*National Radio, Television, and Cinema Association*] [*Colorado*] (LA)
ANRAO ..... Australian National Radio Astronomy Observatory
ANRC .... Australian National Railways Commission
ANRC .... Australian National Research Council (ADA)
ANRD .... Alianza Nacional de Restauracion Democratica [*National Alliance for Democratic Restoration*] [*Equatorial Guinea*] (AF)
ANRD .... Alianza Nacional de Restauracion Democratica de Guinea Ecuatorial [*National Alliance for Democratic Restoration in Equatorial Guinea*] [*Switzerland*] (EAIO)
ANRDGE .. Alianza Nacional de Restauracion Democratica de Guinea Ecuatorial [*Political party*] (EY)
Anreg .... Anregung [*Stimulation*] [*German*] (GCA)
Anreicher ... Anreicherung [*Enrichment*] [*German*] (GCA)
ANRF .... Australian Nomads Research Foundation (ADA)
ANRI .... Australian Neurological Research Institute
ANRL .... Association of Norwegian Research Librarians (EAIO)
ANRPC ...... Association of Natural Rubber Producing Countries [*Kuala Lumpur, Malaysia*] (EAIO)
ANRR .... Australian National Register of Records
ANRS .... Assembly for Continuous Pouring of Steel (RU)
ANRT .... Association Nationale de la Recherche Technique [*National Association of Technical Research - NATR*] [*France*] [*Information service or system*] (IID)
ANS .... Afrikaans-Nasionale Studentebond [*Afrikaans National Student Union*] [*South Africa*] (AF)
ANS .... Air Navigation Service (RU)
ANS .... Alaska North Slope (OMWE)
ANS .... American-Nicaraguan School
ANS .... Andahuaylas [*Peru*] [*Airport symbol*] [*Obsolete*] (OAG)
ans .... An Das [*As The, To The, On The*] [*German*]
ANS .... Anotaton Navtikon Symvoulion [*Supreme Naval Council*] [*Greek*] (GC)
Ans .... Ansicht [*View*] [*German*]
ANS .... Archiv Narodniho Shromazdeni [*Archives of the National Assembly*] (CZ)
ANS .... Armee Nationale Sihanoukiste [*Cambodia*] (EY)
ANS .... Asociacion de Ninos Sandinistas [*Association of Sandinist Children*] [*Nicaragua*] (LA)
ANS .... Australian Numismatic Society (ADA)
ANS .... Transportes Aereos Norte-Sur Ltda. [*Chile*] [*ICAO designator*] (FAAC)
ANSA .... Agenzia Nazionale Stampa Associata [*National Associated Press Agency*] [*Italian*] (WER)
ANSA .... Agricultura Nacional SA [*Mexico*] (DSCA)
ANSA .... Antibiotik ve Ilac Ham Maddeleri Sanayii AS [*Antibiotics and Medicinal Raw Materials Industry Corp.*] (TU)
ANSA .... Association Nationale des Societes par Actions [*France*] (FLAF)

ANSA .... Australian National Shipping Agencies
ANSA .... Australian National Spearfishing Association
ANSA .... Australian National Sportfishing Association   (EAIO)
ANSA .... Australian National Sportsfishing Association   (ADA)
ANSARL... Association Nationale des Societes a Responsabilite Limitee [*France*]   (FLAF)
ANSCA...... Algodoneros Nicaraguenses Sociedad Cooperativa Anonima [*Leon, Nicaragua*]   (LAA)
anschl........ Anschliessend [*Following, Subsequent*] [*German*]
ANSCO ..... Asociacion Nacional de Supervisores del Cobre [*National Association of Copper Supervisors*] [*Chile*]   (LA)
ANSEAU... Association Nationale des Services d'Eau [*Belgium*]   (DSCA)
ANSESAL ... Salvadoran National Security Agency
ANSETT ... Ansett Airlines of Australia
ANSI........ Associazione Nazionale per la Scuola Italiana [*Italian*]   (SLS)
ANSL........ Australian National Standards Laboratory   (ADA)
ANSO/I..... Anouc Songrama I [*General mobilization unit*] [*Cambodia*]   (CL)
ANSOL ..... Australian National Social Sciences Library   (ADA)
ANSP........ Agency for National Security Planning [*South Korea*]   (ECON)
ANSP........ Asociacion Nacional de Scout de Panama [*National Scouts Association of Panama*]   (EAIO)
ANSP........ Australian National Socialist Party   (ADA)
ANSPI....... Agrupacion Nacional Sindical de Pinturas [*Spain*]   (PDAA)
Anspr .... Anspruch [*Requirement*] [*German*]
ANSSMFE ... Australian National Society of Soil Mechanics and Foundation Engineering   (PDAA)
ANSSSR.... Akademija na Naukite SSSR [*Academy of Sciences of the USSR*]   (YU)
Anst............ Anstalt [*Institute*] [*German*]
ANSTALT ... Baden Wuerttembergische Fortliche Versuchs-und Forschungs [*Germany*]   (DSCA)
ANSTEL ... Australian National Scientific and Technological Library   (ADA)
ANSTI....... African Network of Scientific and Technological Institutes [*Kenya*] [*Research center*]
ANSTIS..... Australian National Scientific and Technological Information Service   (ADA)
ANSTO ..... Australian Nuclear Science and Technology Organisation [*Formerly, AAEC*] [*Research center*] [*Australia*]   (IRC)
Anstreich ... Anstreichungen [*Marks*] [*Publishing*] [*German*]
ansv .... Ansvarig [*Responsible*] [*Sweden*]
ANSW .... Air New South Wales [*Australia*]
ANSWCU ... Association of New South Wales Credit Unions Ltd. [*Australia*]
ANT.......... Aircraft Designed by A. N. Tupolev   (RU)
Ant .... Anteil [*Part*] [*German*]
Ant .... Antenne [*Antenna*] [*German*]   (GCA)
ant .... Anteriore [*Anterior, Front*] [*Publishing*] [*Italian*]
ant .... Antico [*Old*] [*Italian*]
Ant .... Antienne [*Anthem*] [*French*]
ant .... Antigo [*Antique*] [*Portuguese*]
ant .... Antiguo [*Old*] [*Spanish*]
ant .... Antiikki [*Antiquity*] [*Finland*]
ant .... Antimeridiano [*Forenoon*] [*Italian*]   (GPO)
ant .... Antique [*Tooled*] [*Publishing*] [*French*]
ANT.......... Antrieb Neuer Technologie [*New Technology Power Plant*]
ANT.......... Armee Nationale Tchadienne [*Chadian National Army*]   (AF)
ANT.......... Arme Nucleaire Tactique [*Tactical Nuclear Weapon*] [*French*]   (WER)
ANT.......... Assemblee Nationale du Togo
ANT.......... Australian Nouveau Theatre
ANT.......... Netherlands Antilles [*ANSI three-letter standard code*]   (CNC)
ANTA .... Agence Nationale d'Information "Taratra" [*"Taratra" National Information Agency*] [*Malagasy*]   (AF)
ANTA .... Asociacion Nacional de Trabajadores del Arte [*National Art Workers Association*] [*Peru*]   (LA)
ANTA .... Asociacion Nicaraguense de Talleres Automotores [*Nicaraguan Association of Auto Repair Shops*]   (LA)
ANTA .... Associazione Nazionale Termotecnici e Aerotecnini [*Italy*]
ANTA .... Australian National Travel Association   (ADA)
ANTA .... Australian Natural Therapists Association
ANTA .... Australian Natural Therapists Association Ltd.
ANTAR .... Petroles de l'Atlantique SA [*Petroleum of the Atlantic*] [*French*]
Antarc .... Antarctic
Antarc .... Antarctica   (BARN)
ANTBIRLIK ... Antalya Tarim Satis Kooperatifleri Birligi [*Antalya Agricultural Sales Cooperatives' Union*]   (TU)
ant-bl......... Anteckningsblad [*Note Page*] [*Publishing*] [*Sweden*]
ANTC .... Asociacion Nicaraguense de Transportistas de Carga [*Nicaraguan Association of Cargo Carriers*]   (LA)
ANTC .... Australian National Television Council   (ADA)
ANTCC ..... Asociacion Nacional de Trabajadores Cientificos de Cuba [*National Association of Scientific Workers of Cuba*]   (LA)
ANTDEFCOM ... Antilles Defense Command   (MCD)
anteckn....... Anteckning [*Note*] [*Publishing*] [*Sweden*]

ANTED ..... Association of Psychologists and Educators for New Technologies of Education and Development [*Former USSR*]   (EAIO)
ANTEL...... Administracion Nacional de Telecomunicaciones [*National Telecommunications Administration*] [*El Salvador*]   (LA)
ANTEL...... Administracion Nacional de Telecomunicaciones [*National Telecommunications Administration*] [*Uruguay*]   (LA)
ANTELCO ... Administracion Nacional de Telecomunicaciones [*National Telecommunications Administration*] [*Paraguay*]   (LAA)
antep .... Anteportada [*Half-Title Page*] [*Publishing*] [*Spanish*]
ANTEP...... Association for Non-Traditional Education in the Philippines   (EAIO)
anter.......... Anteriore [*Anterior, Front*] [*Publishing*] [*Italian*]
ANTGWDPEC ... Association of National Trade Groups of Wood and Derived Products in the EEC [*European Economic Community*] Countries [*Denmark*]   (EAIO)
anth/khos .. Anthypoploiarkhos [*Lieutenant Junior Grade*] [*Navy*]   (GC)
Anthol .... Anthologie [*Anthology*] [*German*]
anthrop....... Anthhropologie [*French*]   (TPFD)
anthrop....... Anthropology   (TPFD)
Anthropol... Anthropologie [*Anthropology*] [*German*]
ANTI .... Associazione Nazionale Teleradio-Diffusioni Indipendenti [*National Private Radio-TV Broadcasting Network*] [*Italian*]   (WER)
antiallerg.... Antiallergisch [*Antiallergic*] [*German*]   (GCA)
antich .... Antique   (RU)
Antifa .... Antifaschistisch [*Anti-Fascist*] [*German*]   (EG)
ANTIKOR ... Preduzece za Proizvodnju, Promet, i Servisne Usluge Antikorozione Zastite [*Establishment for the Production, Trade, and Servicing of Anticorrosives*] [*Belgrade*]   (YU)
ANTIKVA ... Narodni Podnik pro Vyvoz a Dovoz Starozitnosti [*National Enterprise for the Export and Import of Antiques*]   (CZ)
antilog .... Antilogarithm   (RU)
ANTILOPE ... Antwerpse Inventaris van Lopende Periodieken [*Netherlands*]
ANTIOPE ... L'Acquisition Numerique et Televisualisation d'Images Organisees en Pages d'Ecriture [*French videotex system*]
antip .... Antiporta [*Frontispiece*] [*Publishing*] [*Italian*]
antiq .... Antiquite [*French*]   (TPFD)
antiq .... Antiquity   (TPFD)
antirelig...... Antireligious   (RU)
ANTIS .... Australian National Technical Information Service
ANTO........ Antarctic Treaty Organization   (ASF)
ANTO........ Aviation Scientific and Technical Society   (RU)
anton .... Antonimo [*Antonym*] [*Portuguese*]
ANTOS ...... Aviation Scientific and Technical Society of Students   (RU)
ANTOSTRAT ... Antarctic Offshore Seismic Stratigraphy Project [*Australia*]
antr............. Antroponimo [*Portuguese*]
antrop......... Anthropology   (BU)
Antrop........ Antropologia [*Anthropology*] [*Portuguese*]
ANTS........ Asociacion Nacional de Trabajadores Sociales [*National Social Workers Association*] [*Costa Rica*]   (LA)
ANTSCI .... Association Nationale de Travailleurs Sociaux de la Cote-D'Ivoire
ANTT .... Aboriginal National Theatre Trust [*Australia*]
ANTTS ...... Automatic Network Travel Time System [*Australia*]
ANTUF ..... All-Nigerian Trade Unions Federation
antw.......... Antwoord [*Answer*] [*Afrikaans*]
Antw.......... Antwort [*Answer*] [*German*]
antw bet..... Antwoord Betaal [*Reply Paid*] [*Afrikaans*] [*Business term*]
ANU .... Anadolu Universitesi [*Anatolia University*]   (TU)
ANU .... Antigua [*IYRU nationality code*] [*Airport symbol*]
ANU .... Australian National University [*National Union Catalogue of Australia symbol*]
ANU .... Automatic Navigation Equipment   (RU)
anual .... Anualmente [*Annually*] [*Spanish*]
ANUAS ..... Australian National University Atheist Society
ANUC........ Asociacion Nacional de Usuarios Campesinos [*National Association of Consumer Peasants*] [*Colorado*]   (LA)
ANUCAG ... Asociacion Nacional de Uniones de Credito Agricola y Ganadero [*Mexico*]   (DSCA)
ANUCC..... Australian National University Caving Club   (ADA)
Anude........ Asamblea Nicaraguense de Unidad Democratica [*Nicaraguan Assembly Democratic Unity*]   (PD)
ANUIES.... Asociacion Nacional de Universidades e Institutos de Ensenanza Superior [*The Mexican Association of Universities and Public Institutes of Higher Education*]   (CROSS)
ANUkrSSR ... Akademiya Nauk Ukrainskoi SSR Academy of Sciences of the Ukrainian SSR [*Former USSR*]   (DSCA)
ANULIS..... Australian National University Library and Information Service
ANUMC..... Australian National University Mountaineering Club
ANUP........ Australian National University Press   (ADA)
ANU-P....... Australian National University, Research School of Physical Sciences   (PDAA)
ANU:P....... Australian National University - Research School of the Social Sciences [*National Union Catalogue of Australia symbol*]
ANUROM ... Asociatia pentru Natiunile Unite din Romania [*Romanian Association for the United Nations*]   (RO)

ANUSA ..... Australian National University Staff Association
ANUSA ..... Australian National University Students' Association
ANUSSCG ... All-Nigerian Universities Staff Sports Clubs Games
ANUVIBHA ... Anuvrat Vishva Bharati [*Anuvrat Global Organization*] [*India*]   (EAIO)
ANUzSSR ... Akademiya Nauk Uzbekskoi SSR Academy of Sciences of the Uzbek SSR [*Former USSR*]   (DSCA)
ANV .... Accion Nacional Vasca [*Basque National Action*] [*Spain*] [*Political party*]   (PPE)
ANV .... Algemeen Nederlands Verbond [*Universal Dutch Union*] [*Afrikaans*]
ANV .... Asociacion Nacional de Vitivinicultores [*Mexico*]   (DSCA)
ANV .... Continuous Vulcanization Unit   (RU)
ANVA .... Australian Nuclear Veterans Association   (PDAA)
ANVAR ..... Agence Nationale de Valorisation de la Recherche [*National Agency for the Promotion of Research*] [*Information service or system*]   (IID)
ANVED ..... Associazione Nazionale Vendite per Corrispondenza e a Distanza [*Italy*]
ANVM .... Association Nationale des Veterinaires du Maroc [*National Veterinary Association of Morocco*]   (EAIO)
ANVSG ..... Algemene Nederlandse Vereniging voor Sociale Gezondheidszorg [*Netherlands*]   (SLS)
ANVW .... Algemene Nederlandse Vereniging voor Wijsbegeerte [*Netherlands*]   (SLS)
Anw .... Anwaerter [*Candidate (for a job)*] [*German*]
Anw .... Anwalt [*or Anwaltschaft*] [*Lawyer or Attorneyship*] [*German*]
Anw .... Anweisung [*Directive, Instruction*] [*German*]
Anw .... Anwendung [*Application*] [*German*]
ANW .... Aviacion del Noroeste SA de CV [*Mexico*] [*ICAO designator*]   (FAAC)
Anwend ...... Anwendung [*Application*] [*German*]   (GCA)
Anwesenh... Anwesenheit [*Presence*] [*German*]   (GCA)
ANWF .... Australian National Word Festival
ANWU....... African Newspaper Workers Union
ANWV .... Algemeen Nederlands Werklieden Verbond [*Netherlands*]   (BAS)
ANX .... Anax Aviation [*France*] [*ICAO designator*]   (FAAC)
ANX .... Andenes [*Norway*] [*Airport symbol*]   (OAG)
anyagell...... Anyagellatas [*Supply of Materiel*]   (HU)
anyaggazd .. Anyaggazdalkodas [*Supply Management Department*]   (HU)
anyagv........ Anyagvizsgalat [*Material Testing*]   (HU)
ANYE .... Anotati Navtiki Ygeionomiki Epitropi [*Supreme Naval Medical Board*] [*Greek*]   (GC)
ANYOLP... Arab Nationalist Youth Organization for the Liberation of Palestine   (ME)
ANZ........... Air New Zealand   (PDAA)
ANZ........... Air New Zealand Ltd. [*ICAO designator*]   (FAAC)
ANZ........... Algemeen Nederlands Zangverbond [*General Dutch Singing Society*] [*Belgium*]   (EAIO)
Anz............. Anzahl [*Number*] [*German*]
Anz............. Anzeige [*or Anzeiger*] [*Advertisement or Announcer*] [*German*]
ANZ........... Armee Nationale du Zaire [*National Army of Zaire*]   (AF)
ANZ........... Australia and New Zealand Banking Group Ltd.   (ADA)
ANZA .... Australian, New Zealand, African [*Radio network*]
ANZA .... Australian-New Zealand Association
ANZAAB... Australian and New Zealand Association of Antiquarian Booksellers
ANZAAS... Australian and New Zealand Association for the Advancement of Science
ANZAB ..... Australian and New Zealand Association of Bellringers
ANZAC ..... Australia-New Zealand Army Corps
ANZAC ..... Australian-New Zealand Army Corps   (VNW)
ANZACS... Australian and New Zealand Association for Canadian Studies
ANZAEVH ... Australian and New Zealand Association of Educators of the Visually Handicapped
ANZALDATA ... Australian and New Zealand Academic Library Statistics [*Database*]
ANZALS... Australian and New Zealand Association of Law Schools
ANZALS... Australian and New Zealand Association of Law Students   (ADA)
ANZAM.... Australia, New Zealand, and Malaysia [*Defense pact*]   (BARN)
ANZAME ... Australasian and New Zealand Association for Medical Education
ANZAMRS ... Australasian and New Zealand Association for Medieval and Renaissance Studies   (ADA)
ANZANAC ... Australian and New Zealand Association of Nurses in AIDS [*Acquired Immune Deficiency Syndrome Care*]
ANZAOMS ... Australian and New Zealand Association of Oral and Maxillofacial Surgeons
ANZAPPL ... Australian and New Zealand Association of Psychiatry, Psychology, and the Law
ANZAR ..... Australian and New Zealand Association of Radiology   (ADA)
ANZART... Australia New Zealand Artists Encounter
ANZASA... Australian and New Zealand American Studies Association   (ADA)

ANZAScA ... Australia and New Zealand Architectural Science Association   (SLS)
ANZATS... Australian and New Zealand Association of Theological Schools
ANZATS... Australian and New Zealand Association of Theological Studies
ANZATVH ... Australian and New Zealand Association of Teachers of the Visually Handicapped
ANZAWV ... Australians and New Zealanders Against the War in Vietnam   (ADA)
ANZBA ..... Australian and New Zealand Burn Association
ANZBC...... Australia-New Zealand Business Council
ANZCAN .. Australian-New Zealand-Canada [*Cable*]
ANZCCART ... Australian and New Zealand Council for the Care of Animals in Research and Teach
ANZCER... Australia New Zealand Closer Economic Relationship
ANZCERTA ... Australia-New Zealand Closer Economic Relations Trade Agreement   (BARN)
ANZCIES ... Australian and New Zealand Comparative and International Education Society
ANZCL...... Australia-New Zealand Container Line
ANZCP...... Australian and New Zealand College of Psychiatrists   (ADA)
ANZDL ..... Australia-New Zealand Direct Line
ANZEC...... Australia/New Zealand Environment Council
ANZECC... Australian and New Zealand Environment and Conservation Council
ANZECS... Australia/New Zealand/Europe Container Service
ANZEFA... Australia and New Zealand Emigrant and Families Association   (ADA)
ANZELA... Australian and New Zealand Education Law Association
ANZESC... Australian and New Zealand Eastern Shipping Conference   (ADA)
ANZF .... Australia/New Zealand Foundation
ANZFAS... Australian and New Zealand Federation of Animal Societies
ANZFM .... Australia and New Zealand Funds Management [*Banking*]
ANZHES... Australian and New Zealand History of Education Society   (ADA)
ANZMA .... Australia and New Zealand Marketing Association   (ADA)
ANZSERCH ... Australian and New Zealand Society for Epidemiology and Research in Community Health
ANZSES ... Australian and New Zealand Schools Exploring Society
ANZSES ... Australian and New Zealand Scientific Exploration Society
ANZSES ... Australian and New Zealand Solar Energy Society
ANZSNM ... Australian and New Zealand Society of Nuclear Medicine   (ADA)
ANZSOM ... Australian and New Zealand Society of Occupational Medicine   (ADA)
ANZSOS... Australian and New Zealand Society of Oral Surgeons   (ADA)
ANZSRL... Australian and New Zealand Scientific Research Liaison
ANZSSA... Australian and New Zealand Student Services Association   (ADA)
ANZSTS ... Australian and New Zealand Society for Theological Studies
ANZTLA... Australian and New Zealand Theological Library Association
ANZTUCC ... Australian and New Zealand Trade Union Coordinating Committee
ANZUK ..... Australia, New Zealand, and United Kingdom
ANZUS ..... Australia, New Zealand, and the United States [*Signatories to the Tripartite Security Treaty of 1951*]
ANZWONA ... Australian and New Zealand Web Offset Newspaper Association   (ADA)
AO .... AbgabenOrdnung [*Tax regulations*] [*German*]
AO .... Acridine Orange   (RU)
AO .... Adjudant-Offisier [*Adjutant-Officer*] [*Afrikaans*]
AO .... Administrative Department   (RU)
a/o............. Advance Report   (RU)
AO .... Aerial Fragmentation Bomb   (RU)
AO .... Aeromere SpA [*Italy*] [*ICAO aircraft manufacturer identifier*]   (ICAO)
AO .... Air Detachment   (RU)
AO .... Air Section   (RU)
AO .... Aktivni Opatreni [*Active Measures or Covert Action*]   (CZ)
AO .... Alempi Oikenstutkinto [*Finland*]
AO .... Algemeen Ouderdomswet [*General Old Age Insurance Act*] [*Netherlands*]   (WEN)
ao................ Allatorvos [*Veterinarian*]   (HU)
AO .... Ambulance Officer
ao................ Ammattiosasto [*Finland*]
AO .... Anatheoritiki Omada [*Revisionist Group*]   (GC)
aO .... An der Oder [*On the Oder River*] [*German*]   (EG)
AO .... Angola [*ANSI two-letter standard code*]   (CNC)
AO .... Anonim Ortaklari [*Partnership*] [*TAO*] [*See also*]   (TU)
AO .... Anonim Ortakligi [*Joint-Stock Partnership*] [*Turkey*]   (CED)
AO .... Anordnung [*Order*] [*German*]   (WEN)
AO .... Aosta [*Car registration plates*] [*Italian*]
AO .... Armijska Oblast [*Army Region*]   (YU)
ao................ Army Train   (BU)
AO .... Artillery Section   (BU)
ao................ Asianomainen [*Finland*]

AO .... Asian Outreach International [*Missionary association*] [*Hong Kong*]
AO .... Astronomical Observatory (RU)
AO .... Athlitikos Omilos [*Athletic Club*] [*Plus initial letter of club name*] (GC)
AO .... Atomic Orbital (RU)
AO .... Atomic Weapons (RU)
AO .... Auslandsorganisation [*Foreign Organization*] [*of the Nazi Party*]
ao .... Ausserordentlich [*Extraordinary*] [*German*]
AO .... Australian Opera (ADA)
AO .... Authority to Officiate [*Church of England in Australia*]
AO .... Automatic Optimizer [*Computers*] (RU)
AO .... Automatic Pumping Unit (RU)
AO .... Autonomous Oblast (RU)
AO .... Avanguardia Operaia [*Worker's Vanguard*] [*Italy*] [*Political party*] (PPE)
AO .... Aviation Equipment [*Aircraft maintenance*] (RU)
AO .... Avtonomyni Okrug (Autonomus Okrug) [*Commonwealth of Independent States*] (EECI)
AO .... Joint-Stock Company (RU)
AO .... Officer of the Order of Australia (ADA)
AO .... Operational Airfield (RU)
AOA .... Action Outdoor Association [*Australia*]
AOA .... African Overseas Agency
AOA .... Airlines of Australia
AOA .... Antioxidant Activity (RU)
AOA .... Asociacion Odontologica Antioquera [*Colombia*] (COL)
AOA .... Asociacion Odontologica Argentina [*Dental Association of Argentina*] [*Buenos Aires*] (LAA)
AOA .... Australian Onion Association
AOA .... Australian Optometrical Association (ADA)
AOA .... Australian Orthopaedic Association (ADA)
AOA .... Australian Osteopathic Association
AOABH .... Assault Occasioning Actual Bodily Harm [*Criminology*]
aoabr .... Army Gun-Artillery Brigade (BU)
AOACEurope ... Association of Official Analytical Chemists - Europe [*Bennekom, Netherlands*] (EAIO)
AOAD ...... Arab Organisation for Agricultural Development
AOAD ...... Arab Organization for Agricultural Development (EAIO)
AOAITM .. Asociatia Oamenilor de Arta din Institutiile Teatrale si Muzicale [*Association of Artists in Theatrical and Musical Institutions*] (RO)
AOANS ..... Asociacion de Organismos de Agricultores del Norte de Sonora [*Mexico*] (DSCA)
AOAPC ..... Association des Organisations Africaines de Promotion Commerciale [*Association of African Organizations for Trade Promotion*] (AF)
AOAS .... Arab Organization of Administrative Sciences (EAIO)
AOATC ..... Atlantic Ocean Air Traffic Control [*NATO*] (NATG)
AOB .... Aerial Fragmentation Bomb (RU)
AOB .... Association des Originaires de Bandounga [*Association of Natives of Bandounga*]
AOB .... Atlanta Olympic Band (OLYM)
AOB .... Atlanta Olympic Broadcasting (OLYM)
AOB .... Aziatische Ontwikkelingsbank [*Benelux*] (BAS)
AOBC .... American Overseas Book Co.
AOBF .... Australian Outward Bound Foundation
AOBO .... Australian Opera and Ballet Orchestra
AOC .... Alianca Operaria Camponesa [*Peasants and Workers Alliance*] [*Portugal*] [*Political party*] (PPE)
AOC .... Alvis Owners Club [*North Droitwich, Worcestershire, England*] (EAIO)
AOC .... Appellation d'Origine Controlee [*French*]
AOC .... Arabian Oil Company Ltd. [*Riyadh, Saudi Arabia*] (ME)
AOC .... Associated Overseas Countries of the European Economic Community
AOC .... Ataturk Orman Ciftligi [*Ataturk Forest Farm*] (TU)
AOC .... Atlanta Organizing Committee (OLYM)
AOC .... Attock Oil Company [*Pakistan*]
AOC .... Australian Olympic Committee
AOC .... JV Avcom [*Russian Federation*] [*ICAO designator*] (FAAC)
AOCA .... Australian Oilseed Crushers' Association
AOCA .... Australian Owned Companies Association
AOCC .... Australian Onion Coordinating Committee
AOCC .... Australian Overseas Construction Council
AOCCOS... Australian Organisations Co-Ordinating Committee for Overseas Students in New South Wales (ADA)
AOCRS...... African Organization of Cartography and Remote Sensing [*Algeria*] (EAIO)
AOD .... Aerial Sprayer (RU)
AOD .... Alliance of Oil Development [*Australia*] (ADA)
AODA........ Ananeotiki Omada Dimokratikis Aristeras [*Restorative Group of the Democratic Left*] [*Greek*] (GC)
AODC .... Argentine Oceanographic Data Center (ASF)
AODC .... Australian Oceanographic Data Centre (ADA)
AODRO..... Australian Overseas Disaster Response Organization

AOE .... Africa Occidental Espanola
AOE .... Allatorvostudomanyi Egyetem [*Veterinary Science, University of Budapest*] [*Hungary*] (ARC)
AOE .... Astronomical Observatory Imeni V. P. Engel'gardt (RU)
AOE .... Avance a l'Ouverture d'Echappement [*French*] (MTD)
AOEA .... Awards for Outstanding Export Achievement [*Australia*]
AOEK .... Avtonomos Organismos Ellinikou Kapnou [*Autonomous Greek Tobacco Organization*]
AOEK .... Avtonomos Organismos Ergatikis Katoikias [*Autonomous Organization for Workers' Housing*] [*Greek*] (GC)
AOeR .... Anstalt des Oeffentlichen Rechts [*Institution Incorporated under Public Law*] (EG)
AOF .... Afrique Occidentale Francaise [*French West Africa*] (AF)
AOF .... Arbejdernes Oplysningsforbound [*Workers' Educational Association*] [*Denmark*] (WEN)
AOF .... Association des Orientalistes de France [*Orientalist Association of France*] (EAIO)
AOF .... Association d'Oceanographie Francaise
AOF .... Australian Oilseeds Federation
AOF .... Australian Olympic Federation (ADA)
AOF .... Australian Orchid Foundation
AOFO .... Australian Odd Feet Organisation
AOG .... Arbeitsgemeinschaft Oesterreichischer Entomologen [*Austria*] (SLS)
AOG .... Australian Oil and Gas Corp. (ADA)
AOGA .... Assembly of God in Australia
AOGZ .... Austriski Opsti Gradanski Zakonik [*Austrian General Civil Code*] (YU)
AOH .... Automatic Number Identification (RU)
AOI .... Academia Ophthalmologica Internationalis (EAIO)
AOI .... Ancona [*Italy*] [*Airport symbol*] (OAG)
AOI .... Arab Organization for Industrialization
AOI .... Associazione Ottica Italiana [*Italian*] (SLS)
AOIC .... Arab Oil Investments Company (ME)
AOIP .... Association Ouvriers Instruments Precision [*Association of Precision Instrument Operatives*] [*France*] (PDAA)
AOIP .... Australian Organizations Industrial Policy
AOIS .... Australian Overseas Information Service
AOIUU...... Adyge Oblast Institute for the Advanced Training of Teachers (RU)
AOJ .... Aero-Jet SA [*Switzerland*] [*ICAO designator*] (FAAC)
AOJ .... Aomori [*Japan*] [*Airport symbol*] (OAG)
AOK .... Aerovias del Atlantico Ltd. [*Colombia*] [*ICAO designator*] (FAAC)
AOK .... Allgemeine Ortskrankenkasse [*General Health Insurance Fund*] [*German*] (WEN)
AOK .... Armeeoberkommando [*Army High Command*] [*German*]
AOK .... Karpathos [*Greece*] [*Airport symbol*] (OAG)
AOKhB ..... Aerial Fragmentation Chemical Bomb (RU)
AOKosmeta ... Autonomna Oblast Kosovo-Metohija [*Autonomous Region of Kosovo-Metohija*] [*Serbia*]
AOKosovometohija ... Autonomna Oblast Kosovo-Metohija [*Autonomous Region of Kosovo-Metohija*] [*Serbia*] (YU)
AOKP .... Asfalistikos Organismos Kindynon Polemou [*War Risks Insurance Organization*] (GC)
AOL .... Aeidinkielen Opettajain Liitto [*Finland*] (SLS)
AOL .... African Ocean Lines Ltd. [*Nigeria*]
AOL .... Air Exel Executive [*France*] [*ICAO designator*] (FAAC)
AOL .... Australian Ocean Lines Proprietary Ltd.
AOL .... Paso De Los Libres [*Argentina*] [*Airport symbol*] (OAG)
AOLG .... Australian [*Commonwealth*] Office of Local Government [*National Union Catalogue of Australia symbol*]
AOLGU ..... Astronomical Observatory of the Leningrad State University (RU)
AOLIN ..... Australian Open Learning Information Network
AOM .... Associes d'Outre-Mer [*France*] (FLAF)
AOM .... Australian Options Market
AOM .... Naval Operational Air Station (RU)
AOMA .... Arab Organization for the Manufacture of Armaments (PDAA)
AOMC .... Associated Ores Mining Company [*Nigeria*]
AOMK .... Association des Ouvriers et Manoeuvres Khmers [*Cambodian Workers and Unskilled Laborers Association*] (CL)
AON .... Academy of Social Sciences at the TsK KPSS (RU)
AON .... Aero Trade International [*Romania*] [*ICAO designator*] (FAAC)
AON .... Anorthotiki Organosis Neon [*Restorative Organization of Youth*] [*Cyprus*] (GC)
AON .... Special-Purpose Artillery (RU)
AON .... Special-Purpose Aviation (RU)
AONA........ Australian Office of National Assessments [*National Union Catalogue of Australia symbol*]
AONA........ Australian Orthopaedic Nurses' Association
AONBP-CE ... Association des Organisations Nationales de la Boulangerie et de la Patisserie de la CE [*Association of National Organizations in the Bakery and Confectionery Trade in the European Community*] [*Belgium*] (EAIO)
AONSU ..... Academy of Social Sciences and Social Management (BU)

AOO .... Airfield Lighting Equipment   (RU)
AOOA .... Avtonomos Oikodomikos Organismos Axiomatikon [*Officers'*
                Autonomous Construction Organization] [*Greek*]   (GC)
AOOB .... Australian Order of Old Bastards
AOOC .... Albertville Olympic Organizing Committee [*Albertville, France*]
                (EAIO)
AOOI .... Associazione Otologica Ospedaliera Italiano [*Italian*]   (SLS)
AOP .... Aeropiloto-Sociedade Exploradora de Servicos Aereos Lda.
                [*Portugal*] [*ICAO designator*]   (FAAC)
AOP .... Asociacion Ornitologica del Plata [*Argentina*]   (DSCA)
AOP .... Austrian Liberation Party   (RU)
AOP .... Main Astronomical Observatory in Pulkovo   (RU)
AOPA .... Aircraft Owners and Pilots Association of Australia   (ADA)
AOPA ofSA ... Aircraft Owners' and Pilots' Association of South Africa
                (AA)
AOPC .... Australian Overseas Projects Corporation   (ADA)
AOPM .... Australian Office of Parliamentary [*Counsel*] [*National Union
                Catalogue of Australia symbol*]
AOPO .... African Oilseed Producers' Organisation
Ao Prof ...... Ausserordentlicher Professor [*Assistant Professor*] [*German*]
                (GCA)
AOPU .... Asian Oceanic Postal Union [*Later, APPU*] [*China, Korea,
                Philippines, Thailand*]
AOQ .... Australian Organisation for Quality
AOQC .... Australian Organisation for Quality Control   (ADA)
AOQC .... Australian Organization for Quality Control
AOR .... Abnormal Occurrence Report
AOR .... Administrativno-Operativni Rukovodilac [*Administrative-
                Operational Supervisor*] [*Military*]   (YU)
AOR .... Alor Setar [*Malaysia*] [*Airport symbol*]   (OAG)
AOR .... Arabskii Obshchii Rynok
AOR .... Association of Rehabilitation Ltd.
AOR .... Australian Oil Refining Proprietary Ltd.   (ADA)
AORA .... Australian Organisation for the Relief of AIDS
AORN .... Automatic Optimum Load Distribution Device   (RU)
AORTA ..... Australian Organization of Retired Teachers Associations
AOS .... Acoustic Feedback   (RU)
AOS .... Allied Ordnance Co. of Singapore
AOS .... Anotaton Oikonomikon Symvoulion [*Supreme Economic
                Council*]   (GC)
AOS .... Antifasisticka Omladina Srbije [*Anti-Fascist Youth of Serbia*]
                (YU)
AOS .... Apostleship of the Sea [*See also AM*] [*Vatican City, Vatican City
                State*]   (EAIO)
AOs .... Artiljeriski Osmatrac [*Artillery Observer*]   (YU)
AOS .... Asociatia Oamenilor de Stiinta [*Roman Catholic religious order*]
                (SLS)
AOS .... Ataturk Ogrenci Sitesi [*Ataturk Student Dormitory*] [*Istanbul
                University*]   (TU)
AOS .... Australian Optical Society
AOS .... Automatic Simultaneous Jettison Device [*Fuel tanks*]   (RU)
AOS .... Automatic Windshield Heater   (RU)
AOS .... Servicios Aereos del Sol SA de CV [*Mexico*] [*ICAO designator*]
                (FAAC)
AOSARIO ... Association des Originaires de la Seguia El Hamra et du Rio De
                Oro [*Association of Natives of Seguia El Hamra and Rio De
                Oro*] [*Saharan*]   (AF)
AOSAS ...... Aboriginal and Torres Strait Islander Study Award Scheme
                [*Australia*]
AOSC .... Arab Organization for Space Communications
AOSIS .... Alliance of Small Island States
AOSPK ...... Association des Originaires du Srok de Prey Krabas [*Association
                of Natives of Srok (District), Prey Krabas*]   (CL)
AOT .... Asociacion Obrera Textil [*Textile Workers Association*]
                [*Argentina*]   (LA)
AOT .... Deutsche Forschungs-and Versuchsanstalt fur Luft EV
                [*Germany*] [*ICAO designator*]   (FAAC)
AOTA .... American Society of Travel Agents [*ASTA*]   (RU)
AOTA .... Australian Oversea Transport Association   (ADA)
AOTC .... Australian and Overseas Telecommunications Corp.
AOTC .... Australian Overseas Trading Corporation   (ADA)
AOTH .... Algemene Ooreenkoms oor Tariewe en Handel [*General
                Agreement on Tariffs and Trade - GATT*] [*Afrikaans*]
AOTS .... Advanced Orbital Test Satellite [*European Space Agency*]
AOU .... Air Reinforcement Detachment   (RU)
AOU .... Australasian Ornithologists' Union   (ADA)
AOVDQS .. Appellation d'Origine Vin de Qualite Superieure [*Trademark for
                Vintage Wine of Superior Quality*]
AOVP .... Australian Ordnance Vehicle Park   (ADA)
AOW .... Algemene Ouderdomswet [*Benelux*]   (BAS)
AOW .... Asia-Oceania Workshop [*Computer science*]   (TNIG)
AOX .... Aerotaxi del Valle [*Colombia*] [*ICAO designator*]   (FAAC)
AOZ .... Automobilove Opravarenske Zavody [*Automobile Repair Shops*]
                (CZ)
ap .... Aamupaivalla [*Before Noon*] [*Finland*]   (GPO)
Ap .... Abpraller [*Ricochet*] [*German*]   (GCA)

AP .... Academisch Proefschrift [*Benelux*]   (BAS)
AP .... Access Permittee [*Access Permit*] [*Nuclear energy*]   (NRCH)
AP .... Accion del Pueblo [*Costa Rica*] [*Political party*]   (EY)
AP .... Accion Popular [*Popular Action*] [*Spain*] [*Political party*]   (PPE)
AP .... Accion Popular [*Popular Action*] [*Peru*] [*Political party*]   (PPW)
AP .... Accueil et la Promotion
AP .... Action Publique [*French*]   (FLAF)
AP .... Adalet Partisi [*Justice Party - JP*]   (TU)
AP .... Aerolineas Peruanas [*Cali-Sucursal*]   (COL)
AP .... Aero Spacelines [*ICAO aircraft manufacturer identifier*]   (ICAO)
AP .... Agen Polisi [*Policeman*]   (IN)
AP .... Agonistiki Protoporeia [*Struggling Vanguard*]   (GC)
AP .... Agrarian Party [*Albania*] [*Political party*]   (EY)
a/p .... Airport   (RU)
AP .... Air Regiment   (RU)
ap .... Alempi Palkkausluokka [*Finland*]
AP .... Algemeen Politieblad van het Koninkrijk der Nederlanden
                [*Netherlands*]   (BAS)
AP .... Alianza para el Progreso [*Alliance for Progress*] [*Washington,
                DC*]
AP .... Alianza Patriotica [*Bolivia*] [*Political party*]   (EY)
AP .... Alianza Popular [*Popular Alliance*] [*Madrid, Spain*]   (PPW)
AP .... Alianza Productiva [*Productive Alliance*] [*El Salvador*]   (LA)
AP .... Alliance Party [*Fiji*] [*Political party*]   (EY)
ap .... Allomasparancsnok [*Garrison Commander, Railroad Transport
                Officer*]   (HU)
AP .... Amerikanisches Patent [*American Patent*] [*German*]
AP .... Aminopterin   (RU)
AP .... Amsterdams Peil [*Amsterdam Ordnance Datum*] [*Netherlands*]
                (GPO)
AP .... Analog Converter   (RU)
AP .... Anavatan Partisi [*Motherland Parties*]   (EAIO)
AP .... Andhra Pradesh [*State in southeast India*]
AP .... Angkutan Pertambangan [*Commercial firm*]   (DS)
AP .... Anglo-Pacific Shipping Ltd. [*Australia*]
AP .... Anilinpunkt [*Aniline Point*] [*German*]   (GCA)
ap .... Anno Passato [*Last Year*] [*Italian*]   (GPO)
AP .... Antenna Switch, Duplexer   (RU)
AP .... Antimony Products [*Chemical plant*] [*South Africa*]
ap .... Apartamento [*Apartment*] [*Portuguese*]
ap .... Aparte [*Apart, Aside*] [*Spanish*]
ap .... Apostol [*Apostle*] [*Spanish*]
Ap. .... Apotheke [*or Apotheker*] [*Pharmacy or Pharmacist*] [*German*]
AP .... A Protester [*To Be Protested*] [*French*]
AP .... Arbeitsprogramm [*Work Program*] [*German*]   (ADPT)
AP .... Arkhigeion Pyrovolikou [*Artillery Command*]   (GC)
AP .... Armia Polska [*Polish Army*] [*Poland*]
AP .... Artillery Preparation   (RU)
AP .... Artillery Range   (RU)
AP .... Artillery Regiment   (RU)
AP .... Ascoli Piceno [*Car registration plates*] [*Italian*]
AP .... Asia Pacific Container Terminal, Inc. [*Taiwan*]
AP .... Asociacion Proverista [*"For the Truth" Association*] [*Spanish*]
                (WER)
AP .... Assistance Publique [*French*]
AP .... Association en Participation [*French*]   (FLAF)
AP .... Associative Memory   (RU)
AP .... Astronomical Point   (RU)
AP .... Astynomia Poleon [*City Police*] [*Greek*]   (GC)
a/p .... Atmoploion [*Steamship*]   (GC)
AP .... Auftragspuffer [*Instructional Nudgeri*] [*German*]   (ADPT)
AP .... Australia Party   (ADA)
AP .... Australia Post   (ADA)
AP .... Automatic Pilot, Autopilot, Gyropilot   (RU)
AP .... Automatic Sampler   (RU)
AP .... Automatic Switch   (RU)
AP .... Automatic Translation   (RU)
AP .... Automatic Tuning   (RU)
AP .... Automobile Industry   (RU)
AP .... Automobilklub Polski [*Polish Automobile Club*]   (POL)
AP .... Autonomna Pokrajina [*Autonomous Province*]   (YU)
AP .... Autorisations de Programme
AP .... Avant-Poste [*Outpost*] [*Military*] [*French*]   (MTD)
ap .... Avaries Particulieres [*French*]
AP .... Aviation Populaire [*France*]
a/p .... Aviopoletanje [*Takeoff*] [*Aviation*]   (YU)
AP .... Department of Primary Industries and Energy - Central Library
                [*National Union Catalogue of Australia symbol*]
AP .... Regimental Artillery   (RU)
Ap. .... Submersible Artesian Pump   (RU)
AP .... Subscriber's Panel   (RU)
AP .... Territorio do Amapa [*Portuguese*]
AP .... Truck Trailer   (RU)
AP .... Yielding Arch Support [*Mining*]   (RU)
APA .... Aboriginal Protection Association
APA .... Aborigines Progress Association [*Australia*]   (ADA)

APA .... Aborigines Protection Association
APA .... Accion Patriotica Argentina [*Argentine Patriotic Action*]   (LA)
APA .... Acetone Producers Association [*Belgium*]   (EAIO)
APA .... Adoptive Parents Association [*Australia*]
APA .... Aerovias Panama [*Bogota-Agencia*]   (COL)
APA .... African Purchase Areas
APA .... Airport Mobile Power Unit   (RU)
APA .... Albanian People's Army
APA .... All Parties Administration [*Australia*]   (ADA)
APA .... Apachito [*Race of maize*] [*Mexico*]
apa............. Apostolica [*Apostolic*] [*Spanish*]
APA .... Approved Pathology Authority [*Australia*]
APA .... Asociacion del Personal Aeronautica [*Airline Personnel Association*] [*Argentina*]   (LA)
APA .... Asociacion de Proveedores Agricolas [*Association of Agricultural Suppliers*] [*El Salvador*]   (LA)
APA .... Asociacion Paleontologica Argentina Buenos Aires [*Argentina*]   (SLS)
APA .... Asociacion para la Prevencion de Accidentes [*Association for the Prevention of Accidents*] [*Spain*]   (PDAA)
APA .... Asociacion Peruana de Astronomia [*Peru*]   (SLS)
APA .... Associacao de Amizade Portugal-RP Angola [*Portugal-Angola Friendship Association*]   (EAIO)
APA .... Associacao Paulista de Avicultura [*Brazil*]   (DSCA)
APA .... Associacao Protetora de Animais [*Portuguese*]
APA .... Association des Producteurs Agricoles [*Haiti*]   (EY)
APA .... Association of Paediatric Anaesthetists of Great Britain and Ireland [*Birmingham, England*]   (EAIO)
APA .... Association of Physicians of Australasia   (ADA)
APA .... Association of Practicing Accountants
APA .... Astrakhan' Party Archives   (RU)
APA .... Australian Paediatric Association   (ADA)
APA .... Australian Peace Alliance
APA .... Australian Perendale Association
APA .... Australian Physiotherapy Association   (ADA)
APA .... Australian Podiatry Association
APA .... Australian Population Association
APA .... Australian Postmasters' Association   (ADA)
APA .... Australian Pre-School Association   (ADA)
APA .... Australian Press Association
APA .... Australian Provincial Assurance   (ADA)
APA .... Austria Presse Agentur [*Austria Press Agency*] [*Vienna*]   (WEN)
APA .... Avrupa Para Anlasmasi [*European Monetary Agreement*]   (TU)
APAA .... Adelaide [*Australia*] [*ICAO location identifier*]   (ICLI)
APAA .... ASEAN [*Association of South East Asian Nations*] Port Authorities Association   (DS)
APAA .... Asian Patent Attorneys Association   (EA)
APAA .... Association of Professional Aestheticians of Australia   (ADA)
APAAE..... Asia-Pacific Association for Agricultural Education
APAAL..... Association Professionnelle des Artistes et Artisans d'Art Lao [*Lao Professional Artists and Artisans Association*]   (CL)
APAAP...... Association de la Presse Anglo-Americaine de Paris [*Anglo-American Press Association of Paris*]   (EAIO)
APABA..... Australian Pig Artificial Breeding Association
APAC........ Air Pollution Appeal Committee [*South Africa*]   (AA)
APAC........ Asociacion Peruana para el Avance de la Ciencia [*Peruvian Association for the Advancement of Science*] [*Lima*]   (LAA)
APAC........ Asociacion de Profesionales de Accion Catolica [*Professionals Catholic Action Association*] [*Argentina*]   (LA)
APAC........ Associacao Paranaense de Cafeicultores [*Brazil*]   (DSCA)
APAC........ Australian Pesticides Analytical Committee
APAC........ Australian Prison After-Care Council   (ADA)
APACA...... Australian Preservation and Conservation Abroad Group
APACE...... Appropriate Technology and Community Environment Group [*Australia*]   (ADA)
APACE...... Asian Pacific Alliance for Creative Equality
APACI....... Association for the Promotion of African Community Initiatives   (EAIO)
APAD........ Adelaide [*Australia*] [*ICAO location identifier*]   (ICLI)
APADA ..... Asociacion de Productores Agrarios del Delta Argentino [*Argentina*]   (LAA)
APADA ..... Australian Petroleum Agents and Distributors Association
APADI....... Asosiasi Perpustakaan, Arsip dan Dokumentasi Indonesia
APAE........ Asociacion de Productores de Aceites Esenciales [*Essential Oils Producers Association*] [*Guatemala*]   (LA)
APAEIM ... Association des Parents et Amis des Enfants Inadaptes du Maroc [*Morocco*]
APAG .... Association Europeenne des Producteurs d'Acides Gras [*European Association of Fatty Acid Producing Companies*]   (EAIO)
APAG .... Atlantic Policy Advisory Group [*Belgium*]   (EAIO)
APAG .... Atlantic Political Advisory Group [*NATO*]
APAGRO .. Asociacion de Productores Agricolas del Guarico [*Venezuela*]   (DSCA)
APAI......... Australian Public Affairs Information Service [*AUSINET database*]   (ADA)

APAIATM ... Associacao Portuguesa dos Armazenistas e Importadores de Acos, Tubos, e Metais [*Portugal*]   (EAIO)
apais........... Apaisado [*Oblong*] [*Publishing*] [*Spanish*]
APAIS .... Australian Public Affairs Information Service [*National Library of Australia*]   (PDAA)
APAJ .... Asia Pacific Association of Japan
APAK .... Association Professionnelle Apolitique du Katanga [*Nonpolitical Professional Association of Katanga*]
APAL........ Albany [*Australia*] [*ICAO location identifier*]   (ICLI)
APAL........ Asociacion de Padres de Alumnos de Liceo [*Association of Parents of Secondary School Students*] [*Uruguay*]   (LA)
APAL........ Asociacion Psiquiatrica de la America Latina [*Venezuela*]   (SLS)
APAM .... Associacao Politica do Arquipelago da Madeira [*Political Association of the Madeira Archipelago*] [*Portuguese*]   (WER)
APAN .... Administracion de los Parques Nacionales [*Venezuela*]   (DSCA)
APANAC... Panamanian Association for the Advancement of Science   (EAIO)
Apanc........ Armia Pancerna [*Armoured Army*] [*Poland*]
AP & P....... Accounting Practices and Principles [*Australia*]
APAO .... Asia-Pacific Academy of Ophthalmology [*Tokyo, Japan*]   (EAIO)
APAP........ Asociacion Paraguaya de Administracion del Personal [*Asuncion, Paraguay*]   (LAA)
APAP........ Asociacion Peruana de Agencias de Publicidad [*Association of Peruvian Advertising Agencies*]   (LA)
APAP........ Association Interdepartementale pour la Promotion des Agriculteurs dans le Parc Naturel Regional du Vercors [*France*]
APAPHAM ... Association Professionnelle des Armateurs a la Peche Hauturiere au Maroc
APAR........ Adelaide [*Australia*] [*ICAO location identifier*]   (ICLI)
apart......... Apartamento [*Separation*] [*Portuguese*]
APAS........ Asociacion de Productores Avicolas Sur [*Uruguay*]   (DSCA)
APAS........ Association of Personal Assistants and Secretaries [*Leamington Spa, Warwickshire, England*] [*Defunct*]   (EAIO)
APAS........ Association of Public Authority Surveyors [*Australia*]
APASCO ... Australian Planning and Systems Company   (ADA)
apat........... Apatite Mines [*Topography*]   (RU)
APAT........ Australasian Porcelain Art Teachers [*An association*]
APATU...... All-Poland Alliance of Trade Unions   (EAIO)
APAU .... Andhra Pradesh Agricultural University [*India*]   (DSCA)
APAU .... Association Professionnelle de l'Administration Universitaire [*Professional Association of University Adminstration*] [*Algeria*]
APAVIT .... Asociacion Panamena de Agencias de Viajes y Turismo   (EY)
APAVIT .... Asociacion Peruana de Agencias de Viajes y Turismo [*Peruvian Association of Travel and Tourist Agencies*]   (LA)
APAX........ Adelaide [*Australia*] [*ICAO location identifier*]   (ICLI)
APB .... Aanvullende Personele Belastingen [*Benelux*]   (BAS)
APB .... Aboriginal Protection Board [*Australia*]
AP/B .... Additional Pension/Benefit
APB .... Agriculture Protection Board [*Western Australia*]
APB .... Air Atlantique Air Publicite [*France*] [*ICAO designator*]   (FAAC)
APB .... Aircraft Design Office   (RU)
APB .... Associacao Paulista de Bibliotecarios [*Brazil*]   (SLS)
APB .... Associacao Portuguesa de Bancos [*Portugal*]   (EY)
APB .... Association Professionnelle des Banques [*Employers' organization*] [*Burkina Faso*]
APB .... Australian Publishers' Bureau
APBA........ Asia Pacific Business Association
APBA........ Asociacion de Periodistas de Buenos Aires [*Buenos Aires Newsmen's Association*] [*Argentina*]   (LA)
APBA........ Australasian Power Boat Association
APBA........ Australian Pig Breeders' Association
APBC........ Australia Philippines Business Council
APBD .... Association Professionnelle des Bibliothecaires et Documentalistes [*Belgium*]   (SLS)
APBEF ...... Association Professionnelle des Banques et Etablissements Financiers [*Burkina Faso*]   (EY)
APBH .... Broken Hill [*Australia*] [*ICAO location identifier*]   (ICLI)
apble......... Apreciable [*Valued*] [*Spanish*]
APBM....... Superheavy Artillery Regiment   (RU)
APBN .... Anggaran Pendapatan dan Belandja Negara [*Estimate of State Expenditures and Income (National budget)*]   (IN)
APBPA....... Australian PaintBall Players' Association
APBR........ Broome [*Australia*] [*ICAO location identifier*]   (ICLI)
APBS .... Association of Permanent Building Societies [*Australia*]   (ADA)
APBS .... Australian Pig Breeders' Society
APC .... Abadan Petrochemical Company   (ME)
APC .... Adelaide Potters' Club [*Australia*]
APC .... African Peanut Council
APC .... Agence Presse Comores
APC .... Agricultural Prices Commission [*India*]   (PDAA)
APC .... Aircraft Production Commission [*Australia*]   (ADA)

APC .... Alianza Popular Conservadora [*Nicaragua*] [*Political party*] (EY)

APC .... Alianza Popular Cristiana [*Popular Christian Alliance*] [*Ecuador*] (LA)

APC .... Alliance des Pays Producteurs de Cacao [*Cocoa Producers' Alliance*] [*Use COPAL*] (AF)

APC .... All-People's Congress [*Sierra Leone*] [*Political party*] (PPW)

APC .... Altona Petrochemical Company Ltd. [*Australia*] (ADA)

APC .... Arunachal People's Conference [*India*] [*Political party*] (PPW)

APC .... Assemblee Populaire Communale [*People's Communal Assembly*] [*Algeria*] (AF)

APC .... Associacao Paulista de Cafeicultores [*Brazil*] (DSCA)

APC .... Association des Planteurs de Caoutchouc [*Rubber Planters Association*] [*Cambodia*] (CL)

APC .... Association for Progressive Communications [*Australia*]

APC .... Association of Property Conveyancers [*Australia*]

APC .... Association "Pierres Carrees" [*France*] (EAIO)

APC .... Associu di Patrioti Corsi [*Association of Corsican Patriots*] [*France*] [*Political party*] (PPE)

APC .... Atelier de Production et Creation [*French fashion label*]

APC .... Australasian Petroleum Co.

APC .... Australian Parents' Centre (ADA)

APC .... Australian Parents' Council (ADA)

APC .... Australian Peace Committee

APC .... Australian People's Congress

APC .... Australian Pioneers' Club

APC .... Australian Podiatry Council

APC .... Australian Police College (ADA)

APC .... Australian Polo Council

APC .... Australian Postal Commission (ADA)

APC .... Australian Press Council (ADA)

APC .... Australian Production Committee

APC .... Australian Productivity Council

APC .... Australian Prostitutes Collective

APC .... Autoridad Portuaria de Corinto [*Nicaragua*] (LAA)

APC .... Azote and Produits Chimiques SA

APCA .... Asamblee Permanente des Chambres d'Agriculture [*France*] (DSCA)

APCA .... Asociacion de Periodicos Centroamericanos [*Association of Central American Newspapers*] (LA)

APCA .... Assemblee Permanente des Chambres d'Agriculture [*Industrial organization*] [*France*] (EY)

APCA .... Australian Payments Clearing Association

APCA .... Australian Pest Controllers Association

APCA .... Australian Physical Culture Association (ADA)

APCA .... Australian Port Charge Additional

APCA .... Australian Postgraduate Course Awards

APCAS ...... Asia and the Pacific Commission on Agricultural Statistics [*Formerly, Asia and the Far East Commission on Agricultural Statistics*] (EA)

APCB .... Associacao Paranaense de Criadores de Bovinos [*Brazil*] (DSCA)

APCB .... Associacao Paulista de Criadores de Bovinos [*Brazil*] (DSCA)

APCC .... American-Paraguayan Cultural Center [*Paraguay*] (EAIO)

APCC .... Animal and Plant Control Commission [*Australia*]

APCC .... Aral Philanthropic Commercial Center (EAIO)

APCC .... Asian and Pacific Coconut Community [*Jakarta, Indonesia*] (EAIO)

APCC .... Asociacion Pro-Cultura China [*Pro-Chinese Culture Association*] [*Mexico*] (LA)

APCC .... Assessoria de Planejamento Coordenacao e Controle [*Natal, Brazil*] (LAA)

APCC .... Associacao Paulista dos Criadores de Charoles [*Brazil*] (DSCA)

APCC .... Association des Planteurs de Caoutchouc du Cambodge [*Cambodian Rubber Planters Association*] (CL)

APCC .... Australian Pony Club Council

APCC .... Australian Professional Consultants Council

APCC .... Cocos Islands [*Australia*] [*ICAO location identifier*] (ICLI)

APCChE .... Asian Pacific Confederation of Chemical Engineering (EAIO)

APCCI ...... Assemblee Permanente des Chambres de Commerce et d'Industrie [*Chambers of Commerce of Industry*] [*France*]

APCD .... Ceduna [*Australia*] [*ICAO location identifier*] (ICLI)

apce .... Apostolice [*Spanish*]

APCE .... Assemblee Populaire Communale Elargie [*Expanded People's Communal Assembly*] [*Algeria*] (AF)

APCEMA ... Air Pollution Control Equipment Manufacturers' Association

APCET ...... Association Professionnelle des Cooperants de l'Enseignement Technique [*Professional Association of Technical Studies Advisors*] [*Algeria*] (AF)

APCh .... Antifriction Porous Pig Iron (RU)

APCh .... Automatic Frequency Control (RU)

APChG ...... Automatic Heterodyne Frequency Control (RU)

APCh i F .... Automatic Frequency and Phase Control (RU)

APCJ .... Agrupacion Politica Catorce de Junio [*14 June Political Group*] [*Dominican Republic*] (LA)

APCL .... Australian Portland Cement Limited (ADA)

APCLA ...... Australian Professional Colour Laboratories Association

APCLCCMM ... Associacao Profissional dos Capitaes de Longo Curso e de Cabotagem da Marinha Mercante [*Brazil*] (EAIO)

APCM .... Asia Pacific Christian Mission

APCO .... Application de Procedes de Construction [*Morocco*]

APCO .... Arab Political and Cultural Organization [*Iran*] (PD)

APCOL....... Asian Parasite Control Organization [*Japan*] (EAIO)

APCOL....... All-Pakistan Confederation of Labor

APCOL....... Alternative Publishing Cooperative [*Australia*] (ADA)

APCP........ Asociacion Panamericana de Cirugia Pediatrica [*Mexico*] (SLS)

APCP........ Australian Prime Cattle Project

APCR........ Carnarvon [*Australia*] [*ICAO location identifier*] (ICLI)

APCRC ...... Australian Petroleum Cooperative Research Centre

APCS .... Association pour la Promotion de la Culture Sepharade [*Association for the Promotion of the Sephardic Culture*] [*France*] (EAIO)

APCT........ Association des Planteurs des Cultures Tropicales [*Tropical Crop Planters Association*] [*Cambodia*] (CL)

APCTCC ... Association of Playing Card and Tarot Card Collectors [*France*] (EAIO)

APCTT ...... Asian and Pacific Centre for Transfer of Technology [*India*] (EAIO)

APCVM..... Association of Photo, Cinema, and Video Materials [*France*] (EAIO)

APD .... Aide Publique au Developpement

APD .... Asia Pacific Distribution [*Australia*] [*ICAO designator*] (FAAC)

APD .... Associacao Portuguesa de Defidientes [*Portuguese Association of Disabled Peoples*] (EAIO)

APD .... Autoridad Portuaria Dominicana [*Dominican Port Authority*] [*Dominican Republic*] (LA)

APD .... Data Transmission Equipment (RU)

apda........... Apreciada [*Valued*] [*Spanish*]

APDA .... Australian Poll Dorset Association

APDA .... Australian Porcelain Decorators' Association

APDA .... Australian Production Designers' Association

APDA .... Australian Protestant Defence Association (ADA)

APDAYC... Asociacion Peruana de Autores y Compositores [*Association of Peruvian Authors and Composers*] (EAIO)

APDB .... Derby [*Australia*] [*ICAO location identifier*] (ICLI)

APDC .... Asian and Pacific Development Centre (EAIO)

APDD........ Long-Range Air Regiment (RU)

APDEN ..... Association pour la Protection et le Developpement de l'Economie Nationale [*Association for the Protection and Development of the National Economy*] [*Laotian*] (CL)

APDEP ...... Associacao Portuguesa para o Desenvolvimento Economico Popular [*Portuguese Association for Popular Economic Development*] (WER)

APDF........ Africa Project Development Facility [*United Nations*] (EY)

APDF/APRO ... Asian Pacific Dental Federation/Asian Pacific Regional Organisation (EAIO)

APDH........ Asamblea Permanente por los Derechos Humanos [*Permanent Assembly for Human Rights*] [*Argentina*] (EAIO)

APDH........ Asociacion pro Derechos Humanos de Espana [*Spanish Human Rights Association*]

APDHE ..... Asociacion pro Derechos Humanos de Espana [*Spanish Human Rights Association*] (EAIO)

APDILA .... Association des Pharmaciens Directeurs de Laboratoires d'Analyses Biologiques [*French*] (SLS)

APDKM .... Activist Group for Assistance to the Militia Children's Room (RU)

Apdo........... Apartado [*Post Office Box*] [*Spanish*]

APDPN ..... Acetylpyridine Diphosphopyridine Nucleotide (RU)

APDR .... Long-Range Air Reconnaissance Regiment (RU)

APDSA ...... Asian Pacific Dental Students' Association [*Singapore, Singapore*] (EAIO)

Apdusa .... African People's Democratic Union of South Africa (PD)

APDVE...... Aide aux Personnes Deplacees et Ses Villages Europeens [*Aid to Displaced Persons and Its European Villages*] (EAIO)

APE .... Amalgamated Power Engineering (Australia) Ltd. (ADA)

APE .... Amphibious Pionier Erkundungsfahrzeug [*Amphibious Engineer Reconnaissance Vehicle*] [*German*] (MCD)

APE .... Asociacion de Prensa Extranjera [*Foreign Press Association*] [*Chile*] (LA)

APE .... Asociacion de Profesionales Especializados en Estados Unidos [*Colombia*] (COL)

APE .... Asociacion Proverista Espanola [*Spanish "For the Truth" Association*] (WER)

APE .... Assemblea Parlamentare Europea [*European Parliamentary Assembly*] [*Italian*] (WER)

APE .... Assemblee Parlementaire Europeenne [*European Parliamentary Assembly*] [*French*]

APE .... Associacao Portuguesa de Escritores [*Portuguese*] (SLS)

APE .... Athinaikon Praktoreion Eidiseon [*Athens News Agency*] [*Ath Pr*] [*See also*] (GC)

APEA........ Asociacion Peruana de Economistas Agricolas [*Peru*] (DSCA)

APEA........ Association de la Presse Eurafricaine [*Eurafrican Press Association*] [*Belgium*]

APEA......... Association des Producteurs Europeens d'Azote [*European Association of Nitrogen Manufacturers*] (EAIO)
APEA........ Association of Professional Engineers (Australia) (ADA)
APEA........ Australian Petroleum Exploration Association (ADA)
APEABA .. Association pour les Echanges Bretagne - Pays Arabes
APEC........ American Petrofina Exploration Company [*North African*]
APEC........ Apparels Export Promotion Council [*India*]
APEC........ Asia Pacific Economic Cooperation [*Forum*]
APEC........ Asociacion de Profesionales Electronicos de Colombia [*Colombia*] (COL)
APEC........ Australia Post Express Courier
APECA...... Asociacion de Periodistas de Centro-America [*Central American Newsmen's Association*] (LA)
APECA...... Association des Parents et Amis de l'Enseignement Catholique
APECC...... Asia Pacific Economic Cooperation Council
APECO...... Asociacion de Pequenos Comerciantes [*Colombia*] (COL)
APED .... Edinburgh [*Australia*] [*ICAO location identifier*] (ICLI)
APEDA...... Ananeotiki Parataxi Epangelmation Dikigoron Athinon [*Renewal Faction of Practicing Attorneys of Athens*] (GC)
APEDE...... Asociacion Panamena de Ejecutivos de Empresas [*Panamanian Business Executives Association*] (LA)
APEE .... Association for Pediatric Education in Europe (PDAA)
APEEF ...... Association Professionnelle des Entreprises et Etablissements Financiers [*France*] (FLAF)
APEF .... Association des Pays Exportateurs de Mineral de Fer [*Association of Iron Ore Exporting Countries*] [*Switzerland*] (EAIO)
APEFRAC ... Association Professionnelle des Enseignants Francais Residants au Cambodge [*Professional Association for French Teachers Living in Cambodia*] (CL)
APEG........ Area de Pesquisas Ecologicas de Guara [*Brazil*] (DSCA)
APEG........ Asia Pacific Economic Group
APEGE...... Asamblea Permanente de Entidades Gremiales Empresariales [*Permanent Assembly of Union Management Organizations*] [*Argentina*] (LA)
APEH .... Asociacion de Paises Exportadores de Hierro [*Association of Iron Exporting Countries*] (LA)
APEIA ...... Asociacion Profesional de Empleados Industriales Argentinos [*Professional Association of Argentine Industrial Employees*] (LA)
APEKE ...... Association des Parents des Etudiants Khmers a l'Etranger [*Association of Parents of Cambodian Students Abroad*] (CL)
APEL......... Asociacion Progreso en Libertad [*Progress with Liberty Association*] [*Venezuela*] (LA)
APEL........ Association des Parents d'Eleves de l'Enseignement Libre [*French*]
APEM........ Associacao Portuguesa de Educacao Musical [*Portuguese Association of Music Education*] (EAIO)
APEM........ Australian Political Economy Movement (ADA)
APEMA..... Association pour l'Etude des Marches d'Assurances
APEN .... Asociacion de Periodistas y Escritores Nacionales [*National Journalists and Writers Association*] [*Honduras*] (LA)
APENC..... Austrian PEN Centre (EAIO)
APENPLAN ... Asian and Pacific Energy Planning Network [*of the Asian and Pacific Development Centre*] (EAIO)
APEP........ Agencia de Prensa Espanola Popular [*People's Spanish Press Agency*] (WER)
APEP......... Asociacion de Periodistas Escolares de Peru [*Association of Peruvian Student Journalists*] (LA)
APERGS ... Associacao de Pesquisadores do Rio Grande do Sul [*Brazil*] (DSCA)
APERU...... Asociacion pro Ensenanza Rural Universitaria [*Argentina*] (LAA)
APES .... Asociacion de Periodistas de El Salvador [*El Salvador Journalists Association*] (LA)
APES .... Asociacion de Profesores de Ensenanza Secundaria [*Secondary School Teachers Association*] [*Uruguay*] (LA)
APES .... Association Professionnelle de l'Enseignement Superieur [*Advanced Education Professional Association*] [*Algeria*] (AF)
APESA ...... Apoti Agropecuaria SA [*Brazil*] (DSCA)
APESA ...... Association of Professional Engineers and Scientists, Australia
APESB ...... Associacao Portuguesa para Estudos de Saneamento Basico [*Portuguese Association on Water, Wastewater and Solid Wastes Research*] (EAIO)
APESCA.... Asociacion Colombiana de Pescadores e Industriales de Pesca [*Colombia*] (DSCA)
APESEG.... Asociacion Peruana de Empresas de Seguros [*Peruvian Association of Insurance Companies*] (LA)
APESGE.... Association du Personnel Enseignant et Scientifique des Grands Ecoles [*Association of Teachers and Scientists of Higher Learning*] [*Zaire*]
APESMA .. Association of Professional Engineers, Scientists, and Managers, Australia
APESS....... Association des Professeurs de l'Enseignement Secondaire et Superieur du Grand-Duche de Luxembourg [*Luxembourg*] (SLS)

APETA...... Australian Primary English Teachers Association
APETI .... Asociacion Profesional Espanola de Tradutores e Interpretes [*Spanish Professional Association of Translators and Interpreters*]
APEUCh.... Asociacion de Profesores y Empleados de la Universidad de Chile [*Association of Professors and White-Collar Employees of the University of Chile*] (LA)
APEX........ Advanced Passenger Excursion
APEX........ Associate of Professional, Executive, Clerical and Computer Staffs [*Australia*]
APF........... Aboriginal Publications Foundation
APF........... African Peace Force
APF........... Alianza Popular Familiar [*People's Family Alliance*] [*Spanish*] (WER)
APF........... Alianza Popular Federalista [*Popular Federalist Alliance*] [*Argentina*] (LA)
APF........... Anglican Pacifist Fellowship [*Oxford, England*] (EAIO)
APF........... Asia-Pacific Fellowship
APF........... Asparagine Polysaccharide Fragment (RU)
APF........... Associacao Portuguesa de Fundicao [*Portuguese*] (SLS)
APF........... Australian Parachute Federation (ADA)
APF........... Australian Pensioners Federation
APF........... Australian Permanent Forces
APF........... Australian Petanque Federation
APF........... Australian Pharmaceutical Formulary (ADA)
APF........... Australian Powerlifting Federation
APF........... Australian Products First [*An association*]
APF........... Automatic Phase Control (RU)
APF........... Phage-Inhibiting Agents (RU)
APF........... Transporte de Carga Aeropacifico SA de CV [*Mexico*] [*ICAO designator*] (FAAC)
APFA........ All People's Freedom Alliance [*Liberia*] (AF)
APFA........ Associated Poultry Farmers of Australia (ADA)
APFA........ Association des Professeurs de Francais en Afrique [*Association of French Teachers in Africa - AFTA*] [*Khartoum, Sudan*] (EAIO)
APFA........ Australian Picture Framers' Association
APFACTS ... Association of Parents and Friends of Australian Capital Territory Schools
APFC......... Asia-Pacific Forestry Commission (ADA)
APFC......... Asociacion de Peritos Forestales Centroamericanos [*Guatemala*] (DSCA)
APFM....... Australian Postgraduate Federation in Medicine (ADA)
APFOL...... All Pakistan Federation of Labour
APFRL ..... Association des Professeurs Francais Residants au Laos [*Association of French Teachers Living in Laos*] (CL)
APFS .... African Peasant Farming Scheme
APFS .... Australian Pacific Friendly Society
APFT .... Forrest [*Australia*] [*ICAO location identifier*] (ICLI)
APFTU..... All Pakistan Federation of Trade Unions
APFV....... Asociacion de Peritos Forestales de Venezuela [*Venezuela*] (DSCA)
APG .... Aboriginal Provisional Government [*Australia*]
APG .... ACLANT [*Allied Command, Atlantic*] Planning Guidance [*NATO*]
APG .... Aerotaxis Pegaso SA de CV [*Mexico*] [*ICAO designator*] (FAAC)
APG .... Agu Pflanzungs-Gesellschaft
APG .... Army Mobile Hospital (RU)
APG .... Asamblea Popular Galega [*Galician People's Assembly*] [*Spanish*] (WER)
APG .... Asociacion de Periodistas de Guatemala [*Guatemalan Journalists Association*] (LA)
APG .... Australian Performing Group (ADA)
APG .... Australian Property Group
APGA .... Apple and Pear Growers' Association [*Australia*] (ADA)
APGA .... Australian Pistacio Growers' Association
APGA .... Australian Protea Growers' Association
APGASA ... Apple and Pear Growers' Association of South Australia
APGF .... Perth [*Australia*] [*ICAO location identifier*] (ICLI)
APGM....... Autonomous Precision-Guided Munition [*NATO*]
APGN....... Geraldton [*Australia*] [*ICAO location identifier*] (ICLI)
APGOMS ... Association du Personnel de Geneve OMS [*Geneva Staff Association World Health Organization*] [*Switzerland*] (EAIO)
APGR .... Automatic Recorder of Clay Mud Parameters (RU)
APH........... Asociacion de Prensa Hondurena [*Honduran Press Association*] (LA)
APH........... Asociacion Peruana de Hospitales [*Peruvian Hospital Association*] (EAIO)
APH........... Automobilove Pohonne Hmoty [*Motor Vehicle Fuels*] (CZ)
APHA....... Aged Persons Homes Act [*Australia*]
APHA....... Australian Pneumatic and Hydraulic Association (ADA)
APHA....... Australian Poll Hereford Association
APHA....... Australian Private Hospitals Association
APHA........ Australian Psychology and Hypnotherapy Association

APHA .... Australian Public Health Association   (ADA)
APHC .... Halls Creek [*Australia*] [*ICAO location identifier*]   (ICLI)
APHCA ..... Animal Production and Health Commission for Asia [*Australia*]
APHEDA .. Australian People for Health, Education, and Development Abroad
APHG .... Association des Professeurs d'Histoire et de Geographie de l'Enseignement Public [*French*]   (SLS)
APHH .... Port Hedland [*Australia*] [*ICAO location identifier*]   (ICLI)
APHLC ..... All-Party Hill Leaders' Conference [*India*] [*Political party*]   (PPW)
APHS .... Australian Poll Hereford Society   (ADA)
APHS .... Australian Printing Historical Society
APHS .... Australian Psychology and Hypnotherapy Association   (ADA)
API .... Accion Popular Independiente [*Independent Popular Action*] [*Chile*]   (LA)
API .... Agence Angolaise de Presse et d'Information [*Angolan Press and Information Agency*]
API .... Agence de Presse Ivoirienne [*Ivorian Press Agency*]
API .... Agence de Promotion des Investissements [*Agency for the Promotion of Foreign Investments*] [*Tunisia*]
API .... Agence Populaire d'Information
API .... Agencja Prasowo-Informacyjna [*Press and Information Agency*] (POL)
API .... Agencja Publicystyczno-Informacyjna [*Publicity and Information Agency*] [*Poland*]
API .... Agency for Public Information [*Replaced by JIS*] [*Jamaica*] (LA)
API .... Air Panama Internacional [*ICAO designator*]   (FAAC)
API .... Alianza Popular de Izquierdas [*Popular Alliance of Leftists*] [*Spanish*]   (WER)
API .... Alianza Popular Independiente [*Independent Popular Alliance*] [*Venezuela*]   (LA)
API .... Alianza Popular Informativo [*People's Informative Alliance*] [*Spanish*]   (WER)
API .... Allgemeiner Presse-Informationsdienst [*General Press Information Service*]   (EG)
API .... Allied Pacific Investments Ltd.
API .... American Petroleum Institute   (OMWE)
API .... Angkatan Pemuda Indonesia [*Indonesian Youth Corps*]   (ML)
API .... Angkatan Pemuda Insaf [*Awakened Youth Corps*]   (ML)
API .... Anonima Petroli Italiana SpA
API .... Arab Planning Institute [*Kuwait*]   (EY)
API .... Asociacion de Personal Investigador del CSIS [*Spanish*]   (SLS)
API .... Asociatia Petrolifera Internationala [*International Petroleum Association*]   (RO)
API .... Associacao Paulista da Imprensa [*Sao Paulo Press Association*] [*Brazil*]   (LA)
API .... Association Pharmaceutique Interafricaine
API .... Associazione Pescicoltori Italiana [*Italian Fish Farmers Association*]   (ASF)
API .... Associazione Piccole e Medie Industrie di Milano e Provincia [*Italy*]
API .... Australian Petroleum Institute
API .... Australian Pharmaceutical Industries
API .... Australian Planning Institute   (ADA)
API .... Australian Post-Tel Institute   (ADA)
API .... Autorisations Prealables d'Importation [*Advance Import Authorizations*]   (CL)
API .... Azerbaydzhan Pedagogical Institute Imeni V. I. Lenin   (RU)
API .... Import Identification Number [*Indonesia*]   (IMH)
API .... Industrie de Transformation des Produits Agricoles [*Cocoa marketing company*] [*Ivory Coast*]
APIA .... Agence de Promotion des Investissements Agricoles [*Tunisia*]
APIA .... Asociacion Peruana de Ingenieros Agronomos [*Peru*]   (DSCA)
APIA .... Associate of the Plastics Institute of Australia   (ADA)
APIA .... Association pour la Promotion de l'Information Agricole [*French*]
APIA .... Association pour la Promotion Industrie - Agriculture [*Association for the Promotion of Industry - Agriculture*] (EAIO)
APIA .... Associazione Polisportiva Italo-Australiana
APIA .... Australian Photographic Industry Association
APIA .... Australian Pipeline Industry Association
APIA .... Australian Poultry Industries Association   (ADA)
APIA .... Australian Poultry Industry Association
APIAC .... Asociacion de Pequenos Industriales de Articulos de Cuero [*Colombia*]   (COL)
APIAC .... Australian Post-Tel Institute Aero Club   (ADA)
APIA-FH ... Asociacion Peruana de Ingenieros Agronomos [*Peru*]   (DSCA)
APIC .... African Policy Information Center
APIC .... Alleanza dei Patrioti Indipendenti del Congo
APIC .... Allied Press Information Center [*NATO*]   (NATG)
APIC .... Amicale des Postiers Indigenes Congolais
APIC .... Armements des Peches Ivoiriennes Cotieres
APIC .... Asamblea Permanent d'Intellectuals Catalans [*Permanent Assembly of Catalan Intellectuals*] [*Spanish*]   (WER)

APIC .... Asian Packaging Information Centre [*Hong Kong Packaging Council*]
APIC .... Association des Patrons et Ingenieurs Catholiques [*Association of Catholic Employers and Engineers*] [*Belgium*]   (WER)
APIC .... Association du Personnel Indigene du Congo Belge et du Rwanda-Urundi
APIC .... Australian Population and Immigration Council   (ADA)
APIC .... Australian Potato Industry Council
APICA .... Association pour la Promotion des Initiatives Communautaires Africaines [*Association for the Promotion of African Community Initiatives - APACI*]   (EAIO)
APICCAPS ... Associacao Portuguesa dos Industriais de Calcado, Componentes, e Artigos de Pele e Seus Sucedaneos [*Portugal*]   (EY)
APICE .... Asociacion Panamericana de Instituciones de Credito Educativo [*Pan American Association of Educational Credit Institutions - PAAECI*]   (EAIO)
APICE .... Associazione Produttori Italiani di Calcestruzzi per l'Edilizia [*Italy*]   (EAIO)
APICI .... Association Professionnelle des Informaticiens de Cote-D'Ivoire
APICOL .... Agro-Pecuaria Industria e Comercio Ltd [*Brazil*]   (DSCA)
APICOL .... Apicultura Colombiana Ltda. [*Colombia*]   (COL)
APICORP ... Arab Petroleum Investments Corp.   (ECON)
APICORP ... Arab Petroleum Investments Corporation [*of the Organization of Arab Petroleum Exporting Countries*]
APID .... Agence de Production, d'Information, et de Documentation
APIDC .... Andhra Pradesh Industrial Development Corp. [*India*]   (PDAA)
APIDEN .... Association Professionnelle des Inspecteurs Departementaux de l'Education Nationale [*Professional Association of Departmental Inspectors for National Education*] [*Algeria*]
APIE .... Administracao do Parque Imobiliaria do Estado [*Administration of State Lands and Property*] [*Mozambique*]   (AF)
APIEAS ..... Asociacion Peruana de Instituciones de Educacion Agricola Superior [*Peru*]   (DSCA)
APIF .... Asociacion para la Integracion Familiar [*Guatemala*]
APIFA .... Association Professionnelle des Instituteurs Francais en Algerie [*Professional Association of French Teachers in Algeria*]   (AF)
APIJAC ..... Australian Pet Industry Joint Advisory Council
APIL .... Asociacion pro Integracion Latinoamericana   (LAA)
APIM .... Association Professionnelle Internationale des Medecins [*France*]   (FLAF)
APIMO ..... Associazione Professionale Italiana Medici Oculisti [*Italian*]   (SLS)
APIMONDIA ... Federation Internationale des Associations d'Apiculture [*International Federation of Beekeepers' Associations*] [*ICSU*]
APIN .... Alianza Popular de Integracion Nacional [*Bolivia*] [*Political party*]   (PPW)
APIN .... Association for Programmed Instruction in the Netherlands (PDAA)
APIN .... System of Computerized Processing of Scientific Information [*Technical University of Wroclaw*] [*Information service or system*]   (IID)
APINESS .. Asia-Pacific Information Network in Social Sciences
APINMAP ... Asian and Pacific Information Network on Medicinal and Aromatic Plants [*UNESCO*] [*United Nations*]   (DUND)
APIPOL .... Regional Association of Beekeepers [*Poland*]   (EAIO)
APIRA .... Asociacion de Profesionales Interamericana en Reforma Agraria (LAA)
APIRA ...... Australian Petroleum Industry Research Association
APIRC .... Australian Pig Industry Research Committee
APIS .... Australian Patent Information Service   (ADA)
APIS .... Australian Photographic Information Service   (ADA)
APISZ .... Allami Papiripari Szovetkezet [*State Paper Cooperative Enterprise*]   (HU)
APITCO .... Andhra Pradesh Industrial and Technical Consultancy Organisation [*Industrial Development Bank of India*]
APIZ .... Alliance des Proletaires Independants du Zaire [*Political party*]
APJ .... Agent de Police Judiciaire [*French*]   (FLAF)
ap J-C ...... Apres Jesus-Christ [*After Jesus Christ*] [*French*]
APJT .... Perth/Jandakot [*Australia*] [*ICAO location identifier*]   (ICLI)
APK .... African Trade-Union Confederation   (RU)
APK .... Afrikanskaia Profsoiuznaia Konfederatsiia
APK .... Agen Polisi Kepala [*Senior Policeman*]   (IN)
APK .... Agroindustrial Complex   (BU)
APK .... Allami Pincegazdasagok Kozpontja [*State Wine Cellar Center*] (HU)
apk .... Allomasparancsnok [*Garrison Commander, Railway Transport Officer*]   (HU)
APK .... Apataki [*French Polynesia*] [*Airport symbol*]   (OAG)
APK .... Arbetarpartiet Kommunisterna [*Communist Workers' Party*] [*Sweden*]   (PPE)
APK .... Asia Pacific Air Cargo PTE Ltd. [*Singapore*] [*ICAO designator*]   (FAAC)
APK .... Association de la Presse Khmere [*Cambodian Press Association*] (CL)

APK .... Propionic Acid Amide   (RU)
APKA .... Karratha [Australia] [ICAO location identifier]   (ICLI)
APKG .... Kalgoorlie [Australia] [ICAO location identifier]   (ICLI)
APKh .... Association of Proletarian Artists   (RU)
APKU .... Kununurra [Australia] [ICAO location identifier]   (ICLI)
APL............ Academia Panamena de la Lengua [Panamanian Academy of
     Language]   (EAIO)
APL............ Academia Paulista de Letras [Brazil]   (SLS)
APL............ Aircraft Preheater Lamp   (RU)
APL............ Albanian Party of Labor [Political party]
APL............ Assessment of Prior Learning
apl .... Ausserplanmaessig [Not According to Schedule] [German]
APL............ Australian Pensioners League   (ADA)
APL............ Automatic Production Line   (RU)
APL............ Nampula [Mozambique] [Airport symbol]   (OAG)
APL............ Nuclear Powered Submarine, Atomic Submarine   (RU)
APLA........ Asia-Pacific Lawyers Association
APLA........ Asociacion Petroquimica Latinoamericana [Argentina]   (EAIO)
APLA........ Association of Parliamentary Librarians of Australasia
APLA........ Australian Product Liability Association
APLA........ Automatic Programing of Logical Algorithms   (RU)
APLA........ Azanian People's Liberation Army [South Africa]   (ECON)
APLAC..... Asia Pacific Laboratory Accreditation Cooperation
APLAN..... Agencia Journalistica do Planalto [Planalto News Agency]
     [Brazil]   (LA)
APLC .... Australian Peace Liaison Committee
APLC........ Australian Plague Locust Commission
APLC........ Leigh Creek [Australia] [ICAO location identifier]   (ICLI)
APLF........ Alliance of Progressive and Left-Wing Forces [Greek]   (PPE)
APLI .... African People's League for Independence
aplic.......... Aplicaciones [Appliques] [Publishing] [Spanish]
APLIS...... Automated Parliamentary Library Information Service [New
     South Wales, Australia]
APLM....... Learmonth [Australia] [ICAO location identifier]   (ICLI)
APLR........ Armee Populaire de Liberation Rwandaise
APLS .... Armee Populaire de Liberation Sahraouie [Saharan People's
     Liberation Army]   (AF)
APLS .... Australian Capital Territory Library Service [National Union
     Catalogue of Australia symbol]
APLTR ...... Asian Pacific Law and Tax Review [A publication]
APLV .... Association des Professeurs de Langues Vivantes de
     l'Enseignement Public [French]   (SLS)
APM .... Adelaide Produce Market [Australia]
APM .... Air Pacific Airlines [ICAO designator]   (FAAC)
APM .... Akcja Porzadkowania Miasta [City Cleaning Drive]   (POL)
APM .... Armenian Pan-National Movement [Political party]   (EY)
APM .... Association of Proletarian Musicians   (RU)
APM .... Attached Pressurized Module [European Space Agency]
APM .... Australian Pacific Minerals
APM .... Australian Paper Manufacturers Ltd.   (ADA)
APM .... Australian People's Movement   (ADA)
APM .... Australian Police Medal
APM .... Truck-Mounted Shop   (RU)
APMA .... Asociacion Paraguaya Maderera y Afines [Paraguay]   (DSCA)
APMA .... Australian Packaging Machinery Association
APMA .... Australian Pharmaceutical Manufacturers Association
APMA .... Australian Plastic Modellers' Association
APMA ...... Australian Postmasters' Association
APMA ...... Australian Professional Musicians Agency
APMA ...... Australian Pump Manufacturers Association   (ADA)
APMAA .... Aggregative Programming Model of Australian Agriculture
     (ADA)
APMC .... Andhra Pradesh Mining Corp. [India]   (PDAA)
APMC .... Associated Pan Malaysia Cement   (ML)
APMCA..... Asian Pacific Materials and Corrosion Association
APMCSOG ... Australian Police Ministers' Council, Senior Officers' Group
APMD .... Australian Prime Minister [and Cabinet] [National Union
     Catalogue of Australia symbol]
APME....... Association of Plastics Manufacturers in Europe   (EA)
APMEP..... Association des Professeurs de Mathematiques de
     l'Enseignement Public [French]   (SLS)
APMF....... Australian Paint Manufacturers Federation   (ADA)
APMH...... Association of Professions for the Mentally Handicapped [South
     Africa]
APMIS ..... Aboriginal Programs Management Information System
     [Australia]
APML........ Acao Popular Marxista-Leninista [Marxist-Leninist Popular
     Action] [Brazil]   (LA)
APMMA ... Australasian Presentation and Multi-Media Association
APMM-EEC ... Association of Preserved Milk Manufacturers of the EEC
     [European Economic Community] [France]   (EAIO)
APMP........ Association pour la Promotion de Medecine Preventive
APMR ...... Meekatharra [Australia] [ICAO location identifier]   (ICLI)
APMRS..... Associacao dos Produtores de Madeiras da Regiao Serrana
     [Brazil]   (DSCA)
APN .... Academy of Pedagogical Sciences, RSFSR   (RU)

APN .... Administracion Postal Nacional [National Postal
     Administration] [Colorado]   (LA)
APN .... Aerovia del Altiplano SA de CV [Mexico] [ICAO designator]
     (FAAC)
APN .... Afrikanskaia Partiia Nezavisimosti
APN .... Agentstvo Pechati Novosti [News agency] [Former USSR]
APN .... Armee Populaire Nationale [National People's Army] [Congo]
     (AF)
APN .... Assemblee Populaire Nationale [Haiti] [Political party]   (EY)
APN .... Assemblee Populaire Nationale [Algeria] [Political party]
APN .... Association Prachea Niyum [Humanitarian Association]
     [Cambodia]   (CL)
APN .... Australian Product Number
APN .... Australian Provincial Newspapers
APN .... Submersible Artesian Pump   (RU)
APNA .... Association des Professionnels Navigants de l'Aviation [French]
APNA .... Australian Product Number Association
APNG .... Australia - Papua New Guinea [Submarine cable]
     [Telecommunications]
APNGBCC ... Australia-Papua New Guinea Business Cooperation Committee
APNGFA ... Australia-Papua New Guinea Friendship Association
AP No 4 .... Association Professionnelle Numero 4 [Professional Association
     Number 4]   (CL)
APNP .... Mobile Artillery Observation Post   (RU)
APNR .... Association for the Protection of Native Races [Australia]
APO .... Abteilungsparteiorganisation [Party Organization Division]
     [German]
APO .... African People's Organisation
APO .... African People's Organization   (WDAA)
APO .... Agitation and Propaganda Department   (RU)
Apo............ Apartado [Post Office Box] [Correspondence] [Spanish]
Apo............ Apoderado [Empowered, Attorney] [Spanish]
apo............ Apostolico [Apostolic] [Spanish]
APO .... Arbeitsgemeinschaft fuer Psychotechnik in Oesterreich
     [Association for Psychotechnology in Austria]   (SLS)
APO .... Architectural Planning Department   (RU)
APO .... Asian Productivity Organization [Japan]   (EAIO)
APO .... Asociacion Panamericana de Oftalmologia [Panamerican
     Association of Ophthalmology] [Washington, DC]
ApO .... Ausserparlamentarische Opposition [Extra-Parliamentary
     Opposition] [German]   (WEN)
APO .... Australian Patents Office
APO .... Australian Post Office   (ADA)
APOA .... Australian Purchasing Officers Association   (PDAA)
APOC .... Anglo-Persian Oil Company [Later, British Petroleum]   (MENA)
apof .... Apofasis [Decision, Decree]   (GC)
APOL .... Australian Political Register [Australian Consolidated Press]
     [Database]
APOPEC ... Agence de Presse de l'OPEC [OPEC News Agency - OPECNA]
     [Vienna, Austria]   (EAIO)
APORCAE ... Association of Principal Officers of Regional Colleges of
     Advanced Education [Australia]   (ADA)
aportg......... Aportuguesamento [Made Portuguese] [Portuguese]
apos........... Apostolica [Spanish]
APOS........ Australian Protestant Orphan Society   (ADA)
APOS........ Cocos Islands [Australia] [ICAO location identifier]   (ICLI)
apost.......... Apostol [Apostle] [Spanish]
APOSTCI ... All Pakistan Organization of Small Traders and Cottage
     Industries   (EAIO)
APP............ Accident Prevention Plan
APP............ Accion Politica Progresista [Progressive Political Action]
     [Ecuador] [Political party]   (PPW)
APP............ Action Pro-Populaire [Pro-People's Action] [Cambodia]   (CL)
APP............ Action Psychologique et Propagande [Algeria]
APP............ Aerolineas Pacifico Atlantico SA [Spain] [ICAO designator]
     (FAAC)
APP............ African People's Party [Kenya]   (AF)
APP............ African Progressive Party
APP............ Agence Parisienne de Presse [Parisian Press Agency] [French]
     (AF)
APP............ Agence pour la Protection des Programmes [France]
APP............ Alianza para el Progreso [Colombia]   (COL)
APP............ Anguilla People's Party [Later, ADP] [Political party]   (PPW)
App .... Apparat [Extension, Apparatus] [German]   (WEN)
app .... Appellant [Appellant] [Afrikaans]
app .... Appendice [Appendix] [Publishing] [French]
App .... Appendix [Appendix] [Publishing] [German]
APP............ Area de Propiedad del Pueblo [People's Ownership Sector]
     [Nicaragua]   (LA)
app .... Army Forwarding Station   (RU)
APP............ Artillery in Support of Infantry   (RU)
APP............ Asociacion de Periodistas del Peru [Peruvian Journalists
     Association]   (LA)
APP............ Asociacion Politica Proverista ["For the Truth" Political
     Association] [Spanish]   (WER)
APP............ Associated Press of Pakistan   (FEA)

APP............ Association of Proletarian Writers   (RU)
APP............ Athinon, Peiraios, Perikhoron [*Of Athens, Piraeus, Suburbs*]
          (GC)
APP............ Atmospheric Physics Programme [*International Council of
          Scientific Unions*]
APP............ Australian Psychologists Press [*A publication*]
APP............ Automatic Reclosing   (RU)
APP............ Breakthrough Artillery Regiment   (RU)
App .... Cour d'Appel [*Benelux*]   (BAS)
app .... Landing Strip   (RU)
APPA........ African Petroleum Producers' Association [*Gabon*]
APPA........ Asociacion Colombiana para Perros Pastores Alemanes
          [*Colombia*]   (COL)
APPA .... Associate of the Professional Photographers Association
          [*Australia*]
APPA........ Association des Pilotes et Proprietaires d'Aeronefs [*Association of
          Private Aircraft Owners*] [*France*]   (PDAA)
APPA........ Association pour la Prevention de la Pollution Atomspherique
          [*Association for the Prevention of Atmospheric Pollution*]
          [*French*]   (SLS)
APPA........ Australasian [*or Australian*] Provincial Press Association   (ADA)
APPA........ Australian Primary Principals Association
APPA........ Port Hedland [*Australia*] [*ICAO location identifier*]   (ICLI)
APPAN...... Asociacion de Pequenos Panaderos [*Colombia*]   (COL)
APPBF....... Asociacion Puertorriquena Pro Bienestar de la Familia [*Puerto
          Rico*]   (EAIO)
APPC........ Alliance des Pays Producteurs de Cacao [*Cocoa Producers'
          Alliance*] [*Use COPAL*]   (AF)
APPC........ Associacao Portuguesa para o Progresso das Ciencias [*Portugal*]
          (DSCA)
APPC........ Australia Pacific Projects Corp. Proprietary Ltd.
APPCN...... Association des Pays Producteurs de Caoutchouc Naturel
          [*Association of Natural Rubber-Producing Countries*]   (CL)
app corr ..... Chambre des Appels Correctionnels [*French*]   (FLAF)
APPD........ Port Hedland [*Australia*] [*ICAO location identifier*]   (ICLI)
APPE........ Association of Petrochemical Producers in Europe   (ECON)
APPE........ Association of Petrochemicals Producers in Europe [*Brussels,
          Belgium*]
APPE........ Pearce [*Australia*] [*ICAO location identifier*]   (ICLI)
APPEC ...... Asia-Pacific Petroleum Conference
APPEN...... Asia-Pacific People's Environment Network [*Penang, Malaysia*]
          (EAIO)
append........ Appendice [*Appendix*] [*Publishing*] [*Italian*]
append........ Appendice [*Appendix*] [*Publishing*] [*French*]
APPER ...... African Priority Programme for Economic Recovery
APPF .... Adelaide/Parafield [*Australia*] [*ICAO location identifier*]   (ICLI)
APPF .... Australian Pork Producers' Federation
App Fabr.... Apparatefabrik [*Apparatus Manufacturing Plant*] [*German*]
          (GCA)
APPG........ Australian Pensioner Pressure Group
APPH .... Perth/International [*Australia*] [*ICAO location identifier*]   (ICLI)
APPI......... Association Internationale d'Etudes pour la Promotion et la
          Protection des Investissements Prives en Territoires
          Etrangers [*France*]   (FLAF)
APPI......... Association of the Pulp and Paper Industry [*Former
          Czechoslovakia*]   (EAIO)
APPI......... Australian Pulp and Paper Institute [*Monash University*]
          [*Australia*]
APPITA..... APPITA - Technical Association for the Australian and New
          Zealand Pulp and Paper Industry [*Formerly, Australian
          Pulp and Paper Industry Technical Association*] [*Australia*]
          (EAIO)
APPITA..... Australian Pulp and Paper Industry Technical Association
          (ADA)
appl .... Applous [*Applause*] [*Afrikaans*]
APPL........ Court of Appeal Judgements [*Database*] [*Australia*]
applan .... Applantus [*Flattened*] [*Latin*]   (MAE)
APPM....... Associated Pulp and Paper Mills Ltd. [*Australia*]   (ADA)
APPM....... Association of Pre-School Play Groups in Malawi   (EAIO)
APPM....... Australian Project Planning and Management
APPMECI ... Association Professionnelle des Petites et Moyennes Entreprises
          de Cote-D'Ivoire
APPO .... Anti-Fascist Secret Patriotic Organization [*1942-1945*]   (RU)
APPO .... Department of Agitation, Propaganda and Press   (RU)
APPP........ Asamblea Provincial del Poder Popular [*Provincial People's
          Government Assembly*] [*Cuba*]   (LA)
APPP........ Perth [*Australia*] [*ICAO location identifier*]   (ICLI)
APPPC ...... Asia and Pacific Plant Protection Commission [*Formerly, Plant
          Protection Committee for the Southeast Asia and Pacific
          Region*]   (EA)
Appr.......... Approbiert [*Certified, Approved*] [*German*]
Appr.......... Approuve [*Benelux*]   (BAS)
APPR........ Perth [*Australia*] [*ICAO location identifier*]   (ICLI)
approf........ Apulaisprofessori [*Finland*]
approx........ Approximately   (EECI)
Ap PrudBrux ... Jugement Conseil de Prud'hommes d'Appel de Bruxelles
          [*Belgium*]   (BAS)

APPS .... Alianca Portuguesa para o Progresso Social [*Portuguese Alliance
          for Social Progress*] [*Portuguese*]   (WER)
APPS .... Association for Public Policy Studies [*Taiwan*]
APPS .... Australasian [*or Australian*] Plant Pathology Society   (SLS)
APPS .... Australian Physiological and Pharmacological Society   (ADA)
APPS .... Automated Purchase and Payment System [*United Nations*]
          (DUND)
APPSA ..... Association of Plastics Processors of South Africa   (AA)
APPSO ...... Asociacion de Profesionales de la Planta Siderurgica del Orinoco
          [*Association of Orinoco Iron and Steel Mill Professionals*]
          [*Venezuela*]   (LA)
Appt .... Appartement [*Apartment*] [*French*]
Appt .... Approvisionnement [*Victualing, Supply*] [*Military*] [*French*]
          (MTD)
App Trib .... Appeals Tribunal
APPTU...... All-Pakistan Post and Telegraph Union
APPU........ Asian-Pacific Parliamentary Union
APPU........ Asian-Pacific Postal Union [*Manila, Philippines*]   (EAIO)
APPU........ Australian Primary Producers' Union   (ADA)
APPUG...... Carrier-Based Antisubmarine Hunter-Killer Group   (RU)
apPVO ...... Antiaircraft Artillery Regiment   (RU)
APQ .... Air Philippines Corporation, Inc. [*ICAO designator*]   (FAAC)
APQI .... Associacao Portuguesa para a Qualide Industrial [*Portuguese
          Association for Quality Control*]   (PDAA)
APR .... Accion Popular Revolucionaria [*Colorado*]   (LAA)
APR .... Accion Publica del Regionalismo [*Public Regionalism Action*]
          [*Spanish*]   (WER)
APR .... Algemene Practische Rechtsverzameling [*Benelux*]   (BAS)
apr .... April [*Netherlands*]   (GPO)
Apr .... April [*German*]   (GPO)
apr .... April [*Denmark*]   (GPO)
Apr .... Aprile [*April*] [*Italian*]
apr .... Aprilis [*April*]   (HU)
APR .... Association pour le Ravitaillement des Produits de Premiere
          Necessite de Phnom Penh et des Provinces [*Association for
          Supplying Phnom Penh and the Provinces with Necessities*]
          [*Cambodia*]   (CL)
APR .... Automobilni Prepravni Rad [*Automobile Traffic Regulations*]
          (CZ)
APR .... Density Distribution Analyzer   (RU)
APR .... Societe Nouvelle d'Exploitation Air Provence [*France*] [*ICAO
          designator*]   (FAAC)
APRA........ Alianza Popular Revolucionaria Americana [*American Popular
          Revolutionary Alliance*] [*Peru*] [*Political party*]   (PPW)
APRA........ American Popular Revolutionary Alliance [*Peru*] [*Political
          party*]
APRA........ Association for the Protection of Rural Australia
APRA........ Australasian Performing Right Association   (EAIO)
APRA........ Australian Plastics Research Association   (PDAA)
APRA........ Australian Postgraduate Research Awards
APRA........ Australian Professional Rodeo Association
APRAA...... Auto Parts Recyclers Association of Australia
APRACA ... Asian and Pacific Regional Agricultural Credit Association   (EA)
APRAD...... Association des Professionnels Agrees en Douanes du Benin
          (EY)
APRAGAZ ... Association des Proprietaires de Recipients a Gaz Comprimes
          [*Belgium*]   (PDAA)
APR(AR) ... Autodopravni Prapor (Rota) [*Truck Battalion (Company)*]   (CZ)
APRCG...... Asia-Pacific Railway Cooperation Group   (MHDB)
APRE........ Accion Popular Revolucionaria Ecuatoriana [*Ecuadorean
          Popular Revolutionary Action*]   (LA)
APRE........ Alianza Popular Revolucionaria Ecuatoriana [*Ecuadorean
          Popular Revolutionary Alliance*] [*Political party*]   (PPW)
aprec.......... Apreciado [*Valued*] [*Spanish*]
APREF ...... Asia-Pacific Real Estate Federation
APREMA ... Angkatan Pemuda Revolusi Malaya [*Malayan Youth
          Revolutionary Forces*]   (ML)
APREP ...... Asociacion de Productores Rurales del Estado Portuguesa
          [*Venezuela*]   (DSCA)
APRF........ All-Pakistan Railwaymen's Federation
APRF........ Perth [*Australia*] [*ICAO location identifier*]   (ICLI)
APRG .... Air Pollution Research Group [*South Africa*] [*Research center*]
          (IRC)
APRI.......... Angkatan Perang Republik Indonesia [*Combat Forces of the
          Republic of Indonesia*]   (IN)
APRI.......... Asia Pacific Research Institute (Macquarie University)
APRI.......... Australian Particleboard Research Institute
APRI.......... Austrian Peace Research Institute
APRI.......... Autorisations Prealables d'Importation
APRIA ...... Association pour la Promotion Industrie Agriculture   (ASF)
APRI(Aust) ... Associate of the Public Relations Institute of Australia   (ADA)
APRIGA .... Agence pour la Promotion Industrielle de la Guadeloupe [*Agency
          for the Industrial Promotion of Guadeloupe*]   (LA)
APRIM...... Truck-Mounted Engineering Repair Shop   (RU)
APRIMA ... Australian Public Risk Insurance Management Association
APRISA..... Ahorro, Prestamos, e Inversiones Sociedad Anonima [*El
          Salvador*]   (EY)

apr J-C....... Apres Jesus-Christ [*After Jesus Christ*] [*French*]

APRL......... Aeroklub Polskiej Rzeczypospolitej Ludowej [*Aero Club of the Polish People's Republic*]

APRM .... Adelaide [*Australia*] [*ICAO location identifier*]   (ICLI)

APRO .... Asian and Pacific Regional Organization [*International Confederation of Free Trade Unions*]   (EY)

APROBA... Association Professionelle pour l'Accroissement de la Productive dans l'Industrie du Batiment [*Association for Increasing Productivity in the Building Industry*] [*France*]   (PDAA)

APROBANA ... Asociacion de Productores Bananeros del Ecuador   (EY)

APROCAL ... Asociacion de Profesores de Ensenanza Secundaria de Caldas [*Manizales*]   (COL)

APROCEL ... Asociacion de Profesionales de la Comision Ejecutiva Hidroelectrica del Rio Lempa [*Professional Association of the Rio Lempa Hydroelectric Executive Commission*] [*El Salvador*]   (LA)

APROCOLIN ... Association Professionnelle de Colons Individuels [*Professional Association of Colonials*]

APRODEBA ... Association des Progressistes et Democrates Burundi de Gitega

APRODECO ... Association pour le Promotion de la Defense de l'Economie Congolaise [*Assocation of the Advancement and Protection of the Congolese Economy*]

APROFAM ... Asociacion Pro Sienestar de la Familia [*Family Welfare Association*] [*Guatemala*]   (LA)

APROH..... Asociacion para el Progreso de Honduras [*Association for the Progress of Honduras*] [*Political party*]

APROLECHE ... Asociacion de Productores de Leche [*Association of Milk Producers*] [*Dominican Republic*]   (LA)

APROM .... Atelierul de Prototipuri si Serii Feromobila [*Workshop for Prototype and Mass Production of Iron Furniture*]   (RO)

APROMACI ... Association des Producteurs et Manufacturiers de Caoutchouc en Cote-D'Ivoire [*Ivory Coast Rubber Producers and Manufacturers Association*]   (AF)

APROMAQUINAS ... Asociacion Colombiana de Productores de Maquinas de Oficina [*Colombia*]   (COL)

APRONA .. Association des Producteurs Nationaux [*Haiti*]   (EY)

APROPATACHIRA ... Asociacion de Productores Rurales del Estado Tachira [*Venezuela*]   (DSCA)

APROQUI ... Compania Organizadora de Abonos y Productos Quimicos [*Colombia*]   (DSCA)

APROS...... Australian and Pacific Researchers in Organisation Studies

APROSE ... Associacao Portuguesa dos Produtores de Seguros [*Insurance representative body*] [*Portugal*]   (EY)

APROSECEM ... Asociacion de Productores de Semillas Certificada de Maiz [*Peru*]   (DSCA)

APROSIGUA ... Asociacion de Productores del Sistema Guarico [*Venezuela*]   (DSCA)

APROSOMA ... Association pour la Promotion Sociale de la Masse [*Association for the Social Betterment of the Masses*] [*Burundi and Rwanda*]   (AF)

APROVENCE ... Asociacion Venezolana de Productores de Cementos [*Venezuelan Association of Cement Producers*]   (LAA)

APROZAR ... Aprovizionarea cu Zarzavaturi [*State Vegetable Supply Organization*]   (RO)

APRP........ Aged Persons' Residential Program [*Australia*]

APRP........ All Peoples' Republican Party [*Ghana*]   (AF)

APRSS...... Australian Photogrammetric and Remote Sensing Society

APRSU...... All Penang Revolutionary Students Union   (ML)

APRU .... Associacao dos Portugueses Refugiados do Ultramar [*Association of Portuguese Refugees from Overseas*]   (WER)

APRU .... Australian Population Research Institute

APRUALA ... Asociacion de Productores Rurales de Unidad Agropecuaria de Los Andes [*Venezuela*]   (DSCA)

APRUNA .. Asociacion Productores Rurales de la Cuenca del Unare [*Venezuela*]   (DSCA)

APRURD... Asociacion de Profesores del Recinto Universitario Ruben Dario [*Ruben Dario University Professors Association*] [*Nicaragua*]   (LA)

APRV........ Algemene Praktische Rechtsverzameling [*Benelux*]   (BAS)

APRW .... Australian Price Waterhouse - Government Liaison Services Library [*National Union Catalogue of Australia symbol*]

APS........... Aborigines' Protection Society [*Malaysia*]   (ML)

APS........... Aborigines' Protection Society [*Australia*]   (ADA)

APS........... Accion Politica Socialista [*Socialist Political Action*] [*Peru*] [*Political party*]   (PPW)

APS........... Accion Popular Socialista [*Socialist Popular Action*] [*Peru*]   (LA)

APS........... Administracion de Programas Sociales [*Puerto Rico*]   (DSCA)

APS........... Aerotransporte Peruanos Internacionales SA [*Peru*] [*ICAO designator*]   (FAAC)

APS........... Agonistiki Parataxi Spoudaston [*Student Fighting Faction*] [*Greek*]   (GC)

aps............. Air Communications Regiment   (RU)

aps............. Air Regiment Liaison   (BU)

APS........... Algerie Presse Service [*Algerian Press Service*]   (AF)

APS........... All Africa Press Service

APS........... Alliance pour le Progres Social [*Alliance for Social Progress*] [*Cambodia*]   (CL)

APS........... Anfangspunkt der Strecke [*Starting Point of a Flight*]   (EG)

APS........... Anotaton Peitharkhikon Symvoulion [*Supreme Disciplinary Council*] [*Greek*]   (GC)

ApS............ Anpartsselskab [*Private Limited Company*] [*Sweden*]

APS........... Arab Press Service

APS........... Arkhigeion Pyrosvestikou Somatos [*Fire Corps Headquarters*] [*Greek*]   (GC)

APS........... Armazens do Provo Socomin [*People's Store*] [*Guinea-Bissau*]

aps............. Army Food Depot   (RU)

APS........... Army Signal Regiment   (RU)

APS........... Associacao Portuguesa de Seguros [*Insurance representative body*] [*Portugal*]   (EY)

APS........... Association of Polish Archivists   (EAIO)

APS........... Association Professionnelle Sucriere [*Morocco*]

APS........... Atmospheric Pressure Sensor

APS........... Australian Perinatal Society

APS........... Australian Pig Society   (ADA)

APS........... Australian Prosthodontic Society

APS........... Australian Psychoanalytical Society

APS........... Australian Psychological Society   (ADA)

APS........... Australian Public Service   (ADA)

APS........... Automatic Deicer   (RU)

APS........... Automatic Signal Transmitter   (RU)

APS........... Homing Station   (RU)

APS........... Stechkin Automatic Pistol   (RU)

APSA........ Aerolineas Peruanas [*Peruvian Airlines*]   (LA)

APSA........ Aerolineas Peruanas Sociedad Anonima [*Peruvian Air Lines*]

APSA........ Association of Potters of South Africa

APSA........ Association of Professional Scientists of Australia   (ADA)

APSA........ Australasian [*or Australian*] Political Studies Association   (ADA)

APSA........ Australian Peak Shippers' Association

APSA........ Australian Pharmaceutical Sciences Association   (ADA)

APSA........ Australian Pig Science Association

APSA........ Australian Pre-School Association

APSA........ Australian Professional Surfers' Association

APSA........ Australian Public Service Association   (ADA)

APSA(FDO) ... Australian Public Service Association (Fourth Division Officers)

APSARA ... Australian Peace Studies and Research Association

APSB .... Australian Pony Stud Book

APSB .... Australian Public Service Bureau [*Commission*] [*Library*] [*National Union Catalogue of Australia symbol*]

APSBS...... Australian Pony Stud Book Society   (ADA)

APSBSI .... Australian Public Service Benevolent Society Inc.

APSBU...... Australian Public Sector and Broadcasting Union

APSC........ Adelaide Pistol Shooting Club [*Australia*]

APSC........ Air Power Studies Centre [*Royal Australian Air Force*]

APSC........ Arab Petroleum Services Company [*of the Organization of Arab Petroleum Exporting Countries*]

APSC........ Asian-Pacific Society of Cardiology   (EA)

APSC........ Australian Payments System Council

APSC........ Australian Police Staff College

APSCO...... Arabian Petroleum Supply Co. [*Saudi Arabia*]

APSDEP... Asian and Pacific Skill Development Programme

APSDIN .... APSDEP Information Network [*Islamabad, Pakistan*] [*Information service or system*]   (IID)

APSDIN .... Asian and Pacific Skill Development Information Network [*ILO*] [*United Nations*]   (DUND)

APSE .... Asociacion de Profesores de Segunda Ensenanza [*Secondary School Teachers Association*] [*Costa Rica*]   (LA)

APSEC ...... Asociacion de Productores de Semilla Certificada [*Colombia*]   (DSCA)

APSECS .... Australasian and Pacific Society for Eighteenth Century Studies   (ADA)

APSEDC ... Association for Pre-School Education of Deaf Children

APSF .... Australian Public Service Federation   (ADA)

APSFC...... Andhra Pradesh State Financial Corp. [*India*]   (PDAA)

APSG........ Association pour le Socialisme au Gabon [*Political party*]   (EY)

APSI .... Australian Professional Security Institute   (ADA)

APSIG .... Asia and Pacific Special Interest Group [*Australian Library and Information Association*]

APS-IPRS ... Asian-Pacific Section - IPRS [*International Confederation for Plastic and Reconstructive Surgery*] [*Singapore*]   (EAIO)

APSLF....... Association de Psychologie Scientifique de Langue Francaise [*French-Language Association of Scientific Psychology*]   (EAIO)

APSM........ Association de Prehistoire et de Speleologie de Monaco [*Monaco*]   (SLS)

APSM........ Automatic Letter-Sorting Machine   (RU)

APSO........ Afro-Asian People's Solidarity Organisation

APSO........ Asian Physical Society   (PDAA)

APSO........ Asia-Pacific Socialist Organization [*Political party*] [*Tokyo, Japan*]   (EAIO)

APSO........ Association of Personnel Service Organisations of South Africa (AA)
APSO........ Automatic Print Drier   (RU)
APSP .... Anotati Panellinios Synomospondia Polyteknon [*Supreme Panhellenic Confederation of Parents of Large Families*] [*Greek*]   (GC)
APS/RGK ... Air Communications Regiment of the High Command Reserve (RU)
APsS.......... Australian Psychological Society
APSSA....... Associate Member of the Pharmaceutical Society of South Africa (AA)
APSSEAR ... Association of Pediatric Societies of the Southeast Asian Region (EA)
APSSIDC .. Andhra Pradesh Small Scale Industrial Development Corp. [*India*]   (PDAA)
APSTC ...... Andhra Pradesh State Road Transport Corp. [*India*]   (PDAA)
APSU........ Amateur Pistol Shooting Union of Australia
APS/W ...... Asia Pacific Seminar/Workshop [*International Association of Scholarly Publishers*]
APsyOI...... Association des Psychologues de l'Ocean Indien   (EAIO)
APT .... Action for Public Transport [*Australia*]
APT .... African Personal Tax
APT .... African Petroleum Terminals Ltd.
APT .... Africa Publications Trust [*British*]
APT .... Agence de Presse Tunisienne [*Tunisian Press Agency*]
APT .... Albanian Labor Party   (RU)
APT .... Albanian Workers' Party   (BU)
apt .... Apartman [*Apartment, Flat*] [*Turkey*]   (CED)
Apt .... Apartment   (SCAC)
APT .... Artillery in Support of Tanks   (RU)
APT .... Asia-Pacific Telecommunity [*Thailand*] [*Telecommunications*]
APT .... Asset Privatization Trust [*Philippines*]
APT .... AT & T Philips Telecommunications
APT .... Australia Prophetical Truth Centre
APT .... Lineas Aereas Petroleras [*Colombia*] [*ICAO designator*]   (FAAC)
apt .... Pharmaceutical   (BU)
APTA........ Antigua Paddle Tennis Association   (EAIO)
APTA........ Asian Pineapple Traders Association   (PDAA)
APTA........ Asociacion de la Prensa Tecnica Argentina [*Argentina*]   (LAA)
APTA........ Australian Planning and Training Associates Proprietary Ltd.
APTA........ Australian Professional Triathletes Association
APTAV...... Asociation de Pilotos y Trabajadores de la Aviacion [*Association of Pilots and Aviation Workers*] [*Venezuela*]   (LA)
APTCH ..... Asociacion Postal-Telegrafica de Chile [*Postal and Telegraph Association of Chile*]   (LA)
APTEU...... Amalgamated Printing Trades Employees' Union [*Australia*] (DGA)
APTh .... Aristoteleion Panepistimion Thessalonikis [*Salonica Aristoteleion University*]   (GC)
APTI......... Arab Petroleum Training Institute [*Defunct*]   (EA)
APTIC ...... African Pyrethrum Technical Information Centre
APTIRC .... Asian-Pacific Tax and Investment Research Centre [*Singapore*] (EA)
APTIS....... Asia-Pacific Technology Information System [*ESCAP*] [*United Nations*]   (DUND)
APTL........ Administracion Publica de Transportes de Lima [*Lima Municipal Transportation Administration*] [*Peru*]   (LA)
APTLF...... Association de Psychologie du Travail de Langue Francaise [*French-Language Association of Work Psychology*] (EAIO)
Apto .... Apartamento   (SCAC)
APTR........ Antitank Artillery Reserve   (RU)
APTR........ Artillery Antitank Reserve   (BU)
APTU .... African Postal and Telecommunications Union   (AF)
APTU .... Australian Postal and Telecommunications Union   (ADA)
APTU .... Steam-Turbine Nuclear Propulsion Engine, Steam-Turbine Atomic Power Plant   (RU)
APTUC...... All Pakistan Trade Union Congress
APTUF...... All-Pakistan Trade Union Federation
APTUN ..... Association of Professional Trade Unionists of Nigeria   (AF)
APU .... Aeropuma SA [*El Salvador*] [*ICAO designator*]   (FAAC)
APU .... African Parliamentary Union
APU .... Akademija Primenjenih Umetnosti [*Academy of Applied Arts*] [*Belgrade*]   (YU)
APU .... Akademija za Pozorisnu Umetnost [*Academy of Theatrical Art*] [*Belgrade*]   (YU)
APU .... Alianca Popular Unida/Alianca Povo Unido [*United People's Alliance*] [*Portugal*] [*Political party*]   (PPW)
APU .... Angkatan Perpaduan Ummah [*Muslim Unity Movement*] [*Malaysia*] [*Political party*]   (EY)
APU .... Arab Postal Union
APU .... Architectural Planning Administration   (RU)
APU .... Arcidiecesni Pastoracni Ustredi [*Archdiocesan Pastoral Center*] (CZ)
APU .... Asia Parliamentary Union   (CL)
APU .... Asociacion de Prensa Uruguaya [*Uruguayan Press Association*] (LA)

APU .... Autocollimation Instrument for Checking Angular Measures (RU)
APU .... General-Purpose Truck Trailer   (RU)
APUA .... Association du Peuple pour l'Unite et l'Action [*Algeria*] [*Political party*]   (EY)
APUDAH ... Agence de Publicite Dahomeene
APUG .... Carrier-Based Hunter-Killer Group   (RU)
APUK .... Apurinic Acid   (RU)
APUMAG ... Asociacion de Profesionales Universitarios del Ministerio de Agricultura y Ganaderia de la Nacion [*Argentina*]   (LAA)
APUR .... Atelier Parisien d'Urbanisme [*Paris Office of Urbanization*] [*France*] [*Information service or system*]   (IID)
apuv............ Apuverbi [*Auxiliary verb*] [*Finland*]
APUV .... Universal Pneumatic Impact Fuze [*Aviation*]   (RU)
APV .... Agence Presse Voltaique [*Upper Voltan Press Agency*]   (AF)
APV .... Algemene Politieverordening [*Benelux*]   (BAS)
APV .... Automatic Reclosing   (RU)
APV .... Autonomna Pokrajina Vojvodina [*Autonomous Province of Vojvodina*]   (YU)
APV b/s .... Automatic Reclosing without Controlling Synchronism   (RU)
APVN .... Armee Populaire du Viet-Nam [*Vietnam People's Army*] [*Use VPA North Vietnamese*]   (CL)
APV-NRS ... Autonomna Pokrajina Vojvodina, Narodna Republika Srbija [*Autonomous Province of Vojvodina, Serbia*]   (YU)
APVO .... Soviet Air Defense Aviation   (MCD)
APVOS..... Automatic Reclosing with Synchronism Expectation   (RU)
APVRD...... Atomic Ramjet Engine   (RU)
APVS .... Automatic Reclosing with Self-Synchronization   (RU)
APVT........ Actes Tenant Lieu de Proces-Verbaux et de Transaction [*Instruments Taking the Place of Proceedings and Transactions*]   (CL)
APVUS...... Automatic Reclosing with Synchronism-Catch Arrangement (RU)
APW .... Apia [*Samoa Islands*] [*Airport symbol*]   (OAG)
APW .... Assemblee Populaire des Wilayate [*Governorate Popular Assembly*] [*Algeria*]   (AF)
APWA ...... Australian Plaiters and Whipmakers' Association
APWR .... Woomera [*Australia*] [*ICAO location identifier*]   (ICLI)
APWSS ..... Asian Pacific Weed Science Society   (EA)
APWU .... Amalgamated Postal Workers' Union [*Australia*]   (ADA)
APX .... Atelier de Construction de Puteaux [*Groupement Industriel des Armements Terrestres*] [*France*]   (PDAA)
APXM .... Christmas Island [*Australia*] [*ICAO location identifier*]   (ICLI)
APY .... APA Internacional [*Dominican Republic*] [*ICAO designator*] (FAAC)
APYF........ Asian Pacific Youth Forum   (EA)
APYFL...... Asian Pacific Youth Freedom League [*Tokyo, Japan*]   (EAIO)
APYSDE ... Anotera Perifereiaka Ypiresiaka Symvoulia Dimotikis Ekpaidevseos [*Higher Regional Service Councils for Elementary Education*] [*Greek*]   (GC)
APZ .... Barrage Balloon   (RU)
APZ .... Zapala [*Argentina*] [*Airport symbol*]   (OAG)
Aq.............. Aequivalent [*Equivalent*] [*German*]   (GCA)
AQ.............. Air Queensland [*Australia*]
AQ.............. Antarctica [*ANSI two-letter standard code*]   (CNC)
AQ.............. Aquila [*Car registration plates*] [*Italian*]
AQA.......... Approved Quality Assurance [*Australia*]
AQA.......... Araraquara [*Brazil*] [*Airport symbol*] [*Obsolete*]   (OAG)
AQA.......... Asociacion Quimica Argentina [*Argentina*]   (DSCA)
AQA.......... Australian Quadraplegic Association   (ADA)
AQA.......... Australian Quilters' Association
AQAC .... Australian Quality Assurance Consultants
AQAP .... Allied Quality Assurance Provision [*NATO*]   (MCD)
AQAP .... Allied Quality Assurance Publication [*NATO*]   (NATG)
AQBBA ..... Australian Queen Bee Breeders' Association
AQC .... Allied Queensland Coal [*Australia*]
AQCA .... Australian Quality Circle Association
AQD.......... Aquacultural Department [*SEAFDEC*] [*Philippines*] [*Research center*]   (IRC)
AQE.......... Air Aquitaine [*France*] [*ICAO designator*]   (FAAC)
AQHA ...... Australian Quarter Horse Association   (ADA)
AQI .... Qaisumah [*Saudi Arabia*] [*Airport symbol*]   (OAG)
AQI .... Quartalsberichterstattung fuer Arbeitskraefte in der Industrie [*Quarterly Report on the Industrial Labor Force*]   (EG)
AQIS......... Australian Quarantine and Inspection Service
AQJ .... Aqaba [*Jordan*] [*Airport symbol*]   (OAG)
AQMC....... Association of Quality Management Consultants [*British*] (EAIO)
AQN .... Air Queensland [*Australia*] [*ICAO designator*]   (FAAC)
AQP.......... Arequipa [*Peru*] [*Airport symbol*]   (OAG)
AQPC .... Australian Quaker Peace Committee
AQS .... Australian Quarantine Service
AQS .... Saqani [*Fiji*] [*Airport symbol*]   (OAG)
AQSASA ... Aleemiyah Qaderiyyah Spiritual Assembly of South Africa [*South Africa*]   (EAIO)
AQSH........ Arkivi Qendror Shteteror [*Albanian*]

Aqu............ Aequivalent [*Equivalent*] [*German*] (GCA)
AQU .... Aquair Luftfahrt GmbH [*Germany*] [*ICAO designator*] (FAAC)
aqu............. Aquarelle [*Watercolor*] [*Publishing*] [*French*]
AQUACOP ... Aquaculture Programme du Centre Oceanologique du
Pacificue [*French*] (MSC)
Aque.......... Aqueduc [*Aqueduct*] [*Military map abbreviation World War I*]
[*French*] (MTD)
Aquiv-Gew ... Aequivalentgewicht [*Equivalent Weight*] [*German*] (GCA)
AR............. Academische Raad [*Netherlands*]
AR............. Acting Rector [*Church of England in Australia*]
AR............. Activated Ore (RU)
AR............. Adelaide Rifles [*Australia*] (DMA)
AR............. Aerial Reconnaissance (RU)
AR............. Aeronca Manufacturing [*ICAO aircraft manufacturer identifier*]
(ICAO)
AR............. Agencja Reutera [*Reuters Agency*] [*Poland*]
AR............. Agencja Robotnicza [*Workers' Press Agency*] (POL)
AR............. Air Reserve (RU)
AR............. Akkumulatives Register [*Storage Register*] (ADPT)
AR............. Algemeen Rijksarchief [*Netherlands*]
AR............. Alger [*Algiers*] [*On cartridge bags*] [*Military*] [*French*] (MTD)
AR............. Allard Register (EA)
AR............. Altesse Royale [*Royal Highness*] [*French*]
AR............. Altezza Reale [*Royal Highness*] [*Italian*]
AR............. Amilcar Register (EA)
AR............. Amis de la Roche (EAIO)
AR............. Analogrechner [*Analog Calculator*] (ADPT)
AR............. Animal Rights [*An association*] [*Australia*]
ar.............. Arabe [*or Arabico*] [*Arabian or Arabic*] [*Portuguese*]
ar.............. Arabian, Arabic (RU)
ar.............. Arabic (BU)
ar.............. Arabisch [*Arabic*] [*German*] (GCA)
Ar............. Arad [*Arad*] (RO)
Ar............. Arapca [*Arabic*] (TU)
Ar............. Arapcadan [*From Arabic*] (TU)
Ar............. Arazi [*Land Surface, Terrain*] (TU)
AR............. Arbitrale Rechtspraak [*Benelux*] (BAS)
ar.............. Archaic (TPFD)
ar.............. Archaique [*French*] (TPFD)
AR............. Archeologicke Rozhledy [*Archeological Annals*] (CZ)
Ar............. A Retard [*Military*] [*French*] (MTD)
AR............. Arezzo [*Car registration plates*] [*Italian*]
AR............. Argentina [*ANSI two-letter standard code*] (CNC)
Ar............. Argon [*Argon*] [*Chemical element*] [*German*]
ar.............. Aromatisch [*Aromatic*] [*German*] (GCA)
AR............. Arrete [*Decision, Ordinance, By-law*] [*French*]
AR............. Arrete Royal [*Royal Decree*] [*French*] (FLAF)
AR............. Arriere [*Home Front*] [*Military*] [*French*] (MTD)
AR............. Arrondissementsrechtbank [*Benelux*] (BAS)
ar.............. Artillery (BU)
AR............. Artillery Reconnaissance (RU)
AR............. Asociacion Regionalista [*Regionalist Association*] [*Spanish*]
(WER)
AR............. Assembleia da Republica [*Assembly of the Republic*] [*Portuguese*]
(WER)
AR............. Associacao Rural [*Brazil*] (DSCA)
AR............. Aufsichtsrat [*Supervisory Board*] [*German*]
AR............. Augustinian Recollect Sisters [*An association*] [*Australia*]
AR............. Australian Ratings Proprietary Ltd.
AR............. Australian Republican
AR............. Automatic Control (RU)
AR............. Autonomous Recording Device (RU)
A/R............. Avis de Reception [*Return Receipt*] [*French*]
AR............. Emergency Breaker (RU)
AR............. Fountain Pen (RU)
AR............. Intelligence through Secret Agents (RU)
ar.............. Irrigation Ditch [*Topography*] (RU)
ar.............. Motor Transport Company, Truck Company (RU)
AR............. Nitrogen Equilibrium (RU)
AR............. Repair Service (BU)
ARA .... Accao Revolucionaria Armada [*Armed Revolutionary Action*]
[*Portuguese*] (WER)
ARA .... Accion Revolucionaria Agraria [*Agrarian Revolutionary Action*]
[*Ecuador*] (LA)
ARA .... Accion Revolucionaria Anticommunista [*Anticommunist
Revolutionary Action*] [*Argentina*] (LA)
ARA .... Aerobeira, Sociedade de Transportes Aeros [*Portugal*] [*ICAO
designator*] (FAAC)
ARA .... Algemeen Rijksarchief [*Benelux*] (BAS)
ARA .... Amateurs Radio Algeriens [*Amateur Radio Society of Algeria*]
(PDAA)
ARA .... Anti-Rightist Alliance (ML)
ARA .... Antwerp-Rotterdam-Amsterdam [*Oil refining region*]
[*Netherlands*]
ARA .... Arab Roads Association [*Cairo, Egypt*] (EAIO)

ARA .... Armada de la Republica Argentina [*Navy of the Republic of
Argentina*] (LAA)
ARA .... Asian Recycling Association (EAIO)
ARA .... Assistance Routiere et Assurance (FLAF)
ARA .... Associacao Rural de Arceburgo [*Brazil*] (DSCA)
ARA .... Association of Radiologists of Australasia (ADA)
ARA .... Australian Racquetball Association
ARA .... Australian Reading Association (ADA)
ARA .... Australian Regular Army (ADA)
ARA .... Australian Renderers' Association
ARA .... Australian Retailers Association (ADA)
ARA .... Australian Robot Association (EAIO)
ARA .... Australian Romney Association
ARA .... Auto Recovery Association of New South Wales [*Australia*]
ARAB .... Academie Royale +d'Archeologie de Belgique [*Royal Academy
of Archaeology of Belgium*] (EAIO)
arab .... Arabiaa [*or Arabiaksi*] [*Finland*]
arab .... Arabialainen [*Finland*]
arab .... Arabic (BU)
Arab .... Arabies [*Arabian*] [*Afrikaans*]
ARAB .... Association Royale des Actuaires Belges [*Royal Association of
Belgian Actuaries*] (SLS)
ARAB .... Association Royale des Actuaires Belges [*Association of Belgian
Actuaries*] (EAIO)
ARAB .... Australian Radio Advertising Bureau (ADA)
ARABHA .. Arab Historians Association (EAIO)
ARABIC ... Ar-Rajhi Banking & Investment Co. [*Saudi Arabia*] (EY)
ARABS ...... Australian Racing and Breeding Stables Ltd.
ARABSAT ... Arab Satellite Communications Organization [*Saudi Arabia*]
[*Telecommunications*]
arabsk .... Arabian, Arabic (RU)
ARAC .... Antarctic Research Advisory Council
ARAC .... Australasian Register of Agricultural Consultants
ARAC .... Australian Refugee Advisory Council
ARACI ...... Associate of the Royal Australian Chemical Institute
arad .... Army Artillery Reconnaissance Battalion (RU)
ARAD .... Association des Radio Amateurs de Djibouti [*Association of
Radio Amateurs of Djibouti*] (PDAA)
Aradet .... Arab (OMWE)
ARADET... Arab Company for Chemical Detergents [*Iraq*]
Aradet .... Arab Company for Detergent Minerals (OMWE)
ARADO ..... Arab Administrative Development Organization [*Jordan*]
(EAIO)
arae .... Airplane on Artillery Mission (BU)
ARAEN ..... Appareil de Reference pour la determination de l'Affaiblissement
Equivalent pour la Nettete [*Reference Apparatus for the
Determination of AEN*] (PDAA)
ARAF........ Accademia Romana delle Arti Figurative [*Italian*] (SLS)
ARAI .... Automotive Research Association of India [*Research center*]
(IRC)
ARAIA...... Associate of the Royal Australian Institute of Architects (ADA)
Aral m .... Aral Sea (RU)
Aramco...... Arabian American Oil Company (OMWE)
ARAMIS... Agencement en Rames Automatisees de Modules Independants
dans les Stations [*Arrangement in automated trains of
independent modules in stations*] [*A satirical novel by Bruno
Latour*] [*Based on an actual Personal Rapid Transit
program pursued by the French government*]
ARAN-D.... Dispatcher's Automatic Active Load Distributor (RU)
ARAN-S.... Power Plant Automatic Active Load Distributor (RU)
ARANZ ..... Archives and Records Association of New Zealand (EAIO)
aranzh .... To Arrange [*Music*] (BU)
ARAPB...... Association Royale des Artistes Professionels de Belgique [*Royal
Association of Professional Artists of Belgium*] (EAIO)
ARAPH ..... Automated Reading Aid for the Physically Handicapped
[*Australia*]
ARAPI...... Affiliate of the Royal Australian Planning Institute
ARAR .... Algemeen Rijksambtenaren Reglement [*Benelux*] (BAS)
ARAR .... Azienda Rilievo e Alienazione Residuati [*Organization for the
Resale of Army Surplus Stores*] [*Italian*]
ARAS........ Agricultural Research and Advisory Station [*New South Wales,
Australia*]
Aras........... Arastirma [*Research*] (TU)
ARATE...... Australian Financial Markets Database
ARATECO ... Arabian Trading and Equipment Company [*Saudi Arabia*]
(ME)
ARAU .... Atelier de Recherche et d'Action Urbaines [*The Workshop for
Urban Research and Action*] [*Belgium*]
ARAU .... Australian Rural Adjustment Unit
ARAVA ..... Asuntorakennustuotannon Valtuuskunta [*State Housing
Construction Commission*] [*Finland*] (WEN)
ARAWA .... Amateur Rowing Association of Western Australia
ARAZP...... Australasian Regional Association of Zoological Parks and
Aquaria
ARB .... Agricultural Requirements Board [*Queensland, Australia*]
ARB .... Air Maintenance Base (BU)

ARB .... Air Reservation Bureau [*New South Wales, Australia*]
ARB .... Alianza Revolucionaria Barrientista [*Bolivia*] [*Political party*] (PPW)
ARb .... Allgemeine Bedingungen fuer Bahnamtliche Rollfuhrbetriebe [*General Terms for Railroad Trucking Enterprises*] (EG)
arb .... Arbeid [*Work*] [*Publishing Danish/Norwegian*]
Arb .... Arbeider [*Labor (Party)*] [*Afrikaans*]
Arb .... Arbeidsblad [*Benelux*] (BAS)
Arb .... Arbeit [*or Arbeiter*] [*Work or Worker*] [*German*]
arb .... Arbete [*Work*] [*Sweden*]
Arb .... Arbitrale Beslissing [*Belgium*] (BAS)
Arb .... Arbre [*Tree*] [*Military map abbreviation World War I*] [*French*] (MTD)
ARB .... Arubair [*Aruba*] [*ICAO designator*] (FAAC)
ARB .... Motor Vehicle Repair Base (RU)
ARB .... Wet Administratieve Rechtspraak Bedrijfsorganisatie [*Benelux*] (BAS)
ARBA .... Australian Right to Bear Arms Association
ArbAHV .... Arbitrage Algemene Handelsvoorwaarden [*Benelux*] (BAS)
Arb AusglG ... Gesetz u. d. Ausgleichs und Schiedsverfahren Arbeitsstreitigkeiten [*Law on Labor Arbitration*] [*German*] (ILCA)
ArbBloemb ... Arbitrage van de Vereniging voor de Bloembollenhandel [*Benelux*] (BAS)
ArbCvG...... Arbitrage van het Comite van Graanhandelaren [*Benelux*] (BAS)
ArbDNC .... Arbitrage over het Duitsch-Nederlandsch Contract [*Netherlands*] (BAS)
ARBED...... Acieries Reunies de Burbach-Eich-Dudelange [*Luxembourg*] [*Business term*]
Arbeitg .... Arbeitgeber [*Employer*] [*German*]
Arbeitsgem ... Arbeitsgemeinschaft [*Study Group*] [*German*]
ARBel .... Wet Administratieve Rechtspraak Belastingzaken [*Benelux*] (BAS)
Arb et Sec... Arbitrage et Securite (FLAF)
Arb G .... Arbeitsgericht [*Labor Court*] [*German*] (DLA)
ArbGBHV ... Arbitrage van de Bond voor de Handel in Vetten [*Benelux*] (BAS)
Arb GG ...... Arbeitsgerichtsgesetz [*Law on labor courts*] [*German*] (ILCA)
ArbGronKorenbeurs ... Arbitrage van de Groningse Korenbeurs [*Benelux*] (BAS)
ARBICA ..... Arab Regional Branch of the International Council on Archives
arbit............ Arbitrage [*French*] (FLAF)
ARBN .... Australian Registered Body Number
ArbNGZI... Arbitrage van de Nederlandse Vereniging van Graan- en Zaadimporteurs [*Netherlands*] (BAS)
ArbNHLB ... Arbitrage van de Vereniging Nederlandsche Huideden Lederbeurzen [*Netherlands*] (BAS)
ArbRKorenbeurs ... Arbitrage van de Rotterdamse Korenbeurs [*Netherlands*] (BAS)
ArbRspr ..... Arbitrale Rechtspraak [*Benelux*] (BAS)
ARBV .... Architects' Registration Board of Victoria [*Australia*]
ArbVBoekhandel ... Arbitrage van de Vereniging tot Behartiging van de Belangen van de Boekhandel [*Benelux*] (BAS)
ArbVK .... Arbitrage van de Vereniging voor de Koffiehandel [*Benelux*] (BAS)
ArbvKat ..... Arbitrage van de Vereniging voor de Katoenhandel [*Benelux*] (BAS)
ArbVVO .... Arbitrage van de Vereniging voor de Handel in Vetten en Olien [*Benelux*] (BAS)
ArbVZ(V) .. Arbitrage van de Vereniging voor de Handel in Zuidvruchten [*Benelux*] (BAS)
ARC .... Abortion Rights Coalition [*Australia*]
ARC .... Accounting Research Centre [*University of Sydney*] [*Australia*]
ARC .... Action pour la Renaissance de Corse [*Action for the Rebirth of Corsica*] [*French*]
ARC .... Action Revolutionnaire Corse [*Corsican Revolutionary Action*] (PD)
ARC .... Adelaide Racing Club [*Australia*]
ARC .... Administrative Radio Conference [*International Telecommunications Union*]
ARC .... Administrative Reforms Commission [*India*]
ARC .... Aeronautical Research Committee [*CSIR*] [*India*] (PDAA)
ARC .... African Representative Council
ARC .... Agricultural Refinancing Corporation [*India*]
ARC .... Agricultural Research Center [*Egypt*] (IRC)
ARC .... Agricultural Research Council [*Zimbabwe*] (ARC)
ARC .... Air Routing International Corp. [*ICAO designator*] (FAAC)
ARC .... Alexandria Racing Club [*Egypt*]
ARC .... Alianza Regional de Castilla y Leon [*Regional Alliance of Castile and Leon*] [*Spanish*] (WER)
ARC .... Alliance of Revolutionary Communists
ARC .... Alliance Revolutionnaire Caraibe [*Guadeloupe*] [*Political party*] (EY)
ARC .... Alpine Resorts Comminnsoin [*Victoria, Australia*]
ARC .... Annual Review Committee [*NATO*] (NATG)

ARC .... Antrepriza Romana pentru Constructii [*Romanian Construction Enterprise*] (RO)
ARC .... Applied Research Corp. [*Singapore*] (IRC)
ARC .... Aqaba Railway Corp. [*India*]
arc .... Arcaico [*Archaic*] [*Portuguese*]
ARC .... Archive and Records Centre [*Geneva, Switzerland*] [*United Nations*] (ECON)
Arc .... Arcivescovo [*Archbishop*] [*Italian*]
ARC .... Arctic (WDAA)
ARC .... Artemia Reference Center [*Research center*] [*Belgium*] (IRC)
ARC .... Associacao Rural de Cantagalo [*Brazil*] (DSCA)
ARC .... Associacao Rural de Concordia [*Brazil*] (DSCA)
ARC .... Assurances et Reassurances du Congo [*Insurance*]
ARC .... Atma Jaya Research Center [*Indonesia*] [*Research center*] (IRC)
ARC .... Australian Capital Territory Recycling Campaign
ARC .... Australian Registrars Committee
ARC .... Australian Reinforced Concrete (ADA)
ARC .... Australian Repertory Company
ARC .... Australian Research Council
ARC .... Australian Resuscitation Council
ARC .... Australian Review Council
ARC .... Australian Rostrum Council
ARC .... Australian Rowing Council
ARC .... Autoklub Republiky Ceskoslovenske [*Automobile Club of the Czechoslovak Republic*] (CZ)
ARC .... Automatyczna Regulacja Czestotliwosci [*Automatic Frequency Control*] [*Poland*]
ARC .... Azzawiya Refinery Company [*Libya*]
ARC .... Laboratory of Aquaculture and Artemia Reference Center [*Belgium*] (IRC)
ARC .... Rainbow Group [*Party group in the European Parliament*] (ECED)
ARC .... Societe Nationale d'Assurance du Congo
ARCA .... Aerovias Colombianas [*Colombia*] (COL)
ARCA .... Asbestos Removalists Contractors Association [*Australia*]
ARCACI .... Association des Representants des Compagnies Aeriennes de Cote-D'Ivoire
ARCAFA ... Applied Research Center for Archeology and Fine Arts [*Cambodia*] (CL)
ARCAM .... Assemblee Representative du Cameroun
ARCBA...... Australian Registered Cattle Breeders' Association
ARCC .... Africa Regional Coordinating Committee
ARCCA...... Agricultural Research Council of Central Africa
ARCCCWA ... Association of Registered Child Care Centers of Western Australia
ARCCEC ... Al-Rajhi Co. for Currency Exchange and Commerce [*Saudi Arabia*]
ARCE......... Associazione per le Relazioni Culturali con l'Estero [*Association for Cultural Relations with Foreign Countries*] [*Italian*] (WER)
ARCEDEM ... African Regional Centre for Engineering Design and Manufacturing (EA)
ARCES ...... Armement Cesbron
arch .... Archaeology (TPFD)
ARCH....... Archduke (WDAA)
arch .... Archeologie [*French*] (TPFD)
Arch .... Archipielago [*Archipelago*] [*Spanish*] (NAU)
Arch .... Architekt [*Architect*] [*German*]
Arch .... Architektur [*Architecture*] [*German*] (GCA)
Arch .... Architetto [*Architect*] [*Italian*]
Arch .... Archiv [*Archive*] [*German*]
arch .... Archivum [*Archives*] [*Hungary*] (HU)
ARCH....... Association to Resource Co-op Housing [*Australia*]
ARCH....... Australian Architectural Database [*Stanton Library*] [*Information service or system*] (IID)
ARCh .... Automatic Frequency Control (BU)
ARCh .... Automatic Sensitivity Control (RU)
Archa .... Alianza Chilena Anticomunista (WGAO)
Archaol ...... Archaeologie [*Archeology*] [*German*] (GCA)
ARCHEDDA ... Architectures for Heterogeneous European Distributed Databases
ARChERANUP ... Automatic Frequency Control and Economical Active Load Distribution Allowing for Network Losses (RU)
ARCHI ...... Asociacion de Radiodifusoras de Chile [*Chilean Broadcasting Association*] (LA)
Archip .... Archipelag [*Archipelago*] [*Poland*]
ARChM ..... Automatic Frequency and (Active) Power Control (RU)
Arch MedLeg ... Archives Belges de Medecine Legale [*Belgium*] (BAS)
Arch PhilDr ... Archives de Philosphie du Droit [*French*] (BAS)
ARCI......... Applied Research Center of Iran (WED)
ARCI......... Association Regionale Caraibeenne des Infirmieres [*Martinique*] (EAIO)
ARCI......... Associazione Ricreativa Culturale Italiana [*Italian Cultural-Recreational Association*] (WER)
ARCI......... Atelier de Rectification de Cote-D'Ivoire
ARCIC-II... Anglican-Roman Catholic International Commission

ARCN .... Agricultural Research Council of Norway   (EAIO)

ARCO .... Accion Revolucionaria Campesina y Obrera [*Peasant and Worker Revolutionary Action*] [*Ecuador*]   (LA)

ARCO .... Aerolineas Colonia SA [*Airline*] [*Uruguay*]

ARCO .... Arcato [*With the Bow*] [*Music*]   (ROG)

arco .... Arcebispo [*Archbishop*] [*Portuguese*]

ARCO .... Associacao Riograndense de Criadores de Ovinos [*Brazil*]   (DSCA)

ARCOA ..... Agence de Representation Consignation pour l'Ouest Africain

ARCOA ..... Asociacion Rosarina de Criadores de Ovejeros Alemanes [*Argentina*]   (LAA)

ARCOB ..... Verdi Arcobaleno [*Italy*] [*Political party*]   (ECED)

ARCOIN ... Arquitectura Construcciones. Ingenieria [*Colombia*]   (COL)

ARCOM ... Antrepriza Romana de Constructii-Montaj [*Romanian Enterprise for Construction-Assembly*]   (RO)

ARCOMA ... Atelier Regional de Construction de Materiel Agricole

ARCOMET ... Area Commanders' Meeting [*NATO*]   (NATG)

ARCONZ .. Queen Elizabeth II Arts Council of New Zealand   (EAIO)

ARCOPLAN ... Arquitectura Construccion Planeamiento Ingenieria Ltda. [*Cucuta*]   (COL)

ARCOS ...... All-Russian Cooperative Society [*English equivalent of AMTORG*]

ARCP .... Aerodrome Reference Code Panel [*ICAO*]   (DA)

ARCRAN .. Agricultural Research Council of Rhodesia and Nyasaland

ARCS .... Aeroklub Republiky Ceskoslovenske [*Aero Club of the Czechoslovak Republic*]

ARCS .... Afghan Red Crescent Society [*Afghanistan*]   (EAIO)

ARCS .... Association of Regulatory and Clinical Scientists

ARCS .... Australian Red Cross Society   (ADA)

ARCS .... Automatisiertes Reproduktions-,Copier-und Sortiersystem [*Automated Reproduction Copier and Sort System*] [*German*]   (ADPT)

ARCSOLA ... AACOBS [*Australian Advisory Committee on Bibliographical Services*] Regional Committee - Sub-Committee on Library Automation   (ADA)

ARCSS ...... Center for Social Science Research and Documentation for the Arab Region [*UNESCO*] [*Information service or system*]   (IID)

ARCT .... African Regional Centre for Technology [*See also CRAT*]   (EA)

Arct .... Arctic

ARCV .... Association de Recherche en Chirurgie Vasculaire [*Association for Research in Vascular Surgery*] [*France*]   (EAIO)

ARCWU .... Australian Rope and Cordage Workers' Union

arcybp .... Arcybiskup [*Archbishop*] [*Poland*]

arcyks........ Arcyksiaze [*Archduke*] [*Poland*]

ARD........... Accion Radical Democrata [*Democratic Radical Action*] [*Guatemala*]   (LA)

ARD........... Algemeen Reglement voor den Dienst op de Spoorwegen [*Benelux*]   (BAS)

ARD........... Alor [*Indonesia*] [*Airport symbol*]   (OAG)

ARD........... Arbeitsgemeinschaft der Oeffentlichrechtlichen Rundfunkanstalten der Bundesrepublik Deutschland [*Working Association of the Statutory Broadcasting Corporations of the Federal Republic of Germany*]   (WEN)

ARD........... Ardent   (DSUE)

ard.............. Artillery Reconnaissance Battalion   (RU)

ARD........... Ata-Aerocondor Transportes Aereos Ltda. [*Portugal*] [*ICAO designator*]   (FAAC)

ARD........... Atomic Jet Engine   (RU)

ARD........... Automatic Pressure Regulator   (RU)

ARDA .... Agricultural and Rural Development Authority [*Rhodesian*]   (AF)

ARDB .... Australian Resources Development Bank Ltd.   (ADA)

ARDC .... Agricultural Refinance and Development Corp. [*India*]   (PDAA)

ARDC .... Air Research and Development Council [*NATO*]   (NATG)

ARDC .... Aswan Regional Development Centre

ARDC .... Australian Racing Drivers Club   (ADA)

ARDCES ... Arab Regional Documentation Centre for the Economic and Social Sciences [*Proposed*]

ARDD........ Ananeotiki Kinisi Dimokratikon Dikigoron [*Restorative Movement of Democratic Lawyers*]   (GC)

ARDE .... Accion Republicana Democratica Espanola [*Spanish Democratic Republican Action*]   (WER)

ARDE .... Alianza Revolucionaria Democratica [*Democratic Revolutionary Alliance*] [*Nicaragua*] [*Political party*]   (PD)

ARDE .... Armament Research and Development Establishment [*India*]   (PDAA)

ARDE .... Associazione Romana di Entomologia [*Italian Association of Entomology*]   (SLS)

ARDECOMAG ... Association Regionale de Developpement de la Cooperation Maritime aux Antilles-Guyane [*Regional Association for Developing Maritime Cooperation in the Antilles-French Guiana*]   (LA)

ARDEN ..... Association Regionale pour le Developpement et l'Etude des Energies Nouvelles [*Regional Association for the Development and Study of Nonconventional Energies*] [*France*]

ARDES...... Accion Revolucionaria de Estudiantes de Secundaria [*Revolutionary Action of Secondary School Students*] [*El Salvador*]   (LA)

ARDES...... Association pour la Recherche Demographique, Economique, et Sociale [*Algeria*]

ARDF .... Association Reunion Departement Francais [*Association for Reunion as a French Department*] [*Political party*]   (PPW)

ARDG .... Automatic Gas Pressure Regulator   (RU)

ARDGT .... Automatic Gas Pressure Regulator for Terminal Lines   (RU)

ARDIC....... Agence de Representations Directes pour la Defense des Interets Commerciaux

ARDIC....... Association pour la Recherche et le Developpement en Informatique Chimique [*Association for Research and Development of Chemical Informatics*] [*Information service or system*]   (IID)

ARDL .... Algemeen Reglement voor den Dienst op de Locaalspoorwegen [*Benelux*]   (BAS)

ARD-L ...... Algierska Republika Demokratyczno-Ludowa [*Algerian People's Democratic Republic*] [*Poland*]

Ardo .... Ardito [*Ardently*] [*Music*]

Ardre .... Ardoisiere [*Slate Quarry*] [*Military map abbreviation World War I*] [*French*]   (MTD)

ARDRI...... Agricultural and Rural Development Research Institute [*South Africa*]   (ARC)

ARDS........ Aboriginal Resource and Development Services [*Australia*]

Ardt........... Arrondissement [*Rounding Off*] [*French*]

ARDU .... Aircraft Research and Development Unit [*Australia*]

ARDXC ..... Australian Radio DX [*Long Distance*] Club

ARE .... Accion Republicana Espanola

ARE .... Aires, Aerovias de Integracion Regional SA [*Colombia*] [*ICAO designator*]   (FAAC)

are .... Air Radio Squadron   (BU)

ARE .... Alianza Revolucionaria Ecuatoriana [*Ecuadorean Revolutionary Alliance*]   (LA)

ARE .... Alianza Revolucionaria Estudiantil [*Student Revolutionary Alliance*] [*Peru*]   (LA)

ARE .... Arab Republic of Egypt   (ME)

ARE .... Arabskaia Respublika Egipet [*Arab Republic of Egypt*]

ARE .... Army Air Reconnaissance Squadron   (RU)

Are .... Aromatischer Kohlenwasserstoffrest [*Aromatic Hydrocarbon Radical*] [*German*]   (GCA)

ARE .... Assemblee des Regions d'Europe [*Later, AER*]   (EAIO)

ARE .... Assembly of European Regions [*Later, AER*]   (EAIO)

ARE .... Atelier de Construction de Roanne [*Groupement Industriel des Armements Terrestres*] [*France*]   (PDAA)

ARE .... Austrian Rain Engineering [*Commercial firm*]

ARE .... United Arab Emirates [*ANSI three-letter standard code*]   (CNC)

AREA .... Agrupacion Reformista de Estudiantes de Agricultura [*Agriculture Students Reform Group*] [*Argentina*]   (LA)

AREA .... Association for Research, Exploration, and Aid [*Australia*]

AREA .... Australian Remedial Education Association   (ADA)

AREA .... Australian Resources and Environmental Assessment

AREAM .... Australian Resources and Environmental Assessment Model

AREBO ..... Association pour le Developpement de la Region de Bonoua [*Bonoua Region Development Association*] [*Ivory Coast*]   (AF)

AREC........ Arab Engineering Company [*Technical support and professional training firm*] [*Abu Dhabi*]   (MENA)

AREC........ Association des Ressortissants de l'Enclave de Cabinda

ARECS ..... Australian Real Estate Computer Systems

AREDI-ABIDJAN ... Africaine de Representation et Diffusion Abidjan

AReg......... Arrete du Regent [*French*]   (BAS)

AREI........ Associate of the Real Estate and Stock Institute of Australia   (ADA)

AREIA ...... Associate of the Real Estate Institute of Australia

AREL........ Ingenieros Electricistas [*Colombia*]   (COL)

ARELAP ... Asociacion Regional Latinoamericana de Puertos del Pacifico [*Latin American Regional Association of Pacific Coast Ports*]   (LA)

ARELS-FELCO ... Association of Recognised English Language Schools and Federation of English Language Course Organisations Ltd. [*European*]

AREMA .... Antoky ny Revolosiona Malagasy [*Vanguard of the Malagasy Revolution*]   (PPW)

AREMA .... Avantgarde de la Revolution Malgache [*Vanguard of the Malagasy Revolution*] [*Political party*]   (PPW)

aremb .... Motor Vehicle Repair Battalion   (RU)

AREMG .... Association Regionale d'Expansion Musicale de la Guyane [*Regional Association for Expanding French Guianese Music*]   (LA)

Aremkuz .... Automobile Body Repair Plant   (RU)

AREMZ..... Automobile Repair Plant   (RU)

ARENA .... Alianca Renovadora Nacional [*Alliance for National Renewal*] [*Brazil*] [*Political party*]   (PPW)

ARENA .... Alianza Republicana Nacionalista [*Nationalist Republican Alliance*] [*El Salvador*] [*Political party*]   (PPW)

ARENCO .. Architects, Engineers, and Constructors [*Tunisia*]

ARENSA... Asociacion Regional Episcopal del Norte Sud Americano [*Regional Episcopal Association of Northern South America*]

ARENTO .. Arab Republic of Egypt National Telecommunications Organization   (IMH)

AREO .... Agence Regionale d'Editions Officielles [*France*]   (FLAF)

AREP........ Aboriginal Rural Education Programme [*Australia*]

AREP........ Association Reunionnaise d'Education Populaire [*Reunionese Association for Popular Education*]   (AF)

AREPRA ... Asociacion de Rectores de la Ensenanza Privada de la Republica Argentina [*Association of Private School Rectors of the Argentine Republic*]   (LA)

ARER........ Asociatia de Radio Emitatori si Receptori [*Association of Radio Transmitter and Receiver Operators*]   (RO)

ARER........ Automatic Regulator of Electrical Conditions   (RU)

ARES........ Alianza Revolucionaria Estudiantil Socialista [*Socialist Students Revolutionary Alliance*] [*Dominican Republic*]   (LA)

ARES........ Applications de Recherches sur l'Energie et la Societe [*Applied Research on Energy and Society*] [*French*]   (ARC)

ARES........ Australian Army Reserve

ARESA...... Association pour le Recherche sur l'Energie Solaire en Algerie

ARESBANK ... Banco Arabe Espanol [*Syria*]

ARESS...... Association Reunionnaise d'Education Sanitaire et Sociale

ARETO ..... Arab Republic of Egypt Telecommunications Organization   (PDAA)

AREX........ Partido de Accion Regional Extremena [*Party of Extremaduran Regional Action*] [*Spanish*]   (WER)

ARF .... Accountancy Research Foundation [*Australia*]

ARF .... Aerofer, SL [*Spain*] [*ICAO designator*]   (FAAC)

ARF .... Alliance of Reform Forces [*Macedonia*] [*Political party*]

arf............. Arfolyam [*Current Price, Rate of Exchange, Quotation*]   (HU)

ARF .... Armenian Revolutionary Federation [*Political party*]   (EY)

ARF .... ASEAN [*Association of Southeast Asian Nations*] Regional Forum   (ECON)

ARF .... Australian Retirement Fund

ARF .... Australian Road Federation   (ADA)

ARF .... Automatic Phase Control   (RU)

ARF .... Autoriserte Reklamebyraers Forening [*Association of Authorized Advertising Agencies*] [*Norway*]   (IMH)

ARFA........ Allied Radio Frequency Agency [*Formerly, ERFA*] [*Brussels, Belgium*] [*NATO*]

ArFFA .... Armed Forces Federation of Australia

ARFI........ Association de Recherche et Formation pour l'Insertion [*Association of Research and Training for Integration*] [*France*]   (EAIO)

ARFI........ Association for Research into the Folklore of Imagination [*French*]   (ECON)

ARFL........ Australian Rugby Football League   (ADA)

ARFL........ Australian Rules Football League   (ADA)

ARFLS...... Australian Rules Football League of Sydney

ARFS........ Australian Religious Film Society   (ADA)

ARFSU ...... Australian Rugby Football Schools Union

ARFU .... Australian Rugby Football Union   (ADA)

arg .... Aargang [*Volume, Year*] [*Publishing Danish/Norwegian*]

ARG .... Aerolineas Argentinas [*Argentina*] [*ICAO designator*]   (FAAC)

ARG .... Aethylen-Rohrleitungs-Gesellschaft

ARG .... Africa Research Group

ARG .... Argaisme [*Archaism*] [*Afrikaans*]

arg .... Argang [*Annual Volume, Year*] [*Publishing*] [*Sweden*]

ARG .... Argentina [*ANSI three-letter standard code*]   (CNC)

arg .... Arginine   (RU)

Arg .... Argument [*French*]   (FLAF)

ARg .... Arrete du Regent [*French*]   (BAS)

Ar G .... Arriere Garde [*Rear Guard*] [*French*]   (MTD)

ARG .... Artillery Reconnaissance Group   (BU)

ARG .... Association for Research on Germany   (EAIO)

ARG .... Automatic Volume Control   (RU)

arg .... Field Artillery Group   (BU)

ArgA .... Argentine Angel [*Record label*]

ARGAB ..... Asociacion Regional de Ganaderos del Guayabo [*Venezuela*]   (DSCA)

ARGAD ..... Action-Oriented Research Group on African Development [*Sweden*]

Arg Art....... Argument Tire de l'Article [*French*]   (FLAF)

ARGAS...... Arabian Geophysical and Surveying Company [*Jeddah, Saudi Arabia*]

ARGB .... Association Royale des Gaziers Belges [*Belgium*]   (BAS)

ArgC .... Argentine Columbia [*Record label*]

ARGC .... Asociacion Regional de Ganaderos de Carabobo [*Venezuela*]   (DSCA)

ARGC .... Australian Research Grants Committee   (ADA)

ARGCI...... Agence de Representation Generale en Cote-D'Ivoire

ArgD .... Argentine Decca [*Record label*]

ARGE .... Arbeitsgemeinschaft der Verbande der Europaischen Schloss-und Beschlagindustrie [*European Federation of Associations of Lock and Builders' Hardware Manufacturers*]   (EAIO)

ARGE .... Arbeitsgemeinschaft Meerestechnik [*Germany*]   (PDAA)

ARGEALP ... Arbeitsgemeinschaft Alpenlaender [*Working Group of Alpine Regions*]   (EAIO)

Arged .... Wojewodzkie Przedsiebiorstwo Hurtu Artykulow Gospodarstwa Domowego [*Voivodship Enterprise of the Wholesale Trade in Household Goods*]   (POL)

ARGEG ..... Asociacion Regional de Ganaderos del Estado Guarico [*Venezuela*]   (DSCA)

argent......... Argentine, Argentinean   (RU)

Argent .... Argentinien [*Argentina*] [*German*]

ARGEOL.... Argeologie [*Archaeology*] [*Afrikaans*]

ARGEUFI ... ArbeitsGemeinschaft Unabharngiger Friedens Initiativen [*Association for Independent Peace Initiatives*] [*Austria*]

ARGIT....... Argitektuur [*Architecture*] [*Afrikaans*]

ARGK .... Artillery Reserve of the High Command   (RU)

ArgLon .... Argentine London [*Record label*]

ARGMM ... Agence de Representation Generale Manutention Mauritanie

Argo .... Argo Sozu [*Argot, Slang*]   (TU)

ARGO .... Australian Regional Governmental Organisation

ArgOd .... Argentine Odeon [*Record label*]

ArgP........... Argentine Parlophone [*Record label*]

ARGPA...... Associacao Riograndense de Protecao aos Animais [*Brazil*]   (DSCA)

ArgPat .... Argentine Pathe [*Record label*]

ARGPLC ... Asociacion Regional de Ganaderos y Productores de Leche del Estado de Carabobo [*Venezuela*]   (DSCA)

ARGS........ Australian Research Grants Scheme

ARgt........... Arrete du Regent [*French*]   (BAS)

ArgV .... Argentine Victor [*Record label*]

arh............. Aarhundrede [*Century*] [*Danish/Norwegian*]

ARH .... Administracao de Recursos Hidricos [*Water Resources Administration*] [*Brazil*]   (LA)

a/Rh .... Am Rhein [*On the Rhine River*] [*German*]

ARHBF...... Association pour la Rehabilitation des Handicapes du Burkina Faso [*Association for the Rehabilitation of the Handicapped of Burkina Faso*]   (EAIO)

ArhD .... Drzavni Arhiv u Dubrovniku [*State Archives in Dubrovnik*]   (YU)

ArheolmS... Arheoloski Muzej u Splitu [*Archaeological Museum in Split*]   (YU)

ARHIV ...... Arhivatal [*Price Office*]   (HU)

ArhivMP.... Arhiv Ministarstva Poljoprivrede [*Archives of the Ministry of Agriculture*] [*Belgrade*]   (YU)

ARHRF ..... Australian Rotary Health Research Fund

ARHS........ Australian Railway Historical Society   (ADA)

ArhZ .... Drzavni Arhiv u Zadru [*State Archives in Zadar*]   (YU)

ARI .... Active Retirees in Israel [*An association*]

ARI .... Aero Vics SA de CV [*Mexico*] [*ICAO designator*]   (FAAC)

ARI .... African Research Institute [*La Trobe University*] [*Australia*]

ARI .... Animal Research Institute [*Ghana*]   (PDAA)

ARI .... Arica [*Chile*] [*Airport symbol*]   (OAG)

ARI .... Artist-Run Initiative [*Australia*]

ARI .... Asociacion de Relaciones Industriales [*Industrial Relations Association*] [*Peru*]   (LA)

ARI .... Asociacion de Revistas de Informacion [*Spanish*]

ARI .... Astronomisches Recheninstitut [*Information retrieval*]

ARI .... Australian Radioisotopes

ARI .... Australian Road Index   (ADA)

ARIA .... Agentia Romana de Impresariat Artistic [*Romanian Artistic Booking Agency*]   (RO)

ARIA .... Australian Record Industry Association   (ADA)

ARIBEV .... Association Reunionnaise Inter-Professionnelle du Betail et des Viandes [*Reunionese Interoccupational Cattle and Meat Association*]   (AF)

ARIC........ Agricultural Research Information Centre [*Indian Council of Agricultural Research*]   (IID)

ARIC........ Australian Railways Industry Commission

ARICON ... Arab Industrial Consultants [*Iraq*]

ARID .... Australian Resources Industry Database

ARIFA ...... Asociacion de Rehabilitacion del Impedido Fisico de Asuncion [*Paraguay*]   (EAIO)

arifm........... Arithmetic   (RU)

ARIG .... Arab Insurance Group BSC [*Kuwait, Libya, and United Arab Emirates*]   (MENA)

ARIL........ Airfield Radio-Testing Laboratory   (RU)

ARIMA...... Association de Recherche sur les Arts Martiaux Institutionnels et Similaires [*Association for Research on Institutional Martial Arts*] [*France*]   (EAIO)

ARIMA...... Association of Risk and Insurance Managers of Australia

ARINFI ..... Arab International Finance SA

ARINI....... Agricultural Research Institute of Northern Ireland   (IRC)

ARIPPS.... Australian Region of the International Plant Propagators' Society

ARIS........ Aboriginal and Torres Strait Islander Commission Regional Information Syste

ARIS........ Adult Basic Education Resource and Information Service [*Australia*]

ARIS......... Australian Recreation Information System   (ADA)

ARIS......... Australian Resources Information System
Ar-Is........... Turkiye Muzisyenler Sendikasi [*Turkish Musicians Union*]
                (TU)
ARISA .... Agricultural Research Information for Australia
ARISF....... Association des Federations Internationales de Sports Reconnues
                par le CIO [*Comitato Internazionale Olimpico*] [*South Korea*]   (EAIO)
ARISF....... Association of the IOC Recognized International Sports
                Federations [*Seoul, Republic of Korea*]   (EAIO)
ARISTOTE ... Association de Reseaux Informatique en Systeme Totalement
                et Tres Elabore [*Association of Information Networks in a
                Completely Open and Very Elaborate System*] [*France*]
                [*Computer science*]   (TNIG)
Arit............ Aritmetica [*Arithmetic*] [*Portuguese*]
ARITECSA ... Arquitectura Ingenieria Tecnica Sanitaria [*Colombia*]   (COL)
arithprot..... Arithmos Protokollou [*Registry Number*]   (GC)
ARIV.......... Algemene Rijksinkoopvoorwaarden [*Benelux*]   (BAS)
ARIV.......... Automatic Radio Anemometer   (RU)
ARIV.......... Automatic Radio Information Stations of Reservoirs   (RU)
ARJ........... Aerojet de Costa Rica SA [*ICAO designator*]   (FAAC)
ARJ........... Anciens de la Resistance Juive   (BJA)
arj.............. Arjegyzek [*Price List, Catalog*] [*Hungarian*]   (HU)
ARK.......... Air Corse [*France*] [*ICAO designator*]   (FAAC)
ARK.......... Aircraft Radio Compass   (RU)
ARK.......... Anglo-Russian Committee of Unity   (RU)
ARK.......... Ankara Rotary Kulubu [*Ankara Rotary Club*]   (TU)
Ark............ Arkeoloji [*Archaeology*]   (TU)
ark............. Arkikielta [*Colloquialism*] [*Finland*]
ark............. Arkki(a) [*Finland*]
ark............. Arkusz [*Sheet of Paper, Signature of a Book*] [*Poland*]   (POL)
ARK.......... Association of Revolutionary Cinematography   (RU)
ARK.......... Automatic Radio Compass   (RU)
ARK.......... Ship-Based Arctic Reconnaissance Aircraft   (RU)
ARKA .... Algemene Rooms-Kath. Ambtenarenorganisatie [*Benelux*]
                (BAS)
arkeol........ Arkeologia [*Archaeology*] [*Finland*]
arkh........... Archaeological, Archaeology   (RU)
arkh........... Archaism   (RU)
arkh........... Archipelago   (RU)
arkh........... Architect, Architectural, Architecture   (RU)
arkh........... Architect, Architecture   (BU)
arkh........... Archival   (BU)
arkh........... Archival, Archives   (RU)
arkhed........ Archival Unit   (BU)
arkheol....... Archaeology   (BU)
Arkhimpromstroy ... Armenian Construction Trust of the Chemical Industry
                (RU)
arkhit......... Architect, Architectural   (RU)
arkhit .... Architecture   (BU)
Arkhitstroy ... Administration of Urban, Rural, and Industrial Construction
                (RU)
Arkhmorput' ... Arkhangel'sk Administration of Sea Routes   (RU)
Arkhoblgiz ... Arkhangel'sk Oblast State Publishing House   (RU)
Arkhplan.... Architectural Planning Commission   (RU)
arkh sb........ Archival Collection   (BU)
ArkKand .... Master's Degree in Architecture [*Finland*]
arkkit .... Arkkitehtuuri [*Architecture*] [*Finland*]
arkom........ Army Commissar   (RU)
ar kor......... Arany Korona [*Gold Crown (Hungarian currency before World
                War I, still used to estimate real estate values)*]   (HU)
arkt............ Arktisch [*Arctic*] [*German*]   (RU)
Arktikstroy ... Construction and Installation Trust of the Glavsevmorput'
                (RU)
arktikugol' ... Trust for Coal Mining in the Arctic   (RU)
ARL .... Aeronautical Research Laboratories [*Melbourne, Australia*]
                (ERC)
ARL .... Airlec [*France*] [*ICAO designator*]   (FAAC)
ARL .... Akademie fuer Raumforschung und Landesplanung   (SLS)
ARL .... Albanska Republika Ludowa [*Albanian People's Republic*]
                [*Poland*]
ARL .... Arabian Research Ltd. [*Cyprus*]   (IRC)
Arl............. Arctic Preheater Lamp   (RU)
ARL .... Associacao Rural de Londrina [*Brazil*]   (DSCA)
ARL .... Australian Radiation Laboratory   (ADA)
ARL .... Australian Rugby League   (ADA)
ARLA .... Arab Latin American Bank [*Peru*]
ARLHS...... Australasian [*or Australian*] Railway and Locomotive Historical
                Society   (ADA)
ARLIS/ANZ ... Art Libraries Society, Australia and New Zealand   (ADA)
ARLO .... Arab Regional Literacy Organization
ARLO .... Australian Reference Libraries Overseas   (ADA)
ARLP........ Alliance Republicaine pour les Libertes et le Progres [*Republican
                Alliance for Liberties and Progress*] [*France*] [*Political
                party*]   (PPE)
ARLP........ Associacao Rural do Litoral Paulista [*Brazil*]   (DSCA)
ARLP........ Association of Rugby League Players [*Australia*]

ARLS......... Artillery Radar Station   (RU)
ARLUS...... Asociatia Romana pentru Legaturile de Prietenie cu Uniunea
                Sovietica [*Romanian Association for Ties of Friendship
                with the Soviet Union*]   (RO)
ARM......... Aeromarket Express [*Spain*] [*ICAO designator*]   (FAAC)
ARM......... African Resistance Movement [*South Africa*]   (PD)
ARM......... Aircraft Repair Shop   (RU)
ARM......... Allergy Recognition and Management, Inc. [*Australia*]
ARM......... Alliance Reformee Mondiale [*World Alliance of Reformed
                Churches - WARC*] [*Geneva, Switzerland*]   (EAIO)
arm............ Armenian   (RU)
ARM......... Armidale [*Australia*] [*Airport symbol*]   (OAG)
arm............ Army   (BU)
ARM......... Army Repair Shop   (RU)
ARM......... Artillery Repair Shop   (RU)
ARM......... Assistent-Resident-Magistraat [*Afrikaans*]
ARM......... Associacao Rural de Maca [*Brazil*]   (DSCA)
ARM......... Associacao Rural de Mococa [*Brazil*]   (DSCA)
ARM......... Australian Reform Movement   (ADA)
ARM......... Australian Republican Movement
ARM......... Australian Rights Movement
ARM......... Australian Rural Management Ltd.
ARM......... Automatic Power Control   (RU)
Arm.......... Fittings Plant [*Topography*]   (RU)
ARMA ...... Australian Records Management Association
ARMA ...... Australian Rubber Manufacturers Association   (PDAA)
ARMAA ... Associate of the Records Management Association of Australia
ARMAPP.. Armavir Association of Proletarian Writers   (RU)
ARMASAL ... Armadora Maritima Salvadorena, SA [*National Association of
                Ship-Owners*] [*El Salvador*]
Armatur ..... Fittings Plant [*Topography*]   (RU)
ARMAVEN ... Armas Venezolanas, CA
ARMB ...... Academie Royale de Medecine de Belgique [*Belgium*]   (SLS)
ARMCA .... Australian Royal Military College - Bridges Memorial Library
                [*National Union Catalogue of Australia symbol*]
ARMCANZ ... Agriculture and Resource Management Council of Australia
                and New Zealand
Armceta ..... Armiska Ceta [*Army Company*]   (YU)
ARME ...... Electrical Anemorhumbometer, Anemovane   (RU)
ARMED .... Artileri Medan [*Field Artillery*]   (IN)
Armelektro ... Armenian Electromechanical Plant   (RU)
Armenenergo ... Armenian Regional Administration of Power System
                Management   (RU)
ARMETAL ... Artisans du Metal
ArmFAN.... Armenian Branch of the Academy of Sciences, USSR   (RU)
ARMGA .... Australian Risk Management Graduates Association
armgen .... Armadni General [*Army General*] [*US equivalent: General*]
                (CZ)
Armgiprotsvetmet ... Armenian State Institute for the Planning of
                Establishments of Nonferrous Metallurgy   (RU)
Armgiz ...... State Publishing House of Armenia   (RU)
Armgosizdat ... State Publishing House of the Armenian SSR   (RU)
ARMH...... Association for Research in Modern History [*Germany*]   (EAIO)
ARMIA ...... Associate of the Retail Management Institute of Australia
Armid........ Armidale [*Australia*]   (ADA)
Armier........ Armierung [*Reinforcement*] [*German*]   (GCA)
ARMIT...... Associate of the Royal Melbourne Institute of Technology
                [*Australia*]   (ADA)
ARMNIIG i M ... Armenian Scientific Research Institute of Hydraulic
                Engineering and Reclamation   (RU)
Armniikhimproyekt ... Kirovakan Scientific Research and Planning Institute of
                Chemistry of the Council of the National Economy,
                Armenian SSR   (RU)
ArmNIITK ... Armenian Scientific Research Institute of Industrial Crops
                (RU)
ArmNIIZ ... Armenian Scientific Research Institute of Agriculture   (RU)
ArmNIIZhV ... Armenian Scientific Research Institute of Livestock Breeding
                and Veterinary Science   (RU)
ARMO....... Servicio Nacional de Adiestramiento Rapido de la Mano de Obra
                [*Rapid Manpower Training*] [*Mexico*]   (LAA)
armpod....... Army Jurisdiction   (BU)
ARMS....... Association of Relinquishing Mothers [*Australia*]
ARMS....... Automatic Radio Meteorological Station   (RU)
ARMSCOR ... Armaments Development and Production Corporation [*South
                Africa*]
Armset' ...... State All-Union Trust for the Planning, Production, Supply of
                Complete Sets, and Marketing of Network Fixtures,
                Insulators, and Assembly Equipment for the Construction
                of High-Voltage Transmission Lines and Substations   (RU)
ArmSSR..... Armenian Soviet Socialist Republic   (RU)
ARMT....... Australian Register of Massage Therapists
ArmTAG.... Armenian News Agency   (RU)
ARMTC..... Associate of the Royal Melbourne Technical College [*Australia*]
armu.......... Army Medical Reinforcement Company   (RU)
armuchpedgiz ... Armenian State Publishing House of Textbooks and
                Pedagogical Literature   (RU)

ArmVNITOE ... Armenian Branch of the All-Union Scientific, Engineering, and Technical Society of Power Engineers   (RU)
Armvodkhoz ... Administration of Water Management of the Armenian SSR   (RU)
Armw .... Armenwet [*Benelux*]   (BAS)
armyan .... Armenian   (RU)
Armzaktag ... Armenian Branch of the Transcaucasian News Agency   (RU)
ARN .... Accion Radical Nacionalista [*Nationalist Radical Action*] [*Guatemala*]   (LA)
ARN .... Acido Ribonucleico [*Ribonucleic Acid*] [*Spanish*]
ARN .... Armata Revoluzione Nucleare [*Armed Revolutionary Nucleus*] [*Italy*]
Arn .... Arnavutcu [*Albanian*]   (TU)
ARN ... Association of Radiographers of Nigeria   (EAIO)
ARN .... Australian Radio Network
ARN .... Automatic Voltage Regulation, Automatic Voltage Regulator   (RU)
ARN .... Stockholm [*Sweden*] Arlanda Airport [*Airport symbol*]   (OAG)
ARNA .... Arab Revolution News Agency [*Libya*]   (ME)
ARNA .... Australian Rehabilitation Nurses Association
ARNAHIS ... Archivo Nacional de Historia [*Ecuador*]
ARNE .... Accion Revolucionaria Nacional Ecuatoriana [*National Revolutionary Action*] [*Ecuador*] [*Political party*]
ARNE .... Accion Revolucionaria Nacionalista Ecuatoriana [*Ecuadorean Nationalist Revolutionary Action*]   (LA)
ARnI .... Association of Rhodesian Industries   (AF)
ARNM .... Arnhem [*Botanical region*] [*Australia*]
ARO .... Agriculture Research Organization [*Israel*]
ARO .... Arboletas [*Colombia*] [*Airport symbol*]   (OAG)
aro .... Artillery Battalion   (BU)
ARO .... Asian Regional Organization   (RU)
ARO .... Assurance, Reassurance, Omnibranches [*Insurance, Reinsurance, Omnibranch*] [*Malagasy*]   (AF)
ARO .... Automatic Cutoff Control   (RU)
ARO .... Motor Vehicle Repair Section   (RU)
AROA .... Applied Research of Australia Proprietary Ltd.
AROCA ..... Alfa Romeo Owners' Club of Australi
AROEVEN ... Association Regionale des Oeuvres Educatives et des Vacances de l'Education Nationale [*French*]   (SLS)
AROF .... Association Reunionnaise d'Orientation Familiale
ar ogn sk .... Artillery Ammunition Depot   (BU)
AROL .... Anexartiti Rizospastiki Organosis Lemesou [*Independent Radical Organization of Limassol*] [*Cyprus*]   (GC)
AROMAR ... Asociatia Romana de Marketing [*Romanian Marketing Association*]   (RO)
aromat .... Aromatisch [*Aromatic*] [*German*]   (GCA)
aromatich ... Aromatic   (RU)
AROP .... Association pour le Rayonnement de l'Opera de Paris [*France*]
AROWF .... Association of Retailer-Owned Wholesalers in Foodstuffs [*Later, ACROWE*]   (EAIO)
ARoy .... Arrete Royal [*French*]   (BAS)
ARP .... Accademia di Relazioni Pubbliche [*Italian*]   (SLS)
ARP .... Active Retired Persons Club [*Australia*]
ARP .... Agence Rwandaise de Press [*Rwandan Press Agency*]
arp .... Air Radio Regiment   (BU)
ARP .... Albanian Republican Party [*Partia Republikane Shqiptare*] [*Political party*]   (EY)
ARP .... Alliance Rurale Progressiste
ARP .... Alternativa Racional a las Pseudociencias [*Rational Alternative to Pseudosciences*] [*Spain*]   (EAIO)
ARP .... Alternativa Revolucionaria del Pueblo [*Bolivia*] [*Political party*]   (EY)
ARP .... Amur River Steamship Line   (RU)
ARP .... Antarctic Research Programs   (MSC)
ARP .... Anti-Revolutionaire Partij - Evangelische Volkspartij [*Antirevolutionary Party*] [*Netherlands*] [*Political party*]   (PPW)
ARP .... Aragip [*Papua New Guinea*] [*Airport symbol*]   (OAG)
ar p .... Arany Pengo [*Gold Pengo (Hungarian currency in 1925-45, still used to estimate real estate values)*]   (HU)
ARP .... Armee Revolutionnaire Populaire Ougandaise
Arp .... Arpeggio [*Record label*] [*Italy*]
arp .... Artillery Park   (BU)
ARP .... Australian Recommended Retail Price
ARP .... Australian Republican Party   (ADA)
ARP .... Automatic Radio Direction Finder   (RU)
ARP .... Automatic Reporting Post [*Air defense*] [*NATO*]   (NATG)
ARP .... Aviation Regulatory Proposal [*Australia*]
ARP .... Emergency Repair Station   (RU)
ARP .... Societe d'Exploitation Aeropostale [*France*] [*ICAO designator*]   (FAAC)
ARPA .... Alianza Revolucionaria Patriotica [*Revolutionary Patriotic Alliance*] [*Venezuela*]   (LA)
ARPA .... Asociacion de Radioemisoras Privadas Argentinas [*Private Radio Stations Association of Argentina*]   (LA)
ARPA .... Associatia Romana pentru Propaganda Aviatiei [*Romania*]

ARPA .... Australian Reinforced Plastics Association
ARPA .... Australian Religious Press Association   (ADA)
ARPA .... Australian Retinitis Pigmentosa Association
ARPA .... Australian Retired Persons Association
ARPA .... Australian Rural Publishers' Association
ARPAC ..... Antarctic Research Policy Advisory Committee [*Australia*]
ARPC .... Australia Radio Propagation Committee
ARPCBA ... Australian Red Poll Cattle Breeders' Association
ARPCCA ... Association for Regional Parks and Countryside Commissions of Australia   (ADA)
ARPEL ...... Asistencia Reciproca Petrolera Estatal Latinoamericana [*Mutual Assistance of the Latin American Government Oil Companies*]   (EAIO)
ARPEL ...... Associacao de Assistencia Reciproca Petroleira Latino-Americana [*Latin American Petroleum Industry Mutual Aid Association*] [*Montevideo, Uruguay*]   (LA)
ARPI .... Atelier de Reproduction de Plans Ivoiriennes
ARPLA ...... Asian Regional Project for Strengthening Labour and Manpower Administration
ARPLOE ... Association des Reeducateurs de la Parole et du Langage Oral et Ecrit [*French*]   (SLS)
ARPNET ... Advance Research Projects Agency Network [*Australia*]
ARPO .... Association of Railway Professional Officers of Australia   (ADA)
ARPOA ..... Association of Railway Professional Officers of Australia   (ADA)
ARPPIS .... African Regional Postgraduate Programme in Insect Science
ARPS .... Aborigines Rights Protection Society
ARPS .... Abortion Rights Protection Society
ARPS .... Arab Physical Society [*Lebanon*]   (PDAA)
ARPS .... Australian Radiation Protection Society   (ADA)
ARPS .... Australian Red Poll Society
Arq .... Arquipelago [*Archipelago*] [*Portuguese*]   (NAU)
Arq .... Arquitecto [*Architect*] [*Spanish*]
ARQ .... Australian Resources Quarterly [*A publication*]
ARQC .... Australian Rope Quoit Council
Arqueol ..... Arqueologia [*Archaeology*] [*Portuguese*]
Arquit .... Arquitetura [*Architecture*] [*Portuguese*]
ARR .... Academically-Related Research
ARR .... Aerora SA [*Mexico*] [*ICAO designator*]   (FAAC)
ARR .... Alto Rio Senguerr [*Argentina*] [*Airport symbol*]   (OAG)
ARR .... Amsterdamsche Relais Rekenmachine [*Amsterdam Relay Calculating Machine*] [*German*]   (ADPT)
ARR .... Arab Report and Record
Arr .... Arrecife [*Reef*] [*Spanish*]   (NAU)
arr .... Arrest [*Benelux*]   (BAS)
Arr .... Arrete [*Decision, Order*] [*French*]   (ILCA)
arr .... Arroba [*Thirty-Two Pound Weight*] [*Portuguese*]
arr .... Arrondissement [*District*] [*French*]
ARR .... Australian Rainfall and Runoff [*Meteorology*]
ARR .... Australian Rifle Regiment   (DMA)
ARR .... Automatische Relaisrechenmaschine [*Automatic Relay Calculating Machine*] [*German*]   (ADPT)
ARR .... Motor Vehicle Repair Company   (RU)
ARRA .... Australian Rough Riders' Association   (ADA)
Arr Adv RSt ... Arresten en Adviezen van de Raad van State [*Benelux*]   (BAS)
Arr AvCons Etat ... Arrets et Avis du Conseil d'Etat [*French*]   (BAS)
ARRB .... Australian Road Research Board [*Information service or system*]   (IID)
ARRC .... Army Reserve Review Committee
Arr Cass .... Arresten van het Hof van Cassatie [*Benelux*]   (BAS)
ARRCO ..... Association des Regimes de Retraites Complementaires [*France*]   (FLAF)
ARRD .... Australian Road Research Documentation [*Australian Road Research Board*] [*Information service or system*]   (IID)
ARRDO ..... Australian Railway Research and Development Organisation   (ADA)
ARRENDAVEN ... Arrendadora Industrial Venezolana, CA [*Venezuela*]
ARRF .... Australian Reading Research Federation   (ADA)
Arr G .... Arriere-Garde [*Rear-Guard*] [*Military*] [*French*]   (MTD)
ARRG .... Australian Regional Research Grant   (ADA)
Arr G-Duc ... Arrete Grand-Ducal [*French*]   (BAS)
Arr GouvProv ... Arrete du Gouvernement Provisoire [*Benelux*]   (BAS)
ArrHofVerbr ... Arresten van het Hof van Verbreking [*Benelux*]   (BAS)
ARRI .... Alligator Rivers Research Institute [*Australia*]
ARRINSA ... Arrendamientos Industriales, Sociedad Anonima [*Industrial Leasings Corporation*] [*El Salvador*]
ARRIP .... Australian Rural Research in Progress [*Database*]
ARRK .... Association of Workers in Revolutionary Cinematography   (RU)
Arr-L .... Arrete-Loi [*French*]   (BAS)
Arr Min ...... Arrete Ministeriel [*French*]   (BAS)
ARRO .... Afro-Asian Rural Reconstruction Organization   (EAIO)
Arro .... Arroyo [*Stream*] [*Spanish*]   (NAU)
ARROLIMA ... Arroceros del Tolima y del Huila [*Ibague*]   (COL)
ARROND ... Arrondissement [*District*] [*French*]
arross .... Arrossato [*With Reddish Spots*] [*Publishing*] [*Italian*]
ARRP .... Associacao Rural de Ribeirao Preto [*Brazil*]   (DSCA)

ARRP........ Australian Recommended Retail Price
Arr PrSouv ... Arrete du Prince Souverain [*French*]   (BAS)
Arr Reg ...... Arrete du Regent [*French*]   (BAS)
Arr Roy ...... Arrete Royal [*French*]   (BAS)
ArrSecrGen ... Arrete des Secretaires Generaux [*French*]   (BAS)
ARRSTC ... Asian Regional Remote Sensing Training Center
ARRU .... Army Reserve Recruiting Unit
ARS........... Accion Revolucionaria Salvadorena [*Salvadoran Revolutionary Action*]   (LA)
ARS........... Accion Revolucionaria Socialista [*Socialist Revolutionary Action*] [*Peru*] [*Political party*]   (PPW)
ARS........... Action Republicaine et Sociale [*Republican and Social Action*] [*France*] [*Political party*]   (PPE)
ARS........... Air Communications Company   (RU)
ARS........... Air Sardinia International [*ICAO designator*]   (FAAC)
ARS........... Akademie Remscheid fuer Musische Bildung und Medienerziehung   (SLS)
ARS........... Anodal Opening Contraction   (RU)
ARS........... Anti-Revolutionaire Staatkunde [*Benelux*]   (BAS)
ARS........... Aragarcas [*Brazil*] [*Airport symbol*]   (OAG)
ARS........... Arrete du Resident Superieur [*Decree of the Resident Superior*] [*Used in historical material*]   (CL)
Ars .... Arsiv [*Archive, File*]   (TU)
ARS........... Asociacie Rusistov na Slovensku [*Association of Teachers of Russian in Slovakia*]   (SK)
ARS........... Atelier de Construction de Rennes [*Groupement Industriel des Armaments Terrestres*] [*France*]   (PDAA)
ARS........... Australian Rangeland Society   (ADA)
ARS........... Automatic Control Rod [*Nuclear physics and engineering*]   (RU)
ARS........... Automatic Self-Adjusting Regulator   (RU)
ARS........... Automatic Speed Control   (RU)
ARS........... Ayr Research Station [*Queensland, Australia*]
ARS........... Gasoline-Filling Station   (BU)
ARS........... Stationary Aerosol Radiometer   (RU)
ARS........... Truck-Mounted Spraying Unit   (RU)
ARSA........ Aeroportos de Rio De Janeiro, Sociedade Anonima [*Rio De Janeiro Airports, Incorporated*] [*Brazil*]   (LA)
ARSA(NSW) ... Associate of the Royal Society of Arts (New South Wales) [*Australia*]
ARSAP ...... Agricultural Requisites Scheme for Asia and the Pacific [*Thailand*]
ARSASA ... Associate of the Royal South Australian Society of Artists
ARSC........ Academie Royale des Sciences Coloniales
ARSC......... African Remote Sensing Council
ARSC......... Association Royale Sportive Congolaise [*Congolese Royal Sporting Association*]
ARSC......... Australian Royal [*Air Force*] Staff College [*National Union Catalogue of Australia symbol*]
ARSFC ...... Australian Recreational and Sport Fishing Confederation
ARSG........ African Rhino Specialist Group [*Switzerland*]   (EAIO)
arsh .... Arshin   (RU)
Arsl .... Arsenal [*Arsenal*] [*Military map abbreviation World War I*] [*French*]   (MTD)
ARSO .... African Regional Organization for Standardization [*Kenya*]
ARSO .... Amenagement de la Region du Sud-Ouest
ARSO .... Armament Supply Officer [*British Navy slang*] [*World War II*]   (DSUE)
ARSO .... Autorite pour l'Amenagement de la Region du Sud-Ouest [*Southwest Region Development Authority*] [*Ivory Coast*]   (AF)
ARSOM .... Academie Royale des Sciences d'Outre-Mer
ARSOM .... Mortar Detection Artillery Station   (RU)
ARSOV...... Motor Delivery of Persistent Chemical Agents [*Military term*]   (RU)
ARSP........ Action Reconciliation/Services for Peace [*An association*] [*Germany*]   (EAIO)
ARSP........ African Regional Remote Sensing Programme
ARSPACO ... Arab Spacescene Corporation [*Subsidiary of ARABSAT*]
ARSR........ Academia Republicii Socialiste Romania [*Academy of the Socialist Republic of Romania*]   (RO)
ARSt .... Anti-Revolutionaire Staatkunde [*Benelux*]   (BAS)
ART .... Aerotal Aerolineas Territoriales de Colombia Ltd. [*ICAO designator*]   (FAAC)
ART .... Agency for Rural Transformation [*Grenada*]   (LA)
ART .... Anggaran Rumah Tangga [*Bylaws*]   (IN)
A Rt .... Arrete du Regent [*Benelux*]   (BAS)
art.............. Artel   (RU)
Art.............. Article [*French*]   (FLAF)
Art.............. Articolo [*Article*] [*Italian*]
art.............. Articulo [*Article*] [*Spanish*]
art.............. Artigo [*Article*] [*Portuguese*]
Art.............. Artikel [*Article*] [*German*]   (GPO)
Art.............. Artikel [*Article*] [*Netherlands*]
ART .... Artileri [*Artillery*]   (IN)
art.............. Artilharia [*Artillery*] [*Portuguese*]
art.............. Artilheiro [*Artilleryman*] [*Portuguese*]

Art.............. Artillerie [*Artillery*] [*French*]   (MTD)
art.............. Artillery   (RU)
art.............. Artist   (RU)
art.............. Artykul [*Article, Item*]   (POL)
art.............. Artysta [*Artist*] [*Poland*]
ART .... Assemblee Representative du Togo
ART .... Association for the Retarded of Thailand   (EAIO)
ART .... Automatic Fuel Distributor   (RU)
ART .... Automatic Temperature Regulator   (RU)
ART .... Automobilni Registracny Trenazer [*Automobile Driver Trainer*]   (CZ)
ART .... Ordnance Depot   (RU)
ART .... Spray Chamber   (RU)
Art 1 Div .... Artillerie de la Premiere Division [*Military*] [*French*]   (MTD)
ARTA .... Artillery Radiotechnical Academy   (RU)
ARTANES ... Aids and Research Tools in Ancient Near Eastern Studies
ART-B ...... Ammunition Depot   (RU)
artbat........ Artillery Battery   (RU)
art BB .... Short-Range Artillery   (RU)
artbr .... Artillery Brigade   (RU)
Art C .... Artillerie de Corps [*Military*] [*French*]   (MTD)
ARTCA..... Asbestos Removal and Treatment Contractors' Association [*Australia*]
ARTCA..... Association of Round Tables of Central Africa
artdiv .... Artillery Battalion   (RU)
ARTECOLOMBIA ... Artesanias de Colombia SA [*Colombia*]   (COL)
ARTELANA .. Fabrica de Tejidos de Lana [*Colombia*]   (COL)
ARTEMETAL ... Industria de Articulos Metalicos [*Colombia*]   (COL)
Artemgres .. Artem State Regional Electric Power Plant   (RU)
ARTEMIS ... Association de Recherche Technique pour l'Etude de la Mer Interieure Saharienne
ARTENE... Artesanato do Nordeste [*Brazil*]   (LAA)
ARTEP ...... Asian Regional Team for Employment Promotion
ARTEP ...... Projet Regional Asien de Promotion de l'Emploi [*Asian Regional Project for Employment Promotion*]   (CL)
ARTF........ Australian Road Transport Federation   (ADA)
ARTFL ...... American and French Research on the Treasury of the French Language [*University of Chicago*] [*Research center*]   (RCD)
ARTG .... Australian Register of Therapeutic Goods
ARTI......... Aeronautical Research and Test Institute [*Former Czechoslovakia*] [*Research center*]   (IRC)
ARTI......... Agrarian Research and Training Institute [*Sri Lanka*]   (ARC)
ARTI......... Arab Regional Telecommunication Institute [*Saudi Arabia*]   (PDAA)
ARTI......... Association of Research and Training for Integration [*France*]   (EAIO)
ARTIA....... Podnik Zahranicniho Obchodu pro Dovoz a Vyvoz Kulturnich Statku [*Foreign Trade Enterprise for the Import and Export of Cultural Articles*]   (CZ)
ARTIC...... Australian Road Transport Industry Conference
artigl......... Artiglieria [*Artillery*] [*Italian*]
artill .... Artillery   (RU)
artiller ...... Artillery   (RU)
ARTIS ...... African Regional Trade Information System [*ECA*] [*United Nations*]   (DUND)
art k.......... Artesian Well [*Topography*]   (RU)
Artl........... Artillerie [*Artillery*] [*German*]
artletnab.... Artillery Observer Pilot   (RU)
art mal....... Artysta Malarz [*Painter*] [*Poland*]
Artn.......... Artesien [*Artesian*] [*Military map abbreviation World War I*] [*French*]   (MTD)
ARTN .... Artillery Observation   (RU)
artnpp........ Artillery in Direct Support of Infantry   (RU)
arto........... Articulo [*Article*] [*Spanish*]
ARTOC .... Arab European International Trading Company   (ME)
ARTOP...... Arakli Toprak ve Gida Sanayii AS [*Arakli Land and Food Industry Corporation*]   (TU)
artpod........ Artillery Preparation   (RU)
artpp......... Artillery in Support of Infantry   (RU)
art rzez ..... Artysta Rzezbiarz [*Sculptor*] [*Poland*]
arts .... [*In The*] Arts   (TPFD)
ARTS....... Arts Documentation Service [*Australian Council Library*] [*Information service or system*]
ARTS....... Arts, Research, Training, and Support Ltd. [*Australia*]   (ADA)
arts .... Langage des Arts [*French*]   (TPFD)
ARTS &P ... Australian Radio and Technical Services and Patents Co.   (ADA)
ARTSDOC ... Arts Documentation Service [*Australian Council Library*] [*Information service or system*]   (IID)
ARTT........ Annual Review Traveling Team [*NATO*]   (NATG)
artt........... Artikelen [*Articles*] [*Dutch*]   (ILCA)
Art T .... Artillerie Territoriale [*Military*] [*French*]   (MTD)
ARTU .... Armada Tugas [*Naval Task Force*]   (IN)
artuch........ Artillery School   (RU)
Artv .... Artillery Observation Tower   (RU)
ARTVK...... Automatic Cabin Temperature Control   (RU)

ARTVS...... Australian Rocket Test Vehicle Simulator
ARU.......... Aboriginal Reconciliation Unit [*Australia*]
ARU.......... Aboriginal Resource Unit [*University of New England*] [*Australia*]
ARU.......... Air Aruba [*ICAO designator*]   (FAAC)
ARU.......... Applied Research Unit [*Botswana*]   (IRC)
ARU.......... Aracatuba [*Brazil*] [*Airport symbol*]   (OAG)
ARU.......... Asociacion Rural de Uruguay [*Rural Association of Uruguay*] (LA)
ARU.......... Association of Urbanist Architects   (RU)
ARU.......... Australian Railways Union   (ADA)
ARU.......... Australian Rugby Union   (ADA)
ARU.......... Automatic Amplification Control   (BU)
ARU.......... Automatic Level Control   (RU)
aruatv........ Aruatvevo [*Inspector (Standards of quality)*]   (HU)
ARUC........ Atelier de Reparatie Utilaj de Constructie [*Workshop for Repair of Construction Equipment*]   (RO)
aruforg....... Aruforgalmi [*Trade (adjective)*]   (HU)
ARUG........ Atelier de Reparatie Utilaj Greu [*Workshop for Repair of Heavy Equipment*]   (RO)
ARUGC..... Atelier de Reparatie Utilaj Greu de Constructie [*Workshop for Repair of Heavy Construction Equipment*]   (RO)
ARUL........ Arsiv ve Ulastirma Dairesi Genel Mudurlugu [*Archives and Communications Office Directorate General*] [*of Foreign Affairs Ministry*]   (TU)
ARUM....... Atelier de Reparatie Utilaj Minier [*Workshop for Repair of Mining Equipment*]   (RO)
ARUV........ Administracion de Renovacion Urbana y Vivienda [*Puerto Rico*] (DSCA)
ARV.......... Algemeen Reglement voor het Vervoer op de Spoorwegen [*Benelux*]   (BAS)
ARV.......... Anglican Retirement Village [*Australia*]
arv............. Arveres [*Auction*]   (HU)
Arv............ Arvoisa [*Esteemed*] [*Finland*]   (GPO)
ARV.......... Automatic Excitation Control   (RU)
ARV.......... Automatic Humidity Regulator   (RU)
ARV.......... Motor Vehicle Repair Platoon   (RU)
ARVB........ Army Maintenance and Recovery Battalion   (RU)
ARVC........ Agricultural Research and Veterinary Centre [*New South Wales, Australia*]
ARVGK..... Artillery Reserve of the Supreme Command   (RU)
ARVIA....... Associate of the Royal Victorian Institute of Architects [*Australia*]   (ADA)
ARVL........ Algemeen Reglement voor het Vervoer op de Locaalspoorwegen [*Benelux*]   (BAS)
ARVN........ Armee de la Republique du Viet-Nam [*Army of the Republic of Vietnam*] [*South Vietnamese Army*] [*Also,*]   (CL)
ARVNSEAL... Army of the Republic of Vietnam Sea, Air, and Land Team (VNW)
ARVP......... Automatic Internal Overvoltage Recorder   (RU)
ARVR........ Motor Vehicle Repair and Reconstruction Company   (RU)
ARVR 22.... Anno Regni Victoriae Regina Vicesimo Secundo   (DLA)
ARVS........ Association for Research in Vascular Surgery [*France*]   (EAIO)
ARW.......... Arad [*Romania*] [*Airport symbol*]   (OAG)
ARW.......... Automatyczna Regulacja Wzmocnienta [*Automatic Gain Control*] [*Poland*]
ARW.......... Autoreparaturwerkstatt [*Automobile Repair Shop*]   (EG)
ARX.......... Artists' Regional Exchange [*Australia*]
ARY.......... Ararat [*Australia*] [*Airport symbol*] [*Obsolete*]   (OAG)
ARY.......... Australian Rural Youth
ARYA........ Asociacion Rural Yerbatera Argentina [*Argentina*]   (DSCA)
ARYa........ Automatic Brightness Control   (RU)
ARYT........ Aryt Optronics Industries Ltd. [*NASDAQ symbol*]
ARZ.......... Air Resorts [*ICAO designator*]   (FAAC)
ARZ.......... Aleksandrov Radio Plant   (RU)
arz............. Arzobispo [*Archbishop*] [*Spanish*]
ARZ.......... Automatic Load Regulator   (RU)
ARZ.......... Automobile Repair Plant   (RU)
ARZ.......... Motor Vehicle Repair Plant   (BU)
ARZ.......... N'Zeto [*Angola*] [*Airport symbol*]   (OAG)
arzbpo....... Arzobispo [*Archbishop*] [*Spanish*]
ARZhK...... Airfield Liquid Oxygen Storage   (RU)
Arzi........... Hed-Arzi [*Israel*] [*Record label*]
arztl........... Aerztlich [*Medical*] [*German*]
as............... Aanstaande [*Of the Next Month*] [*Afrikaans*]
AS............. Abortion Sydney [*An association*] [*Australia*]
AS............. Ackerschlepper [*Field Tractor*]   (EG)
AS............. Afrolit Society [*Defunct*]   (EAIO)
As............. Agregation de l'Enseignement Superieur [*French*]
AS............. Aircraft Radio   (RU)
AS............. Aircraft Sextant   (RU)
AS............. Air Force   (BU)
as............... Akciova Spolecnost [*Joint-Stock Company*]
AS............. Akoustiki Sykhnotis [*Audio Frequency*]   (GC)
A/S........... Aksjeselskap [*Joint-Stock Company*] [*Norway*]   (GPO)
A/S........... Aktieselskab [*Joint-Stock Company*] [*Sweden*]

A/S............ Aktieselskab [*Joint-Stock Company*] [*Denmark*]   (GPO)
AS............. Alandsk Samling [*Aland Coalition (Party)*] [*Finland*]   (WEN)
AS............. Albania Society [*New Zealand*]   (EAIO)
AS............. Alianza Sindical [*Trade Union Alliance*] [*Spanish*]   (WER)
AS............. Alkan Society [*Surrey, England*]   (EAIO)
AS............. Allgemeines Sekretariat [*General Secretariat*]   (EG)
AS............. Altesse Serenissime [*Serene Highness*] [*French*]
AS............. Altezza Serenissima [*Serene Highness*] [*Italian*]
AS............. American Samoa [*Postal code*] [*ANSI two-letter standard code*] (CNC)
AS............. Amerika Serikat [*United States*]   (IN)
AS............. Ammunition Depot   (RU)
AS............. Ampere-Segundo [*Ampere-Second*] [*Portuguese*]
AS............. Ampere Stunde [*Ampere-Hour*] [*German*]
AS............. Anatomical Society [*Germany*]   (EAIO)
a/S........... An der Saale [*On the Saale River*] [*German*]
AS............. Anexartitos Syndesmos [*Independent Association*] [*Greek*]   (GC)
As............. Angel-Saksies [*Anglo-Saxon*] [*Afrikaans*]
AS............. Angiosarcoma   (RU)
AS............. Anglo-Saxon Real Estate Agency Ltd. [*Israel*]
AS............. Anonim Sirketi [*Corporation, Joint-Stock Company*]
AS............. Anthologie Sonore [*Record label*] [*France*]
AS............. Anti-Revolutionaire Staatkunde [*Benelux*]   (BAS)
AS............. Arhijerejski Sabor [*Synod of Bishops*] [*Serbian Eastern Orthodox Church*]   (YU)
AS............. Arkhigeion Stratou [*Army Command*] [*Greek*]   (GC)
As............. Armadni Sbor [*Army Corps*]   (CZ)
as............. Army Depot   (BU)
As............. Arsen [*Arsenic*] [*Chemical element*] [*German*]
as............. Arsenal   (BU)
As............. Arsenio [*Arsenic*] [*Chemical element*] [*Portuguese*]
AS............. Artillery Supply   (RU)
As............. Asagi [*Lower*]   (TU)
As............. Asbest [*Asbestos*] [*German*]   (GCA)
as............. Asema [*Finland*]
AS............. Asisten [*Assistant*]   (IN)
As............. Asker [*or Askeri*] [*Military*]   (TU)
AS............. Asociatia Studenteasca [*Student Association*]   (RO)
AS............. Assemblersprache [*Assembly Language*] [*German*]   (ADPT)
AS............. Association Sportive [*Athletic Association*] [*French*]
AS............. Assurances Sociales [*Social Security*] [*French*]
AS............. Astronomisk Selskab [*Danish Astronomical Association*]   (EAIO)
as............. Asukasta [*Finland*]
as............. Asunto [*Finland*]
AS............. Ausbildung und Schulung [*Training and Schooling*]   (EG)
AS............. Auslieferungsschein [*Delivery Permit, Certificate of Delivery, Delivery Order*] [*German*]   (EG)
AS............. Austenitic Steel   (RU)
AS............. Australia
AS............. Australiana Society
AS............. Australian Skeptics   (EAIO)
AS............. Australian Standard   (ADA)
AS............. Australian Swimming [*An association*]
AS............. Austrian Schilling [*Monetary unit*]
AS............. Automatic Synchronization   (RU)
AS............. Automatic Welding   (RU)
A/S........... Aux Soins De [*Care Of, c/o*] [*French*]
AS............. Aviation   (BU)
AS............. Hawker Siddeley Aviation Ltd. [*British*] [*ICAO aircraft manufacturer identifier*]   (ICAO)
AS............. Landplane Airfield   (RU)
AS............. L'Annee Sociologique   (FLAF)
AS............. Selective Lubricating Oil   (RU)
ASA.......... Absorption Spectral Analysis   (RU)
ASA.......... Accion Sindical Argentina [*Argentine Trade Union Action*]   (LA)
ASA.......... Accordion Society of Australia   (EAIO)
ASA.......... Administracion de Servicios Agricolas [*Puerto Rico*]   (DSCA)
ASA.......... Aeropuertos y Servicios Auxiliares [*Airports and Auxiliary Services*] [*Mexico*]   (LA)
ASA.......... African Students Association [*South Africa*]   (AF)
ASA.......... Aged Services Association [*Australia*]
ASA.......... Air Ambulance Airfield   (RU)
ASA.......... Airlines of South Australia
ASA.......... Air Service Agreement [*Australia*]
ASA.......... Air Starline AG [*Switzerland*] [*ICAO designator*]   (FAAC)
ASA.......... Alianza Socialista de Andalucia [*Socialist Alliance of Andalucia*] [*Spanish*]   (WER)
ASA.......... Amateur Softball Association   (OLYM)
ASA.......... Angus Society of Australia
ASA.......... Anotaton Stratiotikon Arkhigeion [*Higher Military Command*] [*Greek*]   (GC)
ASA.......... Anotaton Symvoulion Aeroporias [*Supreme Air Force Council*] [*Greek*]   (GC)
ASA.......... Anotaton Symvoulion Anasyngrotiseos [*Supreme Reconstruction Council*] [*Greek*]   (GC)
ASA.......... Asian Students' Association [*Kowloon, Hong Kong*]   (EAIO)

ASA .... Asian Surgical Association (EAIO)
ASA .... Asociacion de Scouts de Argentina [*Scout Association of Argentina*] (EAIO)
ASA .... Asociacion Salvadorena de Agricultores [*Salvadoran Association of Farmers*] (LA)
ASA .... Asociacion Semilleros Argentinos [*Argentina*] (LAA)
ASA .... Asociacion Sindical Antioquena [*Colombia*] (COL)
ASA .... Assab [*Ethiopia*] [*Airport symbol*] (OAG)
ASA .... Association de l'Asie du Sud-Est [*Association of South East Asia*] (FLAF)
ASA .... Association of Social Anthropologists of the Commonwealth [*British*] (EAIO)
ASA .... Association of South East Asia [*Later, ASEAN*]
ASA .... Astronomical Society of Australia (ADA)
ASA .... Atheist Society of Australia (ADA)
ASA .... Audiological Society of Australia
ASA .... Australian Salvadorian Association
ASA .... Australian Science Action
ASA .... Australian Scots Association (ADA)
ASA .... Australian Shareholders' Association (ADA)
ASA .... Australian Shipbuilders' Association
ASA .... Australian Shooting Association
ASA .... Australian Society of Accountants (ADA)
ASA .... Australian Society of Anaesthetists (ADA)
ASA .... Australian Society of Archivists (ADA)
ASA .... Australian Society of Authors (ADA)
ASA .... Australian Sociological Association
ASA .... Australian Songwriters' Association
ASA .... Australian Steel Association
ASA .... Australian Studies Association
ASA .... Australian Sunflower Association
ASA .... Australian Surfers' Association
ASA .... Australian Surfriders' Association
ASA .... Austrian Space Agency (IRC)
ASA .... Autocostruzioni Societa per Azione [*Automobile manufacturing company*] [*Italy*]
ASAA .... Amputee Sports Association of Australia
ASAA .... Asian Studies Association of Australia
ASAA .... Australian Ski Areas Association
ASAASD ... Australian Society for the Advancement of Anaesthesia and Sedation in Dentistry
ASAAT ...... Austrian Society of Acupuncture and Auricular Therapy [*Multinational organization*] (EAIO)
ASAAWE .. Association of South Asian Archaeologists in Western Europe (EAIO)
ASAB .... Association des Informaticiens de Belgique [*Belgium*] (SLS)
ASAC .... Asian Securities Analysts Council [*See also CAAF*] [*Japan*] (EAIO)
ASAC .... Asian Standards Advisory Committee (PDAA)
ASAC .... Assistance Sociale au Congo
ASAC .... Association des Societes d'Assurance au Cameroun
ASAC .... Australian Science Advisory Committee
ASAC .... Australian Sport Aviation Confederation
ASAC .... Australian Statistics Advisory Council (ADA)
ASACORRI ... Associate Member of the South African Corrosion Institute (AA)
ASACUT ... Academic Staff Association of Curtin University of Technology [*Australia*]
ASADEGA ... Asociacion de Abastecedores de Ganado Mayor [*Colombia*] (COL)
ASADPO... Australian Strategic Analysis and Defence Policy Objectives
ASAE........ Australian Society of Association Executives
ASAED...... Association Senegalaise d'Assistance aux Enfants Drepanocytaires [*Senegal*] (EAIO)
ASAF........ Australian Sports Acrobatic Federation
ASAFED ... Association Africaine d'Education pour le Developpement [*African Association of Education for Development*] (AF)
ASAFOP ... Association des Amis des Forets et des Peches [*Association of Friends of Forests and Fishing*] [*Cambodia*] (CL)
ASAG .... Aerial Sports Association of Guatemala (EAIO)
ASAG .... Australian Staffing Assistance Group (ADA)
ASAGI....... Assosiasie van Suid-Afrikaanse Geregistreerde Ingenieurstegnici [*Association of South African Registered Engineering Technicians*] (EAIO)
ASAI......... Associazione per lo Sviluppo delle Attivita Ittiologiche [*Italian*] (ASF)
ASAIA ...... Associate of the South Australian Institute of Architects
ASAIB ...... Associate Member of the South African Institute of Building (AA)
ASAICHE ... Associate Member of the South African Institution of Chemical Engineers (AA)
ASAIHL .... Association of Southeast Asian Institutions of Higher Learning [*Bangkok, Thailand*]
ASAIM...... Associate Member of the South African Institute of Management (AA)

ASAIMECHE ... Associate Member of the South African Institute of Mechanical Engineers (AA)
ASAJA ...... Asociacion Agraria de Jovenes Agricultores [*Spain*] (EY)
ASAL........ Asociacion Antioquena de Licenciados [*Colombia*] (COL)
ASAL........ Association for the Study of Australian Literature (ADA)
ASALA ...... Armenian Secret Army for the Liberation of Armenia [*Turkey*] (PD)
ASAM ...... Amicale des Secretaires d'Administration en Service a la Commune de Dakar
ASAMACON ... Asociacion Antioquena de Constructores [*Colombia*] (COL)
ASAMANI ... Association des Agents de Marques Automobiles du Niger
AS & TS..... Associated Scientific and Technical Societies of South Africa (EAIO)
ASANESCA ... Association des Anciens Eleves et Eleves de l'Ecole Superieure de Chimie Appliquee [*Association of Alumni and Students of the Higher School of Applied Chemistry*] [*Cambodia*] (CL)
ASANT...... Australian School of Nuclear Technology (WND)
ASANU ..... Academic Staff Union of Nigerian Universities
ASANU ..... All South Africa Netball Union (AA)
ASAO .... Arbeitsschutzanordnung [*Accident Prevention Order*] (EG)
ASAO .... Association of Swedish Amateur Orchestras (EAIO)
ASAOTT ... Australian Society of Anaesthetic and Operating Theatre Technicians
ASAP........ Aboriginal Service Action Plan [*Australia*]
ASAP........ Akciova Spolecnost pro Automobilovy Prumysl [*Automobile Industry Joint-Stock Company*] (CZ)
ASAP........ All-Student Alliance Party
ASAP........ Arab Socialist Action Party
ASAP........ Asociacion Salvadorena de Agencias de Publicidad [*Salvadoran Association of Advertising Agencies*] (LA)
ASAP........ Association d'Anciens Eleves des Peres Jesuites
ASAP........ Association of Swedish Agricultural Producers [*Finland*] (EAIO)
ASAP........ Australian Science Archives Project
ASAP........ Australian Seniors Action Plan
ASAP........ Australian Society for Aero-Historical Preservation (ADA)
ASAP........ Australian Society of Animal Production (ADA)
ASAPRA ... Asociacion Americana de Profesionales Aduaneros [*American Association of Professional Customs Employees*] (LA)
ASAPRO ... Association Africaine pour la Promotion de Main-d'Oeuvre [*African Association for Manpower Advancement*] [*France*] (AF)
ASAQ .... Ambulance Superintendents' Association of Queensland [*Australia*]
ASAQS...... Association of South African Quantity Surveyors (EAIO)
ASARA ..... Australian Small-Bore and Air Rifle Association
ASARET ... Association of South African Registered Engineering Technicians (EAIO)
ASAS........ Academia de Stiinte Agricole si Silvice [*Academy of Agricultural and Forestry Sciences*] (RO)
ASAS........ Agostiniani Secolari Agustinos Seculares [*Order Secular of St. Augustine - OSSA*] [*Rome, Italy*] (EAIO)
ASAS........ Amsterdam Security Account System [*Amsterdam stock exchange*] [*Netherlands*]
ASAS........ Australian Science and Application Spacecraft
ASAS........ Australian Special Air Services (VNW)
ASAS........ Australian Staffing Assistance Scheme
ASAS 50 .... Angkatan Sasterawan 1950 [*1950 Literature Generation*] (ML)
ASASA ...... Action South and Southern Africa (AF)
ASASA ...... African Students Association of South Africa (AF)
ASASM .... Associate of the South Australian School of Mines (ADA)
ASAT........ Arbeitsgemeinschaft Satellitentragersystem [*German*]
ASAT........ Australian Scholastic Aptitude Test (ADA)
ASATA ..... Association of Southern Africa Travel Agents
ASATOM ... Association pour les Stages et l'Accueil des Techniciens d'Outre-Mer [*Association for the Reception and Instruction of Overseas Technicians*]
ASAUCUNSW ... Academic Staff Association of University College, University of New South Wales [*Australia*]
ASAVA...... Australian Small Animals Veterinary Association (ADA)
ASA(VB) ... Anthroposophical Society in Australia, Victorian Branch
ASAWI..... African Studies Association of the West Indies
ASAZGUA ... Asociacion de Azucareros de Guatemala [*Guatemala*] (EY)
ASB........... Afrikaanse Studentebond [*Afrikaans Students Union*] [*South Africa*] (AF)
ASB........... Albania Society of Britain [*British*] (EAIO)
asb............. Apostilb (RU)
ASB........... Arap Sosyalist Birligi [*Arab Socialist Union*] (TU)
ASB........... Archaeological Society of Berlin [*Germany*] (EAIO)
asb............. Asbestos Mine [*Topography*] (RU)
asb............. Asbestos Plant [*Topography*] (RU)
ASB........... Ashkhabad [*Former USSR*] [*Airport symbol*] (OAG)
ASB........... Asociacion de Silvicultura "Bosques" [*Chile*] (DSCA)
asb............. Asseblief [*If You Please*] [*Afrikaans*]
Asb............. Assubay [*Noncommissioned Officer*] (TU)
ASB........... Ateliers et Scieries de Batalimo

ASB............ Australian Savings Bonds (ADA)
ASB............ Australian Shipbuilding Board (ADA)
ASB............ Australian Space Board
ASB............ Australian Studies Books (ADA)
asb............. Motor Ambulance Battalion (BU)
ASB............ Special Libraries Association [*SLA*] (RU)
ASB............ Studio Equipment Unit (RU)
ASBA......... Australian Sheep Breeders' Association
ASBA......... Australian Simmental Breeders Association (ADA)
ASBA......... Australian Small Business Association
ASBA......... Australian Small Business Awards
ASBA......... Australian Spina Bifida Association
ASBAD...... Association Senegalaise des Bibliothecaires, Archivistes, et
            Documentalistes [*Senegalese Association of Librarians,
            Archivists, and Documentalists*] (EAIO)
ASBANA... Asociacion Bananera Nacional [*National Banana Growers
            Association*] [*Costa Rica*] (LA)
ASBBS...... Australian Society of Breeders of British Sheep
ASBC........ Australian Second Board Consultants Proprietary Ltd.
ASbH........ Arbeitsgemeinschaft Spina Bifida und Hydrocephalus eV
            [*Association for Spina Bifida and Hydrocephalus*] (SLS)
ASBIAPRI ... Asesores de Bibliotecas, Archivos, y Publicaciones [*Colombia*]
            (COL)
ASBIB ...... Association of Special Libraries and Information Bureaus
            [*ASLIB*] (RU)
ASBIC ...... Australian School Bibliographic Centre
ASBK........ Sydney/Bankstown [*Australia*] [*ICAO location identifier*] (ICLI)
ASBL........ Association sans But Lucratif [*Nonprofit Organization*] [*French*]
            (WER)
ASBOLFI.. Asociacion Boliviana para el Fomento del Intercambio [*Bolivian
            Trade Development Association*] (LA)
ASBORA ... Asociacion Boliviana de Radiodifusoras [*Bolivian Radio
            Broadcasting Association*] (LA)
ASBR........ Emergency Bomb Release (RU)
ASBS .... Australian Systematic Botany Society (ADA)
ASBT .... Australian Society of Blood Transfusion
ASBU....... Arab States Broadcasting Union [*Tunis, Tunisia*]
ASBUG...... Australian Synchrotron Beam Users' Group
ASBw........ Amt fuer die Sicherheit der Bundeswehr [*Office for the Security of
            the Armed Forces*] (WEN)
ASC........... Academie de Sports de Combats [*Algeria*]
ASC........... Accounting Society of China (EAIO)
ASC........... Acoustical Society of China (EAIO)
ASC........... Adelaide Steamship Company [*Australia*]
ASC........... Advertising Standards Council [*Canada Australia*]
ASC........... African Settlement Convention
ASC........... African Studies Center
ASC........... Alexandria Sporting Club [*Egypt*]
ASC........... Alianza Socialista de Castilla [*Socialist Alliance of Castille*]
            [*Spanish*] (WER)
ASC........... American Studies Centre [*University of Sydney*] [*Australia*]
ASC........... Arab Sports Confederation [*Saudi Arabia*] (EAIO)
ASC........... Arbitrajul de Stat Central [*Central State Arbitration Office*]
            (RO)
Asc........... Ascenseur [*Elevator*] [*French*]
ASC........... Ascension [*Bolivia*] [*Airport symbol*] [*Obsolete*] (OAG)
ASC........... Asian Studies Council [*Australia*]
ASC........... Association Sportive Communale [*Algeria*]
ASC........... Association Sportive et Culturelle
ASC........... Australian Schools Commission (ADA)
ASC........... Australian Securities Commission
ASC........... Australian Seeds Committee
ASC........... Australian Seismological Center
ASC........... Australian Shiatsu College
ASC........... Australian Shippers Council (ADA)
ASC........... Australian Shipping Commission
ASC........... Australian Signal Corps
ASC........... Australian Singing Competition
ASC........... Australian Society of Calligraphers
ASC........... Australian Sports Commission
ASC........... Australian Staff Corps
ASC........... Australian Studies Centre [*University of Queensland*]
ASC........... Australian Submarine Corp.
ASC........... Austral Standard Cables [*Australia*] (ADA)
ASC........... Austrian Shippers Council (DS)
ASC........... Movimiento de Accion Social Cristiana [*Christian Social Action
            Movement*] [*Dominican Republic*] [*Political party*] (PPW)
ASC........... Swedish Choral Association (EAIO)
ASCA........ Advanced Satellite for Cosmology and Astrophysics [*Japanese
            spacecraft*]
ASCA........ Airlines Sports and Cultural Association (EA)
ASCA........ Association for Science Cooperation in Asia (ADA)
ASCA........ Association of Suppliers of Concrete Admixtures [*Denmark*]
            (EAIO)
ASCA........ Australian Sister Cities Association
ASCA........ Australian Speech Communication Association (ADA)

ASCA......... Canberra [*Australia*] [*ICAO location identifier*] (ICLI)
ASCAC...... Association for the Study of Classical African Civilizations (EA)
ASCAF ...... Association pour le Developpement des Carburants par
            Fermentation [*France*]
ASCAL ...... Anti-Sickle Cell Anemia League [*Haiti*] (EAIO)
ASCANIC ... Asociacion de Caneros de Nicaragua [*Nicaraguan Association of
            Sugar Producers*] (LA)
ASCAR...... Associacao Sulina de Credito e Assistencia Rural [*Brazil*] (LAA)
ASCAR...... Centrul de Asistenta a Cardiacilor [*Care Center for Cardiac
            Patients*] (RO)
ASCAT ...... Association Internationale des Editeurs de Catalogues de
            Timbres-Poste [*International Association of Publishers of
            Postage Stamp Catalogues*] (EA)
ASCATEP ... Arab States Centre for Educational Planning and Administration
ASCATTECK ... Association Camerounaise pour le Transfert des
            Technologies
ASCB........ Canberra [*Australia*] [*ICAO location identifier*] (ICLI)
ASCC........ Armstrong Siddeley Car Club [*Australia*]
ASCC........ Asian Studies Co-Ordinating Committee [*Australia*]
ASCC........ Australian Schoolboys Cricket Council
ASCC........ Australian Schools' Cricket Council
ASCC........ Australian Society of Cosmetic Chemists (ADA)
ASCC........ Australian Sporting Car Club (ADA)
ASCCLH .. Ataturk Supreme Council for Culture, Language and History
            [*Turkey*] (EAIO)
ASCCOP ... Asociacion Colombiana de Cooperativas [*Colombia*] (COL)
ASCD........ Automatic Speed Control Device
ASCE........ Asociacion de Seguros para Creditos en el Exterior (LAA)
ASCED..... Australian Standard Classification of Education
ASCEH...... Australian Society for Clinical and Experimental Hypnosis
            (ADA)
ASCEP ..... Australasian Society of Clinical and Experimental
            Pharmacologists (ADA)
ASCF .... Australian Sport Climbing Federation
ASCH .... Association of Supportive Care Homes
ASCH .... Australian Society of Clinical Hypnotherapists (ADA)
ASCH .... Coffs Harbour [*Australia*] [*ICAO location identifier*] (ICLI)
ASCHIMICI ... Assoziazione dell'Industrie Chimica Italiana
ASCI......... Administrative Staff College of India (PDAA)
ASCI......... Association Scientifique de Cote-D'Ivoire [*Ivory Coast*]
ASCI......... Association Suisse des Commerces de Gros et Importateurs de la
            Branche Autom obile [*Switzerland*] (EAIO)
ASCI......... Associazione Scoutistica Cattolica Italiana [*Catholic Boy Scouts*]
            [*Italian*]
ASCIDEC ... Australian Science Distance Education Consortium
ASCILLANOS ... Asociacion de Comerciantes e Industriales de los Llanos
            Orientales [*Villavicencio*] (COL)
ASCIN....... Asociacion Social Cristiana de Integracion Revolucionaria
            [*Social Christian Association for Revolutionary Integration*]
            [*Guatemala*] (LA)
ASCIS........ Australian School Catalogue Information Service (ADA)
ASCIS........ Australian Schools Cooperative Information Service
ASCITRUS ... Asociacion de Citricultores [*Citrus Growers Association*]
            [*Chile*] (LA)
ASCJ .... Amalgamated Society of Carpenters and Joiners [*Australia*]
            (ADA)
ASCJA....... Amalgamated Society of Carpenters and Joiners of Australia
ASCL........ Australia Straits Container Line Proprietary Ltd.
ASCM........ Australian Student Christian Movement (ADA)
ASCM........ Cooma [*Australia*] [*ICAO location identifier*] (ICLI)
ASCN .... Camden [*Australia*] [*ICAO location identifier*] (ICLI)
ASCNEB ... Association des Stagiares du College National des Experts
            Compatables de Belgique [*Association of Accountancy
            Students of Belgium*] (PDAA)
ASCNI....... Advisory Committee on the Safety of Nuclear Installations
            (WGAO)
ASCNSW .. Agricultural Societies Council of New South Wales [*Australia*]
ASCO .... Arab Satellite Communications Organization [*League of Arab
            States*] [*Riyadh, Saudi Arabia*] (EAIO)
ASCO .... Asian Science Communicators' Organization [*International
            Council of Scientific Unions*]
ASCO .... Australian Services Canteen Organisation
ASCO .... Australian Standard Classification of Occupations
ASCO .... Canberra [*Australia*] [*ICAO location identifier*] (ICLI)
ASCOBIC ... African Standing Conference on Bibliographic Control (PDAA)
ASCODOC ... Association des Commissionnaires en Douane du Cambodge
            [*Association of Customs Commissioners in Cambodia*]
            (CL)
ASCOFAM ... Association Mondiale de Lutte Contre la Faim
ASCOFAME ... Asociacion Colombiana de Facultades de Medicina
            [*Colombian Medical Schools Association*] (LA)
ASCOFOM ... Associacao Brasileira Contra a Fome [*Rio De Janeiro, Brazil*]
            (LAA)
ASCOIN.... Asociacion Colombiana Indigenista [*Colombia*] (COL)
ASCOLBI ... Asociacion Colombiana de Bibliotecarios [*Colombia*] (COL)
ASCOLCO ... Asociacion Colombiana de Comerciantes [*Colombia*] (COL)

ASCOLPA ... Asociacion Colombiana de Cultivadores de Papa [*Colombia*] (COL)

ASCOLSI ... Asociacion Colombiana de Sistemas [*Colombia*] (DSCA)

ASCOM .... Arvi Satellite Communication Project [*India*] (PDAA)

ASCON ..... Administrative Staff College of Nigeria

ASCONA .. Asociacion Costarricense para la Conservacion de la Naturaleza [*Costa Rican Association of Nature Conservation*] (LA)

ASCONTRY ... Asesoria Contable y Tributaria [*Colombia*] (COL)

ASCOOP... Association Cooperative [*Cooperative Association*] [*Algeria*] (AF)

ASCOOPER ... Associacao das Cooperativas do Rio Grande do Sul [*Brazil*] (DSCA)

ASCOP...... Association Cooperative de Recherches des Hydrocarbures [*Algeria*]

ASCOPE ... ASEAN [*Association of South East Asian Nations*] Council on Petroleum [*Indonesia*]

ASCOTRIBUTI ... Associazione Nazionale fra i Concessionari del Servizio di Riscossione dei Tributi [*Italy*] (EY)

ASCOVE... Asociacion Colombiana de Veteranos [*Colombia*] (COL)

ASCOVEN ... Asociacion de Colombianos en Venezuela [*Association of Colombians in Venezuela*] (LA)

ASCP........ Aboriginal Staff Cadetship Program [*Australia*]

ASCP........ Air Standardization Coordination Program [*NATO*]

ASCPA ...... Australian Society of Certified Practising Accountants

ASCRIA .... African Society for Cultural Relations with Independent Africa [*Guyana*] (LA)

ASCS .... Australian Society for Classical Studies

ASCT......... Agricultural Show Council of Tasmania [*Australia*]

ASCT .... Australasian Smaller Companies Trust

ASCT........ Australian Society of Corporate Treasurers

ASCUBI .... Asociacion Cubana de Bibliotecarios [*Cuban Association of Librarians*] (EAIO)

ASCUN ..... Asociacion Colombiana de Universidades [*Colombian Universities Association*] [*Colombia*] (LA)

ASCVD...... Advisory Committee on Safety in Vehicle Design [*Australian Transport Advisory Council*] (PDAA)

ASCWSA .. Association of Scientific Workers of South Africa

ASD .... Accao Social Democratica [*Social Democratic Action*] [*Portugal*] [*Political party*] (PPE)

ASD .... Accion Social Democrata [*Social Democratic Action*] [*Spanish*] (WER)

ASD .... Administrative Services Department [*Queensland, Australia*]

ASD .... Air Sinai [*Egypt*] [*ICAO designator*] (FAAC)

ASD .... Alianza Social Democrata [*Social Democratic Alliance*] [*Dominican Republic*] (LA)

ASD .... Alliance pour la Social-Democratie [*Benin*] [*Political party*] (EY)

ASD .... Andros Town [*Bahamas*] [*Airport symbol*] (OAG)

ASD .... Armadni Stredisko Dukly [*Dukla Army Sports Center*] (CZ)

ASD .... Association des Senegalais Democrates [*Association of Senegalese Democrats*] (AF)

ASD .... Association Suisse de Documentation

ASD .... Automatic Parts Counter (RU)

ASD .... Automatic Range Tracking (RU)

ASD .... Axel Springer Inlandsdienst [*Axel Springer Domestic News Service*] (WEN)

ASD .... Dorogov's Antiseptic Stimulant (RU)

ASDA .... Associate of Speech and Drama, Australia

ASDA .... Association Suisse de Droit Aerien et Spatial [*Switzerland*] (SLS)

ASDA .... Australasian Stamp Dealers Association (ADA)

ASDA .... Australian Screen Directors' Association

ASDA .... Australian Soft Drink Association

ASDA .... Australian Sports Drug Agency

ASDAK...... Anotati Stratiotiki Dioikisis Amynis Kyprou [*Supreme Military Command for Cyprus Defense*] (GC)

ASDAN ..... Anotati Stratiotiki Dioikisis Attikis kai Nison [*Supreme Military Command of Attica and the Islands*] (GC)

ASDB........ Association for the Support and Defense of the Bedouin [*Israel*] (EAIO)

ASDBA ...... Australian South Devon Breeders Association (ADA)

ASDC........ Association Social-Democrate du Cameroun [*Political party*] (EY)

ASDC........ Australian Sports Drug Commission

ASDEC...... Association des Exportateurs de Cafe [*Haiti*] (EY)

ASDEN...... Anotera Stratiotiki Dioikisis Esoterikou kai Nison [*Higher Military Command for the Interior and Islands*] (GC)

ASDEP ...... Anotaton Symvoulion Dioikiseos Ekpaidevtikou Prosopikou [*Supreme Administrative Council of Teachers*] (GC)

ASDER...... Asociacion Salvadorena de Radiodifusores [*Salvadoran Association of Broadcasters*] (LA)

ASDES ...... Asociacion Medica de Especialistas [*Colombia*] (COL)

ASDES ...... Asociacion para el Desarrollo de Tolima [*Ibague, Colombia*] (LAA)

ASDEST.... Australian Space Debris Emergency Search Team

ASDF......... Air Self Defense Force

ASDI......... Asociation de Scouts Dominicanos [*Dominican Scout Association*] [*Dominican Republic*] (EAIO)

ASDI......... Associacao Social Democrata Independente [*Independent Social Democrat Association*] [*Portugal*] [*Political party*] (PPE)

ASDI......... Associazione Didattica Italiana tra Fabbricanti Importatori Distributori di Materiale Didattico

ASDIK....... Adesmevti Syndikalistiki Dimosioypalliliki Kinisi [*Free Civil Servants Trade Union Movement*]

ASDINARCO ... Asociacion Sindical de Ingenieros y Arquitectos Colombianos [*Colombia*] (COL)

ASDIS .... Adesmevti Syndikalistiki Dimokratiki Synergasia [*Nonaligned Democratic Trade Union Coalition*] [*Greek*] (GC)

ASDO .... Association "Sedifor" pour la Diffusion de l'Orgonomie [*Association "SEDIFOR" for the Study of Orgonomy*] [*France*] (EAIO)

ASDOAS... Asociacion Odontologica Sindical [*Colombia*] (COL)

ASDT........ Australian Society of Dairy Technology (ADA)

ASDT........ Timorese Social Democratic Association [*Indonesia*] (PD)

ASDU .... Accion Social Democratica Universitaria [*Social Democratic University Action*] [*Spanish*] (WER)

ASDU .... Dubbo [*Australia*] [*ICAO location identifier*] (ICLI)

ASDW .... Admiralty Sailing Directions for the World (BARN)

ASDY .... Anotaton Symvoulion Dimosion Ypiresion [*Supreme Council of Civil Services*] [*Greek*] (GC)

ASDZ........ Avstrijski Splosni Drzavljanski Zakonik [*Austrian General Civil Code*] (YU)

ASE........... Academia de Studii Economice [*Academy of Economic Studies*] (RO)

ASE........... Agence Spatiale Europeenne [*European Space Agency*] (EAIO)

ASE........... Aide Sociale a l'Enfance [*French*] (FLAF)

ASE........... Andikommounistiki Stavroforia Ellados [*Anticommunist Crusade of Greece*] (GC)

ASE........... Anotaton Symvoulion Ergasias [*Supreme Labor Council*] [*Greek*] (GC)

Ase .... Asile [*Asylum*] [*Military map abbreviation World War I*] [*French*] (MTD)

ASE........... Association Suisse des Electriciens (MCD)

ASE........... Australasian Society of Engineers (ADA)

ASE........... Australian Society of Endodontology (SLS)

ASE........... Australian Stock Exchange Indices [*Database*] [*Sydney Stock Exchange*] [*Information service or system*] (CRD)

ASEA........ Allemanna Svenska Elektriska Aktiebolaget [*Swedish General Electric Corporation*] (WEN)

ASEA........ Anotaton Symvoulion Ethnikis Amynis [*Supreme National Defense Council*] [*Greek*] (GC)

ASEA........ Association pour la Sauvegarde de l'Enfance Africaine

ASEA........ Australian Shorthorn Export Association

ASEA........ Australian Society for Education through Art (ADA)

ASEA........ Australian Speak Easy Association

ASEACOLK ... Association des Eleves et Anciens Eleves du College et du Lycee de Kompong Cham [*College and Lycee Kompong Cham Students and Alumni Association*] [*Cambodia*] (CL)

ASEAED ... Anotati Syndonistiki Epitropi Athlitismou Enoplon Dynameon [*Armed Forces Supreme Coordinating Committee for Sports*] [*Greek*] (GC)

ASEAN...... Association of Southeast Asian Nations (ECON)

ASEAN-ABC ... ASEAN [*Association of South East Asian Nations*] - Australia Business Council

ASEANAM ... ASEAN [*Association of South East Asian Nations*] Association of Museums (EAIO)

ASEANIS ... Association of South East Asian Nations: Indonesia-Singapore [*Submarine cable*] [*Telecommunications*]

ASEAQ...... Association of Special Education Administrators in Queensland [*Australia*]

ASEAUS ... Association of Southeast Asian University Students (CL)

ASEB......... Assam State Electricity Board [*India*] (PDAA)

ASEB......... Association pour la Mise en Valeur du Patrimoine Historique Sous-Marin [*Association for the Preservation of Underwater Historical Heritage*] [*France*] (EAIO)

ASEBANCIAL ... Asociacion de Empleados del Banco Comercial Antioqueno [*Colombia*] (COL)

ASEC........ Albert Schweitzer Ecological Centre [*Switzerland*] (EAIO)

ASEC........ Alice Springs Education Centre [*Australia*]

ASEC........ Association des Stagiaires et Etudiants Comoriens [*Association of Comoro Trainees and Students*] (AF)

ASECANA ... Agency for the Security of Aerial Navigation in Africa

ASECIC..... Asociacion Espanola de Cine Cientifico [*Spanish*] (SLS)

ASECNA... Agence pour la Securite de la Navigation Aerienne en Afrique et Madagascar [*Agency for Air Navigation Safety in Africa and Madagascar*] (AF)

ASECO...... Association d'Etudiants Comoriens [*Association of Comoro Students*] (AF)

ASECOL ... Asesoria Colombiana de Cultivos Tropicales [*Colombia*] (COL)

ASECOLDA ... Asociacion Colombiana de Companias de Seguros [*Colombian Insurance Companies Association*] (LA)

ASED......... Ammoniaque Synthetique and Derives [*Belgium*]

ASED......... Andifasistikos Syndesmos Ellinon Dimosiografon [*Antifascist Union of Greek Journalists*] (GC)

ASED......... Anotaton Symvoulion Enoplon Dynameon [*Supreme Armed Forces Council*] [*Greek*] (GC)

ASEDAMA ... Seguros Tequendama SA [*Colombia*] (COL)

ASEDB...... Australian Solar Energy Database

ASEDEC ... Asesoria Economica de Colombia [*Colombia*] (COL)

ASEEAI..... Anotati Syndonistiki Epitropi Ethnikon Agonon Ipeirou [*Supreme Coordinating Committee for the National Struggles of Ipeiros*] [*Greek*] (GC)

AsEF......... Asia Evangelistic Fellowship

ASEFNS.... Association of South East Field Naturalists Societies

ASEFT....... Australian Society for Education in Film and Television (ADA)

ASEG......... Army Clearing Evacuation Hospital (RU)

ASEG......... Australian Society of Exploration Geophysicists (ADA)

ASEI......... Association for the Support of Ecological Initiatives (EAIO)

ASEI......... Association of Swedish Engineering Industries (EAIO)

ASEI......... Australian Sports and Economics Institute

ASEI......... Automated Epidemiological Information System (BU)

ASEIBI...... Asociacion de Egresados de la Escuela Interamericana de Bibliotecologia [*Colorado*] (LA)

ASEIG ...... Asociacion Salvadorena de Empresarius de Industrias Graficas [*Salvadoran Association of Printing Industry Owners*] (LA)

a-sek.......... Ampere-Second (RU)

ASELCA.... Asociacion Espanola de la Lucha Contra la Contaminacion Ambiental [*Spanish*] (SLS)

ASELEC.... Asesoramientos Electricos [*Consulting electrical engineers*] [*Affiliated with Union Internationale des Laboratoires Independants*] [*Argentina*]

ASELT ...... Association Europeenne pour l'Echange de la Litterature Technique dans le Domaine de la Siderurgie [*European Association for the Exchange of Technical Literature in the Field of Ferrous Metallurgy - EAETLFFM*] (EAIO)

ASEM....... Asociacion Ecuatoriana de Museos [*Ecuador*] (SLS)

ASEMOLPRO ... Asociacion Nacional de Molineros de Trigo [*Colombia*] (COL)

ASEMUCH ... Asociacion Nacional de Empleados Municipales de Chile [*Chilean National Association of Municipal Employees*] (LA)

ASEO .... Anexartitai Synergazomenai Ergatoypallilikai Organoseis [*Independent Cooperating Employee Organizations*] [*Greek*] (GC)

ASEP......... Agence Senegalaise d'Edition et de Publicite

ASEP......... Anotaton Symvoulion Ekpaidevtikou Programmatos [*Supreme Council of the Educational Program*] [*Greek*] (GC)

ASEP......... Asociacion Salvadorena de Ejecutivos de Empresas Privadas [*Salvadoran Association of Executives of Private Corporations*]

ASEP......... Associacao de Seguradores Privados em Portugal [*Insurance representative body*] [*Lisbon, Portugal*] (EY)

ASEP......... Association Sportive d'Entretien Physique

ASEP......... Australian Science Education Project (ADA)

ASEPAS.... Association des Exportateurs de Produits Agricoles du Senegal

ASEQUA... Association Senegalaise pour l'Etude du Quaternaire de l'Ouest Africain

ASER......... Asesores de Relaciones Publicas y Publicidad Ltda. [*Colombia*] (COL)

ASERCA .. Aeroservicios Carabobo CA [*Venezuela*] [*ICAO designator*] (FAAC)

ASERCA ... Association for Strengthening Agricultural Research in Eastern and Central Africa (ECON)

ASERJ...... Association Senegalaise d'Etudes et de Recherches Juridiques

AS-EROS .. Adriatic Sea Expanded Regional Oceanological Studies (MSC)

ASERP ...... Asociacion Salvadorena de Ejecutivos de Relaciones Publicas [*Salvadoran Association of Public Relations Executives*] (LA)

ASES .... Agency for the Economic Development of Somalia [*Italian*]

ASES .... Asociacion Salvadorena de Empresas de Seguros [*Salvadoran Association of Insurance Companies*] (LA)

ASET .... Anambra State Education and Technology [*Nigeria*]

ASET .... Australian Society of Educational Technology (ADA)

ASET .... Australian, Sport, Environment and Territories [*Department*] [*National Union Catalogue of Australia symbol*]

ASETA ...... Asociacion de Empresas Estatales de Telecomunicaciones del Acuerdo Subregional Andino [*Association of State Telecommunication Undertakings of the Andean Subregional Agreement*] [*Ecuador*] (EAIO)

ASETA ...... Association Suisse pour l'Equipement de l'Agriculture [*Swiss Association for Agricultural Technology*] (PDAA)

ASETEPEXPORT ... Asociacion de Exportadores y Tecnicos en Promocion de Exportaciones [*Association of Exporters and Specialists for the Promotion of Exports*] [*Bolivia*] (LA)

ASETT ...... Arts, Sport, the Environment, Tourism, and Territories [*Portfolio*] [*Australia*]

ASETT ...... Australians Supporting European Transfer Treaty

ASE-USA .. Association of Space Explorers - USA (EAIO)

ASEV .... Anangastikos Synetairismos Engeion Veltioseon [*Emergency Association of Land Reclamation*] [*Plus the initial letter of the district in which located*] [*Greek*] (GC)

ASEVALLE ... Aseguradora del Valle [*Colombia*] (COL)

ASEVENTAS ... Asesoria y Ventas de Colombia [*Colombia*] (COL)

ASEVIK..... Association des Etudes du Vieux Khmer [*Ancient Cambodian Studies Association*] [*Samakom Niek Seksa Pheasa Khmer Boran*] [*Also,*] (CL)

ASEWA ..... Application of Sciences in Examination of Works of Art

ASF............ Acoustical Society of Finland (EAIO)

ASF............ Agricultural Special Fund [*Asian Development Bank*] [*United Nations*] (EY)

ASF............ Aktion Suehnezeichen/Friedensdienste [*Action Reconciliation/ Services for Peace*] [*Germany*] (EAIO)

ASF............ Arab Sugar Federation [*Khartoum, Sudan*] (EAIO)

ASF............ Asfaleia [*Security*] [*Athens General Security Subdirectorate*] (GC)

asf.............. Asphalt (RU)

asf.............. Asphalt Plant [*Topography*] (RU)

ASF............ Associated Securities Finance Ltd. [*Australia*] (ADA)

ASF............ Australian Ski Federation

ASF............ Australian Soccer Federation (ADA)

ASF............ Australian Softball Federation

ASF............ Australian Speleological Federation (ADA)

ASF............ Austrian Science Foundation (EAIO)

ASF............ Aviation sans Frontieres [*Humanitarian organization*] [*France*] (EY)

ASFA .... Associatie van Surinaamse Fabrikanten [*Surinam Manufacturers' Association*] (EY)

ASFA .... Association of Superannuation Funds of Australia (ADA)

ASFA .... Association pour la Solidarite Franco-Algerienne [*Association for Franco-Algerian Solidarity*] [*French*] (AF)

ASFA .... Association pour la Solidarite Franco-Arabe

ASFAC ...... Association Syndicale des Fonctionnaires et Agents du Cameroun

ASFACO ... Asociacion de Fabricantes de Conservas [*Association of Canned Foods Manufacturers*] [*Chile*] (LA)

ASF &OC ... Amateur Sports Federation and Olympic Committee of Hong Kong (EAIO)

ASFAP ...... AIDS Society for Asia and the Pacific

ASFB .... Australian Society for Fish Biology (ADA)

ASFC .... AeroSports Federation of China (EAIO)

ASFEC...... Arab States Fundamental Education Centre

ASFFI....... Association des Societes et Fonds Francais d'Investissement [*France*] (EAIO)

ASFINCO ... Asociacion Financiadora Comercial [*Commercial Financing Association*] [*Chile*] (LA)

ASFIS........ Aquatic Sciences and Fisheries Information System [*Food and Agriculture Organization*] [*United Nations*] (IID)

ASFL .... Associated Securities Finance Limited

ASFNRJ.... Akademski Savet Federativne Narodne Republike Jugoslavije [*Academic Council of the Federal People's Republic of Yugoslavia*] (YU)

ASFO......... Association Sportive des Fonctionnaires

ASFO......... Truck Superfilter with Sedimentation Trap (RU)

ASFOMENTO ... Asociacion de Fomento Comercial Ltda. [*Colombia*] (COL)

AS:FOR ..... Australian CSIRO [*Commonwealth Scientific Research Organisation*] Forestry [*Division - Canberra Laboratory*] [*National Union Catalogue of Australia symbol*]

ASFROBEL ... Association Belge du Commerce des Fromages [*Belgian Association of Chesse Wholesalers*] (EAIO)

ASFS .... Australia-Soviet Friendship Society (ADA)

ASG .... Acetylsulfanilguanidine (RU)

ASG .... African Seabird Group [*South Africa*] (EAIO)

ASG .... Agrarsoziale Gesellschaft eV [*Agrarian Social Society*] (ARC)

ASG .... Air Service Gabon (EY)

ASG .... Akademia Sztabu Generalnego [*General Staff Academy*] (POL)

ASG .... Aktion Soziale Gemeinschaft, die Partei der Sozialversicherten Arbeitnehmer und Rentner [*Social Community Action (Party of Socially Insured Employees and Pensioners)*] [*Germany*] [*Political party*] (PPW)

ASG .... Alekseyevskiy Student Settlement (RU)

ASG .... Arbeitsgemeinschaft der Sozialdemokraten im Gesundheitswesen [*Association of Social Democrats in Health Organizations*] (SLS)

ASG .... Armeesportgemeinschaft [*Army Sports Association*] (EG)

ASG .... Army Fuel Depot (RU)

ASG .... Assessment Subgroup [*NATO*] (NATG)

ASG .... Association of Swiss Graphic Designers (EAIO)

ASG .... Association Suisse de Golf [*Swiss Golf Association*] (EAIO)

ASG .... Ausruestungen fuer Schwerindustrie und Geraetebau (VVB) [*Equipment for Heavy Industry and Equipment Construction (VVB)*] (EG)

ASG .... Australasian Seabird Group (EA)

ASG .... Australasian Share/Guide Ltd.

ASGA .... Association des Services Geologiques Africains [*Association of African Geological Surveys - AAGS*] [*ICSU*]   (EAIO)
ASGA .... Australian Sporting Goods Association
ASGAP..... Association of Societies for Growing Australian Plants
ASGAT...... Astronomie Gamma a Themis [*France*]
ASGAV...... Associacao Gaucha de Avicultura [*Brazil*]   (DSCA)
ASGAZ...... Anadolu Sinai Gazlar Anonim Sirketi [*Anatolian Industrial Gases Corp.*] [*Izmit*]   (TU)
ASGC......... Australian Standard Geographic Classification
ASGER...... Assesoria Geral [*Brazil*]   (DSCA)
ASGILCO ... Assistant Secretary General for Infrastructure, Logistics, and Council Operations [*NATO*]
ASGME..... Anotati Synomospondia Goneon Mathiton Ellados [*Supreme Confederation of Parents of Students of Greece*]   (GC)
ASGP........ Association of Secretaries General of Parliaments   (EA)
ASGP........ Australian Society of General Practitioners   (ADA)
ASGS........ Aboriginal Study Grants Scheme [*Australia*]   (ADA)
ASh .... Aircraft Engine Designed by A. D. Shvetsov   (RU)
ASh .... Anthracite Dust   (RU)
ASH .... Armadni Sportovni Hry [*Armed Forces Athletic Games*]   (CZ)
ASH .... Astronomical Society of the Hunter [*Australia*]   (ADA)
ASH .... Australian School of Hypnotherapy
ASH .... Australian Society of Herpetologists   (ADA)
ASH .... Australian Stationary Hospital   (ADA)
ASh .... Collapsible-Whip Antenna   (RU)
ASh .... Hinged Arch Support [*Mining*]   (RU)
ASHA .... African Self Help Association [*South Africa*]   (AA)
ASHA .... Association for the Application of Science to Human Affairs [*India*]   (PDAA)
ASHA .... Australian Society for Historical Archaeology
ASHA .... Australian Software Houses Association
ASHB .... Australian School of Health and Beauty
ASHC .... Aeronautics and Space Historical Center   (EA)
ASHC .... Australian Scottish Heritage Council
AShch .... Antenna Panel   (RU)
AShchP...... Instrument Switchboard   (RU)
ASHEC....... Australian Slimming and Health Education Centre
Ashges ...... Ashkhabad Hydroelectric Power Plant   (RU)
AShK .... Automatic Wrench   (RU)
AShKhB .... Ashkhabad Railroad   (RU)
ASHL .... ASCIS [*Australian School Catalogue Information Service*] Subject Headings List
ASHM ...... Australasian Society for HIV [*Human Immunodeficiency Virus*] Medicine
AShO .... Aviation School of the Osoaviakhim   (RU)
AShP.......... Afro-Shirazskaia Partiia [*Afro-Shirazi Party*] [*Tanzania*]
AS:HQ....... Australian CSIRO [*Commonwealth Scientific and Research Organisation*] Headquarters [*Corporate Library and Information Service*] [*National Union Catalogue of Australia symbol*]
AShS.......... Aerial Navigator's Handbook   (RU)
ASHS........ Association of Sacred Heart Schools [*Australia*]
ASHS........ Australian Society of Horticultural Science
ASHS........ Australian Stock Horse Society
ASHW ...... Holsworthy [*Australia*] [*ICAO location identifier*]   (ICLI)
ASI............ Agregation de l'Enseignement Secondaire Inferieur [*French*]
ASI............ Agricultural Society of Iceland   (EAIO)
ASI............ Air Service Ivoirien
ASI............ Althydusamband Islands [*Icelandic Federation of Labor*]
ASI............ Anti-Slavery International [*England*]   (EAIO)
ASI............ Arbeitsgemeinschaft Sozialwissenschaftlicher Institute eV [*Association of Social Science Institutes*]   (SLS)
ASI............ Archaeological Survey of India
ASI............ Armaments Standardization and Interoperability [*NATO*]   (NATG)
ASI............ Asian Statistical Institute [*Japan*]   (PDAA)
ASI............ Asosiasi Semen Indonesia [*Indonesia Cement Association*]   (EAIO)
ASI............ Association Stomatologique Internationale [*French*]   (SLS)
ASI............ Astronomy Society of India   (PDAA)
ASI............ Australian Shipbuilding Industries Ltd.
ASI............ Australian Skeptics, Inc. [*An association*]
ASI............ Australian Society of Indexers
ASI............ Australian Supermarket Institute
ASI............ Australian Swimming, Inc.
ASI............ Pulse-Height Selector   (RU)
ASiA .... Academy of Construction and Architecture   (RU)
ASIA .... Airlines Staff International Association   (EAIO)
ASIA .... Asociacion de Antiguos Alumnos de la Compania de Jesus [*Colombia*]   (COL)
ASIA .... Asociacion Salvadorena de Ingenieros y Arquitectos [*Salvadoran Association of Engineers and Architects*]   (LA)
ASIA .... Associate, Security Institute of Australia   (ADA)
ASIA .... Association Suisse de l'Industrie Aeronautique [*Switzerland*]
ASIA .... Australian Scientific Industry Association
ASIA .... Australian Security Industry Association

ASIA .... Australian Stevedoring Industry Authority   (ADA)
ASIAC ...... Australian Seed Industry Advisory Council
ASIAC ...... Australian Society for Intercountry Aid (Children)
ASIAC ...... Australian Society for Inter-Country Aid for Children   (ADA)
ASIAC ...... Australian Surveying Industry Advisory Committee
ASIAL ...... Australian Security Industry Association Limited   (ADA)
ASIAPACK ... South East Asia International Exhibition of Packaging Machinery and Materials and Food Processing Machinery
ASIATEX ... South East Asia's International Exhibition of Textile and Garment Machinery and Fabrics Trade
ASIC .... Association Scientifique Internationale du Cafe [*International Scientific Association of Coffee*]   (EAIO)
ASIC .... Association Suisse d'Ingenieurs-Conseils [*Swiss Association of Consulting Engineers*]   (EAIO)
ASIC .... Australian Standard Industrial Classification   (ADA)
ASICA ...... Agrupacion Sindical de Caucion para las Actividades Agrarias [*Spain*]   (DSCA)
ASICH....... Asociacion Sindical de Chile [*Chilean Trade Union Association*] [*Santiago*]   (LA)
ASICOL .... Asociacion de Ingenieros Contratistas Ltda. [*Colombia*]   (COL)
ASID......... Australian Society of Implant Dentistry   (ADA)
ASID......... Australian Society of Infectious Diseases
ASIDUOS ... Asociacion de Ingenieros de la Universidad Industrial de Santander [*Bucaramanga*]   (COL)
ASIES........ Asociacion de Sindicatos Independientes [*Association of Independent Trade Unions*] [*El Salvador*]   (EY)
ASIFA .... Association Internationale du Film d'Animation [*International Animated Film Association*]   (EAIO)
ASIFA .... Australian Society of Investment and Financial Advisers
ASII .... Australian Science Index [*AUSINET database*]   (ADA)
ASILAC..... Asociacion de Industrias Lacteas [*Association of Dairy Industries*] [*Chile*]   (LA)
ASIM........ Arbeitsgemeinschaft fuer Simulation [*Germany*]   (PDAA)
ASIM........ Australian Scientific Instrument Manufacturers
ASIMAD... Asociacion de Industriales Madereros [*Association of Wood Products Manufacturers*] [*Chile*]   (LA)
ASIMCO... Associazione Italiana degli Imbottigliatori
ASIMCOL ... Asociaciones de Impresores de Colombia [*Colombia*]   (COL)
ASIMET ... Asociacion de Industriales Metalurgicos [*Metallurgical Manufacturers Association*] [*Chile*]   (LA)
ASIN......... Accion de Sistemas de Informacion Nacional [*National Information Systems Activity*] [*Venezuela*]   (LA)
ASINCA .... Asociacion de Industriales de Cautin [*Chile*]   (LAA)
ASINCAL ... Asociacion de Industriales de Calzado de Chile [*Chilean Association of Shoe Manufacturers*]   (LA)
ASINEL .... Asociacion de Investigacion Industrial Electrica [*Spain*]   (PDAA)
ASIO......... Australian Secret Intelligence Organization   (LAIN)
ASIO......... Australian Security Intelligence Organisation   (PD)
ASIP .... Agriculture Sector Implementation Project
ASIP .... Asociatia Sindicala a Industriei Pielei [*Trade Union Association of the Leather Industry*]   (RO)
ASIP .... Associazione per lo Sviluppo dell'Istruzione e della Formazione Professionale [*Italian*]   (SLS)
ASIPI........ Asociacion Interamericana de la Propiedad Industrial [*Inter-American Association of Industrial Property - IAAIP*]   (EAIO)
ASIPI........ Association Interamericaine de Propriete Industrielle   (FLAF)
ASIPLA.... Asociacion de Industriales del Plastico [*Association of Plastics Industries*] [*Chile*]   (LAA)
ASIQUIM ... Asociacion de Industriales Quimicos [*Association of Chemical Manufacturers*] [*Chile*]   (IMH)
ASIS .... Agac Esya Iscileri Sendikasi [*Wood Products Workers Union*]   (TU)
AS-IS .... Agac Sanayii Iscileri Birligi [*Wood Industry Workers Union*]   (TU)
Asis .... Asistan [*Assistant*]   (TU)
ASIS .... Australian Secret Intelligence Service   (ADA)
ASIS .... Socialist Art Association   (RU)
ASISA .... Israel Goat Breeders' Association   (EAIO)
ASISS........ Alpine Science Information Service [*Information service or system*]   (IID)
asist........... Assistant   (BU)
ASIT .... Asociatia Stiintifica a Inginerilor si Tehnicienilor [*Scientific Association of Engineers and Technicians*]   (RO)
AS:IT .... Australian CSIRO [*Commonwealth Scientific and Industrial Research Organisation*] Information Technology [*Division of Information Technology*] [*National Union Catalogue of Australia symbol*]
ASIVA ...... Asociacion de Industriales de Valparaiso y Aconcagua [*Valparaiso and Aconcagua Manufacturers Association*] [*Chile*]   (LA)
AsIz.......... Askeri Inzibat [*Military Police*] [*Turkish Cypriot*]   (GC)
ASJ .... AB Svenska Jarnvagsverkstaderna [*Swedish Railroad Workshops*]   (WEN)
ASJ .... Accion Social Juvenil [*Youth Social Action*] [*Costa Rica*]   (LA)
ASJ .... Alianca Socialista de Juventude [*Socialist Youth Alliance*] [*Portugal*] [*Political party*]   (PPE)

ASJ .... Amami O Shima [*Japan*] [*Airport symbol*]   (OAG)
ASJA .... Anjuman Sunnatul Jamaat Association of Trinidad and Tobago
ASJL........... Association for the Study of Jewish Languages [*Haifa, Israel*]
                  (EAIO)
ASJU .... African Sports Journalists Union
ASK .... Adana Sinema Kultur Dernegi [*Adana Cinema Cultural
                  Association*]   (TU)
ASK .... Agricultural Society of Kenya
ASK .... Alerting Search Service from Kinokuniya [*Kinokuniya Co. Ltd.*]
                  [*Japan*] [*Information service or system*]   (IID)
ASK .... Algemene Sendingkommissie [*Afrikaans*]
ASK .... Anotati Skholi Kinimatografon [*Supreme Cinematographers'
                  School*] [*Greek*]   (GC)
ASK .... Anotaton Symvoulion Kriseos [*Supreme Rating Council*]   (GC)
ASK .... Antiimperialistische Solidaritaetskomitee fuer Afrikan, Asien,
                  und Lateinamerika
ASK .... Arbeitsschutzkommission [*Accident Prevention Commission*]
                  (EG)
ASK .... Armee-Sport-Klub [*Army Sport Club*]   (EG)
ASK .... Army Sports Club   (RU)
Ask........... Asker [*or Askeri*] [*Soldier or Military*]   (TU)
ASK .... Available Seat-Kilometres [*Air travel*]
ASK .... Reinforced Graded Bit   (RU)
ASK .... Studio Equipment Complex   (RU)
ASK .... Sudania Aviation Co. [*Sudan*] [*ICAO designator*]   (FAAC)
ASK .... Yamoussoukro [*Ivory Coast*] [*Airport symbol*]   (OAG)
ASKA........ Association Khmere des Agences de Voyage et de Tourisme
                  [*Cambodian Association of Travel and Tourism Agencies*]
                  (CL)
ASKA........ Australian Shotokan Karate Association   (ADA)
ASKDF ...... Amator Spor Kulupleri Dernegi Federasyonu [*Federation of
                  Amateur Sports Clubs Associations*]   (TU)
ASKF .... Amator Spor Kulupleri Federasyonu [*Federation of Amateur
                  Sports Clubs*]   (TU)
ASKhI....... Azerbaydzhan Agricultural Institute   (RU)
ASKhN ...... Academy of Agricultural Sciences   (RU)
ASKM....... Australian Society for Keyboard Music   (ADA)
ASKS .... Sydney [*Australia*] [*ICAO location identifier*]   (ICLI)
ASKT .... Anotati Skholi Kalon Tekhnon [*Supreme Fine Arts School*]
                  [*Greek*]   (GC)
ASKZ........ Automatic Cathodic Protection Unit   (RU)
ASL........... Antistreptolysin   (RU)
ASL........... Associated Securities Limited [*Australia*]   (ADA)
ASL........... Australian Socialist League   (ADA)
ASL........... Australian Society for Limnology   (ADA)
asl.............. Transfer Machine   (RU)
ASLA .... Amerikan Suomen Lainan Apurahat [*American Finnish Loan
                  Scholarships*]   (WEN)
ASLA .... Armenian Secret Liberation Army
ASLA .... Associazione Siciliana per le Lettere e le Arti [*Italian*]   (SLS)
ASLA .... Australian School Library Association   (ADA)
ASLAF ...... Association of Swedish-Language Authors in Finland   (EAIO)
ASLAT ...... Association Senegalaise de Lutte Antituberculeuse
ASLF .... Australian Student Labor Federation   (ADA)
ASLH .... Lord Howe Island [*Australia*] [*ICAO location identifier*]   (ICLI)
ASLK........ Algemene Spaar- en Lijfrentekas [*State-owned bank*] [*Belgium*]
                  (EY)
ASLK-CGER ... Algemene Spaar- en Lijfrentekas - Caisse Generale d'Eparque
                  et de Retraite [*Bank*] [*Brussels, Belgium*]
ASLK-CGER ... Algemene Spaar- en Lijfrentekas/Caisse Generale d'Espargne
                  et de Retraite [*Commercial bank*] [*Belgium*]   (EY)
ASLLP...... Australian Second Language Learning Program
ASLO........ Australian Scientific Liaison Office   (ADA)
ASLP .... Association of Special Libraries of the Philippines   (SLS)
ASLP .... Australian Society of Legal Philosophy   (EAIO)
ASLPR ...... Australian Second Language Proficiency Ratings
ASLS .... Association for Scottish Literary Studies [*Aberdeen, Scotland*]
                  (EAIO)
ASLS .... Associazione Sindacati Lavoratore della Somalia [*Workers'
                  Trade Union Association of Somalia*]
ASLV .... Assurance sur la Vie [*Life Insurance*] [*French*]
ASLV .... Augmented Satellite Launch Vehicle [*India*]
ASM .... Academia de Stiinte Medicale [*Academy of Medical Sciences*]
                  (RO)
ASM .... Activated Finely Porous Silica Gel   (RU)
ASM .... African Service Medal
ASM .... African Student Movement
ASM .... Agregation de l'Enseignement Secondaire Moyen [*French*]
ASM .... Aircraft Survival Measures Programme [*NATO*]
ASM .... American Samoa [*ANSI three-letter standard code*]   (CNC)
ASM .... Antisousmarine [*Antisubmarine*] [*French*]   (WER)
ASM .... Asmara [*Ethiopia*] [*Airport symbol*]   (OAG)
ASM .... Asmara Airport
ASM .... Assembleur [*Assembler*] [*French*]   (ADPT)
ASM .... Association of Spectacle Makers [*Australia*]
ASM .... Australian Society for Microbiology   (ADA)

ASM .... Australian Society of Magicians   (EAIO)
ASM .... Australian St Mark's [*National Theological Centre - St Mark's
                  Library*] [*National Union Catalogue of Australia symbol*]
ASM .... Avenir Sportif de la Marsa [*Tunisia*]
ASM .... Modern Music Association   (RU)
ASM .... SCTA Air St. Martin [*ICAO designator*]   (FAAC)
ASMA .... Australian Adhesives and Sealants Manufacturers' Association
ASMA .... Australian Small Magazine Association   (ADA)
ASMA .... Australian Speedway Media Association
ASMA .... Australian Stipendiary Magistrates Association   (ADA)
ASMAE..... Anotati Synomospondia Mikroidioktiton Avtokiniton Ellados
                  [*Supreme Confederation of Small Vehicle Owners of Greece*]
                  (GC)
ASMAF ..... Association Scientifique des Medecins Acupuncteurs de France
                  [*French*]   (SLS)
As Mah...... Askeri Mahkeme [*Military Court, Tribunal*]   (TU)
ASMAI...... Archivio Storico dell'ex Ministero dell'Africa Italiana
ASMAR.... Astilleros y Maestranzas de la Armada [*Naval Docks and Yards*]
                  [*Chile*]   (LA)
ASMAS .... Asbest Madencilik ve Sanayi Anonim Sirketi [*Asbestos Mining
                  and Industry Corporation*]   (TU)
ASMC....... Association of Stores and Materials Controllers   (EAIO)
ASMC....... Australian Sugar Milling Council
ASME....... Australian Society for Music Education   (ADA)
ASMEC..... Australian Society for Microbiology Environment and
                  Community Group
ASMECCANICA ... Associazione Nazionale di Meccanica [*Italian*]   (SLS)
ASMEDAS ... Asociacion Medica Sindical Colombiana [*Colombian Medical
                  Union Association*]   (LA)
ASMEDICA ... Asociacion Medica Odontologica [*Colombia*]   (COL)
ASMEVEZ ... Asociacion Nacional de Medicos Veterinarios Zootecnistas
                  Colorado   (DSCA)
ASMF........ Australian Sports Medicine Federation [*or Foundation*]   (ADA)
ASMF........ Australian Street Machine Federation
ASMIC...... Australian Surveying and Mapping Industry Conference
ASMIC...... Australian Surveying and Mapping Industry Council
ASMIPAC ... Association des Importateurs de Pneumatiques et d'Articles en
                  Caoutchouc Manufacture [*Morocco*]
ASMO .... Arab Organisation for Standardisation and Metrology
ASMO .... Arab Organization for Standardization and Metrology   (EAIO)
ASMO .... Arab Standardization and Metrology Organization   (DS)
ASMO .... Association of State Medical Officers [*Western Australia*]
ASMO .... Canberra [*Australia*] [*ICAO location identifier*]   (ICLI)
ASMP........ Air-Sol Moyenne Portee [*Air-to-Ground Medium-Range Missile*]
                  [*French*]
ASMP........ Australasian Species Management Plan
ASMP........ Austrian Medical Society of Psychotherapy   (EAIO)
ASMR........ Australian Society for Medical Research   (ADA)
ASMS........ Australian Steel Mill Services
ASMW ...... Amt fuer Standardisierung Messwesen und Warenpruefung
                  [*Standardization, Measurement, and Commodity Testing
                  Office*] [*German*]   (EG)
ASN .... Aatteellisten Sahkoinsinoorijarjestojen Neuvottelukunta
                  [*Consulting Committee of the Professional Electroengineers'
                  Organizations in Finland*]   (EAIO)
ASN .... Acoustical Society of the Netherlands   (EAIO)
ASN .... Advertising Services Network [*Australia*]
ASN .... Agencia de Seguridad Nacional [*National Security Agency*]
                  [*Costa Rica*]   (LA)
ASN .... Air Services Nantes [*France*] [*ICAO designator*]   (FAAC)
ASN .... Association des Sourds du Niger
ASN .... Australasian Steam Navigation Co.   (ADA)
ASNA .... Australian Suburban Newspapers Association   (ADA)
ASNC .... Alexandria Shipping and Navigation Company
ASNC .... Australasian Steam Navigation Co.
ASNCo....... Australasian Steam Navigation Company
ASNEMGE ... Association des Societes Nationales, Europeennes, et
                  Mediterraneennes de Gastroenterologie [*Association of
                  National, European, and Mediterranean Societies of
                  Gastroenterology*]   (EAIO)
ASNF........ Norfolk Island [*Australia*] [*ICAO location identifier*]   (ICLI)
ASNIBI ..... Asociacion Nicaraguense de Bibliotecarios [*Nicaragua*]   (SLS)
ASNLH ..... Association for the Study of Negro Life and History
ASNM .... Archiv Slovenskeho Narodneho Muzea [*Archives of the Slovak
                  National Museum*]   (CZ)
ASNOCh ... Anti-Fascist Assembly of People's Liberation of Montenegro
                  (RU)
ASNOM .... Antifasisticko Sobranie na Narodnoto Osloboduvanje na
                  Makedonija [*Anti-Fascist Assembly of National Liberation
                  of Macedonia*]   (YU)
ASNOS...... Antifasisticka Skupstina Narodnog Oslobodenja Srbije [*Anti-
                  Fascist Assembly of National Liberation of Serbia*]   (YU)
ASNOVA .. Association of Modern Architects [*1923-1932*]   (RU)
ASNT........ Australian School of Nuclear Technology   (NRCH)
ASNU .... Association Senegalaise pour les Nations-Unies
ASNW .... Nowra [*Australia*] [*ICAO location identifier*]   (ICLI)

ASO .... Air Sarthe Organisation - Societe [*France*] [*ICAO designator*] (FAAC)
ASO .... Air Support Officer [*Military*]
ASO .... Alianza Sindical Obrera [*Workers Trade Union Alliance*] [*Spanish*] (WER)
ASO .... Anexartiti Sosialistiki Omada [*Independent Socialist Group*] (GC)
ASO .... Ankara Sanayi Odasi [*Ankara Chamber of Industry*] (TU)
ASO .... Arab Socialist Organization [*Egypt*] (ME)
ASO .... Arbeidsgiverforeningen for Skip og Offshorefartoyer [*Norwegian Shipping and Offshore Federation*] (EAIO)
ASO .... Asosa [*Ethiopia*] [*Airport symbol*] (OAG)
ASO .... Australian Safeguards Office
ASO .... Australian Society of Orthodontists (ADA)
ASO .... Australian Space Office
ASO .... Australian Survey Office
ASO .... Australia's Strategic Outlook
ASO .... Automatic Target Range Equipment (RU)
ASO .... Automobile Service Station (RU)
ASO .... Avtonomos Stafidikos Organismos [*Autonomous Currant Organization*] [*Greek*] (GC)
ASO .... Breakdown Rescue Department (BU)
ASOA .... Australasian Steamship Owners Association (DS)
ASOA .... Australian Serviced Offices Association
ASOA .... Australian Shipping Officers' Association (ADA)
ASOB .... Asociacion Salvadorena de Oficiales Bancarios [*Salvadoran Association of Banking Officials*] (LA)
ASOBAN... Asociacion de Bancos e Instituciones Financieras de Bolivia (EY)
ASOBANC ... Asociacion Bancaria [*Bankers Association*] [*Colorado*] (LA)
ASOBANCARIA ... Asociacion Bancaria de Colombia [*Colombian Banking Association*] (COL)
ASOC .... Armstrong Siddeley Owners Club (EA)
ASOC .... Artists' Society of Canberra [*Australia*]
ASOCAJAS ... Asociacion Nacional de Cajas de Compensacion Familiar [*National Association of Family Compensation Funds*] [*Colorado*] (LA)
ASOCAL... Asociacion de Oficinistas de Cali (COL)
ASOCANA ... Asociacion de Cultivadores de Cana de Azucar de Colombia [*Colombian Sugar Growers Association*] (LA)
ASOCAR... Asociacion Colombiana de Carreteras [*Colombia*] (COL)
ASOCEM ... Association of Cement Producers [*Peru*] (EAIO)
ASOCHOIN ... Asociacion de Choferes Independientes [*Association of Independent Drivers*] [*Dominican Republic*] (LA)
ASOCO ..... Asociacion Colombiana de Criadores de Ganado Ovino [*Colombia*] (COL)
AsOCOA ... Asia-Oceania Clinical Oncology Association
ASOCOPI ... Asociacion Colombiana de Profesores de Ingles. Universidad del Valle [*Colombia*] (COL)
ASOCRENAL ... Asesoria de Credito Nacional Ltda. [*Colombia*] (COL)
ASocSc....... Associateship of Social Science [*Australia*]
ASODAS... Asociacion Odontologica Sindical (COL)
ASODEFO ... Asociacion de Empleados Forestales [*Dominican Republic*] (DSCA)
ASODIRVALL ... Asociaciones de Directores de Droguerias del Valle del Cauca [*Colombia*] (COL)
ASODOBI ... Asociacion Dominicana de Bibliotecarios [*Dominican Republic*] (SLS)
ASOE .... Australian Society of Engineers
ASOEE...... Anotati Skholi Oikonomikon kai Emborikon Epistimon [*Supreme School of Economic and Commercial Sciences*] [*Greek*] (GC)
ASOELVA ... Asociacion de Electricistas del Valle [*Colombia*] (COL)
ASOEXPORT ... Asociacion Nacional de Exportadores de Cafe [*National Association of Coffee Exporters*] [*Colorado*] (LA)
ASOF......... Australasian Steamship Owners' Federation (ADA)
ASOFARCO ... Asociacion Farmaceutica de Colombia [*Colombia*] (COL)
ASOFER ... Asociacion Colombiana de Ferreteros [*Colombia*] (COL)
AsOFNM .. Asia-Oceania Federation of Nuclear Medicine
ASOHI ...... Asosiasi Obat Hewan Indonesia [*Indonesia Veterinary Drug Association*] (EAIO)
ASOIF .... Association ofSummer Olympic International Federation (OLYM)
ASOLIVA ... Agrupacion Espanola de la Industria y Comercio Exportador de Aceite de Oliva [*Spain*] (EY)
ASOM .... Academie des Sciences d'Outre-Mer [*French*] (SLS)
ASOM .... Association of Marketers [*South Africa*] (AA)
ASOMAR ... Asociacion de Marinos de Colombia [*Colombian Seamen's Association*] (LA)
ASOMEDIOS ... Asociacion Nacional de Medios de Communicacion [*Colorado*] (EY)
ASOMERIDA ... Asociacion de Productores Rurales del Estado Merida [*Venezuela*] (DSCA)
ASOMEVA ... Asociacion de Medicos del Valle [*Colombia*] (COL)
ASOMEX ... Association of American Schools in the Republic of Mexico (EAIO)

ASOMHOCOL ... Asociacion Medica Homeopata Colombiana [*Colombia*] (COL)
ASONADI ... Asociacion Nacional de Inhabilitados [*Colombia*] (COL)
ASONAV .. Asociacion Nacional de Agentes Navieros [*Colombia*] (COL)
ASONIDA ... Asociacion Nacional de Industriales del Arroz [*Venezuela*] (DSCA)
ASOO .... Anotati Skholi Oikiakis Oikonomias [*Supreme Home Economics School*] [*Name of location usually follows name of school*] [*Greek*] (GC)
ASOPA...... Australian School of Pacific Administration (ADA)
ASOPEF.... Athinaikos Syllogos Oikogeneion Politikon Exoriston kai Fylakismenon [*Athenian Association of Families of Political Exiles and Prisoners*] (GC)
ASOPROBAR ... Asociacion Productores Rurales de Barlovento [*Venezuela*] (DSCA)
ASOPROLE ... Asociacion de Productores de Leche [*Venezuela*] (DSCA)
ASOQUIM ... Asociacion de Fabricantes de Productos Quimicos [*Association of Chemical Manufacturers*] [*Venezuela*] (LA)
ASOR .... Australian Society for Operations Research, Inc. (ADA)
ASOR .... Automated System of Work Organization (RU)
ASOS........ Association Suisse d'Organisation Scientifique [*Swiss Association for Scientific Management*] (PDAA)
ASOS........ Australian Society of Orthopaedic Surgeons
ASOSCOL ... Asociacion de Simpatizantes de la Orquesta Sinfonica de Colombia [*Colombia*] (COL)
ASOSH ..... Association of Societies for Occupational Safety and Health [*South Africa*] (AA)
ASOTA...... Association pour le Soutien du Khet Takeo [*Association to Support Takeo Province*] [*Cambodia*] (CL)
ASOTRANCOL ... Asociacion de Transportadores de Colombia [*Colombian Transport Workers Association*] (LA)
ASOVA ...... Asociacion de Odontologos del Valle [*Colombia*] (COL)
ASOVAC... Asociacion Venezolana para el Avance de la Ciencia [*Venezuelan Association for the Advancement of Science*] (LA)
ASOVIARO ... Asociacion de Agentes Viajeros de Occidente [*Colombia*] (COL)
ASOVIM... Asociacion Venezolana de Impedidos Motores (EAIO)
ASP........... Aboriginal Studies Press [*Australia*]
ASP........... Accao Socialista Portugues [*Portuguese Socialist Action*] (PPE)
ASP........... Accepte sans Protet [*Accepted without Protest*] [*French*] [*Business term*]
ASP........... Accepte sous Protet [*Accepted under Protest*] [*French*] [*Business term*]
ASP........... Accion Sindical Panamena [*Panamanian Trade Union Action*] (LA)
ASP........... Accion Social Patronal [*Employers Social Welfare Association*] [*Spanish*] (WER)
ASP........... African Studies Program
ASP........... Afro-Shirazi Party [*Tanzania*] (AF)
ASP........... Akademia Sztuk Pieknych [*Academy of Fine Arts (1950-1957)*] (POL)
ASP........... Akademia Sztuk Plastycznych [*Academy of Plastic Arts*] (POL)
ASP........... Akcja Sanitarno-Porzadkowa [*Cleaning and Sanitation Drive*] (POL)
ASP........... Alianza Socialista Popular [*Popular Socialist Alliance*] [*Venezuela*] (LA)
ASP........... Alice Springs [*Australia*] [*Airport symbol*] (OAG)
ASP........... Allied Standing Procedure [*NATO*] (NATG)
ASP........... American Selling Price
ASP........... Anotati Skholi Polemou [*Superior War School (Army)*] (GC)
ASP........... Arab Socialist Party [*Egypt*] [*Political party*] (PPW)
ASP........... Arab Socialist Party [*Syria*] [*Political party*] (PPW)
ASP........... Arbeitsspeicher [*German*] (ADPT)
ASP........... Artillery Signal Post (RU)
asp............. Aspartic Acid (RU)
Asp............. Aspirant [*Officer Cadet (Recently candidate for a degree)*] (CZ)
asp............. Aspirante [*Midshipman*] [*Portuguese*]
ASP........... Assistant Superintendent of Police
ASP........... Associated Steamships Proprietary Ltd. [*Australia*]
ASP........... Association Scientifique de la Precontrainte [*French*] (SLS)
ASP........... Association Suisse de Pneu [*Association of the Swiss Tire Industry*] (PDAA)
ASP........... Australasian [*or Australian*] Socialist Party (ADA)
ASP........... Australian Shooters Party [*Political party*]
ASP........... Australian Society for Parasitology (ADA)
ASP........... Australian Society of Periodontology (ADA)
ASP........... Australian Society of Prosthodontists (ADA)
ASP........... Autonomous Economic Enterprise (BU)
asp............. Motor Ambulance Regiment (BU)
ASP........... Panel Station [*Aviation*] (RU)
ASP........... Truck-Drawn Dump Trailer (RU)
ASP90...... Australia's Strategic Planning in the Nineties [*An association*]
ASPA........ Accion Social Patriotica [*Patriotic Social Action*] [*Colorado*] (LA)
ASPA........ Alloy Steel Producers Association [*India*] (PDAA)
ASPA........ Argentinian Society for Philosophical Analysis (EAIO)
ASPA........ Asociacion de Productividad Agraria [*Spain*] (DSCA)

ASPA......... Association of South Pacific Airlines [*Fiji*]   (EY)
ASPA......... Associazione Scientifica di Produzione Animale [*Italian*]   (SLS)
ASPA......... Astikai Syngoinoniai Periokhis Athinon [*Athens Area Urban Communications*]   (GC)
ASPA......... Australasian Student Philosophy Association
ASPA......... Australian Saddle Pony Association
ASPA......... Australian Sales Promotion Association
ASPA......... Australian Scrabble Players' Association
ASPA......... Australian Ski Patrol Association   (ADA)
ASPA......... Australian Student Philosophy Association
ASPA......... Australian Sugar Producers Association   (ADA)
ASPAC...... Asian and Pacific Council
ASPAC...... Asian-Pacific Section [*International Union of Local Authorities*] [*Australia*]
ASPAC...... Australian Soil and Plant Analysis Council
ASPACLS ... Australian and South Pacific Association for Comparative Literary Studies
ASPACO ... Associacao Paulista de Criadores de Ovinos [*Brazil*]   (DSCA)
ASPAEN ... Asociacion para la Ensenanza [*Colombia*]   (COL)
ASPAL ...... Association pour la Promotion des Artistes Lao [*Association for the Promotion of Lao Artists*]   (CL)
AsPALMS ... Asian-Pacific Association of LASER Medical Surgery
ASPAM..... Association des Producteurs d'Agrumes du Maroc [*Association of Citrus Growers of Morocco*] [*Casablanca*]   (AF)
ASPAN...... Association Suisse pour le Plan d'Amenagement National [*Swiss Association for the National Development Plan*]   (PDAA)
ASPAS...... Asociacion para el Fomento de Estudios sobre la Patata [*Spain*]   (DSCA)
ASPAS...... Asociacion Sindical de Pilotos Aviadores Salvadorenos [*Union Association of Salvadoran Airline Pilots*]   (LA)
AsPASL...... Asian-Pacific Association for the Study of the Liver
ASPAU...... African Scholarship Program of American Universities
ASPAU...... Asociacion de Profesionales Agricolas Universitarios [*El Salvador*]   (DSCA)
AsPAvMA ... Asia-Pacific Aviation Medicine Association
ASpB......... Arbeitsgemeinschaft der Spezialbibliotheken eV   (SLS)
ASPB......... Archiv Svazu Protifasistickych Bojovniku [*Archives of the Union of Fighters of Fascism*]   (CZ)
ASPBAE.... Asian-South Pacific Bureau of Adult Education   (ADA)
ASPC........ Australian Seed and Plant Club   (ADA)
ASPC........ Australian Softwood Producers' Council
AsPCDE.... Asian-Pacific Society for Digestive Endoscopy
ASPE......... Anotati Synomospondia Polemiston Ellados [*Supreme Confederation of Combatants of Greece*]   (GC)
ASPEA...... Association Suisse pour l'Energie Atomique [*Switzerland*] [*Nuclear energy*]   (NRCH)
ASPEC...... Association of Sorbitol Producers in the European Community   (EAIO)
ASPECT.... Australian Services in Pollution and Environmental Control Technology [*Research center*]   (ERC)
ASPEI....... Association of South Pacific Environmental Institutions
ÆSPEICP .. Associated Schools Project in Education for International Cooperation and Peace [*UNESCO*] [*Paris, France*]   (EAIO)
ASPEN...... Asian Physical Education Network [*Malaysia*]   (PDAA)
ASPENA ... Association des Anciens Eleves de la Section "Production" de l'Ecole Nationale d'Assurances [*France*]   (FLAF)
ASPER ...... Australasian Society for Photographic Education and Research   (ADA)
ASPES....... Association du Personnel de l'Enseignement Secondaire (Enseignants Francais du Maroc) [*North African*]
ASPESA.... Australian and South Pacific External Studies Association   (ADA)
ASPESCA ... Asociacion Colombiana de Pescadores [*Colombia*]   (COL)
ASPF .... Australian Society of Perfumers and Flavourists   (PDAA)
ASPFA ...... Association of Superannuation and Provident Funds of Australia   (ADA)
ASPG........ Australasian Study of Parliament Group
ASPH .... Australian Society of Professional Hypnotherapists   (ADA)
asphalt ...... Asphaltig [*Asphaltic*] [*German*]   (GCA)
ASPHER ... Association of Schools of Public Health in the European Region   (EAIO)
ASPIDA .... Axiomatikoi, Sosate Patrida, Idanika Dimokratias kai Axiokratia [*Officers, Save Fatherland, Ideals of Democracy, and Meritocracy*] [*Greek*]   (GC)
ASPIN ...... Asociacion Peruana de Ingenieria Naval [*Peru*]   (LAA)
aspir .... Aspirant   (RU)
ASPL .... Arastirma ve Siyaset Planlama Dairesi Genl Mudurlugu [*Research and Political Planning Office Directorate General*] [*of Foreign Affairs Ministry*]   (TU)
ASPLM ..... Association des Sommeliers de Provence et du Littoral Mediterraneen [*France*]   (EAIO)
ASPM....... Association of Surgeons and Physicians of Malta   (SLS)
A spol .... A Spolecnost [*and Company*] [*Czech*]   (BARN)
asport .... Asportazione [*Removal*] [*Publishing*] [*Italian*]
asportaz...... Asportazione [*Removal*] [*Publishing*] [*Italian*]
ASPP .... Aeronautical Fixed Systems Planning for Data Interchange Panel [*ICAO*]   (DA)

ASPP .... Australian Society of Plant Physiologists   (SLS)
ASPPC....... Accepte sous Protet pour Compte [*Accepted under Protest for Account*] [*French*] [*Business term*]
ASPQ........ Association Suisse pour la Promotion de la Qualite [*Association for Quality Improvement*] [*Sweden*]   (PDAA)
ASPRI .... Asisten Pribadi [*Personal Aide*]   (IN)
ASPROCO ... Asesores, Proyectistas, Constructores [*Colombia*]   (COL)
ASPROMEDICA ... Asociacion de Practica Medica de Grupo [*Colombia*]   (COL)
ASPS .... African Succulent Plant Society
ASPS .... Association Sportive des Professions de Sante [*France*]   (EAIO)
ASPS .... Azerbaydzhan Trade-Union Council   (RU)
AsPSC .... Asian-Pacific Society of Cardiology
AsPSIR ...... Asia-Pacific Society for Impotence Research
AsPSN .... Asian-Pacific Society of Nephrology
AsPSPGN ... Asian-Pacific Society of Paediatric Gastroenterology and Nutrition
ASPSS....... Asian Studies Postgraduate Scholarship Scheme [*Australia*]
ASPTE ...... Anotati Synomospondia Polemiston-Travmation Ellados [*Supreme Confederation of Wounded Combatants of Greece*]   (GC)
aspte.......... Aspirante [*Midshipman*] [*Portuguese*]
ASPTT ...... Association Sportive des Postes, Telegraphe, et Telephone
ASPU........ Asociacion Sindical de Profesores Universitarios [*University Professors Association*]   (COL)
ASPUV...... Asociacion de Profesores de la Universidad del Valle [*Colombia*]   (COL)
ASPWBPSA ... Association of Sometimes Professional Wiffle Ball Players on the Spaceship Aarde (Earth) [*Netherlands*]   (EAIO)
ASPYL ...... Afro-Shirazi Party Youth League [*Tanzania*]
ASQ .... Air Service [*Poland*] [*ICAO designator*]   (FAAC)
ASQ .... Australian String Quartet
ASQ .... Deutsche Arbeitsgemeinschaft fur Statistische Qualitatskontrolle [*German Society for Statistical Quality Control*]   (PDAA)
ASR........... Accion Socialista Revolucionaria [*Peru*] [*Political party*]   (EY)
ASR........... Advanced Systems Research Proprietary Ltd. [*Australia*]
ASR........... Army Medical Company   (RU)
ASR........... Australian Society of Rheology
ASR........... Australian Synthetic Rubber Co. Ltd.
ASR........... Kayseri [*Turkey*] [*Airport symbol*]   (OAG)
asr .... Motor Ambulance Company   (BU)
ASR........... Motorized Medical Company   (RU)
ASRA........ Anti-Shark Research Association [*South Africa*]   (SLS)
ASRA........ Asociacion de Bacteriologos   (COL)
ASRA........ Australasian Sound Recordings Association
ASRA........ Australian Squash Racquets Association
ASRB........ Australian Sales Research Bureau   (ADA)
ASRB........ Australian Society for Reproductive Biology   (ADA)
ASRC........ Australian Standard Research Classification
ASRCT...... Applied Scientific Research Corp. of Thailand
ASREAV ... Australian Society of Real Estate Agents and Valuers
ASRES....... Association Sorgem pour la Recherche Economique et Sociale [*French*]   (EAIO)
ASRET ...... Affiliation of Societies Representing Engineering Technicians [*ICSU*]
ASRF .... Australian Soccer Referees Federation
ASRF .... Sydney [*Australia*] [*ICAO location identifier*]   (ICLI)
ASRFU ...... Australian Schools' Rugby Football Union
ASRG........ Australian Ship Repairers Group
ASRI .... Academy of Sciences Research Institute [*Ghana*]
ASRI .... Akademi Seni Rupa Indonesia
ASRI .... Richmond [*Australia*] [*ICAO location identifier*]   (ICLI)
ASRK........ Air Sea Rescue Kit [*Military*]
ASRL .... Australian Scientific Research Liaison [*British*]
ASRR .... Academy of the Socialist Republic of Romania   (EAIO)
ASRR .... Australian States Regional Relations Committee   (ADA)
ASRR .... Autonomiczna Socjalistyczna Republika Radziecka [*Autonomous Soviet Socialist Republic*] [*Poland*]
ASRRF ...... Australian Special Rural Research Fund
ASRS .... Amalgamated Society of Railway Servants [*New Zealand*]
ASRS .... Australian Sex Role Scale
ASRT........ Academy of Scientific Research and Technology [*Egypt*]   (ASF)
ASRT........ Atlantic Salmon Research Trust   (MSC)
ASRU .... Australian Schools Rugby Union
ASRY .... Arab Shipbuilding and Repair Yard Co. [*Bahrain*]   (MENA)
ASS........... Acoustical Society of Scandinavia [*Formerly, Nordic Acoustics Society*]   (EA)
ASS........... African Supply Service
ASS........... Agregation de l'Enseignement Secondaire Superieur [*French*]
ASS........... Air-Launched Cruise Missile   (RU)
ASS........... Akademicke Spevacke Sdruzenie [*Student Choral Society*]   (CZ)
ASS........... Akateeminen Sosialistiseura [*Academic Socialist Society*] [*Finland*]   (WEN)
ASS........... Analytic Self-Adjusting System   (RU)
ASS........... Anotaton Stratiotikon Symvoulion [*Supreme Military Council*] [*Greek*]   (GC)

ASS............ Anotaton Syndonistikon Symvoulion [*Supreme Coordination Council*] [*Greek*]   (GC)
ASS............ Approved Study Structure
ASS............ Arabskii Sotsialisticheskii Soiuz
ASS............ Asociatia Stiintifica de Studenti [*Scientific Association of Students*]   (RO)
Ass............ Assemblee Generale du Contentieux, Conseil d'Etat [*France*]   (ILCA)
Ass............ Assessor [*Assistant, Assessor*] [*German*]
ass............. Assicelle [*Boards*] [*Publishing*] [*Italian*]
ass............. Assinado [*Signed*] [*Portuguese*]
Ass............ Assistent [*Assistant*] [*German*]
ASS............ Association Sportive de Sale [*Morocco*]
Ass............ Assurance [*Insurance*] [*French*]   (ILCA)
ass............. Assuransie [*Assurance*] [*Afrikaans*]
ASS............ Australian Sahiwal Society
ASS............ Australian Secret Service
ASS............ Australian Seminar Services
ASS............ Australian Synchronised Swimming
ASS............ Avionska Signalna Stanica [*Airplane Signal Station*] [*Military*]   (YU)
ASS............ Emergency Rescue Service [*Military term*]   (RU)
A'SS.......... Proton Soma Stratou [*First Army Corps*] [*Greek*]   (GC)
ASSA....... Academy of the Social Sciences in Australia   (SLS)
ASSA....... Adjontes Sanitaires et Sociales Auxiliaires [*Algeria*]
ASSA....... Aeronautical Society of South Africa   (AA)
ASSA....... Anatomical Society of Southern Africa   (EAIO)
ASSA....... Astronomical Society of South Africa
ASSA....... Australian School Surfing Association
ASSA....... Australian Screen Studies Association
ASSA....... Australian Society of Security Analysts   (ADA)
ASSA....... Australian Society of Sport Administrators
ASSA....... Australian Stevedoring Supervisors' Association
ASSA....... Austrian Solar and Space Agency [*Research center*]   (IRC)
ASSAB..... Australasian Society for the Study of Animal Behaviour
ASSABAF ... Association pour l'Africanisation de la Culture Bananiere et Fruitiere
ASSALZOO ... Associazione Nazionale tra i Produttori di Alimenti Zootecnici [*Italy*]
ASSAM ..... Association des Anciens Militaires et Auxiliaires Militaires [*Association of Veterans and Military Auxiliaries*] [*Cambodia*]   (CL)
ASSANEF ... Association des Anciens Eleves des Ecoles des Freres Chretiennes [*Association of Former Students of Catholic Schools*]
ASSAPA.... Australian Scientific Societies and Professional Associations
ASSB........ Anti-Secret Society Branch   (ML)
ASSBA ...... Association of Stud Sheep Breeders of Australia
ASSBB....... Associazione per lo Sviluppo degli Studi di Banca e Borsa [*Italian*]   (SLS)
ASSBIOTEC ... Associazione Nazionale per lo Sviluppo delle Biotecnologie [*Italy*]
ASSBRA.... Association Belge des Brasseries [*Belgian Association of Breweries*]   (PDAA)
ASSC .... Accounting Standards Steering Committee [*Australia*]
ASSC .... Accounting Standards Sub-Committee [*Australia*]
ASSC .... Australian Schools Sports Council
ASSC .... Australian Sports Science Council
Assce......... Assurance [*Insurance*] [*French*]
ASSCHIMICI ... Associazione Nazionale Industria Chimica [*National Chemical Industry Association*] [*Italy*]   (PDAA)
ASSCI....... Association des Scientifiques de Cote-D'Ivoire
asscn .... Association   (EECI)
ASSCOM.. Association of Chambers of Commerce of South Africa   (IMH)
ASSCT...... Australian Society of Sugar Cane Technologists
ASSD........ Australian Social Security Department [*Central Library*] [*National Union Catalogue of Australia symbol*]
ASSE .... Administracion de los Seguros Sociales por Enfermedad [*Social Security Health Benefits Administration*] [*Uruguay*]   (LA)
ASSE .... Anotati Synomospondia Syndaxioukhon Ellados [*Supreme Confederation of Pensioners of Greece*]   (GC)
ASSE .... Association Suisse des Syndicats Evangeliques [*Swiss Federation of Protestant Trade Unions*]
asse .... Assurance [*Insurance*] [*French*]
ASSE .... Australian Society of Senior Executives   (ADA)
ASSEA ...... Association of Surgeons of South East Asia   (EAIO)
ASSEA ...... Association Senegalaise pour la Sauvegarde de l'Enfance et de l'Adolescence
ASSEBA.... Association des Etudiants Bahutu
ASSECA.... Association for the Educational and Cultural Advancement of Africans [*South Africa*]   (AF)
ASSEDIC.. Association pour l'Emploi dans l'Industrie et le Commerce [*Association for Promotion of Employment in Industry and Business*] [*French*]   (WER)
ASSEDIT .. Association des Etudiants de l'Institut de Technologie Tertiaire

ASSEKAT ... Association des Entreprises du Katanga [*Association of Kotanga Businesses*] [*Zaire*]
As-Sen ...... Kibris Turk Askeri Mustahdemler Sendikasi [*Turkish Cypriot Military Employees' Union*] [*KTAMS*] [*See also*]   (TU)
ASSERT.... Australian Society of Sex Educators, Researchers, and Therapists
ASSET...... Australian Superannuation Savings Employment Trust
ass extr...... Assemblee Extraordinaire [*French*]
ASSF .... Arbetarnas och Smabrukarnas Socialdemokratiska Foerbund [*Social Democratic League of Workers and Smallholders*] [*Finland*] [*Political party*]   (PPE)
AS:SG........ Australian CSIRO [*Commonwealth Scientific and Industrial Research Organisation*] Stored Grain [*Research Laboratory - Division of Entomology*] [*National Union Catalogue of Australia symbol*]
ASSGME .. Anotati Synomospondia Syllogon Goneon Mathiton Ellados [*Supreme Confederation of Associations of Parents of Students of Greece*]   (GC)
ASSH........ Australian Social Sciences and Humanities Information Systems   (ADA)
ASSH........ Australian Society for Sports History
ASSh......... Automatic Glass Ball Machine   (RU)
ASSIAD .... Associazione Italiana Produttori di Additivi per Calcestruzzo e de Malte Speciali [*Italy*]   (EAIO)
ASSIBRA .. Associacao dos Servidores do Instituto Brasileiro de Reforma Agraria [*Brazil*]   (DSCA)
ASS ICA.... Associazione degli Industriali delle Carni [*Italy*]
ASSID .... Australian Society for the Study of Intellectual Disability   (EAIO)
ASSIDER ... Associazione Industrie Siderurgiche Italiane [*Iron and Steel Industries Association*] [*Italy*]   (EY)
ASSIFACT ... Associazione fra le Societa di Factoring Italiane
ASSIFONTE ... Association de l'Indsutrie de la Fonte de Fromage [*Association of the Processed Cheese Industry*]   (PDAA)
ASSIG ...... Assignation   (DSUE)
ASSIG ...... Australian Serials Special Interest Group [*Library Association of Australia*]
ASSILEA .. Associazione Italiana Leasing
ASSILEC .. Association de l'Industrie Laitiere de la CE [*European Community Dairy Trade Association*] [*Belgium*]   (EAIO)
Assimilat.... Assimilation [*German*]   (GCA)
ASSIMPREDIL ... Associazione Imprese Edili e Complementari della Provincia di Milano [*Italy*]
assin .... Assinatura [*Signature, Subscription*] [*Publishing*] [*Portuguese*]
assinat....... Assinatura [*Signature, Subscription*] [*Publishing*] [*Portuguese*]
Ass Ind...... Assam, India   (ILCA)
ASSINEZ ... Association pour l'Industrialisation du Nord-Est du Zaire [*Association for the Industrialization of Northeastern Zaire*]   (AF)
ASSINSEL ... Association Internationale des Selectionneurs pour la Protection des Obtentions Vegetales [*International Association of Plant Breeders for the Protection of Plant Varieties - IAPBPPV*]   (EAIO)
Ass Int........ Association Internationales [*International Associations*] [*French*]   (BAS)
ASSIPORT ... Association des Interets Portuaires
assist .... Assistant   (RU)
Assist .... Assistent [*Assistant*] [*German*]
ASSITALIA ... Assicurazioni d'Italia [*Le*] [*Insurance*]   (EY)
ASSITEJ... Association Internationale du Theatre pour l'Enfance et de la Jeunesse [*International Association of Theatre for Children and Youth*]   (EAIO)
ASSITOL.. Associazione Italiane dell'Industria Olearia [*Italy*]
ASSIUC..... Australian South Sea Islander United Council   (ADA)
ASSLA..... Anambra State School Libraries Association [*Nigeria*]   (EAIO)
ASSLH...... Australian Society for the Study of Labour History   (ADA)
ASSM....... Antisurface Ship Missile [*NATO*]   (MCD)
AssNAS..... Associazione Nazionale Assistenti Sociali [*Italian*]   (SLS)
ASSNAT ... All-Union Association of Naturalists   (RU)
Ass Nat ..... Assemblee Nationale [*France*]   (FLAF)
ASSO .... Association of Swedish Symphony Orchestras   (EAIO)
ASSO......... Association "Sedifor" for the Study of Orgonomy [*France*]   (EAIO)
ASSOBANCA ... Associazione Bancaria Italiana [*Italian Bankers' Association*]   (WER)
ASSOBASE ... Associazione di Industrie del Settore della Chimica di Base Inorganica e Organica [*Italy*]
ASSOBELA ... Association des Batetela de Lodja [*Association of Batetelas of Lodja*]
assoc.......... Associate   (EECI)
Assoc......... Association   (PWGL)
ASSOCARTA ... Associazione Italiana fra gli Industriali della Carta, Cartoni e Paste per Carta
ASSOCASA ... Associazione Nazionale Prodotti per la Casa [*Italy*]
AssocDipAbComMgt & Dev ... Associate Diploma in Aboriginal Community Management and Development
AssocDipAbHlth ... Associate Diploma in Aboriginal Health
AssocDipAcctg ... Associate Diploma in Accounting
AssocDipAdvrt ... Associate Diploma in Advertising

AssocDipAgProd ... Associate Diploma in Agricultural Production
AssocDipAgr ... Associate Diploma in Agriculture
AssocDipAgServs ... Associate Diploma in Agricultural Services
AssocDipAppSci(Ag) ... Associate Diploma in Applied Science (Agriculture)
AssocDipAppSci(AnimalSc) ... Associate Diploma in Applied Science (Animal Science)
AssocDipAppSci(AnimalTech) ... Associate Diploma in Applied Science (Animal Technology)
AssocDipAppSci(GrainMgmt) ... Associate Diploma in Applied Science (Grain Management)
AssocDipArchDraft ... Associate Diploma in Architectural Drafting
AssocDipArchTech ... Associate Diploma in Architectural Technology
AssocDipArts(AppPhotog) ... Associate Diploma in Arts (Applied Photography)
AssocDipArts(ComArt) ... Associate Diploma in Arts (Commercial Art)
AssocDipAsianSt ... Associate Diploma in Asian Studies
AssocDipBiolSc(AnimalTech) ... Associate Diploma in Biological Science (Animal Technology)
AssocDipBuildCons ... Associate Diploma in Building Construction
AssocDipBus ... Associate Diploma in Business
AssocDipEd ... Associate Diploma in Education
AssocDipFor ... Associate Diploma in Forestry
AssocDipFurnTechnology ... Associate Diploma in Furniture Technology
AssocDipHorseMgmt ... Associate Diploma in Horse Management
AssocDipHort ... Associate Diploma in Horticulture
AssocDipHumanSt ... Associate Diploma in Human Studies
AssocDipIntTrade ... Associate Diploma in International Trade
AssocDipLegPrac ... Associate Diploma in Legal Practice
AssocDipMedLabTech ... Associate Diploma in Medical Laboratory Technology
AssocDipMktg ... Associate Diploma in Marketing
AssocDipMktgJap ... Associate Diploma in Marketing and Japanese
AssocDipMMT ... Associate Diploma of Mining and Mineral Technology
AssocDipModLang ... Associate Diploma of Modern Languages
AssocDipMus ... Associate Diploma in Music
AssocDipOccHlth&Saft ... Associate Diploma in Occupational Health and Safety
AssocDipOffAdmin ... Associate Diploma in Office Administration
AssocDipPolSt ... Associate Diploma in Political Studies
AssocDipSc ... Associate Diploma in Science
AssocDipSc(AnimalScience) ... Associate Diploma in Science (Animal Science)
AssocDipSc(SystemsAg) ... Associate Diploma in Science (Systems Agriculture)
AssocDipSocSc ... Associate Diploma of Social Science
AssocDipSurv ... Associate Diploma of Surveying
AssocDipSurvMap ... Associate Diploma in Surveying and Mapping
AssocDipTrainDev ... Associate Diploma in Training and Development
ASSOCHAM ... Associated Chambers of Commerce and Industry [*India*] (PDAA)
AssocICSETT ... Associate Member of the Institute of Civil Service Engineering Technicians and Technologists [*South Africa*] (AA)
AssocInter ... Associations Internationales [*International Associations*] [*French*] (BAS)
AssocLUA ... Associate of the Life Underwriters Association of Australia
ASSOCOM ... Association of Chambers of Commerce of South Africa
ASSOCOMAPLAST ... Associazione Nazionale Costruttori di Macchine per Materie Plastiche e Gomma [*Association of makers of plastic and rubber manufacturing machinery*] [*Italy*] (EY)
ASSOCONCIMI ... Associazione Nazionale Produttori Concimi [*Italy*]
AssocSAIEE ... Associate Member of the South African Institute of Electrical Engineers (AA)
AssocSAIETE ... Associate Member of the South African Institute of Electrical Technician Engineers (AA)
ASSODEL ... Associazione Nazionale Distribuzione Elettronica [*Italy*]
ASSOFECAM ... Association pour l'Emancipation de la Femme Camerounaise [*Association for the Emancipation of Cameroonian Women*]
ASSOFELT ... Associazione Italiana Fabbricanti di Feltri per Cartiere e Cemento Amianto
ASSOFERLEGHE ... Associazione Produttori Italiani di Ferroleghe ed Affini [*Ferro-alloy producers association*] [*Italy*] (EY)
ASSOFERMET ... Associazione Nazionale Commercianti in Ferro e Acciai, Metalli Non-Ferrosi, Rottami Ferrosi, Ferramenta e Affini [*Italy*] (EAIO)
ASSOFIBRE ... Associazione Italiana Produttori Fibre Chimiche
ASSOFOND ... Associazione Nazionale delle Fonderie [*Foundries association*] [*Italy*] (EY)
ASSOFOTO ... Associazione Italiana Fabbricanti Articoli Foto-Cine
ASSOGASTECNICI ... Associazione Nazionale delle Industrie dei Gas Tecnici e Medicali [*Italy*]
ASSOGOMMA ... Associazione Nazionale fra le Industrie della Gomma [*National Association of the Rubber Industry*] [*Italy*] (PDAA)
ASSOGOMMA ... Associazione Nazionale fra le Industrie della Gomma, Cavi Elettrici e Affini [*Italy*]

ASSOGRAFICI ... Associazione Nazionale Italiana Industrie Grafiche, Cartotecniche, e Trasformatrici
ASSOGRASSI ... Associazione Nazionale Produttori Grassi e Proteine Animali [*Italy*]
ASSOLATTE ... Associazione Italiana Lattiero Casearia [*Italian Milk and Dairy Industries Association*] (EAIO)
ASSOLOMBARDA ... Associazione Industriale Lombarda [*Lombardy Manufacturers' Association*] [*Italian*] (WER)
ASSOMAC ... Associazione Nazionale Costruttori Italiani Macchine e Accessori per Calzature, Calzaturifici, e Pelletteria
ASSOMARMI ... Associazione dell'Industria Marmifera Italiana e delle Industrie Affini
ASSOMEP ... Associazione Nazionale Industria dell'Ottica, Meccanica Fine, e di Precisione [*Optical and Precision Instrument Manufacturers Association*] [*Italy*] (EY)
ASSOMET ... Associazione Nazionale Industrie Metalli Non-Ferrosi [*Non-Ferrous Metal Industries Association*] [*Italy*] (EY)
ASSOMINERARIA ... Associazione Mineraria Italiana
ASSOMIZO ... Association Mutuelle des Ressortissants de Zombo
ASSOMODA ... Associazione Lombarda Rappresentanti Moda [*Italy*]
ASSOMUBA ... Association de Secours Mutuel de la Jeunesse Bantanu
ASSONIME ... Associazione fra le Societa Italiane per Azioni [*Italy*] (EY)
ASSOPIASTRELLE ... Associazione Nazionale dei Produttori di Piastrelle di Ceramica e di Materiali Refrattari [*Italy*] (EAIO)
ASSOPLAST ... Associazione di Industrie del Settore delle Materie Plastiche e Resine Sintetiche [*Italy*]
ASSORECO ... Association des Ressortissants du Haut-Congo
ASSORENI ... Associazione per la Ricerca Scientifica fra Societa del Gruppo ENI
ASSOSIRACI ... Association des Sinistres et Repatries de Cote-D'Ivoire [*Association of the Wounded and Repatriates of the Ivory Coast*]
ASSOSPORT ... Associazione Nazionale Produttori Articoli Sportivi [*Italy*]
assots .... Association (RU)
ASSOURMUVOIX ... Association pour le Sourds-Muets et Mutiles de la Voix
ASSOVETRO ... Associazione Nazionale degli Industriali del Vetro [*Italy*]
ASSOZUCCHERO ... Associazione Nazionale fra gli Industriali dello Zucchero dell'Alcool e del Lievito [*Italy*]
ASSP .... Academia de Stiinte Sociale si Politice [*Academy of Social and Political Sciences*] (RO)
ASSP .... Actes Sous-Seing Prive [*French*] (FLAF)
ASSP .... African Social and Environmental Studies Programme [*Formerly, African Social Studies Programme*] [*Kenya*] (EAIO)
ASSP .... African Social Studies Programme (EA)
ASSP .... Agronomic Scientific Society of Portugal (EAIO)
ASSP .... Australian Studies in Student Performance
ASSP .... Australian Studies Schools Project
ASSPA ...... Aboriginal Sacred Sites Protection Authority [*Northern Territory, Australia*]
ASSPA ...... Australian Symposium on Signal Processing and Applications
ASSPHR ... Anti-Slavery Society for the Protection of Human Rights (EA)
Ass PlenCiv ... Assemblee Pleniere Civile de la Cour de Cassation [*France*] (FLAF)
ASSR ...... Adzhar Autonomous Soviet Socialist Republic (RU)
ASSR ...... Autonomna Sovjetska Socijalisticka Republika [*Autonomous Soviet Socialist Republic*] (YU)
ASSR .... Autonomni Sovetska Socialisticka Republika [*Autonomous Soviet Socialist Republic*] (CZ)
ASSR .... Autonomous Soviet Socialist Republic (EECI)
ASSR .... Azerbaydzhan Soviet Socialist Republic (RU)
ASSR .... Sydney [*Australia*] [*ICAO location identifier*] (ICLI)
ASSRNP .... German Volga Autonomous Soviet Socialist Republic (RU)
ASSS .... Association for Swedish Specialized Press (EAIO)
ASSS .... Australian Society of Soil Science, Inc. (ADA)
ASSS .... Sydney [*Australia*] [*ICAO location identifier*] (ICLI)
ASSSI .... Australian Society of Soil Science, Incorporated (SLS)
Asst .... Assistant (PWGL)
asst .... Assistent [*Assistant*] [*Afrikaans*]
ASST .... Azienda di Stato per i Servizi Telefonici [*National Telephones State Board*] [*Italy*] (WER)
asste .... Assistente [*Assistant*] [*Afrikaans*]
AS STER ... Associazione Italiana per la Sterilizzazione Volontaria [*Italian Association for Voluntary Sterilization*] (SLS)
ASSU .... Association Sportive Scolaire et Universitaire [*Algeria*]
ASSUC ...... Association des Organisations Professionnelles du Commerce des Sucres pour les Pays de la Communaute Economique Europeenne [*Association of Sugar Trade Organizations for the European Economic Community Countries*] [*Belgium*]
ASSURBANISTI ... Associazione Nazionale degli Urbanisti [*Italian*] (SLS)
ASSURLUX ... Assurances Reunies du Luxembourg [*Les*] [*Insurance agency Luxembourg*] (EY)
ASSVAN ... Association pour la Sante sans Vaccination [*Association for Health without Vaccination*] [*France*] (EAIO)
ASSX .... Sydney [*Australia*] [*ICAO location identifier*] (ICLI)
ASSY .... Sydney/Kingsford Smith International [*Australia*] [*ICAO location identifier*] (ICLI)

AST............ Accion Sindical de Trabajadores [*Workers' Trade Union Action*] [*Spanish*]   (WER)

AST............ Action Sociale Tchadienne

AST............ Advanced Skills Teacher [*Australia*]

AST............ Aerogeophysical Station   (RU)

AST............ Aerolineas del Oeste SA de CV [*Mexico*] [*ICAO designator*] (FAAC)

a St............. Alten Stils [*Old Style*] [*German*]

AST............ Ankara Sanat Tiyatrosu [*Ankara Theatre of Art*]   (TU)

AST............ Archery Society of Tasmania [*Australia*]

AST............ Armadni Soutez Tvorivosti [*Armed Forces Creative Activities Contest*]   (CZ)

AST............ Artillery Stereoscopic Telescope   (RU)

AST............ Asociatia Stiintifica de Tehnicieni [*Scientific Association of Technicians*]   (RO)

AS-T .... Aspartic-Glutamic Transaminase   (RU)

AST............ Associates of Science and Technology   (EAIO)

Ast............. Astronomi [*Astronomy*]   (TU)

ast.............. Astuccio [*Box, Slipcase*] [*Publishing*] [*Italian*]

AST............ Aufgabenstellung (Bau) [*Project Specifications (Construction)*] (EG)

AST............ Australian Synthesis Telescope

AST............ Aviation Standard   (RU)

AST............ Self-Hardening Acrylate   (RU)

AST............ Tank-Accompanying Artillery   (RU)

ASTA........ Aerospace Technologies of Australia Proprietary Ltd.

AStA .... Allgemeiner Studentenausschuss [*General Student Committee (of a university)*]   (WEN)

ASTA........ Astatic Ammeter   (RU)

ASTA........ Australian Science Teachers Association   (ADA)

ASTA........ Australian Sogetsu Teachers' Association

ASTA........ Australian Sports Trainers Association

ASTA........ Australian String Teachers' Association

ASTALCO ... Asociacion Colombiana de Criadores de Reses de Lidia   (COL)

ASTANO... Astilleros y Talleres del Noroeste [*Spain*]   (PDAA)

ASTARSA ... Astilleros Argentinos Rio De La Plata, Sociedad Anonima [*Argentine River Plate Shipyards, Incorporated*]   (LA)

ASTARTE ... Avion-Station-Relais de Transmission Exceptionnelle [*Exceptional Air-Station-Relay Transmission*] [*Aircraft*] [*French*]

ASTAS ...... Azot Sanayii Turk Anonim Sirketi [*Turkish Nitrogen Industry Corporation*]   (TU)

ASTC........ Administrative Section for Technical Cooperation [*United Nations*]

ASTC........ Asociacion Sandinista de Trabajadores de la Cultura [*Sandinist Association of Cultural Workers*] [*Nicaragua*]   (LA)

ASTC........ Associate of the Sydney Technical College [*Australia*]   (ADA)

ASTC........ Australian Silky Terrier Club

ASTCON... Australian Science and Technology Counsellor Network

ASTDB...... Australian Scientific and Technological Database

ASTE........ African Selection Trust Exploration Ltd.

ASTE........ Association pour le developpement des Sciences et Techniques de l'Environment [*Association for the Development of Environmental Sciences and Techniques*] [*France*]   (PDAA)

ASTEC ...... Australian Science and Technology Council

ASTECA ... Associacao dos Agronomos Veterinarios e Tecnicos Rurais de Camaqua [*Brazil*]   (DSCA)

ASTECO ... Asociacion Tecnico Comercial [*Colombia*]   (COL)

ASTEF...... Association pour l'Organisation des Stages de Techniciens Etrangers dans l'Industrie Francaise

ASTELBO ... Asociacion de Tecnicos Electricitas de Bogota   (COL)

ASTEM ..... Association Scientifique et Technique pour l'Exploitation de la Mediterranee [*Scientific and Technical Association for the Exploitation of the Mediterranean*] [*French*]   (ASF)

ASTENG... Asia Tenggara [*Southeast Asia*]   (IN)

ASTEO...... Association Scientifique et Technique pour l'Exploitation des Oceans [*Scientific and Technical Association for the Exploitation of the Oceans*] [*French*]   (ASF)

Aster-Is...... Askeri Tersane ve Askeri Isyerleri Sendikasi [*Military Shipyard and Military Installation Workers' Union*]   (TU)

A St G .... Adalbert Stifter-Gesellschaft [*Adalbert Stifter Society*] [*Austria*] (SLS)

ASTI......... Arbetsstudietekniska Institutet [*Sweden*]

ASTI......... Armement Sardinier Thonier Ivoirien

ASTI......... Association Suisse des Traducteurs et Interpretes [*Swiss Association of Translators and Interpreters*]

ASTIN...... Actuarial Studies in Non-Life Insurance [*of the International Actuarial Association*] [*Brussels, Belgium*]   (EA)

ASTINAVE ... Astilleros Venezolanos, SA [*Venezuelan Shipyards, Inc.*]   (LA)

ASTINFO ... Asian Scientific and Technological Information Network (EAIO)

ASTIS........ Australian Science and Technology Information Service

ASTISA..... Asesoramiento y Servicios Tecnicos Industriales Sociedad Anonima [*Mexico*]   (EY)

ASTM........ Australian Scientific and Technical Mission

ASTMA..... Astatic Milliammeter   (RU)

ASTNO ..... Astilleros Telleres del Noroeste [*Spain*]   (PDAA)

ASTOA...... Australian Shipping and Travel Officers Association

ASTOK...... Astika Oikistika Kendra [*Urban Housing (Development) Centers*] (GC)

ASTOUKIN ... Association Kinoise de Tourisme

ASTOVOCT ... Association Togolaise des Volontaires Chretiens au Travail

ASTOVOT ... Association Togolaise de Volontaires du Travail [*Togolese Association of Labor Volunteers*]   (AF)

ASTP .... Advanced Systems and Technology Programme [*European Space Agency*]

ASTP .... Australian System of Tariff Preferences for Developing Countries

A/STP .... Alor Star [*Malaysia*] [*ML*]

AStR .... Arbeitseinkommen-Steuerrichtlinien [*Income Tax Guidelines*] [*German*]   (EG)

Astr .... Astronomia [*Astronomy*] [*Portuguese*]

astr .... Astronomical Point [*Topography*]   (RU)

Astr .... Astronomico [*Astronomical*] [*Portuguese*]

Astr .... Astronomie [*Astronomy*] [*German*]   (GCA)

astr .... Astronomie [*Astronomy*] [*Afrikaans*]

astr .... Astronomo [*Astronomer*] [*Portuguese*]

astr .... Astronomy, Astronomical   (RU)

ASTR........ Australian Scientific and Technological Reports [*AUSINET database*]   (ADA)

ASTRA ...... Aktion Strafvollzug [*Prisoners' Union*] [*Switzerland*]   (WEN)

ASTRA ...... Application of Science and Technology to Rural Areas [*India*]

ASTRA ...... Applications of Space Technology Panel to Requirements of Civil Aviation [*ICAO*]   (DA)

ASTRA ...... Asociatia Transilvana pentru Literatura si Cultura Poporului Roman [*Transylvanian Association for the Literature and Culture of the Romanian People*]   (RO)

ASTRA ...... Association in Scotland to Research into Astronautics   (SLS)

ASTRA ...... Australian Space Technology and Research Authority

ASTRACO ... Associated Transtech Contracting [*Jordanian-Syrian joint construction venture*]

ASTRAD ... Advisory Services in Technology Research and Development [*University of Sierra Leone*]

ASTRO...... Anstalt fuer Stroemungsmaschinen GmbH [*State Research Institute for Hydraulic Machinery*] [*Research center*] [*Austria*]   (IRC)

ASTRO...... Association Internationale des Enterprises Publiques dans les Pays en Voie de Developpment [*International Association of State Trading Organizations of Developing Countries*] [*Samoa*]   (EAIO)

ASTRO...... International Association of State Trading Organizations of Developing Countries [*Ljubljana, Yugoslavia*]   (EAIO)

Astrol .... Astrologia [*Astrology*] [*Portuguese*]

astrol .... Astrologie [*French*]   (TPFD)

astrol .... Astrology   (TPFD)

astrom .... Astronomie [*French*]   (TPFD)

astron .... Astronomy   (TPFD)

Astrosovet ... Astronomical Council (of the Academy of Sciences, USSR) (RU)

ASTRU ..... Associazione Italiana Strumenti e Attrezzature Scientifico-Medicali

Astrybvtuz ... Astrakhan' Technical Institute of the Fish Industry and Fisheries (RU)

ASTS .... Associated Scientific and Technical Societies of South Africa

ASTS .... Association Suisse pour la Technique de Soudage [*Swiss Association for the Technique of Welding*]   (PDAA)

ASTs.......... Automatic Target Tracking   (RU)

ASTT .... Agricultural Society of Trinidad and Tobago [*Trinidad and Tobago*]   (DSCA)

ASTU........ Advanced Studies for Teachers Unit [*New Zealand*]

ASTU........ Anti-Stock Theft Unit [*Kenya*]   (AF)

ASTV .... Astatic Voltmeter   (RU)

AStVO ...... Allgemeine Steuerverordnung [*General Tax Decree*]   (EG)

ASTW....... Australian Society of Travel Writers

ASTW....... Tamworth [*Australia*] [*ICAO location identifier*]   (ICLI)

ASU .... Accion Sindical Uruguaya [*Uruguayan Trade Union Action*] (LA)

ASU .... Agrupacion Socialista Universitaria [*Socialist University Group*] [*Spanish*]   (WER)

ASU .... Airborne Self-Propelled Gun

asu.............. Allt som Utkommit [*All Published*] [*Sweden*]

ASU .... Amalgamated Shearers Union [*Australia*]   (ADA)

ASU .... Amateur Swimming Union of Australia   (ADA)

ASU .... Ankara Sular Idaresi Genel Mudurlugu [*Ankara Hydraulics Administration Directorate General*]   (TU)

ASU .... Arab Socialist Union [*Libya*] [*Political party*]   (ME)

ASU .... Arab Socialist Union [*Syria*] [*Political party*]   (PPW)

ASU .... Architectural Science Unit [*University of Queensland*] [*Australia*] (WED)

ASU .... Asuncion [*Paraguay*] [*Airport symbol*]   (OAG)

ASU .... Atomic Power Plant   (RU)

ASU .... Australian Swimming Union   (ADA)

ASU .... Automated Control Systems   (BU)

ASU .... Automatic Angle Tracking   (RU)

ASU .... Automatic Control System   (RU)

ASU .... Automatic Self-Service Information Unit   (RU)
ASU .... Compania Aerea del Sur SA [*Uruguay*] [*ICAO designator*]
    (FAAC)
ASU .... Emergency Rescue Service at Sea   (RU)
ASU .... General-Purpose Automatic Synchronizer   (RU)
Asuag .... Allgemeine Schweizerische Uhrenindustrie [*Swiss watch
    manufacturer*]
ASUAP...... Asociacion Uruguaya de Administracion Publica [*Uruguay*]
    (LAA)
ASUB........ Asociacion de Universitarios de Bucaramanga   (COL)
ASUCC...... Arab Socialist Union Central Committee
ASUE........ Arbeitsgemeinschaft fuer Sparsamen und Umweltfreundlichen
    Energieverbrauch eV [*Association for Economical and
    Ecological Use of Energy*]   (SLS)
ASUG .... Ausruestungen-Schwerindustrie und Getriebebau [*Equipment for
    Heavy Industry and Transmission Production*]   (EG)
ASUNORTE ... Asociacion de Universitarios del Norte de Santander [*Cucuta*]
    (COL)
ASUPA...... Aluminium Sulphate Producers Association [*Belgium*]   (EAIO)
ASUR .... Association Sportive Universitaire de Rabat [*Morocco*]
ASUS .... Associazione Studentesca Universitaria della Somalia [*University
    Students' Association of Somalia*]
ASUSA ...... African Students Union of South Africa   (AF)
ASUU .... Academic Staff Union of Universities [*Nigeria*]
ASUV .... Automatic Troop Control System   (RU)
ASUVA...... Asociacion de Universitarios del Valle [*Colombia*]   (COL)
ASUVD ..... Automated Foreign Trade Activities Management System   (BU)
ASV .... Agrupacion Socialista Valencia [*Socialist Group of Valencia*]
    [*Spanish*]   (WER)
ASV .... Air Savoie [*France*] [*ICAO designator*]   (FAAC)
ASV .... Arabe Standard Voyelle
ASV .... Ardal og Sundal Verk [*Norway*]   (PDAA)
ASV .... Armadni Sokolsky Vybor [*Armed Forces Sokol Committee*]
    (CZ)
ASV .... Association des Scolaires Voltaiques de Dakar
ASV .... Atterrissage sans Visibilite [*Blind Landing*] [*Aviation*] [*French*]
ASV .... Automatische Sprecher-Verifikation [*Automatic Speech
    Verification*] [*German*]   (ADPT)
ASV .... Motorized Medical Platoon   (RU)
ASVAHL... Association pour la Valorisation des Huiles Lourdes
asvb .... Army Liaison Battalion   (BU)
ASVE......... Amt zum Schutze des Volkseigentums [*Office for the Protection of
    Public Property*]   (EG)
ASVE......... Anotati Synomospondia Viotekhnon Ellados [*Supreme
    Confederation of Craftsmen of Greece*]   (GC)
ASVG........ Allgemeines Sozialversicherungsgesetz [*General Social Security
    Laws*] [*German*]
ASVILMET ... Associazione Italiana per lo Sviluppo degli Studi Sperimentali
    sulla Lavorazione dei Metalli [*Italian Association for the
    Promotion of Metalworking Research*]   (PDAA)
ASvNS .... Akciova Spolecnost v Narodni Sprave [*Corporation under
    National Administration*]   (CZ)
ASVO .... Australian Society of Viticulture and Oenology
ASVSA ...... Aansteeklike Siektesvereniging van Suider Afrika [*Infectious
    Diseases Society of Southern Africa*]   (EAIO)
ASW .... Absatzwirtschaft Data Bank [*Dusseldorf, Federal Republic of
    Germany*] [*Database producer*] [*Information service or
    system*]   (IID)
ASW .... Akademicka Spoldzielnia Wydawnicza [*Student Publishing
    Cooperative*]   (POL)
ASW .... Anwendersoftware [*Processing Software or Application Software*]
    [*German*]   (ADPT)
ASW .... Association of Salvadoran Women [*Costa Rica*]   (EAIO)
ASW .... Aswan [*Egypt*] [*Airport symbol*]   (OAG)
ASWA .... Anthropological Society of Western Australia   (SLS)
ASWA ...... Australian Sports Writers Association   (ADA)
ASWAPA .. Association of Swedish Wholesalers of Automotive Parts and
    Accessories   (EAIO)
ASWAS..... Antisubmarine Warfare Area System [*Italy*]
ASWC....... Antisubmarine Warfare Center [*NATO*]   (NATG)
ASWEA..... Association for Social Work Education in Africa [*See also AESA*]
    (EAIO)
ASWEC..... Australian Software Engineering Conference
ASWG .... Wagga Wagga [*Australia*] [*ICAO location identifier*]   (ICLI)
ASWGA..... Australian Superfine Wool Growers' Association
ASWI........ Antisubmarine Warfare Installations [*NATO*]   (NATG)
ASWM ...... Williamtown [*Australia*] [*ICAO location identifier*]   (ICLI)
AS:WR....... Australian CSIRO [*Commonwealth Scieitific and Industrial
    Research Organisation*] Wildlife e Resources [*and Ecology
    Division*] [*National Union Catalogue of Australia symbol*]
ASWRC..... Antisubmarine Warfare Research Center [*NATO*]   (NATG)
ASWRECEN ... Antisubmarine Warfare Research Center [*NATO*]
ASWU .... Australian Social Welfare Union   (ADA)
ASWU .... Australian Sugar Workers Union   (ADA)
ASX........... Air Special [*Czechoslovakia*] [*ICAO designator*]   (FAAC)
ASX........... Australian Stock Exchange
ASY........... Royal Australian Air Force [*ICAO designator*]   (FAAC)

AS-YA-IS .. Ankara Askeri Yardim Isyerleri Iscileri Sendikasi [*Ankara
    Military Aid Employment Locations Workers Union*]
    (TU)
ASYD........ Ankara Spor Yazarlari Dernegi [*Ankara Sports Writers'
    Association*]   (TU)
ASYE........ Anotati Stratiotiki Ygeionomiki Epitropi [*Supreme Army
    Medical Board*] [*Greek*]   (GC)
ASYGT...... Askeri Yargitay [*Military Court of Cassation*]   (TU)
ASYL........ Afro-Shirazi Youth League [*Tanzania*]   (AF)
asym.......... Asymmetrisch [*Asymmetric*] [*German*]
asymm....... Asymmetrisch [*Asymmetric*] [*German*]
ASYNBA... Association des Syndicats du Benin [*Employers' organization*]
    [*Benin*]   (EY)
asyst .... Asystent [*Assistant*] [*Poland*]
ASZ........... Air Sardinia SpA [*Italy*] [*ICAO designator*]   (FAAC)
ASZ........... Armadni Strelecke Zavody [*Armed Forces Marksmanship
    Matches*]   (CZ)
ASZERF.... Altalanos Szerelsi Feltetelek (Kolcsonos Gazdasagi Segitseg
    Tanacsa) [*General Conditions for Assembly (Council for
    Mutual Economic Assistance)*]   (HU)
ASZF .... Aruszallitasok Altalanos Feltetelei (Kolcsonos Gazdasagi Segitseg
    Tanacsa) [*General Terms for Freight Shipments (Council for
    Mutual Economic Assistance)*]   (HU)
ASZFALTUTEP V ... Aszfaltutepito Vallalat [*Asphalt Road Building
    Enterprise*]   (HU)
ASZSZ....... Allamigazgatasi Szamitogepes Szolgalat [*State Administration
    Computer Service*]   (HU)
ASZSZK... Autonom Szovjet Szocialista Koztarsasag [*Autonomous Soviet
    Socialist Republic (ASSR)*]   (HU)
ASZTE ...... Ahmed Seleh Al Zahrani Trading Establishment [*Saudi Arabia*]
    [*Commercial firm*]
AT.............. Accidents du Travail [*French*]   (FLAF)
AT.............. Administration Territoriale
AT.............. Admission Temporaire [*French*]
AT.............. Aerial Torpedo   (RU)
AT.............. Aerial Tours [*Australia*]
AT.............. Aerological Theodolite   (RU)
AT.............. Airport Traffic [*ICAO*] [*Information service or system United
    Nations*]   (DUND)
AT.............. Akku Triebwagen [*Battery-Operated Rail Motor Car*]   (EG)
at .... Allami Tulajdon [*State Property, State-Owned*]   (HU)
AT.............. Alta Tensao [*High Tension*] [*Portuguese*]
AT.............. Altes Testament [*Old Testament*] [*German*]
AT.............. Alt Tuberculin [*Old Tuberculin*] [*German*]
AT.............. Amatol with Trotyl Plug   (RU)
at .... Ampere-Tours [*Ampere-Turns*] [*French*]
AT.............. Amplitude-Modulated Radiotelegraphy   (RU)
AT.............. Amtstag [*Court Day*] [*German*]
AT.............. Ancien Testament [*Old Testament*] [*French*]
At .... Antibody   (RU)
AT.............. Antico Testamento [*Old Testament*] [*Italian*]
AT.............. Angkatan Tugas [*Task Force*]   (IN)
At .... Antibody   (RU)
AT.............. Arama Transport Ltd. [*Papua New Guinea*]
AT.............. Arkhigeion Tethorakismenon [*Armored Command*] [*Greek*]
    (GC)
AT.............. Army Rear Area   (RU)
AT.............. Army Telegraph   (RU)
At .... Arret [*Halt*] [*Military map abbreviation World War I*] [*French*]
    (MTD)
AT.............. Artillerie de Tranchee [*Military*] [*French*]   (MTD)
AT.............. Artillerie Territoriale [*Military*] [*French*]   (MTD)
AT.............. Asia Tenggara [*Southeast Asia*]   (ML)
AT.............. Assemblees des Travailleurs [*Workers Assemblies*] [*Algeria*]
    (AF)
At .... Astatinio [*Astatine*] [*Chemical element*] [*Portuguese*]
At .... Astaton [*Astatine*] [*Chemical element*] [*German*]
AT.............. Asti [*Car registration plates*] [*Italian*]
AT.............. Asynchronous Generator Tachometer   (RU)
AT.............. Asynchronous Transformer   (RU)
At .... Atasoz [*Proverb*]   (TU)
AT.............. Ataxia Telangiectasia   (PDAA)
At .... Atmosphaere [*Atmosphere*] [*German*]
at .... Atoll [*Topography*]   (RU)
At .... Atom [*Atom*] [*German*]
at .... Atomfizika [*Nuclear Physics*]   (HU)
at .... Atomic   (RU)
At .... Atomo [*Atom*] [*Portuguese*]
At .... Atom Prozent [*Atomic Percent*] [*German*]
at .... Atono [*Unaccented*] [*Portuguese*]
at .... Attache [*French*]
AT.............. Australian Tourism [*Department*] [*National Union Catalogue of
    Australia symbol*]
AT.............. Austria [*ANSI two-letter standard code*]   (CNC)
AT.............. Automatic Titrimeter   (RU)
AT.............. Automatic Transformer Switch   (RU)
AT.............. Autoridad de Tierras [*Puerto Rico*]   (DSCA)

AT .... Autorisation de Transferts [French]
AT .... Autotransformer (RU)
AT .... Aydin Tekstil [Aydin Textile Corp.] (TU)
AT .... Height Pattern, Isobaric Topography (RU)
AT .... Industrija Alata, Trebinje [Tool Industry, Trebinje] (YU)
AT .... Motor Vehicle and Tractor Depot (RU)
AT .... Subscriber's Telegraph (RU)
at .... Technical Atmosphere (RU)
ATA .... Aboriginal Teaching Assistant [Australia]
ata .... Absolute Atmosphere (RU)
ATA .... Administrateur Territorial Assistant [Assistant Territorital Adminstrator] [Zaire]
ATA .... Admission Temporaire/Temporary Admission [Customs] (IMH)
ATA .... African Travel Association
ATA .... Agence Touristique Algerienne [Algerian Tourist Agency] (AF)
ATA .... Agricultural Technologists of Australasia (ADA)
ATA .... Air Technical Aircraft [Royal Australian Navy]
ATA .... Albanian Telegraphic Agency [News agency] (EY)
ATA .... Alternative Technology Association [Australia]
ATA .... Anta [Peru] [Airport symbol] (OAG)
ATA .... Antarctica [ANSI three-letter standard code] (CNC)
ATA .... Anwendungstechnische Abteilung [Department for Technical Application] [German] (EG)
ATA .... Arkhigeion Taktikis Aeroporias [Tactical Air Force Command] [Greek] (GC)
ATA .... Asia Teachers' Association (ADA)
ATA .... Asociacion de Tecnicos Azucareros [Venezuela] (DSCA)
ATA .... Asociacion de Teleradiodifusoras Argentinas [Argentina] (EY)
ATA .... Associate in Teaching Art [Australia]
ATA .... Association Algerienne des Transports Automobiles [Algerian Automobile Transport Association] [Algeria]
ATA .... Association du Traite Atlantique [Atlantic Treaty Association] (EAIO)
ATA .... Associazione Tecnica dell'Automobile [Association of Automotive Technology] [Italian] (SLS)
ata .... Atado Allomas [Clearing Station, Relay Station] (HU)
ATA .... Atlantic Treaty Association (EA)
ata .... Atmospheres [Absolute Pressure] [German]
ATA .... Australian Taekwondo Association
ATA .... Australian Taxpayers' Association
ATA .... Australian Toolmakers Association (ADA)
ATA .... Australian Touch Association
ATA .... Australian Toy Association
ATA .... Australian Trainers Association
ATA .... Australian Transcontinental Airways
ATA .... Australian Translators Association (ADA)
ATA .... Australian Transport Association (ADA)
ATA .... Australian Tunnelling Association (ADA)
ATA .... Australia-Thailand Association
ATA .... Automatic Teleprinter Exchange (RU)
ATA .... Avtomati Timarithmiki Anaprosarmogi [Automatic Cost of Living Readjustment] (GC)
ATA .... Societe Africaine de Transports Auxiliaires
ATAAC...... Australian Travel Agents Administration Charge
ATAACT ... Agricultural Teachers' Association of the Australian Capital Territory
ATAB........ Antwerps Teer - and Asphaltbedrijf NV [Belgium]
ATAC .... Asociacion de Tecnicos Azucareros de Cuba [Cuban Society of Sugar Cane Technologists]
ATAC .... Asociacion Tecnica Argentina de Ceramica [Argentina]
ATAC .... Australian Television Advisory Committee (ADA)
ATAC .... Australian Time Assignment Committee
ATAC .... Australian Transport Advisory Council
ATACES ... Asociacion de Trabajadores Agropecuarios y Campesinos de El Salvador [Salvadoran Association of Agricultural Workers and Peasants] (LA)
ATADSIA ... Allied Tactical Data Systems Interoperability Agency [NATO] (NATG)
ATAEA...... Australian Theatrical and Amusement Employees Association (ADA)
ATAF........ Advanced Technology Applications Facility [UNCIIS] [United Nations] (DUND)
ATAF........ Allied Tactical Air Force [NATO]
ATAF........ Association des Transporteurs Aeriens de la Zone Franc [Association of Air Transporters of the Franc Zone] (AF)
ATAFG...... African Region Traffic Analysis Forecasting Group [ICAO] (DA)
ATAGUA .. Asociacion de Tecnicos Azucareros de Guatemala [Guatemalan Association of Sugar Technicians] (LA)
ATAIU...... Australian Timber and Allied Industries Union
ATALA...... Asociacion para la Transformacion Armada de America Latina [Association for the Armed Transformation of Latin America] [Ecuador] (LA)

ATALA...... Association pour le Traitement Automatique de Langues [Association for Automatic Language Processing] [France] (EAIO)
ATALA...... Association pour l'Etude et le Developpement de la Traduction Automatique et de la Linguistique Appliquee
ATAM .... Asociacion sw Tecnicos en Alimentos de Mexico [Mexico] (DSCA)
AT &MOEA ... Australian Tramway and Motor Omnibus Employees' Association (ADA)
ATANSW ... Airedale Terrier Association of New South Wales [Australia]
ATAP........ Administrateur Territorial Assistant Principal [Principal Assistant Territorial Administrator] [Zaire]
ATAPEX ... African Timber and Plywood
ATAPR...... Asociacion de Tecnicos Azucareros de Puerto Rico [Puerto Rico] (DSCA)
ATAQ....... Australian Travel Agents Qualification
ATAS........ Advance Technology Alert System [United Nations] (DUND)
ATAS........ Agencia de Colocacao de Trabalhadores para a Africa do Sul
ATAS........ Amerikan-Turk Anonim Sirketi [American-Turkish Corporation Refinery] [Izmir] (TU)
ATAS........ Anadolu Tasfiyehanesi Anonim Sirketi [Anatolian Refinery Corporation] [Mersin] (TU)
ATAS........ Anatolian Refinery Co. (MENA)
ATASM...... Association Tunisienne d'Aide aux Sourds-Muets
ATAV .... Association Tunisian d'Action Volontaire [Tunisian Association of Voluntary Work] (EAIO)
ATAVE...... Asociacion de Tecnicos Azucareros de Venezuela [Venezuelan Association of Sugar Technicians]
ATAX .... Australian Taxation Studies Program [University of New South Wales]
ATB .... Air Technical Base (RU)
ATB .... Allami Terv Bizottsag [State Planning Commission] (HU)
ATB .... Arab Tunisian Bank
ATB .... Arap-Turk Bankasi [Arab-Turkish Bank] [Istanbul] (TU)
ATB .... Assistance Technique Belge [Belgian Technical Assistance] [Zaire]
ATB .... Association des Travailleurs du Bini
ATB .... Association of Tropical Biology [Costa Rica] (ASF)
ATB .... Atbara [Sudan] [Airport symbol] (OAG)
ATB .... At the Time of Bombing [Radiation Effects Research Foundation, Japan]
ATB .... Australian Tobacco Board
ATB .... Motor Transport Base, Motor Pool (RU)
ATB .... Motor Transport Battalion (RU)
ATBAT...... Atelier des Batisseurs [Architectural firm founded by Le Corbusier]
ATBC........ Australian Tenpin Bowling Congress (ADA)
ATBC........ Australia-Taiwan Business Council
ATBC........ Australia-Thailand Business Council
ATBOA..... Australian Tuna Boat Owners' Association
atbr............. Air Technical Brigade (RU)
ATBSA...... Aceros y Tuberias Sociedad Anonima [Colombia] (COL)
ATC .... Aboriginal Treaty Committee [Australia]
ATC .... Activity Therapy center
ATC .... African Timbers Company
ATC .... Agence des Transports du Congo
ATC .... Agence Transcongolaise des Communications [Trans-Congolese Communications Agency] (AF)
ATC .... Agence Transequatoriale des Communications [Trans-Equatorial Communications Agency]
ATC .... Air Tanzania [ICAO designator] (FAAC)
ATC .... Air Tanzania Corporation
ATC .... Air Technical Communications [Royal Australian Navy]
ATC .... Air Transport Council [New South Wales, Australia]
ATC .... Alianza de Trabajadores de la Comunidad Cubana [Cuban Community Workers Alliance] (LA)
ATC .... Alpine Tourist Commission [See also TGA] [Switzerland] (EAIO)
ATC .... Appropriate Technology Centre [Kenya]
ATC .... Argentina Televisora Color [Argentina] (EY)
ATC .... Arthur's Town [Bahamas] [Airport symbol] (OAG)
ATC .... Asociacion de Trabajadores del Campo [Agricultural Workers Association] [Nicaragua] (LA)
ATC .... Aureol Tobacco Development Company [Sierra Leone]
ATC .... Australian Tariff Council (ADA)
ATC .... Australian Taxi Council (ADA)
ATC .... Australian Telecommunications Commission (ADA)
ATC .... Australian Tibet Council
ATC .... Australian Tonnage Committee
ATC .... Australian Tourist Commission (ADA)
ATC .... Automatska Telefonska Centrala [Automatic Telephone Exchange] (YU)
ATC .... Automobile Technical Association [Netherlands] (EAIO)
ATCA .... Allied Tactical Communications Agency [Brussels, Belgium] [NATO] (NATG)
ATCA .... Australian Tuberculosis and Chest Association (PDAA)

ATCA .... Australian Turkish Cultural Association
ATCA .... Automovel e Touring Clube de Angola
ATCAM .... Assemblee Territoriale du Cameroun
ATCAR...... Association des Tshokwe de Congo Belge, de l'Angola, et de la Rhodesie [*Association of Belgian Congolese, Angolan, and Rhodesian Tshokwe*]
ATCAS ..... African Training Centre for Agricultural Statistics
ATCAS ...... Air Traffic Control Automatic System [*Sweden*]
ATCC......... Agence Telegraphique Centrale Coreenne [*Korean Central News Agency*] [*Use KCNA*]   (CL)
ATCC......... Australian Touring Car Championship   (ADA)
ATCC......... Automovil Club de Costa Rica [*Automobile Club of Costa Rica*]   (EAIO)
ATCCI ...... Agence de Transactions Commerciales de Cote-D'Ivoire
ATCE......... Automobile et Touring Club d'Egypte [*Automobile and Touring Club of Egypt*]   (EAIO)
ATCER...... Appropriate Technology Workshops [*Kenya*]   (EAIO)
ATCF........ Australian Teachers' Christian Fellowship   (ADA)
ATCF........ Australian Technological Change Forum
ATCF........ Automobile and Touring Club of Finland   (EAIO)
ATCFITC.. Australian Textile, Clothing, and Footwear Industry Training Council
ATCh .... Air Maintenance Unit   (BU)
ATCO .... Australian Tourism Commission
ATCP .... Antarctic Treaty Consultative Parties
ATCP......... Asociacion Mexicana de Tecnicos de las Industrias de la Celulosa y del Papel [*Mexican Association for the Technology of the Wood Pulp and Paper Industry*]   (PDAA)
ATCP......... Asociacion Tecnica de la Celulosa y Papel [*Pulp and Paper Technical Association*] [*Chile*]   (EAIO)
ATCS........ Aerial Transport Co. of Siam Ltd.
ATCS........ Associate of the Town Clerks' Society [*Australia*]
ATCT........ Association des Techniciens Congolais des Telecommunications [*Association of Congolese Telecommunications Technicians*] [*Zaire*]
ATCV......... Australian Trust for Conservation Volunteers
ATD.......... Aerotours Dominican, C por A [*Dominican Republic*] [*ICAO designator*]   (FAAC)
atd .... Air Maintenance Division   (BU)
atd .... Air Technical Division   (RU)
ATD.......... Anti-Tuberkulozni Dispanzer [*Antituberculosis Dispensary*]   (YU)
atd .... A Tak Dale [*And So Forth, Etc.*] [*Former Czechoslovakia*]
ATD.......... Australian Treasury Directorate [*Information Services*] [*National Union Catalogue of Australia symbol*]
ATD.......... Avtonomos Tourkiki Dioikisis [*Autonomous Turkish Administration*]   (GC)
ATDA .... Appropriate Technology Development Association [*India*] [*Research center*]   (IRC)
ATDA .... Australian Telecommunications Development Association   (ADA)
ATDA .... Australian Tyre Dealers' Association
ATDC .... Austin Ten Drivers Club [*High Wycombe, Buckinghamshire, England*]   (EAIO)
ATDH........ Agrupacion de Tropas de Defensa de La Habana [*Havana Defense Troops*] [*Cuba*]   (LA)
ATDI .... Appropriate Technology Development Institute [*Papua New Guinea*]   (ARC)
ATDO........ Appropriate Technology Development Organization [*Pakistan*]
atdolg .... Atdolgozas [*Adaptation*] [*Hungary*]
ATDU .... Appropriate Technology Development Unit [*SPATF*] [*Papua New Guinea*]
ATE .... Agrotiki Topiki Enosis [*Agrarian Local Union*] [*Name applied to Pan Agrarian Union of Cyprus locals*]   (GC)
ATE .... Agrotiki Trapeza Ellados [*Agricultural Bank of Greece*]   (GC)
ATE .... Anti-Terrorismo ETA [*Anti-ETA Terrorism*] [*Spanish*]   (PPE)
ATE .... Antithrombotic Unit   (RU)
ATE .... Asociacion de Trabajadores del Estado [*State Workers Association*] [*Argentina*]   (LA)
ATE .... Association of Tanganyika Employers
ATE .... Atelier de fabrication de Toulouse [*Groupement Industriel des Armements Terrest res*] [*France*]   (PDAA)
At E .... Atomische Einheit [*Atomic Unit*] [*German*]   (GCA)
ATE .... Australian Tourism Exchange
ATE .... Automatic Test Equipment
ATE .... Moscow Automobile and Tractor Electrical Equipment Plant   (RU)
ATEA........ Australian Teacher Education Association   (EAIO)
ATEA........ Australian Telecommunications Employees Association   (ADA)
ATEAI...... Assessoria Tecnico-Economica Agro-Industrial [*Brazil*]   (DSCA)
ATEC........ Agence Transequatoriale des Communications [*Trans-Equatorial Communications Agency*] [*Africa*]   (AF)
ATEC........ Appropriate Technology Extension Centre [*Nepal*]
ATEC........ Association pour le Developpement Technique des Transports de l'Environnement et de la Circulation
ATEC........ Atlantic Treaty Education Committee [*NATO*]   (NATG)
ATEC........ Atomic Energy Commission [*Australia*]

ATEC........ Australian Technology Export Committee
ATECC...... Australian Technology, Education, and Creativity Centre [*Armidale*]
ATECI .... Asociacion Tecnica Espanola de la Contruccion Industrialialzada [*Spanish Technical Association of Industrialised and Prefabricated Building*]   (PDAA)
ATECMA ... Agrupacion Tecnica Espanola de Constructores de Material Aeroespacial [*Spain*]
ATEE......... Association for Teacher Education in Europe [*Belgium*]   (EAIO)
ATEF......... Asociacion de Trabajadores en Embarques de Frutas [*Association of Fruit Shipment Workers*] [*Ecuador*]   (LA)
ATEGIPE ... Association Technique pour l'Etude de la Gestion des Institutions Publiques et des Entreprises Privees [*French*]   (SLS)
ATEKAD... Akademi Tehnik Angkatan Darat [*Indonesian*]
ATEL......... Aare-Tessin Ag fuer Elektrizitaet [*Switzerland*] [*Nuclear energy*]   (NRCH)
ATEL......... Aar et Tessin SA d'Electricite [*Switzerland*]   (WND)
Atel .... Atelye [*Shop, Workshop*]   (TU)
ATEM .... Association for the Teaching of English in Malawi
A Tem .... A Tempo [*In Strict Time*] [*Music*]
ATEN .... Association Technique de l'Energie Nucleaire [*Nuclear energy*] [*French*]   (NRCH)
ATENA ..... Associazione Italiana di Tecnica Navale [*Italian*]   (SLS)
ATENAGRO ... Ateneo Nacional Agronomico [*Mexico*]   (LAA)
ATENE...... Association for Theological Education in the Near East [*Later, ATIME*]
ATEP......... Aboriginal Teacher Education Programme [*Australia*]   (ADA)
ATEP......... Asociacion Tecnica Espanola del Pretensado [*Spanish Technical Association of Prestressed Concrete*]   (EAIO)
ATEPAM .. Asistencia Tecnica, Esfuerzo Propio, y Ayuda Mutua [*Argentina*]   (LAA)
ATERB...... Australian Telecommunications and Electronics Research Board
ATES .... Anoteres Tekhnikes Epangelmatikes Skholes [*Higher Technical Training Schools*] [*Greek*]   (GC)
ATES .... Asociacion Salvadorena de Transportistas [*Salvadoran Association of Drivers*]   (LA)
ATESA ...... Aerotaxis Ecuatorianos, Sociedad Anonima [*Ecuador*]   (EY)
ATESA ...... Association Technique du Secteur d'Animation [*France*]   (EAIO)
ATESA ...... Australian Tertiary Education Sports Association
ATESEA.... Association for Theological Education in South East Asia   (EAIO)
ATETA ...... Anti-Terorista de ETA [*Anti-Terrorist Group of ETA*] [*Spanish*]   (WER)
ATETs .... Atomic Thermal-Electric Power Plant   (BU)
ATEX........ Allami Textilkiskereskedelmi Vallalat [*State Textile Retail Trade Enterprise*]   (HU)
ATF........... Adenosine Triphosphate   (RU)
ATF........... Air Transport Force
ATF........... Association of Total Fashion [*Japan*]   (EAIO)
ATF........... Association Technique de la Fonderie [*French*]   (SLS)
ATF........... Australian Task Force
ATF........... Australian Tax Forum
ATF........... Australian Teachers' Federation   (SLS)
ATF........... Australian Turkey Federation
ATF........... Compania Aerotecnicas Fotograficas [*Spain*] [*ICAO designator*]   (FAAC)
ATF........... French Southern and Antarctic Lands [*ANSI three-letter standard code*]   (CNC)
ATF-aza..... Adenosinetriphosphatase   (RU)
ATFC........ American-Turkish Friendship Council
ATFC........ Association of Tasmanian Forum Clubs [*Australia*]
ATFCA ...... Asian Track and Field Coaches Association [*India*]   (EAIO)
ATFCNN... Allied Task Force Commander, North Norway [*NATO*]   (NATG)
ATFCV ...... Australian Trust for Conservation Volunteers
ATFS .... Association of Track and Field Statisticians [*British*]   (EAIO)
ATG .... Afrikaanse Taalgenootskap [*Afrikaans*]
ATG .... Air Transport Group [*Australia*]
ATG .... Allgemeine Transportgesellschaft [*General Forwarding Company*]
ATG .... Antigua-Barbuda [*ANSI three-letter standard code*]   (CNC)
ATG .... Assistance Technique Generale [*General Technical Assistance*] [*Zaire*]   (AF)
ATG .... Association Technique de l'Industrie du Gaz en France [*French*]   (SLS)
At-G .... Atom Gewicht [*Atomic Weight*] [*German*]
ATG .... Autotransportgemeinschaft [*Automotive Transport Association*]   (EG)
ATG .... Auxiliary Turbogenerator   (RU)
ATG .... Avia Technique Gabon
At-Gew...... Atom Gewicht [*Atomic Weight*] [*German*]
ATGGA ..... Australian Table Grape Growers' Association
Atgm .... Astegmen [*Second Lieutenant*]   (TU)
ATGRI....... Australian Turf Grass Research Institute   (ADA)
ATGSL ...... Appropriate Technology Group of Sri Lanka

ATGW .... Anti-Tank Guided Weapon
ATGWU .... Amalgamated Transport and General Workers Union [*Uganda*] (AF)
ath .... Aetherisch [*Ethereal*] [*German*]
ATH .... Air Travel Corp. [*ICAO designator*] (FAAC)
ATH .... Athens [*Greece*] [*Airport symbol*] (OAG)
ATHCOM ... Australasian [*or Australian*] Tertiary Handbook Collection on Microfiche
ather .... Aetherisch [*Ethereal*] [*German*] (GCA)
AThP .... Avtou Theiotati Panagiotis [*His (Most Divine) Holiness*] [*Used for Patriarch of Constantinople only*] (GC)
Ath Pr .... Athinaikon Praktoreion [*Athens (News) Agency*] [*See also APE*] (GC)
ATHRA ..... Australian Trail Horse Riders Association (ADA)
ATHS .... Australian Theatre Historical Society
ATHU .... Association Tunisienne des Historiens Universitaires
ATI .... Aero Transporti Italiani SpA [*Italy*] [*ICAO designator*] (FAAC)
ATI .... Allami Terkepeszeti Intezet [*State Institute of Cartography*] (HU)
ATI .... Anotaton Tekhnologikon Instituton [*Supreme Technological Institute*] (GC)
ATI .... Ansett Transport Industries [*Australia*] (ADA)
ATI .... Artigas [*Uruguay*] [*Airport symbol*] (OAG)
ATI .... Association of Thai Industries (DS)
ATI .... Athinaikon Tekhnologikon Institouton [*Athens Technological Institute*] (GC)
ATI .... Automobile and Tractor Institute (RU)
ATI .... Aviation Technological Institute (RU)
ati .... Gage Atmosphere (RU)
ATI .... Industrial Asbestos Products (RU)
ATI .... Telemetry Equipment (RU)
ATIA .... Australian Taxi Industry Association
ATIA .... Australian Tourism Industry Association
ATIA .... Australian Transport Industry Association (ADA)
ATIA .... Australian Travel Industry Association
ATIBT .... Association Technique Internationale des Bois Tropicaux [*International Technical Tropical Timber Association*] (EAIO)
ATIC .... Associacao Tecnica da Industria do Cimento [*Portuguese*] (SLS)
ATIC .... Association Technique de l'Importation Charbonniere [*North African*]
ATIC .... Associazione Tecnica Italiana per la Cinematografia [*Italian*] (SLS)
ATIC .... Australian Tin Information Centre (ADA)
ATICCA .... Australian Tertiary Institutions' Consulting Companies Association
ATICELA ... Associazione Tecnica Italiana per la Cellulosa e la Carta [*Italian Technical Association for Wood Pulp and Paper*] (PDAA)
ATICLCA ... Associazione Tecnica Italiana per la Cellulosa e la Carta [*Italian*] (SLS)
ATID .... Australian Transport Information Directory [*Australia Bureau of Transport Economics*] [*Information service or system*] (CRD)
ATIE .... Associacao dos Tradutores e Interpretes do Estado do Rio De Janeiro [*Association of Translators and Interpreters of the State of Rio De Janeiro*] [*Brazil*]
ATIEL .... Association Technique de l'Industrie Europeenne de Lubrifiants [*Technical Association of European Lubricant Manufacturers*] (PDAA)
ATIF .... Australian Timber Importers' Federation
ATIF .... Australian Turkish Islamic Federation
ATIFAS ..... Associazione Tessiture Italiano Artificiali e Sintetiche [*Italian Associaton for Weaving Artificial and Synthetic Fabrics*] (PDAA)
ATIG .... Associazione Tecnica del Gas [*Italy*]
ATIGA ...... Asociacion de Trabajadores de la Industria Gastronomica de Antioquia [*Colombia*] (COL)
ATIGF .... Association de l'Industrie du Gaz en France
ATII .... Australian Transport Index [*AUSINET database*] (ADA)
ATILH .... Association Technique de l'Industrie des Liants Hydrauliques [*Technical Association for the Hydraulic Binders Industry*] (IID)
ATILRA .... Asociacion de Trabajadores de la Industria Lechera de la Republica Argentina [*Argentine Dairy Industry Workers Association*] (LA)
ATIM .... Asociacion de Tecnicos en Alimentos de Mexico [*Mexico*] (DSCA)
ATIM .... Automatic Maximal Heat-Sensitive Alarm (RU)
ATIM .... Aviation Heat-Insulating Material (RU)
ATIME ...... Association of Theological Institutes in the Middle East (EAIO)
ATIN .... Andean Trade Information Network [*Peru*] (EAIO)
ATIP .... Algemeen Tarief Interlokaal vervoer Partijgoederen [*Benelux*] (BAS)
ATIP .... Association Technique de l'Industrie Papetiere [*French*] (SLS)
ATIPCA .... Asociacion de Tecnicos de la Industria Papelera y Celulosica Argentina [*Technical Association of the Pulp and Paper Industry - TAPPI*] [*Argentina*] (LAA)

ATIPE .... Action Thematique et Incitative sur Programme et Equipe [*France*]
ATIRA .... Ahmedabad Textile Industry's Research Association [*India*] [*Research center*] (IRC)
ATIS .... Appropriate Technology Information Service [*International Council of Scientific Unions*]
ATIS .... Association of Teachers in Independent Schools [*Australia*]
ATISA .... Asesoria Tecnica e Inspeccion, Sociedad Anonima [*Mexico*] (LAA)
ATISM ...... Associazione Teologica Italiana per lo Studio della Morale [*Italian*] (SLS)
ATISS .... Asociacion de Trabajadores de la Industrial Siderurgica y Similares [*Association of Steel and Related Industry Workers*] [*Venezuela*] (LA)
ATITA .... Association Technique des Industries Thermiques et Aerauliques [*French*] (SLS)
ATJ .... Air Traffic GmbH [*Germany*] [*ICAO designator*] (FAAC)
ATJ .... Association Territorial pour la Protection de la Jeunesse
ATJL .... Adriatico Tirreno Jonio Ligure [*Shipping*] [*Italy*] (EY)
ATK .... Administrateur de Territoire de Katanga
ATK .... Aerotaxi Casanare Ltda. [*Colombia*] [*ICAO designator*] (FAAC)
ATK .... Agrar-Technische Konstruction [*Technical Designing for Agriculture*] (EG)
ATK .... Air Transport Column (RU)
ATK .... Akademia Teologii Katolickiej [*Academy of Catholic Theology*] (POL)
ATK .... Allattenyesztesztesi es Takarmanyozasi Kutatokozpont [*Animal Husbandry and Nutrition Investigation Center*] [*Hungary*] (ARC)
ATK .... Amt fuer Technische Kontrolle [*Office for Technical Supervision*] (EG)
ATK .... Arkhi Tilepikoinonion Kyprou [*Cyprus Telecommunications Authority*] [*See also CYTA*] (GC)
ATK .... Armadni Telovychovny Klub [*Armed Forces Physical Education Club*] (CZ)
ATK .... Automaattinen Tietojenkasittely [*Automatic Data Processing*] [*Finland*]
ATK .... Automobile Transportation Office (RU)
ATK .... Autotransformer of Magnetic Comparator (RU)
ATK .... Aviation Turbine Kerosene
ATK .... Turbocompressor Unit (RU)
ATKAT ..... Association des Tshokwe du Katanga
ATKh .... Automobile Transportation Establishment (RU)
ATKV .... Afrikaanse Taal- en Kultuurvereniging [*Afrikaans*]
ATL .... Advanced Technology Laboratories Proprietary Ltd. [*Australia*]
ATL .... Akosombo Textiles Limited
ATL .... Arewa Textiles Ltd. [*Nigeria*]
atl .... Atlante [*Atlas*] [*Publishing*] [*Italian*]
atl .... Atlas (RU)
ATL .... Auspuff-Turbolaeder [*Exhaust turbocharger*] [*German*] [*Automotive engineering*]
ATL .... Automatic Totalisators Limited [*Australia*] (ADA)
ATL .... Avant Toute Lettre [*Before All the Lettering*] [*Engraving*] [*French*]
ATLA .... Air Transport Licensing Authority [*Hong Kong*]
ATLA .... American Theological Library Association
ATLA .... Asociacion Textil Latinoamericana [*Montevideo, Uruguay*] (LAA)
ATLA .... Australian Toy Library Association
ATLANCO ... Compagnie Atlantique de Conserves
AtlantNIRO ... Atlanticheskij Nauchno-Issledovatel'skij Institut [*Atlantic Research Institute of Marine Fisheries and Oceanography*] (ASF)
ATLAS ...... Asociacion de Trabajadores de America Latina [*Association of Latin American Workers*] (LA)
ATLAS ...... Assises Internationale de la Traduction Litteraire en Arles [*1985*] [*France*]
ATLAS ...... Australian Travel and Leisure Automated Systems
ATLAS ...... Australian Travel, Leisure, and Sports Club Ltd.
ATLAS ...... [*A*] Tactical, Logistical, and Air Simulation [*NATO*] (NATG)
ATLF .... Association of Literary Translators of France
ATLIS .... Australian Transport Literature Information System [*Australia Bureau of Transport Economics*] [*Information service or system*] (CRD)
AtlO .... Atlantic Ocean
ATLS .... Association of TAFE [*Technical and Further Education*] Library Staff [*Australia*]
ATLS .... Australian Transport Literature Informatin System [*Database on AUSINET*] (NITA)
ATLS .... Australian Transport Literature Information System [*Database*]
ATLSOL ... Association of Teachers of Languages to Speakers of Other Languages [*Australia*]
ATLU .... Antigua Trades and Labour Union [*Affiliated with the Antigua Labour Party*] (EY)
ATM .... Abastecimiento Tecnico-Militar [*Military Technical Supply*] [*Cuba*] (LA)
ATM .... Aide au Tiers Monde (EAIO)

ATM	Airlines of Tasmania [Australia] [ICAO designator] (FAAC)
ATM	Airspace and Traffic Management [ICAO] (DA)
ATM	Altamira [Brazil] [Airport symbol] (OAG)
ATM	Amici Thomae Mori [Angers, France] [An association] (EA)
ATM	Angkatan Tentera Malaysia [Malaysian Armed Forces] (ML)
ATM	Antarctic Treaty Meeting
ATM	Antifriction Heat-Conducting Material (RU)
atm	Aprovizionare Tehnico-Materiala [Technical-Material Supply] (RO)
ATM	Archiv fuer Technische Messen [Archives for Technical Fairs] (EG)
ATM	Asociatia Oamenilor de Arta din Institutiile Teatrale si Muzicale [Association of Artists in Theatrical and Musical Institutions] (RO)
ATM	Association of Teachers of Mathematics [Derby, England] (EAIO)
ATM	Atmosfeer [Atmosphere] [Afrikaans]
Atm	Atmosfer [Atmosphere] (TU)
atm	Atmosfera [Atmosphere] [Portuguese]
atm	Atmosfera [Atmosphere Unit] [Poland]
Atm	Atmosphaere [Atmosphere] [German]
Atm	Atmosphere [Atmosphere] [French] (MTD)
atm	Atmospheres (BU)
atm	Atmospheric (RU)
ATM	Australian Road Research Board Technical Manual (ADA)
ATM	Australian Teachers of Media [An association]
ATM	Australian Tube Mills Proprietary Ltd. (ADA)
ATM	Corrosion-Resistant Heat-Conducting Material (RU)
atm	Physical Atmosphere (RU)
ATMA	Associated Tie Manufacturers of Australia
ATMA	Association Technique, Maritime, et Aeronautique [French]
ATMA	Australian Association of Taxation and Management Accountants
ATMA	Australian Technical Millers Association (ADA)
ATMA	Australian Tire Manufacturers' Association
Atm abs	Atmosphaere Absolut [Absolute Pressure in Atmospheres] [German]
ATMAC	Australian Tobacco Marketing Advisory Committee
ATMIL	Atase Militer [Military Attache] (IN)
ATMN	Amalgamated Tin Mines of Nigeria Ltd.
atmo	Atentisimo [Yours Truly] [Correspondence] [Spanish]
ATMOEA	Australian Tramway and Motor Omnibus Employees' Association
ATMS	Australian Traditional Medicine Society
ATMS	Automatic Telemetry Meteorological Station (RU)
ATN	Air Transport International [ICAO designator] (FAAC)
ATN	Amalgamated Television Services Proprietary Ltd. [Australia] (ADA)
ATN	Arts Training New South Wales [An association] [Australia]
at n	Atomic Number (RU)
ATN	Australian Television Network
ATN	Namatanai [Papua New Guinea] [Airport symbol] (OAG)
ATN	Turbine-Driven Artesian Pump (RU)
ATNA	Australasian Trained Nurses' Association (ADA)
ATNE	Applications des Techniques Nouvelles en Electronique [Research center] [French] (ERC)
ATNF	Australia Telescope National Facility
ATNSW	Adoptive Triangle New South Wales [Australia] [An association]
ATO	Afghan Tourist Organization (MENA)
ATO	African Timber Organisation
ATO	African Timber Organization (EAIO)
ATO	Airfield Technical Support (RU)
ATO	Air Tonga [ICAO designator] (FAAC)
ATO	Antarctic Treaty Organization (ASF)
ATO	Arab Telecommunications Organization
ATO	Arab Towns Organization [Safat, Kuwait] (EAIO)
ATO	Associated Tour Operators
ato	Atencioso [Kind, Thoughtful] [Portuguese]
Ato	Atento [Attentive] [Spanish]
ato	Atento [Attentive] [Portuguese]
ATO	Athinaikos Tekhnologikos Omilos [Athens Technological Club] (GC)
ATO	Australian Taxation Office
ato	Automatic Tankborne Flamethrower (RU)
ATO	Auto Transport de l'Ouest [Western Auto Transport] [Madagascar]
ATOA	Australian Transport Officers Association (ADA)
ATOC	Acoustic Thermometry of Ocean Climate [International oceanographic project]
ATOC	Agence Togolaise d'Opinion Commerciale
ATOC	Air Tactical Operations Center [Military]
ATOCI	Association de Traducteurs et Reviseurs des Organisations et Conferences Intergouvernementales
ATOF	Almanyadaki Turk Ogrenciler Federasyonu [Turkish Student Federation in Germany] (TU)
ATOF	Australian Transport Officers Federation (ADA)
ATOI	Alliance Touristique de l'Ocean Indien
ATOM	Against Testing on Mururoa [An association] [Australia]
ATOM	Anti-Terrorist Operations in Malaya (ML)
ATOM	Australian Teachers of Media
Atomgew	Atomgewicht [Atomic Weight] [German]
Atomizdat	Publishing House of the State Committee of the Council of Ministers, USSR, for the Use of Atomic Energy (RU)
ATOMKI	Atommag Kutato Intezet [Nuclear Research Institute] (HU)
ATONU	Assistance Technique de l'Organisations des Nations Unies
ATOP	Aboriginal Teacher Orientation Program [Australia]
ATOP	Agence Togolaise de Presse [Togolese Press Agency] (AF)
ATOWA	Australian Tug-of-War Association
ATP	Adult Training Program [Australia]
ATP	Aerotransportes Especiales Ltda. [Colombia] [ICAO designator] (FAAC)
ATP	African Timber and Plywood Ltd.
ATP	Agence Tchadienne de Presse [Chadian Press Agency] (AF)
ATP	Agence Transcontinentale de Presse [Transcontinental Press Agency] [France] (AF)
ATP	Agence Tunisienne de Publicite [Tunisian Advertising Agency] (AF)
ATP	Agreement for the International Transport of Perishable Products
ATP	Air Technical Regiment (RU)
ATP	Aitape [Papua New Guinea] [Airport symbol] (OAG)
ATP	Allied Tactical Publication [Army] [NATO]
ATP	Allied Technical Publication [Navy] [NATO]
ATP	Amt fuer Technisches Pruefwesen [Office for Technical Testing] (EG)
ATP	Association des Tennismen Professionnels [Tunisia]
atp	A Tout Prix [At Any Cost] [French]
ATP	Australian Trade Practices [Commission] [National Union Catalogue of Australia symbol]
ATP	Authority to Prospect [Australia]
ATP	Automatic Telephone Project [Saudi Arabia] (ME)
ATP	Automation of Technological Planning (RU)
ATP	Autorisation de Transferts Prealables [French]
ATP	Motor Transport Regiment (RU)
ATPA	Andean Trade Preference Act
ATPA	Australian Tin Producers' Association
ATPA	Australian Tomato Processors' Association
ATPC	Association of Tin Producing Countries [Australia]
ATPC	Association of Tin Producing Countries [Inaugurated in October, 1983] [Kuala Lumpur, Malaysia]
ATPC	Australian Tin Producers' Council
ATPF	Action Tunisienne dans le Domaine du Planning Familial
ATPI	Association of Public Translators and Interpreters of Brazil
ATPLO	Army of Tripura People's Liberation Organization [India] (PD)
ATPOA	Australian Telephone and Phonogram Officers [or Operators] Association (ADA)
ATPW	Air Transit of the Printed Word [Australia]
ATQ	Air Transport Schiphol [Netherlands] [ICAO designator] (FAAC)
ATQ	Amritsar [India] [Airport symbol] (OAG)
ATR	Airfield Technical Company (RU)
ATR	Akademia Techniczno-Rolnicza im Jana i Jedrzeja Sniadeckich w Bydgoszczy [Academy of Technology and Agriculture, Bydgoszcz] [Poland] (ERC)
ATR	Anti-Torture Research [Copenhagen, Denmark] [An association] (EAIO)
ATR	Atar [Mauritania] [Airport symbol] (OAG)
ATR	Australian Technology Resources
ATR	Australian Training Resources
ATR	Avions de Transport Regional [Regional Transport Aircraft]
ATR	Motor Transport Company
ATR	Subscriber's Manually Operated Telegraph Set (RU)
ATr	Wind Tunnel (RU)
ATRA	Ateliers de Reparation Radiateurs
ATRA	Austrade [National Union Catalogue of Australia symbol]
ATRA	Australian Tape Recordist Association
ATRACA	Association des Transporteurs de Carburants, Lubrifiants, et Tous Produits Petroliers [Association of Transporters of Motor Fuel, Lubricants, and Petroleum Products] [Cambodia] (CL)
ATRACO	Accra Training College
ATRAM	Australian Trade and Manufacturing Proprietary Ltd. (ADA)
ATRC	Agricultural Tools Research Centre [India] (IRC)
ATRCH	Association to Resource Co-Operative Housing [Australia]
ATRCW	African Training and Research Centre for Women
ATRD	Atomic Turbojet Engine (RU)
ATREM	Association Technique de la Refrigeration et de l'Equipement Menager [French] (SLS)
ATRF	Australian Tax Research Foundation
ATRF	Australian Transport Research Forum
ATRI	Australian Timber Research Institute
ATRI	Australian Tourism Research Institute
ATRI	Australian Turf Grass Research Institute

ATRIP .... Asociacion Internacional para el Progreso de la Ensenanza y de la Investigacion de la Propiedad Intelectual [*International Association for the Advancement of Teaching and Research in Intellectual Property*]   (EAIO)

ATRIP .... Australian Transport Research in Progress [*Australia Bureau of Transport Economics*] [*Information service or system*]   (CRD)

ATRIP .... International Association for the Advancement of Teaching and Research in Intellectual Property   (EA)

ATRM .... Motor Vehicle and Tractor Repair Shop [*Military term*]   (RU)

atro .... Absolut Trocken [*Absolutely Dry*] [*German*]

ATRP .... Air Transport Regulation Panel [*ICAO*]   (DA)

ATrP .... Allied Training Publications [*NATO*]   (NATG)

ATRS........ Association Togolaise de la Recherche Scientifique [*Togolese Scientific Research Association*]   (AF)

ATRS........ Australian Tape Recording Society   (ADA)

ATRZ........ Automobile and Tractor Repair Plant   (RU)

ats.............. Acetone   (RU)

ATS........... Active Turbulent Stratum [*Meteorology*]   (BU)

ATS........... African Travel System

ATS........... Agence Telegraphique Suisse [*Swiss News Agency*] [*Berne, Switzerland*]

ATS........... Air Technical Service   (RU)

ATS........... Air Technical Supply   (RU)

ATS........... Air Transport Service [*Zaire*] [*ICAO designator*]   (FAAC)

ATS........... Air Transport Statistics

ATs .... Analog-to-Digital [*Converter*]   (RU)

ATS........... Aniema Transport Services (Nigeria) Ltd.

ATS........... Antarctic Treaty System

ATS........... Appropriate Technology Section [*Ministry of Cooperatives and Rural Development*] [*Lesotho*]   (WED)

ATS........... Armadni Telovychovny Svaz [*Armed Forces Physical Education Union*]   (CZ)

ATS........... Armiska Transportna Sluzba [*Army Transport Service*]   (YU)

ATS........... Artillery Medium Prime Mover   (RU)

ATS........... Artillery Topographic Service   (BU)

ATS........... Asiatic Territory of the USSR   (RU)

ATS........... Association Technique de la Siderurgie Francaise [*French*]   (SLS)

ATs .... Astronomical Circular   (RU)

ATS........... Atelier de Construction de Tarbes [*Groupement Industriel des Armaments Terrestres*] [*France*]   (PDAA)

ATS........... Atomtekniska Saellskapet i Finland [*Nuclear energy*]   (NRCH)

ATS........... Australian Academy of Technological Sciences and Engineering   (EAIO)

ATS........... Australian Television Society   (ADA)

ATS........... Australian Traineeship System

ATS........... Automated Titles System [*Australia*]

ATS........... Automatic Telephone Exchange   (RU)

ATS........... Automobili Turismo Sport [*Auto manufacturing company*] [*Italy*]

ATS........... Aviation Transport Services [*Italy*] [*ICAO designator*]   (FAAC)

ATS........... Aviotehnicka Sluzba [*Air Technical Service*] [*Air Force*]   (YU)

ATs .... Cellulose Acetate   (RU)

ATs .... Central Control Room   (RU)

ATS........... Dial Telephone Exchange   (BU)

ATS........... Suomen Atomiteknillinen Seura [*Finland*]   (SLS)

ATS........... Telephone Subscribers' Office   (RU)

ATSA......... Aerial Transport of South Australia

ATSA......... Australian Transplant Sports Association

ATS &GWTU ... All Trinidad Sugar and General Workers Trade Union [*Trinidad and Tobago*]   (EAIO)

ATSB .... Avrupa Turk Sosyalistler Birligi [*Union of European Turkish Socialists*]   (TU)

ATSC......... Air Traffic Service Centre [*Civil Aviation Authority*] [*Australia*]

ATSC......... Australian Tree Seed Centre

ATSDR....... Attente [*Leave on*] [*Knitting term*] [*French*]   (BARN)

ATSEFWU ... All-Trinidad Sugar Estates and Factory Workers' Union

ATSEGWTU ... All-Trinidad Sugar Estates and General Workers' Trade Union   (EY)

atset ch .... Acetyl Value   (RU)

ATSG......... Australian Transport Study Group   (ADA)

Atsges .... Adzharis-Tskali Hydroelectric Power Plant   (RU)

ATSH .... Agjencia Telegrafike Shqiptare [*Albanian Telegraph Agency*]

ATSIC .... Aboriginal and Torres Strait Islander Commission [*National Union Catalogue of Australia symbol*]

ATSIC .... Aboriginal and Torres Strait Islander Curriculum Information [*Australia*]

ATSICDC ... Aboriginal and Torres Strait Islander Development Commission [*Australia*]

ATSICLAS ... Aboriginal and Torres Strait Islanders Corp. for Legal Aid Services [*Australia*]

ATsIIS....... Analog Cyclic Information and Measuring System   (RU)

ATSILRN ... Aboriginal and Torres Strait Islander Library and Resource Network [*Australia*]

ATSILS ..... Aboriginal and Torres Strait Islander Legal Service [*Australia*]

ATSIR ...... Aboriginal and Torres Strait Islanders Research [*Australia*]

ATSK........ Crossbar-Type Telephone Exchange   (RU)

ATsM .... Modernized Tank Truck   (RU)

ATsP .... Analog-to-Digital Converter   (RU)

ATsP .... Asbestos Cement Production   (BU)

ATsP .... Tank-Truck Trailer   (RU)

ATsPu .... Alphanumeric Printer   (RU)

ATSR........ Air Ambulance Company   (RU)

ATsR........ Automatic Centrifugal Regulator   (RU)

ATsRB...... Central Army Repair Base   (RU)

ATsRM...... Central Army Repair Shop   (RU)

ATsS .... Antireticular Cytotoxic Serum   (RU)

ATSSR...... Tatar Autonomous Soviet Socialist Republic   (RU)

ATsVM...... Analog [*or Automatic*] Digital Computer   (RU)

ATS VRS ... Intrarayon Automatic Telephone Exchange   (RU)

ATsZ........ Asbestos Cement Plant   (BU)

ATsZhNG ... Tank Truck for Transporting Liquefied Gas   (RU)

ATT .... Adresse Table Travail [*Address Table Work*]   (ADPT)

ATT .... Aer Turas Teoranta [*Republic of Ireland*] [*ICAO designator*]   (FAAC)

ATT .... Artillery Heavy Prime Mover   (RU)

ATT .... Assemblee Territoriale du Togo

att .... Atomic Weight   (BU)

Att .... Attache [*Attached*] [*French*]   (MTD)

ATTA......... Association of Thai Travel Agents   (EAIO)

atta .... Atenta [*Attentive*] [*Spanish*]

ATTA......... Australian Table Tennis Association

ATTC........ Anglo-Taiwan Trade Committee

ATTC........ Associate Teachers' Training Certificate [*Australia*]

atte .... Atenciosamente [*Thoughtfully*] [*Portuguese*]

atte .... Atentamente [*Attentively*] [*Spanish*]

ATTE........ Australian Tea Tree Estate Proprietary Ltd.

attez........... Atomska Tezina [*Atomic Weight*]   (YU)

ATTF........ African Table Tennis Association

ATTF........ Avrupa Turkiyeli Toplumcular Federasyonu [*European Turkish Socialists Federation*]   (TU)

ATTF........ Avrupa Turk Talebe Federasyonu [*European Turkish Student Federation*]   (TU)

ATTIC ...... Association of Trinidad and Tobago Insurance Companies   (EAIO)

Atti Parl .... Atti Parlamentari [*Parliamentary Acts*] [*Italian*]   (ILCA)

ATTJ .... Association Tunisienne: Tourisme et Jeunesse [*Tunisian Association: Tourism and Youth*]

Attn .... Austroton [*Austria, Germany, etc.*] [*Record label*]

atto .... Atentisimo [*Yours Truly*] [*Correspondence*] [*Spanish*]

Atto .... Atento [*Attentive*] [*Spanish*]

Atto y SS.... Atento y Seguro Servidor [*(Yours) Very Truly*] [*Correspondence*] [*Spanish*]

attr............. Attributief [*Attributive*] [*Afrikaans*]

attr............. Attributiivisena [*Attributive*] [*Finland*]

attr............. Attribuutti [*Finland*]

ATTRP...... Australian Travel Training Review Panel

ATTs......... Dial Telephone Exchange   (BU)

ATU.......... African Telecommunications Union

ATU.......... Air Toulon [*France*] [*ICAO designator*]   (FAAC)

ATU.......... Air Trials Unit [*Australia*]

ATU.......... Arab Telecommunications Union   (EA)

ATU.......... Assemblee des Travailleurs de l'Unite [*Plant Workers Assembly*] [*Algeria*]   (AF)

ATU.......... Association of Trade Unions [*Philippines*]   (FEA)

ATU.......... Ataturk Universitesi [*Ataturk University*]   (TU)

Atu .... Atmosphaere Ueberdruck [*Atmospheric Excess Pressure*] [*German*]

ATU.......... Australasian Typographical Union   (ADA)

ATU.......... Australian Teachers Union

ATU.......... Automobile Transportation Administration [*or Sector*]   (RU)

atu .... Driving School   (BU)

ATU.......... Standard Television Antenna   (RU)

atual .... Atualizado [*Brought Up to Date*] [*Portuguese*]

ATUC .... Aden Trades Union Congress

ATUC .... African Trade Union Confederation [*Later, OATUU*]

ATUC(SR) ... African Trades Union Congress of Southern Rhodesia

atue........... Atmosphaeren-Ueberdruck [*Atmospheric Excess Pressure*] [*German*]   (WEN)

ATUESP ... Acordo Trigo entre a Uniao e o Estado de Sao Paulo [*Brazil*]   (DSCA)

ATUF........ Agricultural Trade Union Federation [*Federata Sindikale e Bujqesise*] [*Albania*]   (EY)

ATUF........ Austrian Trade Union Federation

ATUG........ Australian Telecommunications Users Group

ATUKI....... Autokozlekedesi Tudomanyos Kutato Intezet [*Scientific Research Institute for Automobile Transportation*]   (HU)

ATV .... Abonnee Televisie [*Surinam*]   (EY)

ATV .... Abwassertechnische Vereinigung eV   (SLS)

ATV .... Afrikaanse Taalvereniging [*Afrikaans*]

ATV .... Agence de Tourisme et Voyages

ATV .... Agence de Transit et de Voyages [*Central African Republic*]
ATV .... Akademiet foer de Tekniske Videnskaber [*Academy of Technical Sciences*] [*Denmark*] [*Research center*] (WEN)
ATV .... Asian Television Ltd. [*Hong Kong*]
ATV .... Asociacion Textil Venezolana [*Venezuela*] (DSCA)
at v.............. Atomic Weight (RU)
atv............... Atvitel [*Balance Brought Forward*] (HU)
ATV .... Autotransportvereinigung [*Automobile Transport Association*] [*German*] (EG)
ATV .... Avanti Air [*Austria*] [*ICAO designator*] (FAAC)
ATVI........ Australia Television International
ATW .... Australian Theatre Workshop (ADA)
ATW .... Australian Training Workshops Proprietary Ltd.
ATWC ...... Alaska Tsunami Warning Center (MSC)
ATWS........ Alaska Tsunami Warning System (MSC)
ATWU ...... Australian Textile Workers Union (ADA)
ATWU .... Australian Timber Workers Union
ATY .... International Airports Authority of India [*ICAO designator*] (FAAC)
ATYe......... Administrative Territorial Subdivision (RU)
at yed......... Atomic Unit (RU)
ATYP........ Australian Theatre for Young People (ADA)
ATZ .... Altay Tractor Plant Imeni M. I. Kalinin (RU)
ATZ .... Automatische Telefonzentrale [*Automatic Telephone Exchange*] (WEN)
ATZ .... Nitrogen Fertilizer Plant (BU)
ATZ .... Refueling Truck (RU)
ATZ .... Tyumen' Battery Plant (RU)
ATZT........ Association des Techniciens Zairois des Telecommunications [*Association of Zairian Telecommunications Technicians*] (AF)
AU.............. Active Carbon, Activated Carbon, Activated Charcoal (RU)
AU.............. Administration of Archives (RU)
au................ Allt som Utkommit [*All Published*] [*Sweden*]
AU.............. Amplitude Indicator (RU)
AU.............. Angkatan Udara [*Air Force*] (IN)
AU.............. Ankara Universitesi [*Ankara University*] (TU)
AU.............. Arbetsutskottet [*Working Committee, Executive Committee*] [*Sweden*] (WEN)
AU.............. Archelolgicky Ustav [*Institute of Archeology*] (CZ)
AU.............. Arithmetic Unit [*Computers*] (RU)
AU.............. Artillery Directorate (RU)
AU.............. Artillery School (RU)
AU.............. Associative Unit [*Computers*] (RU)
AU.............. Astronomic Theodolite (RU)
AU.............. Aunes [*French Ells*]
Au.............. Auro [*Gold*] [*Chemical element*] [*Portuguese*]
AU.............. Australia [*ANSI two-letter standard code*] (CNC)
AU.............. Author Index (RU)
AU.............. Automatic Control (RU)
AU.............. Automobilne Uciliste [*Automobile Training Center*] (CZ)
AU.............. Autonomous Control (RU)
AU.............. Autosaobracajno Poduzece [*Motor Transport Establishment*] (YU)
AU.............. Disaster Level (of water) (RU)
AU.............. Pharmaceutical Administration (BU)
AUA.......... African Union of Architects [*South Africa*]
AUA.......... Aruba [*Netherlands Antilles*] [*Airport symbol*]
AUA.......... Associate of the University of Adelaide [*Australia*] (ADA)
AUA.......... Association des Ulemas Algeriens [*Algeria*]
AUA.......... Association des Universites Africaines [*Association of African Universities - AAU*] (EAIO)
AUA.......... Atelier d'Urbanisme et d'Architecture
aua.............. Auch under Andern [*Also among Others*] [*German*]
AUA.......... Australian Ultralight Association
AUA.......... Austrian Airlines [*ICAO designator*] (FAAC)
AUA.......... Austrian Airways [*Oesterreichische Luftverkehrs AG*]
AUA(Com) ... Associate of the University of Adelaide (Commerce) [*Australia*] (ADA)
AuAU-AR ... University of Adelaide, Mawson Institute for Antartic Research, Adelaide, SA, Australia [*Library symbol*] [*Library of Congress*] (LCLS)
AUB.......... American University of Beirut [*Lebanon*]
AUB.......... Asociacion de Universidades Bolivianas [*Bolivian Universities Association*] (LA)
AUB.......... As U Blief [*Please*] [*Afrikaans*]
AUBC .... All-Union Book Chamber (EAIO)
Aubge........ Auberge [*Inn*] [*Military map abbreviation World War I*] [*French*] (MTD)
AUBI .... Automatische Bibliofoonuitlening
aubo............ Aussenbord [*Outboard*] [*German*] (GCA)
AUBRCC... Australian Uniform Building Regulations Co-Ordinating Council
AUC.......... Abidjan University Club
AUC.......... American University of Cairo
AUC.......... Anno Urbis Conditae [*In the Year from the Founding of the City (Rome) 753BC*] [*Latin*] (GPO)

AUC.......... Arauca [*Colombia*] [*Airport symbol*] (OAG)
AUC.......... Asociacion de Universidades del Caribe [*Association of Caribbean Universities and Research Institutes*] (EAIO)
AUC.......... Australian United Corporation Ltd. (ADA)
AUC.......... Australian Universities Commission (ADA)
AUC.......... Australian University of Canberra [*National Union Catalogue of Australia symbol*]
AUCA .... Asociacion de Universitarios del Cauca [*Popayan*] (COL)
AUCAM .... Association Universitaire Catholique d'Amitie Mondiale
AUCANUKUS ... Australia, Canada, United Kingdom, United States (ADA)
AUCBM .... Arab Union for Cement and Building Materials [*See also UACMC*] (EAIO)
AUCCTU .. All-Union Central Council of Trade Unions [*Former USSR*]
AUCh........ Arithmetic Number Unit (RU)
AUCIHD ... Australia-UNESCO Committee for the International Hydrological Decade (ADA)
AUCOLDI ... Asociacion Colombiana de Autores de Obras Didacticas [*Colombia*] (COL)
AUCOS ..... Autoservicios Comunitarios [*Community Self-Services*] [*Chile*] (LA)
AUCSM..... All-Russian Committee of Soldiers' Mothers [*Formerly, All-Union Committee of Soldiers' Mothers*] (EAIO)
AUCTA ..... Australian Underground Construction and Tunnelling Association
AUD.......... Accion Universitaria Democrata de la Facultad de Derecho y Ciencias Sociales [*Democratic University Action of the School of Law and Social Services*] [*Paraguay*] (LA)
AUD.......... Aktionsgemeinschaft Unabhaengiger Deutscher [*Action Group of Independent Germans*] [*Germany*] [*Political party*] (PPE)
AUD.......... Armadni Umelecke Divadlo [*Armed Forces Theater*] (CZ)
Aud............ Audiencia [*Spanish*]
Aud............ Auditeur au Conseil d'Etat [*France*] (FLAF)
aud............. Audycja [*Hearing*] [*Poland*]
AUD......... Augustus Downs [*Australia*] [*Airport symbol*] [*Obsolete*] (OAG)
AUD......... Australian Dollar [*Monetary unit*]
AUDAVI ... Asociacion Uruguaya de Agencias Viajes [*Association of Uruguayan Travel Agencies*] (LA)
AUDBM .... African Union of Development Bank Management [*Benin*] (EAIO)
AUDEA ..... Asociacion de Universitarios de Antioquia [*Colombia*] (COL)
AUDEBA .. Asociacion de Universitarios de Barrancabermeja (COL)
AUDECAM ... Association Universitaire pour le Developpement de l'Enseignement et de la Culture en Afrique et a Madagascar [*University Association for the Development of Teaching and Culture in Africa and Madagascar*] [*Paris, France*] (AF)
AUDET ..... Associatie van Uitgevers van Dagbladen en Tijdschriften [*Netherlands*] (ECON)
AUDI .... Arab Urban Development Institute (EA)
AUDKSC... Archiv Ustavu Dejin Komunisticke Strany Ceskoslovenska [*Archives of the Institute for the History of the Communist Party of Czechoslovakia*] (CZ)
AUDKSS ... Archiv Ustavu Dejin Komunistickej Strany Slovenska [*Archives of the Institute for the History of the Communist Party of Slovakia*] (CZ)
Aud Sol ...... Audience Solennelle [*French*] (FLAF)
AUETSA ... Association of University English Teachers of Southern Africa (AA)
AUF .... Assemblee de l'Union Francaise [*France*] (FLAF)
AUF .... Auftragsabwicklung [*Instructional Development*] [*German*] (ADPT)
AUF .... Australian Ultralight Federation
AUF .... Australian Underwater Federation [*or Foundation*]
AUF .... Australian Union Federation (ADA)
AUF .... Australian United Fresh Fruit and Vegetables Association
AUF .... Austrian Union of Foresters (EAIO)
Aufarbeit.... Aufarbeitung [*Finishing*] [*German*] (GCA)
Aufber........ Aufbereitung [*Preparation*] [*German*] (GCA)
Aufbereit.... Aufbereitung [*Preparation*] [*German*] (GCA)
Aufbring..... Aufbringung [*Application*] [*German*] (GCA)
Auff .... Auffuehrung [*Performance*] [*German*]
auffall......... Auffaellig [*Remarkable*] [*German*] (GCA)
Auffull....... Auffuellung [*Filling*] [*German*] (GCA)
AUFFVA ... Australian United Fresh Fruit and Vegetable Association
Aufg .... Aufgabe [*Task*] [*German*]
aufgen........ Aufgenommen [*Accepted*] [*German*] (GCA)
aufges......... Aufgesetzt [*Patched, Mounted*] [*Publishing*] [*German*]
aufgez........ Aufgezogen [*Mounted*] [*Publishing*] [*German*]
Aufhell ...... Aufhellung [*Clarification*] [*German*] (GCA)
Aufkl......... Aufklaerung [*Elucidation*] [*German*] (GCA)
Aufl .... Auflage [*Edition*] [*German*] (GPO)
Auflg .... Auflage [*Edition*] [*Publishing*] [*German*]
Auflos........ Aufloesen [*Dissolution*] [*German*] (GCA)
Auflos........ Aufloesung [*Dissolution*] [*German*] (GCA)
Aufnahmefahigk ... Aufnahmefaehigkeit [*Absorptivity*] [*German*] (GCA)
Aufrechterh ... Aufrechterhaltung [*Maintenance*] [*German*] (GCA)
Aufrechterhalt ... Aufrechterhaltung [*Maintenance*] [*German*] (GCA)

AUFS........ American Universities Field Staff
Aufs........... Aufsatz [*Essay*] [*German*]
Aufs........... Aufseher [*Foreman*] [*German*]
Aufs........... Aufsicht [*Supervision*] [*German*]
Aufschlamm ... Aufschlaemmung [*Suspension*] [*German*]   (GCA)
Aufschliess ... Aufschliessung [*Decomposition*] [*German*]   (GCA)
Aufst .... Aufstellung [*Statement*] [*German*]
Aufstell ...... Aufstellung [*Erection*] [*German*]   (GCA)
Auftr.......... Auftrag [*Order*] [*German*]
Aufz.......... Aufzeichnung [*Note*] [*German*]
Aug........... August [*German*]   (GPO)
aug............. August [*Denmark*]   (GPO)
aug............. Augustus [*August*] [*Netherlands*]   (GPO)
aug............. Augusztus [*August*]   (HU)
AUG.......... Australian United Gold No Liability
AUG.......... Carrier-Based Attack Group   (RU)
AUG........... CPA Cesar Augusto de la Cruze Lepe [*Mexico*] [*ICAO designator*]   (FAAC)
augenblickl ... Augenblicklich [*Instantly*] [*German*]   (GCA)
augm.......... Augmentation [*Increase*] [*Knitting*] [*French*]
augm.......... Augmente [*Enlarged*] [*Publishing*] [*French*]
AUH .... Abu Dhabi [*United Arab Emirates*] [*Airport symbol*]   (OAG)
AUH .... American University Hospital [*Lebanon*]
AUHA .... Australian Underwater Hockey Association
AUHC .... Adelaide University History Club [*Australia*]
AUHC .... Adelaide University Hockey Club [*Australia*]
AUI .... Action d'Urgence Internationale [*International Emergency Action - IEA*] [*Paris, France*]   (EAIO)
AUI .... Air Ukraine International [*ICAO designator*]   (FAAC)
AUI .... Association Universitaire Interamericaine [*Interamerican University Association*] [*France*]
AUI .... Aua [*Papua New Guinea*] [*Airport symbol*]   (OAG)
AUI .... Australian United Investments Co.
AUI .... Australian Urban Investments   (ADA)
AUIDP ...... Australian Universities International Development Program
AUJ .... Ambunti [*Papua New Guinea*] [*Airport symbol*]   (OAG)
AUJ .... Aujourd'hui [*Today*] [*French*]
AUJENGI ... Association de la Jeunesse Ngidingienne
AUJS .... Australasian Union of Jewish Students   (ADA)
AUK.......... Aliupseerikoulu [*Finland*]
AUK .... Aminoacetic Acid   (RU)
AUL .... Agrupacion Universitaria Liberacion [*University Liberation Group*] [*Argentina*]   (LA)
AUL .... Artillery Training Camp   (RU)
AUL .... Aur [*Marshall Islands*] [*Airport symbol*]   (OAG)
AULF .... Australian Universities Liberal Federation   (ADA)
AULLA ...... Australasian Universities Language and Literature Association   (EAIO)
AULLA ...... Australian Universities Languages and Literature Association   (ADA)
AULN .... Association of University Librarians in the Netherlands   (EAIO)
AULSA ...... Australasian Universities Law Schools Association   (ADA)
AUM......... Air Atlantic Uruguay [*ICAO designator*]   (FAAC)
aum .... Aumentado [*Enlarged*] [*Publishing*] [*Spanish*]
aum .... Aumentado [*Enlarged*] [*Publishing*] [*Portuguese*]
aum .... Aumentado [*Enlarged*] [*Spanish*]   (BARN)
aum .... Aumentato [*Enlarged*] [*Publishing*] [*Italian*]
AUM......... Mantissa Arithmetic Unit [*Computers*]   (RU)
AUM......... Self-Balancing Bridge   (RU)
AUMA....... Association des Ulema Musulmans Algeriens
AUMA....... Ausstellungs- und Messe-Ausschuss der Deutschen Wirtschaft eV [*German Committee on Fairs and Exhibitions*]   (IMH)
AUME....... Association pour l'Union Monetaire de l'Europe [*Association for the Monetary Union of Europe*] [*France*]   (EAIO)
AUMLA .... Australasian Universities Modern Language Association   (ADA)
AUN .... Afirmacion Universitaria Nacional [*National University Affirmation*] [*Spanish*]   (WER)
AUN .... Agrupacion Universitaria Nacional [*National University Group*] [*Argentina*]   (LA)
AUN .... Aviones Unidos SA de CV [*Mexico*] [*ICAO designator*]   (FAAC)
AUNA....... Asociacion de Universidades Nacionales y Autonomas [*Association of National and Autonomous Universities*] [*Bolivia*]   (LA)
AUNA....... Australian United Nations Assembly   (ADA)
AuNL........ National Library of Australia, Canberra, ACT, Australia [*Library symbol*] [*Library of Congress*]   (LCLS)
AUNSW .... Associate of the University of New South Wales [*Australia*]
AUO .... African Unity Organisation
AUO .... Arithmetic Remainder Unit [*Computers*]   (RU)
AUO .... Atlantic Union Oil Co. Ltd. [*Australia*]   (ADA)
AUO .... Empresa Aero Uruguay SA [*ICAO designator*]   (FAAC)
AUOD .... Alliance Universelle des Ouvriers Diamantaires [*Universal Alliance of Diamond Workers - UADW*] [*Antwerp, Belgium*]   (EAIO)
AUP .... Academy of the Coal Industry   (RU)
AUP .... African Union of Physics [*See also UAP*]   (EAIO)

AUP .... Agrupamentos de Unidades Producao [*Production Unit Groups*] [*Angola*]   (AF)
AUP .... Aguan [*Papua New Guinea*] [*Airport symbol*]   (OAG)
AUP .... Australian United Press
AUP .... Number Sequence Arithmetic Unit [*Computers*]   (RU)
AUPAC ..... Asociacion Universitaria para la Accion Comunal [*University Community Action Association*] [*Colorado*]   (LA)
AUPELF ... Association des Universites Partiellement ou Entierement de Langue Francaise [*Association of Wholly or Partially French Language Universities*] [*Montreal, PQ*]   (EA)
AUPS........ Verband der Schweizerischen Volkshochschulen [*Switzerland*]   (SLS)
AUPT .... Australian Urban Passenger Train   (ADA)
AUQ .... Atuona [*Marquesas Islands*] [*Airport symbol*]   (OAG)
AUR.......... Active Unattached Reserve [*Royal Australian Navy*]
AUR .. Administrative Expenditures   (RU)
AUR.......... Agence d'Urbanisme de la Reunion
AUR.......... Aurillac [*France*] [*Airport symbol*] [*Obsolete*]   (OAG)
AURA .... Atelier d'Urbanisme de la Region d'Abidjan
AURA .... Ateliers d'Usinage Mecanique et de Rectification Automobile
AURA .... Australian Rock Art Research Association
AURA .... Australian Ultra Runners Association
AURDR..... Australian Urban and Regional Development Review
AURE .... Agrupacion Universitaria Reformista [*University Reformist Association*] [*Argentina*]   (LA)
AUREG ..... Association de Recherches Geographiques et Cartographiques [*French*]   (SLS)
AUREL...... Australian Religious Film Society   (ADA)
AURI .... Angkatan Udara Republik Indonesia [*Republic of Indonesia Air Force*]   (IN)
AURI .... Ankatan Udara Republik Indonesia
AURISA .... Australian Urban and Regional Information Systems Association   (ADA)
AURP .... Institut d'Amenagement et d'Urbanisme de la Region Parisienne
AURS .... Guided Aircraft Rocket   (RU)
AUS .... Aerodynamic Drift Angle   (RU)
AuS .... Also Sundays and Holidays [*Train schedules*]   (EG)
AUS .... Arbeit und Sozialfuersorge (Aemter der DDR) [*Labor and Social Welfare (GDR Government Offices)*]   (EG)
AUS .... Armadni Umelecky Soubor [*Armed Forces Artistic Ensemble*]   (CZ)
AUS .... Asociacion Uruguaya de Seguridad [*Uruguayan Security Association*]   (LA)
aus............. Ausgeschaltet [*Eliminated*] [*German*]
AUS .... Australia [*ANSI three-letter standard code*]   (CNC)
AUS .... Australian Airlines [*ICAO designator*]   (FAAC)
AUS .... Australian Union of Students   (ADA)
AUS .... Automatic Tracking Device   (RU)
AUS .... Carrier-Based Strike Force   (RU)
AUS .... Modular System Automatic Control   (RU)
AUSA .... Australian Universities Sports Association   (ADA)
AUSAE...... Australian Society of Association Executives
AusAID...... Australian Agency for International Development
AUSAT...... Australian Satellite Users Association
Ausb.......... Ausbeute [*Yield*] [*German*]   (GCA)
Ausb.......... Ausbildung [*Education*] [*German*]
AUSB........ Australian Business [*Australian Consolidated Press*] [*Information service or system*]
AUSBC...... ASEAN [*Association of South East Asian Nations*] - United States Business Council [*Bangkok, Thailand*]   (EAIO)
Ausbess...... Ausbesserung [*Repair*] [*German*]
AUSBF...... Ankara Universitesi Siyasi Bilgiler Fakultesi [*Ankara University Faculty of Political Science*]   (TU)
Ausbreit ..... Ausbreitung [*Expansion*] [*German*]   (GCA)
AUSCANUKUS ... Australia, Canada, United Kingdom, United States   (MCD)
Ausdehnungskoeff ... Ausdehnungskoeffizient [*Coefficient of Expansion*] [*German*]   (GCA)
Ausdex .... Australian Defence Export Group
AUSDIL.... Australian Dangerously Ill List [*Scheme*]
AUSDOC .. Australian Document Exchange   (ADA)
AusDrama St ... Australasian Drama Studies
AUSEAnet ... Australasia and South East Asia Network [*Computer science*]   (TNIG)
AUSECO... Australian Ecology
AUSED...... Australian Ethnic Democrats [*An association*]
AUSELGRID ... Australian Electricity Grid
AUSF........ Australian Universities Sports Federation
Ausflock..... Ausflockung [*Flocculation*] [*German*]   (GCA)
AUSFS...... Australian Union of Students Friendly Society   (ADA)
Ausfuhr...... Ausfuehrung [*Execution Procedure*] [*German*]   (GCA)
ausfuhrl...... Ausfuehrlich [*Detailed*] [*Publishing*] [*German*]
Ausg.......... Ausgabe [*Edition*] [*German*]
ausg............ Ausgegeben [*Published*] [*German*]   (GCA)
ausg............ Ausgewaehlt [*Selected*] [*German*]
ausgeb .... Ausgebessert [*Repaired*] [*Bookbinding*] [*German*]

ausgebess ... Ausgebessert [*Repaired*] [*Bookbinding*] [*German*]
ausgeg .... Ausgegeben [*Published*] [*German*]   (GCA)
ausgegeb..... Ausgegeben [*Published*] [*German*]   (GCA)
ausgeschn... Ausgeschnitten [*Cut Out*] [*Publishing*] [*German*]
ausgeschnitt ... Ausgeschnitten [*Cut Out*] [*Publishing*] [*German*]
ausgew........ Ausgewaehlt [*Selected*] [*Publishing*] [*German*]
ausgezeichn ... Ausgezeichnet [*Excellent*] [*German*]
AuSh .... Australian Serum Hepatitis   (ADA)
AUSHEP... Australian Institute of High Energy Physics
AUSHEP... Australian Institute of Higher Energy Physics
AusIMM ... Australian Institute of Mining and Metallurgy   (ADA)
AUSINET ... Australian Information Network   (NITA)
AUSINTEL ... Australian International and Ethnic Library   (ADA)
AUSIRC .... Australian Sport Information Resource Centre   (ADA)
AUSIT....... Australian Institute of Interpreters and Translators
Auskleid..... Auskleidung [*Coating*] [*German*]   (GCA)
ausl............ Auslaendisch [*Foreign*] [*German*]   (GCA)
Ausl............ Ausland [*or Auslaendisch*] [*Foreign, Export*] [*German*]
ausland...... Auslaendisch [*Foreign*] [*German*]   (GCA)
Auslang...... Australian Supply Language
Ausleihsp ... Ausleihspuren [*Marks of Lending*] [*Publishing*] [*German*]
AUSLIG .... Australian Surveying and Land Information Group
AUSLIT .... Australian Literary Database [*Australian Defence Force Academy*]
Auslosch .... Ausloeschung [*Extinction*] [*German*]   (GCA)
AUSMARC ... Australian Machine-Readable Cataloging Records   (ADA)
AUSMARC ... Australian MARC [*Machine readable catalogue*]   (NITA)
AUSMEAT ... Authority for Uniform Specification of Meat and Livestock [*Australia*]
AUSMIMPS ... Australian Standard Material Issue and Movement Priority System
AUSMIN... Australian-United States Ministerial Talks [*Conference*]
AUSNCo ... Australasian Union Steam Navigation Company   (ADA)
Ausnutz...... Ausnutzung [*Utilization*] [*German*]   (GCA)
AUSPELD ... Australian Council of Speld Associations   (ADA)
AUSPHARM ... Australian Pharmaceutical Interests
Auspress .... Auspressen [*Pressing*] [*German*]   (GCA)
AUSQS...... Australian Unlisted Securities Quotation System
Ausr .... Ausruestung [*Equipment*] [*German*]   (GCA)
AUSRAPID ... Australian Sport and Recreation Association for People with an Intellectual Disability
AUSREP ... Australian Ship Reporting System
Ausrest....... Ausruestung [*Equipment*] [*German*]   (GCA)
AUSRS...... All-Union Scientific Rheumatology Society [*Russian*]   (SLS)
auss .... Aeusserlich [*External*] [*German*]   (GCA)
AUSS........ Andrews University Seminary Studies
AUSSAT ... Australian Domestic Communications Satellite
AUSSAT ... Australian Satellite [*Telecommunications*]   (NITA)
AUSSAT ... Australia's Communication Satellite
AUSSAT ... Austrialian National Satellite System   (PDAA)
Aussch ...... Ausschuss [*Committee*] [*German*]
Ausschalt... Ausschaltung [*Elimination*] [*German*]   (GCA)
Ausscheid... Ausscheidung [*Elimination*] [*German*]   (GCA)
ausschl ...... Ausschliesslich [*Excluding, Exclusive*] [*German*]   (EG)
ausschliessl ... Ausschliesslich [*Exclusive*] [*German*]
Ausschn ..... Ausschnitt [*Clipping*] [*German*]
ausserd....... Ausserdem [*Furthermore*] [*German*]
Aussetz....... Aussetzung [*Exposure*] [*German*]   (GCA)
AusSI .... Australian Society of Indexers   (SLS)
AUSSI .... Australian Union of Senior Swimmers International
AUSSIP..... African University Student Services Internship Program
AUS-SLEEP ... Australasian Sleep Association
Aussp .... Aussprache [*Pronunciation*] [*German*]   (GCA)
Ausspr........ Aussprache [*Pronunciation*] [*German*]
Ausst......... Ausstellung [*Exhibition*] [*German*]
AUSST ...... Australian Union of Students Student Travel
AUSSTOCK ... Australian Stock Exchanges Share Prices [*Database*]
AUST........ Allied Unions Superannuation Trust [*Australia*]
Aust........... Australia [*or Australian*]   (ADA)
AUST......... Australian
AusT .... Austrian Telefunken [*Record label*]
AUSTA...... Australian String Teachers' Association
AUSTA...... Australian Studies Association
AUSTACCS ... Australian Tactical Command and Control System   (PDAA)
AUSTAT ... Australian Society of Teachers, Alexander Technique
AUSTCARE ... Australians Care for Refugees   (ADA)
AUSTCIVPOL ... Australian Civil Police
Aust CollPhys Ed ... Australian College of Physical Education
Aust CollTheol ... Australian College of Theology
Aust CoNo ... Australian Company Number
AustCP ...... Australian Country Party [*Political party*]
AUSTEL ... Australian Telecommunications Authority
AUSTENERGY ... Australian Energy Systems Exporters Group
AUSTEO... Australian Eyes Only [*For*]
AUSTEXT ... Australian Teletext Network
AustIMM .. Australasian Institute of Mining and Metallurgy

AustIntCorps ... Australian Intelligence Corps
AUSTIS..... Australian Timber Industry Stabilization Conference
AUSTL...... Australasia   (BARN)
AUSTL...... Australia
AUSTLIT ... Australian Literary Database
AustMaritime Coll ... Australian Maritime College
AUSTOCK ... Australian Stock Exchanges Share Prices [*Database*]
Aust P .... Australisches Patent [*Australian Patent*] [*German*]   (GCA)
AUSTPAC ... Australian Packet-Switching Network   (PDAA)
AUSTR...... Australia
austr .... Australialainen [*Australia*] [*Finland*]
Austr .... Australien [*Australia*] [*German*]   (GCA)
AUSTRADE ... Australian Trade Commission
Austral...... Australasia [*or Australasian*]   (ADA)
AUSTRAL ... Australia
AUSTRALIS ... Australian Technical, Research, and Library Information Service [*CSIRO*]
AUSTRIATOM ... Osterreichische Interessengemeinschaft fur Nukleartechnik [*Austrian Nuclear Industry Group*]   (PDAA)
AUSTROADS ... National Association of Australian Road Authorities
AUSTROP ... Australian Tropical Research Foundation
AUSTSIA ... Australasia   (ADA)
AUSTSN..... Australasian   (ADA)
Austswim ... Australian Council for the Teaching of Swimming and Water Safety
AUSVETPLAN ... Australian Veterinary Emergency Plan
AUSVN ..... Armadni Umelecky Soubor Vita Nejedleho [*Vit Nejedly Armed Forces Artistic Ensemble*]   (CZ)
Ausw .... Auswaertiges [*Nonresident*] [*German*]
Ausw .... Auswage [*Quantity Weighed Out*] [*German*]   (GCA)
Ausw .... Auswahl [*Selection*] [*German*]
Auswasch... Auswaschung [*Erosion*] [*German*]
Auswirk...... Auswirkung [*Effect*] [*German*]   (GCA)
Ausz .... Auszug [*Excerpt*] [*German*]   (GCA)
AUT .... Association of Ukrainians in Tasmania [*Australia*]
AUT .... Austral Lineas Aereas [*Argentina*] [*ICAO designator*]   (FAAC)
AUT .... Austria [*ANSI three-letter standard code*]   (CNC)
aut .... Auteur [*Author*] [*Publishing*] [*French*]
aut .... Autografo [*Autograph*] [*Publishing*] [*Italian*]
aut .... Autographe [*Autograph*] [*Publishing*] [*French*]
AUT .... Automatic Fuze Setter [*Artillery*]   (RU)
aut .... Automatika [*or Automatikus*] [*Automatic or Automation*]   (HU)
aut .... Automatyczny [*Automatic*] [*Poland*]
Aut .... Autore [*Author*] [*Italian*]
aut .... Autorisiert [*Authorized*] [*German*]
aut .... Autour [*Authorized*] [*Publishing*] [*French*]
AUTB .... Ankara Universitesi Talebe Birligi [*Ankara University Student Union*]   (TU)
AUTE .... Agrupacion de Funcionarios de la Administracion General de las Usinas Electricas y los Telefonos del Estado [*Union of UTE (General Administration of State Electric Power and Telephones) Workers*] [*Uruguay*]   (LA)
AUTEB...... Asociacion de Universitarios de la Universidad Tecnologica de Boyaca [*Tunja*]   (COL)
AUTECO .. Autotecnica Colombiana Ltda. [*Colombia*]   (COL)
AUTEVO .. Automatisierung der Technologischen Produktionsvorbereitung [*Automation of Technological Product Preparation*] [*German*]   (ADPT)
auth .... Authorized   (EECI)
authent....... Authentisch [*Authentic*] [*German*]   (GCA)
AUTIMPEX ... China National Automotive Industry Import/Export Corporation [*China*]   (IMH)
auto .... Autoilu [*Motoring*] [*Finland*]
AUTOCALDAS ... Automotores de Caldas Ltda. [*Manizales*]   (COL)
AUTOCOL ... Automotora Colombiana Ltda. [*Colombia*]   (COL)
AUTOFEM ... Autofelszereles es Femtomegcikk KSz [*Small Cooperative for Automobile Accessories and Mass-Produced Metal Articles*]   (HU)
autog .... Autographe [*Autograph*] [*Publishing*] [*French*]
autogr .... Autografo [*Autograph*] [*Publishing*] [*Italian*]
Autogr .... Autograph [*Autograph*] [*Publishing*] [*German*]
autogr .... Autographe [*Autograph*] [*Publishing*] [*French*]
AUTOIMPORT ... Empresa Central de Abastecimiento y Venta de Equipos de Transporte Ligero [*Central Enterprise for Supply and Sales of Light Automotive Equipment*] [*Cuba*]   (LA)
AUTOKER ... Auto- es Alkatreszkereskedelmi Vallalat [*Auto and Spare Parts Trade Enterprise*]   (HU)
Autoklavier ... Autoklavierung [*Autoclave Treatment*] [*German*]   (GCA)
Autoko .... Automatische Korpsstamunetz [*Tactical Communications System*] [*Germany*]
autokozl...... Autokozlekedesi [*Automobile Transport (adjective)*]   (HU)
Autokut...... Autoipari Kutato Intezet [*Automotive Industry Research Institute*] [*Budapest, Hungary*] [*Research center*]   (ERC)
autom .... Automatisch [*Automatic*] [*German*]
AUTOMAGDA ... Automotora del Magdalena Ltda. [*Santa Marta*]   (COL)

AUTOMAN ... European Automated Manufacturing Exhibition and Conference [*British Robot Association*]
AUTOMASIA ... South East Asian International Automated Manufacturing Technology and Robotics Show and Conference
AUTONAL ... Automotora Nacional SA [*Colombia*]   (COL)
AUTOPACIFICO ... Automotriz del Pacifico Ltda. [*Colombia*]   (COL)
AUTOPREVOZ ... Preduzece za Automobilski Prevoz Robe i Putnika [*Establishment for Motor Transport of Goods and Passengers*]   (YU)
autor .... Autorise [*Authorized*] [*Publishing*] [*French*]
autor .... Autorisiert [*Authorized*] [*Publishing*] [*German*]
autoris .... Autorisiert [*Authorized*] [*Publishing*] [*German*]
AUTOSRBIJA ... Serbian Motor Vehicles Establishment [*Belgrade*]   (YU)
Autotrans ... Auto Transport [*Rijeka*]   (YU)
AUTOTURIST ... Pretprijatie za Turisticki Saobrakaj [*Establishment for Tourist Traffic*] [*Skopje*]   (YU)
AUTOVILL ... Autovillamossagi Felszerelesek Gyara [*Automotive Electrical Equipment Factory*]   (HU)
Autoxydat .. Autoxydation [*Autoxidation*] [*German*]   (GCA)
AUT(S) ...... Association of University Teachers (Scotland)   (SLS)
AUU .... Aurukun Mission [*Australia*] [*Airport symbol*]   (OAG)
AUUG .... Australian Unix Users Group
AUV .... Automatic Fuze Setter [*Artillery*]   (RU)
AUVIS ...... Authorised Unregistered Vehicle Inspection Station [*Australia*]
AUVPS ...... Army Directorate of Military Field Construction   (RU)
AuWWA .... Australian Water and Wastewater Association
AUX .... Araguaina [*Brazil*] [*Airport symbol*]   (OAG)
aux .... Auxiliaire [*Auxiliary*] [*Knitting*] [*French*]
aux .... Auxiliar [*Portuguese*]
aux .... Auxiliary   (TPFD)
AUXERAP ... Societe Auxiliaire de la Regie du Petrole   (MENA)
AUXI-ATOME ... Societe Auxiliaire pour l'Energie Atomique [*Nuclear energy*] [*French*]   (NRCH)
AUXIMAD ... Societe Auxiliaire Maritime de Madagascar
AUXINI ..... Empresa Ausiliar de la Industria [*Spain*]   (PDAA)
AUXITRANS ... Societe Auxiliaire Transafric
auxo .... Auxilio [*Portuguese*]
AUY .... Aerolinas Uruguayas SA [*Uruguay*] [*ICAO designator*]   (FAAC)
AUY .... Aneityum [*Vanuata*] [*Airport symbol*]   (OAG)
AUZ .... Aliance Unitarskych Zen [*Alliance of Unitarian Women*]   (CZ)
AUZ .... Aus-Air [*Australia*] [*ICAO designator*]   (FAAC)
AUZ .... Automatic Recording Control   (RU)
AV .... Advance Victoria [*Australia*]
AV .... Aerial Bomb Fuze   (RU)
AV .... Aircraft Armament [*Aircraft maintenance*]   (RU)
AV .... Aircraft Carrier   (RU)
AV .... Akcni Vybor [*Action Committee*]   (CZ)
av .... Aknaveto [*Trench Mortar, Mine Thrower*]   (HU)
AV .... Algemeene Voorschriften [*Benelux*]   (BAS)
AV .... Algemene (Administratieve) Voorwaarden [*Benelux*]   (BAS)
AV .... Algemene Vergadering van Aandeelhouders [*Benelux*]   (BAS)
AV .... Allami Vallalat [*State Enterprise*]   (HU)
AV .... Allgemeiner Verkaufspreis [*General Sales Price*] [*German*]   (EG)
AV .... Allgemeine Verwaltungsvorschrift [*or Vorschrift*] [*General Administrative Regulation*] [*German*]   (ILCA)
AV .... Alta Voltagem [*Portuguese*]
av .... Ampere-Turn   (RU)
AV .... Antarctic Air   (RU)
AV .... Antennenverstaerker [*Antenna Booster*] [*German*]   (EG)
av .... Apsolutna Visina [*Absolute Altitude*] [*Aviation*]   (YU)
AV .... Arbeitsvorbereitung [*Work Preparation*] [*German*]   (ADPT)
AV .... Arctic Air   (RU)
AV .... Arrete Viziriel [*Morocco*]   (FLAF)
AV .... Ascension Verse [*Astronomy*] [*French*]
AV .... Aseguradora del Valle SA [*Colombia*]   (COL)
AV .... Attenuation Equalizer   (RU)
AV .... Auslandsvertretung [*Foreign Representation*] [*German*]   (EG)
av .... Autovasar [*Auto Fair*]   (HU)
AV .... Avant [*Front*] [*Military*] [*French*]   (MTD)
av .... Avec [*With*] [*French*]   (GPO)
AV .... Avellino [*Car registration plates*] [*Italian*]
Av .... Avenida [*Avenue*] [*Spanish*]
av .... Avenida [*Avenue*] [*Portuguese*]   (CED)
av .... Avenue [*Avenue*] [*French*]   (CED)
Av .... Avesta [*Language, etc.*]
av .... Aviacao [*Aviation*] [*Portuguese*]
av .... Aviador [*Aviator*] [*Portuguese*]
av .... Aviation   (BU)
AV .... Avion Liviano [*Light Aircraft*] [*Chile*]
a/v .... A Vista [*At Sight*] [*Spanish*]
Av .... Avocat [*French*]   (FLAF)
AV .... Avoir [*Credit*] [*French*]
av .... Avril [*April*] [*French*]
AV .... Avtomat Kalashnikov [*Kalashnikov automatic*] [*Soviet assault rifle*]
a/v .... A Vue [*At Sight*] [*French*]

Av .... Avukat [*Attorney*]   (TU)
AV .... Bus Terminal   (RU)
AV .... Emergency Switch   (RU)
AV .... Hawker Siddeley Aviation Ltd. [*British*] [*ICAO aircraft manufacturer identifier*]   (ICAO)
AV .... Oesterreichischer Astronomischer Verein [*Austria*]   (SLS)
AV .... Propeller [*Aviation*]   (RU)
av .... Wave Amplitude   (RU)
AVA .... Aerodynamische Versuchsanstalt [*Aerodynamic Research Institute*]   (EG)
AVA .... Aerovais del Valle [*Costa Rica*]   (PDAA)
AVA .... African Voice Association
AVA .... Agence de Voyage Algerienne
AVA .... Agence Voltaique d'Assurances
ava .... Algemene Vergadering van Aandeelhouders [*Benelux*]   (BAS)
AVA .... Andre, Vidal & Associes
AVA .... Arbeitsgemeinschaft zur Verbesserung der Agrarstruktur in Hessen   (SLS)
AVA .... ASEAN [*Association of South East Asian Nations*] Valuers Association [*Kuala Lumpur, Malaysia*]   (EAIO)
AVA .... Asociacion Vitivinicola Argentina [*Argentina*]   (LAA)
AVA .... Auctioneers and Valuers Association of Australia
AVA .... Auftrags-Vergabe-Abrechnung [*German*]   (ADPT)
AVA .... Aurora Vivar Association [*Peru*]   (EAIO)
AVA .... Australian Veterinary Association   (ADA)
AVA .... Australian Volleyball Association
AVA .... Australian Volunteers Abroad   (ADA)
AVA .... Avianca, Aerovias Nacionales de Colombia SA [*ICAO designator*]   (FAAC)
AVAA .... African Violet Association of Australia
AVAA .... Auctioneers and Valuers Association of Australia
AVAD .... Australian Veterans' Affairs Department [*Central Library*] [*National Union Catalogue of Australia symbol*]
AVADSC ... Australian Veterans and Defense Services Council [*Also, AVDSC*]
AVAE .... Association for Voluntary Action in Europe [*See also AVE*]   (EAIO)
AVAOSB ... Australian Volunteers Abroad: Overseas Service Bureau Program   (EAIO)
AVARD ..... Association of Voluntary Agencies for Rural Development [*India*]   (PDAA)
Avas .... Afwezigheid van Alle Schuld [*Benelux*]   (BAS)
AVASA ...... Audiovisual Association of Southern Africa   (AA)
AVAWA .... Auctioneers and Valuers' Association of Western Australia
AVB .... Air Base   (RU)
AVB .... Allgemeine Versicherungsbedingungen [*General conditions of insurance*] [*German*]   (ILCA)
AVB .... Armiska Veterinarska Bolnica [*Army Veterinary Hospital*]   (YU)
AVB .... Autorite pour l'Amenagement de la Vallee du Bandama [*Bandama Valley Development Authority*] [*Ivory Coast*]   (AF)
AVB .... Truck-Mounted Drill Rig   (RU)
AVBA .... Australian/Victorian Biathlon Association
AVBC .... Australia Vietnam Business Council
avbildn ...... Avbildning [*Illustration*] [*Danish/Norwegian*]
avbildn ...... Avbildning [*Illustration*] [*Sweden*]
AVBLN ..... Asociacion de Vendedores de Billetes de la Loteria Nacional [*Association of National Lottery Ticket Sellers*] [*El Salvador*]   (LA)
AVC .... Aeronautica Venezolana, CA [*Venezuela*] [*ICAO designator*]   (FAAC)
AVC .... Agricultural and Veterinary Chemical
AVC .... Algemene Vervoerconditties [*Benelux*]   (BAS)
AVC .... Asociacion Venezolana de Cafecultores [*Venezuelan Coffee Growers Association*]   (LA)
AVC .... Australian Vocational Certificate
Av C .... Avanti Cristo [*Before Christ*] [*Italian*]
AVCA .... Agricultural and Veterinary Chemicals Association of Australia
AVCA .... Australian Video Copyright Association
AVCA .... Australian Volunteer Coastguard Association   (ADA)
AVCAA .... Agricultural and Veterinary Chemicals Association of Australia
AVCASA ... Agricultural and Veterinary Chemicals Association of South Africa   (EAIO)
AVCAT ..... Aviation Carrier Turbine Fuel
AVCAT ..... Aviation Fuel, High-Flash Point [*NATO*]
AVCC .... Australian Vice-Chancellors' Committee   (ADA)
Av C d'Et ... Avis du Conseil d'Etat [*France*]   (FLAF)
Avce .... Avance [*Advance*] [*French*]
AVCGA ..... Australian Volunteer Coast Guard Association   (ADA)
AVCGC ..... Asociacion Venezolana de Criadores de Ganado Cebu [*Venezuela*]   (DSCA)
AVCM .... Associate of the Victorian College of Music [*Australia*]
AVCS .... Australian Visual Copyright Society
AVCU .... Agricultural and Veterinary Chemicals Unit
AVD .... Air Vendee [*France*] [*ICAO designator*]   (FAAC)
AvD .... Automobilclub von Deutschland [*Germany*]   (EAIO)

avd............ Avdeling [*Part, Section*] [*Publishing Danish/Norwegian*]
avd............ Avdelning [*Part, Section*] [*Publishing*] [*Sweden*]
avd............ Avdode [*Deceased*] [*Norway*]   (GPO)
AVDA........ Asociacion Veinticinquena de Apicultores [*Argentina*]   (DSCA)
AVDA........ Asociacion Venezolana de Derecho Agrario [*Venezuela*]   (DSCA)
Avda.......... Avenida [*Avenue*] [*Spanish*]
av-dern....... Avant-Dernier [*French*]   (FLAF)
Av-Dev...... Aviation Developments [*Australia*]
Avdp.......... Avoirdupois [*Weight*] [*French*]
AVDSC...... Australian Veterans and Defence Services Council [*Also, AVADSC*]
av dt........... Avec Droit [*French*]
AVE........... Aceites Vegetales Ecuatorianos [*Ecuador*]   (DSCA)
AVE........... Asociacion de Vivienda Economica [*Argentina*]   (EAIO)
AVE........... Asociacion Venezolana de Exportadores [*Venezuelan Exporters Association*]   (LA)
AVE........... Asocio de Verduloj Esperantistaj [*Association of Esperantist Greens*] [*Belgium*]   (EAIO)
AVE........... Association pour le Volontariat a l'Acte Gratuit en Europe [*Association for Voluntary Action in Europe - AVAE*]   (EAIO)
Ave............ Avenida [*Avenue*] [*Spanish*]
Ave............ Avenija [*Avenue*] [*Commonwealth of Independent States*]   (EECI)
AVE........... Avensa Aerovias Venezolanas SA [*Venezuela*] [*ICAO designator*]   (FAAC)
Ave............ Avenue [*Avenue*] [*French*]
AVEC......... Asociacion Venezolana de Educadores Catolicos [*Venezuelan Association of Catholic Educators*]   (LA)
AVEC......... Association of Poultry Processors and Poultry Import- and Export-Trade in the EEC Countries   (EAIO)
AVECI....... Asociacion Venezolana de Cooperacion Intermunicipal [*Venezuelan Association for Intermunicipal Cooperation*]   (LA)
AVEFAM.. Asociacion Venezolana de Facultades de Medicina [*Venezuela*]   (SLS)
AVEGUIVOL ... Asociacion Venezolana de Guias Voluntarios [*Venezuela*]   (DSCA)
AVEMECA ... Asociacion Venezolana de Medicos Catolicos [*Venezuelan Association of Catholic Physicians*]   (LA)
AVENCULTA ... Asociacion Venezolana de Cultivadores de Tabaco [*Venezuelan Tobacco Growers Association*]   (LA)
AVENEXCAF ... Asociacion Venezolana de Exportadores de Cafe [*Venezuela*]   (DSCA)
AVENSA... Aerovias Venezolanas Sociedad Anonima [*Airline*] [*Venezuela*]
AVERE...... Association Europeenne des Vehicules Electriques Routiers [*European Electric Road Vehicle Association*]   (EAIO)
AVES......... Australian Voluntary Euthanasia Society   (ADA)
AVESCA ... Aerovias Especiales de Carga Ltda. [*Colombia*] [*ICAO designator*]   (FAAC)
AVEX........ Asociacion Venezolana de Exportacion [*Venezuelan Export Association*]   (LA)
AVF........... Afrikaner Volkfront [*An association*]
AVF........... Arabskii Valiutn Fond
AVF........... Australian Volleyball Federation
AVF........... Austrian Volleyball Federation   (EAIO)
AVF........... Autovillamossagi Felszerelesek Gyara [*Automotive Electrical Equipment Factory*]   (HU)
avg............ Algemeenheid van Goederen [*Benelux*]   (BAS)
AVG.......... Angestelltenversicherungsgesetz [*Unemployment Insurance*] [*German*]
AVG.......... Asociacion Venezolana de Ganaderos [*Venezuela*]   (DSCA)
avg............ August   (BU)
Av G......... Avant Garde [*Vanguard*] [*Military*] [*French*]   (MTD)
AVG.......... Avialgarve, Taxis Aereos do Algarve Ltd. [*Portugal*] [*ICAO designator*]   (FAAC)
AVGC....... Association of Victorian Greyhound Clubs [*Australia*]
Av Gen...... Avocat General [*District Attorney*] [*French*]   (ILCA)
AVGF....... Australian Vegetable Growers' Federation
AVGMP.... Asociacion Venezolana de Geologia, Minas, y Petroleo [*Venezuela*]   (DSCA)
AVH.......... Alexander von Humboldt-Stiftung [*Alexander von Humboldt Foundation*] [*Germany*]   (PDAA)
AVH.......... Allamvedelmi Hatosag [*State Security Authority (of the Ministry of Interior)*]   (HU)
AVH.......... Allamvedelmi Hivatal [*Hungarian secret police*]
avh............ Avhandling [*Dissertation, Thesis*] [*Sweden*]
AVH.......... Aviser SA [*Spain*] [*ICAO designator*]   (FAAC)
AVHOLD ... Anglovaal Holdings [*South Africa*]
AVHU....... Archiv Vojenskeho Historickeho Ustavu [*Archives of the Military Institute of History*]   (CZ)
AVI........... Accion Venezolana Independiente [*Independent Venezuelan Action*]   (LA)
AVI........... Anglovaal Industries Ltd. [*South Africa*]
AVI........... Arhiv Vojnoistoriskog Instituta [*Archives of the Institute of Military History*]   (YU)

AVI........... Asociacion Venezolana de Inversionistas [*Venezuelan Association of Investors*]   (LA)
AVI........... Association of Veterinarians of Indonesia [*Indonesia*]   (DSCA)
AVI........... Association Universelle d'Aviculture Scientifique [*World's Poultry Science Association - WPSA*]   (EAIO)
AVI........... Audio-Visual Institute of Australia   (ADA)
AVI........... Australian Veterinarians in Industry
AVI........... Aviorrenta SA [*Mexico*] [*ICAO designator*]   (FAAC)
AVIA........ Adult Video Industry Association of Australia
AVIA........ Australian Videotex Industry Association
AVIACO... Aviacion y Comercio SA [*Aviation and Trade Corporation*] [*Airline*] [*Spain*]
Aviadarm ... Field Directorate of Aviation and Aeronautics of Fighting Forces [*1919-1921*]   (RU)
aviadiviziya ... Air Division   (RU)
AVIAIMPORT ... Empresa Cubana Importadora de Aviacion [*Cuban Enterprise for Aircraft Import*]   (LA)
Aviakhim... Obshchestvo Sodeystviya Aviatsyonnokhimicheskomu Stroitelstvu v SSSR [*Society for Assistance to the Aviation and Chemical Construction of the USSR*] [*1925-1927*]   (RU)
Aviamashtekhsnab ... Moscow Technical Supply Office of the Glavsnab of the Ministry of the Aircraft Industry, USSR   (RU)
aviamet....... Air Weather Station   (RU)
AVIANCA ... Aerovias Nacionales de Colombia [*Colombian National Airways*]
aviap.......... Air Park, Aircraft Park   (RU)
aviapochta ... Air Mail   (RU)
aviapribor... Aircraft Instrument   (RU)
aviaprom... Aircraft Industry   (RU)
AVIASAN ... Aviatia Sanitara [*Health Aviation Service*]   (RO)
AVIASNAB ... All-Union Office for Aviation Supply (of the Narkomtyazhprom)   (RU)
AVIATECA ... Empresa Guatemalteca de Aviacion [*Airline*] [*Guatemala*]
aviats.......... Aviation   (BU)
Aviavnito.... All-Union Aviation Scientific, Engineering, and Technical Society [*1932-1941*]   (RU)
aviazent...... Aviation Canvas   (RU)
AVIC......... Aviation Industries of China   (ECON)
AVID......... Agriculture Victoria-Library Catalogue [*Victoria Department of Agriculture and Rural Affairs*] [*Australia*] [*Information service or system*]   (IID)
AVIEAS.... Asociacion Venezolana de Instituciones de Educacion Agricola Superior [*Venezuela*]   (DSCA)
AVIEM...... Asociacion Venezolana de Ingenieria Electrica y Mecanica [*Venezuela*]   (SLS)
AVIFO....... Administracion de Viveros Forestales [*Venezuela*]   (DSCA)
AVIG......... Autokozlekedesi Vezerigazgatosag [*Directorate of Automotive Transportation*]   (HU)
AVIHA...... Asociacion Veterinaria Internacional de Higiene de la Alimentacion [*Netherlands*]   (DSCA)
AVINOVA ... Avicultores del Norte del Valle Ltda. [*Cartago*]   (COL)
aviomarsh .. Aviators' March   (BU)
AVIP......... Avicola Industrial Piracicaba [*Brazil*]   (DSCA)
AVIPA....... Australian Videotex Information Providers Association
AVIPLA .... Asociacion Venezolana de Industrias Plasticas [*Venezuela*]   (DSCA)
AVIROM .. Asociatia Generala a Crescatorilor de Pasari si Animale Mici din RSR [*General Association of Breeders of Fowl and Small Animals in the Socialist Republic of Romania*]   (RO)
AVIRT....... Allami Villamosmuvek Reszvenytarsasag [*State Electricity Works Limited*]   (HU)
AVIS......... Associazione Volontari Italiani del Sangue [*Association of Voluntary Italian Blood Donors*]
AVISA...... Asociacion Venezolana de Ingenieria Sanitaria y Ambental [*Venezuelan Chapter of the Inter-American Association of Sanitary Engineering*]   (EAIO)
AVISA...... Associazione Vernici, Inchiostri, Sigillanti, e Adesivi [*Italy*]
AVISCO.... Avicultura Industria e Comercio [*Brazil*]   (DSCA)
AVIVALLE ... Avicultores del Valle Ltda. [*Colombia*]   (COL)
AVJ........... Aeroviajes Ejecuitvos SA de CV [*Mexico*] [*ICAO designator*]   (FAAC)
av J-C......... Avant Jesus-Christ [*Before Jesus Christ*] [*French*]
AVK.......... Arhiv Visokog Komesarijata [*Archives of the High Commissariat*]   (YU)
AVK.......... Automatic High-Frequency Concentration Meter   (RU)
AVK.......... Automatic Volume Control   (RU)
AVk.......... Continental Arctic Air   (RU)
AVK.......... Output Switching Devices   (RU)
AVKh......... Arkhigeion Vasilikis Khorofylakis [*Royal Gendarmerie Headquarters*] [*Greek*]   (GC)
avkl........... Avklippet [*Clipped Off*] [*Publishing Danish/Norwegian*]
AVL.......... Aerovial [*Chile*] [*ICAO designator*]   (FAAC)
AVL.......... Army Veterinary Hospital   (RU)
AVL.......... Small Aircraft Carrier   (RU)
AVLC........ Aesthetics and Visual Literacy Council [*Australia*]

AVLS........ Automatisches Verkehrserfassungs-und Lenkungssystem [*Automatic Traffic Registration and Guidance System*] [*German*] (ADPT)

AVLW .... Association of Vatican Lay Workers   (EAIO)

AVM.......... Analog Computer   (RU)

AVM.......... Aqualung   (RU)

AVM.......... Atelier de Vitrification de Marcoule [*France*]   (PDAA)

AVM.......... Audio-Visuele Media

AVM.......... Automatic Computer   (RU)

AVM.......... Aviacion Ejecutiva Mexicana SA [*Mexico*] [*ICAO designator*] (FAAC)

AVm.......... Maritime Arctic Air   (RU)

AV-MF...... Aviatsiya Voennomorskovo Flota [*Naval Air Force*] [*Russian*] (PDAA)

AVMF .... Naval Aviation   (RU)

AVMS....... Naval Aviation [*USSR designation*]

AVN........... Air Vanuatu [*ICAO designator*]   (FAAC)

AVN.......... Avignon [*France*] [*Airport symbol*]   (OAG)

AVN.......... High-Voltage Equipment   (RU)

AVNA....... Australian Visiting Nurses Association   (ADA)

AVNF .... Akcni Vybor Narodni Fronty [*Action Committee of the National Front*]   (CZ)

AVNII....... Arkhangel'sk Scientific Research Institute of Algae   (RU)

AVNK....... Aviation Nationale Khmere [*Cambodian National Air Force*] [*AVRK*] [*Formerly,*]   (CL)

AVNOJ ..... Antifasisticko Vece Narodnog Oslobodenja [*Anti-Fascist Council of National Liberation of Yugoslavia*]   (YU)

AVNOYu... Anti-Fascist Popular Assembly of People's Liberation of Yugoslavia [*1942-1945*]   (RU)

AVO.......... Aerovias Oaxaquenas SA [*Mexico*] [*ICAO designator*]   (FAAC)

a-vo........... Agency   (RU)

AVO.......... Air Detachment   (RU)

AVO.......... Australian Valuations Office

AVO.......... (Magyar Allamrendorseg) Allamvedelmi Osztalya [*State Security Department (of the Hungarian State Police)*]   (HU)

avometr .... Multimeter   (RU)

avost........ Alarm Stop, Emergency Stop   (RU)

AVOZVOTS ... Average Australian Voters

AVP .... Agence Voltaique de Presse

AvP .... Air Park, Aircraft Park   (RU)

AVP .... Aktionsgemeinschaft Vierte Partei [*Fourth Party Action Group*] [*Germany*] [*Political party*]   (PPW)

AVP .... Allgemeiner Verkaufspreis [*General Sales Price*]   (EG)

AVP .... Apparatus for Rotating Test Tubes   (RU)

AVP .... Arubaanse Volks Partij [*Aruban People's Party*] [*Netherlands Antilles*] [*Political party*]   (PPW)

AVP .... Asociacion Venezolana de Periodistas [*Venezuelan Journalists Association*]   (LA)

AVP .... Automatic Pilot, Autopilot, Gyropilot   (RU)

Av P .... Avant-Poste [*Outpost*] [*French*]   (MTD)

AVP .... Aviation Enterprises [*Denmark*] [*ICAO designator*]   (FAAC)

avp............. Aviation Park   (BU)

AVP .... Avoirdupois   (ADA)

AVP .... Foreign Policy Archives (of Russia)   (RU)

AVPA .... Asociacion Venezolana de Peritos Agropecuarios [*Venezuela*]   (DSCA)

AVPA .... Australian Veterinary Poultry Association

AVPC........ Asociacion Venezolana de Productores de Cacao [*Venezuela*]   (DSCA)

AVPC........ Asociacion Venezolana de Productores de Cementos [*Venezuelan Association of Cement Producers*]   (LA)

AVPES ...... Asociacion de Vendedores Profesionales de El Salvador [*Association of Salvadoran Professional Salesmen*]   (LA)

AVPP........ Very Peculiar Practice [*A*] [*BBC television program*]

AVPR........ Foreign Policy Archives of Russia   (RU)

AVPS........ Asociatia Vinatorilor si Pescarilor Sportivi [*Association of Sport Hunters and Fishermen*]   (RO)

avr .... Air Reserve   (RU)

AVR .... Arbeitsgemeinschaft Versuchsreaktor [*Test Reactor Working Group*] [*Germany*]   (EG)

AVR .... Arteriovenous Difference   (RU)

AVR .... Automatic Reserve Switching   (RU)

AVR .... Automatische Verstaerkungsregelung [*Automatic Reinforcement Control*] [*German*]   (ADPT)

avr .... Aviation Repair Shop   (BU)

AVR .... Avior Pty Ltd. [*Australia*] [*ICAO designator*]   (FAAC)

AVRAC...... Agricultural and Veterinary Research Advisory Committee

AVRB .... Australian Veteran's Review Board [*National Union Catalogue of Australia symbol*]

AVRDC ..... Asian Vegetable Research and Development Center   (EA)

AVRI......... Association of Video Recording Importers [*Indonesia*]

AVRK .... Aviation Royale Khmere [*Royal Cambodian Air Force*] [*AVNK*] [*Later,*]   (CL)

AVRL........ Automatic Reserve Line Switching   (RU)

AVRN .... Automatic Reserve Pump Switching   (RU)

AVRO .... Algemeen Vereniging Radio Omroep [*General Broadcasting Association*] [*Netherlands*]   (WEN)

AVRT .... Automatic Reserve Transformer Switching   (RU)

AVS .... Aboriginal Visitors' Scheme [*Australia*]

AVS .... Aeroklub Vysokoskolskeho Studentstva [*Aero Club of University Students*]   (CZ)

AVS .... Algemene Vereniging van Schoolleiders bij het Voortgezet Onderwijs [*General Association of Secondary Heads and Deputy-Heads*] [*Netherlands*]   (EAIO)

AVS .... Anotati Viomikhaniki Skholi [*Supreme Industrial School*] [*Piraeus*]   (GC)

AVS .... Anotera Viomikhaniki Skholi [*Superior Industrial School (Followed by name)*]   (GC)

AVS .... Army Clothing and Equipment Depot   (RU)

avs .... Army Veterinary Depot   (RU)

AVS .... Atomic Hydrogen Welding   (RU)

AVS .... Australian Vegetarian Society

AVS .... Australia-Vietnam Society

AVS .... Aviation Seychelles Ltd. [*ICAO designator*]   (FAAC)

AVS .... Nitrogen-Hydrogen Mixture   (RU)

AVS .... Recording Aneroid Altimeter   (RU)

AVS .... Simonov Automatic Rifle   (RU)

AVSA .... African Violet Society of Australia

AVSA .... Afrikatalevereniging van Suider-Afrika [*South Africa*]   (AA)

AVSA .... Aptekersvereniging van Suid-Afrika [*South Africa*]   (AA)

AVSA .... Australian Victorian Studies Association

AVSAP...... Asociatia Voluntara pentru Sprijinirea Apararii Patriei [*Voluntary Association to Support the Defense of the Fatherland*]   (RO)

AVSEC ...... Aviation Security Panel [*ICAO*]   (DA)

AVSECOM ... Aviation Security Command [*Philippines*]

AVSh .... Attack Aircraft Fuze   (RU)

avsh .... Flying School   (BU)

AVSM....... Austrian Variant of the Scandinavian Model

AVSSA ...... Association for Voluntary Sterilization of South Africa   (AA)

avstr .... Austrian   (RU)

avstral .... Australian   (RU)

avt............... Air Force Unit Train   (BU)

AVT .... Analog Computer Engineering   (RU)

AVT .... Atmospheric-Vacuum Pipe Still   (RU)

avt............... Author   (RU)

avt............... Automobile   (RU)

avt............... Automobile Plant [*Topography*]   (RU)

avt............... Automobilism   (RU)

avt............... Autonomous   (RU)

AVT .... Large Aircraft Carrier   (RU)

AVTAG ..... Aviation Fuel [*Gasoline/Kerosene*] [*NATO*]

avtb .... Motor Transport Battalion   (BU)

avtb .... Motor Transport Battalion, Truck Battalion   (RU)

avtbr........... Motor Transport Brigade   (BU)

avt l........... Author's Sheet [*40,000 printed characters*]   (RU)

avtob.......... Autobiographical, Autobiography   (RU)

avtob.......... Motor Transport Battalion   (RU)

avtobat ...... Motor Transport Battalion, Truck Battalion   (RU)

avtobaza .... Motor Pool   (RU)

avtobiogr.... Autobiographical, Autobiography   (RU)

avtobiogr.... Autobiography   (BU)

avt obl........ Autonomous Oblast   (RU)

avtochasti... Motor Vehicle Parts   (BU)

avtodispetcher ... Automatic Supervisor, Automation Dispatcher   (RU)

Avtodor ...... Society for Furthering the Development of Automobilism and Road Improvement [*1927-1935*]   (RU)

avtogara ..... Motor Vehicle Station   (BU)

avtogr......... Autograph   (BU)

AVTOMAKEDONIJA ... Macedonian Motor Vehicle Establishment [*Skopje*]   (YU)

Avtomatprom ... Rustavi Planning and Design Institute for the Automation of Production Processes   (RU)

avtomob...... Automobile   (RU)

avtopark..... Vehicular Depot [*for a motor vehicle fleet*]   (BU)

AVTOPROMET ... Avtoprevoznisko Podjetje [*Motor transport establishment*]   (YU)

avtoref........ Author's Abstract   (RU)

avtoriz .... Authorized   (BU)

avtostantsiya ... Automobile Station   (BU)

AVTOTEK ... Automobile Transportation and Forwarding Office   (RU)

avtotek....... Motor Vehicle Transport and Forwarding Office   (BU)

avtotrakt .... Automobile and Tractor   (RU)

Avtotransizdat ... Scientific and Technical Publishing House of Automobile Transportation Literature   (RU)

Avtovneshtrans ... All-Union Office for Automobile Transportation of Export and Import Freight of the Ministry of Foreign Trade, USSR   (RU)

avtozavod ... Automobile Plant   (BU)

avtp .... Motor Transport Regiment   (BU)

avtp .... Motor Transport Regiment, Truck Regiment   (RU)

AVTR .... Motor Transport [*Military term*]   (RU)
avtr .... Motor Transport Company   (BU)
avtrb .... Motor Transport Battalion   (BU)
AVTS .... Allocation aux Vieux Travailleurs Salaries [*Algeria*]
AVTS .... Australian Vocational Training System
avt-sost .... Author-Compiler   (RU)
avt svid ...... Author's Certificate   (RU)
avtur .... Automatic Level Controller   (RU)
AVU .... Akademie Vytvarnych Umeni [*Academy of Creative Arts*]   (CZ)
AVU .... Analog Computer   (RU)
AVU .... Avia Sud [*France*] [*ICAO designator*]   (FAAC)
AVU .... Avu Avu [*Solomon Islands*] [*Airport symbol*]   (OAG)
Avue .... Avenue [*Avenue*] [*Military map abbreviation World War I*] [*French*]   (MTD)
AVUP .... Association for Vegetables under Protection [*South Africa*]   (AA)
Avv .... Algemeen-Verbindendverklaring [*Benelux*]   (BAS)
avv .... Avverbio [*Adverb*] [*Italian*]
AVV .... Avvocato [*Solicitor*] [*Italian*]   (EY)
AVV-C .... Algemeen Verbond van Vrije Vakverenigingen-Curacao [*National Confederation of Curacao Trade Unions*] [*Netherlands Antilles*]   (EY)
AVVG .... Ausfuehrungsvorschriften zum Viehseuchengesetz [*Implementing Regulations to the Animal Diseases Law*] [*German*]   (EG)
AVVIT .... Affiliasie van Verenigings Verteenwoordigend van Ingenieurswesetegnici [*South Africa*]   (AA)
AVVS .... Algemeen Verbond van Vakverenigingen in Surinam "De Moederbond" [*Surinam*]
AVW .... Aviator SA [*Greece*] [*ICAO designator*]   (FAAC)
AVWA .... Auctioneers and Valuers of Western Australia [*An association*]
AVWVT ..... Australian Vietnam War Veterans' Trust
AVWWA ... Australian Vietnam Women's Welfare Association
AVX .... Avcon AG [*Switzerland*] [*ICAO designator*]   (FAAC)
avx ar .... Avxon Arithmos [*Serial Number*]   (GC)
AVYP .... Apothiki Vaseos Ylikou Polemou [*Base Ordnance Depot*] [*Greek*]   (GC)
AVZ .... Altay Railroad Car Plant   (RU)
AVZ .... Sound-Reproduction Unit   (RU)
AW .... Aangehaalde Werk [*In the Work Cited*] [*Afrikaans*]
AW .... Addierwerk [*Addition Work*] [*German*]   (ADPT)
AW .... Aeroklub Warszawski [*Warsaw Aeroclub*]   (POL)
aW .... Aeussere Weite [*Outside Diameter*] [*German*]
AW .... Aisin Warner [*Automotive industry supplier*] [*Japan*]
AW .... Aktion Widerstand [*Resistance Action*]   (WEN)
AW .... Ambtenarenwet [*Benelux*]   (BAS)
AW .... Amperewindung [*Ampere Winding*] [*German*]
AW .... Anweisung [*Directive, Instruction*] [*German*]   (EG)
AW .... Arbeidswet [*Benelux*]   (BAS)
AW .... Archiwum Wojewodzkie [*Voivodship Archives*]   (POL)
AW .... [*The*] Artists World Ltd. [*Papua New Guinea*]
AW .... Aruba [*ANSI two-letter standard code*]   (CNC)
AW .... Aussenwirtschaft [*Foreign Economic Relations*] [*German*]   (EG)
AW .... Australian White [*Cattle*]
Aw .... Auteurswet [*Benelux*]   (BAS)
AWA .... African West Air [*Senegal*] [*ICAO designator*]   (FAAC)
AWA .... Albinism World Alliance
AWA .... Amalgamated Wholesalers Association [*Australia*]
AWA .... Amalgamated Wireless (Australasia)   (ADA)
AWA .... Amalgamated Wireless Australasia Ltd. [*Telecommunications service*]
AWA .... Amalgamated Workers' Association [*Australia*]   (ADA)
AWA .... Anglican Women of Australia
AWA .... Anstalt zur Wahrung der Auffuehrungsrechte auf dem Gebiet der Musik [*Institute for Protection of Musical Performance Rights*] [*German*]   (EG)
AWA .... Anstalt zur Wahrung der Autorenrechte [*Literary Copyrights Institute*] [*German*]   (EG)
AWA .... Army Wives Association
AWA .... Australasian Women's Association   (ADA)
AWA .... Australian Waterbird Association
AWA .... Australian Wheelchair Athletes [*An association*]
AWA .... Australian Wide Array of Geomagnetic Stations
AWA .... Australian Windscreen Association
AWAAU ... Australian Women's Amateur Athletic Union   (ADA)
AWACS .... Australian Water and Coastal Studies
AWADI ..... Amalgamated Wireless Australasia Defence Industries Ltd.
AWAFC .... American West African Freight Conference   (AF)
AWAG .... Australian Writers-Authors Group
AWAGS .... Australian Wide Array of Geomagnetic Stations
AWAHF .... Adjustment With a Human Face [*UNICEF phrase to describe African adjustment programs*]
AWAIR ...... Arab World and Islamic Resources and School Services   (EA)
AWALCO ... AWAL Contracting and Trading Co. [*Bahrain*]
AWAM .... Association of West African Merchants
AWAR .... Australian Women Against Rape   (ADA)
AWARD .... Australian Writers and Art Directors Association   (ADA)

AWARE .... Australian Wildlife Ambulance Rescue and Emergency Service
AWAS .... Ansett Worldwide Aviation Services [*Australia*]
AWAS .... Australian Women's Army Service   (ADA)
AWASA .... Australian Women's Army Service Association   (ADA)
AWASM .... Associate of the Western Australian School of Mines   (ADA)
AWAY .... Australia-Wide Adventuring Youth
AWB .... Aboriginal Welfare Board [*New South Wales, Australia*]
AWB .... Adelaide Wool Brokers' Association [*Australia*]
AWB .... Afrikaner Weerstandsbeweging [*Afrikaner Resistance Movement*] [*South Africa*] [*Political party*]   (ECON)
AWB .... Airways International, Inc. [*ICAO designator*]   (FAAC)
AWB .... Australian Wheat Board   (ADA)
AWB .... Australian Wine Board   (ADA)
AWB .... Australian Wool Board [*or Bureau*]   (ADA)
AWBA .... American World's Boxing Association   (BARN)
AWBC ...... Australian Wine and Brandy Corporation
AWBC ...... Australian Women's Bowling Council
AWBC ...... Australian Women's Broadcasting Cooperative   (ADA)
AWBPA .... Australian Wine and Brandy Producers' Association
AWBZ ...... Algemene wet Bijzondere Ziektekosten [*Benelux*]   (BAS)
AWC .... Algemeen Weekblad voor Christendom en Cultuur [*Benelux*]   (BAS)
AWC .... American Women's Club - Argentina   (EAIO)
AWC .... August 13 Working Committee [*Germany*]   (EAIO)
AWC .... Australian Watching Company   (ADA)
AWC .... Australian Whaling Commission   (ADA)
AWC .... Australian Wildlife Club
AWC .... Australian Wool Commission
AWC .... Australian Wool Corporation   (ARC)
AWCC ...... Australian Women's Cricket Council
AWCC ...... Austrian Wandering and Climbing Club   (EAIO)
AWCCQ .... Association of Wall and Ceiling Contractors of Queensland [*Australia*]
AWCCV ..... Association of Wall and Ceiling Contractors of Victoria [*Australia*]
AWCCWA ... Association of Wall and Ceiling Contractors of Western Australia
AWCL .... Australian Women's Chess League   (ADA)
AWD .... Automatischer Waehldienst [*Automatic Selection Service*] [*German*]   (ADPT)
AWD .... Automatische Waehleinrichtung fuer Datenverkehr [*Automatic Selection Equipment for Data Traffic*] [*German*]   (ADPT)
AWDA .... Algemene wet Inzake de Douane en de Accijnzen [*Benelux*]   (BAS)
AWE .... Association for World Education [*Denmark*]   (SLS)
AWE .... Australian Work Ethic Scale
AWE .... Automatische Wiedereinschaltung [*Automatic Reclosing*] [*Electrical*] [*German*]   (EG)
AWE .... Automobil-Werke Eisenach [*Automobile manufacturer*] [*Germany*]
AWE .... Automobilwerk Eisenach (VEB) [*Eisenach Automobile Plant (VEB)*] [*German*]   (EG)
AWEC ...... Albury-Wodonga Environment Center [*Australia*]
AWEC ...... Australian Women's Education Coalition   (ADA)
AWEG ...... Australian Writers and Editors' Guide [*A publication*]
AWEP .... Aboriginal Work Experience Program [*Australia*]
AWES .... Association of West European Shipbuilders [*London, England*]   (EAIO)
AWEUS ..... Association of Women Employees of the University of Sydney [*Australia*]
Awewa .... Armeewetterwarte [*Meteorological Observatory*] [*German*]
AWF .... African Workers Federation [*Kenya*]   (AF)
AWF .... Agriculture Workers Federation [*San Marino*]   (EAIO)
AWF .... Akademia Wychowania Fizycznego [*Academy of Physical Education*]   (POL)
AWF .... Algemeen Werkloosheids Fonds [*Benelux*]   (BAS)
AWF .... Anglican Women's Fellowship [*South Africa*]   (AA)
AWF .... Arab Air Cargo [*Jordan*] [*ICAO designator*]   (FAAC)
AWF .... Ausschuss fuer Wirtschaftliche Fertigung [*Economic Production Board*] GN   (EG)
AWF .... Australian Weightlifting Federation
AWF .... Australian Wheat Forecasters
AWF .... Australian Wheatgrowers' Federation
AWF .... Australian Wildlife Fund
AWF .... Australian Wine Foundation
AWF .... Australian Winemakers' Forum
AWF .... Austrian Water Ski Federation   (EAIO)
AWFA .... Animal Welfare Federation of Australia
AWFA .... Arab Wings Flying Ambulance (Service)
AWFCA ..... Association of Women's Forum Clubs of Australia
AWG .... Agriculture Working Group
AWG .... Airtaxi Wings AG [*Switzerland*] [*ICAO designator*]   (FAAC)
AWG .... Allgemeine Werkzeugmaschinen Gesellschaft [*General Machine-Tool Company*] [*German*]   (EG)
AWG .... Aquaculture Working Group [*EEC*]   (MSC)

AWG......... Arbeiterwohnungsbaugenossenschaft [*Workers' Housing Construction Cooperative*] [*German*] (EG)
AWG......... Aussenwirtschaftsgesetz [*Nature's Law*] [*German*]
AWG......... Australian Writers Guild (ADA)
AWG......... Auswertungs-Programm-Generator [*Analysis Program Generation*] (ADPT)
AWGC...... Australian Woolgrowers' and Graziers' Council (ADA)
Awgie........ Australian Writers' Guild Award (ADA)
AWGP...... American Women's Group in Paris [*France*] (EAIO)
AWH........ Australian Women's Hospital
AWHA...... Australian Women's Hockey Association
AWHA...... Australian Women's Home Army (ADA)
AWHAM... Association of Wives of Heads of African Missions
AWHP...... Archiwum Wojewodzkie Historii Partii [*Voivodship Archives of (Communist) Party History*] (POL)
AWHP...... Australian Wool Harvesting Programme (ADA)
AWI.......... Alfred-Wegener-Institut fuer Polar- und Meeresforschung [*Alfred Wegener Institute for Polar and Marine Research*] [*Germany*] (EAS)
AWI.......... Asian Women's Institute [*Pakistan*] (EAIO)
AWI.......... Australian Welding Institute (ADA)
AWI.......... Australian Wire Industries Proprietary Ltd.
AWI.......... Australia Wide Industries
AWIAV...... Aluminium Window Industry Association of Victoria [*Australia*]
AWIC....... Australian Wool Industry Council
AWIR....... Annual Worldwide Industry Review (IMH)
AWIRS..... Australian Workplace Industrial Relations Survey
AWIS........ Automatisches Wartungs-Informations-system [*Automatic Waiting-Information System*] (ADPT)
AWJF....... Australian Women's Judo Federation (ADA)
AWL......... Anti-War League [*Australia*]
AWL......... Art and Working Life [*Australia*]
AWL......... Auswahllogik [*Selection Logic*] [*German*] (ADPT)
AWLA...... Australian Women's Land Army
AWLC...... Australian Women's Lacrosse Council
AWLSA..... Animal Welfare League of South Australia
AWM........ Askar Wataniah Malaysia [*Malaysian Territorial Army*] (ML)
AWM........ Australian Wallcovering Manufacturers (ADA)
AWM........ Australian War Memorial (ADA)
AWMA...... Australian Waste Management Association
Awmn........ Airwoman
AWMPF.... Australian Wool and Meat Producers' Federation (ADA)
AWMR...... Nepal Association for the Welfare of the Mentally Retarded (EAIO)
AWN......... Air Niger [*ICAO designator*] (FAAC)
AWN......... Alton Downs [*Australia*] [*Airport symbol*] [*Obsolete*] (OAG)
AWNL...... Australian Women's National League (ADA)
AWO......... Angolan Writers Union (EAIO)
AWO......... Arbeiterwohlfahrt Bundesverband [*Germany*] (EAIO)
AWOLDA ... Aboriginal Writers, Oral Literature, and Dramatists Association [*Australia*]
AWOTE .... Average Weekly Ordinary Time Earnings [*Australia*]
AWP......... Akademia Wojskowo-Polityczna [*Academy of Military and Political Sciences*] (POL)
AWP......... Albania Workers' Party [*Political party*]
AWP......... ALCAN [*Aluminum Co. of Canada Ltd.*] World Price [*Obsolete*] (FEA)
AWP......... Allied Weather Publications [*NATO*] (NATG)
AWP......... Arbeitsgemeinschaft fur Wissenschaft und Politik [*Association for Sciences and Politics*] (EAIO)
AWPA...... Australian Women Pilots Association (PDAA)
AWPA...... Australian Wood Panels Association
AWPC...... Australian Wildlife Protection Council
AWPC...... Australian Wool Processors' Council
AWPL....... Australia-West Pacific Line (ADA)
AWPPA..... Arctic Water Pollution Prevention Act [*1970*] (MSC)
AWPT....... Australia Wide Property Trust
AWR......... Algemene wet Inzake Rijksbelastingen [*Benelux*] (BAS)
AWR......... Association for the Study of the World Refugee Problem [*Vaduz, Liechtenstein*] (EAIO)
AWR......... Association of Women Religious of Southern Africa (AA)
AWR......... Ausgabewortregister [*Output Word Register*] [*German*] (ADPT)
AWR......... Australian Wire Rope Works Proprietary Ltd. (ADA)
AWRA...... Australian Welding Research Association (ADA)
AWRA...... Australia Wool Realisation Agency (ADA)
AWRC...... Australian Water Resources Council (ADA)
AWRI....... Australian Wine Research Institute
AWRIS..... Arab War Risk Syndicate [*Began operation in 1981*] [*Insurance*] (IMH)
AWRS....... Australian War Records Section
AWRSA..... Australian Window Roller Shutter Association
AWS .... Animal Welfare Society of South Africa (AA)
AWS .... Arab Wings Co. [*Jordan*] [*ICAO designator*] (FAAC)
AWS .... Australian Warships Systems Pty. Ltd.
AWSA ...... Arab Women Solidarity Association [*Egypt*] (EAIO)
AWSA .... Australian Water Ski Association (ADA)

AWSA ...... Australian Women's Soccer Association
AWSA ...... Australian Wool Surveillance Authority
AWSBEF... Australian Wool Selling Brokers Employers' Federation
AWSC...... Australian Women's Service Corps (ADA)
AWSF....... Australian Wheelchair Sports Federation
AWSKA.... Australian Water Ski Association
AWSPA.... Australian Wheat Starch Producers' Association
AWSRA.... Australian Women's Squash Rackets Association
AWST....... Australian Western Standard Time
AWT......... Arbeitsgemeinschaft Waermebehandlung und Werkstoff-Technike eV (SLS)
AWT .... Australian Writers' Theatre
AWTA ...... Australian Women's Tennis Association
AWTA ...... Australian Wool Testing Authority (ARC)
AWTC ...... Amman World Trade Center [*Jordan*] (EAIO)
AWTOMM ... Australian Workshop on the Theories of Machines and Mechanisms
AWU......... Agricultural Workers Union
AWU......... Antigua Workers Union (LA)
AWU......... Australian Workers' Union (ADA)
AWU......... Australian Wrestling Union
AWV .... Algemene Werkgevers-Vereniging [*General Industrial Employers Association*] [*Netherlands*] (EAIO)
AWV .... Amalgamated Wireless Valve Co. Proprietary Ltd. [*Australia*] (ADA)
AWV .... Arbeitsgemeinschaft fuer Wirtschaftliche Verwaltung eV (SLS)
AWVA ...... Australian Women's Vigoro Association
AWVH...... Australia Woden Valley Hospital [*Medical Library*] [*National Union Catalogue of Australia symbol*]
AWVPRFPP ... Association of War Veterans of the Polish Republic and of Former Political Prisoners (EAIO)
AWW......... Algemeen Weduwen-en Wezenwet [*General Widows and Orphans Act*] [*Netherlands*] (WEN)
AWWA..... Australian Water and Wastewater Association (ADA)
AWWV..... Abeitsgemeinschaft der Wasserwirtschafsverbaende [*Water Utilisation Research Association*] [*Germany*] (PDAA)
AWWWL .. Ansett World Wide Wet Leasing [*Australia*]
AWZ......... Ahwaz [*Iran*] [*Airport symbol*] [*Obsolete*] (OAG)
AWZ......... Automobilwerk Zwickau [*Zwickau Automobile Plant*] [*Audi Kraftfahrwerke*] [*Formerly,*] (EG)
Ax............. Wytwornia Aparatow Numer X [*Number X Apparatus Plant*] (POL)
AXA .... Anguilla [*West Indies*] [*Airport symbol*] (OAG)
AXC .... Aramac [*Australia*] [*Airport symbol*] (OAG)
AXD .... Alexandroupolis [*Greece*] [*Airport symbol*] (OAG)
AXE .... Executive Air [*Zimbabwe*] [*ICAO designator*] (FAAC)
AXI .... Aeron International Airlines, Inc. [*ICAO designator*] (FAAC)
AXIS......... Auxiliary System for Interactive Statistics [*Sweden*] [*Information service or system*] (IID)
ax/kos .... Axiomatikos [*Commissioned Officer*] (GC)
AXL .... Air Exel Netherlands BV [*ICAO designator*] (FAAC)
AXM......... Armenia [*Colombia*] [*Airport symbol*] (OAG)
AXP .... Air Express AS [*Norway*] [*ICAO designator*] (FAAC)
AXP .... Allied Exercise Publications [*NATO*]
AXP .... Spring Point [*Bahamas*] [*Airport symbol*] (OAG)
AXR .... Axel Rent SA [*Mexico*] [*ICAO designator*] (FAAC)
AXT .... Akita [*Japan*] [*Airport symbol*] (OAG)
AXU .... Axum [*Ethiopia*] [*Airport symbol*] (OAG)
AXX .... Avioimpex [*Yugloslavia*] [*ICAO designator*] (FAAC)
AY............. Aeritalia SpA [*Italy*] [*ICAO aircraft manufacturer identifier*] (ICAO)
AY............. Anglo-Yugoslav Shipping Co.
AyA .... Aquine & Aranzabal [*Gun manufacturer*]
AYA .... Ashanti Youth Association
AYaM .... Amur-Yakutsk Highway (RU)
AYaPM .... Portable Absolute Nuclear Resonance Magnetometer (RU)
AYASA...... Aviacion y Agricultura SA [*Ecuador*] (DSCA)
AY/ASQ.... Arthur Young/Audit Smarter Quicker [*Computer science*] [*Australia*]
AYB .... Avrupa Yatirim Bankasi [*European Investment Bank*] [*Turkish*] (TU)
AYC .... African Youth Command [*Ghana*] (AF)
AYC .... Australian Youth Choir
AYC .... Aviacion y Comercio SA [*Spain*] [*ICAO designator*] (FAAC)
AYCC .... Australian Yugoslav Community Centre
AYE .... Anotati Ygeionomiki Epitropi [*Supreme Medical Board*] [*Greek*] (GC)
AYe .... Antigenic Unit (RU)
AYe .... Antitoxic Unit (RU)
a ye .... Astronomical Unit (RU)
AyEE .... Agua y Energia Electrica [*Argentina*] (IMH)
AYeM .... Atomic Mass Unit (RU)
AYF .... Australian Yachting Federation (ADA)
AYFR........ Autonomist Youth Front of Reunion
AYG .... Yuguara [*Colombia*] [*Airport symbol*] (OAG)
AYGA .... Goroka [*Papua New Guinea*] [*ICAO location identifier*] (ICLI)

AYHA....... Australian Youth Hostels Association   (ADA)
AYI .... Yari [*Colombia*] [*Airport symbol*]   (OAG)
AYIA .... Association of Young Irish Archaeologists   (SLS)
AYIG .... Australian Youth Initiatives Grant
Ayk-Is........ Antalya Yag Kurumu [*Antalya (Vegetable) Oil Industry Workers Union*]   (TU)
AYKO......... Kibris Turk Kooperatif Ayakkabi Fabrikasi [*Turkish Cypriot Cooperative Shoe Factory*]   (TU)
AYL .... Australian Young Labor   (ADA)
AYLA......... Lae [*Papua New Guinea*] [*ICAO location identifier*]   (ICLI)
AYLP......... African Youth Leadership Program
AYM.......... Anayasa Mahkemesi [*Constitutional Court*]   (TU)
AYMD........ Madang [*Papua New Guinea*] [*ICAO location identifier*]   (ICLI)
AYMH....... Mount Hagen [*Papua New Guinea*] [*ICAO location identifier*]   (ICLI)
AYMN....... Australian Youth Music Network
Aym upr ..... Aimak Administration [*Topography*]   (RU)
ayn mll .... Ayni Muellif [*The Same Author*] [*Turkey*]   (GPO)
AYNZ........ Nadzab [*Papua New Guinea*] [*ICAO location identifier*]   (ICLI)
AYO........... Australian Youth Orchestra   (ADA)
AYOD........ Ankara Yuksek Ogrenim Dernegi [*Ankara Association of Higher Learning*]   (TU)
AYOKD ..... Ankara Yuksek Ogrenim Kultur Dernegi [*Ankara Higher Education Cultural Association*]   (TU)
AYOTB ..... Ankara Yuksek Okullar Talebe Birligi [*Ankara Advanced Schools Student Union*]   (TU)
AYP .... Amerikaniki Ypiresia Pliroforion [*United States Information Service*]   (GC)
AYP .... Ayacucho [*Peru*] [*Airport symbol*]   (OAG)
AYPAA...... Australian Youth Performing Arts Association   (ADA)
AYPY........ Port Moresby [*Papua New Guinea*] [*ICAO location identifier*]   (ICLI)
AYQ.......... Ayers Rock [*Australia*] [*Airport symbol*]   (OAG)
AYRB........ Rabaul [*Papua New Guinea*] [*ICAO location identifier*]   (ICLI)
AYRS........ Amateur Yacht Research Society [*Turnchapel, Plymouth, England*]   (EAIO)
AYS........... Anotaton Ygeionomikon Symvoulion [*Supreme Health Council*] [*Greek*]   (GC)
AYSM........ Association of Yugoslav Societies for Microbiology [*Samoa*]   (EAIO)
AYSME..... Anotaton Ypiresiakon Symvoulion Mesis Ekpaidevseos [*Supreme Administrative Council for Secondary Education*] [*Greek*]   (GC)
AYSSE...... Anotaton Ypiresiakon Symvoulion Stoikheiodous Ekpaidevseos [*Supreme Administrative Council for Elementary Education*] [*Greek*]   (GC)
AYT .... Antalya [*Turkey*] [*Airport symbol*]   (OAG)
AYTA .... Association of Yugoslav Travel Agencies   (YU)
AYU........... Aiyura [*Papua New Guinea*] [*Airport symbol*] [*Obsolete*]   (OAG)
AYWK ...... Wewak [*Papua New Guinea*] [*ICAO location identifier*]   (ICLI)
AYWS........ Australian Yugoslav Welfare Society
AYYeSYsK ... Lokal'nyy Komitet Mezhdunarodnoy Assotsiatsii Studentov, izuchayushchikh Eko nomiku i Upravleniy [*Local Committee of the International Association of Economics and Management Students*] [*Former USSR*]   (EAIO)
AZ............. Academy of Zoology [*Uttar Pradesh, India*]   (EA)
AZ............. Acetylzahl [*Acetyl Number*] [*German*]   (GCA)
AZ............. Aerial Incendiary Bomb   (RU)
AZ............. Air Zaire   (AF)
Az............. Aktenzeichen [*File Number*] [*German*]   (WEN)
AZ............. Aktywizacja Zatrudnienia [*Activation of Employment*]   (POL)
AZ............. ALITALIA [*Aerolinee Italiane Internazionali*] [*Italian airline*] [*ICAO designator*]
AZ............. Alkoholzahl [*Alcohol Number*] [*German*]   (GCA)
Az............. Amperozwoj [*Ampere Turn*] [*Poland*]
AZ............. Artillery Weapons Plant   (RU)
Az............. Aufschlag-Zuender [*Percussion Fuse or Primer*] [*Military*] [*German*]   (MTD)
AZ............. Auf Zeit [*On Credit*] [*German*]
AZ............. Automatic Load Control   (RU)
AZ............. Automatic Start   (RU)
AZ............. Automobile Plant   (RU)
AZ............. Automobilove Zavody, Narodni Podnik [*Automobile Works, National Enterprise*]   (CZ)
AZ............. Azerbaydzhan Railroad   (RU)
az............. Azimuth   (RU)
az............. Azinhaga [*Lane*] [*Portuguese*]   (CED)
AZ............. Azote [*Nitrogen*] [*French*]
Az............. Azymut [*Azimuth*] [*Poland*]
AZ............. Barrage Balloon   (RU)
AZ............. Core [*Nuclear physics and engineering*]   (RU)
AZ............. Flight [*Air Force unit*]   (RU)
AZ............. Localized Gasoline   (RU)
AZ............. Scram System [*Nuclear physics and engineering*]   (RU)
AZ............. Storage-Batteries Plant   (BU)

AZA .... Alitalia-Linee Aeree Italiane SpA [*Italy*] [*ICAO designator*]   (FAAC)
AZA .... Antiaircraft Artillery   (BU)
AZA .... Atelje za Arhitekturo [*Studio for Architecture*] [*Ljubljana*]   (YU)
AZA .... Australian Zebu Association
Aza .... Azasi [*Member*]   (TU)
AZACCO... Azanian Co-Ordinating Committee [*South Africa*] [*Political party*]   (EY)
AZAG .... Army Antiaircraft Artillery Group   (RU)
AZAP......... Agence Zaire-Presse [*Zairian Press Agency*]   (AF)
AZAP......... Army Antiaircraft Artillery Regiment   (RU)
AZAPO ..... Azanian People's Organization [*South Africa*]   (PPW)
AzAPP....... Azerbaydzhan Association of Proletarian Writers   (RU)
AZASO ...... Azanian Students' Organization
AZAT .... Association Zairoise de Tourisme [*Zairian Tourism Association*]   (AF)
AZB .... Aerial Incendiary Bomb   (RU)
azb............. Alphabetic   (BU)
AZB .... Amazon Bay [*Papua New Guinea*] [*Airport symbol*]   (OAG)
AZB .... Azamat [*Kazakhstan*] [*ICAO designator*]   (FAAC)
AZC .... Archiv Zeme Ceske [*Archives of the Province of Bohemia*]   (CZ)
AZCB .... Association Zairoise des Compagnons Batisseurs [*Zaire*]   (EAIO)
AZCHERNIRO ... Azovsko-Chernomorskiy Nauchno-Issledovatel'skiy Institut Morskogo Rybnogo Khozyaystva i Okeanografii [*Azov-Black Sea Scientific Research Institute of Marine Fisheries and Oceanography*] [*Russian*]   (MSC)
AZD.......... Yazd [*Iran*] [*Airport symbol*]   (OAG)
AZDA .... Agence Zairoise de Distribution Automobile
AZDA .... Australian Zinc Development Association   (ADA)
AZE .... Aranzadi Zientzi Elkartea [*Spain*]   (EAIO)
AZE .... Arcus-Air-Logistic GmbH [*Germany*] [*ICAO designator*]   (FAAC)
AZED .... Electric Motor Protective Device   (RU)
AZEM .... Azinliklar ve Emlak Ofisi Genel Mudurlugu [*Minorities and Properties Office Directorate General*] [*of Foreign Affairs Ministry*]   (TU)
Azenergo .... Azerbaydzhan Regional Administration of Power System Management   (RU)
azeotrop...... Azeotropisch [*Azeotropic*] [*German*]   (GCA)
Azerb.......... Azerbaijani   (BARN)
azerb.......... Azerbaydzhan
Azeruchpedgiz ... Azerbaydzhan State Publishing House of Textbooks and Pedagogical Literature   (RU)
Azervin....... Azerbaydzhan Wine-Making Trust   (RU)
AzFAN....... Azerbaydzhan Branch of the Academy of Sciences, USSR   (RU)
AzFV.......... Anhang zu den Fahrdienstvorschriften [*Appendix to Train Service Regulations*]   (EG)
AZG.......... Academisch Ziekenhuis Groningen
AzG........... Azimut Gadanja [*Azimuth of Fire*] [*Army*]   (YU)
Azgaz......... Azerbaydzhan Gas Industry Trust   (RU)
AzGIFK...... Azerbaydzhan State Institute of Physical Culture Imeni S. M. Kirov   (RU)
AzGIK....... Azerbaydzhan State Quality Inspection of Agricultural Products   (RU)
Azgiprovodkhoz ... Azerbaydzhan State Institute for the Planning of Water-Management and Reclamation Construction   (RU)
Azgiz .... State Publishing House of the Azerbaydzhan SSR   (RU)
AzGNII...... Azerbaydzhan State Scientific Research Institute   (RU)
AzGNIIP ... Azerbaydzhan State Scientific Research Institute of Pedagogy   (RU)
AzGONTI ... Azerbaydzhan State United Scientific and Technical Publishing House   (RU)
Azgosarkhproyekt ... Azerbaydzhan State Architectural Planning Institute   (RU)
Azgospromproyekt ... Azerbaydzhan State Institute for the Planning of Industrial Establishments   (RU)
Azgosstrakh ... Azerbaydzhan State Insurance Administration   (RU)
Azgostekhizdat ... Azerbaydzhan State Technical Publishing House   (RU)
AzGPU ...... State Political Administration of the Azerbaydzhan Soviet Socialist Republic   (RU)
AzGU .... Azerbaydzhan State University Imeni S. M. Kirov   (RU)
AZH.......... Association Zairoise des Handicapes [*Zaire*]   (EAIO)
AZh........... Rigid Arch Support [*Mining*]   (RU)
AZhRD....... Nuclear Liquid-Propellant Rocket Engine   (RU)
AZI .... Allami Zeneiskola [*State Music School*]   (HU)
AZI .... Association Zen Internationale [*International Zen Association - IZA*]   (EAIO)
aziat........... Asian, Asiatic   (RU)
AZII.......... Azerbaydzhan Industrial Institute Imeni M. Azizbekov   (RU)
AzINEFTEKhIM ... Azerbaydzhan Institute of Petroleum and Chemistry Imeni M. Azizbekov   (RU)
AzINMASh ... Azerbaydzhan Scientific Research Institute of Petroleum Machinery   (RU)
AzINTI ...... Azerbaydzhan Institute of Scientific and Technical Information   (RU)
AzIS........... Azerbaydzhan Scientific Research Institute of Building Materials and Structures   (RU)

AZJO......... All Zanzibar Journalists' Organization
AZKG .... Automobilove Zavody Klementa Gottwalda [*Klement Gottwald Automobile Plants*] [*Mlada Boleslav*] (CZ)
AZKMGR ... Azerbaydzhan Office of Marine Geophysical Exploration (RU)
Azkombank ... Azerbaydzhan Municipal Bank (RU)
AzKOMSTARIS ... Azerbaydzhan Committee for the Preservation of Relics of Antiquity, Art, and Nature (RU)
Azkoopinsoyuz ... Azerbaydzhan Union of Cooperative Associations of Disabled Persons (RU)
AZL .... Air Zanzibar [*Tanzania*] [*ICAO designator*] (FAAC)
AZL .... Automobilove Zavody Letnany [*Letnany Automobile Works*] (CZ)
AZLK........ Avtomobilei Zavod Lenin Komsomol [*Lenin Collective Automobile Works*] [*Former USSR*]
AZM .... Aerocozumel SA [*Mexico*] [*ICAO designator*] (FAAC)
AZMMYO ... Ankara Zafer Muhendislik ve Mimarlik Ozel Yuksek Okulu [*Ankara Zafer (Victory) Engineering and Architectural Private Advanced School*] (TU)
Azmorput'.. Azov Basin Administration of Sea Routes (RU)
Azmuzgiz.... Azerbaydzhan State Music Publishing House (RU)
Az m v .... Aufschlagzuender mit Verzoegerung [*Delayed-Action Fuse*] [*German*]
Azneft'........ All-Union Trust of the Azerbaydzhan Petroleum and Gas Industry [*1934-1935*] (RU)
Azneftegeofizika ... Azerbaydzhan Administration of Geophysical Exploration of the Ministry of the Petroleum Industry (RU)
Aznefteizdat ... Azerbaydzhan Publishing House of Petroleum and Scientific and Technical Literature (RU)
Aznefterazvedka ... Azerbaydzhan Petroleum Geological Exploration Trust [*1936-1937*] (RU)
Azneftezavody ... Association of Azerbaydzhan Petroleum-Processing Plants (RU)
AZNII........ Azerbaydzhan Scientific Research Petroleum Institute Imeni V. V. Kuybyshev (RU)
AzNIIDN... Azerbaydzhan Scientific Research Institute for Petroleum Production (RU)
AZNIIGeofiziki ... Azerbaydzhan Scientific Research Institute of Geophysics (RU)
AzNIIGIM ... Azerbaydzhan Scientific Research Institute of Hydraulic Engineering and Reclamation (RU)
AzNIIMASh ... Azerbaydzhan Scientific Research Institute of Petroleum Machinery (RU)
AzNIIMN ... Azerbaydzhan Scientific Research Institute of Perennial Plantings (RU)
AzNIINP ... Azerbaydzhan Scientific Research Institute for Petroleum Processing Imeni V. V. Kuybyshev (RU)
AZNIIRKH ... Azovskiy Nauchno-Issledovatel'skiy Institut Rybnogo Khozyaystva [*Azov Scientific Research Institute of Fisheries*] [*Russian*] (MSC)
AzNIKhI.... Azerbaydzhan Scientific Research Institute of Cotton Growing (RU)
AzNIKI ...... Azerbaydzhan Clinical Scientific Research Institute (RU)
AzNITON ... Azerbaydzhan Branch of the All-Union Scientific, Engineering, and Technical Society of Petroleum Workers (RU)
AzNIVI...... Azerbaydzhan Veterinary Scientific Research Institute (RU)
Aznivos ...... Azerbaydzhan Scientific Research Veterinary Experimental Station (RU)
AzNKh....... Azerbaydzhan Petroleum Industry (RU)
AZNP .... Automobilove Zavody, Narodni Podnik [*Automobile Works, National Enterprise*] [*Mlada Boleslav*] (CZ)
AzNTO ...... Azerbaydzhan Republic Administration of the Scientific and Technical Society (RU)
AzNTONGP ... Azerbaydzhan Scientific and Technical Society of the Petroleum and Gas Industry (RU)
AZO.......... Antiaircraft Defense (RU)
AZO.......... Artillery Barrage (RU)
AZO.......... Automated Zonal Observatory (RU)
AzONTI..... Azerbaydzhan United Scientific and Technical Publishing House (RU)
AzOP .... Azimut Osnovnog Pravca [*Azimuth of Main Direction*] [*Army*] (YU)
Azotier .... Azotierung [*Azotization*] [*German*] (GCA)
Azovstal' ... Azov Metallurgical Plant (RU)
AZP .... Antiaircraft Artillery Regiment (RU)
AZP .... Automatic Antiaircraft Sight (RU)
AZP .... Filling Station (RU)
Azpartizdat ... Party Publishing House of the Azerbaydzhan SSR (RU)
AZPB........ Andrychowskie Zaklady Przemyslu Bawelnianego [*Andrychow Cotton Mill*] (POL)
Azpoligrafizdat ... Azerbaydzhan Administration for Printing, Publishing, and the Book Trade (RU)
AZPP........ Aleksandrowskie Zaklady Przemyslu Ponczoszniczego [*Aleksandrow Hosiery Mill*] (POL)
AZR .... Adrar [*Algeria*] [*Airport symbol*] (OAG)
AZR .... Air Zaire, Societe [*ICAO designator*] (FAAC)
AZR .... Ausgabezielregister [*Output Target Register*] [*German*] (ADPT)
AZR .... Documents of Western Russia (RU)

AZRC........ Arid Zone Research Centre [*Australia*] (DSCA)
AZRI......... Arid Zone Research in Iraq
Azryba....... Azerbaydzhan State Fish Industry Trust (RU)
AZS........... Akademickie Zrzeszenie Sportowe [*Student Sport Association*] (POL)
AZS........... Akademicki Zwiazek Sportowy [*Student Sport Union*] (POL)
AZS........... Anodal Closure Contraction (RU)
AZS........... Antiaircraft Equipment, Antiaircraft Weapons (RU)
AZS........... Arabski Zwiazek Socjalistyczny [*Arab Socialist Union*] (POL)
AZS........... Automatic Circuit Protection [*Circuit breaker*] (RU)
AZS........... Azot Sanayii Turk Anonim Sirketi [*Turkish Nitrogen Industry Corporation*] (TU)
AZS........... Battery-Charging Station (RU)
AZS........... Communications Flight [*Air Force unit*] (RU)
AZS........... Filling Station (RU)
AZS........... Students' Agrarian Union (BU)
AzSO .... Anhang zur Signal-Ordnung [*Appendix to the Signal Regulations*] (EG)
AzSSR ...... Azerbaydzhan Soviet Socialist Republic (RU)
Azstankostroy ... Azerbaydzhan Machine Tool Plant (RU)
AZT .... Azimut SA [*Spain*] [*ICAO designator*] (FAAC)
AzTAG...... Azerbaydzhan News Agency (RU)
AZTE .... Altay Tractor Electrical Equipment Plant (RU)
AZTM ...... Alma-Ata Heavy Machinery Plant (RU)
Aztorg .... Azerbaydzhan State Retail Trade Association (RU)
AZTRA..... Azucarera Tropical Americana, SA [*American Tropical Sugar Mill, Inc.*] [*Ecuador*] (LA)
Az TsAU... Azerbaydzhan Central Administration of Archives (RU)
AzTsIK ..... Central Executive Committee of Azerbaydzhan SSR (RU)
AZU.......... Academisch Ziekenhuis Utrecht
AZU.......... Afrikanische Zahlungsunion
AZU.......... Air Star Zanzibar [*Tanzania*] [*ICAO designator*] (FAAC)
AZU.......... Akademija Znanosti in Umetnosti [*Academy of Sciences and Arts*] [*Slovenian Academy Ljubljana*] (YU)
AZU.......... Associative Storage, Associative Memory (RU)
AZU.......... Azul [*Race of maize*] [*Mexico*]
AZU.......... High-Speed Tin-Plating Unit (RU)
AZUCARLITO ... Azucareras del Litoral SA [*Uruguay*] (DSCA)
AZUCOL... Azucarera Colombiana [*Colombia*] (COL)
AZUFRON ... Industria Azucarera de la Frontera SA [*Chile*] (DSCA)
AZUMT .... Azerbaydzhan Administration of Local Transportation (RU)
AZV .... Zodiac Air [*Bulgaria*] [*ICAO designator*] (FAAC)
AZVF........ Azov Naval Flotilla (RU)
Azvin........ Azerbaydzhan State Wine-Making Trust (RU)
AZVU .... Academisch Ziekenhuis Universiteit [*Netherlands*]
AZW .... Air Zimbabwe [*ICAO designator*] (FAAC)
Azw .... Amperozwoj [*Ampere Turn*] [*Poland*]
AZWK ...... Amt fuer Zoll und Warenkontrolle [*Office for Customs and Commodity Control*] (EG)
AZWM ...... Akademicki Zwiazek Walki Mlodych [*Student Union of the Struggle of Youth*] (POL)
azz .... Azzurro [*Blue*] [*Italian*]
AzZII .... Azerbaydzhan Industrial Correspondence Institute (RU)

B

B .... Armor, Armored   (RU)
B .... Aviation Gasoline   (RU)
B .... Baai [*Bay*] [*Netherlands*]   (NAU)
B .... Baccalaureat [*French*]
B .... Baccalaureat en Theologie [*Fribourg*] [*French*]
B .... Baccalaureos [*Egypt*]
B .... Bacharel [*Bachelor*] [*Portuguese*]
B .... Bacharelato [*Academic degree*] [*Portuguese*]
B .... Bachiller [*Bachelor*] [*Academic degree*] [*Spanish*]
B .... Bacillus Breslaviensis   (RU)
B .... Bahia [*Bay*] [*Ba*] [*See also*]   (NAU)
B .... Baht [*Monetary unit*] [*Thailand*]
B .... Baia [*Bay*] [*Portuguese*]   (NAU)
B .... Baia [*Bay*] [*Italian*]   (NAU)
B .... Baie [*Bay*] [*French*]   (NAU)
B .... Bajaj Auto Ltd. [*India*]
B .... Bakalaureus [*or Bakalaurat*] [*Academic degree Indonesian*]
B .... Baker [*Phonetic alphabet*] [*World War II*]   (DSUE)
b .... Bal [*Left*]   (HU)
B .... Balboa [*Monetary unit*] [*Panama*]
b .... Balle [*Bale*] [*French*]
b .... Band [*Volume*] [*Sweden*]   (GPO)
B .... Bandar [*Harbour*] [*Persian*]   (NAU)
B .... Bani [*Monetary unit*] [*Romania*]
b .... Bar [*German*]   (GCA)
B .... Baracke [*Barracks*] [*German*]
B .... Barcelona [*Spain*]
b .... Bardzo [*Very*] [*Poland*]
b .... Baria [*Portuguese*]
b .... Barometerstand [*Barometric Pressure*] [*German*]   (GCA)
B .... Baron [*Baron*] [*French*]
B .... Base   (RU)
b .... Basophil, Basophile   (RU)
B .... Basse [*Shoal*] [*French*]   (NAU)
B .... Bati [*West*]   (TU)
B .... Battery   (RU)
B .... Bay [*Mister*]   (TU)
b .... Bay, Cove   (RU)
B .... Beacon, Buoy [*Topography*]   (RU)
B .... Beato [*Blessed*] [*Spanish*]
B .... Beato [*Blessed*] [*Italian*]
B .... Beco [*Lane*] [*Correspondence*] [*Portuguese*]
B .... Beer [*Phonetic alphabet*] [*Pre-World War II*]   (DSUE)
b .... Begge [*Both, Either*] [*Danish/Norwegian*]
b .... Bei [*or Beim*] [*Near, With, Care Of*] [*German*]   (GPO)
b .... Bel   (RU)
B .... Belga [*Monetary unit*] [*Belgium*]
B .... Belgia [*Belgium*] [*Poland*]
B .... Belgium [*International automobile identification tag*]
b .... Benefice [*Profit*] [*French*]
B .... Beobachtung [*Observation*] [*German*]
B .... Beslissingen in Belastingzaken [*Benelux*]   (BAS)
B .... Besluit [*Benelux*]   (BAS)
B .... Betrieb [*Operations*] [*All measures and procedures required for the assembly, operation, and breaking up of trains*] [*German*]   (EG)
B .... Bey [*Mister*] [*Turkey*]   (GPO)
b .... Bianco [*Blank, White*] [*Italian*]
B .... Biegeprobe [*Bending Test*] [*German*]   (GCA)
B .... Bienheureux [*Blessed*] [*French*]
B .... Big, Large, Great   (RU)
B .... Bildung [*Education*] [*German*]
b .... Billet [*Bill*] [*French*]
B/ .... Billet a Ordre [*Promissory Note*] [*French*]
b .... Bind [*Binding, Volume*] [*Publishing Danish/Norwegian*]
b .... Birlik [*Unit*] [*Military*]   (TU)
b .... Ble [*Wheat*] [*Used in contexts having to do with flour French*]   (CL)

B .... [*The*] Boeing Co. [*ICAO aircraft manufacturer identifier*]   (ICAO)
B .... Bois [*Wood*] [*Military map abbreviation World War I*] [*French*]   (MTD)
B .... Bolivar [*Monetary unit*] [*Venezuela*]
B .... Boliviano [*Monetary unit*] [*Bolivia*]
B .... Bolometer   (RU) ,
b .... Bom [*Good*] [*Portuguese*]
B/ .... Bomber   (RU)
b/ .... Bon [*Good For*] [*French*]
b .... Bonification [*Improvement*] [*French*]
B .... Bookline Enterprise [*Malaysia*]
B .... Bor [*Boron*] [*Chemical element*] [*German*]
B .... Boreal [*Northern*] [*French*]
b .... Born   (EECI)
B .... Boro [*Boron*] [*Chemical element*] [*Portuguese*]
B .... Bouchet [*Powder Works*] [*French*]   (MTD)
b .... Bougie [*Candlepower*] [*French*]
B .... Bouwe [*Benelux*]   (BAS)
B .... Bravo [*International phonetic alphabet*]   (DSUE)
B .... Brevet [*Certificate, Diploma*] [*French*]
B .... Brevete d'Etat-Major [*Of officer who has passed staff course*] [*French*]   (MTD)
B .... Brief [*Currency*] [*German*]
b .... Brigade   (BU)
b .... Broche [*Stitched*] [*Publishing*] [*French*]
b .... Brochura [*Pamphlet*] [*Publishing*] [*Portuguese*]
b .... Brossura [*Paper-Cover Binding*] [*Publishing*] [*Italian*]
B .... Brunei   (BARN)
B .... Brunswick [*Record label*] [*Great Britain*]
B .... Bucht [*Bay*] [*German*]   (NAU)
B .... Bueno [*On an Examination: Good*] [*Spanish*]
B .... Bugt [*Bay, Bight*] [*Denmark*]   (NAU)
B .... Bukhta [*Bay, Inlet*] [*Russian*]   (NAU)
B .... Bukt [*Bukta*] [*Bay, Bight*] [*Norway*]   (NAU)
B .... Bukt [*Bay, Bight*] [*Sweden*]   (NAU)
B .... Bulletin   (RU)
B .... Bund [*Union*] [*German*]
B .... Buoy [*Topography*]   (RU)
B .... Burgerlijk Wetboek [*Civil Code*] [*Netherlands*]   (DLA)
B .... Butter [*Phonetic alphabet*] [*Royal Navy World War I*]   (DSUE)
B .... Butut [*Monetary unit*] [*Gambia*]
b .... Byly [*Former*]   (POL)
B .... Cobblestone [*Topography*]   (RU)
B .... Fast [*Nuclear physics and engineering*]   (RU)
B .... Former   (RU)
B .... Melon Field [*Topography*]   (RU)
B .... Obus a Balles [*On base of projectiles*] [*French*]   (MTD)
B .... Railroad Guard's Cabin [*Topography*]   (RU)
B .... Ravine, Valley [*Topography*]   (RU)
B .... Stopien Baume [*Degree Baume*] [*Poland*]
BA .... Armored Car   (RU)
ba .... Author's Note   (BU)
BA .... Automatic Battery [*Artillery*]   (RU)
BA .... Aviation Gasoline   (RU)
BA .... Baccalaureat es Arts [*Bachelor of Arts*] [*French*]
BA .... Bachelor of Arts   (PWGL)
BA .... Bachiller Academico [*Academic degree*] [*Spanish*]
Ba .... Bag [*or Baglar*] [*Vineyard or Vineyards*]   (TU)
Ba .... Bahia [*Bay*] [*B*] [*See also*] [*Spanish*]   (NAU)
BA .... Balneum Arenae [*Sand Bath*] [*Medicine*]
Ba .... Bana [*Cape, Point*] [*Ha*] [*See also*] [*Japan*]   (NAU)
BA .... Banco Agricola [*Agricultural Bank*] [*Dominican Republic*]   (LA)
BA .... Banco Amazonas [*Amazon Bank*] [*Ecuador*]
BA .... Banco Avellane da SA [*Bank*] [*Argentina*]
BA .... Banque Agreee [*Accredited Bank*] [*Cambodia*]   (CL)
BA .... Banque d'Algerie [*Bank of Algeria*]
BA .... Bari [*Car registration plates*] [*Italian*]

137

Ba .... Bario [*Barium*] [*Chemical element*] [*Portuguese*]
BA .... Base Aerienne [*Air Base*] [*Cambodia*]   (CL)
BA .... Basketball Australia [*An association*]
B-A .... Basses-Alpes [*French*]
BA .... Bataillon d'Afrique
BA .... Battalion Artillery   (RU)
BA .... Belle Arti [*Fine Arts*] [*Italian*]
BA .... Benzoylacetone   (RU)
BA .... Bergakademie Freiberg/Sachsen [*Freiberg Mining Academy*]   (EG)
BA .... Berita Atjara [*Official Report or Record*]   (IN)
BA .... Berperkte Aansprakelijkheid [*Benelux*]   (BAS)
BA .... Besuchsanregung [*Frequency Stimulation*] [*German*]   (ADPT)
BA .... Bevorratungsartikel [*Items for Stockpiling*]   (EG)
ba .... Bez Autora [*Anonymous*]   (POL)
BA .... Bibliotheca Aegyptia
BA .... Bicycle Australia [*An association*]
BA .... Bintara [*Noncommissioned Officer*]   (IN)
BA .... Bipe Association [*France*]   (EAIO)
BA .... Birma [*Myanmar*] [*Poland*]
BA .... Blocking Anticyclone   (RU)
BA .... Bolshoi Ballet Academy [*Former USSR*]
BA .... Bombardment Aviation   (RU)
BA .... Bomber Command   (BU)
BA .... Bonne Action [*Good Deed*] [*French*]
BA .... Bousquet-Afrique
ba .... Boven Aangehaald [*Benelux*]   (BAS)
BA .... British Aircraft Corp. Ltd. [*ICAO aircraft manufacturer identifier*]   (ICAO)
BA .... British Airways [*British*] [*ICAO designator*]   (ICDA)
BA .... Brong Ahafo
BA .... Buchungsautomat [*German*]   (ADPT)
BA .... Buenos Aires [*Capital of Argentina*]
BA .... Building Application [*Australia*]
BA .... Bundesanwalt [*Public Prosecutor or Attorney General*] [*German*]   (ILCA)
BA .... Bundesanwaltschaft [*The Office of Public Prosecutor*] [*German*]   (ILCA)
BA .... Bundesverband Deutscher Autoren eV   (SLS)
BA .... Bureau Arabe
BA .... Bushman Alliance [*Namibia*]
BA .... Butyl Acetate   (RU)
BA .... Coast Artillery   (RU)
BA .... Estado da Bahia [*State of Bahia*] [*Brazil*]
BA .... Establissements Bruno Aduier
BA .... Large Astrograph   (RU)
BA .... Office of Automation   (RU)
ba .... Submachine-Gun Battalion   (RU)
BAA .... Bank of America Australia
BAA .... Bialla [*Papua New Guinea*] [*Airport symbol*]   (OAG)
BAA .... Blindmakers' Association of Australia
BAA .... Boomerang Association of Australia
BAA .... Bosnaair [*Yugoslavia*] [*ICAO designator*]   (FAAC)
BAA .... Bursary Association of Australia
BAA .... Societe Biscuiterie et Alimentation Africaine
BAAA .... Bahamas Amateur Athletic Association   (EAIO)
BAAA .... Botswana Amateur Athletics Association
BAAA .... Brunei Amateur Athletic Association [*Brunei Darussalam*]   (EAIO)
BAAC .... Bank for Agriculture and Agricultural Cooperatives [*Thai*]   (GEA)
BAAH .... Bureau d'Aide et d'Assistance Humanitaire [*Humanitarian Aid and Relief Office*] [*Cambodia*]   (CL)
BAAI .... Bureau d'Aide et d'Assistance aux Sinistres de l'Inondation [*Office of Aid and Relief for Flood Victims*] [*Cambodia*]   (CL)
BAAM .... Banque Arabe Africaine en Mauritanie [*African Arab Bank in Mauritania*]   (AF)
BAAP .... Bureau d'Aide et d'Assistance a la Population [*Office of Aid and Relief for the Population*] [*Cambodia*]   (CL)
BAAZ .... Begeleidings-Commissie Academische Ziekenhuizen
bab .... Air Bombardment Base   (BU)
BAB .... Banco Agricola de Bolivia [*Agricultural Bank of Bolivia*]   (LAA)
BAB .... Barristers' Admission Board [*Australia*]   (ADA)
BAB .... Betriebsabrechnungsbogen [*Master Summary Sheet, Operations Sheet, Cost Control Sheet*] [*See also BB*] [*German*]   (EG)
BAB .... Boissons Africaines de Brazzaville
BAB .... Bureau Afvoer Burgerbevolking [*Benelux*]   (BAS)
BAB .... Ontwerp Beroep Administratieve Beschikkingen [*Benelux*]   (BAS)
BAB .... Wet Beroep Administratieve Beschikkingen [*Benelux*]   (BAS)
BABA .... Botswana Amateur Boxing Association
BABEL ...... Baltic and Bothnian Echoes from the Lithosphere [*Collaborative seismic project*] [*Britain, Denmark, Finland, Germany, and Sweden*]

BABTarim Is ... Bati Anadolu Bolgesi Tarim Sanayii, Ziraii Arastirma, ve Orman Isletmeleri Iscileri Sendikasi [*Western Anatolian Region Agriculture Industry, Agricultural Research, and Forestry Operations Workers' Union*]   (TU)
BABW .... Beratender Ausschuss fur Bildungs-und Wissenschaftspolitik [*Advisory Commission for Education and Science Policy*] [*Germany*]   (PDAA)
Bac .... Bacac [*Mortar*] [*Military*]   (YU)
BAC .... Baccalaureat [*Baccalaureate*] [*French*]
BAC .... Banco Agricola de Cantagalo [*Brazil*]   (DSCA)
BAC .... Bank of the Arab Coast Ltd. [*United Arab Emirates*]
BAC .... Bantu Affairs Commission [*South Africa*]   (AF)
BAC .... Basutoland African Congress
BAC .... Biblioteca Agropecuaria de Colombia [*Colombia*]   (COL)
BAC .... Bill Acceptance Corp. [*Australia*]
BAC .... Birlesik Arap Cumhuriyeti [*United Arab Republic - UAR*]   (TU)
BAC .... Black Affairs Center
BAC .... Bois Africains Contreplaques
BAC .... Building Advisory Committee
BAC .... Burdekin Agricultural College [*Australia*]
BAC .... Burma Airways Corp. [*Rangoon*]   (EY)
BAC .... Business Arts Connection [*Australia*]
BAC .... Ghana Bauxite Company
BAC(AG)... Beleids Advies College (Automatisering Gezondheidszorg)
BACC .... Building and Construction Council [*Australia*]
bacc en dr ... Baccalaureat en Droit [*Bachelor in Law*] [*French*]
bacc es l ...... Baccalaureat es Lettres [*Bachelor of Literature*] [*French*]
bacc es sc... Baccalaureat es Sciences [*Bachelor of Science*] [*French*]
BACCI .... Beton Arme Constructions Civiles et Industrielles
BACE .... Board of Adult and Community Education [*New South Wales, Australia*]
BACE .... Brazilian Aeronautical Commission in Europe
BACGA ..... British-Australian Cotton Growing Association   (ADA)
BACh .... Number Address Unit [*Computers*]   (RU)
BACI .... Banque Atlantique de Cote-D'Ivoire
BACME..... Baza de Aprovizionare pentru Constructii si Montaje Energetice [*Supply Base for Power Plant Construction and Installation*]   (RO)
BACON ..... Backfile Conversion Project [*European Patent Office*]
BA(Creative) ... Bachelor of Creative Arts
BACS .... Ben Asia Container Services   (DS)
BACTAG ... Beecroft and Cheltenham Tollway Action Group [*Australia*]
Bacter .... Bacteriologia [*Bacteriology*] [*Portuguese*]
bad .... Air Bombardment Division   (BU)
BAD .... Banco Asiatico de Desarrollo [*Asian Development Bank - ADB*] [*Spanish*]
BAD .... Banque Africaine de Developpement [*African Development Bank*] [*Use ADB*]   (AF)
BAD .... Banque Algerienne de Developpement [*Algerian Development Bank*]   (AF)
BAD .... Banque Asiatique de Developpement [*Asia Development Bank*] [*Use ADB*]   (CL)
BAD .... Baza de Aprovizionare si Desfacere [*Base for Supply and Distribution*]   (RO)
BAD .... Belgian Association of Dieticians   (EAIO)
BAD .... Bomber Division   (RU)
BAD .... Bulgarian Society of Architects   (BU)
BADC .... Barbados Agricultural Development Corporation   (GEA)
BADC .... Brackishewater Aquaculture Development Centre [*Indonesian*]   (ASF)
BADEA...... Banque Arabe pour le Developpement Economique en Afrique [*Arab Bank for African Economic Development*] [*Khartoum, Sudan*]   (AF)
BADEAC... Banque de Developpement des Etats de l'Afrique Centrale [*Development Bank of the Central African States*]   (AF)
BADEP...... Banco de Desenvolvimento do Parana, SA [*Brazil*]   (LAA)
BADESP ... Banco de Desenvolvimento do Estado de Sao Paulo [*Sao Paulo State Development Bank*] [*Brazil*]   (LA)
BADESP ... Banco de Desenvolvimento do Estado de Sao Paulo SA [*Brazil*]   (EY)
BADESUL ... Banco de Desenvolvimento do Estado do Rio Grande Do Sul SA [*Brazil*]   (EY)
BADOSZ... Banyaipari Dolgozok Szakszervezete [*Trade Union of Mine Workers*]   (HU)
BADPRK... Badminton Association of the Democratic People's Republic of Korea   (EAIO)
BADR .... Banque de l'Agriculture & du Developpement Rural [*Algeria*]
bae .... Air Bombardment Squadron   (BU)
BAE .... Betriebswirtschaftliche Analysen, Einzelhandel [*Business Management Analysis, Retail Trade*] [*German*]   (ADPT)
BAE .... Bomber Squadron   (RU)
BAeA .... British Aerospace Australia
BAEC........ Bangladesh Atomic Energy Commission   (EY)
BAEE .... Ethyl Ester of Benzoylarginine   (RU)
BAEMTP .. Budget Annexe d'Exploitation du Materiel de Travaux Publics
BAER........ Base Airfield   (RU)

BAF............ Bananeraies Africaines
BAF............ Banco Agrario de Financiamento, Sociedade Cooperativa de Responsabilidade Ltd [*Brazil*] (DSCA)
BAF............ Benzylaminophenol (RU)
BAF............ Burmese Air Force
BAFCO...... Bahrain Fishing Co. (IMH)
BAFED...... Basutoland Factory Estate Development Company
BAfEuV ..... Bundesamt fuer Eich-und Vermessungswesen [*Federal Office of Metrology and Surveying*] [*Federal Ministry of Construction and Technology*] [*Austria*] [*Research center*] (EAS)
BA f EV...... Bundesamt fuer Eichung Vermessungswesen [*Federal Office for Standardized Measurements*] [*German*]
BAFIP........ Banque Financiere Parisienne [*France*]
BAFISUD ... Banco Financiero Sudamericano [*South American Financial Bank*] (LA)
BAFMA..... British and Foreign Maritime Agencies (BARN)
BAFO .... Byurakan Astrophysical Observatory (RU)
BAFoeG ..... Bundesausbildungsfoerderungsgesetz [*Federal Law for the Advancement of Education*] [*German*] (WEN)
BAFQD...... Banco Agricola y Fertilizantes Quimicos Dominicanos [*Dominican Republic*] (DSCA)
BAFS .... Beton Armat du Fibra de Sticla [*Concrete Reinforced with Glass Fibers*] (RO)
BAfW &B ... Bundesamt fuer Wehrtechnik und Beschaffung [*Federal Office for Weapons Technology and Procurement*] (WEN)
BAG .... Bagian [*Division, Section, Component*] (IN)
BAG .... Baguio [*Philippines*] [*Airport symbol*] (OAG)
BAG .... Black Action Group [*Australia*]
BAG .... Bloc Africain de Guinee
BAG .... Brigadna Artiljeriska Grupa [*Brigade Artillery Group*] [*Military*] (YU)
BAG .... Bundesarbeitsgericht [*Federal Supreme Labour Court*] [*German*] (DLA)
BAG .... Bureau d'Achat du Gouvernement [*Government Purchasing Office*] [*Laotian*] (CL)
BAG .... Deutsche Ba Luftfahrtgesellschaft MBH [*Germany*] [*ICAO designator*] (FAAC)
BAGES...... Baku City Electric Power Network (RU)
BAGFAS ... Bandirma Gubre Fabrikalari Anonim Sirketi [*Bandirma Fertilizer Factories Corporation*] (TU)
Bag-Kur ..... Esnaf ve Sanatkarlar ile Bagimsiz Calisanlar Sosyal Guvenlik Kurumu [*Social Security Association Relating to Tradesmen, Artisans, and Independent Workers*] (TU)
BAGO........ Bloque Antiguerrillero del Oriente [*Eastern Anti-Guerrilla Bloc*] [*El Salvador*] (PD)
BAGO........ Bureau Aanvoer van Goederen van Overzee [*Benelux*] (BAS)
bagomsl...... Bagomslag [*Back Wrapper*] [*Publishing Danish/Norwegian*]
BAgrEcon .. Bachelor of Agricultural Economics
BAgResEcon ... Bachelor of Agricultural Research and Economics
BAGRICOLA ... Banco Agricola de la Republica Dominicana [*Dominican Republic*] (DSCA)
BAG/WfB ... Arbeitsgemeinschaft der Werkstaetten fuer Behinderte in der Bundesrepublik Deutschland eV [*Association of Workshops for the Handicapped in the Federal Republic of Germany*] (SLS)
BAH.......... Amiri Flight-Bahrain [*ICAO designator*] (FAAC)
BAH.......... Bahrain Islands [*Airport symbol*] (OAG)
BAH.......... Banco Ambrosiano Holding [*Italy*]
BAH.......... Biologische Anstalt Helgoland [*Biological Institute of Helgoland*] (ASF)
BAHS .... British-Australian Heritage Society
BA I........... Bahama Islands (WDAA)
BAI .... Bahrain Atomisers International (IMH)
BAI .... Banca d'America e d'Italia [*Bank*] [*Italian*]
BAI .... Barair SA [*Spain*] [*ICAO designator*] (FAAC)
BAI .... Book Association of Ireland (BARN)
BAI .... Builders Association of India
BAI .... Bureau des Affairs Indigenes
BAIA......... Banca de Agricultura si Industrie Alimentara [*Bank for Agriculture and Food Industry*] (RO)
BAIBK....... Beta-Aminoisobutyric Acid (RU)
BAIC........ Bahamas Agricultural and Industrial Corporation (EY)
BAII.......... Banque Arabe et Internationale d'Investissement [*France*]
BAIMK...... Beta-Aminoisobutyric Acid (RU)
Ba Is......... Bahama Islands (BARN)
BAISP........ Banco Agro Industrial de Sao Paulo, Sociedade Cooperativa [*Brazil*] (DSCA)
BAJ........... Bali [*Papua New Guinea*] [*Airport symbol*] (OAG)
BAJSR....... Board of Australian Journals of Scientific Research
Bak............ Bakim [*Maintenance, Upkeep*] (TU)
Bak............ Bakiniz [*Look, Please Refer To, See*] (TU)
BAK .... Baku [*Former USSR*] [*Airport symbol*] (OAG)
BAK .... Ballonabwehrkanone [*Antiaircraft*] [*German*]
bak .... Beacon, Buoy (RU)
BAK .... Bomber Corps (RU)
BAK .... Bundesaerztekammer [*Republic Doctors Bureau*] (SLS)

BAK .... Bundesassistenkonferenz [*Federal University Assistants Conference*] [*Germany*] (PDAA)
BAK .... Bundesaufsichtsamt fur das Kreditwesen [*Federal Supervisory Office for Credit*] [*Germany*]
BAK .... Instruction Address Unit (RU)
BAKER..... Badan Kerdja [*Working Committee*] (IN)
BAKER..... Barisan Kemerdeka'an Rakyat Brunei [*Brunei People's Freedom Front*] (ML)
BAKIN....... Badan Koordinasi Intelidjen Negara [*State Intelligence Coordination Agency*] (IN)
BAKITA .... Baraza la Kiswahili la Taifa [*National Kiswahili Council*] [*Tanzania*] (EAIO)
BAKITWAN ... Balai Penelitian Penyakit Hewan [*Animal Diseases Research Institute*] [*Indonesian*] (ARC)
bakomsl...... Bakomslag [*Back Wrapper*] [*Publishing Danish/Norwegian*]
BAKOSURTANAL ... Badan Koordinasi Survey dan Pemetaan [*National Coordination Agency for Surveys and Mapping*] [*Indonesia*] [*Research center*] (IRC)
Bakport...... Baku Commercial Seaport (RU)
Baksanges ... Baksan Hydroelectric Power Plant (RU)
bakt........... Bacteriological (RU)
bakt........... Bacteriologist, Bacteriology (BU)
bakt........... Bakteriologisch [*Bacteriological*] [*German*] (GCA)
BAKWATA ... Baraza Kuu la Waislamu [*Supreme Council of Moslems*] [*Tanzania*] (AF)
Bal............. Balance [*Accounting*] [*French*]
bal .... Balans [*Balance*] [*Afrikaans*]
BAL .... Berichten aan Luchtvarenden [*Netherlands*]
BAL .... Blok Automatique Lumineux
BAL .... Boston Australia Ltd. [*Australia*]
bal .... Ravine, Valley [*Topography*] (RU)
BALCC ...... Belgo-Arab Luxembourg Chamber of Commerce
balce .... Balance [*Balance*] [*Accounting*] [*French*]
BALCO...... Bahrain-Saudi Aluminium Marketing Company [*Manama, Bahrain*] (MENA)
BALEAR ... Baltic Environmental and Acoustic Range (MSC)
BALEXCO ... Bahrain Aluminium Extrusion Company WLL [*Supplier to the construction industry*] [*Manama*] (MENA)
BALF .... Blue Army of Our Lady of Fatima [*Later, World Apostolate of Fatima - WAF*] (EA)
BALIB ...... Banque Arabe-Libyenne-Burkinabe pour le Commerce et le Developpement (EY)
BALIMA ... Banque Arabe Libyo-Malienne pour le Commerce Exterieur et la Developpement [*Bank*] [*Mali*]
BALINEX ... Banque Arabe Libyenne Nigerienne pour le Commerce Exterieur et le Developpement [*Libya-Niger Arab Bank for External Trade and Development*] [*Nigeria*]
Bal Isls....... Balearic Islands
balk .... Balkanski [*Balkan*] [*Poland*]
Balkanbas ... Central Balkan Basin (BU)
Balkanizdat ... Balkan Publishing House (BU)
Balkanturist ... State Economic Enterprise for Excursions and Travel (BU)
Ball............ Balliol College [*Oxford, England*] (BARN)
Ballist........ ballistik [*Ballistics*] [*German*] (GCA)
BALM....... Banque Arabe Libyenne-Mauritanienne pour le Commerce Exterieur et le Developpement [*Libyan-Mauritanian Arab Bank for External Trade and Development*]
B Alp........ Basses-Alpes [*Lower Alps*] [*French*] (BARN)
Bal Pak ...... Baluchistan, Pakistan (ILCA)
Bals .... Balboas [*Monetary unit*] [*Panama*]
BALS .... Bandas Armadas de Liberacion del Sahara [*Armed Bands for the Liberation of the Sahara*] (AF)
BALSA ..... Black Action for the Liberation of South Africa
Balt............ Baltic (RU)
balt............ Baltycki [*Baltic*] [*Poland*]
BALTAP ... Allied Forces Baltic Approaches [*NATO*]
BALTEX ... Banque Arabe Libyenne-Togolaise du Commerce Exterieur [*Libyan-Togolese Arab Bank for External Trade*]
Baltflot....... Baltic Fleet (RU)
Baltmorput' ... Baltic Administration of Sea Routes (RU)
BALTNIRO ... Baltiyskiy Nauchno-Issledovatel'skiy Institut Morskogo Rybnogo Khozyaystva i Okeanografii [*Baltic Scientific Research Institute of Marine Fisheries and Oceanography*] [*Russian*] (MSC)
Baltzavod ... Baltic Shipyard (RU)
BALUBAKAT ... Association des Baluba du Katanga [*Association of the Baluba People of Katanga*] [*Zaire*]
BAM .... Badminton Association of Malta (EAIO)
BAM .... Baikal-Amur Railway [*Russian*]
BAM .... Banco Agricola Mercantil [*Guatemala*] (DSCA)
BAM .... Bank of Africa-Mali
BAM .... Belize Action Movement (PD)
BaM .... Boite-a-Musique, Paris [*Record label*] [*France*]
BAM .... Brigada Antonio Maceo [*Antonio Maceo Brigade*] [*Cuba*] (LA)
BAM .... Bundesanstalt fuer Materialforschung und -Pruefung [*Federal Institute for Materials Research and Testing*] [*Database producer*] [*Germany*] [*Information retrieval*] (IID)

BAM .... Bundesanstalt fuer Materialprufung Unter den Eichen [*International Association for Structural Mechanics in Reactor Technology*]   (EAIO)
BAM .... Bureau des Affaires Musulmanes
BAMAG .... Societe Banguienne de Grands Magasins
BAMAS ..... Buyuk Anadolu Madenleri Anonim Sirketi [*Greater Anatolian Mines Corporation*]   (TU)
BAMB .... Botswana Agicultural Marketing Board
Bamer .... Banco de America [*Bank of America*] [*Nicaragua*]   (GEA)
BAMERT .. Banyagepgyar [*Mining Machines Factory*]   (HU)
BAMES ..... Banque Malgache d'Escompte et de Credit [*Malagasy Discount and Credit Bank*]   (AF)
BAMF .... Bundesamt fuer Militarflugplatze [*Switzerland*] [*ICAO designator*]   (FAAC)
BAMG .... Banco Agricola de Minas Gerais [*Brazil*]   (DSCA)
BAMI .... Brothers to All Men International   (EA)
BAMIN ..... Banco Minero de Bolivia [*Mining Bank of Bolivia*]   (LA)
BAMIS ...... Banque al-Baraka Mauritanienne Islamique   (EY)
BAMREL .. Bureau Africain et Malgache de Recherches et d'Etudes Legislatives [*African and Malagasy Office for Legislative Research and Studies*]   (AF)
BAMUNAS ... Badan Musjawarah Pengusaha Nasional Swasta [*Consultative Council of National Private Businessmen*]   (IN)
BAN .... Balgarska Akademija na Naukite [*Bulgarian Academy of Sciences*]   (EAIO)
Ban .... Banyo [*Bath*]   (TU)
BAN .... Base d'Aeronautique Navale [*French*]
BAN .... Belaruskaja Akademija Navuk [*Belorussian Academy of Sciences*]   (RU)
BAN .... Bulgarska Akademija na Naukite [*Bulgarian Academy of Sciences*] [*Sofia*]   (YU)
BAN .... Bundeseinheitliche Artikel-Nummer [*Federal Unified Article Number*] [*German*]   (ADPT)
BAN .... Library of the Academy of Sciences, USSR   (RU)
BANABel ... Library of the Academy of Sciences, Belorussian SSR   (RU)
BANADE .. Banco Nacional de Desarrollo [*National Development Bank*] [*Argentina*]   (LA)
BANADESA ... Banco Nacional de Desarrollo Agricola [*National Agricultural Development Bank*] [*Honduras*]   (LA)
BANAFI .... Banco Nacional de Fomento Industrial [*El Salvador*]   (EY)
BANAFIBRA ... Sacos de Fibra de Banano [*Ecuador*]   (DSCA)
BANAFOM ... Banco Nacional de Fomento [*National Development Bank*] [*Tegucigalpa, Honduras*]   (LAA)
BANAFRIQUE ... Banque d'Afrique et d'Outre-Mer
BANAGAS ... Bahrain National Gas Co. [*State enterprise*]   (EY)
BANAICO ... Banco Agro-Industrial y Comercial de Panama [*Bank*] [*Panama*]
Banamex .... Banco Nacional de Mexico [*National Bank of Mexico*]
BANANIC ... Empresa Nicaraguense de Banano [*Nicaraguan Banana Enterprise*]
BANANOL ... Derivados del Banano SA [*Ecuador*]   (DSCA)
BANAP ...... Banco Nacional de Ahorro y Prestamo [*National Savings and Loan Bank*] [*Venezuela*]   (LA)
BAN-Arkheoli ... BAN [*Bulgarian Academy of Sciences*] Institute of Archaeology   (BU)
BAN-ArkheolMuzey ... BAN [*Bulgarian Academy of Sciences*] Archaeological Museum   (BU)
BANArm ... Library of the Academy of Sciences, Armenian SSR   (RU)
BAN-Ashkh ... Library of the Academy of Sciences (Ashkhabad)   (RU)
BANAz ...... Library of the Academy of Sciences, Azerbaydzhan SSR   (RU)
BANBel ..... Library of the Academy of Sciences, Belorussian SSR   (RU)
BANBOGOTA ... Banco de Bogota Tlg. [*Bank of Bogota*]   (COL)
BAN-BotGr ... BAN [*Bulgarian Academy of Sciences*] Botanical Garden   (BU)
BANC .... Biblioteca Agricola Nacional de Colombia [*Colombia*]   (DSCA)
BANCA ...... Banco Cafetero [*Colombia*]
BANCAHORRO ... Banco de el Ahorro Hondureno SA [*Honduras*]   (EY)
BANCAHSA ... Banco la Capitalizadora Hondurena Sociedad Anonima [*Honduras*]   (EY)
BANCALDAS ... Banco de Caldas [*Manizales*]   (COL)
BANCATLAN ... Banco Atlantida SA [*Honduras*]   (EY)
BANCEPAC ... Bancos Centrales del Pacto Andino [*Andean Pact Central Banks*]   (LA)
BANCOAMERICA ... Banco de America Latina [*Colombia*]   (COL)
BANCOBU ... Banque Commerciale du Burundi   (EY)
BANCOCCI ... Banco de Occidente SA [*Honduras*]   (EY)
BANCOLAT ... Banco de Latinoamerica, SA [*Panama*]   (EY)
BANCOLOM ... Banco de Colombia [*Colombia*]   (COL)
BANCOMER ... Banco Comercial [*Bank of Commerce*] [*Mexico*]   (LA)
BANCOMER ... Banco de Comercio SA [*Honduras*]   (EY)
BANCON ... Banco Continental SA [*Honduras*]   (EY)
BANCON ... Banco Latino de Fomento de la Construccion [*Peru*]   (EY)
BANCOPLAN ... Cooperativa dos Plantadores de Cana de Pernambuco Ltd. [*Brazil*]   (DSCA)
BANCOQUIA ... Banco Comercial Antioqueno [*Colombia*] Tlg.   (COL)
BANCOSTA ... Banco de la Costa SA [*Barranquilla*] Tlg.   (COL)
BANCOTRAB ... Banco de los Trabajadores SA [*Honduras*]   (EY)

BAND .... Businesses Against Non-Deductibility [*Australia*]
BANDA ..... Bureau of Anti-Narcotics and Drug Abuse [*Bangladesh*]   (EAIO)
BANDAGRO ... Banco de Desarrollo Agropecuario [*Agricultural and Livestock Development Bank*] [*Venezuela*]   (LA)
B&BRSWW ... Bed & Breakfast Reservation Services World-Wide [*An association*]
B & CA .... Business and Consumer Affairs Department [*New South Wales, Australia*]
B & Cie .... Bordier & Compagnie [*Bank*] [*Switzerland*]
B & Co .... Baladi and Co. [*Switzerland*]
BANDEGUA ... Compania de Desarrollo Bananero de Guatemala Ltda. [*Guatemala Banana Development Company Ltd.*]   (LA)
BANDELCO ... Banco del Comercio SA [*Colombia*] Tlg.   (COL)
BANDEPE ... Banco do Desenvolvimento do Estado de Pernambuco [*Recife, Brazil*]   (LAA)
BANDES ... National Bank for Social and Economical Development [*Cuba*]
BANDESA ... Banco Nacional de Desarrollo [*National Development Bank*] [*Guatemala*]   (LA)
Bandesa ..... Banco Nacional de Desarrollo Agricola [*National Agricultural Development Bank*] [*Honduras*]   (GEA)
BANDESABANA ... Banco de la Sabana [*Colombia*] Tlg.   (COL)
BANDESCO ... Banco de Desarrollo de la Construccion [*Construction Development Bank*] [*Peru*]   (GEA)
BANDEVI ... Banco de Desarrollo de la Vivienda [*Chile*]   (LAA)
B & RD .... Department of Business and Regional Development [*New South Wales, Australia*]
B & S .... Bank and Savill Line [*Australia*]   (ADA)
BANEB ...... Banco de Estado da Bahia [*Brazil*]   (DSCA)
BANERJ ... Banco do Estado do Rio De Janeiro SA [*State commercial bank*] [*Brazil*]
BANERJ ... Banco do Estado do Rio de Janiero SA [*Brazil*]   (EY)
BANESPA ... Banco do Estado de Sao Paulo [*Brazil*]   (EY)
BANEst ..... Library of the Academy of Sciences, Estonian SSR   (RU)
BANESTADO ... Banco del Estado [*Popayan*] Tlg.   (COL)
BANESTES ... Banco do Estado do Espirito Santo [*Espirito Santo State Bank*] [*Brazil*]   (LA)
BANESTO ... Banco Espanol de Credito [*Spanish Credit Bank*]
BAN-EtnogrMuzey ... BAN [*Bulgarian Academy of Sciences*] Ethnographic Museum   (BU)
BANEXI .... Banque pour l'Expansion Industrielle [*Industrial Development Bank*] [*France*]   (EY)
BAN-F .... Library of the Academy of Sciences (Frunze)   (RU)
BANFAIC ... Banco de Fomento Agricola e Industrial de Cuba [*Cuba*]   (DSCA)
BANFOCO ... Banco Nacional de Fomento Cooperativo [*National Cooperative Development Bank*] [*Mexico*]   (LA)
Bang .... Bangladesh   (ILCA)
BANGr ...... Library of the Academy of Sciences, Georgian SSR   (RU)
BANHCAFE ... Banco Hondureno del Cafe [*Honduras*]   (EY)
BANHICO ... Banco Hipotecario de la Construccion SA [*The Dominican Republic*]   (EY)
BAN-IArkh ... BAN [*Bulgarian Academy of Sciences*] Institute of Archives   (BU)
BAN-IArkhit ... BAN [*Bulgarian Academy of Sciences*] Institute of Architecture   (BU)
BAN-IBiol ... BAN [*Bulgarian Academy of Sciences*] Institute of Biology   (BU)
BAN-IBot .. BAN [*Bulgarian Academy of Sciences*] Botanical Institute   (BU)
BAN-IBulgEz ... BAN [*Bulgarian Academy of Sciences*] Institute for the Bulgarian Language   (BU)
BANIC .... Banco Nicaraguense [*Nicaraguan Bank*]   (LA)
BAN-IEksKhumMed ... BAN [*Bulgarian Academy of Sciences*] Institute of Experimental Medicine   (BU)
BAN-IEkspVetMed ... BAN [*Bulgarian Academy of Sciences*] Institute of Experimental Veterinary Medicine   (BU)
BAN-IFilos ... BAN [*Bulgarian Academy of Sciences*] Institute of Philosophy   (BU)
BAN-IFiz ... BAN [*Bulgarian Academy of Sciences*] Institute of Physics   (BU)
BAN-IGeogr ... BAN [*Bulgarian Academy of Sciences*] Geographic Institute   (BU)
BAN-IGeol ... BAN [*Bulgarian Academy of Sciences*] Geological Institute   (BU)
BAN-IIkon ... BAN [*Bulgarian Academy of Sciences*] Institute of Economics   (BU)
BAN-IIst .... BAN [*Bulgarian Academy of Sciences*] Institute of History   (BU)
BAN-IIzobrIzk ... BAN [*Bulgarian Academy of Sciences*] Institute of Representative Arts   (BU)
BAN-IKhim ... BAN [*Bulgarian Academy of Sciences*] Institute of Chemistry   (BU)
BAN-ILit ... BAN [*Bulgarian Academy of Sciences*] Institute of Literature   (BU)
BAN-IMat ... BAN [*Bulgarian Academy of Sciences*] Institute of Mathematics   (BU)
BAN-IMikrobiol ... BAN [*Bulgarian Academy of Sciences*] Institute of Microbiology   (BU)
BAN-IMuz ... BAN [*Bulgarian Academy of Sciences*] Institute of Music   (BU)

BAN-IPedag ... BAN [*Bulgarian Academy of Sciences*] Institute of Education (BU)
BAN-IPochv ... BAN [*Bulgarian Academy of Sciences*] Soil Institute (BU)
BAN-IPrilBiol ... BAN [*Bulgarian Academy of Sciences*] Institute of Applied Biology (BU)
BAN-IR ..... Library of the Academy of Sciences (Irkutsk) (RU)
BAN-ISotsMed ... BAN [*Bulgarian Academy of Sciences*] Institute of Social Medicine (BU)
BAN-ITekhn ... BAN [*Bulgarian Academy of Sciences*] Institute of Technology (BU)
BAN-IZhiv ... BAN [*Bulgarian Academy of Sciences*] Institute of Animal Husbandry (BU)
BAN-IZool ... BAN [*Bulgarian Academy of Sciences*] Institute of Zoology (BU)
bank .... Bank (RU)
bank .... Banking (BU)
BAN-K....... Library of the Academy of Sciences (Kazan') (RU)
BANKaz..... Library of the Academy of Sciences (Kazakh) (RU)
BAN-Kish ... Library of the Academy of Sciences (Kishinev) (RU)
BAN-Kl...... Library of the Academy of Sciences (Klyuchi) (RU)
Bankotrud ... Union of Credit Institution Workers (RU)
bank sch..... Bank Bookkeeping (BU)
Bank-Sen ... Kibris Turk Banka Iscileri Sendikasi [*Turkish Cypriot Bank Workers' Union*] (TU)
BAN-KT .... Library of the Academy of Sciences (Kurgan-Tyube) (RU)
bankw........ Bankwet [*Benelux*] (BAS)
BAN-L...... Library of the Academy of Sciences Leningrad (RU)
BANLat ...... Library of the Academy of Sciences, Latvian SSR (RU)
BANLit ...... Library of the Academy of Sciences, Lithuanian SSR (RU)
BAN-L'v ... Library of the Academy of Sciences, Ukrainian SSR (L'vov) (RU)
BAN-M...... Library of the Academy of Sciences (Moscow) (RU)
Banma........ Banco Municipal Autonomo [*Autonomous Municipal Bank*] [*Honduras*] (GEA)
BAN-MK... Library of the Academy of Sciences (Makhachkala) (RU)
BAN-Mur.. Library of the Academy of Sciences (Murgab) (RU)
BAN-N...... Library of the Academy of Sciences (Nikolayev) (RU)
BAN-Nch... Library of the Academy of Sciences (Novocherkassk) (RU)
BAN-Ns..... Library of the Academy of Sciences (Novosibirsk) (RU)
BANOBRAS ... Banco Nacional de Obras y Servicios Publicos SA [*Bank*] [*Mexico*]
BANOCO ... Bahrain National Oil Co. [*State enterprise*] (EY)
BAN-Osh... Library of the Academy of Sciences (Osh) (RU)
BANPECO ... Banco Peruano de los Constructores [*Bank*] [*Peru*]
BANPOPULAR ... Banco Popular [*Colombia*] (COL)
BAN-PrirMuzey ... BAN [*Bulgarian Academy of Sciences*] Natural History Museum (BU)
Banq.......... Banque [*Bank*] [*French*]
BANRURAL ... Banco Nacional de Credito Rural SA [*Bank*] [*Mexico*]
BAN-S ...... Library of the Academy of Sciences (Stalinabad) (RU)
BANSANTANDER ... Banco de Santander [*Bucaramanga*] Tlg. (COL)
BANSDOC ... Bangladesh National Scientific and Technical Documentation Centre (PDAA)
BAN-Shch ... Library of the Academy of Sciences (Shcherbakov) (RU)
BAN-Sim .. Library of the Academy of Sciences (Simeiz) (RU)
BAN-Simf .. Library of the Academy of Sciences (Simferopol') (RU)
BAN-Sv ..... Library of the Academy of Sciences (Sverdlovsk) (RU)
BANSW..... Blindmakers' Association of New South Wales [*Australia*]
BANSW..... Board of Architects of New South Wales [*Australia*]
BANSW..... Boxing Authority of New South Wales [*Australia*]
BANSW..... Brewers' Association of New South Wales [*Australia*]
BAN-Sykt ... Library of the Academy of Sciences (Syktyvkar) (RU)
BANTA ..... Basutoland African National Teachers' Association
Bantral ...... Banco Central de Honduras [*Central Bank of Honduras*] (GEA)
BANU....... Library of the Academy of Sciences, Ukrainian SSR (RU)
BANU-L'v ... Library of the Academy of Sciences, Ukrainian SSR, (L'vov) (RU)
BANUz...... Library of the Academy of Sciences,(Uzbek) (RU)
BAN-V...... Library of the Academy of Sciences (Vladivostok) (RU)
Banvi......... Banco Nacional de la Vivienda [*National Housing Bank*] [*Guatemala*] (GEA)
bany.......... Banyaszat [*Mining*] (HU)
BAN-Ya..... Library of the Academy of Sciences (Yakutsk) (RU)
BANYATERV ... Banyaszati Tervezo Intezet [*Planning Institute of Mining*] (HU)
Banykut .... Banyaszati Kutato Intezet [*Mining Research Institute*] (HU)
BAN-YuS .. Library of the Academy of Sciences (Yuzhno-Sakhalinsk) (RU)
BANZ .... Booksellers' Association of New Zealand
BANZARE ... British-Australian-New Zealand Antarctic Research Expedition [*1929-31*]
BAN-ZoolGr ... BAN [*Bulgarian Academy of Sciences*] Zoological Garden (BU)
bao.......... Air Base Battalion (BU)
BAO.......... Airfield Service Battalion (RU)
BAO.......... Banque d'Afrique Occidentale [*Bank of French West Africa*]
BAO.......... Bayer Afrique de l'Ouest

BAO.......... Beijing Astronomical Observatory [*Chinese Academy of Sciences*] [*Research center*] (EAS)
BAO.......... Betriebs-Absatzorganisation [*Plant Sales Organization*] (EG)
BAOM....... Bibliotheque d'Afrique et d'Outre-Mer
Baon........ Batalion [*Battalion*] [*Poland*]
bap .... Air Bombardment Regiment (BU)
BAP .... Baibara [*Papua New Guinea*] [*Airport symbol*] (OAG)
BAP .... Banco Agricola y Pecuario [*Agriculture and Livestock Bank*] [*Venezuela*] (LA)
BAP .... Bankers Association of the Philippines (DS)
BAP .... Banque Agricole Paysanne [*Farmers Agricultural Bank*] [*Cambodia*] (CL)
BAP .... Billet a Payer [*Bill Payable*] [*French*] [*Business term*]
BAP .... Bomber Regiment (RU)
BAP .... Brazilian Agricultural Prices
BAP .... Brevet d'Aptitude Pedagogique [*French*]
BAP .... Brigade Active du Port [*Regular Port Brigade*] [*Cambodia*] (CL)
BAP .... Brigades Attelees de Production
BAP .... Bulgarian Agrarian Party [*Political party*] (PPW)
BAP .... Bureau Algerien des Petroles
BAPCO...... Bahrain Petroleum Company Ltd. (ME)
BAPD .... Belizean Assembly of and for Persons with Disabilities (EAIO)
BAPEBTI .. Badan Pelaksana Bursa Komoditi [*Indonesian Commodity Exchange Board*] (EAIO)
BAPEPAM ... Badan Pelaksana Pasar Modal [*Capital Market Executive Agency*] [*Stock exchange Indonesia*] (FEA)
BAPERDA ... Badan Perentjanaan Daerah [*Regional Planning Board*] (IN)
BAPERNAS ... Badan Perentjanaan Nasional [*National Planning Board*] (IN)
BAPETCO ... Badreddin Petroleum Co. [*Egypt*]
BAPH .... Brisbane, Adelaide, Perth, Hobart [*Australia*]
BAPI......... Barcelona, Spain - Pisa, Italy [*Submarine cable*] [*Telecommunications*]
BAPINDO ... Bank Pembangunan Indonesia [*Indonesian Development Bank*] (IN)
BAPP........ Bulgarian Agrarian People's Party [*Political party*] (PPW)
BAPP........ Bureau Arabe de Presse et de Publications
BAPPENAS ... Badan Perentjanaan Pembangunan Nasional [*National Development Planning Board*] (IN)
BAppScInfo ... Bachelor of Applied Science - Information
BAppSci(Optom) ... Bachelor of Applied Science (Optometry)
BAppSci(SocEcol) ... Bachelor of Applied Science (Social Ecology)
BAPSA ...... Brigade d'Assistance aux Personnes sans Abri [*French*]
BAPSC ...... Badeku Agricultural Production and Supply Company
bapt .... Baptista [*Baptist*] (HU)
BAPU .... Bulgarian Agrarian People's Union-United [*Political party*] (EY)
BAPU-NP ... Bulgarian Agrarian People's Union - Nikola Petkov [*Political party*]
BAPV........ High-Speed Automatic Reclosing (RU)
BAQ.......... Bar Association of Queensland [*Australia*]
BAQ.......... Barranquilla [*Colombia*] [*Airport symbol*] (OAG)
BAQ.......... Board of Architects of Queensland [*Australia*]
BAR .... Barometer [*Afrikaans*]
bar............ Barometryczny [*Barometric*] [*Poland*]
bar............ Baron [*Baron*] [*Poland*]
Bar .... Barone [*Baron*] [*Italian*]
BAR .... Barque [*Bark, Boat*] [*French*] (ROG)
Bar .... Barrack [*Topography*] (RU)
BAR .... Berliner Aussenring [*Berlin Outer Ring*] (EG)
BAR .... Billet a Recevoir [*Bill Receivable*] [*French*] [*Business term*]
BAR .... Binnenaanvaringsreglement [*Benelux*] (BAS)
BAR .... Board of Airline Representatives [*Australia*]
BAR .... Brigade Aeroportee Renforcee [*Reinforced Airborne Brigade*] [*Zaire*] (AF)
BARA .... Barisan Rakyat [*People's Front*] [*Brunei*] (ML)
BARA .... Board of Airline Representatives of Australia
BARA .... Bureau d'Analyse et de Recherche Appliquees [*Bureau of Analysis and Applied Research*] [*French*]
BARABA ... Narodni Podnik pro Stavbu Tunelu [*National Enterprise for the Construction of Tunnels*] (CZ)
BARB........ Barbados (ROG)
BARB........ Cooperativa Banco Agricola de Rio Bonito Ltd. [*Brazil*] (DSCA)
BArbG .... Bundesarbeitsgericht [*Federal Labor Court*] [*German*] (ILCA)
BARC........ Bangladesh Agricultural Research Council [*Research center*] (IRC)
BARC........ Berger Ardoin & Compagnie
BARC........ Bhabha Atomic Research Centre [*India*]
BARC........ Bhabha Atomic Research Centre [*India*]
BARC........ Brewery Agro & Research Company [*Jos International Breweries*] [*Nigeria*]
BARC........ Bureau d'Affretement Routier Centrafricain (EY)
BARC........ Bus Apartheid Resistance Committee
BARCEP ... Barclays Australia Investment Services Consensus Earnings Profile
BArchSt..... Bachelor of Architectural Studies

BArchStudies ... Bachelor of Architectural Studies
BARD .... Bangladesh Academy for Rural Development [*Research center*] (IRC)
BARD .... Binational Agricultural Research and Development Fund [*US-Israeli*] [*Research center*] (IRC)
Bar-Der-Is ... Bagirsak ve Deri Iscilerin Sendikasi [*Animal Casings and Leather Workers Union*] (TU)
BAREM ..... Bureau Algerien de Recherches et d'Exploitation Miniere
barev .... Barevny [*In Color*] [*Publishing Former Czechoslovakia*]
BARG .... Building Action Review Group [*Australia*]
BaRI .... Ballistics Research Institute [*Turkey*] (ERC)
BARI .... Bangladesh Agricultural Research Institute (ARC)
BARIF .... Banjarbaru Research Institute for Food Crops [*Indonesia*] [*Research center*] (IRC)
BARIF .... Banjarmasin Research Institute for Food Crops [*Indonesian*] [*Research center*] (IRC)
BARIG ...... Board of Airline Representatives in Germany
BARIM ...... Bureau d'Achat de la Republique Islamique de Mauritanie [*Islamic Republic of Mauritania Purchasing Office*] (AF)
BARJASA ... Barisan Ra'ayat Jati Sarawak [*Sarawak Indigenous People's Front*] (ML)
BARK .... Bicentennial Australian Revolutionary Kommandos
BARKISAN ... Bartin Kirec Sanayii AS [*Bartin Lime Industry, Inc.*] [*Zonguldak*] (TU)
BARN .... Biologisch Agrarische Reactor Nederland [*Netherlands Biological Agrarian Reactor*] (WEN)
Barna .... Barcelona [*Spain*]
BARNACS ... Barbados National Association of Cooperative Societies (EY)
BARNOD .. Barnod [*Barbados*] (EAIO)
barom .... Barometer [*Barometer*] (HU)
barr .... Barrique [*Barrel*] [*French*]
BARRA ...... Barisan Revolusi Rakyat [*People's Revolution Front*] (ML)
BARRC ...... Bicol Consortium for Agriculture and Natural Resources Research and Development [*Philippines*] (IRC)
BARS .... Bangladesh Amateur Radio Society (PDAA)
B/ART .... Bataillon d'Artillerie [*Artillery Battalion*] [*Cambodia*] (CL)
BArtEd ...... Bachelor of Art Education
BArtTh ...... Bachelor of Art Theory
BARU .... High-Speed Automatic Gain Control (RU)
barwn .... Barwny [*Colorful*] [*Poland*]
BAS .... Aero Services [*Barbados*] [*ICAO designator*] (FAAC)
BAS .... Bahrain Airport Services
BAS .... Balalae [*Solomon Islands*] [*Airport symbol*] (OAG)
BAS .... Bangladesh Academy of Sciences (EAIO)
BAS .... Barbados Astronomical Society (SLS)
bas .... Basane [*Sheepskin*] [*Publishing*] [*French*]
BAS .... Basel [*Bale*] [*Switzerland*] [*Seismograph station code, US Geological Survey*]
bas .... Basin, Reservoir [*Topography*] (RU)
bas .... Basisch [*Basic*] [*German*] (GCA)
Bas .... Basutoland (BARN)
BAS .... Bataljon Aerodromski Sluzbe [*Airport Service Battalion*] (YU)
BAS .... Bavarian Academy of Sciences [*Germany*] (EAIO)
BAS .... Befreiungsaktion fuer Suedtirol [*Liberation Group for South Tyrol*] [*Austria*] (WEN)
BAS .... Bomber Unit (RU)
BAS .... Border Agricultural Society [*South Africa*] (EAIO)
BAS .... Brussels American School [*Belgium*]
BAS .... Bulgarian Academy of Sciences (EAIO)
BAS .... Dry B Battery (RU)
BASA .... Babysitting Association of South Australia
BASA .... Bahnselbstanschlussanlage [*(GDR) Railroad Automatic Telephone System*] (EG)
BASA .... Banco da Amazonia [*Bank of Amazonia*] [*Brazil*] (LA)
BASA .... British-Australian Studies Association
BASC .... Business Advisory Service Centre [*Townsville, Australia*]
BASCON ... Basso Continuo [*Continued Bass*] [*Music*] (ROG)
BASD .... Banque Asiatique de Developpement [*Asian Development Bank - ADB*] [*French*]
BASE .... Bureau Africain des Sciences de l'Education [*African Bureau for Science Education*] [*Zaire*]
BASES ...... Building and Solar Energy Service [*New Zealand*]
BASF .... Badische Anilin und Soda-Fabrik [*Automotive industry supplier*]
BASF .... Badische Anilin- und Sodafabrik AG [*Baden Aniline and Soda Factory*] (EG)
BASG .... Blacktown Agoraphobia Support Group [*Australia*]
BashASSR ... Bashkir Autonomous Soviet Socialist Republic (RU)
Bashgosizdat ... Bashkir State Publishing House (RU)
bashk .... Bashkir (RU)
BashASSR ... Bashkir Autonomous Soviet Socialist Republic (RU)
Bashknigoizdat ... Bashkir Book Publishing House (RU)
Bashles .... Kombinat of Lumber Industry Establishments of Bashkir ASSR (RU)
BashLOS ... Bashkir Forest Experimental Station (RU)
Bashneft' .... Association of the Bashkir Petroleum Industry (RU)

BashNIINP ... Bashkir Scientific Research Institute for Petroleum Processing (RU)
BashNIIStroy ... Bashkir Scientific Research Institute for Construction (RU)
BashSSR .... Bashkir Soviet Socialist Republic
BASI .... Bundesarbeitsgemeinschaft fuer Arbeitssicherheit [*Study Group for Job Security*] (SLS)
BASI .... Bureau of Air Safety Investigation [*Australia*]
BAsianStudies ... Bachelor of Asian Studies
BASIC .... Bank of Small Industries and Commerce [*Bangladesh*] (EY)
Basin-Is ...... Turkiye Gazeteciler ve Basin Sanayii Iscileri Sendikasi [*Turkish Journalists and Press Industry Workers Union*] (TU)
BASJE .... Bolivian Air Shower Joint Experiment (PDAA)
Bas Kom ..... Bas Komiser [*Chief Commissioner (of police)*] (TU)
Baskomflot ... Basin Committee of the Trade Union of Workers of the Maritime and River Fleets (RU)
Baskommor ... Basin Committee of the Marine Transportation Workers' Trade Union (RU)
Baskomrech ... Basin Committee of the River Transportation Workers' Trade Union (RU)
BASL .... Banco Agricola de Sete Lagoas SA [*Brazil*] (DSCA)
BASMTB .. Belgian Association for the Study, Modification and Therapy of Behavior (EAIO)
Bas Muf ..... Bas Mufettis [*Chief Inspector*] (TU)
Bas Ogrt ..... Bas Ogretmen [*Head Teacher*] (TU)
BASOMED ... Basutoland Socio-Medical Services
bass .... Basin, Reservoir [*Topography*] (RU)
BASS .... Bendigo Agricultural Show Society [*Australia*]
BASSA ...... Bangladesh-Australia Society of South Australia
BASSCON ... Basso Continuo [*Continued Bass*] [*Music*]
BASSP .... Bicentennial Australian Studies Schools Project
BASSR ...... Bashkir Autonomous Soviet Socialist Republic (RU)
BASSR ...... Buryat Autonomous Soviet Socialist Republic (RU)
bast .... Bastante [*Sufficiently*] [*Portuguese*]
BASt .... Bundesanstalt fuer Strassenwesen [*Federal Highway Research Institute*] [*Database producer*] [*Germany*] [*Research center*] (IRC)
Bastand ...... Barometerstand [*Barometric Pressure*] [*German*] (GCA)
BASUCOL ... Barranquilla Supply Company Limited [*Barranquilla*] (COL)
BAT .... Badminton Association of Thailand (EAIO)
BAT .... Banque d'Algerie et de la Tunisie
Bat .... Bataillon [*Battalion*] [*Military*] [*French*] (MTD)
bat .... Bataljon [*Battalion*] [*Afrikaans*]
Bat .... Bateau [*Boat*] [*Military map abbreviation World War I*] [*French*] (MTD)
bat .... Bateria [*Battery*] [*Poland*]
Bat .... Bateria [*Battery*] [*Portuguese*]
Bat .... Batiment [*Building*] [*French*]
BAT .... Bois Africains Tropicaux
BAT .... Bolshoi Alt-Azimuth Telescope [*Former USSR*]
BAT .... Brevet d'Aptitude Technique
BAT .... Bureau de l'Assistance Technique
BAT .... Bureau of Air Transport [*Philippines*] (DS)
BAT .... Butler Air Transport [*Australia*] (ADA)
Bata .... Batallon [*Battalion*] [*Spanish*]
BATAL ...... Banque Tchado-Arabe Libyenne pour le Commerce et le Developpement [*Chadian-Libyan Arab Bank for Trade and Development*] (AF)
BATAN ..... Badan Tenaga Atom Nasional [*National Atomic Energy Agency*] (IN)
BATAN ..... Bangkok Tanner (Group) Co. Ltd. [*Thailand*]
BATC .... Brussels Air Terminal Co. [*Belgium*]
BATCO ...... Bauxite and Alumina Trading Company of Jamaica (LA)
BATELCO ... Bahamas Telecommunications Corporation (LA)
BATELCO ... Bahrain Telecommunications Co.
BATI .... Bintara Tinggi [*Warrant Officer*] (IN)
BATICO .... Batiment et Construction Societe Anonyme
Batie .... Batterie [*Battery*] [*Military map abbreviation World War I*] [*French*] (MTD)
BATIM ...... Bureau Africain des Travaux d'Interet Militaire
BATIMA ... Societe Batiments et Materiaux
BATIMETAL ... Entreprise Nationale de Batiments Industrialises [*Nationalized industry*] [*Algeria*] (EY)
BATL .... Business Apprentices Training Ltd. [*Australia*]
BATMAAGA ... Baza de Aprovizionare Tehnico-Materiala pentru Agricultura cu Ambalaje si Gospodaria Ambalajelor [*Base for Technical-Material Supply of Packaging to Agriculture and Packaging Management*] (RO)
BATMMB ... Baza de Aprovizionare Tehnico-Materiala a Municipiului Bucuresti [*Technical-Material Supply Base for Bucharest Municipality*] (RO)
bat-n .... Battalion (RU)
BATO .... Airfield Technical Support Battalion (RU)
BATO .... Britain-Africa Trade Organisation
batr .... Artillery Battery (RU)
batr .... Battery (BU)

BATRAL ... Batiment de Transport Leger [*Light Transport Ship*] [*French*] (WER)
batr b/o ...... Recoilless Gun Battery (BU)
batr FR...... Photogrammetric Reconnaissance Battery (BU)
batrPTURS ... Antitank Guided Missile Battery (RU)
batr RTR... Electronic Reconnaissance Battery (BU)
batr RU ..... Reconnaissance Battery Command and Control (BU)
Batr SAU ... Battery of Self-Propelled Guns (RU)
batr s/o...... Battery of Self-Propelled Guns (RU)
batr TR...... Topographic Battery [*Artillery*] (BU)
batr ZR ..... Sound-Ranging Battery (BU)
BATSB ...... Bundesanstalt fuer Tierseuchenbekaempfung in Moedling [*Federal Institute for the Control of Infectious Diseases in Animals*] [*Austria*] (ARC)
batshd .... Baterie Samohybnych Del [*Battery of Self-Propelled Artillery*] (CZ)
batsr .... Artillery Ordnance Supply and Repairs Battalion (BU)
Batt .... Batterie [*Battery*] [*French*] (MTD)
Batt .... Batterie [*Battery*] [*German*] (GCA)
BATT........ Battery [*Afrikaans*]
Battr........ Batterie [*Battery*] [*German*] (GCA)
BATU .... Brotherhood of Asian Trade Unionists [*Philippines*]
BATYL ..... Building Apprentices Training Ltd. [*Australia*]
BAU .... Bangladesh Agricultural University (PDAA)
BAU .... Bauru [*Brazil*] [*Airport symbol*] (OAG)
BAU .... Bulgarian Agrarian Union [*Political party*]
Bau-BG ..... Bau-Berufsgenossenschaft [*State Insurance Organization for Building*] [*Germany*] (PDAA)
BAUFO ..... Bauforschungsprojekte [*Building Research Projects*] [*Fraunhofer Society*] [*Information service or system*] (IID)
Baumstr ..... Baumeister [*Master Builder*] [*German*]
BAURES ... Bangladesh Agricultural University Research System [*Research center*] (IRC)
Bauw .... Bauwesen [*Constructional Engineering*] [*German*] (GCA)
BAUXIVEN ... Bauxita Venezolana, CA [*Venezuela*] (LA)
BAV .... Air Varna Co. [*Bulgaria*] [*ICAO designator*] (FAAC)
BAV .... Bachelier en Arts Visuels [*Bachelor of Visual Arts*] [*French*]
BAV .... Baotou [*China*] [*Airport symbol*] (OAG)
BAV .... Barium-Aluminum-Vanadium Catalyst (RU)
BAV .... Bavaria [*State in West Germany*] (ROG)
BAV .... Bereit zur Arbeit und zur Verteidigung des Friedens (Sportleistungsabzeichen) [*Ready for Work and for the Defense of Peace (Sport Achievement Medal)*] [*German*] (EG)
BAV .... Bizomanyi Aruhaz Vallalat [*Retail Store for Sales on Commission*] (HU)
BAV .... Boucherie Arsenique Vert
BAV .... Bulharska Akademie Ved [*Bulgarian Academy of Sciences*] (CZ)
BAV .... Large Amphibian Truck (RU)
BAVK .... Besluit Algemeen Vestigingsverbod Kleinbedrijf [*Benelux*] (BAS)
BAW .... Beijing Auto Works [*China*]
BAW .... Bremer Ausschuss fuer Wirtschaftsforschung [*Bremen Commission for Scientifc Research*] (SLS)
BAW .... Bundesamt fuer Gewerbliche Wirtschaft [*Federal Office for Trade and Industry*]
BAW .... Bundesanstalt fuer Wasserbau [*Federal Center for Waterway Engineering*] [*Research center*] [*Germany*] (EAS)
BAW .... Bureau of Animal Welfare [*Victoria, Australia*]
BAWA .... Badminton Association of Western Australia
BAWAG .... Bank fuer Arbeit und Wirtschaft Aktiengesellschaft [*Bank for Work and Management Joint Stock Company*] [*Austria*]
BAWC ...... Brisbane Amateur Winemakers' Club [*Australia*]
BAWI....... Bundesamt fuer Aussenwirtschaft [*Switzerland*]
BAWU ...... Black Allied Workers Union [*South Africa*] (AF)
BAWV ...... Bundesarbeitsgemeinschaft Wirtschaftswissenschaftlicher Vereinigungen [*Society for Scientific Economic Study*] (SLS)
BAY .... Baia Mare [*Romania*] [*Airport symbol*] (OAG)
BAY .... Bay Air Aviation [*New Zealand*] [*ICAO designator*] (FAAC)
Bay........... Bayern [*Bavaria*] [*German*]
BAYA .... Brong Ahafo Youth Association
Bayan........ Bagong Alyansang Makabayan [*Philippines*] [*Political party*] (EY)
BAYBA..... Bayindirlik Bakanligi [*Public Works Ministry*] (TU)
Bayr .... Bayrisch [*Bavarian*] [*German*]
Baysen-Is... Ministry of Public Works Directorate General of Construction Activities Workers Union (TU)
BAYWA .... Bayerische Warenvermittlung Landwirtschaftlicher Genossenschaften Aktiengesellschaft [*Bavarian Commodity Supply and Agricultural Association*]
BAZ .... Automobile Made by the Belorussian Automobile Plant (RU)
baz............ Basalt (RU)
baz............ Bazzana [*Sheepskin*] [*Publishing*] [*Italian*]
BAZ .... Belorussian Automobile Plant (RU)
BAZ .... Biuro Angazowania Zalog [*Crew Hiring Office*] (POL)

BAZ .... Bogoslovsk Aluminum Plant [*Karpinsk*] (RU)
BAZ .... Character Analysis Unit (RU)
BAZA .... Banque du Zaire
BAZIL ...... Office of Automation of the Moscow Automobile Plant Imeni Likhachev (RU)
BAZIS ...... Office of Automation of the Moscow Automobile Plant Imeni Stalin (RU)
bazkom...... Base Committee (RU)
bazotsentrir ... Base-Centered (RU)
BAZS........ Union of Bulgarian University Students of the Agrarian Party (BU)
BB .... Bahusbanken [*Bank*] [*Swaziland*]
BB .... Baloldali Blokk [*Coalition of the Left*] (HU)
BB .... Banca Brignone [*Italy*]
BB .... Banco de Bilbao [*Italian*]
BB .... Banco de Bilbao [*Spain*]
BB .... Banco do Brasil [*Bank of Brazil*]
BB .... Bangkok Bank [*Thailand*]
BB .... Bangsa Bersatu [*United Nations*] (ML)
BB .... Bankim Barotra [*Commerce Bank*] [*Malagasy*] (AF)
BB .... Barbados [*ANSI two-letter standard code*] (CNC)
BB .... Barclaycard [*Credit card*]
BB .... Battalion Base (RU)
BB .... Baugrunduntersuchung Berlin [*Office for Construction-Site Surveys in Berlin*] [*German*] (EG)
BB .... Bayindirlik Bakanligi [*Public Works Ministry*] (TU)
bb .... Beacon Keeper's Cabin [*Topography*] (RU)
BB .... Bedrijfsbelasting [*Benelux*] (BAS)
BB .... Belgian Boerenbond (EAIO)
BB .... Beobachtung [*Observation*] [*German*]
BB .... Bergen Bank [*Norway*]
BB .... Beruhazasi Bank [*Investment Bank*] (HU)
BB .... Besuchsbericht [*Frequency Report*] [*German*] (ADPT)
BB .... Betriebsabrechnungsbogen [*Master Summary Sheet, Operations Sheet, Cost Control Sheet*] [*BAB*] [*Also,*] [*German*] (EG)
BB .... Betriebsberichterstattung [*Enterprise Reporting*] [*German*] (EG)
BB .... Bevolkingsboekhouding [*Benelux*] (BAS)
bb .... Bez Broja [*No Number*] (YU)
Bb .... Bijblad op het Staatsblad [*Benelux*] (BAS)
BB .... Billet de Bank [*Bank Note*] [*French*] (GPO)
bb .... Bojni Brod [*Battleship*] (YU)
BB .... Bombordo [*Port*] [*Portuguese*]
BB .... Boys' Brigade [*British*]
BB .... Brasseries de Brazzaville
BB .... Brisbane Basketball
BB .... Brisbane Biennial
bb .... Broeder [*Brother*] [*Afrikaans*]
BB .... Budapest Bajnoksag [*Budapest Championship*] (HU)
BB .... Bundesbahnen [*Federal Railway*] [*German*]
BB .... Burgan Bank [*Kuwait*]
BB .... Der Betriebs-Berater [*Germany*] (FLAF)
BB .... Hawker Siddeley Aviation Ltd. [*British*] [*ICAO aircraft manufacturer identifier*] (ICAO)
BB .... Hospital Base (BU)
BB .... Short-Range Bomber (RU)
BB .... Turret Battery (RU)
BBA .... Bahrain Badminton Association (EAIO)
BBA .... Balmaceda [*Chile*] [*Airport symbol*] (OAG)
BBA .... Banco Boliviano Agropecuario [*Bolivian Farming Bank*] (LA)
BBA .... Banque Belge d'Afrique [*Belgian Bank of Africa*]
BBA .... Barclays Bank Australia
BBA .... Berichterstattung zum Plan der Berufsausbildung [*Report on the Vocational Training Plan*] [*German*] (EG)
BBA .... Betaling by Aflewering [*Cash on Delivery*] [*Afrikaans*]
BBA .... Biologische Bundesanstalt fuer Land- und Forstwirtschaft [*Federal Biological Research Center for Agriculture and Forestry*] (ARC)
BBA .... Bolnicka Baza Armije [*Army Hospital Base*] (YU)
BBA .... Bolshoi Ballet Academy [*Moscow*]
BBA .... Botswana Bowling Association
BBA .... Brain & Brown Airfreighters [*Australia*]
BBA .... Buitenbewoon Besluit Arbeidsvorhoudingen [*Benelux*] (BAS)
BBA .... Short-Range Bombardment Aviation (RU)
BBAA....... Bloodhorse Breeders Association of Australia (ADA)
BBAB....... Banque Belgo-Africaine du Burundi [*Commercial bank*] [*Bujumbura*]
BBAD ...... Short-Range Bomber Division (RU)
BBAG .... Brown Boveri AG [*Commercial firm*]
BBAN ...... Library of the Bulgarian Academy of Sciences (BU)
BBAP....... Short-Range Bomber Regiment (RU)
BBB .... Balair AG [*Switzerland*] [*ICAO designator*] (FAAC)
BBB........... Blanke Bevrydingsbeweging [*White Protection Movement*] [*South Africa*] [*Political party*] (EY)
B-B-B .... Burn-Bash-Bury [*Australian trash disposal policy in Vietnam*] (VNW)
BBBG........ Britse en Buitelandse Bybelgenootskap [*Afrikaans*]

BBC............ Banahaw Broadcasting Corporation [*Philippines*]
BBC............ Bangkok Bible College [*Thailand*]
BBC............ Bangladesh Biman [*ICAO designator*]   (FAAC)
BBC............ Biblioteca de la Bolsa de Cereales [*Argentina*]   (DSCA)
BBC............ Biplabi Bangla Congress [*India*] [*Political party*]   (PPW)
BBC............ Boxing Board of Control
BBC............ Brisbane Bushwalkers Club
BBC............ Brown Boveri & Compagnie [*German-Swiss builder of electrical-engineering and electronic equipment, nuclear power plants, and machinery*]   (EG)
BBC............ Buchanan Borehole Collieries Proprietary Ltd. [*Australia*]
BBCCI .... Brunei Bumiputra Chamber of Commerce and Industry [*Brunei Darussalam*]   (EAIO)
BBD .... Balgarsko Botanicesko Druzestvo [*Bulgarian Botanical Society*]   (EAIO)
BBD .... Banque Beninoise pour le Developpement [*Beninese Development Bank*]   (AF)
BBD .... Buero der Betreuung der Diplomaten [*Service Office for Diplomats*]   (EG)
BBE............ Short-Range Bomber Squadron   (RU)
BBehavSci ... Bachelor of Behavioral Sciences
BBEIUWWA ... Breweries and Bottleyard Employees' Industrial Union of Workers of Western Australia
Bbespr........ Boekbespreking [*Benelux*]   (BAS)
bbetr........... Concrete Construction Battalion   (RU)
bbetr........... Concrete Works Battalion   (BU)
BBEU.......... Breweries and Bottleyards Employees' Union [*Australia*]
BBF............ Bangladesh Badminton Federation   (EAIO)
BBF............ Bangladesh Baptist Fellowship   (EAIO)
BBF............ Belgian Badminton Federation   (EAIO)
BBF............ Bulgarian Badminton Federation   (EAIO)
BBF............ Front Hospital Base   (BU)
BBG .... Bayerische Botanische Gesellschaft [*Bavarian Botanical Society*]   (SLS)
BBG .... Biro Bantuan Guaman [*Legal Aid Bureau*]   (ML)
BBG .... Bodenbearbeitungsgeraete, Leipzig [*Leipzig Agricultural Machines and Implements Plant*]   (EG)
BBG .... Butaritari [*Kiribati*] [*Airport symbol*]   (OAG)
BBGS.......... Bund der Baptistengemeinden in der Schweiz [*Union of Baptist Churches in Switze rland*]   (EAIO)
BBH .... Al-Baha [*Saudi Arabia*] [*Airport symbol*]   (OAG)
BBH .... Berichten over de Buitenlandse Handel [*Benelux*]   (BAS)
BBH .... Bond Brewing Holdings [*Australia*]
BBHS......... Australian Business Brief and Hansard Service [*Australian Chamber of Commerce*] [*Information service or system*] [*Defunct*]   (IID)
BBI............ Barbara Bain International
BBI............ Bereich Bezirksgeleitete Industrie [*Area or Field of District Managed Industry*]   (EG)
BBI............ Bhubaneswar [*India*] [*Airport symbol*]   (OAG)
BBI............ Boma-Bisma-Indra [*Manufacturing company*] [*Indonesia*]   (IMH)
BBI............ Boral Basic Industries [*Australia*]   (ADA)
BBI............ Bulgarian Bibliographic Institute   (BU)
BBIEP........ Elin Pelin Bulgarian Bibliographic Institute   (BU)
BBiomed .... Bachelor of Biomedical Sciences
BBIP .... British Books in Print [*Whitaker & Sons, Ltd.*] [*Information service or system*]   (IID)
BBK .... Bank of Bahrain and Kuwait [*Bahrain*]   (EY)
BBK .... Beroepsvereniging Beeldende Kunstenaars [*Professional Association of Plastic Artists*] [*Netherlands*]   (WEN)
BBK .... Bezirksbankkontor [*District Banking Office*] [*German*]   (EG)
BBK .... Bibliotechno-Bibliograficheskaya Klassifikatsiya [*Library Bibliographical Classification*] [*Russian Federation*]   (NITA)
BBK .... Bibliotehkarisch-Bibliographische Klassifikation
BBK .... Bolnicka Baza Korpusa [*Corps Hospital Base*] [*Military*]   (YU)
BBK .... Bundesverband Bildender Kuenstler [*Society of Graphic Artists*]   (SLS)
BBK .... White Sea-Baltic Canal   (RU)
BBL............ Baltic Bankers Ltd. [*Finland*]
BBL............ Banque Bruxelles Lambert [*Belgium*]   (ECON)
BBL............ Baubetriebsleitung [*Construction Management*]   (EG)
BBL............ IBM, Euroflight-Operations [*Switzerland*] [*ICAO designator*]   (FAAC)
BBM .... Mandela Bush Negro Liberation Movement [*Suriname*] [*Political party*]   (EY)
BBMB........ Bank Bumiputra Malaysia Berhad   (FEA)
BBME......... British Bank of the Middle East
BBN .... Bario [*Malaysia*] [*Airport symbol*]   (OAG)
BBN .... Belize Broadcasting Network   (EY)
BBN .... Bond van Bedrijfsautoverkeer in Nederland [*Netherlands*]   (BAS)
BBNP........ Botany Bay National Park [*Australia*]
BBO .... Berbera [*Somalia*] [*Airport symbol*]   (OAG)

BBO .... Binnenschiffs-Besetzungsordnung [*Inland Water Transport Crew Regulations*]   (EG)
BBO .... Coast Defense Base   (RU)
BBO .... Coast Defense Battleship   (RU)
BBO .... Gesamtverband Bueromaschinen, Buromoebel, Organisationsmittel EV [*Comprehensive Collection, Office Machines, Office Furniture, Organizational Devices*] [*German*]   (ADPT)
BBP .... Bagersko-Brodarsko Preduzece [*Dredging and Shipping Establishment*]   (YU)
BBP .... Baie Belangrike Persoon [*Very Important Person*] [*Afrikaans*]
BBP .... Bechuanaland Border Police
BBP .... Short-Range Bomber Regiment   (RU)
BBQ .... Barbuda [*West Indies*] [*Airport symbol*]   (OAG)
BBR .... Babarci Buzatermelesi Rendszer [*Babarci Wheat Growing System*]   (HU)
BBR .... Babcock-Brown Boveri Reacktor, GmbH [*Nuclear energy*]   (NRCH)
BBR .... Basse-Terre [*Guadeloupe*] [*Airport symbol*]   (OAG)
BBRA........ Bezoldiginsbesluit Burgerlijke Rijksambtenaren [*Benelux*]   (BAS)
BBRD .... Banana Board Research Department [*Jamaica*]   (DSCA)
BBRI.......... Brain Behaviour Research Institute [*Australia*]
BBRPDC ... Botany Bay Regional Planning and Development Committee [*Australia*]
BBRU .... Bituminous Binder Research Unit
BBS............ Band-Betriebssystem [*Band Business System*]   (ADPT)
BBS............ Barber Blue Sea [*Commercial firm*]   (DS)
BBS............ Bermuda Biological Station for Research, Inc. [*Research center*]   (IRC)
BBS............ Besluit Buitengewoon Strafrecht [*Benelux*]   (BAS)
BBS............ Betriebsberufsschule [*Factory Training School*] [*Germany*]
BBS............ Bhutan Broadcasting Service   (EY)
BBS............ Biblioteka Beletrystyki Sportowej [*Sport Fiction Series*]   (POL)
BBS............ Bioloska Borbena Sredstva [*Biological Combat Equipment*]   (YU)
BBS............ Borodino Biological Station   (RU)
BBS............ Bulgarian Botanical Society   (EAIO)
BBS............ Burma Broadcasting Service
BBS............ Short-Range Bomber Unit   (RU)
BBSAWS... Babiker Badri Scientific Association for Women's Studies [*Sudan*]   (EAIO)
BBSFC....... Beach Boys Stomp Fan Club   (EAIO)
BBSR .... Bermuda Biological Station for Research   (ASF)
BBSS .... Bielsko-Bialska Spoldzielnia Spozywcow [*Bielsko-Biala Consumers' Cooperative*]   (POL)
BBT............ Balai Besar Penelitian dan Pengembangan Industri Tekstil [*Institute for Research and Development of Textile Industry*] [*Indonesia*]
BBT............ Barbados Board of Tourism   (GEA)
BBT............ Barbier, Bernard, et Turenne
BBT............ Bhaktivedanta Book Trust [*Publisher*] [*India*]
BBT............ Bundesverband Buerotechnik [*Federal Union Office Technology*] [*German*]   (ADPT)
BBTP .... Banque du Batiment et des Travaux Publics [*Bank of Public Building and Construction*] [*France*]
BBU .... Bucharest [*Romania*] Banesa Airport [*Airport symbol*]   (OAG)
BBUD .... Bornova Buyuk Ulkucu Dernegi [*Bornova Greater Idealist Association*]   (TU)
BBuilding... Bachelor of Building
BBusAdmin ... Bachelor of Business Administration
BBusMgmt ... Bachelor of Business Management
BBV .... Bacteriological Warfare Agent   (RU)
BBV .... Banco Bilbao Vizcaya   (ECON)
BBV .... Bayerische Biologische Versuchsanstalt [*Nuclear energy*]   (NRCH)
BBV .... Bybel- en Bidvereniging [*Afrikaans*]
BBVSA ...... Brand-Beskermings-Vereniging van Suider-Afrika [*Fire Protection Association of Southern Africa*]   (EAIO)
BBW .... Bundesausschuss Betriebswirtschaft [*National Committee on Management*]   (SLS)
BBWA .... Bank of British West Africa
BBWI......... Black Business Women - International [*French*]   (EAIO)
BBWR........ Bezpartyjny Blok Wspolpracy z Rzadem [*Non-Party Bloc of Cooperation with the Government*] [*Poland*] [*Political party*]   (PPE)
BBYP .... Birinci Bes Yillik Plani [*First Five-Year Plan*]   (TU)
BBZ............ Barclays Bank of Zimbabwe
BBZ............ Large Concrete Plant   (RU)
BBZ............ Zambezi [*Zambia*] [*Airport symbol*]   (OAG)
BBZG........ Bielsko-Bialski Zaklady Gastronomiczne [*Bielsko-Biala Restaurant Enterprises*]   (POL)
Bc .... Bacau [*Bacau*]   (RO)
BC .... Backpackers Club [*Reading, Berkshire, England*]   (EAIO)
BC .... Baha'i Community [*Australia*]
BC .... Baja California [*Mexico*]
Bc .... Banc [*Bank*] [*French*]   (NAU)

BC .... Banco Central do Brasil [*Central Bank of Brazil*] [*Rio De Janeiro*]   (LAA)
BC .... Bataillon des Chasseurs [*Infantry Battalion*] [*Cambodia*]   (CL)
bc .... Beco [*Cul-de-Sac*] [*Portuguese*]   (CED)
BC .... Before Christ   (EECI)
BC .... Belastingsconsulent [*Benelux*]
BC .... Berner Conventie [*Copyright*] [*Benelux*]   (BAS)
BC .... Biblioteca Central [*Chile*]   (DSCA)
BC .... Bibliotheque Congo
BC .... Bilingual Counsellor
BC .... Blue Crescent [*Later, BCI*] [*An association*]   (EAIO)
BC .... Brevet Commercial
BC .... Broadcasting Council [*Australia*]
Bc .... Brzina Cilja [*Target Speed*] [*Military*]   (YU)
BC .... Buecker Flugzeugbau GmbH & Hagglund-Soner [*Germany*] [*ICAO aircraft manufacturer identifier*]   (ICAO)
BC .... Buero-Computer [*Office Computer*] [*German*]   (ADPT)
BC .... Smokeless Powder for Field Guns [*Symbol*] [*French*]   (MTD)
BCA .... Badgery's Creek Airport [*Australia*]
BCA .... Baltic Council of Australia   (EAIO)
BCA .... Bamenda Cooperative Association
BCA .... Banco de Credito da Amazonia SA [*Belem*] [*Brazil*]   (LAA)
BCA .... Banque Centrafricaine Arabe
BCA .... Banque Centrale d'Algerie [*Central Bank of Algeria*]   (AF)
BCA .... Banque Commerciale Africaine [*African Commercial Bank*]
BCA .... Baracoa [*Cuba*] [*Airport symbol*]   (OAG)
bca .... Barrica [*Barrel*] [*Spanish*]
BCA .... Bataillon de Commandement et d'Appui [*Headquarters and Support Battalion*] [*Algeria*]   (AF)
BCA .... Bliss Classification Association [*London, England*]
BCA .... Bouchonnerie et Capsulerie d'Algerie
BCA .... British Commonwealth Alliance   (ADA)
BCA .... British Council in Australia
BCA .... Building Code of Australia
BCA .... Building Contractors' Association [*Hong Kong*]
BCA .... Bulgarian Air Cargo [*ICAO designator*]   (FAAC)
BCA .... Bureau de Credito Agricole [*Port-Au-Prince, Haiti*]   (LAA)
BCA .... Bureau of Co-Ordination of Arabization   (EA)
BCA .... Bush Church Aid Society [*Australia*]
BCA .... Business Council of Australia
BCAA .... Bahrain Contemporary Art Association   (EAIO)
BCAA .... Banco Cooperativo Agrario Argentino Ltd. [*Argentina*]   (DSCA)
BCAA .... Building Control Accreditation Authority [*Victoria, Australia*]
BCAB .... Banco Comercial e Agricola do Brasil [*Brazil*]   (DSCA)
BCAD .... Banque de Credit Agricole et de Developpement [*Central African Republic*]   (EY)
BCAET ...... Bureau Central Africain d'Etudes Techniques
BCAI .... Banco de Credito Agricola e Industrial [*Dominican Republic*]   (DSCA)
BCAIF .... Agricultural, Industrial, and Mortgage Credit Bank [*Lebanon*]   (ME)
B Cal .... British Caledonian Airways   (DCTA)
BC & GS .... Bureau of Coast and Geodetic Survey [*Philippines*]   (MSC)
BC & I .... Banca Popolare Commercio & Industria [*People's Bank of Commerce & Industry*] [*Italy*]
BCANSW ... Bus and Coach Association of New South Wales
BCASA ...... Bush Church Aid Society of Australia
BCB .... Ballet Contemporani de Barcelona
BCB .... Banque Commerciale du Benin [*Benin Commercial Bank*]   (AF)
BCB .... Banque de Credit du Bujumbura [*Bujumbura Credit Bank*] [*Burundi*]   (AF)
BCB .... Banque du Congo Belge [*Bank of the Belgian Congo*]
BCB .... Biographie Coloniale Belge
BCB .... Bureau Congolais des Bois
BCBA .... Beef Cattle Breeders' Association [*Israel*]   (EAIO)
BCC .... Bahamas Chamber of Commerce   (EAIO)
BCC .... Banjul City Council
BCC .... Banque Commerciale Congolaise [*Congolese Commercial Bank*]   (AF)
BCC .... Bataillon des Chasseurs Cambodgiens [*Cambodian Infantry Battalion*]   (CL)
BCC .... Bede Cosse Chicaya
BCC .... Benue Cement Co. Ltd. [*Nigeria*]
BCC .... Bharat Coking Coal Ltd. [*India*]   (PDAA)
BCC .... Botswana Christian Council
BCC .... Brazilian Chamber of Commerce   (DS)
BCC .... Brigada Coheteril Central [*Central Missile Brigade*] [*Cuba*]   (LA)
BCC .... Bureau Central de Compensation [*Central Bureau of Compensation - CBC*]   (EAIO)
BCC .... Business Cooperation Center [*EC*]   (ECED)
BCCA .... Bank of Credit and Commerce Australia
BCCA .... Belgian Chamber of Commerce for Australia
BCCB .... British Coordinating Committee for Biotechnology
BCCBRU ... Banque Centrale du Congo Belge et du Ruanda-Urundi [*Central Bank of the Belgian Congo and Rwanda-Urandi*]

BCCC .... Bank of Credit and Commerce Cameroon SA
BCCDA ...... Berbice Chamber of Commerce and Development Association [*Guyana*]
BCCF .... Bearded Collie Club de France   (EAIO)
BCCI .... Bahrain Chamber of Commerce and Industry   (EAIO)
BCCI .... Bank of Credit & Commerce International [*Facetious Translation: Bank of Crooks and Criminals International*]   (ECON)
BCCI .... Bhutan Chamber of Commerce and Industry   (EAIO)
BCCIA .... Banco de Credito Commercial e Industrial de Angola
BCCJ .... British Chamber of Commerce in Japan
BCCL .... Bharat Coking Coal Ltd. [*India*]   (PDAA)
BCCN .... Bank of Credit and Commerce Niger   (EY)
BCCN .... Bureau de Controle de la Construction Nucleaire [*Nuclear Construction Control Bureau*] [*France*]   (WND)
BCCNSW .. Building and Construction Council, New South Wales [*Australia*]
BCCO .... Bureau pour la Creation, le Controle, et l'Orientation des Entreprises et Exploitations [*Office for the Establishment, Supervision, and Guidance of Enterprises and Operations*] [*Congo*]   (AF)
BCCQ .... Border Collie Club of Queensland [*Australia*]
BCD .... Bacolod [*Philippines*] [*Airport symbol*]   (OAG)
BCD .... Banco de Construccion y Desarrollo [*Bogota-Agencia*]   (COL)
BCD .... Banque Cambodgienne pour le Developpement [*Cambodian Development Bank*]   (CL)
BCD .... Banque Camerounaise de Developpement [*Cameroonian Development Bank*]   (AF)
BCD .... Base-Catalysed Dechlorination
BCD .... Base Commune de Donnees [*Common Data Base*]   (ADPT)
BCD .... Bureau du Commerce et du Developpement [*UNCTAD*]   (ASF)
BCDA .... Bureau Communautaire de Developpement Agricole [*Community Agricultural Development Office*]   (AF)
BCDD .... Boost-Controlled Decelerating Device
BCDI .... Bureau Communautaire de Developpement Industriel [*Community Industrial Development Office*]   (AF)
BCE .... Baikal Commodity Exchange [*Russian Federation*]   (EY)
bce .... Balance [*French*] [*Accounting*]
BCE .... Banco Central del Ecuador [*Ecuador*]   (LAA)
BCE .... Bilingual Community Educator
BCE .... Bishops' Committee for Education [*Australia*]
BCE .... Bloc Catala d'Estudiants [*Catalan Students Bloc*] [*Spanish*]   (WER)
BCEAEC ... Banque Centrale des Etats de l'Afrique Equatoriale et de Cameroun [*Central Bank of the States of Equatorial Africa and Cameroon*]   (AF)
BCEAO ..... Banque Centrale des Etats de l'Afrique de l'Ouest [*Central Bank of the West African States*] [*Dakar, Senegal*]   (AF)
BCEDI .... Banque Congolaise d'Equipement et de Developpement Industriel
BCEEOM ... Bureau Central d'Etudes pour les Equipements d'Outre-Mer [*Central Studies Office for Overseas Equipment*] [*French*]
BCEIA .... Beijing Conference and Exhibition on Instrumental Analysis [*China*]
BCEL .... Banque du Commerce Exterieur Lao [*Lao Foreign Trade Bank*]   (GEA)
BCEN .... Banque Commerciale pour l'Europe du Nord [*Commercial Bank for North Europe*] [*French*]   (WER)
BCEOM .... Bureau Central d'Etudes pour les Equipements d'Outre-Mer [*Central Study Office for Overseas Equipment*] [*French*]   (AF)
BCF .... Belfast Car Ferries Ltd.   (DS)
BCF .... Bond Corp. Finance [*Australia*]
BCF .... Boxer Club de France   (EAIO)
BCFA .... Britain-China Friendship Association   (BI)
BCG .... Beira Corridor Group [*Africa*]
BCG .... Bemichi [*Guyana*] [*Airport symbol*]   (OAG)
BCGT .... Banque Commerciale du Ghana-Togo
BCH .... Banco Central de Honduras [*Centro de Informacion Industrial*] [*Honduras*]
BCH .... Banco Central Hipotecario [*Central Mortgage Bank*] [*Colorado*]   (LA)
BCh .... Bataliony Chlopskie [*Peasants' Battalions (1940-1944)*]   (POL)
BCH .... Bond Corporation Holdings Ltd. [*Australia*]
BCh .... Combat Operational Unit [*on a naval vessel*]   (RU)
bch .... For the Most Part, Mostly   (RU)
B Ch D ...... Baccalaureus Chirurgiae Dentium [*Bachelor of Dental Surgery*]
Bche .... Bouche [*Mouth*] [*Military map abbreviation World War I*] [*French*]   (MTD)
Bches-Du-R ... Bouches-Du-Rhone [*French*]
BChF .... Frequency Filter Unit   (RU)
BCHK .... Baptist Convention of Hong Kong   (EAIO)
BChK .... Bulgarian Red Cross   (BU)
BChK .... Great Chu Canal   (RU)
b-chka .... Small Library, Series of Small Books   (RU)
BChL .... Bojove Chemicke Latky [*Chemical Warfare Agents*]   (CZ)
BCHL .... Bond Corp. Holdings Ltd. [*Australia*]
BChS .... Baltic - Black Sea Seiner   (RU)

BCI............ Banca Centrala de Investitii [*Central Investment Bank*] (RO)
BCI............ Banca Commerciale Italiana [*Italy*]
BCI............ Banco de Comercio e Industria [*Portuguese*]
BCI............ Banque Centrafricaine d'Investissement [*Central African Investment Bank*]
BCI............ Barcaldine [*Australia*] [*Airport symbol*] (OAG)
BCI............ Blue Crescent International (EAIO)
BCI............ Bond Corp. International Ltd. [*Hong Kong*]
BCI............ Bureau of Criminal Intelligence [*Victoria, Australia*]
BCI............ Business Competitive Intelligence
BCIA......... Bishops' Committee for Industrial Affairs [*Australia*]
B-cia........... Bracia [*Brothers*] [*Poland*]
BCIA......... Brake and Clutch Industries Australia Proprietary Ltd.
BCIAWPRC ... Belgian Committee of the International Association on Water Pollution Research and Control (EAIO)
BCIB.......... Bloque de Campesinos Independientes de Bolivia [*Bloc of Independent Peasants of Bolivia*] (LA)
BCIC........... Building and Construction Industry Council [*Australia*]
BCICE....... Bangladesh Council for International Correspondence and Exchanges (EAIO)
BCIE.......... Banco Centroamericano de Integracion Economica [*Central American Bank of Economic Integration*] [*Tegucigalpa, Honduras*] (LA)
BCIE......... Banque Centramericaine d'Integration Economique [*Central American Bank of Economic Integration - CABEI*] [*French*]
BCIL........ Bond Corp. International Ltd. [*Hong Kong*] (ECON)
BCILSB..... Building and Construction Industry Long Service Leave Board [*Australia*]
BCINA....... British Commonwealth International News Agency
BCIP......... Belgian Centre for Information Processing
BCIS......... Building Cost Information Service [*Royal Institute of Chartered Surveyors*] [*Information service or system*] (IID)
BCIS......... Bureau Central International de Seismologie [*International Central Seismological Bureau*] (MSC)
BCJDP...... Bishop's Committee for Justice, Development, and Peace [*Australia*]
BCK .... Bolworra [*Australia*] [*Airport symbol*] [*Obsolete*] (OAG)
BCK .... Compagnie de Chemin de Fer Bas-Congo-Katanga [*Lower Congo-Katanga Railway*] [*Zaire*]
BCKR........ Bulgarski Centralny Komitet Rewolucyjny [*Bulgarian Central Revolutionary Committee*] (POL)
BCL........... Bamangwato Concessions Limited
BCL........... Barra Colorado [*Costa Rica*] [*Airport symbol*] (OAG)
BCL........... British Caribbean Airways Ltd. [*ICAO designator*] (FAAC)
BCL........... Bureau Central Laitier
BCL........... Business in the Community Ltd. [*Australia*]
BCLV........ Brown Coal Liquefaction (Victoria) Proprietary Ltd. [*Australia*]
BCM .... Bacau [*Romania*] [*Airport symbol*] (OAG)
BCM .... Bachelor of Computer and Mathematical Sciences
BCM .... Banque Centrale de la Mauritanie [*Central Bank of Mauritania*] (AF)
BCM .... Banque Centrale du Mali
BCM .... Banque Commerciale du Maroc
BCM .... Berendi Cement Muvek [*Berend Cement Works*] (HU)
BCM .... Black Consciousness Movement [*South Africa*]
BCM .... Courier-Mail (Brisbane) [*A publication*]
bcm............ Thousand Million Cubic Metres (OMWE)
BCMEA..... Bureau Commun du Machinisme et de l'Equiment Agricole [*France*] (PDAA)
BCMGA .... Biblioteca Central [*Uruguay*] (DSCA)
BCMN....... Bureau Central de Mesures Nucleaires [*Central Office for Nuclear Measures*] [*Belgium*] (PDAA)
BCMSA..... Black Consciousness Movement of South Africa (AF)
BCN .... Banco Central de Nicaragua [*Central Bank of Nicaragua*] (LA)
BCN .... Banco de Credito Nacional SA [*Private bank*] [*Brazil*] (EY)
BCN .... Barcelona [*Spain*] [*Airport symbol*] (OAG)
BCN .... Biblioteca del Congreso de la Nacion [*National Congress Library*] [*Buenos Aires, Argentina*] (LAA)
BCNBP...... Belgian College of Neuropsychopharmacology and Biological Psychiatry
BCNN....... Broadcasting Company of Northern Nigeria Ltd.
BCNT .... Bushfires Council of the Northern Territory [*Australia*]
BCNZ .... Bible College of New Zealand
Bco .... Banco [*Bank*] [*Spanish*] (NAU)
Bco .... Banco [*Bank*] [*Italian*] (NAU)
bco............. Banco [*Bank*] [*French*]
BCO .... Biblioteca Conmemorativa Orton [*Instituto Interamericano de Ciencias Agricolas*] [*Costa Rica*] (LAA)
BCom(Acc) ... Bachelor of Commerce (Accounting)
BCom-LLB ... Bachelor of Commerce-Bachelor of Laws
BCommSc .. Bachelor of Commercial Science
BComp ...... Bachelor of Computing
BCompSc ... Bachelor of Computer Science
BCompScEng ... Bachelor of Computer Science and Engineering
BComSysEng ... Bachelor of Computer Systems Engineering

BCON........ Branzowy Centralny Osrodek Normalizacyjny [*Central Standardization Point for Production Divisions*] (POL)
BConstrucEc ... Bachelor of Construction Economics
BCP........... Banco Comercial Portugues [*Portuguese Commercial Bank*] (ECON)
BCP........... Banco de Credito Popular [*People's Credit Bank*] [*Nicaragua*] (GEA)
BCP........... Banque Centrale Populaire [*Morocco*] (IMH)
BCP........... Baptist Conference of the Philippines (EAIO)
BCP........... Basotho Congress Party [*Lesotho*] [*Political party*] (PPW)
BCP........... Black Community Program
BCP........... Borneo Communist Party (ML)
BCP........... Boucherie-Charcuterie-Perigourdine
BCP........... Bougainville Copper Proprietary [*Australia*] (ADA)
BCP........... British Commonwealth Pacific Airlines Ltd. (ADA)
BCP........... Bulgarian Communist Party [*Bulgarska Komunisticheska Partiia*] [*Political party*] (PPW)
BCP........... Bund-Communist Party [*Political party*] (BJA)
BCP........... Burma Communist Party [*"White Flag" party*] [*Political party*] (PD)
BCPCP ...... Banco Cooperativo de Plantadores de Cana de Pernambuco Ltd. [*Brazil*] (DSCA)
BCPOU ..... Bahamas Communications and Public Officers Union (LA)
BCPP .... Bureau Communautaire de Produits de la Peche
BCPSI........ Biological Cultivation of Plants Society of India (EAIO)
BCQB .... Building Control Qualifications Board [*Victoria, Australia*]
BCR .... Banco Central de Reserva [*El Salvador*] (LAA)
BCR .... Banco Central de Reservas [*Central Reserve Bank*] [*Peru*] (LA)
BCR .... Banque Commerciale du Rwanda [*Commercial Bank of Rwanda*] (AF)
BCR .... Base Central de Reparacoes (do Estado Maior das FAPLA) [*Center for Repairs (of the FAPLA General Staff)*] [*Angola*] (AF)
BCR .... Belmont Common Railway [*Australia*] (ADA)
BCR .... Botswana Council of Refugees
BCR .... Community Bureau of Reference [*Belgium*]
BCRA........ Banco Central de la Republica Argentina [*Central Bank of the Argentine Republic*] (LA)
BCRA........ Bureau Central des Renseignements et d'Action [*French Resistance organization*]
BCRB........ Banco da Republica do Brasil [*Central Bank of the Republic of Brazil*] [*Rio De Janeiro*] (LAA)
BCRC........ Banco Central de la Republica de Chile [*Santiago, Chile*] (LAA)
BCreativeArts ... Bachelor of Creative Arts
BCRG .... Banque Centrale de la Republique de Guinee [*Central Bank of the Republic of Guinea*] (AF)
BCRP........ Banco Central de Reserva del Peru [*Peru*] (DSCA)
BCRS........ Bureau de Credito Rural Supervise [*Port-Au-Prince, Haiti*] (LAA)
BCS........... Bangladeshiyo Cha Sangsad [*Tea Association of Bangladesh*] (EAIO)
BCS........... Banque Centrale de Syrie [*Central Bank of Syria*] (BJA)
BCS........... Banque Commerciale du Senegal (EY)
BCS........... Baptist Community Service [*Australia*]
BCS........... Baptist Counselling Service [*Australia*]
BCS........... Barbados Cancer Society (EAIO)
BCS........... Basic Carriage Service [*Telecommunications*]
BCS........... Bataillon de Commandement et des Services [*Command and Service Battalion*] [*French*] (WER)
BCS........... Bugisu Coffee Scheme
BCS........... Bureau of Ceylon Standards [*Sri Lanka*]
BCS........... Byroja e Cmimeve dhe e Standardeve [*Albanian*]
BCS........... European Air Transport [*ICAO designator*] (FAAC)
BCSA....... Book Collectors' Society of Australia
BCSA....... Botswana Civil Servants Association
BCSA(NSW) ... Book Collectors' Society of Australia (New South Wales Branch)
BCSA(Vic) ... Book Collectors' Society of Australia (Victorian Branch)
BCSBANSW ... Black and Coloured Sheep Breeders' Association of New South Wales [*Australia*]
BCSIR .... Bangladesh Council of Scientific and Industrial Research [*Research center*] (IRC)
BCSP .... Bolsa de Cereais de Sao Paulo [*Brazil*] (DSCA)
BCSR........ Bureau de Commercialisation et de Stabilisation des Prix du Paddy et des Riz [*Rice and Paddy Marketing and Stabilization Office*] [*Malagasy*] (AF)
BCSR........ Bureau of Crime Statistics and Research [*New South Wales, Australia*]
BCSS .... Breast Cancer Support Service [*Australia*]
BCSSTI ..... Beijing Center of Space Science and Technology Information [*China*] (IRC)
bcst............ Broadcast
BCSz KutInt ... Bor-, Cipo-, es Szormeipari Kutato Intezet [*Research Institute for the Leather, Shoe, and Fur Industries*] (HU)
BCT........... Banque Centrale de Tunisie [*Central Bank of Tunisia*] (AF)

BCT........... Banque des Connaissances et des Techniques [*Knowledge and Technique Bank*] [*National Agency for the Promotion of Research*] [*Information service or system*]   (IID)

BCT........... British Caribbean Territory

BCT........... Bureau Central des Traitements [*Central Salary Office*] [*Zaire*]   (AF)

BCT........... Bureau de Controle Technique [*Algeria*]

BCTA........ Bangladesh College Teachers' Association

BCTAC...... Building Control Technical Advisory Council [*Victoria, Australia*]

BCTU .... Basutoland Congress of Trade Unions

BCU .... Banco Central del Uruguay [*Central Bank of Uruguay*]   (LA)

BCU .... Biblioteca Centrala Universitara [*Central University Library*]   (RO)

BCU .... Botswana Cooperative Union

BCU .... British Commonwealth Union   (ADA)

BCU .... Bugisu Cooperative Union Ltd.

BCV .... Baltic Council of Victoria [*Australia*]

BCV .... Banco Central de Venezuela [*Central Bank of Venezuela*]   (LA)

BCV .... Banco de Cabo Verde [*Bank of Cape Verde*]   (EY)

BCV .... Belgian Circle in Victoria [*An association*] [*Australia*]

Bcvs........... Bascavus [*Master Sergeant*]   (TU)

BCW .... Bachelor of Community Welfare

BCW .... Bachelor of Community Work

bcw .... Bogie Cattle Wagon [*Australia*]

BCW .... Botswana Council of Women

BCZ .... Banque Commerciale Zairoise [*Zairian Commercial Bank*]   (AF)

b-czka........ Biblioteczka [*Little Library*] [*Often used for a series of books*]   (POL)

BD .... Baccalaureat en Droit [*French*]

Bd .... Bad [*Spa*] [*German*]

BD .... Bahrain Dinar [*Monetary unit*]   (BJA)

BD .... Band [*Volume*] [*German*]

bd .... Band [*Volume*] [*Sweden*]   (GPO)

BD .... Bande Dessinee [*Comic strip*] [*French*]

BD .... Bangladesh [*ANSI two-letter standard code*]   (CNC)

b/d .... Barrels per Day   (EECI)

BD .... Base de Donnees [*Data Base*]   (ADPT)

BD .... Besturende Direkteur [*Managing Director*] [*Afrikaans*]

BD .... Betriebsdirektion [*Plant Management*]   (EG)

bd .... Bez Daty [*Undated*] [*Poland*]

bd .... Bind [*Volume*] [*Denmark*]   (GPO)

BD .... Birlesik Devletler [*United States*] [*Turkey*]   (GPO)

BD .... Blattdrucker [*Page Printer*] [*German*]   (ADPT)

Bd .... Board   (PWGL)

bd .... Bomber Division   (RU)

bd .... Boulevard [*Boulevard*] [*French*]   (CED)

Bd .... Bulevardi [*Commonwealth of Independent States*]   (EECI)

bd .... Bulevardul [*Boulevard*] [*Romanian*]   (CED)

BD .... Bulgarian State   (BU)

BD .... Bureau Departemental [*Algeria*]

BD .... Combat Patrol   (RU)

BD .... Flank Patrol   (RU)

BD .... High Pressure   (RU)

BDA .... Baluchistan Development Authority [*Pakistan*]   (GEA)

BDA .... Banco de Desarrollo Agropecuario [*Agricultural and Livestock Development Bank*]   (LA)

BDA .... Barbados Dental Association   (EAIO)

BDA .... Basotho Democratic Alliance [*Lesotho*] [*Political party*]   (EY)

BDA .... Bermuda [*Airport symbol*]   (OAG)

BDA .... Bermuda Dental Association   (EAIO)

BDA .... Bibliotheek & Documentatie Akademie

BDA .... Bintulu Development Authority [*Malaysia*]

BDA .... Boomerangs Disabled Association [*Australia*]

BDA .... Border Airways [*South Africa*] [*ICAO designator*]   (FAAC)

bda .... Brygada [*Brigade*] [*Poland*]

BDA .... Bund Deutscher Architekten [*League of German Architects*]   (EG)

BDA .... Bundesvereinigung der Deutschen Arbeitgeberverbaende [*Confederation of German Employers Associations*]   (WEN)

BDA .... Confederation of German Employers' Associations   (EAIO)

BDA .... Hamilton [*Bermuda*] [*Airport symbol*]

BDAC .... Biological Diversity Advisory Committee [*Australia*]

BDAD .... Bibliotheek & Documentatie Akademie Deventer

BdA/DDR ... Bund der Architekten der Deutschen Demokratischen Republik [*Society of Architects of the German Democratic Republic*]   (SLS)

BDAE .... Banque de Developpement de l'Afrique de l'Est [*East African Development Bank - EADB*]   (EAIO)

BDAF........ British Defence and Aid Fund for South Africa [*London*]

BDAG........ Bibliotheek & Documentatie Akademie Groningen

BDAO........ Banque de Developpement de l'Afrique de l'Ouest

BDAS........ Bibliotheek & Documentatie Akademie Sittard

BDASA..... Building Design Association of South Australia

BDAT .... Bibliotheek & Documentatie Akademie Tilburg

BDB .... Bahamas Development Bank   (GEA)

BDB .... Bahrain Development Bank   (EY)

BdB .... Bank der Bondsspaarbanken [*Bank*] [*Netherlands*]

BDB .... Barbados Development Bank   (LA)

BDB .... Bundaberg [*Australia*] [*Airport symbol*]   (OAG)

BDB .... Bund Deutscher Baumeister, Architekten, und Ingenieure [*German Society of Master Builders, Architects, and Engineers*]   (SLS)

BDB .... Bundesvereinigung Deutscher Bibliotheksverbande [*Federation of German Library Associations*]   (EAIO)

BDB .... Byelorussian Democratic Bloc [*Political party*]

BDB .... High-Speed Landing Barge   (RU)

BDBL........ Belgische Dienst voor Bedrijfsleven en Landbouw [*Belgium*]   (BAS)

BDC .... Bachelier en Droit Canonique [*Bachelor of Canon Law*] [*French*]

BDC .... Banco de Desarrollo del Caribe [*Caribbean Development Bank - CDB*] [*Spanish*]

BDC .... Banque de Developpement des Caraibes [*Caribbean Development Bank - CDB*] [*French*]

BDC .... Banque de Developpement des Comoros [*Development Bank of the Comoros*]   (GEA)

BDC .... Baza pentru Desfacerea Cartii [*Base for Book Distribution*]   (RO)

BDC .... Biroul de Compensatii [*Compensation Office*]   (RO)

BDC .... Bloc Democratique Camerounais

BDC .... Botswana Development Corporation

Bdch .... Baendchen [*Pamphlet*] [*Publishing*] [*German*]

BDCh .... Frequency Division Unit   (RU)

Bdchn........ Baendchen [*Pamphlet*] [*Publishing*] [*German*]

BDD .... Balgarsko Dermatologichno Drujestvo [*Bulgarian Dermatological Society*]   (EAIO)

BDD .... Banque Dahomeenne de Developpement [*Dahomean Development Bank*]

BDD .... Bulgarian Dermatological Society   (SLS)

BdD .... Bund der Deutschen [*League of Germans*]   (WEN)

Bde .... Baende [*Volumes*] [*German*]

BDE .... Betriebsdatenerfassung [*Employment Data Registration*] [*German*]   (ADPT)

Bde .... Borde [*Farm*] [*Military map abbreviation World War I*] [*French*]   (MTD)

Bde .... Brigade [*Brigade*] [*Military*] [*French*]   (MTD)

BDE .... British Document Exchange

BDE .... Bundesverband Deutscher Eisenbahnen [*Union of Non-Federal Railways, Bus-Services, and Cable-Ways*]   (EY)

BDE .... Bund fuer Deutschlands Erneuerung [*League for the Renewal of Germany*]   (EG)

BDEAC...... Banque de Developpement des Etats de l'Afrique Centrale [*Development Bank of the Central African States*]   (AF)

BDEAP..... Bedienungs-Ein/Ausgabe-Programm [*Service In/Output Program*] [*German*]   (ADPT)

B de B........ Banco de Bogota [*Colombia*]   (COL)

BDEGL..... Banque de Developpement des Etats des Grands Lacs [*Development Bank of the Great Lakes States*] [*Burundi, Rwandan, Zairian*]   (AF)

BDEGL..... Banque de Developpement des Etats du Grand Lac [*Development Bank of the Great Lakes States*]   (EAIO)

BDentistry ... Bachelor of Dentistry

BDesign ..... Bachelor of Design

B des S ..... Bachelier des Sciences [*Bachelor of Science*] [*French*]

BDET........ Banque de Developpement Economique de la Tunisie [*Bank for the Economic Development of Tunisia*] [*Tunis*]   (AF)

BDF .... Belize Defense Forces [*Military*]

B d F.......... Bildmeldung der Flieger [*Photographic Report by Aviator*] [*German*]

BDF .... Botswana Defence Force

BDF .... Bund Deutscher Forstleute [*Germany*]   (EAIO)

BDFC........ Bhutan Development Finance Corp.   (EY)

Bdfu.......... Bordfunker [*Radio Operator*] [*Aviation*] [*Navy*]   (EG)

BDG .... Banque de Developpement du Gabon [*Development Bank of Gabon*]   (AF)

BDG .... Bloc Democratique de Gorgol

BDG .... Bloc Democratique de Guinee-Bissau

BDG .... Bloc Democratique Gabonais [*Gabonese Democratic Bloc*] [*Later, PDG*]

BDG .... Bois Deroules Gabon

BDG .... Bund Deutscher Grafik-Designer eV [*Society of German Graphic Designers*]   (SLS)

BdG .... Bundesgesetz [*Federal Act or Statute*] [*German*]   (ILCA)

BDGD........ Bund Deutscher Grafik-Designer [*Germany*]   (EAIO)

BdGes .... Bundesgesetz [*Federal Act or Statute*] [*German*]   (ILCA)

BDH .... Bandar Lengeh [*Iran*] [*Airport symbol*]   (OAG)

BDI .... Bird Island [*Seychelles Islands*] [*Airport symbol*]   (OAG)

BDI .... Bundesverband der Deutschen Industrie [*Federation of German Industries*]   (WEN)

BDI .... Bureau de Developpement Industriel [*Industrial Development Office*] [*Ivory Coast*]   (AF)

BDI .... Burundi [*ANSI three-letter standard code*]   (CNC)

BDIA .... Bund Deutscher Innenarchitekten [*Germany*]   (EAIO)

BDIC......... Bibliotheque de Documentation Internationale Contemporaine

BDJ............ Banjarmasin [*Indonesia*] [*Airport symbol*]   (OAG)

BDK .... Bank for Long-Term Industrial Credit   (RU)

BDK .... Bezirksdirektion fuer den Kraftverkehr [*District Directorate for Automotive Traffic*]   (EG)

Bdk............ Bodenkultur [*Agriculture*] [*German*]

BDK .... Bondoukou [*Ivory Coast*] [*Airport symbol*]   (OAG)

bdk .... Brigade of Landing Ships   (BU)

BDK .... Bruesseler Dezimal Klassifikation

BDK .... Bulgarian State Conservatory   (BU)

BDK .... Bureau for Services to the Diplomatic Corps   (BU)

BDK .... Infinitely Long Cable   (RU)

BDKDD ..... Bingol Devrimci Kultur ve Dayanisma Dernegi [*Bingol Revolutionary Cultural and Solidarity Association*]   (TU)

BDKJ .... Bund der Deutschen Katholischen Jugend [*League of German Catholic Youth*]   (WEN)

BDkmA...... Bundesdenkmalamt [*Federal Monument Office*] [*German*]

BdkProf ..... Professor der Hochschule fuer Bodenkultur [*Professor of the High School for Agriculture*] [*German*]

BDL .... Banque de Developpement du Laos [*Development Bank of Laos*]   (CL)

BDL .... Banque de Developpement Local [*Algeria*]   (EY)

BDL .... Banque de Donnees Locales [*Local Area Data Bank*] [*National Institute of Statistics and Economic Studies*] [*Information service or system*]   (IID)

BDL .... Bulgarian State Lottery   (BU)

BDL .... Bund der Deutschen Landjugend [*German Federation of Rural Youth*]   (EAIO)

BDLI......... Bundesverband der Deutschen Luftfahrt-, Raumfahrt- und Ausruestungsindustrie eV [*Aerospace industries association*]   (EY)

bdm .... Area Decontamination Battalion   (BU)

BDM......... Banque de Developpement du Mali [*Development Bank of Mali*]

BDM......... Brazil Democratic Movement [*Political party*]

BDM......... Bund Deutscher Maedchen [*League of German Women*]

BDMG....... Banco de Desenvolvimento de Minas Gerais [*Minas Gerais Development Bank*] [*Brazil*]   (LA)

BDMG....... Banco de Desenvolvimento de Minas Gerais SA [*Brazil*]   (EY)

BDMH....... Bundesverband der Deutschen Musikinstrumenten Hersteller [*National Association of German Musical Instrument Manufacturers*]   (EAIO)

BDN.......... Badana [*Saudi Arabia*] [*Airport symbol*] [*Obsolete*]   (OAG)

Bdn............ Baende [*Volumes*] [*Publishing*] [*German*]

BDN.......... Banco di Napoli [*Italy*]

BDN.......... Bank Dagang Negara [*State Commerce Bank*]   (IN)

BDN.......... Saturation Choke Unit   (RU)

BDO.......... Bandung [*Indonesia*] [*Airport symbol*]   (OAG)

BDO.......... Bois Deroules de l'Ocean

BDO.......... Bund Deutscher Offiziere [*League of German Officers*]   (EG)

BDOB .... Butyl Diiodohydroxybenzoate   (RU)

B d Oe L..... Betrieb der Oertlichen Landwirtschaft [*Local Agricultural Enterprise*]   (EG)

BDOP .... Belgisch Dienst Opvoering Produktiviteit [*Belgium*]   (BAS)

BDOT........ British Department of Transport

BDP .... Bahamian Democratic Party [*Political party*]   (PPW)

BDP .... Banque du Peuple [*People's Bank*] [*Zaire*]   (AF)

BDP .... Bath and Disinfection Train   (RU)

BDP .... Battalion Administrative Point   (BU)

BDP .... Bechuanaland Democratic Party

BDP .... Beogradsko Dramsko Pozoriste [*Belgrade Dramatic Theatre*]   (YU)

BDP .... Berufsverband Deutscher Psychologen eV   (SLS)

BDP .... Bhadrapur [*Nepal*] [*Airport symbol*]   (OAG)

BDP .... Bophuthatswana Democratic Party [*Political party*]   (PPW)

BDP .... Botswana Democratic Party [*Political party*]   (PPW)

BDP .... British Democratic Party [*Political party*]

BDPA .... Bureau pour le Developpement de la Production Agricole [*Bureau for the Development of Agricultural Production*] [*Congo*]   (AF)

BDPI......... Bureau de Developpement et de Promotion Industriels [*Bureau of Industrial Promotion and Development*] [*Malagasy*]

BDQ.......... Vadodara [*India*] [*Airport symbol*]   (OAG)

Bdr .... Bandar [*Bendar*] [*Seaport Malaysia*]   (NAU)

bdr .... Bedruckt [*Printed*] [*Publishing*] [*German*]

BDR .... Blue Danube Radio [*Austrian radio program*]

BDRC .... Barwon Disability Resource Council [*Australia*]

BDRI......... Brick Development Research Institute [*Australia*]

BDRN .... Banque de Developpement de la Republique du Niger [*Development Bank of the Republic of Niger*]   (AF)

BdS .... Banco di Sicilia [*Italy*]

BDS .... Bloc Democratique Senegalais [*Senegal*] [*Political party*]   (PPW)

BDS .... Brindisi [*Italy*] [*Airport symbol*]   (OAG)

BDS .... Bulgarian Dermatological Society   (EAIO)

BDS .... Bulgarian State Standard   (BU)

BDS .... Bund Deutscher Segler [*League of German Yachtsmen*]   (EG)

BDS .... Remote Signaling Unit   (RU)

BDSANZ... Blonde D'Aquitaine Society of Australia and New Zealand

BDSG......... Bundesdatenschutzgesetz [*Federal Data Protection Law*] [*German*]   (ADPT)

BDSh .... Bulgarski Durzhavni Zhelezhitsi [*Bulgarian National Railroads*]   (EG)

BDSh .... Large Smoke Pot   (RU)

BDSI......... Bangladesh Standards Institution

BDT .... Bado Lite [*Zaire*] [*Airport symbol*]   (OAG)

BDT .... Banque de Developpement du Tchad [*Development Bank of Chad*]   (AF)

BDT .... Buero-und Datentechnik [*Office & Data Technology*] [*German*]   (ADPT)

BDT .... Building Disputes Tribunal [*Australia*]

BDT .... Bureau of Domestic Trade [*Philippines*]   (DS)

BDT .... Telecommunications Development Bureau [*United Nations*]   (DUND)

BDTC........ Baringo Development Training Centre

BDTC........ British Dependent Territories Citizen [*Hong Kong*]

Bdtg.......... Bedeutung [*Definition*] [*German*]

BDTM .... Bulgarian State Tobacco Monopoly   (BU)

BDTRA..... Baza de Deservire Tehnica si Reparatii Aeroportuare [*Airport Technical Services and Repair Base*]   (RO)

BDU.......... Banque de Donnees Urbaines de Paris et de la Region d'Ile-De-France [*Urban Data Bank of Paris and the Paris Region*] [*Paris Office of Urbanization France*] [*Information service or system*]   (IID)

BDU.......... Bardufoss [*Norway*] [*Airport symbol*]   (OAG)

BDU.......... Bromodeoxyuridine   (RU)

BDU.......... Bundesverband der Dolmetscher und Uebersetzer eV [*Federal Association of Interpreters and Translators*]

BDU.......... Remote-Control Unit   (RU)

BDV .... Bremen Demokratische Volkspartei [*Bremen Democratic People's Party*] [*Germany*] [*Political party*]   (PPE)

BDV .... Brussels Definition of Value   (IMH)

BDVB .... Bundesverband Deutscher Volks- und Betriebswirte eV   (SLS)

BDVC .... Botswana Diamond Valuing Company

BDVP........ Bezirksbehoerde der Deutschen Volkspolizei [*District Office of the German People's Police*]   (EG)

BDWi........ Bund Demokratischer Wissenschaftler [*Association of Democratic Scientists*] [*Federal Republic of Germany*]   (EG)

BdZ .... Bodenzuender [*Base Percussion Fuze, Base Detonator Fuze*]   (EG)

BDZ .... Bulgarski Durzhavni Zhelezhitsi [*Bulgarian State Railways*]   (EG)

BDZ .... Bundesverband der Deutschen Zahnaerzte eV   (SLS)

BDZh .... Bulgarski Durzhavni Zhelezhitsi [*Bulgarian State Railways*]   (BU)

BE .... Albumin Extract, Protein Extract   (RU)

Be .... Baeume [*Trees*] [*German*]

Be .... Baie [*Bay*] [*B*] [*See also*] [*French*]   (NAU)

BE .... Bedrijfseconoom [*Benelux*]   (BAS)

BE .... Beech Aircraft Corp. [*ICAO aircraft manufacturer identifier*]   (ICAO)

BE .... Belgium [*ANSI two-letter standard code*]   (CNC)

Be .... Bengal Regiment [*India*] [*Army*]

BE .... Berechnungsgrundlagen fuer Eisenbahnbruecken [*Basic Computation Data for Railroad Bridges*]   (EG)

Be .... Berilio [*Beryllium*] [*Chemical element*] [*Portuguese*]

Be .... Beryllium [*Chemical element*]

BE .... Brevet Elementaire [*A primary school certificate granted to a teacher who passes French government examinations*] [*French*]

BE .... Budapesti Eromu [*Budapest Power Plant*]   (HU)

BE .... Bukti Ekspor [*Export Certificate*]   (IN)

BE .... Butyl Ethyl Acetate [*Solvent*]   (RU)

BE .... Electric Razor   (RU)

be.............. Protein Equivalent   (RU)

Be2 .... Beriev [*Russian aircraft designation*]   (DOMA)

BEA .... Banque Exterieure d'Algerie [*Algerian Foreign Bank*]   (AF)

BEA .... Barbados Environmental Association   (EAIO)

BEA .... Bereina [*Papua New Guinea*] [*Airport symbol*]   (OAG)

BEA .... Board of Ethnic Affairs [*Queensland, Australia*]

BEA .... British East Africa

BEAAC..... British East Africa Army Corps

BEAC........ Banque des Etats de l'Afrique Centrale [*Bank of Central African States*]   (AF)

BEAC........ Budapesti Egyetemi Atletikai Club [*University Athletic Club of Budapest*]   (HU)

BEACON .. Building Engineering and Construction Co. [*Sierra Leone*]

bead............ Coast Artillery Battalion   (BU)

BEAG .... Budapesti Elektroakusztikai Gyar [*Budapest Electroacoustics Factory*]   (HU)

BEAL........ Banco Europeu para a America Latina [*Bank*] [*Portuguese*]   (EY)

BEAL........ Banque Europeenne pour l'Amerique Latine [*Bank*] [*French*]   (EY)

BEAN .... Bloc d'Esquerra d'Alliberament Nacional [*Left Bloc for National Liberation*] [*Spain*]   (PPW)
BE & C ...... British Empire and Commonwealth
Beanspruch ... Beanspruchung [*Strain*] [*German*]   (GCA)
beap............ Coast Artillery Regiment   (BU)
BEAR........ Bourns Electronic Artificial Respirator [*Australia*]
bearb .... Bearbeidet [*Revised*] [*Publishing Danish/Norwegian*]
Bearb........ Bearbeiter [*Editor*] [*German*]   (BARN)
bearb .... Bearbeitet [*Revised*] [*Publishing*] [*German*]
Bearb........ Bearbeitung [*Processing*] [*German*]   (GCA)
bearb .... Bearbetad [*Revised*] [*Publishing*] [*Sweden*]
bearb .... Bearbetning [*Adaptation*] [*Sweden*]
beau........... Bordereau [*Statement*] [*French*] [*Business term*]
Beau & Fl ... [*Francis*] Beaumont and [*John*]Fletcher [*17th century English dramatists*]   (BARN)
beauftr........ Beauftragt [*Authorized*] [*German*]
BEB........... Banco Economico da Bahia [*Brazil*]   (DSCA)
BEB........... Benbecula [*Hebrides Islands*] [*Airport symbol*]   (OAG)
BEB........... Be- und Entladebetriebe [*Loading and Unloading Enterprises*] (EG)
BEB........... Buitenlandse Economische Betrekkingen [*Benelux*]   (BAS)
BEC........... Bahamas Electricity Corporation   (LA)
BEC........... Banco do Estado do Ceara [*Ceara State Bank*] [*Brazil*]   (LA)
BEC........... Banque Europeenne de Credit [*Belgium*]
BEC........... Barnax Engineering Co. (Nigeria) Ltd.
BEC........... Book Exporters Council - Singapore   (EAIO)
BEC........... Brevet d'Enseignement Commercial [*Commercial Education Certificate*]   (CL)
BEC........... Brevet d'Enseignement Complementaire [*French*]
BEC........... Bureau de l'Enseignement Catholique [*Catholic Teaching Bureau*] [*Zaire*]
BEC........... Bureau d'Execution et de Controle [*Application and Control Office*] [*Cambodia*]   (CL)
BEC........... Bureau Europeen de Coordination des Organisations Internationales de Jeunesse [*European Coordination Bureau for International Youth Organizations - ECB*] (EAIO)
BEC........... Bureau Europeen du Cafe [*European Coffee Bureau*]
BEC........... Business Enterprise Center [*Australia*]
BECEG....... Bureau Europeen de Controle et d'Etudes Generales
BECIBA .... Societes des Betons et Ciments de Bassa
BECIP .... Bureau d'Etudes Industrielles et de Cooperation de l'Institut Francais du Petrole [*Industrial Studies and Cooperation Office of the French Petroleum Institute*]
BECO .... Banana Export Co. [*Jamaica*]   (EY)
BECOT....... Bureau d'Etudes et de Controle Technique
BECS........ Bulk Electronic Clearance System
BECSP....... Bureau des Examens et Concours Scolaires et Professionnels [*Scholastic and Professional Examinations and Competitions Office*] [*Cambodia*]   (CL)
Bed .... Bedeutung [*Significance*] [*German*]
BED .... Bureau Episcopal de Developpement
BED .... Bureau of Energy Development [*Philippines*]   (DS)
BEDA .... Better Environment Development Association [*Australia*]
BEDA .... Bureau of European Designers Associations   (EA)
Bedampf.... Bedampfung [*Vapor Treatment*] [*German*]   (GCA)
BEDAS ...... Betriebs-Daten-System [*Employment Data System*] [*German*] (ADPT)
BEDCO ..... Basotho Enterprise Development Corporation
BEDE........ Banco de Desarrollo del Ecuador [*Development Bank of Ecuador*] (LA)
Bedeut .... Bedeutung [*Importance*] [*German*]   (GCA)
Bedford ..... Bedfordshire [*England*]   (BARN)
BEDFPU ... Brigada de Estudos da Defesa Fitosanitaria dos Productos Ultramarinos [*Task Force for the Phytosanitary Defense of Overseas Products*]   (ASF)
Beding........ Bedingung [*Condition*] [*German*]   (GCA)
BEd(Prelim) ... Bachelor of Education (Preliminary Studies)
BEDR .... Bedrag [*Amount*] [*Afrikaans*]
BEd(TAS) ... Bachelor of Education (Technological and Applied Studies)
BEDU .... Botswana Enterprise Development Unit [*Gaborone*]   (AF)
bed verm..... Bedeutend Vermehrt [*Much Enlarged*] [*German*]
BEE........... Banco Exterior de Espano Group [*Business library*] [*Spanish*]
BEE........... Bureau Europeen de l'Environnement [*European Environmental Bureau - EEB*] [*Belgium*]   (SLS)
BEE........... Busy Bee of Norway AS [*ICAO designator*]   (FAAC)
BEEC........ Brevet d'Enseignement Economique et Commercial [*Economic and Commercial Education Certificate*]   (CL)
bee cee ...... Birger Christensen [*Commercial firm*]
BEEF .... British Egyptian Expeditionary Force
Beeinfluss .. Beeinflussung [*Influence*] [*German*]   (GCA)
BEEN .... Bureau d'Etude de l'Energie Nucleaire [*Belgium*]
BEEP .... Bureau Europeen de l'Education Populaire [*European Bureau of Adult Education - EBAE*]   (EAIO)
bef .... Befejezes [*End, Conclusion*]   (HU)
BEF........... Borneo Evangelical Fellowship

BEFA .... Beobachtende Fahndung [*Observation and Research*]
Befama....... Bydgoska Fabryka Maszyn [*Bydgoszcz Machinery Plant*]   (POL)
Befestig...... Befestigung [*Attachment*] [*German*]   (GCA)
Befeucht ..... Befeuchtung [*Moistening*] [*German*]   (GCA)
BEFIEX ..... Comissao para Concessao de Beneficios Fiscais a Programas Especiais de Exportacao [*Commission for the Concession of Fiscal Benefits to Special Export Programs*] [*Brazil*]   (LA)
BEFOURRA ... Belgian Fourragere [*Military decoration*]
BEG .... Banco do Estado da Guanabara [*Guanabara State Bank*] [*Brazil*] (LA)
BEG .... Belgrade [*Former Yugoslavia*] [*Airport symbol*]   (OAG)
BEGA .... Bureau d'Etudes Gabonais d'Architecture
BEGL........ Begleitung [*Accompaniment*] [*Music*]
begr .... Begruendet [*Established*] [*German*]
Begrw .... Begrafeniswet [*Benelux*]   (BAS)
BEGS........ British and European Geranium Society   (EAIO)
begy h........ Begyujto Hely [*Collecting Station*]   (HU)
BEGYM.... Begyujtesi Miniszterium/Miniszter [*Ministry/Minister for Collection of Agricultural Produce and Livestock*]   (HU)
begyujt .... Begyujtesi [*Collecting (Adjective)*]   (HU)
beh............ Behandeln [*Treat, Handle*] [*German*]
beh............ Behandla [*Deal With*] [*Publishing*] [*Sweden*]
Beh .... Behelf [*Makeshift*] [*German*]   (GCA)
Beh .... Behelfsmaessig [*Temporary*] [*German*]   (EG)
Beh .... Beher [*Each*]   (TU)
Beh .... Behoerde [*Authority*] [*German*]   (GCA)
beh............ Behozatal [*Import, Imports*] [*Hungarian*]   (HU)
Behandl...... Behandlung [*Treatment*] [*German*]   (GCA)
BEHC .... Bureau d'Etudes Henri Chomette
Beheiz .... Beheizung [*Heating*] [*German*]   (GCA)
Beherrsch.... Beherrschung [*Domination*] [*German*]   (GCA)
BEI........... Banca Europea degli Investimenti [*European Investment Bank - EIB*] [*Italian*]
BEI........... Banco Europeo de Inversion [*European Investment Bank - EIB*] [*Spanish*]
BEI........... Banco Expansion Industrial [*Industrial Expansion Bank*] [*Spanish*]
BEI........... Banque Europeenne d'Investissement [*European Investment Bank - EIB*] [*French*]
BEI........... Beica [*Ethiopia*] [*Airport symbol*]   (OAG)
BEI........... Benair [*Italy*] [*ICAO designator*]   (FAAC)
BEI........... Brevet d'Enseignement Industriel
BEI........... Office for Research and Experiments [*ORE*] of the International Railroad Union   (RU)
BEI........... Standard-Pulse Unit   (RU)
Beibl.......... Beiblatt [*or Beiblaetter*] [*Supplement or Supplements (to a periodical)*] [*German*]   (EG)
BEICIP...... Bureau d'Etudes Industrielles et de Cooperation de l'Institut Francais du Petrole [*Industrial Studies and Cooperation Office of the French Petroleum Institute*]   (AF)
Beida .... Beijing Daxue [*Beijing University*] [*China*]
beidseit....... Beidseitig [*On Both Sides*] [*Publishing*] [*German*]
beif .... Beifolgend [*Enclosed*] [*German*]   (EG)
beiflgd .... Beifolgend [*Enclosed*] [*German*]
beigeb........ Beigebunden [*Bound With*] [*German*]   (BARN)
beigedr .... Beigedruckt [*Printed With*] [*German*]
Beih .... Beihefte [*Supplements*] [*German*]
Beil........... Beilage [*or Beiliegend*] [*Enclosure or Enclosed*] [*German*]
BEIPU .... Belize Export and Investment Promotion Unit [*Chamber of Commerce and Industry*]
Beis .... Bachareis [*Portuguese*]
Beis .... Beisitzer [*Assessor*] [*German*]
BEISP....... Beispiel [*Example*] [*Music*] [*German*]
Beitr .... Beitrag [*Contribution*] [*Publishing*] [*German*]
bej............. Bejarat [*Entrance*]   (HU)
bej............. Bejegyzett [*Registered, Incorporated*] [*Hungarian*]   (HU)
BEJ .... Berau [*Indonesia*] [*Airport symbol*]   (OAG)
BEJA .... Brigada Contra el Trafico de Estupefacientes y Juegos de Azar [*Drug Traffic and Gambling Control Squad*] [*Chile*]   (LA)
BEK .... Bakanliklararasi Ekonomik Kurul [*Inter-Ministry Economic Council*]   (TU)
Bek............ Bekanntmachung [*Announcement*] [*German*]   (GCA)
bek............ Bekezdes [*Paragraph*]   (HU)
BEK .... Betriebsmitteleingabe-Karte [*Means of Employment Input Card Operational Inputs Card*] [*German*]   (ADPT)
BEK .... Biuro Elektryfikacji Kolei [*Railroad Electrification Office*] (POL)
BEK .... Budapesti Eotvos Lorand Tudomanyegyetem Konyvtara [*Library of the Lorand Eotvos University of Budapest*] (HU)
BEK .... Bureau de l'Enseignement Kimbanguiste [*Kimbanguist Teaching Bureau*] [*Zaire*]
Bekampf.... Bekaempfung [*Attack*] [*German*]   (GCA)
BEKDDR... Bund der Evangelischen Kirchen in der Deutschen Demokratischen Republik [*Federation of Protestant Churches in the German Democratic Republic*]   (EY)

bekl .... Beklaagde [*Accused*] [*Afrikaans*]
bekr .... Bekrachtigd [*Benelux*]   (BAS)
BEKULA ... Berliner Kraft- und Licht (Bewag)-Aktiengesellschaft [*Berlin Power and Light Joint Stock Company*]
Bel .... Bacharel [*Bachelor*] [*Portuguese*]
BEL .... Baha'i Esperanto-League [*Luxembourg*]   (EAIO)
Bel .... Belediye [*Municipality*]   (TU)
Bel .... Beleg [*Documentary Evidence*] [*German*]   (GCA)
BEL .... Belem [*Brazil*] [*Airport symbol*]   (OAG)
Bel .... Belge [*Document*]   (TU)
Bel .... Belgic [*Language*]   (BARN)
BEL .... Belgium [*ANSI three-letter standard code*]   (CNC)
Bel .... Belize   (BARN)
BEL .... Bell-Air Executive Air Travel Ltd. [*New Zealand*] [*ICAO designator*]   (FAAC)
BEL .... Belorussian Railroad   (RU)
BEL .... Bharat Electronics Ltd. [*India*]   (PDAA)
BEL .... Biuro Ewidencji Ludnosci [*Population Registration Office*]   (POL)
BEL .... British Electrotechnical Committee   (BARN)
bel .... Note   (BU)
bel .... White   (RU)
BELAIR ..... Belgian Air Staff [*NATO*]   (NATG)
BelAPP ...... Belorussian Association of Proletarian Writers   (RU)
BelAZ .... Belorussian Automobile Plant   (RU)
Bel Ber .... Belasting Berichten [*Benelux*]   (BAS)
Belbesch ..... Belastingsbeschouwingen [*Benelux*]   (BAS)
BELC .... Bureau pour l'Enseignement de la Langage et de la Civilisation Francaises a l'Etranger [*French*]
BELC .... Buyuk Elci [*Ambassador*]   (TU)
BELDE-IS ... Belediye Iscileri Sendikasi [*Municipal Workers Union*] [*Sakarya*]   (TU)
Belediye-Is ... Turkiye Belediyeler ve Genel Hizmetler Iscileri Sendikasi [*Municipal workers union*] [*Turkey*]   (MENA)
Beleucht ..... Beleuchtung [*Illumination*] [*German*]   (GCA)
belf .... Belfoldi [*Domestic, Internal*]   (HU)
BELFAST ... Programmsystem fuer Zeitschiftengrosshandel, Bezugsregulierung, Lieferscheine, Fakturierung, Statistiken [*Program System for Wholesale Magazine Trade, Salary Regulations Delivery Receipts, Manufacturing, Statistics*] [*German*]   (ADPT)
BELFOX ... Belgian Futures and Options Exchange [*Stock exchange*] [*Belgium*]   (EY)
bel'g .... Belgian   (RU)
BELG .... Belgie [*Belgium*] [*Afrikaans*]
Belg Col ..... Belgique Coloniale et Commerce International [*Belgium*]   (BAS)
Belgiprodor ... Belorussian State Planning Institute for the Surveying and Planning of Highways and Related Structures   (RU)
Belgiprosel'stroy ... Belorussian State Institute for the Planning of Rural Construction   (RU)
Belgiprotorf ... Belorussian State Institute for the Planning of Peat Establishments   (RU)
Belgiz .... Belorussian State Publishing House   (RU)
BELGOLAISE ... Banque Belgo-Zairoise [*Belgian-Zairian Bank*]   (AF)
Belgosizdat ... Belorussian State Publishing House   (RU)
BELGOSPACE ... Assocation Belge Interprofessional des Activities Spatiales [*Belgium*]   (PDAA)
Belgosproyekt ... Belorussian State Planning Institute   (RU)
Belgosuniversitet ... Belorussian State University Imeni V. I. Lenin   (RU)
Belg P .... Belgisches Patent [*Belgian Patent*] [*German*]   (GCA)
Belgres .... Belorussian State Regional Electric Power Plant   (RU)
BelgTijdsSoc Zekerh ... Belgish Tijdschrift voor Sociale Zekerheid [*Belgium*]   (BAS)
belieb .... Beliebig [*Arbitrary*] [*German*]   (GCA)
BELIMINES ... Benino-Arabe-Libyenne des Mines [*Societe*]   (EY)
BELINDIS ... Belgian Information and Dissemination Service [*Ministry of Economic Affairs*]   (PDAA)
Belinksel'mash ... Belinskiy Agricultural Machinery Plant   (RU)
BELIPECHE ... Societe Benino-Arabe Libyenne de Peche
belker .... Belkereskedelem [*Domestic Trade*]   (HU)
BELKERIG ... Belkereskedelmi Igazgatosag [*Domestic Trade Directorate*]   (HU)
BelkerMin ... Belkereskedelmi Miniszterium/Miniszter [*Ministry/Minister of Domestic Trade*]   (HU)
BELKM ..... Belkereskedelmi Miniszterium/Miniszter [*Ministry/Minister of Domestic Trade*]   (HU)
Belkoopsoyuz ... Cooperative Union of the Belorussian SSR   (RU)
belliss .... Bellissimo [*Most Beautiful*] [*Italian*]
BELNAV ... Belgian Naval Staff [*NATO*]   (NATG)
BelNIILKh ... Belorussian Scientific Research Institute of Forestry   (RU)
BelNIIMiVKh ... Belorussian Scientific Research Institute of Reclamation and Water Management   (RU)
BelNITOE ... Belorussian Branch of the All-Union Scientific, Engineering, and Technical Society   (RU)
BelOKS ...... Belorussian Society for Cultural Relations with Foreign Countries   (RU)

Belomor ...... White Sea   (RU)
Belomorkanal ... White Sea-Baltic Canal   (RU)
Belonitomash ... Belorussian Branch of the All-Union Scientific, Engineering, and Technical Society of Machinery Manufacture   (RU)
belorussk .... Belorussian   (RU)
Belpromsovet ... Belorussian Council of Producers' Cooperatives   (RU)
BELSPED ... Belfoldi Szallitmanyozasi Vallalat [*Domestic Transport Enterprise*]   (HU)
BELT .... Belokranjska Zelezolivarna in Kovinska Tovarna [*Bela Krajina Iron and Metal Foundry*] [*Crnomelj*]   (YU)
BELT .... Boloko Enterprises Limited
BELTA ...... Belorussian News Agency   (RU)
Beluft .... Belueftung [*Ventilation*] [*German*]   (GCA)
BELVAC ... Societe Belge de Vacuologie et de Vacuotechnique [*Belgian Society for Vacuum Science and Technology*]   (PDAA)
BelVO .... Belorussian Military District   (RU)
BEM .... Banya- es Energiaugyi Miniszterium/Miniszter [*Ministry/ Minister of Mines and Power*]   (HU)
BEM .... Belgian Evangelical Mission
Bem .... Bemerkung [*Note, Comment, Observation*] [*German*]   (EG)
BEM .... Borsodi Ercelokeszito Muvek [*Borsod Ore Dressing Plant*]   (HU)
BEM .... Bourses d'Etudes du Mayombe
BEM .... Brevet d'Enseignement Moyen [*French*]
bem .... Brigade of Navy Destroyers   (BU)
bemaerkn ... Bemaerkninger [*Remarks*] [*Publishing Danish/Norwegian*]
Bemerk .... Bemerkung [*Remark*] [*German*]   (GCA)
Bemess .... Bemessung [*Size Determination*] [*German*]   (GCA)
BEMFAM ... Sociedade Civil Bem Estar Familiar no Brasil [*Brazil*]   (EAIO)
BEMI .... Biciklista Esperantista Movado Internacia [*International Movement of Esperantist Bicyclists - IMEB*]   (EAIO)
BEMIS ...... Besin ve Misir Sanayii AS [*Provisions and Corn Products Industry Corp.*]   (TU)
BEMZ .... Baku Electromechanical Plant   (RU)
Ben .... Beneficiat [*Beneficiary*] [*German*]
ben .... Benevens [*Including*] [*Publishing*] [*Netherlands*]
BEN .... Benghazi [*Libya*] [*Airport symbol*]   (OAG)
BEN .... Benin [*ANSI three-letter standard code*]   (CNC)
ben .... Benutzt [*Used*] [*German*]
BEN .... Bureau d'Etudes Nucleaires [*Belgium*]
BEN .... Bureau Executif National [*National Executive Bureau*]
BEN .... Buro Ejecutivo Nacional [*National Executive Bureau*] [*Peru*]   (LA)
BENBO ..... Bureau for Economic Research on Bantu Development [*South Africa*]   (AF)
BENC .... Bencubbin [*Botanical region*] [*Australia*]
Bend .... Bendigo College of Advanced Education [*Australia*]
BendigoCAE ... Bendigo College of Advanced Education [*Australia*]
B en Dr .... Bachelier en Droit [*Bachelor of Laws*] [*French*]
BENECHAN ... BENELUX [*Belgium, Netherlands, Luxembourg*] Subarea Channel [*NATO*]   (NATG)
BENELUX ... Belgium, Netherlands, Luxembourg [*Economic union*]
Benetz .... Benetzung [*Wetting*] [*German*]   (GCA)
BenS .... Bibliotheek en Samenleving
B en W .... Burgemeester en Wethouders [*Mayor and Aldermen*] [*Netherlands*]   (WEN)
BEO .... Balesetelharito es Egeszsegvedo Ovorendszabaly [*Safety Rules for Prevention of Accidents and Health Protection*]   (HU)
BEO .... Belmont [*Australia*] [*Airport symbol*]
BEO .... Bureau d'Etudes Oceanographiques [*French*]   (MSC)
BEOA .... British and European Osteopathic Association [*Sutton, Surrey, England*]   (EAIO)
Beob .... Beobachter [*or Beobachtung*] [*Observer or Observation*] [*German*]
Beobacht .... Beobachtung [*Observation*] [*German*]   (GCA)
BEP .... Battalion Etranger de Parachutistes [*Foreign Battalion of Parachutists*] [*French Foreign Legion*]
Bep .... Bepaling [*Provision in statute or contract*] [*Netherlands*]   (ILCA)
bep .... Beperkt [*Limited*] [*Netherlands*]
BEP .... Biomolecular Engineering Program [*EC*]   (ECED)
BEP .... Brevet d'Enseignement Professionnel [*French*]
BEP .... Brevet d'Etudes Professionnelles [*French*]
BEP .... Brnenska Elektrarna a Plynarna [*Brno Electric and Gas Works*]   (CZ)
BEP .... Bureau d'Edition et de Publicite
BEP .... Bureau de l'Enseignement Protestant [*Protestant Teaching Bureau*] [*Zaire*]
BEP .... Bureau d'Etude et des Plans [*Study and Planning Office*] [*Cambodia*]   (CL)
BEP .... Combat Echelon of Motor Park   (RU)
BeP .... Flashless Powder   (RU)
BEPA .... Buro vir Ekonomiese Politiek en Analise [*University of Pretoria*] [*South Africa*]   (AA)
BEPC .... Beijing Electron-Positron Collider [*High-energy physics*] [*China*]
BEPC .... Brevet d'Etudes du Premier Cycle [*Elementary School Diploma*] [*French*]   (WER)

BEPI .... Bureau d'Etudes et de Participations Industrielles [*Office of Industrial Studies and Investments*] [*Morocco*] (AF)

BEPM .... Bureau d'Exploitation Petroliere Marocain

BEPO .... Armored Train (RU)

bepp .... Bepalingen [*Benelux*] (BAS)

BEPS .... Bund Evangelischer Pfarrer in der DDR, Schwerin [*League of Protestant Pastors in the GDR, Schwerin*] (EG)

BEPTOM ... Bureau d'Etudes des Postes et Telecommunications d'Outre-Mer [*Overseas Postal and Telecommunications Studies Office*] [*France*] (AF)

BER .... Air Berlin, USA [*Germany*] [*ICAO designator*] (FAAC)

ber .... Berechnet [*or Berechnung*] [*Calculated or Calculation*] [*German*]

Ber .... Bericht [*Report*] [*German*]

Ber .... Berichtigung [*Settlement (of an account), Adjustment (of a bill), Correction*] [*German*] [*Business term*] (EG)

ber .... Berieben [*Scraped*] [*Publishing*] [*German*]

BER .... Berlin [*Germany*] [*Airport symbol*] (OAG)

Ber .... Beruf [*Profession*] [*German*]

ber .... Birch (RU)

BER .... Brevet Elementaire de Radio

BER .... Bureau d'Economie Rurale [*Rural Economics Center*] [*Belgium*] (ARC)

BER .... Bureau of Economic Research [*Bangladesh*] [*Research center*] (IRC)

ber .... Coast, Shore (RU)

BER .... Roentgen Equivalent Man (RU)

BERA .... Bureau d'Etudes des Realites Africaines

BERAMETAL ... Compania Metalurgica Bera de Colombia SA [*Colombia*] (COL)

berat .... Beratend [*Consulting*] [*German*] (GCA)

Berat Ing .... Beratender Ingenieur [*Consulting Engineer*] [*German*] (GCA)

BERB .... Banque d'Emission du Rwanda et du Burundi

BERC .... Biochemical Engineering Research Centre [*India*] (IRC)

BERCON ... Berlin Contingency [*NATO*] (NATG)

BERD .... East European Development Bank [*Acronym is based on foreign phrase*]

BERDIKARI ... Berdiri Diatas Kaki Sendiri [*Standing on One's Own Feet (Self-sufficiency)*] (IN)

Berechn ...... Berechnung [*Calculation*] [*German*] (GCA)

BEREG ...... Bureau d'Engineering, de Recherches, et d'Etudes Generales [*Algeria*]

berend .... Berendezes [*Equipment*] (HU)

BERES ...... Bureau d'Etudes pour la Renovation de l'Enseignement Secondaire

Berginst ...... Berginstitut [*Mining Institute*] [*German*] (GCA)

bergm .... Bergmaennisch [*Relating to Miners*] [*German*]

BERI .... Biomolecular Engineering Research Institute [*Formerly, PERI*] [*Japan*]

BERI .... Bureau d'Etudes et de Realisations Industrielles [*Office of Industrial Studies and Achievements*] [*Algeria*] (AF)

Berichtig .... Berichtigung [*Correction*] [*German*] (GCA)

berieb .... Berieben [*Scraped*] [*Publishing*] [*German*]

BERIM ...... Bureau d'Etudes et de Recherches d'Industrie Miniere [*Office of Mining Industry Studies and Exploration*] [*Algeria*] (AF)

Ber Is .... Bermuda Islands (BARN)

BERJAYA ... Bersatu Rakyat Jelata Sabah [*Sabah People's Union*] [*Malaysia*] [*Political party*] (PPW)

Berks .... Berkshire (IDIG)

BERM .... Armored Evacuation and Repair Vehicle (RU)

berm .... Bermentve [*Postage Paid*] (HU)

BermudaLRC ... Law Reform Committee, Bermuda (DLA)

BERNAMA ... Berita Nasional Malaysia [*Malaysian National News Agency*] (IN)

BerS .... Berufsschule [*Trade School*] [*German*]

BERU .... Bureau d'Etudes de Realisations Urbaines [*Urban Projects Studies Office*] [*Algeria*] (AF)

Berucksichtig ... Beruecksichtigung [*Consideration*] [*German*] (GCA)

BES .... Aero Services Executive [*France*] [*ICAO designator*] (FAAC)

bes .... Besending [*Consignment*] [*Afrikaans*]

Bes .... Beseri [*Human, Mankind*] (TU)

bes .... Besitlik [*Possessive*] [*Afrikaans*]

Bes .... Besitzer [*Proprietor*] [*German*]

bes .... Besonders [*Especially*] [*German*] (GPO)

bes .... Besorgt [*Attends To*] [*German*] (GCA)

bes .... Bestimmt [*Definite*] [*German*] (GCA)

BES .... Bioelectrochemical Society (EA)

BES .... Bipolar Electrolyte-Exchange Resin (RU)

BES .... Brest [*France*] [*Airport symbol*] (OAG)

BES .... Bureau of Emergency Services [*Queensland, Australia*]

B es A .... Bachelier es Arts [*Bachelor of Arts*] [*French*]

BESA .... British Ex-Services Association [*Australia*]

Bes/Bel ...... Beslissingen in Belastingzaken [*Benelux*] (BAS)

besch .... Beschadigd [*Damaged*] [*Publishing*] [*Netherlands*]

besch .... Beschaedigt [*Damaged*] [*Publishing*] [*German*]

besch .... Beschikking [*Decree*] [*Netherlands*] (BAS)

beschad ...... Beschadigd [*Damaged*] [*Publishing*] [*Netherlands*]

beschad ...... Beschaedigt [*Damaged*] [*Publishing*] [*German*]

Beschaff ..... Beschaffung [*Acquisition*] [*German*] (GCA)

Beschaffenh ... Beschaffenheit [*Condition*] [*German*] (GCA)

Beschick ..... Beschickung [*Charging*] [*German*] (GCA)

Beschleunig ... Beschleunigung [*Acceleration*] [*German*] (GCA)

beschn .... Beschnitten [*Cut Down*] [*German*]

Beschr .... Beschreibung [*Description*] [*German*] (GCA)

BESCL .... Banco Espirito Santo e Comercial de Lisboa [*Espirito Santo Commercial Bank of Lisbon*] [*Portuguese*] (WER)

BESD .... Bank Economic and Social Database [*World Bank*] [*United Nations*] (DUND)

Beseitig ...... Beseitigung [*Removal*] [*German*] (GCA)

Besetz .... Besetzung [*Personnel*] [*German*] (GCA)

BESFA .... Bakery Employees and Salesmen's Federation of Australia

Besin-Is ...... Turkiye Et, Ekmek, ve Besin Sanayii Iscileri Sendikasi [*Turkish Meat, Bread, and Food Industry Workers Union*] (TU)

BES-IS .... Bursa Elektrik ve Su Iscileri Birligi [*Bursa Municipal Electric Power and Water Workers Union*] (TU)

Besitzverm ... Besitzvermerk [*Notation of Ownership*] [*Publishing*] [*German*]

besk .... Beskaaret [*Trimmed*] [*Publishing Danish/Norwegian*]

besk .... Beskadiget [*Damaged*] [*Publishing Danish/Norwegian*]

BESK .... Beskuldigde [*Accused*] [*Afrikaans*]

beskad .... Beskadiget [*Damaged*] [*Publishing Danish/Norwegian*]

beskhoz ...... Ownerless Property, Property in Abeyance (RU)

B es L .... Bachelier es Lettres [*Bachelor of Literature*] [*French*]

Besl .... Besluit [*Decree or Resolution*] [*Netherlands*] (BAS)

BESL .... Herring-Fishing Expeditionary Base (RU)

Besl I B ...... Besluit Inkomstenbelasting [*Benelux*] (BAS)

besl Ib .... Besluit Loonbelasting [*Benelux*] (BAS)

BesluitVpb ... Besluit op de Vennootschapsbelasting [*Benelux*] (BAS)

BesluitWB ... Besluit op de Winstbelasting [*Benelux*] (BAS)

BESM .... High-Speed Electronic Computer (RU)

BESONU ... Bureau des Affaires Economiques et Sociales des Nations Unies

BESP .... Banco do Estado de Sao Paulo [*Brazil*] (DSCA)

besp .... Non-Party, Non-Party Man (RU)

bespl .... Free of Charge, Gratis (RU)

Bespr .... Besprechung [*Discussion*] [*German*] (GCA)

bespr .... Bespreking [*Benelux*] (BAS)

B es S .... Bachelier es Sciences [*Bachelor of Science*] [*French*]

BESSA .... Biomedical Engineering Society of South Africa (AA)

B es SC ...... Bachelier es Sciences [*Bachelor of Science*] [*French*] (ROG)

BESSY .... Betriebsdaten-Erfassungs-und Steuerungssystem [*Employment Data - Registration& Taxation System*] [*German*] (ADPT)

BEST .... Beit Ettamwil Saudi Tounsi [*Bank*] [*North and West Africa*]

Best .... Bestand [*Amount*] [*German*]

Best .... Bestandteil [*Ingredient*] [*German*] (GCA)

Best .... Bestellung [*Order*] [*German*]

best .... Bestimmt [*Definite*] [*German*]

Best .... Bestimmung [*Determination*] [*German*]

best .... Bestossen [*Bruised, Injured*] [*Publishing*] [*German*]

Best .... Bestuurswetenschappen [*Benelux*] (BAS)

bestan .... Bestaendig [*Resistant*] [*German*]

Bestandigk ... Bestaendigkeit [*Resistance*] [*German*] (GCA)

Bestaub ...... Bestaeubung [*Pollination*] [*German*] (GCA)

Best Nr .... Bestellnummer [*Order Number*] [*German*] (EG)

bestoss .... Bestossen [*Bruised, Injured*] [*Publishing*] [*German*]

Bestrahl ..... Bestrahlung [*Irradiation*] [*German*] (GCA)

Bestuursw .. Bestuurswetenschappen [*Benelux*] (BAS)

BestW .... Bestuurswetenschappen [*Benelux*] (BAS)

Bestz .... Bestellzettel [*Order Form*] [*German*] (GCA)

bes vnw ...... Besitlike Voornaamwoord [*Possessive Pronoun*] [*Afrikaans*]

BESW(UK)A ... British Ex-Services Womens (United Kingdom) Association

besz .... Beszamolo [*Proceedings, Report*] [*Hungary*]

besz .... Beszerzes [*Purchase*] [*Hungarian*] (HU)

BESZKART ... Budapest Szekesfovarosi Kozlekedesi Reszvenytarsasag [*Metropolitan Transit Company of Budapest*] (HU)

beszolg .... Beszolgaltatasi [*Agricultural Produce Collection*] (HU)

BET .... Barbados External Telecommunications

BET .... Betaal [*Pay*] [*Afrikaans*]

bet .... Betekenis [*Meaning*] [*Afrikaans*]

BET .... Billet [*Bill*] [*French*] [*Business term*] (ROG)

BET .... Board of External Trade [*Tanzania*]

BET .... Borkou-Ennedi-Tibesti [*Chad*] (AF)

BET .... Brigadas Estudiantiles de Trabajo [*Student Labor Brigades*] [*Cuba*] (LA)

BET .... Brunauer, Emmett, and Teller [*Method*] (RU)

BET .... Business Experience Training (BARN)

bet .... Concrete (RU)

bet .... Concrete Plant [*Topography*] (RU)

BETAB ...... Concrete-Piercing Aerial Bomb (RU)

BETAS ...... Betonarme Elemanlari Sanayi ve Ticaret Anonim Sirketi [*Reinforced Concrete Workers Industry and Trade Corporation*] (TU)

Betaub .... Betaeubung [*Narcosis*] [*German*] (GCA)

BETC .... Bureau d'Etudes Techniques de Construction

b(e)td .... Betaal(d) [*Paid*] [*Afrikaans*]

BE-TE-HA ... Biuro Techniczno-Handlowe [*Engineering and Trade Office*] (POL)

BETEX ...... Budapesti Textilnagykereskedelmi Vallalat [*Wholesale Textile Enterprise of Budapest*] (HU)

BETONPROIZVOD ... Gradsko Poduzece za Proizvodnju Betonskih Preradevina [*Municipal Establishment for Concrete Manufacture*] (YU)

BETONSAN ... Konut Sanayi ve Ticaret AS [*Reinforced Concrete Housing Industry and Trade Corp.*] (TU)

BETP .... Base-Escola de Tropas Paraquedistas [*Paratroopers School/Base*] [*Portuguese*] (WER)

BETPA ...... Bureau d'Etudes Techniques de Projets Agricoles

Betr .... Betrag [*Amount*] [*German*] (GCA)

betr .... Betraut [*Entrusted*] [*German*]

betr .... Betreffende [*Benelux*] (BAS)

Betr .... Betreffs [*or Betreffend*] [*Concerning*] [*German*] (GPO)

betr .... Betreklik [*Relative*] [*Afrikaans*]

Betr .... Betrieb [*Operation*] [*German*] (GCA)

betr .... Betrifft [*Concerns*] [*German*] (GCA)

Betra .... Betriebs- und Bauanweisungen der Reichsbahn [*GDR railroad regulations for operation and construction*] (EG)

Betr Abt ..... Betriebsabteilung [*Operations Section*] [*German*] (GCA)

BETRACO ... Societe de Consignation et de Transit du Benin

betriebsmass ... Betriebsmaessig [*Commercial*] [*German*] (GCA)

Betr O .... Betriebsordnung [*Operating Regulations*] [*German*] (GCA)

BetrRG....... Betriebsrategesetz [*Law on Works Councils*] [*German*] (ILCA)

BetrVG....... Betriebsverfassungsgesetz [*Law on the Representation of Workers and Works Councils*] [*German*] (ILCA)

BETT .... Bureau d'Etudes et de Travaux Topographiques

BETU......... Bureau Etudes Tunnel [*Tunnel Design Bureau*] [*France*]

BEU .... Bedourie [*Australia*] [*Airport symbol*] [*Obsolete*] (OAG)

BEU .... BENELUX Economische Union [*Belgium, Netherlands, and Luxembourg Economic Union*] (EAIO)

BEUB........ Bureau d'Etudes pour l'Urbanisme et le Batiment [*City Planning and Building Construction Studies Office*] [*Malagasy*] (AF)

BEUC .... Bureau Europeen des Unions de Consommateurs [*European Bureau of Consumers' Unions*] (EAIO)

Beug .... Beugung [*Bending*] [*German*] (GCA)

beurl........... Beurlaubt [*Granted a Leave of Absence*] [*German*]

Beurt .... Beurteilung [*Judgement*] [*German*] (GCA)

Beurteil ...... Beurteilung [*Judgement*] [*German*] (GCA)

BEV .... Banco Ecuatoriano de Vivienda [*Ecuadorean Housing Bank*] (LA)

BEV .... Banyaszati Epito Vallalat [*Mining Construction Enterprise*] (HU)

BEV .... Beersheba [*Israel*] [*Airport symbol*] [*Obsolete*] (OAG)

bev.............. Bevarad [*Preserved*] [*Publishing*] [*Sweden*]

bev.............. Bevestigend [*Benelux*] (BAS)

bev.............. Bevetel [*Income, Proceeds*] (HU)

bev.............. Bevezetes [*Introduction*] [*Hungary*]

Bev .... Bevoelkerung [*Inhabitants*] [*German*]

BEV .... Bevolking [*Population*] [*Afrikaans*]

bev............. Bevollmaechtigt [*Authorized*] [*German*]

Bev .... Billion Electron Volt

BEV .... Budapesti Elovarosi Vasut [*Budapest Suburban Railways*] (HU)

BEV .... Bundesamt fuer Eich- und Vermessungswesen-Gruppe Eichwesen [*Federal Office of Metrology and Surveying-Metrology Service*] [*Austria*]

bev.............. Nitrogen-Free Extractive (RU)

BEVEKA ... Belgisch Verbond van de Kaashandel [*Belgium*] (EAIO)

BEVFET.... Bureau of Employment, Vocational, and Further Education Training [*Queensland, Australia*]

BEW .... Beira [*Mozambique*] [*Airport symbol*] (OAG)

BEW .... Berliner Elektromotorenwerk [*Berlin Electric Motor Plant*] [*German*] (EG)

Bew............. Bewachung [*Guard*] [*German*] (GCA)

bew............. Beweglich [*Mobile*] [*German*] (GCA)

Bew............. Beweis [*Evidence*] [*German*] (GCA)

bew............. Bewerkt [*Edited*] [*Publishing*] [*Netherlands*]

BEW .... Biuro Ewidencji Wczasowiczow [*Resort Visitors' Registration Office*] (POL)

BEWAG .... Berliner Elektrizitaetswerke Aktiengesellschaft [*Berlin Electric Power Works Corporation*] [*German*] (EG)

BEWAG(Ost) ... Berliner Kraft- und Licht AG (Ost) [*Berlin Power and Light Corporation (East)*] (EG)

Bewasser.... Bewaesserung [*Irrigation*] [*German*] (GCA)

BewaV........ Dienstvorschrift fuer den Bahnbewachungsdienst [*Service Regulations for Railroad Guards*] (EG)

bewegl .... Beweglich [*Mobile*] [*German*] (GCA)

Beweglichk ... Beweglichkeit [*Flexibility*] [*German*] (GCA)

Bewert........ Bewertung [*Estimation*] [*German*] (GCA)

BEX .... Benin Air Express [*ICAO designator*] (FAAC)

BEXA........ Business Efficiency Exhibition [*Business Equipment Association of South Africa*]

BEY .... Beirut [*Lebanon*] [*Airport symbol*] (OAG)

BEZ............ Beru [*Kiribati*] [*Airport symbol*] (OAG)

Bez .... Bezahlt [*Paid, Salaried*] [*German*] (EG)

bez .... Bezeichnet [*or Bezeichnung*] [*Designated or Designation Publishing*] [*German*]

bez .... Beziehungsweise [*And, And/Or, Or, Respectively*] [*German*]

Bez .... Bezirk [*One of 14 large GDR administrative districts*] (EG)

bez .... Bezogen [*Covered*] [*Publishing*] [*German*]

bez .... Bezogen Auf [*Based On*] [*German*]

bez .... Bezorgd [*Edited*] [*Publishing*] [*Netherlands*]

BEZ............ Bezueglich [*Concerning*] [*German*]

BEZ............ Bratislavske Elektrotechnicke Zavody [*Bratislava Electrical Engineering Factories*] (CZ)

BEZALKO ... Preduzece za Proizvodnju Bezalkoholnih Pica [*Establishment for Production of Nonalcoholic Beverages*] (YU)

Bezeich....... Bezeichnung [*Designation*] [*German*] (GCA)

bezFw......... Bezuegliches Fuerwort [*German*]

Bez G.......... Bezirksgericht [*District Court*] [*German*] (DLA)

Bez Ger ...... Bezirksgericht [*District Court*] [*German*] (DLA)

bezgl........... Bezueglich [*With Reference To*] [*German*] (GCA)

bezgw.......... Beziehungsweise [*And, And/Or, Or, Respectively*] [*German*]

Bezhetskel'mash ... Bezhetsk Agricultural Machinery Plant (RU)

Bezieh .... Beziehung [*Respect*] [*German*] (GCA)

bezl............. Bezueglich [*Concerning*] [*German*]

bezl............. Impersonal (RU)

Bezpieka .... Ministerstwo Bezpieczenstwa Publicznego [*Ministry of Public Security*] (POL)

bezpl........... Free of Charge (BU)

bezugl.......... Bezueglich [*Concerning*] [*German*]

bezv............. Anhydrous, Water-Free (RU)

bezv .... Calm, Windless (RU)

Bezvodn...... Anhydrous, Water-Free (RU)

bezw .... Beziehungsweise [*And, And/Or, Or, Respectively*] [*German*] (GPO)

Bezymyanlag ... Bezymyanka Corrective Labor Camp (RU)

BF .... Baha'i Faith

Bf............... Bahnhof [*Railroad Station*] (EG)

BF .... Bakelite-Phenol [*Adhesive*] (RU)

BF .... Baltic Fleet (RU)

BF .... Banque de France [*Bank of France*]

BF .... Bassa Forza [*Other Ranks*] [*Italian*]

BF .... Bassa Frequenza [*Low Frequency*] [*Use LF*] [*Italian*] (WER)

BF .... Basse Frequence [*Base Frequency*] [*French*]

Bf............... Bastfaser [*Bast Fiber*] [*German*] (GCA)

Bf............... Befehlsform [*Order Form*] [*German*]

BF .... Bellerive Foundation (EAIO)

BF .... Betonelement-Foreningen [*Danish Precast Concrete Federation*] (EAIO)

BF .... Bibliotekarforbundet [*Denmark*] (SLS)

bf............... Bie Fjala (Per Shembull) [*Albanian*]

Bf............... Biophysics (RU)

bf............... Board Foot (RU)

BF .... Boas Festas [*Happy New Year*] [*Portuguese*]

Bf............... Brief [*Currency*] [*German*]

BF .... Burkina Faso [*ANSI two-letter standard code*] (CNC)

BF .... Fixing Unit [*Computers*] (RU)

BF .... Small-Arm Smokeless Powder [*Symbol*] [*French*] (MTD)

BFA............ Banco de Fomento Agropecuario [*Agricultural and Livestock Development Bank*] [*El Salvador*] (LA)

BFA............ Banco Financiero Argentino [*Bank*] [*Argentina*]

BFA............ Banque Franco-Allemande SA

BFA............ Belgian Franchising Association (IMH)

BFA............ Bicycle Federation of Australia

BFA............ Biological Farmers of Australia

BFA............ Bocce Federation of Australia

BFA............ Boucherie France-Afrique

BfA............ Bundesstelle fuer Aussenhandelsinformation [*Federal Office for Export Trade Information*]

BFA............ Bureau of Financial Analysis [*University of Pretoria*] [*South Africa*] (AA)

BFA............ Burkina Faso [*ANSI three-letter standard code*] (CNC)

BFAC.......... Bush Fires Advisory Committee [*Australia*] (ADA)

BfAi........... Bundesstelle fuer Aussenhandelsinformation [*Federal Office of Foreign Trade Information*] [*German Ministry of Economics*] (IID)

BFAN .... Bashkir Branch of the Academy of Sciences, USSR (RU)

BF & AR .... Bureau of Fisheries and Aquatic Resources [*Philippines*] (MSC)

BF & W...... Behoudens Foute en Weglatinge [*Errors and Omissions Excepted*] [*Afrikaans*]

BFAP......... Banco de Fomento Agropecuario del Peru [*Peru*] (DSCA)

BFAR........ Bundesforschungsanstalt fuer Rebenzuchtung Geilweilerhof [*German Federal Research Institute for Viticulture*]

BFAR........ Bureau of Fisheries and Aquatic Resources [*Philippines*] (ASF)

BFB............ Banco Fonsecas & Burnay [*Fonsecas & Burnay Bank*] [*Portugal*]

BFB............ Bowater Faculty of Business [*Deakin University*] [*Australia*]

BFB............ British Forces Borneo (ML)

BFB............ Bush Fires Board [*Western Australia*]

BFBWA ..... Bush Fire Board of Western Australia
BFC .... Banque Francaise pour le Commerce [*French Commercial Bank*] (AF)
BFc .... Belgian Franc [*Monetary unit*]
BFC .... Board of Fire Commissioners [*New South Wales, Australia*]
BFC .... Bush Fire Committee [*or Council*] [*Australia*] (ADA)
BFCD .... Bureau of Flood Control and Drainage [*Philippines*] (DS)
BFCE .... Banque Francaise du Commerce Exterieur [*French state-owned bank*]
BFCIB .... Banque pour le Financement du Commerce et des Investissements du Burkina (EY)
BFCMMFI ... Belgian Federation of the Cotton and Man-Made Fibre Industry (EAIO)
BFCNSW .. Board of Fire Commissioners, New South Wales [*Australia*]
BFCNT ...... Bush Fire Council of the Northern Territory [*Australia*]
BFCO .... Bank/Fund Conferences Office [*World Bank, IMF*]
BFCOI .... Banque Francaise Commerciale Ocean Indian [*Reunion*] (EY)
BFD .... Bund Freies Deutschland [*Free Germany Federation*] (WEN)
BFD .... Burma Fisheries Department (MSC)
BFDA .... Brisbane Funeral Directors' Association [*Australia*]
BFDB .... Bast Fibres Development Board
BFdW .... Bund Freiheit der Wissenschaft [*Association for the Freedom of Science*] (WEN)
Bfe .... Buero fuer Erfindungs- und Vorschlagswesen [*Office for Inventions and Suggestions*] (EG)
BFE .... Bundesforschungsanstalt fuer Ernaehrung [*Federal Research Center for Food and Nutrition*] [*Karlsruhe, West Germany*] [*Information retrieval*] (ARC)
Bf E .... Bundesstelle fuer Entwicklungshilfe [*Federal Republic of Germany Agency for Development Aid*] (EG)
BFEC .... Banking Federation of the European Economic Community [*Belgium*] (EAIO)
BFEEC ...... Banking Federation of the European Economic Community [*Belgium*] (EAIO)
BFEP .... Bicentennial Futures Education Project [*Australia*]
BFF .... Brazilian Film Foundation (EAIO)
BFF .... Bundesforschungsanstalt fuer Fischerei [*Database producer*] [*Germany*]
BFF .... Bund fuer Frieden und Einheit [*League for Peace and Unity*] (EG)
BFF .... Bureau of Flora and Fauna [*Australia*]
BFG .... Bahrain FibreGlass Co. Ltd.
BfG .... Bank fuer Gemeinwirtschaft [*Germany*]
BfG .... Bank fuer Gemeinwirtschaft Aktiengesellschaft [*Bank*]
BFG .... British Forces Germany [*NATO*]
BfG .... Bundesanstalt fuer Gewasserkunde [*Federal Institute of Hydrology*] [*Research center*] [*Germany*] (EAS)
BFGA .... Biodynamic Farming and Gardening Association [*Australia*]
BFH .... Bundesfinanzhof [*Federal Supreme Fiscal Court*] [*German*] (DLA)
BFH .... Bundesforschungsanstalt fuer Forst- und Holzwirtschaft [*Federal Research Center for Forestry and Forest Products*] [*Hamburg, West Germany*] [*Information retrieval*]
BFHE .... Entscheidungen des Bundesfinanzhofs [*German*] (DLA)
BFI .... Baltic Freight Index [*of spot market rates*] [*Shipping*] (DS)
BFI .... Betriebsforschungsinstitut [*Institute for Industrial Research*] [*German Iron and Steel Engineers Association Dusseldorf*] [*Information service or system*] (IID)
BFin .... Bachelor of Finance
BFIRI .... Badminton Federation, Islamic Republic of Iran (EAIO)
BFISL .... Bunadarfelag Islands [*Agricultural Society of Iceland*] (EAIO)
BFJ .... Ba [*Fiji*] [*Airport symbol*] (OAG)
BFK .... Benzofurancarboxylic Acid (RU)
BFK .... Great Fergana Canal (RU)
BFKP .... Flag Headquarters Ashore (RU)
BFL .... Basutoland Federation of Labour
BFL .... Betonforskningslaboratoriet [*Concrete Research Laboratory*] [*Sweden*] (PDAA)
BFL .... Biophysical Laboratory (RU)
BFLC .... Billings Family Life Center [*Australia*]
BFM .... Beamtenfonds voor het Mijnbedrijf [*Benelux*] (BAS)
BFM .... British Forces Malaya (ML)
BFMRG ..... Belgium-Flemish Minority Rights Group (EAIO)
BFN .... Banco do Fomento Nacional
BFN .... Bloemfontein [*South Africa*] [*Airport symbol*] (OAG)
BfN .... Buero fuer Neurerbewegung [*Office for the Innovator Movement*] (EG)
BFN .... Compagnie Nationale Naganagani [*Burkina Faso*] [*ICAO designator*] (FAAC)
BFNC .... Barrier Field Naturalists Club [*Australia*] (ADA)
BFNC .... Bloc Federal National Congolais
BFO .... Balneological and Physiotherapeutic Association (RU)
BFO .... Berufsverband Freiberuflich Taetiger Tieraerzte Oesterreichs [*Austria*] (SLS)
BFO .... Buffalo Range [*Zimbabwe*] [*Airport symbol*] (OAG)
BFP .... Basutoland Freedom Party

BFP .... Overflow Fixing Unit (RU)
BFPA .... Brisbane Forest Park Administration [*Australia*]
Bfr .... Belgian Franc
BFR .... Biennial Flight Review [*Department of Aviation*] [*Australia*]
BFR .... Combat Photoreconnaissance (RU)
BFR .... Statens Rad foer Byggnadsforskning [*Swedish Council for Building Research*] (WED)
BFRI .... Bangladesh Forest Research Institute
BFS .... Base Facilities for SACLANT [*NATO*] (NATG)
BFS .... Benelux Falcon Service [*Belgium*] [*ICAO designator*] (FAAC)
BFS .... British Frontier Service (BARN)
BFS .... Bromophenol Blue [*Indicator*] (RU)
BFS .... Bundesamt fur Statistik [*Federal Statistical Office*] [*Information service or system*] (IID)
BFS .... Bundesanstalt fur Flugsicherung [*Air-Traffic Control Authority*] [*Germany*] (PDAA)
BFS .... Business Funding Scheme
BFSC .... Building Fire Safety Committee [*South Australia*]
BFSL .... Burma Five Star Line (DS)
BFSSH ...... Bashkimi i Fizkulturisteve dhe i Sportisteve te Shqiperise [*Albanian*]
BFSV .... Beratungs- und Forschungsstelle fuer Seemaessige Verpackung (SLS)
BFSz .... Bekescsabai Forgacsolo Szerszamgyar [*Cutting Tool Factory of Bekescsaba*] (HU)
BFSzIB ..... Betakaritasi es Felvasarlasi Szallitasokat Intezo Bizottsag [*Committee for Collection and Purchase of Agricultural Produce*] (HU)
BFSzV .... Baranyai Foldmuvesszovetkezetek Szolgaltato Vallalata [*Supply Enterprise of the Farmers' Cooperatives of Baranya County*] (HU)
BFT .... Bank for Foreign Trade of the USSR
BFT .... Budapest Fovaros Tanacsa [*Municipal Council of Budapest*] (HU)
BFT .... Bureau of Foreign Trade [*Philippines*] (DS)
BFTT .... British Federation of Textile Technicians (DCTA)
BFTU .... Botswana Federation of Trade Unions
BFTUC ...... Bangladesh Free Trade Union Congress (EAIO)
BFU .... Franc [*Monetary unit*] [*Burundi*]
BFUS .... Control Signal Forming Unit (RU)
BFV .... Banky Fampandrosoana ny Varotra [*National Trade Bank*] [*Madagascar*]
BFV .... Buddhist Foundation of Victoria [*Australia*]
BfV .... Bundesamt fuer Verfassungsschutz [*Federal Office for the Protection of the Constitution*] [*West German counterintelligence agency*]
BFW .... Bayerische Flugzeug Werke [*Bavarian Airplane Works*] [*German*]
BfW .... Buero fuer Wirtschaftsfragen [*Office of Economic Affairs*] [*German*] (EG)
BFW .... Bund Freiheit der Wissenschaft [*Association for the Freedom of Science*] (WEN)
BFX .... Bafoussam [*Cameroon*] [*Airport symbol*] (OAG)
bg .... Ballistic Galvanometer (RU)
BG .... Banca del Gottardo [*Gotthard Bank*] [*Switzerland*]
BG .... Bandgeschwindigkeit [*Tape Bind Speed*] [*German*] (ADPT)
BG .... Baris Gucu [*Peace Force*] [*Turkish armed forces on Cyprus*] (GC)
BG .... Bataviash Genootschap [*Benelux*] (BAS)
BG .... Bela Garda [*White Guard*] [*Slovenia*] [*World War II*] (YU)
BG .... Belastinggids [*Benelux*] (BAS)
BG .... Bengal [*or Bengalese*] (WDAA)
Bg .... Berg [*Mountain*] [*Sweden*] (NAU)
Bg .... Berg [*Mountain*] [*Netherlands*] (NAU)
Bg .... Berg [*Mountain*] [*German*] (NAU)
Bg .... Berg [*Mountain*] [*Norway*] (NAU)
BG .... Bergamo [*Car registration plates*] [*Italian*]
Bg .... Bergegut [*Flotsam*] [*German*]
BG .... Berufsgericht [*Court of Appeal*] [*German*] (ILCA)
BG .... Best Game [*Billiards*] (BARN)
BG .... Bezirksgericht [*District Court*] [*German*] (EG)
BG .... Blocking Oscillator (RU)
Bg .... Bogen [*Bow*] [*Music*]
BG .... Bogenoemd(e) [*Above-Mentioned*] [*Afrikaans*]
bg .... Borgata [*Suburban Tenement District*] [*Italian*] (CED)
bg .... Borgo [*Village*] [*Italian*] (CED)
Bg .... Bourg [*Large Village*] [*Military map abbreviation World War I*] [*French*] (MTD)
BG .... Breguet-Dassault [*Societe Anonyme des Ateliers d'Aviation Louis Breguet*] [*France*] [*ICAO aircraft manufacturer identifier*] (ICAO)
BG .... Bulgaria [*ANSI two-letter standard code*] (CNC)
BG .... Bundesgericht [*Federal Supreme Court*] [*German*] (DLA)
BG .... Bundesgesetz [*Federal Act or Statute*] [*German*] (ILCA)
Bg .... Bundesgymnasium [*Federal Secondary School*] [*German*]
BG .... Combat Group, Combat Team (RU)

bg............... Commanding General of a Brigade   (BU)

BG............... Fuel Base   (RU)

BG............... Groupe de Brigade [*Brigade Group*] [*Cambodia*]   (CL)

b g............... Next Year   (RU)

Bg............... No Date [*Year of publication not given*]   (RU)

BG............... Oscillator Unit   (RU)

BG............... Tactical Ridge [*Topography*]   (RU)

BGA........... Bolsa de Generos Alimenticios do Rio de Janeiro [*Brazil*]   (DSCA)

BGA........... Bucaramanga [*Colombia*] [*Airport symbol*]   (OAG)

BGA........... Bulgarian Civil Aviation   (BU)

BGIS........... Bundesgesundheitsamt [*Federal Health Office*] [*Germany*]

BGA........... Bundesverband des Deutschen Gross-und Aussenhandels [*Federation of German Wholesalers and Foreign Traders*] (EAIO)

BGA........... Bureau de Gerances d'Affaires

BGAB....... Bolidens Gruvaktiebolag [*Boliden Mining Company*] [*Sweden*]   (WEN)

BGAG....... Beteiligungsgesellschaft fuer Gemeinwirtschaft

B/gal......... Brigadier General [*Brigadier General*] [*Use Brig Gen*]   (CL)

BGAM...... Angmagssalik [*Greenland*] [*ICAO location identifier*]   (ICLI)

BGAS........ Angissoq [*Greenland*] [*ICAO location identifier*]   (ICLI)

BGAS........ Bulolo Goldfields Aeroplane Service [*Australia*]

BGASH..... Botanic Gardens of Adelaide and State Herbarium [*Australia*]

BGAT....... Aputiteq [*Greenland*] [*ICAO location identifier*]   (ICLI)

BGATs....... Automatic Hump Unit Centralization [*Railroads*]   (RU)

BGB .... Bankgesellschaft Berlin [*Germany*]   (ECON)

BGB .... Bauern-, Gewerbe-, und Buergerpartei [*Farmers, Artisans, and Citizens Party*] [*Switzerland*]   (WEN)

Bgb............. Bergbau [*Mining*] [*German*]   (GCA)

BGB .... Booue [*Gabon*] [*Airport symbol*]   (OAG)

BGB .... Boulangerie de Grand Bassam

BGB .... Buergerliches Gesetzbuch [*Civil Code*] [*German*]   (EG)

bgb .... Deep-Drilling Battalion   (RU)

BGBl........... Bundesgesetzblatt [*Federal Code Newspaper*] [*German*]

BGBW .... Narssarssuaq [*Greenland*] [*ICAO location identifier*]   (ICLI)

BGC .... Benemerita Guardia Civil [*Meritorious Civil Guard*] [*Use Civil Guard GC Peru*] [*See also*]   (LA)

BGC .... Braganca [*Portugal*] [*Airport symbol*]   (OAG)

BGCA .... Bean Growers Cooperative Association [*Australia*]

BGCE........ Banque Guineenne du Commerce Exterieur [*Guinean Bank of Foreign Commerce*]   (AF)

BGCH........ Christianshab [*Greenland*] [*ICAO location identifier*]   (ICLI)

BGCO........ Constable Point [*Greenland*] [*ICAO location identifier*]   (ICLI)

BGD .... Bachelor of Graphic Design

BGD.......... Bangladesh [*ANSI three-letter standard code*]   (CNC)

BGD.......... Banque Gabonaise de Developpement [*Gabonese Development Bank*]   (AF)

BGD.......... Bedrijfsgeneeskundige Dienst [*Benelux*]   (BAS)

Bgd............. Beograd [*Belgrade*]   (YU)

BGD.......... Bulolo Gold Dredging [*Australia*]

BGD.......... Stichting Bureau voor Gemeenschappelijke Diensten [*Office of Joint Services*] [*Netherlands*]   (ARC)

BGDB .... Daneborg [*Greenland*] [*ICAO location identifier*]   (ICLI)

BGDH....... Danmarkshavn [*Greenland*] [*ICAO location identifier*]   (ICLI)

Bgdr............ Brigadier [*Brigadier*] [*German*]

BGDU........ Dundas [*Greenland*] [*ICAO location identifier*]   (ICLI)

Bge .... Barrage [*Dam*] [*Military map abbreviation World War I*] [*French*]   (MTD)

BGE .... Entscheidungen des Schweizerischen Bundesgerichtes [*Switzerland*]   (DLA)

bGeg........... Bei Gegenwart [*In the Presence Of*] [*German*]

BGEM .... Egedesminde [*Greenland*] [*ICAO location identifier*]   (ICLI)

BGES .... Board of Governors of the European Schools [*Belgium*]   (EAIO)

BGF .... Banco Gubernamental de Fomento [*Puerto Rico*]   (DSCA)

BGF .... Bangui [*Central African Republic*] [*Airport symbol*]   (OAG)

BGF .... Benzoylglycylphenylalanine   (RU)

BGF .... Bobby Goldsmith Foundation [*Australia*]

BGFC........ Banana Growers' Federation Cooperative [*Australia*]

BGFC........ Banana Growers Federation Cooperative, Ltd. [*Australia*]   (DSCA)

BGFD .... Frederiksdal [*Greenland*] [*ICAO location identifier*]   (ICLI)

BGFH .... Frederikshab [*Greenland*] [*ICAO location identifier*]   (ICLI)

BGG .... Department of Biology, Geology, and Geography   (BU)

BGGD........ Gronnedal [*Greenland*] [*ICAO location identifier*]   (ICLI)

BGGF......... Bedrijfschap Groothandel Groenten en Fruit [*Netherlands*]   (EAIO)

BGGF......... Department of Biology, Geology, and Geography (of Sofia University)   (BU)

BGG fak.... Department of Biology, Geology, and Geography   (BU)

BGGH........ Godthab [*Greenland*] [*ICAO location identifier*]   (ICLI)

BGGL........ Sondrestrom [*Greenland*] [*ICAO location identifier*]   (ICLI)

BGGN........ Godhavn [*Greenland*] [*ICAO location identifier*]   (ICLI)

BGG/P....... Berufsverband Gepruefter Graphologen/Psychologen eV   (SLS)

BGH........... Bundesgerichtshof [*Federal Supreme Court*] [*German*]   (DLA)

BGH........... Turkiye Belediye Hizmetlileri Sendikasi [*Turkish Municipal Service Workers Union*] [*Istanbul*]   (TU)

BGHB....... Holsteinsborg [*Greenland*] [*ICAO location identifier*]   (ICLI)

BGI .... Barbados [*Airport symbol*]   (OAG)

BGI .... Brasseries et Glacieries Internationales [*French brewery*]

BGI .... Bureau Gravimetrique International [*International Gravimetric Bureau*] [*Research center*] [*French*]   (IRC)

BGI .... Scientific Research Institute of Biogeography (of the State University Imeni A. A. Zhdanov)   (RU)

BGI .... Societe des Brasseries et Glacieres de l'Indochine [*Indochinese Brewery and Refrigeration Plant Company*] [*French*]   (CL)

BGIFK...... Belorussian State Institute of Physical Culture   (RU)

BGIS......... Isortoq [*Greenland*] [*ICAO location identifier*]   (ICLI)

BGIT .... Ivigtut [*Greenland*] [*ICAO location identifier*]   (ICLI)

BGITIS..... Belorussian State Institute of Theatrical Art   (RU)

BGIUV ...... Belorussian State Institute for the Advanced Training of Physicians   (RU)

BGJ........... Borgarfjordur [*Iceland*] [*Airport symbol*]   (OAG)

BGJH....... Julianehab [*Greenland*] [*ICAO location identifier*]   (ICLI)

BGJN....... Jakobshavn [*Greenland*] [*ICAO location identifier*]   (ICLI)

BGK .... Bangkok [*Thailand*]   (WDAA)

BGK .... Bank Gospodarstwa Krajowego [*Bank of the National Economy*]   (POL)

BGKD .... Kap Dan [*Greenland*] [*ICAO location identifier*]   (ICLI)

BGKh....... Benzene Hexachloride   (RU)

BGKhL ..... Biogeochemical Laboratory (of the Academy of Sciences, USSR)   (RU)

BGKK .... Kulusuk [*Greenland*] [*ICAO location identifier*]   (ICLI)

BGKM ...... Kungmiut [*Greenland*] [*ICAO location identifier*]   (ICLI)

BGKT .... Kap Tobin [*Greenland*] [*ICAO location identifier*]   (ICLI)

BGL .... Baglung [*Nepal*] [*Airport symbol*]   (OAG)

BGL .... Banque du Gabon et du Luxembourg

BGL .... Bell Group Ltd. [*Australia*]

BGL .... Betriebsgewerkschaftsleitung [*Plant Labor Union Executive Board*]   (EG)

Bgl............. Bogoslovski Glasnik [*Theological Bulletin*]   (YU)

Bgl............. Burgenland [*or Burgenlaendisch*] [*German*]

BGL .... Light Hydraulic Bulldozer   (RU)

BGL .... Societe Brasserie et Glaciere du Laos [*Lao Brewery and Refrigeration Plant Company*]   (CL)

Bgld............ Burgenland [*or Burgenlaendisch*] [*German*]

BGM.......... BENELUX Group on Mortality   (EAIO)

Bgm............ Buergermeister [*Mayor*] [*German*]

BGM........... Bugesera, Gisaka, et Mikongo

bgm............. Without Year and Place of Publication   (BU)

BGMI .... Beijing General Machinery Research Institute [*China*]   (IRC)

BGMM...... Marmorilik [*Greenland*] [*ICAO location identifier*]   (ICLI)

BGMP .... Baltic State Maritime Steamship Line   (RU)

BGMP .... Hydrometeorological Forecasting Bureau   (RU)

BGMV .... Mesters Vig [*Greenland*] [*ICAO location identifier*]   (ICLI)

BGNN....... Nanortalik [*Greenland*] [*ICAO location identifier*]   (ICLI)

BGNS....... Narssaq [*Greenland*] [*ICAO location identifier*]   (ICLI)

BGO .... Bergen [*Norway*] [*Airport symbol*]   (OAG)

BGOS .... Orssuiorssuaq [*Greenland*] [*ICAO location identifier*]   (ICLI)

BG (OV).... Bezirksgericht [*District Court*] [*German*]

BGPC........ Prins Christian Sund [*Greenland*] [*ICAO location identifier*]   (ICLI)

BGPI.......... Bel'tsy State Pedagogical Institute   (RU)

BGPS........ Bauddha-Grantha-Prakasana Samitiya [*Buddhist Publication Society*] [*Sri Lanka*]   (EAIO)

BGQ......... Bulk Grains Queensland [*An association*] [*Australia*]

BGQS .... Qutdligssat [*Greenland*] [*ICAO location identifier*]   (ICLI)

bgr .... Battle Group   (BU)

Bgr .... Bibliography, Bibliographic   (BU)

BGR .... Bulgaria [*ANSI three-letter standard code*]   (CNC)

BGR .... Bundesanstalt fuer Geowissenschaften und Rohstoffe [*Federal Institute for Geosciences and Natural Resources*] [*Research center*]   (IRC)

BGR .... Sigi Air [*Bulgaria*] [*ICAO designator*]   (FAAC)

BGRIMM ... Beijing General Research Institute of Mining and Metallurgy [*China National Non-Ferrous Metals Industry Corp.*] [*Research center*]   (EAS)

BGRS......... Ravns Storo [*Greenland*] [*ICAO location identifier*]   (ICLI)

BGS........... Bank Gospodarstwa Spoldzielczego [*Bank of Cooperative Economy*]   (POL)

BGS........... Bauersachs Genealogical Society   (EAIO)

BGS........... Betriebsgewerkschaftsschule [*Enterprise Labor Union School*]   (EG)

BGS........... Botswana Geological Survey

BGS........... Bulgarian Geological Society   (SLS)

BGS........... Bundesgrenzschutz [*Federal Border Police*]   (WEN)

BGS........... Bundesgrenzschutz [*Germany*] [*ICAO designator*]   (FAAC)

BGS........... Coast and Geodetic Survey [*USCGS*]   (RU)

BGSC........ Scoresbysund [*Greenland*] [*ICAO location identifier*]   (ICLI)

BGSF .... Sondre Stromfjord [*Greenland*] [*ICAO location identifier*]   (ICLI)

BGSG........ Sermiligaq [Greenland] [ICAO location identifier]   (ICLI)
BGSH .... Bashkimi i Grave te Shqiperise [Albanian]
BGSL........ Bakhrabad Gas Systems Ltd.
BGSM....... Fuel and Lubricants Base   (RU)
BGSO .... Be Ready for Sanitary Defense   (RU)
BGSO .... Ready for Health Defense   (BU)
BGST........ Sukkertoppen [Greenland] [ICAO location identifier]   (ICLI)
Bgt............ Berget [Mountain] [Sweden]   (NAU)
BGT .... Bodensee-Geratetechnik   (MCD)
BGTD........ Beigetretene Teile Deutschlands [Newly Adhered Parts of
               Germany] [Name given to former East German territory
               after unification]
BGTL........ Thule Air Base [Greenland] [ICAO location identifier]   (ICLI)
BGTM .... Tingmiarmiut [Greenland] [ICAO location identifier]   (ICLI)
BGTN .... Tiniteqilaq [Greenland] [ICAO location identifier]   (ICLI)
BGTO .... Be Ready for Labor and Defense   (RU)
BGTO .... Ready for Labor and Defense [Badge slogan]   (BU)
BGTS........ Bhutan Government Transport Service   (FEA)
BGTV .... Budapesti Geodeziai es Terkepeszeti Vallalat [Budapest Geodesy
               and Cartography Enterprise]   (HU)
BGU .... Bashkir State University Imeni Fortieth Anniversary of the
               October Revolution   (RU)
BGU .... Belorussian State University Imeni V. I. Lenin   (RU)
BGUM .... Unanak [Greenland] [ICAO location identifier]   (ICLI)
BGUP .... Upernavik [Greenland] [ICAO location identifier]   (ICLI)
BGV .... Beroepsgholfspelersvereniging [Professional Golfers' Association]
               [Afrikaans]
BGW .... Baghdad [Iraq] [Airport symbol]   (OAG)
Bgw .... Bergwerk [Mine] [German]
BGW .... Bundeskammer der Gewerblichen Wirtschaft [Federal Chamber
               of Commerce and Industry] [Austria]   (WEN)
BGW .... Bundesverband der Deutschen Gas- and Wasserwirtschaft eV
BGWO....... Botswana General Workers Organization   (AF)
BGWU .... Bank and General Workers Union [Grenada]   (LA)
BGX .... Bage [Brazil] [Airport symbol]   (OAG)
BGY .... Bergamo [Italy] [Airport symbol]   (OAG)
BH .... Bahrain [IYRU nationality code] [ANSI two-letter standard code]
               (CNC)
BH............. Bank Handlowy [Bank of Commerce]   (POL)
BH............. Banska a Hutni Spolecnost, Narodni Podnik [Mining and
               Metallurgical Society, National Enterprise]   (CZ)
Bh............. Beiheft [Supplement] [German]   (GCA)
BH............. Bezirkshauptmannschaft [District Captaincy] [German]
BH.......... Blackwood Hodge (Ghana) Ltd.
BH............. Bonne Humeur [Good Humor] [French]
BH............. Bosna i Hercegovina [Bosnia and Hercegovina]   (YU)
BH............. Broken Hill [Australia]   (ADA)
BH............. BuralHess Construction and Trade Co. Ltd. [Somalia]
BH............. Wet Belastingsherziening [Benelux]   (BAS)
BHA .... Banco Hispano Americano [Spanish]
BHA .... Barbados Hotel Association   (LA)
BHA .... Better Hearing Australia   (EAIO)
BHA .... Breeders and Hatchermen's Association [Australia]
BHA .... Bulk Handling Authority [Australia]
BHAP .... Business Health Assessment Program
BHAS .... Broken Hill Associated Smelters [Australia]   (ADA)
BHBFC...... Bangladesh House Building Finance Corp.   (EY)
BHC .... Bahamas Hotels Corporation   (GEA)
BHC .... Bank for Housing and Construction [Ghana]
BHC .... Bermuda Housing Corporation   (GEA)
BHC .... Better Health Commission [Australia]
BHC .... Black Hebrew Community
BHC .... Botswana Housing Corporation   (AF)
BHC .... Societe Bois Hydraulique du Cameroun
BHCC .... Broken Hill Chamber of Commerce [Australia]
BHCFC..... Buddy Holly and the Crickets Fan Club   (EAIO)
BHD.......... Berhad [Public Limited Company] [Malaysia]   (FEA)
Bhd........... Brotherhood   (ILCA)
BHE .... Blenheim [New Zealand] [Airport symbol]   (OAG)
BHE.......... Bund der Heimatvertriebenen und Entrechteten [Society of
               Exiles and Those Deprived of Rights] [German]
BHEL .... Bharat Heavy Electricals Ltd. [India]
BHESCO... Building, Hardware, and Electrical Supplies Company Ltd.
BHEV .... Budapesti Helylerdeku Vasut [Suburban Railways of Budapest]
               (HU)
Bhf .... Bahnhof [Railroad Station] [German]   (EG)
BHF .... Baie Hoe Frekwensie [Very-High Frequency] [Use VHF]   (AF)
BHF .... Berliner Handels- & Frankfurter Bank [Berlin & Frankfurt Bank]
BHF .... Besonder Hoe Frekwensie [Very High Frequency] [Afrikaans]
BHG .... Baeuerliche Handelsgenossenschaft [Peasants' Trade
               Cooperative]   (EG)
BHG.......... Beloiannisz Hiradastechnikai Gyar [Beloiannisz
               Telecommunication Factory]   (HU)
BHG.......... Nederlandse Bond van Huis- en Grondeigenaren [Netherlands]
               (BAS)
BHH .... Bisha [Saudi Arabia] [Airport symbol]   (OAG)

BHH .... Broken Hill Holdings Ltd. [Australia]
BHI .... Bahia Blanca [Argentina] [Airport symbol]   (OAG)
BHI .... Bureau Hydrographique International [International
               Hydrographic Organization]   (EAIO)
BHIF......... Banco Hipotecario de Fomento Nacional [Bank] [Chile]
BHJ .... Bhuj [India] [Airport symbol]   (OAG)
BHK.......... Bezirks-Hochwasserkommission [District Flood Control
               Commission]   (EG)
BHK.......... Bukhara [Former USSR] [Airport symbol]   (OAG)
BHL.......... Bernard-Henri Levy [French writer and philosopher]
BHM......... Bolge Hareket Merkezi [Regional Operations Center]   (TU)
BHM......... Broken Hill Metals [Australia]
BHMMGM ... Bas Hukuk Musavirligi ve Muhakemat Genel Mudurlugu
               [Chief Legal Adviser and Judgments Directorate General]
               (TU)
BHMS .... Bishop's Home Mission Society [Australia]
BHN .... Banco Hipotecario Nacional [National Mortgage Bank]
               [Argentina]   (LAA)
BHNOOS ... Bosansko-Hercegovacki Narodnooslobodilacki Omladinski
               Savez [Bosnian and Hercegovinian National Liberation
               Youth Federation]   (YU)
BHNV........ Balatoni Hajozasi Nemzeti Vallalat [Lake Balaton National
               Navigation Enterprise]   (HU)
BHO .... Bhoja Airlines [Pakistan] [ICAO designator]   (FAAC)
BHO .... Bhopal [India] [Airport symbol]   (OAG)
BHortSci.... Bachelor of Horticultural Science
BHospitality ... Bachelor of Hospitality
BHP........... Bezpieczenstwo i Higiena Pracy [Industrial Safety and Hygiene]
               (POL)
BHP........... Bhojpur [Nepal] [Airport symbol]   (OAG)
BHP........... Broken Hill Proprietary Co. Ltd. [Australia]   (ADA)
BHPIT....... Broken Hill Proprietary Information Technology [Australia]
BHPP........ Broken Hill Proprietary Petroleum [Australia]
BHPS........ Byro Hlavni Politicke Spravy [Bureau of the Main Political
               Directorate]   (CZ)
BHPV .... Bharat Heavy Plate and Vessels Ltd. [India]
BHQ .... Broken Hill [Australia] [Airport symbol]   (OAG)
BHR.......... Bahrain [ANSI three-letter standard code]   (CNC)
BHR.......... Bharatpur [Nepal] [Airport symbol] [Obsolete]   (OAG)
BHS .... Bahamas [ANSI three-letter standard code]   (CNC)
BHS .... Bahamasair Holdings Ltd. [Bahamas] [ICAO designator]
               (FAAC)
BHS .... Bahamas Historical Society   (EAIO)
BHS .... Bane a Hute na Slovensku, Narodny Podnik [Mines and
               Metallurgical Works in Slovakia, National Enterprise]
               (CZ)
BHS .... Banque de l'Habitat du Senegal
BHS .... Bathurst [Australia] [Airport symbol]   (OAG)
BHS .... British Home Stores [Retail chain]
BHSc......... Bachelor of Health Science
BHSNSW ... Baptist Historical Society of New South Wales [Australia]
BHT.......... Baht [Monetary unit] [Thailand]
BHT.......... Bogazici Hava Tasimacilik AS [Turkey] [ICAO designator]
               (FAAC)
BHT.......... Braunkohlen-Hochtemperaturkoks [Brown Coal High-
               Temperature Coke]   (EG)
BHthSc...... Bachelor of Health Science
BHU .... Banaras Hindu University [India]   (PDAA)
BHU .... Banco Hipotecario del Uruguay [Mortgage Bank of Uruguay]
               (LAA)
BHU .... Banco Holandes Unido [Dutch Union Bank] [Ecuador]
BHU .... Bhavnagar [India] [Airport symbol]   (OAG)
Bhu............ Bhutan
BHUMMVT ... Bachelor of Human Movement
BHV.......... Balatoni Hajozasi Vallalat [Lake Balaton Navigation Enterprise]
               (HU)
BHV.......... Brandbestrydingstoerusting Handelaars Vereniging [South
               Africa]   (AA)
BHVK........ Bezirks-Havarie-Verhuetungskommission [District Sea-Damage
               Prevention Commission]   (EG)
BHVSA...... Beroepshigiene Vereniging van Suid-Afrika [South Africa]   (AA)
BHW......... Berliner Halbzeug-Werke [Berlin Semi-Finished Products
               Factory]   (EG)
BHY.......... Birgenair [Turkey] [ICAO designator]   (FAAC)
BHY.......... Bursa Hava Yollari Sirketi [Bursa Airlines Corporation]   (TU)
BHZ.......... Belo Horizonte [Brazil] [Airport symbol]   (OAG)
BHZ.......... Berliner Handelszentrale [Berlin Trade Center] [German]   (EG)
Bhz............ Wet Belastingsherziening [Benelux]   (BAS)
B Hz B....... Bolge Hizmet Birligi [Regional (or Area) Service Unit]   (TU)
Bi.............. Baai [Bay] [B] [See also] [Netherlands]   (NAU)
BI .... Banca de Investitii [Investment Bank]   (RO)
BI .... Banca d'Italia [Bank of Italy]   (WER)
BI .... Banco Industrial [Industrial Bank] [Venezuela]   (LAA)
BI .... Banco Internacional [International Bank] [Ecuador]
BI .... Bankin'ny Indostria [Industrial Bank] [Malagasy]   (AF)
BI .... Bank Inwestycyjny [Investment Bank]   (POL)

BI .... Banque de l'Indochine
BI .... Baptist Independent Church [*Also, BIC*]
BI .... Befrienders International [*Later, BISW*]   (EAIO)
BI .... Bezirksinspektor [*District Inspector*] [*German*]   (ADPT)
BI .... Bibliographisches Institut [*Bibliographic Institute*]   (EG)
BI .... Biologiju Institut [*Former Yugoslavia*]   (MSC)
BI .... Biology   (DSUE)
BI .... Bioloski Institut [*Biological Institute*]   (YU)
BI .... Bioteknisk Institut [*Biotechnical Institute*] [*Denmark*]   (ARC)
BI .... Bismuth Institute [*Brussels, Belgium*]   (EAIO)
Bi .... Bismuto [*Bismuth*] [*Chemical element*] [*Portuguese*]
BI .... Bladamannafelag Islands [*Union of Icelandic Journalists*]   (EAIO)
BI .... Bobs International [*An association*]   (EAIO)
BI .... Botanical Institute   (BU)
BI .... Brevet Industrielle
BI .... Brigade d'Infanterie [*Infantry Brigade*] [*Cambodia*]   (CL)
BI .... Brother Industries [*Microwave-oven manufacturer*] [*Japan*]
B-I .... Broz-Ivekovic, Rjecnik Hravatska Jezika [*Dictionary of the Croatian Language by Ivan Broz and Franjo Ivekovic*]   (YU)
BI .... Bureau Interdepartemental [*Algeria*]
BI .... Burundi [*ANSI two-letter standard code*]   (CNC)
Bi .... Byochi [*Anchorage*] [*Japan*]   (NAU)
BI .... Inspection Barometer   (RU)
BI .... Institute of Biology of the Bulgarian Academy of Sciences   (BU)
BI .... Integrating Unit   (RU)
BIA .... Baldan-Implementos Agricolas SA [*Brazil*]   (DSCA)
BIA .... Baltic International Airlines [*Latvia*] [*ICAO designator*]   (FAAC)
BIA .... Bankers Institute of Australasia   (ADA)
BIA .... Bastia [*Corsica*] [*Airport symbol*]   (OAG)
BIA .... Bilingual Information Assistant [*Australia*]
BIA .... Boletim de Industria Animal [*Brazil*]   (DSCA)
BIA .... Bomber-Fighter Aviation   (RU)
BIA .... Bouraq Indonesia Airlines   (FEA)
BIA .... Bread Industry Authority [*Queensland, Australia*]
BiA .... Budownictwo i Architektura [*Construction and Architecture*] [*Publisher*]   (POL)
BIA .... Bulgarian Historical Archives of the V. Kolarov State Library   (BU)
BIA .... Bulgarian Industrial Association
BIA .... Bureau d'Investissement en Afrique [*Office of Investments in Africa*] [*France*]   (AF)
BIA .... Bureau Industriel Africain
BIA .... Bureau Industriel d'Algerie
BIA .... Bureau International Afghanistan   (EA)
BIA .... Burma Independence Army   (FEA)
BIA .... Business International Assistance
BIA .... Real-Aerovias Brasil [*Brazilian international airline*]
BIA .... Union of Bulgarian Engineers and Architects   (BU)
BIAA .... Beef Improvement Association of Australia
BIAA .... Beijing Institute of Aeronautics and Astronautics [*China*]   (PDAA)
BIAC .... Building Industry Advisory Council [*Australia*]
BIAC .... Business and Industry Advisory Committee [*NATO*]   (NATG)
BIAD .... Bulgarian Society of Engineers and Architects   (BU)
BIAD .... Bureau International d'Anthropologie Differentielle [*Switzerland*]   (SLS)
BIA-DBVK ... Bulgarian Historical Archives of the V. Kolarov State Library   (BU)
BIADI .... Bureau Inter-Administration de Documentation Informatique [*Inter-Administration Bureau of Information Documentation*] [*French*]   (ADPT)
BIAE .... Bunbury Institute of Advanced Education [*Australia*]
BIAG .... Banque Internationale pour l'Afrique en Guinee   (EY)
BIAM .... Banque d'Informations Automatisees sur les Medicaments [*Data Bank for Medicaments*] [*Information service or system*]   (IID)
BIAM PA .. Banque d'Information Automatisee sur les Medicaments Principes Actifs [*Databank on active ingredients of drugs*] [*French*]   (NITA)
BIANSW ... Baking Industry Association of New South Wales [*Australia*]
BIANSW ... Boating Industry Association of New South Wales [*Australia*]
BIAO .... Banque Internationale pour l'Afrique Occidentale [*International Bank for West Africa*] [*France*]   (AF)
BIAO-CI.... Banque Internationale pour l'Afrique Occidentale - Cote d'Ivoire   (EY)
BIAP .... Bureau de l'Industrie de l'Artisanat et de la Peche [*Artisan Industry and Fisheries Bureau*] [*Martinique*]   (GEA)
BIAP .... Bureau International d'Audiophonologie [*International Office for Audiophonology - IOA*] [*Brussels, Belgium*]   (EA)
BIAPE .... Banco Interamericano de Ahorro y Prestamos [*Inter-American Savings and Loan Bank*]   (LA)
BIAQ .... Boating Industry Association of Queensland [*Australia*]
BIAR .... Akureyri [*Iceland*] [*ICAO location identifier*]   (ICLI)

BIAS .... Bibliotheks Ausleihverwaltungsystem [*Library circulation system*] [*Federal Republic of Germany*]   (NITA)
BIAS .... Bremer Institut fuer Angewandte Strahlenforschung
BIASA ...... Boating Industry Association of South Australia
BIAT .... Banque Internationale Arabe de Tunisie [*International Arab Bank of Tunisia*]   (AF)
BIAT .... Banque Internationale pour l'Afrique au Tchad [*International Bank for Africa in Chad*]
BIAT .... British Institute of Architectural Technicians   (EAIO)
BIAWA ...... Boating Industry Association of Western Australia
BIAZ .... Banque Internationale pour l'Afrique au Zaire [*International Bank for Africa in Zaire*]   (AF)
BIB .... Bahamas Institute of Bankers   (EAIO)
BIB .... Bahrain International Bank
BIB .... Balatoni Intezo Bizottsag [*Lake Balaton Managing Committee (Tourism)*]   (HU)
BIB .... Banco de Investimento do Brasil [*Brazilian Investment Bank*]   (LA)
BIB .... Banque Internationale du Burkina [*Burkina Faso*]   (EY)
BIB .... Berliner Institut fur Betriebsfuhrung [*Berlin Business Management Institute*] [*Germany*]   (PDAA)
BiB .... Beslissingen in Belastingzaken [*Benelux*]   (BAS)
Bib .... Bible [*Bible*] [*French*]
Bib .... Bibliotheque [*Library*] [*French*]
BIB .... Bulgarian Historical Library [*Series*]   (BU)
BIB .... Bulgarian Investment Bank   (BU)
BIB .... Bulgarian Mortgage Bank   (BU)
BIBA .... Balai Penelitian dan Pengembangan Industri Banda Aceh [*Laboratory and Testing Institute for Industrial Products - Banda Aceh*] [*Indonesia*]
bi banka ..... Bulgarian Investment Bank   (BU)
bibl .... Biblical   (BU)
bibl .... Bibliografia [*Bibliography*] [*Portuguese*]
bibl .... Bibliografia [*Bibliography*] [*Hungary*]
bibl .... Bibliografico [*Bibliographical*] [*Portuguese*]
Bibl............ Bibliographie [*Bibliography*] [*German*]
Bibl............ Biblioteca [*Library*] [*Portuguese*]
bibl .... Bibliotheek [*Library*] [*Netherlands*]
Bibl............ Bibliothek [*or Bibliotheker*] [*Library (or Librarian)*] [*German*]
bibl .... Bibliotheque [*Library*] [*Publishing*] [*French*]
bibl .... Biblique [*French*]   (TPFD)
Bibl............ Biblisch [*Biblical*] [*German*]
Bibl............ Bibliyografya [*Bibliography*]   (TU)
BIBL .... Blonduos [*Iceland*] [*ICAO location identifier*]   (ICLI)
bibl .... Library, Library's   (BU)
BIBLIOCANAPI ... Biblioteca Camara Nacional de Artesania y Pequena Industria de Costa Rica [*Costa Rica*]
bibliogr....... Bibliografi [*Bibliography*] [*Publishing Danish/Norwegian*]
bibliogr....... Bibliografia [*Bibliography*] [*Poland*]
bibliogr....... Bibliografisk [*Bibliographic*] [*Sweden*]
bibliogr....... Bibliographisch [*Bibliographic*] [*Publishing*] [*German*]
bibliogr....... Bibliography, Bibliographic   (BU)
bibliogradres ... Publication Data [*Library cataloging*]   (BU)
bibliot........ Biblioteca [*Library*] [*Italian*]
biblioth....... Bibliotheque [*Library*] [*Publishing*] [*French*]
biblst .... Bibliotheekstempel [*Library Stamp*] [*Publishing*] [*Netherlands*]
bibl-uppl.... Bibliofilupplaga [*Book Collector's Edition*] [*Sweden*]
BIBM .... Bureau International du Beton Manufacture [*International Bureau for Precast Concrete*]   (EAIO)
BIBOR ...... Bahrain Interbank Offered Rate
BIBSKI ...... Buyuk Istanbul Bolgesel Su ve Kanalizasyon Idaresi Genel Mudurlugu [*Greater Istanbul Regional Water and Sewage Administration Directorate General*]   (TU)
BIC............ Bahrain Insurance Co.   (IMH)
BIC............ Banana Industry Committee [*New South Wales, Australia*]
BIC............ Banco Industrial Colombiano [*Colombia*]   (COL)
BIC............ Banco Internacional de Credito [*Portugal*]   (EY)
BIC............ Banque Internationale des Comores   (EY)
BIC............ Bantu Investment Corporation [*South Africa*]   (AF)
BIC............ Baptist Independent Church [*Also, BI*]
BIC............ Barrier Industrial Council [*Australia*]   (ADA)
BIC............ Beatles Information Center [*Sweden*]   (EAIO)
BIC............ Belgian International Air Carriers [*ICAO designator*]   (FAAC)
BIC............ Benefices Industriels et Commerciaux [*Industrial and Business Profits*] [*French*]   (WER)
BIC............ Boulangerie Industrielle de Cotonou
BIC............ Brigade d'Infanterie de Choc [*Infantry Shock Brigade*] [*Cambodia*]   (CL)
BIC............ Briqueterie Industrielle du Chari
BIC............ Bureau International des Containers [*International Container Bureau*] [*Paris, France*]   (EAIO)
BIC............ Bureau of International Commerce   (ADPT)
BIC............ Bushveld Igneous Complex [*South Africa*]
BIC............ Business and Innovation Centre [*European Community*]
BIC............ Business in the Community [*Australia*]
BICA.......... Reykjavik [*Iceland*] [*ICAO location identifier*]   (ICLI)

BICASA..... Banco de Industria y Comercio Sociedad Anonima [*Mexico*] (LAA)
BICC......... Reykjavik [*Iceland*] [*ICAO location identifier*]   (ICLI)
BICE.......... Banca Internationala de Colaborare Economica [*International Bank for Economic Cooperation - IBEC*] [*Romanian*] (RO)
BICE.......... Banca Internazionale per la Cooperazione Economica [*International Bank for Economic Cooperation - IBEC*] [*Italian*]   (WER)
BICE.......... Bureau International Catholique de l'Enfance [*International Catholic Child Bureau - ICCB*] [*Geneva, Switzerland*] (EA)
BICEDA .... Beijer Institute Centre for Energy and Development in Africa [*Kenya*] [*Research center*]   (WED)
BICELL..... Bimbresso Cellulose SA
BICEPS ..... Basic Inservice Computer Education for Primary Schools [*Australia*]
BICh .... Aircraft Designed by B. I. Cheranovskiy   (RU)
bich .... Bichado [*Wormholed*] [*Publishing*] [*Portuguese*]
BICI .... Banque Internationale pour le Commerce et l'Industrie [*International Bank of Commerce and Industry*]   (AF)
BICIA .... Banque Internationale pour le Commerce, l'Industrie et l'Agriculture [*International Bank for Trade, Industry, and Agriculture*] [*Burkina Faso*]   (GEA)
BICIA-BF ... Banque Internationale pour le Commerce, l'Industrie, et l'Agriculture du Burkina Faso [*International Bank for Trade, Industry, and Agriculture of Burkina Faso*]
BICIA-HV ... Banque Internationale pour le Commerce, l'Industrie, et l'Agriculture de Haute Volta [*International Bank of Commerce, Industry, and Agriculture of Upper Volta*] [*BICIA-BF*] [*Later,*]   (AF)
BICIC .... Banque Internationale pour le Commerce et l'Industrie du Cameroun [*International Bank of Commerce and Industry of Cameroon*]   (AF)
BICIC .... Banque Internationale pour le Commerce et l'Industrie du Congo [*International Bank of Commerce and Industry of the Congo*]   (AF)
BICICI...... Banque Internationale pour le Commerce et l'Industrie de la Cote-D'Ivoire [*International Bank of Commerce and Industry of the Ivory Coast*]
BICIG .... Banque Internationale pour le Commerce et l'Industrie du Gabon [*International Bank of Commerce and Industry of Gabon*]   (AF)
BICIN....... Banque Internationale pour le Commerce et l'Industrie du Niger [*International Bank of Commerce and Industry of Niger*]
BICIS........ Banque Internationale pour le Commerce et l'Industrie du Senegal [*International Bank of Commerce and Industry of Senegal*]
BICIT .... Banque Internationale pour le Commerce et l'Industrie du Tchad [*International Bank of Commerce and Industry of Chad*]
BICMG...... Brothers of the Immaculate Conception of the Mother of God [*See also CBH Netherlands*]   (EAIO)
BICMOS ... Bipolar Complementary Metal Oxide Semiconductor [*Electronics*]   (BARN)
bicol........... Bicolore [*Bicolored*] [*Italian*]
BICP .... Bureau of Industrial Costs and Prices [*India*]   (ECON)
bicr .... Bicromia [*Bichrome*] [*Italian*]
BICT.......... Banque Ivoirienne de Construction et de Travaux Publiques [*Construction and Public Works Bank of the Ivory Coast*]   (GEA)
BID .... Banco Interamericano de Desarrollo [*Inter-American Development Bank*] [*Spanish*]
BID .... Banque Interamericaine de Developpement [*Inter-American Development Bank*] [*French*]
BID .... Banque Islamique de Developpement [*Islamic Development Bank*] [*Use IDB*]   (AF)
BID .... Bibliografia di Informatica e Diritto [*Bibliography of Legal/Rights Information*] [*CSC-Corte Suprema di Cassazione*] [*Italy*]   (NITA)
BID .... Buitenlandse Inlichtingendienst [*Foreign Intelligence Service*] [*Netherlands*]   (WEN)
BID .... Office for Inventions   (RU)
BIDC......... Banque Internationale du Congo
BIDC......... Barbados Industrial Development Corporation   (GEA)
BIDC........ Bureau Interafricain de Developpement et de Cooperation [*Inter-African Development and Cooperation Office*]   (AF)
BIDCO ...... Bauxite Industry Development Company [*Guyana*]   (LA)
Bide........... Bastide [*Country House, Redoubt*] [*Military map abbreviation World War I*] [*French*]   (MTD)
BIDECAL ... Bicicletas de Caldas [*Pereira*]   (COL)
BIDI.......... Banque Ivoirienne de Developpement Industriel [*Ivorian Bank for Industrial Development*]   (AF)
BIDiLc ...... Bureau International de la Didactique des Langues Classiques [*Belgium*]   (SLS)
BiDN......... Osrodek Bibliografii i Dokumentacji Naukowej [*Center of Bibliography and Scientific Documentation*]   (POL)
BIDR......... Banque Internationale de Developpement et de Reconstruction

bidr............ Bidrag [*Contribution*] [*Publishing Danish/Norwegian*]
BIDS......... Bangladesh Institute of Development Studies [*Dhaka, Bangladesh*]
BIDV......... Djupivogur [*Iceland*] [*ICAO location identifier*]   (ICLI)
Bie .... Batterie [*Battery*] [*Military*] [*French*]   (MTD)
BIE............ Beijing Institute of Electromachining [*China*]   (IRC)
Bie .... Bergerie [*Sheepfold*] [*Military map abbreviation World War I*] [*French*]   (MTD)
BIE............ Bijblad Industriele Eigendom [*Benelux*]   (BAS)
BIE............ Bureau International d'Education [*International Bureau of Education - IBE*]   (EAIO)
BIE............ Bureau International des Expositions [*International Bureau of Exhibitions*]   (EAIO)
BIE............ Bureau Ivoirien d'Engineering
BIE............ Bureau voor de Industriele Eigendom [*Benelux*]   (BAS)
BIE............ Royal Institute of Research [*Greece*]   (DSCA)
BIEANSW ... Bakery Industry Employees' Association of New South Wales [*Australia*]
BIEC .... Beijing International Exhibition Center [*China*]
Bieg .... Biegung [*Bending*] [*German*]   (GCA)
BIEG......... Egilsstadir [*Iceland*] [*ICAO location identifier*]   (ICLI)
biegs .... Biegsam [*Flexible*] [*German*]
BIEM........ Bureau International des Societes Gerant les Droits d'Enregistrement et de Reproduction Mecanique [*French*]
BIESANSW ... Bread Industry Employees and Salespersons' Association of New South Wales [*Australia*]
BIETA ...... Biblioteca Interamericana de Estadistica Teorica y Aplicada [*Washington, DC*]   (LAA)
BiF .... Borneo International Furniture Co. Ltd. [*South Korea*]
BIFA .... Birlesik Alman Ilac Fabrikalari Turk Ltd. Sti. [*United German Pharmaceutical Factories*]   (TU)
BIFA .... British International Freight Association   (EAIO)
BIFAD...... Board for International Food and Agricultural Development
BIFAP....... Bourse Internationale de Fret Aerien de Paris [*France*]
BIFE .... Banco Interamericano de Fomento Economico [*Inter-American Bank for Economic Development*]   (LA)
BIFEN ...... Banque Internationale pour le Financement de l'Energie Nucleaire
BIFF .... Battlefield Identification Friend or Foe
BIFFEX .... Baltic International Freight Futures Exchange [*London, England*]
BIFM........ Fagurholsmyri [*Iceland*] [*ICAO location identifier*]   (ICLI)
BIFNRJ..... Bibliografski Institut FNRJ [*Federativna Narodna Republika Jugoslavija*] [*Bibliographic Institute of Yugoslavia*]   (YU)
BIFOA...... Betriebswirtschaftliches Institut fur Organisation und Automation [*Germany*]   (PDAA)
BIFOR....... Building Industry's Federation of Rhodesia
BIFSA....... Building Industries Federation of South Africa   (AA)
BIFU......... Banking Insurance and Finance Union [*Formerly, National Union of Bank Employees - NUBE*] [*British*]   (DCTA)
BIG .... Banque Internationale de Gestion [*Bank*] [*Switzerland*]
BIG .... Bois Industriels du Gabon
BIG .... Breastfeeding Information Group [*Kenya*]   (EAIO)
BIGA .... Bundesamt fur Industrie, Gewerbe und Arbeit [*Switzerland*]   (PDAA)
BIGFON.... Breitbandiges Integriertes Glasfaser-Fernmeldeortsnetz [*Brand-Bonded Integrated Telephone Exchange Net*] [*German*]   (ADPT)
BIGR......... Grimsey [*Iceland*] [*ICAO location identifier*]   (ICLI)
BIGRAP .... Gradezno Pretprijatie Bitola [*Bitola Construction Establishment*]   (YU)
BIGWU ..... Barbados Industrial and General Workers Union   (LA)
BIGZ......... Beogradski Izdavacko-Graficki Zavod [*Publisher*] [*Serbia*]   (EY)
BiH .... Bosna i Hercegovina [*Bosnia and Hercegovina*]   (YU)
BIH .... Budapesti Izraelita Hitkozseg [*Jewish Religious Community of Budapest*]   (HU)
BIH .... Bureau International de l'Heure [*International Time Bureau*]   (EAIO)
BIHE .... Benue Institute of Higher Education
BIHN......... Hofn/Hornafjordur [*Iceland*] [*ICAO location identifier*]   (ICLI)
BIHU........ Husavik [*Iceland*] [*ICAO location identifier*]   (ICLI)
BII............. Banca Internationala de Investitii [*International Investment Bank*]
BII............. Basle Institute for Immunology [*Switzerland*]
BII............. Bureau of Internal Investigation
BIICC .... Bureau International d'Information des Chambres de Commerce
BIIL.......... Banque Industrielle et Immobiliere de Libye
BIIS .... Isafjordur [*Iceland*] [*ICAO location identifier*]   (ICLI)
BIIZhT ...... Belorussian Institute of Railroad Transportation Engineers   (RU)
BIJ .... Banque Inadana Jati [*Inadana Jati (Enn'tean Cheat; National Commerce) Bank*] [*Cambodia*]   (CL)
Bijbl IE ...... Bijblad Industriele Eigendom [*Benelux*]   (BAS)
Bijbl IndEig ... Bijblad bij de Industrieele Eigendom [*Benelux*]   (BAS)
bijdr........... Bijdrage [*Contribution*] [*Publishing*] [*Netherlands*]
Bijdr .... Bijdragen tot de Kennis van het Staats-, Provinciaal en Gemeentebestuur in Nederland [*Netherlands*]   (BAS)
bijgeb......... Bijgebonden [*Bound In*] [*Publishing*] [*Netherlands*]

bijgev......... Bijgevoegd [*Appended*] [*Publishing*] [*Netherlands*]
bijgew......... Bijgewerkte [*Benelux*]   (BAS)
bijl............. Bijlage [*Appendix, Supplement*] [*Publishing*] [*Netherlands*]
Bijl HandTw K der St Gen ... Bijlagen bij de Handelingen van de Tweede Kamer der Staten Generaal [*Benelux*]   (BAS)
bijv............ Bijvoorbeeld [*Benelux*]   (BAS)
BijvStb....... Bijvoegsel Staatsblad [*Benelux*]   (BAS)
bijz.............. Bijzonder [*Benelux*]   (BAS)
Bijz Rvc...... Bijzondere Raad van Cassatie [*Benelux*]   (BAS)
BIK............. Basin Ilan Kuruma [*Press Advertisement Organization*]   (TU)
BIK............ Biak [*Indonesia*] [*Airport symbol*]   (OAG)
BIK............ Bomb-Run True Heading   (RU)
BIK............ Borsodvideki Ipari Kozpont [*Industrial Center of the Borsod Area*]   (HU)
BIKF......... Keflavik [*Iceland*] [*ICAO location identifier*]   (ICLI)
BIKh.......... Office of Tool Supply   (RU)
BIKP.......... Kopasker [*Iceland*] [*ICAO location identifier*]   (ICLI)
BIKR.......... Saudarkrokur [*Iceland*] [*ICAO location identifier*]   (ICLI)
BIKSAN ... Birlesik Kablo Sanayii ve Ticaret AS [*United Cable Industry and Trade Corp.*]   (TU)
BIL............. Bank in Liechtenstein
BIL............. Banque Internationale a Luxembourg SA   (ECON)
BIL............. Bilangan [*Number*]   (ML)
BIL............. Brierley Investments Ltd. [*Australia*]
BILBY .... Books I Loved Best Yearly [*Award*] [*Australia*]
Bild............ Bildung [*Education*] [*German*]
BILD.......... Bureau International de Liaison et de Documentation [*French*]   (SLS)
Bildg.......... Bildung [*Education*] [*German*]
Bildl........... Bildlich [*Pictorial*] [*German*]
Bildn.......... Bildnis [*Portrait*] [*Publishing*] [*German*]
Bildtaf....... Bildtafel [*Illustrated Plate*] [*Publishing*] [*German*]
bilh............ Bilhete [*Ticket, Note*] [*Portuguese*]
bili............. Biljardipeli [*Billiards*] [*Finland*]
b ili m .... More or Less   (RU)
bilj............. Biljeska [*Note*]   (YU)
Bilkokoop .. Cooperative for Medicinal Herbs   (BU)
bill............. Billede [*Illustration*] [*Publishing Danish/Norwegian*]
BILLS....... Current Commonwealth Bills [*Database*] [*Australia*]
BIM.......... Ballet Intensive from Moscow
BIM........... Banco Industrial del Mediterraneo [*Industrial Bank of the Mediterranean*] [*Spain*]
BIM........... Bank of Industry and Mines [*Iran*]   (GEA)
BIM........... Beriged Infanteri Malaysia [*Malaysian Infantry Brigade*]   (ML)
BIM........... Bimini [*Bahamas*] [*Airport symbol*]   (OAG)
BIM........... Binter-Mediterraneo [*Spain*] [*ICAO designator*]   (FAAC)
BIM........... Bonneterie Industrielle du Maghreb
BIM........... Brigada de Institutos Militares [*Military Institutes Brigade*] [*Colorado*]   (LA)
BIM.......... Large Ivanovo Textile Mill   (RU)
BIMA .... Banque Internationale pour la Mauritanie [*International Bank for Mauritania*]   (AF)
BIMA .... Bosques e Industrias Madereras, SA [*Timber and Lumber Industries, Inc.*] [*Chile*]   (LA)
BIMA .... British International Motorcycle Association   (EA)
BIMAS ..... Bimbingan Massa [*Mass Guidance (Name of government-supported agricultural production projects)*] [*INSUS*] [*Later,*]   (IN)
BIMAS ...... Birlesik Insaat ve Muhendislik Anonim Sirketi [*United Construction and Engineering Corporation*]   (TU)
BIMC......... [*The*] Baltic and International Maritime Conference
BIMC......... Brega International Marketing Co. [*Libya*]
BIMCO ..... Baltic and International Maritime Conference [*or Council*] [*Copenhagen, Denmark*]   (EAIO)
BIMD .... Balai Industri Medan [*Laboratory and Testing Institute for Industrial Products - Medan*] [*Indonesia*]
bimen .... Bimensual [*Semimonthly*] [*Spanish*]
BIMET ...... Building Industry Management Education and Training [*Australia*]
BIMI......... Baptist International Mission
BIMP........ Banque Industrielle et Mobiliere Privee [*French*]
BIMP........ Beijing Institute of Modern Physics [*China*]
BIMP........ Brunei, Indonesia, Malaysia, Philippines [*International trade*]
BIMP-EAGA ... Brunei, Indonesia, Malaysia, Philippines East Asian Growth Area [*International trade*]
BIMS........ Bain Investment Management Services [*Australia*]
BIMSA ...... Bilgi Islem Merkezi Ticaret ve Sanayi AS [*Data Processing Center Trade Corp.*]   (TU)
BIn............. Bachelor of Informatics
BIN............ Bamian [*Afghanistan*] [*Airport symbol*] [*Obsolete*]   (OAG)
BIN............ Banco Inmobilario [*Nicaragua*]   (EY)
Bin............. Barin [*Military map abbreviation*] [*World War I*] [*French*]   (MTD)
bin............. binaer [*Binary*] [*German*]   (GCA)
BIN .... Biological Institute   (RU)

BIN .... Botanical Institute Imeni V. L. Komarov (of the Academy of Sciences, USSR)   (RU)
BIN .... Bulgarian Institute of Standards   (BU)
BINA .... Bangladesh Institute of Nuclear Agriculture [*Research center*]   (IRC)
BINABOC ... Societe Binard et Bocconi
Binb............ Binbasi [*Major*]   (TU)
bind............ Bindning [*Binding*] [*Publishing*] [*Sweden*]
Bind........... Bindung [*Bond*] [*German*]   (GCA)
BIndDes..... Bachelor of Industrial Design
Bindg.......... Bindung [*Binding*] [*Publishing*] [*German*]
BINE......... Beijing Institute of Nuclear Engineering [*China*]   (IRC)
BINEA....... Le Bureau Ivoirien des Nouvelles Editions Africaines [*Publishing house*] [*The Ivory Coast*]   (EY)
BINF......... Nordfjordur [*Iceland*] [*ICAO location identifier*]   (ICLI)
BInfoSc..... Bachelor of Information Science
BInfoSys ... Bachelor of Information Systems
B Ing .... Baccalaureus in die Ingenieurswese [*Bachelor of Engineering*] [*Afrikaans*]
BING .... Federation of European Rigid Polyurethane Foam Associations   (EAIO)
BINGI....... Batalion de Inteligencia y Contra-Inteligencia [*Intelligence and Counterintelligence Battalion*] [*Colorado*]   (LA)
BINK .... Berliner Industrie- und Handelskontor [*Berlin Industrial and Commercial Office*]   (EG)
BINT......... Office of Foreign Science and Technology   (RU)
BIO .... Bilbao [*Spain*] [*Airport symbol*]   (OAG)
BIO .... Bilingual Information Officer [*Australia*]
bio .... Biology   (TPFD)
BIO .... British Imperial Oil Co. Ltd. [*Australia*]
BIO .... Brit Ivrit Olamit [*World Association for Hebrew Language and Culture*]   (EAIO)
BIO .... Bureau d'Information et d'Orientation [*Office of Information and Orientation*] [*Ministry of Education*] [*France*]
BIOA .... Biuro Inkasowe Oplat Abonamentowych [*Office for the Collection of Subscription Fees*] [*Post Office*]   (POL)
bioch........... Biochimie [*French*]   (TPFD)
biofak .... Biology Division   (RU)
Biofis........... Biofisica [*Biophysics*] [*Portuguese*]
biofiz........... Biophysical, Biophysics   (RU)
biogeokhim ... Biogeochemistry   (RU)
biogr .... Biografi [*Biography*] [*Sweden*]
biogr .... Biografia [*Biography*] [*Hungary*]
biogr .... Biographic   (BU)
biogr .... Biographical, Biography   (RU)
biogr .... Biographisch [*Biographical*] [*Publishing*] [*German*]
biokhim....... Biochemical, Biochemistry   (RU)
Biol............ Biologia [*Biology*] [*Portuguese*]
biol .... Biologia [*Biology*] [*Finland*]
biol .... Biological, Biology   (RU)
Biol............ Biologie [*Biology*] [*German*]   (GCA)
BIOL.......... Biologie [*Biology*] [*Afrikaans*]
Biol st .... Biological Station [*Topography*]   (RU)
BIOMASS ... Biological Investigations of the Marine Antarctic System and Stocks [*ICSU*]   (MSC)
Biomedgiz .. State Publishing House of Biological and Medical Literature   (RU)
biomel .... Biological Reclamation   (RU)
biomet .... Biometric, Biometry   (RU)
Bioquim....... Bioquimica [*Biochemistry*] [*Portuguese*]
BIOQUIP ... Biotechnology Equipment Suppliers [*Deutsche Gesellschaft fuer Chemisches Apparatewesen, Chemische Technik, und Biotechnologie eV*] [*Germany*]   (IID)
BIOREP .... Biotechnical Research Project [*EC*]   (ECED)
BIOS......... Centro Italiano di Biostatistica [*Italian*]   (SLS)
BIOS......... Near Infrared Region of the Spectrum   (RU)
BIOSHELF ... Study of Shelf and Continental Divide [*Russian*]   (MSC)
BIOT......... British Indian Ocean Territory
BIOTALASSA ... Study of Oceanological Basis for Bioproductivity of Prospective Open-Ocean Fishing Grounds [*Russian*]   (MSC)
BIOTECH ... National Institutes of Biotechnology and Applied Microbiology [*Philippines*]   (ARC)
Biotip .... Biotipologia [*Portuguese*]
BIOTROP ... Regional Center for Tropical Biology [*SEAMEO*] [*Indonesia*] [*Research center*]   (IRC)
BIOTROP ... Tropical Biology [*Center*] [*ICSU*]   (CL)
BIP........... Banco Industrial del Peru [*Industrial Bank of Peru*]   (LAA)
BIP........... Banque International de Placement
BIP............ Biuro Informacji i Propagandy [*Office of Information and Propaganda*] [*World War II*]   (POL)
BIP........... Borbena Izvidacka Patrola [*Combat Reconnaisance Patrol*]   (YU)
BIP............ Botswana Independence Party [*Political party*]   (PPW)
BIP............ Brazilian Industrial Prices

BIP............ Buergerinitiative Parlament [*Citizens' Parliamentary Initiative*] [*Austria*] [*Political party*]   (EY)

BIP............ Bulimba [*Australia*] [*Airport symbol*] [*Obsolete*]   (OAG)

BIP............ Bureau International de Presse [*International Press Office*] [*French*]   (AF)

BIP............ Business Information Processing

BIP............ Combat and Political Training   (RU)

BIP............ Combat Information Center   (RU)

BIP............ Coreless Induction Furnace   (RU)

BIP............ Office of Tools and Devices   (RU)

BIPA......... Patreksfjordur [*Iceland*] [*ICAO location identifier*]   (ICLI)

BIPAC...... Britian Israel Public Affairs Centre

BIPAC...... British Israel Public Affairs Committee

BIPALINDO ... Biro Pengapalan Indonesia [*Indonesian Shipping Bureau*]   (IN)

BIPAR....... Bureau International des Producteurs d'Assurances et de Reassurances [*International Association of Insurance and Reinsurance Intermediaries - IAIRI*] [*Paris, France*]   (EAIO)

BIPAVER ... Bureau International Permanent des Associations des Vendeurs et Rechapeurs de Pneumatiques [*Permanent International Bureau of Tire Dealers and Retreaders Associations*] [*Switzerland*]

BIPB .... Banana Industry Protection Board [*Australia*]

BIPC .... Bureau of Information and Public Communication [*Commonwealth Scientific and Industrial Research Organization*] [*Australia*]

BIPCA ...... Bureau International Permanent de Chimie Analytique pour les Matieres Destinees a la Alimentation de l'Homme et des Animaux [*Permanent International Bureau of Analytical Chemistry of Human and Animal Food - PIBAC*] [*French*]   (ASF)

BIPE .... Bureau d'Informations et de Previsions Economiques [*Office of Economic Information and Forecasting*] [*Information service or system*]   (IID)

BIPG......... Banque Internationale pour le Gabon [*International Bank for Gabon*]   (AF)

BIPIK .... Bimbingan dan Pengembangan Industri Kecil [*Promotion and Development of Small Industry*] [*Indonesia*]

BIPM........ Bureau International des Poids et Mesures [*International Bureau of Weights and Measures*] [*Sevres, France*]   (EA)

BIPPI........ Bureau International pour la Protection de la Propriete Industrielle [*France*]   (FLAF)

Biprohut.... Biuro Projektow Urzadzen Przemyslu Hutniczego [*Metallurgical Industry Equipment Project Bureau*]   (POL)

BIPROWLOK ... Biuro Studiow i Projektow Przemyslu Wlokienniczego [*Textile Industry Study and Design Office*] [*Poland*]

BIPT .... Banque Ivoirienne d'Epargne et de Developpement des Postes et Telecommunications [*Ivorian Postal and Telecommunications Savings and Development Bank*]

BIQ .... Biarritz [*France*] [*Airport symbol*]   (OAG)

BIQH .... Bureau Independante pour les Questions Humanitaires [*Independent Bureau for Humanitarian Issues*] [*Switzerland*]   (EAIO)

BIR............ Banco de Intercambio Regional [*Argentina*]

BIR............ Banque d'Information sur les Recherches [*INSERM Research Information Bank*] [*National Institute for Health and Medical Research*] [*Information service or system*]   (IID)

BIR............ Banque Internationale de Reconstruction [*International Bank for Reconstruction*]

BIR............ Biratnagar [*Nepal*] [*Airport symbol*]   (OAG)

bir............. Birosag [*Law Court*]   (HU)

BIR............ Bureau International de la Recuperation [*International Bureau of Recuperation*] [*Brussels, Belgium*]   (EA)

BIR............ Bureau of Immigration Research [*Australia*]

BIRAC....... Bureau of Immigration Research Advisory Committee [*Australia*]

BIRD......... Banca International de Reconstructie si Dezvoltare [*International Bank for Reconstruction and Development*]   (RO)

BIRD......... Banco Internacional para Reconstrucao e Desenvolvimento [*International Bank for Reconstruction and Development - IBRD*]   (LA)

BIRD......... Banque Internationale pour la Reconstruction et le Developpement [*International Bank for Reconstruction and Development; also known as the World Bank*] [*French*]

BIRD......... Base d'Information Robert Debre [*Robert Debre Information Base*] [*International Children's Center*] [*Information service or system*]   (IID)

BIRD......... Reykjavik [*Iceland*] [*ICAO location identifier*]   (ICLI)

BIRDEM... Bangladesh Institute of Research and Rehabilitation in Diabetes, Endocrine, and Metabolic Disorders [*Research center*]   (IRC)

BIRD-F...... Binational Industrial Research and Development Fund [*US and Israel*]

BIRDS .... Bangladesh Integrated Rural Development Services   (EAIO)

BIRF .... Banco Internacional de Reconstruccion y Fomento [*International Bank for Reconstruction and Development; also known as World Bank*] [*Spanish*]

BIRG......... Raufarhofn [*Iceland*] [*ICAO location identifier*]   (ICLI)

BIRH .... Bureau d'Inventaire des Ressources Hydrauliques

BIRIN....... Biro Industrialisasi [*Industrialization Bureau*]   (IN)

BIRK........ Reykjavik Airport [*Iceland*] [*ICAO location identifier*]   (ICLI)

BIRKO...... Birlesik Koyunlular Ticaret ve Sanayi AS [*United Sheep Raisers Trade and Industry Corp.*]   (TU)

Birl........... Birligi [*Union*]   (TU)

birm.......... Burmese   (RU)

BIRPI .... United International Bureaus for Protection of Intellectual Property

BIRPS....... British Institutions Reflection Profiling Syndicate [*Seismic profiling*]

BIRS .... Biblioteka Instrukcji i Regulaminow Sportowych [*Sport Instruction and Regulation Series*]   (POL)

birt............ Birtokos [*Owner, Owning*]   (HU)

BIS............ Bahamas Information Service   (LA)

BIS............ Bank for International Settlements [*Basel, Switzerland*]   (AF)

BIS............ Bataljonska Intendantska Stanica [*Battalion Quartermaster Station*]   (YU)

BIS............ Bataljonsko Intendantsko Slagaliste [*Battalion Quartermaster Depot*]   (YU)

BIS............ Bayraktarlik Istihbarat Teskilati [*Bayraktar Intelligence Organization*] [*Commander of Turkish forces on Cyprus*]   (TU)

BIS............ Beijing International Society [*Chinese*]

BIS............ Belediye Iscileri Sendikasi [*Municipal Workers Union*] [*Isparta*]   (TU)

BIS............ Betriebswirtschaftliches Informationssystem [*Business Management Information System*] [*German*]   (ADPT)

BIS............ Bibliotheks- und Informationssystem [*Library and Information System*] [*German*]

BIS............ Bois Inter Service

BIS............ Brigade d'Infanterie Speciale [*Special Infantry Brigade*] [*Cambodia*]   (CL)

BI's............ Buergerinitiativen [*Citizens' action groups*] [*Germany*]

BIS............ Bureau d'Information Software [*Bureau of Safeware Information*] [*French*]   (ADPT)

BIS............ Bureau Interafricain des Sols [*Inter-African Soils Office*]   (AF)

BIS............ Bureau of Indian Standards   (IRC)

BISA .... Banco Industrial, Sociedad Anonima [*La Paz, Bolivia*]   (LAA)

BISA .... Bibliographic Information on Southeast Asia [*University of Sydney Library*] [*Database*] [*Information service or system*]   (IID)

BISA .... Botswana Institutions Sports Association

BISA .... Bulgarian Industrial Association   (EY)

BISAN...... Bisiklet Sanayii Limited Sirketi [*Bicycle Industry Corporation*]   (TU)

BISAS....... Bursa Iplik Sanayii Anonim Sirketi [*Bursa Silk Industry Corporation*]   (TU)

BISB .... Institute for Research and Development Industry [*Indonesia*]

BISCLANT ... Bay of Biscay Subarea [*NATO*]

BISCOA .... Building Industry Specialist Contractors Organisation of Australia   (ADA)

BISD.......... Basic Instruments and Selected Documents [*GATT*]   (FLAF)

BISER....... Bureau Interafricain des Sols et de l'Economie Rurale [*Inter-African Soils and Rural Economy Office*]   (AF)

BISFA........ Bureau International pour la Standardisation de la Rayonne et des Fibres Synthetiques [*International Bureau for the Standardisation of Manmade Fibres*]   (EAIO)

BISI .... Siglufjordur [*Iceland*] [*ICAO location identifier*]   (ICLI)

BIS-IS........ Turkiye Devrimici Buro Iscileri Sendikasi [*Turkish Revolutionary Office Workers Union*] [*Ankara*]   (TU)

BISM .... Balai Penelitian dan Pengembangan Industri Semarang [*Laboratory and Testing Institute for Industrial Products*] [*Indonesia*] [*Research center*]   (IRC)

BISM .... Botswana Industrial School of Music

BISp.......... Bundesinstitut fuer Sportwissenschaft [*Federal Institute for Sports Science*] [*Germany*]   (IID)

BISR .... Birla Institute of Scientific Research [*India*]

BISS.......... Battlefield Identification System Study [*NATO*]   (NATG)

BISS.......... Sandskeid [*Iceland*] [*ICAO location identifier*]   (ICLI)

BIST .... Stykkisholmur [*Iceland*] [*ICAO location identifier*]   (ICLI)

BISVOT .... Bibliographic Information Service for Vocational Training [*ILO*] [*United Nations*]   (DUND)

bisw.......... Bisweilen [*Sometimes, Occasionally*] [*German*]   (EG)

BIT............ Baitadi [*Nepal*] [*Airport symbol*]   (OAG)

BIT............ Bendigo Institute of Technology [*Australia*]

BIT............ Bilateral Investment Treaty

BIT............ Birla Institute of Technology [*India*]   (PDAA)

BIT............ Board of Internal Trade

BIT............ Buero-und Informations-Technik [*Office and Information Technology*] [*German*]   (ADPT)

BIT............ Bureau Internacional do Trabalho [*International Bureau of Labor*] [*Portuguese*]

BIT............ Bureau International du Travail [*International Labour Office*] [*French*]

BIT............ Burroughs Integriertes Terminal [*Burrough's Integrated Terminals*] [*German*]   (ADPT)

BITA......... Reykjavik [*Iceland*] [*ICAO location identifier*]   (ICLI)

BITAC....... Bangladesh Industrial Technical Assistance Centre

BITC......... Brain Injury Therapy Centre [*Australia*]

Bitco......... Bahamas International Trust Co. Ltd.   (EY)

BITCO...... Biashara Transport Company Ltd.

BITE......... Thingeyri [*Iceland*] [*ICAO location identifier*]   (ICLI)

BITEJ....... Bureau International pour le Tourisme et les Echanges de la Jeunesse [*International Bureau for Youth Tourism and Exchanges*]   (EAIO)

BITG......... Bureau International Technique des Gelatines   (EAIO)

BITH .... Thorshofn [*Iceland*] [*ICAO location identifier*]   (ICLI)

BITIA .... Bursa Iktisadi ve Ticari Ilimler Akademisi [*Bursa Academy of Economy and Commercial Science*]   (TU)

BITIFP ...... Bureau International Technique des "Inorganic Feed Phosphates" [*Inorganic Feed Phosphates International Technical Bureau - IFPITB*]   (EAIO)

Bitk .... Bitkibilim [*Botanical term*]   (TU)

BITL......... Bureau International Technique de l'ABS [*Acronitrile-Butadiene-Styrene*] [*of the European Council of Chemical Manufacturers' Federations*]   (EAIO)

BITM........ Birla Industrial and Technological Museum [*India*]   (PDAA)

BITM........ Bryansk Institute of Transportation Machinery   (RU)

BITM........ Bureau International Technique du Methanol [*European Council of Chemical Manufacturers' Federations*] [*Belgium*]   (EAIO)

BITP .... Bureau International Technique des Polyesters   (EAIO)

BITPI........ Bureau International Technique des Polyesters Insatures [*of the European Council of Chemical Manufacturers' Federations*]   (EAIO)

BITPR ...... Bureau d'Inspection Technique et Professionnelle, de Recherches, d'Etudes, de Documentation, et de Revue de l'Enseignement Secondaire [*Technical and Professional Inspection, Research, Study, Documentation, and Secondary Education Review Office*] [*Cambodia*]   (CL)

BITS .... Birla Institute of Technology and Science [*India*]

BITS .... Bureau International du Tourisme Social [*International Bureau of Social Tourism - IBST*]   (EAIO)

BITU......... Bustamante Industrial Trade Union [*Jamaica*]   (LA)

BIU .... Bermuda Industrial Union

BIU .... Beta-Ray Level Gauge   (RU)

BIU .... Bildudalur [*Iceland*] [*Airport symbol*]   (OAG)

biul.......... Biuletyn [*Bulletin*]   (POL)

BIUN .... Bloque Integral de Unificacion Nacionalista [*Nationalist Integral Unification Bloc*] [*Venezuela*]   (LA)

BIV............ Banco Industrial de Venezuela [*Industrial Bank of Venezuela*]   (LA)

BIV............ Banque Internationale des Voltas [*International Bank of the Voltas*] [*Burkina Faso*]   (AF)

Biv............ Bivouac [*Bivouac*] [*Military*] [*French*]   (MTD)

BIV............ Budapesti Ipari Vasar [*Budapest Industrial Fair*]   (HU)

BIV............ Contactless Weigher   (RU)

BIVM........ Vestmannaeyjar [*Iceland*] [*ICAO location identifier*]   (ICLI)

BIVO........ Vopnafjordur [*Iceland*] [*ICAO location identifier*]   (ICLI)

BIVSA .... Biomediese Ingenieursvereniging van Suid-Afrika [*South Africa*]   (AA)

Biw .... Biwak [*Bivouac*]   (EG)

BIW1........ Bermuda Inshore Waters Investigation

BIWS .... Bureau of International Whaling Statistics [*Norway*]   (ASF)

BIY............ Baska Ihtiyac Yok [*No Further Need (for someone or something)*]   (TU)

Biyo.......... Biyoloji [*Biology*]   (TU)

Biyog......... Biyografya [*Biography*]   (TU)

BIZ............ Bank fuer Internationalen Zahlungsausgleich [*Bank for International Settlements*] [*German*]

BiZ............ Bau-Informationszentrum Muenchen

BIZ............ Biuro Inwentaryzacji Zabytkow [*Office of Registration of Historical Relics*]   (POL)

biz............. Bizalmas [*Confidential*]   (HU)

biz............. Bizottsag [*Committee*] [*Hungary*]   (HU)

Bizair......... Business Aircraft Users' Association [*Airline call sign*]

B i Zh .... Concrete and Reinforced Concrete   (RU)

bizt .... Biztositas [*Insurance, Safety*]   (HU)

BJ.............. Bataillons de la Jeunesse   (BJA)

BJ.............. Belgique Judiciaire [*Belgium*]   (BAS)

BJ.............. Benin [*ANSI two-letter standard code*]   (CNC)

BJ.............. Bharatiya Janata Party [*Indian People's Party*] [*Political party*]

BJ.............. Biblioteka Jagiellonska [*The Jagiellonian Library*] [*Poland*]

BJA........... Bejaia [*Algeria*] [*Airport symbol*]   (OAG)

BJA........... Bund Juedischer Akademiker   (BJA)

BJA........... Unifly [*Italy*] [*ICAO designator*]   (FAAC)

BJATM ..... Baza Judeteana de Aprovizionare Tehnico-Materiala [*County Base for Technical-Material Supply*]   (RO)

BjBI............ Balkan-ji-Bari International [*Children's Own Garden International - COGI*]   (EAIO)

BJC........... Beijing Jeep Corp. [*China*]

BJC........... Brisbane Jazz Club [*Australia*]

BJD........... Bakkafjordur [*Iceland*] [*Airport symbol*]   (OAG)

BJEP......... Bureau on Jewish Employment Problems

BJF........... Batsfjord [*Norway*] [*Airport symbol*]   (OAG)

BJGA........ Bangladesh Jute Goods Association   (EAIO)

BJH .... Bajhang [*Nepal*] [*Airport symbol*]   (OAG)

BJK........... Besiktas Jimnastik Kulubu [*Besiktas Gymnastic Club*] [*Istanbul*]   (TU)

BJL........... Banjul [*Gambia*] [*Airport symbol*]   (OAG)

BJM........... Bujumbura [*Burundi*] [*Airport symbol*]   (OAG)

BJM........... Bureau de Justice Militaire [*Etat-Major*] [*France*]   (FLAF)

BJMA........ Bangladesh Jute Mills Association

BJMT........ Bolyai Janos Matematikai Tarsulat [*Janos Bolyai Society of Mathematics*]   (HU)

BJOC........ Federation Francaise de la Bijouterie, Joaillerie, Orfevrerie du Cadeau, Diamants, Pierres, et Perles, et Activites qui S'y Rattachent [*France*]   (EY)

BJP........... Bharatiya Janata Party [*Indian People's Party*] [*Political party*]   (PPW)

BJR........... Bahar Dar [*Ethiopia*] [*Airport symbol*]   (OAG)

BJR........... Battaillon des Jeunes Ruraux [*Rural Youth Battalion*] [*Zaire*]

BJR........... Bundesjugendring [*Federal Youth Circle*] [*Austria*]   (WEN)

BJRI......... Bangladesh Jute Research Institute   (ARC)

BJ = 's .... Blue-Johnnies [*Australian slang for "delirium tremens"*]

BJSA......... Bangladesh Jute Spinners Association   (EAIO)

BJSL......... Bangladesh Jatio Sramik League

BJVN........ Dokumentationszentrum des Bundes Judischer Verfolgter des Naziregimes [*Jewish Documentation Centre - JDC*]   (EAIO)

BJW.......... Bajawa [*Indonesia*] [*Airport symbol*]   (OAG)

BJZ........... Badajoz [*Spain*] [*Airport symbol*]   (OAG)

BK .... Antiboat Battery   (RU)

BK .... Bahnknoten [*Railroad Junction*]   (EG)

Bk .... Bakiniz [*Look, Please Refer To, See*]   (TU)

bk .... Bakken [*Side Street*] [*Norway*]   (CED)

BK .... Balancing Network   (RU)

BK .... Ballistic Cable   (BU)

Bk............. Bank [*Dutch*]   (NAU)

Bk............. Bank [*Swedish*]   (NAU)

bk............. Bank [*Hungarian*]   (HU)

Bk............. Banke [*Bank*] [*Danish*]   (NAU)

BK .... Bank Komunalny [*Communal Bank*]   (POL)

BK .... Banque de Kinshasa

BK .... Banyankole Kweterana

BK .... Barque

BK .... Bediendekamer [*Servant's Room*] [*Afrikaans*]

BK .... Benzoic Acid   (RU)

BK .... Berliner Konferenz Europaischer Katholiken [*Berlin Conference of European Catholics*] [*Germany*]   (EAIO)

Bk............. Berquelio [*Chemical element*] [*Portuguese*]

BK .... Bibliotheca Kiado [*Bibliotheca Publishing House*]   (HU)

BK .... Blocking Contact   (RU)

bk .... Boek [*Book*] [*Afrikaans*]

Bk............. Boluk [*Company*] [*Military*]   (TU)

BK .... Borclar Kanunu [*Liabilities Law*]   (TU)

BK .... Bundeskanzler [*Federal Chancellor*] [*German*]   (ILCA)

BK .... Bundeskanzleramt [*Federal Chancery*] [*German*]   (ILCA)

bk............. Burgerlijke Kamer [*Benelux*]   (BAS)

BK .... Bursa Beton Kiremit Ticaret ve Sanayi Ltd. Sti. [*Bursa Concrete Tile Industry and Trade Corp.*]   (TU)

BK .... Drill Carriage, Drill Truck   (RU)

BK .... Firing Track (of a Tank), Bomb Run   (RU)

BK .... Koch's Bacillus   (RU)

BK .... Library of Congress [*United States*]   (RU)

BK .... Protein Plasma Substitute   (RU)

b k .... Sentry Box [*Topography*]   (RU)

BK .... Switching Unit   (RU)

BK .... Tower Crane   (RU)

BK .... Unit of Fire   (RU)

BKA .... Armored Cutter   (RU)

b-ka .... Bank   (BU)

Bka .... Banka [*Bank*] [*Russian*]   (NAU)

BKA .... Bank fuer Kredit und Aussenhandel AG [*Bank for Credit and Export Trade*] [*German*]

b-ka .... Bank, Shoal [*Topography*]   (RU)

b-ka .... Biblioteka [*Library*] [*Often used for a series of books*]   (POL)

BKA .... Bundeskanzleramt [*Office of the Federal Chancellor*] [*German*]

BKA .... Bundeskartellamt [*Federal Cartel Office*] [*German*]   (ILCA)

BKA .... Bundeskriminalamt [*Federal Criminal Police Bureau*] [*Germany*]

b-ka .... Library   (RU)

BKAA .... Badan Koordinasi Amalan Agama [*Committee for the Coordination of Religious Practices*]   (IN)

B/ka svKliment ... [*The*] Sveti Kliment Library   (BU)
BKAV .... Boarding Kennels Association of Victoria [*Australia*]
Bkb .... Balkan Coal Basin   (BU)
BKB .... Bangladesh Krishi Bank   (EY)
BKB .... Braunschweigische Kohlen-Bergwerke AG [*Electronics company*]
BKB .... Bus-Koppel-Baustein [*Bus Belt Building Stone*] [*German*]
(ADPT)
BKB .... Office of Majority Committees (of the RSDRP)   (RU)
BKBPT ..... Brotherhood of Knights of the Black Pudding Tasters   (EA)
BKC .... Banque Khmere pour le Commerce [*Cambodian Commercial Bank*]   (CL)
BKCC .... Brazil Kennel Club Confederation   (EAIO)
BK-CK ...... Bibliograficky Katalog - Ceska Kniha [*Bibliographical Catalog - The Czech Book*]   (CZ)
BKD .... Bugarsko Knizovno Druzestvo [*Bulgarian Literary Society*]   (YU)
BKDA .... Bund Katholischer Deutscher Akademikerinnen   (SLS)
BKDH .... Bupati/Kepala Daerah [*Regent/Chief of Region*]   (IN)
BKED .... Bund Katholischer Erzieher Deutschlands   (SLS)
BKF .... Balkanska Komunisticka Federacija [*Balkan Communist Federation*]   (YU)
BKF .... Biblioteka Kultury Fizycznej [*Physical Culture Series*]   (POL)
BKG .... Ballistocardiogram, Ballistocardiography   (RU)
BKGS .... Tower Crane for Hydraulic Engineering Construction   (RU)
BKGY .... Budapesti Konzervgyar [*Budapest Cannery*]   (HU)
Bkh .... Biochemistry   (RU)
BKhM .... Chemical Warfare Vehicle   (RU)
BKhP .... Chemical Warfare Post   (RU)
bkhrr .... Chemical and Radiation Reconnaissance Battalion   (BU)
BKhS .... Chemical Warfare Agent   (RU)
BKhSS .... Combating the Embezzlement of Socialist Property and Speculation   (RU)
BKhV .... Chemical Warfare Agent   (RU)
bkhz .... Chemical Defense Battalion   (BU)
Bki .... Banki [*Banks*] [*Russian*]   (NAU)
BKI .... Banyaszati Kutato Intezet [*Mining Research Institute*]   (HU)
BKI .... Biro Klasifikasi [*Indonesian*]
BKI .... Kota Kinabalu [*Malaysia*] [*Airport symbol*]   (OAG)
BKIA .... Balai Kesedjahteraan Ibu dan Anak [*Welfare Clinic for Mothers and Children*]   (IN)
BKIC .... Bahrain-Kuwait Insurance Co.   (IMH)
b-kite .... Libraries   (BU)
BKK .... Bakanliklararasi Koordinasyon Kurullari [*Inter-Ministry Coordination Committees*]   (TU)
BKK .... Bangkok [*Thailand*] [*Airport symbol*]   (OAG)
BKK .... Braunkohlenkombinat Lauchhammer (VEB) [*Lauchhammer Brown Coal Combine (VEB)*]   (EG)
BKK .... Bulgarian Constitution Clubs   (BU)
BKK .... Channel Switching Unit   (RU)
BKK .... Compass Heading on Bomb Run   (RU)
BKKhZ ...... Bagley By-Product Coke Plant   (RU)
BKKI .... Badan Kongress Kebathinan Indonesia
BKKL .... Banyaszati Kemiai Kutatolaboratoriuma [*Chemical Research Laboratory for Mining*] [*Hungary*]   (EAS)
BKL .... Baikal [*Russian Federation*] [*ICAO designator*]   (FAAC)
B Kl .... Bass Klarinette [*Bass Clarinet*] [*Music*]
Bkl. .... Beklagter [*Defendant*] [*German*]   (WEN)
BKLY .... Barkly [*Botanical region*] [*Australia*]
BKM .... Bakalalan [*Malaysia*] [*Airport symbol*]   (OAG)
BKM .... Bataljonska Komanda Mesta [*Battalion Command Post*]   (YU)
Bkm. .... Bekanntmachung [*Announcement*] [*German*]   (WEN)
BKM .... Bel- es Kulkereskedelmi Miniszterium/Miniszter [*Ministry/Minister of Domestic and Foreign Trade*]   (HU)
BKM .... Belkereskedelmi Miniszterium/Miniszter [*Ministry/Minister of Domestic Trade*]   (HU)
BKME ...... Bank of Kuwait & the Middle East   (ECON)
BKME ...... Contactless Magnetic Element   (RU)
BKMG ...... Biuro Konstrukcji Maszyn Gorniczych [*Mining Machinery Designing Office*]   (POL)
BKMS .... Bulgarian Communist Youth Union   (BU)
BKN .... Airborne Sky Chart   (RU)
BKn .... Bulgarski Knigopis [*Bulgarian Bibliography*] [*A periodical*]   (BU)
BKNII .... Buryat Complex Scientific Research Institute   (RU)
BKN-Yu .... Airborne Sky Chart of the Southern Hemisphere   (RU)
BKO .... Bamako [*Mali*] [*Airport symbol*]   (OAG)
BKO .... Bezpecnostni Koordinacni Odbor [*Security Coordination Department*]   (CZ)
BKO .... Budget Control Section   (BU)
bkovr .... Naval Brigade for District Defense   (BU)
BKP .... Bangkok Airways [*Thailand*] [*ICAO designator*]   (FAAC)
BKP .... Battalion Command Post   (RU)
BKP .... Battery Command Post   (RU)
BKP .... Belgian Communist Party   (BU)
BKP .... Belgische Kommunistische Partij [*Belgian Communist Party*]   (WEN)

BKP .... Bolgar Kommunista Part [*Bulgarian Communist Party*]   (HU)
BKP .... Bromocresol Purple [*Indicator*]   (RU)
BKP .... Bugarska Komunisticka Partija [*Bulgarian Communist Party*]   (YU)
BKP .... Bulgarian Coastal Navigation   (BU)
BKP .... Bulgarska Komunisticheska Partiia [*Bulgarian Communist Party*] [*Political party*]   (PPE)
BKP .... Bulgarya Komunist Partisi [*Bulgarian Communist Party*]   (TU)
BKP .... Burmese Congress of Trade Unions   (RU)
BKP .... Lateral Command Post   (RU)
BKP .... Postal Money Order Control Office   (RU)
BKP .... Shore Command Post   (RU)
BKPM .... Badan Koordinasi Penamanaman Model [*Capital Investment Coordinating Board*] [*Indonesian*]   (GEA)
BKPM .... Biuro Konstrukcyjne Przemyslu Motoryzacyjnego [*Automotive Industry Designing Office*]   (POL)
BKP(ts) ...... Bulgarian Communist Party (Left Wing)   (BU)
BKPZYe .... Office of Communist Parties of Western Europe   (RU)
BKQ .... Blackall [*Australia*] [*Airport symbol*]   (OAG)
BKR .... Bajai Kukorica Termelesi Rendszer [*Baja Corn Growing System*]   (HU)
bkr .... Bez Kraja [*Without End*]   (YU)
BKR .... Check and Decision Unit   (RU)
BKR .... Compensation and Control Unit   (RU)
BKS .... Badan Kerdja Sama [*Cooperating Committee*]   (IN)
BKS .... Bengkulu [*Indonesia*] [*Airport symbol*]   (OAG)
BKS .... Blutkorpersenkung [*Blood Sedimentation Rate*] [*German*] [*Medicine*]
BKS .... Brilliant Cresyl Blue   (RU)
BKS .... Bromocresol Blue [*Indicator*]   (RU)
BKS .... Commutation and Synchronization Unit   (RU)
BKS .... Hip and Large Joints   (RU)
BKSAKSI .. Badan Kerdja Sama Antar Kotapradja Seluruh Indonesia [*All-Indonesia Inter-Municipal Cooperating Committee*]   (IN)
BK-SK .... Bibliograficky Katalog - Slovenska Kniha [*Bibliographical Catalog - The Slovak Book*]   (CZ)
BKSKh ...... Tower Crane for Agricultural Use   (RU)
BKSM .... Bulgarian Young Communist League   (RU)
BKSM .... Construction and Assembly Tower Crane   (RU)
BKSS .... Bangladesh Karma Shibir Samity [*Bangladesh Work Camps Association*]   (EAIO)
BKT .... Bulgarian Confederation of Labor   (BU)
BKT .... Communist Labor Brigade   (RU)
BKTC .... Bagimsiz Kibris Turk Cumhuriyeti [*Independent Turkish Cypriot Republic*]   (TU)
BKTD .... Bagimsiz Kibris Turk Devleti [*Independent Turkish Cypriot State*]   (GC)
BKTM .... Biuro Konstrukcyjne Taboru Morskiego [*Marine Designing Office*]   (POL)
BKU .... Betioky [*Madagascar*] [*Airport symbol*]   (OAG)
BKV .... Betriebskollektivvertrag [*Enterprise Collective Labor Contract*]   (EG)
BKV .... Braunkohlenverwaltung [*Brown Coal Administration*] [*See BV*]   (EG)
BKV .... Budapesti Kozlekedesi Vallalat [*Budapest Transportation Enterprise*]   (HU)
BKV .... Life and Culture of the East   (RU)
BKVO .... Berufskrankheitenverordnung [*Regulation on Occupational Diseases*]   (WEN)
BKVRD ...... Ramjet Engine   (RU)
BkW .... Bahnkraftwerk [*Railroad Power Plant*] [*German*]   (EG)
BKW .... Bernische Kraftwerke, AG [*Switzerland*] [*Nuclear energy*]   (NRCH)
BKW .... Biuro Kontroli Wojskowej [*Office of Military Control*]   (POL)
BKW .... Braunkohlenwerk [*Brown Coal Enterprise*]   (EG)
BKW .... Forces Motrices Bernoises SA [*Switzerland*]   (WND)
BKY .... Bukavu [*Zaire*] [*Airport symbol*]   (OAG)
BKZ .... Barnaul Boiler Plant   (RU)
BKZ .... Bukoba [*Tanzania*] [*Airport symbol*]   (OAG)
BKZ .... Lateral Logging   (RU)
BL .... Barackenlager [*Barracks*] [*German*]
BL .... Barat Laut [*Northwest*]   (ML)
bl .... Baril [*Barrel*] [*French*]
BL .... Base Infirmary   (RU)
BL .... Bellanca Aircraft Corp. [*ICAO aircraft manufacturer identifier*]   (ICAO)
BL .... Belluno [*Car registration plates*] [*Italian*]
BL .... Betriebsleiter [*Plant Manager*] [*German*]   (EG)
bl .... Blad [*Leaf, Sheet*] [*Publishing*] [*Sweden*]
bl .... Blad [*Leaf, Sheet*] [*Publishing Danish/Norwegian*]
bl .... Bladsy [*Page*] [*Afrikaans*]
bl .... Bladzijde [*Benelux*]   (BAS)
bl .... Blanc [*Blank, White*] [*Publishing*] [*French*]
bl .... Blanco [*Blank, White*] [*Spanish*]
bl .... Blank [*Blank*] [*Publishing Danish/Norwegian*]
Bl .... Blasinstrumente [*Wind Instruments*] [*Music*]

Bl.............. Blatt [*Newspaper, Sheet*] [*German*]   (BJA)
bl .... Blindage, Dugout [*Topography*]   (RU)
Bl.............. Blindgaenger [*Dud*] [*German*]   (GCA)
Bl.............. Blockhaus [*Blockhouse*] [*Military map abbreviation World War I*] [*German*]   (MTD)
BL.............. Blocklaenge [*Block Length*] [*German*]   (ADPT)
Bl.............. Block Signal Box, Block Station [*Topography*]   (RU)
bl .... Blogoslawiony [*Blessed*] [*Poland*]
bl .... Blok [*Block*] [*Turkey*]   (CED)
Bl.............. Blok [*Block of Houses*] [*Poland*]
Bl.............. Bolge [*Region*] [*Geographical area within the country*]   (TU)
Bl.............. Boluk [*Company, Squadron*] [*Military*]   (TU)
BL.............. Border Landbouvereniging [*Border Agricultural Society*] [*South Africa*]   (EAIO)
BL.............. Border Leicester [*Sheep*]
bl .... Brilliance   (RU)
Bl.............. Bulletin [*German*]   (GCA)
BL.............. Drum Winch   (RU)
BL.............. Naval Base Infirmary   (RU)
BL.............. State Library of the USSR Imeni V. I. Lenin   (RU)
BLA .... Barcelona [*Venezuela*] [*Airport symbol*]   (OAG)
BLA .... Belize Library Association   (EAIO)
bl a........... Bland Andra [*Among Other Things*] [*Sweden*]   (GPO)
bl a........... Bland Annat [*Among Other Things*] [*Sweden*]   (GPO)
bla .... Blandt Andet [*Among Other Things*] [*Denmark*]   (GPO)
bla .... Blandt Andre [*Among Other Things*] [*Denmark*]   (GPO)
bl a........... Blant Annet [*Among Others*] [*Norway*]   (GPO)
BLA .... British Library Association   (BARN)
BLA .... Bundeslehranstalt [*Federal Educational Establishment*] [*German*]
BLA .... Bureau de Liaison des Syndicats Europeens (CEE) des Produits Aromatiques [*Liaison Bureau of the European and EEC Unions of Aromatic Products*]   (EAIO)
BLA .... Pilotless Aircraft
BLACT ...... Bureau de Liaison des Agents de Cooperation Technique
BLADA...... Bloque Latinoamericano de Actores [*Latin American Actors Group*]   (LA)
BLADEX ... Banco Latinoamericano de Exportaciones SA
BLAdmin ... Bachelor of Law Administration
bladz.......... Bladzijde [*Page*] [*Publishing*] [*Netherlands*]
BLAE........ Banco Latinoamericano de Exportacion [*Latin American Export Bank*]   (LA)
BLandInfo ... Bachelor of Land Information
BLandResSc ... Bachelor of Land Resource Science
BLAPL ...... Belgian and Luxembourg Association of Penal Law   (EAIO)
blas........... Blason [*Armorial Shield*] [*Publishing*] [*French*]
BLASA ...... Belgian-Luxembourg American Studies Association [*Belgium*]   (EAIO)
BLASZ ...... Budapesti Labdarugok Alszovetsege [*Subassociation of the Soccer Teams of Budapest*]   (HU)
BLAT........ Blatter Herbarium [*St. Xavier College*] [*India*]
Blattdung ... Blattduengung [*Leaf Fertilizing*] [*German*]   (GCA)
blattgr .... Blattgross [*Full-Page*] [*Publishing*] [*German*]
BLB........... Atlantic Air BVI Ltd. [*British*] [*ICAO designator*]   (FAAC)
BLB........... Badische Landesbibliothek
BLB........... Bookmakers' Licensing Board [*South Australia*]
BLB........... Bundesvereinigung Lebenshilfe fur Geistig Behinderte [*National Association for Persons with Mental Handicap*] [*Germany*]   (EAIO)
BLBS .... Bundesverband der Lehrer an Beruflichen Schulen eV im Deutschen Beamtenbund   (SLS)
BLC........... Bali [*Cameroon*] [*Airport symbol*]   (OAG)
BLC........... Ben Line Containers Ltd.   (DS)
BLC........... Brasil-Central Linhas Aereas Regional SA [*Brazil*] [*ICAO designator*]   (FAAC)
BLC........... Brisbane Latvian Club [*Australia*]
BLC........... Bulwer-Lytton Circle   (EAIO)
BLCC........ Basic Law Consultative Committee [*China*]
B-LCC....... Belgium-Luxembourg Chamber of Commerce [*Australia*]
BLCC........ Belo-Luxembourg Chamber of Commerce   (DS)
BLD .... Bharatiya Lok Dal [*India*] [*Political party*]   (PPW)
Bld............ Bild [*Picture*] [*German*]
bld .... Boulevard [*Boulevard*] [*French*]
BLD .... Brno-Lisen Draha [*Brno-Lisen Railroad*]   (CZ)
BLD .... Building and Lands Department [*Hong Kong*]
bld .... Bulevardul [*Boulevard*] [*Romanian*]   (CED)
BLDC........ Basic Law Drafting Committee [*Hong Kong*]
BLDC........ Botswana Livestock Development Corporation   (GEA)
Bldg.......... Bildung [*Formation*] [*German*]   (GCA)
Bldg.......... Building   (PWGL)
Ble .... Balle [*Bale*] [*French*]
BLE .... Borlange [*Sweden*] [*Airport symbol*]   (OAG)
BLE .... Budhana Ligo Esperantista [*Buddhist League of Esperantists - BLE*] [*German*]   (EAIO)
BLEC .... Business Law Education Centre [*Australia*]
BLegSt .... Bachelor of Legal Studies

Bleianm...... Bleianmerkungen [*Pencil Notes*] [*Publishing*] [*German*]
Bleist........ Bleistift [*Pencil*] [*German*]
BLeisureStud ... Bachelor of Leisure Studies
BLEO........ British Leyland Europe and Overseas [*Commercial firm*]
BLEU........ Belgium-Luxembourg Economic Union [*Political party*]   (PPE)
BLF .... Baluchistan Liberation Front [*Pakistan*] [*Political party*]   (PD)
blf .... Blaetterfoermig [*Flakes*] [*German*]
BLF .... Builders' Labourers' Federation [*Australia*]
BLF .... Bulgarian Lucky Flight [*ICAO designator*]   (FAAC)
BLFAE ...... Bureau de Liaison France-Afrique-Europe
Blg............ Beilage [*Enclosure*] [*German*]   (GPO)
BLG .... Belaga [*Malaysia*] [*Airport symbol*]   (OAG)
BLG .... Belgavia (Societe de Handling) [*Belgium*] [*ICAO designator*]   (FAAC)
BLG .... Business Land Group [*New South Wales, Australia*]
Blg P .... Belgisches Patent [*Belgian Patent*] [*German*]   (GCA)
BlGrO .... Group Operations Unit   (RU)
BLH........... Bamalete Lutheran Hospital
BLI............ Bank Leumi Le-Israel
BLI............ Belair [*Belarus*] [*ICAO designator*]   (FAAC)
BLI............ Belorussian Forestry Engineering Institute Imeni S. M. Kirov   (RU)
BLI............ Bibliothekar-Lehrinstitut [*Information retrieval*] [*German*]
BLibSt........ Bachelor of Liberal Studies
BLibStudies ... Bachelor of Liberal Studies
BLIC .... Bureau de Liaison des Industries du Caoutchouc de la CEE [*Rubber Industries Liaison Bureau of the EEC*] [*Belgium*]
Blinddr ...... Blinddruck [*Blind Tooling*] [*Bookbinding*] [*German*]
blinddr....... Blinddruk [*Blind Tooling*] [*Bookbinding*] [*Netherlands*]
blindgepr.... Blindgepraegt [*Blind-Tooled*] [*Bookbinding*] [*German*]
Blindprag.... Blindpraegung [*Blind Goffering*] [*Bookbinding*] [*German*]
blindpreg.... Blindpregning [*Blind Tooling*] [*Bookbinding Danish/Norwegian*]
blindtr .... Blindtrykt [*Blind-Tooled*] [*Bookbinding Danish/Norwegian*]
BLIPS........ Basic Learning in Primary Schools [*Australia*]
BLIROI ..... Bureau de Liaison de l'Information Religieuse dans l'Ocean Indien [*Indian Ocean Religious Information Liaison Office*]   (AF)
BLISS........ Betriebswirtschaftliches Literatursuchsystem [*Business Literature Search System*] [*Society for Business Information*] [*Information service or system*]   (IID)
BLIW........ Belgisch-Luxembourgs Instituut voor de Wissel [*Belgium/Luxembourg*]   (IMH)
blizhn .... Near, Close, Neighboring   (RU)
Blk............. Blinkfeuer [*Intermittent Light*] [*German*]   (GCA)
BLK........... Brygada Lekkiej Kawalerii [*Light Cavalry Brigade*]   (POL)
BLL........... Baccalaureus Legum [*Bachelor of Laws*]
BLL........... Bibliographie Linguistique Literatur [*Bibliography of Linguistic Literature*] [*Database*] [*Information retrieval*]
BLL........... Billund [*Denmark*] [*Airport symbol*]   (OAG)
bll .... Blade [*Journals, Leaves, Sheets*] [*Publishing Danish/Norwegian*]
Bll............. Blaetter [*Leaves, Pages*] [*Publishing*] [*German*]
BLL........... Bund fuer Lebensmittelrecht und Lebensmittelkunde eV   (SLS)
BLL........... Buraku Liberation League [*Japan*]
Blle............ Bouteille [*Bottle*] [*French*]
Bllg........... Biologische Loesung [*Biological Solution*] [*German*]   (GCA)
BLLV .... Bayerischer Lehrer- und Lehrerinnenverband   (SLS)
BLM .... Beso la Mano [*(I Kiss Your Hand) Respectfully*] [*Correspondence*] [*Spanish*]
BLMG .... Banco da Lavoura de Minas Gerais [*Brazil*]   (DSCA)
BLN .... Bali International Air Service [*Indonesia*] [*ICAO designator*]   (FAAC)
BLN .... Bank fuer Landwirtschaft und Nahrungsgueterwirtschaft [*Bank for Agriculture and Food Production*]   (EG)
Bln............ Berlin [*Berlin*]   (EG)
BlNP .... Short-Range Observation Post   (RU)
BLNS........ Biblioteka Laureatow Nagrod Stalinowskich [*Stalin Prize Winner Series*]   (POL)
BLO .... Aerotransportes Barlovento SA de CV [*Mexico*] [*ICAO designator*]   (FAAC)
blo .... Balloon Squad   (BU)
BLO .... Besluit Buitengewoon Lager Onderwijs [*Benelux*]   (BAS)
BLO .... Blonduos [*Iceland*] [*Airport symbol*]   (OAG)
BLOC .... Brisbane Light Opera Co. [*Australia*]
BLOCECH ... Bloque Campesino del Estado de Chiapas [*Peasant Bloc of Chiapas State*] [*Mexico*]   (LA)
BLOSIRH ... Bloque de Sindicatos del Ingeniero Rio Haina [*Rio Haina Refinery Union Bloc*] [*Dominican Republic*]   (LA)
BLP........... Bacterial Lipopolysaccharides   (RU)
BLP........... Barbados Labor Party
BLP........... Besa los Pies [*Kiss the Feet*] [*Spanish*]
blp .... Blogoslawionej Pamieci [*Of Blessed Memory*] [*Poland*]
BLP........... Botswana Liberal Party [*Political party*]   (PPW)
BLP........... Bulgarian Liberal Party [*Political party*]
BLQ........... Bologna [*Italy*] [*Airport symbol*]   (OAG)
BLR........... Bangalore [*India*] [*Airport symbol*]   (OAG)
BLR........... Bezirkslandwirtschaftsrat [*District Agricultural Council*]   (EG)

BLR........... Bijzonder Loodsreglement [Benelux]   (BAS)
BLR........... Bolnica Lakih Ranjenika [Hospital for the Lightly Wounded] [Military]   (YU)
BLR........... Light Casualties Hospital   (BU)
BLS........... Balansstaat [Balance Sheet] [Afrikaans]
BLS........... Baykal Limnological Station   (RU)
Bls............. Bolivares [Monetary unit] [Venezuela]
BLS........... BoonLerd Stuff [Thailand] [Commercial firm]
BLS........... Botswana, Lesotho, Swaziland
BLS........... Brigade Legere de Securite [Morocco]
BLS........... Union of Bulgarian Physicians   (BU)
BLSA........ Border Leicester Sheepbreeders' Association [Australia]
BLSANSW ... Border Leicester Sheepbreeders' Association of New South Wales [Australia]
BLT........... Baltic Aviation, Inc. [ICAO designator]   (FAAC)
BLT........... Banque Libyo-Togolaise pour le Commerce Exterieur [Libyan-Togolese Foreign Trade Bank]   (AF)
BLT........... Belfoldi Leveltavirat [Domestic Night Letter (Telegram)]   (HU)
BLT........... Biological Laboratories Teva Ltd. [Israel]   (IRC)
BLT........... Blackwater [Australia] [Airport symbol]   (OAG)
Blt .... Blaettchen [Leaflets] [German]
BLT........... Bureau of Land Transport [Philippines]   (DS)
BLT........... Busola Lakog Tipa [A Light Compass] [Army]   (YU)
BLTI .... Belorussian Forestry Engineering Institute Imeni S. M. Kirov   (RU)
blto .... Air Technical Support Battalion   (BU)
BLU .... Bande Laterale Unique   (ADPT)
BluStV ...... Vorschriften fuer den Block- und Stellwerkdienst [Regulations for Block and Control Tower Operations]   (EG)
BLV........... Bell-View Airlines Ltd. [Nigeria] [ICAO designator]   (FAAC)
BLV........... Bezirkslastverteiler [District (Electric Power) Load Distributor]   (EG)
Blvd........... Boulevard [Boulevard] [French]
Blvd........... Bulevard [Boulevard] [Romanian]
Blvd........... Bulevard [Boulevard] [Bulgarian]
BLW......... Federal Office of Agriculture [Switzerland]
BLWI........ Belgisch-Luxembourg Wissel Instituut [Benelux]
blyansnot ... Blyansnotater [Pencil Notations] [Publishing Danish/Norwegian]
blyantsindstregn ... Blyantsindstregning [Pencil Scoring] [Publishing Danish/Norwegian]
blyantsmrk ... Blyantsmaerke [Pencil Mark] [Publishing Danish/Norwegian]
BLZ........... Aero Barloz SA de CV [Mexico] [ICAO designator]   (FAAC)
BLZ........... Belize [ANSI three-letter standard code]   (CNC)
blz............. Bladzijde [Page] [Publishing] [Netherlands]
BLZ........... Blantyre [Malawi] [Airport symbol]   (OAG)
Blz............. Blattzahl [Number of Sheets] [Publishing] [German]
BLZK........ Bayerische Landeszahnaerztekammer   (SLS)
blzz........... Bladzijden [Pages] [Publishing] [Netherlands]
bm .... Author's Note   (BU)
Bm............ Bahnmeisterei [Railroad Section]   (EG)
bm .... Baixa-Mar [Portuguese]
BM............ Balneum Marinum [Sea-Water Bath] [Medicine]
BM............ Banca Mondiale [World Bank] [Italian]
BM............ Banco Mundial [World Bank] [Spanish]
BM............ Bande Magnetique   (ADPT)
BM............ Banque Mondiale [World Bank] [Use IBRD] [French]   (AF)
BM............ Battalion Mortar   (RU)
Bm............ Baumuster [Type] [German]   (GCA)
bm .... Beeldmerk [Benelux]   (BAS)
BM............ Belugyminiszterium/Miniszter [Ministry/Minister of the Interior]   (HU)
BM............ Bermuda [ANSI two-letter standard code]   (CNC)
bm .... Bez Miejsca [No Place (of publication)] [Poland]
bm .... Bez Mista [No Place (of publication)]   (CZ)
bm .... Bezny Metr [Linear Meter]   (CZ)
BM............ Biblioteka Miejska [Municipal Library]   (POL)
BM............ Bibliotheque du Museon   (BJA)
bm .... Biezacego Miesiaca [The Current Month] [Poland]
BM............ Binocular Microscope   (RU)
BM............ Birlesmis Milletleri [United Nations Organization]   (TU)
BM............ Blockmarke   (ADPT)
BM............ Blue Mountains [Australia]
BM............ Blume [Germany] [ICAO aircraft manufacturer identifier]   (ICAO)
B M........... Bohr Magneton   (RU)
BM............ Boroko Motors [Papua New Guinea] [Commercial firm]
BM............ Boundary Marker [Beacon]   (RU)
BM............ Bouw en Metaal [Hoofdgroep] [Division for Building and Metal Research Netherlands Central Organization for Applied Natural Scientific Research]   (WND)
BM............ Braca Miladinovi [Miladinov Brothers]   (YU)
BM............ Buddhist Mission [Hungary]   (EAIO)
BM............ Bulgarska Misul [Bulgarian Thought] [A periodical]   (BU)
BM............ Buona Memoria [Of Blessed Memory] [Italian]
BM............ Contactless Micrometer   (RU)
BM............ Marine Bathometer   (RU)

BM............. Mechanical Unit   (RU)
b m.............. Next Month   (RU)
bm .... No Place (of Publication Given)   (BU)
BM............. Societa Aero Trasporti Italiani SpA [Italy] [ICAO designator]   (ICDA)
BM............. Superheavy [Artillery]   (RU)
BMA .... Bahrain Monetary Agency   (IMH)
BMA .... Banana Marketing Australia   (ADA)
BMA .... Bangkok Metropolitan Administration [Thailand]   (DS)
BMA .... Bermuda Monetary Authority   (GEA)
BMA .... Berndt Museum of Anthropology [Australia]
BMA .... Bon Marche Africain
BMA .... Bonne Maison d'Afrique
BMA .... Building Management Authority [Western Australia]
BMA .... Bundesministerium fuer Auswaertige Angelegenheiten [German]
BMA .... Butyl Methacrylate   (RU)
BMA .... Stockholm [Sweden] Bromma Airport [Airport symbol]   (OAG)
BMAA ...... Boat Manufacturers' Association of Australia
BMAA ...... Brushware Manufacturers' Association of Australia
BMAC ...... Boeing Military Airplane Company
BMANSW ... Bread Manufacturers' Association of New South Wales [Australia]
BManufTech ... Bachelor of Manufacturing Technology
bmar .... Bez Mista a Roku [No Place and No Date of Publication] [Publishing Former Czechoslovakia]
BMASA..... Bread Manufacturers' Association of South Australia
BMASSR... Buryat-Mongol Autonomous Soviet Socialist Republic [1923-1958]   (RU)
BMAT .... Blind Manufacturers' Association of Tasmania [Australia]
BMaths...... Bachelor of Mathematics
BMAV ...... Bread Manufacturers' Association of Tasmania [Australia]
BMAWA ... Bread Manufacturers' Association of Western Australia
BMAWA ... Building Management Authority of Western Australia
BMB .... Bahrain Middle East Bank
BMB .... Baltic Marine Biologists [Sweden]   (SLS)
BMB .... Bois de M'Balmayo
BMB .... Bumba [Zaire] [Airport symbol]   (OAG)
BMB .... Bundesministerium fuer Bauten und Technik [German]
BMB .... Butter Marketing Board [Queensland, Australia]
BMBNSW ... Barley Marketing Board of New South Wales [Australia]
BMBO ...... Baltic Marine Biology Organization [Also, BMB]   (MSC)
BMBR....... Birlesmis Milletler ve Bogazlar Rejimi Dairesi Genel Mudurlugu [United Nations and Straits Regime Office Directorate General] [of Foreign Affairs Ministry]   (TU)
BMBW ...... Bundesministerium fur Bildung und Wissenschaft [Federal Ministry for Education and Science] [Germany]   (PDAA)
BMC .... Banque de Madagascar et des Comores [Bank of Madagascar and of the Comoro Islands]   (AF)
BMC .... Benguet Management Corp. [Philippines]
BMC .... Bibliotheque Municipale Classee de Tours [France]
BMC .... Bong Mining Company [Liberia]   (AF)
BMC .... Bosna Film, Morava Film, Croacia Film [Bosnia and Hercegovina, Serbian, and Croatian Motion Picture Establishments]   (YU)
BMC .... Botswana Meat Commission [Lobatse]
BMC .... Bush Music Club [Australia]   (ADA)
BMCC .... Blue Mountains City Council [Australia]
BMCD ...... Banque Malienne de Credits et de Depots [Malian Credit and Deposits Bank]   (AF)
BMCE ...... Banque Marocaine pour le Commerce Exterieur [Moroccan Foreign Trade Bank]   (AF)
BMChK .... Bulgarian Junior Red Cross   (BU)
BMD......... Banque Mauritanienne de Developpement [Mauritanian Development Bank]   (AF)
BMD......... Belo [Madagascar] [Airport symbol]   (OAG)
BMDA...... Bahamas Motor Dealers Association   (EAIO)
BMDC...... Banque Mauritanienne pour le Developpement et le Commerce
BMDC...... Biomedical Documentation Centre [Sweden]
BME .... Base Material de Estudios [Study Materials Program] [Cuba]   (LA)
bme............ Bombardment Squadron   (BU)
BME .... Bond Mining and Exploration Co. [Australia]
BME .... Broome [Australia] [Airport symbol]   (OAG)
BME .... Budapesti Muszaki Egyetem [Technical University of Budapest]   (HU)
BME .... Bueromaschinen-Export [Office Machinery Export Foreign Trade Enterprise]   (EG)
BME .... Bundesverband Materialwirtschaft und Einkauf [National Association of Materials Management and Purchasing] [Germany]   (PDAA)
BMEDC..... Bangladesh Mineral Exploration and Development Corp.   (EAS)
Bment........ Batiment [Building] [Military map abbreviation World War I] [French]   (MTD)
BMF .... Bulgarian Maritime Fleet   (BU)
BMF .... Bumiputra Malaysia Finance

BMF .... Bundesministerium fuer Finanzen [*Federal Minister of Finance*] [*German*]

BMfgMgt... Bachelor of Manufacturing Management

BMFOCA ... Blue Mountain Firearms Owners and Collectors Association [*Australia*]

BMFT....... Bundesministerium fuer Forschung und Technologie [*Ministry for Research and Technology*] [*Information service or system*] [*German*]　(IID)

BMFT....... German D-1 Spacelaboratory Payload

BMG .... Baader-Meinhof Group [*Revolutionary group*] [*Germany*]

BMG .... Badan Meteorologi dan Geofisika [*Meteorological and Geophysical Agency*] [*Indonesia*]　(EAS)

BMG .... Banco de Minas Gerais [*Brazil*]　(LAA)

BMG .... Berliner Medizinische Gesellschaft　(SLS)

BMG .... British Military Government

BMG .... Bundesministerium fuer Gesundheit und Umweltschutz [*Federal Minister of Health and Accident*] [*German*]

BMG .... Bureau of Mines and Geo-Sciences [*Philippines*] [*Research center*]　(EAS)

bmg .... No Place and Year of Publication Given　(BU)

BMGK .... Birlesmis Milletler Genel Kurulu [*United Nations General Assembly*]　(TU)

BMH.......... Bank Mees & Hope NV

BMH.......... Berliner Metallhuetten- und Halbzeugwerke [*Berlin Metallurgical and Semifinished Products Works*]　(EG)

BMH......... Bomai [*Papua New Guinea*] [*Airport symbol*]　(OAG)

BMH.......... Bristow Masayu Helicopter PT [*Indonesia*] [*ICAO designator*]　(FAAC)

BMH......... Bundesministerium fuer Handel, Gewerbe, und Industrie [*Federal Minister of Business, Trade, and Industry*] [*German*]

BMHIC ..... [*The*] Blue Mountains' Hiking & Information Centre [*Jamaica*]

BMHP....... Biomedicine and Health Program

BMHS .... Barbados Museum and Historical Society　(EAIO)

BMHW...... Berliner Metallhuetten- und Halbzeugwerke [*Berlin Metallurgical and Semifinished Products Works*]　(EG)

BMI .... Bank Melli Iran

BMI .... Banque Maghrebine d'Information Industrielle [*Morocco*]

BMI .... Bundesministerium fuer Inneres [*Federal Ministry of the Interior*]

BMI .... Large Toolmaker's Microscope　(RU)

BMIA .... Bicycle and Motorcycle Industries Association [*Germany*]　(EAIO)

BMIAA..... Bread Manufacturers' Industrial Association of Australia

BMIC......... Basic Metals Industry Council [*Australia*]

bmig .... No Place, No Date [*Bibliography*]　(RU)

BMIHK ..... Birlesmis Milletler Insan Haklari Komisyonu [*United Nations Human Rights Commission*]　(TU)

BMinELF .. Bundesministerium fuer Ernaehrung Landwirtschaft und Forsten [*Germany*]　(DSCA)

BMin f....... Bundesminister Fuer [*Federal Minister Of*] [*German*]

BMIT........ Biological Museum Imeni K. A. Timiryazev　(RU)

BMITA...... British Malaysian Industry and Trade Association　(DS)

BMJ.......... Baramita [*Guyana*] [*Airport symbol*]　(OAG)

BMJ.......... Bemidji Aviation Services, Inc. [*ICAO designator*]　(FAAC)

BMJ.......... Bundesministerium der Justiz [*Federal Minister of Justice*] [*German*]　(ILCA)

BMJ.......... Bundesministerium fuer Justiz [*Federal Minister of Justice*] [*German*]

BMK .... Banque Militaire Khmere [*Cambodian Military Bank*]　(CL)

BMK .... Bau und Montagekombinat [*Building and Assembly Combine*]　(EG)

BMK .... Borkum [*Germany*] [*Airport symbol*]　(OAG)

BMK .... Magnetic Heading on Bomb Run　(RU)

BMK .... Motor Tugboat　(RU)

BMKGM ... Butce ve Mali Kontrol Genel Mudurlugu [*Budget and Financial Control Directorate General*]　(TU)

BMKhP ..... Central Scientific and Technical Library of the Ministry of the Chemical Industry　(RU)

BMKN .... Badan Meshuarat Kebudayaan Nasional [*National Cultural Council*]　(ML)

BMKP........ Birlesmis Milletler Kalkinma Programi [*United Nations Development Program*]　(TU)

BML .... Bank of Maldives Ltd.　(FEA)

BML .... Barrack Mines Ltd. [*Australia*]

BML .... Belize Mills Ltd.

BML .... Diodeless Magnetic Logical (Element) [*Computers*]　(RU)

BML .... Magnetic-Tape Unit　(RU)

BMLC........ Ballarat Music Lovers' Club [*Australia*]

BMLF .... Bundesministerium fuer Land- und Forstwirtschaft [*Federal Minister of Agriculture and Forestry*] [*German*]

BMLV....... Bundesministerium fuer Landesverteidigung [*Federal Minister of Domestic Defense*] [*German*]

BMM .... Baptist Mid Mission

BMM .... Bitam [*Gabon*] [*Airport symbol*]　(OAG)

BMM......... Brigades Mixtes Mobiles [*Paramilitary force responsible for interrogation*] [*Cameroon*]

BMM .... Burgas Copper Mines　(BU)

BMM .... Buyuk Millet Meclisi [*Grand National Assembly*] [*TBMM*] [*See also*]　(TU)

BMM .... V. V. Mayakovskiy Library-Museum　(RU)

BMMK ...... Baltic and International Maritime Conference [*BIMC*]　(RU)

BMMPIC .. Basic Metals and Minerals Processing Industry Council [*Australia*]

BMNIIK... Buryat-Mongol Scientific Research Institute of Culture　(RU)

BMNIIKE ... Buryat-Mongol Scientific Research Institute of Culture and Economics　(RU)

BMNLF..... Bangsa Moro National Liberation Front [*Philippines*] [*Political party*]　(FEA)

BMNP .... Central Scientific and Technical Library of the Ministry of the Petroleum Industry　(RU)

BMNSW ... Bread Manufacturers of New South Wales [*Australia*]

BMO......... Bhamo [*Myanmar*] [*Airport symbol*]　(OAG)

BMO......... Briqueterie Mecanique du Ouaddai

BMO......... Bureau de Main-d'Oeuvre [*Algeria*]

BMO......... Large Magellanic Cloud　(RU)

BMOI .... Banque Malgache de l'Ocean Indien [*Indian Ocean Malagasy Bank*] [*Madagascar*]　(EY)

BMOP .... Bureau de la Main d'Oeuvre Portaire [*Port Manpower Office*] [*Senegal*]　(AF)

BmoPadre ... Beatisimo Padre [*Most Blessed Father*] [*Spanish*]

Bmo Pe....... Beatisimo Padre [*Most Blessed Father*] [*Spanish*]

BM OTP... Belugyminiszterium, Orszagos Tuzrendeszeti Parancsnoksag [*Ministry of the Interior, National Fire Protection Headquarters*]　(HU)

BMP .... Bank for International Settlements - BIS　(RU)

BMP .... Basutoland Mounted Police

BMP .... Battalion Medical Point　(BU)

BMP .... Battalion Medical Station　(RU)

BMP .... Boevaya Mashina Pekhota [*Infantry Fighting Vehicle*] [*Russian*]

BMP .... Brampton Island [*Australia*] [*Airport symbol*]　(OAG)

BMP .... Brigades Mecanisees de Production

BMP .... Business Migrants Programme [*Australia*]

BMP .... Gasoline Motor Pump　(RU)

BMP .... Inner Marker Beacon　(RU)

BMP .... Marine Battalion　(RU)

BMP .... Microprogram Unit　(RU)

bmp .... Naval Infantry Battalion　(BU)

BMPF....... Bahrain Modern Pentathlon Federation　(EAIO)

BMPU ...... Magnetic Bomb-Run Track Angle　(RU)

BMQ......... Bamburi [*Kenya*] [*Airport symbol*] [*Obsolete*]　(OAG)

BMQUE .... Bread Manufacturers of Queensland Union of Employers [*Australia*]

bmr............ Bez Miejsca i Roku [*Place and Year of Publication Not Given*] [*Poland*]

BMR .... Bureau of Market Research [*South Africa*]　(SLS)

BMR .... Bureau of Mineral Resources [*Australia*]　(NRCH)

BMR .... Contactless Magnetic Relay　(RU)

BMRC .... Bureau of Meteorology Research Centre [*Australia*]　(IRC)

BMRC .... Business Management Research Center [*South Korea*]　(IRC)

BMRDA .... Bombay Metropolitan Region Development Authority [*India*]　(PDAA)

BMRGG .... Bureau of Marine Resources, Geology, and Geophysics [*Australia*]　(MSC)

BMRI........ Baker Medical Research Institute [*Australia*]

BMRT....... Large Refrigerated Fishing Trawler　(RU)

BMRTs...... Route Control Interlocking System　(RU)

bmrw .... Bez Miejsca, Roku Wydania [*Place and Year of Publication Not Given*] [*Poland*]

BMS.......... Baptist Missionary Society

BMS.......... Bharatiya Mazdoor Sangh [*India*]

BMS.......... Bloc des Masses Senegalaises [*Bloc of the Senegalese Masses*]　(AF)

BMS.......... Brazilian Money Supplies

BMS.......... Brumado [*Brazil*] [*Airport symbol*]　(OAG)

BMS.......... Bundesministerium fuer Soziale Verwaltung [*Federal Minister of Social Administration*] [*German*]

BMS.......... Bureau Militaire de Standardisation [*Military Agency for Standardization*] [*NATO*]

BMS.......... Bush Missionary Society [*Australia*]　(ADA)

BMS.......... Fat-Free Detergent　(RU)

BMSA........ Building Material Suppliers Association [*South Africa*]　(AA)

BMSR(HV) ... Betriebsmess-, Steuer- und Regelungstechnik [*Hauptverwaltung*] [*(Main Administration for) Industrial Measuring, Control, and Regulating Technology*]　(EG)

BMSRI ...... Bangladesh Medical Studies and Research Institute　(EAIO)

BMSR-Technik ... Betriebsmess-, Steuer-, und Regelungstechnik [*Industrial Measuring, Control, and Regulating Technology*]　(EG)

BMSS........ Beogradski Medunarodni Slavisticki Sastanak [*International Congress of Slavicists in Belgrade*] [*1955*]　(YU)

BMT .... Brisbane Market Trust [*Australia*]

BMT .... Bureau Marocain du Travail

BMT .... Mikhaylovskiy-Turov Aiming Circle [*Artillery*]　(RU)

BMT .... Small Ship-Hold Bulldozer (RU)
BMTA ...... Bangkok Mass Transit Authority [*Thailand*] (DS)
BMTA ...... Blue Mountains Tourism Authority [*Australia*]
BmtAnlagen ... Betriebsmaschinentechnische Anlagen [*Mechanical and Technical Railroad Installations*] (EG)
BMTD ...... Birlesmis Milletler Turk Dernegi [*United Nations Association of Turkey*] (EAIO)
BMTK ...... Office of Metal and Heat Engineering Structures (RU)
BMtkm ...... Brutto Megatonnen-Kilometer [*Gross Megaton-Kilometer*] [*Metric Ton*] (EG)
BMTM ...... Central Scientific and Technical Library of the Ministry of Heavy Machinery Manufacture (RU)
BM-TNO... Hoofdgroep Bouw en Metaal - Nederlands Centrale Organisatie voor Toegepast-Natuurwetenschappelijk Onderzoek [*Division for Building and Metal Research*] [*Netherlands Central Organization for Applied Natural Scientific Research*] (ERC)
Bmtr .... Beamter [*Official, Civil Servant*] [*German*]
BMTR........ Large Refrigerated Fish-Factory Trawler (RU)
BMTsM.... Central Library of the Ministry of Nonferrous Metallurgy (RU)
BMU......... Balkan Medical Union [*Romania*] (EAIO)
BMU......... Bermuda [*ANSI three-letter standard code*] (CNC)
BMU......... Bima [*Indonesia*] [*Airport symbol*] (OAG)
BMU......... Bundesministerium fuer Unterricht und Kunst [*Federal Minister of Education and Art*] [*German*]
BMU......... High-Speed Magnetic Amplifier (RU)
BMU......... Local-Control Unit (RU)
BMU deA ... Biblioteca Medica Universidad de Antioquia [*Colombia*] (COL)
BMUK....... Botanical Mission of the University of Kyoto [*Japan*] (DSCA)
BMusT..... Bachelor of Music Teaching
BMV .... Bases de Multiplication et de Vulgarisation
BMV .... Beata Maria Virgem [*Blessed Virgin Mary*] [*Portuguese*]
BMV .... Berliner Metallverarbeitung [*Berlin Metalworking Plant*] (EG)
BMV .... Bundesministerium fuer Verkehr [*Federal Minister of Commerce*] [*German*]
BMV .... International Exhibition Bureau (RU)
BMvD .... Bureau Marcel van Dijk, SA [*Information service or system*] (IID)
BMW .... Bayerische Motoren Werke [*Bavarian Motor Works*] [*German automobile manufacturer; initialism used as name of its cars and motorcycles*]
BMW .... Beat Matsushita Whatsoever [*Facetious translation of BMW - Bavarian Motor Works, Originated by Sony Corp.*] (ECON)
bmw .... Bez Miejsca Wydania [*Place of Publication Not Given*] [*Poland*]
BMW .... Bundesministerium fuer Wissenschaft und Forschung [*Federal Minister of Science and Research*] [*German*]
BMWF...... Bundeministerium fur Wissenschaftliche Forschung [*Federal Ministry of Scientific Research*] [*Germany*] (PDAA)
BMWS...... Bundesministerium fuer Wissenschaftliche Forschung [*Germany*] (DSCA)
BMWU..... Black Municipal Workers' Union
BMWW ..... Biuro Miedzynarodowej Wymiany Wydawnictw [*International Bureau for the Exchange of Publications*] [*Poland*]
BMX .... Banco de Mexico [*ICAO designator*] (FAAC)
BMY .... Belep [*New Caledonia*] [*Airport symbol*] (OAG)
BMZ .... Bamu [*Papua New Guinea*] [*Airport symbol*] (OAG)
BMZ .... Berezniki Magnesium Plant (RU)
BMZ .... Bundesministerium fuer Wirtschaftliche Zusammenarbeit [*Federal Ministry for Economic Cooperation*] (EG)
bn .... Author's Note (BU)
BN............. Banco de la Nacion [*National Bank*] [*Peru*]
BN............. Barisan Nasional [*Malaysia*] [*Political party*] (EY)
Bn............. Bassin [*Basin*] [*French*] (NAU)
BN............. Batalion [*Battalion*] (ML)
Bn............. Bayan [*Mrs., Miss, Ms.*] (TU)
BN............. Belgonucleaire [*Nuclear energy*] [*Belgium*] (NRCH)
BN............. Benevento [*Car registration plates*] [*Italian*]
BN............. Berita Negara [*State Journal*] (IN)
BN............. Betriebsnummer [*Enterprise Number*] (EG)
bn .... Bez Nakladatele [*No Publisher Given*] (CZ)
BN............. Biblioteca Nacional [*National Library*] [*Portuguese*]
BN............. Biblioteka Narodowa [*National Library*] (POL)
BN............. Bibliotheque Nationale [*National Library*] [*French*]
bn .... Billion [*Thousand million*] (OMWE)
BN............. Britten Norman (Bembridge) Ltd. [*British*] [*ICAO aircraft manufacturer identifier*] (ICAO)
B'n............. Bruedern [*Brethren*] [*Freemasonry*] [*German*]
BN............. Brunei Darussalam [*ANSI two-letter standard code*] (CNC)
b/n............. Brut pour Net [*French*]
BN............. Buitengewoon Navorderingsbesluit [*Benelux*] (BAS)
BN............. Combat Assignment, Combat Mission (RU)
BN............. Combat Unclassified [*Gas mask*] (RU)
BN............. Fast-Neutron Reactor, Fast Reactor (RU)
BN............. Filament Battery [*Radio*] (RU)

BN............. Malfunction Unit, Error Unit [*Computers*] (RU)
BN............. Petroleum Bitumen (RU)
BN............. Tuning Unit [*Computers*] (RU)
b/n............. Unnumbered (RU)
bn .... Without Beginning [*Book*] (BU)
BN............. Zero-Setting Unit (RU)
BNA.......... Banca Nazionale dell'Agricoltura [*National Bank of Agriculture*] [*Italy*] (ECON)
Bna............. Banchina [*Quay*] [*Italian*] (NAU)
BNA.......... Banco de la Nacion Argentina [*National Bank of Argentina*]
BNA.......... Banco Nacional Agrario [*National Agricultural Bank*] [*Guatemala*] (LAA)
BNA.......... Banco Nacional de Angola [*National Bank of Angola*]
BNA.......... Banque Nationale Agricole [*National Agricultural Bank*] [*Tunisia*] (AF)
BNA.......... Banque Nationale d'Algerie [*National Bank of Algeria*] (AF)
BNA.......... Benzylnicotinamide (RU)
BNA.......... Biblioteca Nacional de Angola [*National Library of Angola*] (PDAA)
BNA.......... Bloc Nigerienne d'Action
BNA.......... Botswana National Airways
BNA.......... Brisbane Netball Association [*Australia*]
BNA.......... British North Atlantic (DS)
BNA.......... Bulgarian People's Army (BU)
BNA.......... Bureau des Normes de l'Automobile [*Bureau of Automobile Standards*] [*France*] (PDAA)
BNA.......... Koninklijke Maatschappij tot Bevordering der Bouwkunst Bond van Nederlandse Architekten [*Netherlands*] (SLS)
BNAe....... Bureau de Normalisation de l'Aeronautique et de l'Espace [*French*]
BNAF .... British North Africa Force
BNAL .... Bundesnotaufnahmelager [*Emergency Reception Camp*] (EG)
BNAS....... Bolivian National Academy of Sciences (EAIO)
BNASS ..... Biennial National Atomic Spectroscopy Symposium
BNASS ..... Bureau National d'Animation du Secteur Socialiste [*National Office for the Promotion of the Socialist Sector*] [*Algeria*] (AF)
BNB .... Banco do Nordeste do Brasil [*Bank of Northeast Brazil*] (LA)
BNB .... Banque Nationale de Belgique [*National Bank of Belgium*]
BNB .... Barbados National Bank (LA)
BNB .... Barclays National Bank [*South Africa*]
BNB .... Beslissingen in Belastingzaken, Nederlandse Belastingrechtspraak [*Netherlands*] (BAS)
Bnb............. Binbasi [*Major (Army), Lieutenant Commander (Navy)*] (TU)
BNB .... Blue Nile Bank Ltd. [*Sudan*]
BNB .... Boende [*Zaire*] [*Airport symbol*] (OAG)
BNB .... Bulgarian National Bank (BU)
BNBA .... Brunei National Badminton Association (EAIO)
BNBC .... British North Borneo Co. (FEA)
BNBE .... Bibliografia Extranjera Depositada en la Biblioteca Nacional [*Ministerio de Cultura*] [*Spain*] [*Information service or system*] (CRD)
BNC .... Banca Nazionale della Comunicazioni [*Bank*] [*Italian*]
BNC .... Banco Nacional de Cuba [*National Bank of Cuba*] (LA)
BNC .... Banque de Nouvelle - Caledonie (EY)
BNC .... Banque Nationale de Credit [*National Credit Bank*] [*Haiti*] (GEA)
BNC .... Banque Nationale du Cambodge [*National Bank of Cambodia*] (CL)
BNC .... Banque Nationale du Congo [*National Bank of the Congo*]
BNC .... Basutoland National Council
BNC .... Benefices Non Commerciaux
BNCA .... Banco Nacional de Credito Agricola SA [*Mexico*] (DSCA)
BNCC .... Banco Nacional de Credito Cooperativo [*National Cooperative Credit Bank*] [*Brazil*] (LA)
BNCCI...... Bengal National Chamber of Commerce and Industry [*India*] (PDAA)
BncCtrl .... Banco Central Hispanoamericano SA [*Associated Press*]
BNCD .... Banque Nationale Centrafricaine de Depots
BNCD .... Banque Nationale Centrafricaine de Developpement [*Central African National Development Bank*] (AF)
BNCE .... Banco Nacional de Comercio Exterior [*National Foreign Trade Bank*] [*Mexico*] (GEA)
BNCF........ Biblioteca Nazionale Centrale, Florence [*Italy*]
BNCI .... Banque Nationale pour le Commerce et l'Industrie [*National Bank for Commerce and Industry*] [*Togo*] [*French*]
BNCIA....... Banque Nationale pour le Commerce et l'Industrie Afrique
BNCIAWPRC ... Brazilian National Committee of the International Association on Water Pollution Research and Control (EAIO)
BNCR .... Banque Nationale de Credit Rural [*Gabon*] (EY)
BND.......... Banco Nacional de Desarrollo [*National Development Bank*] [*Argentina*]
BND.......... Banco Nacional de Desarrollo [*National Development Bank*] [*Nicaragua*] (LA)
bnd .... Band [*Binding, Cover, Wrapper*] [*Publishing*] [*Netherlands*]

BND.......... Bandar Abbas [Iran] [Airport symbol]   (OAG)
BND.......... Banque Nationale de Developpement [National Development Bank] [Burkina Faso]   (AF)
BND.......... Banque Nationale de Developpement de la Republique Centrafricaine [National Development Bank of the Republic of Central Africa]
BNd.......... Betriebsvorschrift fuer den Vereinfachten Nebendienst [Traffic Regulations for Simplified Secondary Railroad Service] (EG)
BND.......... Blocul National Democrat [National Democratic Bloc]   (RO)
BND.......... Bundesnachrichtendienst [Federal Intelligence Service] [Germany]
BND.......... Inertialess Nonlinear Two-Terminal Network   (RU)
BNDA....... Banque Nationale pour le Developpement Agricole [National Agricultural Development Bank] [Ivory Coast]   (AF)
BNDB....... Banque Nationale de Devellopement du Burkina   (EY)
BNDC....... Banque Nationale de Developpement du Congo [National Development Bank of the Congo]   (AF)
BNDC....... Bophuthatswana National Development Corporation
BNDC....... Bureau National de Developpement Communautaire [National Office for Community Development] [Zaire]
BNDD....... Banco Nacional de Deposito y Desarrollo
BNDE....... Banco Nacional do Desenvolvimento Economico [National Economic Development Bank] [Brazil]
BNDE....... Banque Nationale de Developpement Economique [National Economic Development Bank] [France]   (AF)
BNDE....... Banque Nationale pour le Developpement Economique [National Bank for Economic Development] [Morocco] (IMH)
BNDES...... Banco Nacional do Desenvolvimento Economico e Social [National Bank for Economic and Social Development] [Rio De Janeiro, Brazil]   (GEA)
BNDHV..... Banque Nationale de Developpement de la Haute-Volta [National Development Bank of Upper Volta]   (AF)
BNDO....... Bureau National des Donnees Oceaniques [National Bureau for Ocean Data] [European host database system] [France] [Information service or system]   (IID)
BNDP....... Bet-Nahrain Democratic Party [Political party]   (BJA)
BNDP....... Brunei National Democratic Party [Political party]   (FEA)
BNDS....... Banque Nationale de Developpement du Senegal [Senegal National Development Bank]   (AF)
BNDT....... Banque Nationale de Developpement Touristique [National Bank of Tourist Development] [Tunisia]
Bne.......... Borne [Boundary Stone] [Military map abbreviation World War I] [French]   (MTD)
BNE.......... Brisbane [Australia] [Airport symbol]   (OAG)
BNEC....... Banque Nationale pour l'Epargne et le Credit [National Savings and Credit Bank] [Ivory Coast]   (AF)
BNEDER... Bureau National d'Etudes pour le Developpement Rural [Algeria]   (IMH)
BNEL........ Bureau National de l'Enseignement Libre [National Office of Public Education] [Zaire]
BNEP........ Biuro Nadzoru Estetyki Produkcji [Production Aesthetics Supervisory Bureau]   (POL)
BNETD..... Bureau National d'Etudes Techniques de Developpement [National Office for Technical Development Studies] [Ivory Coast]   (AF)
BNF.......... Banco Nacional de Fomento [National Development Bank] [Paraguay]   (LAA)
BNF.......... Banco Nacional de Fomento [National Development Bank] [Ecuador]   (LAA)
BNF.......... Belarusky Narodny Front [Belarussian Popular Front] [Political party]   (EY)
BNF.......... Bewegung Neues Forum [New Forum] [Germany]   (EAIO)
BNF.......... Botswana National Front [Political party]   (PPW)
BNG.......... Ballast Nedam Groep [Land reclamation company] [Netherlands]
BNG.......... Bloque Nacionalista Galego [Galician Nationalist Block] [Spain] [Political party]   (EY)
BNG.......... Blue Nile Grid [Electricity production] [Sudan]   (IMH)
BNG.......... British New Guinea   (ADA)
BNGB....... Bloco Nacional da Guinea-Bissau [National Bloc of Guinea-Bissau] [Portuguese Guinea]   (AF)
BNGL....... Bangladesh   (WDAA)
BNH.......... Banco Nacional de Habitacao [National Housing Bank] [Rio De Janeiro, Brazil]   (LA)
BNI.......... Bankin'ny Indostria [Industrial Bank] [Malagasy]   (AF)
BNI.......... Bank Negara Indonesia [Indonesian State Bank]   (IN)
BNI.......... Beijing Neurosurgical Institute [China] [Research center]   (IRC)
BNI.......... Benin City [Nigeria] [Airport symbol]   (OAG)
BNI.......... Brodarski Naucni Institut [Naval Scientific Institute]   (YU)
BNI.......... Bureau of National Investigation [Ghana]
BNIB........ Biblioteka Narodowa - Instytut Bibliograficzny [National Library - Bibliographical Institute]   (POL)
BNIC........ Bureau of National and International Communications [South Africa]   (AF)
BNIlLKh... Belorussian Scientific Research Institute of Forestry   (RU)

BNIST....... Bureau National de l'Information Scientifique et Technique [National Scientific and Technical Information Bureau] [France] [Information service or system]   (IID)
BNJ.......... Bonn [Germany] [Airport symbol]   (OAG)
BNK......... Ballina [Australia] [Airport symbol]
BNK......... Bolgar Nepkoztarsasag [Bulgarian People's Republic]   (HU)
BNK......... Bulgarian National Committee   (BU)
bnk.......... Without Beginning or End   (BU)
BNKCPA... Bureau National Kamerunais pour la Conference des Peuples Africains [Cameroonian National Bureau for African Peoples Conference]
BNKh........ Standards Management Office   (RU)
BNL.......... Banca Nazionale del Lavoro [National Bank of Labor] [Italy] (ECON)
BNL.......... Banque Nationale du Laos [National Bank of Laos]   (CL)
BNL.......... Base Naval de Lisboa [Lisbon Naval Base] [Portuguese]   (WER)
BNL.......... Borsodnadasdi Lemezgyar [Borsodnadasd Metal Sheet Factory] (HU)
BNLTA...... Botswana National Lawn Tennis Association
BNM......... Banco Nacional de Mexico [National Bank of Mexico]   (LAA)
BNM......... Bank Negara Malaysia [Central Bank of Malaysia]   (ML)
BNM......... Banque Nationale de Mauritanie   (EY)
BNM......... Banque Nationale Malgache de Developpement [Malagasy National Development Bank]   (AF)
BNM......... Biblioteca Nacional de Mocambique [National Library of Mozambique]
BNM......... Black Nationalist Movement
BNM......... Bodinumu [Papua New Guinea] [Airport symbol]   (OAG)
BNM......... Bureau de Normalisation de la Mecanique [French]
BNMG...... Banco Nacional de Minas Gerais [Minas Gerais National Bank] [Brazil]   (LA)
BNMI........ Beijing Nonferrous Metals and Rare Earth Research Institute [China]   (IRC)
BNML....... League of Dutch Marxist-Leninists   (WEN)
BNMO...... Bond Nederlandse Militaire Oorlogsslachtoffers [Federation of Dutch War Victims]   (WEN)
BNMS....... Bulgarian National Maritime Union   (BU)
BNN.......... Banco Nacional de Nicaragua [National Bank of Nicaragua] (LAA)
BNN.......... Bronnoysund [Norway] [Airport symbol]   (OAG)
BNN.......... Pilot Unit for Initial Voltage   (RU)
BNn.......... Smokeless Powder [Symbol] [French]   (MTD)
BNO.......... Beroepsvereniging Nederlandse Ontwerpens [Association of Dutch Designers]   (EAIO)
BNOC....... Bahrain National Oil Company   (ME)
BNOC....... Barbados National Oil Co. [State-owned]   (EY)
BNOC....... British National Oil Corp. [British]   (OMWE)
BNOCL...... Barbados National Oil Co. Ltd.   (EY)
BNOS....... Broadband Network Operating System
BNOSP...... Banco Nacional de Obras y Servicios Publicos [National Bank for Public Works and Services] [Mexico]   (LAA)
BNOV....... Bulgarian National Liberation Army   (BU)
BNP.......... Banco Nacional de Panama [National Bank of Panama]
BNP.......... Bangladesh National Party [Bangladesh Jatiyabadi Dal]   (PPW)
BNP.......... Bannu [Pakistan] [Airport symbol]   (OAG)
BNP.......... Banque Nationale de Paris [National Bank of Paris] [France]
BNP.......... Basotho National Party [Lesotho] [Political party]   (PPW)
BNP.......... Battery Observation Post   (RU)
BNP.......... Biblioteca Nationala de Programe [National Library of Computer Programs]   (RO)
BNP.......... Bruto Nationaal Product [Benelux]   (BAS)
BNP.......... Bureau de Normalisation des Petroles
BNP.......... Combat Observation Post   (RU)
BNPD....... Battalion Combat Observation Post [Artillery]   (RU)
BNPG-PSG ... Bloque Nacional Popular de Galicia - Partido Socialista Gallego [Popular National Bloc of Galicia - Galician Socialist Party] [Political party]   (PPW)
BNPP........ Barisan Nasional Penbebasan Pattani [Thailand] [Political party]
BNPP........ Regimental Combat Observation Post   (RU)
BNPS........ Bulgarian National Pensioners' Union   (BU)
BNR.......... Banque Nationale du Rwanda [National Bank of Rwanda]
BNR.......... Bibliothek der Neuesten und Wichtigsten Reisebeschreibungen
BNR.......... Bulgarian People's Republic   (RU)
BNR.......... Bureau National de Recensement [National Census Bureau] [Senegal]
BNRH....... Banco Nacional de la Republica de Haiti [National Bank of the Republic of Haiti]   (LAA)
BNRSR...... Banca Nationala a Republicii Socialiste Romania [National Bank of the Socialist Republic of Romania]   (RO)
BNS.......... Balanced Nutrient Solution
BNS.......... Barinas [Venezuela] [Airport symbol]   (OAG)
BNS.......... Board of Nursing Studies [Queensland, Australia]
BNS.......... Bond van Nederlandse Stedebouwkundigen [Netherlands]   (SLS)
BNS.......... Dry Filament Battery [Radio]   (RU)
BNS.......... Office of Standardization   (RU)
BNSA........ Baha'i National Spiritual Assembly [Australia]

BnSant .... Banco de Santander Sociedad Anonima de Credito [*Associated Press*]
BNSC......... Botswana National Sports Council
BNSI.......... Barbados National Standards Institute   (LA)
BNSR......... Bukhara People's Soviet Republic [*1920-1924*]   (RU)
BNSW .... Bank of New South Wales [*Australia*]
BNT .... Banco Nacional de Trabajadores [*Paraguay*]   (EY)
BNT .... Banque Nationale de Tunisie [*Tunisian National Bank*]   (AF)
BNT .... Barbados National Trust   (EAIO)
BNT .... Basketball Northern Territory [*Australia*] [*An association*]
BNT .... Bibliotheque Nationale Togo [*National Library of Togo*]
BNT .... Brussels Tariff Nomenclature   (ILCA)
BNT .... Bundi [*Papua New Guinea*] [*Airport symbol*]   (OAG)
BNT .... Quick-Saturation Transformer   (RU)
BNTA .... Brisbane Night Tennis Association [*Australia*]
BNTI.......... Office of Scientific and Technical Information   (RU)
BNTL......... Bibliografie van de Nederlandse Taal- en Literatuurwetenschap
BNU.......... Banco Nacional Ultramarino [*National Overseas Bank*] [*Portuguese*]
BNU.......... Benson Needham Univas [*International advertising network*]
BNU.......... Drilling and Pumping Unit   (RU)
BNUP........ Brunei National United Party [*Political party*]   (EY)
BNUS .... Bibliotheque Nationale et Universitaire de Strasbourg [*France*]
BNV .... Banco de la Vivienda [*Housing Bank*] [*Dominican Republic*]   (LAA)
BNV .... Besloten Naamloze Vennootschap [*Benelux*]   (BAS)
BNV .... Budapesti Nemzetkozi Vasar [*Budapest International Fair*]   (HU)
b nw .... Byvoeglike Naamwoord [*Adjective*] [*Afrikaans*]
BNY .... Bellona Island [*Solomon Islands*] [*Airport symbol*]   (OAG)
BNYE .... Budapesti Nyomdaipari Egyesules [*Industrial Printing Syndicate of Budapest*]   (HU)
BNZ .... Bank of New Zealand
BNZ .... BANZ [*British-Australian-New Zealand*] [*Papua New Guinea*] [*Airport symbol*] [*Obsolete*]   (OAG)
Bnz .... Benzin [*Gasoline*]   (TU)
bnz............ Benzine [*Solvent*]   (RU)
BNZhD....... Bulgarian National Women's Association   (BU)
BNZS........ Bulgarski Naroden Zemedelski Suiuz [*Bulgarian National Agrarian Union*]   (PPE)
BO............ Bacteriological Weapons   (BU)
Bo............. Bajo [*Shoal*] [*Spanish*]
BO............. Banco Obrero [*Workers Bank*] [*Venezuela*]   (LA)
BO............. Bath Detachment   (RU)
Bo............. Beco [*Lane*] [*Portuguese*]
BO............. Bevelvoerende Offisier [*Officer in Command*] [*Afrikaans*]
BO............. Bezne Opravy [*Customary Repairs*]   (CZ)
bo............. Blaai Om [*Please Turn Over*] [*Afrikaans*]
BO............. Bocni Odrad [*Flank Screening Detachment*]   (CZ)
Bo............. Bogha [*Sunken Rock*] [*Gaelic*]   (NAU)
BO............. Bolivia [*ANSI two-letter standard code*]   (CNC)
BO............. Bologna [*Car registration plates*] [*Italian*]
Bo............. Bombay Regiment [*India*] [*Army*]
BO............. Boracki Odred [*Combat Detachment*]   (YU)
BO............. Boulets Ogivaux [*On artillery sights*] [*French*]   (MTD)
BO............. Bulletin Officiel [*French*]
BO............. Close Target   (RU)
BO............. Coast Defense   (RU)
BO............. Coast Guard   (RU)
BO............. Combat Organization   (RU)
BO............. Combat Security Unit, Combat Outpost   (RU)
bo............. Combat Train   (BU)
BO............. Eisenbahn-Bau- und Betriebsordnung [*Railroad Construction and Traffic Regulations*]   (EG)
bo............. Flamethrower Battalion   (RU)
BO............. Flank Guard   (RU)
BO............. Large Submarine Chaser   (RU)
BO............. Lateral Deviation [*Artillery*]   (RU)
BO............. MBB-UV [*Messerschmitt-Boelkow-Blohm*] [*Germany*] [*ICAO aircraft manufacturer identifier*]   (ICAO)
BO............. [*The*] Officer's Library [*Book series*]   (RU)
BO............. Oscilloscope Unit [*Computers*]   (RU)
BO............. Recoilless Gun   (BU)
BO............. Wet op de Bedrijfsorganisatie [*Benelux*]   (BAS)
BOA .... Bank of Africa [*Mali*]   (EY)
BOA .... Base Oceanografica Atlantica [*Atlantic Oceanographic Base*] [*Brazil*]   (MSC)
BOA .... Boulangerie d'Armee [*Military*] [*French*]   (MTD)
BOA .... Boykot Outspan Aktie
BOA .... Brits-Oos-Afrika [*British East Africa*] [*Afrikaans*]
BOA .... Bureau of Agriculture [*Government agency*] [*Taiwan*]   (EY)
BOA .... Butoxyanisole   (RU)
BOA .... Compagnie des Bois de l'Ouest Africain
BOAC .... Bank of the Arab Coast Ltd. [*United Arab Emirates*]   (EY)
BOAD........ Banque Ouest Africaine de Developpement [*West African Development Bank - WADB*]   (EAIO)

BOADICEA ... British Overseas Airways Corp. [*later, British Airways*] Digital Information Computer for Electronic Automation
BOAG........ Bureau d'Ordre et des Affaires Generales [*Appointments and General Affairs Office*] [*Cambodia*]   (CL)
BOAMV .... Office for Warehouse Pest Control   (RU)
BOAR .... Biuro Obrotu Artykulami Rolniczymi [*Farm Products Sales Office*]   (POL)
BOASA...... Bank Officials' Association of South Australia
BOAWA .... Bank Officials' Association of Western Australia
BOB .... Berner Oberland-Bahnen [*Bernese Overland Railways*]
BOB .... Bora-Bora [*French Polynesia*] [*Airport symbol*]   (OAG)
BOB .... Bukhara Oblast Library   (RU)
BOB .... Bundesverband Offentlicher Binnenhafen [*Germany*]   (EAIO)
BOB .... Bureau des Organisations Benevoles
BOBELE ... Boris Becker of Leimen [*Acronym also refers to pretzel produced by German bakers in recognition of this tennis player*]
BOBM ...... Baltic Sea Coast Defense   (RU)
BOC .... Bank of China [*China*]   (IMH)
BOC .... Bank of Communications [*China*]
BOC .... Bird Observers Club [*Australia*]   (SLS)
BOC .... Bocas Del Toro [*Panama*] [*Airport symbol*]   (OAG)
BOC .... Border Operations Committee   (ML)
BOC .... Boulangerie de Campagne [*Military*] [*French*]   (MTD)
BOC .... Bristol Owners' Club   (EA)
BOC .... Brodski Operativni Centar [*Ship Operational Center*] [*Navy*]   (YU)
BOCCA ..... Board for Coordination of Civil Aviation [*NATO*]
BOChM..... Black Sea Coast Defense   (RU)
boch zav ..... Cooperage [*Topography*]   (RU)
BOCI .... Bloque de Obreros, Campesinos, e Intelectuales [*Bloc of Workers, Peasants, and Intellectuals*] [*Costa Rica*]   (LA)
BOCO........ Bestuurlijke Overleg Commissie voor Overheidsautomatisering [*Netherlands*]
BoCom ...... Bank of Communications [*China*]
BOCTC...... Bank of China Trust and Consultancy Co.
BOD.......... Biskupski Ordinarijat u Dakovu [*Chancery of the Catholic Bishopric of Dakovo*]   (YU)
bod............ Bodoniana [*In the Style of Bodoni*] [*Publishing*] [*Italian*]
BOD.......... Bond Air Services Ltd. [*Uganda*] [*ICAO designator*]   (FAAC)
BOD.......... Bordeaux [*France*] [*Airport symbol*]   (OAG)
BOD.......... Data-Processing Unit   (RU)
BODK........ Bureau for Services to the Diplomatic Corps   (BU)
BODO........ Bauobjektdokumentation [*Buildings Documentation*] [*Fraunhofer Society*] [*Germany*] [*Information service or system*]   (IID)
BOE .... Boletin Oficial del Estado [*Official State Gazette*] [*Spanish*]   (WER)
BOE .... Boundji [*Congo*] [*Airport symbol*]   (OAG)
BOE .... Budapesti Orvostudomanyi Egyetem [*Medical University of Budapest*]   (HU)
BOEEOWLA ... Board of Examiners of Engineers and Overseers of Works to Local Authorities [*Australia*]
boekh .... Bockhou [*Bookkeeping*] [*Afrikaans*]
BOEKH ..... Boekhandel [*Book-Trade*] [*Afrikaans*]
BOeL .... Betrieb der Oertlichen Landwirtschaft [*Local Agricultural Enterprise*]   (EG)
BOE(S)...... Board of Examiners (Scaffolding) [*Victoria, Australia*]
BOESEDBA ... Board of Examiners for Steam Engine Drivers and Boiler Attendants [*Victoria, Australia*]
BOE(WBPV) ... Board of Examiners (Welders of Boilers and Pressure Vessels) [*Victoria, Australia*]
BOF .... Australian Bank Officials' Federation
BOF .... Bofo [*Race of maize*] [*Mexico*]
BOFB .... Belgian Organisation for Fish Producers   (EAIO)
B of E .... Bank of England
BOFF .... Biafran Organization of Freedom Fighters
BofG........ Bank of Ghana
Bog .... Bogaz [*Straits, Gorge*]   (TU)
Bog .... Bogen [*Sheet*] [*Publishing*] [*German*]
BOG .... Bogota [*Colombia*] [*Airport symbol*]   (OAG)
BOG.......... Buero-Organisations-Gesellschaft [*German*]   (ADPT)
bogh .... Boghandel [*Book Trade, Bookstore*] [*Publishing Danish/Norwegian*]
Bogosl fak .. School of Theology   (BU)
bogtr.......... Bogtrykt [*Printed*] [*Publishing Danish/Norwegian*]
bohr........... Bohren [*Drill*] [*German*]   (GCA)
Bohr .... Bohrung [*Drilling*] [*German*]   (GCA)
Bohrg .... Bohrung [*Drilling*] [*German*]   (GCA)
BOI .... Aboitiz Air Transport Corp. [*Philippines*] [*ICAO designator*]   (FAAC)
BOIA .... Bund Osterreichischer Innenarchitekten [*Austria*]   (EAIO)
BOJ........... Bank of Japan
BOJ........... Bourgas [*Bulgaria*] [*Airport symbol*]   (OAG)
BOK .... Bank of Korea
BOK .... Bulgarian Olympic Committee   (BU)
bokh .... Bokhandel [*Bookstore*] [*Sweden*]

bokhist ...... Bokhistoria [*History of Books*] [*Publishing*] [*Sweden*]
BOKhR ...... Combat Security Unit, Combat Outpost (RU)
BOKN .... Biuro Odzysku Kabli Nieeksploatowanych [*Office for the Recovery of Unused Cables*] (POL)
boktr .... Boktryckeri [*Printing Firm*] [*Sweden*]
Bol .... Big, Large, Great [*Topography*] (RU)
BOL .... Bojova Otravna Latka [*Chemical Warfare Agent*] (CZ)
bol .... Boletim [*Bulletin*] [*Portuguese*]
BOL .... Bolita [*Race of maize*] [*Mexico*]
BOL .... Bolivia [*ANSI three-letter standard code*] (CNC)
BOL .... Bombardovace Letectvo [*Bomber Airforce*] (CZ)
Bol .... Swamp [*Topography*] (RU)
BOL .... Transportes Aeros Boliviands [*Bolivia*] [*ICAO designator*] (FAAC)
bolg .... Bulgarian (RU)
BOLMAQ ... Bolsa de Maquinaria Industrial Ltda. [*Colombia*] (COL)
BOLMM ... Brothers of Our Lady, Mother of Mercy [*Netherlands*] (EAIO)
bol'n .... Hospital [*Topography*] (RU)
BOLO .... Bilingual Obstetric Liaison Officer
BOLP .... Bydgoski Okreg Lasow Panstwowych [*Bydgoszcz State Forest District*] (POL)
BOLSA ...... Bank of London and South America
BOLSAMED ... Bolsa de Medellin SA (COL)
BOLSIPLAS ... Fabrica de Bolsas Plasticas [*Colombia*] (COL)
BOM .... Bank of Melbourne [*Australia*]
BOM .... Base Oceanologique de Mediterranee [*Mediterranean Oceanographic Base*] [*French*] (MSC)
BOM .... Bombay [*India*] [*Airport symbol*] (OAG)
BOM .... Bureau d'Organisation et de Methode [*Organization and Methods Office*] [*Senegal*] (AF)
BOM .... Bureau of Meteorology [*Australia*]
BOM .... Service Aerien Gouvernmental Ministere des Transports Gouvernment du Quebec [*Canada ICAO designator*] (FAAC)
BOMA .... Bois et Materiaux
BOMA .... Building Owners and Managers Association of Australia
BOMAA .... Building Owners and Managers' Association of Australia
BOMAS ..... Bobin ve Masura Sanayi ve Ticaret Anonim Sirketi [*Bobbin and Shuttle Industry and Trade Corporation*] (TU)
BOMEX .... Barbados Oceanographic and Meteorological Experiment (PDAA)
BOMREP ... Bombing Report [*Military*]
BOMZh ..... Without Fixed Residence (RU)
BON .... Bank of Nauru
Bon .... Baron [*Baron*] [*French*] (MTD)
Bon .... Bataillon [*Battalion*] [*Military*] [*French*] (MTD)
BON .... Bonaire [*Netherland Antilles*] [*Airport symbol*] (OAG)
Bon .... Buisson [*Thicket*] [*Military map abbreviation World War I*] [*French*] (MTD)
Bon .... Buron [*Cheese Factory*] [*Military map abbreviation World War I*] [*French*] (MTD)
Bona .... Ballonnachrichtenabteilung [*Balloon Communication Battalion*] [*German*]
BONA .... Bonneterie de l'Agneby
BONAC ..... Broadcasting Organizations of Non-Aligned Countries (EY)
BONC .... Broadcasting Organizations of Non-Aligned Countries [*Belgrade, Yugoslavia*] (EAIO)
BOND .... Buro vir Ondersteunende Navorsingsdienste [*Human Sciences Research Council*] [*South Africa*] (AA)
BO-Niger ... Societe de Promotion des Boissons Hygieniques du Niger
Bon Mem ... Bonae Memoriae [*of Happy Memory*] [*Reference to a deceased person*] [*Latin*] (BARN)
BONMOT ... Sinnspruche, Aphorismen, und Lebensweisheiten [*Mottos, Aphorisms, and Witticisms*] [*Society for Business Information*] [*Information service or system*] (IID)
Bonne .... Baronne [*Baroness*] [*French*] (MTD)
Bonnet .... Baronne [*Baroness*] [*French*] (BARN)
BONOT ..... Bulgarian Organization for the Scientific Organization of Labor (BU)
BONSF ..... Bulgarian National Students Federation (BU)
BONSS ..... Bulgarian National Students Union (BU)
BOO .... Bodo [*Norway*] [*Airport symbol*] (OAG)
BOOC .... Barcelona Olympic Organizing Committee [*Spain*] (EAIO)
BOP .... Berufsverband Oesterreichischer Psychologen [*Professional Association of Austrian Psychologists*] (SLS)
BOP .... Bezpieczenstwo i Ochrona Pracy [*Industrial Safety*] (POL)
BOP .... Biuro Odbudowy Portow [*Office of Port Reconstruction*] (POL)
BOP .... Bop Air (Pty) Ltd. [*South Africa*] [*ICAO designator*] (FAAC)
BOP .... Brigade de l'Ordre Publique [*Public Order Brigade*] [*Tunisia*] (AF)
BOP .... Budget, Accounting, and Enterprises (BU)
BOP .... Bureau of Post [*Philippines*] (DS)
BOP .... Office for the Organization of Production (RU)
BOP .... Office of Operational Planning (RU)
BOP .... White Sea-Onega Steamship Line (RU)
BOPA .... Botswana Press Agency

BO PEEP ... Bangor [*Wales*] Orange Position Estimating Equipment for Pastures [*Electronic beepers attached to sheep*] (ADA)
BOPLAS ... Botellas Plasticas Ltda. [*Colombia*] (COL)
b opr .... Bez Oprawy [*Unbound*] [*Poland*]
BOPR .... Bureau d'Organisation des Programmes Ruraux
BOptometry ... Bachelor of Optometry
BOQ .... Bank of Queensland Ltd.
BOQ .... Boku [*Papua New Guinea*] [*Airport symbol*] [*Obsolete*] (OAG)
BOR .... Banco de la Republica [*Bank of the Republic*] [*Colorado*] (LA)
BOR .... Belfort [*France*] [*Airport symbol*] (OAG)
BOR .... Board of Optical Registration [*South Australia and Tasmania*]
BOR .... Board of Optometrical Registration [*New South Wales, Australia*]
Bor .... Borneo
BOR .... Budowa Osiedli Robotniczych [*Workers' Settlement Construction Office*] (POL)
BOR .... Flash-Ranging Battery (RU)
BOR .... Orion Air [*Bulgaria*] [*ICAO designator*] (FAAC)
BOR .... Recoilless Gun (RU)
BORCO ..... Bahamas Oil Refining Company (LA)
BORD .... Bordereau [*Statement*] [*French*] [*Business term*]
Bord .... Borduere [*Border*] [*Publishing*] [*German*]
bord .... Bordure [*Ornamental Border*] [*Publishing*] [*French*]
BORDOSZ ... Boripari Dolgozok Szakszervezete [*Trade Union of Workers in the Leather Industry*] (HU)
Bordradist ... Ship's Radio Operator (BU)
Borforg V ... Borforgalmi Vallalat [*Leather Trade Enterprise*] (HU)
BORG .... Basic Operational Requirements and Planning Criteria Group [*ICAO*] (DA)
BORIF .... Bogor Research Institute for Food Crops [*Indonesia*] [*Research center*] (IRC)
bormill .... Borneo United Sawmills [*Southeast Asia*] [*Commercial firm*]
bornetegn ... Boernetegning [*Child's Scribbling*] [*Publishing Danish/ Norwegian*]
BORO .... Biuro Obslugi Ruchu Turystycznego [*Tourist Movement Service Bureau*] (POL)
BORSA ...... Budget Orientiertes Rechnungswesen fuer Staatliche Aufgaben [*German*] (ADPT)
BOR-SAN ... Boru Sanayi [*Pipe Manufacturing Industry*] [*Turkish Cypriot*] (TU)
BORTAN .. Bordeaux-Tananarive
BORUSAN ... Boru Sanayi Sirketi [*Pipe Industry Corporation*] (TU)
BOS .... Bank of Singapore
BOS .... Bau- und Betriebsordnung fuer Schmalspurbahnen [*Construction and Operating Regulations for Narrow-Gauge Railroads*] (EG)
BOS .... Biuro Odbudowy Stolicy [*Office for the Reconstruction of Warsaw (1945-1947)*] (POL)
BOS .... Bloque Opositora del Sur [*Costa Rica*] (EY)
BOS .... Board of Studies [*New South Wales, Australia*]
BOs .... Borbeno Osiguranje [*Combat Security*] (YU)
BOS .... Bosal International Management NV [*Belgium*] [*ICAO designator*] (FAAC)
BOS .... Burgas Oblast Court (BU)
BOS .... Coastal Convoy Detachment [*Navy*] (RU)
BOS .... Feedback Unit [*Computers*] (RU)
BOS .... Northern Coast Defense (RU)
BOS .... Silkworm Experimental Station (BU)
BOSA .... Beplande Ouerskapvereniging van Suiderlike Afrika [*South Africa*] (AA)
BOSCAM ... Bouygues Offshore Cameroon
BOSEX ...... Baltic Open Sea Experiment [*ICSU*]
BOSIC .... Bosch Symbolischer Instruktions-Code [*German*] (ADPT)
BOSLO ...... Board of Studies Liaison Officer [*New South Wales, Australia*]
bosm .... Bosman [*Boatswain*] [*Poland*]
BOSNABARIT ... Bosnian Barite Mine [*Velika Kladusa, BiH*] (YU)
Bosna-Coop ... Bosnian Export-Import Establishment [*Sarajevo*] (YU)
BOSNALIJEK ... Preduzece za Proizvodnju Lijekova [*Bosnian Pharmaceutical Establishment*] [*Sarajevo*] (YU)
BOSNAMETAL ... Bosnian Metallurgical Factory [*Sarajevo*] (YU)
BOSNATRANSPORT ... Udruzenje Transportnih Preduzeca [*Bosnian Association of Transport Establishments*] [*Sarajevo*] (YU)
BOSOM .... Bogotana Sombrerera Ltda. [*Colombia*] (COL)
BOSS .... Basic Operating System Software [*Toshiba Corp.*] [*Japan*]
BOSS .... Bureau of State Security [*South Africa*] (AF)
BOT .... Air Botswana (Pty) Ltd. [*ICAO designator*] (FAAC)
BOT .... Bank of Thailand (IMH)
BOT .... Bank of Tokyo
BOT .... Biuro Obslugi Turystycznej [*Tourist Service Bureau*] (POL)
BOT .... Board of Thailand (DS)
BOT .... Board of Transport [*NATO*] (NATG)
BOt .... Bojni Otrovi [*Poison Gases*] [*Military*] (YU)
Bot .... Botanica [*Botany*] [*Portuguese*]
bot .... Botanie [*Botany*] [*Afrikaans*]
Bot .... Botanik [*Botany*] [*German*] (GCA)
bot .... Botanika [*Botany*] (HU)

bot .... Botanique [*French*]   (TPFD)
bot .... Botanisch [*Botanical*] [*German*]   (GCA)
bot .... Botany, Botanical   (BU)
BOT .... Build-Operate-Transfer [*Infrastructual project developed by the Turkish government*]
BOT .... Butoxytoluene   (RU)
BOTA .... Bank of Tokyo Australia Ltd.
BOTAS ..... Beynelmilel Otelcilik Turk Anonim Sirketi [*International Hotel Management Corporation*]   (TU)
BOTAS ..... Boru Hatlari ile Petrol Tasima Anonim Sirketi [*Pipe Lines and Petroleum Transport Corporation*]   (TU)
BOTE .... Budapest Orvostudomany Egyetem [*Budapest Medical University*]   (HU)
BOTIC ...... Bankarski, Osiguravajuci, Trgovacki, i Industriski Cinovnici [*Bank, Insurance, Commercial, and Industrial Employees*]   (YU)
BOTiI .... Biuro Obslugi Turystycznej i Informacji [*Tourist Service and Information Bureau*] [*Poland*]
BOTOCOL ... Fabrica de Botones de Colombia [*Colombia*]   (COL)
BOTOSTROJ ... Narodni Podnik pro Vyrobu Obuvnickych Stroju [*National Enterprise for the Manufacture of Shoe Machinery*]   (CZ)
BOTP .... Base Operacional de Tropas Paraquedistas [*Paratroopers Operational Base*] [*Air Force*] [*Portugal*]
BOTP .... Belugyminiszterium, Orszagos Tuzrendeszeti Parancsnoksag [*Ministry of the Interior, National Fire Protection Headquarters*]   (HU)
BOTREST ... Botswana Rest [*Mined by Anglo-American Corporation of South Africa*]
BOTU .... Botswana Teachers Union
BOTUB ..... Office for Protection of Labor and Improvement of Living Conditions   (RU)
BOU .... Bouraq Indonesia Airlines PT [*ICAO designator*]   (FAAC)
BOU .... Hopper Directing Device   (RU)
BOUK .... Boukunde [*Architecture*] [*Afrikaans*]
boul .... Boulevard [*Boulevard*] [*French*]
BOURP ..... White Sea-Onega Administration of River Steamship Lines   (RU)
BOUTM .... Biro za Organizaciju i Unapredenje Trgovinske Mreze [*Bureau for the Organization and Development of Commerce*]   (YU)
BOV .... Boang [*Papua New Guinea*] [*Airport symbol*]   (OAG)
bov .... Bovitett [*Enlarged*]   (HU)
BOV .... Chemical Warfare Agent   (RU)
BOV .... "Let Us Rest Joyfully" [*Slogan*]   (RU)
BOVAG ..... Bond van Automobiel-, Garage- en Aanverwante Bedrijven [*Benelux*]   (BAS)
BOVESPA ... Bolsa de Valores de Sao Paulo [*Sao Paulo Stock Exchange*] [*Brazil*]   (LA)
BOW .... Biuro Odszkodowan Wojennych [*War Compensation Bureau*] [*POL*]
BOWA .... Brisbane Overseas Wharfowners' Association [*Australia*]
BOWAL .... Documentatiepool Verontreiniging Bodem, Water, en Lucht [*Netherlands*]
BOWOF .... Bundesverband Osterreichischer Widerstandskampfer und Opfer des Faschismus [*Association of Former Resistance Fighters and Victims of Fascism*] [*Austria*]   (EAIO)
BOX .... Borroloola [*Airport symbol*]
BOY .... Bobo-Dioulasso [*Burkina Faso*] [*Airport symbol*]   (OAG)
boyepit .... Ammunition Supply   (RU)
boyn .... Slaughterhouse, Abattoir [*Topography*]   (RU)
BOYSNC ... Beginning of Year Significant NonCompliers [*Environment*]   (GNE)
Boy-szolg ... Boy-Szolgalat ["*Boy*" *Messenger Service*]   (HU)
BOZ .... Bank of Zambia
BP .... Action Station, Battle Station   (RU)
BP .... Ammunition   (RU)
BP .... Armored Train   (RU)
BP .... Bachiller Profesional [*Academic degree*] [*Spanish*]
BP .... Badan Pimpinan [*Executive Committee*]   (IN)
BP .... Balai Polis [*Police Station*]   (ML)
BP .... Balisticka Planseta [*Ballistic Board*] [*Army*]   (YU)
BP .... Ballistic Converter   (RU)
BP .... Bank Polski [*Bank of Poland*]
BP .... Basse Pression [*Low Pressure*] [*French*]
B-P .... Basses-Pyrenees [*French*]
BP .... Bassposaune [*Bass Trombone*] [*Music*]
BP .... Bataillon Parachutiste [*Parachute Battalion*] [*Cambodia*]   (CL)
BP .... Bayernpartei [*Bavarian Party*] [*Germany*] [*Political party*]   (PPE)
BP .... Bedienungspult [*German*]   (ADPT)
Bp .... Bendicion Papal [*Papal Benediction*] [*Spanish*]
BP .... Bereitschaftspolizei [*Alert Police*] [*German*]   (EG)
BP .... Beschleunigter Personenzug [*Express Passenger Train*] [*German*]
BP .... Betriebspreis [*Enterprise Price*] [*German*]   (EG)
BP .... Bezne Prohlidky [*Customary Inspections*]   (CZ)
BP .... Biblioteca Publica [*Public Library*] [*Portuguese*]
BP .... Bibliotheksprogramm [*German*]   (ADPT)

BP .... BIOSIS Previews [*Information retrieval*]
BP .... Birlik Partisi [*Unity Party - UP*] [*TBP*] [*See also*]   (TU)
bp .... Biskup [*Bishop*] [*Poland*]
BP .... Biuro Planowania [*Planning Office*]   (POL)
BP .... Biuro Polityczne [*Political Bureau*]   (POL)
BP .... Biuro Projektowania [*Planning Office*]   (POL)
bp .... Blogoslawionej Pamieci [*Of Blessed Memory*] [*Poland*]
BP .... Boeren Partij [*Farmers' Party*] [*Netherlands*] [*Political party*]   (PPE)
BP .... Boite Postale [*Post Office Box*] [*French*]
BP .... Bolsevik Part [*Bolshevik Party*]   (HU)
BP .... Bomb Run [*Aviation*]   (RU)
b/p .... Borbeni Poredak [*Combat Formation*]   (YU)
BP .... British Petroleum [*British*]   (OMWE)
BP .... Britis Petrol [*British Petroleum*]   (TU)
BP .... Budapest [*Budapest*]   (HU)
BP .... Buergerpartei [*Citizens' Party*] [*Germany*] [*Political party*]   (PPE)
BP .... Buitenlandsch Personenrecht [*Benelux*]   (BAS)
BP .... Bulgarian Press   (BU)
BP .... Bundespost [*German*]   (ADPT)
Bp .... Bunteto Perrendtartas [*Code of Criminal Procedure*]   (HU)
bp .... Buono Per [*Good For*] [*Italian*]
BP .... Bureau of Weather Forecasts   (RU)
BP .... Burundi Populaire
BP .... Carry Unit   (RU)
BP .... Close-In Homing Radio Station   (RU)
BP .... Combat Training   (RU)
BP .... Drum Switch, Barrel Switch   (RU)
BP .... Field Battery   (RU)
BP .... Float Tank   (RU)
BP .... High-Speed Potentiometer   (RU)
BP .... Lateral Displacement [*Navy*]   (RU)
bp .... Non-Party, Non-Party Man   (RU)
BP .... Operation Order, Combat Order   (RU)
BP .... Partai Bumiputra [*Party of Indigenous Peoples*]   (ML)
BP .... Power Supply Unit, Supply Unit   (RU)
BP .... Program Unit   (RU)
BP .... Storage Unit, Memory Unit [*Computers*]   (RU)
b/p .... Unbound   (RU)
BP .... Unconditional Transfer [*Computers*]   (RU)
BP .... Weather Bureau   (RU)
BPA .... Back Pain Association [*British*] [*Research center*]   (EAIO)
BPA .... Bahn Post Amt [*Railway Post Office*] [*German*]
BPA .... Bahrain Pediatric Association   (EAIO)
BPA .... Banco Portugues do Atlantico [*Portuguese Bank of the Atlantic*]   (ECON)
BPA .... Bank Pembangunan Asia [*Asia Development Bank*]   (ML)
BPA .... Berufsverband der Praktischen Aerzte und Aerzte fuer Allgemeinmedizin Deutschlands eV [*Professional Association of General Practitioners and Doctors for General Medicine of Germany*]   (SLS)
BPA .... Betriebsplanungsausschuss [*Enterprise Planning Committee*]   (EG)
BPA .... Black Parents Association
BPA .... Board of Petroleum Affairs [*Sudan*]   (IMH)
BPA .... Bouake-Pieces d'Autos
BPA .... British Pediatric Association   (BARN)
BPa .... Buergerpartei [*Citizens' Party*] [*Germany*] [*Political party*]   (PPW)
BPA .... Bundespresse- und Informationsamt [*Federal Press and Information Office*]   (WEN)
BPA .... Bureau Permanent des Actions [*German*]   (ADPT)
BPA .... Bush Pilots Airways Ltd. [*Australia*]   (ADA)
BPANZ ...... Book Publishers Association of New Zealand   (EAIO)
BPAO .... Societe des Petroles BP d'Afrique Occidentale
B Para .... Bataillon Parachutiste [*Parachute Battalion*] [*Cambodia*]   (CL)
BPAT .... Bakers and Pastrycooks' Association of Tasmania [*Australia*]
BPAV .... Bus Proprietors' Association, Victoria [*Australia*]
BPB .... Badan Perdjoangan Buruh [*Board for the Defense of Labor Interest*] [*Indonesian*]
BPB .... Balai Polis Bergerak [*Mobile Police Station*]   (ML)
BPB .... Battalion Ammunition Supply Point   (RU)
BPB .... Benutzerprogramm-bibliothek [*German*]   (ADPT)
BPBK .... Biuro Projektow Budownictwa Komunalnego [*Communal Construction Plans Office*]   (POL)
BPBM .... Badan Pembagian Bahan Makanan [*Food Distribution Board*]   (IN)
BPBM .... Biuro Projektow Budownictwa Morskiego [*Maritime Construction Plans Office*]   (POL)
BPBS .... Band/Platte Betriebssystem [*German*]   (ADPT)
BPC .... Barbados Peace Commission   (LA)
BPC .... Basic People's Congress
BPC .... Basrah Petroleum Company   (ME)
BPC .... Bataillon de Parachutistes Coloniaux
BPC .... Black People's Convention [*South Africa*]   (PD)

BPC............ Black Protest Committee [*Australia*]
BPC............ Bombay Productivity Council [*India*]
BPC............ Botswana Power Corporation
BPC............ Brigade Parachutiste de Choc [*Algeria*]
BPCAFVS ... Bookseller and Publisher Cooperative for Agricultural, Food and Veterinary Sciences [*Italy*]   (EAIO)
BPCC......... Bamburi Portland Cement Company Ltd.
BPCh .... Intermediate-Frequency Unit   (RU)
BPCISGH ... Bureau Permanent des Congres Internationaux des Sciences Genealogique et Heral dique [*Permanent Bureau of International Congresses for the Sciences of Genealogy and Heraldry*] [*Denmark*]   (EAIO)
BPCL......... Bharat Petroleum Corp. Ltd.
BPCTN...... Bureau de Planification des Cadres Techniques Nationaux [*Bureau of Planning for National Technical Cadres*] [*Zaire*]   (AF)
BPCU......... Bakers, Pastrycooks, and Confectioners Union [*Australia*]
BPD .... Badan Produksi Daerah [*Regional Production Board*]   (IN)
BPD .... Banco Popular de Desenvolvimento [*People's Development Bank*] [*Mozambique*]   (AF)
BPD .... Bank Pembangunan Daerah [*Regional Development Bank*]   (IN)
bpd .... Barrel per Day   (OMWE)
BPD .... Blocul Partidelor Democratice [*Bloc of Democratic Parties*]   (RO)
BPD .... Bloque Popular Democratico [*Popular Democratic Bloc*] [*Venezuela*]   (LA)
BPD .... Bombrini Parodi-Delfino [*Italy*]   (PDAA)
BPD .... Data Acquisition Unit   (RU)
BPD .... Program-Transducer Unit   (RU)
BPDC........ Bardon Professional Development Centre [*Australia*]
BPDK........ Bakanlik Planlama Danisma Kurulu [*Ministry Planning and Advisory Council*]   (TU)
BPDK........ Unit of Conversion to an Auxiliary Code   (RU)
BPDO .... Bath, Laundry, and Disinfection Service   (RU)
BPDP .... Bath, Laundry, and Disinfection Train   (RU)
BPE........... Bureau du Projet Education
BPEAR ..... Bureau for the Placement and Education of African Refugees
BPENC...... Bulgarian PEN Centre   (EAIO)
BPEQ .... Board of Professional Engineers of Queensland [*Australia*]
BPERA ...... Bureau de Placement et d'Education des Refugies Africains [*Bureau for the Placement and Education of African Refugees - BPEAR*]
Bpest .... Budapest [*Budapest*]   (HU)
BPF .... Belgian Petroleum Federation
BPF .... Bezirks-Post und Fernmeldeamt [*District Postal and Telecommunications Office*]   (EG)
BPF .... Bon pour Francs [*Value in Francs*] [*French*]
BPF .... Bureau de Prospection Forestiere
BPF .... Byelorussian Popular Front [*Political party*]
BPFNA ..... Baptist Peace Fellowship of North America   (EAIO)
BPFP .... Bechuanaland Protectorate Federal Party [*Botswana*]
BPG .... Balai Pendidikan Guru [*Teacher Training School*]   (IN)
BPGF .... Banque Privee de Gestion Financiere [*Bank*] [*France*]
BPGN .... Badan Pendjualan Gula Negara [*State Sugar Sales Board*]   (IN)
BPH .... Badan Pemerintah Harian [*Government Standing Committee (DPRD executive committee)*]   (IN)
BPH .... Balai Penelitian Hutan [*Forest Research Institute*] [*Indonesian*]   (ARC)
BPH .... Bislig [*Philippines*] [*Airport symbol*]   (OAG)
BPHH....... Balai Penelitian Hasil Hutan [*Forest Products Research Institute*] [*Indonesian*]   (ARC)
BPHR .... Bureau of Ports, Harbors, and Reclamation [*Philippines*]   (DS)
BPhysio..... Bachelor of Physiotherapy
BPI............. Banco Portugues do Investimento [*Portuguese Investment Bank*]
BPI............. Bank Pembangunan Indonesia [*Indonesian Development Bank*]   (IN)
BPI............. Belorussian Polytechnic Institute   (RU)
BPI............. Bernard Price Institute of Geophysical Research
BPI............. Bernard Price-Instituut vir Paleontologiese Navorsing [*Bernard Price Institute for Palaeontological Research*] [*University of Witwatersrand*] [*South Africa*]   (AA)
BPI............. Bibliotheque Publique d'Information [*France*]
bp-i............ Budapesti [*Of Budapest*] [*Hungary*]   (GPO)
BPI............. Burma Pharmaceutical Industry   (DS)
BPICA .... Bureau Permanent International des Constructeurs d'Automobiles [*International Permanent Bureau of Motor Manufacturers*]   (EAIO)
BPICM ...... Bureau Permanent International des Constructeurs de Motocycles [*Permanent International Bureau of Motorcycle Manufacturers*]   (EAIO)
BPID......... Bloque Parlamentario de Izquierda Democratica [*Democratic Left Parliamentary Bloc*] [*Ecuador*]   (LA)
BPIEC .... Beijing Publications Import & Export Corp.
BPIF .... British Printing Industries' Federation   (DCTA)
BPIF .... Brunei People's Independence Front [*Political party*]   (FEA)
BPIL .... British Practice in International Law   (FLAF)
BPIT .... Bureau de Promotion Industrielle du Tchad [*Chad*]

BPITT........ Bureau Permanent Inter-Africain de la Tse-Tse et de la Trypanosomiase
bpk .... Antisubmarine Ship Brigade   (BU)
BPK........... Badan Pemeriksa Keuangan [*Financial Audits Agency*]   (IN)
BPK........... Barisan Pemadam Kebakaran [*Fire Department*]   (IN)
BPK........... Bataljonski Partiski Komitet [*Battalion Party Committee*]   (YU)
Bpk........... Beperk [*Limited*] [*South Africa*] [*Business term*]   (AF)
BPK........... Biochemical Oxygen Requirement   (RU)
BPK........... Biological Oxygen Intake   (RU)
BPK........... Boulangerie Patisserie de N'Kembo
BPK........... Bulgarska Partia Komunistyczna [*Bulgarian Communist Party*]   (POL)
BPK........... Direct-Flow Boiler Construction Office   (RU)
BPK........... Office of Steam Boilers   (RU)
BPKB .... Badan Pembina Kesatuan Bangsa [*Committee for the Advancement of National Unity*]   (IN)
BPKBA ..... Badan Penolong Korban Bentjana Alam [*Committee for Assisting Victims of Natural Disasters*]   (IN)
BPKD .... Bakanlik Planlama ve Koordinasyon Dairesi [*Ministry Planning and Coordination Office*]   (TU)
BPKI .... Badan Penjelidikan Karet Indonesia [*Indonesia Rubber Research Council*]   (IN)
BPKK....... Bezirks-Partei-Kontroll-Kommission [*District Party Control Commission*]   (EG)
BPKR .... Badan Penampungan Karet Rakjat [*Smallholders Rubber Collection Agency*]   (IN)
BPL........... Baterie Proti Letadlum [*Antiaircraft Battery*]   (CZ)
BPL........... Bedrijfspensionenfonds voor de Landbouw [*Benelux*]   (BAS)
BPL........... Betriebsparteileitung [*Enterprise Party Management*]   (EG)
BPL........... Bone Phosphate Lime
BPL........... Budowniczy Polski Ludowej [*Builder of People's Poland (Award)*]   (POL)
bpl .... Submarine Brigade   (RU)
B-Plan....... Bahnhofs-Bedienungs Plan [*Station Service Plan*]   (EG)
BPLSA...... Bird Protection League of South Australia
BPM .... Barbuda People's Movement [*Antigua*] [*Political party*]   (PD)
BPM .... Battafsche Petroleum Maatschappij [*Benelux*]   (BAS)
BPM .... Battalion Medical Aid Station   (RU)
BPM .... Biuro Pokazu Mody [*Fashion Show Office*]   (POL)
BPM .... Biuro Projektow Miejskich [*Bureau of Municipal Projects*]   (POL)
BpM........... Buchstaben pro Minute [*Letters per Minute*]   (EG)
BPMA....... Brisbane Produce Merchants' Association [*Australia*]
BPMD ...... Balai Pendidikan Masjarakat Desa [*Village Community Training School*]   (IN)
BPME....... Banco de la Pequena y Mediana Empresa [*Spain*]   (EY)
BPN .... Balikpapan [*Indonesia*] [*Airport symbol*]   (OAG)
BPN .... Bureau Politique National [*National Political Bureau*]   (AF)
BPN .... Conversion Voltage Unit   (RU)
BPNC....... Ba'th Party National Command   (ME)
BPNH....... Biuro Projektow Nowej Huty [*Office of Plans for Nowa Huta Metallurgical Center*]   (POL)
BPO .... Bath and Laundry Detachment   (RU)
BPO .... Betriebsparteiorganisation [*Plant Party Organization*]   (EG)
BPP........... Balai Penelitian Perkebunan [*Research Institute for Estate Crops*] [*Bogor, Indonesia*]   (ARC)
BPP........... Bath and Laundry Train   (RU)
BPP........... Battalion Small-Arms Ammunition Supply Point   (RU)
BPP........... Beach Protection Program [*Australia*]
BPP........... Bechuanaland People's Party
BPP........... Belize Popular Party [*Political party*]   (EY)
BPP........... Bhutan People's Party [*Political party*]
BPP........... Black People's Party [*South Africa*] [*Political party*]   (PPW)
BPP........... Bojova a Politicka Priprava [*Combat and Political Training*]   (CZ)
BPP........... Border Patrol Police [*Thai-Malaysia border*]   (ML)
BPP........... Borge Prien Prove [*Danish intelligence test*]
BPP........... Botswana People's Party [*Political party*]   (PPW)
BPP........... Budowlane Przedsiebiorstwo Powiatowe [*County Construction Enterprise*]   (POL)
BPP........... Interrupt Unit   (RU)
BPP........... Office for Planning Preparation   (RU)
BPP........... Variable-Conductance Unit   (RU)
BPPB .... Balai Penjelidikan Perkebunan Besar Research Institute for Estate Crops [*Indonesia*]   (DSCA)
BPPB .... Banque de Paris et des Pays-Bas
BPPBG ..... Banque de Paris et des Pays-Bas Gabon
BPPBM .... Belgian Pulp, Paper and Board Association   (EAIO)
BPPI .... Badan Pembangunan Perindustrian Indonesia [*Indonesian Industrial Development Board*]   (IN)
BPPL .... Biuro Planow Perspektywicznych Lacznosci [*Communications Long-Range Planning Office*]   (POL)
BPPM........ Balai Penelitian Perkebunan Medan [*Sumatra Planters Association Research Institute*] [*Indonesian*]   (ARC)
BPPOV...... Bud Pripraven k Praci a Obrane Vlasti [*Be Prepared for Work and for National Defense (Badge)*]   (CZ)

BPPP .... Office for Planning the Preparation of Production (RU)
BPPS .... Bangladesh Paribar Parikalpana Samity [*Family Planning Association of Bangladesh*] (EAIO)
BPR .... Badan Penchegah Rasuah [*Agency to Prevent Corruption*] (ML)
BPR .... Biro za Posredovanje Rada [*Employment Agency*] (YU)
BPR .... Bloque Popular Revolucionario [*Popular Revolutionary Bloc*] [*El Salvador*] (PD)
BPr .... Bulgarski Pregled [*Bulgarian Review*] [*A periodical*] (BU)
BPR .... Live Ammunition (BU)
BPr .... Translator's Note (BU)
BPRA .... Book Publishers Representatives in Australia (ADA)
BPRC .... Baath Party Regional Command [*Iraq*]
BPRM .... Close-In Homing Radio Beacon (RU)
BPRS .... Badan Pembrontak Raayat Sabah [*Sabah People's Rebellion Organization*] (ML)
BPRS .... Short-Range Homing Radio Station (BU)
BPS .... Banco de Prevision Social [*Social Security Bank*] [*Uruguay*] (LA)
BPS .... Benelux Phlebology Society (EA)
BPS .... Biro Pusat Statistik [*Central Bureau of Statistics*] (IN)
BPS .... Bloc Populaire Senegalais [*Senegal*] (PPW)
BPS .... Bloc Progressiste Senegalais [*Senegal*]
BPS .... Bratnia Pomoc Studentow [*Students' Fraternal Aid*] (POL)
BPS .... Brigada Pohranicni Straze [*Border Guard Brigade*] (CZ)
BPS .... Brigadas Proletarias Salvadorenas [*Salvadoran Proletariat Brigades*] (LA)
BPS .... Brygada Pracy Socjalistycznej [*Socialist Work Brigade*] [*Poland*] (LA)
BPS .... Buddhist Publication Society [*Multinational association based in Sri Lanka*] (EAIO)
BPS .... Burgas Court of Reconciliation (BU)
BPS .... Concrete-Rolling Stand (RU)
BPS .... Gasoline Transfer-Pumping Station (RU)
BPS .... Porto Seguro [*Brazil*] [*Airport symbol*] (OAG)
BPSA .... Bermuda Public Services Association
BPSANSW ... British Public Schools Association of New South Wales [*Australia*]
BPSG .... Black Priests' Solidarity Group [*South Africa*] (AF)
BPSH .... Bashkimet Profesionale te Shqiperise [*Union of Albanian Trade Unions*]
BPsy .... Bachelor of Psychology
BPT .... Balai Penelitian Ternak [*Research Institute of Animal Production*] [*Indonesia*] [*Research center*] (IRC)
BPT .... Bicentennial Park Trust [*Australia*]
BPT .... Tank-Support Battery (RU)
BPTC .... Bataljonski Protivtenkovski Cvor [*Battalion Antitank Center*] (YU)
BPTC-1 ...... Bataljonski Protivtenkovski Cvor 1 Bataljona [*First Battalion Antitank Center*] (YU)
BPTPM ..... Balai Penelitian Tanaman Pangan Maros [*Maros Research Institute for Food Crops*] [*Indonesian*] (ARC)
BPTRI .... Beijing Printing Technical Research Institute [*China*] (IRC)
BPTs .... Bulgarian Eastern Orthodox Church (BU)
BPTU .... Battalion Antitank Strongpoint (RU)
BPTWG ..... Book and Paper Trades Workers' Group [*Belgium*] (EAIO)
BPU .... Badan Pimpinan Umum [*General Management Board*] (IN)
BPU .... Basisprogrammierunter-stuetzung [*German*] (ADPT)
BPU .... Beijing Polytechnic University [*China*]
BPU .... Botswana Progressive Union
BPU .... Bumiputra Participation Unit [*Ministry of Trade and Industry*] [*Malaysia*]
BPU .... Combat Track Angle (RU)
BPU .... Gasoline Transfer-Pumping Unit (RU)
BPU .... High-Speed Printer (RU)
BPUAO ..... Coastal Battery Post for Artillery Fire Control (RU)
BPubAdmin ... Bachelor of Public Administration
BPubPol .... Bachelor of Public Policy
BPUI .... Badan Permusjawaratan Ummat Islam [*Moslem Community Consultative Council*] (IN)
BPV .... Banco Peruano de la Vivienda [*Peruvian Housing Bank*] (LAA)
BPV .... Buitenlandse Persvereniging [*Foreign Press Association*] [*Netherlands*] (WEN)
bpv .... Field Water Supply Battalion (RU)
BPVCh .... High-Frequency Supply Unit (RU)
BPVMAA ... Boiler and Pressure Vessel Manufacturers' Association of Australia
BPW .... Australian Federation of Business and Professional Women's Clubs (ADA)
BPW .... Wet Buitengewoon Pensioen [*Benelux*] (BAS)
BPWA .... Business and Professional Women's Association [*Bahamas*] (LA)
BPWC .... Business and Professional Women's Club [*Australia*]
BPWCP ..... Business and Professional Women's Club of Perth [*Australia*]
BPY .... Besalampy [*Madagascar*] [*Airport symbol*] (OAG)
BPZ .... Bocni Pochodova Zastita [*Forward March Screening Element*] (CZ)
BPZ .... Constant Delay Unit (RU)

BPZ .... March Flank Guard, March Flank Party (RU)
BPZB .... Bialostockie Przemyslowe Zjednoczenie Budowlane [*Bialystok Industrial Construction Association*] (POL)
BPZB .... Bielskie Przemyslowe Zjednoczenie Budowlane [*Bielsko Industrial Construction Association*] (POL)
BPZB .... Bydgoskie Przemyslowe Zjednoczenie Budowlane [*Bydgoszcz Industrial Construction Association*] (POL)
BPzH .... Bojova Pruzkumna Hl'dka [*Combat Reconnaissance Patrol*] (CZ)
BPzH .... Bojovy Pruzkum Hloubkovy [*Combat Reconnaissance in Depth*] (CZ)
BPZO .... Bud Pripraven k Zdravotnicke Obrane [*Be Prepared for Health Protection (Badge)*] (CZ)
BQKA .... Bashkimi Qendror i Kooperativave te Artizanatit [*Albanian*]
BQKK .... Bashkimi Qendror i Kooperativave te Konsumit [*Albanian*]
BQL .... Bank of Queensland Ltd. [*Australia*]
BQL .... Boulia [*Australia*] [*Airport symbol*] (OAG)
BQN .... Aguadilla [*Puerto Rico*] [*Airport symbol*] (OAG)
BQO .... Bouna [*Ivory Coast*] [*Airport symbol*] (OAG)
BQQ .... Barra [*Brazil*] [*Airport symbol*] (OAG)
Bque .... Banque [*Bank*] [*French*]
Bque .... Baraque [*Hut*] [*Military map abbreviation World War I*] [*French*] (MTD)
BQUE .... Barque [*Bark, Boat*] [*French*]
bque .... Barrique [*Barrel*] [*French*]
BR .... Armor-Piercing (RU)
Br .... Bachiller [*Bachelor*] [*Academic degree*] [*Spanish*]
BR .... Bacteriological Warfare Reconnaissance (BU)
BR .... Balance Relay (RU)
BR .... Ballistic Missile (RU)
BR .... Bandera Roja [*Red Flag*] [*Dominican Republic*] (LA)
BR .... Bandera Roja [*Red Flag*] [*Venezuela*] (LA)
BR .... Bank Rolny [*Agricultural Bank*] (POL)
br .... Baro [*Baron*] (HU)
BR .... Battalion Area (RU)
BR .... Battalion Radio Station (RU)
BR .... Battleship (RU)
BR .... Befehlsregister [*German*] (ADPT)
BR .... Betriebsrat [*Workers' Council*] (EG)
BR .... Bezpecnostni Rada [*Security Council*] [*United Nations*] (CZ)
br .... Bez Roku [*or Brak Roku*] [*No Date Given*] [*Poland*]
br .... Biezacy Rok [*or Biezacego Roku*] [*The Current Year*] (POL)
BR .... Biographical Register [*Australian National University*]
BR .... Blocking Relay, Locking Relay (RU)
BR .... Boksitni Rudnici [*Bauxite Mines*] (YU)
br .... Bradel [*A Cased Binding*] [*Publishing*] [*French*]
br .... Branch (EECI)
Br .... Brat [*Bratul, Bratu*] [*Branch, Arm Romanian*] (NAU)
BR .... Brazil [*ANSI two-letter standard code*] (CNC)
BR .... Brazilian Register [*Ship Classification Society of Brazil*] (DS)
BR .... Brazylia [*Brazil*] [*Poland*]
Br .... Brdo [*Brda*] [*Mountain(s) Former Yugoslavia*] (NAU)
Br .... Breedte [*Latitude*] [*Afrikaans*]
Br .... Breite [*Latitude*] [*German*]
Br .... Brennstoff [*Fuel*] [*German*] (GCA)
Br .... Brevete d'Etat-Major [*Of officer who has passed staff course*] [*French*] (MTD)
BR .... Brigadas Revolucionarias [*Revolutionary Brigades*] [*Portugal*] [*Political party*] (PPE)
Br .... Brigade [*Military*] [*French*] (MTD)
BR .... Brigate Rosse [*Red Brigades*] [*Italy*] (PD)
BR .... Brindisi [*Car registration plates*] [*Italian*]
BR .... British Aircraft Corp. Ltd. [*ICAO aircraft manufacturer identifier*] (ICAO)
Br .... Brits [*British*] [*Afrikaans*]
BR .... Britse Ryk [*British Empire*] [*Afrikaans*]
br .... Brochado [*Stitched in Paper Covers*] [*Publishing*] [*Portuguese*]
br .... Broche [*Stitched*] [*Publishing*] [*French*]
br .... Brochura [*Pamphlet*] [*Publishing*] [*Portuguese*]
br .... Brochure, Pamphlet (RU)
Br .... Broe(de)r [*Brother*] [*Afrikaans*]
Br .... Broj [*Number*] (YU)
Br .... Brom [*Bromine*] [*Chemical element*] [*German*]
Br .... Bromo [*Bromine*] [*Chemical element*] [*Portuguese*]
br .... Broschiert [*Sewn in Pamphlet Form*] [*German*]
Br .... Broschur [*Brochure Binding*] [*Publishing*] [*German*]
br .... Brossura [*Paper-Cover Binding*] [*Publishing*] [*Italian*]
br .... Brosura [*Brochure*] [*Hungary*]
br .... Broszura [*Pamphlet*] [*Publishing*] [*Poland*]
br .... Brothers (BU)
Br .... Broussaille [*Brushwood*] [*Military map abbreviation World War I*] [*French*] (MTD)
Br .... Bruder [*Brother*] [*German*]
Br .... Bruecke [*Bridge*] [*German*] (GCA)
Br .... Brutto [*Gross*] [*German*]
BR .... Buitenlandse Rechtstijdingen [*Benelux*] (BAS)

BR .... Bulgarian Register of Shipping (DS)
BR .... Bulletin de Renseignements [*Military*] [*French*] (MTD)
Br .... Burun [*Cape, Headland, Promontory, Point*] (TU)
BR .... Combat Reconnaissance, Combat Intelligence (RU)
BR .... Contactless Relay (RU)
BR .... Deployment Base (RU)
BR .... Editor's Note (BU)
BR .... Fast Reactor (RU)
Br .... Ford [*Topography*] (RU)
Br .... Gross Weight, Gross (RU)
br .... Number (BU)
BR .... Onboard Recording Device (RU)
BR .... Paper-Cutting Machine (RU)
BR .... Rapid Discharge Circuit (RU)
br .... Stone Blocks [*Road-paving material*] [*Topography*] (RU)
BR .... Wetboek van Burgerlijke Rechtsvordering [*Benelux*] (BAS)
BR .... Worker's Idleness (BU)
BRA .... Barreiras [*Brazil*] [*Airport symbol*] (OAG)
BRA .... Barrier Reef Airways [*Australia*]
BRA .... Base de Reparaciones de Aviacion [*Aviation Repair Base*] [*Cuba*] (LA)
BRA .... Bee Research Association [*Later, IBRA*]
BRA .... Bomber Replenishment Area [*Military*]
BRA .... Bougainville Revolutionary Army [*Papua New Guinea*] [*Political party*] (EY)
BRA .... Braathens South American & Far East Airtransport AS [*Norway*] [*ICAO designator*] (FAAC)
BRA .... Brazil [*ANSI three-letter standard code*] (CNC)
BRA .... Brigada Roja de Ajusticiamiento [*Red Execution Brigade*] [*Honduras*] (LA)
BRA .... Code Address Register Unit (RU)
BRAB........ Armor-Piercing Aerial Bomb (RU)
BRAB(DS) ... Armor-Piercing Aerial Bomb with Additional Velocity Component (RU)
brabr .... Coastal Artillery Rocket Brigade (BU)
BRACAN... Brazil and the Canary Islands [*Submarine telephone cable*] (PDAA)
BRACODI ... Societe des Brasseries de la Cote-D'Ivoire
BRACONGO ... Brasseries du Congo
BRACS ...... Broadcasting for Remote Aboriginal Communities Scheme [*Australia*]
BRACS ...... Budget Rent-a-Car Services [*Australia*]
BRADESCO ... Banco Brasileiro de Descontos SA [*Brazilian Discount Bank*] (LA)
bradi.......... Coastal Artillery-Rocket Division (BU)
BRADUNI ... Brasseries du Niger
BRAG .... Brigadna Artiljeriska Grupa [*Brigade Artillery Group*] (YU)
BRAIN...... Basic Research in Adaptive Intelligence [*EEC*]
BRAIN...... Bio-Oriented Technology Research Advancement Institution [*Japan*]
BRAL........ Bureau de Renseignements et d'Action, Londres [*Free French*]
BRALIM ... Bravarsko Limarsko Preduzece [*Locksmiths' and Plumbers' Establishment*] (YU)
BRALIMA ... Brasseries, Limonaderies, et Malteries Africaines
BRALUP ... Bureau of Resource Assessment and Land Use Planning
BR AM ...... British America (BARN)
BRAMS..... Broome Regional Aboriginal Medical Service [*Australia*]
BRANA ..... Brasserie Nationale [*Zaire*] (IMH)
Branc C...... Groupe de Brancardiers de Corps [*Military*] [*French*] (MTD)
BRANCOSTA ... Branco Costa & Compagnie
BRANIGER ... Societe des Brasseries du Niger
BRANOMA ... Societe des Brasseries du Nord-Marocain
BRANZ ..... Building Research Association of New Zealand (ERC)
brap........... Coastal Artillery-Rocket Regiment (BU)
Bras........... Brasil [*Brazil*] [*Portuguese*]
bras .... Brasileirismo [*Portuguese*]
bras .... Brasileiro [*Brazil*] [*Portuguese*]
BRASILPEC ... Sociedade Comercial de Fomento Agro Pecuario Ltd. [*Brazil*] (DSCA)
BRASIMBA ... Brasseries Simba [*Zaire*] (IMH)
BRASPETRO ... PETROBRAS Internacional SA [*PETROBRAS International, Inc.*] [*Rio De Janeiro, Brazil*] (LA)
BRASSIDER ... Empresa Brasileira de Siderurgia SA [*Brazil Steel Company, Inc.*] (LA)
braunfl....... Braunfleckig [*Brown-Spotted*] [*Publishing*] [*German*]
BRAV .... Radioactive Warfare Contaminant (BU)
BRAVOLTA ... Brasseries de Haute-Volta
BRAWICO ... Brandt, Willig & Co.
brazm .... Mine-Clearing Battalion (BU)
BRB .... Banque de la Republique du Burundi [*Bank of the Republic of Burundi*] (AF)
BRB .... Banque du Royaume du Burundi
BRB .... Barbados [*ANSI three-letter standard code*] (CNC)
BRB .... Barisan Rakyat Brunei [*Brunei People's Front*] (ML)
BRb .... Vonnis van de Burgerlijke Rechtbank [*Benelux*] (BAS)
BRBD .... Short-Range Ballistic Missile (RU)

BRBQ .... Building Registration Board of Queensland [*Australia*]
BR BUR..... British Burma
BRBWA..... Builders' Registration Board of Western Australia [*Australia*]
BRC .... Barley Research Council [*Australia*]
BRC .... Bautura Racoritoare Carbonata [*Carbonated Beverage*] (RO)
BRC .... Bookmakers' Revision Committee [*New South Wales, Australia*]
BRC .... Building Research Centre [*University of New South Wales*] [*Australia*]
BRC .... Bureau de Relations Commerciales
BRC .... San Carlos De Bariloche [*Argentina*] [*Airport symbol*] (OAG)
BRCC........ Barwon Regional Consultative Council [*Australia*]
BRCh........ Number Register [*Computers*] (RU)
BRCNSW.. Barley Research Committee, New South Wales [*Australia*]
Br Col........ Brevet-Colonel
BRCQ .... Barley Research Committee for Queensland [*Australia*]
BRCS .... Bahamas Red Cross Society (EAIO)
BRCSA ..... Barley Research Committee for South Australia
BRCWA..... Barley Research Committee for Western Australia
BRD .... Banque Rwandaise de Developpement [*Rwanda Development Bank*] (GEA)
BRD .... Bundesrepublik Deutschland [*Federal Republic of Germany*]
BRD .... Combat Reconnaissance Patrol (RU)
BRD .... Gunpowder Rocket Engines [*Rocket shells*] (BU)
BRDAC..... Building Research and Development Advisory Committee [*Australia*]
BRDD........ Long-Range Ballistic Missile (RU)
BRDE .... Banco Regional de Desenvolvimento do Extremo Sul [*Regional Development Bank*] [*Rio De Janeiro, Brazil*] (LA)
Bre.............. Barriere [*Barrier, Gate*] [*Military map abbreviation World War I*] [*French*] (MTD)
BRE .... Berridale [*Airport symbol*]
BRE .... Bremen [*Germany*] [*Airport symbol*] (OAG)
BRE .... Bulletin of Export Registration [*Export license*] [*Portugal*] (IMH)
bre .... Roentgen Equivalent Man (RU)
Brec........... Brecknockshire [*Wales*] (BARN)
Brech.......... Brechung [*Fracture*] [*German*] (GCA)
BRED .... Banque Regionale d'Escompte et de Depots [*Bank*] [*French*]
Bred........... Editor's Note (BU)
BREDA...... Bureau Regional pour l'Education en Afrique [*Regional Office for Education in Africa*] (AF)
BREDAT ... Breda Termomeccanica, SpA [*Nuclear energy*] [*Italian*] (NRCH)
bredrand... Bredrandig [*With Wide Margins*] [*Publishing*] [*Sweden*]
BReg .... Besluit van de Regent [*Benelux*] (BAS)
Brenn .... Brennerei [*Distillery*] [*German*] (GCA)
BRES .... Brigadas Revolucionarias Estudiantiles Salvadorenas [*Salvadoran Students Revolutionary Brigades*] (LA)
BRES .... Bryansk Regional Electric Power Plant (RU)
BRESP...... Combating Enemy Radio-Electronic Equipment (BU)
BRESP...... Countermeasures Against Electronic Warfare Weapons (RU)
BRESTCHAN ... Brest Subarea, Channel [*NATO*]
BRET........ Botswana Renewable Energy Technology Project [*Ministry of Mineral Resources and Water Affairs in cooperation with United States Agency for International Development*] [*Research center*]
BREVATOME ... Societe Francaise pour la Gestion des Brevets d'Application Nucleaire [*Nuclear energy*] [*French*] (NRCH)
Brev-Maj.... Brevet-Major
Brevo.......... Vorschriften fuer den Bremsdienst [*Braking Regulations*] (EG)
b-reya........ Battery (RU)
BRF........... Air Bravo [*Uganda*] [*ICAO designator*] (FAAC)
BRF........... Baltic Research Foundation [*Australia*] (EAIO)
BRF........... Belgisches Rundfunk- und Fernsehzentrum der Deutschsprachigen Gemeinschaft [*Broadcasting organization*] [*Belgium*] (EY)
BRF........... Bereich Rundfunk und Fernsehen [*Radio and Television Field*] (EG)
BRF........... Brigades Revolutionnaires Francaises [*Revolutionary French Brigades*] [*French*] (PD)
BRF........... Bulgarian River Fleet (BU)
BRF........... Physical Beryllium Reactor (RU)
BR-FAS .... Bandera Roja - Frente Americo Silva [*Red Flag - Americo Silva Front*] [*Venezuela*] (LA)
BRFEF....... Bureau de la Repression de Fraudes Economiques et Financieres [*Economic and Financial Crimes Repression Office*] [*Cambodia*] (CL)
BRFK........ Budapesti Rendor Fokapitanysag [*Budapest Police Headquarters*]
BRFKGTO ... Bulgarian Republic Physical Culture Program "Ready for Labor and Defense" (BU)
BRG .... Betriebsraetegesetz [*Law Concerning Workers' Councils*] (EG)
BRG .... Budapesti Radiotechnikai Gyar [*Budapest Radio Technology Factory*] (HU)
BRG-FAR ... Bases de Reparaciones Generales de las Fuerzas Armadas Revolucionarias [*Revolutionary Armed Forces General Repair Depots*] [*Cuba*] (LA)

BRGM .... Base de Reparaciones Generales de Municiones [*General Munitions Repair Base*] [*Cuba*]   (LA)

BRGM .... Bureau de Recherches Geologiques et Minieres [*Bureau of Geological and Mining Exploration*] [*French*]   (WER)

BRGM .... Bureau de Recherches Geologiques et Minieres [*Bureau of Geological and Mining Research*] [*Burkina Faso*] [*Information service or system*]   (IID)

BRgt .... Besluit van de Regent [*Benelux*]   (BAS)

BRH .... Banque de la Republique d'Haiti [*Bank of the Republic of Haiti*]   (GEA)

BRH .... Belgische Rechtspraak in Handelszaken [*Belgium*]   (BAS)

BRH .... Biuro Radcy Handlowego [*Trade Adviser's Bureau*] [*Poland*]

BRH .... Braathens Helicopter AS [*Norway*] [*ICAO designator*]   (FAAC)

BRI .... Banca dei Regolamenti Internazionali [*Bank for International Settlements - BIS*] [*Italian*]   (WER)

BRI .... Bank Rakjat Indonesia [*People's Bank of Indonesia*]   (IN)

BRI .... Bari [*Italy*] [*Airport symbol*]   (OAG)

BRI .... Bio-Dynamic Research Institute [*Australia*]

BRI .... Biomolecular Research Institute [*Australia*]

BRI .... Bread Research Institute of Australia   (ARC)

BRI .... Broker Report Index [*Australia*]

BRI .... Building Research Institute [*Poland*]   (IRC)

BRI .... Building Research Institute [*Turkey*]   (ERC)

BRI .... Building Research Institute [*Ministry of Construction*] [*Japan*]   (ERC)

BRI .... Building Research Institute [*Icelandic*]   (IRC)

BRI .... Bureau de Renseignements Internationaux [*International Information Bureau*] [*French*]   (WER)

BRIA .... Bread Research Institute of Australia

BRIAAC .... Burdekin River Irrigation Area Advisory Committee [*Queensland, Australia*]

BRIAN ...... Barrier Reef Image Analysis [*Australia*]

BRIATAC ... Burdekin River Irrigation Area Technical Advisory Committee [*Queensland, Australia*]

BRIB .... Ballarat and Western Victoria Regional Information Bureau [*Australia*]

BRIDGE .... Biotechnology Research for Innovation, Development, and Growth in Europe [*EC*]   (ECED)

BRIE .... Banco de la Republica [*Colombia*]   (DSCA)

Briefbeil ... Briefbeilage [*Supplement of Letter*] [*Publishing*] [*German*]

Brig .... Brigade [*Military*] [*French*]   (MTD)

BRIG .... Brigade [*Military*] [*Afrikaans*]

brig .... Brigadeiro [*Brigadier*] [*Portuguese*]

Brig .... Brigadier   (PWGL)

brigadmil.... Brigade in Support of the Militia   (RU)

BRIGDJEN ... Brigadir Djenderal [*Brigadier General*]   (IN)

brig genl ..... Brigade-Generaal [*Brigade General*] [*Afrikaans*]

BRIGPOL ... Brigadir Polisi [*Police Brigadier*]   (IN)

BRIGPUR ... Brigade Pertempuran [*Combat Brigade*]   (IN)

BRiH .... Bank Rzemiosla i Handlu [*Bank of Handicraft Industry and Trade*]   (POL)

Brikettier ... Brikettierung [*Briquetting*] [*German*]   (GCA)

BRIMOB... Brigade Mobil [*Mobile Brigade (Police)*]   (IN)

Brinckwalux ... Bank MM Warburg-Brinckmann, Wirz International (Luxembourg) SA [*Bank*]

br in X .... Broeder in Christus [*Brother in Christ*] [*Afrikaans*]

br iod ist .... Bromine and Iodine Spring [*Topography*]   (RU)

BRIPDA .... Brigadir Polisi Dua [*Police Brigadier II*]   (IN)

BRIPTU .... Brigadir Polisi Satu [*Police Brigadier I*]   (IN)

Briqie .... Briqueterie [*Brickyard*] [*Military map abbreviation World War I*] [*French*]   (MTD)

Bris............ Brisanz [*High Explosive*] [*German*]   (GCA)

BRIS .... Brisbane [*Australia*]   (DSUE)

bris .... Brisures [*Broken-Grain Rice*]   (CL)

BRISA .... Bienes Raices de El Salvador, SA [*Real Estate of El Salvador Corp.*]

BRISB........ Brisbane [*Australia*]   (ROG)

BrisbaneCAE ... Brisbane College of Advanced Education [*Australia*]

BrisbaneColl Theol ... Brisbane College of Theology [*Australia*]

BRISQ .... Business Reference and Information Service Queensland [*Australia*]

Brit............ Briticism   (BARN)

brit............. British   (RU)

BRITAIR... Brittany Air International [*Airline*] [*France*]

Brit Burm... British Burma   (ILCA)

BRITE ...... Basic Research in Industrial Technologies for Europe

BRITE ...... Basic Research in Industrial Technology for Europe

BRITEC..... British Information Technology Exhibition and Conference on Engineering Software [*Computational Mechanics Institute*]

Brit Gui...... British Guiana   (ILCA)

Brit Hond... British Honduras   (ILCA)

BRITT .... Britannarium [*Of All the Britains*] [*Coin inscription*]   (ROG)

britt .... Brittilainen [*British*] [*Finland*]

BRIZ......... Office for Rationalization and Inventions   (RU)

brizol .... Bitumen-Rubber Waterproofing Material   (RU)

BRIZTI...... Office of Rationalization, Inventions, and Technical Information   (RU)

BRK .... Betriebsfunk-Redaktionskommission [*Enterprise Radio Editorial Commission*]   (EG)

BRK .... Bezirks-Revisionskommission [*District Auditing Commission*]   (EG)

BRK .... Bourke [*Australia*] [*Airport symbol*]   (OAG)

BrK............ Brankovo Kolo [*Sremski Karlovci*] [*A periodical*]   (YU)

brk............. Brigade of Missile Warships   (BU)

Brk............ Bruecke [*Bridge*] [*German*]   (GCA)

BRK .... Bulgarian Revolutionary Committee   (BU)

br k .... Ford for Wheeled Vehicles [*Topography*]   (RU)

BRK .... River Craft Squadron   (RU)

brka........... Brigade of Missile Cutters   (BU)

brkb........... Armored Cavalry Battalion   (BU)

brkbr .... Armored Cavalry Brigade   (BU)

brkhz......... Chemical Defense Brigade   (BU)

BRKKV..... Algemene Bond van Rooms Katholieke Kiesverenigingen [*General League of Roman Catholic Election Societies*] [*Netherlands*]   (PPE)

brkp........... Armored Cavalry Regiment   (BU)

BRL........... Air Bras d'Or [*Canada ICAO designator*]   (FAAC)

BRL........... Bell Resources Ltd. [*Australia*]

BRL........... Bulgarska Republika Ludowa [*Bulgarian People's Republic*] [*Poland*]

BRM .... Banque de la Republique du Mali [*Bank of the Republic of Mali*]   (AF)

BRM .... Barquisimeto [*Venezuela*] [*Airport symbol*]   (OAG)

BRM .... Bimetallic Power-Control Thermostat [*Electric range*]   (RU)

BRM .... Borbene Radioaktivne Materije [*Combat Radioactive Materials*] [*Military*]   (YU)

BRM .... Power Control Unit   (RU)

BRMA ...... Bureau de Recherches Minieres de l'Algerie

BRMD ...... Short-Range Surface-to-Surface Ballistic Missile   (RU)

BRMG ...... Banco Rural de Minas Gerais SA [*Brazil*]   (DSCA)

BR-ML ..... Bandera Roja - Marxista Leninista [*Red Flag - Marxist Leninist Faction*] [*Venezuela*]   (LA)

br mog .... Common Grave [*Topography*]   (RU)

BrMP........ Brigade Medical Aid Station   (BU)

brmp.......... Naval Infantry Brigade, Marines   (BU)

BRN .... Barisan Revolusi Nasional [*Thailand*] [*Political party*]

BRN .... Berne [*Switzerland*] [*Airport symbol*]   (OAG)

BRN .... Book Registration Number

Brn............ Brennerei [*Distillery*] [*German*]   (GCA)

BRN .... Brunei Darussalam [*ANSI three-letter standard code*]   (CNC)

BRO .... Battalion Defense Area   (RU)

BRO .... Brabham Racing Organization [*Australia*]

bro............. Bruto [*Gross*] [*Afrikaans*]

BROC .... Brigade Rouge d'Occitanie [*Red Brigade of Occitania*] [*France*]   (PD)

broch .... Brochado [*Stitched in Paper Covers*] [*Publishing*] [*Portuguese*]

broch .... Broche [*Stitched*] [*Publishing*] [*French*]

broch .... Brochura [*Pamphlet*] [*Publishing*] [*Portuguese*]

BRODOIMPEKS ... Preduzece za Medunarodnu Trgovinu Brodogradevnim Materijalom [*Establishment for International Trade in Shipbuilding Materials*] [*Belgrade*]   (YU)

BRODOSPAS ... Preduzece za Spasavanje i Teglenje Brodova [*Shipping Salvage and Towage Establishment*] [*Split*]   (YU)

Bromier...... Bromierung [*Bromination*] [*German*]   (GCA)

BrOMO .... Brigade Medical Support Detachment   (BU)

Bron .... Buron [*Cheese Factory*] [*Military map abbreviation World War I*] [*French*]   (MTD)

bronkat....... Armored Cutter   (RU)

BrOP......... Brigade Supply Relay Point   (RU)

brosch........ Broschiert [*Sewn in Pamphlet Form*] [*German*]

broschyromsl ... Broschyromslag [*Stitched Wrappers*] [*Publishing Bookbinding*] [*Sweden*]

brosh .... Brochure [*or Pamphlet*]   (BU)

brosh der .... Abandoned Village [*Topography*]   (RU)

bross........... Brossura [*Paper-Cover Binding*] [*Publishing*] [*Italian*]

brosz.......... Broszura [*Pamphlet*]   (POL)

brot........... Coastal Defense   (BU)

BROTRAZ ... Brodarska Transportna Proizvodacka Zadruga [*Shipping Transport and Production Cooperative*]   (YU)

BROU........ Banco de la Republica Oriental de Uruguay [*Bank of Uruguay*]   (LA)

BROU........ Rapid Reduction and Cooling Unit   (RU)

broz .... Brozovany [*Unbound*]   (CZ)

BRP........... Biaru [*Papua New Guinea*] [*Airport symbol*]   (OAG)

BRP........... Brazilian Workers' Party   (RU)

BRP........... Budget Related Papers

BRP........... Bulgarian River Navigation Administration   (BU)

BRP........... Bulgarska Rabotnicheska Partiia [*Bulgarian Workers Party*] [*Political party*]   (PPE)

BRP........... Bureau de Recherches de Petrole [*Petroleum Prospecting Office*] [*French*]   (AF)

BRP............ Burmese Workers' Party   (RU)
BRP............ Close-In Radio Marker Beacon   (RU)
br p............. Ford for Pedestrians [*Topography*]   (RU)
BRP(k)....... Bugarska Radnicka Partija (Komunisti) [*Bulgarian Workers' Party (Communists)*]   (YU)
BRP (k)...... Bulgarian Workers' Party (Communist)   (BU)
BRPL......... Bongaigaon Refinery and Petrochemicals Ltd. [*India*]
BRPM........ Bureau de Recherches et de Participations Minieres [*Mineral Prospecting and Investment Office*] [*Rabat, Morocco*]   (AF)
BRPM........ Bureau de Recherches Petrolieres Marocain
BRPR......... Banca Republicii Populare Romane [*Bank of the Romanian People's Republic*]   (RO)
BRPSH...... Bashkimi i Rinise se Punes se Shqiperise [*Albanian*]
BRP (ts)..... Bulgarian Workers' Party (Left Wing)   (BU)
BRQ.......... Brno [*Former Czechoslovakia*] [*Airport symbol*]   (OAG)
BRR.......... Barra [*Hebrides Islands*] [*Airport symbol*]   (OAG)
BRR.......... Bureau of Rural Resources [*Commonwealth Department of Primary Industries and Energy*] [*Australia*]   (EAS)
BRR.......... Fast Breeder Reactor   (RU)
BRRA........ BMW [*Bavarian Motor Works*] Rolls-Royce AeroEngines [*Commercial firm*]   (ECON)
BRRI......... Bangladesh Rice Research Institute [*Research center*]   (IRC)
BRRI......... Building and Road Research Institute [*Ghana*]   (AF)
BRRO........ Shore-Based Radio Intelligence Detachment   (RU)
BRRTF...... Building Regulation Review Task Force
BRRU........ Business Regulation and Review Unit [*Australia*]
BRS.......... Brazilian Air Force [*ICAO designator*]   (FAAC)
BRS.......... Brisbane [*Totalizator Agency Board code*] [*Australia*]
BRS.......... British Road Services
BRS.......... Bueromaschinenwerk Rheinmetall, Soemmerda [*Rheinmetall Office-Machine Plant, Soemmerda*]   (EG)
BRS.......... Building Research Service [*National Engineering Centre*] [*University of the Philippines*]   (EAS)
BRS.......... Bulgarian Workers' Union   (BU)
BRS.......... Bureau of Rural Science [*Australia*]
brsch......... Broschiert [*Stitched in Paper Covers*] [*Publishing*] [*German*]
BRSD........ Intermediate-Range Ballistic Missile   (RU)
BRSDP...... Bulgarian Workers' Social Democratic Party   (BU)
BRSDP(ts) ... Bulgarian Workers' Social Democratic Party (Left Wing)   (BU)
BrSl.......... Broj Sluzbeno [*Official Number*]   (YU)
BRSR........ Biroul pentru Rezolvarea Sezisarilor si Reclamatiilor [*Bureau for Resolving Notifications and Complaints*]   (RO)
BRSS........ Bashkimi i Republikave Socialiste Sovjetike [*Albanian*]
BRSS........ Bureau for Research Support Services [*Human Sciences Research Council*] [*South Africa*]   (AA)
BRST........ Botswana Roan Selection Trust
Br st.......... British Standard   (RU)
BRT.......... Bathurst Island [*Australia*] [*Airport symbol*]   (OAG)
BRT.......... Bayrak Radyo-Televisyon [*Bayrak Radio-Television*]
BRT.......... Belgische Radio en Televisie [*Belgian Radio and Television - Dutch Service*]
BRT.......... Bruttoregistertonne [*Gross Register Ton*] [*Poland*]
BRT.......... Brutto-Registertonnen [*Gross Register Tons*] [*German*]   (EG)
BRT.......... Brutto Registrovane Tuny [*Gross Register Tons*] [*Maritime weight*]   (CZ)
brt............ Bruttorekisteritonni(a) [*Finland*]
BRT.......... Bulgarian Radio and Television   (BU)
BRT.......... Gross Register Ton, Gross Register Tonnage   (RU)
BRT.......... Large Diesel Fish-Salting Trawler   (RU)
brtbr......... Armored Brigade   (BU)
BrTD........ Armored Division   (RU)
BRTK....... Bayrak Radio & TV Corp. [*Turkish Cyprus*]   (EY)
Br-to......... Gross Weight, Gross   (RU)
brtr.......... Armored Carrier   (RU)
BRTR....... Electronic Reconnaissance Battery   (BU)
BRTR....... Radio Reconnaissance Battery   (RU)
BRTs........ Fast-Setting Expanding Cement   (RU)
BRTsK...... Bulgarian Central Revolutionary Committee   (BU)
BRU......... Belavia [*Belarus*] [*ICAO designator*]   (FAAC)
BRU......... Bilharzia Research Unit
BrU.......... Bromouracil   (RU)
BRU......... Brussels [*Belgium*] [*Airport symbol*]   (OAG)
BRU......... Building Research Unit [*Tanzania*]
BRU......... Contactless Regulating Device   (RU)
BRU......... Contactless Relay   (RU)
BRUC....... Bloque Revolucionario Universitario Cristiano [*Christian Revolutionary University Bloc*] [*Dominican Republic*]   (LA)
Bruchfestigk ... Bruchfestigkeit [*Breaking Strength*] [*German*]   (GCA)
BRUFINA ... Societe de Bruxelles pour la Finance et l'Industrie Brufina SA [*Belgium*]
Brug......... Bruggroep (Dissidente Kommunisten) [*Benelux*]   (BAS)
Brum........ Birmingham [*England*]
Brum........ Brumaire [*Second month of the "calendrier republicain", from October 22 to November 20*] [*French*]   (FLAF)
brunfl........ Brunflaeckad [*Foxed*] [*Publishing*] [*Sweden*]

brunskjold ... Brunskjoldet [*Foxed*] [*Publishing Danish/Norwegian*]
BRUNSW ... Brunswick [*Australia*]   (ROG)
BRurScEd ... Bachelor of Rural Science Education
BRUSTA ... Bureau Regional de l'UNESCO pour la Science et la Technologie en Afrique [*UNESCO Regional Office for Science and Technology in Africa - UNESCO-ROSTA*] [*Nairobi, Kenya*]   (EAIO)
Brux......... Arret de la Cour d'Appel de Bruxelles [*Belgium*]   (BAS)
BRUX....... Bruxelles [*Belgium*] [*City in Belgium*]   (ROG)
BRV.......... Bezirks-Registrierverwaltung [*District Registration Administration*]   (EG)
BRV.......... Bremerhaven [*Germany*] [*Airport symbol*]   (OAG)
BRV.......... Development and Application Base   (BU)
BRV.......... Gross Register Tonnage   (RU)
BRV.......... Radioactive Substance [*Military term*]   (RU)
BRV.......... Radioactive Warfare Contaminant   (BU)
BRV.......... Reactant Warfare Agents   (BU)
BRV.......... Recording and Reproduction Unit   (RU)
BRv.......... Wetboek van Burgerlijke Regtsvordering [*Benelux*]   (BAS)
BRVT........ Bijzonder Reglement voor het Vervoer op de Tramwegen [*Benelux*]   (BAS)
brw.......... Bez Roku Wydania [*Undated, Year of Publication Not Given*] [*Poland*]
BRW......... Bijdragen tot Rechtsgeleerdheid en Wetgeving [*Benelux*]   (BAS)
BRX......... Barahona [*Dominican Republic*] [*Airport symbol*]   (OAG)
Bryg......... Brygada [*Brigade*] [*Poland*]
bryt.......... Brytyjski [*British*] [*Poland*]
BRZ......... Berdsk Radio Plant   (RU)
BRZ......... Bezirksrechenzentrum [*District Computer Center*]   (EG)
BrzA........ Brazilian Angel [*Record label*]
BrzC........ Brazilian Columbia [*Record label*]
BrzCont..... Brazilian Continental [*Record label*]
BrzEli....... Brazilian Elite [*Record label*]
BrzMGM... Brazilian MGM [*Record label*]
BrzOd....... Brazilian Odeon [*Record label*]
BrzV........ Brazilian Victor [*Record label*]
BS........... Adder   (RU)
BS........... Armor-Piercing Projectile, Armor-Piercing Shell   (RU)
BS........... Bacterial Means, Bacterial Agents   (RU)
BS........... Bahamas [*ANSI two-letter standard code*]   (CNC)
BS........... Ballast Resistance   (RU)
BS........... Banco de Sabadell [*Spanish*]
BS........... Banco de Sangue [*Blood Bank*] [*Portuguese*]
BS........... Bancus Superior [*King's Bench*] [*British*] [*Legal term*]   (DLA)
BS........... Barisan Sosialis [*Socialist Front*]   (ML)
BS........... Base System   (RU)
Bs............ Bedrijfschap [*Benelux*]   (BAS)
BS........... Beef Shorthorn [*Cattle*]
BS........... Belgisch Staatsblad [*Belgium*]   (BAS)
BS........... Berezin Synchronized Machine Gun [*Aviation*]   (RU)
BS........... Berufsschule [*Trade School*] [*German*]
BS........... Betriebssystem [*German*]   (ADPT)
BS........... Biblioteka Sportowa [*Sport Series*]   (POL)
BS........... Bijvoegsel tot het Staatsblad [*Benelux*]   (BAS)
BS........... Binder Aviatik, Scheibe-Bruns, Schleicher-Bruns [*Germany*] [*ICAO aircraft manufacturer identifier*]   (ICAO)
BS .... Biochemical Society [*London, England*]   (EAIO)
BS........... Biuro Sprzedazy [*Sales Office*]   (POL)
BS........... Black Sash [*South Africa*]   (EAIO)
BS........... Blanicke Strojirny [*Blanik Engineering Works*]   (CZ)
BS........... Block Station, Blocking Station   (RU)
BS........... Bojove Stanoviste [*Combat Position*]   (CZ)
Bs............ Bolivares [*Venezuelan monetary unit*]
BS........... Book Block Pasting Machine   (RU)
BS........... Bookplate Society [*London, England*]   (EAIO)
BS........... Border Scouts   (ML)
BS........... Boru Sanayii Anonim Sirketi [*Pipe Industry Corporation*] [*Istanbul*]   (TU)
BS........... Bo Seespieel [*Above Sea-Level*] [*Afrikaans*]
BS........... Brescia [*Car registration plates*] [*Italian*]
BS........... Brevet Superieur [*Teaching certificate*] [*French*]
BS........... Broadcast Satellite [*Japan*]
BS........... Broteriana Society [*Portugal*]   (EAIO)
BS........... Burgerlijke Stand [*Benelux*]   (BAS)
BS........... Combat Contact   (RU)
BS........... Combat Firing   (RU)
BS........... Combat Listening Post   (RU)
BS........... Combat Sector   (RU)
BS........... Fixed Battery [*Military term*]   (RU)
BS........... Grupo Banco de Santander [*Spain*]
BS........... Lower Beam, Passing Beam [*Vehicles*]   (RU)
BS........... Nederlandse Binnenlandse Strijdkrachten [*Netherlands Forces of the Interior, 1944*]
BS........... Reading Unit   (RU)
BS........... Shift Unit [*Computers*]   (RU)
BS........... Shore Station, Coast Station   (RU)

BS .... Signal Battalion   (RU)
BS .... Signal Unit   (RU)
BS .... Synchronization Unit [Automation]   (RU)
BS .... The Biometric Society [Switzerland]   (DSCA)
BS .... White Glass   (RU)
BS .... White Light [Fluorescent lamp]   (RU)
BSA............ Bachelier en Sciences Administratives [Bachelor in Administrative Sciences] [French]
BSA............ Betonvereniging van Suidelike Africa [Concrete Society of South Africa]   (EAIO)
BSA............ Bible Society in Australia   (ADA)
BSA............ Blind Spoting Association of New South Wales [Australia]
BSA............ Bonsai Society of Australia
BSA............ Bosaso [Somalia] [Airport symbol]   (OAG)
BSA............ Botswana Softball Association
BSA............ Brazilian Supermarkets Association
BSA............ Brisbane School of Arts [Australia]   (ADA)
BSA............ British South Africa Co.
BSA............ Brits-Suid-Afrika [British South Africa] [Afrikaans]
BSA............ Broadcasting Services Association Proprietary Ltd. [Australia]   (ADA)
BSA............ Budgerigar Society of Australia
BSA............ Building Services Authority [Queensland, Australia]
BSA............ Bund Schweizer Architekten [Swiss Architects Union]   (SLS)
BSA............ Bureau Senegalaise d'Architecture et d'Etudes
BSA............ Ecole d'Aviation Civile [Belgium] [ICAO designator]   (FAAC)
BSAA........ British School of Archeology at Athens   (BARN)
BSAA........ Business Software Association of Australia
BSAB........ Byggandets Samordning AB [Building Coordination Center] [Sweden]   (PDAA)
BSABACT ... Barristers and Solicitors' Admission Board of the Australian Capital Territory
BSABNSW ... Barristers and Solicitors Admission Board of New South Wales [Australia]
BSAC........ British South Africa Co.   (ROG)
BSACP ..... Brazilian Society for Artistic and Cultural Promotion   (EAIO)
BSAM........ Great Soviet World Atlas   (RU)
BSANSW .. Blind Sporting Association of New South Wales [Australia]
BSANZ...... Bibliographical Society of Australia and New Zealand   (ADA)
BSAT .... Vseobshchii Soiuz Alzhirskikh Trudiashchikhsia
bsau.......... Self-Propelled Gun Battalion [Artillery]   (RU)
BSAV........ Blind Soldiers Association of Victoria [Australia]
BSAWA..... Billiards and Snooker Association of Western Australia
BSB.......... Bahraini Saudi Bank   (EY)
BSB........... Bangladesh Shilpa Bank [Industrial Development Bank]   (EY)
BSB........... Bankers' Society of Bahrain   (EAIO)
BSB........... Bayerische Staatsbibliothek [Information retrieval]
BSB........... Betrieb mit Staatlicher Beteiligung [Semi-State Enterprise]   (EG)
BSB........... Border Scouts Borneo   (ML)
BSB........... Brasilia [Brazil] [Airport symbol]   (OAG)
BSB........... British Satellite Beam   (BARN)
BSB........... Bulgarska Sbirka [Bulgarian Collection] [A periodical]   (BU)
BSB........... Burgerlijke Stand en Bevolking [Benelux]   (BAS)
BSBG........ Bibbebschiffahrts - Berufsgenossenschaft [Inland Waterways Authority] [Germany]   (PDAA)
BSBI .... Bureau de Statistiques Baleinieres Internationales [Bureau of International Whaling Statistics - BIWS]   (MSC)
BSBL .... Bangladesh Samabaya Bank Ltd.   (EY)
BSBO........ Border Special Branch Officers   (ML)
BSBP .... Bataljonska Stanica Borbenih Potreba [Battalion Combat Supply Station]   (YU)
BSBW .... Backer Spielvogel Bates Worldwide [Commercial firm] [British]   (ECON)
BSc............ Baccalaureat es Sciences [Bachelor of Science] [French]
BSc............ Bachelor of Science   (PWGL)
BSC........... Bahia Solano [Colombia] [Airport symbol]   (OAG)
BSC........... Bangladesh Shipping Corp.   (DS)
BSC........... Bawarith Shipping Co. [Egypt]
BSC........... Belgian Shippers Council   (DS)
BSC........... Biuro Sprzedazy Ceramiki [Sales Office for Ceramic Wares] [POL]
BSC........... Blue Sky Carrier Co. Ltd. [Poland] [ICAO designator]   (FAAC)
BSC........... Building Services Corp. [New South Wales, Australia]
BSC........... Business Studies Course [Australia]
BScA .... Bachelier es Sciences Appliquees [Bachelor of Applied Science] [French]
BSCAI ...... Building Service Contractors Association International   (EAIO)
BSCC........ Brisbane Sporting Car Club [Australia]
BSCC........ British-Soviet Chamber of Commerce   (DS)
BSCC........ Brunei State Chamber of Commerce   (DS)
BSCE........ Bird Strike Committee Europe [Denmark]   (EAIO)
BSCh........ Bojowe Srodki Chemiczne [Chemical Warfare Materials]   (POL)
BSch.......... Read Unit   (RU)
BschA .... Beschussamt [German]
BSChin ...... Reglement Burgerlijke Stand voor de Chinezen [Benelux]   (BAS)

BSCHMB ... Biuro Sprzedazy Centrali Handlowej Materialow Budowlanych [Sales Office of the Building Materials Trade Center] (POL)
BSCI .... Reglement Burgerlijke Stand voor de Christenindonesiers [Benelux]   (BAS)
BSCIC....... Bangladesh Small and Cottage Industries Corporation   (GEA)
BSc(PE)..... Bachelor of Science in Physical Education
BSD.......... Bangladesh Samajtantrik Dal [Bangladesh Socialist Party] (PPW)
BSD .... Banque Senegalaise de Developpement
BSD .... Baoshan [China] [Airport symbol]   (OAG)
BSD .... Belgian Royal Society of Dermatology and Venerology   (EAIO)
BSD .... Bentara Setia Di-Raja [Medal to the Orders of Chivalry] [Malaysia]   (ML)
bsd............ Besonder [Particular] [German]   (GCA)
BSD .... Bloc pour la Social-Democratie [Benin] [Political party]   (EY)
BSD .... Blutspendedienst [Blood Donor Service]   (EG)
BSD .... Bulgarian-Soviet Society   (BU)
BSDA........ Bureau Senegalais des Droits d'Auteurs [Senegalese Copyright Office]   (AF)
BSDA........ Business Services and Defense Administration [Department of Commerce]   (BARN)
BSDP .... Bulgarska Socialdemokraticheska Partiia [Bulgarian Social Democratic Party] [Political party]   (PPE)
BSDr .... Bulgaro-Suvetska Druzhba [Bulgarian-Soviet Friendship] [A periodical]   (BU)
BSE........... Bahrain Society of Engineers   (PDAA)
BSE........... Black Sea Expedition [1969] [Turkey, US]   (MSC)
BSE........... Board of Secondary Education [New South Wales, Australia]
BSE........... Bombay Stock Exchange [India]
BSE........... Bovine Spongiform Encephalopathy   (EECI)
BSE........... Great Soviet Encyclopedia   (RU)
BSEC........ Brevet Superieur d'Enseignement Commercial [Higher Commercial Education Certificate]   (CL)
BSEC........ Brevet Superieur d'Etudes Commerciales [Algeria]
BSEG........ Broadband Service Expert Group
BSEHR...... Bangladesh Society for the Enforcement of Human Rights (EAIO)
BSERI....... Beijing Solar Energy Research Institute [China]   (WED)
BSerSoc .... Bachelier en Service Social [Bachelor of Social Work] [French]
BSF........... Badmintonsamband Foroya [Faroe Islands]   (EAIO)
BSF .... Border Security Force [India]
BSF .... Business Flight Service [Denmark] [ICAO designator]   (FAAC)
BSF .... US-Israel Binational Science Foundation   (EA)
BSFA .... Building Science Forum of Australia   (ADA)
BSFC .... Bihar State Finance Corp. [India]   (PDAA)
BSFE .... Banque de la Societe Financiere Europeenne [Bank] [French]
BSFL........ Barbados Sugar Factories Limited   (LA)
BSFS......... Bulgarian Union for Physical Culture and Sports   (BU)
BSG........... Betriebs-Sportgemeinschaft [Enterprise Sports Association] (EG)
BSG........... Bundessozialgericht [Federal Court of Social Security] [German] (ILCA)
BSGC........ Barbra Streisand Fan Club   (EAIO)
BSGDG...... Brevete sans Garantie du Gouvernement [Patent without Government Guarantee] [French]
BSGL........ Branch System General License [Information technology]
BSGPA ..... Brisbane Sand and Gravel Producers' Association [Australia]
BSh .... Bickford Fuze, Safety Fuze   (RU)
BSHC .... Bulgarian Ship Hydrodynamics Center [Bulgarian Shipbuilding Industry] [Research center]   (ERC)
BShchP...... Battery Distribution Panel [Telephony]   (RU)
BShtU .... Power Unit Control Panel [Nuclear energy]   (BU)
BSI .... Badminton Association of Iceland   (EAIO)
BSI .... Banca della Svizzera Italiana [Swiss-Italian Bank] [Switzerland]
BSI .... Belize Sugar Industries
BSI .... Botanical Society of Israel   (EAIO)
BSI .... Botanical Survey of India
BSI .... Building Societies' Institute   (BARN)
BSI .... Bulgarian Society of Immunology   (EAIO)
BSI .... Bundesverband der Deutschen Spirituosen-Industrie [Germany] (EAIO)
BSI .... Indicating Light Unit   (RU)
BSI .... Israel Biochemical Society   (EAIO)
BSI .... Pulse-Erasing Unit   (RU)
BSIE .... Budget Special d'Investissement et d'Equipement [Special Investment and Equipment Budget] [Ivory Coast]   (AF)
BSIF......... Bund Schweizerischer Israelitischer Frauenvereine   (BJA)
BSiP......... Biuro Studiow i Projektow [Bureau for Study and Designing] [Poland]
BSIP .... British Solomon Islands Protectorate   (ADA)
BSiPL .... Biuro Studiow i Projektow Lacznosci [Office of Communication Research and Plans]   (POL)
BSiUS....... Biblioteka Sprzetu i Urzadzen Sportowych [Sporting Goods and Equipment Series]   (POL)
BSJ .... Bairnsdale [Australia] [Airport symbol] [Obsolete]   (OAG)

BSJ .... Bocarski Savez Jugoslavije [*Croatia*]   (EAIO)
BSK........... Banque Senegalo-Koweitienne [*Senegal-Kuwait Bank*]
Bsk .... Baskan [*or Baskanlik*] [*Chairman or Chairmanship, Chief*]   (TU)
BSK........... Bereg Slovnoi Kosti
BSK........... Berliner Stadtkontor [*Berlin Municipal Bank*]   (EG)
BSK........... Biskra [*Algeria*] [*Airport symbol*]   (OAG)
BSK........... Braunkohlen-Schwelkoks [*Carbonized Lignite*]   (EG)
BSK........... Butadiene-Styrene Rubber   (RU)
BSKhA....... Belorussian Agricultural Academy   (RU)
BSKhI....... Bashkir Agricultural Institute   (RU)
BSKhI....... Belorussian Agricultural Institute   (RU)
BSL........... Basel/Mulhouse [*Switzerland*] [*Airport symbol*]   (OAG)
BSL........... Bestemmelser om Sikringstjenesten foer Luftfaht [*Norway*]
BSL........... Biblioteka Sportowo-Lekarska [*Sport and Medical Series*]   (POL)
BSL........... Bignier Schmid-Laurent [*Nuclear energy*] [*French*]   (NRCH)
BSL........... Black Star Line
BSL........... Bokaro Steel Ltd. [*India*]   (PDAA)
BSL........... Brotherhood of St. Laurence [*Australia*]
BSL........... Shore Duty, Shore Service   (RU)
BSM.......... Barisan Sosialis Malaysia [*Malaysian Socialist Front*]   (ML)
BSM.......... Belgian Society of Musicology   (EAIO)
BSM.......... Beso Sus Manos [*With Great Respect*] [*Correspondence*] [*Spanish*]
BSM.......... Biuro Spoldzielni Mieszkaniowych [*Office of Housing Cooperatives*]   (POL)
BSM.......... Brigade in Support of the Militia   (RU)
BSMI........ Bureau of Small and Medium Industries [*Philippines*]   (DS)
BSMP....... Specialized Medical Aid Brigade   (RU)
BSMSP...... Bernoulli Society for Mathematical Statistics and Probability [*Voorburg, Netherlands*]   (EA)
BSN .... Boussois Souchon Neuvesel [*French*]
BSN .... Bulgarian Society of Neurosurgery   (SLS)
BSN .... Office of Standardization   (RU)
BSNCIA .... Brazilian Society for Numerical Control and Industrial Automation   (EAIO)
BSNKh ...... Bashkir Council of the National Economy   (RU)
BSNSW ..... Benevolent Society of New South Wales [*Australia*]
BSNSW ..... Bromeliad Society of New South Wales [*Australia*]
BSNSW ..... Buddhist Society of New South Wales [*Australia*]
BSO .... Baluchi Students' Organization [*Pakistan*]   (PD)
BSO .... Basco [*Philippines*] [*Airport symbol*]   (OAG)
BSO .... Black September Organization [*Israel*]
BSO .... Bratislavsky Symfonicky Orchester [*Bratislava Symphonic Orchestra*]   (CZ)
BSO .... Equipment Monitoring Unit   (RU)
BSO .... National Security Organization [*Royal Thai Government*]
Bs Og .... Bas Ogretmen [*Head Teacher*]   (TU)
BSOKRiS ... Balto-Slavyanskoye Obshchestvo Kul'turnogo Razvitiya i Sotrudnichestva [*Latvia*]   (EAIO)
BSOO .... Berlin State Opera Orchestra
BSOT........ Disappearing Armored Emplacement   (RU)
B Soz G ..... Bundessozialgericht [*Federal Supreme Social Security Court*] [*German*]   (DLA)
BSP .... Bahujan Samaj Party [*Political party*] [*Italy*]   (ECON)
BSP .... Barisan Socialist Party [*Singapore*]   (ML)
BSP .... Bayerische Staatspartei [*Bavarian State Party*] [*Germany*]   (PPW)
BSP .... Belgische Socialistische Partij [*Belgian Socialist Party*]   (PPW)
BSP .... Bensbach [*Papua New Guinea*] [*Airport symbol*]   (OAG)
BSP .... Bojowe Srodki Promieniotworcze [*Radioactive Warfare Substances*] [*Poland*]
BSP .... Border Security Police [*NATO*]   (NATG)
BSP .... Bosphorus Hava Yollari Turizm Ve Ticaret AS [*Turkey*] [*ICAO designator*]   (FAAC)
BSP .... Brunei Shell Petroleum Co. Ltd.   (DS)
BSP .... Bulgarian Socialist Party [*Political party*]   (EY)
BSP .... Overflow Signaling Unit   (RU)
BSP .... Smokeless Powder for Siege and Fortress Guns [*Symbol*] [*French*]   (MTD)
BSP .... Subroutine Library [*Computers*]   (RU)
BSPA .... Barbados Sugar Producers Association   (LA)
BSPD........ Bratsko Srpsko Potporno Drustvo [*Serbian Fraternal Welfare Society*]   (YU)
BSpeechTherapy ... Bachelor of Speech Therapy
BSPO........ Badz Sprawny do Pracy i Obrony [*Be Fit for Work and Defense (Badge)*] [*POL*]
BSPP .... Burma Socialist Programme Party [*Political party*]   (PPW)
BSPSC....... Bendel State Public Service Commission
BSQ .... Bach Society of Queensland [*Australia*]
BSQ .... Buddhist Society of Queensland [*Australia*]
BSR........... Basair AB [*Sweden*] [*ICAO designator*]   (FAAC)
BSR........... Brigade de Securite Republicain [*Republican Security Brigade*] [*Cambodia*]   (CL)
BSR........... Brigade Speciale de Recherches (de la Gendarmerie) [*Special Investigation Brigade*] [*Zaire*] [*French*]   (WER)

BSR............ British School at Rome [*Italy*]
BSr............. Comparator   (RU)
BSR............ Flash-Ranging Battery   (RU)
BSRAB ...... British Society of Rheology, Australian Branch
BSRB .... Bandalag Starfsmanna Rikis og Baeja [*Municipal and Governmental Employees' Association*] [*Iceland*]
BSRC .... Bloc Socialista Revolucionari de Catalunya [*Revolutionary Socialist Bloc of Catalonia*] [*Spanish*]   (WER)
BSRDI .... Bulgarian Ship Research and Design Institute [*Research center*]   (ERC)
BSRI .... Brewing Scientific Research Institute [*Japan*]   (DSCA)
BSRR .... Bialoruska Socjalisticzna Republika Radziecka [*Belorussian Soviet Socialist Republic*]   (POL)
BSRS .... Bangladesh Shilpa Rin Sangstha [*Bangladesh Industrial Loan Agency*]   (FEA)
bsrto .... Communications and Technical Support Battalion   (BU)
BSS .... Ballistic Strategic Missile   (RU)
BSS .... Barisan Sosialis Singapura [*Singapore Socialist Front*]   (IN)
bss .... Besser [*Better*] [*German*]   (GCA)
BSS .... Black Students Society
BSS .... Board of Secondary Studies
BSS .... Bram Stoker Society [*Irish*]   (SLS)
BSS .... Brandyske Strojirny a Slevarny [*Brandys Engineering Works and Foundries*]   (CZ)
BSS .... Quick-Setting Mixtures   (RU)
BSS .... Union of Bulgarian Stenographers   (BU)
BSSA .... Beef Shorthorn Society of Australia
BSSA .... Botanical Society of South Africa   (EAIO)
BSSD .... Intermediate-Range Ballistic Missile   (RU)
BSSF......... Bangladesh Sanjukta Sramik Federation
BSSR .... Belorussian Soviet Socialist Republic   (BU)
BSSR .... Bukhara Soviet Socialist Republic [*1924*]   (RU)
BSSSC .... Baltic Sea Salmon Standing Committee [*Denmark, West Germany, Poland, Sweden*]   (MSC)
BST .... Banque Senegalo-Tunisienne   (EY)
BST .... Basic Skills Testing [*Australia*]
BST .... Bessemer Steel   (RU)
BST .... Bostaande [*Above*] [*Afrikaans*]
BST .... Brigade de Surveillance du Territoire [*France*]   (FLAF)
BST .... Byggstandardiseringen [*Building Standards Institution*] [*Research center*] [*Sweden*]   (IRC)
BST .... Large Stereoscopic Telescope, Large Battery Commander's Telescope   (RU)
BST .... Tower Solar Telescope   (RU)
Bstbp......... Bastabip [*Head Doctor*]   (TU)
BSTI .... Bangladesh Standards and Testing Institution [*Research center*]   (IRC)
BSTR .... Befehlsstruktur [*German*]   (ADPT)
BSTU........ Barbados Secondary Teachers Union   (LA)
BSTZ........ Charging Current Stabilization Unit   (RU)
BSU .... Basankusu [*Zaire*] [*Airport symbol*]   (OAG)
BSV........... Bogie Sheep Van [*Australia*]
BSV........... Bromeliad Society of Victoria [*Australia*]
BSv............ Coupling Unit   (RU)
BSv............ Signal Battalion   (RU)
BSW........... Badische Stahlwerke
BSW........... Buitesintuiglike Waarneming [*Extrasensory Perception*] [*Afrikaans*]
BSWA .... Bonsai Society of Western Australia
BSX........... Bassein [*Myanmar*] [*Airport symbol*]   (OAG)
BSY........... Big Sky Airline [*ICAO designator*]   (FAAC)
BSZT .... Borsodi Szenbanyaszati Troszt [*Coal Mining Trust of Borsod*]   (HU)
BSZV .... Belkereskedelmi Szallitasi Vallalat [*Domestic Trade Shipping Enterprise*]   (HU)
BT .... Al Buainain Trading Co. [*Saudi Arabia*]
BT .... Armored   (RU)
BT .... Bachelor of Theatre
BT .... Bankers Trust [*Australia*]
BT .... Bank of Tonga
BT .... Baric Topography   (RU)
BT .... Basse Tension [*Low Tension*] [*French*]
Bt.............. Batarya [*Battery*] [*Military*]   (TU)
BT .... Bea dan Tjukai [*Duties and Customs, Customs Service*] [*Indonesian*]   (IN)
BT .... Beklaednings-og Textilinstituttet [*Clothing and Textile Institute*] [*Denmark*]   (EAIO)
bt .... Bez Tiskare [*No Printing Firm Given*]   (CZ)
BT .... Bhutan [*ANSI two-letter standard code*]   (CNC)
bt .... Billet [*Bill*] [*French*] [*Business term*]
BT .... Binocular Tube   (RU)
BT .... Blasnikova Tiskarna [*Blasnik Printing House*] [*Ljubljana*]   (YU)
BT .... Bodensee-Toggenburg-Bahn [*Switzerland*]   (EY)
BT .... Boissons et Glacieres du Tchad [*Beverage company*] [*Chad*]
bt .... Boucaut [*Barrel*] [*French*]
BT .... Brevet de Technicien [*French*]

bt .... Brez Tiskarne [*Without Printer's Imprint*]   (YU)
bt .... Brut [*Gross (as in produce); Rough, Raw*] [*French*]
BT .... Bruto [*Gross*] [*Afrikaans*]
BT .... Buehrmann-Tetterode NV [*Netherlands*]
BT .... Bukit [*Hill*]   (ML)
BT .... Bulgarski Turist [*Bulgarian Tourist*] [*A periodical*]   (BU)
BT .... Current Unit [*Computers*]   (RU)
BT .... Diesel Tug   (RU)
BT .... High-Speed Tank   (RU)
BT .... Labor Exchange, Employment Agency   (RU)
BT .... Scottish Aviation Ltd. [*ICAO aircraft manufacturer identifier*]
                  (ICAO)
Bt................ Transformer Vault [*Topography*]   (RU)
Bta.............. A Buntetotorvenykonyv Altalanos Resze [*General Section of the Penal Code*]   (HU)
BTA .... Bander Travel and Aviation [*Australian Airlines*] [*Saudi Arabia*]
BTA .... Bangladesh Teachers' Association
BTA .... Bankers Trust Australia Ltd.
BTA .... Barrier Teachers' Association [*Australia*]
BTA .... Bautechnische Abteilung [*Structural Engineering Department*]   (EG)
BTA .... Belize Telecommunications Agency
BTA .... Bertoua [*Cameroon*] [*Airport symbol*]   (OAG)
BTA .... Bois Transformes d'Afrique
BTA .... Book Trade Association of Southern Africa   (EAIO)
BTA .... Bulgarian Telegraph Agency [*News agency*]
BTAA........ Bulgarian Turkish Association of Australia
BTAB........ Concrete-Piercing Aerial Bomb   (RU)
B-Tafel....... Stoerungstafel fuer Massnahmen des Fahrdienstleiters bei Stoerungen im Befehlstellwerk [*Table of Measures to be Taken by the Dispatcher in Case of Interruption in the Control Signaling Device*]   (EG)
BTAO .... Briqueterie Tuilerie de l'Afrique Occidentale
BTASA ..... Bicycle Traders' Association of South Australia
BTB........... Belgische Transport arbeidersbond [*Belgian Transport Workers' Union*]   (EAIO)
BTB........... Berliner Technisches Buero [*Berlin Technical Office*]   (EG)
BTC........... Bahrain Telecommunications Co.   (IMH)
BTC........... Bahrain Tourism Co.   (EY)
BTC........... Ba Technical Centre [*Fiji Institute of Technology*]
BTC........... Bhutan Tourism Corp.   (EY)
BTC........... Botswana Technology Center [*Nonprofit organization*]   (WED)
BTC........... Brigadas de Trabajadores del Campo [*Workers Brigades of the Countryside*] [*El Salvador*]   (LA)
BTC........... Brisbane Technical College [*Australia*]   (ADA)
btca........... Biblioteca [*Library*] [*Spanish*]
BTCC........ Biblioteca Tecnica Cientifica Centralizada [*Venezuela*]
BTCD........ Banque Tchadienne de Credit et de Depots [*Chad*]   (EY)
BTCD........ Banque Tchadienne de Credits et de Depots
BTCE........ Bureau of Transport and Communications Economics [*Austria*] [*Also, an information service or system*]   (IID)
BTCE........ Bureau of Transport and Communications Electronics [*Australia*]
BTCF........ Bureau Technique du Chemin de Fer [*Technical Railroad Office*] [*Gabon*]   (AF)
BTCh......... Armored Unit   (RU)
BTCI......... Banque Togolaise pour le Commerce et l'Industrie [*Togolese Bank for Trade and Industry*]
BTCI......... Bureau Technique de Conseillers Industriels
Bt-Col........ Brevet-Colonel
BTD .... Banque Togolaise de Developpement [*Togolese Development Bank*]   (GEA)
btd .... Betaald [*Paid*] [*Afrikaans*]
BTD .... Brigadni Tezke Dilny [*Brigade Maintenance Shops for Heavy Equipment*]   (CZ)
BTE........... Base de Temps Emission [*French*]   (ADPT)
BTE........... Boite [*Box, Post Office Box*] [*Correspondence*] [*French*]
BTE........... Bonthe [*Sierra Leone*] [*Airport symbol*]   (OAG)
BTE........... Boripari Tudomanyos Egyesulet [*Scientific Association of the Leather Industry*]   (HU)
bte .... Brevete [*Patent*] [*French*]
BTE........... Bureau of Transport Economics [*Australia*] [*Information service or system*]   (IID)
BTE........... Bureau Technique d'Etudes
BTeach...... Bachelor of Teaching
BTEC........ Brucellosis and Tuberculosis Eradication Committee [*Australia*]
BTechEd .... Bachelor of Technology Education
B-teczka.... Biblioteczka [*Little Library*] [*Often used for a series of books*] [*Poland*]
BTEI......... Office of Technical and Economic Information   (RU)
BTENAP ... Biblioteca Tecnica, Empresa Nacional del Petroleo [*Chile*]
BTETs ...... Berezniki Heat and Electric Power Plant   (RU)
BTEUNSW ... Baking Trades Employees' Union of New South Wales [*Australia*]
Btg.............. Batang [*River*] [*Malay*]   (NAU)
BTG .... Botswana Technology Group

BTG .... Butterworths Tax Guide [*A publication*]
BTGM .... Beden Terbiyesi Genel Mudurlugu [*Directorate General of Physical Training*]   (TU)
BTGV .... Belgische Technische Gieterijvereniging [*Belgium*]   (SLS)
BTG(WA) ... Book Trade Group (Western Australia)
BTH .... Barth's Aviation [*France*] [*ICAO designator*]   (FAAC)
BTH .... Batu Besar [*Indonesia*] [*Airport symbol*]   (OAG)
BTH .... Bureau Technique Huguet
BTheol .... Bachelor of Theology
BTI .... Armored Equipment   (RU)
BTI .... Biblijsko Teoloski Institut [*Former Yugoslavia*]
BTI .... Budget Transport Industries [*Australia*]
BTI .... Office of Technical Information
BTI .... Office of Technical Inventory   (RU)
BTIC......... Barbados Tourism Investment Corporation   (GEA)
BTiMV ...... Armored and Mechanized Troops   (BU)
b tit l.......... No Title Page   (RU)
BTJ .... Banda Aceh [*Indonesia*] [*Airport symbol*]   (OAG)
BTJ .... Bibliotekstjanst AB [*Library Service Ltd.*] [*Sweden*] [*Information service or system*]   (IID)
BTJ .... Brigadas Tecnicas Juveniles [*Youth Technical Brigades*] [*Cuba*]   (LA)
BTK .... Bourse de Travail du Katanga
BTK .... Bratsk [*Former USSR*] [*Airport symbol*]   (OAG)
BTK .... Bunteto Torvenykonyv [*Penal Code*]   (HU)
btk .... Motor Torpedo Boat Brigade   (RU)
BTK .... Office of Technical Control   (RU)
BTK .... Office of Technical Cost Accounting   (RU)
BTK .... Trapezoidal-Oscillation Unit   (RU)
BTK .... Tubular Tower Crane   (RU)
btka........... Brigade of Torpedo Boats [*PT boats*]   (BU)
BTKD........ Banque Tuniso-Koweitienne de Developpement [*Tunisia*]
btl .... Batalhao [*Battalion*] [*Portuguese*]
BTL........... Belize Telecommunications Ltd.
BTL........... Bureau Technique de Liaison
BTLAA....... Bankruptcy Trustees and Liquidators Association of Australia
BTM .... Bankin'ny Tantsaha Mpamokatra [*National Bank for Rural Development*] [*Malagasy*]   (AF)
BTM .... Batiment et Travaux du Maghreb
BTM .... Bydgoskie Towarzystwo Muzyczne [*The Bydgoszcz Music Society*] [*Poland*]
BTM .... High-Speed Trench Excavator, High-Speed Ditching Machine   (RU)
BTMot .... Biuro Turystyki Motorowej [*Motor-Touring Office*] [*Poland*]
BTMS....... Brisbane Tramway Museum Society [*Australia*]
BTN .... Bank Tabungan Negara [*State Savings Bank*]   (IN)
BTN .... Basic Telecommunications Needs [*Telecom Australia project*]
Btn............. Bataillon [*Battalion*] [*Military*] [*French*]   (MTD)
BTN .... Bhutan [*ANSI three-letter standard code*]   (CNC)
BTN .... Brussels Tariff Nomenclature [*See also CCCN*] [*EEC Belgium*]
btn .... Bruttorekisteritonni(a) [*Finland*]
BTN .... Brutto-Tara-Netto-Rechner   (ADPT)
BTN .... Bydgoskie Towarzystwo Naukowe [*Poland*]   (SLS)
BTN .... Office of Technical Standardization   (RU)
BTO .... Botopasie [*Surinam*] [*Airport symbol*]   (OAG)
BTO .... Brussels Treaty Organization [*Western European*]   (WEN)
bto .... Bruto [*Gross*] [*Spanish*]
bto .... Bulto [*Size*] [*Spanish*]
B-to .... Gross Weight, Gross   (RU)
BTP........... Bank Tabungan Pos [*Postal Savings Bank*]   (IN)
BTP........... Bataljon Tim Pertempuran [*Battalion Combat Team*]   (IN)
BTP........... Batiment et Travaux Publics [*Algeria*]
BTP........... Beta-Ray Coating Thickness Gauge   (RU)
BTP........... Bulgarian Chamber of Commerce   (BU)
BTP........... Buoni del Tesoro Poliennali [*Italy*]   (ECON)
BTP........... Technical Assistance Board of the UN [*TAB*]   (RU)
BTPP........ Bulgarian Chamber of Commerce and Industry   (BU)
BTPP........ Bulgarian Trade and Industrial Enterprise   (BU)
BTPP........ Office of Technical Preparation of Production   (RU)
BTPS .... Ballarat Tramway Preservation Society [*Australia*]
BTPS .... Batiments et Travaux Publics Senegalais [*Senegalese Building Construction and Public Works*]   (AF)
BTQ .... Ballet Theatre of Queensland [*Australia*]
BTQ-7........ Brisbane TV Ltd. [*Queensland, Australia*] [*Telecommunications service*]
BTQI......... Banque Tuniso-Qatarie d'Investissement [*Bank*] [*Tunisia*]
BTR .... Armored Personnel Carrier   (BU)
BTR .... Base de Temps Reception [*French*]   (ADPT)
BTR .... Belize Transair [*ICAO designator*]   (FAAC)
Btr............. Betrieb [*Operation*] [*German*]   (GCA)
BTR .... Broneje Transporter [*Soviet Armored Personnel Carrier*]
BTR .... Bureau of Tourism Research [*Australia*]
b tr .... Large Transformer   (RU)
BTR .... Stakeless Fabric Tank   (RU)
BTR .... Technical Development Base   (BU)
BTR .... Topographic Reconnaissance Battery   (RU)

B tr .... Transformer Vault [*Topography*]   (RU)
BTRA......... Bombay Textile Research Association [*India*] [*Research center*]
                 (IRC)
BTRGK...... Armored Reserve of the High Command   (RU)
BTRIP .... Bureau for the Technology and Development of Instruments
                 Production   (BU)
BTRM........ Armored Vehicle Repair Shop   (RU)
BTRR......... Armored Repair Shop   (BU)
BTS........... Bairnsdale Technical School [*Australia*]
BTS........... Bible Translation Society
BTS........... Biuro Turystyki Sportowej "Sports Tourist" [*Sport Touring
                 Office "Sports Tourist"*] [*Poland*]
BTS........... Board of Theological Studies
BTS........... Bois Tropicaux de Soubre
BTs............ Bolshevist Center (of the RSDRP)   (RU)
BTS........... Bratislava [*Former Czechoslovakia*] [*Airport symbol*]   (OAG)
BTS........... Brevet de Technicien Superieur [*Advanced Technician's
                 Certificate*] [*French*]   (CL)
BTS........... Brisbane Theosophical Society [*Australia*]
BTS........... British Troops in Sudan
BTS........... Bromothymol Blue [*Indicator*]   (RU)
BTS........... Bulgarian Tourist Union   (BU)
bts.............. Colorless, Achromatic   (RU)
bts.............. Price Not Given, No Price [*Bibliography*]   (RU)
BTS........... Tactical Ballistic Missile   (RU)
Bts............. Unpriced   (BU)
BTs............ White Portland Cement   (RU)
b-tsa .... Hospital   (BU)
BTSB .... Bagimsiz Turkiye Sosyalistleri Birligi [*Union of Independent
                 Turkish Socialists*]   (TU)
BTSB .... Budapesti Testnevelesi es Sportbizottsag [*Budapest Committee
                 for Physical Culture and Sports*]   (HU)
BTsBO...... Bulgarian Central Philanthropic Society   (BU)
BTsDS...... Long-Distance Communications Circuit Unit   (RU)
BTSF .... Budapesti Testnevelesi es Sport Felugyeloseg [*Inspectorate of
                 Physical Culture and Sports of Budapest*]   (HU)
BTsGD...... Bicycloheptadiene   (RU)
BTShch..... Coastal Minesweeper   (RU)
BTSI .... Budapesti Testnevelesi es Sportegeszsegugyi Intezet [*Budapest
                 Institute of Physical Culture and Hygiene*]   (HU)
BTSI .... Budapesti Testnevelesi es Sport Intezet [*Budapest Institute of
                 Physical Culture and Sports*]   (HU)
BTSI .... Budapesti Testnevelesi es Sportorvosi Intezet [*Budapest Institute
                 for Physical Education and Sports Physicians*]   (HU)
BTsK......... Bureau of the Central Committee   (RU)
BTsK......... Office of Central Cataloging   (RU)
bt sk .... Powder Magazine   (RU)
BTsN .... Centrifugal Gasoline Pump   (RU)
BTsRK ...... Bulgarian Central Revolutionary Committee   (BU)
BTST .... Budapesti Testnevelesi es Sport Tanacs [*Council of Physical
                 Culture and Sports of Budapest*]   (HU)
BTsVB ...... Berlin Air Safety Center   (RU)
BTsVS ...... Intercom Circuit Unit   (RU)
BTT........... Beztrzajni Top [*Recoiless Gun*]   (YU)
BTT........... Biroul de Turism pentru Tineret [*Bureau of Tourism for Young
                 People*]   (RO)
BTT........... Business Turnover Tax   (IMH)
BTT........... Telephone and Telegraph Channel Unit   (RU)
BTTDD...... Bati Trakya Turkleri Dayanisma Dernegi [*Association of Mutual
                 Solidarity with the Turks of Western Thrace*]   (TU)
BTTKDD... Bati Trakya Turkleri Kultur ve Dayanisma Dernegi [*Western
                 Thrace Turks' Culture and Mutual Solidarity Association*]
                 (GC)
Btto .... Brutto [*Gross (as in produce)*] [*German*] [*Business term*]
Bttr............. Batterie [*Battery*] [*German*]   (GCA)
BTTRI .... Beijing Television Technology Research Institute [*China*]
                 [*Research center*]   (IRC)
BTTs.......... Fast Hardening Cement   (RU)
BTTsK....... Bulgarian Secret Central Committee   (BU)
BTU .... Armored Troops Directorate   (RU)
BTU .... Basutoland Congress of Trade Unions
BTU .... Bintulu [*Malaysia*] [*Airport symbol*]   (OAG)
BTU .... British Thermal Unit [*British*]   (OMWE)
BTU .... Office of Technical Computation   (RU)
BTU .... Remote-Control Unit   (RU)
BTU .... Tank Angledozer   (RU)
BTUK .... Bangladesh Trade Union Kendra
BTUSA...... Baking Trade Union of South Australia
BTV .... Armored Troops   (RU)
BTV .... Banco de los Trabajadores de Venezuela [*Workers' Bank of
                 Venezuela*]   (GEA)
BTV .... Bangladesh Television   (EY)
BTV .... Beance Tubaire Volontaire [*Voluntary opening of eustachian
                 tubes*] [*Deep-sea diving*] [*French*]
BTV .... Buero fuer Textverarbeitung [*German*]   (ADPT)
BTVH .... Bo Tuc Van Hoa [*Supplementary Education*]

BTW .... Belasting op Toegevoegde Waarde [*Value-Added Tax*] [*Dutch*]
                 (WEN)
BTX .... Bildschirmtext [*Viewdata system*] [*Federal Ministry of Posts and
                 Telecommunications*] [*Germany*]
BTYe.......... British Thermal Unit   (RU)
BTZ........... Belorussian Tractor Plant   (RU)
BTZ........... Bilimbay Pipe-Casting Plant   (RU)
BTZ........... Biuro Turystyki Zagranicznej [*Bureau for Foreign Touring*]
                 [*Poland*]
BTZ........... Bureau Technique Zborowski [*France*]   (PDAA)
BTZ........... Bursa [*Turkey*] [*Airport symbol*] [*Obsolete*]   (OAG)
BTZU .... Remote-Control Contactless Protection Device   (RU)
BU............. Accounting   (RU)
BU............. Ballet School   (BU)
Bu............. Batu [*Rock*] [*Malay*]   (NAU)
BU............. Bau-Union (VEB) [*Construction Enterprise*]   (EG)
BU............. Beatles Unlimited ( )
BU............. Biblioteka Uniwersytecka [*University Library*] [*Poland*]
BU............. Biologicky Ustav [*Institute of Biology*]   (CZ)
BU............. Bogazici Universitesi [*Bosporus Straits University*] [*Robert
                 College*] [*Formerly,*]   (TU)
BU............. Bollettino Ufficiale [*Official Gazette*] [*Italian*]   (WER)
BU............. Brodogradiliste Uljanik [*Uljanik Shipyard*] [*Pula*]   (YU)
BU............. Bromouracil   (RU)
BU............. Bulgarian Register of Shipping   (DS)
BU............. Burma [*ANSI two-letter standard code*]   (CNC)
BU............. Bushmaster Aircraft Corp. [*ICAO aircraft manufacturer
                 identifier*]   (ICAO)
Bu............. Buyuk [*Large, Greater*]   (TU)
BU............. Combat Regulations   (RU)
BU............. Combat Sector, Combat Zone   (RU)
BU............. Control Unit   (RU)
BU............. Drilling Rig   (RU)
BU............. Gasoline-Resistant, Gasoline-Proof   (RU)
BU............. Lateral Deviation, Deflection Error   (RU)
BU............. Steeping Unit [*Clothing decontamination*]   (RU)
BU............. Union Bubi, Equatorial Guinea
b/u............. Used, Not New   (RU)
BUA .... Artillery Combat Regulations   (RU)
Bua .... Bahnunterhaltungs-Arbeiter [*Section Hand*]   (EG)
BUA .... Baptist Union of Australia
BUA .... Bibliotheques Universitaires de l'Afrique
BUA .... Botswana Uniforms Agency
BUA .... Buka Island [*Papua New Guinea*] [*Airport symbol*]   (OAG)
BUA .... Business Aviation AS [*Denmark*] [*ICAO designator*]   (FAAC)
bualosztaly ... Bunugyi Alosztaly [*Criminal Investigation Section*]   (HU)
BUB .... Bau-Union Berlin [*Berlin Construction Enterprise*]   (EG)
BUBA .... Bombardment Aviation Combat Regulations   (RU)
Bubel-Is ..... Bursa ve Cevresi Belediye Iscileri Sendikasi [*Bursa and Environs
                 Municipal Workers' Union*]   (TU)
BUBIV....... Budapesti Butoripari Vallalat [*Budapest Furniture Industry
                 Enterprise*]   (HU)
BUBMV .... Combat Regulations of Armored and Mechanized Troops   (RU)
BUC .... Banque Unie de Credit [*United Credit Bank*] [*Cameroon*]   (AF)
BUC .... Bayero University College
BUC .... Burketown [*Australia*] [*Airport symbol*]   (OAG)
BUC .... MK Burundi Air Cargo [*ICAO designator*]   (FAAC)
BUCA .... Baseball Umpires Council of Australia
BUCC .... Buccaneer Aircraft [*"Banana Bomber"*] [*British*]   (DSUE)
Buchdr ...... Buchdrucker [*Printer*] [*Publishing*] [*German*]
Buchh........ Buchhalter [*Bookkeeper, Accountant*] [*German*]
Buchh........ Buchhandlung [*Bookstore*] [*German*]
Buchst .... Buchstabe [*Letter, Character, Type*]   (EG)
buckr......... Buckram [*Buckram*] [*Publishing*] [*Netherlands*]
BUCT .... Beijing University of Chemical Technology
BUCU .... Business Union Consultation Unit [*Australia*]
BUD.......... Air Budapest Club Ltd. [*Hungary*] [*ICAO designator*]   (FAAC)
BUD........ Baptist Union of Denmark   (EAIO)
BUD........ Budapest [*Hungary*] [*Airport symbol*]   (OAG)
BUD........ Buyuk Ulku Dernegi [*Greater Idealist Society*]   (TU)
Budab........ Business Development Advisory Bureau [*Tuvaluan*]   (GEA)
BUDAPRESS ... MTI Idegen Nyelvu Szerkesztosegenek Bulletin- es
                 Cikkszolgalata [*Bulletin and Article Service of MTI's
                 Foreign Language Editorial Office*]   (HU)
BUDAVOX ... Budavox Hiradastechnikai Kulkereskedelmi Reszvenytarsasag
                 [*Budavox Telecommunications Foreign Trade Company*]
                 (HU)
BUDFIN.... Budget and Finance Division [*NATO*]   (NATG)
Budopiec ... Budowa Piecow Przemyslowych i Kominow [*Enterprise for
                 Industrial Furnace and Chimney Construction*]   (POL)
Budpst........ Budapest   (BARN)
BUDR........ Bromodeoxyuridine   (RU)
BUE .... Banque de l'Union Europeenne [*European Union Bank*] [*France*]
BuE .... Berichtigungen und Ergaenzungen [*Corrections and Additions*]
                 [*German*]   (GCA)
BUE........... Buddhist Union of Europe   (EAIO)

BUE .... Buenos Aires [*Argentina*] [*Airport symbol*] (OAG)
BUe .... Dienstvorschrift fuer Betriebsueberwachungen von Bahnhoefen [*Service Regulations for Supervision of Railroad Station Operations*] (EG)
BUEK .... Boldog Ujevet Kivan [*or Kivanok or Kivannak*] [*Happy New Year*] (HU)
BUET........ Bangladesh Univeristy of Engineering and Technology (PDAA)
BUF .... Black United Front [*South Africa*] (PD)
BUFMAR ... Bureau des Formations Medicales Agrees du Rwand
BUFOFI .... Bundesforschungsanstalt fuer Fischerei [*Federal Research Institute for Fisheries*] (MSC)
BUFVC...... British Universities Film and Video Council [*Information service or system*] (IID)
BUG .... Benguela [*Angola*] [*Airport symbol*] (OAG)
BUG .... Bundesanstalt fuer Unterwasserschall und Geophysik [*Institute for Subsoil Water Noise and Geophysics*] (MSC)
bug............. Hillock, Knoll, Mound [*Topography*] (RU)
BUH .... Baghdad University Herbarium [*Iraq*]
BUH .... Baptist Union of Hungary (EAIO)
BUH .... Bucharest [*Romania*] [*Airport symbol*] (OAG)
BUI .... Bokoudini [*Indonesia*] [*Airport symbol*] (OAG)
BUIA .... Fighter Aviation Combat Regulations (RU)
BUIST .... Beijing University of Iron and Steel Technology [*China*] (ERC)
BuitenlRechtstijd ... Buitenlandse Rechtstijdingen [*Benelux*] (BAS)
BuitenlWetteks ... Buitenlandse Wetteksten [*Benelux*] (BAS)
BUK .... Albuq [*Yemen*] [*Airport symbol*] (OAG)
BUK .... Bayero University, Kano [*Nigeria*]
BUK .... Bratislavsky Umelecky Kabinet [*Bratislava Art Group*] (CZ)
BUK .... Britse Uitssaikorporasie [*British Broadcasting Corporation*] [*Afrikaans*]
BUK .... Tug, Tugboat (RU)
bukh .... Bay [*Topography*] (RU)
bukhg .... Bookkeeping, Bookkeeping Department (RU)
BUKOP ..... Bukoba Coffee Curing Plant
BUKS......... Cable Drilling Rig, Cable Drill (RU)
bukv .... Literally (RU)
BUL .... Blue Airlines [*Zaire*] [*ICAO designator*] (FAAC)
bul .... Boulevard (BU)
bul .... Bulding (TPFD)
BUL .... Bulgaria (WDAA)
BUL .... Bulolo [*Papua New Guinea*] [*Airport symbol*] (OAG)
bul .... Bulvar [*or Bulvari*] [*Boulevard*] [*Turkey*] (CED)
BulascHst ... Bulasici Hastaliklar [*Contagious Diseases*] (TU)
BULF........ Brunei United Labor Front (ML)
Bulg........... Bulgarian (BU)
Bulg........... Radioprom & Orfei (Bulgaria) [*Record label*]
Bulg akadnauk ... Bulgarian Academy of Sciences (BU)
Bulgargeomin ... Bulgarian Specialized Organization for Geological Prospecting, Designing, and Building Mining Projects Abroad (BU)
Bulgarplodeksport ... Bulgarian Enterprise for Export of Fresh and Canned Fruit, Vegetables, and Wine (BU)
Bulgartabak ... Bulgarian Commercial Enterprise for the Export of Tobacco and Tobacco Products (BU)
Bulgartabakeksport ... Bulgarian Enterprise for Tobacco Exports (BU)
Bulg geold-vo ... Bulgarian Geological Society (BU)
BulgTsurk Pregled ... Bulgarski Tsurkoven Pregled [*Bulgarian Church Review*] [*A periodical*] (BU)
Bulg Voin ... Bulgarski Voin [*Bulgarian Soldier*] [*A periodical*] (BU)
BULI.......... [*The*] Bulletin [*Database*] [*Australia*]
Bull............ Bulletin [*German*] (GCA)
BULOC ...... Brisbane University Libraries Office of Cooperation [*Australia*]
BULOGNAS ... Badan Urusan Logistik Nasional [*National Logistics Board*] (IN)
Bult .... Buletin [*Bulletin*] (TU)
BuM .... Belugyminiszterium/Miniszter [*Ministry/Minister of the Interior*] (HU)
BUM .... Booster Unit (RU)
BUM .... Combat Regulations of Mechanized Units (RU)
BUM .... Large Department Store (RU)
bum .... Paper (RU)
bum .... Paper Mill [*Topography*] (RU)
BUMA .... Bureau voor Muziek-Auteursrecht [*Netherlands*]
BUMCO ..... Bureau Minier Congolais
BUMF .... Baltic Administration of the Maritime Fleet (RU)
BUMF .... Bum-Fodder [*Toilet paper*] [*Slang*] [*British*] (DSUE)
BUMICO .. Bureau Minier Congolais [*Congolese Mining Office*] (AF)
BUMIDOM ... Bureau des Migrations d'Outre-Mer [*Overseas Migrations Office*] [*French*] (WER)
BUMIFOM ... Bureau Minier de la France d'Outre-Mer [*Mining Bureau of Overseas France*]
BUMIGEB ... Bureau des Mines de la Geologie du Burkina [*Burkina Faso*] (EY)
Bumiz .... Moscow Paper Plate and Packing Materials Factory (RU)
bum l .... Paper Sheet [*Printing*] (RU)
bumlitiz...... Molded-Pulp Insulation (RU)

Bummash... Paper Machinery Plant (RU)
Bum pr ...... Cotton-Spinning Mill [*Topography*] (RU)
BUMS .... Naval War Exercises (RU)
BUMS .... Navy Combat Regulations (RU)
BUNAP ..... Borneo Utara National Party [*North Borneo National Party*] (ML)
BUNB........ Bunbury [*Australia*] (ROG)
BUND....... Bund der Deutschen Togolaender
BUND....... Bund fuer Umwelt und Naturschutz Deutschland eV (SLS)
BUNEP...... Bureau National d'Etudes des Projets [*National Project Study Office*] [*Rwanda*] (AF)
BUNK........ Bunkum [*Nonsense*] [*Slang*] (DSUE)
BUO.......... Bloque de Unidad Obrera [*Labor Unity Bloc*] [*Mexico*] (LA)
BUO.......... Burao [*Somalia*] [*Airport symbol*] (OAG)
BUO.......... Buro vir Universiteitsonderrig [*Bureau for University Education*] [*University of the Orange Free State*] [*South Africa*] (AA)
BUO.......... Irradiation Control Unit (RU)
BUO.......... Oscilloscope-Control Unit (RU)
BUP .... Banque de l'Union Parisienne
BUP .... Basin Administration of Waterways (RU)
BUP .... Basotho Unity Party [*South Africa*] [*Political party*] (PPW)
BUP .... Bupati [*Regent*] (IN)
BUP .... Converter Control Unit (RU)
BUP .... Infantry Combat Regulations (BU)
BUP .... Infantry Field Manual (RU)
BUPNG ..... Baptist Union of Papua New Guinea (EAIO)
BUPO........ Firefighting Combat Regulations (RU)
BUPPIN .... Biro Urusan Perusahaan Perusahaan Industri Negara [*State Industrial Firms Bureau*] (IN)
BUPTAN... Biro Urusan Perusahaan Tambang Negara [*State Mining Firms Bureau*] (IN)
BUQ.......... Bulawayo [*Zimbabwe*] [*Airport symbol*] (OAG)
BUR.......... Baptist Union of Romania (EAIO)
BUR.......... Bloque de Unidad Reformista [*Reformist Unity Bloc*] [*Dominican Republic*] (LA)
Bur .... Borehole, Drill Hole [*Topography*] (RU)
BUR.......... Bundesverband Unabhaengiger Betriebs- und REFA-Berater eV (SLS)
BUR.......... Burma [*ANSI three-letter standard code*] (CNC)
Bur .... Burun [*Cape, Headland, Promontory, Point*] (TU)
BUR.......... Business Air AG [*Switzerland*] [*ICAO designator*] (FAAC)
bur .... Derrick [*Topography*] (RU)
BUR.......... Disciplinary Barrack (RU)
BUR.......... Fortified Coastal Area (RU)
BUR.......... Safe Angle of Divergence (RU)
Bur .... Surf, Breakers [*Topography*] (RU)
BUrbRegPlan ... Bachelor of Urban and Regional Planning
BURD........ Burdekin [*Botanical region*] [*Australia*]
BUREMI... Bureau de Recherche et d'Exploitation Miniere [*Mining, Prospecting, and Exploitation Office*] [*Niger*] (AF)
BURG .... Burgemeester [*Mayor*] [*Afrikaans*]
BURGEAP ... Bureau d'Etudes de Geologie Appliquee et d'Hydrologie Souterraine
Burgeotrest ... Drilling and Geological Exploration Trust (RU)
Burgiz........ Buryat Book Publishing House (RU)
Burgiz........ Buryat-Mongol State Publishing House (RU)
Burgosizdat ... Buryat Book Publishing House (RU)
BURIDA... Bureau Ivoirien des Droits d'Auteurs
Burlag .... Bureya Railroad Construction Camp [*Corrective labor camps*] (RU)
BURM .... Burma (WDAA)
BURMA ..... Be Undressed, Ready, My Angel [*Correspondence*] (DSUE)
bur-mong.... Buryat-Mongol (RU)
BurMongASSR ... Buryat-Mongol Autonomous Soviet Socialist Republic [*1923-1958*] (RU)
Burmonggiz ... Buryat-Mongol State Publishing House (RU)
BUROBIN ... Tsentralkoye BURO Po OBsulzhivaniyu Inostrantsev [*Bureau of Service to Foreigners*] [*Former USSR*]
BURP........ Bachelor of Urban and Regional Planning
BURP........ Bomb-Run Drift Angle (RU)
BURP........ White Sea River Steamship Line Administration (RU)
bur skv .... Borehole, Drill Hole (RU)
burv .... Drilling Platoon (RU)
burzh .... Bourgeois (RU)
BUS .... Batumi [*Former USSR*] [*Airport symbol*] (OAG)
BUS .... Bulgarian Teachers' Union (BU)
BUS .... Bureau Universitaire de Statistique et de Documentations Scolaires et Professionnelles [*France*] (FLAF)
BUS .... Bureau Universitaire de Statistiques et de Documentation Scolaires et Professionnelles [*French*]
BUSDOM ... Bureau Shell d'Outre-Mer
BUSHCO .. Bushehr Petroleum Co. (MENA)
BUSL......... Baptist Union of Sri Lanka (EAIO)
Busta .... Dienstvorschrift fuer die Statistik der Bahnbetriebsunfaelle [*Service Regulations for Railroad Accident Statistics*] (EG)
BUT .... Bahamas Union of Teachers (LA)

BUT .... Barbados Union of Teachers   (LA)
but .... Batiments [*Building*] [*French*]   (TPFD)
BUT .... Baza de Utilaj Transport [*Base for Transportation Equipment*]   (RO)
BUT .... Biblioteka Uniwersytetu w Toruniu [*Torun University Library*]   (POL)
but .... Bottle   (RU)
BUT .... Business Air Taxi [*Switzerland*] [*ICAO designator*]   (FAAC)
Bute .... Buteshire [*County in Scotland*]   (BARN)
BUTEL ...... Bureau of Telecommunications [*Philippines*]   (DS)
BUTJ .... Biuro Urzadzen Techniki Jadrowej [*Nuclear Technology Equipment Bureau*]   (POL)
BUTORERT ... Butorertekesito Allami Vallalat [*State Enterprise for Sale of Furniture*]   (HU)
buttenahnl ... Buettenaehnlich [*Like Handmade Paper*] [*Publishing*] [*German*]
BUU .... Biro za Unapredenje Ugostiteljstva [*Bureau for Development of Hotel and Catering Trade*]   (YU)
BUU .... Bursa Universitesi [*Bursa University*]   (TU)
BUUD .... Badan Usaha Unit Desa [*Hamlet Unit Enterprise Bodies*] [*Indonesia*]   (FEA)
BUV .... Bactericidal Uviol Lamp   (RU)
BuV .... Betrieb und Verkehr [*Operations and Traffic*]   (EG)
BUV .... Budapesti Uveg- es Porcelanertekesito Vallalat [*Glass and China Commercial Enterprise of Budapest*]   (HU)
BUVATEX ... Budapesti Vatta- es Textilipari Termeloszovetkezet [*Budapest Cotton and Textile Producer Cooperative*]   (HU)
BUVATI .... Budapesti Varosepitesi Tervezo Vallalat [*Budapest Planning Enterprise for Urban Construction*]   (HU)
BUVATI .... Budapesti Varostervezo Intezet [*City Planning Institute of Budapest*]   (HU)
Buvo .... Betriebsunfall-Vorschrift [*Industrial Accident Regulations*]   (EG)
BUVOGEMI ... Bureau Voltaique de la Geologie et des Mines [*Voltan Bureau of Geology and Mines*]   (AF)
BUVVS ...... Air Force Combat Regulations   (RU)
BUW .... Baptist Union of Wales   (EAIO)
BUW .... Bau Bau [*Indonesia*] [*Airport symbol*]   (OAG)
BUW .... Biblioteka Uniwersytetu Warszawskiego [*Library of Warsaw University*]   (POL)
BUW .... Biuro Urbanistyczne Warszawy [*Office for the Urban Development of Warsaw*]   (POL)
BUX .... Bunia [*Zaire*] [*Airport symbol*]   (OAG)
BUY .... Bunbury [*Australia*] [*Airport symbol*]   (OAG)
BuZ .... Buchner Zahl [*Buchner Number*] [*German*]
BUZ .... Bushehr [*Iran*] [*Airport symbol*]   (OAG)
BUZA .... Antiaircraft Artillery Combat Regulations   (RU)
Buzema ...... Bulgarian Farm Machinery School   (BU)
bv .... Anhydrous, Water-Free   (RU)
BV .... Application Base   (BU)
BV .... Baksteenvereniging Bpk [*South Africa*]   (AA)
BV .... Balneum Vaporis [*Vapor Bath*] [*Medicine*]
BV .... Banco de la Vivienda [*Puerto Rico*]   (DSCA)
BV .... Bank of Valletta [*Malta*]
BV .... Barlavento [*Windward*] [*Portuguese*]
BV .... Beata Vergine [*Blessed Virgin*] [*Italian*]
BV .... Bedrijfsvereniging [*Benelux*]   (BAS)
BV .... Benzylviologen   (RU)
BV .... Berliner Volksbank [*Berlin People's Bank*]   (EG)
BV .... Besloten Vennootschap [*Private or Closed Limited Company*] [*Dutch*]
bv .... Bij Voorbeeld [*For Example*] [*Netherlands*]   (GPO)
BV .... Boeing-Vertol Division [*The Boeing Co.*] [*ICAO aircraft manufacturer identifier*]   (ICAO)
BV .... Bosanska Vila [*Sarajevo, 1886-1914*] [*A periodical*]   (YU)
BV .... Bouvet Island [*ANSI two-letter standard code*]   (CNC)
bv .... Boven Vermeld [*Benelux*]   (BAS)
BV .... Braunkohlenverwaltung [*Brown Coal Administration*] [*BKV*] [*See also*]   (EG)
bv .... Brutto Vaha [*Gross Weight*]   (CZ)
bv .... Buntetesvegrehajtas [*An abbreviation preceding the rank of officers of the National Penal Authority*] [*Prison Guards*] [*Formerly,*]   (HU)
BV .... Bureau Veritas [*International register for the classification of shipping and aircraft*]
bv .... Byvoorbeeld [*For Example*] [*Afrikaans*]
BV .... Convalescent Battalion   (RU)
BV .... Near East   (RU)
BV .... Office of Interchangeability   (RU)
BV .... Recovery Unit   (RU)
BVA .... Bachelor of Visual Arts
BVA .... Belgische Vereniging voor Aardrijkskundige Studien [*Belgian Society for Geographical Studies*]   (IRC)
BVA .... Berufsverband der Augenaerzte Deutschlands eV   (SLS)
BVA .... Blohm and Voss Australia
BVA .... Bond van Vlaamse Architekten [*Association of Flemish Architects*] [*Belgium*]   (EAIO)
BVAB .... Bedrijfsvereniging voor het Agrarisch Bedrijf [*Benelux*]   (BAS)

BVAK .... Instruction Address Unit   (RU)
BVAP .... Bureau de Vulgarisation des Activites Pratiques [*Practical Activities Popularization Office*] [*Cambodia*]   (CL)
BVB .... Bacterial Pathogen   (RU)
BVB .... Bedrijfsvergunningenbesluit [*Benelux*]   (BAS)
BVB .... Boa Vista [*Brazil*] [*Airport symbol*]   (OAG)
BVB .... Bulgarian Foreign Trade Bank   (BU)
BVB .... Bundesverband der Bueromaschinen-Importeure [*German*]   (ADPT)
BVC .... Boa Vista [*Cape Verde Islands*] [*Airport symbol*]   (OAG)
BVCh .... High-Frequency Unit   (RU)
BVD .... Binnenlandse Veiligheidsdienst [*Internal Security Service*] [*Netherlands*]   (WEN)
BVD .... Bond van Dienstplichtige [*League of Conscripts*] [*Netherlands*]   (WEN)
BvD .... Bund Vertriebener Deutschen [*Federation of German Expellees*]   (WEN)
BvD .... Bureau + van Dijk, SA   (IID)
BVD .... Data Input Unit   (RU)
BVDN .... Berufsverband Deutscher Nervenaerzte eV   (SLS)
bv dor .... Large Crater in Road [*Topography*]   (RU)
BVdS .... Bevorzugte Versorgung der Schwerpunktbetriebe [*Procurement Priority for Key Enterprises*]   (EG)
BVE .... Batallon Vasco Espanol [*Spanish Basque Battalion*]   (PD)
BVE .... Brive-La-Gaillarde [*France*] [*Airport symbol*]   (OAG)
BVE .... High-Speed Pipeless Electric Drill   (RU)
BVerf. .... Bundesverfassung [*Federal Constitution*] [*German*]
B Verf G ..... Bundesverfassungsgericht [*Federal Constitutional Court*] [*German*]   (DLA)
B Verw G .... Bundesverwaltungsgericht [*Federal Supreme Administrative Court*] [*German*]   (DLA)
BVET .... Board of Vocational Education and Training [*New South Wales, Australia*]
BVET .... Bundesamt fuer Veterinaerwesen [*Federal Veterinary Office*] [*Switzerland*]   (ARC)
BVF .... Berufsverband der Frauenaerzte eV   (SLS)
BVF .... Bua [*Fiji*] [*Airport symbol*] [*Obsolete*]   (OAG)
BVF .... White Sea Fleet   (RU)
BVFA .... Bundesversuchs und Forschungsanstalt Arsenal [*Nuclear energy*] [*Austria*]   (NRCH)
BVFI .... Bokavardafelag Islands [*Iceland*]   (SLS)
BVG .... Bataljonska Vatrena Grupa [*Battalion Fire Group*]   (YU)
BVG .... Berlevag [*Norway*] [*Airport symbol*]   (OAG)
BVG .... Berliner Verkehrs-Gesellschaft [*Berlin Transportation Company (West Berlin)*]   (WEN)
Bvg .... Bewijs van Geschiktheid [*Benelux*]   (BAS)
BVH .... Betriebsvolkshochschule [*Enterprise Adult Education Institute*]   (EG)
BVI .... Birdsville [*Australia*] [*Airport symbol*]   (OAG)
BVI .... Budapesti Vasarrendezo Iroda [*Organization Bureau of the Budapest Fair*]   (HU)
BVI .... Information Selection Unit   (RU)
BVI .... Military Information Bureau   (BU)
BVIK .... Bundesverband der Israelitischen Kultusgemeinden Oesterreichs [*Austria*]   (BJA)
bvk .... Bivouac Commandant   (BU)
BVK .... Borsodi Vegyi Kombinat [*Chemical Combine of Borsod*]   (HU)
BVK .... Office of Weight Checking   (RU)
BVK .... Protein-Vitamin Concentrate   (RU)
Bvl .... Bewijs van Luchtwaardigheid [*Benelux*]   (BAS)
BVL .... Bundesvereinigung Logistik eV   (SLS)
BVM .... Beata Virgem Maria [*Blessed Virgin Mary*] [*Portuguese*]
BVM .... Belmonte [*Brazil*] [*Airport symbol*]   (OAG)
BVM .... Bibliotheques Vertes pour le Monde [*Green Library - GL*] [*Saint Egreve, France*]   (EAIO)
BVM .... Bodenverbesserungsmittel [*Soil Improvement Agent*]   (EG)
BVM .... Britska Vojenska Misse [*British Military Mission*]   (CZ)
BVM .... Bulgarska Voenna Misul [*Bulgarian Military Thought*] [*A periodical*]   (BU)
BVM .... Bundesverband Deutscher Marktforscher eV   (SLS)
BVM .... High-Speed Computer   (RU)
BVM .... Large Computer   (RU)
BVMB ...... Baltic Naval Bases   (RU)
BVMSiIP ... Office of Interchangeability of the Ministry of the Machine Tool and Tool Industry   (RU)
BVN .... Banco de la Vivienda de Nicaragua [*Nicaraguan Housing Bank*]   (LAA)
BVN .... Bund der Verfolgten des Naziregimes [*League of Persecutees of the NAZI Regime*]   (WEN)
BVN .... Number Selection Unit   (RU)
BVO .... Belorussian Military District   (RU)
BVO .... Beogradska Vojna Oblast [*Belgrade Military District*]   (YU)
BVO .... Berufsverband Bildender Kuenstler Oesterreichs [*Austria*]   (SLS)
BVO .... Beweging voor Vrijheid en Onafhankelijkheid [*Movement for Freedom and Independence*] [*Netherlands*]   (WEN)

BvO .... Bond van Orkest+dirigenten [*Association of Conductors in the Netherlands*] [*Netherlands*]   (EAIO)

BVO .... Buchereiverband Osterreichs [*Library Association of Austria*]   (EAIO)

BVO .... Technisch-Wissenschaftlicher Verein Bergmaennischer Verband Oesterreichs [*Austria*]   (SLS)

BVOP .... Buntetesvegrehajtas Orszagos Parancsnoksaga [*National Penal Authority*] [*Prison Guards*] [*Formerly,*]   (HU)

BVP .... Bayerische Volkspartei [*Bavarian People's Party*] [*Germany*] [*Political party*]   (PPE)

bvp .... Been voor Paaltjies (Krieket) [*Leg before Wicket (Cricket)*] [*Afrikaans*]

BVP .... Business Venture Promotion [*Thailand*]

BVP .... Combat Air Patrol   (RU)

BVPA .... Brigade Policiere de la Voie Publique et des Agressions [*France*]   (FLAF)

BVpb .... Besluit Vennootschapsbelasting [*Benelux*]   (BAS)

BVPP .... Concrete Runway   (RU)

BVPU .... Bath, Disinfection, and Laundry Unit   (RU)

BVR .... Bloque de la Vanguardia Revolucionaria [*Bolivia*] [*Political party*]   (PPW)

BVR .... Bureaus for Reciprocal Accounts [*Bulgarian*]   (BU)

BVR .... Byggvaruregistret [*Building Commodity File*] [*Swedish Building Center Stockholm*] [*Information service or system*]   (IID)

BVR .... Clearinghouse [*Banking*]   (RU)

BVS .... Belgische Vereniging voor Suikerzieken [*Belgium*]   (SLS)

BVS .... Bibliothek-Verbund-System [*Library Network System*] [*Siemens AG*] [*Information service or system*]   (IID)

BVS .... Bildverarbeitungssystem [*German*]   (ADPT)

BVS .... Bulgarian Air Routes   (BU)

BVS .... Business Vehicle Survey

BVSA .... Botaniese Vereniging van Suid-Afrika [*Botanical Society of South Africa*]   (EAIO)

BVSI .... Library of the Higher Agricultural Institute   (BU)

BVSK .... Bundesverband der Freiberuflichen und Unabhaengigen Sachverstaendigen fuer das Kraftfahrzeugwesen eV   (SLS)

BVSL .... Bezrucova Vysoka Skola Lidova [*Bezruc People's College*]   (CZ)

BVSNSW .. Board of Veterinary Surgeons of New South Wales [*Australia*]

BVSS .... Bundesverband fuer den Selbstschutz [*Federal Self-Defense Association*]   (WEN)

BVT .... Beke Vilagtanacs [*World Peace Council*]   (HU)

BVT .... Bouvet Island [*ANSI three-letter standard code*]   (CNC)

BVT .... Budapesti Varosi Tanacs [*City Council of Budapest*]   (HU)

BVTL .... Belgische Vereniging voor Toegepaste Linguistiek [*Belgium*]   (SLS)

BVTsK ...... Numerical Code Delivery Unit   (RU)

BVTV .... Budapesti Varosepitesi Tervezo Vallalat [*Budapest Urban Development Planning Enterprise*]   (HU)

BVV .... Budapesti Villamos Vasut [*Budapest Electric Railways*] [*BSZKRT*] [*Formerly,*]   (HU)

BVV .... High Explosive, Blasting Agent   (RU)

BVVFA ...... Barossa Valley Vintage Festival Association [*Australia*]

BVVMI...... Library at the Higher Veterinary Medicine Institute   (BU)

BVW .... Berliner Volkseigene Wohnungsverwaltung [*Berlin State Housing Administration*]   (EG)

BVZ .... Beverly Springs [*Australia*] [*Airport symbol*] [*Obsolete*]   (OAG)

BW .... Baden-Wuerttembergische Bank

Bw .... Bahnbetriebswerk [*Locomotive Light Repair and Maintenance Shop*]   (EG)

BW .... Baltischer Weltrat [*Baltic World Council*]   (EAIO)

Bw .... Baumwolle [*Cotton*] [*German*]   (GCA)

BW .... Besluitwet [*Benelux*]   (BAS)

BW .... Bestuurswetenschappen [*Benelux*]   (BAS)

BW .... Betaalbare Wissels [*Afrikaans*]

BW .... Betriebswerkstatt [*Workshop*]   (EG)

bw .... Bez Wydawcy [*Name of Publisher Not Given*] [*Poland*]

Bw .... Bindewort [*Conjunction*] [*German*]

bw .... Bitte Wenden [*Please Turn Page*] [*German*]   (GPO)

BW .... Botswana [*ANSI two-letter standard code*]   (CNC)

BW .... Buitenlandse Wetteksten [*Benelux*]   (BAS)

BW .... Burgerlijk Wetboek [*Civil Code*] [*Netherlands*]   (ILCA)

bw .... Bywoord [*Adverb*] [*Afrikaans*]

BW .... Trinidad and Tobago Airways Corp. [*Trinidad and Tobago*] [*ICAO designator*]   (ICDA)

BWA .... Bank of West Africa

BWA .... Baptist World Alliance

BWA .... Barossa Winemakers' Association [*Australia*]

BWA .... Betriebswirtschafts-Akademie eV   (SLS)

BWA .... Bhairawa [*Nepal*] [*Airport symbol*]   (OAG)

BWA .... Biuro Wystaw Artystycznych [*Bureau of Art Exhibitions*]   (POL)

BWA .... Botswana [*ANSI three-letter standard code*]   (CNC)

BWA .... British West Africa

BWA .... Standard Bank of West Africa

BWA .... Trinidad and Tobago Airways Corp. [*ICAO designator*]   (FAAC)

BWAC ...... Bridge Wholesale Acceptance Corp. [*Australia*]

BWASA..... Blind Welfare Society of South Australia

BWB .... Boere Weerstandsbeweging [*South Africa*] [*Political party*]   (EY)

BWB .... Bundesamt fuer Wehrtechnik und Beschaffung   (IMH)

BWB .... Bundestamt fur Wehrtechnik und Beschaffund [*Federal Office for Military Technology and Procurement*] [*Germany*]   (PDAA)

BWC .... Black Women's Convention

BWC .... Brisbane Women's Club [*Australia*]

BWCA ...... Bangladesh Work Camps Association   (EAIO)

BWCDF.... Black Women's Community Development Foundation   (AF)

BWCS....... Beauty Without Cruelty Society [*Australia*]

BWCSA .... British White Cattle Society of Australia

BWF........ Brisbane Warana Festival [*Australia*]

BWFAB .... Bangladesh Wireless and Frequency Allocation Board   (PDAA)

BWFC....... Beatles and Wings Fan Club [*Germany*]   (EAIO)

BWFCRS... Brackish Water Fish Culture Research Station [*Australia*]

BWFK....... Brackish Water Fish Farm [*India*]   (ASF)

BWG .... Braunschweigische Wissenschaftliche Gesellschaft   (SLS)

BWG .... Oesterreichische Bankwissenschaftliche Gesellschaft an der Wirtschaftsuniversitaet Wien [*Austria*]   (SLS)

BWH .... Biological Wool Harvesting [*Australia*]

BWHA ...... Brisbane Women's Hockey Association [*Australia*]

BWI .... Perseroan Terbatas Bonded Warehouses Indonesia   (IMH)

BWIA .... British West Indies Airways [*Trinidadian and Tobagan*]   (LA)

BWIU .... Building Workers' Industrial Union [*Australia*]

BWIUA ..... Building Workers' Industrial Union of Australia

BWIU &PF ... Building Workers' Industrial Union and Plasterers' Federation [*Australia*]

BWK .... Bremer Woll-Kaemmerei [*Bremen Carding Combs*]

BWKZ .... Biuro Wspolpracy Kulturalnej z Zagranica [*Foreign Cultural Relations Bureau*] [*Poland*]

BWL .... Banco Wiese Limitado [*Bank*] [*Peru*]

BWMC ..... British Working Men's Club

BWN......... Bandar Seri Begawan [*Brunei*] [*Airport symbol*]   (OAG)

BWO......... Bundesverband der Weinbautreibenden Osterreichs [*Austria*]   (EAIO)

BWP .... Belgische Werkliedenpartij [*Belgian Workers' Party*] [*Later, Belgian Socialist Party*] [*Political party*]   (PPE)

BWP .... Betriebswirtschaftsplan [*Enterprise Economic Plan*]   (EG)

BWP .... Bewani [*Papua New Guinea*] [*Airport symbol*]   (OAG)

BWP .... Biblioteka Wydawnictw Prasowych [*Press Agency Library (Series)*]   (POL)

BWP .... Biblioteka Wydawnictw Prasy [*Press Agency Library*]   (POL)

BWPR....... Biuro Wydawnictw Polskiego Radia [*Publications Office of the Polish Radio*]   (POL)

BWQ......... Brewarrina [*Australia*] [*Airport symbol*]   (OAG)

BWR......... Boiling-Water Reactor

BWRE....... Biological Welfare Research Establishment   (ASF)

BWS.......... Bank of Western Samoa

BWS.......... Basque Workers' Solidarity [*Spain*]   (EAIO)

BWS.......... Bureau of Water Supply [*Philippines*]   (DS)

BWU .... Barbados Workers Union   (LA)

BWUSA..... Blind Workers' Union of South Australia

BWUSWP ... Baptist Women's Union of the South West Pacific [*Australia*]

BWUV ...... Blind Workers' Union of Victoria [*Australia*]

BWV .... Bach Werke-Verzeichnis [*Music*]

BWVO .... Binnenwasserstrassen-Verkehrsordnung [*Inland Waterways Traffic Regulations*]   (EG)

Bww.......... Bahnbetriebswagen-Werk [*Railroad Car Maintenance Shop*]   (EG)

BWW .... Biblioteka Wiedzy Wojskowej [*Military Science Library*]   (POL)

BWWA ...... Business Who's Who of Australia [*R. G. Riddell Pty. Ltd.*] [*Information service or system*]   (IID)

BX .... Compania SPANTAX (Servicios y Transportes Aereos Air Charter) [*Spain*] [*ICAO designator*]   (ICDA)

Bxa............ Baixa [*Shoal*] [*Portuguese*]   (NAU)

BxA............ Beaux Arts [*French*]

BXB .... Babo [*Indonesia*] [*Airport symbol*]   (OAG)

BXD .... Bade [*Indonesia*] [*Airport symbol*]   (OAG)

BXE .... Bakel [*Senegal*] [*Airport symbol*]   (OAG)

BXI .... Boundiali [*Ivory Coast*] [*Airport symbol*]   (OAG)

BXL........... Air Exel Belgique [*Belgium*] [*ICAO designator*]   (FAAC)

Bxo............ Baixo [*Shoal*] [*Portuguese*]   (NAU)

BXO........... Bissau [*Portuguese Guinea*] [*Airport symbol*]   (OAG)

BXS........... Compania Spantax [*Spain*] [*ICAO designator*]   (FAAC)

BXU .... Butuan [*Philippines*] [*Airport symbol*]   (OAG)

BXV .... Breiddalsvik [*Iceland*] [*Airport symbol*]   (OAG)

by............... Bio-Yeda Ltd. [*Israel*]

BY .... Byelorussian Soviet Socialist Republic [*ISO two-letter standard code*]   (CNC)

BY .... Byelorussian SSR [*ANSI two-letter standard code*]   (CNC)

B-ya........... Bulgaria   (BU)

ByB .... Bybel [*Bible*] [*Afrikaans*]

Byb Gesk ... Bybelse Geskiedenis [*Bible History*] [*Afrikaans*]

BYC .... Balatoni Yacht Club [*Balaton Yacht Club*]   (HU)

BYC .... Yacuiba [*Bolivia*] [*Airport symbol*]   (OAG)

BYD .... Bilimsel Yayinlar Dernegi [*Scientific Publications Society*]   (TU)

Bye .... Byelorussia [*Belarus*]   (BARN)
b/ye .... Library Unit   (RU)
b ye .... Protein Unit   (RU)
BYGGDOK ... Institutet foer Byggdokumentation [*Swedish Institute of Building Documentation*] [*Research center*]   (IRC)
BYGM .... Basin-Yayin Genel Mudurlugu [*Press and Publications Directorate General*] [*Under Office of Premier*]   (TU)
BYK .... Bouake [*Ivory Coast*] [*Airport symbol*]   (OAG)
BYKP .... Bes Yillik Kalkinma Plani [*Five-Year Development Plan*]   (TU)
byl .... Bylae [*Enclosure*] [*Afrikaans*]
byl .... Bylina [*Bibliography*]   (RU)
BYM .... Bayamo [*Cuba*] [*Airport symbol*]   (OAG)
BYM .... Born Youth Movement
BYS .... Byelorussian Soviet Socialist Republic [*ISO three-letter standard code*]   (CNC)
BYS .... Byelorussian SSR [*ANSI three-letter standard code*]   (CNC)
BYTB .... Basin, Yayin, ve Turizm Bakanligi [*Ministry of Press, Broadcasting, and Tourism*]   (TU)
BYU .... Bayreuth [*Germany*] [*Airport symbol*]   (OAG)
BYU .... Bayu Indonesia Air PT [*ICAO designator*]   (FAAC)
byudzhsch ... Budget Accounting   (BU)
byul .... Bulletin   (RU)
BYuP .... Office of Young Pioneers   (RU)
byurobin ..... Office of Services to Foreigners   (RU)
byv .... Byvaly [*Former*]   (CZ)
byv .... Byvoeglik [*Adjective*] [*Afrikaans*]
BYV .... Byvoegsel [*Appendix, Supplement*] [*Afrikaans*]
byv .... Former [*Topography*]   (RU)
byvsh ukr ... Abandoned Fortification [*Topography*]   (RU)
BYW .... Bywoord [*Adverb*] [*Afrikaans*]
BYWCA ..... Botswana Young Women's Christian Association   (EAIO)
BYYO .... Basin ve Yayin Yuksek Okulu [*Advanced School for Press and Publications*] [*Attached to Ankara University School of Political Science*]   (TU)
BZ .... Antiaircraft Battery   (RU)
BZ .... Bacteriological Contamination [*Warning*], Bacteriological Infection   (RU)
BZ .... Banque du Zaire [*Bank of Zaire*]   (AF)
BZ .... Belize [*ANSI two-letter standard code*]   (CNC)
Bz .... Benzol [*Benzene*] [*German*]
Bz .... Bestellzettel [*Order Form*] [*German*]
bz .... Bezahlt [*Paid*] [*German*]
bz .... Bezeichnet [*Denoted*] [*German*]   (GCA)
Bz .... Bezirk [*One of 14 large GDR administrative districts*]
bz .... Bez Zmian [*Unchanged*] [*Poland*]
BZ .... Bolzano [*Car registration plates*] [*Italian*]
Bz .... Brenn-Zuender [*Time Fuse or Primer*] [*Military*] [*German*]   (MTD)
BZ .... Buitenlandse Zaken [*Benelux*]   (BAS)
BZ .... Combat Supplies on Hand, Combat Stockpile   (RU)
b z .... No Title [*Bibliography*]   (RU)
BZ .... Order Form, Order Blank   (RU)
BZ .... Refueling Truck   (RU)
BZA .... Binnenzollamt [*Inland Customs Office*]   (EG)
BZAD .... Antiaircraft Artillery Battalion Battery   (RU)
b zav .... Without Verification   (BU)
BZB .... Besluit Bedrijfszelfbescherming [*Benelux*]   (BAS)
BZB .... Bugarska Zemljoradnicka Zadruzna Banka [*Bulgarian Agricultural Cooperative Bank*]   (YU)
BZB .... Bulgarian Agricultural Bank   (BU)
BZC .... Bibliografia Zawartosci Czasopism [*Bibliography of Articles in Periodicals*]   (POL)
BZCB .... Biuro Zbytu Ceramiki Budowlanej [*Sales Office for Building Tiles*]   (POL)
BZDGM .... Bos Zamanlari Degerlendirme Genel Mudurlugu [*Directorate General for Improved Utilization of Spare Time*]   (TU)
BZE .... Belize City [*Belize*] [*Airport symbol*]   (OAG)
BzFstI .... Bezirksforstinspektion [*District Forest Inspection*] [*German*]
BZG .... Botanisch-Zoologische Gesellschaft Liechtenstein-Sargans-Werdenberg [*Liechtenstein*]   (EAIO)
BZG .... Bydgoszcz [*Poland*] [*Airport symbol*] [*Obsolete*]   (OAG)
BzGK .... Bezirksgendarmeriekommando [*District Constabulary Detachment*]
BZGK .... Bohuminske Zelezarny Gustava Klimenta [*Gustav Kliment Iron Works at Bohumin*]   (CZ)
BZGL .... Bezueglich [*In Regard To, With Reference To*] [*German*]
BZH .... Britair SA [*France*] [*ICAO designator*]   (FAAC)
BZh .... Railroad Battery [*Artillery*]   (RU)
BZhNS ...... Bulgarian National Women's Union   (BU)
bzhw .... Beziehungsweise [*Respectively*] [*German*]   (GCA)
BZI .... Baterija Zvukovnog Izvidanja [*Sound Reconnaissance Battery (equipped with listening apparatus)*]   (YU)
BZK .... Code-Protection Unit   (RU)
BZK .... Instruction Storage Unit   (RU)
BZKB .... Bulgarian Agricultural and Cooperative Bank   (BU)
BZKBanka ... Bulgarian Agricultural and Cooperative Bank   (BU)

bzl .... Benzene [*Solvent*]   (RU)
Bzl .... Benzol [*Benzene*] [*German*]   (GCA)
BZMAJ ..... Bavlnarske Zavody Mistra Aloise Jiraska [*Alois Jirasek Cotton Mills*]   (CZ)
BZmR .... Sound-Ranging Battery   (RU)
Bzn .... Benzin [*Benzine*] [*German*]
bzn .... Benzine [*Solvent*]   (RU)
Bzn .... Benzol [*Benzene*] [*German*]
BZN .... Biuro Zbytu Narzedzi [*Tool Sales Office*]   (POL)
BZNS .... Bugarski Zemljoradnicki Narodni Savez [*National Agrarian Union of Bulgaria*]   (YU)
BZNS .... Bulgarian National Agrarian Union   (BU)
BZNS .... Bulgarian People's Agricultural Union   (RU)
BZNS .... Bulgarski Zemedelski Naroden Soyuz [*Bulgarian Agrarian People's Union-United*] [*Political party*]   (EY)
Bzo .... Brazo [*Arm (of the sea)*] [*Spanish*]   (NAU)
BZO .... Correspondence Training Center   (RU)
BZO .... Warhead (of Torpedo)   (RU)
BZP .... Bizant [*Australia*] [*Airport symbol*] [*Obsolete*]   (OAG)
BZP .... Refueling Point   (RU)
BZPG .... Bydgoskie Zaklady Przemyslu Gumowego [*Bydgoszcz Rubber Works*]   (POL)
BZPT .... Bielskie Zaklady Przemyslu Terenowego [*Bielsko Local Industry Plant*]   (POL)
BZPW .... Bialostockie Zaklady Przemyslu Welnianego [*Bialystok Wool Mill*]   (POL)
BZPW .... Bytomskie Zaklady Przemyslu Weglowego [*Bytom (Beuthen) Coal Industry Plant*]   (POL)
BZPW .... Bytomskie Zjednoczenie Przemyslu Weglowego [*Bytom (Beuthen) Coal Industry Association*]   (POL)
BZR .... Befehlszaehlregister [*German*]   (ADPT)
BZR .... Beziers [*France*] [*Airport symbol*]   (OAG)
BZR .... Bialostockie Zaklady Roszarnicze [*Bialystok Flax Processing Plant*]   (POL)
BZR .... Office of Plant Protection   (RU)
BZR .... Sound-Ranging Battery   (RU)
BZS .... Union of Bulgarian Dentists   (BU)
BZT .... Armor-Piercing Incendiary Tracer Bullet   (RU)
BZTM .... Biuro Zagranicznej Turystyki Mlodziezowej [*International Youth Touring Office*] [*Poland*]
BZTPMB .. Bialostockie Zjednoczenie Terenowego Przemyslu Materialow Budowlanych [*Bialystok Association of the Local Building Materials Industry*]   (POL)
BZU .... Buffer Storage   (RU)
BZU .... Bunkering Facilities, Bunkering Gear   (RU)
BZU .... Buta [*Zaire*] [*Airport symbol*]   (OAG)
BZUT .... Bielskie Zaklady Urzadzen Technicznych [*Bielsko Technical Equipment Plant*]   (POL)
BZV .... Brazzaville [*People's Republic of the Congo*] [*Airport symbol*]   (OAG)
BZW .... Barclays de Zoete Wedd [*Investment firm*] [*British*]
bzw .... Beziehungsweise [*And, Or, And/Or, Respectively*] [*German*]   (EG)

C

C .... Cabo [*Cape*] [*Spanish*]   (NAU)
C .... Cabo [*Cape*] [*Portuguese*]   (NAU)
C .... Cadde [*Avenue, Street*] [*Cad, cd*] [*See also*]   (TU)
C/ .... Caisse [*Cash*] [*French*]
c/ .... Caja [*Box, Chest, Safe*] [*Spanish*]
C .... Calcada [*Street*] [*Portuguese*]
C .... Calle [*Street*] [*Spanish*]   (CED)
C .... Campagne [*Country*] [*French*]   (MTD)
C .... Candidato a Doctor en Ciencias [*Spanish*]
C .... Candidature [*Candidature*] [*French*]
c .... Canto [*Song*] [*Portuguese*]
c .... Canton [*District*] [*French*]
C .... Cap [*Cape*] [*French*]   (NAU)
C .... Cap [*Cape*] [*Romanian*]   (NAU)
c .... Capacite [*Capacity*] [*French*]
C .... Capacite en Droit [*Qualification in Law*] [*French*]
C .... Capitolo [*Chapter*] [*Italian*]
c .... Capitulo [*Chapter*] [*Spanish*]
C .... Capo [*Cape*] [*Italian*]   (NAU)
C .... Capo [*The Beginning*] [*Music*]
C .... Carbono [*Carbon*] [*Chemical element*] [*Portuguese*]
c .... Cargo [*Charge, Debit*] [*Spanish*]
C .... Carta [*Folio*] [*Italian*]
c .... Cas [*Hour, Given Moment or Interval of Time*]   (YU)
c .... Casse [*Broken*] [*French*]
C .... Cay [*Stream, Brook*]   (TU)
C .... Cedi [*Monetary unit*] [*Ghana*]
C .... Celsius [*Centigrade*] [*German*]   (GCA)
C .... Celsius [*Centigrade*] [*French*]
C .... Celsiusta [*Celsius, Centigrade*] [*Finland*]
C .... Celsjusz [*Celsius, Centigrade*] [*Poland*]
c .... Cena [*Scene*] [*Portuguese*]
C .... Centavo [*Monetary unit in many Spanish-American countries*]
C .... Centerpartiet [*Center Party*] [*Sweden*]   (WEN)
C .... Centigrade [*Centigrade*] [*French*]
C .... Centime [*Monetary unit*] [*France*]
c .... Centimetre [*Centimeter*] [*French*]
c .... Centimetros [*Centimeters*] [*Spanish*]
c .... Cento [*Hundred*] [*Portuguese*]
c .... Cesky [*or Cestina*] [*Czech or Czech Language*]   (CZ)
C .... Cessna Aircraft Co. [*ICAO aircraft manufacturer identifier*]
                 (ICAO)
C .... Ceta [*Platoon*]   (CZ)
C .... Charlie [*Phonetic alphabet*] [*International since 1956*]   (DSUE)
c .... Child   (364)
c .... Children   (EECI)
c .... Cikk [*or Cikkely*] [*Article or Item or Paragraph*]   (HU)
C .... Cilt [*Volume*]   (TU)
c .... Cim [*or Cimu*] [*Title or Entitled*]   (HU)
c .... Circa   (EECI)
c .... Cislo [*Number*]   (CZ)
C .... Code [*French*]   (FLAF)
c .... Codice [*Code*] [*Italian*]
c .... Coins [*Corners*] [*Publishing*] [*French*]
C .... Col [*With The*] [*Music*]
C .... Colon [*Monetary unit*] [*Costa Rica, El Salvador*]
C .... Columbia [*Record Label*] [*Great Britain, Europe, Australia, etc.*]
c .... Columna [*Column*] [*Spanish*]
c/ .... Com [*With*] [*Portuguese*]
C .... Commandeur [*Commander*] [*French*]
C .... Compania [*Company, Society*] [*Spanish*]
C .... Compte [*Account*] [*Business term*] [*French*]   (GPO)
c .... Con [*With*] [*Spanish*]
C .... Confessore [*Confessor*] [*Italian*]
c/ .... Conta [*Count*] [*Portuguese*]
C .... Conto [*Account*] [*Italian*]
c .... Contra [*Against*] [*Spanish*]
c/ .... Contre [*Against*] [*French*]

c .... Coperta [*Covered*] [*Italian*]
C .... Cordoba [*Monetary unit*] [*Nicaragua*]
c .... Corka [*Daughter*] [*Poland*]
c .... Corso [*Street*] [*Italian*]   (CED)
c .... Corte [*Edge*] [*Publishing*] [*Spanish*]
c .... Coulomb [*French*]
c .... Coulomb [*German*]   (GCA)
C .... Council [*Australia*]
c .... Coupon [*Coupon*] [*French*]
c .... Coupure [*Denomination*] [*Business term*] [*French*]
c .... Courant [*Instant*] [*French*]
c .... Cours [*Quotation, Price*] [*French*]
C .... Court [*Short*] [*Of guns*] [*French*]   (MTD)
C .... Coutume [*Custom*] [*French*]   (FLAF)
C .... Cube [*Cubic*] [*French*]   (MTD)
C .... Cumhuriyet [*Republic, Republican*]   (TU)
C .... Cyprus   (BARN)
C .... Elektrische Kapazitaet [*Electrical Capacity*] [*German*]
C .... Grande Calorie [*Kilogram Calorie*] [*French*]
c .... Petite Calorie [*Gram Calorie*] [*French*]
C .... Stopien Celsjusza [*Degree Celsius*] [*Poland*]
C1O .... Canto Primo [*First Soprano*] [*Music*]
C2 .... Nauru [*Aircraft nationality and registration mark*]   (FAAC)
c^2 .... Negyzetcentimeter [*Square Centimeter*]   (HU)
c^2 .... Quadratzentimeter [*Square Centimeter*]   (EG)
c^3 .... Kobcentimeter [*Cubic Centimeter*]   (HU)
c^3 .... Kubikzentimeter [*Cubic Centimeter*]   (EG)
C5 .... Gambia [*Aircraft nationality and registration mark*]   (FAAC)
C6 .... Bahamas [*Aircraft nationality and registration mark*]   (FAAC)
C9 .... Mozambique [*Aircraft nationality and registration mark*]
                 (FAAC)
C-47 .... Centrale 47 [*Union for bauxite workers*] [*Surinam*]
CA .... Cadmium Association [*British*]   (EAIO)
Ca .... Caesium [*Cesium*] [*Chemical element*] [*German*]
CA .... Cagliari [*Car registration plates*] [*Italian*]
ca .... Caixa Alta [*Old Trunk*] [*Portuguese*]
Ca .... Calcio [*Calcium*] [*Chemical element*] [*Portuguese*]
CA .... California   (IDIG)
Ca .... Cami [*Mosque*]   (TU)
CA .... Canada [*ANSI two-letter standard code*]   (CNC)
CA .... Capeverdean Association [*Portugal*]   (EAIO)
CA .... Caprivi Alliance [*Namibia*]
ca .... Carta [*Map, Paper*] [*Publishing*] [*Italian*]
Ca .... Cay [*or Cayi*] [*Stream or River*] [*Turkey*]   (NAU)
CA .... Centacare Australia
ca .... Centiare [*Centare*] [*French*]   (GPO)
CA .... Central Africa
CA .... Centroamerica [*Central America*] [*Spanish*]   (GPO)
CA .... Certificat d'Aptitude [*French*]
CA .... Cervena Armija [*Red Army*]   (YU)
CA .... Chemistry Associates [*Australia*]
CA .... Chiffre d'Affaires [*French*]   (FLAF)
ca .... Cirka [*About*] [*Sweden*]
ca .... Cirka [*About*] [*German*]
CA .... Citizen Action [*India*]   (EAIO)
CA .... Coastwatchers' Association [*Australia*]
CA .... Colegio Agricola de Camboriu [*Brazil*]   (DSCA)
CA .... Colegio Agricola "Senador Gomes de Oliveira" [*Brazil*]   (DSCA)
CA .... Coll'Arco [*With the Bow*] [*Music*]
CA .... Collectieve Arbeidsovereenkomst [*Benelux*]   (BAS)
CA .... Comites d'Action [*Action Committees*] [*French*]   (WER)
CA .... Commonwealth of Australia
Ca .... Compagnia [*Company*] [*Italian*]   (GPO)
Ca .... Companhia [*Company*] [*Portuguese*]
ca .... Compania [*Company, Society*] [*Spanish*]
CA .... Compania Anonima [*Joint Stock Company*] [*Spanish*]   (CED)
CA .... Composants Acoustiques   (ADPT)
CA .... Concert Artist [*Record label*] [*Great Britain*]

CA .... Confirming Authority [*Australia*]
CA .... Conseil d'Administration [*Board of Directors (of a private organization, company, fund, or governmental or other financial body)*] [*Administrative Council (of a political party, university, or non-financial governmental unit)*] (CL)
CA .... Consejo Agricola de Puerto Rico [*Puerto Rico*]   (DSCA)
c/a .... Conta Aberta [*Unsettled Account*] [*Business term*] [*Portuguese*]
ca .... Contractuele Aansprakelijkheid [*Benelux*]   (BAS)
CA .... Convention Africaine
CA .... Corps d'Armee [*Army Corps*] [*Military*] [*French*]   (MTD)
CA .... Corrente Alternata [*Alternating Current*] [*Italian*]
C/A .... Corrente Anno [*Current Year*] [*Italian*]   (WER)
ca .... Corriente Alterna [*Alternating Current*] [*Spanish*]
CA .... Courant Alternatif [*Alternating Current*] [*French*]
CA .... Cour d'Appel [*French*]
CA .... Cour d'Assises [*French*]   (FLAF)
CA .... Courier Aircrafts Ltd. [*Australia*]
CA .... Credit Agricole [*France*]
CA .... Cromwell Association   (EA)
CA .... Cruising Association [*British*]   (EAIO)
CA .... Crvena Armija [*Red Army*]   (YU)
CA .... Cuenta Abierta [*Open Account*] [*Spanish*] [*Business term*]
CA .... Cuerpo de Aviacion [*Air Corps*] [*Bolivia*]
CA .... Cyprus Airways Ltd.   (IMH)
CA .... Kanada [*Canada*] [*Poland*]
CA .... Mastercharge
CA .... Societe en Commandite par Actions   (FLAF)
CAA .... Caisse Autonome d'Amortissement [*Autonomous Amortization Fund*] [*Ivory Coast*]
CAA .... Campus Activities Australia   (ADA)
CAA .... Caribbean Australian Association
CAA .... Centre Against Apartheid [*United Nations*]   (DUND)
CAA .... Centre d'Apprentissage Agricole
CAA .... Centre for Aboriginal Artists [*Australia*]
CAA .... Centro Azucarero Argentino [*Argentina*]   (DSCA)
CAA .... Chiropractors' Association of Australia
CAA .... Civil Aeronautics Administration [*Taiwan*]   (PDAA)
CAA .... Civil Aviation Agency [*Australia*]
CAA .... Civil Aviation Authority [*Australia*]
CAA .... Civil Aviation Authority [*British*]
CAA .... Colombian Actuarial Association   (EAIO)
CAA .... Comandos Autonomos Anti-Capitalistas [*Spain*] [*Political party*]   (EY)
CAA .... Comitato Anti-Imperialista Antifascista [*Anti-Imperialist, Antifascist Committee*] [*Italian*]   (WER)
CAA .... Commercial Aviation Association of Southern Africa   (AA)
CAA .... Commonwealth Accreditation Agency [*Australia*]
CAA .... Commonwealth Archivists Association [*Later, ACARM*]   (EA)
CAA .... Commonwealth Association of Architects [*British*]   (EAIO)
CAA .... Community Aid Abroad [*Australia*]   (EAIO)
CAA .... Compagnie Africaine d'Accumulateurs [*Algeria*]
CAA .... Conciliation and Arbitration Act [*Australia*]   (ADA)
CAA .... Confederation Arabe d'Athletisme [*Arab Amateur Athletic Federation - AAAF*]   (EAIO)
CAA .... Conseil Africain de l'Arachide [*African Groundnut Council*]   (EAIO)
CAA .... Conseil Africaine de l'Arachide [*African Groundnut Council - AGC*]   (AF)
CAA .... Constitutional Association of Australia   (ADA)
CAA .... Croatian Australian Association
CAA .... Cryonics Association of Australia
CAA .... Cyprus Automobile Association   (EAIO)
CAAA .... Centre d'Activities Artistiques d'Amateurs - Bulgarie [*Centre for Artistic Activities for Amateurs - Bulgaria*]   (EAIO)
CAAA .... Comision Asesora de Asuntos Aduaneros [*Asociacion Latinoamericana de Libre Comercio*]   (LAA)
CAAA .... Corporacion Argentina de Aberdeen-Angus [*Argentina*]   (DSCA)
CAAACT ... Chiropractors' Association of Australia, Australian Capital Territory
CAAB .... Commandement Allie des Approches de la Baltique [*Baltic Approaches Allied Command*] [*NATO*]   (NATG)
CAAB .... Commonwealth Art Advisory Board [*Australia*]   (ADA)
CAA/BADIV ... Business Aviation Division of the Commercial Aviation Association of Southern Africa   (EAIO)
CAABU ..... Council for the Advancement of Arab-British Understanding [*Arab-British Centre*] [*Research center*]   (MENA)
CAAC .... Central Australian Aboriginal Congress   (ADA)
CAAC .... Civil Aviation Administration of China
CAACACT ... Consumer Affairs Advisory Committee of the Australian Capital Territory
CAACE...... Comite des Associations d'Armateurs des Communautes Europeennes [*Committee of the European Communities Shipowners' Associations*] [*Belgium*]   (DS)
CAA-CI...... Caisse Autonome d'Amortissement de la Cote-D'Ivoire [*Autonomous Sinking Fund of the Ivory Coast*]   (AF)

CAACTD... Comite Asesor sobre la Aplicacion de la Ciencia y la Tecnologia al Desarrollo [*Advisory Committee on the Application of Science and Technology to Development - ACASTD*] [*United Nations (already exists in GUS II database)*] [*Spanish*]   (ASF)
CAADE ..... Caisse Autonome d'Amortissement des Dettes de l'Etat [*Autonomous Fund for the Amortization of State Debt*] [*Central African Republic*]   (AF)
CAADES ... Confederacion de Asociaciones Agricolas del Estado de Sinaloa [*Mexico*]   (DSCA)
CAAEA...... Citizens Against Airport Environment Association
CAAEO ..... Commission des Affaires d'Aise et d'Extreme-Orient de la Chambre de Commerce Internationale   (WGAO)
CAAEO ..... Commission des Affaires d'Asie et d'Extreme-Orient [*Chambre de Commerce Internationale*] [*France*]   (FLAF)
CAAF........ Campaign Against AIDS [*Acquired Immune Deficiency Syndrome*] Foundation [*Ghana*]
CAAF........ Conseil Asiatique d'Analystes Financiers [*Asian Council of Securities Analysts - ASAC*] [*Tokyo, Japan*]   (EAIO)
CAAFDP ... Central American Association of Families of Disappeared Persons [*See also ACAFADE*] [*San Jose, Costa Rica*]   (EAIO)
CAAIM...... Cooperative Agricole d'Approvisionnement des Agriculteurs de la Marche   (WGAO)
CAAIS .... Computer-Assisted Action Information System [*NATO*]   (NATG)
CAAK .... Civil Aviation Administration of Korea [*North Korea*]
CAAKK..... Comite d'Aide et d'Assistance aux Khmers Venus du Sud Vietnam [*or Comite d'Aide et d'Assistance aux Khmers Venus du Kampuchea Krom*] [*Khmer Krom Aid and Relief Committee Cambodia*]   (CL)
CAALAS ... Central Australian Aboriginal Legal Aid Scheme
CAALE...... Centro Addrestamento Aviazione Leggera dell'Esercito [*Army Light Avaition Training Center*] [*Italy*]   (PDAA)
CAALG...... Central Australia Adult Literacy Group
CAAM ...... Colegio de Agricultura y Artes Mecanicas [*Puerto Rico*]   (DSCA)
CAAMA ... Central Australian Aboriginal Media Association
CAAMC .... China National Agricultural & Animal Husbandry Machinery Corp.   (TCC)
CAAMD .... Council of Australian Art Museum Directors
CAAMI...... Caisse Auxiliaire d'Assurance Maladie-Invalidite [*French*]   (BAS)
CAAMS..... Chinese Academy of Agricultural Mechanization Sciences [*China*]
CAAN .... Confederacion de Asociaciones Algodoneras de Nicaragua [*Nicaraguan Cotton Associations Confederation*]   (LA)
CAAP........ Centro Andino de Accion Popular [*Ecuador*]   (EAIO)
CAAP........ Consultants in Alternative Agriculture Projects [*Brazil*]   (EAIO)
CAAPA...... China Association of Amusement Parks and Attractions   (EAIO)
CAAPP ...... Cooperative d'Achats des Administrations Publiques et Privees [*Morocco*]
CAAPS ...... Council for Aboriginal Alcohol Program Services [*Australia*]
CAAPU ..... Central Australian Aboriginal Planning Unit
CAAQ .... Customs Agents' Association of Queensland [*Australia*]
CAAR .... Caisse Algerienne d'Assurance et de Reassurance [*Algerian Insurance and Reinsurance Fund*]
CAAR .... Compagnie Africaine des Automobiles Renault
CAARAV... Community Alert against Racism and Violence [*Australia*]
CAARC...... Commonwealth Advisory Aeronautical Research Council [*British*]   (EAIO)
CAARI....... Cyprus American Archaeological Research Institute [*Research center*]   (IRC)
CAARM .... Confederacion de Asociaciones Algodoneras de la Republica Mexicana   (WGAO)
CAARM .... Confederacion de Asociaciones Algodoneras de la Republica Mexicana, AC [*Mexico*]   (DSCA)
CAARP...... Comissao de Antifascistas de Apoio aos Revolucionarios Presos [*Antifascist Committee of Support for Revolutionary Prisoners*] [*Portuguese*]   (WER)
CAAS........ Canadian Association of African Studies
CAAS........ Center for African and African-American Studies
CAAS........ Ceylon Association for the Advancement of Science   (MCD)
CAAS........ Chinese Academy of Agricultural Sciences   (WGAO)
CAAS........ Chinese Association for the Advancement of Science   (WGAO)
CAAS........ Chinese Association of Agricultural Science   (EAIO)
CAAS........ Continence Aids Assistance Scheme [*Australia*]
CAAS........ Cooperativa Agricola Apicola del Sur Ltd [*Chile*]   (DSCA)
CAASA...... Centre Africain d'Application de Statistique Agricole
CAASA...... Community Aid Abroad, Southern Africa Group [*Australia*]
CAASD...... Corporacion del Acueducto y Alcantarilla de Santo Domingo [*Santo Domingo Aqueduct and Sewerage Corporation*] [*Dominican Republic*]   (LA)
CAAT .... Campaign Against Arms Trade   (WGAO)
CAAT .... Centre Afro-Americain du Travail [*Afro-American Labor Center*]   (AF)
CAAV .... Central Association of Agricultural Valuers   (WGAO)
CAAV .... Civil Aviation Administration of Vietnam

CAB .... Caballero [*Cavalier*] [*Spanish*]   (DSUE)
CAB .... Cabinda [*Angola*] [*Airport symbol*]   (OAG)
CAB .... Central Agricultural Board
CAB .... Centro Atomico Bariloche [*Bariloche Atomic Centre*] [*Research center*]   (WND)
CAB .... Chambre des Architectes de Belgique [*Belgium*]   (SLS)
CAB .... Chemiean!agenbau [*Chemical Facilities Construction Enterprise*]   (EG)
CAB .... Christliche Arbeiterwegung   (WGAO)
CAB .... Citizens Advice Bureaux   (WGAO)
CAB .... Club Astronomique de Berce [*France*]   (EAIO)
CAB .... Club Automobile du Burundi
CAB .... Comite des Assurers Belges   (WGAO)
CAB .... Commonwealth Agricultural Bureaux [*Australia*]   (ADA)
CAB .... Community Arts Board [*Australia Council*]
CAB .... Compagnie Africaine des Bois [*African Lumber Co.*] [*Ivory Coast*]
CAB .... Confederation Asiatique Billar   (WGAO)
CAB .... Cooperativa Agricola Bandeirante [*Brazil*]   (DSCA)
CAB .... Cooperativa dos Avicultores de Benfica Ltd [*Brazil*]   (DSCA)
CAB .... Corrosion Advice Bureau   (WGAO)
CABA .... Calisma Bakanligi [*Ministry of Labor*]   (TU)
CABA .... Citizens' Advice Bureau, Adelaide [*Australia*]
CABACT ... Citizen's Advice Bureau, Australian Capital Territory
CABAS ...... City and Borough Architects Society   (WGAO)
CABB .... Citizens' Advice Bureau, Brisbane [*Australia*]
CABC .... Camara Arbitral de la Bolsa de Cereales [*Argentina*]   (DSCA)
CaBC .... Caribbean Broadcasting Corporation   (WGAO)
CABE .... Christian Association of Business Executives   (WGAO)
CABE .... Course of Adult Basic Education [*Australia*]
CABEI .... Central American Bank for Economic Integration
CABEI .... Intergovernmental Committee on the River Plate Basin [*Uruguay*]   (WGAO)
CABEL ...... Cables Electricos, CA [*Venezuela*]   (LAA)
Cabet .... Cabaret [*Small Country Inn*] [*Military map abbreviation World War I*] [*French*]   (MTD)
CABETAT ... Cabinet du Chef de l'Etat [*Office of the Chief of State*] [*Cambodia*]   (CL)
CABFAA ... Coach and Bus First Aid Association   (WGAO)
CABGOC .. Cabinda Gulf Oil Co. [*Africa*]
CAB-IB ...... Centro Atomico Bariloche/Instituto Balseiro [*Bariloche Atomic Center/Balseiro Institute*] [*Argentina*]   (WND)
CABICO.... Cabinet Comptable
CABLAF.... Cablerie Electrique Africaine [*Algeria*]
CABLESCO ... Cables Colombianos SA [*Colombia*] Tlg.   (COL)
CABM .... Commonwealth of Australia Bureau of Meteorology   (ADA)
CABO .... Centrum voor Agrobiologisch Onderzoek [*Center for Agrobiological Research*] [*Netherlands*]   (ARC)
CABO .... Council of American Building Officials   (WGAO)
CABR .... Centre for Applied Business Research [*Australia*]
CABS .... Central African Broadcasting Service
CABS .... Central African Building Society
CABS .... China National Animal Breeding Stock Import and Export Corp.   (EY)
CABUC ...... Cameroon Associated Business Corporation
CABW .... Cercle des Amateurs de Braque de Weimar [*France*]   (EAIO)
CAB(WA) ... Citizens' Advice Bureau of Western Australia
CAC .... Cacahuacintle [*Race of maize*] [*Mexico*]
CAC .... Cairo American College
CAC .... Camara Argentina de la Construccion [*Argentine Construction Board*]   (LA)
CAC .... Campaign Against Censorship   (WGAO)
CAC .... Canterbury Agricultural College [*Lincoln*] [*New Zealand*]   (WGAO)
CAC .... Cascavel [*Brazil*] [*Airport symbol*]   (OAG)
CAC .... Casino Advisory Committee [*Tasmania*] [*Australia*]
CAC .... Cathedrals Advisory Committee for England   (WGAO)
CAC .... Central African Council
CAC .... Central Arbitration Committee   (WGAO)
CAC .... Centre for Agricultural Commerce [*University of New England*] [*Australia*]
CAC .... Centro de Acopiadores de Cereales [*Argentina*]   (DSCA)
CAC .... Champion Arabian Company [*Saudi Arabia*]
CAC .... Codex Alimentarius Commission   (WGAO)
CAC .... Colonial Advisory Council
CAC .... Comite Administratif de Coordination [*Administrative Committee on Coordination - ACC*] [*United Nations French*]   (ASF)
CAC .... Comite Administrativo de Coordinacion [*Administrative Committee on Coordination - ACC*] [*United Nations Spanish*]   (MSC)
CAC .... Comite Amilcar Cabral [*Amilcar Cabral Committee*] [*Angola*]   (AF)
CAC .... Comite d'Action et de Coordination [*Chad*]
CAC .... Comite de Accion Cultural [*Mexico*]   (LAA)
CAC .... Commercial Arbitration Centre [*Northern Territory*] [*Australia*]

CAC .... Commission du Codex Alimentarius [*Joint FAO-WHO Codex Alimentarius Commission*]   (EA)
CAC .... Commonwealth Aircraft Corporation Ltd. [*Australia*]   (MCD)
CAC .... Commonwealth Archives Committee [*Australia*]   (ADA)
CAC .... Commonwealth Association of Architects   (WGAO)
CAC .... Commonwealth Conciliation and Arbitration Commission [*Australia*]
CAC .... Compagnie des Agents de Change [*French Stockbrokers Association*] [*Information Service or System*]   (EAIO)
CAC .... Companhia Agricola Cacaueira da Bahia SA [*Brazil*]   (DSCA)
CAC .... Computer Augmented Communication
CAC .... Confiscated Assets Committee [*Ghana*]
CAC .... Conseil des Arts du Canada [*Canada Council*]   (EAIO)
CAC .... Consumers Advisory Council   (WGAO)
CAC .... Cooperativa Agricola de Campinas [*Brazil*]   (DSCA)
CAC .... Cooperativa Agricola de Cotia [*Cotia Farmer Cooperative*] [*Brazil*]   (LA)
CAC .... Copyright Agency of China
CAC .... Corporate Affairs Commission [*Australia*]
CAC .... Council for Arms Control   (WGAO)
CAC .... Credito Agricola Comunitario [*Chile*]   (LAA)
CACA .... Cambodian Advisory Council of Australia
CACA .... Cement and Concrete Association   (WGAO)
CACA .... Citizens Against Crime Association [*Australia*]
CACAA...... Corporacion Argentina Criadores de Aberdeen Angus [*Argentina*]   (DSCA)
CACAC...... Civil Aircraft Control Advisory Committee   (WGAO)
CACAE...... Commonwealth Advisory Committee on Advanced Education [*Australia*]   (ADA)
CACAM .... Caisse Algerienne de Credit Agricole Mutuel
CACAMAC ... China Association of Computer-Automated Measurement and Control Technology   (EAIO)
CACAOZA ... Cacaoyeres du Zaire   (IMH)
CACAS...... Civil Aviation Council of the Arab States   (WGAO)
CACASW .. China Association of Civil Affairs and Social Welfare   (EAIO)
CACBB...... Commission Administrative Chargee du Basket-Ball [*Morocco*]
CACC........ Civil Aviation Communications Centre   (WGAO)
CACC........ Continental Africa Chambers of Commerce   (WGAO)
CACC........ Council for the Accreditation of Correspondence Colleges   (WGAO)
CAC-CC..... Cooperativa Agricola de Cotia-Cooperativa Central [*Brazil*]   (DSCA)
CAC-CDR ... Comite d'Action et de Concertation du Conseil Democratique Revolutionnaire [*Chad*] [*Political party*]   (EY)
CACCI....... Committee on the Application of Computers in the Construction Industry   (WGAO)
CACCI....... Confederation of Asian Chambers of Commerce and Industry [*Later, Confederation of Asian-Pacific Chambers of Commerce and Industry*]   (IN)
CACCI....... Confederation of Asian-Pacific Chambers of Commerce and Industry [*Taipei, Taiwan*]   (EAIO)
CACCN ..... Confederation of Australian Critical Care Nurses
CACDP...... Council for the Advancement of Communication with Deaf People   (WGAO)
CACDS...... Centre for Advanced Computing and Decision Support [*Council for Scientific and Industrial Research*] [*South Africa*]   (WND)
CACDS...... Commonwealth Advisory Committee on Defence Science   (WGAO)
CACE........ Central Advisory Council for Education   (WGAO)
CACE........ Centro de Analise da Conjuntura Economica [*Brazil*]   (DSCA)
CACE........ Compania Andina de Comercio Exterior   (WGAO)
CACEF....... Centre d'Action Culturelle de la Communaute d'Expression Francaise   (WGAO)
CACEP...... Societe Camerounaise de Commercialisation et d'Exportation de Produits
CACEPA ... Centre d'Actions Concertees des Enterprises de Produits Alimentaires   (WGAO)
CACEU...... Central American Customs and Economic Union
CACEX...... Carteira de Comercio Exterior [*Foreign Trade Department*] [*Brazil*]   (LA)
CACFOA... Chief and Assistant Chief Fire Officers Association   (WGAO)
CACGP...... Commission on Atmospheric Chemistry and Global Pollution [*IAMAP*]   (MSC)
CACH........ Central American Clearing House   (WGAO)
CACH........ Copyright Agency of China in Hongkong
CACHAC .. Community Athenaeum Colleges of the Hellenic Advancement Council [*Australia*]
CACHR ..... Central American Committee for Human Rights [*British*]   (EAIO)
CACHR ..... El Salvador and Guatemala Committees for Human Rights [*British*]   (EAIO)
CACI.......... Caisse Administrative de Circonscription Indigene
CACI......... Chaine Avion Cote-D'Ivoire
CACI......... Civil Aviation Chaplains International   (EAIO)
CACI......... Compagnie Agricole Commerciale Industrielle
CACI......... Compagnie Francaise des Cafes de Cote-D'Ivoire

CACI......... Societe Centrafricaine de Ciment
CACIA....... Compagnie d'Agriculture, de Commerce, et d'Industrie d'Afrique [African Agriculture, Commerce and Industry Co.]
CACIA....... Comptoirs Africains pour le Commerce, l'Industrie, et l'Agriculture
CACIF....... Comite Coordinador de Asociaciones Agricolas, Comerciales, Industriales, y Financieras [Guatemala] (EY)
CACILA .... Calheira Comercio e Industria da Lavoura Ltd [Brazil] (DSCA)
CACIP....... Central American Co-operative Corn Improvement Project (WGAO)
CACIP....... Confederacion Argentina de Comercio, de la Industria, y de la Produccion [Argentina] (DSCA)
CACIRA .... Chambre Syndicale des Constructeurs d'Appareils de Controle Industriel et de Regulation Automatique (WGAO)
CACISS..... Comitato Assistenza Culturale Italiana Scolastica Scozia (WGAO)
CACJ........ Comite de Asuntos Constitucionales y Juridicos (WGAO)
CACJ........ Cooperativa dos Agricultores a Criadores de Jacarepagua [Brazil] (DSCA)
CACL......... Canadian Association of Children's Librarians (WGAO)
CACLB..... Churches Advisory Committee on Local Broadcasting (WGAO)
CACM .... Central American Common Market (BARN)
CACMDBMC ... Community Advisory Committee of the Murray-Darling Basin Ministerial Council [Australia]
CACMI...... Comite Africain pour la Coordination des Moyens d'Information [African Committee for the Coordination of Information Media] (AF)
CACNT ..... Consumer Affairs Council, Northern Territory [Australia]
CACO .... Compagnie Africaine Commerciale de l'Ouest
CACOBRAL ... Companhia Agro-Colonizadora Brasil Central Ltd [Brazil] (DSCA)
CACOCOM ... Cambodian Commercial Company (CL)
CACODS... Commonwealth Advisory Committee on Defence Science [Australia] (PDAA)
CACOM .... Central American Common Market (WGAO)
CACOM .... Cooperative Algeroise de Commercialisation [Algiers Marketing Cooperative] (AF)
CACOM .... Cooperative d'Approvisionnement et de Commercialisation [Supply and Marketing Cooperative] [Algeria] (AF)
CACOMIAF ... Comptoir de l'Automobile et du Cycle, Outillage Materiel Industriel, Agricole, et Forestier
CACP......... Chambre des Agences-Conseils en Publicite [Belgium] (WGAO)
CACPK...... Citizens Alliance for Consumer Protection in Korea [South Korea]
CACRMA ... Caisse Autonome Centrale de Retraites Mutuelles Agricoles (WGAO)
CACS........ Centre for Applied Colloid Science [Australia]
CACS......... China Arts and Crafts Society (EAIO)
CACS......... Commonwealth Accommodation and Catering Services [Australia]
CACS......... Commonwealth Accommodation and Catering Services Ltd. [Australia] (ADA)
CACSA...... Contemporary Art Centre of South Australia
CACSO...... Central American and Caribbean Sports Organization (EAIO)
CACT........ Caribbean Association of Catholic Teachers (WGAO)
CACT........ Centre d'Assistance du Calcul Technique [French] (ADPT)
CACTAL.... Conference on the Application of Science and Technology to Latin America (WGAO)
CACTD...... Council for the Application of Computer Technology for Development
CACTO ..... Cactoblastis [South American moth brought to Australia to destroy the prickly pear] (DSUE)
CACU .... Central Agricultural Cooperative Union [Egypt] (EAIO)
CACUL...... Canadian Association of College and University Libraries (WGAO)
CACW .... Central American Confederation of Workers (EAIO)
cad............. Cadastre [French] (FLAF)
cad............. Cadauno [Each] [Italian]
cad............. Cadde [Road] [Turkey] (CED)
Cad............ Caddesi [Avenue, Street] [C, cd] [See also] (TU)
CAD........... Cadrage a Droite [French] (ADPT)
CAD........... Caisse Algerienne de Developpement [Algerian Development Fund] (AF)
CAD........... Center for Astronomical Data [Academy of Sciences of the USSR] [Information service or system] (IID)
CAD........... Central Activities District [Of a city] [Australia]
CAD........... Centrale Africaine de Diffusion [Morocco]
CAD........... Centralforeningen of Autoreparatorer i Danmark (WGAO)
CAD........... Centres d'Assistance au Developpement
c-a-d .... C'Est-a-Dire [That Is to Say] [French]
CAD........... Chinese Affairs Department (ML)
CAD........... Civil Aid Department [British Army] [Oman]
CAD........... Civil Aviation Department [Brunei] (DS)
CAD........... Civil Aviation Department [Australia]
CAD........... Civil Aviation Department [Sudan]
CAD........... Civil Aviation Department [Saudi Arabia] (ME)
CAD........... Civil Aviation Department [India] (WGAO)

CAD........... Coloured African Department
CAD........... Comite Agricole Departmental (WGAO)
CAD........... Comite d'Aide au Developpement [Committee for Developmental Aid] (AF)
CAD........... Commission for Aboriginal Development [Australia]
CAD........... Compagnie Africaine de Diffusion
CAD........... Conference of African Demographers
CAD........... Consortium Africain de Droguerie
CAD........... Corporacion Azucarera Dominicana [Dominican Republic] (DSCA)
CAD........... Corporate Affairs Department [Western Australia]
CAD........... Corps Adjudan Djenderal [Adjutant General's Corps] (IN)
CAD........... Council for Aboriginal Development [Australia]
CAD........... Culture and Arts Department [Jordan] (EAIO)
CADA .... Campaign Against Drug Addiction (WGAO)
CADA .... Centre d'Analyse Documentaire pour l'Archeologie
CADA .... Comision Administradora del Abasto [Supply Management Commission] [Uruguay] (LA)
CADA .... Compagnie Atlantique d'Assurances et de Reassurances [Morocco] (WGAO)
CADA .... Companhia Angolana de Agricultura [Angolan Agricultural Company] (AF)
CADA .... Compania Administradora de Aeropuertos [Peru]
CADA .... Compania Anonima Distribuidora de Alimentos [Venezuela]
CADA .... Compania Antioquena de Automotores SA [Colombia] (COL)
CADA .... Concerted Action for Development in Africa
CADA .... Confederation of Art and Design Associations (WGAO)
CADA .... Crossbow Archery Development Association (EAIO)
CADAFE ... Compania Anonima de Administracion y Fomento Electrico [Electrical Administration and Development Corporation] [Venezuela] (LA)
CADAL...... Centro di Azione e Documentazione sull'America Latina (WGAO)
CADAL...... Compagnie Africaine Forestiere et des Allumettes (WGAO)
CADAL...... Companhia Industrial de Sabao e Adubos [Brazil] (DSCA)
CADAN..... Centre d'Analyses Documentaires pour l'Afrique Noire
CADASA... Compania Aerea de Desarrollo Agricola [Ecuador] (DSCA)
CADAT ..... Caisse Algerienne d'Amenagement du Territoire [Algerian Territorial Development Fund] (AF)
CADAUMA ... Cooperative Agricole d' Achat et d'Utilisation de Materiel Agricole de l'Aveyron (WGAO)
CADC .... Centro Academico da Democracia Crista [Academic Center for Christian Democracy] [Portugal] [Political party] (PPE)
CADC .... Computer Aided Design Centre (WGAO)
CADCC...... Central American Development Coordination Council
CADDIA.... Cooperation in Automation of Data and Documentation for Imports/Exports and Agriculture [EC] (ECED)
Cade .... Cascade [Waterfall] [Military map abbreviation World War I] [French] (MTD)
CADE .... Coalition Against Dangerous Exports
CADE .... Coalition Against Dangerous Sports (WGAO)
CADE .... Conferencia Annual de Ejecutivos de Empresas [Annual Conference of Business Executives] [Peru] (LA)
CADE .... Conselho Administrativo de Defesa Economica [Administrative Council for Economic Defense] [Brazil] (LA)
CADEB...... Caisse d'Epargne du Burundi [Burundi Savings Bank]
CADEBU... Caisse d'Epargne du Burundi [Burundi Savings Bank] (AF)
CADEC...... Christian Action for Development in the Caribbean
CADEC...... Committee of the Dietetic Association of the Common Market (WGAO)
CADEF...... Centro Argentino de Estudios Forestales [Argentina] (LAA)
CADEG ..... Centro de Abastecimento do Estado da Guanabara [Brazil] (DSCA)
CADEG ..... Consejo Anticomunista de Guatemala [Anticommunist Council of Guatemala] (LA)
CADEGAS ... Compania Antioquena de Gas Ltda. [Colombia] (COL)
CADEL...... Comite d'Action pour la Defense de la Legalite [Committee for Legal Defense] [Dahomey]
CADEM .... Societe de Ciments Artificiels de Meknes [North African]
CADEMIN ... Camara Nacional de Mineria [Bolivia] (LAA)
CADENALCO ... Cadena de Almacenes Colombianos SA [Colombia] (COL)
CADENON ... Radio Cadena del Norte Ltda. [Colombia] (COL)
CADEPAN ... Camara de Defensa del Patrimonio Nacional [Council for Conservation of National Resources] [Uruguay] (LA)
CADER...... Consejo Argentino de Estudios sobre la Reproduccion [Argentina] (LAA)
CADES...... Centro Argentino de Estudios Sociologicos [Argentina] (DSCA)
CADESOI ... Circulo Argentino de Estudios sobre Organizacion Industrial [Buenos Aires, Argentina] (LAA)
CADET...... Centrale d'Achat et de Developpement de la Region Miniere du Tafilalet [Morocco]
CADEX...... Compagnie Africaine des Explosifs [Morocco]
CADEZ...... Caisse d'Epargne du Zaire [Savings Fund of Zaire]
CADEZA... Caisse Generale d'Epargne du Zaire [General Savings Fund of Zaire] (AF)
CADHU..... Comision Argentina de Derechos Humanos [Argentine Human Rights Commission] (LA)

CADI .... Centre Algerien de Diffusion et d'Information [*Algerian Center for Broadcasting and Information*] (AF)
CADI .... Comision Asesora de Desarrollo Industrial [*Uruguay*] (DSCA)
CADI .... Comite Asesor de Desarrollo Industrial [*Advisory Commission on Industrial Development*] [*Asociacion Latinoamericana de Libre Comercio*] (LAA)
CADI .... Comptoir d'Approvisionnement et de Distribution
CADI .... Conseil Asiatique du Developpement Industriel [*Asian Council for Industrial Development*] (CL)
CADIA ...... Centro Argentino de Ingenieros Agronomos [*Argentine Center of Agricultural Engineering*] (LAA)
CADIAM... Societe Centrafricaine Americaine de Diamants
CADICA.... Confederacion Atletica del Istmo Centroamericano [*Costa Rica*] (WGAO)
CADICEC ... Association des Cadres des Dirigeants Chretiens des Entreprises au Congo et au Ruanda-Urundi
CADICI..... Consortium Africain du Disque et du Cinema
CADIEM... Centro Argentino de Investigacion y Ensayo de Materiales [*Argentine Center for Research and Testing of Materials*] (LA)
CADIF .... Camara Argentina de la Industria Frigorifica [*Argentina*] (LAA)
CADIF .... Comite National de Coordination des Associations de Deportes, Internes, et Familles des Disparus
CADIN ...... Camara de Industrias de Nicaragua [*Nicaraguan Chamber of Industries*] (LA)
CADIPPE ... Comite d'Action pour le Developpement de l'Interessement du Personnel a la Productivite des Enterprises (WGAO)
CADIS .... Corporacion Argentina de Discapacitados (EAIO)
CADIST .... Centres d'Acquisition et de Diffusion de l'nformation Scientifique et Technique (WGAO)
CADL .... Camara Argentina de Destiladores (WGAO)
CA-DLP..... Call to Australia - Democratic Labor Party Coalition
CADM .... Camara de Aserraderos y Depositos de Madera [*Argentina*] (DSCA)
CADMOS ... Computer Administrations-und Organisationssysteme fuer Schulen [*German*] (ADPT)
CADNAM ... Computer Aided Design and Numerical Analysis for Manufacture Group
CADO........ Ciments Artificieux d'Oranie [*Algeria*]
CADP .... Centre Africain de Developpement et de Planification [*North African*]
CADRE...... Cumulative Abstracts of Defence Readings [*Department of Defence*] [*Australia*] [*Information service or system*] (IID)
CADS........ Commando Anticomunista del Sur [*Southern Anticommunist Commando*] [*Guatemala*] (PD)
CADS........ Compagnie Africaine des Docks et Silos
CADSE...... Comision Asesora de los Delitos Socio-Economicos [*Consultation Committee on Socioeconomic Crimes*] [*Uruguay*] (LA)
CADU .... Chilalo Agricultural Development Unit
CADU .... Comite de Apoyo a la Democracia Universitaria [*Committee in Support of University Democracy*] [*Honduras*] (LA)
CADYL...... Cooperativa Agropecuaria de Young Limitada [*Young Livestock Cooperative Limited*] [*Uruguay*] (LA)
CAE .... Central African (AF)
CAE .... Centro de Astroanalists Electronico [*Colombia*] (COL)
CAE .... Certificat d'Aptitude de l'Enseignement [*French*] (FLAF)
CAE .... Cobrese al Entregar [*Cash on Delivery*] [*Spanish*]
CAE .... Colleges of Advanced Education [*Australia*]
CAE .... Comision Asesora de Estadisticas [*Asociacion Latinoamericana de Libre Comercio - ALALC*] (LAA)
CAE .... Comision Asesora Ejecutiva [*Executive Advisory Commission*] [*Argentina*] (LA)
CAE .... Comite Atlantique de l'Education (WGAO)
CAE .... Comite d'Accio d'Ensenyants [*Teachers Action Committee*] [*Spanish*] (WER)
CAE .... Commandement Allie Europe (WGAO)
CAe .... Commission d'Aerologie [*French*]
CAE .... Compagnie Europeene d'Automatisme Electronique [*France*] (PDAA)
CAE .... Comunita Agricola Europea [*European Agricultural Community*] [*Italian*] (WER)
CAE .... Consejo Andino de Exportadores [*Andean Council of Exporters*] (LA)
CAE .... Consejo Asesor de Exportacion [*Spain*] (EY)
CAE .... Contre-Assurance Etendue (FLAF)
CAEA .... Campo Agricola Experimental Antunez [*Mexico*] (DSCA)
CAEA .... Central American Economics Association (WGAO)
CAEBB...... Conference Aeronautique des Etats Baltiques et des Balkans
CAEC....... Camara Agricola del Estado Carabobo [*Venezuela*] (DSCA)
CAEC........ Campo Agricola Experimental de Culiacan [*Mexico*] (DSCA)
CAEC........ Central American Economic Community (LAA)
CAEC........ Central American Energy Commission (EAIO)
CAEC........ Comite des Associations Europeennes de Cafe [*Committee of European Coffee Associations*] [*EC*] (ECED)
CAEC........ Committee of the Acta Endocrinologica Countries (WGAO)
CAEC........ Conseil Africain de l'Enseignement de la Communication

CAEC......... County Agricultural Executive Committee (WGAO)
CAECL...... Caisse d'Aide a l'Equipement des Collectivites Locales [*Local Board of Community Equipment Aid*] [*France*]
CAEDA ..... Compressed Air Equipment Distributors Association (WGAO)
CAEE........ Committee on Aircraft Engine Emissions [*ICAO*] (DA)
CAEER...... Centro de Aperfeicoamento, Especializacao, e Extensao Rural [*Brazil*] (DSCA)
CAEES ...... Centre Algerien d'Expansion Economique et Social
CAEET...... Centre Artisanal d'Etudes et de Technique [*France*] (FLAF)
CAEEV...... Compagnie Africaine d'Elevage et d'Exportation de Viande
CAEF......... Comite des Associations Europeennes de Fonderie [*Committee of European Foundry Associations*] (EA)
CAEGE...... Centre Algerien d'Etudes de la Gestion des Entreprises
CAEGT...... Campo Agricola Experimental de General Teran [*Mexico*] (DSCA)
CAEI......... Compagnie Africaine d'Equipement Industriel [*African Industrial Equipment Co.*]
CAEJ .... Communante des Associations d'Editeurs de Journaux [*Community of Associations of Newspaper Publishers*] [*EEC Belgium*] (PDAA)
CAEJ .... Communaute des Associations d'Editeurs de Journaux de la CEE (WGAO)
CAEJ-CEE ... Communaute des Associations d'Editeurs de Journaux de la CEE [*Community of the Newspaper Publishing Associations of the EEC*] [*Belgium*] (EAIO)
CAEM .... Camara Empresarial [*Chamber of Businesses*] [*Guatemala*]
CAEM .... Campo Agricola Experimental de Mexicali [*Mexico*] (DSCA)
CAEM .... Cekmece Arastirma ve Egitim Merkezi [*Cekmece Research and Training Center*] [*CNAEM*] [*See also*] (TU)
CAEM .... Centre Africaine d'Etudes Monetaires [*African Centre for Monetary Studies*] [*Senegal*] (EAIO)
CAEM .... Centro Avanzado de Estudios Militares [*Peru*] (WGAO)
CAEM .... Centro de Altos Estudios Militares [*Center of Advanced Military Studies*] [*Peru*] (LA)
CAEM .... Certificat d'Aptitude a l'Enseignement Moyen [*French*]
CAeM .... Commission for Aeronautical Meteorology [*WMO*] (MSC)
CAEM .... Companhia Auxiliar de Empresos de Mineraca [*Brazil*] (PDAA)
CAEM .... Conseil d'Assistance Economique Mutuelle [*Council for Mutual Economic Assistance - CMEA*] [*French*] (AF)
CAEM .... Consejo de Asistencia Economica Mutual [*Council for Mutual Economic Assistance - CMEA*] [*Spanish*]
CAEMC..... Comite d'Associations Europeennes de Medecins Catholiques [*Committee of European Associations of Catholic Doctors*] [*Belgium*] (SLS)
CAEMI...... Companhia Auxiliar de Empresas de Mineracao [*Mining Enterprises Assistance Corporation*] [*Brazil*] (LA)
CAEMIC ... Comite d'Associations Europeennes de Medecins Catholiques (WGAO)
CAEN .... Centro de Aperfeicoamento de Economistas do Nordeste [*Brazil*] (DSCA)
CAEND ..... Centro Argentino de Ensayos no Destructivos de Materiales [*Center for Non-Destructive Testing of Materials*] [*Argentina*] (PDAA)
CAENE...... Companhia de Aguas e Esgotos do Nordeste [*Brazil*] (LAA)
CAEP......... Certificat d'Aptitude d'Enseignement Primaire [*Primary Education Aptitude Certificate*] [*Tunisia*] (AF)
CAEP........ Chamber d'Agriculture et d'Elevage [*French Polynesia*] (WGAO)
CAEP........ Chambre d'Agriculture et d'Elevage [*French Polynesia*] (FEA)
CAEP........ Communaute des Associations d'Editeurs de Periodique du Marche Commun (WGAO)
CAEP........ Council of Action for Equal Pay [*Australia*]
CAEPC...... Comision Asesora Europea sobre Pesca Continental (WGAO)
CAEPE...... Centre d'Assemblage et d'Essais des Propulseurs et des Engins [*Launchers and Missiles Assembly and Testing Center*] [*France*] (PDAA)
CAEPR...... Centre for Aboriginal Economic Policy Research [*Australia*]
CAER........ Conference Administrative Extraordinaire des Radiocommunications [*1951*] [*Geneva*]
CAER........ Consiliul de Ajutor Economic Reciproc [*Council for Mutual Economic Assistance*]
CAERB...... Campo Agricola Experimental de Rio Bravo [*Mexico*] (DSCA)
Caern.......... Caernarvonshire [*Wales*] (BARN)
CAES........ Central Agricultural Experiment Station
CAES........ Central Association of Experiment Stations [*Indonesia*] (WGAO)
CAES........ Certificat d'Aptitude a l'Enseignement Secondaire [*Secondary Education Aptitude Certificate*] [*French*]
CAES........ Chiba Prefecture Agricultural Experiment Station [*Japan*] (WGAO)
CAES........ Comando Anti-Extorsion y Secuestros [*Anti-Extortion and Kidnapping Command*] [*Colombia*] (LA)
CAES........ Comissao de Aguas e Engenharia Sanitaria [*Water and Sanitary Engineering Commission*] [*Brazil*] (LA)
CAES........ Comite Asesor Economico y Social [*Economic and Social Advisory Committee*] [*Colorado*] (LA)

CAES......... Comite de Asesoramiento Economico y Social [*Economic Social Advisory Committee*] [*Peru*]   (LA)

CAES......... Confederacion Argentina de Estudiantes Secundarios [*Argentine Confederation of Secondary School Students*]   (LA)

CAESAR ... Centre of Advanced European Studies and Research [*Germany*]

CAESE...... Campo Agricola Experimental "Santa Elena" [*Mexico*]   (DSCA)

CAESPCI.. Central Association of Experimental Stations for Perennial Crops in Indonesia [*Indonesia*]   (DSCA)

CAESS....... Centre Armoricain d'Etude Structurale des Socles [*Armorican Center for Study of the Continental Crust*] [*Research center*] [*France*]   (IRC)

CAESS....... Compania de Alumbrado Electrico de San Salvador [*San Salvador Electric Power Company*] [*El Salvador*]

CAETA...... Commonwealth Association for Education and Training of Adults

CAETAP ... Confederacion Argentina de Entidades del Transporte Automotor de Pasajeros [*Argentina*]   (LAA)

CAEU .... Council of Arab Economic Unity [*United Nations (already exists in GUS II database)*]

CAEVR...... Comite d' Action Ecole et Vie Rurale   (WGAO)

CAF........... Caisse d'Allocations Familiales [*Family Allowance Office*] [*French*]   (WER)

CAF........... Central African Federation

CAF........... Central African Republic [*ANSI three-letter standard code*]   (CNC)

CAF........... Centralna Agencja Fotograficzna [*Central Photographic Agency*]   (POL)

CAF........... Centralne Archiwum Filmowe [*Central Film Archives*]   (POL)

CAF........... Club Alpin Francais [*French Alpine Club*]

CAF........... Comptoir Agricole Francais   (WGAO)

CAF........... Concrete Association of Finland   (EAIO)

CAF........... Confederation Africaine de Football [*African Football Confederation - AFC*]   (EAIO)

CAF........... Construcciones y Auxiliar de Ferrocarriles SA [*Spanish*]

CAF........... Convention Africaine

CAF........... Corporacion Andina de Fomento [*Andean Development Corporation*]   (LA)

CAF........... Counseil del l'Agriculture Francaise   (WGAO)

CAF........... Cout, Assurance, Fret [*Cost, Insurance, Freight - CIF*] [*Shipping*] [*French*]

CAF........... Current Affairs Films

CAFA........ Chambre Agricole Franco-Allemande   (WGAO)

CAFA........ Compagnie Africaine Franco-Anglaise

CAFA........ Customs Agents Federation of Australia

CAFAC...... Centrale Africaine d'Achats en Commun

CAFAC...... Commission Africaine de l'Aviation Civile [*African Civil Aviation Commission - AFCAC*]   (EAIO)

CAFADE... Comision Nacional de Administracion del Fondo de Apoyo al Desarrollo Economico [*Argentina*]   (LAA)

CAFAL...... Compagnie Africaine Forestiere et des Allumettes

CAFAM..... Caja de Compensacion Familiar [*Colombia*]   (COL)

CAFAN...... Cooperative Africaine Forestiere et Agricole du Niari

CAFANDINA ... Camara de Fabricantes de Autopartes Andina   (WGAO)

CAFANGOL ... Empresa de Rebeneficio e Exportacao do Cafe de Angola [*National coffee processing and trade organization*] [*Luanda, Angola*]

CAFBANGUI ... Compagnie Cafeiere du Haut Oubangui

CAFC........ Compagnie Agricole et Forestiere du Cameroun [*Forestry and Agricultural Co. of Cameroon*]

CAFCO...... Caisse d' Allociations Familiales des Societies Cooperatives de Consommation et de Production de la Suisse Romande   (WGAO)

CAFCO...... Compagnie Africaine de Commerce et de Commission

CAFCO...... Compagnie Africaine de Constructions et de Travaux Publics

CAFDA...... Commandement Aerien des Forces de Defense Aerienne [*Air Defense Forces Air Command*]   (NATG)

CAFE........ Comite d'Action Feminine Europeenne   (WGAO)

CAFE......... Companhia Agropecuaria de Fomento Economico do Parana [*Brazil*]   (DSCA)

CAFE......... Compariia Americana de Fomento Economico   (WGAO)

CAFE......... Cours Autodidactique de Francais Ecrit

CAFE......... Negotiations on Conventional Armed Forces in Europe

CAFEAICC ... Commission on Asian and Far Eastern Affairs of the International Chamber of Commerce   (WGAO)

CAFEBASA ... Cafe da Bahia SA [*Brazil*]   (DSCA)

CAFEC...... Consortium Africain d'Exploitation de la Chaux [*Senegal*]   (WGAO)

CAFESA.... Compania Costarricense del Cafe   (WGAO)

CAFESA.... Compania Costarricense del Cafe, SA [*Costa Rica*]   (DSCA)

CAFFA...... Comissao Administrativa do Fundo de Fomento de Angola

CAFGE...... Colombian Association of Fresh Cut Flowers Exporters   (EAIO)

CAFGU...... Citizen Armor Forces Geographical Unit [*Philippines*]

CAFHS...... Child, Adolescent, and Family Health Service [*South Australian Health Commission*]

CAFHS...... Child and Family Health Services [*Australia*]

CAFI.......... Commercial Advisory Foundation in Indonesia   (IN)

CAFI.......... Compania Agropecuaria Forestal Industrial [*Industrial, Forest, Agricultural, and Livestock Company*] [*Ecuador*]   (LA)

CAFIC....... Club Agricola Formacion Integral del Campesinado [*Ecuador*]   (DSCA)

CAFIC....... Combined Allied Forces Information Centre   (WGAO)

CAFIC....... Compagnie Agricole, Forestiere, Industrielle, et Commerciale

CAFIC....... Compagnie Algerienne de Fabrication de la Chaussure

CAFIDEC ... Compagnie Franco-Ivoirienne d'Entreprises Commerciales

CAFIECA ... Camara Argentina de Frigorificos Industriales y Exportadores de Carne y Afines [*Argentine Chamber of Industrial Meatpacking Houses and Exporters of Meats and Related Products*]   (LA)

CAFIM...... Confederation des Associations des Facteurs d'Instruments de Musique de la CEE   (WGAO)

CAFISHTRACO ... Cameroon Fishing and Trading Company   (WGAO)

CAFIU....... Chinese Association for International Understanding

CAFL........ Chingola Amateur Football League

CAFL......... Compagnie des Ateliers et Forges de la Loire

CAFM........ Cathedral Films, Inc.

CAFM........ Chief of Air Force Materiel [*Australia*]

CAFMBA .. Campaign Against Foreign Military Bases in Australia   (ADA)

CAFMNA ... Compound Animal Feedingstuffs Manufacturers National Association   (WGAO)

CAFOD ..... Catholic Fund for Overseas Development

CAFOP...... Centre d'Animation et de Formation Pedagogique [*Teachers Promotion and Training Center*]   (AF)

CAFOP...... Centre d'Animation et de Formation Professionnelle

CAFOP...... Chief of Air Force Operations and Plans [*Australia*]

CAFP........ Chief of Air Force Personnel [*Australia*]

CAFP........ Comision Andina de Formacion Profesional   (WGAO)

CAFPTA.... Comision Administradora del Fondo de Promocion de Tecnologia Agropecuaria [*Argentina*]   (DSCA)

CAfr.......... Central Africa

CAFR........ Renseignements Coloniaux et Documents Publiees par le Comite de l'Afrique Francaise et le Comite du Maroc 1932

CAFRA...... Compagnie de l'Afrique Francaise

CAFRAD... Centre Africain de Formation et de Recherche Administrative pour le Developpement [*African Training and Research Center in Administration for Development*] [*Tangiers, Morocco*] [*Research center*]

CAFRAD... Centre Africain de Formation et de Recherche Administratives pour la Developpement [*African Training and Research Center in Administration for Development*]   (IID)

CAFRADES ... Centre Africain de Recherche Appliquee et de Formation en Matiere de Developpement Social [*African Center for Applied Research and Training in Social Development - ACARTSD*]   (EAIO)

CAFRANCO ... Compagnie de l'Afrique Francaise pour le Commerce

CAFRECA ... Cambio de Frecuencia, CA [*Venezuela*]   (LAA)

CAFRICO ... Consortium Africain de Commerce

CAFRILOSA ... Camal Frigorifico Loja SA [*Ecuador*]   (DSCA)

CAFS......... Central Australian Folk Society

CAFS......... Centre for African Family Studies [*Kenya*]   (EAIO)

CAFS......... Centre for African Studies [*International Planned Parenthood Federation*]   (ECON)

CAFSO...... Societe de Cafe Soluble

CAFTA...... Central American Free Trade Association   (WGAO)

CAFTA...... Comision Administradora para el Fondo de Tecnologia Agropecuaria [*Argentina*]   (LAA)

CAFTA...... Council of Australian Food Technology Associations   (ADA)

CAFTEL.... Companie Africaine de Fabrication de Tableux et d'Equipements Electriques [*Ivory Coast*]   (WGAO)

CAFTEX.... Compagnie Africaine de Textile

CAFTRAC ... Companie Africaine de Transactions Commerciales [*Ivory Coast*]   (WGAO)

CAFTRAD ... Centre Africain de Formation et de Recherche Administrative pour Le Developpement   (WGAO)

CAFTS...... Chief of Air Force Technical Services [*Australia*]

CAFUM..... Companhia de Fumigacoes de Mocambique

CAG.......... Cagliari [*Italy*] [*Airport symbol*]   (OAG)

CAG.......... Camara de Agricultores y Ganaderos [*Costa Rica*]   (DSCA)

CAG.......... Caribbean-Atlantic Geotraverse [*IDOE project*]   (MSC)

CAG.......... Centre for Applied Geology [*Saudi Arabia*]   (PDAA)

CAG.......... Clauses Administratives Generales   (FLAF)

CAG.......... Comitetul Antifascist German [*German Anti-Fascist Committee*]   (RO)

CAG.......... Comparative Administrative Group of the American Society for Public Administration   (WGAO)

CAG.......... Comptroller and Auditor General of India

CAG.......... Creative Art Group [*Australia*]

CAG.......... Crisis Assessment Group [*NATO*]   (NATG)

CAGA........ Commercial and General Acceptance Ltd. [*Australia*]   (ADA)

CAGAC..... Civil Aviation General Administration of China   (WGAO)

CAGE....... Central Australian Gold Expedition

cage........... Courtage [*Brokerage*] [*French*]

CAGEO ..... Council of Australian Government Employee Organisations (ADA)
CAGEP ...... Companhia de Armazens Gerais do Estado de Pernambuco [*Brazil*] (DSCA)
CAGESC ... Companhia de Armazens Gerais do Estado de Santa Catarina [*Brazil*] (DSCA)
CAGESP ... Companhia de Armazens Gerais do Estado de Sao Paulo [*Brazil*] (DSCA)
CAGF .... Club des Amateurs de Greyhounds de France (EAIO)
CAGFU ..... Civilian Armed Force Geographical Units [*Paramilitary security force*] [*Philippines*] (ECON)
CAGI .... Consultative Association of Guyana Industries (LA)
CAGIGO ... Companhia Agro Industrial de Goias [*Brazil*] (DSCA)
CAgM .... Commission for Agricultural Meteorology [*WMO*] (MSC)
CAGPM .... Companhia de Armazens Gerais da Producao de Minas [*Brazil*] (DSCA)
CAGS .... Chet Atkins Guitar Society [*British*] (EAIO)
CAGS .... Chinese Academy of Geological Sciences (SLS)
CAGT .... Camara Agricola y Ganadera de Torreon [*Mexico*] (DSCA)
CAH .... Colegio de Abogados de Honduras [*Honduran Bar Association*] (LA)
CAH .... Command Airways [*South Africa*] [*ICAO designator*] (FAAC)
CAH .... Compagnie Africaine d'Hotellerie [*Congo*] (WGAO)
CAH .... Credito Agricola de Habitacion [*Paraguay*] (LAA)
CAHA .... Chamber and Association of Hungarian Architects (EAIO)
CAHB .... Confederation Africaine de Handball
CAHBI ...... Ad hoc Committee of Experts on Bioethics [*Council of Europe*] (WGAO)
CAHDA ..... Camara Hondurena de Aseguradores [*Insurance association*] [*Honduras*] (EY)
CAHE .... Commission for Ancient History and Epigraphy [*Germany*] (EAIO)
CAHI .... Caribbean Association for the Hearing Impaired (WGAO)
CAHIPE .... Committee of the Associations of Honey Importers and Packers of Europe (EAIO)
CAHIS ...... Circulo Afro-Hispano
CAHN .... Cooperative Agricole Haute Normandie (WGAO)
CAHOF .... Canadian Aviation Hall of Fame (WGAO)
CAHPA ..... China Animal Health Products Association (EAIO)
CAHR .... Chinese Association for Human Rights [*Taiwan*] (EAIO)
CAHR .... Colombian Association for Human Rights (EAIO)
CAHS .... Civil Aviation Historical Society [*Australia*]
CAHS .... Council of Australian Humanist Societies
CAHT .... Centre Africain des Hydrocarbures et du Textile de Boumerdes [*African Center for Hydrocarbons and Textiles at Boumerdes*] [*Algeria*] (AF)
CAI .... Cairo [*Egypt*] [*Airport symbol*] (OAG)
CAI .... Cairo Airport
CAI .... Centro Aeronautico de Instrucao
CAI .... Centro Argentino de Ingenieros [*Argentina*] (LAA)
CAI .... Centro de Automatizacion Industrial [*Industrial Automation Center*] [*Cuba*] (LA)
CAI .... Club Alpin Israelien (EAIO)
CAI .... Club Alpino Italiano [*Italian Alpine Club*]
CAI .... Comision Agro-Industrial [*Venezuela*] (DSCA)
CAI .... Comite Arctique International [*International Arctic Committee*] [*Monte Carlo, Monaco*] (EAIO)
CAI .... Comite de Accion Internacional Sindical [*Colombia*] (COL)
CAI .... Comite de Asuntos Internacionales [*Committee for International Affairs*] [*Uruguay*] (LA)
CAI .... Comites Anti-Imperialistas [*Anti-Imperialist Committees*] [*Spanish*] (WER)
CAI .... Compagnia Aeronautica Italiana SPA [*Italy*] [*ICAO designator*] (FAAC)
CAI .... Compagnie Africaine pour le Developpement de l'Informatique
CAI .... Compagnie Africaine pour l'Informatique [*Ivory Coast*] (WGAO)
CAI .... Comptoir d'Approvisionnement Automobile et Industriel
CAI .... Concrete Association of India (PDAA)
CAI .... Confederation of Australian Industry
CAI .... Container Aid International [*Belgium*] (PDAA)
CAI .... Convenio Azucarero Internacional (DSCA)
CAI .... Corporacion Aereo Internacional SA de CV [*Mexico*] [*ICAO designator*] (FAAC)
CAI .... Crochet Association International (WGAO)
CAIA .... Centro Argentino de Ingenieros Agronomos [*Argentine Center of Agricultural Engineering*] [*Buenos Aires*] (LAA)
CAIA .... Congreso Argentino de la Industria Aceitera [*Argentina*] (DSCA)
CAIA .... Customs Agents' Institute of Australia (ADA)
CAIB .... Companhia Agricola e Industrial Brasileira [*Brazil*] (DSCA)
CAIBA .... Centro Artistico Italiano delle Belle Arti [*Italian*] (SLS)
CAIBO ...... Companhia Agricola Industrial Bocaina [*Brazil*] (DSCA)
CAIC .... Caribbean Association of Industry and Commerce [*Barbados*] (LA)
CAIC .... Commission Internationale des Activites Commerciales [*International Commission on Commercial Activities*] (EAIO)

CAIC .... Compagnie d'Agriculture, d'Industrie, et de Commerce
CAIC .... Companhia de Agricultura, Imigracao, e Colonizacao [*Agriculture, Immigration, and Settlement Company*] [*Brazil*] (LA)
CAICYT .... Centro Argentino de Informacion Cientifica y Tecnologica [*Argentine Center for Scientific and Technological Information*] [*Information service or system*] (IID)
CAICYT .... Comision Asesora de Investigacion Cientifica y Tecnica [*Barcelona, Spain*]
CAID .... Comptoir Africain d'Importation et de Diffusion
CAIDAL .... Comision Nacional del Comite de Accion para la Integracion y el Desarrollo de America Latina [*Argentina*] (LAA)
CAIE .... Centro de Analisis e Investigacion Economica [*Participant in the Inter-American Bank Research Network*] [*Mexico*] (CROSS)
CAIEI .... China American International Engineering, Incorporated
CAIEL .... Comercial Agricola, Importadora, e Exportadora Ltda [*Brazil*] (DSCA)
CAIFOM ... Caisse de la France d'Outre-Mer
CAIG .... Companhia Agro Industrial Guaiana [*Brazil*] (DSCA)
CAIH .... Cairo Herbarium [*Egypt*]
CAIH .... Central Australian International Hotels
CAIL .... Coal and Allied Industries Limited [*Australia*] (ADA)
CAIM .... Colonizacao Agricola Industrial Matogrossense Ltd [*Brazil*] (DSCA)
CAIM .... Compagnie Agricole et Industrielle de Madagascar [*Madagascar Agricultural and Industrial Co.*]
CAIM .... Syndicat National des Createurs d'Architectures Interieures et de Modeles (WGAO)
CAIMA ...... Comite Asesor para la Importacion de Maquinaria Agricola y Equipo en General [*Mexico*] (DSCA)
CAIMO ..... Comite Asesor de Investigaciones Meteorologicas Oceanicas [*Advisory Committee on Oceanic Meteorological Research - ACOMR*] [*Spanish*] (MSC)
CAIN .... Computerised AIDS [*Acquired Immune Deficiency Syndrome*] Network [*Medicine*] [*Australia*]
CAINSW ... Chamber of Automotive Industries of New South Wales [*Australia*]
CAIO .... Caribbean American Intercultural Organization (WGAO)
CAIP .... Certificat d'Aptitude a l'Inspection Primaire
CAIR .... Comite d'Action Interallie de la Resistance (WGAO)
CAIR .... Confidential Aviation Incident Reporting Program [*Australia*]
CAIRA ...... Conferencia Administrativa Internacional de Radiocomunicaciones Aeronauticas [*Spanish*]
caire .... Commissionnaire [*Agent*] [*French*]
CAIRE ...... Compagnie d'Applications Industrielles de Recherches et d'Etudes
CAIRM ..... Comite Asesor de Expertos sobre Investigaciones de los Recursos Marinos [*Advisory Committee of Experts on Marine Resources Research - ACMRR*] [*FAO*] [*Spanish*] (ASF)
CAIRM ..... Comite Asesor sobre Investigaciones de los Recursos Marinos (WGAO)
CAIRS .... Close Air Support
CAIRU ...... Colonial Agricultural Insecticides Research Unit (WGAO)
CAIS .... Central Abstracting and Indexing Service (WGAO)
CAIS .... Central American Economic Integration Secretariat [*Guatemala*] (LAA)
CAIS .... Central American Integration Scheme (WGAO)
CAIS .... Centre for Aboriginal and Islander Studies [*Northern Territory*] [*Australia*]
CAIS .... Club de l'Amitie Ivoiro-Senegalaise
CAIS .... Computer-Assisted Action Information System [*NATO*]
CAIS .... Congress of Arabic and Islamic Studies [*Madrid, Spain*] (EA)
CAISA .... Compania Agricola e Industrial, Sociedad Anonima [*Agricultural and Industrial Corporation*] [*El Salvador*]
CAISTAB ... Caisse de Stabilisation et de Perequation des Produits Agricoles [*The Central African Republic*] (EY)
CAITA ...... Compagnie Agricole et Industrielle des Tabacs Africains [*African Tobacco Agricultural and Industrial Company*] (AF)
CAITACI ... Compagnie Agricole et Industrielle des Tabacs de Cote-D'Ivoire [*Ivory Coast Tobacco Agricultural and Industrial Company*]
caith .... Caithness County [*Scotland*] (BARN)
CAITS .... Centre for Alternative Industrial and Technological Systems (WGAO)
CAJ .... Canaima [*Venezuela*] [*Airport symbol*] (OAG)
CAJ .... Comision Andina de Juristas [*Andean Commission of Jurists - ACJ*] (EAIO)
CAJ .... Cooperativa de Avicultores de Jacarepagua [*Brazil*] (DSCA)
CAJ .... Internationale Christliche Arbeiterjugend (WGAO)
CAJAD ...... Center po Atomn. i Jadernum Dannym [*Center for Nuclear Structure and Reaction Data*] [*USSR State Committee on the Utilization of Atomic Energy*] [*Information service or system*] (IID)
CAJANAL ... Caja Nacional de Prevision Social [*National Social Security Fund*] [*Colombia*] (COL)
CAJAT ...... Comissao Agronomica Jose Augusto Trinidad [*Brazil*] (DSCA)
CAJL .... Central-Anzeiger fuer Juedische Literatur, Frankfurt Am Main

CAJP .... Christian Anti-Jewish Party   (BJA)
CAJP .... Clubes Agricolas Juveniles del Peru [*Peru*]   (LAA)
CAK .... Comite des Angolais au Katanga
CAKUR-IS ... Calisma Bakanligi Sosyal Sigortalar, Is ve Isci Bulma Kurumlari Sendikasi Federasyonu [*Labor Ministry Social Insurance, Labor and Employment Organizations' Union Federation*]   (TU)
Cal.............. Calando [*Dying Away*] [*Music*]
Cal.............. Calata [*Wharf*] [*Italian*]   (NAU)
CAL .... Calcraft [*Hangman*] [*Slang*] [*British*]   (DSUE)
Cal.............. Caleta [*Cove*] [*Cta*] [*See also*] [*Spanish*]   (NAU)
Cal.............. Calibre [*Caliber*] [*French*]   (MTD)
cal.............. Caloria [*Calorie*] [*Portuguese*]
cal.............. Caloriagrama [*Grams of Calories*] [*Portuguese*]
CAL .... Camara Agropecuaria Latinoamericana [*Latin American Chamber of Agriculture and Livestock*]   (LA)
Cal.............. Canal [*Canal*] [*Military map abbreviation World War I*] [*French*]   (MTD)
CAL .... Carabine Automatique Legere
CAL .... Cargo Air Lines [*Israel*]   (BJA)
CAL .... Centre d'Amelioration du Logement [*Center for Improved Housing Conditions*] [*French*]   (WER)
CAL .... Centro di Azione Latina   (WGAO)
CAL .... China Airlines [*Taiwan*] [*ICAO designator*]   (FAAC)
CAL .... Colegio de Abogados de Lima [*Lima Bar Association*] [*Peru*]   (LA)
CAL .... Comandos Armados de Liberacion [*Armed Liberation Commandos*] [*Puerto Rico*]   (PD)
CAL .... Comision de Asesoramiento Legislativa [*Legislative Advisory Commission*] [*Argentina*]   (LA)
CAL .... Comite Atlantique du Luxembourg [*Atlantic Committee of Luxembourg*]   (EAIO)
CAL .... Comite d'Action Lyceen [*Lycee Action Committee*] [*French*]   (WER)
CAL .... Commercial Agencies Law [*1977*] [*Oman*]   (IMH)
CAL .... Commonwealth Acoustic Laboratories [*Australia*]   (ADA)
CAL .... Computer Accounting Limited [*Australia*]   (ADA)
CAL .... Confederacion Anticomunista Latinoamericana [*Latin American Anticommunist Confederation*]   (LA)
CAL .... Copyright Agency Ltd. [*Australia*]
Cal.............. Cortal [*Military map abbreviation*] [*World War I*] [*French*]   (MTD)
CAL .... Cuban Association of Librarians   (EAIO)
Cal.............. Grande Calorie [*Kilogram Calorie*] [*French*]
Cal.............. Kilogramm-Calorie [*Kilogram Calorie*] [*German*]
cal.............. Petite Calorie [*Gram Calorie*] [*French*]
CAL .... Pontificia Commissione per l'America Latina   (WGAO)
CALA........ Chinese-American Librarians Association   (WGAO)
CALA........ Christiana Area Land Authority [*West Indies*]   (WGAO)
CALA........ Compania Argentina de Laminacion y Afines, SA [*Argentina*]   (LAA)
CALAIS..... Council of Australian Libraries and Information Services
CALANS ... Caribbean and Latin American News Service   (LA)
CALAR...... Cooperative Arid Lands Agriculture Research Program [*Established by Egypt, Israel, and the US at the University of San Diego in 1981*]
CALB........ Confederation Africano-Levantine de Billard
Calc........... Calcada [*Street*] [*Portuguese*]
calc .... Calciniert [*Calcined*] [*German*]
CALC........ Computer Aided Learning Centre [*Victoria University*] [*Australia*]
CALECOL ... Catalogacion Legible en Computador para Colombia [*Colombia*]   (COL)
CALEMPA ... Compagnie Algerienne d'Emballages en Papier
CALEV ...... Compania Anonima Luz Electrica de Venezuela [*Venezuelan Power and Light Company*]   (LA)
CALFORU ... Cooperativa Agropecuaria de Sociedades de Fomento Rural [*Agricultural and Livestock Cooperative of Rural Development Associations*]   (LA)
CALG .... Compagnie des Landes de Gascogne   (WGAO)
CALI......... Consortium of Arid Lands Institutions
CALIN....... Consejo Asesor para el Licenciamiento de Instalaciones Nucleares [*Advisory Council for Licensing Nuclear Facilities*] [*Argentina*]   (LA)
CALIR ...... Centro de Aperfeicoamento do Lider Rural [*Brazil*]   (DSCA)
Calis .... Calismalar [*Efforts, Activities*]   (TU)
CALIS .... Council of Australian Libraries and Information Services   (ADA)
CALL......... Centre for Australian Languages and Linguistics [*Batchelor College*]
CALL......... Cercle de les Arts i de les Lettres [*Andorra*]   (EAIO)
CALL......... Content Area Literacy and Learning [*Program*]
CALLAS.... Computerangeschlossenes Lernleistungs-Analysesystem [*German*]   (ADPT)
CALLS...... Crown and Lease Land System [*Australia*]
CALM .... Coalition Against Legalised Murder [*Australia*]
CALM .... Comfort and Love Movement [*Australia*]
c-alm .... Contra-Almirante [*Rear Admiral*] [*Portuguese*]

CALM .... Department of Conservation and Land Management [*Australia*]
CALMA..... Chinese Analytical Laboratory Managers' Association
CALMAT.... Calcul Matriciel   (ADPT)
CALNU ..... Cooperativa Agropecuaria del Norte Uruguayo [*Farm Cooperative of Northern Uruguay*]   (LA)
CALNU ..... Cooperativa Agropecuaria Limitada Norte Uruguayo   (WGAO)
CALO .... City Area Leases Ordinance [*Australian Capital Territory*]
CALO .... Cooperative Agricole Lainiere de l'Ouest   (WGAO)
CALOM .... Comptoir Africain de Liaison Outre-Mer
CALP........ Cristalleria Artistica La Piana [*Piana Artistic Crystal Co.*] [*Italy*]
CALPA ...... Cooperativa Agropecuaria Limitada de Paysandu [*Paysandu Agricultural and Livestock Cooperative, Limited*] [*Uruguay*]   (LA)
CALPC ...... Centrala de Aprovizionare si Livrare Produse Chimice [*Central for the Supply and Delivery of Chemical Products*]   (RO)
CALPICA ... Cooperativa Agropecuaria Limitada de Produccion e Industrializacion de Cana de Azucar [*Farm Cooperative for the Cultivation and Processing of Sugar Cane Limited*] [*Uruguay*]   (LA)
CALPROSE ... Cooperativa Agropecuaria Limitada Productores de Semillas [*Uruguay*]   (DSCA)
CALPS...... Council of Australian Labor Party Students   (ADA)
CALQ .... Centro Academico 'Luiz de Queiroz' [*Brazil*]   (WGAO)
CALS .... Committee of Australian Library Schools   (ADA)
CALSAL.... Cooperativa Agropecuaria Limitada de Salto [*Salto Agricultural and Livestock Cooperative Limited*] [*Uruguay*]   (LA)
CALTA ...... Cooperativa Agropecuaria Limitada de Tarariras [*Uruguay*]   (DSCA)
CALTRAM ... Compagnie Algero-Libyenne de Transports Maritimes [*Shipping*] [*Algiers, Algeria*]   (MENA)
CALUSA ... Centre for Applied Linguistics, University of South Australia
CAM .... Camara Argentina de Maderas [*Argentina*]   (DSCA)
CAM .... Camara Argentina de Molineros [*Argentina*]   (DSCA)
CAM .... Cameroon   (WDAA)
CAM .... Cameroon Action Movement
CAM .... Camiri [*Bolivia*] [*Airport symbol*]   (OAG)
CAM .... Central Asian Mission
CAM .... Centre d'Automatisation pour le Management [*French*]   (ADPT)
CAM .... Centro Administrativo Municipal [*Colombia*]   (COL)
CAM .... Centro de Abastecimiento Medico [*Medical Supplies Center*] [*Nicaragua*]   (LA)
CAM .... Cercle Archeologique de Mons [*Belgium*]   (SLS)
CAM .... Certificat d'Aptitude aux Fonctions de Moniteur
CAM .... Certificat d'Aptitude Maritime
CAM .... Ceylon Association of Manufacturers [*Sri Lanka*]   (WGAO)
CAM .... Christian Alternative Movement [*Australia*]
CAM .... Comando Anticomunista de Mendoza [*Mendoza Anticommunist Command*] [*Argentina*]   (LA)
CAM .... Comision Asesora de Asuntos Monetarios [*Asociacion Latinoamericana de Libre Comercio*]   (LAA)
CAM .... Comision para los Asuntos de la Mujer [*Puerto Rico*]   (EAIO)
CAM .... Comite d'Action Marocaine
CAM .... Comite d'Action Musulman [*Moslem Action Committee*] [*Mauritius*]   (AF)
CAM .... Commission for Agricultural Meteorology   (WGAO)
CAM .... Committee for Aquatic Microbiology [*United Nations*]   (ASF)
CAM .... Commonwealth Association of Museums [*Calgary, AB*]   (EAIO)
CAM .... Compagnie Agricole du Mungo
CAM .... Conference Aeronautique de la Mediterranee
CAM .... Consejo Agrarista Mexicano [*Mexican Agrarian Council*]   (LA)
CAMA ...... Cartonnages Marocains
CAMA ...... Central Australian Motels Association
CAMA ...... Children's Aid Movement of Australia   (ADA)
CAMA ...... Christian and Missionary Alliance
CAMA ...... Coated Abrasives Manufacturers Association   (WGAO)
CAMA ...... Commission d'Amelioration des Methodes Administratives   (FLAF)
CAMA ...... Compagnie Africaine de Materiels [*Morocco*]
CAMA ...... Continental Advertising and Marketing Association   (WGAO)
CAMA ...... Control and Automation Manufacturers' Association   (WGAO)
CAMA ...... Council of Australian Museum Associations
CAMAA .... Comptoir Africain de Materiel Abidjan
CAMAB .... Companhia de Adubos e Materiais Agricolas da Bahia [*Brazil*]   (DSCA)
CAMACOL ... Camara Colombiana de la Construccion [*Colombian Chamber of Construction (Medellin)*]   (LA)
CAMACOL ... Camara de Comercio Latina [*Latin Chamber of Commerce*]   (LA)
CAMAD .... Societe Camerounaise de Produits Alimentaires et Dietetiques
CAMAG .... Societe Camerounaise des Grands Magasins
CAMAGENCE ... Agence de Voyages H. De Suares d'Almeyda et Compagnie
CAMAIR... Cameroon Airlines
CAMAL..... Campaign Against Mining on Aboriginal Land [*Australia*]   (ADA)
CAMARCA ... Caisse Mutuelle Autonome de Retraites Complementaires Agricoles   (WGAO)

CAMARTEC ... Center for Agricultural Mechanization and Rural Technology [*Tanzania*] [*Research center*] (IRC)

CAMAS..... Confederation of African Medical Associations and Societies [*Nigeria*] (EAIO)

CAMAS..... Coordinador del Area Maritima del Atlantico Sur [*South Atlantic Maritime Area Coordination*] (LA)

CAMAT .... Compagnie Africaine de Materiel Europeen

CAMAT .... Compagnie d'Assurances Maritimes Aeriennes et Terrestres

CAMAUTO ... Cameroun Automobile

CAMB .... Cambodia (WDAA)

CAMB .... Cuerpo de Aviadores Militares Bolivianos [*Bolivian Military Aviation Corps*]

CAMBA .... China-Australia Migratory Birds Agreement

CAMBADU ... Centro Almaceneros Minoristas, Baristas, y Afines del Uruguay [*Association of Uruguayan Retail Businessmen, Bartenders, and Related Professionals*] (LA)

CAMBL..... Commission Administrative Mixte Belgo-Luxembourgeoise (FLAF)

CAMBOIS ... Societe Camerounaise des Bois (WGAO)

CAMC .... Central American Monetary Council

CAMC .... China National Agricultural Machinery Import & Export Corporation [*China*] (IMH)

CAMC .... Corporacion Argentina de Productores Avicolas [*Argentina*] (DSCA)

CAMCO .... Comite Permanente de Camaras de Comercio del Grupo Andino [*Peru*] (DSCA)

CAMCOLAM ... Camara de Comercio Colombo Americana [*Colombia*] (COL)

CAMCORE ... Central American and Mexico Coniferous Resources Cooperative (GNE)

CAMCS..... Comissao de Analise dos Meios de Comunicacao Social [*Commission for the Analysis of Mass Communication Means*] [*Portuguese*] (WER)

CAMD....... Council of Australian Museum Directors

CAMDA .... Car and Motorcycle Drivers Association (WGAO)

CAMDE .... Campanha da Mulher pela Democracia

CAMDECAF ... Compagnie Camerounaise de Decafeination

CAMDEF ... Societe Camerounaise de Deforestage (WGAO)

CAMDEV ... Cameroon Development Corp.

CAME .... Conference of Allied Ministers of Education (WGAO)

CAME .... Conscripcion Agraria Militar Ecuatoriana [*Ecuadorean Agrarian Military Conscription*]

CAME .... Consejo de Asistencia Mutua Economica [*Council for Mutual Economic Assistance*] [*Use CEMA*] (LA)

CAME .... Consejo de Ayuda Mutua Economica (WGAO)

CAME .... Coordinadora de Actividades Mercantiles [*Coordinating Agency for Mercantile Activities*] [*Argentina*] (LA)

CAMEA .... Comite des Applications Militaires de l'Energie Atomique [*French*]

CAMEC..... Casa Agricola Mercantil y Exportadora de Cafe [*Guatemala*] (DSCA)

CAMEC..... Compagnie Africaine de Metaux et de Produits Chimiques

CAMECA ... Centro Ajujic Mejoracmiento Educacion Superior America (WGAO)

CAMECA ... Compagnie d'Applications Mecaniques a l'Electronique au Cinema et a l'Atomistique [*French company that invented Scopitone, a coin-operated machine that projects musical movies in places of entertainment*]

CAMECEC ... Carpentreria Metalica y Cerrajania de la Construccion [*Spain*] (PDAA)

CAMECO ... Camara Ecuatoriana de la Construccion [*Ecuador*] (LAA)

CaMeCo..... Catholic Media Council [*Aachen, Federal Republic of Germany*] (EAIO)

CAMEI...... China Association for Medical Equipment Industry (EAIO)

CAMEL..... Compagnie Algerienne du Methane Liquide [*Algerian Liquid Methane Company*] (AF)

CAMEN .... Centro Applicazioni Militari Energia Nucleare (WGAO)

CAMEN .... Centro Autonomo Militare Energia Nucleare [*Italian*]

CAMEN .... Centro d'Applicazioni Militari dell' Energia Nucleare [*Center for Military Applications of Nuclear Energy*] [*Italian*] (WER)

CAMEP..... Central Autonoma Metropolitana de Agua Potable [*Autonomous Metropolitan Water Board*] [*Haiti*] (LAA)

CAMEP..... Societe Camerounaise d'Etudes et de Promotion pour l'Afrique (WGAO)

Camer......... Cameroon

CAMER..... Compania Auxiliar Mercantil de Colombia SA [*Colombia*] (COL)

CAMERA ... Commonwealth Advance Movement Encouraging Responsibility towards Alcohol [*Australia*] (ADA)

CAMERI... Coastal and Marine Engineering Research Institute [*Israel*] (ERC)

CAMERINDUSTRIEL ... Compagnie Camerounaise de Representations Industrielles (WGAO)

CAMEROUNCONSULT ... Societe Camerounaise d'Engineering et de Consultation (WGAO)

CAMES..... Conseil Africain et Malgache pour l'Enseignement Superieur [*African and Malagasy Council on Higher Education*] (AF)

CAMETANCHE ... Societe Camerounaise d'Etancheite

CAMFAX ... Civil Aviation Meteorological Facsimile Network (WGAO)

CAMGAZ ... Societe Camerounaise de Gaz Liquefies de Petrole

CAMGOC ... Gulf Oil Company of Cameroon

CAMHADD ... Commonwealth Association for Mental Handicap and Development Disabilities (WGAO)

CAMHDD ... Commonwealth Association of Mental Handicap and Developmental Disabilities (EA)

CAMI .... Cameroon Motors Industries

CAMI .... Central Asian Mission International

CAMI .... Cercle de l'Amitie

CAMI .... Comite Africain des Moyens d'Information

CAMI .... Correo Aereo Militar Internacional [*International Military Air Mail*] [*Venezuela*] (LA)

CAMIA...... Centre for Advanced Manufacturing and Industrial Automation [*University of Wollongong*] [*Australia*]

CAMIA...... Comptoir Algerien de Materiel Industriel et Agricole [*Algerian Industrial and Agricultural Equipment Office*] (AF)

CAMIA...... Correo Aereo Militar Interamericano [*Inter-American Military Air Mail*] [*Venezuela*] (LA)

CAMICO... Comptoir de l'Automobile, du Materiel Industriel, du Cycle, et de l'Outillage

CAMIG ..... Companhia Agricola de Minas Gerais [*Brazil*] (WGAO)

CAMIG ..... Companhia Agricola de Minas Gerais SA [*Brazil*] (DSCA)

CAMIK..... Club des Amis Khmers [*Cambodian Friends Club*] (CL)

CAMILA ... Chicanos Against Military Intervention in Latin America [*Promotes understanding between Mexico and the US at the grassroots level*] (CROSS)

CAMIMEX ... Camara Minera de Mexico

CAMINA .. Compania Anonima Minas de Naricual [*Naricual Mines Company*] [*Venezuela*] (LA)

CAMINFOR ... Societe Camerounaise d'Informatique et de Services (WGAO)

CAMINVEST ... Societe Holding Cameroun Investissement (WGAO)

CAMIRA... Comite d'Application des Methodes Isotopiques aux Recherches Agronomiques [*Belgium*] (WGAO)

CAMITEX ... Societe Camerounaise pour l'Industrie Textile

CAMJ........ Council of Arab Ministers of Justice [*See also CMAJ*] [*Rabat, Morocco*] (EAIO)

CAMJA..... Comision Nacional de Apoyo al Movimiento Juvenil Agrario [*Uruguay*] (LAA)

CAMLA..... Communications and Media Law Association [*Australia*]

CAMLR..... Conservation of Antarctic Marine Living Resources [*International agreement signed in 1982*]

CAMM ...... Compagnie Africaine de Manutentions Mecaniques

CAMMAC ... Canadian Amateur Musicians (EAIO)

CAMO....... Centro de Adiestramiento de Mecanicos y Operadores [*Training Center for Mechanics and Operators*] [*Peru*] (LAA)

CAMOA..... Societe Camerounaise d'Oxygene et d'Acetylene

CAMOBRA ... Societe des Brasseries Modernes de Cameroun (WGAO)

CAMOFI.... Caisse Centrale de Mobilisation et de Financement [*Central Mobilization and Finance Bank*] [*Burundi*] (GEA)

Camp.......... Campeche [*Mexico*] (BARN)

CAMP .... Centre d'Assistance pour la Motorisation des Pirogues de Saint-Louis

CAMP .... Computer Graphics - Anwendungen fuer Management und Produktivitaet [*German*] (ADPT)

CAMP .... Cooperative African Microform [*or Microfilm*] Project

CAMPA..... Comptoir d'Approvisionnements de Materiel et Produits Agricoles [*Morocco*]

CAMPC..... Centre Africain et Mauricien de Perfectionnement des Cadres [*African and Mauritian Center for Training Cadres*] (AF)

CAMPROMAR ... Societe Camerounaise de Produits et Marchandises

CAMPSA .. Compania Arrendataria del Monopolio de Petroleos, Sociedad Anonima [*Leasing Company of the Petroleum Monopoly, Incorporated*] [*Spanish*] (WER)

CAMPSA .. Compania Arrendatoria de Monopolio de Petroleos (WGAO)

CAMR .... Centre for Applied Microbiology and Research (WGAO)

CAMR .... Centro de Administradores y Mayordomos Rurales [*Argentina*] (DSCA)

CAMR .... Ceylon Association for the Mentally Retarded [*Sri Lanka*] (EAIO)

CAMR .... Conference Administrative Mondiale des Radiocommunications

CAMRA .... Campaign for Real Ale (WGAO)

CAMRDC ... Central African Mineral Resources Development Centre [*Congo*] (EAIO)

CAMRODD ... Caribbean Association on Mental Retardation and Other Development Disabilities [*Netherlands Antilles*] (EAIO)

CAMS........ Central African Motors

CAMS........ Central Agency for Mobilization and Statistics [*Egypt*]

CAMS........ Centre d'Analyse et de Mathematique Sociales [*Center for Social Analysis and Mathematics*] [*Research center*] [*France*] (IRC)

CAMS........ Chantiers Aero-Maritimes de la Seine

CAMS....... Chinese Academy of Medical Sciences   (PDAA)
CAMS....... Commission pour l'Abolition de Mutilation Sexuelle [*Commission for the Abolition of Sexual Mutilation*] [*Senegal*]
CAMS....... Confederation of Australian Motor Sport   (EAIO)
CAMS....... Conseil Africain et Malgache du Sucre
Camsa Is .... Cayirova Cam Fabrikasi Iscileri Sendikasi [*Cayirova Glass Factory Workers Union*]   (TU)
CAMSHIPLINES ... Cameroon Shipping Lines SA
CAMSPF... Catholic Archdiocese of Melbourne Schools' Provident Fund [*Australia*]
CAMSSP... Caisse Militaire de Securite Sociale et de Prevoyance [*Algeria*]
CAMSTEEL ... Cameroon Steel Products SA
CAMSUCO ... Cameroon Sugar   (WGAO)
CAMSUCO ... Cameroon Sugar Company, Inc.
CAMT .... Camara Argentina Maderas Terciadas [*Argentina*]   (DSCA)
CAMT .... Centre for Advanced Materials Technology [*Monash University*] [*Australia*]
CAMTEL .. Societe Camerounaise de Telecommunications   (WGAO)
CAMTRON ... Council of Australian Machine Tool and Robotics Manufacturers
CAMVAC ... Centro de Apoyo para Mujeres Violadas [*An association*] [*Mexico*]   (EAIO)
CAMVAL ... Comite d'Amenagement et de Mise en Valeur de l'Alaotra [*Malagasy*]
CAMVOYAGES ... Agence Camerounaise de Voyages
Camwork.... Caribbean Association of Media Workers   (EY)
CAMYGIENE ... Societe Camerounaise d'Hygiene
CAMYP..... Confederacion Argentina de Maestros y Profesores [*Argentine Confederation of Teachers and Professors*]   (LA)
CAN.......... Air Canarias S. Coop Ltd. [*Spain*] [*ICAO designator*]   (FAAC)
CAN.......... Canada [*ANSI three-letter standard code*]   (CNC)
Can............ Canal [*Channel*] [*Portuguese*]   (NAU)
Can............ Canal [*Channel*] [*Spanish*]   (NAU)
Can............ Canale [*Channel*] [*Italian*]   (NAU)
CAN.......... Cannabis Action Network   (EA)
Can............ Canonikus [*German*]
CAN.......... Central Autentica Nacionalista [*Nationalist Authentic Central*] [*Guatemala*] [*Political party*]   (PPW)
CAN.......... Centralforbundet for Alkohol- och Narkotikaupplysning [*Swedish Council for Information on Alcohol and Other Drugs*] [*Information service or system*]   (IID)
CAN.......... Centro Administrativo Nacional [*Colombia*]   (COL)
CAN.......... Climate Action Network [*An alliance of groups that includes Greenpeace, the World Wide Fund for Nature, and The Natural Resources Defense Council*]
CAN.......... Cocoa Association of Nigeria   (WGAO)
CAN.......... Combinado Avicola Nacional [*National Poultry Complex*] [*Cuba*]   (LA)
CAN.......... Comision Asesora de Nomenclatura [*Asociacion Latinoamericana de Libre Comercio*]   (LAA)
CAN.......... Comite de Accion Nacionalista [*Committee of Nationalist Action*] [*Bolivia*]   (LA)
CAN.......... Comite de Alto Nivel para la Reestructuracion del Mercado Comun Centroamericano [*High Level Committee for the Restructuring of the Central American Common Market*]   (LA)
CAN.......... Committee on Aircraft Noise [*ICAO*]   (DA)
CAN.......... Community Arts Network [*Australia*]
CAN.......... Compagnie Africaine de Navigation
CAN.......... Compagnie de l'Afrique Noire
CAN.......... Consejo Agrario Nacional [*Buenos Aires, Argentina*]   (LAA)
CAN.......... Consejo Agropecuario Nacional [*National Agricultural and Livestock Council*] [*Costa Rica*]   (LA)
CAN.......... Convertisseur Analogique Numerique [*French*]   (ADPT)
CANS......... Correio Aereo Nacional [*National Airmail*] [*Portuguese*]
CAN.......... Guangzhou [*China*] [*Airport symbol*]   (OAG)
CANA....... Caribbean News Agency   (LA)
CANA........ Clergy Against Nuclear Arms   (WGAO)
CANA........ Cooperative Agricole la Noelle, Ancenis   (WGAO)
CANACH ... Asociacion Nacional de Campensios de Honduras   (WGAO)
CANACINTRA ... Camara Nacional de la Industria de Transformacion [*National Association of the Processing Industry*] [*Mexico*]   (LA)
CANACO .. Camara de Comercio de la Ciudad de Mexico [*Mexico City Chamber of Commerce*]   (LA)
CANACO .. Camara Nacional de Comercio de la Ciudad de Mexico   (WGAO)
CANACOMIND ... Camara Nacional de Comercio e Industrias de Managua [*Nicaragua*]   (LAA)
CANAI ...... Comiato Artistico Nazionale Accounciatori Italiani   (WGAO)
CANAICA ... Camara Nacional de la Industria de Calzado [*National Chamber of Shoe Industries*] [*Mexico*]   (LA)
CANAIR.... Canary Islands Air
CANAIRFAX ... Maritime Group Headquarters, Halifax, Nova Scotia, Canada
CANAL ..... Kanizkar Le'eyl [*As Mentioned Above*] [*Hebrew*]

CANAM .... Commission d'Aide aux Nord-Africains de la Metropole
CANAMECC ... Camara Nacional de Medios de Comunicacion Colectiva [*Costa Rica*]   (EY)
CANA-OESTE ... Associacao dos Plantadores de Cana do Oeste do Estado de Sao Paulo [*Brazil*]   (DSCA)
CANAPI.... Camara Nacional de Artesania y Pequena Industria de Costa Rica [*Costa Rica*]   (LA)
CANAPP... Comite Asesor Nacional de Adiestramiento Petrolero y Petroquimico [*National Advisory Committee for Petroleum and Petrochemical Training*] [*Venezuela*]   (LA)
CANAPRACOL ... Casa Nacional del Profesor Caldas [*Manizales*]   (COL)
CANAPRO ... Casa Nacional del Profesor-Sociedad Cooperaria [*Colombia*]   (COL)
CANAPRONAR ... Casa Nacional del Profesor Narino [*Pasto*]   (COL)
CANAPROPAM ... Casa Nacional del Profesor [*Pamplona*]   (COL)
CANAPROSUC ... Casa Nacional del Profesor Sucre   (COL)
CANARA .. Camara Nacional de Radio [*National Radio Council*] [*Costa Rica*]   (LA)
CANARI.... Caribbean Natural Resources Institute   (EAIO)
CANAS...... Cellule d'Analyse des Politiques Alimentaires et Nutritionnelles
CANATA .. Canada-Australia Trade Agreement
CANATUR ... Camara Nacional de Turismo [*National Tourism Board*] [*Costa Rica*]   (LA)
CANAVI.... Cooperativa Agropecuaria Nacional de Avicultores Ltda [*Uruguay*]   (DSCA)
Canb.......... Canberra [*Australia*]
Canb.......... University of Canberra [*Australia*]
Canberral Arts ... Canberra Institute of the Arts [*Australia*]
CANC........ Chambre d'Agriculture de Nouvelle Caledonie   (EAIO)
CANCAVA ... Caisse Autonome Nationale de Compensation d'Assurance Viellesse Artisanale [*France*]   (FLAF)
CANCES ... Centre for Advanced Numerical Computation in Engineering and Science [*Australia*]
CAND....... Cantate Domino [*Sing Unto the Lord*] [*Music*]
CANDA ..... Computer Assisted New Drug Application [*Medicine*] [*Australia*]
C & C .... Communication and Cognition   (EA)
C &CA(NZ) ... Cement and Concrete Association of New Zealand   (EAIO)
C & D .... Cultures et Developpement, Louvain
CANDECAF ... Campagnie Camerounaise de Decafeination   (WGAO)
C & F......... Costo y Flete [*Cost and Freight*] [*Shipping*] [*Spanish*]
C & F......... Cout et Fret [*Cost and Freight*] [*Shipping*] [*French*]
C & MA ..... Christian and Missionary Alliance of Australia
C & P.......... Church and Peace [*An association*] [*Germany*]   (EAIO)
CANE .... Campaign Against Nuclear Energy [*Australia*]
CANE .... Citizens Against Nuclear Energy [*India*]   (EAIO)
CANEFA ... Comision Asesora Nacional de Erradicacion de la Febre Aftosa [*Argentina*]   (WGAO)
CANEFA ... Comision Asesora Nacional para la Erradicacion de la Fiebre Aftosa [*Argentina*]   (LAA)
CANESA ... Centrais de Abastecimiento do Nordeste, Sociedad Anonima [*Brazil*]   (LAA)
CANFORCEHED ... Canadian Forces Headquarters [*NATO*]   (NATG)
CANGO..... Committee for Air Navigation and Ground Organization   (WGAO)
CANIRAC ... Camera Nacional de la Industria de Restaurantes y Alimentos Condimentados [*Mexico*]   (WGAO)
CANO........ Compania Anonima Naviera Orinoco [*Venezuela*]   (LAA)
CANOVAL ... Cooperative Agricole du Noyonnaise et du Valois   (WGAO)
CANP .... Campaign Against Nuclear Power [*Australia*]
Can P .... Canadisches Patent [*Canadian Patent*] [*German*]   (GCA)
CANPM .... Centro Associativo dos Negros da Provincia de Mocambique [*Associative Center of the Blacks of Mozambique Province*]   (AF)
CANR .... Chamber of Agriculture and Natural Resources [*Philippines*]   (DS)
CANS .... Cesko-Americke Narodni Sdruzeni [*National Czech-American Federation*]   (CZ)
CANSG .... Civil Aviation Navigational Services Group   (WGAO)
CANSM .... Caisse Autonome Nationale de la Securite dans les Mines   (WGAO)
CANSW..... Careers' Association of New South Wales [*Australia*]
CANSW..... Chess Association of New South Wales [*Australia*]
CANSW..... Christian Assembly of New South Wales [*Australia*]
CA(NSW) ... Court of Appeal (New South Wales) [*Australia*]
cant............ Canto [*Edge*] [*Publishing*] [*Spanish*]
CANT .... Cantonese
Cant......... Cantonnement [*Billet, Quarters*] [*Military*] [*French*]   (MTD)
CANTAS... Cankiri Tuz Urunleri Uretim ve Dagitim Anonim Sirketi [*Cankiri Salt Products Production and Distribution Corporation*]   (TU)
Cantaur ...... Cantuariensis [*of Canterbury*] [*Latin*]   (BARN)
CANTEEN ... Australian Teenage Cancer Patients Society
CANTIERMACCHINE ... Associazione Commercianti Importatori Macchine da Cantiere ed Affini   (WGAO)
CANTO ..... Caribbean Association of National Telecommunications Organization   (WGAO)

CANTV ..... Compania Anonima Nacional de Telefonos Venezolanos [*National Telephone Company of Venezuela*] (LA)
CANTV ..... Compania Anonima Nacional Telefonos de Venezuela (WGAO)
CANU....... Caprivi African National Union [*Namibia*]
CANU....... Convention African National Union [*Nyasaland*]
CANU....... Crnogorska Akademija Nauka i Umjetnosti [*Former Yugoslavia*] (EAIO)
CANUC..... Campaign Against the Namibian Uranium Contract (AF)
CANUMAR ... Compania de Navegacion de Ultramar, SA [*Argentina*] (LAA)
CANUSPA ... Canada, Australia, New Zealand and United States Parents Association (WGAO)
CANYA ..... Cancer and the Young Adult, Inc. [*Australia*]
CANZ........ Canada, Australia and New Zealand
CAO........ Campagne Anti-Outspan
CAO.......... Canadian Association of Optometricists (WGAO)
CAO.......... Coalicion Aranista Organizada [*Organized Aranista Coalition*] [*Guatemala*] (LA)
CAO.......... Collectieve Arbeidsovereenkomst [*Collective Labor Agreement*] [*Netherlands*] (WEN)
CAO.......... Comision Asesora de Origen [*Asociacion Latinoamericana de Libre Comercio*] (LAA)
CAO.......... Commonwealth Archives Office [*Australia*]
CAO.......... Commonwealth Arts Organization (EA)
CAO.......... Conception Assistee par Ordinateur [*Computer-Assisted Design - CAD*] [*French*]
CAO.......... Corporate Affairs Office [*Victoria, Australia*]
CAO.......... Council of African Organizations (AF)
CAO.......... Wet op de Collectieve Arbeidsovereenkomst [*Benelux*] (BAS)
CAOAA ..... Civil Air Operations Officers' Association of Australia
CAOBISCO ... Association des Industries de la Chocolaterie, Biscuiterie-Biscotterie et Confiserie de la CEE [*Association of the Chocolate, Biscuit and Confectionery Industries of the EEC*] (ECED)
CAOBISCO ... Association d'Industries de Produits la Chocolaterie, Biscuiterie-Biscotterie etConfiserie de la CEE (WGAO)
CAO-EC .... Committee of Agricultural Organizations in the European Communities (EAIO)
CAOMI ..... Centre d'Accueil d'Observation des Mineurs Delinquants
CAOOAA ... Civil Air Operations Officers' Association of Australia (ADA)
CAOP .... Centruum voor Arbeids- en Organisatiepsychologisch Onderzoek [*Center for Research in Work and Organizational Psychology*] [*Netherlands*] (IRC)
CAOP .... Companhia de Agricultura e Organizacoes Pecuarias [*Agricultural and Animal Husbandry Organizations Society*] [*Angola*] (AF)
CAOPRI .... Central Arecanut and Oil Palm Research Institute [*India*] (DSCA)
CAORB ..... Civil Aviation Operational Research Branch (WGAO)
CAOSO ..... Cooperative Agricole Ovine du Sud-Ouest (WGAO)
CAP .... Caixa de Aposentadoria e Pensoes [*Portuguese*]
CAP .... Camara Algodonera del Peru [*Peru*] (DSCA)
CAP .... Camara Argentina de Publicaciones (EAIO)
CAP .... Canadian Association of Physicists (WGAO)
Cap......... Capacitariat [*French*]
CAP .... Cap Haitien [*Haiti*] [*Airport symbol*] (OAG)
Cap......... Capitaine [*Captain, Commander*] [*Military*] [*French*] (MTD)
cap........... Capital [*Capital*] [*Business term*] [*French*]
cap........... Capitale [*Capital*] [*French*]
cap........... Capital Letter (TPFD)
Cap........ Capitano [*Captain*] [*Italian*]
cap........... Capitao [*Captain*] [*Portuguese*]
cap........... Capitol [*Chapter*] [*Romanian*]
Cap........ Capitolo [*Chapter*] [*Italian*] (ILCA)
cap........... Capitulo [*Chapter*] [*Spanish*]
cap........... Capitulo [*Chapter*] [*Portuguese*]
cap........... Caporale [*Corporal*] [*Italian*]
Cap........ Captain (PWGL)
CAP .... Central African Party
CAP .... Central African Post
CAP .... Central Agricultural Producers (WGAO)
CAP .... Central America and Panama (IID)
CAP .... Central Azucarero Portuguese [*Venezuela*] (DSCA)
CAP .... Centralne Archiwum Panstwowe [*Central State Archives*] (POL)
CAP .... Centre Aeroporte de Toulouse [*France*] (PDAA)
CAP .... Centre d'Analyse et de Prevision [*Center for Analysis and Forecasting*] [*French*] (WER)
CAP .... Centres d'Alevinage Principaux
CAP .... Centres d'Approvisionnement des Planteurs
CAP .... Centro de Adiestramiento Profesional [*Guatemala*] (LAA)
CAP .... Certificado de Aportacion Patrimonial [*Certificate of Patrimonial Apportion*] [*Mexico*]
CAP .... Certificat d'Aptitude Pedagogique [*For primary schoolmasters*] [*French*]
CAP .... Certificat d'Aptitude Professionelle [*Certificate of Professional Ability*] [*French*] (BARN)
CAP .... Certificat d'Aptitude Professionnelle [*French*]

CAP .... Chaudiere Avancee Prototype [*Advanced Prototype Boiler*] [*French*] (WER)
CaP .... Church and Peace [*Schoeffengrund, Federal Republic of Germany*] (EAIO)
CAP .... Comandos Armados del Pueblo [*People's Armed Commands*] [*Mexico*] (LA)
CAP .... Comision Asesora de Asuntos Agropecuarios [*Asociacion Latinoamericana de Libre Comercio - ALALC*] (LAA)
CAP .... Comision de Administracion Publica [*Commission of Public Administration*] [*Caracas, Venezuela*] (LAA)
CAP .... Comite Antifascista Pameno [*Panamanian Antifascist Committee*] (LA)
CAP .... Comites de Accion Popular [*People's Action Committees*] [*Nicaragua*] (LA)
CAP .... Commission d'Assistance Publique [*French*] (BAS)
CAP .... Commissions d'Assistance Publique [*Commissions for Public Assistance*] [*Belgium*] (WER)
CAP .... Common Agricultural Policy (EG)
CAP .... Commonwealth Association of Planners [*British*] (EAIO)
CAP .... Community Action Party [*Thailand*] [*Political party*] (FEA)
CAP .... Compagnie Africaine d'Armement a la Peche
CAP .... Compagnie Africaine de Placages
CAP .... Compagnie d'Agences de Publicite (WGAO)
CAP .... Compania de Acero del Pacifico [*Pacific Steel Company*] [*Chile*] (LA)
CAP .... Confederacao dos Agricultores de Portugal [*Portuguese Farmers Association*] (WER)
CAP .... Confederate Action Party of Australia [*Political party*]
CAP .... Conference of African Planners
CAP .... Consejo Argentino de la Paz [*Argentine Peace Council*] (LA)
CAP .... Consejo Asesor de Planificacion [*Peru*] (DSCA)
CAP .... Consortium Africaine Pharmaceutique
CAP .... Constructions Africaines Pontenegrines
CAP .... Consumers Association of Penang [*Malaysia*] (EAIO)
CAP .... Contingency Amphibious Plan [*NATO*] (NATG)
CAP .... Continuing Airworthiness Panel [*ICAO*] (DA)
CAP .... Cooperativa Agraria de Produccion [*Agrarian Production Cooperative*] [*Peru*] (LA)
CAP .... Cooperativa Agricola de Productie [*Agricultural Production Cooperative*] (RO)
CAP .... Corporacion Argentina de Productores de Carne [*Argentine Corporation of Meat Producers*] (LA)
CAP .... Corporation of Argentine Meat Producers (WGAO)
CAP .... Crisis Accommodation Programme [*Australia*]
CAP .... Cuerpo de Aviacion del Peru [*Air Corps of Peru*]
CAPA........ Camara Argentina del Papel y Afines [*Argentina*] (DSCA)
CAPA........ Canada-Caribbean-Central America Policy Alternatives [*An association*]
CAPA........ Certificat d'Aptitude a la Profession d'Avocat [*Lawyers Professional Aptitude Certificate*] [*Morocco*] (AF)
CAPA........ Certificat d'Aptitude Professionnelle Agricole
CAPA........ Circulo Argentino de Periodistas Agrarios [*Argentina*] (DSCA)
CAPA........ Comision Aeronautica Permanente Americana
CAPA........ Comision Asesora de Politica Agraria [*Venezuela*] (WGAO)
CAPA........ Comissao de Ampara a Producao Agropecuaria [*Rio De Janeiro, Brazil*] (LAA)
CAPA........ Comite Argentino Permanente de Aeronautica [*Argentina*]
CAPA........ Comite d'Action pour la Productivite en Assurance [*France*] (FLAF)
CAPA........ Commission Aerienne Pan-Americaine (FLAF)
CAPA........ Commission Americaine Permanente Aeronautique (FLAF)
CAPA........ Commonwealth Association of Polytechnics in Africa [*Nairobi, Kenya*] (EAIO)
CAPA........ Compagnie Africaine de Peche Atlantique [*Ivory Coast*] (WGAO)
CAPA........ Compagnie Africaine de Produits Alimentaires
CAPA........ Compagnie d'Achat de Produits Africains
CAPA........ Comptoir Africain de Pieces Automobiles
CAPA........ Confederation of Asian and Pacific Accountants (ADA)
CAPA........ Conference of the Anglican Provinces of Africa
CAPA........ Corporation of Australian Performing Arts
CAPA........ Council of Anglican Provinces of Africa (WGAO)
CAPA........ Council of Australian Postgraduate Associations
CAPA........ Selecion y Comercio de la Patata de Siembra (WGAO)
CAPAA ...... Council of Australian Public Abattoir Authorities
CAPAASA ... Compania de Aviacion Pan American Argentina Sociedad Anonima [*Argentina*]
CAPAB...... Cape Performing Arts Board
CAPAC...... Caisse Auxiliaire de Paiement des Allocations de Chomage [*Benelux*] (BAS)
CAPAC...... Camara Panamena de la Construccion [*Panama Chamber of Construction*] (LA)
CAPAGRO ... Capitales Agropecuarios SA [*Venezuela*] (DSCA)
CAPAM..... Comptoir Africain de Pieces Automobiles de Meknes [*Morocco*]
CAPAM..... Cooperative Agricole de Production des Anciens Moudjahidine [*War Veterans Agricultural Production Cooperative*] [*Algeria*] (AF)

CAPAP...... Confederation of Australasian Performing Arts Presenters
    [*Australia*]
CAPAR...... Catalogue Partage
CAPAR...... Centre d'Animation et de Promotion Agricole et Rurale
    (WGAO)
CAPAS ...... Centre d'Assistance a la Peche Artisanale Senegalaise
CAPASA ... Coordinadora Aerea de Pilotos Agricolas [*Venezuela*]   (DSCA)
CAPB........ Child Abuse Protection Board [*Tasmania*] [*Australia*]
CAPC........ Central African Power Corporation
CAPC........ Certificat d'Aptitude au Professorat des Colleges [*French*]
CAPC........ Certificat d'Aptitude Professionnel Commercial [*Commercial
    Professional Aptitude Certificate*] (CL)
CAPC........ City of Adelaide Planning Commission [*Australia*]
CAPC........ Comision Asesora de Politica Comercial [*Asociacion
    Latinoamericana de Libre Comercio - ALALC*]   (LAA)
CAPC........ Comite Ampliado del Programa y de la Coordinacion   (WGAO)
CAPC........ Czechoslovak Sports Confederation   (EAIO)
CAPCA...... Council of Australian Pest Control Associations
CAPCDC... China Aeronautical Projects Contracting and Development Corp.
    (TCC)
CAPCEG ... Certificat d'Aptitude au Professorat des Colleges d'Enseignement
    General [*French*]
CAPCI ...... Compagnie Africaine de Pneumatiques et de Caoutchouc
    Industriel [*Morocco*]
CAPCIDC ... Czechoslovak Association of Physical Culture, Information, and
    Documentation Centre (EAIO)
CAPCO...... Capsulas Colombianas Ltda. [*Colombia*] Tlg.   (COL)
CAPCO...... Central Africa Power Corporation
CAPCO...... China American Petrochemical Co. Ltd. [*Taiwan*]
CAPCS ...... Cooperative Agricole Polyvalente Communale de Services
    [*Communal Multi-Service Agriculture Cooperative*]
    [*Algeria*]   (AF)
CAPD .... Council for Agricultural Planning and Development [*Taiwanese*]
    [*Research center*]   (IRC)
CAPDAS ... Computer-Aided Polymer Data System   (IID)
CAPDS ...... Christian Aboriginal Parent Directed School [*Australia*]
CAPE ...... Center for Propellant and Missile Completion [*France*]
CAPE........ Centre Africain de Promotion Economique
CAPE........ China Association of Plant Engineering   (EAIO)
CAPE........ Commonwealth AIDS Prevention and Education Program
    [*Australia*]
CAPE........ Council for American Private Education   (WGAO)
CAPEB ...... Confederation de l' Artisanat et des Petites Entreprises du
    Batiment   (WGAO)
CAPEC ...... Centre Africain de Prevention et de Controle [*Morocco*]
CAPECO ... Camara Peruana de la Construccion [*Peruvian Chamber of
    Construction*]   (LA)
CAPEF ...... Cooperative Agricole des Producteurs d'Endives de France
    (WGAO)
capel.......... Capella [*Chapel*] [*Latin*]   (BARN)
CAPEL ...... Centre pour l'Accroissement de la Productivite des Entreprises
    Laitieres   (WGAO)
CAPEL ...... Certificat d'Aptitude Professionnelle pour l'Enseignement dans
    les Lycees
CAPEM..... Certificat d'Aptitude a l'Enseignement Moyen [*Intermediate
    Education Aptitude Certificate*] [*Algeria*]   (AF)
CAPEM ..... Comite d'Amenagement et du Plan d'Equipment de la Moselle
    (WGAO)
CAPEMI ... Caixa de Peculio Militar [*Brazil*]   (WGAO)
CAPENE ... Centre d'Application et de Promotion des Energies Nouvelles
    Ecologiques [*France*]
CAPER ...... Caisse d'Accession a la Propriete et a l'Exploitation Rurales
    [*Algeria*]
CAPERAS ... Comite Argentino para el Estudio de las Regiones Aridas y
    Semiaridas [*Argentina*]   (LAA)
CAPES ...... Certificat d'Aptitude au Professorat de l'Enseignement
    Secondaire [*Secondary School Teaching Certificate*]
    [*French*]   (WER)
CAPES ...... Coordenacao para o Aperfeicoamento de Pessoal de Nivel
    Superior [*Coordination of Advanced Training for Higher-
    Level Personnel*] [*Brazil*]   (LA)
CAPESA.... Cabotaje Peru Sociedad Anonima [*Peru*]   (LAA)
CAPESA.... Central de Abastecimiento de Pernambuco [*Brazil*]   (LAA)
CAPET ...... Certificat d'Aptitude au Professorat de l'Enseignement
    Technique [*French*]
CAPET ...... Certificat d'Aptitude Pedagogique a l'Enseignement Technique
    [*Technical Education Aptitude Certificate*] [*French*]
CAPEXIL ... Chemicals and Allied Products Export Promotion Council
    [*India*]
CAPF .... Council for Agricultural Planning and Development [*Taiwan*]
    (WGAO)
CAPFA ...... Child Accident Prevention Foundation of Australia
CAPFCE.... Comite Administrador del Programa Federal de Construcion de
    Escuelas [*Administrative Committee of the Federal Program
    for the Building of Educational Institutes*] [*Mexico*]
    (PDAA)

CAPFCE.... Comite Administrador del Programa Federal de Construciou de
    Escuels [*Mexico*]   (WGAO)
cap frag ...... Capitao-de-Fragata [*Frigate Captain*] [*Portuguese*]
CAPH .... Continental African Publishing House
CAPI......... Certificat d'Aptitude Professionnelle des Instituteurs [*French*]
CAPI......... Comision de Administracion Publica Internacional   (WGAO)
CAPIA .... Camara Argentina de Productores Industriales Avicolas
    [*Argentina*]   (LAA)
CAPIA .... Companhia Auxiliar de Producao de Insumos [*Brazil*]   (DSCA)
CAPIC .... Campaign Against Psychiatric Injustice and Coercion [*Australia*]
CAPIEL..... Comite de Coordination des Associations de Constructeurs
    d'Appareillage [*Coordinating Committee for Common
    Market Associations of Manufacturers of Electrical
    Switchgear and Controlgear*] [*EC*]   (ECED)
CAPIEL..... Comite de Coordination des Associations de Constructeurs
    d'Appareillage Industriel Electrique du Marche Commun
    (WGAO)
capil........... Capilettera [*Initial Letter*] [*Publishing*] [*Italian*]
CAPIL .... Capital Indexed Loan Pilot Scheme [*Victoria, Australia*]
capilett .... Capilettera [*Initial Letter*] [*Publishing*] [*Italian*]
CAPIM...... Consortium Africain de Produits Industriels et Menagers
CAPIN....... Companhia Agro Pastoril e Industrial [*Brazil*]   (DSCA)
CAPIN....... Companhia Agropecuaria do Inga [*Brazil*]   (DSCA)
CAPINGO ... Companhia Agropecuaria do Norte de Goias [*Brazil*]   (DSCA)
CAPISM.... Comite d'Action Politique et Sociale pour l'Independance de
    Madagascar [*Political and Social Committee for Malagasy
    Independence*]
capit .... Capitolo [*Chapter*] [*Publishing*] [*Italian*]
CAPITB...... Chemical and Allied Products Industry Training Board   (WGAO)
CAPITIB .... Clothing and Allied Products Industry Training Board   (WGAO)
CAPL........ Coastal Anti-Pollution League [*BRIT*]   (WGAO)
CAPL........ Commonwealth Assistance to Public Libraries [*Campaign*]
    [*Australia*]
CAPLA ...... Council of Australian Public Library Associations
CAPLABA ... Cooperative Agricole des Planteurs Bamoun
CAPLABAM ... Cooperative Agricole des Planteurs de Bamboutos
    [*Cameroon*]   (WGAO)
CAPLAME ... Cooperative Agricole des Planteurs de la Menoua [*Cameroon*]
    (WGAO)
CAPLAMI ... Cooperative Agricole des Planteurs de la Misi [*Cameroon*]
    (WGAO)
CAPLO...... Council of Australian Power Lifting Associations
CAPMA..... Cairns Agricultural, Pastoral, and Mining Association [*Australia*]
CAPMA..... Caisse d'Assurance et de Prevoyance Mutuelle des Agriculteurs
    (WGAO)
CAPME..... Centre d'Assistance aux Petites et Moyennes Entreprises [*Center
    for Aid to Small and Medium-Size Businesses*] [*Cameroon*]
    (AF)
CAPME..... Centre National d'Assistance aux Petities et Moyennes Enterprise
    [*Cameroon*]   (WGAO)
cap mg........ Capitao-de-Mar-e-Guerra [*Navy Captain*] [*Portuguese*]
CAPMS ..... Central Agency for Public Mobilisation and Statistics [*Egypt*]
    (PDAA)
capn........... Capitan [*Captain*] [*Spanish*]
capo........... Capitulo [*Chapter*] [*Spanish*]
CAPO .... Complaints Against Police Office [*Hong Kong*]
CAP-OZC ... Centro de Actividad del Programa de Oceanos y Zonas Costeras
    [*Spanish*]
CAPP......... Campaign Against Police Powers [*Australia*]
C App........ Sentenza della Corte di Appello [*Decision of the Court of Appeal*]
    [*Italian*]   (ILCA)
CAPPA ...... Confederation of Australian Professional Performing Arts
CAPPAP.... Commission d'Action Pro-Populaire et d'Action Psychologique
    [*Pro-People's Action and Psychological Action Committee*]
    [*Cambodia*]   (CL)
cappn.......... Capellan [*Chaplain*] [*Spanish*]
CAPPO...... Cabinete de Apoio a Producao Agricola [*Office of Support to
    Agricultural Production*] [*Mozambique*]   (AF)
CAPR........ Centre Artisanal de Promotion Rurale
CAPRA...... Cooperative Agricole de Production de la Revolution Agraire
    [*Agricultural Production Cooperative of the Agrarian
    Revolution*] [*Algeria*]   (AF)
CAPRAL ... Compagnie Africaine de Preparations Alimentaires [*Ivory Coast*]
    (WGAO)
CAPRAL ... Compagnie Africaine de Preparations Alimentaires et
    Dietetiques
CAPRE ...... Comissao de Co-ordenacao das Atividades de Processamento
    Electronico [*Brazil*]   (WGAO)
CAPRE ...... Comissao de Coordenacao das Atividades de Processamento
    Eletronico de Dados [*Electronic Data Processing
    Coordination Committee*] [*Brazil*]   (LA)
CAPREC ... Compagnie Equatoriale d'Equipement [*Equatorial Co.*] [*Congo*]
CAPRECOM ... Caja de Prevision Social de Comunicaciones
    [*Communications Ministry Social Security Fund*]
    [*Colorado*]   (LA)
CAPREF.... Central African Petroleum Refiners

CAPRI ...... Centre d'Application ed de Promotion des Rayonnements Ionisants [*Commissariat a l'Energie Atomique*] [*France*] (PDAA)

CAPRI ...... Centre d'Application et de Promotion des Rayonnements Ionisants (WGAO)

CAPRO ...... Compagnie des Cafes et Produits Coloniaux Francais

CAPS .... Captive Animals' Protection Society (WGAO)

CAPS .... Cesky Amatersky Plavecky Svaz [*Czech Amateur Swimming Union*] (CZ)

CAPS .... Challenge, Achievement, and Pathways in Sport Program [*Australia*]

CAPS .... Child Abuse Prevention Service [*Australia*]

CAPS .... Civil Aviation Purchasing Service [*ICAO*] (DA)

CAPS .... Community and Pharmacy Support Group [*Australia*]

CAPS .... Confederation Agricole des Producteurs de Plantes Saccchariferes (WGAO)

CAPS .... Contents, Abstracts, and Photocopies Services [*India*] [*Information service or system*]

Capsa .... Compania Algodonera Paraguaya (WGAO)

CAPSA ...... Compania Algodonera Paraguaya, Sociedad Anonima [*Paraguay*] (LAA)

CAPSC ...... Campaign Against Public Sector Cuts [*Australia*]

CAPSE ...... Companhia Auxiliar de Prestacao de Servicos [*Brazil*] (DSCA)

CAPSE-NE ... Companhia Auxiliar de Prestacao de Servicos para a Agriculture do Nordeste [*Brazil*] (DSCA)

CAPSE-RJ ... Companhia Auxiliar de Prestacao de Servicos para a Agricultura do Rio de Janeiro [*Brazil*] (DSCA)

CAPSES .... Cooperative Aragonesa da Productores de Semillas Selectas (WGAO)

CAPSOME ... Comite d'Action des Producteurs et Stockeurs d'Oleagineux pour les Marches Exterieurs (WGAO)

Capt .... Captain (EECI)

CAPT .... Child Accident Prevention Trust (WGAO)

CAPT .... Citizens Against the Poll Tax (WGAO)

CAPT .... Citizens for Accessible Public Transport [*Australia*]

CAPT .... Comite 'Association Pays Tiers' (WGAO)

CAPTA ...... China National Aquatic Products Marketing and Supplying Trades Association (EAIO)

CAPTAC ... Conference Africaine des Postes et Telecommunications de l'Afrique Centrale (WGAO)

CAPTAC ... Conference des Administrations des Postes et Telecommunications de l'Afrique Centrale [*Conference of Posts and Telecommunications Administrations of Central Africa*] (PDAA)

Capt(D) ...... Destroyer Captain [*Australia*]

CAPTEAO ... Conference Administrative des Postes et Telecommunications des Etats de l'Afrique de l'Ouest [*Conference of Posts and Telecommunications Administrations of the States of West Africa*]

CAPTEI ..... Cyprus Association of Private Tertiary Educational Institutions (EAIO)

cap-ten .... Capitao-Tenente [*Lieutenant Captain*] [*Portuguese*]

CAPU .... Coast African Political Union

Capv .... Capoverso [*Paragraph*] [*Italian*] (ILCA)

CAQ .... Caucasia [*Colombia*] [*Airport symbol*] (OAG)

CAQ .... Chess Association of Queensland [*Australia*]

CA(Q) .... Council of Agriculture, Queensland [*Australia*]

CAR .... Cadena Argentina de Radiodifusion (EY)

car .... Caractere [*Letter, Type*] [*Publishing*] [*French*]

car .... Carattere [*Letters, Type*] [*Publishing*] [*Italian*]

car .... Carre [*Square*] [*French*]

car .... Cartonne [*Bookbinding*] [*French*]

CAR .... Central African Railway Co.

CAR .... Central African Republic (AF)

C AR .... Central Arriere [*Military*] [*French*] (MTD)

CAR .... Centre of African Studies

CAR .... Centres d'Animation Rurale [*Rural Promotion Centers*] [*Senegal*] (AF)

CAR .... Centro Addestramento Reclute [*Recruit Training Center*] [*Italian*]

CAR .... Certificat d'Aptitude a la Recherche [*French*]

CAR .... Ceskomoravsky Avaz Radiomatero [*Czech-Moravian Union of Radio Amateurs*] (PDAA)

CAR .... Child at Risk [*Australia*]

CAR .... Circonscription Aeronautique Regionale [*French*]

CAR .... Collectivites Autochtones Rurales

CAR .... Comite Agricole Regional (WGAO)

CAR .... Comites d'Action Republicaine (WGAO)

CAR .... Comites de Accion Radical [*Radical (Party) Action Committee*] [*Chile*] (LA)

CAR .... Commissie Automatisering Rijksdienst

CAR .... Commission for Abortion Rights [*Spain*] (EAIO)

CAR .... Confederation of Arab Republics (ME)

CAR .... Conference d'Action Regionale [*French*]

CAR .... Constitutional Association of Rhodesia

CAR .... Corporacion Autoctona Regional de la Sabana de Bogota y de los Valles de Ullate y Chinquinquira [*Colombia*] (WGAO)

CAR .... Corporacion Autonoma Regional de la Sabana de Bogota y de los Valles de Ubate y Chiquinquira [*Bogota Plain and Ubate and Chiquinquira Valleys Autonomous Regional Corporation*] [*Colorado*] (LA)

CAR .... Country Accommodation Registry [*Australia*]

CAR .... Inter RCA [*Central African Republic*] [*ICAO designator*] (FAAC)

CARA .... Canberra Automobile Racing Association [*Australia*]

CARA .... Christian Alternative to Remand Accommodation [*Australia*]

CARA .... Christian Arts Resources Australia (EAIO)

CARA .... Citizen Alternative to Remand Accommodation [*Australia*]

CARA .... Club Athletique Renaissance-Aiglon

CARA .... Comissoes de Apoio a Reforma Agraria [*Agrarian Reform Support Committees*] [*Portuguese*] (WER)

CARA .... Compagnie d'Applications et de Recherches Atomiques [*French*]

CARAC ..... Civil Aviation Radio Advisory Committee (WGAO)

CARACOL ... Cadena Radial Colombiana [*Colombia*] (COL)

CARAE ...... Caribbean Regional Council for Adult Education [*University of the West Indies*] (EAIO)

CARAF ...... Christians Against Racism and Fascism (WGAO)

CARAH ..... Centre Agronomique de Recherches Appliquees du Hainaut [*Agronomic Center of Applied Research, Hainaut*] [*Belgium*] (ARC)

CARAL ...... Societe pour la Construction des Automobiles Renault en Algerie

CARAN ..... Centre d'Accueil et de Recherche des Archives Nationales (WGAO)

CARARA-CIAC ... Camara de Comercio, Industrias, y de Agricultura y Cria del Edo [*Venezuela*] (DSCA)

CARASE ... Centre Algerien de la Recherche Agronomique, Sociologique et Economique (WGAO)

CARATE ... Caribbean Association for the Teaching of English (WGAO)

CARATOM ... Compagnie d'Applications et de Recherches Atomiques [*French*]

caratt .... Carattere [*Letters, Type*] [*Publishing*] [*Italian*]

CARAVA ... Christian Association for Radio and Audio-Visual Aid [*India*] (WGAO)

Carb .... Commission Arbitrale sur les Biens, Droits et Interets en Allemagne (FLAF)

CARBAP ... Confederacion de Asociaciones Rurales de Buenos Aires y La Lampa [*Argentina*] (WGAO)

CARBAP ... Confederacion de Asociaciones Rurales de Buenos Aires y la Pampa [*Confederation of Buenos Aires and the Pampa Rural Associations*] [*Argentina*] (LA)

CARBHOTEL ... Compania del Hotel Caribe SA [*Colombia*] Tlg. (COL)

CARBIA .... Central African Regional Branch of the International Council on Archives

CARBICA ... Caribbean Regional Branch of the International Council on Archives (WGAO)

CARBOAFRIC ... Societe pour l'Etude et l'Application de Combustibles et Carburants Africains

CARBOCOL ... Carbones de Colombia (WGAO)

CARBOCOL ... Carbones de Colombia SA [*Colombian Coal Company, Inc.*] (LA)

CARBOEXPORT ... Banska Prodejna, Narodni Podnik, Odbor pro Vyvoz Uhli [*Coal Export Section of the Mining Products Sales Office, National Enterprise*] (CZ)

CARBOMOC ... Empresa Nacional de Carvao de Mocambique [*Mozambique National Coal Company*] (AF)

CARB-Z ..... Instituto de Carboquimica, Zaragoza [*Zaragoza Institute of Coal Chemistry*] [*Research center*] [*Spain*] (IRC)

CARCAE ... Caribbean Regional Council for Adult Education [*Barbados*] (EAIO)

CARCEPT ... Caisse Autonome de Retraites Complementaires et de Prevoyance du Transport [*France*] (FLAF)

CARCESA ... Carnes y Conservas Espanolas, Sociedad Anonima [*Spanish Meats and Canned Goods, Incorporated*] (WER)

CARCHAMAC ... Exploitations Agricoles Cartier, Charvet, MacDonald

CARCLO ... Confederacion de Asociaciones Rurales del Centro y Litoral Oeste [*Confederation of Central and Western Littoral Rural Associations*] [*Argentina*] (LA)

CARCOR ... Coordinadora de Asociaciones Regionales de Caficultores del Occidente de la Republica [*Guatemala*] (DSCA)

CARD .... Campaign Against Racial Discrimination (WGAO)

card .... Cardeal [*Cardinal*] [*Portuguese*]

Card .... Cardinale [*Cardinal*] [*Italian*]

CARD .... Caribbean Association for the Rehabilitation of the Disabled [*Defunct*] (EAIO)

CARD .... Center for Agricultural and Rural Development

CARDAN .. Centre d'Analyse et de Recherche Documentaires pour l'Afrique Noire [*Documentary Analysis and Research Center for Black Africa*] [*French*] (AF)

CARDATS ... Caribbean Agricultural Rural Development Advisory Training Service (WGAO)

CARDER ... Centre d'Amenagement Regional de Developpement Rural

CARDI .... Cardigan (DSUE)

CARDI .... Caribbean Agricultural Research and Development Institute (LA)

cardl .... Cardenal [*Cardinal*] [*Spanish*]
CARDPB ... Civil Aviation Research and Development Programme Board (WGAO)
CARE .... Bereavement Counselling Advice, Resources, and Education [*Australia*]
CARE .... Campaign Against Racial Exploitation   (EAIO)
CARE .... Cancer Aftercare and Rehabilitation Society   (WGAO)
CARE .... Christian Action Research and Education   (WGAO)
CARE .... Citizens Against Rare Earths [*Australia*]
CARE .... Citizens' Association for Racial Equality
CARE .... Comision Americana de Remesas al Exterior [*Bogota-Agencia*] (COL)
CARE .... Comites de Ayuda a la Resistencia Espanola [*Spanish Resistance Support Committees*]   (WER)
CARE .... Cooperative for American Remittances Everywhere [*Former name*]
CARE .... Cottage and Rural Enterprises Ltd.   (WGAO)
CAREBACO ... Caribbean Regional Badminton Confederation [*Aruba*] (EAIO)
CAREC ...... Caribbean Epidemiology Center [*Trinidadian and Tobagan*] [*Research center*]   (IRC)
CAREC ...... China Association of Railway Engineering Construction   (EAIO)
CARECE ... Confederation des Associations de Residents a l'Etranger de la Communaute Europeenne   (WGAO)
CARECT ... Centre Algerien de Recherches et d'Echanges Culturels et Techniques [*Algerian Center for Cultural and Technical Research and Exchange*]   (AF)
CAREF ...... Centre Algerien de Recherches et Experimentations Forestieres
CAREI ...... China Association of Rural Energy Industry   (EAIO)
CAREME ... Centre Automatique de Reception et d'Emission de Messages [*French*]   (MCD)
CAREMOCI ... Carrelage Revetement, Mosaique de la Cote-D'Ivoire
CARENA ... Compagnie Abidjanaise de Reparation Navale [*Abidjan Ship Repair Company*] [*Ivory Coast*]   (AF)
CARENA ... Compagnie Abidjanaise de Reparations Navales et de Travaux Industriels [*Ivory Coast*]   (WGAO)
CAREP ...... Compagnie Algerienne de Recherche et d'Exploitation Petrolieres [*Algerian Petroleum Exploitation and Prospecting Company*]   (AF)
CARES ...... Centre for Aboriginal Research, Education and Studies [*University of Western Sydney*] [*Australia*]
CARF .... Canadian Amateur Radio Federation   (WGAO)
CARFF ...... Centre Africain de Recherche de Formation pour la Femme [*African Center for Research on Training for Women*] [*Niger*]   (AF)
CARG .... Commonwealth AIDS Research Grant [*Australia*]
CARHB ..... Comite de Coordination d'Aide aux Refugies Hutu du Burundi
CARI .... Central Agricultural Research Institute [*Liberia*]   (IRC)
CARI .... Changchun Automobile Research Institute [*China*]   (IRC)
CARIBANK ... Caribbean Development Bank   (WGAO)
CARIBDOC ... Caribbean Documentation Centre [*Trinidad-Tobago*] (WGAO)
CARIBESA ... Mercantil del Caribe Ltda. [*Colombia*] Tlg.   (COL)
CARIBEX ... Exportadora del Caribe [*Caribbean Export Enterprise*] [*Cuba*] (LA)
caric .... Caricatura [*Caricature*] [*Publishing*] [*Italian*]
CARIC .... Compagnie Africaine de Representations Industrielles et Commerciales
CARICAD ... Caribbean Centre for Development Administration   (WGAO)
CARICAM ... Societe des Carrieres du Cameroun   (WGAO)
CARICARGO ... Caribbean Air Cargo Ltd. [*Barbados*]   (EY)
CARICOM ... Caribbean Commodity Market   (WGAO)
CARICOM ... Caribbean Community [*or Common Market*] [*Barbados, Jamaica, Trinidad-Tobago, Guyana, Belize, Dominica, Grenada, St. Kitts-Nevis-Anguilla, St. Lucia, St. Vincent Guyana*]
CARICOM ... Caribbean Community and Common Market   (SCAC)
CARIFTA ... Caribbean Free Trade Association   (LA)
CARIM ...... Caisse de Retraite des Ingenieurs des Mines [*France*]   (FLAF)
CARIPLO ... Cassa di Risparmio delle Provincie Lombarde [*Savings bank*] [*Italy*]
CARIRI ..... Caribbean Industrial Research Institute [*Trinidad and Tobago*] [*Research center*]   (IRC)
CARIS .... Computerized Agricultural Research Information System (NITA)
CARIS .... Current Agricultural Research Information System [*Food and Agriculture Organization*] [*United Nations Information service or system*]   (IID)
CARISFORM ... Caribbean Institute for Social Formation   (WGAO)
CARISOV ... Caribische Institut voor Social Vorming   (WGAO)
CARISPLAN ... Caribbean Information System for Economic and Social Planning [*ECLAC*] [*United Nations*]   (DUND)
CARITAS ... Conference Internationale des Charites Catholiques   (WGAO)
CARITAS ... Coordinacion Arquidiocesana de Asistencia Social [*Colombia*] (COL)

CARITAS ... International Confederation of Catholic Organizations for Charitable and Social Action [*Vatican*] [*Acronym is based on foreign phrase*]
CARJ .... Catholic Association for Racial Justice   (WGAO)
CARL .... Computer-Assisted Retrieval of the Law [*Australia*]
CARLDS ... Central African Rail Link Development Survey
C ARM ...... Certificate, Australian Risk Management
CARMABI ... Caraibisch Marien-Biologisch Instituut [*Caribbean Marine Biological Institute*] [*Research center*]   (IRC)
CARMS ..... Computer-Aided Records Management System [*Australia*]
carn .... Carneira [*Sheepskin*] [*Publishing*] [*Portuguese*]
CARN .... Comite de Accion para la Reconstruccion de Nicaragua [*Action Committee for the Reconstruction of Nicaragua*]   (LA)
CARNEID ... Caribbean Network of Educational Innovation for Development [*UNESCO*] [*United Nations*]   (DUND)
CARNOSYMA ... Cartel National des Organisations Syndicales Malgaches [*National Coalition of Malagasy Labor Union Organizations*]   (AF)
CARO .... Central Army Records Office [*Australia*]
CARO .... Societe de Fabrication de Carrelages et Revetements au Cameroun
Carp .... Carpathian Mountains   (BARN)
CARP .... Carpentaria [*Botanical region*] [*Australia*]
carp .... Carpentry   (TPFD)
carp .... Carpintaria [*or Carpinteiro*] [*Carpentry or Carpenter*] [*Portuguese*]
CARP .... Casa de Ajutor Reciproc a Pensionarilor [*Pensioners Mutual Assistance Fund*]   (RO)
CARP .... Collegiate Association for the Research of Principles   (WGAO)
CARP .... Comprehensive Agrarian Reform Programme [*Philippines*] (ECON)
CARP .... Council of Australian Religious Parents
CARPA ...... Caisse des Reglements Pecuniaires Effectues par les Avocats a la Cour de Paris [*France*]   (FLAF)
CARPA ...... Caribbean Psychiatric Association   (PDAA)
CARPA ...... Committee Against Repression in the Pacific and Asia [*Australia*]   (EAIO)
CARPAS ... Comision Asesora Regional de Pesca para el Atlantico Sudoccidental [*Regional Fisheries Advisory Commission for the South-West Atlantic*] [*Inactive*]   (EAIO)
CARPLE .... Cartilla Electoral para el Plebiscito [*Colombia*]
CARP M-L ... Comite de Apoio de Reconstrucao do Partido Marxista-Leninista [*Support Committee for the Reconstruction of the Marxist-Leninist Party*] [*Portugal*] [*Political party*]   (PPE)
CARRD ..... Australian Committee to Combat Racism and Racial Discrimination   (ADA)
Carre .... Carriere [*Quarry*] [*Military map abbreviation World War I*] [*French*]   (MTD)
carref .... Carrefour [*Square*] [*In addresses*] [*French*]   (CED)
Carrefr .... Carrefour [*Crossroads*] [*Military map abbreviation World War I*] [*French*]   (MTD)
Cars .... Carsamba [*Wednesday*]   (TU)
CARS .... Central Agricultural Research Station [*Somalia*]   (DSCA)
CARS .... Centre for Agricultural Research in Surinam [*Surinam*]   (DSCA)
CARS .... Coast Agricultural Research Station [*Kenya*]   (DSCA)
CARS .... Confederation Asia of Roller Skating [*Japan*]   (WGAO)
CARS .... Court Assistance and Referral Service [*Australia*]
CARSA .... Comercial Agricola Riojana, SA [*Spain*]   (DSCA)
CARSOSYMA ... Cartel Nationale des Organisations Syndicales de Madagascar
CARSTRIKGRU ... Carrier Striking Group [*NATO*]
CART .... Caribbean Association of Rehabilitation Therapists [*Guyana*] (EAIO)
cart .... Carton [*Cardboard*] [*Publishing*] [*French*]
cart .... Carton [*Cardboard*] [*Publishing*] [*Spanish*]
cart .... Cartonado [*Bound in Boards*] [*Publishing*] [*Portuguese*]
cart .... Cartonato [*Bound in Boards*] [*Publishing*] [*Italian*]
cart .... Cartone [*Cardboard*] [*Publishing*] [*Italian*]
CART .... Championship Auto Racing Team [*Australia*]
CART .... Council for Advancement of Rural Technology [*India*]   (EAIO)
CARTAMOTORES ... Cartagena de Motores Ltda. [*Colombia*]   (COL)
CARTE ...... Centre for Agrarian Research and Training and Education [*India*]   (WGAO)
CARTEZ ... Confederacion de Asociaciones Rurales de la Tercera Zona [*Confederation of Rural Associations of the Third Zone*] (LA)
carton .... Cartonato [*Bound in Boards*] [*Publishing*] [*Italian*]
carton .... Cartonnage [*Board Binding*] [*Publishing*] [*French*]
CARTONAL ... Cartones Nacionales, SA [*Venezuela*]   (LAA)
cartonc .... Cartoncino [*Thin Cardboard*] [*Publishing*] [*Italian*]
CARTONEX ... Conference for the Carton and Case Making Industry (WGAO)
cartonn .... Cartonnage [*Board Binding*] [*Publishing*] [*French*]
CARTOVEN ... Carton de Venezuela, SA [*Venezuela*]   (LAA)
CARV .... Campaign Alert Against Racism and Violence [*Australia*]
CARVA ...... Curtiduria Argentina de Vacunos y Anexos SRL [*Argentina*] (DSCA)

CARVOLT ... Societe de Cartoucherie Voltaique
CAS........... Canberra Archaeological Society [*Australia*]
CAS........... Capricorn Africa Society
CAS........... Careers and Appointments Service [*University of Sydney*] [*Australia*]
CAS........... Caribbean Air Services   (WGAO)
CAS........... Casa Asigurarilor de Stat [*State Insurance Society*]   (RO)
CAS........... Casablanca [*Morocco*] [*Airport symbol*]   (OAG)
CAS........... Casablanca Airport
Cas .... Castel [*Castello*] [*Castle*] [*Italian*]   (NAU)
CAS........... Catgut Acoustical Society   (WGAO)
CAS........... Central Asian States
CAS........... Centralna Akcja Szkoleniowa [*Central Training Course*]   (POL)
CAS........... Centralna Aptek Spolecznych [*Socialized Pharmacies Center*] (POL)
CAS........... Centre for Aboriginal Studies [*Sydney Institute of Education*] [*Australia*]
CAS........... Centre for Aging Studies [*Flinders University*] [*Australia*]
CAS........... Centre for Australian Studies [*Monash University*] [*Australia*]
CAS........... Ceskoslovenska Astronomicka Spolecnost [*Czechoslovak Astronomical Society*]   (CZ)
CAS........... Cesky Abstinentni Svaz [*Czech Temperance Union*]   (CZ)
CAS........... Chinese Astronomical Society   (SLS)
CAS........... Christelijk Arbeidssecretariaat [*Benelux*]   (BAS)
CAS........... Church Adoption Society   (WGAO)
CAS........... Church Archivists Society [*Australia*]
CAS........... Citizenship Automated System [*Australia*]
CAS........... Clean Air Society [*Australia*]
CAS........... Club Alpine Suisse [*Swiss Alpine Club*]
CAS........... Club Alpin Suisse   (WGAO)
CAS........... Commission for Atmospheric Sciences [*WMO*]   (ASF)
CAS........... Committee for the Assurance of Supplies
CAS........... Committee on Atlantic Studies   (WGAO)
CAS........... Computer Accounting Services Proprietary Ltd. [*Australia*] (ADA)
CAS........... Computer Arts Society   (EAIO)
CAS........... Confederation of Australia Sport
CAS........... Conference on African Statistics
CAS........... Confiserie Africaine de Sebikotane
CAS........... Consorcio Agricola del Sur [*Southern Agricultural Association*] [*Chile*]   (LA)
CAS........... Consortium for Atlantic Studies [*Arizona State University*] [*Research center*]
CAS........... Contemporary Art Society   (WGAO)
CAS........... Contemporary Art Society of Australia   (ADA)
CAS........... Contre-Assurance Speciale [*France*]   (FLAF)
CAS........... Convention Assistance Scheme [*Australia*]
CAS........... Cooperativa Algodonera Salvadorena [*El Salvador*]   (DSCA)
CAS........... Council of Arab Students
CAS........... Court of Arbitration of Sport [*See also TAS*] [*Lausanne, Switzerland*]   (EAIO)
CAS........... Credito Agricola Supervisado [*Bolivia*]   (LAA)
CAS........... Current Agricultural Statistics
CAS........... Curriculum and Accreditation Secretariat [*Victoria*] [*Australia*]
CAS........... Czechoslovak Academy of Sciences [*Czechoslovakia*]   (DSCA)
CASA........ Callisthenic Association of South Australia
CASA........ Camping Association of South Australia
CASA........ Centre Against Sexual Assault [*Australia*]
CASA........ Centre Alliance Students' Association [*Australia*]
CASA........ Centre for Advanced Study of Astronomy [*Osmania Univeristy*] [*Pakistan*]   (PDAA)
CASA........ Centro de Accion Social Autonoma [*Autonomous Social Action Center*]   (LA)
CASA........ Centro de Assistencia Socio-Sanitaria
CASA........ Ceylon Association of Steamer Agents [*Sri Lanka*]   (WGAO)
CA (SA) ... Chartered Accountant (South Africa)   (AA)
CASA........ Chiropractic Association of South Africa   (EAIO)
CASA........ Classical Association of South Africa   (AA)
CASA........ Colostomy Association of South Australia
CASA........ Comision Analitica del Sindicalismo Argentino [*Analytical Commission for Argentine Labor Unions*]   (LA)
CASA........ Companies Acquisitions of Shares Act [*Australia*]
CASA........ Confederazione Artigiana Sindacati Autonomi   (WGAO)
CASA........ Confederazione Autonomi Sindacati Artigiani [*Italy*]   (EY)
CASA........ Conseil Africain des Sociologues et des Anthropologues [*African Council of Sociologists and Anthropologists*]   (AF)
CASA........ Construcciones Aeronauticas SA [*Spanish*]   (MCD)
CASA........ Construcciones Aeronauticas, Sociedad Anonima [*Aeronautics Manufacturing Corporation*] [*Spanish*]
CASA........ Construccion y Ahorro [*El Salvador*]   (WGAO)
CASA........ Construccion y Ahorro Sociedad Anonima [*El Salvador*]   (EY)
CASA........ Consumers Association of South Australia
CASA........ Contemporary Art Society of Australia   (ADA)
CASA........ Cornish Association of South Australia
CASA........ Cosecheros Abastecedores Sociedad Anonima [*Harvester Suppliers, Incorporated*] [*Spanish*]   (WER)

CASA........ Council of Academic Staff Associations [*Australia*]
CASA........ Societe Centrale d'Achats Supermarche d'Afrique   (WGAO)
CASAFA ... Interunion Commission on the Application of Science to Agriculture, Forestry, and Aquaculture [*ICSU*] [*Ottawa, ON*]   (EAIO)
CASAFA ... Inter-Union Commission on the Application of Science to Agriculture, Forestry, and Aquaculture   (ARC)
CASAM.... Collective Against Sexual Assault, Melton [*Australia*]
CASAN..... Clean Air Society of Australia and New Zealand   (PDAA)
CASAN..... Concerned Asian Scholars of Australia and New Zealand   (ADA)
CASANZ... Clean Air Society of Australia and New Zealand   (ADA)
CASAS ..... Commonwealth Association of Scientific Agricultural Societies (WGAO)
CASASOL ... Caisse Saharienne de Solidarite
Cas B.......... Cour de Cassation Belge [*Belgium*]   (BAS)
CASC........ Caisse d'Assurances des Cooperatives Suisse de Consommation (WGAO)
CASC........ China Aero-Space Corp.   (ECON)
CASC........ China Aviation Supplies Corp.   (PDAA)
CASC........ Confederacion Autonoma de Sindicatos Cristianos [*Dominican Republic*]
CASC........ Confederacion Autonoma Sindical Clasista [*Autonomous Confederation of Class Trade Unions*] [*Dominican Republic*]   (LA)
CASCO...... Canadian Australian Line
Cas Com..... Arret de la Section Commerciale de la Cour de Cassation [*Decision of the Commercial Section of the Court of Appeal*] [*French*]   (ILCA)
CASCOM ... Casa de Asigurari Sociale si Pensii din Cooperatia Mestesugareasca [*Social Security and Pension Fund in the Artisan Cooperatives*]   (RO)
CASD........ Center for Applied Studies in Development [*University of the South Pacific*] [*Fiji*]
CASDB...... Central African States Development Bank [*Congo*]
CASDS ..... Centre for Advanced Study in the Developmental Sciences (WGAO)
CASE........ Campaign for the Advancement of State Education   (WGAO)
CASE........ CCH [*Commerce Clearing House*] Australian Case Digest Library [*Database*]
CASE........ Centre for Advanced Studies in Environment   (WGAO)
CASE........ Centre for Applications of Solar Energy [*Australia*]
CASE........ Comision Administradora de los Servicios de Estiba [*Administrative Commission of Wood Compressing Services*] [*Uruguay*]   (LA)
CASE........ Comision Asesora de Servicios de Estiba [*Uruguay*]   (LAA)
CASE........ Commision d'Aeronautique Sportive Internationale [*International Aeronautical Sports Commission*]   (PDAA)
CASE........ Committee on the Atlantic Salmon Emergency   (WGAO)
CASE........ Consumers Association of Singapore   (WGAO)
CASEAL.... Companhia de Armazens e Silos do Estado de Alagoas [*Brazil*] (DSCA)
CASEB ...... Companhia de Armazens e Silos do Estado da Bahia [*Brazil*] (DSCA)
CASEC ...... Centre for the Advancement and Study of the European Currency [*France*]   (EAIO)
CASEC ...... Confederation of Associations of Specialist Engineering Contractors   (WGAO)
CASEGO... Companhia de Armazens e Silos do Estado de Goias [*Brazil*] (DSCA)
CASEMBA ... Companhia de Alimentacao, Sementes, e Mercados da Bahia SA [*Brazil*]   (DSCA)
CASEMG .. Companhia de Armazens e Silos do Estado de Minas Gerais [*Brazil*]   (DSCA)
CASEP ...... Companhia de Armazens e Silos do Estado da Paraiba [*Brazil*] (DSCA)
CASEREC ... Canberra and South East Region Environment Centre [*Australia*]
CASES....... Companhia de Armazens e Silos do Espirito Santo [*Brazil*] (DSCA)
CASES...... Criminal Advocacy Support and Enquiry System [*Australia*]
CASEX ...... Combined Aircraft Submarine Exercise [*NATO*]   (NATG)
CASFEC .. Caja de Subsidios Familiares para Empleados de Comercio [*Argentina*]   (LAA)
Cas Fr .... Cour de Cassation Francaise [*France*]   (BAS)
CASHA ..... Centre Africain des Sciences Humaines Appliquees [*African Center for Applied Human Sciences*] [*French*]   (AF)
CASI .... Commission Aeronautique Sportive Internationale   (WGAO)
CASIN....... Center for Applied Studies in International Negotiations [*Switzerland*]   (EAIO)
CASIS........ Chartered Accountants Students Introduction Service   (WGAO)
CASL......... Confederation Africaine des Syndicats Libres [*African Federation of Free Trade Unions*] [*Ivory Coast*]   (AF)
CASL......... Cooperativa Algodonera Salvadorena Limitada [*Salvadoran Cotton Cooperative Limited*]   (LA)
CASL-CI ... Confederation Africaine des Syndicats Libres de Cote d'Ivoire [*African Confederation of Free Trade Unions of the Ivory Coast*]

CASLE ...... Commonwealth Association of Surveying and Land Economy [*British*] (EAIO)
CASLE ...... Commonwealth Association of Surveying and Land Engineering (WGAO)
CASLF....... Comite d'Action pour la Sauvegarde des Libertes Forestieres (WGAO)
CASL-FO .. Confederation Africaine des Syndicats Libres - Force Ouvriere [*African Confederation of Free Trade Unions - Workers' Force*] [*Cameroon, Chad, Gabon*]
CASL-FO-RC ... Confederation Africaine des Syndicats Libres - Force Ouvriere - Republique Centafricaine [*African Confederation of Free Trade Unions - Workers' Force - Central African Republic*]
CASL-HV ... Confederation Africaine des Syndicats Libres de la Haute Volta [*African Confederation of Free Trade Unions of the Upper Volta*]
CASLM ..... Colegio Agricola de Sao Lourenco da Mata [*Brazil*] (DSCA)
CASM........ Centre for Aboriginal Studies in Music [*Australia*] (ADA)
CASMA..... Confederation des Associations et Societes Medicales d'Afrique [*Confederation of African Medical Associations and Societies - CAMAS*] [*Nigeria*] (EAIO)
CASMAC .. Core Australian Specification for Management and Administrative Computing
CASME..... Commonwealth Association of Science and Mathematics Educators (WGAO)
CASMU..... Centro de Asistencia del Sindicato Medico del Uruguay [*Assistance Center of the Medical Union of Uruguay*] (LA)
Casne .... Caserne [*Barracks*] [*Military map abbreviation World War I*] [*French*] (MTD)
CASNO ..... Crnogorska Antifasisticka Skupstina Narodnog Oslobodenja [*Montenegrin Anti-Fascist Assembly of National Liberation*] [*YU*]
CASOC...... California Arabian Standard Oil Co.
Casoc.......... California Arabian Standard Oil Company (OMWE)
CASORAL ... Caisse Sociale de la Region d'Alger [*Algiers Region Social Fund*] [*Algeria*]
CASORAN ... Caisse Sociale de la Region d'Oran [*North African*]
CASOS...... Coastal Air/Sea Operations Support [*Australia*] (ADA)
CASP .... Central American Society of Pharmacology [*Panama*] (EAIO)
CASP .... Civil Aviation Statistics Programme [*ICAO*] [*United Nations*] (DUND)
CASP .... Commodities Assistance Program [*Australian International Development Assistance Bureau*]
CASP .... Compagnie Africaine de Services Publics [*African Public Services Co.*] [*Congo*] [*France*]
CASP .... Companhia Avicola Sao Paulo [*Brazil*] (DSCA)
CASPA ...... Council of Australian Spa and Pool Associations
CASPA ...... Council of Australian Swimming Pool Associations (ADA)
CASR........ Centre for Applied Social Research [*Macquarie University*] [*Australia*]
CASRO...... Commission d'Achat de la Suisse Romande (WGAO)
CASRSS .... Centre of Advanced Study and Research in Social Sciences [*Bangladesh*] (WGAO)
Cass............ Arrest van het Hof van Cassatie van Belgie [*Belgium*] (BAS)
Cass............ Arret de la Cour de Cassation [*Decision of the Court of Appeal*] [*Belgium*] (ILCA)
Cass............ Cassatie [*Appeal to High Court of Justice*] [*Netherlands*] (ILCA)
CASS .... Central Australian Show Society
CASS .... Centrul de Astronomie si Stiinte Spatiale [*Center for Astronomy and Space Sciences*] (RO)
CASS .... Chartered Accountant Students' Society [*Australia*]
CASS .... China's Academy of Social Sciences
CASS .... Combined Australian Superannuation Scheme
Cass............ Corte di Cassazione [*Court of Appeal*] [*Italian*] (DLA)
C Ass.......... Cour d'Assises [*France*] (FLAF)
Cass............ Cour de Cassation [*Court of Appeal*] [*French*] (DLA)
C Ass.......... Sentenza della Corte d'Assise [*Decision of the Assize Court*] [*Italian*] (ILCA)
Cass............ Sentenza della Corte Suprema di Cassazione [*Decision or Judgment of the Supreme Court of Appeals*] [*Italian*] (ILCA)
Cass AssPlen ... Cour de Cassation, Assemblee Pleniere [*France*]
Cass B .... Cour de Cassation de Belgique [*Belgium*] (BAS)
Cass ChReun ... Cour de Cassation, Chambres Reunies [*France*] (ILCA)
Cass ChReunies ... Cour de Cassation, Chambres Reunies [*France*] (FLAF)
Cass Civ ..... Arret de la Chambre Civile de la Cour de Cassation [*Decision of the Court of Appeal, Civil Division*] [*French*] (ILCA)
Cass civ ...... Cour de Cassation, Ch. Civile, Section Civile [*French*]
Cass Civ ..... Sentenza della Sezione Civile della Corte di Cassazione [*Decision of the Court of Appeal, Civil Division*] [*Italian*] (ILCA)
Cass Civ1re ... Cour de Cassation, Premiere Section Civile [*French*] (ILCA)
Cass Civ3e ... Cour de Cassation, Troisieme Section Civile [*French*] (ILCA)
Cass CivCom ... Cour de Cassation, Commerciale [*French*] (ILCA)
Cass Cive2e ... Cour de Cassation, Deuxieme Section Civile [*French*] (ILCA)
Cass CivSoc ... Cour de Cassation, Sociale [*French*] (ILCA)
Cass com ..... Cour de Cassation, Commerciale [*French*]
Cass Com.... Cour de Cassation, Commerciale [*French*] (ILCA)

Cass Crim .. Arret de la Chambre Criminelle de la Cour de Cassation [*Decision of the Court of Appeal, Criminal Division*] [*French*] (ILCA)
Cass Crim .. Cour de Cassation, Chambre Criminelle [*France*] (FLAF)
CassExpropr ... Cour de Cassation, Chambre des Expropriations [*France*] (FLAF)
Cass F .... Cour de Cassation de France [*Benelux*] (BAS)
Cass Fr....... Arrest van het Hof van Cassatie van Frankrijk [*Benelux*] (BAS)
CASSI........ Coastal Accommodation Support Service, Inc. [*Australia*]
Cass It........ Cour de Cassation d'Italie [*Benelux*] (BAS)
Cass Ital.... Cour de Cassation Italienne (FLAF)
Cass Pen .... Sentenza della Sezione Penale della Corte di Cassazione [*Decision of the Court of Appeal, Criminal Division*] [*Italian*] (ILCA)
Cass Req .... Arret de la Chambre des Requetes de la Cour de Cassation [*Decision of the Court of Appeal, Chamber of Requests*] [*French*] (ILCA)
Cass Req .... Cour de Cassation, Chambre des Requetes [*France*] (FLAF)
Cass Soc..... Arret de la Section Sociale de la Cour de Cassation [*Decision of the Social Security and Labor Division of the Court of Appeal*] [*French*] (ILCA)
Cass Soc..... Cour de Cassation, Chambre Civile, Section Sociale [*France*] (FLAF)
CASSU ...... Comites d'Arondissement du Sport Scolaire et Universitaire
Cass Verw .. Cassatie Verworpen Door [*Benelux*] (BAS)
CAST........ Castile [*Spain*]
CAST .... Centre d'Actualisation Scientifique et Technique
CAST .... China Association for Science and Technology
CAST .... China Association of Science and Technology [*ICSU*]
CAST .... Confederation Africaine des Syndicats Libres (WGAO)
CAST .... Consolidated African Selection Trust [*Sierra Leone*] (AF)
CaSTA .... Campionati Sciistici della Truppe Alpini [*Alpini Ski Championships*] [*Italian*]
CASTALA ... Conferencia sobre la Aplicacion de la Ciencia y la Tecnologia al Desarrollo de America Latina [*Conference on the Application of Science and Technology to the Development of Latin America*] [*1965 Santiago, Chile*] (LAA)
CASTARAB ... Conference on the Application of Science and Technology to the Development of the Arab States (MSC)
CASTD ..... Committee on Application of Science and Technology to Development [*ICSU*]
CASTME .. Commonwealth Association of Science, Technology and Mathetics Educators (WGAO)
CASU .... Cooperative Association of Suez Canal Users (WGAO)
CASVAL ... Cooperative d'Approvisionnement des Syndicats Viticoles et Agricoles du Loire a Orleans (WGAO)
CASW........ Committee on the Medical Aspects of the Contamination of Air, Soil and Water (WGAO)
CASW........ Council for the Advancement of Scientific Writing (WGAO)
CASWIG ... Council for the Affairs and Status of Women in Guyana (LA)
CAT .... Cado-Aktions-Terminal (ADPT)
CAT .... Cameroun Air Transport
CAT .... Capsule Ariane Technologique [*Ariane Technological Capsule*] [*French*] (WER)
cat.............. Catalogo [*Catalog*] [*Portuguese*]
cat.............. Catalogus [*Catalog*] [*Publishing*] [*Netherlands*]
CAT .... Catalonian [*Language, etc.*] (ROG)
CAT .... Center for Appropriate Technology [*Delft University of Technology*] [*Netherlands*]
CAT .... Centro Appenninico del Terminillo "Carlo Jucci" [*Italian*] (SLS)
CAT .... Centro de Asistencia Tecnica [*Technical Assistance Center*] [*Cuba*] (LA)
CAT .... Cercle des Arts et Techniques de la Coiffure Francaise [*UK*] (WGAO)
CAT .... Certificado de Abono Tributario [*Tax Credit Certificate*] [*Spanish*]
CAT .... Chahada 'Amma fi al Tarbiya [*Academic qualification*] [*Syria*]
CAT .... Christian Accommodation Trust [*Australia*]
c at.............. Ciezar Atomowy [*Atomic Weight*] [*Poland*]
CAT .... Ciments Artificiels Tunisiens [*Tunisia*] (IMH)
CAT .... Clean Air Transport [*Commercial firm*] [*Sweden*]
CAT .... Clerical Assistant Test [*Australia*]
CAT .... Coffee Authority of Tanzania
CAT .... Comando Aereo Tattico [*Tactical Air Command*] [*Use TAC*] [*Italian*] (WER)
CAT .... Comando de Apoyo Tupamaro [*Tupamaro Support Command*] [*Uruguay*] (LA)
CAT .... Comisaria de Abastecimientos y Transportes [*Commissariat for Supplies and Transportation*] [*Spanish*] (WER)
CAT .... Comision Asesora del Transporte [*Asociacion Latinoamericana de Libre Comercio*] [*Colorado*] (LAA)
CAT .... Comite de l'Assistance Technique (WGAO)
CAT .... Comite de l'Assistance Technique de l'Organisation des Nations Unies
CAT .... Comite Permanent d'Assistance Technique [*Organisme Inter-Gouvernemental*] (FLAF)

CAT .... Committee Against Torture [*See also CCT*] [*Geneva, Switzerland*] (EAIO)
CAT .... Communications Authority of Thailand (DS)
CAT .... Community Access Television [*Australia*]
CAT .... Community Arts Teachers [*Australia*]
CAT .... Compagnie Abidjanaise des Techniques
CAT .... Compagnie Africaine de Transformation [*Togo*] (WGAO)
CAT .... Compagnie Africaine de Transports
CAT .... Compagnie Algerienne de Transports
CAT .... Compagnie Aluminium Togolais (WGAO)
CAT .... Compagnie d'Achat du Togo
CAT .... Comptoir Africain des Textiles
CAT .... Computer Assisted Televideo [*Commercial firm*] [*Netherlands*] (NITA)
CAT .... Confederacion Americana de Tiro
CAT .... Confederation Autonome de Travail [*Autonomous Confederation of Labor*]
CAT .... Conseil Africain de la Teledetection
CAT .... Continental African Travels
CAT .... Contracting and Trading Co. [*Engineering, pipeline, and marine construction contractor*] [*Beirut, Labanon*] (MENA)
CAT .... Coordenacao Autonoma de Trabalhadores [*Brazil*]
CAT .... Copenhagen Airtaxi [*Denmark*] [*ICAO designator*] (FAAC)
CATA .... Cashew-Nut Authority of Tanzania
CATA .... Centre d'Assistance Technique Artisanal [*Handicrafts Technical Assistance Center*] [*Algeria*] (AF)
CATA .... Civil Air Training Academy [*Australia*]
CATA .... Commonwealth Association of Tax Administrators (WGAO)
CATA .... Compagnie Africaine de Transports Automobiles
CATA .... Compania Amazonia Textil de Aniagem [*Commercial firm*] [*Brazil*]
CATAC...... Commandement Aerien Tactique [*French Tactical Air Command*]
CATAC...... Confederacion Argentina del Transporte Automotor de Cargas [*Argentina*] (LAA)
CATALPA ... Coordinating Agency for Training Adult Literacy Personnel in Australia
CATANA .. Compania Anonima Tabacalera Nacional [*Venezuela*] (DSCA)
CATARAC ... Central Area Training Aboriginal Resource Accounting Committee [*Australia*]
CATARC... China Automotive Technology and Research Center (IRC)
CATC........ Caribbean Appropriate Technology Centre (WGAO)
CATC........ Central African Trading Company
CATC........ Commonwealth Air Transport Commission [*or Council*] [*Australia*] (EAIO)
CATC........ Compagnie Africaine de Tissage et de Confection
CATC........ Confederation Africaine des Travailleurs Croyants [*African Confederation of Believing Workers*] [*Burkina Faso*] (AF)
CATCH ..... Cumberland Activity Therapy Centre Human-Potential [*Australia*]
CATCI....... Compagnie Africaine de Transports Cote-D'Ivoire
CATCM..... Centre Administratif des Troupes Coloniales en Metropole
CATCN ..... Societe Africaine de Transportes Cameroun (WGAO)
CATCO ..... Central African Transport Company
CATD .... Confederacion Autentica de Trabajadores Democraticos [*Authentic Confederation of Democratic Workers*] [*Costa Rica*] (LA)
CATE......... Club des Amateurs de Terriers d'Ecosse [*France*] (EAIO)
CATE......... Committee for the Accreditation of Teacher Education (WGAO)
CATE......... Conference de Coordination des Transports Aeriens Europeens (FLAF)
CATECO... Societe Camerounaise d'Automobile, de Technique, et du Commerce [*Cameroonian Automobile, Technological, and Trading Company*] (AF)
CATED...... Centre d'Assistance Technique et de Documentation du Batiment et des Travaux Publique [*Center for Technical Assistance and Documentation for Building and Public Works*] [*Database producer*] [*France*] (PDAA)
CATEES.... Conference Africaine pour les Techniques d'Exploitation des Eaux Sousterraines [*African Conference for Subterranean Waters Exploitation Techniques*] (AF)
CATEHUILSA ... Compagnie Africaine Toutes Enterprises Huilieres des Savanes [*Ivory Coast*] (WGAO)
CATEL...... Compagnie Africaine de Television
CATER...... Centro Andino de Technologia Rural [*Andean Centre for Rural Technology*] [*Ecuador*] (PDAA)
CATES ..... Centres d'Appui Technique et Social
CATESA ... Casas y Terrenos, Sociedad Anonima [*Houses and Lands, Incorporated*] [*Costa Rica*] (LA)
CATET...... Centro Argentino de Tecnicos en Estudios del Trabajo [*Argentina*] (LAA)
CATEX...... Societe Centrafricaine des Textiles pour l'Exportation
CATG .... Compagnie pour l'Application des Techniques Geophysiques
CATH .... Central Autonome des Travailleurs Haitiens [*Autonomous Confederation of Haitian Workers*]
Cathle........ Cathedrale [*Cathedral*] [*Military map abbreviation World War I*] [*French*] (MTD)

CatholicColl Ed Syd ... Catholic College of Education, Sydney [*Australia*]
Catholic ISyd ... Catholic Institute of Sydney [*Australia*]
CATI......... Caribbean Aviation Training Centre (WGAO)
CATI......... Central Autentica de Trabajadores Independientes [*Panama*] (WGAO)
CATI......... Centre Administratif et Technique Interdepartemental [*Prefet de Defense*] [*France*] (FLAF)
CATI......... Centre d'Analyse et de Traitement de l'Ingormation [*French*] (ADPT)
CATI......... Centres Adminstratifs et Techniques Interdepartementaux (WGAO)
CATI......... Confederacion Argentina de Trabajadores Independientes [*Argentine Confederation of Independent Workers*] (LA)
CATI......... Coordenadoria de Asistencia Tecnica Integral [*Brazil*] (DSCA)
CATI......... Coordenadoria de Assitencia Tecnica Integral [*Brazil*] (WGAO)
CATIA....... Central Australian Tourism Industry Association
CATIAC .... Cotton and Allied Textiles Industry Advisory Committee (WGAO)
CATIB....... Civil Air Transport Industry Training Board (WGAO)
CATIC....... China National Aero-Technology Import & Export Corporation [*China*] (IMH)
CATIE....... Centro Agronomico Tropical Investigacion y Ensenanza [*Tropical Agricultural Research and Training Center*] [*Turrialba, Costa Rica*] (EAIO)
CATITB .... Cotton and Allied Textiles Industry Training Board (WGAO)
CATK........ Cesko-Americka Tiskova Kancelar [*Czech-American Press Bureau*] (CZ)
CATMAR ... Comision Asesora de Transporte Maritimo [*Chile*] (LAA)
CATN .... Community AIDS Trials Network [*Australia*]
CATO .... Compania Colombo Americana de Tornillos Ltda. [*Barranquilla*] (COL)
CATOSON ... Compagnie Allemande et Togolaise pour le Sondage
CATP........ Compagnie Africaine de Travaux Publics
CATPA...... Comite d'Action Technique Contra la Pollution Atmospherique [*French*] (ASF)
CATPCE ... Comite d'Action des Transports Publics des Communautes Europeennes (WGAO)
CATRA..... Compagnie Africaine de Travaux
CATRA..... Cutlery and Allied Trades Research Association (WGAO)
CATRE..... Catholic Association of Tertiary Religious Education [*Australia*]
CATRF...... Central Africa Tea Research Foundation
CATRU ..... Centre d'Appui aux Technologies Rurales et Urbaines [*Burkina Faso*]
CATS........ Centre for Advanced Teaching Studies [*Australia*]
CATS........ Centre for Advanced Television Studies (WGAO)
CATS........ Children's Activities Time Society [*Western Australia*]
CATS........ Combined Adelaide Television Stations [*Australia*]
CATT........ Confederacion Argentina de Trabajadores del Transporte [*Argentine Confederation of Transport Workers*] (LA)
CATT........ Consumers' Association of Trinidad and Tobago
c att........... Coupon Attache [*Coupon Attached*] [*French*]
CATTS ...... Committee on Advanced Television Transmission Systems [*Australia*]
CATU .... Ceramic and Allied Trades Union (WGAO)
CATU .... Confederation of Arab Trade Unions
CATUA .... Clothing and Allied Trades Union of Australia
CATUD ..... Central Autonoma de Trabajadores del Uruguay (WGAO)
CAU.......... Cancun Avioturismo SA [*Mexico*] [*ICAO designator*] (FAAC)
CAU.......... Chung-Ang University [*South Korea*] (ERC)
CAU.......... Commis Auxiliaire
CAUCA ..... Codigo Aduanero Uniforme Centroamericano [*Central American Standard Customs Code*] (LAA)
CAUCHAMA ... Cauchos del Amazonas Ltda. [*Colombia*] (COL)
CAUCHOSOL ... Compania Colombiana de Caucho el Sol SA [*Colombia*] (COL)
CAUL .... Committee of Australian University Librarians (ADA)
CAUMAC ... Council of Australian University Museums and Collections
CAUN........ Cuban Association for the United Nations (EAIO)
CAUNC..... Comite d'Action de l'Union Nationale Cabindaise [*Action Committee of the Cabindan National Union*] [*Angola*] (AF)
CAUNC..... Comite de Accao da Uniao Nacional de Cabinda [*Action Committee of the Cabindan National Union*] [*Angola*]
CAUS .... Central de Accion y Unidad Sindical [*Center for Trade Union Action and Unification*] [*Nicaragua*] (LA)
CAUSA...... Colonizadora Agricola e Urbanizadora, Sociedade Anonima [*Brazil*] (DSCA)
CAUSA...... Compania Aeronautica Uruguaya, Sociedad Anonima
CAUTOR .. Central Automotor Ltda. [*Colombia*] Tlg. (COL)
CAV .... Camara Agricola de Venezuela [*Venezuela*] (DSCA)
CAV .... Cambodian Association of Victoria [*Australia*]
CAV .... Camping Association of Victoria [*Australia*]
cav .... Cavalaria [*Cavalry*] [*Portuguese*]
Cav .... Cavalerie [*Cavalry*] [*Military*] [*French*] (MTD)
Cav .... Cavaliere [*Decoration*] [*Italian*]
C AV .... Central Avant [*Military*] [*French*] (MTD)

CAV .... Centro Antonio Valdivieso [*Nicaragua*]   (WGAO)
CAV .... Ceska Akademie Ved [*Czech Academy of Sciences*]   (CZ)
CAV .... Ceskoslovenska Akademie Ved   (WGAO)
CAV .... Ceskoslovensti Amateri Vysilaci [*Czechoslovak Amateur Radio Operators*]
CAV .... Chinese Association of Victoria [*Australia*]
CAV .... Classical Association of Victoria [*Australia*]
CAV .... Comando Anticastrista de Venezuela [*Venezuelan Anti-Castroite Commando*]   (LA)
CAV .... Commando Association, Victoria [*Australia*]
CAV .... Committee on Agricultural Valuation   (WGAO)
CAV .... Corporacion de Ahorro y Vivienda [*Colombia*]   (COL)
CAV .... Corporate Affairs Victoria [*Australia*]
CAV .... Czechoslovak Association of Victoria [*Australia*]
CAVA .... Christian Audio Visual Action [*Publisher*] [*Zimbabwe*]
CAVAG ..... Cursos de Aviacao Agricola [*Brazil*]   (DSCA)
CAVAL...... Cooperative Action by Victorian Academic Libraries [*Australia*] (ADA)
CAVASA ... Corporacion de Abastecimiento del Valle del Cauca [*Colombia*] (COL)
CAVE........ Comptoir Africain de Vente
CAVEDINA ... Camara Venezolana de Industriales de Arroz [*Venezuela*] (DSCA)
CAVEIS..... Comite de Accion de Viviendas y Edificaciones de Interes Social [*Public Housing and Building Action Committee*] [*Uruguay*]   (LA)
CAVELBA ... Cavendes, Lansberg, Brunet & Alcantara, CA [*Venezuela*]
CAVENBA ... Consortium d'Achats et de Ventes des Bois Africains
CAVENDES ... CA Venezolana de Desarrollo [*Venezuela*]   (LAA)
CAVEPA ... Corporacion Trasandina Venezolana de Productores Agropecuarios CA [*Venezuela*]   (DSCA)
CAVI........ Camara Argentina de Vegetales Industriales [*Argentina*]   (LAA)
CAVI......... Centre Audio-Visuel International   (WGAO)
CAVIAR ... Cinema and Video Industry Audience Research   (WGAO)
CAVIC...... Corporacion Agroeconomica Vinicola Industrial y Comercial [*Wine Manufacturing and Sales Agricultural-Economic Corporation*] [*Argentina*]   (LA)
CAVIC...... Corporacion Agroeconomica, Viticola, Industrial y Comercial [*Argentina*]   (WGAO)
CAVIM...... Compania Anonima Venezolana de Industrias Militares [*Military Industries Company*] [*Venezuela*]   (LA)
CAVINEX ... Societe Camerounaise d'Exploitation Vinicole
CAVIS ...... Caisse Assurance-Viellesse
CAVN....... Comite d'Amenagement de la Vallee du Niari
CAVN....... Compania Anonima Venezolana de Navegacion [*Venezuelan Navigation Company*]   (LA)
cavo .... Cavaleiro [*Horseman, Knight*] [*Portuguese*]
CAVO .... Centralgenossenschaft fuer Alkoholfreie Verwertung von Obstprodukten [*Switzerland*]   (WGAO)
CAVP....... Census of Australian Vascular Plants
CAVS........ Camara de Aceites Vegetales y Subproductos [*Argentina*] (DSCA)
Cav T......... Cavalerie Territoriale [*Military*] [*French*]   (MTD)
CAVU .... Ceska Akademie Ved a Umeni [*Czech Academy of Sciences and Arts*]   (CZ)
CAVUB ..... Commissie Algemene Vraagstukken Universitair Bibliotheekwezen ['s-Gravenhage]
CAVV .... Cooperative Aan-en Verkoop Vereniging   (WGAO)
CAVY .... Cooperative Agricole et Viticole du Departement de l'Yonne (WGAO)
CAW .... Campos [*Brazil*] [*Airport symbol*]   (OAG)
CAW .... Central America Week
CAW .... Centralne Archiwum Wojskowe [*Central Military Archives*] (POL)
CAW .... Commericial Air Services (Pty) Ltd. [*South Africa*] [*ICAO designator*]   (FAAC)
CAW .... Coordinating Animal Welfare   (WGAO)
CAWA ...... Consumers' Association of Western Australia
CAWC ...... Central Advisory Water Committee   (WGAO)
CAWISE ... Commonwealth AIDS Workforce, Information and Exchange Program [*Australia*]
CAWPR..... Committee for the Aid to West Papuan Refugees [*Netherlands*] (EAIO)
CAWSS ..... Council of Australian Weed Science Societies
CAX .... Canpax-Air AG [*Switzerland*] [*ICAO designator*]   (FAAC)
CAY .... Cayenne [*French Guiana*] [*Airport symbol*]   (OAG)
CAY .... Cayman Airways Ltd. [*British*] [*ICAO designator*]   (FAAC)
CAYA .... Catholic Association of Young Adults   (WGAO)
CAYA .... Centro Agrario Yerbatero Argentino [*Argentina*]   (DSCA)
CAYC .... Centro de Arte y Communicacion [*Center of Art and Communication*] [*Argentina*]   (EAIO)
CAYCMP.. China Association of Traditional Chinese Medicine and Pharmacology   (EAIO)
CAYCP...... Chinese Association of Youth and Children's Palaces   (EAIO)
CAYKUR... Cay Kurumu [*Tea Producers Organization*] [*Limited economic state enterprise*]   (TU)
CAYO........ Council of Australian Youth Organisations

Cayr .... Cayolar [*Military map abbreviation*] [*World War I*] [*French*] (MTD)
CAYTA...... Colombiana Agricola y Trabajos Aereos SL [*Colombia*]   (DSCA)
CAZ .... Cat Aviation, AG [*Switzerland*] [*ICAO designator*]   (FAAC)
CAZ .... Ceska Akademie Zemedelska [*Czech Agricultural Academy (Since 1969)*]   (CZ)
CAZ .... Ceskoslovenska Akademie Ved Zemedelsky'ch   (WGAO)
CAZ .... Ceskoslovenska Akademie Zemedelska [*Czechoslovak Academy of Agriculture (Until 1969)*]   (CZ)
CAZ .... Ceskoslovenske Automobilove Zavody Praha [*Czechoslovak Automobile Works, Prague*]   (CZ)
CAZ .... Cobar [*Australia*] [*Airport symbol*]   (OAG)
CAZ .... Conservative Alliance of Zimbabwe
CAZ .... Cycling Association of Zambia
CAZACRUZ ... Compania Azucarera Santa Cruz [*Colombia*]   (COL)
CAZF........ Comite des Agences de la Zone Franc [*North African*]
CAZF........ Comite des Agrumes de la Zone Franc   (WGAO)
CAZRI...... Central Arid Zone Research Institute
CB .... Besluit op de Commissarissenbelasting [*Benelux*]   (BAS)
cb............. Cabo [*End*] [*Portuguese*]
CB .... Cairo Barclay's [*Egypt*]
cb............. Caixa Baixa [*Retirement Fund*] [*Portuguese*]
CB .... Campobasso [*Car registration plates*] [*Italian*]
CB .... Cannery Board [*Queensland*] [*Australia*]
cb............. Carta Bianco [*Blank Page*] [*Publishing*] [*Italian*]
CB .... Central Bank [*Philippines*]   (IMH)
CB .... Centro de Botanica [*Portugal*]   (DSCA)
CB .... Cinema Board [*Tasmania*] [*Australia*]
Cb............. Colombio [*Columbium*] [*Chemical element*] [*Portuguese*]
CB .... Commonwealth Bank [*Australia*]   (ADA)
CB .... Comptabilite Budgetaire
CB .... Correspondentieblad, Orgaan der Centrale van Hoogere Rijks- en Gemeente-Ambtenaren [*Benelux*]   (BAS)
CB .... Kongo Belgijskie [*Belgian Congo*] [*Poland*]
CB-21........ Comite Benque 21 de Septiembre [*21 September Benqueno Committee*]   (LA)
CBA .... Cake and Biscuit Alliance   (WGAO)
CBA .... Carbon Black Association [*Japan*]   (EAIO)
CBA .... Caribbean Atlantic Airways   (WGAO)
CBA .... Catholic Biblical Federation [*Germany*]   (EAIO)
CBA .... Central Broadcasting Administration [*China*]
CBA .... Chambre Belge de l'Affichage et Media Connexes   (WGAO)
CBA .... Chef de Bureau Adjoint
CBA .... China Badminton Association   (EAIO)
CBA .... Christian Booksellers Association   (WGAO)
CBA .... Christian Brethren Assemblies [*Australia*]
CBA .... Christian Brothers' Association of Australia
CBA .... Citizens Band Association   (WGAO)
CBA .... Civil Aviation Inspectorate of the Czech Republic [*ICAO designator*]   (FAAC)
CBA .... Clay Brick Association Ltd. [*South Africa*]   (AA)
CBA .... Comite Brasileiro pela Anistia [*Brazilian Amnesty Committee*] (LA)
CBA .... COMLINE Business Analysis [*COMLINE International Corp.*] [*Japan*] [*Information service or system*]   (CRD)
CBA .... Commercial Bank of Africa
CBA .... Commercial Bank of Australia
CBA .... Commercial Bank of Australia Ltd.   (ADA)
CBA .... Commonwealth Broadcasting Association [*London, England*] (EAIO)
CBA .... Companhia Brasileira de Adubos [*Brazil*]   (DSCA)
CBA .... Computer Benefits (Australia) Proprietary Ltd.
CBA .... Concrete Block Association   (WGAO)
CBA .... Confederacao Brasileira de Automobilismo   (EAIO)
CBA .... Consortium des Bois Africains
CBA .... Criminal Bar Association   (WGAO)
CBA .... Czechoslovak Biathlon Association   (EAIO)
CBA .... De Colonne Beaufaict, A., Azande
CBAA .... Christian Booksellers Association of Australia   (ADA)
CBAA .... Christian Brothers Association of Australia
CBAAC...... Centre for Black and African Arts and Civilization [*Nigeria*] (WGAO)
CBABG...... CAB [*Commonwealth Agricultural Bureaux*] International Bureau of Animal Breeding and Genetics   (EAIO)
CBABG...... Commonwealth Bureau of Animal Breeding and Genetics (WGAO)
CBAC........ Commander Base Area Command [*Australia*]
CBACE...... Club du Barbet et Autres Chiens d'Eau [*France*]   (EAIO)
CBACT...... Chiropractic Board of the Australian Capital Territory [*Medicine*]
CBAE....... Commonwealth Board of Architectural Education [*British*] (EAIO)
CBAE....... Commonwealth Bureau of Agricultural Economics   (WGAO)
CBAH....... Commonwealth Bureau of Animal Health   (WGAO)
CBAI......... Comite Belge des Assureurs d'Incendie   (WGAO)

CBAI......... Commissao Brasileira Americana de Educacao Industrial [Brazil] (LAA)
CBAMC..... Chambre Belge de l'Affichage et Media Connexes (WGAO)
CBAN .... Commissie voor de Spelling van Buitenlandse Aardrijkskundige Namen [Benelux] (BAS)
CB & A...... College van Bijstand en Advies voor de Bedrijfsgeneeskunde [Benelux] (BAS)
CBANZ...... Christian Booksellers Association of New Zealand (EAIO)
CBAQ .... Clay Brick Association of Queensland [Australia]
CBAS........ Complexe de Bois Alger Sahel
CBAT........ Central Bureau for Astronomical Telegrams (WGAO)
CBAT........ Centro de Biologia Aquatica Tropical [Portugal] (DSCA)
CBATMU ... Centro de Biologia Aquatica Tropical Ministerio do Ultramar [Center of Biological, Aquatic, and Tropical Ministry of Overseas Colonies] [Portuguese] (MSC)
CBAV........ Cambodian Buddhist Association of Victoria [Australia]
CBB........... Centrale Besturenbond v. Zuivelorganisaties in Nederland (WGAO)
CBB........... Centre Belge du Bois [Belgian Timber Research Center] (PDAA)
CBB........... Centrum voor Bedrijfseconomie en Bedrijfseconometrie [Center for Business Economics and Econometrics] [Research center] [Belgium] (IRC)
CBB........... Cochabamba [Bolivia] [Airport symbol] (OAG)
CBB........... College van Beroep voor het Bedrijfsleven [Benelux] (BAS)
CBB........... Confederation des Betteraviers Belges (WGAO)
CBB........... Confederation des Brasseries de Belgique (WGAO)
CBBA........ Comissao Brasileira de Bibliotecarios Agricolas [Brazil] (DSCA)
CBBMG.... Centralne Biuro Budowy Maszyn Gorniczych [Central Office of Mining Machinery Construction] (POL)
CBC .... Canberra Bridge Club [Australia]
CBC .... Canberra Bushwalkers' Club [Australia]
CBC .... Canberra Business Council [Australia]
CBC .... Carrieres de Basalte du Cayor
CBC .... Catholic Bushwalking Club [Australia]
CBC .... Central Bureau of Compensation [See also BCC] [Belgium] (EAIO)
CBC .... Chad Basin Commission
CBC .... Children by Choice [Australia]
CBC .... Chinese Baptist Convention [Taiwan] (EAIO)
CBC .... Christian Brothers' College [Australia] (ADA)
CBC .... Christian Businessman's Committees [Australia]
CBC .... Civil Budget Committee [NATO] (NATG)
CBC .... Commercial Banking Co. of Sydney [Australia]
CBC .... Commonwealth Bank Cycle Classic [Australia]
CBC .... Commonwealth Banking Corporation [Australia]
CBC .... Consumer Buying Corporation of Zambia Ltd.
CBC .... Cyprus Broadcasting Corp. (IMH)
CBC .... Societe Commerciale des Bois du Cameroun
CBC .... Societe Royale Chambre Belge des Comptales (WGAO)
CBCA........ Caribbean Basin Corrections Association [Cayman Islands] (EAIO)
CBCA........ Children's Book Council of Australia
CBCA........ Customs Brokers' Council of Australia
CBCC........ Canada-British Colombia Consultative Board (WGAO)
CBCC........ Commonwealth Bank Cycle Classic [Australia]
CBCE........ Comite de Bourses de la Communaute Europeenne [Committee of Stock Exchanges in the European Community - CSEE] (EAIO)
CBCI......... Catholic Bishops' Conference of India (EY)
CBCI......... Children's Book Council of Iran [Research center] (IRC)
CBCISS..... Centro Brasileiro de Cooperacao e Intercambio de Servicos Sociais (WGAO)
CBCISS..... Comite Brasileiro da Conferencia Internacional de Servico Social [Brazil] (DSCA)
CBCM .... Confederation of Brewers in the Common Market [Belgium] (EAIO)
cbcm .... Kubikzentimeter [Cubic Centimeter] [German]
CBCP........ Catholic Bishops' Conference of the Philippines
CBCR........ Compania Bananera de Costa Rica [Costa Rica] (DSCA)
CBCS .... Commonwealth Bureau of Census and Statistics [Australia] (ADA)
CBCSM .... Council of British Ceramic Sanitaryware Manufacturers [Now BBC] (WGAO)
CBD .... Centrale Bibliotheek Dienst
CBD .... Centralforeningen af Benzinforhandlere i Danmark (WGAO)
CBD .... Coffee Berry Disease
CBD .... Comite Belge de la Distribution [Belgium] (EAIO)
CBD .... Confederacao Brasileira de Desportos [Brazilian Sports Confederation]
CBD .... Corporacion Boliviana de Desarrollo [Bolivia] (DSCA)
CBDA .... Chad Basin Development Authority
CBDA .... Comissao Brasileira de Documentacao Agricola [Brazil] (SLS)
CBDD .... Cografya Bakimindan Dezavantajli Devletler [Geographically Disadvantaged Nations] (TU)
CBDIC .... Centre Belge de Documentation et d'Information de la Construction (WGAO)

cbdo .... Co Bylo do Okazania [or Okreslenia] [Which Was to Be Proved] [Poland]
CBDST ...... Commonwealth Bureau of Dairy Science and Technology (WGAO)
CBDT........ Confederacao Brasileira de Desportos Terrestres (EAIO)
CBE........... Aerovias Caribe SA [Mexico] [ICAO designator] (FAAC)
CBE........... Centro Brasileiro de Pesquisas Educacionais [Brazil] (LAA)
CBE........... China Business Enterprises
CBE........... Commercial Bank of Ethiopia (AF)
CBE........... Commission for Biological Education [Germany] (WGAO)
CBE........... Corporacion Bancaria de Espana [Spain] (ECON)
CBE........... International Commercial Business Establishment [Saudi Arabia]
CBEA........ Centro Brazileiro de Estatisticas Agropecuarias [Brazil] (DSCA)
CBEA........ Centro Brazileiro de Estatisticas Agropecuarias (WGAO)
CBEA........ Commonwealth Banana Exporters Association [Saint Lucia] (EAIO)
CBEA........ Cyprus Bankers Employers Association (EAIO)
CBECI....... Centre Belge des Echanges Culturels Internationaux
CBEE........ Companhia Brasileira de Energia Eletrica [Brazil] (LAA)
CBEEP ..... Commercial Building Energy Efficiency Program [Australia]
CBEET ..... Commonwealth Board on Engineering Education and Training (WGAO)
CBEFEN ... Comite Belge des Expoisitions et des Foires et d'Expansion Nationale (WGAO)
CBEN .... Comision Boliviana de Energia Nuclear [Bolivian Atomic Energy Commission] [La Paz] (LAA)
CBEVE ...... Central Bureau for Educational Visits and Exchanges (WGAO)
CBF........... Ceskoslovensky Badminton Federation (EAIO)
CBF........... Club du Bouledogue Francais (EAIO)
CBF........... Club du Bouvier des Flandres [France] (EAIO)
CBF........... Club du Braque Francais (EAIO)
CBF........... Confederacao Brasileira de Futebol (WGAO)
CBF........... Corporacion Boliviana de Fomento [Bolivian Development Corporation] [La Paz] (LA)
CBF........... Shenyang Regional Administration of CAA of China [ICAO designator] (FAAC)
CBFC........ Commonwealth Bank Finance Company [Australia] (ADA)
CBFCA ..... Commander, British Forces, Caribbean Area [NATO] (NATG)
CBG........... Campus Booksellers Group [Australia]
CBG........... Chambre Belge des Graphistes (WGAO)
CBG........... Compagnie de Bauxites de Guinee [Guinea Bauxite Company] (AF)
CBG........... Companhia Brasileira de Geofisica (WGAO)
CBGA........ Carpathian Balkan Geological Association [ICSU] [Poland]
CBGFS ...... Commonwealth Bank Group Financial Services [Australia]
CBGS........ Centrum voor Bevolkings- en Gezinsstudien [Center for Population and Family Studies] [Research center] [Belgium] (IRC)
CBH........... Bechar [Algeria] [Airport symbol] (OAG)
CBH........... Central Board of Health [South Australia] [Australia]
CBH........... Club du Basset Hound [France] (EAIO)
CBH........... Club Francais du Braque Hongrois (EAIO)
CBH........... Congregatie Broeders van Huybergen [Brothers of the Immaculate Conception of the Mother of God - BICMG] [Huybergen, Netherlands] (EAIO)
CBHPC..... Commonwealth Bureau of Horticulture and Plantation Crops (WGAO)
CBHV .... Christlicher Bau und Holzarbeiter-Verband (WGAO)
CBI........... Caribbean Basin Initiative (LA)
CBI........... Cement- och Betonginstitutet [Swedish Cement and Concrete Research Institute] [Research center] (IRC)
CBI........... Central Bank of Iran (ME)
CBI........... Centrum voor Bedrijfsinformatie [Center for Company Information] [Flemish Economic Association] [Belgium]
CBI........... Comision Ballenera Internacional [International Whaling Commission - IWC] [Spanish] (ASF)
CBI........... Compagnie de Banque et d'Investissements [Switzerland]
CBI........... Cooperative Business International (WGAO)
CBI........... Corriente Batelista Independiente [Uruguay] (WGAO)
CBI........... Corriente Batllista Independiente [Uruguay] [Political party] (EY)
CBIC.......... Caribbean Basin Business Information Center (IMH)
CBIP.......... Central Board of Irrigation and Power [India] [Research center] (WED)
CBJ........... Caribjet, Inc. [Antigua and Barbuda] [ICAO designator] (FAAC)
CBJO........ Co-Ordinating Board of Jewish Organizations [United Nations (already exists in GUS II database)]
CBK........... Centraal Brouwerij Kantoor (WGAO)
CBK........... Centralne Biuro Konstrukcyjne [Central Designing Office] (POL)
CBKC........ Confederacao do Brasil Kennel Clube (EAIO)
CBKK........ Centralne Biuro Konstrukcji Kotlow [Central Boiler Design Office] (POL)
CBKM .... Centralne Biuro Konstrukcji Maszynowych [Central Machinery Designing Office] (POL)

CBKMiUO ... Centralne Biuro Konstrukcyjne Maszyn i Urzadzen Odlewniczych [*Central Machineryand Foundry Equipment Designing Office*]   (POL)

CBKN .... Centralne Biuro Konstrukcyjne Narzedzi [*Central Tool Designing Office*]   (POL)

CBKO .... Centraal Bureau voor Katholiek Onderwijs

CBKO .... Centralne Biuro Konstrukcji Okretowych [*Central Ship Designing Office*]   (POL)

CBKO .... Centralne Biuro Konstrukcyjne Obrabiarek [*Central Machine Tool Design Office*]   (POL)

CBKO .... Centralne Biuro Kulturalno-Oswiatowe [*Central Office of Culture and Education*]   (POL)

CBKT .... Centralne Biuro Konstrukcji Teletechniznych [*Central Telecommunication Installation Designing Office*]   (POL)

CBKT .... Centralne Biuro Konstrukcyjne Telekomunikacji [*Central Telecommunication Designing Office*]   (POL)

CBKUB...... Centralne Biuro Konstrukcji Urzadzen Budowlanych [*Central Building Equipment Designing Office*]   (POL)

CBKW .... Centralne Biuro Konstrukcji Wagonow [*Central Office for Railroad Car Design*]   (POL)

CBL............ Camara Brasileira do Livro [*Brazilian Chamber of Publishing*]   (EAIO)

CBL............ Carte Blanche [*Freedom of Action*] [*French*]

CBL............ Centraal Bureau Levensmiddelenbedrijf   (WGAO)

CBL............ Cercle Belge de la Librairie   (WGAO)

CBL............ Circulo del Buen Lector [*El*] [*Argentina*]

CBL............ Ciudad Bolivar [*Venezuela*] [*Airport symbol*]   (OAG)

CBL............ Commission Centrale Belge du Lait   (WGAO)

Cbl BrschNot Ned ... Correspondentieblad van de Broederschap der Notarissen in Nederland [*Netherlands*]   (BAS)

CBLIA .... Centro Belgo-Luxembourgeois d'Information de l'Acier   (WGAO)

CBLT .... Centralne Biuro Lozysk Tocznych [*Central Ball Bearings Office*]   (POL)

CBLT .... Commission du Bassin du Lac Tchad [*Lake Chad Basin Commission*] [*Cameroon*]   (AF)

CBM .... Central Bank of Malta

CBM .... Centrale Bond van Meubelfabrikanten   (WGAO)

CBM .... Centre de Biochimie et de Biologie Moleculaire [*Biochemistry and Molecular Biology Center*]   (ARC)

CBM .... Centre Technique et Scientifique de la Brasserie Malterie et des Industries Connexes [*Belgium*]   (WGAO)

CBM .... Centro Bibliografico Medico [*Italian*]   (SLS)

CBM .... Centro Biologia Molecular [*Molecular Biology Center*] [*Spain*]

CBM .... Christian Blind Mission [*Australia*]

CBM .... Congo Balolo Mission

cbm............ Kubikmeter [*Cubic Meter*] [*German*]   (EG)

CBMA .... Concrete Brick Manufacturers Association   (WGAO)

CBMA .... Country Bread Manufacturers' Association [*Western Australia*] [*Australia*]

CBMAWA ... Clay Brick Manufacturers' Association of Western Australia

CBMC .... Communaute de Travail des Brasseurs du Marche Commun   (WGAO)

CBMC .... Confederation des Brasseurs du Marche Commun [*Belgium*]   (EAIO)

CBMCA..... Christian Business Men's Committees Australia

CBMI........ Christian Blind Mission International [*Bensheim, Federal Republic of Germany*]   (EAIO)

CBMIE...... China National Building Materials & Equipment Import and Export Corp.   (TCC)

CBMM ...... Companhia Brasileira de Metalurgia e Mineracao [*Brazilian Mining and Metallurgy Company*]   (LA)

CBMWA ... Country Bread Manufacturers of Western Australia

CBN .... Central Bank of Nigeria

CBN .... Cirebon [*Indonesia*] [*Airport symbol*]   (OAG)

CBN .... Clandestine Broadcasting Network [*Australia*]

CBN .... Comision Bancaria Nacional [*National Banking Commission*] [*Panama*]   (LA)

CBN .... Commission on Biochemical Nomenclature   (WGAO)

CBN .... Commonwealth Broadcasting Network [*Australia*]   (ADA)

CBN .... Commonwealth Bureau of Nutrition   (WGAO)

CBN .... Correspondentieblad van de Broederschap der Notarissen in Nederland [*Netherlands*]   (BAS)

CBNM ...... Central Bureau for Nuclear Measurements [*Research center*]   (IRC)

CBO .... Centrum voor Bedrijfsontwikkeling [*Center for Management and Industrial Development*] [*Netherlands*]

CBO .... Comite de Bases Obreras [*Workers Base Committee*] [*El Salvador*]   (LA)

CBO .... Commissie Bibliografisch Onderzoek

CBO .... Conference of Baltic Oceanographers [*Germany*]   (EAIO)

CBO .... Cotabato [*Philippines*] [*Airport symbol*]   (OAG)

CBOA .... Comite des Bons Offices Angolais [*Angolan Good Offices Committee*]   (AF)

CBOA .... Commonwealth Bank Officers Association [*Australia*]   (ADA)

CBOAR ..... Centralne Biuro Obrotu Artykulami Rolnymi [*Central Agricultural Products Sales Office*]   (POL)

CBOB .... Christelijke Bond van Ondernemers in de Binnenwaart   (WGAO)

CBOB .... Christian Brothers Old Boys [*Australia*]   (ADA)

CBoC......... Central Bank of China

CBOE .... Committee of Butchery Organizations of the EEC   (EAIO)

CBOI .... Centro Biologico del Oceano Indico   (WGAO)

CBOK-ACES ... Christelijke Bond voor de Ondergrondse Kerk/Action Chretienne pour l'Eglise du Silence [*Belgium*]

CBOM .... Centralne Biuro Obrotu Maszynami [*Central Machinery Sales Office*]   (POL)

CBOMB .... Canadian Baptist Overseas Mission Board

CBOR .... Centrala Budowy Osiedli Robotniczych [*Poland*]

CBP............ Caribbean Basin Program   (LA)

CBP............ Centar Bateriskog Polozaja [*Center of Battery Position*]   (YU)

CBP............ Centralne Biuro Planowania [*Central Planning Office*]   (POL)

CBP............ Centralni Biro za Projektiranje [*Central Bureau for Designs (Naval Architecture*)] [*Brodogradnja*]   (YU)

CBP............ Chambre Belge des Podologues   (WGAO)

CBP............ Convencao Baptist Portuguesa   (EAIO)

CBPAE...... Centro Brasileiro de Pesquisas Agrcoles em Elano   (WGAO)

CBPAE...... Centro Brasileiro de Pesquisas Agricolas em Elano [*Brazil*]   (DSCA)

CBPANSW ... Clay Brick and Paver Association of New South Wales [*Australia*]

CBPAV ..... Chambre Belge des Publicites Audio-Visuelles   (WGAO)

CBPBG ...... Commonwealth Bureau of Plant Breeding and Genetics   (WGAO)

CBPBM ..... Centralne Biuro Projektow Budownictwa Miejskiego [*Central Office of Urban Construction Plans*]   (POL)

CBPBW .... Centralne Biuro Projektow Budownictwa Wiejskiego [*Central Office of Rural Construction Plans*]   (POL)

CBPC .... Chambre Belge de la Publicite Cinematographique   (WGAO)

CBPCL ..... Club des Bichons et des Petits Chiens Lions [*France*]   (EAIO)

CBPDA...... China Books and Periodicals Distribution Association   (EAIO)

CBPE .... Centro Brasileiro de Pesquisas Educacionais [*Brazil*]   (ASF)

CBPF .... Centro Brasileiro de Pesquisas Fisicas [*Brazilian Center for Physics Research*]

CBPFC...... Commonwealth Bureau of Pastures and Field Crops   (WGAO)

CBPI .... Centro Boliviano de Productividad Industrial [*La Paz, Bolivia*]   (LAA)

CBPI .... Clay Brick and Paver Institute [*Australia*]

CBPISA..... Clay Brick and Paver Institute of South Australia

CBPiSBP... Centralne Biuro Projektow i Studiow Budownictwo Przemyslowego [*Central Office of Plans and Research in Industrial Construction*]   (POL)

CBPM........ Chambre Belge des Pedicures Medicaux [*Belgium*]   (SLS)

CBPO .... Companhia Brasileira de Projetos e Obras [*Brazil*]

CBPP .... Centralne Biuro Projektow Przemyslu [*Central Office of Plans in the Industry*]   (POL)

CBPPW ..... Centralne Biuro Projektow Przemyslu Weglowego [*Central Office of Plans in the Coal Industry*]   (POL)

CBQ .... Calabar [*Nigeria*] [*Airport symbol*]   (OAG)

CBQ .... Centre Belge pour la Gestion de la Qualite   (WGAO)

CBR .... Biomedical Research Centre [*National Institute of Health Research and Development*] [*Indonesia*]

CBR .... Canberra [*Australia*] [*Airport symbol*]   (OAG)

CBR .... Centraal Bureau voor de Rijweilhandel   (WGAO)

CBR .... Centralina Biblioteka Rolnicza [*Central Agricultural Library*] [*Poland*]   (PDAA)

CBR .... China Business Resources Co. Ltd.   (ECON)

CBR .... Commonwealth Bureau of Roads [*Australia*]   (ADA)

CBR .... Companhia Brasileira de Reflorestamento [*Brazil*]   (DSCA)

CBR .... Conferencia Boliviana de Religiosos   (WGAO)

CBR .... Consejo de Bienestar Rural [*Venezuela*]   (LAA)

CBRB........ Central Bureau voor de Rijnen Binnenvaart   (WGAO)

CBRI........ Central Bee Research Institute [*India*]   (WGAO)

CBRI........ Central Building Research Institute [*India*] [*Research center*]   (IRC)

CBRP........ Centre Belge des Relations Publiques   (WGAO)

CBRPT ...... Confederation of British Road Transport [*Now BBC*]   (WGAO)

CBRPW..... Centralne Biuro Rozliczen Przemyslu Weglowego [*Central Clearing Office of the Coal Industry*]   (POL)

CBRS .... Coffee Board Research Station [*India*]   (WGAO)

CBRTC...... Chengdu Biogas Research Institute / Asian-Pacific Regional Biogas Research and Training Centre [*China*]   (WED)

CBS............ Canberra Blind Society [*Australia*]

CBS............ Canberra Bonsai Society [*Australia*]

CBS............ Canberra Building Society [*Australia*]

CBS............ Centraal Bureau Slachtveeverzekeringen   (WGAO)

CBS............ Centraal Bureau voor de Statistiek [*Central Statistical Bureau*] [*Netherlands*]   (PDAA)

CBS............ Centraal Bureau voor Shcimmelcultures   (WGAO)

CBS............ Central Bank of Seychelles

CBS............ Central Bureau of Statistics [*Information service or system*]   (IID)

CBS............ Ceskoslovenska Botanica Spoleenost   (WGAO)

CBS............ Cesky Bruslarsky Svaz [*Czechoslovak Skating Association*]   (CZ)
CBS............ Chinese Biochemical Society   (EAIO)
CBS............ Christian Brethren Schools [*Australia*]
CBS............ Christian Broadcasting System [*Korean*]
CBS............ Comite de Barrio Sandinista [*Sandinist Neighborhood Committee*] [*Nicaragua*]   (LA)
CBS............ Commission for Basic Systems [*WMO*]   (MSC)
CBS............ Commonwealth Bureau of Soils   (WGAO)
CBS............ Copenhagen Business School [*Denmark*]   (ECON)
CBS............ Croatian Biological Society   (EAIO)
CBS............ Czechoslovak Botanical Society   (EAIO)
CBSA........ Chiropody Board of South Australia [*Medicine*]
CBSA........ Chiropractors' Board of South Australia [*Medicine*]
CBSA........ Citrus Board of South Australia
CBSA........ Clay Bird Shooting Association   (WGAO)
CBSA........ Council of Bank Staff Association   (WGAO)
CBSAA..... Christian Book Selling Association of Australia
CBSE........ Commonwealth Board of Surveying Education [*London, England*]   (EAIO)
CBSI......... Chartered Building Societies Institute   (WGAO)
CBSiPKol .. Centralne Biuro Studiow i Projektow Kolejowych [*Central Office of Railroad Research and Plans*]   (POL)
CBSiPTD... Centralne Biuro Studiow i Projektow Transportu Drogowego [*Central Office of Research and Plans for Road Transportation*]   (POL)
CBSiPTDL ... Centralne Biuro Studiow i Projektow Transportu Drogowego i Lotniczego [*Central Office of Research and Plans for Road and Air Transportation*]   (POL)
CBSKol...... Centralne Biuro Statystyki Kolejowej [*Central Railroad Statistics Office*]   (POL)
CBSN........ Centraal Bureau voor de Schapenfokkerij in Nederland   (WGAO)
CBSN........ Christelijke Bond van Scoenwinkeliers   (WGAO)
CBSPPKP ... Centralne Biuro Statystyki Przewozow Polskich Kolei Panstwowych [*Central Office of Statistics on Polish State Railroad Shipments*]   (POL)
CBSZ........ Comunidad Budista Soto Zen [*Spain*]   (EAIO)
CBT........... Centre Belge de Traductions   (WGAO)
CBT........... Centre for Business Technology [*Australia*]
CBT........... Commission du Bassin du Tchad   (WGAO)
CBT........... Competency-Based Training [*Australia*]
CBTB........ Christelijke Boeren- en Tuindersbond [*Benelux*]   (BAS)
CBTB........ Nederlandse Christelijke Boeren-en Tuindersbond   (WGAO)
CBTC........ Club du Boston Terrier et du Carlin [*France*]   (EAIO)
CBTC........ Confederacao Brasileira de Trabalhandores Cristaos   (WGAO)
CBTDC...... China Building Technology Development Centre [*Beijing*] [*Information service or system*]   (IID)
CBTIP....... Chambre Belge des Traducteurs, Interpretes, et Philologues [*Belgian Chamber of Translators, Interpreters, and Philologists*]
CBTN........ Companhia Brasileira de Tecnologia Nuclear [*Brazilian Nuclear Technology Company*]   (LA)
CBTU .... Companhia Brasileira de Trens Urbanos [*Railway system*] [*Brazil*]   (EY)
CBTUC...... [*The*] Commonwealth of the Bahamas Trade Union Congress   (EY)
CBU .... Caribbean Broadcasting Union   (LA)
CBU .... Clearing Bank Union   (WGAO)
CBURC...... Computer Board for Universities and Research Councils   (WGAO)
CBV .... Centraal Bureau voor de Varkensfokkerij in Nederland   (WGAO)
CBV .... Centraal Bureau voor de Veilingen   (WGAO)
CBV .... Christliche Bayerische Volkspartei - Bayerische Patriotenbewegung [*Christian Bavarian People's Party - Movement of Bavarian Patriots*] [*Germany*] [*Political party*]   (PPW)
CBV .... Computer Benefits (Victoria) Proprietary Ltd. [*Australia*]
CBV .... Conseil des Bourses de Valeurs [*French*]   (ECON)
CBV .... Cooperative Suisse pour l'Approvisionnement en Betail de Boucherie et en Viande   (WGAO)
CBVN .... Centraal Bureau voor de Varkensfokkerij in Nederland   (WGAO)
CBVO .... Centraal Bureau de Verzorging van Oorlogsslachtoffers [*Benelux*]   (BAS)
CBW .... Centralne Biblioteka Wojskowa [*Central Military Library*]   (POL)
CBW .... Centralne Biuro Wystaw [*Central Exhibitions Office*]   (POL)
CBW .... Curacao's Burgerlijk Wetboek [*Benelux*]   (BAS)
CBWA .... Centralne Biuro Wystaw Artystycznych [*Central Art Exhibitions Office*]   (POL)
CBWAS..... Central Bank of the West African States   (WGAO)
CBWG .... Children's Book Writers' Group [*Australia*]
CBX .... Condobolin [*Australia*] [*Airport symbol*]   (OAG)
CBY .... Canobie [*Australia*] [*Airport symbol*] [*Obsolete*]   (OAG)
CBYH .... Christian Brethren Youth Hostel [*Australia*]
cc.............. Calcada [*Street*] [*Portuguese*]   (CED)
CC............. Calcutta Computers [*Software manufacturing company*] [*India*]   (ECON)

CC .... Camara de la Construccion [*Chamber of Construction*] [*Nicaragua*]   (LA)
CC............. Camera di Commercio [*Chamber of Commerce*] [*Italian*]
CC............. Canada Council   (EAIO)
CC............. Canberra Consumers Incorporated [*Australia*]
CC............. Carabinieri [*Italian National Military Police*]   (WER)
CC............. Caribbean Commission   (LAA)
cc .... Carte [*Pages*] [*Publishing*] [*Italian*]
CC............. Casinos Czechoslovakia   (ECON)
CC............. Causa Comun [*Venezuela*]   (WGAO)
cc .... Celni Cent [*Customs Quintal (About 50 kilograms)*]   (CZ)
cc .... Centimetre Cube [*Cubic Centimeter*] [*French*]
CC............. Central Committee   (PWGL)
CC............. Centrale Catalogus [*KB*] [*'s-Gravenhage*]
CC............. Centristas de Cataluna [*Political party*] [*Spain*]   (EY)
CC............. Chancellor College
CC............. Chapter Clerk [*Church of England in Australia*]
CC............. Children's Court [*Australia*]
CC............. Coal Corp. [*Philippine National Oil Co.*]   (DS)
CC............. Cobres de Colombia SA [*Urbanizacion Industrial Acopi-Menga Cali*]   (COL)
CC............. Cocos [*Keeling*] Islands [*ANSI two-letter standard code*]   (CNC)
CC............. Code Civil Francais   (DLA)
CC............. Codice Civile [*Civil Code*] [*Italian*]   (ILCA)
CC............. Coe & Clerici Agenti [*Commercial firm*] [*Italy*]
CC............. Combat Clothing [*NATO*]
cc .... Combustibil Conventional [*Conventional Fuel*]   (RO)
CC............. Comisiones Campesinos [*Rural Workers Commissions*] [*Spanish*]   (WER)
CC............. Comitato Centrale [*Central Committee*] [*Italian*]   (WER)
CC............. Comite Central [*Central Committee*]
CC/........... Comite Central De [*Central Committee Of*] [*Cambodia*]   (CL)
CC............. Comite Consultatif [*French*]   (BAS)
CC............. Comitetul Central [*Central Committee*]   (RO)
CC............. Commande de Controle [*French*]   (ADPT)
CC............. Commanders Call [*Meeting of KODAM commanders*]   (IN)
CC............. Commission de Climatologie   (WGAO)
CC............. Commonwealth Aircraft Corp. Ltd. [*Australia*] [*ICAO aircraft manufacturer identifier*]   (ICAO)
CC............. Compensation Court [*Australia*]
CC............. Compte Courant [*Current Account*] [*French*] [*Business term*]
CC............. Conciliation Committees [*Australia*]
CC............. Conseil Communal [*French*]   (BAS)
CC............. Conseil Constitutionnel [*France*]   (FLAF)
CC............. Consiliul Central [*Central Council*]   (RO)
CC............. Constituency Committee [*Mauritius*]   (AF)
c/c .... Conta Corrente [*Current Account*] [*Portuguese*]
c/c .... Conto Corrente [*Current Account*] [*Italian*]
CC............. Contrat Collectif [*Convention Collective*] [*France*]   (FLAF)
CC............. Coordination Committee for the Transfer of Powers
CC............. Corne de Cerf [*Pharmacy*]
CC............. Corpo Consolare [*Consular Corps*] [*Italian*]
CC............. Corps Consulaire [*Consular Corps*] [*French*]
CC............. Corps de Cavalerie [*Cavalry Corps*] [*Military*] [*French*]   (MTD)
CC............. Corrente Continua [*Direct Current*] [*Italian*]
cc .... Corriente Continua [*Direct Current*] [*Spanish*]
CC............. Corriente Critica [*Mexico*] [*Political party*]   (EY)
CC............. Courant Continu [*Direct Current*] [*French*]
CC............. Cours Complementaire [*French*]
cc .... Cours de Compensation [*French*]
CC............. Credit Corp. (Papua New Guinea) Ltd.
CC............. Crevettes du Cameroun
CC............. Crossword Club [*Romsey, Hampshire, England*]   (EAIO)
C/C .... Cuenta Corriente [*Current Account*] [*Business term*] [*Spanish*]
CC............. Cultural Colombiana Ltda. [*Colombia*]   (COL)
CC............. Cultural Council [*Australia*]
CC............. Curriculum Corporation [*Commercial firm*] [*Australia*]
CC............. Cyfeillion Cymru [*Friends of Wales*] [*Australia*]
CCA .... Air China [*ICAO designator*]   (FAAC)
CCA .... Caisse Congolaise d'Amortisation [*Congolese Sinking Fund*]   (AF)
CCA .... Caja de Colonizacion Agricola [*Santiago, Chile*]   (LAA)
CCA .... Caja de Credito Agricola [*Ecuador*]   (DSCA)
CCA .... Camara de Comercio de las Americas [*Panama*]   (DSCA)
CCA .... Camp and Cabin Association of New Zealand   (EAIO)
CCA .... Canadian Chemical Association   (WGAO)
CCA .... Canberra Classical Association [*Australia*]
CCA .... Caribbean Conservation Association [*St. Michael, Barbados*]
CCA .... Carpet Cleaners Association   (WGAO)
CCA .... Cattle Council of Australia
CCA .... Celktic Council of Australia
CCA .... Cement and Concrete Association   (WGAO)
CCA .... Cemeteries and Crematoria Association [*Australia*]
CCA .... Centre Commercial Africain
CCA .... Centro de Ciencias de la Atmosfera [*Atmospheric Sciences Center*] [*Mexico*]   (EAS)

CCA .... Charter Cruise Air Ltd. [*Australia*]
CCA .... Christian Chiropractors Association   (WGAO)
CCA .... Christian Colportage Association   (WGAO)
CCA .... Christian Conference of Asia   (EA)
CCA .... Civic Catering Association   (WGAO)
CCA .... Clubul Central al Armatei [*Central Army Club*]   (RO)
CCA .... Coastal Cruising Association   (WGAO)
CCA .... Coca-Cola Amatil [*Australia*]
CCA .... Coca-Cola Australia
CCA .... College Caterers Association   (WGAO)
CCA .... Comites Communistes pour l'Autogestion [*Communist Committees for Self-Management*] [*France*] [*Political party*]   (PPW)
CCA .... Commissie Consumenten Aangelegenheden [*Benelux*]   (BAS)
CCA .... Commission Centrale des Arbitres de Football
CCA .... Commissioner for Consumer Affairs [*Australia*]
CCA .... Commission on Crystallographic Apparatus [*International Council of Scientific Unions*]
CCA .... Committee for Cultural Action [*Mexico*]   (LAA)
CCA .... Commonwealth Chess Association   (EA)
CCA .... Commonwealth Correspondents Association [*Australia*]   (ADA)
CCA .... Community Care Australia
CCA .... Compagnie Commerciale Africaine [*African Trading Co.*] [*Ivory Coast*]
CCA .... Companhia de Culturas de Angodre
CCA .... Company Chemists Association   (WGAO)
CCA .... Comptoirs Commerciaux Africains
CCA .... Computer Corp. Australia
CCA .... Conference Chretienne d' Asie Orientale   (WGAO)
CCA .... Conseil du Contentieux Administratif [*France*]   (FLAF)
CCA .... Consejo de Cooperacion Aduanera   (WGAO)
CCA .... Conselho Coordinadora de Abastecimento [*Rio De Janeiro, Brazil*]   (LAA)
CCA .... Consumer Credit Association   (WGAO)
CCA .... Contribution sur les Chiffres d'Affaires [*Turnover tax*] [*Zaire*]   (IMH)
CCA .... Cooperativa Central Agricola [*Brazil*]   (DSCA)
CCA .... Copper Conductors Association   (WGAO)
CCA .... Corporacion de Credito Agricola [*Puerto Rico*]   (DSCA)
CCA .... Corrections Corp. of Australia
CCA .... Court of Criminal Appeal [*Australia*]   (DLA)
CCA .... Covered Conductors Association   (WGAO)
CCA .... Crafts Council of Australia   (ADA)
CCA .... Current Cost Accounts [*London Stock Exchange*]
CCA .... Curriculum Corp. of Australia
CCA .... Cyprus Consumers Association   (WGAO)
CCAA .... Caribbean-Central American Action   (LA)
CCAA .... Cement and Concrete Association of Australia   (ADA)
CCAA .... Couseil de Coordination des Associations Aeroportuaires   (WGAO)
CCAAP...... Central Committee for the Architectural Advisory Panels   (WGAO)
CCAB........ Consultative Committee of Accountancy Bodies   (WGAO)
CCAC........ Central Coast against Chemicals [*Australia*]
CCAC........ Children's Court Advisory Committee [*Australia*]
CCAC........ Commonwealth Conciliation and Arbitration Commission [*Australia*]
CCAC........ Compagnie Commerciale de l'Afrique Centrale
CCACC...... Coordinating Committee of the EC Cooperative Associations   (WGAO)
CCACT...... Crafts Council of the Australian Capital Territory
CCACU ..... Central Coordinating Allocation Committee for University Project Research
CCAE........ Canberra College of Advanced Education [*Australia*]   (ADA)
CCAE........ Comision Consultiva de Asuntos Empresariales [*Asociacion Latinoamericana de Libre Comercio - ALALC*]   (LAA)
CCAEDI .... Convenio Centro-Americano sobre Equiparacao dos Direitos de Importacao   (LAA)
CCAES ...... Central das Cooperativas Agricolas do Espirito Santo [*Brazil*]   (DSCA)
CCAF........ Canberra Community Arts Front [*Australia*]
CCAF........ Comite Central des Armateurs de France   (EAIO)
CCAF........ Compagnie Agricole et Forestiere   (WGAO)
CCAF........ Compagnie Commerciale Agricole et Forestiere [*Commercial Agricultural and Forestry Co.*]
CCAF........ Consejo Central de Asignaciones Familiares [*Family Aid Council*] [*Uruguay*]   (LA)
CCAFMA .. Caisse Centrale d' Allocations Familiales Mutuelles Agricoles   (WGAO)
CCAFRP.... Caisse Centrale d'Allocations Familiales de la Region Parisienne [*France*]   (FLAF)
CCAG .... Companhia Carioca de Armazens Gerais [*Brazil*]   (DSCA)
CCAH........ Commercial & Credit America Holdings [*Arab*]
CCAHC ..... Central Council for Agricultural and Horticultural Cooperation   (WGAO)

CCAI......... Chambre de Commerce, Agriculture, et Industrie [*Chamber of Commerce, Agriculture, and Industry*]   (AF)
CCAI......... Chambre de Commerce, d'Agriculture et l'Industrie [*Mali, Togo*]   (WGAO)
CC-AI .... Communication and Cognition - Artificial Intelligence   (EA)
CCAIM...... Caja de Credito Agrario, Industrial, y Minero [*Bogota, Colombia*]   (LAA)
CCAIT ...... Chambre de Commerce d'Agriculture et d'Industrie du Togo [*Chamber of commerce*] [*Togo*]
CCAJ .... Consiliul Central al Asociatiei Juristilor [*Central Council of the Association of Jurists*]   (RO)
CCAL......... Comision Consultiva de Asuntos Laborales [*Asociacion Latinoamericana de Libre Comercio*]   (LAA)
CCAM .... Cement and Concrete Association of Malaysia   (EAIO)
CCAM .... Centre de Conjoncture Africaine et Malgache
CCAM .... Commission Consultative des Achats et de Marches   (WGAO)
CCAM .... Consorcio de Centros Agricolas de Manabi [*Ecuador*]   (DSCA)
CCAM .... Council for Complementary and Alternative Medicine   (WGAO)
CCAMAA ... Caisse Centrale d'Assurances Mutuelles Agricoles contre de Accidents   (WGAO)
CCAMAG ... Caisse Centrale d' Assurances Mutuelles Agricoles contre la Grele   (WGAO)
CCAMAI... Caisse Centrale d'Assurances Mutuelles Agricoles contre l'Incendie   (WGAO)
CCAMAMB ... Caisse Centrale d'Assurances Mutuelles Agricoles contre la Mortalite du Betail   (WGAO)
CCAMLR .. Commission for the Conservation of the Antarctic Marine Living Resources [*Australia*]   (EAIO)
CCANSW ... Campers and Caravanners' Association of New South Wales [*Australia*]
CCA(NSW) ... Court of Criminal Appeal (New South Wales) [*Australia*]
CCAO .... Chambre de Compensation de l'Afrique de l'Ouest [*West African Clearing House - WACH*]   (EAIO)
CCAP........ Caja Central de Ahorros y Prestamos [*Central Savings and Loan Bank*] [*Chile*]   (LA)
CCAP........ Church of Central Africa Presbyterian
CCAP........ Culture Centre of Algae and Protozoa   (WGAO)
CCAQ .... Consultative Committee on Administrative Questions [*United Nations*]
CCAR .... Compagnie Camerounaise d'Assurances et de Reassurances
CCAS........ Canberra Contemporary Art Space [*Australia*]
CCAS........ Centre for Contemporary Asian Studies   (WGAO)
CCAS........ Comissao Consultiva de Armazens e Silos [*Brazil*]   (DSCA)
CCAS........ Consejo Coordinador Argentino Sindical [*Argentinian Trade Union Coordinating Council*]
CCAS........ Consiliul de Cultura si Arta Socialista [*Council of Socialist Culture and Arts*]   (RO)
CCAS........ Convention for the Conservation of Antarctic Seals [*Australia*]
C Cass deBelgique ... Cour de Cassation de Belgique   (FLAF)
CCAST ...... Cameroon College of Arts, Science, and Technology
CCAST ...... China Center for Advanced Science and Technology
CCASTD ... Comite Consultatif sur l'Application de la Science et de la Technique du Developpement [*Advisory Committee on the Application of Science and Technology to Development - ACASTD*] [*French*]   (ASF)
CCAT........ Central Council for the Amateur Theatre   (WGAO)
CCAT........ Comite de Coordination de l'Assistance Technique   (WGAO)
CCAT........ Comptoir Commercial des Alfas Tunisie
CCAT........ Control de Conmutaciones Automaticas [*Telex-Automatic Switching Control*] [*Cuba*]   (LA)
CCATU...... Central Council of Afghan Trade Unions
CCAU .... Confederation of Central American Universities   (WGAO)
CCAV .... Community Council Against Violence [*Australia*]
CCAVMA ... Caisse Centrale d'Assurance Viellesse Mutuelle Agricole   (WGAO)
CCAWA .... Cleaning Contractors' Association of Western Australia
CCB .... Canberra City Band [*Australia*]
CCB .... Centrala Industriei Confectiilor Bucuresti [*Bucharest Central for the Clothing Industry*]   (RO)
CCB .... Centre Commercial du Benin
CCB .... Civil Cooperation Bureau [*South African covert-operations team*]   (ECON)
CCB .... Code de Commerce Belge   (DLA)
CCB .... Colegio Colombiano de Bibliotecarios [*Colombia*] [*CBC*] [*Formerly,*]   (COL)
CCB .... [*The*] Collective Catalogue of Belgium [*Database*]   (IID)
CCB .... Comite de Comercio de Bogota   (COL)
CCB .... Commercial Crimes Bureau [*Hong Kong*]
CCB .... Commision Canadienne du Ble   (WGAO)
CCB .... Commonwealth Geographical Bureau   (WGAO)
CCB .... Compagnie Camerounaise de Boissons
CCB .... Compagnie Commerciale du Betsileo
CCB .... Comunidades Cristianas de Base [*Christian Base Communities*] [*Spanish*]   (WER)
CCB .... Concorde des Citoyens du Burundi
CCB .... Cooperatieve Centrale Boerenleenbank
CCB .... Co-Operative and Commerce Bank [*Nigeria*]

CCB .... Co-Operative Central Bank [*Malaysia*]
CCB .... Cooperatives des Commercants du Burundi
CCBA........ Centre de Calcul de Beton Arme [*Ivory Coast*]   (WGAO)
CC-Bank.... Bankhaus Central Credit [*Central Credit Bank Company*]
CCBAT...... Comite Central Belge de l' Achevement Textile   (WGAO)
CCBB........ Comite Central de la Bonneterie Belge   (WGAO)
CCBD .... Chambre de Commerce Belgo-Danoise   (WGAO)
CCBE........ Commission Consultative des Barreaux Europeens   (WGAO)
CCBE........ Conseil des Barreaux de la Communaute Europeenne [*Council of the Bars and Law Societies of the European Community*]   (EAIO)
CCBE........ Consultative Committee of the Bars and Law Societies of the European Community   (ILCA)
CCBESP.... Cooperativa Central dos Bananicultores do Estado de Sao Paulo [*Brazil*]   (DSCA)
CCBET ...... Comite Central Belge de Textile l'Ennoblissement   (WGAO)
CCBFE ...... Companhia Central Brasileira de Forca Eletrica [*Brazil*]   (LAA)
CCBG .... Canberra Craft Bookbinders' Guild [*Australia*]
CCBI........ Chambre de Commerce Belgo-Italienne   (WGAO)
CCBI.......... Primo Catalogo Collettivo delle Biblioteche Italiane [*General library catalog*] [*Italy*]
CCBM .... Copper Cylinder and Boiler Manufacturers' Association   (WGAO)
CCBN .... Compagnie des Cultures Bananieres du Nieky
CCBP........ Certificat de Capacite au Bornage et a la Peche
CCBS .... Country Children's Book Service [*Australia*]
CCBSA ...... Central Council of Bank Staff Associations   (WGAO)
CCBV........ Comite Professionnel des Cooperatives des Pays du Marche Commun pour le Betail et la Viande [*France*]   (DSCA)
CCC .... Calculator Collectors Club   (WGAO)
CCC .... Camara Chilena de la Construccion [*Chilean Construction Council*]   (LA)
CCC .... Camara de Comercio de la Republica de Cuba [*Chamber of Commerce of the Republic of Cuba*]   (LA)
CCC .... Camara de Compensacion Centroamericana [*Tegucigalpa, Honduras*]   (LAA)
CCC .... Cameroon Cultural Centre
CCC .... Camping Car Club [*France*]   (EAIO)
CCC .... Campus Crusade for Christ   (WGAO)
CCC .... Canberra Canoe Club [*Australia*]
CCC .... Canberra Chamber of Commerce [*Australia*]
CCC .... Canberra Children's Choir [*Australia*]
CCC .... Canberra Churches Centre [*Australia*]
CCC .... Canine Control Council [*Australia*]
CCC .... Capricorn Conservation Council [*Australia*]
CCC .... Caribbean Conference of Churches   (EAIO)
CCC .... Caribbean Consumer Committee [*Jamaica*]   (WGAO)
CCC .... Caribbean Council of Churches   (LA)
CCC .... Carribbean Conservation Corp.   (WGAO)
CCC .... Carrington Cotton Corporation [*Australia*]
CCC .... Cellules Combattantes Communistes [*Communist Combatant Cells*] [*Belgium*]
CCC .... Cellules Communistes Combattantes [*Terrorist organization*] [*Belgium*]   (EY)
CCC .... Central Classification Committee [*FID*] ['*s-Gravenhage ICSU*]
CCC .... Central Council of Cooperatives [*Czechoslovakia*]   (WGAO)
CCC .... Centrale Cultuurtechnische Commissie [*Benelux*]   (BAS)
CCC .... Centre for Corporate Change (Australian National University)
CCC .... Ceylon Chamber of Commerce [*Sri Lanka*]
CCC .... China Christian Council [*Anglican church mission*]
CCC .... China Container Corp.   (TCC)
CCC .... Chinese Chamber of Commerce   (ML)
CCC .... Chlorcholinchlorid [*Trimethyl Ammonium Chloride*]   (EG)
CCC .... Christian City Church [*Australia*]
CCC .... Christian Community Church [*Australia*]
CCC .... Christian Community Concern [*Australia*]
CCC .... Civil Construction Corps [*Australia*]
CCC .... Club Cricket Conference   (WGAO)
CCC .... Club des Chefs des Chefs   (WGAO)
CCC .... Club des Clubs de Casablanca
CCC .... Clyde Cameron College [*Australia*]
CCC .... Comando de Caca aos Communistas [*Communist Hunters Command*] [*Brazil*]   (LA)
CCC .... Commissione Centrale di Controllo [*Central Control Commission*] [*Italian*]   (WER)
CCC .... Commonwealth Credit Corporation [*Australia*]   (ADA)
CCC .... Compagnie Commerciale Cypriote
CCC .... Compagnie de Cultures Cacayeres
CCC .... Complexe Chimique Camerounais
CCC .... Concerned Christian Candidates [*Australia*]
CCC .... Confederacion de Camara de Comercio [*Chamber of Commerce Confederation*] [*Nicaragua*]   (LA)
CCC .... Confederacion Nacional de Colegio Catolicos [*Colombia*]   (COL)
CCC .... Conseil de la Cooperation Culturelle [*French*]   (BAS)

CCC .... Consolidated Contractors International Company [*United Arab Emirates*]
CCC .... Constitutional Consultative Committee on the Political Future of Nigeria [*Political party*]
CCC .... Consumers' Consultative Committee [*EC*]   (ECED)
CCC .... Council for Cultural Co-Operation [*Council of Europe*]   (EY)
CCC .... Council for the Care of Churches
CCC .... Counseil National du Credit [*Cameroon*]   (WGAO)
CCC .... Custom Credit Corporation [*Australia*]
CCC .... Customs Co-Operation Council [*See also CCD*] [*Brussels, Belgium*]   (EAIO)
CCC .... International Developments in China Cooperative Business Corp.   (TCC)
CCC .... Societe de Commission, de Consignation, et de Courtage de l'Ocean Indien
CCC .... Vanguarda de Comando de Caca aos Comunistas [*Vanguard of the Commando for Hunting Communists*] [*Brazil*]   (PD)
CCCA........ Centre de Cooperation et de Coordination Agricole
CCCA........ Cocoa, Chocolate and Confectionary Alliance   (WGAO)
CCCA........ Comissao de Coordinacao de Credito Agropecuario   (LAA)
CCCA........ Comite Consultivo en Cuestiones Administrativas [*United Nations*]   (WGAO)
CCCA........ Community College of Central Australia
CCCAM..... Caisse Centrale de Credit Artisanal et Maritime
CCCAM..... Centro de Cooperacion Cientifica de Asia Meridional [*India*]   (WGAO)
CCCAS...... Centro de Cooperacion Cientifica de Asia Sudoriental [*Science Co-Operation Office for Southeast Asia - SEASCO*] [*Spanish*]   (ASF)
CCCAV...... Child Care Centres Association, Victoria [*Australia*]
CCCB........ Camara de Comercio Colombo Britanica   (WGAO)
CCCB........ Comissao de Comercio do Cacau da Bahia [*Brazil*]   (DSCA)
CCCB........ Commisao de Comercio do Cacau da Bahia [*Brazil*]   (WGAO)
CCCB........ Cooperative Casamancaise de Construction de Batiments
CCCBR...... Central Council of Church Bell Ringers   (WGAO)
CCCC........ Camara Central de Comercio de Chile [*Central Office of Chilean Commerce*]   (LAA)
CCCC........ Charity Christmas Card Council   (WGAO)
CCCC........ Commission Consultative du Controle et du Contentieux [*French*]   (BAS)
CCCC........ Commonwealth Corporate Credit Card [*Australia*]
CCCC........ Community Child Care Cooperative [*Australia*]
CCCC........ Cross-Channel Coordination Center [*NATO*]   (NATG)
CCCCA...... Confederacion de Cooperativas del Caribe y Centro America [*Costa Rica*]   (WGAO)
CCCCE...... Conseil de la Cooperation Culturelle du Conseil de l'Europe [*Council for Cultural Cooperation of the Council of Europe*]   (EAIO)
CCCCN...... Comissao Coordenadora da Criacao do Cavalo Nacional [*Brazil*]   (DSCA)
CCCCN...... Commissao Coordenadora da Criacao do Cavalo Nacional [*Brazil*]   (WGAO)
CC CCP ..... Central Committee Communist Party of China   (PWGL)
CCCD .... Combating Childhood Communicable Diseases Project [*Agency for International Development*]
CCCE......... Caisse Centrale de Cooperation Economique [*Mauritania*]   (EY)
CCCE......... Caisse Centrale de Cooperation Economique [*Central Fund for Economic Cooperation*] [*Paris, France*]   (AF)
CCCE......... Centre Congolais du Commerce Exterieur
CCCE......... Computer Communication Center Europe   (ADPT)
CCCF......... Chaos Computer Club France   (EAIO)
CCCF......... Chow-Chow Club Francais   (EAIO)
CCCFE ...... Comite Consultatif de Coordination du Financement a moyen terme des Exportations   (WGAO)
CCCH .... Confederation des Cooperatives de Construction et d'Habitation   (WGAO)
CCCHV ..... Cooperative Centrale de Consommation de la Haute-Volta
CCCI.......... Compagnie du Congo pour le Commerce et l'Industrie [*Congo Commerce and Industry Company*]
CCCI.......... Conceal-Control-Command-Instruction [*NATO*]
CCCI.......... Copenhagen Conference on Computer Impact [*Denmark*]   (PDAA)
CCCI.......... Cyprus Chamber of Commerce and Industry   (EAIO)
CCCLA ...... Coordination Council on Control of Liquor Abuse
CCCM .... Cooperativa Central dos Cafeicultores de Mojiana [*Brazil*]   (DSCA)
CCCMA..... Central Coast Country Music Association
CCCMAES ... Consiliul Central de Control Muncitoresc al Activitatilor Economico-Sociale [*Central Council of Worker Control of Socioeconomic Activities*]   (RO)
CCCN .... Customs Co-Operation Council Nomenclature
CCCO .... Committee on Climatic Changes and the Ocean [*Defunct*] [*Paris, France*]   (EAIO)
CCCOCM ... Centro de Cooperacion Cientifica del Oriente Cercano y Medio   (DSCA)

CCCOE...... Comision Coordinadora de las Comisiones de Euzkadi Obreras [*Coordinating Commission for the Basque Workers Commissions*] [*Spanish*] (WER)

CCCP........ Caisse Central du Credit Populaire [*People's Central Credit Fund*] [*Algeria*] (AF)

CC CP....... Central Committee of Communist Party (PWGL)

CCCP........ Combined Conversion of the Catalogues Project [*National Library of Australia*]

CCCP........ Committee for the Communciation of Conservative Policies (WGAO)

CCCP........ Union of Soviet Socialist Republics [*Initialism represents Russian phrase, Soyuz Sotsialistiches Kikh Respublik*]

CCCR........ Coordinating Committee for Career Research (WGAO)

CCCRJ..... Centro do Comercio do Cafe do Rio de Janeiro [*Brazil*] (DSCA)

CCCS........ Certificate in Child Care Studies [*Australia*]

CCCS........ Commonwealth and Continental Church Society [*Australia*] (ADA)

CCCU........ Caribbean Confederation of Credit Unions (WGAO)

CCCV........ Chevrolet Car Club of Victoria [*Australia*]

CCCWA..... Central Citrus Council of Western Australia

CCCWA..... Christian Consultative Council for the Welfare of Animals (WGAO)

CCD.......... Camara de Comercio de la Dorada (COL)

CCD.......... Carlos Cervantes del Rio [*Mexico*] [*ICAO designator*] (FAAC)

CCD.......... Centrale Controle Dienst (WGAO)

CCD.......... Century Computer Deutschland GmbH [*German*] (ADPT)

CCD.......... Certificat de Capacite en Droit [*French*]

CCD.......... Civil Coordination Detachment [*General Air Traffic Element at Operational Traffic and Defense Centers*] [*NATO*]

CCD.......... Comissao Civica Democratica

CCD.......... Comite du Commerce et de la Distribution (WGAO)

CCD.......... Commission Centrale de Discipline [*Tunisia*]

CCD.......... Confederazione dei Coltivatori Diretti [*Confederation of Small Farmers*] [*Italian*] (WER)

CCD.......... Conference of the Committee on Disarmament [*Formerly, ENDC*] [*NATO*]

CCD.......... Conseil de Cooperation Douaniere [*Customs Co-Operation Council - CCC*] (EAIO)

CCD.......... Crisis Controle Dienst [*Benelux*] (BAS)

CCDA........ Canberra Commercial Development Authority [*Australia*]

CCDA........ Commission de Coordination de la Documentation Administrative [*French*]

CCDC........ Capital City Development Corporation

CCDEE...... Compagnie Centrale de Distribution d'Energie Electrique

CCDEE...... Compagnie Coloniale de Distribution d'Energie Electrique

CCDF........ Catholic Church Development Fund [*Australia*]

CCDF........ Co-ordinating Committee of Democratic Forces [*Ghana*] [*Political party*] (EY)

CCDFANZ ... Catholic Church Development Funds of Australia and New Zealand

CCDG .... Civil Coordination Detachment General [*NATO*] (NATG)

CCDG .... Compagnie Commerciale du Gabon

CCDG .... Societe Commerciale du Gabon (WGAO)

CCDI......... Christelijke Centrale van Diverse Industrieen [*Belgium*] (EAIO)

CCDL........ Camera Confederale del Lavoro [*Confederal Chamber of Labor*] [*Trieste, Italy*]

CCDLNE... Commission for Controlling the Desert Locust in the Near East [*United Nations*] (EA)

CCDLNWA ... Commission for Controlling the Desert Locust in North-West Africa [*United Nations*] (EA)

CCDN........ Ciamara de Comercio, Agricultura e Industria del Distrito Nacional [*Dominican Republic*] (WGAO)

CCDN........ Comite Contra la Dependencia y el Neo-Colonialismo [*Committee Against Dependence and Neocolonialism*] [*Venezuela*] (LA)

CCD(OCCE) ... Commonwealth Committee for Defence (Operational Clothing and Combat Equipment) (ADA)

CCDP........ Comision Centroamericana de Desarrollo Pesquero [*Central American Fishery Development Commission*] [*Spanish*] (ASF)

CCDP........ Compagnie Camerounaise de Depots Petroliers

CCDP........ Croatian Christian Democratic Party [*Political party*] (EY)

CCDR .... Compagnie Camerounaise de Developpement Regional

CCDU .... Community Cultural Development Unit [*Australia Council*]

CCDVT..... Caisse Centrale de Depots et Virements de Titres (WGAO)

CCDVT...... Caisse Centrale de Depots et Vriements de Titres

CCE .... Cairo Air Transport Co. [*Egypt*] [*ICAO designator*] (FAAC)

CCE .... Camara de Comercio Espanola [*Taiwan*] (EAIO)

CCE .... Catholic College of Education [*Australia*] (ADA)

CCE .... Central Coast Exploration [*Australia*] (ADA)

CCE .... Centre for Civic Education

CCE .... Centro de Calculo Electronico Universidad Nacional Autonoma de Mexico [*National Autonomous University of Mexico, Data Processing Center*] [*Mexico*]

CCE .... Comhaltas Ceoltoiri Eireann (WGAO)

CCE .... Comite de Cooperacion Economica del Istmo Centroamericano [*Central American Economic Cooperation Committee*]

CCE .... Comite de Coordination et d'Execution [*Algeria*]

CCE .... Commission des Communautes Europeennes [*Commission of the European Communities - CEC*] [*Belgium*]. (EAIO)

CCE .... Compagnie Camerounaise d'Enterprise (WGAO)

CCE .... Compagnie Commerciale d'Electronique

CCE .... Confederation des Compagnonnages Europeens [*European Companions - EC*] [*France*] (EAIO)

CCE .... Conseil des Communes d'Europe (FLAF)

CCE .... Consejo Central de Elecciones [*Central Elections Council*] [*El Salvador*] (LA)

CCE .... Consejo Coordinador Empresarial [*Coordinating Business Council*] [*Mexico*] (LA)

CCE .... Conselho dos Comissariados de Estado

CCE .... Coordinating Committee Executive

CCEA........ Center for Climate and Environmental Assessment

CCEA........ Central Council of Employers of Australia

CCEA........ Commonwealth Council for Education Administration [*Armidale, NSW, Australia*] (EAIO)

CCEAC...... Comite de Cooperation Economique de l'Amerique Centrale (WGAO)

CCEAD...... Consultative Committee on Exotic Animal Diseases [*Australia*]

CCEAE...... Conference des Chefs d'Etat de l'Afrique Equatoriale [*Conference of Heads of State of Equatorial Africa*] (AF)

CCEAFS.... Conference of Central and East African States

CCEB........ Centre for Clinical Epidemiology and Biostasis [*University of Newcastle*] [*Australia*]

CCEB........ Conseil Canadien des Ecoles de Bibliothecaires (WGAO)

CCEC........ Chairman, Communications-Electronics Committee [*NATO*] (NATG)

CCECA...... Cour de Justice de la Communaute Europeenne du Charbon et de l'Acier (FLAF)

CCECC...... China Civil Engineering Construction Corp.

CCECCON ... China Civil Engineering Construction Co. of Nigeria Ltd.

CCECL ...... Christelijke Centrale van Energie, Chemie en Leder [*Belgium*] (EAIO)

CCEE......... Commission de Cooperation Economique Europeenne [*French*]

CCEE......... Consilium Conferentiarum Episcopalium Europae [*Council of European Bishops' Conferences*] (EAIO)

CCEG .... Confederation des Compagnonnages Europeens (WGAO)

CCEHO..... Compagnie Centrafricaine d'Exploitation Hoteliere

CCEI......... Caisse Commune d'Epargne et d'Investissement [*Finance institutions*] [*Cameroon*] (EY)

CCEI......... Comite Consultatif Economique et Industriel aupres de l'OCDE (WGAO)

CCEI......... Conference sur la Cooperation Economique Internationale

CCEIC ...... Comite de Cooperacion Economica del Istmo Centroamericano [*Central American Economic Cooperation Committee*] [*Costa Rica*] (ASF)

CCELF...... Conference des Communautes Ethniques de Langue Francaise [*Standing Committee of French-Speaking Ethnical Communities - SCFSEC*] (EA)

CCEMRI ... Comite Consultatif pour les Standards des Mesurement Radiations Ionizant [*Consultative Committee for the Standards of Measurement of Ionizing Radiations*] [*International Standards Organization*] [*French*] (BARN)

CCEN .... Comision Chilena de Energia Nuclear [*Chilean Nuclear Energy Commission*] (LA)

CCEN .... Cross Campus Education Network [*Australia*]

CCEO .... Caribbean Council of Engineering Organisations [*Jamaica*] (WGAO)

CCEOBHA ... Conference of Chief Executive Officers of Bulk Handling Authorities [*Australia*]

CCEP........ Commission Consultative des Etudes Postales [*de l'Union Postale Universelle*] [*Consultative Commission for the Study of Postal Services*]

CCEP........ Commonwealth Community Employment Program [*Australia*]

CCEP........ Coordinating Committee for Earthquake Prediction [*Japan*] (PDAA)

CCEPI ...... Commission Consultative Europeenne pour les Peches dans les Eaux Interieures (WGAO)

CCEPL ...... Consejo Central Ejecutivo del Partido Liberal [*Central Executive Council of the Liberal Party*] [*Honduras*] (LA)

CCEPTI..... Centrul de Cercetari Economice pentru Promovarea Turismului International [*Economic Research Center for the Promotion of International Tourism*] (RO)

CCER........ Centre de Coordination et d'Exploitation des Renseignements [*Center for Coordinating and Utilizing Intelligence*] [*Chad*] (AF)

CCER........ Comite Comunitario de Extensao Rural [*Brazil*] (DSCA)

CCERO...... Centre d'Etudes de Recherche Operationnelle [*Belgium*] (WGAO)

CCERS ...... Comite Consultative Europeenne de la Recherche sur la Sante (WGAO)

CCES........ Catholic College of Education, Sydney [*Australia*]

CCES........ Centrala Industriei Poligrafice [*Central for the Printing Industry*] (RO)

CCES........ China Civil Engineering Society (SLS)

CCES........ Computer Consulting & Education Services Proprietary Ltd. [*Australia*]

CCES........ Conseil Consultatif Economique et Social de l'Union Economique Benelux [*Belgium*]   (SLS)

CCES........ Consiliul Culturii si Educatiei Socialiste [*Council for Socialist Culture and Education*]   (RO)

CCES........ Council for Christian Education in Schools [*Australia*]

CCETI....... Commission Consultative des Employes et des Travailleurs Intellectuels [*de l'OIT*]

CCETSW... Central Council for Education and Training in Social Work (WGAO)

CCETT...... Centre Commun d'Etudes de Television et de Telecommunications [*Videotex research center*] [*France*]

CCEUREA ... Centre Cooperatif d'Expansion et d'Utilisation Rationnelles d'Equipement Agricole   (WGAO)

CCEWP..... Combat Clothing and Equipment Working Party [*NATO*]

CCF........... Carcassonne [*France*] [*Airport symbol*]   (OAG)

CCF........... Centrale Cultuurfondsen [*Indonesia*]   (WGAO)

CCF........... Centre Culturel Francais

CCF........... Centre for Conservation Farming [*Charles Sturt University*] [*Australia*]

CCF........... Centre for our Common Future [*Switzerland*]   (EAIO)

CCF........... Centrul de Chimie Fizica [*Center for Physical Chemistry*]   (RO)

CCF........... Christian Children's Fund

CCF........... Club du Caniche de France   (EAIO)

CCF........... Comando do Corpo de Fuzileiros [*Marine Corps Command*] [*Portuguese*]   (WER)

CCF........... Commission for the Status of Women [*Portugal*]   (WGAO)

CCF........... Common Communication Format [*Australia*]

CCF........... Congregational Churches Fellowship [*Australia*]

CCF........... Credit Commercial de France [*Commercial Credit of France*]

CCFA........ Caribbean Cane Farmers' Association [*Kingston, Jamaica*] [*Inactive*]   (EAIO)

CCFA........ Chambre de Commerce Franco-Neerlandaise   (WGAO)

CCFA........ Comando Conjunto de la Fuerza Armada [*Joint Command of the Armed Forces*] [*Peru*]   (LA)

CCFA........ Combined Cadet Force Association   (WGAO)

CCFA........ Comptoir Commercial Francais d'Approvisionnement

CCFA........ Comptoir Commercial Franco-Africain [*Franco-African Trade Office*] [*Guinea*]   (AF)

CCFAL...... Chambre de Commerce France-Amerique Latine [*Paris*]   (LAA)

CCFAN...... Conseil de Commandement des Forces Armees du Nord [*Northern Armed Forces Command Council*] [*Chad*]   (AF)

CCFC........ Corporacion Colombiana de Fomento de la Construccion [*Colombia*]   (COL)

CCFD........ Comite Catholique Contre la Faim et pour le Developpement [*France*]

CCFE........ Communaute des Chemins de Fer Europeens [*Belgium*]   (EAIO)

CCFF .... Compensatory and Contingency Financing Facility [*International Monetary Fund*]

CCFGANSW ... Commercial Cut Flower Growers' Association of New South Wales [*Australia*]

CCFI .... Constante Cameroon Fish Industry   (WGAO)

CCFI .... Consultancy Centre for Finance & Investment [*Saudi Arabia*]

CCFL .... Caisse Centrale de la France Libre   (FLAF)

CCFOE...... Central Committee for Forest Ownership in the EEC   (EAIO)

CCFOM..... Caisse Centrale de la France d'Outre-Mer   (WGAO)

CCFOM..... Comite Central Francais pour l'Outre-Mer [*French Central Committee for Overseas Affairs*]   (AF)

CCFPC ...... Comision Coordinadora de Fuerzas Politicas de Cataluna [*Coordinating Commission for Political Forces of Catalonia*] [*Spanish*]   (WER)

CCFPI....... Comite Consultatif de la Fonction Publique Internationale (WGAO)

CCFPI....... Comite Consultatif pour la Fonction Publique Internationale (FLAF)

CCFR........ Coordinating Committee on Fast Reactors [*Euratom*]   (WGAO)

CCFS .... Comitetul de Cultura Fizica si Sporturi [*Committee for Physical Education and Sports*]   (RO)

CCFS .... Compagnie Commerciale Franco-Scandinave [*Senegal*]

CCFST....... Comite Consultatif pour la Formation Scientifique et Technique (WGAO)

CCG .... Camara de Comercio de Guatemala [*Chamber of Commerce of Guatemala*]   (EAIO)

CCG .... Central Coast Gruens [*Political party*] [*Australia*]

CCG .... Comite de Coordination des Experts Budgetaires Gouvernementaux [*Coordinating Committee of Government Budget Experts*] [*NATO*]   (NATG)

CCG .... Conseil de Cooperation du Golfe [*Morocco*]

CCG .... Copyright Convergence Group [*Australia*]

CCGA .... Compagnie de Constructions Generales en Afrique [*Company for General Construction in Africa*] [*French*]   (AF)

CCGA .... Custom Clothing Guild of America

CCGB .... Confrerie des Chevaliers du Goute Boudin [*Brotherhood of Knights of the Black Pudding Tasters - BKBPT*]   (EA)

CCGC .... Cooperative Centrale des Grandes Cultures [*North African*]

CCGEU ..... Confederation of Central Government Employees' Unions [*India*]

CCGM....... Commission de la Carte Geologique du Monde [*Commission for the Geological Map of the World - GMW*]   (EAIO)

CCGP........ Christelijke Centrale der Grafische en Papierbedrijven [*Belgium*] (EAIO)

CCh........... Ceskoslovenske Chemicke Zavody, Narodny Podnik [*Czechoslovak Chemical Plants, National Enterprise*]   (CZ)

CCH........... Chilchota Taxi Aereo SA de CV [*Mexico*] [*ICAO designator*] (FAAC)

CCH........... Combinatul de Celuloza si Hirtie [*Cellulose and Paper Combine*] (RO)

CCH........... Commerce Clearing House Australia Ltd.

CCH........... Compagnie Commerciale Hollando   (WGAO)

CCHA........ Camara de Comercio Hondureno Americana [*Honduras*] (EAIO)

CCHA........ Compagnie Commerciale Hollando-Africaine

CCHAPG .. Conference of Chaplains-General [*Australia*]

CCHB........ Christelijke Centrale van de Houtbewerkers en Bouwvakarbeiders [*Belgium*]   (EAIO)

CCHC........ Camara de Comercio Hispano Colombiana [*Colombia*]   (COL)

CCHC........ Corporacion Chilena del Cobre [*Chile*]   (LAA)

CCHD........ Catholic Committee against Hunger and for Development [*France*]   (WGAO)

CCHE........ Central Council for Health Education   (WGAO)

CCHEN..... Comision Chilena de Energia Nuclear [*Chilean Nuclear Energy Commission*]   (NRCH)

CCHF .... Childrens Country Holidays Fund   (WGAO)

CCHFA...... Combinatul de Celuloza, Hirtie, si Fibre Artificiale [*Cellulose, Paper, and Artificial Fibers Combine*]   (RO)

CCHH .... Churches Council for Health and Heating   (WGAO)

CCHI .... CCH [*Commerce Clearing House*] Tax Index [*Database*] [*Australia*]

CCHMS .... Central Committe for Hospital Medical Services   (WGAO)

CCHO........ Comite Consultatif d'Hydrologie Operationelle [*Advisory Committee for Operational Hydrology - ACOH*] [*French*] (ASF)

CCHR........ Correspondentieblad van de Centrale voor Hogere Rijksambtenaren [*Benelux*]   (BAS)

CCHS .... Christian Community High School [*Australia*]

CCHS .... Community and Child Health Service [*Australia*]

CCHSSA ... Cyprus Computer Hardware and Software Suppliers Association (EAIO)

CChZ .... Ceskoslovenske Chemicke Zavody [*Czechoslovak Chemical Plants*]   (CZ)

CCI............ Camera di Commercio Internazionale [*International Chamber of Commerce - ICC*] [*Italian*]   (WER)

CCI............ Canberra Consumers, Inc. [*Australia*]

CCI............ Cape Chamber of Industries [*South Africa*]   (AA)

CCI............ Central Campesina Independiente [*Independent Peasants Federation*] [*Mexico*]   (LA)

CCI............ Centre de Creation Industrielle [*Center for Industrial Creation*] [*Information service or system*]   (IID)

CCI............ Centre du Commerce International [*International Trade Center - ITC*] [*Geneva, Switzerland*] [*French*]   (EAIO)

CCI............ Centro de Comercio Internacional [*International Trade Center - ITC*] [*Spanish*]

CCI............ Centro de Investigaciones de Ingenieria [*Engineering Research Center*] [*Universidad de San Carlos de Guatemala*]   (WED)

CCI............ Chamber of Commerce and Industry [*Namibia*]   (EAIO)

CCI............ Chamber of Commerce and Industry [*Bolivia*]   (EAIO)

CCI............ Chambers of Commerce and Industry [*ASEAN*]   (DS)

CCI............ Chambre de Commerce et d'Industrie [*Chamber of Commerce and Industry*] [*Guadeloupe*]   (LA)

CCI............ Chambre de Commerce et d'Industrie de Nouvelle-Caledonie [*Chamber of Commerce of New Caledonia*]   (EAIO)

CCI............ Chambre de Commerce Internationale [*The International Chamber of Commerce - ICC*] [*Paris, France*]   (EAIO)

CCI............ Church and Commercial Insurances Ltd.

CCI............ Comites Consultatifs Internationaux

CCI............ Compagnie Camerounaise Industrielle [*Cameroonian Industrial Co.*]

CCI............ Compagnie Commerciale Ivoirienne

CCI............ Compagnie de Construction Internationale [*French*]

CCI............ Compagnie de Constructions Internationales   (WGAO)

CCI............ Compagnie de Cultures de la Cote-D'Ivoire

CCI............ Concordia [*Brazil*] [*Airport symbol*] [*Obsolete*]   (OAG)

CCI............ Coordination Chemistry Institute [*China*]   (EAIO)

CCI............ Cotton Corp. of India   (PDAA)

CCI............ Credit de la Cote-D'Ivoire [*Credit Bank of the Ivory Coast*]

CCIA........ Camera di Commercio, Industria e Agricoltura di Rieti   (WGAO)

CCIA........ Caravan and Camping Industry Association [*Australia*]

CCIA......... Centre de Commerce International d'Abidjan [*Ivory Coast*] (EAIO)

CCIA........ Chambre de Commerce, d'Industrie et d'Agriculture de Tananarive [*Madagascar*]   (WGAO)

CCIA......... China Computer Industry Association   (EAIO)

CCIA.......... Comite Cientifico de Investigaciones Antarticas [*Scientific Committee on Antarctic Research - SCAR*] [*Spanish*] (ASF)

CCIA.......... Comite de Cooperacion para el Istmo Centroamericano [*Cooperation Committee for the Central American Isthmus*] (LA)

CCIA.......... Commission of the Churches on International Affairs [*Switzerland*] (EAIO)

CCIA.......... Comptoir Commercial et Industriel Afrique

CCIA.......... Consejo Coordinador de la Industria de Autopartes [*Auto Parts Industry Coordinating Council*] [*Argentina*] (LA)

CCIAB....... Chambre de Commerce, d'Industrie et d'Artisanat du Burkina [*Burkina Faso*] (EAIO)

CCIAESC ... Coffee Commission of the Inter-American Economic and Social Council [*United States*]

CCIANSW ... Caravan and Camping Industry Association of New South Wales [*Australia*]

CCIASA .... Caravan and Camping Industry Association of South Australia [*Australia*]

CCIASO .... Chambre de Commerce, d'Industrie et d'Artisant de la Region du Senegal Oriental (WGAO)

CCIA/WCC ... Commission of the Churches on International Affairs of the World Council of Churches (WGAO)

CCIB.......... Central Crime Intelligence Bureau [*Australia*]

CCIB.......... Chambre de Commerce et d'Industrie de la Republique Populaire du Benin (EY)

CCIB.......... Chambre de Commerce et d'Industrie du Burundi (WGAO)

CCIB.......... China Commodity Inspection Bureau

CCIBEM ... Christian Center of Intervention for Business Executives and Managers [*Zaire*] (EAIO)

CCIC.......... Centre Catholique International pour l'UNESCO [*France*]

CCIC.......... Comite Catholique International de Coordination aupres de l'Unesco (WGAO)

CCIC.......... Comite Consultatif International du Coton (WGAO)

CCIC.......... Convention Relative a Certaines Institutions Communes aux Communautes Europeennes (FLAF)

CCICAY .... Chamber of Commerce in Cayenne [*French Guiana*]

CCIC-MAROC ... Compagnie Centrale Industrielle et Commerciale [*Morocco*]

CCICMS ... Council for the Coordination of International Congress of Medicine (WGAO)

CCIEM...... Catholic Committee for Intra-European Migration (WGAO)

CCIES....... Camara de Comercio e Industria de El Salvador [*Chamber of Commerce and Industry of El Salvador*] (LA)

CCIEUROTRAG ... Compagnie de Constructions Internationales [*Gabon*] (WGAO)

CCIF.......... Centre Catholique des Intellectuels Francais (WGAO)

CCIF.......... Comite Consultatif International Telephonique (WGAO)

CCIFP....... Chambre de Compensation des Instruments Financiers de Paris

CCIG.......... Chambre de Commerce et d'Industrie de Guyane [*Chamber of Commerce and Industry of French Guiana*] (LA)

CCIH .... Chambre de Commerce et d'Industrie d'Haiti (EY)

CCII .... Crosscurrents International Institute (EAIO)

CCIL.......... Canadian Cooperative Implements Ltd. (WGAO)

CCILMB ... Interim Committee for Coordination of Investigations of the Lower Mekong Basin [*of the United Nations Economic and Social Commission for Asia and the Pacific*] [*Thailand*] (EAIO)

CCIM........ Chamber of Commerce and Industry of Malawi (AF)

CCIM........ Chambre de Commerce et d'Industrie de la Martinique (WGAO)

CCIM........ Chambre de Commerce et d'Industrie de l'Ile Maurice [*Chamber of Commerce and Industry of the Island of Mauritius*] (EAIO)

CCIN .... Catholic Curriculum Information Network [*Australia*]

CCIO .... Comite Cientifico de Investigaciones Oceanicas [*Scientific Committee on Oceanic Research - SCOR*] [*Spanish*] (ASF)

CCIP.......... Camara de Comercio e Industria Portuguesa [*Portuguese Chamber of Commerce and Industry*] (EAIO)

CCIP.......... Certificate of Commercial and Industrial Practice [*Real Estate Institute of Australia*]

CCIP.......... Chambre de Commerce et d'Industrie de Paris [*Paris Chamber of Commerce and Industry*] [*France*] [*Information service or system*] (IID)

CCIP.......... Commission du Commerce International des Produits de Base [*United Nations*]

CCIPB .... Commission du Commerce International des Produits de Base (WGAO)

CCIPB .... Cooperativa Central do Instituto de Pecuaria da Bahia [*Brazil*] (DSCA)

CCIR.......... Camera de Comert si Industrie a Romaniei [*Chamber of Commerce and Industry of Romania*] (EAIO)

CCIR.......... Catholic Council for International Relations (WGAO)

CCIR.......... Centre for Communication and Information Research [*University of New South Wales, Australia*]

CCIR.......... Chambre de Commerce et l'Industrie de la Reunion (WGAO)

CCIR.......... Comite Consultatif International des Radiocommunications [*International Radio Consultative Committee*] [*of the International Telecommunications Union*] [*Switzerland*]

CCIR.......... Comite Consultative International des Radiocommunications (WGAO)

CCIR.......... Consultative Committee on International Radio [*Australia*]

CCIS .... Canberra Council for International Students [*Australia*]

CCIS .... Communications and Information Systems Committee [*NATO*] (EAIO)

CCIS .... Compagnie Commerciale Industrielle du Senegal [*Tunisia*]

CCISA .... Chamber of Commerce and Industry of South Australia

CCISUA .... Coordinating Committee for Independent Staff Unions and Associations of the United Nations System (WGAO)

CCIT......... Comite Consultatif International Telegraphique [*French*] (ADPT)

CCITAC .... Centrul de Cercetare si Inginerie Tehnologica pentru Articole Casnice [*Research and Technical Engineering Center for Household Articles*] (RO)

CCITT .... Comite Consultatif International Telegraphique et Telephonique [*Consultative Committee on International Telegraphy and Telephony*] [*of the International Telecommunications Union*] [*Switzerland*]

CCITT .... Comite Consultivo de la Internacional de Telefonos y Telegrafos [*Consultative Committee on Telegraphy and Telephony*] [*Geneva, Switzerland*] (LA)

CCITU .... Coordinating Committee of Independent Trade Unions (WGAO)

CCIVS .... Coordinating Committee for International Voluntary Service [*France*] (EAIO)

CCIW........ Canada Centre for Inland Waters (WGAO)

CCIWA...... Chamber of Commerce and Industry of Western Australia

CCIZ.......... Centre de Commerce International du Zaire [*International Trade Center of Zaire*] (AF)

CCJ .... Centre for Christian Journalists [*Netherlands*] (EAIO)

CCJ .... Comite Europeen de Cooperation Juridique [*French*]

CCJ .... Council of Christians and Jews (WGAO)

CCJP .... Catholic Commission for Justice and Peace

CCJPD ...... Catholic Commission for Justice, Peace, and Development [*New Zealand*] (EAIO)

CCJPZ....... Catholic Commission for Justice and Peace in Zimbabwe (EAIO)

CCK .... Centrale Catalogus Kartografie [*Utrecht*]

CCK .... Ceskoslovensky Cerveny Kriz [*Czechoslovak Red Cross*] (CZ)

CCK .... Ching Chuan Kang Air Base [*Vietnam*]

CCK .... Cocos [*Keeling*] Islands [*ANSI three-letter standard code*] (CNC)

CCL........... Caribbean Congress of Labor (LA)

CCL........... Centre de la Construction et du Logement

CCL........... Chinchilla [*Australia*] [*Airport symbol*]

CCL........... Comite Central de la Laine [*France*] (FLAF)

CCL........... Comite Clandestino Local [*Local Clandestine Committee*] [*Guatemala*] (LA)

CCL........... Commercial Companies Law [*1974*] [*Oman*] (IMH)

CCI........... Commission for Climatology [*WMO*]

CCL........... Commonwealth Countries' League [*Middlesex, England*] (EAIO)

CCL........... Communications Consultants Limited

CCL........... Concrete Constructions Ltd. [*Australia*]

CCL........... Confederation du Commerce Luxembourgeois (EAIO)

CCL........... Conseil International de Continuation et de Liaison du Congres Mondial des Forces de Paix (WGAO)

CCL........... Continental Aviation Ltd. [*Ghana*] [*ICAO designator*] (FAAC)

CCL........... Cooperativa Central de Laticinios do Estado de Sao Paulo [*Brazil*] (DSCA)

CCL........... Counsel's Chambers Ltd. [*Australia*]

CCLA........ Correspondence Chess League of Australia (ADA)

CCLAMG ... Chicago Committee for the Liberation of Angola, Mozambique, and Guinea

CCLC........ Comision de la Cuenca del Lago Chad [*Lake Chad Basin Commission*] [*Spanish*] (ASF)

CCLCS ...... Centre for Comparative Literature and Cultural Studies [*Monash University*] [*Australia*]

CCLE........ Council for Civil Liberties in Ethiopia [*Political party*]

CCLF........ Club des Congres de Langue Francaise (WGAO)

CCLFA ...... Comite Central de la Laine et des Fibres Associees (WGAO)

CCLGF ...... Consultative Council on Local Government Finance (WGAO)

CCLIL .... Federation Francaise de la Filature de Laine Cardee et Autres Fibres (WGAO)

CCLM........ Committee on Constitutional and Legal Matters (WGAO)

CCLRU...... Cornea and Contact Lens Research Unit [*University of New South Wales*] [*Australia*]

CCLS .... Consumer Credit Legal Service [*Australia*]

CCLU .... Confederation of Citizens' Labor Unions [*Philippines*]

CCLU .... Conference of Citizens Labor Unions [*Philippines*] (WGAO)

CCLWA...... Council for Civil Liberties in Western Australia

CCM .... Camara de Comercio de Mocambique [*Chamber of Commerce of Mozambique*] (EAIO)

CCM .... Capel-Cure Myers [*French market analysis firm*]

CCM .... Caribbean Common Market (LA)
CCM .... Celtic Club Melbourne [Australia]
CCM .... Central Cigarette Manufacturers
CCM .... Central Coast Media [Australia]
CCM .... Centre Cinematographique Marocaine [Morocco Film Center]
CCM .... Centre de Controle Mixte [Joint Control Center] [NATO] (NATG)
CCM .... Centro Comercial de Mocambique
CCM .... Chama Cha Mapinduzi [Revolutionary Party] [Uganda] [Political party] (AF)
CCM .... Chama Cha Mapinduzi [Revolutionary Party] [Tanzania] [Political party] (PPW)
CCM .... Chemical Company of Malaysia
CCM .... Commission Mixte de Reclamation [France] (FLAF)
CCM .... Companions of the Celtic Mission (EAIO)
CCM .... Concerned Citizens' Movement [St. Christopher and Nevis] [Political party] (EY)
CCM .... Corse-Mediterranee Compagnie [France] [ICAO designator] (FAAC)
CCM .... Council of Cultural Ministers [Australia]
CCM .... Credit Corp. (Malaysian) Berhad
CCM .... Crisciuma [Brazil] [Airport symbol] (OAG)
ccm .... Kubikzentimeter [Cubic Centimeter] [German] (EG)
CCMA .... Caise Centrale des Mutuelles Agricoles [France] (WGAO)
CCMA .... City Capital Market Committee (WGAO)
CCMA .... Comite Consultatif Mondial des Amis (WGAO)
CCMA .... Comite de Compradores de Material Aeronautico de America Latina (WGAO)
CCMA .... Contract Cleaning and Maintenance Association (WGAO)
CCMA .... Corrugated Case Materials Association (WGAO)
CCMA .... Cyprus Clothing Manufacturers Association (EAIO)
CCMB .... Centrala de Constructii-Montaj Bucuresti [Bucharest Central for Constructions-Installations] (RO)
CCMB .... Centrale Chretienne des Metallurgistes de Belgique [Belgium] (BAS)
CCMB .... Centre for Cellular and Molecular Biology [India]
CCMB .... Christelijke Centrale der Metaalbewerkers van Belgie [Belgium] (EAIO)
CCMC .... Comite des Constructeurs d'Automobiles du Marche Common [Common Market Automobile Manufacturers Committee] [French]
CCMC .... Comite des Constructeurs d'Automobiles du Marche Commune
CCMC .... Committee of Common Market Automobile Constructors [Belgium] (WGAO)
CCMCC ..... Continuing Committee on Muslim-Christian Cooperation
CCME .... Churches' Committee on Migrants in Europe (EAIO)
CCMEE ..... Comite Consultatif Maghrebin de l'Education et de l'Enseignement
CCMEP ..... Comision Coordinadora de Mercadeo y Estabilizacion de Precios de Centroamerica y Panama [Guatemala] (DSCA)
CCMEU .... Camera de Comercio Mexico-Estados Unidos [United States-Mexico Chamber of Commerce] (EAIO)
CCMIE ...... Comite Catholique pour les Migrations Intraeuropeennes (WGAO)
CCMIRC ... Commonwealth Caribbean Medical Research Council [Jamaica] (WGAO)
CCMIS ...... Contraceptive Commodity Management Information System [United Nations] (ECON)
CCML........ Centro de Ciencias del Mar y Limnologia [Mexico] (ASF)
CCMM ...... Compagnie Camerounaise de Mobilier Metallique
CCMMI.... Commonwealth Council of Mining and Metallurgy Institutions
CCMMI..... Council of Commonwealth Mining and Metallurgical Institutions (WGAO)
CCMP........ Comision Coordinadora de Mercadeo y Estabilizacion de Precios de Centroamerica y Panama [Central American and Panamanian Coordinating Commission for Trade and Stabilization of Prices] [Secretaria Permanente del Tratado General de Integracion Economica Centroamericana - SIECA Guatemala] (LAA)
CCMP........ Coordinating Committee for Moon and Planets [ICSU]
CCMRC..... Caribbean Medical Research Council (LA)
CCMRG .... Commonwealth Committee on Mineral Resources and Geology (WGAO)
CCMRI...... Central Coal Mining Research Institute [China] [Research center] (IRC)
CCMRP..... Centrul de Cercetari pentru Metale Rare si Pure [Research Center for Rare and Pure Metals] (RO)
CCMS........ Committee on the Challenges of Modern Society [Brussels, Belgium] (EA)
CCMSC ..... Caribbean Common Market Standards Council [Georgetown, Guyana] (EAIO)
CCMTU .... Central Council of Mongolian Trade Unions
CCMW ...... Churches Committee on Migrant Workers in Europe (WGAO)
CCN........... Chakcharan [Afghanistan] [Airport symbol] [Obsolete] (OAG)
CCN........... Christian Council of Nigeria
CCN........... Comissao Coordenadora Nacional [National Coordinating Commission] [Portuguese] (WER)

CCN .... Compagnie Camerounaise du N'Goko
CCN .... Compagnie Commerciale du Niger
CCN .... Companhia Comercio e Navegacao [Brazil] (LAA)
CCN .... Compania Cervecera de Nicaragua [Nicaraguan Brewery Company] (LA)
CCN .... Comunidad de Compensacion Minera [Mining Compensation Community] [Peru] (LA)
CCN .... Consulta di i Cumitati Nationalisti [Corsica] (PD)
CCN .... Convention Collective Nationale, Contrat Collectif National [France] (FLAF)
CCN .... Cruzada Civica Nacionalista [Nationalist Civic Crusade] [Venezuela] [Political party] (PPW)
CCN .... Cruzada Civilista Nacional [Panama] [Political party] (EY)
CCNAA ..... Coordinating Council for North American Affairs (WGAO)
CCNADS... Central Committee of National Associations of Disabled in Sweden (EAIO)
CCNCC...... Coordinating Council for Nature Conservation in the Cape [South Africa] (AA)
CCNE .... Conselho Coordenador da Navegacao Exterior [Brazil] (LAA)
CCNEO ..... Compagnie de Commerce et de Navigation d'Extreme Orient
CCNI .... Compania Chilena de Navegacion Interoceanica [Chile] (LAA)
ccnn .... Carte Non Numerate [Unnumbered Pages] [Publishing] [Italian]
CCNN........ Cement Company of Northern Nigeria
CCNPBC ... Comite Consultatif National pour la Protection des Biens Culturels [National Advisory Committee for the Protection of Cultural Property] [Cambodia] (CL)
CCNR .... Central Commission for the Navigation of the Rhine [France] (EAIO)
CCNR .... Conseil Consultatif National pour le Renouveau [National Consultative Council for the Renewal] [Burkina Faso] (AF)
CCNR .... Consultative Committee for Nuclear Research [Council of Europe] (WGAO)
CCNSW..... Cancer Council, New South Wales [Australia]
CCNT .... Conservation Commission of the Northern Territory [Australia]
CCNUD..... Cycle de la Cooperation de Nations Unies pour le Developpement (WGAO)
CCNZ .... Crafts Council of New Zealand (EAIO)
CCO........... Aerolineas Coco Club Hoteles de Mexico SA de CV [ICAO designator] (FAAC)
CCO........... Canberra Community Orchestra [Australia]
CCO........... Centre for Chiropractic and Osteopathy [Macquarie University] [Australia]
CCO........... Centro de Capacitacion Obrera Puerto Cabello [Venezuela] (LAA)
CCO........... Chemicals Control Order [Australia]
CCO........... Clandestine Communist Organization (ML)
CCO........... Coaxial Cables Organisation [Iraq]
CCo............ Codice di Commercio [Commercial Code] [Italian]
CCO........... Comision Colombiana de Oceanografia [Colorado] (MSC)
CCO........... Commonwealth Copyright Office [Australia] (ADA)
CCO........... Consumenten Contact Organ [Benelux] (BAS)
CCO........... Cours Complementaires Officiels
CCOA .... Chinese Cereals and Oils Association (EAIO)
CCOC .... Comite de Coordination des Organisations des Consommateurs (WGAO)
CCOD....... Christelijke Centrale van de Openbare Diensten [Belgium] (EAIO)
CCOJB ...... Comite de Coordination des Organisations Juives de Belgique [Coordinating Committee for Jewish Organizations in Belgium] (WER)
C Col .... Conseil Colonial [French] (BAS)
CCOM .... Caisse Centrale de la France d'Outre-Mer
C COM ...... Code de Commerce [Commercial Code] [French]
CCOO........ Comisiones Obreras [Workers' Commissions] [Spanish] (WER)
CCOO........ Confederacion Sindical de Comisiones Obreras [Spanish Workers' Commissions] [A union] (DCTA)
CCOOACAL ... Comision Coordinadora de Organizaciones de Oberos Agricolas y Campesinos de America Latina (WGAO)
CCOP .... Comite Coordinador de Organizaciones Populares [Popular Organizations Coordinating Committee] [Peru] (LA)
CCOP .... Committee for Coordination of Joint Prospecting for Mineral Resources in Asian Offshore Areas (WGAO)
CCOPA...... Commissao Coordenadora da Obras Publicas de Alentejo (WGAO)
CCOPEA... Committee for Coordination of Joint Prospecting for Mineral Resources in Asian Offshore Areas, East Asia [United Nations]
CCOP/ESCAP ... Committee for Coordination of Joint Prospecting for Mineral Resources in Asian Offshore Areas (MSC)
CCOP/SOPAC ... Committee for Coordination of Joint Prospecting for Mineral Resources in South Pacific Offshore Areas [Fiji] (MSC)
CCOP/SOPAC ... Committee for Co-Ordination of Joint Prospecting for Mineral Resources in South Pacific Offshore Areas (EAIO)
CCOR .... Central Council of the Odinic Rite (WGAO)
CCOSA...... Christian College of Southern Africa

CCOSOP... Consultative Committee on Safety in the Offshore Petroleum Industry [*Australia*]

C Cost .... Corte Costituzionale [*Constitutional Court*] [*Italian*] (DLA)

CCOTACAL ... Conseil Coordinateur des Organisations des Travailleurs Agricoles et des Paysansd'Amerique Latine (WGAO)

CCOV .... Comite de Coordination de l'Opposition Voltaique [*Coordination Committee of the Voltan Opposition*] (AF)

CCOWE .... Chinese Coordination for World Evangelism [*Publisher*] [*Hong Kong*]

CCP............ Camara de Comercio de Pereira (COL)

CCP............ Catalogue Collectif des Periodiques [*A bibliographic publication*]

CCP............ Centrale Catalogus van Periodieken [*KB*] [*'s-Gravenhage*]

CCP............ Centre de Cheques Postaux [*French*]

CCP............ Centro Catolico Portugues [*Portuguese Catholic Center*] [*Political party*] (PPE)

CCP............ Cercle Culture et Progres [*Culture and Progress Club*] [*Benin*] (AF)

CCP............ Chilean Communist Party [*Political party*]

CCP............ Chinese Communist Party [*Political party*] (PD)

CCP............ Club Canino de Panama (EAIO)

CCp............ Codice di Procedura Civile [*Code of Civil Procedure*] [*Italian*]

CCP............ Comite Cafetalero del Peru [*Peru*] (DSCA)

CCP............ Commissao Coordenadora do Programa [*Program Coordinating Commission*] [*Mozambique*] (AF)

CCP............ Commission Constitutionnelle Provisoire [*France*] (FLAF)

CCP............ Committee on Commodity Problems [*Rome, Italy*] [*United Nations*] (ASF)

CCP............ Commonwealth Centre Party [*Australia*] (ADA)

CCP............ Compagnie de Commerce et de Plantations

CCP............ Compagnie des Caoutchoucs de Pakidie

CCP............ Compte Courant Postal [*Current Postal Account*]

CCP............ Comptes Cheques Postaux [*French*]

CCP............ Concepcion [*Chile*] [*Airport symbol*] (OAG)

CCP............ Confederacao do Comercio Portugues [*Portugal*] (EY)

CCP............ Confederacion Cientifica Panamericana [*Pan-American Scientific Federation*] [*Buenos Aires, Argentina*] (LAA)

CCP............ Confederacion de Campesinos del Peru [*Peasants Confederation of Peru*] (LA)

CCP............ Confederacion de Campesinos Peruanos (WGAO)

CCP............ Confederation of Construction Professions (WGAO)

CCP............ Conference Chretienne pour la Paix [*Christian Peace Conference - CPC*] [*Prague, Czechoslovakia*] (EAIO)

CCP............ Conferenza Cristiana della Pace [*Christian Peace Conference*] [*Use CPC*] [*Italian*] (WER)

CCP............ Consultative Committee on Publications [*European Economic Community*] (WGAO)

CCP............ Conto Corrente Postale [*Current Postal Account*] [*Italian*]

CCP............ Council for the Child in Placement [*Israel*] (EAIO)

CCP............ Country Centres Project [*Australia*]

CCP............ Couples Communication Program [*Australia*]

CCP............ Cuban Communist Party [*Political party*]

CCP............ Cultural Center of the Philippines (EAIO)

CCPA......... Cabinet Committee on Political Affairs [*Home Ministry*] [*India*]

CCPA......... Centrale Cooperative des Productions Animales (WGAO)

CCPA......... Centro Cultural Paraguayo Americano [*Paraguayan-American Cultural Center*] (EAIO)

CCPA......... Chinese Catholic Patriotic Association (WGAO)

CCPA......... Choline Chloride Producers Association [*Belgium*] (EAIO)

CCPA......... Consultative Committee of Plantation Associations [*India*] (PDAA)

CCPA......... Cursos de Classificacao de Produtos Agricolas [*Brazil*] (DSCA)

CCPAA..... Cooperativa Central dos Produtores de Acucar e Alcool [*Brazil*] (DSCA)

CCPALV ... Centrul de Cercetari pentru Protecti Anticorozive, Lacuri si Vopsele, Bucaresti [*Romania*] (WGAO)

CCPB......... Commonwealth Cinema and Photographic Branch [*Australia*]

CCPC......... Comite de Coordination des Plans Civils d'Urgence [*Civil Emergency Coordinating Committee*] [*NATO*] (NATG)

CCPC......... Committee on Crime Prevention and Control [*Economic and Social Council of the UN*] [*Vienna, Austria*] (EAIO)

CCPC......... Cooperative Credit Purchasing Co. [*Company that buys banks' bad debts*] [*Japan*] (ECON)

CCPCAEP ... Comissao de Combate as Pragas da Cana de Acucar no Estado de Pernambuco [*Brazil*] (DSCA)

CCPCE ...... Comissao de Coordenacao da Politica da Compras no Exterior [*Commission for the Coordination of a Policy for Purchases Abroad*] [*Brazil*] (LA)

CCPCI .... Cuirs, Caoutchoucs, Plastiques de Cote-D'Ivoire

CCPCJ....... Commission on Crime Prevention and Criminal Justice [*Austria*] (EAIO)

CCPDF ...... Committee for the Co-Ordination of Patriotic and Democracy-Loving Forces [*Thailand*] (PD)

CCPE......... Centre for Chinese Political Economy [*Macquarie University*] [*Australia*]

CCPE......... Council of European Conferences of Priests (WGAO)

CCPEOF ... Consulting Committee of the Professional Electroengineers' Organizations in Finland (EAIO)

CCPF .... Comite Central de la Propriete Forestiere [*Central Committee for Forest Ownership in the EEC - CCFOE*] (EAIO)

CCPF .... Comite Central de la Propriete Forestiere de la CEE (WGAO)

CCPF .... Comite de Coordination de la Production Frutiere (WGAO)

CCPFCI..... Caisse de Compensation des Prestations Familiales de la Cote-D'Ivoire

CCPI .... Consultative Committee for Public Information [*United Nations*]

CCPIT .... China Council for the Promotion of International Trade (PDAA)

CCPKI ...... Central Comite Partai Komunis Indonesia [*Central Committee of the Indonesian Communist Party*] (IN)

CCPL......... Cooperativa Central dos Produtores de Leite [*Brazil*] (DSCA)

CCPM........ Comite Central des Peches Maritimes [*French*] (ASF)

CCPM........ Comite Consultatif Permanent Maghrebin [*Maghreb Permanent Consultative Committee*] [*North African*] (AF)

CCPM........ Comite de Coordination pour la Prospection en Mer [*Ocean Prospecting Coordination Committee*] [*Cambodia*] (CL)

CCPM........ Consultative Committee for Programme Management [*EEC*] (WGAO)

CCPMA..... Caisse Centrale de Prevoyance Mutuelle Agricole (WGAO)

CCPMFS... Centrul de Cercetari si Proiectari Mecanica Fina si Scule [*Research and Design Center for Precision Machinery and Tools*] (RO)

CCPMNO ... Comite de Coordination des Ports Mediterraneens Nord-Occidental (WGAO)

CCPMO .... Consultative Council of Professional Management Organizations (WGAO)

CCPO .... Comite Central Permanent de l'Opium

CCPP .... Caisse Commune des Pensions du Personnel des Nations Unies (WGAO)

CCPP .... Centro de Consignatarios de Productos del Pais [*Argentina*] (DSCA)

CCPP .... Centrul de Cercetari si Proiectari Pompe [*Center for Pump Research and Design*] (RO)

CCPR........ Central Council for Physical Recreation (WGAO)

CCPR........ Codex Committee on Pesticide Residues [*Australia*]

CCPR........ Cooperativa Central de Productores Rurais de Minas Gerais Ltd [*Brazil*] (DSCA)

CCPR........ Cooperativa de Cafeteros de Puerto Rico [*Puerto Rico*] (DSCA)

CCPR........ Cooperative de Cafeteros de Puerto Rico (WGAO)

CCPS .... Commission Permanente du Pacifique Sud (WGAO)

CCPS .... Consultative Committee for Postal Studies (WGAO)

CCPS .... Consultative Council for Postal Studies [*Universal Postal Union*] (EY)

CCPSO ...... Council of Commonwealth Public Service Organisations [*Australia*] (ADA)

CCPT .... Centrul de Cercetari in Problemele Tineretului [*Center for Research into Youth Problems*] (RO)

CCPT .... Comite de Coordination des Plans de Transport [*Coordinating Committee for Transport Planning*] [*NATO*] (NATG)

CCPTF....... Centrul de Cercetare si Proiectare Tehnologia pentru Fabricatie [*Technological Research and Design Center for Manufacturing*] (RO)

CCPTO...... Christelijke Centrale van het Personeel bij het Technisch Onderwijs [*Belgium*] (EAIO)

CC-PU ...... Conference Reguliere sur les Problemes Universitaires [*Standing Conference on University Problems*] [*Council of Europe*] [*Strasbourg, France*] (EAIO)

CCPW........ Catholic Council for Polish Welfare (WGAO)

CCPY......... Comissao pela Criacao do Parque Yanomami [*Brazil*] (WGAO)

CCQA .... Comite Consultatif pour les Questions Administratives [*France*] (FLAF)

CCQAB...... Comite Consultatif pour les Questions Administratives et Budgetaires (WGAO)

CCR .... Carga Aerea Venezolana Caraven SA [*Venezuela*] [*ICAO designator*] (FAAC)

CCR .... Center Commun de Recherche (WGAO)

CCR .... Centrale Commissie voor de Rijnvaart (WGAO)

CCR .... Centre for Conflict Resolution [*Macquarie University*] [*Australia*]

CCR .... Centre for Cultural Research [*Germany*] (IRC)

CCR .... Centrul de Control al Radiocomunicatiilor [*Center for the Control of Radiocommunications*] (RO)

CCR .... Christian Council of Rhodesia

CCR .... Comision Central para la Nevegacion del Reno [*Central Commission for the Navigation of the Rhine*] [*Spanish*] (ASF)

CCR .... Comites Communaux de la Revolution [*Communal Committees of the Revolution*] [*Benin*] (AF)

CCR .... Commission Centrale de Reglements [*Tunisia*]

CCR .... Commission Centrale pour la Navigation du Rhin [*Central Commission for the Navigation of the Rhine*] [*French*] (ASF)

CCR .... Compagnie Centrale de Reassurance [*Algeria*] (IMH)

CCR .... Company Credit Reports [*Teikoku DataBank Ltd.*] [*Japan*] [*Information service or system*] (CRD)

CCR .... Confrerie de la Chaine des Rotisseurs [*France*] (EAIO)

CCR .... Conseil Communal de la Revolution [*Communal Council of the Revolution*] [*Benin*]   (AF)
CCR .... Conseil de Commandement de la Revolution [*Revolution Command Council*] [*Chad*]   (AF)
CCRA .... Canadian Research Centre for Anthropology   (WGAO)
CCRA .... Centre Cooperatif de la Reforme Agraire [*Agrarian Reform Cooperative Center*] [*Algeria*]   (AF)
CCRA .... Comptoir Commercial de Representations Africaines
CCRAO ..... Communaute Chretienne Rurale de l'Afrique Orientale [*Christian Rural Fellowship of East Africa*] [*Use CRFEA*]   (AF)
CCRB........ Cooperatieve Centrale Raiffeisen-Bank   (WGAO)
CCRC........ Canberra Civil Rehabilitation Committee [*Australia*]
CCRE........ Comptoir Commercial de Radio-Electricite Radiodisc
CCRF........ Comite Central Rayonnement Francais   (WGAO)
CCRH........ Couseil Canadien de Recherches sur les Humanites   (WGAO)
CCRI........ Central Coffee Research Institute [*India*]   (DSCA)
CCRI........ Comite Consultatif de Recherche en Informatique [*Advisory Committee for Data Processing*] [*France*]   (PDAA)
CCRIA....... Comite Consultatif de la Recherche en Informatique et Automatique [*French*]   (ADPT)
CCRJ........ Consultative Committee on Relations with Japan [*Australia*]
CCRM .... Comite Clandestin des Resistants Metro [*Metro Clandestine Committee of Resisters*] [*Guadeloupe*]   (PD)
CCR M-L... Comites Comunistas Revolucionarios, Marxistas-Leninistas [*Marxist-Leninist Revolutionary Communist Committees*] [*Portugal*] [*Political party*]   (PPE)
CCRMO .... Comite Consultatif de la Recherche Meteorologique Oceanique [*Advisory Committee on Oceanic Meteorological Research - ACOMR*] [*French*]   (MSC)
CCRN .... Centre Commun de Recherches Nucleaires [*Euratom*]   (WGAO)
CCRN .... Comite para la Conservacion de los Recursos Naturales [*Panama*]   (DSCA)
CCROI....... Comptoir de Commerce et de Representation pour l'Ocean Indien
CCRP........ Commission Centrale des Reserves et Penalites
CCRP........ Corporacion Cetro Regional de Poblacion [*Colombia*]   (WGAO)
CCRR........ Comite de Coordination des Reacteurs Rapides [*Euratom*]   (WGAO)
CCRRM..... Comite Consultatif de la Recherche sur les Ressources de la Mer   (WGAO)
CCRRM..... Comite Consultatif des Experts de la Recherche sur les Ressources de la Mer [*Advisory Committee of Experts on Marine Resources Research - ACMRR*] [*FAO*] [*French*]   (ASF)
CCRRMM ... Ordo Clericorum Regularium Melkitarum   (WGAO)
CCRS........ Central Coconut Research Station [*India*]   (DSCA)
CCRSA...... Confederation of the Canons Regular of Saint Augustine [*Italy*]   (EAIO)
CCRST ...... Corporacion Catalande Radio y Television   (WGAO)
CCRTD...... Committee for Coordination of Cathode Ray Tube Development   (WGAO)
CCRTV...... Corporacio Catalana de Radio i Televisio [*Spain*]   (EY)
CCRVDF ... Codex Committee on Residues of Veterinary Drugs in Food [*Australia*]
CCS........... Cahier des Charges Speciales [*List of Special Charges*] [*Cambodia*]   (CL)
CCS........... Caracas [*Venezuela*] [*Airport symbol*]   (OAG)
CCS........... Caroline Chisholm Society [*Australia*]
CCS........... Carpentaria Community Services [*Australia*]
CCS........... Castlecrag Conservation Society [*Australia*]
CCS........... Central Co-Operative Society Council [*Rangoon, Burma*]   (EY)
CCS........... Centre of Christian Spirituality [*Australia*]
CCS........... Centro Calculo Sabadell [*Sabadell Computing Center*] [*Information service or system*]   (IID)
CCS........... Centro de Campesinos Salvadorenos [*Salvadoran Peasants Center*]   (LA)
CCS........... Charge Card Service
CCS........... Chinese Chemical Society   (EAIO)
CCS........... Christian Community Schools [*Australia*]
CCS........... Cirkev Ceskoslovenska [*Czechoslovak Church*]   (CZ)
CCS........... Combined Catholic Schools [*Australia*]
CCS........... Comite Coordinador de Sindicatos [*Trade Union Coordinating Committee*] [*El Salvador*]   (LA)
CCS........... Commemorative Collectors Society [*Long Eaton, Nottinghamshire, England*]   (EAIO)
CCS........... Commercial Communications Satellite [*Japan*]
CCS........... Commercial Company of Siam Ltd. [*Thailand*]
CCS........... Compagnie de Commandement et des Services [*Command and Service Company*] [*French*]   (WER)
CCS........... Comptoir Commercial du Senegal
CCS........... Computer-Chemistry-System [*Yokogawa Hewlett Packard Ltd.*] [*Japan*]
CCS........... Consiliul Central al Sindicatelor [*Central Council of Trade Unions*]   (RO)
CCS........... Contact Children's Services [*Australia*]
CCS........... Co-Operative Credit Scheme

CCS........... Corporation of Secretaries   (WGAO)
CCS........... Council of the City of Sydney
CCS........... Countryside Commission for Scotland
CCS........... Covenant Christian School [*Australia*]
CCS........... Czechoslovak Chemical Society   (EAIO)
CCSA......... Christian Concern for Southern Africa   (AF)
CCSA......... Climbers' Club of South Australia
CCSA......... Comite Chretien de Service en Algerie
CCSA......... Conseil Central des Syndicats Afghanistan   (EAIO)
CCSA......... Conservation Council of South Australia   (ADA)
CCSA......... Council of Churches, South Australia
CCSATU ... Coordinating Council of South African Trade Unions   (AF)
CCSBSIF... Consejo Centroamericano de Superintendentes de Bancos, de Seguros y de otras Instituciones Financieras [*Guatemala*]   (WGAO)
CCSC........ Camara de Comercio de Santiago de Chile [*Chamber of Commerce of Santiago, Chile*]
CCSC........ Confederation Camerounaise des Syndicats Chretiens [*Confederation of Believing Workers of the Cameroon*]
CCSC........ Confederation Camerounaise des Syndicats Croyants [*Cameroonian Confederation of Believing Workers Unions*]   (AF)
CCSC........ Coordinating Committee for Satellite Communication [*Switzerland*]   (NITA)
CCSD........ Camadoam Council on Social Development   (WGAO)
CCSDPT.... Committee for Coordination of Services to Displaced Persons in Thailand
CCSDPT.... Committee for the Coordination of Services to Displaced Persons in Thailand [*Australia*]
CCSERC.... Conservation Council for the South East Region and Canberra [*Australia*]
CCSFA ...... Comissao Coordenadora de Sargentos da Forca Aerea [*Air Force Sergeants' Coordinating Committee*] [*Portuguese*]   (WER)
CCSFB....... Centrul de Calculii pentru Sistemul Financiar-Bancar [*Computation Center for the Financial and Banking System*]   (RO)
CCSHS...... Crippled Children's Seaside Home Society [*Australia*]
CCSI......... China Corp. Shipbuilding Industry
CCSL......... Charge Card Services Limited [*Australia*]   (ADA)
CCSL......... Confederation Congolaise des Syndicats Libres [*Congolese Confederation of Free Unions*] [*Brazzaville*]
CCSM....... Centrul de Cercetare pentru Securitate Miniera [*Research Center for Mine Safety*]   (RO)
CCSM....... Comite de Coordination des Syndicats du Mali [*Coordinating Committee of the Trade Unions of Mali*]   (AF)
CCSM....... Confederation Chretienne des Syndicats Malgaches [*Christian Federation of Malagasy Trade Unions*]   (AF)
CCSM....... Czechoslovak Committee for Scientific Management   (WGAO)
CCSMA..... Caisse Centrale de Secours Mutuels Agricoles   (WGAO)
CCSMDG ... Coordinating Committee of the Societies of Mineral-Deposits Geology   (WGAO)
CCSMDG ... Coordination Council of Societies of Mineral Deposits Geology [*International*] [*Spanish*]
CCSMDG ... International Coordination Council of Societies of Mineral Deposits Geology
CCSN......... Caroline Chisholm School of Nursing [*Monash University*] [*Australia*]
CCSO......... Compagnie Commerciale Sangha-Oubangui [*Sangha-Oubangui Trading Co.*] [*Congo*]
CCS ofSA ... Critical Care Society of Southern Africa   (AA)
CCSP......... Coca Cola South Pacific [*Commercial firm*]
CCSPPU.... Comision Costarricense de Solidaridad con los Presos Politicos de Uruguay   (EAIO)
CCSQ........ Consultative Committee on Substantive Questions [*United Nations*]
CCSR......... Centre for Computer Security Research [*University of New South Wales, Australia*]
CCSS .... Caja Costarricense de Seguro Social [*Costa Rican Social Security Institute*]   (LA)
CCSS .... Chilean Computer Science Society   (EAIO)
CCSSA ...... Coalition of Children's Services in South Australia
CCSSA ...... Control and Command Systems Support Agency [*NATO*]   (NATG)
CCST .... Coordinating Committee on Science and Technology [*Australia*]
CCST .... Counseil des Caraibes pour la Science et la Technologie   (WGAO)
CCSU........ Captain Cook Study Unit [*American Topical Association*]   (EA)
CCSU........ Council of Civil Service Unions   (WGAO)
CCSV........ Comite Central Socialista Vasca [*Basque Socialist Central Committee*] [*Spanish*]   (WER)
CCSVI ...... Comite de Coordination du Service Volontaire International [*Coordinating Committee for International Voluntary Service - CCIVS*] [*Paris, France*]   (EA)
CCT .... CCI Comite Consultatif Transporteurs   (WGAO)
CCT .... Center of Culture "Time"   (EAIO)
Cct............. Centi-Stoc [*Centistoke*]

CCT .... Centrale Kranten en Tijdschriften Catalogus [*Van West-Vlaanderen*]
CCT .... Certificati di Credito del Tesoro [*Italy*]   (ECON)
CCT .... Chamber of Coal Traders   (WGAO)
CCT .... Christian Council of Tanzania   (AF)
CCT .... Church of Christ in Thailand
CCT .... Citty Taxi Aereo Nacional SA de CV [*Mexico*] [*ICAO designator*]   (FAAC)
CCT .... Club des Chiens de Tibet [*France*]   (EAIO)
CCT .... Combat Control Team [*Australia*]
CCT .... Comision Centroamericana de Telecomunicaciones   (LAA)
CCT .... Comissao Coordenadora de Trabalhadores [*Workers' Coordinating Commission*] [*Portuguese*]   (WER)
CCT .... Comite Consultatif de Thermemotrie   (WGAO)
CCT .... Comite Contre la Torture [*Committee Against Torture - CAT*] [*Switzerland*]   (EAIO)
CCT .... Comite de Coordination des Telecommunications [*Coordinating Committee for Communications*] [*NATO*] [*France*]   (NATG)
CCT .... Commission Centrale Technique [*Tunisia*]
CCT .... Compagnie Cherifienne de Transit
CCT .... Compagnie de Circulation et des Transports
CCT .... Compulsory Competitive Tendering [*Australia*]
CCT .... Confederacion Centroamericana de Trabajadores [*Central American Workers Confederation*] [*Costa Rica*]   (LA)
CCT .... Confederacion Costarricense del Trabajo   (WGAO)
CCT .... Confederacion Cristiana de Trabajadores [*Christian Confederation of Workers*] [*Paraguay*]   (LA)
CCT .... Confrerie des Chevaliers du Tastevin [*France*]   (EAIO)
CCT .... Consejo Centroamericana de Turismo   (WGAO)
CCT .... Consumer Claims Tribunal [*New South Wales, Australia*]
CCT .... Coordinated Caribbean Transport [*US shipping line*]   (IMH)
CCT .... Crimes Compensation Tribunal [*Victoria*] [*Australia*]
CCTA........ Central Computer and Telecommunications Agency   (WGAO)
CCTA........ Centrale Chemisch-Technische Afdeling [*Indonesia*]   (WGAO)
CCTA........ Centre de Controle Tactique Aerien [*Air Tactical Control Center*] [*NATO*]   (NATG)
CCTA........ Comision de Coordinacion de Tecnologia Andina [*Peru*]   (WGAO)
CCTA........ Commission de Cooperation Technique en Afrique [*Commission for Technical Cooperation in Africa*]
CCTAFE.... Canberra College of Technical and Further Education [*Australia*]   (ADA)
CCTAN ..... Confederacion de Campesinos y Trabajadores Agricolas de Nicaragua [*Nicaragua*]   (DSCA)
CCTC........ Centro Cultural de Trabajadores del Callao [*Workers Cultural Center of Callao*] [*Peru*]   (LA)
CCTD .... Catholic Council of Thailand for Development   (WGAO)
CCTD .... Confederacion Costarricense de Trabajadores Democraticos [*Costa Rican Confederation of Democratic Workers*]   (LA)
C/Cte .... Cuenta Corriente [*Current Account*] [*Business term*] [*Spanish*]
CCTEM..... Consejo Coordinador de Trabajadores Estatales y Municipales [*El Salvador*]   (WGAO)
CCTI......... Centre Commun de Traitement de l'Information [*French*]   (ADPT)
CCTI......... Centro Cooperativo Tecnico Industrial [*Tegucigalpa, Honduras*]   (LAA)
CCTI......... Centro de Cooperacion Tecnica Industrial [*Managua, Nicaragua*]   (LAA)
CCTKB...... Centrale Chretienne des Travailleurs du Textile et du Vetement de Belgique [*EAIO*]
CCTP........ Compagnie de Construction et de Travaux Publics
CCTP........ Coordination Committee for Transport Planning [*NATO*]   (NATG)
CCTSC ...... China Computer Technical Service Corp.   (PDAA)
CCTT........ Congres des Chefs Traditionnels du Togo
CCTU .... Central Council of Trade Unions [*Bulgaria*]
CCTU .... Congolese Confederation of Trade Unions   (EAIO)
CCTV........ China Central Television [*The national Chinese network*]
CCU .... Calcutta [*India*] [*Airport symbol*]   (OAG)
CCU .... Caribbean Consumers Union [*Antigua-Barbuda*]   (EAIO)
CCU .... Centro Cooperativista Uruguayo [*Uruguay*]   (DSCA)
CCU .... Centro de Calculos Universitario [*University Computer Center*] [*Cuba*]   (LA)
CCU .... Comision para la Carga Unitaria [*Container Cargo Committee*] [*Cuba*]   (LA)
CCU .... Communication Credit Union [*Australia*]
CCU .... Croatian Catholic Union [*Hrvatski Katolicki Savez*]   (YU)
CCUA .... Catholic Central Union of America   (WGAO)
CCUC .... Camara Chilena Norteamericana de Comercio, AG [*Chilean-North American Chamber of Commerce*]   (EAIO)
CCULES ... Comite de Coordinacion y Unificacion de las Luchas Estudiantiles Secundarias [*Committee to Coordinate the Struggles of Secondary School Students*] [*Peru*]   (LA)
CCUMES.. Comite Coordinador y Unificador del Movimiento Estudiantil Secundario [*Committee to Coordinate and Unify the Secondary School Student Movement*] [*Peru*]   (LA)

CCUML..... Comite Comunista Unificado Marxista-Leninista [*Peru*] [*Political party*]   (EY)
CCUP .... Commission Consultative Universitaire de Pedagogie [*Belgium*]
CCV .... Canada Club of Victoria [*Australia*]
CCV .... Christelijke Centrale der Vervoerarbeiders [*Benelux*]   (BAS)
CCV .... Coal Corp. of Victoria [*Research center*] [*Australia*]   (EAS)
CCV .... Coal Corporation of Victoria [*Australia*] [*Commercial firm*]
CCV .... Cotonniere du Cap Vert [*Senegal*]   (WGAO)
CCV .... Craft Council of Victoria [*Australia*]
CCV .... Craig Cove [*Vanuatu*] [*Airport symbol*]   (OAG)
CCV .... Societe Cotonniere du Cap-Vert
CCVAR..... Chrui Changvar [*Cambodia*]   (CL)
CCVD .... Christelijke Centrale Voeding en Diensten [*Belgium*]   (EAIO)
CCVM ...... Centrale Commissie voor Melk Hygiene   (WGAO)
CCVRP...... Caisse de Compensation de la Securite et des Allocations Familiales des Voyageurs et Representants de Commerce [*France*]   (FLAF)
CCVV........ Clarissimi Viri [*Illustrious Men*] [*Latin*]   (BARN)
CCW .... Caribbean Church Woman   (WGAO)
CCW .... International Committee on Chemical Warfare   (WGAO)
CCWA .... Climbers' Club of Western Australia
CCWA .... Conference of Churches of Western Australia [*Australia*]
CCWA .... Crafts Council of Western Australia
CCWB....... Commission Consultative des Barreaux de la Communaute Europeenne   (WGAO)
CCWC .... Cambodian Community Welfare Centre [*Australia*]
CCWC .... Catholic Child Welfare Council   (WGAO)
CCWM ..... Congregational Council for World Missions
CCWT ...... Chama Cha Wapangaji Tanzania   (EAIO)
CCWU ...... Clerical and Commercial Workers Union [*Guyana*]   (LA)
CCX .... Caceres [*Brazil*] [*Airport symbol*]   (OAG)
CCX .... Indian Ocean Airlines [*Australia*] [*ICAO designator*]   (FAAC)
CCYL........ Chinese Communist Youth League
CCZ .... Christian Council of Zambia
CCZ .... Chub Cay [*Bahamas*] [*Airport symbol*]   (OAG)
c cz............. Ciezar Czasteczkowy [*Molecular Mass*] [*Poland*]
cd............... Caddesi [*Avenue, Street*] [*C, Cad*] [*See also*]   (TU)
Cd.............. Cadmio [*Cadmium*] [*Chemical element*] [*Portuguese*]
CD.............. Cambio Democratico [*Democratic Change*] [*Spanish*]   (WER)
CD.............. Census Collection District [*Australia*]
CD.............. Centre Democratique [*Democratic Center*] [*Later, Center of Social Democrats*] [*France*] [*Political party*]   (PPE)
CD.............. Centrum-Demokraterne [*Center Democrats*] [*Denmark*] [*Political party*]   (PPE)
CD.............. Centrum Demokratyczne   (WGAO)
CD.............. Ceskoslovenske Doly, Narodni Podnik [*Czechoslovak Mines, National Enterprise*]   (CZ)
CD.............. Cevljarska Delavnica [*Shoemaker's Shop*]   (YU)
CD.............. Christian Democrats [*European political movement*]   (ECON)
cd.............. Ciag Dalszy [*Continued*] [*Poland*]
CD.............. Classification Decimale [*Benelux*]   (BAS)
CD.............. Claude Dornier [*German aircraft designer, 1884-1969*]
CD.............. Clearance Diver [*Royal Australian Navy*]
CD.............. Club Delahaye [*An association*] [*France*]   (EAIO)
CD.............. Club Deportivo [*Sports Club*] [*Spanish*]
CD.............. Coalicion del Centro Democratico [*Nicaragua*] [*Political party*]   (EY)
CD.............. Coalicion Democratica [*Democratic Coalition*] [*Spain*] [*Political party*]   (PPE)
CD.............. Commission du Danube [*Danube Commission - DC*]   (EAIO)
CD.............. Conseil de Direction [*Algeria*]
CD.............. Consigliere Delegato [*Managing Director*] [*Italian*]
CD.............. Convergencia Democratica [*Democratic Convergence*] [*El Salvador*] [*Political party*]   (EY)
CD.............. Cooperation et Developpement, Paris
CD.............. Coordinacion Democratica [*Democratic Coordination*] [*Spain*] [*Political party*]   (PPE)
CD.............. Coordinadora Democratica [*Democratic Coordinating Board*] [*Nicaragua*]   (PPW)
CD.............. Corpo Diplomatico [*Diplomatic Corps*] [*Portuguese*]
CD.............. Corpo Diplomatico [*Diplomatic Corps*] [*Italian*]
CD.............. Corps Diplomatik [*Diplomatic Corps*]   (IN)
CD.............. Corps Diplomatique [*Diplomatic Corps*] [*French*]
CD.............. Croisement a Droite [*Knitting*] [*French*]
CD.............. Cultuurtechnische Dienst   (WGAO)
CD.............. Department of Productivity [*Government Aircraft Factory*] [*Australia*] [*ICAO aircraft manufacturer identifier*]   (ICAO)
cd............... Kandela [*Candela*] [*Poland*]
CD.............. Societe Claud Delmotte & Cie.
CDA .... Capital Development Authority
CDA .... Catholic Daughters of Australia   (ADA)
CDA .... Cattle Development Authority [*Solomon Islands*]   (WGAO)
CDA .... Centro de Defesa Amazonia [*Brazil*]   (WGAO)
CDA .... Centro de Documentacao Agraria [*Mozambique*]   (WGAO)
CDA .... Centro di Documentazione Alpina [*Italian*]   (SLS)
CDA .... Centro per la Documentazione Automatica [*Italian*]   (SLS)

CDA .... Chemists Defence Association (WGAO)
CDA .... Child Disability Allowance [*Australia*]
CDA .... Christen Democratisch Appel [*Christian Democratic Appeal*] [*Netherlands*] [*Political party*] (PPW)
CDA .... Christian Democratic Action [*Namibia*]
CDA .... Christian Democratic Action for Social Justice [*Namibia*] [*Political party*] (EY)
CDA .... Civic Democratic Alliance [*Former Czechoslovakia*] [*Political party*] (EY)
CDA .... Combined Disabilities Association [*Jamaica*] (EAIO)
CDA .... Comision pro Derecho al Aborto [*Spain*] (EAIO)
CDA .... Compania Dominicana de Avaicion SA [*Dominican Republic*] (PDAA)
CDA .... Compania Dominicana de Aviacion (WGAO)
CDA .... Company Directors' Association of Australia
CDA .... Consultoria de Desenvolvimento e Administracao [*Rio De Janeiro, Brazil*] (LAA)
CDA .... Control Data Australia Proprietary Ltd. (ADA)
CDA .... Cooperative Development Agency (WGAO)
CdA .... Corpo d'Armata [*Army Corps*] [*Italian*]
CDA .... Corporacion Dominicana de Aviacion [*Dominican Aviation Corporation*] [*Airline Dominican Republic*]
CDA .... Croation Defense Association [*Political party*] (EE)
CDA .... Czechoslovak Diabetes Association (EAIO)
CDA .... Le Connaissance Direct Aller [*French*] (BAS)
CDA .... South African Copper Development Association (Pty) Ltd. (AA)
CDAA .... Cave Divers Association of Australia
CDAA .... Cellular Dealers Association of Australia
CDAA .... Churches Drought Action in Africa (WGAO)
CDAA .... Company Directors' Association of Australia
CDAB .... Compagnie de Developpement des Agro-Industries et des Biotechnologies [*Biotechnology investment company*] [*Belgium*]
CDAC .... Centre for the Development of Advanced Computing [*India*] (WGAO)
CDACH ..... Centro de Demostracion Agropecuaria "Chipiriri" [*Bolivia*] (DSCA)
CDACH ..... Centro de Demostraciones Agropecuarias de Chinoli [*Bolivia*] (DSCA)
CDACT ...... Centre for the Development of Advanced Computer Technology [*India*]
CDAE .... Centro de Desarrollo Agrario del Ebro [*Spain*] (DSCA)
CDAF .... Compagnie des Dirigeants d'Approvisionmement et Acheteurs de France (WGAO)
CDAG .... Confederacion Deportiva Autonoma de Guatemala [*Autonomous Athletic Confederation of Guatemala*] (LA)
CDAHS ..... Compagnie Diamantifere et Aurifere de la Haute-Sangha
CDAO .... Co-Operating Danish Amateur-Orchestras (EAIO)
CDAP .... Centre de Developpement pour l' Asie et le Pacifique (WGAO)
CDAP .... Centro para el Desarrollo de la Administracion [*Public Administration Development Center*] [*Guatemala*] (LA)
CDAS .... Canberra and District Aquarium Society [*Australia*]
CDAT .... Comite Directeur pour Amenagement du Territoire (WGAO)
CDB .... Cameroon Development Bank
CDB .... Canberra Development Board [*Australia*]
CDB .... Caribbean Development Bank [*St. Michael, Barbados*]
CDB .... Cattle Development Board
CDB .... Caves de Bordeaux
CDB .... Centro de Documentacion y Bibliografia. Universidad Industrial de Santander [*Bucaramanga*] (COL)
CDB .... Comite de Liaison des Producteurs de Bois Divers
CDB .... Commonwealth Development Bank [*Australia*] (ADA)
CDB .... Compagnie de Benin [*Togo*] (WGAO)
CDB .... Compagnie du Benin [*Manufacturer of manioc flour and tapioca*] [*Togo*]
CDB .... Comptoirs de Bordeaux
CDB .... Cyprus Development Bank (GEA)
CDBA .... Commonwealth Development Bank of Australia
CDBL .... Cyprus Development Bank Limited
CDBR .... Campaign to Defend Black Rights [*Australia*]
CDBR .... Committee to Defend Black Rights [*Australia*]
CDC .... Cairo Demographic Center [*Egypt*]
CDC .... Caisse des Depots et Consignations [*Financial institution*] [*French*]
CDC .... Cameroon Development Corporation (AF)
CDC .... Caribbean Documentation Centre [*Port-Of-Spain, Trinidad and Tobago*]
CDC .... Centre de Detection et de Control [*French air defense command and control center*]
CDC .... Centro de Documentacao Cientifica [*Scientific Documentation Center*] [*Portugal*] (PDAA)
CDC .... China Development Corp. (WGAO)
CDC .... Church Development Commission [*Ethiopia*] (AF)
CDC .... Club Discomano Colombiano [*Colombia*] (COL)
CDC .... Colonial Development Corporation
CDC .... Coloured Development Corporation

CDC .... Comision de Documentacion Cientifica [*Argentina*] (WGAO)
CDC .... Commonwealth Development Corporation (ML)
CDC .... Compagnie des Compteurs (WGAO)
CDC .... Compagnie Generale des Produits Dubonnet, Cinzano, Byrrh
CDC .... Comunidad Democratica Centroamericana [*Central American Democratic Community*] (EAIO)
CDC .... Concertacion Democratica Cubana [*Political party*] (EY)
CDC .... Conselho de Desenvolvimento Comercial [*Government advisory body*] [*Brazil*] (EY)
CDC .... Constitution Drafting Committee [*Nigeria*]
CDC .... Convergencia Democratica de Catalunya [*Democratic Convergence of Catalonia*] [*Spain*] [*Political party*] (PPE)
CdC .... Corte dei Conti (WGAO)
CDC .... Croatian Democratic Community [*Political party*]
CDC .... Cyngor Defnyddwyr Cymru (WGAO)
CDCA .... Centre de Depouillement des Cliches Astronomiques [*Astronomical Plate Measuring Center*] [*Institut National d'Astronomie et de Geophysique*] [*Research center*] [*France*] (ERC)
CDCAS ...... Centrul de Documentare pentru Constructii, Arhitectura, si Sistematizare [*Documentation Center for Constructions, Architecture, and Systematization*] (RO)
CDCB .... Caisse des Depots et Consignations du Benin [*Depot and Storage Office of Benin*] (AF)
CDCC .... Caribbean Development and Cooperation Committee [*Economic Commission for Latin America*]
CDCC .... Comite de Desarrollo y Cooperacion del Caribe [*Committee for Development and Cooperation in the Caribbean*] (LA)
CDCC .... Conseil de la Cooperation Culturelle [*CCE*] (WGAO)
CDCC .... Conseil de la Cooperation Culturelle du Conseil de l'Europe [*Council for Cultural Cooperation of the Council of Europe*] [*France*] (EAIO)
CDCD .... Climate Data - Compact Disc [*Bureau of Meteorology*] [*Australia*]
CDCIN ...... Curriculum Development Centre Information Network [*Australia*]
CDCJ .... Comite Europeen de Cooperation Juridique [*CCE*] (WGAO)
CDCM .... Centrale Data Communicatie Machine
CDCN .... Commonwealth Development Corporation Nigeria
CDC-OCCE ... Commonwealth Defence Conference - Operational Clothing and Combat Equipment (EA)
CDCP .... Construction and Development Corporation of the Philippines (DS)
CDCT .... Centro de Documentacao Cientifica e Tecnica [*Scientific and Technical Documentation Center*] [*Portugal*] [*Information service or system*] (IID)
CDCTM .... Centro de Documentacion Cientifica y Tecnica de Mexico (WGAO)
CDCU .... Centro de Documentacao Cientifica Ultramarina [*Portugal*] (DSCA)
CDD .... Carrefour de Developpement [*African*]
CDD .... Centralny Dom Dziecka [*Central Children's Home*] [*Department store*] (POL)
CDD .... Come Dovevasi Dimostrare [*Which Was to Be Demonstrated*] [*Italian*]
CDD .... Committee in Defense of Democracy [*Guyana*] (LA)
CDD .... Comptoir Dahomeen de Distribution
CDDA .... Conseil Departemental de Development Agricole (WGAO)
CDDC .... Central District Development Committee
CDDC .... Comission de Documentacion Cientifica [*Argentina*] (WGAO)
CDDCA ..... Comite de Defense des Droits Culturels en Algerie
CDDH .... Comite Directeur pour les Droits de l'Homme [*CCE*] (WGAO)
CDDL .... Conference of Directors of Danube Lines [*Budapest, Hungary*] (EAIO)
CDDN .... Comite de Defensa de la Democracia en Nicaragua [*Committee for the Defense of Democracy in Nicaragua*] (LA)
CDDPH ..... Conselho de Defesa dos Direitos da Pessoa Humana [*Human Rights Defense Council*] [*Brazil*] (LA)
CDDPW .... Centrala Dostaw Drzewnych dla Przemyslu Weglowego [*Central Lumber Supply Office of the Coal Industry*] (POL)
CDdWC .... Cymdeithas Ddawns Werin Cymru [*Welsh Folk Dance Society*]
CDE .... Caledonia [*Panama*] [*Airport symbol*] (OAG)
c/de .... Casa De [*Care Of*] [*Spanish*]
CDE .... Centre de Documentation Economique [*CCIP*] (WGAO)
CDE .... Centre de Documentation et d'Etudes [*Bureau du President de la Republique, Service Presidentiel d'Etudes*] [*Zaire*]
CDE .... Centre for the Development of Entrepreneurs [*Australia*]
CDE .... Centro de Desarrollo de la Educacion
CDE .... Centrul de Documentare Energetica [*Center for Energy Documentation*] (RO)
CDE .... Chemical Defence Establishment [*MOD*] (WGAO)
CDE .... Club Dirigenti Esportazione (WGAO)
CDE .... Coal Development Establishment (WGAO)
CDE .... Comissao Democratica Eleitoral [*Democratic Electoral Committee*] [*Portugal*] [*Political party*] (PPE)
CDE .... Comitetul Democratic Evreiesc [*Jewish Democratic Committee*] (RO)

CDE .... Commission for Development and Exchange [*International Council of Scientific Unions*]
CDE .... Compagnie Dolisienne d'Entreprises
CDE .... Congo Diesel Electric
CDE .... Conselho de Desenvolvimento do Estado [*Brazil*]
CDE .... Conselho de Desenvolvimento Economico [*Economic Development Council*] [*Brasilia, Brazil*]   (LA)
CDE .... Consortium d'Entreprises
cde .... Corde [*With Bands*] [*Publishing*] [*French*]
CDE .... Corporacion Dominicana de Electricidad [*Dominican Republic*] (IMH)
CDE .... Croisement a Droite a l'Endroit [*Knitting*] [*French*]
CDE .... Croix des Evades [*Belgian military decoration*]
CDEA .... Centro de Dinamizacao e Esclarecimento da Armada [*Navy Dynamization and Enlightenment Center*] [*Portuguese*] (WER)
CDEA .... Comite Deportivo de los Ejercitos Amigos [*Friendly Armies Sports Committee*] [*Cuba*]   (LA)
C de C........ Carton de Colombia [*Colombia*]   (COL)
CDEC .... Centro di Documentazione Ebraica Contemporanea [*Italian*] (SLS)
C de C........ Cour de Cassation [*Highest Court of Appeals*] [*French*]
C deCASS ... Cour de Cassation [*Court of Appeal*] [*French*]
CDEET ...... Commonwealth Department of Employment, Education, and Training [*Australia*]
c de g .... Centre de Gravite [*Center of Gravity*] [*French*]
C de G .... Croix de Guerre [*French military decoration*]
CDEI........ Club des Exportateurs Ivoiriens
C de J .... Compania de Jesus [*Society of Jesus*] [*Jesuits*] [*Spanish*]
CDELI .... Centre de Documentation et d'Etude sur la Langue Internationale   (WGAO)
CDEM .... Civic Development Movement [*Sierra Leone*] [*Political party*] (EY)
CDEN .... Caisse de Developpement de l'Elevage du Nord
CdePA........ Club de Petanque d'Adelaide [*Australia*]
C de Pref .... Conseil de Prefecture [*France*]   (FLAF)
CDEPS ...... Centre Departemental d'Education Populaire et Sportive
CDERE...... Centre Departemental d'Etudes et de Recherches sur l'Environnement [*France*]
CDET........ Council for Dance Education and Training   (WGAO)
C d'Etat B .. Conseil d'Etat de Belgique [*Belgium*]   (BAS)
CDEU .... Christian Democratic European Union   (WGAO)
C de V .... Carte de Visite [*Visiting Card*] [*French*]
CDF .... Capital Development Fund [*United Nations*]
CDF .... Caribbean Development Facility   (LA)
CDF .... Catholic Development Fund [*Australia*]
CDF .... Centralni Devisni Fond [*Central Foreign Exchange Fund*] [*YU*]
CdF .... Charbonnages de France [*France*]
C d F........... Chemin de Fer [*Railway*] [*French*]   (MTD)
CDF .... Chief of Defence Forces [*Australia*]
CDF .... Community Development Foundation, Inc.
CDF .... Creative Development Fund [*Australia*]
CDFA........ Christian Dance Federation of Australia
CDFA........ Christian Dance Fellowship of Australia   (EAIO)
CDFAA..... Commission Dyers and Finishers' Association of Australia
CDFC........ Commonwealth Development Finance Company [*Australia*] (ADA)
CDFC........ Commonwealth Development Finance Corp.   (WGAO)
CDFM .... Committee of Direction of Fruit Marketing [*Queensland*] [*Australia*]
CDG.......... Caisse de Depot et de Gestion [*Morocco*]
CDG.......... Campaign for Democracy in Ghana [*Political party*]
CDG.......... Carl Duisberg-Gesellschaft   (WGAO)
CDG.......... Cellulose du Gabon
CDG.......... Centres Departementaux de Gestion
CdG........... Compagnia di Gesu [*Society of Jesus*] [*Italian*]
CDG.......... Council for Democratic Government [*Japan*]   (ECON)
CDG.......... Croix de Guerre [*French military decoration*]
CDG.......... Paris [*France*] Charles De Gaulle Airport [*Airport symbol*] (OAG)
CDGM .... Centro de Demostracion Ganadera "Magdalena" [*Bolivia*] (DSCA)
CDGS .... Conference des Directeurs de Gymnases Suisses   (EAIO)
CDGSA...... Centro de Demostracion Ganadera "Santa Ana" [*Bolivia*] (DSCA)
CDGSJ ...... Centro de Demostracion Ganadera "San Javier" [*Bolivia*] (DSCA)
CDH .... Center pour les Droits de l'Homme [*Center for Human Rights*] [*Switzerland*]   (EAIO)
CDH .... Centralvereinigung Deutscher Handelsvertreter- und Handelsmakler-Verbaende   (EY)
CDH .... Comite Dominicano de los Derechos Humanos [*Dominican Committee of Human Rights*]   (EAIO)
CDH .... Commonwealth Department of Health [*Australia*]
CDH .... Corte Interamericana Derechos Humanos   (WGAO)
CDH .... Cour Europeenne des Droits de l'Homme   (WGAO)

CDHAR..... Comites Departementaux de l'Habitat et de l'Amenagement Rural   (WGAO)
CDHC....... Canberra and District Home Care [*Australia*]
CDHES ..... Comision de Derechos Humanos de El Salvador [*Spain*]
CDHNRU ... Committee for the Defence of Human and National Rights in Ukraine [*Australia*]
CDHR....... Comite Departmental de l'Habitat Rural   (WGAO)
CDHRCA .. Commission for the Defense of Human Rights in Central America   (EA)
CDHS .... Canberra and District Historical Society [*Australia*]
CDHS .... CERN [*Conseil European pour la Recherche Nucleaire*]-Dortmund-Heidelberg-Saclay Collaboration
CDI .... Centraal Diergeneeskundig Instituut [*Central Veterinary Institute*] [*Netherlands*]   (ARC)
CDI .... Central za Dokumentaciju i Informacije   (WGAO)
CDI .... Centre de Diffusion de l'Innovation [*ANVAR*]   (WGAO)
CDI .... Centre de Documentation et d'Information [*Comite Interafricain d'Etudes Hydrauliques*] [*Burkina Faso*]
CDI .... Centre Economique Development Industriel Afrique, Caraibes, Pacifique Communaute   (WGAO)
CDI .... Centre pour le Developpement Industriel [*Centre for the Development of Industry*]   (EAIO)
CDI .... Centro de Desarrollo Industrial [*Programa de Tecnologias Rurales*] [*Honduras*]
CDI .... Centro de Desarrollo Infantil [*Child Development Center*] [*Nicaragua*]   (LA)
CDI .... Centro de Documentacao e Informacao [*Brazil*]   (WGAO)
CDI .... Centro de Documentacion y Informacion [*Centro Nacional de Productividad de Mexico*] [*Mexico*]
CDI .... Christian Democrat International   (EAIO)
CDI .... Comision de Derecho Internacional [*International Law Commission - ILC*] [*Spanish*]   (ASF)
CDI .... Comissao do Desenvolvimento Industrial [*Rio De Janeiro, Brazil*]   (LAA)
CDI .... Commission du Droit International [*United Nations*]
CDI .... Commission for Discipline Inspection [*China*]
CDI .... Conselho de Desenvolvimento Industrial [*Industrial Development Council*] [*Brasilia, Brazil*]   (LA)
CDI .... Cotton Development International   (WGAO)
CDIA .... Cosmetics and Detergent Industry Association [*Finland*] (EAIO)
CDICP .... Centrul de Documentare al Industriei Chimice si Petroliere [*Documentation Center for the Chemical and Petroleum Industry*]   (RO)
CDIE.......... Centre de Documentation, d'Etudes, et d'Information [*Documentation, Studies, and Information Center*] [*Algeria*]   (AF)
CDIEA...... Centre de Developpement Industriel pour les Etats Arabes [*Egypt*]   (WGAO)
CDIL.......... Centrul de Documentare pentru Industria Lemnului [*Documentation Center for the Wood Industry*]   (RO)
CDIN .... Comite pour la Defense des Interets Nationaux [*Committee for the Defense of National Interests*] [*Use CDNI Replaced by NMDF Laotian*]   (CL)
CDIP........ Community Development Infrastructure Program [*Australia*]
CDIS .... Consumer Drug Information Service [*Australia*]
CDIS .... Curriculum Development Institute of Singapore   (DS)
CDISA ...... Centre de Documentation et d'Information de la Societe des Africanistes   (WGAO)
CDIU .... Centrale Dienst voor de Inen Uitvoer [*Benelux*]   (BAS)
CDIU .... Central Import and Export Agency [*Netherlands*]   (IMH)
CDIUPA.... Centre de Documentation des Industries Utilisatrices des Produits Agricoles [*French*]
CDIUPA.... Centre de Documentation Internationale des Industries Utilisatrices de Produits Agricoles [*International Documentation Center for Industries Using Agricultural Products*] [*Database producer*] [*Information service or system*]   (IID)
CDIV .... Cum Dividendo [*With Dividend*] [*Stock exchange term*]   (ADA)
CDJ............ Comandos 18 de Julio [*18 July Commandos*] [*Spanish*]   (WER)
CDJ............ Conceicao Do Araguaia [*Brazil*] [*Airport symbol*]   (OAG)
CDJA........ Centralni dom Jugoslovenske Armije [*Central House of the Yugoslav Army*] [*YU*]
CDJA........ Cercle Departemental des Jeunes Agriculteurs   (WGAO)
CDJA........ Circulos Doctrinales Jose Antonio [*Jose Antonio Doctrinal Circles*] [*Spanish*]   (WER)
CDK .... Centralny Dom Ksiazki [*Central Publishing House*]   (POL)
CDK .... Centralny Dom Kultury [*Central House of Culture*]   (POL)
CdL .... Camera del Lavoro [*Chamber of Labor*] [*Italian*]   (WER)
CDL .... Centrala Drift Ledningen [*Central Power Operating Board*] [*Sweden*]   (PDAA)
CDL .... Centre for Distance Learning [*University of Central Queensland*] [*Australia*]
CDL .... Comissao para a Defesa de Liberdade [*Committee for Defense of Liberty*] [*Portuguese*]   (WER)
CDL .... Comite de Liaison des Industries de Metaux Non-Ferreux de la Communaute Europeenne   (WGAO)

CDL .... Computer Development Laboratory [*Fujitsu Ltd., Hitachi Ltd., and Mitsubishi Corp.*] [*Japan*]
CDL .... County and Democratic League [*Australia*]　(WGAO)
CDLDK ..... Comite Liaison des Kinesitherapeutes de la CEE　(WGAO)
CDLDM .... Comite de Defense des Libertes Democratiques au Mali [*Committee for the Defense of Democratic Liberties in Mali*] (PD)
CDLP......... Centre de Diffusion du Livre et de la Presse [*Center for Book and Press Dissemination*] [*French*]　(WER)
CDLP......... Christian Democratic Labour Party [*Grenada*] [*Political party*] (EY)
CDLR......... Committee for the Defense of Legitimate Rights [*Saudi Arabia*] (ECON)
CDLS......... Confederazione Democratica dei Lavoratori Sammarinesi [*Democratic Confederation of San Marino Workers*]
CDM .... Carga Aerea Dominicana [*Dominican Republic*] [*ICAO designator*]　(FAAC)
CDM......... Central de Documentare Medicala [*Romania*]　(WGAO)
CDM......... Centralny Dom Mlodziezy [*Central Youth House*]　(POL)
CDM......... Centre de Documentation de la Mecanique [*Documentation Center for Mechanics*] [*Technical Center for Mechanical Industries*] [*Information service or system*]　(IID)
CDM......... Centro Democratico de Macau [*Macao Democratic Center*] (PPW)
CDM......... Centrul de Documentare Medicala [*Medical Documentation Center*]　(RO)
CdM.......... Chant du Monde [*Record label*] [*France*]
CDM......... Christian Democratic Movement [*Former Czechoslovakia*] [*Political party*]　(EY)
CdM .... Chrysler de Mexico SA [*Chrysler Corp.*]
CDM......... Companhia de Desenvolvimento Mineiro [*Mozambique*]　(EY)
CDM......... Consolidated Diamond Mines (Proprietary) Ltd.　(AF)
CDM......... Convergencia Democrata de Mocambique [*Democratic Convergence of Mozambique*]　(AF)
CDM......... Corps Dokter Militer [*Army Medical Corps*]　(IN)
CDMA ...... Catholic Dutch Migrant Association [*Australia*]
CDMB ...... Corporacion de Defensa de la Meseta de Bucaramanga　(COL)
CDME ...... Compagnie de Distribution de Materiel Electrique [*France*] (ECON)
CDMI .... Centre de Documentation de Musique Internationale　(WGAO)
CDMSCS .. Committee for the Development and Management of Fisheries in the South China Sea [*Thailand*]　(EAIO)
CDMT ...... Centrale Democratique Martiniquaise des Travailleurs [*Martinique*]
CDN.......... Centro Dramatico Nacional　(WGAO)
CDN.......... Centro Dyarek-Nyumba [*Dyarek-Nyumba Center*] [*Publisher*] [*Spain*]
CDN.......... Certificat de Navigabilite [*Certificate of Airworthiness*] [*French*]
cdn.............. Ciag Dalszy Nastapi [*To Be Continued*] [*Poland*]
CDN.......... Comitato di Difesa Nazionale [*National Defense Committee*] [*Italian*]　(WER)
CDN.......... Commission de Defense Nationale [*National Defense Commission*]
CDN.......... Coordinadora Democratica Nicaraguense Ramiro Sacasa [*Nicaragua*] [*Political party*]　(EY)
CDN.......... To Be Continued [*Polish underground publishing house begun by author Czeslaw Bielecki*] [*Acronym represents Polish phrase*]
CDNI .... Committee for the Defense of National Interests [*Replaced by NMDF*] [*Laotian*]　(CL)
CDNL........ Conference of Directors of National Libraries [*Australia*]
CDNLAO .. Conference of Directors of National Libraries in Asia and Oceania [*Australia*]
CDO.......... Cargo Dor Ltd. [*Ghana*] [*ICAO designator*]　(FAAC)
CDO.......... Civil Defense Organization [*United Nations*]
CDOA........ Christian Democratic Organisation of America [*Venezuela*] (EAIO)
CDOIPS .... Central Dispatching Organization of the Interconnected Power Systems [*Former Czechoslovakia*]　(EAIO)
CDOPES ... Centralni Dispecerska Organizace Propojenych Energetickych Soustav [*Former Czechoslovakia*]　(EAIO)
CDOS .... Conseils Departementaux Olympiques et Sportifs
C-DOT....... Centre for Development of Telematics [*India*]
CDoT .... Centre for the Development Of Telematics [*India*]
CDP .... Centre Development of Peoples [*Netherlands*]　(EAIO)
CDP .... Centre pour Democratie et Progres [*Center for Democracy and Progress*] [*Later, Center of Social Democrats*] [*France*] [*Political party*]　(PPE)
CDP .... Christian Democratic Party [*Italy*] [*Political party*]
CDP .... Christian Democratic Party [*Jamaica*] [*Political party*]　(LA)
CDP .... Christian Democratic Party [*Namibia*] [*Political party*]　(AF)
CDP .... Christian Democrat Party [*Australia*] [*Political party*]
CDP .... Civic Democratic Party [*Former Czechoslovakia*] [*Political party*]　(EY)
CDP .... Club Democratie et Progres [*Democracy and Progress Club*] [*Senegal*]　(AF)

CDP .... Commercial Data Processing Proprietary Ltd. [*Australia*] (ADA)
CDP .... Committee of Directors of Polytechnics　(WGAO)
CDP .... Compagnie Camerounaise de Depots Petroliers
CDP .... Conselho de Desenvolvimento Politico [*Political Development Council*] [*Brazil*]　(LA)
CDP .... Construction and Development Corporation of the Philippines (GEA)
CDP .... Convention Democratic Party [*Liberia*] [*Political party*]　(EY)
CDP .... Coordinadora de Pobladores [*Guatemala*]　(WGAO)
CDP .... Croatian Democratic Party [*Political party*]　(EY)
CDPEC...... Commonwealth Dairy Produce Equalization Committee [*Australia*]　(ADA)
CDPH........ Centre de Developpement du Potenial Humain [*France*] (WGAO)
CDPI.......... Centro de Desarrollo y Productividad Industrial [*Panama*] (LAA)
CDPM .... Comissao para os Direitos do Povo Maubere [*Portugal*]　(EAIO)
CDPN .... Centrul de Documentare si Publicatii Nucleare [*Center for Nuclear Documentation and Publications*]　(RO)
CDPNRH .. Centar za Naucnu i Tehnicku Dokumentaciju i Produktivnost Narodna Republika Hrvatska [*Center for Scientific and Technical Documentation and Productivity of Croatia*] (YU)
CDPP......... Centrala de Desfacere a Produselor Petroliere [*Central for the Sale of Petroleum Products*]　(RO)
CDPP......... Christian Democratic People's Party [*Hungary*] [*Political party*] (EY)
CDPPP ...... Center for Development Planning, Projections, and Policies [*United Nations*]
CDPPP ...... Centre for Development Planning, Projections and Policies [*United Nations*]　(WGAO)
CDPSP ...... Centro de Demostracion y Produccion de Semillas de Papa [*Bolivia*]　(DSCA)
CDPT......... Centrul de Documentare si Propaganda Technica [*Romania*] (WGAO)
CDPT......... Centrul de Documentare si Publicatii Tehnice [*Center for Technical Publications and Documentation*]　(RO)
CDPT......... Conseil de Defense du Pacte de Tripoli [*North African*]
CDPT......... Council of the Disabled People of Thailand　(EAIO)
CDPV .... Council of Disabled Persons - Victoria [*Australia*]
CDQ.......... Croydon [*Australia*] [*Airport symbol*] [*Obsolete*]　(OAG)
CDR .... Career Development Review [*Australia*]
CdR........... Cassa di Risparmio [*Savings Bank*] [*Italian*]
CDR .... Center for Development Research [*Research center*] [*Denmark*] (IRC)
CDR .... Centre de Documentation Rurale　(WGAO)
CDR .... Centre for Development Research/Center for Udviklingsforskning [*Denmark*]　(WGAO)
CDR .... Centre for Documentation on Refugees [*UNHCR*] [*Information service or system*]　(IID)
CDR .... Comitato per la Difesa della Repubblica [*Committee for the Defense of the Republic*] [*San Marino*] [*Political party*] (PPW)
CDR .... Comite d'Action pour la Defense de la Republique [*Action Committee for the Defense of the Republic*] [*French*] (WER)
CDR .... Comite de Defensa de la Revolucion [*Committee for the Defense of the Revolution*] [*Cuba*]　(LA)
CDR .... Comite de Defense de la Revolution [*Committee for the Defense of the Revolution*] [*Congo*]　(AF)
CDR .... Comite de Defense de la Revolution [*Committee for the Defense of the Revolution*] [*Benin*]　(AF)
CDR .... Comite Directivo Regional [*Regional Directive Committee*] [*Nicaragua*]　(LA)
CDR .... Comites para a Defesa da Revolucao [*Committees for the Defense of the Revolution*] [*Portuguese*]　(WER)
CDR .... Comites para la Defensa de la Revolucion [*Committees for the Defense of the Revolution*] [*Peru*]　(LA)
CDR .... Comites pour la Defense de la Revolution [*Committees for the Defense of the Revolution*] [*Burkina Faso*]
CDR .... Commission des Reparations [*Reparation Commission*] [*France*]
CDR .... Committee for the Defence of the Revolution [*Ghana*]
CDR .... Committee for the Defense of the Revolution [*Cuba*]
CDR .... Conseil Democratique Revolutionnaire [*Democratic Revolutionary Council*] [*Chad*]　(PD)
CDRA .... Central Districts Racing Association [*Australia*]
CDRA .... Committee of Directors of Research Associations and Federation of Technology Centres [*Later,*]　(WGAO)
CDRC .... Canberra Drag Racers Club [*Australia*]
CDRC .... Curriculum Development and Research Centre
Cdr(D)....... Commander, Destroyer Flotilla
Cdr(E)........ Commander, Engineering [*Australia*]
Cdre .... Commodore　(EECI)
CDRI .... Central Drug Research Institute [*Council of Scientific and Industrial Research*] [*India*] [*Research center*]

CDRIA....... Centre de Developpement Rural Integre pour l'Afrique [*FAO*] (WGAO)
CDRL......... Canberra District Rugby League [*Australia*]
CDRM....... Comite Directeur pour les questions Regionales et Municipales [*CCE*] (WGAO)
CDRN....... Comite de Defense de la Race Negre
CDRO........ Comite de Desarrollo del Oriente [*Committee on Development of the East*] [*Peru*] (LA)
CDS .... Center for Development Studies [*Ghana*] (IRC)
CDS .... Central Department of Statistics [*Saudi Arabia*] (ME)
CDS .... Centre de Documentation Siderurgique (WGAO)
CDS .... Centre de Donnees Stellaires [*Stellar Data Center*] [*France*] [*Information service or system*] (IID)
CDS .... Centre des Democrates Sociaux [*Center of Social Democrats*] [*Reunion*] [*Political party*] (EY)
CDS .... Centre des Democrates Sociaux [*Center of Social Democrats*] [*Mayotte*] [*Political party*] (EY)
CDS .... Centre des Democrates Sociaux [*Center of Social Democrats*] [*France*] [*Political party*] (PPW)
CDS .... Centre for Development Studies [*Flinders University*] [*Australia*]
CDS .... Centre for Development Studies [*India*] [*Research center*] (IRC)
CDS .... Centro Democratico y Social [*Democratic and Social Center*] [*Spain*] [*Political party*] (PPE)
CDS .... Centrul de Documentare Sciintifica (WGAO)
CDS .... Ceskoslovenska Dermatovenerologicka Spolecnost [*Czechoslovak Dermatovenerological Society*] (EAIO)
CDS .... Chief Defence Scientist [*Australia*]
CDS .... Chief of Defence Staff
CDS .... Comite de Defensa Sandinista [*Sandinista Defense Committee*] [*Nicaragua*] (LA)
CDS .... Comite de Defense et de Securite [*Committee for Defense and Security*] [*Chad*] (AF)
CDS .... Community Development Service
CDS .... Community Development Support [*Australia*]
CDS .... Computergesteuertes Datendrucksystem [*German*] (ADPT)
CDS .... Conference des Directeurs des Ecoles Professionnelles et de Metier de la Suisse (WGAO)
CDS .... Conseil de Defense et de Securite
CdS .... Conseil de Securite [*United Nations (already exists in GUS II database)*] (FLAF)
CDS .... Conselho de Desenvolvimento Social [*Government advisory body*] [*Brazil*] (EY)
CDS .... Conserveries du Senegal
CDS .... Consiglio di Stato (WGAO)
CDS .... Partido do Centro Democratico Social [*Party of the Social Democratic Center*] [*Portugal*] [*Political party*] (PPE)
CDSA........ Centre for Development Studies and Activities [*India*] (EAIO)
CDSAA...... Centro di Documentazione Storica per l'Alto Adige [*Italian*] (SLS)
CDSAC...... Chief Defence Scientist's Advisory Committee [*Australia*]
CDSC......... Communicable Disease Surveillance Centre (WGAO)
CDSCE...... Centro di Documentazione e Studi sulle Comunita Europea (WGAO)
CDSH .... Centre de Documentation Sciences Humaines [*Documentation Center for Human Sciences*] [*France*] [*Information service or system*] (IID)
CDS/ISIS ... Computerized Documentation Service/Integrated Set of Information Systems [*UNESCO*] (IID)
CDSM .... Comite sur les Defis de la Societe Moderne [*OTAN*] (WGAO)
CDSM .... Committee on Dental and Surgical Materials [*DOH*] (WGAO)
CDSN .... Chinese Digital Seismograph Network
CDSN .... Comite European pour la Sauvegarde de la Nature et des Resources Naturelles [*CE*] (WGAO)
CDSO .... Commonwealth Defence Science Organisation [*Australia*]
CDSP......... China Democratic Socialist Party [*Political party*] (EY)
CDSP......... Comite Europeen de la Sante Publique (WGAO)
CDSP......... Compagnie de Dirigeants de Services du Personnel [*Belgium*] (WGAO)
CDSR......... Centre for Deafness Studies and Research [*Griffith University*] [*Research center*] [*Australia*]
CDSS......... Comision de Deportes de la Seccion Sindical [*Local Union Sports Committee*] [*Cuba*] (LA)
CDSSU...... Comites Departementaux du Sport Scolaire et Universitaire
CDST......... Centre de Documentation Scientifique et Technique [*Center for Scientific and Technical Documentation*] [*ICSU*] [*Research center*] [*French*] (IRC)
CDSUE...... Centro di Documentazione e Studi per l'Unione Europea (WGAO)
CDSVF ...... Comite de Defense Scientifique du Vin Francais (WGAO)
CDT .... Central Democratica de Trabajadores [*Democratic Workers' Center*] [*Chile*]
CDT .... Centralna Dyrekcja Teatrow [*Central Administration of Theatres*] (POL)
CDT .... Centralny Dom Towarowy [*Central Department Store*] (POL)
CDT .... Centrul de Documentatie Tehnica [*Center for Technical Documentation*] (RO)
CDT .... Clearance Diving Team [*Australia*]

CDT .... Comites de Defensa de los Trabajadores [*Committees for the Defense of Workers*] [*Nicaragua*] (LA)
Cdt .... Commandant [*Commander*] [*Military*] [*French*] (MTD)
CDT .... Confederacion Dominicana de Trabajadores [*Dominican Workers Confederation*] [*Dominican Republic*]
CDT .... Confederation Democratique du Travail [*Morroco*] (EY)
CdT .... Conseil de Tutelle [*United Nations (already exists in GUS II database)*] (FLAF)
CDTC .... Confederation Dahomeenne des Travailleurs Croyants [*Dahomean Confederation of Believing Workers*] [*Trade union Benin*]
CDTG .... Centrale Democratique des Travailleurs de la Guyane [*French Guiana*]
CDTI......... Centro para el Desarrollo Tecnologica y Industrial [*Spain*]
CDTI......... Centro para el Desarrollo Tecnologico e Industrial (WGAO)
CDTL......... Centralny Dom Teatrow Ludowych [*Central House of People's Theaters*] (POL)
CDTL......... Centralny Dom Tworczosci Ludowej [*Central House of People's Art*] (POL)
CDTN .... Centro de Desenvolvimento de Tecnologia Nuclear [*Nuclear Technology Development Center*] [*Brazil*] (LA)
CDTOF...... Centralna Dyrekcja Teatrow, Oper, i Filharmonii [*Central Administration of Theares, Opera Houses, and Philharmonic Orchestras*] (POL)
CDTPM..... Campaign for the Defence of the Turkish Peace Movement [*British*]
CDTT......... Comite para el Desarrollo Economico de Trinidad y Tobago [*Committee for Economic Development of Trinidad and Tobago*] (LAA)
CDU.......... Caribbean Democratic Union (WGAO)
CDU.......... Christelijk-Democratische Unie [*Christian Democratic Union*] [*Netherlands*] (PPE)
CDU.......... Christian Democratic Union [*Namibia*]
CDU.......... Christlich-Demokratische Union [*Christian Democratic Union*] [*Germany*] [*Political party*] (PPW)
CDU.......... Classification Decimale Universelle [*Universal Decimal Classification*]
CDU.......... Cocoa Development Unit
CDU.......... Coligacao Democratico Social [*Portugal*] [*Political party*] (ECED)
CDU.......... Coligacao Democratico Unitaria (WGAO)
CDU.......... Convergencia Democratica en Uruguay [*Democratic Convergence in Uruguay*] (PD)
CDU.......... Creative Development Unit [*Australian Film Commission*]
CDU.......... Croatian Democratic Union [*Political party*] (EY)
CDU-BH .... Croatian Democratic Union of Bosnia-Herzegovina [*Political party*] (EY)
CDUCE ..... Christian Democratic Union of Central Europe [*Former Czechoslovakia*] (EAIO)
CDU/CSU ... Christlich Demokratische Union/Christlich Soziale Union [*Christian Democratic Union/Christian Social Union*] [*Germany*] [*Political party*] (PPE)
C du G........ Commissaire du Gouvernement [*France*] (FLAF)
CDU-PAV ... Civic Democratic Party - Public Against Violence [*Former Czechoslovakia*] [*Political party*] (EY)
CDV .... Carte de Visite [*Visiting Card*] [*French*]
CDV .... Compagnie Delmas Vieljeux
CDV .... Council of Disabled Persons, Victoria [*Australia*]
CDVA .... Commission Droit et Vie des Affaires [*French*] (BAS)
CDVFGFC ... Commonwealth Dried Vine Fruits Grade Fixing Committee [*Australia*]
CDVM .... Centrale Data Verwerkende Machine
CDVM .... Club Dirigenti Vendite e Marketing (WGAO)
CDVPA...... Comite Departemental de la Vulgarisation et du Progres Agricole (WGAO)
CDVTPR ... Centre de Documentation du Verre Textile et des Plastiques Renforces [*Documentation Center of Glass Fiber and Reinforced Plastics*] [*France*] (PDAA)
CDW.......... Centrum Derde Wereld [*Center for Development Studies*] [*Research center*] [*Belgium*] (IRC)
CDW.......... Colonial Development and Welfare
CDWA ...... Colonial Development and Welfare Act
CDZ.......... Ceskoslovenske Drevarske Zavody, Narodni Podnik [*Czechoslovak Lumber Industries, National Enterprise*] (CZ)
CE .... Avions Mudry & Cie. [*France*] [*ICAO aircraft manufacturer identifier*] (ICAO)
CE .... Carnuntum Excavations [*Austria*] (EAIO)
CE .... Caserta [*Car registration plates*] [*Italian*]
CE .... Centar Eksplosije [*Center of Explosion*] (YU)
Ce .... Cerio [*Chemical element*] [*Portuguese*]
CE .... Comercio Exterior, Mexico
CE .... Comitato Esecutivo [*Executive Committee*] [*Italian*]
CE .... Comite Executive [*Executive Committee*] [*Malagasy*] (AF)
CE .... Communaute EURAIL [*EURAIL Community*] [*An association*] [*Netherlands*] (EAIO)

CE .... Communaute Europeenne [*European Community*] [*Use EC*] (AF)
CE .... Communidades Europeas [*European Communities*] [*Use EC*] (LA)
Ce .... Compagnie [*Company*] [*French*]
CE .... Complexe d'Emballages [*Algeria*]
CE .... Conductive Education [*Australia*]
CE .... Congress of Estonia (EAIO)
CE .... Connaissances Economiques (FLAF)
CE .... Conseil de l'Entente [*Entente Council - EC*] (EAIO)
CE .... Conseil de l'Europe [*Council of Europe*] (FLAF)
CE .... Conseil d'Etat [*Council of State*] [*French*] (ILCA)
CE .... Council of Europe (NUCP)
CE .... Coupe Einspritz [*Coupe Fuel-Injection*] [*German*]
CE .... Cours Elementaire [*North African*]
CE .... Cukurova Elektrik [*Hydroelectric company*] [*Turkey*]
CE .... Electronic Frequency Counter (RU)
CE .... Estado do Ceara [*State of Ceara*] [*Brazil*]
CE .... Republic of Singapore Air Force [*ICAO designator*] (ICDA)
CEA .... Central Electricity Authority (WGAO)
CEA .... Centre d'Economique Alpine (WGAO)
CEA .... Centre de l'Etude de l'Azote (WGAO)
CEA .... Centre des Etudes Andines [*France*] (WGAO)
CEA .... Centre d'Etude de l'Azote Nitrogen Study Centre [*Switzerland*] (DSCA)
CEA .... Centre d'Etude et d'Arbitrage de Droit Europeen (FLAF)
CEA .... Centre Est Aeronautique (WGAO)
CEA .... Centre for Electronics in Agriculture [*University of New England*] [*Australia*]
CEA .... Centres d'Enseignement Agricole [*Algeria*]
CEA .... Centres d'Etudes Architecturales [*Belgium*] (WGAO)
CEA .... Centro de Ensenanza Agricola [*Mexico*] (DSCA)
CEA .... Centro de Estudios Agrarios [*Agrarian Studies Center*] [*Chile*] (LA)
CEA .... Centro de Estudios y Accion [*Action and Studies Center*] [*Argentina*] (LA)
CEA .... Centro de Estudos Agricolas [*Brazil*] (WGAO)
CEA .... Cercle d'Etudes Africain (WGAO)
CEA .... Chemistry Education Association [*Australia*]
CEA .... Cinematograph Exhibitors' Association [*Australia*]
CEA .... College d'Enseignement Agricole [*North African*]
CEA .... Combustion Engineering Association (WGAO)
CEA .... Comite Europeen des Assurances [*European Insurance Committee - EIC*] [*France*]
CEA .... Commissariat a l'Energie Atomique [*Atomic Energy Commission - AEC*] [*France*] [*Research center*]
CEA .... Commission de l'Energie Atomique [*United Nations*] (WGAO)
CEA .... Commission Economique (des Nations Unies) pour l'Afrique [*(United Nations) Economic Commission for Africa*] [*Use ECA*] (AF)
CEA .... Commission Economique pour l'Afrique [*Economic Commission for Africa - ECA*] (EAIO)
CEA .... Commissioner for Enterprise Agreements [*New South Wales*] [*Australia*]
CEA .... Commonwealth Education Association
CEA .... Communaute Est-Africain [*East African Community*] [*Use EAC*] (AF)
CEA .... Community Electoral Assistant [*Australia*]
CEA .... Compagnie d'Exploitation Automobile
CEA .... Compania Ecuatoriana de Aviacion [*Ecuadorean Aviation Company*] (LA)
CEA .... Computer Engineering Applications Proprietary Ltd. [*Australia*] (ADA)
CEA .... Confederacion de Educadores Americanos [*Confederation of Latin American Educators*] (LA)
CEA .... Confederacion de Empresarios de Andalucia [*Spain*] (EY)
CEA .... Confederacion Economica Argentina [*Argentina*] (DSCA)
CEA .... Confederation Europeenne de l'Agriculture [*European Confederation of Agriculture*] (EAIO)
CEA .... Consejo Empresario Argentino [*Argentine Business Council*] (LA)
CEA .... Consejo Estatal de Azucar [*State Sugar Council*] [*Dominican Sugar Corp. Dominican Republic*] [*Formerly,*] (LA)
CEA .... Consultores de Empresas Asociados [*Colombia*] (COL)
CEA .... Coordination des Animaux Europeen (WGAO)
CEA .... Corporacion Estatal del Azucar, Republica Dominicana [*State Sugar Corporation, Dominican Republic*] (LAA)
CEA .... Czechoslovak Economic Association (EAIO)
CEAA .... Centre Europeen d'Aviation Agrciole (WGAO)
CEAA .... Childbirth Education Association of Australia
CEAA .... West Africa Economic Community
CEAAC...... Catholic Education Aboriginal Advisory Committee [*Australia*]
CEAAL...... Consejo de Educacion de Adultos de America Latina [*Santiago, Chile*] (EAIO)
CEAB........ Crown Employees Appeal Board [*Australia*] (ADA)
CEABH ..... Centre Eurafricain de Biologie Humaine (WGAO)

CEABI ...... Centro de Especialistas de Analisis Biologicos [*Argentina*] (DSCA)
CEABRAS ... Comercio Exterior Agropecuario Ltd [*Brazil*] (DSCA)
CEAC........ Centro de Estudos de Antropologia Cultural [*Portugal*] (DSCA)
CEAC........ Civil Engineering Advisory Council [*South Africa*] (AA)
CEAC........ Colonial Economic Advisory Committee
CEAC........ Comision de Energia Atomica Cuba [*Cuba*] (EY)
CEAC........ Comissao Executiva de Assistencia a Cafeicultura [*Brazil*] (DSCA)
CEAC........ Commission Europeenne de l'Aviation Civile [*European Civil Aviation Conference - ECAC*] (EAIO)
CEAC........ Committee for European Airspace Coordination [*NATO*]
CEAC........ Compagnie d'Exploitation Automobile au Cameroun
CEAC........ Compagnie d'Exploitation d'Automobile et de Camions
CEAC........ Compagnie Euro-Africaine de Commerce
CEACRO... Comision de Energia Atomica de Costa Rica (WGAO)
CEACS ..... Centre for East Asian Cultural Studies [*Japan*] (WGAO)
CEAD .... Community, Environment, Art, and Design Project [*Australia Council*]
CEADO...... Centro Argentino de Datos Oceanograficos [*Argentina*] (MSC)
CEADS..... Central European Air Defense Sector
CEADS..... Centro de Educacion en Administracion de Salud [*Colorado*] (SLS)
CEADS..... Confederation Europeenne des Activities en Dechets Speciaux (WGAO)
CEAE........ Circulo Espanol de Amigos de Europa [*Spanish Circle of Friends of Europe*] (WER)
CEAEECT ... Chambre Europeenne Arbitres Extrajudicaires et des Experts Conseillers Techniques (WGAO)
CEAEN...... Centre d'Etudes pour les Applications de l'Energie Nucleaire (WGAO)
CEAEO...... Commission Economique pour l'Asie et l'Extreme-Orient [*Economic Commission for Asia and the Far East - ECAFE*] (CL)
CEAEX...... Comite Empresarial de Apoio as Exportacoes [*Export Promotion Business Committee*] [*Brazil*] (LA)
CEAF........ Comite Europeen des Associations de Fonderies (WGAO)
CEAF........ Publications du Comite des Etudes Historiques et Scientifiques de l'Afrique Occidentale Francaise
CEAGESP ... Companhia de Entrepostos e Armazens Gerais do Estado de Sao Paulo [*State of Sao Paulo General Warehouse and Supply Station Company*] [*Brazil*] (LA)
CEAGRI.... Conselho Estadual de Agricultura [*Brazil*]
CEAI........ Centre d'Etude et d'Action Internationales
CEAI........ Cercle d'Echanges Artistiques Internationaux (WGAO)
CEAIE....... Chinese Education Association for International Exchanges (EAIO)
CEAIO...... Comite Europeen de l'Association Internationale de l'Ozone [*European Committee of the International Ozone Association*] (EAIO)
CEAL........ Centro de Estudio de Accion Liberal [*Colombia*] (COL)
CEAL........ Comite Europe-Amerique Latine [*Belgium*]
CEAL........ Commission Economique pour l'Amerique Latin [*Chile*] (WGAO)
CEALDO... Comite de Expertos en Ajustes por Lugar de Destimo Oficial [*United Nations*] (WGAO)
CEALL ...... Consejo de Educacion de Adultos de America Latina (WGAO)
CEALM..... Comissao de Estudo do Aprovatomento do Letto do Mar [*Portuguese*] (MSC)
CEALSA.... Central Almacenadora Sociedad Anonima [*Guatemala*] (IMH)
CEAM .... Centre d'Experiences Aeriennes Militaires [*Military Air-Experimentation Center*] [*French*] (WER)
CEAM .... Certificat d'Etudes d'Administration Municipal [*Certificate in Municipal Administration*] [*French Guiana*] (LA)
CEAM .... Confederation des Employeurs et Artisans de Mauritanie
CEAMP..... Centrale d'Equipement Agricole et de Modernisation du Paysannat
CEAMSE .. Cinturon Ecologico del Area Metropolitana, Sociedad del Estado [*State Ecological Belt of the Metropolitan Area*] [*Argentina*] (LA)
CEAN .... Centre d'Etude d'Afrique Noire [*Center for the Study of Black Africa*] [*University of Bordeaux*] [*France*] (FLAF)
CEAN .... Centre d'Etudes pour les Applications de l'Energie Nucleaire [*Belgium*]
CEAN .... Centro de Estudios y Afirmaciones Nacionales [*National Reaffirmation and Studies Center*] [*Argentina*] (LA)
CEAO .... Commission Economique (des Nations Unies) pour l'Asie Occidentale [*United Nations Economic Commission for Western Asia - ECWA*] [*French*]
CEAO .... Commission Economique pour l'Asie Occidentale [*ONU*] (WGAO)
CEAO .... Communaute Economique de l'Afrique de l'Ouest [*West African Economic Community*] [*UDEAO*] [*Ouagadougou, Burkina Faso*] [*Formerly,*] (AF)
CEAO .... Comunidad Economica de Africa del Oeste [*West African Economic Community*] [*Spanish*]

CEAO .... Confederation des Etudiants d'Afrique Occidentale [*West African Students Confederation*] [*Use WASC*]   (AF)

CEAP .... Catholic Educational Association of the Philippines   (EAIO)

CEAP .... Certificat Elementaire d'Aptitude Pedagogique

CEAP .... Comite d'Entente et d'Action Politique [*Committee for Understanding and Political Action*]

CEAP .... Comite d'Etat d'Administration de la Province [*State Committee for Province Administration*] [*Benin*]   (AF)

CEAPE ...... Confederacion Espanola de Asociaciones Pesqueras [*Industrial association*] [*Spain*]   (EY)

CEARC ...... Computer Education and Applied Research Centre   (WGAO)

CEAS .... Central Economic Advisory Service [*South Africa*]

CEAS .... Centre Ecologique Albert Schweitzer [*Albert Schweitzer Ecological Centre*] [*Switzerland*]   (EAIO)

CEAS .... Centro de Estudios e Acao Social [*Brazil*]   (EAIO)

CEAS .... Centro de Estudos e Acao Social [*Brazil*]   (WGAO)

CEAS .... Centro Erboristico Appenninico Sperimentale   (WGAO)

CEAS .... Comissao Executiva de Armazens e Silos [*Rio De Janeiro, Brazil*]   (LAA)

CEAS .... Cooperative Educational Abstracting Service [*IBE*]   (WGAO)

CEAS .... Cukurova Elektrik Anonim Sirketi [*Cukurova Electric (Power) Corporation*]   (TU)

CEASA ...... Celulosas de Asturias Sociedad Anonima [*Spain*]

CEASA ...... Centro Estadual de Abastecimento Sociedade Anonima [*State Supplies Center, Incorporated*] [*Brazil*]   (LA)

CEASA ...... Commercial and Economic Advisory Service of Australia   (ADA)

CEASC ...... Committee for European Airspace Coordination [*NATO*]   (NATG)

CEASPECT ... Camera Europea degli Arbitri Stragiudiziali e dei Periti Esperti Consulenti Tecnici [*European Chamber of Extra-Judicial Adjudicators and Expert Technical Advisors*]   (EAIO)

CEAT .... Centre d'Essais Aeronautiques de Toulouse [*France*]

CEAT .... Centre d'Etudes Aerodynamiques de Toulouse   (WGAO)

CEAT .... Centre d'Etudes Aerodynamiques et Thermiques [*France*]   (PDAA)

CEAT .... Cycle d'Enseignement d'Agriculture Tropicale

CEATM ..... Comite Estatal de Abastecimiento Tecnico-Material [*State Committee for Technical and Material Supply*] [*Cuba*]   (LA)

Ceaux .... Faisceaux [*Pile (of arms)*] [*Used in commands*] [*French*]   (MTD)

CEAV .... Career Education Association of Victoria [*Australia*]

CEAV .... Centro de Ensino Audio-Visual

CEAVG ...... Comite d'Entr'aide et d'Assistance des Victimes de Guerre [*Committee for Welfare and Relief to War Victims*] [*Cambodia*]   (CL)

CEB .... Casa do Estudante do Brasil [*Student Housing of Brazil*]

CEB .... Cebu [*Philippines*] [*Airport symbol*]   (OAG)

CEB .... Central Electricity Board [*Mauritius*]   (AF)

CEB .... Club de l'Epagneul Breton [*France*]   (EAIO)

CEB .... Comite Electrotechnique Belge

CEBLS .... Comite Euro-International du Bruleurs   (WGAO)

CEB .... Comite European du Beton   (WGAO)

CEB .... Comite Europeen des Constructeurs de Broleurs [*European Committee of Manufacturers of Burners*]   (EA)

CEB .... Comite Europeen des Constructeurs de Bruleurs   (WGAO)

CEB .... Communaute Electrique Benin   (WGAO)

CEB .... Communaute Electrique du Benin [*Community Electric Co. of Benin*]

CEB .... Communaute Europeenne des Cuisiniers   (WGAO)

CEB .... Communidades Eclesiais de Base [*Brazil*]

CEB .... Compagnie Equatoriale des Bois

CEB .... Comunidades Eclesiales de Base [*Spanish*]

CEB .... Comunitatea Evreieasca din Bucuresti [*Bucharest Jewish Community*]   (RO)

CEB .... Confederation Europeenne de Billard   (WGAO)

CEB .... Conferences du Centre d'Etudes Bancaires [*French*]   (BAS)

CEB .... Conferencia Episcopal Boliviana [*Bolivian Episcopal Conference*]   (LA)

CEB .... Construction Engineers and Builders

CEB .... Counter-Espionage Bureau [*Australia*]   (ADA)

CEBA .... Comite Economique Belgo-Arabe   (WGAO)

CEBA .... Confederation Europeenne de Baseball Amateur [*European Amateur Baseball Confederation - EABC*]   (EA)

CEBAC ...... Centro de Edafologia y Biologia Aplicada del Cuarto [*Edaphology and Applied Biology Center, Cuarto*] [*Spanish*]   (ARC)

CEBAC ...... Comision Economica Brasileira-Argentina de Comercio [*Argentine-Brazilian Economic Commission on Trade*]   (LA)

CEBAC ...... Comision Especial Brasileno-Argentina de Coordinacion [*Special Brazilian-Argentine Coordination Commission*]   (LAA)

CEBAC ...... Comissao Especial Brasileira-Argentina de Coordenacao [*Special Brazilian-Argentine Coordination Commission*]   (LA)

CEBANOR ... Comite Regional d'Expansion Economique de la Basse-Normandie   (WGAO)

CEBAP ...... Centro de Estudios de Bosques Andimo-Patagonicos [*Argentina*]   (WGAO)

CEBAP ...... Centro de Estudios de Bosques Andino-Patagonicos [*Argentina*]   (DSCA)

CEBAS ...... Centre d'Etudes Biologiques des Animaux Sauvages [*Center for Biological Studies of Wild Animals*] [*French*]   (IRC)

CEBE .... Compagnie d'Exploitation des Bois Exotiques

CEBEA ...... Centre d'Etudes Burundais en Energies Alternatives [*Burundi Center for Studies on Alternative Energy*] [*Research center*]   (IRC)

CEBEA ...... Centre Emile Bernheim pour l'Etude des Affaires [*Belgium*]   (WGAO)

CEBEC ...... Conseil des Eglises Baptiste et Evangelique du Cameroun

CEBECO ... Nationale Cooperatieve Aan- en Verkoopvereniging voor Land-en Tuinbouw   (WGAO)

CEBECOR ... Centre Belge d'Etude de la Corrosion [*Belgium*]

CEBEDAIR ... Centrale Belge d'Etudes et de Documentation de l'Air   (WGAO)

CEBEDEAU ... Centre Belge d'Etude et de Documentation de l'Eau [*Belgian Center for Documentation and Water Research*] [*Research center*]   (IRC)

CeBeDeM ... Centre Belge de Documentation Musicale [*Belgian Center of Musical Documentation*]

CEBELA .... Centro Brasileiro de Estudos Latino-Americans   (WGAO)

CEBELCOR ... Centre Belge d'Etude de la Corrosion [*Belgian Center for the Study of Corrosion*] [*Nuclear energy*] [*Belgium*]   (NRCH)

CEBEMO ... Centrale Bemiddeling bij Medefinanciering Ontuikkelingsprogramma's [*Netherlands*]

CEBEMO ... Centrale voor Bemiddeling bij Medefinanciering van Ontwikkelingsprogramma's   (WGAO)

CEBEMO ... Katholieke Organisatie voor Mede Financiering van Ontwikkelings Programma's [*Catholic Organization for Joint Financing of Development Programmes*] [*Netherlands*]   (EAIO)

CEBERENA ... Centre Belge de Recherches Navales   (WGAO)

CEBES ...... Centre for European Business Education Studies   (WGAO)

CEBES ...... Centro Boliviano de Estudios Sociales [*Bolivian Social Studies Center*]   (LA)

CEBETID ... Comite Belge du Tissage et des Industries Textiles Diverses   (WGAO)

CEBEVITO ... Laduree & Cie., Entreprise de Beton Vibre Togolais

CEBF .... Centre d'Etudes Bancaires et Financieres [*French*]   (BAS)

CEBI .... Comite Europeen des Bureaux d'Ingenerie

CEBI .... Societe Forestiere Tanoh Affing Louis de Commercialisation et d'Exploitation desBois Ivoriens   (WGAO)

CEBIAE .... Centro Boliviano de Investigation y Acion Educativas   (WGAO)

Cebiloz .... Centralne Biuro Lozysk Tocznych "Cebiloz" [*Central Ball Bearings Office "Cebiloz"*]   (POL)

CEBITUR ... Centro Brasileiro de Informacao Turistica [*Brazil*]   (EY)

CEBJ .... Commission of Editors of Biochemical Journals   (WGAO)

CEBKN ...... Compagnie d'Exploitation des Bois du Kouilou Niari

CEBLANCO ... Cemento Blanco de Colombia SA [*Puerto Berrio*]   (COL)

CEBLS .... Council of EEC Builders of Large Ships   (WGAO)

CEBOSINE ... Centrale Bond van Scheepsbouwmeesters in Nederland   (WGAO)

CEBRACO ... Centro Brasileiro de Informacao do Cobre [*Brazil*]   (LAA)

CEBRAP ... Centro Brasileiro de Analise e Planejamento [*Brazilian Analysis and Planning Center*]   (LA)

CEBRECNA ... Centre Belge de Recherches Navales   (WGAO)

CEBS .... Centro de Estudios de Bosques Subtropicales [*Argentina*]   (DSCA)

CEBS .... Centro de Estudios del Bosque Subtropical, La Plata [*Argentina*]   (WGAO)

CEBS .... Church of England Boys' Society [*Australia*]   (ADA)

CEBS .... Commonwealth Experimental Building Station [*Australia*]   (ADA)

CEBs .... Comunidades Eclesiasticas de Base [*Ecclesiastic Base Communities*] [*Brazil*]   (LA)

CEBSO ...... Comite d'Expansion Economique Bordeaux Sud-Ouest   (WGAO)

CEBSP .... Centre d'Etude Belge de Publicite   (WGAO)

CEBST .... Church of England Boys' School in Tasmania [*Australia*]

CEBS(Tas) ... Church of England Boys' Society in Tasmania [*Australia*]

CEBTP ...... Centre Experimental de Recherches et d'Etudes du Batiment et des Travaux Publics [*Algeria*]

CEBUCO ... Centraal Bureau voor Courantenpubliciteit van de Ned Dagbladpers [*Central Advertising Bureau of the Netherlands Daily Press*]   (EY)

CEBUCO ... Centraal Bureau voor Courantenpubliciteit van de Nederlandse Dagbladpers   (WGAO)

CEBV .... Communaute Economique du Betail et de la Viande [*Economic Community for Livestock and Meat - ECLM*] [*Burkina Faso*]   (AF)

CEBWU ..... Central Electricity Board Workers Union [*Mauritius*]   (AF)

CEC .... Canberra Entertainment Centre [*Australia*]

CEC .... Canterbury Engineering Co. Ltd. [*New Zealand*]

CEC .... Caribbean Economic Community

CEC .... Caribbean Employers Confederation [*Trinidad and Tobago*] (EAIO)
CEC .... Caribbean Employers Conference (LA)
CEC .... Casa de Economii si Consemnatiuni [*Savings and Loan Bank*] [*Bucharest, Romania*] (RO)
CEC .... Catholic Education Council (WGAO)
CEC .... Catholic Enquiry Centre [*Australia*]
CEC .... Center for Educational Computing [*Japan*]
CEC .... Centrale Economische Commissie [*Benelux*] (BAS)
CEC .... Centrale Examen Commissie [*GO*] [*'s-Gravenhage*]
CEC .... Central Executive Committee [*Congress of South African Trade Unions*]
CEC .... Centre d'Etudes du Commerce (WGAO)
CEC .... Centre Europeen de la Culture [*European Cultural Centre - ECC*] (EAIO)
CEC .... Centre Extra-Coutumier
CEC .... Centre for Economic Cooperation [*United Nations*] (WGAO)
CEC .... Centro de Estudios Colombianos [*Colombian Studies Center*] (LA)
CEC .... Centro de Exportadores de Cereales [*Argentina*] (DSCA)
CEC .... Centro Oficial de Estudos Cientificos [*Brazil*] (DSCA)
CEC .... China Export Corporation (EG)
CEC .... Circulo Estudiantil de Comercio [*Business Students Club*] [*Panama*] (LA)
CEC .... Citizens Electoral Council [*Political party*] [*Australia*]
CEC .... Collectif Europeen de la Conscientisation (WGAO)
CEC .... Collectif Europeen de la Culture (WGAO)
CEC .... Commission Europeenne de la Corseterie [*European Corsetry Commission - ECC*] (EAIO)
CEC .... Commission Europeenne des Industries de la Corsetrie (WGAO)
CEC .... Commission of the European Communities [*See also CCE*] (EAIO)
CEC .... Commonwealth Economic Committee [*Australia*] (ADA)
CEC .... Commonwealth Education Conference [*Australia*] (ADA)
CEC .... Commonwealth Education Cooperation
CEC .... Commonwealth Employees Compensation [*Australia*]
CEC .... Commonwealth Engineers Council [*See also CAICB*] [*British*] (EAIO)
CEC .... Computer Embroidery Co. Ltd. [*Thailand*]
CEC .... Confederation Europeenne de l'Industrie de la Chaussure [*European Confederation of the Footwear Industry*] [*EC*] (ECED)
CEC .... Confederation Europeenne des Cadres [*European Confederation of Managers*] [*EC*] (ECED)
CEC .... Conference of European Churches (EA)
CEC .... Conseil Europeen de Coordination pour le Developpement des Essais de Performance des Combustibles et des Lubrifiants pour Moteurs [*Coordinating European Council for the Development of Performance Tests for Lubricants and Engine Fuels - CEC*] (EAIO)
CEC .... Conseil Europeen de l'Enseignement par Correspondence [*Belgium*] (SLS)
CEC .... Consejo Economico Centroamericano [*Central-American Economic Council*] (LAA)
CEC .... Consiglio Economica Corporativa
CEC .... Coordinacion Educativa Centroamericana (WGAO)
CEC .... Coordinating European Council for the Development of Performance Tests for Lubricants and Engine Fuels (EA)
CEC .... Cotton Export Corporation [*Pakistan*]
CEC .... Council for Education in the Commonwealth (EAIO)
CEC .... European Council for Education by Correspondence
CECA .... Carbonisation et Charbons Actifs
CECA .... Centro de Estudios Catolicos Argentinos [*Argentine Catholic Studies Center*] (LA)
CECA .... Cercle d'Epanouissement Corps et Ame [*An association*] (EAIO)
CECA .... Committee of European Coffee Associations (EAIO)
CECA .... Communaute Europeenne du Charbon et de l'Acier [*European Coal and Steel Community - ECSC*] [*French*]
CECA .... Compagnie d'Exploitations Commerciales Africaines
CECA .... Compagnie d'Exploitations de Carriere
CECA .... Comunidad Europea del Carbon y del Acero [*European Coal and Steel Community - ECSC*] [*Spanish*] (LA)
CECA .... Comunita Europea del Carbone e dell'Acciaio [*European Coal and Steel Community - ECSC*] [*Italian*] (WER)
CECA .... Confederacion Espanola de Cajas de Ahorro [*Spanish Confederation of Savings Banks*] (EY)
CECA .... Cyprus Employers Consultative Organization (WGAO)
CECACI .... Compagnie d'Explorations Commerciales et Automobiles en Cote-d'Ivoire
CECADE... Centro de Capitacion para el Desarrollo [*Mexico*] (WGAO)
CECAES.... Central das Cooperativas Agricolas do Espirito Santo [*Brazil*] (DSCA)
CECAF ...... Committee for the Eastern Central Atlantic Fisheries [*FAO*] (WGAO)
CECAF ...... Fishery Committee for the Eastern Central Atlantic [*FAO*] [*Senegal*] [*United Nations (already exists in GUS II database)*] (ASF)

CECAFA ... Confederation of East and Central African Football Associations
CECA-GADIS ... Compagnie d'Exploitations Commerciales Africaines - Societe Gabonaise de Distribution
CECAL ...... Comite Europeene de Cooperation avec l'Amerique Latine [*Paris*] [*French*] (LAA)
CECAL ...... Comite Europeo de Cooperacion con la America Latina [*Paris*] [*Spanish*] (LAA)
CECALGERIE ... Carbonisation et Charbon Actif d'Algerie
CECAPI..... Commission Europeenne des Constructeurs d'Appareillage Electrique d'Installations [*European Commission of Manufacturers of Electrical Installation Equipment*] (EAIO)
CECARA ... Centro de Capacitacion en Reforma Agraria [*Agrarian Reform Training Center*] [*Dominican Republic*] (LA)
CECAS ...... Conference of East and Central African States
CECAT...... Centre for Agricultural Education and Cooperation [*Italy*] (WGAO)
CECAT...... Centro dos Estudantes dos Cursos Agro-Tecnicos [*Brazil*] (DSCA)
CECAT...... Committee for the Eastern Central Atlantic
CECATI ... Centro de Capacitacion para el Trabajo Industrial (LAA)
CECAUF... Comptoir d'Echanges Commerciaux avec l'Union Francaise
CECAVI .... Confederation Europeenne des Categories Auxiliaires des Activites Viti-Vinicole [*European Confederation of Auxiliary Occupations in the Wine Trade*] [*Common Market*]
CECB........ Conseil Europeen du Cuir Brut [*France*] (DSCA)
CECC........ Cenelec Electronic Components Committee [*EEC*] (WGAO)
CECC........ CENELEC [*Comite Europeen de Normalisation Electrotechnique*] Electronic Components Committee (DS)
CECC........ Communaute Europeene des Cooperatives de Consummateurs (WGAO)
CECC........ Communaute Europeenne de Credit Communal (FLAF)
CECC........ Compagnie d'Elevage et de Cultures du Cameroun (WGAO)
CECC........ Comunita Europea di Credito Comunale [*Italy*] (DSCA)
CECC........ Coordinadora Educativa y Cultural Centroamericana [*Nicaragua*] (WGAO)
CECCAM ... Centro de Estudios para el Cambio del campo en Mexico [*A Mexican think tank which works on policies and training for growers*] (CROSS)
CECCB...... Chambres des Experts-Comptable et des Comptables de Belgique (WGAO)
CECCG...... Confederation Europeenne du Commerce de la Chaussure en Gros (WGAO)
CECD .... Confederation Europeenne du Commerce de Detail [*European Federation for Retail Trade*] (EAIO)
CECDC...... Committee on Economic Cooperation among Developing Countries [*United Nations*] (WGAO)
CECDV...... Centro de Estudio y Control del Desarrollo de la Vivienda [*Housing Development Study and Control Center*] [*Cuba*] (LA)
CECE......... Centre d'Etude et d'Exploitation des Calculateurs Electroniques [*Center for the Study and Use of Electronic Computers*] [*Belgium*] (PDAA)
CECE......... Comision Especial para Estudiar la Formulacion de Nuevas Medidas de Cooperacion Economica [*Special Committee to Study the Formulation of New Measures of Economic Cooperation*] [*Organizacion de Estados Americanos - OEA*] (LAA)
CECE......... Comision Especial para la Formulacion de Nuevas Medidas de Cooperacion Economica International (WGAO)
CECE......... Comite Estatal de Colaboracion Economica [*State Committee for Economic Cooperation*] [*Cuba*] (LA)
CECE......... Comite Europeen pour la Communication sur l'Environnement (WGAO)
CECE......... Committee for European Construction Equipment [*British*] (EAIO)
CECEC ...... China Electro-Ceramic Export Allied Corp.
CECEC ...... Communaute Europeene Culturelle des Etudiants en Chimie (WGAO)
CECED...... Conseil Europeen de la Construction Electrodomestique [*European Committee of Manufacturers of Electrical Domestic Equipment*] (EA)
CECF .... Chinese Export Commodities Fair
CECF .... Commission Europeenne des Communes Forestieres et Communes de Montagne (WGAO)
CECG .... Confederation Europeenne du Commerce de la Chaussure en Gros [*Belgium*] (WGAO)
CECG .... Consumers in the European Community Group
CECH .... Comite Europeen de la Culture du Houblon [*France*] (DSCA)
CECHA ..... Confederacion de Entidades de Comercio de Hidrocarburos y Afines [*Confederation of Retailers of Hydrocarbons and Related Products*] [*Argentina*] (LA)
CECHIL .... Celulosas de Chile SA [*Chile*] (DSCA)
CECI.......... Centre Europeen de Cooperation Internationale [*European Center for International Cooperation*] [*France*]

CECI .... Centre Europeen du Commerce International   (WGAO)
CECIC .... Comite Ejecutivo del Consejo Interamericano Cultural [*Executive Committee of the Inter-American Cultural Council*] [*Organizacion de Estados Americanos*]   (LAA)
CECIF .... Chambre Europeenne pour le Developpement du Commerce, de l'Industrie, et des Finances [*European Chamber for the Development of Trade, Industry, and Finances*] [*Brussels, Belgium*]   (EAIO)
CECIL .... Centro Esperantista Contro l'Imperialismo Linguistico [*Italian*]   (SLS)
CECIL .... Centro Europeo per il Coordinamento Istruzione Lavoro [*Italian*]   (SLS)
CECIL .... Comissao Estadual de Comercio e Industrializacao do Leite [*Brazil*]   (DSCA)
CECIMO ... Comite Europeen de Cooperation des Industries de la Machine Outil [*European Committee for Cooperation of the Machine Tool Industries*] [*EC*]   (ECED)
CECINE .... Centro de Ensino de Ciencias do Nordeste [*Brazil*]   (DSCA)
CECIOS .... Conseil Europeen du Comite International de l'Organisation Scientifique   (WGAO)
CECIP .... Comite Europeen des Constructeurs d'Instruments de Pesage [*European Committee of Weighing Instrument Manufacturers - ECWIM*]   (EAIO)
CECIRNA ... Centro de Coordinacion de Investigaciones de Recursos Naturales y su Aplicacion [*Universidad Nacional del Sur*] [*Argentina*]   (LAA)
CECITEM ... Centro de Educacion en Ciencia y Tecnologia del Mar de Mazatlan [*Mexico*]   (ASF)
CECLA ...... Comision Especial de Coordinacion Latinoamericana [*Special Latin American Coordinating Commission*]   (LA)
CECLANT ... French Commander-in-Chief, Atlantic [*NATO*]
CECLB ...... Comite European de Controle Laitier-Beurrier   (WGAO)
CECLES .... Conseil Europeen pour la Construction de Lanceures d'Engins Spatiaux [*European Council for the Construction of Spacecraft Launching Areas*] [*France*]
CECLES .... Conseil Europeen pour la Mise au Point et la Construction de Lanceurs d'Engins Spatiaux   (FLAF)
CECM .... Commission pour l'Etude de la Construction Metallique [*Commission for the Study of Metal Building*] [*Belgium*]   (PDAA)
CECM .... Convention Europeenne de la Construction Metallique [*EC*]   (ECED)
CECMA ..... Comite Europeen des Constructeurs de Materiel Aeraulique   (WGAO)
CECMA ..... Compagnie pour l'Exploitation de Centraux Mecanographiques en Afrique
CECMAS .. Centre d'Etudes des Communications de Masse   (WGAO)
CECMED ... French Commander-in-Chief, Mediterranean [*NATO*]
CECO .... Centro de Estudios Costeira e Oceanica   (MSC)
CECO .... Coordinadora de Euzkadi de Comisiones Obreras [*Basque Coordinating Staff of Workers Commissions*] [*Spanish*]   (WER)
CECOAAP ... Central de Cooperativas Agrarias de Produccion Azucarera del Peru [*Peruvian Central of Agrarian Sugar Production Cooperatives*]   (LA)
CECOAAP ... Peruvian Sugar Cooperatives Association   (WGAO)
CECOCO .. Chuo Boeki Goshi Kaisha [*Central Commercial Co.*] [*Japan*]   (WGAO)
CECOD ..... Comite de Fabricants Europeens d'Installations et de Distribution de Petrole [*Committee of European Manufacturers of Petroleum Measuring and Distributing Equipment*] [*EC*]   (ECED)
CECODE... Centre de Cooperation au Developpement [*Belgium*]   (WGAO)
CECODE... Centre Europeen du Commerce de Detail [*European Center of the Retail Trade*] [*Common Market*]
CECODEC ... Conseil Europeen des Constructeurs de Cuisine   (WGAO)
CECOF ...... Cabinet d'Entreprise Comptable et Fiscale
CECOF ...... European Committee of Industrial Furnace and Heating Equipment Associations [*EC*] [*Germany*]   (EAIO)
CECOJEF ... Cabinet d'Etudes Comptables, Juridiques, et Fiscales
CECOLDO ... Centro Colombiano de Datos Oceanograficos [*Colombia*]   (ASF)
CECOM .... Central European Mass Communication Research Documentation Centre [*Poland*]   (WGAO)
CECOMA ... Centre Commercial du Maroc Alimentation
CECOMA ... Confederation Europeenne des Commerces de Mobilier, Machines de Bureau et Accessoires   (WGAO)
CECOMAF ... Comite Europeen des Constructeurs de Materiel Frigorifique [*European Committee of Manufacturers of Refrigeration Equipment*]   (EAIO)
CECOME ... Centro par le Cooperazione Mediterranea
CECON ..... Comision Especial de Consulta y Negociacion [*Special Commission for Consultation and Negotiation*]   (LA)
CECONA .. Centrala de Contractari Achizitii [*Central for Contract Purchases*]   (RO)

CECONDEVI ... Centro de Estudio y Control del Desarrollo de la Vivienda [*Center for the Study and Control of Housing Development*] [*Cuba*]   (LA)
CECOP...... Comite Europeen des Cooperatives de Production et de Travail Associe [*European Committee of Workers' Cooperatives*] [*EC*]   (ECED)
CECOP...... Council of Engineering Consultants of the Philippines   (DS)
CECOPANE ... Centre de Commercialisation des Produits Agricoles du Nord-Est [*Marketing Center for Agricultural Products of the Northeast*] [*Zaire*]   (AF)
CECOPE ... Centro Coordinador de Proyectos Ecumenicos [*Promotes exchanges between Mexico, US, and Canada*]   (CROSS)
CECOPHIL ... Council of Engineering Consultants of the Philippines   (EAIO)
CECORA... Central de Cooperativas de la Reforma Agraria [*Agrarian Reform Cooperatives Headquarters*] [*Colombia*]   (LA)
CECORE... Centre de Commandements du Reseau [*French*]
CECOT..... Centro de Estudos e Consultas Tecnicas Lda.
CECOTEPE ... Centre de Cooperation Technique et Pedagogique [*Technical and Educational Cooperation Center*] [*Belgium*]   (ARC)
CECOTOS ... Comite Europeen de Coordination du Tourisme Social   (WGAO)
CECOTRAD ... Centrale d'Education et de Cooperation des Travailleurs pour le Developpement [*Rwanda*]   (EY)
CECOTRET ... Centre de Cooperation Technique et de Recherche de Suisse
CECP......... Club Egyptien de Chasse et de Peche
CECP......... European Communist Parties   (WER)
CECPA ...... Comite Europeen du Commerce des Produits Amylaces et Derives [*European Center for Trade in Starch Products and Derivatives*] [*Common Market*]
CECPI .... Commission Europeenne Consultative pour les Peches dans les Eaux Interieures [*European Inland Fisheries Advisory Commission - EIFAC*] [*French*]   (ASF)
CECPRA ... Centre d'Etudes de la Commission Permanente du Risque Atomique   (WGAO)
CECRA...... Comite Europeen du Commerce et de la Reparation Automobiles [*European Committee for Motor Trades and Repairs*] [*EC*]   (ECED)
CECRI .... Central Electrochemical Research Institute [*India*] [*Research center*]   (IRC)
CECS .... Centro de Estudios Cientificos de Santiago [*Santiago Center for Scientific Studies*] [*Chile*] [*Research center*]   (IRC)
CECS .... Communications-Electronics Coordinating Section [*NATO*]
CECSA ...... Compania de Electronica y Comunicaciones, Sociedad Anonima [*Spanish*]
CECSA ...... Compania Editorial Continental [*Mexico*]   (WGAO)
CECSFM... Commission d'Enquete et de Controle de la Situation Financiere et Materielle [*Commission for Investigation and Control of the Financial and Material Situation*] [*Chad*]   (AF)
CECT........ Comite Estatal de la Ciencia y Tecnologia [*State Committee for Science and Technology*] [*Cuba*]   (LA)
CECT........ Comite Europeen de la Chaudronnerie et Tuyauterie   (WGAO)
CECTAL ... Centre for English Cultural Tradition and Language   (WGAO)
CECTAL ... Centro para a Aplicacao da Ciencia e da Tecnologia ao Desenvolvimento da America Latina [*Center for the Application of Science and Technology to the Development of Latin America*] [*Brazil*]   (LA)
CECTK ...... Committee for Electro-Chemical Thermodynamics and Kinetics [*Belgium*]   (WGAO)
CECUA...... Confederation of European Computer Users Associations   (EAIO)
CECUA...... Conference of European Computer User Association   (WGAO)
CECUTIVOS ... Centro de Ejecutivos de Quito [*Ecuador*]   (LAA)
Ced .... Cedola [*Dividend, Interest*] [*Business term*] [*Italian*]
CED .... Ceduna [*Australia*] [*Airport symbol*]   (OAG)
CED .... Centre d'Etudes et de Documentation du Parti Social Chretien [*French*]   (BAS)
CED .... Centre Europeen de Documentation Internationale   (WGAO)
CED .... Centro de Encuentros y Dialogos [*Member of RMALC*]   (CROSS)
CED .... Centro de Esploro kaj Dokumentado pri la Monda Lingvo-Problemo [*Center for Research and Documentation on International Language Problems*]   (EAIO)
CED .... Centro de Estudiantes de Derecho [*Law Students Center*] [*Panama*]   (LA)
CED .... Comite para el Desarrollo Economico [*Argentina*]   (DSCA)
CED .... Communaute Europeenne de Defense [*European Defense Community*] [*French*]
CED .... Comunita Europea di Difesa [*European Defense Community*] [*Use EDC*] [*Italian*]   (WER)
CED .... Confederation Europeen de la Droguerie   (WGAO)
CED .... Conselho Estadual de Desenvolvimento [*Paraiba, Brazil*]   (LAA)
CED .... Corporation for Economic Development [*South Africa*]   (AF)
CED .... Council of Education of the Deaf [*Australia*]
CEDA .... Caisse d'Equipement pour le Developpement de l'Algerie [*Equipment Fund for the Development of Algeria*]   (AF)
CEDA .... Catering Equipment Distributors Association   (WGAO)

CEDA .... Central Dredging Association (EA)
CEDA .... Centre d'Edition et de Diffusion Africaines [*Ivory Coast*]
CEDA .... Centre d'Etudes et de Developpement du Cafe Arabusta
CEDA .... Centre for Economic Development and Administration [*Katmandu, Nepal*]
CEDA .... Centro de Desarrollo Agropecuario [*Center for Agricultural Development*] [*El Salvador*] (LA)
CEDA .... Committee for Economic Development of Australia [*Research center*] (IRC)
CEDA .... Confederacion Espanola de Derechas Autonomas [*Spanish Confederation of Autonomous Rightist Forces*] [*Political party*] (PPE)
CEDAC ...... Commissao de Estudos de Desenvolvimento da Aviacao Civil [*Study Commission for Civil Aviation Development*] (AF)
CEDADE ... Cercle Europeen des Amis de l'Europe (WGAO)
CEDADE ... Circulo Ecuatoriano de Amigos de Europa (WGAO)
CEDADE ... Circulo Espanol de Amigos de Europa [*Spanish Circle of Friends of Europe*] (PD)
CEDADEC ... Centre National de Developpement des Entreprises Cooperatives
CEDAF ...... Centre d'Etude et de Documentation Africaine [*Center for African Studies and Documentation*] [*Belgium*]
CEDAG ..... Centre d'Etudes et de Diffusion de l'Agriculture de Groupe [*France*] (DSCA)
CEDAG ..... Companhia Estadual de Aguas da Guanabara [*Guanabara State Water Company*] [*Brazil*] (LA)
CEDAL ...... Centro de Estudios Democraticos de America Latina [*San Jose, Costa Rica*] (LAA)
CEDAM .... Casa Editrice Dott. Antonio Milani (WGAO)
CEDAM .... Centre for Educational Development and Academic Methods [*Australian National University*]
CEDAMEL ... Centre d'Etudes et de Distribution des Appareils et du Materiel de l'Enseignement Linguistique (WGAO)
CEDAN ..... Conference Europeenne des Associations Nationales de Relations Publiques [*CERP*] (WGAO)
CEDAOM ... Centre d'Etudes et de Documentation sur l'Afrique et l'Outre-Mer [*Studies and Documentation Center for Africa and Overseas Areas*] [*French*] (AF)
CEDAP ...... Centro de Desarrollo de Administracion Publica [*Guatemala*] (DSCA)
CEDAP ...... Centro de Desarrollo de Administration Publica [*Guatemala*] (WGAO)
CEDAP ...... Comite Europeen d'Application et de Developpement des Relations Publiques [*CERP*] (WGAO)
CEDATOS ... Compania Ecuatoriana de Datos [*Ecuadorean Data Company*] (LA)
CEDAW .... Committee on the Elimination of Discrimination Against Women [*United Nations*]
CEDB .... Central Engineering and Design Bureau (WGAO)
CEDB .... Centre Europeen de Documentation du Batiment (FLAF)
CEDB .... Comissao Executiva de Defesa da Borracha [*Brazil*] (DSCA)
CEDC .... Central European Development Corp.
CEDC .... Centro de Estudos de Servico Social e Desenvolvimento Comunitario [*Portugal*] (DSCA)
CEDC .... Centro Europeo per la Diffusione della Cultura [*Italian*] (SLS)
CEDC .... Committe on Economic Cooperation among Developing Countries [*United Nations*] (WGAO)
CEDCA ...... Centre d'Etudes de Droit Compare Africain
CEDCA ...... Centro de Estudios Dirigidos de Ciencias Agropecuarias [*Supervised Studies Center for Agricultural and Animal Sciences*] [*Cuba*] (LA)
CEDDA ..... Centre for Experiment Design and Data Analysis [*NOAA*] (WGAO)
CEDDU ..... Centro de Estudios Demograficos y de Desarrollo Urbano [*Center for Demographic and Urban Development Studies*] [*Research center*] [*Mexico*] (IRC)
CEDE .... Centro de Desarrollo, Experimentacion, y Control Poligrafico [*Departamento de Informacion Cientifico-Tecnica*] [*Cuba*]
CEDE .... Centro de Estudios sobre Desarrollo Economico [*Columbia*] (WGAO)
CEDE .... Centro Europeo dell'Educazione [*European Center for Education*] [*Research center*] [*Italian*] (IRC)
CEDE .... Conseil Europeen du Droit de l'Environnement (ASF)
CEDE .... European Centre for Leisure and Education [*Czechoslovakia*] (WGAO)
CEDE .... European Council in Environmental Law (WGAO)
CEDEAO ... Communaute Economique des Etats de l'Afrique de l'Ouest [*Economic Community of West African States*] [*Use ECOWAS*] [*French*] (AF)
CEDEC ...... Confederacion Evangelica de Colombia (WGAO)
CEDEC ...... Coordenacao da Defesa Civil [*Civil Defense Administration*] [*Brazil*] (LA)
CEDECAL ... Compania Explotadora de Cal SA [*Guasca-Cundi*] (COL)
CEDECE ... Commission pour l'Etude des Communautes Europeennes (FLAF)
CEDED ...... Centro de Documentacion Educativa. Universidad de Antioquia [*Colombia*] (COL)

CEDEFOP ... Centre Europeen pour le Developpement de la Formation Professionnelle [*European Centre for the Development of Vocational Training*] (EAIO)
CEDEFOP ... Centro Europeo para el Desarrollo de la Formacion Profesional [*European Center for the Development of Vocational Training*] [*Spanish*]
CEDEFT ... Experimental Centre for the Development of Technical Training [*Mexico*] (WGAO)
CEDEGE ... Comision de Estudios para el Desarrollo de la Cuenca de Guayas [*Study Commission for the Development of the Guayas Basin*] [*Ecuador*] (LA)
CEDEI .... Confederacion Esnapola de Asociaciones de Electronica e Informatica (EY)
CEDEICO ... Centro de Especializacion Tecnica e Intensiva de Contabilidad [*Colombia*] (COL)
CEDEIN .... Centre Europeen de Documentation et d'Information (WGAO)
CEDEL ...... Centrale de Livraison de Valeurs Mobilieres
CEDELA ... Cercle pour le Developpement Economique et Social de la Prefecture de Lakota
CEDELCA ... Centrales Electricas del Cauca [*Electric Power Plants of Cauca*] [*Colorado*] (LA)
CEDEM ..... Centro de Estudios Demograficos [*Center for Demographic Studies*] [*Cuba*] (LA)
CEDEM ..... Centro de Estudios Estadisticos Matematicos [*Santiago, Chile*] (LAA)
CEDEN ..... Comite Evangelico de Desarrollo y Emergencia Nacional [*Evangelical Committee of Development and National Emergency*] [*Honduras*]
CEDEP ...... Centre Europeen d'Education Permanente [*French*] (SLS)
CEDEP ...... Centro de Desarrollo Popular [*Santiago, Chile*] (LAA)
CEDEP ...... Centro de Estudios para el Desarrollo y la Participacion [*Center for Studies of Development and Participation*] [*Peru*]
CEDEPAL ... Colombiana de Papeles Limitada [*Colombia*] (COL)
CEDEPLAR ... Centro de Desenvolvimento e Planejamento Regional, Belo Horizonte [*Brazil*] (WGAO)
CEDES ...... Centre d'Etude du Developpement Economique et Social [*Morocco*] (WGAO)
CEDES ...... Centre d'Etudes Demographiques et Sociales [*Center for Demographic and Social Studies*] [*Mauritania*] (IRC)
CEDES ...... Centro de Estudios de Estado y Sociedad, Buenos Aires [*Argentina*] (WGAO)
CEDES ...... Centro de Estudos de Educacao e Sociedade, Sao Paulo [*Brazil*] (WGAO)
CEDES ...... Centro Experimental de Estudios Superiores [*Venezuela*] (DSCA)
CEDES ...... Centros de Estudios para una Democracia Social [*Study Centers for a Social Democracy*] [*Argentina*] (LA)
CEDES ...... Corps Europeen de Developpement Economique et Social [*European Corps for Economic and Social Development*] [*Belgium*] (AF)
CEDESA ... Centre de Documentation Economique et Sociale Africaine [*African Economic and Social Documentation*] [*Belgium*]
CEDESA ... Centre de Documentation en Sciences Sociales de l'Afrique [*Belgium*] (WGAO)
CEDESA ... Comite de Sindicatos Autonomos [*Committee of Autonomous Unions*] [*Caracas, Venezuela*] (LAA)
CEDESCO ... Centro de Desarrollo Comunitario [*Chile*] (DSCA)
CEDESE .... Communaute Europeenne des Etudiants en Sciences Economiques
CEDETIM ... Centre d'Etudes Anti-Imperialistes [*France*]
CEDETIM ... Centre Socialiste de Documentation et d'Etudes sur les Problemes du Tiers-Monde [*North African*]
CEDETRAN ... Compania Especial de Transportes SA [*Colombia*] (COL)
CEDEV ...... Centre d'Etudes des Problemes des Pays en Developpement [*Center for the Study of Problems of Developing Countries*] [*Belgium*] (AF)
CEDEX ...... Centro de Estudios y Experimentacion [*Spain*]
CEDEX ...... Courrier d'Entreprise a Distribution Exceptionnelle [*French*]
CEDFPU ... Centro de Estudos de Defesa Fitossanitaria dos Produtos Ultramarinos [*Center for Pest Infestation Control of Tropical Stored Products*] [*Portuguese*] (ARC)
CEDH .... Commission Europeenne des Droits de l'Homme [*European Commission of Human Rights - ECHR*] (EA)
CEDH .... Convention Europeenne des Droits de l'Homme (WGAO)
CEDH .... Cour Europeenne des Droits de l'Homme (FLAF)
CEDI .... Centre Europeen de Documentation et d'Information (FLAF)
CEDI .... Centre Protestant d'Editions et de Diffusion [*Publisher*] [*Zaire*]
CEDI .... Centro Ecumenico de Documentacao e Informacao [*Ecumenical Center of Documents and Information*] [*Brazil*] (LA)
CEDI .... Centro Ecumenico de Documentacao, Sao Paulo [*Brazil*] (WGAO)
CEDI .... Confederation Europeenne des Independants [*European Confederation of the Self Employed*] [*EC Germany*] (ECED)
CEDIA .... Centre d'Etudes pour l'Extension des Debouches Industriels de l'Agriculture (WGAO)

CEDIA....... Centro de Estudio, Documentacion e Informacion de Africa [*Spain*] (WGAO)

CEDIA....... Centro Experimental de Investigaciones Amazonicas [*Colombia*] (DSCA)

CEDIAL.... Centro de Estudios para el Desarrollo e Integracion de America Latina

CEDIAS.... Centre d'Etudes, de Documentation, d'Information, et d'Action Sociales [*French*] (SLS)

CEDI-BVD... Confederation Europeen des Independants-Europaverband der Selbstandigen [*Germany*] (EAIO)

CEDIC....... Centro de Desarrollo Integral Canero [*Center for the Integral Development of the Sugar Industry*] (LA)

CEDIC....... Centro de Investigacion Industrial del Cuero [*Bogota, Colombia*] (LAA)

CEDIC....... Centro Ecuatoriano de Organizaciones Clasistas [*Ecuadorean Center for Class Organizations*] (LA)

CEDIC....... Centro Espanola de Informacion de Cobre [*Spanish Center for Information on Copper*] (PDAA)

CEDIC....... Comite Europeen des Ingenieurs-Conseils [*European Committee of Consulting Engineers*] [*EC*] (ECED)

CEDIC....... Comite Europeen des Ingenieurs-Conseils du Marche Commun (WGAO)

CEDICE.... Centre d'Education et d'Information pour la Communaute Europeenne (FLAF)

CEDICON... Centro de Diseno y Contruccion Ltda. [*Colombia*] (COL)

CEDIE....... Centro de Documentacion e Investigacion Educativa, Universidad Catolica Madre y Maestra [*Dominican Republic*] (WGAO)

CEDIE....... Centro de Documentacion e Investigacion Educativa, Universidad Catolica Madre y Maestra [*Dominican Republic*] (WGAO)

CEDIE....... Centro de Documentacion sobre Investigacion y Ensenanza Superior Agropecuaria [*Argentina*] (DSCA)

CEDIES..... Centre d'Etudes, de Documentations, et d'Informations Economiques et Sociales [*Morocco*] (SLS)

CEDIF....... Compagnie Europeenne pour le Developpement Industriel et Financier [*Belgium*] (WGAO)

CEDIGAZ... Centre International d'Information sur le Gaz Naturel et tous Hydrocarbures Ga zeux [*International Information Center on Natural Gas and Gaseous Hydrocarbons*] [*France*] (PDAA)

CEDIJ....... Centre d'Information Juridique (WGAO)

CEDIM...... Centre d'Etudes de Droit International Medical (FLAF)

CEDIM...... Comite d'Etudes pour le Developpement de l'Industrie Morutiere (WGAO)

CEDIM...... Comite Europeen des Federations Nationales de la Maroquinerie, Articles de Voyages, et Industries Connexes (EAIO)

CEDIM...... Compania Explotadora de Industrias Metalicas Ltda. [*Colombia*] (COL)

CEDIMAR... Centro de Documentacion e Informacion en Ciencias del Mar [*Colorado*] (ASF)

CEDIMES... Centre d'Etudes du Developpement International et des Mouvements Economiques et Sociaux (WGAO)

CEDIMEX... Societe Centrafricaine de Distribution-Importation-Exportation

CEDIMO... Centro Nacional de Documentacao e Informacao de Mocambique [*National Documentation and Information Center of Mozambique*]

CEDIMOM... Centre Europeen pour le Developpement Industriel et la Mise en Valeur de l'Outre-Mer [*European Center for Overseas Industrialization and Development*] (AF)

CEDIN...... Centre de Documentation et d'Information du Commerce Exterieur

CEDIN...... Centro de Documentacao e Informacao Technologica, Instituto Nacional da Propriedade Industrial [*Brazil*]

CEDINTEC... Centro para o Desenvolvimento e Inovacao Tecnologica [*Portugal*] (EY)

CEDIP....... Centro de Estudos de Dinamica Populaciona [*Brazil*] (WGAO)

CEDIPCA... Centro Dominicano de Investigacion Pecuaria con Cana de Azucar [*Dominican Center for Livestock Research with Sugarcane*] [*Dominican Republic*] (ARC)

CEDIS...... Conferenica Espanola de Institutos Secularos (WGAO)

CEDIT....... Centro Didattico Telefonico [*Telephone Teaching Center*] [*Italian*]

CEDIT....... Committee for Economic Development of Trinidad and Tobago [*Trinidad and Tobago*] (DSCA)

CEDITEC... Central de Divulgacion Tecnica [*Chile*] (DSCA)

CEDITEX... Centrale de Diffusion de Textile

CEDJ......... Centre d'Etude de la Delinquance Juvenile [*Belgium*] (BAS)

CEDLA...... Centre d'Etudes et de Documentation Legislatives Africaines [*African Legislative Studies and Documentation Center*] (AF)

CEDLA...... Centro de Estudios y Documentacion Latinoamericanos [*Netherlands*] (LAA)

CEDO........ Centre for Educational Development Overseas

CEDO........ Centro de Datos Oceanograficos [*Mexico*] (MSC)

CEDO........ Centro de Documentacion e Intercambio de Casos [*Universidad Escuela de Administracion y Finanzas y Tecnologias*] [*Colorado*]

CEDO........ Centro Espanol de Datos Oceanograficos [*Spanish*] (MSC)

CEDOADO... Centro de Documentacion Agropecuaria Dominicana [*Instituto Superior de Agricultura*] [*Dominican Republic*]

CEDOC..... Central Ecuatoriana de Organizaciones Clasistas [*Ecuadorean Central of Classist Organizations*] (LA)

CEDOC..... Centrale Dienst voor Onderwis- en Culturfilms (WGAO)

CEDOC..... Centre Belge de Documentation et d'Information de la Construction (WGAO)

CEDOC..... Centre de Documentation [*Documentation Center*] [*Gabon*] (AF)

CEDOC..... Centro de Documentacion Cientifica [*Argentina*] (WGAO)

CEDOC..... Confederacion Ecuatoriana de Obreros Catolicos [*Ecuadorean Confederation of Catholic Workers*] (LA)

CEDOC..... Confederacion Ecuatoriana de Organizaciones Clasistas (WGAO)

CEDOCAR... Centre de Documentation de l'Armement [*ICSU*]

CEDOCOS... Centre de Documentation sur les Combustibles Solides [*Belgium*] (WGAO)

CEDODEC... Centre d'Etudes et de Documentation sur le Developpement Culturel [*Research and Documentation Center for Cultural Development*] [*Tunisia*] (IRC)

CEDOH..... Centro de Documentacion de Honduras [*Honduras Documentation Center*] (EAIO)

CEDOINPRO... Centro de Documentacion e Informacion Tecnica, Instituto Venezolano de Productividad [*Venezuela*]

CEDOIT.... Centro de Documentacion e Informacion Tecnica [*Peru*] (DSCA)

Cedok......... Ceskoslovenska Dopravni Kancelar [*Czechoslovak Travel Bureau*] (CZ)

CEDOM.... Centre of Documentation and Teaching Materials [*Peru*] (WGAO)

CEDOM.... Centro de Documentacion [*Asociacion Latinoamericana de Instituciones Financieras de Desarrollo*] [*Peru*]

CEDOP...... Centro de Documentacion, Oficina de Planificacion Nacional y Politica Economica [*Costa Rica*]

CEDOPEX... Centro Dominicano de Promocion de Exportaciones [*Dominican Center for Export Development*] (LA)

CEDOPI.... Centre d'Etudes Documentaries de Propriete Industrielle (WGAO)

CEDOR..... Centre Demographique [*ONU*] (WGAO)

CEDOR..... Centrul Demografic ONU. Romania [*UN Demographic Center in Romania*] (RO)

CEDORES... Centre de Documentation et de Recherche Sociales [*Belgium*] (WGAO)

CEDOSA... Cultivos y Extraccion de Oleaginosas SA [*Ecuador*] (DSCA)

CEDP........ Centre d'Etudes et de Documentation Paleontologique (WGAO)

CEDP........ Centre Europeen du Diamant et des Pierres Precieuses (WGAO)

CEDP........ Community Employment Development Programme [*Philippines*]

CEDR........ Comite Europeen de Droit Rural [*France*]

CEDR........ Conference on Electron Device Research (WGAO)

CEDRASEMI... Centre de Documentation et de Recherches sur l'Asie du Sud-Est et le Monde Insulindien (WGAO)

CEDRE..... Centre d'Etudes de Documentation, de Recherches, et d'Experimentation [*French*] (MSC)

CEDRES... Centro di Documentazione e Ricerche Economiche e Sociali (WGAO)

CEDRI....... Comit Europeen pour la Defense des Refugies (WGAO)

CEDRIC.... Centre d'Etudes de Documentation et de Recherches pour l'Industrie du Chaufage, du Conditionnement d'Air et des Branches Connexes [*Center for Research Studies and Documentation on Heating and Air Conditioning*] [*Belgium*] (PDAA)

CEDRO..... Comite de Desarrollo del Oriente [*Committee on Development of the East*] [*Peru*] (LA)

CEDSA...... Centro de Documentation del Sector Agrario [*Peru*] (WGAO)

CEDT........ Comite Europeen du The [*European Tea Committee*] [*EC*] (ECED)

CEDT........ Confederation Europeenne des Detaillants en Tabac [*European Federation of Tobacco Retail Organizations*] (EAIO)

CEDTA...... Cia Ecuatoriana de Transportes Aereos [*Ecuador*] (EY)

CEDTA...... Compania Ecuatoriana de Transportes Aereos (WGAO)

CEDUCEE... Centre d'Etudes et de Documentation sur l'URSS, la Chine, et l'Europe de l'Est [*Center for Research and Documentation on the USSR, China, and Eastern Europe*] [*Research center*] [*France*] (IRC)

CEDUS...... Centre d'Etudes et de Documentation du Sucre [*France*]

CEDUS...... Centre d'Etudes et de Documentation pour L'Utilisation du Sucre (WGAO)

CEDVAR... Centre National d'Etudes, de Documentation, de Vulgarisation Technique de l'Artisanat Rural (WGAO)

CEDYS...... Centro de Estudios de Democracia y Sociedad [*Center for Democratic and Social Studies*] [*Peru*] (IRC)

CEE........... Caisses Enregistreuses Electroniques

CEE........... Central and Eastern Europe
CEE........... Centro de Ensino e Extensao [*Brazil*]   (DSCA)
CEE........... Centro de Estudios Ecumenicos [*Center for Ecumenical Studies*] [*Mexico*]   (EAIO)
CEE........... Centro de Estudios Educativos [*Center for Educational Studies*] [*Research center*] [*Mexico*]   (IRC)
CEE........... Centro de Estudios Entomologicos [*Chile*]   (DSCA)
CEE........... Centro de Estudios Estrategicos [*Center for Strategic Studies*] [*Mexico*]   (CROSS)
CEE........... Cercle Egyptien d'Escrime et de Tir
CEE........... Comite Estatal de Estadisticas [*State Committee for Statistics*] [*Cuba*]   (LA)
CEE........... Comite Europeen d'Enterprise [*CCE*]   (WGAO)
CEE........... Commission Economique pour l'Europe [*Economic Commission for Europe - ECE*] [*French*]
CEE........... Commission Internationale de Certification de Conformite de l'Equipement Electrique [*International Commission for Conformity Certification of Electrical Equipment*] [*French*]   (EA)
CEE........... Commission Internationale de Reglementation en veu de l'Approbation de l'Equipement Electrique [*International Commission on Rules for the Approval of Electrical Equipment*]   (PDAA)
CEE........... Communaute Economique Europeenne [*European Economic Community*]
CEE........... Comunidad Economica Europea [*European Economic Community - EEC*] [*Spanish*]   (LA)
CEE........... Comunita Economica Europea [*European Economic Community - EEC*] [*Italian*]   (WER)
CEE........... Comunitatea Economica Europeana [*European Economic Community - EEC*]   (RO)
CEE........... Conference des Eglises Europeennes   (WGAO)
CEE........... Corporacion de Empresas Estatales [*State Enterprise Corporation*] [*CORDE Dominican Republic*] [*See also*] (LA)
CEE........... Council for Environmental Education   (WGAO)
CEE........... International Commission for Conformity Certification of Electrical Equipment [*Netherlands*]   (SLS)
CEEA........ Centro de Estudios para Empresas Agricolas [*Chile*]   (LAA)
CEEA........ Centro de Estudos de Economia Agraria   (WGAO)
CEEA........ Comision Ecuatoriana de Energia Atomica [*Ecuadorean Atomic Energy Commission*] [*Research center*]   (LA)
CEEA........ Commissione Europea per l'Energia Atomica [*European Atomic Energy Commission*] [*Use EURATOM*] [*Italian*]   (WER)
CEEA........ Communaute Europeenne de l'Energie Atomique [*Nuclear energy*] [*French*]
CEEA........ Confederation of European Economic Asociations   (WGAO)
CEEA........ Conseil des Etudes Africaines en Europe   (WGAO)
CEEAC..... Communaute Economique des Etats de l'Afrique Centrale [*Economic Community of Central African States - ECCAS*] [*Bangui, Central African Republic*]   (EAIO)
CEEAS ...... Centre Europeen d'Etudes de l'Acide Sulfurique [*European Center for Studies of Sulfuric Acid*]   (EA)
CEEBA ...... Centre d'Etudes Ethnologiques de Bandundu [*Center for Ethnological Studies of Bandundu*] [*Zaire*]   (IRC)
CEEC......... Central and Eastern European Country   (ECON)
CEEC......... Comite Europeen des Economistes de la Construction [*European Committee of Construction Economists*]   (EA)
CEEC......... Comite Europeen pour l'Enseignement Catholique [*European Committee for Catholic Education*]   (EAIO)
CEEC........ Commission Episcopale pour l'Ecole Catholique [*Libya*]   (WGAO)
CEEC........ Construction Economics European Committee   (EAIO)
CEECO...... Comite d'Expansion Economique du Centre-Ouest   (WGAO)
CEECSN ... Comissao Especial de Estudo das Condicoes Sociais do Nordeste [*Special Commission for Studies of Social Conditions in the Northeast*] [*Brazil*]   (LA)
CEED........ Centro de Estudios Economicos y Demograficos [*Colegio de Mexico*] [*Mexico*]   (LAA)
CEEDI .... China Electronics Engineering Design Institute   (IRC)
CEEDIA .... Centre d'Etudes pour l'Extension des Debouches Industriels de l'Agriculture   (WGAO)
CEEE......... Centro de Estudios en Economia y Educacion [*Center for Studies in Economics and Education*] [*Mexico*]   (IRC)
CEEE......... Comissao Estadual Energia Electrica [*State Electric Power Commission*] [*Brazil*]   (LA)
CEEE......... Companhia Estadual de Energia Eletrica [*Brazil*]   (LAA)
CEEFA ...... Centre d'Etudes et d'Echanges Francophones en Australie [*Australia*]
CEEG........ Certificat d'Etudes Economiques Generales [*French*]
CEEGFP.... Centre d'Etudes d'Economie et de Gestion de la Foret Privee (WGAO)
CEEH .... Centre Europeen d'Ecologie Humaine [*Switzerland*]   (SLS)
CEEIM ...... Centre Europeen d'Etude et d'Information sur les Societes Multinationales [*Belgium*]   (SLS)

CEEMA..... Centre d'Experimentation et d'Enseignement du Machinisme Agricole, Division du Machinisme Agricole du Genie Rural [*Mali*]
CEEMA..... Centro de Ensenanza y Experimentacion de la Maquinaria Agricola [*Argentina*]   (LAA)
CEEMA..... Committee for Engineering Education of Middle Africa [*Nigeria*]   (WGAO)
CEEMA..... Conference Europeene des Experts Meteorologistes de l'Aeronautique   (WGAO)
CEEMAC.. Certification of Electrical Equipment for Mining, Advisory Council [*IISE*]   (WGAO)
CEEMAT .. Centre d'Etudes et d'Experimentation du Machinisme Agricole Tropical [*Center for the Study and Experimentation of Tropical Agriculture Machinery*] [*International Cooperation Center of Agricultural Research for Development*] [*Information service or system*] [*France*]   (IID)
CEEN .... Centre d'Etude de l'Energie Nucleaire [*Also known as NERC or SCK*] [*Belgium*]
CEEN .... Centre Europeen d'Etudes Nucleaires   (WGAO)
CEENA...... Central and East European News Agency   (ADA)
CEEO .... Centro de Estudios Sobre Europa Occidental [*Center for West European Studies*] [*Cuba*]   (LA)
CEE/ONU ... Commission Economique pour l'Europe/Organisation des Nations Unies [*Economic Commission for Europe/United Nations Organization*]   (EAIO)
CEEP........ Centre Europeen de l'Entreprise Publique [*European Center of Public Enterprise - ECPE*]   (EAIO)
CEEP........ Centre Europeen d'Etudes de Population   (WGAO)
CEEP........ Centro Studi di Politica Economica [*Italian*]   (SLS)
CEEP........ Commonwealth Employees' Employment Provisions Act [*Australia*]   (ADA)
CEEP........ Confederation Europeene d'Etudes de Phytopharmacie   (WGAO)
CEEPPA.... Centre d'Etudes Economiques pour les Produits Agricoles (WGAO)
CEEPS...... Communaute Europeenne de l'Education Physique Scolaire (WGAO)
CEER........ Center for Energy and Environment Research [*Puerto Rican*] [*Nuclear energy*]   (NRCH)
CEERA...... Conference Europeenne des Experts Radiotelegraphistes de l'Aeronautique   (WGAO)
CEERI ...... Central Electronics Engineering Research Institute [*India*] [*Research center*]   (IRC)
CEES .... Centro de Estudios de Estado y Sociedad [*State and Society Studies Center*] [*Argentina*]   (LA)
CEES .... Comite Europeen d'Etude du Sel [*European Committee for the Study of Salt - ECSS*]   (EA)
CEES .... Conferencia Episcopal de El Salvador [*Episcopal Conference of El Salvador*]   (LA)
CEESP...... Centro de Estudios Economicos del Sector Privado [*Private Sector Center for Economic Studies*] [*Mexico*]   (LA)
CEESTEM ... Centro de Estudios Economicos y Sociales del Tercer Mundo [*Center for Third World Economic and Social Studies*] [*Mexico*]   (LA)
CEESTM... Centros Estudios Economicos y Sociales del Tercer Mundo [*Mexico*]   (WGAO)
CEET........ Compagnie Energie Electrique du Togo [*Togo Electric Power Co.*]
CEETA ...... Centre d'Etude et d'Experimentation des Technologies Appropriees [*Zaire*]
CEETB ...... Comite Europeen des Equipements Techniques du Batiment [*European Committee for Building Technical Equipment - ECBTE*]   (EAIO)
CE et S .... Conseil Economique et Social [*United Nations*]
CEEU .... Coordinadora Estatal de Estudiantes Universitarios [*Spanish*]
CEF........... Caixa Economica Federal [*Federal Economic Bureau*] [*Portuguese*]
CEF........... Campaign for Earth Federation [*Malta*]   (WGAO)
CEF........... Central European Federalists   (WGAO)
CEF........... Centro de Estudios Filosoficos [*Nicaragua*]   (SLS)
CEF........... Comite Estatal de Finanzas [*State Committee for Finance*] [*Cuba*]   (LA)
CEF........... Commission Europeenne des Forets   (WGAO)
CEF........... Consejo Ejecutivo Federal [*Federal Executive Council*] [*Panama*]
CEF........... Conservation des Eaux et Forets   (WGAO)
CEF........... Czech Air Force [*ICAO designator*]   (FAAC)
CEFA......... Centro de Ensenanza de las Fuerzas Armadas [*Armed Forces Training Center*] [*Dominican Republic*]   (LA)
CEFA......... Centro de Estudios de las Fuerzas Armadas [*Armed Forces Studies Center*] [*El Salvador*]   (LA)
CEFA......... Centro Educacional Femenino de Antioquia [*Colombia*]   (COL)
CEFA......... Child Evangelism Fellowship of Australia
CEFA......... Compagnie d'Exploitations Forestieres Africaines
CEFAC ...... Centre de Formations des Assistants Techniques du Commerce et des Consultants Commerciaux   (WGAO)
CEFACD ... Comite Europeen des Fabricants d'Appareils de Chauffage et de Cuisine Domestique   (WGAO)

CEFACEF ... Comite Europeen des Fabricants d'Appareils de Chauffage en Fonte   (PDAA)

CEFAG ...... Centre d'Etudes et de Formation Agricole de Gagnoa

CEFAM ..... Centre de Formation pour l'Administration Municipale a Buea

CEFB .... Centre d'Etudes des Fontes de Batiment [*Research Center for Cast Iron in Building*] [*France*]   (PDAA)

CEFCA ...... Centre Francaise de Cooperation Agricole   (WGAO)

CEFD .... Centro de Estudios de Filosofica del Derecho [*Venezuela*] (WGAO)

CEFDA ...... Central European Forces Distribution Agency [*NATO*]   (NATG)

CEFDI .... Compagnie d'Exploitation Forestiere de Divo

CEFEB ...... Centre d'Etudes Financieres, Economiques, et Bancaires [*Financial, Economic, and Banking Study Center*] [*French*] (AF)

CEFEB ...... Controle des Etudes de Fin d'Enseignement de Base [*Basic Education End Studies Control*] [*Benin*]   (AF)

CEFEI .... Committee of European Financial Executives Institutes [*EC*] (ECED)

CEFEM ..... Compagnie Francaise du Methane

CEFEMINA ... Centro Feminista de Informacion y Accion [*Costa Rica*] (EAIO)

CEFEN ...... Certificat de Fin d'Etudes Normales [*Certificate of Completion of Normal School*] [*French*]   (WER)

CEFER ...... Centro de Estudos de Fertilizantes [*Fertilizer Research Center*] [*IPT*] [*Research center*] [*Brazil*]   (IRC)

CEFI .... Comision Interministerial de Exposiciones y Ferias Internacionales [*Interministerial Commission for International Fairs and Expositions*] [*Uruguay*]   (LA)

CEFIC .... Conseil Europeen des Federations de l'Industrie Chimique [*European Council of Chemical Manufacturers Federations - ECCMF*] [*Belgium*]   (EAIO)

CEFIF .... Centre Europeen du Conseil International des Femmes   (WGAO)

CEFIGRE ... Centre de Formation Internationale pour la Gestion des Ressources en Eau [*Center for International Training in Water Resources Management*] [*ASF*]

CEFILAC .. Companie du Filage des Metaux et des Joints Curty [*Nuclear energy*] [*French*]   (NRCH)

CEFIM ...... Carl en Emily Fuchs-Instituut vir Mikroelektronika [*Carl and Emily Fuchs Institute for Microelectronics*] [*University of Pretoria*] [*South Africa*]   (AA)

Cefis .... Ceskoslovenska Filmova Spolecnost [*Czechoslovak Motion Picture Company*]   (CZ)

CEFISEM ... Centre de Formation et d'Information des Personnels concernes par la Scolarisation des Enfants de Migrants   (WGAO)

CEFITEN ... France Neige International Agency for Snow Techniques (EAIO)

CEFNOMEX ... Centro de Estudios Fronterizos del Norte de Mexico (WGAO)

CEFOE ...... Curso Especial de Formacion de Oficiales del Ejercito [*Special Army Officer Training Course*] [*Venezuela*]   (LA)

CE Fr .... Conseil d'Etat de France [*State Council of France*]   (BAS)

CEFRACOR ... Centre Francais de la Corrosion

CEFRAS .... Centre Europeen de Formation et de Recherche en Action Sociale [*European Centre for Social Welfare Training and Research - ECSWTR*] [*United Nations*]   (EAIO)

CEFRES .... Centre Europeen Feminin de Recherche sur l'Evulation de la Societe [*French*]   (SLS)

CEFRI .... Centrais de Estocagem Frigorificada [*Cold Storage Plants*] [*Brazil*]   (LA)

CEFRI .... Centre de Formation aux Realites Internationales

CEFS .... Comite Europeen des Fabricants de Sucre [*European Committee of Sugar Manufacturers*] [*Common Market*]

CEFTA ...... Central European Free Trade Agreement   (EECI)

CEFTAA ... Campaign Exposing Frame-ups and Targeting Abuses of Authority [*Australia*]

CEFTRI ..... Central Food Technological Research Institute [*India*]   (WGAO)

CEFV .... Centro de Estudios del Futuro de Venezuela   (WGAO)

CEG .... Campo Experimental de Guanipa [*Venezuela*]   (DSCA)

CEG .... Catholic Evidence Guild   (WGAO)

CEG .... Cave Exploration Group [*Australia*]

CEG .... Centre d'Etudes de Gramat [*DTAT*]   (WGAO)

CEG .... Certificate d'Education Generale [*General Education Certificate*] [*Algeria*]   (AF)

CEG .... Clough Engineering Group [*Australia*]

CEG .... College d'Enseignement General [*Secondary General Education School*] [*French*]   (AF)

CEG .... Computer Education Group [*Australia*]

CEGAGADIS ... Compagnie d'Exploitations Commerciales Africaines, Societe Gabonaise de Distribution   (WGAO)

CEGAM .... Confederation Europeenne des Grandes Association Musicales (WGAO)

CEGAP ...... Comite Europeen des Architectes Paysagistes   (WGAO)

CEGAT ...... Centro de Estudios Ganaderos de Areas Tropicales [*Argentina*] (LAA)

CEGB .... Central Electricity Generating Board   (WGAO)

CEGCL ...... Comision Especial de Ganaderia de Carne del Litoral [*Ecuador*] (DSCA)

CEGD .... Centre d'Etudes Geologiques et de Developpement [*Geological and Development Studies Center*] [*Djibouti*]   (AF)

CEGEDA ... Compagnie Generale de Distribution et d'Approvisionnement

CEGEDUR ... Compagnie Generale de Duralumin et de Cuivre

CEGEP ...... College d'Enseignement General et Professionnel [*French*]

CEGEPAR ... Compagnie Generale de Participations et d'Entreprises

CEGERS ... Centre Guyanais d'Etudes et de Reflexions sur la Sante [*French Guianese Center for Health Studies and Research*]   (LA)

CEGET ...... Centre d'Etudes en Geographie Tropicale [*Centre of Studies in Tropical Geography*] [*France*]

CEGET ...... Compagnie Gabonaise d'Entreprise

CEGEX ...... Centre d'Etudes de Gestion et d'Expansion

CEGI .... Compagnie d'Etudes Economiques et de Gestion Industrielle

CEGIR .... Centre d'Etudes de Gestion d'Information et de Recherches

CEGOC ..... Centro de Estudos de Gestao e Organizacao Cientifica [*Portugal*] (WGAO)

CEGOS ...... Commission d'Etudes Generales de l'Organisation Scientifique

CEGOS ...... Commission Generale d'Organisation Scientifique [*General Commission on Scientific Organization*] [*French*]   (WER)

CEGP .... Centro de Estudos da Guine Portuguesa

CEGROB ... Communaute Europeenne des Associations du Commerce de Gros Biere des Pays Members de la CEE   (WGAO)

CEGS .... Church of England Girls' School [*Australia*]

CEGS .... Comptoir d'Electricite Generale du Senegal

CEGUI .... Compania Espanola del Golfo de Guinea

cegv .... Cegvezeto [*Manager*]   (HU)

CEGV .... Computer Education Group of Victoria [*Australia*]

CEH .... Centre on Environment for the Handicapped   (WGAO)

CEH .... Centro de Estudios Hidrograficos [*Hydrographic Studies Center*] [*Madrid, Spain*] [*Research center*]   (ERC)

CEH .... Conference Euorpeenne des Horaires et des Services Directs [*European Conference of Time-tables and Direct Services*] (PDAA)

CEH .... Conference Europeenne des Horaires des Trains de Voyageurs [*European Passenger Timetable Conference*] [*Switzerland*]

CEHC .... Comite d'Etudes du Haut-Congo

CEHF .... Centre for Ergonomics and Human Factors [*Australia*]

CEHI .... Centre d'Etudis Historics Internationals [*Center for International Historical Studies*]   (EA)

CEHILA .... Comisio de Estudios de Historia de la Iglesia en America Latina (WGAO)

CEHILA .... Comision de Estudios de Historia de la Iglesia en Latinoamerica [*Commission of the Studies of History of the Church in Latin America*] [*Mexico*]

CEHMP .... Centro de Estudios Historicos Militares del Peru [*Peruvian Military History Studies Center*]   (LA)

CEHO .... Compagnie Centrafricaine d'Exploitation Hoteliere

CEHP .... Comite Europeen de l'Hospitalisation Privee [*European Committee of Private Hospitalization*] [*EC*] [*Belgium*] (ECED)

CEI .... Bois Confederation Europeenne des Industries du Bois   (WGAO)

CEI .... Central European Initiative   (EECI)

CEI .... Centre d'Etudes Industrielles [*Center for education in international management*] [*Switzerland*]   (DCTA)

CEI .... Centre for Education in International Management [*Switzerland*] (WGAO)

CEI .... Centro de Estudios Interplanetarios [*Spain*]   (EAIO)

CEI .... Chambre d'Etudes Industrielles [*North African*]

CEI .... Chiang Rai [*Thailand*] [*Airport symbol*]   (OAG)

CEI .... Comisia de Electronica Internationala [*International Electronics Commission*]   (RO)

CEI .... Comitato Elettrotechnico Italiano

CEI .... Comite Economique Interministeriel [*Interministerial Economic Committee*] [*France*]   (CL)

CEI .... Comite Espanole de Iluminacion   (WGAO)

CEI .... Commission Electrotechnique Internationale [*International Electrotechnical Commission - IEC*] [*Switzerland*]   (EAIO)

CEI .... Commission Europe de l'IOMTR   (WGAO)

CEI .... Committee for Environmental Information [*United Nations*] (WGAO)

CEI .... Communaute Europeene Information [*French*]

CEI .... Compagnia Editrice Italiana   (WGAO)

CEI .... Compagnia Edizioni Internazionali SPA

CEI .... Compagnia Elettrotecnica Italiana [*Italian electrotechnical company*]

CEI .... Comte Espanol de Illuminacion [*Spain*]   (PDAA)

CEI .... Confederation of the Engineering Industry [*India*]   (EY)

CEI .... Conference of the Electronics Industry   (WGAO)

CEI .... Congreso Eucaristico Internacional [*Colombia*]   (COL)

CEI .... Constructions et Entreprises Industrielles [*Industrial Construction and Enterprise Company*] [*Belgium*]   (WER)

CEI .... Cuerpo del Ejercito Independiente de Pinar Del Rio [*Pinar Del Rio Independent Army Corps*] [*Cuba*]   (LA)

CEIA .... Centre d'Entr'aide Intellectuelle Africaine

CEIA .... Centre Economique Ital-Afrique

CEIA .... Centro Economico Italia Africa [*Italian-African Economic Center*]   (AF)

CEIA......... Comite Especial de Investigaciones Antarticas   (WGAO)
CEIA......... Comunidad de Espanoles con Intereses en Africa
CEIA......... Cooperative d'Elevage et d'Insemination Artificielle   (WGAO)
CEIB......... Centre d'Exploitation Industrielle du Betail [Center for the Industrial Exploitation of Livestock] [Ivory Coast]   (AF)
CEIB......... Confederation Europeenne des Industries du Bois [European Confederation of Woodworking Industries]
CEI-BOIS ... Confederation Europeenne des Industries du Bois [European Confederation of Woodworking Industries]   (EAIO)
CEIBS....... China Europe International Business School
CEIC........ Centro Europeo d'Iniziative Culturali   (WGAO)
CEIC........ Confederacion de Empleados de Industria y Comercio [Industrial and Business Employees Confederation] [Chile]   (LA)
CEIC........ Conseil Economique International du Cur   (WGAO)
CEICA...... Construcciones Electricas Industriales, CA [Venezuela]   (LAA)
CEICN....... Centre Europeen d'Information pour la Conservation de la Nature   (WGAO)
CEIE........ Centre d'Etudes et d'Information sur l'Enseignement   (WGAO)
CEIE......... Cuerpo de Ejercito Independiente del Este [Independent Army Corps of the East] [Cuba]   (LA)
CEIEC....... China National Electronics Import & Export Corporation [China]   (IMH)
CEIF........ Conseil des Federations Industrielles d'Europe   (WGAO)
CEIF........ Council of European Industrial Federations   (WGAO)
CEIG........ Centro de Estudios e Investigaciones Geotecnicas [Center for Geotechnical Studies and Investigations] [San Salvador, El Salvador]   (LAA)
CEIGA...... Comite de Empresarios Industriales del Grupo Andino [Committee of Andean Industrialists] [Ecuador]   (LA)
CEIL........ Combinat pentru Exploatarea si Industrializarea Lemnului [Combine for the Exploitation and Industrialization of Wood]   (RO)
CEILS....... CAVAL [Cooperative Action by Victorian Academic Libraries] Expensive Item Listing Service [Australia]
CEIM....... Centre d'Etudes Industrielles du Maghreb [North African]
CEIM....... Confederacion Empresarial Independiente de Madrid de la Pequena, Mediana, y Gran Empresa [Employers' organization] [Spain]   (EY)
CEIM....... Conservative Evagelicals in Methodism   (WGAO)
CEIMA...... Centro de Estudios de Investigacion sobre Mercadeo Agropecuario. Universidad JTL [Colombia]   (COL)
CEIMSA ... Compania Exportadora e Importadora Sociedad Anonima [Mexico]   (LAA)
CEIN .... Centril Experimental pentru Ingrasaminte Bacteriene [Rumania]   (WGAO)
CEINAR.... Centro de Estudios Internacional Argentinos   (WGAO)
CEIO .... Cuerpo Ejercito Independiente del Oeste [Independent Army Corps of the West] [Cuba]   (LA)
CEIPA ...... Comite d'Etudes et d'Informations sur les Produits Agricoles   (WGAO)
CEIPE ...... Centro Industrial Experimental [Venezuela]   (DSCA)
CEIPI........ Centre d'Etudes Internationales de la Propriete Industrielle [France]   (WGAO)
CEIR......... Centre d'Etudes et d'Initiative Revolutionnaire [Center for Revolutionary Studies and Initiative] [French]   (WER)
CEIR......... Civil Emergency Information Room [NATO]   (NATG)
CEIR......... Comite Europeen de l'Industrie de la Robinetterie [European Committee for the Valves and Fittings Industry] [EC] [Germany]   (ECED)
CEIS .... Caribbean Energy Information System [UNESCO]   (DUND)
CEIS .... Centro de Estudios de Ingenieria de Sistemas [Systems Engineering Study Center] [Havana, Cuba]   (LA)
CeIS .... Centro Italiano di Solidarieta [Italian]   (SLS)
CEISAL..... Consejo Europeo de Investigaciones Sociales sobre America Latina   (WGAO)
CEIST........ Centro Europeo Informazione Scientifiche e Tecniche [Italy]   (WGAO)
CEIT .... Centro de Estudios e Investigaciones Tecnicas de Guipuzcao [Guipuzcoa Technical Studies Research Center] [Spain]   (SLS)
CEITA .... Calcutta Import and Export Trade Association [India]   (PDAA)
CEITJA ..... Centre d'Eutde Internationale sur le Travail des Jeunes dans l'Agriculture   (WGAO)
CE/IWT .... Central Europe Inland Waterways Transport [NATO]   (NATG)
CEJ .... Centre Europeen de la Jeunesse [CE]   (WGAO)
CEJ .... Confederacion Espanola de Organizaciones de Empresarios del Juego   (WGAO)
CEJ .... Confederation Europeenne du Jouet [France]   (EAIO)
CEJ .... Corporacion Area Ejecutiva SA de CV [Mexico] [ICAO designator]   (FAAC)
CEJA .... Conseil Europeen des Jeunes Agriculteurs [European Committee of Young Farmers] [Common Market]
CEJEDP..... Central Europe Joint Emergency Defense Plan [NATO]   (NATG)
CEJG .... Certificat d'Etudes Juridiques Generales [French]
CEJH........ Communaute Europeenne des Jeunes de l'Horticulture   (WGAO)
CEJH........ Communaute Europeennes des Jeunes de l'Horticulture [France]   (DSCA)

CEJI .... Cour Etudiante de Justice Internationale [A la Faculte de Droit d'Aix-en-Provence]   (FLAF)
CEK .... Cocuk Esirgeme Kurumu [Child Protection Association] [TCEK] [See also]   (TU)
CEK .... Societe Seca [France] [ICAO designator]   (FAAC)
CEKOM .... Central European Mass Communication Research Documentation Centre   (WGAO)
CEL........... Celaya [Race of maize] [Mexico]
CEL........... Ceneast Airlines Ltd. [Kenya] [ICAO designator]   (FAAC)
CEL........... Central Electronics Ltd. [India] [Research center]   (WED)
CEL........... Centre d'Essais des Landes (de Biscarosse) [Landes Testing Center] [French]   (WER)
CEL........... China Esperanto League   (EAIO)
Cel............ Colonel [Colonel] [Military] [French]   (MTD)
CEL........... Comision Ejecutiva Hidroelectrica del Rio Lempa [Lempa River Hydroelectric Executive Commission] [El Salvador]   (LA)
CEL........... Comite Executif de la Lutte [Executive Struggle Committee] [Guinea]   (AF)
CEL........... Commission Executive et de Liaison [En matieres postales] [France]   (FLAF)
CEL........... Communications & Entertainment Ltd. [Australia]
CEL........... Compagnie d'Energetique Lineaire [France]   (PDAA)
CEL........... Conseil European des Loisirs   (WGAO)
CEL........... Conselho Executivo da Luta
Cel............ Coronel [Colonel] [Portuguese]
CELA........ Centre d'Etudes de Litterature Africaine [Zaire]   (SLS)
CELA........ Centro de Estudios Latinoamericanos [Center for Latin American Studies] [Research center] [Mexico]   (IRC)
CELA........ Centro de Estudios Latinoamericanos [Center for Latin American Studies] [Panama]   (PDAA)
CELA........ Comision Economica para America Latina [Economic Commission for Latin America - ECLA] [Santiago, Chile]   (LA)
CELAC...... Centre de Recherche et de Controle Lainier et Chimique   (WGAO)
CELAC...... Comite d'Etudes et de Liaison des Amendements Calcaires [French]   (SLS)
CELAC...... Committe for Exports to Latin America and the Caribbean [BNEC]   (WGAO)
CELADE ... Centro Latinoamericana de Demografia [Latin American Demographic Center] [Economic Commission for Latin America and the Caribbean Chile] [United Nations]
CELADE ... Centro Latinoamericano de Demografia [Latin American Center on Demography] [Santiago, Chile]   (LA)
CELADEC ... Comision Evangelica Latinoamericana de Educacion Cristiana   (WGAO)
CELADEC ... Comissao Evangelica Latinoamericana de Educo Crista [Brazil]   (SLS)
CELAM..... Conferencia Episcopal Latinoamericana [Latin American Bishops Conference]   (LA)
CELAM..... Consejo Episcopal Latinoamericano [Latin American Episcopal Council]   (EAIO)
CELAME .. Comite de Liaison et d'Action des Syndicats Medicaux Europeens   (WGAO)
CELAP ...... Centro Latinoamericano de Poblacion [Santiago, Chile]   (LAA)
CELAP ...... Centro Latinoamericano de Poblacion y Familia [Chile]   (WGAO)
CELAPI.... Centro Latinoamericano para la Pequena Industria [Quito, Ecuador]   (LAA)
CELAR...... Centre d'Electronique de l'Armament [Electronics System Command] [French Air Force]   (PDAA)
CELATS.... Centro Latinoamericano de Trabajo Social   (WGAO)
CELB........ Companhia Electrica do Lobito e Benguela [Angola]
CELC........ Commonwealth Education Liaison Committee   (WGAO)
CELC........ Foundation pour le Centres Europeens Langues et Civilisations   (WGAO)
CELCA ...... Centro Latinoamericano de Credito Agricola [Latin American Center for Agricultural Credit]   (LAA)
CELCAA ... Comite Europeen de Liaison des Commerces Agro-Alimentaires [European Liaison Committee for Agricultural and Food Trades]   (EAIO)
CELCAIRO ... Cementos el Cairo SA [Colombia]   (COL)
CELCIT..... Centro Latinoamericano de Creacion e Investigacion Teatral [Latin American Center for Theatrical Production and Research]   (LA)
CELCO...... Controles Electricos Colombianos [Colombia]   (COL)
CELD........ Central External Liaison Department [Chinese Secret Service]
CELE .... Centre Europeen pour Loisir et l'Education   (WGAO)
CELE .... Centro Coordinamento Elettronica   (WGAO)
CELEDESCO ... Cooperativa Industrial Lechera de Colombia Ltda. [Barranquilla]   (COL)
CELEF....... Centre d'Etude des Litteratures d'Expression Francaise
CELEG ...... Centre d'Etude des Litteratures d'Expression Graphique
CELEMA .. Central Lechera de Manizales   (COL)
CELESA.... Centro de Exportacion de Libros Espanoles [Center for the Export of Spanish Books] [Ministry of Culture Spain]

CELEX ...... Communitatis Europae Lex [*European Community Law*] [*Commission of the European Communities*] [*Information service or system*]   (IID)

CELF .... Centre d'Etudes Litteraires Francophones [*France*]   (WGAO)

CELG........ Centrais Eletricas de Goias

CELG......... Certificat d'Etudes Litteraires Generales [*French*]

CELHTO... Centre d'Etude Linguistique par Tradition Orale

CELHTO... Centre d'Etudes Linguistiques et Historique par la Tradition Orale [*Niger*]

CELIB .... Comite d'Etudes et de Liaison des Interets Bretons   (WGAO)

CELIBRIDE ... Comite de Liaison Internationale des Broderies, Rideaux et Dentelles   (WGAO)

CELICA..... Comite Europeen de Liason des Cadres de l'Agriculture   (WGAO)

CELIDA .... Comite d'Etudes et de Liaison Interprofessionnel du Departement de l'Aisne [*French*]   (SLS)

CELIF........ Centrala de Exploatare a Lucrarilor de Imbunatatiri Funciare [*Center for the Execution of Land Improvement Work*]   (RO)

CELIHM... Comite d'Etudes et de Liaison Interprofessionnel de la Haute-Marne [*French*]   (SLS)

CELIMAC ... Comite Europeen de Liaison des Industries de la Machine a Coudre [*European Liaison Committee for the Sewing Machine Industries - ELCSMI*] [*Defunct*]   (EAIO)

CELL .... Centre for English Language Learning [*Royal Melbourne Institute of Technology*] [*Australia*]

Celli........... Violoncelli [*Cellos*] [*Music*]

CELLUCAM ... Societe de Cellulose du Cameroun

CELLUNAF ... Compagnie Nord Africaine de Cellulose

CELME..... Centro Sperimentale Lavorazione Metalli [*Research Insitute for Metalworking*] [*Italy*]   (PDAA)

CELNA...... Compania Electrica Nacional Ltda. [*Itagui-Antioquia*]   (COL)

CELNUCO ... Comite Europeen de Liaison des Negociants et Utilisateurs de Combustibles   (WGAO)

CELOS ...... Centrum voor Landbouwkundig Onderzoek in Suriname   (WGAO)

CELP......... Centro de Estudios Laborales del Peru [*Labor Study Center of Peru*]   (LA)

CELPA ...... Centrais Electricas do Para, SA [*Para Electric Powerplants, Inc.*] [*Brazil*]   (LA)

CELPA ...... Centro de Experimentacion y Lanzamiento de Proyectiles Autopropulsados [*Rocket Testing and Launching Center*] [*Argentina*]   (LA)

CELPA ...... Centro Espacial de Lanzamientos para la Prospeccion Atmosferica [*Argentina*]   (WGAO)

CELPAP.... Entreprise Nationale de Cellulose et de Papier [*Nationalized industry*] [*Algeria*]   (EY)

CELPUF.... Comite d'Etudes de Liaison du Patronat de l'Union Francaise   (WGAO)

CELRA ...... Conference des Eveques Latins dans les Regions Arabes [*Israel*]   (WGAO)

CELRA ...... Conference of Latin Bishops of Arab Regions [*Jersalem, Israel*]   (EAIO)

CELRIA .... Centre des Litteratures Romanes d'Inspiration Africaine

CELSA ..... Comite d'Etudes des Legislations Sociales Algeriennes   (FLAF)

CELTA ...... Centre de Linguistique Theorique et Appliquee [*Center for Theoretical and Applied Linguistics*] [*Zaire*]   (SLS)

CELTE ...... Constructeurs Europeens de Locomotives Thermiques et Electriques [*European Manufacturers of Thermal and Electric Locomotives*]   (EAIO)

CELTIC..... Concentrateur Exploitant les Temps d'Inactivite des Circuits [*French*] [*Telecommunications*]

CELU........ Commonwealth Education Liaison Unit   (WGAO)

CELU........ Confederation of Ethiopian Labor Unions   (AF)

CELZA ...... Cultures et Elevage du Zaire

Cem............ Cemiyeti [*Society, Association*]   (TU)

CEM .... Center for Entrepreneurship and Management [*Ethiopia*]   (AF)

CEM .... Centre d'Essais de la Mediterranee [*Mediterranean Test Center*] [*French*]   (WER)

CEM .... Centre for Environmental Management [*University of Newcastle*] [*Australia*]

CEM .... Centre for Environmental Mechanics [*Commonwealth Scientific and Industrial Research Organization*] [*Australia*]

CEM .... Centre of Excellence in Mineralogy [*University of Baluchistan*] [*Pakistan*]   (EAS)

CEM .... Centres d'Etudes Marxistes [*Centers for Marxist Studies*] [*French*]

CEM .... Centro de Ensenanza Militar [*Military Training Center*] [*Cuba*]   (LA)

CEM .... Centro de Estudios de la Mujer [*Women's Studies Center*] [*Argentina*]   (EAIO)

CEM .... Centro de Estudios para la Mujer   (WGAO)

CEM .... Centro Electromecanico [*Colombia*]   (COL)

CEM .... Chefe do Estado Maior [*Chief of Staff*] [*Portuguese*]   (WER)

CEM .... Christian Education Movement   (WGAO)

CEM .... College d'Enseignement Moyen [*College of Intermediate Studies*] [*Algeria*]   (AF)

CEM .... Comissao Eleitoral Monarquica [*Monarchy Electoral Committee*] [*Portugal*]   (PPE)

CEM .... Compagnie des Experts Maritimes et en Transports

CEM .... Compagnie Electromecanique [*Swiss-German electrical equipment company*]

CEM .... Compagnie Electro-Mecanique [*Electromechanical Equipment Company*] [*French*]   (WER)

CEM .... Compagnie Equatoriale des Mines

CEM .... Companhia de Electricidade de Macau [*Macao Electrical Company*]

CEM .... Confederation Europeenne de Maires   (WGAO)

CEM .... Conferacion Evangelica Mundial   (WGAO)

CEM .... Conference Europeenne des Horaires des Trains de Marchandises [*European Freight Timetable Conference*]   (EAIO)

CEM .... Congo Evangelistic Mission

CEM .... Council of European Municipalities   (WGAO)

CEM .... Croisade d'Evangelisation Mondale   (WGAO)

CEMA .... Catering Equipment Manufacturers Association   (WGAO)

CEMA .... Centrale Marketing-Gesellschaft der Deutschen Agrarwirtschaft [*German Agriculture Central Marketing Association*]   (WEN)

CEMA .... Centre d'Etudes et de Modernisation Agricoles   (WGAO)

CEMA .... Centre d'Etudes Marines Avancees [*French*]   (MSC)

CEMA .... Centres d'Education aux Methodes Actives [*Centers for Training in Methods of Action*] [*French*]   (WER)

CEMA .... Centro de Enlace para el Medio Ambiente [*Kenya*]   (WGAO)

CEMA .... Centro de Estudios Macroeconomicos de Argentina [*Macroeconomics Studies Center of Argentina*]   (LA)

CEMA ...... Centro de Mecanica Aplicada [*Brazil*]   (LAA)

CEMA ...... Centro Relacionador de Centros de Madres [*Santiago, Chile*]   (LAA)

CEMA ...... Centros Maternales [*Mothers Centers*] [*Chile*]   (LA)

CEMA ...... Chefe de Estado Maior da Armada [*Navy Chief of Staff*] [*Portuguese*]   (WER)

CEMA ...... China Enterprise Management Association [*China*]   (IMH)

CEMA ...... Comite Europeen des Groupements de Constructeurs du Machinisme Agricole [*European Committee of Associations of Manufacturers of Agricultural Machinery*]   (EAIO)

CEMA ...... Comite pour l'Etude des Maladies et de l'Alimentation du Betail [*Belgium*]   (WGAO)

CEMA ...... Consejo de Ayuda Mutua Economica [*Council for Mutual Economic Assistance*] [*Cuba*]   (LA)

CEMA ...... Council for Economic Mutual Assistance [*Also known as CMEA, COMECON*] [*Communist-bloc nations: Poland, Russia, East Germany, Czechoslovakia, Romania, Bulgaria, Hungary Dissolved 1991*]

CEMAA .... Council of Egg Marketing Authorities of Australia   (ADA)

CEMAC..... Committee of European Associations of Manufacturers of Active Electronic Components   (ADPT)

CEMAC..... Comptoir Electro-Mecanique du Maroc

CEMACC ... Centro de Matematica Aplicada y Computacion de la Construccion [*Applied Mathematics and Computation Center for Construction*] [*Cuba*]   (LA)

CEMACO ... Central Distribuidora de Materiales de Construccion [*Colombia*]   (COL)

CEMAFON ... Comite Europeen des Materiels et Produits pour la Fonderie [*European Committee of Foundry Materials and Products*]   (EAIO)

CEMAG .... Centre d'Etude de la Mecanisation en Agriculture [*Center for the Study of Mechanization in Agriculture*] [*Belgium*]   (PDAA)

CEMAG .... Centre d'Etude de la Mecanisation en Agriculutre de Gembloux [*Belgium*]   (WGAO)

CEMAGREF ... Centre National du Machinisme Agricole, du Genie Rural des Eaux, et des Forets [*National Center of Agricultural and Forestry Engineering and Water Management*] [*Research center*] [*French*]   (IRC)

CEMAL..... Consejo Empresarial Mexicano para Asuntos Internacionales [*The Mexican Business Council for International Affairs*]   (CROSS)

CEMAM ... Centre d'Etudes pour le Monde Arabe Moderne [*Beirut*]

CEMAN .... Centro de Estudios Audiovisuales. Universidad Nacional [*Colombia*]   (COL)

CEMAP..... Comission Europeenne des Methods d'Analyse des Pesticides   (DSCA)

CEMAP..... Commission Europeenne des Methodes d'Analyse des Pesticides   (WGAO)

CEMAT..... Centrais Eletricas Matogrossenses SA [*Brazil*]   (DSCA)

CEMAT..... Centre d'Etudes Mecanographiques et d'Assistance Technique [*French*]   (ADPT)

CEMAT..... Centro de Estudios Mesoamericano sobre Tecnologia Apropiada [*Guatemala*]   (WGAO)

CEMAT..... Centro Mesoamericano de Estudios sobre Tecnologia Apropiada [*Mesoamerican Study Center on Appropriate Technology*] [*Guatemala*] [*Research center*]

CEMAT..... Conference Europeenne des Ministres Responsables de l'Amenagement du Territoire   (WGAO)

CEMAT..... Societa per la Construzione e l'Esercizio dei Mezzi Ausiliari del Transporte (WGAO)
CEMATEX ... Comite Europeen des Constructeurs de Materiel Textile [European Committee of Textile Machinery Manufacturers] (EAIO)
CEMAV..... Church of England Missionary to the Aborigines of Victoria [Australia]
CEMB........ Comite Europeen pour le Mini-Basketball [European Committee for Mini-Basketball - ECMB] [Munich, Federal Republic of Germany] (EAIO)
CEMB........ Compagnie des Experts Maritimes du Benin
CEMBRAL ... Compania Elaboradora de Metales Barbosa Limitada [Colombia] (COL)
CEMBS ..... Committee for European Marine Biological Symposia [European Marine Biological Association] (MSC)
CEMBUREAU ... Cement Statistical and Technical Organization [France] (PDAA)
CEMBUREAU ... European Cement Association (EAIO)
CEMC .... Central Election Management Committee [Korean]
CEMCC..... China Enterprise Management Consulting Corp.
CEMCI ...... Compagnie des Experts Maritimes de Cote-D'Ivoire
CEMD .... Compagnie des Experts Maritimes du Dahomey
CEMDOC ... Centro Multinacional de Documentacion Cientifica sobre Geologia, Geofisica de Colombia (WGAO)
CEMDOC ... Centro Multinacional de Documentacion Cientifica sobre Geologia y Geofisica de Colombia [Colombia] (DSCA)
CEME........ Central de Medicamentos [Central Enterprise for Medicines] [Brazil] (LA)
CEME........ Centro Italiano per Stuido delle Relazioni Economiche e dei Mercati Esteri (WGAO)
CEME........ Centro per gli Studi sui Mercati Esteri [Italian] (SLS)
CEME........ Comite des Eglises Aupres des Migrants en Europe [Churches' Committee on Migrants in Europe] (EA)
CEME........ Commisao Estadual de Material Excedente [State Surplus Materials Commission] [Brazil] (LA)
CEME........ Confederacion Espanola de Mujures Empresarias (WGAO)
CEME........ Construcora Colombiana de Maquinaria Ltda. [Colombia] (COL)
CEMEA..... Centre d'Entrainement aux Methodes d'Education Active
CEMEACI ... Centre d'Entrainement aux Methodes d'Education Active de Cote-D'Ivoire
CEMEC..... Cementos Ecuatorianos [Ecuadorean Cement Enterprise] (LA)
CEMEC..... Centro Europeo per la Medicina della Catastrofi (WGAO)
CEMEC..... Committee of European Associations of Manufacturers of Electronic Components [EC] [Italy] (ECED)
CEMEDA ... Centro Multinacional de Educacion de Adultos [Costa Rica] (WGAO)
CEMEDETO ... Centro de Mejora y Deomstracion de las Tecnicas Olecolas [Spain] (WGAO)
CEMEDOM ... Centre Medical d'Interentreprises d'Outre-Mer
CEMENCO ... Liberian Cement Corporation
CEMENTERA ... Fabrica Nacional de Cemento [Nicaragua] (WGAO)
CEMENTIR ... Cementerie del Tirreno SpA [Spanish]
CEMEP..... European Committee of Manufacturers of Electrical Machines and Power Electronics [France] (EAIO)
CEMF........ Chambre Syndicale des Editeurs de Musique (WGAO)
CEMGC..... Comite Europeen des Materiels de Genie Civil [Committee for European Construction Equipment - CECE] (EAIO)
CEMGFA ... Chefe do Estado Maior General das Forcas Armadas [Armed Forces Chief of Staff] [Portuguese] (WER)
CEMH....... Centre d'Essais des Moteurs et Helices [French]
CEMI......... China-Europe Management Institute
CEMI........ Commission Europeenne de Marketing Industriel [European Commission for Industrial Marketing] [Brixham, Devonshire, England] (EAIO)
CEMI........ Conseil Europeen pour le Marketing Industriel (WGAO)
CEMIE...... Centro Multinacional de Investigacion Educativa [Multinational Center for Educational Research] [Costa Rica] [Research center] (IRC)
CEMIG...... Central Eletrica de Minas Gerais, SA [Minas Gerais Electric Power Plant, Inc.] [Brazil] (LA)
CEMIQ...... Centro Mexicano de Informacion Quimica [Laboratorios Nacionales de Fomento Industrial] [Mexico]
CEMIZPLO ... Centro Mexicano de Informacion del Zinc y Plomo [Mexico]
CEMJA ..... Centre d'Entrainement des Moniteurs de la Jeunesse d'Algerie
CEMLA..... Centro de Estudios Monetarios Latinoamericanos [Center for Latin American Monetary Studies] [Mexico City, Mexico] (EAIO)
CEMM ...... Compagnie des Experts Maritimes de Madagascar
CEMN .... Comite d'Entente des Mouvements Nationaux
CEMN .... Compagnie des Experts Maritimes du Niger
CEMO .... Commission Economique pour le Moyen-Orient [United Nations] (WGAO)
CEMP........ Centre d'Etude des Matieres Plastiques [Research Center for Plastics] [France] (PDAA)
CEMP........ Centre d'Etudes et de Mesure de la Productivite (WGAO)

CEMP........ Coastal Environmental Management Plan [Advisory Committee on Pollution of the Sea]
CEMP........ Commonwealth Energy Management Program
CEMPA..... Comision Europea-Mediterranea para el Estudio de la Organizacion de Aguas (WGAO)
CEMPE..... Commission Europe-Mediterranee de Planification pour les Problemes de l'Eau (WGAO)
CEMPEX .. Comissao de Emprestimos Externos [Foreign Loans Commission] [Brazil] (LA)
CEMPN..... Centre d'Expertise Medicale du Personnel Navigant [North African]
CEMR .... Council of European Municipalities and Regions
CEMS........ Centre d'Etude de la Meteorologie Spatiale [Center for Space Meteorology Studies] (PDAA)
CEMS........ Compagnie des Experts Maritimes du Senegal
CEMS........ Constructions Electro-Mecaniques de Sologne [French]
CEMSA ..... Centro de Mejoramiento de Semillas Agamicas [Agamic Seeds Improvement Center] [Cuba] (LA)
CEMSA ..... Cooperation Eglises et Missions en Suisse Alemanique [Switzerland] (EAIO)
CEMSE ..... Comite Europeen des Fabricants de Materiels de Soudage Electrique (WGAO)
CEMSZOV ... Cementaru- es Mukoipari KTSZ [Kisipari Termeloszovetkezet] [Artisans Cooperative of Cement Products and Artificial Stone Industry] (HU)
CEMT........ Compagnie des Experts Maritimes du Togo
CEMT........ Conference Europeenne des Ministres des Transports [European Conference of Ministers of Transport - ECMT] [France]
CEMTAS .. Celik Makina Sanayi ve Ticaret Anonim Sirketi [Steel Machinery Industry and Trade Corporation] (TU)
CEMU .... Centro Sperimentale per le Macchine Utensili (WGAO)
CEMUBAC ... Centre Medical de l'Universite de Bruxelles au Congo (WGAO)
CEMUBAC ... Centre Scientifique et Medical de l'Universite de Bruxelles en Afrique Centrale [Scientific and Medical Center of the University of Brussels in Central Africa] [Belgium] (AF)
Cen............ Central (EECI)
CEN .... Central Electronuclear [Thermonuclear Power Plant] [Cuba] (LA)
CEN .... Centre d'Etude de l'Energie Nucleaire [Nuclear Energy Research Center] [Belgium] (WER)
CEN .... Centre d'Etudes Nucleaires (WGAO)
CEN .... Centro di Studi dell'Energia Nucleare [Nuclear Energy Research Center] [Italian] (WER)
CEN .... Centro Nacionalista [Nationalist Center] [Bolivia] [Political party] (PPW)
Cen............ Cenup [South] (TU)
CEN .... Cercle d'Etudes Numismatiques [Belgium] (SLS)
CEN .... Ciudad Obregon [Mexico] [Airport symbol] (OAG)
CEN .... Comando Estrategico Nacionalista [Nationalist Strategic Command] [Argentina] (LA)
CEN .... Comision de Energia Nuclear [National Nuclear Energy Commission] [Mexico] (LA)
CEN .... Comision Estatuaria Nacional [National Statutes Commission] [Peru] (LA)
CEN .... Comite Ejecutivo Nacional [National Executive Committee (of the Institutional Revolutionary Party)] [Mexico] (LA)
CEN .... Comite Ejecutivo Nacional (de Accion Democratica) [National Executive Committee (of Democratic Action)] [Venezuela] (LA)
CEN .... Comite Estatal de Normacion [State Committee for Standardization] [Cuba] (LA)
CEN .... Comite Europeen de Coordination des Normes [European Committee for Coordination of Standards]
CEN .... Comite Europeen de Normalisation [European Committee for Standardization] [Belgium]
CEN .... Commissariat aux Energies Nouvelles [Atomic Energy Commission] [Algeria] (EY)
CEN .... Commission Executive Nationale [National Executive Commission] [Algeria] (AF)
CEN .... Commission pour l'Etude des Nuages [OMI]
CEN .... Conseil Executif National [National Executive Committee] [Zaire] (AF)
CEN .... Consejo de Economia Nacional (WGAO)
CEN .... Consejo Ejecutivo Nacional (Partido Radical) [Chile] (LAA)
CEN .... Consejo Nacional de Economia [National Council on Economy] [Venezuela] (LA)
CEN .... Consiliul Energetic National [National Energy Council] (RO)
CEN .... Corporacion de Empresas Nacionales [National Business Corporation] [Argentina] (LA)
CENA .... Centre d'Etudes Nord-Africaines (WGAO)
CENA .... Centre d'Experimentation de la Navigation Aerienne [French]
CENA .... Centro de Energia Nucleaira Agricultura (WGAO)
CENA .... Centro de Energia Nuclear na Agricultura [Center for Use of Nuclear Energy in Agriculture] [Brazil] (LA)
CENA .... Club des Epagneuls Nains Anglais [France] (EAIO)
CENAC ..... Centro Nacional de Calculo [Mexico] (DSCA)

CENACE... Cercle National Chretien d'Education [*National Christian Educational Club*] [*Malagasy*]   (AF)

CENACO .. Centro Nacional de Computacion [*National Computation Center*] [*Bolivia*]   (IMH)

CENAD ..... Centre National d'Archives et de Documentation   (WGAO)

CENADA .. Centro Nacional de Datos Oceanograficos [*Mexico*]   (MSC)

CENADEC ... Centre National de Developpement des Entreprises Cooperatives

CENADEM ... Centro Nacional de Desenvolvimento do Gerenciamento da Informacao [*National Center for Information Management Development*] [*Brazil*] [*Information service or system*]   (IID)

CENADEM ... Centro Nacional de Desenvolvimento Micrografico [*Brazil*]   (WGAO)

CENADI.... Central Nacional de Distribucion [*National Distribution Headquarters*] [*Chile*]   (LA)

CENAFOP ... Centre National de Formation Professionnelle Continuee

CENAFOR ... National Center for Development of Technical Teacher Training [*Brazil*]

CEN AFRREP ... Central African Republic   (WDAA)

CENAGRI ... Centro Nacional de Informacao Documental Agricola [*National Center for Agricultural Documentary Information*] [*Ministry of Agriculture Brazil*] [*Information service or system*]   (IID)

CENAL...... Comissao Executiva Nacional do Alcool [*National Alcohol Executive Commission*] [*Brazil*]   (LA)

CENALC ... Centro Educacional y de Capacitacion Comercial [*Colombia*]   (COL)

CENAM .... Centre National de l'Artisanat Malagasy [*Malagasy National Handicraft Center*]   (AF)

CENAMI... Centro Nacional de Ayuda a Mexicanos Indigenas   (WGAO)

CENAP...... Centre d'Apprentissage Professionnel [*Vocational Apprenticeship Center*] [*Cambodia*]   (CL)

CENAP...... Centro Nacional de Productividad [*National Productivity Center*] [*El Salvador*]   (LA)

CENAP...... Corriente Estudiantil Nacionalista Popular [*Popular Nationalist Student Current*] [*Argentina*]   (LA)

CENAPEC ... Centre National de Promotion des Entreprises Cooperatives

CENAPEC ... National Centre for Promotion of Cooperative Enterprises [*Ivory Coast*]   (WGAO)

CENAPER ... Centro Nacional de Perfeccionamiento Educativo [*Colombia*]   (COL)

CENAPHI ... Centre de Formation Professionnelle pour les Handicapes et Invalides Physiques [*Vocational Training Center for Invalids and the Physically Handicapped*] [*Zaire*]   (AF)

CENAPIA ... Centro Nacional de Promocion de la Pequena Industria y Artesania [*Ecuador*]

CENAPLANF ... Centro Nacional de Planificacion Natural de la Familia [*National Center for Natural Family Planning*] [*Uruguay*]   (LA)

CENAPO... Centro Nacional de Pobladores [*Santiago, Chile*]   (LAA)

CENAPRO ... Centro Nacional de Productividad de Mexico [*Mexico*]

CENARESO ... Centro Nacional de Reeducacion Social [*National Social Reeducation Center*] [*Argentina*]   (LA)

CENAREST ... Centre National de la Recherche Scientifique et Technologique [*National Center for Scientific and Technological Research*] [*Gabon*] [*Research center*]   (IRC)

CENARGEN ... Centro Nacional de Pesquisa de Recursos Geneticos e Biotecnologia [*National Research Center for Genetic Resources and Biotechnology*] [*Brazil*]   (IRC)

CENARGEN ... Centro Nacional de Recursos Geneticos [*Brazil*]   (WGAO)

CENAT...... Comissao Executiva do Sistema Tiete-Parana [*Tiete-Parana System Executive Commission*] [*Brazil*]   (LA)

CENATRA ... Centre National d'Assistance Technique et Recherche Applique [*National Center for Technical Assistance and Applied Research*] [*Belgium*]   (PDAA)

CENATRIN ... Centre National de Traitement de l'Information

CENAZUCA ... Centrales Azucareros [*Sugar Refineries*] [*Venezuela*]   (LA)

CEN-CA .... Centre d'Etudes Nucleaires de Cadarache [*Cadarache Nuclear Research Center*] [*French*]   (EY)

CENCAFOR ... Centro de Capacitacion y Experimentacion Forestal [*Training and Forestry Experiment Center*] [*Ecuador*]   (LA)

CENCER... Association Cerification Comite European de Normalisation   (OSI)

CENCI....... Centro de Estadisticas Nacionales y Comercio Internacional [*Center of Domestic Statistics and International Trade*] [*Uruguay*]   (LAA)

CENCI....... Centro de Nacionales y Comercio Internacional del Uruguay [*Uruguay*]   (SLS)

CENCIRA ... Centro Nacional de Capacitacion e Investigacion de la Reforma Agraria [*National Center for Agrarian Reform Training and Research*] [*Peru*]   (LA)

CENCLES ... Cooperativa de Leiterias do Espirito Santo [*Brazil*]   (DSCA)

CENCOA .. Central de Cooperativas Agrarias de Occidente [*Colombia*]   (COL)

CENCOP... Centro de Control Pecuario [*Livestock Control Center*] [*Cuba*]   (LA)

CENCOS... Centro Nacional de Communicacion Social [*National Mass Media Center*] [*Mexico*]   (LA)

CENCRA ... Centro Nacional de Capacitacao em Reforma Agraria [*Brazil*]   (DSCA)

CENCRA ... Centro Nacional de Capicitacao em Reforma Agraria [*Brazil*]   (WGAO)

CENDA ..... Centro de Desarrollo Agropecuario [*Agricultural Development Center*] [*Dominican Republic*]   (LA)

CENDA ..... Centro Nacional de Derechos de Autor [*National Center of Authors Rights*] [*Cuba*]   (LA)

CENDEC... Centro de Treinamento e Pesquisa para o Desenvolvimento Economico [*Training and Research Center for Economic Development*] [*Brazil*]   (LA)

CENDES ... Centro de Desarrollo Industrial del Ecuador [*Industrial Development Center of Ecuador*]   (LA)

CENDES ... Centro de Estudios del Desarrollo [*Development Studies Center*] [*Venezuela*]   (LA)

CENDES ... Centro de Estudios para el Desarrollo Social de Colombia [*Center of Studies for the Social Development of Colombia*]   (LA)

CENDES-UCV ... Centro de Estudios del Desarrollo de la Universidad Central de Venezuela [*Venezuela*]   (SLS)

CENDHRRA ... Center for the Development of Human Resources in Rural Asia   (EAIO)

CENDIE.... Centro Nacional de Documentacion e Informacion Educativa [*Argentina*]   (WGAO)

CENDIM... Centro Nacional de Documentacion e Informacion en Medicina y Ciencias de la Salud [*Uruguay*]   (WGAO)

CENDINOR ... Centro de Documentacion, Instituto Nacional de Normalizacion [*Chile*]

CENDIP.... Centro Nacional de Documentacion e Informacion Pedagogica [*Colombia*]   (COL)

CENDIS .... Centre de Documentation et d'Information Interuniversitaire en Sciences Sociales [*Interuniversity Documentation and Information Center for the Social Sciences*] [*Information service or system*]   (IID)

CENDIT.... Centre for Development of Industrial Technology [*New Delhi, India*]

CENDOC .. Centor Nacional de Documentacion [*Colombia*]   (WGAO)

CENDOC .. Centro Nacional de Datos Oceanograficos [*Chile*]   (MSC)

CENDOMAR ... Centro de Documentacion Maritima [*Colorado*]   (ASF)

CENDOPU ... Centro de Documentacion y Publicaciones. Universidad del Valle [*Colombia*]   (COL)

CENDRET ... Centro de Drenaje y Recuperacion de Tierras [*Peru*]   (DSCA)

CENE .... Centro de Energia Nuclear del Ecuador [*Nuclear Energy Center of Ecuador*]   (LA)

Cenebad ..... Centro Nacional de Educacion Basica a Distancia   (WGAO)

CENECA ... Centre National des Expositions et Concours Agricoles   (WGAO)

CENECA ... Centro de Estudios y Experimentacion de la Creacion Artistica   (EAIO)

CENECO... Centre d'Entrainement a l'Economie   (WGAO)

CENECO... Centre National des Expositions et Concours Agricoles   (WGAO)

CENED .... Centro Nacional de Educadores [*National Educators Center*] [*Colorado*]   (LA)

CENEEMA ... Centre National d'Etude et d'Experimentation des Machines Agricoles

CENEL...... Comite Europeen de Coordination des Normes Electriques [*European Electrical Standards Coordinating Committee*]

CENELEC ... Comite European de Normalisation Electrotechnique [*European Committee for Electrotechnical Standardization*]   (EAIO)

CENELEC ... Comite Europeen de Normalisation Electrotechnique [*European Committee for Electrotechnical Standardization*] [*Belgium*]   (SLS)

CENESPAC ... Centro de Estudios Socio-Economicos del Sector Privado Potosino [*San Luis Potosi*] [*Mexico*]   (LAA)

CENET...... Centro Nacional de Electronica y Telecomunicaciones [*National Electronics and Telecommunications Center*] [*Chile*]   (LA)

CENFAM ... Centro Nazionale di Fisica della Atmosfera e Meteorologia   (WGAO)

CENFAM ... Centro Nazionale per la Fisica della Atmosfera e la Meteorologia [*National Center for the Study of Meteorology and the Atmosphere*] [*Italian*]   (ASF)

CENFAR... Centre d'Etudes Nucleaires de Fontenay-Aux-Roses [*Nuclear energy*] [*French*]   (NRCH)

CENFOCAT ... Centre de Formation des Cadres Techniques [*Technical Employee Training Center*] [*Since 1972, CENFOCATAP Cambodia*]   (CL)

CENFOCATAP ... Centre pour la Formation des Cadres Techniques et pour l'Accroissement de la Productivite [*Center for Technical Employee Training and for Increased Productivity*] [*Before 1972, CENFOCAT Cambodia*]   (CL)

CENFOREAD ... Centre for Reading Education [*Australia*]   (ADA)

CENG .... Centre d'Etudes Nucleaires de Grenoble [*Grenoble Nuclear Research Center*] [*French*]   (WER)

CEngAust .. Institution of Chartered Engineers [*Australia*]

CENIAP .... Centro Nacional de Investigaciones Agropecuarias [*National Center for Agricultural and Livestock Research*] [*Research center*] [*Venezuela*]   (IRC)

CENIC....... Centro Nacional de Investigaciones Cientificas [*National Scientific Research Center*] [*Cuba*] (LA)
CENICAFE ... Centro Nacional de Investigaciones de Cafe [*Colorado*]
CENICANA ... Centro de Investigacion de la Cana de Azucar de Colombia [*Sugarcane Research Center of Colombia*] [*Research center*] (IRC)
CENICIT... Centro de Informacion Cientifica y Tecnologica, Instituto Dominicano de Tecnologia Industrial [*Dominican Republic*]
CENICIT... Centro Nacional de Informacion Cientifica y Tecnica [*Venezuela*] (WGAO)
CENID ...... Centro Nacional de Informacion y Documentacion [*National Information and Documentation Center*] [*Santiago, Chile*] (LAA)
CENIDE.... National Centre for Educational Development and Research [*Spain*] (WGAO)
CENIDIM ... Centro Necional de Informacion, Documentacion e Investigacion Musicales [*Mexico*] (WGAO)
CENIDS.... Centro Nacional de Informacion y Documentacion en Salud [*National Center for Health Information and Documentation*] [*Mexico*] [*Information service or system*] (IID)
CENIET .... Centro Nacional de Informacion y Estadisticas de Trabajo [*Mexico*] (WGAO)
CENIM...... Centro Nacional de Informacao Cientifica en Microbiologia [*Brazil*] (ASF)
CENIM...... Centro Nacional de Investigaciones Metalurgicas [*National Center for Metallurgical Research*] [*Research center*] [*Spanish*] (IRC)
CENIMAR ... Centro de Informacoes da Marinha [*Naval Intelligence Center*] [*Brazil*] (LA)
CENIP....... Centro Nacional de Investigaciones Pesqueras [*National Fisheries Research Center*] [*Research center*] [*Spanish*] (IRC)
CENIP....... Centro Nacional de Productividad [*National Productivity Center*] [*Peru*] [*Research center*] (IRC)
CENIT....... Centro Nicaraguense de Informacion Tecnologica [*Nicaraguan Center for Technological Information*] (LA)
CENITAL ... Centro Nacional de Inseminacion Artificial [*Colombia*] (COL)
CENITEC ... Centro de Investigaciones Tecnologicas y Cientificas [*Publishing house*] [*El Salvador*] (EY)
CENOPROM ... Centres Operationnels de Programmation Multinationale [*Multinational Programing Operational Centers*] (AF)
CENORI.... Centre Normand de Recherche en Informatique [*French*] (ADPT)
CENORTE ... Companhia de Eletrificacao Centro Norte do Ceara [*Brazil*] (DSCA)
Cenosid ...... Genocide (TU)
CENPAR.... Centre National de Promotion de l'Artisanat Rural (WGAO)
CENPES.... Centro de Pesquisas e Desenvolvimento [*Research and Development Center*] [*Brazil*] (LA)
CENPES.... Centro de Pesquisas e Desenvolvimento Leopoldo A. Miguez De Mello [*Leopoldo A. Miguez De Mello Research and Development Center*] [*Research center*] [*Brazil*] (IRC)
CENPHA .. Centro Nacional de Pesquisas Habitacionais [*Rio De Janeiro, Brazil*] (LAA)
CENPI....... Centro Nacional de Productividade na Industria [*Rio De Janeiro*] (LAA)
CENPLA ... Centro de Estudos, Pesquisa e Planejamento [*Brazil*] (WGAO)
CENPLACA ... Centro de Acopio de Platano [*Venezuela*] (DSCA)
CENPRO... Centro de Promocion de Inversiones y Exportaciones [*Investment and Exports Promotion Center*] [*Costa Rica*] (LA)
CENPRO... Centro Nacional de Formacion y Promocion [*Colombia*] (COL)
CENPRO... Centro Nacional de Productividad [*National Productivity Center*] [*Costa Rica*] (LAA)
CENRA ..... Centro Nacional de Capacitacion en Reforma Agraria [*Lima, Peru*] (LAA)
CENRADERU ... Centre National de la Recherche Appliquee au Developpement Rural
CENS........ Centre d'Etudes Nucleaires de Saclay [*Saclay Nuclear Research Center*] [*French*]
CENSA...... Centro Nacional de Salud Animal [*National Animal Health Center*] [*Cuba*] (LA)
CENSA...... Council of European and Japanese National Shipowners Associations [*England*] (EAIO)
CENSAT ... Centro Nazionale Studi Amministrative e Tributari per il Personale Finanziario [*Information retrieval*] (SLS)
CENSAV ... Centro de Sanidad Vegetal [*Plant Health Center*] [*Cuba*] (LA)
CEN/SCK ... Centre d'Etude de l'Energie Nucleaire/Studiecentrum voor Kernenergie [*Belgium*] (EY)
CENSERI ... Centro de Servicios Rurales Integrados [*Center for Integrated Rural Services*] [*Dominican Republic*] (LA)
CENSIS..... Centre for Spatial Information Studies [*Australia*] (IRC)
CENSIS..... Centro Studi Investimenti Sociali [*Italy*] (DSCA)
CENSOCULCO ... Centro Social y Cultural de Comercio (COL)
CENSUPE ... Centro Superior de Estudios Penales [*Barranquilla*] (COL)

CEN-SY-BOUL ... City East Environment and Creation of Sydney Boulevarde Society [*Australia*]
cent............ Centavo [*Monetary unit*] [*Portugal*]
cent............ Centiare [*Hundredth*] [*French*]
cent............ Centieme [*Hundredth*] [*French*]
CENT .... Centime [*Monetary unit*] [*France*]
cent............ Centimetre [*Centimeter*] [*French*]
cent............ Centimo [*Centime*] [*Monetary unit*] [*Portugal*]
CENT .... Centre Nucleaire Trico [*Trico Nuclear Center*] [*Zaire*] (AF)
CENTA...... Centro Nacional de Technologia Alimentaria [*Peru*] (WGAO)
CENTA...... Centro Nacional de Tecnificacion Agricola [*Salvador*] (WGAO)
CENTA...... Centro Nacional de Tecnologia Agropecuaria [*National Center of Agricultural Technology*] [*El Salvador*] (ARC)
CENTA...... Combined Edible Nut Trade Association (WGAO)
CENTACA ... Centro de Acopio de Cafe CA [*Venezuela*] (DSCA)
CENTAG... Central [*European*] Army Group [*NATO*]
CENTEC ... Gesellschaft fuer Centrifugentechnik (WGAO)
CENTEXBEL ... Centre Scientifique et Technique de l'Industrie Textile Belge [*Scientific and Tehnical Center for the Belgian Textile Industry*] (PDAA)
CENTI....... Centre pour le Traitement de l'Information
centig......... Centigrade [*Centigrade*] [*French*]
centig......... Centigramme [*Centigram*] [*French*]
centigr .... Centigrade [*Centigrade*] [*French*]
centigr........ Centigramme [*Centigram*] [*French*]
centil .... Centilitre [*Centiliter*] [*French*]
centim........ Centimetre [*Centimeter*] [*French*]
CENTLANT ... Central Subarea, Atlantic [*NATO*]
CENTO ..... Central Treaty Organization [*Also, CTO*] [*Formerly, Baghdad Pact*]
CENTOB... Centre National de Tri d'Oceanographie Biologique [*French*] (MSC)
centr .... Centrale [*Center*] [*Knitting*] [*French*]
centr .... Centralny [*Central*] (POL)
CENTRABOIS ... Societe Centrafricaine de Travaux du Bois
CENTRACO ... Societe Centrafricaine pour le Commerce et l'Industrie
CENTRACUIRS ... Societe Centrafricaine des Cuirs
CENTRAG ... Societe Centrafricano-Arabe d'Agriculture
CENTRAGO ... Societe Centrafricaine pour le Developpement de l'Agro-Industrie (WGAO)
CENTRA-HYDRO ... Societe Centrafricaine des Hydrocarbures
CENTRALCER ... Central de Cervejas, EP [*Portugal*] (EY)
CENTRALCO ... Central Colombiana Autoagricola Ltda. [*Colombia*] (COL)
CENTRAMINES ... Compagnie Centrafricaine des Mines
CENTRANSPORT ... Societe Centrafricaine-Arabe de Transports
CENTRAPALM ... Societe Centrafricaine de Palmiers a Huile [*Central African Republic*] (EY)
CentrbC ..... Centralna Biblioteka u Cetinju [*Central Library in Cetinje*] [*Montenegro*] (YU)
CENTREDIL ... Centro Regionale dei Costruttori Edili Lombardil (WGAO)
CENTREDOC ... Swiss Center of Documentation in Microtechnology [*Information service or system*] (IID)
CENTRI .... Centro de Treinamento Rural de Ipanema [*Brazil*] (DSCA)
CENTRIFAN ... Centre d'Institut Francais d'Afrique Noire
CENTROBANCA ... Banca Centrale di Credito Populare (WGAO)
CENTROC ... Central Western Regional Organisation of Councils [*New South Wales, Australia*]
CENTROCARTA ... Centro Cartario Italiano per il Mercato Comune Europeo (WGAO)
CENTROCOOP ... Uniunea Centrala a Cooperativelor de Consum [*Central Union of Consumer Cooperatives*] (RO)
Centrofarm ... Centrala Handlu Farmaceutycznego [*Pharmaceutical Sales Center*] (POL)
CENTROFARM ... Oficiul Central Farmaceutic [*Central Pharmaceutical Office*] (RO)
CentroICTA ... Centro Provinciale Impiego Combinato Tecniche Agricole [*Italian*] (SLS)
CENTROKOMISE ... Podnik Zahranicniho Obchodu pro Dovoz a Vyvoz Potravin [*Foreign Trade Enterprise for the Import and Export of Foodstuffs*] (CZ)
CENTROMIN ... Empresa Minera del Centro del Peru [*Central Peruvian Mining Enterprise*] (LA)
CENTROMINPERU ... Empresa Minera del Centro del Peru [*Central Peruvian Mining Enterprise*] (LA)
Centrosan... Centrala Handlowa Farmaceutyczno-Sanitarna [*Pharmaceutical and Sanitary Goods Sales Center*] (POL)
CENTROSPED ... Medunarodna Spedicija i Transporti [*International Shipment and Transport Center*] (YU)
Centrosprzet ... Centrala Sprzetu Lekarsko-Sanitarnego [*Medical and Health Protection Supply Center*] (POL)
CENTROTEKSTIL ... Preduzece za Izvoz i Uvoz Tekstila [*Establishment for Import and Export of Textiles*] (YU)
CENTROTEX ... Podnik Zahranicniho Obchodu pro Dovoz a Vyvoz Textilniho a Kozeneho Zbozi [*Foreign Trade Enterprise for the Import and Export of Textiles and Leather Goods*] (CZ)

CENTROVITAL ... Central Colombiana de Vittalium [*Colombia*] Tlg. (COL)

Centrowet... Centrala Zaopatrzenia Weterynaryjno-Zootechniczna [*Veterinary and Animal Husbandry Supply Center*] (POL)

CENTSCO ... Centro Tecnico Superior de la Construccion [*Higher Technical Center for Construction*] [*Cuba*] (LA)

CENUSA... Centrales Nucleares SA [*Spain*] (WGAO)

CENUSA... Centrales Nucleares Sociedad Anonima [*Nuclear energy*] [*Spain*] (EY)

CEN-VALRHO ... Centre d'Etudes Nucleaires de la Vallee du Rhone [*France*] (EY)

CENYC...... Council of European National Youth Committees (EA)

cenz .... Cenzura [*Censorship*] [*Hungary*]

CEO .... Centre d'Etudes et d'Organisation

CEO .... Chief Education Officer [*Australia*]

CEO .... Chief Executive Officer (EECI)

CEO .... Comite Europeen de l'Outillage [*European Tool Committee - ETC*] (EA)

CEO .... Waco Kungo [*Angola*] [*Airport symbol*] (OAG)

CEOA .... Central Europe Operating Agency [*Versailles, France*] [*NATO*]

CEOAH..... Comite Europeen de l'Outillage Agricole et Horticole [*European Committee for Agricultural and Horticultural Tools and Implements - ECAHTI*] (EA)

CEOBM .... Centre pour l'Etude Oceanographique et Biologique Marine [*French*] (MSC)

CEOBOI.... Centro de Documentacion [*Bolivia*] (WGAO)

CEOC .... Centre d'Etudes de l'Orient (WGAO)

CEOC .... Confederation Europeenne d'Organismes de Controle (EAIO)

CEOCOR .. Comite d'Etude de la Corrosion et de la Protection des Canalisations [*Committee for the Study of Pipe Corrosion and Protection*] (EAIO)

CEOCOR .. Commission Europeenne de Corrosion des Conduites Souterraines [*Brussels, Belgium*] (EAIO)

CEOE .... Confederacion Espanola de Organizaciones Empresariales [*Spanish Confederation of Employers' Organizations*] [*Spain*] (EY)

CEOM .... Catholic Education Office, Melbourne [*Australia*]

CEON .... Centro de Estudios y Orientacion Nacional [*Center of Studies and National Orientation*] [*Bolivia*] (LA)

CEOP .... Communaute Europeenne des Organisations de Publicitaires [*European Community of Advertising Organizations*]

CEOS........ Cia Espanola de Ordenadores y Systemas SA [*French*] (ADPT)

CEOS........ County Education Offices Society (WGAO)

CEOSL ..... Confederacion Ecuatoriana de Organizaciones Sindicales Libres [*Ecuadorean Confederation of Free Union Organizations*] [*Quito*] (LA)

CEOST ..... Committee on Equal Opportunities in Science and Technology [*NSF*] (WGAO)

CEOT .... Centre d'Education Ouvriere du Togo [*Workers Education Center of Togo*] (AF)

CEOWA .... Catholic Education Office of Western Australia

CEP............ Caisse d'Epargne et de Prevoyance [*French*]

CEP............ Center of Experimentation in the Pacific Ocean (BARN)

CEP............ Centraal Economisch Plan [*Central Economic Plan*] [*Netherlands*]

CEP............ Centre d'Essais des Propulseurs [*Aerospace Engines Test Center*] [*France*] (PDAA)

CEP............ Centre d'Etudes de Prevention

CEP............ Centre d'Etudes des Matieres Plastiques [*Belgium*] (WGAO)

CEP............ Centro de Estudios Publicos [*Center for Policy Studies*] [*Chile*] [*Research center*] (IRC)

CEP............ Centro de Estudios y Publicaciones [*Peru*] (WGAO)

CEP............ Centro de Estudos de Planeamento [*Center for Planning Studies*] [*Portuguese*] (WER)

CEP............ Centro de Estudos do Pessoal [*Personnel Studies Center*] [*Brazil*] (LA)

CEP............ Centros de Educacion Popular [*Popular Education Centers*] [*Nicaragua*] (LA)

Cep............ Cependant [*French*] (FLAF)

CEP............ Cercle d'Etudes Pediatriques [*French*] (SLS)

CEP............ Certificat d'Etudes Primaires [*Primary Studies Certificate*] (CL)

CEP............ Chile-Ecuador-Peru (MSC)

CEP............ Christian Education Publications [*Australia*]

CEP............ Civil Emergency Planning [*NATO*] (NATG)

CEP............ Colloque Europeen des Paroisses (WGAO)

CEP............ Comite Ejecutivo Permanente [*Standing Executive Committee*] [*Asociacion Latinoamericana de Libre Comercio*] (LAA)

CEP............ Comite Estatal de Precios [*State Committee for Prices*] [*Cuba*] (LA)

CEP............ Comite Estudiantil Peruano [*Peruvian Student Committee*] (LA)

CEP............ Commission d'Enquete Parlementaire

CEP............ Commission on Environmental Planning [*IUCN*] (WGAO)

CEP............ Commonwealth Employment Program [*Australia*]

CEP............ Compagnie d'Encouragement a la Peche

CEP............ Compagnie d'Exploration Petroliere [*Petroleum Exploration Company*] [*Algeria*] (AF)

CEP............ Compagnie Equatoriale de Peintures

CEP............ Compagnie Equatoriale des Pentures [*Cameroon*] (WGAO)

CEP............ Compagnie Europeenne de Publication [*French*]

CEP............ Comptoir d'Exportation du Poisson

CEP............ Concepcion [*Bolivia*] [*Airport symbol*] (OAG)

CEP............ Confederation Europeenne d'Etudes Phystosanitaires [*European Confederation for Plant Protection Research*] [*France*] (PDAA)

CEP............ Country Economic Profiles [*I. P. Sharp Association Pty. Ltd.*] [*Australia*] [*Information service or system*] (CRD)

CEP............ Federation des Organisations Nationales des Grossistes, Importateurs et Exportateurs en Poisson de la CEE (WGAO)

CEPA........ Centrale des Employeurs du Port d'Anvers [*Belgium*] (BAS)

CEPA........ Central Europe Pipeline Agency [*Later, CEOA*] [*NATO*] (NATG)

CEPA........ Centre d'Etudes des Problemes Agricoles (WGAO)

CEPA........ Centro de Educacion y Promocion Agraria [*Agrarian Education and Promotion Center*] [*Nicaragua*] (LA)

CEPA........ Centro Experimental de Produccion Agropecuaria [*Center for Agricultural-Livestock Experimental Production*] [*Nicaragua*] (LA)

CEPA........ Cercle d'Etudes de la Productivite Agricole (WGAO)

CEPA........ Comision Economica para Africa [*Economic Commission for Africa - ECA*] [*United Nations (already exists in GUS II database)*] [*Spanish*] (ASF)

CEPA........ Comision Ejecutiva Portuaria Autonoma [*Autonomous Executive Port Commission*] [*El Salvador*] (LA)

CEPA........ Comite d'Experts pour les Ajustements [*United Nations*] (WGAO)

CEPA........ Commercial Egg Producers' Association [*Australia*]

CEPA........ Commission d'Etudes Pratiques d'Aviation [*French*]

CEPA........ Commission Economique pour l'Afrique [*Economic Commission for Africa - ECA*] [*United Nations (already exists in GUS II database)*] [*French*]

CEPA........ Conference of Fire Protection Associations (WGAO)

CEPA........ Conseil Europeen pour la Protection des Animaux [*European Council for Animal Welfare - ECAW*] (EA)

CEPA........ Consolidated Electric Power Asia (ECON)

CEPA........ Consumers Education and Protective Association International [*United States*] (WGAO)

CEPA........ Corporacion Entrerrianade Productores Avicolas [*Argentina*] (DSCA)

CEPAC .... Centre d'Etudes Politiques en Afrique Centrale [*Zaire*] (SLS)

CEPAC ..... Centro di Produccion Adiovisual para la Capacitacion [*Peru*] (WGAO)

CEPAC ...... Confederation Europeenne de l'Industrie de Pates, Papiers, et Cartons [*European Confederation of Pulp, Paper, and Board Industries*] (EAIO)

CEPAC ...... Conference des Eveques du Pacifique (WGAO)

CEPAC ...... Conferentia Episcopalis Pacifici [*Episcopal Conference of the Pacific*] (EAIO)

CEPACC ... Chemical Education Planning and Coordinating Committee [*ACS*] (WGAO)

CEPAD...... Comite Evangelico pro Ayuda al Desarrollo [*Evangelical Committee for Development Aid*] [*Nicaragua*] (LA)

CEPAD...... Comite Evangelico Pro-Ayuda y Desarrollo [*Nicaragua*] (WGAO)

CEPADES ... Centro Paraguayo de Estudios de Desarrollo Economico y Social [*Paraguayan Center for Economic Social Development Studies*] (LAA)

CEPAF ...... Comite Europeen pour la Protection des Animaux a Fourrure (WGAO)

CEPAJ....... Concurso Estadual de Produtividade Agricola para Jovens [*Brazil*] (DSCA)

CEPAL ...... Comision Economica para America Latina y el Caribe [*Economic Commission for Latin America and the Caribbean - ECLAC*] [*Santiago, Chile*] [*United Nations*] (EAIO)

CEPAL ...... Commission Economique pour l'Amerique Latine [*Economic Commission for Latin America - ECLA*] [*French*] (ASF)

CEPAL ...... Cooperativa Esportazione Produtti Agricoli (WGAO)

CEPALC.... Comision Economica para America Latina y el Caribe [*Economic Commission for Latin America and the Caribbean - ECLAC*] [*Spanish*]

CEPALC.... Commission Economique pour l'Amerique Latine et les Caraibes [*Economic Commission for Latin America and the Caribbean - ECLAC*] [*French*]

CEPAM ..... Centro Ecuatoriano para la Promocion y Accion de la Mujer (WGAO)

CEPAO...... Comision Economica de las Naciones Unidas para el Asia Occidental [*United Nations Economic Commission for Western Asia - ECWA*] [*Spanish*]

CEPAO...... Comision Economica para el Asia Occidental [*ONU*] (WGAO)

CEPAS ...... Centre d'Etudes pour l'Action Sociale

CEPAS ...... Centro di Educazione Professionale per Assistenti Sociali (WGAO)

CEPAZE ... Centre d'Echange et Promotion Artisanal en Zones a Equiper (WGAO)

CEPB .... Civil Emergency Planning Bureau [*NATO*]   (NATG)

CEPB .... Confederacion de Empresarios Privados de Bolivia [*Employers' association*] [*Bolivia*]   (EY)

CEPC .... Central European Pipeline Committee   (WGAO)

CEPC .... Centro de Pesquisas do Cacao [*Cocoa Research Center*] [*Brazil*]   (LAA)

CEPC .... Certificat d'Etudes Primaires Complementaires de l'Enseignement National [*National Education Further Primary Studies Certificate*] [*Laotian*]   (CL)

CEPC .... Comite Elargi du Programme et de la Coordination [*UNDP*]   (WGAO)

CEPCAM .. Centre d'Etudes de Prevention Cameroun   (WGAO)

CEPCEO ... Comite d'Etude des Producteurs de Charbon d'Europe Occidentale [*Association of the Coal Producers of the European Community*]   (EAIO)

CEPCh ...... Confederacion de Empleados Particulares de Chile [*Chilean Confederation of Private Sector Employees*]   (LA)

CEPCIES .. Comision Ejecutiva Permanente del Consejo Interamericano Economico y Social   (WGAO)

CEPD .... Centro de Estudios de Poblacion y Desarrollo [*Peru*]   (DSCA)

CEPD .... Communications-Electronics Policy Directives [*NATO*]   (NATG)

CEPD .... Cooperacion Economica entre Paises en Vias de Desarrollo [*Economic Cooperation among Developing Countries - ECDC*] [*Spanish*]

CEPD .... Cooperation Economique entre Pays en Developpement [*Economic Cooperation among Developing Countries - ECDC*] [*French*]

CEPD .... Council for Economic Planning and Development [*Taiwanese*]   (GEA)

CEPDAC ... Comite d'Etudes pour la Defense et l'Amelioration des Cultures (WGAO)

CEPDECCLA ... Comision Especial de Programacion y Desarrollo de la Educacion, la Ciencia, y la Cultura en America Latina [*Organizacion de Estados Americanos - OEA*]   (LAA)

CEPE .... Centre d'Etudes des Programmes Economiques

CEPE .... Centre d'Etudes Phytosociologiques et Ecologiques [*Center for Phytosociological and Ecological Studies*] [*Under the CNRS*] [*French*]   (WER)

CEPE .... Certificat d'Etudes Primaires et Elementaires [*Primary and Elementary Studies Certificate*] [*Malagasy*]   (AF)

CEPE .... Comision Economica para Europa [*Economic Commission for Europe - ECE*] [*Spanish*]   (ASF)

CEPE .... Comite Eetbaar Plantaardig Eiwit   (WGAO)

CEPE .... Comite Europeen des Associations de Fabricants de Pentures, d'Encres d' Imprimerie et de Couleurs d'Art   (WGAO)

CEPE .... Comite Europeen des Associations des Fabricants de Peinture, d'Encres d'Imprimerie, et de Couleurs [*European Committee of Paint, Printing Ink, and Artists' Colours Manufacturers Associations*]   (EAIO)

CEPE .... Compagnie d'Electronique et de Piezo-Electricite   (WGAO)

CEPE .... Corporacion Estatal Petrolera Ecuatoriana [*Ecuadorean State Petroleum Corporation*]   (LA)

CEPEB ...... Centre d'Etudes et de Promotion des Entreprises Beninoises

CEPEC ...... Centro de Pesquisas do Cacau [*Cacao Research Center*] [*Research center*] [*Brazil*]   (IRC)

CEPEC ...... Committee of European Associations of Maufacturers of Passive Electronic Components   (WGAO)

CEPECA ... Centrul de Perfectionare a Pregatirii Cadrelor de Conducere din Intreprinderi [*Center for Advanced Training of Management Personnel in Enterprises*]   (RO)

CEPECOM ... Centrul de Perfectionare a Lucrarilor din Comert [*Center for Improving Work in Trade*]   (RO)

CEPECOOP ... Centrul de Perfectionare a Cadrelor din Cooperatia de Consum [*Center for Advanced Training of Personnel in the Consumer Cooperative System*]   (RO)

CEPED ...... Centro de Pesquisas e Desenvolvimento [*Research and Development Center*] [*Research center*] [*Brazil*]   (IRC)

Cepede ...... Centrala Importowo-Eksportowa Przemyslu Drzewnego [*Central Import-Export Office of the Lumber Industry*]   (POL)

CEPEIGE ... Centro Panamericano de Estudios e Investigaciones Geograficas [*Pan American Center for Geographical Studies and Research - PACGSR*]   (EAIO)

CEPEIT ..... Centrul pentru Perfectionarea Personalului Didactic din Invatamintul Profesional si Tehnic [*Center for the Advanced Training of Teaching Cadres in Vocational and Technical Education*]   (RO)

CEPEM ..... Centre d'Etude Europeenne pour les Problemes de l'Environnement Marine [*European Center for Marine Environmental Problems*] [*French*]   (MSC)

CEPEM ..... Centre d'Etudes Europeen pour les Problems de l'Environement Marin   (WGAO)

CEPEM ..... Centro de Preparacion de Especialistas Menores [*Training Center for Junior Specialists*] [*Cuba*]   (LA)

CEPEN ...... Centro de Preparacion de Especialistas Navales [*Naval Specialists Training Center*] [*Cuba*]   (LA)

CEPEP ...... Centro Paraguayo de Estudios de Poblacion   (WGAO)

CEPEPA.... Comite Economique de la Prune d'Ente et du Pruneau d'Agen (WGAO)

CEPER ...... Centre d'Edition et de Production pour l'Enseignement et la Recherche [*Publisher*] [*Cameroon*]

CEPER ...... Centre d'Etudes et de Perfectionnement [*ANDCP*]   (WGAO)

CEPERN ... Centro Panamericano de Entrenamiento para Evaluacion de Recursos Naturales [*Brazil*]   (WGAO)

CEPERN ... Centro Panamericano de Entrenamiento para la Evolucion de los Recursos Naturales [*Pan American Training Center for Evaluation of Natural Resources*] [*Rio De Janeiro, Brazil*]   (LAA)

CEPES .... Centre d'Etudes Politiques, Economiques et Sociales [*Belgium*] (BAS)

CEPES .... Centre Europeen pour la Promotion et la Formation en Milieu Agricole et Rural [*Belgium*]   (WGAO)

CEPES .... Centre Europeen pour l'Enseignement Superieur [*European Centre for Higher Education*]   (EAIO)

CEPES .... Centro de Estudios Politicos, Economicos, y Sociales [*Center for Political, Economic, and Social Studies (of the PRI)*] [*Mexico*]   (LA)

CEPES .... Comissao Especial para Execucao do Plano de Melhoramento e Expansao do Ensino Superior [*Rio De Janeiro, Brazil*]   (LAA)

CEPES .... Comitato Europeo per il Progresso Economico e Sociale [*European Committee for Economic and Social Development*] [*Italian*]   (WER)

CEPES .... Comite Europeen pour le Progres Economique et Social [*European Committee for Economic and Social Progress*]

CEPES .... European Centre for Higher Education [*Romania*]   (WGAO)

CEPET ...... Centro de Formacion y Adiestramiento Petrolero y Petroquimico [*Venezuela*]

CEPEX ...... Centre de Promotion des Exportations [*Export Promotion Center*] [*Tunisia*]

CEPEX ...... Centro de Exportacion de la Agrupacion de Fabricantes de Calzado [*Trade association*] [*Spain*]   (EY)

CEPEX ...... Centro de Promocion de las Exportaciones [*Paraguay*]   (IMH)

CEPEX ...... Centro Promotor de Exportadores de la Ficia   (WGAO)

CEPFAR.... Centre Europeen pour la Promotion de la Formation Milieu Agricole et Rural [*European Training and Development Centre for Farming and Rural Life - ETDCFRL*]   (EAIO)

CEPFL ...... Economic Community of the Great Lakes Countries [*Rwanda*]

CEPGL ...... Communaute Economique des Pays des Grands Lacs [*Economic Community of the Great Lakes Countries - ECGLC*] [*Gisenye, Rwanda*]   (EAIO)

CEPH .... Center for the Study of Human Polymorphism [*France*]

CEPH .... Centre d'Etude du Polymorphisme Humain [*Center for the Study of Human Polymorphism*] [*France*]

CEPHAG... Centre d'Etudes des Phenomenes Aleatoires et Geophysiques [*Geophysical and Random Phenomena Study Center*] [*France*]   (EAS)

CEPHH ..... Centro de Estudos e Pesquisas de Hidraulica e Hidrologia [*Brazil*]   (DSCA)

CEPHR...... Comite d'Etude pour la Promotion de l'Habitat Rural   (WGAO)

CEPI .... Centre d'Etudes de Prevention Ivoirien

CEPI .... Centre d'Etudes et de Promotion Industrielles [*Mali*]

CEPI .... Centre four l'Ecouragement de l'Epargne et des Placements Immobiliers [*Benelux*]   (BAS)

CEPI .... Circulo de Escritores y Poetas Iberoamericanos   (WGAO)

CEPI .... Convenios de Especificaciones de Productos Internos [*Agreements on Specifications for Domestic Products*] [*Cuba*]   (LA)

CEPIA .... Caisse d'Encouragement a la Peche

CEPIA .... Centre d'Etudes Pratiques d'Informatique et d'Automatique [*French*]   (ADPT)

CEPIA .... Centre Francais de Promotion Industrielle en Afrique   (WGAO)

CEPIC .... Centre Politique des Independants et Cadres Chretiens [*Political Center of Christian Independents and Cadres*] [*Belgian, French*]   (WER)

CEPIECC .. Comision Ejecutiva Permanente Consejo Interamericano para la Educacion, la Ciencia y la Cultura   (WGAO)

CEPII .... Centre d'Etudes Prospectives et d'Informations Internationales [*Center for International Prospective Studies*] [*Research center*] [*French*]   (IRC)

CEPIS .... Centro de Educacao Popular Instituto Sedes Sapientiae [*Brazil*]   (WGAO)

CEPIS .... Centro Panamericano de Ingenieria Sanitaria y Ciencias del Ambiente [*Pan American Center for Sanitary Engineering and Environmental Sciences*] [*Peru*] [*Research center*]   (IRC)

CEPISA ..... Centrais Eletricas do Piani, Sociedad Anonima [*Brazil*]   (LAA)

CEPITRA ... Centre de Perfectionnement des Industries Textiles [*French*]   (SLS)

CEPITRA ... Centre de Perfectionnement des Industries Textiles Rhone-Alpes (WGAO)

CEPL......... Comite Espanol de Plasticos en Agricultura (WGAO)
CEPL......... Conference Europeenne des Pouvoirs Locaux (WGAO)
CEPLA...... Centro de Planeamiento [*Chile*] (LAA)
CEPLA...... Comision de Estudio para la Promocion de la Lana Argentina [*Argentina*] (LAA)
CEPLA...... Comite Espanol de Plasticos en Agricultura [*Spain*] (DSCA)
CEPLAC.... Comissao Executiva do Plano da Lavoura Cacaueira [*Executive Commission for the Cocoa Production Plan*] [*Brazil*] (LA)
CEPLAC.... Comissao Executiva do Plano de Recuperacao Economico-Rural da Lavoura Cacaueira [*Executive Committee for the Economic Recovery of the Cocoa Culture*] [*Rio De Janeiro, Brazil*] (LAA)
CEPLAES ... Centro de Planificacion y Estudios Sociales, Quito [*Ecuador*] (WGAO)
CEPLAN ... Comissao Estadual do Planejamento do Governo do Estado do Rio [*Brazil*] (DSCA)
CEPM....... Centre d'Exploitation Postal Metropolitain [*French Postal Department*] (PDAA)
CEPM....... Comite d'Etudes Petrolieres Marines [*French*] (MSC)
CEPMAE .. Centre d'Edition et de Production Manuels et d'Auxiliaires de l'Enseignement
CEPMMT ... Centre Europeen pour les Previsions Meteorologiques a Moyen Terme (WGAO)
CePO .... Centrala Poszukiwan Osob [*Central Office of Missing Persons*] (POL)
CEPO .... Central Engineering Projects Office [*NATO*] (NATG)
CEPO .... Central Europe Pipeline Office [*NATO*]
CEPO .... County Emergency Planning Officers Society (WGAO)
CEPOI....... Centre d'Etudes des Pays de l'Ocean Indien (WGAO)
CEPOM..... Centre d'Etudes des Problemes d'Outre-Mer [*Center for the Study of Overseas Problems*] [*France*] (AF)
CEPPAF.... Comite Europeen pour la Protection des Phoques et autres Animaux a Fourrure (WGAO)
CEPPC ...... Central Europe Pipeline Policy Committee [*NATO*]
CEPr .... Centre d'Essais des Propulseurs [*Aircraft Motor Testing Center*] [*French*] (WER)
CEPR........ Centre for Economic Policy Research [*Australian National University*] [*Economics*] [*Australia*]
CEPR......... Cercle des Etudiants Progressistes Rwandais [*Rwandan Progressive Students Club*] (AF)
CEPRA ...... Cooperative d'Elevage Pastorale de la Revolution Agraire [*Stock Breeding Cooperative of the Agrarian Revolution*] [*Algeria*] (AF)
CEPRIG .... Centre de Perfectionnement pour la Recherche Industrielle et sa Gestion [*Center for Improving Industrial Research and its Management*] [*France*] (PDAA)
CEPRO...... Centre d'Etudes des Problemes Humains du Travail
CEPROFI ... Certificado de Promocion Fiscal [*Mexico*] (IMH)
CEPRON... Centro de Productividade do Nordeste [*Fortaleza, Brazil*] (LAA)
CEPS .... Central Europe Pipeline System [*NATO*] (NATG)
CEPS .... Centre for European Policy Studies (ECON)
CEPS .... Centro de Estudos e Pesquisas de Sociologia [*Brazil*] (WGAO)
CEPS .... Commission Europeenne pour la Promotion de Soie (WGAO)
CEPS .... Customs, Excise, and Preventive Service [*Ghana*]
CEPSA ...... Centro Studi di Psicologia e Sociologia Applicate ad Indirizzo Adleriano [*Italian*] (SLS)
CEPSA ...... Compania Espanola de Petroleos SA (WGAO)
CEPSA ...... Compania Espanola de Petroleos, Sociedad Anonima [*Spanish Petroleum Company*] (WER)
CEPSC....... Centre d'Etudes des Problemes Sociaux Congolais
CEPSE....... Centre d'Etudes Politiques et Sociales Europeennes (FLAF)
CEPSE....... Centre d'Etudes Politques et Sociales Europeenes (WGAO)
CEPSE....... Centre d'Execution de Programmes Sociaux et Economiques [*Zaire*] (SLS)
CEPSE....... Centro Empresarial de Perfeccionamiento Socio-Economico [*Mexico*] (DSCA)
CEPSI........ Centre d'Etude des Problemes Sociaux Indigenes [*Center for the Study of Indigenous Social Problems*] [*Zaire*] (AF)
CePsiPeDi ... Centro Psico-Pedagogico Didattico [*Italian*] (SLS)
CEPT .... Centro de Estudos de Pedologia Tropical [*Tropical Pedology Research Center*] [*Portuguese*] (ARC)
CEPT .... Conference Europeenne des Administrations des Postes et des Telecommunications [*Conference of European Postal and Telecommunications Administrations*] [*Telecommunications*] (EAIO)
CEPTI .... Comite de Estudios del Proyecto de Tinajones [*Peru*] (DSCA)
CEPVDVM ... Centre d'Etude des Problems Viticoles et de Defense des Vins Meridionaux (WGAO)
CEPYME .. Confederacion Espanola de Pequena y Mediana Empresa [*Employers' organization*] [*Spain*] (EY)
CEPYRDE ... Cuerpo Especial de Prevencion y Represion de Delitos Economicos [*Special Force for the Prevention and Repression of Economic Crimes*] [*Uruguay*] (LA)
CER .... Cancer-Environment Register [*Sweden*]
CER .... Celmar Servicios Aereos SA de CV [*Mexico*] [*ICAO designator*] (FAAC)

CER .... Centre for Economic Research
CER .... Centres d'Enseignement Revolutionnaire [*Revolutionary Education Centers*] [*Guinea*] (AF)
CER .... Centres d'Expansion Rurale [*Rural Expansion Centers*] [*Senegal*] (AF)
cer.............. Ceramics (TPFD)
cer.............. Ceramique [*French*] (TPFD)
Cer.............. Cerrahiye [*Surgical Ward, Surgery*] (TU)
CER .... Cherbourg [*France*] [*Airport symbol*] (OAG)
CER .... Closer Economic Relationship [*Australia and New Zealand*]
CER .... College d'Enseignement Rural
CER .... Comissao de Estudos Rodoviarios [*Road Studies Commission*] [*Mozambique*] (AF)
CER .... Comite d'Expansion Regional [*French*]
CER .... Commission d'Etudes et de Recherches [*Study and Research Commission*] [*Cambodia*] (CL)
CER .... Community of European Railways [*Belgium*] (EAIO)
CER .... Conferencia Ecuatoriana de Religiosos (WGAO)
CER .... Consultative Environmental Review [*Australia*]
CER .... Council of European Regions (EAIO)
CERA........ Centrale Raiffieisenkas [*Belgium*] (WGAO)
CERA........ Centre d'Etudes des Recherches Arabe-Islamiques (WGAO)
CERA........ Centre d'Etudes des Religions Africaines [*Studies Center for African Religions*] [*Zaire*] (AF)
CERA........ Centre d'Etudes du Risque Atomique [*Switzerland*] (WGAO)
CERA........ Centre d'Etudes et de Recherches en Automatisme [*Study and Research Center on Automation*] [*French*] (WER)
CERA........ Centre d'Etudes et de Recherches sur l'Aquiculture [*Belgium*] (ASF)
CERA........ Centros de Reforma Agraria [*Agrarian Reform Centers*] [*Chile*] (LA)
CERA........ Comision Especial de Expertos para el Estudio de las Necesidades Financieras que Plantea la Ejecucion de Planes de Reforma Agraria [*Consejo Interamericano Economico y Social*] [*Washington, DC*]
CERA........ Comptoirs d'Equipements et de Reparations Automobiles
CERABATI ... Compagnie Generale de la Ceramique du Batiment [*French*]
CERAC...... Centre d'Etudes pour le Ruralisme et l'Amenagement des Campagnes (WGAO)
CERAC...... Comite d'Expansion Regionale et d'Amenagement de la Champagne (WGAO)
CERACHIM ... Centre de Recherche, d'Analyse, et de Controle Chimiques [*Research, Analysis, and Chemical Control Center*] [*Research center*] [*Belgium*] (IRC)
CERAFER ... Centre National d'Etudes Techniques et de Recherches Technologiques pour l'Agriculture, l'Equipment Rural et les Forets [*National Center for Technical Studies and Technological Research for Agriculture, Rural Equipment and Forests*] [*France*] (PDAA)
CERAFER ... Centre National d'Etudes Techniques et de Recherches Technologiques pour l'Agriculture, les Forets et l'Equipement Rural (WGAO)
CERAG...... Centre d'Etudes et de Recherches Agricoles [*Algeria*]
CERAG...... Centre d'Etudes Regionales Antilles-Guyane (WGAO)
CERAM..... Centre d'Enseignement et de Recherche de la Chambre de Commerce et d'Industrie de Nice et des Alpes-Maritimes a Sophia-Antipolis
CERAMBRUX ... European Centre for Medical Application and Research (EAIO)
CERAMEUNIE ... Bureau de Liaison des Industries Ceramique du Marche Commun [*Belgium*] (WGAO)
CERAMGABON ... Societe Gabonaise de Ceramique (WGAO)
CERAO ..... Conference Episcopale Regionale de l'Afrique de l'Ouest Francophone (WGAO)
CERAR...... Centre d'Education Rurale et Artisanale au Rwanda
CERAT...... Centre de Recherche sur le Politique, l'Administration, et le Territoire [*Research Center for Political, Administrative, and Regional Studies*] [*Research center*] [*France*] (IRC)
CERAT...... Centre d'Etude et de Recherche sur l'Administration Economique et l'Amenagement du Territoire (WGAO)
CERB........ Centre d'Etudes et de Recherche Biophysiologiques Appliquees a la Marine [*France*]
CERB........ Conseil Economique Regional pour le Brabant [*Belgium*] (WGAO)
CERBE...... Centrum voor Rationele Bedrijfsvoering Zuidhollandse Eilanden (WGAO)
CERBH ..... Cycle d'Etude et de Recherche en Biologie Humaine [*French*]
CERBHA... Centre d'Etudes et de Recherches en Biologie Humaine et Animale [*Algeria*] (SLS)
CERBI .... Centro de Referencia y Biblioteca [*Instituto Nacional de Fomento Municipal*] [*Colorado*]
CERBOM ... Centre d'Etudes et de Recherches de Biologie et d'Oceanographie Medicale [*Center for Investigations and Biological Research and Medical Oceanography*] (ASF)
CERC........ Centre d'Etudes des Revenus et des Cots (WGAO)
CERC........ Civil Engineering Research Council (WGAO)

CERC......... Coastal Environment Resource Centre [*New South Wales, Australia*]

CERC......... Comite Europeen des Representants de Commerce Group CEE (WGAO)

CERC......... Commonwealth Employees' Rehabilitation and Compensation Act [*Australia*]

CERCA...... Centre d'Enseignement Rural par Correspondance d'Angers (WGAO)

CERCA...... Centre de Recherches pour Combustibles Atomiques [*French*]

CERCA...... Centre d'Etudes et de Recherches Catalanes des Archives (WGAO)

CERCA...... Compagnie pour l'Etude et la Realisation de Combustible Atomique [*Company for the Study and Manufacture of Atomic Fuel*] [*French*]   (WER)

CERCG...... Centre d'Etudes et de Realisations Cartographiques Geographiques [*Geographical Cartography Center*] [*Centre National de la Recherche Scientifique*] [*French*]   (EAS)

CERCHAR ... Centre d'Etudes et Recherches des Charbonnages de France [*Coal Mining Research and Development Center of France*] (WER)

CERCI....... Centre for Educational Resources in the Construction Industry (WGAO)

CERCI....... Compagnie d'Etudes et Realisations de Cybernetique Industrielle [*France*]   (PDAA)

CERCI....... Cooperativa de Educacao e Reabilitacao das Criancas Inadaptadas   (WGAO)

CERCLE.... Centre d'Etudes et de Recherches sur les Collectives Locales en Europe   (WGAO)

CERCOA... Centre d'Etudes et de Recherches de Chimie Organique Appliquee [*French*]   (SLS)

CERCOL... Centre de Recherches Scientifiques et Techniques des Conserves de Legumes et desIndustries Connexes [*Scientific and Technical Research Center for the Vegetable Canning and Allied Industries*] [*Belgium*]   (PDAA)

CERCOL... Centre de Recherches Techniques et Scientifiques de Conserves de Legumes [*Belgium*]   (WGAO)

CERCON .. Cerramientos de Construccion [*Colombia*]   (COL)

CERCOR... Centre Europeen de Recherches sur les Organisations et Ordres Religieux   (WGAO)

CERCOVINS ... Centrale Regionale de Conditionnement et de Commercialisation de Vins et Spiritueux

CERD .... Comite Europeen de Recherche et de Developpement [*Belgium*] (SLS)

CERD .... Committee on the Elimination of Racial Discrimination [*Switzerland*]   (EAIO)

CERDA...... Centre d'Etudes et de Recherches sur le Developpement Regional [*Algeria*]   (SLS)

CERDAC... Centre d'Etudes et de Recherches Documentaires pour 'Afrique Centrale [*Zaire*]   (SLS)

CERDAC... Centre d'Etudes et de Recherches Documentaires sur Afrique Centrale [*Zaire*]   (WGAO)

CERDAC... Centro Regional de Documentacion para el Desarrollo Agricola de America Central [*Costa Rica*]   (WGAO)

CeRDAC... Centro Richerche e Documentazione sull'Antichita Classica [*Italian*]   (SLS)

CERDAS ... Centre de Coordination des Recherches et de la Documentation en Science Sociale Desservant l'Afrique Sud-Saharienne [*Center for Coordination of Social Science Research and Documentation for Sub-Saharan Africa*]   (AF)

CERDAS ... Centre de Coordination des Recherches et de la Documentation en Sciences Sociales en Afrique Sub-Saharienne [*UNESCO*] (WGAO)

CERDEC ... Center for Research and Documentation on the European Community [*American University*] [*Research center*] (RCD)

CERDEM ... Centre d'Etudes et de Recherches sur le Droit et l'Environnement Marin [*French*]   (MSC)

CERDI....... Centre d'Etudes et de Recherches sur le Developpement International [*Center forStudies and Research on International Development*] [*France*]   (IRC)

CERDIA .... Centre de Documentation des Industries Utilisatices de Produits Agricoles   (WGAO)

CERDIA .... Centre d'Etude, Recherche, et Documentation des Industries Agricoles et Alimentaires [*France*]

CERDIC.... Centre de Recherches et de Documentation des Institutions Chretiennes [*Christian Institutions Research and Documentation Center*] [*France*] [*Information service or system*]   (IID)

CERDO ..... Centre d'Etudes et de Recherche sur le Developpement Regional [*Algeria*]   (SLS)

CERDOC... Centre d'Etudes et de Recherches Documentaires [*French*]

CERDOTOLA ... Centre Regional de Documentation sur les Traditions Orales et les Langues Africaines [*Regional Center for Documentation on Oral Traditions and African Languages*] (AF)

CERDOTOLA ... Centre Regional de Recherche et de Documentation pour les Traditions Orales et le Developpement des Langues Africaines [*Center for Research and Documentation on Oral Traditions and the Development of African Languages*] [*Cameroon*] [*Research center*]   (IRC)

CERDP...... Centre Europeen de Recherche et de Documentation Parlementaires [*European Centre for Parliamentary Research and Documentation - ECPRD*] [*Luxembourg*] (EAIO)

CERDS...... Charter of Economic Rights and Duties of States [*United Nations*]

CERE........ Centre d'Essais Regional Europeen [*European Regional Test Center*] [*NATO*]   (NATG)

CERE........ Centre d'Etudes et de Recherches de Environnement [*Center for Environmental Study and Research*] [*Belgium*]   (PDAA)

CERE........ Comite Europeen pour les Relations Economiques   (FLAF)

CEREA...... Centre de Regroupement Africain [*Center for African Grouping*] [*Algeria*]

CEREA...... Centre National de Recherches pour l'Etude des Animaux Nuisibles ou Utiles a l'Agriculture [*Belgium*]   (WGAO)

CEREA...... Comision Especial de Representantes de Entidades Agropecuarias [*Argentina*]   (LAA)

CEREBE.... Centre de Recherche sur le Bien-Etre   (WGAO)

CEREC...... Centre Europeen de Recherches Economiques et Commerciales (FLAF)

CERED...... Centre de Recherches d'Etudes Demographiques [*Morocco*] (WGAO)

CERED...... Centre de Recherches d'Etudes Deniographiques [*Research Center for Demographic Studies*] [*Morocco*]   (PDAA)

CEREEQ... Centre Experimental de Recherches et d'Etudes pour l'Equipement [*Senegal*]

CEREFAQ ... Comision Ejecutiva de Repoblacion Educacion Forestal Agropecuaria [*Cuba*]   (WGAO)

CEREGE... Centre de Recherches en Economie et Gestion des Enterprises [*Belgium*]   (WGAO)

CEREL...... Centro de Estudios de la Realidad Latinoamericana [*Venezuela*] (WGAO)

CEREMADE ... Centre de Recherche de Mathematiques de Decision

CEREN...... Centre d'Etudes Regionales sur l'Economie de l'Energie (WGAO)

CEREN...... Centro de Estudios de la Realidad Nacional [*Chile*]   (LAA)

CERENA... Comissao de Estudos de Recursos Naturais Renovaveis do Parana [*Brazil*]   (DSCA)

CEREOPA ... Centre d'Etudes et de Recherche sur l'Economie et l'Organisation des ProductionsAnimales   (WGAO)

CEREP ...... Centro de Estudios de la Realidad Puertorriquena   (WGAO)

CEREQ...... Centre d'Etudes et de Recherches sur les Enseignements et les Qualifications [*French*]

CEREQ...... Centre d'Etudes et de Recherches sur les Qualifications   (WGAO)

CERER...... Comite d'Etudes et de Recherches Economiques Rurales [*France*]   (FLAF)

CERES ...... Centre d'Assais et de Recherches d'Engins Speciaux   (WGAO)

CERES ...... Centre de Recherches Socio-Religieuses [*Burundi*]   (WGAO)

CERES ...... Centre d'Essais et de Recherches d'Engins Speciaux [*Center for Test and Research of Missiles*] [*France*]   (PDAA)

CERES ...... Centre d'Etude, de Recherche, et d'Education Socialistes [*Center for Socialist Study, Research, and Education*] [*Senegal*] (AF)

CERES ...... Centre d'Etudes et de Recherches Economiques et Sociales [*Economic and Social Research and Studies Center*] [*French*]   (AF)

CERES ...... Centres d'Etudes et de Recherches et d'Education Socialiste (WGAO)

CERES ...... Centro de Estudios de la Realidad Economica y Social [*Bolivia*] (WGAO)

CERES ...... Centro de Estudios y Reformas Economico-Sociales [*Quito, Ecuador*]   (LAA)

CERES ...... Centro de la Realidad Economica y Social [*Bolivia*]

CERES ...... Centro di Richerche Economiche e Sociali [*Labor economics research center*] [*Italian*]   (SLS)

CERES ...... Comite d'Etudes Regionales Economiques et Sociales

CERES ...... Controlled Environment Research Laboratory [*CSIRO*] [*Australia*]   (ASF)

CERESD ... Center of Social Democratic Studies and Thought [*Portuguese*] (WER)

CERESIS .. Centro Regional de Sismologia para America del Sur [*Regional Seismology Center for South America*] [*Peru*] [*Research center*]   (IRC)

CERF........ Centre d'Etudes et de Recherches en Fonderies [*Belgium*] (WGAO)

CERF........ Centre d'Experimentation, de Recherche, et de Formation [*North African*]

CERF........ Comptoir Electro Radio-Froid [*Morocco*]

CERF........ Council of Europe Resettlement Fund

CERFA...... Centre d'Enregistrement et de Revision des Formulaires Administratifs [*France*]   (FLAF)

CERFA...... Compagnie des Experts Reunis France Afrique

CERFACS ... Centre Europeen de Recherche et de Formation Avancee en Calcul Scientifique [*Institute for research and training in numerical analysis*] [*French*]

CERFER.... Centre de Formation pour Entretien Routier

CERG .... Chemical Engineering Research Group [*Council for Scientific and Industrial Research*] [*South Africa*] (AA)

CERGA...... Centre d'Etudes et de Recherches Gazieres [*Gas Research and Study Centre*] [*Belgium*] (WED)

CERGA...... Centre d'Etudes et de Recherches Geodynamiques et Astronomiques [*Geodynamics and Astronomy Research Center*] [*Centre National de la Recherche Scientifique*] [*France*] (EAS)

CERGE...... [*The*] Center for Economic Research and Graduate Education [*Prague*] (ECON)

CERGEC ... Centre de Recherche Geographique et de Production Cartographique [*Research Center for Geography and Cartography*] [*Congo*] (IRC)

CERGIV .... Centre d'Economie Rurale et de Gestion d'Ille et Vilaine (WGAO)

CERGRENE ... Centre d'Enseignement et de Recherche pour la Gestion des Ressources Naturelles et l'Environnement [*Management of Natural Resources and Environment Study Center*] [*Paris, France*] [*Research center*] (ERC)

CERH .... Comite Europeen de Rink Hockey [*European Committee for Rink Hockey*] (EAIO)

CERI.......... Center for Educational Research and Innovation [*Research center*] [*French*] (IRC)

CERI.......... Central Education Research Institute [*Korea*] (WGAO)

CERI.......... Centre d'Etude des Relations Internationales (WGAO)

CERI.......... Centre d'Etudes et de Recherches en Informatique [*Computer Study and Research Center*] [*Algeria*] (AF)

CERI.......... Centre d'Etudes et de Recherches Internationales [*Center of International Studies and Research*]

CERI.......... Centre d'Etudes et de Recherches par Irradiation [*Centre for Studies and Research by Irradiation*] [*France*] (WND)

CERI.......... Centre d'Etudes sur la Recherche et l'Innovation (WGAO)

CERI.......... Centre Europeen de Recherches sur l'Investissement (EAIO)

CERI.......... Centre Europeen de Recherche sur l'Investissement Prive (WGAO)

CERI.......... Centre for Educational Research and Innovation (EAIO)

CERIA .... Centre d'Enseignement et de Recherches des Industries Alimentaires et Chimiques [*Center for Research and Training in Food Science and Technology*] [*Research center*] [*Belgium*] (IRC)

CERIB .... Centre d'Etudes et de Recherches de l'Industrie du Beton [*Study and Researc h Center of the Concrete Industry*] [*France*] (PDAA)

CERIC .... Consortium d'Etudes et de Realisations Industrielles et Commerciales

CERICAM ... Ceramiques Industrielles du Cameroun (WGAO)

CERICAM ... Societe Ceramique Industrielle du Cameroun

CERIES..... Centre de Recherches et Investigations Eridermiques et Sensorielles [*The Epidermal and Sensory Research and Investigation Center*] [*Funded by Chanel*] [*France*]

CERILH .... Centre d'Etudes et de Recherches de l'Industrie des Liants Hydrauliques [*Research and Development Center for the Hydraulic Binder Industry*] [*France*]

CERIN....... Centre d'Etrudes des Relations Interethniques de Nice (WGAO)

CERINECA ... Centre International d'Etudes et de Recherches sur l'Integration Economique de l'Afrique [*International Center for Studies and Research on the Economic Integration of Africa*] (AF)

CERIS .... Centro de Estatisticas Religiosas e Investigacao Social [*Religious Statistics and Social Research Center*] [*Brazil*] (LA)

CERISIE ... Centro di Ricerca e di Sviluppo nell'Impiego degli Elastomeri [*Research and Development Center for the Use of Elastomers*] [*Research center*] [*Italian*] (IRC)

CERK........ Centre d'Etudes et de Recherches de Kara

CERL........ Central Electricity Research Laboratories (WGAO)

CERLAL.... Centro Regional para el Fomento del Libro en America Latina [*Colorado*] (SLS)

CERLALC ... Centro Regional para el Fomento del Libro en America Latina y El Caribe [*Colombia*] (WGAO)

CERM .... Centre d'Etudes et de Recherches Marxistes [*Center for Marxist Study and Research*] [*French*] (WER)

CERMA..... Centre d'Etudes et de Recherches de Medecine Aeronautique [*French*]

CERMA..... Centre d'Etudes et de Recherches du Machinisme Agricole (WGAO)

CERMAC ... Centre d'Enseignement et de Recherche en Materiaux de Construction [*Construction Materials Research and Teaching Center*] [*Research center*] [*France*] (IRC)

CERMAC ... Centre de Recherches sur le Monde Arabe Contemporain

CERMACOM ... Compagnie pour l'Exploitation des Ressources Maritimes et le Commerce

CERMAP.. Centre d'Etudes Mathematiques pour la Planification (WGAO)

CERMAT ... Centre de Recherche Mecanique Appliquee au Textile [*Applied Mechanics Research Center for Textiles*] [*Research center*] [*French*] (ERC)

CERMES .. Centre d'Enseignement et de Recherche en Mecanique des Sols [*Soil Mechanic s Research and Study Center*] [*France*] (EAS)

CERMES .. Centre de Recherches sur les Meningites et les Schistomiases [*Niger*] (WGAO)

CERMO .... Centre d'Etudes et de Recherches de la Machine-Outil [*Machine Tool Research and Study Center*] [*France*] (PDAA)

CERMOC ... Centre d'Etudes et de Recherches sur le Moyen-Orient Contemporain [*Center for Contemporary Studies and Research on the Middle East*] [*Beirut, Lebanon*] [*Research center*] (IRC)

CERMTRI ... Centre d'Etude et de Recherches sur les Mouvements Trotskystes et Revolutionnaires Internationaux (WGAO)

CERN .... Centre Europeen des Recherches Nucleaires [*European Center for Nuclear Research*] [*French*]

CERN .... China International Research Network

CERN .... Conseil Europeen pour la Recherche Nucleaire [*European Council for Nuclear Research*] [*ICSU Geneva, Switzerland*]

CERN .... Consiglio Europeo per le Ricerche Nucleari [*European Council for Nuclear Research*] [*Use ECNR*] [*Research center*] [*Italian*] (WER)

CERN .... Organisation Europeenne pour la Recherche Nucleaire [*European Organization for Nuclear Research*] [*Acronym represents previous name, Conseil Europeen pour la Recherche Nucleaire*] (EAIO)

CERNA ..... Conference des Eveques de la Region Nord de l'Afrique [*North African Episcopal Conference*] (EAIO)

CERNA ..... Conference Episcopale Regionale du Nord de l'Afrique (WGAO)

CERNAS... Comissao Executiva da Rede Nacional de Armazens e Silos [*Brazil*] (DSCA)

CERNE...... Companhia de Eletrificacao Rural do Nordeste [*Northeast Rural Electrification Company*] [*Brazil*] (LA)

CERP........ Cente d'Etudes et de Recherches Psychotechniques (WGAO)

CERP........ Centre d'Etudes des Reformes Politiques [*Center for the Study of Political Reforms*] [*Belgium*] (WER)

CERP........ Centre Europeen des Relations Publiques [*European Public Relations Center*]

CERP........ Centro de Estudios de Relaciones Publicas [*Public Relations Studies Center*] [*Colorado*] (LA)

CERP........ Confederation Europeenne des Relations Publiques [*European Confederation of Public Relations*] (EAIO)

CERPA ...... Centre d'Etude et de Recherche sur la Pollution Atmospherique [*Belgium*] (WGAO)

CERPA ...... Centro de Estudios y de Investigaciones Peruanas y Andinas [*Center for Peruvian and Andean Studies and Research*] (LA)

CERPE ...... Centro de Reflexion y Planificacion Educativa [*Venezuela*] (WGAO)

CERPER.... Empresa Publica de Certificaciones Pesqueras [*Public Enterprise for Fishing Certificates*] [*Peru*] (LA)

CERPER.... Empresa Publica de Certificaciones Pesqueras del Peru (WGAO)

CERPHOS ... Centre d'Etudes et de Recherches des Phosphates Mineraux [*Morocco*]

CERQUA .. Centre de Developpement des Certificatins des Qualities Agricoles et Alimentaires (WGAO)

CERR........ Centre d'Ecologie des Ressources Renouvelables [*Ecology of Renewable Resources Center*] [*Centre National de la Recherche Scientifique*] [*France*] (EAS)

CERR........ Comite Europeen de Reflexion sur les Retraites [*European Pension Committee*] [*Paris, France*] (EAIO)

CERR........ Commonwealth Employees Redeployment and Retirement Act [*Australia*] (ADA)

CERRACOL ... Cerraduras de Colombia SA [*Colombia*] (COL)

CERRAMETAL ... Cerraduras Metalicas Medellin (COL)

CERRAT ... Commonwealth Employees Redeployment and Retirement Appeals Tribunals [*Australia*]

CE/RRT .... Central Europe Railroad Transport [*NATO*] (NATG)

CeRS.......... Centre de Recherches Sociologiques [*Center for Sociological Research*] [*France*] (IRC)

CERS........ Centre d'Etudes et de Recherches Scientifiques (WGAO)

CERS........ Centre Europeen de Recherches Spatiales (FLAF)

CERSE ...... Centre National d'Etudes et de Recherches Socio-Economiques [*Benelux*] (BAS)

CERSG ...... Centro Emilia-Romagna per la Storia del Giornalismo [*Italian*] (SLS)

CE/RT .... Central Europe Road Transport [*NATO*] (NATG)

CERT........ Centre d'Etudes et de Recherches de Toulouse [*Toulouse Research and Study Center*] [*France*] (WED)

CERT........ Charities Effectiveness Review Trust [*NCVO*] (WGAO)

CERT........ Combined Employees Redundancy Trust [*Australia*]

CERT........ Comite de Roubaiz-Torcoing d'Etudes et d'Actions Economiques et Sociales (WGAO)

CERT........ Comite Europeen des Enterprises de Traitements de Surface (WGAO)

CERT........ Committee on Energy, Research and Technology of the European Parliament (WGAO)
CERT........ Compagnie d'Etudes et de Realisations de Travaux
CERT........ Comptoir d'Etudes Radio Techniques (WGAO)
CERT........ Construction Employees Redundancy Trust [Australia]
certam........ Certamente [Certainly] [Italian]
CERTES.... Centre d'Enseignement et de Recherche Techniques et Societes [Technology and Society Management and Research Center] [Paris, France] [Research center] (ERC)
CERTEX ... Certificados de Exportacion [Export Certificates] [Peru] (LA)
certif.......... Certificat [Certificate] [French]
CERTN...... Centre of Excellence for Research into Transport Noise [Australia]
CERTS ...... Centre d'Etudes et Recherches en Technologie Spatiale [Aerospace Technology Study and Research Center] [France] (PDAA)
CERTSM .. Centre d'Etudes et de Recherches Techniques Sous-Marines [French] (MSC)
CertTesol ... Certificate in Teaching English to Speakers of Other Languages [Australia]
CERU .... Centro de Estudos Rurais e Urbanos [Center for Rural and Urban Studies] [Research center] [Brazil] (IRC)
CERUR...... Centro de Estudios Regionales Urbanos Rurales [Center for Regional Urban and Rural Studies] [Dominican Republic] (LA)
CERUSS.... Comite Permanent International des Techniques et de l'Urbanisme Souterrains et Spatials (WGAO)
CERVA...... Consortium Europeen de Realisation et de Vente d'Avions (WGAO)
Cervarm ..... Cervena Armija [Red Army] (YU)
CERVECOL ... Cerveceria Colombo Alemana SA [Colombia] (COL)
CERVED... Centri Elettronici Reteconnessi Valutazione Elaborazione Dati [Central Electronic Network for Data Processing and Analysis] [Information service or system] (IID)
CERVED... Societa Nazionale di Informatica delle Camere di Commerces Italiane [National Information Company of Italian Chambers of Commerce] [Information service or system] (IID)
CERVED... Societa Nazionale di Informatica delle Camere di Commercio per la Gestione dei Centri Elettronici Reteconnessi Valutazione Elaborazione Dati [Italian] (SLS)
CERVL...... Centre d'Etude et de Recherche sur La Vie Locale (WGAO)
CERVUNION ... Cerveceria Union [Colombia] (COL)
CES............ Cadena de Emisoras Sindicales (WGAO)
CES............ Center for Ecumenical Studies [Mexico] (EAIO)
ces .... Centimes [Monetary unit] [France] (GPO)
CES............ Central Experiment Station [Trinidadian] (ARC)
CES............ Centre d'Etudes Sociales [Belgium]
CES............ Centre d'Etudes Sociologiques
CES............ Centre d'Etudes Superieurs
CES............ Centre Europeen des Silicones [of the European Council of Chemical Manufacturers' Federations] (EAIO)
CES............ Centre for Environmental Studies [Australia] (IRC)
CES............ Centre for European Studies [Monash University] [Australia]
CES............ Centro de Estudios Politicos y Sociales [Political and Social Studies Center] [Uruguay] (LA)
CES............ Centro de Estudos de Solos [Brazil] (DSCA)
CES............ Certificat d'Etudes Secondaires [Certificate of Secondary Studies] [French]
CES............ Certificat d'Etudes Superieures [Certificate of Higher Studies] [French]
CES............ Cessnock [Australia] [Airport symbol] (OAG)
CES............ China Eastern Airlines [ICAO designator] (FAAC)
CES............ Coast Earth Station [INMARSAT]
CES............ College d'Enseignement Secondaire [French]
CES............ Comando Estrategico de Sabotaje [Strategic Sabotage Command] [Venezuela] (LA)
CES............ Comite Economique et Social [Benelux] (BAS)
CES............ Comite Electrotechnique Suisse [Switzerland]
CES............ Comites de Estudiantes Socialistas [Socialist Student Committees] [Spanish] (WER)
CES............ Commission d'Etudes Salariales
CES............ Committee of European Shipowners (DS)
CES............ Commonwealth Employment Service [Australia] (ADA)
CES............ Communaute Europeenne Sans-Abri (WGAO)
CES............ Confederation Europeenne de Scoutisme [European Confederation of Scouts - ECS] (EAIO)
CES............ Confederazione Europea dei Sindacati [European Trade Union Confederation - ETUC] [Italian] (WER)
CES............ Conference of European Statisticians [United Nations] (WGAO)
CES............ Conferentia Episcopalis Scandiae [Scandinavian Episcopal Conference - SEC] (EAIO)
CES............ Conseil Economique et Social
CES............ Conservation des Eaux et des Sols
CES............ Croatian Ethnic School [Australia]
CES............ Crop Experiment Station [South Korean] [Research center] (IRC)

CES............ Cuerpo Especial de Seguridad [Special Security Corps] [Honduras] (LA)
CESA........ Canberra Ex-Servicewomen's Association [Australia]
CESA........ Central Ecuatoriana de Reforma Agraria [Ecuador] (DSCA)
CESA........ Central Ecuatoriana de Servicios Agraria (WGAO)
CESA........ Centre d'Enseignement Superieur des Affaires
CESA........ Centre d'Etudes Sociales Africaines
CESA........ Comissao Estadual de Silos e Armazens [Brazil] (DSCA)
CESA........ Comite Europeen des Syndicats de l'Alimentation du Tabac et de l'Industrie Hoteliere [CEE] (WGAO)
CESA........ Committee of EEC [European Economic Community] Shipbuilders' Associations (EAIO)
CESA........ Community Employment Support Agency [Australia]
CESA........ Consumer Electronic Suppliers Association [Australia]
CESA........ Council of Estonian Societies in Australia
CESA........ Cultural Exchange Society of America (WGAO)
CESA........ Czechoslovak Ex-servicemen's Association [Australia]
CESAC...... Commonwealth Employment Service Advisory Committee [Australia]
CESAH...... Comite Ecumenico Salvadoreno de Ayuda Humanitaria [Salvadoran Ecumenical Committee for Humanitarian Aid]
CESAI ...... Centro de Formacao Profissional de Informatica (WGAO)
CESAMP .. Group of Experts on the Scientifc Aspects of Marine Pollution (WGAO)
CESAO...... Centre d'Etudes Economiques et Sociales de l'Afrique Occidentale [West African Economic and Social Studies Center] (AF)
CESAO...... Commission Economique et Sociale pour l'Asie Occidentale [Economic and Social Commission for Western Asia - ESCWA] (EAIO)
CESAP ...... Commission Economique et Sociale des Nations Unies pour l'Asie et le Pacifique (WGAO)
CESAP ...... Commission Economique et Sociale pour l'Asie et le Pacifique [Economic and Social Commission for Asia and the Pacific] [French United Nations] (DUND)
CESARROZ ... Comissao Estadual de Sementes de Arroz no Rio Grande do Sul [Brazil] (DSCA)
CESB .... Centre d'Enseignement Superieur de Brazzaville (WGAO)
CESB .... Centre d'Etudes Superieures de Banque [France] (FLAF)
CESB .... Confederacion de Estudiantes de Secundaria de Bolivia [Bolivian Confederation of Secondary Schools] (LA)
CESBRA.... Companhia Estanifera do Brasil [Brazilian Tin Co.] (EAS)
CESC .... Centre for European Security and Cooperation [Netherlands]
CESC .... Certificat d'Etudes Superieures Commerciales [Commercial Advanced Studies Certificate] (CL)
CESC .... Conference on European Security and Cooperation (WGAO)
CESCA ...... Comunidad Economica y Social Centroamericana [Central American Socioeconomic Community] (LA)
CESCE ...... Comite Europeen des Services de Conseillers d'Enterprises (WGAO)
CESCE ...... Comite Europeen des Services des Conseillers [European Committee for Consultant Services - ECCS] (EAIO)
CESCE ...... Compania Espanola de Seguros de Credito a la Exportacion [Export credit agency] [Spanish]
CESCJ ...... Couseil Europeen des Services Communautaires Juifs (WGAO)
CESCO...... Centro de Estudios del Cobre y la Mineria [Center for Copper and Mining Studies] [Chile] (IRC)
CESD......... Centre Europeen de Formation des Statisticiens Economistes des Pays en Voie de Developpement [European Center for Training Statisticians and Economists from Developing Countries]
CESD......... Centre Europeen pour la Formation de Statisticiens-Economistes pur les Pays en Voie de Developpement (WGAO)
CESDA...... Confederation of European Soft Drink Associations [Switzerland] (EY)
CESDE ...... Centro de Estudios Superiores para el Desarrollo [Center of Higher Studies for Development] [Colorado] (LA)
CESDIS..... Centro Studi di Diritto Sportivo [Italian] (SLS)
CESDIT..... Centro per gli Studi sui Sistemi Distributivi e il Turismo [Italian] (SLS)
CESE .... Centre d'Etudes de la Socio-Economie (WGAO)
CESE .... Centre Economique de Secours Europeens [European Economic Relief Committee] [NATO] (NATG)
CESE .... Centro Studi Economici [Italian] (SLS)
CESE .... Comision Ecumenica de Servicio [Brazil] (WGAO)
CESE .... Comparative Education Society in Europe (EAIO)
CESE .... Council for Environmental Science and Engineering (WGAO)
CESEAR.... Commission d'Entraide et de Service des Eglises et d'Assurance aux Refugies (WGAO)
CESEC ...... Centro de Estudios Socio-Economicos (Universidad de Chile) [Centro de Estudios Socio-Economicos - CESO] [Santiago, Chile] [Formerly,] (LAA)
CESEC ...... Centro Studi Economici [Italian] (SLS)
CESEDEN ... Centro Superior de Estudios de la Defensa Nacional [Highest National Defense Studies Center] [Spanish] (WER)
Ceseden...... Centro Superior de Estudios de la Defense Nacional (WGAO)

cesell .... Cesellato [Chiseled] [Publishing] [Italian]

CESEM ..... Centre d'Etudes Superieures Europeenes de Management (WGAO)

CESERFO ... Centro Studi e Ricerche Fondiarie (WGAO)

CESES ...... Centro Studi e Ricerche su Problemi Economico-Sociali [Italian] (SLS)

CESES .... Centro Studio Economico e Sociale [Studies Center for Economic and Social Affairs] [Of the PCI] [Italian] (WER)

CeSET ...... Centro Studi di Estimo e di Economia Territoriale [Italian] (SLS)

CESETA .... Centro de Servicios Tecnicos Automotrices [Automotive Technical Services Center] [Cuba] (LA)

CESG .... Commonwealth Extension Services Grant [Australia] (ADA)

CESH .... Centre d'Etudes de Sciences Humaines [Zaire] (WGAO)

CESI .... Centre d'Etudes Superieures Industrielles [France]

CESI .... Centre for Economic and Social Information [United Nations]

CESI .... Centro Elettrotecnico Sperimentale Italiano Giacinto Motta SpA [Italian Experimental Electrotechnical Center] [Ente Nazionale per l'Energia Elettrica - ENEL] [Research center] (ERC)

CESI .... Chinese Electronics Standardization Institute (IRC)

CESIA ...... Centre d'Etudes des Systemes d'Information des Administrations [Center for the Study on Information Systems in Government] [Information service or system] (IID)

CESIA ...... Centre d'Etudes Superieures d'Industrie Automobiles

CESIC .... Catholic European Study and Information Centre [France] (WGAO)

CESID ...... Centro Superior de Informacion de la Defensa [Spanish]

CESID ...... Centro Sviluppo Impiego Diesel [Italian] (SLS)

CESIDE ..... Centro de Estudios Superiores para el Desarrollo [Colombia] (WGAO)

CESII .... Centro de Sociologia Industrial e do Trabalho [Brazil] (WGAO)

CESIL .... China Entertainment Strategic Investment Ltd. [Hong Kong]

CESIN ...... Centro Economico Scambi Italo-Nipponici (WGAO)

CESIO .... Comite Europeen des Agents de Service et leurs Intermediares Organiques (WGAO)

CESIT .... Centro de Sociologia Industrial e do Trabalho [Brazil] (DSCA)

CESIT .... Centro Studi e Ricerche Sistemi di Trasporto Collettivo [Transport Research Center] [Societa Finanziaria Meccanica - FINMECCANICA] [Research center] [Italian] (ERC)

CESITRADO ... Central Sindical de Trabajadores Dominicanos [Dominican Workers Federation] [Dominican Republic] (LA)

CeSL .... Centro Studi Lombardo [Italian] (SLS)

CESL .... Confederacion Ecuatoriana de Sindicatos Libres [Ecuadorean Confederation of Free Trade Unions] (LA)

CESL .... Conseil Europeen de la Jeunesse Syndicale (WGAO)

CESLAMD ... Comite de Liaison des Secretariats Latino-Americaines des Moyens de Diffusion (WGAO)

CESM .... Centro Espacial San Miguel [San Miguel Space Center] [Argentina] (EAS)

CESMAD ... Association des Transporteurs Routiers Internationaux Tschecoslovaques (WGAO)

CESMAD ... Sdruzeni Ceskoslovenskych Mezinarodnich Automobilovych Dopravcu [Association of Czechoslovak International Truckers] (CZ)

CESMAD ... Sdruzeni Ceskoslovenskych Mezinaronich Automobilovych Dopravcu [Former Czechoslovakia] (EAIO)

CESMAG .. Companhia Espirito Santo e Minas de Armazens Gerais [Brazil] (DSCA)

CESMAT .. Centre d'Etudes Superieures des Matieres Premieres

CESME ..... Centro de Servicios Metalurgicos [Metallurgical Services Center] [Chile] (LA)

CESMI ...... Centro Economico e Sociale per il Mezzogiorno d'Italia [Italian] (SLS)

CESNAV ... Centro de Estudios Superiores Navales [Naval War College] [Mexico] (LA)

CESNE ...... Centro de Estudios de Sociologia del Noreste [Center for Studies of Northeast Sociology] [Argentina] (LAA)

CESNEF .... Centro di Studi Nucleari Enrico Fermi [Nuclear Engineering Institute - Enrico Fermi Nuclear Center] [Italy] (NRCH)

CESNU ...... Conseil Economique et Social des Nations-Unies [United Nations Economic and Social Council]

CESO .... Canadian Executive Services Overseas (WGAO)

CESO .... Centro de Estudios Socioeconomicos [Socioeconomic Studies Center] [Chile] (LA)

CESO .... Centrum voor de Studie van het Onderwijs in Ontwikkelingslanden [Centre for Study of Education in Developing Countries] [Netherlands] (EAIO)

CESO .... Concorde Engines Support Organization (WGAO)

CESOM ..... Confederacao Europeia dos Espoliados do Ultramar [European Confederation of Persons Exploited Overseas] [Portuguese] (WER)

CESP .... Centrais Eletricas de Sao Paulo, SA [Sao Paulo Electric Powerplants, Inc.] [Brazil] (LA)

CESP .... Centre d'Etude des Supports Publicitaires [Center for the Study of Advertising Support] [Database producer Paris, France]

CESP .... Centre d'Etudes des Supports de Publicite [Center for the Study of Advertising Support] [French]

CESP .... Companhia Energetica de Sao Paulo [Sao Paulo Electric Company] [Brazil] (LA)

CESP .... Confederation Europeenne des Syndicats Nationaux et Associations Professionnelles de Pediatres [Belgium] (WGAO)

CESP .... Confederation of European Specialists in Pediatrics (EAIO)

CESPA ...... Campaign for Equal State Pension Ages (WGAO)

CESPAO ... Comision Economica y Social para Asia Occidental [Economic and Social Commission for Western Asia] [Spanish United Nations] (DUND)

CESPAP .... Comision Economica y Social para Asia y el Pacifico [Economic and Social Commission for Asia and the Pacific] [Spanish United Nations] (DUND)

CESPASD ... Comite Charge d'Etudier et de Suivre les Problemes de Prix, d'Approvisionnement, de Stockage, et de Distribution [Committee in Charge of Studying and Following Price, Supply, Stocking, and Distribution Problems] [Cambodia] (CL)

CESPC .... Compania Ecuatoriana de Sal y Productos Quimicos SA [Ecuador] (DSCA)

CESPE .... Centro Studi di Politica Economica [Center for Studies in Economic Policy] [Of the PCI] [Italian] (WER)

CESPQ ...... Compana Ecuatoriana de Sal y Productos Quimicos (WGAO)

CESPROP ... Centro de Estudios y Promocion Popular [El Salvador] (WGAO)

CESR .... Centre d'Etude Spatiale des Rayonnements [Space Radiation Research Center] [France] (EAS)

CESRF ...... Canberra Regional Committee for Employer Support of Reserve Forces [Australia]

CESRF ...... Christian Economic and Social Research Foundation (WGAO)

CESSA .... Cemento de El Salvador, Sociedad Anonima [Cement of El Salvador Corporation]

CESSAC .... Church of England Soldiers Sailors and Airmen's Clubs [BRIT] (WGAO)

CESSID ..... Centre d'Etudes Superieures de la Siderurgie [Center for Advanced Steel Research] [French] (WER)

CESSIM .... Centre d'Etudes des Supports d'Information Medical (WGAO)

CESSTW .. Center for the Economic and Social Study of the Third World [Mexico] (WGAO)

CESTA ...... Center for Appropriate Technology [El Salvador]

CESTA ...... Centre d'Etudes des Systemes et des Technologies Avancees [French]

CESTA ...... Centre d'Etudes Scientifiques et Techniques d'Aquitaine [France]

CESTA ...... Conference on Education and Scientific and Technical Training in Relation to Development in Africa (WGAO)

CESTI .... Centre d'Etudes des Sciences et Techniques de l'Information [Center for the Study of Information Sciences and Techniques] [Senegal] (AF)

CESTRAR ... Centrale des Syndicale des Travailleurs du Rwanda (EAIO)

CESU .... Ceylon Estates Staffs' Union

CESU .... Consejo de Estudiantes Secundarios Uruguayos [Council of Uruguayan Secondary School Students] (LA)

CESUP ...... Centre d'Enseignement Superieur

CESUP ...... Centre d'Etudes Superieures

CESVIET .. Centro di Studio e Documentazione sul Vietnam e il Terzo Mondo [Italian] (SLS)

CET .... Ceeta-Kel Air [France] [ICAO designator] (FAAC)

CET .... Centrala Energie Termala [Thermoelectric Power Plant] (RO)

CET .... Centre Europeen de Traduction (FLAF)

CET .... Certificat d'Etudes Techniques

Cet .... Cetar [Sergeant] (CZ)

Cet .... Cetra [Record label] [Italy]

Cet .... Cetus [Whale constellation] [Latin] (BARN)

Cet .... Cetvel [Table] [As a statistical table] (TU)

CET .... Club Europeen du Tourisme

CET .... College d'Enseignement Technique [French]

CET .... Commission Europeenne de Tourisme [European Travel Commission - ETC] [Paris, France]

CET .... Common External Tariff [for EEC countries] [Also, CXT]

CET .... Confederation Europeenne dex Taxis [Belgium] (EAIO)

CET .... Contraband Enforcement Team [Australia]

CETA .... Centre d'Entrainement des Troupes Aeroportees [Airborne Troops Training Center] [Zaire] (AF)

CETA .... Centre Economique et Technique de l'Artisanat [Economic and Technical Crafts Center] [Malagasy] (AF)

CETA .... Centres d'Etudes Techniques Agricoles [France] (FLAF)

CETA .... Centro des Estudos Technicos de Automocion [Center for Technical Studies on Automation] [Spain] (PDAA)

CETA .... Comite Especifico Tarifario Centro-Americano (WGAO)

CETA .... Compagnie Equatoriale de Tabacs et Allumettes

CETA .... Conference des Eglises de Toute l'Afrique [All Africa Conference of Churches - AACC] (EAIO)

CETA .... Conference of Engineering Trades Associations (WGAO)

CETAL ...... Centro de Estudios en Technologies Apropiadas para America Latina [*Chile*]   (WGAO)

CETAL ...... Confederacion de Trabajadores de America Latina [*Confederation of Latin American Workers*]   (LA)

CETAM..... Centre d'Etudes de Techniques Agricoles Menageres   (WGAO)

CETAM..... Centre d'Etudes et d'Applications Mecanographiques [*French*] (ADPT)

CETAMA ... Commission d'Establissement des Methodes d'Analyse [*France*] (PDAA)

CETAMEX ... Centro de Estudios de Technologia Apropiada para Mexico (WGAO)

Cetasp .... Cetar Aspirant [*Sergeant Cadet*]   (CZ)

CETATE ... Centro de Treinamento, Assistencia Tecnica e Ensino [*Brazil*] (DSCA)

CETAUTO ... Centro Tecnico Automovel

CETBGE ... Centre d'Etude et de Traitement des Bois Gorges d'Eau   (WGAO)

CETC......... SPC Community Education Training Centre [*Fiji*]   (WGAO)

CETCA...... Centre d'Enseignement Technique du Credit Agricole   (WGAO)

CETDC...... China Engineering Technology Development Corp.   (TCC)

CETDC...... China External Trade Development Council [*Taiwan*]   (WGAO)

CETE........ Centre d'Etudes Techniques de l'Equipement [*Equipment Technical Studies Center*] [*French*]   (WER)

CETEC ...... Centre Technique des Energies et du Chauffage [*Technical Center for Research on Energy Management and Heating*] [*France*]   (WED)

Cetec .... Centro de Estudios Tecnologicos [*Dominican Republic*]

CETEC ...... Fundacao Centro Tecnologico de Minas Gerais [*Minas Gerais Technological Center*] [*Brazil*]   (WED)

CETEC ...... Sector de Documentacao e Informacao, Fundacao Centro Tecnologico de Minas Gerais [*Brazil*]

CETEC ...... Universidad Centro de Estudios Tecnicos [*Dominican Republic*] (WGAO)

CETEHOR ... Centre Technique de l'Industrie Horlogere [*Clock and Watch Industry Technical Center*]   (PDAA)

CETEL ...... Companhia Estadual de Telefonos da Guanabara [*Guanabara State Telephone Company*] [*Brazil*]   (LA)

CETEM ..... Centre d'Enseignement des Techniques d'Etude de Marche (WGAO)

CETEM ..... Centre d'Enseignement des Techniques d'Etudes de Marches [*France*]   (FLAF)

CETEM ..... Centre d'Enseignement Technique d'Etudes Municipales [*Center for Technical Education in Municipal Administration*] [*French Guiana*]   (LA)

CETEM ..... Centre d'Etudes des Techniques Economiques Modernes

CETEM ..... Centro de Tecnologia Mineral [*Center for Mineral Technology*] [*Brazil*]   (IRC)

CETEMA .. Centre d'Etudes Techniques et Economiques des Matieres Grasses

CETENAL ... Comision de Estudios del Territorio Nacional [*Mexico*]   (MSC)

CETEPA.... Centre Professional Technique d'Etudes de la Pollution Atmospherique   (WGAO)

CETESB.... Companhia de Tecnologia de Saneamento Basico [*Basic Sanitation Technology Company*] [*Brazil*]   (LA)

CETEX ...... Comision de Empresas Textiles Exportadoras [*El Salvador*] (WGAO)

CETEX ...... Comissao Executiva Textil [*Brazil*]   (LAA)

CETF .... Centre d'Etudes des Techniques Forestieres   (WGAO)

CETG........ Consejo Ejecutivo del Tratado General [*Secretaria Permanente del Tratado General de Integracion Economica Centroamericana - SIECA*]   (LAA)

CETHEDEC ... Centre d'Etudes Theoriques de la Detection et des Communications   (WGAO)

CETI .... Centre d'Echanges Technologiques Internationaux [*French*]

CETI .... Centre d'Etude et de Traitement de l'Informatique

CETI .... Comissao de Estudos Tributarios e Internacionais [*Tax and International Studies Commission*] [*Brazil*]   (LA)

CETI .... Cooperative d'Entreprises de Transport Internationaux [*Switzerland*]   (PDAA)

CETIC ...... Centre d'Elaboration et de Traitement de l'Information Commerciale [*Algeria*]   (IMH)

CETIC ...... College d'Enseignement Technique, Industriel, et Commercial

CETICE..... Centre d'Ecologie et de Toxicologie de l'Industrie Chimique Europeenne [*European Chemical Industry Ecology and Toxicology Center - ECETOC*]   (EAIO)

CETIE .... Centre Technique International de l'Embouteillage et du Conditionnement   (WGAO)

CETIE .... Centre Technique Internationale de l'Embouteillage [*International Technical Center of Bottling*] [*France*] (PDAA)

CETIEF.... Centre Technique des Industries de l'Estampage   (WGAO)

CETIF........ Consortium de Recherches d'Etudes pour l'Information et la Formation [*Senegal*]   (WGAO)

CETIH...... Centre d'Etudes Techniques des Industries de l'Habillement [*France*]   (EAIO)

CETIL .... Committe of Experts for the Transfer of Information between Community Languages [*EEC*]   (WGAO)

CETIM...... Centre Europe-Tiers Monde [*Switzerland*]

CETIM ...... Centre Technique des Industries Mecaniques [*Technical Center for Mechanical Industries*] [*France*]   (IRC)

CETIOM... Centre Technique Interprofessionnel des Oleagineux Metropolitains [*Interprofessional Technical Center for Oilseed Crops*] [*Research center*] [*France*]   (IRC)

CETIS........ Centre de Traitement de l'Information Scientifique [*Benelux*] (BAS)

CETIS........ Centre Europeen de Traitement de l'Information Scientifique [*Luxembourg*]

CETISA..... Compania Espanola de Editorales Tecnologicas Interacionales (WGAO)

CETLANTIC ... Ceramica Atlantico [*Barranquilla*]   (COL)

CETMA..... Centre d'Ethno-Technologie en Milieu Aquatiques [*French*] (ASF)

CETMA..... Centre d'Etudes Techniques Menageres et Agricoles   (WGAO)

CETME..... Centro de Estudios Tecnicos de Materieles Especiales [*Spain*] (PDAA)

CETME..... Comite des Eglises aupres des Travaileurs Migrants en Europe (WGAO)

CETO .... Centre for Educational Television Overseas   (WGAO)

CETOP...... Comite Europeen des Transmissions Oleohydrauliques et Pneumatiques [*European Hydraulic and Pneumatic Committee*] [*France*]   (SLS)

CETOPES ... Centre d'Etudes des Techniciens de l'Organisation Professionnelle   (WGAO)

CETP......... Competitive Employment and Training Programs [*Australia*]

CETP......... Confederation Europeenne pour la Therapie Physique [*French*] (SLS)

CETP......... Confederation Europeenne Therapeutique Physique [*European Confederation for Physical Therapy*]   (EAIO)

Cetra .... China External Trade Development Council   (GEA)

CETRA..... Compagnie Equatoriale des Travaux

CETRAC.... Centrale de Transports en Commun

CETRAL ... Centre de Recherche sur l'Amerique Latine et le Tiers-Monde [*France*]

CETRAMAR ... Consortium Europeen de Transports Maritimes [*Shipping company*] [*France*]   (EY)

CETRAMET ... Compagnie Equatoriale pour la Transformation des Metaux en Republique Centrafricaine   (WGAO)

CETRAMETCONGO ... Compagnie Equatoriale pour la Transformation des Metaux au Congo   (WGAO)

CETRE ...... Centro Pratico de Treinamento [*Brazil*]   (DSCA)

CETREC ... Centro de Adiestramento de Campinas [*Brazil*]   (LAA)

CETREDE ... Centro de Entrenamiento para el Desarrollo Economico Regional [*Fortaleza*] [*Brazil*]   (LAA)

CETREINO ... Centro de Treinamento para o Nordeste [*Brazil*]   (DSCA)

CETREISUL ... Centro de Treinamento e Informacao do Sul [*Brazil*]   (DSCA)

CETREMFA ... Centro de Treinamento e Desenvolvimento do Pessoal do Ministerio da Fazenda [*Center for the Training and Development of Finance Ministry Personnel*] [*Brazil*]   (LA)

CETRHU .. Centro de Estudios y Capacitacion en Recursos Humanos [*Brazil*]   (LAA)

CETRI .... Centre Tricontinential [*Belgium*]   (WGAO)

CETRIC.... Consortium d'Etudes Techniques et de Realisations Industrielles du Cameroun

CETS .... Conference Europeenne des Telecommunications par Satellites [*Benelux*]

CETSAP.... Centre d'Etudes Transdisciplinaires (Sociologie, Anthropologie, Politique) [*Center of Interdisciplinary Studies (Sociology, Anthropology, Politics)*] [*France*]   (IRC)

CETSAS..... Centre d'Etudes Transdisciplimaires Sociologie, Anthropoligie, Semiologie   (WGAO)

CETSS ...... Comite Estatal de el Trabajo y Seguro Social [*State Committee for Labor and Social Security*] [*Cuba*]   (LA)

CETT .... Centro de Entreamiento para Tecnicos en Telecomunicaciones [*Training Center for Telecommunications Technicians*] [*Venezuela*]   (PDAA)

CETT .... Compagnie Europeenne de Teletransmissions   (WGAO)

CETU .... Centre d'Etudes des Tunnels [*Tunnels Research Center*] [*Ministere des Transports*] [*Research center*] [*French*] (ERC)

CETUC...... Centro du Estudos en Telecomunicacoes da Universidade Catolica [*Center for Studies in Telecommunications of the Catholic University*] [*Brazil*]   (PDAA)

CETURIS ... Corporacion Ecuatoriana del Turismo [*Ecuadorean Corporation for Tourism*]   (LA)

CETV......... Church of England Television Society [*Australia*]   (ADA)

CEU .... Central European University [*Hungary*]

CEU .... Centro de Estudiantes Universitarios [*University Students Center*]   (LA)

CEU .... Centro de Estudios Universitarios   (WGAO)

CEU .... Ceuta Unida [*Political party*]   (EY)

CEU .... China Experimental University

CEU .... Computer Education Unit [*Department of Education*] [*New South Wales, Australia*]

CEUC .... Confederacion de Estudiantes Universitarios de Colombia [*Confederation of University Students of Colombia*]   (LA)

CEUCA...... Centro de Estudios Universitarios Colombo-Americanos [*Colombia*]   (DSCA)
CEUCA...... Centros de Estudios Universitarios Colombo Americano [*Colombia*]   (COL)
CEUCA...... Confederacion de Estudiantes Universitarios de Centroamerica [*Confederation of University Students of Central America*] (LA)
CEUCORS ... Centre Europeen de Documentation en Sciences Sociales (WGAO)
CEUD....... Comissao Eleitoral para a Unidade Democratico [*Electoral Committee for Democratic Unity*] [*Portugal*] [*Political party*]   (PPE)
CEUMA .... Christian European Visual Media Association   (WGAO)
CEUPAM ... Centre Europeen pour le Promotion des Activites Medicales [*French*]   (SLS)
CEUR .... Centro de Estudios Urbanos y Regionales [*Argentina*]   (WGAO)
CEUR .... Centro de Estudios Urbanos y Regionales del Instituto Torcuato Di Tella [*Center for Urban and Regional Studies*] [*Research center*] [*Argentina*]   (IRC)
CEV .... Centre d'Essais en Vol [*In-Flight Testing Center*] [*French*]   (WER)
CEV .... Ceskoslovenske Energeticke Vyrobny [*Czechoslovak Electric Power Producing Enterprises*]   (CZ)
Cev .... Ceviri [*or Ceviren*] [*Translation or Translator*]   (TU)
CEV .... Colegio de Economistas de Venezuela [*Venezuela*]   (LAA)
CEV .... Confederacion Empresarial Valenciana [*Spain*]   (EY)
CEV .... Cooperatieve Eierveiling van de ABTB   (WGAO)
CEVA........ Cementarny a Vapenky [*Cement and Lime Works*]   (CZ)
CEVA........ Centre d'Essaies Vehicule Automobile [*Motor Vehicle Test Center*] [*French*]
CEVAL...... Cementos del Valle SA [*Colombia*]   (COL)
CEVAL...... Centrale de Livraison de Valeurs Mobilieres [*Independent company, incorporated in Luxembourg and operating worldwide*]
CEVE........ Centro Experimental de Vivienda Economica [*Argentina*]   (EAIO)
CEVECO... Centrale Organisatie van Veeafzet-en Vleesverwerkings-cooperaties   (WGAO)
CEVER...... Centro de Educacion Vocacional Evangelico y Reformado [*Honduras*]
CEVMA..... Christian European Visual Media Association   (EAIO)
CEVNO ..... Centre for International Education [*Netherlands*]   (EAIO)
CEVOI...... Comptoir d'Exportation de Vanille de l'Ocean Indien
CEW .... Career Education for Women [*Technical and further education course*] [*Australia*]
CEW .... Commissions Electorales de Wilaya [*Governorate Electoral Commissions*] [*Algeria*]   (AF)
CEW .... Continuing Education West [*University of Sydney*] [*Australia*]
CEWA .... Central Water and Electricity Administration [*Sudan*]
CEWAL..... Central West Africa Lines   (AF)
CEWC....... Council for Education in World Citizenship   (WGAO)
CEWLRA .. Commission on Education of the World Leisure and Recreation Association   (EAIO)
CEXCUT ... Comite Exterior-Central Unica de Trabajadores [*Central Union of Workers-External Committee*] [*Chile*]
CEXIM...... Carteira de Exportacao e Importacao [*Export and Import Department*] [*Brazil*]   (LA)
Cey .... Ceylon
Ceypetco .... Ceylon Petroleum Corporation   (GEA)
CEZ .... Centrale des Enseignants Zairois
CEZ .... Centre European pour la Formation dans l'Assurance [*Switzerland*]   (WGAO)
CEZ .... Ceskoslovenske Energeticke Zavody, Narodni Podnik [*Czechoslovak Power Plants, National Enterprise*]   (CZ)
CEZA........ Comite Europeen des Etudes de Zoologie Agricole   (WGAO)
CEZAC...... Centre Zairois de Commerce Exterieur [*Zairian Foreign Trade Center*]   (AF)
CEZAREP ... Centre Zairois des Relations Publiques [*Zairian Public Relations Center*]   (AF)
CEZAS ...... Centrala Zaopatrzenia Szkol [*Central Supply Office for Schools*]   (POL)
CEZOO ..... Centre de Recherches Zoologiuqes Appliquees [*Belgium*]   (WGAO)
CEZUS...... Compagnie Europeenne du Zirconium Ugine-Sandvik [*France*]   (PDAA)
Cf............. Californio [*Chemical element*] [*Portuguese*]
CF .... Capitaine de Fregate [*French*]   (MTD)
CF .... Caribbean Finance Ltd. [*Nigeria*]
CF .... Central African Republic [*ANSI two-letter standard code*]   (CNC)
CF .... Centrum voor Fondsenadministratie BV [*Amsterdam, 1946*] [*Private company in Holland, controlled by the Amsterdam Stock Exchange and founded to simplify the handling of securities coupons*]
CF .... Ceska Filharmonie [*Czech Philharmonic Orchestra*]   (CZ)
CF .... ChangFu Industrial Ltd. [*Taiwan*]
CF .... Christian Endeavour   (WGAO)
CF .... Citizen Force [*South Africa*]

CF .... Club de Futbol [*Football Club*] [*Spanish*]
CF .... Comite des Forets   (WGAO)
CF .... Commonwealth Foundation   (EAIO)
CF .... Commonwealth Fund [*Australia*]   (ADA)
CF .... Communaute Francaise
CF .... Compania de Aviacion "Faucett" SA [*Peru*] [*ICAO designator*]   (ICDA)
CF .... Compassionate Friends   (WGAO)
cf............. Confer [*Compare*]   (SCAC)
Cf............. Conferez [*Confer*] [*French*]
cf............. Confesor [*Confessor*] [*Spanish*]
cf............. Confira [*Portuguese*]
cf............. Confirma [*In old documents*] [*Spanish*]
cf............. Confronte [*Compare*] [*Portuguese*]
cf............. Confronte [*French*]
Cf............. Confrontez [*French*]   (FLAF)
CF .... Conseil Economique   (WGAO)
CF .... Council of Europe   (WGAO)
CF .... Les Colonies Francaises
CF .... Sveriges Civilingenjoersfoerbund [*Sweden*]   (SLS)
CFA .... Caminho de Ferro de Amboim [*Amboim Railroad*] [*Angola*]   (AF)
CFA .... Caribbean Federation of Aeroclubs   (EA)
CFA .... Centre de Formation Administrative [*Algeria*]
CFA .... Chemins de Fer Algeriens
CFA .... Chinese Forestry Association   (SLS)
CFA .... Club Francais des Aviateurs [*France*]
CFA .... Colonies Francaises d'Afrique
CFA .... Comite Francais des Aerosols   (WGAO)
CFA .... Commission des Foreits pour l'Afrique [*FAO*]   (WGAO)
CFA .... Committee on Food Aid Policies and Programmes [*FAO/WFP*]   (WGAO)
CFA .... Commonwealth Foremen's Association [*Australia*]   (ADA)
CFA .... Commonwealth Forestry Association [*Oxford, England*]   (EAIO)
CFA .... Communaute Financiere Africaine [*African Financial Community*]   (AF)
CFA .... Communaute Francaise d'Afrique [*French*]
CFA .... Compagnie Financiere Africaine
CFA .... Compagnie Forestiere Africaine
CFA .... Compagnie Forestiere d'Azingo
CFA .... Compagnie France-Amerique [*Ivory Coast*]
CFA .... Compagnie Franco-Africaine
CFA .... Comptoir Francais de l'Azote   (WGAO)
CFA .... Confederation Francaise de l'Artisanat   (WGAO)
CFA .... Confederation Francaise de l'Aviculture   (WGAO)
CFA .... Conference des Femmes Africaines [*Conference of African Women*]   (AF)
CFA .... Congregatio Fratrum Cellitarum seu Alexianorum   (WGAO)
CFA .... Conseils Associes en Afrique
CFA .... Contact Furnishing Association   (WGAO)
CFA .... Continence Foundation of Australia
CFA .... Contract Flooring Association   (WGAO)
CFA .... Cookery and Food Association   (WGAO)
CFA .... Cooperation Financiere en Afrique Centrale [*Central Africa*]   (EY)
CFA .... Corporacion Fruticola Argentina [*Argentina*]   (LAA)
CFA .... Cote Francaise d'Afrique
CFA .... Council for Acupuncture   (WGAO)
CFA .... Council of Ironfoundry Associations   (WGAO)
CFA .... Credit Foncier d'Afrique
CFAA......... Coloured Film Artists' Association
CFAA......... Compagnie Commerciale Franco-Africaine et Antillaise
CFAD........ Centre de Formation d'Auto-Defense [*Algeria*]
CFAD........ Consejo Fundaciones Americans Desarrollo   (WGAO)
CFAE........ Centre de Formation en Aerodynamique Experimentale
CFAE........ Chemins de Fer Algeriens de l'Etat
CFAE........ Compagnie Francaise de l'Afrique Equatoriale
CFAF........ Credit Foncier de l'Afrique Francaise
CFAF........ Francs de la Communaute Financiere Africaine
CFAL........ Comision Forestal Latinoamericana   (WGAO)
CFAN .... Commission Forestiere pour l'Amerique du Nord [*FAO*]   (WGAO)
CFAO .... Compagnie Francaise de l'Afrique Occidentale [*French Company of West Africa*]   (AF)
CFAP........ Commission des Forets pour l'Asie et la Region du Pacifique [*FAO*]   (WGAO)
CFAPAL.... Compagnie Franco-Africaine de Produits Alimentaires
CFAR........ Centres de Formation d'Animateurs Ruraux
CFAS .... Commandement des Forces Aeriennes Strategiques [*Strategic Air Forces Command*] [*France*]
CFAT........ Centre de Sidi-Fredj de Formation en Art Traditionnel
CFAT........ Credit Foncier d'Algerie et de Tunisie [*Loan Bank of Algeria and Tunisia*]
CFAT &DT ... Club Francais de l'Airedale et Divers Terriers   (EAIO)
CFB........... Caminho de Ferro de Benguela [*Benguela Railroad*] [*Angola*]   (AF)
CFB........... Central Freight Bureau   (DS)

CFB........... Club du Fauve de Bretagne [*France*] (EAIO)
CFB........... Clube Filatelico do Brasil [*Philatelic Club of Brazil*]
CFB........... Commercial Farmers Bureau
CFB........... Commonwealth Fire Board
CFB........... Commonwealth Forestry Bureau (WGAO)
CFB........... Compagnie Forestiere de Bika
CFB........... Conselho Federal de Biblioteconomia [*Brazil*] (SLS)
CFB........... Council of the Corp. of Foreign Bondholders (WGAO)
CFBA........ Club Francais du Braque Allemand (EAIO)
CFBB........ Country Fire Brigades Board [*Australia*]
CFBE........ Club des Amis du Colley [*France*] (EAIO)
CFBN........ Chemin de Fer Benin-Niger [*Benin-Niger Railroad*] (AF)
CFC........... Canberra Fishermans Club [*Australia*]
CFC........... Caribbean Food Corp. [*An association*] (EAIO)
CFC........... Centre Francais du Copyright (WGAO)
CFC........... Centres de Formation de Cadres
CFC........... Chemins de Fer du Cambodge [*Cambodian Railroads*] [*Replaced CFRC*] (CL)
CFC........... Colegio de Farmaceuticos de Chile [*College of Pharmacists*] [*Santiago, Chile*] (LAA)
CFC........... Commercial Facilities Company [*Kuwait*]
CFC........... Committee for a Free China (WGAO)
CFC........... Compagnie Forestiere du Congo
CFC........... Confederation Generale des Cadres (WGAO)
CFC........... Congregatio Fratrum Christianorum (WGAO)
CFC........... Construction Forecasting Committee [*Australia*]
CFC........... Cooperative Federation of Ceylon (WGAO)
CFC........... Corporacion Financiera Colombiana [*Colombian Financial Corporation*] (LA)
CFC........... Corporacion Financiera de Caldas [*Manizales*] [*Colorado*] (LAA)
CFC........... Credit Foncier du Cameroun [*Financial Credit of Cameroon*]
CFCA........ China Fashion Colour Association (EAIO)
CFCA........ Confederation Francaise de la Cooperation Agricole (WGAO)
CFCAM..... Caisse Forestierre de Credit Agricole Mutuel et de Garantie Incendie Forestiere (WGAO)
CFCB........ Commonwealth Film Censorship Board [*Australia*]
CFCB........ Compagnie Francaise de Credit et de Banque [*North African*]
CFCBB...... Club Francais du Chien Berger Belge (EAIO)
CFCCA...... Centre de Formation des Cadres pour Cooperatives Agricoles
CFCCE...... Club Francais du Chihuahua et du Chien Exotique (EAIO)
CFCD........ Compagnie Fonciere et Commerciale de Distribution
CFCD........ Compagnie Francaise des Charbonnages de Dakar
CFCD........ Compagnons du Feu, Fernand Cronel
CFCDCI .... Compagnie Fonciere et Commerciale de Distribution de Cote-d'Ivoire (WGAO)
CFCDNIGER ... Compagnie Fonciere et Commerciale de Distribution du Niger (WGAO)
CFCE........ Centre Francais du Commerce Exterieur [*French*]
CFCE........ Conseil des Federations Commerciales d'Europe [*Council of European Commercial Federations*]
CFCE........ Conselho Federal do Comercio Exterior [*Portuguese*]
CFCG........ Compagnie Forestiere et Commerciale du Gabon
CFCI.......... Centre de Formation et de Cooperation Internationale [*France*]
CFCI.......... Compagnie Francaise de la Cote-D'Ivoire
CFCIA....... Chambre Francaise de Commerce de d'Industrie en Algerie (EY)
CFCIM...... Chambre Francaise de Commerce et de l'Industrie du Maroc [*French Chamber of Commerce and Industry in Morocco*] (AF)
CFCN........ Child and Family Care Network [*Australia*]
CFCN........ Club Francais des Chiens Nordiques (EAIO)
CFCO........ Chemin de Fer Congo-Ocean [*Congo-Ocean Railroad*] (AF)
CFCP........ Compagnie Francaise de Cultures et de Participation
CFCPC...... Comite Fruits a Cidre et des Productions Cidricoles (WGAO)
CFCS........ Caribbean Food Crops Society [*Isabela, Puerto Rico*] (EAIO)
CFCTN...... Club Francais du Chien de Terre Neuve (EAIO)
CFD........... Centralnamnden for Fastighetsdata [*Central Board for Real Estate Data*] [*Sweden*]
CFD........... Christlicher Friedensdienst [*Christian Peace Service*] (EG)
CFD........... Civil Forfeiture Division [*State Drug Crime Commission*] [*New South Wales, Australia*]
CFD........... Club Francais du Disque [*Record label*] [*France*]
CFD........... Comite Francais de Documentation
CFD........... Comitetul Femeilor Democratice [*Committee of Democratic Women*] (RO)
CFD........... Compagnie Forestiere Dolisienne
CFD........... Congress for Democracy [*India*]
CFDC......... Cane Farming Development Corp. [*Guyana*] (WGAO)
CFDC......... Centre Francais de Droit Compare (WGAO)
CFDE......... Compagnie Forestiere du Cameroun
CFDE......... Centre de Formation et de Documentation sur l'Environnement (WGAO)
CFDL........ Confederation Francaise Democratique du Travail [*French Democratic Confederation of Labor*] (BARN)

CFDP........ Compagnie Forestiere Durecu Pontabry
CFDPA...... Compagnie Francaise de Distribution des Petroles en Afrique
CFDT........ Compagnie Francaise pour la Diffusion des Techniques
CFDT........ Compagnie Francaise pour le Developpement des Fibres Textiles [*French Company for the Development of Textile Fibers*] (AF)
CFDT........ Confederation Francaise Democratique du Travail [*French Democratic Confederation of Labor*] [*Paris*] (WER)
CFDT........ Union Departemental des Syndicats [*Martinique*] (WGAO)
CFDV........ Compagnie Financiere Delmas-Vieljeux
CFE........... Clermont-Ferrand [*France*] [*Airport symbol*] (OAG)
CFE........... Comision Federal de Electricidad [*Federal Electricity Commission*] [*Mexico*] (LA)
CFE........... Compagne Belge de Chemins de Fer et d'Enterprises [*Belgium*] (WGAO)
CFE........... Compagnie du Chemin de Fer Franco-Ethiopien [*Franco-Ethiopian Railroad Company*] (AF)
CFE........... Compagnie Forestiere de l'Equateur [*Gabon*] (WGAO)
CFE........... Compagnie Forestiere d'Eseka
CFE........... Compagnie Francaise d'Entreprises [*French*]
CFE........... Compteur Frappe Erronee [*French*] (ADPT)
CFE........... Confederation Fiscale Europeenne [*European Fiscal Confederation*] (EAIO)
CFE........... Confederation Francaise d'Encadrement (WGAO)
CFE........... Conference on Forces in Europe
CFE........... Conselho Federal de Educacao [*Federal Education Council*] [*Brazil*] (LA)
CFE........... Conventional Forces in Europe (EECI)
CFE........... Negotiations on Conventional Armed Forces in Europe
CFEA........ Comptoir Fournitures Electriques Automobiles Ets. Weydert
CFEB........ Central Forestry Examination Board (WGAO)
CFEHD...... Centre for Early Human Development [*Monash University*] [*Australia*]
CFEI......... Centre de Formation et d'Echanges Internationaux (WGAO)
CFEJ........ Comision Forestal del Estado de Jalisco [*Mexico*] (DSCA)
CFEL........ Continental Far East Lines (DS)
CFEM....... Comision Forestal del Estado de Michoacan [*Mexico*] (DSCA)
CFEM....... Compagnie Francaise d'Entreprises Metalliques
CFEN........ Certificat de Fin d'Etudes Normales
CFEP........ Centre Francais de Protection de l'Enfance (WGAO)
CFEP........ Certificat de Fin d'Etudes Pedagogics
CFEPI....... Comite de Fomento Economico y Promocion Industrial [*Durango*] [*Mexico*] (LAA)
CFEPP...... Comite Francais pour Etude des Phenomenes Paranormaux (EAIO)
CFERDAP ... Centre for Forestry Education Research and Development for the Asia/Pacific Region [*Philippines*] (ARC)
CFES .... Comite Francais d'Education pour la Sante (WGAO)
CFETC ...... Central Fisheries Extension Training Centre [*India*] (ASF)
CFEU........ Conseil Francais pour l'Europe Unie (WGAO)
CFF........... Chemins de Fer Federaux (Suisses) [*French*]
CFF........... Civilforsvars-Forbundet (WGAO)
CFF........... Conselho Florestal Federal [*Brazil*] (DSCA)
CFF........... Cooperative Financing Facility [*Export-Import Bank*]
CFF........... Credit Foncier de France (FLAF)
CFF........... Croatian Franciscan Fathers [*Chicago*] (YU)
CFFA........ Commonwealth Families and Friendship Association (WGAO)
CFFA........ Conselho do Fundo Federal Agropecuario [*Brazil*] (DSCA)
CFFA........ Credit Foncier et Financier d'Afrique
CFFV........ Cooperative Forestiere du Fernan-Vaz
CFG .... Chemins de Fer de Guinee [*Guinea Railroad*] (AF)
CFG .... Chemins de Fer du Gabon [*Gabonese Railroad*] (AF)
CFG .... Cienfuegos [*Cuba*] [*Airport symbol*] [*Obsolete*] (OAG)
CFG .... Compagnie Forestiere du Gabon [*Gabonese Forestry Company*] (AF)
CFG .... Compagnie Francaise du Gabon
CFG .... Comunn Forbairt na Gaidhealtachd [*Highland Development League*] [*Scottish*]
CFG .... Condor Flugdienst GmbH [*Germany*] [*ICAO designator*] (FAAC)
CFGG .... Comite Francais des Grandes Chasses (EAIO)
CFGG .... Compagnie Forestiere du Golfe de Guinee [*Gulf of Guinea Forestry Co.*] [*Cameroon*]
CFH .... Clifton Hills [*Australia*] [*Airport symbol*] [*Obsolete*] (OAG)
CFH .... Congregatie Broeders van Huybergen [*Netherlands*] (EAIO)
CFH .... International Information Centre of the Swiss Watchmaking Industry (WGAO)
CFHBC...... Compagnie Francaise du Haut et Bas Congo
CFHC........ Compagnie Francaise du Haut-Congo
CFHCI....... Chambre Franco-Haitienne de Commerce et d'Industrie (EY)
CFHP........ Compagnie Fermiere des Huileries de Palme
CFHQ .... Canadian Forces Headquarters [*NATO*]
CFHTA...... Centre de Formation Hoteliere et Touristique d'Abidjan
cfi .... Caile Ferate Inguste [*Narrow-Gauge Railroads*] (RO)
CFI .... Clothing and Footwear Institute [*British*] (EAIO)
CFI .... Compagnie Forestiere de l'Indenie

CFI............ Consejo Federal de Inversiones [*Argentina*] (LAA)
CFI............ Controles Financiers Internationaux (FLAF)
CFI............ Control Financial Intern [*Internal Financial Control*] (RO)
CFI............ Coordinacion Financiera Internacional [*Lima, Peru*] (LAA)
CFI............ Corporacion de Fomento Industrial [*Industrial Development Corporation*] [*Dominican Republic*] (LA)
CFI............ Corporacion Financiera Internacional [*International Finance Corporation - IFC*] [*Spanish*]
CFI............ Court of First Insurance [*EEC*] (WGAO)
CFI............ Credit Foncier et Immobilier
CFI............ Societe Cafeiere Franco-Ivoirienne
CFIA........ China Forging Industry Association (EAIO)
CFIA........ Comision de Fomento e Investigaciones Agricolas [*Chile*] (DSCA)
CFIC......... Compagnie Fonciere et Immobiliere du Cameroun
CFIC......... Congregatio Filii Immaculatae Conceptionis (WGAO)
CFIE......... Conseil des Federations Industrielles d'Europe [*Council of European Industrial Federations*]
CFIE......... Conseil des Federations Industrielles d'Europe, Consejo de las Federaciones Industriales de Europa (WGAO)
CFIEX....... Compagnie Francaise d'Importation et d'Exportation
CFIOP...... International Organization of Psychophysiology (WGAO)
CFIS........ Canned Food Information Service [*Australia*]
CFIUS....... Committee on Foreign Investment in the United States (WGAO)
CFJP......... Commission Francaise Justice et Paix (EAIO)
CFK........... Christliche Friedenskonferenz [*Christian Conference for Peace*] (EG)
CFK........... Compagnie Forestiere de Kango
CFK........... Compagnie Forestiere Kritikos [*Cameroon*] (WGAO)
CFK........... Credit Foncier Khmer [*Cambodian Real Estate Bank*] (CL)
CFKR........ Comite des Femmes Khmeres Republicaines [*Cambodian Republican Women's Committee*] (CL)
CFL............ Caminho de Ferro de Luanda [*Luanda Railroad*] [*Angola*] (AF)
CFL............ Ceylon Federation of Labour [*Sri Lanka*]
CFL............ Chemins de Fer des Grands Lacs [*Great Lakes Railroad Company*] [*Zaire*] (AF)
CFL............ Chemins de Fer Luxembourgeois (WGAO)
CFL............ Chinese Federation of Labour [*Taiwan*]
CFL............ Club Francais du Livre [*French Book Club*]
CFL............ Compagnie des Chemins de Fer du Congo Superieur et des Grands Lacs [*Zaire*]
CFL............ Confektionsfabrikanternes Landsforbund (WGAO)
CFL............ Consolidated Fertilisers Ltd.
CFL............ Department of Conservation, Forests, and Lands [*Victoria, Australia*]
CFL............ Societe Nationale des Chemins de Fer Luxembourgeois [*Luxembourg*] (BAS)
CFLA......... Comision Forestal Latinoamericana (WGAO)
CFLAC...... China Federation of Literary and Art Circles (EAIO)
CFLF........ Comptoir des Filasses de Lin Francaises (WGAO)
CFLLP...... Commission on Folk Law and Legal Pluralism [*of the International Union of Anthropological and Ethnological Sciences*] (EAIO)
CFLMG..... Companhia Forca e Luz de Minas Gerais [*Brazil*] (LAA)
CFLN........ Comite Francais de Liberation Nationale [*Algeria*]
CFLNB...... Companhia Forca e Luz Nordeste do Brasil [*Brazil*] (LAA)
CFLP........ Central Fire Liaison Panel (WGAO)
CFLP........ Companhia Forca e Luz do Parana [*Brazil*] (LAA)
CFM......... Caminhos de Ferro do Mocambique [*Mozambique Railroad*] (AF)
CFM......... Centre de Formation Maritime
CFM......... Chemin de Fer de Mayumbe
CFM......... Christiane Fabre de Morlhon [*Information service name CFM Documentazione*] (IID)
CFM......... Comision Femenil Mexicana Nacional (WGAO)
CFM......... Committee for a Free Mozambique
CFM......... Commonwealth Funds Management [*Australia*]
CFM......... Compagnie Financial Michelin [*Michelin Financial Company*] [*Switzerland*]
CFM......... Compagnie Francaise du Methane [*French Methane Company*] (WER)
cfm........... Conform [*German*] (GCA)
CFM......... Consortium Forestier et Maritime [*Forestry and Maritime Consortium*] [*French*] (WER)
CFM......... Contingency Financing Mechanism [*International Monetary Fund*]
CFM......... Council of Foreign Ministers
CFM......... Empresa dos Caminbos de Ferro de Mocambique (WGAO)
CFM......... Ports, Railways, and Transport Services [*Morocco*] (AF)
CFMA....... Chair Frame Manufacturers Association (WGAO)
CFMA....... Cyprus Footwear Manufacturers Association (EAIO)
CFMB....... Compagnie Forestiere Michel Brouillet
CFMC....... Caribbean Fishery Management Council (MSC)
CFME........ Comite Francais des Manifestations Economiques a l'Etranger [*France*]

CFME........ Compagnie Franco-Malgache d'Entreprises
CFMEU.... Construction, Forestry, and Mining Employees Union [*Australia*] (EAIO)
CFMK....... Chemin de Fer Matadi-Kinshasa
CFML....... Chemin de Fer de Matadi-Leopoldville
CFMR....... Centre de Formation de Monitrices Rurales
CFMSA ..... Commonwealth Committee of Foreign Ministers on Southern Africa [*Australia*]
CFMU .... Compagnie Francaise des Minerais d'Uranium [*French Uranium Ores Company*] (AF)
CFMVA..... Centre de Formation de Moniteurs et de Vulgarisateurs Agricoles (WGAO)
CFN .... Commission du Fleuve Niger [*Niger River Commission*] (AF)
CFN .... Compagnie Forestiere du Niari [*Niary Forestry Co.*] [*Congo*] (AF)
CFN .... Compagnie Forestiere du Nombo
CFN .... Cooperative Federation of Nigeria (WGAO)
CFN .... Corporacion Financiera Nacional [*National Financial Corporation*] [*Ecuador*] (LA)
CfN .... Council for Nature (WGAO)
CFNA .... Comision Forestal Norteamericana [*FAO*] (WGAO)
CFN&HCP ... Centre for Nursing and Health Care Practices [*Southern Cross University*] [*Medicine*] [*Australia*]
CFNCL...... Comite Federal National de Controle Laitier (WGAO)
CFNFMPR ... Centre Familial National pour la Formation Menagere Professionnelle Rurale (WGAO)
CFNI......... Caribbean Food and Nutrition Institute [*Jamaica*] [*Research center*] (LA)
CFNIS .... Consolidated Food and Nutrition Information System
CFNR....... Compagnie Francaise de Navigation Rhenane
CfNRI .... Centre for Nursing Research, Inc. [*Australia*]
CFNSW ...... Challenge Foundation of New South Wales [*Australia*] (EAIO)
CFO .... Algemeen Christelijke Federatie van Bonden van Personeel, Werkzaam bij de Overheid en in de Sectoren Gezondheidszorg en Maatschappelijk (WGAO)
CFO .... Commonwealth Fisheries Offices [*Australia*] (ADA)
CFOA .... Chief Fire Officers Association (WGAO)
CFOA .... Credit Foncier de l'Ouest Africain
CFOD .... Cyprus Federation of the Organizations of Disabled (EAIO)
CFOM .... Centre de Formation des Officiers de Marine
CFP .... Centre de Formation Professionnelle de la Police
CFP .... Centrul de Fizica Pamintului [*Center for Earth Physics*] (RO)
CFP .... Chinese Freedom Party [*Political party*] (EY)
CFP .... Club Filatelico de Portugal (WGAO)
CFP .... Combinatul Fondului Plastic [*Combine of the Plastics Fund*] (RO)
CFP .... Comissao de Financiamento da Producao [*Production Financing Commission*] [*Brazil*] (LA)
CFP .... Common Fisheries Policy [*1983*] [*EEC*] (EY)
CFP .... Compagnie Francaise des Petroles [*French Petroleum Company*] (AF)
CFP........... Compania de Aviacion Faucett SA [*Peru*] [*ICAO designator*] (FAAC)
CFP........... Comptoirs Francais du Pacifique
CFP........... Concentracion de Fuerzas Populares [*Concentration of Popular Forces*] [*Ecuador*] [*Political party*] (PPW)
CFP........... Concentration des Forces Populaires [*Concentration of Popular Forces*]
CFP........... Confederation Francaise de la Photographie (WGAO)
CFP........... Congregatio Fratrum Pauperum Sancti Francisci Seraphici (WGAO)
CFP........... Cooperation for Peace [*Sweden*] (EAIO)
CFP........... Franc des Colonies Francaises du Pacifique (FLAF)
CFPA .... Caribbean Family Planning Affiliation (EAIO)
CFPA .... Centre de Formation et de Perfectionnement Administratif
CFPA .... Centre de Formation Professionelle des Adultes [*Adult Vocational Training Center*] [*Algeria*] (AF)
CFPA .... Centre de Formation Professionnelle Agricole [*North African*]
CFPA .... China Film Production Association (EAIO)
CFP-A........ Compagnie Francaise des Petroles - Algerie [*French Petroleum Company - Algeria*] (AF)
CFPC .... Centre Chretien des Patrons et Dirigeants d'Entreprise Francais (WGAO)
CFPC .... Centre Francais du Patronat Chretien (FLAF)
CFPC .... Computer Funding Priorities Committee [*Australia*]
CFPC .... Consell de Forces Politiques de Catalunya [*Council of Political Forces of Catalonia*] [*Spanish*] (WER)
CFPD........ Compagnie Francaise Powell Duffryn (WGAO)
CFPFAO ... Centre Forestier Pilote de la FAO
CFPFLC .... Confederation Francaise des Producteurs de Fruits, Legumes et Champignons (WGAO)
CFPG......... Consello de Forzas Politicas Galegas [*Galician Political Forces Council*] [*Spanish*] (WER)
CFPI .... Central Family Planning Institute [*India*] (WGAO)
CFPI .... Centro de Fomento y Productividad Industrial [*Industrial Productivity and Development Center*] [*Guatemala*] (LA)
CFPI .... Commission de la Fonction Publique Internationale (WGAO)

CFPI .... Compagnie Francaise des Produits Industriels [*France*]
CFPL .... Centro Federado de Periodistas de Lima [*Federated Center of Journalists of Lima*] [*Peru*]   (LA)
CFPLI .... Club Francais du Petit Levrier Italien   (EAIO)
CFPM .... Centro de Formacao de Pilots Militares [*Military Pilots Training Center*] [*Brazil*]   (LA)
CFPM .... China Food Processing and Packaging Machinery Technical Developing Centre   (TCC)
CFPMA ..... China Food and Packaging Machinery Industry Association   (EAIO)
CFPO .... Commission des Forets pour le Proche-Orient
CFPPA ...... Cend de Formation et de Perfectionnement Professionnel Agricole   (WGAO)
CFPPT .... Centre de Formation et Perfectionnement des Planteurs de Tabac   (WGAO)
CFPPU ...... Comite de Familiares de Presos Politicos Uruguayos [*Relatives' Committee for Uruguayan Political Prisoners*] [*Malmo, Sweden*]   (EAIO)
CFPR .... Centre de Formation Professionnelle Rapide
CFPS .... Captain, Fishery Protection Squadron [*NATO*]
CFPS .... Compagnie Francaise de Prospection Sismique [*North African*]
CFR .... Caen [*France*] [*Airport symbol*]   (OAG)
CFR .... Caile Ferate Romane [*Romanian Railways Board*] [*Department of Railways*]
CFR .... Centre des Faibles Radioactivities [*Low Radioactivity Research Center*] [*France*]   (WND)
CFR .... Comite des Femmes Revolutionnaires [*Committee of Revolutionary Women*] [*Benin*]   (AF)
CFR .... Commander on the Order of the Federal Republic [*Nigeria*]
CFR .... Committee on Family Research [*Sweden*]   (SLS)
CFR .... Compagnie Francaise de Raffinage [*French*]
cfr .... Confira [*Portuguese*]
cfr .... Confronte [*Compare*] [*Portuguese*]
CFRAI .... Comite Francais des Relations Agricoles Internationales   (WGAO)
CFRC .... Chemins de Fer Royaux du Cambodge [*Royal Cambodian Railroads*] [*Replaced by CRC*]   (CL)
CFRG .... Centre Francais de Recherches sur la Gravitation [*French Gravitation Research Center*]   (EAS)
CFRI .... Central Fuel Research Institute [*India*]   (WGAO)
CFRO .... Centre Francais de Recherche Operationnelle
CFRP .... Comite Francais de la Recherche sur la Pollution de l'Eau   (EAIO)
CFRS .... Canada-France Redshift Survey [*Astronomy*]
CFRS .... Central Farm Research Station [*British Honduras*]   (DSCA)
CFRTI .... Centre Francais de Renseignements Techniques Industriels   (WGAO)
CFRTI .... Centre Francais des Renseignements Techniques et Industriels   (FLAF)
CFRTU ...... Chinese Federation of Railway Worker's Union   (WGAO)
CFRZ .... Centre Federal de Recherches Zootechniques
CFS .... Central Flying School [*RAF*] [*British*] [*Australia*]
CFS .... Ceskoslovenska Filmova Spolecnost [*Czechoslovak Motion Picture Company*]   (CZ)
CFS .... China Fisheries Society   (EAIO)
CFS .... Civil Flying Services [*Australia*]
CFS .... Coastal Farmers Cooperative Society [*Australia*]   (ADA)
CFS .... Coffs Harbour [*Australia*] [*Airport symbol*]   (OAG)
CFS .... Committee on World Food Security [*United Nations*]   (EA)
CFS .... Compagnie Financiere de Suez [*Suez Financial Co.*] [*France*]
CFS .... Compagnie Forestiere de Sangatanga
CFS .... Compagnie Forestiere de Sassandra
CFS .... Comptoir Foncier du Senegal   (WGAO)
CFS .... Comptoir Francais des Superphosphates   (WGAO)
CFS .... Congregatio a Fraternitate Sacerdotrali   (WGAO)
CFS .... Franc de la Cote Francaise des Somalis [*Francs Djibouti*]   (FLAF)
CFSBDT .... Club Francais du Saint Bernard et Dogue du Tibet   (EAIO)
CFSG .... Compagnie Forestiere du Sud-Gabon
CFSI .... Centre de Formation de Specialistes de l'Information [*Information Media Specialists Training Center*] [*Malagasy Republic*]   (AF)
CFSI .... Comite Francais de la Semoulerie Industrielle   (WGAO)
CFSI .... Confederation Francaise des Syndicats Independants [*French Confederation of Independent Unions*]
CFSL .... Central Forensic Science Laboratory   (WGAO)
CFSO .... Compagnie Forestiere Sangha-Oubangui [*Sangha-Oubangui Forestry Co.*] [*Cameroon*]
CFSP .... Club Francais du Schnauzer et du Pinscher   (EAIO)
CFSTF .... Sveriges Civilingenjorsforbund   (WGAO)
CFT .... Centrul de Fizica Tehnica [*Center for Technical Physics*]   (RO)
CFT .... Chemin de Fer du Togo
Cft .... Cift [*Pair (Of)*]   (TU)
CFT .... Compagnie Forestiere Tere
CFT .... Compagnie Forestiere Tropicale
CFT .... Confederation Francaise du Travail [*French Confederation of Labor*]   (WER)

CFT .... Corporacion Financiera del Transporte [*Transport Financial Corporation*] [*Colorado*]   (LA)
CFTA .... Club Francais des Touristes Aeriens [*France*]
CFTB .... Commonwealth Forestry and Timber Bureau [*Australia*]   (ADA)
CFTC .... Commonwealth Fund for Technical Cooperation [*Australia*]   (ADA)
CFTC .... Confederation Francaise des Travailleurs Chretiens [*French Confederation of Christian Workers*] [*Paris*]   (WER)
CFTD .... Confederation Francaise du Travail Democratique [*French National Trade Union Confederation*]   (DCTA)
CFTF .... Centre Technique Forestier Tropical [*France*]   (WGAO)
CFTF .... Children's Film and Television Foundation   (WGAO)
CFTH .... Compagnie Francaise Thomson Houston [*French*]
CFTI .... Centre de Formation aux Techniques de l'Information
CFTP .... Compagnie Franco-Tunisienne de Petrole [*Franco-Tunisian Petroleum Company*]   (AF)
CFTPA .... Centro de Formacao e Treinamento de Professores Agricolas [*Brazil*]   (DSCA)
CFTRI .... Central Food Technological Research Institute [*India*]   (PDAA)
CFTTP .... Centre de Formation des Techniciens des Travaux Publics [*Public Works Technician Training Center*] [*Laotian*]   (CL)
CFTU .... Ceylon Federation of Trade Unions [*Sri Lanka*]
CFTU .... Confederation of Free Trade Unions [*India*]
CFTV .... Centre de Formation de Techniciens de Vulgarisation   (WGAO)
CFU .... Caribbean Football Union   (WGAO)
CFU .... Ceskoslovensky Filmovy Ustav [*Czechoslovak Motion Picture Institute*]   (CZ)
CFU .... Commercial Farmers Union
CFU .... Commonwealth Film Unit [*Australia*]   (ADA)
CFU .... Corfu [*Greece*] [*Airport symbol*]   (OAG)
CFUP .... Comite Francais de l'Union Paneuropeenne   (WGAO)
CFV .... Comite des Forces Vives - Hery Velona [*Madagascar*] [*Political party*]   (EY)
CFV .... Corporacion Venezolana de Fomento   (WGAO)
CFVA .... Centre de Formation et de Vulgarisation Agricoles de Kaedi [*Mauritania*]
CFVU .... Cesky Fond Vytvarnych Umelcu [*Czech Creative Artists' Fund*]   (CZ)
CFW .... Club Francais du Whippet [*French Whippet Club*]   (EAIO)
CFW .... Committee for the Free World [*United States*]   (WGAO)
CFW .... Concern for Family and Womanhood   (WGAO)
CFW .... Confederation of Filipino Workers   (EY)
CFWCA ..... Child and Family Welfare Council of Australia   (ADA)
CFX .... Congregatio Fratrum a Sancto Francisco Xaverio   (WGAO)
CFZ .... Colon Free Zone [*Free Trade Zone*] [*Panama*]   (IMH)
CFZV .... Centrala Farmaseutica Zoo-Veterinara [*Romania*]   (WGAO)
Cg .... Caglayan [*Waterfall*]   (TU)
CG .... Carl Gustav [*King of Sweden*]
cg .... Centigrama [*Centigram*] [*Portuguese*]
cg .... Centigramm [*Centigram*]   (HU)
cg .... Centigramme [*Centigram*] [*French*]
cg .... Centigramo [*Centigram*] [*Spanish*]
CG .... Centrale Grondkamer [*Benelux*]   (BAS)
CG .... Chemische Gesellschaft [*Chemical Society*]   (EG)
CG .... Coalicion Galega [*Spain*] [*Political party*]   (EY)
CG .... Coalition des Gauches [*Left Unity*] [*Transnational party group in the European Parliament*]   (ECED)
CG .... Congo [*ANSI two-letter standard code*]   (CNC)
CG .... Connradh na Gaedhilge [*The Gaelic League, founded in 1893*]
CG .... Conseil General [*General Council*]   (LA)
CG .... Console Generale [*Consul-General*] [*Italian*]
CG .... Consul General [*General Council*] [*French*]   (MTD)
CG .... Consultative Group [*NATO*]
CG .... Contadora Group [*Mexico*]   (EAIO)
CG .... Cowper Greens [*Political party*] [*Australia*]
CG .... Crna Gora [*Montenegro*]   (YU)
CG .... Croisement a Gauche [*Knitting*] [*French*]
CG .... Cruiser, Guided Missile [*NATO*]
cg .... Senttigramma(a) [*Centigram*] [*Finland*]
cg .... Zentigramm [*Centigram*] [*German*]
CGA .... Chinese Garment Association   (EAIO)
CGA .... Clove Growers' Association
CGA .... Comandancia General de Aeronautica [*Peru*]
CGA .... Commonwealth General Assurance Corp. Ltd. [*Australia*]   (ADA)
CGA .... Compagnie Gaziere d'Afrique
CGA .... Compagnie Generale Africaine
CGA .... Compagnie Generale d'Aeronautique [*French*]
CGA .... Compagnie Generale d'Automatisme [*French*]
CGA .... Composers Guild of Australia
CGA .... Comptoir General d'Approvisionnement
CGA .... Confederation Generale de l'Agriculture [*General Confederation of Agriculture*] [*French*]   (WER)
CGA .... Conseil General de l'Agriculture   (WGAO)
CGA .... Country Gentlemen's Association   (WGAO)

CGA .... Cyprus Geographical Association   (SLS)
CGAC .... China General Aviation Corp. [*ICAO designator*]   (FAAC)
CGAD .... Confederation Generale de l'Alimentation en Detail   (WGAO)
CGADIP .... Compagnie Gaziere d'Afrique et de Distribution de Primagaz
CGAE .... Compagnie Generale Africaine d'Electricite
CGAF .... Confederation Generale de l'Artisanat Francais
CGAF .... Confederation Generale des Architectes Francais   (WGAO)
CGAMEEC ... Committee of Glutamic Acid Manufacturers of the European Economic Community   (EAIO)
CGAP .... Comite General d'Action Paysanne   (WGAO)
CGARA ..... Commission Generale de l'Assurance du Risque Atomique [*Paris, France*]   (EAIO)
CGAT .... Confederation Generale Africaine du Travail [*African General Confederation of Labor*]
CGB .... Christlicher Gewerkschaftsbund Deutschlands [*Confederation of German Christian Trade Unions*]
CGB .... Commonwealth Geographical Bureau   (EA)
CGB .... Confederation Generale des Planteurs de Betteraves   (WGAO)
CGB .... Cuiaba [*Brazil*] [*Airport symbol*]   (OAG)
CGBBB ...... Club du Griffon Bruxellois, Belge, Brabancon [*France*]   (EAIO)
CGBCE ...... Christliche Gewerkschaft Bergbau-Chemie-Energie   (WGAO)
CGBE .... Christliche Gewerkschaft Bergbau und Energie   (WGAO)
CGC .... Cape Gloucester [*Papua New Guinea*] [*Airport symbol*]   (OAG)
CGC .... Commonwealth Grants Commission [*Australia*]
CGC .... Compagnie Generale de Carrelages
CGC .... Compagnie Generale de Chauffe [*French energy-management group*]
CGC .... Compagnie Generale de la Chaussure [*North African*]
CGC .... Confederation Francaise de l'Encadrement   (EAIO)
CGC .... Confederation Generale des Cadres [*General Confederation of Supervisory Employees*] [*France*]
CGC .... Cruiser, Guided Missile and Command [*NATO*]
CGCC .... Chinese General Chamber of Commerce [*Hong Kong*]   (EAIO)
CGCCET ... Comisia Guvernamentala pentru Colaborare si Cooperare Economica si Tehnica [*Governmental Commission for Economic and Technical Collaboration and Cooperation*] (RO)
CGCE .... Centre Gabonais de Commerce Exterieur   (EY)
CGCE .... Comptoir Guineen du Commerce Exterieur [*Guinean Foreign Trade Agency*]
CGCED ..... Caribbean Group for Cooperation in Economic Development (LA)
CGCh .... Cahier General des Charges [*Benelux*]   (BAS)
CGCI .... Confederation Generale du Commerce et de l'Industrie (WGAO)
CGCL .... Consejo General de Castilla y Leon   (WGAO)
CGCP .... Confederacion General de Campesinos del Peru [*General Confederation of Peasants of Peru*]   (LA)
CGCRI ...... Central Glass and Ceramic Research Institute [*India*] [*Research center*]   (IRC)
CGCS .... Commonwealth Games Council for Scotland   (WGAO)
CGCT .... Compagnie Generale de Construction Telephonique [*General Telephone Construction Co.*] [*Morocco*]
CGCT .... Confederation Generale Camerounaise du Travail [*Cameroonian General Confederation of Workers*]
CGCTP ...... Compagnie Gabonaise de Construction et Travaux Publics
CGD .... Caixa Geral de Depositos [*General Deposit Bank*] [*Portuguese*] (GEA)
CGD .... Christliche Gewerkschaftsbewegung Deutschlands [*Christian Trade Union Movement of Germany*] [*Germany*]
CGD .... Commissariat General au Developpement [*General Development Commission*] [*Niger*]   (AF)
CG/DDR ... Chemische Gesellschaft der Deutschen Demokratischen Republik [*Chemical Society of the German Democratic Republic*]   (SLS)
CGDE .... Christliche Gewerkschaft Deutscher Eisenbahner   (WGAO)
CGDK .... Coalition Government of Democratic Kampuchea
CGDLS ...... Confederazione Generale Democratica dei Lavoratori Sanmarines [*San Marino*]   (WGAO)
CGDORIS ... Compagnie Generale pour les Developpements Operationnels de Richesses Sous-Marines
CGE .... Compagnie Generale d'Electricite [*General Electric Company*] [*France*]
CGE .... Confederacion General Economica [*General Economic Confederation*] [*Argentina*]   (LA)
CGE .... Confederation Generale l'Epargne   (WGAO)
CGE .... Conference des Grandes Ecoles
CGE .... Croisement a Gauche a l'Endroit [*Knitting*] [*French*]
CGE .... Nelson Aviation College [*New Zealand*] [*ICAO designator*] (FAAC)
CGEA .... Centre de Gestion des Exploitations Agricoles [*North African*]
CGEA .... Commissariat General de l'Energie Atomique [*General Atomic Energy Commission*] [*Zaire*]   (AF)
CGEA .... Confederation Generale Economique Algerienne [*Algerian General Economic Confederation*]   (AF)
CGEC .... Confederacion General de Empleados de Comercio [*General Confederation of Business Employees*] [*Argentina*]   (LA)

CGECI .... Compagnie Generale d'Electricite de Cote-D'Ivoire
CGEE .... Compagnie Generale de l'Equipement Electrique [*General Electrical Equipment Company*] [*French*]   (WER)
CGEEOM ... Compagnie Generale des Eaux pour l'Etranges et l'Outre-Mer
CGEM .... Confederation Generale des Employeurs de Mauritanie   (EY)
CGEM .... Confederation Generale Economique Marocaine [*Moroccan General Economic Federation*] [*Casablanca*]   (AF)
CGER .... Caisse Generale d'Epargne et de Retraite [*State-owned bank*] [*Belgium*]   (EY)
CGER .... Centre de Gestion et d'Economie Rurale   (WGAO)
CGERA ...... Confederacion General de Educadores de la Republica Argentina [*General Teachers Confederation of the Argentine Republic*] (LA)
CGES .... Compagnie Generale des Eaux du Senegal
CGET .... Chamber of Geological Engineers of Turkey   (EAIO)
cgf .... Centigrama-Forca [*Centigrams of Force*] [*Portuguese*]
CGF .... Czech Government Flying Service [*ICAO designator*]   (FAAC)
CGFA .... Consolidated Gold Fields Australia   (ADA)
CGFPI .... Consultative Group on Food Production and Investment in Developing Countries [*United Nations*]
CGFTL ...... Confederation Generale des Filateurs et Tisseurs de Lin (WGAO)
CGG .... Compagnie Generale de Geophysique [*North African*]
CGGE .... Compagnie Generale Guineenne d'Electricite
CGGM .... Centre Geologique et Geophysique de Montpellier [*Geology and Geophysics Center*] [*France*]   (EAS)
CGGSNPA ... Compagnie General de Geophysique a la Societe Nationale des Petroles d'Aquitaine
CGH .... Castle of Good Hope Decoration
CGH .... Sao Paulo [*Brazil*] Congonhas Airport [*Airport symbol*]   (OAG)
CGI .... Code General des Impots [*French*]
CGI .... Comissao Geral de Investigacoes [*General Investigations Committee*] [*Brazil*]   (LA)
CGI .... Comitato Glaciologico Italiano [*Italian*]   (SLS)
CGI .... Commisione Geodetica Italiana   (WGAO)
CGI .... Compagnie Generale d'Informatique [*French*]   (ADPT)
CGI .... Compagnie Generale Immobiliere [*North African*]
CGI .... Compagnie Generale Industrielle [*Ivory Coast*]   (WGAO)
CGI .... Confederacion General de la Industria [*General Confederation of Industry*] [*Argentina*]   (LA)
CGI .... Congres Geologique International   (WGAO)
CGI .... Corticene-Grabber's Itch [*Refers to desire to "hit the deck" during bombing attacks*] [*Australian Navy slang*]   (DSUE)
CGIA .... Confederazione Generale Italiana del' Artigianato   (WGAO)
CGIAR .... Consultative Group for International Agricultural Research [*United Nations (already exists in GUS II database)*]
CGIC .... Caisse Generale Interprofessionnelle des Cadres [*France*] (FLAF)
CGIC .... Comisaria General de Investigacion Criminal [*Commissariat General of Criminal Investigation*] [*Spanish*]
CGIC .... Comite General Interprofessionnel Chanvrier   (WGAO)
CGICA ...... Credit Guarantee Insurance Corporation of Africa
CGIL .... Confederazione Generale Italiana del Lavoro [*General Confederation of Labor*] [*Italian*]   (DCTA)
CGIOR ...... Centro General de Instruccion de Oficiales de Reserva [*General Training Center for Reserve Officers*] [*Uruguay*]   (LA)
CGIS .... Comisaria General de Investigacion Social [*General Headquarters of Social Studies*] [*Spanish*]   (WER)
CGK .... Cihelny Gustava Klimenta [*Gustav Kliment Brick Works*]   (CZ)
CGKT .... Confederation Generale Kamerunaise du Travail [*Cameroonian General Confederation of Labor*]   (AF)
CGL .... Camelot Ghana Ltd.
CGL .... Centro Gerontologico Latino [*An association*]   (EA)
CGL .... Colourgraphic Programmiersprache [*German*]   (ADPT)
CGL .... Confederation Generale du Logement   (WGAO)
CGL .... Confederazione Generale di Lavora [*General Confederation of Labor*] [*Italy*]
CGLO .... Commonwealth Geological Liaison Office   (WGAO)
CGLS .... Camara Gremial de la Legumbre Seca [*Argentina*]   (DSCA)
CGLS .... Confederazione Generale dei Lavoratori della Somalia [*General Confederation of Somali Workers*]   (AF)
CGM .... Cairo Geological Museum [*Egypt*]
CGM .... Cargoman [*Oman*] [*ICAO designator*]   (FAAC)
CGM .... Compagnie Generale de Madagascar
CGM .... Compagnie Generale des Moteurs
CGM .... Compagnie Generale Maritime [*State-controlled shipping group*] [*French*]
CGM .... Confederatia Generala a Muncii [*General Confederation of Labor*]   (RO)
CGM .... Congo Gospel Mission
CGMA .... Casein Glue Manufacturers Association   (WGAO)
CGMA .... Consolidated Gold Mining Areas [*Australia*]
CGMSA ..... Camara Gremial de Molinos Semoleros y Afines [*Argentina*] (DSCA)
CGMW ...... Commission for the Geological Map of the World [*International Union of Geological Sciences*] [*Paris, France*]

CGN.......... Centrum voor Genetische Bronnen [*Center for Genetic Resources*] [*Netherlands*] (IRC)
CGN.......... Cologne/Bonn [*Germany*] [*Airport symbol*] (OAG)
CGN.......... Compagnie Generale du Niger
CGN.......... Coordinadora Guerrillera Nacional [*Colorado*] (EY)
CGO.......... Compagnie Generale d'Organisation
CGO.......... Contango [*Premium or interest paid*] [*London Stock Exchange*]
CGO.......... Zhengzhou [*China*] [*Airport symbol*] (OAG)
CGOT....... Compagnie Generale des Oleagineux Tropicaux
CGP .... Caisse Generale de Perequation des Prix des Produits et Marchandises de Grande Consommation [*Burkina Faso*] (WGAO)
CGP .... Camara Gremial del Pasto [*Argentina*] (DSCA)
CGP .... Camara Guatemalteca de Periodismo [*Guatemala*] (EY)
CGP .... Centre Gabonais de Prevention
CGP .... Chittagong [*Bangladesh*] [*Airport symbol*] (OAG)
CGP .... Comando Guerrilleros del Pueblo [*Guerrilla group*] [*Guatemala*] (EY)
CGP .... Commando de Guerra Popular [*Popular War Command*] [*Venezuela*] (LA)
CGP .... Commissariat General a la Productivite (WGAO)
CGP .... Commissariat General au Plan (WGAO)
CGP .... Confederacion General de Profesionales [*General Confederation of Professionals*] [*Argentina*] (LA)
CGP .... Conseil de la Guerre Politique [*Political Warfare Council*] [*Cambodia*] (CL)
CGP .... Cuerpo General de Policia [*General Police Corps*] [*Spanish*] (WER)
CGP .... Cumhuriyet Guvenlik Partisi [*Republican Reliance Party*] (TU)
CGPB....... Confederacao General dos Pescadores do Brasil (WGAO)
CGPB....... Confederacao Geral dos Pescadores do Brasil [*Brazil*] (DSCA)
CGPB....... Confederation Generale des Planteurs de Betteraves (WGAO)
CGPCC..... Confederation Generale des Planteurs de Chicoree a Cafe (WGAO)
CGPEL..... Confederation Generale des Producteurs de Fruits et Legumes (WGAO)
CGPF........ Confederation Generale de la Production Francaise [*France*] (FLAF)
CGPF........ Confederation Generale du Patronat Francais [*General Confederation of French Employers*] [*Now CNPF*] (WER)
CGPIF ...... Compagnie Generale de Participation Industrielle et Financiere
CGPJ........ Consejo General del Poder Judicial (WGAO)
CGPLBIR ... Confederation Generale des Producteurs de Lait de Brebis et des Industriels de Roquefort (WGAO)
CGPM ...... Conference Generale des Poids et Mesures [*General Conference on Weights and Measures*]
CGPM ...... Conseil General des Peches pour la Mediterranee [*General Fisheries Council for the Mediterranean - GFCM*] [*French*] (ASF)
CGPM ...... Consejo General de Pesca del Mediterraneo [*General Fisheries Council for the Mediterranean - GFCM*] [*FAO*] [*Spanish*] (ASF)
CGPME..... Confederation Generale des Petites et Moyennes Entreprises [*France*] (FLAF)
CGPP........ Confederazione General dei Produttori di Patate (WGAO)
CGPPO...... Compagnie Generale des Plantations et Palmeraies de l'Ogooue [*Gabon*]
CGPPT ...... Confederation General des Producteurs de Pommes de Terre (WGAO)
CGPS........ Caisse Gabonaise de Prevoyance Sociale
CGPT........ Confederation des Paysans Travailleurs (WGAO)
CGQ.......... Changchun [*China*] [*Airport symbol*] (OAG)
CGR .... Campo Grande [*Brazil*] [*Airport symbol*] (OAG)
cgr .... Centigrade [*Centigrade*] [*French*]
cgr .... Centigrado [*Centigrade*] [*Portuguese*]
CGR .... Compagnie Generale de Radiologie
CGR .... Contraloria General de la Republica [*National General Accounting Office*] [*Colorado*] (LA)
CGRA .... China and Glass Retailers Association (WGAO)
CGRA .... Consortium General des Recherches Aeronautiques (WGAO)
CGRB .... Capital Gains Research Bureau (WGAO)
CGRB .... Combinatie Groningen v. Rationele Bedrijfsvoering (WGAO)
CGRECOA ... Camara Gremial de Recibidores y Entregadores de Cereales, Oleaginosos y Afines [*Argentina*] (DSCA)
CGRH........ Centre for Genetic Resources and Heritage [*Australia*]
CGRI......... Central Glass and Ceramic Research Institute [*India*] (PDAA)
CGrkamer ... Centrale Grondkamer [*Benelux*] (BAS)
CGRL......... Central Gippsland Regional Library [*Australia*]
CGS .... CAP-Gemini-Sogeti [*Software manufacturer*]
CGS .... Cegesimal [*Spanish*]
cgs .... Centimetre-Gramme-Seconde [*Centimeter-Gram-Second*] [*French*]
CGS .... Centimetro, Grama, e Segundo [*Centimeters, Grams, and Seconds*] [*Portuguese*]
CGS .... Centymetr-Gram-Sekunda [*Centimeter-Gram-Second*] [*Poland*]
CGS .... Clinical Genetics Society (WGAO)
CGS .... Commonwealth Government Securities [*Australia*]

CGS .... Confederacion General de Sindicatos [*General Confederation of Trade Unions*] [*El Salvador*] (LA)
CGS .... Confederation Generale des Syndicats [*General Confederation of Trade Unions*] [*French*]
CGS .... Confederation Generale des Syndicats [*General Confederation of Trade Unions*] [*Congo - Leopoldville*]
CGSB....... Coordinadora Guerrillera Simon Bolivar [*Colorado*] [*Political party*] (EY)
CGSCOP ... Confederation Generale des Societes Cooperatives Ouvrieres de Production (WGAO)
CGSI......... Confederation Generale des Syndicats Independents [*General Confederation of Independent Unions*] [*Algeria*]
CGSL....... Compagnie Generale Sangha-Likouala
CGSL....... Confederazione Generale Somala dei Lavoratori [*Somali General Workers Confederation*] (AF)
CGSLB ...... Centrale Generale des Syndicats Liberaux de Belgique [*General Organization of Belgian Liberal Labor Unions*] [*Ghent*] (WER)
CGSP........ Centrale Generale des Services Publics [*Benelux*] (BAS)
CGSSSA .... Catholic Girls' Secondary Schools Sports Association [*Australia*]
CGSTMMICC ... Confederacion General de Sindicatos de Trabajadores Metalurgicos, Mineros, Industrias y Comercio de Chile (EAIO)
CGSU .... Confederation Generale des Syndicats Unifies [*France*] (FLAF)
CGT .... Central General de Trabajadores [*General Confederation of Workers*] [*Dominican Republic*]
CGT .... Central General de Trabajadores [*General Workers Federation*] [*Honduras*] (LA)
CGT .... Central Geral dos Trabalhadores [*Workers' General Confederation*] [*Brazil*]
CGT .... Centro de Geografia Tropical [*Ecuador*] (DSCA)
CGT .... Cheguitti [*Mauritania*] [*Airport symbol*] (OAG)
CGT .... Comando Geral dos Trabalhadores [*Union Headquarters*] [*Brazil*] (LA)
CGT .... Commissariat General au Tourisme [*Belgium*] (WGAO)
CGT .... Compagnie Generale des Constructions Telephoniques [*General Telephone Construction Company*] [*French*] (WER)
CGT .... Compagnie Generale de Transports Aeriens [*Algeria*]
CGT .... Compagnie Generale Transatlantique [*General Transatlantic Shipping Company*] [*French*] (WER)
CGT .... Confederacao Geral de Trabalho [*General Confederation of Labor*] [*Portuguese*] (WER)
CGT .... Confederacion General del Trabajo [*National Confederation of Labor*] [*Spain*] (EY)
CGT .... Confederacion General del Trabajo [*General Confederation of Labor*] [*Argentina*] (PD)
CGT .... Confederacion General del Trabajo [*General Confederation of Labor*] [*El Salvador*]
CGT .... Confederacion General del Trabajo [*General Confederation of Labor*] [*Colorado*] (LA)
CGT .... Confederacion General del Trabajo [*General Confederation of Labor*] [*Nicaragua*] (LA)
CGT .... Confederacion General de Sindicatos de Trabajadores Metalurgicos, Mineros, Industrias, y Comercios de Chile [*Chile*]
CGT .... Confederacion General de Trabajadores [*General Confederation of Workers*] [*Mexico*]
CGT .... Confederacion General de Trabajadores [*General Confederation of Workers*] [*Chile*] (EY)
CGT .... Confederacion General de Trabajadores de Venezuela [*General Confederation of Workers of Venezuela*]
CGT .... Confederation Generale des Travailleurs [*South Vietnamese*]
CGT .... Confederation Generale du Travail [*General Confederation of Labor*] [*Luxembourg*] (WER)
CGT .... Confederation Generale du Travail [*General Confederation of Labor*] [*Martinique*] (PPW)
CGT .... Confederation Generale du Travail [*General Confederation of Labor*] [*France*] (PPE)
CGT .... Contaduria General de Transportes [*Brazil*] (LAA)
CGTA .... Compagnie Generale de Transports Aerien [*Algeria*]
CGTA .... Confederation Generale des Travailleurs Africains [*General Confederation of African Workers*] [*Former French Equatorial Africa*]
CGTA .... Confederation Generale des Travailleurs de l'Angola [*General Confederation of Workers of Angola*] (AF)
CGTAE...... Compagnie Generale de Transports en Afrique Equatoriale [*Equatorial Africa General Transport Company*] [*Congo*] (AF)
CGTAP...... Compagnie Generale de Transports en Afrique et de Participations
CGTB........ Canadian Government Travel Bureau (WGAO)
CGTB........ Confederacion General de Trabajadores de Bolivia [*General Confederation of Labor of Bolivia*] (EY)
CGTB........ Confederation Generale du Travail Burkinabe [*General Confederation of Labor of Burkina Faso*] (EY)
CGTB........ Confederation Generale du Travail de Belgique [*General Confederation of Belgian Labor*]

CGTB........ Confederation Generale du Travail du Burundi [*General Confederation of Labor of Burundi*] (AF)
CGTC .... Central General di Trahadonan di Corsow [*General Centre of Workers of Curacao*] [*Netherlands Antilles*]
CGTC .... Confederacion General de Trabajadores Costarricenses [*General Confederation of Costa Rican Workers*] (LA)
CGTC .... Confederation Generale des Travailleurs Congolais [*General Confederation of Congolese Workers*] [*Zaire*]
CGTDS...... Confederation Generale des Travailleurs Democrates du Senegal [*General Confederation of Democratic Workers of Senegal*] (AF)
CGTFB...... Confederacion General de Trabajadores Fabriles de Bolivia [*General Confederation of Bolivian Factory Workers*] (LA)
CGT-FO .... Confederation Generale du Travail - Force Ouvriere [*General Confederation of Labor - Workers' Force*] [*French*] (AF)
CGTG .... Confederation Generale du Travail de la Guadeloupe [*General Confederation of Labor of Guadeloupe*]
CGTG .... Co-Ordinadora General de Trabajadores de Guatemala [*Guatemala*]
CGT-I .... Confederacion General de Trabajo (Independiente) [*General Confederation of Labor - Independent*] [*Nicaragua*]
CGTK .... Confederation Generale du Travail du Kamerun
CGTL........ Confederation Generale des Travailleurs du Liban [*Trade union federation*] [*Beirut, Labanon*] (MENA)
CGTL........ Confederation Generale du Travail de Luxembourg [*General Confederation of Labor of Luxembourg*] (BAS)
CGTM .... Compagnie Generale des Turbo-Machines [*French*]
CGTM .... Confederation Generale du Travail de la Martinique [*General Confederation of Labor of Martinique*]
CGTP........ Confederacao Geral dos Trabalhadores Portugueses [*General Confederation of Portugese Workers*] (EY)
CGTP........ Confederacion General de Trabajadores del Peru [*General Confederation of Workers of Peru*] (LA)
CGTP........ Construction Generale et Travaux Publics
CGTP-IN... Confederacao Geral dos Trabalhadores Portugueses-Intersindical Nacional [*Portugal*]
CGTR .... Confederation Generale du Travail de la Reunion [*General Confederation of Labor of Reunion*] (AF)
CGTR .... Confederation Generale du Travail du Ruanda [*General Confederation of Rwandan Workers*]
CGTRA...... Compagnie Gabonaise de Transport et de Reparation Automobile
CGTREO... Compagnie Generale de Travaux de Recherches et d'Exploitation Oceaniques [*General Society for Research and Oceanic Exploitation*] [*French*] (ASF)
CGTS........ Confederacion General de Trabajadores Salvadorenos [*General Confederation of Salvadoran Workers*] (LA)
CGTS........ Confederation Generale du Travail du Senegal [*General Confederation of Labor of Senegal*] (AF)
CGTT........ Confederacion General de Trabajadores del Transporte Terrestre y Afines de Chile [*Trade union*] (EY)
CGTTA...... General Confederation of African Workers (WGAO)
CGTU .... Confederation General de Trabajadores del Uruguay [*General Confederation of Uruguayan Workers*] (LA)
CGTU .... Confederation Generale du Travail Unitaire [*France*] (FLAF)
CGTU .... General Confederation of Trade Unions [*Syria*] (ME)
CGU .... Ceremonial Guard Unit [*Singapore*] (ML)
CGU .... Cesky Geologicky Urad [*Czech Geological Office*] (CZ)
CGU .... Computergesteuerter Unterricht [*German*] (ADPT)
CGU .... Confederacion General Universitaria [*Brazil*] (WGAO)
CGUP .... Comite Guatemalteca de Unidad Popular (WGAO)
CGUP .... Comite Guatemalteco de Unidad Patriotica [*Guatemalan Committee of Patriotic Unity*] (PD)
CGV .... Centre de Gravite Verticale [*Vertical Center of Gravity*] [*Shipping*] [*French*]
CGV .... Confederation Generale de la Vieillesse (WGAO)
CGV .... Confederation Generale des Vignerons (WGAO)
CGV .... Consejo General Vasco (WGAO)
CGVCO ..... Confederation Generale des Vignerons du Centre-Ouest (WGAO)
CGVSO...... Confederation Genrale des Vignerons du Sud-Ouest (WGAO)
CGVT .... Commission Gastronomique, Vinicole, et Touristique (EA)
CGW .... Great Wall Airlines [*China*] [*ICAO designator*] (FAAC)
CGWIC...... China Great Wall Industry Corp. (TCC)
CGWU ...... Commercial and General Workers' Union [*Rhodesia and Nyasaland*]
CGY .... Cagayan De Oro [*Philippines*] [*Airport symbol*] (OAG)
CH .... Bellanca Aircraft Corp., Champion Aircraft Corp. [*ICAO aircraft manufacturer identifier*] (ICAO)
CH .... Centrala Handlowa [*Sales Center*] (POL)
CH .... Ceskoslovenske Hute, Narodni Podnik [*Czechoslovak Metallurgical Works, National Enterprise*] (CZ)
CH .... Challenge Air Services [*Airline code*] [*Australia*]
Ch.............. Chambre [*French*] (FLAF)
ch.............. Chant [*Song*] [*French*]
ch.............. Chapitre [*Chapter*] [*French*]
ch.............. Chaque [*Each*] [*French*]

ch.............. Chaussee [*Road*] [*French*] (CED)
Ch.............. Chef [*Chief*] [*German*] (GCA)
Ch/ .... Chef De [*Chief Of*] [*Cambodia*] (CL)
Ch.............. Chemie [*Chemistry*] [*German*]
ch.............. Cheque [*Check*] [*Spanish*]
ch.............. Chervonets [*Monetary unit; 1922-1947*] [*Russian*]
ch.............. Cheval [*Horse*] [*French*]
Ch.............. Chevaux [*Horses*] [*Military*] [*French*] (MTD)
CH .... Chieti [*Car registration plates*] [*Italian*]
ch.............. Chiffre [*Numbered*] [*Publishing*] [*French*]
Ch.............. Chitalishte [*Library*] [*A periodical*] (BU)
CH .... Cin-Ho [*Yunnanese Chinese*]
CH .... Confederatio(n) Helveti(que) [*Switzerland*] [*International automobile identification tag*]
ch.............. Date (BU)
Ch.............. H-Hour, Time of Attack (BU)
ch.............. Hour (BU)
Ch.............. Library (BU)
ch.............. Man, Men (RU)
ch.............. Number (BU)
ch.............. Number, Date (RU)
ch.............. Part, Section (BU)
ch.............. Part, Unit (RU)
ch.............. Pure (RU)
CH .... Switzerland [*ANSI two-letter standard code*] (CNC)
ch.............. Via (RU)
CHA.......... Caribbean Hotel Association (WGAO)
CHA.......... Centrale van Hogere Ambtenaren
CHA.......... Committee of Heads of Administration [*NATO*] (NATG)
CHA.......... Countrywide Holidays Association (WGAO)
CHA.......... Cyprus Hotel Association (EAIO)
ChA........... Red Army (BU)
CHACA ..... Classic and Historic Automobile Club of Australia
ch acc.......... Chambre des Mises en Accusation (FLAF)
CHACONA ... Chantier des Constructions Navales [*Naval Shipyard*] [*Congo*] (AF)
CHADA..... Societe Chimique et Industrielle Africaine du Dahomey
CHADECJA ... Stronnictwo Chrzescijanskiej Demokracji [*Christian Democratic Party*] [*Poland*] (PPE)
CHAE........ Centre d'Histoire de l'Aeronautique et de l'Espace [*Aeronautics and Space Historical Center - ASHC*] (EAIO)
CHAFREC ... Chambre Syndicate Francaise de l'Enseignement Prive par Correspondance (WGAO)
chag............ Chagrin [*Shagreen*] [*Publishing*] [*French*]
chagr .... Chagrin [*Shagreen*] [*Publishing*] [*French*]
chagr .... Chagrin [*Shagreen*] [*Publishing Danish/Norwegian*]
CHAGRID ... Association Nationale Suisse de Genie Rural, Irrigations et Drainage (WGAO)
CHAGS ..... International Conference on Hunting and Gathering Societies [*Australia*]
CHAIDIS .. Chaine Africaine d'Importation, de Distribution, et d'Exportation [*Senegal*]
Chair .... Chairman [*or Chairwoman*] (EECI)
Chair .... Chairman/woman (IDIG)
Chair .... Chairmen/women (IDIG)
CHAIS...... Consumer Hazards Analysis (WGAO)
CHAKA ..... Chama Cha Kiswahili Africa
CHAL........ Christian Health Association of Liberia
CHALLPESCA ... Empresa Mixta Pesquera Peruano-Japonesa [*Peru-Japan Mixed Fisheries Enterprise*] (LA)
CHALUTCAM ... Societe de Chalutage du Cameroun (WGAO)
CHAMA.... Chama Cha Mapinduzi [*Revolutionary Party*] [*Tanzania*] (AF)
Chamb....... Chambellan [*Chamberlain*] [*French*] (MTD)
CHAMCOM ... Chambre de Commerce d'Agriculture et de l'Industrie de la Republique du Tchad (WGAO)
CHAMINE ... Ghana Chamber of Mines (EAIO)
CHAN....... Chandler Insurance Co. Ltd. [*NASDAQ symbol*]
chancel .... Chancelaria [*Chancery*] [*Portuguese*]
CHANCOM ... Channel Committee [*NATO*] (NATG)
CHANCOMTEE ... Channel Committee [*NATO*] (NATG)
CHANETA ... Tanzania Amateur Netball Association
CHANGE ... Coalition of Hawkesbury and Nepean Groups for the Environment [*Australia*]
CHANIC ... Chantier Naval et Industriel du Congo
CHANS ..... Chanson [*Song*] [*Music*]
CHANSEC ... Channel Committee Secretary [*NATO*] (NATG)
ChAO........ Chuvash Autonomous Oblast [*1920-1925*] (RU)
ChAO........ Quaternary Ammonium Compound (RU)
ChAP .... Automatic Frequency Control (RU)
Chap.......... Chapelle [*Chapel*] [*French*] (NAU)
chap............ Chapitre [*Chapter*] [*French*]
Ch App...... Chambre d'Appel [*French*] [*Legal term*] (DLA)
Ch AppCorr ... Chambre des Appels Correctionnels [*France*] (FLAF)
CHAR........ Campaign for the Homeless and Rootless (WGAO)
charak .... Charakteristisch [*Characteristic*] [*German*] (GCA)
charakterist ... Charakteristisch [*Characteristic*] [*German*] (GCA)

charn .... Charniere [*Hinge, Joint*] [*Publishing*] [*French*]
ChARS ...... Automatic Reader with a Shift Register (RU)
CHAS .... Catholic Housing Aid Society (WGAO)
CHAS .... Centrala Handlu Artykulami Sportowymi [*Sports Goods Trade Center*] (POL)
Chas .... Chapel [*Topography*] (RU)
CHAS .... Co-Operative Housing Advice Service [*Victoria, Australia*]
CHASA ..... Committee of Heads of Architecture Schools of Australasia [*Australia*]
CHASA ..... Community Health Association of Southern Africa (AA)
CHASA ..... Council of Hungarian Associations in South Australia
CHASP ...... Community Health Accreditation and Standards Project [*Australia*]
chasprom ... Watchmaking Industry (RU)
CHASS ...... Conference of Heads of Assisted Secondary Schools
CHAST ...... Centre for Human Aspects of Science and Technology [*University of Sydney*] [*Australia*]
CHASYCA ... Chambre Syndicale des Abattage et Confitionnement de Produits de Basse-Cour (WGAO)
Chat .... Chateau [*Castle*] [*French*] (NAU)
ChAT .... Chrzescijanska Akademia Teologiczma (WGAO)
CHATN ..... Community HIV [*Human Immunodeficiency Virus*]/AIDS Trials Network [*Australia*]
CHATO ..... Societe Chimique et Industrielle Africaine du Togo
Chau .... Chateau [*Castle, Country House*] [*Military map abbreviation World War I*] [*French*] (MTD)
CHAWA .... Council of Hungarian Associations in Western Australia
chayn .... Tea Factory [*Topography*] (RU)
ChAZ .... Chelyabinsk Abrasives Plant (RU)
CHB .... Central Housing Board
CHB .... Christlicher Holz- und Bauarbeiterverband der Schweiz [*Christian Building and Woodworkers of Switzerland*] (EY)
CHB .... Commonwealth Heraldry Board [*Papatoetoe, New Zealand*] (EAIO)
CHB .... Compagnie Honeywell Bull [*German*] (ADPT)
CHB .... Corps Perhubungan [*Signal Corps*] (IN)
ChBm .... Church of the Brethren Mission
Chbre .... Chambre [*Chamber*] [*French*]
ChBT .... Black and White Television (System) (RU)
ChBT .... Pulse Frequency Towed Thermograph [*Oceanography*] (RU)
ChBVP ...... Black Sea - Baltic Sea Waterway (RU)
CHC .... Centrala Handlowa [*or Handlu*] Ceramiki [*Ceramic Products Sales Center*] (POL)
CHC .... Child Health Centre [*Australia*]
CHC .... China Ocean Helicopter Corp. [*ICAO designator*] (FAAC)
CHC .... Christchurch [*New Zealand*] [*Airport symbol*] (OAG)
CHC .... Commonwealth Housing Commission [*Australia*]
CHC .... Societe Cameroon Hotels Corporation
CHCB .... Companhia Hidroelectrica de Cabora Bassa [*Mozambique*]
CHCF .... Catholic Handicapped Childrens Fellowship (WGAO)
chch .... Parts, Units (RU)
Ch Civ .... Chambre Civile [*Cour de Cassation*] [*France*] (FLAF)
CHCNSW ... Catholic Health Care Association of New South Wales [*Australia*]
Ch Comm ... Chambre Commerciale et Financiere [*Cour de Cassation*] [*France*] (FLAF)
Ch Cons ..... Chambre de Conseil [*France*] (FLAF)
ChCons ...... Ordonnance de la Chambre du Conseil [*French*] (BAS)
CHCRISP ... Courrier Hebdomadaire. Centre de Recherche et d'Information Socio-Politiques [*Benelux*] (BAS)
CHD .... Cagdas Hukukcular Dernegi [*Contemporary Jurists' Organization*] (TU)
CHD .... Computer Haus Darmstadt [*German*] (ADPT)
ChD .... Frequency Discriminator (RU)
ChD .... Point of Advance Guard (BU)
ChD .... Rate of Respiration (RU)
chda .... Analytically Pure (RU)
Ch d'aff ..... Charge d'Affaires [*French*] (MTD)
ch de f .... Chemin de Fer [*Railway*] [*French*] (GPO)
Ch d f .... Chemin de Fer [*Railway*] [*French*] (MTD)
CHE .... Campaign for Homosexual Equality (WGAO)
CHE .... Centrala Hidroelectrica [*Hydroelectric Power Plant*] (RO)
CHE .... Comite d'Hygiene et d'Eau (WGAO)
CHE .... Comite Hygiene et Eau [*French*] (ASF)
CHE .... Council for Higher Education [*US and Israel*]
ChE .... Number Equivalent (RU)
ChE .... Sensitive Element (RU)
CHE .... Switzerland [*ANSI three-letter standard code*] (CNC)
CHEA .... Centre des Hautes Etudes Administratives [*France*] (FLAF)
CHEA .... Commonwealth Hansard Editors Association (EAIO)
CHEAM .... Centre des Hautes Etudes Administratives sur l'Afrique et l'Asie Modernes [*Center for Advanced Administrative Studies on Modern Africa and Asia*] [*French*] (AF)
CHEAM .... Centre des Hautes Etudes sur l'Afrique et l'Asie Modernes (WGAO)

CHEAR .... Council on Higher Education in the American Republics (WGAO)
CHEC .... Central Hidroelectrica de Caldas [*Manizales*] (COL)
CHEC .... China Harbours Engineering Co. (TCC)
CHEC .... Commonwealth Human Ecology Council [*British*] (EAIO)
Chechengosizdat ... Chechen-Ingush State Publishing House (RU)
Chechoblizdat ... Chechen-Ingush Oblast Publishing House (RU)
CHECI .... China Highway Engineering Consultants, Inc. (TCC)
CHED .... Children and Education Unit [*Australian Broadcasting Corp.*]
Chee .... Chaussee [*Road*] [*Military map abbreviation World War I*] [*French*] (MTD)
CHEHA ..... Centre for Human Ecology and Health Advancement [*University of Newcastle*] [*Australia*]
CHEKA ..... Chrezvychainaya Komissiya po Borbe s Kontrrevolutisiei i Sabotazhem [*Extraordinary Commission for Combating Counterrevolution and Sabotage; Soviet secret police organization, 1917-1921*]
chekhosl ..... Czechoslovak (RU)
chel .... Man, Men (RU)
chel-ch .... Man-Hour (RU)
CHEM .... Chemical Hazards and Emergency Management [*Australia*]
Chem .... Chemie [*or Chemiker*] [*Chemistry or Chemist*] [*German*]
CHEM ...... Chemie [*Chemistry*] [*Afrikaans*]
chem .... Chemistry (TPFD)
CHEMAK ... Zjednoczenie Przemyslu Budowy Aparatury Chemicznej [*Association of Chemical Equipment Construction Industry*] (POL)
CHEMAPOL ... Podnik Zahranicniho Obchodu pro Dovoz a Vyvoz Chemickych Vyrobku a Surovin [*Foreign Trade Enterprise for the Import and Export of Chemical Products and Raw Materials*] (CZ)
CHEMASIA ... Asian International Chemical and Process Engineering and Contracting Show and Conference
CHEMFICO ... Chemical International Finance & Consulting [*Belgium*]
Chemifa ..... Chemie- und Pharmazie-GmbH [*Chemical and Pharmaceutical Co.*] (EG)
CHEMODROGA ... Narodni Podnik pro Prodej Drog a Kosmetickych Vyrobku [*National Enterprise for the Retail Sale of Drugs and Cosmetic Products*] (CZ)
CHEMOKOMPLEX ... CHEMOKOMPLEX Vegyipari Gep es Berendezes Export-Import Vallalat [*CHEMOKOMPLEX Export-Import Enterprise for Chemical Industry Machinery and Equipment*] (HU)
CHEMU .... Chemical Hazards and Emergency Management Unit [*Queensland*] [*Australia*]
ChEMZ ..... Cheboksary Electromechanical Plant (RU)
ChEMZ ..... Frequency Electromagnetic Sounding (RU)
Chen .... Chenal [*Channel*] [*French*] (NAU)
ChENIS ...... Black Sea Experimental Scientific Research Station (RU)
CHENOP .. Companhia Hidro-Electrica do Norte de Portugal (WGAO)
CHEP .... Commonwealth Handling Equipment Pool [*Australia*]
CHEQ .... Cheque [*British*] (ROG)
cherep .... Tile Factory [*Topography*] (RU)
Chern m ..... Black Sea (RU)
Chernomorneft' ... Association of the Black Sea Region Petroleum Industry (RU)
Cheroblnatsizdat ... Cherkess Oblast National Publishing House (RU)
CHERP ...... Central Health Education Register of Programs [*Australia*]
CHERP ...... Companhia Hidro-Eletrica do Rio Pardo [*Brazil*] (DSCA)
Cherpen ..... Cherita Pendek [*Short Story*] (ML)
chert .... Drawing, Diagram (RU)
chert .... Sketch, Drawing (BU)
cherv .... Chervonets [*Monetary unit; 1922-1947*] (RU)
CHESF .... Companhia Hidroeletrica do Sao Francisco [*Sao Francisco Hydroelectric Company*] [*Brazil*] (LA)
chesh .... Czech (BU)
CHESS ...... Children's Health, Education, and Safety Services [*Australia*]
CHESS ...... Clearing House Electronic Subregister System [*Australian Stock Exchange*]
CHEST ...... Combined Higher Education Software Teams (WGAO)
Chet .... Chalet [*Swiss Cottage*] [*Military map abbreviation World War I*] [*French*] (MTD)
chet. .... Even (RU)
Cheteka ...... Czechoslovak Telegraph Agency (BU)
Chev .... Chevalier [*Knight*] [*French*] (MTD)
CHEVAP .... Companhia Hidroeletrica do Vale do Paraiba [*Paraiba Valley Hydroelectric Company*] [*Brazil*] (LA)
ChF .... Black Sea Fleet (RU)
ch f .... Change Fixe [*Fixed Exchange*] [*French*]
CHF .... Congregation of the Sisters of the Holy Faith [*Australia*]
CHF .... Consumers' Health Forum [*Australia*]
chf .... Pair (BU)
ChFAP ...... Automatic Frequency - Phase Control (RU)
chg .... Chagrin [*Shagreen*] [*Publishing*] [*French*]
Chg .... Chiang [*River, Shoal, Harbor, Inlet, Channel, Sound*] [*Chinese*] (NAU)
CHG .... Compagnie de la Haute Gambie

CHG.......... Helicopter Ship, Missile-Armed [*NATO*]
ChGK........ Extraordinary State Commission for the Determination and Investigation of Crimes Committed by the German Fascist Aggressors (RU)
ChGMP..... Black Sea State Steamship Line (RU)
ChGPI....... Cherkassy State Pedagogical Institute (RU)
chgr .... Chagrin [*Shagreen*] [*Publishing*] [*French*]
ChGS........ Black Sea Hydrophysical Station (RU)
ChGU........ Chernovtsy State University (RU)
CHH .... Airlines of Hainan Province [*China*] [*ICAO designator*] (FAAC)
CHH .... Chaplain of His Holiness
Ch-H .... Chemiehandel [*Trade in Chemicals*] (EG)
CHH .... Commission d'Histoire de l'Historiographie [*Commission of the History of Historiography*] [*Ceret, France*] (EAIO)
CHHS........ Coffs Harbour Historical Society [*Australia*]
CHHVC.... Cairns and District Historic Vehicle Club [*Australia*]
CHIA .... Craft and Hobby Industry Association (WGAO)
Chiarmo ..... Chiarissimo [*Form of address used when writing to distinguished persons*] [*Italian*]
ChIASSR... Chechen-Ingush Autonomous Soviet Socialist Republic (RU)
CHIBCHA ... Colombia Human Rights Information Committee (EA)
Chic........... Chihuahua [*Mexico*] (BARN)
CHIDRAL ... Central Hidroelectrica del Rio Anchicaya, Limitada [*Colombia*] (WGAO)
CHIDS...... Cholistan Institute of Desert Studies [*Pakistan*] (IRC)
CHIEF...... Customs Handling of Import and Export Freight [*EC*] (ECED)
chif........... Chiffre [*Numbered*] [*Publishing*] [*French*]
ChIK .... Number-Pulse Code (RU)
CHILECTRA ... Compania Chilena de Electricidad Ltda. [*Chilean Electric Company Ltd.*] [*Santiago*] (LAA)
chim .... Chimica [*Chemistry*] [*Italian*]
ChIM .... Pulse Frequency Modulation (RU)
CHIMAF... Societe Gabonaise de Produits Chimiques et Industriels
ChIMESKh ... Chelyabinsk Institute of Rural Mechanization and Electrification (RU)
CHIMI-KHMER ... Societe Khmere d'Industrie Chimique [*Cambodian Chemical Industries Company*] (CL)
Chin .... Chemin [*Way, Road*] [*Military map abbreviation World War I*] [*French*] (MTD)
chin .... Chinesisch [*Chinese*] [*German*] (GCA)
CHINAPACK ... China National Packaging Import & Export Corp. (IMH)
CHINATEX ... China National Textiles Import & Export Corp. [*China*] (IMH)
CHINATUHSU ... China National Native Produce & Animal Byproducts Import & Export Corp. [*China*] (IMH)
chines .... Chinesisch [*Chinese*] [*German*] (GCA)
CHIP .... Allied Command Channel Intelligence Plan [*NATO*] (NATG)
CHIP .... Community Housing and Infrastructure Program [*Australia*]
CHIPF....... Children of High Intellectual Potential Foundation [*Australia*]
CHIPRODAL ... Compania Chilena de Productos Alimenticios [*Chilean Food Products Company*] (LA)
CHIPS....... Christian International Peace Service (WGAO)
Chir .... Chirurg [*Surgeon*] [*German*]
CHIRANA ... Narodni Podnik pro Vyrobu Lekarskych Stroju a Nastroju [*National Enterprise for the Production of Medical Appliances and Surgical Instruments*] (CZ)
Chirchiksel'mash ... Chirchik Agricultural Machinery Plant (RU)
CHIS......... Central Health Interpreter Service [*Victoria, Australia*]
CHIS......... Chinese Intelligence Service Operative
Chis........... Chisholm Institute of Technology [*Australia*]
ChIS.......... Pulse Frequency System (RU)
ChisholmIT ... Chisholm Institute of Technology [*Australia*]
chisl........... Numeral (BU)
chislkolich ... Cardinal Number (RU)
chisl por ..... Ordinal Number (RU)
chisl sobir... Collective Numeral (RU)
CHISS .... Centre Haiten d'Investigation en Sciences Sociales (WGAO)
ChISS .... Frequency Selection Seismic Station (RU)
CHIT .... Child Head Injury Trust (WGAO)
CHIT .... Chitarrone [*Large Guitar*] [*Music*]
CHITEAA ... Clearing House of the Interpreters/Translators Educator Association of Australia
Chitkoop .... Library Cooperative (BU)
Chitkori...... Chitalishtni Korespondenti [*Library Correspondents*] [*A periodical*] (BU)
CHIVE....... Council for Hearing-Impaired Visits and Exchanges (WGAO)
ChIZ.......... Chelyabinsk Measuring Instruments Plant (RU)
CHJV......... Coronation Hill Joint Venture [*Australia*]
ChK.......... Chrezvychainaya Komissiya po Borbe s Kontrrevolutisiei i Sabotazem [*Extraordinary Commission for Combating Counter-Revolution and Sabotage*] [*Soviet secret police organization, 1918-1922*] (RU)
ChKKh....... Frequency-Contrast Characteristic (RU)
ChKLB...... Extraordinary Commission for the Liquidation of Illiteracy (RU)
ChKP .... Czechoslovak Communist Party (BU)

ChKZ........ Chelyabinsk Kirov Plant (RU)
ChKZ........ Member of the College of Attorneys (RU)
chl .... Article [*Legal document*] (BU)
CHL.......... Chalqueno [*Race of maize*] [*Mexico*]
ch-l........... Chef-Lieu [*Country Town*] [*French*]
CHL.......... Chile [*ANSI three-letter standard code*] (CNC)
chl .... Member [*of a society*] (BU)
ch-l............. Something, Anything, Whatever (RU)
chl chl........ Articles [*Legal document*] (BU)
chl chl........ Members [*of a society*] (BU)
Chlf........... Chloroform [*German*] (GCA)
CHLJ........ Chaplain of the Order of St Lazarus of Jerusalem [*Australia*]
chl kollzashch ... Member of the College of Attorneys (RU)
chl-kor....... Corresponding Member (RU)
Chlle.......... Chapelle [*Chapel*] [*Military map abbreviation World War I*] [*French*] (MTD)
Chlorier...... Chlorierung [*Chlorination*] [*German*] (GCA)
ChLTs....... Iron Foundry Shop (RU)
ChLZ .... Cast Iron Foundry (BU)
chl zor........ Corresponding Member (BU)
CHM........ Aero Chombo SA [*Mexico*] [*ICAO designator*] (FAAC)
ChM.......... Arret de la Chambre des Mises en Accusation [*French*] (BAS)
CHM.......... Cape Horn Methanol [*Chile*]
CHM.......... Centre d'Hebergement des Misereux [*Indigent Shelter Center*] [*Cambodia*] (CL)
Chm........... Chemie [*Chemistry*] [*German*]
CHM.......... Chimbote [*Peru*] [*Airport symbol*] [*Obsolete*] (OAG)
ChM.......... Clockwork (RU)
ChM.......... Extremely Soft (RU)
ChM.......... Ferrous Metallurgy (RU)
ChM.......... Frequency-Modulated, Frequency Modulation (RU)
ChM.......... Frequency Modulation (BU)
ChM.......... Sensitive Manometer (RU)
chm........... Triannual Publication (BU)
CHMA....... Colegia Hispanomusulman "Averroes" [*Averroes Spanish Muslim College*]
CHMB....... Centrala Handlowa Materialow Budowlanych [*Building Materials Sales Center*] (POL)
ChM/ChM ... Frequency-Modulated Carrier/Frequency-Modulated Subcarrier Type System [*FM/FM*] (RU)
ch met........ Ferrous Metallurgy Plant [*Topography*] (RU)
ChMG....... Frequency Modulation Generator (RU)
ChMises .... Arret de la Chambre des Mises en Accusation [*French*] (BAS)
Ch MisesAcc ... Chambre des Mises en Accusation [*Arret de la Cour d'Appel*] [*France*] (FLAF)
CHMN ...... Centrala Handlowa Metali Niezelaznych [*Non-Ferrous Metals Sales Center*] (POL)
ChMN........ Cranial Nerve (RU)
ChMS .... High-Speed Combing Machine (RU)
ChMT .... Black Sea Trawler (RU)
ChMTU ... Technical Specifications for Ferrous Metallurgy (RU)
ChMZ........ Chelyabinsk Metallurgical Plant (RU)
ChMZ........ Cherepovets Metallurgical Plant (RU)
ChMZAP... Chelyabinsk Machinery Plant for Motor Vehicle and Tractor Trailers (RU)
ChN .... Chemicky Nacelnik [*Chief of Chemical Service*] (CZ)
CHN .... China [*ANSI three-letter standard code*] (CNC)
ChN .... Chirurgicka Nemocnice [*Surgical Hospital*] (CZ)
Chne.......... Chaine [*Military map abbreviation*] [*World War I*] [*French*] (MTD)
Chnee .... Cheminee [*Chimney*] [*Military map abbreviation World War I*] [*French*] (MTD)
ChNII .... Cherkess Scientific Research Institute of Language, Literature, and History (RU)
ChNIIGD .. Chelyabinsk Scientific Research Institute of Mining (RU)
ChNN .... Peak-Load Hour [*Telephony*] (RU)
ChNP........ Low-Pressure Component (RU)
ChO .... Advance Detachment (BU)
CHO .... Centrala Handlu Opalem [*Fuel Sales Center*] (POL)
CHO .... Christelike Hoeer Onderwys [*Christian Higher Education*] [*Afrikaans*]
CHO .... Ciga Hotels Aviation SpA [*Italy*] [*ICAO designator*] (FAAC)
ChOA........ Chkalov Oblast Archives (RU)
CHOBISCO ... Chambre Syndicale des Grossiers en Confiserie Chcolaterie, Biscuits et Autres Derives du Sucre [*Belgium*] (WGAO)
CHOCOCAM ... Chocolaterie et Confiserie Camerounaise
CHOCOCAMC ... Chocolaterie-Confiserie Camerounaise (WGAO)
CHOCODI ... Chocolaterie et Confiserie de Cote-D'Ivoire
ChOd .... Chilean Odeon [*Record label*]
CHOGM ... Commonwealth Heads of Government Meeting (ADA)
CHOGRM ... Commonwealth Heads of Government Regional Meeting [*Australia*] (ADA)
CHOiW ..... Centrala Handlu Owocami i Warzywami [*Fruit and Vegetable Sales Center*] (POL)
CHOKE..... Concern for the Health of Our Kids and the Environment [*Adelaide*] [*Australia*]

ChOKPROD ... Extraordinary Oblast Food and Supply Committee (RU)
ChOMGI ... Black Sea Branch of the Marine Hydro-Physical Institute (RU)
CHOMI ..... Clearinghouse on Migration Issues [*Australia*]
ChON .... Chasti Osobogo Naznacheniia [*Elements of Special Designation*] [*Political police units attached to the armed forces (1918-1924)*] [*Former USSR*]
chor .... Chorazy [*Ensign*] [*Poland*]
Chovnitovt ... Black Sea Branch of the All-Union Scientific, Engineering, and Technical Society of Water Transportation (RU)
CHP .... Aviacion de Chiapas [*Mexico*] [*ICAO designator*] (FAAC)
ChP .... Black Sea Steamship Line (RU)
CHP .... Centrala Handlowa Przemyslu [*Industry Sales Center*] (POL)
CHP .... Chapalote [*Race of maize*] [*Mexico*]
CHP .... Community History Program [*School of History, University of New South Wales*] [*Australia*]
CHP .... Cumhuriyet Halk Partisi [*Republican Peoples' Party - RPP*] (TU)
ChP .... Drawing Instrument (RU)
ChP .... Extraordinary Event (RU)
ChP .... Magnifying Projector for Watch Parts (RU)
ChP .... Pulse Rate (RU)
CHPA .... Combined Heat and Power Association (WGAO)
CHPC .... Centrala Handlowa Przemyslu Ceramicznego [*Ceramic Industry Sales Center*] (POL)
CHPCh ...... Centrala Handlowa Przemyslu Chemicznego [*Chemical Industry Sales Center*] (POL)
CHPD .... Comite d'Hygiene et de Securite [*De l'Entreprise*] (FLAF)
CHPE .... Centrala Handlowa Przemyslu Elektrotechnicznego [*Electric Engineering Industry Sales Center*] (POL)
CHPH .... Centrala Handlowa Przemyslu Hutniczego [*Metallurgical Industry Sales Center*] (POL)
ChPI .... Chelyabinsk Polytechnic Institute (RU)
ChPI .... Repetition Rate (RU)
ChPK .... Black Sea Coast of the Caucasus (RU)
CHPM .... Centrala Handlowa Przemyslu Metalowego [*Metal Industry Sales Center*] (POL)
CHPM .... Centrala Handlowa Przemyslu Muzycznego [*Commercial Center for Music Industry*] [*Poland*]
CHPO .... Centrala Handlowa Przemyslu Odziezowego [*Clothing Industry Sales Center*] (POL)
CHPP .... Centrala Handlowa Przemyslu Papierniczego [*Paper Industry Sales Center*] (POL)
CHPS .... Centrala Handlowa Przemyslu Skorzanego [*Leather Industry Sales Center*] (POL)
ChPV .... Preignition Number (RU)
ChPZ .... Advance Party (BU)
CHQ .... Chania [*Greece*] [*Airport symbol*] (OAG)
Chq .... Cheque [*Check*] [*French*]
CHR .... Air Charter Services [*Zaire*] [*ICAO designator*] (FAAC)
CHR .... Calculateur Hybride a Reseau [*French*] (ADPT)
CHR .... Centralforeningen af Hotelvaerter og Restauratorer i Danmark (EAIO)
Chr .... Christschall [*Record label*] [*Austria*]
Chr .... Christus [*Christ*] [*German*]
Chr .... Chronik [*Chronicle*] [*German*]
CHR .... Chronique [*Chronicle*] [*French*]
CHR .... Commission Internationale de l'Hydrologie du Bassin du Rhin (WGAO)
CHR .... Commission on Human Rights [*Geneva, Switzerland*] (EAIO)
CHR .... Compagnie hors Rang [*Headquarters Company*] [*French*]
CHR .... Conference Haitienne des Religieux (WGAO)
CHR .... Correspondentieblad van Hogere Rijksambtenaren [*Benelux*] (BAS)
ChR .... Czechoslovak Republic (BU)
chr .... Partly Soluble (RU)
CHRAC ..... Construction and Housing Research Advisory Council (WGAO)
ChrComm ... Chronique de la Communaute, La Documentation Francaise [*France*] (FLAF)
Ch Repres .. Chambre des Representants [*France*] (FLAF)
Ch Reun ..... Arret de la Cour de Cassation Toutes Chambres Reunies [*Decision of the Full Court of the Court of Appeal*] [*French*] (ILCA)
Ch Reun ..... Arret des Chambres Reunies de la Cour de Cassation [*France*] (FLAF)
Ch ReunR ... Arret des Chambres Reunies de la Cour de Cassation qui Rejette [*France*] (FLAF)
Ch RevInt ... China Review International
Chrezpolpred ... Plenipotentiary Extraordinary (RU)
chrezv .... Extraordinary, Special (RU)
ChRF .... Partial Recursive Function (RU)
CHRIS .... Cheque Reconciliation and Information System [*Australia*]
Chr Is .... Christian Israelite
CHRIS .... Customised Human Resource Information System [*Australia*]
ChristWerkg ... Christelijke Werkgever [*Benelux*] (BAS)
ChRL .... Chinska Republika Ludowa [*Chinese People's Republic*] (POL)

chromo .... Chromolithographie [*Color Lithograph*] [*Publishing*] [*French*]
chromol ...... Chromolithographie [*Color Lithograph*] [*Publishing*] [*French*]
chromolith ... Chromolithographiert [*Chromolithographed*] [*Publishing*] [*German*]
chron .... Chronisch [*Chronic*] [*German*] (GCA)
CHRONOR ... Narodni Podnik pro Tuzemskou Distribuci Hodin a Zlatnickeho Zbozi [*National Enterprise for Domestic Distribution of Watches and Jewelry Products*] (CZ)
Chron PolEtrang ... Chronique de Politique Etrangere [*French*] (BAS)
ChronTransp ... Chronique des Transports [*France*] (FLAF)
ChrP .... National Palace Museum, Wai-shuang-hsi, Shih-lin, Taipei, Taiwan, China [*Library symbol*] [*Library of Congress*] (LCLS)
Chr PolEt ... Chronique de Politique Etrangere [*French*] (BAS)
Chr PolEtr ... Chronique de Politique Etrangere [*Belgium*] (FLAF)
ChRTS .... Private Manual Exchange (RU)
chrv .... Net Register Tonnage (RU)
CHS .... Canberra Horticultural Society [*Australia*]
ChS .... Carrier Telegraphy (RU)
CHS .... Centralni Hospodarske Skladiste [*Central Warehouse*] (CZ)
CHS .... Challenge Aviation Pty Ltd. [*Australia*] [*ICAO designator*] (FAAC)
ChS .... Chemicky Spolek, Narodni Podnik [*Chemical Society, National Enterprise*] (CZ)
CHS .... Clydesdale Horse Society (WGAO)
CHS .... Comite d'Hygiene et de Securite [*De l'Entreprise*] (FLAF)
CHS .... Congress Health Service [*Australia*]
ch s .... Private Collection (RU)
CHSA .... Chest Heart and Stroke Association (WGAO)
ChSA .... Human Serum Albumin (RU)
ChSAN ..... Czechoslovak Academy of Sciences (RU)
CHSANSW ... Cooperative Housing Societies Association of New South Wales [*Australia*]
ChSD .... Medium-Pressure Component (RU)
chshch .... Calyx (RU)
chshl .... Sepal (RU)
ch-shte .... Library (BU)
CHSKH ..... Chung Hua Sheng Kung Hui [*Holy Catholic Church in China*] [*Church of England*]
ChSM .... Czechoslovak Youth League (RU)
ch sp .... Pure Alcohol (RU)
ChSR .... Czechoslovak Republic (RU)
CHSS .... Centrala Handlowa Sprzetu Sportowego [*Sport Equipment Sales Center*] (POL)
ChSS .... Chrzescijanskie Stowarzyszenie Spoleczne (WGAO)
CHSSA ...... Church History Society of Southern Africa (AA)
ChSSR ...... Czechoslovak Socialist Republic (BU)
CHSSS ...... Centrala Handlowa Sprzetu Sportowego i Szkutniczego [*Sport and Boating Equipment Sales Center*] (POL)
ChT .... Carrier Telegraphy (RU)
CHT .... Centrala Handlowo-Techniczna [*Technical Trade Center*] (POL)
cht .... Chetvert [*Measures*] (RU)
CHT .... Chittagong Hill Tracts [*Bangladesh*]
ChT .... Christelijk Historisch Tijdschrift [*Benelux*] (BAS)
ChT .... Extremely Hard (RU)
Cht .... Read, Reading [*Computers*] (RU)
cht .... Thursday (RU)
CHTA .... Contract Heat Treatment Association (WGAO)
ChTA .... Czechoslovak News Agency (RU)
CHTI .... Caribbean Hotel Training Institute (WGAO)
ChTPD ...... Chlopskie Towarzystwo Przyjaciol Dzieci [*Peasants' Society of Children's Friends*] (POL)
ChTPZ .... Chelyabinsk Pipe-Rolling Plant (RU)
ChTR .... Chervena Tribuna [*Red Tribune*] [*A periodical*] (BU)
ChTs .... Number of Centers [*of Recrystallization*] (RU)
ChTS .... Technical Supply Unit (RU)
ChTT .... Number of Theoretical Plates (RU)
chtv .... Thursday (RU)
ChTZ .... Chelyabinsk Tractor Plant (RU)
ChTZ .... Specific Technical Task (RU)
CHU .... Centre Hospitalier Universitaire [*University Hospital Center*] [*French*] (WER)
ChU .... Chemicky Ustav [*Chemical Institute*] (CZ)
CHU .... Christelijk-Historische Unie [*Christian-Historical Union*] [*Netherlands*] [*Political party*] (PPW)
ChU .... Reader, Reading Device [*Computers*] (RU)
chug .... Iron Foundry [*Topography*] (RU)
chuk .... Chukchi, Chuckchee (RU)
Chuppie ..... Chinese Urban Professional [*Hong Kong Yuppie*] [*Lifestyle classification*]
CHURITSUROREN ... Churitsu Rodo Kumiai Renraku Kaigil [*Federation of Independent Unions of Japan*] (FEA)
Churokyoto ... Churo Kyotokaigi [*Joint Council of Garrison Forces Labor Unions*] [*Japan*]

ChUSTO ... Extraordinary Plenipotentiary of the Council of Labor and Defense (RU)
chuv .... Chuvash (RU)
ChuvAO ..... Chuvash Autonomous Oblast [*1920-1925*] (RU)
Chuvashgiz ... Chuvash State Publishing House (RU)
Chuvashgosizdat ... Chuvash State Publishing House (RU)
ChuvASSR ... Chuvash Autonomous Soviet Socialist Republic (RU)
CH-V .... Cheval-Vapeur [*Horsepower*] [*French*]
ChV .... Chilean Victor [*Record label*]
ch vap .... Cheval-Vapeur [*Horse-Power*] [*French*]
chv-ch .... Man-Hour (RU)
ChVD .... High-Pressure Component (RU)
chv-d .... Man-Day (RU)
ChVO .... Military Guard Unit (RU)
ChVS .... Member of the Military Council (RU)
ChVSK .... Extraordinary Military Medical Commission (RU)
CHW .... Citizens Highway Watch [*Australia*]
CHW .... Jiuquan [*China*] [*Airport symbol*] (OAG)
CHX .... Air Charter Express [*France*] [*ICAO designator*] (FAAC)
CHX .... Changuinola [*Panama*] [*Airport symbol*] (OAG)
chx .... Chevaux [*Horsepower*] [*French*] (MTD)
CHY .... China Air Cargo [*ICAO designator*] (FAAC)
CHY .... Choiseul Bay [*Solomon Islands*] [*Airport symbol*] (OAG)
CHy .... Commission for Hydrology [*WMO*] (MSC)
CHZ .... Centrala Handlu Zagranicznego [*Commercial Center for Foreign Trade*] [*Poland*]
CHZ .... Centralni Higijenski Zavod [*Central Institute of Hygiene*] (YU)
ChZ .... Chemicka Zaloha [*Chemical Reserve*] (CZ)
ChZ .... Chemicke Zavody [*Chemical Works*] (CZ)
Chz .... Cihaz [*Device, Instrument*] (TU)
ChZ .... Light Dimming, Dimout [*In blackout*] (RU)
chz .... Reading Room (RU)
CHZFuzine ... Crpna Hidroelektrana Fuzine [*Fuzine Pumped Storage Hydroelectric Station*] (YU)
CHZiS .... Centrala Handlowa Zelasa i Stali [*Iron and Steel Sales Center*] (POL)
ChZJD .... Chemicke Zavody Juraja Dimitrova [*Juraj Dimitrov Chemical Works*] (CZ)
ChZPW ..... Chorzowskie Zaklady Przemyslu Weglowego [*Chorzow Coal Enterprises*] (POL)
ChZS .... Chemicke Zavody na Slovensku, Narodny Podnik [*Chemical Plants in Slovakia, National Enterprise*] (CZ)
ChZWP ..... Chemicke Zavody Wilhelma Piecka [*Wilhelm Pieck Chemical Works*] (CZ)
CI .... Caritas Internationalis [*International Confederation of Catholic Organizations for Charitable and Social Action*] [*Vatican City, Vatican City State*] (EAIO)
CI .... Carte d'Identite [*Identification Card*] (CL)
CI .... Carte d'Importation [*Import License*] [*Cambodia*] (CL)
CI .... Cassa Integrazione [*Italy*]
CI .... Centre d'Instruction [*Instruction Center*] [*Cambodia*] (CL)
CI .... Centro de Informacion [*Instituto Mexicano de Investigaciones Siderurgicas*] [*Mexico*]
CI .... Certificat d'Investissement [*Stock exchange*] [*French*]
CI .... Channel Islands (EY)
CI .... Circonscription Indigene
CI .... Circuit Imprime (ADPT)
CI .... Circuit Integre [*French*] (ADPT)
CI .... C. Itoh & Co. Ltd. [*Hong Kong*]
CI .... Comite Interimaire [*Provisional Committee*] [*Chad*] (AF)
CI .... Commonwealth Institute [*Australia*] (ADA)
CI .... Community Interpreter [*Australia*]
CI .... Comunita Internazionale [*Italy*] (FLAF)
CI .... Conselho de Imprensa [*Press Council*] [*Portuguese*] (WER)
CI .... Consiliul Intercooperatist [*Intercooperative Council*] (RO)
CI .... Consumer Interpol (EA)
CI .... Corps Intendans [*Quartermaster Corps*] (IN)
CI .... Counterintelligence
CI .... Credit d'Impot [*French*] (BAS)
CI .... Credito Italiano [*Bank*] [*Italian*]
CI .... Crux Iberica [*Iberian Cross*] [*Spanish*] (WER)
CI .... Institum Iosephitarum Gerardmontensium (WGAO)
CI .... Ivory Coast [*ANSI two-letter standard code*] (CNC)
CIA .... Canberra Institute of the Arts [*Australia*]
CIA .... Cancer Information Association (WGAO)
CIA .... Carpet Institute of Australia
CIA .... Catering Institute of Australia (ADA)
CIA .... Cement Industry Authority [*Philippines*] (DS)
CIA .... Centrala a Industriei Alimentare [*Food Industry Central*] (RO)
CIA .... Central Intelligence Agency (PWGL)
CIA .... Centre d'Insemination Artificielle (WGAO)
CIA .... Centre for Image Analysis [*Charles Sturt University*] [*Australia*]
CIA .... Centre International d'Aviation Agricole (WGAO)
CIA .... Centro de Inseminacion Artificial [*Puerto Rico*] (DSCA)
CIA .... Centro de Investigaciones Agrarias [*Agricultural Research Center*] [*Venezuela*] (LA)

CIA .... Centro de Investigaciones Agrarias [*Agricultural Research Center*] [*Mexico*] (LA)
CIA .... Centro de Investigaciones Agricolas [*Agricultural Research Center*] [*Uruguay*] (LAA)
CIA .... Centro de Investigaciones Agronomicas [*Venezuela*] (WGAO)
CIA .... Centro de Investigaciones Aplicadas. Universidad del Cauca [*Popayan*] (COL)
CIA .... Chemical Industries Association (WGAO)
CIA .... Christmas Island Arbitrator
CIA .... Collegium Internationale Allergologicum [*Berne, Switzerland*] (EA)
CIA .... Colored, Indian, and African [*South Africa*]
CIA .... Colostomy and Ileostomy Association [*Medicine*]
CIA .... Comision Internacional del Alamo [*FAO*] (WGAO)
CIA .... Comision Internacional del Alamo [*Italy*] (DSCA)
CIA .... Comision Internacional del Arroz (DSCA)
CIA .... Comision Internatinal del Arroz [*Thailand*] (WGAO)
CIA .... Comitato Italiano Atlantico [*Italian Atlantic Committee*] (EAIO)
CIA .... Comite International d'Auschwitz
CIA .... Comite Intersyndical d'Automatisation [*French*] (ADPT)
CIA .... Commission Internationale d'Aerostation [*International Ballooning Commission*] (PDAA)
CIA .... Commonwealth Industries Association (WGAO)
CIA .... Community Information Association [*Australia*]
Cia .... Compagnia [*Company*] [*Italian*]
CIA .... Compagnia Industriale Aerospaziale [*Italy*] (PDAA)
CIA .... Compagnie Immobiliere Algerienne [*Algerian Real Estate Company*] (AF)
Cia .... Companhia [*Company*] [*Portuguese*]
CIA .... Compania [*Company*] [*Spanish*]
CIA .... Composites Institute of Australia
CIA .... Concrete Institute of Australia (ADA)
CIA .... Confederacion Intercooperativa Agropecuaria [*Argentina*] (DSCA)
CIA .... Confederation Internationale des Accordeonistes (WGAO)
CIA .... Confederation Nationale Belge du Commerce Independant de l'Alimentation (WGAO)
CIA .... Conseil International des Archives
CIA .... Construccion e Inversiones Astoria [*Colombia*] (COL)
CIA .... Construccion, Ingenieria, Arquitectura [*Colombia*] (COL)
CIA .... Corresponsal Internacional Agricola [*Germany*] (DSCA)
CIA .... Curtain Industry Association of Victoria [*Australia*]
CIA .... Rome [*Italy*] Ciampino Airport [*Airport symbol*] [*Obsolete*] (OAG)
CIAA .... Centre International d'Aviation Agricole (FLAF)
CIAA .... Christmas Island Administration and Assembly [*Australia*]
CIAA .... Colegio de Ingenieros, Arquitectos, y Agrimensores de Puerto Rico [*Puerto Rico*] (DSCA)
CIAA .... Comite International d'Assistance Aeroportuaire (WGAO)
CIAA .... Comptoir Industriel et Agricole Abidjan
CIAA .... Confederation des Industries Agro-Alimentaires de la CEE [*Confederation of the Food and Drink Industries of the ECC*] (EAIO)
CIAAB .... Centro de Investigaciones Agricolas Alberto Boerger [*Alberto Boerger Agricultural Research Center*] [*Uruguay*] (ARC)
CIAA del'UNICE ... Confederation des Industries Agro-Alimentaires de l'Union des Industries de la Communaute Europeenne [*Commission of the Agricultural and Food Industries of the Union of Industries of the European Community*] (EAIO)
CIAAU ...... Comptoir Ivoirien d'Accessoires Automobiles
CIAAUNICE ... Commission des Industries Agricoles et Alimentaires de l'Union des Industries dela CEE (WGAO)
CIAB .... Centro de Investigaciones Agricolas de El Bajio [*Mexico*] (DSCA)
CIAB .... Conseil International des Agences Benevoles [*International Council of Voluntary Agencies - ICVA*] (EA)
CIABA .... Compagnie Immobiliere de l'Avenue Barthe
CIABB .... Centro de Ingenieros Agronomos de Bahia Blanca [*Argentina*] (DSCA)
CIABC .... Centre d'Instruction de l'Arme Blinde Cavaleries [*Armoured Cavalry Training Center*] [*French Army*] (PDAA)
CIABRA .... Centro Integrado de Abastecimento de Brasilia [*Brasilia Integrated Supply Center*] [*Brazil*] (LA)
CIAC .... Centrala Industriei Articolelor Casnice [*Central for the Household Articles Industry*] (RO)
CIAC .... Centrale Ivoirienne d'Achats et de Credit (WGAO)
CIAC .... Centre d'Inter-Action Culturelle [*Center for Inter-Cultural Action*] (EAIO)
CIAC .... Centre International d'Action Culture [*Belgium*] (WGAO)
CIAC .... Ceramics Industry Advisory Committee (WGAO)
CIAC .... Changchun Institute of Applied Chemistry [*China*]
CIAC .... Comision Interamericana de Arbitraje Comercial [*Inter-American Commercial Arbitration Commission*] (LA)
CIAC .... Commonwealth Immigration Advisory Council [*Australia*]
CIAC .... Compagnie des Industries Africaines du Caoutchouc
CIAC .... Compagnie Industrielle et Agricole au Cameroun

CIAC......... Corporacion de la Industria Aeronautica Colombiana [Colombia]   (COL)

CIACA....... Commission Internationale d'Aeronefs de Construction Amateur [FAI]   (WGAO)

CIACA....... International Committee for Amateur-Built Aircraft   (EA)

CIACAE..... Commonwealth Institutions Accreditation Committee for Advanced Education

CIACAM..... Compagnie Industrielle d'Automobiles au Cameroun

CIACOL.... Compana de Ingenieros Agronomos de Colombia   (WGAO)

CIACOL.... Compania de Ingenieros Agronomos de Colombia [Colombia]   (DSCA)

CIACOP.... Centro Interamericano de Adiestramiento en Communicaciones para Poblacio [Costa Rica]   (WGAO)

CIACUT.... Centrala Industriei Articolelor Casnice si Utilajelor Tehnologice [Central for the Household Articles and Technical Equipment Industry]   (RO)

CIAD......... Coalition Internationale pour l'Action au Developpement [International Coalition for Development Action - ICDA] (EAIO)

CIADE....... Centro de Investigaciones en Administracion de Empresas [Chile]   (LAA)

CIADEC.... Centro Nacional de Entrenamiento e Investigacion Aplicada para el Desarrollo de la Comunidad [Center for Training and Applied Research in Community Development] [Venezuela] (LAA)

CIADFOR ... Centre Interafrican pour le Developpement de la Formation Professionnelle [Inter-African Center for the Development of Professional Training] [Abidjan, Ivory Coast]   (EAIO)

CIADFOR ... Centro Interafricano para el Desarrollo de la Formacion Profesional [Inter-African Center for the Development of Professional Training] [Spanish]

CIADSR .... Comite International sur l'Alcool, les Drogues et la Securite Routiere [International Committee on Alcohol, Drugs, and Traffic Safety]   (EAIO)

CIAE......... Capricornia Institute of Advanced Education [Australia]   (ADA)

CIAE......... Central Institute of Agricultural Engineering [India] [Research center]   (IRC)

CIAE......... Compania Italo-Argentina de Electricidad [Italo-Argentine Electric Power Company] [Buenos Aires]   (LA)

CI-AEA...... Certificat d'Importation sur l'Aide Economique Americaine [Import Certificate on American Economic Aid] [Cambodia]   (CL)

CIAECOSOC ... Consejo Interamericano Economico y Social   (WGAO)

CIAEF .... Comision Intersectorial de Asuntos Economicos y Financieros [Intersectorial Committee on Economic and Financial Affairs] [Peru]   (LA)

CIAEM...... Comite Interamericano Educacion Matematica   (WGAO)

CIAF......... Centro Interamericano de Fotointerpretacion [Colombia] (COL)

CIAF......... Centro Internazionale di Analisi Finanziaria [Italian]   (SLS)

CIAF......... Congres International d'Etudes Africaines   (WGAO)

CIAFMA ... Centre International de l'Actualite Fantastique et Magique (WGAO)

CIAG .... Commission Internationale d'Aviation Generale [FAI]   (WGAO)

CIAG .... Construction Industry Advisory Council   (WGAO)

CIAGA...... Confederacion Interamericana de Ganaderos [Inter-American Cattlemen's Confederation]   (LAA)

CIAGE....... Centro Internacional de Agencias, Lda.

CIAGO ...... Chemische Industrie AKU [Algemene Kunstzidie Unie]-Goodrich [Belgium]

CIAGP....... Commission Internationale des Aumoniers Generaux des Prisons [International Commission of Catholic Prison Chaplains - ICPC]   (EA)

Ciagro .... Centro Integrado de Informacoes Agrometeorologicas [Brazil] (WGAO)

CIAH......... Centro de Investigaciones de la Huasteca [Mexico]   (DSCA)

CIAI........... Conference Internationale des Associations d'Ingenieurs [International Federatiio of Engineering Associations] (PDAA)

CIAJ .... Communications Industries Association of Japan [Telecommunications]

CIAL......... Comercial e Industrial Agricola Ltd [Brazil]   (DSCA)

Cial............ Commercial [French]

CIAL......... Credit Industriel d'Alsace et de Lorraine [France]   (EY)

CIALA ...... Inter-Faculty Centre for African Anthropology and Linguistics

CIAM .... Caisse Industrielle d'Assurance Mutuelle [France]   (EY)

CIAM .... Centro de Ingenieros Agronomos de Mendoza [Argentina] (LAA)

CIAM .... Centro Internazionale di Animazione Missionario   (WGAO)

CIAM .... Colegio de Ingenieros Agronomos de Mexico [Mexico]   (DSCA)

CIAM .... Commission International d'Aeromodelisme [International Aeromodelling Commission]   (PDAA)

CIAM .... Congres Internationaux d'Architecture Moderne [Defunct]

CIAMAN .. Confederacion Internacional de Asociaciones de Medicinas Alternativas Naturales [Spanish]

CIAMAN .. Confederatiuon Internationale des Associations des Medecines Alternatives Naturelles   (WGAO)

CIAME...... Commission Interministerielle pour les Appareils de Mesures Electriques et Electroniques [France]   (PDAA)

CIAN .... Comite International pour l'Afrique Noire   (WGAO)

CIAN .... Fabrica de Monturas para Anteojos [Colombia]   (COL)

CIANA ..... Comision Ibero-Americano de Navegacion Aerea [Spanish]

CIANA ..... Comision Interprovincial del Agua del Noroeste de Argentina [Argentina]   (LAA)

CIANE....... Centro de Investigaciones Agricolas del Noreste [Mexico] (WGAO)

CIANE....... Comite Interminsterielle d'Action pour la Nature et l'Environment [Inter Ministerial Action Committee for Nature and the Environment] [France]   (PDAA)

CIANO...... Centro de Investigaciones Agricolas del Noroeste [Mexico] (DSCA)

CIANORTE ... Companhia de Armazens Gerais do Norte do Parana [Brazil] (DSCA)

CIANS...... Collegium Internationale Activitatis Nervosae Superioris [Milan, Italy]   (EAIO)

CIAO .... Compagnie Industrielle et Agricole Oubangui

CIAO .... Conference Internationale des Africanistes de l'Ouest

CIAP......... Cambodia-IRRI [International Rice Research Institute]-Australia Project

CIAP......... Centre d'Information Agricole des Planteurs   (WGAO)

CIAP......... Centre d'Information de l' Aviation Privee   (WGAO)

CIAP......... Centro de Investigaciones en Administracion Publica [Argentina] (WGAO)

CIAP......... Comite Interamericain de l'Alliance pour le Progres [Inter-American Committee on the Alliance for Progress - ICAP] [French]

CIAP......... Comite Interamericano de la Alianza para el Progreso [Inter-American Committee on the Alliance for Progress] [Use ICAP] [Spanish]   (LA)

CIAP......... Commission Internationale de l'Atlas de Folklore Europeen (WGAO)

CIAP......... Commission Internationale des Arts et Traditions Populaires (WGAO)

CIAP......... Compagnie Indusdtrielle et Agricole de l'Oubangui [Central Africa]   (WGAO)

CIAP......... Compagnie Ivoirienne d'Armement a la Peche

CIAP......... Conseil Interafricain de Philosophie   (WGAO)

CIAPESC.. Companhia Amazonica de Pesca [Brazil]   (DSCA)

CIAPG....... Confederation Internationale des Anciens Prisonniers de Guerre [International Confederation of Former Prisoners of War] [Paris, France]   (EAIO)

CIAPT .... Centre d'Instruction et d'Application de Police de Tchibanga

CIAPY ...... Centro de Investigacion Agricolas de la Peninsula de Yucatan [Mexico]   (WGAO)

CIAPY ...... Centro de Investigaciones Agricolas La Peninsula de Yucatan [Mexico]   (DSCA)

CIARA....... Centro de Capacitacion e Investigacion Aplicada en Reforma Agraria [Foundation for Training and Research Applied to Agrarian Reform] [Venezuela]   (LAA)

CIARA....... Conference Internationale sur l'Assistance aux Refugies en Afrique [International Conference on Assistance for Refugees in Africa - ICARA] [United Nations Geneva, Switzerland]   (EAIO)

CIARA....... Fundacion para la Capacitacion e Investigaacion Aplicada a la Reforma Agraria [Venezuela]   (WGAO)

CIARCO.... Colombiana de Ingenieros Arquitectos Constructores Ltda. [Colombia]   (COL)

CIARD....... Comite Francais des Concours d'Inventions et Innovations Adaptees aux Regions en Developpement [French Committee for Competitions Relating to Inventions and Innovations Suitable for Use in Third World Areas]   (AF)

CIAREL .... Comercio e Industria Agricola, Representacoes e Exportacao Ltd. [Brazil]   (DSCA)

CIArh........ Chartered Institute of Arbitrators   (WGAO)

CIAS......... Centro de Investigaciones Administrativas y Sociales [Venezuela]   (WGAO)

CIAS......... Centro de Investigaciones Agricolas de Sinaloa [Mexico] (WGAO)

CIAS......... Centro de Investigacion y Accion Social [Social Research and Action Center] [Colombia]   (COL)

CIAS......... Centro de Investigacion y Accion Social [Social Research and Action Center] [Peru]   (LA)

CIAS......... Centro de Investigacion y Accion Social [Social Research and Action Center] [Argentina]   (LA)

CIAS......... Centro de Investigacion y Accion Social [Social Research and Action Center] [Santiago, Chile]   (LAA)

CIAS......... Comitato Interministeriale per Ricerche Spaziali [Interministerial Committee for Space Research] [Italian] (WER)

CIAS......... Comite de Investigacion Agua Subterranea [Argentina]   (LAA)

CIAS......... Conference of Independent African States

CIAS......... Conseil International de l'Action Sociale [International Council on Social Welfare - ICSW] [Vienna, Austria]   (EA)

CIAS......... Consejo Interamericano de Seguridad   (WGAO)

CIASA .... Caju Industrial de Alagoas SA [*Brazil*]   (DSCA)
CIASA .... Compania Industrial Azucarera "San Aurelio" SA [*Santa Cruz, Bolivia*]
CIASA .... Compania Internacional Aerea SA [*Ecuador*]   (PDAA)
ciasc .... Ciascuno [*Each*] [*Italian*]
CIASE .... Centro de Investigaciones Agricolas del Surest [*Mexico*] (WGAO)
CIASE .... Centro de Investigaciones Agricolas del Sureste [*Mexico*] (DSCA)
CIASI .... Comite Interministeriel d'Amenagement des Structures Industrielles [*Interministerial Committee for Planning Industrial Structures*] [*Guadeloupe*]   (LA)
CIASTR..... Commission Internatinale d'Astronautique [*FAI*]   (WGAO)
CIAT.......... Centrala Industriei de Autovehicule si Transport [*Central of the Motor Vehicle and Transportation Industry*]   (RO)
CIAT.......... Centre Interamericain d'Administration du Travail [*Inter-American Center for Labor Administration*] [*French*]
CIAT.......... Centres d'Informatique Appliquee aux Transports [*French*] (ADPT)
CIAT.......... Centro de Investigacion Agricola Tropical [*Tropical Agriculture Investigation Center*] [*Bolivia*]   (ARC)
CIAT.......... Centro Interamericano de Administracion del Trabajo [*Inter-American Center for Labor Administration*] [*Lima, Peru*] (EAIO)
CIAT.......... Centro Interamericano de Administradores Tributarios [*Inter-American Center of Tax Administrators*]   (EAIO)
CIAT.......... Centro Internacional de Agricultura Tropical [*International Center for Tropical Agriculture*] [*ICSU*]   (LA)
CIAT.......... Comision Interamericana del Atun Tropical [*Inter-American Tropical Tuna Commission*] [*Spanish*]   (LA)
CIAT.......... Comite des Industries de l'Ennoblissement Textile des Pays de la CEE   (WGAO)
CIAT.......... Comite Interministeriel de l'Amenagement du Territoire [*Morocco*]
CIAT.......... Compagnia Italiana Autoservizi Turistici
CIAT.......... Comptoir Immobilier de l'Afrique Tropicale
CIATE .... Cooperativa Industrial Agricola Tropical Ecuatoriana [*Industrial and Agricultural Cooperative of Tropical Ecuador*] [*Quito*] (LAA)
CIATF .... Comite International des Associations Techniques de Fonderie [*International Committee of Foundry Technical Associations*]   (EAIO)
CIATI .... Centre Inter-Administratif de Traitement de l'Information [*Inter-Administrative Center for Information Processing*] [*Tunisia*]   (AF)
CIATI .... Centro de Investigacion y Asistencia Tecnica de la Industria [*Center for Industrial Research and Technical Assistance*] [*INTI*] [*Research center*] [*Argentina*]   (IRC)
CIATO .... Centre International d'Alcoologie / Toxixomanies [*International Center of Alcohol/Drug Addiction*]   (PDAA)
CIAV.......... Comite International pour l'Archetecture Vernaculaire [*ICOMOS*]   (WGAO)
CIAVER .... Centre International Audiovisuel d'Etudes et de Recherches [*Belgium*]   (WGAO)
CIB............. Cambodian Investment Board   (ECON)
CIB............. Centra-European-International Bank Ltd. [*Hungary*]   (IMH)
CIB............. Central European International Bank   (WGAO)
CIB............. Centre Interamerican de Biostatistique   (WGAO)
CIB............. Centro de Investigaciones Basicas [*Mexico*]   (WGAO)
CIB............. Centro de Investigaciones Biologicas [*Biological Investigations Center*] [*Research center*] [*Spanish*]   (IRC)
CIB............. Centro Interamericano de Bioestadistica   (LAA)
CIB............. Centro Internacional Bibliografico   (WGAO)
CIB............. Centrum voor Informatie Beleid [*Netherlands Center for Information Policy*] [*The Hague*] [*Information service or system*]   (IID)
CIB............. Ceramique Industrielle du Benin
CIB............. Chartered Institute of Bankers [*London, England*]   (EAIO)
CIB............. Children's Interests Bureau [*Australia*]   (EAIO)
CIB............. China Investment Bank
CIB............. Classification Internationale des Brevets
CIB............. Comite Interprofessionel du Bourgogne [*French*]
CIB............. Comite Interprofessionnel Bananier
CIB............. Commission Internationale de la Baleine [*International Whaling Commission - IWC*]   (MSC)
CIB............. Commonwealth Investigation Branch [*Australia*]
CIB............. Communaute International Baha'ie
CIB............. Compagnie Industrielle du Bois [*Ivory Coast*]   (IMH)
CIB............. Compagnie Ivoirienne de Boissons
CIB............. Confederation des Immobiliers de Belge   (WGAO)
CIB............. Conseil Interfederal du Bois   (WGAO)
CIB............. Conseil International du Batiment pour la Recherche, l'Etude, et la Documentation [*International Council for Building Research, Studies, and Documentation*]   (EAIO)
CIB............. Conseil International du Ble [*International Wheat Council - IWC*]   (EAIO)
CIB............. Corporation of Insurance Brokers   (WGAO)

CIB............. ICC [*International Chamber of Commerce*] Counterfeiting Intelligence Bureau   (EA)
CIB............. Societe Congolaise Industrielle des Bois   (WGAO)
CIBA......... Corporation of Insurance Brokers of Australia   (ADA)
CIBA......... Society of Chemical Industry in Basel [*Switzerland*]   (DSCA)
CIBAL .... Centre International de l'Information et Sources de l'Histoire Balkanique et Mediterraneenne [*Bulgaria*]   (WGAO)
CIBC.......... Church of India, Burma, and Ceylon [*Anglican Church*]
CIBC.......... Commonwealth Institute of Biological Control [*Trinidad and Tobago*]   (DSCA)
CIBC.......... Confederation Internationale de la Boucherie et de la Charcuterie (WGAO)
CIBC.......... Cook Islands Broadcasting Corp.   (EY)
CIBDOC.... International Council for Building Documentation   (WGAO)
CIBE.......... Compagnie Intercommunale Bruxelloise des Eaux [*Brussels Water Company*] [*Belgium*]   (ARC)
CIBE.......... Confederation Internationale des Betteraviers Europeens [*International Confederation of European Sugar-Beet Growers*]   (EAIO)
CIBEP .... Association du Commerce International de Bulbes a Fleurs et de Plantes   (WGAO)
CIBER .... Centre Interafricain d'Information et de Liaison sur le Bien-Etre Rural
CIBER .... Inter-African Centre for Information and Liaison in Rural Welfare   (WGAO)
CIBESTAL ... Societe de Constructions Industrielles de Batiment de l'Est-Algerien
CIBET .... Groupement Interuniversitaire Benelux des Economistes des Transports [*Belgium*]   (WGAO)
CIBFV .... Cinema Industry Benevolent Fund of Victoria [*Australia*]
CIBJO .... Confederation Internationale de la Bijouterie, Joaillerie, Orfevrerie, des Diamants, Perles et Pierres   (WGAO)
CIBM......... Centro de Investigacion de Biologia Marina [*Argentina*]   (LAA)
CIBOAF ... Compagnie d'Importation des Bois Africains
CIBPP........ Confederation Internationale de Jeu de Balle Pelote Paume (WGAO)
CIBPU .... Comissao Interestadual da Bacia Parana-Uruguai [*Interstate Commission on Parana-Uruguay Basin*] [*Brazil*]   (LA)
CIBRA .... Comercio e Industria de Produtos Agricolas do Brasil Ltd. [*Brazil*]   (DSCA)
CIBRA .... Concerico e Industria de Produtos Agricolas do Brasil   (WGAO)
CIBRASCEX ... Companhia Brasileira de Comercio Exterior [*Brazilian Foreign Trade Company*]   (LA)
CIBRAZEM ... Companhia Brasileira de Armazenamento [*Brazilian Warehousing Company*]   (LA)
CIBS .... Center for International Business Studies [*Research center*] (RCD)
CIBSE........ Chartered Institution of Building Services Engineers   (EAIO)
CIBSL........ Centro de Investigacion Biologica Sanchez Labrador [*Argentina*] (DSCA)
CIBTC .... China International Book Trading Corporation
CIBTIC...... Centro de Informacion Bibliografica Tecnica para Ingenieros Civiles [*Cuba*]   (DSCA)
CIBV.......... Consejo Internacional de Buena Vecindad, AC [*International Good Neighbor Council - IGNC*] [*Monterrey, Mexico*] (EAIO)
CIC............. Cala Izba Cywilna [*The Full Civil Chamber of the Supreme Court*]   (POL)
CIC............. Camara de Industria y Comercio [*Bolivia*]   (EAIO)
CIC............. Capital Issues Committee [*Malaysian stock exchange*]
CIC............. Caribbean Investment Corporation [*St. Lucia*]   (LA)
CIC............. Central de Inversion y Credito SA [*Investment and Credit Center, Inc.*] [*Spanish*]   (WER)
CIC............. Central Incentives Committee [*Guyana*]   (LA)
CIC............. Centre d'Information de la Couler   (WGAO)
CIC............. Centre d'Informations Catholiques   (WGAO)
CIC............. Centre for International Communication [*Netherlands*] (WGAO)
CIC............. Centre International de Calcul [*Switzerland*]   (SLS)
CIC............. Centres d'Initiative Communiste [*Centers of Communist Initiative*] [*French*]   (WER)
CIC............. Centro de Informaciones y Control [*Information and Control Center*] [*Bolivia*]   (LA)
CIC............. Centro de Informaciones y Control [*Information and Control Center*] [*Chile*]   (LA)
CIC............. Centro de Investigacion y Capacitacion [*Research and Training Center*] [*Peru*]   (LA)
CIC............. Ceramic Industries Corporation [*Myanmar*]   (DS)
CIC............. China Isotope Corp.
CIC............. Christian Israelite Church [*Australia*]
CIC............. Cinema International Corp.   (WGAO)
CIC............. College Internationale des Chirurgiens   (WGAO)
CIC............. Combinat de Ingrasaminte Chimice [*Chemical Fertilizer Combine*]   (RO)
CIC............. Combined Industry Committee [*Australia*]
CIC............. Comision de Investigaciones Cientificas [*Argentina*]
CIC............. Comitato Italiano di Co-Ordinamento [*Italian*]

CIC............ Comite Intergubernamental de los Paises Coordinador de la Cuenca del Plata [*Argentina*] (WGAO)
CIC............ Comite International de Coordination pour l'Initiation a la Science et le Developpement des Activites Scientifiques Extra-Scolaires [*International Coordinating Committee for the Presentation of Science and the Development of Out-of-School Scientific Activities - ICC*] (EAIO)
CIC............ Comite International de la Conserve (WGAO)
CIC............ Comite International des Associations d'Analystes Financiers (WGAO)
CIC............ Comite International des Camps [*UIRD*] (WGAO)
CIC............ Commission Internationale de Supervision et de Controle [*International Supervisory and Control Commission*] [*Use ISCC*] (CL)
CIC............ Commission Internationale du Chataignier [*FAO*] (WGAO)
CIC............ Committee for Industrial Co-Operation [*European Economic Community/African, Caribbean, and Pacific States*] (DS)
CIC............ Commonwealth Industrial Court [*Australia*] (ADA)
CIC............ Commonwealth Information Centre [*Australia*] (ADA)
CIC............ Compagnie Immobiliere du Congo
CIC............ Compagnie Internationale de Commerce
CIC............ Compania de Industrias Chilenas [*Chilean Industries Company*] (LA)
CIC............ Confederation Internationale de la Coiffure (WGAO)
CIC............ Confederation Internationale des Cadres [*International Confederation of Executive Staffs*] [*Paris, France*] (EAIO)
CIC............ Conseil International de la Chasse et de la Conservation du Gibier [*International Council for Game and Wildlife Conservation*] (EAIO)
CIC............ Conseil International des Compositeurs (FLAF)
CIC............ Conseil Ivoirien des Chargeurs
CIC............ Consejo Interamericano Cultural [*Organizacion de Estados Americanos - OEA*] (LAA)
CIC............ Consejo Internacional de Curtidores (WGAO)
CIC............ Consejo Internacional del Cafe [*International Coffee Council*] (LA)
CIC............ Conselho de Imigracao e Colonizacao [*Council of Immigration and Colonization*] [*Portuguese*]
CIC............ Construction Industry Council [*Australia*]
CIC............ Coordinacion Investigacion Cientifica [*Mexico*] (ASF)
CIC............ Council for International Contact (WGAO)
CIC............ Creation Industrial Co. Ltd. [*Taiwan*]
CIC............ Credit Industriel et Commercial (WGAO)
CIC............ Credit Industriel et Commercial de Paris [*French*]
CICA......... Campbell Information Consultants Australia
CICA......... Canadian Institute of Chartered Accountants (WGAO)
CICA......... Centro de Investigacao Cientifica Algodoeira
CICA......... Centro de Investigaciones Ciencias Agronomicas [*Scientific Agricultue Research Center*] [*Argentina*] (PDAA)
CICA......... Centro Information y Computo SA [*Columbia*] (WGAO)
CICA......... Centro Interamericano de Ciencias Adminstrativas (WGAO)
CICA......... Circulo Colombiano de Artistas [*Colombia*] (COL)
CICA......... Comite Interconfederal de Cordination de l'Artisanat (WGAO)
CICA......... Comite International Catholique des Aveugles (EAIO)
CICA......... Comite International de la Croisade des Aveugles (WGAO)
CICA......... Comite International des Critiques d'Architecture (WGAO)
CICA......... Comite Internationale de la Crise Alimentaire (WGAO)
CICA......... Comite International pour le Cite Antique (WGAO)
CICA......... Commerciale Italiane Cooperative Agricole (WGAO)
CICA......... Compagnie Industrielle de Conserves Alimentaires
CICA......... Compagnie Internationale de Commerce et d'Approvisionnement (WGAO)
CICA......... Confederation Internationale du Credit Agricole [*International Confederation of Agricultural Credit*] [*Zurich, Switzerland*] (EAIO)
CICA......... Confederation of International Contractors' Associations [*Paris, France*] (EAIO)
CICA......... Conference Internationale des Controles d'Assurances des Etats Africains [*International Conference of African States on Insurance Supervision*] (EAIO)
CICA......... Conference Internationale des Controles d'Assurances des Etats Africains, Francais, et Malgache [*International Conference of African, French, and Malagasy States on Insurance Supervision*] (AF)
CICA......... Construction Industry Computing Association (WGAO)
CICA......... Societe Commerciale et Industrielle de la Cote-d'Afrique
CICAA....... Comision Internacional para la Conservacion del Atun del Atlantico [*International Commission for the Conservation of Atlantic Tunas - ICCAT*] [*Spanish*] (MSC)
CICABE .... Centre International de la Culture Africaine et du Bien-etre de l'Enfance (WGAO)
CICADES ... Centro Interamericano de Cooperacion Academica para el Desarrollo Economico y Social (WGAO)
CICAE....... Confederation Internationale des Cinemas d'Art et d'Essai [*International Experimental and Art Film Theatres Confederation*] [*France*]

CICAF .... Caisse Inter-Professionnelle de Compensation des Allocations Familiales [*Interoccupational Family Allowance Compensation Fund*] [*Cambodia*] (CL)
CICAF .... Camara Industrial, Comercial, y Agricola del Estado Falcon [*Venezuela*] (DSCA)
CICAF .... Centre International de Creation Audiovisuella Francophones [*France*] (WGAO)
CICAF .... Compagnie Industrielle de Combustibles Atomiques Frittes [*French*]
CICAF .... International Committee for the Cinema and the Figurative Arts
CICAH ...... Comite de l'Industrie et des Activities Connexes de la Region Havraise (WGAO)
CICAJ .... Centre International de Coordination de l'Assistance Juridique (FLAF)
CICAL....... Construtora Industrial e Comercial Agricola Ltd. [*Brazil*] (DSCA)
CICALIM ... Compagnie Industrielle et Commerciale d'Alimentation [*Morocco*]
CICAM...... Cotonniere Industrielle du Cameroun (WGAO)
CICAM...... Societe Cotonniere Industrielle du Cameroun
CICAP .... Centre Interamericano de Capacitacion en Administracion Publica [*Argentina*] (WGAO)
CICAP .... Centro Interamericano de Capacitacion en Administracion Publica (de la Organizacion de Estados Americanos) [*Inter-American Center for Training in Public Administration (of the Organization of American States)*] (LAA)
CICAP .... Comercio e Industria Cafeeira Alta Paulista [*Brazil*] (DSCA)
CICAR....... Corporacion Industrial Comercial Agropecuaria [*Argentina*] (WGAO)
CICAR....... Corporacion Industrial Comercial Agropecuaria Regional [*Argentina*] (LAA)
CICARWS ... Commission on Inter-Church Aid, Refugee and World Service (WGAO)
CICASI...... Centro de Investigaciones Carboniferas y Siderurgicas [*Venezuela*]
CICAT .... Center for International Cooperation and Appropriate Technology [*Netherlands*] (IRC)
CICATI ..... Comissao de Intercambio e Coordenacao da Assistencia Tecnica Internacional [*Brazil*] (DSCA)
CICATI ..... Division of the Exchange and Coordination of International Technical Assistance [*Brazil*] (WGAO)
CICATIRS ... Comite International de Coordination et d'Action des Groupements de Techniciens des Industries de Revetements de Surface [*International Committee to Coordinate Activities of Technical Groups in Coatings Industry - ICCATCI*] (EAIO)
CICATUR ... Centro Interamericano de Capacitacion Turistica [*Argentina*] (WGAO)
CICAV....... Conseil International de Coordination des Associations d'Etudes et d'Action en Matiere de Viellissement (WGAO)
CICB........ Center International des Civilisations Bantu (EAIO)
CICB........ Chambre des Ingenieurs-Conseils de Belgique (WGAO)
CICB........ Confederacion Independiente de Campesinos de Bolivia (WGAO)
CICB........ Societe Royale Chambre des Ingenieurs Conseils de Belgique (WGAO)
CICC......... Cayman Islands Chamber of Commerce (EAIO)
CICC......... Centre International de Criminologie Comparee [*International Center for Comparative Criminology - ICCC*] [*Montreal, PQ*] (EA)
CICC......... Centro Internazionale di Coordinazione Culturale (WGAO)
CICC......... Compagnie Immobiliere et Commerciale du Cameroun
CICCA ...... Centre International de Coordination pour la Celebration des Anniversaries (WGAO)
CICCA ...... Committee for International Cooperation between Cotton Associations (WGAO)
CICCC .... Commission Internationale Contre les Camps de Concentration (WGAO)
CICCE .... Comite des Industries Cinematographiques des Communautes Europeennes [*Committee of the Cinematography Industries in the European Communities*] (EAIO)
CICCH....... Centre International Chretien de la Construction d'Habilitation (WGAO)
CICCOPN ... Centro de Formacao Professional da Industria de Construcao e Obras Publicas do Norte (WGAO)
CICCYB .... Centre International de Cyto-Cybernetique [*International Center of Cyto-Cybernetics*] [*French*] (SLS)
CICD......... Campaign for International Cooperation and Disarmament [*Australia*]
CICD......... Collegium Internationale Chirurgiae Digestivae [*Rome, Italy*] (EAIO)
CICE......... Centre d'Information des Chemins de Fer Europeens (FLAF)
CICE......... Centre International de Calcul Electronique [*International Computation Center*] [*French*] (ASF)
CICE......... Centre Ivoirien du Commerce Exterieur [*Ivorian Center for Foreign Trade*] (AF)

CICE .... Centro de Investigaciones en Ciencias de la Educacion (del Instituto Torcuato di Tella) [*Buenos Aires*] [*Argentina*] (LAA)

CICE .... Centro Internacional de Calculos Electronicos [*International Computation Center*] [*Spanish*] (ASF)

CICE .... Club International de Correspondance Ekong [*Ekong International Correspondence Club*] (EAIO)

CICE .... Comite de Informacion y Contacto Externo para Empresarios Privados [*Committee on Information and External Contacts for Private Business Owners*] [*Ecuador*] (LA)

CICE .... Comite de l'Industrie Cinematographique Europeenne (WGAO)

CICE .... Comite International des Createurs en Email [*International Committee of Enamelling Creators*] [*France*] (EAIO)

CICE .... Compagnie Industrielle des Ceramiques Electroniques (WGAO)

CICE .... Conferencia Internacional Catolica de Escultismo (WGAO)

CICE .... Corriente Izquierdista en las Ciencias Economicas [*Leftist Trend Economic Sciences*] [*Argentina*] (LA)

CICE .... Council for International Congresses of Entomology [*London, England*] (EA)

CICE .... Cumann Innealtoiri Comhairle na Eireann [*Association of Consulting Engineers of Ireland*]

CICEIPB ... Comite Interimaire de Coordination des Echanges Internationaux de Produits de Base (WGAO)

CICELC..... Comite International du Cinema l'Enseignement et de Culture (WGAO)

CICELPA.. Centro de Investigacion de Celulosa y Papel [*Pulp and Paper Research Center*] [*Argentina*] (LAA)

CICEO ...... China International Cultural Exchange Organization

CICEP .... Conseil Interamericain du Commerce et de la Production (FLAF)

CICEPLA.. Confederacion Industrial de Celulosa y Papel Latinoamericana [*Latin American Cellulose and Paper Industrial Confederation*] (LA)

CICER .... Companhia Industrial de Cervejas e Refrigerantes da Guine [*The Brewery Company of Guinea-Bissau*] (AF)

CICERO .... The Center for International Climate and Environmental Research - Oslo [*University of Oslo*] [*Norway*]

CICESE..... Centro de Investigacion Cientifica y de Educacion Superior de Ensenada [*Mexico*] (ASF)

CICF .... Centre International du Commerce de Gros (WGAO)

CICF .... Chambre des Ingenieurs - Conseils de France

CICF .... Confederation Internationale des Cadres Fonctionnaires (FLAF)

CICFRI...... Central Inland Capture Fisheries Research Institute [*India*] (IRC)

CICG......... Centre International de Conferences de Geneve [*International Conference Center of Geneva*] [*Switzerland*] (PDAA)

CICG......... Conference Internationale Catholique du Guidisme [*International Catholic Conference of Guiding*] (EAIO)

CICG......... Conference Internationale du Commerce de Gros (WGAO)

CICH .... Centro de Informacion Cientifica y Humanistica [*Center for Scientific and Humanistic Information*] [*Mexico*] [*Information service or system*] (IID)

CICH .... Comite International de la Culture du Houblon [*International Hop Growers Convention - IHGC*] (EAIO)

CICHE...... British Council Committee for International Cooperation in Higher Education (WGAO)

CICHE...... Committee for International Co-Operation in Higher Education

CICH/UNAM ... Centro de Informacion Cientifica y Humanistica/Universidad Nacional Autonoma de Mexico [*Center for Scientific and Humanistic Information/National Autonomous University of Mexico*]

CICI .... Centre d'Information sur les Carrieres liees a l'Informatique [*French*] (ADPT)

CICI .... Centre Industriel Centrafricano-Israelien

CICI .... Commission Internationle de Cooperation Intellectuelle (WGAO)

CICI .... Confederation of Information Communication Industries (WGAO)

CICI .... Consortium Ivorien de Commerce et d'Industrie (WGAO)

CICIAMS ... Comite International Catholique des Infirmieres et Assistantes Medico-Sociales [*International Committee of Catholic Nurses - ICCN*] [*Vatican City, Vatican City State*] (EAIO)

CICIBA ..... Centre International des Civilisations Bantu [*International Center for the Bantu Civilizations*] [*Gabon*] [*Research center*] (IRC)

CICIEM .... Chambre Islamique de Commerce, d'Industrie et d'Echange des Marchandises [*Islamic Chamber of Commerce, Industry, and Commodity Exchange - ICCICE*] [*Karachi, Pakistan*] (EAIO)

CICIG .... Commissione Italiana del Comitato Internazionale di Geofisica (WGAO)

CICIH....... Confederation Internationale Catholique des Institutions Hospitalieres (WGAO)

CICIHA ..... Centro de Investigacion de la Construccion Industrializada en el Habitat [*Instituto Nacional de Tecnologia Industrial*] [*Argentina*]

CICILS ...... Confederation Internationale du Commerce et des Industries des Legumes Secs [*International Pulse Trade and Industry Confederation*] [*EC*] (ECED)

CICIND..... Comite International des Cheminees Industrielles

CICIREPATO ... Committee for International Coopeation in Information Retrieval among Examining Patent Offices (WGAO)

CICITE...... Conseil International du Cinema et de la Television (WGAO)

CICJU .... Centro de Informacion y Cultura Judaica [*Zionist organization in Venezuela*]

CICL .... Chambre des Ingenieurs-conseils du Grand-Duche de Luxembourg (WGAO)

CICLA .... Corporacion de Integracion Cultural Latinoamericana [*Latin American Cultural Integration Corporation*] [*Chile*] (LA)

CICLU .... Ceylon Indian Congress Labor Union

CICM........ Centro de Investigaciones de Ciencias Marinas [*Colombia*] (COL)

CICM........ Commission Internationale Catholique pour les Migrations [*International Catholic Migration Commission - ICMC*] [*Geneva, Switzerland*] (EAIO)

CICM........ Congregatio Immaculati Cordis Mariae (WGAO)

CICO .... Conference of International Catholic Organizations [*Geneva, Switzerland*] (EAIO)

CICODEC ... Compania Colombiana de Calzado [*Colombia*] (COL)

CICOL...... Compania Comercial Ltda. [*Popayan*] (COL)

CICOLAC ... Compania Colombiana de Alimentos Lacteos [*Colombia*] (COL)

CICOLPAGRO ... Compania Comercial de Productos Agropecuarios [*Colombia*] (COL)

CICOLPLAS ... Compania Colombiana de Plasticos [*Colombia*] (COL)

CICOM ..... Centro Interamericano de Capacitacao e Comercializacao (WGAO)

CICOMO .. Companhia Industrial de Cordoarias de Mocambique

CICON ...... Centro de Informacion a la Construccion [*Facultad de Ingenieria de la Universidad de San Carlos de Guatemala*] [*Guatemala*]

CICON ...... Consolidated Investment & Contracting Co. [*United Arab Emirates*]

CICOOP.... Centrul de Calcul si Informatica al Cooperativelor de Consum [*Computation and Data Processing Center of the Consumer Cooperatives*] (RO)

CICOPA.... Comite International des Cooperatives de Production et Artisanales [*International Committee of Producers' Cooperatives*] (EAIO)

CICOTEPHAR ... Centre Technique International de Coordination Pharmaceutique (WGAO)

CICOTP .... Compagnie Ivoirienne de Construction des Travaux Publics

CICP......... Comite Internacional para la Cooperacion de los Periodistas [*International Committee for Cooperation of Journalists*] [*Use ICCJ*] (LA)

CICP......... Confederation Internationale du Credit Populaire [*International Confederation of Popular Credit - ICPC*] [*Paris, France*] (EAIO)

CICPA .... Chinese Institute of Certified Public Accountants (EAIO)

CICPE .... Comite d'Initiative pour le Congres du Peuple Europeen (WGAO)

CICPLB..... Comite International pour le Controle de la Productivite Laitiere du Betail [*International Committee for Recording the Productivity of Milk Animals - ICRPMA*] (EAIO)

CICPND.... Comitato Italiano di Coordinamento par le Prova Non-Distruttiva [*Italian Committee for the Coordination of Non-Destructive Testing*] (PDAA)

CICPR .... Confederation Internationale pour la Chirurgie Plastique et Reconstructive [*International Confederation for Plastic and Reconstructive Surgery*] (EAIO)

CICR......... Comitato Interministeriale per il Credito e Risparmio [*Interministerial Committee for Credit and Savings*] [*Italian*] (WER)

CICR......... Comite Internacional de la Cruz Roja [*International Committee of the Red Cross - ICRC*] [*Spanish*]

CICR......... Comite International Contre la Repression [*International Committee Against Repression*] [*Paris, France*] (EAIO)

CICR......... Comite International de la Croix-Rouge [*International Committee of the Red Cross*] [*French*] (WER)

CICR......... Committee on Information and Cultural Relations (EAIO)

CICRA .... Centre International de Coordination des Recherches sur l'Autogestion [*France*] (WGAO)

CICRA .... Centre International pour la Cooperation dans les Recherches en Agriculture [*Switzerland*] (DSCA)

CICRA .... Centre International pour la Cooperation des Recherches en Agriculture [*France*] (WGAO)

CICRC....... Commission Internationale Contre le Regime Concentrationnaire [*International Commission Against the Regime of Concentration Camps*] [*France*]

CICRED .... Comite International de Cooperation dans les Recherches Nationales en Demographie [*Committee for International Cooperation in National Research in Demography*] (EAIO)

CICREF..... Club Informatique des Grandes Entreprises Francaises [*French*] (ADPT)
CICRIS...... Cooperative Industrial and Commercial Reference and Information Service   (WGAO)
CICRODEPORTES ... Circulo de Cronistas Deportivos de Antioquia [*Colombia*]   (COL)
CICRU....... Camara Internacional de Comercio del Rio Uruguay [*Uruguay*] (LAA)
CICS .... Centre for Industrial Control Science [*University of Newcastle*] [*Australia*]
CICS .... Commission Internationale Catholique de la Sante [*Switzerland*] (SLS)
CICS .... Committee for Index Cards for Standards [*IOS*]   (WGAO)
CICS .... Compagne Industrielle et Commerciale du Senegal   (WGAO)
CICS .... Conference Internatiionale Catholique du Scoutisme   (WGAO)
CICSA .... Centro de Informacion y Computo Sociedad Anonima [*Colombia*]   (COL)
CICSETT .. Corporate Member of the Institute of Civil Engineering Technicians and Technologists [*South Africa*]   (AA)
CICSSA..... Comision Industrial Comercial del Sur SA [*Uruguay*]   (DSCA)
CICT......... Commission on Internatinal Commodity Trade [*UNCTAD*] (WGAO)
CICT......... Conseil International du Cinema et de la Television   (WGAO)
CICTA .... Commission Internationale pour la Conservation des Thonides de l'Atlantique [*International Commission for the Conservation of Atlantic Tunas - ICCAT*] [*French*]   (ASF)
CICTEE..... China International Center for Technical and Economic Exchange
CICTM...... Combinatul de Ingrasaminte Chimice Turnu Magurele [*Chemical Fertilizer Combine of Turnu Magurele*]   (RO)
CICTP .... Companie Industrielle de Constructions, d'Amenagements et du Travaux Publics [*Ivory Coast*]   (WGAO)
CICTRAN ... Computer Information Centre for Transportation [*South Africa*] (WGAO)
CICTUS .... Centro de Investigaciones Cientificas y Tecnologicas de la Universidad de Sonora [*Mexico*]   (ASF)
CICY......... Centre Internationale de Cyto-Cybernetique   (WGAO)
CICYP .... Consejo Interamericano de Comercio y Produccion [*Inter-American Council of Commerce and Production - IACCP*] (LA)
CICYT....... Comite Interamericano de Ciencia y Tecnologia   (WGAO)
CICYT .... Comite Interministerial de Ciencia y Tecnologia   (WGAO)
CICYT .... Inter-American Committee on Science and Technology [*Organization of American States*]   (ASF)
CICZ......... Comision Interministerial Coordinadora de Zoonosis [*Argentina*]   (DSCA)
CID .... Association de Consultants Internationaux en Droits de l'Homme [*Association of International Consultants on Human Rights*] [*Geneva, Switzerland*]   (EAIO)
CID .... Center for Industrial Development [*European Economic Community/African, Caribbean, and Pacific States*]   (DS)
CID .... Central for Industrial Development   (WGAO)
CID .... Centre d'Information Documentation Moyen-Orient   (WGAO)
CID .... Centre d'Information et de Documentation [*EG*] [*Luxembourg*]
CID .... Centre d'Information et de Documentation du Congo et du Ruanda-Urundi
CID .... Centre for Industrial Democracy [*Australia*]
CID .... Centre for Information and Documentation [*Euratom*]   (WGAO)
CID .... Centre for Innovation Development [*Australia*]
CID .... Centre for the Development of Industry [*Formerly, Centre for Industrial Development*]
CID .... Centre Interinstitutionnel pour la Diffusion de Publications en Sciences Humaines   (WGAO)
CID .... Centre International de Documentation des Producteurs de Scories Thomas [*Belgium*]   (SLS)
CID .... Centre International pour le Developpement [*International Center for Development*] [*French*]   (AF)
CID .... Centro de Informacao e Documentacao [*Fertilizantes Vale do Rio Grande*] [*Brazil*]
CID .... Centro de Informacion Bibliografica y Documentacion [*Servicio Industrial de la Marina Callao*] [*Peru*]
CID .... Centro de Informacion y Documentacion [*Information and Documentation Center*] [*Argentina*]   (LA)
CID .... Centro de Informacion y Documentacion [*Information and Documentation Center*] [*Colorado*]
CID .... Centro de Informaction de Archivos [*Spain*]   (PDAA)
CID .... Centro de Integracion y Desarrollo [*Integration and Development Center*] [*Bolivia*]   (LA)
CID .... Centro de Investigacion Documentaria [*Buenos Aires, Argentina*]
CID .... Centro de Investigaciones Digitales [*Computer Research Center*] [*Cuba*]   (LA)
CID .... Centro de Investigaciones para el Desarrollo [*Universidad de Colombia*] [*Bogota, Colombia*]   (LAA)
CID .... Centro Internacional para el Desarrollo   (WGAO)

CID .... Centrum voor Informatie en Documentatie [*Center for Information and Documentation*] [*Netherlands Organization for Applied Scientific Research Delft*] [*Information service or system*]   (IID)
CID .... Centrum voor Technische en Wetenschappelijke Informatie en Dokumentatie [*Center for Technical and Scientific Information and Documentation*] [*Netherlands*]   (WED)
CID .... Coalicion Institucionalista Democratica [*Democratic Institutional Coalition*] [*Ecuador*] [*Political party*]   (PPW)
CID .... Comite International de la Detergence   (WGAO)
CID .... Comite International du Dachau
CID .... Committee for Industrial Development [*United Nations*]
CID .... Compagnie Industrielle du Disque [*Record label*] [*France*]
CID .... Conseil International de la Danse   (WGAO)
CID .... Consortium for International Development
CID .... Council of Intellectual Disabilities [*Australia*]   (EAIO)
CID .... Criminal Investigation Department   (WGAO)
CID .... Criminal Investigation Division [*Mauritius*]   (AF)
CID .... Criminal Investigation Division [*New South Wales Crime Commission*] [*Australia*]
CID .... Czechoslovak Industrial Design   (CZ)
CIDA .... Canadian International Development Agency   (WGAO)
CIDA .... Centre d'Information de Documentation et de l'Alimentation (WGAO)
CIDA .... Centre d'Information et Documentation Automatique   (WGAO)
CIDA .... Centre d'Informatique et Documentation Automatique [*Center for Automated Information and Documentation*] [*France*] [*Information service or system*]   (IID)
CIDA .... Centre International de Development de l'Aluminium   (WGAO)
CIDA .... Centre International de Documentation Arachnologique [*International Centre for Arachnological Documentation*] (EAIO)
CIDA .... Centre l'Infrometiun et Documentation Atlantique   (WGAO)
CIDA .... Centro de Investigaciones de Astronomia "Francisco J. Duarte" [*Francisco J. Duarte Center for Research in Astronomy*] [*Venezuela*]   (IRC)
CIDA .... Centro de Investigacion y Difusion Aeronautico-Espacial [*Aeronautics and Space Research Center*] [*Uruguay*] [*Research center*]   (IRC)
CIDA .... Comision Interprofesional de Antioquia [*Antioquia Interprofessional Commission*] [*Colorado*]   (LA)
CIDA .... Comite Interamericano de Desarrollo Agricola [*Inter-American Committee for Agricultural Development*]   (LA)
CIDA .... Comite Intergouvernemental du Droit d'Auteur [*Intergovernmental Copyright Committee - IGC*] [*UNESCO*]   (EAIO)
CIDA .... Commission Internationale des Industries Agricoles   (WGAO)
CIDA .... Community Information Development Association [*Australia*]
CIDA .... Companhia Industrial de Desenvolvimento da Amazonia [*Brazil*]   (WGAO)
CIDA .... Confederazione Italiana die Dirigenti di Azienda [*A union for executives*] [*Italy*]   (DCTA)
CIDA .... Council of Intellectual Disability Agencies [*Victoria*] [*Australia*]
CIDA .... Inter-American Centre for Archives Development [*Argentina*] (WGAO)
CIDAA....... Inter-American Commission for Environmental Law and Administration [*Colombia*]   (WGAO)
CIDAC...... Centre International de Documentation et d'Animation Culturelle [*France*]
CIDAC...... Centro de Informacao e Documentacao Amilcar Cabral [*Portugal*]
CIDAC...... Centro de Informacao e Documentacao Anticolonial [*Anticolonial Information and Documentation Center*] [*Portuguese*]   (WER)
CIDAC...... Centro de Investigaciones Demograficas de America Central [*Central-American Demographic Research Center*]   (LAA)
CIDAC...... Centro de Investigacion para el Desarrollo [*Mexican government funded political and economic research center*]   (CROSS)
CIDADEC ... Confederation Internationale des Associations d'Experts et de Conseils   (WGAO)
CIDAECA ... Comite International pour le Developpement des Activities Educatives et Culturelles en Afrique
CIDAF....... Centro Italiano di Azione Forense [*Italian*]   (SLS)
CIDAK...... Centre d'Information de Dakar
CIDAL....... Centro de Informacion y Documentacion para America Latina (WGAO)
CIDALC .... Comite International pour la Diffusion des Arts et des Lettres par le Cinema [*International Committee for the Diffusion of Arts and Literature through the Cinema*]   (EAIO)
CIDAN ...... Compagnie Immobiliere d'Afrique Noire
CIDAP....... Centro Interamericano de Artesanias Popular [*Ecuador*] (WGAO)
CIDAPA .... Comptoir International d'Automobiles, Pieces Detachees, et Accessoires [*Morocco*]
CIDAPAR ... Companhia de Desenvolvimento Agropecuario, Inddustrial e Mineral do Estado do Para [*Brazil*]   (DSCA)

CIDAPAR ... Compannia de Desenvolvimento Agropecuario, Industrial e Mineral do Estado do Para [*Brazil*]   (WGAO)

CIDAS .... Centre d'Information et Documentation pour l'Agriculture et la Sylviculture [*Rumania*]   (WGAO)

CIDAS .... Centro Italiano Documentazione, Azione, Studi [*Italian Center for Documentation, Action, and Studies*]   (WER)

CIDAS .... Centrul de Informare si Documentare pentru Agricultura si Silvicultura [*Information and Documentation Center for Agriculture and Silviculture*]   (RO)

CIDAS .... Conference on Industrial Development in Arab States

CIDAT .... Centre d'Informatique Appliquee au Developpement et a l'Agriculture Tropicale [*Center for Informatics Applied to Development and Tropical Agriculture*] [*Royal Museum of Central Africa*] [*Information service or system*]   (IID)

CIDB .... Centre d'Information et du Documentatin du Batiment (WGAO)

CIDB .... Chemie-Information und Dokumentation Berlin [*Chemical Information and Documentation - Berlin*] [*Information service or system*] [*German*]   (IID)

CIDB .... Conseil International de Documentation du Batiment   (WGAO)

CIDB .... Construction Industry Development Board [*Singapore*]

CIDC .... Centre Islamique pour le Developpement du Commerce [*Islamic Center for Development of Trade - ICDT*] [*Casablanca, Morocco*]   (EAIO)

CIDC .... Comite International de Droit Compare   (FLAF)

CIDC .... Consorci d'Informacio i Documentacio de Catalunya [*Spain*] (WGAO)

CIDC .... Consortium Interafricain de Distribution Cinematographique [*Inter-African Moving Picture Distribution Consortium*] [*OCAM Ouagadougou, Burkina Faso*]   (AF)

CIDCMA ... Committee Internationale pour la Definition des Caracteristiques Microbiologiques des Aliments [*International Commission on Microbiological Specifications for Foods*] [*Switzerland*] (EAIO)

CIDD .... Conseil International de la Danse [*International Dance Council - IDC*] [*France*]   (SLS)

CIDE .... Centre Iberoamericain de Documentation Europeenne   (FLAF)

CIDE .... Centro de Informacion y Documentacion Economica   (WGAO)

CIDE .... Centro de Investigaciones de Desarrollo Economico. Universidad del Valle [*Colombia*]   (COL)

CIDE .... Centro de Investigacion y Desarrollo de la Educacion [*Santiago, Chile*]   (LAA)

CIDE .... Centro de Investigacion y Docencia Economica [*Institute which focuses on Mexica n/US relations*]   (CROSS)

CIDE .... Centro Informativo de la Edificacion [*Information Center on Building*] [*Spain*]   (PDAA)

CIDE .... Comision de Inversiones y Desarrollo Economico [*Uruguay*]

CIDE .... Commission Intersyndicale des Deshydrateurs Europeens [*European Dehydrators Association*] [*Common Market Paris, France*]

CIDE .... Confederation Internationale des Etudiants   (WGAO)

CIDE .... Conseil International pour le Droit de l'Environnement (WGAO)

CIDEA .... Consejo Interamericano de Educacion Alimenticia [*Venezuela*] (DSCA)

CIDEC .... Cofederazione Italiana degli Esercenti e Cummercianti   (WGAO)

CIDEC .... Comite Interamericano de Cultura [*United States*]   (WGAO)

CIDEC .... Conseil International pour le Developpement du Cuivre [*International Copper Development Council*]   (AF)

CIDECAF ... Compagnie Ivoirienne de Decafeination   (WGAO)

CIDECO .... Consortium des Industries du Deoupage et de l'Emboutissage du Centre-Ouest   (WGAO)

CIDECT .... Comite Internationale pour le Developpement et l'Etude de la Construction Tubulaire   (WGAO)

CIDEF .... Comite International des Etudes Francaises et du Dialogue des Cultures   (WGAO)

CIDEF .... Commonwealth Industrial Development Fund

CIDEFEG ... Conference Internationale des Doyens de Facultes et des Directeurs d'Ecoles de Gestion   (WGAO)

CIDELCA ... Compania Importadora del Caribe [*Colombia*]   (COL)

CIDELTRA ... Compania Industrial del Transporte Ltda. [*Neiva*]   (COL)

CIDEM ...... Centre d'Informacio i Desenvolupment Empresarial [*Department of Industry and Energy of the Generalitat of Catalonia*]

CIDEM ...... Centro de Investigaciones y Desarrollos Espaciales Mendoza [*Center for Space Research, Mendoza*] [*Argentina*]   (EAS)

CIDEM ...... Consejo Interamericano de Musica [*Inter-American Music Council*]   (EA)

CIDEM ...... Consejo Internacional de Mujeres   (WGAO)

CIDEMA ... Compania Importadora de Materiales Ltda. [*Cartagena-Bogota*] (COL)

CIDEP .... Centre Interdisciplinaire pour le Developpement et l'Education Permanente [*Interdisciplinary Center for Development and Permanent Education*] [*Zaire*]   (AF)

CIDEP .... Centre International de Documentation et d'Etudes Petrolieres (WGAO)

CIDER .... Centro Interdisciplinario Estudios Regionales [*Interdisciplinary Center for Regional Studies*] [*Colombia*]   (IRC)

CIDERE .... Corporacion Industrial para el Desarrollo Regional [*Chile*] (LAA)

CIDES .... Centro de Investigacion para el Desarrollo Economico Social [*Research Center for Socioeconomic Development*] [*Argentina*]   (IRC)

CIDESA .... Centre International de Documentation Economique et Sociale Africaine [*International Center for African Economic and Social Documentation*]   (AF)

CIDESCO ... Comite Internationale d'Esthetique et de Cosmetologie [*International Committee of Aesthetics and Cosmetology*] [*Switzerland*]   (EY)

CIDET .... Cooperation Internationale en Matiere de Documentation sur l'Economie des Transports [*International Cooperation in the Field of Transport Economics Documentation*] [*France*] [*Information service or system*]   (IID)

CIDEX .... Compagnie Commerciale d'Importation et d'Exportation

CIDH .... Centrul de Informare si Documentare Hidrotehnica [*Center for Hydrotechnology Information and Documentation*]   (RO)

CIDH .... Comision Interamericana de Derechos Humanos [*Washington, DC*]   (LAA)

CIDHAL .... Communicacion Intercambio Desarrollo Humano Americano Latino   (WGAO)

CIDHEC .... Centre Intergouvernemental de Documentation sur l'Habitat et l'Environnement [*Intergovernmental Center for Documentation on Dwellings and the Environment*] (PDAA)

CIDHEC .... Centre Intergouvernmental de Documentation sur l'Habitat et l'Environnement pour les Pays de la Commission Economique pour l'Europe des Nations Unies   (WGAO)

CIDI .... Centre Internationale de Documentation et d'Information

CIDI .... Centro de Informacion de Drogas y Intoxicantes [*Drug and Poison Information Center*] [*Dominican Republic*] [*Research center*]   (IRC)

CIDI .... Centro de Informacion sobre Contaminacion Ambiental Urbana, Centro de Investigaciones para el Desarrollo Integral [*Universidad Pontificia Bolivariana*] [*Colombia*]

CIDI .... Centro de Investigacion del Diseno Industrial y Grafico [*Research Center for Industrial and Graphic Design*] [*INTI*] [*Research center*] [*Argentina*]   (IRC)

CIDI .... Centro de Investigaciones para el Desarrollo Integral [*Integrated Development Research Center*] [*Research center*] [*Colombia*]   (IRC)

CIDI .... Centrul de Informare si Documentare a Invatamintului [*Information and Documentation Center for Education*] (RO)

CIDI .... Cote Ivoirienne d'Importation et de Distribution

CIDIA .... Centro Interamericano de Documentacion e Informacion Agricola [*Inter-American Center for Documentation and Agricultural Information*] [*Inter-American Institute for Cooperation on Agriculture*] [*Information service or system*] (IID)

CIDIA .... Consejo Inter-Americano de Educacion Alimenticia   (WGAO)

CIDIA .... Consejo Interamericano de Instruccion Alimenticia [*Inter-American International Council for Education on Nutrition*]   (LAA)

CIDIAT ..... Centro Interamericano para el Desarrollo Integral de Aguas y Tierras [*Interamerican Center for the Integral Development of Land and Water Resources*]   (ASF)

CIDIC .... Comite Interprofessionnel de Developpement de l'Industrie Chevaline   (WGAO)

CIDIE .... Committee of International Development Institutions on the Environment   (WGAO)

CIDIM .... Centro Italiano di Iniziativa Musicale [*Italian Center of Music*] (IRC)

CIDISE ...... Comite Interministeriel pour le Developpement de l'Investissement et de l'Emploi   (WGAO)

CIDITVA .. Centre International de Documentation de l'Inspection Techniques des Vehicles Automobiles   (WGAO)

CIDJ .... Centre d'Information et de Documentation Jeunesse   (WGAO)

CIDM .... Conseil International de Musique [*UNESCO*] [*Record label*]

CIDMA ..... Centro de Investigaciones y Desarrollo de la Maquinaria Agropecuaria [*Agricultural Machinery Research and Development Center*] [*Cuba*]   (LA)

CIDNET .... Consortium for International Development Information Network

CIDNT ...... Centralny Instytut Dokumentacji Naukowo-Technicznej [*Central Institute of Scientific and Technical Documentation*]   (POL)

CIDO .... Conseil International de la Danse   (WGAO)

CIDOB ...... Centro de Informacion y Documentacion, Barcelona   (WGAO)

CIDOB ...... Centro de Informacion y Documentacion Boliviano   (WGAO)

CIDOC ...... Centro Intercultural de Documentacion [*Mexico*]   (DSCA)

CIDOLOU ... Cimenterie Domaniale de Loutete

CIDP .... Centre International de Documentation Parlementaire [*International Center for Parliamentary Documentation*] (EAIO)

CIDP......... Confederation Internationale pour le Desarmement et la Paix [*International Confederation for Disarmament and Peace - ICDP*] [*London, England*]   (EA)
CIDPA....... Conference Internationale de Droit Prive Aerien   (FLAF)
CIDR .... Comite Infantil de Defensa de la Revolucion [*Children's Committee for Defense of the Revolution*] [*Cuba*]   (LA)
CIDR .... Compagnie Internationale de Developpement Rural [*International Rural Development Company*] [*French*]   (AF)
CIDRA...... Comercial Industrial de Automotores SA [*Colombia*]   (COL)
CIDRE....... Centro de Informacion, Documentacion, y Referencia [*Consejo Venezolano de la Industria*] [*Venezuela*]
CIDS.......... Changi International Distribution Services Pte. Ltd. [*Singapore*]
CIDSE....... Cooperation Internationale pour le Developpement et la Solidarite [*International Cooperation for Development and Solidarity*] [*Formerly, Cooperation Internationale pour le Developpement Socio-Economique*]   (EAIO)
CIDSP....... Centrul de Informare si Documentare in Stiintele Sociale si Politice [*Information and Documentation Center for the Social and Political Sciences*]   (RO)
CIDSS ...... Comite International pour la Documentation des Sciences Sociales [*International Committee for the Documentation of Social Sciences*] [*French*]   (SLS)
CIDSS ...... Comite International pour l'Information et la Documentation des Sciences Sociales   (WGAO)
CIDST .... Centre d'Information et de Documentation Scientifique et Technique [*Madagascar*]   (EAIO)
CIDST .... Comite d'Information et de Documentation Scientifique et Techniques [*EEG*] [*Belgium*]
CIDST .... Committee for Scientific and Technical Information and Documentation [*EEC*]   (WGAO)
CIDT......... Compagnie Ivoirienne pour le Developpement des Textiles
CID-TNO .. Centrum voor Technische en Wetenschappelijke Informatie en Dokumentatie-Nederlands Centrale Organisatie voor Toegepast-Natuurwetenschappelijk Onderzock [*Center for Technical and Scientific Information and Documentation-Netherlands Central Organization for Applied Natural Scientific Research*] [*Research center*]   (ERC)
CIDU .... Centro Interdisciplinario de Desarrollo Urbano y Regional (de Universidad Catolica de Chile) [*Santiago, Chile*]   (LAA)
CIDUNATI ... Comite d'Information et de Defense de l'Union Nationale des Artisans et Travailleurs Independants [*French*]
CIDV .... Compagnie Ivoirienne pour le Developpement des Cultures Vivrieres [*The Ivory Coast*]   (EY)
CIE............ Cartographie des Invertebres Europeens   (WGAO)
CIE............ Centre for International Economics [*Australia*]
CIE............ Centre International de l'Enfance [*International Children's Centre*] [*Paris, France*]   (EAIO)
CIE............ Centre International de l'Environnement [*International Center for the Environment - ICE*] [*French*]   (ASF)
CIE............ Centro de Informacao do Exercito [*Army Intelligence Center*] [*Brazil*]   (LA)
CIE............ Centro de Investigaciones Economicas [*Economic Research Center*] [*Argentina*]   (LA)
CIE............ Centro de Investigaciones Economicas. Universidad de Antioquia [*Colombia*]   (COL)
CIE............ Centro de Investigaciones Espaciales [*Space Research Center*] [*Argentina*]   (LA)
CIE............ Centro Islamico de Espana [*Islamic Center of Spain*]
CIE............ Centro Italiano dell'Edilizia [*Italy*]
CIE............ Chinese Institute of Economics
CIE............ Chinese Institute of Engineers
CIE............ Comite Interafricain de Statistiques   (WGAO)
CIE............ Comite Interamericano de Educacion   (WGAO)
CIE............ Comite International des Echanges   (WGAO)
Cie............ Commissie [*Benelux*]   (BAS)
CIE............ Commission Internationale de l'Eclairage [*International Commission on Illumination*] [*Vienna, Austria*]   (EA)
CIE............ Commonwealth Institute of Entomology   (WGAO)
Cie............ Compagnie [*Company*] [*French*]
Cie............ Compagnie [*Company*] [*German*]   (GCA)
CIE............ Compagnie Ivoirienne des Etiquettes
CIE............ Compagnie Ivoirienne d'Etudes
CIE............ Compania Industrial de Estructuras Ltda. [*Barranquilla*]   (COL)
CIE............ Confederation of Icelandic Employers   (EAIO)
CIE............ Congres International des Editeurs [*International Congress of Publishers*]
CIE............ Conseil International de l'Etain [*International Tin Council - ITC*] [*Defunct*]   (EAIO)
CIE............ Consejo Interamericano do Escultismo [*Inter-American Scout Committee - IASC*] [*San Jose, Costa Rica*]   (EAIO)
CIE............ Consejo Internacional de Enfermeras   (WGAO)
CIE............ Consejo Internacional de Estano [*International Tin Council - ITC*]   (LA)
CIE............ Consorcio de Ingenieria Electromecanica [*Electromechanical Engineering Consortium*] [*Paraguay*]   (LA)
CIE............ Culturally Inclusive Education [*Australia*]

CIEA......... Centrala Industriala de Electronica si Automatizare [*Industrial Central for Electronics and Automation*]   (RO)
CIEA......... Centre International de l'Elevage pour l'Afrique   (WGAO)
CIEA......... Centre International d'Etudes Agricoles   (WGAO)
CIEA......... Centre International pour Education Artistique [*International Centre for Art Education*]   (EAIO)
CIEA......... Centro de Investigacion y Estudios Avanzados [*Mexico*]   (MSC)
CIEA......... Commission Internationale de l'Enseignement Aeronautique et Spatial [*FAI*]   (WGAO)
CIEA......... Conseil International d'Education des Adultes   (WGAO)
CIEACH.... Centro de Investigaciones y Extension Agropecuarios de la Chontalpa [*Mexico*]   (DSCA)
CIEAS ...... Committee on International Education in Agricultural Sciences [*See also SVLB*] [*Deventer, Netherlands*]   (EAIO)
CIEB......... Centro de Informacion Economica de Bogota [*Colombia*]   (DSCA)
CIEBA ...... Compagnie Industrielle d'Exploitation des Bois Africains
CIEC......... Centre International des Engrais Chimiques   (WGAO)
CIEC......... Centre International d'Etudes Criminologiques [*International Center of Criminological Studies*] [*Paris, France*]
CIEC......... Centre International pour les Etudes Chimiques [*International Center for Chemical Studies - ICCS*]   (EAIO)
CIEC......... China International Economic Consultants, Inc. [*China*]   (IMH)
CIEC......... Comite International des Etudes Creoles   (WGAO)
CIEC......... Comite Nacional de Lucha contra el Cancer [*Colombia*]   (WGAO)
CIEC......... Commission Internationale de l'Etat Civil [*International Commission on Civil Status - ICCS*]   (EAIO)
CIEC......... Confederacion Interamericana de Educacion Catolica [*Colombia*]   (COL)
CIEC......... Conference on International Economic Cooperation   (AF)
CIEC......... Conseil International des Employeurs du Commerce [*International Council of Commerce Employers*]
CIEC......... Consejo de Iglesias Evangelicas de Cuba [*Council of Evangelical Churches of Cuba*]   (LA)
CIECA ...... Commission Internationale des Examens de Conduite Automobile [*International Driving Tests Committee*]   (EAIO)
CIECA ...... Comptoir Import-Export Casablancais
CIECA ...... Consejo de Integracion Economica Centroamericana [*Managua, Nicaragua*]   (LAA)
CIECC ...... Comite Interamericano para la Educacion, la Ciencia, y la Cultura [*Inter-American Educational, Scientific, and Cultural Committee*] [*OAS*]   (LA)
CIECC ...... Consejo Interamericano para la Educacion, la Ciencia y la Cultura   (WGAO)
CIECE ...... Centre d'Information et d'Etudes sur les Communautes Europeennes [*Belgium*]   (WGAO)
CIECH...... Centrala Importowo-Eksportowa Chemikalii i Aparatury Chemicznej [*Import-Export Center for Chemicals and Chemical Equipment*]   (POL)
CIECMM ... Comision Internacional para la Exploracion Cientifica del Mar Mediterraneo
CIED.......... Centre International d'Echanges de Dakar
CIED.......... Compagnie Industrielle des Entrepots de Dakar
CIEDART ... Centro Internazionale per l'Educazione Artistica della Fondazione Giorgio Cini [*Italian*]   (SLS)
CIEDLA .... Centro Interdisciplinario de Estudios sobre el Desarrollo Latinoamericano [*Argentina*]   (WGAO)
CIEDOP.... Centre Interdisciplinaire d'Etudes et de Documentation Politiques [*Zaire*]   (SLS)
CIEDUR.... Centro Interdisciplinario de Estudios del Desarrollo, Uruguay [*Interdisciplinar y Center for Development Studies, Uruguay*]   (IRC)
CIEDUR.... Centro Interdisciplinario de Estudios sobre el Desarrollo Ururgay   (WGAO)
CIEE......... Centro de Informacion sobre Envase y Embalaje [*Instituto Mexicano de Asistencia a la Industria, Secretaria de Patrimonio y Fomento Industrial*] [*Mexico*]
CIEE......... Consejo Internacional de Preparcion para la Ensenanza   (WGAO)
CIEE......... Council on International Educational Exchange
CIEEPP.... Comite Illusionniste d'Expertise et d'Experimentation des Phenomenes Paranormaux [*France*]   (EAIO)
CIEES...... Centre Interarmees d'Essais d'Engins Speciaux (de Colomb-Bechar) [*Inter-Service Center for Testing Special Devices (At Colomb-Bechar)*] [*French*]   (WER)
CIEET ...... Centrala Industriala a Energiei Electrice si Termice [*Industrial Central for Thermal and Electric Power*]   (RO)
CIEF .... Centro de Investigaciones y Estudios Familiares [*Family Research and Study Center*] [*Uruguay*]   (LA)
CIEF .... Centro Interamericano de Ensenanza de Estadistica Economica y Financiera [*Centro Interamericano de Ensenanza de Estadistica*] [*Santiago, Chile*] [*Later,*]   (LAA)
CIEF .... Comite International d'Enregistrement des Frequences   (WGAO)
CIEF .... Commission Importation Exportation Francaise
CIEFC ...... China Imported Equipment Fittings Co.

CIEFL........ Central Institute of English and Foreign Language [*India*]
CIEFR....... Centre International d'Etudes de la Formation Religieuse (WGAO)
CIEH......... Comite Interafricain d'Etudes Hydrauliques [*Inter-African Committee for Hydraulic Studies - ICHS*] [*Ouagadougou, Burkina Faso*] (EAIO)
CIEHV....... Conseil International pour l'Education des Handicapes de la Vue [*International Council for Education of the Visually Handicapped - ICEVH*] (EAIO)
CIEI.......... Centro de Investigaciones en Economia Internacional [*Center for Research in International Economics*] [*Cuba*] (LA)
CIEI.......... Comision Investigadora Contra el Enriquecimiento Ilicito de Funcionarios y Empleados Publicos [*Committee Investigating the Illegal Use of Public Funds by Public Officials and Employees*] [*Venezuela*] (LA)
CIEIA........ Centro Internazionale per degli Studi sull'Irrigazione (WGAO)
CIEIA........ Centro Internazionale per gli Studi sull'Irrigazione [*Italy*] (DSCA)
CIEL......... Centre International d'Etudes du Lindane [*International Research Centre on Lindane - IRCL*] (EAIO)
CIEL......... Centre International d'Etudes Latines [*French*] (SLS)
CIEL......... Centre International d'Etudes Loisir (WGAO)
CIEL......... Commercial Importadora Exportadora [*Canary Islands*] (WGAO)
CIEL......... Computerized Industrial Environmental Legislation [*UNEP*] [*United Nations*] (DUND)
CIEL......... Constructions Installations Electriques du Littoral
CIEL......... Construtora e Incorporadora Eldorado
CIELDA.... Construcciones y Estudios Electricos Ltda. [*Colombia*] (COL)
CIEM........ Center for Information and Immigration Studies [*Mexico*] (CROSS)
CIEM........ Centre de Recherches et de Production pour l'Information et l'Education des Masses
CIEM........ Comision Intergremial de Educadores de Montevideo [*Interunion Commission of Montevideo Educators*] [*Uruguay*] (LA)
CIEM........ Commission Internationale pour l'Enseignement des Mathematiques [*International Commission on Mathematical Instruction - ICMI*] (EA)
CIEM........ Compagnie Ivoirienne d'Elevage Marin
CIEM........ Confederation Internationale des Editeurs de Musique (WGAO)
CIEM........ Conseil International d'Education Mesologique des Pays de Langue Francaise (WGAO)
CIEM........ Conseil International pour l'Exploration de la Mer [*International Council for the Exploration of the Sea - ICES*] [*French*] (ASF)
CIEM........ Consejo Internacional para la Exploracion del Mar [*International Council for the Exploration of the Sea - ICES*] [*Spanish*] (ASF)
CIEMA...... Centre International des Etudes de la Musique Ancienne
CIEMA...... Comptoir d'Importation et d'Exportation de Materiel Automobile
CIEMA...... Constructions Industrielle Electro Mecanique d'Algerie
CIEMAT... Centro de Investigaciones Energeticas, Medioambientales, y Tecnologicas [*Spain*] (EY)
CIEMEN... Centre Internacional Escarre per a les Minories Etniques i Nacionalitats (EAIO)
CIEN........ Centro de Investigaciones Economicas Nacionales [*Center for Research in National Economics*] [*Guatemala*] [*Research center*] (IRC)
CIEN........ Comisao Interamericano de Energia Nuclear (WGAO)
CIEN........ Comision Interamericana de Energia Nuclear [*Inter-American Nuclear Energy Commission*] [*Use IANEC*] [*Spanish*] (LA)
CIEN........ Commissione Italiana per l'Europa Nucleare [*Italian Committee for Nuclear Europe*] (WER)
CIEN........ Commission Interamericaine d'Energie Nucleaire [*Inter-American Nuclear Energy Commission - IANEC*] [*French*] (ASF)
CIENER.... Centro de Investigacion Economica de la Energia [*Energy Economics Research Center*] [*Research center*] [*Spanish*] (IRC)
CIENES.... Centro Interamericano de Ensenanza Estadistica [*Inter-American Statistical Training Institute*] (LA)
CIENTAL... Centro de Investigaciones y Estudios Internacionales para la America Latina [*Ecuador*] (WGAO)
CIEO......... Catholic International Education Office [*Belgium*]
CIEP......... Centre International d'Etudes Pedagogiques [*French*] (SLS)
CIEP......... Centro de Investigacion y Experimentacion Pedagogica [*Uruguay*] (WGAO)
CIEP......... Commission Internationale de l'Enseignement de la Physique [*International Commission on Physics Education - ICPE*] (EAIO)
CIEP......... Consorcio dos Industriais de Equipaduento Pesado (WGAO)
CIEP......... Corporacion Instituto de Educacion Popular [*Santiago, Chile*] (LAA)
CIEP......... Council of International Economic Policy (EG)

CIEPA....... Centro de Investigacion Economica para la Accion [*Center for Action-Oriented Economic Research*] [*Peru*] (LA)
CIEPAT..... Centre Inter-Etats de Promotion de l'Artisanat d'Art et de Tourisme Culturels [*Benin*] (WGAO)
CIEPC....... Commission Internationale d'Etudes de la Police de Circulation (WGAO)
CIEPE....... Fundacion Centro de Investigaciones del Estado para la Produccion Experimental Agroindustrial [*Venezuela*]
CIEPI........ Comite Interprofessionnel Europeen des Professions Intellectuelles [*French*] (SLS)
CIEPLAN ... Corporacion de Investigaciones Economicas para Latinoamerica [*Latin American Economic Research Corporation*] [*Chile*] [*Research center*] (IRC)
CIEPP........ Comite Illusionniste d'Expertise des Phenomenes Paranormaux [*International PSI Committee of Magicians - IPSICM*] (EAIO)
CIEPRC..... Confederation Internationale des Institus Catholiques d'Education des Adultes Ruraux (WGAO)
CIEPS........ Centre International pour l'Enregistrement des Publications en Serie
CIEPS........ Conseil Intergouvernemental pour l'Education Physique et le Sport (WGAO)
CIEPSA..... Compania de Investigacion and Exploraciones Petroliferas SA
CIEPSS..... Conseil International pour l'Education Physique et la Science du Sport [*International Council of Sport Science and Physical Education - ICSSPE*] (EAIO)
CIEQE....... Comite International pour l'Etude des Questions Europeennes (WGAO)
CIER......... Centre International d'Etudes Romanes [*French*] (SLS)
CIER......... Centre Internationale d'Etudes Recherches [*Belgium*] (WGAO)
CIER......... Centro Interamericano de Educacion Rural [*Inter-American Center of Rural Education*] (LAA)
CIER......... Comision de Integracion Electrica Regional [*Commission of Regional Electrical Integration*] (EAIO)
CIER......... Commission for International Educational Reconstruction (WGAO)
CIER......... Conseil International des Economies Regionales [*International Council for Local Development*] (EAIO)
CIERA...... Center for International Education and Research in Accounting [*University of Illinois, Urbana-Champaign*] [*Research center*] (RCD)
CIERA...... Centro de Investigacion y Estudio de Reforma Agraria [*Nicaragua*]
CIERA...... Club Ivoirienne d'Etudes et de Recherche Appliquee
CIERA...... Compagnie Ivoirienne d'Etudes et de Realisations en Informatique et Automatisme (WGAO)
CIERE....... Centre International d'Etudes et de Recherches Europeennes (WGAO)
CIERE....... Centre International d'Etudes et de Recherches sur l'Europe [*Luxembourg*] (BAS)
CIERIE...... Compagnie Ivoirienne d'Etudes et de Realisations Informatiques et Economiques
CIERO....... Centre Interafricain d'Etudes en Radio Rurale [*Inter-African Rural Radio Studies Center*] (AF)
CIERP....... Centre Intersyndical d'Etudes et de Recherches de Productivite
CIERRO.... Centre Interafrican d'Etudes en Radio Rural de Ouagadougou [*Burkina Faso*] (WGAO)
CIERSES.. Centre International d'Etudes et de Recherches en Socio-Economie de la Sante [*International Health Centre of Socioeconomics, Researches and Studies - IHCSERS*] [*Lailly En Val, France*] (EAIO)
CIES......... Centre d'Information Economique et Sociale des Nations Unies (WGAO)
CIES......... Centre International d'Enseignement de la Statistique (WGAO)
CIES......... Comitato Italiano per l'Educazione Sanitaria [*Italian*] (SLS)
CIES......... Comite International des Entreprises a Succursales (WGAO)
CIES......... Comite Inter-Unions de l'Enseignement des Sciences (WGAO)
CIES......... Commission Internationale des Etudes Slaves (WGAO)
CIES......... Conseil Interamericain Economique et Social (FLAF)
CIES......... Consejo Interamericano Economico y Social [*Inter-American Economic and Social Council*] [*Use IA-ESOSOC*] (LA)
CIES......... International Center for Companies of the Food Trade and Industry [*Formerly, International Association of Chain Stores*] (EAIO)
CIESC........ Chemical Industry and Engineering Society of China
CIESC........ Inter-American Council of Education, Science, and Culture [*Organization of American States*] (ASF)
CIESCO...... China Communications Import and Export Service Co. (TCC)
CIESE........ Centro de Investigaciones y Estudios Socioeconomicos [*Ecuador*] (WGAO)
CIESEF..... Centre Interamericaine d'Enseignement de Statistique Economique et Financiere (WGAO)
CIESIN...... Consortium for International Earth Science Information Network [*Information service or system*] (IID)
CIESJ........ Centre International d'Enseignement Superieur de Journalisme [*UNESCO*] (NTCM)

CIESJ .... Centre International d' Enseignement Superieur de Journalisme (WGAO)
CIESM ...... Commission Internationale d'Exploration Sous-Marine dans la Mer Mediterranee
CIESM ...... Commission Internationale pour l'Exploration Scientifique de la Mer Mediterranee [*International Commission for the Scientific Exploration of the Mediterranean Sea - ICSEM*] [*Monaco*] [*Research center*] (IRC)
CIESMM .. Commission Internationale d'Exploration Sous-Marine dans la Mer Mediterranee
CIESP .... Centro das Industrias do Estado de Sao Paulo [*Sao Paulo State Industry Center*] [*Brazil*] (LA)
CIESPAL .. Centro Internacional de Estudios Superiores de Periodismo de America Latina [*International Center of Higher Journalism Studies for Latin America*] (LA)
CIESS .... Centre Interamericain d'Etudes de la Securite Sociale (WGAO)
CIESS .... Centro Interamericano de Estudios de Seguridad Social [*Inter-American Center of Social Security Studies*] (LA)
CIEST .... Centre International des Etudes Superieures de Tourisme [*International Center of Advanced Tourism Studies*] [*Use ICATS*] (CL)
CIESTPM ... College International pour l'Etude Scientifique des Techniques de Production Mecanique [*International Institute for Production Engineering Research*] (EAIO)
CIESU .... Centro de Informaciones y Estudios del Uruguay (WGAO)
CIET .... Campaign for an Independent East Timor [*Australia*] (ADA)
CIET .... Centre d'Instruction et d'Etudes Techniques [*Technical Studies and Instruction Center*] [*French*] (CL)
CIET .... Centro Interamericano de Estudios Tributarios [*Buenos Aires, Argentina*] (LAA)
CIET .... Chinese Institute of Engineers of Taiwan (MCD)
CIETA ...... Calcutta Import and Export Trade Association [*India*] (WGAO)
CIETA ...... Centrala Industriala de Echipamente de Telecomunicatii si Automatizari [*Industrial Central for Telecommunications and Automation Equipment*] (RO)
CIETA ...... Centre International d'Etude des Textiles Anciens [*International Center for the Study of Ancient Textiles*] [*France*] (SLS)
CIETA ...... Centre International d'Etudes des Textiles Anciens [*International Center for the Study of Ancient Textiles*] [*Lyon, France*] (SLS)
CIETAP ..... Comite Interprofessionnel d'Etudes des Techniques Agricoles et Pesticides (WGAO)
CIETB .... Centre Intercontinental d'Etudes de Techniques Biologiques [*Intercontinental Center of Biological Research*] [*French*] (ASF)
CIETC .... Centrala Industriala de Electronica si Tehnica de Calcul [*Industrial Central for Electronics and Computer Technology*] (RO)
CIETT .... Confederation Internationale des Entreprises de Travail Temporaire (WGAO)
CIEU .... Centre Interdisciplinaire d'Etudes Urbaines [*Interdisciplinary Center for Urban Studies*] [*France*] (IRC)
CIEU .... Centro de Investigaciones Economicas [*Chile*] (WGAO)
CIEUA .... Congres International de l'Enseignement Universitaire pour Adultes (WGAO)
CIEUC .... Centro de Investigaciones Economicas (de la Universidad Catolica) [*Santiago, Chile*] (LAA)
CIEx .... Centro de Informacoes do Exercito [*Army Intelligence Center*] [*Brazil*] (LA)
ciez .... Ciezar [*Weight*] [*Poland*]
CIF .... Camara de la Industria Frigorifica [*Chamber of the Meatpacking Industry*] [*Uruguay*] (LA)
CIF .... Cameroon Industrial Forest
CIF .... Centre Inter-Enterprises de Formation et d'Etudes Superieures Industrielles
CIF .... Centro de Integracion Familiar [*Family Integration Center*] [*Guatemala*] (EAIO)
CIF .... Centro de Investigacion Forestal [*Forestry Research Center*] [*Cuba*] (ARC)
CIF .... Centro Europeo di Informatica Giuridico-Fiscale SRL [*Italian*] (SLS)
CIF .... Chemical Industry Federation [*Finland*]
CIF .... Chifeng [*China*] [*Airport symbol*] (OAG)
CIF .... Children in Families Project [*Australia*]
Cif .... Ciftlik [*Farm, Ranch*] (TU)
CIF .... Commission Interamericaine des Femmes (WGAO)
CIF .... Committee on Industry and Finance [*NEDC*] (WGAO)
CIF .... Compagnia Italiana della Frutta [*Italy*] (DSCA)
CIF .... Companhia Itau de Fertilizantes [*Brazil*] (DSCA)
CIF .... Comptoir d'Importations Francaises [*Morocco*]
CIF .... Confederation Internationale de Fonctionnaires (WGAO)
CIF .... Conseil International des Femmes [*International Council of Women - ICW*] [*Paris, France*] (EA)
CIF .... Cork Industry Federation (WGAO)
cif .... Cost, Insurance and Freight (EECI)
CIF40 .... Conseil International Formule 40 [*International F-40 Council*] [*Paris, France*] (EAIO)
CIFA .... Camara de Importadores de Frutas Afines [*Argentina*] (DSCA)

CIFA .... Comite International de Recherche et d'Etude de Facteurs de l'Ambiance [*Belgium*] (SLS)
CIFA .... Committee for Inland Fisheries of Africa
CIFA .... Companhia Industrial de Fibras Artificiais [*Industrial Company of Artificial Fibers*] [*Portuguese*] (WER)
CIFA .... Consociazione Italiani Federazioni Autotrasporti (WGAO)
CIFA .... Corporation of Insurance and Financial Advisers (WGAO)
CIFAC .... Confederation Internationale des Fabriques Artistiques et Creatives (WGAO)
CIFAO .... Compagnie Industrielle et Financiere d'Entreprises (WGAO)
CIFARA .... Camara de Industriales Fabricantes de Repuestos Automotrices [*Chamber of Auto Parts Manufacturers*] [*Argentina*] (LA)
CIFAS .... Centre d'Instruction des Forces Aeriennes Strategiques [*Strategic Air Forces Instruction Centre*] [*France*]
CIFAS .... Franco-German Consortium for Symphonie Satellite (WER)
CIFAVE ..... Camara de la Industria Farmaceutica [*Chamber of Pharmaceutical Industry*] [*Venezuela*] (LA)
CIFC .... Centre for Interfirm Comparisons (WGAO)
CIFC .... Centro de Investigacao das Ferrugens do Cafeeiro [*Center for the Study of Coffee Rusts*] [*Research center*] [*Portuguese*] (IRC)
CIFC .... China International Forestry Corp. (TCC)
CIFC .... Consolidated Investment and Finance Corp. Proprietary Ltd. [*Australia*]
CIFC .... Council for the Investigation of Fertility Control (WGAO)
CIFCA .... Centro Internacional de Formacion en Ciencias Ambientales para Paises de Habla Espanol [*International Center for the Preparation of Personnel in Environmental Sciences in Spanish-Speaking Countries*] [*Spain*]
CIFDA .... Canberra International Folk Dancing Association [*Australia*]
CIFE .... Central Institute of Fisheries Education [*India*] (ASF)
CIFE .... Centre International de Formation Europeenne [*France*]
CIFE .... Centro Italiano di Formazioine Europea (WGAO)
CIFE .... Comision Interministerial de Fomento Economico [*Peru*] (WGAO)
CIFE .... Compagnie Industrielle et Financiere d'Entreprises
CIFE .... Conference for Independent Further Education (WGAO)
CIFE .... Conseil des Federations Industrielles d'Europe (FLAF)
CIFEG .... Centre International pour la Formation et les Echanges Geologiques [*International Center for Training and Exchanges in the Geosciences*] (EAIO)
CIFEI .... Compagnia Italiana Forniture Elettro Industrialia (WGAO)
CIFEJ .... Centre International du Film pour l'Enfance et la Jeunesse [*French*] (SLS)
CIFEL .... Companhia Industrial de Fundicao e Laminagem [*Mozambique*]
CIFEN .... Compagnie Internationale pour le Financement de l'Energie Nucleaire (WGAO)
CIFEN .... Compania Industrial Financiera Empresa Nacional [*National Industrial Financial Company Enterprise*] [*Argentina*] (LA)
CIFES .... Comite International du Film Ethnographique et Sociologique (WGAO)
CIFF .... Centro Incremento Frutticoltura Ferraresa (WGAO)
CIFFCH .... Centrala Industriala de Fire si Fibre Chemice Savinesti [*Industrial Central for Chemical Yarns and Fibers in Savinesti*] (RO)
CIFH .... Comite International des Films de l'Homme [*French*] (SLS)
CIFHV .... Centro de Investigacion en Fruticultura, Horticultura, y Viticultura [*Uruguay*] (DSCA)
CIFI .... Centres Interentreprises de Formation Industrielle
CIFi .... Collegio degli Ingegneri Ferroviari Italiani [*Italian*] (SLS)
CIFI .... Collegio Ingegneri Ferroviari Italiani (WGAO)
CIFI .... Consorzio Industriali Fontomeccanici Italiani (WGAO)
CIFIM .... Compagnie Ivoirienne de Financement de l'Immobilier
CIFNET .... Central Institute of Fisheries Nautical and Engineering Training [*India*] (ASF)
CIFOOT .... Cameroon International Football
CIFOR .... Center for International Forestry Research
CIFOS .... Compagnie Immobiliere et Fonciere du Senegal (WGAO)
CIFP .... Comite International pour le Fair Play [*International Fair Play Committee*] [*Paris, France*] (EAIO)
CIFPSE ..... Catholic International Federation for Physical and Sports Education [*See also FICEP*] [*Paris, France*] (EAIO)
CIFREDH ... Centre de Formation et de Recyclage des Enseignants des Droits de l'Homme [*France*]
CIFRES ..... Centre International de Formation, de Recherches et d'Etudes Sericicoles [*France*] (WGAO)
CIFRI .... Central Inland Fisheries Research Institute [*India*] [*Research center*] (IRC)
CIFRS .... Common Market Group of International Rayon and Synthetic Fibres Committee (EAIO)
CIFT .... Central Institute of Fisheries Technology [*India*] (ASF)
CIFT .... Centro Internazionale di Fisica Teorica [*International Center for Theoretical Physics - ICTP*] (EAIO)
CIFT .... Committee on Invisibles and Financing Related to Trade [*UNCTAD*] (WGAO)

CIFTA .... Comite Internatioal des Federations Theatrales d'Amateurs de Langue Francaise (WGAO)

CIG .... Cataloguing and Indexing Group (WGAO)

CIG .... Centre d'Information Generale [*General Information Center*]

CIG .... College d'Informatique et de Gestion [*French*] (ADPT)

CIG .... Comite Intergouvernemental Nations (WGAO)

CIG .... Comite Internacional de Geofisica [*International Geophysical Committee - IGC*] [*Spanish*] (ASF)

CIG .... Comite International de Geophysique [*International Geophysical Committee - IGC*] [*French*] (ASF)

CIG .... Commonwealth Industrial Gases [*Australia*] (ADA)

CIG .... Computer-Informationsdienst Graz [*Graz Computer-Information Service*] [*Austria*] (IID)

CIG .... Conference Internationale du Goudron [*International Tar Conference - ITC*] (EAIO)

CIG .... Construction Industry Information Group (WGAO)

CIG .... Credit Immobilier du Gabon [*Gabon Real Estate Credit Bank*] (AF)

CIG .... Curriculum Interest Group [*Australia*]

CIG .... International Helicopter Committee [*FAI*] (WGAO)

CIGA .... Centro de Investigacion de Grasas y Aceites (LAA)

CIGA .... Compagnia Italiana del Grandi Alberghi [*Italian hotel chain*]

CIGAS .... Cambridge Intercollegiate Graduate Application Scheme (WGAO)

CIGB .... Commission Internationale des Grands Barrages [*International Commission on Large Dams - ICOLD*] (EAIO)

CIGC .... Comite Imergouvernemental de Coordination pour la Planification del la Population et du Developpement en Asie du Sud-Est (WGAO)

CIGC .... Comite Interprofessionnel du Gruyere du Comte (WGAO)

CIGDL .... Chmabre Immobiliere du Grand-Duche de Luxembourg (WGAO)

CIGE .... Centre Ivoirien de Gestion des Entreprises [*Ministere de l'Enseignement Technique et de la Formation Professionnelle Association Interprofessionnelle des Employeurs de la Cote-D'Ivoire*] [*Ivory Coast*]

CIGE .... Centro de Instrucao de Guerra Electronica [*Electronic Warfare Training Center*] [*Brazilian Army*] (PDAA)

CIGEB ...... Compagnie Ivoirienne de Gestion d'Enterprise de Boulangerie (WGAO)

CIGEL .... Compagnie Ivoirienne de Gestion et d'Etudes de Logements (WGAO)

CIGGA ...... Cigarette [*Australian slang*] (DSUE)

CIGH .... Confederation Internationale de Genealogie et d'Heraldique [*International Confederation of Genealogy and Heraldry - ICGH*] [*Paris, France*] (EAIO)

CIGI .... Comitato Italiano Gioco Infantile [*Italian Committee for Child Development*] (EAIO)

CIGM .... Centrala Industriala de Gaz Metan [*Industrial Central for Methane Gas*] (RO)

CIGMA ..... Comitato Italiano per la Giornata Mondiale dell'Alimentazione

CIGMA ..... Compagnie Internationale des Grands Magasins (WGAO)

CIGP .... Conference Internationale sur la Guerre Politique (WGAO)

CIGR .... Chilean Institute of Genealogical Research (EAIO)

CIGR .... Commission Internationale du Genie Rural [*International Commission of Agricultural Engineering*] [*ICSU*] (EAIO)

CIGRE .... Conference Internationale des Grands Reseaux Electriques a Haute Tension [*International Conference on Large High Voltage Electric Systems*] (EAIO)

CIGS .... Centre International de Gerontologie Sociale [*International Center of Social Gerontology - ICSG*] [*Paris, France*] [*Defunct*]

CIGS .... Curso Intensivo de Guerrilla nas Selvas [*Intensive Guerrilla Jungle Training Course*] [*Brazil*] (LA)

CIGTRG .... Centre d'Instruction du Groupement de Transport de Reserves Generales [*Algeria*]

CIH .... Changzhi [*China*] [*Airport symbol*] (OAG)

CIH .... Comite Professionnel Interregional de l'Horlogerie (WGAO)

CIH .... Commonwealth Institute of Helminthology (WGAO)

CIH .... Credit Immobilier et Hotelier [*Morocco*]

CIHA .... Comite International d'Histoire de l'Art (EAIO)

CIHAN ...... Central Institut ter Bevordering v.d. Buitenlandse Handel (WGAO)

CIHE .... Council for Industry and Higher Education (WGAO)

CIHEAM .. Centre International des Hautes Etudes Agronomiques Mediterraneennes [*International Center for Advanced Mediterranean Agronomic Studies*] [*Paris, France*] [*Research center*]

CIHEC .... Commission Internationale d'Histoire Ecclesiastique Comparee (WGAO)

CIHGLF .... Comite International d'Historiens et Geographes de Langue Francaise [*International Committee of French-Speaking Historians and Geographers - ICFHG*] (EAIO)

CIHL .... Comision Internacional de Historiadores Latinoamericanistas y del Caribe (WGAO)

CIHM .... Commission Internationale d'Histoire Militaire [*International Commission of Military History*] (EAIO)

CIHM .... Commission Internationale d'Historie Maritime (WGAO)

CIHV .... Centre International Humanae Vitae [*International Centre Humanae Vitae*] [*Paris, France*] (EAIO)

CII .... Centro de Informacion Industrial [*Departamento de Tecnologia*] [*Universidad Nacional Autonoma de Honduras Honduras*]

CII .... Centro de Investigaciones de Ingenieria [*Engineering Research Centre*] [*Universidad de San Carlos Guatemala*]

CII .... Centro Internacional de la Infancia (WGAO)

CII .... Compagnie Internationale pour l'Informatique [*French*]

CII .... Confederation of Indian Industry (EY)

CII .... Confederation of Irish Industry (WGAO)

CII .... Conseil International des Infirmieres [*International Council of Nurses - ICN*] [*Geneva, Switzerland*] (EA)

CII .... Construction Industry Institute [*Australia*]

CII .... Cook Islands International [*New Zealand*] [*ICAO designator*] (FAAC)

CIIA .... Centro de Investigacion de Ingenieria Ambiental [*Argentina*] (LAA)

CIIA .... Comision Internacional de las Industrias Agricolas y Alimentarias [*International Commission for Food Industries*] [*Research center*] [*Spanish*] (ASF)

CIIA .... Commission Internationale des Industries Agricoles et Alimentaires [*International Commission for Food Industries*] (EAIO)

CIIA .... Cook Islands International Airline (EY)

CIIA .... Council of Independent Inspecting Authorities (WGAO)

CIIB .... Cooerdinatiecommissie Internationale Informatie-Betrekkingen [*Netherlands*]

CIIC .... Centre d'Information de l'Industrie des Chaux et Ciments (WGAO)

CIIC .... Centro Internacional de Investigaciones sobre el Cancer (WGAO)

CIID .... Centro Internacional de Investigaciones para el Desarrollo [*International Development Research Center - IDRC*] [*Spanish*]

CIID .... Commission Internationale des Irrigations et du Drainage [*International Commission on Irrigation and Drainage - ICID*] (EAIO)

CIIDS .... Childhood Immunisation and Infectious Diseases Survey [*Australia*]

CIIE .... Centre International de l'Industrie et pour l'Environnement (WGAO)

CIIG .... Centro Internazionale per l'Iniziativa Giuridica [*Italian*] (SLS)

CIIHB .... Compagnie Internationale pour l'Informatique Honeywell-Bull [*Computer manufacturer*] [*France*]

CIIM .... Centre for Intelligent Information Management [*Charles Sturt University-Riverina*] [*Australia*]

CIIM .... Centro de Investigacion para las Industrias Minerales [*Research Center for the Mineral Industries*] [*INTI*] [*Research center*] [*Argentina*] (IRC)

CIIM .... Cyprus International Institute of Management (ECON)

CIIMP .... Centro Internazionale di Ipnosi Medica e Psicologica [*International Center for Medical and Psychological Hypnosis*] [*Italy*] (IRC)

CIINTE ..... Centralny Institut Informacji Naukow-Technicznei i Ekonomiczney [*Central Institute for Scientific, Technical and Economic Information*] [*Poland*] (PDAA)

CI-INTEC ... Centro de Informacion y Documentacion - Instituto de Investigaciones Tecnologicas [*Chile*]

CIIP .... Centro de Informacion de la Industria Petrolera [*Colombia*] (COL)

CIIP .... Commissione Italiana Iustitia et Pax [*Italian Justice and Peace Commission*] (EAIO)

CIIR .... Catholic Institute for International Relations [*British*] (EAIO)

CIIS .... Central Industrial Information Services [*Cement Research Institute of India*]

CIIS .... Comitato Interministeriale per le Informazioni e la Sicurezza [*Interministerial Committee on Intelligence and Security*] [*Italian*] (WER)

CIIS .... Community Interpreter, and Information Service [*Ethnic Affairs Commission*] [*New South Wales, Australia*]

CIIS .... Conferenza Italiana degli Istituti Secolari (WGAO)

CIIT .... Centre of Innovation and International Trade [*University of Western Sydney, Macarthur*] [*Australia*]

CIITC .... Confederation Internationale des Industries Techniques du Cinema (WGAO)

CIJ .... Cobija [*Bolivia*] [*Airport symbol*] (OAG)

CIJ .... Commissao Interamericana Juridica (de la OEA) [*Organizacion de Estados Americanos*] (LAA)

CIJ .... Commission Internationale de Juristes [*International Commission of Jurists - ICJ*] [*Switzerland*]

CIJ .... Corte Internacional de Justicia [*International Court of Justice*] [*Spanish United Nations*] (DUND)

CIJ .... Cour Internationale de Justice [*International Court of Justice*] [*North African*]

CIJ .... Curtea Internationala de Justitie [*International Court of Justice*] [*RO*]

CIJA .... Centro para la Independencia de Jueces y Abogados [*Switzerland*]

CIJF........... Commission de l'Industrie des Jus de Fruits et de Legumes de la CEE (WGAO)

CIJL........... Centre for the Independence of Judges and Lawyers [*See also CIMA*] [*Geneva, Switzerland*]

CIJM .... Comite International des Jeux Mediterraneens [*Athens, Greece*] (EAIO)

CIJM .... Comite Internationale des Jeux Mediterraneens [*North African*]

CIJM .... Comite Internatonal des Jeux Mediterraneens (OLYM)

CIJN .... Club International des Jeunes Naturistes [*Paris, France*] (EAIO)

CIJP........... Carte d'Identite des Journalistes Professionnels [*France*] (FLAF)

CIJRec....... Cour Internationale de Justice, Recueil des Arrets, Avis Consultatifs et Ordonnances [*Benelux*] (BAS)

CIJS........... Copenhagen International Junior School

CIK .... Centralny Instytut Kultury [*Central Institute of Culture*] (POL)

CIK .... Cestovna Informacna Kancelaria [*Travel Information Bureau*] (CZ)

CIL............ Centro de Investigaciones Literarias [*Center of Literary Studies*] [*Cuba*] (LA)

CIL............ Centro de la Industria Lechera [*Argentina*] (DSCA)

CIL............ Chief Inspectorate of Electronics [*Ministry of Defense*] [*India*] (PDAA)

CIL............ Coal India Ltd.

CIL............ Combinatul de Industrializare a Lemnului [*Combine for the Industrialization of Wood*] (RO)

CIL............ Comites Interprofessionnels de Logement [*France*] (FLAF)

CIL............ Compagnie Ivoirienne Lamoulere

CIL............ Computers in Libraries [*Australia*]

CIL............ Confederation Nationale du Secteur Immobilier et du Logement [*Belgium*] (WGAO)

CIL............ Confederazione Italiana dei Lavoratori [*Italian Confederation of Workers*]

CIL............ Consortium Investments Limited [*Australia*]

CILA......... Centro Interamericano de Libros Academicos [*Inter-American Scholarly Book Center*] [*Mexico*] (LAA)

CILA......... Chartered Institute of Loss Adjustors (WGAO)

CILA......... Companhia Industrial de Lacticinios do Ceara [*Brazil*] (DSCA)

CILA......... Companhia Industrializadora do Leite de Alagoas [*Brazil*] (DSCA)

CILA......... Consortium International des Librairies d'Afrique

CILACC .... Comite International de Lutte et d'Action contre le Communisme (WGAO)

CILAD....... Colegio Ibero-Latino-Americano de Dermatologia [*Ibero Latin American College of Dermatology - ILACD*] (EA)

CILAF .... Comite International de Liaison des Associations Feminines [*International Liaison Committee of Women's Organizations*] [*French*]

CILAM...... Compagnie Ivoirienne de Location Automobile et de Materiel

CILAS .... Centro de Investigacion Laboral y Asesoria Sindical [*Member of RMALC*] [*Mexico*] (CROSS)

CILAS .... Compagnie Industrielle des Lasers

CILAS .... Consejo Internacional para la Investigacion en Agrosilvcultura [*Kenya*] (WGAO)

CILB .... Comite Interprofessional du Lait de Brebis (WGAO)

CILB .... Commission Internationale de Lutte Biologique Contre les Ennemis des Cultures [*ICSU*]

CILC .... Confederation Internationale du Lin et du Chanvre [*International Linen and Hemp Confederation*] (EAIO)

CILEA ...... Consorzio Interuniversitario Lombardo per l'Elaborazione Automatica [*Lombard Interuniversity Consortium for Data Processing*] [*Information service or system*] (IID)

CILECT..... Centre International de Liaison des Ecoles de Cinema et de Television [*International Liaison Centre for Film and Television Schools*] (EAIO)

CILEDCO ... Cooperativa Industrial Lechera de Colombia Ltda. [*Barranquilla*] (COL)

CILEH....... Centro de Investigaciones Literarias Espanolas y Hispanoamericanas (WGAO)

CILES........ Central Information, Library, and Editorial Section [*CSIRO*] [*Information service or system*] [*Australia*] (IID)

CILF .... Conseil International de la Langue Francaise [*International Council of the French Language - ICFL*] (EAIO)

CILG......... CIRIA Information Liaison Group (WGAO)

CILICE...... Centro Interbancario Latinoamericano de Information sobre Comercio Exterior [*Colombia*] (WGAO)

CILIP........ Civil Liberties and Police [*Germany*]

CILO......... Centraal Instituut voor Landbouwkundig Onderzoek (WGAO)

CILO......... Comites de Industrias Locales [*Local Industry Committees*] [*Cuba*] (LA)

CILO......... Coeordinatiegroep Informatiesystemen Lopend Onderzoek [*Netherlands*]

CILOG....... Cooperative Investigations of a Large Ocean Gyre [*Proposed*] (MSC)

CILOMI .... Compagnie Internationale pour la Location de Materiel Informatique [*French*] (ADPT)

CILOP....... Conversion-in-Lieu-of-Production Pirating

CILP .... Centrale de l'Industrie du Livre et Papier [*Book and Paper Trades Workers' Group*] [*Belgium*] (EAIO)

CILPE........ Companhia de Industrializacao do Leite de Pernambuco [*Brazil*] (DSCA)

CILRECO ... Comite International de Liaison pour la Reunification et la Paix en Coree [*International Liaison Committee for Reunification and Peace in Korea*] (EAIO)

CILS .... Comite d'Information sur la Lutte Solidarite [*Portugal*]

CILSIG...... Computers in Libraries Special Interest Group [*Australia*]

CILSS........ Comite Permanent Interetats de Lutte Contre la Secheresse dans le Sahel [*Permanent Interstate Committee for Drought Control in the Sahel*] (EAIO)

CILT .... Centre for Information on Language Teaching (WGAO)

CIM .... Carte Internationale du Monde (WGAO)

CIM .... Centrala Industriei Matasii [*Silk Industry Central*] (RO)

CIM .... Centre d'Instruction Militaire [*Military Training Center*] [*French*] (WER)

CIM .... Centro de Industriales de la Madera [*Uruguay*] (DSCA)

CIM .... Centro de Informacion Metalurgica [*Asesoria Tecnica Industrial*] [*Mexico*]

CIM .... Centro de Instruccion de la Marina [*Naval Training Center*] [*Uruguay*] (LA)

CIM .... Centro Internacional del Medio Ambiente [*International Center for the Environment - ICE*] [*Spanish*] (ASF)

CIM .... Chief Industrial Magistrate [*Australia*]

CIM .... China Inland Mission

CIM .... Cimitarra [*Colombia*] [*Airport symbol*] (OAG)

CIM .... Coetus Internationalis Ministrantium (WGAO)

CIM .... Comision Interamericana de Mujeres [*Inter-American Women's Commission*] (LA)

CIM .... Comite Intergouvernemental pour les Migrations [*Switzerland*] (WGAO)

CIM .... Comite Intergubernamental para las Migraciones [*Intergovernmental Committee for Migration - ICM*] [*Spanish*]

CIM .... Comite International de Mauthausen (WGAO)

CIM .... Comite International du Mini-Basketball [*International Committee for Mini-Basketball*] [*Munich, Federal Republic of Germany*] (EAIO)

CIM .... Comite Intersectoral Mexico [*Mexico*] (LAA)

CIM .... COMLINE Industrial Monitor [*COMLINE International Corp.*] [*Japan*] [*Information service or system*] (CRD)

CIM .... Commission for Industry and Manpower (WGAO)

CIM .... Commission Internationale de Marketing [*International Marketing Commission - IMC*] [*Brixham, Devonshire, England*] (EAIO)

CIM .... Companhia Industrial de Matols

CIM .... Congregatio Iesu et Mariae [*Eudistarum*] (WGAO)

CIM .... Congres International des Fabrications Mecaniques (WGAO)

CIM .... Congreso Islamic de Mozambique [*Mozambique Islamic Congress*] (EAIO)

CIM .... Conseil International de la Musique [*French*] (SLS)

CIM .... Conservative Immigration Movement [*Australia*] (ADA)

CIM .... Consorzio Italiano fra Macellatori Industriali Produttori Importatori Bestiame Carni e Affini (WGAO)

CIM .... Convention Internationale Concernant le Transport des Merchandises par Chemins de Fer [*North African*]

CIM .... Convention Internationale des Marchandises [*French*]

CIM .... Cooperative Investigations in the Mediterranean [*IOC*]

CIMA .... Centrala Industriala de Masini Agricole [*Industrial Central for Agricultural Machinery*] (RO)

CIMA .... Centre for Industrial Microelectronics Applications [*Australia*]

CIMA .... Centre Interdisciplinaire d'Etude du Milieu Naturel et de l'Amenagement Rural (WGAO)

CIMA .... Centre pour l'Independance des Magistrats et des Avocats [*Centre for the Independence of Judges and Lawyers - CIJL*] (EA)

CIMA .... Centro Italiano di Musica Antica [*Italian*] (SLS)

CIMA .... Chartered Institute of Management Accountants [*South Africa*] (AA)

CIMA .... Comercio e Industria de Maquinas Agricolas Ltd. [*Brazil*] (DSCA)

CIMA .... Comision Interministerial del Medio Ambiente [*Interministerial Commission on the Environment*] [*Spanish*] (WER)

CIMA .... Comite Intergovernamental para as Migracoes Europeias [*Intergovernmental Committee for European Migrations*] [*Portuguese*] (WER)

CIMA .... Commission Internationale de Meteorologie Aeronautique

CIMA .... Commission Internationale de Micro Aviation

CIMA .... Compagnie Industrielle de Miroiterie en Afrique

CIMA .... Compagnie International des Machines Agricoles (WGAO)

CIMA .... Companhia Industrial das Mahotas Lda.

CIMA .... Comptoir Ivoirien de Materiel

CIMAA...... Cellulose Insulation Manufacturers and Agents Association [*Australia*]

CIMAC...... Conseil International des Machines a Combustion [*International Council on Combustion Engines*] [*Paris, France*] (EAIO)

CIMACO... Compania Industrial de Materiales para Construccion [*Colombia*] (COL)

CIMADE... Comite Inter-Mouvement Aupres des Evacues [*France*]

CIMAF...... Centro de Cooperacao dos Industriais de Maquinas-Ferramentas [*Cooperative Centre r for Machine Tool Manufacturers*] [*Portuguese*] (PDAA)

CIMAFRIC... Societe Africaine des Ciments

CIMAG..... Societe des Grands Magasins de la Cote-D'Ivoire

CIMA-IS... Ege Bolgesi Civa, Izole Maden Arama Iscileri Sendikasi [*Aegean Region Mercury, Insulation Ore Exploration Workers' Union*] [*Izmir*] (TU)

CIMAL...... Centre d'Information Mondiales Antilepre

CIMALOR... Societe des Ciments de l'Algerie Orientale

CIMANGOLA... Empresa de Cimento de Angola [*Cement producing and exporting enterprise*] [*Luanda, Angola*]

CIMAO..... Les Cimeteries de l'Afrique de l'Ouest [*Ghana, Ivory Coast, Togo*] (WGAO)

CIMAO..... Societe des Ciments de l'Afrique de l'Ouest [*Cement Company of West Africa*] (AF)

CIMAP...... Commission Internationale des Methodes d'Analyse des Pesticides [*Collaborative International Pesticides Analytic Council - CIPAC*] (EAIO)

CIMAP...... Computer-Integrated Manufacturing Automation Protocol [*Manufacturing communications*]

CIMAR...... Centro de Investigaciones del Mar [*Universidad Catolica de Valparaiso*] [*Chile*] (ASF)

CIMAR...... Compagnie Industrielle des Petroles du Maroc

CIMARA... Camara de Instituciones Medicas de la Republica Argentina [*Chamber of Medical Institutions of the Argentine Republic*] (LA)

CIMAS...... Conference Internationale de la Mutualite et des Assurances Sociales (WGAO)

CIMASA... Construcoes e Industria Metalurgica Amazonia SA [*Amazon Metal Industry and Construction, Inc.*] [*Brazil*] (LA)

CIMATAO-YS... Compagnie Malienne de Montage et d'Exploitation Automobiles

CIMATEC... Cote Ivoirienne de Materiels Techniques

CIMAV...... Comite International de Medecine d'Assurances sur la Vie [*International Committee for Life Assurance Medicine*] [*France*] (EAIO)

CIMAVE... Sociedade Comercio e Industria de Material Avicola Ltd. [*Brazil*] (DSCA)

CIMB........ Construction Industry Manpower Board (WGAO)

CIMC......... Cercle International Massotherapie Chinoise (WGAO)

CIMC......... Colombian Internal Medical Congress (WGAO)

CIMC......... Committee for International Municipal Cooperation (WGAO)

CIMCA...... Compania Industrial Maderera, CA [*Dominican Republic*] (DSCA)

CIMCCL... Centrala Industriala de Medicamente, Cosmetice, Coloranti, si Lacuri [*Industrial Central for Drugs, Cosmetics, Dyes, and Lacquers*] (RO)

CIMCEE... Comite des Industries de la Moutarde de la CEE (WGAO)

CIMCLG... Construction Industry Metric Change Liaison Group (WGAO)

CIMCO..... Compagnie des Ciments du Congo Francais

CIME........ Centro de Investigacion de Metodos y Tecnicas para Pequenas y Medianas Empresas [*Research Center for Small- and Medium-Scale Industries*] [*INTI*] [*Research center*] [*Argentina*] (IRC)

CIME........ Centro de Investigaciones en Microelectronica [*Microelectronics Research Center*] [*Instituto Superior Politecnico Jose Antonio Echeverria Havana, Cuba*] [*Research center*] (ERC)

CIME........ China International Medical Exhibition

CIME........ Comitato Internazionale per le Migrazioni Europee [*International Committee for European Migrations*] [*Use ICEM*] [*Italian*] (WER)

CIME........ Comite Intergouvernemental pour les Migrations Europeennes (FLAF)

CIME........ Comite Intergubernamental para la Migracion Europea [*Intergovernmental Committee for European Migration*] [*Use ICEM*] [*Spanish*] (LA)

CIME........ Committee for International Investment and Multinational Enterprises [*OECD*] (WGAO)

CIME........ Compagnie Industrielle des Metaux Electroniques (WGAO)

CIME........ Confederation Internationale de Musique Electroacoustique [*International Confederation for Electroacoustic Music - ICEM*] (EAIO)

CIME........ Conseil International des Moyens d'Enseignement (WGAO)

CIME........ Conseil International des Moyens du Film d'Enseignement [*French*] (SLS)

CIME........ Council of Industry for Management Education (WGAO)

CIMEA...... Comite International des Mouvements d'Enfants et d'Adolescents [*International Committee of Children's and Adolescents' Movements*] [*Budapest, Hungary*] (EAIO)

CIMEC...... Comite des Industries de la Mesure Electrique et Electronique de la Communaute [*CEE*] (WGAO)

CIMED...... Centro de Investigaciones in Metodos Estadisticos para Demogratia [*Colombia*] (PDAA)

CIMELTA... Constructions Mecaniques et Electriques de Tananarive

CIMENCAM... Cimenterie du Cameroun [*Cameroon Cement Plant*] (AF)

CIMENCAM... Societe des Cimenteries du Cameroun (WGAO)

CIMENCO... Societe de la Cimenterie du Congo

CIMENTAL... Cimenteries d'Albertville

CIMETEL... Centro de Investigaciones y Mediciones en Telecomunicaciones [*Center for Telecommunications Research and Measurements*] [*INTI*] [*Research center*] [*Argentina*] (IRC)

CIMEX...... Control de Creditos Importacion y Exportacion [*Cucuta*] (COL)

CIMG........ Colloque International de Marketing Gazier [*International Colloquium about Gas Marketing - ICGM*] (EA)

CIMH........ Comite International pour la Metrologie Historique [*International Committee for Historical Metrology*] (EAIO)

CIMHER... Centro de Investigaciones de Maquinas-Herramienta [*Research Center for Machines and Tools*] [*INTI*] [*Research center*] [*Argentina*] (IRC)

CIMI......... Centre of Industrial Microbiological Investigations [*Argentina*] (WGAO)

CIMI......... Compagnia Italiana Montaggi Industriali, SpA [*Nuclear energy*] [*Italian*] (NRCH)

CIMI......... Conselho Indigenista Missionario [*Native Missionary Council*] [*Brazil*] (LA)

CIMIL....... CSIRO [*Commonwealth Scientific and Industrial Research Organisation*] Inquiry into Mechanization in Libraries [*Australia*]

CIMIT....... Compagnie Industrielle de Materiel de Transport [*France*] (WGAO)

CIMJI....... Committee for Inquiry of Missing Japanese in Indochina (CL)

ciml........... Cimlap [*Title Page*] [*Hungary*]

CIMM....... Centro de Investigacion de Materiales y Metrologia [*Center for Materials Research and Metrology*] [*INTI*] [*Research center*] [*Argentina*] (IRC)

CIMM....... Centro de Investigacion Minera y Metalurgica [*Mining and Metallurgical Research Center*] [*Chile*] [*Research center*] (IRC)

CIMM....... Chambre Internationale de la Marine Marchande (WGAO)

CIMM....... Comite International de Medecine Militaire [*International Committee of Military Medicine*] [*Belgium*] (EAIO)

CIMMYT... Centro Internacional de Mejoramiento de Maiz y Trigo [*International Maize and Wheat Improvement Center*] [*ICSU*] (EAIO)

CIMNR..... Centrala Industriala pentru Metale Neferoase si Rare [*Industrial Central for Nonferrous and Rare Metals*] (RO)

CIMO........ Central Institut voor Materiaalonderzoek (WGAO)

CIMO........ Commission des Instruments et des Methodes d'Observation [*Commission for Instruments and Methods of Observation*] [*OMI*]

CIMO........ Confederation of Importers and Marketing Organizations in Europe of Fresh Fruit and Vegetables [*Brussels, Belgium*] (EA)

CIMP........ Centro de Instruccion Militar de Peru [*Military Training Center of Peru*] (LA)

CIMP........ Commission Internationale de la Meteorologie Polaire [*AIMPA*] (WGAO)

CIMP........ Commission Internationale Medico-Physiologique [*International Medico-Physiological Commission*] (PDAA)

CIMPA...... Centre International de Mathematiques Pures et Appliquees [*International Center for Pure and Applied Mathematics - ICPAM*] [*United Nations*] (EA)

CIMPEC... Centro Interamericano de Produccion de Material Educativo y Cientifico para la Prensa [*Inter-American Center for the Production of Press Information on Educational and Scientific Matters*] (LA)

CIMPM..... Comite International de Medecine et de Pharmacie Militaires [*International Committee of Military Medicine and Pharmacy - ICMMP*] [*Liege, Belgium*] (EA)

CIMPO...... Central Indian Medicinal Plants Organization (PDAA)

CIMPOR... Cimentos de Portugal, EP [*Portugal*] (EY)

Cimre......... Cimetiere [*Cemetery*] [*Military map abbreviation World War I*] [*French*] (MTD)

CIMRST.... Comite Interministeriel de la Recherche Scientifique et Technique [*France*] (PDAA)

CIMS......... Centro de Investigaciones Motivacionales y Sociales [*Argentina*] (WGAO)

CIMS......... Centro de Investigaciones Multidisciplinarias de Sistemas de Bienestar Social [*Colombia*] (COL)

CIMS......... Consociatio Internationalis Musicae Sacrae [*Rome, Italy*] (EAIO)

CIMSA...... Compagnie d'Informatique Militaire, Spatiale, et Aeronautique [*Research center*] [*French*] (ERC)

CIMSCEE ... Comite des Industries des Mayonnaises et Sauces Condimentaires de la CEE [*Committee of the Industries of Mayonnaises and Table Sauces of the European Economic Community*]

Cimse-Is ..... Turkiye Cimento, Seramik, ve Toprak Sanayii Iscileri Sendikasi [*Turkish Cement, Ceramics, and Earthenware Industry Workers' Union*]   (TU)

CIMT .... Centre International des Marees Terrestres [*International Centre for Earth Tides*]   (EAIO)

CIMT .... Commission Internationale de la Medecine du Travail [*International Commission of Occupational Health - ICOH*] [*Information service or system*]   (IID)

CIMTAC ... Committee for International Marine Telecommunications and Aviation Coordination   (WGAO)

CIMTE ...... Centro de Investigaciones Multidisciplinarias en Tecnologia y Empleo [*Center for Multidisciplinary Technological Research*] [*Research center*] [*Colorado*]   (IRC)

CIMTOGO ... Societe des Ciments du Togo

CIMTP ...... Congres Internationaux de Medecine Tropicale et de Paludisme

CIMU .... Centrala Industriala de Masini Unelte [*Industrial Center for Machine Tools*]   (RO)

CIMUIU .... Centrala Industriala de Masini si Utilaje pentru Industria Usoara [*Industrial Center for Machines and Equipment for Light Industry*]   (RO)

CIMUMFS ... Centrala Industriala de Masini Unelte, Mecanica Fina, si Scule [*Industrial Center for Machine Tools, Precision Machinery, and Tools*]   (RO)

CIMUR ..... Comite d'Information pour le Developpement des Facades Legeres et Cloisons Industrialisees

CIMUSET ... Comite International des Musees des Sciences et Technologies   (WGAO)

CIN .... Centro de Informacoes Nucleares [*Center for Nuclear Information*] [*Brazil*] [*Information service or system*]   (IID)

CIN .... Centro de Integracion Nacional [*National Integration Center*] [*Bolivia*]   (LA)

CIN .... Centro de Investigaciones Nucleares [*Nuclear Research Center*] [*Uruguay*]   (LA)

cin .... Cinema [*French*]   (TPFD)

CIN .... Comision Iberoamericana de Normalizacion   (LAA)

CIN .... Commission Internationale de Numismatique [*International Numismatic Commission*] [*Oslo, Norway*]   (EA)

CIN .... Curriculum Information Network [*Formerly, Australian Curriculum Information Netwo rk*]

CINA .... Centralinstitut for Nordisk Asienforskning [*Scandinavian Institute of Asian Studies*] [*Later, NIAS*]   (EAIO)

CINA .... Commission Internationale de la Navigation Aerienne   (FLAF)

CINA .... Confederacion Industrial Argentina [*Argentina*]   (EY)

CINAB ...... Comite des Instituts Nationaux des Agents en Brevets   (WGAO)

CINABA .... Comercio, Industria, e Navegacao Bandeirante, SA [*Brazil*]   (LAA)

CINAG ...... Centro de Informatica Nacional Aplicada a la Gestion [*National Applied Data Processing Center*] [*Cuba*]   (LA)

CINAM ..... Compagnie d'Etudes Industrielles et d'Amenagement du Territoire

CINAN ...... Centro de Informacion Aplicada a la Normalizacion [*Applied Standardization Data Center*] [*Cuba*]   (LA)

CINAREMA ... Comite Inter-Sindical Nacional de Radioelectricidad, Metalurgica, y Afines [*National Inter-Union Committee of Radioengineering and Metallurgical Workers*] [*Uruguay*]   (LA)

CINAT .... Cimenterie Nationale [*National Cement Plant*] [*Zaire*]   (AF)

CINAV ...... Commission Internationale de la Nomenclature Anatomique Veterinaire [*International Committee on Veterinary Anatomical Nomenclature - ICVAN*] [*Zurich, Switzerland*]   (EAIO)

C-in-C .... Commander-in-Chief   (EECI)

CINCAFMED ... Commander-in-Chief, Allied Forces, Mediterranean [*NATO*]

CINCAU ... Centro de Informacion sobre Contaminacion Ambiental Urbana [*Centro de Investigaciones para el Desarrollo Integral, Universidad Pontificia Bolivariana*] [*Colorado*]

CINCC .... Coal Industry National Consultative Council   (WGAO)

CINCCENT ... Commander-in-Chief, Allied Forces, Central Europe [*NATO*]

CINCEASTLANT ... Commander-in-Chief, Eastern Atlantic Area [*NATO*]

Cinch .... Cinchona [*Quinine*] [*Pharmacology*]   (ROG)

CINCH ...... Computerised Information from National Criminological Holdings [*Australian Institute of Criminology Library*] [*Database*] [*Information service or system*]   (IID)

CINCMEAF ... Commander-in-Chief, Middle East Air Forces

CINCMELF ... Commander-in-Chief, Middle East Land Forces

CINCNELM ... Commander-in-Chief, US Naval Forces, Eastern Atlantic and Mediterranean

CINCNORTH ... Commander-in-Chief, Allied Forces, Northern Europe [*NATO*]

CINCO ...... Compania de Ingenieros Contratistas Ltda. [*Colombia*]   (COL)

CINCOL .... Compania Industrial y Comercial Ltda. [*Colombia*]   (COL)

CINCSOUTH ... Commander-in-Chief, Allied Forces, Southern Europe [*NATO*]

CINCWESTLANT ... Commander-in-Chief, Western Atlantic Area [*NATO*]

CINCWIO ... Cooperative Investigations in the North and Central Western Indian Ocean   (MSC)

CINDA ...... Centro Interuniversitario por Desarrollo Andino [*Chile*]   (WGAO)

CINDACOL ... Consorcio Industrial Aleman para Colombia [*Colombia*]   (COL)

CINDACTA ... Centro Integrado de Defesa Aerea e de Controle de Trafico Aereo [*Combined Air Safety and Air Traffic Control Center*] [*Brazil*]   (LA)

CINDER .... Centro Interamericano para el Desarrollo Regional [*Inter-American Center for Regional Development*] [*Venezuela*]   (EAIO)

CINDESS ... Curso Interamericano de Estadistica de Seguridad Social   (LAA)

CINDESTRUC ... Compania Industrial Aleman para Colombia Ltda. [*Barranquilla*]   (COL)

CINE .... Cinematografia [*Ministerio de Cultura*] [*Spain*] [*Information service or system*]   (CRD)

CINECA .... Cooperative Investigations of the Northern Part of the Eastern Central Atlantic [*FAO*]   (WGAO)

CINECO .... Cine Colombia SA [*Colombia*]   (COL)

CINEP .... Centro de Investigacion y Educacion Popular [*Center of Research and Popular Education*] [*Colorado*]

CINE-PERU ... Empresa de Cinematografia del Peru [*Peruvian Motion Picture Enterprise*]   (LA)

CINF .... Commission Intersyndicale de l'Instrumentation et de le Mesure Nucleaire Francaise   (WGAO)

CINFR .... Central Institute for Nutrition and Food Research [*Netherlands*]   (MCD)

C-Infre .... Charente-Inferieure [*French*]

CING .... Commission Internationale des Neiges et Glaces   (WGAO)

CINGRA .... Coordenacao de Assuntos Internacionais da Agricultura [*Coordination of International Agricultural Issues*] [*Brazil*]   (LA)

CINIDREP ... Centro Interamericano de Investigacion y Documentacion de Relaciones Publicas   (WGAO)

CINIME .... Centro de Informacion de Medicamentos [*Spanish Drug Information Center*] [*Information service or system*]   (IID)

Cin-Kur ...... Cinko-Kursun Fabrikasi [*Zinc-Lead Factory*] [*Kayseri*]   (TU)

CIN-KUR .. Cinko-Kursun Metal Sanayii AS [*Zinc and Lead Metal Industry Corp.*] [*Ankara*]   (TU)

CINM .... Camara Internacional de Navegacion Maritima   (WGAO)

Cinnam .... Cinnamomum [*Cinnamon*] [*Pharmacology*]   (ROG)

CINOA ...... Confederation Internationale des Negociants en Oeuvres d'Art [*International Confederation of Art Dealers*]   (EAIO)

CINOCA ... Compania Industrias Nacionales Oxigeno, Canos Acero [*Montevideo, Uruguay*]   (LAA)

CINOR ...... Centrul de Informatica si Organizare [*Center for Data Processing and Organization*]   (RO)

CINP .... Chambre Interdepartmentale des Notaires de Paris   (WGAO)

CINP .... Collegium Internationale Neuro-Psychopharmacologicum   (WGAO)

CINP .... Collegium International Neuro-Psychopharmacologicum

CINP .... Comite International de Liaison pour la Navigation de Plaisance [*Pleasure Navigation International Joint Committee - PNIC*] [*The Hague, Netherlands*]   (EAIO)

CINPEC .... Comite Interdiocesain des Pelerinages Catholiques

CINPEXAM ... Centre d'Information pour l'Expansion Africaine, Malgache, et Mauricienne [*Information Center for African, Malagasy, and Mauritian Development*]   (AF)

CINPROS ... Commission Internationale des Professionals de la Sante   (EAIO)

CINPROS ... Commission Internationale des Professionels de la Sante [*International Commission of Health Professionals for Health and Human Rights - ICHP*]   (EA)

CINPROS ... Commission Internationale des Professionnels pour la Sante et les Droits de l'Homme   (WGAO)

CINS .... Collegium Internationale Activitatis Nervosae Superioris   (SLS)

CINSA .... Compania Insular del Nitrogeno SA [*Spanish*]

CINSE .... Centro Italo-Nipponico di Studi Economici [*Italian*]   (SLS)

CINSELA ... Comite de Investigaciones sobre Ejecutivos Latinoamericanos   (LAA)

C Instr Cr ... Code d'Instruction Criminelle [*Code of Criminal Procedure*]   (DLA)

CInstRE(Aust) ... Companion of the Institution of Radio Engineers (Australia)   (ADA)

CINTE .... Centrum Informacij Naukowej, Technicznej i Ekonomicznej   (WGAO)

CINTECA ... Centro de Informacion Tecnica Cafetalera [*Brazil*]   (WGAO)

CINTERFOR ... Centre Interamericain de Recherche et de Documentation sur la Formation Professionnelle [*Inter-American Center for Research and Documentation on Vocational Training*] [*French*]

CINTERFOR ... Centro Interamericano de Investigacion y Documentacion sobre Formacion Profesional [*Inter-American Centre for Research and Documentation on Vocational Training - IACRDVT*] (EAIO)
CINTERPLAN ... Centro Interamericano de Estudios e Investigaciones para el Planeamiento de la Educacion [*Venezuela*] (WGAO)
CINTRACINTEL ... Sindicato de Trabajadores de Cine [*Colombia*] (COL)
CINU .... Centre d'Information des Nations Unies (FLAF)
CINU .... Centro de Informacion e las Naciones Unidas para Colombia, Ecuador, y Venezuela [*UN Information Center for Colombia, Ecuador, and Venezuela*] (LA)
CINVA ...... Centro Interamericano de Vivenda [*Colombia*] (WGAO)
CINVA ...... Centro Interamericano de Vivienda y Planeamiento [*Inter-American Housing and Planning Center*] [*Bogota, Colombia*] (LAA)
CINVE....... Centro de Investigaciones Economicas [*Uruguay*] (WGAO)
CINWA ..... Community Information Network of Western Australia
CINZ .... Commission Internationale de Nomenclature Zoologique [*International Commission on Veterinary Anatomical Nomenclature*] [*British*] (EAIO)
CIO .... Centar za Industrijsko Oblikovanje (WGAO)
CIO .... Central Intelligence Organization [*South Africa*]
CIO .... Church Information Office (WGAO)
CIO .... Comitato Internazionale Olimpico [*International Olympics Committee*] [*Italian*]
CIO .... Comite International Olympique [*North African*]
CIO .... Commissione Italiana per la Oceanografica [*Italian*] (MSC)
CIO .... Commission Internationale d'Optique [*International Commission for Optics - ICO*] (EAIO)
CIO .... Compania Industrial de Occidente [*Colombia*] (COL)
CIO .... Congressus Internationalis Ornithologicus [*International Ornithological Congress - IOC*] (EA)
CIOA .... Centro Italiano Assidatori Anodici (WGAO)
CIOAC...... Central Independiente de Obreros Agricolas y Campesinos [*Independent Central Organization of Agricultural Workers and Peasants*] [*Mexico*] (LA)
CIOB .... Chartered Institute of Building (WGAO)
CIOC .... Cayman Islands Olympic Committee (EAIO)
CIOFF ...... Comite International des Organisateurs de Festivals de Folklore et d'Arts Traditionnels (WGAO)
CIOFF ...... Conseil International des Organisations de Festivals de Folklore et d'Arts Traditionnels [*International Council of Folklore Festival Organizations and Folk Art - ICFFO*] (EAIO)
CIOG .... Central Islamic Organisation of Guyana (EAIO)
CIOH........ Centro de Investigaciones Oceanograficas y Hidrograficas [*Colorado*] (MSC)
CIOIC....... Centre d'Information des Organisations Internationales Catholiques (WGAO)
CIOIC....... Commission Interimaire de l'Organisation Internationale du Commerce (FLAF)
CIOJ .... Centre d'Information et Documentation de la Jeunesse (WGAO)
CIOM .... Confederation Internationale des Officers-Medicins (WGAO)
CIOMR ..... Comite Interallie des Officiers Medecins de Reserve (WGAO)
CIOMS..... Council for International Organizations on Medical Sciences [*Geneva, Switzerland*] (EA)
cion............. Commission [*Commission*] [*French*]
CIOP......... Centralny Instytut Ochrony Pracy [*Central Institute of Labor Safety*] (POL)
CIOP......... Commissie Informatie-Opleiding [*Netherlands*]
CIOPI .... Centro de Investigacion Operativa y Procesamiento de Informacion (LAA)
CIOPORA ... Communaute Internationale des Obtenteurs de Plantes Ornementales et Fruitieres a Reproduction Asexuee [*International Community of Breeders of Asexually Reproduced Fruit Trees and Ornamental Varieties*] [*Geneva, Switzerland*] (WGAO)
CIOR .... Confederation Interalliee des Officiers de Reserve [*Interallied Confederation of Reserve Officers*] (EAIO)
CIOS......... Centro Italiano di Orientamento Sociale (WGAO)
CIOS......... Comisia pentru Incercarea si Omologarea Soiurilor [*Commission for the Testing and Approval of Seed Varieties*] (RO)
CIOS......... Comitato Internazionale Organizzazione Scientifica [*International Committee for Scientific Organization*] [*Italian*] (WER)
CIOS......... Comite International pour l'Organisation Scientifique [*World Council of Management*] (WGAO)
CIOS......... Conseil International pour l'Organisation Scientifique [*International Council for Scientific Management*] [*ICSU*] [*French*]
CIOS......... World Council of Management [*Netherlands*]
CIOSL....... Confederacion Internacional de Organizaciones Sindicales Libres [*International Confederation of Free Trade Unions*]
CIOSL....... Conferencia Internacional de Organizaciones Sindicales Libres [*International Conference of Free Trade Union Organizations*] [*Use ICFTUO*] (LA)
CIOSM...... Counseil International des Organisations des Sciences Medicales (WGAO)

CIOSTA .... Comite International d'Organisation Scientifique du Travail en Agriculture (WGAO)
CIOSTA .... Commission Internationale pour l'Organisation Scientifique du Travail en Agriculture [*Germany*] (DSCA)
CIOT .... Centro Internacional de Operacion Telegrafica [*Argentina*] (WGAO)
CIOT .... Chisholm Institute of Technology [*Research center*] [*Australia*] (ERC)
CIOT .... Commerce et Industrie de l'Oubangui et du Tchad
CIOT .... Compagnie Industrielle d'Ouvrages en Textiles
CIOVNI..... Centro de Investigacion de Objetos Voladores No Identificados [*Unidentified Flying Objects Research Center*] [*Uruguay*] (LA)
CIP............. Carte d'Identite Professionnelle (FLAF)
CIP............. Catholic International Press (WGAO)
CIP............. Central Industrial Prison [*Australia*] (ADA)
CIP............. Centre d'Information de Presse [*Press agency*] [*Belgium*]
CIP............. Centre d'Instruction des Parachutistes [*Paratroop Training Center*] [*Zaire*] (AF)
CIP............. Centre for International Policy (WGAO)
CIP............. Centre International de Paris (WGAO)
CIP............. Centro de Informacion de Pesca [*Mexico*] (MSC)
CIP............. Centro de Investigaciones Pesqueras [*Fishing Research Center*] [*Cuba*] (LA)
CIP............. Centro de Investigaciones Pesqueras [*Venezuela*] (WGAO)
CIP............. Centro de Investigacion para la Paz [*Peace Research Center*] [*Spain*]
CIP............. Centro Industrial de Productividad [*Mexico*] (LAA)
CIP............. Centro Informacion Preinversion America Latina Caribe (WGAO)
CIP............. Centro Internacional de la Papa [*International Potato Center*] [*ICSU*] (EAIO)
CIP............. Centro Internazionale della Pace [*Italian*] (SLS)
CIP............. Centro Internazionale di Psicobiofisica [*Italian*] (SLS)
CIP............. Centro Italiano di Parapsicologia [*Italian*] (SLS)
CIP............. Certificats d'Investissement Privileges [*French securities*]
CIP............. Chipata [*Zambia*] [*Airport symbol*] (OAG)
CIP............. Club Internacional de Prensa (WGAO)
CIP............. Collection de l'Institut Pasteur [*French*]
CIP............. College International de Podologie (WGAO)
CIP............. Comandos Incontrolados Patrioticos [*Patriotic Autonomous Commandos*] [*Spanish*] (WER)
CIP............. Comision Interamericana de Paz [*Organizacion de Estados Americanos*] [*Washington, DC*] (LAA)
CIP............. Comision Internacional de Paz (WGAO)
CIP............. Comitato Interministeriale Prezzi [*Interministerial Price Committee*] [*Italian*] (WER)
CIP............. Comite Inter-Etats Permanent
CIP............. Comite Internacional Preparatorio [*International Preparatory Committee*] [*Cuba*] (LA)
CIP............. Comite Internationale de Photobiologie [*International Committee of Photobiology*] [*French*] (ASF)
CIP............. Commission Internatinale de Phytogpharmacie (WGAO)
CIP............. Commission International du Peuplier (WGAO)
CIP............. Commission Internationale Permanente pour l'Epreuve des Armes a Feu [*Permanent International Commission for the Proof of Small-Arms - PICPSA*] (EAIO)
CIP............. Compagnie d'Investissements de Paris [*Paris Investment Co.*] [*Banque Nationale de Paris*] [*France*]
CIP............. Companhia Industrial de Plasticos
CIP............. Comptoir Ivoirien des Papiers
CIP............. Confederacao da Industria Portuguesa [*Portuguese Industry Confederation*] [*Lisbon*] (WER)
CIP............. Confederacion Internationale des Parents (WGAO)
CIP............. Conselho Interministerial de Precos [*Interministerial Price Council*] [*Rio De Janeiro, Brazil*] (LA)
CIP............. Cook Islands Party [*Political party*] (PPW)
CIP............. Coordinadora Internacional Publicitaria [*Colombia*] (COL)
CIP............. Cote-D'Ivoire Plastique
CIP............. Council of Iron Producers (WGAO)
CIPA .... Centro de Investigacion y de Promocion Amazonica [*Center for Investigation and Promotion of the Indigenous Peoples of the Amazon*] [*Peru*] (EAIO)
CIPA .... Centrul de Instruirea Personalului Aeronautic [*Center for the Instruction of Aeronautical Personnel*] (RO)
CIPA .... Chartered Institute of Patent Agents (WGAO)
CIPA .... Comision Interdepartamental de Politica Agricola [*Venezuela*] (DSCA)
CIPA .... Comitato Interministeriale per l'Ambiente [*Inter-Ministerial Committee for the Environment*] [*Italy*] (PDAA)
CIPA .... Comite Interamericano de Proteccion Agricola (LAA)
CIPA .... Comite Interamericano Permanente Anti-Acridiano [*Permanent Inter-American Anti-Locust Committee*] [*Buenos Aires, Argentina*] (LAA)
CIPA .... Comite International de Photogrammetrie Architecturale [*International Committee of Architectural Photogrammetry*] (EAIO)

CIPA.......... Comite International de Plastiques en Agriculture [*International Committee of Plastics in Agriculture*]   (EAIO)

CIPA.......... Compagnie Industrielle des Piles Electriques   (WGAO)

CIPA.......... Compagnie Ivoirienne de Produits Alimentaires

CIPA.......... Confederazione Generale Italiana dei Professionisti e Artisti [*Artists and Professional People*] [*Italy*]   (EY)

CIPA.......... Cook Islands Party Alliance [*Political party*]   (FEA)

CIPAC....... Collaborative International Pesticides Analytical Council Ltd. [*See also CIMAP*] [*Wageningen, Netherlands*]   (EAIO)

CIPACI...... Societe Commerciale et Industrielle des Produits Animaux en Cote d'Ivoire   (WGAO)

CIPA/ICPA ... Comite International de Prevention des Accidents du Travail de la Navigation Interieure/International Committee for the Prevention of Work Accidents in Inland Navigation   (EAIO)

CIPAIM .... Cellule d'Intervention contre la Pollution dans les Alpes-Maritimes   (WGAO)

CIPAL .... Centro de Informaciones para la America Latina [*Latin American Information Center*]   (LA)

CIPAL .... Comercio e Industria de Produtos Alimenticios Ltd. [*Brazil*]   (DSCA)

CIPAL .... Companhia Industrial de Produtos Alimentares, SARL

CIPAL .... Compania Industrial de Productos de Acero [*Colombia*]   (COL)

CIPAM...... Centro de Investigaciones de Plantas y Animales Medicinales [*Mexico*]   (DSCA)

CIPAN....... Comision Internacional de Pesquerias del Atlantico Noroeste [*International Commission for the Northwest Atlantic Fisheries - ICNAF*] [*Spanish*]   (ASF)

CIPAN....... Commission Internationale des Pecheries de l'Atlantique Nord-Ouest [*International Commission for the Northwest Atlantic Fisheries - ICNAF*] [*French*]   (ASF)

CIPAO....... Compagnie Industrielle des Petroles de l'Afrique Occidentale [*Petroleum Industry Company of West Africa*] [*Senegal*]   (AF)

CIPAPE..... Companhia Industrial de Produtos Alimenticios de Pernambuco [*Brazil*]   (DSCA)

CIPAR .... Centro de Investigaciones Parasicologicas [*Colombia*]   (COL)

CIPAS .... Cimento Pazarlama Anonim Sirketi [*Cement Marketing Corporation*]   (TU)

CIPASE..... Commission Internationale des Peches de l'Atlantique Sud-Est [*International Commission for the Southeast Atlantic Fisheries - ICSEAF*] [*Madrid, Spain*]   (EAIO)

CIPASH .... Committee for an International Program in Atmospheric Sciences and Hydrology [*United Nations*]

CIPASO .... Comision Internacional de Pesquerias del Atlantico Sudoriental [*International Commission for the Southeast Atlantic Fisheries - ICSEAF*] [*Spanish*]   (ASF)

CIPAT .... Conseil International sur les Problemes de l'Alcoolisme et des Tosicomanies [*Switzerland*]   (SLS)

CIPB .... Commission du Commerce International des Produits de Base [*CNUCED*]   (WGAO)

CIPBC .... Centre National Interprofessinnel des Produits de Basse-Cour   (WGAO)

CIPBC .... Church of India, Pakistan, Burma, and Ceylon [*Anglican*]

CIPC .... Central Institut v. Physisch-Chemische Constanten   (WGAO)

CIPC .... Centre d'Instruction Para-Commando

CIPC .... Centre International de Phenomenologie Clinique   (EAIO)

CIPC .... Centrul de Investitii Proiectari si Constructii [*Center for Construction and Design Investments*]   (RO)

CIPC .... Comite Internacional Permanente de la Conserva [*Permanent International Committee on Canned Foods*] [*Spanish*]   (ASF)

CIPC .... Comite International Permanent de la Conserve [*Permanent International Committee on Canned Foods*] [*French*]   (ASF)

CIPC .... Compagnie Ivoirienne de Plomberie et Chaudronnerie

CIPCA .... Centro de Investigacion y Promocion del Campesinado [*Bolivia*]   (WGAO)

CIPCC .... Comite Internatinal Permanent du Carbon Carburant   (WGAO)

CIPCE .... Centre d'Information et de Publicite des Chemins de Fer Europeens [*Information and Publicity Center of the European Railways*] [*Italy*]

CIPCE .... Information and Publicity Centre of the European Railways   (WGAO)

CIPCEL..... Comite International de la Pellicule Cellulosique   (WGAO)

CIPCMP.... Centrala Industriala de Prelucrare Cauciuc si Mase Plastice [*Industrial Central for the Processing of Rubber and Plastic*]   (RO)

CIPCO....... Compagnie Ivoirienne de Poisson Congele

CIPCRO .... Comite Intersecretarial sobre Programas Cientificos Relacionados con la Oceanografia [*Inter-Secretariat Committee on Scientific Programs Relating to Oceanography - ICSPRO*] [*Spanish*]   (ASF)

CIPDEM ... Comite Internacional pro Defensa de la Democracia [*International Committee for the Defense of Democracy*] [*Venezuela*]   (LA)

CIPE .... Centro Interamericano de Promocion de Exportaciones [*Inter-American Export Promotion Center*]

CIPE .... College International de Phonologie Experimentale [*French*]   (SLS)

CIPE .... Comitato Interministeriale per la Programmazione Economica   (WGAO)

CIPE .... Comitato Interministeriale Programmazione Economica [*Interministerial Committee for Economic Planning*] [*Italy*]

CIPE .... Conseil International de la Preparation a l'Enseignement   (WGAO)

CIPEA .... Centre Internationale pour l'Elevage en Afrique

CIPEC .... Compagnie Camerounaise des Instruments de Pesage et des Coffres-Forts

CIPEC .... Conseil Intergouvernemental des Pays Exportateurs de Cuivre [*Intergovernmental Council of Copper Exporting Countries - ICCEC*]   (EAIO)

CIPEC .... Consejo Intergubernamental de Paises Exportadores de Cobre [*Intergovernmental Council of Copper-Exporting Countries - ICCEC*] [*LA*]

CIPEC .... Consortium International Pharmaceutique et Chimique   (WGAO)

CIPECPT .. Centre International Perfectionnement Cadres Postes Telecommunications   (WGAO)

CIPEET..... Centrala Industriala pentru Productia Energiei Electrice si Termice [*Industrial Center for the Production of Electric and Thermal Power*]   (RO)

CIPEL........ Compagnie Industrielle des Piles Electriques

CIPEM ...... Comite International pour les Etudes Myceniennes [*Standing International Committee for Mycenaean Studies*]   (EAIO)

CIPEPC..... Commission Internationale Permanente d'Etudes de la Police de la Circulation   (WGAO)

CIPES........ Comitato Italiano Permanente per l'Educazione Stradale [*Italian*]   (SLS)

CIPET .... Central Institute of Plastics Engineering and Tools [*India*] [*Research center*]   (IRC)

CIPEXI...... Compagnie Ivoirienne de Promotion pour l'Exportation et l'Importation

CIPF .... Confederation Internationale du Commerce des Pailles, Fourrages, Tourbes et Derives [*International Straw, Fodder and Peat Trade Confederation*] [*EC*]   (ECED)

CIPFA .... Chartered Institute of Public Finance and Accountancy   (WGAO)

CIPFE........ Comite d'Initiative pour le Parti Federaliste Europeen [*France*]   (FLAF)

CIPH .... Comite International des Pharmaciens Homeopathiques [*International Committee of Homeopathic Pharmacists*] [*Karlsruhe, Federal Republic of Germany*]   (EAIO)

CIPH .... Comite International Pharmaciens Homeopathes   (WGAO)

CIPHP....... Comision Internacional de Pesquerias del Hipogloso del Pacifico   (WGAO)

CIPI .... Centre for International Public Issues   (WGAO)

CIPI .... Comitato Interministeriale per la Politica Industriale [*Interministerial Committee for Industrial Policy Coordination*] [*Italian*]   (WER)

CIPI .... Comitato Interministeriale Politics Industriale [*Interministerial Committee for Industrial Policy*] [*Italy*]

CIPI .... Comite Interministeriel de Politque Industrielle   (WGAO)

CIPI .... Compagnie Ivoirienne de Peche et d'Industrie   (WGAO)

CIPI .... Compagnie Ivoirienne de Peche Industrielle

CIPIK .... Compagnie Industrielle de Pikine

CIPIMM ... Centro de Investigaciones para la Industria Minera-Metalurgica [*Research Center for the Mining-Metallurgical Industry*] [*Cuba*]   (LA)

CIPIST ...... Centre International pour l'Information Scientifique et Technique   (WGAO)

CIPL .... Comite International Permanent des Linguistes [*Permanent International Committee of Linguists*]   (EAIO)

CIPLA .... Confederacion Industrial Papelera Latinoamericana [*Latin American Paper Industry Confederation*] [*Mexico*]   (LA)

CIPM.......... Centrala Industriala de Prelucrari Metalurgice [*Industrial Central for Metallurgical Processing*]   (RO)

CIPM........ Comite International des Poids et Mesures [*International Committee on Weights and Measures*]

CIPMA...... Centro de Investigacion y Planificacion del Medio Ambiente [*Center for Research and Planning in Environment*] [*Chile*]   (IRC)

CIPME...... Committee on International Policy in the Marine Environment   (MSC)

CIPMP ...... Commission Internationale pour la Protection de la Moselle Contre la Pollution [*International Commission for the Protection of the Moselle Against Pollution - ICPMP*]   (EA)

CIPO........ Comite International pour la Preservation des Oiseaux   (WGAO)

CIPO......... Conseil International pour la Preservation des Oiseaux [*International Council for Bird Preservation - ICBP*] [*French*]   (MSC)

CIPO.......... Corporacion Industrial de Productos [*Argentina*]   (WGAO)

CIPOL....... Centre International de Publications Oecumeniques des Liturgies (WGAO)
CIPP.......... Comision Internacional de Problemas Pesqueros [*Apostolatus Maris*] [*Spanish*] (ASF)
CIPP.......... Commission Indo-Pacific des Peches [*Indo-Pacific Fishery Commission - IPFC*] (EAIO)
CIPP.......... Commission Indo-Pacifique des Peches [*Indo-Pacific Fisheries Commission - IPFC*] [*Indo-Pacific Fisheries Council*] [*Formerly,*] [*French*] (ASF)
CIPP.......... Conseil Indo-Pacifique des Peches (DSCA)
CIPP.......... Conseil Indo-Pacifiques des Peches [*FAO*] (WGAO)
CIPPAS..... Comite International Provisoire de Prevention Acridienne au Soudan Francais
CIPPN....... Commission Internationale des Pecheries du Pacifique Nord (WGAO)
CIPPT....... Centre International de Perfectionnement Professionnel et Technique [*International Center for Advanced Technical and Vocational Training - ICATVT*] [*French*]
CIPPT....... Centre International des Perfectionnement Professionnel et Technique (WGAO)
CIPPT....... Centro Internacional de Perfeccionamiento Profesional y Tecnico [*International Center for Advanced Technical and Vocational Training - ICATVT*] [*Spanish*]
CIPQ.......... Centre International de Promotion de la Qualite (WGAO)
CIPR........ Comision Internacional de Proteccion Contra las Radiaciones [*International Commission on Radiological Protection - ICRP*] [*Spanish*] (ASF)
CIPR.......... Commission Internationale de Protection Contre les Radiations [*International Commission on Radiological Protection - ICRP*] [*French*] (MSC)
CIPR.......... Commission Internationale pour la Protection contre les Radiations (WGAO)
CIPRA....... Camara de Industrias de Procesos de la Republica Argentina [*Processing Industries Association of the Argentine Republic*] (LA)
CIPRA....... Clothing Industry Productivity Resources Agency (WGAO)
CIPRA....... Commission Internationale pour la Protection des Regions Alpines [*International Commission for the Protection of Alpine Regions*] (EAIO)
CIPRE....... Centre d'Initiative Progressiste Europeen (WGAO)
CIPREA.... Circulation et Production a l'Equateur Atlantique [*Guinea*] (MSC)
CIPRES..... Centre Ivoirien de Reparation a la Promotion Renault Saviem
CIPRO....... Compagnie Ivoirienne de Produits
CIPROFILM ... Centre Interafricain de Production de Films [*Inter-African Film Production Center*] [*OCAM Ouagadougou, Burkina Faso*] (AF)
CIPROVA ... Comite Interprofessionnel pour la Promotion des Ventes des Produits Agricoles et Alimentaires (WGAO)
CIPS.......... Comite Interprofessionnel des Productions Sacchariferes (WGAO)
CIPS.......... Commonwealth International Philatelic Society (WGAO)
CIPS.......... Confederation Internationale de la Peche Sportive (ASF)
CIPSA....... Compania Iberica de Prospeccion, Sociedad Anonima [*Spanish*]
CIPSEP..... Comptoir Ivoirien de Prestation de Services et d'Electricite et de Plomberie
CIPSH....... Conseil International de la Philosophie et des Sciences Humaines [*International Council for Philosophy and Humanistic Studies*] (EAIO)
CIPSO....... Compagnie Industrielles de Plastiques Semi-Ouvres (WGAO)
CIPSRO .... Conseil Intersecretariat des Programmes Scientifiques Relatifs a l'Oceanographie [*Inter-Secretariat Committee on Scientific Programs Relating to Oceanography - ICSPRO*] [*French*] (ASF)
CIPT.......... Centre International de Physique Theorique [*Italian*] (WGAO)
CIPT.......... Comite International des Telecommunications de Presse (EAIO)
CIPV.......... Comite Permanent des Industries du Verre [*CEE*] (WGAO)
CIQ............ Comite de Industria Quimica [*Mexico*]
CIQ............ Confoederatio Internationalis ad Qualitates Plantarum Edulium Perquirendas [*Germany*] (DSCA)
CIQUINE ... Compania de Industrias Quimicas do Nordeste [*Brazil*]
CIR............ Arctic Circle Service, Inc. [*ICAO designator*] (FAAC)
CIR............ Center for International Relations [*University of California, Los Angeles*] [*Research center*] (RCD)
CIR............ Centralny Instytut Rolniczy [*Central Agricultural Institute*] (POL)
CIR............ Centre International de l'Eau et l'Assainissement [*IRC International Water and Sanitation Centre*] (EAIO)
CIR............ Centre International de Reference (WGAO)
CIR............ Centro Italiano Riscaldamento [*Italian*] (SLS)
CIR............ Centros de Instrucao Revolucionaria [*Centers for Revolutionary Instruction*] (AF)
CIR............ Circulos de Instruccion Revolucionaria [*Revolutionary Training Circles*] [*Cuba*] (LA)
cir.............. Cirilica [*Cyrillic Alphabet*] (YU)
Cir............. Cirurgia [*Surgery*] [*Portuguese*]
CIR............ Citizen Initiated Referendums [*Political party*] [*Australia*]

CIR .... Comission Internationale du Riz (DSCA)
CIR .... Comite de Innovadores y Racionalizadores [*Innovators and Efficiency Experts Committee*] [*Cuba*] (LA)
CIR .... Comite Integracionista Revolucionario [*Revolutionary Integration Committee*] [*Venezuela*] (LA)
CIR .... Comite Intergouvernemental pour les Refugies
CIR .... Comite International de la Radioelectricite (WGAO)
CIR .... Comite International Rom (WGAO)
CIR .... Commissie voor Internationaal Recht [*United Nations*]
CIR .... Commission for Industrial Relations (WGAO)
CIR .... Commission Internationale du Riz [*International Rice Commission - IRC*] [*United Nations*] (EAIO)
CIR .... Compagnia Industriali Riunite [*Italy*]
CIR .... Conference Internationale des Reparations
CIR .... Convention des Institutions Republicaines [*Convention of Republican Institutions*] [*France*] [*Political party*] (PPE)
CIR .... Coordinator for International Relations [*Australia*]
CIR .... Council of Industrial Relations (WGAO)
CIRA.......... Cast Iron Research Association (WGAO)
CIRA.......... Centrala Industriala de Reparatii Auto [*Industrial Central for Auto Repairs*] (RO)
CIRA.......... Centre for Research into Revolutionary Activities [*Rand Afrikaans University*] [*South Africa*] (AA)
CIRA.......... Centre International de Recherches sur l'Anarchisme [*International Research Center on Anarchism*] [*Geneva, Switzerland*] (EAIO)
CIRA.......... Centro Interamericano de Reforma Agraria [*Colombia*] (COL)
CIRA.......... Centro Italiano Radiatori Alluminio (WGAO)
CIRA.......... Citizen Initiated Referendum Alliance [*Australia*] [*Political party*]
CIRA.......... Commission Internationale pour la Reglementation des Ascenseurs et Monte-Charge [*International Committee for Lift Regulations - ICLR*] (EAIO)
CIRA.......... Confederation of Industrial Research Associations (WGAO)
CIRA.......... Consejo Inter-Sindical Renovador Argentino [*Argentina Inter-Union Reform Council*] (LA)
CIRA.......... Cooperativa Integral de Reforma Agraria [*Integral Land Reform Cooperative*] [*Brazil*] (LA)
CIRAD...... Centre de Cooperation Internationale en Recherche Agronomique pour le Developpement [*International Cooperation Center of Agricultural Research for Development*] [*Research center*] [*France*] (IRC)
CIRAF....... Conseil International pour la Recherche en Agroforesterie [*International Council for Research in Agroforestry*] (EAIO)
CIRAL....... Centro Regional para America Latina [*Regional Center for Latin America*] [*World Assembly of Youth Lima, Peru*] (LAA)
CIRAT....... Centre for Industrial Research and Analytical Technology [*University of Western Sydney, Nepean*] [*Australia*]
CIRB.......... Centre International de Recherche Biologique (WGAO)
CIRB.......... Centre International de Recherches sur le Bilinguisme [*International Center for Research on Bilingualism*] [*Universite Laval, Quebec*] [*Canada*]
CIRB.......... Companhia Industrial de Rochas Betuminosas [*Shale Oil Company*] [*Brazil*] (LA)
CIRC.......... Centre for International Research Cooperation [*CSIRO*] [*Research center*] [*Australia*] (IRC)
CIRC.......... Centre International de Recherche sur le Cancer [*International Center for Cancer Research*] [*French*] (SLS)
CIRC.......... Centro Italiano Rinnovamento Catolico [*Catholic Italian Renewal Center*]
circ............. Circulaire [*Circular*] [*French*] (BAS)
circ............. Circulation (EECI)
CIRC.......... Comite Internacional de la Cruz Roja [*Switzerland*]
CIRC.......... Comite International de Reglementation du Caoutchouc (WGAO)
CIRCA....... Centre International de Recherche, de Creation, et d'Animation [*France*]
CIRCAS..... Comitato Italiano delle Risorse Communitarie d'Assistenza Sociale
CIRCCE .... Confederation Internationale de la Representation Commerciale de la Communaute Europeenne (FLAF)
CircChanc ... Circulaire de la Chancellerie [*Ministere de la Justice*] [*France*] (FLAF)
CIRCE .... Centre d'Information et de Recherche Documentaire des Communautes Europeennes [*Later, SII*] (WGAO)
CIRCE .... Centro Italiano di Ricerche sul Commercio Estero [*Italian*] (SLS)
CIRCEA .... College of Investigative Remedial and Consulting Engineers of Australia
CIRCIT...... Centre for International Research on Communication and Information Technology [*Australia*]
CIRCLE..... Cultural and Information Research Centres in Europe (WGAO)
CIRCOM... Centre International de Recherches sur les Communautes Cooperatives Rurales (WGAO)
CIRCOM... Cooperative Internationale de Recherche et d'Action en Matiere de Communication (EAIO)

CIRD .... Centre International de l'Echerches Dermatologiques [*France*]
CIRD .... Centre International de Recherches Dermatologiques (WGAO)
CIRD .... Centro Italiano Ricerche e Documentazione (WGAO)
CIRD .... Comite Interservice de Recherche et de Developpement [*CEE*]
       (WGAO)
CIRD .... Compagnie Internationale de Riz et de Denrees
CIRDA ...... Centre for Integrated Rural Development for Africa
CIRDAFRICA ... Centre for Integrated Rural Development for Africa
CIRDAfrica ... Centre on Integrated Rural Development for Africa [*FAO*]
       (WGAO)
CIRDAP .... Centre for Integrated Rural Development for Asia and the Pacific
CIRDEC .... Centre International de Recherche et de Documentation en
       Education Continue (WGAO)
CIRDI .... Centre International pour le Reglement des Differends Relatifs
       aux Investissements
CIRDOM .. Centre Interuniversitaire de Recherche et de Documentation sur
       les Migrations (WGAO)
CIRE .... Caisse Israelite de Relevement Economique [*Morocco*]
CIRE .... Confederacion Internacional de Remolacheros Europeos
       [*France*] (DSCA)
CIREA .... Commission Interministerielle des Radioelements Artificiels
       [*Nuclear energy*] [*French*] (NRCH)
CIREC .... Centre International de Recherches et d'Etudes Chreiologiques
       (WGAO)
CIRED .... Centre International de Recherche sur l'Environnement et le
       Developpement [*International Research Center on
       Environment and Development*] [*Research center*] [*French*]
       (IRC)
CIRED ...... Congres Internationale des Reseaux Electriques de Dstiribution
       (WGAO)
CIRELFA .. Conseil International pour le Recherche en Linguistique
       Fondamentale et Appliquee [*International Research
       Council on Pure and Applied Linguistics - IRCPAL*] (EA)
CIRES .... Centre Ivoirien de Recherches Economiques et Sociales [*Ivorian
       Economic and Social Research Center*] (AF)
CIRES .... Companhia Industrial de Resinas Sinteticas
CIRESS ..... Centre International d'Etudes et de Recherches Socio-Samitaires
       [*Belgium*] (WGAO)
CIRET .... Center for International Research on Economic Tendency
       Surveys [*Research center*] (IRC)
CIRET .... Centre for International Research on Economic Tendency
       (WGAO)
CIRF .... Centre International d'Information et de Recherche sur la
       Formation Professionnelle [*Bureau International du
       Travail*] (FLAF)
CIRF .... Consejo Internacional de Recursos Fitogeneticos [*FAO*]
       (WGAO)
CIRFED .... Centre International de Recherche et de Formation en vue du
       Developpement Harmonise (WGAO)
CIRFP .... Centre International d'Information et de Recherche sur la
       Formation Policiere (WGAO)
CIRFS .... Comite International de la Rayonne et des Fibres Synthetiques
       [*International Rayon and Synthetic Fibres Committee -
       IRSFC*] (EAIO)
CIRG .... Commonwealth Internet Reference Group [*Information service
       or system*]
CIRIA .... Construction Industry Research and Information Association
       (WGAO)
CIRIC .... Centre International de Reportages et d'Information Culturelle
       [*Switzerland*] (WGAO)
CIRIEC ..... Centre International de Recherches et d'Information sur
       l'Economic Publique, Sociale et Cooperative (WGAO)
CIRIEC ..... Centre International de Recherches et d'Information sur
       l'Economie Publique, Sociale, et Cooperative [*International
       Centre of Research and Information on Public and Co-
       Operative Economy*] [*Belgium*] (SLS)
CIRIEC ..... Centro Italiano di Ricerche e d'Informazione sull'Economia delle
       Imprese Pubbliche e di Pubblico Interesse [*International
       Centre of Research and Information on Public and Co-
       Operative Economy*] [*Italian*] (SLS)
CIRIL .... Centre Interdisciplinaire de Recherches avec les Ions Lourds
       [*Interdisciplinary Heavy Ion Research Center*] [*France*]
       (WND)
ciril .... Cirilica [*Cyrillic Alphabet*] (YU)
CIRIL .... College International de Recherches Implantaires et Lariboisiere
       [*Rouen, France*] (EAIO)
CIRIOL ..... Comitato Italiano di Rappresentanza Internazionale per
       l'Organizzazione del Lavoro (WGAO)
CIRIP .... Centre d'Instruction du Renseignement et d'Interpretation
       Photographique [*Center for Intelligence Training and Photo
       Interpretation*] [*French*] (WER)
CIRIT .... Comite Interprofessionel de Renovation de l'Industrie Textile
       (WGAO)
CIRL .... Central Investigation and Research Laboratory [*Australia*]
CIRM .... Centro Internazionale Radio-Medico (WGAO)
CIRM .... Comissao Interministerial de Recursos do Mar [*Interministerial
       Commission for Ocean Resources*] [*Brazil*] (LA)

CIRM .... Comite Internacional Radiomaritimo [*International Radio
       Maritime Committee*] [*Spanish*] (ASF)
CIRM .... Comite International Radio Maritime [*International Maritime
       Radio Association*] (EAIO)
CIRM .... Conferencia de Institutos Religioses de Mexico (WGAO)
CIRMA ...... Centro de Investigaciones Regionales de Mesoamerica (WGAO)
CIRMF .... Centre International de Recherches Medicales [*Gabon*] (WGAO)
CIRMF .... Centre International de Recherches Medicales de Franceville
CIRN .... Centre d'Imformation et de Recherches sur les Nuisances
       (WGAO)
CIRN .... Comite de l'Industrie et des Ressources Naturelles [*Committee
       on Industry and Natural Resources*] [*Cambodia*] (CL)
CIRNA ...... Compagnie pour l'Ingenierie des Reacteurs au Sodium [*France*]
       (PDAA)
CIRO .... Centre Interarmees de Recherche Operationnelle [*Inter-Service
       Operational Research Center*] [*French*] (WER)
CIRP .... Central de Instituciones Regionales del Peru [*Center for Peruvian
       Regional Institutions*] (LA)
CIRP .... College International de Recherches pour la Production [*Later,
       CIESTPM*] (EAIO)
CIRP .... College International pour l'Etude Scientifique des Techniques
       de Production Mecanique (WGAO)
CIRP .... Comite Interamericano de Representantes de los Presidentes
       [*Inter-American Committee of Presidential Representatives*]
       (LAA)
CIRP .... Conseil International des Ressources Phytogenetiques
       [*International Board for Plant Genetic Resources - IBPGR*]
       (EAIO)
CIRPA .... Comercio Industrial Produtos Agro-Pecuarios Ltd. [*Brazil*]
       (DSCA)
CIRPHO.... Cercle International de Recherches Philosophiques par
       Ordinateur [*French*] (SLS)
CIRPO .... Conference Internationale des Resistants dans les Pays Occupies
       (WGAO)
CIRSA .... Centro Internazionale Ricerche sulle Strutture Ambientali "Pio
       Manzu" [*Italian*] (SLS)
CIRSA .... Centro Italiano Ricerche e Studi Assicurativi [*Italian*] (SLS)
CIRSA .... Comite Internacional Regional de Sanidad Agropecuaria [*El
       Salvador*] (DSCA)
CIRSE .... Cardiovascular and Interventional Radiology Society of Europe
       (EA)
CIRSEA..... Compagnia Italiana Ricerche Sviluppo Equipaggiamenti
       Aerospaziali [*Italy*] (PDAA)
CIRSOC .... Centro de Investigacion de los Reglamentos Nacionales de
       Seguridad para Obras Civiles [*Research Center for National
       Security Codes in Civil Engineering*] [*INTI*] [*Research
       center*] [*Argentina*] (IRC)
CIRSS .... Centre International de Recherches Sahariennes et Saheliennes
       [*International Center for Saharian Research*] [*France*]
       (IRC)
CIRSS .... Centro Italiano per la Ricerca Sanitaria e Sociale [*Italian*] (SLS)
CIRSTA..... Centro Italiano Ricerche e Studi Trasporto Aereo [*Italian*]
       (SLS)
CIRT .... Centre International de Creations Theatrales (WGAO)
CIRT .... Centre Ivoirien de Recherches Technologiques [*Ivory Coast
       Technological Research Center*] (WED)
CIRT .... Compagnie Industrielle de Radio et de Television
CIRTEF..... Conseil International des Radios-Televisions d'Expression
       Francaise [*International Association of Broadcasting
       Manufacturers - IABM*] (EAIO)
cirvall .... Circonvallazione [*Outer Circle*] [*In addresses*] [*Italian*] (CED)
CIRVE .... Conferenza Italiana de Rappresentanti de Vettori d'Emigrazione
       (WGAO)
CIRZ......... Centro Italiano di Ricerche Zooeconomiche (WGAO)
CIS............ Caribbean Information System [*Proposed*]
CIS............ Catalogiseren in Samenwerking
CIS............ Centrala Industriala Siderurgica [*Industrial Central for Iron and
       Steel*] (RO)
CIS............ Centralny Inspektorat Standaryzacji [*Central Inspectorate for
       Standardization of Imports and Exports*] (POL)
CIS............ Centre d'Informations Scientifiques [*Center for Scientific
       Information*] [*French*] (EAIO)
CIS............ Centre d'Informations Spectroscopiques [*Spectroscopic
       Information Center*] [*Group for the Advancement of
       Spectroscopic Methods and Physicochemical Analysis*]
       [*Information service or system*] (IID)
CIS............ Centre for Independent Studies [*Research center*] [*Australia*]
       (IRC)
CIS............ Centre for Information on Standardization and Metrology
       [*Information service or system*] (IID)
CIS............ Centre for Information Services [*Council for Scientific and
       Industrial Research*] [*South Africa*] (WED)
CIS............ Centre for Information Studies [*Riverina-Murray Institute of
       Higher Education*] [*Australia*]
CIS............ Centre for International Security (WGAO)
CIS............ Centre Interafricain de Sylviculture (WGAO)
CIS............ Centre International de Semiologie (WGAO)

CIS............. Centre International des Stages
CIS............. Centre International de Synthese   (WGAO)
CIS............. Centre International d'Informations de Securite et d'Hygiene du Travail [*International Occupational Safety and Health Information Center*] [*International Labour Office*]   (IID)
CIS............. Centre International pour la Culture et l'Instruction par Image et le Son [*Belgium*]   (WGAO)
CIS............. Centro de Industriales Siderurgicos [*Iron and Steel Industrialists Center*] [*Argentina*]   (LA)
CIS............. Centro de Investigaciones Sociales [*Social Research Center*] [*Buenos Aires, Argentina*]   (LAA)
CIS............. Centro de Investigaciones Sociales [*Social Research Center*] [*Colorado*]
CIS............. Centro de Investigaciones Sociales [*Social Research Center*] [*Bolivia*]   (IRC)
CIS............. Centro de Investigaciones Submarinas [*Underseas Research Center*] [*Chile*]   (LA)
CIS............. Centro Internacional de Informacion sobre Seguridad e Higiene del Trabajo [*International Occupational Safety and Health Information Center*] [*Spain*]
CIS............. Centro Italiano di Sessuologia [*Italian*]   (SLS)
CIS............. Cestovni Informacni Sluzba [*Travel Information Service*] [*Prague*]   (CZ)
CIS............. Cetna Intendantska Stanica [*Company Quartermaster Station*] [*YU*]
CIS............. Chaillotine Air Service [*France*] [*ICAO designator*]   (FAAC)
CIS............. Chinese Industrial Standards
cis............. Cisele [*Chiseled*] [*Publishing*] [*French*]
cis............. Cislo [*Issue, Number*] [*Publishing Former Czechoslovakia*]
CIS............. Coal Industry Society   (WGAO)
CIS............. Combined Independent Schools [*Australia*]
CIS............. Comitato Internazionale degli Scambi Presso la Camera Internazionale di Commercio [*International Trade Committee of the International Chamber of Commerce*] [*Italian*]   (WER)
CIS............. Comite Inter-Sindical [*Inter-Trade Union Committee*] [*El Salvador*]   (LA)
CIS............. Commonwealth Investigation Service [*Australia*]   (ADA)
CIS............. Commonwealth of Independent States [*Formerly, Soviet Union*]
CIS............. Compagnie Ivoirienne de Sciages
CIS............. Compatibles Informationssystem   (ADPT)
CIS............. Computer Investor Services [*Australia*]
CIS............. Consejo Interamericano de Seguridad [*New York*]   (LAA)
CIS............. Constructeurs Inga-Shaba [*Inga-Shaba Engineers*] [*Zaire*]   (AF)
CIS............. Copenhagen International School
CIS............. Court Information Service [*South Australia*]
CIS............. Credit Information Service [*Iran*]   (ME)
CIS............. Credito Industriale Sardo [*Sardinian*]
CIS............. Criminal Investigation Service [*Philippines*]
CIS............. Current Information Service [*Australia*]
CIS............. Institute of Chartered Secretaries and Administrators   (WGAO)
CISA.......... Centro de Informacion sobre el Alcoholismo [*Colombia*]   (COL)
CISA.......... Centro de Informacoes e Seguranca da Aeronautica [*Air Force Intelligence and Security Center*] [*Brazil*]   (LA)
CISA.......... Centro di Informazioni Sterilizzazione e Aborto [*Italian*]   (SLS)
CISA.......... Centro Italiano di Studi Aziendali [*Italian*]   (SLS)
CISA.......... Commission Internationale de Secours Alpin   (WGAO)
CISA.......... Confederation Internationale des Syndicats Arabes [*International Confederation of Arab Trade Unions - ICATU*]   (AF)
CISA.......... Congresos Internacionales SA   (WGAO)
CISA.......... Consejo Indio de Sud America [*Indian Council of South America*] [*Peru*]   (EAIO)
CISA.......... Crucible and Tool Steel Association   (WGAO)
CISAC....... Clinical Imaging Services Advisory   (WGAO)
CISAC....... Confederation Internationale des Societes d'Auteurs et Compositeurs [*French*]   (SLS)
CISAD....... Consel International des Services d'Aide a Domicilo   (WGAO)
CISAE....... Congres International des Sciences Anthropologiques et Ethnologiques   (WGAO)
CISAF....... Conseil International des Services d'Aide Familiale [*International Council of Homehelp Services - ICHS*] [*Driebergen-Rijsenburg, Netherlands*]   (EAIO)
CISAL ...... Companhia Industrial do Sisal [*Brazil*]   (DSCA)
CISAL ...... Confederazione Italiana dei Sindacati Autonomi Lavoratori [*Italian Confederation of Autonomous Labor Unions*]   (DCTA)
Cisalp......... Centre Internationale de Secours Alpins
CISAN....... Turkiye Cimento Sanayii TAS [*Turkish Cement Industry Corporation*]   (TU)
CISAS....... Centro Italiano Studi sull'Arte dello Spettacolo [*Italian*]   (SLS)
CISAVIA... Civil Service Aviation Association   (WGAO)
CISB .... Centrala Industriala Siderurgica Bucuresti [*Bucharest Industrial Central for Iron and Steel*]   (RO)
CISC .... Comite International de Sociologie Clinique [*International Committee on Clinical Sociology - ICCS*]   (EA)
CISC .... Comite International pour la Solidarite avec Chypre [*Finland*]   (WGAO)

CISC .... Commission Internationale de Supervision et de Controle [*International Supervisory and Control Commission*] [*Use ISCC*]   (CL)
CISC .... Confederacion Internacional de Sindicatos Cristianos [*International Federation of Christian Trade Unions - IFCTU*]   (LA)
CISC .... Confederation Internationale des Syndicats Chretiens [*International Federation of Christian Trade Unions - IFCTU*]   (AF)
CISC .... Conference Internationale du Scoutisme Catholique   (WGAO)
CISC .... Groupe International de Sociologie   (EAIO)
CISCCV..... Centre Technique de la Salaison de la Charcuterie et des Conserves de Viande   (WGAO)
CISCE........ Comite International pour la Securite et la Cooperation Europeennes [*International Committee for European Security and Co-Operation - ICESC*]   (EAIO)
CISCF....... Centrala Industriei Sticlei si Ceramicii Fine [*Center of the Glass and Fine Ceramics Industry*]   (RO)
CISCL........ Commission Internationale de Supervision et de Controle au Laos [*International Supervisory and Control Commission for Laos*] [*Use ISCC for Laos*]   (CL)
CISCO .... Centro Italiano Studi Containers   (WGAO)
CISCO .... Civil Service Catering Organization   (WGAO)
CISCO .... Compagnie Industrielle et Commerciale du Sud-Ouest
CISCOP ... Centre d'Investigation sur le Colonialisme Portugais
CISCS....... Centre International Scolaire de Correspondance Sonore Solidarite avec la Jeunesse Algerienne
CISCS....... Centro Internazionale dello Spettacolo e della Comunicazione Sociale [*Italian*]   (SLS)
CISDCE..... Centro Internazionale di Studi e Documentazione sulle Comunita Europee [*European Communities Information Office*] [*Italian*]   (SLS)
CISDCE..... Centro Internazionale Studi Documentazione sulle Comunita Europee   (WGAO)
CISDEN ... Centro Italiano di Studi di Diritto dell'Energia Nucleare [*Nuclear energy*] [*Italian*]   (NRCH)
CISDO....... Comitato Italiano per lo Studio del Dolore in Oncologia [*Italian*]   (SLS)
CISE .... Centre for International Sports Exchanges   (WGAO)
CISE .... Centro Informazioni Studi Esperienze [*Center of Information, Studies, and Experiments*] [*Research center*] [*Italian*]   (IRC)
CISE .... Centro Italiano di Studi Europei "Luigi Einaudi" [*Italian*]   (SLS)
CISE .... Centro Italiano Studi Erboristici [*Italian*]   (SLS)
CISE .... Council of the Institution of Structural Engineers   (WGAO)
CISE .... Cuerpo Internacional de Servicios Ejecutivos [*International Executives Service Corps*] [*El Salvador*]
CISEPA..... Centro de Investigaciones Sociales, Economicas, Politicas, y Antropologicas [*Lima, Peru*]   (LAA)
CISES....... Centro Italiano Studi Esperienze Sanitarie [*Italian*]   (SLS)
CISET........ Centro Internazionale di Studi sull'Economia Turistica [*International Center of Studies on the Tourist Economy*] [*University of Venice*] [*Italy*]
CISF .... Centro Internazionale Studi Famiglia [*Italian*]   (SLS)
CISF .... Confederation Internationale des Sages-Femmes   (WGAO)
CISGO....... Commonwealth Interchange Study Group Operations   (WGAO)
CISH......... Comite International des Sciences Historiques [*French*]   (SLS)
CISH......... Comite International de Standardisation en Hematologie [*International Committee for Standardization in Haematology*]   (EAIO)
CISH......... Conseil International des Sports pour Handicapes   (WGAO)
CISI .... Centro Iniziative Studi Internazionali   (WGAO)
CISI .... Compagnie Internationale de Services et Informatique [*International Information Services Company*] [*Information service or system*]   (IID)
CISIA .... Centro Italiano Sviluppo Impieghi Acciaio [*Italian*]   (SLS)
CISIC........ Centro Internazionale Sociale Istituzione Clero   (WGAO)
CISI-ELECNUL ... Compagnie Internationale de Services en Informatique-Electrical and Nuclear Energy [*France*] [*Information service or system*]   (NITA)
CISI-IAI .... Compagnie Internationale de Services en Informatique [*Information service or system*] [*France*]   (NITA)
CISIP .... Centro Internazionale Studi Irrigazione a Pioggia   (WGAO)
CISIP .... Centro Internazionale Studi Irrigazione a Pioggia [*Italy*]   (DSCA)
CISIR........ Center for Industrial Statistics, Information, and Research [*Industrial Economics and Planning Division, Ministry of Industry*] [*Thailand*]
CISIR........ Ceylon Institute of Scientific and Industrial Research [*Sri Lanka*] [*Research center*]   (IRC)
Cisitalia...... Consorzio Industriale Sportivo Italia [*Italian sporting goods company*]
CISJA........ Comite International de Solidarite avec la Jeuness Algerienne
CISL .... Confederatia Internationala a Sindicatelor Libere [*International Confederation of Free Trade Unions - ICFTU*]   (RO)
CISL .... Confederation Internationale des Syndicats Libres [*International Confederation of Free Trade Unions*]

CISL .... Confederazione Italiana dei Sindacati Lavoratori [*Italian Confederation of Labor Unions*] [*Rome*] (WER)

CISL .... Confederazione Italiana di Sindacati Liberi [*Italian Confederation of Free Workers*] (PPE)

CISL .... Groupe des Syndicate de l'Alimentation du Tabac et de l'Industrie Hoteliere clans la CEE (WGAO)

CISLB....... Comite International pour la Sauveguarde de la Langue Bretonne [*International Committee for the Defense of the Breton Language - ICDBL*] (EAIO)

CISLE....... Centre International des Syndicalistes Libres en Exil [*International Center of Free Trade Unionists in Exile*] [*Defunct*]

CISLORA ... Confederation Internationale des Syndicats Libres Organization Regionale Asienne (WGAO)

CISLORE ... Organisation Regionale Europeenne de la Confederatin Internationale des Syndicats Libres (WGAO)

CISM........ Centre for Information on Standardization and Metrology [*Poland*] (EAIO)

CISM........ Centre International des Sciences Mecaniques

CISM........ Centro de Investigaciones Sociales por Muestreo [*Lima, Peru*] (LAA)

CISM........ Centro de Investigacion y Servicios Museologicos [*Center for Research and Museum Services*] [*Research center*] [*Mexico*] (IRC)

CISM........ Centro Informazione e Studi sul Mercato Comune Europeo (WGAO)

CISM........ Centro Internazionale di Scienze Meccaniche [*Italian*] (SLS)

CISM........ Centro Internazionale Studi Musicali [*Italian*] (SLS)

CISM........ Confederation Internationale des Societes Musicales [*International Confederation of Societies of Music - ICSM*] (EA)

CISM........ Conference Internationale pour l'Etude (WGAO)

CISM........ Conferenza Italiana dei Superiori Maggiori (WGAO)

CISM........ Conseil International du Sport Militaire [*International Military Sports Council*] [*Belgium*]

CISM........ International Centre for Mechanical Sciences [*ICSU*]

CISMEC.... Centro Informazioni e Studi sulla Comunita Europea (Milano) [*Italian*] (SLS)

CISMI .... Confederazione Italiana dei Sindacati Nazionali dei Lavoratori (WGAO)

CISNAL .... Confederazione Italiana Sindacati Nazionali Lavoratori [*Italian Confederation of National Workers' Unions*]

CISNAR .... Commission for Integrated Survey of Natural Resources [*Chinese Academy of Sciences State Planning Commission*] (EAS)

CISNU...... Confederation of Iranian Students [*Germany*] (PD)

CISO......... Comite International des Sciences Onomastiques [*International Committee of Onomastic Sciences*]

CISOR....... Centro de Investigaciones en Ciencias Sociales [*Venezuela*] (SLS)

CISOR....... Centro de Investigaciones Sociales y Religiosas [*Buenos Aires, Argentina*] (LAA)

CISOR....... Centro de Investigaciones Sociales y Sociorreligosas [*Venezuela*] (WGAO)

CISP .... Centro de Informacion y Solidaridad con el Paraguay [*Switzerland*]

CISP .... Centro d'Informazione e Studi Previdenziali e Pensionistici [*Italian*] (SLS)

CISP .... Comitato Interministeriale per gli Studi dei Problemi Spaziali [*Interministerial Committee for Space Research*] [*Italian*] (WER)

CISP .... Comitato Italiano per lo Studio dei Problemi della Popolazione [*Italian*] (SLS)

CISP .... Comitato Italiano per lo Studio des Probleme della Porcellanati (WGAO)

CISP .... Converts to Islam Society of the Philippines (EAIO)

CISPCI ...... Commission Internationale pour la Sauvegarde du Patrimoine Culturel Islamique [*International Commission for the Preservation of Islamic Cultural Heritage - ICPICH*] (EA)

CISPE........ Centro Internazionale per lo Studio dei Papiro Ercolanesi [*Italian*] (SLS)

CISPEL ..... Confederazione Italiana dei Servizi Pubblici degli Enti Locali [*Italian Confederation of Public Services of Local Government*] (WER)

CISPES ..... Centro Italiano Studi Politici Economici Sociali [*Italian*] (SLS)

CISPLAN ... Caribbean Information System for Economic and Social Planning (WGAO)

CISPM ...... Confederation Internationale des Societes Populaires de Musique (WGAO)

CISPP........ Centro Italiano di Studi e Programmazioni per la Pesca [*Italian National Center for Fisheries Research*] (ASF)

CISPR........ Comite International Special des Perturbations Radioelectriques [*International Special Committee on Radio Interference*] (EAIO)

CISR .... Commonwealth Inscribed Stock Registry [*Australia*] (ADA)

CISR .... Conference Internationale de Sociologie des Religions [*French*] (SLS)

CISRI........ Central Iron and Steel Research Institute [*China*]

CISRS........ Christian Institute for the Study of Religion and Society [*India*] (WGAO)

CISS .... Cancer Information and Support Society [*Australia*]

CISS .... Centre for International and Strategic Studies [*York University*] [*Research center*] (RCD)

CISS .... Centre for International Sports Studies (WGAO)

CISS .... Centro Internazionale di Studi Sardi [*Italian*] (SLS)

CISS .... Comite International des Sports des Sourds [*International Committee of Sports for the Deaf*] (EAIO)

CISS .... Comite Permanente Interamericano de Seguro Social [*Mexico*] (WGAO)

CISS .... Conference Internationale de Service Social (WGAO)

CISS .... Conferencia Interamericana de Seguridad Social [*Inter-American Conference on Social Security - IACSS*] (EAIO)

CISS .... Conseil International des Sciences Sociales [*International Social Science Council - ISSC*] (EAIO)

CISSA....... Community Information Support Service of South Australia

CISSAM.... Centro Italiano per lo Studio e lo Sviluppo dell'Agopuntura Moderna e dell'Altra Medicina [*Italian*] (SLS)

CISSEG ..... Centro Italiano di Studi Sociali Economici e Giuridici [*Italian*] (SLS)

CISSEG ..... Centro Italiano per lo Studio e lo Sviluppo della Psicoterapia e dell'Autogenes Training (WGAO)

CISSIG ...... Cataloguing and Indexing Systems Special Interest Group [*Australian Library and Information Association*]

CISSL........ Comissoes Integradoras dos Servicos de Saude Locais [*Local Health Services Coordinating Commissions*] [*Portuguese*] (WER)

CIST .... Centro Internazionale della Stampa Turistica (WGAO)

CIST .... Centro Internazionale di Studi sui Trasporti [*International Center for Transportation Studies - ICTS*] (EAIO)

CISTE........ Congres International pour la Creation d'Une Societe [*Commerciale*] de Type Europeen (FLAF)

CISTI........ Canada Institute for Scientific and Technical Information (SLS)

CISTIP...... Committee on International Scientific and Technical Information Programs [*Commission on International Relations*] (PDAA)

CISTIT ...... Centre d'Information Scientifique et Technique et de Transferts Technologiques [*Algeria*] (WGAO)

CISTOD .... Confederation of International Scientific and Technological Organizations for Development [*ICSU*] [*Paris, France*] [*Defunct*] (EAIO)

CISV .... Children's International Summer Villages International Association [*Newcastle-Upon-Tyne, England*] (EAIO)

CISV .... Childrens's International Summer Villages (WGAO)

CISW........ Christians in Social Work/Social Welfare [*Australia*]

CISWO..... Coal Industry Social Welfare Organisation (WGAO)

CIT............ Advisory Committee for Innovation and Technology Transfer [*EC*] (ECED)

CIT............ Canberra Institute of Technology [*Australia*]

CIT............ Caulfield Institute of Technology [*Australia*] (ADA)

CIT............ Central Institute of Technology [*New Zealand*] (WGAO)

CIT............ Central Istmena de Trabajadores [*Isthmian Workers Federation*] [*Panama*] (LA)

CIT............ Centre International de Transactions [*Benin*] (WGAO)

CIT............ Centre International du Tabac (WGAO)

CIT............ Centre of Industrial Tribology [*Australia*]

CIT............ Centro de Informacao e Turismo [*Information and Tourist Center*] [*Mozambique*] (AF)

CIT............ Centro de Informacion Tecnica [*Instituto de Investigaciones Electricas*] [*Mexico*]

CIT............ Centro de Informacion Tecnologica [*Instituto de Investigacion Tecnologica Industrial y de Normas Tecnicas*] [*Peru*]

CIT............ Centro de Informacion Tecnologica [*Instituto Tecnologico de Costa Rica*]

CIT............ Centro de Investigaciones Textiles [*Textile Research Center*] [*INTI*] [*Research center*] [*Argentina*] (IRC)

CIT............ Chartered Institute of Transport [*South Africa*] (SLS)

CIT............ Chartered Institute of Transport [*Australia*] (ADA)

CIT............ Chisholm Institute of Technology [*Australia*]

cit .... Citacao [*Citation, Summons*] [*Portuguese*]

cit .... Citada [*or Citado*] [*Portuguese*]

Cit .... Citation [*Mention in Dispatches*] [*Military*] [*French*] (MTD)

cit .... Citato [*Cited*] [*Publishing*] [*Italian*]

CIT............ City-Jet Luftverklehrsges, GmbH [*Austria*] [*ICAO designator*] (FAAC)

CIT............ Coal Industry Tribunal [*Australia*]

CIT............ Comite International des Transports [*French*] (BAS)

CIT............ Comite International des Transports Ferroviaires [*International Rail Transport Committee*] (EAIO)

CIT............ Comite International de Television [*International Committee of Television*] [*French*] (SLS)

CIT............ Comite International Tzigane [*French*] (SLS)

CIT............ Compagnia Italiana Turismo [*Italian Tourist Organisation*]

CIT............ Compagnie Industrielle des Telecommunications (WGAO)

CIT............ Compagnie Industrielle de Telecommunication [*Computer manufacturer*] [*France*]

CIT............. Compagnie Italiana Transatlantica (WGAO)
CIT............. Compagnie Ivoirienne de Transports
CIT............. Computer Industry Training and Technology Corp. Ltd. [*Australia*]
CIT............. Computer Information Technology Centre [*New South Wales Technical and Further Education*] [*Australia*]
CIT............. Confection Industrielle Tchadienne
CIT............. Confederacion Interamericana de Trabajadores [*Inter-American Workers Confederation*] [*ORIT*] [*Later,*] (LA)
CIT............. Confederation Internationale du Travail [*North African*]
CIT............. Congres International Teletrafic (WGAO)
CIT............. Conseil International des Tanneurs [*International Council of Tanners - ICT*] (EAIO)
CIT............. Consejo Internacional del Trigo [*International Wheat Council - IWC*] (EAIO)
CIT............. Cooperative Ivoirienne des Transporteurs
CIT............. Customer Imput Terminal [*Royal Jockey Club*] [*Hong Kong*]
CITA......... Centre d'Information et de Tourisme d'Angola [*French*]
CITA......... Centro de Informacao e Turismo de Angola [*Portuguese*]
CITA......... Centro de Investigaciones en Tecnologia de Alimentos [*Food Technology Research Center*] [*Costa Rica*] [*Research center*] (IRC)
CITA......... Chartered Institute of Transport in Australia
CITA......... Comite International de l'Inspection Technique Automobile [*International Motor Vehicle Inspection Committee*] [*Verviers, Belgium*] (EAIO)
CITA......... Confederacion Interamericana de Transporte Aero [*Inter-American Air Transport Confederation*] (LA)
CITA......... Confederation Internationale des Ingenieurs et Techniciens de l'Agriculture [*International Confederation of Agricultural Engineers and Technicians*] [*Switzerland*]
CITA......... Conference Internationale des Trains Speciaux d'Agences de Voyages [*International Conference on Special Trains for Travel Agencies*] (EAIO)
CITA......... Consejo Interamericano de Archiveros [*Inter-American Archivists' Council*] [*Mexico*] (LAA)
CITAB....... Compagnie Industrielle des Tabacs de Madagascar
CITAC...... Centro de Investigacion de la Tecnologia Aplicada a la Construccion [*Argentina*] (LAA)
CITAM..... Centre International de la Tapisserie Ancienne et Moderne [*Switzerland*]
CITAV....... Centro Informacion Tecnicade Aplicaciones de Vidrio [*Technical Information Center on the Use of Glass*] [*Spain*] (PDAA)
CITB......... Carpet Industry Training Board (WGAO)
CITB......... Construction Industry Training Board (WGAO)
CITC........ Caltex International Technical Centre [*Australia*] (ADA)
CITC........ Caribbean Interim Tourism Committee (WGAO)
CITC........ Cathay Investment & Trust Co. [*Taiwan*]
CITC........ Centre for Information Technology and Communications [*Queensland*] [*Australia*] [*Information service or system*]
CITC........ China International Television Services Corp.
CITC........ Christian Industrial Training Centre
CITC........ Comision de Investigaciones Tecnicas y Cientificas [*Scientific, Technical, and Research Commission - STRC*] [*Spanish*] (ASF)
CITC......... Confederation Internationale des Industries Techniques du Cinema (WGAO)
CITCA...... Committee of Inquiry into Technological Change in Australia (ADA)
CITCARB ... Caulfield Institute of Technology Computer Abuse Research Bureau [*Australia*] (ADA)
CITD......... Committee for Industrial Technology Development [*Ministry of Industry*] [*Thailand*]
CITD......... Computer and Information Services Industry Training Division [*New South Wales Technical and Further Education*] [*Australia*]
CITDEE .... Centrala Industriala pentru Transportul si Distributia Energiei Electrice [*Industrial Center for the Transportation and Distribution of Electric Power*] (RO)
CITE......... Centre d'Information Technique et Economique [*Technical and Economic Information Center*] [*Malagasy*] (AF)
CITE......... Centro de Instruccion de Tropas Especiales [*Special Forces Training Center*] [*Bolivia*] (LA)
Cite........... Citerne [*Cistern, Well*] [*Military map abbreviation World War I*] [*French*] (MTD)
CITE......... Compagnie d'Ingenieurs et Techniciens d'Etudes
CITE......... Compagnie Ivoirienne de Travaux et d'Entreprises
CITE......... Confederacion Intersectorial de Trabajadores del Estado [*Peru*] (WGAO)
CITE......... Confederacion Intersectorial de Trabajadores Estatales [*Union of Public Sector Workers*] [*Peru*] (EY)
CITEAA .... Conference of the Interpreter Translator Education Association of Australia
CITEC....... Centro de Investigacion de Tecnologia del Cuero [*Research Center for Leather Technology*] [*INTI*] [*Research center*] [*Argentina*] (IRC)
CITEC .... Compagnie de l'Industrie Textile Cotonniere (WGAO)

CITEC ...... Compagnie Industrielle and Technique d'Echangeurs
CITEC ...... Compagnie pour l'Information et les Techniques Electroniques de Controle (WGAO)
CITECA .... Centro de Investigacion y Tecnologia de Carnes [*Meat Research and Technology Center*] [*INTI*] [*Research center*] [*Argentina*] (IRC)
CITEC-huilerie ... Societe des Huiles et Savons de Haute-Volta
CITEF........ Centro de Investigacion Tecnologia de Frutas y Hortalizas [*Research Center for Fruit and Vegetable Technology*] [*Argentina*] (LAA)
CITEFA..... Centro de Investigaciones Cientificas y Tecnicas de las Fuerzas Armadas [*Armed Forces Scientific and Technical Research Center*] [*Argentina*] (LA)
CITEFA..... Cientificas y Tecnicas de las Fuerzas Armadas [*Argentina*] (WGAO)
CITEJA..... Comite International Technique d'Experts Juridiques Aeriens (FLAF)
CITEL ...... Comision Interamericana de Telecommunicaciones [*United States*] (WGAO)
CITEL ...... Compagnie Internationale de Teleinformastique [*French*] (ADPT)
CITEL ...... Conference on Inter-American Telecommunications [*Organization of American States*] [*Telecommunications*]
CITEM ...... Center for International Trade Exhibitions and Missions [*Ministry for Trade*] [*Philippines*]
CITEN ...... Comite International de la Teinture et du Nettoyage a Sec (WGAO)
CITEP ...... Centro de Investigaciones de Tecnologia Pesquera [*Argentina*] (ASF)
CITEP ...... Centro de Investigacion y Tecnicas Politicas [*Center for Political Research and Techniques*] [*Spanish*] (WER)
CITEPA..... Camara de Industriales de Tejidos de Punto y Anexos [*Argentina*]
CITEPA..... Centre Interprofessionnel Technique d'Etudes de la Pollution Atmospherique [*French*] (ASF)
CITERAC ... Chisholm Institute of Technology, Engineering Research and Advisory Centre [*Australia*]
CITERE..... Centre d'Information Tempi Reel Europe (WGAO)
CITES........ Convention on International Trade in Endangered Species [*Of wild fauna and flora*]
CITES........ Convention on International Trade in Endangered Species of Wild Fauna and Flora (ASF)
CITG......... Coal Industry Triparite Group (WGAO)
CITGV....... Circuits Integres a Tres Grande Vitesse
CITH .... Centre d'Information Textile Habillement [*Textile and Clothing Information Center*] [*Information service or system*] (IID)
CITHA ..... Confederation of International Trading Houses Associations [*The Hague, Netherlands*] (EAIO)
CITI.......... Centro de Informacao Tecnica para a Industria [*Technical Information Center for Industry*] [*National Laboratory for Engineering and Industrial Technology*] [*Portugal*]
CITI.......... Classification Internationale Type, par Industrie [*De Toutes les Branches d'Activites Economiques*] (FLAF)
CITI.......... Confederation Internationale des Travailleurs Intellectuels [*French*] (SLS)
CITIC .... Centro de Investigacion Tecnologica de la Industria del Caucho [*Rubber Industry Technological Research Center*] [*Research center*] [*Argentina*] (IRC)
CITIC .... China International Trust Investment Corp.
CITIL........ Centro de Investigaciones Tecnologicas de la Industria Lactea [*Dairy IndustryTechnological Research Center*] [*Research center*] [*Argentina*] (IRC)
CITIP........ Centro de Investigaciones Tecnologicas para la Industria Plastica [*INTI*] [*Research center*] [*Argentina*] (IRC)
CITLA ...... Camara Industrial Textil Lanera [*Argentina*] (LAA)
Citlle .... Citadelle [*Citadel*] [*Military map abbreviation World War I*] [*French*] (MTD)
CITLO....... Centrum voor Informatieverwerking op het Gebied van Tropische Landbouw en Ontwikkeling [*Belgium*] (WGAO)
CITM........ College International du Tiers-Monde (WGAO)
CITM........ Compagnie Ivoirienne de Transit et de Manutention
CITMA..... Centrala Industriala de Tractoare si Masini Agricole [*Industrial Central for Tractors and Agricultural Machinery*] (RO)
CITMADE ... Centro de Investigaciones en Tecnicas Matematicas Aplicadas a la Direccion de Empresas [*Argentina*] (LAA)
CITO .... Centro de Investigaciones Tecnologicas de Oriente [*Eastern Technological Research Centre*] [*Research center*] [*Venezuela*] (IRC)
CITO .... Conference Internationale des Techniques Oleicoles (WGAO)
CITP......... Comite International des Telecommunications de Presse [*International Press Telecommunications Council - IPTC*] (EAIO)
CITP......... Community Infrastructure Training Program
CITP......... Computer Industry Training Program [*Australia*]
CITP......... Conseil International des Telecommunications de Presse (WGAO)

CITPA .... International Committee of Paper and Board Converters in the Common Market   (ECED)

CITPA .... International Confederation of Paper and Board Converters in the European Commuity [*Germany*]   (EA)

CITPPM.... Confederation des Industries de Traitement des Produits des Peches Maritimes   (WGAO)

CITR .... Centre for Information Technology Research [*University of Queensland*] [*University of Wollongong*] [*Australia*]

CITR .... Compagnie Ivoirienne de Transports Routiers

CITR .... Conseil International des Transports Routiers   (FLAF)

CITRA ...... Compagnie Industrielle de Travaux [*Morocco*]

CITRA ...... Conference Internationale de la Table Ronde des Archives   (WGAO)

CITRAM ... Compagnie Industrielle de Travaux du Maroc [*Morocco*]

CITRAP .... Societe de Construction de l'Immobilier et de Travaux Publiques [*Ivory Coast*]   (WGAO)

CITRE .... Centro Impianti Tecnici Rame Edilizia [*Italian*]   (SLS)

CITREMPAC ... Planta Empacadora de Citricos [*Venezuela*]   (DSCA)

CITROA .... Compagnie Internationale de Terrassements Routes et Ouvrages d'Art

CITS .... China International Travel Service

CITS .... Commission Internationale Technique de Sucrerie [*International Commission of Sugar Technology*]   (EAIO)

CITS .... Companhia Internacional Tratamentos de Superficies   (WGAO)

CITSAFE .. Centro de Investigacion Tecnologica de la Provincia de Santa Fe [*Technological Research Center of the Province of Santa Fe*] [*INTI*] [*Research center*] [*Argentina*]   (IRC)

CITSS .... Centre International pour la Terminologie des Sciences Sociales [*France*]   (EAIO)

CITT .... Commission Interamericaine de Thon Tropical [*Inter-American Tropical Tuna Commission - IATTC*] [*French*]   (ASF)

CITTA .... Confederation Internationale des Fabricants de Tapis et de Tissus d'Ameublement [*International Confederation of Manufacturers of Carpets and Furnishing Fabrics*]   (EAIO)

CITTA .... Confederation Internationale des Fabricants de Tapis Velours et Tissus d'Ameublement   (WGAO)

CIT-TAFE ... Caulfield Institute of Technology, TAFE [*Technical and Further Education*] Division [*Australia*]

CITTC ...... Computer Industry Training and Technology Corp., Inc. [*Commercial firm*] [*Australia*]

CITU......... Centre of Indian Trade Unions [*India*]

CITU......... Confederation of Independent Trade Unions   (EAIO)

CITUB...... Confederation of Independent Trade Unions in Bulgaria   (EE)

CITUC...... Council of International Trade Union Cooperation [*Sweden*]   (EAIO)

CITV .... [*The*] China International Television Collaboration Corp.   (TCC)

City Art I.... City Art Institute [*Sydney, Australia*]

CIU .... Chlorella International Union [*Later, MIU*]

CiU........... Convergencia i Unio [*Convergence and Union*] [*Spain*] [*Political party*]   (PPE)

CIU .... Crime Intelligence Unit [*Australia*]   (ADA)

CIUA .... Chemisches Institut fuer Umweltanalytik Dr. W. Jaeger [*Chemical Institute for Environmental Analysis Dr. W. Jaeger*]   (SLS)

CIUC .... Consejo Internacional de Uniones Cientificas [*International Council of Scientific Unions - ICSU*] [*Spanish*]   (ASF)

CIUDCO ... Comision Permanente Inter-Universitaria de Desarrollo de la Comunidad [*Colombia*]   (COL)

CIUEMC... Centrala Industriala de Utilaj Energetic, Metalurgic, si pentru Constructii [*Industrial Center for Power, Metallurgical, and Construction Equipment*]   (RO)

CIUEMMR ... Centrala Industriala de Utilaj Energetic, Metalurgic, si Masini de Ridicat [*Industrial Center for Power and Metallurgical Equipment, and for Hoisting Machines*]   (RO)

CIUF......... Conseil Interuniversitaire de la Communaute Francaise   (WGAO)

CIUFFAS .. Comitato Italiano Utilizzatori Filati di Fibre Artificiali e Sintetiche   (WGAO)

CIUL......... Congress of Industrial Unions of Liberia   (AF)

CIUL......... Council for International Urban Liaison   (WGAO)

CIUMR ..... Commission Internationale des Unites et Mesures Radiologiques [*International Commission of Radiological Units and Measures*]   (PDAA)

CIUP......... Centro de Investigaciones Universidad Pedagogica [*Colombia*]   (WGAO)

CIUPST..... Commission Interunions de la Physique Solaire et Terrestre [*CIUS*]   (WGAO)

CIUR .... Comite Interministeriel d'Intervention d'Urgence des Secours aux Refugies [*Interministerial Committee for Urgent Provision of Aid to Refugees*] [*Cambodia*]   (CL)

CIUS......... Conseil International des Unions Scientifiques [*International Council of Scientific Unions - ICSU*] [*French*]   (ASF)

CIUS......... Consiglio Internazionale delle Unioni Scientifiche [*International Council of Scientific Unions*] [*Use ICSU*] [*Italian*]   (WER)

CIUSS ...... Catholic International Union for Social Service

CIUTCPM ... Centrala Industriala de Utilaj Tehnologic, Chimic, Petrolier, si Minier [*Industrial Central for Technological, Chemical, Petroleum, and Mining Equipment*]   (RO)

CIUTI........ Conference Internationale Permanente de Directeurs d'Instituts Universitaires pour la Formation de Traducteurs et d'Interpretes [*Standing International Conference of the Directors of University Institutes for the Training of Translators and Interpreters*]   (EAIO)

CIUTMR.... Centrala Industriala de Utilaj Tehnologic si Material Rulant [*Industrial Central for Technological Equipment and Rolling Stock*]   (RO)

Civ............. Arret de la Chambre Civile de la Cour de Cassation [*Decision of the Court of Appeal, Civil Division*] [*French*]   (ILCA)

CIV .... Centro de Investigaciones Veterinarias [*Venezuela*]   (DSCA)

CIV .... Civil Aviation Authority of New Zealand [*ICAO designator*]   (FAAC)

Civ............. Code Civil [*Civil Code*] [*French*]

CIV .... Colegio de Ingenieros de Venezuela [*Venezuelan Engineers Association*]   (LA)

CIV .... Commerce Industrie Voltaique

CIV .... Commission Internationale du Verre [*International Commission on Glass - ICG*]   (EAIO)

CIV .... Commonwealth Institute of Valuers [*Australia*]   (ADA)

CIV .... Convention Internationale Concernant le Transport des Voyageurs et des Baggages par Chemins de Fer

CIV .... Convention Internationale sur le Transport des Voyageurs et des Bagages par Chemins de Fer   (WGAO)

CIV .... Cooperatieve Centrale Landbouw In -en Verkoopvereniging

CIV .... Ivory Coast [*ANSI three-letter standard code*]   (CNC)

Civ............. Tribunal Civil [*Benelux*]   (BAS)

CIVA .... Commission Internationale de Voltige Aerienne [*FAI*]   (WGAO)

CIVA .... Compagnia Italiana Viaggi Aerei [*Italy*]

CIVACC .... Comercio e Industria de Vidros e Acabamentos de Construcao Civil Lda.

CIVAM...... Centre d'Information et de Vulgarisation Agricole et Menager   (WGAO)

CIVAS ...... Comite Interprofessionnel des Vins d'Anjou-Saumur   (WGAO)

CIVAT....... Comissao Interestadual dos Vales do Araguaia e Tocantins [*Brazil*]   (DSCA)

CIVB......... Comite Interprofessionnel des Vins de Bergerac   (WGAO)

CIVB......... Comite Interprofessionnel des Vins de Bordeaux   (WGAO)

CIVB......... Conseil Interprofessionel du Vin de Bordeaux [*Professional Council of Bordeaux Wines*] [*France*]

Civ Brux.... Jugement du Tribunal Civil de Bruxelles [*Belgium*]   (BAS)

Civ C .... Arret de la Chambre Civile de la Cour de Cassation qui Casse [*France*]   (FLAF)

CIVC......... Comite Interprofessionnel des Vins de Champagne   (WGAO)

CIVCP ...... Comite Interprofessionnel des Vins des Cotes de Provence   (WGAO)

CIVCR ...... Comite Interprofessionnel des Vins des Cotes-du-Rhone   (WGAO)

CIVDN ..... Comite Interprofessionnel des Vins Doux Naturels   (WGAO)

CIVE......... International Centre of Winter Maintenance [*Italian*]   (WGAO)

CIVEM...... Constructions Ivoiriennes Electro-Mecaniques

CIVEXIM .. Compagnie Ivoirienne d'Exportation et d'Importation

CIVG .... Comite Interprofessionnel des Vins de Gaillac   (WGAO)

CIVI.......... Centraal Instituut voor Industrie-Ontwikkeling [*Netherlands*]

CIVI.......... Central Institute for Industrial Development [*Netherlands*]   (WGAO)

CIVICIMA ... Comite International du Vocubulaire des Institutions et de la Communication Intellectuelle au Moyen Age   (WGAO)

CIVIJU...... Association des Producteurs de Cidre, Vins, Jus de Fruits et des Embouteilleurs de Jus de Fruits [*Belgium*]   (WGAO)

CIVILCO... Civil Contracting Company Oman

CIVILCO... Construcciones Civiles Ltda. [*Colombia*]   (COL)

CIVINEX ... Compagnie Ivoirienne d'Exploitation Vinicole

CIVINEX .. Societe Ivoirienne d'Exploitation Vinicole   (WGAO)

CIVL......... Center International de Vol Libre [*Aguessac, France*]   (EAIO)

CIVO .... Centraal Instituut voor Voedingsonderzoek   (WGAO)

CIVPN....... Comite Interprofessionnel des Vins du Pays Nantais   (WGAO)

Civr .... Arret de la Chambre Civile de la Cour de Cassation qui Rejette [*France*]   (FLAF)

CIVRES..... Congres International des Techniques de Vide en Recherche Spatiale [*International Congress for Vacuum Techniques in Space Research*]   (PDAA)

CIVT......... Comite Interprofessionel des Vins de Touraine   (WGAO)

CIVV......... Centro Ittiologico Valli Venete [*Research Laboratory for Venetian Fish Culture*] [*Italian*]   (ASF)

CIW .... Community Information Week [*Australia*]

CIWF........ Centralny Instytut Wychowania Fizycznego [*Central Institute of Physical Education*]   (POL)

CIWLT...... Comite Permanent des Syndicates de Travailleurs de la Compagnie International des Wagon-Lits et du Tourisme   (WGAO)

CIWU .... Commercial and Industrial Workers Union [*Grenada*]   (LA)

CIX .... Chiclayo [*Peru*] [*Airport symbol*]   (OAG)

cj .... Cislo Jednaci [*File Number*]   (CZ)

CJ .... Comision de Jornaleros [*Commission of Day Laborers*] [*In Andalusia; dominated by the Labor Party and the ORT*] [*Spanish*]   (WER)

CJ .... Conseil de la Jeunesse [*Youth Council*] [*Senegal, Mali, Upper Volta, Niger, and Dahomey*]

CJ .... Court of Justice of the European Communities

c/j .... Courts Jours [*Short-Dated Bills*] [*French*]

CJA .... Cajamarca [*Peru*] [*Airport symbol*]   (OAG)

CJA .... Commonwealth Journalists Association [*British*]   (EAIO)

CJA .... Conseil de la Jeunesse d'Afrique [*African Youth Council*] [*Senegal*]

CJB .... Coimbatore [*India*] [*Airport symbol*]   (OAG)

CJBL .... Centre for Japanese Business Language [*Australia*]

CJC .... Calama [*Chile*] [*Airport symbol*]   (OAG)

CJC .... Canberra Jazz Club [*Australia*]

CJC .... Conseil de la Jeunesse Catholique [*Catholic Youth Council*] [*Belgium*]   (EAIO)

CJC .... Criminal Justice Commission [*Queensland, Australia*] [*Proposed*]

CJCA .... Cour de Justice de l'Amerique Centrale   (FLAF)

CJCC .... Commonwealth Joint Communications Committee   (WGAO)

CJCC .... Coordinating Justice for Cyprus Committee [*Australia*]

CJCE .... Cour de Justice des Communautes Europeennes [*French*]   (BAS)

CJCI .... Conseil de la Jeunesse de Cote d'Ivoire   (WGAO)

CJCS .... Center for Jewish Community Studies [*Israel*]   (IRC)

CJD .... Canadian Journalism Data Base [*University of Western Ontario*]   (IID)

CJD .... Candilejas [*Colombia*] [*Airport symbol*]   (OAG)

CJD .... Centrala Jajczarsko-Drobiarska [*Egg and Poultry Center*]   (POL)

CJD .... Centre des Jeunes Dirigeants d'Entreprise [*Center for Young Businessmen*] [*France*]   (EY)

CJEC .... Court of Justice of the European Communities   (DLA)

CJEFS .... Consiliul Judetean al Educatiei Fizice si al Sportului [*County Council for Physical Education and Sports*]   (RO)

CJEPC ...... Central Joint Education Policy Committee   (WGAO)

CJES .... Centre for Japanese Economic Studies [*Macquarie University*] [*Australia*]

CJF .... Chief Justice of the Federation [*Nigeria*]   (DLA)

CJFA .... Comite Juridique Francais de l'Aviation [*France*]

CJFA .... Commander of Joint Forces of Australia

CJG .... Council of Jews from Germany [*British*]   (EAIO)

CJG .... Zhejiang Airlines [*China*] [*ICAO designator*]   (FAAC)

CJI .... Comissao Juridica Interamericana [*Inter-American Juridical Committee*] [*Portuguese*]   (LA)

CJI .... Comite Juridico Interamericano [*Inter-American Juridical Committee*] [*Spanish*]   (LA)

CJIA .... Comite Juridique International de l'Aviation   (FLAF)

CJIE .... Comite des Jeux Internationaux des Ecoliers   (OLYM)

CJIT .... Consiliul Judetean al Inginerilor si Tehnicienilor [*County Council of Engineers and Technicians*]   (RO)

CJL .... Chitral [*Pakistan*] [*Airport symbol*] [*Obsolete*]   (OAG)

CJM .... Code de Justice Militaire [*Military Law*] [*Military*] [*French*]   (MTD)

CJM .... Confederacion de la Juventud Mexicana [*Mexican Youth Confederation*]   (LA)

CJM .... Congres Juif Mondial   (WGAO)

CJMV .... Christelike Jongemannevereniging [*YMCA*] [*Afrikaans*]

CJN .... Chief Justice of Nigeria   (DLA)

CJP .... Centre de Jeunes Patrons [*Young Employers' Center*] [*French*]   (WER)

CJP .... Comissao de Justica e Paz [*Brazil*]   (WGAO)

CJP .... Commission Justice et Paix [*Justice and Peace Commission*] [*Belgium*]   (EAIO)

CJPCMA... Commonwealth Jam Preserving and Condiment Manufacturers' Association [*Australia*]

CJPN .... Commissie Justitia et Pax Nederland [*Justice and Peace Commission of the Netherlands*]   (EAIO)

CJR .... Chaurjahari [*Nepal*] [*Airport symbol*]   (OAG)

CJR .... Circulos de Jovenes Revolucionarios [*Revolutionary Youth Circles*] [*Spanish*]   (WER)

CJRC .... Civil Justice Research Centre [*Australia*]

CJS .... Ciudad Juarez [*Mexico*] [*Airport symbol*]   (OAG)

CJS .... Confederation des Jeunesses Socialistes [*Confederation of Socialist Youth*] [*Belgium*]   (WER)

CJTF .... Combined Joint Task Forces [*NATO*]   (ECON)

CJU .... Cheju [*South Korea*] [*Airport symbol*]   (OAG)

C JustEur ... Cour de Justice des Communautes Europeennes [*Benelux*]   (BAS)

CJV .... Christelike Jongeliedevereniging

CK .... Centralna Komisja [*Central Board*] [*Poland*]

CK .... Centralni Komitet [*Central Committee*]   (YU)

CK .... Centralny Komitet [*Central Committee*]   (POL)

CK .... Cerveny Kriz [*Red Cross*]   (CZ)

ck .... Cesarsko-Krolewski [*Poland*]

CK .... Channel Bay   (RU)

CK .... Chawangan Khas [*Special Branch*]   (ML)

Ck .... Cikmaz [*Dead-End Street, Impasse*]   (TU)

ck .... Cisarsky Kralovsky [*Imperial Royal (In reference to the Austro-Hungarian Empire)*]   (CZ)

CK .... Compagnie du Kasai

CK .... Cook [*Royal Australian Navy*]

CK .... Cook Islands [*ANSI two-letter standard code*]   (CNC)

CK .... Corvina Kiadovallalat [*Corvina Publishing Enterprise*]   (HU)

CK .... Crven Krst [*Red Cross*]   (YU)

CK .... Cyklisticky Klub [*Cycling Club*]   (CZ)

CKAQ .... Creche and Kindergarten Association of Queensland [*Australia*]

CKB .... Christelijke Kruideniers Bond   (WGAO)

CKBA .... Centralna Komisja Brakowania Akt [*Central Commission for the Destruction of Records*]   (POL)

CKBKP ..... Centralni Komitet Bugarske Komunisticke Partije [*Central Committee of the Bulgarian Communist Party*]   (YU)

CKBRP(komunisti) ... Centralni Komitet Bugarske Radnicke Partije (Komunisti) [*Central Committee of the Bulgarian Workers' Party (Communists)*]   (YU)

CKC .... Canberra Kennel Club [*Australia*]

CKC .... Cesky Klub Cyklistu [*Czech Cycling Club*]   (CZ)

CKC .... Cyprus Kennel Club   (EAIO)

CKC .... Samozaryadnyy Karabin Simonov [*Simonov Semi-Automatic Carbine*] [*Use SKS*]   (CL)

CKCh .... Ceska Katolicka Charita [*Czech Catholic Charity Society*]   (CZ)

CKD .... Ceskomoravska - Kolben - Danek, Narodni Podnik [*Ceskomoravska - Kolben - Danek, National Enterprise*] [*Heavy machinery plants*]

CKF .... Centerns Kvinnoforbund [*Women's Association of the Centre Party*] [*Sweden*] [*Political party*]   (EAIO)

CKG .... Central Kalgoorlie Gold [*Australia*]

CKG .... Centralni Komitet Grcke [*Central Committee of Greece*]   (YU)

CKG .... Chongqing [*China*] [*Airport symbol*]   (OAG)

CKH .... Centrale Kamer van Handelsbevordering   (WGAO)

CKH .... Centrale Kamer voor Handelsbevordering [*Netherlands*]

CKH .... Corps Kehakiman [*Military Justice Corps*]   (IN)

CKHBC ..... Capital Kang Hua Bodybuilding Club [*China*]

CKIA .... China Knitting Industry Association   (EAIO)

C(K)IAC .... Cocos (Keeling) Islands Administration and Council [*Australia*]

C(K)ICS .... Ccos (Keeling) Islands Cooperative Society [*Australia*]

CKIOAB.... Caglayan Kucukler Ilkokulu Okul Aile Birligi [*Caglayan Kucukler Elementary School Family Union*] [*Turkish Cypriot*]   (GC)

CKK .... Centralna Komisja Kwalifikacyjna [*Central Qualification Commission*]   (POL)

CKK .... Cesky Klub Kanoistu [*Czech Canoe Club*]   (CZ)

CKKP........ Centralna Komisja Kontroli Partyjnej [*Central Party Control Commission*]   (POL)

CKKP........ Centralni Komitet Komunisticke Partije [*Central Committee of the Communist Party*]   (YU)

CKKPA...... Centralni Komitet Komunisticke Partije Albanije [*Central Committee of the Communist Party of Albania*]   (YU)

CKKPB ..... Centralni Komitet Komunisticke Partije Bugarske [*Central Committee of the Communist Party of Bulgaria*]   (YU)

CKKPBiH ... Centralni Komitet Komunisticke Partije Bosne i Hercegovine [*Central Committee of the Communist Party of Bosnia and Hercegovina*]   (YU)

CKKPC...... Centralni Komitet Komunisticke Partije Cehoslovacke [*Central Committee of the Communist Party of Czechoslovakia*]   (YU)

CKKPCG... Centralni Komitet Komunisticke Partije Crne Gore [*Central Committee of the Communist Party of Montenegro*]   (YU)

CKKPG...... Centralni Komitet Komunisticke Partije Grcke [*Central Committee of the Communist Party of Greece*]   (YU)

CKKPH ..... Centralni Komitet Komunisticke Partije Hrvatske [*Central Committee of the Communist Party of Croatia*]   (YU)

CKKPJ....... Centralni Komitet Komunisticke Partije Jugoslavije [*Central Committee of the Communist Party of Yugoslavia*]   (YU)

CKKPM..... Centralni Komitet Komunisticke Partije Makedonije [*Central Committee of the Communist Party of Macedonia*]   (YU)

CKKPP...... Centralni Komitet Komunisticke Partije Poljske [*Central Committee of the Communist Party of Poland*]   (YU)

CKKPS ..... Centralni Komite Komunisticne Partije Slovenije [*Central Committee of the Communist Party of Slovenia*]   (YU)

CKKPS ..... Centralni Komitet Komunisticke Partije Srbije [*Central Committee of the Communist Party of Serbia*]   (YU)

CKKPSS .... Centralni Komitet Komunisticke Partije Sovjetskog Saveza [*Central Committee of the Communist Party of the Soviet Union*]   (YU)

CKKPSZ.... Centralni Komite Komunisticne Partije Sovjetske Zveze [*Central Committee of the Communist Party of the Soviet Union*]   (YU)

CKKR .... Centralna Komisja Kontrolno Rewizyjna   (WGAO)

CKL .... Centralny Komitet Ludowy [*Central People's Committee*]   (POL)

CKL .... Commissie voor Keuring Luchtvaartmaterieel [*Commission for the Investigation of Aircraft Materials*] [*Netherlands*]

CKLMJ ..... Centralni Komite Ljudske Mladine Yugoslavije [*Central Committee of the People's Youth of Yugoslavia*]   (YU)

CKLMS ..... Centralni Komite Ljudske Mladine Slovenije [*Central Committee of the People's Youth of Slovenia*]   (YU)

CKM .... Centrale Kamer voor Handelsbevordering [*Benelux*]   (BAS)

CKM .... Chawangan Keselamatan Medan [*Field Security Branch*]   (ML)

CKM .... Ciezki Karabin Maszynowy [*Heavy Machine Gun*]   (POL)

CKMP .... Cumhuriyet Koylu Millet Partisi [*Republican Peasants Nation Party - RPNP*] [*MHP*] [*See also*]   (TU)

CKMPT ..... Centralni Komitet Madarske Partije Trudbenika [*Central Committee of the Hungarian Workers' Party*]

CKNMM ... Centralni Komitet na Narodnata Mladina na Makedonija [*Central Committee of the People's Youth of Macedonia*]   (YU)

CKNO .... Centralni Komitet Narodne Omladine [*Central Committee of the People's Youth*]   (YU)

CKO .... Centrale van Kapiteins en Officieren ter Koopvaardij [*Benelux*]   (BAS)

CKO .... Centralna Komisja Odwolawcza [*Central Appeals Commission*]   (POL)

CKO .... Cesky Komorni Orchestr [*Czech Chamber Music Ensemble*]   (CZ)

CKO .... Cornelio Procopio [*Brazil*] [*Airport symbol*]   (OAG)

CKOM .... Communaute Khmere d'Outre Mer [*Overseas Cambodian Community*]   (CL)

CKOS .... Centralny Komitet Opieki Spolecznej [*Central Committee on Social Welfare*]   (POL)

CKP .... Centrala Kolportazu Prasy [*Center for Press Circulation*]   (POL)

CKP .... Cinli Komunist Partisi [*Chinese Communist Party*]   (TU)

CKPiWRuch ... Centrala Kolportazu Periodykow i Wydawnictw "Ruch" ["*Ruch" Center for Circulation of Periodicals and Publications*]   (POL)

CK PZPR ... Centralny Komitet Polskiej Zjednoczonej Partii Robotniczej [*Polish United Workers' Party Central Committee*]   (POL)

CKR .... Centralna Komisja Rewizyjna [*Central Review Commission*]   (POL)

CKRRP ...... Centralni Komitet Rumunske Radnicke Partije [*Central Committee of the Romanian Labor Party*]   (YU)

CKRSDRP ... Centralni Komitet Ruske Socijal-Demokratske Radnicke Partije [*Central Committee of the Russian Social-Democratic Workers' Party*]   (YU)

CKS .... Ceska Kardiologicka Spolecnost [*Czech Cardiological Society*]   (CZ)

CK SD .... Centralny Komitet Stronnictwa Demokratycznego [*Central Committee of the Democratic Party*]   (POL)

CKSE .... Centralna Komisja Slownictwa Elektrycznego [*Central Commission on Electric Terminology*]   (POL)

CKSKBiH ... Centralni Komitet Saveza Komunista Bosne i Hercegovine [*Central Committee of the League of Communists of Bosnia and Hercegovina*]   (YU)

CKSKJ ...... Centralni Komitet Saveza Komunista Jugoslavije [*Central Committee of the League of Communists of Yugoslavia*]   (YU)

CKSKM ..... Centralni Komitet Saveza Komunista Makedonije [*Central Committee of the League of Communists of Macedonia*]   (YU)

CKSKMJ ... Centralni Komitet na Sojuzot na Komunistickata Mladina na Jugoslavija [*Central Committee of the Union of Communist Youth of Yugoslavia*]   (YU)

CKSKOJ .... Centralni Komitet Saveza Komunisticke Omladine Yugoslavije [*Central Committee of the Union of Communist Youth of Yugoslavia*]   (YU)

CKSKP(b) ... Centralni Komitet Sovjetske Komunisticke Partije (Boljsevika) [*Central Committee of the Soviet Communist Party (Bolsheviks)*]   (YU)

CKSKP(b) ... Centralni Komitet Svesavezne Komunisticke Partije (Boljsevika) [*Central Committee of the All-Union Communist Party (Bolsheviks)*]   (YU)

CKSKS ...... Centralni Komitet Saveza Komunista Srbije [*Central Committee of the League of Communists of Serbia*]   (YU)

CKSS .... Ceskoslovenska Keramicka a Sklarska Spolecnost [*Czechoslovak Ceramics and Glass Company*]   (CZ)

CKSW .... Centrala Krajowych Surowcow Wlokienniczych [*Domestic Textile Materials Center*]   (POL)

CKT .... Chahada Khassa fi al Tarbiya [*Academic qualification*] [*Syria*]

CKT .... Compagnie Khmere de Tabacs [*Cambodian Tobacco Company*]   (CL)

CKTP .... Cumhuriyet Kibris Turkiye Partisi [*Turkish Cypriot Republican Party*]   (TU)

CKU .... Corps Keuangan [*Finance Corps*]   (IN)

CKUAP ...... Centralna Komisja Usprawnienia Administracji Publicznej [*Central Commission for the Improvement of Public Administration*]   (POL)

CKV .... Cesky Klub Velocipedistu [*Czech Cycling Club*]   (CZ)

CKV .... Cesky Klub Veslaru [*Czech Rowing Club*]   (CZ)

CKVKP(b) ... Centralni Komite Vsesvezne Komunisticne Partije (Boljsevikov) [*Central Committee of the All-Union Communist Party (Bolsheviks)*]   (YU)

CKVMRO ... Centralni Komitet Unutrasnje Makedonske Revolucionarne Organizacije [*Central Committee of the Internal Macedonian Revolutionary Organization*]   (YU)

CKVO .... Ceskoslovensky Komitet pro Vedeckou Organisaci [*Czechoslovak Committee for the Organization of Scientific Work*]   (CZ)

CKVR .... Ceskoslovensky Komitet pro Vedecke Rizeni [*Czechoslovak Committee for Scientific Management*]   (CZ)

CKW .... Centralny Komitet Wykonawczy [*Central Executive Committee*]   (POL)

CKW .... Forces Motrices de la Suisse Centrale [*Switzerland*]   (WND)

CKWPPS ... Centralny Komitet Wykonawczy Polskiej Partii Socjalistycznej [*Central Executive Committee of the Polish Socialist Party*]   (POL)

CKY .... Conakry [*Guinea*] [*Airport symbol*]   (OAG)

CKZ .... Ceskoslovenske Keramicke Zavody, Narodni Podnik [*Czechoslovak Ceramic Works, National Enterprise*]   (CZ)

CKZKMJ .. Centralni Komite Zvezekomunisticne Mladine Jugoslavije [*Central Committee of the Union of Communist Youth of Yugoslavia*]   (YU)

CKZKS ...... Centralni Komite Zveze Komunistov Slovenije [*Central Committee of the League of Communists of Slovenia*]   (YU)

CKZP .... Centralny Komitet Zydow w Polsce [*Central Committee of Jews in Poland*]   (POL)

CKZZ .... Centralny Komitet Zwiazkow Zawodowych [*Central Committee of Trade Unions*]   (POL)

CL .... Caltanissetta [*Car registration plates*] [*Italy*]

CL .... Canadair Ltd. [*Canada ICAO aircraft manufacturer identifier*]   (ICAO)

cl .... Centiliter [*Centiliter*]   (HU)

cl .... Centilitre [*Centiliter*] [*French*]

cl .... Centilitro [*Centiliter*] [*Portuguese*]

cl .... Centilitro [*Centiliter*] [*Spanish*]

CL .... Centre Left [*Australian Labor Party*] [*Political party*]

cl .... Centylitr [*Centiliter*] [*Poland*]

CL .... Chawangan Laut [*Marine Branch*]   (ML)

CL .... Chile [*ANSI two-letter standard code*]   (CNC)

Cl .... Chlor [*Chlorine*] [*Chemical element*] [*German*]

cl .... Cimlap [*Title Page*] [*Hungary*]

CL .... Cirkevne Listy [*Church News*] [*A periodical*]   (CZ)

cl .... Clanek [*Article*]   (CZ)

Cl .... Cloro [*Chlorine*] [*Chemical element*] [*Portuguese*]

CL .... Commercial List [*Australia*]

CL .... Comunione e Liberazione [*Italian Catholic association*]

CL .... Conseil de Legislation [*French*]   (BAS)

CL .... Convention Liberale [*Cameroon*] [*Political party*]   (EY)

CL .... Council for Libya

CL .... Credit Lyonnais [*Bank*] [*French*]

CL .... Criminel Wetboek Landmacht [*Benelux*]   (BAS)

c/l .... Curso Legal [*Legal Procedure*] [*Spanish*]

cl .... Senttilitra(a) [*Finland*]

CLA .... Canadian Library Association   (SLS)

CLA .... Canadian Linguistic Association   (SLS)

CLA .... Canadian Lung Association   (SLS)

CLA .... Circolo dei Librai Antiquari   (WGAO)

CLA .... College Language Association [*Barbados*]   (SLS)

CLA .... Columbia [*Italy*] [*ICAO designator*]   (FAAC)

CLA .... Comite Latinoamericano (de la Federacion Internacional de Documentacion - FID)   (LAA)

CLA .... Commercial Law Association of Australia   (ADA)

CLA .... Commercial Life Assurance Ltd. [*Australia*]

CLA .... Commonwealth Lawyers' Association [*British*]   (EAIO)

CLA .... Commonwealth Library Association [*Jamaica*]   (WGAO)

CLA .... Confederacion Lanera Argentina   (WGAO)

CLA .... Consejo Latinoamericano y del Caribe para le Autogestion   (WGAO)

CLA .... Conselho de Libertacao de Angola

CLA .... Cooperativa de Lacticinios de Avare [*Brazil*]   (DSCA)

CLA .... Copyright Licensing Agency   (WGAO)

CLA .... Council of Labor Affairs [*Taiwan*]

CLA .... Country Landowners Association   (WGAO)

CLA .... Credit Licensing Authority [*Victoria*] [*Australia*]

CLA .... Crown Leasehold Association [*New Zealand*]   (EAIO)

CLAA .... Centre Lyonnais d'Applications Atomiques [*French*]

CLAA .... Commercial Law Association of Australia

Cl A au N ... Clause d'Assimilation au National   (FLAF)

CLAB .... Centro de Investigaciones Agricolas de El Bajio [*Mexico*]   (WGAO)

CLAB .... Centro Latinoamericana de Automatizacion Bancaria [*Colombia*]   (WGAO)

CLAB .... Centro Latinoamericano de Ciencias Biologicas [*Latin American Center of Biological Sciences*] [*Research center*] [*Venezuela*]   (IRC)

CLAB........ Confederacion Latinoamericana Box (WGAO)
CLABD...... Congresso Latino-Americano de Bilbloteconomia e
　　　　　　Documentacao [Brazil] (WGAO)
CLAC........ Caisettes de Livres de l'Association Albert Camus
CLAC........ Centre de Loisirs et d'Animation Culturelle
CLAC......... Centro Latinoamericano de Adiestramiento Censal (del IASI)
　　　　　　[Inter-American Statistical Institute] [Lima, Peru] (LAA)
CLAC........ Comision Latinoamericana de Aviacion Civil [Latin American
　　　　　　Civil Aviation Commission - LACAC] (EAIO)
CLAC........ Comites Lutadoras Anticolonista [Anticolonial Struggle
　　　　　　Committees] [Portuguese] (WER)
CLAC........ Commonwealth Legal Aid Commision [Australia]
CLAC........ Commonwealth Legal Aid Council [Australia]
CLACE...... Centro Latinoamericano de Coordinacion de Estudios [Brazil]
　　　　　　(WGAO)
CLACJ....... Confederacion Latinoamericana de Asociaciones Cristianas de
　　　　　　Jovenes [Latin American Confederation of YMCAs -
　　　　　　LACYMCA] (EAIO)
CLACSO ... Consejo Latinoamericano de Ciencias Sociales [Latin American
　　　　　　Social Sciences Council - LASSC] (EAIO)
CLAD .... Centre de Linguistique Appliquee de Dakar
CLAD .... Centro Latinoamericano de Administracion para el Desarrollo
　　　　　　[Latin American Center for Development Administration]
　　　　　　[Research center] [Venezuela] (IRC)
CLADE...... Conferencia Latinoamericana de Ejecutivos [Latin American
　　　　　　Executives Conference] (LA)
CLADEA ... Consejo Latinamericano de Escuelas de Administracion [Latin
　　　　　　American Council of Schools of Administration]
CLADEM ... Centro Latinoamericano de Estudios de Comercializacion o
　　　　　　Marketing (LAA)
CLADER ... Centre Latino-Americaine de Documentation Etude et
　　　　　　Recherche (WGAO)
CLADES ... Centro Latinoamericano de Documentacion Economica y Social
　　　　　　[Latin American Center for Economic and Social
　　　　　　Documentation] [Economic Commission for Latin America
　　　　　　and the Caribbean] [United Nations] [Information service
　　　　　　or system] (IID)
CLAE......... Congreso Latino Americano de Estudiantes [Latin American
　　　　　　Students Congress] (LA)
CLAEH ..... Centro Latino Americano Economia Humana (WGAO)
CLAEU...... Comite de Liaison des Architectes de l'Europe Unie [Liaison
　　　　　　Committee of the Architects of United Europe] [EC]
　　　　　　(ECED)
CLAF .... Centro Latinoamericano de Fisica [Latin American Center for
　　　　　　Physics] [Cuba] (LA)
CLAF .... Comite Latinoamericano de la Fe [Latin American Committee of
　　　　　　the Faith] [Brazil] (LAA)
CLAF .... Commission Latino-Americaine des Forets (WGAO)
CLAFE ...... Consejo Latinoamericano de Fisica Espacial (LAA)
CLAG .... Conference of Latin Americanist Geographers (WGAO)
CLAH .... Conference on Latin American History [USA] (WGAO)
CLAI......... Consejo Latinoamericano de Iglesias [Latin American Council of
　　　　　　Churches] (EAIO)
CLAID....... Comision Latino Americano de Irigacion y Drenaje (WGAO)
CLAIET..... Comite de Liaison des Associations Internationales d'Entreprises
　　　　　　Touristiques (WGAO)
CLAIM...... Christian Literature Association in Malawi
CLAIP .... Consejo Latinoamericano de Investigacion para la Paz
　　　　　　(WGAO)
CLAIR .... Computerised Library of Analysed Igneous Rocks [Australia]
　　　　　　[Information service or system] (IID)
CLAIS .... Committee on Latin American and Iberian Studies [Harvard
　　　　　　University] [Research center]
CLAL......... Comptoir Lyon Alemand Louyot [French]
CLAM .... Centro Latinoamericano de Mandioca (LAA)
CLAM .... Comite de Liaison de l'Agrumiculture Mediterraneenne [Liaison
　　　　　　Committee for Mediterranean Citrus Fruit Culture -
　　　　　　LCMCFC] (EAIO)
CLAMA..... Centro Latinoamericano de Mandioca [Brazil] (DSCA)
CLAMOP ... Centre Latino-American d'Opinion Publique (WGAO)
CLAMPI ... Confederacion Latinoamericana de Pequena y Mediana Industria
　　　　　　[Latin American Confederation of Small and Medium
　　　　　　Industries] (LA)
CLAMUC ... Consejo Latinoamericano de Mujeres Catolicas [Latin American
　　　　　　Council of Catholic Women] (EAIO)
CLAN .... Clean Air Society in the Netherlands (EAIO)
CLAN .... Comision Liberal de Accion Nacional [Liberal National Action
　　　　　　Commission] [Colorado] (LA)
CL&CGB ... Church Lads' and Church Girls' Brigade (WGAO)
CLANEB ... Centro Latino-Americano do Nordeste do Brasil [Brazil]
　　　　　　(DSCA)
CLANG ..... Community Language Audio Book [Australia]
CLANN ..... College Libraries Activities Network [Australia] [CLANN Ltd.]
　　　　　　[Information service or system] (CRD)
CLANN ..... College Libraries Activities Network in New South Wales
　　　　　　[Australia] (ADA)
CLANN ..... College Library Activity Network in New South Wales

CLANN ..... Cooperating Libraries Action Network New South Wales
　　　　　　[Australia]
CLANSW .. Corporate Lawyers' Association of New South Wales [Australia]
CLAO .... Christian Legal Aid Office [El Salvador] (EAIO)
CLAO .... Conseil Latino-Americaini d'Oceanographie [Latin American
　　　　　　Council on Oceanography] [French] (ASF)
CLAO .... Consejo Latinoamericano de Oceanografia [Latin American
　　　　　　Council on Oceanography] [Spanish] (ASF)
CLAP......... Centro Latinoamericano Perinatologia y Desarrollo Humano
　　　　　　(WGAO)
CLAPA ...... Cleft Lip and Palate Association (WGAO)
CLAPCS.... Centro Latinoamericano de Pesquisas en Ciencias Sociais
　　　　　　[Brazil] (LAA)
CLAPF ...... Comite Latinoamericano de Productos Forestales [Chile]
　　　　　　(DSCA)
CLAPN...... Comite Latinoamericano de Parques Nacionales (LAA)
CLAPTUR ... Confederacion Latinoamericana de Prensa Turistica [Latin
　　　　　　American Confederation of Touristic Press] [Medellin,
　　　　　　Colombia] (EAIO)
CLAPU ...... Confederacion Latinoamericana de Profesionales Universitarios
　　　　　　[Latin American Conference of University Professionals]
　　　　　　(LA)
CLAQ .... Centro Latinoamericano de Quimica [Latin American Center for
　　　　　　Chemistry] (PDAA)
CLAR........ Confederacion Latinoamericana de Religiosos [Latin American
　　　　　　Confederation of Religious Men] [Brazil] (LAA)
CLAR........ Conferencia Latinoamericana de Religiosas [Latin American
　　　　　　Conference of Religious Women] (LA)
CLARA...... China's Liberated Areas Rehabilitation Administration
CLARA...... Comite Latinoamericano para las Regiones Aridas (WGAO)
CLARA...... Consejo Latinoamericano para el Estudio de las Regiones Aridas
　　　　　　(LAA)
CLARC...... Consejo Latino-Americano de Radiacon Cosmica [Latin-
　　　　　　American Council on Cosmic Radiation] [Bolivia] (PDAA)
CLARCFE ... Consejo Latino Americano de Radiacion Cosmica y Fisica del
　　　　　　Espacio (WGAO)
CLARM..... International Center for Living Aquatic Resources Management
　　　　　　(EAIO)
CLARTE ... Centre de Liaison des Activites Regionales, Touristiques et
　　　　　　Economiques (WGAO)
CLAS .... Confederacion Latino Americana de Sindicatos [Latin American
　　　　　　Confederation of Trade Unions] (LA)
CLASA ...... Chief Librarians Association of South Australia
CLASA ...... Confederacion Latinoamericana de Sociedades de Anestesia
　　　　　　(WGAO)
CLASA ...... Confederacion Latinoamericana de Sociedades de Anestesiologia
　　　　　　[Colorado] (SLS)
CLASC ...... Confederacao Latino-Americana dos Sindicalistas Cristaos
　　　　　　[Latin American Federation of Christian Trade Unionists]
　　　　　　[Portuguese] (LA)
CLASC ...... Confederacion Latinoamericana de Sindicalistas Cristianos
　　　　　　[Latin American Federation of Christian Trade Unionists]
　　　　　　[Spanish] (LA)
CLASEP.... Comision Latinoamericana Servidores Publicos (WGAO)
CLASS....... Concrete Lintel Association (WGAO)
CLASS....... Confederation of Labor and Allied Social Services [Philippines]
　　　　　　(EY)
CLASS....... Crown Lands Assessment and Status System [Australia]
CLASSIC .. Covert Local Area Sensor System for Intruder Classification
　　　　　　[Military] [Australia]
CLAT........ Central Latinamericana de Trabajadores [Latin American
　　　　　　Central of Workers] (EA)
CLAT........ Central Latinoamericana de Trabajadores [Latin American
　　　　　　Workers Federation] (LA)
CLAT........ Confederation of Latin-American Teachers
CLATE ...... Confederacion Latino Americana de Trabajadores Estatales
　　　　　　[Latin American Confederation of Government Employees]
　　　　　　(LA)
CLATEC ... Comision Latinoamericana de Trabajadores de la Educacion
　　　　　　[Venezuela]
CLATES.... Latin American Center for Educational Technology in Health
CLATRAMM ... Coordinacion Latinoamericana de Trabajadores
　　　　　　Metallurgicos y Mineros (WGAO)
CLATRAMM ... Coordinacion Latinoamericana de Trabajadores Minero-
　　　　　　Metalurgicos [World Federation for the Metallurgic
　　　　　　Industry - Latin America] [Trade union]
CLATT ...... Comite Latinoamericano de Textos Teologicos (WGAO)
CLAUPAE ... Comite de Lineas Aereas de la Union Postal de las Americas y
　　　　　　Espana [Air Lines Committee of the Postal Union of the
　　　　　　Americas and Spain] (LA)
CLAVA...... County Land Agents' and Valuers Association (WGAO)
CLAVE...... Centro Latinoamericano de Venezuela
CLAWS..... Canine Livestock Animals Welfare Service [Australia]
CLB........... Centro do Livro Brasileiro (WGAO)
Cl B .... Clarinette Basse [Bass Clarinet] [Music]
CLB........... Commissie Literatuurdocumentatie Bouwwezen

CLBC........ Confederacion Latinoamericana de Bioquimica Clinica [*Latin American Confederation of Clinical Biochemistry - LACCB*] (EAIO)
CLBDA...... Cyprus Land and Building Developers Association (EAIO)
CLBN........ Credit Lyonnais Bank Nederland [*Credit Lyonnais' Dutch subsidiary*] (ECON)
CLC........... Capitaine au Long Cours
CLC........... Caribbean Labour Congress (WGAO)
CLC........... Centrale Landbouwcatalogus [*LHS*] [*Wageningen*]
CLC........... Chinese Liaison Committee (ML)
CLC........... Christian Life Centre [*Australia*]
Clc............. Classic [*Record label*] [*France*]
CLC........... Classic Air AG [*Switzerland*] [*ICAO designator*] (FAAC)
CLC........... Comite de Liaison des Industries Cimentieres de la CEE [*Liaison Committee of the Cement Industries in the EEC*] (ECED)
CLC........... Commonwealth Liaison Committee [*Australia*] (ADA)
CLC........... Communications Law Centre [*Australia*]
CLC........... Community Legal Centre [*Australia*]
CLC........... Conseil pour la Liberation du Congo-Kinshasa [*Council for the Liberation of the Congo-Kinshasa*] [*Zaire*] (PD)
CLC........... Consejo Latinoamericano de Cultura [*Argentina*] (WGAO)
CLC........... Convention on Civil Liability for Oil Pollution Damage (DS)
CLCA........ Comite de Liaison de la Construction Automobile [*Liaison Committee for the Motor Industry in the EEC Countries*] [*Brussels, Belgium*] (EAIO)
CLCA........ Comite de Liaison de la Construction Automobile des Pays des Communautes Europeennes (WGAO)
Cl CB .... Clarinette Contre Basse [*Contrabass Clarinet*] [*Music*]
CLCCR ...... Comite de Liaison de la Construction de Carrosseries et de Remorques [*Liaison Committee of the Body- and Trailer-Building Industry*] (EAIO)
CLCF .... Centro Linguistico Colombo Frances [*Colombia*] (COL)
CLCF .... Children's Leukemia and Cancer Foundation [*Australia*]
CLC(I) .... Christian Literature Crusade (International) [*Australia*]
CLCI......... Comptoir Lorrain de la Cote-D'Ivoire
CLCS .... Chinese Language Computer Society [*Taiwan*] (EAIO)
CLD .... Agency for Christian Literature Development (WGAO)
CLD .... Comite de Liaison Commerce de Detail [*Liaison Committee of European Retail Trade Associations*] (EAIO)
CLD .... Comite de Liaison des Associations Europeennes du Commerce de Detail (WGAO)
CLD .... Crown Law Department [*Western Australia*]
CLDC........ Centru de Librarii si Distributie de Carti [*Center for Bookstores and Book Distribution*] (RO)
CLE........... Caribbean Council for Legal Education (WGAO)
CLE........... Centre de Liaison pour l'Environnement [*Kenya*] (WGAO)
CLE........... Centre de Litterature Evangelique
CLE........... Centre Europeen pour les Loisirs et l'Education [*European Centre for Leisure and Education - ECLE*] (EAIO)
CLE........... Comando de Lucha Estudiantil [*Student Struggle Command*] [*Ecuador*] (LA)
CLE........... Comunidad Latinoamericana de Escritores [*Mexico*] (WGAO)
CLE........... Council of Legal Education (WGAO)
CLEA........ Centro Latinoamericano de Educacion de Adults [*Chile*] (WGAO)
CLEA........ Comision Liquidadora de Entidades Aseguradoras [*Spain*] (EY)
CLEA........ Commonwealth Legal Education Association (EAIO)
CLEA........ Council of Local Education Authorities (WGAO)
CLEAA ...... Comite de Liaison Entr'Aide et Action [*Help and Action Coordinating Committee*] (EAIO)
CLEAPSE ... Consortium of Local Education Authorities for the Provision of Science Equipment (WGAO)
CLEAR ...... Campaign for Lead-Free Air (WGAO)
CLEC........ Comite de Liaison de l'Engineering Chimique Francais (WGAO)
CLECAT ... Comite de Liaison Europeen des Commissionnaires et Auxiliaires de Transports du Marche Commun (WGAO)
CLECAT ... Comite de Liaison Europeen des Commissionnaires et Auxiliaires de Transport [*European Liaison Committee of Forwarders*] (EAIO)
CLEDI ...... Comite de Legislation Etrangere et de Droit International (FLAF)
CLEDIPA ... Comite de Liaison Europeen de la Distribution Independante de Pieces de Rechange et Equipements pour Automobiles [*European Liaison Committee for the Independent Distribution of Spare Parts and Equipment for Motor Cars*] [*EC*] (ECED)
CLEF .... Club des Lecteurs d'Expression Francaise
CLEFTPALS ... Cleft Palate and Lip Society [*Australia*]
CLEI......... Centro Latinoamericano Estudios Informatica (WGAO)
CLEIC ...... Comite de Liaison et d'Etude de l'Industrie de la Chaussure de la CEE (WGAO)
CLEJFL..... Centre de Liaison et d'Etude pour les Jus de Fruits et de Legumes [*France*] (WGAO)
CLEO .... Agricultural Economics Research Centre, Catholic University of Louvain [*Belgium*] (ARC)
CLEO .... Comite de Liaison Europeen des Osteopathes [*European Liaison Committee for Osteopaths - ELCO*] (EA)

CLEO .... Commonwealth Legal Education Office [*Australia*]
CLEPA ...... Comite de Liaison de la Construction d'Equipements et de Pieces d'Automobiles [*Liaison Committee of Manufacturers of Motor Vehicle Parts and Equipment*] (EAIO)
CLEPR ...... Council on Legal Education for Professional Responsibility (WGAO)
Cler .... Clocher [*Steeple*] [*Military map abbreviation World War I*] [*French*] (MTD)
CLER........ Comite de Liaison des Etudiants Revolutionnaires [*Revolutionary Students Liaison Committee*] [*French*] (WER)
CLER........ Comites de Luchas de Estudiantes Revolucionarios [*Struggle Committees of Revolutionary Students*] [*Venezuela*] (LA)
CLERES..... Centre de Liaison des Etudes et Recherches Economiques et Sociales [*French*]
CLES .... Centre for Local Economic Strategies (WGAO)
CLESAV.... Cooperative Libraria Editrice per le Scienze Agrarie, Alimentarie, e Vetrinar ie [*Bookseller and Publisher Cooperative for Agricultural, Food, and Veterinary Sciences*] [*Italy*] (EAIO)
Cl et B .... Jurisprudence des Tribunaux de Premiere Instance, par Cloes et Bonjean [*Benelux*] (BAS)
CLETC ...... China Light Industrial Corporation for Foreign Economic and Technical Cooperation (IMH)
CLEW....... Community Legal Education for Welfare Project [*Australia*]
CLF........... Comite Linier de France (WGAO)
CLF........... Commonwealth Literary Fund [*Australia*] (ADA)
clg............. Kologarytm [*Cologarithm*] [*Poland*]
CLG........... Societe Chaleng Air [*France*] [*ICAO designator*] (FAAC)
CLGA .... Customary Law Group of Australia
CLH .... Conventions de La Haye (FLAF)
CLH .... Croix de la Legion d'Honneur [*Cross of the Legion of Honor*] [*French*]
CLH .... Lufthansa Cityline [*Germany*] [*ICAO designator*] (FAAC)
CLI .... Centre de Liaison Interprofessionnel de l'Industrie, du Commerce et del l'Artisanat de l'Indre (WGAO)
CLI............ Corps Legers d'Intervention
CLIC......... Canberra Library and Information Consultants [*Australia*]
CLICEC.... Comite de Liaison International des Cooperatives d'Epargne et de Credit [*International Liaison Committee on Co-Operative Thrift and Credit - ILCCTC*] [*Paris, France*] (EA)
CLIETA..... Comite de Liaison de l'Industrie Europeenne des Tubes d'Acier [*Liaison Committee of the EEC Steel Tube Industry*] (EAIO)
CLIF .... Comite Latinoamericano de Investigaciones Forestales [*Chile*] (DSCA)
CLII .... Centrul de Lupta Impotriva Intoxicantiilor [*Poison Control Center*] (RO)
CLIMA...... Centro Laminadores Industriales Metalurgicos Argentinos [*Buenos Aires, Argentina*] (LAA)
CLIMM...... Commission de Liaison Inter-Nations Mars et Mercure (WGAO)
CLIMMAR ... Centre de Liason International des Marchands de Machines Agricoles et Reparateurs [*France*] (DSCA)
CLIMO...... Comite Europeen de Liaison des Importateurs de Machines-Outils (WGAO)
CLINES..... CSIRO [*Commonwealth Scientific and Industrial Research Organisation*] Library Network System [*Australia*]
CLINIMED ... Societe des Cliniques Medicales
CLIP......... Centre for Legal Information and Publications [*College of Law, Sydney*] [*Australia*]
CLIRS........ Computerised Legal Information Retrieval System [*CLIRS Ltd.*] [*Information service or system*] (IID)
CLIS .... Centre for Library and Information Studies [*Canberra College of Advanced Education*] [*Australia*]
CLIS .... Comite de Liberation des Iles Sao Tome et Principe [*Committee for the Liberation of the Islands of Sao Tome and Principe*] (AF)
CLITAM ... Centre de Liaison des Industries de Traitement des Algues Marines de la CEE [*Liaison Center of the Industries for the Treatment of Seaweeds in the European Economic Community*]
CLITAM ... Chadian Livestock Tanning and Manufacturing Industries
CLITRAVI ... Centre de Liaison des Industries Transformatrices de la CEE [*Liaison Center of the Meat Processing Industries of the EEC*] [*Belgium*]
CLITRAVI ... Centre de Liaison des Industries Transformatrices de Viandes de la CEE (WGAO)
Clj.............. Cluj [*Cluj*] (RO)
CLJ .... Cluj-Napoca [*Romania*] [*Airport symbol*] (OAG)
clkor .... Clen Korespondent [*Corresponding Member*] (CZ)
CLL........... Aerovias Castillo SA [*Mexico*] [*ICAO designator*] (FAAC)
CLL........... Confederation of Lebanese Labor (ME)
CLL........... Copyright Licensing Limited [*New Zealand*] (WGAO)
CLLA........ Comite Laboral Latinoamericano [*Latin American Labor Committee*] [*Mexico*] (LA)

CLLC .... Centre for Literacy and Linguistic Computing [*University of Newcastle*] [*Australia*]
cllo .... Cuartillo [*A unit of measure*] [*Spanish*]
CLLR .... International Symposium on Computing in Library and Linguistic Research (WGAO)
CLM .... Compagnie Lyonnaise de Madagascar
CLM .... Confederacion Latinoamericana de Marinos Mercantes (LAA)
CLM .... Croatian Liberation Movement [*Australia*]
CLN .... Committee of National Liberation: Italian All-Party Coordinating Organization for Resistance
CLN .... Conseil de Liberation Nationale
CLN .... Conseil Legislatif National [*National Legislative Council*] [*Zaire*] (AF)
CLNAI .... Comitato de Liberazione Nazionale per l'Alta Italia [*Committee of National Liberation for Upper Italy*]
CLNAI .... Comitato di Liberazione Nazionale alta Italia (WGAO)
Cl Nlpf ...... Clause de la Nation la Plus Favorisee [*France*] (FLAF)
CLO .... Cali [*Colombia*] [*Airport symbol*] (OAG)
CLO .... Campaign for Law and Order (WGAO)
CLO .... Central Agricultural Organisation [*Netherlands*] (WGAO)
CLO .... Centrale Landsdienaren Organisatie [*Central Organization for Civil Service Employees*] [*Surinam*]
CLO .... Centralne Laboratorium Optyki [*Central Optical Laboratory*] (POL)
CLO .... Centrum Landbouwkundig Onderzoek [*Belgium*] (WGAO)
CLO .... Centrum voor Literatuuronderzoekers ['s-*Gravenhage*]
CLO .... Crown Lands Office [*Australia*] (ADA)
CLO .... Rijkscentrum voor Landbouwkundig Onderzoek - Gent [*Government Agricultural Research Center - Ghent*] [*Belgium*] (ARC)
CLOA .... Chief Leisure Officers Association (WGAO)
CLOCCI .... Comite de Liaison des Organismes Chretiens de Cooperation Internationale (EAIO)
CLODO ..... Comite Liquidant ou Detournant les Ordinateurs [*Committee to Liquidate or Neutralize Computers*] [*France*] (PD)
clog .... Kologarytm [*Cologarithm*] [*Poland*]
CLOG-A .... Chief of Logistics - Army [*Australia*]
CLOING ... Comite de Liaison des Organisations Internationales Non-Gouvernementales (WGAO)
CLONG-CE ... Comite de Liaison des Organisations Non-Gouvernmentales de Developpement aupres des Communautes Europeennes [*Liaison Committee of Development Non-Governmental Organizations to the European Communities*] (EAIO)
CLONGV .. Comite de Liaison des OrganizationSs Non-Gouvernmentales de Volontariat [*Committee for the Liaison of Non-Governmental Voluntary Organizations*] [*France*] (EAIO)
CLOP .... CSIRO [*Commonwealth Scientific and Industrial Research Organisation*] List of Publications
CLOR .... Centraine Laboratorium Ochrony Radiologiczenj [*Poland*] (PDAA)
CLOSP ...... Comite de Liaison des Organisations Syndicales et Professionnelles du Personnel des Communautes Europeenes (WGAO)
CLOTI .... Comite de Liaison des Organisations de Travailleurs Immigrants [*Liaison Committee of the Immigrant Workers Organization*] [*French*] (WER)
CLP .... Centre de Liaison Politique [*Center for Political Liaison*] [*French*] (WER)
CLP .... China Light and Power Co. Ltd. [*Hong Kong*]
CLP .... Christian Liberation Party [*Political party*] [*Malawi*]
CLP .... Christian Literature Press [*Zambia*]
CLP .... Club der Luftfahrtpublizisten [*Austria*] (WGAO)
CLP .... Coating, Laminating and Polypropylene [*Israel*] [*Commercial firm*]
CLP .... Comite de Luchas Populares [*Popular Struggle Committee*] [*Venezuela*] (LA)
CLP .... Commonwealth Liberal Party [*Australia*] (ADA)
CLP .... Communal Liberation Party [*IRNC*] (WGAO)
CLP .... Confederation of Labor in the Philippines
CLP .... Congress Liberation Party [*Malawi*] [*Political party*]
CLP .... Congress Liberation Party [*Nyasaland*] [*Political party*]
CLP .... Country Liberal Party [*Australia*] (ADA)
CLPCE ...... Comite de Liaison des Podologues de la CE [*Liaison Committee of Podologists of the Common Market*] (ECED)
CLPCE ...... Comite de Liaison des Podologues de la Communaute Europeenne (WGAO)
CLPD .... Centralne Laboratorium Przemyslu Drzewnego [*Central Laboratory of the Lumber Industry*] (POL)
CLPG .... Chretiens pour la Liberation du Peuple Guadeloupeen [*Guadeloupe*] (PD)
CLPO .... Centralne Laboratorium Przemyslu Odziezowego [*Central Laboratory of the Clothing Industry*] (POL)
CLPR .... Cooperative League of Puerto Rico (WGAO)
CLPS .... Centralne Laboratorium Przemyslu Szklarskiego [*Central Laboratory of the Glass Industry*] (POL)
CLR .... Cinska Lidova Republika [*Chinese People's Republic*] (CZ)
Cl R .... Clause de Reciprocite [*France*] (FLAF)

CLR .... Council of Law Reporting [*Australia*]
CLRA .... Consumers' Law Reform Association [*Australia*]
CLRAE ...... Standing Conference of Local and Regional Authorities of Europe (WGAO)
CLRAQ ...... Consumers' Law Reform Association, Queensland [*Australia*]
CLRC .... Co-Operative League of the Republic of China [*Taiwan*] (EAIO)
CLRC .... Copyright Law Review Committee [*Australia*]
CLRD .... Criminal Law Review Division [*New South Wales*] [*Australia*]
CLRI .... Central Leather Research Institute [*India*] [*Research center*] (IRC)
CLRNSW .. Council of Law Reporting of New South Wales [*Australia*]
CLRU .... Cambridge Language Research Unit (WGAO)
CLS .... Canon Law Society of America (WGAO)
CLS .... Caribbean Labor Solidarity Organization (LA)
CLS .... Centrale der Liberale Syndicaten [*Benelux*] (BAS)
CLS .... Centre for Language Studies [*University of Newcastle*] [*Australia*]
CLS .... Ceska Logopedicka Spolecnost [*Czech Logopedic Society*] (CZ)
CLS .... Ceskoslovenska Letecka Spolecnost [*Czechoslovak Airlines*] (CZ)
CLS .... China Linguistic Society (EAIO)
CLS .... Christian Lawyer's Society [*Victoria, Australia*]
CLS .... Comites de Lucha Sindical [*Union Struggle Committees*] [*Nicaragua*] (LA)
CLS .... Computer Listing Services (Australia) Proprietary Ltd. (ADA)
CLSA .... Contact Lens Society of Australia (ADA)
CLSC .... Confederation Luxembourgeoise des Syndicats Chretiens [*Confederation of Christian Trade Unions of Luxembourg*]
CLSI .... Computer Library Services International (Australia) Pty. Ltd.
CLSM .... Caribbean Labor Solidarity Movement (LA)
Cl Soc .... Clause Relative aux Societes [*France*] (FLAF)
CLSRC ...... Company Law and Securities Review Committee [*Australia*]
CLSS .... Club Leopold Sedar Senghor
CLSTP .... Comite de Liberation de Sao Tome e Principe [*Liberation Committee of Sao Tome and Principe*] (AF)
CLSUM ..... Chinese Language Society of the University of Malaya (ML)
CLT .... Caribbean Air Transport Co., Inc. [*Netherlands*] [*ICAO designator*] (FAAC)
CLT .... Centrale Laitiere de Tananarive
CLT .... Comite de Lucha de los Trabajadores [*Workers Struggle Committee*] [*Nicaragua*] (LA)
CLT .... Community Language Teaching [*Australia*]
CLT .... Compagnie Libanaise de Television [*Lebanese Television Company*]
CLT .... Compagnie Luxembourgeoise de Telediffusion [*Luxembourg broadcasting group*]
CLT .... Consolidacao das Leis Trabalho [*Consolidated Labor Laws*] [*Brazil*] (LA)
CLT .... Cooperative League of Thailand (WGAO)
CLTADP ... Comite de Libertacao dos Territorios Africanos Sub o Dominio Portugues
CLTAV ...... Clinical Language Teachers Association of Victoria [*Australia*]
CLTB .... Commonwealth Land Transport Board [*Australia*]
CLTC .... Central and Local Trades Committees [*Australia*]
CLTC .... Confederacion Latinoamericana de Trabajadores de Comunicaciones (WGAO)
CLTC .... Congreso Latinoamericano de Trabajadores de Comunicaciones [*Latin American Congress of Communications Workers*] (LA)
CLTK .... Cesky Lawn-Tennisovy Klub [*Czech Lawn Tennis Club*] (CZ)
CLTRI .... Central Leprosy Teaching and Research Institute [*indianaia*] (WGAO)
CLT-RTL .. Compagnie Luxembourgeoise de Telediffusion - Radio Television Luxembourg
CLU .... Central Labor Union [*Thai*]
CLUC .... Combined Library Unions Committee [*Australia*]
CLUP .... Comites de Lucha Universidad Popular [*Committees of Popular University Struggle*] [*Spanish*] (WER)
CLUSA ...... Cooperative League of the USA (WGAO)
CLUTS ...... Canberra Land Use and Transportation Study [*Australia*]
CLV .... Cal Aviation SA [*Greece*] [*ICAO designator*] (FAAC)
CLV .... Cooperative Landbouwvereniging (WGAO)
CLX .... Cargolux Airline International [*Luxembourg*] [*ICAO designator*] (FAAC)
CLY .... Calvi [*Corsica*] [*Airport symbol*] (OAG)
CLZ .... Aerotaxis Calzada SA de CV [*Mexico*] [*ICAO designator*] (FAAC)
CLZ .... Calabozo [*Venezuela*] [*Airport symbol*] (OAG)
CLZ .... Ceske Lnarske Zavody [*Czech Flax Mills*] (CZ)
CLZ .... Conseil de Liberation du Zimbabwe
CM .... Cable Makers Association (WGAO)
CM .... Calvary Mission [*Nigeria*]
CM .... Camair [*Division of Cameron Iron Works, Inc.*] [*ICAO aircraft manufacturer identifier*] (ICAO)
CM .... Cameroon [*ANSI two-letter standard code*] (CNC)
CM .... Carmelite Missionaries [*Rome, Italy*] (EAIO)
CM .... Caroline Movement (WGAO)

CM............. Cechy-Morava [*Bohemia-Moravia*] (CZ)
CM............. Celamerck GmbH & Co. KG [*Celamerck Limited Liability Co.*] (ARC)
cm............. Centimeter [*Centimeter*] [*Albanian*]
Cm............. Centimetre [*Centimeter*] [*French*] (MTD)
cm............. Centimetre(s) (SCAC)
cm............. Centimetro [*Centimeter*] [*Spanish*]
cm............. Centimetro [*Centimeter*] [*Portuguese*] (GPO)
CM............. Centrala Miniera [*Mining Central*] (RO)
cm............. Centymetr [*Centimeter*] [*Poland*]
cm............. Cesko-Moravsky [*Czech-Moravian*] (CZ)
CM............. Ceskoslovenske Mlyny [*Czechoslovak Flour Mills*] (CZ)
CM............. Chamber of Mines of South Africa
CM............. Chambre des Metiers (WGAO)
CM............. Chambre des Mises en Accusation [*France*] (FLAF)
CM............. Chief Minister [*Australia*]
CM............. Circulaire Ministerielle [*France*] (FLAF)
CM............. Civic Movement [*Former Czechoslovakia*] [*Political party*] (EY)
CM............. Compagnie de Mitrailleuses [*Military*] [*French*] (MTD)
CM............. Conciertos Mexicanos [*Record label*] [*Mexico*]
CM............. Congregatio Missionis (WGAO)
CM............. Conseil des Ministres [*Cabinet*] [*Cambodia*] (CL)
CM............. Conselho de Ministros [*Council of Ministers*] [*Portuguese*] (WER)
cm............. Corrente Mese [*Instant*] [*Italian*] (GPO)
c/m............. Cours Moyen [*Average Price*] [*French*]
CM............. Crna Metalurgija [*Iron and Steel Industry*] (YU)
CM............. Cyrilo-Metodejska (Bohoslovecka Fakulta) [*Cyril and Methodius (School of Divinity)*] (CZ)
CM............. Landsbond der Christelijke Mutualiteiten [*Benelux*] (BAS)
CM............. Minelayer [*Navy symbol*] [*NATO*]
C-M............. North Atlantic Council Memorandum [*NATO*]
CM............. Office of the Chief Minister [*Australian Capital Territory*]
cm............. Senttimetri(a) [*Finland*]
Cm............. Zentimeter [*Centimeter*] (EG)
Cm²............. Centimetre Carre [*Square Centimeter*] [*French*] (MTD)
cm²............. Centymetr Kwadratowy [*Square Centimeter*] [*Poland*]
cm²............. Neliosenttimetri(a) [*Finland*]
Cm³............. Centimetre Cube [*Cubic Centimeter*] [*French*] (MTD)
cm³............. Centimetro Cubico [*Cubic Centimeter*] [*Spanish*]
cm³............. Centymetr Szescienny [*Cubic Centimeter*] [*Poland*]
cm³............. Kuutiosenttimetri(a) [*Finland*]
CMA............. Cable Makers Australia (ADA)
CMA............. Canadian Museums Association (WGAO)
CMA............. Canberra Mathematical Association [*Australia*]
CMA............. Capital Markets Authority [*Egypt*] (IMH)
CMA............. Carrot Marketing Association (WGAO)
CMA............. Cement Manufacturers Association [*India*] (PDAA)
CMA............. Central European Airlines [*Czechoslovakia*] [*ICAO designator*] (FAAC)
CMA............. Central Mapping Authority [*Australia*] (ADA)
CMA............. Centre de Transport International par Vehicules Automobiles [*Yugoslavia*] (WGAO)
CMA............. Centro de Mecanica Agricola [*Brazil*] (DSCA)
CMA............. China Mining Association (EAIO)
CMA............. Chinese Manufacturers' Association [*Hong Kong*]
CMA............. Chinese Manufacturers Association of Hong Kong (WGAO)
CMA............. Chinese Medical Association (SLS)
CMA............. Christian and Missionary Alliance of Africa
CMA............. Church Music Association (WGAO)
CMA............. Club Managers' Association [*Australia*]
CMA............. Coal Mines Authority Ltd. [*India*] (PDAA)
CMA............. Colegio Militar de Aviacion [*Military Aviation College*] [*Bolivia*]
CMA............. Comando Militar da Amazonia [*Brazil*] (WGAO)
CMA............. Combined Maritime Agencies (Nigeria) Ltd.
CMA............. Commonwealth Magistrates' Association [*British*] (EAIO)
CMA............. Commonwealth Medical Association [*British*] (EAIO)
CMA............. Communication Managers Association (WGAO)
CMA............. Compania Mexicana de Aviacion [*Mexican Aviation Company*] (LA)
CMA............. Computer Microfilming of Australia Ltd. (ADA)
CMA............. Concrete Masonry Association [*South Africa*] (EAIO)
CMA............. Confectionery Manufacturers of Australia
CMA............. Confection Moderne Africaine
CMA............. Conseil Mondial de l'Alimentation [*World Food Council*] [*French United Nations*] (DUND)
CMA............. Consejo Mundial de la Alimentacion [*World Food Council*] [*Spanish United Nations*] (DUND)
CMA............. Cooperatives Marocaines Agricoles (WGAO)
CMA............. Corporacion de Mercadeo Agricola [*Venezuela*]
CMA............. Country Mayors' Association [*New South Wales*] [*Australia*]
CMA............. Country Music Association (WGAO)
CMA............. Credit Mutuel Agricole (WGAO)
CMA............. Cunnamulla [*Australia*] [*Airport symbol*] (OAG)
CMA............. Egyptian Capital Market Authority

CMA............. Societe de Carrosserie Moderne Artisanale
CMAA............. Ceramic Manufacturers' Association of Australia
CMAA............. Cocoa Merchants Associations of America (WGAO)
CMAA............. Communication Management Alumni Association [*Kuring-gai College of Advanced Education*] [*Australia*]
CMAA............. Crane Manufacturers Association of America (WGAO)
CMAAC............. Concrete Masonry Association of Australia Cooperative
CMAAO............. Confederation of Medical Associations in Asia and Oceania (ADA)
CMAB............. Centro Medico Argentino-Britanico (WGAO)
CMAC............. Catchment Management Advisory Committee [*Australia*]
CMAC............. Catholic Marriage Advisory Council (WGAO)
CMA-C............. Certified Medical Assistant-Clinical
CMAD............. Computer Manufacture and Design Proprietary Ltd. [*Australia*]
CMAe............. Commission de Meteorologie Aeronautique [See also CAeM] [*French*]
CMAEC............. Conseil Mondial des Associations d'Education Comparee [*World Council of Comparative Education Societies - WCCES*] (EA)
CMAg............. Commission de Meteorologie Agricole [*OMM*] (WGAO)
CMAHK............. Chinese Manufacturers Association of Hong Kong (EAIO)
CMAI............. Clothing Manufacturers Association of India (EAIO)
CMAJ............. Conseil des Ministres Arabes de la Justice [*Council of Arab Ministers of Justice - CAMJ*] [*Rabat, Morocco*] (EAIO)
CMANSW............. Ceramic Manufacturers' Association of New South Wales [*Australia*]
CMANSW............. Country Meatworks Association of New South Wales [*Australia*]
CMAO............. Consejo Mundial de Artes y Oficios (WGAO)
CMAP............. Census Collectors' Maps [*Australian Bureau of Statistics*]
CMAP............. Commission Mondiale d'Action Professionnelle [*World Committee for Trade Action - WCTA*] (EA)
CMAR............. Comite Maghrebin d'Assurances et de Reassurances
CMAS............. Cement Manufacturers Association of Singapore (EAIO)
CMAS............. Confederacion Mundial de Actividades Subacuaticas [*World Underwater Federation - WUF*] [*Spanish*] (ASF)
CMAS............. Confederation Mondiale des Activites Subaquatiques [*World Underwater Federation - WUF*] [*ICSU Paris, France*] (EAIO)
CMA/SME............. Composites Manufacturing Association of the Society of Manufacturing Engineers (EAIO)
CMAT-A............. Chief of Materiel - Army [*Australia*]
CMATA............. Compagnie Maritime et Aerienne de Transports et d'Affretement [*Morocco*]
CMAV............. Coalition Mondiale pour l'Abolition de la Vivisection (WGAO)
CMAWA............. Cabinetmakers' Association of Western Australia
CMB............. Centrala Materialow Budowlanych [*Building Materials Center*] (POL)
CMB............. Centrale des Metallurgistes de Belgique (WGAO)
CMB............. China Motor Bus Co. Ltd. [*Hong Kong*]
CMB............. Christelijk Bedrijfsbond voor de Metaalnijverheid en Elektrotechnische Industrie [*Benelux*] (BAS)
CMB............. Christelijke Middenstandsbond [*Benelux*] (BAS)
CMB............. Christian Mission to Buddhists [See also NKB] [*Arhus, Denmark*] (EAIO)
CMB............. Club Francais du Bullmastiff et du Mastiff [*French Association of Bullmastiffs and Mastiffs*] (EAIO)
CMB............. Cocoa Marketing Board
CMB............. Colombo [*Sri Lanka*] [*Airport symbol*] (OAG)
CMB............. Compagnie Maritime Belge [*Belgium*]
CMB............. Confederation des Metalurgistes Belges [*Confederation of Belgian Metallurgists*] (WER)
CMB............. Continental Merchant Bank [*Nigeria*]
CMB............. Corp. of Mortgage, Finance and Life Assurance Brokers [*Later,*] (WGAO)
CMB............. Corporacion Minera de Bolivia [*Mining Corporation of Bolivia*]
CMB............. Cotton Marketing Board [*Australia*]
CMB............. Counseil Mondial de la Boxe (WGAO)
CMB............. Cuyas Manos Beso [*Very Respectfully*] [*Correspondence*] [*Spanish*]
CMBA............. Confectionery and Mixed Business Association of Australia
CMBANZ............. Confectionery and Mixed Business Association of Australia and New Zealand
CMBEFS............. Consiliul Municipal Bucuresti pentru Educatie Fizica si Sport [*Bucharest Municipality Council for Physical Education and Sports*] (RO)
CMBI............. Caribbean Marine Biological Institute (BARN)
CMBI............. Citrus Marketing Board of Israel (PDAA)
CmBK............. Commercial Bank of Kuwait
CMBM............. Centre for Molecular Biology and Medicine [*Monash University*] [*Australia*]
CMBU............. Confederation of Metal and Building Unions [*South Africa*] (AF)
CMC............. Caractere Magnetique Code [*French*] (ADPT)
CMC............. Catholic Media Council (WGAO)
CMC............. Cement Marketing Co. [*Oman*]

CMC .... Centrala Materialelor de Constructie [*Central for Construction Materials*] (RO)
CMC .... Central Military Commission [*China*]
CMC .... Christian Medical Commission (EA)
CMC .... Christian Ministry Centre [*Australia*]
CMC .... Colegio Medico de Chile [*Chilean Medical Association*]
CMC .... Collective Measures Commission [*United Nations*] (DLA)
CMC .... Collective Measures Committee [*United Nations*] (WGAO)
CMC .... Commission Medicale Chretienne [*Christian Medical Commission*] [*Geneva, Switzerland*] (EA)
CMC .... Commonwealth Motoring Conference [*Australia*]
CMC .... Compagnie Malgache de Cabotage
CMC .... Compagnie Maritime Camerounaise SA [*Shipping line*] (EY)
CMC .... Compagnie Miniere de Conakry [*Conakry Mining Company*] [*Guinea*] (AF)
CMC .... Computer Maintenance Corp. [*India*] (WGAO)
CMC .... Conference Mondiale sur le Climat [*OMM*] (WGAO)
CMC .... Congregation de la Mere du Carmel [*Congregation of Mother of Carmel*] [*Alwaye Kerala, India*] (EAIO)
CMC .... Consejo Monetario Centroamericano [*San Jose, Costa Rica*] (LAA)
CMC .... Cooperatieve Melk Centrale (WGAO)
CMC .... Cooperativa Muratori & Cementisti di Ravenna [*Brick & Cement Corporation of Ravenna*] [*Italy*]
CMC .... Cooperative Multimedia Centre [*Australia*]
CMC .... Cooper Motor Car Ltd. [*Kenya*]
CMC .... Corporate Management Committee [*Australia*]
CMC .... Cultural Ministers Council [*Australia*]
CMC .... Curriculum Materials Committee [*Australian Education Council*]
CMC .... Cutlery Manufacturing Company [*Nigeria*]
CMC .... Groupement des Producteurs de Carreaux Ceramiques du Marche Commun [*Grouping of Ceramic Tile Producers of the Common Market*] (ECED)
CMC .... Syndicat National des Constructeurs de Materiel de Chauffage Central (WGAO)
CMC7 .... Caractere Magnetique Code a 7 Batonnets [*French*] (ADPT)
CMCA .... Campervan and Motorhome Club of Australia
CMCA .... Comite Mundial de la Consulta de los Amigos (WGAO)
CMCA .... Commission of Mediation, Conciliation, and Arbitration
CMCA .... Constructions Metallurgiques de Centrafrique
CMCA .... Constructions Metalliques du Centrefrique (WGAO)
CMCAT..... Caisse Mutuelle de Credit Agricole de Tunisie
CMCC .... Coastal Management and Coordination Committee [*Victoria*] [*Australia*]
CMCC .... Credit de Mobilisation des Creances Commerciales [*Credit secured by payments receivable*] [*French*] (IMH)
CMCCJ ..... Confederation Mondiale de Centres Communautaires Juifs [*World Confederation of Jewish Community Centers*] (EAIO)
CMCE .... Centre Malien du Commerce Exterieur
CMCE .... Comite Ministeriel de Coordination Economique [*Benelux*] (BAS)
CMCENGRAIS ... Comite Marche Commun de l'Industrie des Engrais Azotes et Phosphates (WGAO)
CMCES ..... Comite Ministeriel de Coordination Economique et Sociale [*Ministerial Committee for Economic and Social Coordination*] [*Belgium*] (WER)
CMCF....... Campagne Mondiale contre la Faim [*Italy*] (DSCA)
CMCF....... Comite Mondial Contre le Faim [*World Committee to Combat Hunger*] [*French*] (CL)
CMCF/AD ... Campagne Mondiale Contre la Faim/Action pour Developpement [*Freedom from Hunger Campaign/Action for Development - FFHC/AD*] [*French*] (ASF)
CMcGSA... Clan McGillivray Society, Australia
CMCH....... Campana Mundial Contra el Hambre [*Freedom from Hunger Campaign - FFHC*] [*Spanish*]
CMCH/AD ... Campana Mondial Contra el Hambre/Accion por Desarrollo [*Freedom from Hunger Campaign/Action for Development - FFHC/AD*] [*Spanish*] (ASF)
CMCH/AD ... Campana Mundial contra el Hambre/Accion pro Desarrollo (WGAO)
CMCI........ Centrala de Mecanizare pentru Constructii Industriale [*Mechanization Central for Industrial Constructions*] (RO)
CMCI........ Children's Medical Center of Israel [*Tel Aviv*]
CMCIB...... Centrala de Mecanizare pentru Constructii Industriale, Bucuresti [*Industrial Constructions Mechanization Central, Bucharest*] (IMH)
CMCM ...... Centre for Machine Condition Monitoring [*Monash University*] [*Australia*]
CMCM ...... Chairman, Military Committee Memorandum [*NATO*]
CMCM ...... Croatian Male Choir, Melbourne [*Australia*]
CMCO ...... Chinese Malayan Communist Organization (ML)
CMCO ...... Complexe de Materiaux de Construction d'Oran [*Algeria*]
CMCP....... Compagnie Marocaine des Cartons et Papiers
CMCPT..... Comite Maghrebin de Coordination des Postes et Telecommunications

CMCQ...... Commercial Mariculture Council of Queensland [*Australia*]
CMCR ...... Compagnie Maritime des Chargeurs Reunis
CMCRI..... Comptoir Malgache de Courtage, de Representation, et d'Importation
CMCV ...... Classic Motorcycle Club of Victoria [*Australia*]
CMCW ..... Christian Mission to the Communist World [*Australia*]
CMD......... Centrala Maszyn Drogowych [*Road Building Machinery Center*] (POL)
CMD......... Centrale Melkcontrole Dienst (WGAO)
CMD......... Centralforeningen af Malermestre i Danmark (WGAO)
CMD......... Centre Mondiale de Donnees [*World Data Center*] (MSC)
CMD......... Ceskomoravske Statni Drahy [*Czech-Moravian State Railroads*] (CZ)
CMD......... Chemicals and Mineral Division [*Industrial Technology Development Institute*] [*Philippines*] (IRC)
CMD......... Chief Minister's Department [*Australian Capital Territory*] [*Australia*]
CMD......... Comite de Mujeres Democraticas [*Committee of Democratic Women*] [*Colorado*] (LA)
CMD......... Comite Militaire pour le Developpement [*Military Development Committee*] [*Malagasy*] (AF)
CMD......... Compagnie Marocaine de Distribution
CMD......... Council of Music and Drama [*Queensland*] [*Australia*]
CMD......... Courrier Mensuel Defauts [*French*] (ADPT)
CMDC ...... Central Milk Distributive Committee (WGAO)
CMDC ...... Consejo Metropolitano del Distrito Central [*Central District Metropolitan Council*] [*Honduras*] (LA)
CMDI .... China Media Development, Inc. (TCC)
CMDIK ..... Centrum Medycyny Doswiadczalnej i Klinicznej Pan (WGAO)
CMDLRS .. Cirilmetodijsko Drustvo Katoliskih Duhovnikov Ljudska Republika Slovenija [*Cyril and Methodius Society of the Catholic Priests of Slovenia*] (YU)
CMDM...... Compagnie Malgache de Manutention
CMDPA .... Centrul de Material Didactic si Propaganda Agricola [*Center for Teaching Materials and Agricultural Propaganda*] (RO)
Cmdr .... Commander (PWGL)
CMDT .... Compagnie Malienne pour le Developpement des Textiles
CME .... Ciudad Del Carmen [*Mexico*] [*Airport symbol*] (OAG)
CME .... Comite Mixte Economique [*Joint Economic Committee*] [*Cambodia*] (CL)
CME .... Compagnie Mauritanienne d'Entreprises
CME .... Condor Minerals and Energy Ltd. [*Australia*]
CME .... Conference Mondiale de l'Energie [*World Energy Conference - WEC*] (EAIO)
CME......... Conseil Mondial d'Education [*World Council for Curriculum and Instruction*]
CME......... Contracting Marine Engineering [*United Arab Emirates*] (MENA)
CME......... Cumann na Meanmhuinteoiri, Eire [*Association of Secondary Teachers, Ireland*]
CMEA .... Council for Mutual Economic Assistance [*Also known as CEMA, COMECON*] [*Communist-bloc nations: Poland, Russia, East Germany, Czechoslovakia, Romania, Bulgaria, Hungary Dissolved 1991*] [*Former USSR*]
CMEAA .... Construction and Mining Equipment Association of Australia
CMEAOC ... Conference Ministerielle des Etats d'Afrique de l'Ouest et du Centre sur les Transports Maritimes [*Ministerial Conference of West and Central African States on Maritime Transportation - MCWCS*] [*Abidjan, Ivory Coast*] (EAIO)
CMEAOC ... Conference Ministerielle d'Etats Afrique Ouest Centre Transport Maritimes (WGAO)
CMEC .... China National Machinery and Equipment Import and Export Corp. (TCC)
CMEF....... Centro Mexicano de Estudios de Farmacodependencia [*Mexican Center for Studies of Drug Addiction*] (LA)
CMELTA .. Constructions Mecaniques et Electriques de Tananarive
CMEM ...... Centros Militares de Ensenanza Media [*Military Centers for Secondary Education*] [*Cuba*] (LA)
CMER .... Comite Municipal de Extensao Rural [*Brazil*] (DSCA)
CMERA..... Centre Maghrebin d'Etudes et de Recherches Administratives
CMERD .... Centre for Medical Education, Research, and Development [*University of New South Wales*] [*Australia*] (ADA)
CMERI...... Central Mechanical Engineering Research Institute [*Council of Scientific and Industrial Research*] [*India*] (ERC)
CMESC ..... China Mechanical and Electrical Equipment Supplies Corp. (TCC)
CMET....... Comite Maghrebin de l'Emploi et du Travail [*North African*]
CMET....... Committee for Middle East Trade (WGAO)
CMET....... Council on Middle East Trade
CMEWA ... Chamber of Mines and Energy of Western Australia
CMF .... Cast Metal Federation (WGAO)
CMF .... Cement Makers Federation [*Later, BCA*] (WGAO)
CMF .... Chambery [*France*] [*Airport symbol*] (OAG)
CMF .... Christian Missionary Foundation [*Nigeria*]
CMF .... Congregatio Missionariorum Filiorum Immaculati Cordis BMV 'Claretiani' (WGAO)

CMF .... Cordis Mariae Filius (Misioneros Hijos del Corazon de Maria) [*Colombia*] (COL)
CMFA .... Carpet Manufacturers' Federation of Australia
CMFE .... Committee for Mapping the Flora of Europe [*Finland*] (EAIO)
CMFI ..... Central Metal Forming Institute [*India*]
CMFRI ..... Central Marine Fisheries Research Institute [*India*] (MCD)
CMG .... Camargue Air Transport [*France*] [*ICAO designator*] (FAAC)
cm g .... Centimetro-Grama-Forca [*Centimeter Grams of Force*] [*Portuguese*]
CMG .... Comite Mixte Gabonaise [*Gabonese Joint Committee*] (AF)
CMG .... Commission for Marine Geology [*of the International Union of Geological Sciences*] (EAIO)
CMG .... Constructions Mecaniques Generales
CMG .... Constructions Metalliques Generales
CMG .... Corumba Mato Grosso [*Brazil*] [*Airport symbol*] (OAG)
CMGA ...... Country Music Guild of Australasia [*Australia*]
CMGM ...... Comite du Monitoring des Grands Malades [*CEE*] (WGAO)
CMH .... China Merchant Holdings (ECON)
CMH .... Commission de Meteorologie Hydrologique [*OMM*] (WGAO)
CMHN ...... Consejo Mexicano de Hombres de Negocios [*Mexico*] (EY)
Cmh Rs ..... Cumhur Reisi [*President*] [*of Republic*] (TU)
CMHV .... Communaute Musulmane de Haute-Volta [*Upper Volta Moslem Community*] (AF)
CMI .... Caribbean Institute for Meteorology and Hydrology [*Caribbean Meteorological Institute*] [*Acronym is based on former name,*] (EAIO)
CMI .... Caribbean Meteorological Institute [*University of the West Indies*] [*Barbados*] (EAS)
CMI .... Chamber of Manufactures Insurance [*Australia*]
CMI .... Christian Michelsens Institutt for Videnskap og Andsfrihet [*Christian Michelsen Institute of Science and Intellectual Freedom*] [*Research center*] [*Norway*] (ERC)
CMI .... Comite Maritime International [*International Maritime Committee - IMC*] [*Antwerp, Belgium*] (EAIO)
CMI .... Comite Meteorologique International (WGAO)
CMI .... Commission Mixte Internationale pour la Protection des Lignes de Telecommunication et des Canalisations Souterraines (WGAO)
CMI .... Commission Mixte Internationale pour les Experiences Relatives a la Protection des Lignes de Telecommunication et des Canalisations Souterraines [*Joint International Commission for the Protection of Telecommunication Lines and Underground Ducts*] [*Switzerland*]
CMI .... Commonwealth Mining Investments (Australia) Ltd. (ADA)
CMI .... Commonwealth Mycological Institute (WGAO)
CMI .... Communications et Media Internationaux (WGAO)
CMI .... Compagnies Mobiles d'Intervention [*Mobile Intervention Companies*] [*Morocco*] (AF)
CMI .... Conference of African Ministers of Industry
CMI .... Congregatio Fratrum Carmelitarum Beatae Virginis Mariae Immaculatae (WGAO)
CMI .... Consejo Mundial de Iglesias [*Switzerland*]
CMI .... Consolidated Metallurgical Industries [*South Africa*]
CMI .... Continental Micronesia, Inc. [*Guam*] [*ICAO designator*] (FAAC)
CMI .... Creative Ministries International [*Australia*]
CMIA .... Cyprus Metal Industry Association (EAIO)
CMIAP ...... Comite Militaire Inter-Armee Provisoire [*Provisional Joint Military Committee*] [*Chad*] (AF)
CMIB .... Comite d'Organisation du Congress Mondial d'Implantologie des Biomateriaux [*Organizing Committee of the World Congress on Implantology and Biomaterials*] [*France*] (EAIO)
CMIC .... Chicken Meat Industry Committee [*Queensland*] [*Australia*]
CMID .... Ceskomoravska Impregnace Dreva [*Czech-Moravian Wood Impregnating Enterprise*] (CZ)
CMIDOM ... Centre Militaire d'Information et de Documentation sur l'Outre-Mer [*Military Center for Overseas Information and Documentation*] [*French*] (AF)
CMIE .... Centre for Monitoring the Indian Economy (ECON)
CMIEA ...... Conference of Minister for Immigration and Ethnic Affairs [*Australia*]
CMIEB ...... Centre Mondial d'Information sur l'Education Bilingue [*World Information Centre for Bilingual Education - WICBE*] (EAIO)
CMIEC ...... China National Metallurgical Import & Export Corporation [*China*] (IMH)
CMI-EC ..... Committee for the Mustard Industry of the European Communities [*Belgium*] (EAIO)
CMIM .... Constructions Metalliques et Industrielles Mecaniques
CMIS .... Computerorientiertes Management-Informationssystem [*French*] (ADPT)
CMIS .... Conferenza Mondale degli Istituti Secolari [*Italy*] (WGAO)
CMIT .... Committee on Capital Movements and Invisible Transactions [*OECD*] (WGAO)
CMITU ...... Centre Mondial d'Informations Techniques et d'Urbanisme [*FMVJ*] (WGAO)

CMIUW .... Coal Miners' Industrial Union of Workers [*Australia*]
CMJA .... Commonwealth Magistrates and Judges Association (WGAO)
CMJP .... Centre Marocain des Jeunes Patrons
CMJP .... Centre Marocain des Jeunes Patrons et des Cardres Dirigeants (WGAO)
CMKD .... Consortium Marocain-Kuwaitien de Developpement [*Moroccan-Kuwaiti Development Consortium*] (AF)
CML .... Camara Municipal de Lisboa [*Lisbon City Hall*] [*Portuguese*] (WER)
CML .... Coles Myer Ltd. [*Australia*]
CML .... Collegium Musicum di Latina [*Italian*] (SLS)
CML .... Colonial Mutual Life Assurance Society Ltd. [*Australia*] (ADA)
CML .... Comite Marxista Leninista
CML .... Companhia Mineira de Lobito
CML .... Council Moslem League [*Pakistan*] [*Political party*]
CMLA ...... Chief Martial Law Administrator [*Pakistan*] [*Facetious translation: "Cancel My Last Announcement"*] (ECON)
CMLA ...... Communications and Media Law Association [*Australia*]
CMLAWA ... Civilian Maimed and Limbless Association of Western Australia
CMLN ...... Comite Militaire de Liberation Nationale [*Military National Liberation Committee*] [*Mali*] (AF)
CMLO ...... Central Medical Library Organization [*Australia*] (ADA)
CMLO ...... Chief Martial Law Office [*Pakistan*]
CM-LP ...... Comite Marxista-Leninista Portugues [*Portuguese Marxist-Leninist Committee*] (PPE)
CMM .... Center for Molecular Medicine [*Germany*]
CMM .... Century Minerals and Mining [*Australia*]
CMM .... Certified Marketing Manager [*Australia*]
CMM .... Civil and Mechanical Maintenance Proprietary Ltd. [*Australia*] (ADA)
CMM .... Comision de Meteorologia Marina [*Commission for Marine Meteorology - CMM*] [*World Meteorological Organization*] [*Spanish*] (ASF)
CMM .... Comissao de Marinha Mercante [*Merchant Marine Commission*] [*Brazil*] (LA)
CMM .... Comite du Cahier Medical de Madagascar
CMM .... Commission de Meteorologie Maritime [*Commission for Marine Meteorology - CMM*] [*World Meteorological Organization*] [*French*] (ASF)
CMM .... Commission for Maritime Meteorology [*World Meteorological Organization*]
CMM .... Compagnie des Messageries Maritimes
CMM .... Compagnie Marseillaise de Madagascar
CMM .... Compagnie Metallurgique et Miniere
CMM .... Compagnie Miniere de la Moufumbi
CMM .... Congregatio Missionariorum de Mariannhill [*Congregation of Mariannhill Missionaries*] [*Mariannhill Fathers*] [*Roman Catholic religious order*] [*Italy*]
CMM .... Consolidated Modderfontein Mines [*South Africa*] [*Commercial firm*]
CMM .... Constructions Metalliques de Mauritanie
CMM .... Marine Mammals Committee [*IUCN*] (ASF)
CMM .... Technical Commission for Marine Meteorology [*WIIO*] [*Geneva, Switzerland*] (EAIO)
CMMA ...... Company of Master Mariners of Australia
CMMA ...... Concrete Mixer Manufacturers Association (WGAO)
CMMBE ..... Comissao Militar Mista Brasil-Estados Unidos [*Portuguese*]
CMMC ...... Commonwealth Mining and Metallurgical Congress (WGAO)
CMMC ...... Moulding Materials Co. [*China*] (TCC)
CMMEI ..... Chamber of Mines, Metals, and Extractive Industries [*Australia*]
CMMI ...... Commonwealth Mining and Metallurgical Institutions (WGAO)
CMMICTUC ... Confederation of Metallurgical, Mineral, Industrial, and Commercial Trade Unions in Chile (EAIO)
CMML ...... Christian Missions in Many Lands
CMMN ...... Centrala Minereurilor si Metalurgiei Neferoase [*Central for Nonferrous Ores and Metallurgy*] (RO)
CMMR ...... Centrala Mecanica de Material Rulant [*Machine Central for Rolling Stock*] (RO)
CMN .... Casablanca-Mohamed V [*Morocco*] [*Airport symbol*] (OAG)
CMN .... Centro de Mujeres de Nigeria [*Women's Centre of Nigeria*] (EAIO)
CMN .... Chamber of Mines of Namibia (EAIO)
CMN .... Comisia pentru Ocrotirea Monumentelor Naturii (WGAO)
CMN .... Compagnie Malgache de Navigation
CMN .... Compagnie Malienne de Navigation
CMN .... Conselho Monetario Nacional [*National Monetary Council*] [*Brazil*] (LA)
CMN .... Constructions Mecaniques de Normandie [*France*] (PDAA)
CMNPO .... Common Market Newspaper Publishers' Organization [*See also CAEJ*] [*Brussels, Belgium*] (EAIO)
CMNR .... Comite Militaire de Redressement National [*Military Committee for National Recovery*] [*Use CMRN Mauritania*] (AF)
CMNT .... Comissao Mista Nacional de Telecomunicacoes [*National Mixed Commission of Telecommunications*] [*Portuguese*] (WER)
CMO .... Career Medical Officer [*Australia*]
CMO .... Caribbean Meteorological Organisation [*Formerly, Caribbean Meteorological Service*] (EA)

CMO......... Central Melkhandelaren Organisatie (WGAO)
CMO......... Central Meteorological Office [*Korean*] (MSC)
CMO......... Chemin de Fer du Maroc Oriental
CMO......... Citizen's Municipal Organisation [*Australia*]
CMO......... Colonia Militar de Oiapoque [*Brazil*] (WGAO)
CMO......... Commonwealth Medical Officer [*Australia*]
CMO......... Cootamundra [*Australia*] [*Airport symbol*] (OAG)
CMO......... Ocean Minelayer [*NATO*]
CMOA....... Commonwealth Medical Officers' Association [*Australia*]
CMOD....... Centre Mondial d'Orientation Documentaire (WGAO)
CMOO....... Compagnie Miniere de l'Oubangi Oriental
CMOPE..... Confederation Mondiale des Organisations de la Profession Enseignante [*World Confederation of Organizations of the Teaching Profession - WCOTP*] (EAIO)
CMOT....... Confederation Maghrebine des Operateurs de Tourisme [*North African*]
CMP .... Campo Alegre [*Brazil*] [*Airport symbol*] (OAG)
CMP .... Centre Meteorologique Principal [*Main Meteorological Office*] [*French*]
CMP .... Chamber of Mines of the Philippines (DS)
CMP .... Christian Movement for Peace [*See also MCP*] [*Brussels, Belgium*] (EAIO)
CMP .... Comite Militaire du Parti
CMP .... Comite Militaire du PCT [*PCT Military Committee*] [*Congo*] (AF)
CMP .... Compagnie Malgache des Petroles
CMP .... Compania Panamena de Aviacion SA [*Panama*] [*ICAO designator*] (FAAC)
CMP .... Conseil Mondial de la Paix [*World Peace Council - WPC*] (EAIO)
CMP .... Consejo Mundial de Paz [*World Peace Council*] [*Use WPC*] [*Spanish*] (LA)
CMP .... Consiglio Mondiale della Pace [*World Peace Council*] [*Use WPC*] [*Italian*] (WER)
CMP .... Continental Margins Program [*Australia*]
CMPA ...... Chinchilla Pelt Marketing Association (WGAO)
CMPA ...... Cyprus Master-Printers Association (EAIO)
CMPAA..... Certified Milk Producers Association of America (WGAO)
CMPC........ Compania Manufacturera de Papeles y Cartones [*Paper and Cardboard Manufacturing Company*] [*Chile*] (LA)
CMPCO .... Comite Mixta sobre Programas Cientificos Relacionados con la Oceanografica (WGAO)
CMPD .... Comite Militaire pour le Developpement [*Military Development Committee*] [*Use CMD*] (AF)
CMPE........ Comite Medical Permanent Europeen (WGAO)
CMPE........ Contractors Mechanical Plant Engineers (WGAO)
CMPFE ..... Centre Malagasy de Production de Films Educatifs [*Malagasy Center for Production of Educational Films*] (AF)
CMPFT ..... Centro de la Mujer Peruana Flora Tristan [*Flora Tristan Peruvian Center for Women*] (EAIO)
CMPI......... Consejo Mundial de Pueblos Indigenos (WGAO)
CMPO .... Calcutta Metropolitan Planning Organisation [*India*] (WGAO)
CMPP........ Comite Maghrebin des Produits Pharmaceutiques [*North African*]
CMPR........ Centre Militaire de Preformation de la Reunion [*Basic Military Training Center of Reunion*] (AF)
CMPR........ Chambre Syndicale des Fabricants de Tuiles et de Briques du Poitou-Charentes-Limousin (WGAO)
CMPR........ Comptoir Malgache de Pieces de Rechange
CMPS........ Combined Military Planning Staff
CMPS........ Crooks Michell Peacock Stewart Proprietary Ltd. [*Australia*]
CMQ......... Clermont [*Australia*] [*Airport symbol*] (OAG)
CMQB ...... Coal Mining Qualifications Board [*New South Wales*] [*Australia*]
CMR .... Cameroon [*ANSI three-letter standard code*] (CNC)
CMR .... Cape Mounted Rifles
CMR .... Central Mortgage Registry [*Australia*]
CMR .... Centre Meteorologique Regional [*Regional Meteorological Center - RMC*] [*French*] (ASF)
CMR .... Centro Meteorologico Regional [*Regional Meteorological Center - RMC*] [*Spanish*] (ASF)
CMR .... Centrul Metodologic de Reumatologie [*Methodology Center for Rheumatology*] (RO)
CMR .... Chretiens dans le Monde Rural (WGAO)
CMR .... Christelike Maatskaplike Raad [*Afrikaans*]
CMR .... Colmar [*France*] [*Airport symbol*] (OAG)
CMR .... Comite Militaire de la Revolution [*Military Committee of the Revolution*] [*Benin*] (AF)
CMR .... Comites Militares Regionales [*Regional Military Committees*] [*Cuba*] (LA)
CMR .... Convention Relative au Transport International de Marchandises par Route (FLAF)
CMRAAS.. Commission for Music Research of the Austrian Academy of Sciences
CMRADR ... Conference Mondiale sur la Reforme Agraire et Developpement Rural [*FAO*] (WGAO)
CMRC .... Colonial Medical Research Committee (WGAO)
CMRD....... Committee on Migration, Refugees, and Demography (EA)

CMRDC .... Chicken Meat Research and Development Council [*Australia*]
CMRDI..... Central Metallurgical Research and Development Institute [*Egypt*] [*Research center*] (IRC)
CMRI........ Children's Medical Research Institute [*Australia*]
CMRI........ Colonial Microbiological Research Institute [*Port Of Spain, Trinidad*] (LAA)
CMRLS .... Caulfield-Malvern Regional Library Service [*Australia*] (ADA)
CMRN ...... Comite Militaire de Redressement National [*Military Committee for National Recovery*] [*Mauritania*] (AF)
CMRN ...... Military Committee for National Recovery [*Central Africa*] (PD)
CMRP....... Cesky a Moravsky Rudny Pruzkum [*Mineral Prospecting in Bohemia and Moravia*] (CZ)
CMRPN .... Comite Militaire de Redressement pour le Progres National [*Military Committee for Redress and National Progress*]
CMRS....... Central Mining Research Station [*Council of Scientific and Industrial Research*] [*India*] [*Research center*] (ERC)
CMRS....... Conference of Major Religious Superiors (WGAO)
CMRSS .... Conseil Mediterraneen de Recherches en Sciences Sociales (DSCA)
CMS .... Canberra Montessori Society [*Australia*]
CMS .... Canberra Mothercraft Society [*Australia*]
CMS .... Caribbean Meteorological Service (WGAO)
CMS .... Catholic Missionary Society (WGAO)
C-M-S....... Cechy - Morava - Slovensko [*Bohemia - Moravia - Slovakia*] (CZ)
cm/s .... Centimetro por Segundo [*Centimeters per Second*] [*Portuguese*]
cms .... Centimetros [*Centimeters*] [*Spanish*]
CMS .... Centre for Multicultural Studies [*Flinders University*] [*Australia*]
CMS .... Centrul de Mecanica a Solidelor [*Center for the Mechanics of Solids*] (RO)
cm/s .... Centymetr na Sekunde [*Centimeter per Second*] [*Poland*]
CMS .... Ceska Matice Skolska [*Czech Educational Foundation*] (CZ)
CMS .... Ceskomoravske Sklarny, Narodni Podnik [*Czech-Moravian Glass Factories, National Enterprise*] (CZ)
CMS .... Ceskoslovenska Mykologicka Spolecnost [*Czechoslovak Mycological Society*] (CZ)
CMS .... Chinese Masonic Society [*Australia*]
CMS .... Chinese Mathematical Society (SLS)
CMS .... Chinese Meteorological Society (EAIO)
CMS .... Church Missionary Society (WGAO)
CMS .... Church Monuments Society (EA)
CMS .... Club Micro Son [*France*] (EAIO)
CMS .... Comite Maghrebin des Sports
CMS .... Commission de Meteorologie Synoptique [*See also CSM*] [*French*]
CMS .... Conseil Militaire Supreme [*Supreme Military Council*] [*Niger*] (AF)
CMS .... Corps Mondial de Secours (WGAO)
CMS .... Czech Medical Society (EAIO)
CMSA....... Chinese Motor Sport Association (EAIO)
CMSA....... Church Missionary Society of Australia
CMS & A... C. M. Steele & Associates [*Australia*]
CMSB....... Confederation Mondiale du Sport de Boules (WGAO)
CMSC....... Council of Moslem School Proprietors
CMSEF .... Congregatio Missionaria Sancti Francisci Assissensis (WGAO)
CMSER ..... Commission on Marine Science, Engineering and Resources (WGAO)
CMSF .... Centre for Molecular Structure and Function [*Australian National University*]
CMSL-FO ... Confederation Malgache des Syndicats Libre - Force Ouvriere
CMSM ...... Conferonica Melitensis Superiorum Maiorum [*Malta*] (WGAO)
CMSN ...... Comite Militaire de Salut National [*Military Committee for National Salvation*] [*Mauritania*] (AF)
CMSP........ Confederacion de Militares en Servicio Pasivo [*Federation of Retired Servicemen*] [*Ecuador*] (LA)
CMSRBA .. Conference of Major Superiors of Religious Brothers of Australia
CMSS........ Caisse Mutuelle de Securite Sociale [*Morocco*]
CMSTTKU ... College of Marine Science and Technology, Tokai University (MSC)
CMSWA.... Conference of Major Superiors of Women's Religious Institutes of Australia
CMSWA.... Convention on the Conservation of Migratory Species of Wild Animals (ASF)
CMT .... Centraal Medisch Tuchtcollege [*Benelux*] (BAS)
CMT .... Centrala de Masini Textile [*Romania*] (EY)
CMT .... Centros de Mantenimiento de Transmision [*Transmission Maintenance Centers*] [*Cuba*] (LA)
CMT .... Ceska Matice Technicka [*Czech Foundation for Advancement of Technology*] (CZ)
CMT .... Comite Maghrebin du Tourisme
CMT .... Common Market Travel Association (EAIO)
CMT .... Community Management Training Scheme [*Australia*]
CMT .... Confederacion Multigremial del Trabajo [*Confederation of Business and Professional Associations*] [*Chile*] (LA)
CMT .... Confederation Mauricienne des Travailleurs [*Mauritius Confederation of Labor*]

CMT .... Confederation Mondiale du Travail [*World Confederation of Labour - WCL*] [*Brussels, Belgium*] (EAIO)
CMT .... Construction Metallique Tropicale
CMT .... MM/CMT Federation Mondiale de le Metallurgie (WGAO)
CMTA ...... Comite Maghrebin des Transports Aeriens
CMTD ...... Center for Market and Trade Development [*China*]
Cmte.......... Committee (PWGL)
CMTI........ Central Machine Tool Institute [*National Information Centre for Machine Tools and Production Engineering*] [*India*]
CMTM ..... Comite Maghrebin des Transports Maritimes
CMTMA ... Cyprus Mosaic and Tiles Manufacturers Association (EAIO)
CMTR ...... Comite Maghrebin des Transports Routiers
CMTR ...... Compagnie Malienne des Transports Routiers
CMTS ...... Community Management Training Service [*Australia*]
CMTT....... Commission Mixte pour les Transmissions Televisuelles (WGAO)
CMTT....... Consortium Marocain de Transit et de Transports
CMTTCW ... Christian Mission to the Communist World [*Australia*]
CMTU ...... Confederation of Malta Trade Unions (WGAO)
CMTU ...... Confederation of Trade Unions [*Malta*]
CMU......... Canadian Maritime Union (BARN)
CMU......... Central Mindanao University [*Philippines*] (ARC)
CMU......... Ceza Mahkemeleri (Kanunu) Usul [*Criminal Courts' Procedural Law*] (TU)
CMU......... Combined Mining Unions [*Australia*] (ADA)
CMU......... Commandement Militaire Unifie [*Unified Military Command*] [*Angola*] (AF)
CMU......... Cumhuriyet Muddei Umumisi [*Public Prosecutor*] (TU)
CMU......... Kundiawa [*Papua New Guinea*] [*Airport symbol*] (OAG)
CMUF ...... Compagnie Miniere de l'Uranium de Franceville
CMUK....... Ceza Mahkemeleri Usul Kanunu [*Criminal Courts' Procedural Law*] (TU)
CMV .... Celostatni Mirovy Vybor [*All-State Peace Committee*] (CZ)
CMV .... Christlicher Metallarbeiterverband [*Switzerland*] (WGAO)
CMV .... Christlicher Metallarbeiterverband der Schweiz [*Christian Metalworkers Association of Switzerland*] (EY)
CMV .... Comite Militaire de Vigilance [*Military Vigilance Committee*] [*Benin*] (AF)
CMV .... Congregatione Mechitarista di Vienna (WGAO)
CMV .... Council of the Museum of Victoria [*Australia*]
CMVKD .... Celostatni Mirovy Vybor Katolickeho Duchovenstva [*All-State Peace Committee of the Catholic Clergy*] (CZ)
CMVV ...... Colegio de Medicos Veterinarios de Venezuela [*Venezuela*] (DSCA)
CMW........ Camaguey [*Cuba*] [*Airport symbol*] (OAG)
CMWA...... Chamber of Mines of Western Australia
CMWPT.... Coal Mine Workers' Pension Tribunal [*Victoria*] [*Australia*]
CMX .... Compania Mexicana de Taxis Aereos SA [*Mexico*] [*ICAO designator*] (FAAC)
CMZ .... Compagnie Maritime Zairoise [*Zairian Shipping Company*] (AF)
Cn............. Black Powder [*Symbol*] [*French*] (MTD)
CN............. Certificat de Nationalite [*France*] (FLAF)
CN............. China [*ANSI two-letter standard code*] (CNC)
CN............. Circulo Nacional de Prensa [*Guatemala*] (EY)
CN............. Cirkevne Nakladatelstvo [*Religious Literature Publishing House*] (CZ)
CN............. Coalicion Nacionalista [*Spain*] [*Political party*] (ECED)
CN............. Combined Nomenclature [*EC*] (ECED)
CN............. Commande Numerique [*French*] (ADPT)
c/n............. Compte Nouveau [*New Account*] [*Business term*] [*French*]
C-N............ Conico Norteno [*Race of maize*] [*Mexico*]
CN............. Conselho Nacional
CN............. Country National Party [*Political party*] [*Australia*]
c/n............. Cours Nul [*French*]
CN............. Credit du Niger
CN............. Credit National [*National Credit Bank*] [*Guinea, Luxembourg*] (AF)
CN............. Cuneo [*Car registration plates*] [*Italy*]
CNA.......... Caisse Nationale Autoroutes [*National Motorways Fund*] [*France*]
CNA.......... Camp New Amsterdam [*Netherlands*]
CNA.......... Cartel dos Nationalistas Angolanos
CNA.......... Centennial [*Spain*] [*ICAO designator*] (FAAC)
CNA.......... Centrale Nucleaire des Ardennes
CNA.......... Central News Agency Ltd.
CNA.......... Centre National d'Agriculture [*National Agricultural Center*] [*Senegal*] (AF)
CNA.......... Centre National d'Alphabetisation [*Algeria*]
CNA.......... Centrul National Aeronautic [*Romania*] (EY)
CNA.......... Ceramisti Novesi Associati (WGAO)
CNA.......... Cesky Narodni Aeroklub [*Czech National Aero Club*] (CZ)
CNA.......... Charbonnages Nord-Africains [*Morocco*]
CNA.......... Chemicals Notation Association [*Later,*] (WGAO)
CNA.......... China Notaries' Association (EAIO)
CNA.......... Chin National Army [*Myanmar*] [*Political party*] (EY)

CNA.......... Coalition of National Agreement [*Croatia*] [*Political party*]
CNA.......... Code de la Nationalite Algerienne
CNA.......... Colegio Nacional de Arquitectos de Cuba [*National Association of Cuban Architects*] (LA)
CNA.......... College of Nursing Australia
CNA.......... Combined New Australia Party [*Political party*]
CNA.......... Comision Nacional del Arroz [*Ecuador*] (DSCA)
CNA.......... Comissao Nacional de Alimentacao [*Brazil*] (DSCA)
CNA.......... Comissao Nacional de Avicultura [*Brazil*] (DSCA)
CNA.......... Comissao Nacional do Alcool [*National Alcohol Commission*] [*Brazil*] (LA)
CNA.......... Comite Nacional de Abastos [*National Supply Committee*] [*Nicaragua*] (LA)
CNA.......... Comite National pour l'Etude et la Prevention de l'Alcoolisme et des Autres Toxicomanies [*Belgium*] (SLS)
CNA.......... Commission de la Navigation Aerienne [*France*] (FLAF)
CNA.......... Compagnie Nationale d'Assurances [*Insurance*] [*Ivory Coast*]
CNA.......... Compagnie Nationale d'Assurances [*Insurance*] [*Cameroon*]
CNA.......... Compania Nacional de Aviacion [*Peru*]
CNA.......... Confederacao Nacional da Agricultura [*National Agriculture Confederation*] [*Brasilia, Brazil*] (LA)
CNA.......... Confederacao Nacional de Agricultura [*Brazil*] (DSCA)
CNA.......... Confederacion Nacional Agraria [*National Agrarian Confederation*] [*Peru*] (LA)
CNA.......... Confederation Nationale de l'Artisanat (WGAO)
CNA.......... Confederazione Nazionale dell'Artigianato [*Italy*] (EY)
CNA.......... Conseil National de l'Aeronautique
CNA.......... Consejo Nacional Agrario [*Peru*] (LAA)
CNA.......... Consejo Nacional Agrario [*National Agrarian Council*] [*Honduras*] (LA)
CNA.......... Consiliul National al Apelor [*National Water Council*] (RO)
CNA.......... Consiliul National de Agricultura [*National Council for Agriculture*] (RO)
CNA.......... Convertisseur Numerique Analogique [*French*] (ADPT)
CNA.......... Corporacion Nacional de Abastecimientos [*Peru*] (WGAO)
CNA.......... Cyprus News Agency
CNAA....... Camara Nacional de Agricultura y Agroindustria [*National Chamber of Agriculture*] [*Costa Rica*] (EAIO)
CNAA....... Comite National d'Action Agricole (WGAO)
CNAA....... Corporation Nationale de l'Agriculture et de l'Alimentation (WGAO)
CNAA....... Council for National Academic Awards (WGAO)
CNAAC..... Comite National d'Aide et d'Assistance aux Combattants [*National Aid and Relief Committee for Combatants*] [*Cambodia*] (CL)
CNAAFERT ... China National Advertising Association for Foreign Economic Relations and Trade
CNAAG..... Centre National d'Astronomie, d'Astrophysique, et de Geophysique [*Algeria*] (SLS)
CNAAG..... Comite National d'Astronomie d'Astrophysique et de Geographique [*Algeria*] (WGAO)
CNAB....... Confederation Nationale de Administrateurs de Biens (WGAO)
CNABRL... Compagnie Nationale d'Amenagement du Bas-Rhone et Languedoc (WGAO)
CNAC....... China National Aviation Corp. (WGAO)
CNAC....... Comision Nacional de Accion Conservadora [*Conservative National Action Commission*] [*Colorado*] (LA)
CNAC....... Comision Nacional de la Academia de Ciencias [*National Commission of the Academy of Sciences*] [*Cuba*] (LA)
CNAC....... Comite National d'Action Communal
CNAC....... Compagnie Nationale d'Assurances du Cambodge [*National Insurance Company of Cambodia*] (CL)
CNACSC... China National Automation Control System Corp. (TCC)
CNAD....... Conference of National Armaments Directors [*NATO*]
CNAD....... Conseil National des Arts Dramatiques (WGAO)
CNAE....... Campanha Nacional de Alimentacao Escolar [*National School Lunch Drive*] [*Brazil*] (LA)
CNAE....... Comissao Nacional de Atividades Espaciais [*National Space Activities Commission*] [*INPE*] [*Later,*] [*Brazil*] (LA)
CNAE....... Companhia Nacional de Alimentacao Escolar [*Brazil*] (WGAO)
CNAEE...... Conselho Nacional de Aguas e Energia Eletrica [*National Council on Water and Electric Power*] [*Brazil*] (LA)
CNAEM .... Cekmece Nucleer Arastirma ve Egitim Merkezi [*Cekmese Nuclear Research and Training Center*] (TU)
CNAF .... Confederation Nationale de l'Aviculture Francaise (WGAO)
CNAFAT... Caisse Nationale d'Allocations Familiales et des Accidents du Travail [*National Welfare and Workmen's Compensation Fund*] [*Malagasy*] (AF)
CNAFM .... Conseil National des Associations des Femmes de Madagascar [*National Council of Women's Associations of Madagascar*] (AF)
CNAG....... Centro Nacional de Agricultura y Ganaderia [*Honduras*] (DSCA)
CNAG....... Comite National d'Assainissement General [*National General Cleanup Committee*] [*Cambodia*] (CL)
CNAG....... Commission Nationale d'Amelioration Genetique (WGAO)
CNAG....... Comunn na Gaidhlig (WGAO)

CNAH........ Centre National pour l'Amelioration de l'Habitat   (WGAO)
CNAIC........ China National Automotive Industry Corporation
CNAIC........ Chinese National Association of Industry and Commerce
        [*Taiwan*]   (EAIO)
CNAIIDC.. China National Automotive Industry Investment &
        Development Corp.
CNAIOS.... Consociazione Nazionale delle Infermiere / Infermierri de Altri
        Operatori Sanitorio   (WGAO)
CNALCM ... Comite National d'Action et de Liaison des Classes Moyennes
        (WGAO)
CNAM........ Confederation Nationale de l'Artisanat et des Metiers   (WGAO)
CNAM........ Congreso Nacional Africano de Mocambique
CNAM........ Conservatoire National des Arts et Metiers de Paris [*France*]
        (PDAA)
CNAM........ Conservatoire National des Arts et Mietiers   (WGAO)
CNAMC.... China Nanchang Aircraft Manufacturing Co.
CNAN........ Compagnie Nationale Algerienne de Navigation [*Algerian
        National Shipping Company*]   (AF)
CNAO........ Comite Nacional de Auscultacion y Organizacion [*National
        Committee for Auscultation and Organization*] [*Mexico*]
        (LA)
CNAOP..... Comision Nacional de Aprendizaje y Orientacion Profesional
        [*Argentina*]   (LAA)
CNAP........ Centre National Anti-Pollution [*National Antipollution Center*]
        [*Gabon*]   (AF)
CNAP........ Centre National d'Animation et de Promotion   (WGAO)
CNAP........ Centro de Nutricao Animal e Pastagens [*Brazil*]   (DSCA)
CNAP........ Combined New Australia Party [*Political party*]
CNAP........ Comitetul National pentru Apararea Pacii [*National Committee
        for the Defense of Peace*]   (RO)
CNAPC...... Comite National d'Action pour la Paix et la Concorde [*National
        Action Committee for Peace and Concord*] [*Cambodia*]
        (CL)
CNAPCM ... Comite National d'Action pour la Paix et la Concorde [*National
        Action Committee for Peace and Concord*] [*Use CNAPC
        Cambodia*]   (CL)
CNAPD..... Comite National d'Action pour la Paix et le Developpement
        [*National Action Committee for Peace and Development*]
        [*Belgium*]   (WER)
CNAPF...... Centre National des Academies et Associations Litteraires et
        Savantes des Provinces Francaises   (WGAO)
CNAPS...... Caisse Nationale de Prevoyance Sociale [*National Social Welfare
        Fund*] [*Malagasy*]   (AF)
CNAPT...... Ceylon National Association for the Prevention of Tuberculosis
        (WGAO)
CNAR........ Caisse Nationale d'Assurance et de Reassurance [*Insurance*]
        [*Mali*]   (EY)
CNAR........ Compagnie Nationale d'Assurances et de Reassurances [*Ivory
        Coast*]
CNAR........ Confederation Nationale des Artisans Ruraux   (WGAO)
CNAR........ Confederation Nationale pour l'Amenagement Rural   (WGAO)
CNAREM ... Centre National des Recherches Metallurgiques   (WGAO)
CNAS........ Research Center for Nepal and Asian Studies   (IRC)
CNASA...... Centre National d'Amenagements des Structures Agricoles
        (WGAO)
CNASEA ... Centre National pour l'Amenagement des Structures des
        Exploitations Agricoles   (WGAO)
CNAT........ Centre National d'Animation des Entreprises et de Traitement
        des Informations du Secteur de la Construction [*Algeria*]
        (IMH)
CNAT........ Comissao Nacional de Assistencia Tecnica [*National Technical
        Assistance Commission*] [*Brazil*]   (LA)
CNAT........ Commission Nationale d'Amenagement du Territoire [*France*]
        (FLAF)
CNAT........ Confederation Nord-Africaine des Transports [*Morocco*]
        (WGAO)
CNAV........ Christlinationaler Angestelltenverband der Schweiz   (WGAO)
CNAVA..... Caisse Nationale Assurance Vieillesse Agricole [*France*]   (FLAF)
CNAVMA ... Caisse Nationale d'Assurance Vieillesse Mutuelle Agricole
        (WGAO)
CNAVS...... Cesky Narodni Aeroklub Vysokoskolskeho Studentstva [*Czech
        National Aero Club of University Students*]   (CZ)
CNB.......... Air Columbus SA [*Portugal*] [*ICAO designator*]   (FAAC)
CNB.......... Canberra [*Australia*]
CNB.......... Centrale Nucleaire Belge [*Nuclear reactor*] [*Belgium*]   (NRCH)
CNB.......... Central Normalisatiebureau   (WGAO)
CNB.......... Citizens National Bank [*South Korea*]   (IMH)
CNB.......... Comite National Belge   (WGAO)
CNB.......... Confederation Nationale de la Boulangerie et Boulangerie
        Patisserie   (WGAO)
CNB.......... Coonamble [*Australia*] [*Airport symbol*]   (OAG)
CNB.......... Coordinador Nacional de Bases [*National Coordination of Bases*]
        [*Colorado*]   (PD)
CNBB........ Confederacao Nacional dos Bispos do Brasil   (WGAO)
CNBB........ Conferencia Nacional dos Bispos do Brasil [*National Conference
        of Brazilian Bishops*]   (LA)

CNBE .... Comite National Belge de l'Eclairage [*Belgian National Lighting
        Committee*]   (WED)
CNBF........ Caisse Nationale des Barreaux Francais   (FLAF)
CNBF........ Centre National des Bles de Force   (WGAO)
CNBF........ Centre National des Bureaux de Fret [*Ivory Coast*]
CNBF........ Confederation Nationale de la Boucherie Francaise   (WGAO)
CnBK .... Central Bank of Kuwait
CNBOS...... Comite National Belge de l'Organisation Scientifique [*Belgium*]
        (SLS)
CNBP........ Comision Nacional de Badminton del Peru [*National Badminton
        Commission of Peru*]   (EAIO)
CNBT .... Conseil National de la Blanchisserie et de la Teinturerie
        (WGAO)
CNBU .... Commission Nationale du Burundi pour l'UNESCO
CNBV .... Comissao Nacional de Bolsas de Valores [*National Stock
        Exchange Commission*] [*Brazil*]   (LA)
CNBVSL ... Confederation Nationale Belge des Industries et du Commerce
        des Vins, Spirituex et Liqueurs   (WGAO)
CNC .... Camara Nacional de Comercio [*National Chamber of
        Commerce*] [*Bolivia*]   (EAIO)
CNC .... Camara Nicaraguense de la Construccion [*Nicaraguan Chamber
        of Construction*]   (LA)
CNC .... Capitaine de Navigation Cotiere
CNC .... Central Nacional Campesina [*Venezuela*]   (EY)
CNC .... Centre for National Culture [*Ghana*]   (EAIO)
CNC .... Centre National Cinematographique [*National Cinematographic
        Center*] [*Algeria*]   (AF)
CNC .... Centre National de la Cinematographie [*France*]   (FLAF)
CNC .... Centre National du Cinema [*National Motion Picture Center*]
        [*Burkina Faso*]   (AF)
CNC .... Centrul National de Chimie [*National Center for Chemistry*]
        (RO)
CNC .... Chambre Nationale de Commerce [*Algeria*]   (EY)
CNC .... Chantiers Navals de la Ciotat [*France*]   (PDAA)
CNC .... Clinical Nurse Consultants [*Australia*]
CNC .... Comision Nacional Campesina [*Trade union*] [*Chile*]   (EY)
CNC .... Comision Nacional de Cultura [*National Commission for
        Cultural Activities*] [*Buenos Aires, Argentina*]   (LAA)
CNC .... Comision Nacional del Cacao [*Ecuador*]   (WGAO)
CNC .... Comite National de Coordination
CNC .... Comite National de la Consommation [*French*]
CNC .... Commande Numerique par Calculateur [*French*]   (ADPT)
CNC .... Compagnie Nouvelle de Cadres [*Morocco*]
CNC .... Confederacao Nacional do Comercio [*National Confederation of
        Commerce*] [*Brasilia, Brazil*]   (LA)
CNC .... Confederacion Nacional Campesina [*National Peasant
        Confederation*] [*Mexico*]   (LA)
CNC .... Confederacion Nacional Campesina [*National Peasant
        Confederation*] [*Chile*]   (LA)
CNC .... Confederacion Nacional de Campesinos [*Mexico*]   (WGAO)
CNC .... Confederacion Nacional de la Construccion [*Spain*]   (EY)
CNC .... Confederation Nationale de la Construction [*Civil Engineering,
        Road and Building Contractors, and Auxiliary Trades
        Confederation*] [*Brussels, Belgium*]   (EY)
CNC .... Confederation Nationale des Cadres [*National Confederation of
        Cadres*] [*Trade union*] [*Belgium*]   (WER)
CNC .... Congreso Nacional de Canarias [*Spain*] [*Political party*]   (EY)
CNC .... Conseil National Consultatif [*National Advisory Committee*]
        [*Mauritania*]   (AF)
CNC .... Conseil National des Charbonnages [*Benelux*]   (BAS)
CNC .... Conseil National du Commerce [*France*]   (FLAF)
CNC .... Conseil National du Credit   (WGAO)
CNC .... Conseil National du Cuir   (WGAO)
CNC .... Consejo Nacional de Campesinos [*National Council of Peasants*]
        [*Chile*]   (LA)
CNC .... Consejo Nacional de la Cultura [*National Culture Council*]
        [*Cuba*]   (LA)
CNC .... Consejo Nacional Campesino [*Costa Rica*]   (WGAO)
CNC .... Conselho Nacional de Cooperativismo [*Rio De Janeiro, Brazil*]
        (LAA)
CNC .... Conselho Nacional do Comercio   (WGAO)
CNC .... Consell Nacional Catala [*National Council of Catalonia*]
        [*Spanish*]   (WER)
CNC .... Consorzio Nazionale Canapa   (WGAO)
CNC .... Corporacion Aereo Cencor SA de CV [*Mexico*] [*ICAO
        designator*]   (FAAC)
CNCA .... Caisse Nationale de Credit Agricole [*National Agricultural Credit
        Bank*] [*Ivory Coast*]   (AF)
CNCA .... Caisse Nationale de Credit Agricole [*National Agricultural Credit
        Bank*] [*Togo*]   (AF)
CNCA .... Caisse Nationale de Credit Agricole [*National Agricultural Credit
        Bank*] [*Benin*]   (AF)
CNCA .... Caisse Nationale de Credit Agricole [*National Agricultural Credit
        Bank*] [*Morocco*]   (AF)
CNCA .... Centre National de la Cooperation Agricole
CNCA .... Centre National du Cinema Algerien [*Algerian National Motion
        Picture Center*]   (AF)

CNCA .... Chambre Nationale de Commerce - Algeria [*National Chamber of Commerce - Algeria*] (EAIO)
CNCA .... Compagnie Nationale de Credit Agricole [*North African*]
CNCA .... Compania Nacional Cubana de Aviacion [*Cuba*]
CNCA .... Consejo Nacional de Conciliacion Agraria [*Peru*] (EY)
CNCA .... Conselho Nacional Consultativo de Agricultura [*Brasilia, Brazil*] (LAA)
CNCAB ..... Caisse Nationale de Credit Agricole du Burkina (EY)
CNCA-BF ... Caisse Nationale de Credit Agricole du Burkina Faso
CNCACI ..... Caisse Nationale de Credit Agricole de la Cote-D'Ivoire
CNCAF ...... Conseil National de la Cooperation Agricole Francaise (WGAO)
CNCAS ...... Caisse Nationale de Credit Agricole du Senegal [*Commercial bank*] [*Senegal*]
CNCATA .... Centre National Cooperatif Agricole de Traitements Antiparasitaires (WGAO)
CNCBP ...... Centre National de Cooperation des Bibliotheques Publiques (WGAO)
CNCC .... Confederation Nationale du Commerce Charbonnier (WGAO)
CNCC .... Conseil National des Chargeurs du Cameroun
CNCCC ...... China National Chemical Construction Corporation [*China*] (IMH)
CNCCEF ... Comite National des Conseillers du Commerce Exterieur de la France (WGAO)
CNCCL ...... China National Center for Clinical Laboratory
CNCCMM ... Chambre Nationale des Constructeurs de Caravanes et de Maisons Mobiles (WGAO)
CNCD .... Centre National de Cooperation au Developpement [*Belgium*] (WGAO)
CNCD .... Confederazione Nationale dei Coltivatori Diretti (WGAO)
CNCD .... Confederazione Nazionale Coltivatori Diretti [*National Confederation of Small Farmers*] [*Italy*] (EAIO)
CNCDC ..... China National Coal Development Corporation [*China*] (IMH)
CNCE .... Centre National Algerien du Commerce Exterieur [*Algeria*] (MENA)
CNCE .... Centre National du Commerce Exterieur (WGAO)
CNCE .... Comite National de Coordination des Eleves [*National Student Coordination Committee*] [*Malagasy*] (AF)
CNCE .... Consejo Nacional de Comercio Exterior [*National Foreign Trade Council*] [*Venezuela*] (LA)
CNCECT ... Comision Nacional de Colaboracion Economica y Cientifico-Tecnica [*National Commission for Economic, Scientific, and Technical Cooperation*] [*Cuba*] (LA)
CNCF .... College National des Chirurgiens Francais [*National College of French Surgeons*] (SLS)
CNCF .... Confederation Nationale de la Charcuterie de France (WGAO)
CNCI .... Ceylon National Chamber of Industries [*Sri Lanka*] (EAIO)
CNCI .... Confederacion Nacional de Comunas Industriales [*National Confederation of Industrial Communes*] [*Peru*] (LA)
CNCI .... Societe Commerciale du Nord de la Cote-D'Ivoire
CNCIA .... Confederation Nationale des Commerces et Industries de l'Alimentation (WGAO)
CNCIAWPRC ... Chilean National Committee of the International Association on Water Pollution Research and Control (EAIO)
CNCIAWPRC ... Cyprus National Committee of the International Association on Water Pollution Research and Control (EAIO)
CNCIAWPRC ... Czechoslovak National Committee of the International Association on Water Pollution Research and Control (EAIO)
CNCIEC .... China National Chemicals Import and Export Corp. (PDAA)
CNCIEC .... China National Coal Import & Export Corporation [*China*] (IMH)
CNC-IFAC ... Canadian National Committee for the International Federation of Automatic Control (EAIO)
CNCK .... Comite National de Coordination du Karate
CNCL .... Commission National des Communications et Libertes [*National Commission of Communication and Free Speech*] [*France*]
CNCL .... Commission Nationale de la Communication et des Libertes (WGAO)
CNCM ...... Confederation Nationale du Credit Mutuel (WGAO)
CNCM ...... Council of Nature Conservation Ministers [*Australia*]
CNCMA .... Centre National de la Cooperation et de la Mutualite Agricoles
CNCMCA ... Confederation Nationale de la Cooperation de la Mutualite et du Credit Agricoles (WGAO)
CNCNSW ... Captive Nations' Council of New South Wales [*Australia*]
CNCO .... China Navigation Co. (DS)
CNCO .... Compagnie Nantaise des Chargeurs de l'Ouest
CNCO .... Coordinadora Nacional de Comisiones Obreras [*National Coordinator of Workers Commissions*] [*Spanish*] (WER)
CNCOR ..... Chinese National Committee for Ocean Resources (MSC)
CNCP .... Caisse Nationale de Credit Professionnel [*Benelux*] (BAS)
CNCP .... Comision Nacional Consultiva de Pesca [*Mexico*] (MSC)
CNCPIR .... Chambre Nationale du Commerce du Pneumatique et de l'Industrie du Rechapage (WGAO)
CNCR .... Caisse Nationale de Credit Rurale [*Gabon*] (EY)
CNCrA .... Caisse Nationale de Credit Agricole (WGAO)

CNCS .... Consiliul National de Cercetari Stiintifice [*National Council for Scientific Research*] (RO)
CNCSH ..... Comite Nordique des Commissions des Sciences Humaines [*Nordic Committee of the Research Councils for the Humanities - NCRCH*] (EAIO)
CNCT .... Consejo Nacional de Ciencia y Tecnologia [*National Council for Science and Technology*] [*Cuba*] (LA)
CNCT .... Coordenacao Nacional das Classes Trabalhadores [*Trade union*] [*Brazil*] (EY)
CNCU .... Comision Nacional Cubana de la UNESCO [*Cuban National UNESCO Commission*] (LA)
CNCU .... Commission Nationale Congolaise pour l'UNESCO
CNCV .... Confederacion Nacional Campesina de Venezuela [*Venezuelan National Peasant Confederation*] (LA)
CNCV .... Confederacion Nacional de Cooperativas de Venezuela (WGAO)
CNCV .... Confederation Nationale des Cooperatives Vinicoles (WGAO)
CND.......... Campaign for Nuclear Disarmament (WGAO)
CND.......... Centre National de Documentation [*National Documentation Center*] [*Laotian*] (CL)
CND.......... Centre National de Documentation [*National Documentation Center*] [*Zaire*] (AF)
CND.......... Ceskoslovenske Naftove Doly [*Czechoslovak Petroleum Fields*] (CZ)
CND.......... Club National du Disque [*Record label*] [*France*]
CND.......... Club Nation et Developpement [*Nation and Development Club*] [*Senegal*] (AF)
CND.......... Club Nautique de Dakar
CND.......... Colegio Nacional de Decoradores y Disenadores de Interior (WGAO)
CND.......... Comisia Nationala de Demografie [*National Commission for Demography*] (RO)
CND.......... Comision Nacional de Desarrollo [*Commission for National Development*] [*Dominican Republic*] (LA)
CND.......... Comite National de Documentation [*National Committee for Coordinating Government Information*] [*France*] (PDAA)
CND.......... Comptoir National du Diamant
CND.......... Concord Airlines Nigeria Ltd. [*ICAO designator*] (FAAC)
CND.......... Confrerie de Notre-Dame
CND.......... Conseil National de Discipline [*National Discipline Council*] [*Cambodia*] (CL)
CND.......... Conseil National du Developpement [*National Development Council*] [*Niger*] (AF)
CND.......... Constanta [*Romania*] [*Airport symbol*] (OAG)
CNDA .... Centre National de Documentation Agricole, Tunisia [*AGRIS*] (WGAO)
CNDA .... Cherished Numbers Dealers Association (WGAO)
CNDACLMG ... Comite National de Direction des Actions Communes de Lutte dans le Cadre de la Mobilisation Generale [*National Committee for Directing Joint Campaigns for General Mobilization*] [*Cambodia*] (CL)
CNDC .... Ciskei National Development Corporation
CNDC .... Comision Nacional de Desarrollo Comuna [*Peru*] (WGAO)
CNDC .... Consiglio Nazionale dei Dottori Commercialisti (WGAO)
CNDC .... Corps National de Defense Civile [*National Civil Defense Corps*] [*Congo*] (AF)
CNDCT ..... Centro Nacional de Documentacion Cientifica y Tecnologica [*Universidad Boliviana Mayor de San Andres*] [*Bolivia*]
CNDE........ Consejo Nacional de Desarrollo Economico [*Peru*] (DSCA)
CNDEP...... Comite Nacional para la Defensa de la Economia Popular [*National Committee for Defending the Popular Economy*] [*Mexico*] (LA)
CNDEP...... Conseil National des Detectives et Enqueteurs Prives (WGAO)
CNDES...... Centre National de Documentation Economique et Sociale [*Ministere de la Planification et de l'Amenagement du Territoire*] [*Algeria*]
CNDES...... Consejo Nacional de Desarrollo Economico y Social [*Peru*] (LAA)
CNDF .... Compagnie de Navigation Denis Freres
CNDFA ..... Conseil National Democratique des Forces Armees [*National Democratic Council of Armed Forces*] [*Algeria*] (AF)
CNDH .... Centre National de Documentation Horticole (WGAO)
CNDH .... Comision Nacional de Derechos Humanos [*National Commission of Human Rights*] [*Paraguay*] (LA)
CNDI .... Caisse Nationale des Depots et des Investissements [*National Deposits and Investments Fund*] [*Burkina Faso*] (AF)
CNDI .... Consiglio Nazionale Donne Italiane (WGAO)
CNDIE ...... Centro Nacional de Documentacion e Informacion Educativa [*Argentina*] (DSCA)
CNDO........ Centro Nacional de Datos Oceanograficos [*Argentina*] (MSC)
CNDP........ Centre National de Documentation Pedagogique [*National Center for Pedagogical Documentation*] [*Ministry of Education*] [*Information service or system*] (IID)
CNDPK ..... Centre National de Peche a Kinkole [*National Fishing Center at Kinkole*] [*Zaire*] (AF)

CNDR........ Comite National de Defense de la Revolution [*National Committee for the Defense of the Revolution*] [*Algeria*] (AF)

CNDR........ Comite National de Defense de la Revolution [*National Committee for the Defense of the Revolution*] [*Mali*] (AF)

CNDR........ Consiglio Nazionale delle Ricerche [*National Research Council*] [*Research center*] [*Italian*]

CNDRP ..... Centre National de Documentation et de Recherche en Pedagogie [*Algeria*] (SLS)

CNDS .... Council of Nordic Dental Students (WGAO)

CNDST...... Centre National de Documentation Scientifique et Technique [*National Scientific and Technical Documentation Center*] [*Royal Library of Belgium Belgium*] [*Information service or system*] (IID)

CNDV........ Confederation Nationale des Distilleries Vinicoles (WGAO)

Cne .... Cabane [*Cabin*] [*Military map abbreviation World War I*] [*French*] (MTD)

CNE........... Caisse Nationale de l'Energie [*France*] (FLAF)

CNE........... Caisse Nationale d'Epargne [*National Savings Bank*] [*Burkina Faso*] (AF)

CNE........... Caisse Nationale d'Equipement [*National Equipment Bank*] [*Cambodia*] (CL)

CNE........... Camara Nacional de Exportadores [*National Chamber of Exporters*] [*Bolivia*] (EAIO)

CNE........... Centrala Nucleara de Energie [*Nuclear Power Plant*] (RO)

CNE........... Centrale Nationale des Employes [*Employees' National Center*] [*Belgium*] (WER)

CNE........... Centro Nacional de Economia [*Nicaragua*] (WGAO)

CNE........... Chantier Naval de l'Estuaire

CNE........... Comision Nacional de Electricidad [*San Jose, Costa Rica*] (LAA)

CNE........... Comision Nacional de Emulacion [*National Emulation Committee*] [*Cuba*] (LA)

CNE........... Comision Nacional de Energia [*Managua, Nicaragua*] (LAA)

CNE........... Comision Naval de Energia [*Naval Commission for Energy*] [*Chile*] (LA)

CNE........... Comissao Nacional de Energia [*National Energy Commission*] [*Brazil*] (LA)

CNE........... Comissao Nacional Eleitoral [*National Electoral Commission*] [*Portuguese*] (WER)

CNE........... Comissao Nacional Executivo

CNE........... Comite Nacional de Emergencia [*National Emergency Committee*] [*Nicaragua*] (LA)

CNE........... Comite Nacional de Emergencia [*National Emergency Committee*] [*El Salvador*] (LA)

CNE........... Comite National d'Entr'aide [*National Welfare Committee*] [*Cambodia*] (CL)

CNE........... Comptoir National d'Escompte [*French*]

CNE........... Confederacion Nacional de Estudiantes [*National Confederation of Students*] [*Mexico*] (LAA)

CNE........... Confederation Nationale de l'Elevage (WGAO)

CNE........... Consejo Nacional de Educacion [*National Education Council*] [*La Paz, Bolivia*] (LAA)

CNE........... Consejo Nacional de Educacion [*National Education Council*] [*Cuba*] (LA)

CNE........... Consejo Nacional de la Energia [*Venezuela*] (DSCA)

CNE........... Conselho Nacional de Economia [*National Economic Council*] [*Brazil*] (LA)

CNE........... Conselho Nacional de Estatistica [*Brazil*] (DSCA)

CNE........... Constructions Nautiques Eburneennes

CNEA .... Centre National d'Etudes Agricoles [*Tunisia*]

CNEA .... Comision Nacional de Energia Atomica [*National Atomic Energy Commission*] [*Buenos Aires, Argentina*] (LA)

CNEA .... Comision Nacional de Energia Atomica [*National Atomic Energy Commission*] [*Mexico*]

CNEA .... Comision Nacional de Energia Atomica [*National Atomic Energy Commission*] [*Uruguay*] (LA)

CNEAF...... Comite National des Exploitants Agricoles Forestiers (WGAO)

CNEAF...... Confederatin Nationale des Experts Agricoles et Fonciers (WGAO)

CNEARC... Centre National d'Etudes Agronomiques des Regions Chaudes [*Ministry of Agriculture*] [*France*]

CNEAT...... Centre National d'Etudes d'Agronomie Tropicale (ASF)

CNEC .... Centre National d'Enseignement par Correspondance [*National Center for Instruction by Correspondence*] [*Algeria*] (AF)

CNEC .... Centro Nacional de Estudios Cooperativos [*Rio De Janeiro, Brazil*] (LAA)

CNEC .... Christian Nationals' Evangelism Council [*Australia*]

CNEC .... Confederacion Nacional de Ex Combatientes [*National Confederation of Veterans*] [*Spanish*] (WER)

CNEC .... Conseil National de l'Education et de la Culture [*National Education and Culture Council*] [*Cambodia*] (CL)

CNEC .... Consorcio Nacional de Engenheiros Consultores [*Brazil*] (WGAO)

CNECA ..... Comision Nacional de Estudio de la Cana y del Azucar [*National Commission for Studying Sugar and Sugarcane*] [*Bolivia*] (LA)

CNECB...... College National des Experts Comptables de Belgique (WGAO)

CNECI....... Caisse Nationale d'Epargne et de Credit Immobiliere [*National Savings and Real Estate Credit Fund*] [*Zaire*] (AF)

CNED........ Confederacion Nacional de Estudiantes Democraticos [*National Confederation of Democratic Students*] [*Mexico*] (LA)

CNEDES ... Centre National d'Etudes et de Documentation Economique et Sociale

CNEE .... Comision Nacional del Espacio Exterior [*National Commission for Outer Space*] [*Mexico*]

CNEEJA ... Centre National d'Etudes Economiques et Juridiques Agricoles (WGAO)

CNEEMA ... Centre National d'Etudes et d'Experimentation de Machinisme Agricole [*National Design and Experimental Center for Agricultural Machinery*] [*France*] (PDAA)

CNEF........ Camara Nacional de Exploitacion Forestal [*Bolivia*] (WGAO)

CNEF........ Camara Nacional de Explotacion Forestal [*Bolivia*] (DSCA)

CNEF........ Compagnie Nationale des Experts Forestiers (WGAO)

CNEFS ...... Consiliul National pentru Educatie Fizica si Sport [*National Council for Physical Education and Sports*] (RO)

CNEG .... Centre National d'Enseignement Generalise

CNEH........ Centre National d'Etudes Historiques [*National Center for Historic Studies*] [*Algeria*] (IRC)

CNEH........ Confederation Nationale des Enseignants Haitiens (EY)

CNEI .... Centre National d'Etudes Industrielles [*National Industrial Studies Center*] [*Tunisia*] (AF)

CNEIA...... Comite National d'Expansion pour l'Industrie Aeronautique (WGAO)

CNEIC....... China Nuclear Energy Industry Corp. [*China*] (IMH)

CNEIL....... Centre National d'Etudes et d'Initiatives du Logement (WGAO)

CNEIL....... Centre National d'Etudes et l'Initiatives en Faveur du Logement [*France*] (FLAF)

CNEJ .... Conseil National de l'Education et de la Jeunesse [*National Education and Youth Council*] [*Malagasy*] (AF)

CNEL........ Caisse Nationale d'Epargne Logement [*Tunisia*]

CNEL........ Chambre Nationale Syndicale des Experts du Grand-Duche de Luxembourg (WGAO)

CNEL........ Consiglio Nazionale dell'Economia e del Lavoro [*National Council for Economy and Labor*] [*Italian*] (WER)

CNEL........ Consiglio Nazionale Economiche e Lavoro (WGAO)

CNELAJ ... Centre National d'Etudes et de Liaison des Associations de Jeunesse

CNEM .... Comite National de l'Epargne Mobiliere [*Benelux*] (BAS)

CNEN........ Comision Nacional de Energia Nuclear [*National Nuclear Energy Commission*] [*Mexico*]

CNEN........ Comissao Nacional de Energia Nuclear [*National Commission for Nuclear Energy*] [*Brazil*] [*Information service or system*] (IID)

CNEN........ Comitato Nazionale per l'Energia Nucleare [*National Nuclear Energy Commission*] [*Italy*] (WER)

CNEN........ Conseil National de l'Energie Nucleaire [*Luxembourg*] [*Nuclear energy*] (NRCH)

CNENA ..... Centro Nacional de Energia Nuclear na Agricultura [*National Center of Nuclear Energy in Agriculture*] [*Brazil*] (LAA)

CNEOT ..... Centre National d'Education Ouvriere du Togo [*National Workers Education Center of Togo*] (AF)

CNEP........ Caisse Nationale Algerienne d'Epargne et de Prevoyance [*Algerian National Savings and Insurance Bank*] (AF)

CNEP........ Caisse Nationale d'Epargne et de Prevoyance [*National Savings and Insurance Bank*] [*North African*]

CNEP........ Centre National d'Etude Politique (WGAO)

CNEP........ Comision Nacional para el Erradicacion del Paludismo (WGAO)

CNEP........ Comptoir National d'Escompte de Paris [*France*] (FLAF)

CNEPA...... Centro Nacional de Ensino e Pesquisas Agronomicas [*National Center for Agricultural Instruction and Information*] [*Brazil*] (LAA)

CNEPCE ... Consejo Nacional de Evaluacion, Programacion, y Capacitacion Educativa [*National Council of Educational Evaluation, Programming, and Training*] [*Nicaragua*] (LA)

CNEPDA... Comite National d'Etude des Problems du Developpement Agricole (WGAO)

CNEPS...... Centre National d'Education Physique et Sportive [*Algeria*]

CNER .... Campanha Nacional de Educacao Rural [*Brazil*] (WGAO)

CNER .... Conseil National des Economies Regionales (WGAO)

CNERA ..... Centre National d'Etudes et des Recherches Aeronautiques [*Belgium*] (WGAO)

CNERAD .. Centre National pour l'Etude, la Recherche et l'Application du Developpement (WGAO)

CNERAT... Centre National d'Etudes et de Recherches en Amenagement du Territoire [*Algeria*]

CNERIA.... Centre National d'Etudes et de Recheres des Industries Agricoles (WGAO)

CNERNA .. Centre National de Coordination des Etudes et Recherches sur la Nutrition Animale (WGAO)

CNERNA .. Centre National de Coordination des Etudes et Recherches sur la Nutrition et l'Alimentation [*France*]

CNERP...... Centre National d'Etude et de Recherche au Paysage (WGAO)

CNERP...... Conseil National des Economies Regionales et de la Productivite (WGAO)
CNERTP ... Centre National d'Essais et de Recherches des Travaux Publics [*National Public Works Test and Research Center*] [*Benin*] (AF)
CNERV...... Centre National de l'Elevage et de la Recherche Veterinaire
CNES........ Centre National d'Etudes Scientifiques [*National Center for Scientific Studies*] [*French*]
CNES........ Centre National d'Etudes Spatiales [*National Center for Space Studies*] [*France*]
CNES........ Conseil National Economique et Social [*National Economic and Social Council*] [*Algeria*] (AF)
CNES........ Consejo Nacional de Educacion Superior [*National Council of Higher Education*] [*Bolivia*] (LA)
CNES........ Consejo Nacional de Educacion Superior [*National Council of Higher Education*] [*Nicaragua*] (LA)
CNES........ Consejo Nacional de Ensenanza Secundaria [*National Council of Secondary Education*] [*Uruguay*] (LA)
CNESER ... Conseil National de l'Enseignement Superieur et de la Recherche (WGAO)
CNET .... Centre National d'Etudes des Telecommunications [*France*] [*ICAO designator*] (FAAC)
CNET .... Centre National d'Etudes des Telecommunications [*National Center for Telecommunications Studies*] [*French*] (WER)
CNETEA... Centre National d'Etudes Techniques et Economiques de l'Artisanat (WGAO)
CNEU .... Comite National d'Evaluation des Universites [*National Committee for Evaluation of Universities*] [*French*]
CNEUPEN ... Commission Nationale pour l'Etude de l'Utilisation Pacifique de l'Energie Nucleaire [*Belgium*]
CNEV .... Conseil National des Entreprises Voltaiques [*National Council of Voltan Enterprises*] (AF)
CNEWA .... Catholic Near East Welfare Association (WGAO)
CNEXCA... Confederacion Nacional de Ex Cautivos [*National Confederation of Ex-Prisoners*] [*Spanish*] (WER)
CNEXO ..... Centre National pour l'Exploitation des Oceans [*National Center for Exploitation of the Oceans*] [*French*] (WER)
CNF .... Cameroon's National Federation
CNF .... Centre National de Floristique
CNF .... Chin National Front [*Myanmar*] [*Political party*] (EY)
CNF .... Code de la Nationalite Francaise [*North African*]
CNF .... Comision Nacional Forestal [*Chile*] (DSCA)
CNF .... Comite National Francais (FLAF)
CNF .... Commonwealth Nurses Federation (WGAO)
CNF .... Compagnie du Niger Francais
CNF .... Consiliul National al Femeilor [*National Council of Women*] (RO)
CNFA .... Centre National de Formation Administrative [*National Administration Training Center*] [*Malagasy*] (AF)
CNFA .... Coalition for a Nuclear-Free Australia
CNFB........ Conseil National des Femmes Belges [*Belgian Women's National Council*] (WER)
CNFC........ Centre National de Formation Cooperative
CNFC........ China National Fisheries Corp. (TCC)
CNFI........ Chinese National Federation of Industries [*Taiwan*] (EAIO)
CNFL........ Compania Nacional de Fuerza y Luz [*San Jose, Costa Rica*] (LAA)
CNFLRH... Comite National Francais de Liaison pour la Readaption des Handicapes (WGAO)
CNFM .... Comite National Francaise des Mathematiciens (WGAO)
CNFP........ Consejo Nacional de Fomento Pesquero [*Venezuela*] (DSCA)
CNFPT ...... Centre National de la Fonction Publique Terrioriale (WGAO)
CNFR........ Confederation Nationale de la Famille Rurale (WGAO)
CNFRA...... Centre National Francaise de la Recherche Antarctique (WGAO)
CNFRA...... Comite National Francais des Recherches Antarctiques (ASF)
CNFRE....... Comite National Francaise de Recherches dans l'Espace [*France*] (PDAA)
CNFRO ..... Comite National Francaise de Recherche Oceanique [*French National Committee for Oceanographic Research*] (PDAA)
CNFSFACM ... Committee of the National Ferrous Scrap Federations and Associations of the Common Market [*See also COFENAF*] (EAIO)
CNFTC...... Centre National de Formation aux Techniques de Conditionnement des Boissons et Denrees Alimentaires (WGAO)
CNFUS...... Consiliul National al Frontului Unitatii Socialiste [*National Council of the Socialist Unity Front*] (RO)
CNG.......... Centrala Navala Galati [*Romania*] (EY)
CNG.......... Central Norseman Gold Corp. Ltd. [*Australia*]
CNG.......... Christlichnationaler Gewerkschaftsbund der Schweiz [*Christian-National Trade Union Federation of Switzerland*] [*Berne*] (WEN)
CNG.......... Comhdhail Naisunta na Gaeilge [*National Gaelic Congress*]
CNG.......... Comite National des Guerrillas [*National Committee of Guerrillas*] [*Guinea*] (AF)
CNG.......... Community Newspapers Group [*Australia*]

CNG.......... Compagnie de Navigation Gabonaise
CNG.......... Confederacion Nacional Ganadara [*Mexico*] (WGAO)
CNG.......... Conseil National du Gouvernement [*Haiti*] (WGAO)
CNG.......... Consejo Nacional de Gobierno [*National Council of Government*] [*Uruguay*] (LA)
CNG.......... Conselho Nacional de Geografia [*National Geography Council*] [*Brazil*] (LAA)
CNG.......... Consiglio Nazionale dei Geometri (WGAO)
CNG.......... Coordinadora Nacional Guerrillero [*Columbia*] (WGAO)
CNG.......... Cumberland Newspaper Group [*Australia*]
CNGE .... Conseil National des Grandes Ecoles (WGAO)
CNGIAPL ... Czechoslovak National Group of International Association of Penal Law (EAIO)
CNGRDC .. China National Garments Research and Designing Center (IRC)
CNGRSR ... Comitetul National al Geologilor din Republica Socialista Romana [*Roman Catholic religious order*] (SLS)
CNGSE...... Commission Nationale pour la Gestion Socialiste des Entreprises [*National Commission for the Socialist Management of Businesses*] [*Algeria*] (AF)
CNGU........ Commission Nationale Gabonaise pour l'UNESCO
CNH .... Centre National Hospitalier de Tokoin
CNH .... Concours National d'Habilitation [*French*]
CNHC........ Cape Natural History Club [*South Africa*] (EAIO)
CNHE........ Consejo Nacional de Hombres de Empresa [*National Council of Businessmen*] [*Dominican Republic*] (LA)
CNHG ...... Chung Nip Hwe Gwan [*Korea Polio Foundation*] (EAIO)
CNHOO .... Chinese Naval Hydrographic and Oceanographic Office (MSC)
CNHR....... Comite National de l'Habitat Rural (WGAO)
CNHRAC .. Confederation Nationale pour l'Habitat Rural et l'Amenagement des Champagnes (WGAO)
CNI .... Carte Nationale d'Identite [*France*] (FLAF)
CNI .... Centrale Nucleaire Interescaut [*A nuclear power station*] [*Belgium*]
CNI .... Centre National de l'Informatique [*National Center for Informatics*] [*Tunisia*] [*Research center*] (IRC)
CNI .... Centre National des Independants [*National Center of Independants*] [*France*] [*Political party*] (PPE)
CNI .... Centre National des Independants et des Paysans [*National Centre of Independents and Peasants*] (EAIO)
CNI .... Centro Nacional de Informaciones [*National Information Center*] [*Supersedes DINA Chile*]
CNI .... Church of North India [*Anglican*]
CNI .... Comision Nacional Intersindical [*National Inter-Trade Union Commission*] [*Argentina*] (LA)
CNI .... Comision Nacional Intersindical [*National Inter-Trade Union Commission*] [*Nicaragua*] (LA)
CNI .... Commissariat National a l'Informatique [*National Data-Processing Commission*] [*Algeria*] (AF)
CNI .... Commission Nationale d'Investissements [*National Investment Committee*] [*Algeria*] (AF)
CNI .... Compagnie Nationale de Navigation Interieure [*Transport company*] [*Gabon*]
CNI .... Companhia Nordeste de Industrializacao [*Brazil*] (DSCA)
CNI .... Confederacao Nacional da Industrias [*National Confederation of Industries*] [*Brasilia, Brazil*] (LA)
CNI .... Conseil National des Ingenieurs (WGAO)
CNI .... Consejo Nacional de Inversion [*Investment Council of Panama*] (IMH)
CNI .... Consejo Nacional de Inversiones [*Panama*] (WGAO)
CNI .... Consejo Nacional de Investigacion [*National Research Council*] [*Peru*] (LA)
CNI .... Conselho Nacional de Imigracao [*National Council for Immigration*] [*Brazil*] (LA)
CNI .... Consiglio Nazionale degli Ingegneri (WGAO)
CNI .... Construction Navale Ivoirienne
CNI .... Corporacion Nicaraguense de Inversiones [*Managua, Nicaragua*] (LAA)
CNI .... Council for the National Interest [*Australia*]
CNIA .... Centro Nacional de Investigaciones Agropecuarias [*Argentina*] (LAA)
CNIA .... Centro Nacional de Investigaciones Agropecuarias [*Dominican Republic*] (LAA)
CNIA .... Comite National Interprofessionnel de l'Amande (WGAO)
CNIA .... Compagnie Nordafricaine et Intercontinentale d'Assurances [*Insurance company*] [*Morocco*] (MENA)
CNIA .... Conseil National Interprofessionnel de l'Aviculture (WGAO)
CNIA .... Consejo Nacional de Investigaciones Agricolas [*Venezuela*] (WGAO)
CNIAA ...... Camara Nacional de las Industrias Azucarera y Alcoholera [*Mexico*] (WGAO)
CNIB .... Confederation Nationale des Industries du Bois (WGAO)
CNI-BAN .. Scientific Information at the Bulgarian Academy of Sciences and Social Sciences (SLS)
CNIC .... Centre National de l'Information Chimique [*National Center for Chemical Information*] [*Information service or system*] (IID)
CNIC .... Centro Nacional de Investigaciones Cientificas [*Cuba*] (WGAO)

CNIC .... Centro Nacional de Investigaciones de Cafe [*Colombia*]
(WGAO)
CNIC .... Centro Nacional para la Investigacion Cientifica [*National Scientific Research Center*] [*Cuba*]   (LA)
CNIC .... Confederacion Nacional de la Industria de la Construccion [*National Construction Workers Confederation*] [*Uruguay*]   (LA)
CNIC .... Conseil National de l'Industrie du Charbon   (WGAO)
CNIC .... Cuban National Center for Scientific Investigations
CNICI .... Consejo Nacional de Investigaciones Cientificas y Tecnicas [*Argentina*] [*Uruguay*]   (WGAO)
CNICT .... Comision Nacional de Investigacion Cientifica y Tecnologica [*National Commission for Scientific and Technological Research*] [*Santiago, Chile*]   (LAA)
CNICT .... Consejo Nacional de Investigaciones Cientificas y Tecnicas [*National Council for Scientific and Technical Research*] [*Argentina*]   (LA)
CNICT .... Consejo Nacional de Investigaciones Cientificas y Tecnologicas [*National Council for Scientific and Technological Research*] [*ICSU Caracas, Venezuela*] [*Research center*]   (LAA)
CNICT .... Consejo Nacional para la Investigacion Cientifica del Trabajo [*National Scientific Labor Research Council*] [*Cuba*]   (LA)
CNICTEI ... Comitato Nazionale Italiano per la Cooperazione Tecnico Economico Internazionale   (WGAO)
CNID .... Centro Nacional de Informacion y Documentacion [*National Information and Documentation Center*] [*Ministry of Labour*] [*Information service or system*]   (IID)
CNID .... Congres National d'Initiative Democratique [*Mali*] [*Political party*]   (EY)
CNIDICT .. Centro Nacional de Informacion y Documentacion Cientifica y Technologica   (WGAO)
CNIDJ .... Centro Nacional de Informacion y Documentacion de Juventud [*National Center of Information and Documentation on Youth*] [*Spain*]
CNIDS .... Camara Nacional de las Industrias Derivadas de la Silvicultura [*Mexico*]   (WGAO)
CNIE .... Comision Nacional de Investigaciones Espaciales [*National Commission for Space Research*] [*Buenos Aires, Argentina*] [*Research center*]   (LA)
CNIEC ...... China National Import and Export Corp.   (WGAO)
CNIEC ...... China National Non-Ferrous Metals Import and Export Corp. (EY)
CNIEC .... China Nuclear Instrumentation and Equipment Corp.   (TCC)
CNIEL .... Centre National Interprofessionnel de l'Economie Laitiere [*France*]   (EAIO)
CNIF .... Conseil National des Ingenieurs Francais [*National Council of French Engineers*]   (EAIO)
CNIH .... Camara Nacional de la Industria Hulera [*Mexico*]   (DSCA)
CNIH .... Comite National Interprofessionnel de l'Horticulture Florale et Ornementale et des Pepinieres non Forestieres   (WGAO)
CNIH .... Comite National Interprofessionnel du Houblon   (WGAO)
CNIIEC ...... China National Instruments Import and Export Corp.   (EY)
CNIIIC ...... China Ningxia Islamic International Investment Co.
CNIL .... Comite National Interprofessionnel de la Laine   (WGAO)
CNIL .... Commission Nationale d'Informatique et des Libertes [*France*]
CNIM .... Centre Naturaliste International de la Mediterranee
CNIM .... Confederation Nationale des Instituteurs Malgaches [*National Confederation of Malagasy Teachers*]
CNIM .... Consejo Nacional de la Industria Maquiladora [*National Council of the Maquiladora Industry*] [*Mexican/US business organization*]   (CROSS)
CNIM .... Constructions Navales et Industrielles de la Mediterranee [*North African*]
CNIMZ ..... Tsentar za Nauchna Informacija po Meditsina i Zdraveopazvane [*Center for Scientific Information in Medicine and Public Health*] [*Medical Academy*] [*Information service or system*] (IID)
CNIOS ...... Comitato Nazionale Italiana per l'Organizzazione Scientifica del Lavoro   (WGAO)
CNIP .... Centre for Networked Information and Publishing [*Australian National University*]
CNIP .... Centre National des Independants et des Paysans [*National Center of Independents and Peasants*] [*France*] [*Political party*]   (PPW)
CNIP .... Ciskei National Independence Party [*South Africa*]
CNIPA ...... Committee of National Institutes of Patent Agents   (WGAO)
CNIPBC .... Comite National Interprofessionnel des Produits de Basse-Cour (WGAO)
CNIPE ...... Centre National d'Information pour la Productive des Enterprises   (WGAO)
CNIPE ...... Centre National d'Information pour la Productivite des Entreprises [*French*]   (ADPT)
CNIPI .... Comision Nacional de Productividad Industrial   (WGAO)
CNIPT .... Centre National d'Instruction des Postes, Telegraphes, et Telephones [*National Post, Telegraph, and Telephone Training Center*] [*Niger*]   (AF)

CNIPT .... Comite National Interprofessionnel de la Pomme de Terre (WGAO)
CNIPTI ..... Caisse Nationale Interprofessionnelle de Pension des Travailleurs Independants [*Benelux*]   (BAS)
CNIR .... Centre National Interprofessionnel du Rhum   (WGAO)
CNIR .... Conferencia Nacional dos Institutos Religiosos   (WGAO)
CNISF .... Conseil National des Ingenieurs et des Scientifiques de France [*French National Council of Scientific Engineers*]   (EAIO)
CNIST ...... Centre National d'Informations Scientifiques et Techniques [*French*]   (ADPT)
CNIT .... Camara Nacional de la Industria de Transformacion [*National Association of the Processing Industry*] [*Mexico*]   (LAA)
CNIT .... Centre National des Industries et Techniques [*French*]
CNIT .... Confederation Nationale Independante des Travailleurs [*National Independent Confederation for Workers*] [*Belgium*]
CNIT .... Consiliul National al Inginerilor si Tehnicienilor [*National Council of Engineers and Technicians*]   (RO)
CNITE .... Centro Nazionale Italiano per le Tecnologia Educative [*Italian*] (SLS)
CNIZA .... Centro Nacional de Investigacion para el Desarrollo de Zonas Aridas
CNJ .... Cloncurry [*Australia*] [*Airport symbol*]   (OAG)
CNJ .... Comite National de Jumelage [*National Committee for Town/City Twinning*] [*France*]   (EAIO)
CNJ .... Conseil National de la Jeunesse [*National Youth Council*] [*Zaire*] (AF)
CNJ .... Conseil National de la Jeunesse [*National Youth Council*] [*Congo*]   (AF)
CNJ .... Consejo Nacional de Justicia [*National Justice Council*] [*Peru*] (LA)
CNJA .... Centre National des Jeunes Agriculteurs [*National Young Farmers Center*] [*French*]   (WER)
CNJC .... Centre National des Jeunes Cadres   (WGAO)
CNJD .... Confederacion Nacional de Jovenes Democraticos [*National Confederation of Democratic Youths*] [*Mexico*]   (LA)
CNJM .... Conseil National de la Jeunesse Mauricienne [*National Mauritian Youth Council*]   (AF)
CNJPHP ... Cercle National des Jeunes Producteurs de l'Horticulture et des Pepinieres   (WGAO)
CNJS .... Conseil National de la Jeunesse et des Sports [*Morocco*]
CNJT .... Centre National Action Sociale pour les Jeunes Travailleurs (WGAO)
CNK .... Confederation of Khmer Nationalists [*Cambodia*]   (PD)
CNKi .... Comite National de Kivu
CNL .... Centre National des Lettres [*France*]
CNL .... Colodense Nigeria Limited
CNL .... Comite National de Liberation [*National Liberation Committee*] [*Zaire*]   (AF)
CNL .... Commission Nationale de Linguistique [*National Linguistics Commission*] [*Benin*]   (AF)
CNL .... Commonwealth National Library [*Australia*]   (ADA)
CNL .... Confederation Nationale Laitiere   (WGAO)
CNL .... Conferentie der Nederlandse Letteren
CNL .... Conseil National de Liberation
CNL .... Conselho Nacional de Libertacao
CNLA .... Centre Nationale de Lutte Antiparasitaire   (WGAO)
CNLGE ...... Cruzada Nacional de Liberacion de la Guinea Ecuatorial
CNLM .... Comite National Lao du Mekong [*Lao National Mekong Committee*]   (CL)
CNLP .... Caribbean National Labor Party [*Trinidadian and Tobagan*] (LA)
CNLS .... Comite Nationale de Lutte Contre le SIDA [*National Committee on the Fight Against AIDS*] [*Mauritania*]   (EAIO)
CNL-SIDA ... Comite Nationale de Lutte Contre le SIDA [*National Committee on the Fight Against AIDS*] [*Burkina Faso*] (EAIO)
CNM .... Caribbean Nationalist Movement   (LA)
CNM .... Comite National de la Musique [*National Music Committee*] [*France*]   (EAIO)
CNM .... Compagnie de Navigation Mixte
CNM .... Confederacao Nacional dos Metalurgicos [*Brazil*]   (WGAO)
CNM .... Conseil National des Moudjahidines [*National War Veterans Council*] [*Algeria*]   (AF)
CNM .... Consejo Nacional de Magistros [*Guatemala*]   (WGAO)
CNMA .... Caisse Nationale de Mutualite Agricole [*National Farmers Mutual Bank*] [*Algeria*]   (AF)
CNMA .... Centro Nazionale Meccanico Agricolo [*Italy*]   (DSCA)
CNMA .... Comitato Nazionale di Meccanica Agraria   (WGAO)
CNMA .... Communications Network for Manufacturing Applications [*Europe*]
CNMART ... Comite National contre les Maladies Respiratoires et la Tuberculose   (WGAO)
CNMB .... Central Nuclear Measurements Bureau [*EEC*]   (WGAO)
CNMC .... Chinese Naval Meteorology Center   (MSC)
CNMC .... Council of Nordic Master-Craftsmen [*Oslo, Norway*]   (EAIO)
CNMDSA ... Community Nursing Minimum Data Set Australia

CNME....... Caisse National des Marches et l'Etat
CNME....... Comite National de la Meanerie d'Exportation
CNMHS.... Caisse Nationale des Monuments Historiques et des Sites (WGAO)
CNMI....... Camera Nazionale della Moda Italiana (WGAO)
CNMI....... Comite National de la Meunerie Industrielle (WGAO)
CNMI....... Commissie Nucleaire en Metallurgische Informatieverzorging [*Netherlands*]
CNMI....... Commonwealth of the Northern Mariana Islands (WGAO)
CNMP....... Comite National Malgache pour la Paix [*Malagasy National Peace Committee*] (AF)
CNMT....... Centre National de Medecine Traditionnelle [*Office Malien de Pharmacie*] [*Mali*]
CNMU...... Commission Nationale Marocaine pour l'UNESCO
CNN.......... Chantiers Navals de Nianing
CNN.......... Companhia Nacional de Navegacao [*Shipping company*] [*Portugal*] (EY)
CNNA....... Clan Napier in North America [*An association*]
CNNC....... China National Nonferrous Metals Industry Corp. (TCC)
CNO.......... Christelijke Nasionale Onderwys
CNO.......... Comision Nacional del Olivo [*Mexico*] (DSCA)
CNO.......... Comite National d'Organisation [*Cameroon*]
CNO.......... Comites Nationaux Olympiques
CNO.......... Commission Nationale Operationelle [*National Operational Commission*] [*Algeria*] (AF)
CNO.......... Commonwealth Nursing Officer [*Australia*]
CNO.......... Conseil National des Opticiens (WGAO)
CNO.......... Council of National Organisations (WGAO)
CNO.......... Crnogorska Narodna Omladina [*People's Youth of Montenegro*] (YU)
CNO.......... Crnogorski Narodni Odbor [*People's Committee of Montenegro*] (YU)
CNOC....... Coordinadora Nacional de Organizaciones Cafetaleras [*National network of small coffee producers*] [*Mexico*] (CROSS)
CNODDT ... China National Opera and Dance Drama Theater
CNOE....... Comites Nationaux Olympiques Europeens (WGAO)
CNOF........ Comite National de l'Organisation Francaise [*Association Francaise de Management*] (WGAO)
CNOis........ Centrala Nasiennictwa Ogrodniczego i Szkolkarstwa [*Garden and Nursery Seeds Center*] (POL)
CNOM....... Consiliul National al Oamenilor Muncii [*National Council of Workers*] (RO)
CNOOC..... China National Offshore Oil Corp. (PDAA)
CNOP........ Confederacion Nacional de Organizaciones Populares [*National Confederation of Popular Organizations*] [*Mexico*] (LA)
CNOP........ Conseil National de l'Ordre des Pharmaciens (WGAO)
CNOP........ Consiliul National al Organizatiei Pionierilor [*National Council of the Organization of Pioneers*] (RO)
CNOPAR .. Confederation Nationale des Organismes de Promotion Agricole et Rurale (WGAO)
CNOPU..... Crnogorsko Narodnooslobodilacki Partizanski Udarni [*Montenegrin National Liberation Partisan Shock Detachment*] (YU)
CNOS........ China Nationalities Orchestra Society (EAIO)
CNOS........ Comitato Nazionale per l'Organizzazione Scientifica [*National Committee for Scientific Administration*] [*Italy*] (PDAA)
CNOSA..... Centro Nazionalle Organizazione Scientifica in Agricoltura [*Italy*] (DSCA)
CNOSA..... Centro Nazionel per l'Organizzazione Scientifica in Agricoltura [*Italy*] (WGAO)
CNOSF..... Conseil National Olympique et Sportif Francais (WGAO)
CNOT........ Comite National Olympique Togolais
CNOU ...... Centre National des Oeuvres Universitaires
CNOUS..... Centre National des Oeuvres Universitaires et Scolaires [*French*]
CNOV....... Comite National des Producteurs d'Oeufs a Couver et des Volailles dites d'un Jour (WGAO)
CNP.......... Caisse Nationale d'Epargne de Paris
CNP.......... Central North Pacific Ocean
CNP.......... Centre National de Pret
CNP.......... Centre National Pilote [*National Pilot Center*] [*Zaire*] (AF)
CNP.......... Ciskei National Party [*South Africa*]
CNP.......... Colegio Nacional de Periodistas [*National Journalists Association*] [*Colorado*] (LA)
CNP.......... Comision Nacional Permanente [*Nicaragua*] (WGAO)
CNP.......... Comissao Nacional do Plano [*National Planning Commission*] (AF)
CNP.......... Comitato Nazionale per la Producttivita [*National Council for Productivity*] [*Italy*] (PDAA)
CNP.......... Comite National des Prix (WGAO)
CNP.......... Commissariat National du Parti [*National Party Commission*] [*Algeria*] (AF)
CNP.......... Compagnie de Navigation Paquet
CNP.......... Compagnie Navale des Petroles
CNP.......... Companhia Nacional de Petroquimica [*National Petrochemical Company*] [*Lisbon, Portugal*] (WER)
CNP.......... Comptoir National de Peche [*North African*]

CNP.......... Consejo Nacional de Produccion [*National Council for Production*] [*Costa Rica*] (LA)
CNP.......... Conselho Nacional de Pesquisas [*Rio De Janeiro, Brazil*] (LAA)
CNP.......... Conselho Nacional de Petroleo [*National Petroleum Council*] [*Brasilia, Brazil*] (LA)
CNP.......... Corporation Nationale Paysanne (WGAO)
CNP.......... Council for National Parks (WGAO)
CNP.......... Country Nationalist Party [*Australia*] [*Political party*]
CNP.......... Country National Party [*Australia*] (ADA)
CNPA....... Centro Nacional de Patologia Animal [*Peru*] (DSCA)
CNPA....... Centro Nacional de Pesquisa de Algodao [*National Research Center for Cotton*] [*Brazil*] (ARC)
CNPA....... Centro Nazional de Patologia Animal [*Peru*] (WGAO)
CNPA....... Comision Nacional de Politica Aeronautica [*Uruguay*] (EY)
CNPA....... Comissao Nacional de Politica Agraria [*Brazil*] (WGAO)
CNPA....... Coordinadora Nacional Plan de Ayala [*National Coordinating Board for the Ayala Plan*] [*Mexico*] (LA)
CNPA-EEC ... Community of the Newspaper Publishing Associations of the European Economic Communities [*Belgium*] (EAIO)
CNPAF...... Centro Nacional de Pesquisa de Arroz e Feijao [*National Research Center for Rice and Beans*] [*Brazil*] (ARC)
CNPAR..... Centre National de Progres Agricole et Rural (WGAO)
CNPB........ Conseil Nordique de la Preservation du Bois (WGAO)
CNPC........ Centre National de Production Cinematographique [*National Moving Picture Production Center*] [*Mali*] (AF)
CNPC .... Centro Nacional de Pesquisa de Caprinos [*National Research Center for Goats*] [*Brazil*] (ARC)
CNPC .... Centrul National pentru Promovarea Prieteniei si Colaborarii cu Alte Popoare [*National Center for the Promotion of Friendship and Cooperation with Other Peoples*] (RO)
CNPC .... Comision Nacional Peruana de Cooperacion con la UNESCO [*Peruvian National Commission for the United Nations Educational, Scientific and Cultural Organization*] [*Peru*] (EAIO)
CNPC .... Comite National de la Production et de la Commercialisation Agricoles [*National Committee for Agricultural Production and Marketing*] [*Benin*] (AF)
CNPCC...... Confederation National des Planteurs de Chicoree a Cafe (WGAO)
CNPCF...... Chambre Nationale des Paysagistes Conseils de France [*Later, ANAPAL*] (WGAO)
CNPD........ Conseil National de la Paix et le Developpement [*National Council for Peace and Development*] [*Benin*] (AF)
CNPD........ Conseil National Populaire du Developpement [*People's National Development Council*] [*Malagasy*] (AF)
CNPE......... Caisse Nationale des Pensions pour Employes [*Benelux*] (BAS)
CNPE......... Consejo Nacional de Planificacion Economica [*National Economic Planning Council*] [*Guatemala*] (LAA)
CNPEM..... Centre National de Production et d'Etude des Substances d'Origine Microbienne [*National Center for the Production and Study of Microbial Substances*] [*Belgium*] (ARC)
CNPESCA ... Comision Nacional de Pesca [*Cuba*] (LAA)
CNPF........ Confederation Nationale des Parachutistes Francais (WGAO)
CNPF........ Conseil National du Patronat Francais [*National Council of French Employers*] [*Paris*] (WER)
CNPFP...... Comite National de Propagande en Faveur du Pain (WGAO)
CNPFV...... Comite National de Propagande en Faveur du Vin (WGAO)
CNPG........ Conseil National du Patronat Gabonais (EY)
CNPGC...... Centro Nacional de Pesquisa de Gado de Corte [*National Research Center for Meat*] [*Brazil*] (ARC)
CNPGL...... Centro Nacional de Pesquisa de Gado de Leite [*National Research Center for Milk*] [*Brazil*] (ARC)
CNPI......... Comision Nacional de Productividad Industrial [*Spain*] (DSCA)
CNPI......... Conselho Nacional de Protecao aos Indios [*National Council for Protecting the Indians*] [*Brazil*] (LA)
CNPIC....... China National Publications Import Corp. [*Later,*] [*CNPIEC*] (WGAO)
CNPIEC .... China National Publications Import and Export Corp. (TCC)
CNPIO ...... Comissao Nacional Portuguesa para Investigacao Oceanografico [*Portuguese National Committee for Oceanographic Research*] (PDAA)
CNPITC .... China National Publishing Industry Trading Corp. (WGAO)
CNPL........ Centre National de Pastorale Liturgique [*National Center of Pastoral Liturgy*] [*France*] (EAIO)
CNPL........ Comissao Nacional da Pecuaria do Leite [*Brazil*] (DSCA)
CNPL........ Confederacao Nacional das Profissoes Liberais [*Liberal Professions Confederation*] [*Brazil*] (EY)
CNPMF..... Centro Nacional de Pesquisa de Mandioca e Fruticultura [*National Center for Cassava and Fruit Crops Research*] [*Brazil*] (ARC)
CNPMS..... Centro Nacional de Pesquisa de Milho e Sorgo [*National Research Center for Millet and Sorghum*] [*Brazil*] (ARC)
CNPP......... Centre National de Prevention et de Protection [*National Center for Prevention and Protection*] [*France*] (WED)
CNPP........ Consejeria Nacional de Promocion Popular [*Santiago, Chile*] (LAA)

CNPPA...... Comite Nacional de la Pequena Produccion Agropecuaria [*National Committee of Small Agricultural-Livestock Producers*] [*Nicaragua*]   (LA)

CNPPA...... Commission on National Parks and Protected Areas [*of the International Union for Conservation of Nature and Natural Resources*]   (EAIO)

CNPPLF.... Comite National de Propagande des Produits Laitiers Francais   (WGAO)

CNPPME.. Centre National de Promotion des Petites et Moyennes Entreprises [*Togo*]

CNPP-PSD ... Convention Nationale des Patriotes Progressistes-Parti Social-Democrate [*Burkina Faso*] [*Political party*]   (EY)

CNPq .... Conselho Nacional de Desenvolvimento Cientifico e Tecnologico [*National Council of Scientific and Technological Development*] [*Research center*] [*Brazil*]   (IRC)

CNPq .... Conselho Nacional de Pesquisas [*Rio De Janeiro, Brazil*]

CNPR .... Centre National de Promotion Rural   (WGAO)

CNPRS...... Caisse Nationale des Pensions de Retraite et de Survie [*Benelux*]   (BAS)

CNPRST ... Centre National de Planification de la Recherche Scientifique et Technologique   (WGAO)

CNPS......... Caja Nacional de Prevision Social [*National Social Security Fund*] [*Colorado*]   (LA)

CNPS......... Centro Nacional de Pesquisa de Soja [*National Research Center for Soy Beans*] [*Brazil*]   (ARC)

CNPS......... Club Nautique de Port-Said

CNPS......... Confederation Nationale des Produits du Sol et Derives   (WGAO)

CNPS......... Conseil National de la Politique Scientifique [*Benelux*]   (BAS)

CNPS......... Conselho Nacional de Politica Salarial [*National Wage Policy Council*] [*Brazil*]   (LA)

CNPSA...... Centro Nacional de Pesquisa de Suinos e Aves [*National Research Center for Swine and Birds*] [*Brazil*]   (ARC)

CNPSD...... Centro Nacional de Pesquisa de Seringueira e Dende [*National Research Center for Rubber and Palm Nut Oil*] [*Brazil*]   (ARC)

CNPSEPC ... Confederation Nationale des Produits du Sol Engrais et Products Connexes   (WGAO)

CNPSo....... Centro Nacional de Pesquisa de Soja [*National Center for Soybean Research*] [*Brazil*]   (IRC)

CNPT......... Centro Nacional de Pesquisa de Trigo [*National Research Center for Wheat*] [*Brazil*]   (ARC)

CNPTAC ... China National Postal and Telecommunications Appliances Corp.   (TCC)

CNPTI .... Centre National de Prevention et de Traitement des Intoxications [*National Poison Control Center*] [*Information service or system*]   (IID)

CNPU .... Comissao Nacional de Politica Urbana [*National Urban Policy Commission*] [*Brazil*]   (LA)

CNPU .... Committee for National Peace and Unity [*Rwanda*]

CNPV .... Colegio Nacional de Periodistas de Venezuela [*National Association of Venezuelan Journalists*]   (LA)

CNPV .... Comite National des Producteurs de Viande   (WGAO)

CNPVE...... Confederation Nationale des Producteurs de Vins et Eaux-de-Vie de Vin a Appellations d'Orgine Controlees   (WGAO)

CNQ.......... Corrientes [*Argentina*] [*Airport symbol*]   (OAG)

CNR.......... Caisse Nationale de Reassurances [*Cameroon*]   (WGAO)

CNR.......... Caisse Nationale de Reassurances SA

CNR.......... Cantieri Navali Riunti, Ufficio Ricerca e Sviluppo [*Canteri Navali Riuniti, Research and Development Group*] [*Genoa, Italy*]

CNR.......... Ceska Narodni Rada [*Czech National Council*]   (CZ)

CNR.......... Coalicion Nacional Republicana [*Ecuador*] [*Political party*]   (EY)

CNR.......... Colombian National Railroads   (LAA)

CNR.......... Compagnie Nationale du Rhone   (FLAF)

CNR.......... Conseil National de la Recuperation [*Switzerland*]   (WGAO)

CNR.......... Conseil National de la Resistance [*National Council of the Resistance*] [*French*]   (WER)

CNR.......... Conseil National de la Revolution [*National Council of the Revolution*] [*Congo*]   (AF)

CNR.......... Conseil National de la Revolution [*National Council of the Revolution*] [*Guinea*]   (AF)

CNR.......... Conseil National de la Revolution [*National Council of the Revolution*] [*Burkina Faso*]

CNR.......... Conseil National de la Revolution [*National Council of the Revolution*] [*Benin*]   (AF)

CNR.......... Consejo Nacional de Rectores [*Colombia*]   (COL)

CNR.......... Consiglio Nazionale delle Ricerche [*National Research Council*] [*Italy*] [*Information service or system*]   (IID)

Cnr .... Corner   (SCAC)

CNRA .... Cameroon National Railway Authority

CNRA .... Centre National de Recherches Agronomiques [*National Agronomic Research Center*] [*Niger*]   (AF)

CNRA .... Certificat de Navigabilite Restreint d'Avions   (FLAF)

CNRA .... Commission Nationale de la Revolution Agraire [*National Commission of the Agrarian Revolution*] [*Algeria*]   (AF)

CNRA .... Conseil National de la Republique Algerienne [*Algeria*]

CNRA .... Conseil National de la Revolution Algerienne [*National Council of the Algerian Revolution*]   (AF)

CNRA .... Consejo Nacional de Reforma Agraria [*Bolivia*]   (DSCA)

CNRB .... Ceskoslovenska Narodni Rada Badatelska [*Czechoslovak National Research Council*]   (CZ)

CNRC .... Centre National du Registre du Commerce [*National Center of Trade Register*] [*Algeria*]   (IMH)

CNRC .... Centro Nacional de Radiacion Cosmica [*Argentina*]   (WGAO)

CNRDO...... Centro Nazionale Raccolta Dati Oceanografici [*Italian*]   (MSC)

CNREBTP ... Centre National de Recherche et d'Experimentation pour le Batiment et les Travaux Publics [*Ministere des Transports et des Travaux Publics*] [*Mali*]

CNREF...... Centre National de Recherche et d'Experimentation Forestiere [*Algeria*]

CNRET...... Centre for Natural Resources, Energy, and Transport [*United Nations*]

CNRF......... Centre National de Recherches Forestieres

CNRG........ Conseil National de la Resistance Guadeloupeenne [*Political party*]   (EY)

CNRG........ Conseil National de la Revolution de la Guinee Dite Portugaise [*National Revolutionary Council of So-Called Portuguese Guinea*]

CNRHVU ... Commission Nationale de la Republique de Haute-Volta pour l'UNESCO

CNRI .... National Research and Investigations Center [*Zaire*]   (PD)

CNRIR....... Comite National pour la Renovation des Institutions Republicaines [*National Committee for the Restoration of Republican Institutions*] [*Malagasy*]   (AF)

CNRM .... Centre National de Recherches Metallurgiques [*Belgium*]

CNRM .... Comite National de Reforme et de Modernisation

CNRM .... Commission Nationale de la Republique Malgache

CNRN........ Comitato Nazionale per le Ricerche Nucleari [*National Committee for Nuclear Research*] [*CNEN*] [*Later,*] [*Italian*]   (WER)

CNRN........ Comite National pour une Republique Nouvelle [*National Committee for a New Republic*] [*Malagasy*]   (AF)

CNROP ..... Centre National de Recherches Oceanographiques et des Peches [*Ministere des Peches et de l'Economie*] [*Mauritania*]

CNRPM .... Centre National de Recherches Pharmaceutiques de Madagascar [*National Pharmaceutical Research Center of Madagascar*]   (AF)

CNRPS...... Caisse Nationale de Retraite et de Prevoyance Sociale [*Tunisia*]

CNRS......... Centre de Recherches sur la Physio-Chimie des Surfaces Solides [*French*]   (SLS)

CNRS......... Centre National de la Recherche Scientifique [*National Center for Scientific Research*] [*Paris, France*] [*Research center*]   (WER)

CNRS......... Centre National des Republicains Sociaux [*National Center of Social Republicans*] [*France*] [*Political party*]   (PPE)

CNRS......... Conseil National de Recherche Scientifique [*International Council of Scientific Unions*]

CNRSH ..... Centre Nigerien de Recherches en Sciences Humaines [*Nigerien Center for Research in the Social Sciences*] [*Niger*]   (AF)

CNRST ..... Centre National de la Recherche Scientifique et Technique   (WGAO)

CNRST ..... Comite National de la Recherche Scientifique et Technique [*National Scientific and Technical Research Committee*] [*Malagasy*]   (AF)

CNRZ .... Centre National de Recherche Zootechnique [*Algeria*]

CNRZA ..... Centre National de Recherche sur les Zones Arides [*National Center for Research on Arid Zones*] [*Algeria*] [*Research center*]   (IRC)

CNS .... Cairns [*Australia*] [*Airport symbol*]   (OAG)

CNS .... Central Nacional Sindical [*National Labor Union Federation*] [*Spanish*]   (WER)

CNS .... Centralno Narodno Sveuciliste [*Central People's University*] [*Zagreb*]   (YU)

CNS .... Centre National des Sports [*Algeria*]

CNS .... Compagnies Nationales de Securite [*National Security Companies*] [*Algeria*]   (AF)

CNS .... Complexe National Sportif [*National Sports Complex*] [*Cambodia*]   (CL)

CNS .... Conseil National de Securite [*National Security Council*] [*Algeria*]   (AF)

CNS .... Conseil National des Sports

CNS .... Conseil National des Syndicates [*Luxembourg*]   (WGAO)

CNS .... Coordinadora Nacional de Sindicatos [*National Coordinating Board of Trade Unions*] [*Costa Rica*]   (LA)

CNS .... Co-Ordinadora Nacional Sindical [*National Trade Union Co-Ordinating Body*] [*Chile*]   (PD)

CNS .... Council for Nuclear Safety [*South Africa*]   (AA)

CNS .... Cyprus Numismatic Society [*Cyprus*]   (SLS)

CNS .... Czechoslovak Neurological Society   (EAIO)

CNSA .... Chirurgiese Navorsingvereniging van Suidelike Afrika [*Surgical Research Society of Southern Africa*]   (EAIO)

CNSC......... China National Seed Corp.   (TCC)

CNSC........ Confederacion Nacional Sindical Campesina [*National Peasant Trade Union Confederation*] [*Chile*] (LA)

CNSD .... Confederation Nationale des Syndicats Dentaires [*French*] (SLS)

CNSH .... Conseil National des Succuralistes de l'Habillement [*France*] (EAIO)

CNSL......... Confederation Nationale des Syndicats Libres [*Trade union*] [*Benin*]

CNSLR ...... Confederatia Nationala a Sindicatelor Libere din Romania [*National Free Trade Union Confederation of Romania*] (EY)

CNSM .... Comision Nacional de los Salarios Minimos [*National Commission on Minimum Wages*] [*Mexico*] (LA)

CNSM .... Confederation Nationale des Syndicats du Mali [*National Confederation of Malian Unions*]

CNSM .... Conservatoire National Superieur de Musique (WGAO)

CNSNS...... Comision Nacional de Seguridad Nuclear y Salvaguardias [*Mexico*] [*Nuclear energy*] (NRCH)

CNSO .... Confederacion Nacional de Sindicatos Obreros [*Chile*] (WGAO)

CNSP......... Comite Nicaraguense de Solidaridad con los Pueblos [*Nicaraguan Committee of Solidarity with Peoples*] (LA)

CNSP......... Comite Nicarguense por la Solidaridad con los Pueblos (WGAO)

CNSP......... Conselho Nacional de Seguros Privados [*Brazil*] (EY)

CNSS......... Caisse Nationale de Securite Sociale [*Morocco*]

CNSS......... Caja Nacional de Seguro Social [*National Social Security Fund*] [*Bolivia*] (LA)

CNSS......... Comite National de Solidarite Sociale [*National Committee for Social Solidarity*] [*Tunisia*] (AF)

CNST......... Consiliul National pentru Stiinta si Tehnologie [*National Council for Science and Technology*] (RO)

CNT .... Center of New Technologies [*Ukraine*] (EAIO)

CNT .... Central Nacional de Trabajadores [*National Central Organization of Workers*] [*El Salvador*] (LA)

CNT .... Central Nacional de Trabajadores [*Trade union*] [*Guatemala*] (EY)

CNT .... Centre National d'Etudes des Telecommunications [*France*] [*ICAO designator*] (FAAC)

CNT .... Code de la Nationalite Tunisienne

CNT .... Comando Nacional de Trabajadores [*National Workers' Command*] [*Chile*]

CNT .... Comision Nacional del Trabajo [*National Commission of Workers*] [*Argentina*] (PD)

CNT .... Comision Nacional de Trigo [*Ecuador*] (LAA)

CNT .... Commission for the New Towns (WGAO)

CNT .... Commission Nationale des Tarifs [*Medicaux en Securite Sociale*] (FLAF)

CNT .... Compagnie Nigerienne de Television

CNT .... Confederacion Nacional del Trabajo [*National Confederation of Labor*] [*Spain*] (PPE)

CNT .... Confederacion Nacional de Trabajadores [*National Confederation of Workers*] [*Peru*] (LA)

CNT .... Confederacion Nacional de Trabajadores [*National Confederation of Workers*] [*Colorado*] (LA)

CNT .... Confederacion Nacional de Trabajadores [*National Confederation of Workers*] [*Costa Rica*]

CNT .... Confederation Nationale des Travailleurs [*National Confederation of Labor*] [*Burkina Faso*] (EY)

CNT .... Confederation Nationale du Travail [*National Confederation of Labor*] [*Zaire*] (AF)

CNT .... Confederation Nationale du Travail [*National Confederation of Labor*] [*French*] (WER)

CNT .... Conselho Nacional do Trabalho [*Brazil*]

CNT .... Convencion Nacional de Trabajadores [*National Convention of Workers*] [*Uruguay*] (LA)

CNT .... Convergencia Nacional de Timor [*Timorese National Convergence*] [*Portugal*] (EAIO)

CNT .... Co-Ordinacion Nacional de Trabajadores [*Paraguayan confederation of workers*]

CNT .... Corporacion Nacional de Turismo [*National Tourism Corporation*] [*Colombia*] (COL)

CNT .... Corporation Nationale du Transport

CNTA .... City and New Territories Administration [*Hong Kong*]

CNTA .... Comptoir National Technique Agricole (WGAO)

CNTA .... Council of Nordic Teachers' Associations [*Copenhagen, Denmark*] (EAIO)

CNTB .... Confederation Nationale des Travailleurs Burkinabe [*Burkina Faso National Confederation of Laborers*] (EY)

CNTC .... Central Nacional de los Trabajadores del Campo [*National Congress of Rural Workers*] [*Honduras*]

CNTC .... Confederacao Nacional dos Trabalhadores no Comercio [*National Confederation of Commercial Workers*] [*Brasilia, Brazil*] (LA)

CNTC .... Confederacion Nacional de Transporte por Carretara Viajeros y Mercancias (WGAO)

CNTC .... Confederation Nationale des Travailleurs Croyants du Senegal [*National Confederation of Believing Workers of Senegal*]

CNTC .... Confederation Nationale des Travailleurs du Centrafrique

CNTCB ...... Confederacion Nacional de Trabajadores Campesinos de Bolivia [*Bolivian National Peasant Workers Confederation*] (LA)

CNTCCI .... Centrale Nationale des Travailleurs Croyants de Cote d'Ivoire [*National Union of Believing Workers of the Ivory Coast*]

CNTCS ...... Confederation Nationale des Travailleurs Croyants du Senegal [*National Confederation of Believing Workers of Senegal*] (AF)

CNTD .... Confederacion Nacional de Trabajadores Dominicanos [*National Confederation of Dominican Workers*] [*Dominican Republic*]

CNTD .... Confederacion Nacionalista de Trabajadores Democraticos [*National Confederation of Democratic Workers*] [*Nicaragua*] (LA)

CNTD .... Consejo Nacional de Trabajadores Democraticas [*Guatemala*] (WGAO)

CNTE .... Central Nacional de Trabajadores de Euzkadi [*National Federation of Basque Workers*] [*Spanish*] (WER)

CNTE .... Centre National de Tele-Enseignement [*French*]

CNTE .... Coordinadora Nacional de Trabajadores de la Educacion [*National Coordinating Board of Education Workers*] [*Mexico*] (LA)

CNTEEC ... Confederacao Nacional dos Trabalhadores em Estabelecimentos de Educacao e Cultura [*National Confederation of Education and Cultural Workers*] [*Brasilia, Brazil*] (LA)

CNTG .... Confederation Nationale des Travailleurs de Guinee [*National Confederation of Guinean Workers*] (AF)

CNTG .... Confederation Nationale des Travailleurs Gabonais [*National Confederation of Gabonese Workers*] (AF)

CNTG .... Confederation Nationale des Travailleurs Guineens (WGAO)

CNTI .... Confederacao Nacional dos Trabalhadores na Industria [*National Confederation of Industrial Workers*] [*Brasilia, Brazil*] (LA)

CNTIB....... Confederation Nationale 'Les Travailleurs Independants' de Belgique (WGAO)

CNTIC....... China National Technical Import Corp. (PDAA)

CNTL........ National Council of Tourism in Lebanon (EY)

CNTMAF ... Confederacao Nacional dos Trabalhadores Maritimos, Aereos, e Fluviais [*National Confederation of Maritime, Air, and River Transport Workers*] [*Brazil*] (LA)

CNTMC .... China National Textile Machinery Corp. (TCC)

CNTMR .... Comite National Contre la Tuberculose et les Maladies Respiratoires [*French*] (SLS)

CNTP......... Central Nacional de Trabajadores de Panama [*National Center of Panamanian Workers*]

CNTPI .... Centro Nacional de Tecnologia y Productividad Industrial [*Uruguay*]

CNTR .... Compagnie Nationale des Transports Routiers

CNTS........ Centre National de Transfusion Sanguine [*National Blood Transfusion Center*] [*Cambodia*] (CL)

CNTS........ Confederation Nationale des Travailleurs Senegalais [*National Confederation of Sengalese Workers*]

CNTSC ...... China National Tree Seed Corp. (TCC)

CNTSM..... Cooperacion Nacional de Trabajadores de Servicios Multiplos [*Venezuela*] (WGAO)

CNTSM..... Cooperativa Nacional de Trabajadores de Servicios Multiples [*Venezuela*] (EY)

CNTT .... Confederacao Nacional dos Transportes Terrestres [*Brazil*] (EY)

CNTT .... Confederation Nationale des Travailleurs du Togo [*National Confederation of Togolese Workers*] (AF)

CNTTA...... Centre National de Traduction et de Terminologie Arabe [*Algeria*] (SLS)

CNTTMFA ... Confederacao Nacional dos Trabalhadores em Transportes Maritimos, Fluvais, e Aereos [*Maritime, River, and Air Transport Workers Confederation*] [*Brazil*] (EY)

CNTTT ...... Confederacao Nacional dos Trabalhadores em Transportes Terrestres [*National Confederation of Land Transport Workers*] [*Brasilia, Brazil*] (LA)

CNTU .... Commission Nationale Tunisienne pour l'UNESCO

CNTUR ..... Conselho Nacional de Turismo [*National Tourism Council*] [*Rio De Janeiro, Brazil*] (LA)

CNTV .... Confederation Nationale des Travailleurs Voltaiques [*National Confederation of Voltan Workers*] (AF)

CNTYPI .... Centro Nacional de Tecnologia y Productividad Industrial [*National Center for Industrial Productivity and Technology*] [*Uruguay*] (LA)

CNU.......... Cameroon National Union [*Political party*]

CNU.......... Clubul Nautic Universitar [*University Sailing Club*] (RO)

CNU.......... Comando Nacionalista Universitario [*Nationalist University Command*] [*Ecuador*] (LA)

CNU.......... Comando Nacional Urbano [*National Urban Command*] [*Venezuela*] (LA)

CNU.......... Concentracion Nacional Universitaria [*National University Concentration*] [*Argentina*] (LA)

CNU.......... Conseil National d'Union [*National Council of Unity*] [*Chad*] (AF)

CNU........... Consejo Nacional de Universidades [*National University Council*] [*La Habana, Cuba*]   (LAA)
CNU........... Consiglio Nazionale Universitario [*National University Council*] [*Italian*]   (WER)
CNUAC..... China National United Advertising Corp.   (TCC)
CNUAH .... Centro de las Naciones Unidas para los Asentamientos Humanos [*United Nations Centre for Human Settlements*] [*Spanish*]   (DUND)
CNUCD..... Conference des Nations Unies pour le Commerce et le Developpement [*United Nations Conference on Trade and Development - UNCTAD*] [*French*]
CNUCE ..... Centro Nazionale Universitario di Calcolo Elettronico   (WGAO)
CNUCED .. Conference des Nations Unies pour le Commerce et le Developpement   (WGAO)
CNUCED .. Conference des Nations Unies sur le Commerce et le Developpement [*United Nations Conference on Trade and Development - UNCTAD*] [*French*]   (WER)
CNUDCI ... Commission des Nations Unies pour le Droit Commercial International [*United Nations Commission for International Commercial Law*] [*French*]
CNUEH..... Centre des Nations Unies pour les Etablissements Humains [*United Nations Centre for Human Settlements*] [*French*]   (DUND)
CNUJ .... Committee for Nordic Universities of Journalism [*See also RNJ*]   (EAIO)
CNUP........ Consejo Nacional Provisorio de Universidades [*National Provisional Council of Universities*] [*Venezuela*]   (LA)
CNUPEA... Comision Nacional para el Uso Pacifico de la Energia Atomica [*National Commission for the Peaceful Use of Atomic Energy*] [*Cuba*]   (LA)
CNUR........ Corriente Nacionalista de Unidad y Reconciliacion [*Nicaragua*] [*Political party*]   (EY)
CNUS .... Comite Nacional de Unidad Sindical [*National Committee of Trade Union Unity*] [*Guatemala*]   (LA)
CNUS .... Comite National de l'Unite Syndicale
CNUT........ Conference Nationale des Usagers des Transports   (WGAO)
CNUTS...... Central Nacional Unificada de Trabajadores de la Salud [*National Federation of Health Workers*] [*Peru*]   (LA)
CNUURC.. Commission des Nations Unies pour l'Unification et le Relevement de la Coree   (WGAO)
CNV........... Canavieiras [*Brazil*] [*Airport symbol*]   (OAG)
CNV........... Christelijk Nationaal Vakverbond [*Christian National Federation of Trade Unions*] [*Netherlands*]
CNV........... Christelijk Nationaal Vakverbond in Nederland   (WGAO)
CNV........... Comision Nacional de Valores [*National Securities Commission*] [*Mexico, Panama*]   (LA)
CNV........... Comite National Vietnam [*National Vietnam Committee*] [*French*]   (WER)
CNVE .... Conseil National des Volontaires Etudiants [*National Council of Student Volunteers*] [*Algeria*]   (AF)
CNVF .... Comite National des Vins de France   (WGAO)
CNVPA...... Conseil National de la Vulgarisation du Progres Agricole   (WGAO)
CNVS......... Comite Nacional de Vanguardia Socialista [*National Committee of Socialist Vanguard*] [*Colorado*]   (LA)
CNVS......... Confederation Nationale des Industries et Commerces en Gros des Vins, Cidres, Sirops, Spiritueux et Liqueurs de France   (WGAO)
CNVSA...... Chirurgiese Navorsingsvereniging van Suider-Afrika [*South Africa*]   (AA)
CNW......... Canada Northwest Australia   (ADA)
CNW......... China Northwest Airlines [*ICAO designator*]   (FAAC)
CNX......... Chiang Mai [*Thailand*] [*Airport symbol*]   (OAG)
CNZ.......... Casova Norma Zasob [*Supply Schedule*]   (CZ)
CNZ.......... Ceskoslovenske Naftove Zavody, Narodni Podnik [*Czechoslovak Petroleum Industries, National Enterprise*]   (CZ)
CO............. Cabinet Office [*New South Wales*] [*Australia*]
c/o .... Care of   (EECI)
CO............. Centrala Odziezowa [*Clothing Center*]   (POL)
CO............. Centrala Ogrodnicza [*Horticultural Center*]   (POL)
CO............. Centralne Ogrzewanie [*Central Heating*] [*Poland*]
CO............. Centralni Odbor [*Central Committee*]   (YU)
CO............. Cerkvena Obcina [*Parish*]   (YU)
Co............. Cerro [*Hill*] [*Spanish*]   (NAU)
CO............. Civilni Obrana [*Civil Defense*]   (CZ)
CO............. Clerical Officer [*Australia*]
Co............. Cobalto [*Cobalt*] [*Chemical element*] [*Portuguese*]
Co............. Code de Commerce [*French*]
CO............. Colombia [*ANSI two-letter standard code*]   (CNC)
CO............. Colonial Office
CO............. Comites Obreros [*Workers' Committees*] [*Spanish*]   (WER)
CO............. Commonwealth Ombudsman [*Australia*]
Co............. Compagnie [*Company*] [*French*]
co............. Compagno [*Partner*] [*Italian*]
Co............. Compania [*Company, Society*] [*Spanish*]
Co............. Company   (PWGL)
c/o .... Compte Ouvert [*Open Account*] [*French*] [*Business term*]

Co.............. Country   (EECI)
CO............. Crown Office [*Australia*]
CO............. Kolumbia [*Colombia*] [*Poland*]
co.............. Tribunal de Commerce [*French*]
CO1O .... Canto Primo [*First Soprano*] [*Music*]
COA........... Centre Operationnel des Armees [*Armed Forces Operations Center*] [*French*]   (WER)
COA........... Comite Obrero Antipolitico [*Antipolitical Workers Committee*] [*Of "Bunkerist" tendency*] [*Spanish*]   (WER)
COA........... Commissie ter Bevordering van het Kweken en het Onderzock van Nieuwe Aardappelrassen Committee for the Advancement of Potato Breeding [*Netherlands*]   (DSCA)
COA........... Commissie ter Bevordering v het Kweken en het Onderzoek y Nieuwe Aardappelrassen   (WGAO)
COA........... Commonwealth of Australia
COA........... Compagnie d'Ouvriers d'Administration [*French*]
COA........... Confederacion Obrera Argentina [*Argentine Worker Confederation*]   (LA)
COA........... Cote Occidentale d'Afrique
COA........... Council of Agriculture [*Taiwan*] [*Research center*]   (IRC)
COA........... Council of Agriculture [*Queensland*] [*Australia*]
COA........... Operational Command in Angola
COA........... Sydney Jewish Centre on Ageing [*Australia*]
COAA .... Customs Officers' Association of Australia
COAC .... College Ouest Africaine des Chirurgiens [*West African College of Surgeons - WACS*]   (EAIO)
COACAL... Centrum voor Onderzoek van het Arabisch en de Cultuur van de Arabische Landen [*CRACAC*] [*Ghent, Belgium*]   (MENA)
CO-ACTION ... Co-Operative Action Programme [*UNESCO*]   (EA)
COAER ..... Union Construttori Apparecchiature ed Impianti Aeraulici [*Italy*]   (WGAO)
COAF .... La Commerciale de l'Afrique Francaise
COAG........ Committee on Agriculture [*Food and Agricultural Organization*] [*United Nations*]
COAKA ..... Coalition Kasaienne
COALBRA ... Companhia Coque e Alcool de Madeira [*Brazil*]   (EY)
COALDATA ... European Coal Data Bank [*DECHEMA*] [*Germany*] [*Information service or system*]   (IID)
COALSA ... Compania Almacenadora Sociedad Anonima [*Guatemala*]   (IMH)
COAM....... Colegio Oficial de Arquitectos de Madrid [*Official Association of Architects of Madrid*] [*Spanish*]   (WER)
COAMA .... Coordenacao da Amazonia [*Amazon Basin Administration*] [*Brazil*]   (LA)
COAP .... Comissao de Abastecimento e Precos [*Supply and Price Commission*] [*Brazil*]   (LA)
COAP .... Comite de Asesoramiento de la Presidencia de la Republica [*Advisory Committee of the Presidency*] [*Peru*]   (LA)
COAR .... Comando Obrero de Accion Revolucionaria [*Workers Commando of Revolutionary Action*] [*Spanish*]   (WER)
COARIN ... Commitee on Arabic in Informatics [*Computer science*]   (ADPT)
COARPIMAR ... Compania de Artifices en Piedra y Marmol [*Colombia*]   (COL)
COAS .... Council of the Organisation of American States   (WGAO)
COAV .... Comisiones Obreras Anticapitalistas de Valencia [*Anticapitalist Workers Commissions of Valencia*] [*Spanish*]   (WER)
COB........... Central Obrera Boliviana [*Bolivian Workers Confederation*]
COB........... Centre Oceanologique de Bretagne [*CNEXO*] [*French*]   (ASF)
COB........... Chevalier Old Boys [*Australia*]   (ADA)
COB........... Cinematograph Operators' Board [*Victoria*] [*Australia*]
cob............. Cobra [*Snake*] [*Portuguese*]
COB........... Comisiones Obreras de Barrio [*Workers City District Commissions*] [*Spanish*]   (WER)
COB........... Comite Olimpico Boliviano [*Bolivian Olympic Committee*]   (EAIO)
COB........... Commission des Operations de Bourse [*Operations Commission of the Stock Exchange*] [*France*]
COB........... Confederation of Business [*Rhodesian*]   (AF)
COB........... Conseil des Operations de Bourse [*French*]   (ECON)
COB........... Contractorgaan Beroepsvervoer [*Benelux*]   (BAS)
COBAC ...... Cooperative Ouvriere Belge   (WGAO)
COBAC .... Compagnie Belge d'Assurance-Credit SA [*Belgium*]   (EY)
COBAE...... Comissao Brasileira de Actividades Espaciais [*Brazilian Space Activities Commission*] [*Brazil*]   (LA)
COBAFI .... Companhia Bahiana de Fibras [*Brazil*]
COBAFRUIT ... Cooperative Bananiere et Fruitiere de la Cote-D'Ivoire
COBAG ...... Cooperative Bananiere Guineenne
COBAKWA ... Abako Cooperative
COBAL...... Companhia Brasileira de Alimentos [*Brazilian Foods Company*]   (LA)
COBAM .... Confection-Bonneterie Africaine et Malgache
COBAP...... Comissao da Bacia do Plata [*River Plate Basin Commission*] [*Brazil*]   (LA)
COBAST ... Companhia Brasileira Administradora de Servicos Tecnicos [*Brazil*]   (LAA)
COBAUTOS ... Cooperativa Boyacense de Autos Ltda. [*Tunja*]   (COL)
COBAZ ..... Council of Governing Bodies of Australian Zoos

COBBA...... Council of Brass Bands Association (WGAO)
COBCCEE ... Comite des Organisations de la Roucherie et de la Charcuterie de la CEE (WGAO)
COBCOE... Council of British Chambers of Commerce in Continental Europe (WGAO)
COBEC...... Companhia Brasileira de Entrepostos e Comercio [*Brazilian Warehouses and Trade Company*] (LA)
COBECEP ... Comite Belge des Constructeurs d'Equipement Petrolier (WGAO)
COBECHAR ... Comptoir Belge des Charbons (WGAO)
COBELDA ... Compagnie Belge d'Electronic et d'Automation [*Belgium*] (PDAA)
COBELEXFO ... Comite Belge des Expositions, des Foires et d'Expansion Nationale [*Belgium*] (BAS)
COBELMIN ... Compagnie Belge d'Entreprise Minieres
COBELPA ... Association des Fabricants de Pates, Papiers et Cartons de Belgique [*Belgian Association of Pulp, Paper and Carton Manufacturers*] (PDAA)
COBELTO ... Consortium Belge pour le Togo
COBELTOUR ... Compagnie Belge de Tourisme (WGAO)
COBEMAG ... Cooperative Beninoise de Materiel Agricole [*Benin Cooperative for Agricultural Supplies*] (AF)
COBEN ..... Colegio de Biologos y Ecologos de Nicaragua [*College of Biologists and Ecologists of Nicaragua*] (EAIO)
COBENAM ... Compagnie Beninoise de Navigation Maritime [*Beninese Maritime Navigation Company*] (AF)
COBI .... Council on Biological Information (WGAO)
COBICA.... Campanhia Brasileria de Industrializacao da Castanha do Caju (WGAO)
COBICA.... Companhia Brasileira de Industrializacao da Castanha do Caju [*Brazil*] (DSCA)
COBIDOC ... Commissie voor Bibliografie en Documentatie [*Netherlands Bibliographical and Documentary Committee*] [*Information service or system*] (IID)
COBISCAL ... Complexe de l'Industrie de la Biscuiterie et de la Chocolaterie [*North African*]
COBLAMED ... Cooperative Black and Mediterranean Sea Study (MSC)
COBLSA ... Committee to Oppose Bank Loans to South Africa
COBOEN .. Comision Boliviana de Energia Nuclear [*Bolivian Nuclear Energy Commission*] (LA)
COBOLCA ... Comite Boliviano del Cafe [*Bolivia*] (EY)
COBOLIVAR ... Compania de Seguros Bolivar [*Colombia*] (COL)
COBOMA ... Compagnie des Bois du Mayumba
COBOPAL ... Boulangerie, Patisserie, et Alimentation [*Tunisia*]
COBQ........ Chiropractors' and Osteopaths' Board of Queensland [*Australia*]
COBR .... Centralny Osrodek Badawczy Rozwojowy (WGAO)
COBRA ..... Chiang Mai Old Burma Retirement Association [*Thailand*]
COBRA ..... Computadores e Sistemas Brasileiros SA [*Brazilian Computers and Systems, Inc.*] (LA)
COBRA ..... Conference for Basic Human Rights in the ASEAN [*Associaton of South East Asian Nations*] Countries [*British*]
COBRA ..... Continent, Britain & Asia [*Commercial firm*] (DS)
COBRAG .. Companhia Brasileira de Agricultura [*Brazil*] (DSCA)
COBRAG .. Companhia Brasileira de Agricultura (WGAO)
COBRAPI ... Companhia Brasileira de Projetos Industriais [*Brazil*]
COBRASA ... Companhia Brasileira de Silos e Armazems [*Rio De Janeiro, Brazil*] (LAA)
COBRASMA ... Companhia Brasileira de Material Ferroviario [*Sao Paulo, Brazil*] (LAA)
COBRAZIL ... Companhia de Mineracao e Metalurgia Brasil [*Brazil Mining and Metallurgy Company*] (LA)
COBRECAF ... Compagnie Bretonne de Cargos Frigorifiques
COBRPO... Centralny Osrodek Badawczo-Rozwojowy Przemyslu Odziezowego [*Research Development Center for the Polish Clothing Industry*]
COBSEA ... Co-Ordinating Body on the Seas of East Asia
COBSTRU ... COBOL [*Common Business Oriented Language*]-Struktur [*Computer science*] (ADPT)
COBU........ Credit Libanais [*Cyprus*] (WGAO)
COBUILD ... Collins Birmingham University International Language Database
COC.......... Canberra Christian Outreach Centre [*Australia*]
COC.......... Central Obrera Colombiana [*Colombian Workers Federation*] (LA)
COC.......... Centro do Operaciones Conjuntas [*Joint Operations Center*] [*Venezuela*] (LA)
COC.......... Circulos Obreros Comunistas [*Communist Workers Circles*] [*Spanish*] (WER)
COC.......... Comisia pentru Organizarea Cooperativelor [*Commission for Organizing Cooperatives*] (RO)
COC.......... Comite Olimpico Colombiano [*Colombian Olympic Committee*] [*Colombia*] (COL)
COC.......... Comite Olimpico Cubano [*Cuban Olympic Committee*] (LA)
COC.......... Commission Officielle de Controle des Semeces et Plants (WGAO)

COC.......... Committee on Carcinogencity in Chemicals in Food, Consumer Products and the Environment [*Dept. of Health*] [*BRIT*] (WGAO)
COC.......... Compagnie Ouest-Cameroun
COC.......... Concordia [*Argentina*] [*Airport symbol*] (OAG)
COC.......... Confederacion Obrera Centroamericana [*Trade union*] [*El Salvador*]
COC.......... Conference of Omnibus Companies (WGAO)
COC.......... Credito Orientado de Capitalizacion [*Chile*] (LAA)
COC.......... Cyprus Olympic Committee (EAIO)
COCADA .. Compagnie des Commercants Africains du Dahomey
COCADAC ... Compagnie Camerounaise Danoise de Construction (WGAO)
COCADAC SA ... Compagnie Camerounaise Danoise de Construction SA
COCAM .... Contreplaques du Cameroun [*Cameroon Plywood Corporation*]
COCAP...... Comissao de Coordenacao da Alianca para o Progresso [*Alliance for Progress Coordinating Commission*] [*Brazil*] (LA)
COCARZI ... Comite d'Organisation pour le Carnaval de la Ville de Ziguinchor
COCAST ... Council for Overseas Colleges of Arts, Science and Technology (WGAO)
COCATRAM ... Comision Centroamericana de Transporte Maritimo [*Central American Commission of Maritime Transport*] [*Organization of Central American States*] [*San Salvador, El Salvador*] (EAIO)
COCC .... Cahiers d'Observations de la Cour des Comptes [*Benelux*] (BAS)
COCC .... Centrul de Organizare si Cibernetica in Constructii [*Center for Organization and Cybernetics in Constructions*] (RO)
COCC .... Confederacion de Obreros y Campesinos Cristianos [*Christian Workers and Peasants Confederation*] [*Costa Rica*] (LA)
COCCEE... Comite des Organizations Commerciales des Pays de la Communaute Economique Europeenne [*Benelux*] (BAS)
COCDYC .. Conservative and Christian Democratic Youth Community (WGAO)
COCE .... Coalicion Obrera-Campesina-Estudiantil [*Worker-Peasant-Student Coalition*] [*Mexico*] (LA)
COCEA ..... Comite de Coordinacion de la Ensenanza Agricola [*Committee on Agricultural Education*] [*Haiti*] (LAA)
COCEA ..... Companhia Central de Abastecimento do Estado da Guanabara [*Central Supply Company of the State of Guanabara*] [*Brazil*] (LA)
COCEAN .. Compagnie d'Etudes et d'Exploitation des Techniques Oceans [*France*] (PDAA)
COCEI...... Coalicion Obrera, Campesina, Estudiantil del Istmo [*Labor, Peasant, Student Coalition of the Isthmus*] [*Mexico*] (LA)
COCEI...... Compagnie Central d'Etudes Industrielles [*Central Industrial Research Company*] [*French*] (WER)
COCELBA ... Cooperativaa Central dos Lavradores Baianos [*Brazil*] (DSCA)
COCEMA ... Comite des Constructeurs Europeen de Materiel Alimentaire et de Materiel de Conditionnement (WGAO)
COCEMA ... Comite des Constructeurs Europeens de Materiel Alimentaire [*Committee of European Plant Manufacturers for the Food Industry*] [*Common Market*]
COCEOLA ... Comercializacion de Cereales Oleaginosos y Afines [*Argentina*] (DSCA)
COCEPRA ... Comptoir Commercial d'Exchanges des Products Africains [*Senegal*] (WGAO)
COCERAL ... Comite du Commerce des Cereales et des Aliments du Betail de la CEE (WGAO)
COCERAL ... Comite du Commerce des Cereales et des Aliments du Betail de la Communaute Economique Europeenne [*Committee of the Cereals and Animal Feed Trade of the European Economic Community*]
COCESNA ... Corporacion Centroamericana de Servicios de Navegacion Aerea [*Central American Corporation for Aerial Navigation Services*] [*Honduras*] (LAA)
COCESNA ... Corporacion Centroamericana de Servicios de Navegacion Aerea [*Central American Corporation for Aerial Navigation Services*] [*Guatemala*] (SLS)
COCESNA ... Corporation Centro-Americaine pour la Securite de la Navigation Aerienne (FLAF)
COCHEPA ... Compagnie Cherifienne d'Emballages en Papier
COCHEREX ... Compagnie Cherifienne d'Explosifs
COCHIME ... Compagnie Chimique de la Mediterranee
Coch Ind..... Cochin, India (ILCA)
COCHOSAM ... Cooperativa de Choferes de Taxis de Santa Marta Ltda. (COL)
COCI .... Consortium des Agrumes et Plantes a Parfum de Cote-D'Ivoire
COCI .... Consortium on Chemical Information (WGAO)
COCIC....... Comision Coordinadora de las Investigaciones Cientificas [*Coordinating Commission for Scientific Investigation*] (MSC)
COCIC....... Comision de Coordinacion de Investigaciones Cientificas de la Comision Permanente del Pacifico Sur [*Spanish*] (ASF)
COCIDEPRO ... Comite Civico de Desarrollo y Progreso [*Civic Committee for Development and Progress*] [*Bolivia*] (LA)

COCINA ... Coordinadora Civilista Nacional [*Panama*] [*Political party*] (EY)
COCIR....... Comite Consultatif International des Radio-Communications (WGAO)
COCIR....... Coordinamento delle Industrie Radiologiche ed Elettromedicali [*Coordination Committee of the Radiological and Electromedical Industries*] [*EC*] (ECED)
COCITAM ... Compagnie Cote-D'Ivoirienne pour Tous Appareillages Mecaniques
COCITEX ... Compagnie Camerounaise d'Importation d'Articles Textiles
COCITRA ... Compagnie Ivoirienne de Transports
COCIZA.... Cooperativa Agricola Mista da Zona de Araraguara [*Brazil*] (DSCA)
COCLA...... Coordinating Committee for the Liberation of Africa
COCMIB... Comite d'Organisation du Congres Mondial d'Implantologie des Biomateriaux [*Organizing Committee of the World Congress on Implantology and Bio-Materials - OCWCIB*] [*Rouen, France*] (EAIO)
COCMM ... Confederation des Organisations de Credit Maritime Mutuel (WGAO)
COCOA..... Council to Outlaw Contrived and Outrageous Acronyms [*Australia*]
COCOBANK ... United Coconut Planters' Bank [*Philippines*]
COCOBBRO ... Coordinative van Cultuur en Onderzoek van Broodgraan (WGAO)
COCOBOD ... Cocoa Board [*Ghana*] (EY)
COCOBOD ... Cocoa Marketing Board [*Ghana*] (WGAO)
COCOCAM ... Comite de Coordination Camerounaise [*Committee for Cameroonese Coordination*]
COCODI ... Compagnie de Commerce de la Cote-D'Ivoire
COCOES... Comite de Coordination des Enquetes Statistiques (WGAO)
COCOES... Comite de Coordination des Etudes Statistiques [*Statistical Research Coordination Committee*] [*Morocco*] (AF)
COCOM... Coordinating Committee on Export Controls [*NATO*] (WGAO)
COCOMBO ... Comptoir Commercial de M'Boss
COCOMI .. Comunidad de Compensacion Minera [*Community for Mining Compensation*] [*Peru*] (LA)
COCONEX ... Commission Confederal Executive [*Executive Committee of the Confederation Syndicale Congolaise*] [*Congo*] (AF)
COCOP ..... Comite de Organizaciones Populares [*Committee of People's Organizations*] [*Peru*] (LA)
COCOP ..... Red Latinoamericana de Coordinacion y Promocion de Tecnologia Apropriada (WGAO)
COCOR..... Commission de Coordination pour la Nomenclature des Produits Siderurgiques [*Commission for Coordinating the Naming of Metallurgical Products*] (PDAA)
COCOS ..... Coordinating Committee for Manufacturers of Static Converters in the Common Market Countries (WGAO)
COCPCIA ... Centrul de Organizare Calcul si Perfectionarea Cadrelor pentru Industria Alimentara [*Center for the Computer Organization and Advanced Training of Cadres for the Food Industry*] (RO)
COCRIL.... Council of City Research and Information Libraries (WGAO)
COCSA...... Compana Organizadora del Consumo SA (WGAO)
COCSU ..... Council of Civil Service Unions (WGAO)
COCTA ..... Committee on Conceptual and Terminological Analysis [*IPSA*] (WGAO)
COCTI....... Conference des Institutions Catholique de Theologie (WGAO)
COCU........ Comision Organizadora del Congreso Universitario [*Mexico*] (WGAO)
COCUSA... Chamber of Commerce of the United States (WGAO)
COD........... Central Obrera Departamental [*Department Labor Federation*] [*Bolivia*] (LA)
COD........... Central Obrera Dominicana [*Dominican Workers' Center*] [*Dominican Republic*]
COD........... Centro de Orientacion Docente [*Colombia*] (COL)
COD........... Coalition de l'Opposition Democratique [*Togo*] [*Political party*] (EY)
cod.............. Codice [*Codex*] [*Portuguese*]
Cod.............. Codigo [*Code*] [*Portuguese*]
COD........... Comites de Distritos [*District Committees*] [*Spanish*] (WER)
COD........... Committee of Direction of Fruit Marketing [*Australia*] (WGAO)
COD........... Congress of Democrats
COD........... Co-ordination de l'Opposition Democratique [*Gabon*] [*Political party*] (EY)
COD........... Council of Defence
CODA........ Centro do Operacaos do Defensa Aerea [*Air Defense Operations Center*] [*Military*] [*Portugal*]
CODA........ Corporation for Olympic Development in Atlanta (OLYM)
CODACERO ... Compania de Productos de Acero Ltda. [*Colombia*] (COL)
CODAGRO ... Comissao de Desenvolvimento do Agreste Ocidental [*Pernambuco, Brazil*] (LAA)
CODAI ...... Companhia de Desenvolvimento Agro-Industrial [*Brazil*] (DSCA)
CODAL ..... Comptoir Industriel de Produits Alimentaires [*Malagasy*]
CODAM.... Companhia de Destroncas e Aluguer de Maquinas
CODAP ..... Compagnie Dakaroise de Peches

CODAPAG ... Compagnie Dakaroise de Produits Agricoles
CODAR ..... Codage Arabe
CODAR ..... Confederation des Associations Republicaines (WGAO)
CODARTE ... Compania Nacional de Artefactos Electricos [*Colombia*] (COL)
CODARU ... Codage Arabe Unifie
CODAS ..... Council of Departments of Accounting Studies (WGAO)
CODATA .. Comite de Datos para la Ciencia y la Tecnologia [*Committee on Data for Science and Technology*] [*Spanish*] (ASF)
CODATA .. Committee on Data for Science and Technology [*ICSU*] [*Paris, France*]
CODATAL ... Compagnie Daho-Togolaise des Allumettes
CODATU .. Conference de Dakar sur les Transports Urbains
CODAUTO ... Companhia Distribuidora de Automoveis
CODDETREISA ... Compania de Desarrollo Turistico, Residencial, e Industrial, Sociedad Anonima [*Dominican Republic resort development company*]
CODE........ Confederacion Democratica [*Democratic Confederation*] [*Chile*] [*Political party*]
CODEAGRO ... Amasonas Agricultural Development Co. [*Brazil*] (WGAO)
CODEAL... Companhia de Desenvolvimento de Alagoas [*Maceio, Brazil*] (LAA)
CODEBRAS ... Coordenacao do Desenvolvimento de Brasilia [*Brasilia Development Coordination*] [*Brazil*] (LA)
CODEC ..... Companhia do Desenvolvimento Economico do Ceara [*Fortaleza, Brazil*] (LAA)
CODECA .. Caribbean Corporation for Economic Development [*Puerto Rican*] (ASF)
CODECA .. Corp. for Economic Development in the Caribbean (WGAO)
CODECAL ... Corporacion Integral de Desarrollo Cultural y Social [*Colombia*] (WGAO)
CODECAL ... Corporacion Integral para el Desarrollo Cultural y Social [*Corporation for Cultural and Social Development*] [*Colombia*] (EAIO)
CODECARGA ... Corporacion del Transporte Automotor [*Colombia*] (COL)
CODECI.... Corporacion para el Desarrollo de la Ciencia [*Chile*] (SLS)
Codeco........ Coordinadora Opositora Demoncratica Constitucional [*Honduras*] (WGAO)
CODECOP ... Comite de Defensa de Comensales en los Comedores Populares [*Committee to Defend Eaters in Relief Canteens*] [*Peru*] (LA)
CODECOS ... Colombiana de Construccion [*Colombia*] (COL)
CODEFF ... Comite Nacional pro Defensa de la Flora y Fauna [*Chile*] (SLS)
CODEFI ... Comite Interdepartementaux d'Examen des Problemes de Fonctionnement des Enterprises (WGAO)
CODEH..... Comite para la Defensa de Derechos Humanos [*Committee for the Defence of Human Rights*] [*Honduras*]
CODEHUCA ... Comision de Defensa de los Derechos Humanos en Centroamerica (WGAO)
CODEHUCA ... Comision para la Defensa de los Derechos Humanos en Centroamerica [*Commission for the Defense of Human Rights in Central America - CDHRCA*] (EA)
CODEJ...... Comite pour le Developpement de l'Espace pour le Jeu [*France*] (EAIO)
CODEJA ... Companhia Mista de Desenvolvimento do Jaguaribe [*Brazil*] (DSCA)
CODEJU... Comision Nacional pro Derechos Juveniles [*National Commission for Children's Rights*] [*Chile*] (LA)
CODEL ..... Compania Colombiana de Elementos Electricos [*Colombia*] (COL)
CODEL ..... Coordination for Development, Inc.
CODELAM ... Comite de Desarrollo Departamental [*Departmental Development Committee*] [*Peru*] (LA)
CODELCA ... Compania Odontologica del Caribe [*Barranquilla*] (COL)
CODELCO ... Corporacion del Cobre [*Copper Corporation*] [*Chile*] (LA)
CODELCO ... Corporacion Nacional del Cobre de Chile (WGAO)
CODELSINA ... Coalicion del Sindicalismo Nacional [*National Labor Coalition*] [*Argentina*] (LA)
CODEMAC ... Comite des Demenageurs du Marche Commun (WGAO)
CODEMACO ... Compania Colombiana de Maderas Compensadas [*Colombia*] (COL)
CODEMIN ... Panama Mining Orgnisation [*Acronym is based on foreign phrase*] (WGAO)
CODEMY ... Comite de Developpement Auto-Centre de l'Arrondissement de Massangam, Annexe de Yaounde
CODEN..... Colombiana de Negocios Ltda. [*Colombia*] (COL)
CODENA .. Council for the Development of the North-East of Brazil (WGAO)
CODENAL ... Confederacion pro Defensa Nacional [*Confederation for National Defense*] [*Bolivia*] (LA)
CODENAL ... Corporacion de Accion Comunal [*Colombia*] (COL)
CODENE .. Comite pour le Desarmement Nucleaire en France [*Committee for Nuclear Disarmament in France*] (PDAA)
CODENO ... Conselho do Desenvolvimento do Nordeste [*Northeast Development Council*] [*Brazil*] (LA)
CODEP ..... Compania Distribuidora de Equipos Petroleros Ltda. [*Colombia*] (COL)

CODEPALE ... Ley Organica para la Ensenanza Secundaria [*Organic Law for Secondary Education*] [*Uruguay*] (LA)

CODEPAR ... Companhia de Desenvolvimento Economico do Parana [*Parana Economic Development Company*] [*Brazil*] (LA)

CODEPE ... Comissao de Desenvolvimento Economico de Pernambuco [*Brazil*] (DSCA)

CODEPE ... Conselho de Desenvolvimento da Pesca [*Brazil*] (DSCA)

CODER ..... Commission de Developpement Economique Regional [*Regional Economic Development Commission*] [*French*] (WER)

CODERA .. Comite de Desarrollo de la Reforma Agraria [*Agrarian Reform Development Committee*] [*Chile*] (LA)

CODERESA ... Colombiana de Repuestos Ltda. [*Colombia*] (COL)

CODERESA ... Conseil pour le Developpement de la Recherche Economique et Sociale en Afrique [*Council for the Development of Economic and Social Research in Africa*] (AF)

CODERJ ... Companhia de Desenvolvimento Economico do Estado do Rio De Janeiro [*Niteroi*] [*Brazil*] (LAA)

CODERN .. Companhia de Desenvolvimento do Rio Grande do Norte [*Brazil*] (DSCA)

CODES ...... Centre for Ore Deposit and Exploration Studies [*Australia*] (IRC)

CODES ...... National Centre for Ore Deposit and Exploration [*University of Tasmania*] [*Australia*]

CODESA ... Centro Operacional del Desarrollo [*Operational Center for Development*] [*Colombia*]

CODESA ... Confederacion de Sindicatos Autonomas [*Venezuela*] (WGAO)

CODESA ... Confederacion de Sindicatos Autonomos de Venezuela [*Confederation of Autonomous Venezuelan Unions*]

CODESA ... Consejo de Desarrollo de Salta [*Argentina*] (WGAO)

CODESA ... Corporacion de Desarrollo, SA [*Development Corporation, Inc.*] [*Costa Rica*] (LA)

CODESAIMA ... Companhia de Desenvolvimento de Roraima [*Brazil*] (WGAO)

CODESARROLLO ... Corporacion Social de Desarrollo y Bienestar [*Colombia*] (COL)

CODESCO ... Convention des Democrates Socialistes

CODESF ... Comissao de Desenvolvimento Economico de Sao Francisco [*Brazil*] (LAA)

CODESK ... Compagnie d'Exploitation Sfax-Kerkennah [*Offshore oil exploration company*] [*Tunisia*]

CODESPAL ... Comissao de Desenvolvimento Economico e Social de Palmares [*Brazil*] (LAA)

CODESRIA ... Council for the Development of Economic and Social Research in Africa [*Dakar, Senegal*] (EAIO)

CODEST ... Committee for the European Development of Science and Technology (WGAO)

CODESUL ... Companhia de Desenvolvimento de Sul [*Brazil*] (WGAO)

CODESUL ... Conselho de Desenvolvimento do Extremo Sul [*Council for Development of the Far South*] [*Brazil*] (LA)

CODESUR ... Comision para el Desarrollo del Sur [*Committee for the Development of the South*] [*Venezuela*] (LA)

CODETAFCAM ... Compagnie d'Etancheite Africaine au Cameroun (WGAO)

CODETAF-CI ... Compagnie d'Etancheite Africaine en Cote-D'Ivoire

CODETAR ... Comite de Obras Publicas y Desarrollo de Tarija [*Public Works and Development Committee of Tarija*] [*Bolivia*] (LA)

CODETOUR ... Compagnie pour le Developpement de l'Hotellerie de du Tourisme (WGAO)

CODETRAN ... Compania Especial de Transportes SA [*Colombia*] (COL)

CODEV ..... Commerce et Developpement

CODEV ..... Communications for Development [*Malta*] (WGAO)

CODEV ..... Communications for Development Foundation [*Rome, Italy*]

CODEVAP ... Comissao de Desenvolvimento Economico do Vale do Pajeu [*Brazil*] (LAA)

CODEVASF ... Companhia de Desenvolvimento do Vale do Sao Francisco [*Brazil*] (EY)

CODEVI .... Compagnie pour le Developpement de l'Industrie Cameroun (WGAO)

CODEVINTEC ... Compagnie pour le Developpement Industriel et Technique (ASF)

CODEX ..... Customers of Dynix Exchange [*Australia*]

CODEX ..... Exercise Code Word [*NATO*] (NATG)

CODEXAL ... Conseil Europeen du Codex Alimentarius (WGAO)

CODI .... Centro de Operacoes de Defesa Interna [*Internal Defense Operations Center*] [*Brazil*] (LA)

CODI .... Colombianos Distribuidores de Combustibles SA [*Colombia*] (COL)

CODIA ...... Colegio de Ingenieros Agronomos [*Agronomic Engineers Association*] [*Dominican Republic*] (LA)

CODIA ...... Comite de Industrializacion de Algas [*Argentina*] (WGAO)

CODIA ...... Comite pour l'Organisation et le Developpement des Investissements Intellectuels en Afrique et a Madagascar

CODIA ...... Customers of Dynix in Australia

CODIAM .. Comite de Organisation et Developpement d'Investissments Intellectuels d'Afrique (WGAO)

CODIAM .. Comite pour le Developpement des Activities Intellectuelles en Afrique et Madagascar [*Committee for the Development of Intellectual Activities in Africa and Madagascar*] [*French*] (AF)

CODIANZ ... Customers of Dynix in Australia and New Zealand

CODICA .... Compania Distribuidora de Calzado Ltda. [*Colombia*] (COL)

CODICAF ... Conseil des Directeurs des Compagnies Aeriennes en France (PDAA)

CODICE .... Comissao Dinamizadora Central [*Central Dynamization Commission*] [*Portuguese*] (WER)

CODIESEE ... Reseau de Cooperation en Matiere de Recherche et de Developpement pour l'Innovation Educative dans le Sud-Est Europeen [*Unesco*] (WGAO)

CODIF .... Societe Commerciale de Diffusion

CODIFA .... Comite de Developpement des Industries Francaises de l'Ameublement (WGAO)

CODIFAC ... Comite de Development d'Industrie de la Chaussure et des Articles Chaussants [*Committee for the Development of the Footwear Industry*] [*France*] (PDAA)

CODIFINCI ... Compagnie Financiere de la Cote d'Ivoire (WGAO)

CODIG ...... Associacio per a la Creacio del Collegi de Dissenyadors Grafics [*Association to Create the Graphic Designers Professional Union*] [*Spain*] (EAIO)

CODIL .... Colombiana de Importadores Ltda. [*Colombia*] (COL)

CODILOL ... Colombiana Distribuidora de Loterias Limitada [*Colombia*] (COL)

CODIM ..... Cooerdinatiegroep Documentatie en Informatie Milieu-Hygieene Nederland

CODIMA .. Societe Commerciale de Diffusion de Marques [*Ivory Coast*] (WGAO)

CODIMA .. Union Commerciale de Diffusion de Marques en Cote-D'Ivoire

CODIMCO ... Compania Distribuidora de Materiales de Construccion Ltda. (COL)

CODIMPA ... Compagnie Francaise Industrielle et Miniere du Pacifique (WGAO)

CODINA ... Compania Distribuidora Nacional [*National Distributing Company*] [*Chile*] (LA)

CODINP ... Confederacion de Investigadores Profesionales [*Colombia*] (COL)

CODIP .... Compagnie de Distribution Internationale de Periodiques [*International Periodical Distribution Company*] [*Mauritius*] (AF)

CODIP .... Conference de la Haye de Droit International Prive [*Hague Conference on Private International Law*] (EA)

CODIPESCA ... Companhia Distribuidora de Pescados [*Brazil*] (DSCA)

CODIPETROLEOS ... Colombianos Distribuidores de Combustibles SA [*Bucaramanga*] (COL)

CODIPLAM ... Comissao de Divulgacao do Plano Global para a Amazonia [*Brazil*] (WGAO)

CODIPRA ... Companhia Distribuidora de Produtos Alimenticios [*Brazil*] (DSCA)

CODIPRAL ... Compagnie de Distribution de Produits Alimentaires [*Senegal*]

CODIS .... Continentale de Distribution

CODISCOS ... Compania Colombiana de Discos Ltda. [*Colombia*] (COL)

CODITEX ... Compania Distribuidora Textil Ltda. [*Colombia*] (COL)

CODIVAL ... Compagnie Ivoirienne de Securite

CODKO ..... Centralny Osrodek Doskonalenia Kadr Oswiatowych [*Central Institute for the Improvement of Teaching Personnel*] (POL)

Codos .... Commandos Rouges [*Military group*] [*Chad*] (EY)

CODREMAR ... Corporacion para el Desarrollo y Administracion de los Recursos Marinos Lacustres y Fluviales de Puerto Rico (ASF)

CODRESS ... Coded Address [*NATO*]

CODUL ..... Companhia de Desenvolvimento Urbano Lda.

CODUSUCO ... Compania Distribuidora de Subsistenci, Conasupo [*Mexico*] (WGAO)

COE .... Chamber Orchestra of Europe (WGAO)

COE .... Coalition on Employment [*Australia*]

COE .... Comisiones Obreras de Empresa [*Workers Commissions of Enterprises*] [*Spanish*] (WER)

COE .... Comite Europeen de l'Outillage [*European Tool Committee*] [*France*] (EAIO)

COE .... Commonwealth Office of Education [*Australia*] (ADA)

COE .... Conseil Oecumenique des Eglises [*World Council of Churches*] [*Use WCC*] [*French*] (AF)

COE .... Council of Europe

COEA .... Consejo de la Organizacion de los Estados Americanos [*Council of the Organization of American States*] [*Washington, DC*] (LAA)

COEC .... Comite Central d'Oceanographie et d'Etude des Cotes [*French*] (ASF)

COEC .... Council Operations and Exercise Committee [*NATO*]

COECE ...... Coordinacion de Organismos Empresariales de Comercio Exterior [*Mexican Business Coordinating Council for NAFTA*] (CROSS)

COEHS ..... Church of England Historical Society [*Australia*]

COELBA ... Companhia de Eletricidade do Estado da Bahia
COEMA .... Confederacion de Obreros y Empleados Municipales de la Argentina [*Confederation of Municipal Workers and Employees of Argentina*] (LA)
COEMAR ... Commission on Ecumenical Mission and Relations
COEMPAQUES ... Compania Andina de Empaques Ltda. [*Colombia*] (COL)
COEMSAVAL ... Cooperativa de Ahorro y Credito. Empleados de Salud del Valle [*Colombia*] (COL)
COEN .... Comision Boliviana de Energia Nuclear [*Bolivian Nuclear Energy Commission*] (LA)
CoEnCo ...... Council for Environmental Conservation (WGAO)
COENER ... Comision Nacional de Politica Energetica [*National Commission for Energy Policy*] [*Dominican Republic*] (WED)
COES .... Centro Obrero de Estudios Sociales [*Worker Center for Social Studies*] [*Nicaragua*] (LA)
COES .... Comite Organizador de Estudiantes Secundarios [*Secondary School Students Organizing Committee*] [*Peru*] (LA)
COES .... Consiliul Organizarii Economico-Sociale [*Council for Socioeconomic Organization*] (RO)
COES .... Cooperativa Estudiantil de Ahorro y Credito. Universidad del Valle [*Colombia*] (COL)
COEX .... Direccion General de Comercio Exterior [*Uruguay*]
COEXPORT ... Comite de Exportadores de El Salvador [*Committee of Exporters of El Salvador*]
COEXPORT ... Corporacion de Exportadores de El Salvador (WGAO)
COF .... Christian Outreach Fellowship [*Ghana*]
COF .... Comite Olympique Francaise (WGAO)
COF .... Comites d'Organisation des Femmes [*Women's Organization Committees*] [*Benin*] (AF)
COF .... Coordinadora de Organizaciones Feministas [*Coordination of Feminist Organizations*] [*Puerto Rico*] (EAIO)
COFA .... Commonwealth and Overseas Families Association (WGAO)
C of A .... Commonwealth of Australia
COFA .... Compagnie Francaise pour l'Afrique Equatoriale
COFA .... Comptoir Francais Agricole (WGAO)
COFABA ... Cooperativa Mista dos Fazendeiros de Cacau da Bahia [*Brazil*] (DSCA)
COFACE ... Comite des Organisations Familiales aupres des Communautes Europeennes [*Committee of Family Organizations in the European Communities*] [*Common Market*] [*Belgium*]
COFACE ... Compagnie Francaise d'Assurance pour le Commerce Exterieur [*French Insurance Company for Foreign Trade*] (AF)
COFACE ... Compagnie Francaise pour l'Assurance du Commerce Exterieur
COFACE ... Confederation des Organisations Familiales de la Communaute Europeenes (WGAO)
COFACICO ... Compagnie Financieres Africaine Cinematographiques et Commerciales [*Congo*]
COFACICO ... Enterprises Financieres Cinematographiques et Commerciales [*Congo*] (WGAO)
COFADEH ... Comite de las Familias de los Detenidos-Desaparecidos Hondurenos [*Committee of the Families of the Detained-Disappeared of Honduras*]
COFADENA ... Corporacion de las Fuerzas Armadas para el Desarrollo Nacional [*Armed Forces National Development Corporation*] [*La Paz, Bolivia*] (LA)
COF AE ..... Coordinating Office for Asian Evangelism [*Singapore*]
COFAF ...... Committee on Food, Agriculture, and Forestry [*Association of South East Asian Nations*] [*Jakarta, Indonesia*] (EAIO)
COFAG ..... Comite des Fabricants d'Acide Glutamique de la CEE [*Committee of Glutamic Acid Manufacturers of the European Economic Community*] (EAIO)
COFAGRI ... Societe de Conditionnement et de Formulation Agricola [*Cameroon*] (WGAO)
COFALEC ... Comite des Fabricants de Levure de Panification de la CEE (WGAO)
COFAMA ... Comptoirs Franco-Africains de Materiaux
COFAP ...... Comissao Federal de Abastecimento e Precos [*Federal Supply and Price Commission*] [*Portugal*]
COFAP ...... Comissao Federal de Abastecimento e Precos [*Federal Supply and Price Commission*] [*Brazil*]
COFAP ...... Comite Francaise des Applications du Pyrethre (WGAO)
COFAPEFIRE ... Comptoir Familial Pere et Fils Reunis
COFARMA ... Consorcio Farmaceutico Colombiano Ltda. [*Barranquilla*] (COL)
COFARMA ... Cooperation Pharmaceutique Malgache
COFAS ...... Centre de l'Operation des Forces Aeriennes Strategiques
COFAZ ...... Compagnie Francaise de l'Azote
COFCA ...... Coffee and Cacao Institute of the Philippines [*Philippines*] (DSCA)
COFCE ...... Comite pour l'Orientation et Formation des Cadres d'Entreprises (WGAO)
COFCE ...... Comite pour l'Orientation et la Formation des Cadres de l'Economie [*Committee for the Guidance and Training of Economic Cadres*] [*Belgium*] (AF)
COFDET ... Corporacion de Fomento y Desarrollo Economico de Tacna [*Peru*] (DSCA)

COFE .... Confederacion de Organizaciones de Funcionarios de Estado [*Confederation of State Civil Service Organizations*] [*Uruguay*] (LA)
COFE .... Confederacion de Organizaciones de Funcionarios de Estado [*Confederation of State Civil Service Organizations*] [*Venezuela*] (LA)
C of E AgrPI ... General Agreement on Privileges and Immunities of the Council of Europe (DLA)
COFEB ...... Centre Ouest-Africain de Formation et d'Etudes Bancaires
COFEB ...... Confederation Europeenne des Fabricants de Baignoires (WGAO)
COFEB ...... Confederation of European Bath Manufacturers (EAIO)
COFECH ... Consejo de Organizaciones Femeninas de Chile [*Chile*] (LAA)
COFEGES ... Conseil Federal des Groupements Economiques du Senegal [*Federal Council of Economic Groups of Senegal*] (AF)
COFEL ...... Cooperative des Fruits et Legumes [*Fruit and Vegetable Cooperative*] [*Algeria*] (AF)
COFELI ..... Comite Femenino de Liberacion [*Women's Committee for Liberation*] [*Honduras*] (LA)
COFENAF ... Commission des Federations et Syndicats Nationaux des Entreprises de Recuperation de Ferrailles du Marche Commun [*Committee of the National Ferrous Scrap Federations and Associations of the Common Market - CNFSFACM*] (EAIO)
COFHAUT ... Confederation Francaise pour l'Habitation l'Urbanisme et l'Amenagement du Territoire (WGAO)
Cofhylux .... Compagnie Fonciere et Hypothecaire du Luxembourg (BAS)
COFI .... Committee on Fisheries [*Food and Agriculture Organization*] (ASF)
COFIAGRO ... Corporacion Financiera de Fomento Agropecuario y Exportaciones [*Agriculture and Livestock Development and Exports Financing Corporation*] [*Colorado*] (LA)
COFIBOIS ... Compagnie Forestiere et Industrielle du Bois
COFIBOIS ... Nouvelle Compagnie Forestiere et Industrielle du Bois [*Congo*] (WGAO)
COFICA .... Compagnie pour le Financement de l'Industrie du Commerce et de l'Agriculture (WGAO)
COFICA .... Comptoir Francais des Industries de la Conserverie Alimentaire [*French Agency for Food Canning Industries*] (WER)
COFICOM ... Compagnie Financiere pour le Commerce [*Financial Trading Company*] [*Guinea*] (AF)
COFICOMEX ... Compagnie Financiere pour le Commerce Exterieur [*Financial Foreign Trade Company*] [*French*] (AF)
COFIDA .... Comite pour les Fonds Internationaux de Droit d'Auteur [*FIPC*] (WGAO)
COFIDE .... Corporacion Financiera de Desarrollo [*Financial Development Corporation*] [*Peru*] (LA)
Cofide .... Corporacion Financiera de Desarrolo [*Peru*] (WGAO)
COFIE .... Comissao de Fusao e Incorporacao de Empresas [*Mergers and Incorporations Commission*] [*Brazil*] (GEA)
COFIEC .... Compania Financiera Ecuatoriana [*Ecuadorean Finance Company*] (LA)
COFIEC .... Compania Financiera Ecuatoriana de Desarrollo (WGAO)
COFIFA .... Compagnie Financiere France-Afrique
COFIGEST ... Compagnie Financiere d'Information et de Gestion
COFILLA ... Corporacion Financiera de los Llanos [*Financial Corporation of the Plains*] [*Venezuela*] (LA)
COFIMEG ... Compagnie Francaise d'Investissements Immobiliers et de Gestion [*French*]
COFIMER ... Compagnie Financiere pour l'Outre-Mer [*Overseas Finance Company*] [*French*] (AF)
COFIMER ... Nouvelle Compagnie Financiere pour l'Outre-Mer (WGAO)
COFIMPA ... Compagnie Francaise Indistrielle et Miniere du Pacifique (WGAO)
COFIMPAC ... Compagnie Francaise Industrielle et Miniere du Pacifique [*French commercial firm*]
COFINA .... Corporacion Financiera Nacional [*National Financial Corporation*] [*Panama*] (LA)
COFINANCIERA ... Corporacion Financiera Colombiana de Desarrollo Industrial [*Colombia*] (COL)
COFINANCIERA ... Corporacion Financiera Columbiana (WGAO)
COFINATOME ... Compagnie de Financement de l'Industrie Atomique [*French*]
COFINCI .. Compagnie Financiere de la Cote-D'Ivoire
COFINDE ... Conferencia para el Financiamiento y el Desarrollo de America Latina y el Caribe [*Conference for the Financing and Development of Latin America and the Caribbean*] (LA)
COFINEX ... Comite Consultatif de Coordination du Financement a Moyen Terme des Exportations [*Benelux*] (BAS)
COFININDUS ... Compagnie Financiere et Industrielle
COFINORTE ... Corporacion Financiera del Norte [*Barranquilla*] (COL)
COFIPECHE ... Compagnie Industrielle Ivoirienne de Filets de Peche
COFIREP ... Compagnie Financiere de Recherches Petrolieres [*French*]
COFISA .... Corporacion Costarricense del Financiamiento Industrial, Sociedad Anonima [*Costa Rican Industrial Finance Corporation*] (LAA)
COFIT .... Compagnie Financiere et Touristique [*Tunisia*] (IMH)

COFITEX ... Compagnie Marocaine de Filature et de Textiles [*Saharan*]
COFITOUR ... Compagnie Financiere et Touristique [*Tunisia*]
COFLA ...... Comision Forestal Latinoamericana [*Chile*]   (DSCA)
COFLONORTE ... Cooperativa de Flota Norte Ltda. [*Quintana-Boyaca*]   (COL)
COFLUMA ... Compagnie Fluviale et Maritime de l'Ouest Africain
COFNA ..... Comision Forestal Norteamericana [*Mexico*]   (DSCA)
COFNA ..... Comision Forestal Norteamericana [*Mexico*]   (WGAO)
COFO .... Committee on Forestry [*Food and Agricultural Organization*] [*United Nations*]
COFOCI .... Compagnie Forestiere de la Cote-D'Ivoire
COFOR ..... Compagnie Generale de Forages [*French*]
COFORCES ... Confederation Modiale Forces Culturelles Economiques Sociales   (WGAO)
COFORGA ... Compagnie Forestiere Gabonaise
COFORIC ... Compagnie Forestiere et Industrielle du Congo
COFRABLACK ... Compagnie Francaise du Carbon Black SA
COFRAL ... Comite Francais Agricole de Liaison pour le Developpement International   (WGAO)
COFRAL ... Compagnie du Froid Alimentaire
COFRAMET ... Compagnie Franco-Americaine des Metaux et des Minerals
COFRAMINES ... Compagnie Francaise des Mines   (WGAO)
COFRANIMEX ... Compagnie Francaise pour l'Exportation et l'Importation des Animaux Reproducteurs   (WGAO)
COFRAPAL ... Compagnie Franco-Africaine de Produits Alimentaires
COFRAS ... Compagnie Francaise d'Assistance Specialisee [*French*]
COFRASED ... Comite France-Asie pour la Sante et le Developpement [*France-Asia Committee for Health and Development*]   (CL)
COFREDA ... Compagnie pour Favoriser la Recherche et l'Elargissement des Debouches Agricoles   (WGAO)
COFREM ... Compagnie pour la Fabrication d'Elements Mecaniques
COFRENA ... Comite Francaise de l'Equipement Naval [*French Marine Equipment Committee*]   (PDAA)
COFREND ... Cosmite Francaise pour l'Etude des Essais Non Destructifs   (WGAO)
COFROI .... Comptoir Franco-Ivoirien
COFROR ... Compagnie Francaise d'Organisation
COFRUBA ... Comptoir de Fruits et Bananes [*Morocco*]
COFRUCI ... Cooperative Agricole de Production Bananiere et Fruitiere de Cote-D'Ivoire [*Ivory Coast Agricultural Cooperative for Banana and Fruit Production*]   (AF)
COFRUIT ... Compagnie des Fruits et Legumes du Senegal
COFRUITEL ... Cooperative des Producteurs pour la Commercialisation des Fruits et Legumes de la Cote d'Ivoire   (WGAO)
COFRUMAD ... Cooperative Fruitiere de Madagascar [*Malagasy Fruit Cooperative*]   (AF)
COFSA ...... Commonwealth and Overseas Fire Services Association   (WGAO)
COFUPA ... Comptoir de Fumage de Produits Alimentaires
COG .... Canberra Ornithologists' Group [*Australia*]
Cog .... Cografya [*Geography*]   (TU)
COG .... Comite Olimpico Guatemalteco [*Guatemalan Olympic Committee*]   (EAIO)
COG .... Commissie van Overleg Goederenvervoer [*Benelux*]   (BAS)
COG .... Committee on Oceanography and GARP [*SCOR*]   (WGAO)
COG .... Condoto [*Colombia*] [*Airport symbol*]   (OAG)
COG .... Confederacion Obrera de Guayas [*Guayas Labor Confederation*] [*Ecuador*]   (LA)
COG .... Congo [*ANSI three-letter standard code*]   (CNC)
COG .... Coordination Group of Nongovernmental Organisations in the Field of the Manmade Environment   (WGAO)
COG .... Current Operational Group [*NATO*]   (NATG)
COGAL ..... Consul General [*Consul General*] [*Cambodia*]   (CL)
COGATEL ... Compagnie Gabonaise de Telecommunications   (WGAO)
COGDEM ... Council of Gas Detection Equipment Manufacturers   (WGAO)
COGEAA .. Commercial Orchid Growers' and Exporters' Association [*Australia*]
COGEAC .. Compagnie Generale de l'Afrique Centrale
COGEB ..... Compatibilite Generale et Budgetaire [*French*]   (ADPT)
COGECA .. Comite General de la Cooperation Agricole de la CE [*General Committee of Agricultural Cooperation in the EC*]   (EAIO)
COGECA .. Comite General de la Cooperation Agricole de la CEE   (WGAO)
COGECAM ... Constructions Generales Camerounaise
COGECI .... Comptoir General pour le Commerce et l'Industrie [*Benin*]   (WGAO)
COGEDA .. Compagnie Generale de Distribution et d'Approvisionnement
COGEDEP ... Association pour la Cogestion des Deplacements a But Educatif de Jeunes
COGEDRO ... Comptoirs Generaux Reunis de Droguerie Produits Chimiques, Peintures, Colorants
COGEFAR ... Costruzioni Generali Farsura
COGEFI .... Conseil en Orgnaisation de Gestion Economique et Financieere d'Enterprises   (WGAO)
COGEFIC ... Compagnie Generale de Financement et de Credit
COGEGA .. Comptoirs Generaux du Gabon
COGEI ...... Comitato dei Geografi Italiani   (WGAO)

COGEI ...... Compagnie de Gestion d'Investissements Internationaux
COGEL ...... Comptoir General Commercial [*Morocco*]
COGEMA ... Compagnie Generale des Matieres Nucleaires [*French*]
COGEMAC ... Compagnie Generale Marocaine
COGEMAT ... Compagnie Generale de Materiels et de Materiaux [*Gabon*]   (WGAO)
COGENE .. Committee on Genetic Experimentation [*ICSU*]
COGEODATA ... Commission on Storage, Automatic Processing, and Retrieval of Geological Data   (EAIO)
COGEODOC ... Commission on Geological Documentation [*IUGS*]   (WGAO)
COGEQUIN ... Confederation Generale de la Quincaillerie   (WGAO)
COGER ..... Compagnie Gabon ELF [*Essences et Lubrifiants de France*] de Raffinage
COGERA .. Compagnie Generale d'Etudes Economiques et de Recherches Appliquees
COGERAF ... Compagnie Generale d'Etudes et Recherches pour l'Afrique [*General Company for African Studies and Research*] [*French*]   (AF)
COGERAN ... Societe de Courtage et de Gerance
COGERCO ... Comite de Gerance de la Caisse des Reserves Cotonnieres [*Bujumbura, Burundi*]
COGERCO ... Comite de Gerance de la Reserve Cotonniere [*Burundi*]   (WGAO)
COGEREC ... Comptoir General de Representation Commerciale [*Morocco*]
COGERIM ... Societe de Commerce General en Republique Islamique de Mauritanie
COGESA ... Compania General de Ediciones SA [*Mexico*]   (DSCA)
COGETA ... Cooperative Generale de Takeo [*General Cooperative of Takeo Province*] [*Cambodia*]   (CL)
COGETEXIM ... Compagnie Generale Togolaise d'Export Import
COGETRANS ... Compagnie Generale de Transit et de Transport
COGETRO ... Compagnie Generale des Transports Routiers
COGEX ..... Comptoirs Generaux d'Exploitations
COGEXIM ... Compagnie Generale Import-Export [*Ivory Coast*]   (WGAO)
COGI .... Children's Own Garden International [*See also BjBI*]   (EAIO)
COGICOM ... Consortium General Industriel et Commercial
COGIM ..... Compagnie Generale Ivoirienne de Maintenance   (WGAO)
COGIMEX ... Comptoir General d'Importation et d'Exportation
COGIP .... Compagnie Generale Ivoirienne de Piles Electriques
COGISA .... Compagnie Generale Immobiliere SA
Coglu .... Cagaloglu [*Quarter of Istanbul*]   (TU)
COGMA ... Concrete Garage Manufacturers Association   (WGAO)
cogn .... Cognome [*Cognomen, Surname*] [*Portuguese*]
COGRA ..... Compania Colombiana de Grasas [*Colombia*]   (COL)
COGRANJAS ... Cooperativa dos Proprietarios de Granjas de Pernambuco [*Brazil*]   (DSCA)
COGROPA ... Comercio Grossista de Produtos Alimentares [*Food supplier*] [*Mozambique*]
CoGroWa ... Commissie Grondwaterleidingsbedrijven   (WGAO)
COGS .... Canberra Organic Growers Society [*Australia*]
COGS .... Committee on General Staffing [*Australia*]
COGS .... Computer Oriented Geological Society   (WGAO)
COGSO ..... Northern Territory Council of Government School Organisations [*Australia*]
COGUISA ... Colonizadora de la Guinea Continental, Sociedad Anonima
COH .... Comite Olimpico Hondureno [*Honduran Olympic Committee*]   (EAIO)
COH .... Comite Olympique Hongrois [*Hungarian Olympic Committee*]   (EAIO)
COHAB ..... Companhia de Habitacao Popular [*Low-Cost Housing Company*] [*Brazil*]   (LA)
COHACA ... Compagnie Havraise Camerounaise
COHATA ... Compagnie Haitienne de Transports Aeriens   (WGAO)
COHBANA ... Corporacion Hondurena del Banano [*Honduran Banana Corporation*]   (LA)
COHC .... China Ocean Helicopter Corp. [*ICAO designator*]   (FAAC)
COHDEFOR ... Corporacion Hondurena de Desarrollo Forestal [*Honduran Corporation for Forest Development*]   (LA)
COHEBE .. Companhia Hidroeletrica da Boa Esperanca [*Brazil*]   (LAA)
COHEP ..... Consejo Hondureno de la Empresa Privada [*Honduran Private Enterprise Council*]   (LA)
COHETA .. Conseil pour l'Homologation des Etablissements Theologiques en Afrique [*Accrediting Council for Theological Education in Africa - ACTEA*]   (EAIO)
COHI .... Caribbean Operational Hydrology Institute   (WGAO)
COHO .... Council of Heritage Organisations [*New South Wales, Australia*]
COHRED ... Council on Health Research for Development [*Switzerland*]   (ECON)
COHSE ..... Confederation of Health Service Employees
COI .... Central Office of Information   (WGAO)
COI .... Comision de Orientacion Ideologica [*Ideological Orientation Commission*] [*Cuba*]   (LA)
COI .... Comision Oceanografica Intergubernamental [*Intergovernmental Oceanographic Commission - IOC*] [*Spanish*]   (ASF)

COI .... Commission Oceanographique Intergouvernementale [*Intergovernmental Oceanographic Commission - IOC*] (EAIO)

COI .... Conseil Oleicole International [*International Olive Oil Council - IOOC*]   (EAIO)

COI .... Consejo Oleicola Internacional [*Spain*]   (DSCA)

COIC .... Careers and Occupational Information Centre   (IID)

COIC .... Comite d'Organisation de l'Industrie Cinematographique [*France*]   (FLAF)

COID .... Council of Industrial Design   (WGAO)

COID .... Council on International Development   (WGAO)

COIDIEA .. Conseil des Organisations Internationales Directement Interessees a l'Enfance et a l'Adolescence [*Council of International Organizations Directly Interested in Children and Youth*] [*Geneva, Switzerland*]   (EAIO)

COIE .... Committee on Invisible Exports   (WGAO)

COIE .... Continentale d'Import Export

COIF .... Control of Intensive Farming   (WGAO)

Co Imo .... Come Primo [*As at First*] [*Music*]

COIN .... Construcciones Industriales Ltda. [*Colombia*]   (COL)

COIN .... Counterinsurgency Operations [*South Africa*] [*Military*]

COINDUSTRIAL ... Control e Instrumentacion Industrial Ltda. [*Colombia*] (COL)

COINFOR ... Compania de Ingenieros Forestales [*Colombia*]   (DSCA)

COINIM ... Centralny Osrodek Informacji Normalizacyjnej i Metrologicznej [*Center for Information on Standardization and Metrology*] [*Poland*]   (EAIO)

COINS .... Committee on the Improvement of National Statistics [*Inter-American Statistical Institute*] [*United States*]   (LAA)

COINTRASUR ... Cooperativa de Transportadores del Sur del Tolima Ltda. [*Chaparral-Tolima*]   (COL)

COINZOSUR ... Comision de Investigacion Zona Sur del Lago [*Venezuela*] (DSCA)

COIOEQ ... Coal Operators' Industrial Organisation of Employers, Queensland [*Australia*]

COIP .... Corporacion Industrial del Pueblo [*People's Industrial Corporation*] [*Nicaragua*]   (LA)

COIPM ...... Comite International Permanent pour la Recherche sur la Preservation des Materiaux en Milieu Marin [*Permanent International Committee for Research on Corrosion in a Marine Environment*]   (PDAA)

COIS .... Committee on International Standardization [*National Researh Council*]   (NUCP)

COIS .... Committee on International Standardization [*ASTM*]   (WGAO)

COISM ...... Conseil des Organisations Internationales des Sciences Medicales (WGAO)

COISTD .... Confederation des Organisations Internationales Scientifiques et Techniques pourla Developpement   (WGAO)

COJ .... Comites d'Organisation des Jeunes [*Youth Organization Committees*] [*Benin*]   (AF)

COJ .... Coonabarabran [*Australia*] [*Airport symbol*]   (OAG)

COJCK ...... Centralni Odbor Jugoslovenskog Crvenog Krsta [*Central Committee of the Yugoslav Red Cross*]   (YU)

COJE .... Comite d'Organisation des Jeux Africains d'Alger

COJE .... Conseil Oecumenique de Jeunesse en Europe [*Ecumenical Youth Council in Europe*] [*Northern Ireland*]   (EAIO)

COJEV ...... Comite des Organisations de Jeunesses Europeennes Volontaires (WGAO)

COJM .... Comite d'Organisation des Jeux Mediterraneens [*Algeria*]

COJO .... Albertville Olympic Organizing Committee   (OLYM)

COK .... Ceskoslovenska Obchodni Komora [*Czechoslovak Chamber of Commerce*]   (CZ)

COK .... Ciskei International Airways Corp. [*South Africa*] [*ICAO designator*]   (FAAC)

COK .... Cochin [*India*] [*Airport symbol*]   (OAG)

COK .... Cook Islands [*ANSI three-letter standard code*]   (CNC)

COL .... Ceskoslovenska Obec Legionarska [*Czechoslovak Legion*]   (CZ)

col .... Colaboracion [*Collaboration*] [*Spanish*]

col .... Colecao [*Series*] [*Publishing*] [*Portuguese*]

col .... Coleccion [*Collection*] [*Publishing*] [*Spanish*]

COL .... Colombia [*ANSI three-letter standard code*]   (CNC)

Col .... Colonel [*Colonel*] [*French*]   (MTD)

col .... Colonia [*Spanish*]

col .... Colonne [*Column*] [*Publishing*] [*French*]

col .... Colophon [*Publishing*] [*Netherlands*]

col .... Colorado [*Colored*] [*Spanish*]

col .... Colore [*Colored*] [*French*]

col .... Colore [*Colored*] [*Italian*]

col .... Colorido [*Colored*] [*Portuguese*]

col .... Coloris [*Color*] [*Knitting*] [*French*]

col .... Columna [*Column*] [*Spanish*]

col .... Coluna [*Column*] [*Portuguese*]

cola .... Colonia [*Spanish*]

cola .... Columna [*Column*] [*Spanish*]

COLAC ...... Comite Latinoamericano de Manejo de Cuencas de Torrentes (WGAO)

COLAC ...... Comite Latinoamericano de Manejo de Cuencas y Correccion de Torrentes [*Chile*]   (DSCA)

COLAC ...... Confederacion Latinoamericana de Cooperativas de Ahorro y Credito [*Latin American Confederation of Savings and Loan Cooperatives*]   (EAIO)

COLACEROS ... Compania Colombiana de Aceros SA [*Bucaramanga*] (COL)

COLACOT ... Confederation Latinoamericana de Cooperatives de Trabajadores   (WGAO)

COLACTI ... Cooperativa Central de Lacticinios da Regiao Sudeste do Rio Grande do Sul [*Brazil*]   (DSCA)

COLADIN ... Commissie voor Landbouwdocumentatie en Informatie TNO

COLAF ...... Colombiana Asesora y Financiera Ltda. [*Colombia*]   (COL)

COLAR ...... Compania Colombiana de Arrabio [*Colombian Pig Iron Company*]   (LA)

COLAROMA ... Colombiana de Aromaticos Ltda. [*Colombia*]   (COL)

colat .... Colature [*Filtering*] [*Pharmacy*]

COLAT ...... Colectivo Latinoamericano de Trabajo Psico-Social [*Belgium*]

COLATAM ... Council for Latin America, Inc. [*New York*]   (LAA)

COLATRADE ... Commision Latinoamericana de Trabajadores de la Energia (WGAO)

COLBAV ... Colegio de Bibliteconomas y Archivistes de Venezuela (WGAO)

COLBIENES ... Colombiana de Bienes [*Colombia*]   (COL)

COLC .... Comite de Liaison et de Coordination du Travail et de la Mobilisation Generale [*Liaison and Coordination Committee for Labor and General Mobilization*] [*Cambodia*]   (CL)

COLCADENAS ... Industria Colombiana de Cadenas Ltda. [*Colombia*] (COL)

COLCAFE ... Industria Colombiana de Cafe [*Colombia*]   (COL)

COLCAR ... Colombiana de Carrocerias Ltda. [*Colombia*]   (COL)

COLCEMENTO ... Colombiana de Cementos SA [*Colombia*]   (COL)

COLCERRAM ... Colombiana de Cerraduras Metalicas [*Colombia*]   (COL)

COLCIENCIAS ... Centro Colombiano de Investigaciones Cientificas y Proyectos Especiales Francisco Jose De Caldas [*Francisco Jose De Caldas Colombian Organization for Scientific Research and Special Products*]   (COL)

COLCIENCIAS ... Fondo Colombiano de Investigaciones Cientificas y Proyectos Especiales [*Colombian Fund for Scientific Research and Special Projects*] [*Colombia*] [*Information service or system*]   (IID)

COLCIENCIAS ... Instituto Colombiano para el Desarrollo de la Ciencia y la Tecnologia [*Colombian Institute for the Development of Science and Technology*]   (IRC)

COLCITRICOS ... Compania Colombiana de Citricos [*Colombia*]   (COL)

COLCREDITOS ... Compania Colombiana de Creditos y Cobranzas Ltda. [*Colombia*]   (COL)

COLCULTURA ... Instituto Colombiano de Cultura [*Colombian Cultural Institute*]   (LA)

COLDAMPAROS ... Cooperativa Colombiana de Prevision y Amparos Ltda. [*Bucaramanga*]   (COL)

COLDEINAR ... Colombiana de Inseminacion Artificial [*Colombia*]   (COL)

COLDEMAR ... Compania Colombiana de Navegacion Maritima [*Colombia*] (COL)

COLDEPORTES ... Instituto Colombiano de la Juventud y el Deportes [*Colombian Institute for Youth and Sports*]   (LA)

COLDESA ... Compania Colombiana de Desarrollo Agricola SA [*Colombia*] (COL)

COLDESIVOS ... Colombiana de Adhesivos Ltda. [*Colombia*]   (COL)

COLDEST ... Colombiana de Servicios Tecnicos [*Bucaramanga*]   (COL)

COLDEX ... Colombiana de Exportaciones Ltda. [*Colombia*]   (COL)

COLDICON ... Compania Colombiana de Inversiones y Construcciones [*Colombia*]   (COL)

COLDIGRASAS ... Sociedad Colombiana de Industriales de Grasas Vegetales [*Colombia*]   (COL)

COLEACP ... Comite de Liaison des Fruits Tropicaux et Legumes de Contresaison Originaires des Etats ACP

COLECHE ... Cooperativa de Leches de Santander [*Bucaramanga*]   (COL)

COLECHERA ... Cooperativa de Productos de Leche del Atlantico [*Barranquilla*]   (COL)

COLEGAS ... Colegio Antioqueno de Abogados [*Colombia*]   (COL)

COLENCERA ... Compania Colombiana de Encerados SA [*Colombia*] (COL)

COLESAL ... Compania Lechera de la Sabana SA [*Colombia*]   (COL)

COLESTE ... Grupo de Coordenacao do Comercio com os Paises Socialistas da Europa Oriental [*Coordinating Group for Trade with the Socialist Countries of Eastern Europe*] [*Brazil*]   (LA)

COLFECAR ... Confederacion de Transporte de Carga [*Confederation of Cargo Transport Workers*] [*Colorado*]   (LA)

COLFICOM ... Colombiana de Fomento Industrial y Comercial Ltda. [*Colombia*]   (COL)

COLFIM ... Compania Colombiana de Financiamientos [*Colombia*]   (COL)

COLFIN .... Compania Colombiana de Financiamiento SA [*Colombia*] (DSCA)

COLFIN .... Compania Columbiana de Financiamiento   (WGAO)

COLFINANZAS ... Compania Colombiana de Finanzas y Creditors [*Colombia*]   (COL)
COLFRA ... Societe du Fruit Colonial Francais
COLG .... Commonwealth Office of Local Government [*Australia*]
COLGAS ... Compania Colombiana de Gas SA   (COL)
COLGRO .. Verband Schweizerischer Grossisten der Kolonialwarenbranche (WGAO)
COLIBI ..... Comite de Liaison des Fabricants de Bicyclettes   (EA)
COLIDIRETTI ... Confederazione Nazionale Coltivatori Diretti [*National Confederation Board of Farmers*] [*Italy*]
COLIER .... Comite de Liaison des Interets Economiques de la Reunion (WGAO)
COLIM ...... Colombiana de Limas Ltda. [*Manizales*]   (COL)
COLIME ... Comite de Liaison des Industries Metaliques Europeennes (FLAF)
COLIME ... Comite de Ligazon de Industrias Metalurgicas   (LAA)
COLIMO .. Comite de Liaison des Constructeurs de Motorcycle des Pays de la CEE   (WGAO)
COLIMO .. Comite de Liaison des Fabricants de Motocyclettes [*Liaison Committee of European Motorcycle Manufacturers*] [*Belgium*]   (EAIO)
COLINA .... Coalicion de Liberacion Nacional [*Panama*] [*Political party*] (EY)
COLINAC ... Comite de Liaison National des Associations Culturelles (WGAO)
COLINAL ... Compania Litografica Nacional Ltda. [*Colombia*]   (COL)
COLINAV ... Conference des Lignes de Navigation
COLINDA ... Colombiana de Industrias y Agencias Ltda. [*Colombia*]   (COL)
COLINDUC ... Compania Colombiana para Industria y Comercio Ltda. [*Colombia*]   (COL)
COLING ... International Conference on Computational Linguistics (WGAO)
COLIPA .... Comite de Liaison des Associations Europeennes de l'Industrie de la Parfumerie, des Produits Cosmetiques, et de Toilette [*European Federation of the Perfume, Cosmetics, and Toiletries Industry*] (EAIO)
COLIPED ... Comite de Liaison des Fabricants de Pieces et Equipements de Deux Roues des Pays de la CEE [*Liaison Committee of Manufacturers of Parts and Equipment for Two-Wheeled Vehicles*]   (EAIO)
COLIPED ... Commission de Liaison des Pieces et Equipements de Deux Roues des Pays de la CEE   (WGAO)
COLISE ..... Comptoir de Literie du Senegal
coll .... Collection [*Collection*] [*Publishing*] [*French*]
Coll .... College   (PWGL)
coll .... Collquial   (TPFD)
collaz .... Collazione [*Collation*] [*Publishing*] [*Italian*]
collect .... Collectif [*French*]   (TPFD)
collect .... Collective   (TPFD)
collez .... Collezione [*Collection*] [*Publishing*] [*Italian*]
Coll I DrComp ... Colloque International de Droit Compare [*International Symposium on Comparative Law*]   (DLA)
Coll'Ott ...... Coll'Ottava [*With the Octave*] [*Music*]
CollvB .... College van Beroep vor het Bedrijfsleven [*Benelux*]   (BAS)
COLMALLAS ... Colombiana de Mallas [*Colombia*]   (COL)
COLMAQUINAS ... Industria Colombiana de Maquinaria Ltda. [*Colombia*] (COL)
COLMEDICAL ... Colombian Medical Industrial Equipment Ltda. [*Colombia*]   (COL)
COLMENA ... Consorcio Metalurgico Nacional SA [*Colombia*]   (COL)
COLMETAL ... Compania Colombiana de Metales Ltda. [*Colombia*]   (COL)
COLMIL ... Colegio Militar [*Military College*] [*Bolivia*]   (LA)
COLMINAS ... Colombiana de Mineria   (EY)
COLMINERA ... Corporacion Minera Colombiana SA [*Colombia*]   (COL)
COLMOTORES ... Fabrica Colombiana de Automotores [*Colombia*]   (COL)
COLMOVIL ... Colombiana de Automotores Limitada [*Colombia*]   (COL)
COLMUEBLES ... Compania Colombiana de Muebles [*Colombia*]   (COL)
COLN .... Commissie Onderzoek Landbouwwaterhuishouding Nederland (WGAO)
COLNEON ... Compania Colombiana de Neon Ltda. [*Colombia*]   (COL)
Colo .... Colegio [*School, College*] [*Portuguese*]
COLO .... Comisiones Obreras de Loita Obreira [*Workers' Commissions of Loita Obreira*] [*Spanish*]   (WER)
Colom .... Colombia
COLOMBATES ... Compania Colombiana de Empaques Bates SA [*Colombia*]   (COL)
COLOMBEX ... Compania Colombiana de Comercio Exterior [*Columbian Foreign Trade Company*] [*Colombia*]   (COL)
Colombr ..... Colombier [*Dovecote*] [*Military map abbreviation World War I*] [*French*]   (MTD)
color .... Colorato [*Colored*] [*Italian*]
color .... Colore [*Colored*] [*Publishing*] [*French*]
COLOSA ... Comite de Lineas (Navieras) Operativas en Sud America [*London*]   (LAA)
COLP .... Comite Latino Americano de Pargues Nacionales y de Vida Silvestre [*Chile*]   (DSCA)

COLP .... Comite Latino Americano de Parques Nacionales y de Vida Silvestre   (WGAO)
COLPA ...... Colombiana de Publicidad Ltda. [*Colombia*]   (COL)
COLPAEF ... Comite de Liaison du Patronat de l'AEF
COLPAPELES ... Compania Industrial de Papeles [*Colombia*]   (COL)
COLPATRIA ... Compania Colombiana de Capitalizacion y Seguros Patria [*Colombia*]   (COL)
COLPET ... Colombiana de Petroleos [*Colombian Petroleum Company*] [*Colombia*]   (COL)
COLPETROL ... Colombian Petroleum Company SA [*Cucuta*]   (COL)
COLPIELES ... Compania Colombiana de Pieles [*Colombia*]   (COL)
COLPIN ... Colombiana de Pinturas Ltda. [*Colombia*]   (COL)
COLPOZOS ... Colombiana Perforadora de Pozos [*Colombia*]   (COL)
COLPPOSUMAH ... Colegio Profesional de Subimiento Magisterio Hondureno [*Professional Association for the Improvement of Teaching in Honduras*]   (LA)
COLPROSUMAH ... Colegio Profesional Superior Magisterial Hondureno [*Honduran College of Teachers in Higher Education*]
COLPUERTOS ... Empresa de Puertos de Colombia [*Colombian Ports Enterprise*]   (LA)
COLQUIMICA ... Compania Colombiana de Productos Quimicos [*Colombia*]   (COL)
COLRESIN ... Colombiana de Resinas [*Colombia*]   (COL)
cols .... Colones [*Costa Rican monetary unit*] [*Spanish*]
cols .... Colunas [*Columns*] [*Portuguese*]
COLSEGUROS ... Compania Colombiana de Seguros [*Colombia*]   (COL)
COLTABACO ... Compania Colombiana de Tabaco [*Colombian Tobacco Company*]   (LA)
COLTED ... Comissao do Livro Tecnico e do Livro Didatico [*Textbook and Technical Book Commission*] [*Rio De Janeiro, Brazil*] (LAA)
COLTEJER ... Compania Colombiana de Tejidos [*Colombian Textile Company*]   (LA)
COLTEPUNTO ... Compania Colombiana de Tejidos de Punto [*Colombia*] (COL)
COLTEXCO ... Colombiana de Textiles y Confecciones Ltda. [*Colombia*] (COL)
COLTOLIMA ... Compania Automotora del Tolima Ltda. [*Ibague*]   (COL)
COLTRADA ... Compania General Transportadora Ltda. [*Colombia*]   (COL)
COLTRAP ... Compania Colombiana de Trabajos Publicos [*Colombia*] (COL)
COLTUBOS ... Colombiana de Tubos [*Colombia*]   (COL)
COLTUR ... Colombiana de Turismo [*Colombia*]   (COL)
COLUCHO ... Comite de Lucha Choferil [*Drivers Struggle Committee*] [*Dominican Republic*]   (LA)
COLUDE .. Committee for the Democratic Struggle [*Mexico*]
COLUG ..... Canberra Online Users Group [*Australia*]
colum .... Columna [*Column*] [*Spanish*]
COLUMA ... Comite Francais de Lutte contre les Mauvaises Herbes [*France*] (DSCA)
COLURANIO ... Empresa Colombiana de Uranio   (EY)
COLVAPORES ... Colombiana Internacional de Vapores [*Colombia*]   (COL)
COLVENTAS ... Compra y Venta de Propiedad Raiz [*Colombia*]   (COL)
COLVEX ... Conservas California Ltda. [*Barranquilla*]   (COL)
COLVIDRIOS ... Compania Colombiana de Vidrios [*Colombia*]   (COL)
COLVINOS ... Compania Colombiana de Vinos Ltda. [*Colombia*]   (COL)
COLVIVIENDAS ... Compania Colombiana de Viviendas [*Colombia*] (COL)
COLYMAD ... Comptoir Lyon-Madagascar [*Lyon-Madagascar Bank*]   (AF)
COM .... Centraal Orgaan ter Bevordering van de Bouw van Middenstandsbedrijfspanden [*Benelux*]   (BAS)
COM .... Centraal Orgaan voor Melkhygiene   (WGAO)
COM .... Centrala Obrotu Maszynami [*Machinery Sales Center*]   (POL)
COM .... Centralny Osrodek Metodyczny [*Central Methodological Institute*]   (POL)
com .... Comandante [*Commandant, Leader*] [*Portuguese*]
com .... Comendador [*Commander*] [*Portuguese*]
com .... Comentario [*Commentary*] [*Spanish*]
COM .... Comiteco [*Race of maize*] [*Mexico*]
com .... Commerce [*Trade*] [*French*]
com .... Commission [*Commission*] [*French*]
COM .... Commission on Ore Microscopy [*IMA*]   (WGAO)
COM .... Committee on Mutagenicity of Chemicals in Food, Consumer Products and the Environment [*Dept. of Health*]   (WGAO)
COM .... Communist Party of Australia [*Political party*]
COM .... Comoros [*ANSI three-letter standard code*]   (CNC)
COM .... Confederacion Obrera de Mexico [*Mexican Labor Confederation*]   (LA)
COM .... Consiliul Oamenilor Muncii [*Council of Workers*]   (RO)
COM .... Council of Ministers [*European Economic Commission*]   (DLA)
COMA ...... Coke Oven Managers Association   (WGAO)
COMAAFV ... Commander, Australian Army Forces, Vietnam
COMABU ... Cooperative des Maraichers de Bugarama
COMACEE ... Comite CEE de l'Union Internationale des Agents Commerciaux et des Courtiers   (WGAO)
COMACERO ... Compania Manufacturera de Muebles Colombiana [*Barranquilla*]   (COL)

COMACh ... Confederacion Maritima de Chile [*Chilean Maritime Confederation*] (LA)

COMACI... Comptoir Marocain Commercial et Industrial

COMACI... Confection Masculine de Cote-D'Ivoire

COMACI... Societe de Commission et d'Approvisionnement de la Cote-D'Ivoire

COMACO ... Compagnie de Manutention et de Chalandage d'Owendo

COMACO ... Compagnie Maritime et Commerciale [*Morocco*]

COMACOP ... Compagnie Mauritano-Coreenne pour la Peche (WGAO)

COMACT ... Commonwealth Acts [*Database*] [*Australia*]

COMADAN ... Corporacion de Mercado Agricola de Antioquia [*Colombia*] (COL)

COMADEV ... Consortium Maghrebin de Developpement Economique [*Maghreb Economic Development Consortium*] [*North African*] (AF)

COMADIEX ... Comptoir Abidjanais d'Import-Export

COMAF .... Comite des Constructeurs de Material Frigorifique de la CEE (WGAO)

COMAF .... Commercial Sud-Est Afrique

COMAFAK ... Compagnie Malienne des Ets. Fakhry

COMAFCI ... Compagnie Maritime Africaine Cote d'Ivoire (WGAO)

COMAFRA ... Comptoir Africain d'Assurances

COMAFRIQUE ... Societe Ivoirienne d'Expansion Commerciale

COMAFRUTA ... Companhia de Amadurecimento de Frutas Lda.

COMAF-SENEGAL ... Compagnie Maritime Africaine - Senegal

COMAFV ... Commander, Australian Forces, Vietnam

COMAG.... Societe Malgache de Constructions Metalliques et du Materiel Agricole

COMAGRI ... Compagnie Marocaine de Gestion des Exploitations Agricoles [*Morocco*]

COMAGRICOLA ... Associazione Nationale Commercianti di Prodotti per l'Agricoltura (WGAO)

COMAHA ... Cooperative Marocaine des Huileries Alimentaires [*Moroccan Cooperative for Edible Oils*]

COMAIA .. Comptoir Automobile, Industriel, et Agricole

COMAIP... Cia Maritima Isla de Pascua, SA [*Chile*] (EY)

COMAL .... Compagnie Commerciale Camerounaise de l'Alumine et de l'Aluminium

COMALFA ... Comptoir Maghrebin de l'Alfa [*Maghreb Alfa Agency*] [*North African*] (AF)

COMALFI ... Sociedad Columbiana de Control de Malezas y Fisiologia Vegetal (WGAO)

COMAMIDI ... Associazione Italiana dei Commercianti e degli Utilizzatori di Amidi Fecole e Prodotti Derivati (WGAO)

COMANATRA ... Compagnie Mauritanienne de Navigation et de Transports (WGAO)

COMANAV ... Compagnie Malienne de Navigation [*Malian Navigation Company*]

COMANAV ... Compagnie Marocaine de Navigation [*Moroccan Navigation Company*] [*Casablanca*]

COMANDOS ... Construction and Management of Distributed Office Systems [*ESPRIT*] (NITA)

COMANIGUA ... Cooperativa de Productores de Mani [*Venezuela*] (DSCA)

COMANOR ... Comite Marocain de Normalisation [*Morocco*] (WGAO)

COMAP .... Comite Maghrebin des Agrumes et Primeurs [*North African*]

COMAPAN ... Cooperativa de Maestros Panaderos [*Cooperative of Master Bakers*] [*El Salvador*] (LA)

COMAPE ... Companhia de Mecanizacao Agricola de Pernambuco [*Brazil*] (DSCA)

COMAPEG ... Compagnie Malgache de Participations et de Gestion

COMAPI... Comite d'Action pour l'Isolation et l'Insonorisation (WGAO)

COMAPIC ... Compagnie Mauritanienne pour l'Armement, la Peche, l'Industrie, et le Commerce

COMAPOCO ... Comando de Accion Politica-Conservadora [*Conservative Political Action Command*] [*Colorado*]

COMAPOPE ... Compagnie Mauritanienne Portugaise des Peches

COMAPOPE ... Compagnie Mauritano-Portugaise des Peches (WGAO)

COMAPRA ... Compagnie Marocaine de Commercialisation et de Produits Agricoles

COMAR .... Comando Aereo Regional [*Brazil*] (WGAO)

COMAR .... Committee on Man and Radiation [*IEEE*] (WGAO)

COMAR .... Committee on Man and Radiation [*National Research Council*] (NUCP)

COMAR .... Compagnie Mauritanienne des Armements

COMAR .... Companhia Mocambicana de Ar Condicionado Lda.

COMAR .... Compania Maritima Internacional [*Colombia*] (COL)

COMARAN ... Compagnie Maritime de l'Afrique Noire

COMARINE ... Compagnie Marocaine d'Agences Maritimes [*Morocco*] (MENA)

COMARNA ... Comision Nacional para la Proteccion del Ambiente y Conservacion de los Recursos Naturales [*National Committee for Environmental Protection and Conservation of Natural Resources*] [*Cuba*] (LA)

COMARSA ... Compradora de Maravilla, Sociedad Anonima [*Santiago, Chile*] (LAA)

COMA-S ... Belgian Solidarity Committee with Malaysia and Singapore

COMASCI ... Societe Commerciale d'Applications Scientifiques [*Belgium*] (WGAO)

COMASE ... Companhia Agricola de Sergipe [*Brazil*]

COMASSO ... Association of Plant Breeders of the EEC (WGAO)

COMATA ... Companhia de Mecanizacao Agricola [*Brazil*] (DSCA)

COMATAM ... Compagnie Malienne pour Tous Appareillages Mecaniques

COMATAS ... Committee for Monitoring Agreements on Tobacco Advertising and Sponsorship (WGAO)

COMATEX ... Compagnie Malienne de Textiles

COMATOR ... Comite Maghrebin de Tourisme (WGAO)

COMATRANSIT ... Compagnie Malienne de Transit

COMAUBEL ... Chambre Syndicale du Commerce Automobile de Belgique (WGAO)

COMAUNAM ... Compagnie Mauritanienne de Navigation Maritime [*Mauritanian Shipping Company*] (AF)

COMAUNAV ... Compagnie Mauritano-Algerienne de Navigation Maritime (WGAO)

COMAUR ... Societe des Commercants de Mauritanie

COMAURAL ... Comptoir Mauritano Algerien

COMBALTAP ... Allied Command Baltic Approaches [*NATO*]

COMBAT ... Association to Combat Huntington's Chorea (WGAO)

COMBISLANT ... Commander, Bay of Biscay Atlantic Subarea [*NATO*]

COMBOFLA ... Comite Boliviano de Fomento Lanero [*Bolivia*] (LAA)

COMBOIS ... Interessengemeinschaft fuehrender Holzbe- und Verarbeitungsmaschinengrosshaendler (WGAO)

COMBOIS ... Internationale Gemeinschaft fuer Holz-technologie-Transfer [*International Community for Wood-Technology Transfer*] (EAIO)

COMBRAD ... Companhia Brasileira de Racoes e Abudos [*Brazil*] (DSCA)

COMCABI ... Comunidade Cabindense

COMCANLANT ... Commander, Canadian Atlantic Subarea [*NATO*]

COMCAR ... Commonwealth Car [*Australia*]

COMCARE ... Commission for the Safety, Rehabilitation, and Compensation of Commonwealth Employees [*Australia*]

COMCEC ... Standing Committee for Commercial and Economic Cooperation [*OIC*] (WGAO)

COMCEN ... Communications Center [*NATO*] (NATG)

COMCENTLANT ... Commander, Central Atlantic Subarea [*NATO*]

ComCES .... Comitetul pentru Cultura si Educatie Socialista [*Committee for Socialist Culture and Education*] (RO)

COMCIEC ... Comunidad Cientifica Ecuatoriana [*Ecuadorian Scientific Community*] (EAIO)

COMCOL ... Confederation of Music Copyright Owners Limited [*Australia*]

COMCORDE ... Comision Coordinadora para el Desarrollo Economico [*Coordinating Committee for Economic Development*] [*Uruguay*] (LA)

COMCORDET ... Standing Committee for Coordination of Research, Development, Evaluation and Training [*REC*] [*India*] (WGAO)

COMCOS ... Comando Costeiro [*Coastal Command*] [*Air Force*] [*Brazil*]

Com D .... Commercial Division [*New South Wales Supreme Court*] [*Australia*]

COMDAC ... Comite d'Action en France

COMDESA ... Banco de Desarrolo del Paraguay (WGAO)

COMDEV ... Commonwealth Development Corporation

COMDEV ... Commonwealth Development Finance Co. [*Australia*] (ADA)

come .... Comadre [*Godmother*] [*Portuguese*]

COME ... Committee on the Ministry of Elders [*Australia*]

COME .... Conference Mondiale d'Energie (WGAO)

COMEBA ... Cooperatives des Menuisiers Burundi

COMECAFCO ... Commerciale Europeenne de Cafes et Cacaos

COMECE ... Commission des Episcopats de la Communaute Europeenne [*Association of Episcopacies of the European Community*] (EA)

COMECON ... Comite d'Entraide Economique [*North African*]

COMECON ... Council for Mutual Economic Assistance [*Also known as CEMA, CMEA*] [*Communist-bloc nations: Poland, Russia, East Germany, Czechoslovakia, Romania, Bulgaria, Hungary Dissolved 1991*]

COMEDA ... Conseil Mondial d'Ethique des Droits de l'Animal (WGAO)

COMEDOR ... Comite Permanent d'Etudes de Developpement, d'Organisation, et d'Amenagement de l'Agglomeration d'Alger [*Permanent Committee for Development, Organization, and Planning Studies for the Algiers Metropolitan Area*] (AF)

COMEFA ... Constructions Metalliques Ferronnerie d'Art

COMEL..... Comite de Coordination des Constructeurs de Machines Tournantes Electriques du Marche Commun (WGAO)

COMEL..... Consorcio de Maquinas e Electricidade Lda.

COMELEC ... Comite Maghrebin de l'Energie Electrique [*North African Electric Power Committee*] (AF)

COMELEC ... Commission on Elections [*Philippines*]

COMELEC ... Compagnie Malienne d'Electricite et d'Equipement

COMEMA ... Comite d'Expansion Economique de Marovoay

COMENER ... Comision Centroamericana de Energia [*Central American Energy Commission*] (EAIO)

COMEPA ... Comite European de Liaison du Commerce de Gros des Papiers et Cartons [*European Liaison Committee of Wholesalers of Paper and Cardboard*]   (PDAA)

COMEPA ... Companhia de Melhoramentos do Paraibuna [*Brazil*]   (DSCA)

COMEPLAST ... Compagnie Malgache de Produits Metallurgiques et Plastiques

COMERAL ... Comercial de Alimentos [*Colombia*]   (COL)

COMERCO ... Compagnie Commerciale Congolaise

COMERCOL ... Comercial Colombia [*Colombia*]   (COL)

COMERGAN ... Compania de Comercializacion del Ganado [*Colombia*]   (COL)

COMERWA ... Cooperative de Manuiserie du Rwanda

COMES..... Comite de l'Energie Solaire   (WGAO)

COMES..... Cooperation Mediterraneenne pour l'Energie Solaire

COMES..... Cooperativa de Ahorro y Credito Maizena y Empresas Similares [*Colombia*]   (COL)

COMES..... Societe Commerciale du Methane Saharien [*Saharan Methane Trading Company*] [*Algeria*]   (AF)

COMESA ... Committee on Meteorological Effect of Stratospherical Aircraft   (WGAO)

COMESTRA ... Comissao Especial de Estudo de Reforma Administrativa [*Special Commission for Studies of Administrative Reform*] [*Brazil*]   (LA)

COMET .... Collegium Medicorum Theatri   (EA)

COMET .... Comite d'Organization des Manifestations Economiques et Touristiques   (WGAO)

COMET .... Council on Middle East Trade

COMETAL ... Complexe Metallurgique Algerois

COMETAL ... Talleres de Construcciones Metalicas [*Barranquilla*]   (COL)

COMETE ... Compagnie Mauritanienne des Etudes Techniques et Economiques

COMETEC-GAZ ... Comite d'Etudes Economiques de l'Industrie du Gaz [*Economic Research Committee of the Gas Industry*]

COMETRA ... Compagnie Financiere et de Gestion pour l'Etranger

COMETRAP ... Cooperativa Metropolitana del Transporte [*Metropolitan Transport Cooperative*] [*Panama*]   (LA)

COMETT ... Community Program for Education and Training in Technology [*EC*]   (ECED)

COMEURIM ... Commission Europeenne Immigres [*Belgium*]   (WGAO)

COMEUROCAFE ... Union des Cafetiers-Limondiers de la Communaute Economique Europeene   (WGAO)

COMEX .... Commonwealth Expedition   (WGAO)

COMEX .... Compagnie Maritime d'Expertise [*Maritime Appraisal Company*] [*French*]   (WER)

COMEX .... Compagnie Mauritanienne d'Explosifs

COMEX .... Compana Exportadora Espanola   (WGAO)

COMEX .... Compania Colombiana de Comercio Exterior [*Colombian Foreign Trade Company*] [*Colombia*]   (LA)

COMEX .... New York Commodity Exchange   (WGAO)

COMEXAZ ... Comite de Mexico y Aztlan   (EA)

COMEXO ... Comite d'Exploitation des Oceans   (WGAO)

COMEXO ... Committee for Exploitation of the Oceans   (BARN)

COMEXPO ... Commerciale d'Exploitation et d'Importation

COMEXPORT ... Comercio de Exportadores Metalurgicos SA [*Colombia*]   (COL)

COMFACI ... Compagnie Maritime Africain Cote d'Ivoire   (WGAO)

COMFENALCO ... Caja de Compensacion Familiar de Fenalco [*Cucuta*]   (COL)

COMFER ... Comite Federal de Radiodifusion [*Federal Committee for Broadcasting*] [*Argentina*]   (LA)

COMGAR ... Comando Geral do Ar [*Brazilian Air Force*]

COMGAS ... Companhia Gas Estado Sao Paulo [*Sao Paulo Gas Co.*] [*Brazil*]

COMGE ... Nederlandse Vereniging van Computer Gebruikers   (WGAO)

COMHA .... Committee on Mental Health Advocacy [*Australia*]

COMHOTEB ... Compagnie Hoteliere de Bouake

COMIAC ... Islamic Standing Committee for Information and Cultural Affairs [*OIC*]   (WGAO)

COMIAO .. Compagnie Commerciale et Industrielle de l'Afrique de l'Ouest

COMIBERLANT ... Commander, Iberian-Atlantic Area [*Portuguese*]   (WER)

COMIBIOL ... Corporation Minera de Bolivia   (WGAO)

COMIBOL ... Corporacion Minera de Bolivia [*Mining Corporation of Bolivia*] [*La Paz*]   (LA)

COMIEX ... Compagnie Ivoirienne d'Import-Export

COMIEXCO ... Compania Minera Exportadora de Colombia Ltda. [*Colombia*]   (COL)

COMIG ..... Companhia Agro-Industrial Igarassu [*Brazil*]   (DSCA)

COMIGAL ... Commissariat General [*General Commissariat*] [*Cambodia*]   (CL)

COMIGEM ... Combinat Industriel de Gemens

COMIL...... Compagnie Marocaine par l'Industrie du Liege

COMIL...... Compostos Quimicos Industriais Lda.

COMILOG ... Compagnie Miniere de l'Ogooue [*Ogooue Mining Company*] [*Gabon*]   (AF)

COMIMPRA ... Compagnie Mauritanienne d'Importation de Produits Alimentaires

COMINA .. Compagnie Miniere d'Andriamena

COMINAK ... Compagnie Miniere d'Akouta [*Akouta Mining Company*] [*Niger*]   (AF)

COMINARMAR ... Compagnie Internationale d'Armement Maritime, Industriel, et Commercial

COMINES ... Comptoir des Mines Ivoiriennes

COMINFIL ... Communist Infiltration [*Name of 1960's FBI campaign against infiltrators*]

COMINFORM ... Information Bureau of Communist Parties and Workers   (WGAO)

COMINIERE ... Societe Commerciale et Miniere du Congo

COMINIF ... Irano-France Investment Company   (ME)

COMINKHMER ... Compagnie Industrielle du Cambodge [*Cambodian Industrial Company*]   (CL)

COMINKHMERE ... Compagnie Industrielle du Cambodge [*Cambodian Industrial Company*] [*Use COMIN KHMER*]   (CL)

COMINO ... Nouvelle Societe Commerciale et l'Immobiliere

COMINOA ... Comptoir des Mines et des Grands Travaux de l'Ouest Africain

COMINOR ... Complexe Minier du Nord [*Mining Complex of the North*] [*French*]   (WER)

COMINPRA ... Compagnie Mauritanienne de Produits Alimentaires

Comintern.. Communist International   (PPE)

COMIP...... Comision Mixta del Rio Parana [*Parana River Joint Commission*] [*Argentine, Brazilian, Paraguayan*]   (LA)

COMIP...... Compagnie Mauritanienne des Industries de Peches

COMIPAL ... Comision Mixta de Palmar [*Palmar Joint Commission*] [*Uruguay*]   (LA)

COMIPEZ ... Comisariato-Industria Pescados y Mariscos Congelados Ltda. [*Barranquilla*]   (COL)

COMIPHOS ... Compagnie Miniere et Phosphatiere

COMIPLAN ... Commissariat General du Plan [*General Commissariat for Planning*] [*Cambodia*]   (CL)

COMIPOL ... Comision Militar Politica [*Political Military Commission*] [*Argentina*]   (LA)

COMIR ..... Compagnie Marocaine d'Equipements Industriels et Routiers

COMIREC ... Comite Interprofessionnel de la Recuperation et du Recyclage des Papers et Cartons   (WGAO)

Comis........ Comisario [*Commissioner*] [*Spanish*]

COMISE ... Comptoir Industriel du Senegal   (WGAO)

COMISIREK ... Comite Charge de Suivre l'Evolution de l'Esprit et de l'Idee de la Republique [*Committee to Oversee the Evolution of the Spirit and the Concept of the Republic*] [*Cambodia*]   (CL)

comiso........ Comisario [*Spanish*]

COMIT ..... Banca Commerciale Italiana   (WGAO)

COMITA... Income Tax Assessment Act [*Database*] [*Australia*]

COMITAS ... Compagnia Italiana di Assicurazioni   (WGAO)

COMITEXTIL ... Comite de Coordination des Industries Textiles de la Communaute Economique Europeenne [*Coordination Committee for the Textile Industries in the European Economic Community*] [*Brussels, Belgium*]   (EAIO)

COMITRA ... Comite des Transporteurs au Congo

COMIVAL ... Cooperativa de Militares en Retiro del Valle del Cauca Ltda. [*Colombia*]   (COL)

COMIVOIRE ... La Commercile Ivoirienne

COMIZA... Communaute Islamique au Zaire [*Islamic Community of Zaire*]   (AF)

COMLA .... Commonwealth Library Association [*Australia*]   (ADA)

COMLA .... Commonwealth Library Association [*Jamaica*]   (SLS)

Comm........ Commandeur [*or Commandant*] [*Commander*] [*French*]   (MTD)

comm.......... Commentaire [*Commentary*] [*Publishing*] [*French*]

comm.......... Commente [*Annotated*] [*Publishing*] [*French*]

comm.......... Commerce [*French*]   (TPFD)

comm.......... Commercio [*Trade*] [*Italian*]

Comm........ Commission   (IDIG)

comm.......... Comparative   (TPFD)

Comm........ Jugement du Tribunal de Commerce [*Benelux*]   (BAS)

COMMAIRCENTLANT ... Commander, Maritime Air Central Subarea [*NATO*]

COMMAIRCHAN ... Commander, Allied Maritime Air Force Channel [*NATO*]

COMMAIREASTLANT ... Commander, Maritime Air Eastern Atlantic Area [*NATO*]

COMMAIRGIBLANT ... Commander, Maritime Air Gibraltar Subarea [*NATO*]   (NATG)

COMMAIRNORECHAN ... Commander, Maritime Air Northeast Subarea Channel [*NATO*]

COMMAIRNORLANT ... Commander, Maritime Air Northern Subarea [*NATO*]

COMMAIRPLYMCHAN ... Commander, Maritime Air Plymouth Subarea Channel [*NATO*]

CommArbit Loyers ... Commission Arbitrale des Loyers [*France*]   (FLAF)

CommArr Assur Soc ... Commission d'Arrondissement des Assurances Sociales [*France*]   (FLAF)

CommBanc ... Commission Bancaire [*Benelux*]   (BAS)

Commbel.... Commissarissenbelasting [*Benelux*]   (BAS)

COMMBOND ... Commonwealth Bank Bond Index [*Database*] [*Australia*]

CommBrux ... Jugement du Tribunal de Commerce de Bruxelles [*Belgium*] (BAS)
Commdr ..... Commander (EECI)
Commdt ..... Commandant (EECI)
Comm duGouv ... Commissaire du Gouvernement [*France*] (FLAF)
comment ..... Commentaar [*Commentary*] [*Publishing*] [*Netherlands*]
comment ..... Commentaire [*Commentary*] [*Publishing*] [*French*]
COMMET ... Council of Mechanical and Metal Trade Associations (WGAO)
COMMIGAL ... Commissariat General [*General Commissariat*] [*Cambodia*] (CL)
COMMIGAL MOBIGALE ... Commissariat General de Mobilisation Generale [*General Commissariat for General Mobilization*] [*Cambodia*] (CL)
CommMkt ... Common Market (DLA)
CommPrem Inst ... Commission de Premiere Instance de Securite Sociale [*France*] (FLAF)
Commr .... Commissioner (EECI)
Comm Ref .. Commission de Reforme [*France*] (FLAF)
Comm RefC Civ ... Travaux de la Commission de Reforme du Code Civil [*France*] (FLAF)
CommRegion Secur Soc ... Commission Regionale d'Appel de la Securite Sociale [*France*] (FLAF)
CommReg Sec Soc Nantes ... Commission Regionale de Securite Sociale de Nantes (FLAF)
Comm SecSoc ... Commission de Premiere Instance de la Securite Sociale [*France*] (FLAF)
CommSpec ... Commission Speciale [*France*] (FLAF)
CommSup de Cass ... Commission Superieure de la Cour de Cassation [*France*] (FLAF)
CommSup Domm Guerre ... Commission Superieure des Dommages de Guerre [*France*] (FLAF)
COMNADEFLANT ... Commander, North American Defense Force, Atlantic [*NATO*]
COMNET ... International Network of Centres for Documentation and Communication Research and Policies (EAIO)
COMNET ... International Network of Communication Documentation Centres [*Formerly, International Network of Centers for Documentation and Communication Research and Policies*] [*France*] (EAIO)
COMNET ... International Network of Documentation Centres on Communication Research and Policies (WGAO)
COMNOMET ... Corporacion Nicaraguense de Minerales No Metalicos [*Nicaraguan Corporation of Nonmetallic Minerals*] (LA)
COMNORASDEFLANT ... Commander, North American Antisubmarine Defense Force, Atlantic [*NATO*]
COMNORLANT ... Commander, Northern Atlantic Subarea [*NATO*]
COMO .... Committee of Marketing Organisations (WGAO)
COMO .... Comptoir du Mono
COMOCEANLANT ... Commander, Ocean Atlantic Subarea [*NATO*]
COMODHOR ... Comptoir Moderne d'Horlogerie
COMOROCLANT ... Commander, Maritime Forces, Morocco
COMOTEL ... Societe Comorienne de Tourisme et d'Hotellerie [*National tourist agency*] [*Comoros*]
COMOUNA ... Compagnie Commerciale de l'Ouhame-Nana
comp .... Companhia Militar [*Military Company*] [*Portuguese*]
comp .... Comparatif [*French*] (TPFD)
comp .... Comparativo [*Comparative*] [*Italian*]
comp .... Comparese [*Confer*] [*Spanish*]
Comp .... Comparez [*French*] (BAS)
comp .... Compartiments [*Panel Sections*] [*French*]
comp .... Compartimientos [*Paneled Design*] [*Publishing*] [*Spanish*]
comp .... Compilado [*Compiled*] [*Portuguese*]
comp .... Complet [*Complete*] [*Publishing*] [*French*]
COMP .... Compositor [*Printers' term*] (DSUE)
comp .... Composto [*Composed, Compound*] [*Portuguese*]
COMPA ...... College Moderne Prive d'Adzope
compa .... Compania [*Company, Society*] [*Spanish*]
COMPAC ... Commonwealth Trans-Pacific Telephone Cable [*Australia*] (ADA)
COMPAC ... Compania de Productos de Acero [*Santiago, Chile*] (LAA)
COMPACO ... Compania Profesional Agropecuaria y Comercial [*Guatemala*] (DSCA)
COMPANIC ... Complejo Paplero Nicaraguense (WGAO)
compar .... Comparativo [*Comparative*] [*Portuguese*]
COMPARE ... Companhia de Abastecimento do Recife [*Brazil*] (DSCA)
compart ...... Compartiments [*Panel Sections*] [*French*]
Compart ..... Compartimientos [*Paneled Design*] [*Publishing*] [*Spanish*]
COMPAS ... Comite por la Paz, el Anti-Imperialismo, y la Solidaridad entre los Pueblos [*Mexican Committee for Peace, Anti-Imperialism, and Solidarity among Nations*] (LA)
COMPASS ... Computer-Assisted Yeast Identification System [*AFRC Institute of Food Research*] [*Information service or system*] (IID)
COMPASS ... Computer Pruefungs-Analysesystem fuer Schulen [*German*] (ADPT)

COMPAU ... Comision Tecnica Mixta del Puente entre Argentina y Uruguay [*Joint Technical Commission for the Argentina-Uruguay Bridge*] (LA)
compe .... Compadre [*Friend*] [*Portuguese*]
COMPER ... Companhia de Desenvolvimento de Pernambuco [*Pernambuco Development Company*] [*Brazil*] (LA)
COMPESCA ... Companhia Brasileira de Pesca [*Brazil*] (DSCA)
COMPESCA ... Companhia Brasileria de Pesca (WGAO)
COMPETA ... Computer and Peripherals Equipment Trade Association (WGAO)
CompIIE .... Companion of the South African Institute of Industrial Engineers (AA)
COMPILE ... Customs On-Line Method of Preparing from Invoices Lodgeable Entries [*Australia*]
compl .... Compleet [*Complete*] [*Publishing*] [*Netherlands*]
compl .... Complement [*French*] (BAS)
compl .... Complessivo [*Including*] [*Publishing*] [*Italian*]
compl .... Complet [*Complete*] [*Publishing*] [*French*]
Compl .... Complete [*French*] (FLAF)
compl .... Completo [*Complete*] [*Italian*]
COMPLAN ... Comissao de Planejamento, Coordenacao e Desenvolvimento Social e Economico e Produtividade [*Brazil*] (WGAO)
COMPLAN ... Comissao de Planejamento, Coordenacao, e Desenvolvimento Social e Economico e Produtividade [*Brazil*] (DSCA)
COMPLANT ... China National Complete Plant Export Corp. (TCC)
COMPLES ... Cooperation Mediterraneenne pour l'Energie Solaire
compless ..... Complessivo [*Including*] [*Publishing*] [*Italian*]
COMPO .... Compensation [*Australian slang*] (DSUE)
COMPOL ... Commonwealth Police [*Australia*]
compr .... Compreso [*Including*] [*Publishing*] [*Italian*]
COMPRO ... Comite pour la Simplification des Procedures du Commerce International [*CEE*] (WGAO)
COMPROBA ... Compania de Produccion Bananera [*Banana Production Company*] [*Ecuador*] (LA)
COMPRx .. Comprehensive Prescription House Association (WGAO)
comps .... Companeros [*Companions*] [*Spanish*]
COMPSAC ... International Computer Software and Applications Conference (WGAO)
COMPSTAT ... Conference on Computational Statistics (WGAO)
compt .... Comptabilite [*Accountancy*] [*French*]
compt .... Comptant [*Cash*] [*French*] [*Business term*]
ComptesRend ... Comptes Rendus [*Proceedings*] [*French*]
COMPUMAG ... Conference on Computations of Magnetic Fields (WGAO)
COMR .... Comite Organizador del Movimiento de la Revolucion [*Organizing Committee of the Revolutionary Movement*] [*Peru*] (LA)
ComReclam ... Commission de Reclamation [*Benelux*] (BAS)
COMREG ... Commonwealth Statutory Rules [*Database*] [*Australia*]
COMREP ... Commonwealth Acts: Pamphlet Reprints [*Database*] [*Australia*]
COMRO .... Central Organisation of Military Reserve Officers [*Sweden*] (EAIO)
COMRO .... Chamber of Mines of South Africa Research Organization (EAS)
ComSAIEE ... Companion of the South African Institute of Electrical Engineers (AA)
COMSAT ... Union Internationale des Communications par Satellites [*North African*]
COMSC .... Caribbean Council of Quality Standards (WGAO)
ComSec ...... Commonwealth Secretariat (WGAO)
Com SecSoc ... Commission de Securite Sociale [*France*] (FLAF)
COMSER ... Commission on Marine Science and Engineering Research [*United Nations*] (WGAO)
COMSTATS ... Commonwealth Statistics Office [*Australia*]
COMSTECH ... Standing Committee for Scientific and Technical Cooperation [*OIC*] (WGAO)
COMSTEEL ... Commonwealth Steel Company Ltd. [*Australia*]
COMSTSELMAREA ... Commander, Military Sea Transportation Service, Eastern Atlantic and Mediterranean Area
COMSUBCOMNELM ... Commander, Subordinate Command, United States Naval Forces, Eastern Atlantic and Mediterranean
COMSUBMED ... Commander, Submarines Mediterranean
COMSUBMEDNOREAST ... Commander, Submarines Northeast Mediterranean
COMSUFRHIN ... Commander, French Rhine River Squadron [*NATO*]
Com SupCass ... Commission Superieure de Cassation [*France*] (FLAF)
Com SupPens ... Commission Superieure des Pensions de Vieillesse [*Benelux*] (BAS)
Comt .... Commandant [*Commander*] [*Military*] [*French*] (MTD)
COMTAG ... International Commission on Measurement, Theory, and Application in Geomorphology [*IGU*] [*Israel*] [*Research center*] (IRC)
COMTEC ... Compagnia Tecnica di Progettazione
COMTEC/RAT ... Comision Tecnica de la Red Andina Telecomunicaciones [*Technical Commission for the Andean Telecommunication Network*] (PDAA)
COMTEL ... Comision Nacional de Telecommunications [*Chile*] (WGAO)

COMTELCA ... Comision Tecnica de Telecomunicaciones de Centroamerica [*Technical Commission of Telecommunications in Central America*] [*Tegucigalpa, Honduras*] (LAA)

COMTOVAL ... Le Comptoir du Valo [*Senegal*]

COMTRADE ... Compressed International Trade Database [*United Nations*]

COMUF .... Compagnie des Mines d'Uranium de Franceville [*Franceville Uranium Mining Company*] [*Gabon*] (AF)

COMUNBANA ... Commercializadora Multinacional Banano (WGAO)

ComunInt ... Comunita Internazionale [*Italy*] (FLAF)

COMURHEX ... Societe pour la Conversion de l'Uranium en Metal et en Hexafluorure [*France*] (PDAA)

COMUVIR ... Institut d'Etudes Internationales de la Communication sur l'Environnement (WGAO)

COMVE .... Committee on Motor Vehicle Emissions [*Australia*] (PDAA)

CON.......... Commander of the Order of the Niger

Con............ Commission [*French*] [*Business term*]

con............ Conego [*Canon*] [*Portuguese*]

CON.......... Congo (WDAA)

CON.......... Conico [*Race of maize*] [*Mexico*]

con............ Conjunction (TPFD)

CON.......... Constantinople [*Later, Istanbul*] [*Turkey*] (ROG)

Con............ Coron [*Miner's House*] [*Military map abbreviation World War I*] [*French*] (MTD)

CON 8VA .. Con Ottava [*With the Octave*] [*Music*] (ROG)

CONA........ Comite Oceanografico Nacional [*National Oceanographic Committee*] [*Chile*] (MSC)

CONAC..... Comision Nacional de Accion Comunitaria [*Uruguay*] (WGAO)

CONAC..... Comision Organizadora Nacional de Accion Comunitaria [*Uruguay*] (DSCA)

CONAC..... Confederacion Nacional de Asentamientos Campesinos [*National Confederation of Peasant Settlements*] [*Panama*] (LA)

CONAC..... Consejo Nacional de la Cultura [*National Culture Council*] [*Venezuela*] (LA)

CONAC..... La Continentale Agricole du Cameroun (WGAO)

CONAC..... Societe la Continentale Agricole du Cameroun

CONACA .. Comision Nacional de Aqueductos y Alcantarillado [*National Waterworks and Sewerage Commission*] [*Cuba*] (LA)

CONAC-ACOR ... Comision Nacional de Accion Comunitaria y Regional [*National Organizing Commission for Community Action*] [*Uruguay*] (LAA)

CONACAJP ... Comite Nacional de Clubes Agricolas Juveniles Peru [*Peru*] (DSCA)

CONACE .. Comite Nacional pro Construccion de Escuelas [*National Committee for School Construction*] [*Guatemala*] (LA)

CONACED ... Confederacion Nacional de Centros Docentes [*Colombia*] (COL)

CONACEX ... Consejo National de Comercio Exterior [*Mexico*] (WGAO)

CONACI ... Confederacion Nacional de Comunidades Industriales [*National Confederation of Industrial Communities*] [*Peru*] (LA)

CONACIONAL ... Compania Nacional de Fosforos Ltda. [*Manizales*] (COL)

CONACO ... Confederacion Nacional de Comerciantes [*National Confederation of Merchants*] [*Peru*] (LA)

CONACO ... Confederation Nationale des Associations Congolaises

CONACO ... Convention Nationale Congolaise [*Congolese National Convention*]

CONACOLTNATORI ... Confederazoine Nazionale Coltivatori Diretti (WGAO)

CONACYT ... Consejo Nacional de Ciencia y Tecnologia [*National Council for Science and Technology*] [*ICSU*] [*Mexico*] [*Research center*] (LA)

CONACYT ... Consejo Nacional de Ciencia y Tecnologia [*National Council for Science and Technology*] [*Argentina*] (LA)

CONACYT ... Consejo National de Ciencia y Tecnologia [*National Council for Science and Technology*] [*Ecuador*] (LA)

CONADE .. Comision Nacional de Energia [*National Commission for Energy*] [*Organizacion Latinoamericana de Energia Panama*] (WED)

CONADE .. Comite Nacional de Defensa de la Democracia [*National Committee for Defending Democracy*] [*Bolivia*] (LA)

CONADE .. Consejo Nacional de Desarrollo [*National Development Council*] [*Argentina, Ecuador*] (LA)

CONADE .. Corporacion Nacional de Desarrollo [*National Development Corporation*] [*Honduras*] (LA)

Conadeca.... Comision Nacional del Cacao [*Mexico*] (EY)

CONADEF ... Comite Nacional de Desarrollo Fronterizo [*National Committee for Border Development*] [*Honduras*] (LA)

CONADEP ... Comision Nacional sobre la Desaparacion de Personas [*Argentina*] (WGAO)

CONADEP ... Conseil National de Developpement et Planification [*National Council for Development and Planning*] [*French*] (LAA)

CONADEP ... Conseil National de Developpement et Planification [*National Council for Development and Planning*] [*Haiti*] (LA)

CONADEP ... Consejo Nacional de Desarrollo y Planificacion [*National Council for Development and Planning*] [*Spanish*] (LAA)

CONADESE ... Consejo Nacional de Desarrollo y Seguridad [*National Development and Security Council*] [*Argentina*] (LA)

CONADESOPAZ ... Comite Nacional de Defensa de la Soberania y la Paz [*National Committee for the Defense of Sovereignty and Peace*] [*Panama*] (LA)

Conadi........ Corporacion Nacional de Inversiones [*National Investment Corporation*] [*Honduras*] (GEA)

CONADIN ... Corporacion Nacional de Inversiones [*National Investment Corporation*] [*Honduras*] (LA)

CONADIS ... Compania Nacional de Distribucion Ltda. [*Colombia*] (COL)

CONAE..... Consejo Nacional de Educacion [*National Education Council*] [*Uruguay*] (LA)

CONAE..... Convocatoria Nacional Empresaria [*National Business Assembly*] [*Argentina*] (LA)

CONAE-CENID ... Consejo Nacional de Educacion Centro Nacional de Informacion y Documentacion [*Uruguay*] (SLS)

CONAES... Colegio Nicaraguense de Administradores de Empresa [*Nicaraguan College of Business Managers*] (LA)

CONAF ..... Comite Nacional de Federaciones [*Trade union*] [*Chile*]

Conaf......... Corporacion Nacional Forestal [*National Forestry Corporation*] [*Chile*] (GEA)

CONAFE... Comite Nacional de Ferias [*Nicaragua*] (WGAO)

CONAFER ... Corporacion Nacional de Fertilizantes [*Peru*] (LAA)

CONAFLEMA ... Comision Nacional de Fletes Maritimos [*National Commission of the Maritime Fleet*] [*Mexico*] (LAA)

Conafrut..... Comision Nacional de Fruticultura [*Mexico*] (EY)

CONAGE.. Coordenacao Nacional dos Geologos [*Brazil*] (WGAO)

CONAHOTU ... Corporation Nacional de Hoteles y Turismo [*Venezuela*] (WGAO)

CONAI...... Comision Nacional de Asuntos Indigenas [*National Commission for Indian Affairs*] [*Costa Rica*] (LA)

CONAI...... Consultoria Agricola e Industrial [*Brazil*] (DSCA)

CONAIM.. Comision Nacional de la Industria del Maiz [*National Commission of the Corn Industry*] [*Mexico*] (LA)

CONAIN... Comision Nacional del Ano Internacional del Nino [*National Commission for the International Year of the Child*] [*Peru*] (LA)

CONAKAT ... Confederation des Associations du Katanga [*Confederation of Katangan Associations*]

CONAL..... Comision Nacional del Algodon [*National Cotton Commission*] [*Nicaragua*] (LA)

CONAL..... Comite Nacional de Asesoramiento y Legislacion [*National Legislative Advisory Committee*] [*Bolivia*] (LA)

CONALALC ... Comision Nacional de Asociacion Latinoamericana de Libre Comercio [*Latin American Free Trade Association National Commission*] [*Venezuela*] (LA)

CONALBO ... Corporacion Colegio Nacional de Abogados [*National Bar Association*] [*Colorado*] (LA)

CONALBOS ... Corporacion Colegio Nacional de Abogados [*National Bar Association*] [*Colorado*] (COL)

CONALBUSES ... Corporacion Nacional de Buses [*National Bus Corporation*] [*Colorado*] (LA)

CONALCO ... Cooperativa Nacional de Consumo Ltda. [*Colombia*] (COL)

CONALFE ... Confederacion Nacional Femenina [*National Confederation of Women*] [*Colorado*] (LA)

CONALPES ... Coonacional los Alpes Ltda. [*Colombia*] (COL)

CONALPRUN ... Cooperativa Nacional de Profesionales Unidos Ltda. [*Colombia*] (COL)

CONALTRA ... Corporacion Nacional de Transportes Ltda. (COL)

CONALVIDRIOS ... Compania Nacional de Vidrios [*Colombia*] (COL)

CONAM.... Confederacion Nacional de Municipalidades [*National Confederation of Municipalities*] [*Chile*] (LA)

CONAMAG ... Comite Nacional de Mercadeo Agropecuario [*Caracas*] [*Venezuela*] (LAA)

CONAMAR ... Consejo Nacional Maritimo [*National Maritime Council*] [*Bolivia*] (LA)

CONAMCOS ... Consejo Nacional de Comunicacion Social [*National Mass Media Council*] [*Peru*] (LA)

CONAME ... Consejo Nacional de Menores [*National Advisory Board for Minors*] [*Bolivia*] (LA)

CONAN..... Companhia de Navegacao do Norte [*Shipping company*] [*Brazil*] (EY)

CON AN.... Con Anima [*With a Soulful Feeling*] [*Music*] (ROG)

CONAN..... Consejo Nacional para el Desarrollo de la Industria Nuclear [*National Council for Development of the Nuclear Industry*] [*Venezuela*] (LA)

CONANCRA ... Comite National Contre le Racisme et l'Apartheid [*National Committee Against Racism and Apartheid*] [*Malagasy*] (AF)

CONANDEX ... Consejo Andino Exportadores (WGAO)

CONANDINA ... Confederacion Andina Industrias (WGAO)

CONANI... Consejo Nacional para la Ninez [*National Council for Children*] [*Dominican Republic*] (LA)

CONAP..... Consejo Nacional de la Publicidad [*National Council for Publicity*] [*Guatemala*] (LA)

CONAP..... Corporacion Nacional de Abastecimientos del Peru [*Peru*] (DSCA)

CONAP..... Corporation Nacional de Abastecimientos del Peru (WGAO)

CONAPAC ... Companhia Nacional de Produtos Alimenticios Cearenses [*Brazil*]   (DSCA)
CONAPAN ... Confederacion Nacional de Sindicatos de Trabajadores de la Industria del Pan, Ramos Conexos y Organismos Auxiliares [*Trade union*]   (EY)
CONAPE... Comision Nacional del Petroleo [*El Salvador*]   (WGAO)
Conape .... Comision Nacional de Petroleo [*National Petroleum Commission*] [*El Salvador*]   (GEA)
CONAPE... Consorcio Naviero Peruano [*Peru*]   (LAA)
CONAPLAN ... Consejo Nacional de Planificacion y Coordinacion Economica [*National Economic Planning and Coordination Council*] [*El Salvador*]   (LA)
CONAPOL ... Consejo Nacional Politico y Social [*National Council for Political and Social Affairs*] [*Bolivia*]   (LA)
CONAPRO ... Comite National Provisoire
CONAPRO ... Confederacion Nacional de Asociaciones Profesionales [*National Confederation of Professional Associations*] [*Nicaragua*]   (LA)
CONAPROLE ... Cooperativa Nacional de Productores de Leche [*National Milk Producers Cooperative*] [*Uruguay*]   (LA)
CONAPS... Comision Nacional de Propiedad Social [*National Social Property Commission*] [*Peru*]   (LA)
CONARA .. Comision Nacional de Reformas Administrativas [*National Administrative Reform Commission*] [*Chile*]   (LA)
CONARA .. Concilio Nacional de la Reconstrucion Administrativa [*National Council for Administrative Reconstruction*] [*Argentina*]   (LA)
CONARCA ... Comision Nacional de Renovacion de Cafetales [*National Committee for Renovating Coffee Lands*] [*Nicaragua*]   (LA)
CONARE .. Consejo Nacional de Reformas [*National Council for Structural Reforms*] [*Bolivia*]   (LA)
CONAREPA ... Comision Nacional de Recuperacion Patrimonial [*National Commission for Patrimonial Recovery*] [*Argentina*]   (LA)
CONAREX ... Consortium Africain de Realisation et d'Exploitation
CONARG ... Consejo Nacional de Registros Genealogicos [*Nicaragua*]   (DSCA)
CONART .. Consejo Nacional de Radiodifusion y Television [*National Radiobroadcasting and Television Council*] [*Argentina*]   (LA)
CONASE... Consejo Nacional de Seguridad [*National Security Council*] [*Argentina*]   (LA)
CONASEV ... Comision Nacional Supervisora de Empresas y Valores [*National Enterprises and Securities Supervisory Commission*] [*Peru*]   (LA)
CONASIDA ... Comite Nationale de Lutte Contre Le Sida [*National Committee on AIDS*] [*Panama*]   (EAIO)
CONASTIL ... Compania Colombiana de Astilleros Ltda.   (WGAO)
CONASUPO ... Compania Nacional de Subsistencias Populares [*Government Basic Commodities Company*] [*Mexico*]   (LA)
CONAT ..... Coordinadora Nacional de Agrupaciones "Augustin Tosco" [*Argentina*]
CONATEL ... Conseil National des Telecommunications [*Haiti*]   (EY)
CONATO ... Consejo Nacional de Trabajadores Organizados [*National Council of Organized Workers*] [*Panama*]
CONATON ... Comision Nacional de Toxicomania y Narcoticos [*National Commission on Addiction and Narcotics*] [*Argentina*]   (LA)
CONATRACH ... Confederacion Nacional de Federaciones y Sindicatos de Interempresas y Empresas de Trabajadores del Transporte Terrestre y Afines de Chile [*Trade union*]   (EY)
CONATRADECO ... Confederacion Nacional de Federaciones y Sindicatos de Trabajadores del Comercio de Chile [*Trade union*]   (EY)
CONATRAL ... Confederacion Nacional de Trabajadores Libres [*Dominica*]   (WGAO)
CONATRAL ... Congreso Nacional de Trabajadores Libres [*Dominican Republic*]   (DSCA)
CONATRAP ... Confederacion Nacional de Sindicatos de Trabajadores de la Industria del Plastico y Ramos Conexos [*Trade union*] [*Chile*]   (EY)
CONATRAP ... Coordinadora Nacional de Trabajadores de Prensa [*National Coordinating Board of Press Workers*] [*Argentina*]   (LA)
CONATUR ... Comite Nacional de Turismo [*National Committee on Tourism*] [*El Salvador*]   (EY)
CONAVAL ... Astilleros Construcciones Navales Ltda. [*Colombia*]   (COL)
CONAVE .. Compania Nacional de Ventas Ltda. [*Colombia*]   (COL)
CONAVI ... Confederacion Nacional de Vinateros [*Argentina*]   (LAA)
CONAVI ... Consejo Nacional de Vivienda [*National Housing Council*] [*Bolivia*]   (LA)
CONAZU ... Confederacion Nacional de Azucareros [*National Sugar Producers Confederation*] [*Chile*]   (LA)
CONBA ..... Council of National Beekeeping Assoiactions of the United Kingdom   (WGAO)
CONBOS .. Comite National Belge de l'Organisation Scientifique   (WGAO)
CONC....... Australian Conferences: Complete [*Database*]
CONC....... Comision Obrera Nacional de Catalunya [*Catalonia National Workers Commission*] [*Spanish*]   (WER)
CONCA ..... Comite Nacional de Comercializacion del Arroz [*Bolivia*]   (LAA)

CONCA ..... Consejo Nacional de Credito Agricola [*Chile*]   (LAA)
CONCAB .. Conseil du Cabinet [*Cambodia*]   (CL)
CONCACAF ... Confederacion Norte, Centroamericana, y del Caribe de Futbol [*North and Central American and Caribbean Football Confederation*]   (EAIO)
CONCACAF ... Confederacion Norte-Centro America y del Caribe de Futbol [*North and Central American and Caribbean Soccer Confederation*]   (LA)
CONCACAF ... Confederation d'Amerique du Nord d'Amerique Centrale et des Caraibes de Futbal [*Guatemala*]   (WGAO)
CONCAMIN ... Confederacion de Camaras Industriales [*Confederation of Industrial Chambers*] [*Mexico*]   (LA)
CONCAMIN ... Confederacion de Camaras Industriales de los Estados Unidos Mexicanos   (WGAO)
CONCANACO ... Confederacion de Camaras Nacionales de Comercio [*Confederation of National Chambers of Commerce*] [*Mexico*]   (LA)
CONCANACO ... Confederacion de Camaras Nacionales de Comercio Servicios y Turismo [*Mexico*]   (WGAO)
CONCAP .. Confederacion de Campesinos Peruanos [*Confederation of Peruvian Peasants*]   (LA)
CONCAP .. Consejo de Iglesias Luteranas en Centroamerica y Panama   (WGAO)
CONCAWE ... Oil Companies' European Organization for Environmental and Health Protection   (EA)
CONCE ..... Comision Nacional Coordinadora de Extension [*Venezuela*]   (DSCA)
CONCENTRAL ... Cooperativa Central de Distribucion [*Colombia*]   (COL)
CONCENTRANABANGUI ... Compagnie Nationale Centrafricaine de Navigation Maritime   (WGAO)
CONCERN ... Congregational Outreach Network Concerned with Elderly Residents of Nursing Homes
CONCERT ... Consultative Group on Certification [*CEN*] [*France*]   (WGAO)
CONCERTA ... Concessionaire de la Route Tahoua-Arlit
CONCEX .. Conselho Nacional de Comercio Exterior [*National Council on Foreign Trade*] [*Brasilia, Brazil*]   (LA)
Conciln .... Conciliation [*Australia*]
CONCIVILES ... Construcciones Civiles Ltda. [*Colombia*]   (COL)
concl .... Conclusie [*Benelux*]   (BAS)
Concl .... Conclusions [*French*]   (FLAF)
Concl .... Conclusions du Ministere Public [*Benelux*]   (BAS)
CONCLAP ... Conselho Superior das Classes Produtoras [*Higher Board of Producer Groups*] [*Brazil*]   (LA)
CONCLAT ... Conferencia Nacional das Classes Trabalhadores [*National Conference of the Working Classes*] [*Brazil*]   (LA)
CONCLAT ... Congresso Nacional de Classe Trabalhadora [*Brazil*]   (WGAO)
ConclCom Gouv ... Conclusions du Commissaire du Gouvernement [*France*]   (FLAF)
ConclContr ... Conclusions Contraires [*French*]   (FLAF)
Conc Med... Concours Medical   (FLAF)
CONCO ..... Concrete Co. [*Saudi Arabia*]   (WGAO)
CONCOM ... Council of Nature Conservation Ministers [*Australia*]
CONCORDE ... Comision Coordinadora para el Desarrollo Economico [*Uruguay*]   (WGAO)
CONCORDE ... Consejo de Coordinacion para el Desarrollo [*Coordinating Council for Development*] [*Honduras*]   (LA)
CONCORDE ... Corporacion Coordinadora para el Desarrollo Popular [*Santiago, Chile*]   (LAA)
CONCORP ... Construction Corp. [*Myanmar*]   (DS)
CONCP ..... Conference des Organisations Nationalistes des Colonies Portugaises [*Conference of National Organizations of Portuguese Colonies*]   (LA)
CONCP ..... Conferencia de Organizacoes Nacionalistas das Colonias Portuguesas [*Morocco*]
CONCRENAL ... Control Nacional de Credito [*Colombia*]   (COL)
CONCUERO ... Confecciones de Cuero Ltda. [*Colombia*]   (COL)
cond .... Condicional [*Conditional*] [*Portuguese*]
cond .... Condizione [*Condition*] [*Italian*]
cond .... Condutor [*Conductor, Driver*] [*Portuguese*]
CONDAL .. Comision Nacional de Algodon [*National Cotton Commission*] [*Ecuador*]   (LAA)
Con De .... Canon Declasse [*Military*] [*French*]   (MTD)
CONDECA ... Consejo de Defensa Centroamericana [*Central American Defense Council*] [*Guatemala, Guatemala*]   (EAIO)
CONDEMINA ... Corporacion Nicaraguense de Minas [*Nicaraguan Corporation of Mines*]   (LA)
CONDEP .. Consejo Nacional de Desarrollo Pecuario [*Brazil*]   (LAA)
CONDEP .. Conselho de Desenvolvimento da Pecuaria [*Livestock Development Council*] [*Brazil*]   (LA)
Condepa ..... Conciencia de Patria [*Bolivia*] [*Political party*]   (EY)
CONDEPALE ... Ley Organica para la Ensenanza Secundaria [*Organic Law for Secondary Education*] [*Uruguay*]   (LA)
CONDEPE ... Conselho Nacional de Desenvolvimento Pecuario [*Government advisory body*] [*Brazil*]   (EY)
CONDEPE ... Instituto de Desenvolvimento de Pernambuco [*Brazil*]   (SLS)
CONDESA ... Consorcio de Diarios Espanoles, Sociedad Anonima [*News agency*] [*Spanish*]

CONDESE ... Conselho de Desenvolvimento Economico de Sergipe [*Brazil*]

CONDEVE ... Con Devotione [*With Devotion*] [*Music*] (ROG)

CONDIMA ... Compania para el Desarrollo de la Zona Industrial de Maracaibo [*Venezuela*] (DSCA)

condiz......... Condizione [*Condition*] [*Italian*]

CONDOC ... Consortium to Develop an Online Catalog [*European Community*] (MHDB)

CONDOL ... Con Dolore [*With Sadness*] [*Music*] (ROG)

CONDOR ... Confederacion Dominicana de Religiosos (WGAO)

CONE........ Comision Obrera Nacional de Euzkadi [*Basque National Workers Commission*] [*Spanish*] (WER)

CONECI.... Consortium d'Enterprises de Cote-Ivoire (WGAO)

CONECOB ... Comite National des Experts-Comptables de Belgique (WGAO)

CONEE ..... Comision Nacional del Espacio Exterior [*National Commission for Outer Space*] [*Mexico*] (LA)

CONEFO .. Conference of the New Emerging Forces (IN)

CONELA... Confraternidad Evangelica Latinoamericana [*Confraternity of Evangelicals in Latin America*] [*Argentina*] (EAIO)

CONELCA ... Conductores Electricos de Centroamerica, SA [*Electric Conductors of Central America Corp.*] [*El Salvador*]

CONEMPA ... Consorcio de Empresas Constructoras Paraguayas [*Consortium of Paraguayan Construction Companies*] (LA)

CONEN..... Comision Nacional de Energia Nuclear [*National Nuclear Energy Commission*] [*Guatemala*] (LAA)

CONEP ..... Comissao Nacional de Estimulos e Estabilizacao de Precos [*National Commission for Incentives and Price Stabilization*] [*Brazil*] (LA)

CONEP ..... Consejo Nacional de la Empresa Privada [*National Council of Private Enterprise*] [*Panama*] (LA)

CONEPLAN ... Consejo Nacional de Economia y Planificacion [*National Economic and Planning Council*] [*Bolivia*] (LA)

CONES...... Consejo Nacional Economicoe Social [*Argentina*] (WGAO)

CONES...... Consejo Nacional Economico y Social [*National Economic and Social Council*] [*Argentina*] (LA)

CONESCAL ... Centro Regional de Construcciones Escolares para America Latina [*Mexico*] (LAA)

CONESCAR ... Convenio de Cooperacion Tecnia Estadistica y Cartograffa [*Peru*] (WGAO)

CONESG... Companhia Nordestina de Servicos Gerais [*Brazil*] (LAA)

CONESP... Companhia Nordestina de Sondagens e Perfuracoes [*Brazil*] (LAA)

CONESPR ... Con Espressione [*With Expression*] [*Music*]

CONESTCAR ... Convenio de Cooperacion Tecnica Estadistica y Cartografia [*Peru*] (DSCA)

CONESTUDIOS ... Construcciones y Estudios Ltda. [*Colombia*] (COL)

CONET ..... Consejo Nacional de Educacion Tecnica [*National Technical Education Council*] [*Argentina*] (LA)

CONET ..... National Council of Technical Training [*Argentina*]

CONEXITO ... Concentrados Exitos Ltda. [*Colombia*] (COL)

CONF........ Australian Conferences: Current [*Database*]

conf............. Conferatur [*Compare*] [*French*]

CONF........ Conferences in Energy, Physics, and Mathematics [*Fachinformationszentrum Karlsruhe GmbH*] [*Germany*] [*Information service or system*] (CRD)

Conf............ Conforme [*French*] (FLAF)

CONFACT ... Confederation of Australian Capital Territory Industry

CONFAGRICOLTURA ... Confederazione Generale dell'Agricoltura Italiana (WGAO)

CONFAPI ... Confederazione Italiana della Piccola e Media Industria [*Small and Medium Industry*] (EY)

CONFCOMMERCIO ... Confederazione Generale Italiana del Commercio e del Turismo (WGAO)

CONFCONSIRZI ... Confederazione Italiana Coltivatori (WGAO)

CONFCOOP ... Confederazione Cooperative Italiana (WGAO)

CONFCOOPERATIVE ... Confederazione Cooperative Italiane [*Cooperative Confederation of Italy*] (EY)

CONFECAMARAS ... Confederacion Columbiana de Camaras de Comercio (WGAO)

CONFECAMARAS ... Confederacion de Camaras de Comercio [*Confederation of Chambers of Commerce*] [*Colombia*] (LA)

Confed........ Confederation (SCAC)

CONFEDEM ... Confederacion Nacional de Empresarios de la Mineria y de la Metalurgia [*Industrial association*] [*Spain*] (EY)

CONFEDILIZIA ... Confederazione Italiana della Proprieta Edilizia [*Property and Building*] (EY)

CONFEDORAFI ... Unione Italiana delle Federazioni Nazionali ed Associazioni Territoriali di Categoria tra Fabbricani, Commercianti, Artigiani, Orafi, Gioellieri, Argentieri,Orologiai, Banci Metalli Preziosi, Pietre Preziose (WGAO)

CONFEJES ... Conference des Ministres de la Jeunesse et des Sports des Pays d'Expression Francaise

CONFEMEN ... Conference des Ministres d'Education National des Pays d'Expression Francaise

CONFEMEN ... Conference des Ministres de l'Education des Pays d'Expression Francaise

CONFEMETAL ... Confederacion Espanola de Organizaciones Empresariales del Metal [*Spain*] (EY)

CONFEN .. Consello Federal de Entorpecentes [*Brazil*] (WGAO)

CONFENACOOP ... Confederacion Nacional de Cooperativas [*National Confederation of Cooperatives*] [*Peru*] (LA)

CONFER... Confederacion Espanola de Religiosos (WGAO)

CONFER... Confederacion Nicaraguense de Escuelas Catolicas [*Nicaraguan Confederation of Catholic Schools*] (LA)

CONFER... Conferencia de Religiosos de Nicaragua (WGAO)

CONFER... Consejo de Superioras Mayores de Argentina (WGAO)

CONFER... Consejo Federal de Radiodifusion [*Federal Broadcasting Council*] [*Argentina*] (LA)

CONFEREMO ... Conferencia das Religiosas [*Mozambique*] (WGAO)

CONFERH ... Conferencia de Religiosos de Honduras (WGAO)

CONFERRE ... Conferencia de Religiosos de Chile (WGAO)

CONFERS ... Confederacion de Religiosos de El Salvador (WGAO)

CONFETRA ... Confederazione Generale del Traffico e dei Transporti (WGAO)

CONFICOMARC ... Confederazione Italiana Commercianti Agenti Rappresentanti di Commercio (WGAO)

CONFIEP ... Confederacion de Empresas Privadas [*Confederation of Private Businesses*] [*Peru*] (EY)

CONFIEP ... Confederacion Nacional de Instituciones de la Empresa Privada [*Peru*] (WGAO)

CONFIGI.. Confiturerie de Gihindamuyaga

CONFIN ... Consejo de Fomento e Investigaciones Agricolas [*Chile*] (LAA)

CONFINDUSTRIA ... Confederazione Generale dell'Industria Italiana (WGAO)

CONFINORTE ... Corporacion Financiera del Norte [*Barranquilla*] [*Colorado*] (LAA)

CONFISIA ... Confederazione Italiana dei Sindacati Ingegneri e Architetti (WGAO)

CONFITARMA ... Confederazione Italiana degli Armatori Liberi (WGAO)

Confl .... Arret du Tribunal des Conflits [*France*] (FLAF)

confl .... Confluent [*Tributary*] [*French*]

CONFORM ... Continuous Forms Manufacturers Association of South Africa (PDAA)

CONFRATEL ... Compagnie Francaise des Telephones (WGAO)

CONFREGUA ... Confederacion de Religiosos de Guatemala (WGAO)

CONFUO ... Con Fuoco [*With Force*] [*Music*] (ROG)

CONFUR ... Con Furia [*With Fury*] [*Music*] (ROG)

cong.......... Congiunzione [*Conjunction*] [*Italian*]

Cong........... Congolese

CONGEMAR ... Confederacion de Gente de Mar, Maritimos, Portuarios, y Pesqueros de Chile [*Trade union*] (EY)

CONGITA ... Confederation General Italienne de la Technique Agricole (WGAO)

CONGO .... Conference of Non-Governmental Organisations in Consultative Status with UNESCO (WGAO)

CONGO .... Conference on Non-Governmental Organizations in Consultative Status with the United Nations Economic and Social Council (EAIO)

CONGOBOIS ... Compagnie Congolaise des Bois

CONGOLAP ... Societe Congolaise d'Appareillage Electrique (WGAO)

CONGO-MECA ... Societe Congolaise de Mecanographie

CONGOMER ... Societe Congolaise de Commerce

CONGONA ... Compagnie Congolaise de Navigation

CONGOOD ... Confederation of Non-Governmental Organizations for Overseas Development

CONGRA ... Con Grazia [*With Grace*] [*Music*] (ROG)

CONGU ... Council of National Golf Unions (WGAO)

CONGUST ... Con Gustoso [*With Taste*] [*Music*] (ROG)

CONI........ Comitato Olimpico Nacionale Italiano (WGAO)

CONIA ...... Consejo Nacional de Investigaciones Agricolas [*Venezuela*] (DSCA)

CONIA ...... Consejo Nacional de Investigaciones Agricoles [*Venezuela*] (WGAO)

CONIAC ... Construction Industry Advisory Committee [*HSE*] (WGAO)

CONIBIR.. Corporacion Nicaraguense de Bienes Raices [*Nicaraguan Corporation of Real Estate*] (LA)

CONICET ... Consejo Nacional de Investigaciones Cientificas y Tecnologicas [*National Council for Scientific and Technological Research*] [*ICSU*] [*Argentina*] (LA)

CONICIT .. Consejo Nacional de Investigaciones Cientificas y Technologicas [*Costa Rica*] (EAIO)

CONICIT .. Consejo Nacional de Investigaciones Cientificas y Tecnologicas [*National Council for Scientific and Technological Research*] [*ICSU*] [*Research center*] [*Venezuela*] (LA)

CONICYT ... Comision Nacional de Investigacion Cientifica y Tecnologica [*National Commission for Scientific and Technological Research*] [*Chile ICSU*] [*Research center*] (LA)

CONICYT ... Consejo Nacional de Investigaciones Cientificas y Tecnicas [*National Council for Scientific and Technical Research*] [*Uruguay*] (EAS)

CONIDA ... Comision Nacional de Investigacion y Desarrollo Aerospacial [*National Commission for Aerospace Research and Development*] [*Peru*] (PDAA)

CONIE ...... Comision Nacional de Investigacion del Espacio [*National Space Research Commission*] [*Spanish*]

CONIEL.... Compagnia Imprese Elettriche dell'Eritrea

CONIEXCO ... Compagnie Nigerienne d'Expansion Commerciale

CONIF....... Corporacion Nacional de Investigaciones Foretales [*National Corporation for Forestry Research*] [*Colorado*] (LA)

CONIF....... National Corporation for Forestry Research and Development in Colombia (WGAO)

CONINAGRO ... Confederacion Intercooperativa Agropecuaria [*Argentina*] (WGAO)

CONINAGRO ... La Confederacion Intercooperativa Agropecuaria [*Agricultural and Livestock Intercooperative Confederation*] [*Argentina*] (LA)

CONINDUSTRIA ... Consejo Venzolano de la Industria (WGAO)

CONIP ...... Consejo Nacional de la Iglesia Popular [*El Salvador*] (WGAO)

CONIRGUA ... Cooperativa de Servicios Agropecuarios Nirgua RL [*Venezuela*] (DSCA)

CONISTO ... Comite National Inter-Syndical du Togo [*Inter-Union National Committee of Togo*] (AF)

CONITAL ... Consorzio Italiano Allevatori (WGAO)

CONITE.... Comision Nacional de Inversiones y Tecnologia Extranjeras [*National Commission for Foreign Investments and Technology*] [*Peru*] (LA)

CONITO ... Comite National Intersyndical du Togo

conj............ Conjonction [*French*] (TPFD)

conj............ Conjuncao [*Conjunction*] [*Portuguese*]

conj............ Conjuntivo [*Subjunctive*] [*Portuguese*]

CONLAC .. Empresa Consolidada de Industria Lactea [*Dairy Industry Consolidated Enterprise*] [*Cuba*] (LA)

CONLARDEPE ... Confederacion Latinoamericana de Expendedores de Derivados del Petroleo [*Latin American Confederation of Oil Derivative Merchants*] (LA)

CONLATINGRAF ... Confederacion Latinoamericana de la Industria Grafica y Afines [*Buenos Aires, Argentina*] (LAA)

CONLATINGRAF ... Latin American Confederation of the Graphics Industry (WGAO)

CONMEBOL ... Confederacion Sudamericana de Futbol [*Peru*] (WGAO)

CONMETAL ... Construcciones Metalicas SA [*Bucaramanga*] (COL)

CON MO... Con Moto [*With the Movement*] [*Music*] (ROG)

ConNSW ... Conservatorium of Music, New South Wales [*Australia*]

CONNT..... Connaissement [*Bill of Lading*] [*Legal term*] [*French*]

CONOBRAS ... Compania Constructora de Obras de Ingenieria Ltda. [*Colombia*] (COL)

CONOCA ... Consejo Centroamericano de Organizaciones Campesinas [*Central American Council of Peasant Organizations*] (LA)

CONOCO ... Continental Oil Company

CONORTE ... Comision Coordinadora para la Zona Norte [*Chile*] (DSCA)

CONOTON ... Centro Nacional de Narcoticos y Sustancias Peligrosas [*National Center for Narcotics and Dangerous Drugs*] [*Argentina*] (LA)

Conpan....... Consejo Nacional para la Alimentacion y la Nutricion [*National Council for Food and Nutrition*] [*Chile*] (GEA)

CONPANCOL ... Compania Consultante Panamericana de Colombia Ltda. [*Colombia*] (COL)

CONPES... Consejo Nacional de Politica Economica y Social [*National Economic and Social Policy Council*] [*Colorado*] (LA)

CON-PLAC ... Contreplacages, Placages Camerounais

CONPROBA ... Consorcio de Productores Bananeros [*Ecuador*] (DSCA)

CONREDEC ... Consulting, Research, and Development Centre [*Cyprus Professional Engineers' Association*]

CONRUB.. Comision Nacional de Reordenamiento de la Universidad Boliviana [*National Council for Restructuring the Bolivian University*] (LA)

CONS .... Central Obrera Nacional Sindicalista [*National Workers Trade Union Confederation*] [*Of Hedillist tendency*] [*Spanish*] (WER)

Cons .... Conseil [*Council*] [*French*] (DLA)

Cons .... Conseiller [*Councillor, Judge*] [*French*] (ILCA)

Cons .... Consejo [*Council*] [*Spanish*]

cons .... Conselheiro [*Counselor, Adviser*] [*Portuguese*]

CONS .... Conservative and Unionist Party [*British*] [*Political party*]

cons .... Conservato [*Well-Preserved*] [*Publishing*] [*Italian*]

Cons .... Conservatoire [*Conservatory*] [*French*]

cons .... Conservazione [*State of Preservation*] [*Publishing*] [*Italian*]

cons .... Conserve [*Preserved*] [*French*]

Cons .... Considerant [*Whereas, In View*] [*French*] (ILCA)

cons .... Consoante [*Consonant*] [*Portuguese*]

Cons .... Consultez [*French*] (BAS)

CONSAFRIQUE ... Consortium European pour le Developpement des Ressources Naturelles de l'Afrique

CONSAL... Conference of Southeast Asian Librarians (ADA)

CONSAL... Congress of Southeast Asian Librarians (EAIO)

CONSALD ... Committee on South Asian Libraries and Documentation [*Australia*] (ADA)

CONSANE ... Conselho Nacional de Saneamento Basico [*National Basic Sanitation Council*] [*Brazil*] (LA)

CONSAS... Constellation of Southern African States [*South Africa*]

CONSCARIBE ... Compania Constructora del Caribe Ltda. [*Colombia*] (COL)

ConsConst ... Conseil Constitutionnel [*Constitutional Council*] [*French*] (DLA)

Consd'Adm ... Conseil d'Administration (FLAF)

Cons d'Et ... Conseil d'Etat [*French*]

Consd'Etat ... Arret ou Avis du Conseil d'Etat [*French*] (BAS)

CONSEMACh ... Confederacion de Sindicatos de Empleadores Agricolas de Chile [*Confederation of Unions of Agriculture Employers*] (LA)

CONSEMP ... Consultores de Empresas [*Rio De Janeiro, Brazil*] (LAA)

CONSENA ... Consejo de Seguridad Nacional [*Uruguay*] (WGAO)

CONSENSUS ... Cooperative North Scandinavian Enalapril Survival Study [*Medicine*]

CONSEPP ... Confederacion de Servidores Publicos del Peru [*Confederation of Civil Servants of Peru*] (LA)

conservaz.... Conservazione [*State of Preservation*] [*Publishing*] [*Italian*]

CONSFA... Consejo Superior de Fomento Agropecuario [*Higher Council for Agricultural and Livestock Development*] [*Chile*] (LA)

Cons Fam... Conseil de Famille (FLAF)

CONSICOL ... Confederacion Sindical de Colombia [*Trade Union Confederation of Colombia*] [*Colombia*] (LA)

CONSIDER ... Conselho Nacional de Nao-Ferrosos e de Siderurgica [*Brazil*] (WGAO)

CONSIDER ... Conselho Nacional de Nao-Ferrosos e Siderurgia [*National Nonferrous Metals and Steel Council*] [*Brasilia, Brazil*] (LA)

CONSIGUA ... Confederacion Sindical de Guatemala [*Guatemalan Trade Union Confederation*] (LA)

CONSILP ... Confederazione Sindacale Italiana Libere Professioni [*Liberal Professions*] (EY)

CONSILP ... Confederazione Sindicale Italiana Liberi Professionisti (WGAO)

Cons IntPref ... Conseil Interdepartemental de Prefecture (FLAF)

CONSINTRA ... Conselho Sindical dos Trabalhadores [*Labor Union Council*] [*Brazil*] (LA)

CONSISAL ... Consejo Sindical Salvadoreno [*Salvadoran Trade Union Council*] (LA)

ConsNP...... Conservative Nationalist Party [*Australia*] [*Political party*]

ConsNSW ... Conservatorium of Music, New South Wales [*Australia*]

conso .... Consejo [*Council*] [*Spanish*]

conso .... Conselheiro [*Counselor, Adviser*] [*Portuguese*]

CONSOB .. Commissione Nazionale per le Societa e la Borsa [*National Commission for Companies and the Stock Exchange*] [*Italian counterpart of the American Securities and Exchange Commission Milan*] (WER)

CONSOM ... Federation Syndicale des Consommateurs (WGAO)

CONSORPERSCA ... Consorzio Nazionale fra Cooperative Pescatori ed Affini (WGAO)

Cons Perf... Arrete du Conseil de Prefecture [*France*] (FLAF)

CONSPLAN ... Conselho do Planejamento [*Planning Council*] [*Brazil*] (LA)

ConsPrud'h Jonzac ... Conseil de Prud'hommes de Jonzac (FLAF)

Cons Rep.... Conseil de la Republique [*France*] (FLAF)

Cons SupInstr Publ ... Conseil Superieur de l'Instruction Publique [*France*] (FLAF)

Const .... Constitucion [*Constitution*] [*Spanish*]

Const .... Constitution [*Benelux*] (BAS)

Constit........ Constitution (FLAF)

constl........ Constitucional [*Constitutional*] [*Spanish*]

constr .... Construcao [*Construction, Building*] [*Portuguese*]

Constr .... Construction [*Construction*] [*French*]

CONSTRAL ... Construtores Associados Lda.

CONSTRONIC ... Conference on Mechanical Aspects of Electronic Design (WGAO)

CONSTRUIMPORT ... Empresa Cubana Importadora de Maquinarias y Equipos de Construccion [*Cuban Enterprise for the Import of Construction Machinery and Equipment*] (LA)

CONSTRUNAVES ... Asociacion de Constructores Navales Espanoles (WGAO)

CONSTRUNAVES ... Constructores Navales Espanoles [*Madrid, Spain*]

Cons Tut .... Conseil des Tutelles (FLAF)

CONSUCASA ... Constructora de Casas Consucasa Ltda. [*Colombia*] (COL)

CONSUEL ... Comite National pour la Securite des Usagers de l'Electricite [*National Committee for the Safety of Users of Electricity*] [*France*] (PDAA)

CONSULT ... Community, Industry, Accounting and Legal Consultants [*Database*] [*Australia*]

CONSULTEC ... China Economic and Trade Consultants Corp. (TCC)

CONSULTECA ... Consultora Tecnico Administrativa Ltda. [*Colombia*] (COL)

CONSUMIMPORT ... Empresa Cubana Importadora de Articulos de Consumo General [*Cuban Enterprise for the Import of General Consumer Goods*] (LA)

CONSUPE ... Consejo Superior de Planificacion Economica [*Supreme Council for Economic Planning*] [*Comayaguela, Honduras*] (LAA)

Consuplane ... Consejo Superior de Planificacion Economica [*Supreme Council for Economic Planning*] [*Comayaguela, Honduras*] (GEA)

CONSUPLANE ... Consejo Superior de Planification Economica [*Honduras*] (WGAO)

CONSURCO ... Cooperativa Surcolombiana Ltda. [*Colombia*] (COL)

CONSUSENA ... Consejo Superior de Seguridad Nacional [*National Security Council*] [*Chile*] (LA)

Consw......... Wet tot Regeling van de Bevoegdheid der Consulaire Ambtenaren tot Hetopmaken van Burgerlijke Akten en van de Consulaire Rechtsmacht [*Benelux*] (BAS)

CONT........ Centralni Odbor Narodne Tehnike [*Central Committee of the People's Technology Society*] [*YU*]

Cont............ Contabilidade [*Bookkeeping*] [*Portuguese*]

Cont............ Contador (SCAC)

cont............. Contemptuous (TPFD)

cont............. Contenant [*Containing*] [*Publishing*] [*French*]

cont............. Continuer [*Continue*] [*Knitting*] [*French*]

CONT....... Continuo [*Thorough Bass*] [*Music*]

CONTAG .. Confederacao Nacional dos Trabalhadores na Agricultura [*National Farmworkers Confederation*] [*Brasilia, Brazil*] (LA)

CONT(AH) ... Continent, Antwerp-Hamburg Range [*Shipping*] (DS)

CONTAP... Conselho de Cooperacao Tecnica da Alianca para o Progresso [*Alliance for Progress Technical Cooperation Council*] [*Brazil*] (LA)

CONT(BH) ... Continent, Bordeaux-Hamburg Range [*Shipping*] (DS)

CONTCOP ... Confederacao Nacional dos Trabalhadores em Comunicacoes e Publicidade [*Communications and Advertising Workers Confederation*] [*Brazil*] (EY)

CONTEC... Confederacao Nacional dos Trabalhadores nas Empresas de Credito [*National Confederation of Credit Institution Workers*] [*Brazil*] (LA)

CONTEC... Confederacion de Trabajadores Establecimientos Bancarios y Credito [*Confederation of Workers of Banks and Credit Firms*] [*Uruguay*] (LA)

CONTEF... Consultoria Tecnica de Assuntos Economicos e Financeiros [*Technical Office for Economic and Financial Affairs*] [*Brazil*] (LA)

CONTEL... Conselho Nacional de Telecomunicacoes [*National Telecommunications Council*] [*Brazil*] (LA)

contemp...... Contemporain [*Contemporary*] [*French*]

contemp...... Contemporaneo [*Contemporary*] [*Italian*]

CONTEXTIL ... Confederacion Nacional de Federaciones y Sindicatos de Trabajadores Textiles y Ramos Similares y Conexos de Chile [*Trade union*] (EY)

CONT(HH) ... Continent, Havre-Hamburg Range [*Shipping*] (DS)

CONTICyT ... Comision Nacional de Investigacion Cientifica y Technologica [*Chile*] (WGAO)

CONTIGUMMI ... Continental Gummi-Werke Aktiengesellschaft [*Continental Rubber Works Joint Stock Company*]

contin .... Continuo [*Continuous*] [*Italian*]

CONTINENTAL-SENEGAL ... Continental Oil Company of Senegal

CONTONAP ... Societe Beninoise de Distribution d'Appareils Electriques (WGAO)

contr .... Contracao [*Contraction*] [*Portuguese*]

Contra .... Contraire [*French*] (BAS)

CONTRA .. Contrario [*Opponent or Enemy*] [*Spanish*]

Contra .... Solution Contraire (FLAF)

contraff....... Contraffazione [*Counterfeit*] [*Publishing*] [*Italian*]

CONTRAGUA ... Confederacion de Trabajadores de Guatemala [*Confederation of Guatemalan Workers*] (LA)

CONTRAN ... Conselho Nacional Transito [*National Traffic Council*] [*Brazil*] (LA)

CONTRANAL ... Cooperativa de Transportes Nacionales de Pamplona Ltda. (COL)

Contr Dir.... Contributions Directes (FLAF)

Contr Ind.... Contributions Indirectes (FLAF)

Cont Syn .... Contact Syndical [*Benelux*] (BAS)

CONTTMAF ... Confederacao Nacional dos Trabalhadores em Transportes Maritimos, Fluviais, e Aereos [*Trade union*] [*Brazil*] (EY)

CONUAR ... Combustibles Nucleares Argentinos, SA [*Argentine Nuclear Fuel Corporation, Inc.*] (LA)

CONUB..... Conferencia de la Universidad Boliviana [*Conference of the Bolivian University*]

CONUCOD ... Conferencia de las Naciones Unidas sobre Comercio y Desarrollo (WGAO)

CONUEP .. Consejo Nacional de Universidades y Escuelas Politecnicas [*Ecuador*]

CONUP..... Consejo Nacional de la Universidad Peruana [*National Council of Peruvian Universities*] (LA)

CONUPIA ... Confederacion Gremial Nacional Unida de la Mediana y Pequena Industria Serviciosy Artesanado [*Chile*] (WGAO)

CONUPIA ... Confederacion Nacional Unica de la Pequena Industria y el Artesanado [*National Single Confederation of Small Industry and Crafts*] [*Chile*] (LA)

CONUPRO ... Consejo Nacional Provisorio de Universidades [*National Provisional Council of Universities*] [*Venezuela*] (LA)

CONURBANAS ... Compania Colombiana de Construcciones Urbanas SA [*Colombia*] (COL)

CONUS ..... Comite Nacional de Unidad Sindical Guatemalteca (WGAO)

CONUS ..... Consejo Nacional de Unidad Sindical [*National Committee for Trade Union Unity*] [*Guatemala*]

CONUTEC ... Consultores Uruguayos en Tecnologia Avanzada [*Uruguayan Advanced Technology Consultants*] (LA)

Conv .... Convention [*French*] (BAS)

conv .... Converti [*Converted*] [*French*]

conv .... Convex [*Convex*] (HU)

CONVELE ... Consejo Venezolano de la Leche [*Venezuela*] (WGAO)

CONVELE ... Consejo Venezolano de la Leche [*Venezuela*] (DSCA)

CONVER .. Conferencia Venezolana de Relgiosos (WGAO)

CONVERS ... Conversazione [*Conversation*] [*Italian*] (ROG)

CONVERTA ... Suomen Paperin-J ja Kartonginjalostajain Yhdistys (WGAO)

Conv FJ...... European Community Convention on the Jurisdiction of the Courts and Enforcement of Judgments in Civil and Commercial Matters [*27 Sept. 1968*] (DLA)

convte .... Conveniente [*Convenient*] [*Spanish*]

CONZUPLAN ... Consejo Zuliano de Planificacion y Coordinacion [*Venezuela*] (SLS)

CONZUPLAN ... Consejo Zuliano de Planificacion y Promocion [*Venezuela*] (LAA)

COO .... Chief of Outpost [*CIA officer in charge of a field office*]

COO .... Commissie van Openbare Onderstand [*Benelux*] (BAS)

COO .... Cotonou [*Benin*] [*Airport symbol*] (OAG)

COOB....... Barcelona Olympic Organizing Committee (OLYM)

COOC....... Calgary Olympic Organizing Committee [*Calgary, AB*] (EAIO)

COOCHOTAS ... Empresa de Transporte de la Cooperativa de Taxis del Atlantico [*Barranquilla*] (COL)

COOD .... Centralny Osrodek Oswiaty Doroslych [*Adult Education Center*] (POL)

COOEMSAVAL ... Cooperativa de Ahorro y Credito de Empleado de Salud del Valle [*Colombia*] (COL)

COOFAVA ... Cooperativa Quimica Farmaceutica del Valle del Cauca [*Colombia*] (COL)

COOFOR .. Cooperativa Forestal de Produccion y Servicio [*Chile*] (DSCA)

COOGRANCOL ... Cooperativa Grancolombiana de Credito Ltda. [*Colombia*] (COL)

COOHACREDITO ... Cooperativa de Habitaciones y Credito Ltda. [*Colombia*] (COL)

COOL........ Canberra's Own Outstanding List [*Children's book awards*] [*Australia*]

COOL-CAT ... CAVAL [*Cooperative Action by Victorian Academic Libraries*] Operated Online Catalogue [*Australia*]

COOMEVA ... Cooperativa de Ahorro y Credito Medico del Valle [*Colombia*] (COL)

COOMPOR ... Cooperativa de Mao-de-Obra do Pessoal de Trafego Portuario [*Port Traffic Employees Labor Cooperative*] [*Portuguese*] (WER)

COONACOVEN ... Confederacion Nacional de Cooperativas de Venezuela [*Venezuela*] (DSCA)

COONACOVEN ... Societe Cooperative Forestiere d'Administration et de Gestion (WGAO)

COONORTE ... Cooperativa Nortena de Transportes [*Colombia*] (COL)

COOP........ Comite de Organizaciones Populares [*Committee for People's Organizations*] [*Peru*] (LA)

COOP........ Cooper [*Botanical region*] [*Australia*]

COOP........ Cooperativa, Preduzece za Uvoz i Izvoz Poljoprivrednih Proizvoda i Stocne Hrane [*Cooperative for Import and Export of Agricultural Products and Fodder*] (YU)

coop............ Cooperativo [*Cooperative*] [*Spanish*]

COOPAHA ... Cooperative Agricole de Houin-Agame

COOPANCOL ... Cooperativa de Panificadores de Colombia [*Colombia*] (COL)

COOPANKAM ... Cooperative Agricole des Planteurs du Nkam

COOPASEL ... Cooperativa de Pequenos Agricultores de Sisal del Estado de Lara [*Venezuela*] (COL)

COOPCAHN ... Cooperative des Planteurs de Cafe Arabica du Haut-Knam [*Cameroon*] (WGAO)

COOPEINDUMA ... Cooperativa de Trabajadores de la Industria de la Madera Ltda. [*Colombia*] (COL)

COOPEMAD ... Cooperatives de Moudjahidine et Ayants-Droit

COOPENAGRO ... Cooperativa Nacional de Mercadeo Agropecuario Limitada [*Colombia*] (DSCA)

COOPENAL ... Cooperativa Nacional de Creditos y Servicios Especiales Ltda. [*Colombia*] (COL)

COOPENGAGRO ... Cooperativa Nacional de Mercadeo Agropecuario Limitada [*Colombia*] (WGAO)

COOPENORTE ... Cooperativa de Transportes del Norte de Santander [*Cucuta*] (COL)

COOPERADIAL ... Cooperativa Radial Colombiana Ltda. [*Colombia*] (COL)
COOPERMAROC ... Societe Marocaine de Cooperation Pharmaceutique
COOPERTOLCA ... Cooperativa de Transportadores y Transportes del Norte del Tolima y Oriente de Caldas Ltda. (COL)
COOPESA ... Cooperative de la Solidarite Africaine
COOPETRA ... Cooperative de Travaux Publics et Particuliers du Cameroun
COOPETRABAN ... Cooperativa de Trabajadores de Antioquia Ltda. [*Colombia*] (COL)
COOPHARMA ... Cooperation Pharmaceutique Khmere [*Cambodian Pharmaceutical Cooperative*] (CL)
COOPI ... Cooperative Ouvriere Publication Impression [*Tunisia*]
COOPIBO ... Cooperation en Developpement Internationale Bouworde [*Belgium*] (WGAO)
COOPIGRA ... Cooperativa de Provision para Industriales Graficos, Ltda. [*Argentina*] (LAA)
COOPILLANTAS ... Cooperativa de Trabajadores de Icollantas [*Colombia*] (COL)
COOPLAINIERE ... Cooperative Lainere de l'ile de France (WGAO)
COOPLEG ... Co-Operative Legislation [*ILO*] [*United Nations Information service or system*] (DUND)
CO-OPPLABAM ... Cooperative des Planteurs Bamilike
COOPRODUTTS ... Groupement Cooperatif de Ventes Internationales des Produits du Burkina Faso (WGAO)
COOPTRANSCART ... Cooperativa Especializada de Transportes de Carga [*Colombia*] (COL)
coopver ... Cooperatieve Vereniging [*Benelux*] (BAS)
Coopw ... Wet tot Regeling der Cooperatieve Vereenigingen [*Benelux*] (BAS)
COORBUQUIN ... Cooperativa de Buses Urbanos del Quindio Ltda. [*Armenian*] (COL)
COORCOM ... Comite de Coordination des Hauts Fonctionnaires des Pays du Sud-Est Asiatique sur les Transports et Communications [*Southeast Asian High-Level Government Employees Coordination Committee on Transportation and Communication*] [*Use COORDCOM*] (CL)
coord ... Coordenativa [*Portuguese*]
CoordAPR ... Verzameling van de Samengeordende Onderrichtingen Betreffende de Aanvullende Personele Belasting [*Benelux*] (BAS)
Coord BB ... Verzameling van de Samengeordende Onderrichtingen Betreffende de Bedrijfsbelasting [*Benelux*] (BAS)
COORDCOM ... Comite de Coordination des Hauts Fonctionnaires des Pays du Sud-Est Asiatique sur les Transports et Communications [*Southeast Asian High-Level Government Employees Coordination Committee on Transportation and Communication*] (CL)
CoordMB ... Verzameling van de Samengeordende Onderrichtingen Betreffende de Mobilienbelasting [*Benelux*] (BAS)
CoordwetSoc Verz ... Coordinatiewet Sociale Verzekering [*Benelux*] (BAS)
COOTRAINGASCOL ... Cooperativa de Ahorro y Credito de Trabajadores de la Industria Gaseosa de Colombia [*Colombia*] (COL)
COOTRANSAL ... Cooperativa de Transportadores de Saldana Ltda. (COL)
COOTRANSHUILA ... Cooperativa de Transportes de Huila [*Neiva*] (COL)
COOTRANSO ... Cooperativa de Transportadores de Soacha [*Colombia*] (COL)
COOTRANSPAL ... Cooperativa Integral de Transportadores Palmeras Ltda. [*Palmira*] (COL)
COOTRANSUCOL ... Cooperativa de Transportadores Unidos de Colombia Ltda. [*Colombia*] (COL)
COOTRAVAL ... Cooperativa de Trabajadores del Valle Ltda. [*Colombia*] (COL)
COOV ... Centraal-Orgaan voor de Ongevallen-Verzekering [*Benelux*] (BAS)
COP ... Centralny Okreg Przemyslowy [*Central Industrial District*] (POL)
COP ... Central Optique Photo
COP ... Centre d'Orientation Pratique [*Practical Work Orientation Center*] [*Mali*] (AF)
COP ... Centre Oceanologique du Pacifique [*French*] (MSC)
COP ... Combined Opposition Party [*Pakistan*] [*Political party*] (FEA)
COP ... Comite Olimpico Peruano [*Peruvian Olympics Committee*] (LA)
COP ... Commissie Ontwikkelings-Plan [*NOBIN*]
COP ... Commissie Opvoering Produktiviteit [*SER*] [*Netherlands*]
Cop ... Commission on Privatization [*Philippines*]
COP ... Companias de Orden Publico [*Public Order Companies*] [*Panama*] (LA)
COP ... Conference of the Parties [*Governments which have ratified UN climate change convention of 1992*]
COp ... Congregatio pro Operariis Christianis a Sancto Josepho Calasantio (WGAO)
COP ... Consejo Obrero del Paraguay [*Trade union*] [*Paraguay*]
COP ... Contactgroep Opvoering Productiviteit (WGAO)
Cop ... Copacabana [*Record label*] [*Brazil*]
cop ... Copertina [*Cover*] [*Publishing*] [*Italian*]
cop ... Copiado [*Portuguese*]

COPA ... Canadian Office Products Association
COPA ... Comite des Organisations Professionnelles Africoles de la Communaute Economique Europeenne [*Benelux*] (BAS)
COPA ... Comite des Organisations Professionnelles Agricoles de la CEE [*EEC*] (FLAF)
COPA ... Compania Panamena de Aviacion (WGAO)
COPA ... Compania Panamena de Aviacion SA [*Panama*] (EY)
Copa ... Copacabana [*Record label*] [*Brazil*]
COPABA ... Confederacion Panamericana de Basquetbol (WGAO)
COPAC ... Comite Mixte pour la Promotion de l'Aide aux Cooperatives [*FAO*] (WGAO)
COPAC ... Committee on Publications and Communications [*International Council of Scientific Unions*]
COPAC ... Community Patent Appeal Court [*EEC*] (WGAO)
COPACA ... Congresos Panamericanos de Carreteras (WGAO)
COPACAR ... Corporacion Paraguaya de Carnes [*Asuncion, Paraguay*] (LAA)
COPACE ... Comite des Peches pour l'Atlantique Centre-Est [*Committee for the Eastern Central Atlantic Fisheries - CECAF*] [*Senegal*] (MSC)
COPACEL ... Confederation Francaise de l'Industrie des Papiers Cartons et Celluloses (WGAO)
COPACI ... Cooperative des Planteurs d'Ananas de la Cote-D'Ivoire
COPACO ... Commission de Peches pour l'Atlantique Centre-Ouest (WGAO)
COPACO ... Commission des Pecheries de l'Atlantique Centre-Ouest [*West Central Atlantic Fisheries Commission - WECAFC*] [*French*] (ASF)
COPADI ... Compagnie de Participations and Developpement Industriel [*France*]
COPAGRO ... Companhia Paraense de Mecanizacao Industrializacao e Comercializacao Agropecuaria [*Brazil*] (WGAO)
COPAL ... Agencia Comercial de Porto Amelia
COPAL ... Cocoa Producers Alliance (AF)
COPAL ... Comision de Industrias de Productos Alimenticios, de Bebidas, y Afines [*Commission of Foods, Drinks, and Related Products*] [*Argentina*] (LA)
CO PAL ... Counts Palatine [*Rulers of historical region now part of Germany*]
COPAM ... Companhia Portuguesa de Amidos [*Portuguese Amide Company*] (WER)
COPAMO ... Consorcio Paulista de Monomero SA [*Brazil*]
COPAN ... Consejo por la Paz y Amistad con Nicaragua [*Council for Peace and Friendship with Nicaragua*] [*Honduras*] (LA)
COPAN ... Consorzio Fabbricanti Compensati Paniforti Listellari e Affini (WGAO)
COPANT ... Comision Panamericana de Normas Tecnicas [*Pan American Standards Commission - PASC*] (EAIO)
COPANU ... Compania Paraguaya de Navegacion de Ultramar [*Paraguay*] (LAA)
COPAP ... Commission Permanente de l'Administration Publique [*Permanent Public Administration Commission*] [*Zaire*] (AF)
COPAR ... Comite Parisien des Oeuvres Scolaires et Universitaires [*Parisian Committee for Assistance to Universities and Schools*] (WER)
COPARCO ... Societe Congolaise de Perfumerie et Cosmetiques (WGAO)
COPAREX ... Compagnies de Participations, de Recherches, et d'Exploitations Petrolieres [*Petroleum Investments, Research, and Exploitation Company*] [*Algeria*] (AF)
COPARMEX ... Confederacion Patronal de la Republica Mexicana [*Employers Confederation of the Mexican Republic*] (LA)
COPARROZ ... Cooperativa de Productores de Arroz de Tacuarembo [*Uruguay*] (WGAO)
COPAS ... Companhia Paulista de Adubos [*Brazil*] (DSCA)
COPAS ... Cooperativa de Pesca Atlantica de Santos [*Brazil*] (DSCA)
COPASA ... Companhia Paranaense de Silos e Armazens [*Brazil*] (DSCA)
COPASCO ... Confecciones de Papel Shellmar de Colombia SA [*Colombia*] (COL)
COPASOPRI ... Comite Panameno de Solidaridad con Puerto Rico [*Panamanian Committee of Solidarity with Puerto Rico*] (LA)
COPAT ... Comite pro Autodeterminacion Tecnologica [*Committee for Technological Self-Determination*] [*Venezuela*] (LA)
COPATRA ... Cooperativa Antioquena de Transportadores Ltda. (COL)
COPAVIO ... Cooperativa de Agentes Viajeros [*Colombia*] (COL)
COPCIA ... Centrul de Organizare Calcul, si Perfectionare a Cadrelor pentru Industria Alimentara [*Center for the Computer Organization and Advanced Training of Cadres for the Food Industry*] (RO)
COPCIZ ... Comite Permanent des Congres Internationaux de Zoologie (WGAO)
COPCO ... Committee on Consumer Policy [*ISO*] (WGAO)
COPCON ... Comando de Operacoes do Continente [*Continental Operations Command*] [*Portugal*]
COPE ... Cadena de Ondas Populares Espanola [*Broadcasting organization*]
COPE ... Coastal Observation Program - Engineering [*Australia*]
COPE ... Commission on Public Ethics [*Australia*]

COPE .... Compagnie Orientale des Petrole d'Egypte [*Egyptian-Italian Oil Company*]

COPE .... Compagnie Orientale des Petroles [*Egypt*] (WGAO)

Cope .... Congress of the People [*South Africa*] [*Political party*] (PPW)

COPEBRAS ... Companhia Petroquimica Brasilieira [*Brazil*] (PDAA)

COPEBUSES ... Cooperativa de Transportes Medellin-Bello Ltda. (COL)

COPEC ...... Compania de Petroleos de Chile [*Chilean Oil Company*] (LA)

COPEC ...... Conference of Politics, Economics and Christianity (WGAO)

COPECI .... Conserveries et Pecheries de la Cote-D'Ivoire

COPECIAL ... Comite Permanent des Congres Internationaux pour l'Apostolat des Laics [*Permanent Committee of International Congresses for the Lay Apostolate*] [*Italy*]

COPECO... China Offshore Platform Engineering Corp. (TCC)

COPECODECA ... Comision Permanente del Consejo de Defensa Centroamericano [*Permanent Commission of the Central American Defense Council*] (LA)

COPECOL ... Cooperativa Colombiana de Transportes [*Colombia*] (COL)

COPEDESMEL ... Comision Permanente de Planeamiento del Desarrollo de los Metales Livianos [*Permanent Commission for Planning the Development of Light Metals*] [*Argentina*] (LA)

COPEDIP ... Compagnie Petroliere d'Interets and de Participations

COPEFA ... Compagnie des Petroles France-Afrique [*France-Africa Petroleum Company*] [*Algeria*] (AF)

COPEFA ... Consejo Permanente de la Fuerza Armada [*Permanent Council of the Armed Forces*] [*El Salvador*] (LA)

COPEG...... Companhia Progresso do Estado da Guanabara [*Guanabara State Progress Company*] [*Brazil*] (LA)

COPEGAN ... Cooperativa de Transportadores de Ganado [*Villavicencio-Bogota*] (COL)

COPEI .... Comite de Organizacion Politica Electoral Independiente [*Committee of Independent Political Electoral Organization*] [*Use Social Christian Party*] [*Venezuela*] (LA)

COPEL ...... Companhia Paranasense de Energia Eletrica [*Brazil*] (WGAO)

COPEL ...... Spanish Prisoners' Trade Union (PD)

COPEMA ... Compagnie Eburneenne des Peches Maritimes

COPEMACO ... Corporacion Civil de Medianos y Pequenos Agricultores de Colombia [*Colombia*] (COL)

COPEMAR ... Compagnie de Peche et de Mareyage (WGAO)

COPEMAR ... Cooperative des Pecheurs Maritimes [*Maritime Fishermen's Cooperative*] [*Cambodia*] (CL)

COPEMAR ... Societe Congolaise de Peches Maritimes [*National fishing industry*] [*Congo*]

COPEMCI ... Conference Permanente Mediterraneenne pour la Cooperation Internationale [*Standing Mediterranean Conference for International Cooperation*] (EA)

COPEMH ... Colegio de Profesores de Educacion Media de Honduras [*Professional Association of High School Teachers of Honduras*] (LA)

COPEN ..... Comite Permanente de Emergencia Nacional [*Permanent National Emergency Committee*] [*Honduras*] (LA)

COPENAL ... Cooperativa Nacional de Choferes [*Colombia*] (COL)

COPENE... Companhia Petroquimica do Nordeste SA [*Brazil*]

COPENO .. Companhia de Pesca do Nordeste [*Brazil*] (DSCA)

COPENOR ... Compagnie Petrochimique du Nord [*QGPC*] [*Qatar*] (MENA)

COPENUR ... Comite Permanent pour l'Enrichissement de l'Uranium [*CCE*] (WGAO)

COPEP ...... Commission Permanente de l'Electronique au Commissariat General du Plan (WGAO)

COPERBO ... Companhia Pernambucana de Borracha Sintetica [*Pernambuco Synthetic Rubber Company*] [*Brazil*] (LAA)

COPERCANA ... Cooperativa dos Plantadores de Cana do Oeste do Estado de Sao Paulo [*Brazil*] (DSCA)

COPERE ... Comite de Programacion Economica y de Reconstruccion [*Economic Programing and Reconstruction Institute*] [*Chile*] (LAA)

COPERS ... Commission Preparatoire Europeenne de Recherches Spatiales [*European Preparatory Commission for Space Research*]

COPERSUCAR ... Cooperativa dos Produtores de Acucar e do Alcool do Estado de Sao Paulo [*Sao Paulo Cooperative of Sugar and Alcohol Producers*] [*Brazil*] (LA)

copert .... Copertina [*Cover*] [*Publishing*] [*Italian*]

COPESA ... Consorcio Periodistico de Chile, SA [*Chilean Newsmen's Association, Inc.*] (LA)

COPESA ... Corporacion Pesquera Ecuatoriana [*Ecuadorean Fishing Corporation*] (LA)

COPESBRA ... Companhia de Pesca do Norte do Brasil [*Brazil*] (DSCA)

COPESCA ... Proyecto Integrado de Turismo [*Integrated Tourism Project*] [*Peru*] (LA)

COPESCAL ... Comision de Pesca Continental para America Latina [*Commission for Inland Fisheries of Latin America*] [*FAO*] [*Italy*] (ASF)

COPESUL ... Companhia Petroquimica do Sul SA

COPESVAL ... Compania Pesquera del Valle [*Colombia*] (COL)

COPETAO ... Compagnie des Petroles Total Afrique Ouest [*French*]

COPETRAN ... Cooperativa Santandereana de Transportes Ltda. [*Colombia*] (COL)

COPEVA... Companhia de Produtos de Petroleo e Derivados [*Brazil*] (DSCA)

COPEXO... Comite pour l'Expansion de l'Huile d'Olive (WGAO)

COPEXTEL ... Corporacion Productora y Exportadora de Tecnologia Electronica [*Cuba*] (EY)

COPFS ...... Canberra One Parent Family Support, Birthright [*Australia*]

COPIA .... Centrala Obslugi Przedsiebiorstw i Instytucji Artystycznych [*Center of Services to Art Enterprises and Agencies*] (POL)

COPIBAT ... Compagnie de Promotion Immobiliere et d'Industrialisation du Batiment [*Ivory Coast*] (WGAO)

COPICA.... Comite de Propagande pour les Industries et les Commerces Agricoles et Alimentaires (WGAO)

COPIDER ... Comite de Promotores de Investigaciones para el Desarrollo Rural [*Mexico*] (WGAO)

COPILA .... Conselho de Produtores e Industriais de Leite de Alegrete [*Brazil*] (DSCA)

COPIME... Cooperativa de Pequenos Industriales Metalarios [*Colombia*] (COL)

COPIMETAL ... Cooperativa de Industrias Metalurgicas del Valle [*Colombia*] (COL)

COPISEE ... Conference Permanente des Ingenieurs du Sud-Est de l'Europe (WGAO)

COPIZ .... Conseil Permanent de l'Informatique au Zaire [*Permanent Data Processing Council in Zaire*] (AF)

COPLAG... Comissao de Planejamento Agropecuario [*Brazil*] (LAA)

COPLAMAR ... Coordinacion General del Plan Nacional de Zonas Deprimidas y Grupos Marginados [*General Coordinating Board of the National Plan for Depressed Areas and Marginal Groups*] [*Mexico*] (LA)

COPLAN... Comissao de Planejamento Nacional [*National Planning Commission*] [*Brazil*] (LA)

COPLAN... Development Planning Commission [*Brazil*] (WGAO)

COPLANAR ... Construccion, Planificacion, Arquitectura [*Colombia*] (COL)

COPLANARH ... Comision del Plan Nacional de Aprovechamiento de los Recursos Hidraulicos [*Commission for the National Plan of Water Resources Development*] [*Venezuela*] (LA)

COPLASTIC ... Compagnie Generale Industrielle de Plastiques [*Morocco*]

COPMEC ... Comite des Petites et Moyennes Entreprises Commerciales des Pays de la CEE (WGAO)

COPMEC ... Comite des Petites et Moyens Enterprises Commerciales [*Committee of Small and Medium Commercial Enterprises*] [*EEC*] (PDAA)

COPNEU .. Compagnie Industrielle du Pneumatique [*Cameroon*] (WGAO)

COPNEU .. Compagnie Industrielle et Commerciale du Pneumatique

COPO .... Centralny Osrodek Przygotowan Olimpijskich [*Olympic Games Arrangements Center*] [*Poland*]

COPOL ..... Council of Polytechnic Librarians (WGAO)

COPORTCHAD ... Cooperative des Transporteurs Tchadiens

COPPAL ... Conferencia Permanente de Partidos Politicos de America Latina [*Permanent Conference of Latin American Political Parties*] (LA)

COPPE ...... Coordenacao dos Programas de Pos-Graduacao em Engenharia [*Coordination of Postgraduate Programs in Engineering*] [*Brazil*] (LA)

COPPSO ... Conference of Professional and Public Service Organisations (WGAO)

COPQ .... Committee on Overseas Qualifications [*Australia*] (WGAO)

COPR .... Centre for Overseas Pest Research

COPR .... Comision Permanente para la Racionalizacion Administrativa [*Permanent Commission for Administrative Efficiency*] [*Argentina*] (LA)

COPRA ...... Conference of Private Residents Associations (WGAO)

COPRA ...... Les Constructeurs Professionnels Associes [*Ivory Coast*] (WGAO)

COPRACAM ... Societe Industrielle du Coprah Camerounais

COPRAF ... Compagnie des Produits d'Afrique

COPRAI .... Comissao de Produtividade da Associaco Industrial Portuguesa [*Productivity Committee of the Portuguese Industrial Association*] (PDAA)

COPRAM ... Companhia Progresso do Amapa [*Brazil*] (WGAO)

COPRAPOSE ... Confederacion Panamericana de Productores de Seguros [*Venezuela*] (WGAO)

COPRAQ .. Cooperative Programme of Research on Aquaculture [*FAO*] (WGAO)

COPREFA ... Comite de Prensa de las Fuerzas Armadas [*Press Committee of the Armed Forces*] [*El Salvador*] (LA)

COPREFIL ... Empresa Comercial y de Producciones Filatelicas [*Cuba*] (EY)

COPRIN.... Comision de Productividad Precios e Ingresos [*Venezuela*] (WGAO)

COPROA .. Comptoir des Produits Africains

COPROARTE ... Cooperativa Nacional de Profesiones, Artes, Oficios, e Industrias Ltda. [*Colombia*] (COL)

COPROBIC ... Comite National pour la Protection des Biens Culturels en Cas de Conflit Arme [*National Committee for the Protection of Cultural Property in Case of Armed Conflict*] [*Cambodia*] (CL)

COPROCI ... Compagnie des Produits de la Cote-D'Ivoire

COPRODE ... Consejo Provincial de Desarrollo [*Buenos Aires, Argentina*] (LAA)
COPRODUITS ... Groupement Cooperatif de Ventes Internationales des Produits de Haute
COPROMA ... Compagnie des Produits du Mali
COPRON .. Comissao de Coordenacao da Protecao ao Programa Nuclear Brasileiro [*Coordinating Commission for Protecting the Brazilian Nuclear Program*] (LA)
COPRONA ... Compania Productora Nacional de Aceites [*National Production Company of Edible Oils*] [*Chile*] (LA)
COPRO-Niger ... Societe Nationale de Commerce et de Production du Niger [*National Trade and Production Company of Niger*] (AF)
COPROPAR ... Cooperativa Limitada de Cultivadores de Papas del Estado Lara [*Venezuela*] (DSCA)
COPRORIBU ... Cooperative des Producteurs du Riz au Burundi
COPROSA ... Comision de Promocion Social de la Iglesia [*Nicaragua*]
COPS........ Centre of Policy Studies [*Australia*]
COPS-A..... Chief of Operations - Army [*Australia*]
COPSA...... Compania Oleaginosa del Peru SA [*State Vegetable Oil Company of Peru, Inc.*] (LA)
COPTAL ... Comite Permanente Tecnico para Asuntos del Asuntos del Trabajo Latinoamerica (WGAO)
COPTAL ... Comite Permanente Tecnico para Asuntos del Trabajo, America Latina (LAA)
COPUOS... Committee on the Peaceful Uses of Outer Space [*United Nations*] (WGAO)
COPUS...... Committee on the Public Understanding of Science (WGAO)
COPVIDU ... Conferencia Permanente Centroamericana de Vivienda y Desarrollo Urbano [*Permanent Conference on Central American Housing and Urban Development*] (LA)
COPWE..... Commission for Organizing the Party of the Working People of Ethiopia (PD)
COPYME ... Corporacion de la Pequena y la Mediana Empresa [*Small and Medium Enterprise Corporation*] [*Argentina*] (LA)
COQ........... Conquista [*Brazil*] [*Airport symbol*] (OAG)
coq.............. Coquatur [*Cook*] [*Pharmacy*]
COR.......... Calabar-Ogoja-Rivers
COR.......... Ceska Odborova Rada [*Czech Trade Union Council*] (EY)
CoR.......... Club of Rome [*France*] (EAIO)
COR.......... Comite de Organizaciones Revolucionarias [*Committee of Revolutionary Organizations*] [*Peru*] (LA)
COR.......... Committee of the Regions [*Belgium*] (ECON)
COR.......... Commonwealth Oil Refineries Ltd. [*Australia*] (ADA)
COR.......... Confederacion Obrera Revolucionaria [*Revolutionary Labor Confederation*] [*Mexico*] (LA)
COR.......... Conferencia de Religiosos de Puerto Rico (WGAO)
COR.......... Cordoba [*Argentina*] [*Airport symbol*] (OAG)
cor .... Coroa [*Crown*] [*Portuguese*]
Cor .... Corolario [*Corollary*] [*Portuguese*]
cor .... Corollaire [*Corollary*] [*French*]
COR.......... Departamento de Orientacion Revolucionaria [*Revolutionary Orientation Department*] [*See DOR*] [*Cuba*] (LA)
CORA .... Coconut Oil Refiners Association [*Philippines*]
CORA .... Cooperatives de Reforme Agraire [*Agrarian Reform Cooperatives*] [*Algeria*] (AF)
CORA .... Corporacion de Reforma Agraria [*Agrarian Reform Corporation*] [*Chile*] (LA)
CORAA ..... Council of Regional Arts Associations (WGAO)
CORACREVI ... Corporacion de Ahorro y Credito para la Vivienda [*Housing Savings and Loan Corporation*] [*Venezuela*] (LA)
CORAD..... Construtora Radio Electrica Lda.
CORADEP ... Corporacion de Radiodifusion del Pueblo [*People's Radio Broadcasting Corporation*] [*Nicaragua*] (LA)
CORAL...... Colombian Oil Refiners Additives Limitada [*Colombia*] (COL)
CORAL...... Consorcio Geral de Comercio Limitada
CORAL...... Corporacion Algodonera del Litoral [*Cotton Corporation of the Coast*] [*Colorado*] (LA)
CORAL...... Corporation of Coastal Cotton Growers [*Colombia*] (WGAO)
CORAM .... Colles et Resines Adhesives du Midi [*French*]
CORANORD ... Compagnie Regionale d'Applications Mecanographiques de Nord [*German*] (ADPT)
CORAPRO ... Controle-Radioprotection [*Nuclear energy*] [*Belgium*] (NRCH)
CORAT ..... Christian Organisations Research and Advisory Trust (WGAO)
CORAUTO ... Corporacion Automotora Ltda. [*Colombia*] (COL)
CORB .... Children's Overseas Reception Board [*Australia*]
CORB .... Chiropractors'and Osteopaths' Registration Board [*Victoria*] [*Australia*]
CORC .... Central Organisation for Rural Cooperatives [*Iran*] (WGAO)
CORC .... Central Organization for Rural Co-Operatives of Iran [*Founded in 1963*] [*Teheran*] (MENA)
CORCOP... Corporacion Comercial del Pueblo [*People's Commercial Corporation*] [*Nicaragua*] (LA)
CORD........ Centre for Organisational Research and Design [*University of New South Wales*] [*Australia*]
CORD........ Collegium Orbis Radiologiae Docentium [*Italian*] (SLS)
cord .... Cordoni [*Bands*] [*Publishing*] [*Italian*]

CORDA..... Coronary Artery Disease Research Organization (WGAO)
CORDAC .. Corporation Radiodiffusion de l'Afrique Centrale
CORDE ..... Corporacion de Empresas Estatales [*State Enterprise Corporation*] [*CEE Dominican Republic*] [*See also*] (LA)
CORDE ..... Corporacion Dominicana de Empress Estatales (WGAO)
CORDECO ... Corporacion de Desarrollo de Cochabamba [*Development Corporation of Cochabamba*] [*Bolivia*] (LA)
CORDECRUZ ... Corporacion Regional de Desarrollo de Santa Cruz [*Bolivia*]
CORDELLANOS ... Corporacion de Desarrollo de los Llanos Orientales [*Colombia*] (DSCA)
CORDEMEX ... Cordeleria Mexicana [*Mexico*] (DSCA)
CORDENTAL ... Corporacion Dental Ltda. [*Colombia*] (COL)
CORDEPAZ ... Corporacion Regional de Desarrollo de la Paz [*Bolivia*] (WGAO)
CORDES... Comite d'Organisation des Recherches Appliquees sur le Developpement Economique et Social (WGAO)
CORDI ...... Comite Consultatif pour la Recherche et le Developpement Industriels [*CCE*] (WGAO)
CORDINA ... Coordinadora Industrial [*Colombia*] (COL)
CORDIPLAN ... Oficina de Coordinacion y Planificacion [*Office of Coordination and Planning*] [*Venezuela*] (LA)
CORDIVENTAS ... Coordinadora de Ventas Ltda. [*Colombia*] (COL)
CORE .... Centre for Operation Research and Econometrics
CORE .... Coalition of Residents for the Environment [*Australia*]
CORE .... Committee [*or Congress*] on Racial Equality
CORE .... Common Register of Development Projects [*United Nations*]
CORE .... Confederation of Rhodesian Employers
CO-RE....... Co-Respondent (DSUE)
CORE .... CSIR Committee on Research Expenditure
CORE .... International Centre of Operations Research and Econometrics (WGAO)
COREB...... Conference des Ordinaires du Rwanda et du Burundi
CORECA... Comite pour la Reunification du Camaroon [*Committee for the Reunification of the Cameroons*]
CORECI .... Compagnie de Regulation et de Controle Industriel [*France*] (PDAA)
COREDE... Communaute Romande de l'Economie d'Entreprise (WGAO)
COREDIAL ... Comite Regional Encargado del Convenio de Convalidacion de Estudios, Titulas y Diplomas de Educacion Superior en America Latina y El Caribe (WGAO)
COREDIF ... Compagnie de Realisations d'Usines de Diffusion Gazeuse [*Gaseous Diffusion-Factory Construction Company*] [*French*] (WER)
COREDIF ... Compagnie de Recherche et d'Etude sur la Diffusion Gazeuse [*Gaseous Diffusion Research Company*] [*French*] (WER)
COREDO .. Commercants Reunis de Diedieng
COREG ..... Compagnie de Recherches Geophysiques [*North African*]
COREGA .. Constructions et Realisations au Gabon
CORELCA ... Corporacion Electrica de la Costa Atlantica [*Electric Corporation of the Atlantic Coast*] [*Colorado*] (LA)
COREM .... Compagnie Rwandaise d'Exploitation Miniere
COREM .... Conferences Regionales de Metiers (WGAO)
COREMA ... Corporacion de Repuestos y Maquinaria Ltda. [*Colombia*] (COL)
COREMO ... Comite Revolutionnaire du Mocambique [*Mozambique Revolutionary Committee*] (AF)
COREN ..... Combustibili per Reattori Nucleari [*A nuclear power company*] [*Italian*]
COREN ..... Council of Registered Engineers of Nigeria
COREPER ... Commission of Representants Permanents [*Committee of Permanent Representatives*] [*EEC*]
CORES...... Coal Ore Reserves Evaluation System
CORESTA ... Centre de Cooperation pour les Recherches Scientifiques Relatives au Tabac [*Cooperation Center for Scientific Research Relative to Tobacco*] [*Paris, France*] (EA)
COREZI.... Comite pour la Renovation de la Ville de Ziguinchor
CORFACO ... Comptoir Franco-Comorien
CORFIN.... Corporacion Financiera de Nicaragua [*Nicaraguan Financial Corporation*] (LA)
CORFINA ... Corporacion Financiera Nacional [*National Financial Corporation*] [*Guatemala*] (LA)
CORFINANSA ... Corporacion Financiera de Santander [*Bucaramanga*] (COL)
CORFIRA ... Corporacion Financiera de la Reforma Agraria [*Peru*] (DSCA)
CORFO ..... Corporacion de Fomento de la Produccion [*Production Development Corporation*] [*Chile*] (LA)
CORFODEC ... Corporacion de Fomento del Centro [*Central Development Corporation*] [*Ecuador*] (LA)
CORFONOR ... Corporacion de Fomento del Norte [*Northern Development Corporation*] [*Ecuador*] (LA)
CORFOP... Corporacion Forestal del Pueblo [*People's Forestry Corporation*] [*Nicaragua*] (LA)
CORFUCI ... Cooperative Agricole de Production Bananiere et Fruitiere de Cote-D'Ivoire
CORGI ...... Confederation for the Registration of Gas Installers (WGAO)
CORH........ Committee on Operations Research-Hungary [*MTA*] (WGAO)

CORHABIT ... Corporacion de Servicios Habitacionales [*Housing Services Corporation*] [*Chile*]   (LA)
CORI .... Compagnia Ricerche Idrocarburi [*or Idrocarburanti*] [*Italian*]
CORICAFRIC ... Comptoir de Representation Industrielle et Commerciale en Afrique
CORINA-CARACAS ... Corredores Internacionales Asociados Caracas, CA [*Venezuela*]
CORINCA ... Corporacion Industrial Centroamericana, SA [*Industrial Corporation of Central America*] [*El Salvador*]
CORIP .... Comite de Recherches de l'Industrie Pharmaceutique [*Belgium*]   (WGAO)
CORIS .... Computerized Registry Information System [*UNIDO*] [*United Nations*]   (DUND)
CORLAM ... Corporacion de Desarrollo de Lambayeque [*Peru*]   (DSCA)
CORMA .... Corporacion Chilena de la Mandera   (WGAO)
CORMA .... Corporacion Chilena de Madera [*Chilean Lumber Corporation*]   (LA)
CORMU.... Corporacion de Mejoramiento Urbano [*Urban Renewal Corporation*] [*Chile*]   (LA)
corn .... Cornice [*Border*] [*Publishing*] [*Italian*]
CORNICAL ... Corporacion Nacional de Industriales del Calzado [*Colombia*]   (COL)
COROI ...... Comptoir de Commerce et de Representation pour l'Ocean Indien [*Bank of Commerce and Representation for the Indian Ocean*] [*Malagasy*]   (AF)
Corp .... Corp.   (PWGL)
CORP .... Corporacion para el Fomento de Investigaciones Economicas [*Colombia*]   (WGAO)
CORPA...... Corporacion Publicitaria Nacional [*Venezuela*]
CORPAC... Corporacion de Aeropuertos y Aviacion Comercial [*Airports and Commercial Aviation Corporation*] [*Peru*]   (LA)
CORPAC... Corporacion Peruana de Aeropuertos y Aviacion Comercial   (WGAO)
CORPACERO ... Corporacion del Acero [*Colombia*]   (COL)
CORPAGUAS ... Corporacion de Agua Potable y Alcantarillado [*Potable Water and Sewerage Corporation*] [*Bolivia*]   (LAA)
CORPAL ... Corporacion Proveedora de Instituciones de Asistencia Social [*Colombia*]   (COL)
CORPE...... Comite de la Revolucion Peruana [*Committee of the Peruvian Revolution*]   (LA)
CORPECOM ... Corporacion Colombiana de Pequenos Comerciantes [*Colombian Small Businessmen's Association*]   (LA)
CORPESCA ... Corporacion de Pesca [*Fishing Corporation*] [*Chile*]   (LA)
CORPLIB ... Corporate Library and Information Service [*City of Melbourne Libraries*] [*Australia*]
Corpn .... Corporation   (EECI)
CORPOANDES ... Corporacion de los Andes [*Andes Corporation*] [*Venezuela*]   (LA)
CORPOBUSES ... Corporacion de Buses Urbanos del Departamento del Valle [*Colombia*]   (COL)
CORPOFRUT ... Corporacion de Productores de Frutas de Rio Negro [*Argentina*]   (LAA)
CORPOINDUSTRIA ... Corporacion de Desarrollo de la Pequena y Medina Industria [*VNZ*]   (WGAO)
CORPOINDUSTRIA ... Corporacion para el Desarrollo de la Pequena y Mediana Industria [*Venezuela*]
CORPOMERCADEO ... Corporacion de Mercadeo Agricola [*Venezuela*]   (WGAO)
CORPOPULAR ... Corporacion Financiera Popular SA [*Colorado*]
CORPORIENTE ... Corporacion de Desarrollo de la Region Nor-Oriental [*Venezuela*]
CORPOSANA ... Corporacion de Obras Sanitarias [*Sanitary Works Corporation*] [*Paraguay*]   (LAA)
CORPOTURISMO ... Corporacion de Turismo de Venezuela [*Venezuelan Tourist Corporation*]
CORPOVEN ... Subsidiary of PETROVEN [*4*]   (LA)
CORPOZULIA ... Corporacion de Desarrollo de la Region del Zulia [*Venezuela*]
CORPRAGRO ... Corporacion Agricola del Valle del Cauca [*Colombia*]   (COL)
CORPROCOM ... Cooperativa de Produccion y Consumo de Cali Ltda.   (COL)
CORPSA ... Corporacion Papelera [*Nicaragua*]   (WGAO)
CORPUNO ... Corporacion de Fomento y Desarrollo de Puno [*Puno Promotion and Development Corporation*] [*Peru*]   (LA)
Corr............ Correctionele Rechtbank [*Benelux*]   (BAS)
corr............. Correctionnel   (FLAF)
corr............. Corregido [*Corrected*] [*Publishing*] [*Spanish*]
Corr........... Correspondentieblad der Broederschap van Notarissen [*Benelux*]   (BAS)
corr............. Corretto [*Corrected*] [*Italian*]
corr............. Corrige [*Corrected*] [*Publishing*] [*French*]
Corr........... Jugement du Tribunal Correctionnel [*Benelux*]   (BAS)
corr............. Korrigiert [*Corrected*] [*German*]   (GCA)
Corr........... Tribunal Correctionnel [*Court of First Instance in Penal Matters*] [*Belgium*]   (ILCA)

CORRA ..... Council for Partnership on Rice Research in Asia [*A consortium of agricultural research institutes*]
Corr Blad ... Correspondentieblad van de Broederschap der Notarissen in Nederland [*Netherlands*] [*Benelux*]   (BAS)
Corr Brux... Jugement du Tribunal Correctionnel de Bruxelles [*Belgium*]   (BAS)
corred .... Corredato [*Furnished With*] [*Publishing*] [*Italian*]
corros .... Corrosione [*Chafing*] [*Publishing*] [*Italian*]
corrte......... Corriente [*Current*] [*Spanish*]
CORS........ Canadian Operational Research Society   (SLS)
CORS........ Copyright Owners' Reproduction Society Ltd. [*Australia*]   (ADA)
cors........... Corsivo [*Cursive, Italic*] [*Publishing*] [*Italian*]
CORSA...... Cosmic Ray Satellite [*Japan*]
CORSAG... Corporacion Santiaguena de Ganaderos [*Argentina*]   (DSCA)
CORSAIN ... Corporacion Salvadorena de Inversiones [*El Salvador*]   (EY)
CORSI ...... Operational Research Society of India   (WGAO)
CORSI .... Societa Cooperativa per la Radiotelevisione nella Svizzera Italiana   (WGAO)
CORSM..... Calabar-Ogoja-Rivers State Movement
CORSO ..... Council of Relief Services Overseas [*New Zealand*]   (WGAO)
CORT .... Consortium on Rural Technology [*India*]   (EAIO)
cort........... Corte [*Edge*] [*Publishing*] [*Spanish*]
Cort .... Cortex [*German*]   (GCA)
CORT .... Council of Regional Theatres   (WGAO)
CORT .... Council of Repertory Theatres   (WGAO)
CORTURISMO ... Corporacion Nacional de Turismo [*National Tourism Corporation*] [*Bogota, Columbia*]   (LA)
CORU....... Consejo de Organizaciones Revolucionarias Unidas [*Council of United Revolutionary Organizations*] [*Exiles*] [*Cuba*]   (LA)
CORVI...... Corporacion de la Vivienda [*Housing Corporation*] [*Chile*]   (LA)
COS .... Centralny Osrodek Sportu   (WGAO)
COS .... Central Orchid Society   (WGAO)
COS .... Ceska Obec Strelecka [*Czech Rifleman Organization*]   (CZ)
COS .... Ceskoslovenska Obec Sokolska [*Czechoslovak Sokol (An athletic and gymnastic organization)*]   (CZ)
COS .... Ceskoslovenska Obilni Spolecnost [*Czechoslovak Grain Company*]   (CZ)
COS .... Cinema Organ Society   (WGAO)
COS .... Comite de Coordination Speciale [*Special Coordination Committee*] [*Cambodia*]   (CL)
COS .... Comite Olympique Suisse [*Swiss Olympic Committee*]   (EAIO)
COS .... Comite Olympique Syrien [*Syrian Olympic Committee*]   (EAIO)
COS .... Coordinadora de Organizaciones Sindicales [*Coordinating Body of Trade Union Organizations*] [*Spanish*]   (WER)
cos .... Coseno [*Cosine*] [*Portuguese*]
cos .... Cosinus [*Cosine*] [*French*]
COS .... Cyprus Ornithological Society   (EAIO)
Cos .... Kosinus [*Cosine*] [*German*]
COSA .... Camara Oficial Sindical Agraria [*Spain*]   (DSCA)
COSA .... Centraal Orgaan voor het Scheppend Ambacht [*Benelux*]   (BAS)
COSA .... Christian Brothers Council on the Overseas Apostolate
COSA .... Clinical Oncological Society of Australia   (ADA)
COSA .... Conseils Olympiques et Sportifs d'Arrondissement
COSAC.... Commonwealth-State Apprenticeship Committee [*Australia*]
COSAF..... Compania Sud Americana de Fosfatos, SA [*Chile*]   (ARC)
COSAG ..... Concerned South Africans Group   (ECON)
COSAGRA ... Compania Santandereana de Grasas Ltda. [*Bucaramanga*]   (COL)
COSAL...... Servicio de Contactos para la Investigacion de las Ciencias Sociales en America Latina (Fundacion Volkswagen) [*Spanish*]   (LAA)
COSAL...... Servico de Contatos para a Pesquisa das Ciencias Sociais na America Latina [*Portuguese*]   (LAA)
COSALFA ... Centro Panamericano de Fiebre Aftosa [*South American Commission for the Control of Foot-and-Mouth Disease*]   (EAIO)
COSALFA ... Comision Sudamericana para la Lucha contra la Fiebre Aftosa   (WGAO)
CoSAMC ... Commission for Special Applications of Meteorology and Climatology [*World Meteorological Organization*]
COSANDI ... Compania Santandereana de Importaciones Ltda. [*Bucaramanga*]   (COL)
COSAS...... Congress of South African Students
COSAT...... Confederacion Sudamericana de Tenis [*Argentina*]   (WGAO)
COSATA ... Cooperative Supply Association of Tanzania
COSATAN ... Compania Salitrena Tarapaca [*Chile*]   (DSCA)
COSATE ... Commission Syndicale Technique [*OEA*]   (WGAO)
COSATU ... Congress of South African Trade Unions
COSAWR ... Committee on South African War Resistance [*Defunct*]   (EAIO)
COSBA...... Computer Services and Bureaus Association   (WGAO)
COSBOA..... Council of Small Business Organisations of Australia
COSC........ Cambridge Overseas School Certificate
COSC........ Club Olympique et Sportif des Cooperants
COSC......... Commandement Operationnel Sud-Casamance [*Southern Casamance Operational Command*] [*Senegal*]   (AF)

COSCA...... Council of Senior Citizens Associations [*Australia*]
COSCHEM ... Society of Cosmetic Chemists of South Africa   (AA)
COSCO ..... China Ocean Shipping Co.
COSCV...... Comissao Organizadora dos Sindicatos Caboverdianos
[*Commission to Establish Cape Verdian Trade Unions*]
(AF)
COSDEGUA ... Confederacion de Sacerdotes Diocesanos de Guatemala
[*Confederation of Guatemalan Diocesan Priests*] (LA)
COSDO ..... Consejo Sindical de Obreros [*Trades Union Council of Workers*]
[*El Salvador*] (LA)
COSEAB ... Compagnie Senegalaise d'Exploitation d'Arachides de Bouche
COSEBI .... Corporacion de Servicios Bibliotecarios [*Puerto Rico*] (WGAO)
COSEC...... Companhia de Seguro e Creditos [*Credit Insurance Company*]
[*Portuguese*] (WER)
cosec.......... Cosecante [*Cosecant*] [*French*]
COSECA ... Compagnie Senegalaise de Construction Automobile
COSECO... Copperbelt Secondary Teachers Association [*Zambia*] (WGAO)
COSEDIA ... Consortium Senegalais pour la Diffusion de l'Automobile
(WGAO)
COSEDIR ... Compagnie Senegalaise pour le Developpement Industriel
Rationnel (WGAO)
COSEH ..... Comite de Secours aux Hopitaux [*Hospital Aid Committee*]
[*Cambodia*] (CL)
COSEM..... Compagnie Generale des Semi-Conducteurs [*France*] (PDAA)
COSEM..... Cooperative de Semence de Tunisie [*Tunisian Seed Cooperative*]
(AF)
COSEM..... Cooperative Seed Corn Society of Tunis (WGAO)
COSEMA ... Comptoirs des Secheries de Mauritanie
COSEMCO ... Comite des Semences du Marche Commun [*Seed Committee of
the Common Market*]
COSEN...... Comision Salvadorena de Energia Nuclear [*El Salvador*] (EY)
COSENA... Compagnie Senegalaise de Navigation
COSENA... Consejo de Seguridad Nacional [*National Security Council*]
[*Uruguay*] (LA)
COSENAM ... Compagnie Senegalaise de Navigation Maritime
COSENEGALAIS ... Commerce Senegalais
COSEP ...... Consejo Superior de la Empresa Privada [*Higher Council of
Private Enterprise*] [*Nicaragua*] (LA)
COSERCOL ... Corporacion de Servicios Colectivos Ltda. [*Colombia*] (COL)
COSERU... Comite Secreto da Restauracao da Udenamo
COSETAM ... Compagnie Senegalaise pour Tous Appareillages Mecaniques
COSG .... Centralni Odbor Sindikata Graficara [*Central Committee of the
Trade-Union of Workers in the Graphic Trades*] (YU)
COSIBRA ... Companhia de Sisal do Brasil [*Brazil*] (DSCA)
COSICA .... Comptoir Senegalais de l'Industrie des Conserves Alimentaires
COSIGUA ... Companhia Siderurgica da Guanabara [*Guanabara Iron and
Steel Company*] [*Brazil*] (LA)
COSIMEX ... Compagnie Senegalaise d'Importation et d'Exportation
COSINE.... Cooperation for Open Systems Interconnection Networking in
Europe (OSI)
COSINE.... Cooperation for OSI Networking in Europe (WGAO)
COSIPA .... Companhia Siderurgica Paulista [*Sao Paulo Iron and Steel
Company*] [*Brazil*] (LA)
COSIRT .... Comite Scientifique International pour la Recherche sur la
Trypanosomiase (WGAO)
COSLITAM ... Confederation des Syndicats Libres des Travailleurs de
Madagascar [*Confederation of Malagasy Workers Free
Labor Unions*] (AF)
COSMIC... Commonwealth/State Migration Committee [*Australia*]
COSMIVOIRE ... Omnium Chimique et Cosmetique
COSMOGRAFICAS ... Cooperativa Integral de Artes Graficas Cosmos Ltda.
[*Colombia*] (COL)
COSMWST ... Coal and Shale Mine Workers' Superannuation Tribunal
[*Australia*]
COSNUP... Committee for a Sane Nuclear Policy [*India*] (EAIO)
COSO .... Central Obrera Sindical de Occidente [*Trade Union Workers
Central Organization of the West*] [*El Salvador*] (LA)
Co So.......... Come Sopra [*As Above*] [*Music*]
COSOB ..... Comite de Organizacion Socialista Obrera de Bogota [*Socialist
Workers Organization Committee of Bogota*] [*Colorado*]
(LA)
COSOFAM ... Comision de Solidaridad con las Familiares de Presos Politicos,
Desaparecidos y Matados en Argentina
COSOMA ... Comite de Solidarite de Madagascar [*Solidarity Committee of
Madagascar*] (AF)
COSONAV ... Cooperativa de Suboficiales Navales Ltda. [*Colombia*] (COL)
COSOUP... Cooperative Sfaxienne Ouvriere de Production [*Sfax Worker
Production Cooperative*] [*Tunisia*] (AF)
COSPA ...... Comite de Solidaridad con el Pueblo Argentino [*Spain*]
COSPAR .... Committee on Space Research [*Paris, France*] [*ICSU*]
COSPE ...... Comite Peruano de Solidaridad con los Patriotas Espanoles
[*Peruvian Committee of Solidarity with Spanish Patriots*]
(LA)
COSPES.... Associazione Centri di Orientamento Scolastico Professionale, e
Sociale [*Italian*] (SLS)
COSPIT..... Centro Orientamento Studi e Propaganda Irrigua (WGAO)
COSPOIR ... National Sports Council [*Eire*] (WGAO)

COSPPZPR ... Centralny Osrodek Szkolenia Partyjnego Polskiej
Zjednoczonej Partii Robotniczej [*Central Institute for Party
Training of the Polish United Workers Party*] (POL)
COSPR...... Comprehensive and Coordinated Scientific Program
[*Intergovernmental Oceanographic Commission*] (MSC)
COSQC ..... Central Organization for Standardization and Quality Control
[*Iraq*]
COSRAA... Conference of State Road Authorities of Australia (ADA)
COSREG ... Compagnie Shell de Recherche et d'Exploration au Gabon
COSS........ Centralny Osrodek Szkolenia Sportowego [*Central Institute of
Sport Training*] (POL)
COSS........ Ceskoslovensky Odborny Spolek Slevarensky [*Czechoslovak
Foundry Specialists Association*] (CZ)
COSS........ Committee to Organize Support for a Settlement
COSS........ Cost of Social Security [*International Labor Organization*]
[*Information service or system United Nations*] (DUND)
COSSA ...... CSIRO [*Commonwealth Scientific and Industrial Research
Organisation*] Office for Space Science and Applications
[*Australia*]
COSSH...... Centralni Odbor Saveza Sindikata Hrvatske [*Central Committee
of the Council of Trade-Unions of Croatia*] (YU)
COSSJ....... Centralni Odbor Saveza Sindikata Jugoslavije [*Central
Committee of the Council of Trade-Unions of Yugoslavia*]
(YU)
COSSMIL ... Corporacion del Seguro Social Militar [*Corporation for Military
Social Security*] [*Bolivia*] (LA)
COSSO...... Vereinging Computer Service-en Software Bureaus (WGAO)
COSST ...... Council of Social Service, Tasmania [*Australia*]
COST........ Centre on Scientific and Technical Information [*Israel*] (NITA)
COST........ Committee for Overseas Science and Technology (WGAO)
COST........ Committee on Science and Technology [*India*] (WGAO)
COST........ Cooperation Europeene dans la Domaine de la Recherche
Scientifique et Technique [*European Cooperation in the
Field of Scientific and Technical Research*] (MSC)
COSTA...... Council of Subject Teaching Associations (WGAO)
COSTAS ... Centro de Estudios para el Desarrollo y Manejo de la Zona
Costera [*Research Center for the Development and
Management of the Coastal Zone*] [*Colorado*] (IRC)
COSTED ... Committee on Science and Technology in Developing Countries
[*Italy*] (DSCA)
COSTI .... Centre on Scientific and Technical Information [*Israel*]
(WGAO)
COSTI .... National Center of Scientific and Technological Information
[*National Council for Research and Development*] [*Israel
Also, CSTI*] (IID)
COSTIC .... Comite Scientifique et Technique de l'Industrie de Chauffage, de
la Ventilation et du Conditionnement d'Air [*Heating,
Ventilation and Air Conditioning Scientific and Technical
Committee*] [*France*] (PDAA)
COSTRAR ... Confederation Syndicale des Travailleurs du Rwanda [*Trade
union*]
COSU .... Coordination de l'Opposition Senegalaise Unie [*Coordination of
the United Senegalese Opposition*] (AF)
COSU .... Correspondence and Open Studies Unit
COSUF...... Conseil des Organisations Syndicales de l'Union Francaise
[*Council of Labor Unions of the French Union*]
COSUFA... Consejo Superior de las Fuerzas Armadas [*Armed Forces'
Superior Council*] [*Honduras*]
COSUFFAA ... Consejo Superior de las Fuerzas Armadas [*Senior Council of
the Armed Forces*] [*Honduras*] (LA)
COSUKO .. Compagnie Sucriere de Koumassi
COSUMA ... Compagnie Sucriere Marocaine
COSUMA ... Conference des Superieurs Majeurs [*Burundi Rwanda*]
(WGAO)
COSUMAR ... Compagnie Sucriere Marocaine et de Raffinage [*Morocco*]
(WGAO)
COSUMAR ... Compagnie Sucriere Marocaine et de Raffinage SA
[*Casablanca, Morocco*]
COSUPEBAN ... Consejo Superior de Estudiantes de Bachillerato Nocturno
[*Colombia*] (COL)
COSUPI .... Comision Supervisora de Planes de Institutos [*Brazil*] (LAA)
COSUPI .... Comissao Supervisora do Plano dos Institutos [*Brazil*] (WGAO)
COSUR ..... Cooperative de Surveillance des Produits Exportes [*Export
Products Supervisory Cooperative*] [*Cambodia*] (CL)
COSVN ..... Central Office for South Vietnam (CL)
COSWA .... Conference on Science and World Affairs (WGAO)
COSY......... Computergesteuertes Satzsystem [*German*] (ADPT)
COSYGA... Confederation Syndicale Gabonaise [*Gabonese Trade Union
Confederation*] (AF)
COSYM..... Council of Students and Youth Movements [*Mauritius*] (EAIO)
COSZ........ Centralny Osrodek Szkolenia Zadowowego [*Chief Vocational
Training Center*] (POL)
COT .... Centrale Organisatie in de Tweewielerbranche (WGAO)
COT .... Central Obrera Tucumana [*Tucuman Workers Union*]
[*Argentina*] (LA)
COT .... Centrum voor Onderzoek en Technisch Advies [*Center for
Surface Technology*] [*Netherlands*] (IRC)

COT .... Centrum voor Oppervlaketechnologie [*Center for Surface Treatment Technology*] [*Netherlands*]   (PDAA)

COT .... Ceskoslovenska Obec Turisticka [*Czechoslovak Tourist Association*]   (CZ)

COT .... Club Olympique des Transports [*Tunisia*]

COT .... Commissioner of Taxes [*Northern Territory*] [*Australia*]

COT .... Compagnie Oubangui Transports

COT .... Congreso Obrero Textil [*Congress of Textile Workers*] [*Uruguay*]   (LA)

cot .... Cotangente [*Cotangent*] [*French*]

COT .... Curacao Oil Terminal

COTA .... Caribbean Organisation of Tax Administration   (WGAO)

COTA .... Caribbean Organization of Tax Administrators   (EAIO)

COTA .... Census of the Americas   (LAA)

COTA .... Collectif d'Echanges pour la Technologie Appropriee [*Belgium*]

COTACEX ... Comite Technique des Assureurs-Credit a l'Exportation de la CEE   (WGAO)

COTAH ..... College of Tourism and Hospitality [*Brisbane, Australia*]

COTAL ...... Confederacion de Organizaciones Turisticas de la America Latina [*Confederation of Latin American Tourist Organizations*]   (LA)

COTAL ...... Confederacion de Organizaciones Turisticas de l' America Latina [*Confederation of Latin American Travel Organizations*] [*Spanish*]   (BARN)

COTAL ...... Confederation des Organisations Touristiques d'Amerique Latine [*Morocco*]

COTAM .... Commandement du Transport Aerien Militaire

COTAM .... Military Air Transport Command [*France*]

COTANCE ... Confederation des Associations Nationales de Tanneurs et Megissiers de le CEE   (WGAO)

COTANCE ... Confederation of Tanners' Associations in the European Community [*Brussels, Belgium*]   (EAIO)

COTANSW ... Council on the Aging, New South Wales [*Australia*]

COTAR ..... Sociedad Cooperativa de Tamberos de la Zona de Rosario [*Argentina*]   (DSCA)

COTB .... Centrale des Ouvriers Textiles de Belgique [*Belgium*]   (EAIO)

COTC .... China Overseas Trade Co.   (TCC)

COTCO ..... Committee on Technical Committee Operations [*ASTM*]   (WGAO)

COTDC ..... Canberra Old Time Dance Club [*Australia*]

COTEBU... Complexe Textile de Bujumbura

COTEC..... Centre de Cooperation Technique

COTEF..... Complexe Textile de Fes [*Fez, Morocco*]

COTEF ...... Consultoria Tecnica de Assuntos Economicos e Financeiros [*Technical Office for Economic and Financial Affairs*] [*Brazil*]   (LA)

COTELCO ... Corporacion Hotelera de Colombia [*Colombian Hotels Corporation*]   (LA)

COTEMA ... Compagnie Technique Mauritanienne

COTEQ ..... Comptoir Tunisien d'Equipement Industriel [*Tunisia*]

COTEVO .. Compagnie de Textiles de la Volta

COTIF .... Comite Technique International de Prevention et d'Extinction du Feu   (WGAO)

COTIMIP ... Comite Technique Interministeriel pour l'Industrie Miniere et Petroliere [*Interministerial Technical Committee for the Mining and Petroleum Industry*] [*Niger*]   (AF)

COTIRC .... Comision Tecnica Interprovincial del Rio Colorado [*Argentina*]   (LAA)

COTIV....... Compagnie de Transports Ivoiriens

COTIVO.... La Cotonniere Ivoirienne [*Ivory Coast*]

COTMA .... Council of Tramway Museums of Australasia   (ADA)

COTMAN ... Cotton Marketers' Association of Nigeria

CO/TNO ... Centrale Organisatie/Toegepast Natuurwetenschappelijk Onderzoek [*Netherlands*]

COTOA ..... Compagnie Textile de l'Ouest Africain

COTODICACS ... Compagnie Togolaise de Diffusion le Coprah Dacomsons

COTOMET ... Compagnie Togolaise des Metaux

COTOMIB ... Compagnie Togolaise des Mines du Benin

COTONA ... Cotonniere d'Antsirabe [*Antsirabe Cotton Industry*] [*Malagasy*]   (AF)

COTONA ... La Cotonniere d'Antsirabe [*Madagascar*]   (WGAO)

COTONAF ... Societe Francaise des Cotons Africains

COTONANG ... Companhia Geral dos Algodoes de Angola [*State industrial enterprise*]

COTONCO ... Compagnie Cotonniere Congolaise

COTONFRAN ... Societe Cotonniere Franco-Tchadienne

COTONTCHAD ... Societe Cotonniere du Tchad

COTOUBANGUI ... Societe Cotonniere du Haut-Oubangui

COTOUNA ... Compagnie Cotonniere de l'Ouhame-Nana

COTPAL ... Comite Tecnico Permanente sobre Asuntos Laborales (del CIES) [*Consejo Interamericano Economico y Social*] [*Permanent Technical Committee on Labor Matters Inter-American Economic and Social Council*]   (LAA)

COTRA ..... Compagnie des Transports [*Transport Company*] [*Guinea*]   (AF)

COTRABOIS ... Compagnie de Transports de Bois

COTRACAIME ... Cooperativa de Transportes de Cajamarca y Amaime Ltda. [*Cajamarca-Tolima*]   (COL)

COTRACOLDA ... Cooperativa de Transportadores de Colombia Ltda. [*Colombia*]   (COL)

COTRAGAB ... Compagnie des Traverses Gabonaises [*Gabonese Railroad Tie Company*]   (AF)

COTRAM ... Compagnie Togolaise de Transit Transport et Agence Maritime   (WGAO)

COTRAM ... La Congolaise de Transport Maritime   (EY)

COTRAM ... Union des Constructeurs de Materiel de Travaux Publics et de Manutention   (WGAO)

COTRAMA ... Societe Civile Cooperative d'Etudes des Transports et de Manutention   (WGAO)

COTRANAL ... Cooperativa de Transportes Nacionales [*Cucuta*]   (COL)

COTRANS ... Cooperativa Auto-Transporte Ltda. [*Malaga-Santander*]   (COL)

COTRAO .. Communaute de Travail des Regions des Alpes Occidentales   (WGAO)

COTRASANA ... Cooperativa de Transportes de San Antonio Ltda. [*Colombia*]   (COL)

COTRATLANTICO ... Cooperativa Transportadora del Atlantico Ltda. [*Barranquilla*]   (COL)

COTRAULTOL ... Transportes del Servicio Urbano del Tolima Ltda. [*Ibague*]   (COL)

COTRAVAUX ... Association de Cogestion pour le Travail Volontaire des Jeunes

COTREL ... Comite d'Associations de Constructeurs de Transformateurs du Marche Commun   (WGAO)

COTRICO ... Societe Camerounaise de Tricotage et de Confection Industrielle

COTRIJUI ... Cooperativa Regional Triticula Serra Ltda. of Ijui [*Brazil*]   (WGAO)

COTRINAG ... Comisso de Organizacao de Triticultura Nacional e Armazenamento Geral [*Fortaleza, Brazil*]   (LAA)

COTS........ Childlessness Overcome Through Surrogacy [*An association*]   (WGAO)

COTSOM ... Compagnie de Travaux Sous-Marins [*Cameroon*]   (WGAO)

COTSOM ... Compagnie de Travaux Sous-Marins du Cameroun

COTT .... Central Organisation for Trade Testing

COTT .... Central Organization for Technical Training [*South Africa*]   (WGAO)

COTTI ...... Commission du Traitement et de la Transmission de l'Information [*Commission for Data Handling and Transmission*] [*France*]   (PDAA)

COTTIA .... Complexe Telegraphique et Telex International Automatique d'Abidjan

COTU .... Central Organization of Trade Unions [*Kenya*]   (AF)

COTU-K.... Central Organization of Trade Unions of Kenya

Cotunace .... Compagnie Tunisienne d'Assurance de Commerce Exterieur [*Tunisian Foreign Trade Insurance Company*]   (GEA)

COTUNANCE ... Compagnie Tunisienne pour l'Assurance du Commerce Exterieur   (WGAO)

COTUSAL ... Compagnie Generale des Salines de Tunisie [*Tunisia*]

COU.......... Centrala Odpadkow Uzytkowych [*Usable Waste Materials Center*]   (POL)

COU.......... Comites Obreros Unitarios [*Unitary Workers Committees*] [*Spanish*]   (WER)

COU.......... Corporation de Obras Urbanas [*Urban Works Corporation*] [*Chile*]

COU......... Curso de Orientacion Universitaria [*Spanish*]

coul............ Couleur [*Color*] [*Publishing*] [*French*]

coul............ Coulomb [*Coulomb*] [*French*]

coup........... Coupon [*French*]

coup........... Coupure [*Denomination*] [*French*] [*Business term*]

coup arr ...... Coupon Arriere [*French*]

cour .... Courant [*Of the Current Month*] [*French*]

CourMilit ...... Cour Militaire [*French*]   (BAS)

Cours InstEtudes Pol ... Cours de l'Institut des Hautes Etudes Politiques [*France*]   (FLAF)

Cour SupArbitr ... Cour Superieure d'Arbitrage [*France*]   (FLAF)

court........... Courtage [*Brokerage*] [*French*] [*Business term*]

couv .... Couvert [*Cover*] [*Publishing*] [*Netherlands*]

couv .... Couverture [*Cover*] [*Publishing*] [*French*]

Couvt......... Couvent [*Convent*] [*Military map abbreviation World War I*] [*French*]   (MTD)

COV .... Ceskoslovensky Olympijsky Vybor [*Czechoslovak Olympic Committee*]   (CZ)

COV .... Christen Onderwijzers Verbond [*Belgium*]   (WGAO)

COVAM .... Centraal Overleg Voorlichting Audio-Visuele Media [*Netherlands*]

COVAP ..... Comissao do Vale Do Paraiba do Sul [*Paraiba Do Sul Valley Commission*] [*Brazil*]   (LA)

COVAS...... Cooperatieve Vereniging voor de Afzet van Suikerbieten

COVATRANS ... Cooperativa Vallecaucana de Transportadores Ltda. [*Colombia*]   (COL)

COVE .... Coalition Opposed to Violence and Extremism

COVECO .. Centrale Organisatie van Veeafzeten en Vleesverwerkings-Cooperaties

COVEG ..... Stichting Centraal Orgaan voor de Voedings-en Genotmiddelenbranche   (WGAO)

COVEMA ... Comando de Vengadores de Los Martires [*Avengers of the Martyrs*] [*Chile*]
COVEMI... Compagnie Voltaique d'Exploitation Miniere
Covena .... Comando Vengadores de Martires [*Chile*]
COVENAL ... Corporacion Venezolana de Aluminio (WGAO)
COVENAL ... Corporacion Venezolana de Aluminio CA [*Venezuela*] (DSCA)
COVENEXTA ... Cooperativa Venezolana de Exportadores de Tabaco [*Venezuela*] (DSCA)
COVENIN ... Comision Venezolana de Normas Industriales [*Caracas, Venezuela*] (LAA)
COVENSA ... Corporacion de Venta de Salitre y Yodo [*Chile*] (LAA)
COVENTA ... Cooperativa Venezolana de Tabacaleros [*Venezuela*] (LAA)
COVEPRO ... Cooperativa Venezolana de Productores [*Venezuela*] (DSCA)
COVESPRO ... Sociedad Anonima Colombo-Venezolana de Estudios y Promociones (LAA)
COVIAJES ... Corporacion de Viajes [*Colombia*] (COL)
COVICA.... Compania Colombiana de Vivienda Ltda. [*Colombia*] (COL)
COVIEMCALI ... Cooperativa de Vivienda de Emcali Ltda. [*Colombia*] (COL)
COVIM ..... Societe des Concentres de Viande de Madagascar
COVIMA .. Compagnie de Commercialisation des Viandes de Mauritanie
COVIMER ... Compagnie Vinicole Meridionale
COVINA ... Compagnie Vinicole de l'Ouest Africain
COVINA ... Companhia Vidreira Nacional (WGAO)
COVINCA ... Corporacion Venezolana para el Desarrollo de la Industria Naval [*Venezuelan Corporation for Development of the Shipbuilding Industry*] (LA)
COVINEX ... Societe Congolaise d'Exploitation Vinicole (WGAO)
COVINOC ... Compania de Vigilancia Nacional de Credito [*Colombia*] (COL)
COVKS(b) ... Centralni Odbor Vsezvezne Komunisticne Stranke (Boljsevikov) [*Central Committee of the All-Union Communist Party (Bolsheviks)*] (YU)
COVODIAM ... Compagnie Voltaique de Distribution Automobile et de Materiel
COVOLCO ... Comptoir Voltaique pour le Commerce
COVOLCO ... Cooperativa Santandereana de Volquetas de Colombia [*Bucaramanga*] (COL)
COVON..... Cooperatieve Vereniging van Ondernemers in het Natuursteenbedrijf (WGAO)
COVOS ..... Comite d'Etudes des Consequences des Vols Stratospheriques
COVOTEX ... Comptoir Voltaique des Textiles
COVOZADE ... Corps Volontaire Zairois au Developpement [*Zaire*] (EAIO)
COW......... Centralny Osrodek Werbunkowy [*Recruiting Center*] (POL)
COW......... Centrum voor Onderzoek Waterkeringen [*Netherlands*] (WGAO)
COW......... Committee of the Whole [*United Nations*]
CoWaBo..... Commissie inzake Wateronttrekking aan de Bodem (WGAO)
COWAC..... Continental West Africa Conference (AF)
COWAD.... Corps Wanita Angkatan Darat [*Women's Army Corps*] (IN)
COWAR .... Committee on Water Research [*ICSU*]
COWAR .... Coordinating Committee for Water Research [*ICSUUATI*] (WGAO)
COWAR .... Joint ICSU-UATI Coordinating Committee on Water Research (EAIO)
COWEC .... Company Welfarism through Employer's Contribution [*Singapore*]
COWT .... Council of World Tensions [*Switzerland*] (WGAO)
COWV .... Centraal Orgaan voor de Werklieden-Verzekering [*Benelux*] (BAS)
COX.......... Coxswain [*Royal Australian Navy*]
COY.......... Transportes Aereos Coyhaique [*Chile*] [*ICAO designator*] (FAAC)
COZ........... Corair [*France*] [*ICAO designator*] (FAAC)
COZA .... Combined Operations Headquarters, Zara [*Former Yugoslavia*] [*World War II*]
COZAC ..... Conservation Zone Advisory Committee [*Australia*]
COZH........ Centrala Obrotu Zwierzetami Hodowlanymi [*Pedigreed Animals Sales Center*] (POL)
COZS........ Ceskoslovensky Ovocnarsky a Zahradkarsky Svaz [*Czechoslovak Fruit and Garden Union*] (CZ)
CP .... Avions Mudry & Cie. [*France*], Lockheed Aircraft Corp. [*ICAO aircraft manufacturer identifier*] (ICAO)
cp............... Cai Putere [*Horse Power*] (RO)
CP .... Caixa Postal [*Post Office Box*] [*Correspondence*] [*Portuguese*]
CP .... Caja Postale [*Post Office Box*] [*Correspondence*] [*Spanish*]
CP .... Caminhos de Ferro Portugueses [*Railway*] [*Portugal*] (EY)
CP .... Cape Province [*South Africa*]
CP .... Carinski Pregled [*Customs Inspection*] (YU)
CP .... [*The*] Carnations [*An association*] [*Germany*] (EAIO)
CP .... Casella Postale [*Post Box*] (IDIG)
CP .... Case Postale [*Post Office Box*] [*Correspondence*] [*French*] (WER)
CP .... Casetta Postale [*Post Office Box*] [*Correspondence*] [*Italian*]
CP .... Centerpartiet [*Center Party*] [*Finland*] [*Political party*] (PPE)
CP .... Centerpartiet [*Center Party*] [*Sweden*] [*Political party*] (PPE)
cP............... Centipoise [*German*] (GCA)

CP .... Centralkommiten for Produktivitetsfragor (WGAO)
CP .... Centre Party
CP .... Centrum Partii [*Center Party*] [*Netherlands*] [*Political party*] (EY)
CP .... Centrum Partij (WGAO)
CP .... Ceskoslovenska Posta [*Czechoslovak Postal Service*] (CZ)
CP .... Charoen Pokphand [*Thailand*] [*Commercial firm*]
cp............... Charte-Partie [*French*]
CP .... Chawangan Penyiasatan [*Investigation Department*] (ML)
CP .... Christian Projects [*Australia*]
CP .... Christmas for Peace [*An association*] [*Switzerland*] (EAIO)
cp............... Cislo Popisne [*House Number*] (CZ)
CP .... Coalicion Popular [*Popular Coalition*] [*Spain*] [*Political party*] (PPW)
CP .... Commercial Printers Ltd. [*Western Samoa*]
CP .... Commission de Paris [*Paris Commission - PARCOM*] (EAIO)
CP .... Commission des Presidents [*Benelux*] (BAS)
CP .... Commonwealth Party [*Gibraltar*] [*Political party*] (PPE)
CP .... Communist Party (PWGL)
CP .... Compagnie Portee [*Algeria*]
CP .... Companhia dos Caminhos de Ferro Portugueses [*Portuguese Railroad Company*] (WER)
cp............... Compare [*Compare*] [*Portuguese*]
CP .... Computergesteuerte Programmierhilfe [*German*] (ADPT)
CP .... Confederate Party
CP .... Congregatio Passions Jesu Christi (WGAO)
CP .... Congregazione della Passione [*Congregation of the Passion*] (EAIO)
CP .... Congress Party [*India*] [*Political party*]
CP .... Conseil des Prud'hommes [*Benelux*] (BAS)
CP .... Conseil Provincial [*Benelux*] (BAS)
CP .... Conservative Party [*Uganda*] [*Political party*] (PPW)
CP .... Conservative Party [*South Africa*] [*Political party*]
CP .... Constitutionalist Party [*Malta*] [*Political party*] (PPE)
CP .... Contestacion Pagada [*Reply Paid*] [*Correspondence*] [*Spanish*]
CP .... Convention Patronale de l'Industrie Horlogere Suisse (WGAO)
CP .... Coordinating Panel [*NATO*]
cp............... Copertina [*Cover*] [*Publishing*] [*Italian*]
CP .... Country Party [*Political party*] [*Australia*] (BARN)
CP .... Cours Preparatoire
CP .... Credits de Paiement [*French*]
CP .... Cumhuriyetci Partisi [*Republican Party*] (TU)
CPA .... Australian Commercial Parachute Association
CPA .... Cadmium Pigments Association (EAIO)
CPA .... Caja Postal de Ahorros (WGAO)
CPA .... Calico Printers Association
CPA .... Canadian Philosophical Association (SLS)
CPA .... Canadian Postmasters Association (WGAO)
CPA .... Canadian Psychiatric Association (WGAO)
CPA .... Canadian Psychological Association (WGAO)
CPA .... Cape Palmas [*Liberia*] [*Airport symbol*] (OAG)
CPA .... Cape Pomological Association [*South Africa*] (AA)
CPA .... Cape Provincial Administration [*South Africa*] (AA)
CPA .... Caribbean Press Association (NTCM)
CPA .... Carpet Planners Association (WGAO)
CPA .... Celula Parlamentaria Aprista [*Aprista Parliamentary Bloc*] [*Peru*] (LA)
CPA .... Centrala Przemyslu Artystycznego [*Central Office of Art Crafts*] (POL)
CPA .... Centrale Persoons Administratie [*Netherlands*]
CPA .... Central Personnel Agency [*Ethiopia*] (AF)
CPA .... Centre de Perfectionnement dans l'Administration des Affaires
CPA .... Centre de Preparation aux Affaires (WGAO)
CPA .... Centre for Policy on Ageing (WGAO)
CPA .... Centro de Productividad de la Argentina [*Buenos Aires, Argentina*] (LAA)
CPA .... Certified Practising Accountant [*Australia*]
CPA .... Chick Producers Association (WGAO)
CPA .... China Publishers Association (EAIO)
CPA .... Chinese Psychological Association (SLS)
CPA .... Chipboard Promotion Association (WGAO)
CPA .... City Parks Administration [*Australia*]
CPA .... Cocoa Producers' Alliance (EAIO)
CPA .... Comissao Portuguesa do Atlantico [*Portugal*] (EAIO)
CPA .... Comite des Paysans Africains [*African Farmers Committee - AFC*] (EAIO)
CPA .... Comite Permanent Argicole [*BIT*] (WGAO)
CPA .... Commissione Pontificia di Assistenza [*Pontifical Commission of Assistance*] [*Italian*] (WER)
CPA .... Commonwealth Parliamentary Association [*British*] (EAIO)
CPA .... Commonwealth Pharmaceutical Association [*British*] (EAIO)
CPA .... Commonwealth Postal Administration (WGAO)
CPA .... Commonwealth Postgraduate Allowance [*Australia*]
CPA .... Communist Party of Arakan [*Myanmar*] [*Political party*]
CPA .... Communist Party of Argentina [*Political party*]
CPA .... Communist Party of Armenia [*Political party*] [*Defunct*]

CPA .... Communist Party of Australia [*Political party*] (PPW)
CPA .... Communist Party of Azerbaidzhan [*Political party*]
CPA .... Compagnie de Petrole d'Algerie [*Algerian Petroleum Company*] (AF)
CPA .... Companhia Paulista de Adubos [*Brazil*] (DSCA)
CPA .... Compania de Productos Agricolas SA [*Argentina*] (DSCA)
CPA .... Concrete Pipe Association (WGAO)
CPA .... Conference Parlementaire Association [*Benelux*] (BAS)
CPA .... Conseil des Prud'hommes d'Appel [*Benelux*] (BAS)
CPA .... Conseil du Peuple Angolais [*Angolan People's Council*]
CPA .... Conselho de Promocoes da Armada [*Navy Promotions Board*] [*Portuguese*] (WER)
CPA .... Conselho do Povo Angolano [*Angolan People's Council*] (AF)
CPA .... Conservative Party of Australia [*Political party*]
CPA .... Constant Phase Angle [*Electronics*] (BARN)
CPA .... Construction Plant-hire Association (WGAO)
CPA .... Consumer Protective Association
CPA .... Contractors Plant Association (WGAO)
CPA .... Cooperativa de Produccion Agropecuaria [*Agricultural and Livestock Cooperative*] [*Cuba*] (LA)
CPA .... Cour Permanente d'Arbitrage [*Permanent Court of Arbitration - PCA*] [*Hague, Netherlands*] (EAIO)
CPA .... Craftsmen Potters Association (WGAO)
CPA .... Credit Populaire d'Algerie [*People's Credit Bank of Algeria*] (IMH)
CPA .... Cyprus Ports Authority (IMH)
CPA .... National Association of Creamery Proprietors and Wholesale Dairymen (WGAO)
CPAA........ Centro de Pesquisa Agroflorestal da Amazonia [*Research Center for Amazon Agroforestry*] [*Brazil*] (IRC)
CPAA........ Commission for Prevention of Abuse of Authority [*Nepal*]
CPAA........ Concrete Pipe Association of Australia
CPAA........ Cultured Pearl Association of America (WGAO)
CPAC........ Centro de Pesquisa Agropecuaria do Cerrados [*Agricultural Research Center of Pastures*] [*Brazil*] (ARC)
CPAC........ Comision Permanente de la Asamblea de Cataluna [*Permanent Commission of the Catalonian Assembly*] [*Spanish*] (WER)
CPAC........ Consumer Protection Advisory Committee [*DTI*] (WGAO)
CPAC........ Corrosion Prevention Advisory Centre (WGAO)
CPAC........ International Collaborative Pesticides Analytical Committee (WGAO)
CPACE...... Comite des Peches pour l'Atlantique Centre-Est [*Committee for the Eastern Central Atlantic Fisheries - CECAF*] [*French*] (MSC)
CPACO...... Comite de Pesca de la FAO para el Atlantico Centro-Oriental (WGAO)
CPACO...... Comite de Pesca para el Atlantico Centro-Oriental [*Committee for the Eastern Central Atlantic Fisheries - CECAF*] [*Spanish*] (ASF)
CPAD .... Comite de Concertation sur l'Alcool et les Autres Drogues (WGAO)
CPAD .... Comite Preparatorio do Accao Directa
CPAG .... Child Poverty Action Group (WGAO)
CPAGSME ... Council for the Protection of Arab Gulf States Marine Environment
CPAL........ Centre de Productivite des Industries de l'Ameublement et de la Literie (WGAO)
CPAL........ Comitetul pentru Problemele Administratiei Locale [*Committee for Problems of Local Administration*] (RO)
CPAL........ Creosote Producers Association (WGAO)
CPAM .... Caisse Primaire d'Assurance Maladie [*French*] (DLA)
CPA(M/L) ... Communist Party of Australia (Marxist/Leninist) (ADA)
CPAMM ... Camara Portuguesa dos Armadores da Marinha Mercante [*Portugal*] (EAIO)
CPANE...... Comision de Pesquerias del Atlantico Nordeste [*North-East Atlantic Fisheries Commission - NEAFC*] [*Spanish*] (ASF)
CPANE...... Commission des Pecheries de l'Atlantique Nord-Est [*Northeast Atlantic Fisheries Commission - NEAFC*] [*French*] (MSC)
CPANE...... Commission des Peches de l'Atlantique Nord-Est (WGAO)
CPANSW .. Concrete Paviors' Association of New South Wales [*Australia*]
CPANSW .. Country Press Association of New South Wales [*Australia*]
CPANSW .. Croquet Players' Association of New South Wales [*Australia*]
CPANT...... Comite Panamericano de Normas Tecnicas [*Uruguay*] (DSCA)
CPAP........ Comissao de Producao Agro Pecuaria [*Brazil*] (DSCA)
CPAPD...... Chinese People's Association for Peace and Disarmament
c par .... Cieplo Parowania [*Heat of Evaporation*] [*Poland*]
C Paris ...... Cour d'Appel de Paris (FLAF)
CPAS........ Centre Publique d'Aide Sociale [*Public Center for Social Aid*] [*Belgium*] (WER)
CPAS........ Church Pastoral Aid Society (WGAO)
CPASA ..... Country Press Association of South Australia
CPASL...... Ceskoslovenska Plarba Akciova Spolecnost Labska [*Czechoslovak Elbe River Navigation Joint-Stock Company*] (CZ)
CPASNSW ... Cancer Patients' Assistance Society of New South Wales [*Australia*]

CPATSA.... Centro de Pesquisa Agropecuaria do Tropico Semi-Arido [*Agricultural Research Center of the Semi-Arid Tropics*] [*Brazil*] (ARC)
CPATU...... Centro de Pesquisa Agropecuaria do Tropico Umido [*Agricultural Research Center of the Humid Tropics*] [*Brazil*] (ARC)
CPAV........ Childbirth and Parenting Association of Victoria [*Australia*]
CPAV........ Combined Pensioners' Association of Victoria [*Australia*]
CPAV........ Council of Progress Associations of Victoria [*Australia*]
CPAWA.... Country Press Association of Western Australia
CPB......... Centraal Planbureau [*Central Planning Bureau*] [*Netherlands*]
CPB......... Centralni Projektanski Biro [*Central Industrial Design Bureau*] (YU)
CPB......... Centre de Pedologie Biologique [*Biological Pedology Center*] [*National ScientificResearch Center*] [*France*] (EAS)
CPB......... Circulo de Periodistas de Bogota [*Bogota Press Club*] [*Colorado*] (LA)
CPB......... Classification of Publications Board [*South Australia*]
CPB......... Coast Protection Board [*South Australia*]
CPB......... Colombo Plan Bureau [*Sri Lanka*] (EAIO)
CPB......... Comissao Popular de Bairro [*People's Neighborhood Commission*] [*Angola*] (AF)
CP (B) ...... Communist Party (Bolsheviks) [*Political party*]
CPB......... Communist Party of Bangladesh (WGAO)
CPB......... Communist Party of Belgium [*Political party*]
CPB......... Communist Party of Burma [*Political party*] (EY)
CPB......... Communist Party of Byelorussia [*Political party*]
CPB......... Community Programs Branch [*Australian Capital Territory*]
CPB......... Companhia Paulista de Bananicultores [*Brazil*] (DSCA)
CPB......... Confederacao dos Professores do Brasil [*Brazilian Teachers' Confederation*]
CPB......... Confederacion Panamericana de Badminton [*Panamerican Badminton Conferation - PBC*] (EAIO)
CPB......... Confederacion Panamericana de Basketball [*Pan American Basketball Confederation - PABC*] (EAIO)
CPB......... Crown Property Bureau [*Thailand*]
CPB......... Cuyos Pies Beso [*Very Respectfully*] [*Formal correspondence*] [*Spanish*]
CPBA........ Caribbean Press and Broadcasting Association (LA)
CPBA........ Caribbean Publishers and Broadcasting Association (WGAO)
CPBC........ Convention of Philippine Baptist Churches (EAIO)
CPBCA .... Cooperative des Planteurs Bamoun du Cafe Arabica [*Cameroon*]
CPBF .... Campaign for Press and Broadcasting Freedom (WGAO)
CPBG........ Compagnie des Placages en Bois Gabonais
CPBM........ Communist Party of Bohemia and Moravia [*Former Czechoslovakia*] [*Political party*] (EY)
CPBP .... Comision Protectora de Bibliotecas Populares [*Commission for the Protection of People's Libraries*] [*Buenos Aires, Argentina*] (LAA)
CPBP .... Comite Professionel du Butane and du Propane [*France*]
CPBS .... Central Peoples Broadcasting Station [*China*] (WGAO)
CPB-TNO ... Centraal Proefdierenbedrijf - Nederlands Centrale Organisatie voor Toegepast-Natuurwetenschappelijk Onderzoek [*Central Institute for the Breeding of Laboratory Animals - Netherlands Central Organization for Applied Natural Scientific Research*] (ARC)
CPC........... Aero Campeche SA de CV [*Mexico*] [*ICAO designator*] (FAAC)
CPC........... Caisse des Pensions Civiles [*Civilian Pension Fund*] [*Cambodia*] (CL)
CPC........... Cameroon Protestant College
CPC........... Campaign against Pornography and Censorship (WGAO)
CPC........... Caribbean Press Council (WGAO)
CPC........... Caring Professions Concern (WGAO)
CPC........... Centros Populares de Cultura [*People's Cultural Centers*] [*Nicaragua*] (LA)
CPC........... Certified Personnel Consultant [*South Africa*] (AA)
CPC........... Ceskoslovensky Prumysl Cukrovarnicky, Narodni Podnik [*Czechoslovak Sugar Industry, National Enterprise*] (CZ)
CPC........... Ceylon Petroleum Company [*Sri Lanka*] (PDAA)
CPC........... Chapelco [*Argentina*] [*Airport symbol*] (OAG)
CPC........... Cherry Processors' Cooperative [*Australia*]
CPC........... Child Protection Council [*New South Wales*] [*Australia*]
CPC........... China PEN Centre (EAIO)
CPC........... Chinese Petroleum Corporation (MSC)
CPC........... Christian Peace Conference [*See also CCP*] [*Prague, Czechoslovakia*] (EAIO)
CPC........... Clouterie Pointerie Camerounaise
CPC........... Coffee Promotion Council (WGAO)
CPC........... Combined Policy Committee [*NATO*] (NATG)
CPC........... Comite del Program y la Coordinacion [*Committee for Program Coordination - CPC*] [*Economic and Social Council*] [*United Nations (already exists in GUS II database)*] [*Spanish*] (ASF)
CPC........... Comite du Programme et de la Coordination [*Committee for Program Coordination - CPC*] [*Economic and Social Council*] [*United Nations (already exists in GUS II database)*] [*French*] (ASF)

CPC............ Committee for Program Coordination [*Economic and Social Council*] [*United Nations (already exists in GUS II database)*] (ASF)

CPC............ Committee for Programme and Coordination [*ECOSOC*] (WGAO)

CPC............ Communist Party of China [*Chung-Kuo Kung-Ch'an Tang*] [*Taiwan*] [*Political party*] (PPW)

CPC............ Communist Party of Colombia [*Political party*] (PPW)

CPC............ Community Patent Convention [*EEC*] (WGAO)

CPC............ Compagnie des Phosphates du Congo

CPC............ Compagnie des Potasses du Congo

CPC............ Companhia Petroquimica Camacari [*Brazil*]

CPC............ Comptoir Pharmaceutique du Cambodge [*Cambodian Pharmaceutical Warehouse*] (CL)

CPC............ Congolese Protestant Council

CPC............ Congres Panafricain du Cameroun [*Political party*] (EY)

CPC............ Consejo Provincial de Cultura [*Provincial Council of Culture*] [*Cuba*] (LA)

CPC............ Conservative Political Centre (WGAO)

CPC............ Construcciones y Prefabricados Colombianos [*Colombia*] (COL)

CPC............ Copperbelt Power Company

CPC............ Cotton Public Corporation [*Sudan*] (GEA)

CPCA........ Centre for Philippine Concerns, Australia

CPCA........ Comite de Pesca Continental para Africa [*Committee for Inland Fisheries of Africa - CIFA*] (MSC)

CPCA........ Comite des Peches Continentales pour l'Afrique [*Committee for Inland Fisheries of Africa - CIFA*] [*French*] (ASF)

CPCA........ Cyprus Photogrammetric and Cartographic Association (WGAO)

CPCAB...... Cooperative des Planteurs de Cafe Arabica de Bafoussam

CPCAG...... Consorcio Provincial de Centros Agricolas del Guayas [*Ecuador*] (DSCA)

CPCAM..... Cooperative des Planteurs de Cafetiers de Mbounda [*Cameroon*] (WGAO)

CPCAN...... Comissao do Plano do Carvao Nacional [*Commission of the National Coal Plan*] [*Rio De Janeiro, Brazil*] (LA)

CPCAS ...... Commission Permanente de Coordination des Associations Specialisees [*FNSEA*] (WGAO)

CPCAT...... Centre de Perfectionnement des Cadres de l'Administration du Travail [*Labor Administration Cadre Retraining Center*] [*Cameroon*] (AF)

CPCC........ Caithness Paperweight Collectors Club (WGAO)

CPCCI .... Conference Permanente des Chambers de Commerce et l'Industrie de la CEE (WGAO)

CPCD........ Comissoes Provinciais dos Conselhos de Producao [*Provincial Commissions of the Production Councils*] [*Mozambique*] (AF)

CPCDM..... Centrala de Prelucrarea si Colectarea Deseurilor Metalice [*Central for Processing and Collecting Metallic Waste*] (RO)

CPCDMR ... Centrala de Prelucrarea si Colectarea Deseurilor Metalice si Refractare [*Central for Processing and Collecting Metallic and Refractory Waste*] (RO)

CPCE........ Comite des Patriotes Cambodgiens d'Europe [*Committee of Cambodian Patriots in Europe*] (CL)

CPCEA ...... Caisse de Prevoyance des Cadres d'Exploitations Agricoles (WGAO)

CPCEAISD ... Comite Permanent du CE de l'Association Internationale de la Savonnerie et de la Detergence [*Standing EEC Committee of the International Association of the Soap and Detergent Industry - SEECCIASDI*] [*Brussels, Belgium*] (EAIO)

CPCERMPS ... Comision Permanente para la Conservacion y Explotacion de los Recursos Maritimos del Pacifico Sur [*Permanent Commission of the South Pacific - PCSP*] [*Spanish*] (MSC)

CPCGSO ... Committee of Protestant Churches in Germany for Service Overseas (EAIO)

CPCI .... Centre de Perfectionnement Pratique des Cadres Commerciaux dans l'Industrie (WGAO)

CPCIP .... Commission Permanente de la Convention Internationale des Peches [*Permanent Commission of the International Fisheries Convention*] [*Political party*] (MSC)

CPCISF ..... Conseil Permanent de la Convention Internationale de Stresa sur les Fromages (EAIO)

CPCIU .... Commonwealth Police Crime Intelligence Unit [*Australia*]

CPCIZ .... Comite Permanent des Congres Internationaux de Zoologie [*Permanent Committee of International Zoological Congresses*] [*France*]

CPCL........ Caisse de Prets aux Collectivites Locales

CPCM........ Comite Permanent Consultatif du Maghreb [*Maghreb Permanent Consultative Committee*] [*North African*] (AF)

CPCMU..... Central Province Cooperative Marketing Union

CPCO .... Chief Parliamentary Counsel's Office [*Victoria*] [*Australia*]

CPCP .... Comite Preparatoire du Congres Populaire Angolais [*Preparatory Committee for the People's Congress of Angola*] (AF)

CPCPM ..... Comisia pentru Controlul Poluției Mediului [*Commission for Control of Environmental Pollution*] (RO)

CPCR........ Center for the Protection of Children's Rights [*Thailand*] (EAIO)

CPCR........ Congregatio Cooperatorum Paroeialium Christi Regis (WGAO)

CPCRI ...... Central Plantation Crops Research Institute [*India*] (PDAA)

CPCS .... Christian Parent-Controlled Schools [*Australia*]

CPCS .... Commissione Pontificia per le Comunicazioni Sociali (WGAO)

CPCT........ Caisse de Prets aux Collectivites Territoriales [*Local Collective Loans Fund*] [*Niger*]

CPCU .... Compagnie Parisienne de Chauffage Urbain [*French*]

CPCWIU ... Chemical, Paper, and Ceramic Workers' Industrial Union [*Germany*] (EAIO)

CPCZ........ Communist Party of Czechoslovakia [*Political party*] (EY)

CPD .... Cable Price Downer Ltd. [*New Zealand*]

CPD .... Centro de Procesamiento de Datos (de la Tesoreria General de la Republica) [*Santiago, Chile*] (LAA)

CPD .... Ceskoslovenska Plavba Dunajska [*Czechoslovak Danube River Navigation Lines*] (CZ)

CPD .... Comite de Planification du Developpement

CPD .... Comite Privado de Desarrollo [*Bogota, Colombia*] (LAA)

CPD .... Commonwealth Parliamentary Debates [*Australia*] (ADA)

CPD .... Communist Party of Denmark [*Political party*]

CPD .... Concertacion de los Partidos de la Democracia [*Chile*] [*Political party*] (EY)

CPD .... Connectez Poste de Donnees [*German*] (ADPT)

CPD .... Continuing Professional Development [*Australia*]

CPD .... Convention a Paiement Differe [*Deferred Payment Agreement*] [*French*] [*Business term*] (WER)

CPD .... Coober Pedy [*Australia*] [*Airport symbol*] (OAG)

CPD .... Courier and Periodicals Division [*Later, UNESCO Publications and Periodicals*]

CPD .... Popular Democratic Coalition [*Ecuador*] [*Political party*] (PPW)

CPDA .... Centro Paulista de Debates Agronomicos [*Brazil*] (DSCA)

CPDA .... Clay Pipe Development Association (WGAO)

CPDC........ China Petrochemical Development Corp.

CPDCET ... Centre de Perfectionnement pour le Developpement et la Cooperation Economique et Technique [*French*]

CPDE........ Commission Permanente de Developpement de l'Elevage (WGAO)

CPDE........ Compagnie Parisienne de Distribution de l'Electricite [*French*]

CPDF......... Caribbean Project Development Facility (WGAO)

CPDHN ..... Comision Permanente de Derechos Humanos de Nicaragua [*Nicaragua*] (EAIO)

CPD(HR)... Commonwealth Parliamentary Debates (House of Representatives) [*Australia*] (ADA)

CPDM .... Cameroon People's Democratic Movement [*Political party*]

CPDOC ..... Centro de Pesquisa e Documentacao [*Brazil*] (WGAO)

CPDP......... Comite Professionnel du Petrole (WGAO)

CPD(R)...... Commonwealth Parliamentary Debates (House of Representatives) [*Australia*] (ADA)

CPDS........ Centre for Policy and Development Studies [*Philippines*] (ARC)

CPD(S) ..... Commonwealth Parliamentary Debates (Senate) [*Australia*] (ADA)

CPDT......... Centre de Preparation Documentaire a la Traduction [*Center for Translation Documentation*] [*Information service or system*] (IID)

CPDT......... Centre de Preparation Documentarie a la Traduction [*French*]

CPE........... Cameroun Publi-Expansion (WGAO)

CPE........... Campaign for Promotion of Education [*Grenada*] (LA)

CPE........... Campeche [*Mexico*] [*Airport symbol*] (OAG)

CPE........... Center for Popular Education [*Grenada*] (LA)

CPE........... Centrally Planned Economy [*Arab*]

CPE........... Centre de la Petite Enfance (WGAO)

CPE........... Centre de Prospective et d'Evaluation [*Feasibility and Evaluation Center*] [*France*] (PDAA)

CPE........... Centre de Protection a l'Enfance [*Children's Protection Center*] [*Cambodia*] (CL)

CPE........... Centrum voor Postoraal in Europa [*Centre for Pastoral Work in Europe*] (EAIO)

CPE........... Cercle Populaire Europeen [*European Popular Circle - EPC*] (EAIO)

CPE........... Chamber of Professional Engineers [*Malta*] (WGAO)

CPE........... Chronique de Politique Etrangere [*Benelux*] (BAS)

CPE........... Comissao de Planejamento Economico [*Salvador, Brazil*] (LAA)

CPE........... Comite de Politique Economique [*OCDE*]

CPE........... Comite de Prospective et d'Evaluation [*Committee on Forcasting and Evaluation*] [*French*] (WER)

CPE........... Committee on Population and the Economy (WGAO)

CPE........... Committees for Popular Education [*Grenada*] (LA)

CPE........... Communist Party of Ecuador [*Political party*]

CPE........... Communist Party of Estonia [*Political party*]

CPE........... Congres du Peuple Europeen (FLAF)

CPE........... Contribution Personnelle d'Etat [*Tunisia*]

CPE........... Council of Public Education [*Victoria*] [*Australia*]

CPE........... Fundacao Centro de Pesquisas e Estudos [*Brazil*] (SLS)

CPEA........ Coconut Products Exporters' Association [*Sri Lanka*] (EAIO)
CPEA........ Confederation of Professional and Executive Associations (WGAO)
CPEA........ Cyprus Professional Engineers' Association
CPECB...... China National Complete Plant Export Corp., Building Materials Industry Branch (TCC)
CPECC...... China Petroleum Engineering Construction Corp. (TCC)
CPECRPS ... Comision Permanente para la Exploracion y Conservacion de los Recursos del Pacifico Sur [*Permanent Commission for the Exploration and Conservation of the Resources of the South Pacific*] [*Spanish*] (ASF)
CPECRPS ... Commission Permanente pour l'Exploration et la Conservation des Ressources du Pacifique Sud [*Permanent Commission for the Exploration and Conservation of the Resources of the South Pacific*] [*French*] (ASF)
CPED........ Commission de la Participation des Eglises au Developpement [*Switzerland*] (WGAO)
CPEFIBA .. Conference Permanente de l'Europe de la Federation Internationale de Basketball [*Standing Conference for Europe of the International Basketball Federation*] (EAIO)
CPEI........ Centro de Promocion de Exportaciones e Inversiones [*Export and Investment Promotion Center*] [*Costa Rica*] (GEA)
CPEI......... Preparation Centre for International Exchanges [*France*] (MENA)
CPEIP....... Center for Training, Experimentation, and Research on Education (IID)
CPEJE...... Cooperation Paneuropeenne de la Jeunesse et des Etudiants (WGAO)
CPEL........ Centro de Pesquisas de Energia Eletrica [*Electricity Research Center*] [*Brazil*] (WED)
CPEM........ Centro de Preparacion de Especialistas Menores [*Junior Specialists Training Center*] [*Cuba*] (LA)
CPEM........ Certificat Preparatoire aux Etudes Medicales [*Medical Studies Preparatory Certificate*] (CL)
CPEMA..... Comite de Prospective et d'Evaluation du Ministere des Armees [*Committee on Forecasting and Evaluation of the Ministry of the Armies*] [*French*] (WER)
CPEMPN .. Centre Principal d'Expertise Medicale du Personnel Navigant [*Main Center for Medical Expertise for Navigation Personnel*] (WER)
CPEN........ Centro de Preparacion de Especialistas Navales [*Naval Specialists Training Center*] [*Cuba*] (LA)
C pen.......... Code Penal [*Penal Code*] [*French*]
CPEN........ Cyprus PEN (EAIO)
CPENCI ..... Centre de PEN de Cote d'Ivoire [*Ivory Coast*] (EAIO)
CPENR....... Centrul PEN Roman [*Romania*] (EAIO)
CPEPA ...... Comite de la Prune d'Entre et du Pruneau d'Agen (WGAO)
CPERS-A .. Chief of Personnel - Army [*Australia*]
CPES .... Centre de Preparation aux Enseignements Superieurs
CPES .... Centres Preparatoires aux Etudes Superieurs [*North African*]
CPES .... Centro Paraguayo de Estudios Sociologicos (WGAO)
CPET .... Centre for Protein and Enzyme Technology [*La Trobe University*] [*Australia*]
CPF............ Central Provident Fund [*Singapore*] (WGAO)
CPF............ Centre de Promotion Feminine [*Women's Advancement Center*] [*Guinea*] (AF)
CPF............ Centre de Protection Familiale [*Family Protection Center*] [*Zaire*] (AF)
CPF............ Charoen Pokphand Feedmill [*Thailand*] [*Commercial firm*]
CPF............ Comissao de Politica Florestal [*Forestry Policy Commission*] [*Brazil*] (LA)
CPF............ Comite Provisoire des Frequences [*French*]
CPF............ Commonwealth Police Force [*Australia*] (ADA)
CPF............ Communist Party of Finland [*Political party*]
CPF............ Community Projects Foundation (WGAO)
CPF............ Compagnie du Polyisoprene Francais
CPF............ Cooperation Pharmaceutique Francaise (WGAO)
CPF............ Cooperative Productive Federation
CPFA .... Centro Panamericano de Febre Aftosa [*Brazil*] (DSCA)
CPFC .... Comision de Proteccion Fitosanitaria para el Caribe [*Caribbean Plant Protection Commission - CPPC*] (EAIO)
CPFCN ...... Centro de Pesquisas Florestais e Conservacao da Natureza [*Brazil*] (DSCA)
CPFCS....... Child Protection and Family Crisis Service [*New South Wales*] [*Australia*]
CPFF .... Christian Pro-Family Forum [*Australia*]
CPFIA .... China Phosphate Fertilizer Industry Association (EAIO)
CPFS .... Council for the Promotion of Field Studies (WGAO)
CPG .... Bureau of Conference Planning and General Services [*UNESCO*] (WGAO)
CPG .... Centro Studi Problemi Giovanili [*Italian*] (SLS)
CPG .... Chemisch-Physikalische Gesellschaft [*Austria*] (WGAO)
CPG .... Commonwealth Procurement Guidelines [*Australia*]
CPG .... Communist Party of Georgia [*Political party*]
CPG .... Communist Party of Germany [*Political party*] (EAIO)
CPG .... Compagnie des Phosphates de Gafsa [*Tunisia*]
CPG .... Computer Power Group [*Australia*]

CPG .... Confederation Patronale Gabonaise [*Gabon*] (EAIO)
CPGA .... Comite Professionnel des Galeries d'Art (WGAO)
CPGB........ Centro de Pesquisas Geograficas do Brasil [*Brazil*] (DSCA)
CPGPA...... Caisse Professionnele de Garantie des Producteurs Agricoles (WGAO)
CPH.......... Census Population and Housing
CPH.......... Communistische Partij Holland [*Communist Party of Holland*] [*Netherlands*] (PPE)
CPH.......... Computergesteuerte Programmierhilfe [*German*] (ADPT)
CPH.......... Consolidated Press Holdings Ltd. [*Australia*] (ADA)
CPH.......... Copenhagen [*Denmark*] [*Airport symbol*] (OAG)
CPhA........ Canadian Pharmaceutical Association (SLS)
CPHEA...... Cooperative des Produits de l'Huilerie d'Etat d'Alokoegbe
CPHERI .... Central Public Health Engineering Research Institute [*India*] (PDAA)
CPHL .... Central Public Health Laboratory (WGAO)
CPHP .... Confederation Patronale des Hautes-Pyrenees (WGAO)
CPI............ Caltex Pacific Indonesia (OMWE)
CPI............ Centrale Penitentiaire Inrichiting in Suriname [*Benelux*] (BAS)
CPI............ Central Personnel Institution [*Namibia*] (AF)
CPI............ Chinese Press Institute [*Taiwan*] (EAIO)
CPI............ Comissao Parlamentar de Inquerito [*Congressional Investigating Committee*] [*Brazil*] (LA)
CPI............ Commission Permanente Internationale Europeenne des Gaz Industriels et du Carbure de Calcium [*Permanent International European Commission on Industrial Gases and Calcium Carbide*] (EAIO)
CPI............ Commission Phytosanitaire Interafricaine
CPI............ Communist Party of India [*Political party*] (PPW)
CPI............ Communist Party of Indonesia [*Political party*] (PD)
CPI............ Communist Party of Iraq (ME)
CPI............ Communist Party of Ireland [*Political party*] (PPW)
CPI............ Confederation of Photographic Industries (WGAO)
CPI............ Confederation of Portugese Industry (EAIO)
CPI............ Conseil de Prefecture Interdepartemental [*France*] (FLAF)
CPI............ Conseil Phytosanitaire Interafricain (WGAO)
CPI............ Consortium Property and Investments Proprietary Ltd.
CPI............ Constituent Particulars Index [*Australia*]
CPI............ Continuous Printing Industry
CPI............ Stichting Cooperatief Pluimveefokkers Institute (WGAO)
CPIA .... Commission Permanente Internationale d'Aeronautique
CPIA .... Conference Pedagogique Internationale d'Approvisionnement (WGAO)
CPIAC ...... Comissao Pro-Indio do Acre [*Brazil*] (WGAO)
CPIB .... Corrupt Practices Investigation Bureau [*Singapore*] (ML)
CPIC .... China Pacific Insurance Co. (EY)
CPIC .... Communist Party of Indo-China [*Political party*] (PPW)
CPIC .... Comprehensive Pig Information Centre (WGAO)
CPIE .... Centre de l'Information Europeenne (WGAO)
CPIH .... Compagnie de Participation et d'Investissement Holding SA
CPI(M)...... Communist Party of India (Marxist) [*Political party*] (PPW)
CPI(ML).... Communist Party of India (Marxist-Leninist) [*Political party*] (PD)
CPI M-L ... Communist Party of Ireland (Marxist-Leninist) [*Political party*] (PPW)
CPIN.......... Canadian Press Information Network (IID)
CP Ind....... Central Provinces, India (DLA)
CPIP.......... Consejo de Pesca Indo-Pacifico (WGAO)
CPIRC ...... China Population Information and Research Centre (IRC)
CPISP....... Comissao Pro-Indio de Sao Paulo [*Brazil*] (EAIO)
CPISP....... Comissao Pro-Indio do Sao Paulo [*Brazil*] (WGAO)
CPISRA..... Cerebral Palsy International Sports and Recreation Association [*Arnhem, Netherlands*] (EAIO)
CP-ISRA ... Cereral Palsy International Sports and Recreation Association (OLYM)
CPISS........ Comite Permanente Interamericano de Seguridad Social [*Inter-American Conference on Social Security - IACSS*] [*Spanish*]
CPISS........ Comite Permanent Interamericain de Securite Sociale [*Inter-American Conference on Social Security - IACSS*] [*French*]
CPITUS..... Comite Permanent International des Techniques et de l'Urbanisme Souterrains (WGAO)
CPIUS .... Comite Permanent Internacional de Tecnios y de Urbanismo Subterraneo (WGAO)
CPIV .... Comite Permanent des Industries du Verre de la CEE [*Brussels, Belgium*] (EAIO)
CPIV .... Comite Permanent International du Vinaigre [*Marche Commun*] (WGAO)
CPJ .... Club du Pekinois et du Japonais [*France*] (EAIO)
CPJ .... Committee to Protect Journalists (WGAO)
CPJ .... Communist Party of Jamaica (LA)
CPJI.......... Cour Permanente de Justice Internationale [*French*]
CPK .... Ceskoslovenska Presidlovaci Komise [*Czechoslovak Commission for Population Resettlement*] (CZ)
CPK .... Cesky Plavecky Klub [*Czech Swimming Club*] (CZ)
CPK .... Chawangan Penyiasatan Khas [*Special Investigation Branch*] (ML)

CPK .... Communist Party of Kampuchea [*Political party*] (PD)
CPK .... Communist Party of Kazakhstan [*Former USSR*] [*Political party*]
cPk .... Continental Polar Cold Air Mass (BARN)
cpl............... Carpel [*Botany*] (BARN)
CPL............ Cats Protection League (WGAO)
CPL............ Centre Paritaire du Logement (WGAO)
CPL............ Ceskoslovenska Plavba Labska [*Czechoslovak Elbe River Navigation Lines*] (CZ)
CPL............ Ceskoslovenske Podniky Lihovarnicke, Narodni Podnik [*Czechoslovak Alcohol Distilling Industries, National Enterprise*] (CZ)
CPL............ Chawangan Polis Laut [*Marine Police Branch*] (ML)
CPL............ Combinatul de Prelucrarea Lemnului [*Wood Processing Combine*] (RO)
CPL............ Commonwealth Parliamentary Library [*Australia*]
CPL............ Communist Party of Latvia [*Political party*]
CPL............ Communist Party of Lebanon (ME)
CPL............ Communist Party of Lesotho [*Political party*] (PD)
CPL............ Communist Party of Lithuania [*Political party*]
CPL............ Communist Party of Luxembourg [*Political party*]
CPL............ Confederation des Professions Liberales (WGAO)
CPL............ Conference Europeenne des Pouvoirs Locaux
CPL............ Conference Permanente des Pouvoirs Locaux et Regionaux de l'Europe (WGAO)
CPL............ Corps Peralatan [*Ordnance Corps*] (IN)
CPL............ Croatian Party of Law [*Political party*]
CPLA......... Cordillera People's Liberation Army [*Philippines*] [*Political party*] (EY)
CPLA......... Country Public Libraries Association [*New South Wales, Australia*]
CPLANSW ... Country Public Libraries Association, New South Wales [*Australia*]
CPLCM ..... Centrul de Proiectare pentru Lucrari de Constructii-Montaj [*Design Center for Construction-Installation Projects*] (RO)
CPLF .... Congres des Psychanalystes de Langue Francaise [*Congress of Romance Language Psychoanalysts*] (EAIO)
CPLiA........ Centrala Przemyslu Ludowego i Artystycznego [*Central Office of Folk and Art Crafts*] (POL)
CPLIM ...... Centrul de Perfectionare a Lucratorilor din Industria Metalurgica [*Center for Advanced Training of Workers in the Metallurgical Industry*] (RO)
CPLK........ Comite Permanent de Liaison des Kinesitherapeutes de la CEE [*Standing Liaison Committee of Physiotherapists within the EEC - SLCP*] [*Copenhagen, Denmark*] (EAIO)
CPLO........ Ceskoslovenska Plavba Labskooderska [*Czechoslovak Elbe-Oder River Navigation Lines*] (CZ)
CPLO........ Consortium Photo Lunetterie Optique
CPLS .... Canberra Public Library Service [*Australia*] (ADA)
CPLS .... Centre for Petrology and Lithospheric Studies [*Macquarie University*] [*Australia*]
CPLS .... Centrul de Proiectari pentru Lucrari Speciale de Constructii Montaj in Constructiile de Masini [*Design Center for Special Construction Installation Projects in Machine Building*] (RO)
CPLS .... Cleft Palate and Lip Society [*Australia*]
cplt .... Compleet [*Complete*] [*Publishing*] [*Netherlands*]
CPM .... Central Pacific Minerals [*Australia*]
CPM .... Centre de Pyrolyse de Marienau [*Marienau Pyrolysis Center*] [*France*] (IRC)
CPM .... Certified Property Manager [*Australia*]
CPM .... College of Petroleum and Minerals [*Saudi Arabia*] (WGAO)
CPM .... Comision del Pacifico Meridional [*South Pacific Commission - SPC*] [*Spanish*] (ASF)
CPM .... Comite du Patrimoine Mondial [*World Heritage Committee - WHC*] (EAIO)
CPM .... Comite pro Maria [*An association*] [*Belgium*] (EAIO)
CPM .... Commission Permanente des Mandats [*France*] (FLAF)
CPM .... Commonwealth Procurement Manual [*Australia*]
CPM .... Communist Party of India - Marxist [*Political party*] (FEA)
CPM .... Communist Party of Malaya [*Political party*] (PD)
CPM .... Communist Party of Malta [*Political party*]
CPM .... Communist Party of Moldavia [*Political party*]
CPM .... Complement de Precompte Mobilier [*Benelux*] (BAS)
CPM .... Conference Permanente d'Etudes sur les Civilisations du Monde Mediterraneen [*Standing Conference of Studies on the Civilisations of the Mediterranean World*] (EAIO)
CPM .... Conference Permanente Mediterraneenne pour la Cooperation Internationale [*Standing Mediterranean Conference for International Cooperation - COPEMCI*] (EAIO)
CPM .... Congregatio Presbyterorum a Misericordia (WGAO)
CPM .... Consumer Product Marketing Proprietary Ltd. [*Australia*]
CPM .... Coordinadora Politico-Militar [*Political-Military Coordinator*] [*El Salvador*] (LA)
CPM .... Corpo de Policia do Mocambique [*Mozambique Police Corps*] (AF)

CPM .... Corporacion ProCrusada Mundial (WGAO)
CPM .... Corps Polisi Militer [*Military Police Corps*] (IN)
CPM .... Cour Permanente des Mandats
CPM .... Swedish Fellowship of Reconciliation (EAIO)
CPMA ...... Cape Province Municipal Association [*South Africa*] (AA)
CPMB........ Consiliul Popular al Municipiului Bucuresti [*People's Council of Bucharest Municipality*] (RO)
CPMC....... Comite Permanent pour le Marche Commun de la Federation Internationale de la Construction (WGAO)
CPMC....... Commission Permanente de Marche Commun de Bureau International des Producteurs d'Assurances et de Reassurances (WGAO)
CPMCT ..... Comite Provincial Malgache Contre le Tuberculose
CPME....... Committee in Postgraduate Medical Education [*University of New South Wales*] [*Australia*]
CPME....... Conseil Parlementaire du Mouvement Europeen (FLAF)
CPME....... Council for Postgraduate Medical Education [*Later, SCPME*] (WGAO)
CPME....... Council on Podiatric Medical Education (WGAO)
CPMEE..... Comite Permanent des Foires et Manifestations Economiques a l'Etranger (WGAO)
CPMG ...... Carrosserie Parisienne-Mecanique Generale
CPMJO.... Conference of Presidents of Major Jewish Organizations
CPMM ...... Comite de la Protection du Milieu Marin [*OMCI*] (WGAO)
CPM-ML... Communist Party of Malaya - Marxist-Leninist [*Political party*] (PD)
CPMOAC ... Comite Permanent de Mise en Oeuvre des Aides Commercialisees [*Permanent Committee for the Application of Commercialized Aid*] [*Cambodia*] (CL)
CPMP....... Comissariado Provincial da Mocidade Portuguesa
CPMP....... Commission Permanente des Marches Publics [*Benelux*] (BAS)
CPMP-AP ... Commission Permanente des Marches Publics - Assemblee Pleniere [*Benelux*] (BAS)
CPMP-GT ... Commission Permanente des Marches Publics - Groupe de Travail [*Benelux*] (BAS)
CPMR....... Conference of Peripheral Maritime Regions of the EEC (EAIO)
CPM-RF.... Communist Party of Malaya - Revolutionary Faction [*Malaysia*] [*Political party*] (PD)
CPN .... Cape Rodney [*Papua New Guinea*] [*Airport symbol*] (OAG)
CPN .... Centrala Produktow Naftowych [*Petroleum Products Center*] (POL)
CPN .... Centrala Przemyslu Naftowego [*Petroleum Industry Center*] (POL)
CPN .... Coalicion Patriotica Nacional [*Panama*] (LAA)
CPN .... Comissao de Politica Nacional [*National Policy Committee*] [*Portuguese*] (WER)
CPN .... Comite Politico Nacional [*National Political Committee (of Accion Democratica)*] [*Venezuela*] (LA)
CPN .... Commission Paritaire Nationale [*Benelux*] (BAS)
CPN .... Commonwealth Procurement Notice [*Australia*]
CPN .... Communistische Partij van Nederland [*Communist Party of the Netherlands*] (PPE)
CPN .... Communist Party of Nepal [*Political party*] (FEA)
CPN .... Communist Party of Norway [*Political party*]
CPN .... Consejo Politico Nacionalista [*Nationalist Political Council*] [*Bolivia*] (LA)
Cpn............. Copenhagen (BARN)
CPN .... Country Progressive National Party [*Australia*] [*Political party*]
CPN .... Cuerpo de la Policia Nacional (WGAO)
CPNA .... Commission Paritaire Nationale pour les Enterprises Agricoles (WGAO)
CPNB........ Collective Propaganda van het Nederlandse Boek (WGAO)
CPNC .... Cameroon People's National Congress
CPNC .... Cameroon People's National Convention [*Political party*] (AF)
CPNCEP ... Chambre Professionnelle Nationale des Conseillers de l'Economie Prive (WGAO)
CPNHMR ... National Heritage Conservation Commission [*Zambia*] (EAIO)
CPNK .... Communist Party of North Kalimantan (ML)
CPNLAF ... Cambodian People's National Liberation Armed Forces (CL)
CPNSW ..... Council of Professions, New South Wales [*Australia*]
CPNT .... Comite Panamericano de Normas Tecnicas [*Argentina*] (DSCA)
CPNU .... Conference des Plenipotentiaires
CPNZ .... Communist Party of New Zealand [*Political party*]
CPO .... Cartes Perforees Ordinateurs [*French*] (ADPT)
CPO .... Central Planning Organization [*Prime Minister's Office*] [*Yeman Arab Republic*]
CPO .... Centre for Chiropractic and Osteopathy [*Macquarie University*] [*Australia*]
CPO .... Centre Pluridisciplinaire d'Oncologie [*University of Lausanne*] [*Switzerland*]
CPO .... Centrum voor Plantenfysiologisch Onderzoek (WGAO)
CPO .... Ceskoslovenska Plavba Oderska [*Czechoslovak Oder River Navigation Lines*] (CZ)
CPO .... Chief Personnel Officer [*Trinidadian-Tobagan*] (LA)
CPO .... Circulo Paulista de Orquidofilos [*Brazil*] (DSCA)
CPO .... Civilna Protiletecka Obrana [*Civil Air Defense*] (CZ)
CPO .... Commonwealth Producers Organization [*Australia*] (ADA)

CPO .... Community Project Officer [Australia]
CPOA .... Commonwealth Police Officers' Association [Australia]
CPOATA ... Chief Petty Officer Air Technical Aircraft [Military] [Australia]
CPO ATC .. Chief Petty Officer Air Technical Communication [Military] [Australia]
CPO CD..... Chief Petty Officer Clearance Diver [Military] [Australia]
CPOCOX ... Chief Petty Officer Coxswain [Military] [Australia]
CPODEN ... Chief Petty Officer Dental [Military] [Australia]
CPO ETC .. Chief Petty Officer Electronic Technical Communications [Military] [Australia]
CPO ETP .. Chief Petty Officer Electrical Technical Power [Military] [Australia]
CPOETW ... Chief Petty Officer Electrical Technical Weapons [Military] [Australia]
CPO EW.... Chief Petty Officer Electronic Warfare [Military] [Australia]
CPO FC..... Chief Petty Officer Fire Control [Military] [Australia]
CPO FF ..... Chief Petty Officer Firefighter [Military] [Australia]
CPOI......... Comision de Pesca para el Oceano Indico [Indian Ocean Fishery Commission - IOFC] [Spanish]   (ASF)
CPOI......... Commission des Peches pour l'Ocean Indien [Indian Ocean Fishery Commission - IOFC] [French]   (ASF)
CPOIR....... Commission Permanente de l'Organisation Internationale pour les Refugies
CPOM .... Centro de Preclasificacion Oceanica de Mexico [Mexican Oceanic Sorting Center]   (ASF)
CPOMED ... Chief Petty Officer Medical [Military] [Australia]
CPOMET ... Chief Petty Officer Meteorology [Military] [Australia]
CPOMTD ... Chief Petty Officer Motor Transport Driver [Military] [Australia]
CPOMTH ... Chief Petty Officer Marine Technical Hull [Military] [Australia]
CPOMTP ... Chief Petty Officer Marine Technical Propulsion [Military] [Australia]
CPOMUSN ... Chief Petty Officer Musician [Military] [Australia]
CPO MW .. Chief Petty Officer Mine Warfare [Military] [Australia]
CPO PH .... Chief Petty Officer Photography [Military] [Australia]
CPOQMG ... Chief Petty Officer Quartermaster Gunner [Military] [Australia]
CPOR .... Centro de Preparacao de Oficiais da Reserva [Reserve Officers Training Center] [Brazil]   (LA)
CPO RO .... Chief Petty Officer Radio Operator [Military] [Australia]
CPO RP..... Chief Petty Officer Radio Plotter [Military] [Australia]
CPO SE ..... Chief Petty Officer Survival Equipment [Military] [Australia]
CPO SIG ... Chief Petty Officer Signalman [Military] [Australia]
CPO SN ..... Chief Petty Officer Stores Naval [Military] [Australia]
CPO SR ..... Chief Petty Officer Survey Recorder [Military] [Australia]
CPO SV ..... Chief Petty Officer Stores Victualling [Military] [Australia]
CPO UC .... Chief Petty Officer Underwater Control [Military] [Australia]
CPO WS... Chief Petty Officer Work Study [Military] [Australia]
CPP........... Cambodian People's Party [Political party]   (ECON)
CPP........... Center for the Progress of Peoples   (EAIO)
CPP........... Centralna Poradnia Przeciwgruzlicza [Central Anti-Tuberculosis Counseling Office]   (POL)
CPP........... Christian People's Party [Norway]
CPP........... Code de Procedure en Matiere Penale [Penal Procedure Code] [Cambodia]   (CL)
CPP........... Commonwealth Parliamentary Papers [Australia]   (ADA)
CPP........... Communist Party of the Philippines [Political party]
CPP........... Convention People's Party [1949-1966] [Ghana]
CPP........... Cornwall People's Party [Jamaica]   (LA)
CPP........... Croatian Peasants Party [Political party]   (EY)
CPPA........ Cadmium Pigments Association [Belgium]   (EAIO)
CPPA........ Coal Preparation Plant Association   (WGAO)
CPPA........ Comissao de Planejamento da Politica Agraria [Rio De Janeiro, Brazil]   (LAA)
CPPA........ Corpo de Policia Popular de Angola [Angolan People's Police Corps]   (AF)
CPPB........ Comite de Problemas de Productos Basicos [Committee on Commodity Problems] [Italy]   (ASF)
CPPB........ Commonwealth Prickly Pear Board [Australia]   (ADA)
CPPC........ Caribbean Plant Protection Commission [Trinidad and Tobago]   (EAIO)
CPPC........ Centrul de Productie, Prestari, si Constructii [Center for Production, Service, and Constructions]   (RO)
CPPC........ China Pictorial Publishing Co.   (TCC)
CPPC........ Conseil Portugais pour la Paix et le Cooperation [Portuguese Council for Peace and Cooperation]   (EAIO)
CPPCA ...... Colour Printed Pottery Collectors Association   (EAIO)
CPPCC ...... Chinese People's Political Consultative Conference
CPPCh....... Centrala Prywatnego Przemyslu Chemicznego [Central Office of the Privately-Owned Chemical Industry]   (POL)
CPPER ...... Commonwealth Program for the Promotion of Excellence in Research [Australia]
CPPG........ Cable Programme Providers Group   (WGAO)
CPPI .... Consultative Panel on Public Information [United Nations (already exists in GUS II database)] [Telecommunications]

CPPIM ...... Center for Preservation and Propagation of Iranian Music   (EAIO)
CPPL .... Companhia Porto de Pesca de Laguna [Brazil]   (DSCA)
CPP/ML.... Communist Party of the Philippines/Marxist-Leninist [Political party]
CPPPD ...... Centre de la Planification, des Projections et des Politiques Relatives au Developpement [United Nations]   (WGAO)
CPP-PFIP ... [The] Christian People's Party - Progressive and Fishing Industry Party [Kristiligi Folkaflokkurin, Foroya Framburds- og Fiskivinnuflokkurin] [The Faroe Islands] [Political party]   (EY)
CPPS .... Centrala Prywatnego Przemyslu Spozywczego [Central Office of the Privately-Owned Food Industry]   (POL)
CPPS .... Comision Permanente del Pacifico Sur [Permanent Commission for the South Pacific - PCSP]   (EAIO)
CPPS .... Comision Permanente para la Explotacion y Conservacion de las Riquezas Maritimas del Pacifico Sur [Permanent Commission for the Conservation and Exploitation of the Maritime Resources of the South Pacific] [Quito, Ecuador]   (LAA)
CPPS .... Commission Permanente du Pacifique Sud [Permanent Commission for the South Pacific - PCSP] [French]   (ASF)
CPPS .... Congregatio Missionariorum Pretiossimi Sanguinis   (WGAO)
CPPT .... Cooperative Program Planning and Teaching [Australia]
CPQ .... Campinas [Brazil] [Airport symbol]   (OAG)
CPR.......... Centrale Personregister [Personal number certificate] [Denmark]
CPR.......... Centre du Perfectionnement et de Recyclage [Training and Retraining Center] [Cambodia]   (CL)
CPR.......... Centre for Policy Research [India] [Research center]   (IRC)
CPR.......... Centres Pedagogiques Regionaux [Regional Teacher Training Centers] [Cambodia]   (CL)
CPR.......... Chantiers Populaires de Reboisement [Popular Projects for Reforestation] [Algeria]   (AF)
CPR.......... Comite de Politique Regionale [CEE]   (WGAO)
CPR.......... Commission Paritaire Regionale [Benelux]   (BAS)
CPR.......... Conferencia Peruana de Religiosos   (WGAO)
CPR.......... Conseil Populaire de Redemption
CPR.......... Conseil Provincial de la Revolution [Provincial Council of the Revolution] [Benin]   (AF)
CPR.......... Croatian Party of Rights [Political party]
CPr........... Preparatory Classes [French]
CPRA........ Chinese Public Relations Association   (WGAO)
CPRA........ Comite Permanent de la Racherche Agricole [CEE]   (WGAO)
CPRAD...... Corps Pemeliharaan Rochani Angkatan Darat [Army Chaplains Corps]   (IN)
CPRC........ Coloured Persons' Representative Council [South Africa]   (PPW)
CPRC........ Corporate Plan and Review Committee [Library Association of Australia]
CPRI.......... Central Potato Research Institute [India]   (ARC)
CPRI.......... Central Power Research Institute [India]
CPrI .... Complement de Precompte Immobilier [Benelux]   (BAS)
CPRM........ Companhia de Pesquisas de Recursos Minerais (MINEROBRAS) [Mineral Resources Prospecting Company] [Brazil]   (LAA)
CPRM........ Companhia Portuguesa Radio Marconi [Portuguese Radio Marconi Co.] [Lisbon] [Information service or system]   (IID)
CProg........ Country Progressive Party [Australia]   (ADA)
CPRP........ Ciskei People's Rights Protection Party [South Africa] [Political party]   (EY)
CPRS .... Committee for the Promotion of Scientific Research [Belgium]   (ARC)
CPRU .... Colonial Pesticides Research Unit
CPS........... Canberra Philharmonic Society [Australia]
CPS........... Canberra Photographic Society [Australia]
CPS........... Canberra Pre-School Society [Australia]
CPS........... Caractere Par Seconde [French]   (ADPT)
CPS........... Cargo & Passenger Air Services Ltd. [Switzerland] [ICAO designator]   (FAAC)
CPS........... Cargo Packing Services [Saudi Arabia]
CPS........... Celostatni Plachtarske Zavody [All-State Glider Contest]   (CZ)
CPS........... Centre for Policy Studies [Monash University] [Australia]
CPS........... Centrul de Proiectare si Scularie [Center for Design and Tooling]   (RO)
CPS........... Ceska Protifasisticka Spolecnost [Czech Anti-Fascist Society]   (CZ)
CPS........... Ceskoslovenske Pivovary a Sladovny, Narodni Podnik [Czechoslovak Breweries and Malt Factories, National Enterprise]   (CZ)
CPS........... Cesky Pevecky Sbor [Czech Choral Society]   (CZ)
CPS........... Children's Protection Society
CPS........... Christian Psychological Services [Australia]
CPS........... Citizens Protection Society   (WGAO)
CPS........... Colombian Pedriatric Society   (EAIO)
CPS........... Comision del Pacifico Sur [South Pacific Commission - SPC] [Spanish]   (MSC)

CPS........... Commission du Pacifique Sud [*South Pacific Commission - SPC*] (EAIO)
CPS........... Committee for Penicillin Sensitivity (WGAO)
CPS........... Commonwealth Public Service [*Australia*] (ADA)
CPS........... Communist Party of Slovakia [*Political party*]
CPS........... Communist Party of Syria (ME)
cps............. Companeros [*Companions*] [*Spanish*]
CPS........... Court of Petty Sessions [*Australia*]
CPS........... Credit Populaire du Senegal
CPS........... Cristianos por el Socialismo [*Christians for Socialism*] [*Spanish*] (WER)
CPS........... Cyprus Pediatric Society (EAIO)
CPS........... Missionary Sisters of the Precious Blood [*Italy*]
CPSA........ Caribbean Public Services Association [*Barbados*] (EAIO)
CPSA........ Civil and Public Services Association (WGAO)
CPSA........ Clay Pigeon Shooting Association (WGAO)
CPSA........ Comite Permanent des Structures Agricoles [*CEE*] (WGAO)
CPSA........ Commonwealth Public Service Association [*Australia*] (ADA)
CPSA........ Communist Party of South Africa [*Political party*] (PD)
CPSA........ Compromiso Politico, SA [*Political Compromise, Inc.*] [*Spanish*] (WER)
CPSA........ Conservative Party of South Africa [*Konserwatiewe Party van Suid-Afrika*] [*Political party*] (PPW)
CPSA........ Consiliul Politic Superior al Armatei [*Higher Political Council of the Army*] (RO)
CPSA........ Consumer Product Safety Association [*Japan*]
CPSAA...... Commonwealth Public Service Artisans' Association [*Australia*] (ADA)
CPSASA.... Clay Pigeon Shooting Association of Southern Africa
CPSCDN ... Centrul pentru Specializarea Cadrelor in Domeniul Nuclear [*Center for Specialization of Personnel in the Nuclear Field*] (RO)
CPSD........ Club de Peche Sportive de Dakar
CPSDHRK ... Commission Parlementaire Speciale pour la Defense de l'Honneur de la Republique Khmere [*Special Parliamentary Committee to Defend the Honor of the Khmer Republic*] [*Cambodia*] (CL)
CPSE .... Committee on Plant Supply and Establishment (WGAO)
CPSEAQ ... Community Pre-School Employers' Association of Queensland [*Australia*]
CPSG........ Children of Prisoners Support Group [*Australia*]
CPSG........ China Policy Study Group (WGAO)
CPSL .... Ceskoslovenska Paroplavebni Spolecnost Labska [*Czechoslovak Elbe River Lines*] (CZ)
CPSL .... Communist Party of Slovakia [*Former Czechoslovakia*] [*Political party*] (EY)
CPSL .... Communist Party of Sri Lanka [*Political party*] (FEA)
CPSL .... Communist Party of Syria and the Lebanon [*Political party*] (BJA)
CPSNSW .. Cat Protection Society of New South Wales [*Australia*]
CPSP .... Caisse de Perequation et de Stabilisation des Prix [*Price Equalization and Stabilization Fund*] [*Senegal*]
CPSR........ Centre for Public Sector Research [*University of Canberra*] [*Australia*]
CPSS........ Compagnie des Pretres de St. Sulpice [*Society of the Priests of St. Sulpice - SPSS*] [*France*] (EAIO)
CPSS........ Congreso Panamericano de Servicio Social (LAA)
CPSSAE.... Centro Polesano di Studi Storici Archeologici, Etnografici [*Italian*] (SLS)
CPSSU ...... Civil and Public Services Staff Union [*Eire*] (WGAO)
CPST .... Comite de la Politique Scientifique et Technologie [*OCDE*] (WGAO)
CPSU........ Communist Party of the Soviet Union [*Political party*] (PPW)
CPSU........ Community and Public Sector Union [*Australia*]
CPSV........ Cat Protection Society of Victoria [*Australia*]
CPT........... Cape Town [*South Africa*] [*Airport symbol*] (OAG)
CPT........... Centennial Park Trust [*Australia*]
CPT........... Central Puertorriquena de Trabajadores [*Puerto Rican Workers' Center*]
CPT........... Centre for Precision Technology [*Australia*]
CPT........... Comissao Pastoral da Terra [*Pastoral Land Commission*] [*Brazil*] (LA)
CPT........... Communist Party of Tadzhikistan [*Political party*]
CPT........... Communist Party of Thailand [*Political party*] (PD)
CPT........... Communist Party of Turkey [*Political party*] (PD)
CPT........... Communist Party of Turkmenistan [*Political party*]
cpt .... Comptant [*Cash*] [*French*] [*Business term*]
CPT........... Confederacion Paraguaya de Trabajadores [*Paraguayan Workers Federation*] (LA)
CPT........... Confederation of British Road Passenger Transport (WGAO)
CPT........... Congreso Permanente de los Trabajadores [*Nicaragua*] (EY)
Cpt .... Contrepoint [*Record label*] [*France*]
CPTA......... China Printing Technology Association (EAIO)
CPTB......... Clay Products Technical Bureau (WGAO)
CPTC......... China Productivity and Trade Centre (WGAO)
CPTC......... Commission Politique des Travailleurs Chretiens [*Benelux*] (BAS)

CPTE......... Comite Permanent des Transports Europeens (WGAO)
cpte............ Compte [*Account*] [*French*] [*Business term*]
CPTE......... Societe pour la Coordination de la Production et du Transport d'Energie Electrique [*Benelux*] (BAS)
cpte ct........ Compte Courant [*Current Account*] [*French*] [*Business term*]
CPTI .... Computer Power Training Institute [*Australia*]
CPTL .... Compagnie des Petroles Total Libye
CPTR .... Cetni Protivtenkovski Reon [*Company Antitank Sector*] (YU)
CPTT .... Central Panamena de Trabajadores del Transporte [*Federation of Panamanian Transport Workers*] (LA)
CPTU........ Council of Progressive Trade Unions [*Trinidadian and Tobagan*] (LA)
CPU .... Centro de Planificacion y Urbanismo (de la Universidad de los Andes) [*Colorado*] (LAA)
CPU .... Centro Nacional de Productividad del Uruguay (LAA)
CPU .... Ceskoslovensky Plavebni Ustav [*Czechoslovak Institute for Navigation*] (CZ)
CPU .... Comite Patriotico Unificado [*United Patriotic Committee*] [*Dominican Republic*] (LA)
CPU .... Commonwealth Press Union [*London, England*] (EAIO)
CPU .... Communist Party of Ukraine [*Political party*]
CPU .... Complexe Polytechnique Universitaire
CPUBINFO ... Chief of Public Information Division [*NATO*] (NATG)
CPUN .... Comite pour la Paix et l'Unite Nationale
CPUSOFBLNJ ... Committee on Peaceful Uses of the Sea-Bed and Ocean Floor Beyond Limits of National Jurisdiction [*United Nations*] (EA)
CPUSTAL ... Congreso Permanente de Unidad Sindical de los Trabajadores de America Latina [*Latin American Workers Permanent Congress for Trade Union Unity*] (LA)
CPUz......... Communist Party of Uzbekistan [*Political party*]
CPV .... Campaign for Peace in Vietnam [*Australia*]
CPV .... Campina Grande [*Brazil*] [*Airport symbol*] (OAG)
CPV .... Cape Verde [*ANSI three-letter standard code*] (CNC)
CPV .... Centrale Proefstations Vereniging (WGAO)
CPV .... Chinese Communist People's Volunteers (MCD)
CPV .... Communist Party of Venezuela [*Political party*]
CPV .... Consorcio de Publicidad y Ventas [*Colombia*] (COL)
CPV .... Corporacion Peruana de Vapores [*Peruvian Shipping Corporation*] (LA)
CPVZ........ Celostatne Patranie po Vojenskom Zbehovi [*National Search for Military Deserters*] (CZ)
CPWC....... Central Peoples Workers Council [*Burma*] (WGAO)
CPWD....... Central Public Works Department [*India*] (WGAO)
CPWOA .... Cape Peninsula Welfare Organization of the Aged
CPX........... Culebra [*Puerto Rico*] [*Airport symbol*] (OAG)
CPY........... Communist Party of Yugoslavia
CPZ........... Cargo & Passenger Air Services Ltd. [*Switzerland*] [*ICAO designator*] (FAAC)
CPZ........... Celni Pochodova Zastita [*Forward March Screening Element*] (CZ)
cq............... Casu Quo [*Benelux*] (BAS)
CQ............. Central Queensland [*Australia*]
CQ............. Chef de Quart
CQA........... Coast Air Ltd. [*Kenya*] [*ICAO designator*] (FAAC)
CQA........... Companhia Quimica de Alagoas [*Brazil*]
CQACCA... Central Queensland Aboriginal Corporation for Cultural Activities [*Australia*]
CQALCA... Central Queensland Articled Law Clerks' Association [*Australia*]
CQC........... Central Queensland Cement [*Australia*]
CQCA .... Central Queensland Coal Associates [*Australia*] (ADA)
CQCA .... Central Queensland Consumers Association [*Australia*]
CQCJ......... Comite des Questions Constitutionnelles et Juridiques [*FAO*] (WGAO)
CQEE .... Conseil du Quebec de l'Enfance Exceptionnelle (WGAO)
CQEMB .... Central Queensland Egg Marketing Board [*Australia*]
CQFD .... Ce Qu'il Fallait Demontrer [*The Thing to Be Proved*] [*French*]
cqfd........... Ce Qu'il Fallait Dire [*French*] (FLAF)
CQG.......... Compagnie de Quartier General
CQGSMB ... Central Queensland Grain Sorghum Marketing Board [*Australia*]
CQRG .... Central Queensland Regional Group [*Australian Library and Information Association*]
CQRI .... Centre Quebecois de Relations Internationales (WGAO)
CQSA .... Commonwealth-Queensland Sugar Agreement [*Australia*] (ADA)
CQSS........ Central Queensland Speleological Society [*Australia*]
CQT.......... Caquetania [*Colombia*] [*Airport symbol*] (OAG)
CQU.......... Central Queensland University [*Australia*]
CR............. Calendrier Republicain [*Republican Calendar*] [*French*]
CR............. Centraal Rassenregister [*Benelux*] (BAS)
CR............. Centrala Rybna [*Fish Center*] (POL)
CR............. Centrale Raad van Beroep [*Benelux*] (BAS)
CR............. Centre for Robotics [*Chisholm Institute of Technology*] [*Australia*]
CR............. Ceskoslovensky Rozhlas [*Czechoslovak Broadcasting*] (CZ)
CR............. Chambre des Representants [*Benelux*] (BAS)

CR .... Chargeurs Reunis
CR .... China Corporation Register (Taiwan) [*Chinese ship classification society*] (DS)
Cr .... Chrom [*Chromium*] [*Chemical element*] [*German*]
CR .... Civilekonomernas Riksforbund [*Sweden*] (EAIO)
CR .... Collegium Romanicum [*Switzerland*] (SLS)
CR .... Comandos de la Resistencia [*Commandos of the Resistance*] [*Dominican Republic*] (LA)
CR .... Commission Restreinte [*Benelux*] (BAS)
CR .... Commission Rogatoire [*France*] (FLAF)
CR .... Commonwealth Railways [*Australia*] (ADA)
CR .... Community of the Resurrection [*CofE*] (WGAO)
CR .... Compagnons de la Revolution
CR .... Compte Rendu [*D'Ouvrage ou d'Article dans une Revue*] (FLAF)
CR .... Compte Rendu des Seances de la Chambre des Deputes du Grand-Duche de Luxembourg (BAS)
CR .... Congregatio a Resurrectione (WGAO)
CR .... Conseil de la Republique [*France*] (FLAF)
CR .... Conselho da Revolucao [*Council of the Revolution*] [*Portuguese*] (WER)
CR .... Costa Rica [*ANSI two-letter standard code*] (CNC)
cr .... Credit [*or Crediteur*] [*Creditor*] [*French*]
CR .... Credito Romagnolo [*Bank*] [*Italian*]
Cr .... Crimen - Tijdschrift voor Criminologie en Criminalistiek [*Benelux*] (BAS)
Cr .... Cromo [*Chromium*] [*Chemical element*] [*Portuguese*]
CR .... Cruzeiro [*Monetary unit*] [*Brazil*]
CR .... Cuadernos Rojos [*Red Notebooks*] [*Spanish*] (WER)
C/R .... Cuenta y Riesgo [*For Account and Risk Of*] [*Spanish*] [*Business term*]
CR .... Ordo Clericorum Regularium vulgo Theatinorum (WGAO)
CRA .... Central Research Agency [*Cuc Nghien-Chu Trung-Uong*] [*North Vietnamese intelligence agency*]
CRA .... Centre de la Recherche Appliquee
CRA .... Centre de Recherche Africaine
CRA .... Centre de Recherches Agronomiques de Gembloux [*Agricultural Research Center of Gembloux*] [*Research center*] [*Belgium*] (IRC)
CRA .... Centres de la Recherche Appliquee [*Zaire*] (WGAO)
CRA .... Centres de Recherches Agronomiques (WGAO)
CRA .... Centro Richerche Aerospaziali [*Italian*]
CRA .... Centros de Reforma Agraria [*Agrarian Reform Centers*] [*Chile*] (LA)
CRA .... Cereal Ryegrowers' Association [*Australia*]
CRA .... Chemical Recovery Association (WGAO)
CRA .... Christian Research Association
CRA .... City Resources Asia [*Metals company*] [*Hong Kong*]
CRA .... Civil Rights Association [*Northern Ireland*]
CRA .... Clinical Research Associate [*Australia*]
CRA .... College of Radiologists of Australasia (ADA)
CRA .... Colostomy Rehabilitation Association [*Australia*] (ADA)
CRA .... Comision de Reforma Agraria [*Agrarian Reform Commission*] [*Panama*] (LAA)
CRA .... Commercial Rabbit Association (WGAO)
CRA .... Commission Permanente du Controle et de la Repression de la Circulation des Automobiles [*Permanent Automobile Traffic Control Commission*] [*Cambodia*] (CL)
CRA .... Commission Regionale d'Appel de Securite Sociale [*France*] (FLAF)
CRA .... Compagnie Riunite di Assicurazione [*Insurance*] [*Italy*] (EY)
CRA .... Companhia Riograndense de Adubos [*Brazil*] (DSCA)
CRA .... Compte-Rendu Analytique des Travaux du Conseil Colonial, Puis Conseil de Legislation [*Benelux*] (BAS)
CRA .... Confederaciones Rurales Argentinas [*Argentine Rural Confederations*] (LA)
CRA .... Conzinc Riotinto of Australia Ltd. (ADA)
CRA .... Coronado Aerolineas Ltda. [*Colombia*] [*ICAO designator*] (FAAC)
CRA .... Craiova [*Romania*] [*Airport symbol*] (OAG)
CRA .... Credit Reference Association of Australia Ltd.
cra .... Criada [*Servant (Feminine)*] [*Portuguese*]
CRA .... Crime Reporters Association (WGAO)
CRA .... Croissant Rouge Algerien [*Algerian Red Crescent*] (AF)
CRAA .... Centre de Recherche Agro-Alimentaire [*Agro-Industrial Research Center*] [*Zaire*] (IRC)
CRAA .... Credit Reference Association of Australia
CRAAM .... Centro de Radio-Astonomia e Astrofisica Universidade Mackenzie [*Brazil*] (WGAO)
CRAB........ Centro Ricerche Applicazione Bioritmo [*Italian*] (SLS)
CRAB........ Crustacean Reprobiology and Aquaculture Bureau [*India*] (ASF)
CRAC .... Careers Research and Advisory Centre (WGAO)
CRAC .... Centre Regional d'Action Culturelle [*Togo*] (WGAO)
CRAC .... Centre Reunionnais d'Action Culturelle
CRAC .... Centro de Rehabilitacion para Adultos y Ciegos [*Colombia*] (COL)

CRAC .... Comite Regional Africain de Coordination (pour l'Integration de la Femme au Developpement) [*African Regional Committee for Coordination (for the Integration of Women in Development)*] (AF)
CRAC .... Community Renewal and Action Council
CRAC .... Conferencia Regional de Aviacion Civil (LAA)
CRACAC... Center for Research on Arabic and the Culture of the Arab Countries [*COACAL*] [*Ghent, Belgium*] [*See also*] (MENA)
CRACAP... Centre National de Recherche, d'Animation et de Creation pour les Arts Plasti ques [*France*] (EAIO)
CRACCUS ... Comite Regional de l'Afrique Centrale et l'Utilisation du Sol
CRACCUS ... Comite Regional de l'Afrique Centrale pour la Conservation et l'Utilisation des Sols (WGAO)
CRACFT ... Centre Regional Africain de Conception et de Fabrication Techniques [*Nigeria*] (EAIO)
CRAD .... Centre de Recherches Appliques du Dahomey
CRAD .... Centres Regionaux d'Assistance Technique pour le Developpement [*Regional Centers for Technical Development Assistance*] [*Senegal*] (AF)
CRAD .... Centro di Ricerca Applicata e Documentazione [*Italian*] (SLS)
CRAD .... Comite Revolutionnaire d'Administration du District [*Revolutionary Committee for District Administration*] [*Benin*] (AF)
CRAD .... Committee for Research into Apparatus for the Disabled (WGAO)
CRADAT... Centre Regional Africain d'Administration du Travail [*African Regional Labor Administration Center*] (AF)
CRADS...... Comite Republicain d'Action Democratique et Sociale [*Republican Committee for Democratic and Social Action*] [*Reunionese*] (AF)
CRADY ..... Compania Radial de Yarumal Ltda. [*Yarumal-Antioquia*] (COL)
CRAE........ Center for Research and Application in Ergonomics [*France*] (IRC)
CRAE........ Centre de Recherches Agronomiques d'Etat [*Belgium*] (WGAO)
CRAE........ Committee for the Reform of Animal Experimentation (WGAO)
CRAE........ CRA [*Conzinc Riotinto of Australia*] Exploration Ltd.
CRAE........ CRA [*Conzinc Rio-Tinto of Australia*] Exploration Proprietary Ltd.
CRAF........ Centre de Recherches Africaines (WGAO)
CRAF........ Comite Regional d'Arboriculture Fruitiere du Bassin Parisien (WGAO)
CRAF........ Comptoir de Representation et d'Agences de Fabriques
CRAF........ Comptoirs Reunis d'Afrique
CRAFOP... Centre de Recherche Appliquee Fondamentale et de Formation Permanente [*Universite Nationale du Rwanda*]
CRAFT ...... Centre Regional Africain de Conception et de Fabrication Techniques [*African Regional Centre for Engineering Design and Manufacturing - ARCEDEM*] (EAIO)
CRAFT ...... Commonwealth Rebate for Apprentice Full-Time Training [*Australia*] (ADA)
CRAG .... Cellular Radio Advisory Group (WGAO)
CRAG .... Centre National de Recherches et d'Application des Geosciences [*Algeria*] (SLS)
CRAG .... Cyclists' Rights Action Group [*Australia*]
CRAIC....... Centre de Recherches Economiques Agricoles Industrielles et Commerciales (WGAO)
CRAL........ Centre de Recherches Agronomiques de Lebamba [*Gabon*] (DSCA)
CRAL........ Comando Revolucionario para America Latina [*Revolutionary Command for Latin America*] (LA)
CRAM .... Centre de Recherches de Montpellier [*Montpellier Research Center*] [*French*] (ARC)
CRAM .... Centre de Recherches sur l'Afrique Mediterraneene [*North African*]
CRAM .... Centre de Renovation de l'Agriculture Malgache
CRAM .... Centre for Research into Asian Migration (WGAO)
CRAM .... Centro Revolucionario d'Aplicacao Militar
CRAM .... Collectivites Rurales Autochones Modernisees a Madagascar
CRAME..... Compania Radio Eerea Maritima Espanola [*Spain*] (PDAA)
CRAMRA ... Convention on the Regulation of Antarctic Mineral Resource Activities [*Australia*]
CRAN .... Cadena Radial Andina [*Colombia*] (COL)
CRANA ..... Council of Remote Area Nurses of Australia
CRANZ ..... Coal Research Association of New Zealand, Inc. [*Research center*] (IRC)
CrAO .... Crimean Astrophysical Observatory [*USSR Academy of Sciences*] [*Research center*] (EAS)
CRAOCA .. Cercle Royal des Anciens Officiers des Campagnes d'Afrique
CRAOCUS ... Comite Regional de l'Afrique Occidentale pour la Conservation et l'Utilisation du Sol
CRAP........ Centralian Range Assessment Program [*Australia*]
CRAP........ Centre de la Recherche en Anthropologie Prehistorique [*Prehistoric Anthropology Research Center*] [*Algeria*] (AF)
CRAP........ Centres Regionaux d'Action Pedagogique [*French*]

CRAPE...... Centre de Recherches Anthropoligiques, Prehistoriques et Ethnographiques [*Algeria*] (SLS)
CRARA...... Comissao Revolucionaria de Apoio a Reforma Agraria [*Revolutionary Commission for Support to the Agrarian Reform*] [*Portuguese*] (WER)
CRAS......... Centre for Radiobiology and Radiation Protection [*Netherlands*] (WGAO)
CRAS......... Centro Regional de Aguas Subterraneas [*Regional Center for Underground Water*] [*Argentina*] (LA)
CRAS......... Comisia Romana pentru Activitati Spatiale [*Romanian Commission for Space Activities*] (RO)
CRAS......... Comunas Revolucionarias de Accion Socialista [*Revolutionary Communes of Socialist Action*] [*Spanish*] (WER)
CRASH...... Citizens Revolt against Sound Harassment [*Australia*]
CRASTE.... Committee to Review Australian Studies in Tertiary Education
CRAT......... Centre Regional Africain de Technologie [*African Regional Centre for Technology - ARCT*] (EA)
CRAT......... Centro Regional de Ayuda Tecnica [*Mexico*] (DSCA)
CRATEMA ... Centro di Ricerca di Assistenza Tecnica e Mercantile alle Aziende (WGAO)
CRATO ..... Centre Regionale de Recherche et de Documentation pour la Tradition Orale (WGAO)
CRAU .... Centre de Recherches Appliquee pour l'Architecture et Urbanisme [*French*]
CRAU .... Centre de Recherches d'Architecture et d'Urbanisme [*Belgium*] (WGAO)
CRAV .... Comision de la Reforma Agraria y la Vivienda [*Peru*] (LAA)
CRAV .... Compania Refineria de Azucar Vina del Mar [*Chile*] (LAA)
CRB .... Cassa di Risparmio di Biella [*Bank*] [*Italian*]
CRB .... Centre Suisse de Rationalisation du Batiment (WGAO)
CRB .... Centro di Ricerche Biopsichiche [*Italian*] (SLS)
CRB .... Chemical, Radiological, Biological Warfare [*NATO*] (NATG)
CRB .... Chiropractors' Registration Board [*Australia*]
CRB .... Confederacao Rural Brasileira [*Rio De Janeiro, Brazil*] (LAA)
CRB .... Conferencia dos Religiosos do Brasil (WGAO)
CRB .... Conselho Regional de Biblioteconomia (WGAO)
CRB .... Cross River Breweries [*Nigeria*]
CRBF .... Commission Royale Belge de Folklore (WGAO)
CRBM .... Centre Regional de Biologie Marine [*Regional Marine Biological Center - RMBC*] [*French*] (ASF)
CRBM .... Centro Regional de Biologia Marina [*Regional Marine Biological Center - RMBC*] [*Spanish*] (ASF)
CRBT........ Centre de Recherches sur les Ressources Biologiques Terrestres [*Research Center for Natural Resources*] [*Algeria*] [*Research center*] (IRC)
CRBV........ Chiropodists' Registration Board of Victoria [*Australia*]
Cr C........... Arret de la Chambre Criminelle de la Cour de Cassation qui Rejette (FLAF)
Cr C........... Arret la Chambre Criminelle de la Cour de Cassation qui Casse (FLAF)
CRC .... Cairo River Club [*Egypt*]
CRC .... Canberra Rifle Club [*Australia*]
CRC .... Cancer Research Campaign (WGAO)
CRC .... Cartago [*Colombia*] [*Airport symbol*] (OAG)
CRC .... Center for Research and Communication [*Philippines*]
CRC .... Centre de Recherches et d'Etudes des Chefs d'Entreprise [*French*] (SLS)
CRC .... Centre de Recherches Techniques et Scientifiques Industries de la Tannerie, de la Chaussure, de la Pantoufle et des autres Industries Transformatrices du Cuir [*Belgium*] (WGAO)
CRC .... Centre d'Etudes et de Recherches des Chefs d'Enterprises (WGAO)
CRC .... Chemical Rubber Co. (WGAO)
CRC .... Chemistry Resource Centre [*Phillip Institute of Technology*] [*Australia*]
CRC .... China Record Co.
CRC .... Civilian Rule Committee [*Sierra Leone*] (AF)
CRC .... Coastal Resource Centre [*Australia*]
CRC .... Colored Persons Representative Council [*South Africa*] (AF)
CRC .... Comalco Research Centre [*Comalco Aluminium Ltd.*] [*Australia*] (EAS)
CRC .... Comite Revolutionnaire Cabindais
CRC .... Community Recreation Council [*Victoria*] [*Australia*]
CRC .... Comptoirs Reunis du Cameroun
CRC .... Conferencia de Religosos de Colombia (WGAO)
CRC .... Conseil de la Revolution Centrafricaine [*Council of the Central African Revolution*] (AF)
CRC .... Constitution Review Committee [*Nigeria*]
CRC .... Cooperative Regionale de Commerce [*Tunisia*]
CRC .... Cooperative Research Centre [*Australia*]
CRC .... Cotton Research Corp. (WGAO)
CRC .... Criminology Research Council [*Australia*]
CRC .... Cruz Roja Colombiana [*Colombian Red Cross*] (LA)
CRCA .... Caisse Regionale de Credit Agricole (WGAO)
CRCA .... Caisse Reunionnaise de Credit Agricole [*Reunion Agricultural Credit Bank*] (AF)
CRCA .... Central Region Cultural Authority [*South Australia*]

CRCA .... Comissao Reguladora do Comercio de Arroz [*Portugal*] (DSCA)
CRCAM..... Caisse Regionale de Credit Agricole Mutuel [*Regional Fund for Mutual Agricultural Credit*] [*Benin*] (AF)
CRCAWA ... Country Regional Councils' Association of Western Australia
CRCB......... Comissao Reguladora do Comercio de Bacalhau [*Codfish Trade Regulatory Commission*] [*Portuguese*] (WER)
CRCC........ Clarence River County Council [*Australia*]
CRCC........ Cooperative Research Centres Committee [*Australia*]
CRCCH ..... Centre for Research and Conservation of Cultural Heritage [*Ministry of Culture*] [*Ethiopia*]
CRCE........ Centre for Research into Communist Economies (WGAO)
CRCEC...... Commonwealth Research Centres of Excellence Committee [*Australia*]
CRCERT ... Cooperative Research Centre for Eye Research Technology [*Australia*]
CRCP........ Conference of Rivers Chiefs and Peoples
CRCP........ Costa Rican Cocoa Products Co. (WGAO)
CRCP........ Costa Rican Cocoa Produts Co. [*Costa Rica*] (DSCA)
CRCV........ Cooperative Research Centre for Viticulture [*Australia*]
CRD .... Aerolineas Cordillera Ltda. [*Chile*] [*ICAO designator*] (FAAC)
CRD .... Centre de Recherches et de Documentation de l'Association Universelle pour l'Esperanto (WGAO)
CRD .... Commission Regionale de Developpement [*Regional Development Commission*] [*Senegal*] (AF)
CRD .... Committee on Energy Research and Development [*OECD*] (WGAO)
CRD .... Comodoro Rivadavia [*Argentina*] [*Airport symbol*] (OAG)
CRD .... Compte-Rendu de Defaut [*French*] (ADPT)
CRD .... Conseil Revolutionnaire de District [*District Revolutionary Council*] [*Benin*] (AF)
CRD .... Corporacion del Rio Dulce [*Argentina*] (DSCA)
CRD .... Cruz Roja Dominicana [*Dominican Red Cross*] [*Dominican Republic*] (LA)
CRDA .... Christian Relief and Development Association
CRDB .... Committee for Restoration of Democracy in Burma (EA)
CRDB .... Co-Operative and Rural Development Bank [*State bank*] [*Tanzania*]
CRDC .... Chemical Research and Development Center [*Philippines*] [*Research center*] (IRC)
CRDC .... Communications Research and Development Consultancy [*Ghana*] (IRC)
CRDCS...... Contingency Rerouting of Communications [*NATO*] (NATG)
CRDEC...... Center for Research and Documentation on the European Community [*American University*] [*Research center*]
CRDEWPA ... Center for Research Documentation and Experimentation on Water Pollution Accidents [*France*] (EAIO)
CRDI .... Cement Research and Development Institute [*Pakistan*] (IRC)
CRDI .... Centre de Recherche pour le Developpement International [*International Development Research Center*] [*French*]
CRDLP...... Centre for Research and Documentation of the Language Problem (WGAO)
CRDM .... Centro Ricerche Didattiche "Ugo Morin" [*Italian*] (SLS)
CRDME .... Committee for Research into Dental Materials and Equipment (WGAO)
CRDP........ Central Rangelands Development Project
CRDP........ COCIN Rural Development Program [*Nigeria*] (EAIO)
CRDS........ Centre de Recherches et de Documentation du Senegal [*Research and Documentation Center of Senegal*] (AF)
CRDT .... Convention Relative aux Dispositions Transitoires [*Du Traite Instituant la CECA*] (FLAF)
CRDTO ..... Centre de Recherche et de Documentation pour la Tradition Orale [*Research and Documentation Center for Oral Tradition*] [*Niger*] (AF)
CRDTO ..... Regional Documentation Centre for Oral Tradition [*Niger*] (WGAO)
CRE .... Cadena Radial Ecuatoriana (EY)
CRE .... Caisse de Retraites des Expatries
Cre............. Calvaire [*Calvary, Wayside Cross*] [*Military map abbreviation World War I*] [*French*] (MTD)
CRE .... Centre for Resource Ecology [*University of the Witwatersrand*] [*South Africa*] (AA)
CRE .... Centre Rencontes Europeenes (WGAO)
CRE .... Coal Research Establishment (WGAO)
CRE .... Commercial Relations Export Department (WGAO)
CRE .... Commission for Racial Equality (WGAO)
CRE .... Conference of the Regions of Europe (WGAO)
CRE .... Conference Permanente des Recteurs, Presidents, et Vice Chanceliers des Universites Europeennes (EAIO)
CRE .... Conseil des Regions d'Europe [*Council of European Regions - CER*] (EAIO)
CRE .... Standing Conference of Rectors Presidents and Vice-Chancellors of the European Universities [*Switzerland*] (WGAO)
CREA........ Center for Anthropological Studies and Research [*Cameroon*] [*Research center*] (IRC)
CREA........ Centre de Recherches Economiques Appliquees [*Center of Applied Economics*] [*Senegal*] [*Research center*] (IRC)
CREA........ Centre de Recherches et d'Etudes Agricoles (WGAO)

CREA........ Centre for Regional Economic Analysis [*Australia*]

CREA........ Centro de Reconversion Economica del Austro [*Ecuador*]   (EY)

CREA........ Centro Regional de Education de Adultos [*Venezuela*]   (WGAO)

CREA........ Centros Regionales de Experimentacion [*Regional Experimentation Centers*] [*Uruguay*]   (LA)

CREA........ Consejo Nacional de Recursos para le Atencion de la Juventud [*Mexico*]   (WGAO)

CREA........ Consorcios Regionales de Experimentacion Agricola [*Argentina*]   (LAA)

CREA........ Cooperative Regionale d'Equipement Agricole   (WGAO)

CREAA...... Centre d'Etudes et de Recherches en Economie Apliquee [*Center for Studies and Research in Applied Economics*] [*Algeria*]   (IRC)

CREAA...... Conseil Regional d'Education et Alphabetisation des Adultes d'Afrique   (WGAO)

CREACUS ... Comite Regional de l'Afrique Orientale pour la Conservation et l'Utilisation du Sol   (WGAO)

CREAGRAF ... Centro Regional de Estudios Especializados Artes Graficas [*Costa Rica*]   (WGAO)

CREAI...... Carteira de Credito Agricola e Industrial [*Brazil*]   (WGAO)

CREAI...... Carteira de Credito Agricola e Industrial do Banco do Brasil [*Agricultural and Industrial Credit Department of the Bank of Brazil*]   (LA)

CREAM..... Centre Regional d'Enseignement et d'Apprentissage Maritime

CREAT...... Centro Regional de Experimentacion Agropecuaria del Tulumayo [*Peru*]   (DSCA)

CREC........ Centre Rural d'Education Communautaire [*Rural Community Education Center*] [*Laotian*]   (CL)

CREC........ Comissao Revolucionaria do Enclave de Cabinda [*Revolutionary Committee of the Cabinda Enclave*] [*Angola*]   (AF)

CRECENA ... Centro Regional de Capacitacion en Economia Alimentaria y Nutricion Aplicada [*Colombia*]   (DSCA)

CRECI....... Comptoir Radiophonique et Electricite de la Cote-D'Ivoire

CRECINCO ... Fondo de Crecimiento Industrial Colombiano [*Colombia*]   (COL)

CRECINCO ... Fondo de Inversiones Industriales y Comerciales [*Industrial and Commercial Investment Fund*] [*Chile*]   (LA)

CRECIT..... Centre de Recherches Essais et Controles Scientifiques pour l'Industrie Textile [*Belgium*]   (WGAO)

crecte......... Creciente [*Spanish*]

CRED .... Center for Research on Economic Development

CREDAL... Centre de Recherche et de Documentation sur l'Amerique Latine [*Center for Research and Documentation on Latin America*] [*France*]   (IRC)

CREDEC ... Centre Regional de Recherche et de Documentation pour le Developpement Culturel [*Regional Research and Documentation Center for Cultural Development*] [*Senegal*] [*Research center*]   (IRC)

CREDES ... Centre de Recherches et d'Etudes du Developpement Economique et Social

CREDIBANCO ... Credito Bancario [*Colombia*]   (COL)

CREDICODI ... Credit de la Cote-D'Ivoire

CREDIF .... Centre de Recherche et d'Etude pour la Diffusion du Francais [*French*]

CREDILA ... Centre de Recherches d'Etudes et de Documentation sur les Institutions et la Legislation Africaines

CREDIOP ... Consorzio di Credito per le Opere Pubbliche [*Financial institution*] [*Rome, Italy*]   (EY)

CREDISA ... Credito Immobiliario [*El Salvador*]   (WGAO)

CREDISA ... Credito Inmobiliario SA [*Real Estate Loans Corp.*] [*El Salvador*]

CREDITARIO ... Caja de Credito Agrario, Industrial, y Minero [*Colombia*]   (COL)

CREDOC... Centre de Recherche, d'Etude, et de Documentation sur la Consommation [*French*]

CREDOC... Centre de Recherche Documentaire [*Documentary Research Center*] [*Information service or system*]   (IID)

CREDOC... Centre de Recherches et de Documentation sur la Consommation   (WGAO)

CREDOC... Centrum voor Rechts-Documentatie [*Netherlands*]

CREDOP... Centre de Recherche d'Etude et de Documentation en Publicite [*Belgium*]   (WGAO)

CREE........ Centro de Recursos para la Ensenanza. Universidad del Valle [*Colombia*]   (COL)

CREE........ Conseil des Relations Economiques Exterieures [*Council of Foreign Economic Relations*] [*Lebanon*]   (GEA)

CREEA...... Comite Regional d'Expansion Economique de l'Auvergne   (WGAO)

CREFAL.... Centro Regional de Alfabetizacion Funcional en las Zonas Rurales de America Latina [*Regional Fundamental Education Center for Community Development in Latin America*] [*Centro Regional de Educacion Fundamental para el Desarrollo de la Comunidad en America Latina*] [*Formerly*] [*Mexico*]   (LAA)

CREFAL.... Centro Regional de Edicacion Fundamental para la America Latina [*Mexico*]   (WGAO)

CREFAL.... Centro Regional de Educacion de Adultos y Alfabetizacion Funcional para America Latina [*Regional Center for Adult Education and Functional Literacy for Latin America*] [*Mexico*]   (EAIO)

CREFE ...... Centre Regional d'Etudes et de Formation Economique [*France*]   (FLAF)

CREFOGA ... Credit Foncier du Gabon

CREGCI .... Comptoir Radiophonique et Electricite Generale de la Cote-D'Ivoire

CREI......... Centro Regional para la Ensenanza de la Informatica [*Spain*]   (WGAO)

CREIA...... Concours de Recrutement des Eleves-Inspecteurs Adjoints

CREIPAC ... Centre de Rencontres et d'Echanges Internationaux du Pacifique [*Center of International Cultural and Linguistic Exchanges in the Pacific*] [*Noumea, New Caledonia*]   (EAIO)

CREIPAC ... Centre de Rencontres et d'Echanges Internationaux du Pacifique Sud   (WGAO)

CREM .... Centre Congolaise de Recyclage des Professeurs en Mathematiques Modernes

CREM .... Centro Regional de Entrenamiento Militar [*Regional Military Training Centre*] [*Honduras*]

CREN .... Centre Regional d'Etudes Nucleaires [*Zaire*]

CRENK...... Centre Regional d'Etudes Nucleaires de Kinshasa [*Kinshasa Regional Nuclear Studies Center*] [*Zaire*]

CRENO ..... Centre Nationale d'Etudes et de Recherche en Energies Renouvelables, Organisme National de la Recherche Scientifique [*Algeria*]

CRENO ..... Conference des Regions de l'Europe du Nord-Ouest   (WGAO)

CRENWE ... Conference of Regions of North-West Europe   (WGAO)

CREO .... Centre de Recherches et d'Etudes Oceanographiques [*French*]   (ASF)

CREOC...... Centro Ricerche Economiche ed Operative della Cooperazione [*Italian*]   (SLS)

CREP......... Centre de Recherche Economique sur l'Epargne   (WGAO)

CREPAL.... Centre Regional d'Elevage et de Production d'Animaux de Laboratoire [*Breeding and Production of Laboratory Animals Regional Center*] [*French*]   (ARC)

CREPEM .. Centre de Recherches et d'Etudes pour une Education Mondialiste   (WGAO)

CREPHAR ... Centre de Recherches et de Pharmacologie Albert Roland [*French*]

CREPLA.... Centre Regional de Promotion du Livre en Afrique

Crepopal .... Credit Populaire d'Algerie [*Popular Credit of Algeria*]   (GEA)

CREPS....... Centre Regional d'Education Physique et Sportive   (WGAO)

CREPS....... Compagnie de Recherches et d'Exploitation de Petrole au Sahara [*Saharan Petroleum Exploration and Exploitation Company*] [*Algeria*]   (AF)

CREPUQ... Conference des Recteurs et des Principaux des Universites du Quebec

C Req .... Cour de Cassation, Chambre des Requetes [*France*]   (FLAF)

CRERMA ... Conseillers Regionaux d'Etude de la Rentabilite du Machinisme Agricole   (WGAO)

CRERU...... Carteira de Credito Rural [*Brazil*]   (DSCA)

CRES........ Centre de Recherche Elf de Solaize [*Elf Research Center at Solaize*] [*France*]   (WED)

CRES........ Centre de Recherches Economiques et Sociales   (WGAO)

CRES........ Centre for Renewable Energy Sources [*India*]   (EAIO)

CRES........ Centre Regional d'Energie Solaire [*Mali*]   (WGAO)

CRES........ Centre Regional pour l'Energie Solaire [*Regional Center for Solar Energy*] [*Mali*]

CRES........ Chief of Army Reserves [*Australia*]

Cres........... Crescent   (IDIG)

CRESA ...... Centre de Recherches Economiques et Sociales Appliquees   (WGAO)

CRESA ...... Centro di Ricerca per l'Economia, l'Organizzazione, e l'Amministrazione della Sanita [*Italian*]   (SLS)

CRESA ...... Centro Ricerca per l'Economia, l'Organizzazione, e l'Amministrazione della Sanita   (WGAO)

CRESA ...... Cuarzo Radioelectrico Espanol SA [*Spain*]   (PDAA)

CRESAL.... Centre de Recherches et d'Etudes Sociologiques Appliquees de la Loire [*Center for Applied Sociological Studies of the Loire*] [*Research center*] [*France*]   (IRC)

CRESALC ... Centro Regional de Educacion Superior en America Latine y el Caribe [*UNESCO*]   (WGAO)

CRESALC ... Centro Regional para la Educacion Superior en America Latina y el Caribe [*Regional Center for Higher Education in Latin America and the Caribbean-Venezuela*] [*United Nations*]   (IID)

CRESALC ... Comite Regional de Educacion Sexual para Latinoamerica y el Caribe [*Colombia*]   (WGAO)

CRESEMILLAS ... Semillas e Credito [*Colombia*]   (DSCA)

CRESEX.... Camara de Representantes de Casas Extranjeras [*Chamber of Representatives of Foreign Enterprises*] [*Costa Rica*]   (LA)

CRESHS ... Centre de Recherches en Sciences Humaines et Sociales [*Haiti*]   (WGAO)

CRESM ..... Centre de Recherche et d'Etudes sur les Societes Mediterraneennes [*Center for Research and Studies on Mediterranean Societies*] [*Information service or system*] (IID)

CRESM ..... Centre de Recherches et d'Etudes sur les Societes Musulmanes (WGAO)

CRESME .. Centro Ricerche Economiche Sociologiche e di Mercato nell'Edilizia [*Italian*]   (SLS)

CRESPA .... Centre Regional d'Etudes Superieures pour la Preparation aux Affaires   (WGAO)

CRESR ...... Centre Regional d'Etudes Socio-Religieuses   (WGAO)

CRESS ...... Center for Research in Social Systems

CRESS ...... Centro Ricerche e Studi Sindacali [*Italian*]   (SLS)

CRESSIDA ... Center for Regional, Ecological, and Science Studies in Development Alternatives [*Calcutta, India*]

CREST ...... Comite de Recherche Scientifique et Technique [*Scientific and Technical Research Committee*] [*European Community*]

CREST ...... Core Research for Evolutional Science and Technology [*Japan*]

CRESU ...... Consejo Representativo del Sistema Universitario [*Representative Council of the University System*] [*Peru*] (LA)

CRET .... Commission Regionale Europeenne de Tourisme   (WGAO)

CRETE ...... Association des Correspondants des Radios et des Televisions Etrangeres   (WGAO)

CRETE ...... Association des Correspondants des Radios et Televisions Etrangeres a Paris [*Association of Foreign Radio and Television Correspondents in Paris*] [*French*]   (AF)

CRETP ...... Centre de Recherche et d'Experimentation des Travaux Publics [*Cameroon*]   (IMH)

CRETRINA ... Comite de Reception des Aides Etrangeres [*Foreign Aid Receiving Committee*] [*Cambodia*]   (CL)

CREVICO ... Credito de Viajes Populares [*Colombia*]   (COL)

CREW .... Centre for Research in Education and Work [*Macquarie University*] [*Australia*]

CREW .... Centre for Research on European Women [*Belgium*]   (EAIO)

CRF .... Cannabis Research Foundation [*Australia*]   (ADA)

CRF .... Centrala Rozpowszechniania Filmow [*Center for Film Distribution*]   (POL)

CRF .... Centro Ricerche Fiat SpA [*Fiat Research Center*] [*Italian*] (ERC)

CRF .... Christian Revival Fellowship [*Australia*]

CRF .... Coffee Research Foundation [*Kenya*]   (ARC)

CRF .... Comite pour la Renaissance de France [*Algeria*]

CRF .... Community Radio Federation Ltd. [*Australia*]

CRF .... Conseil Presidentiel de la Federation

CRF .... Croix-Rouge Francaise [*French Red Cross*]   (WER)

CRFA .... Chongwe River Farmers Associations

CRFA .... Conseil Revolutionnaire des Forces Armees

CRFB .... Centre de Recherches du Fer-Blanc [*Tinplate Research Center*] [*France*]   (PDAA)

CRFEA ...... Christian Rural Fellowship of East Africa   (AF)

CRFER ...... Centre Regional de Formation pour Entretien Routier

CRFM .... Comite de Coordination de la Recherche Forestiere Mediterraneenne   (WGAO)

CRFP .... Centre National de Recherches Forestieres et Piscicoles

CRFS .... Comites Revolutionnaires des Forces de Securite [*Revolutionary Committees of the Security Forces*] [*Benin*]   (AF)

CRFT .... Comitetul Roman de Fotogrammetrie si Teledetectie   (WGAO)

CRFTLA .... Centre Regional de Formation aux Techniques des Leves Aeriens [*Regional Center for Training in Aerial Surveys - RECTAS*] (EAIO)

CRFTLA .... Centre Regional de Formation aux Techniques des Leves Aerospatiaux [*Nigeria*]   (EAIO)

CRG .... Centre de Recherches de Gorsem [*Gorsem Research Center*] [*Belgium*]   (PDAA)

CRG .... Centre de Recherches Geophysiques [*Geophysical Research Center*] [*France*]   (WED)

CRG .... City-Link Airlines Ltd. [*Nigeria*] [*ICAO designator*]   (FAAC)

CRG .... Collaborative Research Group [*Of scientific institute*]

CRG .... Comites Revolutionnaires de Garnison [*Garrison Revolutionary Committees*] [*Benin*]   (AF)

CRG .... Compagnie Reynolds de Geophysique

CRG .... Comptoir de Representations Generales

CRG .... Conditien van de Rotterdamsche Graanbeurs [*Netherlands*] (BAS)

CRGE .... Companhias Reunidas de Gas e Electricidade [*Unified Gas and Electricity Companies*] [*Portuguese*]   (WER)

CRGM .... Centre de Recherches Geologiques et Minieres [*Geological and Mining Research Center*] [*Zaire*]   (IRC)

CRGM .... Comite de la Recherche Geologique et Miniere [*FEGECE*] (WGAO)

CRHBMC ... China Rural House Building Materials Corp.   (TCC)

CRHRE ..... Center for Research of Human Resources and the Environment [*Indonesia*] [*Research center*]   (IRC)

CRHS .... Clarence River Historical Society [*Australia*]

CRHS .... Commonwealth Regional Health Secretariat   (EA)

CRI .... Caisse de Retraites Interentreprises [*France*]   (FLAF)

CRI .... Canari Airlines [*Israel*] [*ICAO designator*]   (FAAC)

CRI .... Carribbean Research Institute [*University of the Virgin Islands*] (PDAA)

CRI .... Cement Research Institute [*India*]   (WGAO)

CRI .... Cement Research Institute of India [*Research center*]   (IRC)

CRI .... Central Research Institute [*India*]   (WGAO)

CRI .... Centre de Recherches et d'Irradiations [*French*]

CRI .... Centre de Recherches Industrielles [*Industrial Research Center*] [*Belgium*]   (IRC)

CRI .... Centre Regional d'Instruction [*Regional Instruction Center*] [*Cambodia*]   (CL)

CRI .... Centro Regional de Informacion [*Corporacion de Desarrollo de la Region Nor-Oriental*] [*Venezuela*]

CRI .... Children in Residential Institutions Program [*Australia*]

CRI .... Children's Relief International

CRI .... Clinical Research Institute [*Korea*] [*Research center*]   (IRC)

CRI .... Coconut Research Institute [*Sri Lanka*]   (ARC)

CRI .... Comite de Recherche en Informatique [*French*]   (ADPT)

CRI .... Comite de Rescate Internacional [*Spanish*]

CRI .... Commando Regional Independiente [*Independent Regional Command*] [*Venezuela*]   (LA)

CRI .... Commission Regionale d'Investissements [*Regional Investment Commission*] [*Algeria*]   (AF)

CRI .... Conference of Religious of India   (WGAO)

CRI .... Conservation Resources International [*Australia*]

CRI .... Costa Rica [*ANSI three-letter standard code*]   (CNC)

CrI .... Credit d'Impot [*French*]   (BAS)

CRI .... Crimean

CRI .... Croce Rossa Italiana   (WGAO)

CRI .... Croix-Rouge Internationale [*International Red Cross*]   (CL)

CRI .... Crooked Island [*Bahamas*] [*Airport symbol*]   (OAG)

CRI .... Crops Research Institute [*Ghana*]   (AF)

CRI .... Custom Resources International [*Australia*]

CRIA .... Caisse de Retraite Interenterprises Agricoles   (WGAO)

CRIA .... Centre de Recherches sur les Trypanosomiases Animales [*Central Africa*]   (WGAO)

CRIA .... Centro Regional de Investigaciones Agropecuarias [*Venezuela*] (DSCA)

CRIA .... Communication Research Institute of Australia

CRIAA .... Collectif de Recherche et d'Information sur Afrique Australe (WGAO)

CRIABD .... Centre International Chretien de Recherche d'Information et d'Analyse de la Bande Dessinee   (WGAO)

CRIAC .... Centre des Recherches Industrielles en Afrique Centrale [*Industrial Research Center in Central Africa*]   (AF)

CRIAD .... Centre de Relations Internationales Entre Agriculteurs pour le Developpement

CRIAMS ... Comite Regional Intersectorial de Apoyo a la Movilizacion Social [*Intersectoral Regional Committee for Support of Social Mobilization*] [*Peru*]   (LA)

CRIBC ...... Central Research Institute of Building and Construction [*China*] (IRC)

CRIBUCA ... Comite Regional de Integracion de Bibliotecas Universitarias de la Costa Atlantica [*Cordoba*]   (COL)

CRIC .... Centre de Recherches de l'Industrie Belge de la Ceramique (WGAO)

CRIC .... Centre de Recherches Industrielles sur Contrats   (WGAO)

CRIC .... Centre de Reflexion et d'Information sur la Cooperation Internationale avec le Tiers Monde

CRIC .... Centre de Relations Internationales Culturelles   (WGAO)

CRIC .... Centre National de Recherches Scientifiques et Techniques pour l'Industrie Cimentiere [*National Center of Scientific and Technical Research of the Cement Industry*] [*Belgium*] (IRC)

CRIC .... Commercial Radio International Committee   (WGAO)

CRIC .... Congregatio Canonicorum Regularium Immaculatae Conceptionis Beatae Virginis Mariae   (WGAO)

CRIC .... Consejo Regional Indigena del Cauca [*Colombia*]   (WGAO)

CRICA .... Caisse de retraite par Repartition, des Ingenieurs, Cadres et Assimiles [*France*]   (FLAF)

CRICCAL ... Centre de Recherches Interuniversitaire sur les Champs Cultures en Amerique Latine   (WGAO)

CRID .... Central Revolutionary Investigation Department [*Security and counterinsurgency agency*] [*Ethiopia*]

CRID .... Centre pour la Recherche Interdisciplinaire sur le Developpement [*Center for Interdisciplinary Research Development*] [*Belgium*]   (IRC)

CRID .... Centro di Riferimento Italiano DIANE [*Italian Reference Center for EURONET DIANE*] [*National Research Council*] [*Information service or system*]   (IID)

CRIDAOL ... Centro Regional de Investigacion y Desarrollo Agraria de Galicia   (WGAO)

CRIDE .... Centre de Recherches Inter-Disciplinaires Droit-Economie [*Benelux*]   (BAS)

CRIDE .... Centre de Recherches Interdisciplinaires pour le Developpement de l'Education

CRIDEV .... Centre Rennais d'Information pour le Developpement et la Liberation des Peuples [*France*]
CRIDON ... Centre de Recherche d'Information et de Documentation Notariel [*French*] (ADPT)
CRIDON ... Centre de Recherches d'Information et de Documentation Notariales (WGAO)
CRIE......... Center for Research in Islamic Education [*Saudi Arabia*] (EAIO)
CRIE......... Centre pour la Recherche et l'Innovation dans l'Enseignement [*France*] (EAIO)
CRIE......... Centro Regional de Informaciones Ecumenicas [*Mexico*] (WGAO)
CRIE......... Comision de Represion de Ilicitos Economicos [*Committee for Repression of Economic Crimes*] [*Uruguay*] (LA)
CRIEL .... Comite Interprofessional des Eaux-de-vie du Languedoc (WGAO)
CRIEPI...... Central Research Institute for Electric Power Industry [*Japan*] (WED)
CRIES .... Coordinadora Regional de Investigaciones Economicas y Sociales [*Regional Coordinator of Social and Economic Research*] [*Nicaragua*] (IRC)
CRIET .... Comites Reunis de l'Industrie de l'Ennoblissement Textile dans le CE [*EC*] (ECED)
CRIF .... Centre de Recherches Scientifiques et Techniques de l'Industrie des Fabrications Metalliques [*Center for Scientific and Technical Research for the Metal Manufacturing Industry*] [*Information service or system*] (IID)
CRIF .... Centre for Research in Finance [*University of New South Wales*] [*Information service or system*] (IID)
CRIF .... Conseil Representatif des Institutions Juives en France
CRIFC ...... Central Research Institute for Food Crops [*Indonesia*] [*Research center*] (IRC)
CRIFCUZCO ... Corporacion de Reconstruccion y Fomento del Cuzco [*Peru*] (DSCA)
CRIFRI...... Comitato Interministeriale per il Risanamento Finanziario e la Rinascita Industriale [*Interministerial Committee for Financial Recovery and Industrial Rebirth*] [*Italian*] (WER)
CRIG......... Cocoa Research Institute of Ghana
CRII.......... Cement Research Institute of India
CRII.......... Centre de Recherches sur les Institutions Internationales [*Switzerland*] (WGAO)
CRIJAF ..... Central Research Institute for Jute and Allied Fibres [*India*] (IRC)
CRIK......... Centre de Regroupement pour les Interets du Kwango
CRILJ........ Centre de Recherche et d'Information sur la Litterature de Jeunesse (WGAO)
Crim .... Arret de la Chambre Criminelle de la Cour de Cassation [*Decision of the Court of Appeal, Criminal Division*] [*French*] (ILCA)
Crim .... Chambre Criminelle [*Criminal Court*] [*French*]
Criminol..... Criminologie [*Criminology*] [*French*] (DLA)
CRIN .... Cacao Research Institute of Nigeria (WGAO)
CRIN .... Centre de Recherche en Informatique de Nancy [*Computer Science Research Center*] [*Centre National de la Recherche Scientifique*] [*French*] (ERC)
CRIN .... Cocoa Research Institute of Nigeria
CRINA....... Centre de Recherche International de Nutrition Animale (WGAO)
CRIP......... Australian Computing Research in Progress [*Information service or system*] (ADA)
CRI/RUL .. Centraal Rekeninstituut/Rijksuniversiteit, Leiden
CRIS .... Centre for Research on Intelligent Systems [*Deakin University*] [*Australia*]
CRIS .... Centro di Ricerca Idraulica e Strutturale [*Hydraulic and Structural Research Department*] [*Italy*] (EAS)
CRIS .... Centro Ricerche Interdisciplinari sul Suicidio [*Interdisciplinary Research Center on Suicide*] [*Italy*] (EAIO)
CRISOL .... Cristianos Solidarios [*Nicaragua*] (WGAO)
CRISP........ Car Radio Industry Specialists Association (WGAO)
CRISP........ Centre de Recherche et d'Information Socio-Politiques [*Center for Socio-Political Research and Information*] [*Belgium*] (WER)
CRISP........ Centre for Information Studies Publications [*Kuring-Gai College of Education*] [*Australia*]
CRIT......... Centre de Recherche Interdisciplinaire sur les Transformations Sociales [*Interdisciplinary Research Center on Social Change*] [*Research center*] [*France*] (IRC)
CRIT......... Coordinating Centre for Regional Information Training
CRIVA...... Commissie Reken- en Informatieverwerkende Apparatuur
CRIWG..... Central Region Interface Working Group [*NATO*] (NATG)
CRIWI...... Research Institute of the Wood Industry [*China*] [*Research center*] (IRC)
CRJ........... Commission for Racial Justice (WGAO)
CRJT .... Centre Reunionnais d'Information, d'Etudes, et d'Action Sociale pour les Jeunes Travailleurs [*Reunionese Information, Study, and Social Action Center for Young Workers*] (AF)
CRK .... Air Pacific Crake [*Philippines*] [*ICAO designator*] (FAAC)

CRK .... Centraal Registratie-Kantoor Detailhandel-Ambacht (WGAO)
CRK .... Croix-Rouge Khmere [*Cambodian Red Cross*] (CL)
CRL........... Canonici Regolari della Congregazione del Sanctissimo Salvatore Lateranense (WGAO)
CRL........... Centralni Rizeni Letounu [*Central Aircraft Control*] (CZ)
CRL........... Centre de Recherche de Lacq [*Lacq Research Center*] [*France*] (EAS)
CRL........... Cholera Research Laboratory [*Bangladesh*] (WGAO)
CRL........... Civil Rights League [*South Africa*] (EAIO)
CRL........... Commercial Register Law [*1974*] [*Oman*] (IMH)
CRL........... Communications Research Laboratory [*Tsunchin-Sougu Kenkyuu-sho*] [*Ministry of Posts and Telecommunications*] [*Japan*] (EAS)
CRL........... Conseil Revolutionnaire Local pour les Villages et Quartiers de Villes [*Local Revolutionary Council for Villages and City Districts*] [*Benin*] (AF)
CRL........... Consolidated Rutile Ltd. [*Australia*]
CRL........... Copper Refineries Ltd. [*Australia*]
Crl............ Coral [*Record label*] [*USA, Europe*]
CRL........... Corse Air International [*France*] [*ICAO designator*] (FAAC)
CRLC........ Cooperative Regionale Lainere du Centre (WGAO)
CRLR........ Civil Rights and Law Reform [*Australia*]
CRLS .... Coastguard Radio Liaison Station (WGAO)
CRM .... Catarman [*Philippines*] [*Airport symbol*] (OAG)
CRM .... Centrale Road voor de Mileuhygiene (WGAO)
CRM .... Centre de Recherches Metallurgiques [*Nuclear energy*] [*Belgium*] (NRCH)
CRM .... Centre de Recherches Metallurgiques/Centrum voor Researsh in de Metallurgie [*Center for Metallurgical Research*] [*Research center*] [*Belgium*] (IRC)
CRM .... Centre de Reflexion sur le Monde Non Occidental [*Center for the Study of the Non-Occidental World*] (EA)
CRM .... Centre for Resource Management [*University of Canterbury/Lincoln College*] [*New Zealand*] (WED)
CRM .... Centre Recherche Macromolecules (Strasbourg) [*France*]
CRM .... Centro Regional Meteorologico [*Chile*] (LAA)
CRM .... Centrum voor Research in de Metallurgie [*Nuclear energy*] [*Belgium*] (NRCH)
CRM .... Citizens' Rights Movement [*Israel*] [*Political party*] (ECON)
CRM .... Clerics Regular Minor [*Italy*] (EAIO)
CRM .... Comite Revolucionario de Mozambique
CRM .... Comite Revolutionnaire Militaire [*Political party*] [*Benin*]
CRM .... Commander Mexicana SA de CV [*Mexico*] [*ICAO designator*] (FAAC)
CRM .... Compagnie Radio Maritime
CRM .... Compte-Rendu de Mouvement [*French*] (ADPT)
CRM .... Comptoir Radio le "Mono"
CRM .... Coordinacion Revolucionaria de las Masas [*Revolutionary Coordination of the Masses*] [*El Salvador*] (PD)
CRM .... Coordinadora Revolucionaria de Masas [*El Salvador*] (WGAO)
CRM .... Credit Research and Management GMBH [*Germany*]
CRM .... Croissant Rouge Maroc
CRM .... Cultuur, Recreatien, Maatschappelijk Werk [*Ministry of Culture, Recreation, and Social Work*] [*Netherlands*] (WEN)
CRMAC.... Centre de Recherche sur le Monde Arabe [*Belgium*] (WGAO)
CRMC ...... Coastal Resources Management Council [*United Nations*]
CRMC2 ..... Centre de Recherche sur les Mecanismes de la Croissance Cristalline [*Center of Crystal Growth Mechanisms*] [*Centre National de la Recherche Scientifique; Universite d'Aix-Marseille III*] [*Research center*] [*French*] (ERC)
CRME .... Centre Regional de Mouvements d'Energie (WGAO)
CRME .... Council for Research in Music Education (WGAO)
CRMF....... Clunies Ross Memorial Foundation [*Australia*] (ADA)
CRMK ...... Confederation Royale Marocaine de Karate
CRMM ..... Centre de Reeducation Motrice de Madagascar [*Musculo-Skeletal Reeducation Center*] [*Malagasy*] (AF)
CRMP....... Comite Revolutionnaire de Milice Populaire [*Revolutionary Committee of the Popular Militia*] [*Guinea*] (AF)
CRMP....... Commission for the Rights of the Maubere People [*Portugal*] (EAIO)
CRMR ...... Compte-Rendu de Mise en Route [*French*] (ADPT)
CRMS....... Canberra Recorded Music Society [*Australia*]
CRMS....... Centro Ricerche Malattie della Selvaggina (WGAO)
CRMS....... Charles Rennie Mackintosh Society (EAIO)
CRMS....... Clerks Regular, Ministers of the Sick [*Rome, Italy*] (EAIO)
CRMSA .... Caisse Regionale de Mutualite Sociale Agricole [*Regional Agricultural and Social Mutual Fund*] [*Algeria*] (AF)
CRMSL ..... Civil Rights Movement of Sri Lanka (EAIO)
CRN .... Comite de Reconciliation Nationale
CRN .... Comite de Reconstruccion Nacional [*National Reconstruction Committee*] [*Guatemala*] (LA)
CRN .... Comite de Renovation Nationale [*National Renewal Committee*] [*Benin*] (AF)
CRN .... Conflict Resolution Network [*Australia*]
CRN .... Constructions Reparations Navales
crn .... Corner (IDIG)
CRN .... Empresa Aerocaribbean SA [*Cuba*] [*ICAO designator*] (FAAC)

CRNA .... Campaign for the Restoration of the National Anthem and Flag (WGAO)
CRNA .... Comite da Revolucao Nacional de Angola
CRNE .... Comite Regional de Normas Electricas (del Subcomite Centroamericano de Electrificacion y Recursos Hidraulicos) [*Regional Committee on Electrical Standards*] (LAA)
CRNL .... Chalk River Nuclear Laboratories [*AECL*] (WGAO)
CRNNR ..... Consejo de Recursos Naturales no Renovables [*Mexico*] (DSCA)
CRO .... Central Records Office [*Sudan*]
CRO .... Central Research Organization [*Myanmar*] (DS)
CRO .... Centre de Recherches Oceanographiques [*Oceanographic Research Center*] [*Abidjan, Ivory Coast*] (MSC)
CRO .... Centro di Riferimento Oncologico [*Center for the Study of Tumors*] [*Italy*] (PDAA)
CRO .... Christian Renewal Outreach [*Australia*]
CRO .... Commissie voor Rassenonderzoek van Groenvoedergewassen
CRO .... Commonwealth Relations Office
CRO .... Companies Registration Office (WGAO)
CRO .... Conseil de la Recherche Oceanologique [*Oceanographic Research Council*] [*French*] (MSC)
cro .... Criado [*Servant (Masculine)*] [*Portuguese*]
CRO .... Croatia (ECON)
CROACUS ... Comite Regional de l'Afrique Occidentale pour la Conservation et l'Utilisation du Sol (WGAO)
Croat .... Croatia
CROATIAFILM ... Croatian Film Establishment [*Zagreb*] (YU)
CROATIAPETROL ... Croatian Petrol Derivatives Establishment [*Zagreb*] (YU)
CROC .... Confederacion Revolucionaria de Obreros y Campesinos [*Revolutionary Confederation of Workers and Peasants*] [*Mexico*] (LA)
CRODT ..... Centre de Recherches Oceanographiques de Dakar-Thiaroye [*Dakar-Thiaroye Center for Oceanographic Research*] [*Senegal*] [*Research center*] (IRC)
CROM .... Confederacion Regional Obrera Mexicana [*Workers' Regional Confederation of Mexico*] (LAA)
crom .... Cromolitografia [*Chromolithography*] [*Publishing*] [*Italian*]
CROMACOL ... Cromados Colombia y Cia. Ltda. [*Colombia*] (COL)
cromo .... Cromolitografia [*Chromolithography*] [*Publishing*] [*Spanish*]
Cron .... Cronologia [*Chronology*] [*Portuguese*]
cron .... Cronologico [*Chronological*] [*Portuguese*]
CRONWE ... Conferentie voor Regionale Ontwikkeling in Noord-West Europa (WGAO)
CROP .... Centre de Recherches Oceanographiques et des Peches [*Algeria*] (SLS)
CROPS ..... Concerned Residents Opposing the Pulp Siting [*Australia*]
croq .... Croquis [*Sketch*] [*Publishing*] [*French*]
CROS .... Ceska Rada Odborovych Svazu [*Czech Council of Trade Unions*] (CZ)
cros .... Crostoso [*Rough-Grained*] [*Publishing*] [*Italian*]
CROSA ...... Cave Research Organisation of South Africa (AA)
CROSS ...... Comprehensive Rural Operations Service Society [*India*] (WGAO)
CROSSA ... Centre Regional Operationnel de Surveillance et de Sauvetage pour l'Atlantique [*Regional Operational Center for Atlantic Search and Rescue*] [*French*] (PDAA)
CROSSMA ... Centre Regional Operationnel de Surveillance et de Sauvetage pour la Manche [*Regional Operationa Center for the English Channel Search and Rescue*] [*French*] (PDAA)
CROUS ..... Centre Regional des Oeuvres Universitaires et Scolaires [*Regional Center for Assistance to Universities and Schools*] [*French*] (WER)
CROW .... Campaign for the Rehabilitation of Wildlife [*South Africa*]
CROWC .... Central Rights of Way Committee (WGAO)
CRP .... Aerotaxis Corporativo SA de CV [*Mexico*] [*ICAO designator*] (FAAC)
CRP .... Centre de Recherche Physique (WGAO)
CRP .... Centre Regional de Planification et l'Administration de l'Education pour les Pays Arabes [*North African*]
CRP .... Cercle pour le Renouveau et le Progres [*Gabon*] [*Political party*] (EY)
CRP .... Cetna Ranjenicka Prihvatnica [*Company First Aid Station*] (YU)
CRP .... Chinese Republican Party [*Political party*] (EY)
CRP .... Christian Republican Party [*Bulgaria*] [*Political party*]
CRP .... Civil Rights Party [*South Korea*] [*Political party*] (PPW)
CRP .... Comando de Resistencia Popular Javier Carrera [*Javier Carrera Popular Resistance Commando*] [*Chile*] (PD)
CRP .... Comandos Revolucionarios del Pueblo [*Peru*] [*Political party*] (EY)
CRP .... Comite Regional Provisoire
CRP .... Community Release Program [*Australia*]
CRP .... Country Residents Party [*Australia*]
CRP .... C.Rudolf Poensgen Stiftung zur Foerderung von Fuehrungskraften in der Wirtschaft e V. (WGAO)

CRPA .... Centro Regional da Reforma Agraria [*Regional Agrarian Reform Center*] [*Portuguese*] (WER)
CRPAO ..... Comision Regional de Pesca para el Africa Occidental
CRPB .... Comite de Relevement du Peuple Bassa [*Committee for the Aid of the Bassa People*]
CRPE .... Centre de Recherches en Physique de l'Environmentment Terrestre et Solaire (WGAO)
CRPE .... Centre de Recherches en Physique de l'Environnement Terrestre et Planetaire [*Research Center for Terrestrial and Planetary Physics*] [*Research center*] [*French*] (IRC)
CRPF .... Central Reserve Police Force [*India*]
CRPG .... Centre de Recherches Petrographiques et Geochimiques [*Center for Petrographic and Geochemical Research*] [*Research center*] [*French*] (IRC)
CRPG .... Conseil Regional du Patronat de la Guadeloupe (WGAO)
CRPHN ..... Centre for Research into Public Health and Nursing [*La Trobe University*] [*Australia*]
CRPL .... Copper Refineries Proprietary Limited [*Australia*]
CRPLF .... Communaute des Radios Publiques de Langue Francaise (EAIO)
CRPM .... Conference des Regions Peripheriques Maritimes de la CEE (WGAO)
CRPP .... Centre de Recherches en Physique des Plasmas [*Plasma Physics Research Center*] [*Switzerland*] (IRC)
CRPPH ...... Committee for Radiation Protection and Public Health [*EURATOM*] (NUCP)
CRPPH ...... Committee on Radiation Protection and Public Health [*Organization for Economic Cooperation and Development*] (ERC)
CRPQF ...... Comissao Reguladora dos Productos Quimicos e Farmaceuticos [*Portugal*] (WGAO)
CRPS .... Conseil Regional pour la Promotion Sociale [*Regional Council for Social Welfare*] [*Zaire*] (EAIO)
CRPTA ...... College Royal Preparatoire aux Technique Aeronautiques [*Morocco*]
CRR .... Central Register of Restrictions [*New South Wales Land Titles Office*] [*Australia*]
CRR .... Centre de Recherches Rizicoles de Djibelor [*Rice Research Center of Djibelor*] [*Senegal*] [*Research center*] (IRC)
CRR .... Centre de Recherches Routieres [*Belgium*]
CRR .... Commission de Recours des Refugies [*France*] (FLAF)
CRR .... Council Recycling Debate [*Australia*]
CRRAG ..... Countryside Recreation Research Advisory Group (WGAO)
CRRERIS .. Commonwealth Regional Renewable Energy Resources Information Service (IID)
CRRG .... Comisia Republicana de Rezerve Geologice [*National Commission of Geological Reserves*] (RO)
CRRI .... Central Rice Research Institute [*India*] (MCD)
CRRI .... Central Road Research Institute [*India*] [*Research center*] (IRC)
CRRIA .... Cliffs Robe River Iron Associates [*Australia*] (ADA)
CRRID ...... Centre for Research in Rural and Industrial Development [*India*]
CRRL .... Central Reference and Research Library [*Ghana*] (WGAO)
CRRL .... Cosmic Ray Research Laboratory [*Nagoya University*] [*Japan*] (EAS)
CRRM .... Centre for Rural Research Management [*University of New England*] [*Australia*]
CRR/OCW ... Centre de Recherches Routieres/Opzoekingscentrum voor de Wegenbouw [*Belgian Road Research Centre*] (ERC)
CRRS .... Central Rainlands Research Station [*Sudan*]
Crrta .... Carretera [*Highway*] [*Spanish*] (CED)
CRRU .... Cosmic Rays Research Unit
Crs .... Carsi [*Market*] (TU)
CRS .... Catholic Record Society (WGAO)
CRS .... Catholic Relief Services (CL)
CRS .... Centrala Rolnicza Spoldzielni [*Agricultural Cooperative Center*] (POL)
CRS .... Centrala Rolnicza Spoldzielni "Samopomoc Chlopska" [*Agricultural Centre of the Co-Operative "Peasants' Self-Help"*] [*Poland*]
CRS .... Centralna Rada Spoldzielcza [*Central Cooperative Council*] (POL)
CRS .... Centre for Remote Sensing [*James Cook University*] [*Australia*]
CRS .... Cereals Research Station (WGAO)
CRS .... Ceskoslovenska Radiologicka Spolecnost [*Former Czechoslovakia*] (EAIO)
CRS .... Cesky Rohovnicky Svaz [*Czech Boxing Association*] (CZ)
CRS .... Chief Radio Supervisor [*Australia*]
CRS .... Chipinga Research Station [*Zimbabwe*] (ARC)
CRS .... Circulo Radial Santandereano [*Bucaramanga*] (COL)
CRS .... Clerics Regular of Somasca [*Italy*] (EAIO)
CRS .... Comercial Aerea SA de CV [*Mexico*] [*ICAO designator*] (FAAC)
CRS .... Commonwealth Record Series [*Australia*]
CRS .... Commonwealth Rehabilitation Service [*Australia*]
CRS .... Commonwealth Reporting Service [*Australia*]
CRS .... Compagnies Republicaines de Securite [*Republican Security Companies*] [*State Mobile Police*] [*French*] (WER)

CRS............ Consiglio Rivolucionario Supremo [*Supreme Revolutionary Council*] [*Use SRC Somali*]   (AF)
CRS............ Corps Republicain de la Securite [*Republican Security Corps*] [*French*]
CRS............ Czechoslowacka Republika Socjalistyczna [*Poland*]
CRS............ Ordo Clericorum Regularium a Somascha   (WGAO)
CRSA........ China Radio Sports Association   (PDAA)
CRSA........ Cold Rolled Sections Association   (WGAO)
CRSA........ Ordo Canonicorum Regularium Sancti-Augustini   (WGAO)
CRSAB...... Centro Ricerche di Storia e Arte Bitontina [*Italian*]   (SLS)
CRSAS...... Centro Regional de Sismologia para America del Sur [*Regional Center for Seismology for South America - RCSSA*]   (EAIO)
CRSC........ Chemicals Review Sub-Committee [*Australia*]
CRSCM..... Centre de Recherches sur la Synthese et la Chimie des Mineraux [*Mineral Synthesis and Chemistry Research Center*] [*Centre National de la Recherche Scientifique*] [*France*]   (EAS)
CRSESFPI ... Centre de Recherches Statistiques, Economiques, et Sociales et de Formation pour les Pays Islamiques [*Statistical, Economic, and Social Research and Training Center for Islamic Countries*] [*Turkey*]
CRSI........ Calisma, Rehabilitasyon, ve Sosyal Isler Bakanligi [*Ministry of Labor, Rehabilitation, and Social Affairs of the Turkish Cypriot Federated State*]   (GC)
CRSIM ...... Centre de Recherches Scientifiques Industrielles et Maritimes   (WGAO)
CRSL........ Coffee Research Station Lyamungu [*Tanzania*]   (DSCA)
CRSOA..... County Road Safety Officers Association   (WGAO)
CRSP........ Clerics Regular of St. Paul [*Italy*]
CRSPPA.... International Pen-Pals Association [*Cross River State Pen-Pals Association*] [*Acronym is based on former name,*]   (EAIO)
CRSR........ Centre for Rural Social Research [*Charles Sturt University*] [*Australia*]
CRSS .... Caisses Regionales de Securite Sociale [*France*]   (FLAF)
CRSS .... Community Refugee Settlement Scheme [*Australia*]
CRSSA ...... Centre de Recherches du Service de Santa des Armees [*Army Medical Service Research Center*] [*France*]   (PDAA)
CRSSA ...... Centre de Recherches du Service de Sante des Armees   (WGAO)
CRSSCh .... Centrala Rolnicza Spoldzielni "Samopomoc Chlopska" [*Agricultural Cooperative Center of the "Peasant's Mutual Aid"*]   (POL)
CRSSGF .... Comptes Rendus des Seances de la Societe Geologique de France
CRSSI....... Council for the Rationalization of the Shipbuilding and Shipping Industries [*Japan*]   (PDAA)
CRSSPPU ... Costa Rican Commission in Solidarity with Political Prisoners in Uruguay   (EAIO)
CRST........ Commission de Recherches Scientifiques et Techniques [*OUA*]   (WGAO)
CRSV........ Centre de Recherches Science Vie   (WGAO)
CRSVI .... Conference Regionale du Service Volontaire International [*Regional Conference on International Voluntary Service*]   (EAIO)
CRT .... Caribintair SA [*Haiti*] [*ICAO designator*]   (FAAC)
CRT .... Cassa di Risparmio di Torino [*Bank*] [*Italian*]
CRT .... Center for Regional Information Training [*Africa*]
CRT .... Central Regional de Trabajadores [*Regional Labor Federation*] [*Venezuela*]   (LA)
CRT .... Centre de Recherches Tchadienne
CRT .... Centro di Ricerca per il Teatro [*Italian*]   (SLS)
CRT .... Centro Regional de Telecomunicaciones [*Chile*]   (LAA)
CRT .... Chicago Research & Trading Bank   (ECON)
CRT .... Combined Rural Traders Ltd. [*Australia*]
CRT .... Confederacion Revolucionaria de Trabajadores [*Revolutionary Confederation of Workers*] [*Mexico*]   (LA)
CRT .... Conselho Revolucionario dos Trabalhadores [*Revolutionary Workers' Councils*] [*Portuguese*]   (WER)
CRT .... Contract Regulation Tribunal [*New South Wales*] [*Australia*]
CRT .... Croix Rouge Togolaise [*Togolese Red Cross*]   (AF)
CRTA........ Centre de Recherches sur les Trypanosomoses Animales [*Research Center for Animal Trypanosomiasis*] [*Burkina-Faso*] [*Research center*]   (IRC)
CRTA........ Colombo Rubber Traders Association [*Sri Lanka*]   (WGAO)
CRTC....... Clay Roofing Tile Council   (WGAO)
CRTCI....... Caisse de Retraite des Travailleurs Salaries de Cote-D'Ivoire
CRTO .... Centre Regional de Teledetection [*Regional Center for Remote-Sensing*] [*Burkina Faso*]   (AF)
CRTS........ Commonwealth Reconstruction Training Scheme [*Australia*]   (ADA)
Crts .... Consorts [*Benelux*]   (BAS)
CRTSM..... Secretariado Nacional Pro-Conselhos Revolucionarios de Trabalhadores, Soldados, e Marinheiros [*National Secretariat for Revolutionary Councils of Workers, Soldiers, and Sailors*] [*Portuguese*]   (WER)
CRTV........ Cameroon Radio Television
CRTVG...... Compania de Radio Television de Galicia [*Spain*]   (EY)
CRU .... Cancer Research Unit [*Flinders University*] [*Australia*]
CRU .... Carriacou [*Windward Islands*] [*Airport symbol*]   (OAG)
CRU .... Centre de Recherche d'Urbanisme   (WGAO)

CRU .... Collective Reserve Unit
CRU .... Commodities Research Unit
CRU .... Community Residential Unit [*Victoria*] [*Australia*]
CRU .... Criminology Research Unit [*Australia*]
CRUA .... Comite Revolutionnaire d'Unite et d'Action [*Revolutionary Unity and Action*] [*FLN*] [*Later,*]
CRUA .... Conference des Recteurs des Universites Africaines
CRUCH...... Consejo de Rectores de Universidades Chilenas [*Chile*]   (SLS)
CRUEA ..... Centre de Recherche sur l'Utilisation des Energies Alternatives [*Center for Research on the Utilization of Alternative Energy*]
CRUEI....... Centre Italien pour les Relations Universitaires avec l'Etranger [*Italian*]
CRUESI .... Centre de Recherches pour l'Utilisation de l'Eau Salee en Irrigation
CRUFA..... Conference des Recteurs des Universities Francophones d'Afrique   (WGAO)
CRUMA..... Council of Retired Union Members Associations [*Australia*]
CRUP .... Consejo de Rectores de Universidades Privadas [*Council of Private Universities Rectors*] [*Argentina*]   (LA)
CRUS........ [*The*] Consultancy and Research Unit, University of Sheffield [*England*] [*Information service or system*]   (IID)
Cruse........... National Organization for the Widowed and their Children   (WGAO)
CRUSHH .. Concerned Residents Under Siege in Hunters Hill [*Australia*]
CRUTAC... Centro Rural Universitario de Treinamento e de Acao Comunitaria [*University Rural Center for Training and Community Action*] [*Brazil*]   (LA)
CRUTEPO ... Commission Regionale de l'Utilisation des Terres et des Eaux au Proche-Orient [*Regional Commission on Land and Water Use in the Near East - RCLWUNE*]   (EAIO)
CRUV .... Corporacion de Renovacion Urbana y Vivienda [*Puerto Rico*]   (DSCA)
Cruz............ Cruzeiro [*Monetary unit*] [*Brazil*]
CRV .... Croix Rouge Vietnamienne [*Vietnamese Red Cross*]   (EAIO)
Crvarm....... Crvena Armija [*Red Army*]   (YU)
CRvB......... Centrale Raad van Beroep [*Benelux*]   (BAS)
Crvkr......... Crveni Krst [*Red Cross*]   (YU)
CRWCS..... Canning Rvier Wetlands Conservation Society [*Australia*]
CRWLRA .. Commission on Research of the World Leisure and Recreation Association [*France*]   (EAIO)
CRWR .... Centre for Rural Welfare Research [*Riverina-Murray Institute of Higher Education*] [*Australia*]
Crx .... Croix [*Cross*] [*Military map abbreviation World War I*] [*French*]   (MTD)
CRX .... Cross Air AG [*Switzerland*] [*ICAO designator*]   (FAAC)
CRYDI....... Corporacion de Reconstruccion y Desarrollo del Departamento de Ica [*Peru*]   (DSCA)
CRYF......... Corporacion de Reconstruccion y Fomento [*Reconstruction and Development Corporation*] [*Peru*]   (LA)
CRYM .... Comision Reguladora de la Produccion y Comercio de la Yerba Mate [*Argentina*]   (LAA)
CRYRZA ... Comision de Reconstruccion y Rehabilitiacion de la Zona Afectada [*Commission for the Reconstruction and Rehabilitation of the Affected Zone*] [*Peru*]   (LA)
CRZ .... Centre de Recherches Zootechniques
CRZ .... Servicios Aereos Cruzeiro do Sul SA [*Brazil*] [*ICAO designator*]   (FAAC)
CRZA........ Centre de Recherches sur les Zones Africaines [*Algeria*]
CRZZ........ Centralna Rada Zwiazkow Zawodowych [*Central Council of Trade Unions*] [*Poland*]   (POL)
CS .... Caledonian Society [*Australia*]
CS .... Cameroon Socialists [*Political party*]
CS .... Canberra Skeptics [*Australia*]
CS .... Caractere Special [*French*]   (ADPT)
CS .... Celostatni Spartakiada [*All-State Spartakiad*] [*National sport and athletic competition*]   (CZ)
cs .... Centimos [*Spanish*]
CS .... Centrala Spozywcow [*Consumer's Center*]   (POL)
CS .... Centralna Szkola [*Central School*]   (POL)
Cs .... Cesio [*Cesium*] [*Chemical element*] [*Portuguese*]
CS .... Ceskoslovensko [or Ceskoslovensky] [*Czechoslovakia or Czechoslovak*]   (CZ)
CS .... Ceskoslovensky Spisovatel [*The Czechoslovak Writer*] [*A publishing house*]   (CZ)
Cs .... Cesme [*Spring*]   (TU)
CS .... Chawangan Siasatan [*Investigation Branch*]   (ML)
CS .... Coleopterists Society   (WGAO)
CS .... Colophon Society [*Australia*]
CS .... Commandite Simple [*France*]   (FLAF)
CS .... Commonwealth Secretariat [*Australia*]
CS .... Commonwealth Secretariat [*British*]   (EAIO)
CS .... Communications Satellite [*Japan*]
CS .... Competitive Strategies [*NATO*]
CS .... Confederacion Socialista [*Socialist Confederation*] [*Spanish*]   (WER)

CS .... Congregatio Missionariorum a Sancto Carolo Scalabriniani (WGAO)
CS .... Congregation of Salesians [*Australia*]
CS .... Conseil de Securite [*United Nations*]
CS .... Conservation Society   (WGAO)
CS .... Con Sordino [*With Mute*] [*Music*]
CS .... Construcciones Aeronauticas SA [*Spain*] [*ICAO aircraft manufacturer identifier*]   (ICAO)
CS .... Corriente Socialista [*Socialist Current*] [*Mexico*]   (LA)
CS .... Corse Air International [*France*] [*ICAO designator*]   (ICDA)
CS .... Cosenza [*Car registration plates*] [*Italy*]
Cs .... Cottbus [*Cottbus*] [*One of the eight reichsbahn directorates*] (EG)
cs .... Cours [*Quotation, Price*] [*French*] [*Business term*]
CS .... Cran Sonar [*Colombia*]   (COL)
CS .... Credit Suisse [*Bank*]
CS .... Cristianos por el Socialismo [*Christians for Socialism*] [*Spanish*] (WER)
CS .... Crkveni Sud [*Ecclesiastical Court*]   (YU)
CS .... Crown Solicitor [*Australia*]
cs .... Csapat [*Troop, Company, Detachment, Squadron*]   (HU)
cs .... Cuartos [*Rooms*] [*Spanish*]
CS .... Cumhuriyet Senatosu [*Republican Senate*]   (TU)
cs .... Cum Suis [*French*]   (BAS)
CS .... Czechoslovakia [*ANSI two-letter standard code*]   (CNC)
CS .... Czechoslowacja [*Former Czechoslovakia*] [*Poland*]
CSA .... Campaign for a Scottish Assembly   (WGAO)
CSA .... Canadian Standards Association   (WGAO)
CSA .... Cancer Support Association [*Australia*]
CSA .... Canoe South Australia
CSA .... Caribbean Studies Association [*Puerto Rico*]   (EAIO)
CSA .... Carillon Society of Australia
CSA .... Casualty Surgeons Association   (WGAO)
CSA .... Centrale Syndicale Angolaise
CSA .... Centralfoerbundet foer Socialt Arbete [*Central Committee for Social Work*] [*Sweden*]   (SLS)
CSA .... Central South Africa Railway
CSA .... Central South Australia   (ADA)
CSA .... Centro Studi Adriatici [*Italian*]   (SLS)
CSA .... Centro Studi Aeronautici [*Aeronautic Study Center*] [*Research center*] [*Italian*]   (ERC)
CSA .... Ceskoslovenska Armada [*Czechoslovak Army*]   (CZ)
CSA .... Ceskoslovenske Aerolinie [*Czechoslovak Airlines*] [*Prague*] (CZ)
CSA .... Ceskoslovenske Spolky v Americe [*Czechoslovak Organizations in America*]   (CZ)
CSA .... Cesky Severozapadni Aeroklub [*Czech Northwestern Aero Club*] (CZ)
CSA .... Chambre Syndicale de l'Amiante   (WGAO)
CSA .... Charolais Society of Australia
CSA .... Chemical Structure Association   (WGAO)
CSA .... Child Support Agency [*Australia*]
CSA .... Christian Schools' Association [*Australia*]
CSA .... Christliche-Sozialistische Arbeitsgemeinschaft [*Christian Social-Workers' Community*] [*Lithuania*] [*Political party*]   (PPE)
CSA .... Civil Service Association [*St. Lucia*]   (LA)
CSA .... Club du Setter Anglais [*English Setter Club*] [*France*]   (EAIO)
CSA .... Club Sportif d'Atakpame
CSA .... Club Suisse d'Aviation [*Switzerland*]
CSA .... Coeliac Society of Australia
CSA .... College of Surgeons of Australasia   (ADA)
CSA .... Comite de Soutien de l'Angola
CSA .... Comite Superieur Arabe [*North African*]
CSA .... Comitetul de Stat al Apelor [*State Water Committee*]   (RO)
CSA .... Commission Federale pour la Securite des Installations Atomiques [*Atomic Installations Safety Commission*] [*French*]   (WER)
CSA .... Commonwealth Sugar Agreement   (ADA)
CSA .... Communaute Suisse de Travail pour l'Aphasie   (WGAO)
CSA .... Computer Sciences of Australia Proprietary Ltd.   (ADA)
CSA .... Computer Sciences of Australia Pty. Ltd. [*Information service or system*]   (IID)
CSA .... Computing Services Association   (WGAO)
CSA .... Confederacion Socialista Argentina [*Socialist Confederation of Argentina*]   (LA)
CSA .... Confederacion Sudamericana de Atletismo [*South American Athletic Confederation - SAAC*]   (EAIO)
CSA .... Confederation Syndicale Africaine [*African Trade Union Confederation*]
CSA .... Confederation Syndicale des Avocats   (WGAO)
CSA .... Conseil Scientifique pour l'Afrique [*Scientific Council for Africa*] (AF)
CSA .... Conseil Superieur de l'Agriculture   (WGAO)
CSA .... Conseil Superieur de l'Audioviseul [*France*]   (EY)
CSA .... Contal Shipping Agencies [*Ghana*]
CSA .... Cornish Scottish Australia [*Mine*]
CSA .... Cour Superieure d'Arbitrage [*France*]   (FLAF)
CSA .... Creative Services Association   (WGAO)
CSA .... Cryogenic Society of America   (WGAO)
Cs A .... Csepeli Autogyar [*Automobile Factory of Csepel*]   (HU)
CSA .... Current Science Association [*India*]   (DSCA)
CSA .... Cyprus Scouts Association   (EAIO)
CSAA .... Canadian Sociology and Anthropology Association   (WGAO)
CSAA .... Cold Storage Association of Australia   (ADA)
CSAA .... Confederacion Sudamericano de Atletismo   (WGAO)
CSAA .... Coopworth Sheep Society of Australia
CSAAR ...... Centre for the Study of Australian-Asian Relations
CSAB .... Civil Service Appeal Board   (WGAO)
CSABrBtr .. Centro di Studi Archeologici di Boscoreale e Boscotrecase [*Italian*]   (SLS)
CSAC .... Alliance Cocoa Scientific Advisory Committee   (WGAO)
CSAC .... Companies and Securities Advisory Committee [*Australia*]
CSAC .... Correctional Services Advisory Council [*South Australia*]
CSACSO ... Council of South Australia College Students Organisations
CSAD .... Ceskoslovenska Automobilova Doprava [*Czechoslovak Automobile Transportation*]   (CZ)
CSAD .... Ceskoslovenska Statni Automobilova Doprava [*Czechoslovak State Automobile Transportation*] [*Prague*]   (CZ)
CSAES ...... Centre for South Australian Economic Studies [*Flinders University*] [*Australia*]
CSAF .... Centro di Sperimentazione Agricola e Forestale [*Agricultural and Forest Research Center*] [*Italian*]   (ARC)
CSAF .... Ceskoslovenska Asociace Footballova [*Czechoslovak Soccer Association*]   (CZ)
CSAG .... Commonwealth-State Advisory Group [*Australia*]
CSAI .... Italian Automobile Sporting Commission   (WGAO)
CSAIMARENA ... Companion of the South African Institute of Marine Engineers and Naval Architects   (AA)
CSAJ .... Cartel Suisse des Associations de Jeunesse [*Switzerland*]
CSAK .... Ceskoslovensky Aeroklub [*Czechoslovak Aero Club*]   (CZ)
CSAL .... Cadbury Schweppes Australia Ltd.
CSAL .... Club Sportif Automobile du Littoral
CSAM .... Conseil Superieur de l'Aviation Marchande [*Air Transport Advisory Board*] [*France*]   (PDAA)
CSANT ...... Cold Storage Association of the Northern Territory [*Australia*]
CSANZ ...... Cardiac Society of Australia and New Zealand   (ADA)
CSAO .... Centro di Studi e Applicazioni di Organizzazione Aziendale della Produzione e dei Trasporti [*Italian*]   (SLS)
CSAO .... Ceskoslovenske Automobilove Opravny [*Czechoslovak Automobile Repair Shops*]   (CZ)
CSAP .... Child Sexual Assault Program [*Australia*]
CSAP .... Child Survival Assistance Program [*Agency for International Development*]
csap .... Csapat [*Troop, Company, Detachment, Squadron*]   (HU)
CSAPP ...... Committee of Solidarity with Arab Political Prisoners [*France*]
CSAPS .... Ceskoslovensky Amatersky Plavecky Svaz [*Czechoslovak Amateur Swimming Association*]   (CZ)
CSAQ .... Cold Storage Association of Queensland [*Australia*]
CSAR .... Central South Africa Railway
CSAR .... Compagnie Senegalaise d'Assurance et de Reassurances
CSARE ...... Centro per gli Studi e le Applicazioni delle Risorse Energetiche [*Italian*]   (SLS)
CSAS .... Centre for Southeast Asian Studies [*Monash University*] [*Australia*]
CSAT .... Cold Storage Association of Tasmania [*Australia*]
CSAT .... Colegio Superior de Agricultura Tropical [*Mexico*]   (DSCA)
CSATA ...... Centro Studi e Applicazioni in Tecnologia Avanzata [*Italian*] (SLS)
csatl .... Csatlakozas [*Connection*]   (HU)
CSATM ..... Confederation Sudamericaine de Tennis de Table [*Uruguay*] (WGAO)
CSAV .... Ceskoslovenska Akademie Ved [*Czechoslovak Academy of Sciences*] [*Research center*]   (CZ)
CSAV .... Compania Sud Americana de Vapores [*Chile*]   (LAA)
CSAWA .... Cold Storage Association of Western Australia
CSAWA .... Country Shires Association of Western Australia
CSAZ .... Ceskoslovenska Akademie Zemedelska   (WGAO)
CSAZ .... Ceskoslovenska Akademie Zemedelstvi [*Czechoslovak Agricultural Academy*]   (CZ)
CSAZV ...... Ceskoslovenska Akademie Zemedelskych Ved [*Czechoslovak Academy of Agricultural Sciences*]   (CZ)
CSB .... Centrala Sprzetu Budownictwa [*Building Equipment Center*] (POL)
CSB .... Centro Simon Bolivar [*Venezuela*]
CSB .... Christian Services for the Blind [*Australia*]
CSB .... Christliche Sozialbewegung der Schweiz [*Swiss Christian Social Movement*]   (WEN)
CSB .... Comite Solidarite-Burundi
CSB .... Common Schools Board [*Australia*]
CSB .... Commonwealth Savings Bank [*Australia*]   (ADA)
CSB .... Community Services Board [*Australia*]

CSB............ Confederation Syndicale Burkinabe [*Trade union*] [*Burkina Faso*]
CSB............ Congregation of Saint Basil (WGAO)
CSB............ Consejo Superior Bancario (WGAO)
csb............. Csapatbajnoksag [*Team Championship*] (HU)
CSBA........ Commonwealth Savings Bank of Australia
CSBISSS ... Commission on Soil Biology of the International Society of Soil Science (EAIO)
CSBkS .... Ceskoslovenska Bioklimatologicka Spolecnost [*Czechoslovak Bioclimatological Society*] [*Multinational association*] (EAIO)
CSBNTP.... Chambre Syndicale Belge des Negociants en Timbres Poste (WGAO)
CSBP .... Cetna Stanica Borbenih Potreba [*Company Combat Supply Station*] (YU)
CSBP .... Chambre Syndicale des Banques Populaires de France (WGAO)
CSBr .... Crkveni Sud Broj [*Ecclesiastical Court Number*] (YU)
CSBS .... Ceskoslovenska Botanicka Spolecnost [*Former Czechoslovakia*] (EAIO)
CSBS .... Ceskoslovensky Basketballovy Svaz [*Czechoslovak Basketball Association*] (CZ)
CSBUSSS ... Commission on Soil Biology of the International Society of Soil Science [*Netherlands*] (EAIO)
CSBVF....... Chambre Syndicale de la Boulonnerie et de la Visserie Forgees (WGAO)
CSBZ......... Cold Storage Board of Zambia
CSc............ Candidatus Scientiae [*Candidate for Doctor of Science*] (CZ)
CSC........... Cartel des Syndicats Caledoniens [*Federation of New Caledonian Trade Unions*]
CSC........... Catholic Students Council (WGAO)
CSC........... Central Standardization Committee
CSC........... Centro Sperimentale de Cinematografia [*Television and video school*] [*Italian*]
CSC........... Centro Studi Cinematografici [*Italian*] (SLS)
CSC........... Chiefs of Staff Committee [*Australia*]
CSC........... Children's Service Council [*Australian Capital Territory*]
CSC........... Chile Solidarity Campaign
CSC........... Civil Service Commission (WGAO)
CSC........... Cold Storage Commission
CSC........... Comite Suisse de la Chimie (WGAO)
CSC........... Comite Superieur de Controle [*Benelux*] (BAS)
CSC........... Comite Syndical de Coordination
CSC........... Commissioner of Soil Conservation [*Western Australia*]
CSC........... Commission Syndicale Consultative (WGAO)
CSC........... Commonwealth Schools Commission [*Australia*]
CSC........... Commonwealth Science Council [*London, England*] (EAIO)
CSC........... Commonwealth Scientific Committee (WGAO)
CSC........... Compagnie Senegalaise de Carrieres (WGAO)
CSC........... Confederacion Sindical de Colombia [*Trade Union Confederation of Columbia*] [*Colombia*] (COL)
CSC........... Confederation des Syndicats Chretiens [*Confederation of Christian Trade Unions*] [*Belgium*] (WER)
CSC........... Confederation des Syndicats Chretiens de la Suisse (WGAO)
CSC........... Confederation Syndicale Congolaise [*Congolese Trade Union Confederation*] (AF)
CSC........... Congregatio a Sancto Cruce (WGAO)
CSC........... Conspicuous Service Cross [*Australia*] (ADA)
CSC........... Consumer Safety Committee [*Queensland*] [*Australia*]
CSC........... Convergencia Socialista Cataluna [*Socialist Convergence of Catalonia*] [*Spanish*] (WER)
CSC........... Coup sur Coup [*In Small Doses at Short Intervals*] [*French*]
CSC........... Cycle-Speedway Council (WGAO)
CSC.......... Sichuan Airlines [*China*] [*ICAO designator*] (FAAC)
CSCA........ Chambre Syndicale des Constructeurs Automobiles [*France*]
CSCA........ Cinderella Stamp Club of Australia
CSCA........ Consejo Superior de los Colegios de Arquitectos de Espana (WGAO)
CSCA........ Country Shire Councils' Association [*Australia*]
CSCAS ...... Comitetul de Stat pentru Constructii, Arhitectura, si Sistematizare [*State Committee for Constructions, Architecture, and Systematization*] (RO)
CSCAW .... Catholic Study Circle for Animal Welfare (WGAO)
CSCB........ Committee of Scotish Clearing Bankers
CSCB........ Confederacion Sindical de Choferes de Bolivia [*Trade Union Confederation of Bolivian Drivers*] (LA)
CSCB........ Confederation des Syndicats Chretiens de Belgique [*Belgium*] (EAIO)
CSCC........ Centre for the Study of Communication and Culture (WGAO)
CSCC........ City of Sydney Cultural Centre [*Australia*]
CSCC........ Cockburn Sound Conservation Council [*Western Australia*]
CSCC........ Commonwealth-State Consultative Committee on Nuclear Codes [*Australia*]
CSCC........ Confederation des Syndicats Chretiens du Congo [*Confederation of Christian Syndicates of the Congo*] [*Leopoldville*]
CSCD........ Committee for the Settlement of Commercial Disputes [*Saudi Arabia*]

CSCD........ Committee on Studies for Cooperation in Development [*Colombo, Sri Lanka*]
CSCDG...... Commission Superieure de Cassation des Dommages de Guerre [*France*] (FLAF)
CSCE........ Centre Senegalais du Commerce Exterieur [*Senegalese Centre for External Trade*] (GEA)
CSCE........ Conference on Security and Cooperation in Europe (PD)
CSCEC...... China State Construction Engineering Corp.
CSCF .... Cast Stone and Concrete Federation (WGAO)
CSCF .... Curtea Superioara de Control Financiar [*Higher Court for Financial Control*] (RO)
CSCFE....... Civil Service Council for Further Education (WGAO)
CSCG........ Centre Socio-Culturel Guyanais [*French Guianese Socio-Cultural Center*] (LA)
CSCh......... Cahier Special des Charges [*Benelux*] (BAS)
CSCHK..... Committee for Science Coordination of Hong Kong
CSCITM.... Centrul de Studii si Cercetari de Istorie si Teorie Militara [*Center for Studies and Research in Military History and Theory*]
CSCK........ Ceskoslovensky Cerveny Kriz [*Czechoslovak Red Cross*] (CZ)
CSCN........ Chambre Syndicale des Constructeurs de Navires et de Machines Marines (WGAO)
CSCo......... Caisse de Stabilisation Cotoniere [*Zaire*] (WGAO)
CSCO........ Caisse de Stabilisation Cotonniere [*Cotton Stabilization Fund*] [*Zaire*] (AF)
CSCOCINE ... Consejo Superior de las Camaras Oficiales de Comercio, Industria y Navegacion d e Espana [*Spain*] (EAIO)
CSCP .... Commission Speciale de Cassation des Pensions [*France*] (FLAF)
CSCPA ...... Comitetul de Stat pentru Colectarea Produselor Agricole [*State Committee for the Collection of Agricultural Products*] (RO)
CSCPAC.... Commonwealth-State Consumer Products Advisory Committee [*Australia*]
CSCPB...... Central Sugar Cane Prices Board [*Queensland*] [*Australia*]
CSC/PRC .. Committee for Scholarly Communication with the People's Republic of China (PDAA)
CSCS .... Commonwealth Students' Children's Society
CSCS .... Crusader Swire Container Service (DS)
CSCSGY.... Csepeli Csogyar [*Pipe Factory of Csepel*] (HU)
CSCSU ...... Common Service Civil Servants Union [*Uganda*] (AF)
CSCT .... Comite Suisse Contre la Torture [*Swiss Committee Against Torture*] (EAIO)
CSCZ......... Ceskoslovenske Cihlarske Zavody [*Czechoslovak Brick Works*] (CZ)
CSD .... Canberra Skydivers [*Australia*]
CSD .... Centralised Services Division
CSD .... Central Semen Depot [*Poland*] (ARC)
CSD .... Central Supplies Department [*Singapore*] (DS)
CSD .... Ceskoslovenska Socialni Demokracie [*Czechoslovak Social-Democratic Party*] (CZ)
CSD .... Ceskoslovenske Statni Drahy [*Czechoslovak State Railroads*] (CZ)
CSD .... Chartered Society of Designers (WGAO)
CSD .... Civil Service Department (WGAO)
CSD .... Coast Study Division [*Israel*] (MSC)
CSD .... Colombian Society of Dermatology (EAIO)
CSD .... Commissioner of Stamp Duties [*Australia*]
CSD .... Commissione Suprema di Difesa [*Supreme Defense Board*] [*Italian*] (WER)
CSD .... Commonwealth Society for the Deaf [*British*] (ADA)
CSD .... Computergestuetzte Systementwicklung und Dokumentation [*German*] (ADPT)
CSD .... Conference Suisse des Directeurs des Ecoles Professionnelles et des Metiers (WGAO)
CSD .... Consejo Superior de Deportes (WGAO)
CSD .... Consejo Superior de la Defensa [*Superior Defense Council*] [*Honduras*] (LA)
CSD .... Consultative Sub-Committee on Surplus Disposal [*FAO*] (WGAO)
CSD .... Convergencia Social Democratica [*Equatorial Guinea*]
CSD .... Correctional Services Department [*Hong Kong*]
CSD .... Court Services Department [*South Australia*]
CSDB........ Corporacion Social de Desarrollo y Bienestar [*Colombia*] (DSCA)
CSDCA .... Centro Studi e Documentazione della Cultura Armena [*Italian*] (SLS)
CSDE........ Ceskoslovenska Socialni Demokracie v Exilu [*Czechoslovak Social Democratic Party*] (EAIO)
CSDEM..... Chambre Syndicale de l'Edition Musicale [*Publisher's Association*] [*France*] (EY)
CSDES ..... Consiliul Suprem al Dezvoltarii Economice si Sociale [*Supreme Council for Economic and Social Development*] (RO)
CSDHA ..... Centre for Social Development and Humanitarian Affairs [*United Nations*] (WGAO)
CSDI......... Changjiang Ship Design Institute [*China*] (IRC)

CSdL .... Confederazione Sammarinese del Lavoro [*Trade union*] [*San Marino*]   (EY)
CSDO .... Children's Services Development Officer [*Australia*]
CSDP .... Ceskoslovenske Dopravni Podniky [*Czechoslovak Transportation Enterprises*]   (CZ)
CSDPP ...... Chambre Syndicale de la Distribution des Produits Petroliers   (WGAO)
CSDS .... Ceskoslovenska Demograficka Spolecnost [*Czechoslovak Demographic Society*]   (CZ)
CSDV .... Chilean Society of Dermatology and Venereology   (EAIO)
CSDVT ...... Ceskoslovenska Spolecnost pro Dejiny Ved a Techniky [*CSAV*]   (WGAO)
CSDWP/WNG ... Committee for Self-Determination West Papua/West New Guinea [*Netherlands*]   (EAIO)
Cse .... Cense [*Farm*] [*Military map abbreviation World War I*] [*French*]   (MTD)
CSE .... Central Studies Establishment [*Research center*] [*Australia*]   (ERC)
CSE .... Centre de Sante Elementaire
CSE .... Centre de Sociologie Europeenne [*Center for European Sociology*] [*Research center*] [*France*]   (IRC)
CSE .... Centre for Science and Environment [*India*]   (EAIO)
CSE .... Ceskoslovenska Spolecnost Ekonomicka [*Former Czechoslovakia*]   (EAIO)
CSE .... Commission Seismologique Europeenne [*European Seismological Commission - ESC*]   (EAIO)
CSE .... Communications Satellite for Experimental Purposes [*Japan*] [*Telecommunications*]
CSE .... Compagnie Senegalaise d'Entreprises
CSE .... Conference des Statisticiens Europeens   (WGAO)
CSE .... Conference Spatiale Europeenne   (WGAO)
CSE .... Consejo Supremo Electoral [*Venezuela*]
CSE .... Copenhagen Stock Exchange [*Denmark*]
CSEA .... Committee of Student European Associations   (WGAO)
CSEABC .... Chambre Syndicale des Entreprises Artisanales du Batiment   (WGAO)
CSEAL ...... Comitetul de Stat pentru Economie si Administratie Locala [*State Committee for Local Economy and Administration*]   (RO)
CSEB .... Chambre Syndicale des Electriciens Belges   (WGAO)
CSECA ...... Center for Studies and Experimentation in the Creative Arts [*CIVITAS Foundation*]   (EAIO)
CSEDB ...... Chambre Syndicale des Entrepreneurs de Demenagements Belgique   (WGAO)
CSEDC ...... Centre for Study of Education in Developing Countries [*Netherlands*]   (EAIO)
CSEE .... Comite Syndical Europeen des Personnels de l'Education [*European Teachers Trade Union Committee*] [*EC*]   (ECED)
CSEE .... Committee of Stock Exchanges in the European Community [*See also CBCE*]   (EAIO)
CSEE .... Compagnie des Signaux et d'Enterprises Electriques [*France*]   (PDAA)
CSEERI .... Comite Scientifique pour l'Etude des Effets des Radiations Ionisantes
CSEF .... Centro di Studi per l'Educazione Fisica [*Italian*]   (SLS)
CSEHMA ... Cyprus Solar and Electric Heaters Manufacturers Association   (EAIO)
CSEHMADOK ... Csehszlovakiai Magyar Dolgozok Kulturegylete [*Cultural Association of Hungarian Workers in Czechoslovakia*]   (HU)
CSEI .... Centro Studi di Economia Applicata all'Ingegneria [*Italian*]   (SLS)
CSEI .... Chambre Syndicale des Estheticiens Industriels   (WGAO)
c/sek .... Cykl na Sekunde [*Cycle per Second*] [*Poland*]
CSELT ...... Centro Studi e Laboratori Telecomunicazioni [*Telecommunications Research and Study Center*] [*Italian*]   (WER)
CSEM .... Centre Seismologique Europeo-Mediterraneen   (WGAO)
CSEM .... Centre Sismologique Euro-Mediterraneen [*European-Mediterranean Seismological Center*] [*France*]   (EAS)
CSEMADOK ... Csehslovakiat Magyar Dolgozok Kulturegyesulete [*Culture Society of Hungarian Workers in Czechoslovakia*]   (CZ)
CSEMADOK ... Csehszlovakai Magyarok Kulturalis-Tarsadalmi Szovetsege [*Cultural-Social Association of Hungarians in Czechoslovakia*]   (HU)
CSEMKER ... Orszagos Csemegekereskedelmi Vallalat [*National Delicatessen Enterprise*]   (HU)
CSEMP ..... Chambre Syndicale des Emballages en Matieres Plastiques   (WGAO)
CSEN .... Centro Superior de Estudios Nucleares [*Peru*]   (EY)
CSEN .... Comite Sindical de Emergencia Nacional [*National Labor Emergency Committee*] [*El Salvador*]   (LA)
CSEN .... Comitetul de Stat pentru Energia Nucleara [*State Committee for Nuclear Energy*]   (RO)
CSEN .... Conseil Superieur de l'Education Nationale [*Higher Council of National Education*] [*Guinea*]   (AF)

CSEP .... Conseil Superieur de l'Education Populaire   (WGAO)
CSEPE ...... Comite Syndical Europeen des Personnels Enseignants   (WGAO)
CSEPP .... Central Sindical de Empleados Particulares del Peru [*Peruvian Trade Union Federation of Workers in Private Enterprise*]   (LA)
CSER .... Committee on Solar Electromagnetic Radiation   (WGAO)
CSERB ...... Computer Science and Electronics Requirements Board   (WGAO)
CSES .... Comite de Solidaridad con El Salvador [*Committee of Solidarity with El Salvador*] [*Costa Rica*]   (LA)
cs es kir .... Csaszari es Kiralyi [*Imperial and Royal*]   (HU)
CSESS ...... Conseil Suisse des Ecoles de Service Social   (WGAO)
CSETHC ... Comite Syndical Europeen de Textile, de l'Habillement et du Cuir [*Belgium*]   (EAIO)
CSEU .... Civil Service Executive Union [*Eire*]   (WGAO)
CSEU .... Confederation of Shipbuilding and Engineering Unions   (WGAO)
CSF .... Cesky Svaz Footballovy [*Czech Soccer Association*]   (CZ)
CSF .... Civil Service Federation [*San Marino*]   (EAIO)
CSF .... Coil Spring Federation   (WGAO)
CSF .... Comite des Salines de France   (WGAO)
CSF .... Commonwealth Schoolbook Fund
CSF .... Commonwealth Superannuation Fund [*Australia*]   (ADA)
CSF .... Community Support Framework [*EC*]   (ECED)
CSF .... Community Systems Foundation
CSF .... Compagnie Generale de Telegraphie sans Fil [*General Radio Company*] [*French*]   (WER)
CSF .... Confederacion Sudamericana de Futbol   (WGAO)
CSF .... Congregatio a Sacra Familia   (WGAO)
csf .... Costo, Seguro, Fiete [*Cost, Insurance, Freight*] [*Spanish*] [*Business term*]
CSF .... Creation Science Foundation [*Australia*]
CSF(A) ...... Community Systems Foundation (Australia)
CSFA .... Confederation des Societes Francaises d'Architectes   (WGAO)
CSF-B .... Ceskoslovensky Film Bratislava [*Czechoslovak Film Bratislava*]   (CZ)
CSFB .... Credit Suisse First Boston [*Bank*]
CSFCO ...... Coordination Staff Foreign and Commonwealth Office   (WGAO)
CSFIFF ..... Chambre Syndicale Francaise des Industriels Fondeurs de Fromage   (WGAO)
csfk .... Csoportfonok [*Chief/Commander of Group, Troop Detachment, or Special Task Force*]   (HU)
CSFM .... Csepeli Femmu [*Csepel Metal Factory*]   (HU)
CSFN .... Centro Siciliano de Fisica Nucleare   (WGAO)
CSFN .... Centro Siciliano di Fisica Nucleare [*Italy*]   (DSCA)
CSFN .... Ceskoslovenske Filmove Nakladatelstvi [*Czechoslovak Motion Picture Publishing House*]   (CZ)
CSFN .... Congregation of the Sisters of the Holy Family of Nazareth [*Australia*]
CSFP .... Commonwealth Scholarship and Fellowship Plan [*Australia*]
CSFPCPM ... Chambre Syndicale des Fabricants de Papiers a Cigarettes et Autres Papiers Minces   (EAIO)
CSFPN ...... Commission on Soil Fertility and Plant Nutrition [*of the International Society of Soil Science*]   (EA)
CSFR .... Czech and Slovak Federal Republic   (RDA)
CSFR .... Czech and Slovak Federative Republic   (EE)
CSFRA ...... Coil Spring Federation Research Organization   (WGAO)
CSFRI .... Citrus and Subtropical Fruit Research Institute [*South Africa*]   (ARC)
CSFSBA .... Chambre Syndicale des Fabricants de Supports en Beton Arme Destines aux Canalisations Aeriennes   (WGAO)
CSG .... Catholic Stage Guild   (WGAO)
CSG .... Centar Sektora Gadanja [*Center of Firing Sector*] [*Military*]   (YU)
CSG .... Centre Spatial Guyanais [*Guyana Space Center*] [*French*]   (WER)
CSG .... Combinatul Siderurgic Galati [*Galati Iron and Steel Combine*]   (RO)
CSG .... Comite Permanent des Secretaires Generaux [*Standing Committee of Secretaries General*] [*NATO*]   (NATG)
CSG .... Comitetul de Stat pentru Geologie [*State Committee for Geology*]   (RO)
CSG .... Commercial Services Group [*New South Wales, Australia*]
CSG .... Confederacion Sindical Guatemalteca [*Guatemalan Labor Union Federation*]
CSG .... Consejo Sindical de Guatemala [*Union Council of Guatemala*]   (LA)
CSG .... Corporate Services Group [*Australia*]
CSG .... Cumann na Scribheann nGaedhilge [*Established in 1898 to publish ancient Irish texts*] [*Irish*]
CSGCC ..... Commission on Soil Genesis, Classification, and Cartography [*of the International Society of Soil Science*]   (EA)
CSGNSW .. Commercial Services Group, New South Wales [*Australia*]
CSGP .... Community Services Grants Program [*Australia*]
CSGS .... Cekoslovenska Gerontologicka Spolecnost   (WGAO)

CSGS......... Centre de Sedimentologie et de Geochimie de la Surface [*Sedimentology and Surface Geochemistry Center*] [*National Scientific Research Center*] [*France*] (EAS)
CSGS......... Ceskoslovensky Golfovy Svaz [*Czechoslovak Golf Association*] (CZ)
CSH.......... Centralna Skladnica Harcerska [*Scouts' Central Store*] [*Poland*]
CSH.......... Ceskoslovenske Hute [*Czechoslovak Metallurgical Enterprises*] (CZ)
CSH.......... Cesky Svaz Hazene [*Czech Volleyball Association*] (CZ)
CSH.......... Chambre Suisse de l'Horlogerie (WGAO)
CSH.......... Chambre Syndicale Horticole (WGAO)
CSH.......... Combina Siderurgica Hunedoara [*Hunedoara Iron and Steel Combine*] (RO)
CSH.......... Compagnie de Services et d'Hotellerie
CSH.......... Shanghai Airlines [*China*] [*ICAO designator*] (FAAC)
CSHA......... Commonwealth-State Housing Agreement [*Australia*] (ADA)
CSHA(SP) ... Commonwealth-State Housing Agreement (Service Personnel) [*Australia*]
CSHB....... Chambre Syndicale de l'Horticulture Belge (WGAO)
CSHE....... Chinese Society of Chemical Engineering (WGAO)
CSHG....... Collective of Self Help Groups [*Australia*]
CSHI........ Christian Services for the Hearing Impaired [*Australia*]
CSHL........ Club Sportif d'Hammam-Lif [*Tunisia*]
CSHP........ Conference of Societies for the History of Pharmacy [*Madrid, Spain*] (EAIO)
CSHS........ Central Sydney Health Service [*Australia*]
CSHTGMA ... Cyprus Suitcase, Handbag, and Travel Goods Manufacturers Association (EAIO)
CSI............ Cartel des Syndicats Independants des Services Publics [*Belgium*] (WGAO)
CSI............ Casino [*Australia*] [*Airport symbol*] (OAG)
CSI............ Center for Scientific Information [*France*] (EAIO)
CSI............ Centrala Spoldzielni Inwalidow [*Disabled Persons' Cooperatives Center*] (POL)
CSI............ Centro Social Independente [*Independent Social Center*] [*Portuguese*] (WER)
CSI............ Centro Sportivo Italiano (WGAO)
CSI............ Centro Sviluppo Settori d'Impiego [*Research Center for Sectors of Application*] [*Italian*] (ARC)
CSI............ Ceskoslovensko-Sovietsky Institut [*Czechoslovak-Soviet Institute*] [*Bratislava*] (CZ)
CSI............ Chartered Surveyors Institution (WGAO)
CSI............ Christian Solidarity International [*Zurich, Switzerland*] (EAIO)
CSI............ Cinematheque Scientifique Internationale [*Belgium*] (SLS)
CSI............ Circle of State Librarians (WGAO)
CSI............ Commission Sericicole Internationale [*International Sericultural Commission - ISC*] (EAIO)
CSI............ Commission Sportive International (WGAO)
CSI............ Community Services Industry [*Australia*]
CSI............ Computer Sciences International (ADPT)
CSI............ Computer Society of India (PDAA)
CSI............ Conference Suisse sur l'Informatique (WGAO)
CSI............ Conferencia Socialista Iberica [*Iberian Socialist Conference*] [*Spanish*] (WER)
CSI............ Congregatio Sancti Ioseph (WGAO)
CSI............ Conseils et Services en Informatique [*French*] (ADPT)
CSI............ Conseil Superieur des Institutions [*Higher Council of Institutions*] [*Malagasy*] (AF)
CSI............ Consejo de Sindicatos Independientes [*Council of Independent Trade Unions*] [*El Salvador*] (LA)
CSI............ Consorzio per il Sistema Informativo Piemonte [*Piedmont Consortium for Information Systems*] [*Information service or system*] (IID)
CSI............ Construction Surveyors Institute (WGAO)
CSI............ Corrective Services Industries [*New South Wales, Australia*]
CSI............ Council for the Securities Industry [*Stock exchange*] [*London, England*]
CSIA......... Centro di Studi per l'Ingegnaria Agraria [*Italy*] (DSCA)
CSIA......... Chambre Syndicale des Importateurs d'Automobiles Cycles et Industries Annexes (WGAO)
CSIA......... China Semiconductor Industry Association (EAIO)
CSIA......... Classical Studies Institute of Australia
CSIAV....... Cold Storage and Ice Association of Victoria [*Australia*]
CSIB......... Cartel des Syndicats Independants de Belgique [*Cartel of Independent Unions of Belgium*] (WER)
CSIB......... Cooperative Synoptic Investigations of the Baltic (MSC)
CSIC......... Camara Salvadorena de la Industria de Construccion [*Salvadoran Chamber of the Construction Industry*] (LA)
CSIC......... China Standards Information Center (IRC)
CSIC......... Consejo Superior de Investigaciones Cientificas [*Higher Council for Scientific Research*] [*Spain*] [*Research center*] (WER)
CSICOP .... Committee for the Scientific Investigation of Claims of the Paranormal (WGAO)
CSICP........ Centro Studi di Ipnosi Clinica e Psicoterapia, H. Bernheim [*Italian*] (SLS)
CSID......... Centro de Servicios de Informacion y Documentacion [*Mexico*] (WGAO)

CSIE.......... Centro Studi Ingegneria Economica [*Italian*] (SLS)
CSII .... Centre for the Study of Industrial Innovation (WGAO)
CSIJ.......... Comite Sportif International de la Jeunesse (WGAO)
csill............ Csillagaszat [*Astronomy*] (HU)
CSIM........ Centro Studi Terzo Mondo [*Third World Studies Center*] [*Italy*] (IRC)
CSIMV ...... Chambre Syndicale des Industriels Metallurgistes du Vimeu (WGAO)
CSINA....... Conseil Superieur de l'Infrastructure et de la Navigation Aerienne [*French*]
CSIO......... Central Scientific Instruments Organization [*India*]
CSIO......... Centrul de Sudura si Incercari la Oboseala [*Center for Welding and Fatigue Testing*] (RO)
CSIP .... Chambre Syndicale des Industries de la Piscine (WGAO)
CSIPM ...... Centro Studi e Iniziative Pier Santi Mattarella [*Italian*] (SLS)
CSIR......... Centre for the Study of International Relations Stockholm (WGAO)
CSIR......... Council for Scientific and Industrial Research [*India*] [*Research center*]
CSIR......... Council for Scientific and Industrial Research [*Ghana*] [*Research center*] (AF)
CSIR......... Council of Scientific and Industrial Research [*Information service or system*] [*South Africa*] (IID)
CSIRO....... Commonwealth Scientific and Industrial Research Organisation [*Australia*] [*Research center*]
CSIROLCA ... Commonwealth Scientific and Industrial Research Organisation Laboratory Craftsmen's Association [*Australia*] (ADA)
CSIRONET ... Commonwealth Scientific and Industrial Research Organisation Computing Network [*Australia*] (ADA)
CSIRONET ... [*The*] Commonwealth Scientific and Industrial Research Organization Network [*Australia*] [*Computer science*] (TNIG)
CSIROOA ... Association of Officers of the Commonwealth Scientific and Industrial Research Organisation [*Australia*] (ADA)
CSIROTA ... Commonwealth Scientific and Industrial Research Organisation Technical Association [*Australia*] (ADA)
CSIRT .... Comite Scientifique International de Recherches sur les Trypanosomiases
CSIS .... Center for Strategic and International Studies [*Indonesia*] [*United States*] (WGAO)
CSIS .... Centre of Strategic International Studies [*Jakarta, Indonesia*]
CSIS .... Ceskoslovenska Immunologicka Spolecnost (WGAO)
CSIS .... Comisia de Stat pentru Incercarea Soiurilor (WGAO)
CSIS .... Comitetul de Stat pentru Invatamintul Superior [*State Committee for Higher Education*] (RO)
CSIT .... Comite Sportif International du Tavail (OLYM)
CSIT .... Comite Sportif International du Travail [*International Workers Sport Committee*] [*Brussels, Belgium*] (EAIO)
CSITSL ..... Comite Syndical International du Tourisme Social et des Loisirs [*International Trade Unions Committee of Social Tourism and Leisure - ITUCSTL*] (EA)
CSJ .... Chemical Society of Japan
CSJ .... Comisiones Sindicales Juveniles [*Youth Trade Union Committees*] [*Cuba*] (LA)
CSJ .... Congregation of St. Joseph [*Italy*] (EAIO)
CSJ .... Conseil Superieur des Jeunes [*Higher Youth Council*] [*Mauritania*] (AF)
CSJ .... Corte Suprema de Justicia [*Supreme Court*] [*Colorado*] (LA)
CSJ .... Cour Supreme de Justice [*Benelux*] (BAS)
CSJC......... Chartered Societies Joint Committee (WGAO)
CSJS......... Ceskoslovensky Jezdecky Svaz [*Czechoslovak Riding Association*] (CZ)
CSK.......... Cap Skirring [*Senegal*] [*Airport symbol*] (OAG)
CSK.......... Cesky Sermirsky Klub [*Czech Fencing Club*] (CZ)
CSK.......... Cesky Svaz Kanoistu [*Czech Canoe Association*] (CZ)
CSK.......... Chawangan Siasatan Khas [*Special Investigation Branch*] (ML)
CSK.......... Comite Special du Katanga
CSK.......... Committee for Standardization of the Democratic People's Republic of Korea [*State Committee for Science and Technology*] [*North Korea*]
CSK.......... Compagnie Special du Kongo
CSK.......... Cooperative Study of the Kuroshio and Adjacent Regions (MSC)
csk............. Cseh Korona [*Czechoslovak Crown*] (HU)
CSK.......... Csehszlovak Koztarsasag [*Czechoslovak Republic*] (HU)
CSK.......... Czechoslovakia [*ANSI three-letter standard code*] (CNC)
CSKAE ...... Ceskoslovenska Komise pro Atomovou Energii [*Czechoslovak Atomic Energy Agency*] [*Research center*] (WND)
CSKAE ...... Czechoslovak Atomic Energy Commission (WGAO)
CSKF .... Centralna Szkola Kultury Fizycznej [*Central School of Physical Education*] (POL)
CSKM........ Ceskoslovensky Klub Motoristu [*Czechoslovak Motoring Club*] (CZ)
CSKOS ...... Ceska a Slovenska Konfederace Odborovych Svazu [*Czech and Slovak Confederation of Trade Unions*] (EY)

CSKP .... Csehszlovakia Kommunista Partja [*Communist Party of Czechoslovakia*] (HU)
CSL .... Centrale des Syndicats Liberaux [*Benelux*] (BAS)
csl .... Cerkvena Slovanscina [*Church Slavonic*] [*Language*] (YU)
CSL .... Ceskoslovenska Statni Loterie [*Czechoslovak State Lottery*] (CZ)
CSL .... Ceskoslovenska Strana Lidova [*Czechoslovak People's Party*] (PPE)
CSL .... Ceskoslovenske Statni Lesy [*Czechoslovak State Forests*] (CZ)
csl .... Ceskoslovensky [*Former Czechoslovakia*] (CZ)
CSL .... Cesky Svaz Lukostrelecky [*Czech Archery Association*] (CZ)
CSL .... Chemische Werke Saar-Lothringen
CSL .... Commercial Securities Limited [*Australia*] (ADA)
CSL .... Commonwealth Serum Laboratories [*Australia*]
CSL .... Communication Services Ltd. [*Hong Kong*] [*Telecommunications*]
CSL .... Compagnie Senegalaise de Lubrifiants
CSL .... Confederation des Syndicats Libres [*Formerly, Confederation Francaise du Travail*] [*France*] (EY)
CSL .... Confederazione Somala dei Lavoratori [*Somali Confederation of Labor*] (AF)
CSL .... Conseil Superieur de la Lutte [*Supreme Struggle Committee*] [*Guinea*] (AF)
CSLA .... Club des Sloughis et des Levriers d'Afrique [*France*] (EAIO)
CSLA .... Confederation des Syndicats Libres Angolais [*Confederation of Angolan Free Trade Unions*] (AF)
CSLA .... Conferencia Sindical Latinoamericana [*Latin American Trade Union Conference*] (LA)
CSLB .... Confederation des Syndicats Liberaux de Belgique (WGAO)
CSLC .... Confederation des Syndicales Libres du Congo
CSLC .... Confederation des Syndicats Libres du Congo [*Congolese Free Trade Union Federation*]
CSLCCA .... Comite de Soutien a la Lutte Contre le Colonialisme et l'Apartheid [*Committee for Supporting the Struggle Against Colonialism and Apartheid*] [*French*] (WER)
CSLORAF ... Confederation Internationale des Syndicats Libres Organisation Regionale Africaine (WGAO)
CSLP .... Croatian Social-Liberal Party [*Political party*]
CSLRC ...... Companies and Securities Law Review Committee [*Australia*]
CSLS .... China Society of Library Science (EAIO)
CSLSC .... Centro Superiore di Logica e Scienze Comparate [*Italian*] (SLS)
Cslt .... Consulat [*Consulate*] [*French*] (MTD)
CSLTA ...... Ceskoslovenska Lawn-Tennisova Asociace [*Czechoslovak Lawn Tennis Association*] (CZ)
Cslt G .... Consulat-General [*Consulate-General*] [*French*] (MTD)
CSLUS ...... Confederazione Sindacale Lavoratori Uniti della Somalia [*Confederation of United Trade Unions of Somalia*] (AF)
CSLUT ...... Celostatni Soutez Lidove Umelecke Tvorivosti [*Folk Arts Contest*] (CZ)
CSLV .... Council of the State Library of Victoria [*Australia*]
CSM .... Centrala Spoldzielni Mieszkaniowych [*Central Office of Housing Cooperatives*] (POL)
CSM .... Centrale Suikermaatschappij (WGAO)
CSM .... Centre Scientifique de Monaco [*Scientific Centre of Monaco*] (EAS)
CSM .... Centre Superieur Militaire [*Advanced Military Training Center*] [*Zaire*] (AF)
CSM .... Centro Sperimentale Metallurgico (WGAO)
CSM .... Centro Sperimentale Metallurgico SPA [*Metallurgical Research Center*] [*Research center*] [*Italian*] (IRC)
CSM .... Centro Sviluppo Materiali SpA [*Materials Development Center*] [*Research center*] [*Italy*] (IRC)
CSM .... Ceskoslovensky Svaz Mladeze [*Czechoslovak Union of Youth*] (CZ)
CSM .... Church of Scotland Mission
CSM .... Cold Storage (Malaysia)
CSM .... Comite de Solidarite de Madagascar [*Solidarity Committee of Madagascar*] (AF)
CSM .... Commission for Synoptic Meteorology [*WMO*] (WGAO)
CSM .... Commission on Soil Mineralogy [*Australia*] (EAIO)
CSM .... Compagnie Saliniere du Maroc
CSM .... Compagnie Senegalaise de Metallurgie
CSM .... Companhia Siderurgica de Mocambique (EY)
CSM .... Conference Francaise des Superieures Majeures (WGAO)
CSM .... Conseil Special de Ministres [*Benelux*] (BAS)
CSM .... Conseil Superieur de la Magistrature [*France*] (FLAF)
CSM .... Conseil Superieur Militaire [*Supreme Military Council*] [*Chad*] (AF)
CSM .... Conselho Superior de Minas [*Brazil*] (WGAO)
CSM .... Convergencia Socialista de Madrid [*Socialist Convergence of Madrid*] [*Spanish*] (WER)
CSM .... Curacaosche Scheepvaartmij NV
CSM .... NV [*Naamloze Vennootschap*] Centrale Suiker Maatschappij [*Netherlands*]
CSMA .... Caisse de Secours Mutuels Agricoles (WGAO)
CSMA .... Civil Service Motoring Association (WGAO)
CSMA .... Communications Systems Management Association (WGAO)

CSMA .... Congregatio Sancti Michaelis Archangeli [*Poland*] (WGAO)
CSMBF ..... Centre for Studies in Money, Banking, and Finance [*Macquarie University*] [*Australia*]
CSMCRI ... Central Salt and Marine Chemicals Research Institute [*India*]
CSMCS ..... Cuban Society of Mathematics and Computer Science (EAIO)
CSME .... Catholic Society for Marriage Education [*Australia*]
CSME .... Confederation Syndicale Mondiale des Enseignants [*World Confederation of Teachers - WCT*] [*Brussels, Belgium*] (EAIO)
CSMEPP .... Committee for Solidarity with Middle East Political Prisoners
CSMF .... Confederation des Syndicats Medicaux Francais [*French*] (SLS)
CSMF .... Conference des Superieurs Majeurs de France (WGAO)
CSMFF ...... Chambre Syndicale des Mines de Fer de France (WGAO)
CSMG .... Ceskoslovenska Spolecnost pro Mineralogi a Geologi (WGAO)
CSMHC .... Council for the Single Mother and Her Child [*Australia*]
CSMI .... Commission on Small- and Medium-Scale Industries [*Philippines*]
CSMIRMA ... Conferencia dos Superiores Mairoes dos Institutos Religiosos Masculinos de Angola (WGAO)
CSMJ .... Centrala Spoldzielni Mleczarsko-Jajczarskich [*Dairy and Egg Cooperatives Center*] (POL)
CSMJ .... Ceskoslovenska Myslivecka Jednota [*Czechoslovak Hunting Association*] (CZ)
CSMRS ..... Central Soil Mechanics Research Station [*India*] (WGAO)
CSMS .... Ceskoslovenska Meteoricka Spolecnost (WGAO)
CSMS .... Ceskoslovenska Spolecnost pro Mezinarodni Styky (CZ)
CSMS .... Ceskoslovensky Myslivecky Svaz [*Czechoslovak Game Keepers Union*] (CZ)
CSMSK ..... Ceskoslovensko-Madarska Smiesana Komisia [*Czechoslovak-Hungarian Joint Commission*] (CZ)
CSMTS ..... Card Setting Machine Tenters Society (WGAO)
CSN .... Ceskoslovenska Spolecnost Normalisacni [*Czechoslovak Society for Standardization*] (CZ)
CSN .... Ceskoslovenske Normy [*Czechoslovak Standards*] (CZ)
CSN .... Ceskoslovenske Statni Normy [*Czechoslovak State Standards*] (CZ)
CSN .... Chilean Society of Nutrition (EAIO)
CSN .... Comision Sindical Nacional [*National Trade Union Commission*] [*Argentina*] (LA)
CSN .... Commissariat of Nuclear Sciences [*French*]
CSN .... Community Support Network [*Australia*]
CSN .... Companhia Siderurgica Nacional [*Brazil*] (WGAO)
CSN .... Companhia Siderurgica Nacional, SA [*National Iron and Steel Company*] [*Rio De Janeiro, Brazil*] (LA)
CSN .... Conseil Superieur du Notariat (WGAO)
CSN .... Consejo de Seguridad Nuclear [*Nucler Safety Council*] [*Spain*] (EY)
CSN .... Consejor de Seguridad Nuclear [*Nuclear energy*] [*Spanish*] (NRCH)
CSN .... Conselho de Seguranca Nacional [*National Security Council*] [*Brazil*] (LA)
CSN .... Coordinadora Sindical Nacional [*National Trade Union Coordinating Board*] [*Nicaragua*] (LA)
CSN .... Coordinador Sindical de Nicaragua (WGAO)
CSN .... Guangzhou Regional Administration of CAA of China [*ICAO designator*] (FAAC)
CSNA .... Chambre Syndicale Nationale de l'Agencement (WGAO)
CSNA .... Compagnie Senegalaise de Negoce Alimentaire
CSNC .... Chambre Syndicale des Constructeurs de Navires et de Machines Marines (WGAO)
CSNC .... Chemical Societies of the Nordic Countries (EAIO)
CSNC .... Confederation Syndicale de Nouvelle Caledonie [*Trade Union Confederation of New Caledonia*]
CSNCRA ... Chambre Syndicale Nationale du Commerce et de la Reparation Automobile [*France*] (FLAF)
CSNDP ...... Chambre Syndicale Nationale des Agencies Privees de Recheres et Mandataires en Obtention de Renseignements et de Preuves (WGAO)
CSNE .... Chambre Syndicale Nationale de l'Etancheite (WGAO)
CSNE .... Chambre Syndicale Nationale des Fabricants d'Equipements (WGAO)
CSNEIMB ... Chambre Syndicale des Entrepreneurs d'Installations de Magasins et Bureaux et Activites Annexes (WGAO)
CSNESA ... Chambre Syndicale Nationale des Electriciens et Specialistes de l'Automobile (WGAO)
CSNF .... Campaign to Save Native Forests [*Australia*]
CSNFEI ..... Chambre Syndicale Nationale des Fabricants d'Encres d'Imprimerie (WGAO)
CSNFG ...... Chambre Syndicale Nationale des Fournisseurs de Garages [*France*] (WGAO)
CSNFWA .. Campaign to Save Native Forests, Western Australia
CSNH .... Ceska Spolecnost Narodohospodarska [*Czech Economic Society*] (CZ)
CSNHP ...... Chambre Syndicale Nationale des Enterprises et Industries de l'Hygiene Publique (WGAO)
CSNI .... Committee on the Safety of Nuclear Installations [*NEA*] [*OECD*] (WGAO)

CSNI .... Conseil Superieur de la Navigation Interieure [*Benelux*]   (BAS)

CSNIGR .... Chambre Syndicale Nationale des Industries Graphiques de Reproduction   (WGAO)

CSNIP .... Chambre Syndicale Nationale des Industries de Protection   (WGAO)

CSNISE ..... Chambre Syndicale Nationale des Installateurs de Stands et d'Expositions   (WGAO)

CSNL .... Centre for the Study of Nigerian Languages

CSNL .... Chambre Syndicale Nationale de la Literie   (WGAO)

CSNLVI .... Chambre Syndicale Nationale des Loueurs de Vehicules Industriels   (WGAO)

CSNM .... Chambre Syndicale Nationale du Motorcycle   (WGAO)

CSNMPH ... Chambre Syndicale Nationale de la Mecanique de Haute Precision   (WGAO)

CSNPT ...... Ceskoslovensky Soubor Narodnich Pisni a Tancu [*Czechoslovak National Song and Dance Ensemble*]   (CZ)

CSNR .... Ceskoslovenska Narodni Rada [*Czechoslovak National Council*]   (CZ)

CSNRB ...... Ceskoslovenska Narodni Rada Badatelska [*Czechoslovak National Research Council*]   (CZ)

CSNRD ...... Consortium for the Study of Nigerian Rural Development

CSNRRM ... Chambre Syndicale Nationale des Rectifieurs et Reconstructeurs de Moteurs   (WGAO)

CSNS .... Ceskoslovenska Strana Narodnesocialisticka [*Czechoslovak National Socialist Party*]   (CZ)

CSNU .... Chambre Syndicale des Fabricants d'Uniformes   (WGAO)

CSNYV ...... Csongradi Nyomda Vallalat [*Csongrad Printing Enterprise*]   (HU)

CSO .... Canberra Symphony Orchestra [*Australia*]

CSO .... Catholic Schools Office [*Australia*]

CSO .... Centralna Spoldzielnia Ogrodnicza [*Central Gardening Cooperative*]   (POL)

CSO .... Central Seismological Observatory [*India*]   (PDAA)

CSO .... Central Selling Organisation [*South Africa*]

CSO .... Central Selling Organization of Diamond Producers   (WGAO)

CSO .... Central Shipping Organisation [*Australia*]

CSO .... Central Statistical Office [*Ethiopia*]   (AF)

CSO .... Central Statistical Office of Finland   (IRC)

CSO .... Central Statistical Organization [*India*]   (WGAO)

CSO .... Central Statistics Office [*Eire*] [*Iraq*]   (WGAO)

CSO .... Centre de Sociologie des Organisations

CSO .... Ceskoslovenska Orientalisticka Spolecnost [*CSAV*]   (WGAO)

CSO .... Ceskoslovensky Orel [*An athletic and gymnastic organization*]   (CZ)

CSO .... Cesky Symfonicky Orchestr [*Czech Symphony Orchestra*]   (CZ)

CSO .... Circulo Social Obrero [*Workers Social Circle*] [*Cuba*]   (LA)

CSO .... Commonwealth Scientific Office [*Australia*]   (ADA)

CSO .... Communications Systems Officer [*Australia*]

CSO .... Community Service Order [*Australia*]

CSO .... Community Service Organisation [*Australia*]

CSO .... Confederacion Sindical Obrera [*Workers Trade Union Confederation*] [*Spanish*]   (WER)

CSO .... Consejo Sindical de Oriente [*Trade Union Council of the East*] [*El Salvador*]   (LA)

CSO .... Crkveno Skolska Opstina [*Parish School District*]   (YU)

cso .... Csendor [*Gendarme*]   (HU)

CSO .... Cumhurbaskani Senfoni Orkestrasi [*Presidential Symphony Orchestra*]   (TU)

CSO .... Cyprus Sport Organization   (EAIO)

CSOA .... Commonwealth Steamship Owners' Association [*Australia*]

CSOB .... Ceskoslovenska Obchodni Banka [*Czechoslovak Commerce Bank*]   (CZ)

C Soc .... Cour de Cassation, Chambre Civil, Section Sociale [*France*]   (FLAF)

C Soc .... Cour de Cassation, Chambre Sociale [*France*]   (FLAF)

CSOK .... Ceskoslovenska Obchodni Komora [*Czechoslovak Chamber of Commerce*]   (CZ)

CSOL .... Ceskoslovenska Obec Legionarska [*Czechoslovak Legion*]   (CZ)

CSOL .... Chinese Society of Oceanology and Limnology   (SLS)

csom .... Csomag [*Parcel*]   (HU)

CSOMIKERT ... Csongrad Megyei Kerteszeti Vallalat   (WGAO)

CSOP .... Centralna Szkola Oficerow Politycznych [*Central School for Political Army Officers*]   (POL)

CSOP .... Cesky Sazv Ochrancu Prirody [*Czech Union of Nature Conservationists*]   (EE)

CSOP .... Csoport [*Group, Section, Troop Detachment, Special Task Force*]   (HU)

CSOS .... Ceskoslovenska Obec Sokolska [*Czechoslovak Sokol (An athletic and gymnastic organization)*]   (CZ)

CSOV .... Ceskoslovensky Olympijsky Vybor [*Czechoslovak Olympic Committee*]   (CZ)

CSP .... Caisse de Secours et de Prevoyance en Faveur des Marins Naviguant Sous Pavillon Belge [*Belgium*]   (BAS)

CSP .... Catholic Solo Parents [*Australia*]

CSP .... Centrala Spoldzielni Pracy [*Labor Cooperatives Center*]   (POL)

CSP .... Centralna Szkola Partyjna [*Central Party School*]   (POL)

CSP .... Centro de Salud Pecuaria [*Ecuador*]   (DSCA)

CSP .... Ceskoslovenska Posta [*Czechoslovak Postal Service*]   (CZ)

CSP .... Chambre Syndicale de la Phytopharmacie et de la Protection des Plantes   (WGAO)

CSP .... Chartered Society of Physiotherapy   (WGAO)

CSP .... Christlich Soziale Partei [*Christian Social Party*] [*Liechtenstein*] [*Political party*]   (PPW)

CSP .... Civil Service in Pakistan

CSP .... Club Soliman Pacha [*Egypt*]

CSP .... Code du Statut Personnel [*Tunisia*]

CSP .... Comite de Salut Public [*France*]   (FLAF)

CSP .... Comitetul de Stat al Planificarii [*State Planning Committee*]   (RO)

CSP .... Comitetul de Stat pentru Preturi [*State Committee for Prices*]   (RO)

CSP .... Compagnie Saharienne Portee

CSP .... Conseil du Salut du Peuple [*People's Salvation Council*] [*Burkina Faso*]   (PD)

CSP .... Conseil Superieur du Pays

CSP .... Conseil Superieur du Plan [*Higher Planning Council*] [*Cambodia*]   (CL)

CSP .... Cuepo Superior de Policia   (WGAO)

CSP .... Societas Sacerdotum Missionariorum a Sancto Paulo Apostolo   (WGAO)

CSPAA ...... Conseil de Solidarite des Pays Afro-Asiatiques

CSPAQ ...... Crushed Stone Producers' Association of Queensland [*Australia*]

CSPB .... Confederacao dos Servidores Publicos do Brasil [*Confederation of Public Employees of Brazil*]   (LA)

CSPBI .... Comite Special du Programme Biologique International [*ICSU*]   (ASF)

CSPC .... Caisse de Stabilisation des Prix du Coton

CSPC .... Central Sydney Planning Committee [*Australia*]

CSPC .... Centrul Special de Perfectionare a Cadrelor [*Special Center for the Advanced Training of Personnel*]   (RO)

CSPC .... Children's Services Planning Committee [*Australia*]

CSPC .... Coal and Steel Planning Committee [*NATO*]   (NATG)

CSPD .... Ceskoslovenska Plavba Dunajska [*Czechoslovak Danube River Navigation Lines*]   (CZ)

CsPdS .... Ceskoslovenska Pedagogicka Spolecnost [*CSAV*]   (WGAO)

CSPE .... Comite Scientifique pour les Problemes de l' Environnement [*Scientific Committee on Problems of the Environment - SCOPE*] [*French*]   (ASF)

CSPEC .... Confederation of Socialist Parties of the European Community [*Belgium*] [*Political party*]   (EAIO)

CSPECVM ... Chambre Syndicale Patronale des Enseignants de la Conduite des Vehicules a Moteur   (WGAO)

CSPEFF .... Chambre Syndicale des Producteurs et Exportateurs de Films Francais   (WGAO)

CSPES .... Centro Studi per la Programmazione Economica e Sociale [*Italian*]   (SLS)

CSPFLC .... Confederation Nationale des Producteurs de Fruits Legumes et Champignons   (WGAO)

CSPG .... Consejo Superior Profesional de Geologia [*Argentina*]   (DSCA)

CSPH .... Cesky Svaz Pozemniho [*Czech Field Hockey Association*]   (CZ)

CSPI .... Conseil Superieur de la Propriete Industrielle [*France*]   (FLAF)

CSPiR .... Centrala Spoldzielni Przemyslowych i Rzemieslniczych [*Industrial and Handicraft Industry Cooperatives Center*]   (POL)

CSPL .... Ceskoslovenska Statni Plavba Labska [*Czechoslovak State Elbe River Navigation Lines*]   (CZ)

CSPL .... City of Sydney Public Library [*Australia*]   (ADA)

CSPL .... Compagnie Saharienne Portee Legere

CSPLE .... Compagnie Saharienne Portee de la Legion Etrangere

CSPLO ...... Ceskoslovenska Plavebni Spolecnost Labsko-Oderska [*Czechoslovak Elbe-Oder River Navigation Lines*]   (CZ)

CSPM .... Centro Studi e Produzione Missili [*Missile Research and Production Center*] [*Rome, Italy*] [*Research center*]   (ERC)

CSPM .... Centro Studi Problemi Medici [*Italian*]   (SLS)

CSPMS ...... Comitetul de Stat pentru Probleme de Munca si Salarii [*State Committee for Labor and Wage Problems*]   (RO)

CSPNP ...... Conseil Superieur de la Promotion Nationale et du Plan [*Higher Council for National Promotion and Planning*] [*Morocco*]   (AF)

CSPO .... Ceskoslovenska Statni Plavba Oderska [*Czechoslovakia State Oder River Navigation Lines*]   (CZ)

CSPO .... Ceskoslovensky Svaz Pozarni Ochrany [*Czechoslovak Fire Fighting Union*]   (CZ)

CSPOE ...... Comite de Solidarite avec les Opposants des Pays de l'Est [*Switzerland*]   (AF)

CSPP .... Centro di Studi sui Problemi Portuali   (WGAO)

CSPP .... Ceskoslovenska Polni Posta [*Czechoslovak Field Postal Service*]   (CZ)

CSPP .... Ceskoslovenske Paroplavebni Podniky [*Czechoslovak Steamship Lines*]   (CZ)

CSPP .... Ceskoslovenske Plynarenske Podniky [*Czechoslovak Gas Works*]   (CZ)

CSPPA .... Caisse de Stabilisation des Prix des Produits Agricoles

CSPPA....... Comite de Solidarite avec les Prisonniers Politiques Arabes et du Proche Orient [*Solidarity Committee for Arab and Near-Eastern Political Prisoners*]

CSPPA....... Committee for Solidarity with Arab and Middle Eastern Political Prisoners [*Lebanon*]

CSPPI....... Chambre Syndicale Parisienne des Proprietaires d'Immeubles (FLAF)

CSPPN ...... Caisse de Stabilisation des Prix des Produits du Niger [*Product Prices Stabilization Fund of Niger*]

CSPR .... Canberra Stereo Public Radio [*Australia*]

CSPT .... Compagnie Senegalaise des Phosphates de Taiba

CSPU........ Ceskoslovensky Plavebni Ustav [*Czechoslovak Institute for Navigation*] (CZ)

CSPU........ Communist Party of the Soviet Union (WGAO)

CSPV .... Convergencia Socialista del Pais Valencia [*Socialist Convergence of the Valencian Country*] [*Spanish*] (WER)

CSPVA ...... Committee on Student Placement in Voluntary Agencies (WGAO)

CS PZPR ... Centralna Szkola Polskiej Zjednoczonej Partii Robotniczej [*Central School of the Polish United Workers Party*] (POL)

csqn .... Conditio Sine Qua Non [*Benelux*] (BAS)

CSR........... Career Structure Review [*Australia*]

CSR........... Caucasus State Reserve [*Commonwealth of Independent States*]

CSR........... Centrala Spoldzielni Rolniczych [*Agricultural Cooperatives Center*] (POL)

CSR........... Centre for Society and Religion [*Sri Lanka*] (EAIO)

CSR........... Ceska Socialisticka Republika [*Czech Socialist Republic (since 1969)*] (CZ)

CSR........... Ceskoslovenska Republika [*Czechoslovak Republic (until 1960)*] (CZ)

CSR........... Circolo Speleologico Romano [*Italian*] (SLS)

CSR........... Cis-Air [*Czechoslovakia*] [*ICAO designator*] (FAAC)

CSR........... Client Services Review [*Australia*]

CSR........... Club Sportif de Redeyef [*Tunisia*]

CSR........... Colonial Sugar Refining Co. [*Australia*] (ADA)

CSR........... Combinatul Siderurgic Resita [*Resita Iron and Steel Combine*] (RO)

CSR........... Commonwealth Strategic Reserve [*Australia*]

CSR........... Conference Suisse de Securite dans le Trafic Routier (WGAO)

CSR........... Congress for the Second Republic

CSR........... Conseil Supreme de la Republique

CSR........... Conseil Supreme de la Revolution [*Supreme Revolutionary Council*] [*Malagasy*] (AF)

CSR........... Control Section Report [*NATO*]

CSR........... Council Situation Room [*NATO*] (NATG)

CSR........... Cyke- och Sporthandlarnas Riksforbund (WGAO)

CSR........... Czesko-Slowacka Republika [*Czechoslovak Republic*] (POL)

CSRA........ Comite Scientifique pour les Recherches Antarctiques [*Scientific Committee on Antarctic Research*] (MSC)

CSRA........ Committee of Secretaries of Research Associations (WGAO)

Csra............ Committee Of State Road Authorities (AA)

CSRA........ Copper Smelters and Refiners Association (WGAO)

CSRC........ China Securities Regulatory Commission (ECON)

CSRC........ CSR [*Colonial Sugar Refining*] Chemicals Ltd. [*Australia*]

CSRD........ Children's Services Resource and Development [*Australia*]

CSRG........ Commonwealth Specialists Research Group [*Australia*] (ADA)

CSRG........ Commonwealth Special Research Grant Scheme [*Australia*]

CSRIPPED ... China Society for International Professionals Exchange and Development (EAIO)

CSRO........ Comite Scientifique pour les Recherches Oceaniques [*Scientific Committee on Oceanic Research - SCOR*] [*France*] (MSC)

CSROH ..... Revolucniho Odboroveho Hnuti (WGAO)

CSRP .... Chambre Syndicale du Raffinage du Petrole (WGAO)

CSRS .... Centre Suisse de Recherches Scientifiques en Cote-D'Ivoire

CSRS .... Ceskoslovensky Rybarsky Svaz [*Czechoslovak Fishing Union*] (CZ)

CSRS .... Czecho-Slowacka Republika Socjalistyczna [*Czechoslovak Socialist Republic*] (POL)

CSRSA ...... Comite Secreto Revolucionario do Sul de Angola

CSRSOM .. Conseil Superieur des Recherches Sociologiques Outre-Mer (WGAO)

CSRSPT .... Conseil Superieur de la Recherche Scientifique et du Progres Technique [*France*] (FLAF)

CSRT .... Conseil Superieur de la Recherche et de la Technologie [*French*]

CSRV .... Comite de Soutien a la Republique de Vietnam [*Committee for Supporting the Republic of Vietnam*] [*French*] (WER)

CSS .... Cassilandia [*Brazil*] [*Airport symbol*] (OAG)

CSS .... Center for Soviet Studies [*Japan*] (IRC)

CSS .... Centrala Sprzetu Samochodowego [*Automobile Equipment Center*] (POL)

CSS .... Central Statistical Office [*Ethiopia*] (PDAA)

CSS .... Centre for Social Studies [*Bangladesh*] (WGAO)

CSS .... Centro Studi Storici di Mestre [*Italian*] (SLS)

CSS .... Ceskoslovenska Silnicni Sluzba [*Czechoslovak Road Service*] (CZ)

CSS .... Ceskoslovenska Strana Socialisticka [*Czechoslovak Socialist Party*] (PPE)

CSS .... Ceskoslovensky Svaz Studentstva [*Czechoslovak Student Union*] (CZ)

CSS .... Cesky Sermirsky Svaz [*Czech Fencing Association*] (CZ)

CSS .... Child Support Scheme [*Australia*]

CSS .... Chinese Sociological Society (SLS)

CSS .... Club Sportif Sfaxien [*Tunisia*]

CSS .... Commonwealth Scholarship Scheme [*Australia*]

CSS .... Commonwealth Security Service [*Australia*] (ADA)

CSS .... Commonwealth Superannuation Scheme [*Australia*]

CSS .... Compagnie Sucriere Senegalaise

CSS .... Congregatio a Sanctissimi Stigmatibus (WGAO)

CSS .... Conseil Superieur de Statistique [*Belgium*] (SLS)

CSS .... Consiglio Italiano per le Scienze Sociali [*Italian*] (SLS)

CSS .... Consiglio Superiore di Sanita [*Higher Health Council*] [*Italian*] (WER)

CSS .... Consiliul Superior al Sanatatii [*Higher Health Council*] (RO)

CSS .... Corse Aero Service [*France*] [*ICAO designator*] (FAAC)

CSS .... Council for Science and Society (WGAO)

CSS .... County Surveyors Society (WGAO)

CSS .... Zentralverband Schweizerischer Schneidermeister (WGAO)

CSSA .... Chambre Syndicale Suisse de l'Automobile et Branches Annexes (WGAO)

CSSA .... Computer Society of South Africa (AA)

CSSA .... Concrete Society of Southern Africa (AA)

CSSA .... Conseil Superieur du Sport en Afrique [*Supreme Council for Sport in Africa - SCSA*] [*Yaounde, Cameroon*] (EAIO)

CSSACT .... Cactus and Succulent Society of the Australian Capital Territory

CSSB .... Ceskoslovenska Spolecnost Biochemicka [*CSAV*] (WGAO)

CSSBS....... Czechoslovak Association of Liberty and Anti-Fascist Fighters (EAIO)

CSSC .... China State Shipbuilding Corp. (IMH)

CSSC .... Civil Service Sports Council (WGAO)

CSSCD ...... Chinese Students Solidarity Campaign for Democracy [*Australia*]

CSSCH ...... Ceskoslovenska Spolecnost Chemicka [*Former Czechoslovakia*] (EAIO)

CSSCO ...... Cunard Steamship Co. (MHDB)

CSSCT....... Cuban Society of Sugar Cane Technologists [*Asociacion de Tecnicos Azucareros de Cuba*]

CSSD........ Ceskoslovenska Socialnedemokraticka Strana Delnicka [*Czechoslovak Social Democratic Workers' Party*] (PPE)

CSSDCA ... Conference on Security, Stability, Development, and Cooperation in Africa

Csse........... Caisse [*Cash*] [*French*]

CSSE .... Ceskoslovenska Spolecnost Entomologiska [*CSAV*] (WGAO)

CSSE .... Compagnie Senegalaise du Sud-Est

CSSF.......... Ceskoslovenske Statni Filmy [*Czechoslovak State Film Studios*] (CZ)

CSSF.......... Chambre Syndicale de la Serigraphic Francaise (WGAO)

CSSF.......... Chambre Syndicale de la Siderurgie Francaise (WGAO)

CSSF.......... Confederation des Societes Scientifiques Francaises [*French*] (SLS)

CSSGB ...... Congregazione Suore di San Giovanni Baptiste [*Italy*] (EAIO)

CSSiS........ Centrala Sprzetu Sportowego i Szkutniczego [*Sport and Boating Equipment Center*] (POL)

CSSL.......... Ceskoslovenske Statni Lesy [*Czechoslovak State Forests*] (CZ)

CSSLD....... Ceskoslovenska Smiesana Letecka Divizia [*Czechoslovak Combined Air Division*] [*World War II*] (CZ)

CSSL'L...... Ceskoslovensky Svaz L'udoveho Letectva [*Czechoslovak Civil Aviation League*] (CZ)

CSSLRP .... Commonwealth Secondary School Libraries Research Project [*Australia*] (ADA)

CSSM .... Ceskoslovenske Statne Majetky [*Czechoslovak State Farms*] (CZ)

CSSM .... Christian Students Social Movement [*Nigeria*]

CSSM .... Cooperative Study of the Southern Mediterranean (MSC)

CSSMMP ... Congregation des Soeurs de Sainte Marie-Madeleine Postel [*France*] (EAIO)

CSSMotozbyt ... Centrala Sprzetu Samochodowego "Motozbyt" [*"Motozbyt" (Motor Sales) Automotive Equipment Center*] (POL)

CSSMW .... Centrum Szkolenia Specjalistow Marynarki Wojennej [*Navy Specialists Training Center*] (POL)

CSSNSW.... Combined Scottish Society of New South Wales [*Australia*]

CSSO......... Cursos Secundarios de Superacion Obrera [*Workers Secondary Improvement Courses*] [*Cuba*] (LA)

CSSp.......... Congregation of the Holy Spirit [*Italy*] (EAIO)

CSSp.......... Congregatio Sacrissimi Spiritis (WGAO)

CSSP.......... Consejo Superior de Salud Publica [*Managua, Nicaragua*] (LAA)

CS-SPB...... Ceskoslovensky Svaz Bojovniku za Svobodu a Proti Fasismu [*Former Czechoslovakia*] (EAIO)

CSSPPA .... Caisse de Stabilisation et de Soutien des Prix des Productions Agricoles [*Agricultural Produce Prices Stabilization and Support Fund*] [*Ivory Coast*]

CSSPS .... Comite Suisse de Soutien au Peuple Sahraoui [*Swiss Support Committee for the Sahrawi People*] (EAIO)

CSSPT....... Ceskoslovensky Statni Soubor Pisni a Tancu [*Czechoslovak State Song and Dance Ensemble*] (CZ)

CSSPVZ.... Ceskoslovenska Spolecnost pro Sireni Politickych a Vedeckych Znalosti [*Czechoslovak Society for the Dissemination of Political and Scientific Knowledge*]   (CZ)

CSSR .... Centro Studi Sociologia Religiosa   (WGAO)

CSSR .... Ceskoslovenska Socialisticka Republika [*Czechoslovak Socialist Republic*]   (CZ)

CSSR .... Ceskoslovensky Svaz Rugby [*Czechoslovak Rugby Association*] (CZ)

CSSR .... Congregatio Sanctissimi Redemptoris   (WGAO)

CSSR .... Czechoslovak Socialist Republic

CSSR .... Tschechoslowakische Sozialistische Republik [*Czechoslovak Socialist Republic*]   (EG)

CSSRI........ Central Soil Salinity Research Institute [*India*]   (ARC)

CSSRO...... Chambre Syndicale des Soies et Rayonnes Ouvrees   (WGAO)

CSSS......... Cekoslovenska Spektroskopicka Spolecnost [*CSAV*]   (WGAO)

CSSS.......... Ceskoslovenska Spektroskopicka Spolecnost pri CSAV [*Former Czechoslovakia*]   (SLS)

CSSS.......... Ceskoslovenske Statni Statky [*Czechoslovak State Farms*]   (CZ)

CSSS.......... Commonwealth Secondary Scholarship Scheme [*Australia*]

CSSSA....... Crop Science Society of South Australia

CSSSpolem ... Centrala Spoldzielni Spozywcow "Spolem" [*"Spolem" Consumers' Cooperatives Center*]   (POL)

CSST .... Cesky Svaz Stolniho Tenisu [*Czech Ping-Pong Association*] (CZ)

CSSUWA .. Children's Services Support Unit of Western Australia

CSSV .... Ceskoslovensky Svaz Vcelaru [*Czechoslovak Beekeepers Union*] (CZ)

CSSZ .... Ceskoslovenska Spolecnost Zemepisna [*Czechoslovak Geographical Society*]   (CZ)

CSSZ .... Ceskoslovenske Stavebni Zavody [*Czechoslovak Construction Plants*]   (CZ)

CSSZ .... Ceskoslovensky Svaz Zen [*Czechoslovak Union of Women*] (CZ)

cs sz .... Csekk-Szamla [*Bank Account, Checking Account*] [*Hungarian*] (HU)

CSSZK....... Csehszlovak Szocialista Koztarsasag [*Czechoslovak Socialist Republic*]   (HU)

CST .... Castaway [*Fiji*] [*Airport symbol*]   (OAG)

CST .... Centrala Spoldzielni Transportu [*Transportation Cooperatives Center*]   (POL)

CST .... Central Sandinista de Trabajadores [*Sandinist Workers Federation*] [*Nicaragua*]   (LA)

CST .... Centro Studi Talassografici [*Italian*]   (MSC)

CST .... Classification Statistique et Tarifaire [*France*]   (FLAF)

CST .... Clerical Selection Test [*Australia*]

CST .... Coast Air KS [*Norway*] [*ICAO designator*]   (FAAC)

CST .... Comite Superieur du Tarif [*France*]   (FLAF)

CST .... Confederation Senegalaise du Travail [*Senegalese Labor Confederation*]   (AF)

CST .... Confederation Syndicale du Tchad [*Trade union*] [*Chad*]

CST .... Consortium on Soils of the Tropics

CST .... Conventional Stability Talks [*Arms control*]

CST .... Cooperation Scientifique et Technique

CST .... Coordinatora de Solidaridad de los Trabajadores [*El Salvador*] (EY)

CST .... Council for Science and Technology [*Japan*]

CST .... Country Support Team [*United Nations*]

CSTA .... Cesky Svaz Tezke Atletiky [*Czech Athletic Association*]   (CZ)

CSTA .... Chambre Syndicale du Transport Aerien [*France*]   (EY)

CSTA .... Chinese Schoolteachers' Association   (ML)

CSTA .... Commandant Superieur des Troupes en Algerie

CSTA .... Consejo Sindical de Trabajadores Andinos [*Trade Union Council of Andean Workers*]   (LA)

CSTAL ...... Confederacion Sindical de los Trabajadores de America Latina [*Trade Union Confederation of Latin American Workers*] (LA)

CSTAM..... Chinese Society of Theoretical and Applied Mechanics   (EAIO)

CSTAVMS ... China Scientific & Technical Audio-Visual Materials Service

CSTB .... Centre Scientifique et Technique du Batiment [*Technical and Scientific Building Center*] [*French*]

CSTC......... Centre Scientifique et Technique de la Construction [*Scientific and Technical Building Center*] [*Belgium*]   (WED)

CSTC......... Compagnie Senegalaise de Transports en Commun

CSTC......... Confederacion Sindical de Trabajadores de Colombia [*Colombian Workers Trade Union Confederation*]   (LA)

CSTC......... Consejo Sindical de Trabajadores del Caribe [*Trade Union Council of Caribbean Workers*]

CSTCB ...... Confederacion Sindical de Trabajadores de Construccion de Bolivia [*Bolivian Construction Workers Union*]   (LA)

CSTCS....... Centre Scientifique et Technique du Cami Salie [*Cami Salie Science and Technology Center*] [*France*]   (EAS)

CSTD......... Committee on Science and Technology for Development [*United Nations (already exists in GUS II database)*]

CSTD......... Commonwealth Society of Teachers of Dancing [*Australia*]

CSTE .... Centro di Studio per la Termodinamica ed Elettrochimica dei Sistemi Salini Fusi e Solidi [*Research Center for Thermodynamics and Electrochemistry of Molten and Solid Salts*] [*Italy*]   (IRC)

CSTEI........ Centre for Scientific, Technical, and Economic Information [*Bulgarian*]   (ARC)

CSTFTAB ... Confederacion Sindical de Trabajadores Ferroviarios Ramas Anexas y Transportes Aereos de Bolivia   (WGAO)

CSTI .... Centre for Scientific and Technological Information [*Council for Scientific and Industrial Research*] [*Pretoria, South Africa*]

CSTI .... Council of Science and Technology Institutes   (WGAO)

CSTI .... Csepeli Tervezo Intezet [*Csepel Planning Institute*]   (HU)

CsTI .... Csomagolastechnikai Intezet [*Institute of Packaging Technology*] (HU)

CSTID .... Centre of Scientific and Technical Information and Documentation [*Madagascar*]   (EAIO)

CSTIM ...... Calcutta School of Tropical Medicine [*India*]   (WGAO)

CSTIV .... Chambre Syndicale Nationale de la Transformation Industrielle du Verre Plat   (WGAO)

CSTK .... Ceskoslovenska Tiskova Kancelar [*News agency*] [*Former Czechoslovakia*]   (EY)

CSTL .... Central Seed Testing Laboratory [*Indian Agricultural Research Institute*]   (IRC)

CSTM........ Centro Studi Terzo Mondo [*Study Center for the Third World*] [*Italy*]   (EAIO)

CSTM........ Centro Studi Trasporti Missilistici [*Italian*]   (SLS)

CSTM........ Compagnie Senegalaise pour la Transformation des Metaux

CSTN......... Centre des Sciences et de la Technologie Nucleaire [*Algeria*]

CSTP .... Ceskoslovensky Tabakovy Prumysl [*Czechoslovak Tobacco Industry*]   (CZ)

CSTP .... Commite Scientifique et Technique de la Peche [*CEE*]   (WGAO)

CSTP .... Committee for Scientific and Technological Policy [*Organization for Economic Cooperation and Development*]   (ERC)

CSTR .... Ceskoslovenska Tabakova Rezie [*Czechoslovak Tobacco Monopoly*]   (CZ)

CSTR .... Commission Scientifique, Technique, et de la Recherche (de l'OUA) [*Scientific, Technical, and Research Commission (of the OAU)*] [*Use STRC*]   (AF)

CSTS .... Centro Studi Telecommunicazioni Spaziali [*Space Telecommunications Research Center*] [*Research center*] [*Italian*]   (IRC)

CSTS .... Ceskoslovensky Telovychovny Svaz [*Czechoslovak Physical Education Association*]   (CZ)

CSTT .... Chinese School of Table Tennis [*France*]   (EAIO)

CSTT .... Comite Superieur des Transports Terrestres du Conseil de l'Entente [*Niger*]   (WGAO)

CSTT .... Confederation Syndicale des Travailleurs Togolais [*Trade Union Confederation of Togolese Workers*]   (AF)

CSTTA ...... Ceskoslovenska Table-Tennisova Asociace [*Czechoslovak Ping-Pong Association*]   (CZ)

CSTV .... Ceskoslovensky Svaz Telesne Vychovy [*Czechoslovak Union of Physical Training*]   (CZ)

CSTV .... Confederation des Syndicats des Travailleurs du Viet-Nam [*Confederation of Workers' Trade Unions of Viet-Nam*] [*South Vietnamese*]

CSTWU..... Civil Service Technical Workers' Union [*Nigeria*]

CSTWUN ... Civil Service Technical Workers' Union of Nigeria

CSU .... Cesky Statisticky Urad [*Czech Statistical Office*]   (CZ)

CSU .... Charles Sturt University [*Australia*]

CSU .... Chinese Seamen's Union [*Hong Kong*]

CSU .... Christian Social Union [*Germany*]

CSU .... Christian Students' Union of South Africa

CSU .... Christlich-Soziale Union [*Christian Social Union*] [*Bavarian Affiliate of the CDU*]   (WEN)

CSU .... Civil Service Union [*Later, NUCPS*]   (WGAO)

CSU .... Confederacion Sindical del Uruguay [*Confederation of Uruguayan Trade Unions*]   (LA)

CSU .... Confederation des Syndicats Unities de Belgique   (WGAO)

CSU .... Consejo Superior Universitario [*University Higher Council*] [*El Salvador*]   (LA)

CSU .... Consejo Superior Universitario [*University Higher Council*] [*Guatemala*]   (LA)

CSUA .... Ceskoslovenske Ustavy Astronomicke [*Astronomical Institutes of Czechoslovakia*]   (CZ)

CSUC......... Ceskoslovenske Ustredi Cyklistu [*Czechoslovak Central Organization of Cyclists*]   (CZ)

CSUCA...... Confederacion Universitaria Centroamericana [*Confederation of Central American Universities*]   (EAIO)

CSUCA...... Consejo Superior Universitario   (WGAO)

CSU-MAW ... Charles Sturt University - Murray, at Albury Wodonga [*Australia*]

CSU-MB ... Charles Sturt University - Mitchell at Bathurst [*Australia*]

CSUP........ Ceskoslovensky Urad Pamatkovy [*Czechoslovak Office for the Preservation of Historical Monuments*]   (CZ)

CSUP........ Ceskoslovensky Ustav Prace [*Czechoslovak Labor Institute*] (CZ)

C SupArbitr ... Cour Superieure d'Arbitrage [*France*]   (FLAF)

CSU-R .... Charles Sturt University - Riverina [*Australia*]
CSUR......... Conseil Superieur des Universites Royales [*Higher Royal University Council*] [*Cambodia*] (CL)
CSUT........ Confederacion de Sindicatos Unitarios de Trabajadores [*Confederation of Unitary Trade Unions of Workers*] [*Madrid, Spain*] (WER)
csut............ Csutortok [*Thursday*] (HU)
CSUTCB ... Confederacion Sindical Unica de los Trabajadores Campesinos de Bolivia [*Trade union*] (EY)
CSUTHD .. Ceskoslovensky Ustav pro Technickou a Hospodarskou Dokumentaci [*Czechoslovak Institute for Technical and Economic Documentation*] (CZ)
CSUZ........ Civil Service Union of Zambia
CSV........... Calligraphy Society of Victoria [*Australia*]
CSV........... Cambrian Society of Victoria [*Australia*]
CSV........... Centraal Stikstof Verkoopkantoor (WGAO)
CSV........... Central Stikstof Verkoopkantoor [*Central Nitrogen Sales Organization Ltd.*] [*Netherlands*] (DSCA)
CSV........... Chreschtlech-Sozial Vollekspartei [*Christian Social Party*] [*Luxembourg*] [*Political party*] (PPW)
CSV........... Christelike Strewersvereniging [*Afrikaans*]
CSV........... Christen-Studentevereniging [*Afrikaans*]
CSV........... Community Services Victoria [*Australia*]
CSV........... Community Service Volunteers (WGAO)
CSV........... Confederation Syndicale Voltaique [*Voltan Trade Union Confederation*] (AF)
CSV........... Congregatio Clericorum Parochialium seu Catechistarum Sancti Viatoris (WGAO)
CSV........... Coordinatiewet Sociale Verzekering [*Benelux*] (BAS)
CSVA........ Ceskoslovenska Stredisko Vystavoy e Architektury (WGAO)
CSVA........ Csepeli Vas- es Acelontodek [*Iron and Steel Foundries of Csepel*] (HU)
CSVD........ Cesky Svaz Vyrobnich Druzstev [*Czech Union of Production Cooperatives*] (CZ)
CSVF .... Csepeli Vas- es Femmuvek [*Iron and Steel Works of Csepel*] (HU)
CSVK........ Ceskoslovenska Spolecnost pro Vedeckou Kinematografi (WGAO)
CSVNSNSW ... Christian Science Visiting Nurse Service New South Wales [*Australia*]
CSVOD ..... Ceskoslovensky Vybor na Ochranu Deti [*Czechoslovak Committee for the Protection of Children*] (CZ)
CSVOM..... Ceskoslovensky Vybor Obrancu Miru [*Czechoslovak Committee of the Defenders of Peace*] (CZ)
CSVPA ...... Comitetul de Stat pentru Valorificarea Produselor Agricole [*State Committee for the Exploitation of Agricultural Products*] (RO)
CSVS .... Ceskoslovensky Volleyballovy Svaz [*Czechoslovak Volleyball Association*] (CZ)
CSVTS....... Ceskoslovenska Vedecka Technicka Spolecnost [*Czechoslovak Scientific and Technological Society*] (CZ)
CSVV .... Ceskoslovensky Vsesportovni Vybor [*Czechoslovak Athletic Committee*] (CZ)
CSW .... Canberra Spinners and Weavers [*Australia*]
CSW .... Christlicher Studenten-Weltbund (WGAO)
CSW .... Commission on the Status of Women [*Economic and Social Council of the UN*] [*Vienna, Austria*] (EAIO)
CSWAD..... Centre for the Study of Wars, Armaments, and Development [*Germany*] (EAIO)
CSWB........ Central Social Welfare Board [*India*]
CSWiK...... Centrala Spoldzielni Wydawniczych i Ksiegarskich [*Central Office of Publishing and Bookselling Cooperatives*] (POL)
CSWMNS ... Council of Social Welfare Ministers, National Secretariat [*Australia*]
CSWPRC... Chinese Society on Water Pollution Research and Control (EAIO)
CSWRI ...... Central Sheep and Wool Research Institute [*India*] (ARC)
CSWSolidarnosc ... Centrala Spoldzielni Wytworczych "Solidarnosc" [*Central Office of the "Solidarnosc" (Solidarity) Production Cooperatives*] (POL)
CSWU .... Christlich-Soziale Waehler Union im Saarland [*Christian Social Voters' Union in Saarland*] [*Germany*] [*Political party*] (PPW)
CSWV........ Centraal Sociaal Werkgeversverbond [*Central Social Employers' Association*] [*Defunct*] [*Netherlands*] (WEN)
CSX........... Changsha [*China*] [*Airport symbol*] (OAG)
CSX........... Coastair [*Denmark*] [*ICAO designator*] (FAAC)
CSX........... CSIRO [*Commonwealth Scientific and Industrial Research Organisation*] Index [*Information service or system*] (ADA)
CSZ............ Ceskoslovensky Svaz Zen [*Czechoslovak Union of Women*] (CZ)
CSZ............ Cuban Society of Zoology (EAIO)
CSZP .... Ceskoslovenske Zavody Papirenske [*Czechoslovak Paper Mills*] (CZ)
CSZPS....... Ceskoslovenske Zavody Presneho Strojirenstvi [*Czechoslovak Precision Machinery Factories*] (CZ)

CSZS .... Ceskoslovenska Zemepisna Spolecnost [*Czechoslovak Geographical Society*] (CZ)
CT .... Cabine Telephonique [*Telephone Booth*] [*French*]
CT .... Canton [*Canton, District, Section*] [*Military map abbreviation World War I*] [*French*] (MTD)
CT .... Canton and Enderbury Islands [*ANSI two-letter standard code*] (CNC)
CT .... Carbonique de Tanger
CT .... Catania [*Car registration plates*] [*Italy*]
CT .... Celjska Tiskarna [*Celje Printing House*] (YU)
ct................. Centilitre [*Centiliter*] [*French*]
CT .... Centrala Tekstylna [*Textile Center*] (POL)
CT .... Central Tablelands [*Australia*]
CT .... Ceskoslovenska Televise [*Czechoslovak Television*] (CZ)
CT .... Chung-Tung Machine Engineering Co. Ltd. [*Taiwan*]
CT .... Comissao de Trabalhadores [*Workers Committee*] [*Portuguese*] (WER)
CT .... Commercial Tribunal [*South Australia*]
CT .... Communist Terrorist
CT .... Community Transit [*System*] [*Shipping EEC*] (DS)
CT .... Comunion Tradicionalista [*Traditionalist Communion*] [*Spanish*] (WER)
CT .... Congreso del Trabajo [*Labor Congress*] [*Mexico*] (LA)
CT .... Congresul Taranimii [*Congress of the Peasantry*] (RO)
CT .... Conseil de Tutelle [*ONU*] (WGAO)
CT .... Consult Tel [*Jordan*] [*Commercial firm*]
CT .... Countertrade [*Economics*] (IMH)
CT .... Courant [*Of the Current Month*] [*French*]
Ct................. Court (PWGL)
CT .... Credit du Togo [*Credit Bank of Togo*] (AF)
CT .... Credit Tribunal [*Victoria*] [*Australia*]
CT .... Cum Tempore [*15 Minutes After the Time Announced*] [*University*] [*German*]
CTA .... Cable Television Association (WGAO)
Cta.............. Caleta [*Cove*] [*Cal*] [*See also*] [*Spanish*] (NAU)
CTA.............. Call to Australia [*Political party*]
CTA .... Caribbean Tourism Association (WGAO)
CTA .... Catania [*Italy*] [*Airport symbol*] (OAG)
CTA .... Catering Teachers Association (WGAO)
CTA .... Centrala de Transporturi Auto [*Automotive Transportation Central*] (RO)
CTA .... Centrala Teatrow Amatorskich [*Central Office of Amateur Theatres*] (POL)
CTA .... Central de Trabajadores del Estado Aragua [*Federation of Workers of Aragua State*] [*Venezuela*] (LA)
CTA .... Centre Technique de Cooperation Agricole et Rural [*Technical Centre for Agricultural and Rural Cooperation*] (EAIO)
CTA .... Centro de Trabalhadores do Acre [*Brazil*] (WGAO)
CTA .... Centro Tecnico Aereospacial [*Brazil*] (WGAO)
CTA .... Centro Tecnologico da Aeronautica [*Aerospace Technology Center*] [*Brazil*] (LA)
CTA .... Ceylon Tamil Association [*Victoria*] [*Australia*]
CTA .... Channel Tunnel Association (WGAO)
CTA .... Cinema Theatre Association (WGAO)
CTA .... Collegio dei Tecnici dell'Acciaio [*Italian*] (SLS)
Cta.............. Comandita [*Conditional Partnership*] [*Portuguese*] [*Business term*]
CTA .... Commercial Trailer Association (WGAO)
CTA .... Commercial Travellers' Association (WGAO)
CTA .... Commission Technique des Achats [*Technical Purchasing Committee*] [*Cambodia*] (CL)
CTA .... Communiquer a Toutes Adresses [*To Be Circulated to All Addresses*] [*Telecommunications*] [*French*]
CTA .... Compagnie de Transport Aerien [*Switzerland*] [*ICAO designator*] (FAAC)
CTA .... Compagnie de Transports Aeriens [*Airline*] [*Switzerland*]
CTA .... Computer Traders Association (WGAO)
CTA .... Consorcio Tecnico de Aeronautica
Cta.............. Constanta [*Constanta*] (RO)
CTA .... Conurbation Transport Authority (WGAO)
CTA .... Corporate Tax Association [*Australia*]
cta.............. Cuenta [*Count*] [*Spanish*]
CTAA .... Centro Nacional de Pesquisa de Tecnologia Agroindustrial de Alimentos [*National Research Center for Agroindustrial Food Technology*] [*Brazil*] (IRC)
CTAA .... Children's Theatre Association of America (WGAO)
CTAA .... Corporate Tax Association of Australia
CTAB........ Chemisch Technisch Adviesbureau [*Chemical Technology Advisory Bureau*] [*Affiliated with Union Internationale des Laboratoires Independants*] [*Netherlands*]
CTAC........ Comite des Transporteurs Aeriens Complementaires (WGAO)
CTAC........ International Conference on Computational Techniques and Applications [*Australia*]
Cta Crrte .... Cuenta Corriente [*Current Account*] [*Spanish*] [*Business term*]
cta cte .... Cuenta Corriente [*Current Account*] [*Spanish*] [*Business term*]

CTA-DLP ... Call to Australia - Democratic Labor Party Coalition [*Political party*]
CTAF........ Comite des Transporteurs Aeriens Francais (WGAO)
CTAG .... Coalition of Tollway Action Groups [*Australia*]
CTAG .... Cultural Tourism Advisory Group [*Australia*]
CTAL........ Confederacion de Trabajadores de America Latina [*Confederation of Latin American Workers*] (LA)
CTAL........ Container Terminals Australia Limited
Ctal .... Cortal [*Shepherd's Hut*] [*Military map abbreviation World War I*] [*French*] (MTD)
CTAMA .... Caisse Tunisienne d'Assurances Mutuelles Agricoles [*Tunisian Agricultural Insurance Fund*] (AF)
CTAMBJO ... Syndicat National des Cadres Techniciens et Agents de Maitrise de la BijoutgerieJoaillerie Orfevrerie et des Activities qui s'y Rattachent (WGAO)
CT & W...... Commercial Travellers' and Warehousemen's Association [*Australia*]
CTAO .... Charters Towers Australia Modified Seismic Research Observatory (IRC)
CTAPI .... China Technical Association of the Paper Industry (EAIO)
CTAQ .... Commercial Travellers' Association of Queensland [*Australia*]
CTAS........ Centre Technique des Applications de Soudago [*SAF*] (WGAO)
CTASA...... Christian Television Association of South Australia
CTAT........ Centre Technique d'Agriculture Tropicale
CTAVI........ Centre Technique Audio Visuel International (WGAO)
CTAWA...... Commercial Travellers' Association of Western Australia
CTAWU .... Commercial, Technical, and Allied Workers' Union [*St. Vincent and the Grenadines*]
CTB............ Canberra Tourist Bureau [*Australia*]
CTB............ Central de Trabajadores Bolivianos [*Federation of Bolivian Workers*] (LA)
CTB........... Centre Technique du Bois [*Wood Technical Center*] [*French*] (ARC)
CTB........... Centrum voor Toegepaste Biologie [*Center of Applied Biology*] [*Belgium*] (ARC)
CTB........... Ceylon Tourist Board (EAIO)
CTB........... Commonwealth Telecommunications Board [*Later, CTO*] [*British*]
CTB........... Commonwealth Telecommunications Board [*Australia*] (ADA)
CTB........... Commonwealth Trading Bank [*Australia*] (ADA)
CTB........... Companhia Telefonica Brasileira [*A telecommunications company*] [*Brazil*]
Ctb .... Cottbus [*Cottbus*] [*One of the eight reichsbahn directorates*] (EG)
CTBA........ Centre Technique du Bois et de l'Ameublement [*Wood and Furniture Technical Center*] [*Research center*] [*France*] (IRC)
CTBA........ Chinese-Taipei Badminton Association [*Taiwan*] (EAIO)
CTBA........ Commonwealth Trading Bank of Australia
CTBA........ Complexe de Transports Bel Abbesiens
CTBLV ...... Christlicher Textil- Bekleidungs- und Leaderarbeiter-Verband (WGAO)
CTB of A.... Commonwealth Trading Bank of Australia
CTBR........ Committee to Defend Black Rights [*Australia*]
CTBR........ Commonwealth Taxation Board of Review [*Australia*]
CTC .... Canberra Technical College [*Australia*] (ADA)
CTC .... Catamarca [*Argentina*] [*Airport symbol*] (OAG)
CTC .... Catholic Teachers' College [*Australia*] (ADA)
CTC .... Center on Transnational Corporations [*United Nations*]
CTC .... Central de Trabajadores Clasistas [*Class Workers' Center*] [*Dominican Republic*]
CTC .... Central de Trabajadores Costarricenses [*Costa Rican Workers' Union*]
CTC .... Central de Trabajadores de Cuba [*Central Organization of Cuban Trade Unions*] (LA)
CTC .... Centrale Technische Catalogus [*Netherlands*]
CTC .... Central Trading Committee [*Ministry of Finance and Petroleum*] [*Qatar*] (IMH)
CTC .... Central Training Council [*DOE*] (WGAO)
CTC .... Central Trust of China
CTC .... Centre on Transnational Corporations [*United Nations*] (WGAO)
CTC .... Centre Technique de Conserves des Produits Agricoles (WGAO)
CTC .... Centre Technique du Cuir [*France*]
CTC .... Centro de Teatro Colombiano [*Colombia*] (COL)
CTC .... Centro Technologico do Calcado (WGAO)
CTC .... Cia de Telefonos de Chile (EY)
CTC .... City Tattersall's Club [*Australia*]
CTC .... Comando Territorial Central [*Central Territorial Command*] [*Mozambique*] (AF)
CTC .... Commercial Tariff Concession System [*Australia*]
CTC .... Commission on Transnational Corporations [*United Nations*]
CTC .... Compagnie de Transactions Commerciales
CTC .... Compagnie de Transport et de Commerce
CTC .... Compagnie Tchadienne de Construction
CTC .... Compania de Telefonos de Chile (WGAO)

CTC .... Compania de Telefonos de Chile SA [*Santiago*] [*Telecommunications service*]
CTC .... Comptoir Togolais du Commerce
CTC .... Computer Telecommunications Corp. [*Australia*]
CTC .... Confederacion de Trabajadores Constarricenses (WGAO)
CTC .... Confederacion de Trabajadores de Colombia [*Colombian Confederation of Workers*] (LA)
CTC .... Confederacion de Trabajadores de Cuba (WGAO)
CTC .... Confederacion de Trabajadores del Cobre [*Copper Workers Confederation*] [*Chile*] (LA)
CTC .... Container Terminal Company
CTC .... Controle Technique de la Construction [*Algeria*]
CTC .... Control Tehnic de Calitate [*Technical Quality Control*] (RO)
CTC .... Cumann Trachtala Chorcai [*Cork Chamber of Commerce*] [*Founded in 1820 Republic of Ireland*]
CTCA........ Confederacion de Trabajadores de Centroamerica [*Confederation of Central American Workers*] (LA)
CTCA........ Cooperative des Tailleurs et Couturieres d'Abidjan
CTCASS.... Commission for Technical Co-Operation in Africa South of the Sahara
CTCB........ Centre Technique du Cuir Brut (WGAO)
CTCB........ Compagnie de Transit et de Consignation du Benin (EY)
CTCB........ Confederacion de Trabajadores de Comercio de Bolivia (WGAO)
CTCC........ Central Transport Consultative Committee (WGAO)
CTCD .... Centre Technique pour le Controle de la Descendance (WGAO)
CTCE........ Centru Teritorial de Calcul Electronic [*Territorial Center for Electronic Data Processing*] (RO)
CTCE........ Comite de Thermodynamique et de Cinetique Electrochique [*Belgium*] (WGAO)
CTCEE ...... Comisao Tecnica de Cooperacao Economica External (WGAO)
CTCEE ...... Comissao Tecnica de Cooperacao Economica Externa [*Portugal*] (DSCA)
CTCG .... Centrale des Travaileurs Chretiens de La Guyane [*French Guiana*] (WGAO)
CTCh .... Confederacion de Trabajadores de Chile [*Chilean Workers Confederation*] (LA)
CTCI.......... Classification Type pour le Commerce International [*Standard International Trade Classification*] [*French*]
CTCI.......... Confederacion de Trabajadores Colombianos Independientes [*Independent Colombian Workers Confederation*] (LA)
CTCIA .... Compagnie Togolaise de Commerce, d'Industrie, et d'Agriculture
CTCL........ Community and Technical College Libraries [*Australia*]
CTCNC...... Christian Temperance Council for the Nordic Countries (EA)
CTCPA ...... Centre Technique des Conserves de Produits Agricoles [*Canned Agricultural Products Technical Center*] [*French*] (ARC)
CTCR........ Confederacion de Trabajadores Cubanos Revolucionarios [*Cuba*] (LAA)
CTCR........ Confederacion de Trabajadores de Costa Rica [*Confederation of Workers of Costa Rica*]
CTCRI .... Central Tuber Crops Research Institute [*India*] (DSCA)
CTCS......... Catholic Teachers' College, Sydney [*Australia*]
CTCS........ Centre Technique de la Canne et du Sucre [*Technical Center for Cane and Sugar*] [*French Guiana*] (LA)
CTCS......... Comisia Tehnica de Colaboratie Stiintifica [*Technical Commission for Scientific Collaboration*] (RO)
CTCS......... Consejo de Trabajadores del Cono Sur [*WCL*]
CTCSG...... Centre Technique de la Canne et du Sucre de la Guadeloupe [*Guadalupe*] (DSCA)
CTCSM..... Centre Technique de la Canne du Sucre de la Martinique (WGAO)
CTCTSC.... China Trade Consultation and Technical Service Corporation [*Ministry of Foreign Economic Relations and Trade*] [*China*] (IMH)
CTD .... Catalogue des Theses de Doctorat [*A bibliographic publication*] [*France*]
CTD .... Central de Trabajadores Democraticos [*Democratic Workers Center/Confederation*] [*El Salvador*]
CTD .... Centre for Telecommunications Development [*ITU*] [*United Nations*] (DUND)
CTD .... Centre Technique de Developpement de Senegal (WGAO)
CTD .... Certificate for Teachers of the Deaf [*Australia*]
CTD .... Comhluchd Tuathanach Duthchail [*National Farmers' Union*] [*Scottish*]
CTD .... Commission Technique Documentation [*UIC*] (WGAO)
CTD .... Confederacion de Trabajadores Dominicanos [*Confederation of Dominican Workers*] (EY)
CTD .... Cultuurtechnische Dienst [*Benelux*] (BAS)
CTD .... Technical Documentation Centre [*Engineering Laboratory of Mozambique*] [*Ministry of Public Works and Housing*]
CTDC .... Confederacion de Trabajadores Democraticos de Colombia [*Democratic Workers Confederation of Colombia*] (EY)
CTDC .... Copper Technical Data Centre [*Australia*]
CTDEC...... Centre Technique de l'Industrie du Decolletage [*Bar-Turning Industry Technical Center*] [*Research center*] [*French*] (ERC)
CTE........... Air Tenglong [*China*] [*ICAO designator*] (FAAC)

CTE............ Canton and Enderbury Islands [*ANSI three-letter standard code*] (CNC)

CTE............ Carti [*Panama*] [*Airport symbol*] (OAG)

CTE............ Centrala Termoelectrica [*Thermoelectric Power Plant*] (RO)

CTE............ Central de Trabajadores del Ecuador [*Ecuadorean Workers Center*]

CTE............ Certificati del Tesoro in Euroscudi [*Italy*] (ECON)

CTE............ Commission Technique des Ententes [*Benelux*] (BAS)

CTE............ Compagnie de Traitement des Eaux [*Water Treatment Company*] (CL)

CTE............ Compte [*Account*] [*French*] [*Business term*] (ROG)

Cte............ Comte [*Count*] [*French*]

CTE............ Confederacion de Trabajadores Ecuatorianos [*Confederation of Ecuadorean Workers*] (LA)

CTE............ Confederacion de Trabajordores del Ecuador (WGAO)

CTE............ Conselho Tecnico de Economia [*Brazil*] (DSCA)

CTE............ Conselleria de Turisme i Esports [*Andorra*] (EAIO)

Cte............ Corriente [*Current*] [*Spanish*] [*Business term*]

CTEB........ Council of Technical Examining Bodies (WGAO)

CTEC........ City Training and Education Centre [*Sydney, Australia*]

CTEC........ Commonwealth Tertiary Education Commission [*Australia*]

CTECC...... China Textile Engineering Consulting Corp.

CTEE........ Chamber of Turkish Electrical Engineers (EAIO)

CTEEV...... Compagnie Tchadienne d'Elevage et d'Exportation de Viande

CTEF........ Conselho Tecnico de Economia e Financas [*Brazil*] (DSCA)

CTEI........ Centro Tropical de Ensenanza e Investigacion [*Costa Rica*] (DSCA)

CTEP........ Societe Cooperative de Transports de Fret et Personnel de Fort - Archambault

CTERA...... Confederacion de Trabajadores de la Educacion de la Republica [*Confederation of Education Workers of the Argentine Republic*] (LA)

CTESE...... Cengiz Topel Erkek Sanaat Enstitusu [*Cengiz Topel Men's Trade Institute*] [*Turkish Cypriot*] (GC)

CTESSE.... Comtesse [*Countess*] [*French*] (ROG)

CTETOC... Council for Technical Education and Training for Overseas Countries (BARN)

CTEX........ Centro Tecnologico do Exercito [*Brazil*] (WGAO)

CTF............ Catholic Teachers Federation (WGAO)

CTF............ Central de Trabajadores Federados [*Confederation of Federated Workers*] [*Guatemala*] (LA)

CTF............ Cetfa SA [*Spain*] [*ICAO designator*] (FAAC)

CTF............ Coffee Trade Federation (WGAO)

CTF............ Combined Task Force [*NATO*] (NATG)

CTF............ Comite de Tourisme et des Fetes (WGAO)

CTF............ Communaute des Televisions Francophones [*Switzerland*] (WGAO)

CTFA........ Coffee and Tea Federation of Austria (EAIO)

CTFAA...... Cosmetic, Toiletry, and Fragrance Association of Australia

CTFB........ Christian Teachers Federation of Belgium (EAIO)

CTFL........ Centre Technique des Fruits et Legumes (WGAO)

CTFM........ Comite des Transports Ferroviaires du Maghreb [*Morocco*]

CTFMA..... Copper Tube Fittings Manufacturers Association (WGAO)

CTFT........ Centre Technique Forestier Tropical [*Technical Center for Tropical Forestry*] [*Paris, France*] (AF)

CTFTS...... Centre Technique Forestier Tropical du Senegal [*Senegal*] (DSCA)

CTG .... Cabinet de Topographie et Geometrie

CTG .... Cartagena [*Colombia*] [*Airport symbol*] (OAG)

CTG .... Combined Task Group [*NATO*] (NATG)

CTG .... Compagnie des Transports Gabonais

CTG .... Confederation des Travailleurs de Guinee [*Confederation of Workers of Guinea*]

ctg.............. Cotangente [*Cotangent*] [*French*]

ctg.............. Courtage [*Brokerage, Commission*] [*French*]

CTGA .... Ceylon Tea Growers Association (WGAO)

CTGREF ... Centre Technique du Genie Rural des Eaux et des Forets [*French*] (ASF)

CTgS.......... Centralna Telegrafska Stanica [*Central Telegraph Station*] [*Military*] (YU)

CTH .... Chalmers Tekniska Hogskola [*Chalmers Univeristy of Technology*] [*Sweden*] (PDAA)

CTH .... China General Aviation Corp. [*ICAO designator*] (FAAC)

CTH .... Commerce et Transport du Hodh

CTH .... Confederacion de Trabajadores de Honduras [*Honduras Workers' Confederation*] (LA)

CTHA .... China Tourist Hotel Association (EAIO)

CTHK .... Cable Television Hong Kong

CTHS .... Comite des Travaux Historiques et Scientifiques (WGAO)

CTI............ Calculo y Tratamiento de la Informacion [*Spain*] (PDAA)

CTI............ Centraal Technisch Instituut (WGAO)

CTI............ Centre de Traitement de l'Information [*Data Processing Center*] [*Ministry of Economic Affairs*] [*Belgium*] [*Information service or system*] (IID)

CTI............ Centre de Transit International [*International Transit Center*] [*Cameroon*] (AF)

CTI............ Centre Telex International

CTI............ Centro de Trabalho Indigenista [*Brazil*] (WGAO)

CTI............ Centro Tecnologico para Informatica [*Technological Center for Informatics*] [*Research center*] [*Brazil*] (IRC)

CTI............ Clothing and Textile Institute [*Denmark*] (EAIO)

CTI............ Comitato Termotecnico Italiano [*Italian*] (SLS)

CTI............ Comite des Transports [*de la CEE*] (FLAG)

CTI............ Confederation des Travailleurs Intellectuels [*France*] (FLAF)

CTIA........ Conseil Technique Interamericain Archives (WGAO)

CTIAQ...... Caravan Trade and Industries Association of Queensland [*Australia*]

CTIB........ Centre Technique de l'Industrie du Bois [*Belgium*] (WGAO)

CTIC........ Comisiones Tecnicas Inter-Crea [*Argentina*] (LAA)

CTICM...... Centre Technique Industriel de la Construction Metallique [*Industrial Technical Center for Metal Construction*] [*France*] (PDAA)

CTIDB...... China's Travel Information Database [*Information service or system*] (IID)

CTIDP...... Common Technical Interface Design Plan [*Joint technical document developed by the US, UK, and Germany*] [*Military*] (RDA)

CTIF........ Centre Technique des Industries de le Fonderie [*French*]

CTIF........ Comite Technique International de Prevention et d'Extinction du Feu [*International Technical Committee for the Prevention and Extinction of Fire*] (EAIO)

CTIFL...... Centre Technique Interprofessionnel des Fruits et Legumes (WGAO)

CTIM........ Centro de la Tribuna Internacional de la Mujer (WGAO)

CTIO .... Cerro Tololo Inter-American Observatory [*Chile*] [*Research center*] (IRC)

CTIOM ..... Centre Technique Interprofessionnel des Oleagineux Metropolitains (WGAO)

CTIP........ Compagnia Tecnica Industrie Petroli [*Technical Petroleum Industries Company*] [*Italian*] (WER)

CTK .... Ceskoslovenska Tiskova Kancelar [*Czechoslovak Press Bureau*] [*Prague*] (CZ)

CTK .... Ceskoslovenska Tlacova Kancelaria [*Czechoslovak Press Bureau*] (CZ)

CTK .... Tschechoslowakische Nachrichten-Agentur [*Czechoslovak News Agency*] (EG)

CTKA........ Chinese Taipei Korfball Association [*Taiwan*] (EAIO)

ctkm .... Cisty Tunkilometr [*Net Ton-Kilometer*] (CZ)

CTL........... Centre de Tourisme et de Loisirs [*Cameroon*] (WGAO)

CTL........... Ceske Tovarny na Lahve [*Czech Bottle Factories*] (CZ)

CTL........... Charleville [*Australia*] [*Airport symbol*] (OAG)

CTL........... Confederacion de Trabajadores Latinoamericanos [*Confederation of Latin American Workers*] [*Mexico*] (LAA)

CTLA........ Central Transport Licensing Authority

CTM .... Carrieres et Transports de la Mondah

CTM .... Central de Trabajadores Mayoritarias [*Trade union*] [*The Dominican Republic*] (EY)

CTM .... Centre Technique et du Materiel de la Meteorologie [*Meteorology Technology and Materials Center*] [*Ministere des Transports*] [*France*] (EAS)

CTM .... Centro Tecnologico Mineral [*Mineral Technology Center*] [*Brazil*] (LA)

CTM .... Ceske Technicke Museum [*Czech Museum of Technology*] (CZ)

CTM .... Ceskoslovensky Tabakovy Monopol [*Czechoslovak Tobacco Monopoly*] (CZ)

CTM .... Chetumal [*Mexico*] [*Airport symbol*] (OAG)

CTM .... Comision Tecnica Mixta Argentina-Uruguaya de Salto Grande [*Argentine-Uruguayan Joint Commission of Salto Grande*] (LA)

CTM .... Commandement du Transport Aerien Militaire Francais [*France*] [*ICAO designator*] (FAAC)

CTM .... Compagnie Auxiliaire de Transports au Maroc

CTM .... Compagnie de Transports Maritimes

CTM .... Compagnie de Transports Marocains

CTM .... Companhia Portuguesa de Transportes Maritimos (WGAO)

CTM .... Computertechnik Mueller GmbH [*German*] (ADPT)

CTM .... Concordia de Telecommunicacoes de Macau (WGAO)

CTM .... Confederacion de Trabajadores de Mexico [*Confederation of Mexican Workers*] (LA)

CTM .... Confederation des Travailleurs Malgaches [*Madagascar*] (EAIO)

CTM .... Conference Technique Mondiale (WGAO)

CTMA ...... Centre Technique du Machinisme Agricole (WGAO)

CTMA ...... China Textile Machinery and Accessories Association (EAIO)

CTMB....... Canal Transport Marketing Board (WGAO)

CTMB....... Compagnie Togolaise des Mines du Benin [*Togolese Mining Company of Benin*] (AF)

CTMC ...... Centre de Tannage et de Manufacture des Cuirs

CTMC ...... Compagnie pour la Transformation des Metaux au Cameroun

CTMC ...... Confederation des Travailleurs des Madagascar et Comores [*Confederation of Workers of Madagascar and the Comores*]

CTML........ Centre de Traitement des Materiaux par LASER [*Federal Institute of Technology in Lausanne*] [*Switzerland*]
CTMLN..... Compagnie de Transports au Maroc "Lignes Nationales" [*Casablanca, Morocco*]
ctmo........... Centesimo [*Hundredth*] [*Spanish*]
CTMO....... Centesimo [*or Centimo*] [*Monetary unit in many Spanish-American countries*]
ctmo........... Centimo [*Centime*] [*Spanish*]
CTMO....... Community Trade Mark Office [*EC*]   (ECED)
CTN.......... Central de Trabajadores de Nicaragua [*Federation of Nicaraguan Workers*]   (LA)
CTN.......... Central de Trabajadores Nicaraguenses   (WGAO)
CTN.......... Compagnie Tunisienne de Navigation
CTN.......... Computer Telecommunications Network [*Australia*]
CTN.......... Consumers' Telecommunications Network [*Australia*]
CTN.......... Cooktown [*Australia*] [*Airport symbol*]   (OAG)
CTN.......... Corps Tjadangan Nasional [*National Reserve Corps*]   (IN)
CTN.......... Croatia Airlines [*ICAO designator*]   (FAAC)
CTNC....... Code of Conduct for Transnational Corporations
CTNC....... Commission on Transnational Corporations [*United Nations*]
CTNC....... Committee on Transnational Corporations [*United Nations*]   (WGAO)
CTNE .... Compania Telefonica Nacional de Espana [*National Telephone Co. of Spain*] [*Telecommunications*]
CTNRC...... Centre for Thai National Reference Collections [*BRIT*]   (WGAO)
CTNSS ..... Center for Thai National Standard Specifications   (PDAA)
CTNSW.... Commercial Tribunal, New South Wales [*Australia*]
CTO.......... Aerotaxis del Centro SA [*Mexico*] [*ICAO designator*]   (FAAC)
CTO.......... Caribbean Tourism Organization   (EAIO)
CTO.......... Carmelite Third Order [*Rome, Italy*]   (EAIO)
CTO.......... Central Tractor Organisation [*India*]   (WGAO)
CTO.......... Central Transport Organisation
CTO.......... Central Treaty Organization [*Also, CENTO*] [*Formerly, Baghdad Pact*]
CTO.......... Centrum voor Technisch Ondezoek [*Center for Technical Research*] [*Netherlands railways*]   (ERC)
CTO.......... Comite Technique de l'Olivier   (WGAO)
CTO.......... Commonwealth Telecommunications Organization [*England*]
CTO.......... Communist Terrorist Organization   (ML)
CTO.......... Community Transport Organisation [*Australia*]
cto.............. Cuarto [*Room*] [*Spanish*]
CTO/A ...... Chief Technical Officer/Airworthiness [*Australia*]
CTOA .... Commonwealth Telephone Officers Association [*Australia*]   (ADA)
Ct of CrApp ... Court of Criminal Appeal [*Australia*]
CTOI .... Cultural Travel Organizations International   (EA)
CTOS .... Central de Trabajadores Organizados de El Salvador [*Central Organization of Salvadoran Organized Workers*]   (LA)
CTOSSU ... Comite Tunisien d'Organisation des Sports Scolaires et Universitaires
CTP........... Caja de Trabajo Penitenciario [*Venezuela*]   (LAA)
CTP........... Centre Technique de l'Industrie des Papiers, Cartons, et Celluloses [*Paper, Paperboard, and Cellulose Industry Technical Center*] [*Research center*] [*France*]   (IRC)
CTP........... Centrum voor Toeristenpastoraat [*Centre for Pastoral Work in Europe*] [*Netherlands*]   (EAIO)
CTP........... Confederacion de Trabajadores del Peru [*Confederation of Workers of Peru*]   (LA)
CTP........... Confederacion de Trabajadores Peruanos   (WGAO)
CTP........... Corpo de Tropas Paraquedistas [*Paratroopers Corps*] [*Air Force*] [*Portugal*]
CTP........... Cumhuriyetci Turk Partisi [*Republican Turkish Party*] [*Turkish Cyprus*] [*Political party*]   (PPE)
CTPA........ Canberra Taxi Proprietors Association [*Australia*]
CTPA........ Chinese Taipei Pediatric Association [*Taiwan*]   (EAIO)
CTPA........ Cosmetic Toiletry and Perfumery Association   (WGAO)
CTPD........ Cooperacion Tecnica entre Paises en Desarrollo [*Technical Cooperation among Developing Countries - TCDC*] [*Spanish*]
CTPD........ Cooperation Technique entre Pays en Developpement [*Technical Cooperation among Developing Countries - TCDC*] [*French*]
CTPL........ Centre Technique et de Promotion des Laitiers de Haut Fourneau   (WGAO)
CTPL........ Commission Technique et de Promotion des Laitiers de Haute Fourneau [*French*]   (SLS)
CTPOA...... Commonwealth Telephone and Phonogram Officers Association [*Australia*]   (ADA)
CTPP .... Comite Tecnico Permanente de Puertos (de la OEA) [*Organizacion de Estados Americanos*] [*Montevideo, Uruguay*]   (LAA)
CTPS .... Consejo de Trabajo y Prevision Social [*Guatemala*]   (LAA)
CTPS .... Permanent Technical Committee for Plant Breeding [*France*]   (WGAO)
CTPTA ...... Centro Tropical de Pesquisas e Tecnologia de Alimentos [*Brazil*]   (WGAO)

CTPTA ...... Centro Tropical de Pesquisas e Tecnologia de Alimentos [*Brazil*]   (DSCA)
CTR .... Cash Transactions Reporting Act [*Australia*]
Ctr............. Center   (PWGL)
Ctr............. Centner [*100 kilograms*] [*German*] [*Business term*]
Ctr............. Central   (PWGL)
CTR .... Comision de Telecommunicaciones Rurales [*Mexico*]   (WGAO)
ctr.............. Contract [*Benelux*]   (BAS)
CTR .... Country [*Totalisator Agency Board code*] [*Australia*]
CTR .... Court Tir Rapide [*Military*] [*French*]   (MTD)
CTR .... Transport Air Centre [*France*] [*ICAO designator*]   (FAAC)
Ctra .... Carretera [*Highway*] [*Spanish*]   (CED)
CTRA........ Cash Transaction Reports Agency [*Australia*]
C Trav....... Code du Travail [*French*]
CTRC........ Caribbean Tourism Research and Development Centre [*Later, Caribbean Tourism Organization*]   (EAIO)
CTRI......... Central Tobacco Research Institute [*Rajamundry, India*]
CTRIN....... Comercializacao do Trigo Nacional [*National Wheat Marketing Enterprise*] [*Brazil*]   (LA)
CTRJ .... Commission Technique Regionale des Jeunes
CTRL........ Cotton Technological Research Laboratory [*India*] [*Research center*]   (IRC)
CTRM .... Compagnie de Transports Routiers et de Messageries
CTRO .... Compagnie des Transports Routiers de l'Oubangui
CTRP........ Central de Trabajadores de la Revolucion Peruana [*Federation of Workers of the Peruvian Revolution*]   (LA)
CTRP........ Confederacion de Trabajadores de la Republica de Panama [*Confederation of Workers of the Republic of Panama*]   (LA)
CTRPD...... Comite Technique Regional du Plan et du Developpement [*Regional Technical Planning and Development Committee*] [*Malagasy*]   (AF)
CTRS........ Cooperative des Transporteurs Routiers du Senegal
CTRU .... Colonial Termite Research Unit
CTS........... Cambodia Travel Service   (CL)
CTS........... Canadian Thoracic Society [*Canada (already exists in GUS II database)*]   (SLS)
cts.............. Centimes [*Monetary unit*] [*France*]
cts.............. Centimos [*Spanish*]
CTS........... Central de Trabajadores Salvadorenos [*Salvadorean Workers' Confederation*]   (LA)
CTS........... Centralna Telefonska Sluzba [*Central Telephone Service*] [*Military*]   (YU)
CTS........... Centralna Telefonska Stanica [*Central Telephone Station*] [*Military*]   (YU)
CTS........... Cesky Tennisovy Svaz [*Czech Tennis Association*]   (CZ)
CTS........... China Travel Service   (ECON)
CTS........... Chinese Television Service [*Taiwan*]
CTS........... Chinese Television System   (EY)
CTS........... Comando Territorial do Sul [*Southern Territorial Command*] [*Mozambique*]   (AF)
CTS........... Commercial Trademark Services Ltd. [*Investigative agency*] [*Hong Kong*]
CTS........... Committee on the Teaching of Science [*ICSU*]   (WGAO)
CTS........... Commonwealth Teaching Service [*Australia*]   (ADA)
CTS........... Commonwealth Time Service [*Australia*]   (ADA)
CTS........... Community Tenant Scheme [*Australia*]
CTS........... Compagnie de Transports Senegalais
CTS........... Compagnies Tchadiennes de Securite [*Chadian Security Companies*]   (AF)
CTS........... Container-Transport-System   (EG)
CTS........... ContiTire System [*German*]
CTS........... Cooperation Technique Suisse   (WGAO)
CTS........... Country Television Services [*Australia*]
cts.............. Cuartos [*Rooms*] [*Spanish*]
CTS........... Incorporated Catholic Truth Society   (WGAO)
CTS........... Sapporo/Chitose [*Japan*] [*Airport symbol*]   (OAG)
CTSC........ Centre for Technology and Social Change [*Australia*]
CTSIBV ..... Centre Technique et Scientifique de l'Industrie Belge du Verre [*Belgian Glass Industry Technical and Scientific Center*]   (PDAA)
CTSK .... Cetinkaya Turk Spor Klubu [*Cetinkaya Turkish Sports Club*] [*Turkish Cypriot*]   (TU)
CTSRGWA ... Commercial Travellers and Sales Representatives' Guild of Western Australia
CTSSS....... Commonwealth Teaching Service Scholarship Scheme [*Australia*]   (ADA)
CTT........... Administracao-Geral dos Correios, Telegrafos, e Telefones [*General Administration of Post Offices, Telegraphs, and Telephones*] [*Portuguese*]   (WER)
CTT........... Central de Trabajadores Textiles [*Federation of Textile Workers*] [*Venezuela*]   (LA)
CTT........... Centre for Technology Transfer [*National Research Development Corporation of India*]
CTT........... Centre for Technology Transfer [*Australia*]
CTT........... Centro de Tenencia de la Tierra [*Santiago, Chile*]   (LAA)

CTT........... Centrum voor Tuinbouwtechnick Centre of Horticultural Engineering [*Netherlands*] (DSCA)
CTT........... Centrum voor Tuinbouwtechniek (WGAO)
CTT........... Compagnie de Tifnout Tiranimine [*Morocco*]
CTT........... Confederacion de Transporte Terrestre [*Automotive Transportation Confederation*] [*Chile*] (LA)
CTT........... Cooperative des Transports Tchadiens
CTT........... Coras Trachtala [*Irish Export Board*]
CTTA........ Colombo Tea Traders' Association [*Sri Lanka*] (EAIO)
CTTA........ Compagnie de Transports et de Travaux Aeriens
CTTAC..... Clinical Trials and Treatments Advisory Committee [*Australia*]
CTTB........ Centre Technique des Tuiles et Briques [*Technical Center for Clay, Tiles, and Bricks*] [*France*] (EAIO)
CTTC........ Centrale Togolaise des Travailleurs Croyants [*Togolese Federation of Believing Workers*] (AF)
CTTE........ Cyprus Turkish Tourist Enterprises Ltd. (EY)
Cttee......... Committee (EECI)
CTTM....... Cok Tarafli Ticaret Muzekereleri [*Multilateral Trade Negotiations*] [*Turkish*] (TU)
CTTRC..... China Textile Testing and Research Center (SLS)
CTTT........ Compagnie Tunisienne de Tourisme et de Thermalisme
CTU.......... Catholic Theological Union
CTU.......... Central de Trabajadores del Uruguay [*Uruguayan Workers Federation*] (LA)
CTU.......... Chengdu [*China*] [*Airport symbol*] (OAG)
CTU.......... Chilean Temperance Union (EAIO)
CTU.......... Confederacion de Trabajadores Unitaria [*United Workers Confederation*] [*The Dominican Republic*] (EY)
CTU.......... Conservative Trade Unionists (WGAO)
CTUA....... Clothing and Allied Trades Union of Australia
CTUBTCW ... Christian Trade Union of Belgium Textile and Clothing Workers (EAIO)
CTUC .... Central Trade Union Council [*Former Czechoslovakia*]
CTUC .... Commonwealth Trade Union Council [*British*] (EAIO)
CTUF....... Ceylon Trade Union Federation [*Sri Lanka*] (FEA)
CTUHR..... Commission on Trade Union and Human Rights [*Philippines*]
CTUM....... Confederation of Trade Unions of Monaco (EAIO)
CTUY....... Confederation of Trade Unions of Yugoslavia (WGAO)
CTUYM.... Caribbean Trade Union Youth Movement (WGAO)
CTV.......... Cameroon Television
CTV.......... Centro Televisivo Vaticano [*Vatican Television Center*] [*1984*]
CTV.......... China Television Co. (EY)
CTV.......... Comites Toupeiras Vermelhas [*Red Youth Committees*] [*Portuguese*] (WER)
CTV.......... Community Television Sydney [*Australia*]
CTV.......... Computerisierte Textverarbeitung [*German*] (ADPT)
CTV.......... Confederacion de Trabajadores de Venezuela [*Confederation of Workers of Venezuela*] (LA)
CTVANSW ... Christian Television Association of New South Wales [*Australia*]
CTVM .... Centre for Tropical Veterinary Medicine
CTVO .... Centavo [*Cent*] [*Monetary unit in many Spanish-American countries*]
CTWA ...... Commercial Tribunal of Western Australia
CTY .... Club du Terrier du Yorkshire [*France*] (EAIO)
CTY .... Cryderman Air Service [*ICAO designator*] (FAAC)
CTZ .... Cata SACIFI [*Argentina*] [*ICAO designator*] (FAAC)
CTZ .... Ceskoslovenske Textilni Zavody, Narodni Podnik [*Czechoslovak Textile Factories, National Enterprise*] (CZ)
CTZ .... Ceskoslovenske Tukove Zavody [*Czechoslovak Fats Rendering Plants*] (CZ)
c/u............. Cada Uno [*Every One, Each*] [*Spanish*]
CU............. Casualties Union (WGAO)
CU............. Cattlemen's Union of Australia
CU............. Centralny Urzad [*Central Administration, Agency, Office*] (POL)
CU............. Charge Utile [*Useful Load*] [*French*]
CU............. Cirkevna Ustava [*Church Statutes*] (CZ)
CU............. Clavieruebung [*Music*]
CU............. Communaute Urbaine [*France*] (FLAF)
CU............. Corps Urbains de Gardiens de la Paix [*France*] (FLAF)
cu.............. Cours Unique [*Sole Quotation*] [*Stock exchange*] [*French*] [*Business term*]
CU............. Cuba [*ANSI two-letter standard code*] (CNC)
CU............. Cubana Airways (DS)
cu.............. Cubic (EECI)
CU............. Cukurova Universitesi [*Cukurova University*] (TU)
CU............. Cumhuriyet Universitesi [*Republic University*] [*Sivas*] (TU)
CU............. Movimiento Colombia Unida [*United Colombian Movement*] [*Political party*] (EY)
CUA.......... Cattlemen's Union of Australia
CUA.......... China United Airlines [*ICAO designator*] (FAAC)
CUA.......... Clean Up Australia Ltd.
CUA.......... Commercial Union Assurance Company of Australia Ltd.
CUA.......... Conference of University Administrators (WGAO)
CUA.......... Congregational Union of Australia (ADA)

CUA.......... Credit Union Australia Ltd.
CUACSA ... Comite de Unidade de Accao e de Coordinacao Sindical de Angola
cuad........... Cuadrado [*Square*] [*Spanish*]
CUAG....... Centre Universitaire des Antilles-Guyane [*Antilles-French Guiana University Center*] (LA)
CUAG....... Computer Users Association Group (WGAO)
CUAN....... Centro Urbano Antonio Narino [*Colombia*] (COL)
CUAP .... Comision Uruguaya de la Alianza para el Progreso [*Uruguayan Commission for the Alliance for Progress*] (LA)
CUARIC.... Centrala de Automatizare de Utilaje si Reparatii pentru Industria Chimica [*Central for the Automation of Equipment and Repairs for the Chemical Industry*] (RO)
CUAS .... Comite de Unidad de Accion Sindical [*Committee for Unity of Labor Union Action*] [*Colorado*] (LA)
CUASS...... Comite de Unidad de Accion y Solidaridad Sindical [*Committee for Unity of Trade Union Action and Solidarity*] [*Colorado*] (LA)
CUAVES ... Comunidad Urbana Autogestionaria de Villa El Salvador [*Urban Self-Management Community of Villa El Salvador*] [*Peru*] (LA)
CUB .... Carlton and United Breweries [*Australia*]
CUB .... Carlton United Breweries [*Australia*]
CUB .... Centralna Uprava Brodogradnje [*Central Administration of Shipbuilding*] [*YU*]
CUB .... Comitato Unitario di Base [*Local Unitary Committee*] [*Italian*] (WER)
CUB .... Confederacion Universitaria Boliviana [*Bolivian University Confederation*] (LA)
CUB .... Cuba [*ANSI three-letter standard code*] (CNC)
cub.............. Cube [*or Cubique*] [*Cubic*] [*French*]
CUB .... Empresa Cubana de Aviacion [*Cuba*] [*ICAO designator*] (FAAC)
CUBACONTROL ... Empresa Cubana de Control [*Cuban Control Enterprise*] (LA)
CUBAEXPORT ... Empresa Cubana Exportadora de Alimentos y Productos Varios [*Cuban Enterprise for the Export of Foodstuffs and Various Products*] (LA)
CUBAFRUTAS ... Empresa Cubana Exportadora de Frutas Tropicales [*Cuban Tropical Fruit Exporting Enterprise*] (LA)
CUBAINDUSTRIA ... Empresa Cubana Exportadora de Productos Industriales [*Cuban Industrial Products Exporting Enterprise*] (LA)
CUBAINDUSTRIAL ... Empresa Cubana Importadora de Plantas Completas [*Cuban Complete Plant Importing Enterprise*] (LA)
CUBAMETALES ... Empresa Cubana Importadora de Metales [*Cuban Enterprise for the Import of Metals*] (LA)
CUBANA .. Empresa Consolidada Cubana de Aviacion [*State Airline*] [*Cuba*] (PDAA)
CUBANA .. Empresa Cubana de Aviacion (WGAO)
CUBANIQUEL ... Empresa Cubana Exportadora de Minerales y Metales [*Cuban Enterprise for the Export of Minerals and Metals*] (LA)
CUBAPESCA ... Empresa Cubana Importadora de Buques y Equipos de Pesca [*Cuban Enterprise forthe Import of Fishing Ships and Fishing Equipment*] (LA)
CUBARTIMPEX ... Empresa Cubana Exportadora e Importadora de Articulos de Arte y Cultura [*Cuban Enterprise for Export and Import of Items of Art and Culture*] (LA)
CUBATABACO ... Empresa Cubana de Tabaco [*Cuban Tobacco Enterprise*] (LA)
CUBATECNICA ... Empresa de Contratacion de Asistencia Tecnica [*Cuba*] (EY)
CUBATEX ... Empresa Cubana Importadora de Fibras, Tejidos, Cueros, y Sus Productos [*Cuban Enterprise for the Import of Fibers, Fabrics, Leathers, and Their By-Products*] (LA)
CUBATUR ... Empresa de Turismo Nacional e Internacional [*National and International Tourist Enterprise*] [*Cuba*] (LA)
CUBAZUCAR ... Empresa Cubana Exportadora de Azucar y Sus Derivados [*Cuban Enterprise for Export of Sugar and Sugar By-Products*] (LA)
CUBE .... Concertation Unit for Biotechnology [*CCE*] (WGAO)
CUBEPAL ... Coordinadora de Unidades Basicas de Emigrados Peronistas en America Latina [*Coordinator of Basic Units of Peronist Emigres in Latin America*] (LA)
CUBI.......... Centro Nazionale per il Catalogo Unico delle Biblioteche Italiane [*Italian*]
CUBN........ Convent van Universiteitsbibliothecarissen in Nederland [*Netherlands*] (EAIO)
CubV.......... Cuban Victor [*Record label*]
CUC........... Cameroon United Congress [*Political party*]
CUC........... Canberra University College [*Australia*] (ADA)
CUC........... CAVAL [*Cooperative Action by Victorian Academic Libraries*] Union Catalogue [*Australia*]
CUC........... Coal Utilization Council (WGAO)
CUC........... Comite de Unidad Campesina [*Committee of Peasant Unity*] [*Guatemala*] [*Political party*] (PD)

CUC.......... Computers Users' Committee [*UNDP*]   (WGAO)
CUC.......... Cucuta [*Colombia*] [*Airport symbol*]   (OAG)
CUC.......... Cuttington University College [*Liberia*]
CUCA........ Carpet and Upholstery Cleaners Association of Australia
CUCA........ Carpet and Upholstery Cleaning Association [*Australia*]
CUCA........ Cercle Universitaire "Connaissance de l'Afrique"
CUCB........ Chabre des Urbanistes- Conseils de Belgique   (WGAO)
CUCES...... Centre Universitaire de Cooperation Economique et Sociale
                     (WGAO)
CUCI .... Clasificacion Uniforme para el Comercio Internacional
                     [*Guatemala*]   (DSCA)
CUCMS..... Compagnie Universelle du Canal Maritime de Suez
CUCO........ Comite de Unidad Civica Organizado [*Organized Civic Unity
                     Committee*] [*Guatemala*]   (LA)
CUCODEP ... Credit Union of Community Development Personnel
                     [*Cambodia*]   (CL)
CUCW....... Central Union for Child Welfare [*Finland*]   (EAIO)
CUD.......... Caloundra [*Australia*] [*Airport symbol*]   (OAG)
CUD.......... Comite de l'Union Douaniere [*Customs Union Committee*]
                     [*Ivory Coast*]   (AF)
CUD.......... Comite de l'Union Douaniere [*Customs Union Committee*]
                     [*Burkinan*]   (AF)
CUD.......... Cooperation Universitaire au Developpement   (WGAO)
CUDAG..... Comite Unificador Docente de Accion Gremial [*Teachers
                     Unification Committee for Union Action*] [*Argentina*]   (LA)
CUDIP....... Comitato Unitario per il Disarmo e la Pace [*United Committee
                     for Disarmament and Peace*] [*Italy*]
CUDMER ... Comite Unificador del Movimiento Estudiantil Revolucionario
                     [*Unifying Committee of the Revolutionary Student
                     Movement*] [*Peru*]   (LA)
CUDW....... Centralny Urzad Drobnej Wytworczosci [*Central Administration
                     of Small Scale Industry*]   (POL)
CUE.......... Committee for University English   (WGAO)
CUE.......... Cuenca [*Ecuador*] [*Airport symbol*]   (OAG)
CUEA........ Conseil de l'Unite Economique Arabe [*Council of Arab Economic
                     Unity - CAEU*] [*French*]
CUEA........ Consejo de la Unidad Economica Arabe [*Council of Arab
                     Economic Unity - CAEU*] [*Spanish*]
CUEBS...... Commission on Undergraduate Education in the Biological
                     Sciences [*AIBS*]   (WGAO)
CUEC........ China United Electric Export Corp.   (TCC)
CUECE...... Centre Universitaire d'Etude des Communautes Europeennes de
                     Paris [*France*]   (FLAF)
CUED........ Certificat Universitaire d'Etudes de Droit [*French*]
CUEE........ Certificat Universitaire d'Etudes Economiques [*French*]
CUEG........ Centro Universitario de Estudios Generales [*University General
                     Studies Center*] [*Dominican Republic*]   (LA)
CUEL........ Certificat Universitaire d'Etudes Litteraires [*French*]
CUEP........ Central Unit on Environmental Pollution [*DOE*]   (WGAO)
CUEP........ Christian Union for the Estate Profession   (WGAO)
CUEPACS ... Congress of Unions of Employees in Public and Civil Services
                     [*Malaysia*]   (WGAO)
CUEPACS ... Congress of Unions of Employees in the Public Administrative
                     and Civil Services [*Malaysia*]   (EY)
CUES........ Certificat Universitaire d'Etudes Scientifiques [*French*]
CUESG...... Curtin University Environmental Studies Group [*Australia*]
CUF .... Catholicarum Universitatum Foederatio   (WGAO)
CUF .... Companhia Uniao Fabril [*United Manufacturers' Company*]
                     [*Portuguese*]   (AF)
CUFEC...... Curso de Formacion Estadistica del Caribe [*Barranquilla*]
                     (COL)
CUFF........ Comando Unico Frente de Liberacion Nacional - Fuerzas
                     Armadas de Liberacion Nacional [*Single Command of the
                     National Liberation Front - Armed Forces of National
                     Liberation*] [*Venezuela*]   (LA)
CUFLET.... Empresa Cubana de Fletes [*Cuban Freight Enterprise*]   (LA)
CUFOP...... Centre Universitaire de Formation Permanente
CUFSAL.... Credit Union Financial Services (Australia) Limited
CUG.......... Centralny Urzad Geologii [*Central Office of Geology*]   (POL)
CUG.......... Computer Utilization Group [*OECD*]
CUG.......... Orange-Cudal [*Australia*] [*Airport symbol*]   (OAG)
CUGC....... Conference of Unions in Government Corporations [*Philippines*]
                     (WGAO)
CUGCO..... Confederation of Unions in Government Corporations and
                     Offices [*Philippines*]
CUGiK....... Centralny Urzad Geodezji i Kartografii [*Central Administration
                     of Geodesy and Cartography*]   (POL)
CUGK........ Cesky Urad Geodeticky a Kartograficky [*Czech Geodetic and
                     Cartographic Office*]   (CZ)
CUGM....... Centralny Urzad Gospodarki Materialowej [*Central
                     Administration of the Management of Materials*]   (POL)
CUGW....... Centralny Urzad Gospodarki Wodnej [*Central Office for Water
                     Management*]   (POL)
CUHK........ Chinese Univeristy of Hong Kong   (PDAA)
CUIDES .... Consejo Universitario Interamericano para el Desarrollo
                     Economico y Social   (WGAO)
cuill .... Cuilleree [*Spoonful*] [*Pharmacy*]

CUIP.......... Comite Universitario de Investigaciones de Poblacion,
                     Universidad del Valle [*Colombia*]   (COL)
CUIROP.... Confederation Europeenne du Commerce de Cuir en Gros
                     (WGAO)
CUJAE...... Ciudad Universitaria Jose Antonio Echeverria [*Jose Antonio
                     Echeverria University City*] [*Cuba*]   (LA)
CUJiM ...... Centralny Urzad Jokosci i Miar [*Central Quality and Measure
                     Office*]   (POL)
CUK.......... Centralny Urzad Kinematografii [*Central Administration of
                     Motion Pictures*]   (POL)
CUKAC ..... Combined United Kingdom / Australian Long Range Weapons
                     Committee
CUKB .... Cairo University Khartoum Branch
CUKK .... Ceskoslovenske Ustredi Knizni Kultury [*Czechoslovak Book
                     Culture Center*]   (CZ)
CUKOBIRLIK ... Cukurova Pamuk ve Narenciye Tarim Satis Kooperatifleri
                     Birligi [*Cukurova Cotton and Citrus Fruit Agricultural Sales
                     Cooperatives Union*] [*Adana*]   (TU)
CUKOSEN ... Cukurova Pamuk Taris Satis Kooperatifi Sendikasi [*Cukurova
                     Cotton Agricultural Sales Cooperative Union*] [*Adana*]
                     (TU)
CUKREX... Akciova Spolecnost pro Obchod s Cukrem [*Sugar Trading Joint-
                     Stock Company*]   (CZ)
CUKROHURT ... Nadmorska Hurtownia Wyrobow Cukierniczych [*Coastal
                     Confectionary Wholesale House*]   (POL)
CUKT .... Carregie United Kingdom Trust   (WGAO)
CUL .... Culiacan [*Mexico*] [*Airport symbol*]   (OAG)
cul.............. Culinaire [*French*]   (TPFD)
cul.............. Culinary   (TPFD)
CULPAVAL ... Cultivadores de Patata Valdivia   (WGAO)
CULT........ Chinese University Language Translator [*Hong Kong University*]
                     (PDAA)
CULT........ Combined Universities Language Test [*Australia*]
CULTUREX ... Association for Cultural Exchange   (EA)
CUM......... Chinese Unity Movement   (ML)
Cum.......... Concerteum [*Record label*] [*France*]
CUM......... Cooperative Union of Malaysia   (WGAO)
CUM......... Cumana [*Venezuela*] [*Airport symbol*]   (OAG)
cum.......... Cumulatif [*Cumulative*] [*French*]
CUMA....... Cooperative d'Utilisation de Materiel Agricole   (WGAO)
CUMA...... Cooperative d'Utilisation du Materiel Agricole en Commun
CUMATEX ... Associazione Nazionale Rappresentanti Commercianti
                     Macchine e Accessori per l'Industria Tessile Maglierie e per
                     Cucire   (WGAO)
Cumb......... Cumberland College of Health Sciences [*Australia*]
Cumberland CHS ... Cumberland College of Health Sciences [*Australia*]
Cumh......... Cumhuriyet [*Republic*]   (TU)
cumpto....... Cumprimento [*Salutation*] [*Correspondence*] [*Portuguese*]
CUMS .... Council of University Management Schools   (WGAO)
CUN.......... Cancun [*Mexico*] [*Airport symbol*]   (OAG)
CUN.......... Centro UFOlogico Nazionale [*Italian*]
CUN.......... Consiglio Universitario Nazionale [*National University Council*]
                     [*Italian*]
CUNA....... Central Unica Agraria [*Single Agrarian Federation*] [*Peru*]   (LA)
CUNA....... Centro Universitario de Alajuela [*Alajuela University Center*]
                     [*Costa Rica*]   (LA)
CUNA....... Comite de l'Unite Nationale Angolaise [*Angolan National Unity
                     Committee*]   (AF)
CUNA....... Commissione Technica di Unificazione nell' Autoveicolo
                     (WGAO)
CUNA....... Consejo Unitario Nacional Agrario [*Peru*]   (EY)
CUNA....... Co-Operative Union National Association, Inc.
CUNC....... Comite d'Union Nationale des Cabindais [*Cabindan Committee
                     of National Union*] [*Angola*]   (AF)
CUNS .... Center for UN Studies   (EAIO)
CUNYTASA ... Compania Uruguaya de Navegacion y Transportes Aereos,
                     Sociedad Anonima [*Uruguay*]   (LAA)
CUODE..... Clasificacion por Uso o Destino Economico [*Classification of
                     Products by Economic Use of Destination*] [*Comision
                     Economica para America Latina*]   (LAA)
CUOP........ Ceskoslovensky Urad Ochrany Prace [*Czechoslovak Office for
                     Labor Protection*]   (CZ)
CUP .... Carupano [*Venezuela*] [*Airport symbol*]   (OAG)
CUP .... Centralny Urzad Planowania [*Central Planning Administration*]
                     (POL)
CUP .... Ceskoslovensky Ustav Prace [*Czechoslovak Labor Institute*]
                     (CZ)
CUP .... Comites de Unidad Popular [*Committees of Popular Unity*]
                     [*Spanish*]   (WER)
CUP .... Computer Umwelt-Projekt [*German*]   (ADPT)
Cup............ Cupol [*Record label*] [*Sweden*]
CUPASAN ... Cukurova Plastik Ambalaj Sanayi ve Ticaret AS [*Cukurova
                     Plastics Packaging Industry and Trade Corp.*]   (TU)
CUPEN ..... Centro Uruguayo PEN [*International PEN - Uruguay*]   (EAIO)
CUPRA...... Confederazione Unitaria della Produzione Agricole   (WGAO)

CUPROCH ... Confederacion Unica de Profesionales y Tecnicos de Chile [*Single Confederation of Chilean Professionals and Technicians*]   (LA)

CUPS......... Centrala pentru Utilaje si Piese de Schimb [*Central for Equipment and Spare Parts*]   (RO)

CUPSA...... Constructora Urbanizadora del Paris SA

CUPSEP.... Computerunterstuetzte Planung und Steuerung der EDV-Produktion [*German*]   (ADPT)

CUPSIC..... Centrala de Utilaje si Piese de Schimb pentru Industria Chimica [*Central for Equipment and Spare Parts for the Chemical Industry*]   (RO)

CUPUOS... Committee on the Peaceful Uses of Outer Space [*United Nations*]   (NTCM)

CUPW .... Canadian Union of Postal Workers   (WGAO)

CUQ........... Coen [*Australia*] [*Airport symbol*]   (OAG)

CUR........... Centralny Urzad Radiofonii [*Central Administration of the Radio Loudspeaker Network*] [*Poland*]   (POL)

CUR........... Centre Universitaire Regional

CUR........... Comando Urbano Revolucionario [*Guatemala*] [*Political party*]   (EY)

CUR........... Comite de Unidad Revolucionaria [*Committee of Revolutionary Unity*] [*Venezuela*]   (LA)

CUR........... Commisse voor Uitvoering van Research   (WGAO)

CUR........... Curacao [*Netherlands Antilles*] [*Airport symbol*]   (OAG)

CUR........... Det Centrale Uddanneisesrad   (WGAO)

CURAC ..... Coal Utilization Research Advisory Committee [*Australia*]   (WGAO)

CURB .... Campaign on the Use and Restriction of Barbiturates   (WGAO)

CURC .... Cairo University Rowing Club

CURE .... Citizens United for Racial Equality

CURE .... Comite Unico Regional de Estudiantes [*Single Regional Student Committee*] [*Venezuela*]   (LA)

CURE .... Comite Unificado Regional de Estudiantes [*Unified Regional Student Committee*] [*Venezuela*]   (LA)

CUREI....... Centre Universitaire de Recherche Europeenne et Internationale [*University Center for European and International Research*] [*France*]   (IRC)

CUREM .... Centre Universitaire Regional d'Etudes Municipales [*Regional University Center for Municipal Studies*] [*French Guiana*]   (LA)

CURER...... Centre Universitaire de Recherches, d'Etudes, et de Realisations [*University Research and Study Center*] [*Algeria*]

CURL .... Consortium of University Research Libraries   (WGAO)

CURN........ Centro Universitario Regional del Norte [*Regional University Center of the North*] [*Honduras*]   (LA)

CURO........ Christelijke Unie van Personeelsleden bij het Rijksonderwijs [*Belgium*]   (EAIO)

CURPHAMETRA ... Centre Universitaire de Recherche sur la Pharmacopee et la Medecine Traditionnelle [*University Center for Research on Pharmaceuticals*] [*Rwanda*] [*Research center*]   (IRC)

CURS........ Centre Universitaire de Recherche Scientifique [*North African*]

Curt........... Curtin University of Technology [*Australia*]

Curtin UTech ... Curtin University of Technology [*Australia*]

Cus............ Cantus [*Record label*] [*Sweden*]

CUS .... Ceskoslovenska Unitarska Spolecnost [*Czechoslovak Unitarian Society*]   (CZ)

CUS .... Cok Uluslu Sirketler [*Multinational Corporations*]   (TU)

CUS .... Comite de l'Unite Syndicale [*French*]

CUS .... Comite de Unidad Sindical [*Committee for Trade Union Unity*] [*Costa Rica*]   (LA)

CUS .... Comite de Unidad Sindical del Salvador [*Committee for Salvadoran Trade Union Unity*]   (LA)

CUS .... Confederacion de Unificacion Sindical [*Confederation of Trade Union Unification*] [*Nicara*]   (LA)

CUS .... Conference Universitaire Suisse   (WGAO)

CUSA .... Carretas and Urbanismo SA

CUSA .... Congress of Unions of South Africa

CUSA .... Council for United States Aid [*China*]   (WGAO)

CUSA .... Council of Unions of South Africa

CUSA-AZACTU ... Council of Unions of South Africa - Azanian Confederation of Trade Unions

CUSAF ...... Commercial Union Assurance Company of South Africa [*Insurance company*]

CUSB........ Credit Union Stabilisation Board [*South Australia*]

CUSC........ Coastal Union Sports Club

CUSC........ Colegio Universitario del Sagrado Corazon [*Valle del Lily-Cali*]   (COL)

CUSC........ Combined Union and Shop Committee [*Australia*]

CUSCA...... Comite de Unidad Sindical de Centroamerica, Belice, y Panama [*Committee for Trade Union Unity in Central America, Belize, and Panama*] [*Costa Rica*]   (LA)

CUSEGO... Cuellar Serrano Gomez & Cia. Ltda. [*Colombia*]   (COL)

CUSG .... Confederacion de Unidad Sindical de Guatemala [*Guatemala*]

CUSI......... Coordinamento Uruguaiano di Solidarieta in Italia

CUSIC .... Comite Unitario de Sindicalistas Cristianos [*Unified Committee of Christian Trade Unionists*] [*Caracas, Venezuela*]   (LAA)

CUSIC .... Comite Unitario de Sindicalistas Cristianos de Venezuela   (WGAO)

CUSIG...... Computer Users' Special Interest Group [*Australia*]

CUSIP .... Centro Universitario per lo Sviluppo Internazionale

CUSK........ Centralny Urzad Skupu i Kontraktacji [*Central Procurement and Contracting Office*]   (POL)

CUSO .... Canadian University Service Overseas [*Jamaica*]   (LA)

CUSPEA ... China-United States Physics Examination and Application Program

CUSRPG ... Canada-United States Regional Planning Group [*NATO*]

CUSS........ Centre for Urban and Social Studies [*Australia*]

CUSS........ Centre Universitaire des Sciences de la Sante [*University Center for Health Sciences*] [*Burkina Faso*]   (AF)

CUSS........ Centre Universitaire des Sciences Sanitaires [*University Center for Health Sciences*] [*Cameroon*]   (AF)

CUST........ Centre Universitaire des Sciences et Techniques   (WGAO)

CUST........ Chengdu University of Science and Technology [*China*]   (ERC)

cust............ Custodia [*Slipcase*] [*Publishing*] [*Italian*]

custod........ Custodia [*Slipcase*] [*Publishing*] [*Italian*]

CUSURDI ... Council of United States Universities for Rural Development in India   (WGAO)

CUSUSWASH ... Council of US Universities for Soil and Water Development in Arid and Subhumid Areas   (WGAO)

CUSZ........ Centralny Urzad Szkolenia Zawodowego [*Central Vocational Training Agency*]   (POL)

CUT .... Caribbean Union of Teachers   (WGAO)

CUT .... Central Unica de Trabajadores [*Single Federation of Workers*] [*Ecuador*]

CUT .... Central Unica de Trabajadores [*Trade union*] [*Paraguay*]   (EY)

CUT .... Central Unica de Trabajadores [*Single Federation of Workers*] [*Chile*]   (LAA)

CUT .... Central Unica dos Trabalhadores [*Workers' Central Union*] [*Brazil*]   (LA)

CUT .... Central Unitaria de Trabajadores [*Workers' Unity Center*] [*Dominican Republic*]

CUT .... Central Unitaria de Trabajadores [*Workers' Unity Center*] [*Colorado*]   (EY)

CUT .... Chartered Union of Taxpayers   (WGAO)

CUT .... Comite de l'Unite Togolaise [*Committee for Togolese Unity*] [*Defunct*]

CUT .... Comite Pro-Confederacion Unica [*Dominican Republic*]   (WGAO)

CUT .... Confederacion Unitaria de Trabajadores [*United Confederation of Workers*] [*Costa Rica*]   (LA)

CUT .... Cooperative Union of Tanganyika

CUT .... Co-Operative Union of Tanzania

CUT .... Curtin University of Technology [*Australia*]

CUT .... Cutral-Co [*Argentina*] [*Airport symbol*]   (OAG)

CUTA .... Canadian Urban Transport Association   (WGAO)

CUTA .... Conduccion Unica de los Trabajadores Argentinos [*United Leadership of Argentinian Workers*]   (EY)

CUTA .... Confederacion Uruguaya de Transporte Automotor [*Uruguay*]   (LAA)

CUTAL...... Central Unica de Trabajadores de America Latina [*Single Federation of Latin American Workers*]   (LA)

CUTAL...... Confederation Unique des Travailleurs de l'Amerique Latine   (WGAO)

CUTC .... China United Trading Corporation [*Ministry of Foreign Economic Relations and Trade*]   (IMH)

CUTCh ...... Central Unica de Trabajadores de Chile [*Chilean Trade Union Federation*]   (LA)

CUTCSA ... Compania Uruguaya de Transportes Colectivos, Sociedad Anonima [*Uruguayan Bus Company, Incorporated*]   (LA)

CUTE .... Cooperativa Usinas Electricas y Telefonos del Estado [*Uruguayan Electric and Telephone Cooperative*]   (LA)

CUTI......... Cesky Urad pro Tisk a Informace [*Czech Office for Press and Information*]   (CZ)

CUTMA ..... Consejo Colombiano de Usuarios del Transporte Maritimo y Aereo [*Colombian Council of Users of Maritime and Air Transport*]   (LA)

CUTP........ Central Unica de Trabajadores Peruanos [*Trade union*]   (EY)

CUTS........ Confederacion Unitaria de Trabajadores Salvadorenos [*United Confederation of Salvadoran Workers*]   (LA)

CUTT .... Confederacion Uruguaya de Trabajadores del Transporte [*Uruguayan Confederation of Transport Workers*]   (LA)

CUTV .... Central Unitaria de Trabajadores de Venezuela [*Venezuelan Workers' United Centre*]   (LA)

CUU........... Chihuahua [*Mexico*] [*Airport symbol*]   (OAG)

CUU........... Club de Unidad Universitaria [*University Unity Club*] [*Guatemala*]   (LA)

CUU........... Computerunterstuetzter Unterricht [*German*]   (ADPT)

CUUI........ Center for US-USSR Initiatives   (EAIO)

CUUN........ Centro Universitario de la Universidad Nacional Autonoma de Nicaragua [*University Center of the Autonomous National University of Nicaragua*]   (LA)

CUUS .... Comitetul Uniunii Uniunilor de Sanatate [*Committee of the Union of Health Unions*]   (RO)

CUV .... Centar Uprave Vatrom [*Firing Control Center*] [*Military*] (YU)
CUV .... Ciudad Universitaria del Valle [*Colombia*] (COL)
CUV .... Computerunterstuetzte Verwaltung [*German*] (ADPT)
CUV .... Cricket Union of Victoria [*Australia*]
CUVb .... Centar Uprave Vatrom Bataljona [*Firing Control Center of Battalion*] (YU)
CUVISA .... Companias Unidas Vitarte, Victoria, Inca, SA [*The United Companies of Vitarte, Victoria, Inca, Inc.*] [*Peru*] (LA)
CUVS .... Comite Universitario de Vanguardia Socialista [*Socialist Vanguard University Committee*] [*Colorado*] (LA)
CUW .... Centralny Urzad Wydawniczy [*Central Publishing Administration*] (POL)
CUWPGiK ... Centralny Urzad Wydawnictw, Przemyslu Graficznego, i Ksiegarstwa [*Central Administration of Publications, the Printing Industry, and Bookselling*] (POL)
CUWPPiK ... Centralny Urzad Wydawnictw, Przemyslu Poligraficznego, i Ksiegarstwa [*Central Administration of Publications, the Printing Industry, and Bookselling*] (POL)
CUZ .... Ceskoslovensky Ustav Zahranicni [*Czechoslovak Foreign Institute*] (CZ)
CUZ .... Cuzco [*Peru*] [*Airport symbol*] (OAG)
CV .... Air Chathams [*Airline code*] [*Australia*]
CV .... Caballo de Vapor [*Horsepower*] [*Spanish*]
CV .... Callisthenics Victoria [*Australia*]
CV .... Cape Verde [*ANSI two-letter standard code*] (CNC)
CV .... Capitaine de Vaisseau [*Post-Captain*] [*French*] (MTD)
CV .... Carte Vierge [*French*] (ADPT)
cv .... Cas Vysazeni [*Airdrop Time*] (CZ)
cv .... Cavalo-Vapor [*Horsepower*] [*Portuguese*]
CV .... Celozavodni Vybor [*All-Factory Committee (of the Communist Party of Czechoslovakia)*] (CZ)
CV .... Centar Veze [*Communications Center*] [*Military*] (YU)
CV .... Centrale Vereniging voor Openbare Bibliotheken [*Later, NBLC*] [*Netherlands*]
CV .... Centralno Vece [*Central Council*] (YU)
cv .... Cette Ville [*This Town*] [*French*]
CV .... Cheval-Vapeur [*Horsepower*] [*French*]
CV .... Christian Voice [*Australia*]
CV .... Chronologische Verzameling [*Luttenberg*] [*Benelux*] (BAS)
cv .... Cista Vaha [*Net Weight*] (CZ)
CV .... Commanditaire Vennootschap [*Limited Partnership*] [*Dutch*] [*Business term*]
cv .... Compte Vieux [*Old Account*] [*French*] [*Business term*]
CV .... Convention pour l'Unification de Certains Regles Relatives au Transport Aerien International [*Varsovie, 1929*] (FLAF)
CV .... Convoi Automobile [*Military*] [*French*] (MTD)
Cv .... Craiova [*Craiova*] (RO)
CV .... Curriculum Vitae [*French*]
CV .... General Dynamics Corp. [*ICAO aircraft manufacturer identifier*] (ICAO)
CV .... Wet op de Cooperatieve Verenigingen; Cooperatieve Vereniging [*Benelux*] (BAS)
CVA .... Air Transport (Chatham Island) Ltd. [*New Zealand*] [*ICAO designator*] (FAAC)
CVA .... Centre for Visual Arts [*University of New England*] [*Australia*]
CVA .... Chinese Volleyball Association (EAIO)
CVA .... Comite de Vigilance et d'Action [*Vigilance and Action Committee*] [*Algeria*] (AF)
CVA .... Commonwealth Veterinary Association [*Later, CWVA*] (WGAO)
CVAA .... Canberra Visitor Attractions Association [*Australia*]
CVAAR ...... Corpo Voluntario Angolano de Assistencia aos Refugiados
CVAD .... Convoi Administratif d'Armee [*Military*] [*French*] (MTD)
CVAG .... Chelmsford Victims Action Trust [*Australia*]
CVAWWII ... Cyprus Veterans Association World War II (EAIO)
CVAX .... Convoi Auxiliaire [*Military*] [*French*] (MTD)
CVB .... Centraal Veevoederbureau in Nederland (WGAO)
CVB .... Centraal Veevoederbureau in Nederland Central Bureau of Livestock Feeding [*Netherlands*] (DSCA)
CVB .... Centralna Vojna Bolnica [*Central Military Hospital*] (YU)
CvBB .... College van Beroep voor het Bedrijfsleven [*Benelux*] (BAS)
CVBC .... Camara Venezolano-Britanica de Comercio y Industria (WGAO)
CVC .... Chemins de Fer Vicinaux du Congo
CVC .... Continental Venture Capital [*Australia*]
CVC .... Cooperative Viviere Camerounaise
CVC .... Corporacion Autonoma Regional del Valle del Cauca [*Autonomous Regional Corporation of the Cauca Valley*] [*Colorado*] (LA)
CVCB .... Canberra Visitor and Convention Bureau [*Australia*]
CVCC .... Christelijke Vakbond van Communicatiemiddelen Cultuur [*Belgium*] (EAIO)
CVCC .... Classic Vehicles Clubs Committee (WGAO)
CV-CFN .... Comision de Valores - Corporacion Financiera Nacional [*Ecuador*] (LAA)
CVCI .... Comptoir de Vente de Cote-D'Ivoire
CV/CPP ..... Current Value/Constant Purchasing Power [*Accounting*]

CVD .... Cercle de la Voile de Dakar
CVD .... Christelijke Vervoerarbeiders en Diamantbewerkers [*Christian Trade Union of Transport and Diamond Workers*] [*Belgium*] (EAIO)
CVD .... Consejo Voluntario Deportivo [*Volunteer Sports Council*] [*Cuba*] (LA)
CVE .... Cape Verde Escudo
C Ver .... Cooperatieve Vereniging [*Benelux*] (BAS)
C VerdIsls ... Cape Verde Islands
CVF .... Corporacion Venezolana de Fomento [*Venezuelan Development Corporation*] (LA)
CVF .... Courchevel [*France*] [*Airport symbol*] (OAG)
CVFA .... Conseil de la Vie Francaise en Amerique (WGAO)
CvG .... Comite van Graanhandelaren te Rotterdam [*Netherlands*] (BAS)
CVG .... Corporacion Venezolana de Guayana [*Venezuelan Corporation of Guayana*] (LA)
CVH .... Aircraft Carrier, Helicopter [*NATO*]
CVHO .... Vereniging van Docenten bij het Christelijk Voorbereidend Wetenschappelijk en Hogen Algemeen Voortgezet Onderwijs (WGAO)
CVI .... Cassovia Air [*Slovakia*] [*ICAO designator*] (FAAC)
CVI .... Centraal Veevoeder Instituut (WGAO)
CVI .... Consejo Venezolano de la Industria [*Venezuela*]
CVI .... Croix Verte Internationale (WGAO)
CVIAA .... Comite des Volontaires Internationales d'Aide et d'Assistance aux Refugies [*Committee of International Women Volunteers for Aid and Relief to Refugees*] [*Cambodia*] (CL)
CVIAA .... Commercial Vehicle Industry Association of Australia (ADA)
CVIAES ..... College of the Virgin Islands Agricultural Experiment Station (ARC)
CVIASA .... Commercial Vehicle Industry Association of South Australia
CVIAV ...... Commercial Vehicle Industry Association of Victoria [*Australia*]
CVJF .... Christlicher Verband Junger Frauen (WGAO)
CVJM .... Christlichen Vereine Junger Manner (WGAO)
CVJM .... Christlicher Verein Junger Maenner [*Young Men's Christian Association - YMCA*] [*German*]
CVJR .... Centre de Voyages de la Jeunesse Rurale (WGAO)
CVK .... Ceske Valcovny Kovu, Narodni Podnik [*Czech Metal Rolling Mills, National Enterprise*] (CZ)
CVK .... Cetnicka Vrhovna Komanda [*Chetnik Supreme Command*] [*World War II*] (YU)
CVKPL ...... Ceta Velkorazních Kulometu Protiletadlovych [*Platoon of Heavy Antiaircraft Machine-Guns*] (CZ)
CVL .... Cape Vogel [*Papua New Guinea*] [*Airport symbol*] (OAG)
CVL .... Comite Vietnam Lycee [*Lycee Vietnam Committee*] [*French*] (WER)
CVL .... Corps of Volunteers for Liberty
CVLB .... Christelijke Veenkoloniale Landbouwbond (WGAO)
CVM .... Ciudad Victoria [*Mexico*] [*Airport symbol*] (OAG)
CVM .... Club du Vieux Manoir [*France*] (EAIO)
CVM .... Comissao de Valores Mobiliarios [*Equity Shares Commission*] [*Portuguese*] (LA)
CVM .... Company of Veteran Motorists [*Later, GEM*] (WGAO)
CVM .... Controlestation voor Melkproducten (WGAO)
CVM .... Corporacion Autonima Regional de los Valles de Magdalena y Sinu [*Colombia*] (WGAO)
CVM .... Corporacion Autonoma de los Valles del Magdalena y del Sinu [*Barranquilla*] (COL)
CVMA .... Commercial Vehicle Manufacturers' Association [*Australia*]
CVMNO ..... Christelijke Centrale van het Personeel uit het Vrij Middelbaar en Normaalonderwijs [*Belgium*] (EAIO)
CVMP .... Committee for Veterinary Medicinal Products [*European Community*]
CVMS .... Centralna Vazduhoplovna Modelarska Skola [*Central Air Force Model School*] (YU)
CVN .... Bromma Flygskola/Cabair [*Sweden*] [*ICAO designator*] (FAAC)
CVN .... Consejo Venezolano del Nino
CVNW ...... Centrale Vereniging van Nederlandse Wijnhandelaren (WGAO)
CVO .... Cislo Vojenske Odbornosti [*Military Occupation Specialty Number*] (CZ)
CVO .... Commander of the Royal Victorian Order [*Australia*] (ADA)
CVOA .... Commanditaire Venootschap op Aandelen [*Benelux*] (BAS)
CVP .... Celorocni Vyrobni Plan [*One Year Production Plan*] (CZ)
CVP .... Christelijke Volkspartij [*Christian Social Party*] [*Also, PSC*] [*Belgium*] [*Political party*] (PPW)
CVP .... Christlichdemokratische Volkspartei der Schweiz [*Christian Democratic Party of Switzerland*] [*Political party*] (PPE)
CVP .... Christliche Volkspartei [*Christian People's Party*] [*Pre-1945 Germany*] [*Political party*] (PPE)
CVP .... Comite Veterinaire Permanent [*CEE*] (WGAO)
CVP .... Commissie Vergunningen Personenvervoer [*Benelux*] (BAS)
CVP .... Conservative Party of Australia [*Political party*]
CVP .... Corporacion Venezolana del Petroleo [*Venezuelan Petroleum Corporation*] (LA)

CVPCEE.... Comite des Ventes Publiques de Cuirs et Peaux Verts des Pays de la CEE (WGAO)
CVQ.......... Carnarvon [*Australia*] [*Airport symbol*] (OAG)
CVR.......... Corps des Volontaires de la Republique
CVRA........ Comites de Volontariat de la Revolution Agraire
CVRD........ Companhia Vale do Rio Doce, SA [*Rio Doce Valley Company*] [*Mining Rio De Janeiro, Brazil*] (LA)
CVRDE...... Combat Vehicle Research and Development Establishment [*India*] (WGAO)
CVRFA ...... Comissao da Vigilancia Revolucionaria das Forcas Armadas [*Armed Forces Revolutionary Vigilance Committee*] [*Portuguese*] (WER)
CVRS........ Centre Voltaique de la Recherche Scientifique
CVRTC..... Commercial Vehicle and Road Transport Club (WGAO)
Cvs .... Cavus [*Sergeant*] (TU)
CVS.......... Cesky Veslarsky Svaz [*Czech Rowing Association*] (CZ)
CVS........... Club de Vulgarisation Scientifique [*French*] (ADPT)
CVS........... Community Volunteer Services Commission of B'nai B'rith International (EAIO)
CVSA........ Chiropraktiese Vereniging van Suid-Afrika [*Chiropractic Association of South Africa*] (EAIO)
CVSF .... Comissao do Vale do Sao Francisco [*Sao Francisco Valley Commission*] [*Brazil*] (LA)
CVSM....... Central-Verband Schweizerishcher Mobeltransporteurs (WGAO)
CVSS .... Council of Voluntary Social Services [*Belize*] (EAIO)
CVSS .... Council of Voluntary Social Services in Jamaica
CVSSJ .... Centralno Vece Saveza Sindikata Jugoslavije [*Central Assembly of the Council of Trade-Unions of Yugoslavia*] (YU)
CVT .... Centrale de Vente Textiles
CVT .... Centrale Vakgroep Tuinbouw van de Belgische Boerenbond (WGAO)
CVT .... Commissioner for Vocational Training [*New South Wales*] [*Australia*]
c/vta .... Cuenta de Venta [*Sales Account*] [*Spanish*] [*Business term*]
CVTC........ Confederation Vietnamienne du Travail Chretien [*Vietnamese Confederation of Christian Labor*] [*South Vietnamese*]
CVTM .... Compagnie Voltaique pour la Transformation des Metaux
CVUT .... Ceske Vysoke Uceni Technicke [*Czech Institute of Technology*] [*Prague*] (CZ)
CVUT .... Ceskoslovensky Vojensky Ustav Technicky [*Czechoslovak Military Institute of Technology*] (CZ)
CVUV .... Ceskoslovensky Vedecky Ustav Vojensky [*Czechoslovak Institute of Military Science*] (CZ)
CVV .... Cesky Vsesportovni Vybor [*Czech Athletic Committee*] (CZ)
CvV .... Commissie van Voorbereiding [*Benelux*] (BAS)
CVV .... Commissie Vervoervergunningen [*Benelux*] (BAS)
CVV .... Cooperatieve Veeafzetvereniging v Noord-en Zuid-Holland (WGAO)
CVV .... Cooperatieve Venlose Veiling Vereniging (WGAO)
CVV .... Curacaosche Verbond van Vakverenigingen [*Netherlands Antilles*] (WGAO)
CVVTMC ... Council of Veteran, Vintage and Thoroughbred Motor Clubs [*Australia*]
CVWW ...... Council of Voluntary Welfare Work (WGAO)
CVX .... Communaute Mondiale de Vie Chretienne [*World Christian Life Community*] [*Italy*] (EAIO)
CVZ .... Ceske Vlnarske Zavody, Narodni Podnik [*Czech Woolen Mills, National Enterprise*] [*Liberec*] (CZ)
CVZ .... Christelijke Vereniging van Ziekenhuizen en Diakonessenhuizen (WGAO)
CVZ .... Societe des Chemins de Fer Vicinaux du Zaire
CW............ Air Marshall Islands [*Airline code*] [*Australia*]
CW............ Codewort (ADPT)
Cw .... Commonwealth
CW............ Coordinatiewet Sociale Verzekering [*Benelux*] (BAS)
CW............ Curtiss-Wright Corp. [*ICAO aircraft manufacturer identifier*] (ICAO)
Cw .... Wet tot Regeling der Cooperatieve Verenigingen [*Benelux*] (BAS)
CWA.......... Chinese Writers Association (EAIO)
CWA.......... Chung Wah Association [*Australia*]
CWA.......... Communications Workers of America (WGAO)
CWA.......... Country Women's Association [*Australia*] (WGAO)
CWA.......... Crime Writers Association (WGAO)
CWAA .... Country Women's Association of Australia
CWAAL..... Chinese Women's Anti-Aggression League [*Taiwan*] (EAIO)
CWAC .... Clean Waters Advisory Committee [*New South Wales*] [*Australia*]
CWAC .... Community Welfare Advisory Council [*New South Wales*] [*Australia*]
CWAI .... Confederation of West Australian Industry (WGAO)
CWAI .... Confederation of Western Australian Industry, Inc. [*Australia*]
CW &PRD ... Children's Welfare and Public Relief Department [*South Australia*]
CWANSW ... Cambodian Women's Association of New South Wales [*Australia*]

CWAS....... Committee of Women in Asian Studies (WGAO)
CWASRO ... Christian Welfare and Social Relief Organization [*Sierra Leone*] (EAIO)
CWAT .... Community Welfare Appeals Tribunal [*New South Wales, Australia*]
CWB.......... Curitiba [*Brazil*] [*Airport symbol*] (OAG)
CWC.......... Canberra Workers' Club [*Australia*]
CWC.......... Catering Wages Commission (WGAO)
CWC.......... Ceylon Workers' Congress [*Sri Lanka*]
CWC.......... Cuban Women's Club (EA)
CWCA ...... Commission for World Christian Action
CWCC .... Childrens World Community Chest (WGAO)
CWCV ...... Catholic Walking Club of Victoria [*Australia*]
CWD.......... Centrala Wydawnicza Drukow [*Central Publishing Office*] (POL)
CWDE .... Centre for World Development Education (WGAO)
CWDS ...... Centre for Women's Development Studies [*India*] (EAIO)
CWE.......... Centralne Warsztaty Elektryczne [*Central Electrical Workshops*] (POL)
CWE.......... China International Water & Electric Corp. (TCC)
CWE.......... Cooperative Wholesale Establishment [*Sri Lanka*] (WGAO)
CWEP....... Commonwealth Work Experience Program [*Australia*]
CWF.......... Career Women's Forum (EAIO)
CWF.......... Centrala Wynajmu Filmow [*Central Rental Office for Films*] (POL)
CWF.......... Christian Workers Fellowship [*Sri Lanka*] (EAIO)
CWF.......... Commonwealth Weightlifting Federation (WGAO)
CWF.......... Construction Workers Federation [*San Marino*] (EAIO)
CWG.......... Cooperative Women's Guild (WGAO)
CWGC....... Commonwealth War Graves Commission (WGAO)
CWHS ...... Centre for Women's Health Studies [*Cumberland College of Health Sciences*] [*Australia*]
CWI .... Centrum voor Wiskunde en Informatica [*Center for Mathematics and Computer Science*] [*Research center*] [*Netherlands*] (IRC)
CWI .... Christian Witness International [*British*]
CWI .... Clean World International [*Brighton, East Sussex, England*] (EAIO)
CWID .... Coalition of Women for International Development (WGAO)
CWINC ..... Central Waterways Irrigation and Navigation Commission [*India*] (WGAO)
CWINRS ... Central Waterpower Irrigation and Navigation Research Station [*India*] (WGAO)
CWISz .... Centrum Wyszkolenia Instruktorow Szybowcowych [*Center for Training Glider Instructors*] (POL)
CWIU .... Chemical Workers' Industries Union [*South Africa*]
CWK.......... Centralne Warsztaty Koksochemiczne [*Central Coke Chemical Plants*] (POL)
CWKS....... Centralny Wojskowy Klub Sportowy [*Central Military Sport Club*] (POL)
CWL .... Catholic Women's League (WGAO)
CWL .... Centrala Wyszkolenia Lotniczego [*Aeronautical Training Center*] (POL)
cwl .... Ciezar Wlasciwy [*Specific Weight*] [*Poland*]
CWLA .... Catholic Women's League, Australia
CWLA .... Catholic Women's League of Australia [*An association*]
CWLS .... Central Western Law Society [*Australia*]
CWM........ Caribbean Workers Movement (WGAO)
CWM........ Christian Women's Movement [*Bulgaria*] [*Political party*]
CWM........ Contactgroep van Werkgevers in de Mataalindustrie (WGAO)
CWM........ Council for World Mission [*Australia*]
CWMA ..... Country Wool Merchants Association (WGAO)
CWME ...... Commission on World Mission and Evangelism (EAIO)
CWN........ Clausen World News [*Danish television program*]
CWO........ Ceylonese Welfare Organisation [*Australia*]
CWOI........ Council of Women's Organizations in Israel (EAIO)
CWOIH..... Conference of World Organisations Interested in the Handicapped [*Later, ICOD*] (WGAO)
CWP .... Centrum Wyszkolenia Piechoty [*Infantry Training Center*] (POL)
CWP .... Christian Workers Party [*Malta*] [*Political party*] (PPE)
CWP .... Committee of Women for Progress [*Jamaica*] (LA)
CWP .... Coordinating Working Party on Atlantic Fishery Statistics [*Food and Agriculture Organization*] [*United Nations (already exists in GUS II database)*] (ASF)
CWPC........ Central Water and Power Commission [*India*] (WGAO)
CWPR........ Centre for Water Policy Research [*University of New England*] [*Australia*]
CWPRS ..... Central Water and Power Research Station [*Council of Scientific and Industrial Research*] [*India*] (ERC)
CWPU .... Central Water Planning Unit [*DOE*]
CWR .... Conference of Women Religious [*Papua New Guinea*] (WGAO)
CWR .... Crusade for World Revival (WGAO)
CWRL....... Camberwell-Waverley Regional Library [*Australia*]
CWRL........ Citrus Wastage Research Laboratory [*Australia*] (DSCA)

CWS .... Air Swazi Cargo (Pty) Ltd. [*Swaziland*] [*ICAO designator*] (FAAC)
CWS .... Centralne Warsztaty Samochodowe [*Central Automotive Shops*] (POL)
CWS .... Central Western Slopes [*Australia*]
CWS .... Centre for Women's Studies [*Australia*]
CWS .... Centrum Wyszkolenia Sanitarnego [*Medical (Military) Training Center*] (POL)
CWS .... Chilean Wildlife Society (EAIO)
CWS .... Chung Wah Society [*Northern Territory*] [*Australia*]
CWS .... Church World Service
CWS .... Coast and Wetlands Society [*New South Wales*] [*Australia*]
CWS .... Cooperative Wholesale Society (WGAO)
CWSA .... Contract Work Study Association (WGAO)
CWSDSC .. Citizens Welfare Service, Drummond Street Centre [*Australia*]
CWSV .... Citizens Welfare Service of Victoria [*Australia*]
CWT .... Cowra [*Australia*] [*Airport symbol*] (OAG)
cwt .... Hundredweight (EECI)
CWTC .... Community Welfare Training Council [*Australia*]
CWTG .... Computer World Trade Group (WGAO)
CWU .... Christian Workers' Union [*Belize*]
CWU .... Christliche Waehlerunion Bayern [*Christian Voters' Union of Bavaria*] [*Germany*] [*Political party*] (PPW)
CWU .... Communications Workers Union [*Trinidadian and Tobagan*] (LA)
CWU .... Wuhan Airlines [*China*] [*ICAO designator*] (FAAC)
CWUA ...... Confectionery Workers' Union of Australia
CWVA ...... Commonwealth Veterinary Association (WGAO)
CWWA ...... Capricornia Wildlife Welfare Association [*Australia*]
CWWA ...... Coloured Workers Welfare Association
CWWIA ..... Cyprus Wood-Working Industry Association (EAIO)
Cx .... Caixa [*Chest, Case, Trunk*] [*Portuguese*]
CX .... Christmas Island [*ANSI two-letter standard code*] (CNC)
Cx .... Contentieux [*French*] (FLAF)
CXA .... Caicara [*Venezuela*] [*Airport symbol*] (OAG)
CXA .... Xiamen Airlines [*China*] [*ICAO designator*] (FAAC)
CXB .... Cox's Bazar [*Bangladesh*] [*Airport symbol*] (OAG)
CXC .... Caribbean Examinations Council [*St. Michael, Barbados*] (EAIO)
CXI .... Christmas Island [*Kiribati*] [*Airport symbol*] (OAG)
CXN .... China Southwest Airlines [*ICAO designator*] (FAAC)
CXP .... Cilicap [*Indonesia*] [*Airport symbol*] (OAG)
CXR .... Christmas Island [*ANSI three-letter standard code*] (CNC)
CXT .... Charters Towers [*Australia*] [*Airport symbol*] (OAG)
CXT .... Coastal Air Transport [*St. Croix*] [*ICAO designator*] (FAAC)
CXY .... Cat Cay [*Bahamas*] [*Airport symbol*] (OAG)
CY .... Chuan Yung Industrial Co. Ltd. [*Taiwan*]
CY .... Chun-ying [*Leung*] [*Hong Kong politician*]
Cy .... Cyanide Group [*Used in old German chemical formulas in place of CN in cyanogen compounds*] (GCA)
CY .... Cypr [*Cyprus*] [*Poland*]
CY .... Cyprus [*ANSI two-letter standard code*] (CNC)
CYA .... Catholic Youth Association [*Lithuania*] (EAIO)
CYA .... Ceska Yachetni Asociace [*Czech Yacht Association*] (CZ)
CYA .... Concretos y Agregados Ltda. (COL)
CYAC .... Commonwealth Youth Affairs Council (WGAO)
CYAMEX ... Cyana-Mexique (MSC)
Cyanier ...... Cyanierung [*Cyanization*] [*German*] (GCA)
CYAP .... Constrained Youth Allowances Package [*Australia*]
cyat............ Cyathus [*Glassful*] [*Pharmacy*]
CYATCA ... Cyprus Air Traffic Controllers Association (WGAO)
CYB .... Cayman Brac [*West Indies*] [*Airport symbol*] (OAG)
CyBC.......... Cyprus Broadcasting Corp. (WGAO)
CYC .... Catholic Youth Council [*Belgium*] (EAIO)
CYC .... Central Youth Club [*Mauritius*] (AF)
CYC .... Community Youth Centre [*Australia*]
CYC .... Cypair Tours Ltd. [*Cyprus*] [*ICAO designator*] (FAAC)
CYCA .... Cruising Yacht Club of Australia (ADA)
Cyclisier..... Cyclisierung [*Cyclization*] [*German*] (GCA)
CYCLOTCHAD ... Industrie Tchadienne du Cycle et du Motocycle
CYDA .... Confederation of Yemen Development Associations (ME)
CYEC........ Commonwealth Youth Exchange Council (WGAO)
CYFA........ Church Youth Fellowships Association (WGAO)
CYH .... Yunnan Airlines [*China*] [*ICAO designator*] (FAAC)
CYHONC ... Committee of Youth Hostel Organizations in the Nordic Countries (EA)
CYI .... Chiayi [*Taiwan*] [*Airport symbol*] (OAG)
CYK .... Cowethas an Yeth Kernewek [*Cornish Language Society*]
CYL........... Cameroon's Youth League
CYL........... Communist Youth League (WGAO)
CYL........... Congress Youth League
CYM .... Cayman Islands [*ANSI three-letter standard code*] (CNC)
CYM .... Commonwealth Youth Movement (WGAO)
CYM .... Compass Airlines of Australia [*ICAO designator*] (FAAC)
CYMS........ Catholic Young Men's Society (WGAO)
CYN .... Zhongyuan Aviation Co. [*China*] [*ICAO designator*] (FAAC)

CyNA........ Cyprus Nurses Association (WGAO)
CyNS .... Cyprus Numismatic Society (WGAO)
CYO........... Catholic Youth Organization
CYO........... Committee for Youth Organisation
CYOS........ Canberra Youth Orchestra Society [*Australia*]
CYP............ Calbayog [*Philippines*] [*Airport symbol*] (OAG)
CYP............ Commonwealth Youth Programme [*British*]
CYP............ Cyprus [*ANSI three-letter standard code*] (CNC)
CYP............ Cyprus Airways Ltd. [*ICAO designator*] (FAAC)
Cypfruvex .. Kibris Sebze, Meyve Isletmeleri Ltd. [*Cyprus Vegetable and Fruit Processing and Exporting Corp. Ltd.*] (TU)
CYR .... Colonia [*Uruguay*] [*Airport symbol*] (OAG)
CYRA .... Commission's Yellowfin Regulatory Area [*Inter-American Tropical Tuna Commission*] (MSC)
CYRK........ Cape York [*Botanical region*] [*Australia*]
CYS........... Catholic Youth Services (WGAO)
CYS........... Chief Yeoman of Signals [*Australia*]
CYSA........ Cape York Space Agency [*Australia*]
CYSA........ Community Youth Services Association (WGAO)
CYSD........ Center for Youth and Social Development [*India*] (EAIO)
CYSP .... Community Youth Special Projects [*Australia*]
CYSS .... Children's and Youth Services Section [*Australian Library*]
cyt............... Cytat [*or Cytowany*] [*Quotation or Quoted*] [*Poland*]
CYTA........ Christian Youth Travel Association [*Australia*]
CYTA........ Cyprus Telecommunications Authority [*See also ATK*] [*Telecommunications service*] (GC)
CYUK .... Ceza Yargilamalari Usulu Kanunu [*Criminal Suits Procedural Law*] [*CYUY*] [*See also*] (TU)
CYUY .... Ceza Yargilamalari Usulu Yasasi [*Criminal Trials Procedural Law*] [*CYUK*] [*See also*] (TU)
CYWU .... Community Youth Workers Union (WGAO)
CYZ .... Cauayan [*Philippines*] [*Airport symbol*] (OAG)
CZ .... Cankarjeva Zalozba [*Cankar Publishing House*] [*Ljubljana*]
CZ .... Catanzaro [*Car registration plates*] [*Italy*]
CZ .... Centrala Zbytu [*Sales Center*] (POL)
CZ .... Centralny Zarzad [*Central Administration*] (POL)
CZ .... Centralny Zwiazek [*Central Union*] [*Poland*]
CZ .... Centro de Zoologia [*Portugal*] (DSCA)
CZ .... Cervena Zastava [*Red Flag*] (YU)
CZ .... Ceskoslovenska Zbrojovka, Narodni Podnik [*Czechoslovak Munitions Plants, National Enterprise*] (CZ)
CZ .... Civilna Zastita [*Civilian Defense*] (YU)
CZ .... Conservation Zone [*Australia*]
CZ .... Corps Zeni [*Corps of Engineers*] (IN)
CZ .... Crvena Zastava [*Red Flag*] (YU)
cz .... Czasopismo [*Magazine*] [*Poland*]
cz .... Czesc [*Part*] (POL)
cz .... Czyli [*That Is*] [*Poland*]
Cz .... "Czytelnik" Spoldzielnia Wydawniczo-Oswiatowa [*"Czytelnik" (The Reader)*] [*Cooperative Educational Publishing House*] (POL)
CZA .... Centralny Zarzad Aptek [*Central Administration of Pharmacies*] (POL)
CZA .... Ceskoslovensky Zemedelsky Archiv [*Czechoslovak Agricultural Archives*] (CZ)
CZA .... Chichen Itza [*Mexico*] [*Airport symbol*] (OAG)
CZAF........ Czechoslovakian Air Force
CZAL........ Ceskoslovenske Zavody Avia (Letnany) [*Czechoslovak Avia Aircraft Plant*] (CZ)
CZAT........ Centrala Zbytu Artykulow Technicznych [*Technical Goods Sales Center*] (POL)
CZA WP.... Centralny Zespol Artystyczny Wojska Polskiego [*Central Art Team, Polish Army*] (POL)
CZB .... Centralny Zarzad Bibliotek [*Central Administration of Libraries*] (POL)
CZB .... Clubul Ziaristilor din Bucuresti [*Bucharest Newspapermen's Club*] (RO)
CZB .... Cruz Alta [*Brazil*] [*Airport symbol*] (OAG)
CZBDiM ... Centralny Zarzad Budowy Drog i Mostow [*Central Administration of Road and Bridge Construction*] (POL)
CZBL......... Centralny Zarzad Budownictwa Lacznosci [*Central Administration of Communication Construction*] (POL)
CZBM........ Centralny Zarzad Budownictwa Miejskiego [*Central Administration of Urban Construction*] (POL)
CZBM........ Centralny Zarzad Budownictwa Mieszkaniowego [*Central Administration of Residential Construction*] (POL)
CZBM........ Centralny Zarzad Budynkow Mieszkalnych [*Central Administration of Residential Buildings*] (POL)
CZBMC..... Centralny Zarzad Budowy Maszyn Ciezkich [*Central Administration of Heavy Machinery Construction*] (POL)
CZBME..... Centralny Zarzad Budowy Maszyn Elektrycznych [*Central Administration of Electric Machine Building*] (POL)
CZBMG..... Centralny Zarzad Budowy Maszyn Gorniczych [*Central Administration of Mining Machinery Construction*] (POL)

CZBMiO ... Centralny Zarzad Budowy Miast i Osiedli [*Central Administration of City and Settlement Construction*] (POL)

CZBP .... Centralny Zarzad Budownictwa Przemyslowego [*Central Administration of Industrial Construction*] (POL)

CZBPBM .. Centralny Zarzad Biur Projektowych Budownictwa Miejskiego [*Central Administration of Offices of Plans in Municipal Construction*] (POL)

CZBWI ...... Centralny Zarzad Budownictwa Wodno-Inzynieryjnego [*Central Administration of Hydraulic Engineering Construction*] (POL)

CZC .... Centrale Zuivelcommissie (WGAO)

CZC .... Centralny Zarzad Cel (Ministerstwa Handlu Zagranicznego) [*Central Customs Administration (Ministry of Foreign Trade)*] (POL)

CZCB .... Centralny Zarzad Ceramiki Budowlanej [*Central Administration of Building Tiles*] (POL)

CZCC .... Centralny Zarzad Ceramiki Czerwonej [*Central Administration of Red Ceramics*] (POL)

CZCE .... Centre Zairois du Commerce Exterieur [*Zairian Foreign Trade Center*]

CZD .... Centralny Zarzad Dyspozytorski [*Central Managerial Administration*] (POL)

CZD .... Centrum Zdrowia Dziecka [*Children's Health Center*] (POL)

CZD .... Ceskoslovenske Zavody na Zpracovani Dreva, Narodni Podnik [*Czechoslovak Lumber Industries, National Enterprise*] (CZ)

CZDP .... Centralny Zarzad Drog Publicznych [*Central Administration of Public Roads*] (POL)

CZDWS ..... Centralny Zarzad Drog Wodnych Srodladowych [*Central Administration of Inland Waterways*] (POL)

CZE .... Centralny Zarzad Energetyki [*Central Power Administration*] (POL)

CZE .... Ceskoslovenske Zavody Energeticke [*Czechoslovak Power Plants*] (CZ)

CZE .... Coro [*Venezuela*] [*Airport symbol*] (OAG)

CZER .... Centralny Zarzad Elektryfikacji Rolnictwa [*Central Administration of Rural Electrification*] (POL)

CZF .... Canal Zone Forces [*Egypt*]

CZGM ...... Centralny Zarzad Gospodarki Maszynami [*Central Administration of the Allocation of Machinery*] (POL)

CZGP .... Ceskoslovenske Zavody Gumarenske a Plastikarske [*Czechoslovak Rubber and Plastics Works*] (CZ)

CZGZ .... Centralny Zarzad Gospodarki Zlomem [*Central Administration of the Utilization of Scrap Metal*] (POL)

CZH .... Centralny Zarzad Handlu [*Central Trade Administration*] (POL)

CZH .... Corozal [*Belize*] [*Airport symbol*] (OAG)

CZHAGD .. Centralny Zarzad Hurtu Artykulow Gospodarstwa Domowego [*Central Administration of Wholesale Trade in Household Goods*] (POL)

CZHAKid .. Centralny Zarzad Handlu Artykulami Kolonialnymi i Delikatesami [*Central Administration of the Grocery and Delicatessen Trade*] (POL)

CZHG .... Centralny Zarzad Handlu Galanteryjnego [*Central Administration of the Haberdashery Trade*] (POL)

CZHG .... Centralny Zarzad Hurtu Galanteryjnego [*Central Administration of the Haberdashery Wholesale Trade*] (POL)

CZHiPJ ..... Centralny Zarzad Handlu i Przemyslu Jubilerskiego [*Central Administration of the Jewelry Trade and Industry*] (POL)

CZHM .... Centralny Zarzad Handlu Miesem [*Central Administration of the Meat Trade*] (POL)

CZHOiMB ... Centralny Zarzad Handlu Opalem i Materialami Budowlanymi [*Central Administration of the Fuel and Building Materials Trade*] (POL)

CZHOiW ... Centralny Zarzad Handlu Owocami i Warzywami [*Central Administration of the Fruit and Vegetable Trade*] (POL)

CZHOW .... Centralny Zarzad Hurtu Owocarsko-Warzywnego [*Central Administration of the Fruit and Vegetable Wholesale Trade*] (POL)

CZHS .... Centralny Zarzad Hurtu Spozywczego [*Central Administration of the Wholesale Food Trade*] (POL)

CZHU .... Centralny Zarzad Handlu w Uzdrowiskach [*Central Administration of Trade in Health Resorts*] (POL)

CZHwU ..... Centralny Zarzad Handlu w Uzdrowiskach [*Central Administration of Trade in Health Resorts*] (POL)

CZI .... Confederation of Zimbabwe Industries

CZIP .... Centralny Zarzad Instalacji Przemyslowych [*Central Administration of Industrial Installations*] (POL)

CZISP .... Centralny Zarzad Instytucji Sztuk Plastycznych [*Central Administration of Institutions of Plastic Arts*] (POL)

CZIUS .... Centrala Zaopatrywania Instytucji Ubezpieczen Spolecznych [*Central Supply Office for Social Security Institutions*] (POL)

CZJ .... Corazon De Jesus [*Panama*] [*Airport symbol*] (OAG)

CZJD .... Centralny Zarzad Jajczarsko-Drobiarski [*Central Eggs and Poultry Administration*] (POL)

CZK .... Centralny Zarzad Kinematografii [*Central Administration of Motion Pictures*] (POL)

CZK .... Centralny Zarzad Ksiegarstwa [*Central Administration of Bookselling*] (POL)

CZKG .... Ceskoslovenske Zavody Kovodelne a Gumarenske, Narodni Podnik [*Czechoslovak Leather and Rubber Plants, National Enterprise*] (CZ)

CZKHP ...... Centralna Zydowska Komisja Historyczna w Polsce [*Central Jewish Historical Commission in Poland*] (POL)

CZKiKD .... Centralny Zarzad Kamieniolomow i Klinkierni Drogowych [*Central Administration of Quarries and Road Gravel*] (POL)

CZKR .... Centralny Zwiazek Kolek Rolniczych [*Central Union of Agricultural Cooperatives*] [*Poland*]

CZKRZ ...... Centralny Zarzad Kopalnictwa Rud Zelaznych [*Central Administration of Iron Ore Mining*] (POL)

CZKS .... Centralny Zarzad Konstrukcji Stalowych [*Central Administration of Steel Construction Designing*] (POL)

CZKS .... Ceskoslovenske Zavody Kovodelne a Strojirenske, Narodni Podnik [*Czechoslovak Metalworking and Machine Building Plants, National Enterprise*] (CZ)

CZKZP ...... Centralny Zarzad Kolejowych Zakladow Produkcyjnych [*Central Administration of Railway Equipment Plants*] (POL)

CZL .... Constantine [*Algeria*] [*Airport symbol*] (OAG)

CZL .... Controlestation voor Zuivelproducten (WGAO)

CZLK .... Ceskoslovenske Zavody Lehkeho Kovoprumyslu [*Czechoslovak (Light) Metal Industry Plants*] (CZ)

CZLMiK .... Centralny Zarzad Linii Miedzymiastowych i Kabli [*Central Administration of Inter-Urban and Cable Lines*] (POL)

CZLP .... Centralny Zarzad Lasow Panstwowych [*Central Administration of State Forests*] (POL)

CZM .... Centrala Zaopatrzenia Materialowego [*Central Material Supply Office*] (POL)

CZM .... Centralny Zarzad Muzeow [*Central Administration of Museums*] (POL)

CZM .... Ceske Zavody Motocyklove [*Czech Motorcycle Works*] (CZ)

CZM .... Cozumel [*Mexico*] [*Airport symbol*] (OAG)

CZMHD .... Centralny Zarzad Miejskiego Handlu Detalicznego [*Central Administration of the Municipal Retail Trade*] (POL)

CZMHM ... Centralny Zarzad Miejskiego Handlu Miesem [*Central Administration of the Municipal Meat Trade*] (POL)

CZMN ...... Centralny Zarzad Metali Niezelaznych [*Central Administration of Non-Ferrous Metals*] (POL)

CZMO .... Czestochowskie Zaklady Materialow Ogniotrwalych [*Czestochowa Fireproof Material Plants*] (POL)

CZMP .... Centralny Zarzad Mechaniki Precyzyjnej [*Central Administration of Precision Instruments*] (POL)

CZMPW .... Centrala Zaopatrzenia Materialowego Przemyslu Weglowego [*Central Material Supply Office of the Coal Industry*] (POL)

CZMPW .... Centrala Zaopatrzenia Materialowego Przemyslu Wlokienniczego [*Central Material Supply Office of the Textile Industry*] (POL)

CZMUE .... Centralny Zarzad Montazu Urzadzen Elektrycznych [*Central Administration of Assembly of Electrical Equipment*] (POL)

CZOBM .... Centralny Zarzad Ogolnego Budownictwa Maszynowego [*Central Administration of the General Machine Construction Industry*] (POL)

CZOFIM ... Centralny Zarzad Oper, Filharmonii, i Instytucji Muzycznych [*Central Administraion of Opera Houses, Philharmonic Orchestras, and Musical Institutions*] (POL)

CZOOW .... Centralny Zarzad Obrotu Owocami i Warzywami [*Central Administration of Fruit and Vegetable Sales*] (POL)

CZOZ .... Cooperative Zuid- Nederlandse Organisatie van Zuivelvervaardigers (WGAO)

CZOZ Rz ... Centralny Zarzad Obrotu Zwierzetami Rzeznymi [*Center Sales Agency for Slaughter Animals*] (POL)

CZP .... Centrala Zaopatrywania Przemyslu [*Industry Supply Center*] (POL)

CZP .... Centralny Zarzad Poczty (Ministerstwa Lacznosci) [*Central Post Office Administration (of the Ministry of Communication)*] (POL)

CZP .... Centralny Zarzad Przemyslu [*Central Administration of the Industry*] (POL)

CzP .... Statni Knihovna Ceske Socialisticke Republiky [*State Library of the Czech S ocialist Republic*], Klementinum, Czechoslovakia [*Library symbol*] [*Library of Congress*] (LCLS)

CZPA .... Comisia de Zonare a Produselor Agricole (WGAO)

CZPAE ...... Centralny Zarzad Przemyslu Artykulow Elektrotechnicznych [*Central Administration of the Electric Equipment Industry*] (POL)

CZPB .... Centralny Zarzad Przemyslu Bawelnianego [*Central Administration of the Cotton Industry*] (POL)

CZPC .... Centralny Zarzad Przemyslu Ceramicznego [*Central Administration of the Ceramics Industry*] (POL)

CZPC......... Centralny Zarzad Przemyslu Cukrowniczego [*Central Administration of the Sugar Industry*] (POL)

CZPC......... Ceskoslovenske Zavody na Papir a Celulosu, Narodni Podnik [*Czechoslovak Paper and Cellulose Factories, National Enterprise*] (CZ)

CZPCh...... Centrala Zbytu Przemyslu Chemicznego [*Chemical Industry Sales Center*] (POL)

CZPCh...... Centralny Zarzad Przemyslu Chemicznego [*Central Administration of the Chemical Industry*] (POL)

CZPD........ Centralny Zarzad Przemyslu Drzewnego [*Central Administration of the Lumber Industry*] (POL)

CZPDT...... Centralny Zarzad Powszechnych Domow Towarowych [*Central Administration of Department Stores*] (POL)

CZPEl........ Centralny Zarzad Przemyslu Elektrotechnicznego [*Central Administration of the Electric Industry*] (POL)

CZPF........ Centralny Zarzad Przemyslu Farmaceutycznego [*Central Administration of the Pharmaceutical Industry*] (POL)

CZPG........ Centralny Zarzad Przemyslu Garbarskiego [*Central Administration of the Tanning Industry*] (POL)

CZPG........ Centralny Zarzad Przemyslu Gastronomicznego [*Central Administration of the Restaurant Industry*] (POL)

CZPG........ Centralny Zarzad Przemyslu Gorniczego [*Central Administration of the Mining Industry*] (POL)

CZPGG...... Centralny Zarzad Przemyslu Guzikarsko-Galanteryjnego [*Central Administration of the Haberdashery Goods Industry*] (POL)

CZPGR...... Centralny Zarzad Panstwowych Gospodarstw Rolnych [*Central Administration of State Farms*] (POL)

CZPH........ Centralny Zarzad Przemyslu Hutniczego [*Central Administration of the Metallurgical Industry*] (POL)

CZPiUK..... Centralny Zarzad Przedsiebiorstw i Urzadzen Komunalnych [*Central Administration of Communal Enterprises and Establishments*] (POL)

CZPJD...... Centralny Zarzad Przemyslu Jajczarsko-Drobiarskiego [*Central Administration of the Egg and Poultry Industry*] (POL)

CZPK........ Centralny Zarzad Przemyslu Kablowego [*Central Administration of the Cable Industry*] (POL)

CZPK........ Centralny Zarzad Przemyslu Kosmetycznego [*Central Administration of the Cosmetics Industry*] (POL)

CZPKons... Centralny Zarzad Przemyslu Konserwowego [*Central Administration of the Canning Industry*] (POL)

CZPKS...... Centralny Zarzad Panstwowej Komunikacji Samochodowej [*Central Administration of State Motor Transport*] (POL)

CZPL........ Centralny Zarzad Przemyslu Lesnego [*Central Administration of Forestry*] (POL)

CZPM........ Centralny Zarzad Przemyslu Meblarskiego [*Central Administration of the Furniture Industry*] (POL)

CZPM........ Centralny Zarzad Przemyslu Metalowego [*Central Administration of the Metal Industry*] (POL)

CZPM........ Centralny Zarzad Przemyslu Miesnego [*Central Administration of the Meat Industry*] (POL)

CZPM........ Centralny Zarzad Przemyslu Mleczarskiego [*Central Administration of the Dairy Industry*] (POL)

CZPME..... Centralny Zarzad Przemyslu Maszyn Elektrycznych [*Central Administration of the Electric Machinery Industry*] (POL)

CZPMH.... Centralny Zarzad Polskiej Marynarki Handlowej [*Central Administration of the Polish Merchant Marine*] (POL)

CZPMH.... Centralny Zarzad Przewozow Morskich Handlowych [*Central Administration of Maritime Trade Transportation*] (POL)

CZP Mies.. Centralny Zarzad Przemyslu Miesnego [*Central Administration of the Meat Industry*] (POL)

CZPMlecz... Centralny Zarzad Przemyslu Mleczarskiego [*Central Administration of the Dairy Industry*] (POL)

CZPMlyn... Centralny Zarzad Przemyslu Mlynarskiego [*Central Administration of the Flour Industry*] (POL)

CZP Mot.... Centralny Zarzad Przemyslu Motoryzacyjnego [*Central Administration of the Automotive Industry*] (POL)

CZPMR..... Centralny Zarzad Przemyslu Maszyn Rolniczych [*Central Administration of the Agricultural Machine Industry*] (POL)

CZPN........ Centralny Zarzad Przemyslu Naftowego [*Central Administration of the Petroleum Industry*] (POL)

CZPO........ Centralny Zarzad Przemyslu Odziezowego [*Central Administration of the Clothing Industry*] (POL)

CZPO........ Centralny Zarzad Przemyslu Okretowego [*Central Administration of the Shipbuilding Industry*] (POL)

CZPOM.... Centralny Zarzad Panstwowych Osrodkow Maszynowych [*Central Administration of State Agricultural Machine Stations*] (POL)

CZPOW..... Centralny Zarzad Przemyslu Owocowo-Warzywnego [*Central Administration of the Fruit and Vegetable Industry*] (POL)

CZPOZiR... Centralny Zarzad Przetworstwa Odpadkow Zwierzecych i Roslinnych [*Central Administration of the Utilization of Animal and Vegetable By-Products*] (POL)

CZPP........ Centralny Zarzad Produkcji Pomocniczej [*Central Administration of Auxiliary Industry*] (POL)

CZPP......... Centralny Zarzad Produktow Przemyslu [*Central Administration of Industry Products*] (POL)

CZPP......... Centralny Zarzad Przemyslu Papierniczego [*Central Administration of the Paper Industry*] (POL)

CZPPB...... Centralny Zarzad Panstwowych Przedsiebiorstw Budowlanych [*Central Administration of State Construction Enterprises*] (POL)

CZPPP...... Centralny Zarzad Przemyslu Paliw Plynnych [*Central Administration of the Liquid Fuel Industry*] (POL)

CZPPW.... Centrala Zbytu Produktow Przemyslu Weglowego [*Sales Center for the Coal Industry*] (POL)

CZPR........ Centralny Zarzad Przemyslu Rolnego [*Central Administration of the Agricultural Industry*] (POL)

CZPR........ Centralny Zarzad Przemyslu Roszarniczego [*Central Administration of the Flax Industry*] (POL)

CZPR........ Centralny Zarzad Przemyslu Rybnego [*Central Administration of the Fish Industry*] (POL)

CZPRK...... Centralny Zarzad Przedsiebiorstw Robot Komunikacyjnych [*Central Administration of Transportation Work Enterprises*] (POL)

CZPS........ Centrala Zbytu Przemyslu Skorzanego [*Leather Industry Sales Center*] (POL)

CZPS........ Ceskoslovenske Zavody Presneho Strojirenstvi [*Czechoslovak Precision Machinery Factories*] (CZ)

CZPSp....... Centralny Zarzad Przemyslu Spozywczego [*Central Administration of the Food Industry*] (POL)

CZPSS....... Centralny Zarzad Przemyslu Stali Specjalnej [*Central Administration of the Special Steel Industry*] (POL)

CZPT........ Centralny Zarzad Przemyslu Teletechnicznego [*Central Administration of the Communications Supply Industry*] (POL)

CZPT........ Centralny Zarzad Przemyslu Tytoniowego [*Central Administration of the Tobacco Industry*] (POL)

CZPUK...... Centralny Zarzad Przedsiebiorstw i Urzadzen Komunalnych [*Central Administration of Communal Enterprises and Establishments*] (POL)

CZPUOrbis ... Centralny Zarzad Przedsiebiorstw Uslugowych "Orbis" [*Central Administration of the "Orbis" Travel Service Enterprises*] (POL)

CZPW........ Centralny Zarzad Przemyslu Weglowego [*Central Administration of the Coal Industry*] (POL)

CZPW........ Centralny Zarzad Przemyslu Welnianego [*Central Administration of the Wool Industry*] (POL)

CZPW........ Czestochowskie Zaklady Przemyslu Welnianego [*Czestochowa Wool Plant*] (POL)

CZPWB..... Centralny Zarzad Przemyslu Wyrobow Blaszanych [*Central Administration of the Tin Products Industry*] (POL)

CZPWlLykowych ... Centralny Zarzad Przemyslu Wlokien Lykowych [*Central Administration of the Bast Fiber Industry*] (POL)

CZPWM.... Centralny Zarzad Przemyslu Wyrobow Metalowych [*Central Administration of the Metal Products Industry*] (POL)

CZPWP..... Centralny Zarzad Przemyslu Wyrobow Precyzyjnych [*Central Administration of the Precision Instrument Industry*] (POL)

CZR.......... Centrala Zaopatrzenia Rolnictwa [*Agriculture Supply Center*] (POL)

CZR.......... Centralny Zarzad Rybactwa [*Central Administration of Fisheries*] (POL)

CZR.......... Central Zambia Railways

CZRK........ Centralny Zarzad Radiofonizacji Kraju [*Central Administration of Country-Wide Radio Installation*] (POL)

CZRM........ Centralny Zarzad Rybolowstwa Morskiego [*Central Administration of Deep Sea Fisheries*] (POL)

CZRMB..... Centralny Zarzad Remontow Maszyn Budowlanych [*Central Administration of Building Machinery Repairs*] (POL)

CZS........... Centrala Zaopatrzenia Szkol [*School Supply Center*] (POL)

CZS........... Centrala Zwalczania Szkodnikow [*Center for Control of Agricultural Pests*] (POL)

CZS........... Centrala Zwiazkow Spoldzielni [*Central Office of Cooperative Unions*] (POL)

CZS........... Centralny Zwiazek Spoldzielni [*Central Union of Cooperatives*] (POL)

CZS........... Ceskoslovenske Zavody Sklarske [*Czechoslovak Glass Factories*] (CZ)

CZS........... Cruzeiro Do Sul [*Brazil*] [*Airport symbol*] (OAG)

CZSA......... Centralny Zarzad Szkolnictwa Artystycznego [*Central Administration of Art Education*] (POL)

CZSBM...... Centralny Zwiazek Spoldzielni Budownictwa Mieszkaniowego [*Central Housing Construction Cooperative Union*] (POL)

CZSBM..... Central Union of Housing Cooperatives [*Poland*] (EAIO)

CZSK........ Centralny Zarzad Szkolenia Kadr [*Central Administration of Personnel Training*] (POL)

CZ-SLOV.. Czechoslovakia

CZSP......... Centralny Zwiazek Spoldzielczosci Pracy (WGAO)

CZSP......... Centralny Zwiazek Spoldzielni Pracy [*Central Union of Labor Cooperatives*] (POL)

CZSPB....... Centralny Zarzad Spolecznych Przedsiebiorstw Budowlanych [*Central Administration of Local Construction Enterprises*] (POL)

CZSPB....... Centralny Zarzad Stolecznego Przedsiebiorstwa Budowlanego [*Central Administration of the Warsaw Construction Enterprise*] (POL)

CZSS .... Centralny Zarzad Sprzetu Samochodowego [*Central Administration of Automobile Equipment*] (POL)

CZSSWiS ... Centralny Zarzad Skupu Surowcow Wlokienniczych i Skorzanych [*Central Administration of the Purchase of Textile and Leather Raw Materials*] (POL)

CZSZ .... Centralny Zarzad Szkolenia Zawodowego [*Central Vocational Training Board*] (POL)

CZSZb-M ... Centrala Zwalczania Szkodnikow Zbozowo-Macznych [*Grain and Flour Pest Control Center*] (POL)

CZT .... Centralny Zarzad Teatrow [*Central Administration of Theatres*] (POL)

CZT .... Ceskoslovenske Zavody na Umele Jedle Tuky, Narodni Podnik [*Czechoslovak Vegetable Oil Plants, National Enterprise*] (CZ)

CZT .... Ceskoslovenske Zavody Tukove [*Czechoslovak Fats Rendering Plants*] (CZ)

CZTiT........ Centralny Zarzad Telefonii i Telegrafii [*Central Telephone and Telegraph Administration*] (POL)

CZTOiF..... Centralny Zarzad Teatrow, Oper, i Filharmonii [*Central Administration of Theatres, Opera Houses, and Philharmonic Orchestras*] (POL)

CZTOR...... Centralny Zarzad Technicznej Obslugi Rolnictwa [*Central Administration of Engineering Service for Agriculture*] (POL)

CZTP......... Centralny Zarzad Tuczu Przemyslowego [*Central Administration of the Animal Fattening Industry*] (POL)

CZTS .... Ceskoslovenske Zavody Tezkeho Strojirenstvi [*Czechoslovak Heavy Machine Building Plants*] (CZ)

CZU .... Ceske Zemske Ustredi Obci, Mest, a Okresu [*Organization of Communities, Towns, and Districts in the Province of Bohemia*] (CZ)

CZU .... Ceskoslovensky Zahranicni Ustav [*Czechoslovak Foreign Institute*] (CZ)

CZU .... Ceskoslovensky Zuctovaci Ustav [*Czechoslovak Accounting Institute*] (CZ)

CZUK .... Centralny Zarzad Urzadzen Kolejowych [*Central Administration of Railroad Equipment*] (POL)

CZUR .... Centralny Zarzad Urzadzen Rolnych [*Central Administration of Agricultural Establishments*] (POL)

CZW .... Centrala Zbytu Wegla [*Coal Sales Center*] (POL)

CZW .... Centralny Zarzad Wagonow [*Central Railroad Car Administration*] (POL)

CZW .... Centralny Zarzad Weterynarii [*Central Veterinary Administration*] (POL)

CZWM ...... Centralny Zarzad Wodnych Melioracji [*Central Administration of Land Reclamation*] (POL)

CZW-PMG ... Centrala Zbytu Wegla - Przeladunki Morskie Gdansk [*Gdansk (Danzig) Center for Sales and Maritime Shipments of Coal*] (POL)

CZWS........ Centralny Zarzad Warsztatow Szkolnych [*Central Administration of School Workshops*] (POL)

czyt............ Czytaj [*Read*] [*Poland*]

czyt............ Czytelnik [*Reader*] [*Poland*]

CZZ .... Centralny Zarzad Zaopatrzenia [*Central Supply Administration*] (POL)

CZZ .... Centralny Zarzad Zbytu [*Central Sales Administration Of*] (POL)

CZZBMiO ... Centralny Zarzad Zaopatrzenia Budownictwa Miast i Osiedli [*Central Supply Administration of City and Settlement Construction*] (POL)

Cz ZG........ Czestochowskie Zaklady Gastronomiczne [*Czestochowa Restaurant Establishments*] (POL)

CZZH .... Centralny Zarzad Zaopatrzenia Handlu [*Central Administration of Trade Supplies*] (POL)

CZZL........ Centralny Zarzad Zaopatrzenia Lacznosci [*Central Administration of Communication Supplies*] (POL)

CZZMT..... Centralny Zarzad Zaopatrzenia Materialowo-Technicznego [*Central Administration of Engineering Material Supply*] (POL)

CZZP......... Centralny Zarzad Zakladow Prefabrykacji [*Central Administration of Prefabrication Plants*] (POL)

Cz ZPB ...... Czestochowskie Zaklady Przemyslu Bawelnianego [*Czestochowa Cotton Mill*] (POL)

CZZPM..... Centralny Zarzad Zbytu Przemyslu Metalowego [*Central Sales Administration of the Metal Industry*] (POL)

CZZZPZZ ... Centralny Zarzad Zakladow Zbozowych "Panstwowe Zaklady Zbozowe" [*Central Administration of Grain Storage "State Grain Storage"*] (POL)

D

d	Act, Action, Deed, Lawsuit, Affairs (BU)
d	Action (RU)
/D	A Titre Definitif [*Permanent Rank*] [*Used following a military rank in French*] (CL)
D	Battalion [*Artillery*], Divisional (RU)
D	Dag [*Mountain*] (TU)
D	Daire [*Room, Office*] (TU)
d	Dakika [*Minute*] (TU)
D	Dampfschiff [*Steamship*] [*German*] (GCA)
d	Dans [*In*] [*French*]
d	Das [*The*] [*German*]
d	Date [*Date*] [*French*]
D	Dative [*Case*] (RU)
d	Daughter (EECI)
D	Day of Operation (BU)
D	D-Day, Day of Commencement of Operations [*Military*] (RU)
d	De [*Of*] [*Spanish*]
D	Debe [*Debit*] [*Spanish*] [*Business term*]
D	Debit [*Debit*] [*Business term*]
D	Decca [*Record label*] [*Great Britain, Europe, Australia, etc.*]
D	Deckel [*Cover*] [*Publishing*] [*German*]
d	Declinaison [*Declination*] [*Astrology*] [*French*]
D	Decret [*Decree*] [*French*] (ILCA)
D	Decreto [*Decree*] [*Italian*] (ILCA)
d	Deel [*Volume*] [*Publishing*] [*Netherlands*]
D	Del [*South*] [*Hungarian*] (GPO)
d	Del [*Part*] [*Swedish*]
d	Del [*Part*] [*Danish/Norwegian*]
D	Delta [*Phonetic alphabet*] [*International*] (DSUE)
d	Dem [*The*] [*German*]
d	Demande [*Request, Claim*] [*French*]
d	Demi [*Half*] [*French*]
d	Den [*The*] [*German*]
d	Densite [*Density*] [*French*]
D	Deport [*French*]
d	Der [*The*] [*German*]
D	Dere (TU)
d	Des [*Of The*] [*German*]
D	Desaleux [*Type of projectile having a sharp ogive and truncated base*] [*Military*] [*French*] (MTD)
d	Despoinis [*Miss*] (GC)
D	Destra [*Right-Hand Side*] [*Italian*]
D	Deutsch [*German*] (GCA)
D	Deutschland [*Germany*] [*International automobile identification tag*]
D	Deve [*Debit*] [*Portuguese*] [*Business term*]
d	Dezi (ADPT)
D	Dezimalpotenz [*Serial Dilution*] [*German*] (GCA)
d	Dia [*Day*] [*Portuguese*]
d	Dias [*Day*] [*Spanish*]
D	Dichte [*Density, Specific Gravity*] [*German*]
D	Didaktorikon [*Greek*]
d	Die [*The*] [*German*]
D	Dienst [*Service*] [*German*]
D	Diesel (RU)
D	Digno [*Worthy, Deserving*] [*Correspondence*] [*Portuguese*]
d	Dina [*Portuguese*]
D	Dinar [*Monetary unit*] [*Tunisia*]
D2	Dinar Tunisien
D	Diopter (RU)
D	Diploma [*Indonesian*]
D	Diplome [*French*]
D	Direita [*Right Side*] [*Portuguese*]
D	Distance, Range (RU)
d	Division (BU)
D	Docteur en Medecine [*Notation that appears after the name of a pharmacist in the Annuaire de l'Armee*] [*French*] (MTD)
D	Doctoraat [*Academic degree*] [*Netherlands*]
D	Doctorado [*Doctorate*] [*Spanish*]
D	Doctorat [*Doctorate*] [*French*]
D	Doctori [*Doctor of Medicine*] [*Afghanistan*]
D	Doctrine [*French*] (FLAF)
d	Dod [*Dead*] [*Danish*] (GPO)
d	Dod [*Dead*] [*Swedish*] (GPO)
D	Dog [*Phonetic alphabet*] [*World War II*] (DSUE)
D	Dogu [*East*] (TU)
D	Doit [*Debit*] [*French*] [*Business term*]
D	Doivent [*Owing, Due*] [*French*] [*Business term*]
D	Doktor [*Russian*]
D	Doktor [*Swedish*]
D	Doktor [*Poland*]
D	Doktor [*Former Czechoslovakia*]
D	Doktor [*Norwegian*]
D	Doktora [*Academic qualification*] [*Turkey*]
D	Doktorat [*Doctorate*] [*Austria*]
D	Doktor na Naukite [*Doctorate of Science*] [*Bulgarian*]
D	Doktorsprof [*Academic examination*] [*Icelandic*]
D	Dom [*Sir*] [*Portuguese*] (GPO)
D	Dom [*Sir*] [*French*]
D	Dominant [*Biology*] (RU)
D	Don [*Sir*] [*Spanish*]
D	Don [*Phonetic alphabet*] [*Pre-World War II*] (DSUE)
D	Dona [*Lady (title)*] [*Portuguese*]
d	Dore [*Gilt*] [*French*]
D	Dorf (Geschlossener Ort) [*German*]
d	Dorso [*Back, Spine (of a Book)*] [*Publishing*] [*Italian*]
d	Dos [*Back (of a Book)*] [*Publishing*] [*French*]
d	Dose [*Dose*] [*French*]
D	Douane [*Customs*] [*French*]
D	Doutorado [*Doctorate*] [*Portuguese*]
D	Doutoramento [*Academic degree*] [*Portuguese*]
D	Droit [*Right*] [*French*]
D	Droite [*Right Hand*] [*French*]
D	Duff [*Phonetic alphabet*] [*Royal Navy World War I*] (DSUE)
d	Dulo [*Balk between strips of cultivated land, farm road*] (HU)
D	Duna [*Danube*] (HU)
d	Durch [*Through*] [*German*] (GCA)
D	Dusio [*In Cisitalia car model "D46"*]
D	"Dynamo" [*Sports society*] (RU)
D	Dysis [*or Dytikos*] [*West, Western, or Westerly*] (GC)
d	File, Dossier, [*Legal*] Case (RU)
D	Girl [*In questionnaires*] (RU)
d	Hitno [*Urgent*] [*Military code*] (YU)
D	House (RU)
d	Inch (RU)
D	Line-of-Sight Distance (RU)
d	Longitude (RU)
d	Part (BU)
d	Persons (RU)
d	Rechtsdrehend [*Clockwise*] [*German*]
d	Road (RU)
D	Road Machine (RU)
D	Transmitter, Transducer, Pickup (RU)
D	Village [*Topography*] (RU)
D2	Angola [*Aircraft nationality and registration mark*] (FAAC)
D3C	Diplome de Troisieme Cycle [*French*]
D4	Cape Verde [*Aircraft nationality and registration mark*] (FAAC)
D-66	Democraten '66 [*Democrats '66*] [*Netherlands*] (PPW)
D$_4^{20}$	Spezifisches Gewicht bei 20 Bezogen auf Wasser von 4 [*Specific Weight at 20 with Reference to Water at 4*] [*German*]
DA	Arctic Diesel (Fuel) (RU)
DA	Auxiliary Attenuator (RU)
Da	Dag [*Dagi*] [*Mountain Turkish*] (NAU)
DA	Dalniya Aviatsiya [*Long Range Aviation*] [*Soviet Air Force*] (PDAA)

345

DA............. Dansk Agronomforening [Denmark] (SLS)
DA............. Dansk Arbejdsgiverforening (WGAO)
DA............. Dassault-Breguet [Avions Marcel Dassault] [France] [ICAO aircraft manufacturer identifier] (ICAO)
DA............. Datenanalysator [German] (ADPT)
DA............. Degtyarev Aircraft (Machine Gun) (RU)
DA............. Delnicka Akademie [Academy of Labor] (CZ)
DA............. Democratic Alliance [Philippines] [Political party] (FEA)
DA............. Demokratischer Aufbruch [Democratic Awakening] [Later, Christian Democratic Union] [Germany] (EAIO)
d:a............. Den Aldre [Senior] [Sweden] (GPO)
dA............. Der Aeltere [Senior] [Title] [German] (GPO)
d:a............. Det Ar [That Is] [Sweden] (GPO)
da............. Dette Ar [This Year] [Norwegian] (GPO)
da............. Dette Ar [This Year] [Danish] (GPO)
DA............. Deutsches Apothekerbuch [German Pharmacopoeia] (GCA)
DA............. Deutsches Arzneibuch [German Pharmacopoeia] (GCA)
DA............. Development Alternatives [India] (EAIO)
DA............. Development Application [Australia]
DA............. Diabetes Australia
DA............. Dienstanweisung [Service Regulation] (WEN)
DA............. Diethnis Amnistia [Amnesty International] (GC)
DA............. Dievthynsis Allodapon [Aliens Directorate] [Greek] (GC)
DA............. Differentialanalysator [German] (ADPT)
DA............. Dimokratiki Allagi [Democratic Change] [Greek] (GC)
DA............. Dimokratiki Amyna [Democratic Defense] [Greek] (GC)
DA............. Dimokratikos Agonas [Democratic Struggle] [Greek] (GC)
DA............. Dimos Athinaion [Municipality of Athens] [License plate designation] (GC)
DA............. Dinar [Monetary unit] [Algeria]
DA............. Dinar Algerien
DA............. Directeur Administratif [Managing Director] [Cambodia] (CL)
DA............. Directio Administrativa [Romania] (WGAO)
DA............. Direction de l'Armee [Directorate of the Army] [Cambodia] (CL)
DA............. Direction de l'Arriere [Military] [French] (MTD)
DA............. Director's Assistant [Australia]
DA............. Dissociated Ammonia (RU)
DA............. Divisao de Aguas do Departamento Nacional da Producao Mineral (LAA)
DA............. Division Artillery (BU)
D/A............. Documenti Contro Accettazione [Documents Against Acceptance] [Italian] [Business term]
D/A............. Documentos Contra Aceptacion [Documents Against Acceptance] [Spanish] [Business term]
D/A............. Documents Contre Acceptation [Documents Against Acceptance] [French] [Banking]
D/A............. Dokumente Gegen Akzept [Documents Against Acceptance] [German] [Banking]
D/A............. Dokumente Teen Akseptasie [Documents Against Acceptance] [Afrikaans] [Business term]
DA............. Dom Akademicki [Student House] (POL)
Da............. Dona [Lady (title)] [Portuguese]
Da............. Dona [Lady (title)] [Spanish]
DA............. Dopamine (RU)
DA............. Doppelachse [Two-Axle Freight Car] [Unit of freight volume equivalent to that carried by a two-axle freight car] (EG)
DA............. Droit Aerien (FLAF)
DA............. Drzavna Arhiva [State Archives] (YU)
DA............. Duracion Ampliada [Extended Play] [Spanish]
DA............. Le Droit d'Auteur [Switzerland] (FLAF)
DA............. Long-Range Aviation (RU)
DA............. Smoke-Generating Apparatus (RU)
DA '91....... Democratisch Alternatief 1991 [Democratic Alternative 1991] [Suriname] [Political party] (EY)
DAA........... Danish Association of Archivists (EAIO)
DAA........... Danish Astronomical Association (EAIO)
DAA........... Defense Anti-Aerienne
DAA........... Dental Assistants Association of Australia (ADA)
DAA........... Departamento de Agricultura e Abastecimento [Brasilia, Brazil] (LAA)
DAA........... Department of Aboriginal Affairs [Australia] (ADA)
DAA........... Dietitians Association of Australia (SLS)
daa............. Division of Automatic Aerostats (BU)
DAAA....... Alger [Algeria] [ICAO location identifier] (ICLI)
DAAA....... Dental Assistants Association of Australia (ADA)
DAAB....... Blida [Algeria] [ICAO location identifier] (ICLI)
DAAC....... Departamento de Asuntos Agrarios y Colonizacion [Mexico] (LAA)
DAAC....... Direccion Administrativa de Aeronautica Civil [Civil Aeronautics Administrative Directorate] [Bogosta, Colombia] (LA)
DAACT..... Diabetes Association of the Australian Capital Territory
DAAD....... Bou Saada [Algeria] [ICAO location identifier] (ICLI)
DAAD....... Deutscher Akademischer Austauschdienst [German Academic Exchange Service]

DAAE........ Bejaia/Soummam [Algeria] [ICAO location identifier] (ICLI)
DAAE........ Dansk Andels Aegexport (WGAO)
DAAF........ Aoulef [Algeria] [ICAO location identifier] (ICLI)
DAAF........ Direction des Affaires Administratives et Financieres
DAAFAR... Defensa Antiaerea y Fuerza Aerea Revolucionaria [Antiaircraft Defense and Revolutionary Air Force] [Cuba] (LA)
DAAG....... Alger/Houari Boumediene [Algeria] [ICAO location identifier] (ICLI)
DAAJ........ Djanet [Algeria] [ICAO location identifier] (ICLI)
DAAK....... Boufarik [Algeria] [ICAO location identifier] (ICLI)
DAAL....... Alger [Algeria] [ICAO location identifier] (ICLI)
DAALPS ... Detachement d'Armee des Alpes [French]
DAAM....... Telergma [Algeria] [ICAO location identifier] (ICLI)
DAAN....... Reggan [Algeria] [ICAO location identifier] (ICLI)
DAAP....... Illizi [Algeria] [ICAO location identifier] (ICLI)
DAAQ....... Ain Oussera [Algeria] [ICAO location identifier] (ICLI)
DAAS....... Doug Anthony All Stars [Popular Music group] [Australia]
DAAS....... Setif/Ain-Arnat [Algeria] [ICAO location identifier] (ICLI)
DAAT....... Tamanrasset [Algeria] [ICAO location identifier] (ICLI)
DAATL..... Detachement d'Armee de l'Atlantique [French]
DAAV....... Jijell/Taher [Algeria] [ICAO location identifier] (ICLI)
DAAW....... Bordj Omar Driss [Algeria] [ICAO location identifier] (ICLI)
DAAWA.... Dental Assistants' Association of Western Australia
DAAX....... Cheragas [Algeria] [ICAO location identifier] (ICLI)
DAAY....... Mecheria [Algeria] [ICAO location identifier] (ICLI)
DAAyC..... Departamento de Asuntos Agrarios y de Colonizacion [Department of Agrarian Affairs and Colonization] [Mexico] (LA)
DAAZ........ Relizane [Algeria] [ICAO location identifier] (ICLI)
DAB........... Aerial Smoke Bomb (RU)
DAB........... Democratic Alliance of Burma [Myanmar] [Political party] (EY)
DAB........... Design Arts Board [Australia]
DAB........... Deutches Arzneibuch [German Pharmacopoeia] (GCA)
DAB........... Deutsche Athletiek-Bund (WGAO)
DAB........... Deutsches Apothekerbuch [German Pharmacopoeia] (GCA)
DAB........... Deutsches Arzneibuch [German Pharmacopoeia] (WEN)
DAB........... Dimethylaminoazobenzene [Organic chemistry] (RU)
DAB........... Dimethylaminobenzene [Organic chemistry] (RU)
DAB........... Disciplinary Appeal Board [Australia]
DAB........... Distributeur Automatiquee Billets [German] (ADPT)
DAB........... Domestic Appliances & Bicycles Co. Ltd.
DAB........... Dortmunder Aktien-Brauerei [Dortmund Brewery Joint Stock Company]
DABA....... Danish Amateur Boxing Association (EAIO)
DABA....... Deutsche Aussenhandelsbank [German Foreign Trade Bank] (EG)
DABAWAS ... Datenbank fuer Wassergefahrdende Stoffe [Data Bank on Substances Harmful to Water] [Information service or system] [Germany] (IID)
DABB .... Annaba/El Mellah [Algeria] [ICAO location identifier] (ICLI)
DABC .... Constantine/Ain El Bey [Algeria] [ICAO location identifier] (ICLI)
DABCO ..... Domestic Appliances & Bicycles Company Ltd.
DABF....... Danske Antikvarboghandlerforening [Denmark] (EAIO)
DABF....... Deutscher Ausschuss fuer Brennbare Fluessigkeiten
DABIS ...... Gesellschaft fuer Datenbank Informationssysteme (WGAO)
DABP....... Skikda [Algeria] [ICAO location identifier] (ICLI)
DABS........ Tebessa [Algeria] [ICAO location identifier] (ICLI)
DABT .... Batna [Algeria] [ICAO location identifier] (ICLI)
DABU....... Dansk Amator Bokse-Union [Danish Amateur Boxing Association] [Denmark] (EAIO)
DAC........... Dacca [Bangladesh] [Airport symbol]
DAC........... Dalby Agricultural College [Australia]
DAC........... Democratic Action Committee [Pakistan] [Political party]
DAC........... Democratic Action Congress [Trinidad and Tobago] [Political party] (PPW)
DAC........... Demokratik Almanya Cumhuriyeti [German Democratic Republic - GDR] (TU)
DAC........... Departamento de Accion Comunal [Federal District Community Action Department] [Colorado] (LA)
DAC........... Departamento de Aeronautica Civil [Peru]
DAC........... Departamento de Assistencia a Cafeicultura [Brazil] (DSCA)
DAC........... Departamento de Assistencia as Cooperativas [Brazil] (DSCA)
DAC........... Development Assistance Committee [Organization for Economic Cooperation and Development] [Paris, France] (EAIO)
DAC........... Direccion de Aviacion Civil [Office of Civil Aviation] [Ecuador] (LA)
DAC........... Direccion de Aviacion Comercial y Civil [Peru]
DAC........... Direct Acceptance Corporation Ltd. [Australia] (ADA)
DAC........... Directoria de Aeronautica Civil [Civil Aeronautics Directorate] [Brazil] (LA)
DAC........... Disabilities Aids Collective [Australia]
DAC........... Distribution Advisory Committee [Australia]
DAC........... Drugs Advisory Committee [Australian Capital Territory, South Australia]

DAC............ Drzavni Arhiv Cetinje [*State Archives in Cetinje*]   (YU)
DACA........ Disability Advisory Council of Australia
DACA........ Institute for the Development of Agricultural Cooperation Asia [*Japan*]   (WGAO)
DACAB ..... Dutch-Australian Community Assistance Bureau
DACC........ Direccion de Aviacion Comercial y Civil [*Office of Commercial and Civil Aviation*] [*Peru*]
DACH........ Department of Arts and Cultural Heritage [*Australia*]
DACHO .... Dachorganisation des Filschaffenden in Deutschland   (WGAO)
DACON..... Dac Cong [*North Vietnamese combat engineers*]   (VNW)
DACS........ Design and Artists Copyright Society Ltd.   (WGAO)
DACT .... Directorate of Administrative and Computer Training [*Australia*]   (WGAO)
dad .... Dadurch [*Thereby*] [*German*]   (GCA)
DAD.......... Danang [*Vietnam*] [*Airport symbol*]   (OAG)
DAD.......... Department Administratiewe Dienste
DAD.......... Dorado Air [*Dominican Republic*] [*ICAO designator*]   (FAAC)
D Ad.......... Droit Administratif   (FLAF)
DAD.......... Drug and Alcohol Directorate [*New South Wales*] [*Australia*]
DAD.......... Drzavni Arhiv u Dubrovniku [*State Archives in Dubrovnik*]   (YU)
DADB .... Directory of Australian Data Collections [*Database*]
DA-DE....... Dimokratikos Agonas - Dimokratiki Enotita [*Democratic Struggle - Democratic Unity*]   (GC)
dad gek...... Dadurch Gekennzeichnet [*Thereby Characterized*] [*German*]
DADJ .... Den Almindelige Danske Jordemoderforening   (WGAO)
DAdK........ Deutsche Akademie der Kuenste [*German Academy of the Arts*]   (EG)
DADMAKh ... Dialkyldimethylammonium Chloride   (RU)
DADOS..... Deputy Assistant Director of Ordnance Services [*Australia*]
DADP .... Dominica Association of Disabled People   (EAIO)
DADV .... Dutch Association for Dermatology and Venereology   (EAIO)
DAdW .... Deutsche Akademie der Wissenschaften (zu Berlin) [*German Academy of Sciences (in Berlin)*]   (EG)
DAE .... Danish Air Force [*ICAO designator*]   (FAAC)
DAE .... Datenanschlusseinheit [*German*]   (ADPT)
DAE .... Departamento de Aguas e Esgotos [*Department of Water and Sewage*] [*Portuguese*]
DAE .... Departamento de Aguas e Esgotos [*Department of Water and Sewage*] [*Brazil*]   (LA)
DAE .... Department of Atomic Energy [*India*] [*Nuclear energy*]   (NRCH)
DAE .... Diethnis Andikarkiniki Enosis [*International Cancer Union*]   (GC)
DAE .... Diethnis Astronavtiki Etaireia [*International Astronautical Society*]   (GC)
DAE .... Dikastirion Aeroporikon Epitaxeon [*Air Force Requisitions Court*] [*Greek*]   (GC)
DAE .... Direction des Achats a l'Etranger [*Office of Foreign Purchases*] [*Cambodia*]   (CL)
DAEC .... Danish Atomic Energy Commission   (PDAA)
DAEC .... Deutscher Aero Club [*German*]
DAEC .... Direction de l'Action Exterieure et de la Cooperation
DAEE .... Departamento de Aguas e Energia Eletrica [*Water and Electric Power Department*] [*Brazil*]   (LA)
DAEK .... Danmark Atomenergikommissionen   (WGAO)
DAEP .... Directorate of Aircraft Equipment Production   (WGAO)
DAEP .... Division of Atomic Energy Production   (WGAO)
DAER .... Departamento Autonomo de Estradas de Rodagem [*Porto Alegre, Brazil*]   (LAA)
DAF .... Daniel Ancel & Fils, Tamatave
DAF .... Danmarks Automobil-Forhandler-Forening   (WGAO)
DAF .... Dansk Annoncaer-Forening   (WGAO)
DAF .... Dansk Arbejdsgiverforening [*Danish Employers' Association*]   (WEN)
DAF .... Dansk Astronautisk Forening [*Danish Astronautical Society*]
DAF .... Dansk Atletik Forbund [*Danish Athletic Federation*]   (EAIO)
DAF .... Delhi Australia Fund
DAF .... Democratic Antitotalitarian Forum [*Romania*]   (EE)
DAF .... Department of Agriculture and Fisheries [*New South Wales*] [*Australia*]
DAF .... Desert Air Force
DAF .... Deutsche Arbeitsfront [*German Workers' Front*] [*Post-World War II*]
DAF .... Diaminophenol   (RU)
DAF .... Diammonium Phosphate   (RU)
DAFA .... Direction pour l'Administration des Forces Armees [*Directorate of Administration of the Armed Forces*] [*Malagasy*]   (AF)
DAFAR...... Defensa Antiaerea y Fuerza Aerea Revolucionaria [*Revolutionary Air Force and Antiaircraft Defense*] [*Cuba*]   (LA)
DAFECO... Direction des Affaires Exterieures et de la Cooperation d'Electricite de France   (WGAO)
DAFFA ...... Delicatessen and Fine Foods Association   (WGAO)
DAFFO...... Dansk Forening til Fremme af Opfindelser [*Danish Society for Furthering Inventions*]
DAFG .... Deutsch-Albanische Freundschaftsgesellschaft EV [*German Albanian Friendship Society*] [*Germany*]   (EAIO)

DAFH........ Tilrempt/Hassi R'Mel [*Algeria*] [*ICAO location identifier*]   (ICLI)
DAFI.......... Delegation Archeologique Francaise en Iran
DAFI.......... Directorate of Air Force Intelligence [*Australia*]
DAFI.......... Djelfa/Tletsi [*Algeria*] [*ICAO location identifier*]   (ICLI)
DAF-N....... Defence and Aid Fund Nederland   (EAIO)
DAFNRJ ... Drzavna Arhiva Federativna Narodna Republika Jugoslavija [*State Archives of Yugoslavia*]   (YU)
DAFS .... Department of Agriculture and Fisheries for Scotland   (ASF)
DAFSA ...... Societe de Documentation et d'Analyses Financiers [*France*]   (EAIO)
DAfStb....... Deutscher Ausschuss fuer Stahlbeton   (WGAO)
DAG........... Aerial Grenade Rack   (RU)
dag............. Dagestan   (RU)
DAG........... Datenanschlussgeraet [*German*]   (ADPT)
DAG........... Debendox Action Group   (WGAO)
dag............. Decagrama [*Decagram*] [*Portuguese*]
dag............. Decagramme [*Decagram*] [*French*]   (GPO)
DAG........... Department of the Attorney-General [*Commonwealth, Queensland*] [*Australia*]
DAG........... Deutsch-Arabische Gesellschaft [*German-Arab Society*]   (EG)
DAG........... Deutsche Afrika Gesellschaft [*German-African Society*]
DAG........... Deutsche Agrarwissenschaftliche Gesellschaft, Kuehlungsborn [*German Society of Agricultural Sciences, Kuehlungsborn*]   (EG)
DAG........... Deutsche Angestelltengewerkschaft [*German Salaried Employees' Union*] [*Hamburg, West Germany*]   (WEN)
DAG........... Deutsche Atlantische Gesellschaft [*Germany*]   (EAIO)
DAG........... Development Assistance Group   (WGAO)
DAG........... Division Artillery Group   (RU)
DAG........... Diviziska Artiljeriska Grupa [*Artillery Group in a Division*]   (YU)
DAG........... Dynamit AG [*Dynamite AG*]
DAGA .... Deutsche Arbeitsgemeinschaft fuer Akustik   (WGAO)
DagASSR .. Dagestan Autonomous Soviet Socialist Republic   (RU)
DAGFA ...... Deutsche Aerztegesellschaft fuer Akupunktur   (WGAO)
DAGFA ...... Deutsche Aerztegesellschaft fuer Akupunktur eV   (SLS)
Daggiz........ Dagestan State Publishing House   (RU)
DAGK .... Deutschen Arbeitsgemeinschaft Kybernetic [*German Study Group on Cybernetics*]   (PDAA)
Dagknigoizdat ... Dagestan Book Publishing House   (RU)
Daguchpedgiz ... Dagestan State Publishing House of Textbooks and Pedagogical Literature   (RU)
dagv........... Dagvaarding [*Benelux*]   (BAS)
DAGV........ Deutsche Arbeitsgemeinschaft Genealogischer Verbande [*Germany*]   (EAIO)
DAGV........ Deutsche Arbeitsgemeinschaft Vakuum   (SLS)
DAGV........ Deutscher Automaten-Grosshandels-Verband   (WGAO)
DAH .... Air Algerie [*Algeria*] [*ICAO designator*]   (FAAC)
Dah .... Dahili [*Internal, Local (Phone call)*] [*Turkish Cypriot*]   (GC)
DAH .... Danmarks Aktive Handelsrejsende   (WGAO)
DAH .... Deutsche Medizinische Arbeitsgemeinschaft fuer Herd- und Regulations-forschung   (WGAO)
DAH .... Deutsche Medizinische Arbeitsgemeinschaft fuer Herd und Regulationsforschung e V   (SLS)
DAH .... Drustvo Arhitekta Hrvatske [*Society of Architects of Croatia*]   (YU)
DAHOTEX ... Societe Dahomey-Texas du Petrole
DAHW ...... Deutsches Aussaetzigen Hilfswerk eV
DAHW ...... Deutsches Aussaetzingen - Hilfswerk   (WGAO)
DAI .... Departamento Administrativo de Inquilinato [*Tenancy Administration Department*] [*Honduras*]   (LA)
DAI .... Deutscher Architekten- und Ingenieur-Verband   (WGAO)
DAI .... Deutsches Archaeologisches Institut [*German Archaeological Institute*] [*Research center*]   (IRC)
DAI .... Direction des Affaires Internationales [*International Affairs Directorate*]   (WER)
DAI .... State Motor Vehicles Inspectorate   (BU)
DAIA .... Delegacion de Asociaciones Israelitas Argentinas [*Delegation of Argentine Jewish Associations*]   (LA)
DAIA .... Department of Aboriginal and Island Affairs [*Australia*]   (ADA)
DAIA .... Department of Aboriginal and Islander Advancement [*Australia*]   (ADA)
DAIC .... Departamento Administrativo de Intendencias y Comisarias [*Administrative Department for Police Headquarters and Intendencies*] [*Colorado*]   (LA)
DAIC .... Dominica Association of Industry and Commerce [*Dominican Republic*]   (LA)
DAINL ...... Dapo Allied Industries Nigeria Ltd.
DAIR .... Dansk Arbejdsgiverforenings og Industriradetsforbindelseskontor ved De Europaeiske Faellesskaber   (WGAO)
DAIR .... Observation Battalion [*Artillery*]   (RU)
DAIS......... Departmental Accounting and Information Service [*Australia*]
DAIS......... District Agricultural Improvement Stations [*China*]   (WGAO)
DAIWGPE ... Dutch Association of Importers and Wholesalers of Glass, Porcelain and Earthenware   (EAIO)

DAJ .... Direct Air [British] [ICAO designator]   (FAAC)
DAK .... Address-Code Selector [Computers]   (RU)
DAK .... Dakair [France] [ICAO designator]   (FAAC)
Dak .... Daktilo [Typing, Typist]   (TU)
DAK .... Dansk Atomreaktor Konsortium [Denmark]   (PDAA)
DAK .... Datenausgabekanal [German]   (ADPT)
DAK .... Dehydroascorbic Acid   (RU)
DAK .... Demokratisch Aktie-Komite (Vlaanderen) [Democratic Action Committee (Flanders)] [Belgium]   (WEN)
DAK .... De Samvirkende Danske Andels-Kreatureskportforeninger   (WGAO)
DAK .... Deutsche Angestellten Krankenkasse   (WGAO)
DAK .... Deutsche Atomkommission [German]
DAK .... Deutsche Atomkommission Geschaftsfuhrung   (WGAO)
DAK .... Deutsches Afrika Korps
DAK .... Dimokratiki Andifasistiki Kinisi [Democratic Antifascist Movement] [Greek]   (GC)
DAK .... Dnepr Aluminum Kombinat   (RU)
DAK .... Documents of the Archaeological Commission   (RU)
DAK .... Remote-Reading Astrocompass   (RU)
DAK-B .... Remote-Reading Astrocompass of a Bomber   (RU)
DAK-DB .... Remote-Reading Astrocompass of a Long-Range Bomber   (RU)
DAK-I .... Remote-Reading Astrocompass of a Fighter   (RU)
DAKO .... Compagnie Dakaroises de Conserves
DAKOFO .. Danske Korn- Og Foderstof Im- Og Eksportorers Faellesorganisation   (WGAO)
DAKS .... Danske Automobil Komponentfabrikkers Sammenslutning   (WGAO)
DAL .... Danske Arkitekters Landsforbund [Denmark]   (SLS)
dal .... Decalitre   (RU)
dal .... Decalitre [Decaliter] [French]
dal .... Decalitro [Decaliter] [Portuguese]
DAL .... Defender Australia Ltd.
DAL .... Deutsche Akademie der Landwirtschaftswissenschaften [German Academy of Agricultural Sciences]   (EG)
DAL .... Deutsche Anlagen-Leasing [Commercial firm] [Germany]
DAL .... Deutscher Arbeitsring fuer Laermbekaempfung eV   (SLS)
DAL .... Deutscher Arbeitsring fuer Laermbekaempfung   (WGAO)
DAL .... Diabetic Association of Luxembourg   (EAIO)
DAL .... Division of Analytical Laboratories [Department of Health] [New South Wales, Australia]
DALA .... Departemento de Asuntos Latinoamericanos [Cuba]   (WGAO)
DALAA ..... Danske Arkitekters Landsforbund Akademisk Arkitekforening   (WGAO)
DALCAN .. Societe Aluminium Alcan du Dahomey
DALDO ..... Disposite d'Aide a la Designation d'Objectif [Target Designation Aid System] [French]
DALEKOVOD ... Preduzece za Izgradnju Dalekovoda i Trafostanica [Enterprise for the Manufacture of Long-Distance Transmission Lines and Transformer Stations]   (YU)
DALF .... Diplome Approfondi de Langue Francaise [French]
Dal'giz .... Far Eastern State Publishing House   (RU)
DALIA .... Distribuidora Argentina Libro Ibero-Americano [Argentina]   (DSCA)
DALIT .... Ljevaonica Zeljeza i Tvornica Strojeva Daruvar [Daruvar Iron Foundry and Machinery Factory]   (YU)
DALMACIJABILJE ... Poduzece Ljekovitog Bilja [Dalmatian Medicinal Plants Establishment] [Dubrovnik]   (YU)
DALMACIJACEMENT ... Dalmatian Cement Export-Import Establishment   (YU)
DALMACIJATEKSTIL ... Dalmatian Wholesale Textile Establishment   (YU)
dal'n .... Distant, Far   (RU)
Dal'neft' ..... Association of the Far Eastern Petroleum Industry   (RU)
Dal'NIILKh ... Far Eastern Scientific Research Institute of Forestry   (RU)
Dal'NIVI ... Far Eastern Scientific Research Veterinary Institute   (RU)
DALPA ...... Danish Air Line Pilots Association   (WGAO)
DALRO ..... Dramatic, Artistic, and Literary Rights Organisation Ltd.
Dal'rybvtuz ... Far Eastern Technical Institute of the Fish Industry and Fisheries   (RU)
Dal'sel'mash ... Far Eastern Agricultural Machinery Plant   (RU)
Dal'stroy .... Main Construction Administration of the Far North   (RU)
Dal'TA ...... Far Eastern News Agency   (RU)
Dal'yevtsib ... Far Eastern Jewish Central Information Office   (RU)
DAM .... Daerah Militer [Military Region (KODAM)]   (IN)
DAM .... Damascus [Syria] [Airport symbol]   (OAG)
dam .... Decameter   (RU)
dam .... Decametre [Decameter] [French]
dam .... Decametro [Decameter] [Portuguese]
DAM .... Denrees Africaines Manufacturees
DAM .... Diacetylmonoxime   (RU)
DAM .... Diamond Asset Management [Subsidiary of Mitsubishi Bank] [Japan]
DAM .... Diplome d'Assistant Medical [French]
DAM .... Direction des Affaires Maritimes [Malagasy]   (MSC)
DAM .... Direction des Applications Militaires [France]

DAM .... Distribuidora de Articulos Metalicos Ltda. [Colombia]   (COL)
DAM .... Djaksa Agung Muda [Deputy Attorney General]   (IN)
DAM .... Drzaven Arhiv na Makedonija [State Archives of Macedonia]   (YU)
DAMAG .... Societe Dakaroise de Grands Magasins [Senegal]   (WGAO)
DAMAG .... Societe Dakaroise de Grands Magasins "Printania"
DAMDA .... Dairy Appliance Manufacturers and Distributors Association   (WGAO)
Dam-E........ Damasteinband [Damask Binding] [German]
DAMEC .... Drug and Alcohol Multicultural Education Centre [Medicine] [Australia]
dAMF .... Deoxyadenosine Monophosphate   (RU)
DAMFK ... Diisoamyl Ester of Methylphosphinic Acid   (RU)
DAMG....... Deutsches Amt fuer Masse und Gewichte [German Office for Weights and Measures]   (EG)
DAMISTOR ... Societe Dahomeenne de Transistors
DAMK .... Diakheirisis Andalaximon Mousoulmanikon Ktimaton [Administration for Exchangeable Moslem Properties] [Greek]   (GC)
DAMM....... Alger [Algeria] [ICAO location identifier]   (ICLI)
Dampfm..... Dampfmaschine [Steam Engine] [German]   (GCA)
DAMR .... Division of Adult and Management Review [United Nations]   (ECON)
DAMS .... Depot-Atelier Munitions Speciales [French nuclear weapon storage site]
DAMS .... Digital Audio Main Storage [Australia]
DAMS .... State Arbitration of the Council of Ministers   (BU)
DAMW....... Deutsches Amt Fuer Material- und Warenpruefung   (WGAO)
DAMW...... Deutsches Amt fuer Messwesen und Warenpruefung [German Office for Measurement and Commodity Testing]   (EG)
DAN.......... Danair AS [Denmark] [ICAO designator]   (FAAC)
DAN.......... Defensa Armada Nacional [National Armed Defense] [Uruguay]   (LA)
DAN.......... Dimokratiki Andistasis Neon [Democratic Youth Resistance] [Greek]   (GC)
dan .... Doctor of Architectural Sciences   (RU)
DAN.......... Dvizheniia Arabskikh Natsionalistov
DAN.......... Komandan [Commanding Officer]   (IN)
DANA....... Andelsslagteriernes Konserveseksport   (WGAO)
DANA....... Drug and Alcohol Nurses Association [Australia]
DANAGRO ... Danish Agricultural Organizations   (ECON)
DANATOM ... Danish Association for Industrial Development of Atomic Energy [Nuclear energy]   (NRCH)
DANBIF.... Danske Boghandleres Importrfrening [Danish Booksellers Import Association]
DANCOM ... Danube Commission   (BARN)
D & AD .... Drug and Alcohol Directorate [Australia]
DANDAM ... Komandan Daerah Militer [Military Region Commander]   (IN)
D & C .... Development & Commercial Bank [Malaysia]
D & C .... Discusion y Convivencia [Discussion and Coexistence] [Spanish]   (WER)
D & Cie ...... Darier & Compagnie [Bank] [Switzerland]
DANDJEN ... Komandan Djenderal [Commanding General]   (IN)
DANDOK ... Danish Committee for Scientific and Technical Information and Documentation   (EAIO)
D & R .... Douanes et Regies [Customs]   (CL)
DANE....... Departamento Administrativo Nacional de Estadistica [National Administrative Department of Statistics] [Colorado]   (LA)
DANFIP.... Danish Federation for Information Processing and Management
DANFIP.... Dansk Federation for Informationbehandling og Virksomhedsstyring   (WGAO)
DANHORS ... Danish Farmers Export Union   (WGAO)
DANI........ Dimokratia-Anexartisia Nomou Imathias [Democracy-Independence of Imathia Nome]   (GC)
DANIDA .... Danish International Development Agency
DANIS..... Datennachweis Informationssystem [Arbeitsgemeinschaft Sozialwissenschaftlicher Institut] [Germany] [Information service or system] [Defunct]   (CRD)
DANJON .. Komandan Bataljon [Battalion Commander]   (IN)
DANMARC ... Danish Machine-Readable Catalogue   (NITA)
Dan P .... Daenisches Patent [Danish Patent] [German]   (GCA)
DANPATATAS ... Danske Kartoffelavleres og Kartoffeleksportorers Faellesorganisation   (WGAO)
DANPRO .. Danish Committee on Trade Procedures   (PDAA)
DANR........ Department of Agriculture and Natural Resources [Philippines]   (DSCA)
DANRH .... Drzavni Arhiv Narodne Republike Hrvatske [State Archives of Croatia]   (YU)
DANRS ..... Drzavni Arhiv Narodne Republike Srbije [State Archives of Serbia]   (YU)
DANSW .... Diabetes Australia - New South Wales [Medicine] [Australia]
DANTE ..... Delivery of Advanced Network Technology for Europe   (ECON)
DAO .... Disability Adviser's Officer (South Australia) [Medicine]
DAO .... State Pharmaceutical Trust   (BU)
DAOB .... Tiaret [Algeria] [ICAO location identifier]   (ICLI)
DAOC....... Bechar/Ouakda [Algeria] [ICAO location identifier]   (ICLI)
DAOE........ Bou Sfer [Algeria] [ICAO location identifier]   (ICLI)

DAOF........ Tindouf [*Algeria*] [*ICAO location identifier*] (ICLI)
DAOI......... Ech-Cheliff [*Algeria*] [*ICAO location identifier*] (ICLI)
DAOL........ Oran/Tafaroui [*Algeria*] [*ICAO location identifier*] (ICLI)
DAON .... Tlemcen/Zenata [*Algeria*] [*ICAO location identifier*] (ICLI)
DAOO .... Oran/Es Senia [*Algeria*] [*ICAO location identifier*] (ICLI)
DAOR........ Bechar/Ouakda [*Algeria*] [*ICAO location identifier*] (ICLI)
DAOS........ Dolgoprudnyy Agrochemical Experimental Station Imeni D. N. Pryanishnikov (RU)
DAOS........ Sidi Bel Abbes [*Algeria*] [*ICAO location identifier*] (ICLI)
DAOV........ Ghriss [*Algeria*] [*ICAO location identifier*] (ICLI)
DAP.......... Aerovias Dap [*Chile*] [*ICAO designator*] (FAAC)
DAP.......... Aircraft Reciprocating Engine (RU)
DAP.......... Aircraft Smoke Generator (RU)
DAP.......... Deformation Aufgerichteter Phasen [*German*] (ADPT)
DAP.......... Democratic Action Party [*Malta*] [*Political party*] (PPE)
DAP.......... Democratic Action Party [*Malaysia*] [*Political party*] (PPW)
DAP.......... Departamento Administrativo de Planeacion Distrital [*Federal District Administrative Department for Planning*] [*Colorado*] (LA)
DAP.......... Desarrollo Agropecuario del Pais [*National Agriculture and Livestock Development Agency*] [*Cuba*] (LA)
DAP.......... Deutsche Akademie fur Psychoanalyse [*German Academy for Psychoanalysis*] (EAIO)
D Ap.......... Deutsches Apothekerbuch [*German Pharmacopoeia*] (GCA)
DAP.......... Development Academy of the Philippines
DAP.......... Diakheirisis Andallaximou Periousias [*Management of Exchangeable Estates*] [*Greek*] (GC)
DAP.......... Diazopyruvic Acid (RU)
DAP.......... Dimokratiki Ananeotiki Protoporeia [*Democratic Renewal Vanguard*] [*Greek*] (GC)
DAP.......... Division Aeroportee [*Airborne Division*] [*Zaire*] (AF)
DAP.......... Drug Association of the Philippines
DAP.......... House of Antireligious Education (RU)
DAP.......... Servicio de Divulgacion Agricola de Panama [*Panama*] (LAA)
DAP.......... State Motor Vehicle Enterprise [*or Transportation*] (BU)
DAP.......... State Pharmaceutical Enterprise (BU)
DAPCEG... Diplome d'Aptitude Pedagogique au Professorat des Colleges d'Enseignement General [*French*]
DAPD........ Directorate of Aircraft Production Development (WGAO)
DAPE .... Diffusion Affichage Publicite Edition
DAPERA ... Dana Pembangunan Daerah [*Regional Development Fund*] (IN)
DAPG .... Dolphin Action and Protection Group [*South Africa*] (AA)
DAPH........ Department of Animal Production and Health [*Sri Lanka*] (ARC)
DAPIB ...... Dana Pembangunan Irian Barat [*West Irian Development Fund*] (IN)
DAPIS ...... Danish Agricultural Products Information Service (WGAO)
DAPIT....... Besluit tot Vastelling van het Reglement, Houdende Bijzondere Dienstvoorwaarden voor de Ambtenaren bij het Staatsbedrijf der Posterijen, Telegrafie en Telefonie [*Benelux*] (BAS)
DAPP........ Development Aid from People to People (EAIO)
DAPPS ...... Drzavno Avtobusno in Prevoznisko Podjetje Slovenije [*State Autobus and Transport Establishment of Slovenia*] (YU)
DAQ.......... Diabetes Association of Queensland [*Medicine*] [*Australia*]
DAR.......... Danish Army [*ICAO designator*] (FAAC)
DAR.......... Dar Es Salaam [*Tanzania*] [*Airport symbol*] (OAG)
DAR.......... Datenausgaberegister [*German*] (ADPT)
DAR.......... Deutscher Autorenrat (SLS)
DAR.......... Diphenylamine Reaction (RU)
DAR.......... Direccion de Aguas de Regadio [*Peru*] (DSCA)
dar............. Division Artillery (BU)
DAR.......... Divisione Affari Riservati [*Secret Affairs Division*] [*Italian*] (WER)
DAR.......... Drzavni Arhiv u Rijeci [*State Archives in Rijeka*] [*Fiume*] (YU)
DAR.......... Long-Range Arctic Reconnaissance Aircraft (RU)
DARA .... Deutsche Arbeitsgemeinschaft fuer Rechen-Anlagen [*German Working Committee for Computing Machines*]
DARA .... Development and Reconstruction of the African Land Areas
DARAG ..... Deutsche Auslands- und Rueckversicherungs-AG [*German Foreign Insurance and Reinsurance Corporation*] (EG)
DARC........ Deutscher Amateur Radio Club (WGAO)
DARCIMC ... Development and Readiness Command Installation Management Course [*Military*]
DARDO..... Direct Access to Remote Data Bases Overseas [*Italy*] [*Telecommunications*]
DARE .... Data Retrieval [*System for documentation in the social and human sciences*] [*UNESCO*]
DARE .... Disabled Adults Residential Establishments [*Australian Capital Territory*]
DAREX...... Organisace pro Tuzemsky Prodej Exportniho Zbozi za Valuty v Drobnem a Darkovy Vyvoz [*Organization for the Domestic Retail Sale of Export Goods for Foreign Currencies and for the Export of Gifts*] (CZ)
dargest .... Dargestellt [*Represented*] [*German*]
DARH........ Drustvo Arhitekta Republike Hrvatske [*Society of Architects of Croatia*] (YU)

DARL .... Darling [*Botanical region*] [*Australia*]
DARM....... Division Aircraft Repair Shop (RU)
DARM....... Division Artillery Repair Shop (RU)
DARM....... Division Motor Vehicle Repair Shop (RU)
DARM....... Drifting Automatic Radiometeorological Station (RU)
DARMS.... Drifting Automatic Radiometeorological Station (RU)
DARNDR.. Departement de l'Agriculture, des Ressources Naturelles, et du Developpement Rural [*Department of Agriculture, Natural Resources, and Rural Development*] [*Haiti*] (LA)
DARR....... Division Ordnance Repair Shop (BU)
Darst......... Darstellung [*Description, Explanation*] [*German*]
DART........ Dutch Auction Rate Transferable [*Securities*] [*Netherlands*]
DARTEL ... Distribuidora de Artigos Electricos Lda.
DAS .... Dansk Akustisk Selskab (WGAO)
DAS .... Dansk Anaesthesiologisk Selskab (WGAO)
DAS .... Dante Alighieri Society [*Australia*]
Das............. Daselbst [*The Same*] [*German*]
DAS .... Datenausgabesteuerung [*German*] (ADPT)
DAS .... Datenstation [*German*] (ADPT)
DAS .... Den Danske Arkiske Station (WGAO)
DAS .... Departamento Administrativo de Seguridad [*Administrative Department of Security*] [*Colorado*] (LA)
DAS .... Department of Aboriginal Sites [*Australia*]
DAS .... Deutsche Ausleprschrift [*German Patent Application*] (GCA)
DAS .... Directia Asistentei de Sanatate [*Health Care Directorate*] (RO)
DAS .... Discrete Automatic System (RU)
DAS .... Division Ammunition Depot (RU)
DAS .... Division Artillery Dump (BU)
DAS .... Divizisko Artiljerisko Skladiste [*Division Ordnance Depot*] (YU)
DAS .... Doyle's Australian Scouts (DMA)
DAS .... Drug and Alcohol Service [*Australia*]
DAS .... Drustvo Arhitektov Slovenije [*Society of Architects of Slovenia*] (YU)
DAS .... Drzavni Arhiv Narodna Republika Bosne i Hercegovine, Sarajevo [*State Archives of Bosnia and Hercegovina in Sarajevo*] (YU)
DAS .... Dutch Australian Society
DAS .... Long-Distance Automatic Service, Long-Distance Dial Service [*Telephony*] (RU)
DAS .... Motor Vehicle Transportation Directorate (BU)
DAS .... State Court of Arbitration (BU)
DASA .... Dagitim ve Satis AS [*Distribution and Sales Corp.*] [*Istanbul*] (TU)
DASA .... Dental Association of South Africa
DASA .... Deutsche Aerospace (ECON)
DASA .... Dimokratiki Andistasis Spoudaston Athinon [*Democratic Resistance of Athens Students*] (GC)
DASA .... Direccion de Abastecimientos y Servicios Auxiliares [*Board of Logistics and Support Services*] [*Peru*] (LA)
DASA .... Dumping at Sea Act [*1974*]
DASC........ Departamento Administrativo de Servicio Civil [*Civil Service Administrative Department*] [*Colorado*] (LA)
DASC........ Department of Agriculture, Southern Cameroons
DASCA...... Department of Administrative Services and Consumer Affairs [*Tasmania, Australia*]
DASET...... Department of the Arts, Sport, the Environment and Territories [*Australia*]
DASH........ Drishat Shalom [*Best Regards*] [*Hebrew*]
DASI......... Dutch Australian Society (Illawarra)
DASIP .... Diplomatski Arhiv Sekretarijata Inostranih Poslova [*Diplomatic Archives of the Secretariat for Foreign Affairs*] (YU)
DASK........ Dimokratiki Avtonomi Syndikalistiki Kinisi [*Democratic Autonomous Trade Union Movement*] (GC)
DASP........ Danish Association of the Specialist Press (EAIO)
DASP........ Departamento Administrativo do Servico Publico [*Administrative Department of Public Service*] [*Portuguese*]
DASP........ Departamento Administrativo do Servico Publico [*Administrative Department of Public Service*] [*Brazil*] (LA)
DASP........ Drzavno Autobusno Saobracajno Preduzece [*State Autobus Transport Establishment*] [*Serbia*] (YU)
DASP........ State Autonomous Economic Enterprise (BU)
DASPE...... Dimokratiki Aristeri Syndikalistiki Parataxi Elladas [*Democratic Left Labor Faction of Greece*] (GC)
DAS-PSG .. Department of Administrative Services - Purchasing and Sales Group [*Australia*]
DASR........ Deutsche Akademie fuer Staats- und Rechtswissenschaften "Walter Ulbricht" [*"Walter Ulbricht" German Academy of Political Science and Jurisprudence*] (EG)
DASR........ Directorate of Aviation Safety Regulation [*Australia*]
dass .... Dasselbe [*The Same*] [*German*]
D Ass .... Droit des Assurances (FLAF)
DASSR....... Dagestan Autonomous Soviet Socialist Republic (RU)
DAST........ Datenaustauschsteuerung [*German*] (ADPT)
DAST........ Datenstation [*German*] (ADPT)
dast............ Decastere [*Decastere (10 cubic meters)*] [*French*] (GPO)

dast............. Decastereo [*Decastere (10 cubic meters)*] [*Portuguese*]
DASt.......... Deutscher Ausschuss fuer Stahlbau (SLS)
DAST......... Division Administrativa de Servicios de Transporte [*Administrative Division of Transportation Services*] [*Nicaragua*] (LA)
DAST......... Division of Aeronautical Systems Technology [*Council for Scientific and Industrial Research*] [*South Africa*] (ERC)
DASTA...... Daerah Istimewa [*Special Region (Jogjakarta and Atjeh)*] (IN)
DASTTTR ... Direction des Affaires Sociales, de Travail, du Tourisme, de Transport, et des Refugies [*Directorate of Social Affairs, Labor, Tourism, Transport, and Refugees*] [*Cambodia*] (CL)
DASU .... Dansk Automobil Sports Union [*Denmark*] (EAIO)
DASWATI I ... Daerah Swatantra Tingkat I [*First Level Autonomous Region (Former province)*] (IN)
DASWATI II ... Daerah Swatantra Tingkat II [*Second Level Autonomous Region (Former regency)*] (IN)
dat .... Danish (RU)
dat .... Datief [*Dative*] [*Afrikaans*]
Dat .... Dativ [*Dative*] [*German*]
dat .... Dative (RU)
Dat .... Datum [*Date*] [*Afrikaans*]
Dat .... Datum [*Date*] [*German*]
DAT .... Defense Antiaerienne du Territoire [*French*]
DAT .... Delmagyarorszagi Aramtermelo Vallalat [*Electric Power Producing Enterprise of Southern Hungary*] (HU)
DAT .... Delta Air Transport [*Belgium*] [*ICAO designator*] (FAAC)
DAT .... Den, Aoyama, and Takemake [*Early investors in automobile manufacturer Nissan*] [*Initials used in creating automobile name DATSUN*] [*Japan*]
DAT .... Dental Association of Thailand (EAIO)
DAT .... Depot a Terme [*Time Deposit*] [*French*] [*Business term*] (CL)
DAT .... Deutsch-Atlantische Telegraphengesellschaft [*German-Atlantic Telegraph Company*]
DAT .... State Motor Vehicle Transportation (BU)
DATA .... Danish Atlantic Treaty Association (EAIO)
DATAPREV ... Empresa de Processamento de Dados da Previdencia Social [*Social Security Data Processing Enterprise*] [*Brazil*] (LA)
DATAR ..... Delegation a l'Amenagement du Territoire et a l'Action Regionale [*Delegation for Territorial Development and Regional Action*] [*French*] (WER)
DATE .... Debreceni Agrartudomanyi Egyetem [*Debrecen University of Agrarian Sciences*] [*Ministry of Food and Agriculture*] [*Hungary*] (ERC)
DATE .... Departamento de Assistencia Tecnica Especializada [*Brazil*] (DSCA)
dATF......... Deoxyadenosine Triphosphate (RU)
DAtF......... Deutsches Atomforum [*German Nuclear Forum*] (EAIO)
DAtF......... Deutsches Atomforum eV [*German Nuclear Forum*] [*An association*] (NRCH)
DATI .... Departamento de Asistencia Tecnica Internacional [*Oficina de Planificacion Nacional - ODEPLAN*] [*Chile*] (LAA)
DATIMTEX ... Data, Images, and Text [*European Patent Office*]
DATM .... Bordj Mokhtar [*Algeria*] [*ICAO location identifier*] (ICLI)
DATM .... Departamento de Assistencia Tecnica aos Municipios [*Paraiba, Brazil*] (LAA)
DATN........ Defence Automatic Telecommunications Network [*Australia*]
DATS........ Danish Academy of Technical Sciences (EAIO)
DATS........ Department of Agricultural Technical Services [*South Africa*] (DSCA)
DATT .... Dental Association of Trinidad and Tobago (EAIO)
DATT .... Departamento Administrativo de Transito y Transporte [*Administrative Department of Traffic and Transportation*] [*Colorado*] (LA)
DAU.......... Automatic Remote Control (RU)
DAU.......... Dansk Atlet-Union [*Danish Wrestling Federation*] (EAIO)
DAu.......... Dansk Automationsselskab [*Denmark*] (SLS)
DAU.......... Daru [*Papua New Guinea*] [*Airport symbol*] (OAG)
DAU.......... Departamento de Assuntos Universitarios [*Department of University Affairs*] [*Brazil*] (LA)
DAU.......... Development Administration Unit [*Malaysia*] (ML)
DAU.......... Digital/Analog-Umsetzer [*German*] (ADPT)
DAUA....... Adrar/Touat [*Algeria*] [*ICAO location identifier*] (ICLI)
DAUB....... Biskra [*Algeria*] [*ICAO location identifier*] (ICLI)
DAUE....... El Golea [*Algeria*] [*ICAO location identifier*] (ICLI)
DAUG....... Ghardaia/Noumerate [*Algeria*] [*ICAO location identifier*] (ICLI)
DAUH ...... Hassi-Messaoud/Oued Irara [*Algeria*] [*ICAO location identifier*] (ICLI)
DAUI........ In Salah [*Algeria*] [*ICAO location identifier*] (ICLI)
DAUK....... Touggourt/Sidi Mahdi [*Algeria*] [*ICAO location identifier*] (ICLI)
DAUL....... Laghouat [*Algeria*] [*ICAO location identifier*] (ICLI)
DAUO ...... El Oued/Guemar [*Algeria*] [*ICAO location identifier*] (ICLI)
DAUT....... Timimoun [*Algeria*] [*ICAO location identifier*] (ICLI)
DAUU ...... Ouargla [*Algeria*] [*ICAO location identifier*] (ICLI)

DAUZ........ Zarzaitine/In Amenas [*Algeria*] [*ICAO location identifier*] (ICLI)
dav............. Daaraan Volgende [*And the Following*] [*Afrikaans*]
DAV.......... David [*Panama*] [*Airport symbol*] (OAG)
DAV.......... Decolare si Aterizare Verticale [*Vertical Takeoff and Landing*] (RO)
DAV.......... Delmagyarorszagi Aramszolgaltato Vallalat [*Electric Power Service Enterprise of Southern Hungary*] (HU)
DAV.......... Deutscher Alpenverein [*Germany*] (EAIO)
DAV.......... Deutscher Autoren-Verband eV (SLS)
DAV.......... Dirac Aviation [*France*] [*ICAO designator*] (FAAC)
DAV.......... Dunantuli Aramszolgaltato Vallalat [*Electric Power Service Enterprise of Transdanubia*] (HU)
DAVIBO.... Societe Dakaroise des Vins et Autres Boissons
davl............. Pressure (RU)
DAVOR..... Datenbank fuer Forderungsvorhaben [*Ongoing Research Project Data Bank*] [*Ministry for Research and Technology*] [*Information service or system*] (IID)
DAVP .... Directorate of Advertising and Visual Publicity [*India*]
DAW.......... Deutsche Akademie der Wissenschaften [*German Academy of Sciences*] (EG)
DAWA...... Diabetes Association of Western Australia
DAWA...... Divinatory Arts World Association [*See also AMAD*] [*Rillieux-La-Pape, France*] (EAIO)
DAWN....... Development Alternatives with Women for a New Era [*Brazil*] (EAIO)
DAWU....... Dominica Amalgamated Workers Union [*Dominican Republic*] (LA)
DAX.......... Aalborg Airtaxi [*Denmark*] [*ICAO designator*] (FAAC)
DAX.......... Deutscher Aktien Index [*German Index of Stock Prices*] [*A publication*] (BARN)
DAZ.......... Dnepr Aluminum Plant Imeni S. M. Kirov (RU)
DAZ.......... Dnepropetrovsk Automobile Plant (RU)
DAZ.......... Drzavni Arhiv u Zagrebu [*State Archives in Zagreb*] (YU)
DAZ.......... Drzavni Arhiv Zadra [*State Archives in Zadar*] (YU)
DAZ.......... State Motor Vehicles Repair Plant (BU)
dazugeh...... Dazugehoerig [*Matching*] [*German*]
Db............. Battery Range (RU)
DB............. Besluit op de Dividendbelasting [*Benelux*] (BAS)
DB............. Biovular Twins (RU)
DB............. Daimler-Benz [*Name of German engine factory*] [*World War II*]
DB............. Daljina Baterije [*Battery Range*] (YU)
DB............. Danmarks Biblioteksforening [*Denmark*] (SLS)
DB............. Danske Baptistsamfund [*Baptist Union of Denmark*] (EAIO)
db............. Darab [*Piece*] [*Hungary*] (GPO)
D/b............. Debetbrief [*Debit Note*] [*Afrikaans*] [*Business term*]
Db............. Decibel (BU)
DB............. Declaration of Berne [*Switzerland*] (EAIO)
DB............. Decret Beylical (FLAF)
DB............. Delostrelecka Baterie [*Artillery Battery*] (CZ)
DB............. Denizcilik Bank [*Maritime Bank of Turkey*] (TU)
DB............. Der Betrieb [*Germany*] (FLAF)
DB............. Desibel [*Decibel*] [*Afrikaans*]
DB............. Deutsche Bundesbahn [*German Federal Railway*] [*Since 1949*] [*Germany*]
DB............. Deutscher Beamtenbund [*German Civil Servants' League*] (EG)
dB............. Dezibel [*Decibel*] (EG)
DB............. Diakjoleti Bizottsag [*Student Relief Committee*] (HU)
DB............. Die Bahn [*Tourist card for rail travel*] [*Germany*]
DB............. Diesel Ram, Diesel Pile Hammer (RU)
DB............. Differentiator (RU)
DB............. Dignity Battalion [*Paramilitary group formed to bolster the regime of Panamanian strongman, Manuel Noriega*]
DB............. Dinitrobenzene (RU)
DB............. Direktionsbereich [*German*] (ADPT)
DB............. Disisleri Bakanligi [*Foreign Affairs Ministry*] (TU)
DB............. Dispatcher's Office, Control Office (RU)
DB............. Division Blindee [*Armored Division*] [*French*]
Db............. Diviziska Baza [*Division Base*] (YU)
D/B............. Dokumente Teen Betaling [*Documents Against Payment*] [*Afrikaans*] [*Business term*]
DB............. Donets Basin (RU)
DB............. Dunya Bankasi [*World Bank*] [*Turkish*] (TU)
DB............. Durch Boten [*By Messenger*] [*German*]
DB............. Durchfuehrungsbestimmung [*Implementing Regulation*] (WEN)
DB............. Duta Besar [*Ambassador*] (IN)
DB............. Far Eastern Office (RU)
db............. Good Quality, Soundness (RU)
DB............. Long-Range Bomber (RU)
db............. Probably, It Must Be (RU)
DB............. Smoke Bomb (RU)
DB............. Twin-Engine Bomber (RU)
DB............. Weighing Batcher, Weighing Batchbox (RU)
DBA.......... Deutsche Bauakademie [*German Architectural Academy*] (EG)
DBA.......... Dibutyl Azelate (RU)

DBA .... Direction des Bases Aeriennes [*Military*] [*French*]
DBA .... Long-Range Artillery   (RU)
DBA .... Long-Range Bombardment Aviation   (RU)
DBA .... Societe DBA [*Ducellier-Bendix-Lockheed, Air Equipment*] [*French*]
DBACS ...... Drawback Accounting and Computing System [*Australia*]
DBACT ...... Dental Board of the Australian Capital Territory
DBAD .... Long-Range Bomber Division   (RU)
DBAE .... Long-Range Bomber Squadron   (RU)
DBAG .... Daimler-Benz AG [*Manufacturer of Mercedes-Benz cars and trucks*] [*German*]
DBAP .... Long-Range Bomber Regiment   (RU)
DBAT .... Delostrelecka Baterie [*Artillery Battery*]   (CZ)
DBB .... Deutsche Bauernbank [*German Peasant Bank*]   (EG)
DBB .... Deutsche Bundesbahn [*German Federal Railway*] [*Since 1949*] [*Germany*]
DBB .... Deutscher Beamtenbund [*German Civil Servants Federation*]   (WEN)
DBB .... Directeur van Binnenlandsch Bestuur [*Benelux*]   (BAS)
DBBB .... Cotonou/Cadjehoun [*Benin*] [*ICAO location identifier*]   (ICLI)
DBBC .... Cana/Bohicon [*Benin*] [*ICAO location identifier*]   (ICLI)
DBBD .... Djougou [*Benin*] [*ICAO location identifier*]   (ICLI)
DBBF .... Danish Basketball-Federation   (EAIO)
DBBK .... Kandi [*Benin*] [*ICAO location identifier*]   (ICLI)
DBBM .... DeBeers Botswana Mining
DBBN .... Natitingou [*Benin*] [*ICAO location identifier*]   (ICLI)
DBBO .... Porga [*Benin*] [*ICAO location identifier*]   (ICLI)
DBBP .... Parakou [*Benin*] [*ICAO location identifier*]   (ICLI)
DBBR .... Bimbereke [*Benin*] [*ICAO location identifier*]   (ICLI)
DBBS .... Save [*Benin*] [*ICAO location identifier*]   (ICLI)
DBBV .... Cotonou [*Benin*] [*ICAO location identifier*]   (ICLI)
DBC .... Darwin Bushwalking Club [*Australia*]
DBC .... Development Bank of the Caribbean   (LA)
DBC .... Devrimci Birlesik Cephesi [*Revolutionary United Front*]   (TU)
DBCA .... Deaf-Blind Care Association [*Australia*]
DBCE .... Division of Building Construction and Engineering [*Australia*]
DBD .... Demokratische Bauernpartei Deutschlands [*Democratic Farmers' Party of Germany*]   (PPW)
DBE .... Danube-Air Ltd. [*Hungary*] [*ICAO designator*]   (FAAC)
DBE .... Development Bank of Ethiopia   (AF)
DBED .... Dibenzylethylenediamine   (RU)
D Beyl .... Decret Beylical   (FLAF)
DBF .... Dansk Badminton Forbund [*Denmark*]   (EAIO)
DBF .... Dansk Databehandlinsforening [*Danish Data Processing Association*]
DBF .... Dibromophenol   (RU)
DBF .... Dibutyl Phosphate   (RU)
DBF .... Dibutyl Phthalate   (RU)
DBFS .... Department of Bush Fire Services [*New South Wales*] [*Australia*]
DBG .... Deutsche Bunsen-Gesellschaft fuer Physikalische Chemie eV   (SLS)
DBGA .... Dominica Banana Growers Association [*Dominican Republic*]   (LA)
DBGI .... David Brown Gear Industries Ltd. [*Australia*]
DBGLS ...... Development Bank of the Great Lake States [*Zaire*]   (EAIO)
DBGM .... Deutsches Bundes-Gebrauchsmuster [*German Utility Patent*]   (GCA)
DBGPC ...... Deutsche Bunsen-Gesellschaft fur Physikalische Chemie [*Formerly, Elektrochemischegesellschaft*] [*Germany*]   (EAIO)
DBI .... Deutsche Bibliotheks Institut
DBI .... Deutsches Bibliotheksinstitut [*German Library Institute*] [*Information service or system*]   (IID)
DBI .... Donald Beasley Institute [*New Zealand*]   (EAIO)
DBIA .... Weekblad der Directe Belastingen, Invoerrechten en Accijnzen [*Benelux*]   (BAS)
DBIRD ...... Department of Business, Industry, and Regional Development [*Queensland*] [*Australia*]
DBIV .... Ivan Vazov State Library   (BU)
DBK .... Debreceni Boripari Kisipari Tsz [*Leather Industry Production Cooperative of Debrecen*]   (HU)
DBK .... Depoh Besar Kelengkapan [*Central Ordnance Depot*]   (ML)
DBK .... Deutsche Bibliothekskonferenz [*German Libraries Conference*]   (PDAA)
Dbk .... Dubrovnik   (YU)
DBL .... Development Bank of Laos   (CL)
d Bl .... Dieses Blattes [*Of This Paper*] [*German*]
dbm .... Decibel at the One-Milliwatt Level   (RU)
DBM .... Development Bank of Mauritius   (GEA)
DBM .... Dibenzoylmethane   (RU)
DBM .... Dyrekcja Budowy Miasta [*Administration of Municipal Construction*]   (POL)
DBMC .... Dominica Banana Marketing Corporation   (EY)
DBMIST ... Direction des Bibliotheques, des Musees, et de l'Information Scientifique et Technique [*French*]
DBN .... Direct Broadcast Network [*Australia*]

dbn .... Doctor of Biological Sciences   (RU)
Dbn .... Durban [*South Africa*]   (ILCA)
DBNSW .... Dental Board of New South Wales [*Australia*]
DBO .... Daulat Beg Oldi [*Indian military post*]
DBO .... Dubbo [*Australia*] [*Airport symbol*]   (OAG)
DBO .... Dzielnicowe Biura Opalowe [*City Section Fuel Offices*]   (POL)
dbo .... Met Ingang Dag Beediging Opvolger [*Benelux*]   (BAS)
DBO .... Royal Phoenix Airlines [*Nigeria*] [*ICAO designator*]   (FAAC)
DBOR .... Dyrekcja Budowy Osiedli Robotniczych [*Administration of the Construction of Workers' Settlements*]   (POL)
DBP .... Deutsche Bundespost [*Federal German Postal Service*] [*Germany*]   (EG)
DBP .... Deutsches Bundespatent [*German Federal Republic Patent*]   (GCA)
DBP .... Development Bank of the Philippines
DBP .... Dewan Bahasa dan Pustaka [*Language and Literature Council*]   (ML)
DBP .... Dicionario Bibliografico Portugues [*A bibliographic publication*] [*Portugal*]
DBP .... Drzavno Bagersko Preduzece [*State Dredging Establishment*]   (YU)
DBPC .... Demi-Brigade Parachutiste de Choc [*Algeria*]
DB Pd .... State Library, Plovdiv   (BU)
DBQ .... Dental Board of Queensland [*Australia*]
DBR .... Deutsche Bundesrepublik [*German Federal Republic*]   (GCA)
DBR .... Deutscher Bildungsrat [*German Education Council*]   (PDAA)
DBR .... Direckcija Broj [*Direction Number*] [*Railroads*]   (YU)
dbr .... Road Brigade   (RU)
DBRCG ..... Drustvo Biblioteckih Radnika SR Crne Gore [*Former Yugoslavia*]   (EAIO)
DBRS .... Long-Range Ballistic Missile   (RU)
DBS .... Darwin Omnibus Service [*Australia*]
DBS .... Database Access Service [*Eastern Telecommunications Philippines, Inc.*] [*Information service or system*]   (IID)
DBS .... Datenbanksystem [*German*]   (ADPT)
DBS .... Datenbankverwaltungs-system [*German*]   (ADPT)
DBS .... Departamento de Bienestar Social [*Federal District Social Welfare Department*] [*Colorado*]   (LA)
DBS .... Det Danske Bibelselskab [*Denmark*]   (SLS)
DBS .... Deutscher Berufsverband der Sozialarbeiter und Sozialpaedagogen eV   (SLS)
DBS .... Development Bank of Singapore Ltd.
DBS .... Dong-A Broadcasting System [*Korean*]
DBS .... Drustvo Bibliotekariev Slovenije [*Former Yugoslavia*]   (SLS)
DBS .... Long-Range Ballistic Missile   (RU)
DBS .... Long-Range Bomber Unit   (RU)
DBSA .... Dental Board of South Australia
DBSV .... Deutscher Billiard-Sport-Verband [*German Billiard Association*]   (EG)
DBSV .... Deutscher Bobund Schlittensportverband [*Germany*]   (EAIO)
DBT .... Department of Biotechnology [*India*]
DBTC .... Department of Business, Technology, and Communications [*Northern Territory*] [*Australia*]
DBTD .... Dibenzothiazyl Disulfide   (RU)
DBTI .... Dansk Beklaednings og Textil Institut [*Danish Clothing and Textile Institute*] [*Research center*]   (IRC)
DBU .... Dansk Boldspil-Union [*Danish Football Association*]   (EAIO)
DBU .... Dnepr Basin Administration   (RU)
DBV .... Dental Board of Victoria [*Australia*]
DBV .... Deutscher Badminton Verband [*Germany*]   (EAIO)
DBV .... Deutscher Beton-Verein eV   (SLS)
DBV .... Deutscher Bibliotheksverband eV   (SLS)
DBV .... Deutscher Boxer-Verband [*German Boxing Association*]   (EG)
DBV .... Deutscher Bund fuer Vogelschutz eV   (SLS)
DBV .... Deutsches Bucherverzeichnis [*A bibliographic publication*] [*German*]
DBV .... Dienstreglement Betonning, Bebakening en Verlichting [*Benelux*]   (BAS)
DBV .... Dieticians' Board of Victoria [*Australia*]
DBV .... Dubrovnik [*Former Yugoslavia*] [*Airport symbol*]   (OAG)
DBVK .... Vasil Kolarov State Library   (BU)
DBVKBIA ... Vasil Kolarov State Library, Bulgarian Historical Archives   (BU)
DBW .... Deutsche Babcock Wilcox Werke
DBY .... Dalby [*Australia*] [*Airport symbol*]   (OAG)
DBYKP ...... Dorduncu Bes Yil Kalkinma Plan [*Fourth Five-Year Development Plan*]   (TU)
DBYP .... Dorduncu Bes Yillik Plani [*Fourth Five-Year Plan*]   (TU)
DBZ .... Development Bank of Zambia
dc .... Da Capo [*Again*] [*Italian*]
DC .... Damara Council [*Namibia*]
DC .... Danube Commission   (EA)
DC .... Daughters of Charity [*Australia*]
DC .... Decision Conjointe [*Joint Decision*] [*French*]   (CL)
DC .... Defensa Civil [*Colombia*]   (COL)

DC.............. Democracia Cristiana [*Christian Democratic Party*] [*Colorado*] [*Political party*]   (PPW)

DC.............. Democracia Cristiana [*Christian Democratic Party*] [*Paraguay*] [*Political party*]   (PD)

DC.............. Democrats Camerounais

DC.............. Departamento de Caminos [*Santiago, Chile*]   (LAA)

DC.............. Departamento de Comercio [*Puerto Rico*]   (DSCA)

DC.............. Depois de Cristo [*After Christ*] [*Portuguese*]

DC.............. Detention Centre [*Australia*]

DC.............. Developpement Communautaire [*Community Development*] [*Cambodia*]   (CL)

DC.............. Dialogue et Cooperation [*An association*] [*France*]   (EAIO)

DC.............. Dinero Contante [*Cash*] [*Spanish*] [*Business term*]

DC.............. Direkcija za Ceste [*Department of Roads*]   (YU)

DC.............. Disarmament Campaign [*Netherlands*]

DC.............. District of Columbia   (IDIG)

DC.............. Distrik Columbia [*District of Columbia*] [*Afrikaans*]

DC.............. Distrito Central   (IDIG)

DC.............. Division de Cavalerie [*Military*] [*French*]   (MTD)

dc.............. Doble Columna [*Double Column*] [*Publishing*] [*Spanish*]

Dc.............. Doctor Docent in Stiinte [*Academic degree*] [*Romanian*]

DC.............. Dopo Cristo [*After Christ*] [*Italian*]

dc.............. Dos Conserve [*Back (of a Book) Preserved*] [*French*]

DC.............. Double Crown [*Monetary unit*] [*British*]

dc.............. Duna Corp. [*Saudi Arabia*]

DC.............. McDonnell-Douglas Aircraft Co., Inc. [*ICAO aircraft manufacturer identifier*]   (ICAO)

DC.............. Partito della Democrazia Cristiana [*Christian Democrat Party*] [*Italy*] [*Political party*]   (EY)

DC.............. Turkiye Demir ve Celik Isletmeleri [*Turkish Iron and Steel Enterprise*]   (TU)

DC24.......... Drug Crisis 24 Hours [*Television program*] [*Australia*]

DCA.......... Defense Contre Avions [*or Aeronefs*] [*Antiaircraft*] [*French*]

DCA.......... Democratic Congress Alliance [*Gambia*]   (AF)

DCA.......... Demolition Contractors Association [*Australia*]

DCA.......... Departement de la Culture et des Arts [*Culture and Arts Department*] [*Jordan*]   (EAIO)

DCA.......... Department of Civil Aviation [*Rhodesian*]   (AF)

DCA.......... Department of Civil Aviation [*Australia*]

DCA.......... Department of Consumer Affairs [*New South Wales, Australia*]

DCA.......... Department of Courts Administration [*New South Wales*] [*Australia*]

DCA.......... DiLucia Chinese Alphabet [*57-character Chinese type font created for typewriter keyboards*]

DCA.......... Directorate of Civil Aviation [*Jordan*]   (PDAA)

DCA.......... Divadlo Ceskoslovenske Armady [*Czechoslovak Armed Forces Theater*]   (CZ)

DCA.......... Documentatie Centrum Atoomkernenergie [*Documentation Center for Nuclear Energy*] [*Netherlands*]   (WEN)

dca.............. Dowodca [*Chief, Commander*] [*Poland*]

DCAE........ Direction des Constructions Aeronautiques [*France*]   (PDAA)

DCAN....... Direction des Constructions et Armes Navales [*Naval Construction and Weapons Directorate*] [*French*]   (AF)

D Can........ Droit Canonique [*France*]   (FLAF)

DCASA...... Dyers and Colourists Association of South Africa   (PDAA)

DCB.......... Decimal Code Binaire [*Binary Coded Decimal*] [*French*] [*Computer science*]

DCB.......... Decimal Currency Board [*Australia*]   (PDAA)

DCB.......... District Contracts Board [*Australia*]

DCBA........ Deer Breeders' Co-operative Association [*Australia*]

dcbel.......... Decybel [*Decibel*] [*Poland*]

DCC........... Caribbean Air Cargo [*Barbados*] [*ICAO designator*]   (FAAC)

DCC........... Dahir sur la Condition Civile des Francais et des Etrangers Dans le Protectorat du Maroc   (FLAF)

DCC........... Darwin Community College [*Australia*]   (ADA)

DCC........... Defensa Civil Colombiana [*Colombian Civil Defense*]   (LA)

DCC........... Delegation Catholique pour la Cooperation   (EA)

DCC........... Directorate of Covert Collection [*South African secret military-intelligence unit*]   (ECON)

DCCA........ Direccion Central de Construccion y Alojamiento [*Central Directorate for Construction and Housing*] [*Cuba*]   (LA)

DCCAN..... Direction Centrale des Constructions et Armes Navales [*Naval Construction and Weapons Central Directorate*] [*French*]   (WER)

DCCCA...... Direccion de Coordinacion, Credito, y Capacitacion Agraria [*Spain*]   (DSCA)

DCCM....... Direccion Central de Construcciones Militares [*Central Directorate for Military Construction*] [*Cuba*]   (LA)

DCCM....... Disciples of Christ Congo Mission

DCD.......... Definition de Constantes Decimales [*French*]   (ADPT)

DCD.......... Dutch Council of the Disabled   (EAIO)

DCDS........ Deputy Chief Defence Scientist [*Australia*]

DCE.......... Data Consultants of Europe   (NITA)

DCE.......... Direction du Commerce Exterieur [*Directorate of Foreign Trade*] [*Cambodia*]   (CL)

DCE.......... Dnepropetrovsk Commodity Exchange [*Ukraine*]   (EY)

DCEM....... Deuxieme Cycle d'Etudes Medicales [*French*]

DCF.......... Dalmatien Club Francais [*French Dalmation Club*]   (EAIO)

DCF.......... Dansk Cerealforening [*Denmark*]   (SLS)

DCF.......... Democratie Chretienne Francaise [*French Christian Democracy*] [*Political party*]   (PPE)

DCF.......... Developing Countries Foundation of 1962 [*Denmark*]   (EAIO)

DCF.......... Direccion de Coordinacion Federal [*Directorate of Federal Coordination*] [*Argentina*]   (LA)

DCF.......... Directeur des Chemins de Fer [*Military*] [*French*]   (MTD)

DCF.......... Directeurs Commerciaux de France   (FLAF)

DCF.......... Doberman Club de France [*French Doberman Pinscher Club*]   (EAIO)

DCF.......... Dominica-Cane [*West Indies*] [*Airport symbol*]   (OAG)

DCFL........ Department of Conservation, Forests, and Lands [*Victoria*] [*Australia*]

DCFRN..... Developing Countries Farm Radio Network   (EAIO)

DCFTT...... Direction de la Conservation Fonciere et des Travaux Topographiques [*Directorate of Land Conservation and Topographical Works*] [*Ministere de l'Agriculture et de la Reforme Agraire Morocco*]   (EAS)

dcg............. Decygram [*Decigram*] [*Poland*]

DCG.......... Democracia Cristiana Guatemalteca [*Guatemalan Christian Democracy*]   (LA)

DCGG........ Deutsche Continental-Gas-Gesellschaft [*German Continental Gas Company*]

DCGTX..... Direction et Controle des Grands Travaux [*The Ivory Coast*]   (EY)

DCH......... Department of Community Health [*Australia*]

DCH......... Direction Centrale d'Hydraulique

DCh.......... Doppler Frequency   (RU)

dch........... Durch [*Through, By*] [*German*]

DCh.......... Frequency Divider   (RU)

DCh.......... Unit on Duty, Alert Unit   (RU)

Dcha......... Derecha [*Right*] [*Spanish*]

DChA........ State Watch Repair Shop   (BU)

DChD........ Net Income Tax   (BU)

d chl........... Full Member   (RU)

DChM....... Double Frequency Modulation   (RU)

Dcho......... Derecho [*Right*] [*Spanish*]

DChT........ Double Frequency Telegraphy, Two-Channel Frequency Telegraphy   (RU)

DCI........... Daerah Chusus Ibukota [*Special Capital Region (Djakarta)*]   (IN)

DCI........... Defence for Children International Movement [*See also DEI*] [*Database producer*]   (EAIO)

DCI........... Demir ve Celik Isletmesi [*Iron and Steel Enterprise*] [*TDCI*] [*See also*]   (TU)

DCI-I........ Defence for Children International - Israel Section   (EAIO)

D Civ......... Droit Civil [*France*]   (FLAF)

dcl............. Decylitr [*Deciliter*] [*Poland*]

DCL.......... Democratie Chretienne Liegeoise [*Benelux*]   (BAS)

DCL.......... Dental Colombiana Ltda. [*Colombia*]   (COL)

DCLA........ Deputy Chief of Staff, Logistics and Administration [*NATO*]   (NATG)

DCLOG-A ... Deputy Chief of Logistics - Army [*Australia*]

DCLTC...... Dry Cargo Loading Technical Committee [*NATO*]   (NATG)

Dcm........... Decimetre [*Decimeter*] [*French*]   (MTD)

dcm........... Decymetr [*Decimeter*] [*POL*]

DCM......... Delhi Cloth Mills [*India*]

DCM......... Department of the Chief Minister [*Northern Territory*] [*Australia*]

DCM......... Development Capital Market [*South Africa*]

dcm........... Dina Centimetro [*Portuguese*]

DCM......... Direction Centrale des Marches

DCM......... District Court Martial [*Australia*]

DCM......... Dovize Cevrilebilir Mevduat [*Convertible Lira Account*] [*Turkish*] [*Business term*]

DCM......... Dunai Cement Muvek [*Danube Cement Works*]   (HU)

Dcm². .... Decimetre Carre [*Square Decimeter*] [*French*]   (MTD)

Dcm³. .... Decimetre Cube [*Cubic Decimeter*] [*French*]   (MTD)

DCMA........ Danish Ready Mixed Concrete Association   (EAIO)

DCMP....... Depot Central Medico-Pharmaceutique

dcn............. Dalszy Ciag Nastapi [*To Be Continued*] [*Poland*]

DCN.......... Direccion de Cartografia Nacional [*National Cartographic Institute*] [*Ministry of the Environment and Renewable Natural Resources*] [*Research center*] [*Venezuela*]   (EAS)

DCN.......... Direction des Constructions Navales [*Submarine manufacturer*] [*France*]

DCN.......... Discalced Carmelite Nuns [*Italy*]   (EAIO)

DCN.......... Federal Armed Forces of Germany [*ICAO designator*]   (FAAC)

DCNR........ Department of Conservation and Natural Resources [*Victoria*] [*Australia*]

DCNS .... Deputy Commander of Naval Services [*Australia*]

DCNSW .... Disability Council of New South Wales [*Australia*]

DCNSW .... District Court of New South Wales [*Australia*]

DCO............ Defence Contracting Organisation [*Department of Defence*] [*Australia*]
DCO............ Deputy Chief Officer [*Australia*]
DCO............ Deputy Chief of Staff, Operations [*NATO*]   (NATG)
DCO............ Divisao Centro-Oeste [*Center-West Division*] [*of the National Indian Foundations*] [*Brazil*]
DCOC........ Dahir du 12 Aout 1913 Formant Code des Obligations et des Contrats   (FLAF)
D Col.......... Droit Colonial [*France*]   (FLAF)
D Com........ Droit Commercial [*France*]   (FLAF)
D Const...... Droit Constitutionnel [*France*]   (FLAF)
DCOPS-A ... Deputy Chief of Operations - Army [*Australia*]
DCOS........ Directia Caselor de Odihna si Sanatorii [*Directorate of Rest Homes and Sanatoriums*]   (RO)
DCP............ Democratic Congress Party
DCP............ Development Control Plan [*Australia*]
DCP............ Division de Chimie Physique [*Division of Physical Chemistry - DPC*]   (EAIO)
DCPANDP ... Deputy Chief of Staff, Plans and Policy [*NATO*]   (NATG)
DCPEP...... Diplome de Conseiller Pedagogique de l'Enseignement Primaire [*French*]
DCPERS-A ... Deputy Chief of Personnel - Army [*Australia*]
DCPL........ Development Consultants Private Ltd. [*India*] [*Research center*]   (WND)
DCPLL...... Dutch Centre for Public Libraries and Literature   (EAIO)
DCPO........ Deputy Chief of Staff, Personnel and Organization [*NATO*]   (NATG)
DCPOC...... Document Center of the Patent Office of China [*Library*]
DCR............ Democratic Constitutional Rally [*Tunisia*] [*Political party*]   (BARN)
DCR............ District Chief Ruler [*Australia*]
DCRA........ Diploma of the College of Radiologists of Australasia   (ADA)
DCRK........ Democratic Confederate Republic of Koryo [*Reunified Korean state*] [*Proposed*]
DCRU........ Dairy Cattle Research Unit [*New Zealand*] [*Research center*]   (IRC)
DCS............ Danish Chemical Society   (EAIO)
DCS............ Dansk Cardiologisk Selskab [*Denmark*]   (SLS)
DCS............ Data Communication Services [*Regie des Telegraphes et des Telephones*] [*Brussels, Belgium*]
DCS............ Defence Cataloguing System [*Australia*]
DCS............ Definition de Configuration Systeme [*French*]   (ADPT)
DCS............ Democrazia Cristiana Sanmarinese [*Christian Democratic Party of San Marino*] [*Italian*]   (WER)
DCS............ Department of Community Services [*Western Australia*]
DCS............ Department of Correctional Services [*Northern Territory, South Australia*]
DCS............ Department of Corrective Services [*New South Wales, Western Australia*]
DCS............ Diosgyori Csapagygyar [*Bearing Factory of Diosgyor*]   (HU)
DCS............ Directia Centrala de Statistica [*Central Directorate of Statistics*]   (RO)
DCSA........ Divadlo Ceskoslovenske Armady [*Czechoslovak Armed Forces Theater*]   (CZ)
DCS & H..... Department of Community Services and Health [*Australia*]
DCsCK...... Dorost Ceskoslovenskeho Cerveneho Krize [*Czechoslovak Junior Red Cross*]   (CZ)
DCSEC...... Dolphin Correspondence and Stamp Exchange Club [*South Africa*]   (EAIO)
DCSHJ...... Daughters of Charity of the Sacred Heart of Jesus [*See also FCSCJ*] [*France*]   (EAIO)
DCSMW.... Democratic Confederation of San Marino Workers   (EAIO)
DCSR........ Da Capo Senza Replica [*From the Beginning, Playing Only Once the Parts Marked with Repeats*] [*Music*]
DCSV........ Direccion de Circulacion y Seguridad Vial [*Directorate for Traffic and Highway Safety*] [*Peru*]   (LA)
DCT .... Departamento de Correios e Telegrafos [*Postal and Telegraph Department*] [*Portuguese*]
DCT .... Departamento de Correios e Telegrafos [*Postal and Telegraph Department*] [*Brazil*]   (LA)
DCT .... Department of the Capital Territory [*Australia*]   (ADA)
DCT .... Deputy Commissioner of Taxation [*Australia*]
DCTF........ Dil, Cografya, ve Tarih Fakultesi [*Faculty of Language, Geography, and History*] [*of Ankara University*]   (TU)
DCTU........ Danish Confederation of Trade Unions   (EAIO)
DCUNICEF ... Danish Committee for UNICEF [*United Nations (already exists in GUS II database)*]   (EAIO)
DCV............ Division de Cuarentena Vegetal [*Puerto Rico*]   (DSCA)
DCV............ Druzstvo Cestujici Verejnosti [*Public Travel Cooperative*]   (CZ)
DCVH........ Democratic Community of Vojvodina Hungarians [*Former Yugoslavia*] [*Political party*]
DCVP .... Druzina Ceskoslovenskych Valecnych Poskozencu [*Society of Czechoslovak War Victims*]   (CZ)
DCW............ Department of Community Welfare [*South Australia*]
DCWAB .... Diplomatic and Commonwealth Writers Association of Britain   (SLS)

DD .... Association Internationale: Donnees pour le Developpement [*Data for Development International Association - DFD*]   (EA)
dd .... Dags Dato [*The Date of the Day*] [*Denmark*]   (GPO)
d/d............. Daily Ration   (BU)
DD .... Dampfdichte [*Vapor Density*] [*German*]
DD .... Damping Diode   (RU)
d d .... Dandar [*Brigade*]   (HU)
DD .... Decrets [*French*]   (FLAF)
DD .... Dedinske Divadlo [*Village Theater*]   (CZ)
DD .... Defense Democratique
DD .... Delostrelecka Divize [*Artillery Division*]   (CZ)
DD .... Development Decade [*Ten-year plan designed to bring about self-sufficiency in developing countries*] [*United Nations*]
d/d............. Dias de Data [*Portuguese*]
DD .... Diastolic Pressure   (RU)
DD .... Dichten [*Densities*] [*German*]   (GCA)
DD .... Dienst fuer Deutschland [*Service for Germany*] [*DfD*] [*See also*]   (EG)
DD .... Diesel Engine   (RU)
DD .... Differential Range Finder   (RU)
DD .... Dignissimo [*Most Dignified*] [*Correspondence*] [*Portuguese*]
DD .... Diode Decoder   (RU)
DD .... Dionicko Drustvo [*Joint-Stock Company*] [*Yugoslavian*]   (YU)
DD .... Doctores [*Doctors*] [*Spanish*]
dd .... Donne Dans [*Given In*] [*Pharmacy*]
DD .... German Democratic Republic [*ANSI two-letter standard code*]   (CNC)
DD .... Long-Range [*Military term*]   (RU)
DD .... Road Distance   (RU)
dd .... Villages   (RU)
DD .... Vrlo Hitno [*Very Urgent*] [*Military code*]   (YU)
DDA........... Danish Dental Association   (EAIO)
DDA........... Delhi Development Authority [*India*]
DDA........... Departamento de Defensa Agricola [*Chile*]   (DSCA)
DDA........... Deutscher Dampfkesselausschuss   (SLS)
DDA........... Direction Departementale de l'Agriculture
DDA........... Dominica Democratic Alliance [*Political party*]   (PPW)
DDA........... Duty Deposit Account [*Customs*]   (DS)
DDA........... Truck-Mounted Disinfection and Shower Unit   (RU)
DDA........... Two-Arm Sprinkler Apparatus   (RU)
DDAA........ Diplom Dietician Association Austria   (EAIO)
DDACS..... Dandenong and District Aborigines Cooperative Society [*Australia*]
DDAP .... Deutsche Demokratische Arbeiterpartei [*German Democratic Workers' Party*] [*Germany*] [*Political party*]   (PPW)
DDAR .... Differential Diphenylamine Reaction   (RU)
DDASS..... Direction Departmentale des Affaires Sanitaires et Sociales [*France*]
DDB........... Danish Dairy Board   (EAIO)
DDB........... De Dion-Bouton [*Automobile*] [*French*]
DDB........... Dortmund Data Bank [*University of Dortmund*] [*Germany*] [*Information service or system*]   (IID)
DDBJ......... DNA [*Deoxyribonucleic Acid*] Data Bank of Japan
DDC........... Danish Datamatics Center [*Research center*]   (ERC)
DDC........... Desert Development Center [*Egypt*] [*Research center*]   (IRC)
DDC........... District Development Committee [*Malawi*]   (AF)
DDC........... District Development Corporation [*Tanzania*]   (AF)
DDC........... Docteur en Droit Canonique [*Doctor of Canon Law*] [*French*]   (ILCA)
DDC........... Driver Development Centre [*South Australia*]
DdD........... Den Danske Dyrlaegeforening [*Denmark*]   (SLS)
DDD .... Deutscher Depeschen-Dienst [*Press agency*] [*Germany*]
DDD .... Dichlorodiphenyldichloroethane   (RU)
DDD .... Diffusion Pressure Deficit   (RU)
DDD .... Discagem Direta a Distancia [*Direct Long-Distance Dialing*] [*Brazil*]   (LA)
DDD .... Izvanredno Vazno [*Extremely Important*] [*Military code*]   (YU)
DDDD .... Devterovathmion Dioikitikon Diaititikon Dikastirion [*Second Degree Administrative and Arbitration Court*] [*Greek*]   (GC)
DDE........... Dichlorobis(dichlorophenyl)ethylene   (RU)
DDE........... Direction Departementale d'Equipement [*Departmental Equipment Bureau*] [*French*]   (WER)
d de JC...... Despues de Jesucristo [*After Jesus Christ*] [*Spanish*]   (GPO)
DDETsA..... Dvizhenie Demokraticheskoi Evoliutsii Tsentral'noi Afriki
DDF .... Departamento del Distrito Federal [*Federal District Department*] [*Mexico*]   (LA)
DDF .... Dimokratikes Dynameis Foititon [*Student Democratic Forces*] [*Greek*]   (GC)
DDF .... Diocesan Development Fund [*Australia*]
DDFSC..... Dubai Duty Free Shopping Complex [*at Dubai International Airport*]
DDG........... Deutsche Datel GmbH [*Germany*]   (PDAA)
DDG........... Deutsche Dermatologische Gesellschaft [*German Dermatological Society*]   (EAIO)

DDGF .... Dunya Demokratik Genclik Federasyonu [*World Federation of Democratic Youth*]   (TU)

DDGRES... Dneprodzerzhinsk State Regional Electric Power Plant   (RU)

DDH .... Destroyer, Antisubmarine Helicopter [*NATO*]

DDH .... Det Danske Hedeselskab [*Denmark*]   (SLS)

DDH .... Director, Division of Health [*New Zealand*]

DDHSF ..... Darling Downs Health Services Foundation [*Australia*]

DDI .... Daydream Island [*Australia*] [*Airport symbol*]   (OAG)

DDI .... Discagem Direta Internacional [*International Direct Dialing*] [*Brazil*]   (LA)

DDI .... Double-Image Range Finder   (RU)

DDIA .... Departamento de Defesa e Inspecao Agropecuaria [*Rio De Janeiro, Brazil*]   (LAA)

DDIAE ...... Darling Downs Institute of Advanced Education [*Australia*]   (ADA)

DDIP .... Darling Downs Institute Press [*Australia*]   (ADA)

DDK........... Children's Book House   (RU)

ddk .... Del-Delkelet [*South-Southeast*]   (HU)

DDK........... Dimethyldithiocarbamate   (RU)

ddk .... Division of Landing Boats   (BU)

DDK........... Dzielnicowy Dom Kultury [*City Section House of Culture*] (POL)

ddk .... Landing Ship Division   (RU)

DDKD......... Devrimci Demokratik Kultur Dernegi [*Revolutionary Democratic Cultural Association*]   (TU)

DDKD........ Devrimci Dogu Kultur Dernegi [*Revolutionary Eastern Cultural Organization*]   (TU)

DDKO........ Devrimci Dogu Kultur Ocaklari [*Revolutionary Eastern Cultural Hearths*] [*Clubs*]   (TU)

DDL........... Det Danske Luftfartselskab A/S [*Airline*] [*Denmark*]

DDL........... Disegno di Legge [*Draft Bill*] [*Italian*]   (WER)

Ddm .... Diplome de Docteur en Medecine [*French*]

DDMIIS .... David Davies Memorial Institute of International Studies (MSC)

DDMV....... Demokraticheskaia Dvizheniia za Malagasiiskoe Vozrozhdenie

DDN .... Datei Definitionsname   (ADPT)

DDN .... Delta Downs [*Australia*] [*Airport symbol*] [*Obsolete*]   (OAG)

DDN .... Departemen Dalam Negeri [*Department of Internal Affairs*] (IN)

DDN .... Normal Disk Diaphragm   (RU)

d d ny....... Del-Delnyugat [*South-Southwest*]   (HU)

DDP........... Dala Djupgas Provborringar [*Sweden*]

DDP........... Data Distribution Point [*NATO*]   (NATG)

DDP........... Denni Davka Potravin [*Daily Food Ration*]   (CZ)

DDP........... Departamento de Diversoes Publicas [*Public Recreation Department*] [*Brazil*]   (LA)

DDP........... Derecha Democratica Espanola [*Spanish Right-Wing Democratic Party*]   (PPW)

DDP........... Deutsche Demokratische Partei [*German Democratic Party*] [*Political party*]   (PPE)

DDP........... Division de Pesca [*Chile*]   (MSC)

DDP........... Dorado [*Puerto Rico*] [*Airport symbol*]   (OAG)

DDP........... Double Diode-Pentode [*Radio tube*]   (RU)

DDP........... Duodioda-Pentoda [*Double Diode-Pentode (Radio tube)*]   (HU)

DDP........... Erato (Discophiles de Paris Series) [*Record label*] [*France*]

DDP........... Trailer-Mounted Disinfection and Shower Unit   (RU)

DDP........... Wooden Landing-Craft Park [*for river crossing*]   (RU)

DDR........... Deutsche Demokratische Republik [*German Democratic Republic (East Germany)*]

DDR........... Direction du Developpement Regional

DDR........... District Deputy Ruler [*Australia*]

DDR........... Divadelni a Dramaturgicka Rada [*Theater and Drama Council*] (CZ)

DDr............ Doktoren [*Doctors*] [*German*]   (GCA)

DDR........... Duitse Demokratiese Republiek [*German Democratic Republic*] [*Afrikaans*]

DDR........... German Democratic Republic [*ANSI three-letter standard code*] (CNC)

DDRKM .... DDR [*German Democratic Republic*] Komitee fur Menschenrechte   (EAIO)

DDS .... Dansk Dermatologisk Selskab [*Denmark*]   (SLS)

DDS .... Data Dissemination System [*European Space Agency - Information Retrieval Service*] [*Rome, Italy*]

DDS .... Daten-Definitions Spezifikationen [*German*]   (ADPT)

DDS .... Departement de la Documentation et de la Securite [*Secret police*] [*Chad*]

DDS .... Det Danske Staalvalsevaerk [*Steel producing firm*] [*Denmark*] (IMH)

DDS .... Dimethyldichlorosilane   (RU)

DDS .... Direction de la Documentation et de la Securite [*Directorate of Documentation and Security*] [*Chad*]

DDS .... Director of Dental Surgery [*Australia*]

DDS .... Divizni Delostrelecka Skupina [*Division Artillery Group*]   (CZ)

DDSE .... Dioikitikon Dikastirion Stratiotikon Epitaxeon [*Army Requisitions Administrative Court*] [*Greek*]   (GC)

DDSG .... Donau-Dampfschiffahrtsgesellschaft [*Danube Steamship Company*]   (EG)

DDT........... Death Defying Theatre [*Australia*]

DDT.......... Denkmaeler Deutscher Tonkunst [*German*]

DDT.......... Dichlorodifenieltrichloro-etann [*Dichlorodiphenyltrichloroethane*] [*Afrikaans*]

DDT........... Dichlorodiphenyltrichloroethane   (RU)

DDT........... Double Diode-Triode [*Radio tube*]   (RU)

DDT........... Duodioda-Trioda [*Double Diode-Triode (Radio tube)*]   (HU)

DDTK ...... Diethyldithiocarbamate   (RU)

DDTV .... Darling Downs Television [*Australia*]   (ADA)

DDTV .... Darling Downs Television Ltd. [*Australia*]

DDUSCP... Depozitul de Dotare a Unitatilor Sanitare Curativo-Profilactice [*Supply Warehouse for Remedial-Prophylactic Health Units*]   (RO)

DDV........... Dienstdauervorschriften [*Permanent Service Regulations*]   (EG)

DDV........... Direkte Datenverarbeitung [*German*]   (ADPT)

DDY.......... Devlet Demiryollari [*State Railways*] [*TCDD*] [*See also*]   (TU)

DDZ........... Timber Extracting and Processing Plant   (BU)

DE.............. Arc-Suppression Element   (RU)

De.............. Dake [*Mountain, Hill*] [*Te*] [*See also*] [*Japan*]   (NAU)

DE.............. Dansk Eksportfinansieringsfond [*Danish Export Finance Corporation*]

DE.............. Datenerfassung [*German*]   (ADPT)

DE.............. Delegacia de Estrangeiros [*Delegation of Foreigners*] [*Portuguese*]

de.............. Delelott [*Morning, Midmorning*]   (HU)

DE.............. Demokratiki Enosis [*Democratic Union*] [*Greek*]   (PPE)

DE.............. Departamento Estatal   (SCAC)

DE.............. Deputy   (IN)

De.............. Dere [*or Deresi*] [*Valley or Stream Turkish*]   (NAU)

de.............. Det Er [*This Is*] [*Norway*]   (GPO)

de.............. Deve [*Debit*] [*Portuguese*] [*Business term*]

DE.............. Dielektrizitaetskonstante [*Dielectric Constant*] [*German*]

d/e............ Diesel-Electric Ship   (RU)

DE.............. Dimokratiki Enosis [*Democratic Union*] [*Cyprus*]   (GC)

DE.............. Dioikitiki Epitropi [*Administrative Committee*]   (GC)

DE.............. Direction des Etapes [*Military*] [*French*]   (MTD)

DE.............. Disposition Entity [*Philippines*]

DE.............. District of Europe [*Proposed location of an EEC federal capital*]

DE.............. Dizelelektrane [*Diesel-Powered Electric Plants*]   (YU)

DE.............. Dizel-Elektrични Pogon [*Diesel-Electric Power*]   (YU)

De.............. Doctorat d'Etat [*French*]

DE.............. Dokumentationseinheit

DE.............. Drustvena Evidencija [*Budgetary Records*]   (YU)

DE.............. Drustvo Ekonomista [*Society of Economists*]   (YU)

De.............. Durchgangs-Eilgueterzug [*Through Express Freight Train*]   (EG)

DE.............. Durchschalteinheit [*German*]   (ADPT)

DE.............. Federal Republic of Germany [*ANSI two-letter standard code*] (CNC)

DE.............. Other Type of Energy   (BU)

DEA .... ANSA [*Agenzia Nazionale Stampa Associata*]'s Electronic Documentation Service [*ANSA Agency*]   (IID)

DEA .... Danish Economic Association   (EAIO)

DEA .... Delta Aerotaxi [*Italy*] [*ICAO designator*]   (FAAC)

DEA .... Departamento de Economia Agropecuaria [*Dominican Republic*] (DSCA)

DEA .... Departamento de Educacion Agropecuaria [*Ecuador*]   (DSCA)

DEA .... Departement Economique Applique [*Applied Economics Department*] [*French*]   (WER)

DEA .... Department of Education and the Arts [*Tasmania, Australia*]

DEA .... Deutsche Erdoel Aktiengesellschaft [*German*]

DEA .... Diffusione Edizioni Anglo-Americane [*Distributors of English and American Publications*] [*Italian*]

DEA .... Digital Equipment (Australia) Proprietary Ltd.   (ADA)

DEA .... Dimoiria Eidikis Apostolis [*Special Mission Platoon*]   (GC)

DEA .... Dimokratiki Epitropi Andistaseos [*Democratic Resistance Committee*] [*Greek*]   (GC)

DEA .... Diplome d'Etudes Approfondies [*Advanced Study Diploma*] [*French*]   (CL)

DE/A .... Direkt Ein/Ausgabe [*German*]   (ADPT)

DEA .... Division de Educacion Agropecuaria [*Peru*]   (DSCA)

DEA .... Drug Enforcement Agency [*New South Wales, Australia*]

DEA .... Drug Enforcement Agency [*Nigeria*]

DEAC .... Debreceni Egyetemi Atletikai Club [*University Athletic Club of Debrecen*]   (HU)

DEAC .... Disability Employment Action Centre [*Melbourne, Australia*]

DEAE .... Deutsche Evangelische Arbeitsgemeinschaft fuer Erwachsenenbildung

DEAETs .... Diethylaminoethyl Cellulose   (RU)

DEAG .... Deutsche Einfuhr- und Ausfuhrgesellschaft [*German Import and Export Company*]   (EG)

DEAIC....... Direccion de Educacion Artesanal, Industrial, y Comercial [*Venezuela*]   (DSCA)

Deak......... Deakin University [*Australia*]

DEAL .... Dignity, Education, and Language Commmunication Centre [*Melbourne, Australia*]

DEAM ...... Diplome d'Etudes d'Administration Municipale [*Diploma in Municipal Administration*] [*French Guiana*]   (LA)

DEAN....... Diethnis Epitropi Aeronavtilias [*International Air Navigation Commission*] (GC)

DEAP .... Diabetes Education Assessment Programme [*Australia*]

DEAS........ Dialogorientiertes-Energlie-Abrechnungs-System [*German*] (ADPT)

DEAS........ Duke of Edinburgh Award Scheme [*Australia*]

deb............ Debit [*Debit*] [*French*] [*Business term*]

DEB .... Debitoren (ADPT)

DEB .... Distrito Especial de Bogota [*Bogota Federal District*] [*Colorado*] (LA)

DEB .... Drug Evaluation Branch [*Therapeutic Goods Administration*] [*Australia*]

DEB .... Road Maintenance Battalion (RU)

DEBA .... Direccion de la Energia de Buenos Aires [*Buenos Aires Power Administration*] [*Argentina*] (LA)

debit .... Debiteur [*Debtor*] [*French*]

Debr .... Debrecen [*Debrecen*] (HU)

debr .... Debroche [*Unstitched*] [*French*]

Debre .... Debarcadere [*Station, Platform*] [*Military map abbreviation World War I*] [*French*] (MTD)

DEBSA ..... Doctor Edward Bach Society of Australia

Debswana... De Beers Botswana Mining Co.

dec............ Decede [*Deceased*] [*French*]

dec............ December [*Danish*] (GPO)

dec............ December [*Dutch*] (GPO)

dec............ December [*Hungarian*] (GPO)

dec............ Decembre [*December*] [*French*]

dec............ Decime [*Ten Centimes*] [*French*]

dec............ Decoctio [*Decoction*] [*Pharmacy*]

dec............ Decorazione [*Decoration*] [*Italian*]

Dec............ Decort [*Deduct*] [*German*] [*Business term*]

Dec............ Decrescendo [*With a Gradual Decrease in Loudness*] [*Music*]

dec............ Decreto [*Decree, Edict*] [*Portuguese*]

DEC .... Depenses d'Equipement Communal [*Algeria*]

DEC .... Development Equity Corporation [*Australia*]

DEC .... Digital Equipment Corp. Australia Proprietary Ltd.

DEC .... Diplome d'Etudes Complementaires [*Further Studies Diploma*] (CL)

DEC .... Direccion de Estadistica y Censos [*Bureau of Statistics and Census*] [*Chile*] (LA)

DEC .... Direction des Echanges Commerciaux

DEC .... Distance Education Centre [*Australia*]

DEC .... Drzavna Elektricna Centrala [*State Electric Station*] (YU)

DECA .... Driver Education Centre of Australia

DECAD/B ... Departamento de Documentacao, Estatistica, Cadastro e Informacoes Industriais - Biblioteca Roberto Simonsen [*Federacao e Centro das Industrias do Estado de Sao Paulo*] [*Brazil*]

Dec Adm .... Decision de l'Administration de l'Enregistrement [*Benelux*] (BAS)

decag .... Decagramme [*Decagram*] [*French*]

decagr........ Decagramme [*Decagram*] [*French*]

decal .... Decalitre [*Decaliter*] [*French*]

DECALC ... DECHEMA [*Deutsche Gesellschaft fuer Chemisches Apparatewesen, Chemische Technik, und Biotechnologie eV*] Data Calculation System [*Information retrieval*]

decam .... Decametre [*Decameter*] [*French*]

Dec Arb .... Decision Arbitrale [*French*] (BAS)

DECARP ... Desert Encroachment Control and Rehabilitation Programme [*Sudan*]

DECAT...... Departamento de Conservacion y Asistencia Tecnica del Ministerio de Agricultura [*Santiago, Chile*] (LAA)

decbre........ Decembre [*December*] [*French*]

DECCRAF ... Departamento de Conservacion de Recursos Agricolas y Forestales [*Chile*] (DSCA)

DECEE..... Direccion de Estadistica, Catastro, y Estudios Economicos [*Lima, Peru*] (LAA)

Dech.......... Dechant [*Dean*] [*German*]

dech.......... Dechire [*Torn*] [*French*]

DECHEMA ... Deutsche Gesellschaft fuer Chemisches Apparatewesen, Chemische Technik, und Biotechnologie eV [*Database producer*] (IID)

dechir .... Dechire [*Torn*] [*French*]

decig .... Decigramme [*Decigram*] [*French*]

decigr .... Decigramme [*Decigram*] [*French*]

decil.......... Decilitre [*Deciliter*] [*French*]

decim......... Decimetre [*Decimeter*] [*French*]

Decis Min .. Decision Ministerielle [*France*] (FLAF)

Decis MinFin ... Decision du Ministre des Finances [*France*] (FLAF)

Deckbl........ Deckblatt [*Cover Sheet*] [*Publishing*] [*German*]

Deckelill.... Deckelillustration [*Cover Illustration*] [*Publishing*] [*German*]

declin......... Declinaison [*Declination*] [*Astrology*] [*French*]

DECO .... Delegacion Exterior de Comisiones Obreras [*Foreign Delegation of Workers Commissions*] [*Spanish*] (WER)

DECONSULT ... Deutsche Eisenbahn Consulting [*Germany*] (PDAA)

DECOR ..... DECHEMA [*Deutsche Gesellschaft fuer Chemisches Apparatewesen, Chemische Technik, und Biotechnologie eV*] Corrosion Data Base [*Germany*] [*Information service or system*] (CRD)

decor.......... Decorazione [*Decoration*] [*Italian*]

DECORATONY ... Decoracion por Tony Ltda. [*Colombia*] (COL)

Decr............ Decret [*French*] (FLAF)

Decres .... Decrescendo [*With a Gradual Decrease in Loudness*] [*Music*]

Decr-L........ Decret-Loi [*French*] (FLAF)

Decr Org .... Decret Organique [*French*] (FLAF)

DECS........ Designated External Courses of Study [*Australia*]

DECS........ Diplome d'Etudes Comptables Superieurs

DECSA...... Departamento de Conservacion de Suelos y Agua [*Chile*] (DSCA)

DECT........ Digital European Cordless Telecommunications

ded............ Dedica [*Dedication*] [*Italian*]

ded............ Dedicatoria [*Dedication*] [*Spanish*]

ded............ Dedicatoria [*Dedication*] [*Portuguese*]

Ded........... Dedikation [*Dedication*] [*German*]

ded............ Dedikation [*Dedication*] [*Danish/Norwegian*]

ded............ Dedikation [*Dedication*] [*Swedish*]

DED.......... Depenses d'Equipement Departementaux [*French*]

DED........... Deutscher Entwicklungsdienst [*German Development Service (Peace Corps)*] (WEN)

DED.......... Developpement Economique Departemental [*French*]

DEDARS... DECHEMA [*Deutsche Gesellschaft fuer Chemisches Apparatewesen, Chemische Technik, und Biotechnologie eV*] Data Retrieval System [*Information retrieval*]

DEDASZ ... Deldunantuli Aramszolgaltato Vallalat [*Electric Power Service Enterprise of Southern Transdanubia*] (HU)

DEDIB....... Departement de la Documentation et de l'Information en Matiere de Brevets [*Organisation Africaine de la Propriete Intellectuelle*] [*Cameroon*]

dedic.......... Dedicacao [*Dedication*] [*Portuguese*]

dedik .... Dedikasjon [*Dedication*] [*Danish/Norwegian*]

dedo........... Dedicado [*Dedicated*] [*Portuguese*]

DEE .... Datenendeinrichtung [*German*] (ADPT)

DEE .... Departamento de Estudios Economicos [*Camara de Industrias del Uruguay*] [*Uruguay*]

DEE .... Diethnes Emborikon Epimelitirion [*International Chamber of Commerce*] (GC)

DEE .... Dioikisis Exoterikou Emboriou [*Foreign Trade Administration*] [*Greek*] (GC)

DEE .... Distribucija Elektricne Energije [*Distribution of Electric Power*] (YU)

DEEA .... Division de Erradicacion de Enfermedades de Animales [*Puerto Rico*] (DSCA)

DEEAS...... Dievthynsis Epopteias kai Elengkhou Aktoploikon Syngoinonion [*Directorate for Supervision and Control of Coastal Shipping Communications*] [*Greek*] (GC)

deelw .... Deelwoord [*Participle*] [*Afrikaans*]

DEEP........ Development Education Exchange Papers [*FAO*] [*Information service or system United Nations*] (DUND)

DEES........ Departamento de Estudos Economicos e Sociais [*Brazil*] (DSCA)

DEES........ Diethnis Epitropi Erythrou Stavrou [*International Red Cross Committee*] (GC)

DEF .... Dansk Eksportfinancieringfond [*Export credit agency*] [*Denmark*]

DEF .... Defaut [*French*] (ADPT)

def .... Defectuosite [*Defect*] [*French*]

def .... Defeito [*Defect*] [*Portuguese*]

def .... Defekt [*Damaged, Incomplete*] [*German*]

def .... Defini [*French*] (TPFD)

def .... Definido [*Definitive*] [*Portuguese*]

def .... Definisie [*Definition*] [*Afrikaans*]

def .... Definite (TPFD)

DEF .... Delegations Economiques et Financieres [*French*]

DEF .... Diethnis Enosis Foititon [*International Union of Students*] (GC)

DEF .... Differential Figure Elements [*Cybernetics*] (RU)

DEF .... Diplomes d'Etudes Fondamentales [*French*]

def .... Imperfect, Defective (RU)

DEFA........ Deutsche Film Aktiengesellschaft [*German Film Corporation*] (EG)

DEFA........ Dimotiki Epikheirisis Fotaeriou Athinon [*Athens Public Gas Corporation*] (GC)

DEFAR...... Department of Defence, Army [*Australia*]

DEFCOMARS ... Defence Communications Automatic Relay Station

DEFCOMMNET ... Defence Force Communications Network [*Australia*]

Defe........... Defile [*Defile*] [*Military map abbreviation World War I*] [*French*] (MTD)

DEFE........ Destacamento Escuela de Fuerzas Especiales [*Special Forces School Detachment*] [*Ecuador*] (LA)

defect.......... Defectivo [*Defective*] [*Portuguese*]

defect.......... Defectueux [*Defective*] [*French*]

defeit .... Defeito [*Defect*] [*Portuguese*]

def ekz .... Defective Copy, Defective Item (BU)

DEFEN...... Defensivos e Fertilizantes Agricolas Ltd. [*Brazil*] (DSCA)
DEFFC ...... Defence Forces Charter [*Australia*]
DEFI.......... Comite de Developpement et de Promotion du Textile et de l'Habillement [*Paris, France*]
DEFNAV... Department of Defence, Navy [*Australia*]
Deformat.... Deformation [*German*] (GCA)
DEFOSZ ... Dolgozo Parasztok es Foldmunkasok Orszagos Szovetsege [*National Association of Working Peasants and Laborers*] (HU)
DEFP .... Departamento de Educacao e Formacao Professional [*Department of Education and Vocational Training*] [*Mozambique*] (AF)
DEFPA ...... Direction de l'Enseignement et de la Formation Professionnelle Agricole [*French*]
DEFPAC ... Defence Force Pay Accounting Centre [*Department of Defence*] [*Australia*]
Def PropInd ... La Defense de la Propriete Industrielle [*France*] (FLAF)
defr .... Defraichi [*Faded*] [*French*]
DEG .... Derechos Especiales de Giro [*Special Drawing Rights*] [*Argentina*] (LA)
DEG .... Deutsche Entwicklungsgesellschaft [*German Development Company*] (EG)
DEG .... Deutsche Gesellschaft fuer Wirtschaftliche Zusammenarbeit (Entwicklungsgesellschaft) mbH
DEG .... Direction des Etudes Generales [*Morocco*]
DEG .... Directorate of Environmental Geology [*Indonesian*] [*Research center*] (IRC)
DEGC .... Departamento Estadual de Geografia e Cartografia [*Brazil*] (DSCA)
Degebo ...... Deutsche Forschungsgesellschaft fuer Bodenmechanik (SLS)
DeGePo...... Deutsche Gesellschaft fuer Polarforschung (SLS)
De Gids ...... De Gids op Maatschappelijk Gebied [*Benelux*] (BAS)
DEGM........ Din Egitimi Genel Mudurlugu [*Religious Education Directorate General*] (TU)
DEGT .... Deutscher Eisenbahnguetertarif [*German Railway Freight Tariff*] (EG)
DEGU........ Diesel-Electric Drive [*Nautical term*] (RU)
DEGUFA... Deutsche Gummifabrik [*German Rubber Factory*] (EG)
DEGUSSA ... Deutsche Gold- und Silberscheide-Anstalt [*German Gold and Silver Separation Installation*] (WEN)
DEH.......... Departement Etranger Hachette
DEH.......... Department of Environment and Heritage [*Queensland*]
DEH.......... Drustvo Ekonomista Hrvatske [*Society of Economists of Croatia*] (YU)
DEHOGA ... Deutscher Hotel- und Gaststaettenverband [*German Hotel and Catering Trade Association*] (EG)
Dehydratisier ... Dehydratisierung [*Dehydration*] [*German*] (GCA)
Dehydrier... Dehydrierung [*Dehydrogenation*] [*German*] (GCA)
DEI .... Defense des Enfants - International [*Defence for Children International Movement - DCI*] (EAIO)
DEI .... Denis Island [*Seychelles Islands*] [*Airport symbol*] (OAG)
DEI .... Dimosia Epikheirisis Ilektrismou [*Public Power Corporation*] [*Greek*] (GC)
DEI .... Directorate of Economic Intelligence [*Australia*] (ADA)
DEI .... State Electric Power Installation (BU)
DEIA .... Department of Employment and Industrial Affairs [*Victoria, Australia*]
DEIC.......... Departamento de Investigacoes Criminais [*Criminal Investigations Department*] [*Brazil*] (LA)
DEIP .... Dairy Export Incentive Program
DEIP.......... Dewan Ekonomi Indonesia Pusat [*Central Economic Council of Indonesia*] (IN)
DEIP .... Division de Exploraciones e Introduccion de Plantas [*Argentina*] (LAA)
DEIRT ...... Department of Employment, Industrial Relations, and Training [*Tasmania, Australia*]
DEJ .... Delta Jet SA [*Spain*] [*ICAO designator*] (FAAC)
DEJ .... Drustvo Ekonomista Jugoslavije [*Society of Economists of Yugoslavia*] (YU)
DEJG........ Diplome d'Etudes Juridiques Generales [*French*]
DEJIMAS ... Developpement des Industries d'Articles de Sport, Jouets, et Instruments de Musique [*Entreprise Nationale de*] [*Algeria*] (EY)
DEK .... Dansk Elektroteknisk Komite [*Denmark*]
DEK .... Data -och Elektronikkomitten [*Commission on Computers and Electronics*] [*Sweden*] (PDAA)
dek.............. Dean (RU)
DEK .... Debreceni Kossuth Lajos Tudomanyegyetem Konyvtara [*Library of the Louis Kossuth University of Debrecen*] (HU)
dek............. Decare (BU)
dek............. December (RU)
Dek............ Dekanat [*Deanship*] [*German*]
dek............. Dekoration [*Decoration*] [*Sweden*]
DEK .... Demokratiki Enosis Kyprou [*Democratic Union of Cyprus*] [*Political party*] (PPE)
DEK .... Deutsche Elektrotechnische Kommission [*German Electrotechnical Commission*] (PDAA)

DEK .... Dimokratiki Enosis Kendrou [*Democratic Center Union*] [*Greek*] (GC)
DEK .... Dimokratikon Enotikon Komma [*Democratic Union Party*] [*Cyprus*] (GC)
DEK .... Dimokratikon Ethnikon Komma [*Democratic National Party*] [*Cyprus*] (GC)
DEKA .... Dimokratikon Ethnikon Kinima Andistaseos [*Democratic National Resistance Movement*] [*Greek*] (GC)
DEKAGE... Deutsche Kamerun GmbH
DEKAS.... Deputy Kepala Staf [*Deputy Chief of Staff*] (IN)
DEKE .... Dimokratikon Ergatikon Kinima Ellados [*Democratic Labor Movement of Greece*] (GC)
DEKFA ...... Dimokratiki Enosis Kyprion Foititon Athinas [*Democratic Union of Cypriot Students of Athens*] [*Greek*] (GC)
dekl .... Deklinasie [*Declination*] [*Afrikaans*]
Dekl .... Deklination [*Declension*] [*German*]
DEKO....... Demokratiko Komma [*Democratic Party*] [*Greek Cyprus*] [*Political party*] (PPE)
DEKO....... Dominikanska Edice Krystal, Olomouc [*Dominican "Krystal" Publishing House, Olomouc*] (CZ)
dekor .... Dekorasjon [*Decoration*] [*Danish/Norwegian*]
dekor .... Dekorerad [*Decorated*] [*Sweden*]
DEKOR ...... Kirakatrendezo es Reklamkivitelezo KTSz [*Producers' Cooperative of Window Dressers and Advertising Designers Enterprise*] (HU)
dekr .... Decree, Statute (RU)
DEKRA ..... West German Motor Vehicle Standards Institution (PDAA)
Del.............. Delagacion (IDIG)
Del.............. Delegacion (SCAC)
Del.............. Delegate (IDIG)
Del.............. Delhi [*India*] [*Airport symbol*] (OAG)
Del.............. Delostrelectvo [*Artillery*] (CZ)
DEL .... Depenses d'Equipement Local [*Algeria*]
DEL .... Developpement Economique Local
del............... Fission [*Nuclear physics and engineering*] (RU)
del............... Plot, Parcel [*of land*] (RU)
Delbat .... Delostrelecka Baterie [*Artillery Battery*] (CZ)
DELCO ...... Sierra Leone Development Company
DELDAV... Deldunantuli Aramszolgaltato Vallalat [*Electric Power Service Enterprise of Southern Transdanubia*] (HU)
deleg .... Delegation [*Delegation*] [*French*]
DELF .... Diplome Elementaire de Langue Francaise [*French*]
DELG .... Diplome d'Etudes Litteraires Generales [*French*]
DELI......... Desertification Library [*Database*] [*UNEP*] [*United Nations*] (DUND)
Delib .... Deliberation [*French*] (FLAF)
DelibAdm Enreg ... Deliberation de l'Administration de l'Enregistrement [*France*] (FLAF)
DELIMA ... Fundicion de Metales de Lima [*Barranquilla*] (COL)
DELIMCO ... Deutsche Liberian Mining Company
DELITBANG ... Dewan Penelitian dan Pembangunan [*Research and Development Council*] (IN)
DELK........ Deutsche Evangelisch-Lutherische Kirche in Suedwestafrika
delker .... Delkeruleti [*Southern District (Adjective)*] (HU)
DELMAIZ ... Derivados del Maiz, SA [*Colombia*] (COL)
Delodd........ Delostrelecky Oddil [*Artillery Battalion*] (CZ)
DELP......... Department of Environment, Lands, and Planning [*Australian Capital Territory*]
DELPCO ... Delta Petroleum Company [*Egypt*]
Delpluk ...... Delostrelecky Pluk [*Artillery Regiment*] (CZ)
DELTA ...... Developing European Learning through Technological Advance [*EC*] (ECED)
DELTA ...... Development of Learning through Technological Advance [*European Community*] (MHDB)
delv .... Delvis [*Partly*] [*Danish/Norwegian*]
DELWU .... Delegate [*or Delegation*] to Western Union [*NATO*] (NATG)
delyuv......... Diluvial (RU)
dem............. Demain [*Tomorrow*] [*French*]
Dem............ Demande en Interpretation et de Decision Prejudicielle [*Benelux*] (BAS)
DEM .... Dembidollo [*Ethiopia*] [*Airport symbol*] (OAG)
dem............. Deminutiivi [*Finland*]
Dem............ Democrat (SCAC)
Dem............ Democratic (SCAC)
DEM .... Demokraat [*Democrat*] [*Afrikaans*]
dem............. Demokraatti(nen) [*Finland*]
dem............. Demokrata [*or Demokratikus*] [*Democrat or Democratic*] (HU)
dem............. Demonstratif [*French*] (TPFD)
dem............. Demonstrative (TPFD)
dem............. Demonstrativo [*Demonstrative*] [*Portuguese*]
DEM .... Departamento de Exploracao Mineral [*Minerals Exploration Department*] [*Brazil*] (LA)
DEM .... Detective, Enigma, and Mystery [*Publisher*] [*Former USSR*] (ECON)
DeM............ Deus Misereatur [*67th Psalm*] [*Music*]
DEM .... Development Bank of Mauritius

DEM.......... Dievthynsis Enaerion Metaforon [*Air Transport Directorate*] [*Greek*] (GC)
DEM.......... Dievthynsis Ergon Mikhanikou [*Engineering Projects Directorate*] [*Greek*] (GC)
DEMA....... Delegacia Estadual do Ministerio da Agricultura [*Brazil*] (DSCA)
DEMA....... Departamento de Economia y Mercadeo Agropecuario [*Paraguay*] (DSCA)
DEMA....... Departamento de Enhenharia e Mecanica da Agricultura (LAA)
DEMA....... Dewan Mahasiswa [*Student Council*] (IN)
DEMA....... Divisao de Mecanizacao Agricola [*Brazil*] (DSCA)
DEMAK .... Demir-Makina Sanayi ve Ticaret AS [*Iron-Machinery Industry and Trading Corporation*] (TU)
DEMAR .... Fondo de Desenvolvimento Economico de Maranhao [*Brazil*] (LAA)
DEMASZ.. Del-Magyarorszagi Aramszolgaltato Vallalat [*Electric Power Service Enterprise of Southern Hungary*] (HU)
DEMATEL ... Decision-Making and Trial Evaluation Laboratory [*Switzerland*] (PDAA)
DEMBA .... Demerara Bauxite Company Ltd. [*Guyana*] (LA)
DEMC....... District Emergency Management Committee [*New South Wales, Australia*] [*Australia*]
DEMCOP ... Democratic Cooperative Development Party
DEMD....... Devlet Emlak ve Malzeme Dairesi Mudurlugu [*State Properties and Equipment Office Directorate*] [*Turkish Cypriot*] (GC)
DEME .... Diakyvernitiki Epitropi Metanastevseos ex Evropis [*Intergovernmental Committee for European Emigration*] (GC)
DEMETER ... Digital Electronic Mapping of European Territory
demilit........ Demilitarized (RU)
Deminex..... Deutsche ErdoeLversorgungs GmbH (OMWE)
Demiryol-Is ... Turkiye Demiryolu Iscileri Sendikasi [*Railway workers union*] [*Turkey*] (MENA)
DEMISAS ... Dokum Emaye Mamulleri Sanayi Anonim Sirketi [*Enamelled Cast Iron Products Industry Corporation*] (TU)
DEMKO .... Danish Board for Approval of Electrical Equipment (IMH)
DEMKO .... Dansk Elektrische Materialkontrol [*Danish Board for the Approval of Electrical Equipment*] (PDAA)
Demogr ...... Demografia [*Demography*] [*Portuguese*]
DEMOS .... Democratic Opposition of Slovenia [*Political party*] (EY)
DEMOSS.. Demographics Statistics System [*Australia*]
dem pron .... Demonstratiivipronomini [*Demonstrative Pronoun*] [*Finland*]
dem red ...... Demandes Reduites [*French*]
DEMSA .... Demographic Association of Southern Africa (AA)
DEMYC .... Democrat Youth Community of Europe [*Formerly, Conservative and Christian Democrat Youth Community of Europe*] (EA)
den............. Denaturalt [*Denatured*] (HU)
DEN.......... Dental [*Royal Australian Navy*]
DEN.......... Detasemen [*Detachment*] (IN)
DEN.......... Direccion de Educacion Naval [*Mexico*] (MSC)
DEN.......... Directia Energiei Nationale [*National Power Directorate*] (RO)
den............. Doctor of Economic Sciences (RU)
DENAGEO ... Departamento Nacional de Geologia [*Bolivia*] (DSCA)
Denaturier ... Denaturierung [*Denaturation*] [*German*] (GCA)
D en D........ Docteur en Droit [*Doctor of Law*] [*French*]
dendr .... Dendrological (RU)
DENEK ..... Dimokratiki Enosis Neolaias Kyprou [*Democratic Union of Cypriot Youth*] (GC)
DENet........ [*The*] Danish Ethernet Network [*Computer science*] (TNIG)
DENG........ Dimokratiki Enosi Neon Gynaikon [*Democratic Union of Young Women*] [*Greek*] (GC)
DENI .... Departamento Nacional de Investigacion [*National Department of Investigation*] [*Panama*] (LA)
DENI .... Departamento Nacional de Investigaciones [*National Department of Investigations*] [*Chile*] (LA)
DENIP....... Dia Escolar de la No-Violancia y la Paz [*School Day of Non-Violence and Peace*] [*Spain*]
Deniz......... Denizci [*or Denizcilik*] [*Sailor or Maritime*] (TU)
DenizUlas-Is ... Istanbul Deniz Ulas-Is Sendikasi [*Istanbul Maritime Transport Workers' Union*] (TU)
DENKA ..... Diakommatiki Epitropi Neolaion Kypriakou Agonos [*Interparty Committee of Youth for the Cypriot Struggle*] [*Greek*] (GC)
Denkschr ... Denkschrift [*Memoir*] [*German*] (GCA)
DENM....... Denmark
DENMA .... Detasemen Markas [*Headquarters Detachment*] (IN)
Denroren .... Zenkoku Denryoku Rodokumiai Rengokai [*Federation of Electrical Workers' Unions of Japan*]
dent .... Dentelle [*Lacelike design used in tooling bindings*] [*Publishing*] [*French*]
DENTEL... Departamento Nacional de Telecomunicacoes [*National Telecommunications Department*] [*Brazil*] (LA)
Dentsukyoto ... Denki Tsushin Rodokumiai Kyotokaigi [*Joint Council of Telecommunication Industry Trade Unions*] [*Japan*]
DEO.......... District Education Officer
DEO.......... Divisional Executive Officer

DEOC .... District Emergency Operations Controller [*Australia*]
DEOK .... Dimokratiki Ergatiki Omospondia Kyprou [*Democratic Labor Federation of Cyprus*] (GC)
DEON....... Dioikitiki Epitropi Oikou Navtou [*Sailors' Home Administrative Committee*] (GC)
DEOPE...... Director of Equal Opportunity in Public Employment [*Australia*]
DEOPS...... Departamento Estadual de Ordem Politica e Social [*State Department of Political and Social Order*] [*Brazil*] (LA)
DEOS .... Datenerfassungs-Organisationssystem [*German*] (ADPT)
DEP .... Defence and Ex-Services Party of Australia [*Political party*]
DEP .... Departamento de Educacao Politica [*Department of Political Education*] [*Angola*] (AF)
dep............. Departement [*Department*] [*Correspondence*] [*French*]
Dep............ Department (EECI)
DEP .... Department of Export Promotion [*Ministry of Commerce*] - [*Thailand*]
Dep............ Depeche Ministerielle [*Benelux*] (BAS)
dep............. Depliant [*Folding*] [*Publishing*] [*French*]
dep............. Deposited (BU)
dep............. Deposits (SCAC)
dep............. Depot [*Depot*] [*Afrikaans*]
Dep............ Deputy (PWGL)
dep............. Deputy, Representative (RU)
DEP .... Diesel-Electric Drive (RU)
DEP .... Dimosia Epikheirisis Petrelaiou [*Public Petroleum Corporation*] [*Greek*] (GC)
DEP .... Diplome d'Etat de Pharmacien [*French*]
DEP .... Direccion de Educacion Profesional [*Directorate of Professional Education*] [*Cuba*] (LA)
DEP .... Distributivno Elektricno Pretprijatie [*Electric Power Distribution Establishment*] [*YU*]
DeP .... Maanblad de Pacht [*Benelux*] (BAS)
DEP .... Road Maintenance Regiment (RU)
DEP .... State Electric Power Enterprise (BU)
DEPA .... Denmark Environmental Protection Agency
DEPA .... Diplome d'Etudes Pratiques d'Anglaise
DEPAD ..... Departemen Angkatan Darat [*Department of the Army*] (IN)
DEPAG...... Departemen Agama [*Department of Religious Affairs*] (IN)
DEPAIR.... Air Deputy [*NATO*] (NATG)
DEPAL ...... Departemen Angkatan Laut [*Department of the Navy*] (IN)
DEPARI .... Dewan Parawisata Indonesia [*Indonesia Tourism Council*] (IN)
DEPARLU ... Departemen Luar Negeri [*Department of Foreign Affairs*] (IN)
DEPAS ...... Denizli Boru ve Profil Sanayii ve Ticaret Anonim Sirketi [*Denizli Pipe and Construction Steelwork Industry Corporation*] (TU)
DEPAU ..... Departemen Angkatan Udara [*Department of the Air Force*] (IN)
DEPDAG... Departemen Perdagangan [*Department of Commerce*] (IN)
DEPDAGRI ... Departemen Dalam Negeri [*Department of Internal Affairs*] (IN)
DEPE........ Diakheiristiki Epitropi Ploion ex Epanorthoseon [*Administrative Committee of Ships Obtained from Reparations*] [*Greek*] (GC)
DEPE......... Division de Ejecucion de Proyectos Educativos [*Division for the Implementation of Educational Projects*] [*Nicaragua*] (LA)
DEPED...... Departamento de Pesquisas e Desenvolvimento [*Research and Development Department*] [*Brazil*] (LA)
DEPERDAG ... Departemen Perdagangan [*Department of Commerce*] (IN)
DEPERHUB ... Departemen Perhubungan [*Department of Communications*] (IN)
DEPERIN ... Departemen Perindustrian [*Department of Industry*] (IN)
DEPERTAM ... Departemen Pertambangan [*Department of Mining*] (IN)
DEPERTAN ... Departemen Pertanian [*Department of Agriculture*] (IN)
DEPES ...... Diplome d'Etudes Pratiques de l'Enseignement Secondaire
DEPFA ...... Deutsche Pfandbriefanstalt [*Financial institution*]
DEPGAKER ... Departemen Tenaga Kerdja [*Department of Manpower*] (IN)
DEPGAM ... Departemen Agama [*Department of Religious Affairs*] (IN)
DEPHAK .. Departemen Kehakiman [*Department of Justice*] (IN)
DEPHANKAM ... Departemen Pertahanan dan Keamanan [*Department of Defense and Security*] (IN)
DEPKEH... Departemen Kehakiman [*Department of Justice*] (IN)
DEPKES.... Departemen Kesehatan [*Department of Health*] (IN)
DEPKEU... Departemen Keuangan [*Department of Finance*] (IN)
depl .... Depliant [*Folding*] [*Publishing*] [*French*]
DEPLADIS ... Development Planning Documents Information System for ESCAP Countries [*Proposed*]
Deple.......... Departementale [*Departmental*] [*Military map abbreviation World War I*] [*French*] (MTD)
DEPLU....... Departemen Luar Negeri [*Department of Foreign Affairs*] (IN)
Dep Min..... Depeche Ministerielle [*France*] (FLAF)
Dep MinInt ... Depeche du Ministere de l'Interieur [*Benelux*] (BAS)
DEPNAKER ... Departemen Tenaga Kerdja [*Department of Manpower*] (IN)
DEPNAV... Naval Deputy [*NATO*] (NATG)

DEPOS...... Dimosia Epikheirisis Poleodomiseos, Oikismou, kai Stegaseos [*Public Enterprise for Town Planning, Housing, and Shelter*] [*Greek*]   (GC)

DEPP........ Societe Dahomeenne d'Entreposage de Produits Petroliers

DEPPEN... Departemen Penerangan [*Department of Information*]   (IN)

DEPPERHUB ... Departemen Perhubungan [*Department of Communications*]   (IN)

DEPPERIN ... Departemen Perindustrian [*Department of Industry*]   (IN)

Dep Perm... Deputation Permanente [*Benelux*]   (BAS)

DEPPERTAM ... Departemen Pertambangan [*Department of Mining*]   (IN)

Dep prov..... Deputato Provinciale [*Member of the Provincial Parliament*] [*Italian*]   (GPO)

DEPPU...... Departemen Pekerdjaan Umum [*Department of Public Works*]   (IN)

DEPRIN.... Departemen Perindustrian [*Department of Industry*]   (IN)

DEPRONAS ... Dewan Produksi Nasion [*National Production Council*]   (IN)

DEPS........ Departmental Entry Processing Systems [*Customs processing for sea and airports*] [*October, 1981*] [*British*]   (DCTA)

DEPS........ Development Education Projects Scheme [*Australia*]

DEPS........ Diplome d'Etudes Primaires Superieures [*Advanced Primary Studies Diploma*]   (CL)

DEPSOS ... Departemen Sosial [*Department of Social Affairs*]   (IN)

dept .... Departement [*Department*] [*Afrikaans*]

Dept .... Department   (IDIG)

DEPT........ Direction d'Entreaide et de Promotion des Travailleurs [*Algeria*]

DEPTAM ... Departemen Pertambangan [*Department of Mining*]   (IN)

DEPTAN... Departemen Pertanian [*Department of Agriculture*]   (IN)

DEPTRANSKOP ... Departemen Transmigrasi dan Koperasi [*Department of Resettlement and Cooperatives*]   (IN)

DEPTS ...... Commonwealth Government Departments [*Database*] [*Australia*]

DEPU .... Departemen Keuangan [*Department of Finance*]   (IN)

DEQUISA ... Desarollo Quimico de Centroamerica SA [*Nicaragua*]

DER .... Datumeingaberegister [*German*]   (ADPT)

DER .... Departamento de Estradas de Rodagem [*Highway Department*] [*Portuguese*]

DER .... Departamento de Estradas de Rodagem [*Highway Department*] [*Brazil*]   (LA)

DER .... Department for the Export of the Revolution [*Iran*]

DER .... Depenses d'Equipement Rural [*Rural Equipment Expenditures*] [*Algeria*]   (AF)

DER .... Derim [*Papua New Guinea*] [*Airport symbol*]   (OAG)

Der .... Derinlik [*Depth*] [*As in meters*]   (TU)

Der .... Derivat [*Derivative*] [*German*]

der .... Dernier [*Last*] [*French*]

DER .... Deutsches Reisebuero [*German Travel Agency*]   (EG)

DER .... Developpement Economique Rural [*Rural Economic Development*] [*Morocco*]   (AF)

DER .... Divisao de Economia Agricola [*Brazil*]   (DSCA)

Der .... Dokter [*Academic degree*] [*Indonesian*]

Der .... Village   (RU)

Der .... Wooden [*Bridge, sluice, dam*] [*Topography*]   (RU)

DERA .... Directory of Education Research and Researchers in Australia [*Commonwealth Department of Education Research and Youth Affairs*] [*Information service or system*]   (IID)

DERAP...... Development Economics Research and Advisory Project [*Kenya*]

DERBH ..... Diplome d'Etudes et de Recherches en Biologie Humaine [*French*]

derel .... Derelie [*With Binding Gone*] [*French*]

Derg .... Dergi [*or Dergisi*] [*Review As a publication*]   (TU)

dergl .... Dergleichen [*Similar*] [*German*]

Deri-Is........ Turkiye Deri, Debbag, Kundura ve Saraciye Iscileri Sendikasi [*Turkish Leather and Shoe Industry Workers Union*]   (TU)

Deriv .... Derivat [*Derivative*] [*German*]

derm .... Dermatology, Dermatologist   (BU)

dern .... Dernier [*Last*] [*French*]

derr .... Dernier [*Last*] [*French*]

derr............ Derriere [*Behind*] [*Knitting*] [*French*]

DERRO ..... Projet de Developpement Economique et Rural du Rif Occidental [*Economic and Rural Development of the Western Rif*]

ders............ Derselbe [*The Same*] [*German*]   (GPO)

DERT .... Division Electronique, Radioelectricite et Telecommunications [*France*]   (PDAA)

DERTS ..... Departement d'Etudes et de Recherches en Technologie Spatiale

DERU .... Departamento Rural [*Brazil*]   (DSCA)

DERUTRA ... Deutsch-Russische Transport AG [*GDR-Soviet Transport Corp.*]   (EG)

DES .... Arc Welding   (RU)

DES .... Daspoort Experimental Station [*Council for Scientific and Industrial Research*] [*South Africa*]   (AA)

DES .... Datenerfassungssystem [*German*]   (ADPT)

DES .... Datumeingabesteuerung [*German*]   (ADPT)

des .... Decimal   (RU)

DES .... Defektni Sluhom [*Persons with Defective Hearing*] [*Labor*]   (YU)

DES .... Defence and Ex-Services Party of Australia

des .... Desatnik [*Corporal*]   (CZ)

des .... Desdobravel [*Unfolding*] [*Publishing*] [*Portuguese*]

Des .... Desember [*December*] [*Afrikaans*]

des .... Desenho [*Sketch*] [*Portuguese*]

des .... Deser [*Of This*] [*Afrikaans*]

des .... Dessin [*Design, Drawing*] [*French*]

DES .... Diesel Electric Power Plant   (RU)

DES .... Diethnis Erythros Stavros [*International Red Cross*]   (GC)

DES .... Dimosia Emboriki Skholi [*Public Commercial School*]   (GC)

DES .... Diploma de Estudos Superiores [*Polytechnical Higher Studies*] [*Portuguese*]

DES .... Diplome d'Etudes Superieures [*Advanced Studies Diploma*] [*French*]   (WER)

DES .... Direction des Etapes et Services [*Obsolete*] [*Military*] [*French*]   (MTD)

DES .... Divers Emergency Service [*Australia*]

DES .... Drustvo Ekonomista Srbije [*Society of Economists of Serbia*]   (YU)

DES .... Landing Force   (RU)

DESA........ Demir, Kazan, ve Makina Sanayii AS [*Iron, Boilers, and Machinery Industry, Inc.*] [*Subsidiary of Yesar Holding*]   (TU)

DESA........ Desarrollo de Edificaciones Sociales y Agropecuarias [*Farm and Social Building Development Agency*] [*Cuba*]   (LA)

DESAL...... Centro para el Desarrollo Economico y Social de America Latina [*Latin American Center for Socioeconomic Development*]   (LA)

DESAM..... Diplome d'Etudes Superieures Administratives Municipale [*Diploma in Advanced Municipal Administration Studies*] [*French Guiana*]   (LA)

DESARRURAL ... Servicio Cooperativo de Desarrollo Rural [*Comayaguela, Honduras*]   (LAA)

DESAS ...... Dioikousa Epitropi Syllogon Anoteron Skholon [*Administrative Committee of Associations of Higher Schools*] [*Greek*]   (GC)

desasp .... Desatnik Aspirant [*Cadet Corporal*]   (CZ)

DESAURChM ... Decentralized Automatic Frequency and Active Power Control System   (RU)

desc .... Desconto [*Deduction, Discount*] [*Portuguese*] [*Business term*]

DESCO...... Centro de Estudios y Promocion del Desarrollo [*Center for Development Studies and Advancement*] [*Lima, Peru*]

DESCON... Desertification Control   (AF)

descr.......... Descrizione [*Description*] [*Italian*]

DESCTC ... Dewaniya State Cotton Textile Company [*Iraq*]

descto .... Descuento [*Discount*] [*Spanish*]

desd .... Desdobravel [*Unfolding*] [*Publishing*] [*Portuguese*]

desdobr....... Desdobravel [*Unfolding*] [*Publishing*] [*Portuguese*]

DESEC ...... Centro para el Desarrollo Social y Economico [*Center for Social and Economic Development*] [*Bolivia*]   (EAIO)

DESEC ...... Departamento de Estudos Economicos [*Brazil*]   (DSCA)

desencad.... Desencadernado [*Covers Gone, Unstitched*] [*Bookbinding*] [*Portuguese*]

DESG........ Diplome d'Etudes Scientifiques Generales [*French*]

desgl.......... Desgleichen [*Similar*] [*German*]

DESIDOC ... Defence Scientific Inforamation and Documentation Centre [*India*]   (PDAA)

DESIG....... Distance Education Special Interest Group [*Australian Library and Information Association*]

Desinfekt ... Desinfektion [*Disinfection*] [*German*]   (GCA)

DESIS........ Desertification Information System [*UNEP*] [*United Nations*]   (DUND)

DESIYAB ... Devlet Sanayi ve Isci Yatirim Bankasi [*State Industry and Worker Investment Bank*]   (TU)

DESK........ Dimokratiki Enotita Syndikalistikon Kiniseon [*Democratic Union of Trade Union Movements*] [*Greek*]   (GC)

D es L........ Docteur es Lettres [*Doctor of Letters*] [*French*]

DESO .... Landing Detachment   (RU)

Desorpt ..... Desorption [*German*]   (GCA)

DESP........ Departamento Estadual de Seguranca Publica [*State Department of Public Security*] [*Brazil*]   (LA)

desp .... Despesa [*Cost*] [*Portuguese*] [*Business term*]

DESP........ Destacamento Especial de Selva Petrolifera [*Oil Jungle Special Detachment*] [*For security work in Santa Cecilia region Ecuador*]   (LA)

DESP........ Dimokratiki Enotiki Syndikalistiki Parataxi [*Democratic Unifying Trade Union Faction*]   (GC)

DESP........ Diplome de l'Ecole Superieure de Pali [*Pali Higher School Diploma*]   (CL)

DESP........ Diplome d'Etudes Scientifiques Preparatoires [*French*]

DESP........ Primeros Puestos del Deporte Espanol [*Ministerio de Cultura*] [*Spain*] [*Information service or system*]   (CRD)

DESPA ...... Dimokratiki Enotiki Syndikalistiki Parataxi Athinon [*Democratic Unifying Trade Union Faction of Athens*]   (GC)

DESPA ...... Dioikousa Epitropi Syllogon Panepistimiou Athinon [*Administrative Committee of Athens University Associations*] (GC)

despb .... Assault Troop Crossing Battalion (BU)

despb .... River Crossing Assault Battalion (RU)

DESPC ...... Diplome d'Etudes Secondaires du Premier Cycle [*First Cycle Secondary Studies Diploma*] (CL)

despr ...... River Crossing Assault Company (RU)

Despred ...... State Shipping Enterprise (BU)

DESRET ... Division Exploitation, Securite Routiere, Etudes Techniques [*Division of Management, Road Safety, and Technology Studies*] [*France*] [*Research center*] (ERC)

dess .... Desselben [*Of the Same*] [*German*]

dess .... Dessin [*Design, Drawing*] [*French*]

DESS .... Diplome d'Etudes Superieures Specialisees [*Advanced Specialized Studies Diploma*] [*French*] (WER)

D es S .... Docteur es Sciences [*Doctor of Sciences*] [*French*]

DESSO ...... Tapijtafbriek H. Desseaux NV [*Netherlands*]

DEST .... Department of Environment, Sport and Territories [*Australia*]

dest .... Destillation [*Distillation*] [*German*]

DESTI ...... Direction des Etudes Statistiques et du Traitement de l'Information

DESTO ...... Defence Science and Technology Organization [*Pakistan*] (EAS)

DESU ...... Delhi Electric Supply Undertaking [*India*] (PDAA)

desus .... Desusado [*Obsolete*] [*Portuguese*]

DESY .... Deutsches Elektronen-Synchrotron [*German Electron-Synchrotron*] (EG)

des zn .... Decimal Point (RU)

det .... Children's Word (BU)

det .... Child's, Children's (RU)

DET .... Daspoortse Eksperimentele Terrein [*Daspoort Experimental Station*] [*Council for Scientific and Industrial Research*] [*South Africa*] (AA)

DET .... Delta Aviation SA [*Spain*] [*ICAO designator*] (FAAC)

DET .... Department of Education and Training [*South Africa*]

DET .... Department of Education and Training [*Western Australia*]

DET .... Department of Employment and Training [*Victoria*] [*Australia*]

DET .... Department of Establishment and Training [*Government of Swaziland*]

det .... Detache [*Detached*] [*French*]

DET .... Detasemen [*Detachment*] (IN)

det .... Determinativo [*Portuguese*]

DET .... Diesel-Electric Tractor (RU)

DET .... Diethnis Enosis Tilepikoinion [*International Telecommunications Union*] (GC)

DET .... Diethnis Enosis Tourismou [*International Touring Alliance*] (GC)

DET .... Diffuse Emission Nebula (RU)

DET .... Division de Desarrollo Tecnologico [*Colorado*]

det .... Part, Element (RU)

DETA .... Direccao de Exploracao dos Transportes Aereos [*Air Transport Exploitation Directorate*] [*Mozambique*] (AF)

DETAFE ... Department of Employment, Technical and Further Education [*South Australia*]

DETAS ...... Dezentralisierte Textverarbeitung am Sachbearbeiterplatz [*German*] (ADPT)

d et c .... Dos et Coins [*Back and Corners (of a Book)*] [*Publishing*] [*French*]

det d .... Children's Home [*Topography*] (RU)

DETEC ...... Detectivismo Tecnico Particular [*Colombia*] (COL)

DETEQ ...... DECHEMA [*Deutsche Gesellschaft fuer Chemisches Apparatewesen, Chemische Technik, und Biotechnologie eV*] Environmental Technology Equipment Databank [*Information service or system*] [*Germany*] (IID)

deterior ...... Deteriorato [*Deteriorated*] [*Italian*]

determpron ... Determinatiivipronomini [*Determinative Pronoun*] [*Finland*]

DeTeWe ..... Deutsche Telephonwerke und Kabelindustrie [*German*] (ADPT)

DETGIZ .... State Publishing House of Children's Literature (RU)

DETh .... Diethnis Ekthesis Thessalonikis [*Salonica International Fair*] (GC)

DETHERM ... DECHEMA [*Deutsche Gesellschaft fuer Chemisches Apparatewesen, Chemische Technik, und Biotechnologie eV*] Thermophysical Property Data Bank [*Germany*] [*Information service or system*] (CRD)

d et ht .... Dans et Hors Texte [*In and Not in the Text*] [*Publishing*] [*French*]

Detizdat ..... State Publishing House for Children's Books (RU)

Det kol .... Children's Colony [*Topography*] (RU)

Detkom ...... Commission for the Improvement of Children's Living Conditions (RU)

Detmag ...... Children's Store (BU)

DETN .... Departement des Etudes et des Travaux Neufs

DETRA ...... Societe de Distribution et d'Equipement pour l'Industrie et les Transports

Detran .... Departamento de Transito [*Traffic Department*] [*Brazil*] (LA)

DETs .... Diesel Electric Power Plant (BU)

det san .... Children's Sanatorium [*Topography*] (RU)

detszagotovka ... Decentralized Procurement, Local Procurement (RU)

Dett .... Detachement [*Detachment*] [*Military*] [*French*] (MTD)

DETT .... Length of Apparatus Equivalent to a Theoretical Plate (RU)

det tubsan ... Children's Tuberculosis Sanatorium [*Topography*] (RU)

Detyunizdat ... State Publishing House of Children's and Young People's Literature (RU)

DEU .... Federal Republic of Germany [*ANSI three-letter standard code*] (CNC)

DEU .... Road Maintenance Section (RU)

DEUG .... Diplome d'Etudes Universitaires Generales [*French*]

DEULA ..... Deutsche Land Maschinenschulen German Farm Machinery Schools [*Germany*] (DSCA)

DEUP .... Diplome d'Etudes Universitaires Pedagogiques [*French*]

Deuqua ...... Deutsche Quartaervereinigung (SLS)

Deut .... Deuteronomium [*Deuteronomy*] [*Afrikaans*]

deut .... Deutsch [*German*]

Deut .... Deutscher [*German*] (GCA)

Deut .... Deutung [*Interpretation*] (GCA)

DEV .... Derecha Emergente de Venezuela [*Political party*] (EY)

dev .... Devant [*Front*] (BARN)

dev .... Deviza [*Foreign Exchange*] (HU)

DEVA .... Demonstration, Experimentation, et Valorisation de l'Aquaculture (MSC)

deva .... Field Forces (BU)

DEVET ...... Department of Employment, Vocational Education, and Training [*Queensland, Australia*]

DevG .... Devisengesetz [*Law on Exchange Control*] [*German*] (DLA)

DEVGENC ... Turkiye Devrimci Genclik Federasyonu [*Turkish Revolutionary Youth Federation*] [*TDGF*] [*See also*] (TU)

DEV-IS ...... Devrimci Isci Sendikalari Federasyonu [*Revolutionary Trade Unions' Federation*] [*Turkish Cypriot*] (GC)

Dev-Lis ...... Devrimci Liseciler Birligi [*Union of Revolutionary Lycee Students*] (TU)

DevMaden-Sen ... Devrimci Maden Arama ve Isletme Iscileri Sendikasi [*Revolutionary Mineral Research and Exploitation Workers' Union*] [*Belongs to DISK*] (TU)

DEV-MEM ... Devrimci Memurlar Dernegi [*Revolutionary Public Officials Organization*] [*Reformist*] (TU)

DEVNET ... Development Information Network [*Proposed*]

DEVO .... Datenerfassungs-verordnung [*German*] (ADPT)

devo .... Devotado [*Devoted*] [*Portuguese*]

DEVREKTAS ... Devrek Insaat Elemanlari Sanayi ve Ticaret Anonim Sirketi [*Devrek Construction Elements Industry and Trade Corporation*] (TU)

Devt .... Development (EECI)

DEW .... Deutsche Edelstahlwerke Aktiengesellschaft [*German High-Grade Steel Works*] [*Germany*]

DEWAG .... Deutsche Werbe- und Anzeigengesellschaft [*German Promotion and Ad Company*] (EG)

dex .... Dexamenoploion [*Tanker*] [*D/P*] [*See also*] (GC)

DEXIA ...... Dominica Export-Import Agency (EY)

DEY .... Diethnis Ethelondiki Ypiresia [*International Volunteer Service*] (GC)

DEY .... Dievthynsis Englimatologikon Ypiresion [*Criminal Services Directorate*] [*Greek*] (GC)

deyeprich ... Verbal Adverb (RU)

DEYF-Is ...... Demiryollari Isci Sendikalari Federasyonu [*Federation of Railway Worker Unions*] (TU)

deystv .... Active (BU)

deystv .... Active (Voice) (RU)

deystv .... Actual (BU)

deystvchlen ... Active Member (RU)

DEZ .... Deir Ez Zor [*Syria*] [*Airport symbol*] (OAG)

Dez .... Dezember [*December*] [*German*] (GPO)

dez .... Dezembro [*December*] [*Portuguese*] (GPO)

DEZ .... State Lighting Fixtures Plant (BU)

deza .... Misleading Information, Deception [*Military term*] (RU)

dezh .... Duty Officer, Man on Duty, Officer of the Day (RU)

dezhkom ..... Duty Commandant (RU)

dezhoperot ... Operations Duty Officer (RU)

Dezinstitut ... Central Scientific Research Institute of Disinfection (RU)

dezo .... Dezembro [*December*] [*Portuguese*]

DE-ZZU ..... Diesel-Electric Suction Dredge (RU)

DF .... Dah Feng Collapsible Tube Industrial Co. Ltd. [*Taiwan*]

DF .... Danske Fysioterapeuter [*Denmark*] (SLS)

DF .... Datenfeld [*German*] (ADPT)

DF .... Delo Formylar [*Formal Case*] [*Former USSR*]

DF .... Detailhandelens Faellesraad [*Danish Retail Association*] (EAIO)

DF .... Deutscher Forschungsrat [*German Research Council*] (EG)

df .... Dias Fecha [*Days from Date*] [*Spanish*]

DF .... Dias Freres

DF .... Distrito Federal [*Federal District*] [*Portuguese*]

DF .... Distrito Federal [*Federal District*] [*Spanish*] (GPO)

DF .... Djakarta Fair (IN)

DF .... Dnepr Flotilla (RU)

DF .... Dong Feng [*East Wind*] [*Chinese missile*]

DF .... Faux Fret [*French*] (FLAF)
d/f .... Slide Film, Film Strip, Strip Positive (RU)
DFA .... Danish Football Association (EAIO)
DFA .... Defence Force Advocate [*Australia*]
DFA .... Delegacia Federal de Agricultura [*Brazil*] (DSCA)
DFA .... Department for the Arts [*Western Australia*] [*Australia*]
DFA .... Department of Food and Agriculture [*Victoria*] [*Australia*]
DFA .... Diabetes Federation of Australia (ADA)
DFA .... Diphenylamine (RU)
DFA .... Diploma in Foreign Affairs (ADA)
DFA .... Directoria de Fotos Aereos do Ministerio de Aeronautica [*Rio De Janeiro, Brazil*] (LAA)
DFA .... Drive Front Axle
DFA .... Dutch Fashion Institute (EAIO)
DFAI .... Department of Foreign Affairs and Information [*South Africa*]
DFAT .... Department of Foreign Affairs and Trade [*Australia*]
DFB .... Damien Foundation - Belgium (EAIO)
DFB .... Dansk Fabriksbetonforening [*Danish Ready Mixed Concrete Association*] (EAIO)
DFB .... Defence Force Development Committee [*Department of Defense*] [*Australia*] (PDAA)
DFB .... Demokratischer Frauenbund Deutschlands [*Democratic Women's League of Germany*] (EG)
DFB .... Deutsche Frauenbewegung [*German Women's Movement*] [*Germany*] (PPW)
DFB .... Dried Fruits Board [*New South Wales, South Australia, Western Australia*]
DFB .... South African Deciduous Fruit Board
DFBD .... Demokratischer Frauenbund Deutschlands [*Democratic Women's League of Germany*] (EG)
DFBO .... Deutsche Forschungsgesellschaft fuer Blechverarbeitung und Oberflaechenbehandlung eV [*German Research Company for Sheet Metal Work and Surface Treatment*] (SLS)
DFC .... Development Finance Corporation [*Kingston, Jamaica*] (LAA)
DFC .... Development Finance Corporation [*New Zealand*]
DFC .... Development Finance Corporation [*Belize, Guyana*] (LAA)
DFC .... Development Finance Corporation [*Australia*]
DFC .... Division of Physical Chemistry [*France*] (EAIO)
DFCC .... Development Finance Corporation of Ceylon (GEA)
DFCK .... Development Finance Company of Kenya Ltd.
DFC of T .... Deputy Federal Commissioner of Taxation [*Australia*]
DFCS .... Department of Family and Community Services [*South Australia*]
DFCU .... Development Finance Company of Uganda Ltd.
DFD .... Data for Development International Association [*See also DD*] [*Marseille, France*] (EAIO)
DFD .... Demokratischer Frauenbund Deutschlands [*Democratic Women's League of Germany*] (EG)
DFD .... Devterovathmion Forologikon Dikastirion [*Tax Court of the Second Instance*] [*Greek*] (GC)
DfD .... Dienst fuer Deutschland [*Service for Germany*] [*DD*] [*See also*] (EG)
DFDAT ...... Defence Force Discipline Appeal Tribunal [*Australia*]
DFDC .... Defence Force Development Committee [*Australia*]
DFDHIDWA ... Die Furcht des Herrn Ist der Weisheit Anfang [*Fear of the Lord Is the Beginning of Wisdom*] [*(Ps., CXI. 10) Motto of Dorothee Hedwig, Princess of Anhalt (1587-1608); Johann Sigismund, Elector of Brandenburg (1572-1619)*]
DFDS A/S ... Det Forenede Dampskibs-Selskab A/S [*Denmark*]
DFE .... Dansk Forening for Europaret [*Denmark*] (SLS)
DFE .... Delegationen foer Energiforskning [*Energy Research and Development Commission*] [*Ministry of Industry*] [*Sweden*] (WED)
DFE .... Photoelectric Densitometer (RU)
DFEPC ...... Diplome de Fin d'Etudes du Premier Cycle [*French*]
DFF........... Danske Forstkandidaters Forening [*Denmark*] (SLS)
DFF........... Dansk Faegte-Forbund [*Danish Fencing Federation*] (EAIO)
DFF........... Dansk Forfatterforening [*Danish Writers Association*] (EAIO)
DFF........... Design Forum Finland (EAIO)
DFF........... Deutscher Fernsehfunk [*German Television*] (EG)
DFF........... Diisopropylfluorophosphate (RU)
DFFA .... Danish Family Farmers Association (EAIO)
DFFF .... Demokratiska Foerbundet av Finlands Folk [*Finnish People's Democratic League*] (PPE)
DFFG........ De Forenade FNL-Grupperna [*The United National Liberation Front Groups*] [*Sweden*] (WEN)
DFFOH ..... Development Fund Future in Our Hands [*Norway*] (EAIO)
DFG .... Deutsche Forschungsgemeinschaft [*German Research Association*] [*Research center*] (WEN)
DFG .... Deutsche Friedensgesellschaft [*German Peace Society*] (EG)
dfg .... Dienstfaehig [*Fit for Duty*] [*German*] (EG)
DFG .... Diphenylguanidine (RU)
DFG-VK .... Deutsche Friedensgesellschaft - Vereinigte Kriegdienstgegner [*German Peace Society - United War Resisters*] (EAIO)
DFHF .... Direccion de Frutas, Hortalizas, y Flores [*Argentina*] (DSCA)
DFI........... Delegationen foer Vetenskaplig och Teknisk Informationsforsoerjning [*Sweden*] (SLS)

DFI .... Delegationen for Vetenskaplig och Teknisk Informationsforsorjning [*Swedish Delegation for Scientific and Technical Information*] [*Information service or system*] [*Defunct*] (IID)
DFI .... Development Finance Institution [*Kiribati*] (FEA)
DFIS .... Digitised Facilities Information System [*Australia*]
D Fisc .... Droit Fiscal [*French*] (FLAF)
DFJ .... Demokratska Federativna Jugoslavija [*Democratic Federative Yugoslavia*] (YU)
DFK .... Dansk Forening foer Kvalitetsstyring [*Danish Society for Quality Control*] [*Denmark*] (SLS)
DFK .... De Duisburgse Vrachtkonvenie [*Benelux*] (BAS)
DFK .... Differential Photoelectric Calorimeter (RU)
DFK .... Dolnoslaska Fabryka Krosien [*Lower Silesia Loom Factory*] (POL)
DFK .... House of Physical Culture (RU)
DFK .... State Fodder Combine (BU)
DFK .... State Leather Factory (BU)
DFL .... Donauflug Bedarfsfluggesellschaft GmbH [*Austria*] [*ICAO designator*] (FAAC)
Dfl .... Dutch Florin [*Monetary unit*] (IMH)
DFLP .... Democratic Front for the Liberation of Palestine (PD)
DFLR .... Deutsche Forschungsanstalt fuer Luft- und Raumfahrt
D Fluv .... Droit Fluvial [*French*] (FLAF)
DFM .... Direccion de Fabricaciones Militares [*Military Construction Administration*] [*Argentina*] (LA)
DFMDFJ... Demokratska Federalna Makedonija vo Demokratska Federativna Jugoslavija [*Democratic Federative Macedonia in Democratic Federal Yugoslavia*] (YU)
d f-m n .... Doctor of Physical and Mathematical Sciences (RU)
DFMV .... Debreceni Finommechanikai Vallalat [*Precision Machine Enterprise of Debrecen*] (HU)
DFN .... Deutsches Foerschungsnetz [*German*] [*Computer science*] (TNIG)
DFN .... Diphosphopyridine Nucleotide (RU)
dfn .... Doctor of Pharmaceutical Sciences (RU)
dfn .... Doctor of Philological Sciences (RU)
dfn .... Doctor of Philosophical Sciences (RU)
DFO .... Deutsche Forschungsgesellschaft fuer Oberflaechenbehandlung eV [*German Research Institute for Surface Treatment*] (SLS)
DFOM .... Departements Francais d'Outre-Mer
D For .... Droit Forestier [*French*] (FLAF)
DFP .... Demokratische Fortschrittliche Partei [*Democratic Progressive Party*] [*Austria*] (PPE)
DFP .... Dominica Freedom Party [*Political party*] (PPW)
DFPA .... Danish Family Planning Association [*Denmark*] (EAIO)
DFPJ .... Dolnoslaska Fabryka Przemyslu Jedwabniczego [*Lower Silesia Silk Factory*] (POL)
DFPM .... Divisao de Fomento da Producao Mineral [*Rio De Janeiro, Brazil*] (LAA)
DFPS .... Danish Foreign Policy Society (EAIO)
DFPS .... Direction de la Formation Professionnelle et des Stages
DFR........... Defence Force Reserves [*Australia*]
DFr........... Discophiles Francais [*Record label*] [*France*]
DFRDBS ... Defence Force Retirement and Death Benefits Scheme [*Australia*]
DFRDC...... Dried Fruits Research and Development Council [*Australia*]
DFRH .... Drustvo Filmskih Radnika Hrvatske [*Society of Motion Picture Workers of Croatia*] (YU)
DFRRI ...... Directorate of Food, Roads, and Rural Infrastructure [*Nigeria*]
DFS........... Departamento Forestal y de Suelos del Ministerio de Agricultura, Comercio, e Industria [*Panama*] (LAA)
DFS........... Direccion Federal de Seguridad [*Federal Security Office*] [*Mexico*] (LA)
DFS-904 .... Deutscher Freiheitssender 904 [*German Freedom Station 904 (Communist Radio)*] (WEN)
DFSA .... Dansk Fagpresse Service ApS [*Danish Association of the Specialist Press*] (EAIO)
DFSC .... Defence Force Structure Committee Dept of Defence (PDAA)
DFSHW .... Department of Family Services and Housing Welfare [*Queensland*] [*Australia*]
DFSI .... Demokraticna Fronta Slovencev v Italiji [*Slovenian Democratic Front in Italy*] (YU)
DFSM........ Defence Force Service Medal [*Military decoration*] [*Australia*]
DFSP .... Departamento Federal de Seguranca Publica [*Federal Department of Public Security*] [*Brazil*] (LA)
DFSP .... Duennschicht-Filmspeicher [*German*] (ADPT)
DFSS .... Democratic Front for the Salvation of Somalia (PD)
DFT .... Diskrete Fouriertransformation (ADPT)
DFTG .... Deutsche Flussigergas Terminal GmbH
DFTI .... Dansk Fiskeriteknologisk Institut [*Danish Fisheries Technology Institute*] [*Also, an information service or system*] (IID)
DFU .... Datenfernuebertragung [*German*] (ADPT)
DFU .... Deutsche Friedens-Union [*German Peace Union*] (WEN)
DFU .... Dominica Farmers Union [*Dominican Republic*] (LA)
DFV .... Datenfernverarbeitung [*German*] (ADPT)

DF(V)........ Deafness Foundation [*Victoria*] [*Australia*]
DFV .... Deutscher Federball Verband der DDR [*Germany*]   (EAIO)
DFV .... Deutscher Fussball-Verband [*German Soccer League*]   (EG)
DFV .... Dokumentationsstelle fuer Veterinaermedizin [*Information retrieval*] [*German*]
DFVLR...... Deutsche Forschungs- und Versuchsanstalt fuer Luft- und Raumfahrt [*German Research and Development Institute for Air and Space Travel*] [*Research center*]   (EG)
DFVLR...... Deutsche Forschungs und Versuchsanstalt fuer Luft und Raumfahrt [*German Research Institute for Air and Space Travel*] [*An association*]
DfwG........ Deutsche Farbwissenschaftliche Gesellschaft eV [*German Scientific Color Society*]   (SLS)
DFWR ...... Deutscher Forstwirtschaftsrat eV [*German Forestry Board*]   (SLS)
DFX .... Dylan Flight Service SA [*Switzerland*] [*ICAO designator*]   (FAAC)
DFZ .... State Fodder Plant   (BU)
DG............. Arc Converter   (RU)
Dg.............. Dag [*Mountain, Mount*]   (TU)
DG............. Dalasi Gambia
Dg.............. Daljina Gadanja [*Firing Range*] [*Military*]   (YU)
DG............. Damping Gyro   (RU)
Dg.............. Decagramo [*Decagram*] [*Spanish*]
dg.............. Decigram   (RU)
dg.............. Decigrama [*Decigram*] [*Portuguese*]
dg.............. Decigrama-Forca [*Decigram of Force*] [*Portuguese*]
dg.............. Decigramme [*Decigram*] [*French*]
dg.............. Decigramo [*Decigram*] [*Spanish*]
DG............. Declaration de Guerre [*Declaration of War*] [*French*]   (ILCA)
DG............. Decreto Governatoriale [*Governor's Decree*] [*Italian*]   (ILCA)
Dg.............. Degirmen [*Mill*]   (TU)
DG............. Dehydrogenase   (RU)
dg.............. Dekagramm [*Decagram*]   (HU)
DG............. Deoxy-D-Glucose   (RU)
DG............. Departamento de Ganaderia [*Chile*]   (DSCA)
dg.............. Dergestalt [*Such*] [*German*]   (GCA)
dg.............. Dergleichen [*Similar*] [*German*]
dG.............. Des Generalstabs [*or Generalstabsdienstes*] [*German*]
dg.............. Desigram [*Decigram*] [*Afrikaans*]
dg.............. Desigramma(a) [*Finland*]
DG............. Destroyer, Guided Missile [*Surface-to-air*] [*NATO*]
DG............. Deus Guarde [*God Bless You*] [*Portuguese*]
DG............. Deutsche Gemeinschaft [*German Union*]   (EG)
DG............. Deutsche Genossenschaftsbank [*German*]
DG............. Deutsche Gesellschaft fuer Galvanotechnik eV [*German Society for Galvanic Technology*]   (SLS)
dg.............. Dezigramm [*Decigram*] [*German*]
DG............. Diesel Generator   (RU)
DG............. Differentiating Gyro   (RU)
DG............. Diplome de Docteur Ingenieur [*French*]
DG............. Directeur-Generaal [*Benelux*]   (BAS)
DG............. Direkteur-Generaal [*Director-General*] [*Afrikaans*]
Dg.............. Districtsgerecht [*Benelux*]   (BAS)
DG............. Division Hospital   (RU)
DG............. Doppelte Genauigkeit [*German*]   (ADPT)
Dg.............. Durchgangsgueterzug [*Through Freight Train*]   (EG)
dG .... Durch Guete [*Kindness Of*] [*German*]
DG............. For Long-Range Shell [*Sight scale*]   (RU)
DG............. General Aviation Services Ltd. [*British*] [*ICAO designator*]   (ICDA)
dg.............. General Commanding a Division   (BU)
Dg.............. Horizontal Range   (RU)
DG............. State Forests   (BU)
DGA.......... Dangriga [*Belize*] [*Airport symbol*]   (OAG)
DGA.......... Delegation General pour l'Armement [*France*]   (PDAA)
DGA.......... Direccion General de Aeropuertos [*Airports Directorate*] [*Research center*] [*Mexico*]   (ERC)
DGA.......... Directia Generala a Agriculturii [*General Directorate of Agriculture*]   (RO)
DGA.......... Dog Grooming Association of Victoria [*Australia*]
DGAA........ Accra/Kotoka International [*Ghana*] [*ICAO location identifier*]   (ICLI)
DGAA........ Direccion General de Asuntos Agrarios [*Guatemala*]   (LAA)
DGaaE....... Deutsche Gesellschaft fuer Allgemeine und Angewandte Entomologie eV [*German Society for General and Applied Entomology*]   (SLS)
DGAC........ Accra [*Ghana*] [*ICAO location identifier*]   (ICLI)
DGAC........ Direction Generation de l'Aviation Civile [*France*]   (PDAA)
DGAD........ Ada [*Ghana*] [*ICAO location identifier*]   (ICLI)
DGAD........ Directia Generala de Aprovizionare si Desfacere [*General Directorate for Supply and Sales*]   (RO)
DGAD........ Director-General of Army Development [*Australia*]
DGAE........ Direccion General de Aprovisionamiento del Estado [*General Directorate of Government Supplies*] [*Chile*]
DGAE........ Kete-Krachi [*Ghana*] [*ICAO location identifier*]   (ICLI)

DGAFA ..... Deposito Geral de Adidos da Forca Aerea [*General Register of Air Force Attaches*] [*Portuguese*]   (WER)
DGAH .... Ho [*Ghana*] [*ICAO location identifier*]   (ICLI)
DGAHS..... Director-General of Army Health Services [*Australia*]
DGAI .... Deutsche Gesellschaft fuer Anaesthesiologie und Intensivmedizin [*German Society for Anesthesiology and Intensive Medicine*]   (SLS)
DGAK....... Akuse [*Ghana*] [*ICAO location identifier*]   (ICLI)
DGaO .... Deutsche Gesellschaft fuer Angewandte Optik eV [*German Society for Applied Optics*]   (SLS)
DGAP .... Akatsi [*Ghana*] [*ICAO location identifier*]   (ICLI)
DGAP .... Deutsche Gesellschaft fuer Analytische Psychologie eV [*German Society for Analytical Psychology*]   (SLS)
DGAP .... Deutsche Gesellschaft fuer Auswaertige Politik eV [*German Society for Foreign Policy*]   (SLS)
DGAQA..... Director-General of Army Quality Assurance [*Australia*]
DGAS .... Direction Generale des Affaires Sociales [*Directorate General of Social Affairs*] [*Cambodia*]   (CL)
DGAS .... Saltpond [*Ghana*] [*ICAO location identifier*]   (ICLI)
DGAT .... Director-General of Army Training [*Australia*]
DGAT .... Tema [*Ghana*] [*ICAO location identifier*]   (ICLI)
DGAW-A... Director-General of Accommodation and Works - Army [*Australia*]
DGB.......... Deutsche Geographische Blaetter
DGB.......... Deutsche Gesellschaft fur das Badewesen [*German Society For Baths Activities*]   (EAIO)
DGB.......... Deutscher Gewerkschaftsbund [*Confederation of German Trade Unions*] [*Germany*]   (DCTA)
DGB.......... Deutscher Gewerkschaftsbund (fuer das Gebiete der Bundesrepublik Deutschland und Berlin) [*German Trade Union Federation (for the Area of the Federal Republic and Berlin)*] [*Dusseldorf, West Germany*]
DGB.......... Devrimci Genclik Birligi [*Revolutionary Youth Union*]   (TU)
DGBAW .... Der Grosse Baumeister aller Welten [*The Grand Architect of the Universe*] [*Freemasonry*] [*German*]
DGBK .... Deutsche Gesellschaft fuer Baukybernetik eV [*German Society for Construction Cybernetics*]   (SLS)
DGBW ...... Deutsche Gesellschaft fuer Bewaesserungswirtschaft eV [*German Society for Irrigation*]   (SLS)
DGC.......... Deutsche Gesellschaft fuer Chronometrie eV [*German Society for Chronometry*]   (SLS)
DGC.......... Direccion de Geodesia y Cartografia [*Geodetic and Cartographic Survey*] [*Nicaragua*] [*Research center*]   (EAS)
DGCFCP ... Direccion General de Capacitacion y Fomento Cooperativo Pesquero [*Mexico*]   (MSC)
DGCMB .... Directia Generala Comerciala pentru Municipiul Bucuresti [*General Trade Directorate for Bucharest Municipality*]   (RO)
DGCO....... Director-General of Coordination and Organisation [*Australia*]
DGD.......... Demokratik Genclik Dernegi [*Democratic Youth Organization*] [*Turkish Cypriot*]   (GC)
DGD.......... Deutsche Gesellschaft fuer Dokumentation [*German Society for Documentation*] [*Information service or system*]   (IID)
DGD.......... Devrimci Genclik Dernegi [*Revolutionary Youth Association*] [*Turkish Cypriot*]   (GC)
DGD.......... Direccao Geral dos Desportos [*General Directorate of Sports*] [*Portuguese*]   (WER)
DGDAL ..... Directia Generala pentru Dezvoltarea Constructiilor de Locuinte Social Culturale si Administratie Locativa [*General Directorate for the Construction of Socio-Cultural Housing and Housing Administration*]   (RO)
DGDC........ Departamento Geral de Defesa Civil [*General Department of Civil Defense*] [*Brazil*]   (LA)
DG de BB.. Direccion General de Banca y Bolsa [*Institute for control of investment*] [*Spanish*]
DGDP........ Deutsche Gesellschaft fuer Dynamische Psychiatrie [*German Society for Dynamic Psychiatry*]   (SLS)
DGE.......... Deutsche Gesellschaft fuer Elektronenmikroskopie eV [*German Society for Electron Microscopy*]   (SLS)
DGE.......... Deutsche Gesellschaft fuer Ernaehrung eV [*German Society for Nutrition*]   (SLS)
DGE.......... Diethnes Grafeion Ergasias [*International Labor Office*]   (GC)
DGE.......... Direccion General de Electricidad [*Mexico*]   (LAA)
DGE.......... Direccion General de Estadistica [*General Office of Statistics*] [*Venezuela*]   (LA)
DGE.......... Mudgee [*Australia*] [*Airport symbol*]   (OAG)
DGEA....... Dehydroepiandrosterone   (RU)
DGEA....... Direccion General de Economia Agropecuario [*General Directorate of Agricultural Economy*] [*El Salvador*]   (LA)
DGEA....... Direccion General de Extension Agropecuaria [*Ecuador*]   (DSCA)
DGE & T.... Director General of Employment and Training [*India*]
DGEC........ Direccion General de Estadisticas y Censos [*General Statistics and Census Bureau*] [*Uruguay*]   (LA)
DGED........ Direction Generale d'Etudes et de Documentation [*Directorate General of Studies and Documentation*] [*Morocco*]   (AF)

DGEG .... Deutsche Gesellschaft fuer Erd- und Grundbau eV [*German Society for Earthworks and Foundations*] (SLS)
DGEME .... Director-General of Electrical and Mechanical Engineering [*Australia*]
DGEP .... Direccao Geral de Educacao Permanente [*General Directorate of Permanent Education*] [*Portuguese*] (WER)
DGEP .... Direccion General de Establecimientos Penales [*General Directorate of Penal Institutions*] [*Peru*] (LA)
DGER .... Direction Generale des Enquetes et Recherches [*French*]
DGER .... Directorate General of Energy Resources [*Government of Pakistan*] (WED)
DGES........ Deutsche Gesellschaft fuer Eingeborenenschutz
DGES........ Dnepr Hydroelectric Power Plant (RU)
DGF .... Dansk Geofysisk Forening [*Danish Geophysical Society*] (SLS)
DGF .... Dansk Geologisk Forening [*Danish Geological Society*] (SLS)
DGF .... Dansk Geoteknisk Forening [*Danish Geotechnical Society*] (SLS)
dgf .... Decigrama-Forca [*Decigram of Force*] [*Portuguese*]
DGF .... Deutsche Gesellschaft fuer Fettwissenschaft
DGF .... Deutsche Gesellschaft fur Flugwissenschaften [*German Society for Aeronautical Sciences*] (PDAA)
DGF .... Direccion General Forestal [*Guatemala*] (DSCA)
DGF .... State Forestry Resources (BU)
DGfA .... Deutsche Gesellschaft fuer Amerikastudien eV [*German Society for American Studies*] (SLS)
DGFA .... Direccion General de Fomento Agricola [*Ecuador*] (DSCA)
DGFA .... Direccion General de Fomento Agricola [*Argentina*] (DSCA)
DGFB .... Deutsche Gesellschaft fuer Betriebswirtschaft [*German*] (ADPT)
DGFC .... Accra [*Ghana*] [*ICAO location identifier*] (ICLI)
DGfdB........ Deutsche Gesellschaft fuer das Badewesen eV [*German Society for the Spa*] (SLS)
DGfE.......... Deutsche Gesellschaft fuer Erziehungswissenschaft [*German Society for Scientific Education*] (SLS)
DGFFC ...... Directia Generala de Fond Funciar si Cadastru [*General Directorate of Land Resources and Cadastres*] (RO)
DGfH .... Deutsche Gesellschaft fuer Hochschulkunde eV [*German Society for Public High Schools*] (SLS)
DGFH .... Deutsche Gesellschaft fuer Holzforschung eV [*German Wood Research and Development Association*] (ARC)
DGfH .... Deutsche Gesellschaft fuer Hopfenforschung eV [*German Society for Hops Research*] (SLS)
DGfHK ...... Deutsche Gesellschaft fuer Heereskunde eV [*German Public Army Association*] (SLS)
DGFI.......... Deutsches Geodaetisches Forschungsinstitut [*German Geodetic Research Institute*] [*Munich, West Germany*]
DGFIDGK ... Deutsches Geodaetisches Forschungsinstitut der Deutschen Geodaetischen Kommission [*German Geodetic Research Institute of the German Geodetic Commission*] [*Munich, West Germany*] (SLS)
DGFK .... Deutsche Gesellschaft fuer Friedens- und Konfliktforschung [*German Society for Peace and Conflict Research*]
DGfK .... Deutsche Gesellschaft fuer Kartographie eV [*German Society for Cartography*] (SLS)
DGFL......... Deutsche Gesellschaft fuer Logistik eV [*German Society for Logistics*] (SLS)
DGFM .... Direccion General de Fabricaciones Militares [*General Directorate of Military Construction*] [*Argentina*] (LA)
DGFP......... Deutsche Gesellschaft fuer Personalfuhrung [*German Society for Personnel Management*] (PDAA)
DGFP......... Direccion General de Fomento Pecuario [*Ecuador*] (DSCA)
DGfPs .... Deutsche Gesellschaft fuer Psychologie eV [*German Society for Psychology*] (SLS)
DGfS.......... Deutsche Gesellschaft fuer Sexualforschung eV [*German Society for Sexual Research*] (SLS)
DGfZ........... Deutsche Gesellschaft fuer Zuechtungskunde eV (SLS)
DGG.......... Deutsche Gartenbau-Gesellschaft eV [*German Horticultural Society*] (SLS)
DGG.......... Deutsche Geologische Gesellschaft [*German Geological Society*] (SLS)
DGG.......... Deutsche Geophysikalische Gesellschaft eV [*German Geophysical Society*] (SLS)
DGG.......... Deutsche Gesellschaft fuer Gerontologie [*German Society for Gerontology*] (SLS)
DGG.......... Deutsche Glastechnische Gesellschaft eV [*German Technical Glass Society*] (SLS)
DGG.......... Deutsche Gruppenpsychotherapeutische Gesellschaft eV [*German Group Psychotherapy Society*] (SLS)
DGGC .... Direccion General de la Guardia Civil [*Civil Guard General Directorate*] [*Spanish*] (WER)
DGGC .... Directia Generala de Gospodarie Comunala [*General Directorate for the Communal Economy*] (RO)
DGGL......... Deutsche Gesellschaft fuer Gartenkunst und Landschaftspflege eV [*German Society for Horticulture and Landscape Cultivation*] (SLS)
DGGM....... Direccion General de Geografia y Meteorologia [*Mexico*] (DSCA)

DGGM....... Direccion General de Geologia y Minas [*Geology and Mining Directorate*] [*Ecuador*] [*Research center*] (EAS)
DGGV........ Deutsche Gesellschaft fuer Gesundheitsvorsorge eV [*German Society for Health Care*] (SLS)
DGH .... Directia Generala de Hidrometeorologie [*General Directorate of Hydrometeorology*] (RO)
DGH .... Director-General of Health [*New Zealand*]
DGHM ...... Deutsche Gesellschaft fuer Hygiene und Mikrobiologie eV [*German Society for Hygiene and Microbiology*] (SLS)
DGHR .... Directia Generala a Hotelurilor si Restaurantelor [*General Directorate of Hotels and Restaurants*] (RO)
DGHT........ Deutsche Gesellschaft fuer Herpetologie und Terrarienkunde eV [*German Society for Herpetology and Terrariums*] (SLS)
DGI .... Danish Geotechnical Institute [*Research center*] (IRC)
DGI .... Denatured Histone (RU)
DGI .... Direccion General de Industrias [*Ministerio de Economia*] [*Honduras*]
DGI .... Direccion General de Inteligencia [*General Directorate of Intelligence*] [*Cuba*] (LA)
DGI .... Direccion General de Investigaciones [*General Directorate of Investigations*] [*Chile*] (LA)
DGI .... Direccion General de la Inteligencia [*Intelligence agency*] [*Cuba*]
DGI .... Direccion General Impositiva [*General Directorate of Taxation*] [*Argentina*] (LA)
DGI .... Directia Generala a Industriei [*General Directorate of Industry*] (RO)
DGI .... Direction General des Impots [*France*] (PDAA)
DGI .... Direction Generale des Impots [*Ministere des Finances*] [*France*] (FLAF)
DGI .... Director Geral de Informacao [*General Director of Information*] [*Portuguese*] (WER)
DGI .... Dnepropetrovsk Mining Institute Imeni Artem (RU)
DGI .... Donets Mining Institute (RU)
DGIA .... Direccion General de Infrasructura Aeronautica [*Uruguay*] (EY)
DGIA .... Direccion General de Investigaciones Agronomicas [*Directorate of Agricultural Research*] [*El Salvador*] (LAA)
DGIAC ...... Direccion General de Investigaciones Aplicadas a la Construccion [*General Directorate for Construction Research*] (LA)
DGICT....... Direccion General de Investigacion Cientifica y Tecnologica [*Peru*]
DGID .... Direction Generale d'Information et de Documentation [*Directorate General of Information and Documentation*] [*Malagasy*] (AF)
DGIE .... Departamento Geral de Investigacoes Especiais [*General Department of Special Investigations*] [*Brazil*] (LA)
DGIE .... Direccion General de Inmigracion y Extranjeria [*General Directorate of Immigration and Alien Affairs*] [*Venezuela*] (LA)
DGIEA ...... Direccion General de Investigacion y Extension Agricola [*Guatemala*] (DSCA)
DGIET....... Directia Generala a Intreprinderilor Electrotehnice [*General Directorate of Electrotechnical Enterprises*] (RO)
DGIFPI ..... Danske Gruppe af IFPI [*Danish Branch of the International Federation of the Phonograhic Industry*] (EAIO)
DGIM .... Drustvo na Gradeznite Inzeneri na Makedonija [*Society of Construction Engineers of Macedonia*] (YU)
DGIS........... Devrimci Genel Is Sendikasi [*Revolutionary (Reformist) General Workers' Union*] (TU)
DGITH ...... Drustvo Gradevinskih Inzinjera i Tehnicara Hrvatske [*Society of Construction Engineers and Technicians of Croatia*] (YU)
DGITLRS ... Drustvo Gradbenih Inzenirjev in Tehnikov Ljudska Republika Slovenija [*Society of Construction Engineers and Technicians of Slovenia*] (YU)
DGIT naNRM ... Drustvo na Gradeznite Inzeneri i Tehnicari na Narodna Republika Makedonija [*Society of Construction Engineers and Technicians of Macedonia*] (YU)
DGK .... Deutsche Gastspiel- und Konzert-Direktion [*German Play and Concert Management*] (EG)
DGK.......... Deutsche Geodaetische Kommission [*German Geodetic Commission*] (SLS)
DGK.......... Deutsche Gesellschaft fuer Kybernetik [*German Society for Cybernetics*]
DGKA........ Akim Oda [*Ghana*] [*ICAO location identifier*] (ICLI)
DGKC........ Deutsche Gesellschaft fuer Klinischen Chemie
DGKK........ Koforidua [*Ghana*] [*ICAO location identifier*] (ICLI)
DGKP .... Dyrekcja Generalna Kolei Panstwowych [*General Administration of State Railroads*] (POL)
DGL........... Denatured Gliadin (RU)
dgl .... Dergelijke [*Such*] [*Netherlands*] (GPO)
dgl .... Dergelike [*Such*] [*Afrikaans*]
dgl .... Dergleichen [*The Like, Of That Kind*] [*German*] (GPO)
dgl .... Desgleichen [*Likewise*] [*German*] (GCA)
DGLB........ Bole [*Ghana*] [*ICAO location identifier*] (ICLI)
DGLDP-A ... Director-General of Logistic Development and Plans - Army [*Australia*]

DGLE .... Tamale [*Ghana*] [*ICAO location identifier*]   (ICLI)
DGLI .... Directia Generala a Liniilor si Instalatilor [*General Directorate of Lines and Installations*]   (RO)
DGLN .... Navrongo [*Ghana*] [*ICAO location identifier*]   (ICLI)
DGLR .... Deutsche Gesellschaft fuer Luft- und Raumfahrt [*Germany*]
DGLRM .... Deutsche Gesellschaft fuer Luft- und Raumfahrtmedizin [*German Society for Air and Space Travel Medicine*]   (SLS)
DGLW .... Wa [*Ghana*] [*ICAO location identifier*]   (ICLI)
DGLY .... Yendi [*Ghana*] [*ICAO location identifier*]   (ICLI)
DGM.......... Destroyer, Guided Missile [*Surface-to-air/Surface-to-surface*] [*NATO*]
DGM.......... Deutsche Gesellschaft fuer Metallkunde eV [*German Society for Metallurgy*] [*Information retrieval*]   (SLS)
DGM.......... Devlet Guvenlik Mahkemesi [*State Security Court*]   (TU)
DGM.......... Directia Generala de Metrologie [*General Directorate of Metrology*]   (RO)
DGM.......... Direction de la Geologie et des Mines
DGM.......... Divisao de Geologia e Mineralogia [*Brazil*]
DGM.......... Dynamic Magnetic Loudspeaker   (RU)
DGMA....... Deutsche Gesellschaft fuer Messtechnik und Automatisierung [*German Society for Measuring Technology and Automation*]   (EG)
DGMAT-A ... Director-General of Materiel - Army [*Australia*]
dGMF .... Deoxyguanosine Monophosphate   (RU)
DGMFA .... Deposito Geral de Material da Forca Aerea [*Air Force General Material Depot*] [*Portugal*]
DGMG....... Deposito Geral de Material de Guerra [*General War Material Depot*] [*Portuguese*]   (WER)
DGMK...... Deutsche Gesellschaft fuer Mineraloelwissenschaft und Kohlechemie eV [*German Society for Petroleum Science and Coal Chemistry*]   (SLS)
DGMK...... Remote-Reading Gyromagnetic Compass   (RU)
DGMKG.... Deutsche Gesellschaft fuer Mund-, Kiefer-, und Gesichtschirurgie [*German Society for Mouth, Jaw, and Face Surgery*]   (SLS)
dg-mn........ Doctor of Geological and Mineralogical Sciences   (RU)
DGMR...... Directia Generala a Materialelor Refractare [*General Directorate of Refractory Materials*]   (RO)
DGMU ...... Direccion General de Meteorologia del Uruguay [*Uruguay*]   (DSCA)
DGMU-P1 ... Department of Geology, Mandalay University, Primate Specimen [*Jaw fragment*] [*Burmese*]
DGMW....... Deutsche Gesellschaft fuer Missionswissenschaft [*German Society for Missionary Science*]   (SLS)
DGN .... Deutsche Gessellschaft fuer Nuclearmedizin [*German Nuclear Medicine Society*]   (PDAA)
DGN .... Direccion de Geologia de la Nacion [*National Geological Administration*] [*Argentina*]   (LAA)
DGN .... Direccion General de Normas [*National Standards Organization*] [*Mexico*]
dgn .... Doctor of Geographical Sciences   (RU)
DGNP........ Director-General of Naval Production [*Australia*]
DGNRER .. Directorate General of Energy Resources [*Pakistan*] [*Research center*]   (WED)
DGNT....... Direccion General de Normas y Tecnologia [*Bolivia*]
DGO .... Deutsche Gemeindeordnung [*German Municipal Regulations*]   (EG)
DGO .... Deutsche Gesellschaft fuer Osteuropakunde eV [*German Society for Eastern European Study*]   (SLS)
DGO .... Durango [*Mexico*] [*Airport symbol*]   (OAG)
DGOM ...... Direccion General de Obras Maritimes [*Mexico*]   (MSC)
DGON ...... Deutsche Gesellschaft fuer Ortung und Navigation eV [*German Society for Position-Finding and Navigation*]   (SLS)
DGOP........ Direccion General de Obras Portuarias [*Costa Rica*]   (MSC)
DGOP........ Direccion General de Operacion Portuaria [*Mexico*]   (MSC)
DGOP........ Direccion General de Orden Publico [*General Directorate of Public Order*] [*Cuba*]   (LA)
DGOP-A.... Director-General of Operations and Plans - Army [*Australia*]
DGOR........ Deutsche Gesellschaft fuer Operations Research [*German Society for Operational Research*] [*Germany*]
DGOR........ Direccion General de Obras de Riego [*General Directorate of Irrigation Workers*] [*El Salvador*]   (LA)
DGOSM .... Direccion General de Oceanografia y Senalamiento Maritimo [*Mexico*]   (MSC)
DGP .... Data General Portugal
DGP .... Deutsche Gesellschaft fuer Parasitologie eV [*German Society for Parasitology*]   (SLS)
DGP .... Deutsche Gesellschaft fuer Parodontologie [*German Society for Periodontology*]   (SLS)
DGP .... Deutsche Gesellschaft fuer Personalwesen eV [*German Society for Staff Conduct*]   (SLS)
DGP .... Deutsche Grenzpolizei [*German Border Police*]   (EG)
DGP .... Direccion General del Presupuesto [*General Budget Office*] [*Venezuela*]   (LA)
DGP .... Dunya Gida Programi [*World Food Program*]   (TU)
DGPA .... Direccion General de Planificacion y Administracion [*Panama*]   (DSCA)

DGPEI....... Direccion General de Prevencion y Extincion de Incendios [*General Directorate of Fire Fighting and Prevention*] [*Cuba*]   (LA)
DGPh......... Deutsche Gesellschaft fuer Photographie eV [*German Society for Photography*]   (SLS)
DGPI .... Dagestan State Pedagogical Institute Imeni S. Stal'skiy   (RU)
DGPM .... Deutsche Gesellschaft fuer Psychosomatische Medizin eV [*German Society for Psychosomatic Medicine*]   (SLS)
DGPM ...... Direction de la Geologie et de la Prospection Miniere
DGPN........ Deutsche Gesellschaft fuer Psychiatrie und Nervenheilkunde eV [*German Society for Psychiatry and Neurology*]   (SLS)
DGPO-A.... Director-General of Personnel Operations - Army [*Australia*]
DGPP .... Direccion General de Planificacion y Presupuesto [*Ministerio de la Vivienda y Urbanismo*] [*Santiago, Chile*]   (LAA)
DGPP .... State Forestry Industrial Enterprise   (BU)
DGPPA....... Direccion General de la Pequena Propiedad Agricola [*Mexico*]   (DSCA)
DGPPP...... Direccion General de Planeacion y Promocion Pesqueras [*Mexico*]   (MSC)
DGPPT...... Deutsche Gesellschaft fuer Psychotherapie, Psychosomatik, und Tiefenpsychologie eV [*German Society for Psychotherapy, Psychosomatics, and the Subconscious*]   (SLS)
DGPS........ State Forestry Industrial Farm   (BU)
DGPT .... Direccion General de Policia y Transito [*General Directorate of Police and Traffic*] [*Mexico*]   (LA)
DGPT .... Directia Generala a Presei si Tipariturilor [*General Directorate of the Press and Printing*]   (RO)
DGPTC...... Directia Generala a Postelor si Telecomunicatiilor [*General Directorate of Posts and Telecommunications*]   (RO)
DGPYT...... Direccion General de Policia y Transito [*General Directorate of Police and Traffic*] [*Mexico*]   (LA)
DGQ .... Deutsche Gesellschaft fuer Qualitaet eV
DGQ .... Deutsche Gesellschaft fuer Qualitaetsforschung (Pflanzl. Nahrungsmittel) eV [*German Society for Quality Research (Plant Nourishment)*]   (SLS)
DGQ .... Direccao-Geral da Qualidade [*Servico de Normalizacao*] [*Portugal*]
dgr .... Decigrade [*French*]
d Gr .... Der Grosse [*The Great*] [*German*]
DGR.......... Direction du Genie Rural [*Ministere de l'Agriculture*] [*Mali*]
DGRA........ Direccion General de Reforma Agraria [*Panama*]   (DSCA)
DGRAS....... Direction Generale du Renseignement et de l'Action Social
DGRCST ... Direction Generale des Relations Culturelles, Scientifiques, et Techniques [*French*]
DGRH .... Direccion General de Recursos Hidraulicos [*Ecuador*]   (DSCA)
DGRM....... Directia Generala a Rezervelor Muncitoresti [*General Directorate of Labor Reserves*]   (RO)
DGRN........ Direccion General de Recursos Naturales [*Honduras*]   (DSCA)
DGRP .... Direccion General de Regiones Pesqueras [*Mexico*]   (MSC)
DGRR .... Deutsche Gesellschaft fuer Raketentechnik und Raumfahrt [*German Society for Rocketry and Astronautics*]   (EG)
DGRS .... Directia Generala a Rezervelor de Stat [*General Directorate of State Reserves*]   (RO)
DGRSCT ... Direction Generale des Relations Scientifiques, Culturelles, et Techniques [*French*]
DGRST...... Delegation Generale a la Recherche Scientifique et Technique [*General Delegation for Scientific and Technical Research*] [*French*]   (WER)
DGS .... Dansk Grafologisk Selskab [*Denmark*]   (SLS)
DGS .... Destroyer, Guided Missile (Surface-to-Surface) [*NATO*]
DGS .... Det Groenlandske Selskab [*Denmark*]   (SLS)
DGS .... Deutsche Gesellschaft fuer Sonnenenergie eV [*German Society for Solar Energy*]   (SLS)
DGS .... Deutsche Gesellschaft fuer Sprachheilpaedagogik eV [*German Society for Speech Therapy*]   (SLS)
DGS .... Deutsche Gesellschaft Fur Suizidpraevention [*German Association of Suicide Prevention*]   (EAIO)
DGS .... Direccao Geral de Seguranca [*Directorate General for Security*] [*Portuguese*]   (AF)
DGS .... Direccion General de Seguridad [*General Directorate of Security*] [*Spanish*]   (WER)
DGS .... Direction Generale de la Sante [*French Ministry of Health*]
DGS .... State Forestry Farm   (BU)
DGSA .... Dairy Goat Society of Australia
DGSA .... Devlet Guzel Sanatlar Akademisi [*State Fine Arts Academy*] [*GSA*] [*See also*]   (TU)
DGS & D.... Directorate General of Supplies and Disposals [*India*]   (IMH)
DGSB........ Sefwi-Bekwai [*Ghana*] [*ICAO location identifier*]   (ICLI)
DGSE........ Department of Geological Survey and Mineral Exploration [*Myanmar*]   (DS)
DGSE........ Direccion General de la Seguridad del Estado [*General Directorate of State Security*] [*Nicaragua*]   (LA)
DGSE........ Direction Generale de la Securite d'Etat [*Secret police*] [*Congo*]
DGSE......... Direction Generale de la Securite Exterieure [*Formerly, SDECE*] [*French intelligence agency*]
DGSF........ Deutsche Gesellschaft fur Sexualforschung [*German Society for Sex Research*]   (EAIO)

DGSFMM ... Direccao General dos Servicos de Fomento Maritimo Marinho [*Portuguese*] (MSC)

DGSI.......... Kumasi [*Ghana*] [*ICAO location identifier*] (ICLI)

DGSMWRFA ... David G. Stead Memorial Wildlife Research Foundation of Australia (ADA)

DGSN .... Direction General de la Surete Nationale [*Directorate General of National Security*] [*Algeria*] (AF)

DGSN .... Direction Generale de la Surete Nationale [*Directorate General of National Security*] [*Morocco*] (AF)

DGSN .... Sunyani [*Ghana*] [*ICAO location identifier*] (ICLI)

DGSNM .... Direccion General del Servicio Nacional Meteorologico [*Argentina*] (DSCA)

DGSP........ Deutsche Gesellschaft fuer Sozialpaediatrie [*German Society for Social Pediatrics*] (SLS)

DGSP........ Direccion General de Seguridad Personal [*General Directorate for Personal Safety*] [*Cuba*] (LA)

DGSP........ Direccion General de Seguridad Politica [*General Board for Political Security*] [*Ecuador*] (LA)

DGSP........ State Forestry Economic Enterprise (BU)

DGSS........ Deutsche Gesellschaft fuer Sprechwissenschaft und Sprecherziehung eV [*German Society for Speech and Speech Education*] (SLS)

DGSS........ Directia Generala a Securitatii Statului [*General Directorate of State Security*] (RO)

DGST........ Direction Generale pour le Surveillance du Territoire [*Directorate General for Surveillance of the Territory*] [*Morocco*] (AF)

DGSTF ...... Direction Generale des Services Techniques et de Fabrications [*National Directorate of Technical Services and Manufacturing*] [*Central African Republic*] (AF)

DGSUP-A ... Director-General of Supply - Army [*Australia*]

DGSUP-N ... Director-General of Supply - Navy [*Australia*]

DGSV .... Direccion General de Sanidad Vegetal [*Mexico*] (DSCA)

DGSW .... Wenchi [*Ghana*] [*ICAO location identifier*] (ICLI)

DGT.......... Direccion General del Turismo [*State tourist organization*] [*Spanish*]

DGT.......... Directia Generala a Transporturilor [*General Directorate of Transportation*] (RO)

DGT.......... Direction Generale des Telecommunications [*Telecommunications administration*] [*France*]

DGT .... Directorate General of Telecommunications [*Taipei, Taiwan*]

DGT .... Director General of Transport

DGT.......... Dumaguete [*Philippines*] [*Airport symbol*] (OAG)

DGT.......... Duna Gozhajozasi Tarsasag [*Danube Steamship Company*] (HU)

DGT.......... Large German Telescope [*Acronym is based on German phrase*]

DGTC .... Direction Generale des Grands Travaux du Cameroon (EY)

DGTCP...... Departamento de Geografia, Terras, e Colonizacao do Estado do Parana [*Brazil*] (DSCA)

DGTD........ Directorate General of Technical Development [*India*] (PDAA)

dGTF .... Deoxyguanosine Triphosphate (RU)

DGTF .... Directia Generala a Transporturilor Feroviare [*General Directorate of Railway Transportation*] (RO)

DGTF .... Don State Tobacco Factory Imeni Rosa Luxemburg (RU)

DGTI .... Direccion General Tecnica de Investigaciones [*Technical General Directorate of Investigations*] [*Cuba*] (LA)

DGTK .... Takoradi [*Ghana*] [*ICAO location identifier*] (ICLI)

Dgt Nok ..... Dagitim Noktasi [*Distribution Point*] (TU)

DGTP .... Direccion General de Tecnologia Pesquera [*Mexico*] (MSC)

DGTS......... Conference Call, Conference Circuit, Round Call (RU)

DGTs........ Germanium-Cesium Diode (RU)

DGTX .... Axim [*Ghana*] [*ICAO location identifier*] (ICLI)

DGU .... Danmarks Geologiske Undersogelse [*Geological Survey of Denmark*] [*Research center*] (IRC)

DGU .... Dnepropetrovsk State University Imeni Tercentenary of the Reunification of the Ukraine with Russia (RU)

DGU .... Doctor of Griffith University [*Australia*]

DGU .... Far Eastern State University (RU)

DGV.......... Deutsche Gesellschaft fuer Volkskunde eV [*German Society for Folklore*] (SLS)

DGV.......... Deutsche Graphologische Vereinigung eV [*German Graphological Association*] (SLS)

DGV.......... Deutscher Giessereiverband [*Germany*] (EAIO)

DGV.......... Dienst Grondwaterverkenning [*TNO Institute of Applied Geoscience*] [*Information service or system*] [*Netherlands*] (IID)

DGVG........ Directeur General Charge des Victimes de Guerre [*Director General for War Victims*] [*Cambodia*] (CL)

DGVR .... Direction Generale Chargee des Victimes de Guerre et des Refugies [*Directorate General for War Victims and Refugees*] [*Cambodia*] (CL)

DGVT .... Deutsche Gesellschaft fuer Verhaltenstherapie eV [*German Society for Repression Therapy*] (SLS)

DGW........ Deutsche Gesellschaft fuer Wirtschaftliche Fertigung und Sicherheitstechnik eV [*German Society for Efficient Manufacturing and Safety Technology*] (SLS)

DGWT .... Deutsche Gesellschaft fuer Warenkunde und Technologie eV [*German Society for Market Research and Technology*]

DG XIII ..... Directorate-General (Section XIII) [*Council of European Communities*] (NITA)

DGZfP .... Deutsche Gesellschaft fuer Zerstoerungsfreie Pruefung eV (SLS)

DH .... Danmarks Havfiskeriforening [*Danish Sea Fishery Association*] (EAIO)

DH .... Danske Husmandsforeninger [*Danish Family Farmers Association*] (EAIO)

DH .... Dansk Hortonomforening [*Denmark*] (SLS)

dh .... Das Heisst [*That Is, Namely*] [*German*] (GPO)

DH .... Demeure Historique [*An association*] [*France*] (EAIO)

dH .... Deutsche Haerte [*German Hardness*] (EG)

DH .... Dewan Harian [*Standing Committee*] (IN)

DH .... Dirham [*Monetary unit*] [*Morocco*]

DH .... Dolgoz Hibatlanul [*Work without Mistakes (A movement)*] (HU)

DHA .... Darling Harbour Authority [*Australia*]

DHA .... De Havilland Aircraft Proprietary Ltd. [*Australia*]

DHA .... Dhahran [*Saudi Arabia*] [*Airport symbol*] (OAG)

dha .... Dicha [*Spanish*]

DHA .... Drug Houses of Australia (ADA)

Dhab .... Doktor Habilitowany [*Senior Doctor*] [*Poland*]

DHAEMAE ... Disposable Hypodermic and Allied Equipment Manufacturers Association of Europe (EAIO)

DHAG ...... Deutsche Heredo-Ataxia Gesellschaft [*Germany*] (EAIO)

DHAS....... Doctors Health Advisory Service [*Australia*]

DHB.......... Defence Housing Board [*Australia*]

DHB.......... Deutsche Handelsbank [*German Commercial Bank*] (EG)

DH-BW ..... Deutsche Heilpraktikerschaft, Landesverband Baden-Wuerttemberg eV (SLS)

DHC .... Defence Housing Committee [*Australia*]

DHC .... District Health Council [*Australia*]

DHCA....... Kaya [*Burkina Faso*] [*ICAO location identifier*] (ICLI)

DHCB........ Barsalogho [*Burkina Faso*] [*ICAO location identifier*] (ICLI)

DHCC........ Ouahigouya [*Burkina Faso*] [*ICAO location identifier*] (ICLI)

DHCD ...... Didyr [*Burkina Faso*] [*ICAO location identifier*] (ICLI)

DHCE .... Batie [*Burkina Faso*] [*ICAO location identifier*] (ICLI)

DHCG....... Kongoussi [*Burkina Faso*] [*ICAO location identifier*] (ICLI)

DHCI........ Titao [*Burkina Faso*] [*ICAO location identifier*] (ICLI)

DHCJ .... Djibo [*Burkina Faso*] [*ICAO location identifier*] (ICLI)

DHCK....... Koudougou [*Burkina Faso*] [*ICAO location identifier*] (ICLI)

DHCL....... Leo [*Burkina Faso*] [*ICAO location identifier*] (ICLI)

DHCM...... Manga [*Burkina Faso*] [*ICAO location identifier*] (ICLI)

DHCO ...... Boromo [*Burkina Faso*] [*ICAO location identifier*] (ICLI)

DHCP....... Po [*Burkina Faso*] [*ICAO location identifier*] (ICLI)

DHCR....... Poura [*Burkina Faso*] [*ICAO location identifier*] (ICLI)

DHCS .... Department of Health and Community Services [*Northern Territory, Australia*]

DHCS .... Seguenega [*Burkina Faso*] [*ICAO location identifier*] (ICLI)

DHCT....... Tenado [*Burkina Faso*] [*ICAO location identifier*] (ICLI)

DHCU ...... Gourcy [*Burkina Faso*] [*ICAO location identifier*] (ICLI)

DHCY....... Yako [*Burkina Faso*] [*ICAO location identifier*] (ICLI)

Dhd .... Dehydrierung [*Dehydrogenation*] [*German*] (GCA)

DHD .... Durham Downs [*Australia*] [*Airport symbol*] (OAG)

DHEA....... Boulsa [*Burkina Faso*] [*ICAO location identifier*] (ICLI)

DHEB....... Bogande [*Burkina Faso*] [*ICAO location identifier*] (ICLI)

DHEC....... Komin-Yanga [*Burkina Faso*] [*ICAO location identifier*] (ICLI)

DHED....... Diapaga [*Burkina Faso*] [*ICAO location identifier*] (ICLI)

DHEE .... Dori [*Burkina Faso*] [*ICAO location identifier*] (ICLI)

DHEF .... Fada N'Gourma [*Burkina Faso*] [*ICAO location identifier*] (ICLI)

DHEG....... Gorom-Gorom [*Burkina Faso*] [*ICAO location identifier*] (ICLI)

DHEK....... Koupela [*Burkina Faso*] [*ICAO location identifier*] (ICLI)

DHEL....... Departamento de Helicopteros de Mozambique [*Mozambique Helicopter Department*] (AF)

DHEL....... Kantchari [*Burkina Faso*] [*ICAO location identifier*] (ICLI)

DHEM...... Tambao [*Burkina Faso*] [*ICAO location identifier*] (ICLI)

DHEN ...... Garango [*Burkina Faso*] [*ICAO location identifier*] (ICLI)

DHEO ...... Zorgo [*Burkina Faso*] [*ICAO location identifier*] (ICLI)

DHEP .... Pama [*Burkina Faso*] [*ICAO location identifier*] (ICLI)

DHER....... Arli [*Burkina Faso*] [*ICAO location identifier*] (ICLI)

DHERF ..... Dental Health Education and Research Foundation [*Australia*]

DHES .... Sebba [*Burkina Faso*] [*ICAO location identifier*] (ICLI)

DHET....... Tenkodogo [*Burkina Faso*] [*ICAO location identifier*] (ICLI)

DHEY....... Ouargaye [*Burkina Faso*] [*ICAO location identifier*] (ICLI)

DHEZ....... Zabre [*Burkina Faso*] [*ICAO location identifier*] (ICLI)

DHF......... Dag Hammarskjold Foundation [*Sweden*] (EAIO)

DHF .... Dis Hekimligi Fakultesi [*School of Dentistry*] [*Diyabakir University*] (TU)

DHFI .... Deutsches High-Fidelity Institut eV (SLS)

DHfK .... Deutsche Hochschule fuer Koerperkultur [*German Advanced School of Physical Culture*] (EG)

DHG .... Deutsche Handelsgesellschaft [*German Trading Company*]
        (EG)
DHHCS ..... Department of Health, Housing and Community Services
        [*Australia*]
DHHH .... Ouagadougou (Airport) [*Burkina Faso*] [*ICAO location
        identifier*] (ICLI)
DHHV .... Ouagadougou [*Burkina Faso*] [*ICAO location identifier*] (ICLI)
DHI .... Dansk Hydraulisk Institut [*Danish Hydraulic Institute*]
        [*Research center*] (IRC)
DHI .... Decennie Hydrologique Internationale [*International
        Hydrological Decade*] (MSC)
DHI .... Deutsches Handwerksinstitut eV (SLS)
DHI .... Deutsches Hydrographisches Institut [*German Hydrographic
        Institute*]
DHI .... Dhangarhi [*Nepal*] [*Airport symbol*] (OAG)
DHI .... Horowitz (David) Research Institute for Developing Countries
        [*Israel*] [*Research center*] (IRC)
DHJ .... Difaa Hassani Jadidi [*Morocco*]
DHK .... Drustvo Hrvatskih Knjizevnika [*Society of Croatian Writers*]
        [*Zagreb*] (YU)
DHKD .... Devrimci Halk Kultur Dernegi [*Revolutionary People's Cultural
        Association*] (TU)
DHL .... Dag Hammarskjold Library [*United Nations*] (DUND)
DHLG .... Department of Housing and Local Government [*Queensland*]
        [*Australia*]
DHM .... Directoria Hidrografica Maritima [*Romanian*] (MSC)
dhmD .... Des Hoeheren Militaerischen Dienstes [*German*]
DHMG ...... Departmento Hidrografico de la Marina de Guerra (MSC)
DHMI .... Devlet Havayollari Meydanlari Isletmesi [*State Airlines Airfields
        Operations*] (TU)
DHN .... Direccion de Hidrografia y Navegacion [*Bureau of Hydrography
        and Navigation*] [*Venezuela*] (MSC)
DHN .... Direccion de Hidrografia y Navegacion [*Bureau of Hydrography
        and Navigation*] [*Peru*] (MSC)
DHN .... Directoria de Hidrografia e Navegacao [*Bureau of Hydrography
        and Navigation*] [*Brazil*] (LA)
DHO .... Deniz Harb Okul [*Naval Academy*] (TU)
dho .... Dicho [*Spanish*]
DHOA .... Dano [*Burkina Faso*] [*ICAO location identifier*] (ICLI)
DHOB .... Banfora [*Burkina Faso*] [*ICAO location identifier*] (ICLI)
DHOD ...... Dedougou [*Burkina Faso*] [*ICAO location identifier*] (ICLI)
DHOF .... Safane [*Burkina Faso*] [*ICAO location identifier*] (ICLI)
DHOG ...... Gaoua [*Burkina Faso*] [*ICAO location identifier*] (ICLI)
DHOH ...... Hounde [*Burkina Faso*] [*ICAO location identifier*] (ICLI)
DHOL .... Loumana [*Burkina Faso*] [*ICAO location identifier*] (ICLI)
DHON .... Nouna [*Burkina Faso*] [*ICAO location identifier*] (ICLI)
DHOO ...... Bobo-Dioulasso [*Burkina Faso*] [*ICAO location identifier*]
        (ICLI)
DHOR .... Orodara [*Burkina Faso*] [*ICAO location identifier*] (ICLI)
DHOS .... Sideradougou [*Burkina Faso*] [*ICAO location identifier*] (ICLI)
DHOT .... Tougan [*Burkina Faso*] [*ICAO location identifier*] (ICLI)
DHOU .... Diebougou [*Burkina Faso*] [*ICAO location identifier*] (ICLI)
DHOY .... Aribinda [*Burkina Faso*] [*ICAO location identifier*] (ICLI)
DHP .... Demokratik Halk Partisi [*Democratic People's Party*] [*Turkish
        Cyprus*] [*Political party*] (PPE)
DHP .... Deutsche Hannover Partei [*German Hanover Party*] (PPE)
DHP .... Dyrekcja Hoteli Pracowniczych [*Administration of Workers'
        Hotels*] (POL)
DHPV .... Druzstvo pre Hospodarenie Pol'-nohospodarskymi Vyrobkami
        [*Agricultural Produce Cooperative*] (CZ)
DHQ .... Defence Headquarters
DHRA .... Danish Hotel and Restaurant Association (EAIO)
DHS .... Dansk Haematologisk Selskab [*Denmark*] (SLS)
DHS .... Daughters of the Holy Spirit [*Cameroon*]
DHS .... Deutsche Hauptstelle Gegen die Suchtgefahren eV (SLS)
DHS .... Division of History of Science [*ICSU*]
DHS .... Dodavaci Hospodarske Smlouvy [*Economic Delivery Contracts*]
        (CZ)
DHSH .... Department of Human Services and Health [*Australia*]
DHV .... Deutscher Handball-Verband [*German Handball League*] (EG)
DHV .... Deutscher Handels- und Industrieangestellten-Verband
        [*Association of Clerical Employees of Germany*]
DHYC .... Darling Harbour Yacht Club [*Australia*]
DHZ .... Deutsche Handelszentrale [*German Trade Center*] (EG)
DI .... Argo, SA [*Dominican Republic*] [*ICAO designator*] (ICDA)
Di .... Calculated Range (RU)
DI .... Daerah Istimewa [*Special Region (Jogjakarta and Atjeh)*] (IN)
DI .... Darul Islam [*Organization of Moslem Dissidents*] (IN)
DI .... Das Ist [*That Is*] [*German*]
di .... Dat Is [*That Is, Namely*] [*Netherlands*] (GPO)
DI .... Declaration d'Importation [*Bill of Entry*] [*Cambodia*] (CL)
DI .... Delegation a l'Informatique [*Central Office for Data Processing*]
        [*France*] (PDAA)
DI .... Depot Intermediaire [*Military*] [*French*] (MTD)
DI .... Desert Institute [*Egypt*] (PDAA)

DI .... Deutsches Industrieninstitut [*Institute of German Industry*]
        (WEN)
DI .... Devizni Inspektorat (DSPF) [*Foreign Exchange Inspectorate*]
        (YU)
Di .... Dinsdag [*Tuesday*] [*Afrikaans*]
di .... Dioptria [*Dioptric*] [*Unit of reactive power*] [*Portuguese*]
Di .... Diplom [*Russian*]
Di .... Diplom [*Norway*]
Di .... Diplom [*German*]
Di .... Diploma [*Portuguese*]
Di .... Diplomasi [*Turkey*]
Di .... Diplome [*Diploma*] [*French*]
Di .... Diplome d'Etudes Universitaires Pratiques en Economie et en
        Droit [*French*]
DI .... Diplome d'Ingenieur [*French*]
DI .... Diplomi-Insinoori [*Finland*]
DI .... Diplom-Ingenieur [*Diploma Engineer, Engineer*] (EG)
Di .... Diplom za Zavarseno Visse Obrazovanie [*Diploma of Higher
        Education*] [*Bulgarian*]
DI .... Direction de l'Industrie [*Ministere de l'Industrie, des Mines, et de
        l'Energie*] [*Benin*]
DI .... Direkcija za Ishranu (DSPRP) [*Directorate of Supply*] (YU)
DI .... Diritto Internazionale [*Italy*] (FLAF)
Di .... Dissertation [*Dissertation*] [*German*]
di .... Dit Is [*That Is*] [*Afrikaans*]
DI .... Division d'Infanterie [*Infantry Division*] [*French*] (MTD)
DI .... Division Engineer [*Military term*] (RU)
DI .... Dommages-Interets [*French*] (FLAF)
DI .... Dopravni Inspektorat [*Office of the Transportation Inspector*]
        (CZ)
DI .... Dvorak International (EAIO)
DI .... Inductive Pickup, Inductive Transducer (RU)
Di .... Primary Teacher's Diploma [*Greek*]
Di .... State Publishing House (BU)
Di .... Technician's Diploma [*Egypt*]
DI .... Two-Seater Fighter (RU)
DIA .... Daerah Istimewa Atjeh [*Atjeh Special Region*] (IN)
DIA .... Danmarks Ingeniorakademi [*Engineering Academy of Denmark*]
        (ARC)
DIA .... Dehydroisoandrosterone (RU)
DIA .... Departamento de Investigaciones Agropecuarias [*Colorado*]
        (LAA)
DIA .... Department of Industrial Affairs [*Western Australia*]
DIA .... Design Institute of Australia
DIA .... Deutscher Innen- und Aussenhandel [*Inner-German and Foreign
        Trade*] (EG)
dia .... Dialect (TPFD)
Dia .... Diaphon [*Record label*] [*Australia*]
DIA .... Diecasting Institute of Australia (ADA)
DIA .... Dievthynsis Iatrikis Andilipseos [*Directorate of Medical
        Assistance*] [*Greek*] (GC)
DIA .... Digital Imaging Australia
DIA .... Diploma in International Affairs (ADA)
Dia .... Diplome d'Ingenieur Agronome [*French*]
DIA .... Direccion de Investigacion del Ambiente [*Office for
        Environmental Research*] [*Ministry of the Environment and
        Renewable Natural Resources*] [*Venezuela*] (EAS)
DIA .... Direct Air, Inc. [*Germany*] [*ICAO designator*] (FAAC)
DIA .... Division de Investigaciones Agropecuarias [*Colombia*] (DSCA)
DIA .... Documentation et Information Africaines [*African
        Documentation and Information*] [*Vatican*] (AF)
DIA .... Drycleaning Institute of Australia
DIA .... Dubai International Airport
DIA .... Dutch Interchurch Aid and Service to Refugees [*Netherlands*]
DIAA .... Dairy Industry Association of Australia
DIABA .... Desarrollo Integrado de Areas de Base Agropecuaria (LAA)
DIAC .... Dairy Industry Advisory Committee [*Australia*]
DIAC .... Diffusion Industrielle et Automobile par le Credit
DIACA .... Desarrollo Industrial Agricola CA [*Venezuela*] (DSCA)
DIACEMENTO ... Cementos Diamante SA [*Colombia*] (COL)
DIACOS .... Diario de la Costa [*Colombia*] (COL)
DIAD .... Adiake [*Ivory Coast*] [*ICAO location identifier*] (ICLI)
DIAE .... Agboville [*Ivory Coast*] [*ICAO location identifier*] (ICLI)
DIA-FS ...... Design Institute of Australia Federal Secretariat
DIAFUTBOL ... Division Aficionada del Futbol Colombiano [*Colombia*]
        (COL)
Diag .... Diagonal (IDIG)
diag .... Diagram [*Diagram*] [*Danish/Norwegian*]
diag .... Diagramme [*French*] (FLAF)
DIAGONAL ... Distribuidora de Algodon Nacional [*Colombia*] (COL)
DIAGOVEN ... Distribuidora Algodonera Venezolana [*Venezuela*] (DSCA)
diagr .... Diagram [*Hungary*]
diagr .... Diagram [*Former Czechoslovakia*]
diagr .... Diagram [*Netherlands*]
diagr .... Diagrama [*Diagram*] [*Spanish*]
diagr .... Diagramme [*Diagram*] [*French*]

DIAKONIA ... World Federation of Diaconal Associations and Sisterhoods [*Germany*] (EAIO)
dial .... Dialecte [*French*] (TPFD)
dial .... Dialek(ties) [*Dialectal*] [*Afrikaans*]
DIAL........ Distribuidora de Alimentos SA [*Brazil*] (DSCA)
DIAL........ Documentacion Iglesial America Latina [*France*]
DIALEC .... Distribuidora de Equipos Agricolas y Electricos [*Colombia*] (COL)
diam .... Diameter (RU)
DIAMANG ... Companhia de Diamantes de Angola [*Angola Diamond Company*] (AF)
DIAMAT... Dialektischer Materialismus [*Dialectical Materialism*] (EG)
DIANA ...... Dimokratiki Ananeossi [*Greece*] [*Political party*] (ECED)
DIANCA ... Diques y Astilleros Nacionales, Compania Anonima [*National Docks and Shipyards, Incorporated*] [*Venezuela*] (LA)
DIANE ...... Disque pour l'Analyse Economique (IID)
DIAO........ Aboisso [*Ivory Coast*] [*ICAO location identifier*] (ICLI)
DIAP......... Abidjan/Port Bouet [*Ivory Coast*] [*ICAO location identifier*] (ICLI)
DIAPEL .... Distribuidora Agro-Pecuaria Ltd. [*Brazil*] (DSCA)
DIARM ..... Desarrollo de Industria Armerias [*Gun manufacturer*] [*Spain*]
DIAS........ Diensten Internationale Arbeiders Samenwerking
DIAS........ DIMDI's [*Deutsches Institut fuer Medizinische Dokumentation und Information*] Administration System (NITA)
DIASFALTOS ... Distribuidora de Asfaltos Ltda. [*Colombia*] (COL)
DIAT .... Dairy Industry Appeals Tribunal [*Queensland*] [*Australia*]
DIAU........ Abengourou [*Ivory Coast*] [*ICAO location identifier*] (ICLI)
DIAUTOS ... Distribuidora Antioquera de Automotores SA [*Colombia*] (COL)
DIAV .... Abidjan [*Ivory Coast*] [*ICAO location identifier*] (ICLI)
DIA/VEHDIA ... Deutscher Innen- und Aussenhandel/Volkseigenes Handelsunternehmen [*Inner-German and Foreign Trade/ State-Owned Commercial Enterprise*] (EG)
DIAWA ..... Dairy Industry Authority of Western Australia
DIB .... Dana Irian Barat [*West Irian Fund*] (IN)
DIB .... Data Inspection Board [*Europe*]
DIB .... Departamento de Instrumentacion Electronica [*Electronic Instrumentation Department*] (LA)
DIB .... Deutsche Investitionsbank [*German Investment Bank*] (EG)
DIB .... Deutsches Institut fuer Berufsausbildung [*German Vocational Training Institute*] (EG)
DIB .... Deutsches Institut fuer Betriebswirtschaft eV [*German Institute of Business Administration and Economics*] (SLS)
DIB .... Development Industrial Bank [*Egypt*] (IMH)
DIB .... Dibrugarh [*India*] [*Airport symbol*] (OAG)
dib .... Dibujo [*Drawing, Sketch*] [*Spanish*]
DIB .... Directorate of Intelligence Bureau [*Pakistan*]
DIB .... Directory Information Base [*Computer science*] (TNIG)
DIB .... Dis Isleri Bakanligi [*Foreign Affairs Ministry*] (TU)
DIB .... Drogowy Instytut Badawczy [*Road Research Institute*] (POL)
DIB .... Drzavna Investicijska Banka [*State Investment Bank*] [*Former Yugoslavia*] (YU)
DIBAG ...... Diisobutylaluminum Hydride (RU)
DIBC.......... Bocanda [*Ivory Coast*] [*ICAO location identifier*] (ICLI)
DIBI.......... Boundiali [*Ivory Coast*] [*ICAO location identifier*] (ICLI)
DIBI.......... Development and Investment Bank of Iran (ME)
DIBID........ Divisao de Bibliografia e Documentacao [*Comissao Executiva do Plano da Lavoura Cacaueira*] [*Brazil*]
DIBK........ Bouake [*Ivory Coast*] [*ICAO location identifier*] (ICLI)
DIBN .... Bouna/Tehini [*Ivory Coast*] [*ICAO location identifier*] (ICLI)
DIBOR ...... Dubai InterBank Offered Rate
DIBU .... Bondoukou/Soko [*Ivory Coast*] [*ICAO location identifier*] (ICLI)
DIC .... Dainippon Ink & Chemicals [*Japan*]
DIC .... Danish Invention Center [*Technological Institute*]
DIC .... Defence Industries Corporation [*Nigeria*]
DIC .... Democratie Integrale au Cameroun [*Political party*] (EY)
DIC .... Departamento de Informacion Comercial [*Centro Dominicano de Promocion de Exportaciones*] [*Dominican Republic*]
DIC .... Departamento de Investigacion Criminal [*Criminal Investigation Department*] [*Bolivia*] (LA)
dic.............. Dicembre [*December*] [*German*]
dic.............. Diciembre [*December*] [*Spanish*]
dic.............. Dicionario [*Dictionary*] [*Portuguese*]
DIC .... Direccion de Instruccion de Cuadros [*Directorate for Training and Cadres*] [*Cuba*] (LA)
DICA .... Derecho de Importacion Centroamericano [*Central American Import Right*] [*Central American Common Market*] (EY)
DICA .... Direccion de Instrumentacion y Control Automatico [*Directorate of Automated Control and Instrumentation*] [*Cuba*] (LA)
DICA .... Direction des Carburants [*Directorate of the Gas, Oil and Hydrocarbon Processing Industries*] [*France*] (PDAA)
DICA .... Distilleria Italiana Carburanti Affini
DICAMEC ... Director de Armas, Municiones, y Explosivos de Uso Civil [*Paraguay*]
DICARWS ... Division of Inter-Church Aid: Refugees and World Service

DICCASS ... Document and Information Center of the Chinese Academy of Social Sciences
dice............ Diciembre [*December*] [*Spanish*]
dicht .... Dichterisch [*German*]
Dicht .... Dichtung [*Joint*] [*German*] (GCA)
DICMA ..... Division de Capacitacion del Magisterio [*Colombia*] (COL)
DICOCALI ... Distribuidora de Combustibles [*Colombia*] (COL)
DICOFILMS ... Distribuidora Colombiana de Films Mundiales [*Colombia*] (COL)
DICOL...... Distribuidora Colombiana de Libros [*Colombia*] (COL)
DICOLSA ... Distribuidora Comercial de Cigarrillos SA [*Colombia*] (COL)
DICOMA .. Distribuidora Colombiana de Manufacturas [*Colombia*] (COL)
DICONAL ... Distribuidora Nacional de Confecciones Ltda. [*Pereira*] (COL)
DICOPA.... Societe de Distribution de Cosmetiques et Parfumerie
DICOPAL .. Distribuidora de Combustibles Palmira (COL)
DICORE.... Division de Conservacion de Recursos [*Chile*] (DSCA)
DICORTOT ... Societe Diamond Corporation Cote-D'Ivoire Ltd.
DICORWAF ... Diamond Corporation of West Africa
DICOVE ... Distribuidora Colombo Venezolana Ltda. [*Cucuta*] (COL)
DICSA ...... Division de Investigacion de Conservacion de Suelos y Aguas [*Puerto Rico*] (DSCA)
DICT......... Department of Industry, Commerce, and Technology [*Australia*]
DICTA....... Digital Image Computing: Techniques and Applications [*Conference*]
DictionCom ... Dictionnaire Communal [*Benelux*] (BAS)
DICTMA... Delegation Italienne de Cooperation Technique Militaire Aeronautique
DICTUC.... Departamento de Investigaciones Cientificas y Tecnologicas [*Santiago, Chile*] (LAA)
DICWA ..... Defence Industries Council of Western Australia
DID........... Departamento Centro Nacional de Informacion y Documentacion [*Comision Nacional de Informacion Cientifica y Tecnologica*] [*Chile*]
DID........... Department of Commercial and Industrial Development [*Queensland, Australia*]
DID........... Department of Industries and Development [*Northern Territory*] [*Australia*]
DID........... Direccion Departamental de Investigacion [*Departmental Directorate of Investigation*] [*Bolivia*] (LA)
DID........... Division of Information and Documentation [*National Institute of Science and Technology*] [*Philippines*]
DIDA........ Defense Industry Development and Support Administration [*Turkey*]
DIDA........ Direccion de Inspeccion y Defensa Agraria [*Peru*] (DSCA)
DIDA........ Divisao de Informacoes e Divulgacao Agricolas [*Brazil*] (DSCA)
DIDACEROS ... Distribuidora de Hierros y Aceros [*Colombia*] (COL)
DIDAR ...... Direccion de Investigacion de Delitos Aduaneros y de la Renta [*Department for the Investigation of Customs and Tax Crimes*] [*Bolivia*] (LA)
DIDB .... Dabou [*Ivory Coast*] [*ICAO location identifier*] (ICLI)
DIDD........ Department of Industrial Development and Decentralisation [*Australia*]
DIDEA ...... Distribuidora de Automoviles, SA [*Automobile Distributor Corp.*] [*El Salvador*]
DIDECO ... Direccion de Desarrollo Comunal [*Directorate of Communal Development*] [*El Salvador*] (LA)
DIDEFA ... Division de Defensa Agropecuaria [*Chile*] (DSCA)
DIDK .... Dimbokro [*Ivory Coast*] [*ICAO location identifier*] (ICLI)
DIDL .... Daloa [*Ivory Coast*] [*ICAO location identifier*] (ICLI)
didodekaedr ... Diploid, Didodecahedral (RU)
DIDOP ...... Divisao de Documentacao Tecnica e Patentes [*Rio De Janeiro, Brazil*] (LAA)
DIDULCES ... Fabrica de Dulces la Colombiana SA [*Colombia*] (COL)
DIDV .... Divo [*Ivory Coast*] [*ICAO location identifier*] (ICLI)
DIE .... Departamento de Investigaciones Economicas [*Economic Research Department*] [*Bolivia*] (LA)
DIE .... Devlet Istatistik Enstitusu [*State Statistical Institute*] (TU)
DIE .... Diego Suarez [*Madagascar*] [*Airport symbol*] (OAG)
DIE .... Diethnis Ilektrologiki Epitropi [*International Electrological Committee*] (GC)
DiE .... Diplome d'Etat [*French*]
DIE .... Direccion de Inteligencia del Estado [*State Intelligence Directorate*] [*Bolivia*] (LA)
DIE .... Romanian Intelligence Service [*Acronym represents Romanian phrase*]
DIEA .... Department of Immigration and Ethnic Affairs [*Australia*]
DIEESE..... Departamento Intersindical de Estatistica e Estudos Socio-Economicos [*Interunion Department of Statistics and Socioeconomic Studies*] [*Brazil*] (LA)
DIEKA....... Sodium Diethyldithiocarbamate (RU)
DIELCI..... Diffusion Electrique de la Cote-D'Ivoire
Dielektr-Konst ... Dielektrizitaetskonstante [*Dielectric Constant*] [*German*] (GCA)
DiENS .... Diplome des Ecoles Normales Superieures [*French*]
diensw .... Dienswillig [*Obedient*] [*Afrikaans*]
DIEO .... Decennie Internationale d'Exploration des Oceans [*International Decade of Ocean Exploration*] (MSC)

DIEP......... Department of Industry and Economic Planning
DIEPE....... Direccion de Investigacion, Experimentacion, y Perfeccionamiento Educativo [*Directorate of Research, Experimentation, and Educational Improvement*] [*Argentina*] (LA)
dierk.......... Dierkunde [*Zoology*] [*Afrikaans*]
dies............. Dieselbe [*The Same*] [*German*]
dies............. Dieselfde [*The Same*] [*Afrikaans*]
DIESA....... Department of International Economic and Social Affairs [*United Nations Information service or system*] (IID)
diesbez...... Diesbezueglich [*Concerning This*] [*German*] (GCA)
DIEST....... Parti de la Defense des Interets Economiques et Sociaux du Territoire
DIF............ Danish Society of Chemical, Civil, Electrical, and Mechanical Engineers (MCD)
DIF............ Deutsches Instute fur Forderung des Industriellen Fuhrungsnachwuchses [*German Institute for Industrial Management Development*] (PDAA)
dif.............. Diferente [*Different, Distinct*] [*Portuguese*]
dif.............. Differe [*Deferred Stock*] [*French*] [*Business term*]
dif.............. Differential (RU)
DIF............ Diiodofluorescein (RU)
DIF............ Diisopropyl Phosphate (RU)
DIF............ Sistema para el Desarrollo Integral de la Familia [*System for Complete Family Development*] [*Mexico*] (LA)
DIFAD....... Deutsches Institut fuer Angewandte Datenverarbeitung [*German*] (ADPT)
DIFANAL ... Distribuidora de Fabricas Nacionales Ltda. [*Colombia*] (COL)
DIFASA .... Distribuidora de Insecticidas y Fertilizantes Agricolas SA [*Mexico*] (DSCA)
diff............. Differe [*Different*] [*French*]
Diff............ Differenz [*Difference*] [*German*] (GCA)
DIFF.......... Diisopropyl Fluophosphate (RU)
differ.......... Differential (RU)
DIFK......... Del-Vietnami Ideiglenes Forradalmi Kormany [*Provisional Revolutionary Government of South Vietnam*] (HU)
DIFK......... Ferkessedougou [*Ivory Coast*] [*ICAO location identifier*] (ICLI)
DIFMA..... Dresdner International Financial Markets (Australia) Ltd.
DIFMAD.... Diffusion Industrielle de Madagascar
DIFOR....... Dibamba Forestiere
DIFOR...... Division Forestal [*Chile*] (DSCA)
DIfR.......... Deutsches Institut fuer Berufsausbildung [*German Vocational Training Institute*] (EG)
DIFSTL..... State Publishing House for Physical Culture and Sports Publications (BU)
DIFU .... Deutsches Institut fuer Urbanistik
DIFU .... Diphenylacetic Acid (RU)
DIG............ Departement Documentation et Information Geologique [*Geological Information and Documentation Department*] [*Bureau of Geological and Mining Research*] [*Information service or system*] (IID)
Dig .... Digue [*Dam*] [*Military map abbreviation World War I*] [*French*] (MTD)
DIG........... Dominican Institute of Genealogy (EAIO)
dig .... Faites Digerer [*Digest*] [*Pharmacy*]
DIGA .... Department of Infrastructure and Government Assets [*Western Australia*]
DIGA .... Gagnoa [*Ivory Coast*] [*ICAO location identifier*] (ICLI)
DIGECA .... Distribuidora General, CA [*Ecuador*] (LAA)
DIGEDECOM ... Direccion General para el Desarrollo de la Comunidad [*General Directorate for Community Development*] [*Panama*] (LA)
DIGENOR ... Direccion General de Normas y Sistemas de Calidad [*Dominican Republic*]
DIGEP....... Diosgyori Gepgyar [*Diosgyor Machine Factory*] (HU)
DIGEPOL ... Direccion General de Policias [*General Directorate of Police*] [*Venezuela*] (LA)
DIGESA .... Direccion General de Servicios Agricolas [*General Directorate of Agricultural Services*] [*Guatemala*] (LA)
DIGESEPE ... Direccion General de Servicios Pecuarios [*General Directorate of Livestock Services*] [*Guatemala*] (LA)
DIGL .... Guiglo [*Ivory Coast*] [*ICAO location identifier*] (ICLI)
Digmo .... Dignissimo [*Most Dignified*] [*Correspondence*] [*Portuguese*]
DIGN......... Grand Bereby/Nero Mer [*Ivory Coast*] [*ICAO location identifier*] (ICLI)
DIHO .... Delta Instituut voor Hydrobiologisch Onderzoek [*Delta Institute for Hydrobiological Research*] [*Netherlands*] (EAS)
DIHT......... Deutscher Industrie- und Handelstag [*Federation of Chambers of German Industry and Commerce*] (WEN)
DII .... Decision Information Institute [*Japan*]
DII .... Direccion de Informacion e Inteligencia [*Office of Intelligence and Information*] [*Uruguay*] (LA)
DII .... Donets Industrial Institute (RU)
DIII........... Abidjan [*Ivory Coast*] [*ICAO location identifier*] (ICLI)
DIIT.......... Dnepropetrovsk Institute of Railroad Transportation Engineers (RU)
DIJ............. Daerah Istimewa Jogjakarta [*Jogjakarta Special Region*] (IN)

dijszab........ Dijszabalyzat [*Price Register*] (HU)
DIK .... Drvno Industriski Kombinat [*Industrial Combine for Wood Products*] (YU)
DIK .... Remote-Reading Induction Compass (RU)
DIK .... State Industrial Combine (BU)
DIKEP....... Dimokratiki Kinisi Epistimonon [*Democratic Movement of Professionals*] [*Greek*] (GC)
DIKF......... Dansk Institut foer Kritisk Fredsforskning [*Danish Institute for Critical Peace Research*]
DIKIF .... Dimokratiki Kinisi Foititon [*Democratic Student Movement*] [*Greek*] (GC)
DIKO .... Demokratiko Komma [*Democratic Party*] [*Cyprus*] [*Political party*] (EY)
DIKO .... Dimokratiko Komma [*Democratic Party*] [*Cyprus*] (GC)
DIKO .... Korhogo [*Ivory Coast*] [*ICAO location identifier*] (ICLI)
dikovr........ Division of Ships for Defense of a Waterway Area (BU)
dikr............ Cruiser Division (RU)
DIKS......... Discrete Measurement Correlation System (RU)
DIKS......... State Goods Quality Inspectorate (BU)
DIL .... Depenses d'Interet Local [*Algeria*]
DIL .... Dili [*Indonesia*] [*Airport symbol*] (OAG)
DIL .... Directia Industriei Locale [*Local Industry Directorate*] (RO)
DIL .... Directorate of Industrial Liaison [*Pakistan Council of Scientific and Industrial Research*] (WED)
dil .... Faites Diluer [*Dilute*] [*Pharmacy*]
DILAPSA ... Distribuidora Latinoamericana de Publicaciones SA [*Latin American Publications Distributor, Inc.*] [*Chile*] (LA)
DILFA .... Direccion de Lucha Contra la Fiebre Aftosa [*Office for the Prevention of Foot-and-Mouth Disease*] [*Uruguay*] (LA)
DILGEA .... Department of Immigration, Local Government and Ethnic Affairs [*Commonwealth*] [*Australia*]
DILIA .... Ceskoslovensky Divadelni a Literarni Jednatelstvi [*Czechoslovak Theater and Literary Agency*] (CZ)
DILKUR..... Turkiye Dil Kurumu [*Turkish Linguistic Association*] (TU)
DIM........... Dahir sur l'Immatriculation des Immeubles (FLAF)
DIM .... Dardo de Investigacion Meteorologica [*Argentina*]
DIM .... Deportivo Independiente Medellin (COL)
DIM .... Deutsches Institut fuer Marktforschung [*German Institute for Market Research*] (WEN)
dim .... Dimension [*Dimension*] [*French*]
dim .... Dimensione [*Dimension*] [*Italian*]
Dim .... Diminuendo [*With Gradually Diminishing Power*] [*Music*]
dim .... Diminutif [*French*] (TPFD)
dim .... Diminution [*Decrease*] [*Knitting*] [*French*]
dim .... Diminutive (TPFD)
dim .... Diminutivo [*Very Small*] [*Publishing*] [*Italian*]
dim .... Diminutivo [*Diminutive*] [*Portuguese*]
DIM .... Direccion de Inteligencia Militar [*Military Intelligency Directorate*] [*Cuba*] (LA)
DIM .... Distrik Militer [*Military District (KODIM)*] (IN)
DIM .... Division d'Infanterie Marocaine
DIM .... Dnepropetrovsk Scientific Research Institute of Metals (RU)
DIM .... Pulse-Duration Modulation (RU)
DIMA .... Digitalisierung von Massen [*German*] (ADPT)
DIMA .... Distribuidora de Maquinas, SARL
DIMA .... Societe de Developpement Industriel Mecanique et Agricole
DIMAC ..... Distribuidora de Materiais de Construcao [*Building trade enterprise*] [*Mozambique*]
DIMAC ..... Distribuidora de Materiales de Construccion [*Colombia*] (COL)
DIMAFRIC ... Societe de Distribution de Materiel en Afrique
DIMAK ..... Dimokratiki Mathitiki Kinisi [*Democratic Student Movement*] [*Greek*] (GC)
DIMAS...... Deutsches Integriertes Modulares Anwendungssystem [*German*] (ADPT)
DIMATIT ... Societe Nord-Africaine de l'Amiante - Ciment Dimatit
DIMAVAG ... Diosgyori Vas-, Acel-, es Gepgyar [*Diosgyor Iron, Steel, and Machine Factory*] (HU)
DIMAYOR ... Direccion Mayor de Futbol Colombiano [*Colombia*] (COL)
DIMDI ...... Deutsches Institut fuer Medizinische Dokumentation und Information [*German Institute for Medical Documentation and Information*] [*Ministry for Youth, Family, and Health Affairs Database producer*] [*Information service or system*] (IID)
DIME .... Development of Integrated Monetary Electronics [*EC*] (ECED)
DIMELEC ... Direction des Industries Mecaniques, Electriques et Electroniques [*France*] (PDAA)
dimens........ Dimensional [*German*] (GCA)
dimens........ Dimensione [*Dimension*] [*Publishing*] [*Italian*]
DIMENTAL ... Distribuidora Mercantil Nacional [*Colombia*] (COL)
DIMENTALES ... Distribuidora de Metales [*Colombia*] (COL)
DIMES...... Distribution de Materiel Electrique au Senegal
dimin .... Diminutivo [*Diminutive*] [*Portuguese*]
DIMINCO ... National Diamond Mining Company [*Sierra Leone*] Ltd.
DIMINT.... Division de Inteligencia del Ministerio del Interior [*Intelligence Division of the Interior Ministry*] (LA)
DIMN........ Man [*Ivory Coast*] [*ICAO location identifier*] (ICLI)

DIMO........ Danske Interne Medicineres Organisation [*Denmark*] (SLS)
dimonstr..... Dimonstrative [*Demonstrative*] [*Italian*]
DIMP .... Defence Industry and Materiel Policy Division [*Department of Defense*] [*Australia*] (PDAA)
DIMP .... Induced Magnetic Dipole Surveying (RU)
dimp .... Marine Division (BU)
DIMS........ Director, International Military Staff Memorandum [*NATO*] (NATG)
DIMS........ Diving Incident Monitoring Survey [*Australia*]
DIN........... Aerodin SA de CV [*Mexico*] [*ICAO designator*] (FAAC)
DIN........... Demographic Institute (of the Academy of Sciences, USSR) (RU)
DIN........... Departamento de Imprensa Nacional [*Portuguese*]
DIN........... Departamento de Impuestos Nacionales [*National Tax Department*] [*Colorado*] (LA)
DIN........... Departamento de Investigacion Nacional [*Department of National Investigation*] [*Honduras*] (LA)
DIN........... Deutsche Industrie-Norm [*German Industrial Standard*] (WEN)
DIN........... Deutsches Institut fuer Normung [*German Institute for Standardization*] (IID)
DIN........... Dinar [*Monetary unit*] [*Former Yugoslavia*]
Din........... Dinbilgisi [*Religion*] (TU)
DIN........... Direccion de Impuestos Nacionales [*Colombia*] (COL)
din............ Doctor of Art Studies (RU)
din............ Doctor of Historical Sciences (RU)
din............ Dyne (RU)
DINA........ Departamento de Inteligencia Nacional [*National Intelligence Department*] [*Chilean secret police Superseded by CNI*]
DINA........ Diesel Nacional [*National Diesel*] [*Mexico*] (LA)
DINA........ Distribuidora Nacional de Repuestos para Automotores SA [*Colombia*] (COL)
DINA........ Division d'Infanterie Nord-Africaine
DINA........ Japan Database Industry Association [*Tokyo*] [*Information service or system*] (IID)
DINAC...... Empresa Nacional de Comercializacion y Distribucion, SA [*National Marketing and Distribution Enterprise*] [*Chile*] (LA)
DINACOPRIN ... Direccion Nacional de Costes, Precios, e Ingresos [*National Costs, Price, and Income Bureau*] [*Uruguay*] (LA)
DINADECO ... Direccion Nacional de Desarrollo de la Comunidad [*National Community Development Directorate*] [*Costa Rica*] (LA)
DINAGECA ... Direccao Nacional de Geografia e Cadastro [*National Directorate for Geography and Survey*] [*Mozambique*] (AF)
DINALCREDITOS ... Directorio Nacional de Creditos (COL)
DINALIADAS ... Distribuciones Internacionales Aliadas Ltda. [*Colombia*] (COL)
DINAME .. Direccion Nacional de Mecanizacion [*National Mechanization Directorate*] [*Cuba*] (LA)
DINAMIGE ... Direccion Nacional de Mineria y Geologia [*National Directorate of Mines and Geology*] [*Ministry of Industry and Energy Uruguay*] (EAS)
DINAPROPE ... Distribuidora Nacional de Produtos Pecuarios [*National Cattle Products Distributing Company*] [*Angola*] (AF)
DINARO ... Distribuidora Nacional de Rodamientos [*Colombia*] (COL)
DINARP.... Direccion Nacional de Relaciones Publicas [*National Public Relations Bureau*] [*Uruguay*] (LA)
DINASEM ... Direccion Nacional de Semillas [*National Seed Directorate*] [*Cuba*] (LA)
DINATUR ... Direccion Nacional de Turismo [*National Direction of Tourism*] [*Bolivia*] (EAIO)
DINAVI..... Direccion Nacional de Vivienda [*National Office of Housing*] [*Uruguay*] (LA)
DINCOL ... Distribuidora Industrial de Colombia Ltda. [*Colombia*] (COL)
D Ind......... Droit Industriel [*French*] (FLAF)
DINE .... Direccion de Industrias del Ejercito [*Army Industries Board*] [*Ecuador*] (LA)
DINE .... Direccion Nacional de Electricidad [*La Paz, Bolivia*] (LAA)
DINEA ...... Direccion Nacional de Education de Adultos [*Colombia*] (COL)
DINEKT.... Study of Dynamics of Equatorial Currents and Structure of Water [*Russian*] (MSC)
DINES....... Direccion Nacional de Emergencias Sociales [*National Social Emergencies Directorate*] [*Argentina*] (LA)
DINFIA ..... Direccion Nacional de Fabricaciones e Investigaciones Aeronauticas [*Argentina*] (DSCA)
Ding .... Docteur-Ingenieur [*French*]
D Ing......... Doktor in die Ingenieurswese [*Doctor of Engineering*] [*Afrikaans*]
DINIKA..... Civil Engineering Study Enterprise [*Malagasy*] [*Use EEGC*] (AF)
DINIL........ Direccao Nacional da Industria Ligeira [*National Light Industry Authority*] [*Ministerio da Industria Angola*]
DINOK...... Dinitro-Ortho-Cresol (RU)
DINOPROC ... Direccao Nacional da Organizacao da Producao Colectiva [*National Directorate for the Organization of Collective Production*] [*Mozambique*] (AF)
DINSA....... Disability Information Network of South Australia

DINTA ...... Deutsches Institut fuer Technische Arbeitsschulung [*German Institute for Technical Knowledge*] [*Nazi Germany*]
DINTEL.... Distribuidora Nacional de Telas Ltda. [*Colombia*] (COL)
DINTEP ... Divisao de Informacao Tecnica e Propriedade Industrial [*Petroleo Brasileiro*] [*Brazil*]
D Int Priv ... Droit International Prive (FLAF)
D Int Pub ... Droit International Public (FLAF)
DINUPS.... DIMDI's [*Deutsches Institut fuer Medizinische Dokumentation und Information*] Input and Updata System (NITA)
DINZ........ Designers Institute of New Zealand (EAIO)
DIO........... State Industrial Trust (BU)
DIOCC ...... District Intelligence and Operations Coordination Center [*Vietnam*] (VNW)
DIOD........ Odienne [*Ivory Coast*] [*ICAO location identifier*] (ICLI)
DIOF .... Frontline Disinfection Instruction Detachment (RU)
DIOF .... Ouango Fitini [*Ivory Coast*] [*ICAO location identifier*] (ICLI)
DIOM....... Dievthynsis Organoseos kai Methodon [*Organization and Methods Directorate*] [*Greek*] (GC)
Dion .... Direktion [*German*]
DIOO........ State Social Insurance Institute (BU)
DIOPE....... Departamento de Investigaciones y Orientacion Profesional y Educacional (de la Universidad Tecnica del Estado) [*Chile*] (LAA)
diovr .... Harbor Defense Division (RU)
DIP .... Demande d'Informations Prioritaires [*French*] (ADPT)
DIP .... Departamento de Imprensa e Propaganda [*Press and Propaganda Department*] [*Brazil*] (LA)
DIP .... Departamento de Imprensa e Propaganda [*Press and Propaganda Department*] [*Portuguese*]
DIP .... Departamento de Informacao e Propaganda [*Department of Information and Propaganda*] [*Mozambique*] (AF)
DIP .... Department of Industrial Promotion [*Ministry of Industry*] [*Thailand*]
DIP .... Diapaga [*Burkina Faso*] [*Airport symbol*] (OAG)
dip .... Diplomatic (RU)
DiP........... Diplome de Professeur de l'Enseignement Secondaire [*French*]
DIP .... Divisiones de Infanteria Permanente [*Regular Infantry Divisions*] [*Cuba*] (LA)
DIP .... Droit International Prive [*Private International Law*] [*French*] (DLA)
DIP .... Drvno Industrijsko Preduzece [*Industrial Enterprise in Wood Products*] (YU)
DIP .... State Industrial Enterprise (BU)
DIP .... Supplementary Spark Gap (RU)
DIP .... "To Overtake and Surpass" [*Slogan*] (RU)
DIPA........ Division de Informacion Politicas Antidemocraticus [*Argentina*]
DIPA........ Societe Distilleries de la M'Passa
DIPAKFA ... Dimokratiki Parataxi Kyprion Foititon Athinon [*Democratic Faction of Cypriot Students in Athens*] (GC)
DIPAN ...... Directoria de Producao Animal [*Rio Grande Do Sul, Brazil*] (LAA)
DIPAS .... Dialog-Informations-und Personal-Abrechnungs-System [*German*] (ADPT)
DIPAS .... Dialogorientiertes Personalabrechnungs-system [*German*] (ADPT)
DIPC......... Departamento de Investigaciones de la Policia [*Nicaragua*]
DipCS .... Diploma of the Chamber of Shipping [*Australia*]
DIPD .... Departamento de Inteligencia de la Policia Distrital [*Federal District Police Intelligence Department*] [*Mexico*] (LA)
DIPD .... Division de Investigaciones para la Prevencion de la Delincuencia [*Mexico*]
DIPES ...... Division de Pesca [*Chile*] (DSCA)
DIPESCA ... Distribuidora de Pescado Ltd. [*Brazil*] (DSCA)
DIP-FAR ... Direccion Politica de las FAR [*Political Directorate of the Revolutionary Armed Forces*] [*Cuba*] (LA)
DipFHS ..... Diploma in Family Historical Studies [*Australia*]
DIPFokhar ... State Industrial Enterprise for Photographic and X-Ray Paper (BU)
DIPG .... Port Gauthier [*Ivory Coast*] [*ICAO location identifier*] (ICLI)
DipIntAffs ... Diploma in International Affairs
DipIPSA .... Diploma of the Institute of Private Secretaries (Australia)
dipiramid ... Dipyramidal (RU)
dipk .... Division of Antisubmarine Ships (BU)
dipl .... Diploid (RU)
Dipl........... Diplom [*or Diplomiert*] [*German*]
dipl .... Diploma [*Diploma*] [*Portuguese*]
dipl .... Diplomacy (RU)
dipl .... Diplomacy, Diplomatic (BU)
dipl .... Submarine Division (RU)
DIPLAN .... Diretriz Basica de Planejamento [*Basic Planning Directorate*] [*Brazil*] (LA)
Dipl-Dolm ... Diplom-Dolmetsch [*Graduate Translator*] [*German*]
Dipl-HdlL ... Diplom-Handelslehrer [*Graduate Business Teacher*] [*German*]
DIPLIN ..... Distribuidora de Plasticos Industriales [*Barranquilla*] (COL)
Dipl-Ing .... Diplom Ingenieur [*Graduate Engineer*] [*German*]
diplins .... Diplomi-Insinoori [*Finland*]

Diplinz .... Diplomovany Inzenyr [*Certified Engineer*] (CZ)
DiplKaufm ... Diploma in Commerce [*German*]
Dipl-Kaufm ... Diplomkaufmann [*Graduate Tradesman*] [*German*]
Dipl Kfm .... Diploma in Commerce [*German*]
Dipl rerpol ... Diplomatus Rerum Politicarum [*Political Science Diplomate*] (EG)
Dipl-TA ..... Diplom-Tierarzt [*German*]
Dipl-Vw ..... Diplom-Volkswirt [*German*]
DipNSTC .. Diploma of the Nursery School Teachers' College [*Australia*]
DIPOA ...... Direcao Inspecao Productos Origen Animal [*Directorate for the Inspection of Animal Origin Products*] [*Brazil*] (ASF)
DIPP .... Descendants of Immigrants and Indian Party [*Suriname*] (EAIO)
DIPP .... Distribution Ivoirienne de Produits Petroliers
DIPPSA ..... Distribuidora de Productos de Petroleo [*Petroleum Products Distributor Corporation*] [*El Salvador*] (LA)
DIPR .... Deutsches Institut fuer Public Relations eV (SLS)
DIPRE .... Division de Informacion de la Prefectura Naval [*Navy Headquarters Information Division*] [*Uruguay*] (LA)
DIPROA .... Division de Produccion Agropecuaria [*Chile*] (DSCA)
DIPROCO ... Distribuidora de Productos Colombianos Ltda. [*Aguachica-Magdalena*] (COL)
DIPROGAS ... Distribuidora Provincial de Gas [*Ocana*] (COL)
DIPS .... Document Information Search System (RU)
DIPSEA ..... Dievthynsis Politikis Skhediaseos Ektaktou Anangis [*Emergency Policy Planning Directorate*] [*Greek*] (GC)
DipSKTC ... Diploma of the Sydney Kindergarten Teachers' College [*Australia*]
DIPUVEN ... Distribuidora de Publicaciones Venezolanas [*Venezuela*] (DSCA)
DIQUIVENJA ... Distribuidora Quimica Venezolana SA [*Venezuela*] (DSCA)
DIR .... Dimbokro Rangers
DIR .... Directeur [*or Direction*] [*Director or Directorate Used as a prefix Cambodia*] (CL)
Dir .... Director (PWGL)
dir .... Director, Directorate (BU)
dir .... Director, Manager (RU)
DIR .... Dire Dawa [*Ethiopia*] [*Airport symbol*] (OAG)
dir .... Direkt [*Direct*] [*Sweden*]
Dir .... Direktor [*Director*] [*German*]
DIR .... Direktur [*Director*] (IN)
DIR .... Diretoria de Imposto de Renda [*Portuguese*]
DIR .... Dirgantara Air Service PT [*Indonesia*] [*ICAO designator*] (FAAC)
dir .... Orchestra Conductor (BU)
DIRA .... Danish Industrial Robot Association (EAIO)
Dir BelAmst ... Uitspraak van den Raad van Beroep voor de Directe Belastingen te Amsterdam [*Netherlands*] (BAS)
DIRC .... Disability Information Resource Centre [*Australia*]
DIRCAB .... Directeur de Cabinet [*Frequently followed by the abbreviation for a ministry*] (CL)
DIRCABETAT ... Directeur de Cabinet du Chef de l'Etat [*Cambodia*] (CL)
DIRCEN .... Direction des Centres d'Experimentation Nucleaire [*Nuclear Experimentation Centers Directorate*] [*French*] (WER)
DIRCENGENIE ... Direction Centrale du Genie [*Central Directorate of Engineering*] [*Cambodia*] (CL)
Dircenmat .. Direction Centrale du Materiel [*Central Equipment Directorate*] [*Cambodia*] (CL)
Dircensante ... Direction Centrale de Sante [*Central Health Directorate*] [*Cambodia*] (CL)
Dircentrans ... Direction Centrale du Transport [*Central Transportation Directorate*] [*Cambodia*] (CL)
DIRD .... Directorate of Industrial Relations Development [*Australia*]
DIRDJEN ... Direktur Djenderal [*Director General*] (IN)
DIRE .... Department of Industrial Relations and Employment [*New South Wales, Australia*]
DIRECO .... Groupe de Defense des Interets de la Region Cotiere
DIRESSENCE ... Direction d'Essence [*Gasoline Directorate*] [*Cambodia*]
DIRET &FE ... Department of Industrial Relations, Employment, Training and Further Education [*New South Wales, Australia*]
DIREVE .... Directorio Revolucionario Venezolano [*Venezuelan Revolutionary Directorate*] (LA)
Dirgale .... Direction Generale [*Directorate General*] (CL)
dir gen .... Directeur-Generaal [*Benelux*] (BAS)
Dirgenie ..... Direction de la Genie [*Engineering Directorate*] [*Cambodia*] (CL)
Dirgeo .... Direction Geographique [*Geographic Directorate*] [*Cambodia*] (CL)
Dir geol imin prouchv ... Geological and Mining Surveys Directorate (BU)
DIRH .... Dirham [*Monetary unit*] [*Iraq*]
DIRINCO ... Direccion de Industria y Comercio [*Industry and Trade Directorate*] [*Chile*] (LA)
Dirintendance ... Direction de l'Intendance [*Quartermaster Corps Directorate*] [*Cambodia*] (CL)
DIRIVENTAS ... Asociacion de Dirigentes de Ventas [*Colombia*] (COL)

dirizh .... Conductor (RU)
dirk .... Division of Missile Ships (BU)
Dir Mu ..... Direkt Muhabere [*Direct Communication*] (TU)
DIR OP ..... Directie Overheids-Personeelsbeleid [*Netherlands*]
dir-or .... Director, Manager (RU)
DIRPE .... Direccion de Recursos Pesqueros [*Argentina*] (DSCA)
Dir pech ..... Press Directorate (BU)
DIRPOLICE ... Direction de la Police d'Immigration [*(Immigration) Police Directorate*] [*Cambodia*] (CL)
Dir PTT ..... Post, Telegraph, and Telephone Directorate (BU)
DIRRELATIONS ... Direction des Relations (Publiques) [*Directorate of (Public) Relations*] [*Cambodia*] (CL)
DIRSLEARN ... Datenbank fuer Schulung von GRIPS/DIRS3-Anwendern [*Database for Training of GRIPS/DIRS3 Users*] [*Database*] [*Information retrieval*] [*German*]
DIRSTAT ... Federazione fra le Associazioni e i Sindacati Nazionali dei Quadri Direttivi dell'Amministrazione dello Stato [*Italy*]
DIRT .... Deposit-Interest Retention Tax
Dir TlsMu ... Direkt Telsiz Muhabere [*Direct Radio Communication*] (TU)
Dirtrans ..... Direction du Transport [*Transportation Directorate*] [*Cambodia*] (CL)
DIRUT ...... Direktur Utama [*Director in Chief*] (IN)
Dir vdLandb ... Directie van de Landbouw [*Benelux*] (BAS)
DIS .... Defence Information Sciences [*Australia*]
DIS .... Defense Intelligence Service [*Denmark*] (WEN)
DIS .... Development Information System [*United Nations Information service or system*] (IID)
DIS .... Diarkis Iera Synodos [*Standing Holy Synod*] [*Greek*] (GC)
DIS .... Dinas [*Service, Office*] (IN)
DiS .... Diplome de Specialisation [*French*]
dis .... Disegno [*Design*] [*Italian*]
Dis .... Dissertation (BU)
DIS .... Division Intendantske Stanice [*Divisional Quartermaster Station*] (YU)
DIS .... Draft International Standard [*International Standards Organization*]
DIS .... Druzstevni Informacni Sluzba [*Cooperative Information Service*] (CZ)
DIS .... Loubomo [*Congo*] [*Airport symbol*] (OAG)
DIS .... Station Duty Engineer [*Telephony*] (RU)
DISA .... Direccao de Informacao e Seguranca de Angola [*Directorate of Information and Security of Angola*]
DISA .... Distribuciones SA [*Colombia*] (COL)
DISB .... Defence Information Services Branch [*Australia*]
DISB .... Disisleri Bakanligi [*Ministry of Foreign Affairs*] (TU)
Disc .... Discours [*French*] (FLAF)
DISC .... Domestic International Sales Corp. (ADPT)
DISCA .... Division de Investigaciones Sobre Contaminacion Ambiental [*Division of Research on Environmental Pollution*] [*Venezuela*] (LA)
DISCAL .... Distribuidora Comercial [*Colombia*] (COL)
DISCARTONES ... Distribuidora Nacional de Papeles y Cartones [*Colombia*] (COL)
DISCENPOL ... Distribuidora Central de Polietileno [*Colombia*] (COL)
DISCOLANA ... Distribuidora Colombiana de Lanas Ltda. [*Colombia*] (COL)
DISCON .... Defense Integrated Secure Communications Network [*Australia*]
DISCOS .... Dialogisiertes Computer Satzsystem [*German*] (ADPT)
DISDROCOL ... Distribuidora de Drogas Alianza [*Colombia*] (COL)
DISEXTRAS ... Distribuidora de Loterias Extras Ltda. [*Colombia*] (COL)
DISFABRILES ... Distribuidora Fabriles Ltda. [*Colombia*] (COL)
DISFANAL ... Distribuidor de Fabricas Nacionales [*Colombia*] (COL)
DISFOR .... Distribuidora de Repuestos Ford [*Colombia*] (COL)
DISFUENTES ... Fabrica de Discos Fuentes Ltda. [*Colombia*] (COL)
DISG .... Seguela [*Ivory Coast*] [*ICAO location identifier*] (ICLI)
Dishek .... Dishekimligi [*Dental, Dentistry*] (TU)
DISHIDRAL ... Dinas Hidrografi-Angkatan Laut [*Naval Hydrographic Office*] [*Indonesian*] (MSC)
DISI .... Dnepropetrovsk Construction Engineering Institute (RU)
DISIP .... Direccion de Servicios de Inteligencia y Prevencion [*Directorate of Intelligence and Prevention Services*] [*Venezuela*] (LA)
DISIP .... Directorate for Services of Intelligence and Prevention [*Jamaica*] (LA)
DISK .... Devrimci Isci Sendikalari Konfederasyonu [*Confederation of Revolutionary Trade Unions of Turkey*] (PD)
disk .... Diskonto [*Discount*] [*Afrikaans*]
DISKES ..... Dinas Kesehatan [*Health Service*] (IN)
d isk n .... Doctor of Art Studies (RU)
diskr .... Diskret [*Discreet*] [*Danish/Norwegian*]
diskus .... Discussion (RU)
DISMACOL ... Distribuidora de Materiales para Construccion Ltda. [*Colombia*] (COL)
DISMETAL ... Distribuidora Metalurgica de Occidents Ltda. [*Colombia*] (COL)
DISMOTORES ... Distribuidora de Motores Ltda. [*Colombia*] (COL)

DISMUSICAL ... Distribuidora Colombiana de Musica Funcional [*Colombia*] (COL)
DISNEGO ... Distribuciones Negocios Generales [*Colombia*] (COL)
DISNEL .... Distribuidora Nacional de Elementos Electricos [*Colombia*] (COL)
DISNET .... Defence Information Services Network [*Australia*]
DISNET .... Drug Information Systems Network
disp............ Dispensa [*Number*] [*Italian*] (GPO)
disp............ Disponible [*Available*] [*French*]
disp............ Disputats [*Dissertation, Thesis*] [*Publishing Danish/Norwegian*]
DISP.......... Draft International Standardized Profile [*OSI*] (OSI)
DISP.......... San Pedro [*Ivory Coast*] [*ICAO location identifier*] (ICLI)
DISPA ...... Diethnis Synandisis Perifereiakis Anaptyxeos [*International Meeting on Area Development*] [*Greek*] (GC)
Disp Aer..... Dispositions Concernant la Poste Aerienne (FLAF)
DISPAPELES ... Distribuidora de Papeles Ltda. [*Colombia*] (COL)
Dispers....... Dispersion [*German*] (GCA)
DISPIELES ... Distribuidora de Pieles Ltda. [*Colombia*] (COL)
DISPINTURAS ... Distribuidora de Pinturas Ltda. [*Colombia*] (COL)
DISPLAN ... Disaster Plan [*Australia*]
DISPO....... Dis Politika Yazar ve Muhabirleri Birligi [*Union of Foreign Political Writers and Correspondents*] (TU)
DISPROCAL ... Distribucion Pro-Capilar Ltda. [*Colombia*] (COL)
DISPROIM ... Distribuidora de Propaganda Impresa Ltda. [*Colombia*] (COL)
DISPROMECO ... Distribuidora de Productos Farmaceuticos [*Colombia*] (COL)
DISPRON ... Distribucion de Propaganda Ltda. [*Colombia*] (COL)
DISPROQUIL ... Distribuidora de Productos Quimicos [*Colombia*] (COL)
DISS .... Diethnes Instituton Stratigikon Spoudon [*International Institute of Strategic Services*] (GC)
diss............. Disputats [*Dissertation*] [*Danish/Norwegian*]
diss............. Dissertatie [*Dissertation*] [*Netherlands*]
Diss .... Dissertation [*German*]
diss............. Dissilabica [*or Dissilabico*] [*Disyllabic*] [*Portuguese*]
Diss .... Dissoziation [*Dissociation*] [*German*] (GCA)
DISS .... Doppler Speed-and-Drift Meter (RU)
DISS .... Sassandra [*Ivory Coast*] [*ICAO location identifier*] (ICLI)
Dissert........ Dissertation [*German*] (GCA)
dissert .... Dissertation [*French*]
Dissoz .... Dissoziation [*Dissociation*] [*German*] (GCA)
dissud......... Disciplinary Court (RU)
DIST.......... Delegation for Scientific and Technical Information (IID)
DIST.......... Department of Industry, Science, and Technology [*Australia*]
dist .... Distilled (RU)
dist .... Distillez [*Distill*] [*Pharmacy*]
dist .... Distinto [*Outstanding, Special*] [*Italian*]
DIST.......... Distrik [*District*] [*Afrikaans*]
DISTA .... Daerah Istimewa Atjeh [*Atjeh Special Region*] (IN)
DISTAPAS ... Distribuidora de Tapas y Productos Metalicos Ltda. [*Colombia*] (COL)
Distie.......... Distillerie [*Distillery*] [*Military map abbreviation World War I*] [*French*] (MTD)
distill.......... Distilled (RU)
DISTINTAS ... Distribucion de Tintas Ltda. [*Colombia*] (COL)
DISTIS ...... Defence Information Services Technical Information System [*Australia*]
dist(r) .... Distrik [*District*] [*Afrikaans*]
DISTRACOL ... Distribuidora Colombiana Ltda. [*Colombia*] (COL)
DISTRAL ... Distribuidora Industrial Ltda. [*Colombia*] (COL)
DISTRICENTRO ... Distribuidora Central de Confecciones Ltda. (COL)
DISTRICON ... Distribuidora de Confecciones Ltda. [*Colombia*] (COL)
DISTRIPHARM ... Societe de Distribution Pharmaceutique
dists............ Disciplinary (RU)
DISUDA.... Distribuidora Sudamericana [*Colombia*] (COL)
DISY......... Demokratikos Synagermos [*Democratic Rally*] [*Cyprus*] (GC)
DISY.......... Dimokratikos Synagermos [*Democratic Rally*] [*Political party*] (EAIO)
DISYA ...... Dimokratiko Syndikalistiko Kinima [*Democratic Trade Union Movement*] [*Greek*] (GC)
DISZ.......... Dolgozo Ifjusag Szovetsege [*Federation of Working Youth*] (HU)
DIT .... Darwin Institute of Technology [*Australia*]
DIT .... Departamento de Investigacions Tecnicas [*Department of Technical Investigations*] [*Guatemala*]
DIT .... Direccion de Informacion Tecnica [*Ministerio de la Industria Azucarera*] [*Cuba*]
DIT .... Direktorat [*Directorate*] (IN)
dit .... Ditongo [*Diphthong*] [*Portuguese*]
DIT .... Drustvo Inzenirjev in Tehnikov [*Society of Engineers and Technicians*] (YU)
DIT .... Drustvo Inzenirjev in Tehnikov Gozdarstva in Lesne Industrije Ljudska Republika Slovenija [*Society of Engineers and Technicians of Forestry and Wood Industry of Slovenia*] (YU)
DITAC....... Department of Industry, Technology, and Commerce [*Australia*]

DIT&RD.... Department of Industry, Technology and Regional Development [*Australia*]
DITB.......... Tabou [*Ivory Coast*] [*ICAO location identifier*] (ICLI)
DITDIKDAS ... Direktorat Pendidikan Dasar [*Directorate of Basic Education*] (IN)
DITEP....... Divisao de Informacoes Tecnicas [*Companhia Vale do Rio Doce*] [*Brazil*]
DITEX-CA ... Societe de Gerance et de Diffusion Textile pour le Centre-Afrique
DITh .... Diethnis Instituton Theatrou [*International Institute of the Theater*] (GC)
DITH .... Drustvo Inzinjera i Tehnicara Hrvatske [*Society of Engineers and Technicians of Croatia*] (YU)
DITH .... Societe du Domain Industriel de Thies
DI/TII........ Darul Islam/Tentara Islam Indonesia [*State of Islam/Islamic Army of Indonesia*] (IN)
DITJ .... Drustvo Inzinjera i Tehnicara Jugoslavije [*Society of Engineers and Technicians of Yugoslavia*] (YU)
DITLA .... Day in the Life of Australia [*A*] [*Photojournalism project*]
DITM .... Touba/Mahana [*Ivory Coast*] [*ICAO location identifier*] (ICLI)
DITP......... Drustvo Inzenirjev in Tehnikov Papirnistva [*Society of Engineers and Technicians of the Paper Industry*] [*Samoa*] (EAIO)
DITR......... Deutsches Informationszentrum fuer Technische Regeln [*German Information Center for Technical Rules*] [*German Institute for Standardization*] [*Information service or system*] (IID)
DITR......... House of Engineers and Technicians (RU)
DITRAC.... Division des Troupes Aeroportees et de Choc [*Airborne and Shock Troops Division*] [*Zaire*] (AF)
ditrig.......... Ditrigonal (RU)
DITT......... Department of Industry, Trade and Technology [*South Australia*]
DITT......... Drustvo Inzinjera i Tehnicara Tekstilaca [*Society of Textile Engineers and Technicians*] (YU)
DITTH ...... Drustvo Inzinjera i Tehnicara Tekstilaca Hrvatske [*Society of Textile Engineers and Technicians of Croatia*] (YU)
DITTNRS ... Drustvo Inzenjera i Tehnicara Tekstilaca Narodna Republika Srbija [*Society of Textile Engineers and Technicians of Serbia*] (YU)
Dituris........ Direccion General de Turismo [*General Directorate for Tourism*] [*Ecuador*] (GEA)
DIU........... Dispositif Intra-Uterin
div.............. Battalion [*Artillery*], Division , Divisional [*Navy*] (RU)
DIV .... Delpesti Ipari Vizmu [*Industrial Water Works of South Budapest*] (HU)
DIV .... Direction de l'Information de la Valorisation [*Information and Valorization Directorate*] [*National Institute of Agronomic Research*] [*Information service or system*] (IID)
Div............. Diverse [*Various*] [*German*]
div.............. Diverse [*Various*] [*Danish/Norwegian*]
div.............. Dividende [*Dividend*] [*French*] [*Business term*]
div.............. Divisao [*Division*] [*Portuguese*]
DIV .... Divisi [*Division*] (IN)
Div............. Division [*German*] (GCA)
Div............. Division [*Military*] [*French*] (MTD)
Div............. Division d'Infanterie [*Military*] [*French*] (MTD)
div.............. Divisioona [*Finland*]
DIVATERV ... Dinamikus Vallalasi Terszamitasi Modell [*Dynamic Enterprise Plan Computing Model*] (HU)
DI-VB .... Dopravni Inspectorat Verejne Bezpecnosti [*Transportation Inspectorate, Public Security*] (CZ)
Div Bel .... Dividendbelasting [*Benelux*] (BAS)
Divde......... Dividende [*Dividend*] [*French*] [*Business term*] (ILCA)
DIVENAZ ... Distribuidora Venezolana de Azucares SRL [*Venezuela*] (DSCA)
Div enTantbel ... Dividend- en Tantiemebelasting [*Benelux*] (BAS)
DIVERMA ... Societe Nationale d'Importation de Marchandises Diverses
divesmintsev ... Destroyer Division (RU)
DIVETIN .. Dnepropetrovsk Scientific Research Institute for Rehabilitation and Determination of Work Fitness of Disabled Persons (RU)
divinzh........ Division Engineer [*Military term*] (RU)
DIVIVIENDA ... Direccion Colombiana de Ahorro y Vivienda [*Colombian Savings and Housing Association*] (LA)
div-n .... Battalion [*Artillery*], Division [*Navy*] (RU)
DIVSZ .... Demokratikus Ifjusagi Vilagszovetseg [*World Federation of Democratic Youth*] (HU)
divtr............ Division Transport (RU)
DIW .... Deutsches Institut fuer Wirtschaftsforschung [*German Institute for Economic Research*] (WEN)
diw.............. Diwidend [*Dividend*] [*Afrikaans*] [*Business term*]
DIXIT .... Delegation for Scientific and Technical Information, Communication, and Culture [*Information service or system*] (IID)
DIY .... Diyarbakir [*Turkey*] [*Airport symbol*] (OAG)
Diyan .... Diyanet [*Religious*] (TU)

DiyB.......... Diyanet Isleri Baskanligi [*Religious Affairs Chairmanship (under Office of Premier)*]   (TU)
DIYCE....... Do-it-Yourself Continuing Education [*Australia*]
Diyetprodukt ... All-Union Office for the Dietetic Foods Trade   (RU)
DIYO........ Yamoussoukro [*Ivory Coast*] [*ICAO location identifier*]   (ICLI)
DIZ........... Deutsches Institut fuer Zeitgeschichte [*German Institute for Contemporary History*]   (EG)
diz.............. Diesel   (RU)
DIZ........... State Tool Plant   (BU)
Dizel'montazh ... Assembly and Repair Office of the Glavlokomobil'dizel'   (RU)
diz ind........ Diesel Index   (RU)
DJ .... Daughters of Jesus of Kermaria [*France*]   (EAIO)
DJ .... Demokratie Jetzt [*Defunct*] [*Germany*]   (EAIO)
dJ .... Der Juengere [*Junior*] [*German*]   (GPO)
Dj .... Dienstjaar [*Benelux*]   (BAS)
DJ .... Dieses Jahres [*Of This Year*] [*German*]   (ROG)
Dj .... Djebel [*Mountain, Hill*] [*Arabic*]   (NAU)
DJ .... Djibouti [*IYRU nationality code*] [*ANSI two-letter standard code*]   (CNC)
DJA .... Dotations aux Jeunes Agricultuers [*Endowments for Young Farmers*] [*Guadeloupe*]   (LA)
DJABAR ... Djawa Barat [*West Java*]   (IN)
DJAGUNG ... Djaksa Agung [*Attorney General*]   (IN)
DJAPEN ... Djawatan Penerangan [*Information Office*]   (IN)
DJATENG ... Djawa Tengah [*Central Java*]   (IN)
DJATI ...... Djaksa Tinggi [*District Attorney*]   (IN)
DJATIM ... Djawa Timur [*East Java*]   (IN)
DJAYA ... Djakarta Raya [*Greater Djakarta*]   (IN)
DJB........... Air Djibouti [*ICAO designator*]   (FAAC)
DJB........... Drustvo Jugoslovenskih Bibliotekara [*Society of Yugoslav Librarians*]   (YU)
DJB........... Jambi [*Indonesia*] [*Airport symbol*]   (OAG)
DJBFA ...... Danske Jazz, Beat og Folkemusik Autorer [*Danish Society for Jazz, Rock, and Folk Composers*]   (EAIO)
DJC........... Desantni Jurisni Camac [*Landing Attack Boat*]   (YU)
DJE........... Demokratischer Jugendverband Europas [*Democrat Youth Community of Europe*] [*Political party*]   (EAIO)
DJE........ Djerba [*Tunisia*] [*Airport symbol*]   (OAG)
DJE........ Documentation Juridique Etrangere [*Benelux*]   (BAS)
DjelaJA...... Djela, Izdanje Jazu [*Works. Publication of the Yugoslav Academy of Sciences and Arts*]   (YU)
DJEN........ Djenderal [*General (Rank)*]   (IN)
DJERBAR ... Djerman Barat [*Germany*]   (IN)
DJERTIM ... Djerman Timur [*Germany*]   (IN)
DJG .... Djanet [*Algeria*] [*Airport symbol*]   (OAG)
DJH .... Deutsche Jugendherberge [*German Youth Hostel*]
DJH .... Deutsches Jugendherbergswerk-Hauptverband [*German Youth Hostel Association*]   (EAIO)
DJI............. Deutsches Jugendinstitut eV   (SLS)
DJI............. Djibouti [*ANSI three-letter standard code*]   (CNC)
DJJ .... Jayapura [*Indonesia*] [*Airport symbol*]   (OAG)
DJK........... Daughters of Jesus of Kermaria [*See also FJ*] [*Paris, France*]   (EAIO)
DJL........... Djalan [*Street*]   (IN)
DJO .... Daloa [*Ivory Coast*] [*Airport symbol*]   (OAG)
DJO .... Deutsche Jugend des Ostens [*German Youth of the East*] [*West German organization*]   (EG)
DJP........... Democratic Justice Party [*South Korea*] [*Political party*]   (PPW)
DJP........... Democratic Justice Party [*Mauritania*] [*Political party*]   (EY)
DJR........... Deutscher Jugendring [*German Youth Ring*]   (EG)
DJS........... District Jungle Squads   (ML)
DJSI........... Directorate of Joint Service Intelligence [*Australia*]   (ADA)
DJU .... Deutsche Journalisten-Union [*Union of German Journalists*]   (WEN)
DJUBIR .... Djurubitjara [*Spokesman*]   (IN)
DJV........... Deshapremi Janatha Viyaparaya [*Patriotic People's Organisation*] [*Sri Lanka*] [*Political party*]
DJV........... Deutscher Journalisten-Verband eV   (SLS)
DJVK....... Danmarks Jordbrugsvidenskabelige Kandidatforbund [*Denmark*]   (SLS)
DJZ........... Direkcija Jugoslovenskih Zeleznica [*Administration of Yugoslav Railroads*]   (YU)
DK .... Association Committee   (BU)
DK .... Bell-Type Differential Manometer   (RU)
DK .... Dania [*Denmark*] [*Poland*]
DK .... Danmark [*Denmark*] [*International automobile identification tag*]
dk .... Decare   (BU)
DK .... Decimal Classification   (RU)
DK .... Decimalna Klasifikacija [*Decimal Classification*]   (YU)
DK .... Decontamination Kit   (RU)
DK .... Decontamination Rooms   (BU)
DK .... Dedictvi Komenskeho [*Comenius Heritage*] [*A publishing house*]   (CZ)
DK .... Delkelet [*Southeast*] [*Hungary*]   (GPO)

DK............. Denmark [*ANSI two-letter standard code*]   (CNC)
DK............. Depoh Kelengkapan [*Ordnance Depot*]   (ML)
DK............. Deutsche Kennziffer [*German Index Number (For standards)*]   (EG)
DK............. Deutscher Kulturbund [*German Cultural Federation*] [*Germany*]   (PPE)
DK............. Devisa Kredit [*Credit Exchange*] [*Indonesian*]   (IMH)
DK............. Dewan Keamanan [*Security Council (UN)*]   (IN)
DK............. Dezimal Klassifikation [*Netherlands*]
DK............. Diaplanitiko Komma [*Interplanetary Party*] [*Greek*]   (GC)
DK............. Dielektrizitaetskonstante [*Dielectric Constant*] [*German*]   (GCA)
DK............. Diesel Compressor   (RU)
DK............. Diesel Crane   (RU)
DK............. Diesel-Kraftstoff [*Diesel Fuel*] [*German*]   (EG)
DK............. Dimokratiko Komma [*Democratic Party*] [*DIKO*] [*See also*]   (GC)
DK............. Dispatching, Dispatcher Control   (RU)
D K............. Division Cavalry   (BU)
DK............. Dlouhodobe Kursy [*Long-Term Courses*]   (CZ)
DK............. Dom Ksiazki [*Book Store*] [*Poland*]
DK............. Dom Kultury [*House of Culture*]   (POL)
DK............. Drvni Kombinat [*Wood Combine*]   (YU)
DK............. Drzavna Komisija [*State Commission*]   (YU)
DK............. Dukhovna Kultura [*Spiritual Culture*] [*A periodical*]   (BU)
dk............. Good Quality, Soundness   (RU)
DK............. House of Culture   (RU)
DK............. House of the Peasant   (RU)
DK............. Indicating Pocket Dosimeter   (RU)
DK............. Landing Ship   (RU)
DK............. Palace of Culture   (RU)
DK............. Respiratory Quotient   (RU)
DK............. State Combine   (BU)
DK............. State Control   (BU)
DK............. Throttle Valve, Butterfly Valve   (RU)
d-k............. Transmitter, Transducer, Pickup   (RU)
DKA......... Daka [*Kazakhstan*] [*ICAO designator*]   (FAAC)
dka............ Decares   (BU)
DKA......... Deutscher Koordinierungsausschuss [*Coordinating European Council*]
DKA......... House of the Red Army   (RU)
DKAN....... Datenkanal [*German*]   (ADPT)
DKB......... Deutscher Kulturbund [*German Cultural League*]   (EG)
DKB......... Dzielnicowy Komitet Blokowy [*City Section Block Committee*]   (POL)
DKB.......... Road Commandant Battalion   (RU)
dkbr........... Road Commandant Brigade   (RU)
DKC.......... Delnicky Klub Cyklistu [*Workers' Cycling Club*]   (CZ)
DKCM....... Delnicky Klub Cyklistu a Motoristu [*Workers' Cycling and Motoring Club*]   (CZ)
DKD.......... Dewey Decimal Classification   (RU)
DKD.......... Dogu Karadeniz Kultur Dernegi [*Eastern Black Sea Cultural Association*]   (TU)
DKDL........ Kongelige Danske Landhusholdningsselskab [*Royal Agricultural Society of Denmark*]   (EAIO)
DKE......... Deutsche Elektrotechnische Kommission im DIN und VDE   (SLS)
DKEL........ Demokratikon Komma Ergazomenou Laou [*Democratic Party of Working People*] [*Greek*]   (PPE)
DKF.......... Dicalcium Phosphate   (RU)
DKF.......... Dimokratiki Kinisi Foititon [*Democratic Movement of Students*] [*Greek*]   (GC)
DKF.......... Dokumentation Kraftfahrwesen [*Motor Vehicle Documentation*] [*Germany*] [*Information service or system*]   (IID)
DKF.......... Dokumentation Kraftfahrwesen eV [*Database producer and database*] [*Bietigheim - Bissingen*] [*Information retrieval*]
DKF.......... Dyskusyjny Klub Filmowy [*Film Discussion Club*]   (POL)
DKF.......... House of the Red Navy   (RU)
DKF.......... State Cannery   (BU)
DKF.......... State Paper Factory   (BU)
Dkfm......... Diploma in Commerce [*German*]
DKfm........ Diplom-Kaufmann [*German*]
DKfO........ Deutsche Kommission fur Ozeanographic [*German Commission for Oceanography*]   (PDAA)
DKFZ........ Deutsches Krebsforschungszentrum [*German Cancer Research Center*] [*Heidelberg*] [*Information retrieval*]
dkg............. Dekagramma(a) [*Finland*]
DKG.......... Deutsche Kautschuk-Gesellschaft eV   (SLS)
DKG.......... Deutsche Keramische Gesellschaft eV [*German Ceramics Society*]   (SLS)
DKG.......... Deutsche Kinotechnische Gesellschaft fuer Film und Fernsehen   (SLSG)
DKG.......... Deutsche Kolonialgesellschaft
DKG.......... Deutsche Krankenhausgesellschaft [*German Hospital Association*]   (EAIO)
DKG........ Dunantuli Koolajipari Gepgyar [*Transdanubian Petroleum Industry Machine Factory*]   (HU)

DKGF .... House of Culture of the Humanities Divisions of MGU   (RU)
DKGMK .... Cutter Remote-Reading Gyrocompass   (RU)
DKH .... Datuk Keramat Holdings [*Tin-smelting company*] [*Malaysia*]
DKh .... Dimosia Khrisis [*Public Vehicle, Vehicle for Hire*] [*Automobile license plate designation*]   (GC)
DKh .... Dynamic Characteristic, Load Characteristic   (RU)
DKhB .... Bulgarian Painters' Union   (BU)
DKhE .... Dichloroethane   (RU)
DKhFK ...... State Chemical-Pharmaceutical Plant   (BU)
DKhGPl ..... State Art Gallery in Plovdiv   (BU)
DKhK .... State Chemical Combine   (BU)
DKhM .... Dichloral Urea   (RU)
dkhn .... Doctor of Chemical Sciences   (RU)
DKhVD ...... House of Children's Art Education   (RU)
DKhZ .... State Chemical Plant   (BU)
DKhZ .... State Refrigeration Systems Plant   (BU)
DKI .... Deutsches Krankenhausinstitut - Institut in Zusammenarbeit mit der Universitat Dusseldorf [*German Hospital Institute - Institute in Cooperation with the University of Dusseldorf*] [*Research center*]   (IRC)
DKI .... Deutsches Kunststoff-Institut [*German Plastics Institute*] [*Research center*]   (IRC)
DKI .... Dunk Island [*Australia*] [*Airport symbol*]   (OAG)
DKIN .... Deutsches Komitee Instandhaltung eV   (SLS)
DKK .... Dansk Kennel Klub [*Danish Kennel Club*]   (EAIO)
DKK .... Dengan Kawan-Kawannja [*And His Friends, With His Colleagues*]   (IN)
DKK .... Deniz Kuvvetleri Komutanligi [*Naval Forces Command*]   (TU)
DKK .... Dimotikos kai Koinotikos Kodix [*Municipal and Communal Code*] [*Greek*]   (GC)
DKK .... State Canning Combine   (BU)
DKK .... State Ready-Made Clothing Combine   (BU)
DKK .... State Rubber Products Combine   (BU)
DKKF .... Dzielnicowy Komitet Kultury Fizycznej [*City Section Committee on Physical Culture*]   (POL)
DKKFiT ..... Dzielnicowy Komitet Kultury Fizycznej i Turystyki [*District Committee for Physical Culture and Tourism*] [*Poland*]
DKL .... Danske Kunsthandvaerkeres Landssammenslutning [*Denmark*]   (SLS)
DKL .... Das Kommando des Luftschutzes [*Air Defense Command*]   (EG)
dkl .... Dekalitr [*Decaliter*] [*Poland*]
dkl .... Dekalitra(a) [*Finland*]
Dkl .... Dekovil [*Narrow Gauge Railway*]   (TU)
DKL .... Gunboat Division   (RU)
DKM .... Dakomat [*Poland*] [*ICAO designator*]   (FAAC)
DKM .... Dansk Kulturhistorisk Museumsforening [*Denmark*]   (SLS)
dkm .... Decameter   (RU)
dkm .... Dekametr [*Decameter*] [*Poland*]
dkm .... Dekametri(a) [*Finland*]
DKM .... Divizisko Komandno Mesto [*Divisional Command Post*]   (YU)
DKM .... House of Culture of the Metrostroy   (RU)
DKM .... Karjah Kerabat Di-Raja Malaysia [*Royal Order - Malaysia*]   (ML)
DKMEI ...... House of Culture of the Moscow Power Engineering Institute   (RU)
DKmEn ...... Delavska Kmecka Enotnost [*Workers' and Peasants' Unity*] [*A periodical*]   (YU)
DKMM ...... Committee on Marine Science and Technology   (MSC)
DKMS .... Dimitrovski Komunisticheski Mladezhki Suiuz [*Dimitrov Communist Youth Union*] [*Bulgarian*]
DKMZ .... State Cardboard and Pasteboard Plant   (BU)
DKN .... Dansk Kvinders Nationalrad [*Danish National Council of Women*]   (EAIO)
DKN .... Dom Kultury Nauczyciela [*Teacher's House of Culture*]   (POL)
DKN .... House of Culture and Science   (RU)
DK naDSNM ... Association Committee of the Dimitrov People's Youth Union   (BU)
DKNGL ..... Dimokratiko Kinima Neolaias Grigoriou Lambraki [*Grigorios Lambrakis Youth Democratic Movement*]   (GC)
DKNVS ..... Det Kongelige Norske Videnskabers Selskab [*Norway*]   (SLS)
DKO .... Children's Communist Organization   (RU)
DKOV .... Deutscher Kriegsopfer Verband [*League of German War Victims*]   (EG)
DKP .... Alternate Command Post   (RU)
DKP .... Command Post of the Division Commander   (RU)
DKP .... Communist Party of Denmark   (BU)
DKP .... Dania Komunista Partja [*Communist Party of Denmark*] [*Political party*]
DKP .... Danmarks Kommunistiske Parti [*Communist Party of Denmark*] [*Political party*]   (PPW)
DKP .... Democratic Korea Party [*South Korea*] [*Political party*]   (PPW)
DKP .... Depoh Kelengkapan Pangkalan [*Base Ordnance Depot*]   (ML)
DKP .... Deutsche Kommunistische Partei [*German Communist Party*] [*Political party*]   (PPE)
DKP .... Dispatcher Control Points   (BU)

DKP .... Dopravni Komunalni Podnik [*Municipal Transport Enterprise*] [*Prague*]   (CZ)
DKP .... Drobne a Kratkodobe Predmety [*Small and Short Term Items*] (CZ)
DKP .... Mobile Disinfection Chamber   (RU)
DKP .... State Book Printing Enterprise   (BU)
DKP .... State Committee for Planning   (BU)
DKPG .... Democratic Peasants' Party of Germany   (RU)
DKR .... Dakar [*Senegal*] [*Airport symbol*]   (OAG)
Dkr .... Dan Korona [*Danish Crown*] [*Monetary unit*]
DKR .... Dynamic Demagnetization Curve   (RU)
DKR .... Road Commandant Company   (RU)
DKR .... Road Commandant District   (RU)
DKRMP ..... House of Culture of Local Industry Workers   (RU)
DKS .... Dansk Kerneteknisk Selskab [*Danish Nuclear Society*]   (WND)
DKS .... Deutsches Kontor fuer Seefrachten [*German Sea Freight Office*] (EG)
DKS .... House of Culture of Construction Workers   (RU)
DKS .... Road Commandant Service   (RU)
DKSA .... State Committee for Construction and Architecture   (BU)
DKSM .... Dimitrov Young Communist League [*Bulgarian People's Republic*]   (RU)
DkSt .... Dekontaminacione Stanice [*Decontamination Stations*]   (YU)
DKSV .... Deutscher Kanusport-Verband [*German Canoeing League*] (EG)
DKT .... Deutscher Kraftwagentarif [*German Motor Vehicle License Fee*] (EG)
DKT .... Dominican Confederation of Labor   (RU)
DKT .... Dzial Kontroli Technicznej [*Technical Control Department*] (POL)
DKTNRH ... Drustvo Kemicara-Tehnologa Narodne Republike Hrvatske [*Society of Chemical Technologists of Croatia*]   (YU)
DKTs .... Shop Dispatcher's Switchboard   (RU)
DKU .... Danmarks Kommunistisk Ungdom [*Danish Communist Youth*] (WEN)
DKU .... Diosgyori Kohaszati Uzem [*Metalworks of Diosgyor*]   (HU)
DKU .... Road Commandant Section   (RU)
DKV .... Deutscher Kaelte- und Klimatechnischer Verein eV   (SLS)
DKV .... Deutscher Kohlen-Verkauf [*German Coal Sales Office*]   (EG)
DKV .... Deutscher Kraftverkehr [*German Motor Vehicle Transport*] (EG)
DKV .... Dunai Koolajipari Vallalat [*Danubian Petroleum Industry Enterprise*]   (HU)
DKVD .... House of Children's Communist Education   (RU)
DKW .... Dampf-Kraft-Wagen [*Steam-Powered Vehicle*] [*German*]
DKW .... Das Kleine Wunder [*The Little Wonder*] [*Initialism used as name of German automobile, manufactured by Auto Union*]
DKW .... Deutsche Kraftfahrzeugwerke [*German Motor Vehicle Plants*] (EG)
DKZ .... Plant Dispatcher's Switchboard   (RU)
DKZ .... State Boilers Plant   (BU)
DKZ .... State Commission on Reserves [*Military*]   (BU)
DKZ .... State Rubber Products Plant   (BU)
DKZh .... House of Culture of Railroad Workers   (RU)
DK ZIL ..... Palace of Culture of the Automobile Plant Imeni I. A. Likhachev (RU)
DL .... Danske Lov [*Laws in Force*] [*Denmark*]   (ILCA)
Dl .... Decalitro [*Decaliter*] [*Spanish*]
dl .... Decilitre [*Deciliter*] [*French*]
dl .... Decilitro [*Deciliter*] [*Portuguese*]
dl .... Decilitro [*Deciliter*] [*Spanish*]
DL .... Decret-Loi [*Decree-Law*] [*French*]   (ILCA)
DL .... Decreto Legge [*Decree-Law*] [*Italian*]   (ILCA)
dl .... Deel [*Part*] [*Netherlands*]   (GPO)
Dl .... Dekaliter [*Decaliter*] [*Afrikaans*]
DL .... Demarkationslinie [*Line of Demarcation*]   (EG)
DL .... Demokratische Linke [*Democratic Left Party*]   (EG)
DL .... Derecha Liberal [*Liberal Right*] [*Spanish*]   (WER)
dl .... Desilitra(a) [*Finland*]
DL .... Deutsche Literaturzeitung
DL .... Deutscher Landkreistag [*Association of German/County Councils*]
DL .... Deutscher Landwirtschaftsverlag [*German Agricultural Publishing House*]   (EG)
DL .... Deutscher Lehrerverband   (SLS)
DL .... Dienstreglement Loodswezen [*Benelux*]   (BAS)
DL .... Dinar Libyen [*Monetary unit*]
DL .... Division Infirmary   (RU)
DL .... Dixson Library [*Australia*]   (ADA)
dl .... Dlugosc [*Length*]   (POL)
DL .... Dopravni Letectvo [*Transport Air Force Units*]   (CZ)
DL .... Drehringlafette [*Electrically-Operated Rotating Top Turret*] [*German*]   (GCA)
Dl .... Druckluft [*Compressed Air*] [*German*]   (GCA)
DL .... Foreningen af Danske Landskabsarkitekter [*Association of Danish Landscape Architects*]   (EAIO)

DL .... Landing Boat   (RU)
dl .... Length   (RU)
DL .... Summer Diesel (Fuel)   (RU)
DLA .... Air Dolomiti [*Italy*] [*ICAO designator*]   (FAAC)
DLA .... Department of Land Administration [*Western Australia*]
DLA .... Deutsche Landjugend-Akademie Fredeburg   (SLS)
DLA .... Dievthynsis Limenikis Astynomias [*Port Police Directorate*] [*Greek*]   (GC)
DLA .... Douala [*Cameroon*] [*Airport symbol*]   (OAG)
DLA .... Douala Airport
DLAE .... Divisao de Levantamentos e Analise Economica [*Brazil*]   (DSCA)
DL &OTCR ... Drug Listing and Over the Counter Registration Section [*Therapeutic Goods Association*] [*Australia*]
DLANT ..... Department of the Legislative Assembly of the Northern Territory [*Australia*]
d lar .... Long-Range Artillery   (BU)
DLAS........ Department of Labour and Administrative Services [*Northern Territory*] [*Australia*]
DLC .... Dalien [*China*] [*Airport symbol*]   (OAG)
DLCC........ Desert Locust Control Committee [*Food and Agriculture Organization*] [*United Nations*]   (EA)
d lch........... Division Field Hospital   (BU)
DLCO-EA ... Desert Locust Control Organization for Eastern Africa   (AF)
DLDPANSW ... Dental Laboratories and Dental Prosthetists' Association of New South Wales [*Australia*]
DLDS .... Detachement Local de Defense en Surface [*Local Surface Defense Detachment*] [*Cambodia*]   (CL)
DLE .... Dole [*France*] [*Airport symbol*] [*Obsolete*]   (OAG)
DLEP .... Draft Local Environment Plan [*Australia*]
D lesn .... Forester's House [*Topography*]   (RU)
DLF........... Danmarks Laereforening [*Denmark*]   (SLS)
DLF........... Deutschlandfunk [*Radio network*] [*Germany*]
DLF........... Development Loan Fund
DLfM........ Deutsche Liga fuer Menschenrechte [*German League for Human Rights*]   (EG)
DLG .... Datenlesegeraet [*German*]   (ADPT)
D Lg .... Decreto Legislativo [*Legislative Decree*] [*Italian*]   (ILCA)
DLG .... Department of Local Government [*South Australia*]
DLG .... Deutsche Landwirtschaftsgesellschaft [*German Agricultural Society*]   (EG)
dl geogr ..... Dlugosc Geograficzna [*Longitude*] [*Poland*]
DLGIFPI... Deutsche Landesgruppe der IFPI [*German Chapter of the International Federation of the Phonographic Industry*]   (EAIO)
DLH........... Demiryollari, Limanlar, ve Hava Meydanlara Insaat Genel Mudurlugu [*Railways, Harbors, and Airfields Construction Directorate General*] [*Under Public Works Ministry*]   (TU)
DLH.......... Department of Lands and Housing [*Northern Territory*] [*Australia*]
DLH.......... Deutsche Lufthansa AG [*German Lufthansa*] [*Airline*]   (EG)
dlhrfilm...... Dlouhy Hrany Film [*Full Length Film*]   (CZ)
DLI .... Department of Labour and Industry [*Australia*]   (PDAA)
DLI .... Far Eastern Forestry Engineering Institute   (RU)
DLIS .... Department of Library and Information Studies [*Australia*]
DLIS .... Desert Locust Information Service
DLK .... Democratic League of Kosovo [*Albania*] [*Political party*]   (ECON)
DLK .... Dienstleistungskombinat [*Services Combine*] [*Valet-Shop Services*]   (EG)
DLM .... Dalaman [*Turkey*] [*Airport symbol*]   (OAG)
DLM .... Democratic Labour Movement [*Guyana*] [*Political party*]   (PPW)
DLM .... Democratic Labour Movement [*Netherlands Antilles*] [*Political party*]
DLM .... Des Laufenden Monats [*Of the Current Month*] [*German*]
DLM .... Differential Lift Manometer   (RU)
DLM .... Dingo Liberation Movement [*Australia*]
DLM .... Dominica Liberation Movement [*Political party*]   (EY)
DLMA .... Dominican Liberation Movement Alliance [*Dominican Republic*]   (LA)
DLMPS..... Division of Logic, Methodology, and Philosophy of Science [*International Council of Scientific Unions*]
dln .... Delen [*Volumes*] [*Publishing*] [*Netherlands*]
DLN.......... Directorio Liberal Nacional [*National Liberal Directorate*] [*Colorado*]   (LA)
DLO.......... Detachement de Liaison et d'Observation
DLP .... Democratic Labor Party [*Dominican Republic*] [*Political party*]   (LA)
DLP .... Democratic Labor Party [*Trinidad and Tobago*] [*Political party*]   (PPW)
DLP .... Democratic Labor Party [*Australia*] [*Political party*]
DLP .... Democratic Labor Party [*Barbados*] [*Political party*]   (PPW)
DLP .... Democratic Left Party [*Turkey*] [*Political party*]   (MENA)
DLP .... Democratic Liberal Party [*Taiwan*] [*Political party*]   (EY)
DLP .... Democratic Liberal Party [*South Korea*] [*Political party*]

DLP .... Demokraattinen Lehtipalvelu [*Democratic Press Service (Communist SKDL)*] [*Finland*]   (WEN)
DLP .... Dominica Labor Party [*Political party*]   (PPW)
DLP .... Double Refraction, Birefringence   (RU)
DLP .... Dufour, Lacarriere, Pouget [*Stockbroking firm*] [*France*]   (ECON)
DLP .... Light Wooden Park [*Pontoons, bridges*]   (RU)
DLPF........ Democratic Labor Party/Family Life [*Australia*]
DLPG .... DIMDI [*Deutsches Institut fuer Medizinische Dokumentation und Information*] List Program Generator   (NITA)
dlr.............. Delar [*Parts*] [*Sweden*]
DLR .... Deutsche Forschungsanstalt fur Luft- und Raumfahrt [*German Aerospace Research Establishment*]   (IRC)
DLR .... Deutsche Versuchsanstalt fur Luft- und Raumfahrt [*German Aeronautics and Space Laboratory*]   (PDAA)
DLR .... Districts-Loodsreglement [*Benelux*]   (BAS)
DLS........... Danata Land & Sea Co. Ltd. [*Nigeria*]
DLS........... Datenleitstelle [*German*]   (ADPT)
dls.............. Dolares [*Dollars*] [*Monetary unit*] [*Spanish*]
DLS........... House of Detention, Prison   (RU)
DLSU........ De La Salle University [*Philippines*]
dlt .... Dans le Texte [*In the Text*] [*Publishing*] [*French*]
DLT .... Distributed Language Translation [*Project being developed by BSO, a Dutch computer company*]
DLT .... Dual Language Translation [*Chinese University of Hong Kong*]   (NITA)
DLT .... House of Leningrad Trade [*Department store*]   (RU)
dltje .... Deeltje [*Small Volume*] [*Publishing*] [*Netherlands*]
D lu .... Dogumlu Yil [*Year of Birth*]   (TU)
DLUG .... Double Lock Up Garage
DLUM .... Drustvo na Likovnite Umetnici na Makedonija [*Macedonian Society of Representational Artists*]   (YU)
DLV .... Deutscher Landwirtschaftsverlag (VEB), Berlin [*German Agricultural Publishing House (VEB), Berlin*]   (EG)
DLW .... Diesel Locomotive Works [*India*]   (PDAA)
DLY .... Dillon Bay [*Vanuatu*] [*Airport symbol*]   (OAG)
DM............ Amphibious Force   (RU)
DM............ Children's World [*Department store*]   (RU)
DM............ Danske Malermestre [*Federation of Danish Painting Contractors*]   (EAIO)
Dm .... Decametro [*Decameter*] [*Spanish*]
dm .... Decimeter   (RU)
dm .... Decimetre [*Decimeter*] [*French*]
dm .... Decimetro [*Decimeter*] [*Portuguese*]
dm .... Decimetro [*Decimeter*] [*Spanish*]
DM............ Decoder Matrix   (RU)
DM............ Decret Ministeriel [*Benelux*]   (BAS)
DM............ Decreto Ministeriale [*Ministerial Decree*] [*Italian*]   (ILCA)
Dm .... Dekameter [*Decameter*]   (EG)
DM............ Delta-Modulation   (RU)
DM............ Demodulator   (RU)
dm .... Denne Maned [*This Month*] [*Denmark*]   (GPO)
DM............ Depeche Ministerielle [*Benelux*]   (BAS)
dm .... Desimeter [*Decimeter*] [*Afrikaans*]
dm .... Desimetri(a) [*Finland*]
DM............ Destra Mano [*Right Hand*] [*Music*] [*Italian*]
DM............ Deutsche Mark [*German Mark*] [*Monetary unit*]   (EG)
dm .... Dezimeter [*Decimeter*]
DM............ Dieses Monats [*Of This Month*] [*German*]   (ROG)
DM............ Differential Manometer   (RU)
dm .... Dimanche [*Sunday*] [*French*]
Dm .... Dios Mediante [*God Willing*] [*Spanish*]
DM............ Direccion de Meteorologia [*Costa Rica*]   (MSC)
DM............ Disk Magnet [*Weld inspection device*]   (RU)
DM............ D-Markka (Saksan Markka) [*Finland*]
DM............ Docteur en Medecine [*Doctor of Medicine*] [*French*]
DM............ Doctorat en Medecine [*Academic degree*] [*French*]
DM............ Dominica [*ANSI two-letter standard code*]   (CNC)
DM............ Dorothea Mission [*South Africa*]
DM............ Draza Mihailovic [*A Yugoslav General*]   (YU)
dm .... Duim [*Inch*] [*Afrikaans*]
Dm .... Durchmesser [*Diameter*] [*German*]
DM............ Electric Oil-Pump Motor   (RU)
DM............ Ground Position (of an aircraft)   (RU)
dm .... Inch   (RU)
DM............ Machine Parts   (RU)
DM............ Outer Radio Marker Beacon   (RU)
DM............ Patrol Vehicle   (RU)
DM............ Range Finder   (RU)
DM............ Road Mine   (RU)
DM............ Smoke Screening   (RU)
DM............ Sprinkler, Sprinkling Machine   (RU)
DM............ State Mines   (BU)
dm .... Supply Officer   (BU)
DM............ Wooden Bridge   (RU)
dm² .... Decimetre Carre [*Square Decimeter*] [*French*]

dm² .... Square Decimeter   (BU)

dm³ .... Decimetre Cube [*Cubic Decimeter*] [*French*]

DMA.......... Centre d'Experimentation et d'Enseignement du Machinisme Agricole, Division du Machinisme Agricole du Genie Rural [*Mali*]

DMA.......... Dean Martin Association   (EAIO)

DMA.......... Delegation Ministerielle a l'Armement [*French*]

DMA.......... Dimethylaniline   (RU)

DMA.......... Disabled Men's Association of Australia   (ADA)

DMA.......... Dominica [*ANSI three-letter standard code*]   (CNC)

DMA.......... Dominica Manufacturers' Association   (EY)

DMA.......... Maersk Air IS [*Denmark*] [*ICAO designator*]   (FAAC)

DMAA....... Defence Manufacturers Association of Australia

DMA-DTE ... Direction Ministerielle pour l'Armement - Direction Technique des Engins [*Ministerial Directorate for Armaments - Missile Technology Directorate*] [*French*]   (WER)

DMAMYu ... Documents of the Moscow Archives of the Ministry of Justice   (RU)

D Mar .... Droit Maritime [*French*]   (FLAF)

DMB.......... Departamento de Material Belico [*War Materiel Department*] [*Brazil*]   (LA)

DMB.......... Department of Management and Budget [*Australia*]

DMB.......... Deutscher Museumsbund eV   (SLS)

DMB.......... State Mineral Water Bath   (BU)

DMBA........ Dimethylbenzanthracene   (RU)

Dmc........... Decimetre Cube [*French*]   (FLAF)

DMC.......... Defence Movement Coordination Committee [*Australia*]

DMC.......... Delta Motor Corporation [*South Africa*]

DMC.......... Developing Member Country [*Asian Development Bank*]

DMC.......... Direccion Meteorologica de Chile [*Meteorological Directorate of Chile*] [*Research center*]   (EAS)

DMC.......... Diviziski Medicinski Centar [*Divisional Medical Center*] [*Military*]   (YU)

DMC.......... Dollfus Mieg & Company [*France*]

DMCT........ Division of Microelectronics and Communications Technology [*Council for Scientific and Industrial Research*] [*South Africa*]   (WND)

DMD.......... Doomadgee Mission [*Australia*] [*Airport symbol*]   (OAG)

DMD.......... RST Aviation, NV [*Belgium*] [*ICAO designator*]   (FAAC)

DME.......... Department of Minerals and Energy [*Australia*]

DME.......... Dimethoxyethane   (RU)

DME.......... Distant Measuring Equipment   (AF)

DME.......... Moscow [*Former USSR*] [*Airport symbol*]

DME.......... Moscow Domodedovo Airport [*Former USSR*] [*Airport symbol*]   (OAG)

DMEA........ Department of Mineral and Energy Affairs [*South Africa*]   (EAS)

DMEA........ Dimosyndiritoi Monades Ethnofylakis Amynis [*State-Supported National Guard Defense Units*] [*Greek*]   (GC)

DMEF........ Decision du Ministre de l'Economie et des Finances [*France*]   (FLAF)

D mel'n....... Miller's House [*Topography*]   (RU)

DMETI....... Dnepropetrovsk Metallurgical Institute   (RU)

DMF.......... Dansk Mathematisk Forening [*Denmark*]   (SLS)

DMF.......... Dimethylformamide   (RU)

DMF.......... Dimethyl Phthalate   (RU)

DMF.......... Le Droit Maritime Francais   (FLAF)

DMFA........ Dimethylformamide   (RU)

DMFKhS.... Dimethylphenylchlorosilane   (RU)

DMFO........ Danske Mejeriers Faellesorganisation [*Danish Dairy Board*]   (EAIO)

DMG.......... Department of Mines and Geology [*Nepal*] [*Research center*]   (EAS)

DMG.......... Deutsche Malakozoologische Gesellschaft   (SLS)

DMG.......... Deutsche Meteorologische Gesellschaft [*German Meteorological Society*]   (ASF)

DMG.......... Deutsche Mineralogische Gesellschaft eV   (SLS)

DMG.......... Deutsche Morgan Grenfell [*Germany*] [*Banking*]

DMG.......... Deutsche Mozart-Gesellschaft eV   (SLS)

DMG.......... Direction des Mines et de la Geologie

DMG.......... Dom Mlodego Gornika [*House of the Young Miner*]   (POL)

DMG.......... Dynamograph   (RU)

DMH.......... Department of Marine and Harbours [*South Australia, Western Australia*]

DMH.......... Deutsches Medikamenten-Hilfswerk, Action Medeor [*German Medical Welfare Organiz ation, Action Medeor*]   (EAIO)

DMH.......... Dom Mlodego Hutnika [*House of the Young Metallurgist*]   (POL)

DMI.......... Danske Meteorologiske Institut [*Danish Meteorological Institute*]   (MSC)

DMI.......... Dar al Mal al Islami [*Islamic financial institution*]

DMI.......... Department of Military Intelligence [*South Africa*]

DMI.......... Deutscher Medizinischer Informationsdienst eV   (SLS)

DMI.......... Directia Monumentelor Istorice [*Directorate of Historic Monuments*]   (RO)

DMI.......... Directorate of Military Intelligence [*Australia*]

DMI.......... Dnepropetrovsk Metallurgical Institute   (RU)

DMID........ Department of Manufacturing and Industry Development [*Victoria*] [*Australia*]

DM i Kh..... Doctor of Medicine and Surgery   (RU)

DMIN........ Direct Marketing Instituut Nederland   (EAIO)

DMIP........ Democratic Malaysia Indian Party [*Political party*]   (FEA)

DMK.......... Dimokratikon Metarrythmistikon Komma [*Democratic Reform Party*]   (GC)

DMK.......... Dravida Munnetra Kazhagam [*India*] [*Political party*]   (PPW)

DMK.......... State Meat Combine   (BU)

DMKP........ State Mining and Coke Producing Enterprise   (BU)

DMKRNRH ... Drustvo Muzejsko-Konservatorskih Radnika Narodne Republike Hrvatske [*Society of Workers in Museums of Croatia*]   (YU)

DML.......... Dieselmotorenwerk Leipzig (VEB) [*Leipzig Diesel Motor Works (VEB)*]   (EG)

DML.......... Dvizheniia Molodezhi Lagosa

DMM.......... Dimethylurea   (RU)

DMM.......... Drustvo na Muzicarite na Makedonija [*Society of Musicians of Macedonia*]   (YU)

DMMA........ Devlet Mimarlik ve Muhendislik Akademisi [*State Academy of Architecture and Engineering*] [*Istanbul, Turkey*]   (TU)

DMN.......... Darjah Utama Seri Mahkota Negara [*Most Exalted Order of the Crown*]   (ML)

DMN.......... Direction de la Meteorologie Nationale [*Cameroon*]   (MSC)

dmn.......... Doctor of Medical Sciences   (RU)

DMN.......... Dom Mlodego Naukowca [*House of the Young Scholar*]   (POL)

DMNA........ Dimethylnitrosoamine   (RU)

dmo.......... Decare [*In plowing standard units*]   (BU)

DMO.......... Devlet Malzeme Ofisi Genel Mudurlugu [*State Equipment Office Directorate General*] [*Under Finance Ministry*]   (TU)

DMO.......... Dimethyloxazolidinedione   (RU)

DMO.......... Machine/Work Days   (BU)

DMO.......... State Mining Trust   (BU)

dmob.......... Service Train [*Military*]   (BU)

DMO-IS.... Devlet Malzeme Ofisi Iscileri Sendikasi [*State Equipment Office Workers' Union*]   (TU)

DMP.......... Demokratik Merkez Partisi [*Democratic Centre Party*] [*Turkey*] [*Political party*]   (EY)

DMP.......... Demokratik Mucadele Partisi [*Democratic Struggle Party*] [*Turkish Cyprus*] [*Political party*]   (EY)

DMP.......... Deutsche Mittelstandspartei [*German Middle Class Party*]   (PPW)

DMP.......... Division Medical Station   (RU)

DMP.......... Diviziski Medicinski Punkt [*Divisional Medical Point*]   (YU)

DMP.......... Docteur Medecin de la Faculte de Paris [*Doctor of Medicine, Paris*] [*French*]

DMP.......... Domiciliary Midwifery Program [*Australia*]

dmp.......... Male Persons [*Statistics*]   (RU)

DMP.......... Outer Marker Beacon   (BU)

DMP.......... State Assembly Enterprise   (BU)

DMP.......... State Mining Enterprise   (BU)

DMP.......... Wooden-Bridge Park [*Military term*]   (RU)

DMPA........ Danish Magazine Publishers Association   (EAIO)

DMPA........ Dimercaptopropylamine   (RU)

DMpF........ Dansk Musikpaedagogisk Forening [*Denmark*]   (SLS)

DMPP........ State Mining and Processing Enterprise   (BU)

DMPS........ State Motor Transportation Vehicles   (BU)

Dmq.......... Decimetre Carre [*French*]   (FLAF)

DMR.......... Department of Mineral Resources [*Thailand*]   (DS)

DMR.......... Department of Mineral Resources [*New South Wales*] [*Australia*]

DMR.......... Detachement Mobile de Reparation [*Mobile Repair Detachment*] [*Malagasy*]   (AF)

DMR.......... Deutscher Musikrat, Sektion Bundesrepublik Deutschland im Internationalen Musikrat   (SLS)

DMR.......... Dieselmotorenwerk Rostock (VEB) [*Rostock Diesel Motor Works (VEB)*]   (EG)

DMR.......... Diversified Mineral Resources [*Australia*]

DMR.......... Dom Mlodego Robotnika [*House of the Young Worker*]   (POL)

DMR.......... Dom Mlodziezy Robotniczej [*House of Working Youth*]   (POL)

Dmr.......... Durchmesser [*Diameter*] [*German*]   (GCA)

DMRK........ State Ore Mining Combine   (BU)

DMRL........ Defence Metallurgical Research Laboratory [*India*]   (PDAA)

DMS.......... Danmarks Mejeriteknike Selskab [*Denmark*]   (SLS)

DMS.......... Dansk Medicinsk Selskab [*Denmark*]   (SLS)

DMS.......... Dansk Metallurgisk Selskab [*Denmark*]   (SLS)

DMS.......... Digital Metropolitan Service [*Telecom Australia*]

DMS.......... Meteorological Station with Distant-Recording Instruments   (RU)

DMSA........ Direccion de Malariologia y Saneamiento Ambiental [*Venezuela*]   (DSCA)

DMSC........ Disinfected Mail Study Circle   (EA)

DMSh........ State Music School   (BU)

dm sl.......... Administrative Duty [*Military*]   (BU)

DMSO........ State Mining Construction Trust   (BU)

DMSP........ Domaines de la Motte-Saint-Pierre & Cie.

DMSP........ State Mine Salt Extraction Enterprise   (BU)

DMST....... Division of Materials Science and Technology [*Council for Scientific and Industrial Research*] [*South Africa*]   (IRC)

DMSZ .... State Mine Salt Extraction Plant   (BU)

dmt............ Bottom Dead Center   (BU)

DMT......... Dimethyl Terephthalate   (RU)

DMT......... Dimethyl Triphthalate   (RU)

DMT......... Donja Mrtva Tacka [*Lower Dead Center*] [*Engine*]   (YU)

DMTII...... Directorate of Music Composition and Performance   (BU)

DMTN...... Direction du Materiel et des Travaux Neufs [*Directorate of Equipment and New Construction*] [*Cambodia*]   (CL)

DMTS....... Machine-Tractor Stations Directorate   (BU)

DMTSA..... Dohnmerino-Telersgenootskap van Suid Afrika [*Dohne Merino Breed Society of South Africa*]   (EAIO)

DMU .... Dimapur [*India*] [*Airport symbol*]   (OAG)

DMU .... Grid Magnetic Azimuth   (RU)

DMU .... Magnetic Choke-Coupled Amplifier   (RU)

DMU .... State Installations Administration   (BU)

DMUPROMMONTAZH ... State Installations Administration for Industrial Installations   (BU)

DMuzA ...... State Academy of Music   (BU)

DMV......... Decimeter Waves   (BU)

DMV......... Decimetric Waves   (RU)

DMV......... Deur Middel Van [*By Means Of*] [*Afrikaans*]

DMV......... Deutsche Mathematiker-Vereinigung eV   (SLS)

DMV......... Deutscher Markscheider-Verein eV   (SLS)

DMV......... Deutscher Musikverlegerverband [*Association of German Music Publishers*]   (EAIO)

DMV......... Diecesni Mirovy Vybor Katolickeho Duchovenstva [*Diocesan Peace Comittee of the Catholic Clergy*]   (CZ)

DMV......... Disabled Motorists (Victoria) [*Australia*]

DMWU...... Dockers and Marine Workers Union [*Jamaica*]   (LA)

Dmy.......... Demiryol [*Railway*]   (TU)

DMY-IS..... Demiryollari Iscileri Sendikasi [*Railway Workers' Union*]   (TU)

DMZ......... Dnepr Magnesium Plant   (RU)

DMZ......... Magnetic Door Fastening   (RU)

DMZ......... State Machine-Building Plant   (BU)

DMZ......... State Metallurgical Plant   (BU)

DMZ......... Wood Pulp Plant   (RU)

dn .... Active Principle [*Chemistry*]   (RU)

dn .... Battalion [*Artillery*], Division [*Navy*]   (RU)

DN .... Chemin de Fer Dakar-Niger

DN .... Defense Nationale [*National Defense*] [*Cambodia*]   (CL)

DN .... Democracy Now [*Defunct*] [*Germany*]   (EAIO)

DN .... Democrazia Nazionale - Constituente di Destra [*National Democracy - Right Constituent*] [*Italy*] [*Political party*]   (PPE)

DN .... Destra Nazionale [*National Right*] [*Italy*] [*Political party*]   (PPE)

DN .... Deutsche Notenbank [*German Bank of Issue*]   (EG)

DN .... Developing Nation   (AF)

DN .... Dewan Nasional [*National (Operations) Council*]   (ML)

dn .... Diary, Journal   (RU)

DN .... Dimokratiki Neolaia [*Democratic Youth*]   (GC)

DN .... Distrito Nacional   (IDIG)

dn .... Dnia [*Day*]   (POL)

dn .... Dokonczenie Nastapi [*To Be Concluded*] [*Poland*]

Dn .... Don [*Spanish*]

DN .... Drustvo Naroda [*League of Nations*]   (YU)

D-N .... Dulcillo del Noroeste [*Race of maize*] [*Mexico*]

dn .... Dyne   (BU)

DN .... Dyrekcja Naczelna [*Chief Administration*]   (POL)

Dn .... Observation Range   (RU)

DN .... Saturation Choke   (RU)

DN .... Saturation Pressure   (RU)

DN .... Section Chief [*Railroads*]   (RU)

dn .... Today, Today's   (BU)

DN .... Voltage Divider   (RU)

DNA......... Aerodespachos de El Salvador [*ICAO designator*]   (FAAC)

DNA......... Dance Network Australia

DNA......... Del Norske Arbeiderparti [*Norwegian Labor Party*]   (BARN)

DNA......... Department of Native Affairs [*Australia*]

DNA......... Det Norske Arbeiderparti [*Norwegian Labor Party*]   (PPE)

DNA......... Deutscher Normenausschuss [*German Standards Committee*] [*Later, DIN*]   (EG)

DNA......... Direccion Nacional del Antartico [*National Administration for the Antarctic*] [*Argentina*]   (PDAA)

DNA......... Direction de la Navigation Aerienne [*Civil Aviation Administration*] [*France*]   (PDAA)

dna .... Docena [*Dozen*] [*Spanish*]

Dna .... Dona [*Mrs.*] [*Spanish*]   (BARN)

DNA......... People's Army Club   (BU)

DNAA....... Abuja/International [*Nigeria*] [*ICAO location identifier*]   (ICLI)

DNAEE ..... Departamento Nacional de Aguas e Energia Eletrica [*National Water and Electrical Power Department*] [*Brazil*]   (LA)

DNB......... Dai Nippon Butoku-kai [*Great Japan Military Virtue Society*] [*World War II*]

DNB.......... Deutsche Nachrichtenburo [*German News Bureau*]

DNB.......... Deutsche Notenbank [*German Bank of Issue*]   (EG)

DNB.......... Deutsches Nachrichtenbuero [*German Press Agency*]

DNB.......... Direccion Nacional del Banano y Frutas Tropicales [*National Banana and Tropical Fruit Office*] [*Ecuador*]   (LA)

DNB.......... Dunbar [*Australia*] [*Airport symbol*] [*Obsolete*]   (OAG)

DNBE........ Benin [*Nigeria*] [*ICAO location identifier*]   (ICLI)

DNBI........ Bida [*Nigeria*] [*ICAO location identifier*]   (ICLI)

DNBJ........ Abuja [*Nigeria*] [*ICAO location identifier*]   (ICLI)

DnC.......... Den Norske Creditbank [*Norway*]

DNC.......... Departamento Nacional del Cafe [*San Salvador, El Salvador*]   (LAA)

DNC.......... Departamento Nacional do Cafe [*Brazil*]

DNC.......... Direction Nationale de la Construction [*Algeria*]

DNC.......... Direction Nationale des Cooperatives [*Algeria*]

DNC.......... Directorate of National Coordination [*Laotian*]   (CL)

DNC.......... Directorio Nacional Conservador [*Conservative National Directorate*] [*Colorado*]   (LA)

DNC.......... Distributed National Collection [*Library resources*] [*Australia*]

DNC.......... Duits Nederlands Contract [*Netherlands*]   (BAS)

DNCA........ Calabar [*Nigeria*] [*ICAO location identifier*]   (ICLI)

DNCIAWPRC ... Danish National Committee of the International Association on Water Pollution Research and Control   (EAIO)

DNCP........ Direccion Nacional de Construcciones Portuarias y Vias Navegables [*National Directorate of Harbor Construction and Shipping Routes*] [*Argentina*]   (PDAA)

DNCSP...... Directorio Nacional para el Control de Sustancias Peligrosas [*National Directorate for Controlling Dangerous Substances*] [*Bolivia*]   (LA)

DND .... Deutscher Nachrichten Dienst [*German News Service*]   (BARN)

DND .... Eldinder Aviation [*Sudan*] [*ICAO designator*]   (FAAC)

DNDE........ Department of National Development and Energy [*Australia*]   (PDAA)

D/ndis........ Dievthyndis [*Manager, Director*]   (GC)

DN/DMR/ST ... Defense Nationale, Direction de Mobilisation et de Recruitement, Bureau des Stages [*National Defense, Directorate of Mobilization and Recruiting, Training Office*] [*Cambodia*]   (CL)

DNDR........ Direccion Nacional de Desarrollo Rural [*Bolivia*]   (DSCA)

DNE.......... Department of National Education

DNE.......... Diethnis Navtikon Epimelitirion [*International Maritime Chamber*]   (GC)

DNE.......... Dinitroethane   (RU)

dne............. Douane [*Customs, Duty*] [*French*]

DNEC........ Direccion Nacional de Energia y Combustibles [*National Fuels and Energy Board*] [*Argentina*]   (LA)

DNEC........ Direccion Nacional de Estadisticas y Censos [*Statistics and Census Office*] [*Argentina*]   (LAA)

DNEE .... Direccao Nacional de Energia Electrica [*National Administration for Electric Energy*] [*Angola*]   (AF)

DNEF .... Departamento Nacional de Estradas de Ferro [*National Railways Department*] [*Brazil*]   (LA)

DNEN....... Enugu [*Nigeria*] [*ICAO location identifier*]   (ICLI)

Dneproenergo ... State Administration of the Dnepropetrovsk Oblast Power System Management   (RU)

Dneproges ... Dnepr Hydroelectric Power Plant Imeni V. I. Lenin   (RU)

Dneprostroy ... State Dnepr Construction Project   (RU)

DNER........ Departamento Nacional de Estradas de Rodagem [*National Highway Department*] [*Portuguese*]

DNER........ Departamento Nacional de Estradas de Rodagem [*National Highway Department*] [*Rio De Janeiro, Brazil*]   (LA)

DNERU..... Departamento Nacional de Endemias Rurais [*National Rural Endemic Disease Department*] [*Brazil*]   (LA)

DNES .... Department of Nonconventional Energy Sources [*India*]

DNF.......... Defenders of Nature Foundation [*Guatemala*]   (EAIO)

DNF.......... Det Nye Folkepartiet [*New People's Party*] [*Norway*]   (PPE)

DNF.......... Dinitrophenol   (RU)

DNF.......... Directia de Navigatie Fluviala [*Directorate of River Navigation*]   (RO)

DNF.......... Disjunctive Normal Form   (RU)

DNF.......... People's Navy Club   (BU)

DNFA .... Ammonium Dinitrophenolate   (RU)

DNFF........ Del-Vietnami Nemzeti Felszabaditasi Front [*National Front for the Liberation of South Vietnam*]   (HU)

DNFG .... Dinitrophenylhydrazine   (RU)

DNFYuK ... Democratic People's Front in South Korea   (BU)

DNG .... Da Nang [*Vietnam*]   (VNW)

DNG .... De Nederlandse Gemeente [*Netherlands*]   (BAS)

DNGM ..... Direction Nationale de la Geologie et des Mines [*Mali*]

DNGTs....... Dinitroglycerol   (RU)

DNGU....... Gusau [*Nigeria*] [*ICAO location identifier*]   (ICLI)

DNH .... Dunhuang [*China*] [*Airport symbol*]   (OAG)

DNI........... Departamento Nacional de Investigaciones [*National Department of Investigations*] [*Nicaragua Honduras*]   (LA)

DNI........... Direccion Nacional de Impuestos [*National Tax Office*] [*Colorado*]   (LA)

DNI........... Direccion Nacional de Investigaciones [*National Investigations Directorate*] [*Dominican Republic*] (LA)
DNI........... Directorate of Naval Intelligence [*Australia*]
DNI........... Documento Nacional de Identidad [*National Identity Document*] [*Spanish*] (WER)
DNIB......... Ibadan [*Nigeria*] [*ICAO location identifier*] (ICLI)
DNIGL...... Dubovskaya Hydrological Scientific Research Laboratory (RU)
DNIGRI..... Dnepropetrovsk Scientific Research Institute of Ore Mining (RU)
DNII.......... Direccion Nacional de Inteligencia e Informacion [*National Intelligence and Information Bureau*] [*Uruguay*] (LA)
DNIL......... Ilorin [*Nigeria*] [*ICAO location identifier*] (ICLI)
DNIS......... Deniz Nakliyat Iscileri Sendikasi [*Maritime Transport Workers' Union*] (TU)
DNIT......... Direction Nationale de l'Infrastructure des Transports [*Mali*]
DNJ........... Det Norske Justervesen [*Norwegian Bureau of Weights and Measures*] (PDAA)
DNJO........ Jos [*Nigeria*] [*ICAO location identifier*] (ICLI)
DNK.......... Dai Nippon Kokusui-kai [*Great Japan National Essence Society*]
DNK.......... Denmark [*ANSI three-letter standard code*] (CNC)
DNK.......... Deoxyribonucleic Acid (RU)
DNK.......... Nationales Komitee der Weltenergiekonferenz fuer die Bundesrepublik Deutschland (SLS)
DNKA....... Kaduna [*Nigeria*] [*ICAO location identifier*] (ICLI)
DNKaza..... Deoxyribonuclease (RU)
DNKK....... Kano [*Nigeria*] [*ICAO location identifier*] (ICLI)
DNKN....... Kano/Mallam Aminu International [*Nigeria*] [*ICAO location identifier*] (ICLI)
DNKZ........ Datennetzkontrollzentrum [*German*] (ADPT)
DNL.......... Det Norske Luftfartselskap AS [*Norwegian Airlines Ltd.*] (EY)
DNL.......... Dimokratiki Neolaia Lambraki [*Lambrakis Democratic Youth*] [*Greek*] (GC)
DNL.......... Direccion Nacional Liberal [*Liberal National Directorate*] [*Colorado*] (LA)
DNL.......... Pneumatic Landing Boat (RU)
DNLE........ Dimokratiki Neolaia Lambraki Ellados [*Lambrakis Democratic Youth of Greece*] (GC)
DNLF........ Den Norske Laegeforening [*Norway*] (SLS)
DNLL........ Lagos App [*Nigeria*] [*ICAO location identifier*] (ICLI)
DNLP........ Direccion Nacional del Liberalismo Popular [*National Directorate of the Popular Liberal Party*] [*Colorado*] (LA)
DNLRS...... Drustvo Novinarjev Ljudske Republike Slovenije [*Journalists' Society of Slovenia*] (YU)
DNM .... Denham [*Australia*] [*Airport symbol*] (OAG)
DNM .... Den Norske Mikrobionomforening [*Norway*] (SLS)
DNM .... Direccion Nacional de Meteorologia [*National Meteorology Directorate*] [*Ministry of National Defence Uruguay*] (EAS)
DNM .... Directia de Navigatie Maritima [*Directorate of Maritime Navigation*] (RO)
DNM .... Dvizheniia Nigeriiskoi Molodezhi
DNM .... People's Militia Directorate (BU)
DNM .... State People's Militia (BU)
DNMA....... Maiduguri [*Nigeria*] [*ICAO location identifier*] (ICLI)
DNMG .... Direction Nationale de la Geologie et des Mines
DNMK .... Makurdi [*Nigeria*] [*ICAO location identifier*] (ICLI)
DNMM ..... Lagos/Murtala Muhammed [*Nigeria*] [*ICAO location identifier*] (ICLI)
DNMO ...... Departamento Nacional de Mao-de-Obra [*National Manpower Department*] [*Brazil*] (LA)
DNMS....... Director of Naval Medical Services [*Royal Australian Navy*]
DNNH....... Dyrekcja Naczelna Nowej Huty [*Main Administration of Nowa Huta*] [*Metallurgical center*] (POL)
DNO .... Alinord [*Italy*] [*ICAO designator*] (FAAC)
DNO .... Danske Nervelaegers Organisation [*Denmark*] (SLS)
DNO .... Det Norske Oljeselskap A/S
DNO .... Division of People's Militia (RU)
DNOCS ..... Departamento Nacional de Obras Contra as Secas [*National Drought Control Department*] [*Brazil*] (LA)
DNOE........ Direccao Nacional de Obras de Engenharia
DNOS........ Departamento Nacional de Obras e Saneamento [*National Department of Works and Sanitation*] [*Brazil*] (LA)
DNOS........ Oshogbo [*Nigeria*] [*ICAO location identifier*] (ICLI)
DNOS........ State Irrigation and Drainage Systems (BU)
D Not........ Droit Notarial [*French*] (FLAF)
D NouvRep ... Nouveau Repertoire Dalloz [*France*] (FLAF)
DNP.......... Alternate Observation Post (RU)
DNP.......... Dai Nippon Printing Co. Ltd. [*Publisher*] [*Japan*]
DNP.......... Dang [*Nepal*] [*Airport symbol*] (OAG)
DNP.......... Democratic Nationalist Party [*1959-1966*] [*Malta*] [*Political party*] (PPE)
DNP.......... Demokrata Neppart [*Democratic People's Party*] (HU)
DNP.......... Deoxyribonucleoprotamine (RU)
DNP.......... Deoxyribonucleoprotein (RU)
DNP.......... Departamento Nacional de Planeacion [*National Planning Department*] [*Colorado*] (LA)

DNP.......... Direccao Nacional das Pescas [*National Fisheries Authority*] [*Cape Verde*] (GEA)
DNP.......... State Economic Plan (BU)
DNPA .... Departamento Nacional de Producao Animal [*Brazil*] (DSCA)
DNPM....... Departamento Nacional da Producao Mineral [*National Department of Mineral Production*] [*Brasilia, Brazil*] (LA)
DNPO........ Port Harcourt [*Nigeria*] [*ICAO location identifier*] (ICLI)
DNPP .... Direccao Nacional de Propaganda e Publicidade
DNPRINT ... Dai Nippon Printing Company Ltd. [*Research center*] [*Japan*] (ERC)
DNPS .... Departamento Nacional da Providencia Social [*National Social Welfare Department*] [*Brazil*] (LA)
dnPTURS ... Antitank Guided Missile Battalion (BU)
DNPV .... Departamento Nacional da Producao Vegetal [*Rio De Janeiro, Brazil*] (LAA)
DNPVN ..... Departamento Nacional de Portos e Vias Navegaveis [*National Department of Ports and Waterways*] [*Brazil*] (LA)
DNQ .... Deniliquin [*Australia*] [*Airport symbol*] (OAG)
DNR.......... Deutscher Naturschutzring eV (SLS)
dnr............. Dienaar [*Servant*] [*Afrikaans*]
DNR.......... Dinard [*France*] [*Airport symbol*] (OAG)
DNR.......... Direccion Nacional de la Resistencia [*National Directorate of Resistance*] [*Bolivia*] (LA)
DNR.......... Dovas Nordiske Rad [*Nordic Council for the Deaf - NCD*] (EAIO)
DNRu........ Departamento Nacional de Endemias Rurais [*Brazil*] (DSCA)
DNS.......... Dansk Neurologisk Selskab [*Denmark*] (SLS)
DNS.......... Delegacion Nacional de Sindicatos [*Spanish state trade union organization*]
DNS.......... Deoksiribonukleiensuur [*Deoxyribonucleic Acid*] [*Afrikaans*]
DNS.......... Departamento Nacional de Salario [*National Wage Department*] [*Brazil*] (LA)
DNS.......... Department of National Security [*South Africa*] (AF)
DNS.......... Det Norske Luftfartselskap AS [*Norwegian Airlines Ltd.*]
DNS.......... Deus Nosso Senhor [*God Our Lord*] [*Portuguese*]
DNS.......... Direccion Nacional de Seguridad [*National Directorate of Security*] [*Dominican Republic*] (LA)
DNS.......... Docasne Narodne Shromazdenie [*Provisional National Assembly*] (CZ)
DNS.......... Doppler Navigation System (RU)
DNSAP...... Danmarks Nationalsocialistisk Arbejdersparti [*National Socialist Worker's Party of Denmark (or Danish NAZI Party)*] (PPE)
dn SAU ...... Self-Propelled Artillery Battalion (BU)
DNSDC ..... Defence National Storage and Distribution Centre [*Australia*]
DNSE........ Direccion Nacional del Servicio Estadistico [*National Department of Statistics*] [*Argentina*] (LAA)
DNSEP...... Diplome National Superieur d'Expression Plastique [*French*]
DNSF........ Democratic National Salvation Front [*Romania*] [*Political party*] (ECON)
DNSO........ Diakyvernitikos Navtiliakos Symvoulevtikos Organismos [*Intergovernmental Maritime Consultation Organization*] (GC)
DNSO........ Sokoto [*Nigeria*] [*ICAO location identifier*] (ICLI)
DNSP .... Datenuebertragungs-und Netzsteuerprogramm [*German*] (ADPT)
DNSP .... Departamento Nacional de Saude Publica [*Brazil*]
DNT.......... Danistay [*Council of State*] (TU)
DNT.......... Departamento Nacional do Trabalho [*National Department of Labor*] [*Brazil*] (LA)
DNT.......... Diethnes Nomismatikon Tameion [*International Monetary Fund*] (GC)
DNT.......... Dinitrotoluene (RU)
DNT.......... Direccao Nacional de Trabalho [*National Administration of Labor*] (AF)
DNT.......... Dni Novej Techniky [*Promotion (Days) of New Technology*] (CZ)
DNT.......... Drustvo Narodne Tehnike [*People's Technology Society*] (YU)
DNT.......... House of Folk Art (RU)
DNTA........ Direction de la Navigation et des Transports Aeriens (FLAF)
DNTP .... House of Scientific and Technical Propaganda (RU)
DNU .... Department of National Unity (ML)
DNU .... Directorio Nacional Unido [*Guerrilla forces*] [*Honduras*] (EY)
DNU .... Low-Level Discriminator [*Computers*] (RU)
DNUUST .. Danish National Union of Upper Secondary Teachers (EAIO)
DNV.......... Den Norske Veterinaerforening [*Norway*] (SLS)
DnV........... Det Norske Veritas [*Norwegian Ship Classification Society*] (PDAA)
DNVA........ Den Norske Videnskaps-Akademi [*Norwegian Academy of Science and Letters*] (EAIO)
DNVP .... Deutschnationale Volkspartei [*German National People's Party*] (EG)
DNW .... Deutsch-Niederlandischer Windkanal [*German-Dutch Wind Tunnel*] [*Research center*] [*Netherlands*] (ERC)
DNW .... Duits-Nederlandse Windtunnel [*German-Dutch Wind Tunnnel*] [*Netherlands*] [*Research center*]
DNY.......... Danish Navy [*ICAO designator*] (FAAC)

D Ny........... Delnyugat [Southwest] (HU)
DNYO .... Yola [Nigeria] [ICAO location identifier] (ICLI)
DNZ........... Public Health Directorate (BU)
DNZ........... State Petroleum Refinery (BU)
DNZA........ Zaria [Nigeria] [ICAO location identifier] (ICLI)
dO .... Das Obige [The Above Mentioned] [German] (EG)
DO .... Delostrelecky Oddil [Artillery Battalion] (CZ)
dO .... Der Obige [The Above Mentioned] [German] (EG)
do.............. Descuento [Discount] [Spanish]
DO .... Diakotthon [Student Home] (HU)
DO .... Diamine Oxidase (RU)
DO .... Diario Oficial [Official Journal] [Portuguese]
dO .... Die Obige [The Above Mentioned] [German] (EG)
DO .... Dilci Organisace [Branch Organization] [Communist Party]
                  (CZ)
DO .... Dioxane (RU)
DO .... Direkteur van Onderwys [Director of Education] [Afrikaans]
d:o............. Dito [Ditto] [Sweden] (GPO)
do.............. Dito [Ditto] [Portuguese]
do.............. Dito [Ditto] [French]
do.............. Ditto [German] (GPO)
DO .... Dominican Republic [ANSI two-letter standard code] (CNC)
DO .... Dominions Office [Australia]
Do.............. Donderdag [Thursday] [Afrikaans]
Do.............. Dopunske Odredbe [Supplementary Regulations] (YU)
DO .... Dornier-Werke GmbH [Germany] [ICAO aircraft manufacturer
                  identifier] (ICAO)
DO .... Droit Ouvrier [France] (FLAF)
DO .... Dum Osvety [House of Culture] (CZ)
DO .... Dyrekcja Okregowa [District Administration] (POL)
DO .... Hoofdgroep Defensie-Onderzoek [Division for Defence Research]
                  [Netherlands Central Organization for Applied Natural
                  Scientific Research] (WND)
DO .... House of Officers (RU)
DO .... Landing Detachment (RU)
DO .... Landing Operation (RU)
DO .... Long-Range Fire (RU)
DO .... Oiselet [Record label] [France]
DO .... Operational Decoder (RU)
DO .... Patrol Detachment (RU)
DO .... Rest Home, Rest Center (RU)
DO .... Road Detachment (RU)
DO .... State Trusts (BU)
DO .... Turnover Tax (BU)
DOA .... Compania Dominicana de Aviacion SA [Dominican Republic]
                  [ICAO designator] (FAAC)
DOA .... Demokraticheskaia Ob'edineni Afriki
DOA .... Deutsch-Ostafrika [German East Africa] [German]
DOA .... Diethnis Olymbiaki Akadimia [International Olympic Academy]
                  (GC)
DOA .... Diethnis Omospondia Andistasiakon [International Resistance
                  Federation] (GC)
DOA .... Directie Overheidsorganisatie- en Automatisering ['s-
                  Gravenhage]
DOA .... Doany [Madagascar] [Airport symbol] (OAG)
DOA .... Duits-Oos-Afrika [German East Africa] [Afrikaans]
DOAE .... Department of Oriental Antiquities and Ethnology
DOAE .... Diethnis Organismos Atomikis Energeias [International Atomic
                  Energy Agency] (GC)
DOAF .... Dihydroxyaceto Phosphate (RU)
DOAG....... Deutsch Ostafrikanische Gesellschaft
DOAL....... Deutsche Ost Afrika Linie [Kenya] (EY)
DoAl......... Doyer Aluminium Ltd. [New Zealand]
DOAP....... Diethnis Organismos Apokatastaseos Prosfygon (GC)
DOAT....... Diethnis Omospondia Athlitikou Typou [International
                  Federation of Sports Publications] (GC)
DOAV....... Deutscher Oesterreichischer Alpen Verein [Austro-German
                  Alpine Federation]
dob............. Addition [or Supplement] (BU)
dob............. Additional, Supplementary (RU)
DOB......... Devrimci Ogrenci Birligi [Revolutionary Student Union] (TU)
dob............. Division Ammunition Train (BU)
DOB......... Dobrolet Airlines [Russian Federation] [ICAO designator]
                  (FAAC)
dob............. Supplement, Appendix (RU)
DOB......... Turkiye Devrimci Ogretmenler Birligi [Union of Turkish
                  Revolutionary Teachers] (TU)
DOBA .... Diploma of the Orthoptic Board of Australia
dobbeltsid... Dobbeltsidig [Two-Sided] [Publishing Danish/Norwegian]
DOBGM... Devlet Opera ve Balesi Genel Mudurlugu [State Opera and Ballet
                  Directorate General] (TU)
DOBIS....... Dortmunder Bibliothekssystem [Dortmund Bibliographic
                  Information System] [Cataloguing system developed in
                  Germany]
DOBOPS... Director Borneo Ops (ML)
dobr........... Good Quality, Soundness (RU)

Dobrarmiya ... Volunteer Army [1917-1920] (RU)
Dobroflot.... Volunteer Fleet [1870-1922] (RU)
Dobrokhim ... Voluntary Society for Furthering the Construction of the
                  Chemical Industry [1924-1925] (RU)
Dobrolet..... All-Union Society of the Volunteer Air Fleet [1923-1930] (RU)
dobr o-vo .... Voluntary Society (RU)
DOC.......... Centre de Documentation [Bureau Central des Projets] [Benin]
DOC.......... Denominazione di Origine Controllata [Italian wine designation]
DoC.......... Department of Conservation [New Zealand]
DOC.......... Depots Ocean Congo
Doc........... Docent [Albanian]
doc............ Docent [Polish]
doc............ Document [French]
doc............ Documento [Document] [Portuguese]
DOC.......... Norsk Luftambulanse AS [Norway] [ICAO designator] (FAAC)
DoCA....... Department of Communications and the Arts [Australia]
DOCA....... Section Documentation Automatique [CETIS] [Luxembourg]
DOCG....... Denominazione di Origine Controllata e Garantita [Italian wine
                  designation]
DOCIT ...... Department of Computing and Information Technology
                  [Western Australia]
DOCPAL... Sistema de Documentacion sobre Poblacion en America Latina
                  [Latin American Population Documentation System]
                  [Economic Commission for Latin America and the
                  Caribbean] [United Nations] [Information service or
                  system] (IID)
Doct........... Doctor [Doctor] [Spanish]
Doct JurCol ... Doctrine et Jurisprudence Coloniale [Benelux] (BAS)
docum....... Documento [Document] [Spanish]
documto...... Documento [Document] [Spanish]
Doc Vdw...... Documentatie Vadewinckele [Benelux] (BAS)
DOD .... Department of Ocean Development [India]
DOD .... Deutsches Ozeanographisches Datenzentrum [German
                  Oceanographic Data Center] (MSC)
DOD .... Devrimci Ogretmenleri Dernegi [Revolutionary Teachers'
                  Organization] [TDOD] [See also] (TU)
DOD .... Diethnis Omosponida Dimosiografon [International Federation
                  of Journalists] (GC)
dod............ Dodatek [Supplement, Appendix] [Poland]
DOD .... Dodoma [Tanzania] [Airport symbol] (OAG)
DOD .... Gross Income Tax (BU)
DODA ...... Department of Defence, Australia
DOE.......... Departamento de Operaciones Especiales [Department of Special
                  Operations] [Uruguay] (LA)
DOE.......... Department of Electronics [India] (PDAA)
DOE.......... Didaskaliki Omospondia Ellados [Teachers Federation of Greece]
                  (GC)
DOE.......... Diethnis Oikonomiki Epitropi [International Economic
                  Committee] (GC)
DOE.......... Diethnis Oikonomikos Elengkhos [International Economic
                  Control] (GC)
DOE.......... Diethnis Organosis Ergasias [International Labor Organization]
                  (GC)
DOE.......... Direccion de Operaciones Especiales [Directorate of Special
                  Operations] [Cuba] (LA)
DOE.......... Djoemoe [Surinam] [Airport symbol] (OAG)
DOEM....... Diethnis Omospondia Ergaton Metaforas [International
                  Transport Workers Federation] (GC)
DOEO....... Darwin Office of Equal Opportunity [Australia]
DOES .... Diethnis Omospondia ton Ergatikon Syndikaton [International
                  Federation of Trade Unions] (GC)
DOF.......... Dansk Ornithologisk Forening [Denmark] (SLS)
DOF.......... Department of Fisheries [South Australia]
DOF.......... Department of Forestry [Queensland] [Australia]
DOF.......... Dioctyl Phthalate (RU)
DOF........... House of Fleet Officers (RU)
D of A........ Department of Aviation [Australia]
DOFA .... Details of Agreement [NATO] (NATG)
DOFA .... Dihydroxyphenylalanine (RU)
DOFSP ..... Departamento de Obras e Fiscalizacao dos Servicos Publicos
                  [Public Services Works and Control Department] [Brazil]
                  (LA)
DOG .... Deoxyglucose (RU)
DOG .... Deutsche Ophthalmologische Gesellschaft (SLS)
DOG .... Deutsche Orient-Gesellschaft
Dog........... Dogumevi [Maternity Ward] (TU)
Dog............ Dogum Yili [Year of Birth] (TU)
DOG .... Dongola [Sudan] [Airport symbol] (OAG)
DOGI........ Dottrina Giuridica [Consiglio Nazionale delle Ricerche] [Italy]
                  [Information service or system] (CRD)
DoH .... Department of Health [Australia]
DOH .... Doha [Qatar] [Airport symbol] (OAG)
DOHSW... Department of Health, Safety, and Welfare [Western Australia]
DOI........... Democratic Organization for Independence and Socialism
                  [Gambia]

DOI............ Departamento de Operacoes Internas [*Department of Domestic Operations*] [*Brazil*] (LA)

DOI............ Destacamento de Operacoes e Informacoes [*Division of Intelligence Operations*] [*Brazil*]

DOI............ Dispozitive Optice Integrate [*Integrated Optical Devices*] (RO)

DOI............ State Publishing Houses Trust (BU)

DOIC......... Defence Operations and Intelligence Centre [*Australia*]

DOJ........... Dahir sur l'Organisation Judiciaire du Protectorat Francais du Maroc (FLAF)

DOJ........... Department of Justice [*Queensland, Tasmania*] [*Australia*]

DOK........... Danmarks Olympiske Komite [*Olympic Committee of Denmark*] (EAIO)

DOK........... Deoxycorticosterone (RU)

dok.............. Documents (BU)

dok.............. Dokonczenie [*Conclusion*] [*Poland*]

dok.............. Dokumentacio [*Documentation*] (HU)

DOK........... Donetsk [*Former USSR*] [*Airport symbol*] [*Obsolete*] (OAG)

DOK........... Dowodztwo Okregu Korpusu [*District Corps Headquarters*] (POL)

DOK........... Dozer Kolovy [*Wheeled Dozer*] (CZ)

DOK........... Woodworking Kombinat (RU)

DOKA......... Deoxycorticosterone Acetate (RU)

dok csop...... Dokumentacios Csoport [*Documentation Group*] (HU)

DOKD.......... Department Oswiaty i Kultury Doroslych [*Department of Adult Education and Culture*] (POL)

DOKDI........ Documentation Service [*Swiss Academy of Medical Sciences*] [*Information service or system*] (IID)

DOKDI........ Dokumentationsdienst der Schweizerischen Akademie der Medizinischen Wissenschaften [*Bern*]

DokGemi-Is ... Turkiye Liman, Dok, ve Gemi Sanayii Iscileri Sendikasi [*Turkish Harbor, Dock, and Ship Industry Workers Union*] (TU)

DOKh......... Deoxycholate (RU)

DOKhES ... Diethnis Omospondia ton Khristianikon Ergatikon Syndikaton [*International Federation of Christian Trade Unions*] (GC)

doki............. Doktor [*Doctor or Doc*] [*Slang*] (HU)

DOKiP......... Dni Oswiaty, Ksiazki, i Prasy [*Education, Book, and Press Days*] (POL)

DOKIS......... Dokumentations-Informations-System [*German*] (ADPT)

dokl............. Report (RU)

dok nast...... Dokonczenie Nastapi [*To Be Concluded*] [*Poland*]

DOKP......... Dni Oswiaty, Ksiazki, i Prasy [*Education, Book, and Press Days*] (POL)

DOKP......... Dyrekcja Okregowa Kolei Panstwowych [*District Directorate of State Railroads*] (POL)

DOKSA...... Deoxycorticosterone Acetate (RU)

dokt............. Doctoral (RU)

DOKTAS... Dokumculuk Ticaret ve Sanayi Anonim Sirketi [*Weaving Trade and Industry, Incorporated*] [*Bursa*] (TU)

dokt fizmat n ... Doctor of Physical and Mathematical Sciences (RU)

doktordisp ... Doktordisputats [*Doctoral Dissertation*] [*Publishing Danish/Norwegian*]

dokum .... Document, Deed, Record (RU)

DOKZENTBW ... Dokumentationszentrum dem Bundeswehr [*Federal Armed Forces Documentation Center*] [*Germany*] (PDAA)

DOL........... Department of Labour [*South Australia, Victoria*]

DOL........... Department of Lands [*Queensland*] [*Australia*]

DOL........... Department of Law [*Northern Territory*] [*Australia*]

dol.............. Dolar [*Dollar*] [*Monetary unit*] [*Poland*]

dol.............. Dolar [*Dollar*] [*Monetary unit*] [*Portugal*]

dol.............. Dollar [*Monetary unit*] [*French*]

Dol.............. Dollarion [*Dollar*] (GC)

D-O-L........ Plavebni Cesta Dunaj-Odra-Labe [*Danube-Oder-Elbe Waterway*] (CZ)

Dol............. Valley [*Topography*] (RU)

DOLA......... Department of Land Administration [*Western Australia*]

DOLCO...... DooL Co. [*Somalia*]

dolg........... Dolgozo [*or Dolgozok*] [*Working or Workers*] (HU)

dolg........... Longitude (RU)

DOLGAS... Department of Local Government and Administrative Services [*Australia*]

DOLITAC ... US Department of Labor, International Technical Assistance Corps

doll............. Dollar [*French*]

doll............. Dollari(a) [*Finland*]

dolls........... Dollares [*Dollars*] [*Spanish*]

dolm........... Dolmen [*Topography*] (RU)

DOM .... Debreceni Orvosi Muszergyar [*Medical Instrument Factory of Debrecen*] (HU)

DOM .... Departement d'Outre-Mer [*Overseas Department*] [*French*] (WER)

DOM .... Department of Mines [*Tasmania*] [*Australia*]

DOM .... Devizno Obracunsko Mesto [*Foreign Exchange Clearinghouse*] (YU)

DOM .... Diethneis Odikes Metafores [*International Road Transportations*] (GC)

DOM .... Direccao das Organizacoes de Massa [*Directorate for the Organization of the Masses*] [*Angola*] (AF)

Dom............ Domingo [*Sunday*] [*Spanish*]

DOM .... Dominica [*West Indies*] [*Airport symbol*] (OAG)

DOM .... Dominican Republic [*ANSI three-letter standard code*] (CNC)

dom .... Domyslnie [*To Be Understood*] [*Poland*]

DOM .... Dos Mundos [*Dominican Republic*] [*ICAO designator*] (FAAC)

DOM .... Republika Dominikanska [*Dominican Republic*] [*Poland*]

DOMA...... Deep Ocean Minerals Association

DOMA....... Dokumentation Maschinenbau [*Mechanical Engineering Documentation*] [*Technical Information Center*] [*Information service or system*]

DOMAC.... Documentation and Market Promotion Centre [*Forestry Development Authority*] [*Liberia*]

DOMCO.... Al-Dossary Brothers-Maintenance & Transport Co. Ltd. [*Saudi Arabia*]

DomD........ Knjiznica Samostana Dominikanaca u Dubrovniku [*Library of the Dominican Monastery in Dubrovnik*] (YU)

Dome.......... Domaine [*Military map abbreviation*] [*World War I*] [*French*] (MTD)

DOMEI ..... Zen Nihon Rodo Sodomei [*Japanese Confederation of Labor*] (FEA)

DOMENG ... Direccion de Organizacion del Estado Mayor General [*Directorate for Organization and Mobilization of the General Staff*] [*Cuba*] (LA)

DOMESA ... Don't Overlook Mature Expertise, South Australia

DOMEV ... Don't Overlook Mature Expertise, Victoria [*Australia*]

DOMF...... Darwin Overland Maintenance Force [*Australia*]

Domh......... Domherr [*German*]

DOMK...... Dihydroxymaleic Acid (RU)

domkom ..... Apartment House Committee (RU)

Domnz....... Dom Narodnog Zdravlja [*Public Health Center*] (YU)

domo.......... Domingo [*Sunday*] [*Spanish*]

domostr...... House-Building Plant [*Topography*] (RU)

domouprav ... House Manager (RU)

Dom P......... Dominium-Party [*Dominion Party*] [*Afrikaans*]

Domprosvet ... House of Education (RU)

DOMSAT ... Domestic Satellite [*Communications satellite*] [*Australia*]

DOMSAT ... Domestic Satellite System [*Guyana*] (LA)

DOM-TOM ... Departements et Territoires d'Outre-Mer

domzak....... House of Confinement, Prison (RU)

don............. Direction [*Management*] [*French*]

don .... Donem [*Session, Period*] [*As of assembly*] (TU)

DON .... Donets Railroad (RU)

DON .... Long-Range Fire, Distant Concentration (BU)

DON .... Long-Range Harassing Fire, Long-Range Attack [*Artillery*] (RU)

Donbass ..... Donets Coal Basin (RU)

Donbassenergo ... Donbass Power System (RU)

do ne........... Before Christ (RU)

DONG .... Danish Oil and Natural Gas (GEA)

Dongres...... Northern Donets State Regional Electric Power Plant (RU)

DONL......... Dimokratiki Omada Navtilias Londinou [*Democratic Seamen's Group of London*] (GC)

DONNII .... Donets Scientific Research Institute of Pithead Construction (RU)

Donobsoyuz ... Don Oblast Union of Consumers' Societies (RU)

DONS........ Department of National Security [*South Africa*]

DonSoc....... Donizetti Society (EA)

Donsoda .... Northern Donets Soda Plant (RU)

DONT........ Department of the Northern Territory [*Australia*]

DONUGI... Donets Scientific Research Institute of Coal (RU)

DOO .... Dorobisoro [*Papua New Guinea*] [*Airport symbol*] (OAG)

DOO .... Driver-Only Operation [*Railroad*] [*British*]

DOO .... State Social Insurance (RU)

DOO .... Voluntary Hunting Society (RU)

DOOD .... De Olympiade Onder Dectatuur [*The Olympics Under Dictatorship*] [*An exhibition in 1936 by 150 artists protesting Nazi repression*] [*Reconstructed in 1996 by the Amsterdam Municipal Archives*]

DOOR .... Dyrekcja Okregowa Osiedli Robotniczych [*District Housing Administration of Workers' Settlements*] (POL)

dop .... Additional, Complementary, Enlarged, Supplementary, Supplemented (RU)

dop .... Correspondence [*Press*] (BU)

DOP.......... Departamento del Orden Publico [*Department of Public Order*] [*Cuba*] (LA)

DOP.......... Department of Planning [*New South Wales, Australia*]

DOP.......... Depot Pusat [*Central Depot*] (IN)

DOP.......... Detachement Operationnel de Protection [*Algeria*]

DOP.......... Division Supply Relay Point (RU)

DOP.......... Dolnoslaski Okreg Przemyslowy [*Lower-Silesian Industrial District*] [*Poland*]

DOP.......... Dolpa [*Nepal*] [*Airport symbol*] (OAG)

dop .... Dopoledne [*Morning*] (CZ)

dop .... Enlarged, Expanded [*Edition*] (BU)

dop .... Supplement, Addition, Complement (RU)

DOPA .... Diethnis Organismos Politikis Aeroporias [*International Civil Aviation Organization*]   (GC)

DOPA .... Dimosthenikos Omilos Politistikis Anaptyxeos [*Demosthenes Group for Cultural Development*] [*Greek*]   (GC)

DOPAED .. Dokumentationsring Paedagogik   (SLS)

DOP art ..... Division Artillery Supply Relay Point   (RU)

DOPCO ..... Dashtestan Offshore Petroleum Company   (ME)

DOPEM .... Director Operations East Malaysia   (ML)

DOPIE ...... Department of Primary Industries and Energy [*Australia*]

dopl .... Doplyw [*Affluent*] [*Poland*]

DOPM .... Direction d'Oceanographie et des Peches Maritimes [*Senegal*]   (MSC)

DOPMA .... Defense Officer Personnel Management Act

dop otkl ..... Permissible Variation, Tolerance   (RU)

dopp .... Doppelt [*Duplicated, Doubled*] [*Publishing*] [*German*]

Doppelbd ... Doppelband [*Double Volume*] [*Publishing*] [*German*]

Doppelbl ... Doppelblatt [*Double Page*] [*Publishing*] [*German*]

doppelblattgr ... Doppelblattgross [*Double-Page Size*] [*Publishing*] [*German*]

doppels .... Doppelseitig [*Double-Page*] [*Publishing*] [*German*]

Dopp Z .... Doppelzuendung [*Combination Fuse*] [*German*]   (GCA)

DOPR .... Pretrial House of Detention   (RU)

DOPR .... Workhouse   (RU)

DOPS .... Departamento de Ordem Politica e Social [*Department of Political and Social Order*] [*Brazil*]   (LA)

DOPS .... Diffuse Obstruktiewe Pulmonere Sindroom-Navorsingseenheid [*Diffuse Obstructive Pulmonary Syndrome Research Unit*] [*South African Medical Research Council*]   (AA)

DOPS .... Halo and Sun Tracking Probe   (RU)

DOPT .... Dyrekcja Okregowa Poczt i Telekomunikacji [*District Post and Telecommunication Administration*]   (POL)

dop tir .... Additional Printing [*of a publication*]   (BU)

dop tit l ...... Supplementary Title Page   (RU)

dopushch .... Admitted, Authorized   (RU)

DOR .... Departamento de Orientacao Revolucionaria [*Department of Revolutionary Orientation*] [*Angola*]   (AF)

DOR .... Departamento de Orientacion Revolucionaria [*Department of Revolutionary Orientation*] [*Cuba*]   (LA)

Dor .... Doktor [*Academic degree*] [*Indonesian*]

dor .... Dorado [*Gilt*] [*Spanish*]

dor .... Dorato [*Gilt*] [*Italian*]

dor .... Dore [*Gilt*] [*French*]

DOR .... Dori [*Burkina Faso*] [*Airport symbol*]   (OAG)

DOR .... Dornier Reparaturwerft GmbH [*Germany*] [*ICAO designator*]   (FAAC)

DOR .... Dyrekcja Osiedli Robotniczych [*Administration of Workers' Settlements*]   (POL)

dor .... Road   (RU)

DORAA ..... Direccao da Organizacao Regional do Alentejo-Algrave [*Alentejo-Algrave Region Organization Directorate*] [*Portuguese*]   (WER)

DORB .... Direccao da Organizacao Regional das Beiras [*Beiras Region Organization Directorate*] [*Portuguese*]   (WER)

DORBRAS ... Companhia Brasileira de Dormentes [*Brazilian Railway Tie Company*]   (LA)

DORC .... Defence Operational Requirements Committee [*Department of Defense*] [*Australia*]   (PDAA)

dorChK ...... Railroad Extraordinary Commission for Combating Counterrevolution and Sabotage   (RU)

doreb .... Road Maintenance Battalion   (RU)

dorev .... Prerevolutionary   (RU)

DORG .... Departamento de Reconstruccao Nacional [*Department of National Reconstruction*] [*Angola*]   (AF)

Dorgan .... Spoldzielnia Pracy Doradcow Organizacyjnych [*Labor Cooperative of Consultants on Organization*]   (POL)

DORIN ...... Darstellungsmethoden fuer Organisations-und Informationssysteme [*German*]   (ADPT)

DORIS .... Societe de Developpement Operationnel des Richesses Sous-Marines [*French*]   (MSC)

Dorizdat ..... Publishing House of Road Construction Literature   (RU)

dorizul .... Railroad Office of Inventions and Improvements   (RU)

DORK .... Dyrekcja Okregowa Radiofonizacji Kraju [*District Administration for Country-Wide Radio Installation*]   (POL)

Dorkhimzavod ... Dorogomilovskiy Chemical Plant Imeni M. V. Frunze   (RU)

DORKTEK ... Railroad Office for Container Shipments and Transportation and Forwarding Operations   (RU)

DORL .... Direccao da Organizacao Regional de Lisboa [*Lisbon Region Organization Directorate*] [*Portuguese*]   (WER)

DORM .... Direccao da Organizacao Regional do Minho [*Minho Region Organization Directorate*] [*Portuguese*]   (WER)

DORMA .... Departamento de Organizacion y Masas [*Department of Organization and the Masses*] [*Nicaragua*]   (LA)

Dormash .... Road Machinery Repair Plant   (RU)

Dormashina ... Road Machinery Plant   (RU)

Dormost ..... Road and Bridge Administration   (RU)

Dormostmekhanizatsiya ... Trust of the Road and Bridge Construction Administration of the Glavmosstroy   (RU)

Dormostproyekt ... Institute for the Planning of Roads, Bridges, and Embankments   (RU)

Dormoststroy ... Republic Trust of Road and Bridge Construction [*RSFSR*]   (RU)

Dormoststroymaterialy ... Trust of the Road and Bridge Construction Administration of the Glavmosstroy   (RU)

DORN .... Direccao da Organizacao Regional do Norte [*Northern Region Organization Directorate*] [*Portuguese*]   (WER)

DORNII .... Scientific Research Institute of Roads   (RU)

DorNITO ... Scientific, Engineering, and Technical Society of Railroad Transportation   (RU)

dorNTO ..... Railroad Administration of the Scientific and Technical Society of Railroad Transportation   (RU)

DOROR ..... Direccao da Organizacao Regional do Oeste e Ribatejo [*West and Ribatejo Region Organization Directorate*] [*Portuguese*]   (WER)

Dorprofsozh ... Railroad Committee of the Railroad Transportation Workers' Trade   (RU)

dorr .... Road Company   (RU)

DORS .... Dansk Selskab foer Operationsanalyse [*Denmark*]   (SLS)

dorsanupr ... Railroad Medical Administration   (RU)

dorsb .... Road-Building Battalion   (RU)

Dorstroy ..... Road-Building Trust   (RU)

DORTEK .... Railroad Transportation and Forwarding Office   (RU)

DORTS ...... Department of Rapid Transit Systems [*Taipei*]   (ECON)

DoRTS ...... Department of Rapid Transport Systems [*Taiwan*]

DORURS .. Road Administration of Workers' Supply   (RU)

dorv .... Road Platoon   (RU)

Dorzdrav .... Railroad Department of Public Health   (RU)

DOS .... Dansk Ortopaedisk Selskab [*Denmark*]   (SLS)

DOS .... Dansk Oto-Laryngologisk Selskab [*Denmark*]   (SLS)

DoS .... Department of Science [*Australia*]

DOS .... Dioikisis Oikonomikis Synergasias   (GC)

DOS .... Direccion de Obras Sanitarias [*Sanitary Public Works Department*] [*Chile*]   (LA)

DOS .... Directorate of Overseas Surveys

DOS .... Director of Studies [*Australia*]

dos .... Dosentti [*Finland*]

Dos .... Dosierung [*Dosage*] [*German*]   (GCA)

dos .... Dosyn [*Dozen*] [*Afrikaans*]

DOS .... Dutch Orchid Society   (EAIO)

DOS .... Duvanska Ogledna Stanica [*Tobacco Experimental Station*]   (YU)

DOS .... House of Officer Personnel   (RU)

dos .... Permanent Emplacement   (RU)

DOS .... Permanent Emplacement, Fighting Pillbox   (BU)

DOSA .... House of Soviet Army Officers   (RU)

DOSAAF ... Dobrovol'noye Obshchestvo Sodeystviya Armii, Aviatsii, i Floty SSSR [*Voluntary Society for Assistance to the Army, Air Force, and Navy of the USSR*]   (CZ)

DOSARM ... All-Union Voluntary Society for Assistance to the Army of the USSR [*1948-1951*]   (RU)

DOSAV ..... All-Union Voluntary Society for Assistance to the Air Force of the USSR [*1948-1951*]   (RU)

DOSD .... Director of Organisation and Staff Duties [*Australia*]

DOSE .... Department of School Education [*New South Wales, Australia*]

DOSFLOT ... All-Union Voluntary Society for Assistance to the Navy of the USSR [*1948-1951*]   (RU)

doshk .... Preschool   (RU)

DOSK .... Docasna Okresna Spravna Komisia [*Provisional District Administrative Commission*]   (CZ)

dosl .... Doslownie [*or Doslowny*] [*Literally or Literal*]   (POL)

DOSO .... Voluntary Civil Defense Organization   (BU)

DOSO .... Voluntary Society for Assistance to Landscaping   (RU)

DOSOM ..... Voluntary Society for Assisting the Landscaping of the City of Moscow   (RU)

DOSS .... Documentation on Social Security [*ILO*] [*Information service or system United Nations*]   (DUND)

Doss ActSoc Cath ... Les Dossiers de l'Action Sociale Catholique [*Benelux*]   (BAS)

DOS-(VEB) ... Deutsche Oder-Schiffahrt [*German Oder Shipping Enterprise (VEB)*]   (EG)

DOSZ .... Dyrekcja Okregowa Szkolenia Zawodowego [*District Administration of Vocational Training*]   (POL)

DOT .... Department of Telecommunications [*India*]

DOT .... Department of Treasury [*Victoria*] [*Australia*]

DOT .... Doswiadczalny Osrodek Telewizyjny [*Experimental Television Center*]   (POL)

dot .... Dotyczy [*or Dotyczacy*] [*Refers To, Concerning*] [*Poland*]

DOT .... Operational Detachment of Ships of the Baltic Fleet [*1919*]   (RU)

DOT .... Permanent Emplacement   (RU)

DOT .... Reinforced Concrete Pillbox   (BU)

DoTA .... Department of Transport, Australia

DOTAC ..... Department of Transport and Communications [*Australia*]

DoTC......... Department of Transport and Communications [*Philippines*]

DOTE........ Debreceni Orvostudomanyi Egyetem [*Medical University of Debrecen*] (HU)

DOTM....... Director of Naval Ordnance, Torpedoes, and Mines [*Royal Australian Navy*]

dots............ Docent (BU)

dots............ Docent, Lecturer (RU)

DOTs......... Woodworking Shop (RU)

Dott Ing..... Dottore Ingenieur [*Doctor of Engineering*] [*Italian*]

DOU .... Dourados [*Brazil*] [*Airport symbol*] (OAG)

doubl .... Doublure [*Lining*] [*Publishing*] [*French*]

DOUCH .... Departamento de Oceanologia, Universidad de Chile [*Santiago, Chile*] (ASF)

douz............ Douzaine [*Dozen*] [*French*]

DOV.......... Doplnovaci Okresni Velitelstvi [*Military District Command for Records and Reserves*] (CZ)

DOV.......... Supplementary Excitation Winding (RU)

dov rub .... Prewar Ruble (RU)

DOW .... Departement van Openbare Werke [*Public Works Department*] [*Afrikaans*]

DOW .... Dowodztwo Okregu Wojskowego [*Military District Headquarters*] (POL)

DOX.......... Dongara [*Australia*] [*Airport symbol*] (OAG)

Doz........... Dozent [*German*]

DOZ.......... Drzaven Osiguritelen Zavod [*State Insurance Institute*] (YU)

DOZ.......... Patrol (RU)

DOZ.......... State Shoe Manufacturing Plant (BU)

DOZ.......... Woodworking Plant (RU)

DOZAB ..... Dopravne Zavody v Bratislave [*Transportation Enterprises in Bratislava*] (CZ)

dozavuch .... School for Pre-Plant Training (RU)

DOZK....... Ship Patrol (RU)

DOZPL...... Submarine Patrol (RU)

DOZV .... Air Patrol Detachment (RU)

DP............. Arc Furnace (RU)

DP............. Breathing Apparatus (RU)

DP............. Center-Line Plane, Fore-and-Aft Line (of a Ship) (RU)

DP............. Child's Gas Mask (RU)

DP............. Circular Saw (RU)

DP............. Dacha Settlement (RU)

DP............. Dansk Psykologforening [*Denmark*] (SLS)

DP............. Datenuebertragungsprogramm [*Data Transfer Program*] [*German*] (ADPT)

DP............. Decontamination Apparatus (RU)

DP............. Decontamination Area (RU)

DP............. Decontamination Station [*Military*] (BU)

dp .... Decret Parlementaire [*Parliamentary Enactment*] [*French*]

DP............. Defense Passive [*Civil Defense*] [*French*]

DP............. Degtyarev Infantry (Machine Gun) (RU)

DP............. Delostrelecky Pluk [*Artillery Regiment*] (CZ)

DP............. Democracia Popular [*Popular Democracy Party*] [*Ecuador*] (LA)

DP............. Democratic Party [*Lithuania*] [*Political party*] (EAIO)

DP............. Democratic Party [*Kenya*] [*Political party*] (EY)

DP............. Democratic Party [*Cook Island*] [*Political party*] (PPW)

DP............. Democratic Party [*Thailand*] [*Political party*] (PPW)

DP............. Democratic Party [*Poland*] [*Political party*] (PPW)

DP............. Democratic Party [*Uganda*] [*Political party*] (PD)

DP............. Democratische Partij - Bovenwinden [*Democratic Party - Windward Islands*] [*Netherlands Antilles*] [*Political party*] (PPW)

DP............. Democratische Partij van Curacao [*Democratic Party - Curacao*] [*Netherlands Antilles*] [*Political party*] (PPW)

DP............. Democrazia Proletaria [*Proletarian Democracy*] [*Italy*] [*Political party*] (PPE)

DP............. Demokratesch Partei [*Democratic Party*] [*Luxembourg*] [*Political party*] (PPE)

DP............. Demokraticheska Partiia [*Democratic Party*] [*Bulgaria*] [*Political party*] (PPE)

DP............. Demokratiki Parataksis [*Democratic Front*] [*Greek*] (PPE)

DP............. Demokrat Partisi [*Democratic Party*] (TU)

DP............. Departamento de Pesca [*Fisheries Department*] [*Mexico*] (LA)

DP............. Deputy President [*Australia*]

DP............. Detection de Porteuse [*French*] (ADPT)

DP............. Deutsche Partei [*German Party*] [*Political party*] (PPE)

dp .... Deutsche Planungsgesellschaft EG Bonn (SLS)

DP............. Deutsche Post [*German Post Office*] (EG)

dp .... Deutscher Politologen-Verband eV (SLS)

DP............. Deutsches Patent [*German Patent*] (GCA)

DP............. Dewan Pimpinan [*Executive Council*] (IN)

D/P........... Dexamenoploion [*Tanker*] [*dex*] [*See also*] (GC)

DP............. Diagnostic Subroutine (RU)

d/p............. Dias Plazo [*Days' Time*] [*Spanish*]

DP............. Dielectric Constant (RU)

DP............. Dienstprogramm [*Service Program*] [*German*] (ADPT)

DP............. Differential Gear (RU)

DP............. Dimokratiki Parataxi [*Democratic Front*] [*Cyprus*] (GC)

DP............. Dimokratiki Poreia [*Democratic Path*] [*Greek*] (GC)

DP............. Direction des Poudres [*Weapons Powder Directorate*] [*French*] (WER)

DP............. Direkcija za Patista [*Department of Roads*] (YU)

DP............. Dispatcher's Station, Control Post, Dispatch Office (RU)

DP............. Displacement Pickup (RU)

DP............. Distance-Finding Station [*Navy*] (RU)

D/P........... Documenti Contro Pagamento [*Documents Against Payment*] [*Italian*] [*Business term*]

D/P........... Documentos Contra Pago [*Documents Against Payment*] [*Spanish*] [*Business term*]

D/P........... Documents Contre Paiement [*Documents Against Payment*] [*French*] [*Banking*]

DP............. Domaine de Pechpeyrou

DP............. Doppelposten [*Double Sentry*] [*German military - World War II*]

DP............. Dopravni Podniky Hlavniho Mesta Prahy [*Transportation Enterprises of the Capital Prague*] (CZ)

DP............. Dopravoprojekt-Statni Ustav pro Projektovani Dopravnich Staveb [*State Planning Institute for Transport Construction*] (CZ)

DP............. Dosimeter (RU)

DP............. Drustveni Plan [*Economic Plan*] (YU)

DP............. Drzavno Posestvo [*State Agricultural Estate*] (YU)

Dp............. Duga Plovidba [*Ocean Shipping*] (YU)

DP............. Duplex Device (RU)

DP............. Durchschnittspolymerizationsgrad [*Average Degree of Polymerization*] [*German*] (GCA)

DP............. Dywizja Pancerna [*Armored Division*] (POL)

DP............. Enemy Documents (BU)

DP............. Flight Range (RU)

DP............. Hoisting Motor (RU)

DP............. House of Pioneers (RU)

DP............. Long-Range Homing Radio Station (RU)

DP............. Maandblad "De Pacht" [*Benelux*] (BAS)

DP............. Obus a Double Paroi [*Type of shell*] [*Military*] [*French*] (MTD)

DP............. Piston Engine (RU)

DP............. Press Directorate (BU)

DP............. Regimental Duty Officer (RU)

DP............. Remote-Indicating Instrument, Remote-Reading Instrument (RU)

DP............. Remote Transmission (RU)

DP............. State Enterprise (BU)

DP............. State Printing Press (BU)

DP............. Yeast Peptone (RU)

DPA .... Averkiyev Breathing Apparatus (RU)

DPA .... Children's Preventive Clinic (RU)

DPA .... Dampier Port Authority [*Australia*]

DPA .... Darwin Port Authority [*Australia*]

DPA .... Democratic Party of Albania [*Political party*] (EY)

DPA .... Demokraticheskaia Partiia Angoly

DPA .... Departamento de Producao Animal [*Brazil*] (DSCA)

DPA .... Departamento de Promocao Agropecuaria [*Rio De Janeiro, Brazil*] (LAA)

DPA .... Department of Public Administration [*Tasmania, Australia*]

DPa .... Deutsche Patentanmeldung [*German Patent Application*] [*German*]

DPA .... Deutsche Presse Agentur [*German Press Agency*]

DPA .... Deutscher Personalausweis [*German Identity Card*] (EG)

DPA .... Deutsches Patentamt [*German Patent Office*] [*Information retrieval*]

DPa .... Deutsches Patent Angemeldet [*German Patent Pending*] (EG)

DPA .... Dewan Pertimbangan Agung [*Supreme Advisory Council*] (IN)

DPA .... Direccion del Proyecto CN Asco [*Asco Nuclear Power Station Project Bureau*] [*Spanish*] (WER)

DPA .... Direccion Provincial de Acueductos [*Provincial Waterworks Office*] [*Cuba*] (LA)

DPA .... Diretoria de Publicidade Agricola [*Brazil*] (DSCA)

DPA .... Disabled Peoples' Association [*Singapore*] (EAIO)

DPA .... Division Politicoadministrativa [*Political Administrative Division*] [*Cuba*] (LA)

DPA .... House of Party Activists (RU)

DP & C..... Department of Premier and Cabinet [*Victoria, Australia*]

DPAP........ Departamento de Promocao Agropecuaria [*Brazil*] (DSCA)

D-PARC .... Daigo Proving Ground and Research Centre [*Japan*]

DPB .... Defence Production Board [*NATO*] (NATG)

DP-B .... Democratische Partij - Bonaire [*Democratic Party - Bonaire*] [*Netherlands Antilles*] [*Political party*] (EY)

DPB .... Disabled Persons Bureau [*Northern Territory*] [*Australia*]

DPB .... Obus a Double Paroi et a Balles [*Type of shell*] [*Military*] [*French*] (MTD)

DPBG .... Democratic Party for British Gibralter (PPW)

DPBZ........ Dukelske Preteky Brannej Zdatnosti [*Dukla Military Fitness Contest*] (CZ)

DPC .... Dahir du 12 Aout 1913 sur la Procedure Civile (FLAF)

DPC .... Defence Planning Committee [*NATO*] (NATG)

DPC .... Defence Production Committee [*NATO*]   (NATG)
DPC .... Democratic People's Congress
DP-C .... Democratische Partij - Curacao [*Democratic Party - Curacao*] [*Netherlands Antilles*] [*Political party*]   (EY)
DPC .... Department of the Premier and Cabinet [*South Australia, Tasmania, Victoria*] [*Australia*]
DPC .... Direccion de Preparacion Combativa [*Directorate of Combat Training*] [*Cuba*]   (LA)
DPC .... Dubai Petroleum Company   (ME)
DPCA .... Department of Public and Consumer Affairs
DPCB........ Disabled Peoples' Council of Bangladesh   (EAIO)
DPCE........ Drejtoria e Pergjithshme e Centraleve Elektrike [*Albanian*]
DPCF........ Danish Precast Concrete Federation   (EAIO)
DPD .... Delnicke Potravni Druzstvo [*Workers' Consumer Cooperative*]   (CZ)
DPD .... Devlet Personel Dairesi [*State Personnel Office*] [*Under Prime Ministry*]   (TU)
DPD .... Diretoria de Pesquisas e Desenvolvimento [*Bureau of Research and Development*] [*Brazil*]   (LA)
DPD .... Division Decontamination Unit   (RU)
DPD .... Dobrovolno Protivpozarno Drustvo [*Society of Volunteer Firemen*]   (YU)
DPD .... Doppelnitelnye Pod'yomnye Dvigateli [*Extra-Lifting Engines*] [*Suffix letters on Soviet combat aircraft*]
DPD .... Drzavno Poljoprivredno Dobro [*State Agricultural Estate*]   (YU)
DPD .... Volunteer Fire Brigade   (RU)
DPDR .... Departamento de Planeamiento y Obras Rurales [*Peru*]   (DSCA)
DPDS........ DARC [*Description, Acquisition, Retrieval, and Conception*] Pluridata System [*Association for Research and Development of Chemical Informatics*] [*Information service or system*]   (IID)
DPDS........ Drustvo Prijatelja Dubrovacke Starine [*Society of the Friends of Ancient and Historical Dubrovnik*] [*Croatia*]   (EAIO)
DPD"Svoboda" ... Delavsko Prosvetno Drustvo "Svoboda" ["*Svoboda,*" *Workers' Educational Society*]   (YU)
DPDU........ Direccion de Planificacion del Desarrollo Urbano [*Chile*]   (LAA)
Dp E.......... Depot d'Eclopes [*Military*] [*French*]   (MTD)
DPE .... Dieppe [*France*] [*Airport symbol*] [*Obsolete*]   (OAG)
DPEA .... Departamento de Pesquisas e Experimentacao Agropecuaria [*Rio De Janeiro, Brazil*]   (LAA)
DPEC........ Direccion de Planificacion de Equipamiento Comunitario [*Santiago, Chile*]   (LAA)
DPEI.......... Departamento de Prevencion y Extincion de Incendios [*Department of Fire Fighting and Prevention*] [*Cuba*]   (LA)
D Pen .... Droit Penal [*French*]   (FLAF)
DPERPLA ... Delegacion del Parlamento Europeo para las Relaciones con los Paises de Latinoamerica [*Europe-Latin America Interparliamentary Assembly - ELAIA*] [*Luxembourg, Luxembourg*]   (EAIO)
DPES........ Mobile Diesel Electric Power Plant   (RU)
DPETD...... Department of the Premier, Economic and Trade Development [*Queensland*] [*Australia*]
DPF........... Dansk Pelsdyravlerforening [*Danish Fur Breeders' Association*]   (EY)
DPF........... Darfur Progress Front
DPF........... Departamento da Policia Federal [*Federal Police Department*] [*Brazil*]   (LA)
DPF........... Devlet Planlama Fonu [*State Planning Fund*]   (TU)
DPF........... State Land Fund   (BU)
DPFF .... State Pasture and Forage Fund   (BU)
DPFLP...... Democratic Popular Front for the Liberation of Palestine   (BJA)
DPFS .... Divisao de Pedologia e Fertilidade do Solo [*Brazil*]   (DSCA)
DPFTK ...... Disabled Peoples Finance Trust of Kenya   (EAIO)
DPG .... Demokraticheskaia Partiia Guinei [*Democratic Party of Guinea*] [*Russian*]
DPG .... Deutsche Phytomedizinische Gesellschaft eV   (SLS)
DPG .... Deutsche Psychoanalytische Gesellschaft eV   (SLS)
DPG .... Deutsch Pazifische Gesellschaft eV   (SLS)
DPG .... Duetsche Physikalische Gesellschaft [*German Physical Society*]   (SLS)
DPgem ...... Deutsches Patent Angemeldet [*German Patent Pending*]   (EG)
DPH........... Department of Planning and Housing [*Victoria*] [*Australia*]
DPH........... Dewan Pimpinan Harian [*Standing Executive Committee*]   (IN)
DPH........... Direccion de Planificacion Habitacional [*Ministerio de la Vivienda y Urbanismo*] [*Santiago, Chile*]   (LAA)
DPhG........ Deutsche Pharmazeutische Gesellschaft eV   (SLS)
DPhV .... Deutscher Philologen-Verband eV im Deutschen Beamtenbund   (SLS)
DPI .... Data Publishing International [*Netherlands*] [*Information service or system*]   (IID)
DPI .... Department of Primary Industry [*Australia*]
DPI .... Department of Public Information [*United Nations*]
DPI .... Disabled Peoples' International   (EAIO)
DPI .... Don Polytechnic Institute   (RU)
DPIA.......... Disabled Peoples' International [*Australia*]
DPIB.......... Disabled Persons' Information Bureau [*Australia*]

DPICG....... Destacamento Pedagogico Internacionalista "Che" Guevara [*Che Guevara Internationalist Teachers Detachment*] [*Cuba*]   (LA)
DPIE.......... Department of Primary Industries and Energy [*Australia*]
DPIF .... Department of Primary Industry and Fisheries [*Northern Territory, Australia*]
DPIFE .... Department of Primary Industry, Fisheries, and Energy
DPIL.......... Democracy and Peace (Iterim) League [*Myanmar*] [*Political party*]
DPIR.......... Department of Personnel and Industrial Relations [*South Australia*]
DPIS .... Disabled Peoples' International - Sweden   (EAIO)
DPISPS ..... Department of Primary Industries [*Queensland*] Stock Permit System [*Australia*]
DPIT.......... Drustvo Poljoprivrednih Inzenjera i Tehnicara [*Society of Agricultural Engineers and Technicians*]   (YU)
DPJ .... Direction Active de la Police Judiciaire [*Directorate of Criminal Investigation Police*] [*French*]   (WER)
DPK .... Container Position Probe   (RU)
DPK .... Democratic Party of Kurdistan [*Iraq*] [*Political party*]   (PPW)
DPK .... Dimokratiki Panepistimiaki Kinisi [*Democratic University Movement*] [*Greek*]   (GC)
DPK .... Divadlo 5 Kvetna [*May 5th Theater*]   (CZ)
DPK .... Pneumatic Telecompass   (RU)
DPK .... Ship Decontamination Apparatus   (RU)
DPK .... State Planning Commission   (BU)
DPK .... State Printing Combine   (BU)
DPKh.......... Division Field Bakery   (RU)
DPKK .... Dimokratikon Proodevtikon Komma Kyprou [*Democratic Progressive Party of Cyprus*]   (GC)
DPL .... Delostrelectvo Proti Letadlum [*Antiaircraft Artillery*]   (CZ)
DPL .... Department of the Parliamentary Library [*Australia*]
dpl .... Dienstplichtige [*Benelux*]   (BAS)
DPL .... Dipolog [*Philippines*] [*Airport symbol*]   (OAG)
DPL .... Division Field Infirmary   (RU)
DPL .... Dopravni Pluk Letecky [*Air Force Transport Regiment*]   (CZ)
DPL .... Dunedin Public Library [*New Zealand*]
DPL .... Floating Dock   (RU)
DPI............ Planned Idleness [*Machine placed in temporary reserve*]   (BU)
DPL .... Submarine Division   (RU)
DPLG .... Diplome par le Gouvernement [*French*]
DPlKom ..... State Planning Commission   (BU)
DPLR........ Department of Productivity and Labour Relations [*Western Australia*]
DPLRS........ Drustvo Pravnikov Ljudska Republika Slovenija [*Slovenian Lawyers' Society*]   (YU)
DPM .... Dewan Perniagaan Melayu [*Malayan Commercial Council*]   (ML)
DPM .... Diplomatoukhos Politikos Mikhanikos [*Certified (Graduate) Civil Engineer*]   (GC)
DPM .... Directia Porturilor Maritime [*Directorate of Maritime Ports*]   (RO)
DPM .... Dorazna Pomoc Medyczna [*Medical First Aid*]   (POL)
DPM .... First-Aid Medical Station   (RU)
DPM .... Modernized Degtyarev Infantry (Machine Gun)   (RU)
DPMA .... Dairy Products Manufacturers Association [*South Africa*]   (ARC)
DPMA .... Data Processing Management Association   (EA)
DPMA .... Direktorat Penyelidikan Masalah Air [*Institute of Hydraulic Engineering*] [*Directorate-General of Water Resources Development within the Ministry of Public Works and Electric Power Indonesia*]   (EAS)
DPMAWA ... Dairy Products Manufacturers' Association of Western Australia
DPMC .... Department of the Prime Minister and Cabinet [*Australia*]
DPMC .... Diviziska Pekarsko-Mesarska Ceta [*Divisional Bakers' and Butchers' Company*]   (YU)
DPMJ .... Dewan Perniagaan Melayu Johor [*Johor Malayan Commercial Council*]   (ML)
DPMJ .... Direktorat Penyelidikan Masalah Tanah Dan Jalan [*Indonesian Road Research Institute*] [*Directorate General of Highways*]   (ERC)
DPMP .... Dewan Persuratan Melayu Pahang [*Pahang Malayan Literature Council*]   (ML)
DPMS........ Distributed Payphone Management System [*Telecom Australia*]
DPN........... Diphosphopyridine Nucleotide   (RU)
dpn .... Doctor of Pedagogical Sciences   (RU)
DPNC .... Democratic Party of Nigeria and the Cameroons
DPNM....... Direktorat Pemetaan Negara Malaysia [*Directorate of National Mapping Malaysia*] [*Ministry of Land and Regional Development*]   (EAS)
DPO........... Demokratische Partei Oesterreichs [*Democratic Party of Austria*]   (PPE)
DPO........... Departure Prohibition Order [*Australia*]
DPO........... Devonport [*Tasmania*] [*Australia*] [*Airport symbol*]   (OAG)
DPO........... Dimitrov Pioneer Organization   (BU)
DPO........... Direct-Current Motor with Printed-Coil Armature   (RU)

DPO .... Disabled Persons Organization [*Bahamas*] (EAIO)
DPO .... Division Dressing Detachment (RU)
DPO .... House of Party Education (RU)
DPO .... State Printing and Publishing Trust (BU)
DPO .... Voluntary Consumers' Society [*1921-1924*] (RU)
DPO .... Volunteer Fire Society (RU)
DPOC .... Base de Documentos en Politica Criminal [*Criminal Law Documents Data Base*] [*United Nations Latin American Institute for Crime Prevention and Treatment of Offenders*] (IID)
DPolitekh .. State Polytechnical School (BU)
DPolitekhn-IFotogrTopogr ... State Polytechnical School, Institute of Photogrammetry and Topography (BU)
DPolitekhn-IGrad ... State Polytechnical School, Institute of City Planning (BU)
DPolitekhn-IInzhGeol ... State Polytechnical School, Institute of Geological Engineering (BU)
DPolitekhn-IKadZemeustr ... State Polytechnical School, Institute of Cadastral Study and Land Organization (BU)
DPolitekhn-IMel ... State Polytechnical School, Institute of Reclamation (BU)
DPolitekhn-IMelPochv ... State Polytechnical Institute of Soil Reclamation (BU)
DPolitekhn-INeorKhimTekhnol ... State Polytechnical Institute of Inorganic Chemical Technology (BU)
DPolitekhn-IOrKhimTekhnol ... State Polytechnical Institute of Organic Chemical Technology (BU)
DPolitekhn-IPrilElektrotekhn ... State Polytechnical Institute of Applied Electrical Engineering (BU)
DPolitekhn-IPrilGeol ... State Polytechnical Institute of Applied Geodesy (BU)
DPolitekhn-IRudNakh ... State Polytechnical School, Institute of Ore Deposits (BU)
DPolitekhn-ITekhnBot ... State Polytechnical School, Institute of Industrial Botany (BU)
DPolitekhn-ITekhnMekh ... State Polytechnical School, Institute of Applied Mechanics (BU)
DPolitekhn-ITopTekhnTekhTerm ... State Polytechnical School, Institute of Heat Engineering and Technical Thermodynamics (BU)
DPolitekhn-IVodkan ... State Polytechnical School, Institute of Water Supply and Sewage (BU)
DPOS .... "Septemvriyche" Dimitrov Pioneer Organization (BU)
DPOZ .... Dopravna Protiletecka Ochrana Zeleznic [*Mobile Anti-Aircraft Defense of Railroads*] (CZ)
DPP .... Democratic People's Party [*Taiwan*] [*Political party*] (ECON)
DPP .... Democratic Progressive Party [*Taiwan*] [*Political party*]
DPP .... Democratic Progressive Party [*Transkei*] [*Political party*] (PPW)
DPP .... Demokratikus Polgari Part [*Democratic Citizens' Party*] (HU)
DPP .... Dewan Perniagaan dan Perindustrian [*Chamber of Commerce and Industry*] (IN)
DPP .... Dewan Pimpinan Pusat [*Central Executive Council*] (IN)
DPP .... Director of Public Prosecutions [*Jamaica*] (LA)
DPP .... Division Dressing Station (RU)
DPP .... Division Reloading Point, Division Load Transfer Point (RU)
dpp .... Doppelt [*Double*] [*German*] (GCA)
DPP .... House of Party Education (RU)
DPP .... Long-Range Infantry Support (RU)
DPP .... Long-Range Weather Forecast (RU)
DPP .... Political Party Democrats 66 [*Netherlands*] [*Political party*] (EAIO)
DPP .... State Industrial Enterprise (BU)
DPPA .... Divisao de Promocao de Producao Animal [*Rio De Janeiro, Brazil*] (LAA)
DPPNRBiH ... Direkcija za Planinske Pasnjake Narodne Republike Bosne i Hercegovine [*Department for Mountain Pastures of Bosnia and Hercegovina*] (YU)
DPPS .... Divisao da Policia Politica e Social [*Political and Social Police Division*] [*Brazil*] (LA)
DPPS .... Voluntary Fire Fighting Service (BU)
DPPU .... Voluntary Fire Fighting School (BU)
DPPWA ..... Director of Public Prosecutions for Western Australia
DPR .... Dewan Perwakilan Rakjat [*Parliament*] (IN)
dpr .... River Crossing Assault Company (RU)
DPR .... State Livestock Breeding Farm (BU)
DPR .... Workhouse (RU)
DPRA .... Democratic People's Republic of Angola
DPRC .... Departamento Nacional de Portos, Rios, e Canais [*Rio De Janeiro, Brazil*] (LAA)
DPRD .... Dewan Perwakilan Rakjat Daerah [*Regional Legislature*] (IN)
DPRD-GR ... Dewan Perwakilan Rakjat Daerah - Gotong Rojong [*Regional Legislature*] (IN)
DPR-GR ..... Dewan Perwakilan Rakjat - Gotong Rojong [*Parliament*] (IN)
DPRI .... Disaster Prevention Research Institute [*Japan*] (IRC)
D Prior .... Deutsche Prioritaet [*German Priority*] (GCA)
D Priv........ Droit Prive [*French*] (FLAF)

DPRK .... Democratic People's Republic of Korea [*Also known as North Korea*]
DPRM .... Long-Range Homing Radio Beacon (RU)
DPRM .... Outer Marker Beacon (RU)
DPRS .... Long-Range Homing Radio Station (BU)
DPRTF ...... Drought Policy Review Task Force [*Australia*]
DPRZ......... Dnepropetrovsk Locomotive Repair Plant (RU)
D Pr Zak ... Pretrial House of Detention (RU)
DPS........... Dansk Pediatrisk Selskab [*Denmark*] (SLS)
DPS........... Data Processing Services Co. [*Information service or system*] (IID)
DPS........... Dateiparametersatz [*German*] (ADPT)
DPS........... Demokratische Partei Saar [*Democratic Party of the Saar*] [*Germany*] [*Political party*] (PPE)
DPS........... Demokratska Partija Socijalista [*Democratic Party of Socialists*] [*Montenegro*] [*Political party*] (EY)
DPS........... Denpasar [*Indonesia*] [*Airport symbol*] (OAG)
DPS........... Dentures for Pensioners Scheme [*Australia*]
DPS........... Department of Property and Services [*Victoria, Australia*]
DPS........... Detaliczny Punkt Sprzedazy [*Retail Sales Center*] (POL)
DPS........... Dische-Positive Substances (RU)
DPS........... Division Advanced Depot (RU)
DPS........... Division Food Depot (RU)
Dps............ Doppelsalz [*Double Salt*] [*German*] (GCA)
DPS........... Double Flip-Flop Circuit (RU)
DPS........... Dzielnica Przemyslowo-Skladowa [*Industrial and warehouse city section*] (POL)
DPS........... Message Center Duty Officer (RU)
dps............ Semiweekly (BU)
DPSA......... Deputy Public Service Arbitrator [*Australia*]
DPSB......... Defence Production Supply Board [*NATO*] (NATG)
DPSC......... Detainees' Parents Support Committee [*South Africa*] (ECON)
DPSCA ...... Darwin Pensioners and Senior Citizens' Association [*Australia*]
DPSP......... Control Tower for Instrument Landing (RU)
DP-StE ...... Democratic Party - Statia [*Netherlands Antilles*] [*Political party*] (EY)
DP-StM ..... Democratic Party - St. Maarten [*Netherlands Antilles*] [*Political party*] (EY)
DPSV......... Direcao Provincial dos Servicos de Veterinaria [*Mozambique*] (DSCA)
dpt .... Danmarks Socialpaedagogiske Forening [*Denmark*] (SLS)
DPT .... Democratic Party of Tadzhikistan [*Political party*]
DPT .... Devlet Planlama Teskilati [*State Planning Organization*] (TU)
DPT .... Dewan Pimpinan Tjabang [*Branch Executive Council*] (IN)
DPT .... Direct-Current Motor (RU)
DPT .... Division Message Code (RU)
DPT .... Division of Production Technology [*Council for Scientific and Industrial Research*] [*South Africa*] (IRC)
DPT .... Domy Pracy Tworczej [*Houses of Artistic Creation*] (POL)
DPT .... State Tourism Enterprise (BU)
DPTE......... Directoria de Pesquisa e Ensino Tecnico do Exercito [*Army Directorate of Technical Research and Training*] [*Brazil*] (LA)
DPTK........ State Cotton Weaving Combine (BU)
dpto .... Departamento (SCAC)
DPTR........ Diviziske Protivtenkovski Rezerve [*Divisional Antitank Reserves*] (YU)
D -pu .... Deli-Palyaudvar [*Deli (South) Station (in Budapest)*] (HU)
DPU.......... Disabled Persons Unit [*United Nations*] (DUND)
DPU.......... Dispatcher's Control Post (RU)
D Pub .... Droit Public [*French*] (FLAF)
DPUD........ Department of Planning and Urban Development [*Western Australia*] [*Australia*]
DP-UDC .... Democracia Popular - Union Democrata Cristiana [*People's Democracy - Christian Democratic Union*] [*Ecuador*] [*Political party*] (PPW)
DPUT .... Departemen Pekerdjaan Umum dan Tenaga [*Department of Public Works and Power*] (IN)
DPUV .... Delostrelectvo Proti Utocne Vozbe [*Antitank Artillery*] (CZ)
DPV .... Democracia Popular Venezolana [*Venezuelan Popular Democratic Movement*] (LA)
DPV .... Departamento da Producao Vegetal [*Brazil*] (DSCA)
DPV .... Deutsche Psychoanalytische Vereinigung eV (SLS)
DPV .... Dievthinsis Polemikis Viomikhanias [*War Industry Directorate*] (GC)
dPVO .... Antiaircraft Defense Division (BU)
DPVRD ..... Subsonic Ramjet Engine (RU)
DPW.......... Departement van Publieke Werk [*Public Works Department*] [*Afrikaans*]
DPWG .... Defence Planning Working Group [*of Defense Ministers*] [*NATO*] (NATG)
DPWH....... Department of Parks, Wildlife, and Heritage [*Tasmania*] [*Australia*]
DPYa .... Dynamic Polarization of a Nucleus (RU)
DPz .... Delostrelecky Pruzkum [*Artillery Reconnaissance*] (CZ)
DPZ .... Pretrial House of Detention (RU)

DPzH	Dustojnicke Pruzkumne Hlidky [*Officer Reconnaissance Patrols*] (CZ)
DPZI	Deutsches Paedagogisches Zentral-Institut [*German Central Teachers' Institute*] (EG)
DPZKh	State Grain Foods Enterprise (BU)
DPZL	Divizni Prostredky Zabezpeceni Letectva [*Aviation Support by Division Resources*] (CZ)
DPzL	Divizni Pruzkumne Letectvo [*Division Reconnaissance Air Force Units*] (CZ)
DPzLP	Delostrelecky Pruzkumny Letecky Pluk [*Air Reconnaissance Artillery Regiment*] (CZ)
DQ	Dernier Quartier [*Last Quarter*] [*Astronomy*] [*French*]
DQ	Fiji [*Aircraft nationality and registration mark*] (FAAC)
DQA	Dairy Quality Assurance [*Australia*]
DQA	Directorate of Quality Assurance [*Australia*]
DQAGP	Directorate of Quality Assurance - General Products [*Department of Defence*] [*Australia*]
DQAMAR	Defence Quality Assurance Marine [*Australia*]
DQAMARHQ	Defence Quality Assurance Marine - Headquarters [*Australia*]
DQI	Cimber Air, Sonderjyllands Flyveselskab [*Denmark*] [*ICAO designator*] (FAAC)
Dr	Choke (RU)
DR	Company Duty Officer (RU)
dr	Comrade (BU)
Dr	Dahir [*French*] (FLAF)
DR	Danish Reactor [*Nuclear energy*] (NRCH)
DR	Danmarks Radio
DR	Danmarks Rederiforening [*Danish Shipowners Association*] (EAIO)
DR	Danmarks Retsforbund [*Justice Party of Denmark*] (PPE)
dr	Debiteur [*Debtor*] [*French*]
DR	Debiteur [*Debtor*] [*Afrikaans*]
DR	Delnicka Rada [*Workers' Council*] (CZ)
dr	Dernier [*Last*] [*French*]
dR	Der Reserve [*Reserve*] (EG)
dR	Des Ruhestandes [*German*]
DR	Deutsche Reichsbahn [*German Democratic Republic Railway*] (DCTA)
DR	Deutsche Reichspartei [*German National Party*] [*Political party*] (PPE)
DR	Deutsches Recht [*German Law*] (ILCA)
DR	Digitairechner [*Digital Computer*] [*German*] (ADPT)
DR	Dilenska Rada [*Shop Council*] (CZ)
DR	Direccion de Riegos [*Ministerio de Obras Publicas*] [*Santiago, Chile*] (LAA)
d-r	Director, Manager (RU)
DR	Division de Reserve [*Military*] [*French*] (MTD)
Dr	Docteur [*Doctor*] [*French*] (MTD)
Dr	Doctor [*Spanish*]
DR	Dokter [*or Doktor*] [*Doctor*] [*Afrikaans*]
Dr	Doktor [*Doctor*] [*German*]
dr	Doktor [*Doctor*] [*Danish*] (GPO)
d:r	Doktor [*Doctor*] [*Swedish*] (GPO)
Dr	Doktorat [*Doctorate*] [*German*]
Dr	Doktor, Mjek [*Albanian*]
DR	Double Socket (RU)
Dr	Doutor [*Doctor*] [*Portuguese*] (GPO)
dr	Drachm [*Unit of weight*] [*German*]
DR	Dragme [*Unit of Weight*] [*Afrikaans*]
Dr	Drive (IDIG)
dr	Droit de Souscription [*French*]
Dr	Druck [*Pressure*] [*German*] (GCA)
Dr	Druck [*Print*] [*Publishing*] [*German*]
dr	Druk [*Print*] [*Publishing*] [*Poland*]
DR	Druk [*Edition*] [*Afrikaans*]
dr	Druk [*Print*] [*Publishing*] [*Netherlands*]
Dr	Druzhba [*Friendship*] [*A periodical*] (BU)
dr	Druzstvo [*Squad (Military); Cooperative (Economic)*] (CZ)
DR	Duty Radio Operator, Duty Radioman (RU)
DR	European Right [*European Parliament*] (ECED)
dr	Fraction (RU)
dr	Others (BU)
DR	Radio Broadcasting Directorate (BU)
DR	Robin Avions [*Pierre Robin*] [*France*] [*ICAO aircraft manufacturer identifier*] (ICAO)
DRA	Danish Retail Association (EAIO)
DRA	Democratic Republic of Afghanistan (FEA)
dra	Derecha [*Right*] [*Spanish*]
DRA	Diplome de Recherches Approfondies [*French*]
DRA	Direction a la Recherche Agronomique
Dra	Doctora [*Doctor (Feminine)*] [*Spanish*] (GPO)
DRA	Doctoranda [*Doctoral Candidate (Feminine)*] (ML)
d-ra	Doktora [*Doctor (Feminine)*] (POL)
DRA	Doktoranda [*Academic title held by women*] (IN)
Dra	Doutora [*Doctor (Feminine)*] [*Portuguese*] (GPO)

DRA	Etablissements Devanlay Recoing Afrique
DRACOG	Diploma of Royal Australian College of Obstetricians and Gynaecologists (BABM)
DRACULA	Disaster Reaction Awareness in the CAVAL [*Cooperative Action by Victorian Academic Libraries*] Union of Libraries and Associates [*Australia*]
Dr Adm	Droit Administratif [*France*] (FLAF)
DRAE	Long-Range Air Reconnaissance Squadron (RU)
Dr Aff	Le Droit et les Affaires [*France*] (FLAF)
Drag	Dragees [*Dragees*] (EG)
DRAGONAIR	Hong Kong Dragon Airlines (FEA)
dram	Dramatic (RU)
Dramkruzhok	Drama Circle (BU)
DRAP	Decret Portant Reglement d'Administration Publique [*North African*]
DRAP	Long-Range Air Reconnaissance Regiment (RU)
dras	Derechas [*Rights*] [*Spanish*]
Dr Aut	Le Droit d'Auteur [*Switzerland*] (FLAF)
drb	Darab [*Piece*] (HU)
DRB	Derby [*Australia*] [*Airport symbol*] (OAG)
DRB	Deutsche Reichsbahn [*German State Railways*] [*Pre-1945*]
DRB	Drzavno Recno Brodarstvo [*State River Shipping*] (YU)
DrBdk	Doktor der Bodenkultur [*Doctor of Agriculture*] [*German*]
DRC	Danish Refugee Council (EAIO)
DRC	Defence Review Committee [*NATO*] (NATG)
Drc	Derece [*Degree, Grade*] (TU)
Dr C	Dernier Cours [*Closing Price*] [*French*]
DRC	Dictionary Research Centre [*Macquarie University*] [*Australia*]
DRC	Dutch Reformed Church
DRCDF	Directia Retelei Cinematografice si Difuzarii Filmelor [*Directorate of the Movie Network and Film Distribution*] (RO)
Drchfb	Durchfuehrungsbestimmung [*Implementing Regulation*] (EG)
DRCM	Dutch Reformed Church Mission
DRCOG	Diploma of the Royal College of Obstetricians and Gynaecologists [*Australia*]
Dr Com	Droit Commercial [*Commercial Law*] [*French*] (DLA)
DRCS	Defence Research Centre, Salisbury [*Australia*] (ADA)
DRCS	Digital Radio Concentrator System [*Australia*]
DRCSA	Distance Runners Club of South Australia
DRCSAB	Defence Research Centre, Salisbury, Administrative Branch [*Australia*]
DRCSMC	Defence Research Centre, Salisbury, Management Committee [*Australia*]
DRD	Defence Research Directors [*NATO*] (NATG)
DRD	Dorunda Station [*Australia*] [*Airport symbol*] [*Obsolete*] (OAG)
DRDC	Dairy Research and Development Corp. [*Australia*]
DRDL	Defence Research and Development Laboratory [*Hyderabad, India*]
DRDL	Defense Research and Development Laboratory [*India*]
DRDO	Defence Research and Development Organization [*India*] (PDAA)
DRE	Department of Resources and Energy [*Australia*] (PDAA)
DRE	Direction des Relations Exterieures
Dre	Dresden [*One of the eight GDR Reichsbahn directorates*] (EG)
DRE	Long-Range Reconnaissance Squadron (RU)
DREAM	Development Rehabilitation of the Environment through Arts and Media [*Philippines Earth Savers movement*]
DRED	Direction de la Recherche et des Etudes Doctorales [*Ministry of Education directorate*] [*France*]
DREE	Direction des Relations Economiques Exterieures [*Exterior Economic Relations Management*] [*French*]
DREF	Departement de Recherches Economiques et Financieres [*Institut de Recherche Scientifique*] [*Zaire*]
DREF	Directia Regionala a Economiei Forestiere [*Regional Directorate of the Forest Economy*] (RO)
DREGRAP	Drzavno Recno-Gradevinsko Preduzece [*State River Construction Establishment*] (YU)
Dr Eh	Doktor Ehrenhalber [*Honorary Doctor*] [*German*]
Dreh	Drehung [*Rotation*] [*German*] (GCA)
Drehko	Drehkondensator [*Variable Condenser*] (EG)
DRET	Direction des Recherches Etudes et Techniques [*France*] (PDAA)
drev	Woodworking Industry Plant [*Topography*] (RU)
DREVAP	Drzavno Recno Preduzece za Vadenje Potopljenih Objekata [*State River Establishment for Salvage of Submerged Objects*] (YU)
drevn ukr	Ancient Fortification [*Topography*] (RU)
DRF	Dansk Robot Forening [*Danish Industrial Robot Association*] (EAIO)
DRFA	Dyslexia Research Foundation of Australia
Dr Fin	Droit Financier [*France*] (FLAF)
Dr Fisc	Droit Fiscal [*France*] (FLAF)
DRG	Defense Research Group [*NATO*]
DRG	Deutsche Rheologische Gesellschaft e.V. (SLS)
DRG	Deutsche Roentgengesellschaft (SLS)

DRG.......... Deutsches Reichsgesetz [*German State Law*] (GCA)
DRG.......... Direction Active des Renseignements Generaux [*Directorate of General Information*] [*French*] (WER)
DRGB....... German Law Code
drgl............ Dergleichen [*Similar*] [*German*]
DRGM....... Deutsches-Reichsgebrauchsmuster [*German-Registered Design*]
dr-gr.......... Ancient Greek (RU)
dr-grech...... Ancient Greek (RU)
DRH .... Daerah [*Region*] (IN)
DRH .... Departamento de Recursos Humanos [*Recife, Brazil*] (LAA)
DRHA....... Dar Es Salaam Regional Hockey Association
Dr habil..... Doktor (Habilitiert) [*Doctor (Usually Professor)*] (EG)
Dr hc .... Doctor Honoris Causa [*Honorary Doctor*]
DRI .... Central Statistical Office Demographic Research Institute [*Research center*] [*Hungary*] (IRC)
DRI .... Dairy Research Institute [*New Zealand*] (DSCA)
DRI .... Dansk Rumforsknings Institut [*Danish Space Research Institute*]
DRI .... Department of Resource Industries [*Queensland*] [*Australia*]
DRI .... Disaster Research Institute (EAIO)
DRI .... House of Workers in the Arts (RU)
DRI .... New Zealand Dairy Research Institute (ARC)
DRI .... Programa de Desarrollo Rural Integrado [*Integrated Rural Development Program*] [*Colorado*] (LA)
DRIA .... Direction Regionale de l'Industrie [*Regional Industrial Directorate*] [*Algeria*] (AF)
DRIL......... Directorio Revolucionario Iberico de Liberta [*Revolutionary Directorate for Iberian Liberation*]
Dr-Ing .... Doktor der Ingenieurwissenschaften [*Doctor of Engineering*] [*German*] (EG)
DRIPAE .... Direction des Relations Inter-Gouvernementales pour les Aides Exterieures [*Directorate of Intergovernmental Relations for Foreign Aid*] [*Cambodia*] (CL)
DRIVE....... Dedicated Road Infrastructure of Vehicle Safety [*European Community*] (MHDB)
Dr jur .... Doktor der Rechte [*Doctor of Laws (LLD)*] [*German*] (EG)
Dr jur utr ... Doktor Beider Rechte [*Doctor of Both Laws (LLD)*] [*German*] (EG)
DRK.......... Deutsches Rotes Kreuz [*German Red Cross*] (WEN)
DRK.......... Druk Air [*Bhutan*] [*ICAO designator*] (FAAC)
DRK.......... Far Eastern Revolutionary Committee (RU)
drka.......... Battalion of Rocket Boats (BU)
DRKF........ Dansk Populaerautorer [*Danish Songwriters Guild*] (EAIO)
DRKhR...... Radiation and Chemical Reconnaissance Patrol (RU)
DRL .... Deutscher Rat fuer Landespflege (SLS)
DRL .... Donated Records List [*Australia*]
DRL(M)..... Defence Research Laboratory (Materials) [*India*] (PDAA)
DRM......... Deborah Relief Memorial Hospital
DRM......... Departamento de Recursos Minerales [*Panama*] (LAA)
DRM......... Dewan Revolusioner Malaya [*Malayan Revolutionary Council*] (ML)
DRMA...... Democratic Reform Movements in Australia (ADA)
Dr MarFr ... Le Droit Maritime Francais (FLAF)
DRME....... Direction des Recherches et Moyens d'Essais [*Research and Test Methods Directorate*] [*French*] (WER)
dr med .... Doktor Medycyny [*Doctor of Medicine*] [*Poland*]
DRN......... Departamento de Recursos Naturais [*Natural Resources Department*] [*Brazil*] (LA)
DRN......... Departamento de Recursos Naturales [*Natural Resources Department*] [*Spanish*]
DRN......... Dirranbandi [*Australia*] [*Airport symbol*] [*Obsolete*] (OAG)
DRN......... Dzielnicowa Rada Narodowa [*City Section People's Council*] (POL)
drn bv .... Duty Officer in Bivouac Area (BU)
DRNK....... Deoxyribonucleic Acid (RU)
drn k.......... Officer of the Day (BU)
DRNM....... Directia Regionala a Navigatiei Maritime [*Regional Directorate of Maritime Navigation*] (RO)
DRNR....... Departamento de Recursos Naturais Renovais [*Rio De Janeiro, Brazil*] (LAA)
DRNT....... Long-Range Radio Navigation Point (RU)
DRO.......... Danske Roentgendiagnostikeres Organisation [*Denmark*] (SLS)
dro............ Derecho [*Right*] [*Spanish*]
dro............ Dinheiro [*Monetary unit*] [*Portugal*]
DRO.......... Dobrudzha Revolutionary Organization (BU)
dro............ Druzstvo s Rucenim Omezenym [*Limited Liability Cooperative*] (CZ)
DRO.......... Grinding and Crushing Equipment (RU)
DRO.......... Supplementary Workers' Education (RU)
drob fabr ... Stone Crusher Plant [*Topography*] (RU)
DROG........ Drogue
DROM...... Druzstvo pre Obchod Mliekom a Mliecnymi Vyrobkami [*Cooperative for Marketing Milk and Milk Products*] (CZ)
dros.......... Derechos [*Rights*] [*Spanish*]
DROT....... Departamento de Relacoes com os Organismos de Trabalho [*Department of Relations with Labor Organizations*] [*Portuguese*] (WER)

Dr Ouv .... Le Droit Ouvrier [*France*] (FLAF)
drov .... Firewood Yard [*Topography*] (RU)
drozh .... Yeast Plant [*Topography*] (RU)
drp............. And Others, Et Cetera (BU)
DRP .... Democratic Reform Party [*South Africa*] [*Political party*] (EY)
DRP .... Democratic Republican Party [*South Korea*] [*Political party*] (PPW)
DRP .... Deutsche Rechtspartei [*German Party of the Right*] [*Political party*] (PPE)
DRP .... Deutsche Reichspost [*German Postal Service*]
DRP .... Deutsches Reichspatent [*German State Patent*]
DRP .... Disability Reform Package [*Australia*]
DRP .... Divisao de Recursos Pesqueiros [*Recife, Brazil*] (LAA)
DRP .... Dnepr River Steamship Line (RU)
DRP .... Hand-Operated Dynamo (RU)
DRP .... House of Education Workers (RU)
DRP .... Road Repair Station (RU)
Drpaed .... Doctor Paedogogikae [*Doctor of Pedagogy*] (CZ)
Dr Phil ...... Doctor Philosophiae [*Doctor of Philosophy*]
DRPLC..... Departement des Recherches des Plantations Lever au Congo
DRPPE...... Direccion de Promocion Economica y Relaciones Publicas [*Villa Hermosa, Peru*] (LAA)
drr .... Doktors [*Doctor*] [*Afrikaans*]
DRR.......... Durrie [*Australia*] [*Airport symbol*] [*Obsolete*] (OAG)
DRRA .... Tessaoua [*Niger*] [*ICAO location identifier*] (ICLI)
DRRC .... Dogondoutchi [*Niger*] [*ICAO location identifier*] (ICLI)
DRRD .... Dosso [*Niger*] [*ICAO location identifier*] (ICLI)
DRRE .... Tera [*Niger*] [*ICAO location identifier*] (ICLI)
DRRG .... Gaya [*Niger*] [*ICAO location identifier*] (ICLI)
DRRI .... Bilma [*Niger*] [*ICAO location identifier*] (ICLI)
DRRL .... Tilabery [*Niger*] [*ICAO location identifier*] (ICLI)
DRRM ...... Maradi [*Niger*] [*ICAO location identifier*] (ICLI)
DRRN .... Niamey Airport [*Niger*] [*ICAO location identifier*] (ICLI)
DRRP .... La Tapoa [*Niger*] [*ICAO location identifier*] (ICLI)
DRRR .... Niamey [*Niger*] [*ICAO location identifier*] (ICLI)
DRRS........ Radio Relay Communications Duty Officer (RU)
DRRS........ State Fishing and Fish Breeding Farm (BU)
DRRSM.... Mantissa Sum Register Supplemental Digit (RU)
DRRT .... Tahoua [*Niger*] [*ICAO location identifier*] (ICLI)
DRRU .... Ouallam [*Niger*] [*ICAO location identifier*] (ICLI)
Dr RurEcon Agric ... Droit Rural et Economie Agricole [*France*] (FLAF)
DRRV .... Niamey [*Niger*] [*ICAO location identifier*] (ICLI)
DRS .... Dansk Radiologisk Selskab [*Denmark*] (SLS)
DRS .... Democratic Republic of the Sudan
DRS .... Department of Recreation and Sport [*South Australia*]
DRS .... Direction de la Restauration des Sols [*Soil Reclamation Directorate*] [*Algeria*] (AF)
DRS .... Direkcija Recnog Saobracaja [*Administration of River Transport*] (YU)
DRS .... Divisao Regional de Saude [*Regional Health Division*] [*Brazil*] (LA)
DRS .... Doktorandus [*Academic title held by men*] (IN)
Drs .... Doutores [*Doctors*] [*Portuguese*]
DRS .... Drenair [*Spain*] [*ICAO designator*] (FAAC)
DRS .... Dresden [*Germany*] [*Airport symbol*] (OAG)
DRS .... Duty Radioman (RU)
DRS .... Speed Regulator Motor (RU)
DRS .... State Fish Breeding Farm (BU)
DrSc........ Doctor Scientiae [*Doctor of Science*] (CZ)
DRSNSW ... Doctors' Reform Society of New South Wales [*Australia*]
Dr Soc .... Droit des Societes [*France*] (FLAF)
DRST........ Direction de la Recherche Scientifique-Technique [*Office of Scientific and Technical Research*] [*Guinea*] [*Research center*] (IRC)
DRT .... Darta [*France*] [*ICAO designator*] (FAAC)
DRT .... Delegacia [*or Divisao*] Regional do Trabalho [*Regional Labor Headquarters*] [*Brazil*] (LA)
DRT .... Department of Roads and Transport [*Tasmania*] [*Australia*]
DRT .... Department of Road Transport [*South Australia*] [*Australia*]
DRT .... Direction de Recherches Techniques [*Directorate of Technological Research*] [*French*] (WER)
DRT .... Division Reconnaissance Team [*Warsaw Pact forces*]
DRTA .... Darwin Region Tourism Association [*Australia*]
DRTC .... Documentation Research and Training Center [*India*] (PDAA)
d-r tekhnnauk ... Doctor of Technical Sciences (RU)
DRTPC...... Development Research and Technological Planning Center [*Egypt*] [*Research center*] (IRC)
DRTS........ Management of a Radio Wire Broadcasting Network (RU)
DRTT .... Division of Roads and Transport Technology [*Council for Scientific and Industrial Research*] [*South Africa*] (IRC)
Drt TSS ..... Droit du Travail et de la Securite Sociale [*France*] (FLAF)
DR-TV....... Danmarks Radio-Television
DR Tv-BUC ... Directia de Radio si Televiziune Bucuresti [*Bucharest Directorate for Radio and Television*] (RO)
DRU.......... Direccion Revolucionaria Unificada [*Unified Revolutionary Directorate*] [*El Salvador*] (LA)

DRU.......... Direccion Revolucionaria Unificada [*Unified Revolutionary Directorate*] [*Honduras*]   (LA)
Druckerm... Druckermarke [*Printer's Mark*] [*Publishing*] [*German*]
Druckf-V.... Druckfehlerverzeichnis [*Table of Errata*] [*German*]
DRUG-ARM ... Drug Awareness and Relief Movement [*Australia*]
DRUJAT ... Druzstvo Jatecnich Delniku [*Stockyard Workers' Cooperative*] (CZ)
druk.......... Drukarnia [*Printing Shop*]   (POL)
druk.......... Drukarski [*Printing*]   (POL)
druk.......... Drukarz [*Printer*] [*Poland*]
druk.......... Drukowano [*Printed*]   (POL)
DRUKAR .. Druzstvo Mistru Kartacnickych a Stetkarskych [*Brushmakers' Cooperative*]   (CZ)
DRUKOL.. Druzstvo Kolaru [*Wheelwrights' Cooperative*]   (CZ)
DRUO....... Dyrekcja Radiowych Urzadzen Odbiorczych [*Administration of Radio Receiving Installations*]   (POL)
DRUPEKA ... Druzstvo Pekaren [*Bakers' Cooperative*]   (CZ)
D Rur........ Droit Rural [*France*]   (FLAF)
Dr u Vrl...... Druck und Verlag [*Publisher, Printed and Published By*] [*German*]
DRV.......... Democratic Republic of Vietnam   (CL)
DRV.......... Dunantuli Rostkikeszito Vallalat [*Fiber Processing Enterprise of Dunantul*]   (HU)
DRV.......... Radikale Venstre [*Danish Social-Liberal Party*] [*Political party*] (EAIO)
DRVN....... Democratic Republic of Vietnam [*Use DRV*]   (CL)
dr-vo.......... Society, Association, Company   (BU)
DRVV .... Dunantuli Regionalis Vizmu es Vizgazdalkodasi Vallalat [*Transdanubian Regional Water Works and Water Conservation Enterprise*]   (HU)
DRW......... Darwin [*Australia*] [*Airport symbol*]   (OAG)
DRW......... Democratic Revolutionary Welfare
DRW......... Demokratyczna Republika Wietnamu [*Democratic Republic of Vietnam*] [*Poland*]
dRW......... Deutsche Reichswaehrung [*German Standard Currency*]
DRX.......... Drachma [*Monetary unit*] [*Greece*]
DRY.......... Deraya Air Taxi PT [*Indonesia*] [*ICAO designator*]   (FAAC)
dr yevr....... Hebrew, Hebraic   (RU)
DRZ.......... Dienstvorschrift Ueber das Rangierzettelverfahren [*Service Regulations on the Shunting Ticket System*]   (EG)
DRZA .... Agades-Sud [*Niger*] [*ICAO location identifier*]   (ICLI)
DRZD........ Dirkou [*Niger*] [*ICAO location identifier*]   (ICLI)
DRZG .... Goure [*Niger*] [*ICAO location identifier*]   (ICLI)
Drzh......... State   (BU)
DRZ1.......... Iferouane [*Niger*] [*ICAO location identifier*]   (ICLI)
DrzknigNRM ... Drzavno Knigoizdatelstvo na Narodna Republika Makedonija [*Government Publishing House of Macedonia*] (YU)
DRZL........ Arlit [*Niger*] [*ICAO location identifier*]   (ICLI)
DRZM....... Maine-Soroa [*Niger*] [*ICAO location identifier*]   (ICLI)
DRZN....... N'Guigmi [*Niger*] [*ICAO location identifier*]   (ICLI)
DRZR .... Zinder [*Niger*] [*ICAO location identifier*]   (ICLI)
DRZT .... Tanout [*Niger*] [*ICAO location identifier*]   (ICLI)
DS .... Additional Resistance   (RU)
DS .... Binary Counter, Binary Scaler   (RU)
DS .... Compagnie Senegalaise de Transports Aeriens [*Senegal*] [*ICAO designator*]   (ICDA)
d/s .... Dae na Sig [*Afrikaans*]
DS .... Dajnavna Sigurnost [*Bulgarian Secret Police affiliated with the KGB*]
DS .... Dal Segno [*Repeat from the Sign*] [*Music*]
DS .... Danmarks Sproglaereforening [*Denmark*]   (SLS)
ds .... Dans [*In*] [*French*]
DS .... Dansk Samling [*Danish Union*]   (PPE)
DS .... Dansk Standardiseringsrad [*Denmark*]   (SLS)
ds .... Das Sind [*That Is, Namely*] [*German*]
DS .... Datensatz [*German*]   (ADPT)
DS .... Daylight   (RU)
DS .... Decontamination Station   (RU)
DS .... DeeStone [*Thailand*] [*Commercial firm*]
DS .... Delavski Svet [*Workers' Council*]   (YU)
DS .... Delius Society   (EA)
DS .... Delphinium Society   (EA)
DS .... Delta Services [*Bahrain*]
DS .... Democracia Socialista [*Spain*] [*Political party*]   (EY)
DS .... Demokraticheska Sgovor [*Democratic Alliance*] [*Bulgaria*] [*Political party*]   (PPE)
DS .... Demokraticka Strana [*Democratic Party*] [*Former Czechoslovakia*] [*Political party*]   (PPE)
DS .... Demokratikos Sinaspismos [*Democratic Coalition*] [*Greece*] [*Political party*]   (PPE)
DS .... Demokratikos Synagermos [*Democratic Rally*] [*Greek Cyprus*] [*Political party*]   (PPE)
DS .... Demokratischer Sektor [*Democratic Sector*]   (EG)
DS .... Dendrological Society -the Tree and Conservation Society of Southern Africa   (AA)

Ds .... Deus [*God*] [*Portuguese*]
DS .... Deutscher Staedtetag [*Association of German Cities and Towns*]
DS .... Dieresorgvereniging [*South Africa*]   (AA)
DS .... Differential Selsyn   (RU)
DS .... Differential System   (RU)
DS .... Dimokratiki Synergasia [*Democratic Cooperation*]   (GC)
DS .... Dioikitikon Symvoulion [*Administrative Council*]   (GC)
DS .... Diploma de Stat [*Professional qualification*] [*Romanian*]
DS .... Direkcija za Sirovine [*Administration of Raw Materials*]   (YU)
Ds .... Disari [*Outside*]   (TU)
DS .... Divadelni Soubor [*Theater Ensemble*]   (CZ)
Ds .... Doctorat de Specialite [*French*]
Ds .... Doctorat de Specialite de Troisieme Cycle [*French*]
Ds .... Doktoratus [*Hungary*]
DS .... Dokumentation Schweisstechnik [*Welding Documentation*] [*Federal Institute for Materials Testing*] [*Information service or system*]   (IID)
DS .... Dom Studencki [*Student's Home*] [*Poland*]
DS .... DooSan Industrial Co. Ltd. [*South Korea*]
ds .... Do Spraw [*For Affairs*] [*Poland*]
DS .... Dozorci pro Spojeni [*Communications Duty Officer*]   (CZ)
DS .... Dracula Society   (EA)
DS .... Dry Dock   (RU)
DS .... Duty Communications Officer   (RU)
DS .... Duty Signalman, Duty Communications Man   (RU)
DS .... Duty Signal Officer   (BU)
DS .... Far North   (RU)
DS .... High Beam [*Vehicles*]   (RU)
DS .... House of Soviets   (RU)
DS .... Permanent Emplacement, Permanent Installation   (RU)
DS .... Signal Transmitter, Signaler   (RU)
DS .... Soviet Detergent   (RU)
DS .... Special Diesel (Fuel)   (RU)
dS .... State Security   (BU)
DS .... Synchronous Motor   (RU)
DS .... Telecommunication, Long-Distance Traffic   (RU)
DS-70........ Democratische Socialisten [*Democratic Socialist Party*] [*Right-wing party, formed in 1970*] [*Netherlands*]   (WEN)
DSA .... Career Army Service   (RU)
DSA .... Danish Shipowners' Association   (EAIO)
DSA .... Defence Science Administration [*Australia*]
DSA .... Defence Services Academy [*Myanmar*]
DSA .... Democracia Socialista Asturiana [*Asturian Socialist Democracy*] [*Spanish*]   (WER)
DSA .... Deutscher Sport-Ausschuss [*German Sports Committee*]   (EG)
DSA .... Dezentrale Systemarchitektur [*German*]   (ADPT)
DSA .... Diabetes Support Association [*Australia*]
DSA .... Dievthynsis Stratiotikou Arkheiou [*Military Archives Directorate*] [*Greek*]   (GC)
DSA .... Dikigorikos Syllogos Athinon [*Athens Bar Association*]   (GC)
DSA .... Dimokratiki Syndikalistiki Allagi [*Democratic Labor Change*] [*Greek*]   (GC)
DSA .... Diplome Superieur d'Aptitude [*French*]
DSA .... Disability Services Act [*Australia*]
DSA .... Donkey Society of Australia
DSA .... Duplex Synchronous Telegraph   (RU)
DSA .... House of the Soviet Army   (RU)
DSAA .... Dairy Shorthorn Association of Australia
DSAA .... Defense Secretary Assistance Agency
DSAA .... Direct Selling Association of Australia
DSAB........ Deutscher Sportaerztebund   (SLS)
DSAG .... Deutsch-Suedafrikanische Gesellschaft
DSAGWismut ... Deutsch-Sowjetische Aktiengesellschaft Wismut [*German-Soviet Wismut Corporation*]   (EG)
DS-AIK...... Demokratiske Sosialister - Arbeidernes Informasjon Komitte [*Democratic Socialists - Workers' Information Committee*] [*Norway*] [*Political party*]   (PPE)
DSAM .... Dansk Selskab foer Almen Medicin [*Denmark*]   (SLS)
DSAMS..... Danish Society for Ancient and Medieval Studies   (EAIO)
DSANSW ... Down Syndrome Association of New South Wales [*Australia*]
DSAP........ State Medical and Pharmaceutical Enterprise   (BU)
DSAPC...... Directia de Sistematizare, Arhitectura, si Proiectare a Constructiilor [*Directorate for Systematization, Architecture, and Construction Design*]   (RO)
DSAR........ Deutsch-Suedafrikanische Reisebuero
DSAS........ Del Shannon Appreciation Society   (EAIO)
dsau............ Battalion of Self-Propelled Guns   (RU)
DSB .... Air Senegal, Societe Nationale de Transport Aerien [*ICAO designator*]   (FAAC)
DSB .... Danske Stats Baner [*Danish State Railways*]   (WEN)
DSB .... Debit sans Brene [*Charge without Abatement*] [*French*] [*Business term*]
DSB .... Debit sans Brevet [*Debt without Writ*] [*French*] [*Legal term*]   (DLA)
DSB .... Denominational Schools Board [*Australia*]
DSB .... Department of Small Business [*Australia*]

DSB .... Deutscher Sportbund [*German Sports Association*] (EG)
DSB .... Diplomatic Services Bureau [*China*]
DSB .... Road-Building Battalion (RU)
DSB .... Wooden Dry-Cargo Barge (RU)
DSBE......... Direkcija za Suzbijanje Bujica i Erozija [*Administration of Flood and Erosion Control*] (YU)
DSBS .... Diviziona Stanica Borbenih Sredstava [*Divisional Station of Combat Supplies*] (YU)
DSBS .... Droughtmaster Stud Breeders' Society [*Australia*]
DSBSSA.... Dorper Sheep Breeders' Society of South Africa (EAIO)
DSBy......... Dansk Selskab foer Bygningsstatik [*Denmark*] (SLS)
DSC .... Danish Shippers Council (DS)
DSC .... Defense Security Command [*South Korea*]
DSC .... Defense Shipping Council [*NATO*]
DSC .... Delta Steel Co. Ltd. [*Nigeria*]
DSC .... Democracia Social Cristiana [*Social Christian Democracy*] [*Spanish*] (WER)
DSC .... Diploma of the Sydney Conservatorium of Music [*Australia*]
DSC .... Dutch Society of Cardiology (EAIO)
DSCh .... Random Numbers Transducer (RU)
DSCS .... Direct Selling Council [*Singapore*] (EAIO)
DSD .... DECHEMA [*Deutsche Gesellschaft fuer Chemisches Apparatewesen, Chemische Technik, und Biotechnologie eV*] Stoffdaten Dienst [*DECHEMA Physical Property Data Service*] [*Information service or system*] (IID)
DSD .... Dedinske Spotrebne Druzstvo [*Rural Consumer Cooperative*] (CZ)
DSD .... Differential Pressure Warning Device (RU)
DSD .... Diplomatic Service Department [*Brunei*] (DS)
DSD .... Division Medical Battalion (BU)
DSD .... Duales System Deutschland [*German recycling organization*]
DSD .... La Desirade [*Guadeloupe*] [*Airport symbol*] (OAG)
Dsdn......... Dresden (EG)
DSDP........ Deep Sea Drilling Project
DSDP........ Division Sanitary and Decontamination Station (RU)
DSDR .... State Supply and State Reserve (BU)
DSe .... Absolutely Lethal Dose (RU)
DSE .... Dacca Stock Exchange [*Bangladesh*]
DSE .... Datensystementwicklung [*Data System Development*] [*German*] (ADPT)
DSE .... Defense Scientific Establishment [*New Zealand*] (MSC)
DSE .... Departamento de Seguridad del Estado [*Department of State Security*] [*Cuba*] (LA)
DSE .... Department of School Education [*New South Wales, Victoria*] [*Australia*]
DSE .... Designated Spouse Equivalent
DSE .... Dessie [*Ethiopia*] [*Airport symbol*] (OAG)
DSE .... Detection Sequentielle d'Evenements [*French*] (ADPT)
DSE .... Deutsche Stiftung fuer Entwicklungslaender [*German Foundation for Developing Countries*] (EG)
DSE .... Dimokratikos Stratos Ellados [*Democratic Army of Greece*] (GC)
DSEB........ Defense Shipping Executive Board [*NATO*]
DSEB........ Discharged Servicemen's Employment Board [*Victoria*] [*Australia*]
DSEChA.... Dvizhenie Sotsialnoi Evoliutsii Chernoi Afriki
DSEES ...... Diethnis Synomospondia Elevtheron Ergatikon Syndikaton [*International Confederation of Free Trade Unions*] (GC)
DSEG........ Design Studies Evaluation Group [*NATO*]
DSEM........ Dutch Society for Electron Microscopy (EAIO)
DSEN .... Dimosios Skholi Emborikou Navtikou [*Public School for the Merchant Marine*] [*Greek*] (GC)
DSEN .... Directia Sistemului de Energie Natonal [*Directorate of the National Power System*] (RO)
DSER........ Road Construction and Maintenance District (RU)
ds et ht........ Dans et Hors Texte [*In and Not in the Text*] [*Publishing*] [*French*]
DSF........... Crushing and Sorting Factory (RU)
DSF........... Danmarks Skolebiblioteksforening [*Denmark*] (SLS)
DSF........... Danske Studerendes Faellesrad [*National Union of Danish Students*] (WEN)
DSF........... Dansk Fysiurgisk Selskab [*Denmark*] (SLS)
DSF........... Dansk Skattevidenskabelig Forening [*Denmark*] (SLS)
DSF........... Dansk Socialradgiverforening [*Denmark*] (SLS)
DSF........... Deutsch-Sowjetische Freundscraft [*Gesellschaft fuer*] [*German-Soviet Friendship Society*] (EG)
DSFA........ Danish Sea Fishery Association (EAIO)
DSFB .... David Syme Faculty of Business [*Chisholm Institute of Technology*] [*Australia*]
DSFL .... Dansk Selskab foer Fotogrammetri og Landmaling [*Denmark*] (SLS)
DSFN........ Democratic Union of the Finnish People (BU)
DSG .... Danish Songwriters Guild (EAIO)
DSG .... Datenschutzgesetz [*Data Protection Law*] [*German*] (ADPT)
DSG .... Democratie Socialiste de Guinee

DSG .... Deutscher Saatgut-Handelsbetrieb [*German Seed Trading Enterprise*] (EG)
DSG .... Deutscher Staedte und Gemeindebund [*League of German Towns and Local Authorities*]
DSG .... Deutsche Saatzuchtgesellschaft [*German Seed Growing Company*] (EG)
DSG .... Deutsche Schillergesellschaft eV [*German Schiller Association*] (SLS)
DSG .... Diplome Superieur de Gestion [*French*]
DSG .... Division Fuel Depot (RU)
DSGE........ Diretoria do Servico Geografico do Ministerio de Guerra [*Rio De Janeiro, Brazil*] (LAA)
dsgl............ Desgleichen [*Similar*] [*German*]
DSGM .... Director Standing Group Memorandum [*NATO*] (NATG)
DSh .... Decoder, Selector (RU)
DSh .... Detonating Cord (BU)
DSh .... Detonating Fuze (RU)
DSH........... Deutsche Sporthochschule
DSH........... Direktion des Seeverkehrs und der Hafenwirtschaft [*Ocean-Going Traffic and Port Management Directorate*] (EG)
DSh .... Staff Duty Officer (RU)
DSHC .... Defence Service Homes Corp. [*Australia*]
DShI .... Two-Motion Selector [*Telephony*] (RU)
DShK .... Instruction Decoder (RU)
DSHM .... Daewoo Shipbuilding and Heavy Machinery [*Commercial firm*] [*South Korea*]
DShS.......... Two-Motion System [*Telephony*] (RU)
DShtK .... State Personnel Commission (BU)
DShZ .... Dnepropetrovsk Tire Plant (RU)
DSI .... Children's Social Inspection (RU)
DSI .... Dairy Society International [*Santiago, Chile*] (LAA)
DSI .... Dairy Society International [*Australia*]
DSI .... Devlet Su Isleri Genel Mudurlugu [*State Hydraulic Affairs Directorate General*] [*Under Ministry of Energy and Natural Resources*] (TU)
DSI .... Diffusion Selective de l'Information [*Selective Distribution of Information*]
DSI .... Difuzare Selectiva a Informatiilor [*Selective Distribution of Information*] (RO)
DSI .... Diplome en Soins Infirmiers [*French*]
DSI .... Directia de Statistica Industriala [*Directorate of Industrial Statistics*] (RO)
DSI .... State Medical Inspectorate (BU)
DSI .... State Stenographic Institute (BU)
DSIC.......... Documentation and Scientific Information Centre [*National Council for Scientific Research*] [*Zambia*]
DSICA ...... Distilled Spirits Industry Council of Australia
DSIE.......... Deutsche Stiftung fur Internationale Entwicklung [*German Foundation for International Development*] (EAIO)
DSIM........ Dansk Selskab foer Intern Medicine [*Denmark*] (SLS)
DSIP.......... Drzavni Sekretarijat za Inostrane Poslove [*State Secretariat for Foreign Affairs*] (YU)
DSIR......... Department of Scientific and Industrial Research [*New Zealand*]
DSITJ........ Drustvo Sumarskih Inzenjera i Tehnicara Jugoslavije [*Society of Forestry Engineers and Technicians of Yugoslavia*] (YU)
DSIYB .... Devlet Sanayi ve Isci Yatirim Bankasi [*State Industry and Worker Investment Bank*] (TU)
DSJ .... Dunav Sava Jadran [*Danube Sava Adriatic*] (YU)
DSJG........ Dutch Society for Jewish Genealogy (EAIO)
DSJRFC.... Danish Society for Jazz, Rock, and Folk Composers (EAIO)
DSK .... Dacha-Building Cooperative (RU)
DSK .... Daur Schutzluft Klimasystem [*German*]
DSK .... Demokratikon Sosialistikon Komma [*Democratic Socialist Party*] [*Greece*] [*Political party*] (PPE)
DSK .... Demokratski Savez Kosovo [*Democratic Alliance of Kosovo*] [*Serbia*] [*Political party*] (EY)
DSK .... Dera Ismail Khan [*Pakistan*] [*Airport symbol*] (OAG)
DSK .... Diak Sport Kozpont [*Students' Sport Center*] (HU)
DSK .... Dimokratikon Syndikalistikon Kinima [*Democratic Labor Movement*] [*Greek*] (GC)
DSK .... Dokumentacni Stredisko Ceskoslovenskych Zavodu Kovodelnych a Strojirenskych [*Documentation Center of the Czechoslovak Metalworking and Machine-Building Plants*] (CZ)
DSK .... Drustvo Slovenskih Knjizevnikov [*Society of Slovenian Writers*] (YU)
DSK .... House-Building Kombinat (RU)
DSK .... House of Sanitary Culture (RU)
DSK .... State Savings Bank (BU)
d s-kh n ..... Doctor of Agricultural Sciences (RU)
DSL........... Collapsible Landing Boat (RU)
DSL........... Defence Science Laboratory [*India*] (PDAA)
DSL........... Defence Standards Laboratory [*Australia*] (PDAA)
dsl.............. Deleslouzici [*Reenlistee*] (CZ)
DSL........... Department of Supply Laboratories [*Australia*]
DSL........... Det Danske Sprog- og Litteraturselskab [*Denmark*] (SLS)

DSL........... Deutsche Siedlungs- und Landesrentenbank [*Bank/financial institution*]

ds le t......... Dans le Texte [*In the Text*] [*Publishing*] [*French*]

DSLP......... Danish Social-Liberal Party [*Political party*]   (EAIO)

DSLV......... Deutscher Sportlehrerverband eV [*German Sport Teachers Association*]   (SLS)

DSM .... Dansk Selskab for Musikforskning [*Danish Musicological Society*]   (EAIO)

DSM .... Dar Es Salaam [*Tanzania*]

DSM .... Dermatological Society of Malaysia   (EAIO)

DSM .... Dimokratikon Syndikalistikon Metopon [*Democratic Labor Front*]   (GC)

DSM .... Direction de la Securite Militaire [*Directorate of Military Security*] [*French*]   (WER)

DSM .... Divisao de Sementes e Mudas [*Brazil*]   (DSCA)

DSM .... Division of Survey and Mapping [*Victoria, Australia*]

DSM .... State Alcohol Monopoly   (BU)

DSM .... Ten-Key Adding Machine   (RU)

DSMA .... Desarrollo del Sur de Monagas y Anzoategui [*Development of South Monagas and Anzoategui*] [*Venezuela*]   (LA)

DSMK .... Democratic Youth League of Korea [*North Korean*]   (RU)

DSML....... Delft Soil Mechanics Laboratory

DSMO .... State Construction and Installation Trust   (BU)

DSN .... Datensatzname [*German*]   (ADPT)

DSN .... Division First Aid Kit   (RU)

DSN .... Dodecyl Sodium Sulfate   (RU)

DSNED ..... Dimokratikos Syndesmos Neon Epistimonon kai Dianooumenon [*Democratic Association of Young Professionals and Intellectuals*] [*Greek*]   (GC)

DSNF........ Democratic Union of the People of Finland   (RU)

DSNF........ Disjunctive Perfect Normal Form   (RU)

DSNKh...... Don Council of the National Economy   (RU)

DSNM....... Dimitrovski Suiuz na Narodnata Mladesh [*Dimitrov Union of People's Youth*] [*Bulgarian*]

DSNO .... Diakyvernitikos Symvoulevtikos Navtiliakos Organismos [*Intergovernmental Maritime Consultative Organization*]   (GC)

DSNO .... Drzavni Sekretarijat Narodne Odbrane [*State Secretariat for National Defense*]   (YU)

DSNSW..... Deaf Society of New South Wales [*Australia*]

DSNT .... Demokraticheskii Soiuz Naseleniia Togo

DSO.......... Dansk Selskab foer Optometri [*Denmark*]   (SLS)

DSO .... Democratic Students' Organization

DSO .... Diakyvernitikos Symvoulevtikos Organismos [*Intergovernmental Maritime Consultative Organization*]   (GC)

DSO.......... Differential System with Amplitude Limiter   (RU)

DSO.......... Dunya Saglik Orgutu [*World Health Organization - WHO*]   (TU)

DSO.......... Road-Building Department   (RU)

DSO.......... State Construction Trust   (BU)

DSO.......... State Economic Trust   (BU)

DSO.......... State Sports Organization   (BU)

DSO.......... State Symphony Orchestra   (BU)

DSO.......... Voluntary Civil Defense   (BU)

DSO........... Voluntary Sports Organization   (BU)

DSO.......... Voluntary Sports Society   (RU)

D Soc........ Droit Social [*France*]   (FLAF)

DSOM .... Dansk Selskab foer Oldtids- og Middelalderforskning [*Denmark*]   (SLS)

DSOMS..... State Construction Trusts of the Ministry of Construction   (BU)

DSOSokol ... Dobrovolna Sportovni Organisace Sokol [*Sokol Athletic Organization*]   (CZ)

DSOV .... Dansk Selskab foer Opvarmnings- og Ventilationsteknik [*Denmark*]   (SLS)

DSP........... Control Panel of the Station Master on Duty [*Railroads*]   (RU)

DSP........... Datenspeicher [*German*]   (ADPT)

DSP........... Datensystemplanung [*Data System Plan*] [*German*]   (ADPT)

DSP........... Deadly Serious Party of Australia

DSP........... Democratic Left Party [*Turkey*] [*Political party*]   (EAIO)

DSP........... Democratic Socialist Party [*Japan*] [*Political party*]   (PPW)

DSP........... Democratic Socialist Party [*South Korea*] [*Political party*]   (PPW)

DSP........... Democratic Socialist Party [*Ireland*] [*Political party*]   (PPW)

DSP........... Democratic Socialist Party [*Australia*] [*Political party*]

DSP........... Democratic Socialist Party [*India*] [*Political party*]   (PPW)

DSP........... Deutsche Sex Partei [*German*] [*Political party*]

DSP........... Dimokratiki Sosialistiki Parataxi [*Democratic Socialist Faction*]   (GC)

DSP........... Direccion de Salud Pecuaria [*Ecuador*]   (DSCA)

DSP........... Direccion de Seguridad Personal [*Directorate of Personal Security*] [*Cuba*]   (LA)

DSP........... Direction Active de la Securite Publique [*Directorate of Public Security*] [*French*]   (WER)

DSP........... Disability Services Program [*Australia*]

DSP........... Disadvantaged Schools Program [*Australia*]

DSp........... Doctorat Special [*French*]

DSP........... Dom Slowa Polskiego [*Polish Publication and Press Institute*] [*Poland*]

DSP........... Druzstevna Skola Prace [*Agricultural Training School*]   (CZ)

DSP........... Duty Station Master [*Railroads*]   (RU)

DSP........... Duty Switchman [*Railroads*]   (RU)

DSP........... For Official Use   (RU)

DSP........... Individual Decontamination Kit   (RU)

DSP........... Le Droit au Service de la Paix [*Belgium*]   (FLAF)

DSP........... State Construction Enterprise   (BU)

DSP........... State Economic Enterprise   (BU)

DSP........... State Supply Enterprise   (BU)

DSP........... Wood Laminate   (RU)

DspC......... Deputazione di Storia Patria per la Calabria [*Italian*]   (SLS)

DSPF .... Drzavni Sekretarijat za Poslove Finansija [*State Secretariat for Finance*]   (YU)

DSPNO ..... Drzavni Sekretarijat za Poslove Narodne Odbrane [*State Secretariat for National Defense*]   (YU)

DSPNOUIJNA ... Drzavni Sekretarijat za Poslove Narodne Odbrane, Uprava Inzenjerije, Jugoslovenska Narodna Armija [*State Secretariat for National Defense, Administration of Engineer Corps, Yugoslav People's Army*]   (YU)

DSPRP ...... Drzavni Sekretarijat za Poslove Robnog Prometa [*State Secretariat for Trade*]   (YU)

DSPU........ Drzavni Sekretarijat za Pravosodno Upravo [*State Secretariat for the Judiciary*]   (YU)

DSPULRS ... Drzavni Sekretarijat za Pravosodno Upravo Ljudska Republika Slovenija [*State Secretariat for the Judiciary of Slovenia*]   (YU)

DSPV........ Division Prisoner-of-War Collecting Point   (RU)

DSP"Zemsnab" ... State Economic Enterprise for Compulsory Grain Delivery   (BU)

DSQ .... Deaf Society, Queensland [*Australia*]

DSQ .... Diplome de Specialiste Qualifie [*French*]

DSR .... Dairo Air Services Ltd. [*Uganda*] [*ICAO designator*]   (FAAC)

DSR .... Datensammelrechner [*German*]   (ADPT)

DSR .... Department of Sport and Recreation [*Victoria, Australia*]

DSR .... Deutsche Seereederei Rostock [*German Maritime Shipping Company, Rostock*]   (EG)

DSR .... Direzione Studi e Ricerche [*Research and Development Department*] [*Italian Electricity Board*]   (WED)

DSR .... Road-Building District   (RU)

DSRA........ Danish Squash Rackets Association   (EAIO)

DSRC........ Development Studies and Research Centre

DSRF .... Drzaven Sekretarijat za Raboti na Finansite [*State Secretariat for Finance*]   (YU)

DSRI........ Danish Space Research Institute [*Dansk Rumforskningsinstitut*] [*Ministry of Education*]   (EAS)

DSRK........ DDR [*Deutsche Demokratische Republik*] Schiffsrevision und -Klassifikation [*GDR Ship Inspection and Classification Agency*]   (EG)

DSRK........ Deutsche Schiffs Revision und Klassifikation [*German ship classification society*]   (DS)

DSRP .... Democratic and Social Republican Party [*Mauritania*] [*Political party*]   (EY)

DSRV........ Deep Submergence Rescue Vehicle

DSS.......... Datensichtstation [*German*]   (ADPT)

DSS.......... Decision Support Services Program [*Australia*]

DSS.......... Department of State Services [*Western Australia*] [*Australia*]

DSS.......... Dermatological Society of Singapore   (EAIO)

DSS.......... Dokuristsu Seinen Sha [*Independent Youth Society*] [*Japan*]

DSS.......... Drustvo Slovenskih Skladateljev [*Society of Slovenian Composers*]   (YU)

DSS.......... Drustvo Srpske Slovesnosti [*Society of Serbian Literature*]   (YU)

DSS.......... Druzyna Sluzby Socjalistycznej [*Socialist Service Team*]   (POL)

DSS........... State Seed Growing Farm   (BU)

DSSA........ Development Society of Southern Africa   (EAIO)

Dssa .... Dottoressa [*Female Doctor*] [*Italian*]

Dsse .... Duchesse [*Duchess*] [*French*]   (MTD)

DSSh......... Children's Sports School   (RU)

DSSO........ Voluntary Rural Sports Society   (RU)

DSSV........ Deutscher Schwimmsport-Verband [*German Swimming League*]   (EG)

DSSV........ Deutschschweizerischer Sprachverein [*German Swiss Society*]   (SLS)

DST .... Datenstation [*German*]   (ADPT)

DST .... Day Construction Technicum   (RU)

dst.............. Decistere [*French*]   (FLAF)

dst.............. Decistereo [*Portuguese*]

DST .... Departement des Statistiques de Transport [*Transportation Statistics Department*] [*of the SAEI*] [*French*]   (WER)

DST .... Deutsche Schuchtbau- and Tiefbohr GmbH

DST .... Devrimci Sanat Tiyatrosu [*Revolutionary Fine Arts Theatre*] [*Turkish Federated State of Cyprus*]   (GC)

DST .... Diethylstilbestrol   (RU)

DST .... Direction de la Surveillance du Territoire [*Directorate of Territorial Surveillance*] [*France*]

388   **International Acronyms, Initialisms & Abbreviations Dictionary ● 4th Edition**

DST .... Diretoria dos Servicos de Transito [*Traffic Services Administration*] [*Brazil*] (LA)

DST .... Dom Srodowisk Tworczych [*House of Creative Art Associations*] (POL)

dst.............. Dore sur tranches [*With Gilt Edges*] [*Publishing*] [*French*]

DST .... La Direction de la Securite du Territoire [*Directorate of Territorial Security*] [*France*]

DSTB........ Danmarks Statistiks TidsseriedataBank [*Denmark*] [*Information service or system*] (CRD)

DStG .... Deutsche Statistische Gesellschaft [*German Statistical Society*] (SLS)

Dstg............ Dienstgutzug [*Local Service Freight Train*] (EG)

DST I........ Daerah Swatantra Tingkat I [*See DASWATI I*] (IN)

DST II....... Daerah Swatantra Tingkat II [*See DASWATI II*] (IN)

DSTO .... Defence Science and Technology Organisation [*Australia*]

DSTO .... Defence Science and Technology Organization [*Australia*] [*Research center*] (IRC)

Dstp .... Dienstpersonen-Zug [*Service Personnel Train*] (EG)

DSTS........ Dansk Selskab foer Teoretisk Statistik [*Denmark*] (SLS)

DSTU .... Drzavno Sredno Tehnicko Uciliste [*State Secondary Technical School*] (YU)

DSTV........ Deutscher Stahlbau-Verband [*German Steel Girder Construction Association*] (SLS)

DSU .... Children's Self-Government (RU)

DSU .... Danish Shooting Union (EAIO)

DSU .... Danish Skating Union (EAIO)

DSU .... Danmarks Social-Demokratisk Ungdom [*Denmark's Social Democratic Youth*] (WEN)

DSU .... Democratic and Social Union [*Mauritania*] [*Political party*] (EY)

DSU .... Deutscher Schiffahrts- und Umschlagbetrieb [*German Water Transport and Transshipping Enterprise*] (EG)

DSU .... Deutsche Soziale Union [*German Social Union*] (PPW)

DSU .... Diagnostic Scintillation Unit (RU)

DSU .... Differentiating Smoothing Device (RU)

DSU .... Druzstvo Spojenych Umelcu Divadelnich a Filmovych [*Joint Association of Theater and Motion Picture Artists*] (CZ)

DSU .... Drzavni Statisticki Ured [*State Statistical Office*] (YU)

DSU .... State Construction Administration (BU)

DSUPFNRJ ... Drzavni Sekretarijat za Unutrasnje Poslove Federativna Narodna Republika Jugoslavija [*State Secretariat for Internal Affairs of Yugoslavia*] (YU)

DSUPNRBiH ... Drzavni Sekretarijat za Unutrasnje Poslove Narodne Republike Bosne i Hercegovine [*State Secretariat for Internal Affairs of the People's Republic of Bosnia and Hercegovina*] (YU)

DSV .... Datensofortverarbeitung [*German*] (ADPT)

DSV .... Deutscher Schriftstellerverband [*German Writers' Union*] (EG)

DSV .... Deutscher Ski-Verband [*German Ski Union*] (EAIO)

DSV .... Deutscher Sportverband [*German Sports Union*] (EG)

DSV .... Duty Communication Officer [*or Noncommissioned Officer*] (BU)

DSVN .... Duong Sat Viet-Nam [*Vietnam Railway Central Department*] (FEA)

DSVR........ Drzaven Sekretarijat za Vnutrasnji Raboti [*State Secretariat for Internal Affairs*] (YU)

DSVTI ...... Division Materiel Depot (RU)

DSW .... Deutsche Solvay-Werke [*German Solvay Works*] (EG)

DSW .... Dom Sprzedazy Wysylkowej [*Mail Order House (Lodz)*] (POL)

DSWD .... Department of Social Welfare and Development [*Philippines*]

DSZ .... House of Socialist Agriculture (RU)

DSZAI....... Demokraticheskii Soiuz Zashchity Afrikanskikh Interesov

DSZE........ Dunantuli Szojatermelesi Egyutt-Mukodes [*Transdanubian Soya Bean Growing Cooperation*] (HU)

DSZPNP ... Drzavni Sekretarijat za Poslove Narodne Privrede [*State Secretariat for National Economic Affairs*] (YU)

DSZT........ Dorogi Szenbanyaszati Troszst [*Coal Mining Trust of Dorog*] (HU)

DSZTP ...... Delavski Svet, Zeleznisko Transportno Podjetje [*Workers' Council, Railroad Transport Establishment*] (YU)

DT.............. Danmarks Turistrad [*Denmark*] (EAIO)

dt................ Dan Thai Co. Ltd. [*Thailand*]

DT.............. Datentraeger [*German*] (ADPT)

Dt .... Dato (ML)

Dt .... Debit [*or Debiteur*] [*Debit or Debtor*]

DT.............. Degtyarev Tank (Machine Gun) (RU)

DT.............. Delovodski Tehnikum [*Technology for Foremen*] (YU)

DT.............. Demande de Transfer [*French*] (ADPT)

DT.............. Deputies of the Working People (BU)

dt................ Derleme Tarihi [*Date Assembled or Collected*] (TU)

DT.............. Desetinne Trideni [*Decimal Classification System*] (CZ)

dt................ Deutsch [*German*] [*German*]

DT.............. Deutsche Tieraerzteschaft eV [*German Veterinary Association*] (SLS)

Dt .... Dezitonne [*Deciton*] [*100 kilograms (of grain)*] (EG)

DT.............. Diesel Fuel, Diesel Tractor (RU)

DT.............. Dinar Tunisien

DT.............. Diplomatic Corps (BU)

DT.............. Diplome Technique [*French*]

DT.............. Direktni Teretni Vlak [*Direct Freight Train*] (YU)

Dt .... Dis Tabibi [*Dentist*] (TU)

DT.............. Diversional Therapist [*Australia*]

DT.............. Docklands Taskforce [*Victoria*] [*Australia*]

DT.............. Doit [*Debit*] [*French*]

DT.............. Droit de Timbre [*Stamp Duty*] [*Cambodia*] (CL)

DT.............. Fuel-Supply Motor (RU)

dt................ Gas-Expansion Machine (RU)

DT.............. Hybrid Transformer, Hybrid Coil [*Telephony*] (RU)

DT.............. Labor Directorate (BU)

DT.............. TAAG Linhas Aereas de Angola [*Angola*] [*ICAO designator*] (ICDA)

DT.............. Temperature Transmitter, Temperature Gauge, Temperature-Sensing Element (RU)

DTA .... Dakka Tourist Agency [*Israel*]

DTA .... Dar Tadine Al-Umma [*Mining company*] [*Sierra Leone*]

DTA .... Democratic Turnhalle Alliance [*Namibia*] [*Political party*] (EY)

DTA .... Demokratiese Turnhalle Alliansie [*Democratic Turnhalle Alliance*] [*Namibia*] (AF)

DTA .... Diagnosetestablauf [*German*] (ADPT)

DTA .... Diethnis Tameion Anaptyxeos [*International Development Fund*] (GC)

DTA .... Diethnis Trapeza Anasyngrotiseos [*International Bank for Reconstruction and Development*] [*DTAA*] [*See also*] (GC)

DTA .... Differential Thermal Analysis (BU)

DTA .... Direccao dos Transportes Aereos [*Air Transport Directorate*] [*Angola*] (AF)

DTA .... Divisao de Transportes Aereos

DTA .... Double Taxation Agreement [*Australia*]

DTA .... Drug Testing Authority [*Australia*]

DTA .... Drzavna Trgovacka Akademija [*State Commercial Academy*] (YU)

DTA .... Dynameis Takheias Anaptyxeos [*Rapid Deployment Forces*] [*KAD, MMAD*] [*See also*] (GC)

DTA .... TAAG, Linhas Aereas de Angola [*ICAO designator*] (FAAC)

DTAA .... Diethnis Trapeza Anasyngrotiseos kai Anaptyxeos [*International Bank for Reconstruction and Development*] [*DTA*] [*See also*] (GC)

DTAA .... Diversional Therapy Association of Australia

DTAA .... Divisao de Tecnologia Agricola e Alimentar [*Brazil*] (DSCA)

DTAFE...... Department of Technical and Further Education [*Australia*]

DTAS........ Division of Tropical Animal Science [*Australia*]

DTAT .... Direction Technique des Armements Terrestres [*Technical Board of Land Armaments*] [*Ministry of the Army*] [*France*] (PDAA)

DTB .... Danish Tourist Board (EAIO)

DTB .... Danmarks Tekniske Bibliotek [*National Technological Library of Denmark*] [*Information service or system*] (IID)

DTB .... Denkmaeler der Tonkunst in Bayern [*German*]

DTB .... Deutsche Terminboerse [*Derivatives market*] [*Germany*]

DTB .... Dividend- en Tantiemebelasting [*Benelux*] (BAS)

DTB .... Dogan Turk Birligi [*Arising Turkish Union*] [*Soccer team Turkish Cypriot*] (GC)

DTB .... Dominica Tourist Board (EAIO)

DTC .... Danish Terrier Club (EAIO)

DTC .... Darwin Turf Club [*Australia*]

DTC .... Department of Transport and Construction [*Australia*]

DTC .... Deposit-Taking Company [*Generic term that originated in Hong Kong*]

DTC .... Deposit-Taking Cooperative [*Bank*] [*Malaysia*]

DTC .... Development Technology Center [*Indonesian*]

DTC .... Devonport Technical College [*Australia*] (ADA)

DTC .... Dhofar Transport Co. [*Oman*]

DTC .... Diplome de Technicien de Laboratoire [*French*]

DTC .... Direct Trading Co. [*Thailand*] (DS)

DTC .... Document de Transport Combine [*Combined Transport Document*] [*French*] [*Business term*]

DTC .... Documento de Transporte Combinado [*Combined Transport Document*] [*Spanish*] [*Business term*]

DTC .... Documento di Trasporto Combinato [*Combined Transport Document*] [*Italian*] [*Business term*]

DTCA .... Defense Terrestre Contre Avions [*French*]

DTCA .... Direction Technique des Constructions Aeronautiques [*Directorate for Technical Aeronautical Construction*] [*French*] (WER)

DTCF........ Ankara Universitesi Dil ve Tarih-Cografya Fakultesi [*Faculty of Language and History-Geography of Ankara University*] (TU)

DTCh......... Two-Tone Frequency Telegraphy (RU)

DTCN........ Direction Technique de Construction Navale [*Technical Directorate for Naval Construction*] [*French*] (WER)

DTCN........ Direction Technique des Constructions Navales [*French naval design bureau*] (DOMA)

DTC(STC) ... Deaf Teachers Certificate (Sydney Teachers College) [*Australia*]

DTD.......... Dekorasie voor Trouwe Dienst [*Decoration for Devoted Service*] [*Netherlands*]
DTD.......... Departement Tegniese Dienste [*Council for Scientific and Industrial Research*] [*South Africa*] (AA)
dtD............. Des Technischen Dienstes [*German*]
DTD.......... Dunav-Tisa-Dunav (Kanal) [*Danube-Tisza-Danube (Canal)*] [*Vojvodina*] (YU)
D-T-D........ Money-Commodity-Money (RU)
DTDT........ David Taylor Dance Theatre
DTE.......... Departamento de Trabajadores Estatales [*Department of Government Workers*] [*Uruguay*] (LA)
DTE.......... Deutsche Telemecanique GmbH [*German*] (ADPT)
DTE.......... Direction Technique des Engins [*Missile Technology Directorate*] [*French*] (WER)
DTE.......... Tamas Darida Enterprise [*Hungary*] [*ICAO designator*] (FAAC)
DTEC........ Department of Technical and Economic Cooperation [*Thailand*] (DS)
DTEP........ Democratic Tradition Education Project [*Australia*]
DTEV........ Deutsche Telecom eV [*Germany*] [*Telecommunications*]
DTEVT...... Department of Technical Education and Vocational Training [*Zambia*] (AF)
DTF.......... Dansk Tandlaegeforening [*Denmark*] (SLS)
DTF.......... Dansk Tele Forbund [*Denmark*] (EAIO)
DTF.......... Department of Treasury and Finance [*Australia*]
DTF.......... Dessolo Traore Freres
DTF.......... Disabilities Task Force [*Australia*]
DTG.......... Deutsche Togo Gesellschaft
DTG.......... Deutsche Tropenmedizinische Gesellschaft eV [*German Tropical Medicine Association*] (SLS)
DTGM...... Devlet Tiyatrosu Genel Mudurlugu [*State Theatre Directorate General*] (TU)
D Th.......... Der Theorie [*Of the Theory*] [*German*] (GCA)
DTH.......... Dom Techniczno-Handlowy [*Engineering Trade House*] (POL)
DTH Ith..... Dis Ticaret Hacmi ve Ithalat [*Foreign Trade Volume and Imports*] [*Turkish*] (TU)
DThKM..... Dievthynsis Thalassion Kratikon Metaforon [*State Maritime Transport Directorate*] [*Greek*] (GC)
DThM........ Dievthynsis Thalassion Metaforon [*Maritime Transport Administration*] [*Greek*] (GC)
DTI.......... Danish Telecom International
DTI.......... Dansk Textil Institut [*Danish Textile Institute*] [*Research center*] (IRC)
DTI.......... Data Team International (ADPT)
DTI.......... Departamento Tecnico de Investigaciones [*Technical Investigation Department*] [*Cuba*] (LA)
DTI.......... State Trade Inspectorate (BU)
DTIA........ Direction Technique et Industrielle de l'Aeronautique [*Aeronautics Technical-Industrial Directorate*] [*French*] (WER)
DTICA...... Departamento Tecnico Interamericano de Cooperacion Agricola (LAA)
DTIH........ Deutsche Togolandische Industrie und Handelgesellschaft GmbH
DTIP........ Departamento do Trabalho Ideologico do Partido [*Department of Party Ideological Propaganda*] [*Mozambique*] (AF)
DTJ.......... Delnicka Telocvicna Jednota [*Workers' Gymnastic Association*] (CZ)
DTK.......... Dansk Terrier Klub [*Denmark*] (EAIO)
DTK.......... Motor Torpedo Boat Division (RU)
DTK.......... State Textile Combine (BU)
DTK.......... State Tobacco Combine (BU)
DTK.......... State Weaving Combine (BU)
DTKA........ Battalion of Torpedo Boats [*PT boats*] (BU)
dtka.......... Motor Torpedo Boat Division (RU)
DTL.......... Dansk Teknisk Laererforening [*Denmark*] (SLS)
DTLG........ Department of Territories and Local Government [*Australia*]
DTLS........ Diode-Transformer Logical Circuit (RU)
DTM.......... Deutsche Tourenwagen Meisterschaft [*German Touring Car Championship*]
DTM.......... Diploma in Tropical Medicine
DTM.......... Ditolylmethane (RU)
DTM.......... Dortmund [*Germany*] [*Airport symbol*] (OAG)
DTM.......... Druhotne Tezebni Metody [*Secondary Mining Methods*] (CZ)
DTM.......... Duplex Morse Telegraphy (RU)
DTM.......... State Tobacco Monopoly (BU)
DTMB...... Monastir/Habib Bourgiba [*Tunisia*] [*ICAO location identifier*] (ICLI)
DTMS........ Desk Top Marketing System [*Australia*]
dtn.............. Desitonni(a) [*Finland*]
dtn.............. Doctor of Technical Sciences (RU)
DTNW....... Deutsches Textilforschungszentrum Nord-West eV [*German Textile Research Center Northwest*] [*Research center*] (IRC)
DTO.......... Dansk Teknisk Oplysningstjeneste [*Danish Technical Information Service*] (PDAA)
DTO.......... Denkmaeler der Tonkunst in Oesterreich [*German*]
dto.............. Descuento [*Discount*] [*Spanish*]

DTO.......... Drustvo za Telesni Odgoj [*Physical Education Society*] (YU)
DTO.......... Road Transportation Department (RU)
DTO.......... State Commercial Trust (BU)
DTO.......... Streetcars and Lighting Directorate (BU)
DTOX-TNO ... Dwarsverband Toxicologie, Nederlands Centrale Organisatie voor Toegepast-Natuurwetenschappelijk Onderzoek [*Toxicology, Netherlands Central Organization for Applied Natural Scientific Research*] [*Netherlands*] (ARC)
DTP.......... State Commercial Enterprise (BU)
DTPA........ Diethylenetriaminopentaacetic Acid (RU)
DTPK........ Diethylenetriaminopentaacetic Acid (RU)
DTPNarmag ... "People's Store" State Commercial Enterprise (BU)
DTPP........ State Tourist Passenger Shipping Administration (BU)
DTR.......... Danish Air Transport [*ICAO designator*] (FAAC)
DTR.......... Domaca Tvornica Rublja [*Underclothing Manufacturer*] [*Zagreb*] (YU)
DTR.......... Druzina Tipografskih Radenika [*Society of Typographers*] (YU)
DTR.......... Long-Distance Tropospheric Propagation (RU)
DTRD........ Ducted-Fan Turbine Engine, Turbo-Fan (RU)
DTREO..... Departement des Travaux, Recherches, et Exploitation Oceaniques [*French*] (ASF)
DTRI.......... Dairy Training and Research Institute [*Philippines*] (ARC)
DTRT........ Duna-Tenger Hajozasi Reszvenytarsasag [*Danube-Ocean Navigation Company Limited (Prewar)*] (HU)
DTRU........ Demographic Training and Research Unit [*Sri Lanka*] [*Research center*] (IRC)
DTs............ Cement Batcher (RU)
DTs............ Deoxycytidine (RU)
DTs............ Differentiating Circuit (RU)
DTS.......... Diplome de Technicien Superieur [*French*]
DTs............ Direction des Travaux et Services [*North African*]
DTs............ Dispatcher Center (BU)
DTs............ Dispatcher Controlled Signals, Central Traffic Control, Centralized Dispatching Control [*Railroads*] (RU)
DTS.......... Divadlo Tesinskeho Slezska [*Silesian (Tesin Area) Theater*] (CZ)
DTS.......... Diviziska Triazna Stanica [*Divisional Discarding Station*] [*Military*] (YU)
DTS.......... Droits de Tirage Special [*Special Drawing Rights*] [*Use SDR*] (AF)
DTS.......... Road Transportation Council (RU)
DTS.......... Road Transportation Service (RU)
DTS.......... Twin-Arc Welding Tractor (RU)
DTSB........ Deutscher Turn- und Sportbund [*German Gymnastics and Sports Federation*] (EG)
dtsch.......... Deutsch [*German*] (EG)
DTsDA....... Dicyandiamide, Dicyanodiamide (RU)
DTS GK..... Mixture of Three Parts of Calcium Hypochlorite and Two Parts of Calcium Hydroxide [*A*] [*Decontaminant*] (RU)
DTSh........ State Theater School (BU)
DTShch ..... Minesweeper Division (RU)
DTsIK........ Central Executive Committee of Dagestan ASSR (RU)
DTsK .... State Cement Combine (BU)
D-Ts/ka ..... Debit Account (BU)
DTSR........ Department of Tourism, Sport, and Racing [*Queensland*] [*Australia*]
DTSR........ Department of Tourism, Sport, and Recreation [*Tasmania*] [*Australia*]
DTSS........ Diplome de Technicien Superieur de la Sante [*French*]
DTsV........ Decimetric Waves (RU)
DTsZ........ State Cement Plant (BU)
DTTA........ Tunis/Carthage [*Tunisia*] [*ICAO location identifier*] (ICLI)
DTTAB...... Vaccin Antityphoidique et Antiparatyphoidique A et B, Antidiphterique et Tetanique [*French*]
DTTB........ Bizerte/Sidi Ahmed [*Tunisia*] [*ICAO location identifier*] (ICLI)
DTTC........ Tunis [*Tunisia*] [*ICAO location identifier*] (ICLI)
DTTD........ Remada [*Tunisia*] [*ICAO location identifier*] (ICLI)
DTTF........ Gafsa [*Tunisia*] [*ICAO location identifier*] (ICLI)
DTTG........ Gabes [*Tunisia*] [*ICAO location identifier*] (ICLI)
DTTI.......... Bordj El Amri [*Tunisia*] [*ICAO location identifier*] (ICLI)
DTTJ........ Jerba/Zarzis [*Tunisia*] [*ICAO location identifier*] (ICLI)
DTTK........ Kairouan [*Tunisia*] [*ICAO location identifier*] (ICLI)
DTTL........ Kelibia [*Tunisia*] [*ICAO location identifier*] (ICLI)
DTTN........ Jendouba [*Tunisia*] [*ICAO location identifier*] (ICLI)
DTTR........ El Borma [*Tunisia*] [*ICAO location identifier*] (ICLI)
DTTV........ Deutscher Tischtennis-Verband [*German Table-Tennis League*] (EG)
DTTV........ Tunis [*Tunisia*] [*ICAO location identifier*] (ICLI)
DTTX........ Sfax/El Maou [*Tunisia*] [*ICAO location identifier*] (ICLI)
DTTZ........ Tozeur/Nefta [*Tunisia*] [*ICAO location identifier*] (ICLI)
DTU.......... Dominica Trade Union
DTU.......... Doppler Trigger Unit [*Australia*]
DTU.......... Dorozhno-Transportnyy Upravleniye [*Road and Transportation Directorate*] [*Former USSR*] (LAIN)
DTU.......... Road Transportation Administration (RU)
DTuV........ Deutscher Turn-Verband [*German Gymnastics League*] (EG)

DTV .... Deutscher Taschenbuch Verlag [*German trade publisher's cooperative*]
DTV .... Deutsche Treuhand-Verwaltung [*German Trusteeship Administration*] (EG)
DTV .... Doppler Test Vehicle [*Australia*]
DTV .... Drustvo za Telesno Vaspitanje [*Physical Education Society*] (YU)
DTVF .... Danmarks Teknisk-Videnskabelige Forskningsrad [*Danish Council for Technical and Scientific Research*] (WEN)
DTVS .... Dny Telesne Vychovy a Sportu [*Physical Education and Sport Days*] (CZ)
dt v sl .... Active Military Service (BU)
DTW .... Department of Transport and Works [*Northern Territory*] [*Australia*]
DTX .... Deltex [*Slovakia*] [*ICAO designator*] (FAAC)
DTYN .... Dievthynsis Tekhnikis Ypiresias Nomou [*Directorate of the Technical Services of the Nome*] [*Followed by initial letter of the nome*] (GC)
DTZ .... Drustvo Tehnike Zavarivanja [*Society of Welding Technology*] (YU)
Dtz............ Dutzend [*Dozen*] [*German*] (EG)
Dtzd........... Dutzend [*Dozen*] [*German*] (GPO)
DU .... Additional Amplifier, Booster (RU)
DU .... Deakin University [*Australia*]
DU .... Decoder (RU)
DU .... Defensa Universitaria [*University Defense*] [*Spanish*] (WER)
DU .... Delostrelecke Uciliste [*Artillery Training Center*] (CZ)
du .... Delutan [*After Noon*] [*Hungary*] (GPO)
DU .... Demokratisk Ungdom [*Democratic Youth*] [*Sweden*] (WEN)
DU .... Deutsche Union [*German Union*] (EG)
DU .... Devisa Umum [*General Exchange*] [*Indonesia*] (IMH)
DU .... Dienste in Uebersee Arbeitsgemeinschaft Evangelischer Kirchen in Deutschland [*Germany*] (EAIO)
du .... Dienstuntauglich [*Unfit for Military Service*] [*German*]
DU .... Differential Amplifier (RU)
DU .... Direccion Unificada [*Unified Directorate*] [*El Salvador*] (LA)
DU .... Disciplinary Regulations (of the Armed Forces of the USSR) (RU)
DU .... Dispatch Control Unit (RU)
DU .... Dispatcher Control [*Railroads*] (RU)
DU .... Distriktenes Utbyggingsfond [*Regional Development Fund*] [*Norway*] (GEA)
DU .... Diyarbakir Universitesi [*Diyarbakir University*] (TU)
DU .... Dozorci Utvaru [*Regimental Duty Officer*] (CZ)
DU .... Dramatiker-Union eV [*Playwrights Union*] (SLS)
du .... Dulout [*Farm Road*] (HU)
DU .... Dum Umelcu [*House of Artists*] [*Prague*] (CZ)
Du .... Durak [*Railroad Stop*] (TU)
DU .... Dzielnica Urzedowa [*Government Building City District*] (POL)
DU .... House Installation, Home Wiring [*Telephony*] (RU)
DU .... Level Transmitter (RU)
DU .... Remote Control, Remote Handling (RU)
DU .... Remote Indicator (RU)
DU .... Road Administration (RU)
DU .... Road Section (RU)
DUA.......... Doctor of the University of Adelaide [*Australia*]
DUB.......... Dortmunder Union-Brauerei AG [*Dortmund Union Brewery*]
DUB.......... Dubai Airwing [*United Arab Emirates*] [*ICAO designator*] (FAAC)
DUBAL ..... Dubai Aluminum Co. [*United Arab Emirates*] (IMH)
dubbelbl ..... Dubbelblad [*Double Page*] [*Publishing*] [*Netherlands*]
DUBES...... Duta Besar [*Ambassador*] (IN)
dubl .... Duplicate (BU)
DUC.......... Dakar University Club
DUC.......... Devlet Uretme Ciftligi Genel Mudurlugu [*State Stud Farm Directorate General*] [*Turkish Cypriot*] (TU)
DuchFAN .. State Higher School for Financial and Administrative Studies (BU)
DUCOM.... Defence Union Catalogue of Monographs [*Australia*]
DUCOR..... Defence Union Catalogue of Reports [*Australia*]
DUCOS ..... Defence Union Catalogue of Serials [*Australia*]
DUD .... Dunedin [*New Zealand*] [*Airport symbol*] (OAG)
DUE.......... Datenuebertragung [*Data Transfer*] [*German*] (ADPT)
DUE.......... Dundo [*Angola*] [*Airport symbol*] (OAG)
DUEB........ Diplome Universitaire d'Etudes Biologiques [*French*]
DUEE .... Datenuebertragungssteteinrichtung [*Data Transfer Equipment*] (ADPT)
DUEE .... Diplome Universitaire d'Etudes Economiques [*French*]
DUEG....... Diplome Universitaire d'Etudes de Gestion [*French*]
DUEG....... Diplome Universitaire d'Etudes Generales [*French*]
DUEJ........ Diplome Universitaire d'Etudes Juridiques [*French*]
DUEL .... Diplome Universitaire d'Etudes Litteraires [*University Literary Studies Diploma*] [*French*] (CL)
DUEN....... Datenuebermittlungsnetz [*German*] (ADPT)
DUEN........ Delegation Universitaire aux Energies Nouvelles [*Universite de Madagascar*] [*Madagascar*]

DUEPS...... Diplome Universitaire d'Education Physique et Sportive [*French*]
DUES .... Datenuebertragungssystem [*Data Transfer System*] [*German*] (ADPT)
DUES .... Diplome Universitaire d'Etudes Scientifiques [*University Scientific Studies Diploma*] [*French*] (CL)
DUES .... Diplome Universitaire d'Etudes Superieures [*French*]
DUEST...... Datenuebertragungssteuerung [*German*] (ADPT)
DUESTA ... Datenuebertragungssteuerung fuer Aussenstationen [*German*] (ADPT)
DUET .... Diplome Universitaire d'Etudes Technologiques [*French*]
DUEVO..... Datenuebermittlungsstetverordnung [*German*] (ADPT)
DUF.......... Dansk Ungdoms Faellesraad [*Danish Youth Council*] (EAIO)
DUF.......... Dansk Ungdoms Faellesrad [*Joint Council of Danish Youth*] (WEN)
DUGAS .... Dubai Natural Gas Co. [*United Arab Emirates*] (IMH)
DUI........... State Information Administration (BU)
Duk .... Dukkan [*Shop, Store*] (TU)
DUKhI...... Donets Institute of Coal Chemistry (RU)
DUL.......... Development Underwriting Limited [*Australia*] (ADA)
DUL.......... Duitsland [*Germany*] [*Afrikaans*]
DULMO.... Diplome Universitaire de Lettres Modernes [*French*]
DUMA...... Dubai Marine Areas Ltd. (ME)
DUN .... Dockworkers Union of Nigeria
Dunantul ... Transdanubia (HU)
DUNATIM ... Dunavolgyi Timfold Ipar (Magyar-Szovjet Bauxit-Aluminium Reszvenytarsasag) [*Danube Valley Bauxite Industry (Hungarian-Soviet Bauxite-Aluminum Limited)*] (HU)
DUND .... Drzavna Uprava Narodnih Dobara [*State Administration of National Property*] (YU)
dundruked ... Dundrukeditie [*Thin Paper Edition*] [*Publishing*] [*Netherlands*]
DUNF........ Democratic United National Front [*Sri Lanka*] [*Political party*] (ECON)
DUNICEFK ... Dansk UNICEF Komite [*Denmark*] (EAIO)
DUP........... Deakin University Press [*Australia*]
DUP........... Delnicke Ustredni Podniky [*Central Workers' Enterprises*] (CZ)
DUP........... Democratic Unification Party [*South Korea*] [*Political party*] (PPW)
DUP........... Democratic Unionist Party [*Sudan*] [*Political party*] (PD)
DUP........... Democratic Unionist Party [*Northern Ireland*] [*Political party*]
DUP........... Docteur de l'Universite de Paris [*Doctor of the University of Paris*] [*French*] (BARN)
DUP........... Remote Perforator Control (RU)
DUP........... Ulster Democratic Unionist Party [*Northern Ireland*] [*Political party*] (PPW)
DUPBB...... Dewan Ushawan dan Perdagangan Bumiputra Brunei [*Brunei Darussalam*] (EAIO)
Dupdo .... Duplicado [*Duplicate*] [*Spanish*]
Dupetco...... Dubai Petroleum Company (OMWE)
Dupl .... Duplikat [*Duplicate*] [*Publishing*] [*German*]
duplic .... Duplicerad [*Duplicated*] [*Publishing*] [*Sweden*]
duplik........ Duplikeret [*Mimeographed*] [*Publishing Danish/Norwegian*]
DUR.......... Durban [*South Africa*] [*Airport symbol*] (OAG)
Dur............ Durium [*Record label*] [*Italy*]
DURC........ Descriptor Utilisation Review Committee [*Australia*]
Durchfuhr .. Durchfuehrung [*Accomplishment*] [*German*] (GCA)
durchg .... Durchgesehen [*Reviewed*] [*Publishing*] [*German*]
durchgearb ... Durchgearbeitet [*Revised*] [*Publishing*] [*German*]
durchgeh ..... Durchgehend [*Throughout*] [*German*]
durchges..... Durchgesehen [*Reviewed*] [*Publishing*] [*German*]
Durchl .... Durchlaucht [*Highness*] [*German*]
durchlass..... Durchlaessig [*Permeable*] [*German*] (GCA)
Durchlassigk ... Durchlaessigkeit [*Permeability*] [*German*] (GCA)
durchlaufd ... Durchlaufend [*Consecutive*] [*German*]
durchsch..... Durchschossen [*Interleaved*] [*Publishing*] [*German*]
durchschn .. Durchschnittlich [*On the Average*] [*German*]
DURICAM ... Durisotti Cameroun
DURP .... Dnepr River Steamship Line Administration (RU)
DURT .... Dnepr Administration of River Transportation (RU)
Durzh izd ... State Publication (BU)
Durzh k-vo .. State Publishing House (BU)
Durzhpech ... Government Printing Office (BU)
Durzh v ...... Durzhaven Vestnik [*State Gazette*] (BU)
Durzh v-kbr ... State Gazette Issue Number (BU)
Durzhvoen izd ... State Military Publishing House (BU)
DUS .... Defense de l'Unite Senegalaise
DUS .... Diplome Universitaire de Sciences [*French*]
DUS .... Droit Unique de Sortie
DUS .... Dusseldorf [*Germany*] [*Airport symbol*] (OAG)
DUS .... Spin-Rate Meter (RU)
DUS .... Supplementary Drift Angle (RU)
DUSC .... Drug Utilisation Sub-Committee [*Australia*]
DUSJEG ... Diplome Universitaire de Sciences Juridiques, Economiques, et de Gestion [*French*]
DUSO........ Dar Es Salaam University Student Organization [*Tanzania*] (AF)

dust............. Dustojnik [*Officer*] [*Military*] (CZ)
DUSvK ...... Sv. Kiril Slavyanobulgarski State University in Varna (BU)
DUT........... Diplome Universitaire de Technologie [*French*]
DUT........... Drainage Unions and Trusts [*Australia*]
DUTO......... Danish Union of Tourist Officers (EAIO)
Dutz............ Dutzend [*Dozen*] [*German*]
DUV........... Demokratisk Ungdoms Varldsfederation [*World Federation of Democratic Youth*] [*Sweden*] (WEN)
DUV........... Dunai Vasmu [*Danube Iron Works*] (HU)
duv.............. Duverne [*Confidential*] [*Document Classification*] (CZ)
duv.............. Duvernik [*Trustee*] (CZ)
DUW .... Rijksdienst voor de Uitvoering van Werken [*Benelux*] (BAS)
Duz............. Duzelten [*Corrected*] (TU)
DUZN........ Drustvo na Umetnicite, Zurnalistite, i Naucnicite [*Society of Artists, Journalists, and Scientists*] (YU)
DUZSAN .. Duzce Birlik Orman Urunleri Sanayi ve Ticaret AS [*Duzce (of Bolu Province) United Forest Products Industry and Trade Corp.*] (TU)
DV.............. Airborne Force (RU)
dv............... Binary, Double, Dual (Number), Twin (RU)
DV.............. Dalekovod [*Long-Distance Transmission Line*] (YU)
DV.............. Datenverarbeitung [*German*] (ADPT)
DV.............. Decontaminating Agents [*Military*] (BU)
dv............... Den Yngre [*Junior*] [*Sweden*] (GPO)
d/v .... Dias de Vista [*Days after Sight*] [*Portuguese*]
d/v .... Dias Vista [*Days Sight*] [*Spanish*]
Dv.............. Dienstvorschriften [*Service Regulations*] [*Railroad police*] (EG)
DV.............. Dilensky Vybor [*Factory Shop Committee*] (CZ)
Dv.............. Direct Fire Range, Point-Blank Range (RU)
Dv.............. Division [*Military*] (BU)
Dv.............. Doktor Ved [*Former Czechoslovakia*]
DV.............. Domaci Vysetrovani [*House Arrest*] (CZ)
DV.............. Domovy Vychovy [*Reform Schools*] (CZ)
dv............... Dora Vete [*Albanian*]
DV.............. Druzstevni Vestnik [*Cooperative Bulletin*] (CZ)
DV.............. Dunai Vasmu [*Danube Iron Works*] (HU)
DV.............. Durchfuehrungsverordnung [*Implementing Regulation*] (EG)
DV.............. Durzhaven Vestnik [*State Gazette*] (BU)
DV.............. Dutch RCA [*Victor*] [*Record label*]
DV.............. Far East (RU)
Dv.............. Farm [*Topography*] (RU)
DV.............. Long Waves (RU)
DV.............. Smoke Agents [*Military*] (BU)
DV.............. Smoke Agent, Toxic Smoke Agent (RU)
DV.............. Vibration Transducer, Vibration Pickup (RU)
DVA........... Datenverarbeitungstetanlage [*German*] (ADPT)
DVA........... Deutsche Versicherungs-Anstalt [*German Insurance Institute*] (EG)
DVA........... Deutsche Verwaltungsakademie [*German Management Academy*] (EG)
DVA........... Distribuidora Venezolana de Azucares [*Venezuelan Sugar Distributing Enterprise*] (LA)
DVA........... Divinylacetylene (RU)
DVA........... Dunkirk Veterans Association [*Leeds, England*] (EAIO)
DVAG........ Deutscher Verband fuer Angewandte Geographie eV [*German Association for Applied Geography*] (SLS)
DVB........... Divinylbenzene (RU)
DVB........... Divinylbutyral (RU)
DVB........... Diviziska Veterinarska Bolnica [*Divisional Veterinary Hospital*] (YU)
Dvbr........... State Gazette Number (BU)
DV-CENTRO ... Delegacia de Vigilancia-Centro [*Vigilance Center Headquarters*] [*Brazil*] (LA)
DVCS......... Domestic Violence Crisis Service [*Australian Capital Territory*] [*Australia*]
DVD........... Dekorasie van Voortreflike Diens [*Afrikaans*]
DVD........... Deutscher Veranstaltungsdienst [*German Service for Organized Events*] (EG)
DVD........... Deutsche Vereinigung fuer Datenschutz [*German Data Protection Organization*] (EG)
DVD........... Dobrovoljno Vatrogasno Drustvo [*Society of Volunteer Firemen*] (YU)
DVD........... Dytiko-Voreio-Dytikos [*West-Northwest*] (GC)
DVEG........ Derwent Valley Environment Group [*Australia*]
dVerf.......... Der Verfasser [*The Author*] [*German*] (EG)
DVF .... Deutscher Verband Farbe [*German Paint Association*] (SLS)
DVF .... Dnepr Naval Flotilla (RU)
DVF .... Far Eastern Branch of the Academy of Sciences, USSR (RU)
DVF .... Far Eastern Front [*1945*] (RU)
DVFA .... Deutsche Vereinigung fuer Finanzanalyse und Anlageberatung [*German Association for Financial Analysis and Investment Counseling*] (SLS)
DVFAN ..... Far Eastern Branch of the Academy of Sciences, USSR (RU)
DVFFA ...... Deutscher Verband Forstlicher Forschungsanstalten [*German Society of Forestry Research*] (SLS)

DVfVW...... Deutscher Verein fuer Versicherungswissenschaft eV [*German Association for Insurance Knowledge*] (SLS)
DVG........... Deutsche Veterinaermedizinische Gesellschaft eV [*German Veterinary Medicine Association*] (SLS)
DVG........... Deutsche Volkswirtschaftliche Gesellschaft eV [*German Political Economy Association*] (SLS)
dvg.............. Internal Combustion Engine (BU)
DVGI........ Far Eastern Mining Institute (RU)
DVGU........ Far Eastern State University (RU)
DVGW...... Deutscher Verein Gas- und Wasserfachmaenner [*German Society of Gas and Water Technologists*] [*German*]
DVI .... Disaster Victim Identification [*New South Wales police service*] [*Australia*]
DVI .... Standard Time-Interval Pulse-Generating Unit (RU)
DVI .... State Air Navigation Inspectorate (BU)
DVI .... State Military Publishing House (BU)
DVIEV....... Far Eastern Institute of Experimental Veterinary Science (RU)
DVIS......... Deutscher Verein fuer Internationales Seerecht eV [*German Association for International Maritime Law*] (SLS)
DVJ........... Directeur van Justitie [*Benelux*] (BAS)
DVJ........... Dobrovoljacka Vojska Jugoslavije [*Volunteer Army of Yugoslavia*] [*World War II*] (YU)
DVK.......... Druckerei- und Verlagskontor [*Printing and Publishing Office*] (EG)
DVK.......... Far Eastern Kray (RU)
dv kh .... Double Stroke (RU)
DVKhL...... Long-Wave Chlorophyll (RU)
DVKNII..... Far Eastern Kray Scientific Research Institute (RU)
DVL .... Delostrelecke Vyzbrojovani Letectva [*Artillery Arming of Aviation (or Aircraft)*] (CZ)
DVL .... Deutsche Versuchsanstalt fuer Luft- und Raumfahrt [*German Air and Space Travel Research Institute*] (WEN)
Dvlt Mues.. Devlet Muessese [*Government Agency*] (TU)
DVM.......... Deutscher Verband fuer Materialpruefung eV [*German Society for Materials Testing*] (SLS)
DVM.......... De Vierde Macht [*Benelux*] (BAS)
DVM.......... Domovy Vychovy Mladeze [*Reform Schools*] (CZ)
DVN.......... Diabetes Vereniging Nederland [*Dutch Diabetes Association*] (SLS)
dvn.............. Doctor of Military Sciences (RU)
dvn.............. Doctor of Veterinary Sciences (RU)
DVN.......... Two-Rotor Vacuum Pump (RU)
DVNIGMI ... Far Eastern Hydrometeorological Scientific Research Institute (RU)
DVNIISKh ... Far Eastern Scientific Research Institute of Agriculture (RU)
DVO........... Air-Cooled Engine (RU)
d-vo .... Association, Society, Company (BU)
DVO........... Danske Veterinaerhygiejnikeres Organisation [*Denmark*] (SLS)
DVO........... Davao [*Philippines*] [*Airport symbol*] (OAG)
d-vo .... Drustvo [*Society*] (YU)
DVO........... Durchfuehrungsverordnung [*Executive Decree*] [*German*] (ILCA)
DVO........... Far Eastern Military District (RU)
DVO........... Far Eastern Oblast (RU)
DVO........... House of Extramural Education (RU)
DVOS........ Far Eastern Railroad (RU)
DVP.......... Demokratische Volkspartei [*Democratic People's Party*] [*Germany*] (PPE)
DVP .... Deutsche Volkspartei [*German People's Party (1919-1933)*] (PPE)
DVP .... Deutsche Volkspolizei [*German People's Police*] (EG)
DVP .... Druzstevni Vinarske Podniky [*Cooperative Wine Enterprises*] (CZ)
DVP.......... Wood Fiber Slabs (RU)
DVPI......... Far Eastern Polytechnic Institute Imeni V. V. Kuybyshev (RU)
dv pl........... Twinning Plane (RU)
DVPMP..... Deutsche Vereinigung gegen Politischen Missbrauch der Psychiatrie [*Germany*]
Dvp't .... Development (PWGL)
DVPW .... Deutsche Vereinigung fuer Politische Wissenschaft [*German Association for Political Science*] (SLS)
DVR........... Datenverarbeitungsstetvorrechner [*German*] (ADPT)
DVR........... Diamond Valley Railway [*Australia*] (ADA)
DVR........... Division de Vivienda Rural [*Rural Housing Division*] [*Venezuela*] (LAA)
DVR........... Far Eastern Republic [*1920-1922*] (RU)
DVR........... Van Riebeeck Decoration
DVRG........ Deja Vu Research Group (EAIO)
DVRP .... Two-Channel Visual Radio Direction Finder (RU)
DVS .... Datenverarbeitungssystem [*Data Processing System*] [*German*] (ADPT)
dvs.............. Det Vill Saga [*That Is*] [*Sweden*] (GPO)
dvs.............. Det Vil Si [*That Is*] [*Norway*] (GPO)
dvs.............. Det Vil Sige [*That Is*] [*Denmark*] (GPO)
DVS .... Deutscher Verband fuer Schweisstechnik eV [*German Society for Welding Technology*] (SLS)

DVS .... Deutscher Verband fur Schweisstechnik [*Germany*]   (EAIO)
DVS .... Digitales Vermittlungssystem [*German*]   (ADPT)
DVS .... Division Clothing and Equipment Depot   (RU)
DVS .... House of Veterans of the Stage Imeni M. G. Savina   (RU)
DVS .... Internal Combustion Engine   (RU)
DVSA .... Dierkundige Vereniging van Suidelike Afrika [*Zoological Society of Southern Africa - ZSSA*]   (EAIO)
DVSSh .... Self-Propelled Chassis with an Air-Cooled Diesel   (RU)
DVST......... Datenvermittlungsstelle [*German*]   (ADPT)
Dvst............ Dienstvorsteher [*Stationmaster*]   (EG)
DvstV .... Dienstvorsteher Vertreter [*Deputy Stationmaster*]   (EG)
DVT .... Datenverteiler [*German*]   (ADPT)
Dvt .... Deadweight   (RU)
DVT .... Deutscher Verband Technisch-Wissenschaftlicher Vereine [*German Technical Scientific Association*]   (SLS)
DVTA .... Deutscher Verband Technischer Assistenten in der Medizin   (EAIO)
DVTeatrU ... State Higher Theater School   (BU)
DVTK .... State Woolen Textiles Combine   (BU)
DVTK .... State Wool Weaving Combine   (BU)
DVTLRS ... Drustvo za Varilno Tehniko Ljudska Republika Slovenija [*Slovenian Society for Welding Technology*] [*Ljubljana*]   (YU)
DVTU .... Far Eastern Territorial Administration   (RU)
DVTU .... State Higher Theater School   (BU)
DVTWV .... Deutscher Verband Technisch-Wissenschaftlicher Verbands [*German Association of Technological Societies*]   (PDAA)
DVU.......... Deutsche Volksunion [*German People's Union*] [*Political party*]   (PD)
DVU.......... Drevarsky Vyskumny Ustav [*Lumber Research Institute*]   (CZ)
DVU.......... Far Eastern University   (RU)
DVU.......... High-Level Discriminator   (RU)
DVU.......... Orbi [*Former USSR*] [*ICAO designator*]   (FAAC)
DVUFAN .. State Higher School of Finance and Administration   (BU)
dvukhned ... Fortnightly, Two-Week   (RU)
Dvumes ...... Bimonthly   (BU)
dvupr .... Birefringence   (RU)
DVV .... Debreceni Villamosvasut Vallalat [*Electric Railroad Enterprise of Debrecen*]   (HU)
DVV .... Deutscher Volkshochschul-Verband eV [*German Adult Education Association*]   (SLS)
DVV .... Deutsche Vereinigung zur Bekaempfung der Viruskrankheiten eV [*German Association for Combating Viral Diseases*]   (SLS)
DVV .... Dvojni Vatreni Val [*Dual Firing Wave*] [*Military*]   (YU)
DVV .... High Explosive, Blasting Agent   (RU)
DVW .... Deutscher Verein fuer Vermessungswesen eV [*German Association for Surveying*]   (SLS)
DVW .... Deutscher Verlag fuer Wissenschaften [*German Scientific Publishing House*]   (EG)
DVWG ...... Deutche Verkehrswissen-Schaftliche Gesellschaft [*German Transportation Society*]   (PDAA)
DVZ .... State Railroad Car Plant   (BU)
DW .... Deelwoord [*Participle*] [*Afrikaans*]
DW .... Deutsche Welle [*Deutsche Welle (Overseas Radio)*]   (WEN)
DW .... Dienstplichtwet [*Benelux*]   (BAS)
dw .... Dienswillig [*Obedient*] [*Afrikaans*]
DW............. DLT Luftverkehrsgesellschaft mbH [*Germany*] [*ICAO designator*]   (ICDA)
DW............. Doktor der Wissenschaften [*Doctor of Science*] [*German*]
Dw............. Dworzec [*Railway Station*] [*Poland*]
DWA......... Deutsche Waren-Abnahme Gesellschaft [*German Commodity Acceptance Company*]   (EG)
D-Wagen.... Durchgangswagen [*Through Carriage*] [*German*]
DWB......... Deutsch West-Afrikanische Bank [*German West-African Bank*]
DWB......... Doctors Without Borders [*France*]   (EAIO)
DWB......... Soalala [*Madagascar*] [*Airport symbol*]   (OAG)
DWBV .... Deutscher Wanderer- und Bergsteigerverband [*German Hiking and Mountain-Climbing League*]   (EG)
DWC......... Democratic Workers' Congress [*Trade union*] [*Sri Lanka*]   (FEA)
DWC......... Development Works Corporation [*Mauritius*]   (AF)
DWD......... Deutscher Wetterdienst [*German Meteorological Service*] [*Ministry of Transport*] [*Research center*]   (WND)
DWD......... De Wet Decoration
DWD......... Dom Wczasow Dziec`iecych [*Children's Vacation House*]   (POL)
DWF .... Danish Wrestling Federation   (EAIO)
DWG......... Deutsche Werbewissenschaftliche Gesellschaft eV [*German Scientific Recruiting Association*]   (SLS)
DWH .... Dritte Welt Haus [*Germany*]   (EAIO)
DWHG ...... Deutsch-Westafrikanische Handelsgesellschaft
DWI .... Deutsches Wirtschaftsinstitut [*German Economics Institute*]   (EG)
dWiD .... Des Wirtschaftsdienstes [*Of the Economic Service*] [*German*]
DWIFC...... Doctor Who International Fan Club [*Australia*]

DWIKORA ... Dwi Komando Rakjat [*Two Commands of the People (Refers to confrontation with Malaysia)*]   (IN)
DWIN........ Doctor Who Information Network [*Canada*]   (EAIO)
DWK......... Deutsche Gesellschaft fuer Wiederaufarbeitung von Kernbrennstoffen, mbH [*Nuclear energy*]   (NRCH)
DWK......... Deutsches Wissenschaftliche Kommission fuer Meeresforschung [*German Scientific Commission for Sea Fisheries*]   (ASF)
DWK......... Deutsche Wirtschaftskommission [*German Economic Commission*]   (EG)
DWLot....... Dowodztwo Wojsk Lotniczych [*Air Force Command*] [*Poland*]
DWM........ Deutsche Waffen- und Munitionsfabriken [*German Weapons and Munitions Factory*] [*World War II*]
DWM........ Divine Word Missionaries [*See also SVD*] [*Italy*]   (EAIO)
DWME...... Division of World Mission and Evangelism
dwp............ Deadweight Tons   (OMWE)
DWP......... Democratic Workers' Party [*South Africa*]
DWP......... Deutsches Wirtschaftspatent [*German Industrial Patent*]   (EG)
DWP......... Dom Wojska Polskiego [*House of the Polish Army*]   (POL)
DWR......... Department of Water Resources [*Victoria, Australia*]
DWS .... Deutsches Wetterdienst Seewetteramt [*German Weather Service for Oceanographic Weather*]   (MSC)
DWS .... Diplomatic Wives Society [*Sudan*]
dws .... Dit Wil Se [*Afrikaans*]
DWSG .... Defence Widows' Support Group [*Australia*]
DWSN....... Dawson [*Botanical region*] [*Australia*]
DWStK ...... Deutsche Waffen Stillstandkommission [*German Armistice Commission, in France*] [*World War II*]
dwt............ Dead Weight Tons   (EECI)
DWT......... Ded Wate Tonluk [*Dead Weight Tons*] [*As in rail or maritime transport*]   (TU)
DWT......... Deutsche Gesellschaft fuer Wehrtechnik eV [*German Association for Weapons Technology*]   (SLS)
DWT......... Division of Water Technology [*Council for Scientific and Industrial Research*] [*South Africa*]   (IRC)
DWU .... Danish Writers Association   (EAIO)
dwum........ Dwumiesiecznik [*Bimonthly*] [*Poland*]
dwumies..... Dwumiesiecznik [*Bimonthly Publication*] [*Poland*]
DWUN ...... Dock Workers Union of Nigeria
dwustr .... Dwustronny [*Two-Sided*] [*Poland*]
dwuszp ...... Dwuszpaltowy [*Two-Column*] [*Poland*]
dwut........... Dwutygodnik [*Biweekly*] [*Poland*]
dwutyg........ Dwutygodnik [*Biweekly*] [*Poland*]
DWUWA... Disabled Workers' Union of Western Australia
DWV......... Deutsche Warenvertriebsgesellschaft [*German Commodity Trading Co.*]   (EG)
DWWSSN ... Digital World-Wide Standardised Seismograph Network [*Australia*]
dwz............ Dat Wil Zeggen [*Benelux*]   (BAS)
DX............. Document Exchange [*Australia*]   (ADA)
DXAK .... Atakpame/Akpaka [*Togo*] [*ICAO location identifier*]   (ICLI)
DXB .... Dubai [*United Arab Emirates*] [*Airport symbol*]   (OAG)
DXBS........ Bassari [*Togo*] [*ICAO location identifier*]   (ICLI)
DXD.......... Dixie [*Australia*] [*Airport symbol*] [*Obsolete*]   (OAG)
DXDP .... Dapango [*Togo*] [*ICAO location identifier*]   (ICLI)
DXHO .... Hahotoe [*Togo*] [*ICAO location identifier*]   (ICLI)
DXKP .... Anie/Kolokope [*Togo*] [*ICAO location identifier*]   (ICLI)
DX-L......... Datexnetz mit Leitungsvermittlung [*German*]   (ADPT)
DXMG...... Sansanne-Mango [*Togo*] [*ICAO location identifier*]   (ICLI)
DXNG....... Niamtougou [*Togo*] [*ICAO location identifier*]   (ICLI)
DX-P......... Datexnetz mit Paketvermittlung [*German*]   (ADPT)
DXSK........ Sokode [*Togo*] [*ICAO location identifier*]   (ICLI)
DXTA .... Tabligbo [*Togo*] [*ICAO location identifier*]   (ICLI)
DXXX .... Lome/Tokoin [*Togo*] [*ICAO location identifier*]   (ICLI)
DY............. Dee Why [*New South Wales, Australia*]
DY............. Democratic Yemen Airlines (ALYEMDA) [*People's Democratic Republic of Yemen*] [*ICAO designator*]   (ICDA)
DY............. Dimosia Ypiresia [*Civil Service*]   (GC)
DY............. Dimosios Ypallilos [*Civil Servant*]   (GC)
Dy............. Disprosio [*Chemical element*] [*Portuguese*]
DYA.......... Alyemda-Democratic Yemen Airlines [*ICAO designator*]   (FAAC)
DYA.......... Dysart [*Australia*] [*Airport symbol*]   (OAG)
DYaER ...... Electron-Nuclear Double Paramagnetic Resonance   (RU)
DYB .... Devlet Yatirim Bankasi [*State Investment Bank*]   (TU)
DYDM...... Devlet Yayinlari Dokumantasyon Merkezi [*State Publications Documentation Center*] [*Under Ministry of Culture*]   (TU)
DYe........... Capacity Transducer, Capacity Pickup   (RU)
DYE .... Dynamic Air [*Netherlands*] [*ICAO designator*]   (FAAC)
DYeP .... Transfer Unit Length   (RU)
DYFC........ Danish Farm Youth   (EAIO)
DYF-Is....... Turkiye Demiryollari Isci Sendikalar Federasyonu [*Federation of Turkish Railway Worker Unions*] [*DYI-Is*] [*See also*]   (TU)
DYI-Is........ Demiryollari Isci Sendikalari Federasyonu [*Federation of Railway Worker Unions*] [*DYF-Is*] [*See also*]   (TU)
DYK.......... Dynameis Ypovrykhion Katastrofon [*Underwater Demolition Forces*] [*Greek*]   (GC)

DYKFE...... Dimokratiki Yperkommatiki Kinisi Foititon Ellados [*Democratic Supra-Party Movement of Greek Students*] (GC)

DYKO........ Dievthinsis Ypiresion Koinovoulevtikis Omados [*Directorate of Parliamentary Group Services (Parliamentary liaison to the premier)*] (GC)

DYMD....... Demiryolu Memurlari Dernegi [*Railway Employees Organization*] (TU)

DYMM...... Dulian Yang Maha Mulia [*His Majesty*] (ML)

dympribor .. Smoke Generator (RU)

dymzavesa ... Smoke Screen (RU)

DYN.......... Diarios y Noticias [*News agency*] [*Argentina*] (EY)

DYO.......... Durmus Yasar ve Ogullari [*Durmus Yasar and Sons Paint Company*] [*Subsidiary of Yasar Holding Corp.*] (TU)

dyon........... Dywizjon [*Unit or Wing*] [*Poland*]

DYOO .... Deneme Yuksek Ogretmen Okulu [*Experimental Advanced Normal (Teacher's) School*] (TU)

DYP .... Dogru Yol Partisi [*Correct Way Party*] [*Turkey*] [*Political party*] (EY)

dypl .... Dyplomacja [*or Dyplomatyczny*] [*Diplomacy or Diplomatic*] [*Poland*]

dypl .... Dyplomowany [*Certified*] [*Poland*]

DYPSP ...... Disabled Young People's Services Program [*Australia*]

dyr .... Dyrekcja [*Administration, Directorate*] (POL)

dyr .... Dyrektor [*Director*] (POL)

DYSA........ Developmental Youth Services Association [*Australia*]

DYT .... Dzongkhag Yargay Tshochungs [*District Planning Committees*] [*Bhutan*] (FEA)

DYU.......... Dushanbe [*Former USSR*] [*Airport symbol*] (OAG)

DYuBKh .... South Bulgarian Painters' Union (BU)

dyun .... Doctor of Laws (RU)

dyuzh.......... Dozen (RU)

DYWIDAG ... Dyckerhoff und Widman Aktiengesellschaft [*Dyckerhoff and Widman Joint Stock Company*]

DZ.............. Algeria [*ANSI two-letter standard code*] (CNC)

dz............... Dat [*or Dit*] Zijn [*Benelux*] (BAS)

Dz.............. Delavska Zdruzenja [*Workers' Association*] (YU)

Dz.............. Deniz [*Sea, Navy*] (TU)

Dz.............. Derzeit [*At the Moment*] [*German*]

d-z .... Diagnosis (RU)

DZ.............. Dipole Sounding (RU)

DZ.............. Direkcija Jugoslovenskih Zeleznica [*Administration of Yugoslav Railroads*] (YU)

DZ.............. Divadelni Zatva [*Theatrical Harvest Festival*] (CZ)

DZ.............. Divisional, Division (BU)

dz............... Doppelzentner [*100 Kilograms*] [*German*] (EG)

DZ.............. Doppelzuender [*Pressure Igniter*] [*German*] (GCA)

dz............... Douzaine [*Dozen*] [*French*]

DZ.............. Druckzuender [*Pressure Igniter*] [*German military - World War II*]

Dz.............. Drustveni Zivot [*Social Life*] [*Sarajevo A periodical*] (YU)

DZ.............. Drzavne Zeleznice [*State Railroads*] (YU)

DZ.............. Dusanov Zakonik [*Code of the Emperor Dusan*] (YU)

dz............... Duzia [*Dozen*] [*Portuguese*]

Dz.............. Duzine [*Dozen*] (TU)

Dz.............. Dywizja Zmechanizowana [*Mechanized Division*] (POL)

dz............... Dzial [*Section*] [*Poland*]

dz............... Dzien [*The Day*] [*Poland*]

dz............... Dziennie [*A Day*] [*Poland*]

dz............... Dziennik [*Daily*] (POL)

DZ.............. Shutter Motor (RU)

DZ.............. Smoke Screen (BU)

DZ.............. Winter Diesel (Fuel) (RU)

DZA .... Algeria [*ANSI three-letter standard code*] (CNC)

Dza............ Denizalti [*Submarine*] (TU)

DZA .... Deutsches Zentralinstitut fuer Arbeitsmedizin [*German Central Institute for Labor Medicine*] (EG)

DZA .... Dzaoudzi [*Comoro Islands*] [*Airport symbol*] (OAG)

DZAG .... Division Antiaircraft Artillery Group (RU)

Dz Alb....... Deniz Albay [*Navy Captain*] (TU)

Dzauges...... Dzaudzhikau Hydroelectric Power Plant (RU)

DZB .... Dzial Zaopatrzenia Bibliotek [*Department of Library Supply*] (POL)

DZBANK .. Denizcilik Bankasi Turk Anonim Ortakligi [*Turkish Maritime Bank Corporation*] (TU)

DZBM .... Dzielnicowy Zarzad Budynkow Mieszkalnych [*City Section Administration of Apartment Houses*] (POL)

DZBMPW ... Dolnoslaskie Zaklady Budowlano-Montazowe Przemyslu Weglowego [*Lower Silesia Construction and Assembly Establishments of the Coal Industry*] (POL)

DZBUP...... Dolnoslaskie Zaklady Budowy Urzadzen Przemyslowych [*Lower Silesia Industrial Equipment Construction Plant*] (POL)

DZBZ......... Dukelske Zavody Branne Zdatnosti [*Dukla Military Fitness Contest*] (CZ)

Dzd............ Dutzend [*Dozen*] [*German*]

DZD.......... State Cattle Farm (BU)

DZF .... Deutsche Zentrale fuer Filmforschung [*German Center for Film Research*] (EG)

DZfCh........ Deutscher Zentralausschuss fuer Chemie [*German Central Committee for Chemistry*] (SLS)

DZFS......... Dmitrov Milling Machine Plant (RU)

DZG.......... Deutsche Zoologische Gesellschaft eV [*German Zoological Association*] (SLS)

DZGI......... Donets Mining Correspondence Institute (RU)

DZh............ Dirigible, Airship (RU)

dzh............. Joule (RU)

DZh............ Liquid Decontaminating Agent (RU)

DZhD........ Children's Railway (RU)

DZHEZKAZGANGIPROTSVETMET ... Dzhezkazgan State Institute for the Planning of Establishments of Nonferrous Metallurgy (RU)

dzhp............ Female Persons [*Statistics*] (RU)

DZhS......... Democratic Women's Union of Germany (RU)

DZhSG ...... Democratic Women's Union of Germany (RU)

dzhut .... Jute Plant [*Topography*] (RU)

DZI .... State Insurance Institute (BU)

dziek.......... Dziekan [*Dean*] [*Poland*]

dzien........... Dziennik [*Daily*] [*Poland*]

DZII.......... Donets Industrial Correspondence Institute (RU)

DZK .... Deutsches Zentralkomitee zur Bekaempfung der Tuberkulose [*German Central Committee for Combating Tuberculosis*] (SLS)

DZK .... Durchlaufzeitkarten [*German*] (ADPT)

DZK .... Monitoring Dosimeter (RU)

DZK .... State Sugar Combine (BU)

Dz KK .... Deniz Kuvvetler Komutanligi [*Naval Forces Command*] (TU)

Dz Kuv ...... Deniz Kuvvetleri [*Naval Forces*] (TU)

DZL .... Differential Line Protection (RU)

DZM .... Dolnoslaskie Zaklady Metalowe [*Lower Silesia Metal Plant*] (POL)

DZMO........ Dnepropetrovsk Metallurgical Equipment Plant (RU)

DZNAK ..... Deniz Bank Deniz Nakliyat Turk Anonim Sirketi [*Turkish Maritime Bank's Maritime Transport Corporation or Turkish Maritime Transport Corporation*] (TU)

dzne............ Douzaine [*Dozen*] [*French*]

DZNIS .... State Agricultural Scientific Research Station (BU)

DZOS .... Earth and Timber Weapon Emplacement (BU)

DZOS .... Log Emplacement (RU)

DZOT .... Earth and Timber Pillbox (BU)

DZOT .... Log Emplacement (RU)

DZOT .... Permanent Ground Gun Emplacement (BU)

DZPD .... Dolnoslaskie Zaklady Przemyslu Drzewnego [*Lower Silesia Wood-Working Plant*] (POL)

DZPJ .... Dolnoslaskie Zaklady Przemyslu Jedwabnego [*Lower Silesia Silk Mill*] (POL)

DZPW .... Dabrowskie Zaklady Przemyslu Weglowego [*Dabrowa Basin Coal Enterprise*] (POL)

DZPW .... Dabrowskie Zjednoczenie Przemyslu Weglowego [*Dabrowa Basin Coal Industry Association*] (POL)

DZPW .... Dolnoslaskie Zaklady Przemyslu Weglowego [*Lower Silesia Coal Plant*] (POL)

DZRCh ...... State Spare Parts Plant (BU)

DZS .... Direkcija na Zeleznite Skopje [*Railroad Administration, Skopje*] (YU)

DZS .... Drevarske Zavody na Slovensku, Narodny Podnik [*Lumber Mills in Slovakia, National Enterprise*] (CZ)

DZS .... Drzavna Zalozba Slovenije [*Government Publishing House of Slovenia*] [*Ljubljana*] (YU)

DZS .... Drzavno Zemjodelsko Stopanstvo [*State Farm*] (YU)

DZS .... State Farm (BU)

DZS .... State Soda Plant (BU)

dzt.............. Derzeit [*At the Moment*] [*German*]

DZT .... Deutsche Zentrale fuer Tourismus eV [*German National Tourist Board*] (EY)

DZTs......... State Cellulose Plant (BU)

DZU .... Diode Storage, Diode Memory (RU)

Dz U.......... Dziennik Urzedowy [*Regulations Gazette*] [*Poland*]

Dz U.......... Dziennik Ustaw [*Government Regulations and Laws Gazette*] [*Poland*]

DZU.......... Permanent Storage, Permanent Memory (RU)

D-Zug........ Durchgangs-Zug [*Through Train*] [*German*]

DZV .... Air Smoke Screen (RU)

DZV .... Deutscher Zentralverlag [*German Central Publishing House*] (EG)

DZV .... Deutsche Zentrale fuer Volksgesundheitspflege eV [*German National Health Promotion Center*] (SLS)

DZV .... Divisao de Zootecnia e Veterinaria [*Brazil*] (DSCA)

DZW.......... Deutsche Dokumentations Zentrale Wasser [*German Water Documentation Office*] (PDAA)

DZWME ... Dolnoslaskie Zaklady Wytworcze Maszyn Elektrycznych [*Lower Silesia Electric Machinery Plant*] (POL)

DZWUR .... Dolnoslaskie Zaklady Wytworcze Urzadzen Radiowych [*Lower Silesia Radio Equipment Plant*] (POL)

DZZ .... Ground Smoke Screen   (RU)
DZZ .... State Sugar Refinery   (BU)
DZZSO ...... Drzavni Zavod za Socijalno Osiguranje [*State Institute for Social Insurance*]   (YU)

E

E............. East   (EECI)
E............. Eastern
E............. Easy [*Phonetic alphabet*] [*World War II*]   (DSUE)
E............. Eau [*Water*] [*Military map abbreviation World War I*] [*French*]
            (MTD)
E............. Echo [*Phonetic alphabet*] [*International*]   (DSUE)
E............. Eclairage [*Illumination*] [*French*]
E............. Editor [*Editor*] [*Portuguese*]
E............. Edward [*Phonetic alphabet*] [*Royal Navy World War I*]   (DSUE)
E............. Ehren [*Honors*] [*German*]
E............. Eilean [*Island (or Islands)*] [*Gaelic*]   (NAU)
E............. Eilzug [*Fast Train*] [*German*]   (EG)
E............. Eingabe [*German*]   (ADPT)
E............. Einsatzstahl [*Casehardened Steel*] [*German*]   (GCA)
E............. Einschicht [*Insight*] [*German*]
E............. Einsteiniano [*Portuguese*]
E............. Einwohner [*Resident*] [*German*]
E............. Eisenbahn [*Railroad*] [*German*]
E............. Elastizitaetsmodul [*Elasticity Modulus*] [*German*]   (GCA)
E............. Electric Steel   (RU)
e............. Electron   (RU)
E............. Elektromotorische Kraft [*Electromotive Force*] [*German*]
e............. Elott [*Prior To, In Front Of*]   (HU)
E............. Emalangeni [*Monetary unit*] [*Swaziland*]   (BARN)
E............. EMBRAER [*Empresa Brasileira Aeronautica SA*] [*Brazil*] [*ICAO
            aircraft manufacturer identifier*]   (ICAO)
E............. Emekli [*Retired*]   (TU)
E............. Eminence [*Eminence*] [*French*]
E............. Empfindlichkeit [*Sensitivity*] [*German*]   (GCA)
e............. Encadernacao [*Binding*] [*Publishing*] [*Portuguese*]
(E)............ Entgegen [*Opposed*] [*Chemistry*] [*German*]
E............. Entscheidung [*Decision, Judgment*] [*German*]   (ILCA)
E............. Entwurf [*Draft*] [*German*]   (ILCA)
E............. Epreuve [*Surmounted by a crown, and stamped on gun barrels
            after firing test*] [*French*]   (MTD)
E............. Equivalent   (RU)
E............. Equivalent Mecanique de la Chaleur [*Mechanical Equivalent of
            Heat*] [*French*]
e............. Erg [*Erg*] [*Portuguese*]
E............. Ergobank [*Greek*]
E............. Erkekler [*Men*]   (TU)
e............. Erkezik [*Arrives*]   (HU)
E............. Ersatz [*Replacement*] [*German*]   (GCA)
E............. Erstarrungspunkt [*Freezing Point*] [*German*]
e............. Erzbischoeflich [*Archiepiscopal*] [*German*]
E............. Escudo [*Monetary unit*] [*Chile, Portugal*]
E............. Espana [*Spain*] [*International automobile identification tag*]
E............. Especialidad [*Specialty*] [*Spanish*]
E............. Esquerda [*Left Side*] [*Portuguese*]
E............. Est [*East*] [*French*]   (MTD)
e............. Este [*Evening*]   (HU)
E............. Este [*East*] [*Spanish*]
E............. Este [*East*] [*Portuguese*]
e............. Estrada [*Road*] [*Portuguese*]   (CED)
E............. Eszak [*North*] [*Hungary*]   (GPO)
e............. Etat [*Condition*] [*French*]
e............. Ether, Ester   (RU)
e............. Ev [*Year*]   (HU)
E............. Evacuation Tag [*Anti-aircraft and atomic defense*]   (RU)
e............. Evenkent [*Annually*]   (HU)
e............. Evezred [*Thousand Years or Millenium*]   (HU)
E............. Examen [*Sweden*]
E............. Excavator   (RU)
E............. Excellence [*Excellency*] [*French*]
e............. Ezer [*Thousand*]   (HU)
e............. Ezred [*Regiment*]   (HU)
E............. Oersted   (RU)
E............. Screen Grid   (BU)

E............. Spanish [*Language in tables*]   (BARN)
E............. Squadron [*Navy*]   (RU)
E............. Stopien Englera [*Engler Degree*] [*Poland*]
EA............. Airbus Industrie [*France*] [*ICAO aircraft manufacturer identifier*]
            (ICAO)
EA............. East African Airways
EA............. Efedros Axiomatikos [*Reserve Officer*]   (GC)
EA............. Egyptian Army
Ea............. Einander [*Each Other*] [*German*]
E/A........... Eingabe/Ausgabe [*German*]   (ADPT)
ea............. Eloado [*Consultant*]   (HU)
EA............. Emirates Airlines [*United Arab Emirates*]   (MENA)
ea............. En Ander [*And So Forth*] [*Afrikaans*]
ea............. En Andere [*Among Others*] [*Netherlands*]
e a........... En Apostrateia [*Retired*] [*Military*]   (GC)
EA............. Enomeni Aristera [*United Left*] [*Greek*]   (GC)
EA............. Enosi Agoton [*Farmers' Union*]   (GC)
EA............. Enterprise Australia
EA............. Entree Accumulateur [*French*]   (ADPT)
EA............. Environmental Agency [*Japan*]   (PDAA)
EA............. Equinox Association [*France*]   (EAIO)
EA............. Ethniki Allilengyi [*National Solidarity*] [*Greek*]   (GC)
EA............. Ethyl Acetate   (RU)
EA............. Europa-Archiv [*Germany*]   (FLAF)
EA............. Eusko Alkartasuna [*Basque Solidarity*] [*Spain*] [*Political party*]
EA............. Exportauftrag [*Export Order*]   (EG)
EA............. Export Authorisation System [*Hong Kong*]
EAA........... Eagle Aircraft Australia Ltd. [*Australia*]
EAA........... East Africa Association   (EA)
EAA........... East African Airways   (AF)
EAA........... East African Artillery
EAA........... Ecclesiastical Archivists Association [*Italy*]   (EAIO)
EAA........... Ecole d'Aviation d'Algerie [*Algerian Aviation School*]   (AF)
EAA........... EDP [*Electronic Data Processing*] Auditors' Association
EAA........... Elliniki Aeroporiki Astynomia [*Aeronomia*] [*Greek Air Police*]
            [*Later,*]   (GC)
EAA........... Etaireia Anaptyxeos Alieias [*Association for the Development of
            Fishing*] [*Greek*]   (GC)
EAA........... Ethnikon Asteroskopeion Athinon [*Athens National Observatory*]
            (GC)
EAA........... European Academy of Anaesthesiology   (EA)
EAA........... European Accounting Association [*Brussels, Belgium*]   (EAIO)
EAA........... European Aluminium Association [*Germany*]   (EA)
EAA........... European Athletic Association [*Paris, France*]
EAA........... Transporte Aereo Andino SA [*Venezuela*] [*ICAO designator*]
            (FAAC)
EAAC........ East African Airways Corporation
EAAC........ European Agricultural Aviation Centre [*Netherlands*]   (DSCA)
EAAC........ European Association of Audiophonological Centres   (EA)
EAACI....... European Academy of Allergology and Clinical Immunology
            (EAIO)
EAAE........ European Association of Agricultural Economists   (EA)
EAAEC...... East African Army Education Corps
EAAEI....... Epitropi Adeias Askiseos tou Epangelmatos tou Ithopiou [*Actors'
            Licensing Committee*] [*Greek*]   (GC)
EAAF........ Equipo Argentino de Antropologia Forense [*Argentine Forensic
            Anthropology Team*]
EAAFRO... East African Agriculture and Forestry Research Organization
            (AF)
EAAM....... European Association for Aquatic Mammals [*Netherlands*]
            (SLS)
EAAM....... European Association of Automobile Manufacturers [*Belgium*]
            (EAIO)
EAAP........ European Association for Animal Production [*ICSU*] [*Italian*]
            (SLS)
EAAS........ East Asian Art Society
EAAS........ European Association for American Studies [*Italy*]   (EAIO)
EAASCS.... East Asian Art Society Chinese School

395

EAASH ..... European Academy of Arts, Sciences, and Humanities   (EAIO)
EAAVA ...... Enosis Apostraton Axiomatikon Vasilikis Aeroporias [*Union of Retired Royal Air Force Officers*]   (GC)
EAAVE ...... Epitropi Agonos Avtokinitiston Voreiou Ellados [*Struggle Committee of Drivers of Northern Greece*]   (GC)
EAB .... Abbse [*Yemen Arab Republic*] [*Airport symbol*]   (OAG)
EAB .... Eagle Air Ltd. [*Switzerland*] [*ICAO designator*]   (FAAC)
EAB .... East African Breweries
EAB .... Electrical Approvals Board (Victoria)
EAB .... Elektro-Apparatebau, Koenigs Wusterhausen [*Koenigs Wusterhausen Electrical Equipment Plant*]   (EG)
EAB .... Epitoipari Allando Bizottsag [*Standing Committee of the Construction Industry (CEMA)*]   (HU)
EAB .... Escola Agronomica da Bahia [*Brazil*]   (DSCA)
EAB .... Estate Agents Board [*Victoria, Australia*]
EAB .... Europaeische Akademie Berlin eV [*European Academy of Berlin*]   (SLS)
EABC .... European Amateur Baseball Confederation   (EA)
EABC .... European American Banking Corporation
EABC .... European/ASEAN [*Association of Southeast Asian Nations*] Business Council   (DS)
EABL .... East African Breweries Limited
EABT .... European Association for Behavior Therapy   (EA)
EAC .... East African Command
EAC .... East African Community [*Formed in 1967*] [*Formerly, EACSO*]   (AF)
EAC .... East Asiatic Co. [*Denmark*]
EAC .... East Australian Current [*Oceanography*]
EAC .... Economic Advisory Council
EAC .... Education Advisory Committee [*South African Council for Professional Engineers*]   (AA)
EAC .... Electricity Authority of Cyprus   (IMH)
EAC .... Emerald Agricultural College
EAC .... Employee Assistance Centre [*City Rail*] [*New South Wales, Australia*]
EAC .... Entreprise Artisanale de Cocobeach
EAC .... European Advisory Council   (EAIO)
EAC .... European Association of Conservatories   (EA)
EAC .... Evangelical Association of the Caribbean   (EAIO)
EAC .... Exploitations Agricoles Ceppo
EAC .... Treaty of East African Cooperation [*Kenya, Tanzania, Uganda*] [*1977*] [*Terminated*]
EACA .... East African Court of Appeal
EACA .... European Association of Charter Airlines   (EAIO)
EACA .... European Athletics Coaches Association   (EAIO)
EAC-AIA ... EEC Advisory Council of the Asbestos International Association   (EAIO)
EACAT ...... Euro-Arab Centre for Appropriate Technology
EACB .... East African Currency Board
EACC .... East African Cricket Conference
EACC .... East Asia Christian Conference [*Later, Christian Conference of Asia - CCA*]
EACC-USA ... European-American Chamber of Commerce in the United States
EACD .... Ein-Ausgabecodierer [*German*]   (ADPT)
EACE .... East African Certificate of Education
EACE .... European Association of Cognitive Ergonomics   (EAIO)
EACEM ..... European Association of Consumer Electronic Manufacturers [*EEC*]   (PDAA)
EACF .... European-Australian Christian Fellowship
EACH .... East African Command Headquarters
EACHS ...... East African Cargo Handling Services   (PDAA)
EACI .... Electricite Automobile de Cote-D'Ivoire
EACL .... European Association for Chinese Law   (EAIO)
EACM .... East African Common Market
EACM .... Ecole de l'Aviation Civile et de la Meteorologie
EACNSW ... Ethnic Affairs Commission of New South Wales
EACPI .... European Association of Country Planning Institutions   (EAIO)
EACR .... European Association for Cancer Research   (EAIO)
EACROTANAL ... Eastern African Centre for Research on Oral Traditions and African National Languages
eacs .... East African Commercial & Shipping Co. Ltd. [*Kenya*]
EACS .... European Association of Chinese Studies   (EA)
EACSA ...... East African Common Services Authority
EACSO ...... East African Common Services Organization [*Later, EAC*]
EACTA ...... European Association of Cardiothoracic Anaesthesiologists [*Cambridge, England*]   (EAIO)
EACW .... Ein-Ausgabecodewandler [*German*]   (ADPT)
EAD .... Ekonomik Arastirma Dernegi [*Economic Research Association*]   (TU)
EAD .... Engineers Australian Database
EAD .... European Association of Decaffeinators [*France*]   (EAIO)
EAD .... Extended Air Defense [*NATO*]
EADA .... East African Dental Association
EADB .... East African Development Bank [*Uganda*]   (AF)
EADB .... Experimental Arctic Data Buoy   (MSC)

EADCA ..... East African Directorate of Civil Aviation
EADE .... Epitropi Apokatastaseos tis Dimokratias eis tin Ellada [*Committee for the Restoration of Democracy in Greece*]   (GC)
EADE .... Ethniki Andidiktatoriki Dimokratiki Enotis [*National Antidictatorial Democratic Unity*]   (GC)
EADI .... European Association of Development Research and Training Institutes   (EAIO)
EADP .... European Association of Directory Publishers   (EA)
EADPTA ... Exotic Animal Disease Preparedness Trust Account
EAE .... Aerosevicios Ecuatorianos CA [*Ecuador*] [*ICAO designator*]   (FAAC)
EAE .... East African Engineers
EAE .... Ein-/Ausgabeeinheit [*German*]   (ADPT)
EAE .... Elliniki Andikarkiniki Etaireia [*Greek Cancer Society*]   (GC)
EAE .... Elliniki Astronavtiki Etaireia [*Greek Astronautical Society*]   (GC)
EAE .... Emae [*Vanuatu*] [*Airport symbol*]   (OAG)
EAE .... Empresa Agropecuaria Estatal [*Agricultural and Livestock Enterprise*] [*Cuba*]   (LA)
EAE .... Estacion Agricola Experimental de Leon [*Agricultural Experiment Station of Leon*] [*Spanish*]   (ARC)
EAE .... Etats d'Afrique Equatoriale   (FLAF)
EAEC .... East African Economic Community
EAEC .... East African Extract Corporation
EAEC .... East Asian Economic Caucus
EAEC .... Egyptian Atomic Energy Commission
EAEC .... European Atomic Energy Community [*Also, EURATOM*]   (DCTA)
EAEC .... European Automotive Engineers Cooperation
EAEE .... Ellinikai Andidiktatorikai Epitropai Exoterikou [*Greek Antidictatorial Committees Abroad*]   (GC)
EAEE .... European Association for Earthquake Engineering   (PDAA)
EAEE .... Evangelische Arbeitsgemeinschaft fuer Erwachsenenbildung in Europa [*Protestant Association for Adult Education in Europe*]   (EAIO)
EAEG .... East Asian Economic Group [*Australia*]
EAEG .... European Association of Exploration Geophysicists   (EAIO)
EAEM ...... Escola de Agronomia Eliseu Maciel [*Brazil*]   (DSCA)
EAEM ...... European Airlines Electronics Meeting   (PDAA)
EAEME ..... East African Electrical and Mechanical Engineers
EAEN .... Escuela de Altos Estudios Nacionales [*National War College*] [*Bolivia*]   (LA)
EAEP .... Estacion Agricola Experimental de Palmira [*Colombia*]   (DSCA)
EAES .... European Atomic Energy Society [*Denmark*]   (SLS)
EAESP ...... European Association of Experimental Social Psychology   (EA)
EAET .... East African External Telecommunications Co.   (PDAA)
EAETLFFM ... European Association for the Exchange of Technical Literature in the Field of Ferrous Metallurgy [*Luxembourg*]   (EA)
EAF .... East African Federation
EAF .... East African Forces
EAF .... Egyptian Air Force
EAFE .... Europe, Australia, and Far East
EAFFRO .... East African Freshwater Fisheries Research Organisation
EAFIT .... Escuela de Administracion y Finanzas e Instituto Tecnologico [*Colombia*]   (COL)
EAFORD ... International Organisation for the Elimination of All Forms of Racial Discrimination [*Geneva, Switzerland*]   (EAIO)
E Afr .... East Africa
EAFRO ...... East African Fisheries Research Organization
EAFS .... European Academy of Facial Surgery   (EAIO)
EAFV .... Eidgenoessische Anstalt fuer das Forstliche Versuchswesen [*Swiss Federal Institute for Forestry Research*] [*Swiss Federal Institute of Technology*]   (ERC)
EAG .... Ecole d'Application du Genie [*North African*]
EAG .... Economists Advisory Group
EAG .... Elektroakusztikai Gyar [*Electroacoustical Factory*]   (HU)
EAG .... Etablissements Andre Gallais
EAGA .... East Asian Growth Area [*International Trade*]
EAGC .... East African Governors' Conference
EAGC .... Ente Autonomo di Gestione per il Cinema [*Italy*]
EAGE .... Ethniki Akadimia Grammaton kai Epistimon [*National Academy of Letters and Sciences*]   (GC)
EAGE .... Ethniki Akadimia Grammaton kai Tekhnon [*National Academy of Arts and Letters*]   (GC)
EAGLE ...... European Association for Grey Literature Exploitation [*Database producer*]   (EAIO)
EAGLEPEN ... Eagle Pencil de Colombia SA [*Colombia*]   (COL)
EAGS .... European Association of Exploration Geophysics [*International Council of Scientific Unions*]
EAH .... European Academy of History   (EA)
EAHA .... European Association of Hospital Administrators   (EA)
EAHC .... East African Harbours Corporation
EAHC .... East African High Commission [*or Commissioner*]
EAHC .... East Asia Hydrographic Commission   (ASF)

EAHIL....... European Association of Health Information and Libraries [*Stockholm, Sweden*] (EAIO)
EAHM...... European Association of Hospital Managers [*France*] (EAIO)
EAHP........ European Association of Hospital Pharmacists (EAIO)
EAHRA ..... East African Railways and Harbours Administration
EAHTRC... East African Human Trypanosomiasis Research Centre
EAI .... East African Industries
EAI .... Ecole d'Application de l'Infrastructure [*Algeria*]
EAI .... Ellinikon Andikarkinikon Institouton (Agiou Savva) [*Greek Cancer Institute (Ag. Savvas)*] (GC)
EAI .... Equipos Agricolas Interdirecciones [*Venezuela*] (DSCA)
EAIMB..... East African Industries Management Board
EAIMR ..... East African Institute for Medical Research
EAIMTR ... East African Institute of Meteorological Training and Research
EAIMVD... East African Institute of Malaria and Vector-Borne Diseases
EAINC...... East African Indian National Congress
EAIRB ...... East African Industrial Research Board
EAIRO...... East Africa Industrial Research Organization
EAISR ...... East African Institute of Social Research
EAJCC ..... European Association of Jewish Community Centres (EAIO)
EAK .... Egyesult Arab Koztarsasag [*United Arab Republic*] (HU)
EAK .... Enosis Agroton Kyprou [*Union of Cypriot Farmers*] (GC)
EAK .... Ethnikon Agronomikon Komma [*National Agrarian Party*] GK (GC)
EAK .... Europai Atommagkutatasi Kozpont [*European Nuclear Science Research Center*] (HU)
EAK .... Evangelische Arbeitsgemeinschaft zur Betreung der Kriegsdienstverweigerer [*Protestant Association for the Pastoral Service of Conscientious Objectors*] [*Germany*]
EAK .... Evropaiki Amyntiki Koinotis [*European Defense Community*] (GC)
EAKKI ...... Epitoanyagipari Kozponti Kutato Intezet [*Central Research Institute of the Building Materials Industry*] (HU)
EAKN ...... Ethnikon Athlitikon Kendron Neotitos (Agiou Kosma) [*National Youth Athletic Center (Ag. Kosmas)*] [*Greek*] (GC)
EAKS........ Ein/Ausgabe Kontroll-System [*German*] (ADPT)
EAL .... Ecuadorian Academy of Language (EAIO)
EAL .... Elektro-Akustisches Laboratorium [*Electro-Acoustic Laboratory*] (EG)
EAL .... Enosis Agoniston Levkosias [*Union of Nicosia Fighters*] (GC)
EAL .... Equiticorp Australia Ltd.
EAL .... Ethiopian Airlines Share Co. (AF)
EAL .... Europe Africa Line
EALA .... East African Legislative Assembly
EALA .... East African Library Association
EALB .... East Africa Literature Bureau
EALCAE ... Ecumenical Association of Laity Centres and Academies in Europe [*See also OVATE*] [*Germany*] (EAIO)
EALGA..... East Asian Librarians' Group of Australia (ADA)
EALIS....... Egyptian Association of Archives, Librarianship, and Information Science (SLS)
EALM....... European Association of Livestock Markets [*See also AEMB*] [*Belgium*] (EAIO)
EALO .... Ethnic Affairs Liaison Officer [*Australia*]
EALR .... East Africa Protectorate Law Reports
EALRC ..... East African Leprosy Research Centre
EALRGA... East Asian Library Resources Group of Australia
EALS .... East African Literature Service
EAM .... Elektronische Analogmaschine [*Electronic Analog Computer*] (EG)
EAM .... ELF [*Essences et Lubrifiants de France*] Aquitaine Maroc
EAM .... Eniaion Armenikon Metopon [*Armenian United Front*] (GC)
EAM .... Entreprises Ali Mheni [*Construction and civil engineering firm*] [*Tunis, Tunisia*] (MENA)
Ea M .... Epitoanyagipari Miniszterium/Miniszter [*Ministry/Minister of the Building Materials Industry*] (HU)
EAM .... Escolas de Aprendizes-Marinheiros [*Schools For Apprentice Seamen*] [*Brazil*] (LA)
EAM .... Ethnikon Apelephtherotikon Metopon [*National Liberation Front*] [*Greek*] (PPE)
EAM .... European Association of Metals [*Belgium*] (EAIO)
EAM .... Nejran [*Saudi Arabia*] [*Airport symbol*] (OAG)
EAMA .... Etats Africains et Malgache Associes [*Afro-Malagasy States Associated (with the EEC)*] (AF)
EAMAC .... Ecole Africaine de la Meteorologie et de l'Aviation Civile
EAMB .... Exploitation Agricole Mecanisee de Battambang [*Battambang Mechanized Agricultural Enterprise*] [*Cambodia*] (CL)
EAMC .... Entreprise Africaine de Menuiserie et de Construction
EAMCAHS ... European Association of Music Conservatories, Academies, and High Schools [*Switzerland*] (EAIO)
EAMCBP .. European Association of Makers of Corrugated Base Papers (EAIO)
EAMD....... East African Meteorological Department
EAME .... European, African, Middle East Theaters of Operations
EAMEAACS ... Europe, Africa, and Middle East Airways and Communication Service

EAMECM ... European-African-Middle Eastern Campaign Medal
EAMF........ European Association of Music Festivals (EA)
EAMFO ..... East African Marine Fisheries Organisation
EAMFRO ... East African Marine Fisheries Research Organization (MSC)
EAMFS ..... European Association for Maxillo-Facial Surgery (EA)
EAMHMS ... European Association of Museums of the History of Medical Sciences [*See also AEMHSM*] (EAIO)
EAMO....... United Antifascist Youth Organization (BU)
EAMRC..... East African Medical Research Council
EAMRDC ... East African Mineral Resources Development Centre
EAMREA ... Environment Impact Assessments of Mineral Resource Exploration and Exploitation in the Antarctic [*ICSU*] (MSC)
EAMS........ Euro-Arab Management School [*Granada, Spain*] (ECON)
EAMTM ... European Association of Machine Tool Merchants [*British*] (EAIO)
EAMU .... East Africa Malaria Unit
EAMVBD ... East African Institute of Malaria and Vector-Borne Disease [*Tanzania*] (PDAA)
EAMW ...... East African Metal Works Ltd. [*Kenya*]
EAMWS.... East African Muslim Welfare Society
EAN .... Association Internationale de Numerotation des Articles [*International Article Numbering Association*] (EAIO)
EAN .... Effective Atomic Number (RU)
EAN .... Elliniki Andidiktatoriki Neolaia [*Greek Antidictatorial Youth*] (GC)
EAN .... Estacao Agronomica Nacional [*Portugal*] (DSCA)
EAN .... Europaeische Artikel Numerlerung [*German*] (ADPT)
EAN .... Express Airways Nigeria Ltd. [*ICAO designator*] (FAAC)
E & A Co... Eastern & Australian Steamship Company (ADA)
EANDC ..... European American Nuclear Data Committee [*ENEA*] [*France*]
E & PForum ... Oil Industry International Exploration and Production Forum (EA)
EANE .... Ethniki Andikommounistiki Neolaia Ellados [*National Anticommunist Youth of Greece*] (GC)
EANHS ..... East Africa Natural History Society
EANHS ..... East African National Health Service
EANHS ..... East African Natural History Society (EAIO)
EANPC...... European Association for National Productivity Centers [*See also AECNP*] (EAIO)
EANRRC... East African Natural Resources Research Council [*Kenya*] (PDAA)
EANS........ European Article Numbering System (PDAA)
EANS........ European Association of Neurosurgical Societies (EAIO)
EANSL...... East African National Shipping Lines
EAO.......... East African Oxygen Ltd. [*Kenya*]
EAO.......... Egyptian Agricultural Organization
EAO.......... Egyptian Antiquities Organization (EAIO)
EAO.......... Enseignement Assiste par Ordinateur [*French*] (ADPT)
EAO.......... Entreprise Africaine Ortal
EAO.......... Etats d'Afrique de l'Ouest (FLAF)
EAO.......... Ethnikai Andartikai Omades [*National Guerrilla Groups*] [*Greek*] (GC)
EAO.......... Europaeische Akademie Otzenhausen eV [*European Academy of Otzenhouse*] (SLS)
EAOG........ European Association of Organic Geochemists (EAIO)
EAOK........ Ethnika Andikommounistikai Omades Kynigon [*National Anticommunist Hunters' Groups*] (GC)
EAP .... East Africa Protectorate
EAP .... Ecole Europeenne des Affaires [*European School of Management*] [*Paris*]
EAP .... Ecological Agriculture Projects [*See also PAE*] [*Sainte Anne De Bellevue, PQ*] (EAIO)
EAP .... Economic Action Plan [*Liberal Party of Australia*]
eap............. Effet a Payer [*Bill Payable*] [*French*] [*Business term*]
EAP .... Electrical Autopilot (RU)
EAP .... Electronic Acoustic Converter (RU)
EAP .... Employment Access Program [*Australia*]
EAP .... Emulatoranschluss-programm [*German*] (ADPT)
EAP .... Engineered Australian Plan (ADA)
EAP .... English for Academic Purposes [*Australia*]
EAP .... Epitropi Analyseos kai Programmatismou [*Analysis and Planning Committee*] (GC)
EAP .... Epitropi Apokatastaseos Prosfygon [*Refugee Resettlement Committee*] [*Greek*] (GC)
EAP .... Escuela Agricola Panamericana [*Honduras*] (DSCA)
EAP .... Escuela de Administracion Publica [*Venezuela*] (LAA)
EAP .... Estacao Agraria do Porto [*Portugal*] (DSCA)
EAP .... Europaeische Arbeiterpartei [*European Workers' Party*] [*Germany*] [*Political party*] (PPE)
EAPA .... European Asphalt Pavement Association (EA)
EAPA........ Exhibited Animals Protection Act [*Australia*]
EAP & T .... East African Posts and Telecommunications Administration
EAPCC...... European Association of Poison Control Centers (EAIO)
EAPCCCT ... European Association of Poisons Control Centers and Clinical Toxicologists [*Sweden*] (EAIO)

EAPCO...... East African Pesticides Control Organization   (PDAA)
EAPDTh.... Epitropi dia tin Apokatastasin kai Prostasian Dimokratikon Thesmon [*Committee for the Restoration and Protection of Democratic Institutions*] [*Greek*]   (GC)
EAPFBO ... European Association of Professional Fire Brigade Officers   (EA)
EAPG........ Eastern Atlantic Planning Guidance [*NATO*]   (NATG)
EAPH .... East African Publishing House
EAPHSS ... European Association of Programmes in Health Services Studies   (EAIO)
EAPL........ East African Power and Lighting Company Ltd.
EAPL........ East Australian Pipeline Ltd. [*Commercial firm*]
EAPL........ Eastern Africa Publications Limited
EAPM....... European Association of Perinatal Medicine   (EAIO)
EAPM....... European Association of Personnel Management [*Paris, France*]   (EA)
EAPP........ Engineered Australia Plan Party [*Political party*]
EAPP........ European Association for the Promotion of Poetry   (EA)
EAPR........ Europaische Gesellschaft fur Kartoffelforschung [*Netherlands*]   (EAIO)
EAPR........ European Association for Potato Research   (EAIO)
EAPS........ European Association for Population Studies   (EA)
EAPS........ European Association of Professional Secretaries [*Paris, France*]   (EAIO)
EAPTC...... East African Posts and Telecommunications Corporation
EAR .... East African Railways [*Kenya*]   (AF)
ear .... Effet a Recevoir [*Bill Receivable*] [*French*] [*Business term*]
EAR .... Elliniki Anatoliki Roumeli [*Greek Eastern Roumelia*]   (GC)
EAR .... Elliniki Aristera [*Greek Left Party*] [*Political party*]   (EY)
EaR .... Entartungs-Reaktion [*Reaction of Degeneration*] [*German*]
EAR .... European Association of Radiology   (EA)
EARC........ East African Railways Corporation
EARC........ East Africa Royal Commission
EARC........ Electoral and Administrative Review Commission [*Queensland, Australia*] [*Proposed*]
EARCCUS ... East African Regional Committee for the Conservation and Utilisation of the Soil
EARDHE .. European Association for Research and Development in Higher Education [*Austria*]   (SLS)
EARH .... East African Railways and Harbours Authority
EARIC ...... East African Research Information Centre
EARL........ Electronically Accessible Russian Lexicon
EARL........ Esso Australia Resources Ltd. [*Commercial firm*]
EAROPH .. East Asia Regional Organization for Planning and Housing   (ML)
EARPC...... East African Royal Pioneer Corps
EARS........ Egypt Amateur Radio Socity   (PDAA)
EARS........ Eldoret Agricultural Research Station [*Kenya*]   (DSCA)
EARSEL.... European Association of Remote Sensing Laboratories   (EA)
EAs........... East African Shilling [*Monetary unit*]
EAS........... East African Standard [*Nairobi*]
EAS........... Ebonit ve Akumulator Sanayii AS [*Ebonite and Battery Industry Corporation*]   (TU)
EAS........... Eingabe/Ausgabesystem [*Input/Output System*] [*German*]   (ADPT)
EAS........... Electronique Aerospatiale [*France*]
EAS........... Ellinikos Andiapoikiakos Syndesmos [*Greek Anti-Colonialist League*]   (GC)
EAS........... Empresa Antillana de Salvamentos [*West Indian Salvage Company*]   (LA)
EAS........... Energy Advisory Service [*New Zealand*]
EAS........... Ethnikos Andidiktatorikos Stratos [*National Antidictatorial Army*] [*Greek*]   (GC)
EAS........... Ethnikos Apelevtherotikos Stratos [*National Liberation Army*] [*Greek*]   (GC)
EAS........... Ethnikos Apelevtherotikos Synaspismos [*National Liberation Alliance*] [*Cyprus*]   (GC)
EAS........... Europe Aero Service
EAS........... European Accident Statement
EAS........... European Aquaculture Society   (EA)
EAS........... European Astronomical Society
EAS........... European Atherosclerosis Society   (EA)
EAS........... Excutive Aerospace (Pty) Ltd. [*South Africa*] [*ICAO designator*]   (FAAC)
EAS........... Executive Air Services Proprietary Ltd. [*Australia*]   (ADA)
EAS........... Rapid Analyzer of Ultra-Sound Velocity   (RU)
EAS........... San Sebastian [*Spain*] [*Airport symbol*]   (OAG)
EASA........ East African School of Aviation [*Kenya*]   (PDAA)
EASA........ Electronics Association of South Australia
EASA........ Engineers' Association of South Africa
EASA........ Ethniki Akadimia Somatikis Agogis [*National Physical Education Academy*]   (GC)
EASAA...... European Association of South Asian Archaeologists [*British*]   (EAIO)
EASACT ... Employee Assistance Service Australian Capital Territory Ltd.
EASB........ East African Settlement Board
EASC........ East African School Certificate

EASC........ East African Service Corps
EASCO...... East African Common Services Organisation
EASCO...... European Association of Schools and Colleges of Optometry   (EA)
EASD........ European Association for the Study of Diabetes [*See also AEED*]   (EAIO)
EASE........ Entertainment Access Service [*Australia*]
EASE........ Ethnikon Andifasistikon Symvoulion Ergazomenon [*National Antifascist Council of Workers*] [*Greek*]   (GC)
EASE........ European Association for Special Education [*Sweden*]   (SLS)
EASE........ European Association of Science Editors [*European Association of Earth Science Editors and European Life Sciences Editors*] [*Formed by a merger of*]   (EAIO)
EASHP...... European Association of Senior Hospital Physicians   (PDAA)
EASI......... European Association of Shipping Informatics [*Brussels, Belgium*]   (EAIO)
EASIT ...... European Association for Software Access and Infomation Transfer   (PDAA)
EASIT ...... Integrated Automated System for Control and Processing of Transport Information   (BU)
EASK........ Enosis Athlitikon Syndakton Kyprou [*Cypriot Sports Writers Union*]   (GC)
EASKEN ... Eniaia Andidiktatoriki Syndikalistiki Kinisi Ellinon Navtergaton [*United Antidictatorial Labor Movement of Greek Seamen*] [*Organized in Hamburg, Federal Republic of Germany, in July 1967 AESKEN*] [*Also,*]   (GC)
EASL........ Eastern African Shipping Lines
EASL........ European Association for the Study of the Liver   (SLS)
EASO........ Egyptian Arab Socialist Organization
EASP........ Egyptian Arab Socialist Party
EASP........ Escuela de Administracion de Empresas de Sao Paulo [*Brazil*]   (LAA)
EASSG ...... European Accountancy Students Study Group   (PDAA)
EAST........ East Australian Standard Time
EAST........ Euro-Arab Sea Trailer Line [*Saudi Arabia*]
EAST........ European Academy of Science and Technology
EASTLANT ... Eastern Atlantic Area [*NATO*]
EASTLANTMEDCOM ... Eastern Atlantic and Mediterranean Command
EASTROPIC ... Cooperative Survey of the Eastern Tropical Pacific   (MSC)
EASY........ Caucus Committee on Education, Arts, Science and Youth [*Australia*]
EAT .... Air Transport Ltd. [*Slovakia*] [*ICAO designator*]   (FAAC)
EAT .... East African Time
EAT .... Eidikon Anakritikon Tmima [*Special Investigating Section (of ESA)*]   (GC)
EAT .... ELF [*Essences et Lubrifiants de France*] Aquitaine Tunisie
EAT .... Entreprise Africaine de Travaux
EAT .... Ethiopia Aid Tonight [*Australia*]
EAT .... European Advertising Tripartite [*Brussels, Belgium*]   (EA)
EAT .... European Association of Teachers [*See also AEDE*]   (EAIO)
EATA........ East Asia Travel Association   (EAIO)
EATC........ East African Training Centre
EATCHIP ... European Air Traffic Control Harmonization and Integration Program [*Eurocontrol*]
EATCS...... European Association for Theoretical Computer Science   (EAIO)
EATEC...... East African Tanning Extract Company
EATEP...... Equipe de Asistencia Tecnica ao Ensino Primario [*Elementary Education Technical Assistance Team*] [*Rio De Janeiro, Brazil*]   (LAA)
EATIC....... East African Tuberculosis Investigation Centre [*Kenya*]   (PDAA)
EATITU .... East African Tractor and Implement Testing Unit
EATJP...... European Association for the Trade in Jute Products   (EA)
EATM .... ELF Aquitaine Triako Mines Ltd. [*Australia*]
EATO........ Euro-Asia Trade Organisation
EATOP...... Epitropi Avtodioikiseos kai Topikon Provlimaton [*Committee for Local Self-Government and Local Problems*]   (GC)
EATP........ European Association for Textile Polyolefins   (EAIO)
EATRO ..... East African Trypanosomiasis Research Organisation
EAT's....... East African Troops
EATS........ Electronic Automatic Telephone Exchange   (RU)
EATSCO.... Egyptian American Transport & Services Company
EATTA...... East African Tea Trade Association   (EA)
EATTA...... East Africa Tourist Travel Association
EATTRRO ... East African Tsetse and Trypanosomiasis Research and Reclamation Organization
EATUC...... East African Trade Unions Congress
EATWOT ... Ecumenical Association of Third World Theologies [*India*]
EATZ........ Elektronische Automatische Telefonzentrale [*Electronic Automatic Telephone Exchange*]   (EG)
EAU.......... Emirats Arabes Unis
EAU.......... European Association of Urology
EAUDRL... Egyptian Authority for Utilization and Development of Reclaimed Lands
EAUG....... European Atex Users Group [*Deventer, Netherlands*]   (EAIO)
EAUS........ Unified Electronic Subassembly System   (RU)
EAV .... Elliniki Aeroporiki Viomikhania [*Greek Aircraft Industry*]   (GC)

EAV .... Escola de Agronomia e Veterinaria [*Brazil*]   (DSCA)
EAV .... Estacao Agraria de Viseu [*Portugal*]   (DSCA)
EAV .... Eszak-Magyarorszagi Aramszolgaltato Vallalat [*Electric Power Enterprise of Northern Hungary*]   (HU)
EAV .... Evangelische Afrika Verein
EAVA .... European Association of Veterinary Anatomists   (EA)
EAVE .... European Audiovisual Entrepeneurs [*EC*]   (ECED)
EAVRI ...... East African Virus Research Institute
EAVRO ...... East African Veterinary Research Organisation
EAW .... Eingabeauswahl [*Input Selection*] [*German*]   (ADPT)
EAW .... Eisenbahnausbesserungswerk [*Railroad Repair Yard*]   (EG)
EAW .... Elektro-Apparatewerk [*Electrical Apparatus Plant*]   (EG)
EAWAG .... Eidgenoessische Anstalt fuer Wasserversorgung, Abwasserreinigung, und Gewasserschutz [*Swiss Federal Institute for Water Resources and Water Pollution Control*] [*Research center*]   (IRC)
EAWLS ..... East African Wild Life Society [*Kenya*]   (SLS)
EAWP .... Eastern Atlantic War Plan [*NATO*]   (NATG)
EAWP .... Ethnic Aged Working Party [*Australia*] [*Political party*]
EAWR ...... Eingabeauswahlregister [*Input Selection Register*] [*German*]   (ADPT)
EAY .... Emirlikler Anadolu Yatirim [*Emirates-Anatolia Investment Company*] [*Turkey*]
EAZ .... Elektronische Abrechnungszentrale [*Electronic Calculation Center*] [*German*]   (ADPT)
EB .... Butyl Ethyl Acetate [*Solvent*]   (RU)
eb .... Ebarbe [*Trimmed*] [*Publishing*] [*French*]
EB .... Efficiency Beurs [*Netherlands*]
eb .... Egeszborkotes [*Full-Leather Binding*] [*Publishing*] [*Hungary*]
EB .... Egyezteto Bizottsag (Uzem) [*(Plant) Arbitration Committee*] (HU)
EB .... Ekonomski Biro [*Economic Bureau*]   (YU)
EB .... Elektrisk Bureau [*Electric Board*] [*Norway*]
EB .... Element Binaire [*Binary Element*] [*French*]   (ADPT)
EB .... Energiebezirk [*Power District*]   (EG)
EB .... Entwurfsbuero [*Design Office*]   (EG)
EB .... Ere Bouddhique [*Buddhist Era*] [*Cambodia*]   (CL)
EB .... Escadre de Bombardement [*French bomber wing*]
EB .... Escuadron Basico [*Basic Squadron*] [*Bolivia*] [*Military*]
EB .... Eskortni Brodovi [*Escort Ships*] [*Navy*]   (YU)
EB .... Estibordo [*Starboard*] [*Portuguese*]
EB .... Etat Belge [*Belgian State*]   (BAS)
EB .... Ethiopian Birr [*Monetary Unit*]   (BARN)
EB .... Ettore Bugatti [*Auto engineer*] [*French*]
EB .... Europa Bajnoksag [*European Championships*]   (HU)
EB .... Evacuation Hospital   (BU)
EB .... Evako-Bolnice [*Evacuation Hospitals*] [*Military*]   (YU)
EB .... ExtraBoom Enterprise Co. Ltd. [*Taiwan*]
EBA .... Ecole des Beaux Arts [*Paris, France*]
EBA .... Ekonomik Basin Ajansi [*Economic Press Agency*]   (TU)
EBA .... Elba Island [*Italy*] [*Airport symbol*] [*Obsolete*]   (OAG)
EBAA .... European Business Aviation Association
EBAD .... Ecole des Bibliothecaires Archivistes et Documentalistes
EBAE .... European Bureau of Adult Education   (EAIO)
EBAG .... Europaeische Bildungs- und Aktionsgemeinschaft [*European Education and Activity Association*]   (SLS)
EBAL .... Aalst [*Belgium*] [*ICAO location identifier*]   (ICLI)
EBAL .... Editora Brasil-America Limitada [*Publisher*] [*Brazil*]   (EY)
EBAM .... Amougies [*Belgium*] [*ICAO location identifier*]   (ICLI)
EBAM .... Empresa Brasileira Comercial e Industrial de Alem Mar [*Brazilian Overseas Commercial and Industrial Company*]   (LA)
EBAP .... Escola Brasileira de Administracao Publica [*Brazilian School of Public Administration*]   (LA)
ebarb .... Ebarbe [*Trimmed*] [*Publishing*] [*French*]
EBAW .... Antwerp-Anvers [*Belgium*] [*ICAO location identifier*]   (ICLI)
EBB .... Endoskopbau, Berlin [*Berlin Endoscope Plant*]   (EG)
EBB .... Entebbe/Kampala [*Uganda*] [*Airport symbol*]   (OAG)
EBB .... Evakuaciska Bolnicka Baza [*Evacuation Hospital Base*] [*Military*]   (YU)
EBBB .... Brussels [*Belgium*] [*ICAO location identifier*]   (ICLI)
EBBCO ...... Emirates Bunkering & Bitumen Company
EBBD .... Central Data Bank, EUROCONTROL [*Belgium*] [*ICAO location identifier*]   (ICLI)
EBBE .... Beauvechain [*Belgium*] [*ICAO location identifier*]   (ICLI)
EBBL .... Klein Brogel [*Belgium*] [*ICAO location identifier*]   (ICLI)
EBBR .... Brussels/National [*Belgium*] [*ICAO location identifier*]   (ICLI)
EBBS .... Brussels [*Belgium*] [*ICAO location identifier*]   (ICLI)
EBBS .... European Brain and Behaviour Society   (PDAA)
EBBT .... Brasschaat [*Belgium*] [*ICAO location identifier*]   (ICLI)
EBBU .... Brussels [*Belgium*] [*ICAO location identifier*]   (ICLI)
EBBV .... Brussels [*Belgium*] [*ICAO location identifier*]   (ICLI)
EBBX .... Bertrix [*Belgium*] [*ICAO location identifier*]   (ICLI)
EBC .... Aero Ejecutivo de Baja California SA de CV [*Mexico*] [*ICAO designator*]   (FAAC)
EBC .... Electoral Boundaries Commission [*Victoria, Australia*]

EBC .... Enterprise-Based Committee [*Australia*]
EBC .... European Brewery Convention
EBC .... Evakuacioni Bolnicki Centar [*Evacuation Hospital Center*] [*Military*]   (YU)
EBC .... Externer Bildschirmtext-Computer   (ADPT)
EBCI .... Charleroi/Gosselies [*Belgium*] [*ICAO location identifier*]   (ICLI)
EBCI .... European Biological Control Laboratory   (ECON)
EBCS .... European Barge Carrier System   (PDAA)
EBCT .... Empresa Brasileira de Correios e Telegrafos [*State enterprise*] [*Brazil*]   (EY)
EBCV .... Chievres [*Belgium*] [*ICAO location identifier*]   (ICLI)
ebd .... Ebenda [*or Ebendaselbst*] [*In the Same Place*] [*German*]   (EG)
Ebd .... Einband [*Binding*] [*Publishing*] [*German*]
EBD .... El Obeid [*Sudan*] [*Airport symbol*]   (OAG)
ebda .... Ebenda [*In the Same Place*] [*German*]
EBE .... Exportation des Bois Exotiques
ebenf.......... Ebenfalls [*Also*] [*German*]
EBES .... Societes Reunies d'Energie du Bassin et l'Escant [*French*]
EBESSA .... Societe Reunis d'Energie du Bassin de l'Escaut SA [*Belgium*]   (PDAA)
EBF .... Europaeische Baptistische Foderation [*European Baptist Federation - EBF*]   (EAIO)
EBF .... Europaeische Baptistische Frauenunion [*European Baptist Women's Union - EBWU*]   (EAIO)
EBFBRG ... European Bank of Frozen Blood of Rare Groups [*Amsterdam, Netherlands*]   (EAIO)
EBFN .... Koksijde [*Belgium*] [*ICAO location identifier*]   (ICLI)
EBFS .... Florennes [*Belgium*] [*ICAO location identifier*]   (ICLI)
EBFYC ..... European Baptist Federation Youth Committee   (EAIO)
EBG .... Ecobank Ghana   (EY)
EBG .... El Bagre [*Colombia*] [*Airport symbol*]   (OAG)
EBG .... Engin Blinde du Genie [*French*]
EBGB .... Brussels/Grimbergen [*Belgium*] [*ICAO location identifier*]   (ICLI)
EBGL .... Glons [*Belgium*] [*ICAO location identifier*]   (ICLI)
EBGM ...... Eti Bank Genel Mudurlugu [*Eti Bank Directorate General*]   (TU)
EBGT .... Gent/St. Denijs Westrem [*Belgium*] [*ICAO location identifier*]   (ICLI)
EBHN .... Hoevenen [*Belgium*] [*ICAO location identifier*]   (ICLI)
EBI .... Electricite-Batiment-Industrie
EBI .... Elektronisches Besucher-Informationssystem [*Electronic Visitor Information System*] [*German*]   (ADPT)
EBI .... Ethnic Broadcasters, Inc. [*Australia*]
EBI .... European Bioinformatics Institute
EBIC .... EFTA [*European Free Trade Association*] Brewing Industry Council   (EAIO)
EBIC .... European Banks International Company
EBIF .... European Button Industries Federation [*British*]   (EAIO)
E(B)IR ...... Escuela (Basica) de Instruccion Revolucionaria [*(Basic) Revolutionary Training School*] [*Cuba*]   (LA)
EBIS .... ESCAP [*Economic and Social Commission for Asia and the Pacific*] Bibliographic Information System [*Thailand*] [*United Nations Information service or system*]   (IID)
EBJ .... Esbjerg [*Denmark*] [*Airport symbol*]   (OAG)
EBK .... Elektroenergie-Bezugskarte [*Electric Power Consumption Permit*]   (EG)
EBK .... Et ve Balik Kurumu Genel Mudurlugu [*Meat and Fish Association Directorate General*] [*Under Ministry of Commerce*]   (TU)
EBKH .... Balen/Keiheuvel [*Belgium*] [*ICAO location identifier*]   (ICLI)
EBKT........ Kortrijk-Wevelgem [*Belgium*] [*ICAO location identifier*]   (ICLI)
EBL .... European Bridge League   (EAIO)
EBLB .... Elsenborn [*Belgium*] [*ICAO location identifier*]   (ICLI)
EBLG .... Liege/Bierset [*Belgium*] [*ICAO location identifier*]   (ICLI)
EBLH .... Liege/Bierset [*Belgium*] [*ICAO location identifier*]   (ICLI)
EBLUL ...... European Bureau for Lesser Used Languages   (EA)
EBM .... Eisen-, Blech-, und Metallwaren [*Iron, Sheetmetal, and Metalware*]   (EG)
EBM .... Empreendimentos Brasileiros de Mineracao [*Brazilian Mining Enterprises*]   (LA)
EBM .... Enterprise Business Model [*Australia*]
EBM .... Estacion de Biologia Marina [*Marine Biological Station*] [*Vina Del Mar, Chile*]   (LAA)
EBM .... Europaeische Baptistische Mission [*European Baptist Mission*] [*Germany*]   (EAIO)
EBM .... European Baptist Mission   (EAIO)
EBMB........ Melsbroek [*Belgium*] [*ICAO location identifier*]   (ICLI)
EBMI .... Brussels [*Belgium*] [*ICAO location identifier*]   (ICLI)
EB Mitte .... Energiebezirk Mitte [*Central Energy District*]   (EG)
EBMM ...... Estacion de Biologia Marina de Montemar [*Chile*]   (DSCA)
EBMO ...... Moorsele [*Belgium*] [*ICAO location identifier*]   (ICLI)
EBMT........ Munte [*Belgium*] [*ICAO location identifier*]   (ICLI)
EBN .... Elektroenergie-Bezugsnachweis [*Electric Power Consumption Voucher*]   (EG)
EBN .... Empresa Brasileira de Noticias [*Brazilian News Agency*]   (LA)
EBN .... European Business and Innovation Centre Network [*Belgium*]

EBNM .... Namur-Suarlee [*Belgium*] [*ICAO location identifier*] (ICLI)
EB Nord..... Energiebezirk Nord [*North Energy District*] (EG)
EBO .... Jadrova Elektraren Jaslovske Bohunice [*Nuclear Power Plant Jaslovske Bohunice*] (CZ)
EBOS........ Oostende [*Belgium*] [*ICAO location identifier*] (ICLI)
EBPE .... European Biotech Partnering Event
EBPS .... European Baptist Press Service [*of the European Baptist Federation*] (EAIO)
EBR .... East Bengal Regiment [*Pakistani army*]
EBR .... Electric Drill (RU)
EBR .... Engin Blinde de Reconnaissance [*Armored Reconnaissance Vehicle*] [*French*] (WER)
Ebr .... Eparhija Broj [*Eparchy Number*] [*Diocese of Orthodox Eastern Church, Serbian*] (YU)
EBRC........ Economic and Budget Review Committee [*Victoria, Australia*]
EBRD .... European Bank for Reconstruction and Development [*Economic assistance for Eastern Europe*] [*Proposed*]
EBRS .... European Businessman's Readership Survey [*Conducted by the Financial Times*]
EBS............ Eastern Bering Sea
EBS............ Eli-Fly SpA [*Italy*] [*ICAO designator*] (FAAC)
EBS............ Eridania-Beghin Say [*France*] (ECON)
EBS............ Ethiopian Broadcasting System
EBS............ European Book Service [*Netherlands*]
EBSA .... Estuarine and Brackish-Water Sciences Association (EAIO)
EBSC .... European Bird Strike Committee (PDAA)
EBSH........ Saint-Hubert [*Belgium*] [*ICAO location identifier*] (ICLI)
EBSL .... Zutendaal [*Belgium*] [*ICAO location identifier*] (ICLI)
EBSLG ...... European Business School Librarians Group [*London Business School*] [*Information service or system*] (IID)
EBSP .... Spa/La Sauveniere [*Belgium*] [*ICAO location identifier*] (ICLI)
EBST .... Sint-Truiden [*Belgium*] [*ICAO location identifier*] (ICLI)
EBSU .... Saint-Hubert [*Belgium*] [*ICAO location identifier*] (ICLI)
EB Sud ...... Energiebezirk Sued [*South Energy District*] (EG)
EBSZ .... Semmerzake [*Belgium*] [*ICAO location identifier*] (ICLI)
EBTN .... Goetsenhove [*Belgium*] [*ICAO location identifier*] (ICLI)
EBTTC ...... European Baptist Theological Teachers' Conference [*Germany*] (EAIO)
EBTU........ Empresa Brasileira de Transportes Urbanos [*Brazilian Urban Transport Company*] [*Brasilia*] (LA)
EBTX......... Theux-Verviers [*Belgium*] [*ICAO location identifier*] (ICLI)
EBTY......... Tournai/Maubray [*Belgium*] [*ICAO location identifier*] (ICLI)
EBTZ .... Electrical Bathythermograph (RU)
EBU .... European Badminton Union (EA)
EBU .... European Blind Union (EA)
EBU .... European Broadcasting Union [*Switzerland*]
EBU .... Europese Betalingsunie [*Benelux*] (BAS)
EBU .... St. Etienne [*France*] [*Airport symbol*] (OAG)
EBUL......... Ursel [*Belgium*] [*ICAO location identifier*] (ICLI)
EBUM ...... Brussels [*Belgium*] [*ICAO location identifier*] (ICLI)
EBUR .... Brussels [*Belgium*] [*ICAO location identifier*] (ICLI)
EBV .... Erdoel-Bevorratungsverband
EBVA........ Brussels [*Belgium*] [*ICAO location identifier*] (ICLI)
EBWE....... Weelde [*Belgium*] [*ICAO location identifier*] (ICLI)
EB West.... Energiebezirk West [*West Energy District*] (EG)
EBWM ...... Brussels [*Belgium*] [*ICAO location identifier*] (ICLI)
EBWU ...... European Baptist Women's Union (EAIO)
EBY .... Empresa Binacional Yacyreta [*Argentina*] (IMH)
EBY .... Entidad Binacional Yacyreta [*Yacyreta Binational Agency*] [*Argentina*] (LA)
EBY .... European Blue Cross Youth Association (EAIO)
EBZH .... Hasselt [*Belgium*] [*ICAO location identifier*] (ICLI)
EBZR .... Zoersel [*Belgium*] [*ICAO location identifier*] (ICLI)
EBZW....... Genk/Zwartberg [*Belgium*] [*ICAO location identifier*] (ICLI)
EC .... East Caribbean
ec .... Ecaille [*Mottled*] [*Publishing*] [*French*]
EC .... Echanges Compenses [*Compensated Exchange*] [*Cambodia*] (CL)
EC .... Ecole Centrale [*Central School of Engineering*] [*Paris, France*]
EC .... Economic Council, Arab League
Ec .... Ecossais [*Scottish*] [*Freemasonry*] [*French*]
EC .... Ecuador [*ANSI two-letter standard code*] (CNC)
EC .... Elections Communales [*Benelux*] (BAS)
EC .... Electricna Centrala [*Electrical Station*] (YU)
EC .... Electronics Corp. of India Ltd.
EC .... Energy Corp. [*Philippines*] (DS)
EC .... Entente Council [*See also CE*] (EAIO)
EC .... Era Crista [*Portuguese*]
EC .... Escadre de Chasse [*French aircraft attack wing*]
EC .... Esquerra Catalana [*Catalan Left*] [*Spanish*] (WER)
EC .... Estat Catala [*Catalan State*] [*Spanish*] (WER)
EC .... Ethiopian Calendar
EC .... Etudes Camerounaises
EC .... EURAIL [*European Railway*] Community (EAIO)
EC .... Euro-Children (EAIO)
EC .... EuroCity [*Railroad*]

EC .... European Commission
EC .... European Community [*Collective name given to the consolidation of the European Coal and Steel Community, the Common Market, and the European Atomic Energy Community*]
EC .... European Companions (EAIO)
EC .... Exercise Commander [*NATO*] (NATG)
ECA .... Economic Commission for Africa [*Addis Ababa, Ethiopia*] [*See also CEA*] [*United Nations*] (EAIO)
ECA .... Economische Commissie voor Africa [*Economic Commission for Africa*] [*United Nations*]
ECA .... [*The*] Educational Corp. of America (ECON)
ECA .... Empire Centrafricain [*Central African Empire*] [*Use CAE*] (AF)
ECA .... Empresa Colombiana de Aerodromos [*Colombian Airport Corporation*] (LA)
ECA .... Empresa Consolidada de Azucar [*Consolidated Sugar Enterprise*] [*Cuba*] (LA)
ECA .... Empresa Cubana de Artistas [*Cuban Artists Enterprise*] (LA)
ECA .... Empresa de Comercio Agricola [*Agricultural Commerce Enterprise*] [*Chile*] (LA)
ECA .... Ensenanza Cultural para Adultos (Programa) [*Agency for Cultural Education*] [*Bolivia*] (LAA)
ECA .... Entreprise de Conditionnement d'Air [*Algeria*]
ECA .... Entreprise du Centre Afrique
ECA .... Environmental Choice Australia
ECA .... Equipments et Componants pour l'Automobile [*Automobile Equipment and Components*] [*Peugeot-Citroen*] [*France*]
ECA .... Estabilizacion y Conservacion Agricola [*Puerto Rico*] (DSCA)
ECA .... Etablissement Central de l'Armement [*Central Armament Establishment*] [*Research center*] [*French*] (ERC)
ECA .... Eurocypria Airlines Ltd. [*Cyprus*] [*ICAO designator*] (FAAC)
ECA .... European Camac Association [*Belgium*] (SLS)
ECA .... European Catering Association [*Germany*] (EAIO)
ECA .... European Choral Association (EA)
ECA .... European Combat Aircraft (PDAA)
ECA .... European Commission on Agriculture [*FAO*] [*United Nations*]
ECA .... European Co-operation Administration (OMWE)
ECA .... Europe China Association (EA)
ECA .... Exercit Catala d'Alliberament [*Catalonian Liberation Army*] [*Spanish*] (WER)
ECA .... Societe d'Etudes et Constructions Aeronautiques [*French*]
ECA .... Societe Eburneenne de Courtage et d'Assurances
ECAC....... East Coast Armaments Complex [*Australia*]
ECAC........ European Civil Aviation Conference [*See also CEAC*] (EAIO)
ECACC...... European Collection of Animal Cell Cultures [*Cell bank*] (ECON)
ECADR...... Nordic Council for Alcohol and Drug Research (EA)
ECADSS.... Executive Controller Australian Defence Scientific Service
ECAF........ Empresa Consolidada de Aprovechamiento Forestal, Aserrio y Elaboracion de Madera y Carbon Vegetal [*Cuba*] (DSCA)
ECAFE ...... Economic Commission for Asia and the Far East [*Later, ESCAP*] [*United Nations*]
ECAHTI.... European Committee for Agricultural and Horticultural Tools and Implements (EA)
ECAJ .... Executive Council of Australian Jewry (ADA)
ECAM ...... Ecole Centrale des Arts et Metiers [*Arts and Crafts Central School*] [*Belgium*] [*Research center*] (ERC)
ECAM ...... Employers' Consultative Association of Malawi
ECAM ...... Entreprise de Construction d'Automobiles Malgaches
ECAM ...... Escuela de Cadetes Interarmas General Antonio Maceo [*General Antonio Maceo Interservice School*] [*Cuba*] (LA)
ECAM ...... Euro-China Association for Management Development
ECAMA .... European Citric Acid Manufacturers Association [*of the European Council of Chemical Manufacturers' Federations*] (EAIO)
ECAMWP ... European Committee of Associations of Manufacturers of Welding Products (EA)
ECANSW ... Electrical Contractors' Association of New South Wales [*Australia*]
ECAP........ Empresa Consolidada de Almacenes de Ferreteria [*Consolidated Enterprise of Hardware Warehouses*] [*Cuba*] (LA)
ECAP........ European Conflict Analysis Project [*NATO*]
Ec Appl ...... Economie Appliquee [*France*] (FLAF)
ECAR........ Empresa Consolidada de Aguas Minerales y Refrescos [*Consolidated Mineral Water and Soft Drinks Enterprise*] [*Cuba*] (LA)
ECARBICA ... East and Central African Regional Branch, International Council of Archives
ECAS........ East and Central African States
ECA (SA)... Electrical Contractors Association (South Africa) (AA)
ECAT........ Ecole Coloniale d'Agriculture de Tunis
ECAT........ Ecole d'Appui Tactique [*French*]
ECATRA .... European Car and Truck Rental Association (EA)
ECATT ...... Employers' Consultative Association of Trinidad and Tobago (EAIO)
ECAW ...... European Council for Animal Welfare (EA)
ECB........... Economic Co-Operation Bureau [*Foreign Ministry*] [*Japan*]
ECB........... Entreprise Camerounaise de Batiments

ECB........... Environmental and Conservation Bureau [*Australian Capital Territory*]

ECB........... Environment Coordination Board [*United Nations*]

ECB........... European Central Bank

ECB........... European Coordination Bureau for International Youth Organizations G2 [*See also BEC*]   (EAIO)

ECB........... L'Echo de la Bourse [*Benelux*]   (BAS)

ECBA........ European Communities Biologists Association [*Belgium*]   (EAIO)

ECBA........ European Communities Biologists Organization [*University of Bremen*]   (EAIO)

ECBC........ Krasnodar English Club Business Center   (EAIO)

ECBF........ European Community Banking Federation [*Belgium*]   (EAIO)

ECBS........ East Central Broadcasting System

ECBTE...... European Committee for Building Technical Equipment [*See also CEETB*]   (EAIO)

ecc .... Eccetera [*And So On*] [*Italian*]   (GPO)

ecc .... Eccezionale [*Exceptional*] [*Italian*]

ECC .... Emergency Cleansing Corps [*Singapore*]   (ML)

ECC .... End Conscription Campaign [*South Africa*]

ECC .... Esperanto Cultural Centre [*Switzerland*]   (EAIO)

ECC .... European Corsetry Commission [*Belgium*]   (EAIO)

ECC .... European Crystallographic Committee [*International Council of Scientific Unions*]

ECC .... European Cultural Centre [*Geneva, Switzerland*]

ECC .... Ex-Communist Country

ECC .... Exercise Control Centre [*Australia*]

ECCA........ Eastern Caribbean Currency Authority   (LA)

ecca .... Eclesiastica [*Ecclesiastical*] [*Spanish*]

ECCAI....... European Coordinating Committee for Artificial Intelligence   (EAIO)

ECCAS ...... Economic Community of Central African States [*See also CEEAC*] [*Bangui, Central African Republic*]   (EAIO)

ECCB......... Eastern Caribbean Central Bank [*Formerly, East Caribbean Currency Authority*] [*Basseterre, St. Christopher*]   (GEA)

ECCC........ European Communities Chemistry Committee   (EA)

eccess .... Eccessivo [*Excessive*] [*Italian*]

ECCI .... Empresa de Construcoes Civis e Industriais Lda.

ECCJ .... European Communities Court of Justice   (DLA)

eccl .... Ecclesiastico [*Ecclesiastical*] [*Italian*]

eccles.......... ecclesiastical   (TPFD)

eccles.......... Ecclesiastique [*French*]   (TPFD)

ECCLS....... European Committee for Clinical Laboratory Standards [*Kent, England*]

ECCM .... East Caribbean Common Market   (DS)

ECCM .... Empresa Consolidada de Consignatarias Mambisas [*Mambisas Cuban Ship's Agent Enterprise*]   (LA)

ECCMF ..... European Council of Chemical Manufacturers' Federations   (ASF)

ECCNSW .. Ethnic Communities Council of New South Wales [*Australia*]

ecco............. Eclesiastico [*Ecclesiastical*] [*Spanish*]

ECCO .... European Conference of Conscripts Organisations   (EAIO)

ECCO .... European Culture Collections' Organization   (EAIO)

ECC ofACT ... Ethnic Communities Council of the Australian Capital Territory

ECCP........ European Chamber of Commerce of the Philippines   (DS)

ECCR-Afrique ... Etudes, Couritage, Commerce, Representation en Afrique

ECCS .... European Committee for Consultant Services   (EA)

ECCSA ...... Ethnic Communities Council of South Australia

ECCTO..... European Chemical Coastal Tanker Owners

ECCTO..... European Community Cocoa Trade Organization   (EAIO)

ECD .... Environnement de Controle et de Decision [*French*]   (ADPT)

ECDA .... Empresa Colombiana de Anuncios Ltda. [*Colombia*]   (COL)

ECDC .... Economic Cooperation among Developing Countries [*United Nations*]

ECDIN ...... Environmental Chemicals Data and Information Network [*Commission of the European Communities*] [*Chemical databank*]   (IID)

ECDIN ...... European Chemical Data and Infomation Network [*EURATOM*]   (PDAA)

ECDMMRL ... European Committee for the Development of the Meuse and Meuse/Rhine Links   (EAIO)

ECDP........ Early Childhood Development Programme [*Australia*]

ECDU .... European Christian Democratic Union [*Brussels, Belgium Political party*]   (EAIO)

ECE........... East Central Europe   (ECON)

ECE........... Economic Commission for Europe [*United Nations*]   (EECI)

ECE........... Empresa Consolidada de Electricidad [*Consolidated Electric Power Enterprise*] [*Cuba*]   (LA)

ECE........... Empresa de Comercio Exterior [*Ecuador*]   (EY)

ECE........... European Commodities Exchange [*of the European Economic Community*]

ECE........... Export Council for Europe   (ILCA)

ECE........... L'Equipement et la Construction Electrique [*French*]

ECEA........ Economic Community of Eastern Africa

ECEA........ Empresa de Construccion de Equipos Agricolas [*Agricultural Equipment Manufacturing Enterprise*] [*Cuba*]   (LA)

ECEJAETA ... European Chamber of Extra-Judicial Adjudicators and Expert Technical Advisers [*See also CEASPECT*]   (EA)

ECE/JP ..... Early Childhood Education/Junior Primary [*Australia*]

ECEL........ European Council for Environmental Law   (PDAA)

ECEM....... Ecole de Commandement et d'Etat-Major [*Command and Staff School*] [*Zaire*]   (AF)

ECEMAR ... Escola de Comando e Estado-Maior da Aeronautica [*Air Force Command and General Staff School*] [*Brazil*]   (LA)

ECEME..... Escola de Comando e Estado-Maior do Exercito [*Army Command and General Staff School*] [*Brazil*]   (LA)

ECEPLAN ... Escritorio de Planejamento e Controle [*Brazil*]   (DSCA)

ECESDB.... European Commodities Exchange Statistical Database [*United Nations*]   (DUND)

ECETOC ... European Chemical Industry Ecology and Toxicology Centre [*Belgium*]   (PDAA)

Ec et Pol..... Economie et Politique [*France*]   (FLAF)

ECEX........ Empresa de Engenharia e Construcoes Especiais [*Engineering and Special Construction Enterprise*] [*Brazil*]   (LA)

ECF........... Empresa Cubana de Fletes [*Cuban Freight Enterprise*]   (LA)

ECF........... Eurasier Club de France   (EAIO)

ECF........... Eurocopter [*France*] [*ICAO designator*]   (FAAC)

ECF........... European Caravan Federation   (EA)

ECF........... European Coffee Federation   (EAIO)

ECF........... European Cultural Foundation   (EAIO)

ECF........... Evangelize China Fellowship

ECFA........ Engineering Consulting Firms Association [*Japan*]   (PDAA)

ECFA........ European Committee for Future Activities   (PDAA)

ECF-IUF ... European Committee of Food, Catering, and Allied Workers' Unions within the IUF [*International Union of Food and Allied Workers' Associations*]   (EAIO)

ECFS .... Export Credit Facilitation Scheme [*Australia*]

ECFTO ..... Ecuador Confederation of Free Trade Union Organizations   (EAIO)

ECFV .... Electrical Contractors Federation of Victoria [*Australia*]

ECG .... Ecosystem Conservation Group [*United Nations (already exists in GUS II database)*]   (ASF)

ECG .... Electricity Corporation of Ghana

ECG .... European Contact Group on Urban Industrial Mission   (EAIO)

ECG .... European Cooperation Grouping   (DCTA)

ECGC .... Empire Cotton Growing Corporation

ECGC .... Export Credit & Guarantee Corporation Ltd. [*India*]

ECGF........ European Container Glass Federation   (EA)

ECGLC...... Economic Community of the Great Lakes Countries [*See also CEPGL*] [*Gisenye, Rwanda*]   (EAIO)

ECGM .... Ecological Center, Green Movement   (EAIO)

ech.............. Echantillon [*Sample*] [*Business term*] [*French*]

ECh........... Elementary Particles   (RU)

ECH........... Empresa Consolidada de la Harina [*Consolidated Flour Enterprise*] [*Cuba*]   (LA)

ECHAP ..... Empresa Publica de la Comercializacion de Harina y Aceite de Pescado [*Public Enterprise for Marketing Fishmeal and Fish Oil*] [*Peru*]   (LA)

ECHC .... European Colloquium on Heterocyclic Chemistry

ECHO....... Early Childhood Organisation [*Australia*]

ECHO....... European Commission Host Organization [*Commission of the European Communities*] [*Host system*] [*Luxembourg*] [*Information service or system*]   (IID)

ECHO....... Exchange Clearing House Organization [*European bank coalition*]   (ECON)

EChP .... Screened Four-Tube Receiver   (RU)

ECHR .... European Commission of Human Rights   (EA)

ECHSA..... Elderly Citizens Homes of South Australia

ECI............ Early Childhood Institute [*Macquarie University*] [*Australia*]

ECI............ Electronics Corp. of Israel [*Tel-Aviv*] [*Research center*]   (ERC)

ECI............ Equipos y Controles Industriales [*Colombia*]   (COL)

ECI............ European Confederation of Independents [*Germany*]   (EAIO)

ECI............ European Federation of Trade Unions for Energy, Chemical, and Miscellaneous Industries   (EA)

ECIAL....... Ensenanza de las Ciencias y de la Ingenieria en la America Latina   (LAA)

ECICS....... Export Credit Insurance Corp. of Singapore   (FEA)

Ecie .... Ecurie [*Stable*] [*Military map abbreviation World War I*] [*French*]   (MTD)

ECIEL ...... Programa de Estudios Conjuntos sobre la Integracion Economica Latinoamericana [*Program of Joint Studies for Latin American Economic Integration*]   (EAIO)

ECIL .... Empresa de la Industria Lactea [*Dairy Industry Consolidated Enterprise*] [*Cuba*]   (LA)

ECIM......... Estacion Costera de Investigaciones Marinas [*Chile*]

ECIMACT ... Empresa Comercial para Industria de Materiales, Construccion, y Turismo [*Commercial Enterprise for Construction Materials, Building, and Tourism*] [*Cuba*]   (LA)

ECIMETAL ... Empresa Comercial de la Industria Metalurgica y Metal-Mecanica [*Commercial Enterprise for the Metallurgical and Metalworking Industry*] [*Cuba*]   (LA)

EC-IOA ..... European Committee of the International Ozone Association [*See also CEAIO*]   (EA)
ECIP .... European Cooperation in Information Processing   (PDAA)
ECIPP .... Early Childhood Injury Prevention Program [*Australia*]
ECIQUIM ... Empresa Comercial de Industrias Quimicas [*Chemical Industries Commercial Enterprise*] [*Cuba*]   (LA)
ECIRC .... European Computer Industry Research Centre   (PDAA)
ECIS .... Elvis Costello Information Service [*Netherlands*]   (EAIO)
ECIS .... European Colloid and Interface Society
ECIS .... European Council of International Schools   (EA)
ECIT .... Escuelas Cubanas de Instruccion Tecnica [*Cuban Technical Training Schools*]   (LA)
ECITC .... European Committee for IT [*Information Technology*] Testing and Certification   (OSI)
ECJ .... Berlin European [*ICAO designator*]   (FAAC)
ECJ .... Court of Justice of the European Communities   (DLA)
ECJCS .... European Council of Jewish Community Services   (EA)
ECK .... East Coast Airlines Ltd. [*Kenya*] [*ICAO designator*]   (FAAC)
ECK .... Elektrochemisches Kombinat [*Electrochemical Combine*]   (EG)
ECK .... Etude en Commun du Kuro-Shio et des Regions Adjacentes [*Cooperative Study of the Kuroshio and Adjacent Regions - CSK*] [*French*]   (MSC)
ecl .... Eclate [*Broken*] [*Publishing*] [*French*]
ecl .... Ecloga [*Ecloque*] [*Portuguese*]
ECL .... Ecole Centrale de Lyon [*Lyon Central College*] [*Research center*] [*France*]   (ERC)
ECL .... Egyptian Confederation of Labor
ECL .... Enterprise Container Lines
ECLA .... Economic Commission for Latin America [*Database originator*] [*Later, ECLAC*] [*United Nations*]
ECLA .... European Clothing Association [*Belgium*]   (EAIO)
ECLAC ...... Economic Commission for Latin America and the Caribbean [*See also CEPAL*] [*Santiago, Chile*] [*United Nations*]   (EAIO)
ECLAIR .... European Collaborative Linkage of Agriculture and Industry through Research [*EC*]   (ECED)
ECLAS ...... European Commission Library Automated System [*Database*] [*EC*]   (ECED)
eclat .... Eclate [*Broken*] [*Publishing*] [*French*]
ECLAT ...... European Computer Lessors and Trading Association   (PDAA)
ECLATEL ... Empresa Commercial Latinoamericana de Telecommunicaciones [*Latin America Commercial Telecommunications Enterprise*]   (PDAA)
ECLE .... European Centre for Leisure and Education   (EA)
ecles .... Eclesiastico [*Ecclesiastical*] [*Portuguese*]
ECLG .... European Consumer Law Group   (EA)
ECLIM ...... European Conference on LASER Interaction with Matter and LASER Thermonuclear Fusion   (PDAA)
ECLM .... Economic Community for Livestock and Meat [*See also CEBV*]   (EAIO)
ECLP .... Egyptian Communist Labour Party
ECM .... Empresa Consignataria Mambisa [*Mambisa Steamship Enterprise*] [*Cuba*]   (LA)
ECM .... Etude en Commun de la Mediterranee [*Cooperative Investigations in the Mediterranean - CIM*] [*French*]   (MSC)
ECM .... European Christian Mission
ECM .... European Common Market
ECMA .... European Carton Makers Association   (PDAA)
ECMA .... European Catalysts Manufacturers Association [*of the European Council of Chemical Manufacturers' Federation*]   (EAIO)
ECMA .... European Collectors and Modellers Association   (EAIO)
ECMA .... European Computer Manufacturers Association [*Switzerland*]
ECMAL ..... Exxon Coal and Minerals Australia Ltd.
ECMALGOL ... European Computer Manufacturers Association Algorithmic Language
ECMB .... Economic Consequences of Marriage Breakdown [*Survey*] [*Australia*]
ECMB .... European Committee for Mini-Basketball [*See also CEMB*] [*Germany*]   (EAIO)
ECMC .... European Container Manufacturers Committee   (EA)
ECME .... Economic Commission for the Middle East [*United Nations*]   (DS)
ECMES ..... Societe d'Entreprise de Construction, d'Ebenisterie et de Menuiserie du Senegal
ECMF .... European Community Mortgage Federation [*Brussels, Belgium*]   (EA)
ECMo .... Einsatzstahl mit Chrom und Molybdaen [*Casehardened Steel with Chromium and Molybdenum*] [*German*]   (GCA)
ECMRA ..... European Association for Business Research, Planning, and Development in the Chemical Industry [*Formerly, European Chemical Market Research Association*] [*British*]
ECMRWF ... European Centre for Medium-Range Weather Forecasts   (PDAA)
ECMT .... European Conference of Ministers of Transport   (EAIO)
ECMWF .... European Center for Medium-Range Weather Forecasting

ECN .... Einsatzstahl mit Chrom und Nickel [*Casehardened Steel with Chromium and Nickel*] [*German*]   (GCA)
ECN .... Electricity Corporation of Nigeria
ECN .... Energieonderzoek Centrum Nederland [*Netherlands Energy Research Foundation*] [*Research center*]
ECN .... Ercan [*Cyprus*] [*Airport symbol*]   (OAG)
ECNAIS .... European Council of National Associations of Independent Schools [*Denmark*]   (EAIO)
ECNAMP ... East Caribbean Natural Area Management Program   (EAIO)
ECNAMP ... Eastern Caribbean Natural Area Management Program   (LA)
ECNDT ...... European Council for Nondestructive Testing   (EA)
ECNOS ...... Eastern Atlantic, Channel and North Sea Orders for Ships [*NATO*]   (NATG)
ECNR .... European Council for Nuclear Research   (DCTA)
ECNSW ..... Environment Centre, New South Wales [*Australia*]
ECNT .... Environment Centre, Northern Territory [*Australia*]
ECO .... East Coast Airlines [*Australia*] [*ICAO designator*]   (FAAC)
ECO .... Economic Cooperation Office
ECO .... Economic Co-Operation Organization [*Iran, Pakistan, and Turkey*]   (MENA)
ECO .... Entreprise Commerciale de l'Ouest Africain
ECO .... European Consumers Organization [*Belgium*]   (EAIO)
ECOA .... Empresa Constructora de Obras de Arquitectura [*Architectural Projects Construction Enterprise*] [*Cuba*]   (LA)
ECOCARBON ... Empresa Colombiana del Carbon [*National Coal Enterprise*] [*Colorado*]   (LA)
ECOCOM ... Economic Commission for Europe [*United Nations*]   (DS)
ECODES ... Empresa Consolidada de Servicio Electrodomestica [*Consolidated Enterprise for Electric Household Appliance Service*] [*Cuba*]   (LA)
ECOFIN .... Economic and Financial Council of Ministers [*EC*]   (ECED)
ECOI .... Empresa Constructora de Obras de Ingenieria [*Engineering Projects Construction Enterprise*] [*Cuba*]   (LA)
ECOL .... Empresa Colombiana Ltda. [*Colombia*]   (COL)
Ecolo .... Parti Ecologiste [*Ecologist Party*] [*Belgium*]   (PPW)
ECOLOS ... Ecological Coalition on the Law of the Sea   (ASF)
ECOM .... Empresa Nacional de Computacion e Informatica SA [*Chile*]   (EY)
ECOM .... Especialidades Consumidas por la Seguridad Social [*Ministerio de Sanidad y Consumo*] [*Spain*] [*Information service or system*]   (CRD)
ECOMA .... Entreprise Commerciale d'Arrondissement [*District Trading Enterprise*] [*Guinea*]   (AF)
ECOMA .... European Computer Measurement Association
ECOME .... Empresa de Construcoes Metalicos [*Agricultural equipment enterprise*] [*Mozambique*]
ECOMED ... Ecological Mediterranean [*An association*] [*Turkey*]   (EAIO)
ECOMINAS ... Empresa Colombiana de Minas [*Colombian Mining Enterprise*]   (LA)
ECOMOG ... Economic Community Monitoring Group [*West Africa*]
ECOMOL ... Empresa Construtora Mocambicana Lda.
ECOMOR ... Excedent du Cout Moyen Relatif [*Insurance*] [*France*]   (FLAF)
ECOMSA ... Empresa Nacional de Computacion y Informatica Sociedad Anonima [*Santiago, Chile*]
Econ .... Economics   (PWGL)
Econ .... Economie [*Benelux*]   (BAS)
Econ .... Economist   (EECI)
Econ .... Economy   (PWGL)
ECONA ...... Economistas Asociados [*Barranquilla*]   (COL)
ECONEC ... Entreprise de Construction Economique
EcoNet .... Ecological Network of Israel   (EAIO)
ECONIQUEL ... Empresa Colombia de Niquel   (EY)
Econ Pol ..... Economia Politica [*Political Economy*] [*Portuguese*]
ECOP .... Employers' Confederation of the Philippines [*An association*]   (FEA)
ECOPAL ..... Empresa Colombiana de Pavimentos Ltda. [*Colombia*]   (COL)
ECOPETROL ... Empresa Colombiana de Petroleos [*Colombian Petroleum Enterprise*] [*Colombia*]   (LA)
ECOPLAS ... Empresa Colombiana de Plasticos Ltda. [*Colombia*]   (COL)
EcoPol .... Societe d'Economie Poitique de Belgique [*Belgium*]   (BAS)
ECOPREFIL ... Empresa de Correos, Prensa, y Filatelia [*Post, Press, and Postal Stamps Enterprise*] [*Cuba*]   (LA)
ECOPS ...... European Committee on Ocean and Polar Science
ECOR .... Engineering Committee on Oceanic Resources [*Later, SUT*] [*United Nations*]
ecorch .... Ecorche [*Skinned*] [*French*]
ECOREP ... Entreprise Nationale de Construction et Reparation des Bateaux de Peche, d'Approvisionnement, et de Fabrication de Materiels de Peche [*Algeria*]   (IMH)
ECORS ...... Etude de la Croute Continentale et Oceanique par Reflexion et Refraction Sismiques [*France*]
ECOSA ...... European Conference on Optical Systems and Applications   (PDAA)
ECOSOC ... Economic and Social Committee [*EC*]   (ECED)
ECOSOC ... Economic and Social Council [*ICSU*] [*United Nations*]
ECOSOL ... European Centre of Studies on Linear Alkylbenzene [*Belgium*]   (EAIO)

ECOSS ..... European Conference on Surface Science
ECOTEC ... Bureau National d'Etudes Economiques et Techniques [*National Office for Economic and Technical Studies*] [*Algeria*]   (AF)
ECOTECH ... China International Economic and Technical Cooperation Consultants, Inc.   (TCC)
ECOTEX ... Entreprise Nationale des Industries de Confection et de Bonneterie [*Nationalized industry*] [*Algeria*]   (EY)
ECOTROP ... Laboratory of Tropical Ecology [*France*]   (IRC)
ECOWAS ... Economic Community of West African States [*Treaty signed May 28, 1975*]
ECP............ Congolese Progressive Students [*Zaire*]   (PD)
EC/P .... Early Childhood/Primary
ECP............ Ecole Centrale de Pyrotechnie [*French*]   (MTD)
ECP............ Ecole Centrale des Arts et Manufactures (Paris) [*French*]
ECP............ Egyptian Communist Party [*Political party*]   (PD)
ECP............ Entreprise de Canalisation et de Plomberie
ECP............ Ethiopian Communist Party [*Political party*]   (PD)
ECP............ European Organization for Cancer Prevention Studies
ECPA......... Empresa Constructora de Pozos y Acueductos Ltda. [*Barranquilla*]   (COL)
ECPA......... Etablissement Cinematographique et Photographique des Armees [*France*]   (PDAA)
ECPA......... Expert Committee on Post Adjustments [*United Nations*]
ECPC......... Egyptian Company for Prestressed Concrete
ECPCDP ... Euro-Commercial Paper and Certificates of Deposit Programme [*Finance*]
ECPE .... European Centre of Public Enterprise   (EAIO)
ECPH .... Encyclopedia of China Publishing House [*Publisher*] [*China*]
ECPH .... European Committee of Private Hospitals [*Belgium*]   (EAIO)
ECPMAOA ... Executive Committee's Panel on Meteorological Aspects of Ocean Affairs [*WMO*]   (MSC)
ECPP .... Empresa Consolidada de Pulpa y Papel [*Cuba*]   (DSCA)
ECPR......... European Confederation of Public Relations [*France*]   (EAIO)
ECPR......... European Consortium for Political Research [*Colchester, Essex, England*]   (EAIO)
ECPRD...... European Centre for Parliamentary Research and Documentation [*See also CERDP*] [*Luxembourg, Luxembourg*]   (EAIO)
ECPS .... Environment and Consumer Protection Service [*EEC*]   (DS)
ECPS .... European Centre for Population Studies [*Netherlands*]   (SLS)
ECPS .... European Council for Payments Systems
ECPSA ...... European Consumer Product Safety Association [*EC*]   (ECED)
ECPT .... European Confederation for Physical Therapy   (EAIO)
ECPTT ...... Ecole Centrale des Postes et Telecommunications [*Algeria*]
ECR .... Air Charter Express AS [*Norway*] [*ICAO designator*]   (FAAC)
ECR .... Ecoles des Cadets de la Revolution [*Algeria*]
ECR .... Enemy Contact Report [*NATO*]   (NATG)
ECR .... Estacao de Culturas Regadas [*Portugal*]   (DSCA)
ECR .... European Commercial Register [*EC*]   (ECED)
ECRC......... European Computer-Industry Research Centre [*Germany*]   (IRC)
ECRE......... European Consultation on Refugees and Exiles
ECRED...... Equipe de Coordenacao de Credito Rural [*Brazil*]   (DSCA)
ECRIE ...... European Center for Research and Information Exchange [*Belgium*]   (EAIO)
ECRO .... European Chemoreception Research Organization [*Research center*] [*Switzerland*]   (IRC)
ECRT........ European Confederation of Retail Tobacconists [*Luxembourg*]   (EA)
ECS............ Echantillons Commerciaux/Commercial Samples [*International trade*] [*French*]
ECS............ Electronic Control Systems Proprietary Ltd. [*Australia*]   (ADA)
ECS............ Engineering Computer Sales Proprietary Ltd. [*Australia*]
ECS............ Episcopal Church of the Sudan
ECS............ Escadron de Commandement et de Service [*Command and Service Squadron*] [*French*]   (WER)
ECS............ Ethnic Children's Service [*Australia*]
ECS............ European Chemical Society
ECS............ European Communications Satellite   (ADPT)
ECS............ European Confederation of Scouts   (EAIO)
ECS............ European Space Conference
ECS............ Executive Counselling Service [*Australia*]
ECSA........ EEC [*European Economic Community*] Ship Owners Association [*Belgium*]   (EAIO)
ECSA........ European Chips and Snacks Association [*British*]   (EAIO)
ECSA........ European Chlorinated Solvent Association   (EAIO)
ECSA........ European Community Shipowners' Associations [*Belgium*]   (EAIO)
ECSA........ European Computing Services Association
ECSC........ European Coal and Steel Community [*France, West Germany, Italy, BENELUX*]
Ecse........... Ecluse [*Lock, Flood Gate*] [*Military map abbreviation World War I*] [*French*]   (MTD)
ECSEDA ... Eastern Caribbean States Export Development Agency [*Dominica*]   (EY)
ECSF .... European Civil Service Federation   (EAIO)

ECSI .... European CAD [*Computer-Aided Design*] Standardization Initiative [*Computer science*]
ECSLA ...... European Centre of Studies on Linear Alkylbenzene   (EAIO)
ECSMA ..... European Copper Sulphate Manufacturers' Association   (EAIO)
ECSS .... European Committee for the Study of Salt   (EA)
ECSS .... European Communication Satellite System
ECSSA....... European Centre for Studies of Sulfuric Acid   (EAIO)
ECSSID..... European Cooperation in Social Science Information and Documentation
ECST .... European Convention on the Suppression of Terrorism
Ec-St B...... Economisch-Statistische Berichten [*Benelux*]   (BAS)
ECSWTR .. European Centre for Social Welfare Training and Research [*See also CEFRAS*] [*United Nations*]   (EAIO)
ECT .... Empresa de Correios e Telegrafos [*Postal and Telegraph Company*] [*Brazil*]   (LA)
ECT .... Esquerra Catalana dels Treballadors [*Workers Leftist Movement of Catalonia*] [*Spanish*]   (WER)
ECT........... Intreprinderea Electroceramica Turda [*Turda Electroceramics Plant*]   (RO)
ECTA........ Early Childhood Teachers' Association [*Australia*]
ECTA........ East Caribbean Tourism Association
ECTA........ European Cutting Tools Association   (EA)
ECTAA...... Group of National Travel Agents' Associations within the EEC   (EAIO)
ECTCI ...... Entreprise Commerciale et de Transports en Cote-D'Ivoire
ECTEL ...... European Telecommunications and Professional Electronics Industry [*European Conference of Associations of Telecommunications Industries and European Conferente of Radio and Electronic Equipment Associations*] [*Formed by a merger of*]   (EAIO)
ECTF .... Episcopal Commission on Tribal Filipinos [*Philippines*]   (EAIO)
ECTG........ European Channel Tunnel Group
ECTH .... Entreprise de Construction et de Travaux Hydrauliques
ECTI......... Echanges et Consultations Techniques Internationaux
ECTMAC.. East Coast Trawler Management Advisory Council [*Australia*]
ECTPWF... European Confederation for Trade in Paint, Wall- and Floorcoverings   (EAIO)
ECTS .... European Calcified Tissue Society   (EA)
ECTS .... European Conference on Telecommunications by Satellite
ECTT........ Ecole Chinoise de Tennis de Table [*France*]   (EAIO)
ECTV........ Empresa Consolidada de Tiendas de Viveres [*Consolidated Enterprise of Grocery Stores*] [*Cuba*]   (LA)
ECTWT ..... Ecumenical Coalition on Third World Tourism   (EA)
ECU .... Ecuador [*ANSI three-letter standard code*]   (CNC)
ECU .... Edith Cowan University [*Australia*]
ECU .... Egyptian Cultural Union
ECu .... E-Kupfer [*High Conductivity Copper*] [*German*]   (GCA)
ECU .... European Currency Unit [*European monetary system*]   (AF)
ECUASIDER ... Ecuatoriana de Siderurgia [*Ecuadorean Iron and Steel*]   (LA)
ECUCT...... East China University of Chemical Technology
ECUFINSA ... Ecuatoriana de Financiamiento Sociedad Anonima [*Ecuador*]   (IMH)
ECUSA...... Australia-East Coast of USA Shipping Conference   (ADA)
ECUTORIANA ... Compania Ecuatoriana de Aviacion [*Ecuador*]   (PDAA)
ECV .... Esperanto Club of Veterans [*See also VEK*] [*Wolfhagen, Federal Republic of Germany*]   (EAIO)
ECVFI .... European Committee for the Valves and Fittings Industry [*Germany*]   (EAIO)
ECVP........ European Community Visitors Program
ECW .... European Council of Women [*Belgium*]   (EAIO)
ECWA .... Economic Commission for Western Asia [*Later, ESCWA*] [*United Nations*]
ECWA .... Environment Centre of Western Australia [*Australia*]
ECWA .... Evangelical Churches of West Africa
ECWAS..... Economic Community of West African States [*Treaty signed May 28, 1975*]
ECWIM..... European Committee of Weighing Instrument Manufacturers   (EAIO)
ECWP........ Egyptian Communist Workers' Party [*Political party*]   (PD)
ECWS........ European Centre for Work and Society   (EA)
ECYC........ European Confederation of Youth Clubs   (EA)
ECYFC ..... European Committee for Young Farmers and 4H Clubs   (EA)
ECYFC4HC ... European Committee for Young Farmers and 4H Clubs [*Germany*]   (EAIO)
ECYO .... European Community Youth Orchestra [*British*]   (EAIO)
Ecz.............. Eczaci [*or Eczahane*] [*Pharmacist or Pharmacy*]   (TU)
ECZ .... Eglise du Christ au Zaire
ECZ .... Elektricna Cestna Zeleznica [*Electric Streetcar*]   (YU)
ED............. Airship Shed   (RU)
ed............... Edafion [*Paragraph, Verse (of the Bible)*]   (GC)
Ed.............. Edebiyat [*Literature*]   (TU)
Ed.............. Edele [*Honorable*] [*Afrikaans*]
ed............... Edella [*or Edellinen*] [*Preceding or Previous*] [*Finland*]   (GPO)
ed............... Edicao [*Edition*] [*Portuguese*]
ed............... Edicion [*Edition*] [*Spanish*]
ed............... Edisie [*Edition*] [*Afrikaans*]

ed............... Edistyspuolue [*Finland*]
ed............... Editeur [*Editor*] [*Publishing*] [*French*]
ed............... Editie [*Edition*] [*Publishing*] [*Netherlands*]
ed............... Edition [*Edition, Issue, Publication*] [*French*]
ed............... Edito [*Edited*] [*Publishing*] [*Italian*]
ed............... Editor [*Publisher*] [*Spanish*]
Ed.............. Editore [*Editor*] [*Italian*]　(GPO)
Ed.............. Edizione [*Edition*] [*Italian*]　(GPO)
ed............... Edustaja [*Finland*]
ED.............. Efficiency Decoration
ED.............. Electric Detonator　(RU)
ED.............. Electric Differential　(RU)
ED.............. Electric Motor　(RU)
ED.............. Electrode Pickup　(RU)
ED.............. Electrodynamic (Apparatus)　(RU)
ED.............. Electronic Differentiator　(RU)
ed............... En Dergelike [*And So Forth*] [*Afrikaans*]
ED.............. Espera Deferimento [*Portuguese*]
ED.............. Esquerra Democratica [*Democratic Left*] [*Spain*] [*Political party*]　(PPE)
ED.............. Eurodefence
ED.............. European Democratic Group [*European Parliament*]　(ECED)
ED.............. European Documentation
ED.............. Units　(BU)
EDA.......... Aerolinas Nacionales del Ecuador SA [*ICAO designator*]　(FAAC)
EDA.......... Educational Drama Association [*Defunct*]　(EAIO)
EdA.......... Ejercito del Aire [*Military Air Force*] [*Spanish*]　(PDAA)
EDA.......... Electronic Differential Analyzer　(RU)
EDA.......... Enacie Demokratiki Aristera [*United Democratic Left Party*] [*Greek*]　(BARN)
EDA.......... Eniaia Dimokratiki Aristera [*United Democratic Left*] [*Athens, Greece*]　(GC)
EDA.......... Entreprise Decoration et Ameublement [*Algeria*]
EDA.......... Entwicklung Dialogorientiertes Anwendersystem [*German*]　(ADPT)
EDA.......... Environmental and Development Agency [*South Africa*]　(AA)
EDA.......... Epitropai Dimosias Asfaleias [*Public Security Committees*] [*Greek*]　(GC)
EDA.......... European Democratic Alliance [*Political movement*]　(ECON)
EDA.......... European Demolition Association　(EA)
EDA.......... European Desalination Association [*Glasgow, Scotland*]　(EAIO)
EDA.......... European Disposables Association [*Belgium*]　(PDAA)
EDAA........ Frankfurt Am Main, USAFE [*United States Air Force in Europe*] [*Germany*] [*ICAO location identifier*]　(ICLI)
EDAB........ Bitburg [*Germany*] [*ICAO location identifier*]　(ICLI)
EDAC........ Kindsbach [*Germany*] [*ICAO location identifier*]　(ICLI)
EDAD........ Spangdahlem [*Germany*] [*ICAO location identifier*]　(ICLI)
EDAF........ Escuela de Administracion y Finanzas [*School of Administration and Finances*] [*Colorado*]　(LA)
EDAF........ Rhein-Main Air Base [*Germany*] [*ICAO location identifier*]　(ICLI)
EdAgb....... EdelAgbare [*Worshipful*] [*Afrikaans*]
EDAH........ Hahn [*Germany*] [*ICAO location identifier*]　(ICLI)
EDAI........ Empresa de Automatizacion Industrial [*Industrial Automation Enterprise*] [*Cuba*]　(LA)
EDAIC....... Editora Agro-Industrial e Cientifica Ltd. [*Brazil*]　(DSCA)
EDAK....... Kindsbach [*Germany*] [*ICAO location identifier*]　(ICLI)
EDAL....... Sollingen [*Germany*] [*ICAO location identifier*]　(ICLI)
EDAM....... Zweibrucken [*Germany*] [*ICAO location identifier*]　(ICLI)
EDAN....... Epitropi Dimosias Asfaleias Nomou [*Nome Public Security Committee*] [*Greek*]　(GC)
EDAN....... Lahr [*Germany*] [*ICAO location identifier*]　(ICLI)
EDANA..... European Disposables and Nonwovens Association
EDANSW ... Electrical Development Association of New South Wales [*Australia*]
EDAO....... Gates [*Germany*] [*ICAO location identifier*]　(ICLI)
EDAP....... Enosis Dikaiomaton Anthropou kai Politou [*Union of Rights of Man and Citizen*] [*Greek*]　(GC)
EDAP....... Epitropi Diakheiriseos Andallaximou Periousias [*Committee for the Administration of Exchangeable Estates*] [*Greek*]　(GC)
EDAP....... May [*Germany*] [*ICAO location identifier*]　(ICLI)
EDAQ....... Electrical Development Association of Queensland [*Australia*]
EDAQ....... Rotz [*Germany*] [*ICAO location identifier*]　(ICLI)
EDAR....... Ramstein [*Germany*] [*ICAO location identifier*]　(ICLI)
EDAS....... Sembach [*Germany*] [*ICAO location identifier*]　(ICLI)
EDASZ...... Eszak-Dunantuli Aramszolgaltato Vallalat [*Electric Power Service Enterprise of Northern Transdanubia*] [*Hungary*]　(HU)
EDAV....... Electrical Development Association of Victoria [*Australia*]
EDAV....... Siegenberg [*Germany*] [*ICAO location identifier*]　(ICLI)
EDAW....... Wiesbaden [*Germany*] [*ICAO location identifier*]　(ICLI)
EDAWA .... Electrical Development Association of Western Australia [*Australia*]
EDAX....... Ramstein [*Germany*] [*ICAO location identifier*]　(ICLI)
EDB.......... Econometric Data Bank [*University of Melbourne*] [*Australia*] [*Information service or system*]　(CRD)

EDB.......... Economic Development Board [*Singapore*]　(IMH)
EDB.......... Einkaufs- und Dienstleistungsbetrieb [*Purchasing and Service Enterprise*]　(EG)
EDB.......... El Debba [*Sudan*] [*Airport symbol*] [*Obsolete*]　(OAG)
EDB.......... Electrodynamic Unit　(RU)
EDBA....... Berlin [*Germany*] [*ICAO location identifier*]　(ICLI)
EDBB....... Berlin/Tempelhof [*Germany*] [*ICAO location identifier*]　(ICLI)
EDBE....... Export Development Bank of Egypt
EDBG....... Berlin/Gatow [*Germany*] [*ICAO location identifier*]　(ICLI)
EDBSA...... Engine Drivers' Board of South Australia
EDBT....... Berlin/Tegel [*Germany*] [*ICAO location identifier*]　(ICLI)
EDC.......... Economic Development Commission
EDC.......... Educational and Cultural Commission
EDC.......... Education Development Centre
EDC.......... Electricite du Cambodge [*Cambodian Power Company*] [*Energie du Cambodge*] [*Formerly,*]　(CL)
EDC.......... Electricite du Cameroun [*Cameroon Electric Company*]　(AF)
EDC.......... Energie du Cambodge [*Cambodian Power Company*] [*Electricite du Cambodge*] [*Later,*]　(CL)
EDC.......... Esquerra Democratica de Catalunya [*Democratic Left of Catalonia*] [*Spanish*]　(WER)
EDC.......... European Defense Community [*NATO*]
EDC.......... European Documentation Centre
EDC.......... Exploration Data Consultants
EDC.......... Export Development Trading Corp. [*Thailand*]
EDCA....... Gluecksburg [*Germany*] [*ICAO location identifier*]　(ICLI)
EDCB....... Bueckeburg [*Germany*] [*ICAO location identifier*]　(ICLI)
EDCB....... Export Development Corporation of Bhutan　(FEA)
EDCC....... Environmental Dispute Coordination Commission [*Japan*]　(PDAA)
EDCC....... Goch [*Germany*] [*ICAO location identifier*]　(ICLI)
EDCE....... Rheine-Bentlage [*Germany*] [*ICAO location identifier*]　(ICLI)
EDCEE...... Equipo Democrata Cristiano del Estado Espanol [*Christian Democratic Team of the Spanish State*]　(WER)
EDCG....... Eggebek [*Germany*] [*ICAO location identifier*]　(ICLI)
EDCGC.... Elliott District Community Government Council [*Australia*]
EDCH....... Hurth [*Germany*] [*ICAO location identifier*]　(ICLI)
ed ch........ Singular [*Grammar*]　(BU)
EDCI....... Itzehoe Hungriger Wolf [*Germany*] [*ICAO location identifier*]　(ICLI)
ed cit......... Editio Citata [*Edition Cited*] [*Latin*]
EDCK....... Kiel-Holtenau [*Germany*] [*ICAO location identifier*]　(ICLI)
EDCL....... Celle [*Germany*] [*ICAO location identifier*]　(ICLI)
EDCM...... Aachen/Merzbruck [*Germany*] [*ICAO location identifier*]　(ICLI)
EDCN...... Nordholz [*Germany*] [*ICAO location identifier*]　(ICLI)
EDCR...... Rotenburg/Wumme [*Germany*] [*ICAO location identifier*]　(ICLI)
EDCS........ Ecumenical Development Cooperative Society　(EAIO)
EDCS........ Schleswig [*Germany*] [*ICAO location identifier*]　(ICLI)
EDCU....... Butzweilerhof [*Germany*] [*ICAO location identifier*]　(ICLI)
EDCW ...... Werl [*Germany*] [*ICAO location identifier*]　(ICLI)
edd............ Ediderunt; Haben (es) Herausgegeben [*Published By*]　(EG)
EDDA....... Bonn, Frankfurt Am Main [*Germany*] [*ICAO location identifier*]　(ICLI)
EDDA....... Electronic Directory of German Databases [*Information service or system*]　(IID)
EDDD....... Frankfurt Am Main [*Germany*] [*ICAO location identifier*]　(ICLI)
EDDE....... Enosis Dimokratikon Dikigoron Ellados [*Union of Democratic Lawyers of Greece*]　(GC)
EDDF .... Frankfurt Am Main [*Germany*] [*ICAO location identifier*]　(ICLI)
EDDH....... Hamburg [*Germany*] [*ICAO location identifier*]　(ICLI)
EDDK....... Koeln-Bonn [*Germany*] [*ICAO location identifier*]　(ICLI)
EDDL....... Duesseldorf [*Germany*] [*ICAO location identifier*]　(ICLI)
EDDM...... Muenchen [*Germany*] [*ICAO location identifier*]　(ICLI)
EDDN...... Nuernberg [*Germany*] [*ICAO location identifier*]　(ICLI)
EDDS .... Stuttgart [*Germany*] [*ICAO location identifier*]　(ICLI)
EDDU....... Rhein [*Germany*] [*ICAO location identifier*]　(ICLI)
EDDV....... Hannover [*Germany*] [*ICAO location identifier*]　(ICLI)
EDDW...... Bremen [*Germany*] [*ICAO location identifier*]　(ICLI)
EDDY....... Maastricht [*Germany*] [*ICAO location identifier*]　(ICLI)
EDDZ....... Frankfurt Am Main [*Germany*] [*ICAO location identifier*]　(ICLI)
EDE.......... Elliniki Diethnistiki Enosi [*Greek Internationalist Union*]　(GC)
EDE.......... Engineering Development Establishment [*Australia*]
EDE.......... Environmental Data and Ecological Parameters Data Base [*International Society of Ecological Modelling*] [*Information service or system*]　(IID)
EDE.......... Ergatiki Diethnikistiki Enosi (Trotskyite) [*Workers Internationalist Union*] [*Greek*]　(GC)
EDE.......... Esquerda Democratica Estudantil [*Democratic Student Left*] [*Portugal*] [*Political party*]　(PPE)
EDE.......... Ethniki Dimokratiki Enosis [*National Democratic Union*] [*Greek*]　(GC)
EDEA........ Amberg [*Germany*] [*ICAO location identifier*]　(ICLI)

EDEB........ Ansbach [*Germany*] [*ICAO location identifier*] (ICLI)
Edeb........ Edebiyat [*Literature*] (TU)
EDEC........ Aschaffenburg [*Germany*] [*ICAO location identifier*] (ICLI)
EDECN ..... European Development Education Curriculum Network
EDED .... Kaiserslautern [*Germany*] [*ICAO location identifier*] (ICLI)
EDEE........ Enosis Diafimistikon Epikheiriseon Ellados [*Union of Greek Advertising Enterprises*] (GC)
EDEE........ Heidelberg, United States Army [*Germany*] [*ICAO location identifier*] (ICLI)
EDEF........ Babenhausen [*Germany*] [*ICAO location identifier*] (ICLI)
EDEG .... Bad Kissingen [*Germany*] [*ICAO location identifier*] (ICLI)
EDEH........ Bad Kreuznach [*Germany*] [*ICAO location identifier*] (ICLI)
EDEI......... Miesau-West [*Germany*] [*ICAO location identifier*] (ICLI)
EDEJ .... Bamberg [*Germany*] [*ICAO location identifier*] (ICLI)
EDEK .... Baumholder [*Germany*] [*ICAO location identifier*] (ICLI)
EDEK .... Elevthero Dimokratiko Ergatiko Kinima [*Free Democratic Labor Movement*] [*Greek*] (GC)
EDEK .... Ethniki Demokratiki Enosi Kyprou [*United Democratic Union of Cyprus*] (GC)
EDEL........ Bayreuth [*Germany*] [*ICAO location identifier*] (ICLI)
EDELCA ... Electrificacion del Caroni [*Caroni River Electrification Project*] [*Venezuela*] (LA)
EDELVIVES ... Editorial Luis Vives (COL)
EDEM .... Muenchen, Hospital, Perlacher Forst [*Germany*] [*ICAO location identifier*] (ICLI)
EDEMED ... Etaireia Diakheiriseos Eidon Monopolion tou Ellinikou Dimosiou [*Company for the Administration of Commodities Sold by Greek Public Monopolies*] (GC)
EDEN .... Eniaia Dimokratiki Enosis Neon [*United Democratic Union of Youth*] [*Cyprus*] (GC)
EDEN .... Maurice Rose [*Germany*] [*ICAO location identifier*] (ICLI)
EDEO........ Bremerhaven [*Germany*] [*ICAO location identifier*] (ICLI)
EDEP........ Budingen [*Germany*] [*ICAO location identifier*] (ICLI)
EDER .... Crailsheim [*Germany*] [*ICAO location identifier*] (ICLI)
EDES........ Darmstadt [*Germany*] [*ICAO location identifier*] (ICLI)
EDES........ Ellinikos Dimokratikos Ethnikos Syndesmos [*Greek Democratic National League*] (GC)
EDES........ Ethnikos Demokratikos Ellinikos Stratos [*National Democratic Greek Army*] (PPE)
EDESA ..... Economic Development for Equatorial and Southern Africa
EDET........ Erlangen [*Germany*] [*ICAO location identifier*] (ICLI)
EDEU .... Giebelstadt [*Germany*] [*ICAO location identifier*] (ICLI)
EDEUCHEM ... Association of Editors of European Chemistry Journals [*ICSU*]
EDEV........ Friedberg [*Germany*] [*ICAO location identifier*] (ICLI)
EDEW........ Fuerth [*Germany*] [*ICAO location identifier*] (ICLI)
EDEX .... Fulda [*Germany*] [*ICAO location identifier*] (ICLI)
EDEY .... Zweibrucken [*Germany*] [*ICAO location identifier*] (ICLI)
EDEZ........ Germersheim [*Germany*] [*ICAO location identifier*] (ICLI)
EDF .... Economic Development Foundation [*Philippines*]
EDF .... Electricite de France [*French Electric Company*] (WER)
EDF .... Electricity Development Fund [*Australia*]
EdF .... Enroles de Force [*Forced Conscripts*] [*Luxembourg*] (PPE)
EDF .... European Development Fund (EY)
EDFA........ Employer Dentists Federation of Australia
EDFB........ Reichelsheim [*Germany*] [*ICAO location identifier*] (ICLI)
EDFC........ Aschaffenburg-Grossostheim [*Germany*] [*ICAO location identifier*] (ICLI)
EDF-DOC ... Electricite de France [*Bibliographic database*] [*French*]
EDFE........ Egelsbach [*Germany*] [*ICAO location identifier*] (ICLI)
EDFF........ Frankfurt [*Germany*] [*ICAO location identifier*] (ICLI)
EDFG .... Gelnhausen [*Germany*] [*ICAO location identifier*] (ICLI)
EDFK........ Bad Kissingen [*Germany*] [*ICAO location identifier*] (ICLI)
EDFM .... Mannheim-Neuostheim [*Germany*] [*ICAO location identifier*] (ICLI)
EDFN .... Marburg-Schoenstadt [*Germany*] [*ICAO location identifier*] (ICLI)
EDFO .... Economic Development Financing Organization
EDFO .... Michelstadt [*Germany*] [*ICAO location identifier*] (ICLI)
EDFQ .... Allendorf/Eder [*Germany*] [*ICAO location identifier*] (ICLI)
EDFR........ Rothenburg [*Germany*] [*ICAO location identifier*] (ICLI)
EDFS........ Schweinfurt-Sud [*Germany*] [*ICAO location identifier*] (ICLI)
EDFU .... Mainbullau [*Germany*] [*ICAO location identifier*] (ICLI)
EDFV........ Worms [*Germany*] [*ICAO location identifier*] (ICLI)
EDFW........ Wuerzburg-Schenkenturm [*Germany*] [*ICAO location identifier*] (ICLI)
EDFX........ Fuldatal [*Germany*] [*ICAO location identifier*] (ICLI)
EDG .... Emigracion Democratica Guatemalteca [*Guatemalan Democratic Emigration*] (LA)
EDG.......... Europese Defensie Gemeenschap [*Benelux*] (BAS)
EDGB .... Breitscheid/Dillkreis [*Germany*] [*ICAO location identifier*] (ICLI)
EDGEP...... European Democratic Group in the European Parliament [*Brussels, Belgium*] [*Political party*] (EAIO)
EdGestr...... EdelGestrenge [*Right Honorable*] [*Afrikaans*]
EDGK .... Korbach [*Germany*] [*ICAO location identifier*] (ICLI)

EDGL .... Ludwigshafen-Unfallklinik [*Germany*] [*ICAO location identifier*] (ICLI)
EDGM....... Mosbach-Lohrbach [*Germany*] [*ICAO location identifier*] (ICLI)
EDGN........ Nordenbeck [*Germany*] [*ICAO location identifier*] (ICLI)
EDGNSW ... Export Development Group of New South Wales [*Australia*]
EDGO........ Oedheim [*Germany*] [*ICAO location identifier*] (ICLI)
EDGW .... Wolfhagen/Granerberg [*Germany*] [*ICAO location identifier*] (ICLI)
EDHA........ Hamburg [*Germany*] [*ICAO location identifier*] (ICLI)
EDHASA .. Editora y Distribuidora Hispano-Americana Sociedad Anonima [*Publisher's imprint*] [*Spain*]
EDHB........ Grube [*Germany*] [*ICAO location identifier*] (ICLI)
EDHC........ Luchow/Rehbeck [*Germany*] [*ICAO location identifier*] (ICLI)
EDHE........ Uetersen [*Germany*] [*ICAO location identifier*] (ICLI)
EDHG........ Luneburg [*Germany*] [*ICAO location identifier*] (ICLI)
EDHI......... Hamburg/Finkenwerder [*Germany*] [*ICAO location identifier*] (ICLI)
EDHK....... Enose Demokratikou Hellinikou Kentrou [*Union of the Greek Democratic Center*] (PPE)
EDHL........ Luebeck/Blankensee [*Germany*] [*ICAO location identifier*] (ICLI)
EDHM....... Hartenholm [*Germany*] [*ICAO location identifier*] (ICLI)
EDHN....... Neumuenster [*Germany*] [*ICAO location identifier*] (ICLI)
EDHX....... Bad Bramstedt [*Germany*] [*ICAO location identifier*] (ICLI)
EDI .... Economic Development Institute [*United Nations (already exists in GUS II database)*]
e-d-i .... Eszak-Deli [*North-South (Adjective)*] (HU)
EDI .... Evans Deakin Industries Ltd. [*Australia*] (ADA)
EDI .... Societe Electricite Domestique et Industrielle
EDIA .... Giessen [*Germany*] [*ICAO location identifier*] (ICLI)
EDIALGE ... Edificaciones y Almacenes Generales [*Quito, Ecuador*] (LAA)
EDIB........ Goeppingen [*Germany*] [*ICAO location identifier*] (ICLI)
edic .... Edicao [*Edition*] [*Publishing*] [*Portuguese*]
edic .... Edicion [*Edition*] [*Publishing*] [*Spanish*]
EDIC.......... Etablissements Dumarest pour l'Industrie et le Commerce
EDIC.......... Grafenwoehr [*Germany*] [*ICAO location identifier*] (ICLI)
EDICA....... Electronic Data Interchange Council of Australia
EDICESA ... Editora de Ceuta Sociedad Anonima [*Spanish North Africa*] (MENA)
EDICO ...... Entreprise de Distribution Congolaise
EDID .... Hanau [*Germany*] [*ICAO location identifier*] (ICLI)
EDIE.......... Heidelberg [*Germany*] [*ICAO location identifier*] (ICLI)
Edif .... Edificio [*Building*] (SCAC)
EDIF.......... Heilbronn [*Germany*] [*ICAO location identifier*] (ICLI)
EDIFACT ... Electronic Data Interchange for Administration, Commerce, and Transport [*Economic Commission for Europe*]
EDIG .... Feucht [*Germany*] [*ICAO location identifier*] (ICLI)
EDIH .... Hohenfels [*Germany*] [*ICAO location identifier*] (ICLI)
EDII........... Augsburg Hospital [*Germany*] [*ICAO location identifier*] (ICLI)
EDIJ .... Bohmer [*Germany*] [*ICAO location identifier*] (ICLI)
EDIK.......... Enosi Dimokratikou Kendrou [*Democratic Center Union*] [*EK-ND*] [*Formerly,*] [*Greek*] (GC)
EDIK.......... Enossi Dimokratikou Kentrou [*Union of Democratic Centre Party*] [*Greece*] [*Political party*] (EY)
EDIK.......... Illesheim [*Germany*] [*ICAO location identifier*] (ICLI)
edil .... Edilizia [*Building*] [*Italian*]
EDIL.......... Empresa Distribuidora Livreria [*Publisher*] [*Angola*]
EDIL.......... Entreprise Nationale d'Engineering et de Developpement des Industries Legeres [*National Enterprise for Engineering and Development of Light Industries*] [*Algeria*] (GEA)
EDIL.......... Karlsruhe [*Germany*] [*ICAO location identifier*] (ICLI)
EDIM......... Edition Imprimerie du Mali
EDIM .... Kirchgons [*Germany*] [*ICAO location identifier*] (ICLI)
EDIMEC... Empresa de Diseno Mecanico [*Mechanical Design Enterprise*] [*Cuba*] (LA)
EDIMEL ... Empresa Regional de Acquisicao, Producao, Distribuicao de Equipamento e Material Escolar e Didactico [*Regional Enterprise for Acquisition, Production, and Distribution of Educational and Teaching Equipment*] [*Angola*] (AF)
EDIMEL ... Entreprise Nationale de Distribution du Materiel Electrique [*Nationalized industry*] [*Algeria*] (EY)
EDIN .... Elliniki Dimokratiki Neolaia [*Greek Democratic Youth*] [*ELDIN*] [*Also,*] [*Greek*] (GC)
EDIN .... Ente Nazionale per la Diffusione e l'Incremento della Nautica [*Italian*] (SLS)
EDIN .... Kitzingen [*Germany*] [*ICAO location identifier*] (ICLI)
EDIO .... Butzbach (Schloss) [*Germany*] [*ICAO location identifier*] (ICLI)
EDIP.......... European Defense Improvement Program [*NATO*] (MCD)
EDIP.......... Landstuhl [*Germany*] [*ICAO location identifier*] (ICLI)
EDI-PERU ... Empresa de Ediciones del Peru [*Peruvian Publishing Enterprise*] (LA)
EDIPSA..... Editora de Publicaciones Sociedad Anonima [*Publisher*] [*Nicaragua*] (EY)
EDIQ .... Herzo Base [*Germany*] [*ICAO location identifier*] (ICLI)
EDIR.......... Ludwigsburg [*Germany*] [*ICAO location identifier*] (ICLI)

EDIS.......... Empresa Distrital de Servicios Publicos [*Bogota Public Service Co.*] [*Colombia*] (COL)
EDIS.......... Nellingen [*Germany*] [*ICAO location identifier*] (ICLI)
EDISA....... Eletronica Digital SA [*Digital Electronics, Inc.*] [*Brazil*] (LA)
edit .... Editeur [*Editor*] [*Publishing*] [*French*]
edit .... Edition [*Edition, Issue, Publication*] [*French*]
edit .... Editore [*Editor*] [*Publishing*] [*Italian*]
edit .... Editoriale [*Editorial*] [*Publishing*] [*Italian*]
EDIT.......... Nuernberg, Hospital [*Germany*] [*ICAO location identifier*] (ICLI)
EDITABECE ... Editorial ABC [*Colombia*] (COL)
EDITEAST ... South-East Asia Association of Science Editors (PDAA)
EDITERRA ... European Association of Earth Science Editors
EDITEX .... Editeur de Textes [*Text Editor*] [*French*] (ADPT)
EDITOGO ... Etablissement National des Editions du Togo
editor .... Editoriale [*Editorial*] [*Publishing*] [*Italian*]
Editora ...... Empresa Editora del Estado [*State Publishing Enterprise*] [*Peru*] (LA)
EDIU .... Heidelberg [*Germany*] [*ICAO location identifier*] (ICLI)
EDIV.......... Pirmasens [*Germany*] [*ICAO location identifier*] (ICLI)
EDIW .... Wuerzburg, Hospital [*Germany*] [*ICAO location identifier*] (ICLI)
EDIX.......... Schwaebisch Gmuend [*Germany*] [*ICAO location identifier*] (ICLI)
ediz............. Edizione [*Edition*] [*Italian*]
EDIZ.......... Schwabach [*Germany*] [*ICAO location identifier*] (ICLI)
EDJABA ... Edjaan Baru [*New Spelling (of the Indonesian and Malay languages)*] (IN)
EDK .... Eisenbahndrehkran [*Rotary Railroad Crane*] (EG)
EDK .... Ekonomik Danisma Kurulu [*Economic Advisory Board*] [*Turkish Federated State of Cyprus*] (GC)
EDK .... Eliktronische Daten-Kommunikation [*Electronic Data Communication*] [*German*] (ADPT)
EDK .... Ellinikon Dimokratikon Kinima [*Greek Democratic Movement*] (GC)
EDK .... Enose Demokratikou Kentrou [*Union of the Democratic Center*] [*Greek*] (PPW)
EDKB .... Bonn/Hangelar [*Germany*] [*ICAO location identifier*] (ICLI)
EDKD........ Altena/Hegenscheid [*Germany*] [*ICAO location identifier*] (ICLI)
EDKD........ Epitropi Dimosion Kipon kai Dendrostoikheion [*Committee of Public Gardens and Tree Plantings*] (GC)
EDKE .... Dierdorf/Wienau [*Germany*] [*ICAO location identifier*] (ICLI)
EDKE .... Enosis Dimon kai Koinotiton Ellados [*Union of Municipalities and Communes of Greece*] (GC)
EDKF........ Bergneustadt/Auf Dem Dumpel [*Germany*] [*ICAO location identifier*] (ICLI)
EDKh........ Encyclopedia of Housekeeping (RU)
EDKI......... Betzdorf/Kirchen [*Germany*] [*ICAO location identifier*] (ICLI)
EDKL......... Leverkusen [*Germany*] [*ICAO location identifier*] (ICLI)
EDKM .... Meschede/Schuren [*Germany*] [*ICAO location identifier*] (ICLI)
EDKN........ Wipperfurth/Neye [*Germany*] [*ICAO location identifier*] (ICLI)
EDKS......... Siegerland [*Germany*] [*ICAO location identifier*] (ICLI)
EDKV .... Dahlemer Binz [*Germany*] [*ICAO location identifier*] (ICLI)
EDKW .... Werdohl/Kuntrop [*Germany*] [*ICAO location identifier*] (ICLI)
EDKZ .... Meinerzhagen [*Germany*] [*ICAO location identifier*] (ICLI)
EDL .... Eldoret [*Kenya*] [*Airport symbol*] [*Obsolete*] (OAG)
EDL .... Electricite du Laos [*Lao Power Company*] (CL)
EdL .... Electricite du Liban [*Lebanon*]
EDL .... Euro Disneyland [*France*]
EDLA .... Arnsberg [*Germany*] [*ICAO location identifier*] (ICLI)
EDLB......... Borkenberge [*Germany*] [*ICAO location identifier*] (ICLI)
EDLC......... Edwardian Drama and Literature Circle (EA)
EDLC......... Kamp/Lintfort [*Germany*] [*ICAO location identifier*] (ICLI)
EDLD .... Dinslaken/Schwarze Heide [*Germany*] [*ICAO location identifier*] (ICLI)
EDLE .... Essen/Muelheim [*Germany*] [*ICAO location identifier*] (ICLI)
EDLF......... Grefrath/Niershorst [*Germany*] [*ICAO location identifier*] (ICLI)
EDLG .... Muenster/Osnabruck [*Germany*] [*ICAO location identifier*] (ICLI)
EDLH .... Hamm/Lippewiesen [*Germany*] [*ICAO location identifier*] (ICLI)
EDLI.......... Bielefeld/Windelsbleiche [*Germany*] [*ICAO location identifier*] (ICLI)
EDLK......... Krefeld/Egelsberg [*Germany*] [*ICAO location identifier*] (ICLI)
EDLL......... Duesseldorf [*Germany*] [*ICAO location identifier*] (ICLI)
EDLM .... Marl/Loemuhle [*Germany*] [*ICAO location identifier*] (ICLI)
EDLN......... Moenchengladbach [*Germany*] [*ICAO location identifier*] (ICLI)
EDLO .... Oerlinghausen [*Germany*] [*ICAO location identifier*] (ICLI)
EDLP......... Paderborn/Lippstadt [*Germany*] [*ICAO location identifier*] (ICLI)
EDLQ .... Essen [*Germany*] [*ICAO location identifier*] (ICLI)
EDLS......... Stadtlohn/Wenningfeld [*Germany*] [*ICAO location identifier*] (ICLI)
EDLT......... Muenster/Telgte [*Germany*] [*ICAO location identifier*] (ICLI)

EDLW .... Dortmund/Wickede [*Germany*] [*ICAO location identifier*] (ICLI)
EDLX......... Wesel/Romerwardt [*Germany*] [*ICAO location identifier*] (ICLI)
edm............ Early Day Motion [*British*] (BARN)
EDM .... Empresa de Desenvolvimento Mineiro [*Portugal*] (EY)
edm............ En Dergelike (Dies) Meer [*And So Forth*] [*Afrikaans*]
EDM .... Executive Doctorate in Management [*Weatherhead School of Management, Case Western Reserve University*] (ECON)
EDM .... Societe Energie du Mali [*Electric Power Company of Mali*] (AF)
EDMA ...... Augsburg/Muehlhausen [*Germany*] [*ICAO location identifier*] (ICLI)
EDMA ...... Empresa de Desenvolvimento Mineiro do Alentejo [*Nationalized industry*] [*Portugal*] (EY)
EDMA ...... Eniaion Dimokratikon Metopon Anadimiourgias [*United Democratic Regeneration Front*] [*Cyprus*] (GC)
EDMA ...... Ethyldimethacrylamide (RU)
EDMA ...... European Direct Marketing Association [*Jona/SG, Switzerland*] (EAIO)
EDMALC ... European Direct Marketing Association List Council [*Jona/SG, Switzerland*] [*Inactive*] (EA)
EDMB .... Biberach Aerodrome Riss [*Germany*] [*ICAO location identifier*] (ICLI)
EDMC .... Energy Data and Modeling Center [*Institute of Energy Economics*] [*Japan*] [*Database producer*] (IID)
EDME .... Eggenfelden, Nieder Bayern [*Germany*] [*ICAO location identifier*] (ICLI)
EDME .... Endolodokhos Diakheiriseos Mikhanikou Exoplismou [*Administrative Agent for Mechanical Equipment*] [*Greek*] (GC)
EDMF .... Fuerstenzell Bei Passau [*Germany*] [*ICAO location identifier*] (ICLI)
EDMG .... Gunzburg/Donauried [*Germany*] [*ICAO location identifier*] (ICLI)
EDMH....... Gunzenhausen [*Germany*] [*ICAO location identifier*] (ICLI)
EDMI .... Illertissen [*Germany*] [*ICAO location identifier*] (ICLI)
EDMJ........ Jesenwang [*Germany*] [*ICAO location identifier*] (ICLI)
EDMK .... Kempten/Durach [*Germany*] [*ICAO location identifier*] (ICLI)
EDML .... Landshut [*Germany*] [*ICAO location identifier*] (ICLI)
EDMM ...... Muenchen [*Germany*] [*ICAO location identifier*] (ICLI)
EDMMA ... Elazig Devlet Muhendislik ve Mimarlik Akademisi [*Elazig State Engineering and Architecture Academy*] (TU)
EDMMA ... European Dessert Mixes Manufacturers' Association [*EC*] (ECED)
EDMO .... Oberpfaffenhofen [*Germany*] [*ICAO location identifier*] (ICLI)
EDMP .... Vilsbiburg [*Germany*] [*ICAO location identifier*] (ICLI)
EDMQ....... Donauworth/Genderkingen [*Germany*] [*ICAO location identifier*] (ICLI)
EDMR .... Ottobrunn [*Germany*] [*ICAO location identifier*] (ICLI)
Edms.......... Eiendoms [*Property*] [*Afrikaans*]
EDMS........ Straubing/Wallmuehle [*Germany*] [*ICAO location identifier*] (ICLI)
EDMT .... Tanheim [*Germany*] [*ICAO location identifier*] (ICLI)
EDMU .... Muenchen [*Germany*] [*ICAO location identifier*] (ICLI)
EDMV .... Vilshofen [*Germany*] [*ICAO location identifier*] (ICLI)
EDMW ...... Deggendorf/Steinkirchen [*Germany*] [*ICAO location identifier*] (ICLI)
EDMX .... Oberschleissheim [*Germany*] [*ICAO location identifier*] (ICLI)
EDMY .... Muehldorf [*Germany*] [*ICAO location identifier*] (ICLI)
edn............ Edition (EECI)
edn............ Ednina [*Singular*] (YU)
EDN .... Estireno do Nordeste SA [*Brazil*]
EDNA........ Ahlhorn [*Germany*] [*ICAO location identifier*] (ICLI)
EDNB .... Koeln-Wahn [*Germany*] [*ICAO location identifier*] (ICLI)
EDND........ Diepholz [*Germany*] [*ICAO location identifier*] (ICLI)
EDNE .... Enosis Dimokratikis Neolaias Ellados [*United Democratic Youth of Greece*] (GC)
EDNF .... Fassberg [*Germany*] [*ICAO location identifier*] (ICLI)
EDNG .... Geilenkirchen [*Germany*] [*ICAO location identifier*] (ICLI)
EDNH .... Husum [*Germany*] [*ICAO location identifier*] (ICLI)
EDNJ........ Jever [*Germany*] [*ICAO location identifier*] (ICLI)
EDNK .... Koeln-Bonn [*Germany*] [*ICAO location identifier*] (ICLI)
EDNL .... Leck [*Germany*] [*ICAO location identifier*] (ICLI)
EDNLA .... Elliniki Dimokratiki Neolaia Lambraki Avstralias [*Greek Democratic Lambrakis Youth of Australia*] (GC)
EDNM....... Muenster [*Germany*] [*ICAO location identifier*] (ICLI)
EDNN........ Norvenich [*Germany*] [*ICAO location identifier*] (ICLI)
EDNO........ Oldenburg [*Germany*] [*ICAO location identifier*] (ICLI)
EDNP .... Hopsten [*Germany*] [*ICAO location identifier*] (ICLI)
EDNQ........ Hohn [*Germany*] [*ICAO location identifier*] (ICLI)
EDNT .... Wittmundhafen [*Germany*] [*ICAO location identifier*] (ICLI)
EDNV .... Kalkar [*Germany*] [*ICAO location identifier*] (ICLI)
EDNW ...... Wunstorf [*Germany*] [*ICAO location identifier*] (ICLI)
EDNX .... Goch [*Germany*] [*ICAO location identifier*] (ICLI)
EDO........... Economic Development Organization [*Egypt*]
EDO........... Environmental Defender's Office [*Australia*]

EDO.......... Export Development Office [*Department of Commerce*]   (IMH)
EDOA........ Schweinfurt [*Germany*] [*ICAO location identifier*]   (ICLI)
EDOB........ Garlstedt/Clay Kaserne [*Germany*] [*ICAO location identifier*]   (ICLI)
EDOC........ Echterdingen [*Germany*] [*ICAO location identifier*]   (ICLI)
EDOC........ Estudios y Documentacion del Caribe [*Caribbean Studies and Documentation*] [*Dominican Republic*]   (LA)
EDOE........ Ulm [*Germany*] [*ICAO location identifier*]   (ICLI)
EDOEAP... Eniaios Dimosiografikos Organismos Epikourikis Asfaliseos kai Perithalpseos [*United Journalistic Organization of Auxiliary Insurance and Relief*] [*Greek*]   (GC)
EDOF........ United Democratic Fatherland Front   (BU)
EDOF........ Wertheim [*Germany*] [*ICAO location identifier*]   (ICLI)
EDOG........ Bad Cannstatt Hospital [*Germany*] [*ICAO location identifier*]   (ICLI)
EDOH........ Emery [*Germany*] [*ICAO location identifier*]   (ICLI)
EDOI......... Vilseck [*Germany*] [*ICAO location identifier*]   (ICLI)
EDOJ......... Bonn (Bad Godesberg-Plittersdorf) [*Germany*] [*ICAO location identifier*]   (ICLI)
EDOK........ Frankfurt-North [*Germany*] [*ICAO location identifier*]   (ICLI)
EDOL........ Frankfurt City [*Germany*] [*ICAO location identifier*]   (ICLI)
EDOM....... Worms [*Germany*] [*ICAO location identifier*]   (ICLI)
EDON....... Eniaia Dimokratiki Organosis Neon [*or Eniaia Dimokratiki Organosis Neolaias*] [*United Democratic Youth Organization Cyprus*]   (GC)
EDON....... Kaiserslautern [*Germany*] [*ICAO location identifier*]   (ICLI)
EDONSW ... Environmental Defender's Office, New South Wales [*Australia*]
EDOP........ Schwaebisch Hall/Hessental [*Germany*] [*ICAO location identifier*]   (ICLI)
EDOQ........ Heidelberg, United States Army [*Germany*] [*ICAO location identifier*]   (ICLI)
EDOR........ Coleman [*Germany*] [*ICAO location identifier*]   (ICLI)
EDOS........ Kaiserslautern (Kapaun) [*Germany*] [*ICAO location identifier*]   (ICLI)
EDOSZ...... Elelmezesipari Dolgozok Szakszervezete [*Trade Union of Food Industry Workers*]   (HU)
EDOSZ...... Epitoipari Dolgozok Szakszervezete [*Construction Workers' Trade Union*]   (HU)
EDOT........ Finthen [*Germany*] [*ICAO location identifier*]   (ICLI)
EDOU....... Wiesbaden [*Germany*] [*ICAO location identifier*]   (ICLI)
EDOV........ Bad Tolz [*Germany*] [*ICAO location identifier*]   (ICLI)
EDOW....... Wildflecken [*Germany*] [*ICAO location identifier*]   (ICLI)
EDOX........ Augsburg/Gablingen [*Germany*] [*ICAO location identifier*]   (ICLI)
EDOY........ Leighton Barracks [*Germany*] [*ICAO location identifier*]   (ICLI)
EDOZ........ Bad Hersfeld [*Germany*] [*ICAO location identifier*]   (ICLI)
EDP.......... Electricidade de Portugal [*Research center*]
EDP.......... Ellinika Diylistiria Petrelaiou [*Greek Oil Refineries*]   (GC)
EDP.......... Emergency Development Plan
EDP.......... Epikourikon Didaktikon Prosopikon [*Auxiliary Teaching Personnel*]   (GC)
EDPF........ Fritzlar [*Germany*] [*ICAO location identifier*]   (ICLI)
EDPH........ Neuhausen Ob Eck [*Germany*] [*ICAO location identifier*]   (ICLI)
EDPITAF ... Education Development Projects Implementing Task Force [*Philippines*]   (DS)
EDPL........ Altenstadt [*Germany*] [*ICAO location identifier*]   (ICLI)
EDPM....... Laupheim [*Germany*] [*ICAO location identifier*]   (ICLI)
EDPN........ Mendig [*Germany*] [*ICAO location identifier*]   (ICLI)
EDPR........ Roth [*Germany*] [*ICAO location identifier*]   (ICLI)
EDPS........ Straubing/Mitterharthausen [*Germany*] [*ICAO location identifier*]   (ICLI)
EDPSG...... European Diabetes Pregnancy Study Group [*of the European Association for the Study of Diabetes*]   (EAIO)
EDPT........ Niederstetten/Bad Mergentheim [*Germany*] [*ICAO location identifier*]   (ICLI)
EDQC........ Coburg/Brandensteinsebene [*Germany*] [*ICAO location identifier*]   (ICLI)
EDQD........ Bayreuth [*Germany*] [*ICAO location identifier*]   (ICLI)
EDQE........ Burg Feuerstein [*Germany*] [*ICAO location identifier*]   (ICLI)
EDQF........ Ansbach/Petersdorf [*Germany*] [*ICAO location identifier*]   (ICLI)
EDQH........ Herzogenaurach [*Germany*] [*ICAO location identifier*]   (ICLI)
EDQK........ Kulmbach [*Germany*] [*ICAO location identifier*]   (ICLI)
EDQL........ Lichtenfels [*Germany*] [*ICAO location identifier*]   (ICLI)
EDQM....... Hof [*Germany*] [*ICAO location identifier*]   (ICLI)
EDQN........ Neumarkt, Oberpfalz [*Germany*] [*ICAO location identifier*]   (ICLI)
EDQP........ Rosenthal-Field Plossen [*Germany*] [*ICAO location identifier*]   (ICLI)
EDQT........ Hassfurt/Mainwiesen [*Germany*] [*ICAO location identifier*]   (ICLI)
EDQW....... Weiden, Oberpfalz [*Germany*] [*ICAO location identifier*]   (ICLI)
EDQY........ Coburg/Steinrucken [*Germany*] [*ICAO location identifier*]   (ICLI)
EDR.......... Edward River [*Australia*] [*Airport symbol*]   (OAG)
EDR.......... Entwurfsbuero der Reichsbahn [*(GDR) Railroad Design Office*]   (EG)

EDR.......... European Depositary Receipt [*Investment term*]
EDR.......... Experimenterede Danske Radiomatorer [*Danish Amateur Radio Society*]   (PDAA)
EDR.......... Exposure Draft Taxation Ruling [*Australia*]
EDR.......... Lineas Aereas Eldorado Ltd. [*Colombia*] [*ICAO designator*]   (FAAC)
EDRA........ European Digital Road-mapping Association
EDRF........ Bad Duerkheim [*Germany*] [*ICAO location identifier*]   (ICLI)
EDRJ........ Saarlouis/Dueren [*Germany*] [*ICAO location identifier*]   (ICLI)
EDRK........ Koblenz/Winningen [*Germany*] [*ICAO location identifier*]   (ICLI)
EDRL........ Lachen/Speyerdorf [*Germany*] [*ICAO location identifier*]   (ICLI)
EDRP........ European Demonstrtion Reprocessing Plant [*Nuclear energy*]   (NUCP)
EDRS........ European Data Relay Satellite
EDRS........ Saarbruecken [*Germany*] [*ICAO location identifier*]   (ICLI)
EDRT........ Trier/Foehren [*Germany*] [*ICAO location identifier*]   (ICLI)
EDRY........ Speyer [*Germany*] [*ICAO location identifier*]   (ICLI)
EDRZ........ Pirmasens/Zweibruecken [*Germany*] [*ICAO location identifier*]   (ICLI)
EDS.......... Eisenbahndienstsache [*Official Railroad Service Document*]   (EG)
EDS.......... Electromotive Force   (BU)
EDS.......... Elektronisches Datenvermittlungssystem [*Electron Data Exchange System*] [*German*]   (ADPT)
EDS.......... English Dialect Society [*Australia*]   (ADA)
EDS.......... Societe d'Etat Electricite du Senegal
EDSA........ Epifanio de los Santos [*Avenue where Philippine President Marcos' government tanks were stopped by unarmed citizens*] [*In the EDSA Revolution of February, 1986*]
EDSA........ Landsberg [*Germany*] [*ICAO location identifier*]   (ICLI)
EDSB........ Buchel [*Germany*] [*ICAO location identifier*]   (ICLI)
EDSD........ Leipheim [*Germany*] [*ICAO location identifier*]   (ICLI)
EDSE........ Erding [*Germany*] [*ICAO location identifier*]   (ICLI)
EDSECGEN ... Education Secretaries General
EDSF........ Fuerstenfeldbruck [*Germany*] [*ICAO location identifier*]   (ICLI)
EDSG........ Bremgarten [*Germany*] [*ICAO location identifier*]   (ICLI)
EDSI......... Ingoldstadt [*Germany*] [*ICAO location identifier*]   (ICLI)
EDSK........ Kaufbeuren [*Germany*] [*ICAO location identifier*]   (ICLI)
EDSL........ Lechfeld [*Germany*] [*ICAO location identifier*]   (ICLI)
EDSM....... Memmingen [*Germany*] [*ICAO location identifier*]   (ICLI)
EDSN........ Neubiberg [*Germany*] [*ICAO location identifier*]   (ICLI)
Ed Soc....... Education et Socialisme [*French*]   (BAS)
EDSP........ Pferdsfeld [*Germany*] [*ICAO location identifier*]   (ICLI)
EDSSA...... Evreia Dimokratiki Syndikalistiki Synergasia Athinon [*Broad Democratic Labor Collaboration of Athens*]   (GC)
EDSSP...... Evreia Dimokratiki Syndikalistiki Synergasia Peiraios [*Broad Democratic Labor Collaboration of Piraeus*]   (GC)
EDST........ Elastische Diaphragma-Schalt-Technologie [*German*]   (ADPT)
EDSU........ Neuburg [*Germany*] [*ICAO location identifier*]   (ICLI)
EDSV........ Mebstetten [*Germany*] [*ICAO location identifier*]   (ICLI)
EDT.......... Ethylenediamine Tartrate   (RU)
EDTA........ Aalen-Heidenheim/Elchingen [*Germany*] [*ICAO location identifier*]   (ICLI)
EDTA........ Entreprise Durieux de Transports Automobiles
EDTA........ Ethylenediaminetetra-Acetate   (RU)
EDTA........ European Dialysis and Transplant Association [*Italian*]   (SLS)
EDTB........ Baden-Baden [*Germany*] [*ICAO location identifier*]   (ICLI)
EDTC........ European Diving Technology Committee   (MSC)
EDTD........ Donaueschingen/Villingen [*Germany*] [*ICAO location identifier*]   (ICLI)
EDTE........ Schwenningen Am Nickar [*Germany*] [*ICAO location identifier*]   (ICLI)
EDTF........ Freiburg/Breisgau [*Germany*] [*ICAO location identifier*]   (ICLI)
EDTH........ Heubach, Wurttemberg [*Germany*] [*ICAO location identifier*]   (ICLI)
EDTK........ Ethylenediaminetetra-Acetic Acid   (RU)
EDTK........ Karlsruhe/Forchheim [*Germany*] [*ICAO location identifier*]   (ICLI)
EDTM....... Mengen [*Germany*] [*ICAO location identifier*]   (ICLI)
EDTN........ Nabern/Teck [*Germany*] [*ICAO location identifier*]   (ICLI)
EDTNA/ERCA ... European Dialysis and Transplant Nurses Association/European Renal Care Association [*Formerly, European Dialysis and Transplant Nurses Associaton*]   (EA)
EDTO........ Offenburg/Baden [*Germany*] [*ICAO location identifier*]   (ICLI)
EDTPL...... Entreprise de Dragage et de Travaux Publics de la Lowe
EDTX........ Schwaebisch Hall/Weckrieden [*Germany*] [*ICAO location identifier*]   (ICLI)
EDTY........ Friedrichshafen-Lowental [*Germany*] [*ICAO location identifier*]   (ICLI)
EDTZ........ Konstanz [*Germany*] [*ICAO location identifier*]   (ICLI)
EDU.......... Eidgenoessische Demokratische Union [*Federal Democratic Union*] [*Switzerland*]   (WEN)
EDU.......... Ethiopian Democratic Union [*Political party*]   (PD)
EDU.......... Europaeische Demokratische Union [*European Democratic Union*] [*Austria*]   (EAIO)

EDUBA ..... Educacion Basica (Programa) [*Agency for Adult Basic Education*] [*Bolivia*]   (LAA)

EDUCA ..... Editorial Universitaria Centroamericana [*Central American University Publishing House*] [*Nicaragua*]   (LA)

EDUD....... Detmold [*Germany*] [*ICAO location identifier*]   (ICLI)

EDUH ...... Hildesheim [*Germany*] [*ICAO location identifier*]   (ICLI)

EDUK........ Rheindahlen [*Germany*] [*ICAO location identifier*]   (ICLI)

edul............ Entgegengesetzt dem Urzeiger Laufend [*Counterclockwise*] [*German*]

EDUL .... Laarbruch [*Germany*] [*ICAO location identifier*]   (ICLI)

EDUN........ Nordhorn Range [*Germany*] [*ICAO location identifier*]   (ICLI)

EDUO....... Guetersloh [*Germany*] [*ICAO location identifier*]   (ICLI)

EDUP........ Ethiopian Democratic Unity Party [*Political party*]   (EY)

EDUPLAN ... Oficina de Planeamiento Integral de la Educacion [*Venezuela*]   (LAA)

EDUR........ Bruggen [*Germany*] [*ICAO location identifier*]   (ICLI)

EDUS .... Soest [*Germany*] [*ICAO location identifier*]   (ICLI)

EDUW....... Wildenrath [*Germany*] [*ICAO location identifier*]   (ICLI)

EDV .... Double-Range Shielded Wattmeter   (RU)

EDV .... Elektronische Datenverarbeitung [*Electronic Data Processing - EDP*] [*German*]

EDV .... Ethylenediamine Tartrate   (RU)

EDVA .... Bad Gandersheim [*Germany*] [*ICAO location identifier*]   (ICLI)

EDVA .... Elektronische Datenverarbeitungsanlage [*Electronic Data-Processing Equipment*]   (EG)

EDVB .... Braunschweig [*Germany*] [*ICAO location identifier*]   (ICLI)

EDVC .... Celle/Arloh [*Germany*] [*ICAO location identifier*]   (ICLI)

EDVE .... Braunschweig [*Germany*] [*ICAO location identifier*]   (ICLI)

EDVH....... Hodenhagen [*Germany*] [*ICAO location identifier*]   (ICLI)

EDVI......... Hoxter/Holzminden [*Germany*] [*ICAO location identifier*]   (ICLI)

EDVK .... Kassel/Calden [*Germany*] [*ICAO location identifier*]   (ICLI)

EDVL .... Holleberg [*Germany*] [*ICAO location identifier*]   (ICLI)

EDVM ...... Kassel-Mittelfeld [*Germany*] [*ICAO location identifier*]   (ICLI)

EDVN ...... Northeim [*Germany*] [*ICAO location identifier*]   (ICLI)

EDVP........ Peine/Eddesse [*Germany*] [*ICAO location identifier*]   (ICLI)

EDVR .... Rinteln [*Germany*] [*ICAO location identifier*]   (ICLI)

EDVS........ Elektronisches Datenverteilungssystem [*Electronic Data Distribution System*] [*German*]   (ADPT)

EDVS........ Salzgitter/Drutte [*Germany*] [*ICAO location identifier*]   (ICLI)

EDVU .... Uelzen [*Germany*] [*ICAO location identifier*]   (ICLI)

EDVV .... Hannover [*Germany*] [*ICAO location identifier*]   (ICLI)

EDVX .... Gifhorn [*Germany*] [*ICAO location identifier*]   (ICLI)

EDVY .... Porta Westfalica [*Germany*] [*ICAO location identifier*]   (ICLI)

EDWA ...... Norden-Hage [*Germany*] [*ICAO location identifier*]   (ICLI)

EDWB ...... Bremerhaven/Am Luneort [*Germany*] [*ICAO location identifier*]   (ICLI)

EDWC ...... Damme [*Germany*] [*ICAO location identifier*]   (ICLI)

EDWD....... Lemwerder [*Germany*] [*ICAO location identifier*]   (ICLI)

EDWE ...... Emden [*Germany*] [*ICAO location identifier*]   (ICLI)

EDWF....... Leer-Nuttermoor [*Germany*] [*ICAO location identifier*]   (ICLI)

EDWG ...... Wangerooge [*Germany*] [*ICAO location identifier*]   (ICLI)

EDWH...... Oldenburg/Hatten [*Germany*] [*ICAO location identifier*]   (ICLI)

EDWI .... Wilhelmshaven/Mariensiel [*Germany*] [*ICAO location identifier*]   (ICLI)

EDWIN ..... Editorial Word Processing International Network   (DGA)

EDWJ........ Juist [*Germany*] [*ICAO location identifier*]   (ICLI)

EDWL ...... Langeoog [*Germany*] [*ICAO location identifier*]   (ICLI)

EDWM ...... Weser-Wumme [*Germany*] [*ICAO location identifier*]   (ICLI)

EDWN....... Nordhorn/Klausheide [*Germany*] [*ICAO location identifier*]   (ICLI)

EDWO....... Osnabruck/Atterheide [*Germany*] [*ICAO location identifier*]   (ICLI)

EDWQ....... Ganderkesee-Atlas Aerodrome [*Germany*] [*ICAO location identifier*]   (ICLI)

EDWR ...... Borkum [*Germany*] [*ICAO location identifier*]   (ICLI)

EDWS........ Norden/Norddeich [*Germany*] [*ICAO location identifier*]   (ICLI)

EDWT....... Nordenham-Einswarden [*Germany*] [*ICAO location identifier*]   (ICLI)

EDWU ...... Varrelbusch [*Germany*] [*ICAO location identifier*]   (ICLI)

EDWV ...... Verden/Scharnhorst [*Germany*] [*ICAO location identifier*]   (ICLI)

EDWW ...... Bremen [*Germany*] [*ICAO location identifier*]   (ICLI)

EDWY ...... Norderney [*Germany*] [*ICAO location identifier*]   (ICLI)

EDXB .... Heide/Busum [*Germany*] [*ICAO location identifier*]   (ICLI)

EDXC .... European DX Council [*Huntingdon, Cambridgeshire, England*]   (EAIO)

EDXE .... Rheine/Eschendorf [*Germany*] [*ICAO location identifier*]   (ICLI)

EDXF........ Flensburg/Schaferhaus [*Germany*] [*ICAO location identifier*]   (ICLI)

EDXH........ Helgoland/Dune [*Germany*] [*ICAO location identifier*]   (ICLI)

EDXM........ St. Michaelisdonn [*Germany*] [*ICAO location identifier*]   (ICLI)

EDXO........ St. Peter/Ording [*Germany*] [*ICAO location identifier*]   (ICLI)

EDXR .... Rendsburg/Schachtholm [*Germany*] [*ICAO location identifier*]   (ICLI)

EDXW .... Westerland/Sylt [*Germany*] [*ICAO location identifier*]   (ICLI)

EDXY .... Wyk Auf Fohr [*Germany*] [*ICAO location identifier*]   (ICLI)

EDYA .... Ampfing/Waldkraiburg [*Germany*] [*ICAO location identifier*]   (ICLI)

EDYB .... Arnbruck [*Germany*] [*ICAO location identifier*]   (ICLI)

EDYG .... Beilingries [*Germany*] [*ICAO location identifier*]   (ICLI)

EDYL......... Leutkirch/Unterzeil [*Germany*] [*ICAO location identifier*]   (ICLI)

EDYN .... Nittenau/Bruck [*Germany*] [*ICAO location identifier*]   (ICLI)

EDYP........ Etaireia Diakheiriseos Ypengyon Prosodon [*Company for the Administration of Accountable Revenues*] [*Greek*]   (GC)

EDYR .... Regensburg-Oberhub [*Germany*] [*ICAO location identifier*]   (ICLI)

EDYTh .... Enosis Dimosion Ypallilon Thessalonikis [*Salonica Civil Servants Union*]   (GC)

EDYV .... Vogtareuth [*Germany*] [*ICAO location identifier*]   (ICLI)

EDZA .... Mittenwald-Luttensee [*Germany*] [*ICAO location identifier*]   (ICLI)

EDZB........ Bergen-Hohne [*Germany*] [*ICAO location identifier*]   (ICLI)

ED-ZD...... Delayed Action Electric Detonator   (RU)

EDZD...... Ulm [*Germany*] [*ICAO location identifier*]   (ICLI)

EDZE........ Sengwarden [*Germany*] [*ICAO location identifier*]   (ICLI)

EDZF........ Fuerstenfeldbruck [*Germany*] [*ICAO location identifier*]   (ICLI)

EDZG .... Oldenburg [*Germany*] [*ICAO location identifier*]   (ICLI)

EDZH........ Garmersdorf [*Germany*] [*ICAO location identifier*]   (ICLI)

EDZI......... Trier [*Germany*] [*ICAO location identifier*]   (ICLI)

EDZJ........ Idar-Oberstein [*Germany*] [*ICAO location identifier*]   (ICLI)

EDZK .... Karlsruhe [*Germany*] [*ICAO location identifier*]   (ICLI)

EDZL........ Flensburg [*Germany*] [*ICAO location identifier*]   (ICLI)

EDZM .... Muenster-Gievenbeck [*Germany*] [*ICAO location identifier*]   (ICLI)

EDZN .... Koblenz [*Germany*] [*ICAO location identifier*]   (ICLI)

EDZO........ Motne-Centre, Offenbach [*Germany*] [*ICAO location identifier*]   (ICLI)

EDZQ........ Quickborn [*Germany*] [*ICAO location identifier*]   (ICLI)

EDZR .... Aurich [*Germany*] [*ICAO location identifier*]   (ICLI)

EDZS........ Bredstedt [*Germany*] [*ICAO location identifier*]   (ICLI)

EDZT........ Altenstadt [*Germany*] [*ICAO location identifier*]   (ICLI)

EDZU .... Appenweiler [*Germany*] [*ICAO location identifier*]   (ICLI)

EDZW .... Offenbach [*Germany*] [*ICAO location identifier*]   (ICLI)

EDZX .... Traben-Trarbach [*Germany*] [*ICAO location identifier*]   (ICLI)

EDZY .... Weiden [*Germany*] [*ICAO location identifier*]   (ICLI)

EE .... Editores [*Editors*] [*Portuguese*]

EE .... Egitim Enstitusu [*Training Institute*]   (TU)

EE .... Ektelestiki Epitropi [*Executive Committee*]   (GC)

EE .... Elengtiki Epitropi [*Control Committee*]   (GC)

EE .... Elevtheroi Ellines [*Free Greeks*]   (GC)

EE .... En Elders [*And Others*] [*Afrikaans*]

e e .... Enestotos Etous [*Of This Year, Of the Current Year*]   (GC)

EE .... Entropieeinheit [*Entropy Unit*] [*German*]

Ee .... Envoye Extraordinaire [*Envoy Extraordinary*] [*French*]   (MTD)

EE .... Eparkhiaki Epitropi [*District Committee*] [*Cyprus*]   (GC)

EE .... Epitropi Epilogis [*Selection Committee*]   (GC)

EE .... Ergatiki Estia [*Labor Hearth*] [*Greek*]   (GC)

e e .... Eterorrythmos Etaireia [*Limited or Registered Partnership*] [*Greek*]

EE .... Ethniki Enosis [*National Unity Party*] [*Greek*]   (PPE)

EE .... Euzkadiko Ezkerra [*Basque Left*] [*Spain*] [*Political party*]   (PPE)

EE .... Executair Ltd. [*Nigeria*] [*ICAO designator*]   (ICDA)

EEA .... Egyptian Electric Power Authority

EEA .... Empresa Ecuatoriana de Aviacion [*Ecuador*] [*ICAO designator*]   (FAAC)

EEA .... Enosi Efimeridopolon Athinon [*Union of Athens Newspaper Vendors*]   (GC)

EEA .... Enosis Efedron Axiomatikon [*Union of Reserve Officers*]   (GC)

EEA .... Epangelmatikon Epimelitirion Athinon [*Athens Chamber of Commerce*]   (GC)

EEA .... Equipe de Engeharia Agricola [*Brazil*]   (DSCA)

EEA .... Estacion Experimental de Agricultura [*Agricultural Experimental Station*] [*La Paz, Bolivia*]   (LAA)

EEA .... Europaeische Evangelische Allianz [*European Evangelical Alliance - EEA*]   (EAIO)

EEA .... European Economic Area   (ECON)

EEA .... European Environment Agency

EEAA........ Enosis Ellinon Apostraton Axiomatikon [*Union of Retired Greek Officers*]   (GC)

EEAA........ Estacion Experimental Agricola del Altiplano [*Bolivia*]   (DSCA)

EEAA........ Estacion Experimental Agropecuaria Anguil [*Argentina*]   (DSCA)

EEAAV...... Estacion Experimental Agropecuaria Alto Valle de Rio Negro [*Argentina*]   (DSCA)

EEAB........ Estacion Experimental Agropecuaria Balcarce [*Argentina*]   (DSCA)

EEAB......... Estacion Experimental Agropecuaria Bordenave [*Argentina*]   (DSCA)

EEABV ...... Estacion Experimental Agropecuaria Bellavista [*Argentina*]   (DSCA)

EEAC........ Education Exports Advisory Council [*New South Wales, Australia*]

EEAC........ Estacion Experimental Agropecuaria Concordia [*Argentina*] (DSCA)

EEAC........ Estacion Experimental Agropecuaria Corrientes [*Argentina*] (DSCA)

EEACB...... Estacion Experimental Agropecuaria Colonia Benitez [*Argentina*] (DSCA)

EEACM..... Estacion Experimental Agropecuaria Colonia Masicas [*Argentina*] (DSCA)

EEACU...... Estacion Experimental Agropecuaria del Uruguay [*Argentina*] (DSCA)

EEAD .... Estacion Experimental de Aula Dei [*Spain*] (DSCA)

EEADP...... Estacion Experimental Agropecuaria Delta del Parana [*Argentina*] (DSCA)

EEAE........ Elliniki Epitropi Atomikis Energeias [*Greek Atomic Energy Committee*] (GC)

EEAEC...... Estacion Experimental Agropecuaria El Colorado [*Argentina*] (DSCA)

EEAGG ..... Estacion Experimental Agropecuario Gobernador Gregores [*Argentina*] (DSCA)

EEAHA ..... Estacion Experimental Agropecuaria Hilario Ascasubi [*Argentina*] (DSCA)

EEAI .... Estacion Experimental Agricola "Isabela" [*Puerto Rico*] (DSCA)

EEAJ .... Estacion Experimental Agropecuaria Jujuy [*Argentina*] (DSCA)

EEAKh ...... Elliniki Epitropi Allilengyis gia tin Khili [*Greek Committee of Solidarity for Chile*] (GC)

EEAL........ Estacion Experimental Agricola de Lambayeque [*Peru*] (DSCA)

EEALB ...... Estacion Experimental Agropecuaria La Banda [*Argentina*] (DSCA)

EEALB ...... Estacion Experimental Agropecuaria Las Brenas [*Argentina*] (DSCA)

EEALI .... Estacion Experimental Agricola de "La Tamborada" [*Bolivia*] (DSCA)

EEALL .... Estacion Experimental Agricola de los Llanos [*Bolivia*] (DSCA)

EEALM..... Estacion Experimental Agricola de La Molina [*Peru*] (DSCA)

EEALO...... Estacion Experimental Agropecuaria la Consulta [*Argentina*] (DSCA)

EEALT ...... Estacion Experimental Agricola de los Tropicos [*Bolivia*] (DSCA)

EEAM .... Ellinikon Epanastatikon Apelevtherotikon Metopon [*Greek Revolutionary Liberation Front*] (GC)

EEAM .... Ergatikon Ethnikon Apelevtherotikon Metopon [*Workers National Liberation Front*] [*Greek*] (GC)

EEAM .... Estacion Experimental Agricola de Mayaguez [*Puerto Rico*] (DSCA)

EEAM .... Estacion Experimental Agropecuaria Manfredi [*Argentina*] (DSCA)

EEAM .... Estacion Experimental Agropecuaria Mendoza [*Argentina*] (DSCA)

EEAMJ ..... Estacion Experimental Agropecuaria Marcos Juarez [*Argentina*] (DSCA)

EEAN .... Estacion Experimental Agricola del Norte [*Peru*] (DSCA)

EEAO .... Estacion Experimental Agropecuario Oliveros [*Argentina*] (DSCA)

EEAP........ Enterprise Energy Audit Program [*Australia*]

EEAP........ Estacion Experimental Agropecuaria Parana [*Argentina*] (DSCA)

EEAP........ Estacion Experimental Agropecuaria Pergamino [*Argentina*] (DSCA)

EEAPRSP ... Estacion Experimental Agropecuaria Presidencia Rogue Saenz Pena [*Argentina*] (DSCA)

EEAR........ Estacion Experimental Agropecuaria Rafaela [*Argentina*] (DSCA)

EEAR........ Estacion Experimental Agropecuaria Reconquista [*Argentina*] (DSCA)

EEARC...... Estacion Experimental Agropecuaria Rama Caida [*Argentina*] (DSCA)

EEAS........ Estacion Experimental Agropecuaria Salta [*Argentina*] (DSCA)

EEASA...... Engineering Employers' Association, South Australia

EEASA...... Environmental Education Association of Southern Africa (AA)

EEASJ....... Estacion Experimental Agropecuaria San Juan [*Argentina*] (DSCA)

EEASL ...... Estacion Experimental Agropecuaria San Luis [*Argentina*] (DSCA)

EEASP ...... Estacion Experimental Agropecuaria San Pedro [*Argentina*] (DSCA)

EEASTh .... Enosis Ergatoypallilon Astikis Syngoinonias Thessalonikis [*Union of Workers of Salonica Urban Transport*] (GC)

EEASV ...... Estacion Experimental Agronomica [*Cuba*] (DSCA)

EEAT........ Estacion Experimental Agricola del Tulumayo [*Peru*] (DSCA)

EEAT........ Estacion Experimental Agricola de Tucuman [*Experimental Research Station of Tucuman*] [*Argentina*] (LAA)

EEATF ...... Estacion Experimental Agropecuaria Tucuman Famailla [*Argentina*] (DSCA)

EEATM..... Estacion Experimental Agricola de Tingo Maria [*Peru*] (DSCA)

EEAU .... Etat des Emirates Arabes Unis

EEAVA...... Estacion Experimental Agropecuaria Villa Alberdi [*Argentina*] (DSCA)

EEB........... Euroberlin [*France*] [*ICAO designator*] (FAAC)

EEB........... Europaeischer Erziehungsbund eV (SLS)

EEB........... European Environmental Bureau [*Belgium*]

EEBI......... Escuela de Entrenamiento Basico de Infanteria [*Infantry Basic Training School*] [*Nicaragua*] (LA)

EEBP......... Estacao Experimental de Biologia e Piscicultura [*Experimental Station for Biology and Pisciculture*] [*Sao Paulo, Brazil*] (LAA)

EEC........... Commission of the European Communities

EEC........... Electoral Education Centre [*Australia*]

EEC........... Estacao Experimetnal de Curitiba [*Brazil*] (DSCA)

EEC........... Estacion Experimental de Cafe [*Venezuela*] (DSCA)

EEC........... Estacion Experimental de Caucagua [*Venezuela*] (DSCA)

EEC........... Eurocontrol Experimental Centre [*France*] (PDAA)

EEC........... Europa Esperanto-Centro [*European Esperanto Centre - EEC*] (EAIO)

EEC........... European Economic Community [*Common Market*]

EEC........... Ewe Evangelical Church

EECA........ Empresa Estatal de Comercializacion de Alimentos [*State Food Marketing Enterprise*] [*Peru*] (LA)

EECA........ European Electronic Component Manufacturers Association (EAIO)

EEC-ACP .. European Economic Community - African, Caribbean, and Pacific Countries (AF)

EECCS ...... European Ecumenical Commission for Church and Society [*Formerly, Ecumenical Commission for Church and Society*] (EA)

EECE......... Estacao Experimental de Campo Grande [*Brazil*] (DSCA)

EECGDR... Entente Europeenne du Commerce en Gros des Deux-Roues (EA)

EECI......... Energie Electrique de Cote-D'Ivoire [*Ivory Coast Electric Power Company*] (AF)

EEC-LCM ... European Economic Community - Liaison Committee of Midwives (EAIO)

EECM........ East European Chemical Monitor [*Business International*] [*Vienna, Austria*] [*Information service or system*] (IID)

EECMA...... European Electronic Component Manufacturers' Association

EECOD ..... European Ecumenical Organization for Development [*Brussels, Belgium*] (EAIO)

EEC-SLC... European Economic Community - Shipbuilders' Linking Committee [*Brussels, Belgium*] (EAIO)

EECT........ Estacion Experimental de Cultivos Tropicales [*Mexico*] (DSCA)

EED .... Ellinikai Enoploi Dynameis [*Greek Armed Forces*] (GC)

EEDA .... Elliniki Epitropi Dikaiomaton tou Anthropou [*Greek Human Rights Committee*] (GC)

EEDA .... Enosis Epangelmation Dikigoron Athinon [*Union of Professional Attorneys of Athens*] (GC)

EEDAP...... Elliniki Enosis Yper ton Dikaiomaton tou Anthropou kai tou Politou [*Greek Union for the Rights of Man and Citizen*] (GC)

EEDB........ Energy and Economics Data Bank [*IAEA*] [*United Nations*] (DUND)

EEDDA ..... Elliniki Epitropi Diethnous Dimokratikis Allilengiis [*Greek Committee for International Democratic Solidarity*] (GC)

EEDE........ Elliniki Etaireia Dioikiseos Epikheiriseon [*Greek Association for Business Management*] (GC)

EEDE........ Enosis Ellinon Dikaston kai Eisangeleon [*Union of Greek Judges and Prosecutors*] (GC)

EEDI......... Entreprise d'Electricite Domestique et Industrielle

EEDK ......: Eniaion Ethnikon Dimokratikon Komma [*United National Democratic Party*] [*EK Cyprus*] [*See also*] (GC)

EEDS......... European Electrostatic Discharge Association [*British*] (EAIO)

EEDYE...... Elliniki Epitropi dia tin Diethni Yfesin kai Eirinin [*Greek Committee for an International Detente and Peace*] (GC)

EEE........... Elliniki Epitropi Eirinis [*Greek Peace Committee*] (GC)

EEE........... Enosi Ellinon Ethnikiston [*Union of Greek Nationalists*] (GC)

EEE........... Enosis Ellinon Efopliston [*Union of Greek Shipowners*] (GC)

EEE........... Ethniki Enosis Ellinon [*National Union of Greece*] (GC)

EEEDEE ... Ethniki Elliniki Epitropi Diethnous Emborikou Epimelitiriou [*National Greek Committee of the International Chamber of Commerce*] (GC)

EEEE......... Ektelestiki Epitropi Exoterikou Emboriou [*Foreign Trade Executive Committee*] [*Greek*] (GC)

EE-EE....... Ellines Ethnikistai - Ethnikistai Ellines [*Greek Nationalists - National Greeks*] (GC)

EEEE........ Evropaiki Enosis Elevtherou Emboriou [*European Free Trade Association*] (GC)

EEEF .... Elliniki Ethniki Enosis Kata tis Fimatioseos [*Greek National Anti-Tuberculosis Association*] (GC)

EEEL .... Ethniki Etaireia Ellinon Logotekhnon [*National Association of Greek Writers*] (GC)

EEEP .... Enosis Efopliston Epivatikon Ploion [*Union of Passenger Ship Owners*] (GC)

Ee et M pl .. Envoye Extraordinaire et Ministre Plenipotentiaire [*Envoy Extraordinary and Ministry of Plenipotentiary*] [*French*] (MTD)

EEEV......... Elevtheroi Ellines Epanaferoun Vasilea [*Free Greeks Reinstate King*] (GC)

EEF............ Dispositif d'Elimination des Echos Fixes [*French*]

EEF............ Etaireia Ellinon Filologon [*Association of Greek Philologists*] (GC)

EEFC .... Estacion Experimental Forestal y de Conservacion [*Ecuador*] (DSCA)

EEG .... Electroencephalogram, Electroencephalography (RU)

EEG .... Elektroensefalogram [*Electroencephalogram*] [*Afrikaans*]

EEG .... Empresa Electrica de Guatemala, SA (LAA)

EEG .... Energy and Environment Group [*India*] (EAIO)

EEG .... Ensemble Electronique de Gestion [*French*] (ADPT)

EEG .... European Expedition Guild (EA)

EEG .... Europese Economische Gemeenschap [*Netherlands*]

EEGAP...... Estacion Experimental Ganadera del Altiplano "Patacamaya" [*Bolivia*] (DSCA)

EEGC........ Entreprise d'Etudes de Genie Civil [*Civil Engineering Study Enterprise*] [*Malagasy*] (AF)

EEGP........ Estacion Experimental Ganadera de Patacamaya [*Bolivia*] (DSCA)

EEGT........ Estacion Experimental Ganadera de Trinidad [*Bolivia*] (DSCA)

EEHRA ..... Ethiopian Hotel and Restaurant Association (EAIO)

EEI............. Engineering Equipment, Inc. [*Philippines*]

EE-IS........ Basque Left - Left for Socialism (PPW)

EEITC .... Electrical and Electronic Industry Training Committee [*Australia*]

EEK .... Elevtheron Ergatikon Kendron [*Free Labor Center*] [*Abbreviation usually followed by initial of town in which located Cyprus*] (GC)

EEK .... Epitropi tis Evropaikis Koinotitos [*European Community Commission*] (GC)

eek............. Eszak-Eszakkelet [*North-Northwest*] (HU)

EEK .... Ethnikon Enotikon Komma [*National Unifying Party*] [*Greek*] (GC)

EEK .... Evropska Ekonomska Komisija [*Economic Commission for Europe*] [*United Nations (already exists in GUS II database)*] (YU)

EEKA........ Ethniki Epitropi Kypriakou Agonos [*National Committee for the Cypriot Struggle*] [*Greek*] (GC)

EEKETP.... Elliniki Etaireia tis Kosmiteias Ethnikou Topeiou kai Poleon [*Greek Society for National Landscape and Cities Beautification*] (GC)

EEKh .... Enosis Ellinon Khimikon [*Union of Greek Chemists*] (GC)

EEKhPL .... Elliniki Etaireia Khimikon Proiondon kai Lipasmaton [*Greek Chemical Products and Fertilizer Company*] (GC)

EEL............ Enosis Ellinon Logotekhnon [*Association of Greek Writers*] (GC)

EELA .... Equipamentos de Escritorio (Beira) Lda.

EELAP ...... Enosis Eispraktoron Leoforeion Athinon-Peiraios [*Union of Athens-Piraeus Bus Collectors*] (GC)

EELIAS..... Electrical Engineering Literature and Information Advisory System [*Australia*]

EELL .... Estacion Experimental Los Llanos [*Venezuela*] (DSCA)

EELPA ...... Ethiopian Electric Light and Power Authority (AF)

EEM .... Earth Exchange Museum [*Sydney, New South Wales, Australia*]

EEM .... Electricite et Eaux de Madagascar [*Electric Power and Water Company of Madagascar*] (AF)

EEM .... Emission Electron Microscope (RU)

EEM .... Energie Electrique de Madagascar

EEM .... Enosis Ellinon Mousourgon [*Greek Composers Union*] (GC)

EEM .... Ethniki Etaireia Meleton [*National Research Society*] [*Greek*] (GC)

EEMGM ... Eski Eserler ve Muzeler Genel Mudurlugu [*Antiquities and Museums Directorate General*] [*Under Ministry of Culture*] (TU)

EEMOS..... Egtim Enstitusu Mezunu Oretmenler Sendikasi [*Training Institute Graduate Teachers Union*] (TU)

EEMS........ European Environmental Mutagen Society [*Leiden, Netherlands*] (EAIO)

EENA .... Enosis Ellinon Neon Axiomatikon [*Union of Young Greek Officers*] (GC)

EENSL ...... Elliniki Epitropi Navtiliakis Synergasias Londinou [*Greek Committee of London for Maritime Cooperation*] [*ENEL*] [*See also*] (GC)

e e ny .... Eszak-Eszaknyugat [*North-Northwest*] (HU)

EEO .... Compagnie des Eaux et Electricite de l'Ouest Africain

EEO .... Enosis Eisagogeon Osprion [*Union of Legume Importers*] (GC)

EEO .... Estacion Experimental de Occidente [*Venezuela*] (DSCA)

EEO .... Ethniki Ergatiki Omospondia [*National Labor Federation*] [*Cyprus*] (GC)

EEO .... European Electro-Optics Conference and Exhibition

EEOA .... Compagnie des Eaux et Electricite de l'Ouest Africain

EEOC .... Equal Employment Opportunity Coordinator [*Australia*]

EEOCC...... Equal Employment Opportunity Consultative Committee [*Australia*]

EEOE .... Elliniki Etaireia Okeanografikon Erevnon [*Greek Oceanographic Research Society*] (GC)

EEOE .... Enotiki Epitropi ton Oikodomon Ellados [*Unifying Committee of Builders of Greece*] (GC)

EEOO .... Elliniki Etaireia Oinon kai Oinopnevmaton [*Greek Wines and Spirits Association*] (GC)

EEOPO ..... Ergatiki Epitropi Organotikis Protovoulias Oikodomon [*Labor Committee for the Organizational Initiative of Construction Workers*] [*Greek*] (GC)

EEOTh ...... Enosis Ergatotekhniton Oikodomon Thessalonikis [*Union of Construction Technicians of Salonica*] (GC)

EEOU .... Equal Employment Opportunities Unit [*State Service Commission*] [*New Zealand*]

EEP............ Epangelmatikon Epimelitirion Peiraios [*Piraeus Chamber of Commerce*] (GC)

EEP............ Estacion Experimental de Pergamino [*Pergamino Experimental Station*] [*Argentina*] (LAA)

EEP............ Estacion Experimental "Dr. Mario Cassinoni" [*Uruguay*] (DSCA)

EEP............ Estacion Experimental Paine [*Chile*] (DSCA)

EEP............ Evropaiki Enosis Pliromon [*European Payments Union*] (GC)

EEPA .... Esso Exploration and Production Australia Incorporated Ltd.

EEPA .... Estacao Experimental de Producao Animal [*Brazil*] (DSCA)

EEPAP ..... Elliniki Etaireia Prostasias Anapiron Paidon [*Greek Association for the Protection of Handicapped Children*] (GC)

EEPC .... Engineering Export Promotion Council [*India*] (PDAA)

EEPDE ...... Enosis Ellinon Panepistimiakon Dytikis Evropis [*Union of Greek Universitarians of Western Europe*] (GC)

EEPE .... Elliniki Epitropi Pyrinikis Energeias [*Greek Nuclear Energy Commission*] (GC)

EEPF .... Elliniki Etaireia Prostasias tis Fyseos [*Greek Society for the Protection of Nature*] (GC)

EEPF .... Estacao Experimental de Passo Fundo [*Brazil*] (DSCA)

EEPK .... Etaireia Ellinikou Pyritidopoieiou kai Kalykopoieiou [*Greek Gunpowder and Cartridge Manufacturing Company*] (GC)

EEPMK ..... Etaireia Epistimonikon kai Politistikon Meleton Kyprou [*Scientific and Cultural Research Company of Cyprus*] (GC)

EEPOIE .... Ekpaidevtikos, Epistimonikos, kai Politistikos Organismos ton Inomenon Ethnon [*United Nations Educational, Scientific, and Cultural Organization*] (GC)

EEPP .... Epitropi Epanapatrismou Politikon Prosfygon [*Committee for the Repatriation of Political Refugees*] [*Greek*] (GC)

EEPsPs...... Elliniki Etaireia Psykhoanalytikis Psykhotherapeias [*Greek Society for Psychoanalytic Psychotherapy*] (GC)

EEQ .... Empresa Electrica Quito [*Ecuador*] (PDAA)

EER .... Electronic Optimalizing Control (RU)

EERA......... Epitropi Elengkhou Rypanseos tis Atmosfairas [*Air Pollution Control Committee*] [*Greek*] (GC)

Eerw......... Eerwaarde [*Reverend*] [*Afrikaans*]

EES .... Egypt Exploration Society

EES .... Electric Power System (BU)

EES .... Elektricky Energeticky System [*Electric Power System*] (CZ)

EES........... Elevtheron Ergatikon Somateion [*Free Labor Union*] [*Used in reference to Confederation of Cypriot Workers unions Cyprus*] (GC)

EES .... Ellinikos Erythros Stavros [*Greek Red Cross*] (GC)

EES .... Environmental Effects Statement [*Australia*]

EES .... Estacao de Ensaio de Sementes [*Portugal*] (DSCA)

EES .... Etaireia Ellinikon Spoudon [*Association of Greek Studies*] (GC)

EES .... Ethniki ton Ellinon Sotiria [*National Salvation of Greeks*] (GC)

EESAK ...... Elliniki Epitropi Seismologias kai Andiseismikon Kataskevon [*Greek Committee for Seismology and Earthquake-Proof Construction*] (GC)

EESC .... Eastern Europe Solidarity Campaign (EAIO)

EESC .... East European Solidarity Committee [*Defunct*] (EAIO)

EESNA...... Estacion Experimental de la Sociedad Nacional de Agricultura [*Chile*] (DSCA)

EEST/PD .. Emergency Establishment Supplement Table of Personnel Distribution [*NATO*] (NATG)

EESV .... Ethniki Enosi Stemmatos Voreioelladiton [*National Union of Northern Greeks for the Crown*] (GC)

EET............ Eastern European Time (DCTA)

EET........... Eglise Evangelique du Togo

EETA .... Enosis Ergaton Typou Athinon [*Athens Press Workers Union*] (GC)

EETE .... Epitropi Elengkhou Timologiou Exagogon [*Export Price Control Committee*] [*Greek*] (GC)

EEThS....... Etaireia Ellinon Theatrikon Syngrafeon [*Greek Playwrights Association*] (GC)

EETP .... Estacion Experimental Tropical "Pichilingue" [*Ecuador*] (DSCA)

EEU .... Eurofly [*Italy*] [*ICAO designator*] (FAAC)

EEU .... European Esperanto Union (EA)

EEUU .... Estados Unidos de America [*United States of America*] [*Spanish*]

EE UU daA ... Estados Unidos da America [*United States of America*]
  [*Portuguese*] (GPO)
EEV .... Enosis Epangelmation kai Viotekhnon [*Union of Tradesmen and
  Craftsmen*] [*Followed by initial letter of district*] [*Greek*]
  (GC)
EEV .... Estacion Experimental Villamontes [*Bolivia*] (DSCA)
EEVaSS ..... Elliniki Epitropi gia tin Valkaniki Synennoisi kai Synergasia
  [*Greek Committee for Balkan Understanding and
  Cooperation*] (GC)
EEVE .... Estacao Experimental de Viticultura e Enologia [*Brazil*] (DSCA)
EEVF .... East Eifel Volcanic Field [*Geology*] [*Germany*]
EEVFL .... Estacion Experimental de "Vista Florida" [*Vista Florida
  Experimental Station*] [*Peru*] (ARC)
EEVP .... Ektelestiki Epitropi Vasilikis Pronoias [*Royal Welfare Executive
  Committee*] (GC)
EEVS .... Elliniki Epitropi gia tin Valkaniki Synergasia [*Greek Committee
  for Balkan Cooperation*] (GC)
EEVVE ...... Ethniki Enosi Vasilofronon Voreiou Ellados [*National Union of
  Northern Greek Royalists*] (GC)
EEY .... Elliniki Etaireia Ydaton [*Greek Water Company*] (GC)
EEY .... Epitropi Ekpaidevtikis Ypiresias [*Educational Services
  Committee*] (GC)
EEYDAP ... Elliniki Epitropi Yper ton Dikaiomaton tou Anthropou kai
  Politou [*Greek Committee for the Rights of Man and
  Citizen*] (GC)
EEYEE ...... Elliniki Etaireia Ydravlikon kai Exygiantikon Ergon [*Greek
  Association for Water and Sanitation Projects*] (GC)
EEYkaiE.... Elliniki Epitropi gia Yfesi kai Eirini [*Greek Committee for
  Detente and Peace*] (GC)
EEZ .... Estacion Experimental del Zulia [*Venezuela*] (DSCA)
EEZ .... Eurofly SPA [*Italy*] [*ICAO designator*] (FAAC)
EEZ .... Evropska Ekonomska Zajednica [*European Economic
  Community (EEC)*] (YU)
EEZ .... Exclusive Economic Zone [*Offshore sovereignty*] [*ICSU*]
EEZA .... Estacion Experimental de Zonas Aridas [*Venezuela*] (DSCA)
Ef .... Efese [*Ephesus*] [*Afrikaans*]
EF .... Efesiers [*Ephesian*] [*Afrikaans*]
EF .... Eingabefolge [*German*] (ADPT)
EF .... Eksportfinans [*Export Finance*] [*Commercial firm*] [*Norway*]
EF .... Eleftherofronon [*Free Opinion Party*] [*Greek*] (PPE)
EF .... Elektricna Filijala [*Electrical Substation*] (YU)
EF .... Endeavour Forum [*Australia*]
EF .... Endeavour Foundation [*Australia*]
EF .... Era Fascista [*Date used during reign of Mussolini*] [*Italy*]
EF .... Ethniki Froura [*National Guard*] [*Cyprus*] (GC)
EF .... Ethnikon Fos [*National Light*] (GC)
EF .... Etudes Fiscales [*French*] (BAS)
EF .... European File
EF .... European Foundation (DS)
EF .... Eurotransplant Foundation (EA)
EFA .... Earth Foundation Australia
EFA .... Ecole des Forces Aeriennes de Bouake
EFA .... Ecole des Forces Armees [*Armed Forces School*] [*Ivory Coast*]
  (AF)
EFA .... Electoral Funding Authority [*New South Wales, Australia*]
EFA .... Empresa de Fumigacion Aerea [*Colombia*] (COL)
EFA .... Empresa Ferrocarriles Argentinos [*Argentine Railway Enterprise*]
  (LA)
EFA .... Enterprise Flexibility Agreement [*Australia*]
EFA .... Equestrian Federation of Australia
EFA .... Etablissements France-Atlantic
EFA .... European Fairytale Association [*See also EMG*] [*Rheine, Federal
  Republic of Germany*] (EAIO)
EFA .... European Federation of Agricultural Workers' Unions [*EC*]
  (ECED)
EFA .... European Finance Association (EAIO)
EFA .... European Free Alliance [*See also ALE*] [*Brussels, Belgium
  Political party*] (EAIO)
EFA .... Evangelical Fellowship of Asia
EFA .... Exploitations Forestieres de l'Afema
EFA .... Societe d'Etudes et Fabrications Aeronautiques [*French*]
EFAA .... Aavahelukka [*Finland*] [*ICAO location identifier*] (ICLI)
EFAAD ...... European Federation for the Advancement of Anaesthesia in
  Dentistry [*Italy*] (EAIO)
EFAB .... Establissement d'Etudes et de Fabrications d'Armaments de
  Bourges [*Groupement Industriel des Armements Terrestres*]
  [*France*] (PDAA)
EFAC .... Echanges Francs d'Avarie Commune [*Exchange Free from
  General Average*] (CL)
EFAC .... Entreprises Franco-Africaines de Constructions
EFAc .... Exportations, Frais, Accessoires (Comptes) [*Exports, Expenses,
  and Accessories (Accounts)*] (CL)
EFACF ...... European Folk Art and Craft Federation [*Zurich, Switzerland*]
  (EAIO)
EFACI .... Exploitations Forestieres et Agricoles de la Cote-D'Ivoire
EFAD .... European Federation of the Associations of Dietitians (EAIO)

EFAK .... Enosis Filon tou Aravikou Kosmou [*Association of Friends of the
  Arab World*] [*Greek*] (GC)
EFAL .... Alavus [*Finland*] [*ICAO location identifier*] (ICLI)
EFANSW .. Electoral Funding Authority of New South Wales [*Australia*]
EFAP .... Environmentally Friendly Accreditation Program [*Australia*]
EFAPIT ..... Euromarket Federation of Animal Protein Importers and Traders
  (EAIO)
EFAR .... European Federation for AIDS Research
EFB .... Europaeische Foderation Biotechnologie [*European Federation
  of Biotechnology*] (EAIO)
EFB .... Societe d'Exploitation Forestiere de la Bembai
EFBA .... Entreprise Forestiere des Bois Africains
EFBACA ... Entreprise Forestiere des Bois Africains Centrafrique
EFBPBI .... European Federation of the Brush and Paint Brush Industries
  (EA)
  ●
EFBS .... European Federation of Building Societies (EAIO)
EFBWW .... European Federation of Building and Woodworkers (EA)
EFC .... Entreprise Forestiere Camerounaise
EFC .... Escort Force Commander [*NATO*] (NATG)
EFC .... European Federation of Corrosion (EA)
EFC .... Experiment Farm Cottage [*Australia*]
EFCA .... Ecole de Formation des Cadres Auxiliaires
EFCA .... Evangelical Free Church of Australia
EFCAT ...... European Football Commentators Association Television (EA)
EFCATS.... European Federation of Catalysis Societies
EFCB .... Estrada de Ferro Central do Brasil [*Portuguese*]
EFCE .... European Federation of Chemical Engineering [*See also EFCIW*]
  (EAIO)
EFCEM ..... European Federation of Catering Equipment Manufacturers
  (EA)
EFCGU...... European Federation of Chemical and General Workers Unions
  (EAIO)
EFChE....... European Federation of Chemical Engineering
EFCIS........ Societe pour l'Etude et la Fabrication de Circuits Integres
  Speciaux [*France*] (PDAA)
EFCIW ...... Europaeische Foderation fuer Chemie-Ingenieur-Wesen
  [*European Federation of Chemical Engineering - EFCE*]
EFCS .... Ethnographic and Folk Culture Society [*India*] (EAIO)
EFCS .... European Federation for Company Sports (EAIO)
EFCS .... European Federation of Chemical Societies
EFCS .... European Federation of Cytology Societies (EAIO)
EFCSA....... Establecimientos Frigorificos del Cerro SA [*Cerro Packing
  Plants, Inc.*] [*Uruguay*] (LA)
EFCSM ..... European Federation of Ceramic Sanitaryware Manufacturers
  (EA)
EFCT .... European Federation of Chemical Trade [*Montreux,
  Switzerland*]
EFCTEC.... European Fluorocarbon Technical Committee [*Belgium*]
  (EAIO)
EFDA........ European Federation of Data Processing Associations (ADPT)
EFDA........ European Formula Drivers Association (EAIO)
EFDA........ European Funeral Directors' Association (EAIO)
EFE .... Agencia Efe [*Efe Agency*] [*Press Association*] [*Spanish*] (WER)
EFE .... Educational Film Enterprises, Inc.
EFE .... Elliniki Filoteliki Etaireia [*Greek Philatelic Society*] (GC)
EFE .... Elliniki Fotografiki Etaireia [*Greek Photographic Society*] (GC)
EFE .... Ethniki Froura Elladas [*National Guard of Greece*] (GC)
EFEA .... Empresa Ferrocarriles del Estado Argentino [*Argentina*] (LAA)
EFEDOSZ ... Epito-, Fa-, es Epitoanyagipari Dolgozok Szakszervezete [*Trade
  Union of Workers of the Construction, Woodworking, and
  Building Material Industries*] (HU)
EFEE .... Ethniki Foititiki Enosis Ellados [*National Student Union of
  Greece*] (GC)
EFEK .... Ethniki Foititiki Enosis Kyprou [*National Student Union of
  Cyprus*] (GC)
EFEM .... Entwicklung und Fabrikation Elektrischer Messinstrumente
  [*Development and Production of Electrical Measuring
  Instruments*] (EG)
EFEMA ..... Association des Fabricants Europeens d'Emulsifants
  Alimentaires [*Association of European Manufacturers of
  Food Emulsifiers*] (EAIO)
EFEO .... Ecole Francaise d'Extreme Orient [*French School of the Far East*]
EFES .... Tampere [*Finland*] [*ICAO location identifier*] (ICLI)
EFET .... Enontekio [*Finland*] [*ICAO location identifier*] (ICLI)
EFEU......... Eura [*Finland*] [*ICAO location identifier*] (ICLI)
EFEX .... Ypiresia Efodion ek tou Exoterikou [*Foreign Supplies Office*]
  (GC)
eff .... Efface [*Effaced*] [*Publishing*] [*French*]
eff .... Effektiv [*Effective*] [*Business term*] [*German*]
EFF .... Elektronicfabrikantforeningen [*Denmark*] (EAIO)
EFF .... Enterprise, Family, and Freedom [*Australia*] [*Political party*]
EFF .... European Franchise Federation [*France*] (EAIO)
EFF .... Experimental Film Fund [*Australia*]
EFFA .... European Flavour and Fragrance Association [*Belgium*] (EAIO)
Eff a P .... Effet a Payer [*Bill Payable*] [*Accounting*] [*French*]

Eff a R .... Effet a Recevoir [Bill Receivable] [Accounting] [French]
EFFAS ...... European Federation of Financial Analysts' Societies (EA)
EFFDEA .... Empresa Flota Fluvial del Estado Argentino [Argentina] (LAA)
effekt .... Effective, Efficient (RU)
EFFM .... European Federation of Fiber Cement Manufacturers [EC] (ECED)
eff Mossb ... Mossbauer Effect (RU)
EFFO .... Forssa [Finland] [ICAO location identifier] (ICLI)
EFFoST ...... European Federation of Food Science and Technology (EA)
EFFY .... Enterprise Funds for Youth [Scottish Development Agency]
EFG .... Efogi [Papua New Guinea] [Airport symbol] (OAG)
EFG .... Elders Finance Group [Australia]
EFGA .... Exotic Fruit Growers Association [Australia]
EFH .... Entwurfsbuero fuer Hochbau [Design Office for Above-Ground Construction] (EG)
EFHA .... Halli [Finland] [ICAO location identifier] (ICLI)
EFHF .... Helsinki/Helsinki-Malmi [Finland] [ICAO location identifier] (ICLI)
EFHK .... Helsinki/Vantaa [Finland] [ICAO location identifier] (ICLI)
EFHL .... Equiticorp Finance Holdings Ltd. [Australia]
EFHL .... Hailuoto [Finland] [ICAO location identifier] (ICLI)
EFHM .... Hameenkyro [Finland] [ICAO location identifier] (ICLI)
EFHN .... Hanko [Finland] [ICAO location identifier] (ICLI)
EFHP .... Haapavesi [Finland] [ICAO location identifier] (ICLI)
EFHT .... Ahtari [Finland] [ICAO location identifier] (ICLI)
EFHV .... Hyvinkaa [Finland] [ICAO location identifier] (ICLI)
EFI .... Eje Fluvial Industrial [Industrial River Axis] [Argentina] (LA)
EFI .... Elektrisitetsforsyningens Forskninginstitutt [Research Institute of Electricity Supply] [Norway]
EFI .... Employers' Federation of India (FEA)
EFI .... Energiforsyningens Forskningsinstitutt [Electrical Power Research Institute] [Norway] (IRC)
EfI .... Entwurfsbuero fuer Industriebau (VEB) [Design Office for Industrial Construction (VEB)] (EG)
EFI .... Erevanskii Fizcheskii Institut [Former USSR] (PDAA)
EFIA .... European Fertilizer Importers' Associations (EAIO)
EFIAP .... Enosis Fymatikon Isfalismenon Athinon-Peiraios [Athens-Piraeus Union of Insured Tuberculars] (GC)
EFIBANCA ... Ente Finanziario Interbancario SpA [Bank] [Italian]
EFIBCA ..... European Flexible Intermediate Bulk Container Association (PDAA)
EFIC .... Export Finance Insurance Corporation [Australia] (ADA)
EFIFC .... European Federation of Investment Funds and Companies (ECON)
EFII .... I Salmi [Finland] [ICAO location identifier] (ICLI)
EFIK .... Evkaf Finansman ve Inkisaf Korperasyonu Ltd. [Religious Endowments' Financing and Development Corporation Ltd.] [Turkish Cypriot] (GC)
EFIK .... Kiikala [Finland] [ICAO location identifier] (ICLI)
EFIL .... European Federation for Intercultural Learning (EAIO)
EFIL .... Ilmajoki [Finland] [ICAO location identifier] (ICLI)
EFIM .... Ente Partecipazioni e Finanziamento Industria Manifatturiera [Manufacturing Industry Holding and Financial Company] [Rome, Italy] (WER)
EFIM .... Immola [Finland] [ICAO location identifier] (ICLI)
EFIV .... Erfolgs-und Finanzvorschau [German] (ADPT)
EFIV .... Ivalo [Finland] [ICAO location identifier] (ICLI)
EFJC .... Europaische Foderation Junger Chore [European Federation of Young Choirs] (EAIO)
EFJM .... Jamijarvi [Finland] [ICAO location identifier] (ICLI)
EFJO .... Joensuu [Finland] [ICAO location identifier] (ICLI)
EFJP .... Jakalapaa [Finland] [ICAO location identifier] (ICLI)
EFJY .... Jyvaskyla [Finland] [ICAO location identifier] (ICLI)
EFK .... Europaeische Foederation Korrosion (SLS)
EFK .... Evangelical Fellowship of Kenya (EAIO)
EFKA .... Kauhava [Finland] [ICAO location identifier] (ICLI)
EFKE .... Kemi [Finland] [ICAO location identifier] (ICLI)
EFKG .... Kumlinge [Finland] [ICAO location identifier] (ICLI)
EFKH .... Kuhmo [Finland] [ICAO location identifier] (ICLI)
EFKI .... Elektronikai es Finommechanikai Kutato Intezet [Electronics and Precision Mechanics Research Institute] (HU)
EFKJ .... Kajaani [Finland] [ICAO location identifier] (ICLI)
EFKJ .... Kauhajoki [Finland] [ICAO location identifier] (ICLI)
EFKK .... Kruunupyy [Finland] [ICAO location identifier] (ICLI)
EFKL .... Helsinki [Finland] [ICAO location identifier] (ICLI)
EFKM .... Kemijarvi [Finland] [ICAO location identifier] (ICLI)
EFKR .... Karsamaki [Finland] [ICAO location identifier] (ICLI)
EFKS .... Kuusamo [Finland] [ICAO location identifier] (ICLI)
EFKT .... Kittila [Finland] [ICAO location identifier] (ICLI)
EFKU .... Kuopio [Finland] [ICAO location identifier] (ICLI)
EFKV .... Kivijarvi [Finland] [ICAO location identifier] (ICLI)
EFKY .... Kymi [Finland] [ICAO location identifier] (ICLI)
EFL .... Argostolion [Greece] [Airport symbol] (OAG)
EFL .... Egyptian Federation of Labor [Trade union]
EFL .... Exploitation Forestiere de la Lobo
EFLA .... Entreprise Force Lumiere Africaine

EFLA .... European Foundation for Landscape Architecture [EC] (ECED)
EFLA .... Vesivehmaa [Finland] [ICAO location identifier] (ICLI)
EFLEX ...... Estacao Florestal de Experimentacao de Lorena [Brazil] (DSCA)
EFLP .... Lappeenranta [Finland] [ICAO location identifier] (ICLI)
EFM .... Edinburgh Fund Managers [Scotland]
EFM .... Export-Financiering-Maatschappij [Benelux] (BAS)
EFMA .... European Fertilizer Manufacturers Association (EAIO)
EFMA .... European Financial Management and Marketing Association (EAIO)
EFMA .... European Fittings Manufacturers Association (EAIO)
EFMA .... Mariehamn [Finland] [ICAO location identifier] (ICLI)
ef-masl .... Essential Oil Plant [Topography] (RU)
EFMC .... European Federation of Medicinal Chemistry (EAIO)
EFMD .... European Foundation for Management Development (EAIO)
EFME .... Menkijarvi [Finland] [ICAO location identifier] (ICLI)
EFMF .... Environmental Fluid Mechanics Foundation [Monash University] [Australia]
EFMI .... European Federation for Medical Informatics (EAIO)
EFMI .... Mikkeli [Finland] [ICAO location identifier] (ICLI)
EfmoR .... Erntefestmeter ohne Rinde [Crop-Yield in Cubic Meters Not Including the Bark] (EG)
EFMP .... Escuela Formadora de Maestros de Primaria [Primary Teachers Training School] [Cuba] (LA)
EFN .... Energiforskningsnaemnden [Energy Research Commission] [Sweden] (WED)
EFNMS ..... European Federation of National Maintenance Societies [Sweden]
EFNSW ..... Esperanto Federation of New South Wales [Australia]
EFNU .... Nummela [Finland] [ICAO location identifier] (ICLI)
EFO .... Ecole de Formation d'Officiers [Officers Training School] [Zaire] (AF)
EFO .... Etablissements Francais d'Oceanie (FLAF)
EFOA .... Elliniki Filathlos Omospondia Andisfairiseos [Greek Lawn Tennis Athletic Federation] (GC)
EFOA .... European Fuel Oxygenates Association (EAIO)
EFOC/LAN ... European Fiber Optic Communications and Local Area Network Exposition [Information Gatekeepers, Inc.]
EFOEA ...... Elliniki Filathlos Omospondia Epitrapeziou Andisfairiseos [Greek Table Tennis Athletic Federation] (GC)
EFOMP ..... European Federation of Organizations for Medical Physics [EC] (ECED)
EFOP .... Oripaa [Finland] [ICAO location identifier] (ICLI)
EFOR .... Oritkari [Finland] [ICAO location identifier] (ICLI)
EFORTOM ... Ecole de Formation des Officiers de Reserve des Territoires d'Outre-Mer [Overseas Territories Reserve Officers Training School] [French] (AF)
EFOU .... Oulu [Finland] [ICAO location identifier] (ICLI)
EFP .... Epitropi Physikou Perivallondos [Committee for Natural Environment] [EKEP] [See also] (GC)
EFP .... Europaeische Foederalistische Partei [European Federalist Party] [Austria] (PPE)
EFP .... European Federation of Parasitologists (EAIO)
EFP .... European Federation of Purchasing (PDAA)
EFPA .... Enosis Foititon Panepistimiou Athinon [Union of Athens University Students] (GC)
EFPA .... European Food Phosphates Producers' Association (EAIO)
EFPA .... European Food Service and Packaging Association [British] (EAIO)
EFPE .... Pello [Finland] [ICAO location identifier] (ICLI)
EFPI .... European Federation of the Plywood Industry (EA)
EFPI .... Piikajarvi [Finland] [ICAO location identifier] (ICLI)
EFPIA .... European Federation of Pharmaceutical Industries' Associations (EA)
EFPK .... Pieksamaki [Finland] [ICAO location identifier] (ICLI)
EFPO .... Pori [Finland] [ICAO location identifier] (ICLI)
EFPPA .... European Federation of Professional Psychologists Associations (EA)
EFPS .... European Federation of Productivity Services [Stockholm, Sweden] (EA)
EFPS .... Rovaniemi [Finland] [ICAO location identifier] (ICLI)
EFPU .... Pudasjarvi [Finland] [ICAO location identifier] (ICLI)
EFPW .... European Federation for the Protection of Waters [Switzerland] (ASF)
EFPWCM ... European Federation of Pallet and Wooden Crate Manufacturers (EA)
EFPY .... Pyhasalmi [Finland] [ICAO location identifier] (ICLI)
EFQFFM ... European Federation of Quick Frozen Food Manufacturers [Belgium] (EAIO)
EFR .... Eingabefolgeregister [German] (ADPT)
EFR .... Elf Air Ltd. [Russian Federation] [ICAO designator] (FAAC)
EFr .... Energetische Futtereinheit [Energy Feed Unit] (EG)
EFRA .... Rautavaara [Finland] [ICAO location identifier] (ICLI)
EFRAC ...... European Working Party for Fractionation and Reassembly of Biological Units
EFRAPI ..... Exposicao Feira Regional Agropecuaria e Industrial de Crissiumal [Brazil] (DSCA)
EFRH .... Pattijoki [Finland] [ICAO location identifier] (ICLI)

EFRL........ Exploitation Forestiere Robert Lamoulie
EFRN........ Rantasalmi [*Finland*] [*ICAO location identifier*]   (ICLI)
EFRO........ Rovaniemi Airport [*Finland*] [*ICAO location identifier*]   (ICLI)
EFRP........ European Federation for Retirement Provision   (ECON)
EFRT........ European Federation of Retail Traders [*Belgium*]   (EAIO)
EFRV........ Kiuruvesi [*Finland*] [*ICAO location identifier*]   (ICLI)
EFRY........ Rayskala [*Finland*] [*ICAO location identifier*]   (ICLI)
EFS.......... Europe Falcon Service [*France*] [*ICAO designator*]   (FAAC)
EFS.......... Export Facilitation Scheme [*Motor vehicles*] [*Australia*]
EFSA........ Ecole Federale Superieure d'Agriculture
EFSA........ Epistimonikos kai Filologikos Syllogos Ammokhostou [*Famagusta Professional and Literary Association*]   (GC)
EFSA........ European Federation of Sea Anglers   (EAIO)
EFSA........ Savonlinna [*Finland*] [*ICAO location identifier*]   (ICLI)
EFSD........ Exploitations Forestieres et Scieries de Divo
EFSE........ Selanpaa [*Finland*] [*ICAO location identifier*]   (ICLI)
EFSEE....... Ethniki Foititiki Spoudastiki Enosis Ellados [*National Union of Students of Greece*]   (GC)
EFSJ......... Sonkajarvi-Jyrkka [*Finland*] [*ICAO location identifier*]   (ICLI)
EFSO........ Sodankyla [*Finland*] [*ICAO location identifier*]   (ICLI)
EFSO-GD ... Exploitation Forestiere du Sud-Ouest-GD
EFSU........ Suomussalmi [*Finland*] [*ICAO location identifier*]   (ICLI)
EFSUMB .. European Federation of Societies of Ultrasound in Medicine and Biology   (EAIO)
EFT.......... Einheitliche Traegerfrequenz Fernsprecheinrichtung [*Uniform Carrier Frequency Telephone Installation*] [*EG*]
Eft .... Erfurt   (EG)
EFT.......... Evangelical Fellowship of Thailand
EFT.......... Exploitation Forestiere et Agricole de la Tanoe
EFTA........ European Fair Trade Association [*Netherlands*]   (EAIO)
EFTA........ European Flexographic Technical Association   (PDAA)
EFTA........ European Foreign Trade Association
EFTA........ European Free Trade Area   (DS)
EFTA........ European Free Trade Association [*Known as the "Outer Seven" as opposed to the "Inner Six" Common Market nations*] [*Switzerland*]
EFTAL ...... Ecole de Formation Technique et Administrative de la Logistique [*Algeria*]
EFTC........ European Fluorocarbon Technical Committee [*of the European Council of Chemical Manufacturers' Federations*] [*Belgium*]   (EAIO)
EFTC........ European Freight Timetable Conference   (EAIO)
EFTE .... Tervola [*Finland*] [*ICAO location identifier*]   (ICLI)
EFTEC ...... European Fluorocarbon Technical Committee [*of the European Council of Chemical Manufacturers' Federations*]   (EAIO)
efterl.......... Efterladt [*Posthumous*] [*Publishing Danish/Norwegian*]
efterskr...... Efterskrift [*Postscript*] [*Publishing Danish/Norwegian*]
Eftf............ Etterfoelger [*Successors*] [*Norway*]   (CED)
Eftf............ Successors [*Danish*]
Eftf............ Successors [*Swedish*]
EFTP .... Tampere-Pirkkala [*Finland*] [*ICAO location identifier*]   (ICLI)
EFTRO ..... European Federation of Tobacco Retail Organizations   (EAIO)
EFTS .... Teisko [*Finland*] [*ICAO location identifier*]   (ICLI)
EFTTA ..... European Fishing Tackle Trade Association   (EAIO)
EFTU........ Turku [*Finland*] [*ICAO location identifier*]   (ICLI)
EFTUNMW ... European Federation of Trade Unions of Non-Manual Workers [*Belgium*]   (EY)
EFU .... Europaische Frauen Union [*Austria*]   (EAIO)
EFUK........ Elblaska Fabryka Urzadzen Kuziennych [*Elblag (Elbing) Forging Equipment Factory*]   (POL)
EFUT........ Utti [*Finland*] [*ICAO location identifier*]   (ICLI)
EFV.......... Epilepsy Foundation of Victoria [*Australia*]
EFV.......... Equestrian Federation of Victoria [*Australia*]
EFVA........ European Federation of Vending Associations   (EA)
EFVA........ Vaasa [*Finland*] [*ICAO location identifier*]   (ICLI)
EFVI........ Viitasaari [*Finland*] [*ICAO location identifier*]   (ICLI)
EFVL........ Vaala [*Finland*] [*ICAO location identifier*]   (ICLI)
EFVR........ Varkaus [*Finland*] [*ICAO location identifier*]   (ICLI)
EFVU........ Vuotso [*Finland*] [*ICAO location identifier*]   (ICLI)
EFW.......... Egyptian Federation of Workers
EFWB........ Wredeby [*Finland*] [*ICAO location identifier*]   (ICLI)
EFYC........ European Federation of Young Choirs [*See also EFJC*]   (EA)
EFYL........ Ylivieska-Raudaskyla [*Finland*] [*ICAO location identifier*]   (ICLI)
EG.............. Eersgenoemde [*The Former*] [*Afrikaans*]
eg.............. Eerstgenoemde [*The Former*] [*Netherlands*]   (GPO)
EG.............. Egypt [*ANSI two-letter standard code*]   (CNC)
EG.............. Eingabegeraet [*German*]   (ADPT)
EG.............. Eingetragene Genossenschaft [*Registered Cooperative*]   (EG)
Eg.............. Eisessig [*Glacial Acetic Acid*] [*German*]
EG.............. Ektelestikon Grafeion [*Executive Office*]   (GC)
EG.............. Electrogram   (RU)
EG.............. Enso-Gutzeit Oy [*Finland*]
EG.............. Eparkhiakon Grafeion [*District Office*] [*Cyprus*]   (GC)
EG.............. Eparkhiakos Grammatevs [*District Secretary*] [*Cyprus*]   (GC)
EG.............. Epitelikon Grafeion [*Staff Office*]   (GC)

EG.............. Escola de Geologia [*Brazil*]   (DSCA)
EG.............. Esquerra Gallega [*Galician Left*] [*Political party*]   (PPW)
EG.............. Europaeische Gemeinschaften [*European Community*] [*German*] [*Information retrieval*]
EG.............. European Greens [*Brussels, Belgium Political party*]   (EAIO)
EG.............. Europese Gemeenschappen [*Luxembourg*]
EG.............. Evacuation Hospital   (RU)
eg.............. Exempli Gratia [*For example*] [*Latin*]   (EECI)
eg.............. For Example   (TPFD)
EG.............. Natural Science and Geography   (BU)
EGA.......... Ecuato Guineana de Aviacion [*Equatorial Guinea*] [*ICAO designator*]   (FAAC)
EGA.......... Electricite et Gaz d'Algerie
EGA.......... Entreprise Generale Atlantique
EGA.......... Equato-Guinean de Aviacion [*Airline*] [*Equatorial Guinea*]
EGA.......... Europese Gemeenschap voor Atoomenergie [*Benelux*]   (BAS)
EGAA........ Belfast/Aldergrove [*British*] [*ICAO location identifier*]   (ICLI)
EGAAE...... European Group of Artists of the Ardennes and the Eifel   (EAIO)
EGAB........ Enniskillen/St. Angelo [*British*] [*ICAO location identifier*]   (ICLI)
EGAC........ Belfast Harbour [*British*] [*ICAO location identifier*]   (ICLI)
EGACT...... Embroiderers' Guild of the Australian Capital Territory
EGAD........ Newtownards [*British*] [*ICAO location identifier*]   (ICLI)
EGAE........ Etaireia Genikon Apothikon Ellados [*General Warehouses Company of Greece*]   (GC)
EGAE........ Londonderry/Eglinton [*British*] [*ICAO location identifier*]   (ICLI)
EGAK........ Greek Women's Antinuclear Movement   (EAIO)
EGAL........ Langford Lodge [*British*] [*ICAO location identifier*]   (ICLI)
EGAM...... Ente di Gestione per le Aziende Minerarie e Metallurgiche [*Agency for the Management of Mineral and Metallurgical Concerns*] [*Italian*]   (WER)
EGAP........ Entreprise Generale Africaine de Peinture
EGART...... Energiagazdalkodasi Reszvenytarsasag Vallalat [*Power Engineering Enterprise Ltd.*]   (HU)
EGAS........ European Group for Atomic Spectroscopy   (EAIO)
EGAT........ Electricity Generating Authority of Thailand [*State enterprise*]   (IMH)
EGATP........ Entreprise Generale Africaine de Travaux Publics
EGB .... Elektrogeraetebau [*Electrical Equipment Plant*]   (EG)
EGB .... Entreprise Generale de Batiments
EGB .... Europaeischer Gewerkschaftsbund [*European Trade Union Confederation*]   (EG)
EGB .... Europai Gazdasagi Bizottsag [*European Economic Commission*]   (HU)
EGBB........ Birmingham [*British*] [*ICAO location identifier*]   (ICLI)
EGBE........ Coventry [*British*] [*ICAO location identifier*]   (ICLI)
EGBG........ Leicester [*British*] [*ICAO location identifier*]   (ICLI)
EGBJ .... Gloucester and Cheltenham/Staverton [*British*] [*ICAO location identifier*]   (ICLI)
EGBK .... Northampton/Sywell [*British*] [*ICAO location identifier*]   (ICLI)
EGBM .... Tatenhill [*British*] [*ICAO location identifier*]   (ICLI)
EGBN .... Nottingham [*British*] [*ICAO location identifier*]   (ICLI)
EGBO .... Halfpenny Green [*British*] [*ICAO location identifier*]   (ICLI)
EGBP........ Pailton [*British*] [*ICAO location identifier*]   (ICLI)
EGBS........ Shobdon [*British*] [*ICAO location identifier*]   (ICLI)
EGBTP....... Entreprise Generale de Batiments et de Travaux Publics
EGBW ...... Wellesbourne Mountford [*British*] [*ICAO location identifier*]   (ICLI)
EGC........... Bergerac [*France*] [*Airport symbol*] [*Obsolete*]   (OAG)
EGC........... Ecole de Gardes-Cotes
EGC........... Entreprise Generale de Chaudonnerie
EGC........... Entreprise Generale de Construction
EGC........... Ethiopian Grain Corporation
EGCA .... Coal Aston [*British*] [*ICAO location identifier*]   (ICLI)
EGCAP...... Entreprise Generale du Cap Vert de Travaux Publics et Particuliers
EGCB........ Manchester/Barton [*British*] [*ICAO location identifier*]   (ICLI)
EGCC .... Manchester International [*British*] [*ICAO location identifier*]   (ICLI)
EGCD .... Woodford [*British*] [*ICAO location identifier*]   (ICLI)
EGCE .... Wrexham/Borras [*British*] [*ICAO location identifier*]   (ICLI)
EGCF........ Sandtoft [*British*] [*ICAO location identifier*]   (ICLI)
EGCG .... Strubby [*British*] [*ICAO location identifier*]   (ICLI)
EGCH .... Holyhead [*British*] [*ICAO location identifier*]   (ICLI)
EGCI .... Doncaster [*British*] [*ICAO location identifier*]   (ICLI)
EGCJ .... Sherburn-In-Elmet [*British*] [*ICAO location identifier*]   (ICLI)
EGCL........ Fenland [*British*] [*ICAO location identifier*]   (ICLI)
EGCM .... Entreprise Gabonaise de Constructions Metalliques
EGCM ...... European Group for Cooperation in Management   (PDAA)
EGCM ...... European Group of Cellulose Manufacturers [*Defunct*]   (EA)
EGCMC.... European Glass Container Manufacturers' Committee [*British*]   (EAIO)
EGCN .... Northern Area Maintenance Unit [*British*] [*ICAO location identifier*]   (ICLI)
EGCPM..... European Group of Corrugated Paper Makers   (EAIO)

EGCS......... Sturgate [*British*] [*ICAO location identifier*]　(ICLI)
EGCT......... Entreprise Generale de Construction et de Topographie
EGD........... Erkende Geneeskundige Dienst [*Benelux*]　(BAS)
EGD........... Ethylhexanediol　(RU)
EGDA........ Brawdy [*British*] [*ICAO location identifier*]　(ICLI)
EGDA........ Electrohydrodynamic Analogy [*Research method in hydraulics*]　(RU)
EGDB........ Plymouth (Mount Wise) [*British*] [*ICAO location identifier*]　(ICLI)
EGDC........ Chivenor [*British*] [*ICAO location identifier*]　(ICLI)
EGDD........ Royal Air Force Supervisory Centre Communications [*British*] [*ICAO location identifier*]　(ICLI)
EGDG........ St. Mawgan [*British*] [*ICAO location identifier*]　(ICLI)
EGDH........ Royal Air Force 1 Group [*British*] [*ICAO location identifier*]　(ICLI)
EGDJ......... Upavon [*British*] [*ICAO location identifier*]　(ICLI)
EGDK........ Kemble [*British*] [*ICAO location identifier*]　(ICLI)
EGDL........ Lyneham [*British*] [*ICAO location identifier*]　(ICLI)
EGDM....... Boscombe Down [*British*] [*ICAO location identifier*]　(ICLI)
EGDN........ Netheravon [*British*] [*ICAO location identifier*]　(ICLI)
EGDP .... Portland [*British*] [*ICAO location identifier*]　(ICLI)
EGDR .... Culdrose [*British*] [*ICAO location identifier*]　(ICLI)
EGDS........ Bulford/Salisbury Plain [*British*] [*ICAO location identifier*]　(ICLI)
EGDT .... Wroughton [*British*] [*ICAO location identifier*]　(ICLI)
EGDV .... Hullavington [*British*] [*ICAO location identifier*]　(ICLI)
EGDX .... St. Athan [*British*] [*ICAO location identifier*]　(ICLI)
EGDY .... Yeovilton [*British*] [*ICAO location identifier*]　(ICLI)
EGE .... Enosis Gynaikon Ellados [*Union of Greek Women*]　(GC)
EGE .... Entreprise Generale d'Electricite
EGE .... Equatorial Guinea Ekuele
EGEA .... Eidikon Grafeion Exypiretiseos Aeroskafon [*Special Aircraft Services Office*]　(GC)
EGEA .... Etablissement General des Entreprises Anani
EGEB........ Entreprise Generale Entretien Batiment
EGEC........ Egyptian General Electricity Corporation　(ME)
EGEC........ Etablissements Guerin & Compagnie
EGED .... Entreprise Nationale Guineenne d'Exploitation du Diamant
EGEMAC ... Egyptian-German Electrical Manufacturing Company
EGEMAK ... Ege Makina ve Ticaret AS [*Aegean Machinery and Trade Corporation*]　(TU)
EGEPPVE ... Eidikon Grafeion Epanepikismou Paramethorion Periokhon Voreiou Ellados [*Special Office for the Resettlement of Frontier Areas of Northern Greece*]　(GC)
E GER........ East Germany
EGERT...... Entreprise Generale d'Electricite et Radio du Tchad
Egeszs K..... Egeszsegugyi Kiado [*Public Health Publishing House*]　(HU)
EGET.......... Equipement General Electro-Technique [*French*]
EGETRAV ... Entreprise Generale de Travaux
EGEV .... Entreprise Generale des Espaces Verts [*Algeria*]
EGF .... Electricite-Gaz de France [*French Electric and Gas Company*]　(WER)
EGF .... Emprestimos do Governo Federal [*Federal Government Loans*] [*Brazil*]　(LA)
EGF .... Europaeische Go Foderation [*European Go Federation - EGF*] [*Austria*]　(EAIO)
EGF .... European Grassland Federation　(EA)
EGFC........ Cardiff/Tremorfa [*British*] [*ICAO location identifier*]　(ICLI)
EGFE........ Haverfordwest [*British*] [*ICAO location identifier*]　(ICLI)
EGFF........ Cardiff [*British*] [*ICAO location identifier*]　(ICLI)
EGFGB...... Einfuehrungsgesetz zum Familiengesetzbuch [*Introductory Law to the Family Code*]　(EG)
EGFH .... Swansea [*British*] [*ICAO location identifier*]　(ICLI)
EGFI.......... Weston-Super-Mare [*British*] [*ICAO location identifier*]　(ICLI)
EGG.......... Electrogastrogram　(RU)
EGGA .... European General Galvanizers Association　(EA)
EGGA .... London [*British*] [*ICAO location identifier*]　(ICLI)
EGGB .... London [*British*] [*ICAO location identifier*]　(ICLI)
EGGC .... London [*British*] [*ICAO location identifier*]　(ICLI)
EGGD....... Bristol/Lulsgate [*British*] [*ICAO location identifier*]　(ICLI)
EGGE .... Bletchley [*British*] [*ICAO location identifier*]　(ICLI)
EGGF........ Uxbridge [*British*] [*ICAO location identifier*]　(ICLI)
EGGO .... London [*British*] [*ICAO location identifier*]　(ICLI)
EGGP .... Liverpool [*British*] [*ICAO location identifier*]　(ICLI)
EGGQ .... Liverpool [*British*] [*ICAO location identifier*]　(ICLI)
EGGR .... Redhill [*British*] [*ICAO location identifier*]　(ICLI)
EGGW .... Luton [*British*] [*ICAO location identifier*]　(ICLI)
EGGX .... Shanwick [*British*] [*ICAO location identifier*]　(ICLI)
EGH........... Europaische Gesellschaft fuer Herbologie [*European Weed Research Society*]　(EAIO)
EGHA .... Compton Abbas [*British*] [*ICAO location identifier*]　(ICLI)
EGHA .... Ege Haber Ajansi [*Aegean News Agency*] [*Izmir*]　(TU)
EGHC........ Land's End/St. Just [*British*] [*ICAO location identifier*]　(ICLI)
EGHD........ Plymouth/Roborough [*British*] [*ICAO location identifier*]　(ICLI)
EGHE........ Scilly Isles/St. Mary's [*British*] [*ICAO location identifier*]　(ICLI)

EGHG......... Yeovil [*British*] [*ICAO location identifier*]　(ICLI)
EGHH........ Bournemouth/Hurn [*British*] [*ICAO location identifier*]　(ICLI)
EGHI........ Southampton [*British*] [*ICAO location identifier*]　(ICLI)
EGHJ .... Bembridge [*British*] [*ICAO location identifier*]　(ICLI)
EGHK........ Penzance/Eastern Green [*British*] [*ICAO location identifier*]　(ICLI)
EGHL .... Lasham [*British*] [*ICAO location identifier*]　(ICLI)
EGHM .... Hamble [*British*] [*ICAO location identifier*]　(ICLI)
EGHN .... Sandown (Isle Of Wight) [*British*] [*ICAO location identifier*]　(ICLI)
EGHO .... Thruxton [*British*] [*ICAO location identifier*]　(ICLI)
EGHR........ Chichester/Goodwood [*British*] [*ICAO location identifier*]　(ICLI)
EGHS .... East Gippsland Historical Society [*Australia*]
EGHS .... Henstridge [*British*] [*ICAO location identifier*]　(ICLI)
EGI .... Energia Gazdalkodasi Intezet [*Institute of Energy Economy*]　(HU)
EGI .... Entreprise Generale d'Installations Electriques J. Sanchez et A. Martinez
egip............ Egyptian　(BU)
EGISCA .... Empresa General de Industria y Comercio [*Equatorial Guinea*]　(EY)
Egit............ Egitim [*Education*]　(TU)
EGITB .... Escuela de Geologia del Instituto Tecnologico Boliviano [*Bolivia*]　(DSCA)
EGITIM-IS ... Turkiye Egitim Iscileri Sendikasi [*Turkish Educational Workers Union*] [*Istanbul*]　(TU)
EGJA .... Alderney, Channel Islands [*British*] [*ICAO location identifier*]　(ICLI)
EGJB .... Guernsey, Channel Islands [*British*] [*ICAO location identifier*]　(ICLI)
EGJ/IFJ .... European Group of Journalists/International Federation of Journalists [*EC*]　(ECED)
EGJJ.......... Jersey, Channel Islands [*British*] [*ICAO location identifier*]　(ICLI)
EGK .... Electric Gas Valve　(RU)
EGK .... Electrohydraulic Valve　(RU)
EGK .... Europai Gazdasagi Kozosseg [*European Economic Community, Common Market*]　(HU)
EGKA .... Shoreham [*British*] [*ICAO location identifier*]　(ICLI)
EGKB .... Biggin Hill [*British*] [*ICAO location identifier*]　(ICLI)
EGKC .... Bognor Regis [*British*] [*ICAO location identifier*]　(ICLI)
EGKE .... Challock [*British*] [*ICAO location identifier*]　(ICLI)
EGKH .... Lashenden/Headcorn [*British*] [*ICAO location identifier*]　(ICLI)
EGKK .... London/Gatwick [*British*] [*ICAO location identifier*]　(ICLI)
EGKM .... West Malling [*British*] [*ICAO location identifier*]　(ICLI)
EGKR .... Redhill [*British*] [*ICAO location identifier*]　(ICLI)
EGKS .... Europaeische Gemeinschaft fuer Kohle und Stahl [*European Coal and Steel Community*] [*German*]　(DCTA)
EGL .... Electrification de la Region des Grands Lacs [*Electrification of the Great Lakes Region*]　(AF)
EGL .... European Group of Lymphology [*Belgium*]　(EAIO)
EGLA......... Bodmin [*British*] [*ICAO location identifier*]　(ICLI)
EGLB .... Brooklands [*British*] [*ICAO location identifier*]　(ICLI)
EGLD .... Denham [*British*] [*ICAO location identifier*]　(ICLI)
EGLG .... Panshanger [*British*] [*ICAO location identifier*]　(ICLI)
EGLI.......... Esperantista Go-Ligo Internacia [*International Esperantist League for Go - IELG*]　(EAIO)
EGLISI...... Service de Presse de l'Eglise du Silence [*Belgium*]
EGLJ .... Chalgrove [*British*] [*ICAO location identifier*]　(ICLI)
EGLK........ Blackbushe [*British*] [*ICAO location identifier*]　(ICLI)
EGLL......... London City [*British*] [*ICAO location identifier*]　(ICLI)
EGLM .... White Waltham [*British*] [*ICAO location identifier*]　(ICLI)
EGLN .... London/Heathrow [*British*] [*ICAO location identifier*]　(ICLI)
EGLS .... Old Sarum [*British*] [*ICAO location identifier*]　(ICLI)
EGLW .... London [*British*] [*ICAO location identifier*]　(ICLI)
EGM.......... Egypt General Mission
EGM.......... Emniyet Genel Mudurlugu [*Directorate General of Security*] [*Under Interior Ministry*]　(TU)
EGM.......... Entreprise Generale de Menuiserie
EGM.......... Etibank Genel Mudurlugu [*Eti Bank Directorate General*] [*Under Ministry of Energy and Natural Resources*]　(TU)
EGM.......... European Glass Container Manufacturers' Committee [*British*]
EGM.......... Sege [*Solomon Islands*] [*Airport symbol*]　(OAG)
eGmbH ...... Eingetragene Genossenschaft mit Beschraenkter Haftpflicht [*Registered Cooperative with Limited Liability*] [*German*]　(EG)
eGmbH ...... Eingetragene Gesellschaft mit Beschraenkter Haftung [*Registered Company with Limited Liability*] [*German*]　(ILCA)
EGMC .... Southend [*British*] [*ICAO location identifier*]　(ICLI)
EGMD....... Lydd [*British*] [*ICAO location identifier*]　(ICLI)
EGMH....... Manston [*British*] [*ICAO location identifier*]　(ICLI)
Egmp.......... Eilgueterzug mit Personenbefoerderung [*Express Freight Train with Passenger Facilities*] [*German*]　(EG)
EGN........... Ecole de la Garde Nationale [*National Guard School*] [*Tunisia*]　(AF)

EGN............ El Geneina [*Sudan*] [*Airport symbol*]   (OAG)

EGN............ Escola de Guerra Naval [*Naval War College*] [*Brazil*]   (LA)

EGNA........ Hucknall [*British*] [*ICAO location identifier*]   (ICLI)

EGNB........ Brough [*British*] [*ICAO location identifier*]   (ICLI)

EGNC........ Carlisle [*British*] [*ICAO location identifier*]   (ICLI)

EGND........ Huddersfield/Crosland Moor [*British*] [*ICAO location identifier*]   (ICLI)

EGNE........ Repton/Gamston [*British*] [*ICAO location identifier*]   (ICLI)

EGNF .... Nether Thorpe [*British*] [*ICAO location identifier*]   (ICLI)

EGNG........ Preston and Blackburn/Samlesbury [*British*] [*ICAO location identifier*]   (ICLI)

EGNH .... Blackpool [*British*] [*ICAO location identifier*]   (ICLI)

EGNI .... Skegness/Ingoldmells [*British*] [*ICAO location identifier*]   (ICLI)

EGNJ........ Humberside [*British*] [*ICAO location identifier*]   (ICLI)

EGNK........ Egipetskaia Neftianaia Korporatsiia

EGNL .... Barrow/Walney Island [*British*] [*ICAO location identifier*]   (ICLI)

EGNM....... Leeds and Bradford [*British*] [*ICAO location identifier*]   (ICLI)

EGNO....... Warton [*British*] [*ICAO location identifier*]   (ICLI)

EGNR....... Hawarden [*British*] [*ICAO location identifier*]   (ICLI)

EGNS .... Isle Of Man/Ronaldsway [*British*] [*ICAO location identifier*]   (ICLI)

EGNSW .... Embroiderers' Guild of New South Wales [*Australia*]

EGNT....... Newcastle [*British*] [*ICAO location identifier*]   (ICLI)

EGNV....... Tees-Side [*British*] [*ICAO location identifier*]   (ICLI)

EGNW....... Wickenby [*British*] [*ICAO location identifier*]   (ICLI)

EGNX....... East Midlands [*British*] [*ICAO location identifier*]   (ICLI)

EGNY....... Ellinika Grafeia Navtikon Ypiresion [*Greek Maritime Services Offices*]   (GC)

EGO............ Eichgebuehren-Ordnung [*Regulations on Calibration Fees*]   (EG)

EGO............ Elektrik, Havagaz, ve Otobus Isletme Muessesi [*Electric Power, Gas, and Bus Administration*]   (TU)

EGO............ Experimental Gamma-Irradiator   (RU)

EGOB .... Burtonwood [*British*] [*ICAO location identifier*]   (ICLI)

EGO-BURO-IS ... Ankara Elektrik, Havagazi, ve Otobus Isletme Muessesi Buro Iscileri Sendikasi [*Ankara Electric, Gas, and Bus Administration Office Workers Union*]   (TU)

EGOC....... Bishops Court [*British*] [*ICAO location identifier*]   (ICLI)

EGOD....... Llanbedr [*British*] [*ICAO location identifier*]   (ICLI)

EGOE....... Ternhill [*British*] [*ICAO location identifier*]   (ICLI)

Eg Og H..... Egitim ve Ogretim Hizmetleri [*Teaching and Training Duties*]   (TU)

Egonav ...... Egyptian Navigation Co.   (IMH)

EGOQ....... Mona [*British*] [*ICAO location identifier*]   (ICLI)

EGOS .... European Group for Organizational Studies [*British*]   (SLS)

EGOS .... European Group for Organizational Studies [*Denmark*]   (SLS)

EGOS .... Shawbury [*British*] [*ICAO location identifier*]   (ICLI)

EGOTH..... Egyptian General Organisation for Tourism and Hotels

EGOTI....... Egyptian General Organization for Trade and Industry   (PDAA)

EGOV....... Valley [*British*] [*ICAO location identifier*]   (ICLI)

EGOW....... Woodvale [*British*] [*ICAO location identifier*]   (ICLI)

EGOY....... West Freugh [*British*] [*ICAO location identifier*]   (ICLI)

EGP .... Ejercito Guerrillero de los Pobres [*Poor People's Guerrilla Army*] [*Guatemala*]   (LA)

EGP .... Electrohydraulic Converter   (RU)

EGP .... Electrohydraulic Drive   (RU)

EGP .... Energoprojekt [*Power Development Project*]   (CZ)

EGP .... Entreprise Generale de Peinture

EGP .... Entreprise Guineenne de Prefabrication

EGP .... Experimental Geodetic Payload [*Japan*]

EGPA........ Egyptian National Petroleum Authority

EGPA........ European Group of Public Administration [*See also GEAP*] [*Brussels, Belgium*]   (EAIO)

EGPA........ Kirkwall [*British*] [*ICAO location identifier*]   (ICLI)

EGPB........ Sumburgh [*British*] [*ICAO location identifier*]   (ICLI)

EGPC........ Egyptian General Petroleum Corporation [*Cairo*]   (ME)

EGPC........ Emirates General Petroleum Corp. [*United Arab Emirates*]   (EY)

EGPC........ Wick [*British*] [*ICAO location identifier*]   (ICLI)

EGPD .... Aberdeen/Dyce [*British*] [*ICAO location identifier*]   (ICLI)

EGPE........ Inverness/Dalcross [*British*] [*ICAO location identifier*]   (ICLI)

EGPF........ Glasgow [*British*] [*ICAO location identifier*]   (ICLI)

EGPGC...... Exercito Guerrilleiro do Pobo Galego Ceibe [*Guerilla group*] [*Spain*]   (EY)

EGPH .... Edinburgh [*British*] [*ICAO location identifier*]   (ICLI)

EGPI......... Islay/Port Ellen [*British*] [*ICAO location identifier*]   (ICLI)

EGPJ......... Fife/Glenrothes [*British*] [*ICAO location identifier*]   (ICLI)

EGPK........ Prestwick [*British*] [*ICAO location identifier*]   (ICLI)

EGPL........ Benbecula [*British*] [*ICAO location identifier*]   (ICLI)

EGPM .... Scatsta [*British*] [*ICAO location identifier*]   (ICLI)

EGPN .... Dundee (Riverside Park) [*British*] [*ICAO location identifier*]   (ICLI)

EGPO .... Stornoway [*British*] [*ICAO location identifier*]   (ICLI)

EGPQ .... Edinburgh [*British*] [*ICAO location identifier*]   (ICLI)

EGPR .... Barra [*British*] [*ICAO location identifier*]   (ICLI)

EGPS .... Peterhead/Longside [*British*] [*ICAO location identifier*]   (ICLI)

EGPT........ Perth/Scone [*British*] [*ICAO location identifier*]   (ICLI)

EGPU .... Tiree [*British*] [*ICAO location identifier*]   (ICLI)

EGPW ...... Unst (Shetland Isles) [*British*] [*ICAO location identifier*]   (ICLI)

EGPX........ Scottish Air Traffic Control Centre [*British*] [*ICAO location identifier*]   (ICLI)

EGPY....... Dounreay/Thurso [*British*] [*ICAO location identifier*]   (ICLI)

EGQ........... Embroiderers' Guild of Queensland [*Australia*]

EGQB .... Ballykelly [*British*] [*ICAO location identifier*]   (ICLI)

EGQJ........ Machrihanish [*British*] [*ICAO location identifier*]   (ICLI)

EGQK .... Kinloss [*British*] [*ICAO location identifier*]   (ICLI)

EGQL .... Leuchars [*British*] [*ICAO location identifier*]   (ICLI)

EGQM ...... Boulmer [*British*] [*ICAO location identifier*]   (ICLI)

EGQN .... Buchan [*British*] [*ICAO location identifier*]   (ICLI)

EGQP .... Edinburgh [*British*] [*ICAO location identifier*]   (ICLI)

EGQQ .... Prestwick [*British*] [*ICAO location identifier*]   (ICLI)

EGQR .... Saxa Vord [*British*] [*ICAO location identifier*]   (ICLI)

EGQS .... Lossiemouth [*British*] [*ICAO location identifier*]   (ICLI)

EGQT .... Edinburgh [*British*] [*ICAO location identifier*]   (ICLI)

EGR .... Electrohydraulic Speed Regulator of Hydraulic Turbines   (RU)

EGRA .... Extractora de Grasas [*Colombia*]   (COL)

EGRA .... Glasgow [*British*] [*ICAO location identifier*]   (ICLI)

EGRB .... London [*British*] [*ICAO location identifier*]   (ICLI)

EGRC .... Manchester [*British*] [*ICAO location identifier*]   (ICLI)

EGRD .... Bristol [*British*] [*ICAO location identifier*]   (ICLI)

EGRE........ Malvern [*British*] [*ICAO location identifier*]   (ICLI)

EGREM.... Empresa de Grabaciones y Emisiones Musicales [*Musical Recording and Publishing Enterprise*] [*Cuba*]   (LA)

EGRG .... Cardiff City [*British*] [*ICAO location identifier*]   (ICLI)

EGRH .... High Wycombe [*British*] [*ICAO location identifier*]   (ICLI)

EGRI .... Southampton [*British*] [*ICAO location identifier*]   (ICLI)

EGRJ........ Upavon [*British*] [*ICAO location identifier*]   (ICLI)

EGRK .... Ocean Station Vessel Romeo [*British*] [*ICAO location identifier*]   (ICLI)

EGRL .... East Gippsland Regional Library [*Australia*]

EGRL .... Ocean Station Vessel Lima [*British*] [*ICAO location identifier*]   (ICLI)

EGRM ...... Ocean Station Vessel Mike [*British*] [*ICAO location identifier*]   (ICLI)

EGRN .... Norwich [*British*] [*ICAO location identifier*]   (ICLI)

EGRP .... Plymouth [*British*] [*ICAO location identifier*]   (ICLI)

EGRR .... Bracknell [*British*] [*ICAO location identifier*]   (ICLI)

EGRS .... Sullom Voe [*British*] [*ICAO location identifier*]   (ICLI)

EGRT........ Newcastle [*British*] [*ICAO location identifier*]   (ICLI)

EGRU .... Economic Geology Research Group [*University of the Witwatersrand*] [*South Africa*]

EGRU .... Economic Geology Research Unit [*James Cook University of North Queensland*] [*Australia*]

EGRU .... Ocean Station Vessel Charlie [*British*] [*ICAO location identifier*]   (ICLI)

EGRW ...... Nottingham [*British*] [*ICAO location identifier*]   (ICLI)

EGRY .... Leeds [*British*] [*ICAO location identifier*]   (ICLI)

EGS........... Egilsstadir [*Iceland*] [*Airport symbol*]   (OAG)

EGS........... Electrogastrograph   (RU)

EGS........... Enosis Georgikon Synetairismon [*Union of Farm Cooperatives*] [*Followed by initial letter of district name*]   (GC)

EGS........... Eparkhiaki Geniki Synelevsis [*Metropolitan General Assembly*] [*Orthodox Church of Greece*]   (GC)

EGS........... Ethnikos Gymnastikos Syllogos [*National Gymnastic Club*]   (GC)

EGS........... Europaeische Gesellschaft fuer Schriftpsychologie und Schriftexpertise [*European Society of Handwriting Psychology - ESHP*]   (EAIO)

EGS........... Europaeische Gesellschaft fuer Schriftpsychologie und Schriftexpertise eV   (SLS)

EGS........... European Geophysical Society   (EAIO)

EGSA........ Embroiderers' Guild of South Australia

EGSA........ Shipdham [*British*] [*ICAO location identifier*]   (ICLI)

EGSAThPE .. Ethniki Geniki Synomospondia Anapiron kai Thymaton Polemou Ellados [*Greek National General Confederation of Handicapped and Victims of War*]   (GC)

EGSB........ Bedford/Castle Mill [*British*] [*ICAO location identifier*]   (ICLI)

EGSC........ Cambridge [*British*] [*ICAO location identifier*]   (ICLI)

EGSC........ Eastern Group Supply Council [*Australia*]

EGSC........ Enterprise General Services Co. [*Saudi Arabia*]

EGSD........ Great Yarmouth/North Denes [*British*] [*ICAO location identifier*]   (ICLI)

Egse........... Eglise [*Church*] [*Military map abbreviation World War I*] [*French*]   (MTD)

EGSE........ Ipswich [*British*] [*ICAO location identifier*]   (ICLI)

EGSF .... Peterborough (Conington) [*British*] [*ICAO location identifier*]   (ICLI)

EGSG........ Stapleford [*British*] [*ICAO location identifier*]   (ICLI)

EGSH........ Norwich [*British*] [*ICAO location identifier*]   (ICLI)

EGSI......... Enosis Georgikon Synetairismon Irakleiou [*Union of Irakleion Agricultural Cooperatives*]   (GC)

EGSJ .... Polstead [*British*] [*ICAO location identifier*]   (ICLI)

EGSK........ Hethel [*British*] [*ICAO location identifier*] (ICLI)
EGSKP ...... Ethnikon Gnomodotikon Symvoulion Koinonikis Politikis [*National Advisory Council for Social Policy*] (GC)
EGSL........ Andrewsfield [*British*] [*ICAO location identifier*] (ICLI)
EGSL........ Groupe Europeen pour l'Etude des Lysosomes [*Belgium*] (SLS)
EGSM....... Beccles [*British*] [*ICAO location identifier*] (ICLI)
EGSM....... Electric Gas Welding Machine (RU)
EGSN .... Bourn (Cambs) [*British*] [*ICAO location identifier*] (ICLI)
EGSP........ Peterborough/Sibson [*British*] [*ICAO location identifier*] (ICLI)
EGSR....... Earls Colne [*British*] [*ICAO location identifier*] (ICLI)
EGSS .... London/Stansted [*British*] [*ICAO location identifier*] (ICLI)
EGST........ Elmsett [*British*] [*ICAO location identifier*] (ICLI)
EGSW....... Weeley [*British*] [*ICAO location identifier*] (ICLI)
EGSZI ...... Epitesgazdasagi es Szervezesi Intezet [*Institute of Construction Management and Organization*] (HU)
EGT .... Egypt
EGT .... Einheitsgebuehrentarif [*Uniform Rates*] (EG)
EGT .... Embroiderers' Guild of Tasmania [*Australia*]
EGT .... Energotrust [*Power Trust*] (CZ)
EGT .... Entreprise de Gestion Touristique [*Algeria*] (EY)
EGT .... Entreprise Generale de Transports
EGT .... Entreprise Generale de Travaux
EGT .... European Geotraverse [*A collaborative lithosphere study*]
EGTA .... Aylesbury/Thame [*British*] [*ICAO location identifier*] (ICLI)
EGTA .... Entreprise Generale de Travaux en Afrique
EGTA .... European Group of Television Advertising (EA)
EGTB........ Entreprise Generale de Travaux de Batiments
EGTB........ Entreprise Generale du Travail du Bois
EGTB........ Wycombe Air Park/Booker [*British*] [*ICAO location identifier*] (ICLI)
EGTBL ...... Energotrust Bratislava, Rozvodove Zavody Elektrickej Energie [*Bratislava Power Trust, Electric Power Distributing Plants*] (CZ)
EGTC........ Cranfield [*British*] [*ICAO location identifier*] (ICLI)
EGTD .... Dunsfold [*British*] [*ICAO location identifier*] (ICLI)
EGTE........ Exeter [*British*] [*ICAO location identifier*] (ICLI)
EGTF........ Fairoaks [*British*] [*ICAO location identifier*] (ICLI)
EGTG .... Bristol/Filton [*British*] [*ICAO location identifier*] (ICLI)
EGTH .... Entreprise de Grands Travaux Hydrauliques
EGTH .... Hatfield [*British*] [*ICAO location identifier*] (ICLI)
EGTI .... Leavesden [*British*] [*ICAO location identifier*] (ICLI)
EGTK .... Oxford/Kidlington [*British*] [*ICAO location identifier*] (ICLI)
EGTO .... Rochester [*British*] [*ICAO location identifier*] (ICLI)
EGTP .... Entreprise Generale des Travaux Publics
EGTR........ Elstree [*British*] [*ICAO location identifier*] (ICLI)
EGTR........ Societe Anonyme d'Entreprise Generale de Travaux Routiers
EGTT........ London Air Traffic Control Center [*British*] [*ICAO location identifier*] (ICLI)
EGTYF ...... European Good Templar Youth Federation [*Norway*] (EAIO)
EGU.......... Energeticky Ustav Pruzkumu [*Power Research Institute*] (CZ)
EGU.......... Engineering and General Union [*Bahamas*] (LA)
EGUA .... Upper Heyford [*British*] [*ICAO location identifier*] (ICLI)
EGUB .... Benson [*British*] [*ICAO location identifier*] (ICLI)
EGUC .... Aberporth [*British*] [*ICAO location identifier*] (ICLI)
EGUD .... Abingdon [*British*] [*ICAO location identifier*] (ICLI)
EGUF .... Farnborough [*British*] [*ICAO location identifier*] (ICLI)
EGUH .... High Wycombe [*British*] [*ICAO location identifier*] (ICLI)
EGUK .... Waterbeach [*British*] [*ICAO location identifier*] (ICLI)
EGUL .... Lakenheath [*British*] [*ICAO location identifier*] (ICLI)
EGUM....... Manston [*British*] [*ICAO location identifier*] (ICLI)
EGUN .... Mildenhall [*British*] [*ICAO location identifier*] (ICLI)
EGUO........ Oakington [*British*] [*ICAO location identifier*] (ICLI)
EGUP .... Sculthorpe [*British*] [*ICAO location identifier*] (ICLI)
EGUS .... Lee-On-Solent [*British*] [*ICAO location identifier*] (ICLI)
EGUU .... Uxbridge [*British*] [*ICAO location identifier*] (ICLI)
EGUW....... Wattisham [*British*] [*ICAO location identifier*] (ICLI)
EGUY .... Wyton [*British*] [*ICAO location identifier*] (ICLI)
EGV .... Embroiderers' Guild of Victoria [*Australia*]
EGV .... Energovod [*Electrical Engineering Enterprise*] (CZ)
EGVA .... Fairford [*British*] [*ICAO location identifier*] (ICLI)
EGVB .... Bawdsey [*British*] [*ICAO location identifier*] (ICLI)
EGVC .... Northolt [*British*] [*ICAO location identifier*] (ICLI)
EGVG .... Woodbridge [*British*] [*ICAO location identifier*] (ICLI)
EGVI........ Greenham Common [*British*] [*ICAO location identifier*] (ICLI)
EGVJ........ Bentwaters [*British*] [*ICAO location identifier*] (ICLI)
EGVN .... Brize Norton [*British*] [*ICAO location identifier*] (ICLI)
EGVO .... Odiham [*British*] [*ICAO location identifier*] (ICLI)
EGVP........ Middle Wallop [*British*] [*ICAO location identifier*] (ICLI)
EGVT .... Wethersfield [*British*] [*ICAO location identifier*] (ICLI)
EGVW ...... Bedford [*British*] [*ICAO location identifier*] (ICLI)
EGWA ...... Embroiderers' Guild of Western Australia
EGWC ...... Cosford [*British*] [*ICAO location identifier*] (ICLI)
EGWD ...... West Drayton [*British*] [*ICAO location identifier*] (ICLI)
EGWE ...... Henlow [*British*] [*ICAO location identifier*] (ICLI)
EGWI ...... London [*British*] [*ICAO location identifier*] (ICLI)
EGWL ...... North Luffenham [*British*] [*ICAO location identifier*] (ICLI)

EGWN ...... Halton [*British*] [*ICAO location identifier*] (ICLI)
EGWS....... Stanmore Park [*British*] [*ICAO location identifier*] (ICLI)
EGWU ...... Northolt [*British*] [*ICAO location identifier*] (ICLI)
EGWX ...... CINCFLEETWOC [*British*] [*ICAO location identifier*] (ICLI)
EGWZ ...... Alconbury [*British*] [*ICAO location identifier*] (ICLI)
EGXB........ Binbrook [*British*] [*ICAO location identifier*] (ICLI)
EGXC .... Coningsby [*British*] [*ICAO location identifier*] (ICLI)
EGXE........ Leeming [*British*] [*ICAO location identifier*] (ICLI)
EGXG .... Church Fenton [*British*] [*ICAO location identifier*] (ICLI)
EGXH .... Honington [*British*] [*ICAO location identifier*] (ICLI)
EGXI........ Finningley [*British*] [*ICAO location identifier*] (ICLI)
EGXJ .... Cottesmore [*British*] [*ICAO location identifier*] (ICLI)
EGXN .... Newton [*British*] [*ICAO location identifier*] (ICLI)
EGXP........ Scampton [*British*] [*ICAO location identifier*] (ICLI)
EGXS........ Swinderby [*British*] [*ICAO location identifier*] (ICLI)
EGXT........ Wittering [*British*] [*ICAO location identifier*] (ICLI)
EGXU .... Linton-On-Ouse [*British*] [*ICAO location identifier*] (ICLI)
EGXV .... Leconfield [*British*] [*ICAO location identifier*] (ICLI)
EGXW ...... Waddington [*British*] [*ICAO location identifier*] (ICLI)
EGXZ .... Topcliffe [*British*] [*ICAO location identifier*] (ICLI)
egy............. Egyetem [*University*] (HU)
EGY .... Egypt [*ANSI three-letter standard code*] (CNC)
EGYB........ Brampton [*British*] [*ICAO location identifier*] (ICLI)
EGY BE .... Egeszsegugyi Berendezeseket Karbantarto es Javito KSZ [*Cooperative for Maintenance and Repair of Sanitation Equipment*] (HU)
EGYC .... Coltishall [*British*] [*ICAO location identifier*] (ICLI)
EGYD .... Cranwell [*British*] [*ICAO location identifier*] (ICLI)
EGYE........ Barkston Heath [*British*] [*ICAO location identifier*] (ICLI)
egyes .... Egyesulet [*Association, Club*] (HU)
egyes .... Egyesult [*United*] (HU)
egyet.......... Egyetem [*University*] (HU)
egyet.......... Egyetemes [*Universal*] (HU)
egyet mtanar ... Egyetemi Magantanar [*Honorary Lecturer at the University*] (HU)
egyezm ...... Egyezmenyes [*Customary, By Agreement*] (HU)
egyh........... Egyhaz [*Church, Religious Community*] (HU)
EGYH........ Holbeach [*British*] [*ICAO location identifier*] (ICLI)
egy hallg.... Egyetemi Hallgato [*University Student*] (HU)
EGYK .... Elvington [*British*] [*ICAO location identifier*] (ICLI)
EGYM ...... Marham [*British*] [*ICAO location identifier*] (ICLI)
egy ny rktanar ... Egyetemi Nyilvanos Rendkivuli Tanar [*Associate Professor*] (HU)
EGYP........ Mount Pleasant [*British*] [*ICAO location identifier*] (ICLI)
egy ny rtanar ... Egyetemi Nyilvanos Rendes Tanar [*Full Professor*] (HU)
EGYR .... Watton [*British*] [*ICAO location identifier*] (ICLI)
egys .... Egyseg [*Unity*] (HU)
EGYT........ Egyesult Gyogyszer- es Tapszergyar [*United Pharmaceutical and Nutriment Factory*] (HU)
EGYTRANS ... Egyptian Transport & Commercial Services Co. Ltd.
egz .... Egzemplarz [*or Egzemplarze*] [*Copy or Copies*] (POL)
EGZ .... Europaische Gesellschaft fuer Zusammenarbeit [*Belgium*] (DSCA)
EH.............. Economie et Humanism [*Economy and Humanism*] [*An association*] (EAIO)
eh............... E Helyett [*Instead Of, In Place Of*] (HU)
eh............... Ehrenhalber [*Honorary (of a degree)*] [*German*] (WEN)
EH.............. Eigud Hataiasim [*Israel*] (EAIO)
EH.............. Western Sahara [*ANSI two-letter standard code*] (CNC)
EHA........... Egyptian Hotel Association (EAIO)
EHA........... European Helicopter Association (PDAA)
EHAA .... Amsterdam [*Netherlands*] [*ICAO location identifier*] (ICLI)
EHAL........ Ameland [*Netherlands*] [*ICAO location identifier*] (ICLI)
EHAM....... Amsterdam/Schiphol [*Netherlands*] [*ICAO location identifier*] (ICLI)
EHAS .... Euzko Harriak Alderdi Sozialista [*Socialist Party of the Basque People*] [*Spanish*] (WER)
EHB........... Elektronik Hesap Bilimleri Enstitusu [*Electronic Accounting Science Institute*] [*of Istanbul Technical University ITUEHB*] [*See also*] (TU)
EHBD........ Weert/Budel [*Netherlands*] [*ICAO location identifier*] (ICLI)
EHBK .... Maastricht/Zuid-Limburg [*Netherlands*] [*ICAO location identifier*] (ICLI)
EHBO........ Eerste Hulp Bij Ongevallen [*Benelux*] (BAS)
EHC........... Egyptian Hotels Co.
EHC........... European Hotel Corp. (PDAA)
EHCD........ Department of Environment, Housing and Community Development [*Australia*]
EHDB........ De Bilt [*Netherlands*] [*ICAO location identifier*] (ICLI)
EHDL........ Deelen [*Netherlands*] [*ICAO location identifier*] (ICLI)
EHDP........ Venraij/De Peel [*Netherlands*] [*ICAO location identifier*] (ICLI)
EHDR........ Drachten [*Netherlands*] [*ICAO location identifier*] (ICLI)
EHE........... Every Home Evangelism [*Tanzania*]
EheG.......... Ehegesetz [*Marriage Law*] [*German*] (ILCA)
EHEH........ Eindhoven [*Netherlands*] [*ICAO location identifier*] (ICLI)
ehem........... Ehemals [*or Ehemalig*] [*Former or Formerly*] (EG)

EHEP .... Ecole des Hautes Etudes Pratiques
EHESS ...... Ecole des Hautes Etudes des Sciences Sociales [*School of Higher Studies in Social Sciences*] [*French*]
EheVerfO .. Eheverfahrensordnung [*Marriage Rules of Procedure*]   (EG)
EHGC .... European Hop Growers Convention [*France*]   (DSCA)
EHGG .... Groningen/Eelde [*Netherlands*] [*ICAO location identifier*]   (ICLI)
EHGR .... Gilze-Rijen [*Netherlands*] [*ICAO location identifier*]   (ICLI)
EHGV .... 'S Gravenhage [*Netherlands*] [*ICAO location identifier*]   (ICLI)
EHHO .... Hoogeveen [*Netherlands*] [*ICAO location identifier*]   (ICLI)
EHHV .... Hilversum [*Netherlands*] [*ICAO location identifier*]   (ICLI)
EHIA .... European Herbal Infusions Association   (EA)
EHK.......... Eisenhuettenkombinat [*Metallurgical Combine*] [*EKO*] [*See also*]   (EG)
EHK.......... Evropska Hospodarska Komise [*Economic Commission for Europe*] [*United Nations*]   (CZ)
EHKD........ De Kooy (Den Helder) [*Netherlands*] [*ICAO location identifier*]   (ICLI)
EHKP .... Einheitliche Hoehere Kommunikationsprotokolle [*German*]   (ADPT)
EHL........... El Bolson [*Argentina*] [*Airport symbol*]   (OAG)
EHLE .... Lelystad [*Netherlands*] [*ICAO location identifier*]   (ICLI)
EHLW .... Leeuwarden [*Netherlands*] [*ICAO location identifier*]   (ICLI)
Ehm.......... Ehemals [*Formerly*] [*German*]   (EG)
EHMA .... European Hotel Managers Association   (EA)
EHMC .... Nieuw Milligen [*Netherlands*] [*ICAO location identifier*]   (ICLI)
EHML .... Nieuw Milligen [*Netherlands*] [*ICAO location identifier*]   (ICLI)
EHMZ....... Middelburg/Midden Zeeland [*Netherlands*] [*ICAO location identifier*]   (ICLI)
EHN .... European Host Network [*Computer science*]
EHNP........ Emmeloord/Noord-Oostpolder [*Netherlands*] [*ICAO location identifier*]   (ICLI)
EHO .... Elektrarna Hodonin [*Electric Power Plant Hodonin*]   (CZ)
EHO .... Environmental Health Officer [*Australia*]
EHOG .... European Host Operators Group [*EURONET*] [*Luxembourg*]
EHP........... Einzelhandelspreis [*Retail Price*] [*German*]   (EG)
EHP .... European Home Products
EHPA .... Extended Hours Pharmacies Association [*Australia*]
EHPF........ European Health Policy Forum   (EAIO)
EHPM .... European Federation of Associations of Health Product Manufacturers   (EAIO)
EHPRG ..... European High Pressure Research Group   (EA)
EHR .... European Human Rights   (EAIO)
EHRD........ Rotterdam [*Netherlands*] [*ICAO location identifier*]   (ICLI)
EHRS .... European Histamine Research Society   (EAIO)
EHS .... Einzelhandelscomputer [*German*]   (ADPT)
EHS .... Einzelhandelsspanne [*Retail Markup*] [*German*]   (EG)
EHS .... Elitos SpA [*Italy*] [*ICAO designator*]   (FAAC)
EHS .... Estonian Heritage Society   (EAIO)
EHS .... Evropske Hospodarske Spolecenstvi [*European Economic Community*]   (CZ)
EHSA .... Enlatadora del Huerto SA [*Ecuador*]   (DSCA)
EHSB........ Soesterberg [*Netherlands*] [*ICAO location identifier*]   (ICLI)
EHSE......... Hoeven/Seppe [*Netherlands*] [*ICAO location identifier*]   (ICLI)
EHSF........ Economic History Society of Finland   (EAIO)
EHST........ Stadskanaal [*Netherlands*] [*ICAO location identifier*]   (ICLI)
EHStG....... Entwicklungshilfe- Steuergesetz
EHTE .... Deventer/Teuge [*Netherlands*] [*ICAO location identifier*]   (ICLI)
EHTW .... Enschede/Twenthe [*Netherlands*] [*ICAO location identifier*]   (ICLI)
EHTX .... Texel [*Netherlands*] [*ICAO location identifier*]   (ICLI)
EHV.......... Eidgenossisch Hornusserverband [*Switzerland*]   (EAIO)
EHV.......... Europaischer Holzhandelsverband [*European Timber Association*] [*EC*]   (ECED)
EHVB .... Valkenburg [*Netherlands*] [*ICAO location identifier*]   (ICLI)
EHVK .... Volkel [*Netherlands*] [*ICAO location identifier*]   (ICLI)
EHW.......... Eisenhuettenwerk [*Metallurgical Works*]   (EG)
EHW.......... Ethnic Health Worker [*Australia*]
EHWB .... Escola de Horticultura "Wenceslao Bello" [*Brazil*]   (DSCA)
EHWO ...... Woensdrecht [*Netherlands*] [*ICAO location identifier*]   (ICLI)
EHYB .... Ypenburg [*Netherlands*] [*ICAO location identifier*]   (ICLI)
EI .... Ekonomski Institut [*Economic Institute*]   (YU)
EI .... Electric Impulse Generator   (RU)
EI .... Electric Integrator   (RU)
EI .... Electric Power Installations   (BU)
EI .... Elektrogenetski Inspektorat [*Electric Power Inspectorate*]   (YU)
EI .... Elektroinstallationen [*Electrical Installations*]   (EG)
EI .... Elettro-Nucleare Italiana [*Italian Nuclear Electric Industry*]   (WER)
EI .... Emaus Internacional [*Emmaus International*]   (EA)
EI .... Entrepreneurial Institute [*Australia*]
EI .... Entrepreneurs Individuels
EI .... Epilepsy International   (EAIO)
EI .... Eurotherm International [*Manufacturer of industrial electronic control and monitoring equipment*]
EI .... Express Information   (RU)

EI .... Irina Dunn Environment Independents [*Political party*] [*Australia*]
EI .... Power Engineering Institute (of the Siberian Department of the Academy of Sciences, USSR)   (RU)
EIA .... Electronics Importers Association [*Australia*]
EIA .... Engineering Industries Association [*British*]   (EAIO)
EIA .... Environment Institute of Australia
EIA .... Escuela de Ingenieria Agronomica [*El Salvador*]   (DSCA)
EIA .... European Information Association [*EC*]   (ECED)
EIA .... Euskal Iraultzako Alderdia [*Basque Revolutionary Party*]   (PPW)
EIAA .... Ethnikon Idryma Apokatastaseos Anapiron [*National Foundation for Rehabilitation of Handicapped Persons*] [*Greek*]   (GC)
EIA-J .... Electronics Industry Association of Japan   (PDAA)
EIAP......... Escuela Interamericana de Administracion Publica   (LAA)
EIASA .... Extractive Industries Association of South Australia
EIASM ...... European Institute for Advanced Studies in Management [*Information service or system*]   (IID)
EIAV......... Early Intervention Association of Victoria [*Australia*]
EIB........... Economisch Instituut voor de Bouwnijverheid [*Building Industry Economic Institute*] [*Netherlands*]   (PDAA)
EIB........... Egyptian International Bank   (IMH)
EIB........... Elektro-Information Berlin [*Information retrieval*]
EIB........... Entreprise et Industrie du Bois
EIB........... Escuela Interamericana de Bibliotecologia [*Colombia*]   (COL)
EIB........... European Investment Bank   (AF)
EIB........... Europese Investeringsbank [*European Investment Bank*]
EIB........... Extractive Industries Board [*Victoria, Australia*]
EIBA .... European International Business Association [*Brussels, Belgium*]   (EA)
EIBCV .... Entreprise Industrielle des Bois de Construction Voltaique
EIBM........ Escuela Interamericana de Bibliotecologia [*Colombia*]   (LAA)
EIC........... Ecole des Ingenieurs de Commerce [*France*]   (FLAF)
EIC........... Energy Information Centre [*Australia*]
EIC........... Entreprise Ivoirienne de Constructions
EIC........... Etat Independant du Congo
EIC........... European Independents Confederation   (EAIO)
EIC........... European Insurance Committee [*Paris, France*]   (EA)
EICA......... East India Cotton Association
EICC......... Echuca Inspectorate Camp Committee [*Education Department*] [*Victoria, Australia*]
EICF......... European Investment Casters Federation [*Netherlands*]   (PDAA)
Eich........... Eichung [*Calibration*] [*German*]   (GCA)
EICOGE.... Entreprise Industrielle pour la Construction Generale
EICPAC..... Esquadra de Instrucao Complementar de Pilotagem de Avioes da Caca [*Complementary Instruction Squadron for Fighter Pilots*] [*Portugal*]
EID .... Electronic Deformation Meter   (RU)
EID .... Empresa de Investigacao e Desenvolvimento Electronica SARL [*Electronics Research and Development Co.*] [*Portugal*] [*Research center*]   (ERC)
EID .... European Investment Bank   (GNE)
EID .... Export Insurance Division [*of the Ministry of International Trade and Industry*] [*Japan*]
EIDAD ...... Ellinikon Institouton Diethnous kai Allodapou Dikaiou [*Greek Institute of International and Foreign Law*]   (GC)
EIDC......... Experimental International Data Centre [*Australia*]
EIDDC....... Engineering and Industrial Design Development Centre [*Ministry of Industry and Mineral Wealth*] [*Egypt*]
EIDE......... Escuela de Iniciacion Deportiva Escolar [*School for Sports Beginners*] [*Cuba*]   (LA)
EIDE......... Especialidad Industrial de Estampacion [*Colombia*]   (COL)
Eidg........... Eidgenoessisch [*Belonging to the Swiss Confederation*]
EIDP......... Ecumenical Institute for the Development of Peoples [*France*]   (EAIO)
EIDSZSZ .. Elelmezesi Ipari Dolgozok Szabad Szakszervezete [*Free Union of Food Industry Workers*]   (HU)
EIE........... Electronic & Industrial Enterprises [*Japan*]
EIE........... Elektrik Isleri Enstitusu [*Electric Affairs Institute*]   (TU)
EIE........... Elliniki Ilektriki Etaireia [*Greek Electric Company*]   (GC)
EIE........... Ethnikon Idryma Erevnon [*National Research Foundation*] [*VIE*] [*See also*] [*Greek*]   (GC)
EIEA......... Entertainment Industry Employers' Association [*Australia*]
EIEC......... European Institute of Ecology and Cancer [*Formerly, European Institute of Cancerology*]   (EA)
EIEI .... Elektrik Isleri Etud Idaresi [*Electric Affairs Study Administration*]   (TU)
Eiens .... Eiendoms [*Property*] [*Afrikaans*]
EIER......... Ecole Inter-Etats d'Ingenieurs de l'Equipement Rural [*Burkina Faso*]
EIET .... Enosis Idioktiton Eparkhiakou Typou [*Union of Provincial Press Owners*] [*Greek*]   (GC)
EIFAC .... European Inland Fisheries Advisory Commission [*Food and Agriculture Organization*] [*United Nations*]   (ASF)
EIFC......... Etablissement International de Financement et de Credit
EIFI .... Electrical Industries Federation of Ireland   (SLS)
EIFI .... European Industrial Fasteners Institute [*EC*]   (ECED)

eig.............. Eigene [*or Eigener*] [*Own*] [*German*]   (EG)
Eig............. Eigenschaft [*Property*] [*German*]   (GCA)
eig.............. Eigentlich [*Properly*] [*German*]   (EG)
Eig............. Eignung [*Suitability*] [*German*]   (GCA)
eigenh........ Eigenhaendig [*Autograph, Handwritten*] [*Publishing*] [*German*]
eigenh........ Eigenhandig [*Autograph*] [*Publishing*] [*Netherlands*]
eigenhd...... Eigenhaendig [*Autograph, Handwritten*] [*Publishing*] [*German*]
Eigensch .... Eigenschaft [*Property*] [*German*]   (GCA)
Eigg........... Eigenschaften [*Properties*] [*German*]
eighd.......... Eigenhaendig [*Autograph, Handwritten*] [*Publishing*] [*German*]
EIGS........ Ethiopian Institute of Geological Surveys   (IRC)
Eigsch .... Eigenschaft [*Property*] [*German*]
EIGT.......... Ellinikon Institouton Grafikon Tekhnon [*Greek Institute of Graphic Arts*]   (GC)
eigtl .... Eigentlich [*Properly*] [*German*]   (EG)
EIHSW...... European Institute of Hunting and Sporting Weapons   (EAIO)
EII.............. Equity in Industry [*Australia*]
EIIC............ Electronic and Information Industries Chamber [*Australia*]
EIIC........... Entertainment Industry Interim Council [*Australia*]
EIIEA .... Enosis Idioktiton Imerision Efimeridon Athinon [*Union of Athens Daily Newspaper Owners*]   (GC)
EIIEE .... Enosis Idioktiton Imerision Eparkhiakon Efimeridon [*Union of Daily Provincial Newspaper Owners*] [*Greek*]   (GC)
EIII .... Association of the European Independent Informatics Industry   (PDAA)
EIIP .... Engineering Industries Internalisation Program [*Australia*]
EIKON ...... Eikon Gesellschaft der Freunde der Ikonenkunst [*Germany*]   (EAIO)
EIKON ...... Gesellschaft der Freunde der Ikonenkunst   (EAIO)
EIL............ Egyptian International Line   (DS)
EIL............ Eiland [*Island*] [*Afrikaans*]
Eil............. Eiland [*Island*] [*Netherlands*]   (NAU)
EIL............ Engineers India Ltd.   (PDAA)
EIL............ Experiment in International Living
EILC.......... Egg Industry Licensing Committee [*Victoria, Australia*]
Eiln............ Eilanden [*Islands*] [*Netherlands*]   (NAU)
EIM .... Computer   (BU)
EIM .... Economisch Instituut voor de Middenstand [*Benelux*]   (BAS)
EIM .... Economisch Instituut voor het Midden- en Kleinbedrijf [*Benelux*]   (BAS)
EIM .... Elelmiszeripari Miniszterium/Miniszter [*Ministry/Minister of the Food Industry*]   (HU)
EIM .... Ellinikon Institouton Modas [*Greek Fashion Institute*]   (GC)
EIM .... Ente Italiano della Moda
EIM .... European Institute for the Media   (EA)
EIM .... European Interprofessional Market   (ECON)
EIM .... Experimental Data Processor   (RU)
EIMM ...... Estacion de Investigaciones Marinas de Margarita [*Venezuela*]   (MSC)
EIMMA..... East India Metal Merchants Association   (PDAA)
EIMP........ Escuela de Ingenieros de la Madera y Plasticos [*Chile*]   (DSCA)
EIN .... Eindhoven [*Netherlands*] [*Airport symbol*]   (OAG)
EIN .... European Information Network
EIN .... Power Engineering Institute   (RU)
EINAP...... Enosis Iatron Nosokomeion Athinon-Peiraios [*Union of Doctors of Athens-Piraeus Hospitals*]   (GC)
Einb........... Einband [*Binding*] [*Publishing*] [*German*]
Einbandzeichng ... Einbandzeichnung [*Binding Design*] [*Publishing*] [*German*]
einbas........ Einbasisch [*Monobasic*] [*German*]   (GCA)
Einbd......... Einband [*Binding*] [*Publishing*] [*German*]
Einblattdr .. Einblattdruck [*Broadside*] [*Publishing*] [*German*]
E Ind .... East Indies
einf............ Einfach [*Simple*] [*German*]   (GCA)
Einf .... Einfuehrung [*Introduction*] [*Publishing*] [*German*]
einfarb........ Einfarbig [*Single Color*] [*Publishing*] [*German*]
Einfl.......... Einfluss [*Influence*] [*German*]
Einfuhr....... Einfuehrung [*Introduction*] [*German*]   (GCA)
Einf W....... Einfallswinkel [*Angle of Incidence*] [*German*]   (GCA)
Eing........... Eingegangen [*Entered*] [*German*]
eingeb........ Eingebunden [*Bound In*] [*Publishing*] [*German*]
eingedr .... Eingedruckt [*Printed in Text*] [*Publishing*] [*German*]
eingef........ Eingefuehrt [*Prefaced*] [*Publishing*] [*German*]
eingel......... Eingeleitet [*With Introduction*] [*Publishing*] [*German*]
eingem........ Eingemalt [*Painted In*] [*Publishing*] [*German*]
einger .... Eingerissen [*Torn*] [*Publishing*] [*German*]
eingetr .... Eingetragen [*Registered*] [*German*]   (GCA)
Einglieder .. Eingliederung [*Arrangement*] [*German*]   (GCA)
Einh........... Einheit [*Unit*] [*German*]   (GCA)
einheitl .... Einheitlich [*Uniform*] [*German*]
EINIS .... European Integrated Network of Image and Services   (EAIO)
Einl............ Einleitung [*Preface*] [*German*]
Einl............ Einliegend [*Enclosed*] [*Correspondence*] [*German*]
Einlager ...... Einlagerung [*Embedment*] [*German*]   (GCA)
einleit .... Einleitend [*Introductory*] [*Publishing*] [*German*]
einmal .... Einmalig [*Unique*] [*German*]   (GCA)
Einricht...... Einrichtung [*Arrangement*] [*German*]   (GCA)

einschl........ Einschliesslich [*Including, Inclusive*] [*German*]   (EG)
Einspr .... Einspruch [*Objection, Opposition, Caveat*] [*German*]   (ILCA)
Einspritz .... Einspritzung [*Injection*] [*German*]   (GCA)
Einstell....... Einstellung [*Adjustment*] [*German*]   (GCA)
Eint .... Einteilung [*Graduation*] [*German*]   (GCA)
Eintr........... Eintragung [*Entry, Note*] [*Publishing*] [*German*]
Eintrag....... Eintragung [*Entry, Note*] [*Publishing*] [*German*]
Einw .... Einwirkung [*Effect*] [*German*]
Einw .... Einwohner [*Resident*] [*German*]
Einwirk...... Einwirkung [*Action*] [*German*]   (GCA)
Einz........... Einzahl [*Singular*] [*German*]
Einz........... Einzeln [*Single*] [*German*]
Einzbl........ Einzelblatt [*Single Sheet*] [*German*]
Einzelpr...... Einzelpreis [*Price for Each Part*] [*German*]
EIO .... Egyptian Investment Office
EIO .... Elliniki Istioploiki Omospondia [*Greek Sailing Federation*]   (GC)
EIO .... Ellinikos Ippikos Omilos [*Greek Riding Club*]   (GC)
EIOC .... Egyptian Independent Oil Co. SAE
EIOI.......... Expedition Internationale de l'Ocean Indien [*International Indian Ocean Expedition - IIOE*] [*French*]   (MSC)
EIP .... Association Mondiale pour l'Ecole Instrument de Paix [*World Association for the School as an Instrument of Peace*] [*Geneva, Switzerland*]   (EAIO)
EIP............ Ellinikon Institouton Paster [*Greek Pasteur Institute*]   (GC)
EIP............ Employment Initiatives Program [*Australia*]
EIPA.......... Enosis Iptamenon Politikis Aeroporias [*Union of Civil Aviation Flying Personnel*]   (GC)
EIPA.......... Ente Istruzione Professionale Artigiana [*Italian*]   (SLS)
EIPA.......... European Institute of Public Administration   (EA)
EIPC.......... European Institute of Printed Circuits   (EA)
EIPEP........ Ethnikon Idryma Prostasias Ergazomenou Paidiou [*National Foundation for the Protection of the Working Child*]   (GC)
EIPG.......... European Industrial Planning Group [*NATO*]
EIPT.......... Enosis Idioktiton Periodikou Typou [*Union of Owners of the Periodical Press*] [*Greek*]   (GC)
EIR............ Eidgenoessisches Institut fuer Reaktorforschung [*Swiss Federal Institute for Reactor Research*] [*Research center*]   (WEN)
EIR............ Escuela de Instruccion Revolucionaria [*Revolutionary Training School*] [*Cuba*]   (LA)
EIR............ Ethnikon Idryma Radiofonias [*National Radio Institute*] [*EIRT*] [*Later,*] [*Greek*]   (GC)
EIRA.......... Ente Italiano Rilievi Aerofotogrammetrici [*National Authority for Survey by Aerial Photogrammetry*]   (PDAA)
EIRD.......... Engineering Institute of Research and Development [*Chulalongkorn University*] [*Thailand*]   (WED)
EIRDC....... Electronic Industries Research and Development Center [*Egypt*]
EIRENE ...... European Information Researchers Network   (IID)
EIRMA....... European Industrial Research Management Association [*France*]
EIRS .... Ethical Investment Research Service [*London, England*] [*Information service or system*]   (IID)
EIRT.......... Ethnikon Idryma Radiofonias-Tileoraseos [*National Radio-Television Institute*] [*ERT*] [*Later,*] [*Greek*]   (GC)
EIRU .... Early Intervention Resource Unit [*Victoria, Australia*]
EIS............ Educational Institute of Scotland   (SLS)
EIS............ Electronic Information Systems [*Commercial firm*] [*Hong Kong*]
EIS............ Electrotechnical Institute of Communications   (RU)
EIS............ Ellinikoi Ilektrikoi Sidirodromoi [*Greek Electric Railways*]   (GC)
EIS............ Energy Information Systems [*UNIDO*] [*United Nations*]   (DUND)
EIS............ Etaireia Ilektrikon Sidirodromon [*ISP*] [*Greek Electric Railways*] [*Later,*]   (GC)
EIS............ Executive Information System [*Computer science*]
EIS............ Export Inspection Service [*Australia*]
EIS............ Export Intelligence Service
EI-S........... Special Electric Integrator   (RU)
EIS............ Tortola [*British Virgin Islands*] [*Airport symbol*]   (OAG)
EISA.......... European Independent Steelworks Association   (EAIO)
EISE .... Ente Incremento Studi Educativi [*Italian*]   (SLS)
Eisenhuttenk ... Eisenhuettenkunde [*Iron Metallurgy*] [*German*]   (GCA)
EIT............ Computer Technology   (BU)
EIT............ Ecole d'Interpretes et Traducteurs de la Chambre de Commerce de Paris [*School of Interpreters and Translators of the Chamber of Commerce of Paris*]
EIT............ Economisch Instituut Tilburg
EIT............ Enterprise Investments Trust [*Australia*]
EIT............ European Institute for Trans-National Studies in Group and Organizational Development   (EA)
EITC.......... Entreprise d'Installations Techniques et de Constructions
EITIA .... Eskisehir Iktisat ve Ticari Ilimler Akademisi [*Eskisehir Academy of Economics and Commercial Science*] [*IITIA*] [*See also*]   (TU)
EITR.......... Ecumenical Institute for Theological Research [*Israel*]   (EAIO)
EITs........... Computer Center   (BU)
EITS .... Express International Telex Service   (MHDB)

EIU .... Economic Intelligence Unit [*Jamaica*] (LA)
EI-VP......... Ethnikon Idryma-Vasilevs Pavlos [*King Paul National Foundation*] [*Greek*] (GC)
EIVRT .... Egyesult Izzolampa es Villamossagi Reszvenytarsasag [*United Incandescent Lamp and Electrical Company*] (HU)
EIW .... European Institute for Water (EAIO)
EIY............ Ein Yahav [*Israel*] [*Airport symbol*] [*Obsolete*] (OAG)
EIZ............ Engineering Institute of Zambia (PDAA)
ej.............. Ejemplar [*Copy*] [*Publishing*] [*Spanish*]
EJ.............. Enciklopedija Jugoslavije [*Encyclopedia of Yugoslavia*] (YU)
EJ.............. Estradni Jednatelstvi [*Theatrical Agency (of the Center of Music Performers and Entertainers)*] (CZ)
EJA........... Barrancabermeja [*Colombia*] [*Airport symbol*] (OAG)
EJCSC....... European Joint Committee of Scientific Cooperation [*Council of Europe*] (PDAA)
ejem.......... Ejemplar [*Copy*] [*Publishing*] [*Spanish*]
ejemp......... Ejemplar [*Copy*] [*Publishing*] [*Spanish*]
EJF .... Elektricke Zavody Julia Fucika [*Julius Fucik Electric Power Plants*] [*Brno*] (CZ)
EJH .... Wedjh [*Saudi Arabia*] [*Airport symbol*] (OAG)
EJK........... Elhagyott Javak Kormanybiztosa [*Commissioner for Abandoned Property*] (HU)
EJL .... Entreprise Jean Lefebvre
EJLCI....... Entreprise Jean Lefebvre Cote-D'Ivoire
EJOB........ European Joint Optical Bistability Programme [*To develop an optical computer*]
EJPC .... European Justice and Peace Commissions (EAIO)
EJPD .... Eidgenoessisches Justiz- und Polizeidepartement [*Federal Justice and Police Department*] [*Switzerland*] (WEN)
EJT .... Aero Ejecutiva SA [*Mexico*] [*ICAO designator*] (FAAC)
EJT .... Ejercito Juvenil del Trabajo [*Youth Labor Army*] [*Cuba*] (LA)
EJU........... European Judo Union (EAIO)
EK .... Commission of Experts (RU)
ek............. Economic, Economical, Economics (RU)
EK .... Economics Study Center (of the Academy of Sciences, USSR) (RU)
ek............. Eerskomende [*Next*] [*Afrikaans*]
EK .... Eerste Kamer [*Benelux*] (BAS)
EK .... Eerste Kwartier [*First Quarter*] [*Afrikaans*]
EK .... Eisernes Kreuz [*Iron Cross*] [*German*] (EG)
EK .... Electric Boiler, Electric Caldron (RU)
EK .... Electric Heater (RU)
EK .... Electrochemical Corrosion (RU)
EK .... Electrolytic Core Sampling (Method) (RU)
EK .... Electronic Commutator (RU)
EK .... Electronic Contact (RU)
EK .... Electropneumatic Valve (RU)
Ek............. Elektromotorische Kraft [*Electromotive Force*] [*German*] (GCA)
EK .... Energiekonzentration [*Energy Concentration*] (EG)
EK .... Energy Factor (RU)
EK .... Eniaion Komma [*United Party*] [*Cyprus*] (GC)
ek............. Enkelvoudige Kamer [*Benelux*] (BAS)
EK .... Enosi Kentrou [*Center Union (Party)*] [*Nicosia, Cyprus*] (GC)
EK .... Ergatikon Kendron [*Labor Center*] (GC)
e k .... Eszakkelet [*Northeast*] (HU)
eK............. Etter Kristi [*After Christ*] [*Norway*] (GPO)
E K .... Europa Kiado [*Europa Publishing House*] (HU)
EK .... Europa Kupa [*Europe Cup (Sports)*] (HU)
ek............. Ezred Kozvetlen [*Directly Subordinate to the Regiment Commander*] (HU)
e K .... Kerr Effect (RU)
EK .... Power Kombinat (RU)
EK .... Power System [*Maritime term*] (RU)
EKA .... Ekonomicheskaia Komissiia dlia Afriki
EKA .... Elektromos Keszulekek es Anyagok Gyara [*Factory of Electric Appliances and Materials*] (HU)
EKA .... Enosis Klostoyfandourgon Athinon [*Athens Textile Workers Union*] (GC)
EKA .... Enosis Kyprion Agroton [*Union of Cypriot Farmers*] (GC)
EKA .... Enosis Kyprion Anglias [*Union of Cypriots in England*] (GC)
EKA .... Entwicklung und Konstruction fuer Apparatebau [*Development and Design Office for Apparatus Building*] (EG)
EKA .... Ergatikon Kendron Athinon [*Athens Labor Center*] (GC)
EKA .... Ergatikin Kinima Allagis [*Labor Movement for a Change*] [*Greek*] (GC)
EKA .... Etaireia Kypriakon Aerogrammon [*Cyprus Airways*] (GC)
EKA .... Evropaiki Koini Agora [*European Common Market*] (GC)
EKA .... United Nations Economic Commission for Africa [*ECA*] (RU)
EKADV .... United Nations Economic Commission for Asia and the Far East [*ECAFE*] (RU)
EKAE........ Aero [*Denmark*] [*ICAO location identifier*] (ICLI)
EKAE........ Ergatiki Kinisis dia ton Afoplismon kai tin Eirinin [*Labor Movement for Disarmament and Peace*] [*Greek*] (GC)
EKAE........ Evropaiki Koinotis Atomikis Energeias [*European Atomic Energy Community*] (GC)
EKAH....... Tirstrup [*Denmark*] [*ICAO location identifier*] (ICLI)

EKAKh ...... Evropaiki Koinopraxia Anthrakos kai Khalyvos [*European Coal and Steel Community*] (GC)
EKAS........ Ellino-Kypriakos Apelevtherotikos Stratos [*Greek-Cypriot Liberation Army*] [*KRKO EKAS is preferred*] [*See also*] (GC)
EKAT........ Anholt [*Denmark*] [*ICAO location identifier*] (ICLI)
EKATE..... Epimelitirion Kalon Tekhnon [*Chamber of Fine Arts*] (GC)
EKAV .... Avno [*Denmark*] [*ICAO location identifier*] (ICLI)
EKB .... Elektrochemisches Kombinat Bitterfeld (VEB) [*Bitterfeld Electrochemical Combine (VEB)*] (EG)
EKB .... Experimental Design Office (RU)
EKBI........ Billund [*Denmark*] [*ICAO location identifier*] (ICLI)
EKCA....... Kobenhavn [*Denmark*] [*ICAO location identifier*] (ICLI)
EKCH....... Kobenhavn/Kastrup [*Denmark*] [*ICAO location identifier*] (ICLI)
EKD .... Elektryczna Kolej Dojazdowa [*Suburban Electric Railroad*] (POL)
EKD .... Evangelische Kirche in Deutschland [*Evangelical Church of Germany*] [*Hanover, West Germany*] (WEN)
EKDITh.... Ellinikon Kendron Diethnous Institoutou Theatrou [*Greek Center of the International Institute of the Theater*] (GC)
EKDK....... Kobenhavn [*Denmark*] [*ICAO location identifier*] (ICLI)
EKDYE..... Ergatiki Kinisis dia tin Diethni Yfesin kai Eirinin [*Labor Movement for an International Detente and Peace*] [*Greek*] (GC)
EKE .... Ekereku [*Guyana*] [*Airport symbol*] (OAG)
EKE .... Elliniki Ktiniatriki Etaireia [*Greek Veterinary Association*] (GC)
EKE .... Ellinikos Kodix Epangelmaton [*Greek Job Classification Code*] (GC)
EKE .... Energie- und Kraftanlagen Export, Berlin (VEB) [*Berlin Energy and Power Plant Export (VEB)*] (EG)
EKE .... Ethniki Kinisi Ellinon [*National Movement of Greeks*] (GC)
EKE .... Ethnikon Komma Ellados [*National Party of Greece*] (GC)
EKEB........ Esbjerg [*Denmark*] [*ICAO location identifier*] (ICLI)
EKEES ...... Eidiki Koinovoulevtiki Epitropi Epexergasias tou Syndagmatos [*Special Parliamentary Committee for Elaboration of the Constitution*] [*Greek*] (GC)
EKEkaiP.... Elliniko Kinima Eirinis kai Politismou [*Greek Committee for Peace and Civilization*] (GC)
EKEKh ..... Ekpaidevtikon Kendron Efedron Kheiriston [*Reserve Pilots' Training Center*] (GC)
EKEL........ Eniaia Kinisi Ekmetallevomenou Laou [*United Movement of Exploited People*] [*Greek*] (GC)
EKEOP..... Eidikon Kendron Ekpaidevseos Oreivatikou Pyrovolikou [*Special Mountain Artillery Training Center*] [*Greek*] (GC)
EKEP........ Eniaion Komma Ethnikofronou Parataxeos [*Unified Nationalist Alignment Party*] [*Cyprus*] (GC)
EKEP........ Ethnikon Kendrom Perivallondos [*National Center for Environment*] [*EKP*] [*See also*] (GC)
EKES .... Enotiki Kinisi Elevtheron Syndikaliston [*Unifying Movement of Free Trade Unionists*] [*Cyprus*] (GC)
EKF .... Enosis Kyprion Foititon (Londinou) [*Cypriot Student Union (London)*] (GC)
EKFC........ Elvis Is King Fan Club (EAIO)
EKFSE...... Enosis Kyprion Foititon (Sovietikis Enoseos) [*Cypriot Student Union (Soviet Union)*] (GC)
EKG .... Electrocardiogram (BU)
EKG .... Electrocardiogram, Electrocardiography (RU)
Ekg.......... Elektrokardiagram [*Electrocardiogram*] (EG)
EKG .... Elektrokardiogram [*Electrocardiogram*] [*Poland*]
EKG .... Elektrokardiogram [*Electrocardiogram*] [*Afrikaans*]
EKG .... Europejska Komisja Gospodarcza [*European Economic Commission*] (POL)
EKG .... Open-Pit Caterpillar Excavator (RU)
EKGF........ Gormfelt [*Denmark*] [*ICAO location identifier*] (ICLI)
EKGG....... Electrocardiogastrogram (RU)
EKGH....... Gronholt [*Denmark*] [*ICAO location identifier*] (ICLI)
Ekgiz........ State Economics Publishing House
EKGV .... Elelmiszeripari Kozponti Gepjavito Vallalat [*Central Machine Repair Shop of the Food Industry*] (HU)
EKGY .... Elektromos Keszulekek Gyara [*Electrical Apparatus Factory*] (HU)
EKh........... Ethniki Khorofylaki [*National Gendarmery*] (GC)
EKhDEVDG ... Elliniki Khristianiki Dimokratiki Enosi Vasilofronon Dytikis Germanias [*Greek Christian Democratic Union of Royalists of West Germany*] (GC)
EKhE .... Elliniki Khristianokoinoniki Enosis [*Greek Christian Socialist Union*] (GC)
EKhEE....... Enosis Kheirourgikon Etaireion Ellados [*Union of Greek Surgical Societies*] (GC)
EKhG .... Electrochemical Automatic Gas Analyzer (RU)
EKhG .... Electrochordogram (RU)
EKhG .... Ethylene Chlorohydrin (RU)
EKHG........ Herning/Skinderholm [*Denmark*] [*ICAO location identifier*] (ICLI)

EKhKE ...... Ethniko Khristianodimokratikon Komma Ellados [*National Christian Democratic Party of Greece*] (GC)

EKhO .... Electrochemical Water Desalting (RU)

EKHO .... Lindtorp [*Denmark*] [*ICAO location identifier*] (ICLI)

EKhPA ...... Enosis Kheiriston Politikis Aeroporias [*Civil Aviation Pilots Association*] [*Greek*] (GC)

EKhPL .... Etaireia Khorikon Proiondon kai Lipasmaton [*Domestic Products and Fertilizers Company*] [*Greek*] (GC)

EKhS .... Ethniko Khorotaxiko Symvoulio [*National Zoning Council*] (GC)

EKHS .... Hadsund [*Denmark*] [*ICAO location identifier*] (ICLI)

EkhV .... Electrochemical Fuze (RU)

EKHV .... Haderslev [*Denmark*] [*ICAO location identifier*] (ICLI)

EKI .... Electrokymogram (RU)

EKI .... Eregli Komur [*or Komurleri*] Isletmesi [*The Eregli Coal Works*] (TU)

EKI .... Erjedesipari Kutato Intezet [*Fermentation Research Institute*] (HU)

EKI .... Exekutiva Komunisticke Internacionaly [*Executive Committee of the Communist International*] (CZ)

EKIKhIMMASh ... Experimental Institute of Chemical Machinery (RU)

EKIS .... Europa Klub, Sezione Italiana [*Italian*] (SLS)

EKISZ .... Egyenruhazati Kisipari Szovetkezet [*Uniforms Producers' Cooperative Enterprise*] (HU)

EKJ .... Estradni a Koncertni Jednatelstvi [*Theatrical and Concert Agency (of the Center of Music Performers and Entertainers)*] (CZ)

EKK .... Enopoiitiki Kinisi Kentrou [*Unification Movement of the Center*] (GC)

EKK .... Epanastatiko Kommounistiko Komma [*Revolutionary Communist Party*] [*Greek*] (GC)

EKKA .... Ethniki kai Koinoniki Apelevtherosis [*National and Social Liberation (Organization)*] [*Greek*] (GC)

EKKA .... Karup [*Denmark*] [*ICAO location identifier*] (ICLI)

EKKE .... Epanastatiko Kommounistiko Kinima Elladas [*Revolutionary Communist Movement of Greece (Maoist)*] (GC)

EKKE .... Epanastatiko Kommunistiko Komma Ellados [*Revolutionary Communist Party of Greece*] (PPW)

EKKE .... Ethniko Kommounistiko Komma Ellados [*National Communist Party of Greece*] (GC)

EKKE .... Ethnikon Kendron Koinonikon Erevnon [*National Center for Social Research*] [*Greek*] (GC)

EKKI .... Epitoanyagipari Kozponti Kutato Intezet [*Central Research Institute of the Building Materials Industry*] (HU)

EKKL .... Kalundborg [*Denmark*] [*ICAO location identifier*] (ICLI)

EKKM .... Arhus/Kirstinesminde [*Denmark*] [*ICAO location identifier*] (ICLI)

EKKU .... Ekonomi dan Keuangan [*Economic and Financial Affairs*] (IN)

EKLA .... United Nations Economic Commission for Latin America [*ECLA*] (RU)

EKLIP .... Entreprise Khmere de Librairie, d'Imprimerie, et de Papeterie, SARL [*Cambodian Book, Printing, and Paper Company, Inc.*] (CL)

EKLS .... Laeso [*Denmark*] [*ICAO location identifier*] (ICLI)

EKLV .... Lemvig [*Denmark*] [*ICAO location identifier*] (ICLI)

EKM .... Electric Contact Pressure Gauge (RU)

EKM .... Elektromos Keszulekek es Meromuszerek Gyara [*Factory of Electric Apparatus and Measuring Instruments*] (HU)

EkM .... Energie- und Kraftmaschinen [*Energy Generators and Engines*] (EG)

EKM .... Epites- es Kosmunkaugyi Miniszter [*Minister of Construction and Public Works*] (HU)

EKM .... Square Meter Equivalent (RU)

EKM .... Warenzeichen der Volkseigenen Betriebe des Energie- und Kraftmaschinenbaus [*Trademark to Designate a Product of the State Enterprises of the Energy Generating and Engine Construction Branch*] (EG)

EKMB .... Maribo [*Denmark*] [*ICAO location identifier*] (ICLI)

EKMC .... Karup [*Denmark*] [*ICAO location identifier*] (ICLI)

EKME .... Epitoipari es Kozlekedesi Muszaki Egyetem [*Technical University of Construction and Transportation*] (HU)

EKMI .... Danish Meteorological Institute [*Denmark*] [*ICAO location identifier*] (ICLI)

EKMK .... Karup [*Denmark*] [*ICAO location identifier*] (ICLI)

EKMN ...... Koster Vig [*Denmark*] [*ICAO location identifier*] (ICLI)

ekn .... Ev es Kiado Nelkul [*Without Date or Publisher*] [*Hungary*] (GC)

EKN .... Exportkreditnamnden [*Export Credit Agency*] [*Sweden*]

EK-ND ...... Enosis Kendrou-Neai Dynameis [*Center Union - New Forces*] [*EDIK*] [*Later,*] (GC)

EKNE .... El'brus Complex High-Altitude Scientific Expedition (RU)

EKNM ...... Morso [*Denmark*] [*ICAO location identifier*] (ICLI)

EKNS .... Nakskov [*Denmark*] [*ICAO location identifier*] (ICLI)

EKO .... Economics Department (RU)

EKO .... Eisenhuettenkombinat Ost [*East Metallurgical Combine (Eisenhuettenstadt)*] (EG)

Eko .... Eko [*Record label*] [*France*]

EKO .... Ekonomik Konut Organizasyonu ve Insaat AS [*Economic Housing Organization and Construction Corp.*] (TU)

EKO .... Elliniki Kopilatiki Omospondia [*Greek Rowing Federation*] (GC)

EKO .... Evreiskoe Kolonizatsionnoe Obshchestvo [*Jewish Colonization Association*]

EKO .... Internacia Ekologia-Ekonomia Akademio [*International Ecological-Economic Academy*] [*Bulgaria*] (EAIO)

EKOD .... Odense/Beldringe [*Denmark*] [*ICAO location identifier*] (ICLI)

EKOF .... Elliniki Kolymvitiki Omospondia Filathlon [*Greek Swimming Federation (of Sportsmen)*] (GC)

EKOF .... Ethniki Koinoniki Organosis Foititon [*National Social Organization of Students*] [*Greek*] (GC)

EKOFNS ... Elliniki Kopilatiki Omospondia Filathlon Navtikon Somateion [*Greek Rowing Federation of Sportsmen of Boating Clubs*] (GC)

EKoG .... Electrocorticogram, Electrocorticography (RU)

ekol .... Ecologic, Ecological, Ecology (RU)

ekon .... Economic, Economical (RU)

ekon .... Ekonomi [*Finland*]

EKON ...... Ekonomie [*Economy*] [*Afrikaans*]

EKON ...... Elliniki Kommounistiki Neolaia "Rigas Feraios" [*Greek Communist Youth "Rigas Feraios"*] [*RIGAS*] [*Formerly,*] (GC)

Ekonomizdat ... Publishing House of Economic Literature (RU)

Ekoso .... Economic Conference [*1920-1936*] (RU)

EKOSOS ... United Nations Economic and Social Council [*ECOSOC*] (RU)

EKOTE ...... Enosis Kataskevaston Oikodomikon-Tekhnikon Ergon [*Union of Construction and Technical Projects Builders*] [*Greek*] (GC)

EKP .... Einkaufspreis [*Purchase Price*] (EG)

EKP .... Epitropi Kratikon Promitheion [*State Supplies Committee*] [*Greek*] (GC)

EKP .... Ergatikon Kendron Patron [*Patras Labor Center*] (GC)

EKP .... Ergatikon Kendron Peiraios [*Piraeus Labor Center*] (GC)

EKP .... Ethnikon Kendron Perivallondos [*National Center for Environment*] [*EKEP*] [*See also*] (GC)

EKP .... Etsiva Keskuspoliisi [*Central Detective Police*] [*Finland*] (WEN)

EKP .... Evreiskaia Kommunisticheskaia Partiia [*Political party*] (BJA)

EKPAS ...... Ekleme Parcalari Ticaret Anonim Sirketi [*Pipe Fittings Trade Corporation*] (TU)

EKPB .... Krusa-Padborg [*Denmark*] [*ICAO location identifier*] (ICLI)

EKPE .... Evropaikon Kendron Pyrinikon Erevnon [*European Nuclear Research Center*] (GC)

EKPOU ..... Uniform Enterprise, Organization, and Establishment Classifier (BU)

Ekprav .... Economics and Law Department (RU)

EKR .... Eksportkreditradet [*Export Credit Agency*] [*Denmark*]

EKR .... Elektronski Komandni Racunar [*Electronic Command Computer*] [*Military*] (YU)

eKr .... Ennen Kristuksen Syntymaa [*Finland*]

EKRD .... Randers [*Denmark*] [*ICAO location identifier*] (ICLI)

EKRF .... Einheitskontenrahmen der Forstwirtschaft [*Standard Accounts for Forestry*] (EG)

EKRG .... Electrocorticogram (RU)

EKRI .... Einheitskontenrahmen der Industrie [*Standard Accounts for Industry*] (EG)

EKRK .... Kobenhavn/Roskilde [*Denmark*] [*ICAO location identifier*] (ICLI)

EKRL .... Einheitskontenrahmen der Landwirtschaft [*Standard Accounts for Agriculture*] (EG)

EKRN .... Ronne [*Denmark*] [*ICAO location identifier*] (ICLI)

EKRR .... Ro [*Denmark*] [*ICAO location identifier*] (ICLI)

EKRS .... Ringsted [*Denmark*] [*ICAO location identifier*] (ICLI)

Eks .... Eksellensie [*Excellency*] [*Afrikaans*]

eks .... Eksempel [*Example*] [*Denmark*] (GPO)

eks .... Eksemplaar [*Copy*] [*Afrikaans*]

eks .... Eksemplar [*Copy*] [*Publishing Danish/Norwegian*]

EKS .... Ekspedisi [*Expediting, Forwarding, Shipping*] (IN)

Eks .... Ekspresi [*Express*] (TU)

EKS .... Engpasskonzentrierte Strategie [*Bottleneck-focused strategy*] [*German*] [*Business term*]

EKS .... Epanastatikos Kommounistikos Syndesmos [*Revolutionary Communist League*] [*Greek*] (GC)

EKS .... Ermittlungsbogen fuer Kostensenkungen, Beziehungsweise Kostensteigerungen [*Form for Determining Cost Decreases or Increases*] (EG)

EKSB .... Sonderborg [*Denmark*] [*ICAO location identifier*] (ICLI)

EKSD .... Spjald [*Denmark*] [*ICAO location identifier*] (ICLI)

EKSE .... Ekstratevtikon Soma Ellados [*Greek Expeditionary Force*] (GC)

eksempl ...... Eksemplar [*Copy*] [*Publishing Danish/Norwegian*]

EKSK .... Elliniki Koinotiki Synelevsis Kyprou [*Greek Communal Chamber*] [*Cyprus*] (GC)

Ekskavatorzapchast' ... Technical Office for the Production of Excavator Spare Parts (RU)

EKSN .... Sindal [*Denmark*] [*ICAO location identifier*] (ICLI)

eksp .... Expedition, Expeditionary (RU)

EKSP .... Skrydstrup [Denmark] [ICAO location identifier]   (ICLI)
ekspl........... Eksemplar [Copy] [Publishing Danish/Norwegian]
Eksportkhleb ... All-Union Association of the Ministry of Foreign Trade, USSR   (RU)
Eksportles ... All-Union Export-Import Association of the Ministry of Foreign Trade, USSR   (RU)
Eksportobuv' ... Export Footwear Factory   (RU)
ekspr .... Express   (RU)
EKSR .... Electrical Signal Flare Container   (RU)
EKSS .... Samso [Denmark] [ICAO location identifier]   (ICLI)
EKST .... Sydfyn/Tasinge [Denmark] [ICAO location identifier]   (ICLI)
ekstr .... Extract   (RU)
EKSV .... Skive [Denmark] [ICAO location identifier]   (ICLI)
EKT .... Eskilstuna [Sweden] [Airport symbol]
EKTD .... Tonder [Denmark] [ICAO location identifier]   (ICLI)
EKTE .... Ellinikos Kodix Epangelmaton [Greek Job Classification Code]   (GC)
EKTE .... Ethniki Ktimatiki Trapeza tis Ellados [National Land Bank of Greece]   (GC)
EKTEK ...... Ekonomi dan Teknik [Economic and Technical Affairs]   (IN)
EKTEL ...... Enopoiimenon Koinon Tameion Eispraxeon Leoforeion [United Joint Bus Collections Fund] [Greek]   (GC)
EKTENOL ... Ethnoktimatiki Energou Poleodomias [National Land Company for Active City Development]   (GC)
EKTS .... Thisted [Denmark] [ICAO location identifier]   (ICLI)
EKU .... Economic Administration   (RU)
EKU .... Evangelische Kirche der Union [Evangelical Church of the Union] [German]   (WEN)
EKUIN ...... Ekonomi, Keuangan, dan Industri [Economic, Financial, and Industrial Affairs]   (IN)
ek v .... Electron Kilovolt   (EECI)
ekv .... Enkelvoud [Singular] [Afrikaans]
EKVA .... Vandel [Denmark] [ICAO location identifier]   (ICLI)
EKVB........ Viborg [Denmark] [ICAO location identifier]   (ICLI)
EKVD .... Vamdrup [Denmark] [ICAO location identifier]   (ICLI)
EKVG .... Vagar, Faroe Islands [Denmark] [ICAO location identifier]   (ICLI)
EKVH .... Vesthimmerland [Denmark] [ICAO location identifier]   (ICLI)
EKVJ .... Stauning [Denmark] [ICAO location identifier]   (ICLI)
EKVL .... Vaerlose [Denmark] [ICAO location identifier]   (ICLI)
EKVS......... Elliniki Kinisis dia tin Valkanikin Synennoisin [Greek Movement for a Balkan Understanding]   (GC)
ekv vl .... Moisture Equivalent   (RU)
EKW .... Eisenhuettenkombinat West [West Metallurgical Combine]   (EG)
ekw .... Ekwiwalent [Equivalent] [Poland]
EKYe......... United Nations Economic Commission for Europe [ECE]   (RU)
EKYSY ...... Enosis Kyprion Syndaxioukhon [Cypriot Pensioners' Union]   (GC)
EKYT......... Alborg [Denmark] [ICAO location identifier]   (ICLI)
ekz............. Copy   (RU)
EKZ .... Forklift Trucks Plant   (BU)
EL .... Einheits-Lack [Unit Lacquer] [German]
el................ Elaintiede [Zoology] [Finland]
el................ Electrical Engineering   (BU)
el................ Electric, Electrical   (RU)
El............... Electric Power   (BU)
EL .... Electroluminescence   (RU)
EL .... Electron Tube   (RU)
el............... Elegant [Elegant] [French]
el............... Elektriese Lig [Electric Light] [Afrikaans]
el............... Elektrisch [Electric] [German]
El............... Elektrizitaet [Electricity] [German]   (GCA)
el............... Elektromos [Electric]   (HU)
El............... Element [German]   (GCA)
el............... Elemento [Element] [Portuguese]
EL .... Elettronucleare Italiana [Nuclear energy] [Italian]   (NRCH)
el............... Eller [Or] [Norway]   (GPO)
EL .... Sounding Device   (RU)
ELA .... Eastland Air [Australia] [ICAO designator]   (FAAC)
ELA .... Ellinikos Laikos Agonas [Greek Popular Struggle]   (GC)
ELA .... Employed Lawyers' Association [Israel]   (EAIO)
ELA .... Enomenos Laikos Agonas [United People's Struggle] [Greek]   (GC)
ELA .... Epanastatikos Laikos Agonas [Revolutionary Popular Struggle] [Greek]   (GC)
ELA .... Estado Libre Asociado [Commonwealth] [Puerto Rican]   (LA)
ELA .... Ethiopian Library Association   (SLS)
ELA .... European Laser Association   (EA)
ELA .... Exercito de Libertacao de Angola
ELA .... Exploration Licence Application [Australia]
ELAB........ Elektronikklaboratoriet [Norway]   (PDAA)
ELABOSEDAS ... Sociedad Elaborada de Articulos de Seda Ltda. [Colombia]   (COL)
ELAF .... Electrification Africaine
elag............. Elagazas [Junction]   (HU)

ELAG........ European Library Automation Group   (PDAA)
ELAIA .... European Parliament Delegations for Latin America [Luxembourg]   (EAIO)
ELAIA .... Europe-Latin America Interparliamentary Assembly [See also DPERPLA] [Luxembourg, Luxembourg]   (EAIO)
elainl .... Elainlaaketiede [Veterinary Medicine] [Finland]
EL AL .... Every Landing, Always Late [Humorous interpretation of El Al Airlines]
ELAN .... Ethnikon Laikon Apelevtherotikon Navtikon [National People's Liberation Navy] [Greek]   (GC)
ELANA...... Elaboradores de Lana SA [Yumbo-Valle]   (COL)
ELAR......... Egyseges Lakossag Adatfelveteli Rendszer [Uniform Population Survey System]   (HU)
ELAS .... Ellenikos Laikos Apeleutherotikos Stratos [Hellenic People's Army of Liberation] [Military arm of EAM] [Greek]
ELAS .... Escuela Latinoamericana de Sociologia [Facultad Latinoamericana de Ciencias Sociales] [Santiago, Chile]   (LAA)
ELAS .... Ethnikos Laikos Apelevtherotikos Stratos [National People's Liberation Army] [Greek]   (GC)
ELASA ...... Empresa Ladrillera de Soacha [Colombia]   (COL)
elast........... Elastisch [Elastic] [German]   (GCA)
ELA/STV .. Euzko Langilleen Alkartasuna/Solidaridad de Trabajadores Vascos [Basque Workers' Solidarity] [Spain]
ELAT........ Ecole de Lutte Anti-Tse-Tse
elat .... Elatiivi [Finland]
ELAW........ Environmental Lawyers Alliance Worldwide [Australia]
ELB........... El Banco [Colombia] [Airport symbol]   (OAG)
ELC........... Elcho Island [Australia] [Airport symbol]   (OAG)
ELC........... Environment Liaison Centre [Later, ELC]   (EAIO)
ELC........... Estudiantes Libertarios de Cataluna [Anarchist Students of Catalonia] [Spanish]   (WER)
ELC........... Europe's Largest Companies [ELC International] [Information service or system]   (CRD)
ELC........... Evangelical Lutheran Church
ELCA........ European Landscape Contractors Association   (EAIO)
ELCA......... Evangelical Lutheran Church of Australia
ELCI .... Environment Liaison Centre International   (EAIO)
ELCO .... Emirates Lube Oil Co.
ELCO .... European Liaison Committee for Osteopaths   (EA)
ELCSA ...... Evangelical Lutheran Church in Southern Africa   (EY)
ELCSMI.... European Liaison Committee for the Sewing Machine Industries [Defunct]   (EA)
ELCT......... Evangelical Lutheran Church of Tanzania
ELD .... Enosis Laikis Dimokratias [Popular Democratic Union] [Greek]   (GC)
ELD .... Federation of Liberal and Democratic Parties of the European Community [Brussels, Belgium Political party]   (EAIO)
ELDC .... European Lead Development Committee [EC]   (EA)
ELDEC ...... European Lead Development Committee [EC]   (ECED)
ELDO .... European Launcher Development Organization [Superseded by European Space Agency]
ELDR......... European Federation of Liberal, Democratic, and Reform Parties   (EAIO)
ELDYK...... Ellinikai Dynameis Kyprou [Greek Forces of Cyprus]   (GC)
Ele .... Ecole [School] [Military map abbreviation World War I] [French]   (MTD)
ELE........... El Real [Panama] [Airport symbol]   (OAG)
ELE........... Ethniki Laiki Enotis [National Popular Unity]   (GC)
Elec .... Electro [Record label] [Finland]
ELECAM .. Electricite Canalisations du Maroc
elect........... Electricite [French]   (TPFD)
elect........... Electricity   (TPFD)
ELECTA..... Electricidad Tecnica Colombiana Ltda. [Colombia]   (COL)
ELECTRA ... Electrical, Electronic, and Nucleonic Trade Fair
ELECTRAGUAS ... Instituto de Aprovechamiento de Aguas y Fomento Electrico [Institute for the Utilization of Waters and Electric Power Development] [Colorado]   (LA)
ELECTREX ... International Electrotechnical Exhibition [British Electrical and Allied Manufacturers Association]
ELECTRICO ... Electricity Corporation [Saudi Arabia]
ELECTRICOL ... Electromecanica Industrial Ltda. [Colombia]   (COL)
ELECTROGAZ ... Establissement Public de Production, de Transport, et de Distribution d'Electricite, d'Eau, et de Gaz [Public Electricity, Water, and Gas Production, Transport, and Distribution Company] [Rwanda]   (AF)
ELECTRO-PERU ... Empresa del Electricidad del Peru [Peruvian State Electric Power Enterprise]   (LA)
eleg............. Elegant [Swedish]
eleg............. Elegant [Danish/Norwegian]
eleg............. Elegant [French]
ELEK........ Elektrisiteit [Electricity] [Afrikaans]
ELEK........ Elliniko Leninistiko Epanastatiko Kinima [Greek Leninist Revolutionary Struggle]   (GC)
Elekt.......... Elektrizitaet [Electricity] [German]
ELEKTHERMAX ... Villamos Hokeszulekek Gyara, Papa [Thermoelectric Equipment Factory, Papa]   (HU)

elektr.......... Electrical (BU)
elektr.......... Electronics (RU)
ELEKTR.... Elektrisiteit [*Electricity*] [*Afrikaans*]
Elektr......... Elektrizitaet [*Electricity*] [*German*]
elektr.......... Elektromos [*Electric*] (HU)
elektr.......... Elektromossag [*Electricity*] (HU)
ELEKTRIK-IS ... Turkiye Elektrik Istihsali, Nakli, ve Tevzi Isci Sendikalari Federasyonu [*Turkish Electric Power Production, Transmission, and Distribution Worker Unions' Federation*] (TU)
Elektrobank ... Bank for Electrification of the USSR (RU)
ELEKTROBOSNA ... Bosnian Electrochemical Industry [*Jacje*] (YU)
Elektrochasofikatsiya ... State Repair Planning and Installation Office of the Glavchasprom (RU)
ELEKTRODISTRIBUCIJA ... Establishment for Electric Power Distribution (YU)
ELEKTROIMPEX ... ELEKTROIMPEX Hiradastechnikai es Finommechanikai Kulkereskedelmi Vallalat [*ELEKTROIMPEX Foreign Trade Enterprise for Telecommunication and Precision Products*] (HU)
Elektrokomplekt ... Trust for the Supply of Complete Sets of Electrical Equipment (RU)
ELEKTROKOVINA ... Tovarna Elektrokovinskih Izdelkov [*Electric and Metal Products Factory*] [*Maribor-Tezno*] (YU)
elektrol....... Elektrolytisch [*Electrolytic*] [*German*]
ELEKTROMATERIJAL ... Electric Equipment Establishment (YU)
ELEKTROMEDICINA ... Establishment for Trade in Electric Medical Apparatus (YU)
Elektromontazhkonstruktsiya ... Trust of the Glavelektromontazh of the Glavmontazhspetsstroy SSSR (RU)
Elektropromremont ... Industrial Establishment for the Repair of the Industrial Electrical Equipment of the Administration of the Chief Mechanical and Power Engineer (RU)
ELEKTRORAD ... Elektro Instalaterska Radnja [*Electrical Installation Shop*] (YU)
ELEKTROSRBIJA ... Serbian Electric Power Establishment [*Belgrade*] (YU)
ELEKTROSREM ... Otsek za Elektrifikaciju Srema [*Section for the Electrification of Srem*] [*Zemun*] (YU)
elektrostat ... Elektrostatisch [*Electrostatic*] [*German*] (GCA)
Elektrotochpribor ... Precision Electrical Instruments Plant (RU)
Elektrotsink ... Electrolytic Zinc Plant (RU)
Elektrotyazhmash ... Heavy Electrical Machinery Plant (RU)
ELEKTROVODA ... Komunalno Preduzece za Distribuciju Elektricne Energije i Vode [*Communal Establishment for the Distribution of Electricity and Water*] (YU)
Elektrozem ... Rural Electrification Department (RU)
elelm.......... Elelmezes [*Food Supply*] (HU)
Elem........... Element [*German*] (GCA)
Elemko....... Electric Enameling Cooperative (BU)
ELES .... Elektrogospodarska Skupnost Slovenije [*Electric Management Corporation of Slovenia*] [*Ljubljana*] (YU)
eletr........... Eletrajz [*Biography*] [*Hungary*]
Eletr .... Eletricidade [*Electricity*] [*Portuguese*]
eletr........... Eletricista [*Electrician*] [*Portuguese*]
eletr........... Eletrico [*Electrical*] [*Portuguese*]
ELETROBRAS ... Centrais Eletricas Brasileiras, SA [*Brazilian Electric Power Companies, Inc.*] [*Rio De Janeiro*] (LA)
ELETROSUL ... Centrais Eletricas do Sul [*Southern Electric Power Plants*] [*Brazil*] (LA)
elett .... Elettricita [*Electricity*] [*Italian*]
elev........... Grain Elevator [*Topography*] (RU)
ELEVME .. Elliniki Etaireia Viomikhanikon kai Metallevtikon Ependiseon [*Greek Industrial and Mining Investments Company*] (GC)
ELF........... El Fasher [*Sudan*] [*Airport symbol*] (OAG)
ELF........... Eritrean Liberation Front [*Ethiopia*] (PD)
ELF........... Esperanto-Ligo Filatelista [*Philatelic Esperanto League - PEL*] (EAIO)
ELF........... Essences et Lubrifiants de France [*Gasoline and Lubricants Company of France*] (AF)
ELF........... External Financing Limit
ELFCA ...... Ecole de Langue Francaise de la Cote D'Azur [*France*] (ECON)
ELF-ERAP ... Essences et Lubrifiants de France - Entreprise de Recherches et d'Activites Petrolieres
ELFIC....... Elder's Finance and Insurance Co. Ltd. [*Australia*]
ELF-PLF ... Eritrean Liberation Front - Popular Liberation Forces [*Ethiopia*] (PD)
ELF-RC ..... Eritrean Liberation Front - Revolutionary Command [*Ethiopia*] (PD)
ELF-SEREPCA ... Societe ELF [*Essences et Lubrifiants de France*] de Recherches et d'Exploitation des Petroles du Cameroun
ELF-SPAFE ... Societe ELF [*Essences et Lubrifiants de France*] des Petroles d'Afrique Equatoriale [*ELF-Petroleum Company of Equatorial Africa*] [*Gabon*] (AF)
ELFT .... Eotvos Lorand Fizikai Tarsulat [*Lorand Eotvos Physics Society*] (HU)
ELG .... Alpi Eagles SpA [*Italy*] [*ICAO designator*] (FAAC)

ELG .... Einkaufs- und Liefergenossenschaft [*Purchase and Delivery Cooperative (for artisans)*] (EG)
elg.............. Ellenseg [*or Ellenseges*] [*Enemy*] (HU)
ELG .... European Lymphology Group [*See also GEL*] [*Brussels, Belgium*] (EAIO)
ELGEP ...... Elelmiszeripari Gepgyar es Szerelo Vallalat [*Food Industry Machine Factory and Assembly Enterprise*] (HU)
ELGH .... Einkaufs- und Liefergenossenschaft des Handwerks [*Purchase and Delivery Cooperative for Artisans*] (EG)
ELGI.......... Eotvos Lorand Geophysical Institute of Hungary [*Research center*] (EAS)
ELGI.......... European Lubricating Grease Institute [*An association*]
el-grafich.... Electron Diffraction (RU)
ELH .... North Eleuthera [*Bahamas*] [*Airport symbol*] (OAG)
ELI.............. Electron Tube Integrator (RU)
Eli............... Elite [*Record label*] [*Europe*]
ELIA......... European League of Institutes of the Arts [*British*]
ELIC......... Early Literacy in Childhood [*Australia*]
ELIC......... Early Literacy Inservice Course [*Australia*]
ELIMCOR ... Ethiopian Livestock and Meat Corp. Ltd.
Eliminier.... Eliminierung [*Elimination*] [*German*] (GCA)
ELINAMO ... Exercito de Libertacao Nacional de Monomotapa
eliotip........ Eliotipia [*Phototype*] [*Publishing*] [*Italian*]
ELIP .... Elektro-Industrisko Preduzece [*Industrial Electrical Establishment*] [*Zemun*] (YU)
elip .... Elelmiszeripar [*Food Industry*] (HU)
ELIPA .... Experienced Librarians and Information Personnel in the Developing Countries of Asia and Oceania [*Korea Advanced Institute of Science and Technology*] [*Seoul*] [*Information service or system*] (IID)
Elip M........ Elelmiszeripari Miniszterium/Miniszter [*Ministry/Minister of the Food Industry*] (HU)
ELISA........ Electronic Library Information Service at the Australian National University
ELISE........ European Network for the Exchange of Information on Local Employment Initiatives [*EC*] (ECED)
elisra .... Electronic Systems Ltd. (Israel)
ELIT .... Equipamentos para Lavoura, Industria, e Transportes Ltd. [*Brazil*] (DSCA)
ELITOSA ... Empresa Litografica Sociedad Anonima [*Barranquilla*] (COL)
ELIZOMAT ... Fabrika na Elektro Izolacioni Materiali [*Electric Insulating Materials Plant*] [*Prilep*] (YU)
elj .... Eljaras [*Procedure, Process, Proceedings*] (HU)
ELJ .... El Recio [*Colombia*] [*Airport symbol*] (OAG)
ELK............ Eesti Lennukompani [*Estonia*] [*ICAO designator*] (FAAC)
ELK............ Ellinikon Laikon Kinima [*Greek Popular Movement*] (GC)
ELK............ Enosis Laikou Kommatos [*Union of Populist Parties*] [*Greek*] (PPE)
ELK............ Ethniko Laiko Komma [*National Populist Party*] [*Greek*] (PPE)
ELK............ Evangelisch-Lutherische Kirche [*Evangelical Lutheran Church*] [*Namibia*] (AF)
Elka........... Elektrokarren [*Electric Carts*] (EG)
ELKA......... Elyafli Plaka Sanayii TAS [*Fiber Record Industry Corporation*] (TU)
ELKA......... Tvornica Elektricnih Kabela [*Electric Cable Works*] [*Zagreb*] (YU)
ELKAD...... Eidikos Logariasmos Koinonikon Asfaliseon Dodekanisou [*Dodecanese Social Insurance Special Account*] [*Greek*] (GC)
elkall .... Elkallodott [*Missing*] (HU)
ELKAR...... Electrocardiograph (RU)
El Ke Pa ..... Ellinikon Kendron Paragogikotitos [*Greek Productivity Center*] (GC)
el-khim....... Electrochemistry (RU)
Elkhima ..... Electrochemical and Technical Cooperative (BU)
ELKI......... Ellinikon Laikon Kinima [*Greek Popular Movement*] (GC)
ELKO .... Tvornica Elektrokovinskih Proizvodov [*Electrical Equipment Plant*] [*Maribor*] (YU)
elkolt......... Elkoltozott [*Departed, Moved*] (HU)
ELKOOP... Producers Cooperative for Electric Appliances (BU)
ell .... Ellato [*or Ellatas*] [*Supplying or Supply*] (HU)
ell .... Ellenor [*Controller, Inspector*] (HU)
ell .... Eller [*Or*] [*Sweden*] (GPO)
ELL............ Estonian Air [*ICAO designator*] (FAAC)
ELLA......... European Long Lines Agency [*NATO*]
ELLIS........ English Language Learning and Improvement Service [*State Library of South Australia*]
ELLIS........ European Legal Literature Information Service [*London, England*]
ello............. Ellato Osztaly [*Supply Department*] (HU)
ELLX........ Luxembourg/Luxembourg [*ICAO location identifier*] (ICLI)
ELM .... Cathode-Ray Minimizer (RU)
elm............. Elelmezes [*or Elelmezesi*] [*Food Supply, Supplying, Catering*] (HU)
ELM .... Ethiopian Liberation Movement
ELM .... La-Rouche-Sur-Yon [*France*] [*Airport symbol*]
ELM(A).... Electric Light Manufacturers (Australia)

ELMA....... Empresa Lineas Maritimas Argentinas, SA [*Argentine Shipping Lines*] [*Buenos Aires*] (LA)
ELMA........ Tovarna Elektroinstalacijskega Materiala [*Electrical Installation Works*] [*Crnuce*] (YU)
ELMAF ..... Societe des Emballages Legers Metalliques Africains
el-magn ...... Electromagnetic (RU)
el magnyed ... Electromagnetic Unit (RU)
ELME....... Enosis Leitourgon Mesis Ekpaidevseos [*Union of Intermediate School Teachers*] [*Greek*] (GC)
EL-MEK.... Elektro Mekanik Cihazlar Sanayii [*Electromechanical Instruments Industry*] (TU)
ELMES ..... Ellinikai Mesogeiakai Grammai [*Greek Mediterranean Lines*] (GC)
ELMEX..... Elementos Electronics Mexicanos SA [*Mexico*]
el-mikroskopich ... Electron-Microscopic (RU)
EIMK....... Elelmezesugyi Miniszterium Kollegiuma [*Council of the Ministry of Food Supply*] (HU)
ELMO .... Elektromotorenwerk (VEB) [*Electric Motor Plant (VEB)*] (EG)
elmo........... Elelmezesi Osztaly [*Food Provisioning Department, Quartermaster Corps Unit*] (HU)
ELMO .... European Laundry and Dry Cleaning Machinery Manufacturers Organization (EA)
ELMOK .... Ellinikon Monarkhikon Kinima [*Greek Monarchist Movement*] (GC)
ELMP........ Experimental Machine-Translation Laboratory (RU)
ELMS .... Eskisehir Lokomotif ve Motor Sanayii [*Eskisehir Locomotive and Motor Industry*] (TU)
ELN .... Ejercito de Liberacion Nacional [*National Liberation Army*] [*Chile*] (LA)
ELN .... Ejercito de Liberacion Nacional [*National Liberation Army*] [*Argentina*] (LA)
ELN .... Ejercito de Liberacion Nacional [*National Liberation Army*] [*Colorado*] (PD)
ELN .... Ejercito de Liberacion Nacional [*National Liberation Army*] [*Bolivia*] (PD)
ELN .... Ejercito de Liberacion Nacional [*National Liberation Army*] [*Peru*] (PD)
ELN .... Ejercito de Liberacion Nicaraguense [*Nicaraguan Liberation Army*] (LA)
ELN .... Ejercito Liberador Nacional [*National Liberating Army*] [*Argentina*] (LA)
eln............... Elnok [*President*] (HU)
ELN .... Erzeugnis- und Leistungsnomenklatur [*Product and Performance Nomenclature*] (EG)
ELN .... Nordic East International Aircraft, AB [*Sweden*] [*ICAO designator*] (FAAC)
ELNA .... Exercito de Libertacao Nacional de Angola
EINII .... Scientific Research Institute for Electric Locomotive Building (RU)
ELNS........ European League for a New Society [*See also LIENS*] [*Paris, France*] (EAIO)
ELO .... Ecole des Langues Orientales [*School of Oriental Languages*] [*French*]
ELO .... Ecole Speciale des Langues Orientales Vivantes
el-od .... Electrode (RU)
elof............. Elofizeto [*Subscriber*] (HU)
ELOG .... European Landowning Organization Group (EAIO)
ELOK .... Elektricna Lokomotiva [*Electric Locomotive*] (YU)
E-Lok .... Elektrische Lokomotive [*Electric Locomotive*] [*German*]
elok............. Elokuva [*Film, Cinema*] [*Finland*]
ELOK .... Evangelisch-Lutheranische Ovambokavangokirche [*Evangelical-Lutheran Ovambo-Kavango Church*] [*Namibia*]
elop............. Electrooptics Industries Ltd. [*Israel*]
el-optich..... Electron-Optical (RU)
ELOSPINA ... Hijos de Eleazar Ospina & Cia. Ltda. [*Colombia*] (COL)
ELOT........ Ellinikos Organismos Tupopoiesseos [*Hellenic Organization for Standardization*] [*Athens*] (SLS)
ELOU .... Electric Desalination Unit (RU)
ELOV .... Ecole Speciale des Langues Orientales Vivantes
ELP........... Aerolineas Ejecutivas de San Luis Potosi SA de CV [*Mexico*] [*ICAO designator*] (FAAC)
ELP........... Exercito de Libertacao Portugues [*Portuguese Liberation Army*] (WER)
ELPA .... Elliniki Leskhi Periigiseon kai Avtokinitou [*Greek Automobile and Touring Club*] (GC)
ELPEC ...... Entreprise Lao de Promotion et d'Exploitation Cinematographique [*Lao Motion Picture Promotion and Exploitation Company*] (CL)
ELPGA ...... European Liquefied Petroleum Gas Association (EA)
el podst....... Electric Substation (RU)
ELPOH ..... Elektricno Poduzece Hrvatske [*Electrical Establishment of Croatia*] (YU)
ELPROM ... Electric Power Industry Enterprise (BU)
ELQ .... Gassim [*Saudi Arabia*] [*Airport symbol*] (OAG)
ELR........... Educational Lending Right [*Australia*]
ELR........... Elrom Aviation & Investments [*Israel*] [*ICAO designator*] (FAAC)

elra .... European Leisure and Recreation Association (EAIO)
ELRU......... Electronic Recorder (RU)
ELS .... East London [*South Africa*] [*Airport symbol*] (OAG)
els.............. Effective Horsepower (RU)
ELS .... Electronic Lodgement Service [*Australian Taxation Office*]
ELS .... Elektronischer Lochstreifenstanzer [*German*] (ADPT)
ELS .... Elliniki Lyriki Skini [*Greek Lyric Theater*] (GC)
ELS .... El Sal Air [*El Salvador*] [*ICAO designator*] (FAAC)
ELSA .... Electronic Selective Archives [*Swiss News Agency*] [*Information service or system*] (IID)
ELSA .... End Loans to South Africa
ELSA .... Environmental Library Services Association [*Australia*]
ELSA .... Evangelical Lutheran Synod in Australia
ELSAG ...... Elettronica San Giorgio [*Italy*] (PDAA)
El Salv........ El Salvador
ELSAP....... Elektronische Schiessanlace fuer Panzer [*German*]
ELSASSER ... Elsaess-Lothringen Partei [*Alsace-Lorraine Party*] [*German*] (PPE)
ELSC .... Elvis Lucky Seven Club [*Philippines*] (EAIO)
ELSE .... Elliniki Synomospondia Ergasias [*Greek Labor Confederation*] (GC)
ELSE .... European Association of Editors of Life Science
EL-SEN..... Kibris Turk Elektrik Mustahdemleri Sendikasi [*Turkish Cypriot Electric Power Employees Union*] (TU)
Els LothrRZ ... Rechtszeitschrift fuer Elsass-Lothringen [*Germany*] (FLAF)
ELSSA .... English Language and Study Skills Assistance Centre [*University of Technology*] [*Sydney, Australia*]
el-st .... Electric Power Plant [*Topography*] (RU)
el-st yed...... Electrostatic Unit (RU)
ELT........... Cathode-Ray Tube (RU)
ELT........... European Letter Telegram
ELTA .... Ellinika Takhydromeia [*Greek Posts*] (GC)
ELTC .... English Language Teaching Centre [*Royal Melbourne Institute of Technology*] [*Australia*]
ELTC .... European Lubricant Testing Committee
ELTE .... Eotvos Lorand Tudomanyegyetem [*Lorand Eotvos University of Arts and Sciences*] (HU)
ELTEK ...... Elektronik Teknoloji AS [*Electronic Technology Corp.*] (TU)
El-term....... Electrothermics (RU)
ELTERV.... Elelmezesipari Tervezo Vallalat [*Food Industry Planning Enterprise*] (HU)
ELTS .... English Language Testing Service [*Australia*]
ELTSA .... End Loans to South Africa
ELTV .... Eternal Love Television
ELU .... El Oued [*Algeria*] [*Airport symbol*] (OAG)
ELU .... Ethiopian Labor Union
ELV........... Elektrovod [*Electrical Engineering Enterprise*] (CZ)
elv............. Elvalt [*Divorced*] (HU)
ELV........... Etaireia Laikis Vasis [*Public Base Company*] (GC)
ELVA .... Elle Va [*She Goes*] [*Racing car*] [*French*]
ELVIL .... Elliniki Viomikhania Lipasmaton [*Greek Fertilizer Industry (of Kavala, OTE)*] (GC)
elvt............. Elvtars [*Comrade*] (HU)
ELWA .... Eternal Love Winning Africa
ELWE........ Elektromotorenwerk Wernigerode [*Wernigerode Electric Motor Plant*] (EG)
ELY........... El Al-Israel Airlines Ltd. [*ICAO designator*] (FAAC)
ELYPAL.... Elliniki Yperpondios Alieia [*Greek Overseas Fishing*] (GC)
elyuv........... Eluvial, Eluvium (RU)
ELZ........... Electric Bulb Plant (RU)
elzagr.......... Electrified Wire Obstacle Company (RU)
el zhd .... Electric Railroad (RU)
ELZI .... Electroluminescent Character Indicator (RU)
EM............ Destroyer [*Navy*] (RU)
EM............ East Malaysia (ML)
EM............ East Mark [*Monetary unit*] [*Germany*]
EM............ Economische Mededinging [*Benelux*] (BAS)
em............. Edella Mainittu [*Finland*]
EM............ Efficiency Medal
EM............ Electromagnet (RU)
EM............ Electromagnetic (Instrument) (RU)
EM............ Electron Microscope, Electron Microscopy (RU)
em............. Email [*Enamel*] [*French*]
Em............ Emekli [*Retired*] (TU)
em............. Emelet [*Floor*] (HU)
em............. Emeritiert [*Honored*] [*German*]
em............. Emerytowany [*Retired*] [*Poland*]
Em............ Eminence [*Eminence*] [*French*]
EM............ Eminensie [*Eminence*] [*Afrikaans*]
EM............ Emmanuel Mission
EM............ Em Mao [*In Hand*] [*Portuguese*]
em............. Emulsion (RU)
EM............ Encuentro de Mujeres (EAIO)
em............. Ennen Mainittu [*Finland*]
EM............ Enrique de la Mata
EM............ Entente Mauritanienne

EM............. Entfernungsmesser [*Range Finder*]   (EG)
EM............. Epitesugyi Miniszterium/Miniszter [*Ministry/Minister of Construction*]   (HU)
EM............. Escuadron de la Muerte [*Death Squadron*] [*El Salvador*]   (LA)
EM............. Estado Maior [*General Staff*] [*Portuguese*]   (WER)
EM............. Estado Mayor [*Spanish*]
E-M........... Etat-Major [*Headquarters*] [*French*]
EM............. Etats Membres [*Member States*] [*French*]   (BAS)
EM............. Ethnikon Metopon [*National Front*] [*Cyprus*]   (GC)
EM............. Euroopan Mestaruus [*Finland*]
EM............. Evergreen Marine Corp. [*Taiwan*]
EM............. Excerpta Medica [*Netherlands*]
EM............. Exploatatie Miniera [*Mining Exploitation*]   (RO)
EM............. Expose des Motifs [*French*]   (BAS)
EM............. Heli-Air-Monaco [*Monaco*] [*ICAO designator*]   (ICDA)
EM............. Magnetic Clutch   (RU)
EM............. Multibucket Excavator   (RU)
EMA.......... Division of Earth, Marine and Atmospheric Science and Technology [*Council for Scientific and Industrial Research*] [*South Africa*]   (IRC)
EMA.......... Ecole Marocaine d'Administration
EMA.......... Ecole Militaire d'Administration [*Algeria*]
EMA.......... Egyptian Aviation Co. [*ICAO designator*]   (FAAC)
EMA.......... Egyptian Medical Association   (PDAA)
EMA.......... Egyptian Moslem Association [*Australia*]
EMA.......... Einwohnermeldeamt [*Resident Registration Office*]   (EG)
EMA.......... Electromagnetic Analyzer   (RU)
EMA.......... Electro Mecanique Abidjan
EMA.......... Elliniki Mousiki Akadimia [*Greek Music Academy*]   (GC)
Ema.......... Eminencia [*Eminence*] [*Spanish*]
Ema.......... Eminencia [*Eminence*] [*Portuguese*]
EMA.......... Empresa Manufatora de Acos, SA [*Minas Gerais*] [*Brazil*]   (LAA)
EMA.......... Energy Managers' Association [*Australia*]
EMA.......... En Meer Ander [*And Others*] [*Afrikaans*]
EMA.......... Equipe de Mecanizacao Agricola [*Brazil*]   (DSCA)
EMA.......... Estado Maior da Armada [*Navy General Staff*] [*Brazil*]   (LA)
EMA.......... Etat-Major de l'Armee [*Army Headquarters*] [*Military*] [*French*]   (MTD)
EMA.......... Ethyl Methacrylamide   (RU)
EMA.......... European Marketing Association [*Brixham, Devonshire, England*]   (EA)
EMA.......... European Monetary Agreement
EMA.......... Europees Monetair Akkoord [*Benelux*]   (BAS)
EMA.......... Export Music Australia
EMA.......... Medical Electric Equipment (Plant)   (RU)
EMAA....... European Mastic Asphalt Association   (EA)
EMAB .... Entreprise Malienne du Bois
EMAC .... Ecole Africaine de la Meterologie et de d'Aviation Civile [*East African School of Meteorology and Civil Aviation*] [*Republic of Niger*]   (PDAA)
EMAC .... Empresa de Mecanizacao Agricola e Construcoes Ltd. [*Brazil*]   (DSCA)
EMAC .... Empresa Mocambicana de Aviacao Comercial
EMAC .... Entreprise Publique Economique des Manufactures de Chaussures et Maroquinerie [*Nationalized industry*] [*Algeria*]   (EY)
EMAC .... Equipamentos e Materiais de Construcao Lda.
EMAC .... European and Mediterranean Association of Coloproctology   (EAIO)
EMAC .... European Marketing Academy   (EAIO)
EMACI...... Entrepots Miliens en Cote-D'Ivoire
EMAD .... Efippa Mikta Apospasmata Dioxeos [*Mounted Joint Pursuit Detachments*] [*Greek*]   (GC)
EMADI ..... Empresa Administradora de Inmuebles [*Buildings Administrative Enterprise*] [*Peru*]   (LA)
EMAer....... Estado Maior da Aeronautica [*Air Force General Staff*] [*Brazil*]   (LA)
EMAF....... Escola Media de Agricultura Florestal [*Brazil*]   (DSCA)
EMAG .... Elso Magyar Gazdasagi Gepgyar [*First Hungarian Agricultural Machine Factory*]   (HU)
EMAG .... Ethnic Minorities Action Group [*Australia*]
EMAI .... Elizabeth Macarthur Agricultural Institute [*Australia*]
e-mail .... Electronic Mail   (EECI)
EMAIL .... Exportadora Mercantil Agro-Industrial Ltd. [*Brazil*]   (DSCA)
EMAK .... Ethnikon Metopon Agoniston Kyprou [*National Front of Fighters*] [*Cyprus*]   (GC)
EMALEDH ... Union of Ethiopian Marxist-Leninist Organizations   (AF)
EMAP....... Empresa Municipal de Agua Potable [*Ecuador*]   (IMH)
EMAP....... Export Marketing Assistance Program [*Australia*]
EMAPA..... Expansao Mercantil e Agricola do Parana SA [*Brazil*]   (DSCA)
EMAQ....... Engenharia e Maquina, SA [*Brazil*]   (LAA)
EMARC..... Escola Media de Agricultura da Regiao Cacaueira [*Brazil*]   (DSCA)
EMAS........ "El Mouggar" Art et Spectacle
EMAS........ Energy Management Advisory Service [*Australia*]

EMASA..... Electrical Manufacturers' Association of South Australia
EMASA..... Equipos y Maquinarias, Sociedad Anonima [*Equipment and Machinery, Inc.*] [*Chile*]   (LA)
EMASAR .. International Program on Ecological Management of Arid and Semi-Arid Rangelands in Africa
EMASZ..... Eszak-Magyarorszagi Aramszolgaltato Vallalat [*Electric Power Enterprise of Northern Hungary*]   (HU)
EMATEC.. Entreprise Nationale d'Importation de Materiel Technique
EMATER.. Empresa de Assistencia Tecnica e Extenso Rural [*Brazil*]   (EY)
EMB .... Editio Musica Budapest (Budapesti Zenemukiado Vallalat) [*"Editio Musica" (Music Publishing Company, Budapest)*]   (HU)
EMB .... Electromagnetic Blocking   (RU)
emb............ Emboitage [*Case*] [*Publishing*] [*French*]
EMB .... Empresa Brasileira de Aeronautica SA [*Brazil*] [*ICAO designator*]   (FAAC)
EMB .... European Molecular Biology Conference
EMBA .... European Marine Biological Association   (ASF)
EMBAL..... Embalagens de Madeiras de Mocambique Lda.
EMBALI ... Establecimiento Publico Empresas Municipales de Cali [*Colombia*]   (DSCA)
EMBALLAF ... Societe "L'Emballage Africain" [*North African*]
EMBARK ... Embarkation   (DSUE)
EMBC........ European Molecular Biology Conference [*or Council*]
embl .... Embalagem [*Package*] [*Portuguese*]
EMBL........ European Molecular Biology Laboratory [*Research center*] [*Germany*]   (IRC)
EMBO .... European Molecular Biology Organization [*ICSU*] [*Germany*]
emboit .... Emboitage [*Case*] [*Publishing*] [*French*]
EMBOSA ... Empresa Metalurgica Boliviana, Sociedad Anonima [*Bolivian Metallurgical Enterprise, Inc.*]   (LA)
EMBOSALVA ... Embotelladora Salvadorena, SA [*Salvadoran Bottling Corp.*]
Embr .... Embriologia [*Embryology*] [*Portuguese*]
embr .... Embryology   (RU)
EMBRAER ... Empresa Brasileira Aeronautica, SA [*Brazilian Aeronautics Company*]   (LA)
EMBRAFILME ... Empresa Brasileira de Filmes [*Brazilian Film Company*]   (LA)
EMBRAMED ... Empresa Brasileira de Medicamentos [*Brazilian Pharmaceutical Companmy*]   (LA)
EMBRAPA ... Empresa Brasileira de Pesquisa Agropecuaria [*Brazilian Agricultural Research Corporation*] [*Brazil*]   (LA)
EMBRASA ... Empresa Agricola e Industrial Brasil SA [*Brazil*]   (DSCA)
EMBRASID ... Empresa Brasileira de Sistemas de Defesa [*Brazilian Defense Systems Enterprise*]   (LA)
EMBRATEL ... Empresa Brasileira de Telecomunicacoes [*Brazilian Telecommunications Enterprises*]
EMBRATER ... Empresa Brasileira de Assistencia Tecnica e Extensao Rural [*Brazilian Rural Extension and Technical Assistance Enterprise*] [*Brasilia*]   (LA)
EMBRATUR ... Empresa Brasileira de Turismo [*Brazilian Tourism Co.*]   (LA)
Embre .... Embarcadere [*Pier*] [*Military map abbreviation World War I*] [*French*]   (MTD)
Embriol ...... Embryology, Embryological   (BU)
EMBS........ European Marine Biology Symposia   (SLS)
Embure ...... Embouchure [*Mouth*] [*Military map abbreviation World War I*] [*French*]   (MTD)
EMBWA ... Egg Marketing Board of Western Australia
EMC .... Ecumenical Migration Centre [*Australia*]   (EAIO)
EMC .... Elektroniczna Maszyna Cyfrowa [*Digital Computer*]   (POL)
EMC .... Elizabeth Matriculation College [*Australia*]   (ADA)
EMC .... Elso Magyar Cernagyar [*First Hungarian Yarn Factory*]   (HU)
EMC .... Empresa Metalurgica Colombiana SA [*Bucaramanga*]   (COL)
EMC .... Entreprise Miniere et Chimique [*Opencast Mining and Chemistry Organization*] [*Paris, France*]
EMC .... Environmental Medical Centre [*Australia*]
EMC .... Environment Management Committee [*Australia*]
EMC .... Estado Mayor Conjunto [*Joint General Staff*] [*El Salvador*]   (LA)
EMC .... European Mathematical Council   (EA)
EMC .... European Mechanics Committee   (EAIO)
EMC .... Executive Medical Centre [*Australia*]   (ADA)
EMC .... Export Management Company
EMCC .... Escuelas Militares Camilo Cienfuegos [*Camilo Cienfuegos Military Schools*] [*Cuba*]   (LA)
EMCCC ... European Military Communications Co-Ordinating Committee [*NATO*]
EMCF........ European Monetary Co-Operation Fund [*Bank for International Settlements*]   (EY)
EMC/JS.... Etat-Major Central de la Jeunesse Sauvetage [*Salvation Youth Central Headquarters*] [*Cambodia*]   (CL)
EMCO .... Empresa de Produccion de Medios Tecnicos de Computacion [*Enterprise for the Production of Technical Means of Computation*] [*Cuba*]   (LA)
EMCOCABLES ... Empresa Colombiana de Cables SA [*Colombia*]   (COL)
EMCOF..... European Monetary Co-Operation Fund

EMCOLDROMOS ... Empresa Colombiana de Aerodromos [*Colombian Airport Corporation*] (COL)

Emcoper ..... Empresa de Comercializacion de Productos Perecedores [*Perishable Produce Marketing Company*] [*Colorado*] (GEA)

EMCRF ..... European and Mediterranean Cereal Rusts Foundation (EAIO)

EMCTCU ... European-Middle East Channel and Traffic Control Unit

EMCWP .... European Mediterranean Commission on Water Planning (EA)

EMD .... Eidgenoessisches Militaerdepartement [*Swiss Military Department*] (WEN)

EMD .... Electronic Marcel Dassault [*France*]

EMD .... Electronique Marcel Dassault [*Marcel Dassault Electronics*] [*French*] (WER)

EMD .... Emerald [*Australia*] [*Airport symbol*] (OAG)

EMDAI ..... Enosis Mousoulmanon Didaskalon Apofoiton ton Ierospoudastirion [*Union of Moslem Teacher Graduates of the Religious Schools*] (GC)

EMDG .... Euromissile Dynamics Group (PDAA)

EMDG .... Export Market Development Grants [*Australia*]

EMDGA ..... Export Market Development Grants Act [*Australia*]

EMDGS ..... Export Market Development Grants Scheme [*Australia*]

EMDP .... Etaireia Metaforas kai Diyliseos Petrelaion [*Petroleum Transport and Refining Company*] (GC)

EMDY .... Enosis Mikhanikon Dimosion Ypallilon [*Union of Civil Service Engineers*] [*Greek*] (GC)

EME .... Elektrarna Melnik [*Electric Power Plant Melnik*] (CZ)

EME .... Elliniki Mathimatiki Etaireia [*Greek Mathematics Society*] (GC)

EME .... Elliniki Metallevtiki Etaireia [*Hellenic Mines Corporation*] [*Cyprus*] (GC)

EME .... Emden [*Germany*] [*Airport symbol*] (OAG)

EME .... Emerging Market Economy (ECON)

EME .... Empirical Matrix Element (RU)

EME .... Empresa Mocambicana de Empreitadas

EME .... Energomachexport [*Former USSR*]

EME .... Enosis Mousoulmanon Ellados [*Union of Moslems of Greece*] (GC)

EME .... Estado Maior do Exercito [*Army General Staff*] [*Portuguese*] (WER)

EME .... Ethnikon Metopon Ellados [*National Front of Greece*] (GC)

EMEA .... Etaireia Meleton Ethnikis Amynis [*Association for National Defense Studies*] [*Greek*] (GC)

EMEA .... European Medicines Evaluation Agency [*London*]

EMEC .... Empresa Estatal de Construcao [*State Construction Company*] [*Cape Verde*] (AF)

EMEC .... Estado Mayor del Ejercito del Centro [*Staff of the Central Army*] [*Cuba*] (LA)

EMEK .... Ethniki Mathitiki Enosis Kyprou [*National Student Union of Cyprus*] (GC)

EMEKEL .. Eniaion Metopon Ergaton kai Ergazomenou Laou [*United Front of Workers and Working People*] [*Greek*] (GC)

EMELEC .. Empresa Electrica Ecuatoriana [*Ecuadorean Electric Power Enterprise*] (LA)

EMEO .... Esoteriki Makedoniki Epanastatiki Organosis [*Internal Macedonian Revolutionary Organization*] (GC)

EMEP .... Etaireia Meletis Ellinikon Provlimaton [*Society for the Study of Greek Problems*] (GC)

EMEP .... European Monitoring and Evaluation Programme [*OECD*]

EMEPS ..... Ecole Militaire d'EPS [*Enseignements Primaire et Secondaire*]

EMERGE ... Magyar Ruggyantagyar Reszvenytarsasag [*Hungarian Rubber Processing Factory*] (HU)

Emexcon .... Empresa Exportadora de la Construccion [*Construction Export Company*] [*Cuba*] (GEA)

EMF .... Etablissements Martre Freres

EMF .... Ethyl Mercury Phosphate (RU)

EMF .... Europaeische Motel Foderation [*European Motel Federation*] (EA)

EMF .... European Metalworkers' Federation in the Community [*EC*] (ECED)

EMF .... European Missionary Fellowship

EMF .... European Monetary Fund [*Proposed*]

EMF .... Europees Monetair Fonds [*Benelux*] (BAS)

EMFA .... Estado Maior das Forcas Armadas [*Armed Forces General Staff*] [*Brazil*] (LA)

EMFGA ..... Eastern Metropolitan Fruit Growers' Association [*Australia*]

EMFJ .... Europees Muziekfestival voor de Jeugd [*European Music Festival for the Youth*] (EAIO)

EMFS .... Estate Mortgage Financial Services [*Australia*]

EMG .... Economic Monitoring Group [*New Zealand*]

EMG .... Electromyogram, Electromyography (RU)

EMG .... Elektronikus Merokeszulekek Gyara [*Factory for Electronic Measuring Instruments*] (HU)

EMG .... Energy Managers' Group [*Australia*]

EMG .... Estado Mayor General [*General Staff*] (LA)

EMG .... Etablissements Metalliques du Gabon

EMG .... Etat-Major General [*General Staff*] [*French*] (CL)

EMG .... Europaeische Maerchengesellschaft [*European Fairytale Association - EFA*] [*Germany*] (EAIO)

EMGDO .... Evangelische Mission Gesellschaft fuer Deutsch-Ostafrika

EMGE .... Estado Mayor General del Ejercito [*Army General Staff*] [*Cuba*] (LA)

Emgekali ... Magnesiumhaltiges Kali [*Magnesium-Bearing Potash*] (EG)

EMGFA ..... Estado-Maior General das Forcas Armadas [*General Staff of the Armed Forces*] [*Portuguese*] (WER)

EMGI .... Ethiopian Mapping and Geography Institute [*Ethiopia*] (DSCA)

EMGy .... Elektronikus Merokeszulekek Gyara [*Factory for Electronic Measuring Instruments*] (HU)

EMH .... Entreprise d'Equipements Mecaniques and Hydrauliques (LA)

emhaka/MHK ... Munkara Harcra Kesz [*Ready for Work and Combat (Organization)*] (HU)

EMI .... Emirau [*Papua New Guinea*] [*Airport symbol*] (OAG)

EMI .... Empresa de Montajes Industriales [*Industrial Installations Enterprise*] [*Cuba*] (LA)

EMI .... Epitesugyi Minosito Intezet [*Construction Qualification Institute*] (HU)

EMI .... Etat-Major Interarmes [*Algeria*]

EMIA .... Ecole Militaire Interarmes [*Military Inter-Service School*] [*Algeria*] (AF)

EMIA .... Employers' Mutual Indemnity Association Ltd. [*Australia*] [*Commercial firm*]

EMIAC ...... Ecole Militaire Interarmes Camerounaise [*Cameroonian Military Inter-Service School*] (AF)

Emiat .... Empresa Importadora y Exportadora de Suministros Tecnicos [*Import-export board*] [*Cuba*] (EY)

EMIB .... European Master's in International Business

EMIC .... Entreprise Marocaine d'Irrigation et de Canalisation

EMID .... Electromagnetic Inductive Flaw Detector (RU)

EMIDICT ... Empresa Especializada Importadora y Distribuidora para la Ciencia y la Tecnica [*Enterprise Specialized in Importing and Distributing Science and Technology*] [*Cuba*] (LA)

E Min .... Eau Minerale [*Military map abbreviation*] [*World War I*] [*French*] (MTD)

EMINSA ... Empressa Sahara Minera [*Sahara Mining Enterprise*] (AF)

EMINSU ... Emekli Subaylar [*Retired Officers Association*] (TU)

EMINWA ... Environmentally Sound Management of Inland Water [*United Nations*]

EMIR .... EDP [*Electronic Data Processing*]-Microfilm-Integrated-Retrieval [*German Patent Office*]

EMIRTEL ... Emirates Telecommunications Corporation

EMIS .... Ege Bolgesi Maden Iscileri Sendikasi [*Aegean Regional Mine Workers' Union*] [*Zonguldak*] (TU)

EMIT .... Electromagnetic Instrument for Measuring Sea Currents (RU)

EMIZ .... Electromechanical Tool Plant (RU)

EMK .... Electromagnetic Compensator (RU)

EMK .... Electromagnetic Valve (RU)

EMK .... Elektrik, Makine, Kablo [*Electric Power, Machinery, and Cable Directorate*] [*Turkish Copper*] (GC)

EMK .... Elektromotoriese Krag [*Electromotive Force*] [*Afrikaans*]

EMK .... Elektromotorische Kraft [*Electromotive Force*] [*German*] (EG)

EMK .... Epitok Muszaki Klubja [*Engineers Club*] (HU)

EMK .... Europaeischer Mikrofilm-Kongress [*European Microfilm Congress*] [*German*] (ADPT)

EMKA .... Ettehadiyye Markazi Kargarane Iran Central Federation of Trade Unions of Workers and Peasants of Iran

EMKE .... Ethnikon Metarrythmistikon Komma Ellados [*National Reformation Party of Greece*] (GC)

EMKh .... Ethyl Mercury Chloride (RU)

EMKIE ...... Ellinikon Morfotikon Kendron Inomenon Ethnon [*United Nations Educational Center of Greece*] (GC)

EMKL .... Ekspedisi Muatan Kapal Laut [*Maritime Cargo Handling Association*] (IN)

EMKS .... Electronic Crossbar Switch (RU)

EMLB .... Elektronmikroskopisk Laboratorium foer de Biologiske Fag [*Electron Microscopy Laboratory for Biological Science*] [*Research center*] [*Norway*] (IRC)

EMLKB ..... Turkiye Emlak Kredi Bankasi TAS [*Turkish Real Estate Credit Bank Corp.*] (TU)

EMM .... Elektrik Muhendisligi Mecmuasi [*Chamber of Turkish Electrical Engineers*] (EAIO)

EMM .... Entente Medicale Mediterraneenne [*Mediterranean Medical Entente*] (EAIO)

EMM .... Estate Mortgage Managers [*Australia*]

EMM .... Mathematical Methods in Economics (RU)

EMMA .... Empresa Mocambicana de Malhas

emman ...... Emmanchure [*Sleeve-Hole*] [*Knitting*] [*French*]

EMMHO .. Ecole Militaire pour les Metiers d'Hotellerie [*Algeria*]

EMMIU .... Empresa Metropolitana de Mantenimiento de Inmuebles Urbanos [*Metropolitan Enterprise for Maintenance of Urban Property*] [*Cuba*] (LA)

Emmo .... Eminentisimo [*Most Eminent*] [*Spanish*]

Emmo .... Eminentissimo [*Most Eminent*] [*Portuguese*]

EMN .... Ecole Nationale Superieure des Mines de Nancy [*Mining Industry National College of Nancy*] [*France*] (EAS)

Emn .... Emniyet [*Security*] (TU)

EMN......... Escuadron de la Muerte Nuevo [*New Death Squad*] [*El Salvador*] (PD)

EMN......... Nema [*Mauritania*] [*Airport symbol*]   (OAG)

EMO......... Education en Milieu Ouvert [*France*]   (FLAF)

EMO......... Elektrarna Mesta Opavy, Narodni Podnik [*Electric Power Works of the City of Opava, National Enterprise*]   (CZ)

EMO......... Elektrik Muhendisleri Odasi [*Chamber of Electrical Engineers*] (TU)

EMO......... Emo [*Papua New Guinea*] [*Airport symbol*]   (OAG)

EMO......... United Youth Organization   (BU)

EMOCHA ... Empresa Mocambicana de Cha [*Tea production enterprise*] [*Mozambique*]

emol............ Emolumentos [*Profits*] [*Portuguese*]

EM/OP...... Etat Major Operationnel [*Operational Staff*]   (CL)

EMOS .... English for Migrant and Overseas Students [*Program*] [*Australia*]

EMOS .... High School Students Youth Union   (BU)

EMOSE..... Empresa Mocambicana de Seguros

EMOTA .... European Mail Order Traders' Association [*EC*]   (ECED)

emouss ...... Emousse [*Rounded*] [*French*]

E Mp .... Economische Machtspositie [*Benelux*]   (BAS)

EMP .... Electric Installation Train   (RU)

EMP .... Electromechanical Production (of Mosgoraptekoupravleniye) (RU)

EMP .... Electromechanical Transducer   (RU)

EMP .... Electromechanical Transmission   (RU)

EMP .... Elektro-Mehanicko Pretprijatie [*Electro-Mechanical Establishment*] [*Skopje*]   (YU)

EMP .... Elektrotehnicko i Masinsko Preduzece [*Electrical Engineering and Machinery Establishment*] [*YU*]

EMP .... Ellinikon Metsovion Polytekhneion [*Greek Metsovion Polytechnic School*] [*Also referred to as National Technical University of Athens*]   (GC)

EMP .... Em Mao Propria [*Portuguese*]

EMP .... Environmental Monitoring Program

EMPA....... Eidgenoess Materials Pruefungs Amt [*Federal Material Testing Institute*] [*Switzerland*]

EMPA....... Eidgenossiche Materialsprufungs und Versuchsanstalt [*Federal Materials Testing and Experiment Station*] [*Switzerland*] (PDAA)

EMPA....... Eidgenossische Materialprufungs- und Forschungsanstalt [*Federal Laboratories for Materials Testing and Research*] [*Switzerland*]   (IRC)

EMPA....... Empresa Publica de Abastecimentos [*Public Enterprise for Supply*] [*Cape Verde*]   (AF)

EMPACO ... Empaques del Pacifico Ltda. [*Colombia*]   (COL)

EMPACOL ... Empaquetadora de Colombia Ltda. [*Colombia*]   (COL)

EMPE....... Extra Mural Penal Employment

Empf .... Empfaenger [*Recipient*] [*German*]

Empf .... Empfindlichkeit [*Sensitivity*] [*German*]   (GCA)

empfindl..... Empfindlich [*Sensitive*] [*German*]   (GCA)

Empfindlichk ... Empfindlichkeit [*Sensitivity*] [*German*]   (GCA)

EMPI........ Empresa de Promocion Integral [*Integral Promotion Enterprise*] [*Cuba*]   (LA)

EMPI........ European Motor Products, Inc. [*Auto industry supplier*]

EMPI........ Ship Electric Centrifugal Firefighting Pump   (RU)

EMPO .... Equipos Modernos para Oficina   (COL)

EMPOCOL ... Empresa de Puertos de Colombia [*Colombian Ports Enterprise*] (COL)

Empoft .... Empresa Operadora de Fuerza de Trabajo [*Workforce Operating Company*] [*Cuba*]   (GEA)

EMPOR .... Empresa Portuguesa de Representacoes Lda.

EMPORCH ... Empresa Portuaria de Chile [*Port Enterpise of Chile*]   (LA)

EMPORCHI ... Empresa Portuaria de Chile [*Chile*]   (LAA)

EMPREFIL ... Empreendimentos Prediais e Financeiros Lda.

EMPREMAR ... Empresa Maritima del Estado [*State Maritime Enterprise*] [*Chile*]   (LA)

EMPROFAC ... Empresa Nacional de Produtos Farmaceuticos [*Cape Verde*] (EY)

EMPROMECA ... Empresa de Produccion Mecanica Azucarera [*National Mechanical Production Enterprise*] [*Cuba*]   (LA)

EMPS....... Einheitliche Modulare Programmstruktur [*German*]   (ADPT)

EMPT....... Einheitlicher Internationaler Personentarif [*Uniform International Passenger Tariff*]   (EG)

EmpVesic ... Emplastrum Vesicatorum [*A Blister*] [*Medicine*]

EMRC .... European Medical Research Councils [*ESF*]   (PDAA)

EMRK ...... Electromagnetic Resolution Valve   (RU)

EMRO ...... Eastern Mediterranean Regional Office [*World Health Organization*] [*Information service or system*]   (IID)

EMRO ...... Energy and Mining Research and Service Organization [*Taiwan*] [*Research center*]   (IRC)

EMRS....... Emergency Medicine Research Society [*Manchester, England*] (EAIO)

E-MRS ...... European-Materials Research Society   (EAIO)

EMRZ....... Electromechanical Repair Plant   (RU)

EMS......... East Malaysia Shipping Ent. Pty. Ltd.   (DS)

EMS......... Electromechanical Counter   (RU)

EMS........... Elektronisch-Mikroprozessorgesteuertes Speicherprogramm [*German*]   (ADPT)

EMS........... Embessa [*Papua New Guinea*] [*Airport symbol*]   (OAG)

EMS........... Empfaengermessender [*Transceiver Tester*]   (EG)

EMS........... Endothelial-Macrophagic System   (RU)

EMS........... Ente Minerario Siciliano

EMS........... Eroul Muncii Socialiste [*Hero of Socialist Labor*]   (RO)

EMS........... Etaireia Makedonikon Spoudon (Thessaloniki) [*Society of Macedonian Studies (Salonica)*]   (GC)

EMS........... European Monetary System   (AF)

EMS........... Evangelical Missionary Society

EMSA....... Electricidad de Misiones, Sociedad Anonima [*Argentina*]   (LAA)

EMSA....... Empresa Electrometalurgica Nacional, Sociedad Anonima [*Peru*] (LAA)

EMSANIT ... Empresa Sanitaria de Desinfecciones y Fumigaciones de Colombia [*Colombia*]   (COL)

EMSC....... Centre Sismologique Europeo-Mediterraneen [*France*]

EMSC....... European-Mediterranean Siesmology Center

EMSI....... Equipes Medico-Sociales Itinerantes [*Algeria*]

EMSIRVA ... Empresa de Servicios Varios [*Colombia*]   (COL)

EMSIS...... Ege Bolgesi Mensucat Sanayi Iscileri Sendikasi [*Aegean Region Textile Industry Workers Union*]   (TU)

EMSO .... Emergency Medical Services Organisation [*South Australian Health Commission*]

EMSR....... Etat-Major Special Revolutionnaire [*Revolutionary Special Staff*] [*Congo*]   (AF)

EMSS .... Equity and Merit Scholarship Scheme [*Australia*]

EMSSA ...... Electron Microscopy Society of Southern Africa   (AA)

EMSU .... Emirates & Sudan Investment Co.

EMSU .... Europaeiche Mittelstands-Union [*European Medium and Small Business Union*] [*EC*]   (ECED)

EMSU ...... European Medium and Small Business Union   (PDAA)

EMSUME ... Empresa Importadora de Suministros Medicos [*Enterprise for Import of Medical Supplies*] [*Cuba*]   (LA)

EMSZ....... Egyesult Magyar Szenbanyak [*United Hungarian Coal Mines*] (HU)

EMT .... Empresa Municipal de Transportes [*Municipal Transportation Enterprise*] [*Madrid*] [*Spanish*]   (WER)

emt .... Ennen Mainittu Teos [*Finland*]

EMT .... Enosis Mikhanikon Thalassis [*Marine Engineers Union*] [*Greek*] (GC)

EMTAM ... Empresa Mocambicana de Transportes e Aluguer de Maquinas Lda.

EMTAS ..... Elektrik Motor Fabrikasi [*Electric Motor Factory Corporation*] (TU)

EMTDB..... ESCAP [*Economic and Social Commission for Asia and the Pacific*] Maritime Transport Database [*United Nations*] (DUND)

EMTE........ European Machine Tool Exhibition   (PDAA)

EM Tervlg ... Epitesugyi Miniszterium Tervezesi Igazgatosaga [*Ministry of Construction, Planning Directorate*]   (HU)

EMTI........ Eromu Tervezo Iroda [*Planning Office of Electric Power Plants*] (HU)

EMTN .... European Meteorological Telecommunications Network (PDAA)

EMTS....... Electrical Machine and Tractor Station   (RU)

EMU......... Amplidyne   (RU)

EMU......... Easily Movable Unit [*Mobile camera*] [*Australia*]

EMU......... Electronic Simulating Unit   (RU)

EMU......... Energy Management Unit [*Commonwealth Scientific and Industrial Research Organization*] [*Australia*]

EMU........ Environmental Management Unit [*Water Board*] [*Sydney, Australia*]

EMU......... Europaeische Musikschul-Union [*European Music School Union*] [*Linz, Austria*]   (SLS)

EMU......... Europaische Musikschul-Union [*European Union of Music Schools*]   (EAIO)

EMU......... European Malacological Union   (ASF)

EMU......... Experimental Military Unit [*Australia*]

Emulgier .... Emulgierung [*Emulsification*] [*German*]   (GCA)

Emuls........ Emulsion [*German*]   (GCA)

eMv .... Electron Megavolt   (EECI)

EMV .... Elektromechanikai Vallalat [*Electromechanical Installation Enterprise*]   (HU)

EMV .... Empresa Metalurgica Vinto [*Bolivia*]   (EY)

EMV .... Eszakmagyarorszagi Vegyimuvek [*Northern Hungary Chemical Works*]   (HU)

EMVCC..... Escuela Militar Vocacional Camilo Cienfuegos [*Camilo Cienfuegos Military Vocational School*] [*Cuba*]   (LA)

EMVELP .. Elliniki Metallevtiki kai Viomikhaniki Etaireia Lignitorykheion Ptolemaidos [*Greek Mining and Industrial Company of the Ptolemais Lignite Mines*]   (GC)

EMVSA...... Elektronmikroskopievereniging van Suidelike Afrika [*Electron Microscopy Society of Southern Africa*]   (AA)

EMW .... Eisenacher Motorenwerke [*Eisenach Motor Works*] [*BMW Plants*] [*Formerly,*]   (EG)

EMWP ..... Esperantist Movement for World Peace [*See also MEM*] [*Tours, France*] (EAIO)
EMWU ...... European Mine Workers Union
EMX .... El Maiten [*Argentina*] [*Airport symbol*] (OAG)
EMY .... Eidiki Merimna Yperilikon [*Special Care for the Aged*] (GC)
EMY .... Ethniki Meteorologiki Ypiresia [*National Meteorological Service*] [*Greek*] (GC)
emye .... Electromagnetic Unit (RU)
EMYE .... Enosis Mikropoliton Yfandikon Eidon [*Union of Woven Fabrics Merchants*] [*Greek*] (GC)
EMZ .... ECOWAS Monetary Zone
EMZ .... Estado Mayor de la Zafra [*Sugar Harvest Staff*] [*Cuba*] (LA)
EMZ .... Experimental Machine Plant (RU)
EN .... Eastern Airways [*British*] [*ICAO designator*] (ICDA)
EN .... Ecole Nationale [*French*]
EN .... Ecole Normale [*French*]
En .... Eileanan [*Islet or Islets*] [*Gaelic*] (NAU)
EN .... Einsatzstahl mit Nickel [*Casehardened Steel with Nickel*] [*German*] (GCA)
EN .... Ejercito Nacional [*National Army*] [*El Salvador*] (LA)
EN .... Elpidoforoi Neoi [*Young Hopefuls*] [*Greek*] (GC)
EN .... Emborikon Navtikon [*Merchant Marine*] (GC)
EN .... Emissora Nacional [*National Radio*] [*Portuguese*] (WER)
EN .... Enna [*Car registration plates*] [*Italy*]
en .... Era Noastra [*Our Era*] [*In the Year of Our Lord*] (RO)
EN .... Escola Naval [*Naval School*] [*Portuguese*]
EN .... Estrada Nacional [*National Highway*] [*Spanish*] (BARN)
EN .... Euromarkt-Nieuws [*Benelux*] (BAS)
EN .... Europa Nostra [*Historic preservation organization*] (EA)
en .... Ev Nelkul [*No Date Given*] (HU)
ENA .... Eastern News Agency [*Bangladesh*] (FEA)
ENA .... Ecole Nationale Agricole [*National School of Agriculture*] [*Algeria*] (AF)
ENA .... Ecole Nationale d'Administration [*National Administration School*] [*France*]
ENA .... Ecole Nationale d'Agriculture [*Morocco*]
ENA .... Ecole Normale d'Administration [*Morocco*]
ENA .... Ecole Normale d'Agriculture
ENA .... Emaillerie Nouvelle Afrique
ENA .... Emirates News Agency [*Arab*]
ENA .... Empresa Nacional de Arroz [*National Rice Company*] [*Bolivia*] (IMH)
ENA .... Encontro Nacional Anti-Fascista [*National Anti-Fascist Conference*] [*Portuguese*] (WER)
ENA .... Encuentro Nacional de los Argentinos [*National Assembly of Argentines*] (LA)
ENA .... Escuela Nacional de Aeronautica [*Argentina*]
ENA .... Escuela Nacional de Agricultura [*National Agricultural School*] [*Mexico*] (LA)
ENA .... Escuela Nacional de Agronomia [*Chapingo, Mexico*] (LAA)
ENA .... Espana, Direccion General de Aviacion Civil [*Spain*] [*ICAO designator*] (FAAC)
ENA .... Ethiopian News Agency (AF)
ENA .... Euro-National Australia Ltd.
ENA .... European Neuroscience Association (EAIO)
ENA .... European Neurosciences Association [*Bussum, Netherlands*] (SLS)
ENAA .... Ecole Nationale d'Agriculture d'Alger
ENAAN ..... Escuela Nacional de Agricultura "Antonio Narro" [*Mexico*] (DSCA)
ENAB .... Entreprise Nationale d'Approvisionnement en Bois et Derives [*State trading organization*] [*Algeria*] (EY)
ENABA ..... Empresa Nacional de Acopio y Beneficio del Algodon [*National Enterprise for Cotton Harvesting and Processing*] [*Cuba*] (LA)
ENABAS ... Empresa Nacional de Abastacimiento [*Nicaragua*]
ENABAS ... Empresa Nacional de Alimentos Basicos [*National Staple Foods Enterprise*] [*Nicaragua*] (LA)
ENABOL ... Empresa Naviera Boliviana [*Shipping company*] [*Bolivia*] (EY)
ENABUS ... Empresa Nacional de Buses [*National Bus Enterprise*] [*Nicaragua*] (LA)
ENAC .... Ecole Nationale de l'Aviation Civile
ENAC .... Empresa Nacional de Almacenamiento y Commercializacion [*National Storage and Marketing Enterprise*] [*Ecuador*] (LA)
ENAC .... Entreprise Nationale de Canalisation [*Ouargla, Algeria*] (MENA)
ENAC .... Entreprise Nationale de Confection
ENACAR ... Empresa Nacional de Carbon [*National Coal Enterprise*] [*Chile*] (LA)
ENACC ..... Escuela Nacional de Aviacion Civil Colombiana [*Colombia*] (COL)
ENACE ...... Empresa Nuclear Argentina de Centrales Electricas [*Argentine Nuclear Enterprise for Electrical Power Plants*] (LA)
ENACO ..... Empresa Nacional de la Coca [*National Coca Enterprise*] [*Peru*] (LA)
ENACOMO ... Empresa Nacional de Comercializacao, Mozambique

ENACOMO ... Empresa Nacional de Exportacao [*Mozambique*] (EY)
ENACT ...... Epson National Computer Training Programme [*Australia*]
ENAD .... Enosis Neon Agiou Dometiou [*Youth Union of Agios Dometios*] [*Cyprus*] (GC)
ENADE ..... Esfuerzo Nacional para el Desarollo [*National Development Effort*] [*Costa Rica*] (LA)
ENADEC ... Entreprise Nationale de Distribution & d'Exploitation Cinematographiques [*Algeria*]
ENADI ...... Empresa Nacional de Distribucion [*National Distribution Enterprise*] [*Chile*] (LA)
ENADIMSA ... Empresa Nacional Adaro de Investigaciones Mineras SA [*Mining Research National Enterprise*] [*Spain*] (WED)
ENAER ...... Empresa Nacional de Aeronautica [*National Aeronautic Enterprise*] [*Aircraft manufacturer Chile*]
ENAES ...... Ecole Nationale des Assistants Sociaux et Educateurs Specialises
ENAEX ...... Empresa Nacional de Explosivos [*Chile*] (EY)
ENAF .... Empresa Nacional de Fundiciones [*National Smelting Enterprise*] [*LaPaz, Bolivia*] (LA)
ENAFER-PERU ... Empresa Nacional de Ferrocarriles del Peru SA [*National Railway Enterprise of Peru*] (LA)
ENAFLA ... Entreprise Nationale d'Approvisionnement et de Regulation en Fruits et Legumes [*Ministry of Commerce*] [*Algiers, Algeria*] (MENA)
ENAFOR ... Entreprise Nationale de Forage [*Nationalized industry*] [*Algeria*] (EY)
ENAFRI .... Empresa Nacional de Frigorificos, SA [*Chile*] (LAA)
ENAFRUV ... Empresa Nacional de Acopio de Frutos Varios [*National Enterprise for Collection of Assorted Produce*] [*Cuba*] (LA)
ENAG .... Escuela Nacional de Agricultura y Ganaderia [*National School of Agriculture and Livestock*] [*Nicaragua*] (LA)
ENAGAS ... Empresa Nacional del Gas [*Spain*] (EY)
ENAGEO .. Entreprise Nationale de Geophysique [*Algiers, Algeria*] (MENA)
ENAJUC ... Entreprise Nationale des Jus et Conserves Alimentaires [*Nationalized industry*] [*Algeria*] (EY)
ENAL .... Alesund/Vigra [*Norway*] [*ICAO location identifier*] (ICLI)
ENAL .... Empresa Nicaraguense de Algodon [*Nicaraguan Cotton Company*] (GEA)
ENAL .... Ente Nazionale Assistenza Lavoratori [*Italian*]
ENAL .... Entreprise Nationale du Livre [*Book publisher and distributor*] [*Algiers, Algeria*] (MENA)
ENALUF ... Empresa Nacional de Luz y Fuerza [*National Light and Power Enterprise*] [*Nicaragua*] (LA)
ENAM .... Ecole Nationale d'Administration et de Magistrature [*National School of Administration and Magistrature*] [*Cameroon*] (AF)
ENAM .... Entreprise Nationale de Metallurgie
ENAMA .... Entreprise Nationale de Navigation Maritime et Aerienne [*National Sea and Air Transport Enterprise*] [*Algeria*] (AF)
ENAMI ..... Empresa Nacional de Mineria [*National Mining Enterprise*] [*Chile*] (LA)
ENAN .... Andoya [*Norway*] [*ICAO location identifier*] (ICLI)
ENANA ..... Empresa Nacional de Exploracao de Aeroportos e da Navegacao Aerea
ENAOQ ..... Entreprise Nationale d'Approvisionnement en Outillage et Produits de Quincaillerie Generale [*State trading organization*] [*Algeria*] (EY)
ENAP .... Ecole Nationale d'Administration Publique [*National Public Administration School*] [*Morocco*]
ENAP .... Empresa Nacional de Petroleo [*National Petroleum Enterprise*] [*Chile*] (LA)
ENAP .... Empresa Nacional de Puertos [*National Ports Enterprise*] [*Nicaragua*] (LA)
ENAP .... Entreprise Nationale des Peintures [*Algeria*]
ENAPAL ... Entreprise Nationale d'Approvisionnements en Produits Alimentaires [*National Enterprise for Supply of Food Products*] [*Algiers, Algeria*] (GEA)
ENAPC ...... Entreprise Nationale des Emballages en Papier et Cartons [*Nationalized industry*] [*Algeria*] (EY)
ENAPECHES ... Entreprise Nationale des Peches [*Fish importer and exporter*] [*Port D'Alger, Algeria*] (MENA)
ENAPESCA ... Empresa Nacional de Pesca [*National Fishing Enterprise*] [*Venezuela*] (LA)
ENAPHAR ... Entreprise Nationale des Produits Pharmaceutiques [*National Pharmaceutical Products Enterprise*] [*Cambodia*] (CL)
ENAPU ..... Empresa Nacional de Puertos [*National Ports Enterprise*] [*Peru*] (LA)
ENAREC ... Entreprise Nationale de Recuperation [*National Reclamation Firm*] [*Algeria*] (AF)
ENAS .... Ny Alesund (Svalbard) [*Norway*] [*ICAO location identifier*] (ICLI)
ENASA ...... Empresa de Navegacao da Amazonia Sociedade Anonima [*Amazon Shipping Company*] [*Brazil*] (LA)
ENASA ...... Empresa Nacional de Autocamiones SA [*National Truck Manufacturing Company*] [*Spain*]
ENASC ...... Entreprise Nationale d'Ascenseurs [*Nationalized industry*] [*Algeria*] (EY)

ENAT .... Alta [Norway] [ICAO location identifier] (ICLI)
ENAT .... Entreprise Abidjanaise de Terrassements
ENAT .... Entreprise Nationale d'Acconage, Transit, Consignation
ENATA ..... Empresa Nacional de Tabaco [National Tobacco Enterprise] [Peru] (LA)
ENATB...... Entreprise Nationale d'Ammeublement et de Transformation du Bois [Nationalized industry] [Algeria] (EY)
ENATCAR ... Empresa Nacional de Transportes por Carretera [Spain] (EY)
ENATEL ... Empresa Nacional de Telecomunicacoes
ENATHYD ... Entreprise Nationale de Travaux Hydrauliques [Algeria] (IMH)
ENATRA... Societe Nord Africaine de Travaux [Morocco]
ENAUTO.. Empresa Nacional Automotriz [National Automotive Enterprise] [Bolivia] (LA)
ENAVI...... Empresa Nacional de Avicultura [State enterprise for poultry farming] [Cape Verde]
ENAVINAS ... Empresa Nacional de Vinas [National Vineyards Enterprise] [Chile] (LA)
ENAZUCAR ... Empresa Nicaraguense del Azucar [Nicaraguan Sugar Enterprise] (LA)
ENB .... Eneabba [Australia] [Airport symbol] (OAG)
ENBA .... Escuela Nacional de Bellas Artes
ENBA .... Escuela Nacional de Biblioteconomia y Archivonomia
ENBC .... Eastern Nigeria Broadcasting Corporation
ENBD .... Bodo [Norway] [ICAO location identifier] (ICLI)
ENBJ......... Bjornoya [Norway] [ICAO location identifier] (ICLI)
ENBL .... Forde/Bringeland [Norway] [ICAO location identifier] (ICLI)
ENBM ...... Bomoen [Norway] [ICAO location identifier] (ICLI)
ENBN .... Bronnoysund/Bronnoy [Norway] [ICAO location identifier] (ICLI)
ENBO .... Bodo [Norway] [ICAO location identifier] (ICLI)
ENBR .... Bergen/Flesland [Norway] [ICAO location identifier] (ICLI)
ENBS........ Batsfjord [Norway] [ICAO location identifier] (ICLI)
ENBV .... Berlevag [Norway] [ICAO location identifier] (ICLI)
ENC .... Ecole Nationale de la Cooperation [Tunisia]
ENC .... Editora Nacional de Cuba [National Publishing House of Cuba] (LA)
ENC .... Empresa de Navegacion Caribe [Caribbean Navigation Enterprise] [Cuba] (LA)
ENC .... Empresa Nacional de Cabotaje [National Coastal Shipping Enterprise] [Cuba] (LA)
enc .... Encadernacao [Binding] [Publishing] [Portuguese]
enc .... Encadernado [Book Bindery] [Portuguese]
enc .... Encadrement [Border] [Publishing] [French]
enc .... Encuadernacion [Binding] [Publishing] [Spanish]
ENC .... Entreprise Nationale de Commerce [National Commerce Enterprise] [Algeria] (AF)
ENC .... Entreprise Nationale de Construction
ENC .... Escuela Nacional de Cuadros [National Cadres School] [Cuba] (LA)
ENC .... Nancy [France] [Airport symbol] (OAG)
ENCA .... Ecole Nationale des Cadres [National Cadres School] [Malagasy] (AF)
ENCA .... Empresa Nacional del Cafe [National Coffee Enterprise] [Nicaragua] (LA)
ENCA .... European Naval Communications Agency [NATO]
ENCA .... Oslo Caa [Norway] [ICAO location identifier] (ICLI)
encad .... Encadernacao [Binding] [Publishing] [Portuguese]
encadr........ Encadrement [Border] [Publishing] [French]
encadrem.... Encadrement [Border] [Publishing] [French]
encadt........ Encadrement [Border] [Publishing] [French]
ENCAFE ... Empresa Nacional do Cafe [National Coffee Enterprise] [Angola] (AF)
ENCAFE ... Empresa Nicaraguense del Cafe [Nicaraguan Coffee Enterprise] (LA)
encaj.......... Encaje [Inlay] [Publishing] [Spanish]
ENCAR ..... Empresa Nacional de Carbon [National Coal Company] [Chile] (LA)
ENCAR ..... Empresa Nicaraguense de la Carne [Nicaraguan Meat Enterprise] (LA)
encart .... Encartage [Insertion] [Publishing] [French]
ENCAT...... Ente Nazionale Consulenza Assistenza Tecnica
ENCATEX ... Empresa Nacional de Calcado e Texteis [Mozambique] (EY)
ENCB .... Escuela Nacional de Ciencias Biologicas [National School of Biological Sciences] [Mexico] (MSC)
ENCBI...... Entreprise Nationale de Construction de Batiments Industriels
ENCC .... Ente Nazionale Cellulosa e Carta [Italy] (PDAA)
ENCC .... Entreprise Nationale de Charpente et de Chaudronnerie [National Construction & Boilermaking Company] [Algeria]
ENCDP...... Entreprise Nationale de Commercialisation et de Distribution des Produits Petroliers [Nationalized industry] [Algeria] (EY)
ENCEL...... Empresa Nacional de Construcoes Electricas [Angola] (EY)
ENCG .... Entreprise Nationale des Corps Gras [Nationalized industry] [Algeria] (EY)

ENCI .... Empresa Nacional de Comercializacion e Insumos [National Enterprise for the Marketing of Basic Food Products] [Peru] (LA)
Encia .... Eminencia [Eminence] [Spanish]
ENCIAWPRC ... Egyptian National Committee of the International Association on Water Pollution Research and Control (EAIO)
ENCIME... Empresa Nacional de Cimento [Angola] (EY)
ENCN .... Kristiansand/Kjevik [Norway] [ICAO location identifier] (ICLI)
ENCO....... Entreprises Commerciales et Industrielles
ENCOBE... Entreprise Commerciale de Betail [Cattle Trading Enterprise] [Guinea] (AF)
ENCODIPA ... Empresa Nacional de Compra e Distribuicao dos Produtos Agricolas [National Company for Purchase and Distribution of Agricultural Products] [Angola] (EY)
ENCOFRAN ... Entreprise de Construction de Franceville
encol.......... Encolure [Collar Size] [Knitting] [French]
ENCOMA ... Empresa Consolidada de Construccion de Maquinarias [Machine Construction Consolidated Enterprise] [Cuba] (LA)
ENCOOP .. Entente Cooperative Senegalaise
ENCORE... Enrichment of Nutrients on Coral Reefs Experiment [Australia]
ENCOTEL ... Empresa Nacional de Correos y Telegrafos [National Mail and Telegraph Enterprise] [Buenos Aires, Argentina] (LA)
ENCP........ European Naval Communications Plan [NATO] (NATG)
ENCR .... Ecoles Nationales des Cadets de la Revolution [Algeria]
encuad .... Encuadernacion [Binding] [Publishing] [Spanish]
encuader..... Encuadernacion [Binding] [Publishing] [Spanish]
end............. Endast [Only] [Sweden]
end............. Endommage [Damaged] [French]
end............. Endroit [Right Side] [Knitting] [French]
End............. Endustri [Industry] (TU)
END........... Entente Nationale Democratique [National Democratic Entente] [Monaco] [Political party] (PPE)
END........... Equipes Notre-Dame [Teams of Our Lady - TOOL] [Paris, France] (EAIO)
END........... European Nuclear Disarmament [British]
ENDA....... Ecole Nationale d'Administration [Zaire]
ENDA....... ENDA [Envoroment and Development] Caribe [An association] (EAIO)
ENDASA... Empresa Nacional del Aluminio, Sociedad Anonima [National Aluminum Enterprise, Incorporated] [Spanish] (WER)
ENDA-TM ... Environnement et Developpement du Tiers Monde [Environment and Development of the Third World] (EAIO)
ENDC....... Eastern Nigeria Development Corporation (AF)
ENDC....... Eighteen-Nation Disarmament Committee [or Conference] [Later, CCD Convened March 14, 1962; actually attended by 17 nations, with France absent]
ENDE .... Empresa Nacional de Electricidad SA [State electricity company] [Bolivia] (EY)
ENDE .... Empresas Nacionales de Energia [Argentina]
ENDE .... Encuentro Nacional de Desarrollo [Colorado]
ENDE .... Escuela Nacional de Direccion de la Economia [National School of Economic Management] [Cuba] (LA)
ENDECJA ... Stronnictwo Narodowej Demokracji [Nationalist Democratic Party] [Poland] (PPE)
endem........ Endemic, Endemism (RU)
ENDES...... Instituto Cultural Ecuatoriano Frances de Desarrollo de Industrias [Ecuadorean-French Cultural Institute of Development Industries] (LAA)
ENDESA... Empresa Nacional de Electricidad, Sociedad Anonima [National Electric Power Enterprise, Incorporated] [Chile] (WER)
ENDI .... Dagali [Norway] [ICAO location identifier] (ICLI)
ENDIAMA ... Empresa Nacional de Diamantes de Angola [State diamond enterprise] [Luanda, Angola]
ENDISTE ... Empresa Nacional de Distribucion y Servicio de Tractores y Equipos [National Enterprise for Distribution and Service of Tractors and Equipment] [Cuba] (LA)
endl .... Endlich [Finite] [German] (GCA)
ENDLF...... Eelam National Democratic Liberation Front [Sri Lanka] [Political party] (EY)
ENDMC .... Entreprise Nationale de Developpement des Materiaux de Construction [Cement supply and construction company] [Algeria]
ENDMC .... Entreprise Nationale de Developpement et de Recherche Industriels des Materiaux de Construction [Algeria] (EY)
ENDOC..... Environmental Information and Documentation Centres Database [Commission of the European Communities] [Information service or system] (CRD)
endokr........ Endocrinic, Endocrinology (RU)
Endprod ..... Endprodukt [Final Product] [German] (GCA)
endr .... Endroit [Right Side] [Knitting] [French]
ENDS .... Empresa Nacional de Semillas [Chile] (DSCA)
ENDS .... European Nuclear Documentation System [EURATOM] [Luxembourg]
End tel........ Endereco Telegrafico [Telegraphic Address] [Portuguese]

ENDU....... Bardufoss [*Norway*] [*ICAO location identifier*]   (ICLI)
ENE .... Elements Non Endivisionnes [*Military*] [*French*]   (MTD)
ENE .... Empresa Nacional de Electricidade [*Angola*]   (EY)
ENE .... Ende [*Indonesia*] [*Airport symbol*]   (OAG)
ene............. Enero [*January*] [*Spanish*]
ENE .... Entreprise Nationale d'Engineering [*Skikda, Algeria*]   (MENA)
ENE .... Epitropi Nomothetikis Exousiodotiseos [*Legislative Authorization Committee*] [*Greek*]   (GC)
ENE .... Escuela Nacional de Economia [*National School of Economics*] [*Mexico*]   (LA)
ENE .... Escuela Nacional de Enfermeria [*National School of Nursing*] [*Nicaragua*]   (LA)
ENE .... Estenordeste [*East Northeast*] [*Spanish*]
ENE .... Est Nord Est [*East Northeast*] [*French*]   (MTD)
ENE .... Etaireia Neon Epistimonon [*Society of Young Professionals*] [*Greek*]   (GC)
ENE .... Ethniki Neolaia Elladas [*Greek National Youth*] [*Greek*]   (GC)
ENEA .... Comitato Nazionale per la Ricerca e per lo Sviluppo dell'Energia Nucleare e delle Engergie Alternative [*National Committee for Research and Development Nuclear and Alternative Energies*] [*Italy*]   (PDAA)
ENEA .... Ecole Nationale d'Economie Appliquee [*National Applied Economics School*] [*Senegal*]   (AF)
ENEA .... Ente Nazionale per l'Energia Atomica [*Italy*]   (EY)
ENEA .... European Nuclear Energy Agency   (DS)
ENECA..... United Nations Economic Commission for Africa
ENECEA... Entreprise Nouvelle d'Etude de Constructions Eau et Assainissement
ENECOFA... Ecole Normale d'Enseignement Commercial et Familial
ENEDIM... Entreprise Nationale de Developpement des Industries Manufacturieres [*Algeria*]   (EY)
ENEE .... Empresa Nacional de Energia Electrica [*National Electric Power Enterprise*]
ENEF........ Ecole Nationale des Eaux et Forets [*French*]   (ASF)
ENEFES.... Ecole Nationale de Formation d'Educateurs Specialises [*National School for the Training of Specialized Teachers*] [*Algeria*]   (AF)
ENEK .... Ekofisk [*Norway*] [*ICAO location identifier*]   (ICLI)
ENEK .... Enosi Neon Epistimonon Kyprou [*Young Professionals Union of Cyprus*] [*Cyprus*]   (GC)
ENEK .... Enosis Elevtherokoinoniston [*Union of Free Socialists*] [*Greek*]   (GC)
ENEL........ Elliniki Navtiliaki Epitropi Londinou [*Greek Maritime Committee of London*]   (GC)
ENEL........ Ente Nazionale per l'Energia Elettrica [*National Electric Power Agency*] [*Rome, Italy*]   (WER)
ENEL........ Entreprise Nationale des Industries Electrotechniques [*Manufacturer of electrotechnical products*] [*Algeria*]
ENELCAM... Energie Electrique du Cameroun [*Cameroon Electric Power*]   (AF)
ENELCI .... Energie Electrique de Cote-D'Ivoire [*Ivory Coast Electric Power Company*]
ENELCO... Energie Electrique du Congo
ENELEC ... Entreprises Electriques et Industrielles
ENEMA .... Etablissement National pour l'Exploitation Meteorologique et Aeronautique [*Meteorological and Aeronautical Development Office*] [*Algiers, Algeria*]
ENEP........ Enterprise Nationale d'Engineering Petrolier [*Nationalized industry*] [*Algeria*]   (EY)
ENEP........ Etablissement National d'Edition et de Presse
ENEPE...... Etablissement National pour l'Education et la Promotion de l'Enfance [*Algeria*]
ENER .... Energy Directory [*Database*] [*Australia*]
ENERCA... Energie Centrafricaine
energ .... Power Engineering   (RU)
ENERGAS ... Empresa Nacional de Gas [*National Gas Enterprise*] [*Spain*]   (PDAA)
Energeprojekt ... Biuro Projektow Energetycznych [*Office for Power Plans*]   (POL)
Energochermet ... Trust of the Glavmetallurgmontazh of the Ministry of Construction, RSFSR   (RU)
Energoizdat ... Scientific and Technical Publishing House of Power Engineering Literature   (RU)
Energokhidroproekt ... Economic Enterprise for Designing Hydraulic Power Plant Structures   (BU)
Energokhidrostroy ... Economic Enterprise for Hydraulic Power Plant Construction   (BU)
Energolegprom ... State All-Union Trust of the Power System Management of the Ministry of Light Industry, USSR   (RU)
Energoles ... State All-Union Trust for Logging, Woodworking, and Utility Pole Impregnation of the Glavenergostroyprom   (RU)
Energomontazh ... Economic Enterprise for Electric Wiring Installations   (BU)
Energonadzor ... State Inspection for Industrial Power Engineering and for Power Engineering Supervision   (RU)
Energoobedinenie ... Electric Power Production Economic Trust   (BU)
energoprom ... Power Engineering Industry   (RU)

Energosanmontazh ... Trust of the Administration of Capital Construction and Equipment of the Mosoblsovnarkhoz   (RU)
Energoset'proyekt ... All-Union State Planning, Surveying, and Scientific Research Institute of Power Systems and Electric Power Networks   (RU)
Energostroy ... Economic Enterprise for Power Plant Construction   (BU)
Energostroykomplektatsiya ... Technical Office of the Glavenergostroyprom of the Ministry of Construction of Electric Power Plants, USSR   (RU)
Energostroykonstruktsiya ... Trust of the Glavenergostroyprom of the Ministry of Construction of Electric Power Plants, USSR   (RU)
Energostroyzapchast' ... Technical Office of the Glavenergostroymekhanizatsiya of the Ministry of Construction of Electric Power Plants, USSR   (RU)
Energotekhnaladka ... Establishment for the Organization and Rationalization of Power System Management, the Introduction of Means of Automation, Adjustment, Planning, and Repair of Power Engineering Equipment of the Mosoblsovnarkhoz   (RU)
Energozapchast' ... Republic Trust for Supplying Spare Parts to Electric Power Plants and Networks of the Administration of the Municipal Electric Power Systems   (RU)
ENERIC .... Entreprise Nationale d'Etudes et de Realisations des Infrastructures Commerciales [*Algeria*]   (IMH)
Enerji-Is..... Turkiye Enerji Isci Sendikalari Federasyonu [*Energy workers union*] [*Turkey*]   (MENA)
ENES........ European and Near East Section [*Friends World Committee for Consultation*] [*Luxembourg*]
ENESA...... Empresa Nacional de Electricidad, Sociedad Anonima [*Spanish state electricity authority*]
ENESA...... Entreprise Nationale d'Exploitation des Services Aeriens [*National Office of Aerial Development and Services*] [*Algeria*]
ENET .... Ecole Nationale d'Etudes des Telecommunications [*National School for Telecommunications Studies*] [*Algeria*]   (AF)
ENET .... Entreprise Nationale d'Etudes Touristiques [*Algeria*]   (IMH)
ENEV .... Evenes [*Norway*] [*ICAO location identifier*]   (ICLI)
ENEWD ... European Network for East-West Dialogue   (EA)
ENEX-ASIA ... International Electrical and Electronic Engineering Exhibition [*Interfama Pte. Ltd.*]
enf .... Enfermeiro [*Nurse, Orderly*] [*Portuguese*]
ENF .... Enformasyo Ajansi [*Information Agency*] [*Turkish Cypriot*]   (TU)
ENF .... Escola Nacional de Florestas [*Brazil*]   (DSCA)
ENFB........ Oslo/Fornebu [*Norway*] [*ICAO location identifier*]   (ICLI)
ENFD .... Forde [*Norway*] [*ICAO location identifier*]   (ICLI)
ENFE........ Empresa Nacional de Ferrocarriles [*National Railway Enterprise*] [*La Paz, Bolivia*]   (LA)
ENFERSA ... Empresa Nacional de Fertilizantes, Sociedad Anonima [*National Fertilizer Company*] [*Spanish*]   (ARC)
ENFG .... Fagernes/Leirin [*Norway*] [*ICAO location identifier*]   (ICLI)
ENFH....... Entreprise Nationale de Forage Hydraulique [*Algeria*]
ENFI......... Beijing Central Engineering and Research Institute for Nonferrous Metallurgical Industries [*China*] [*Research center*]   (IRC)
ENFL........ Floro [*Norway*] [*ICAO location identifier*]   (ICLI)
ENFO........ Forus [*Norway*] [*ICAO location identifier*]   (ICLI)
ENFOM... Ecole Nationale de la France d'Outre-Mer
ENFPPPM ... Ecole Nationale de Formation et de Perfectionnement de Patrons de Peche et de Mecaniciens [*Algeria*]   (ASF)
ENFR........ Frigg [*Norway*] [*ICAO location identifier*]   (ICLI)
ENFREMA ... Empresa Nacional de Fabricacion y Repuestos de Maquinaria Agricola [*National Enterprise for the Manufacture of Agricultural Equipment and Spare Parts*] [*Chile*]   (LA)
ENFS........ Ecole Nationale de Formation de Sous-Officiers [*National Non-Commissioned Officers Training School*] [*Algeria*]   (AF)
ENFY........ Fyresdal [*Norway*] [*ICAO location identifier*]   (ICLI)
ENFZ........ Fritzoe [*Norway*] [*ICAO location identifier*]   (ICLI)
ENG.......... Electroneurogram   (RU)
eng............. Engedely [*Permission*] [*Hungary*]
eng............. Engedelyezett [*Authorized*] [*Hungary*]
Eng........... Engeland [*England*] [*Afrikaans*]
Eng........... Engels [*English*] [*Afrikaans*]
Eng........... Engenharia [*Engineering*] [*Portuguese*]
Eng........... Engineer   (PWGL)
Eng........... Engineering   (EECI)
eng............. Englisch [*English*] [*German*]
eng............. Ingenierie [*French*]   (TPFD)
ENGA....... Entreprise Generale Abidjanaise
ENGA....... Entreprise Generale Africaine
ENGACO.. Entreprises Gabonaises de Construction
ENGaM ... Enterprise Gabonaise de Montage
ENGCB .... Entreprise Nationale de Genie Civil et Batiments [*Algiers, Algeria*]   (MENA)
ENGECA... Entrepot General du Cameroun
ENGESA... Engenheiros Especializados Sociedade Anonima [*Specialized Engineers, Incorporated*] [*Brazil*]   (LA)

ENGETEC ... Engenharia Tecnica Ltda. [*Technical Engineering Ltd.*] [*Brazil*] (LA)

ENGI .... Entreprise Nationale des Gaz Industriels [*Nationalized industry*] [*Algeria*] (EY)

ENGINE ... Australian Engineering Database [*Information service or system*] (IID)

engl .... Englantia [*or Englanniksi*] [*Finland*]

engl .... Englantilainen [*English*] [*Finland*]

engl .... Englisch [*English*] [*German*]

englj .... Englanninjalka [*Finland*]

ENGM ..... Oslo/Gardermoen [*Norway*] [*ICAO location identifier*] (ICLI)

ENGN .... Grimsmoen [*Norway*] [*ICAO location identifier*] (ICLI)

engo .... Engenheiro [*Engineer*] [*Portuguese*]

Eng P .... Englisches Patent [*British Patent*] [*German*] (GCA)

ENGREF ... Ecole Nationale du Genie Rural des Eaux et des Forets [*National College of Agricultural and Forestry Engineering and Water Management*] [*French*] (ARC)

Eng S .... Engerem Sinne [*A Narrower Sense*] [*German*] (GCA)

ENGTP ...... Entreprise Nationale des Grands Travaux Petroliers [*Oil exploration and development firm*] [*Reghaia, Algeria*] (MENA)

ENH .... Elektrik Nakliyat Hatti [*Electric Power Transmission Line*] (TU)

ENH .... Enshi [*China*] [*Airport symbol*] (OAG)

ENHA .... Hamar/Stafsberg [*Norway*] [*ICAO location identifier*] (ICLI)

ENHB .... Heggebakken [*Norway*] [*ICAO location identifier*] (ICLI)

ENHD .... Haugesund/Karmoy [*Norway*] [*ICAO location identifier*] (ICLI)

ENHER ..... Empresa Nacional Hidroelectrica de Ribagorza [*Ribagorza National Hydroelectric Enterprise*] [*Spanish*] (WER)

ENHF .... Hammerfest [*Norway*] [*ICAO location identifier*] (ICLI)

ENHK .... Hasvik [*Norway*] [*ICAO location identifier*] (ICLI)

ENHM ..... Empresa Nacional de Hidrocarbonetos de Mocambique (EY)

ENHN ...... Harnmoen [*Norway*] [*ICAO location identifier*] (ICLI)

ENHO ...... Hopen [*Norway*] [*ICAO location identifier*] (ICLI)

ENHS .... European Natural Hygiene Society (EAIO)

ENHS .... Hokksund [*Norway*] [*ICAO location identifier*] (ICLI)

ENHV .... Honningsvag/Valan [*Norway*] [*ICAO location identifier*] (ICLI)

ENI .... Ecole Nationale d'Informatique [*National School of Information*] [*French*] (ADPT)

ENI .... Ecole Nationale d'Ingenieurs [*French*]

ENI .... Ecole Normale d'Infirmiers

ENI .... Ecole Normale d'Instituteurs [*French*]

ENI .... Electrische Nijverheids - Installaties NV [*Belgium*] (WND)

ENI .... Electro-Navale et Industrielle SA [*Belgium*] (WED)

ENI .... Ente Nazionale Idrocarburi [*National Hydrocarbons Agency*] [*Rome, Italy*] (WER)

ENI .... Ethiopian Nutrition Institute [*Addis Ababa*] [*Research center*]

ENIA .... Ecole des Ingenieurs Agricoles [*Agricultural Engineers School*] [*Morocco*] (AF)

ENIA .... Empresa Nicaraguense de Insumos Agropecuarios [*Nicaraguan Enterprise for Agricultural-Livestock Investments*] (LA)

ENIAL .... Entreprise Nationale de Developpement et de Coordination des Industries Alimentaires [*Nationalized industry*] [*Algeria*] (EY)

ENIB .... Entreprise Nationale de l'Industrie du Bois [*Algeria*]

ENICA .... Ecole Nationale d'Ingenieurs de Constructions Aeronautiques [*French*]

ENICAB .... Empresa Nicaraguense de Cabotaje [*Nicaraguan Enterprise for Coastal Shipping*] (LA)

ENICAB .... Entreprise Nationale des Industries du Cable [*Nationalized industry*] [*Algeria*] (EY)

ENICAS .... Ecole Nationale des Infirmiers Certifies et de l'Action Sociale

ENIEM ...... Entreprise Nationale des Industries de l'Electro-Menager [*Nationalized industry*] [*Algeria*] (EY)

ENIEPSA ... Empresa Nacional de Investigation y Explotacion de Petroleo SA

ENIG .... Enrolled Nurse Interest Group [*Australia*]

enigsz .... Enigszins [*A Little*] [*Netherlands*]

ENIIZiM ... Estonian Scientific Research Institute of Agriculture and Reclamation (RU)

ENIKMASh ... Experimental Scientific Research Institute of Forging-and-Pressing Machinery (RU)

ENIM .... Ecole Nationale de l'Industrie Minerale

ENIM .... Entreprise Nationale de l'Industrie Metallique [*Algeria*]

enimm .... Enimmakseen [*Mostly*] [*Finland*]

ENIMPORT ... Empresa Nicaraguense de Importaciones [*Nicaraguan Imports Enterprise*] (LA)

ENIMS ...... Experimental Scientific Research Institute of Metal-Cutting Machine Tools (RU)

ENIN .... Power Engineering Institute Imeni G. M. Krzhizhanovskiy (RU)

ENIOS .... Comitato Nazionale Italiana per l'Organizzazione Scientifica [*Italian*] (SLS)

ENIP .... Entreprise Nationale de l'Industrie de Prefabrication [*Algeria*]

ENIP .... Estonian National Independence Party [*Political party*]

ENIPP .... Eksperimental'nyy i Nauchno Issledovatel'skiy Institut Podshipnikovoy Promyshlennosti [*Experimental and Scientific Research Institute of the Bearing Institute*] [*Former USSR*] (PDAA)

ENIPREX ... Empresa Nicaraguense de Exportaciones [*Nicaraguan Exports Enterprise*] (LA)

ENIR .... Entreprise Nationale d'Intervention et de Renovation [*Algeria*] (IMH)

ENIR .... Escuela National de Instruccion Revolucionaria [*National Revolutionary Training School*] [*Cuba*] (LA)

ENIT .... Ecole Nationale des Ingenieurs Tunisiens

ENIT .... Ecole Nationale d'Ingenieurs de Tarbes [*National College of Engineers at Tarbes*] [*France*] (ERC)

ENIT .... Ente Nazionale Italiano per il Turismo [*Italian National Tourist Board*]

ENITA ...... Ecole Nationale des Ingenieurs des Travaux Agricoles de Bordeaux [*National College of Agricultural Engineering at Bordeaux*] [*French*] (ARC)

ENITA .... Ecole Nationale des Ingenieurs et de Techniciens de Bordj-El-Bahri

ENITEF ..... Ecole Nationale des Ingenieurs des Travaux des Eaux et Forets [*National College of Water and Forestry Engineering*] [*French*] (ARC)

ENITRA .... Entreprise Nationale des Travaux [*Algeria*]

ENJ .... Nort Jet [*Spain*] [*ICAO designator*] (FAAC)

ENJA .... Jan Mayen [*Norway*] [*ICAO location identifier*] (ICLI)

ENJB .... Jarlsberg [*Norway*] [*ICAO location identifier*] (ICLI)

ENJC .... Ecole Normale Jacques Cartier

ENJEP .... Ecole Nationale de la Jeunesse et de l'Education Populaire [*National School of Youth and People's Education*] [*Malagasy*] (AF)

enk .... Enkelt [*Plain, Single*] [*Danish/Norwegian*]

ENKA .... Kautokeino [*Norway*] [*ICAO location identifier*] (ICLI)

ENKB .... Kristiansund/Kvernberget [*Norway*] [*ICAO location identifier*] (ICLI)

ENKJ .... Kjeller [*Norway*] [*ICAO location identifier*] (ICLI)

ENKL .... Enklities [*Enclitic*] [*Afrikaans*]

ENKR .... Kirkenes/Hoybuktmoen [*Norway*] [*ICAO location identifier*] (ICLI)

ENL .... Ejercito Nacional de Liberacion [*National Liberation Army*] [*Nicaragua*] (PD)

enl .... Enligt [*According To*] [*Sweden*]

ENLF .... Eelam National Liberation Front [*Sri Lanka*]

ENLF .... Ethiopian National Liberation Front

ENLI .... Lista [*Norway*] [*ICAO location identifier*] (ICLI)

ENLK .... Leknes [*Norway*] [*ICAO location identifier*] (ICLI)

ENLO .... Ecole Nationale des Langues Orientales

ENLOV .... Ecole Nationale des Langues Orientales Vivantes

ENM .... Electric Oil Heater (RU)

ENM .... Empresa de Navegacion Mambisa [*Mambisa Navigation Enterprise*] [*Cuba*] (LA)

ENM .... Empresa Nuclear de Mendoza [*Mendoza Nuclear Enterprise*] [*Argentina*] (LA)

ENM .... Escuela Nacional de Maestros [*National Teachers College*] [*Mexico*] (LA)

ENM .... Evropaiki Nomismatiki Monas [*European Monetary Unit*] (GC)

ENMGP .... Entreprise Nationale de Menuiserie Generale & de Prefabrication [*Wood products supplier*] [*Algeria*]

ENMH ...... Mehamn [*Norway*] [*ICAO location identifier*] (ICLI)

ENMI ...... Olso [*Norway*] [*ICAO location identifier*] (ICLI)

ENMISA ... Empresa Nacional Mineral del Sahara [*Corporation owned by the Spanish government*] [*Fosfatos de Bucraa*] [*Later,*]

ENMIU ..... Empresa Nacional de Mantenimiento de Inmuebles Urbanos [*National Enterprise for Maintenance of Urban Real Estate*] [*Cuba*] (LA)

ENML .... Molde/Aro [*Norway*] [*ICAO location identifier*] (ICLI)

ENMS .... European Nuclear Medical Society (EAIO)

ENMS .... Mosjoen/Kjaerstad [*Norway*] [*ICAO location identifier*] (ICLI)

ENNA .... Banak [*Norway*] [*ICAO location identifier*] (ICLI)

ENNA .... Ecole Normale Nationale d'Apprentissage [*France*] (FLAF)

ENNET ...... Ecole Normale d'Enseignement Technique de Tananarive

ENNICO .... Entreprise Nigerienne de Confiserie

ENNK .... Narvik/Framnes [*Norway*] [*ICAO location identifier*] (ICLI)

ENNM .... Namsos [*Norway*] [*ICAO location identifier*] (ICLI)

ENNO ...... Notodden [*Norway*] [*ICAO location identifier*] (ICLI)

ENO .... Electric Pump Irrigation (RU)

ENO .... Elektrarne Novaky [*Electric Power Plants Novaky*] (CZ)

eno .... Enero [*January*] [*Spanish*]

ENOB .... Bodo Oceanic [*Norway*] [*ICAO location identifier*] (ICLI)

ENOC .... Association of the European National Olympic Committees [*See also ACNOE*] [*Brussels, Belgium*] (EAIO)

ENODC ..... Egyptian National Oceanographic Data Center (MSC)

ENOES ...... Ecole Nouvelle d'Organisation Economique et Sociale [*France*] (DSCA)

ENOF .... Entreprise Nationale de Produits Miniers Non-Ferreux et des Substances Utiles [*Nationalized industry*] [*Algeria*] (EY)

ENOF .... Entreprise Nationale des Non-Ferreux [*National Nonferrous Company*] [*Algeria*]

ENOF .... United People's Liberation Front   (BU)

ENOK .... Ekonomiese Ontwikkelingskorporasie [*First National Development Corporation*] [*Namibia*]   (AF)

Enol .... Enologia [*Oenology*] [*Portuguese*]

ENOL .... Orland [*Norway*] [*ICAO location identifier*]   (ICLI)

ENOPO ...... United People's Social and Political Organization   (BU)

ENOPOOF ... United People's Social and Political Organization of the Fatherland Front   (BU)

ENOS .... Ecole Nouvelle d'Organisation Economique et Sociale [*France*]   (FLAF)

ENOS .... Oslo [*Norway*] [*ICAO location identifier*]   (ICLI)

ENOV .... Orsta-Volda/Hovden [*Norway*] [*ICAO location identifier*]   (ICLI)

ENOWD .... Europaeisches Netzwerk fuer den Ost-West-Dialog [*European Network for East-West Dialogue - ENEWD*]   (EAIO)

ENP .... Empresa Nacional Portuaria [*National Port Enterprise*] [*Honduras*]   (LA)

ENP .... Equivalent Neutral Density   (RU)

ENP .... Escuela Nacional de Policia [*National Police School*] [*Costa Rica*]   (LA)

ENP .... European Neuroscience Programme [*Defunct*] [*France*]   (EAIO)

ENPA .... Ecole Normale des Professeurs Adjoints [*North African*]

ENPA .... Enrolled Nurse Professional Association [*Australia*]

ENPAS ...... Ente Nazionale di Previdenza e Assistenza per i Dipendenti Statali [*National Board of Social Security and Welfare for Civil Servants*] [*Italian*]   (WER)

ENPASA ... Empresa Nacional de Petroleos de Aragon SA

ENPC .... Ecole Nationale des Ponts et Chaussees [*Bridges and Roads National College*] [*Ministere de l'Environnement et du Cadre de Vie*] [*Research center*] [*France*]   (EAS)

ENPC .... Ecole Nationale des Ponts et Chaussees [*Graduate School of International Business*] [*France*]

ENPC .... Entreprise Nationale des Plastiques et de Caoutchouc [*Rubber and plastics producer*] [*Setif, Algeria*]   (MENA)

ENPE .... Entreprise Nationale de Petrochimie et d'Engrais [*Petrochemical and fertilizer firm*] [*Algeria*]   (MENA)

ENPEC ...... Entreprise Nationale des Produits de l'Electrochimie [*Algeria*]

ENPENSA ... Empresa Nacional de Petroleos de Navarra SA

ENPETROL ... Empresa Nacional del Petroleo SA

ENPI .... Ente Nazionale di Prevenire Infortuni [*National Agency for the Prevention of Accidents*] [*Italian*]   (WER)

ENPMH .... Entreprise Nationale de Production des Materiels Hydrauliques [*Algeria*]

ENPPI .... Engineering for the Petroleum and Process Industries [*Petroleum refinery*] [*Egypt*]

ENPROVIT ... Empresa Nacional de Productos Vitales [*National Enterprise for Vital Products*] [*Ecuador*]   (LA)

ENPS .... Ecole Nationale Promotion Sociale

ENPT .... Ecole Nationale des Postes et Telecommunications [*National Posts and Telecommunications School*] [*Zaire*]   (AF)

ENPVP ...... L'Entreprise Nationale Production Vehicules Particuliers [*National Special Vehicle Production Company*] [*France*]

ENR .... Ensor Air [*Czechoslovakia*] [*ICAO designator*]   (FAAC)

ENR .... Ente Nazionale Risi [*Italy*]   (DSCA)

ENR .... Uniform Norms and Rates   (BU)

ENRA .... Mo I Rana/Rossvoll [*Norway*] [*ICAO location identifier*]   (ICLI)

ENRAD-PERU ... Empresa Nacional de Radiodifusion del Peru [*National Radio Broadcasting Enterprise of Peru*]   (LA)

ENRB .... Entreprise Nationale de Realisation de Barrages [*National Barrages Manufacturing Company*] [*Algeria*]

ENRC .... European Nuclear Research Centre   (NUCP)

ENRDP ..... Entreprise Nationale de Raffinage et de Distribution des Produits Petroliers [*Refiner and distributor of petroleum products*] [*Algiers, Algeria*]   (MENA)

ENRESA ... Empresa Nacional de Residuos, SA [*Spain*]   (EY)

ENRI .... Electronic Navigation Research Institute [*Ministry of Transport*] [*Tokyo, Japan*] [*Research center*]   (ERC)

ENRM .... Rorvik/Ryum [*Norway*] [*ICAO location identifier*]   (ICLI)

ENRO .... Roros [*Norway*] [*ICAO location identifier*]   (ICLI)

ENROK .... Maquinaria y Envases Rock Ltda. [*Colombia*]   (COL)

ENRS .... Rost [*Norway*] [*ICAO location identifier*]   (ICLI)

ENRY .... Rygge [*Norway*] [*ICAO location identifier*]   (ICLI)

ENS .... Ecole Nationale de Secretariat

ENS .... Ecole Normale Superieure [*French teacher-training institution*]   (WER)

ENS .... Education News Service [*Australia*]

ENS .... Employer Nomination Scheme [*Australia*]

ENS .... Enosi Neon Sosialiston [*Union of Young Socialists*] [*Greek*]   (GC)

ens .... Ensartet [*Uniform*] [*Danish/Norwegian*]

ENS .... Enschede [*Netherlands*] [*Airport symbol*]   (OAG)

Ens .... Enseada [*Bay, Creek*] [*Portuguese*]   (NAU)

ens .... Ensemble [*Group*] [*French*]

Ens .... Ensenada [*Bay, Creek*] [*Spanish*]   (NAU)

ens .... Ensimmainen [*Finland*]

ens .... Ensovoorts [*And So Forth*] [*Afrikaans*]

Ens .... Enstitusu [*Institute*]   (TU)

ENS .... Europaeische Kernenergie-Gesellschaft [*European Nuclear Society - ENS*]   (EAIO)

ENS .... European Neurological Society [*Switzerland*]

ENS .... European Nuclear Society [*Switzerland*]   (SLS)

ENSA .... Ecole Nationale de Ski et d'Alpinisme

ENSA .... Ecole Nationale Superieure de l'Aeronautique [*French*]

ENSA .... Empresa Nacional de Seguros [*National Insurance Company*] [*Angola*]   (AF)

ENSA .... Endocrine Nurses' Society of Australia

ENSA .... Equipos Nucleares [*Nuclear energy*] [*Spanish*]   (NRCH)

ENSAC ..... Ecole Normale Superieure de l'Afrique Centrale [*Higher Teachers Training School of Central Africa*] [*Congo*]   (AF)

ENSAE ..... Ecole Nationale de la Statistique Appliquee a l'Economie [*National School for Statistics Applied to Economics*] [*French*]   (WER)

ENSAe ...... Ecole Nationale Superieure de l'Aeronautique [*France*]

ENSAIA .... Ecole Nationale Superieure d'Agronomie et des Industries Alimentaires [*Agronomy and Food Industries National College*] [*French*]   (ARC)

ENSAIS .... Ecole Nationale Superieure des Arts et Industrie de Strasbourg [*France*]   (PDAA)

ENSAL ...... Empresa Nacional de Salinas [*National Salt Co.*] [*Venezuela*]   (IMH)

ENSAM ..... Ecole Nationale Superieure Agronomique de Montpellier [*Montpellier National Agricultural College*] [*French*]   (ARC)

ENSAM ..... Ecole Nationale Superieure d'Arts et Metiers [*Technical Skills National College*] [*Paris, France*] [*Research center*]   (ERC)

ENSAT ...... Ecole Nationale Superieure d'Agriculture Tunisienne [*Tunisian National Higher Institute of Agriculture*]   (AF)

ENSB .... Ecole Nationale Superieure de Bibliothecaires [*National College of Librarianship*] [*France*]   (PDAA)

ENSB .... Svalbard/Longyear [*Norway*] [*ICAO location identifier*]   (ICLI)

ENSCA ...... European Natural Sausage Casings Association   (EA)

ENSCP ...... Ecole Nationale Superieure de Chimie Physique

ENSCS ..... Ecole Nationale Superieure de Chimie de Strasbourg [*Strasbourg National College of Chemistry*] [*France*]   (EAS)

ENSD .... Sandane/Anda [*Norway*] [*ICAO location identifier*]   (ICLI)

ENSDF ...... Evaluated Nuclear Structure Data File [*National Nuclear Data Center*] [*Information service or system*]

ENSEA ...... Ecole Normale Superieure d'Agronomie [*Higher Education Normal School of Agriculture*] [*Ivory Coast*]

ENSEARCH ... Environmental Management and Research Association of Malaysia   (EAIO)

ENSEC ...... European Nuclear Steelmaking Club [*British*]   (NUCP)

ENSEM ..... Ecole Nationale Superieure d'Electricite et de Mecanique [*Electricity and Mechanics National College*] [*France*]   (WED)

ENSEME .. Entreprise Senegalaise des Mousses et Plastiques

ENSEP ...... Ecole Normale Superieure d'Enseignement Polytechnique [*Algeria*]

ENSEPORT ... Empresa Nacional de Servicios Portuarios [*National Port Services Enterprise*] [*Chile*]   (LA)

ENSET ...... Ecole Normale Superieure de l'Enseignement Technique [*Advanced Teacher-Training College for Technical Studies*] [*French*]

ENSF .... Statfjord-A [*Norway*] [*ICAO location identifier*]   (ICLI)

ENSG .... Ecole Nationale des Sciences Geodesiques [*Algeria*]

ENSG .... Ecole Nationale des Sciences Geographiques [*National School of Geographic Sciences*] [*French*]   (WER)

ENSG .... Ecole Nationale Superieure de Geologie Appliquee et de Prospection Miniere [*Applied Geology and Mine Prospecting National College*] [*France*]   (EAS)

ENSG .... Sogndal/Haukasen [*Norway*] [*ICAO location identifier*]   (ICLI)

ENSH .... Svolvaer/Helle [*Norway*] [*ICAO location identifier*]   (ICLI)

ENSI .... Ecole Nationale Superieure d'Ingenieurs [*Higher Schools of Engineering*] [*French*]

ENSI .... Energia Nucleare Sud Italia [*Italian nuclear power plant project*]

ENSIA .... Ecole Nationale Superieure des Industries Agricoles et Alimentaires [*Food and Agricultural Industries National College*] [*French*]   (ARC)

ENSIA .... Ecole Nationale Superieure d'Ingenieurs d'Abidjan [*Ivory Coast*]

ENSIC ...... Ecole Nationale Superieure des Industries Chimiques de Nancy

ENSIC .... Empresa Nacional de Saneamento Industria e Comercio [*Brazil*]   (LAA)

ENSIC .... Environmental Sanitation Information Center [*Asian Institute of Technology*] [*Thailand*] [*Information service or system*]   (IID)

ENSIDESA ... Empresa Nacional Siderurgica, Sociedad Anonima [*National Iron and Steel Enterprise, Incorporated*] [*Spanish*]   (WER)

ENSIGC .... Ecole Nationale Superieure d'Ingenieurs de Genie Chimique [*France*]   (ECON)

ENSIL .... Ecole Nationale Superieure d'Ingenieurs de Libreville [*Universite Omar Bongo*] [*Gabon*]

ENSIL .... National School of Engineering [*French*]

ENSJ .... Ecole Nationale Superieure de Journalisme a Alger
ENSK......... Stokmarknes/Skagen [*Norway*] [*ICAO location identifier*]   (ICLI)
ENSM .... Ecole Nationale Superieure de Mecanique [*France*]   (FLAF)
ENSM .... Ecole Nationale Superieure des Mines de Saint-Etienne [*National Mining College of Saint Etienne*] [*Research center*] [*France*] (ERC)
ENSMA..... Ecole Nationale Superieure de Mecanique et d'Aerotechnique [*France*]
ENSMP..... Ecole Nationale Superieure des Mines de Paris [*National Mining College of Paris*] [*Ministere de l'Industrie*] [*Research center*] [*France*]   (EAS)
ENSMSE .. Ecole Nationale Superieure des Mines de Saint-Etienne [*National Mining College of Saint Etienne*] [*France*]   (EAS)
ENSN .... Skien/Geiteryggen [*Norway*] [*ICAO location identifier*]   (ICLI)
ENSO .... Stord [*Norway*] [*ICAO location identifier*]   (ICLI)
ENSP........ Ecole Nationale de Sante Publique
ENSP........ Ecole Nationale Superieure de Police
ENSP......... Ecole Normale Superieure Polytechnique [*Higher Polytechnic Teachers Training School*] [*Algeria*]   (AF)
ENSP........ Entreprise Nationale de Service aux Puits [*Servicer of oil wells*] [*Algiers, Algeria*]   (MENA)
ENSPM..... Ecole Nationale Superieure du Petrole et des Moteurs [*Petroleum and Engines National College*] [*Institut Francais du Petrole*] [*Research center*] [*France*]   (ERC)
ENSPS ...... Ecole Nationale Superieure de Physique [*National College of Physics*] [*Research center*] [*France*]   (ERC)
ENSPY...... Ecole Nationale Superieure Polytechnique, Universite de Yaounde [*Cameroon*]
ENSR........ Sorkjosen [*Norway*] [*ICAO location identifier*]   (ICLI)
ENSS........ Svartnes [*Norway*] [*ICAO location identifier*]   (ICLI)
ENSSAA ... Ecole Nationale Superieure des Sciences Agronomiques Appliquees [*National College of Applied Agricultural Sciences*] [*French*]   (ARC)
ENS-System ... Einheitsnebenstellensystem [*Standard Extension System*]   (EG)
ENST........ Ecole Nationale Superieure des Telecommunications [*National Higher College of Telecommunications*] [*France*]   (PDAA)
ENST........ Sandnessjoen/Stokka [*Norway*] [*ICAO location identifier*]   (ICLI)
ENSTA...... Ecole Nationale Superieure de Techniques Avancees [*National College of Advanced Techniques*] [*France*]   (PDAA)
ENSTI ...... European Network Scientific and Technical Information
ENSTP...... Ecole Nationale Superieure des Travaux Publics [*Public Works National Staff College*] [*Ivory Coast*]   (AF)
ENSUME ... Empresa Cubana Importadora de Equipos-Medicos [*Cuban Enterprise for the Import of Medical Equipment*]   (LA)
ENSV........ Stavanger [*Norway*] [*ICAO location identifier*]   (ICLI)
EN(SVU)... Ekonomicky Namestnik (Stavebni Vyrobni Usek) [*Deputy Economist (Construction and Production Sector)*]   (CZ)
ENSz........ Egyesult Nemzetek Szovetsege [*United Nations Organization*]   (HU)
ENT .... Eastern Nigerian Theatre
ENT .... Ecole Nationale des Telecommunications [*National Telecommunications School*] [*Algeria*]   (AF)
ENT .... Empresa Nacional de Turismo [*National Tourist Company*] [*Mozambique*]   (GEA)
ENT .... Eniwetok [*Marshall Islands*] [*Airport symbol*]   (OAG)
ent .... Entierement [*Entirely*] [*French*]
ent .... Entinen [*Former, Earlier*] [*Finland*]   (GPO)
ent .... Entomologie [*French*]   (TPFD)
ent .... Entomology   (RU)
ENT .... Evropaikon Nomismatikon Tameion [*European Monetary Fund*]   (GC)
ENT .... Holmstrom Flyg AB [*Sweden*] [*ICAO designator*]   (FAAC)
ENTA .... Empresa Nacional de Transportes Aereos [*Costa Rica*]   (LAA)
ENTA .... Entreprise Nationale de Tabacs et de Cigarettes
ENTA .... Entreprise Nouvelle de Transports [*Morocco*]
ENTAC..... Engin Teleguide Anti-Char [*Antitank Missile*] [*French*]
ENTARA... Entreprise Mauritanienne de Travaux Publics, d'Etudes et d'Impression
Entarylier... Entarylierung [*Dearylation*] [*German*]   (GCA)
ENTAS...... Entas Nakliyat ve Turizm Anonim Sirketi [*Entas Transport and Tourism Corporation*]   (TU)
ENTC .... Tromso/Langnes [*Norway*] [*ICAO location identifier*]   (ICLI)
Entdeck...... Entdeckung [*Discovery*] [*German*]   (GCA)
ENTEC...... Esfahan Nuclear Technology Centre [*Iran*]   (PDAA)
ENTECOL ... Convenuto Telegrafico dell'Ente Colonizzazione della Libia
ENTEL...... Empresa Nacional de Telecomunicaciones [*National Telecommunications Company*] [*State enterprise Buenos Aires, Argentina*]   (LA)
ENTEL-PERU ... Empresa Nacional de Telecomunicaciones del Peru [*National Telecommunications Enterprise of Peru*]   (LA)
ENTEX...... Empresa Texteis de Angola   (EY)
entf........... Entfaerbt [*Faded*] [*Publishing*] [*German*]
Entf .... Entfernung [*Distance*] [*German*]   (GCA)
Entfarb...... Entfarbung [*Decolorization*] [*German*]   (GCA)
Entfern...... Entfernung [*Distance*] [*German*]   (GCA)

Entfett........ Entfettung [*Degreasing*] [*German*]   (GCA)
Entflammbark ... Entflammbarkeit [*Inflammability*] [*German*]   (GCA)
Entg........... Entgiftung [*Decontamination*] [*German*]   (GCA)
ENTG .... Euro-NATO Training Group [*An association*]   (EAIO)
Entgas....... Entgasung [*Degasification*] [*German*]   (GCA)
Entgift....... Entgiftung [*Decontamination*] [*German*]   (GCA)
enth .... Enthaltend [*Containing*] [*German*]
entier......... Entierement [*Entirely*] [*French*]
Entkalk...... Entkalkung [*Decalcification*] [*German*]   (GCA)
Entkeim ..... Entkeimung [*Sterilization*] [*German*]   (GCA)
Entkiesel.... Entkieselung [*Desilicification*] [*German*]   (GCA)
Entlad .... Entladung [*Discharge*] [*German*]   (GCA)
ENTO .... Torp [*Norway*] [*ICAO location identifier*]   (ICLI)
Entom........ Entomologia [*Entomology*] [*Portuguese*]
ENTP........ Entreprise Nantaise de Travaux Publics
ENTP........ Entreprise Nationale des Travaux aux Puits [*Oil well construction firm*] [*Algiers, Algeria*]   (MENA)
ENTP........ Entreprise Nigerienne de Travaux Publics
ENTPL...... Entreprise Nationale de Transformation de Produits Longs [*Nationalized industry*] [*Algeria*]   (EY)
Entpolymerisier ... Entpolymerisierung [*Depolymerization*] [*German*]   (GCA)
entr............ Entropy   (RU)
ENTR .... Trondheim [*Norway*] [*ICAO location identifier*]   (ICLI)
ENTRACO ... Entreprise Artisanale de Cocobeach
ENTRAT... Entreprise Nationale de Transports Routiers, d'Acconage, de Transit, et de Consignation Maritime
entrel......... Entrelazados [*Interlaced Fillets*] [*Publishing*] [*Spanish*]
ENTRELCO ... Societe d'Entreprises Electriques au Congo
ENTRELEC ... Compagnie d'Entreprises Electriques [*Cameroon*]
ENTREU... Entreprises Reunionnaises [*Reunionese Enterprises*]   (AF)
Ents .... Entsalzung [*Desalination*] [*German*]   (GCA)
Ents .... Entseuchung [*Disinfection*] [*German*]   (GCA)
Entsch........ Entscheidung [*Decision, Judgment*] [*German*]   (ILCA)
Entschl........ Entschliessung [*Resolution*] [*German*]
Entschwefel ... Entschwefelung [*Desulfurization*] [*German*]   (GCA)
Entsilizier .. Entsilizierung [*Desilicification*] [*German*]   (GCA)
ENTSPR ... Entsprechend [*Corresponding*] [*German*]
Entsteh....... Entstehung [*Origin*] [*German*]
ENTTAS ... Entreprise Togolaise des Techniciens Associes
ENTTPP ... Entreprise Nationale de Tubes et de Transformation de Produits Plats [*Nationalized industry*] [*Algeria*]   (EY)
ENTUR ..... Empresa Nacional de Turismo [*Peru*]
ENTURPERU ... Empresa Nacional de Turismo del Peru [*Peruvian National Tourist Enterprise*]   (LA)
ENTURSA ... Empresa Nacional de Turismo [*Spain*]   (EY)
entw........... Entweder [*Either*] [*German*]
entw........... Entwickelt or Entwickelung [*Developed or Development*] [*German*]
Entw .... Entwurf [*Draft*] [*German*]   (ILCA)
Entwasser .. Entwaesserung [*Dehydration*] [*German*]   (GCA)
Entzund...... Entzuendung [*Ignition*] [*German*]   (GCA)
entzundl ..... Entzuendlich [*Ignitable*] [*German*]   (GCA)
ENU.......... Enugu [*Nigeria*] [*Airport symbol*]   (OAG)
ENU.......... Escuela Nacional Unificada [*National Unified School*] [*Chile*]
ENUSA ..... Empresa Nacional del Uranio, Sociedad Anonima [*National Uranium Enterprise, Incorporated*] [*Madrid, Spain*]   (WER)
ENUSA ..... Energie Nucleaire, Societe Anonyme [*Switzerland*] [*Nuclear energy*]   (NRCH)
ENUWAR ... Environmental Consequences of Nuclear War [*International Council of Scientific Unions*]
ENV .... Ecole Nationale Veterinaire [*National Veterinary School*] [*Algeria*]   (AF)
ENV .... Electric Water Heater   (RU)
env .... Envers [*Back Side*] [*Knitting*] [*French*]
en v .... En Ville [*Locally*] [*Correspondence*] [*French*]
ENV .... Environ [*About*] [*French*]
env............. Envoi [*Dedicatory Note or Inscription*] [*Publishing*] [*French*]
ENV .... Europeenne Norme Vorausgabe [*European Prestandard*]   (OSI)
ENVA .... Trondheim/Vaernes [*Norway*] [*ICAO location identifier*]   (ICLI)
ENVAC..... Envases Colombianos SA [*Barranquilla*]   (COL)
ENVAFLEX ... Envasamientos Flexibles [*Colombia*]   (COL)
ENVD........ Vadso [*Norway*] [*ICAO location identifier*]   (ICLI)
ENVI .... Division of Environmental Engineering [*Asian Institute of Technology*] [*Thai*]
envir .... Environ [*About*] [*French*]
ENVN........ Tromso [*Norway*] [*ICAO location identifier*]   (ICLI)
ENVV........ Bergen [*Norway*] [*ICAO location identifier*]   (ICLI)
ENVY........ Vaeroy [*Norway*] [*ICAO location identifier*]   (ICLI)
E Ny.......... Eszaknyugat [*Northwest*]   (HU)
ENY.......... Yanan [*China*] [*Airport symbol*]   (OAG)
ENYVA ..... Enosis Ypallilon Vrettanikon Arkhon [*Union of British Authorities Employees*] [*Cyprus*]   (GC)
enz............. En Zo Voort [*And So Forth*] [*Netherlands*]   (GPO)
ENZ.......... New Zealand Air Services Ltd. [*ICAO designator*]   (FAAC)
en Zn .... En Zoon [*And Son*] [*Netherlands*]   (CED)

ENZV .... Stavanger/Sola [*Norway*] [*ICAO location identifier*] (ICLI)
EO .... Aero America, Inc. [*ICAO designator*] (ICDA)
EO .... Cathode-Ray Oscillograph (RU)
EO .... Daily Service of Motor Vehicles (BU)
eo .... Edition originale [*Original Edition*] [*Publishing*] [*French*]
eo .... Eervol Ontslagen [*Benelux*] (BAS)
EO .... Egeszsegugyi Osztaly [*Health Department*] (HU)
EO .... Ekonomski Otsek [*Economic Section*] (YU)
EO .... Electoral Office [*Australia*]
EO .... Elementary Operator [*Computers*] (RU)
eo .... Eloors [*Reconnaissance Group, Outpost*] (HU)
EO .... Estacao de Orizicultura [*Portugal*] (DSCA)
E/O .... Est/Ovest [*East/West*] [*Italian*]
EO .... Evacuation Detachment (RU)
EO .... Evacuation Section (RU)
EO .... L'Equippe Ouvriere
EO .... Oscillograph Screen (RU)
EOA .... Ente Opera Assistenziali Presso le Federazioni Fasciste della Libia
EOA .... Epitropi Olymbiakon Agonon [*Olympic Games Committee*] (GC)
EOA .... Ethniki Organosis Axiomatikon [*National Organization of Officers*] (GC)
EOAAYL... Enosis Odigon Avtokiniton Astikon kai Yperastikon Leoforeion [*Union of Drivers of Urban and Suburban Buses*] [*Greek*] (GC)
EOAC .... Etats Ouest Africains de la Communaute
EOAS .... Eleves Officiers d'Active du Service de Sante [*Regular Medical Service Officer Candidates*] [*Cambodia*] (CL)
EOAVB ..... Evakuaciono Odeljenje Armiske Veterinarske Bolnice [*Evacuation Sector of the Army Veterinary Hospital*] (YU)
EOAVE ..... Enosis Odigon Avtokiniton Voreiou Ellados [*Drivers' Union of Northern Greece*] (GC)
EOB .... Equal Opportunity Board [*Victoria, Australia*]
EOC .... Educacion Obrero-Campesina [*Workers and Peasants Education*] [*Cuba*] (LA)
EOC .... Elva Owners Club [*Worthing, West Sussex, England*] (EAIO)
EOC .... Equal Opportunity Commission [*Western Australia*]
EOC .... Europe Olympic Committee (OLYM)
EOCA .... Exhibition Organisers Council of Australia
EOCCD ..... European Organisation for the Control of Circulatory Diseases (PDAA)
EODVL ..... Evacuation Section of a Division Veterinary Hospital (RU)
EODYL ..... Elevthera Organosis Dimotikon Ypallilon Levkosias [*Free Organization of Nicosia Civil Servants*] (GC)
EOE .... European Options Exchange [*Netherlands*]
EOEA .... Elliniki Omospondia Erasitekhnon Alieias [*Greek Federation of Amateur Fishermen*] (GC)
EOEA .... Ethnikai Omades Ellinon Andarton [*National Groups of Greek Guerrillas (Zervas-led)*] (GC)
EOED .... Epistimonikos Omilos Erevnon Diastimatos [*Scientific Association for Space Research*] [*Greek*] (GC)
EOEE .... Epitropi Oikonomikou Elengkhou Endypon [*Committee for Financial Audit of Publications*] (GC)
EOEKh ...... Ethnikos Organismos Ellinikis Kheirotekhnias [*National Organization of Greek Handicrafts*] (GC)
EOEP .... Ethnikos Organismos Ellinon Patrioton [*National Organization of Greek Patriots*] (GC)
EOEP .... Executive Office for Educational Projects [*Yemen*]
EOES .... Europese Organizatie voor Ekonomische Samenwerking [*Benelux*] (BAS)
EOF .... Elementary Evaluative Function (RU)
EOFAP ...... Escuela de Oficials de la Fuerza Aerea del Peru [*Peruvian Air Force Academy*] (LA)
EOGFL ...... Europees Orientatie-en Garantiefonds voor de Landbouw [*Benelux*] (BAS)
EOGM .... Egitim ve Ogretim Genel Mudurlugu [*Education and Teaching Directorate General*] (TU)
EOH .... Egitim Ozel Hizmetleri [*Special Educational Duties*] (TU)
EOHPC ..... European Oil Hydraulic and Pneumatic Committee [*Italy*] (EAIO)
EOI .... Eday [*Orkney Islands*] [*Airport symbol*] (OAG)
EOI .... Edible Oils Industries [*Australia*]
EOI .... Edition de l'Ocean Indien
EOK .... Ethnikos Organismos Kapnou [*National Tobacco Organization*] [*Greek*] (GC)
EOK .... Ethnikos Organismos Katoikias [*National Housing Organization*] [*Greek*] (GC)
EOK .... Evropaiki Oikonomiki Koinotis [*European Economic Community*] (GC)
EOK .... Ostravsko-Karvinske Elektrarny [*Ostrava-Karvin Electric Power Plants*] (CZ)
EOKA .... Ethniki Organosis Kyprion Agoniston [*or Ethniki Organosis Kypriakou Agonos*] [*National Organization of Cypriot Fighters*]
EOKhA ...... Ethnikos Organismos Khristianikis Allilengyis [*National Christian Solidarity Organization*] [*Greek*] (GC)

EOLES ...... Escourteur Oceanque Leger a Effet de Surface [*Light Ocean-Going Surface Effects Ship*] [*French*]
EOM .... Ellinikos Organismos Marketing [*Greek*] (SLS)
EOM .... European Options Market (DCTA)
EOMA .... Epikourikos Organismos Metaforon di'Avtokinitou [*Auxiliary Vehicular Transport Organization*] [*Greek*] (GC)
EOMMEHh ... Ellinikos Organismos Mikromesaion Epikheiriseon kai Kheirotekhnias [*Hellenic Organization of Medium and Small-Size Enterprises and Handicrafts*] (GC)
EOMS .... Engel's Experimental Reclamation Station (RU)
EOMTA .... Enosis Oikogeneion Makhomenon Travmation, Anapiron [*Union of Families of Injured and Disabled Fighters*] [*Greek*] (GC)
EON .... Ethniki Organosis Neolaias [*National Youth Organization*] [*Greek*] (GC)
EONR .... European Organization for Nuclear Reserch (NUCP)
EOOE .... Erreur ou Omission Exceptee [*Error or Omission Excepted*] [*French*]
EOOF .... European Olive Oil Federation [*Italy*] (EAIO)
eoov .... Eervol Ontslag op Verzoek [*Benelux*] (BAS)
EOP .... Elektrarna Opatovice [*Opatovice Electric Power Plant*] (CZ)
EOP .... Elementary Machining Surfaces (RU)
EOP .... Elliniki Omospondia Pygmakhias [*Greek Boxing Federation*] (GC)
EOP .... Ethnikos Organismos Pronoias [*National Welfare Organization*] [*Greek*] (GC)
EOP .... Evropaikos Organismos Paragogikotitos [*European Productivity Organization*] (GC)
EOP .... Evropska Organizacija za Produktivnost [*Organization for European Economic Cooperation (OEEC)*] (YU)
EOP .... Image Converter Tube (RU)
EOPAE...... Ethniki Omospondia Prosopikou Avtokiniton Ellados [*National Federation of Automotive Personnel of Greece*] (GC)
EOPGS...... Ecole et Observatoire de Physique du Globe de Strasbourg [*Strasbourg School and Observatory of Earth Sciences*] [*France*] (IRC)
EOPO .... United Social and Political Organization (BU)
EO POM ... Ekspozytury Organizacyjne Panstwowych Osrodkow Maszynowych [*Organizational Branches of the State (Agricultural) Machine Stations*] (POL)
EOPSA...... Ellinikos Organismos Pnevmatikis kai Somatikis Agogis [*Greek Organization for Mental and Physical Health*] (GC)
EOPTR..... Expeditionary Detachment for Underwater Technical Operations (RU)
EOQ .... European Organization for Quality [*Switzerland*] (EAIO)
EOQC....... European Organization for Quality Control [*Bern, Switzerland*] (SLS)
EOR .... Eleve Officier de Reserve [*Reserve Officer Cadet*] [*French*] (WER)
EOR .... Enhanced Oil Recovery (OMWE)
EORC .... Equal Opportunities Resource Centre [*Perth, Australia*]
EORDC ..... Essential Oils Research and Development Committee [*Tasmania, Australia*]
EORTC..... European Organization for Research on the Treatment of Cancer [*Research center*] [*Switzerland*] (IRC)
EOS .... Egyptian Organisation for Standardization
EOS .... Ellinikos Oreivatikos Syndesmos [*Greek Mountaineering League*] (GC)
EOS .... Energie de l'Ouest Suisse [*Switzerland*] (WND)
EOS .... Erweiterte Oberschule [*Advanced Upper School*] [*German*]
EOS .... Ethnikos Organismos Syndaxeon [*National Pensions Organization*] (GC)
EOS .... European Orthodontic Society (PDAA)
EOS .... Evropske Obranne Spolecenstvi [*European Defense Community*] (CZ)
EOS .... Societe Anonyme Energie de l'Ouest Suisse [*Switzerland*] (PDAA)
EOSD .... Education Officers on Special Duties [*Australia*]
EOSI......... Ethniki Omospondia Syndaxioukhon Idryma Koinonikon Asfaliseon [*National Federation of Social Insurance Foundation Pensioners*] [*Greek*] (GC)
EOSMOR ... European Society for Market and Opinion Research
EOSS........ Emergency Oil Sharing System [*Australia*]
EOT .... Ellinikos Organismos Tourismou [*Greek Tourist Organization*] (GC)
EOTE .... Eleves Officiers Techniciens des Essences [*Fuel Technician Officer Candidates*] [*Cambodia*] (CL)
EOUV........ Ekonomicko-Organizacni Ustav Vlnarskeho Prumyslu [*Economic-Organizational Institute of the Wool Industry*]
EOVS......... Ekonomski Otsek Vrhovnog Staba [*Economic Section of the Supreme Headquarters*] (YU)
eow .... Eerste Op Water [*Afrikaans*]
EOWU ...... Electrical and Other Workers Union [*Mauritius*] (AF)
EOY .... Epitropi Oikonomikon Ypotheseon [*Economic Affairs Committee*] [*Greek*] (GC)

EOYESK ... Eniaia Organosis Ypallilon Epitropis Sitiron [*United Organization of Wheat Board Employees*] [*Cyprus*]   (GC)
EOZ .... Elorza [*Venezuela*] [*Airport symbol*]   (OAG)
EP .... Clearing Station   (RU)
ep .... Diocese   (BU)
EP .... Eastern Province
EP .... Economic Planning. Journal for Agriculture and Related Industries [*A publication*]
EP .... Egyseg Partja [*Party of Unity*] [*Hungary*]   (PPE)
EP .... Ejercito Peruano [*Peruvian Army*]   (LA)
EP .... Electric Heater   (RU)
EP .... Electricke Podniky Hlavniho Mesta Prahy [*Prague Capital Electric Enterprises*]   (CZ)
EP .... Electric Range   (RU)
EP .... Electric Saw   (RU)
EP .... Electric Transmission   (RU)
EP .... Electron Flow   (RU)
EP .... Electron Gun   (RU)
EP .... Elektricno Poduzece [*Electrical Establishment*]   (YU)
EP .... Elektro-Praga Jablonec Nad Nisou [*Electrical Engineering Enterprise, Jablonec Nad Nisou*]   (CZ)
EP .... Energieprojektierung (VEB) [*Project Planning Office for Electric Power (VEB)*]   (EG)
EP .... Englisches Patent [*English Patent*] [*German*]
EP .... Enotiki Parataxis [*Unifying (Pro-Enosis) Faction*] [*Cyprus*]   (GC)
EP .... Environmental Park [*Australia*]
EP .... Epitropi Poleos [*City Committee*]   (GC)
ep .... Epoca [*Time*] [*Italian*]
ep .... Epoque [*Time*] [*French*]
EP .... Ergatiki Pali [*Worker Struggle*]   (GC)
EP .... Erweichungspunkt [*Softening Point*] [*German*]
EP .... Escuadron Primario [*Primary Squadron*] [*Bolivia*] [*Military*]
EP .... Ethniki Parataxi [*National Array*]   (GC)
EP .... Etudes de Presse [*France*]   (FLAF)
EP .... Evacuation Center   (BU)
E-P .... Evaporacija-Padavine [*Evaporation of Precipitation*] [*Meteorology*]   (YU)
EP .... Exploration Permit [*Australia*]
EP .... Potentiometer   (RU)
EP .... Power Supply   (RU)
EP .... Self-Propelled Loader   (RU)
EP .... Vacuum Cleaner   (RU)
EPA .... Ecole Polytechnique d'Assurances [*France*]   (FLAF)
EPA .... Economic Planning Agency [*Japan*]
EPA .... Eisenbahn-Polizei-Amt [*Railroad Police Office*]   (EG)
EPA .... Ejercito Popular de Alfabetizacion [*People's Literacy Army*] [*Nicaragua*]   (LA)
EPA .... Empire Parliamentary Association [*Later, CPA*] [*Australia*]
epa .... En Polemiki Apostrateia [*(In) Standby Reserve (Status)*]   (GC)
EPA .... Environmental Protection Authority [*New South Wales, Australia*]
EPA .... Environment Planning Assessment Act [*Australia*]
EPA .... Epitropi Programatismou kai Anaptyxeos [*Planning and Development Committee*]   (GC)
EPA .... Epitropi Promitheion Anasyngrotiseos [*Reconstruction Supply Committee*] [*Greek*]   (GC)
EPA .... Equipement Pneumatique Africain
EPA .... Escola Practica de Artilharia [*Practical Artillery School*] [*Portuguese*]   (WER)
EPA .... Escritorio de Producao Animal [*Brazil*]   (DSCA)
EPA .... Escuela de Peritos Agronomos [*Bolivia*]   (DSCA)
EPA .... Escuela Particular de Agricultura [*Ciudad Juarez, Mexico*]   (LAA)
EPA .... Estudios de Publicidade Artistica
EPA .... Etaireia Prostasias Anilikon [*Society for the Protection of Minors*] [*Greek*]   (GC)
EPA .... Ethnic Party of Australia [*Political party*]
EPA .... Europaeisches Patentamt [*European Patent Office - EPO*]   (EAIO)
EPA .... European Photochemistry Association   (EAIO)
EPA .... European Productivity Agency [*OECD*]
EPA .... Evropaikon Programma Anorthoseos [*European Recovery Plan*]   (GC)
EPA .... Exparc [*Russian Federation*] [*ICAO designator*]   (FAAC)
EPA .... Export Pound Account [*Special type of currency*] [*United Arab Republic*]
EPA .... Eyre Peninsula Airways [*Australia*]
EPAA .... European Primary Aluminum Association [*Later, European Aluminium Association - EAA*]   (IID)
EPAAL ...... Epitropi Allilengyis pros tous Aravikous Laous [*Committee for Solidarity with the Arab Peoples*] [*Cyprus*]   (GC)
EPABA ...... Empresa de Pesquisa Agropecuaria da Bahia [*State Agricultural Research Corporation of Bahia*] [*Research center*] [*Brazil*]   (IRC)

EPAC .... Escritorio de Planejamento Agricola e Cooperativo [*Brazil*]   (DSCA)
EPACA ...... Empacadora de Camarones y Atun [*Ecuador*]   (DSCA)
EPACT ...... Economic Priorities [*Advisory Committee*] of the Australian Capital Territory
EPAD .... Etablissement Public d'Amenagement de la Defense
EPAEA ...... Epitropi Protovoulias dia tin Anagnorisin tis Ethnikis Andistaseos [*or Epitropi Protovoulias Anagnoriseos Ethnikis Andistaseos*] [*Committee of Initiative for Recognition of the National Resistance*] [*Greek*]   (GC)
EPAEEA ... Eniaia Patriotiki Enosi Ellinon Amvourgou [*United Patriotic Union of Hamburg Greeks (West German)*]   (GC)
EPAF .... Enosi Palis Aristeron Foititon [*Union of Leftist Students Struggle*] [*Greek*]   (GC)
EPAF .... Expertutredningen Angaende Prisreglering av Foersvarsutgifterna [*Sweden*]
EPAL .... Empresa Publica das Aguas de Lisboa [*Public Water Enterprise of Lisbon*] [*Portuguese*]   (WER)
EPAM .... Escola Practica de Administracao Militar (Lisboa) [*Practical School of Military Administration*] [*Portuguese*]   (WER)
epam art ..... Epamaarainen Artikkeli [*Indefinite Article*] [*Finland*]
EPAMIG ... Empresa Agropecuaria de Minas Gerais [*State Agricultural Research Corporation of Minas Gerais*] [*Brazil*]   (LA)
Ep anyMin ... Epitoanyagipari Miniszterium/Miniszter [*Ministry/Minister of the Building Materials Industry*]   (HU)
EPARD ...... East Pakistan Academy for Rural Development   (DSCA)
EPAS .... Enosi Palis Aristeron Spoudaston [*Leftist Student Struggle Union*] [*Greek*]   (GC)
EPAThPE ... Enosis Peripertioukhon Anapiron kai Thimaton Polemou Ellados [*Union of Disabled Kiosk Owners and Victims of the War of Greece*]   (GC)
EPAU .... Ecole Polytechnique d'Architecture et d'Urbanisme [*Polytechnic School of Architecture and Town Planning*] [*French*]
EPB .... Economic Planning Board [*Korea*]
EPB .... Ejercito Popular Boricua [*Puerto Rican Popular Army*]   (PD)
EPB .... Exploitation de Port de Bujumbura
EPB .... Export Promotion Bureau [*Pakistan*]   (GEA)
EPBI .... Export Promotion Bureau of Iran   (ME)
EPBTP .... Entreprise Publique de Batiment et des Travaux Publics [*Algeria*]   (IMH)
EPC .... Conti-Flug Koln/Bonn [*Germany*] [*ICAO designator*]   (FAAC)
EPC .... Ecole Primaires Confessionelles [*Religious Primary Schools*] [*Malagasy*]   (AF)
EPC .... Egyptian Phosphate Company
EPC .... Ejercito del Pueblo Costarricense [*Costa Rica*] [*Political party*]   (EY)
EPC .... Ejercito Popular Catalan [*Catalan Popular Army*] [*Spain*]   (PD)
EPC .... Electric Power Corporation [*Myanmar*]   (DS)
EPC .... Environmental Protection Council [*Tasmania, Australia*]
EPC .... Environment Protection Council of Kuwait   (EAIO)
EPC .... Escola Practica de Cavalaria [*Practical School of Cavalry*] [*Portuguese*]   (WER)
EPC .... Etudiants Progressistes Congolais
EPC .... European Confederation of Plastics Convertors [*EC*]   (ECED)
EPC .... European Pension Committee [*France*]   (EAIO)
EPC .... European Political Cooperation
EPC .... European Popular Circle   (EAIO)
EPC .... Ewe Presbyterian Church
EPCA .... European Petrochemical Association
EPCAG ...... Electronic Publishing Consultative and Advisory Group [*Australia*]
EPCh .... Master Electric Clock   (RU)
EPCHAP ... Empresa Publica de la Comercializacion de Harina y Aceite de Pescado [*Public Enterprise for the Marketing of Fishmeal and Fish Oil*] [*Peru*]   (LA)
EPCI .... Export Promotion Center of Iran   (ME)
EPCOM .... Environmental Pollution Advisory Committee [*Hong Kong*]
EPD .... Elektrarenske Podniky Distribucni [*Electric Power Distribution Enterprises*]   (CZ)
EPD .... En Paz Descanse [*Rest in Peace*] [*Spanish*]
epd .... En Polemiki Diathesimotiti [*(In) Ready Reserve (Status)*]   (GC)
EPD .... Environment Protection Department [*Iran*]   (ME)
EPD .... European Progressive Democrats   (PPE)
EPD .... Evangelische Pressedienst
EPDC .... Electric Power Development Company Ltd. [*Nuclear energy*] [*Japan*]   (NRCH)
EPDC .... Engineering & Power Development Consultants [*Oman*]
EPDCC ...... European Pressure Die Casting Committee   (EA)
EPDM .... Ethiopian People's Democratic Movement [*Political party*]
EPDP .... Eelam People's Democratic Party [*Sri Lanka*] [*Political party*]   (EY)
EPE .... Escritorio de Pesquisas e Experimentacao [*Brazil*]   (DSCA)
epe .... Etaireia Periorismenis Evthynis [*Limited Liability Company*]   (GC)
EPE .... Ethniki Parataxi Ellinidon [*National Faction of Greek Women*] [*Greek*]   (GC)
EPE .... Ethniki Politiki Enosis [*National Political Union*] [*Greek*]   (PPE)

EPE........... Evangelische Pfadfinderschaft Europas [*Germany*] (EAIO)
EPEC........ Environmental Protection and Education Club [*Kenya*] (EAIO)
EPECO...... Entreprise de Production, de Gestion et de Distribution d'Eau de Constantaine [*Regional water authority*] [*Algeria*]
Epedeco...... Egyptian Petroleum Development Company (ME)
EPEF .... Escuela Primaria de Educacion Fisica [*Elementary Physical Education School*] [*Cuba*] (LA)
EPEK........ Ethniki Proodevtiki Enosis Kendrou [*National Progressive Union of the Center*] [*Greek*] (GC)
EPEKA ..... Ethniki Patriotiki Enosis Kypriakou Agonos [*National Patriotic Union of the Cyprus Struggle*] (GC)
EPEL .... Ethniki Parataxis Ergazomenou Laou [*National Working People's Faction*] [*Greek*] (GC)
EPEM........ Equipe de Planejamento do Ensino Medio [*Secondary Education Planning Team*] [*Rio De Janeiro, Brazil*] (LAA)
EPEMA ..... Exposicao Permanente de Maquinas Agricolas [*Brazil*] (DSCA)
EPEN........ Greek National Political Society (PPW)
EPEP .... Empresa de Perforacion y Extraccion de Petroleo [*Petroleum Drilling and Extracting Enterprise*] [*Cuba*] (LA)
EPER........ Entraide Protestante Suisse
EPES .... Ellines Spoudastes Parisiou [*Greek Students of Paris*] (GC)
EPESA ...... Ediciones y Publicaciones Espanolas SA [*Spain*] (DSCA)
EPET .... Ethnikon Programma Erevnon kai Tekhnologias [*National Research and Technology Program*] (GC)
EPEXEV.... Epitropi Exoikonomiseos Energeias stin Viomikhania [*Committee for Energy Conservation in Industry*] (GC)
EPF .... Ecole Polytechnique Federale [*Federal Institute of Technology*] [*Switzerland*]
EPF .... Employees Production Fund [*Iran*] (ME)
EPF .... Employees Provident Fund (ML)
EPF .... Empresa Petrolera Fiscal [*Peru*] (LAA)
EPF .... Environment Problems Foundation [*Turkey*]
EPF .... European Packaging Federation [*Denmark*] (SLS)
EPF .... European Psycho-Analytical Federation (EA)
EPF .... Expeditions Polaires Francaises
EPFA .... European Plasma Fractionation Association
EPFCL....... Elvis Presley Fan Club of Luxembourg (EAIO)
EPFCOV ... Elvis Presley Fan Club of Victoria [*Australia*] (EAIO)
EPFL .... Ecole Polytechnique Federale de Lausanne [*Swiss Federal Institute of Technology, Lausanne*] (ECON)
EPFS........ Equipe de Pedologia e Fertilidade do Solo [*Brazil*] (DSCA)
EPFU .... Epuletanyagfuvarozo Vallalat [*Building Materials Transportation Enterprise*] (HU)
EPG .... Electroplethysmogram (RU)
EPG .... Eminent Persons Group [*South Africa*]
EPG .... Equine Practitioners' Group [*South African Veterinary Association*] (AA)
EPG .... Europaische Produktion Gesellschaft [*Commercial firm*] [*Germany*]
EPG .... European Programme Group [*NATO*]
EPG .... Europese Politieke Gemeenschap [*Benelux*] (BAS)
EPG .... Pontoon Caterpillar Excavator (RU)
EPGD .... Gdansk/Rebiechowo [*Poland*] [*ICAO location identifier*] (ICLI)
EPGE .... Escola de Pos-Graduacao en Economia [*Brazil*] (DSCA)
EPHARMECOR ... Ethiopian Pharmaceuticals & Medical Supplies Corp.
EPHE .... Ecole Pratique des Hautes Etudes [*Practical School of Higher Studies*] [*French*]
EPhi.......... English Philips [*Record label*]
EPhMRA... European Pharmaceutical Marketing Research Association (EAIO)
EPHSOC... Ephemera Society of Australia
EPI........... Engineering Projects India Ltd.
EPI........... Entreprise de Peches Ivoiriennes
EPI........... Etablissements Publics Internationaux [*France*] (FLAF)
EPI........... European Pacific Investments [*New Zealand*]
EPI........... European Participating Industry
EPI........... Evangelical Pedagogical Institute
EPI........... Expanded Programme on Immunization [*World Health Organization*]
EPIC........ Education Program for Infants and Children [*Australia*]
EPIC........ Equatorial Pacific International Co. [*Asia*]
EPIC........ Export Payments Insurance Corporation [*Australia*] (ADA)
EPICS....... European Petrochemical Industry Computerized System [*Parpinelli Tecnon*] [*Italy*] [*Information service or system*] (IID)
epid........... Epidermure [*Scraped Place*] [*Publishing*] [*French*]
EPID......... Extension and Project Implementation Department
epidem...... Epidemiology (RU)
EPIDIS...... Ensemble de Programmes Integres pour la Distribution [*French*] (ADPT)
EPIEA .... Enosis Prosopikou Imerision Efimeridon Athinon [*Union of Athens Daily Newspaper Employees*] (GC)
EPIN......... Ente Promozione Industria par la Difesa Navale
Epip K ...... Epitoipari Kiado [*Construction Industry Publishing House*] (HU)
epist........... Epistola [*Letter, Epistle*] [*Portuguese*]

epit .... Epiteszet [*Architecture*] (HU)
EPK .... Effective Threshold Quantum Number (RU)
EPK .... Electropneumatic Valve (RU)
EPK .... Ethnikon Phileleftheron Komma [*National Liberal Party*] [*Greek*] (PPE)
EPK .... Expert Verification Commission (RU)
EPK .... Partido Comunista de Euzkadi/Euzkadiko Partidu Komunista [*Basque Communist Party*] (PPW)
EPKA .... Epitropi Kypriakou Agonos [*Cyprus Struggle Committee*] (GC)
EPKK .... Krakow/Balice [*Poland*] [*ICAO location identifier*] (ICLI)
EPKL .... European Pan-Keltic League (EA)
EPKU .... Electronic Printing and Coding Device (RU)
EPL .... Einheitliche Prozessrechner-Linie [*German*] (ADPT)
EPL .... Einzelplan [*Individual Plan*] (EG)
EPL .... Ejercito Popular de Liberacion [*Popular Liberation Army*] [*Colorado*] (LA)
EPL .... Ejercito Popular de Liberacion [*Popular Liberation Army*] [*El Salvador*] (PD)
EPL .... Elliniki Periigitiki Leskhi [*Greek Travel Club*] (GC)
EPL .... Entreprise de Progres Local
EPL .... European Program Library (ADPT)
EPL .... Fleet Submarine (RU)
EPLA .... East Pakistan Library Association (PDAA)
EPLA .... Ejercito Popular de Liberacion de America [*Army of Popular Liberation of America*] [*Mexico*] (LA)
EPLA .... Eritrean People's Liberation Army [*Ethiopia*] [*Political party*] (EY)
EPLA .... Exercito Popular de Libertacao de Angola [*People's Army of Liberation of Angola*] (AF)
EPLAF....... European Planning Federation [*British*] (EA)
EPLF .... Eritrean People's Liberation Front [*Ethiopia*] (PD)
EPLIB........ Environment Programme Library [*Database*] [*UNEP*] [*United Nations*] (DUND)
EPLP .... European Parliamentary Labor Party [*European Community*] [*Political party*]
EPLS .... Engineering and Physics in the Life Sciences [*Australia*]
EPM .... Electro Plastique Malgache
EPM .... Ellinikon Patriotikon Metopon [*Greek Patriotic Front*] [*Greek*] (GC)
EPM .... Emigration Portfolio Manager [*Investment term*]
EPM .... En Propia Mano [*In His Own Hand*] [*Spanish*]
EPMARKUP ... European Publishers' Markup User Group
EPMI........ Esso Production Malaysia Inc.
EPMMA.... European Proprietary Medicines Manufacturers Association [*Belgium*] (EAIO)
EPN .... Empresa Periodista Nacional [*National Newspaper Enterprise*] [*Peru*] (LA)
EPN .... Epena [*Congo*] [*Airport symbol*] (OAG)
EPN .... Escuela Politecnica Nacional [*Ecuador*] (DSCA)
EPN .... Hot Plate (RU)
EPN .... Submerged Electric Pump (RU)
Epna.......... Empresa Pesquera Nacional [*National Fisheries Company*] [*Ecuador*] (GEA)
EPO .... Economics and Law Department (RU)
EPO .... Elektrarny Porici [*Electric Power Plants, Porici*] (CZ)
EPO .... Elizabethan Philharmonic Orchestra [*Australia*]
EPO .... Enseignement Programme par Ordinateur [*French*] (ADPT)
EPO .... Environment Protection Organization [*Iran*] (ME)
EPO .... Ethniki Podosfairiki Omospondia [*National Soccer Federation*] (GC)
EPO .... Etud, Egitim, Pazarlama, ve Organizasyon Hizmetleri AS [*Study, Training, Marketing, and Organizational Services Corporation*] (TU)
EPO .... European Patent Office [*Germany*] (PDAA)
EPO .... Exclusive Prospecting Order
EPOA .... External Plant Operators' Association of South Australia
EPOC .... Earthquake Prediction Observation Center [*Japan*] (PDAA)
EPOC .... Eastern Pacific Ocean Conference (ASF)
EPOC .... Entreprise de Peinture pour l'Oubangui-Chari
EPOC .... Equity Policy Center
EPOC .... ESCAP [*Economic and Social Commission for Asia and the Pacific*] Pacific Operations Center [*Vanuatu*]
EPOEIAL ... Ethniki Panelladiki Omospondia Epangelmation Idioktiton Astikon Leoforeion [*National Panhellenic Federation of Operator-Owners of Urban Buses*] (GC)
EPOET ...... Elevthera Pankyprios Organosis Ergatoypallilon Tilepikoinonion [*Free Pan-Cyprian Organization of Telecommunications Workers*] (GC)
EPOG .... Eenheid vir Professionele Opleiding en Dienslewering in die Gedragswetenskappe [*University of the Orange Free State*] [*South Africa*] (GC)
EPOIZO.... Enosis gia tin Poiotita Zois [*Union for Life Quality*] (GC)
EPOK .... Ellinikon Politistikon Kinima [*Greek Cultural Movement*] (GC)
EPOK .... Ellinikos Pnevmatikos Omilos Kyprou [*Greek Cultural Club of Cyprus*] (GC)
EPOL......... Ellinikos Pnevmatikos Omilos Larnakos [*Greek Cultural Club of Larnaca*] (GC)

EPON .... Ethniki Panelliniki Organosis Neon [*National Panhellenic Youth Organization*] (GC)
Epont .... Equipage de Pont [*Military*] [*French*] (MTD)
EPOPAI .... Elevthera Pankyprios Omospondia Prosopikou Arkhis Ilektrismou [*Free Pan-Cyprian Federation of Cyprus Electricity Authority Personnel*] (GC)
EPOPEM .. Equipe de Pollution Pelagique de Marseille [*French*] (ASF)
epoq .... Epoque [*Time*] [*French*]
EP-OR .... Elliniki Epistimoniki Etaireia Organoseos Ergasias [*Greek Scientific Society for Work Organization*]
EPOS .... Elektro-Installations-Programm-und Organisationssystem [*German*] (ADPT)
EPOS-IKA ... Ethniki Panelladiki Epitropi Syndaxioukhon Idryma Koinonikon Asfaliseon [*National Panhellenic Federation of Social Insurance Foundation Pensioners*] (GC)
EPOSZ ...... Egyseges Parasztifjusag Orszagos Szovetseg [*or Egyesult Parasztifjusag Orszagos Szovetsege*] [*National United Peasant Youth Association*] (HU)
EPOYET ... Ergatiki Pankypriaki Omospondia Ypallilon Esoterikon Tilepikoinonion [*Pan-Cyprian Federation of Inland Telecommunications Employees*] (GC)
EPOYSY ... Elevthera Pankypriaki Omospondia Synergatikon Ypallilon [*Free Pan-Cyprian Union of Employees of Cooperatives*] (GC)
EPP .... Ecoles Primaires Publiques [*Public Primary Schools*] [*Malagasy*] (AF)
epp .... Edella Puolenpaivan [*Before Noon*] [*Finland*] (GPO)
EPP .... Editions Phonographiques Parisiennes - Allegro Label [*Record label*] [*France*]
EPP .... Electric Furnace Substation (RU)
EPP .... Electrification of Industrial Establishments (RU)
EPP .... Electropneumatic Converter (RU)
EPP .... Elliniki Polemiki Perithalpsis [*Greek War Relief*] (GC)
epp .... Ennen Puoltapaivaa [*Finland*]
EPP .... Etaireia Prostasias Paidiou [*Child Protection Society*] [*Greek*] (GC)
EPP .... European Pallet Pool (PDAA)
EPP .... European People's Party - Federation of Christian Democratic Parties of the European Community [*Brussels, Belgium*]
EPP .... European Producer Price
EPP .... Recording Potentiometer (RU)
EPPA .... Empresa Peruana de Promocion Artesanal [*Peruvian National Enterprise to Promote Handicrafts*] (LA)
EPPAA ...... European Pure Phosphoric Acid Producers' Association [*Belgium*] (EAIO)
EPPAPA .... European Pure Phosphoric Acid Producers' Association [*Belgium*] (EAIO)
EPPC .... KSEPL Exploration and Production Processing Center [*Research center*] [*Netherlands*] (IRC)
EPPG .... Element with a Rectangular Hysteresis Loop (RU)
EPPIC .... Early Psychosis Prevention and Intervention Centre [*Australia*]
EPPIC .... Environmental Planning Professions Interdisciplinary Committee [*South Africa*]
EPPO .... European and Mediterranean Plant Protection Organization [*See also OEPP*] (EAIO)
EPPO .... Poznan/Lawica [*Poland*] [*ICAO location identifier*] (ICLI)
EPPPD ...... Epitropi dia tin Proaspisin tou Pnevmatikou Politismou kai tis Dimokratias [*Committee for the Defense of Cultural Civilization and Democracy*] [*Greek*] (GC)
EPR .... East Pakistan Rifles [*Pakistani army*]
EPR .... Echtzeit-Prozessrechner [*German*] (ADPT)
EPR .... Economische Politierechter [*Benelux*] (BAS)
EPR .... Electric Drive (RU)
EPR .... Electron Paramagnetic Resonance (RU)
EPR .... Electropneumatic Distributor [*Automation*] (RU)
EPR .... Elektrarny Holesovice [*Electric Power Plants, Holesovice*] (CZ)
epr .... Epreuve [*Proof*] [*Publishing*] [*French*]
EPR .... Esperance [*Australia*] [*Airport symbol*] (OAG)
EPR .... Expreso Aereo [*Peru*] [*ICAO designator*] (FAAC)
EPRA .... Early Planning for Retirement Association [*Australia*]
EPRA .... Ethiopian People's Revolutionary Army [*Political party*]
EPRDF ...... Ethiopian People's Revolutionary Democratic Front [*Political party*] (ECON)
EPRI .... Egyptian Petroleum Research Institute [*Academy of Scientific Research and Technology*]
EPRL .... Warszawa [*Poland*] [*ICAO location identifier*] (ICLI)
EPRLF .... Eelam People's Revolutionary Liberation Front [*Sri Lanka*] [*Political party*]
EPRO .... Ethiopian Proletariats Revolutionary Organization (AF)
EPROB ..... Empresa de Proyectos para las Industrias de la Basica [*Cuba*] (EY)
EPRON ..... Expedition for Special Underwater Operations [*1923-1941*] (RU)
EPROYIV ... Empresa de Proyectos para Industrias Varias [*Cuba*] (EY)
EPRP .... Ethiopian People's Revolutionary Party [*Political party*] (PD)
EPRZ .... Rzeszow/Jasionka [*Poland*] [*ICAO location identifier*] (ICLI)
EPS .... Ecole Primaire Superieure [*Higher Elementary School*] [*French*]

EPS .... Education Physique et Sportive [*Physical and Sports Education*] [*Cambodia*] (CL)
EPS .... Effektive Pferdestaerke [*Effective Horsepower*] (EG)
EPS .... Ejercito Popular Sandinista [*Nicaragua*]
EPS .... Eksploatacija Pristanista i Skladista [*Operation of Ports and Depots*] (YU)
EPS .... Elektricno Preduzece Srbije [*Electrical Establishment of Serbia*] (YU)
EPS .... Empresas de Propiedad Social [*Social Property Enterprises*] [*Peru*] (LA)
EPS .... Endpunkt der Strecke [*Terminal Point of a Flight*] (EG)
EPS .... Enseignements Primaire et Secondaire
EPS .... Estudos de Ciencias Politicas e Sociais (Junta de Investigacoes do Ultramar, Lisbon)
EPS .... Ethnikos Paidikos Stathmos [*National Child Care Center*] [*Plus initial letter of district name*] (GC)
EPS .... European Physical Society (EAIO)
EPS .... Exercise Planning Staff [*NATO*] (NATG)
EPS .... Exotic Pathology Society [*Paris, France*] (EAIO)
EPS .... Service des Engrais, des Pesticides, et des Semences [*Fertilizer, Pesticide, and Seed Department*] [*Replaced Service d'Approvisionnement et de Distribution des Produits Importes Cambodia*] (CL)
EPSA .... Empresa Publica de Servicios Alimenticios [*Public Enterprise for Food Services*] [*Peru*] (LA)
EPSA .... Enosis Podosfairikon Somateion Athinon [*Union of Soccer Clubs of Athens*] (GC)
EPSAP ...... Empresa Publica de Servicios Agropecuarios del Peru [*Public Enterprise for Agricultural and Livestock Services of Peru*] [*Peru*] (LA)
EPSCG ...... Groupe de Contact Parlementaire et Scientifique [*European Parliamentary and Scientific Contact Group*] (EA)
EPSEP .... Empresa Publica de Servicios Pesqueros [*Public Enterprise for Fishing Services*] [*Peru*] (LA)
EPSG .... European Pineal Study Group (EAIO)
EPSHOM ... Etablissement Principal de la Service Hydrographique et Oceanographique de la Marine [*French*] (MSC)
EPSI .... Empresa de Polimeros de Sines SARL [*Portugal*]
EPSI .... Empresa Publica de Servicio de Informaciones [*Public Enterprise for Information Service*] [*Peru*] (LA)
EPSILL ..... Effective Partners in Secondary Literacy Learning [*Program*] [*Australia*]
EPSM .... Environmental Protection Society Malaysia (EAIO)
EPSMA ..... European Association for Manufacturers of Self-Adhesive Materials (PDAA)
EPT .... Electropneumatic Brake (RU)
EPTA .... Ethniki Protoporia Tetartis Avgoustou [*National Vanguard of the Fourth of August*] [*Greek*] (GC)
EPTA .... European Piano Teachers Association (EAIO)
EPTA .... European Power Tool Association (EAIO)
EPTA .... Expanded Program of Technical Assistance [*United Nations*]
EPTEK ...... Epitoipari Termeloeszkozkereskedelmi Vallalat [*Construction Industry Capital Equipment Marketing Enterprise*] (HU)
EPTEL ...... Empresa Publica de Telecommunicacoes [*Public Telecommunications Company*] [*Angola*] (AF)
EPTISA .... Estudios y Proyectos Technicos Industriales SA [*Spain*] (PDAA)
EPTR .... Export Profits Tax Relief
EPTT .... Comite Europeen de l'Internationale du Personnel des Postes, Telegraphes et Telephones [*European Committee of the Postal, Telegraph and Telephone International*] [*EC*] (ECED)
EPU .... Economic Planning Unit [*Generic term*] (DS)
EPU .... European Payments Union
EPU .... Evropska Platna Unija [*European Payments Union*] (YU)
Epugyi K .. Epitesugyi Kiado [*Architectural Publishing House*] (HU)
EPUH .... Empresa de Publicaciones de la Universidad de La Habana [*University of Havana Publications Enterprise*] [*Cuba*] (LA)
EPUL .... Ecole Polytechnique de l'Universite de Lausanne [*Institute of Technology of the University of Lausanne*] [*Switzerland*] (PDAA)
EPURE ...... Etude de la Protection des Usagers de la Route et de l'Environnement [*Study of Road User Safety and Environmental Protection*] [*French*] [*Automotive engineering*]
EPV .... Escritorio de Producao Vegetal [*Brazil*] (DSCA)
EPV .... Evangelische Progressieve Volkspartij [*Evangelical Progressive People's Party*] [*Netherlands*] (PPW)
EPV .... Povazske Elektrarny [*River Vah Electric Power Plants*] (CZ)
EPWA .... Warszawa/Okecie [*Poland*] [*ICAO location identifier*] (ICLI)
EPWAPDA ... East Pakistan Water and Power Development Authority (PDAA)
EPWG .... Energy Production Working Group [*Australia*]
EPZ .... Export Processing Zone
EPZA .... Export Processing Zone Association [*Mauritius*] (AF)
EPZA .... Export Processing Zone Authority

EQL .... Equatorial Airlines of Sao Tome and Principe [*ICAO designator*] (FAAC)
EQS .... Esquel [*Argentina*] [*Airport symbol*]   (OAG)
EQUALANT ... Equatorial Atlantic   (MSC)
EQUATGUI ... Equatorial Guinea   (WDAA)
EQUIGAS ... Equipos y Gas [*Colombia*]   (COL)
EQUIMPEX ... China National Machinery and Equipment Import & Export Corp. [*People'sRepublic of China*]   (IMH)
EQUIP....... Enterprise Quality Improvement Program [*Australia*]
EQUIPESCA ... Empresa Mocambicana de Apetrechamento da Industria Pesqueira [*Fishing equipment trade enterprise*] [*Mozambique*]
EQUITEC ... Equipos Tecnicos de Cali Ltda.   (COL)
equiv.......... Equivalente [*Equivalent To*] [*Portuguese*]
EQUL........ Employment in Queensland Libraries [*Australia*]
ER .... Ecole Rabbinique [*France*]   (BJA)
ER .... Economische Raad [*Benelux*]   (BAS)
ER .... Educational Resources [*Auckland, NZ*]
ER .... Egyptian Railways   (DCTA)
er .... Eienaarsrisiko [*Afrikaans*]
ER .... Ekumenicka Rada [*Ecumenical Council*]   (CZ)
ER .... Elders Resources [*Mining company*] [*Australia*]
ER .... Electronic Relay   (RU)
ER .... Elektronenrechner [*Electron Computer*] [*German*]   (ADPT)
ER .... Elektryfikacja Rolnictwa [*Electrification of Agriculture*]   (POL)
ER .... Enallassomenon Revma [*Alternating Current*]   (GC)
Er .... Erbio [*Chemical element*] [*Portuguese*]
er .... Eredeti [*Original*] [*Hungary*]
Er .... Ermenice [*Armenian*]   (TU)
Er .... Erstarrt [*Solidifies*] [*German*]
Er .... Erstarrungspunkt [*Freezing Point*] [*German*]
ER .... Eskortni Razarac [*Escort Destroyer*] [*Navy*]   (YU)
ER .... Espera Resposta [*Awaiting Reply*] [*Portuguese*]
ER .... European Right [*Political movement*]   (ECON)
ER .... Excess Reserves   (MHDB)
ER .... Wheel Excavator   (RU)
ERA .... Education Review Association [*Australia*]
ERA .... Effective Rate of Assistance [*International trade*]
ERA .... Egyptian Railroad Authority   (IMH)
ERA .... Electronic Research Australia Proprietary Ltd.
ERA .... Eletbiztositasi Rendezesi Alap [*Life Insurance Settlement Fund*] (HU)
ERA .... Elliniki Radiophonia [*Greek radio*]   (EY)
ERA .... Energy Resources of Australia Ltd.
ERA .... Environmental Resources of Australia   (ADA)
Era .... Erato [*Record label*] [*France*]
ERA .... Escritorio de Reforma Administrativa [*Administrative Reform Office*] [*Brazil*]   (LA)
ERA .... Eurocommander SA [*Spain*] [*ICAO designator*]   (FAAC)
ERA .... European Ramblers' Association   (EAIO)
ERA .... European Regional Airlines   (PDAA)
ERA .... European Regional Airlines Association [*British*]   (EAIO)
ERA .... European Rotogravure Association [*Germany*]   (PDAA)
ERA .... European Rum Association   (EAIO)
eraanl .... Eraanlainen [*A Kind Of*] [*Finland*]
ERAC........ Economics Research Advisory Committee [*Australia*]
ERAC........ Energy Research and Advisory Centre [*Australia*]
ERAC........ Engineering Research and Advisory Centre [*Chisholm Institute of Technology*] [*Australia*]
ERAC........ Etablissement Regional d'Amenagement et de Construction [*Morocco*]
ERAC........ Handicap International [*France*]   (EAIO)
erafl .... Eraflure [*Scraped Spot*] [*Publishing*] [*French*]
ERALL ...... Eroforras Allokalo Eljaras [*Resource Allocating Procedure*] (HU)
ER & S .... Electrolytic Refining and Smelting Co. [*Australia*]
ERAP........ Entreprise de Recherches et d'Activites Petrolieres [*Petroleum Activities and Research Enterprise*] [*Subsidiary of Essence et Lubrifiants de France*]   (CL)
ERASMUS ... European Action Scheme for the Mobility of University Students   (EY)
ERASP ...... Ecole Royale Agro-Sylvo-Pastorale [*Royal Agriculture, Livestock, and Forestry School*] [*Laotian*]   (CL)
ERASP ...... Education Resource Allocation in Schools Project [*Australia*]
ERATO ...... Exploratory Research for Advanced Technology [*Japan*]
erb .... Erbitten [*Request*] [*German*]   (GCA)
ER-BA ...... Escritorio Regional da Bahia (de SUDENE) [*Superintendencia do Desenvolvimento Economico do Nordeste*] [*Brazil*]   (LAA)
ERBE .... Eromu Beruhazasi Vallalat (Dunapentele-Sztalinvaros) [*Electric Power Plant Investment Enterprise of Dunapentele Sztalinvaros*]   (HU)
ERBOL...... Escuelas Radiofonicas de Bolivia [*Bolivian Radio Schools*]   (LA)
ERC .... Economics Research Center [*Philippines*] [*Research center*]   (IRC)
ERC .... Educational Research Centre [*Australia*]
ERC .... Education and Resource Centre [*South Australia*]

ERC .... Eligibility Review Committee [*Social security*] [*Australia*]
ERC .... Employee Relations Commission [*Victoria*] [*Australia*]
ERC .... Entreprise Regionale de Commerce [*Regional Trade Enterprise*] [*Guinea*]   (AF)
ERC .... Esquerra Republicana de Catalunya [*Catalan Republican Left*] [*Spain*] [*Political party*]   (PPE)
ERC .... European Registry of Commerce   (DS)
ERC .... Expenditure Review Committee [*Australia*]
ERCA........ Ejercito Rojo Catalan de Liberacion [*Spain*] [*Political party*] (EY)
ERCHCW ... European Regional Clearing House for Community Work (EAIO)
ERCO .... Entreprise de Realisation & de Construction d'Oran [*Electrical transmission systems company*] [*Algeria*]
ERCOA ..... Entreprises [*or Etatiques*] Regionale de Commercialisation Agricole
ERCS........ Egyptian Red Crescent Society   (EAIO)
ERC(Vic) ... Employee Relations Commission (Victoria) [*Australia*]
ERD .... Electrical Rocket Engine   (RU)
ERDA .... Electrical Research and Development Association [*Council of Scientific and Industrial Research*] [*India*]   (WED)
ERDC .... Eastern Region Development Corporation
ERDC .... Energy Research and Development Center [*Philippines*]
ERDC .... Environment, Resources and Development Court [*South Australia*]
ERDC .... Ergonomic Research and Design Centre [*Australia*]
ERDC(SA) ... Environment, Resources and Development Court (South Australia)
ERDE .... Electronics and Radar Development Establishment [*India*] (PDAA)
ERDEMIR ... Eregli Demir ve Celik Fabrikalar AS [*Eregli Iron and Steel Plants Corporation*]   (TU)
ERDERT ... Erdogazdasagi es Faipari Ertekesito es Keszletezo Vallalat [*Marketing and Stockpiling Enterprise for Forestry and Lumber Industry*]   (HU)
ERDF........ European Regional Development Fund [*See also FEDER*] [*Brussels, Belgium*]   (EAIO)
Erdg .... Erdgeschichte [*German*]
Erdg .... Erdgeschoss [*Ground Floor*] [*German*]
ERDIC ...... Energy Research, Development, and Information Centre [*University of New South Wales*] [*Australia*]
ERDIC ...... Entente Republicaine pour la Defense des Interets Communaux
Erdk .... Erdkunde [*German*]
ERDL........ Explosives Research and Development Laboratory [*India*] (PDAA)
erdogazd..... Erdogazdasag [*Forestry*]   (HU)
Erdolforder ... Erdoelfoerderung [*Petroleum Production*] [*German*]   (GCA)
ERDOTERV ... Erdogazdasagi es Faipari Tervezo Iroda [*Forestry and Lumber Industry Planning Office*]   (HU)
ERDP........ Entreprise Nationale de Raffinage et de Distribution des Produits Petroliers [*Algeria*]
ERDRI...... Earth Resources Development Research Institute
ERE .... Ecumenical Research Exchange
ERE .... Erave [*Papua New Guinea*] [*Airport symbol*]   (OAG)
ERE .... Ethniki Rizospastiki Enosis [*National Radical Union*] [*Greek*] (GC)
ERECO...... European Economic Research and Advisory Consortium [*Belgium*]   (EAIO)
ERECOS ... Empresa de Refractarios Colombianos [*Colombia*]   (COL)
EREDEC ... Eastern Regional Development Corporation
EREMIL ... Empresa Retalhista Mista de Luanda
EREN .... Ethniki Rizospastiki Enosis Neolaias [*National Radical Youth Union*]   (GC)
EREP........ Ethniki Reformistiki Ergatoypalliliki Parataxis [*National Reformist Workers Faction*] [*Greek*]   (GC)
ERES........ Erlanger Rechner-Entwurfs-Sprache [*Programming language*] [*1974*]
ere-sekr ..... Ere-Sekretaris [*Honorable Secretary*] [*Afrikaans*]
ERF .... Erfurt [*Germany*] [*Airport symbol*]   (OAG)
ERFA........ European Radio Frequency Agency [*Later, ARFA*] [*NATO*]
erfahr .... Erfahren [*Experienced*] [*German*]   (GCA)
Erfahr .... Erfahrung [*Experience*] [*German*]   (GCA)
Erfass........ Erfassung [*Detection*] [*German*]   (GCA)
ERFEN ..... Estudio Regional del Fenomeno El Nino   (MSC)
ERFL .... Epitropi Rythmiseos Fortoekfortoseon Limenos [*Committee for Regulating Cargo Handling Operations of the Port*] [*Followed by initial letter of the name of the port*]   (GC)
ERFOLG ... Ermittlungssysteme fuer Optimale Lukrative Geldanlage [*German*]   (ADPT)
Erforsch ..... Erforschung [*Exploration*] [*German*]   (GCA)
ERFX .... Epitropi Rythmiseos Fortoekfortoseon Xiras [*Committee for Regulating Freight Handling Operations on Land*] [*Followed by the name of the city*] [*Greek*]   (GC)
ERG .... Electroretinogram   (RU)
Erg .... Ergaenze [*Supplement, Add*] [*German*]   (EG)
Erg .... Ergaenzung [*Amendment, Supplement*] [*German*]   (DLA)
Erg .... Ergebenst [*Truly*] [*Correspondence*] [*German*]

ERG .... Etablissements Robert Gonfreville [*Ivory Coast*]

ERG .... Exportrisikogaraantie [*Export credit agency*] [*Switzerland*]

Erganz....... Ergaenzung [*Supplement*] [*German*]   (GCA)

ERG-AS..... Ergatikos Andifasistikos Syndesmos [*Workers' Anti-Fascist League*] [*Greek*]   (GC)

ErgBd........ Ergaenzungsband [*Supplementary Volume*] [*German*]

Ergebn....... Ergebnis [*Result*] [*German*]   (GCA)

Erg-H .... Ergaenzungsheft [*Supplement*] [*German*]

ERGO .... East Rand Gold and Uranium Co. Ltd. [*South Africa*]

ERGODATA ... Banque de Donnees Internationales de Biometrie Humaine et d'Ergonomie [*International Database of Human Biometrics and Ergonomics*] [*Universite Rene Descartes*] [*France*] [*Information service or system*]   (CRD)

Erh .... Erhaltung [*State of Preservation*] [*Publishing*] [*German*]

erh .... Erhitzt [*or Erhitzung*] [*Heated or Heating*] [*German*]

Erhalt......... Erhaltung [*Maintenance*] [*German*]   (GCA)

Erhart .... Erhaertung [*Hardening*] [*German*]   (GCA)

Erhitz........ Erhitzung [*Heating Up*] [*German*]   (GCA)

Erhoh .... Erhoehung [*Raise*] [*German*]   (GCA)

ERI............. Earthquake Research Institute [*University of Tokyo*] [*Japan*]   (EAS)

ERI............. Electronics Research Institute [*Cairo, Egypt*] [*Research center*]   (ERC)

ERI............. Empresa de Radiocomunicacion Internacional [*International Radio Communications*] [*Cuba*]   (LA)

ERI............. Energy Research Institute [*University of Cape Town*] [*South Africa*] [*Research center*]   (ERC)

ERI............. Executive Resources International

ERIA......... Estudios y Realizaciones en Informatic a Aplicada [*Spain*]   (PDAA)

ERIAD....... Entreprise des Industries Alimentaires, Cerealieres & Derives [*Wheat and cereal producing company*] [*Algeria*]

ERIC.......... Energy Recovery Investment Corporation [*Luxembourg*]

ERIC.......... Environmental Research and Information Centre [*Bulgaria*]   (EE)

ERICA....... European Research into Consumer Affairs [*England*] [*Research center*]   (IRC)

erik............ Erikoinen [*Finland*]

erik............. Erikoisesti [*Especially*] [*Finland*]

ERIME...... Economic Research Institute for the Middle East [*Japanese*]

ERIN .... Environmental Resources Information Network [*Australia*]

ERIS .... Environmental Resource Information Services [*Australia*]

erisn .... Erisnimi [*Proper Noun*] [*Finland*]

Erit .... Eritrea

ERIW......... European Research Institute for Welding   (PDAA)

ERJ .... Eurojet Italia [*Italy*] [*ICAO designator*]   (FAAC)

ERK .... Ergatiki Reformistiki Kinisi [*Workers Reformist Movement*] [*Greek*]   (GC)

Erk .... Erkennung [*Recognition*] [*German*]

erk .... Erkezik [*Arrives*]   (HU)

ErK .... Erkin Kyrgyzstan [*Political party*]   (EY)

ERK .... Ethniko Rizospastiko Komma [*National Radical Party*] [*Greek*]   (PPE)

Erkenn .... Erkennung [*Detection*] [*German*]   (GCA)

erkl............. Erklaert [*Explained, Illustrated*] [*German*]

erklar .... Erklaerend [*Explanatory*] [*Publishing*] [*German*]

ERL........... Electronics Research Laboratory [*Adelaide, South Australia*] [*Research center*]   (ERC)

ERL........... Environmental Research Laboratory [*Zambia*]

Erl .... Erlaeuterung [*Explanation, (Explanatory) Note*] [*German*]   (EG)

Erl .... Erlass [*Decree, Edict, Order*] [*German*]   (ILCA)

ERL .... Euralair [*France*] [*ICAO designator*]   (FAAC)

ERLANG.... Erlangen   (ROG)

ERLSS........ Eastern Riverina Linen and Supply Service [*Australia*]

ERM .... Ecole Royale de Medecine [*Royal School of Medicine*] [*Laotian*]   (CL)

ERM .... Espera Receber Merce [*Hopes to Have His Petition Granted*] [*Portuguese*]

ERM .... Exchange-Rate Mechanism [*European Economic Union*]   (ECON)

ERMCO .... European Ready Mixed Concrete Organization   (EAIO)

ERMIG...... Eletrificacao Rural de Minas Gerais [*Brazil*]   (LAA)

ermit.......... Ermitano [*Spanish*]

Ermittl ...... Ermittlung [*Inquiry*] [*German*]   (GCA)

ERMP........ Empresa para la Recuperacion de Materias Primas [*Enterprise for the Recovery of Raw Materials*] [*Cuba*]   (LA)

ERN .... Emissora Regional do Norte [*Northern Regional Radio*] [*Portuguese*]   (WER)

ERNET....... Education and Research Network [*India*] [*Computer science*]   (TNIG)

ERNK .... Enlya Ruzgariya Netwa Kurdistan [*National Front for the Liberation of Kurdistan*] [*Turkey*] [*Political party*]

ERNO........ Entwicklungsring Nord [*Northern Development Center*] [*Germany*]   (PDAA)

Ernteprod... Ernteprodukt [*Crop*] [*German*]   (GCA)

ERO .... European Regional Organization of the International Dental Federation   (EAIO)

ERO .... Operation and Repair Department   (RU)

ERO .... Sundor International Air Services Ltd. [*Israel*] [*ICAO designator*]   (FAAC)

EROPA...... Eastern Regional Organization for Public Administration GG2 [*Manila, Philippines*] [*See also OROAP*]

EROS........ Eelam Revolutionary Organization [*Sri Lanka*] [*Political party*]

EROS........ Equipements Respiratoires a Oxygene de Secours [*French*]

EROS........ Experience de Recherche d'Objects Sombres [*Astronomy*]

EROTERV ... Eromuveket Tervezo Vallalat [*Designing Enterprise for Electric Power Plants*]   (HU)

ERP .... Effective Radiative Power   (EG)

ERP........... Ejercito Revolucionario del Pueblo [*People's Revolutionary Army*] [*Argentina*]   (PD)

ERP........... Ejercito Revolucionario del Pueblo [*People's Revolutionary Army*] [*El Salvador*]   (PD)

ERP........... Electronic Road Pricing System [*Public transport*] [*Hong Kong*]

ERP........... Estimated Resident Population [*Demographics*] [*Australia*]

ERP.......... European Recovery Program

ERPDB...... Eastern Regional Production Development Board

ERPM........ East Rand Proprietary Mines [*South Africa*]

ERPT .... Etablissements Ruraux des Postes et Telecommunications [*Rural Posts and Telecommunications Offices*] [*Cambodia*]   (CL)

err.............. Errichtet [*German*]

Erreich ...... Erreichung [*Obtaining*] [*German*]   (GCA)

erroneam.... Erroneamente [*Erroneously*] [*Italian*]

ERRRU...... Economic and Regional Restructuring Research Unit [*Australia*]

ERS .... Economic Research Service

ERS........... Electrical Exploration Station   (RU)

ERS........... Electrolytic Refining and Smelting Company [*Australia*] [*Commercial firm*]

ERS........... Emissora Regional do Sul [*Southern Regional Radio*] [*Portuguese*]   (WER)

Ers............ Ersatz [*Replacement*] [*German*]   (GCA)

ERS........... ESA [*European Space Agency*] Remote Sensing Satellite

ERS........... European Rhinologic Society   (EA)

ERS........... Export Return Scheme [*Australia*]

ERS........... Windhoek-Eros [*Namibia*] [*Airport symbol*]   (OAG)

Ersch......... Erscheinung [*Appearance*] [*German*]   (GCA)

ersch.......... Erschienen [*Published*] [*German*]

Erschein..... Erscheinung [*Appearance*] [*German*]   (GCA)

ERShR....... Walking Rail Mounted Wheel Excavator   (RU)

ERSK .... Uniform Republic Sports Classification   (BU)

ERSO........ Electronics Research and Service Organization [*Taiwanese*] [*Research center*]   (IRC)

ERSP .... Eesti Rahvusliku Soltumatuse Partei [*Estonian National Independence Party*] [*Political party*]   (EAIO)

ERSPO...... Estonian Republic Union of Consumers' Societies   (RU)

erst .... Oersted   (RU)

Erstarr ...... Erstarrung [*Solidification*] [*German*]   (GCA)

Erst P........ Erstarrungspunkt [*Freezing Point*] [*German*]

ERSU......... Educational Resource Services Unit [*Technical and Further Education*] [*New South Wales, Australia*]

ERT .... Elliniki Radiofonia kai Tileorasis [*Greek Radio and Television*]   (GC)

ERT .... Ertekesito [*Selling or Sale*]   (HU)

ert .... Ertekezes [*Treatise*]   (HU)

ert.............. Ertekezlet [*Meeting*]   (HU)

ert.............. Ertelmeben [*or Ertelemben*] [*In Accordance With*]   (HU)

ert.............. Ertesites [*Notification*]   (HU)

ERT .... European Round Table   (EAIO)

ERT .... Union Explosivos Rio Tinto SA [*Spanish*]   (WER)

ERTA........ European Road Transport Agreement   (ILCA)

ERTAT...... Expressway and Rapid Transit Authority of Thailand   (DS)

ERTC........ Energy Research and Training Center [*Chulalongkorn University*] [*Thailand*]   (WED)

ERTEC ..... Societe Anonyme d'Etudes et de Realisations Techniques

ertek.......... Ertekezes [*Treatise*] [*Hungary*]

ERTI.......... Erdeszeti Tudomanyos Intezet [*Scientific Institute of Forestry*]   (HU)

ERTO .... Erityisalojen Toimihenkiloeliitto [*Federation of Special Service and Clerical Employees*] [*Finland*]   (EY)

ERTS .... Earth Resources Technology Satellite

ERTS-GEOBOL ... Earth Resources Technology Satellite - Bolivian Geological Service   (LA)

ERTV .... Egyptian Radio and Television Corp.   (MENA)

ERU .... Cathode-Ray Recorder   (RU)

ERU .... Education Review Unit [*South Australia*]

ERU .... Electronic Resolver [*Computers*]   (RU)

ERU .... Environmental Review Unit

ERU .... Erume [*Papua New Guinea*] [*Airport symbol*]   (OAG)

ERU .... Exponential Amplification Control   (RU)

ERUOPUR ... Association Europeene des Fabricants de Mousse Souple de Polyurethane [*Belgium*]   (EAIO)

ERUSA...... Empreendimentos Rurais SA [*Brazil*]   (DSCA)

ERV .... Economische Raad voor Vlaanderen [*Benelux*]   (BAS)

ERV .... Electronic Timing Relay   (RU)

ERV .... Escadre de Ravitaillement en Vol [*French aerial refueling wing*]
ERV .... Europese Rum Vereniging [*European Rum Association*] [*EC*] (ECED)
ERVA .... Empresa de Reflorestamento e Valorizacao Agraria SA [*Brazil*] (DSCA)
erw............. Erwaehnt [*Mentioned*] [*German*]
erw............. Erwaermt [*Heated*] [*German*]
Erw............ Erwartung [*Expectation*] [*German*] (GCA)
erw............. Erweitert [*Enlarged*] [*German*]
Erwag........ Erwaegung [*Consideration*] [*German*] (GCA)
Erweich...... Erweichung [*Softening*] [*German*] (GCA)
erweit......... Erweitert [*Enlarged*] [*German*]
ERWP....... European Railway Wagon Pool (EA)
ERYEA..... Elliniki Etaireia Erevnis Elengkhou Rypanseos Ydaton Edafous Aeros [*Greek Research Association for the Control of Water, Land, and Air Pollution*] (GC)
ERZ .... Electric Locomotive Repair Plant (RU)
Erz............. Erzaehlung [*Story*] [*German*]
ERZ .... Erzurum [*Turkey*] [*Airport symbol*] (OAG)
Erzb........... Erzbishof [*Archbishop*] [*German*]
Erzeug....... Erzeugung [*Production*] [*German*] (GCA)
Erziel........ Erzielung [*Attainment*] [*German*] (GCA)
ES .... Air Squadron (RU)
ES .... Destroyer (RU)
ES .... Economic Conference (RU)
ES .... Economic Council (RU)
ES .... Economisch Statistische Berichten [*Benelux*] (BAS)
ES .... Edinaya Systema [*Unified System*] [*Russian*] [*Computer science*]
ES .... Egyesules [*Joint Enterprise, Association*] (HU)
ES .... Ektakton Symvoulion [*Emergency Council*] [*Greek*] (GC)
ES .... Ektelestikon Symvoulion [*Executive Council*] (GC)
ES .... Electric Power Plant (RU)
ES .... Electric Power System (RU)
ES .... Electric Salinometer (RU)
ES .... Electrostatic Instrument (RU)
ES .... Elektrosrbija [*An establishment for planning, construction, and production of electrical equipment*] [*Belgrade*] (YU)
ES .... Elet es Irodalom [*Life and Literature*] [*Title of a publication*] (HU)
es .... El Hawi Shipping [*Saudi Arabia*]
ES .... Ellinikos Stratos [*Greek Army*] (GC)
ES .... Ellinikos Synagermos [*Greek Rally*] (GC)
ES .... Empresa de Semillas [*Seed Enterprise*] [*Cuba*] (LA)
ES .... Encyclopedic Reference Book (RU)
ES .... Energeticka Sluzba [*Electric Power Supply Service*] [*Civil defense*] (CZ)
ES .... Enseignement Secondaire [*Secondary Education*] [*Cambodia*] (CL)
ES .... Epanastatikoi Sosialistes [*Revolutionary Socialists*] [*Greek*] (GC)
ES .... Epitropi Sitiron [*Wheat Board*] [*Cyprus*] (GC)
e/s .... Erg por Segundo [*Ergs per Second*] [*Portuguese*]
ES .... Ernteschaetzung [*Crop Estimate*] (EG)
ES .... Esegiel [*Ezekiel*] [*Afrikaans*]
es .... Esempio [*Example*] [*Italian*] (GPO)
es .... Esemplare [*Copy*] [*Publishing*] [*Italian*]
Es .... Eski [*Old, Ancient*] (TU)
ES .... Espirito Santo
ES .... Estado do Espirito Santo [*State of Espirito Santo*] [*Brazil*]
ES .... Ethniki Sotiria [*National Salvation*] [*Greek*] (GC)
ES .... Ethnographical Society [*Former Czechoslovakia*] (EAIO)
ES .... EUROSTAT [*Statistical Office of the European Communities*]
ES .... Euzko Socialista [*Basque Socialist Party*] [*Spanish*] (WER)
e/s .... Expedition Vessel (RU)
ES .... Instituto per la Ricerca di Economia Sanitaria [*Italian*] (SLS)
ES .... Screen Grid (RU)
ES .... Spain [*ANSI two-letter standard code*] (CNC)
ES .... Synchronization Element (RU)
ES .... Uniform System (BU)
ES² .... European Silicon Structures [*Proposed Pan-European manufacturer of semiconductors*]
ESA........... Department of Economic and Social Affairs
ESA........... Eastern and Southern African Countries
ESA........... Eastern South America (LAA)
ESA........... Ecole Superieure d'Agriculture
ESA........... Ecole Superieure des Affaires [*High Business School*] [*Information service or system*] (IID)
ESA........... Ecological Society of Australia (ADA)
ESA........... Economic Society of Australia
ESA........... Ejercito Salvadoreno Anticomunista [*Salvadoran Anti-Communist Army*] (PD)
ESA........... Ejercito Segredo Anti-Comunista [*Secret Anti-Communist Army*] [*Guatemala*] (PD)
ESA........... Electric Equipment for Aircraft and Automobiles (RU)
ESA........... Elliniki Stratiotiki Astynomia [*Greek Military Police*] (GC)

ESA........... Emborikos Syllogos Athinon [*Commercial Chamber of Athens*] (GC)
ESA........... Endocrine Society of Australia (ADA)
ESA........... English, Scottish & Australian Bank Ltd. (ADA)
ESA........... Entomological Society of Australia
ESA........... Ergonomics Society of Australia
ESA........... Esa Ala [*Papua New Guinea*] [*Airport symbol*] (OAG)
ESA........... Escola Superior de Agricultura [*Brazil*] (DSCA)
ESA........... Escola Superior de Agrimensura [*Brazil*] (DSCA)
ESA........... European Space Agency [*See also ASE*] (EAIO)
ESA........... European Spice Association [*EC*] (ECED)
ESA........... European Strabismological Association (EAIO)
ESA........... European Suzuki Association [*British*] (EAIO)
ESA........... Seagreen Air Transport [*Antigua and Barbuda*] [*ICAO designator*] (FAAC)
ESAA........ Electricity Supply Association of Australia (ADA)
ESAAT ...... Ecole Superieure d'Application d'Agriculture Tropicale
ESAB........ Elektriska Sventsningsaktiebolaget [*Sweden*]
ESACC ...... Ecole Superieure Africaine des Cadres du Chemin de Fer
ESACT ...... European Society for Animal Cell Technology (EA)
ESACTA ... Ente Specializzato Aerofotogrammetria, Cartografia, Topografia, Aerofotogeologia, [*Specialized Agency for Aerophotogrammetry, Cartography, Topography, and Aerophotogeology*] [*Italian*] (AF)
ESAD........ Ege Bolgesi Seyahat Acenteleri Dernegi [*Aegean Region Travel Agents' Organization*] (TU)
ESADE...... Escuela Superior de Administracion y Direccion de Empresas
ESAE........ European Society of Association Executives (EA)
ESAEI ...... Electric Supply Authority Engineers Institute [*New Zealand*] (PDAA)
ESAF .... Enhanced Structural Adjustment Facility [*IMF*] (ECON)
ESAIDARM ... Eastern and Southern African Initiative in Debt and Reserves Management (ECON)
ESA-IRS... European Space Agency Information Retrieval Service [*Italy*]
ESAK........ Ellinikon Stratiotikon Apospasma Kyprou [*Greek Army Contingent on Cyprus*] (GC)
ESAK........ Eniaia Syndikalistiki Andidiktatoriki Kinisi [*United Antidictatorial Labor Movement*] [*Greek*] (GC)
ESAK-S ..... Eniaia Syndikalistiki Andidiktatoriki Kinisi - Synergazomenoi [*United Antidictatorial Labor Movement - Cooperating*]
ESAL .... Empresa de Saneamiento de Lima [*Lima Sanitation Enterprise*] [*Peru*] (LA)
ESAL .... Escola Superior de Agricultura de Lavras [*Brazil*] (DSCA)
ESALQ ...... Escola Superior de Agricultura "Luiz De Queiros" [*Luiz De Queiros Agricultural College*] [*Piracicaba, Brazil*] (LAA)
ESAM........ Evangelization Society of African Missions
ESAMI ...... Eastern and Southern African Management Institute [*Nigeria*]
ESAMRDC ... Eastern and Southern African Mineral Resources Development Center
ESAMRDC ... Eastern and Southern African Mineral Resources Development Centre [*Tanzania*]
ESAN........ Escuela de Administracion de Negocios [*School of Business Administration*] [*Peru*] (LA)
ESANET ... European Space Agency Information Network (PDAA)
ESANZ...... Economic Society of Australia and New Zealand (ADA)
ESANZ...... Ergonomics Society of Australia and New Zealand (ADA)
ESAO .... Escola de Aperfeicoamento de Oficiais [*Officer Training School*] [*Brazil*] (LA)
ESAO .... European Society for Artificial Organs (EA)
ESAP........ Ecole Superieure d'Agriculture de Purpan [*Purpan College of Agriculture*] [*French*] (ARC)
ESAP........ Egyptian Society of Animal Production
ESAP........ Escuela Superior de Administracion Publica [*Advanced School for Public Administration*] [*Colorado*] (LA)
ESAP........ Escuela Superior de Administracion Publica del Peru [*Advanced School for Public Administration*] [*Peru*] (LA)
ESAP........ Ethnikos Syndesmos Anapiron Polemou [*National League of Persons Disabled by War*] [*Greek*] (GC)
ESAP........ Ethniko Symvoulio Anotatis Ekpaidevseos [*National Council of Supreme Education*] (GC)
ESAPAC... Escuela Superior de Administracion Publica America Central [*Costa Rica*]
ESAPE ...... Ethnikon Symvoulion Anotatis Paideias kai Erevnon [*National Council of Higher Education and Research*] [*Greek*] (GC)
ESARBICA ... Eastern and Southern African Regional Branch of the International Council on Archives [*Nairobi, Kenya*] (EAIO)
ESARDA ... European Safeguards Research and Development Association [*Italian*] (SLS)
ESARIPO ... Industrial Property Organization for English-Speaking Africa [*Nairobi, Kenya*] (EAIO)
ESAS .... Elektrometallurji Sanayii Anonim Sirketi [*Electrometallurgy Industry Corporation*] (TU)
ESASA ...... Ethnic Schools Association of South Australia
ESASI....... European Society of Air Safety Investigators (PDAA)
ESAT .... Ecole Superieure d'Agriculture Tropicale

ESAT .... Enosis Syndakton Athinaikou Typou [*Union of Athens Newspaper Editors*]   (GC)

ESAT .... Laboratory Electronics, Systems, Automation, and Technology [*Research center*] [*Belgium*]   (IRC)

esaur........... Esaurito [*Out of Print*] [*Publishing*] [*Italian*]

ESAURP ... Escola Superior de Agricultura da Universidade Federal Rural de Pernambuco [*Brazil*]   (DSCA)

ESAV .... Einheitssystem der Automatisierten Verfahrenstechnik [*German*]   (ADPT)

ESAV .... Escola Superior de Agricultura e Veterinaria [*High School for Agriculture and Veterinary Science*] [*Brazil*]   (LAA)

ESB .... Ankara-Esenboga [*Turkey*] [*Airport symbol*]   (OAG)

ESB .... Eastern Seaboard [*Thailand*]   (DS)

ESB .... Economisch Statistische Berichten [*Benelux*]   (BAS)

ESB .... Education Support Centre [*Australia*]

ESB .... Einheitssystem Bau [*Standard Construction System*]   (EG)

ESB .... Emergency Services Bureau [*Queensland, Australia*]

ESB .... Energeticke Strojirny [*Electrical Engineering Enterprises*]   (CZ)

ESB .... Escuela Secundaria Basica [*Basic Secondary School*] [*Cuba*]   (LA)

ESB .... European Society of Biomechanics   (EA)

ESBASE .... Empresa Subterraneos de Buenos Aires Sociedad del Estado [*Argentina*]   (IMH)

ESBCY ...... European Society for Blue Cross Youth   (EA)

ESBEC ...... Escuela Secundaria Basica en el Campo [*Basic Secondary Farm School*] [*Cuba*]   (LA)

ESBEEC .... Escuela Secundaria Basica en el Campo [*Basic Secondary Farm School*] [*Cuba*]   (LA)

ESBG .... European Savings Bank Group [*EC*]   (ECED)

ESBP .... European Society of Biochemical Pharmacology [*Belgium*]   (SLS)

ESBR .... Electrical Bomb-Release Mechanism   (RU)

ESBR .... Escuela Secundaria Basica Rural [*Rural Basic Secondary School*] [*Cuba*]   (LA)

ESBUR ...... Escuela Secundaria Basica Urbana [*Urban Basic Secondary School*] [*Cuba*]   (LA)

ESBUWU ... Elementary School Building Unit Workers Union

ESBV .... Escuela Secundaria Basica Vocacional [*Vocational Basic Secondary School*] [*Cuba*]   (LA)

ESBVM ..... Ecumenical Society of the Blessed Virgin Mary   (EA)

ESC .... Comite Economique et Social des Comunautes Europeennes   (SLS)

ESC .... Economic and Social Committee [*EC*]   (ECED)

ESC .... Economic and Social Council [*United Nations*]

ESC .... Elektrarensky Svaz Ceskoslovensky [*Union of Czechoslovak Power Plants*]   (CZ)

ESC .... Elektrotechnicky Svaz Ceskoslovensky [*Czechoslovak Electrical Engineering Association*]   (CZ)

ESC .... Employment Studies Centre [*University of Newcastle, Australia*]

ESC .... Entree/ortie Compteur [*French*]   (ADPT)

Esc............. Escadrille [*Military*]   (BARN)

Esc............. Escadron [*Squadron*] [*Military*] [*French*]   (MTD)

ESC .... Escobilla [*Little Broom*] [*Flamenco dance term*] [*Spanish*]

Esc............. Escola [*School*] [*Portuguese*]

ESC .... Escompte [*Discount, Rebate*] [*French*]

Esc............. Escritorio   (SCAC)

ESC .... Escudo [*Monetary unit*] [*Chile, Portugal*]

Esc............. Escudos   (SCAC)

Esc............. Escuela   (SCAC)

ESC .... European Seismological Commission   (EAIO)

ESC .... European Shippers' Councils [*Netherlands*]   (DS)

ESC .... European Society of Cardiology [*Netherlands*]   (SLS)

ESC .... European Society of Climatotherapy [*See also FEC*] [*Briancon, France*]   (EAIO)

ESC .... European Society of Culture [*See also SEC*]   (EAIO)

ESC .... European Sport Shooting Confederation   (EAIO)

ESCA .... Ecole Superieure de Commerce d'Abidjan

ESCA .... Ecole Superieure de Commerce d'Alger

esca .... Escadrille [*Flotilla*] [*French*]

Esca........... Escadrille d'Avions [*Air Squadron*] [*Military*] [*French*]   (MTD)

ESCA .... Executive Secretaries Club of South Africa   (AA)

ESCAMA .. Escadrille Malgache [*Malagasy Air Squadron*]   (AF)

ESCAP ...... European Society of Child and Adolescent Psychiatry   (EA)

ESCAP ...... United Nations Economic and Social Commission for Asia and the Pacific [*Bangkok, Thailand*]   (EAIO)

ESCAPE.... European Symposium on Computer Aided Process Engineering

ESCC .... Stockholm [*Sweden*] [*ICAO location identifier*]   (ICLI)

ESCD........ Escola Superior de Ciencias Domesticas [*Brazil*]   (DSCA)

ESCE .... European Society for Comparative Endocrinology   (ASF)

ESCELSA ... Espirito Santo Centrais Eletricas [*Brazil*]   (LAA)

ESCERC.... European Semiconductor Device Research Conference

ESCES....... Experimental Satellite Communication Earth Station [*India*]   (PDAA)

ESCF .... Linkoping/Malmen [*Sweden*] [*ICAO location identifier*]   (ICLI)

ESCHC..... Educational, Scientific, Cultural, and Health Commission

ESCI .... European Society for Clinical Investigation   (EAIO)

ESCIL........ Ecole Superieure de Chimie Industrielle de Lyon

ESCK .... Norrkoping/Bravalla [*Sweden*] [*ICAO location identifier*]   (ICLI)

ESCL .... Soderhamn [*Sweden*] [*ICAO location identifier*]   (ICLI)

ESCM .... Equipment Support Center, Mannheim [*Germany*]

ESCM .... Uppsala [*Sweden*] [*ICAO location identifier*]   (ICLI)

ESCMTA .. Escuela Superior de Ciencias Maritimas y Tecnologia de Alimentos   (MSC)

ESCN........ Stockholm/Tullinge [*Sweden*] [*ICAO location identifier*]   (ICLI)

esco........... Escudo [*Monetary unit*] [*Spanish*]

ESCO .... European Satellite Consulting Organization [*France*] [*Telecommunications*]

ESCOLATINA ... Estudios Economicos Latinoamericanos para Graduados [*Santiago, Chile*]   (LAA)

ESCOLOMBIAS ... Escuelas Colombianas de Alto Comercio y Finanzas [*Colombia*]   (COL)

ESCOMO ... Escuela de Comercio Moderno [*Colombia*]   (COL)

ESCOOP... Escuela de Cooperativismo [*Uruguay*]   (DSCA)

ESCOPREFIL ... Empresa de Correos, Prensa, y Filatelia [*Post, Press, and Postal Stamps Enterprise*] [*Cuba*]   (LA)

ESCOW..... Engineering and Scientific Committee on Water [*New Zealand*]   (PDAA)

ESCP .... Ecole Superieure de Commerce de Paris [*Paris College of Commerce*] [*France*]   (PDAA)

ESCPB....... European Society of Comparative Physiology and Biochemistry   (EAIO)

escrit.......... Escritura [*A Writing*] [*Spanish*]

escrnia....... Escribania [*Writing-Set*] [*Spanish*]

escrno........ Escribano [*Court Clerk*] [*Spanish*]

ESCSP....... European Society of Corporate and Strategic Planners [*Belgium*]   (PDAA)

escte .... Escompte [*Discount, Rebate*] [*Business term*] [*French*]

ESCUPA ... Estacion Cuarentenaria de Paraguana [*Venezuela*]   (DSCA)

ESCVS....... European Society for Cardiovascular Surgery   (EAIO)

ESCWA ..... Economic and Social Commission for Western Asia [*Iraq*] [*United Nations Research center*]   (IRC)

ESD .... Electronique Serge Dassault [*Research center*] [*French*]   (ERC)

ESD .... Elektroschaltgeraete Dresden (VEB) [*Dresden Electric Switch Plant (VEB)*]   (EG)

ESDA .... Ljungbyhed [*Sweden*] [*ICAO location identifier*]   (ICLI)

ESDAC...... European Space Data Centre

ESDB........ Angelholm [*Sweden*] [*ICAO location identifier*]   (ICLI)

ESDD .... Regional Military Command Subcenter South [*Sweden*] [*ICAO location identifier*]   (ICLI)

ESDE .... Elevtheri Sosialistiki Dimokratiki Enosis [*Free Socialist Democratic Union*] [*Greek*]   (GC)

ESDE/AM/S ... Elliniki Sosialistiki Dimokratiki Enosis/Apelevtherotiko Metopo/"Spartakos" [*Greek Socialist Democratic Union/ Liberation Front/"Spartakos"*]   (GC)

ESDERC ... European Semiconductor Device Research Conference   (PDAA)

ESDF .... Ronneby [*Sweden*] [*ICAO location identifier*]   (ICLI)

ESDIN....... Elliniki Sosialistiki Dimokratiki Neolaia [*Greek Socialist Democratic Youth*]   (GC)

ES DNC..... Entreprise Socialiste pour le Developpement National de la Construction [*Algeria*]   (IMH)

ESDON ..... Elliniki Sosialdimokratiki Organosi Neon [*Greek Social Democratic Youth Organization*]   (GC)

ESDUCK... Egyptian Society for the Dissemination of Universal Culture and Knowledge   (SLS)

ESDY......... Enosi Syndaxioukhon Dimosion Ypallilon [*Civil Service Pensioners' Union*] [*Cyprus*]   (GC)

ESE .... Avesen SA de CV [*Mexico*] [*ICAO designator*]   (FAAC)

ESE .... Ecole Superieure d'Electricite [*Electricity College*] [*France*]   (WED)

ESE .... Estesudeste [*East Southeast*] [*Spanish*]

ESE .... Estimate of Supplementary Expenditure [*Mauritius*]   (AF)

ESE .... Est Sud Est [*East Southeast*] [*French*]   (MTD)

ESE .... Ethniki Sosialistiki Enosis [*National Socialist Union*] [*Cyprus*]   (GC)

ESE .... Ethnikon Symvoulion Energeias [*National Energy Council*] [*Greek*]   (GC)

ESE .... Ethnikon Symvoulion Erevnon [*National Research Council*] [*Greek*]   (GC)

ESE .... Ethnikos Synagermos Ellinon [*National Rally of Greeks*]   (GC)

ESE .... European Stock Exchange

ESEA .... Enosis Sympolemiston Ethnikou Agonos [*Union of Fellow-Combatants in the National Struggle*] [*Cyprus*]   (GC)

ESEA .... Epitropi Syndonismou tou Enotikou Agonos [*Coordinating Committee for the Enosis Struggle*] [*Cyprus*]   (GC)

ESEA .... Ethnikos Syndesmos Ellinon Axiomatikon [*National League of Greek Officers*]   (GC)

ESEADE ... Escuela Superior de Economia y Administracion de Empresas [*School of Economy and Business Administration*] [*Argentina*]   (LA)

ESEAK ...... Enosis Syllogon Ellinon Apofoiton Kyprou [*Union of Greek Alumni Associations of Cyprus*]   (GC)

ESEC .... Ente Studi Economici per la Calabria [*Italian*]   (SLS)

ESEC........ Escuela Secundaria en el Campo [*Secondary Farm School*]
  [*Cuba*] (LA)
ESEDENA ... Escuela de Seguridad y Defensa Nacional [*National Security and Defense School*] [*Uruguay*] (LA)
ESEDES.... Elliniki Synomospondia Elevtheron Dimokratikon Ergatikon Syndikaton [*Greek Federation of Free Democratic Labor Unions*] (LA)
ESEE........ Ethniki Sosialistiki Enosi Ellados [*National Socialist Union of Greece*] (GC)
ESEEA ...... Ethnikon Symvoulion Epistimonikis Erevnis kai Anaptyxeos [*National Council for Scientific Research and Development*] [*Greek*] (GC)
ESEEC...... Escuela Secundaria en el Campo [*Secondary Farm School*] [*Cuba*] (LA)
ESEF .... Escuela Superior de Educacion Fisica [*Higher School of Physical Education*] [*Cuba*] (LA)
ESEG........ Einheitssystem der Elektronik und des Geraetebaus [*German*] (ADPT)
Eseg........... Esegieel [*Ezekiel*] [*Afrikaans*]
ESEKA ...... Elliniki Syndonistiki Epitropi Kypriakou Agonas [*Greek Coordinating Committee of the Cyprus Struggle*] [*Greek*] (GC)
ESEM........ European Society for Engineering and Medicine
esemp .... Esemplare [*Copy*] [*Publishing*] [*Italian*]
esempl........ Esemplare [*Copy*] [*Publishing*] [*Italian*]
ESEN........ Ekklisiastikon Symvoulion Enoriakou Naou [*Church Parish Council*] [*Greek*] (GC)
ESEN........ Empresa de Seguro Estatal Nacional [*State National Insurance Company*] [*Cuba*] (GEA)
ESEP .... Escuelas Superiores de Educacion Profesional [*Higher Schools for Professional Education*] (LA)
ESEPAS.... Empresa de Servicios Petroleros Asociados [*Associated Petroleum Services Enterprise*] [*Ecuador*] (LA)
ESEPP...... Enosis Syngenon Ellinon Politikon Prosfygon [*Union of Relatives of Political Refugees*] [*Greek*] (GC)
ESER .... Einheitliches System der Elektronischen Rechentechnik [*Uniform Electronic Data Processing System*] [*CEMA*] (EG)
eserc.......... Esercizio [*Exercise*] [*Italian*]
ESETC...... Empresa de Servicios Tecnicos de Computacion de Holguin [*Enterprise for Technical Computation Services of Holguin*] [*Cuba*] (LA)
ESETTM... Ecole Superieure d'Economie et de Technique des Transports Maritimes
ESF .... Ecoles Sans Frontieres [*Education Without Frontiers*] [*An association*] (EAIO)
ESF .... Ecole Superieure de Fonderie [*Foundry Technology College*] [*Research center*] [*French*] (ERC)
ESF .... Economic Support Fund
ESF .... Ekonomiska Samfundet i Finland [*Economic Society of Finland*] (EAIO)
ESF .... Escola Superior de Florestas [*Brazil*] (DSCA)
ESF .... European Schools Federation (EA)
ESF .... European Science Foundation (EAIO)
ESF .... European Security Forum
ESF .... European Simmental Federation (EAIO)
ESF .... European Social Fund (EG)
ESF .... European Surfing Federation (EAIO)
ESF .... Exchange Support Fund [*Cambodia*] (CL)
ESFC .... Employment and Skills Formation Council [*National Board of Employment, Education and Training*] [*Australia*]
ESFC .... Epidemiological Study of Female Circumcision [*Sudan*]
ESFH........ Hasslosa [*Sweden*] [*ICAO location identifier*] (ICLI)
ESFI.......... Knislinge [*Sweden*] [*ICAO location identifier*] (ICLI)
ESFINCO ... Estudios, Financieros, y Contables [*Colombia*] (COL)
ESFJ......... Sjobo [*Sweden*] [*ICAO location identifier*] (ICLI)
ESFM .... Escuela Superior de Fisica y Matematicas [*Mexico*] (LAA)
ESFM .... Moholm [*Sweden*] [*ICAO location identifier*] (ICLI)
ESFOA ...... L'Ecole Speciale de Formation des Officiers d'Active
ESFQ .... Kosta [*Sweden*] [*ICAO location identifier*] (ICLI)
ESFR .... Rada [*Sweden*] [*ICAO location identifier*] (ICLI)
ESFU .... Vaxjo/Urasa [*Sweden*] [*ICAO location identifier*] (ICLI)
ESFY .... Byholma [*Sweden*] [*ICAO location identifier*] (ICLI)
ESG........... Ecole Superieure de Guerre [*Armed Forces War College*] [*French*] (WER)
ESG........... Electronik-Systems-Gesellschaft [*Germany*] (PDAA)
ESG........... Electrostatic Generator (RU)
ESG........... Escola Superior de Guerra [*War College*] [*Brazil*] (LA)
ESG........... European Software Company GmbH (ADPT)
ESG........... Evaluation Steering Group [*General Practice Evaluation Program*] [*Australia*]
ESGA .... Backamo [*Sweden*] [*ICAO location identifier*] (ICLI)
ESGC........ Alleberg [*Sweden*] [*ICAO location identifier*] (ICLI)
ESGG........ Goteborg/Landvetter [*Sweden*] [*ICAO location identifier*] (ICLI)
ESGH .... Herrljunga [*Sweden*] [*ICAO location identifier*] (ICLI)
ESGI......... Alingsas [*Sweden*] [*ICAO location identifier*] (ICLI)

ESGJ .... Jonkoping [*Sweden*] [*ICAO location identifier*] (ICLI)
ESGK........ Falkoping [*Sweden*] [*ICAO location identifier*] (ICLI)
ESGL........ Lidkoping [*Sweden*] [*ICAO location identifier*] (ICLI)
ESGLD...... European Study Group on Lysosomal Diseases (EAIO)
ESGLNLA ... European Support Groups for Liberation and Nonviolence in Latin America (EAIO)
ESGM....... European Society of Gastrointestinal Motility [*Louvain, Belgium*] (EAIO)
ESGM........ TC Emekli Sandigi Genel Mudurlugu [*Retirement Fund Directorate General of Republic of Turkey*] (TU)
ESGO........ Vargarda [*Sweden*] [*ICAO location identifier*] (ICLI)
ESGP .... Epitropi gia to Syndonismo Georgikis Paragogis [*Committee for the Coordination of Agricultural Production*] (GC)
ESGP .... Goteborg/Save [*Sweden*] [*ICAO location identifier*] (ICLI)
ESGQ .... Skovde [*Sweden*] [*ICAO location identifier*] (ICLI)
ESGRAON ... Integrated Civil Registration and Administrative Population Services System (BU)
ESGS........ Stromstad/Nasinge [*Sweden*] [*ICAO location identifier*] (ICLI)
ESGT........ Trollhattan/Vanersborg [*Sweden*] [*ICAO location identifier*] (ICLI)
ESGV .... Varberg [*Sweden*] [*ICAO location identifier*] (ICLI)
ESGX........ Boras-Viared [*Sweden*] [*ICAO location identifier*] (ICLI)
ESGY .... Saffle [*Sweden*] [*ICAO location identifier*] (ICLI)
esh............. Echelon (RU)
ESH .... Human Resources, Institutions, and Agrarian Reform Division [*FAO*] [*United Nations Italy Information service or system*] (IID)
ESh .... Stark Effect (RU)
ESh .... Walking Excavator, Dragline (RU)
ESH .... Western Sahara [*ANSI three-letter standard code*] (CNC)
ESHA .... Abisko [*Sweden*] [*ICAO location identifier*] (ICLI)
ESHB........ Goteborg/Eastern Hospital [*Sweden*] [*ICAO location identifier*] (ICLI)
ESHC .... Stockholm/Southern Hospital [*Sweden*] [*ICAO location identifier*] (ICLI)
EShD .... Electric Step-by-Step Motor (RU)
ESHE .... Landskrona [*Sweden*] [*ICAO location identifier*] (ICLI)
ESHG .... Stockholm/Gamla Stan [*Sweden*] [*ICAO location identifier*] (ICLI)
ESHH........ Helsingborg/Harbour [*Sweden*] [*ICAO location identifier*] (ICLI)
ESHI......... Ingmarso [*Sweden*] [*ICAO location identifier*] (ICLI)
ESHL........ Stockholm/Huddinge Hospital [*Sweden*] [*ICAO location identifier*] (ICLI)
ESHM ...... Malmo/Harbour [*Sweden*] [*ICAO location identifier*] (ICLI)
ESHN .... Nacka [*Sweden*] [*ICAO location identifier*] (ICLI)
ESHO .... Skovde/Hospital [*Sweden*] [*ICAO location identifier*] (ICLI)
EShP........ Electrical Tie Tamper [*Railroads*] (RU)
ESHP........ European Society of Handwriting Psychology (EAIO)
ESHPH ..... European Society for the History of Photography (EA)
ESHR .... Akersberga [*Sweden*] [*ICAO location identifier*] (ICLI)
ESHS........ Sandhamn [*Sweden*] [*ICAO location identifier*] (ICLI)
ESHU .... Uppsala/Akademiska [*Sweden*] [*ICAO location identifier*] (ICLI)
ESHV .... Vaxholm [*Sweden*] [*ICAO location identifier*] (ICLI)
ESHW ...... Vastervik Hospital [*Sweden*] [*ICAO location identifier*] (ICLI)
Esi............. Empresa de Suministros Industriales [*Import-export board*] [*Cuba*] (EY)
ESI............ Espinosa [*Brazil*] [*Airport symbol*] (OAG)
ESIA .... Escuela Superior de Ingenieria y Arquitectura [*Mexico*] (MSC)
ESIA .... Karlsborg [*Sweden*] [*ICAO location identifier*] (ICLI)
ESIAC .... Estructuras. Ingenieria, Arquitectura, y Construcciones [*Colombia*] (COL)
ESIALA..... Eastern States Interim Assets and Liabilities Agency [*Nigeria*] (AF)
ESI-ANDINA ... Empresa de Servicios Informativos Andina [*Andean Information Services Enterprise*] (LA)
ESIB .... Satenas [*Sweden*] [*ICAO location identifier*] (ICLI)
ESIC .... Ecole Superieure Internationale de la Cooperation [*Higher International School for Cooperation*] [*French*] (AF)
ESIC .... Emirates Sudan Investment Company
ESIC .... Employees' State Insurance Corporation [*India*] (GEA)
ESIC .... Environmental Science Information Center [*NOAA*] (ASF)
ESIC .... Europees Studie en Informatie Centrum [*Later, European Center for Research and Information*] [*Belgium*] (EAIO)
ESICUBA ... Empresa de Seguros Internacionales de Cuba [*Cuban Enterprise for International Insurance*] (LA)
ESIEA .... Enosis Syndakton Imerision Efimeridon Athinon [*Union of Athens Daily Newspaper Editors*] (GC)
ESIGA .... Entretien Service Immobilier Gabonais
ESII .... Regional Military Command Subcenter West [*Sweden*] [*ICAO location identifier*] (ICLI)
ESIIO .... European Symposium of Independent Inspecting Organizations (EA)
ESIJY .... Ecole Superieure Internationale de Journalisme de Yaounde [*International Higher School of Journalism of Yaounde*] [*Cameroon*] (AF)

ESIL .... Egyptian Society of International Law
esim .... Esimerkiksi [*For Example*] [*Finland*]   (GPO)
esim .... Esimerkkeja [*Finland*]
ESIME ...... Escuela Superior de Ingenieria Mecanica y Electrica [*Mexico*]   (MSC)
ESIN .... Esin Uluslararasi Nakliyat ve Ticaret Anonim Sirketi [*The Esin International Transport and Trade Corp.*] [*Istanbul*]   (TU)
ESINA .... Exercito Secreto de Intervencao Nacionale de Angola [*Secret Army of National Intervention of Angola*]   (AF)
ESI-PERU ... Empresa de Servicios de Informacion del Peru [*Peruvian Information Services Enterprise*]   (LA)
ESIQIE ...... Escuela Superior de Ingenieria Quimica e Industrias Extractivas [*Mexico*]   (LAA)
ESIS .... European Shielding Information Service [*EURATOM*] [*Databank*]   (IID)
ESIT .... Ecole Superieure d'Interpretation et Traduction [*School of Interpretation and Translation, University of Paris*]
ESITB .... Electricity Supply Industry Training Board [*Australia*]
ESITC .... Electricity Supply Industry Training Committee [*Australia*]
ESITEX ..... Association d'Etudes et de Statistiques de l'Industrie Textile [*Association for the Study of Statistics in the Textile Industry*] [*French*]   (SLS)
ESJ .... Enotni Sindikati Jugoslavije [*United Trade-Unions of Yugoslavia*]   (YU)
ESJ .... Entomological Society of Japan   (DSCA)
ESJL .... Entreprise Senegalaise Jean Lefebvre
ESK .... Electronic Pointer Compensator   (RU)
ESK .... Enosis Syndakton Kyprou [*Union of Cypriot Editors*]   (GC)
ESK .... Epanastatikos Kommounistikos Syndesmos [*Revolutionary Communist Association*] [*Greek*]   (GC)
esk .... Eskader [*or Edkadril or Eskadron*] [*Squadron*] [*Afrikaans*]
ESK .... Evropaiki Sosialistiki Kinisi [*European Socialist Movement*]   (GC)
ESK .... Squadron [*Navy*]   (RU)
ESKA .... Enotiki Syndikalistiki Kinisi Athinon [*Unifying Labor Movement of Athens*]   (GC)
ESKA .... Gimo [*Sweden*] [*ICAO location identifier*]   (ICLI)
ESKB .... Stockholm/Barkarby [*Sweden*] [*ICAO location identifier*]   (ICLI)
ESKC .... Sundbro [*Sweden*] [*ICAO location identifier*]   (ICLI)
ESKD .... Dala-Jarna [*Sweden*] [*ICAO location identifier*]   (ICLI)
ESKE .... Egyptologische Stichting Koningin Elisabeth [*Later, Foundation Egyptologique Reine Elisabeth*] [*Belgium*]   (EAIO)
ESKE .... Eniaion Sosialistikon Komma Ellados [*United Socialist Party of Greece*]
ESKE .... Eniaion Syndikalistikon Kinima Ellados [*United Labor Movement of Greece*]   (GC)
ESKE .... Ergatikon Syndekhniakon Komma Ellados [*Worker Labor Union Party of Greece*]   (GC)
ESKH .... Eksharad [*Sweden*] [*ICAO location identifier*]   (ICLI)
ESKI .... Ettehadiyye Sendikayee Kargarene Iran [*Federation of Iranian Workers' Unions*]
ESKI .... Stockholm [*Sweden*] [*ICAO location identifier*]   (ICLI)
eskim .... Eskimo   (RU)
ESKK .... Karlskoga [*Sweden*] [*ICAO location identifier*]   (ICLI)
ESKL .... Norrkoping [*Sweden*] [*ICAO location identifier*]   (ICLI)
esk-l'ya ...... Squadron [*Aviation*]   (RU)
ESKM .... Mora/Siljan [*Sweden*] [*ICAO location identifier*]   (ICLI)
ESKN .... Nykoping/Oxelosund [*Sweden*] [*ICAO location identifier*]   (ICLI)
ESKO .... Munkfors [*Sweden*] [*ICAO location identifier*]   (ICLI)
Es-Koop ..... Eskisehir Koy Kooperatifler Birligi [*Eskisehir Village Cooperatives' Union*]   (TU)
ESKP .... Crystal Field Stabilization Energy   (RU)
ESKP .... Ethnikon Symvoulion Koinonikis Pronoias [*National Social Welfare Council*] [*Greek*]   (GC)
ESKP .... Ethniko Symvoulio Khorotaxias kai Perivallondos [*National Zoning and Environment Council*]   (GC)
eskpl .... Submarine Squadron   (BU)
ESKR .... Stockholm Radio [*Sweden*] [*ICAO location identifier*]   (ICLI)
ESKS .... Enosis Stafidergostasiarkhon Korinthiakis Stafidas [*Union of Corinthian Currant Processing Plant Owners*] [*Greek*]   (GC)
ESKS .... Strangnas [*Sweden*] [*ICAO location identifier*]   (ICLI)
ESKT .... Tierp [*Sweden*] [*ICAO location identifier*]   (ICLI)
ESKU .... Sunne [*Poland*] [*ICAO location identifier*]   (ICLI)
ESKV .... Arvika [*Sweden*] [*ICAO location identifier*]   (ICLI)
ESKW .... Gavle/Avan [*Sweden*] [*ICAO location identifier*]   (ICLI)
ESKX .... Bjorkvik [*Sweden*] [*ICAO location identifier*]   (ICLI)
ESL .... Eastern Shipping Lines   (DS)
ESL .... Erstellung von Schnittlisten [*German*]   (ADPT)
ESL .... Ethiopian Shipping Lines
ESL .... European Systems Language   (ADPT)
ESL .... Vltavska Elektrarna [*Vltava Electric Power Plant*]   (CZ)
ESLA .... Egyptian School Library Association   (SLS)
ESLA .... English as a Second Language Allowance [*Australia*]
ESLCE .... Ethiopian School-Leaving Certificate Examination

ESLI .... Esperantista Sak-Ligo Internacia [*International Esperantist Chess League - IECL*]   (EAIO)
ESLO .... Ethnic Schools Liaison Officer [*Australia*]
ESLOV ..... Ecole Speciale des Langues Orientales Vivantes
ESM .... Ecole Superieure Militaire
ESM .... Electric Spreading Machine [*Peat industry*]   (RU)
esm .... En So Meer [*And So Forth*] [*Afrikaans*]
ESM .... Entreprise Senegalaise du Mobilier
ESM .... Esmeraldas [*Ecuador*] [*Airport symbol*]   (OAG)
ESM .... Estrecho Su Mano [*I Press Your Hand*] [*Spanish*]
ESM .... Etudiants Socialistes Malgaches [*Malagasy Socialist Students*]   (AF)
ESM .... European Society for Microcirculation   (EA)
ESM .... European Society for Mycobacteriology   (EA)
ESMA .... Emmaboda [*Sweden*] [*ICAO location identifier*]   (ICLI)
ESMACO ... Estado Mayor Conjunto [*Joint Chiefs of Staff*] [*Uruguay*]   (LA)
ESMALCO ... Industrias Metalicas y Esmaltes de Colombia Ltda. [*Colombia*]   (COL)
ESMALUX ... Societe d'Electricite de Sambre et Meuse des Ardenners et du Luxembourg SA [*Belgium*]
ESMATIC ... Einheitliches System fuer Erfassung, Aufbereitung, un Ausgabe von Messwerten [*German*]   (ADPT)
ESMB .... Borglanda [*Sweden*] [*ICAO location identifier*]   (ICLI)
ESMC .... Electronic Structure of Materials Centre [*Flinders University, Australia*]
ESMC .... Karlshamn [*Sweden*] [*ICAO location identifier*]   (ICLI)
ESME .... Eslov [*Sweden*] [*ICAO location identifier*]   (ICLI)
ESMF .... Fagerhult [*Sweden*] [*ICAO location identifier*]   (ICLI)
ESMG .... Ljungby/Feringe [*Sweden*] [*ICAO location identifier*]   (ICLI)
ESMH .... Hoganas [*Sweden*] [*ICAO location identifier*]   (ICLI)
ESMI .... Sovdeborg [*Sweden*] [*ICAO location identifier*]   (ICLI)
ESMJ .... Kagerod [*Sweden*] [*ICAO location identifier*]   (ICLI)
ESMK .... Kristianstad/Everod [*Sweden*] [*ICAO location identifier*]   (ICLI)
ESML .... Landskrona/Viarp [*Sweden*] [*ICAO location identifier*]   (ICLI)
ESMM .... Malmo [*Sweden*] [*ICAO location identifier*]   (ICLI)
ESMN ...... Lund [*Sweden*] [*ICAO location identifier*]   (ICLI)
ESMO .... Consolidated Construction and Installation Trust   (BU)
ESMO .... European Society for Medical Oncology   (EA)
ESMO ...... Oskarshamn [*Sweden*] [*ICAO location identifier*]   (ICLI)
ESMP .... Anderstorp [*Sweden*] [*ICAO location identifier*]   (ICLI)
ESMQ .... Kalmar [*Sweden*] [*ICAO location identifier*]   (ICLI)
ESMR .... Escuela Superior de Medicina Rural [*Mexico*]   (LAA)
ESMR .... Trelleborg [*Sweden*] [*ICAO location identifier*]   (ICLI)
ESMS .... Malmo/Sturup [*Sweden*] [*ICAO location identifier*]   (ICLI)
ESMST ..... European Society of Membrane Science and Technology   (EA)
ESMT .... Halmstad [*Sweden*] [*ICAO location identifier*]   (ICLI)
ESMU .... Turkiye Eski Muharipler Cemiyeti [*Turkish Veterans' Society*]   (TU)
ESMV .... Hagshult [*Sweden*] [*ICAO location identifier*]   (ICLI)
ESMX .... Vaxjo/Kronoberg [*Sweden*] [*ICAO location identifier*]   (ICLI)
ESMY .... Smalandsstenar [*Sweden*] [*ICAO location identifier*]   (ICLI)
ESMZ .... Olanda [*Sweden*] [*ICAO location identifier*]   (ICLI)
ESN .... Ecole Superieure de Navigation d'Attiecoube
ESN .... Elliniki Sosialistiki Neolaia [*Greek Socialist Youth*]   (GC)
ESN .... Erythros Stavros Neotitos [*Youth Red Cross*]   (GC)
ESN .... European Scientific Notes [*Office of Naval Research, London*]   (PDAA)
ESN .... European Society for Neurochemistry   (EA)
ESN .... European Society of Nematologists   (EAIO)
ESN .... European Society of Neuroradiology   (EA)
ESNA .... Eesti Skautlikud Noored Austraalias   (ADA)
ESNA .... Hallviken [*Sweden*] [*ICAO location identifier*]   (ICLI)
ESNACIFOR ... Escuela Nacional de Ciencias Forestales [*National School of Forestry Science*] [*Honduras*]   (LA)
ESNB .... Solleftea [*Sweden*] [*ICAO location identifier*]   (ICLI)
ESNC .... Hede/Hedlanda [*Sweden*] [*ICAO location identifier*]   (ICLI)
ESNCD ..... European Society for Noninvasive Cardiovascular Dynamics   (EA)
ESND .... Sveg [*Sweden*] [*ICAO location identifier*]   (ICLI)
ESNE .... Enosis Sidirodromikon Notiou Ellados [*Union of Railwaymen of Southern Greece*]   (GC)
ESNF .... Farila [*Sweden*] [*ICAO location identifier*]   (ICLI)
ESNG .... Gallivare [*Sweden*] [*ICAO location identifier*]   (ICLI)
ESNH .... Hudiksvall [*Sweden*] [*ICAO location identifier*]   (ICLI)
ESNI .... Escola Nacional de Informacoes [*National Intelligence School*] [*Brazil*]   (LA)
ESNI .... Kubbe [*Sweden*] [*ICAO location identifier*]   (ICLI)
ESNICVD ... European Society for Noninvasive Cardiovascular Dynamics   (EAIO)
ESNJ .... Jokkmokk [*Sweden*] [*ICAO location identifier*]   (ICLI)
ESNK .... Ethnikon Symvoulion Neolaias Kyprou [*National Council of Cypriot Youth*]   (GC)
ESNK .... Kramfors [*Sweden*] [*ICAO location identifier*]   (ICLI)
ESNL .... Lycksele [*Sweden*] [*ICAO location identifier*]   (ICLI)
ESNM .... Optand [*Sweden*] [*ICAO location identifier*]   (ICLI)

ESNN .... Sundsvall-Harnosand [*Sweden*] [*ICAO location identifier*]
　　　　　(ICLI)
ESNO .... Ornskoldsvik [*Sweden*] [*ICAO location identifier*]　(ICLI)
ESNP .... Pitea [*Sweden*] [*ICAO location identifier*]　(ICLI)
ESNQ .... Kiruna [*Sweden*] [*ICAO location identifier*]　(ICLI)
ESNR .... Orsa [*Sweden*] [*ICAO location identifier*]　(ICLI)
ESNS .... Skelleftea [*Sweden*] [*ICAO location identifier*]　(ICLI)
ESNSW ..... Entomological Society of New South Wales [*Australia*]
ESNT .... Sattna [*Sweden*] [*ICAO location identifier*]　(ICLI)
ESNU .... Umea [*Sweden*] [*ICAO location identifier*]　(ICLI)
ESNV .... Vilhelmina [*Sweden*] [*ICAO location identifier*]　(ICLI)
ESO .... Ecole des Sous-Officiers
ESO .... Ege Sanayi Odasi [*Aegean Chamber of Industry*]　(TU)
ESO .... Eisenbahn-Signalordnung [*Railroad Signal Regulations*]　(EG)
ESO .... Elektrik, Su, ve Otobus Idaresi [*Electric Power, Water, and Bus
　　　　　Administration*] [*Of various municipalities*]　(TU)
ESO .... Engineering Salle d'Ordinateur [*French*]　(ADPT)
ESO .... Escuela Superior de Oceanografia [*Mexico*]　(MSC)
ESO .... European Southern Observatory [*ICSU*] [*Research center*]
　　　　　[*Germany*]　(IRC)
ESO .... European Space Organization
ESOA .... European Society of Osteoarthrology [*Former Czechoslovakia*]
　　　　　(SLS)
ESOC .... European Space Operations Center
ESOCAM ... Evolution Sociale Camerounaise
ESOE .... Orebro [*Sweden*] [*ICAO location identifier*]　(ICLI)
ES of A ...... Ergonomics Society of Australia
ESOFEL ..... Equipamentos de Soldaduras e Ferramentas Lda.
ESOH .... Hagfors [*Sweden*] [*ICAO location identifier*]　(ICLI)
ESOKA ..... Ethnikon Symvoulion Oikonomikis kai Koinonikis Anaptyxeos
　　　　　[*National Council of Economic and Social Development*]
　　　　　[*Greek*]　(GC)
ESOL .... English for Speakers of Other Languages [*Australia*]
ESOMAR ... European Society for Opinion and Marketing Research
　　　　　[*Amsterdam, Netherlands*]　(SLS)
ESOMAR ... European Society for Opinion and Market Research
　　　　　[*Netherlands*]
ESON .... Elliniki Sosialistiki Neolaia [*Greek Socialist Youth*] [*ESN*]
　　　　　[*Formerly,*]　(GC)
ESONE ...... European Standards on Nuclear Electronics Committee
　　　　　[*Belgium*]　(SLS)
ESONE ...... European Standards on Nuclear Electronics Committee
　　　　　[*Switzerland*]
ESOP .... Epitropi Syndonismou Oikonomikis Politikis [*Economic Policy
　　　　　Coordinating Committee*] [*Greek*]　(GC)
ESOP .... Ethniki Sosialistiki Organosis Panellinon [*National Socialist
　　　　　Organization of Panhellenes*] [*Greek*]　(GC)
ESOP .... Ethnikon Symvoulion Oikonomikis Politikis [*National
　　　　　Economic Policy Council*] [*Greek*]　(GC)
ESOPRS .... European Society of Ophthalmic Plastic and Reconstructive
　　　　　Surgery　(EAIO)
ESOR .... Rescue Coordination Center [*Sweden*] [*ICAO location identifier*]
　　　　　(ICLI)
ESOS .... Stockholm [*Sweden*] [*ICAO location identifier*]　(ICLI)
ESOT .... Ege Sanayi Odasi Teskilati [*Aegean Chamber of Industry
　　　　　Organization*]　(TU)
ESOW ...... Vasteras/Hasslo [*Sweden*] [*ICAO location identifier*]　(ICLI)
ESP .... Ecole Superieure de Pedagogie [*Advanced Teachers Training
　　　　　School*] [*Laotian*]　(CL)
ESP .... Einzelhandelsspanne [*Retail Markup*] [*EHS*] [*See also*]　(EG)
ESP .... Electric Servodrive　(RU)
ESP .... Emborikos Syllogos Peiraios [*Commercial Chamber of Piraeus*]
　　　　　(GC)
ESP .... Employee Share Plan [*Australia*]
ESP .... Endangered Species Program [*Australia*]
esp .... Espanhol [*Spanish*] [*Portuguese*]
esp .... Espanjaa [*or Espanjaksi*] [*Finland*]
esp .... Espanjalainen [*Spanish*] [*Finland*]
esp .... Espece [*French*]　(FLAF)
Esp .... Especializado [*Academic degree*] [*Spanish*]
esp .... Esperanto　(RU)
ESP .... Ethnic Schools Program [*Australia*]
ESP .... European Society of Pathology　(EAIO)
ESP .... Spain [*ANSI three-letter standard code*]　(CNC)
esp .... Specialement [*Especially*] [*French*]　(TPFD)
ESPA .... Escuela Superior de Perfeccionamiento Atletico [*Advanced
　　　　　School of Athletic Improvement*] [*Cuba*]　(LA)
ESPA .... Establecimiento de Productos Aromaticos Ltda. [*Colombia*]
　　　　　(COL)
ESPA .... Lulea/Kallax [*Sweden*] [*ICAO location identifier*]　(ICLI)
ESPADA ... Escuela Popular Antioquena de Aviacion [*Colombia*]　(COL)
ESPADON ... Etudes des Moyens Spatiaux et Aeriens de l'Ocean [*French*]
　　　　　(MSC)
ESPALSA ... Especialidades Alimenticias SA [*Venezuela*]　(DSCA)
ESPC .... Enseignement Secondaire du Premier Cycle [*Secondary
　　　　　Education, First Cycle*]　(CL)

ESPC .... Ostersund/Froson [*Sweden*] [*ICAO location identifier*]　(ICLI)
ESPD .... Gunnarn [*Sweden*] [*ICAO location identifier*]　(ICLI)
ESPE .... European Society for Pediatric Endocrinology　(EAIO)
ESPE .... United Socialist Alliance of Greece　(PPW)
ESPE .... Vidsel [*Sweden*] [*ICAO location identifier*]　(ICLI)
esper .... Esperanto　(RU)
ESPES ...... Especialidades Farmaceuticas Espanolas Data Bank [*Spanish
　　　　　Pharmaceutical Specialities Data Bank*] [*Spanish Drug
　　　　　Information Center*] [*Information service or system*]　(IID)
ES-PE-WU ... Spoldzielnia Pracy Wytworczo-Uslugowa [*Production and
　　　　　Service Cooperative*]　(POL)
ESPG .... Boden [*Sweden*] [*ICAO location identifier*]　(ICLI)
ESPHI ...... European Society for Paediatric Haematology and Immunology
　　　　　(EAIO)
ESPI .... Ente Siciliano per la Promozione Industriale [*Sicilian Association
　　　　　for the Promotion of Industry*] [*Italian*]　(ASF)
ESPIRAL .. Estudios y Proyeccion Industrial [*Colombia*]　(COL)
ESPJ .... Heden [*Sweden*] [*ICAO location identifier*]　(ICLI)
ESPLAF .... European Strategic Planning Federation [*British*]　(EAIO)
ESPN .... European Society for Pediatric Nephrology [*Switzerland*]　(SLS)
espodlodka ... Fleet Submarine　(RU)
ESPP .... Regional Military Command Subcenter North [*Sweden*] [*ICAO
　　　　　location identifier*]　(ICLI)
ESPR .... Esperance [*Botanical region*] [*Australia*]
Espr .... Espressivo [*With Expression*] [*Music*]
ESPR .... European Society of Paediatric Radiology　(EA)
Espres .... Espressivo [*With Expression*] [*Music*]
ESPRIT .... European Strategic Program for Research and Development in
　　　　　Information Technology and Telecommunications
　　　　　[*Research center*] [*Belgium*]　(IRC)
ESPRS ...... Egyptian Society of Plastic and Reconstructive Surgeons　(EAIO)
ESPT .... Enosis Syndakton Periodikou Typou [*Union of Editors of the
　　　　　Periodical Press*] [*Greek*]　(GC)
esq .... Esquerdo [*Left Side*] [*Portuguese*]
esq .... Esquina [*Corner*] [*Spanish*]
Esq .... Esquire [*Record label*] [*British*]
ESQO .... Arboga [*Sweden*] [*ICAO location identifier*]　(ICLI)
ESQP .... Berga [*Sweden*] [*ICAO location identifier*]　(ICLI)
ESQV .... Visby [*Sweden*] [*ICAO location identifier*]　(ICLI)
ESR .... Eastern Suburbs Railway [*Australia*]　(ADA)
ESR .... Egyptian State Railway　(ROG)
ESR .... Einheitliches System der Rechnertechnik [*German*]　(ADPT)
ESR .... El Salvador [*Chile*] [*Airport symbol*]　(OAG)
ESR .... Excelsior Airlines Ltd. [*Ghana*] [*ICAO designator*]　(FAAC)
ESRA .... Economische en Sociale Raad van Advies [*Benelux*]　(BAS)
ESRA .... Employment Services Regulatory Authority [*Australia*]
ESRA .... Escadrille Saharienne de Reconnaissance et d'Appui
ESRA .... European Society of Regional Anaesthesia　(EA)
ESRB .... European Society for Radiation Biology [*Formerly, Association of
　　　　　Radiobiologists from EURATOM Countries*]　(EA)
ESRC .... European Science Research Council　(NUCP)
ESRF .... European Squash Rackets Federation　(EA)
ESRF .... European Synchrotron Radiation Facility [*High-energy physics*]
　　　　　(ECON)
ESRI .... Economic and Social Research Institute [*Ireland*]　(SLS)
ESRIN ...... European Space Research Institute [*Italian*]
ESRO .... European Space Research Organization [*Superseded by ESA*]
ESRO/ELDO ... European Space Research Organisation/European Launcher
　　　　　Development Organization [*Later, ESA*]
ESRO/SDS ... European Space Research Organisation/Space Documentation
　　　　　Service [*Later, ESA/SDS*]
ESRS .... European Society for Rural Sociology [*Netherlands*]　(DSCA)
ESRS .... European Synchroton Radiation Source　(PDAA)
ESS .... Early School Support [*Australia*]
ESS .... Ecole des Sciences de la Sante
ESS .... Ekonomska Srednja Skola [*Secondary School in Economics*]
　　　　　(YU)
ESS .... Ergatikon Symvoulevtikon Soma [*Labor Advisory Board*]
　　　　　[*Cyprus*]　(GC)
ESS .... Ergonomi Sallskapet, Sverige [*Ergonomic Society of Sweden*]
　　　　　[*Sweden*]　(EAIO)
ess .... Essiivi [*Finland*]
ESS .... Etoile Sportive de Sahel [*Tunisia*]
ESS .... European Spallation Source [*High-energy physics*]　(ECON)
ESS .... European Special Situations Fund [*EEC*]
ESS .... TAES [*Tecnicas Aereas de Estudios y Servicios SA*] [*Spain*]
　　　　　[*ICAO designator*]　(FAAC)
ESSA .... Economic Society of South Africa　(EAIO)
ESSA .... Elliotdale Sheepbreeders' Society of Australia
ESSA .... Enterprise Support Services for Africa [*Funded by CIDA -
　　　　　Canadian International Development Agency*]
ESSA .... Entomological Society of Southern Africa　(EAIO)
ESSA .... Epidemiological Society of Southern Africa　(AA)
ESSA .... European Single Service Association
ESSA .... Stockholm/Arlanda [*Sweden*] [*ICAO location identifier*]　(ICLI)
ESSB .... Stockholm/Bromma [*Sweden*] [*ICAO location identifier*]　(ICLI)

ESSC .... Eskilstuna/Ekeby [*Sweden*] [*ICAO location identifier*]   (ICLI)
ESSC .... European Space Science Committee
ESSC .... European Sport Shooting Confederation   (EAIO)
ESSCIRC .. European Solid-State-Circuits Conference   (PDAA)
ESSD .... Borlange [*Sweden*] [*ICAO location identifier*]   (ICLI)
ESSD .... Enosis Sovietikon Sosialistikon Dimokratn [*Union of Soviet Socialist Republics*]   (GC)
ESSDERC ... European Solid State Device Research Conference   (PDAA)
ESSE .... Etaireia Syntheton, Syngrafeon, kai Ekdoton [*Society of Composers, Authors, and Publishers*] [*Greek*]   (GC)
ESSE .... Stockholm/Ska-Edeby [*Sweden*] [*ICAO location identifier*]   (ICLI)
ESSEC ...... Ecole Superieure des Sciences Economiques et Commerciales [*Advanced School for Economic and Commercial Sciences*] [*French*]   (WER)
ESSF .... Hultsfred [*Sweden*] [*ICAO location identifier*]   (ICLI)
ESSG .... Ludvika [*Sweden*] [*ICAO location identifier*]   (ICLI)
ESSH .... Laxa [*Sweden*] [*ICAO location identifier*]   (ICLI)
ESSI .... Integrated Social Information System   (BU)
ESSI .... Visingso [*Sweden*] [*ICAO location identifier*]   (ICLI)
ESSK .... Gavle-Sandviken [*Sweden*] [*ICAO location identifier*]   (ICLI)
ESSL .... Linkoping/SAAB [*Sweden*] [*ICAO location identifier*]   (ICLI)
ESSM .... Brattforsheden [*Sweden*] [*ICAO location identifier*]   (ICLI)
ESSO .... Ekpaidevtiki Seira Stratevsimon Opliton [*Enlisted Conscript Training Course*]   (GC)
ESSOBA ... Essor Social des Bashi [*Social Development of the Bashi*]
ESSP .... Eniaia Sosialistiki Syndikalistiki Parataxis [*United Socialist Labor Faction*] [*Greek*]   (GC)
ESSP .... Euromoney Swaps Services Poll
ESSP .... Norrkoping/Kungsangen [*Sweden*] [*ICAO location identifier*]   (ICLI)
ESSPA .... Enosis Syllogon Spoudaston Paidagogikon Akadimion [*Union of Societies of Students at Pedagogical Academies*] [*Greek*]   (GC)
ESSQ .... Karlstad [*Sweden*] [*ICAO location identifier*]   (ICLI)
ESSR .... Estonian Soviet Socialist Republic   (RU)
ESSR .... European Society for Surgical Research [*Netherlands*]   (SLS)
ESSS .... Emergency Services Superannuation Scheme [*Victoria, Australia*]
ESSS .... Stockholm Aeronautical Fixed Telecommunication Network Center [*Sweden*] [*ICAO location identifier*]   (ICLI)
ESST .... Eastern Standard Summer Time [*Australia*]
ESST .... [*The*] European Interuniversity Association on Society, Science, and Technology [*Lausanne, Switzerland*]   (ECON)
ESST .... European Master in Society, Science, and Technology [*Swiss Federal Institute of Technology, Lausanne*]   (ECON)
ESST .... Torsby/Fryklanda [*Sweden*] [*ICAO location identifier*]   (ICLI)
ESSTIN ..... Ecole Superieure des Sciences et Technologies de l'Ingenieur de Nancy [*Nancy College of Engineering*] [*France*]   (ERC)
ESSU .... Eskilstuna [*Sweden*] [*ICAO location identifier*]   (ICLI)
ESSV .... Visby [*Sweden*] [*ICAO location identifier*]   (ICLI)
ESSW .... Vastervik [*Sweden*] [*ICAO location identifier*]   (ICLI)
ESSX .... Vasteras/Johannisberg [*Sweden*] [*ICAO location identifier*]   (ICLI)
ESSZ .... Vangso [*Sweden*] [*ICAO location identifier*]   (ICLI)
EST .... Einkommensteuer [*Income Tax*]   (EG)
eSt .... Emotionelle Stellungnahme [*Emotional Attitude*] [*German*]
EST .... Enosis ton Syndikaton Trapezon [*Federation of Bank Unions*] [*Greek*]   (GC)
est .... Established   (EECI)
Est .... Establishment Division [*Home Department*] [*India*]
est .... Estampa [*Print*] [*Publishing*] [*Portuguese*]
est .... Estampado [*Tooled*] [*Publishing*] [*Spanish*]
est .... Estampe [*Print*] [*Publishing*] [*French*]
est .... Estancia [*Station*] [*Portuguese*]
est .... Estante [*Bookcase, Desk*] [*Portuguese*]
Est .... Esteiro [*Creek, Inlet*] [*Portuguese*]   (NAU)
est .... Esterno [*Exterior*] [*Publishing*] [*Italian*]
Est .... Estero [*Creek, Inlet*] [*Spanish*]   (NAU)
est .... Estimada [*Respected, Esteemed*] [*Spanish*]
est .... Estimate   (EECI)
est .... Estonian   (RU)
Est .... Estrada [*Road*] [*Portuguese*]
est .... Estrofe [*Stanza*] [*Portuguese*]
Est .... Estuario [*Estuary*] [*Portuguese*]   (NAU)
Est .... Estuario [*Estuary*] [*Spanish*]   (NAU)
EST .... European Society of Toxicology   (EAIO)
EST .... Flugfelag Austerlands Ltd. Egilsstadir [*Iceland*] [*ICAO designator*]   (FAAC)
ESTA .... Ecole Secondaire des Techniques Administratives [*Secondary School for Administrative Procedures*] [*Burundi*]   (AF)
ESTA .... European Science and Technology Assembly
ESTA .... European Security Transport Association   (EA)
ESTAe ...... Ecole Speciale de Travaux Aeronautiques [*French*]
estamp ...... Estampado [*Tooled*] [*Publishing*] [*Spanish*]
ESTAMTEX ... Estampados Textiles [*Colombia*]   (COL)

ESTB .... Entreprise Senegalaise de Transports Bellassee
ESTC .... East Sydney Technical College [*Australia*]
ESTD .... Integrated Technological Information System   (BU)
ESTE .... Escuela Superior Tecnica del Ejercito [*Army Advanced Technical School*] [*Peru*]   (LA)
ESTEC ...... European Space Technology Center [*Netherlands*]
ESTEG ..... Ecole Superieure de Techniques Economiques et de Gestion [*French*]
Esterifizier ... Esterifizierung [*Esterification*] [*German*]   (GCA)
estet .... Estetiikka [*Aesthetics*] [*Finland*]
EStG .... Einkommensteuergesetz [*Income Tax Law*] [*German*]   (DLA)
Estgosizdat ... Estonian State Publishing House   (RU)
ESTh .... Emborikos Syllogos Thessalonikis [*Salonica Trade Association*] [*Greek*]   (GC)
ESTIT .... Ethnikos Syndesmos Trokhiodromikon kai Ilektrotekhniton Thessalonikis [*National Association of Tramway and Electrical Technicians of Salonica*]   (GC)
ESTIZULIA ... Estireno del Zulia CA [*Venezuela*]
ESTL .... European Space Tribology Laboratory
EstNIIZiM ... Estonian Scientific Research Institute of Agriculture and Reclamation   (RU)
ESTO .... Estonian World Festival
ESTOPL .... Easy Search of Topical Law [*Australia*]
ESTPP .... Entreprise Senegalaise de Travaux Publics et Particuliers
ESTR .... Educational Services and Teaching Resources Unit [*Murdoch University*] [*Australia*]
EStR .... EinkommenSteuerRichtlinien [*Income Tax Regulations*] [*German*]
ESTR .... Equipe Speciale de Travail Revolutionnaire
Estr .... Estrecho [*Strait*] [*Spanish*]   (NAU)
Estr .... Estreito [*Strait*] [*Portuguese*]   (NAU)
ESTRAC .... European Space Satellite Tracking and Telemetry Network   (MCD)
ESTRACK ... European Space Satellite Tracking and Telemetry Network   (BARN)
ESTRALES ... Estructuras Centrales SA [*Colombia*]   (COL)
ESTRO ...... European Society for Therapeutic Radiology and Oncology   (EAIO)
EstSSR ...... Estonian Soviet Socialist Republic   (RU)
ESTUCO ... Ingenieria Civil para Estudios y Construcciones [*Colombia*]   (COL)
ESU .... Efficiency Scrutiny Unit [*Australia*]
ESU .... Electronic Level Indicator   (RU)
ESU .... Electrostatic Accelerator   (RU)
ESU .... English Speaking Union [*British*]   (EAIO)
ESU .... European Showmen's Union [*EC*]   (ECED)
ESUA .... Amsele [*Sweden*] [*ICAO location identifier*]   (ICLI)
ESUB .... Arbra [*Sweden*] [*ICAO location identifier*]   (ICLI)
ESUC .... English Speaking Union of the Commonwealth   (EAIO)
ESUE .... Idre [*Sweden*] [*ICAO location identifier*]   (ICLI)
ESUF .... Fallfors [*Sweden*] [*ICAO location identifier*]   (ICLI)
ESUG .... Gargnas [*Sweden*] [*ICAO location identifier*]   (ICLI)
ESUH .... Harnosand/Myran [*Sweden*] [*ICAO location identifier*]   (ICLI)
ESUIC .... English Speaking Union International Council   (EAIO)
ESUK .... Kalixfors [*Sweden*] [*ICAO location identifier*]   (ICLI)
ESUL .... Ljusdal [*Sweden*] [*ICAO location identifier*]   (ICLI)
ESUM .... Mohed [*Sweden*] [*ICAO location identifier*]   (ICLI)
ESUN .... Sundsvall [*Sweden*] [*ICAO location identifier*]   (ICLI)
ESUNIDAS ... Escuelas Unidas de Comercio [*Manizales*]   (COL)
ESUR .... Ramsele [*Sweden*] [*ICAO location identifier*]   (ICLI)
ESUS .... Asele [*Sweden*] [*ICAO location identifier*]   (ICLI)
ESUT .... Hemavan [*Sweden*] [*ICAO location identifier*]   (ICLI)
ESU/UFE ... European Showmen's Union/Union Foraine Europeenne   (EA)
ESUV .... Alvsbyn [*Sweden*] [*ICAO location identifier*]   (ICLI)
ESUY .... Edsbyn [*Sweden*] [*ICAO location identifier*]   (ICLI)
ESv .... Communications Squadron   (RU)
ESV .... Entomological Society of Victoria [*Australia*]
ESV .... Escuela Secundaria Vocacional [*Vocational Secondary School*] [*Cuba*]   (LA)
ESVA .... Avesta [*Sweden*] [*ICAO location identifier*]   (ICLI)
ESVAL ...... Compania Electro Siderurgica e Industrial de Valdivia [*Chile*]   (LAA)
ESVF .... Frolunda [*Sweden*] [*ICAO location identifier*]   (ICLI)
ESVG .... Gagnef [*Sweden*] [*ICAO location identifier*]   (ICLI)
ESVH .... Hallefors [*Sweden*] [*ICAO location identifier*]   (ICLI)
ESVK .... Katrineholm [*Sweden*] [*ICAO location identifier*]   (ICLI)
ESVM .... Malung [*Sweden*] [*ICAO location identifier*]   (ICLI)
ESVO .... Evropske Sdruzeni Volneho Obchodu [*European Free Trade Association*]   (CZ)
ESVP .... European Society of Veterinary Pathology   (EA)
ESVQ .... Koping [*Sweden*] [*ICAO location identifier*]   (ICLI)
ESVS .... Siljansnas [*Sweden*] [*ICAO location identifier*]   (ICLI)
ESWI .... Norrkoping [*Sweden*] [*ICAO location identifier*]   (ICLI)
ESY .... Executive Aviation Services Ltd. [*Nigeria*] [*ICAO designator*]   (FAAC)

ESYE .... Ethniki Statistiki Ypiresia Ellados [*National Statistical Service of Greece*]   (GC)

ESYOAL ... Ethnikos Syndesmos Ypallilon Odigon Aftokiniton Lesvou [*National League of Employee Drivers of Automobiles of Lesvos*]   (GC)

esz .... Egyesszam [*Singular*]   (HU)

ESZGV ...... Erdogazdasagi Szallito es Gepjavito Vallalat [*Forestry Transportation and Machine Repair Enterprise*]   (HU)

ESZR .... Egyseges Szamitastechnikai Rendszer [*Uniform Computer Technology System*]   (HU)

ESzT .... Ertelmisegi Szakszervezeti Toemoerueles [*Federation of Unions of Intellectual Workers*] [*Hungary*]   (EY)

ESZTER.... Egyseges Szamitogep Tervezesi Rendszer [*Unified Computer Design System*]   (HU)

ET .... Division of Energy Technology [*Thai*]

ET .... Edzok Testulete [*Coaches' Association*]   (HU)

Et .... Eiltriebwagen [*Fast Rail Car*]   (EG)

ET .... Electrical Thermometer   (RU)

ET .... Electric Tractor   (RU)

ET .... Electrothermal (Device)   (RU)

ET .... Elektricne Trakcije [*Electric Traction*]   (YU)

ET .... Elnoki Tanacs [*Presidential Council*]   (HU)

et .... Elvtars [*Comrade*]   (HU)

eT .... Embassy Transport and Tourism Co. [*Egypt*]

ET .... Entrepreneurs Traditionnels

ET .... Erimaki Tokage [*Japanese name for the Australian frill-necked lizard, a national favorite that figured in one of Mitsubishi's advertising campaigns*]

ET .... Escrowed TIGR [*Treasury Investment Growth Receipts*]

Et .... Etage [*Degree, Layer, Stage, Story*] [*French*]

et .... Etat [*Condition*] [*French*]

et .... Etela [*Finland*]

et .... Etelainen [*Finland*]

ET .... Ethiopia [*ANSI two-letter standard code*]   (CNC)

ET .... Ethnikon Typografeion [*National Printing Office*]   (GC)

et .... Etude [*Study*] [*Publishing*] [*French*]

ET .... European Taxation [*Benelux*]   (BAS)

ET .... Ex-Tapol [*Political Prisoner*] [*Indonesia*]

et .... Ezredtartalek [*Regimental Reserves*]   (HU)

ET .... Trench Excavator   (RU)

ETA .... Editores Tecnicos Asocaidos SA [*Spain*]   (DSCA)

ETA .... Egyptian Tourist Authority   (EAIO)

ETA .... Electric Tractor Unit   (RU)

ETA .... Electrothermal Unit   (RU)

ETA .... Elektrotechnische Abteilung [*Electrical Engineering Department*]   (EG)

ETA .... Epitropi Taxikis Allilengyis [*Committee for Class Solidarity*]   (GC)

ETA .... Ergatiki Taxiki Allilengyi [*Working Class Solidarity*]   (GC)

ETA .... Escritorio Tecnico de Agricultura Brasil-Estados Unidos [*Rio De Janeiro, Brazil*]   (LAA)

ETA .... Estonian Telegraph Agency   (EE)

ETA .... Estrellas del Aire SA de CV [*Mexico*] [*ICAO designator*]   (FAAC)

Eta............. Eterna [*Record label*] [*Germany*]

ETA .... Ethiopian Teachers' Association

ETA .... Etudes Administratives [*Administrative Studies*] [*French*]   (BAS)

ETA .... Europaischer Holzhandelsverband [*European Timber Association*] [*EC*]   (ECED)

ETA .... European Taxpayers Association   (EA)

ETA .... European Teachers Association   (BARN)

ETA .... European Tennis Association   (EAIO)

ETA .... European Throwsters Association   (EA)

ETA .... European Thyroid Association   (EAIO)

ETA .... European Tube Association [*EC*]   (ECED)

ETA .... European Tugowners Association   (EAIO)

ETA .... Euzkadi ta Azkatasuna [*Basque Fatherland and Freedom*] [*Spain*]   (PD)

ETA .... Transistorized Autocompensator for Electrical Exploration   (RU)

ETAA........ Educators to Africa Association

ETAA........ Empresa de Transportes Aereos de Angola

Etab.......... Etablissement [*Establishment*] [*Business term*] [*French*]

ETAB........ Expanded Technical Assistance Board [*United Nations*]

Etabl .... Etablissement [*Establishment*] [*Business term*] [*French*]   (CED)

Etabnt .... Etablissement [*Establishment*] [*Military map abbreviation World War I*] [*French*]   (MTD)

etabt .... Etablissement [*Establishment*] [*French*]

ETAC........ Ecole Technique Administrative et Commerciale

ETAC........ Environment Technical Advisory Committee [*Australia*]

ETAD .... Ecological and Toxicological Association of the Dyestuffs Manufacturing Industry [*Basel, Switzerland*]   (EAIO)

ETAE........ Equipe Tecnica de Analises e Estudos Economicos [*Brazil*]   (DSCA)

et-afr .... Etelaafrikkalainen [*South Africa*] [*Finland*]

ETAGE...... Equipe Tecnica para Animais de Grande Porte [*Brazil*]   (DSCA)

ETAGRI .... Escritorio Tecnico de Agrimensura [*Brazil*]   (DSCA)

ETAJ .... Egyseges Termek- es Arjegyzek [*Uniform Product and Price List*]   (HU)

ETAL........ Ente Turistico ed Alberghiero della Libia

et al............ Et Alii [*And Others*] [*Latin*]   (EECI)

ETAM .... Anklam [*Germany*] [*ICAO location identifier*]   (ICLI)

et-am .... Etelaamerikkalainen [*South American*] [*Finland*]

ETAMAR ... Empresa de Talleres Maritimos [*Marine Shops Enterprise*] [*Cuba*]   (LA)

ETAME..... Equipe Tecnica para Animais de Medio Porte [*Brazil*]   (DSCA)

ETAN .... Yugoslav Committee for Electronics and Automation [*Beograd, Yugoslavia*]

ETANAL... Ellinolivyki Alievtiki Etaireia [*Greek-Libyan Fishing Company*] [*Greek*]   (GC)

ETANAL... Etaireia Anaptyxeos Alieias [*Fishing Development Company*] [*Greek*]   (GC)

ETAP........ Entreprise Tunisienne des Activites Petrolieres [*Tunisian Petroleum Activities Enterprise*]   (AF)

ETAP........ Expanded Technical Assistance Program [*United Nations*]

ETAPC ...... European Technical Association for Protective Coatings [*Belgium*]   (SLS)

ETAPE ..... Equipe Tecnica para Animais de Pequeno Porte [*Brazil*]   (DSCA)

ETAS .... Escritorio Tecnico Alejandro Solari [*Brazil*]   (DSCA)

ETASC ...... Educational Turbulence among Australian Servicemen's Children [*Project*]   (ADA)

ETAU .... Bureau Central d'Etudes de Travaux Publics, Architecture, et Urbanisme [*Algeria*]   (IMH)

Et Aut........ Etats Autonomes [*France*]   (FLAF)

ETAWA..... English Teachers' Association of Western Australia

ETB........... Bureau d'Etudes Economiques et Techniques de Batna [*Algeria*]

ETB........... Einheitliche Technische Baubestimmungen [*Uniform Technical Building Regulations*]   (EG)

ETB........... Elastic Top and Bottom [*Military-issue clothing*] [*British*]   (DSUE)

ETB........... English Tourist Board

ETB........... External Trade Bureau [*Guyana*]   (LA)

ETB........... Heavy Bomber Squadron   (RU)

ETBA .... Hellenic Industrial Development Bank [*Greece*]

ETBAA...... Enosis Tekhniton Beton Arme Athinon [*Union of Athens Reinforced Concrete Technicians*]   (GC)

ETBE........ Entreprise Togolaise de Batiments Economiques

ETBH .... Barth [*Germany*] [*ICAO location identifier*]   (ICLI)

ETBN .... Berlin/Schonefeld [*Germany*] [*ICAO location identifier*]   (ICLI)

ETBS .... Berlin/Schonefeld [*Germany*] [*ICAO location identifier*]   (ICLI)

ETC........... Eastern Tool Company (Australia) Proprietary Ltd.

ETC........... Educational Testing Centre [*University of New South Wales*] [*Australia*]

ETC........... Eenheid vir Toegepaste Chemie [*Council for Scientific and Industrial Research*] [*South Africa*]   (AA)

ETC........... Electronic Technical Communications [*Royal Australian Navy*]

ETC........... Empresario de Transporte Combinado [*Combined Transport Operator*] [*Business term*] [*Spanish*]

ETC........... Empresas de Transportes Colectivos del Estado [*Santiago, Chile*]   (LAA)

ETC........... Entrepreneur de Transport Combine [*Combined Transport Operator*] [*Business term*] [*French*]

ETC........... Entreprise Tchadienne de Construction, Romano & Cie.

etc............. Et Cetera   (EECI)

ETC........... Ethiopian Textile Corporation

ETC........... European Tax Confederation   (EAIO)

ETC........... European Taxi Confederation [*Belgium*]   (EAIO)

ETC........... European Tea Committee   (EA)

ETC........... European Tool Committee   (EA)

ETC........... European Toy Confederation [*France*]   (EAIO)

ETC........... European Translations Centre [*Later, International Translations Centre*]

ETC........... Euro Travellers Cheque [*Thomas Cook International*]

ETCA........ Entreprise Togolaise de Construction et d'Ameublement

ETCA........ Etudes Techniques et Constructions Aerospatiales [*Belgium*]   (PDAA)

ETCD........ Entreprise de Transit C. Deodati

ETCD........ Equipment de Terminaison de Circuit de Donnees [*French*]   (ADPT)

ETCF .... European Technical Committee for Fluorine [*of the European Council of Chemical Manufacturers' Federations*] [*Belgium*]   (EAIO)

ETCh .... Electron Transport Particle   (RU)

ETCO .... Cottbus [*Germany*] [*ICAO location identifier*]   (ICLI)

ETCOM .... European Testing and Certification for Office and Manufacturing Protocol   (OSI)

ET Cons .... Eastern Transvaal Consolidated Mines [*South Africa*]

ETCR........ Entreprise Tchadienne de Construction, Romano et Compagnie

Et Crimin .. Etudes Criminologiques [*France*]   (FLAF)

ETD .... Education and Training Division [*Technical and Further Education*] [*New South Wales, Australia*]

ETD .... Ersatzteildienst [*German*]   (ADPT)

ETDC........ Egyptian Tourist Development Company

ETDCFRL ... European Training and Development Centre for Farming and Rural Life   (EA)

ETDDTh ... Enosis Tourkon Didaskalon Dytikis Thrakis [*Union of Turkish Teachers of Western Thrace*]   (GC)

ETDE........ Societe Entreprise Transport et Distribution d'Electricite

Et deScience Crim et de Dr Pen Comp ... Etudes de Science Criminelle et de Droit Penal Compare [*France*]   (FLAF)

ETDN .... Dresden [*Germany*] [*ICAO location identifier*]   (ICLI)

Et DocSoc ... Centre d'Etudes et de Documentation Sociales [*Benelux*]   (BAS)

ETDZ........ Economic and Technical Development Zones [*China*]   (TCC)

ETE........... Emboriki Trapeza Ellados [*Commercial Bank of Greece*]   (GC)

ETE........... Energiagazdalkodasi Tudomanyos Egyesulet [*Scientific Association for Energy Management*]   (HU)

ETE........... Epitoipari Tudomanyos Egyesulet [*Scientific Association of the Construction Industry*]   (HU)

Ete............. Eterna [*Record label*] [*Germany*]

ETE........... Ethniki Trapeza Ellados [*National Bank of Greece*]   (GC)

ETE........... Evropaiki Trapeza Ependyseon [*European Investment Bank*]   (GC)

ETE........... Metemma [*Ethiopia*] [*Airport symbol*]   (OAG)

ETEA........ Equipe Tecnica de Estatistica Agropecuaria [*Brazil*]   (DSCA)

ETEA........ Escuela Superior de Tecnica Empresarial Agricola [*Agricultural Business Administration College*] [*Spanish*]   (ARC)

ETEA........ Etudes et Travaux d'Electrification, d'Eau, et d'Assainissement

ETEAG...... Equipe de Tecnologia Agricola [*Brazil*]   (DSCA)

ETEAP ...... Etaireia Tekhnikou Exoplismou kai Axiopoiiseos (Nopon Georgikon) Proiondon [*Company for Providing Technical Equipment and Marketing Fresh Farm Products*] [*Greek*]   (GC)

ETEAV ...... Equipe Tecnica de Aviacao Agricola [*Brazil*]   (DSCA)

ETEC........ Entreprise de Transport et Exploitation de Carrieres

ETECOF ... Equipe Tecnica de Corretivos e Fertilizantes [*Brazil*]   (DSCA)

ETEDA...... Equipe Tecnica de Defesa Sanitaria Animal [*Brazil*]   (DSCA)

ETEDE...... Equipe Tecnica de Defesa Sanitaria Vegetal [*Brazil*]   (DSCA)

ETEEFO ... Eidikon Tameion Elengkhou kai Epopteias Forologias Oinopnevmatos [*Special Fund for the Control and Supervision of Alcoholic Beverage Taxation*] [*Greek*]   (GC)

ETEF .... Equipe Tecnica de Fruticultura e Olericultura [*Brazil*]   (DSCA)

ETEF .... Erfurt [*Germany*] [*ICAO location identifier*]   (ICLI)

ETEFRIA .. Equipe Tecnica de Fisiopatologia da Reproducao e Inseminacao Artificial [*Brazil*]   (DSCA)

ETEHA ..... Entreprise Togolaise d'Electricite et d'Hydraulique Applique

ETEKPS.... Eidikon Tameion Efarmogis Rythmikon Poleodomikon Skhedion [*Special Fund for Implementing Regulatory and Zoning Plans*]   (GC)

ETEL .... Empreendimentos Tecnicos de Estradas Limitada

ETENA...... Equipe Tecnica de Nutricao Animal e Agrostologia [*Brazil*]   (DSCA)

ETENE...... Escritorio Tecnico de Estudos Economicos do Nordeste [*Technical Office for Economic Studies of the Northeast*] [*Brazil*]   (LA)

ETEO .... Eidikon Tameion Eparkhiakis Odopoiias [*Special Fund for Provincial Road Construction*] [*Followed by initial letter of the nome in which located*]   (GC)

ETEO .... Equipe Tecnica de Operacoes [*Brazil*]   (DSCA)

ETEPEM .. Equipe Tecnica de Pesquisas Meteorologicas [*Brazil*]   (DSCA)

ETEPI....... Equipe Tecnica de Plantas Industriais [*Brazil*]   (DSCA)

ETEPOV ... Equipe Tecnica de Padronizacao, Classificacao, e Inspecao de Produtos de Origem Vegetal [*Brazil*]   (DSCA)

ETEPRE.... Equipe de Treinamento e Programas Rurais Educativos [*Brazil*]   (DSCA)

ETESEM... Equipe Tecnica de Sementes e Mudas [*Brazil*]   (DSCA)

ETET........ Equipe Tecnica de Treinamento [*Brazil*]   (DSCA)

Et et Conj... Etudes et Conjuncture [*France*]   (FLAF)

Et et Doc... Etudes et Documents du Conseil d'Etats [*France*]   (FLAF)

et/ev .... Ezer Tonna Evente [*Thousand Tons per Year*]   (HU)

ETEVA ...... Ethniki Trapeza Ependyseon Viomikhanikis Anaptyxeos [*National Investment Bank for Industrial Development*] [*Greek*]   (GC)

Et Ex......... Etudes et Expansion   (EA)

ETEX........ Societe d'Etudes et d'Exploitations Industrielles

ETF........... Education and Training Foundation [*New South Wales, Australia*]

ETF........... Escola Tecnica Federal [*Federal Technical School*] [*Brazil*]   (LA)

ETF........... Etudes Topographiques et Foncieres

ETF........... European Training Foundation [*EC*]   (ECED)

ETFA .... European Technological Forecasting Association   (PDAA)

ETFAS...... Ente per la Transformazione Fondiaria e Agraria in Sardegna [*Italian*]

ETFL .... Friedland [*Germany*] [*ICAO location identifier*]   (ICLI)

ETG.......... Electric Heat Generator   (RU)

ETG.......... Entreprise de Travaux au Gabon

Etg............. Etang [*Pond*] [*Military map abbreviation World War I*] [*French*]   (MTD)

ETH .... Eidgenossische Technische Hochschule [*Federal Institute of Technology*] [*Switzerland*]   (PDAA)

ETH........... Elat [*Israel*] [*Airport symbol*]   (OAG)

ETH........... Entretien, Transformation, Habitat

ETH........... Ethiopia [*ANSI three-letter standard code*]   (CNC)

ETH........... Ethiopian Airlines Corp. [*ICAO designator*]   (FAAC)

ETHD........ Heringsdorf [*Germany*] [*ICAO location identifier*]   (ICLI)

EThE .... Elliniki Thalassia Enosis [*Greek Maritime Union*]   (GC)

EthEN........ Ethniki Enosis Neon [*National Youth Union*] [*Greek*]   (GC)

ETHIC...... Ethiopian Tourism and Hotel Investment Company   (AF)

EthIGME .. Ethnikon Idryma Geologikon kai Metallevtikon Erevnon [*National Institute of Geological and Mineral Research*] [*Greek*]   (GC)

ETHIOP.... Ethiopic [*Language, etc.*]   (ROG)

ETHZ .... Eidgenoessische Technische Hochschule, Zuerich [*Swiss Federal Institute of Technology, Zurich*] [*Research center*]

ETI............ Economisch Technologisch Instituut [*Benelux*]   (BAS)

ETI............ Egyesitett Tiszti Iskola [*United Officers' School*]   (HU)

ETI............ Elektrarna Tisova [*Electric Power Plant, Tisova*]   (CZ)

ETI............ Emballage og Transportinstituttet [*Danish Packaging and Transportation Research Institute*] [*Research center*]   (IRC)

ETI............ Endustri, Ticaret, ve Isletmecilik Tesebbusleri Ltd. [*Industry, Commerce, and Management Enterprises Ltd.*] [*Turkish Cypriot*]   (TU)

ETI............ Epitestudomanyi Intezet [*Institute of Architecture*]   (HU)

ETI............ Escuela Tecnica Industrial [*Industrial Technical School*] [*Venezuela*]   (LA)

ETI............ European Toy Institute   (EAIO)

ETI............ European Transuranium Institute [*Germany*]

ETI............ Executor and Trustee Institute [*Australia*]

ETIA......... European Tape Industry Associaton   (PDAA)

ETIB......... Eti Bank Genel Mudurlugu [*Eti Bank Directorate General*] [*Under Ministry of Energy and Natural Resources*]   (TU)

ETIL......... Economisch Technologisch Instituut in Limburg [*German*]

ETIM........ Emprese de Transportes Intermunicipal de Cargas e Passageiros

ETIMEX ... Ethiopian Import and Export Corp.

ETINAF .... Etablissements Industriels Africains

ETIPOA .... Equipe Tecnica de Padronizacao, Classificacao, e Inspecao de Produtos de Origem Animal [*Brazil*]   (DSCA)

ETIPTA..... Enosi Tekhnikon Imerisiou kai Periodikou Typou Athinon [*Union of Athens Daily and Periodical Press Technical Workers*]   (GC)

etiq .... Etiquette [*Label*] [*Publishing*] [*French*]

Et Is.......... Et Is Sendikasi [*Butchers' Union*]   (TU)

ETITAS.... Elektrik Techizati Imalati Anomim Sirketi [*Electrical Equipment Manufacturing Corporation*] [*Izmir*]   (TU)

etj .... E Tjera [*or E Tjere*] [*Albanian*]

ETJ.......... Exploitation de Transports Jumeles

Et JurEcon ... Etudes Juridiques et Economiques [*France*]   (FLAF)

ETK .... Epitesugyi Tajekoztatasi Kozpont [*Center for Information on Construction Affairs*] [*Ministry for Building and Urban Development*]   (HU)

ETK .... Estonian Labor Commune [*1918-1919*]   (RU)

ETK .... Technical Operations Office   (RU)

ETKA........ Eparkhiakon Tameion Koinonikon Asfaliseon [*District Social Insurance Fund*] [*Cyprus*]   (GC)

ETKB........ Enerji ve Tabii Kaynaklar Bakanligi [*Ministry of Energy and Natural Resources*]   (TU)

ETKh .... Scientific Research Laboratory of Experimental Chemotherapy   (RU)

ETKO .... Etaireia Kypriakon Oinon [*Cyprus Wines Corporation*]   (GC)

ETKZ........ Kyritz [*Germany*] [*ICAO location identifier*]   (ICLI)

ETL........... Electro Technical Laboratory [*Japan*]   (PDAA)

ETL........... Equipement Terminal de Lignes [*French*]   (ADPT)

etl .... Etelaista Leveytta [*Finland*]

ETL........... European Transport Law [*Benelux*]   (BAS)

Etle............. Etoile [*Star*] [*Military map abbreviation World War I*] [*French*]   (MTD)

ETLM........ Leipzig/Mockau [*Germany*] [*ICAO location identifier*]   (ICLI)

ETLS .... Leipzig [*Germany*] [*ICAO location identifier*]   (ICLI)

ETM .... Entreprise et Travaux de Makokov

ETM .... Etudes Topographiques et Metres

ETMA .... Elliniki Trapeza Mesis Anatolis [*Greek Bank of the Middle East*]   (GC)

ETMAR..... Institut pour l'Etude des Marches en France et a l'Etranger

ETMC....... European Telephone Marketing Council [*of the European Direct Marketing Organization*] [*Jona, Switzerland*]   (EA)

ETMG .... Magdeburg [*Germany*] [*ICAO location identifier*]   (ICLI)

ETMLE ..... Eidikon Tameion Mikhanimaton Limenikon Ergon [*Special Fund for Port Projects Machinery*] [*Greek*]   (GC)

ETMO .... Empresa Terminales Mambisas de Occidente [*Western Mambisas Shipping Enterprise*] [*Cuba*]   (GC)

ETMOA .... Eidikon Tameion Monimon Odostromaton Athinon [*Athens Special Fund for Permanent Road Surfaces*]   (GC)

ETMS........ Electronic Territory Management System [*Australia*]

ETN .... Electronic Heat Pump   (RU)

ETN .... Enosis Tourkikis Neolaias [*Union of Turkish Youth*]   (GC)

etn .... Ethnography, Ethnographic   (BU)

etn .... Etnico [*Ethnic*] [*Portuguese*]
Etn.............. Etnografya [*Ethnography*] (TU)
ETN .... Hinged Trench Excavator (RU)
ETN .... Uniform Labor Norms (BU)
Etno.......... Etnografya [*Ethnography*] (TU)
etnogr........ Ethnography, Ethnographic (BU)
Etnogr .... Etnografia [*Ethnography*] [*Portuguese*]
etnol .... Ethnology (RU)
ETNOL ..... Etnologie [*Ethnology*] [*Afrikaans*]
Etnolog...... Etnologia [*Ethnology*] [*Portuguese*]
ETNVT..... Edinaia Tovarnaia Nomenklatura Vneshney Torgovli
     [*Commodity nomenclature system used in international
     trade*]
ETO .... Ecole Technique Officielle
ETO .... Egyetemes Tizedes Osztalyozas [*Universal Decimal
     Classification*] (HU)
ETO .... Eidikon Tagma Opliton [*Special Soldiers Battalion*] [*Greek*]
     (GC)
ETO .... Ellinikos Tapitourgikos Organismos [*Greek Carpet
     Manufacturers Organization*] (GC)
ETO .... Ethiopian Tourist Organization
ETO .... Express Transportation Organization of Thailand (FEA)
ETOPEC ... Ethiopian Oilseeds and Pulses Export Corp.
ETP............ Ecole des Travaux Publics
ETP............ Electrical Technical Power [*Royal Australian Navy*]
ETP............ Electrotechnical Industry (RU)
ETP............ Electrotonic Potential (RU)
ETP............ Empire Test Pilots School [*British*] [*ICAO designator*] (FAAC)
ETP............ Entreprise Travaux Publics
ETP............ European Training Programme in Brain and Behavior Research
     [*of the European Science Foundation*] [*France*] (EA)
ETP............ Semiconductor Soil Electrical Thermometer (RU)
ETPD......... Entreprise des Travaux pour l'Extension et l'Amenagement du
     Part de Dakar
ETPI.......... Eastern Telecommunications Philippines, Inc. [*Manila*]
ETPM....... Entreprise-GTM pour les Travaux Petroliers Maritimes [*French*]
ETPO........ Entreprise de Travaux Publics de l'Ouest
ETPO........ European Trade Promotion Organization (DS)
etr............. Etranger [*Foreign*] [*French*]
ETR .... Etudes Techniques et Realisations
ETR .... Technical Operations Area (RU)
ETR .... Wheel Trench Excavator (RU)
ETRA........ Empresa de Trabajos Agricolas Ltda. [*Colombia*] (COL)
ETRC........ Education Training and Resource Centre [*Technical and Further
     Education*] [*New South Wales, Australia*]
ETRI........ Electronics and Telecommunications Research Institute
     [*Research center*] [*South Korea*] (IRC)
ETRS .... Engineering Testing and Research Services Proprietary Ltd.
     [*Australia*]
ETRTO..... European Technical Rim and Tyre Organisation (PDAA)
ETRTO..... European Tyre and Rim Technical Organisation [*Belgium*]
ETs............ Electrical Centralization of Switches and Signals [*Railroads*]
     (RU)
ETS........... Entreprise de Transports Senegalais
Ets............ Etablissements [*Establishments*] [*French*] (CED)
Ets............ Ethylcellulose (RU)
et s .... Et Suivants [*And Following*] [*French*] (ILCA)
ETS........... Etudes Senegalaises
ETS........... European Telecommunications Standard (OSI)
ETS........... European Teleprocessing System (ADPT)
ETS........... European Teratology Society (EA)
ETS........... Excursion and Tourist Station (RU)
ETS........... Integrated Transportation System (BU)
ETSA .... Ecole Technique Secondaire Agricole [*Secondary Agricultural
     Technical School*] [*Zaire*]
ETSA .... Empresa de Transportes y Servicio Aereos [*Air Transportation
     and Service Enterprise*] [*Nicaragua*] (LA)
ETSAB ...... Escuela Tecnica y Superior de Arquitectura de Barcelona [*Higher
     Technical School of Architecture of Barcelona*] [*Spain*]
ETSAIMECHE ... Engineering Technician of the South African Institute of
     Mechanical Engineers (AA)
ETSAM .... Escuela Tecnica Superior de Arouitectura de Madrid [*Higher
     Technical College of Architecture, Madrid*] [*Spain*] (ERC)
ETsBG ...... Electrocerebellogram (RU)
ETSEC...... Etablissements Simon et Compagnie
et seqq .... Et Sequentes [*And the Following*] [*Latin*] (BARN)
EtsG.......... Electrocerebrogram (RU)
ETShch...... Ocean Mine Sweeper (RU)
ETSHOS ... Ecole Technique Superieure des Hostesses et Secretaires
ETSI .... European Telecommunications Standards Institute
ETSIA .... Escuela Tecnica Superior de Ingenieros Agronomos [*Spain*]
     (DSCA)
ETSICCPB ... Escuela Tecnica Superior de Ingenieros de Caminos, Canales y
     Puertos [*Higher College of Civil Engineering*] [*Spain*]
     (ERC)

ETSIIB...... Escuela Tecnica Superior de Ingenieros Industriales de Barcelona
     [*Higher Technical College of Industrial Engineering of
     Barcelona*] [*Spain*] (ERC)
ETSIIT ...... Escuela Tecnica Superior de Ingenieros Industriales de Terrassa
     [*Higher Technical College of Industrial Engineering of
     Terrassa*] [*Spain*] (WED)
ETSIM ...... Escuela Tecnica Superior de Ingenieros de Montes [*Spain*]
     (DSCA)
ETSIN ...... Escuela Tecnica Superior de Ingenieros Navales [*Higher
     Technical College of Naval Architects and Marine
     Engineers*] [*Spain*] (ERC)
ETSITB ..... Escuela Tecnica Superior de Ingenieros de Telecomunicacion
     [*Higher Technical College of Telecommunications*] [*Spain*]
     (WED)
ETsM........ Electronic Digital Computer (RU)
ETSMA .... European Tyre Stud Manufacturers Association (PDAA)
ETsN........ Electrical Centrifugal Pump (RU)
etsn............ Etsning [*Etching*] [*Publishing*] [*Sweden*]
ETsNPKMM ... Consolidated Center for the Scientific Training of Cadres in
     Mathematics and Mechanics (BU)
ETs NPKpo biologiya ... Consolidated Center for Scientific Training of
     Cadres in Biology (BU)
ETsO .... United Zionist Organization (BU)
ETsR........ Electronic Digital Recorder (RU)
ETsUM...... Electronic Digital Control Computer (RU)
ETsVM..... Electronic Digital Computer (RU)
ETsVP ...... Electronic Digital Recording Voltmeter (RU)
ETT........... Egeszsegugyi Tudomanyos Tanacs [*Scientific Council of Health*]
     (HU)
ETT........... Einheitlicher Transittarif [*Uniform Transit Tariff*] [*Business
     term*] [*German*] (EG)
ETT........... Electric Skidding Tractor (RU)
ETT........... Entreprise de Travaux Touristiques [*Algeria*] (IMH)
ETT........... Entreprise Travaux-Togo
ETT........... Eska Turizm & Ticaret [*Property company*] [*Turkey*]
ETT........... Uniform Transit Rates (BU)
ETTC........ Engine Test Technology Centre [*Worcester, England*]
ettc.......... Ethiopian Tourist Trading Corp.
ETTD........ Equipment Terminal de Traitement de Donnees [*French*]
     (ADPT)
ETTDC...... Electronics Trade and Technology Development Corp. [*India*]
     (PDAA)
Ette.......... Baionnette [*Bayonet*] [*French*] (MTD)
ETTE......... Ethiopian Tourist Trading Enterprise
Ettf.......... Etterfoelger [*Successors*] [*Norway*] (CED)
ETTU........ European Table Tennis Union (EA)
ETTUC...... European Teachers Trade Union Committee [*EC*] (ECED)
ETU .... Ethiopian Trade Union
ETU .... European Triathlon Union (EA)
ETU .... Technical Operations Administration (RU)
ETU .... Technical Specifications for Export (RU)
ETU .... Universal Electric Tractor (RU)
ETU .... Universal Trench Excavator (RU)
ETUC........ European Trade Union Confederation [*Western Europe*] (WER)
ETUCTCL ... European Trade Union Committee for Textiles, Clothing, and
     Leather [*Belgium*] [*Belgium*] (EAIO)
Etud.......... Etudler [*Studies*] (TU)
EtudesComm ... Collection Etudes de la Commission de la Communaute
     Economique Europeenne [*Benelux*] (BAS)
ETUDIS .... Etudes et Distributions
ETUF........ Egyptian Trade Union Federation [*Cairo*] (MENA)
ETUI......... European Trade Union Institute [*Belgium*]
ETUI......... European Trans-Uranium Institute [*Karlsruhe, Germany*]
ETUP........ Egypto-Tripolitanian Union Party
ETV .... Eskisehir TV Enstitusu [*Eskisehir TV Institute*] (TU)
ETV .... Europaeischer Tabakwaren-Grosshandels-Verband [*European
     Tobacco Wholesalers' Union*] (EAIO)
ETV .... Experimental Test Vehicle [*Australia*]
ETVA....... Elliniki Trapeza Viomikhanikis Anaptyxeos [*Hellenic Industrial
     Development Bank*] (GC)
ETVAA...... Educational Television Association of Australia (ADA)
ETVG .... European Tumour Virus Group (EAIO)
ETVKYA ... Enosis Tekhniton-Voithon Kalorifer-Ydravlikon Athinon [*Union
     of Athens Heating and Plumbing Technicians and Helpers*]
     (GC)
ETW .... Electrical Technical Weapons [*Royal Australian Navy*]
ETW .... Ernst Thaelmann Werke [*Ernst Thaelmann Works*] (EG)
etw........... Etwaig [*Possible*] [*German*] (GCA)
etw........... Etwas [*Something*] [*German*]
ETW .... European Transonic Wind-Tunnel
ETWN ...... Wriezen [*Germany*] [*ICAO location identifier*] (ICLI)
ETY .... Energiataloudellinen Yhdistys [*Finnish Energy Economy
     Association*] (EAIO)
ETY .... Enosis Trapezitikon Ypallilon [*Union of Bank Employees*]
     [*Greek*] (GC)
ETYAP...... Epikourikon Tameion Ypallilon Astynomias Poleon [*City Police
     Employees Auxiliary Fund*] [*Greek*] (GC)

ETYK......... Conference on Security and Cooperation in Europe [*Use CSCE*] [*Finland*] (WEN)

ETYK......... Enosis Trapezitikon Ypallilon Kyprou [*Union of Cyprus Bank Employees*] (GC)

ETYOO ..... Erkek Teknik Yuksek Ogretmen Okulu [*Men's Advanced Teachers School*] [*Ankara*] (TU)

ETYPS...... Eidikon Tameion Ypallilon Pyrosvestikou Somatos [*Special Fund for Employees of the Fire Corps*] [*Greek*] (GC)

ETZ........... Electrical Grain Thermometer (RU)

ETZ........... Electric Hoists Plant (BU)

EU............. Ege Universitesi [*Aegean University*] [*Izmir*] (TU)

EU............. Einzelhandelsumsatz [*Retail Turnover*] (EG)

EU............. Ekonomicky Ustav [*Institute of Economics (of the Czechoslovak Academy of Sciences)*] (CZ)

EU............. Electronic Amplifier (RU)

EU............. Empresa Ecuatoriana de Aviacion [*Ecuador*] [*ICAO designator*] (ICDA)

EU............. Energeticky Ustav [*Power Research Institute*] (CZ)

EU............. Estados Unidos de America [*United States of America*] [*Spanish*]

E-U .... Etats-Unis [*United States*] [*French*]

EU............. European Union [*Formerly, European Community*]

Eu............. Europio [*Chemical element*] [*Portuguese*]

EU............. Extremadura Unida [*Spain*] [*Political party*] (EY)

EU............. Power Plant [*Maritime term*] (RU)

EUA........... Estados Unidos Americanos [*United States of America*] [*Spanish*]

EUA........... Estados Unidos da America [*United States of America*] [*Portuguese*] (GPO)

EUA........... Eua Tonga Island [*South Pacific*] [*Airport symbol*] (OAG)

EUA........... Europe Air [*France*] [*ICAO designator*] (FAAC)

EUA........... European Unit of Account

EUA........... Ewe Unionist Association

EUAIS...... European Union of Arab and Islamic Studies [*See also UEAI*] (EAIO)

EUB .... Estados Unidos do Brasil [*United States of Brazil*]

EUBM .... Egba United Board of Management

EUBS......... European Undersea Biomedical Society (MSC)

EUC .... Eurocontrol [*Belgium*] [*ICAO designator*] (FAAC)

EUC .... European Union of Coachbuilders (EA)

EUCA .... European Federation of Associations of Coffee Roasters (EA)

EUCAPA... European Capsules Association [*EC*] (ECED)

EUCARPIA ... European Association for Research on Plant Breeding (EAIO)

EUCATEL ... European Conference of Associations of Telecommunications Industries (OSI)

EUCEPA ... Europaeischer Verband fuer Zellstoff und Papiertechnik [*European Liaison Committee for Pulp and Paper*] (EAIO)

EUCHEMAP ... European Committee of Chemical Plant Manufacturers [*EC*] (ECED)

EUCLID .... Easily Used Computer Language for Illustration and Drawing [*European Community*] (MHDB)

EUCLID.... European Cooperative Longterm Initiative for Defense [*NATO*]

EUCOFEL ... Union Europeenne du Commerce de Gros en Fruits et Legumes [*European Union of the Fruit and Vegetable Wholesale, Import, and Export Trade*] [*Brussels, Belgium*] (EAIO)

EUCOFF ... European Conference on Flammability and Fire Retardants

EUCOLAIT ... Union Europeenne du Commerce des Produits Laitiers et Derives [*European Union of Importers, Exporters, and Dealers in Dairy Products*] (EAIO)

EUCOMED ... European Confederation of Medical Suppliers Associations (EA)

EUCONEC ... Europaische Konferenz der Industrie Elektrischer Kondensatoren [*European Conference of the Industry of Electrical Capacitors*] [*EC*] (ECED)

Eu Cs.......... Egeszsegugyi Csoport [*Health Group, Sanitary Group*] (HU)

EUD........... European Union of Dentists (PDAA)

EUDC........ European Urban Driving Cycle [*Automotive emissions*]

EUDEBA... Editorial Universitaria de Buenos Aires [*Argentina*] (DSCA)

EUDH .... European Union of Developers and House Builders [*Belgium*] (EAIO)

EUDISED ... European Documentation and Information System for Education [*Council of Europe*] [*Database*] (IID)

EUFODA .. European Food Distributors Association (PDAA)

EufR.......... Knjiznica Samostana Sveti Eufemije na Rabu [*Library of the St. Eufemija Monastery on the Island of Rab*] (YU)

EUFTT ...... European Union of Film and Television Technicians (BARN)

EUG.......... European Union of Geosciences [*Strasbourg, France*]

EUI .... Euravia [*Spain*] [*ICAO designator*] (FAAC)

EUITBF.... Ege Universitesi Iktisadi ve Ticari Bilimler Fakultesi [*Aegean University Faculty of Economy and Commercial Science*] (TU)

EUITIB ..... Escuela Universitaria de Ingenieria Tecnica Industrial de Barcelona [*University College of Industrial Engineering of Barcelona*] [*Spain*] (ERC)

EUITIT ..... Escuela Universitaria de Ingenieria Tecnica Industrial de Terrassa [*University College of Industrial Technical Engineering of Terrassa*] [*Spain*] (ERC)

EUJS .... European Union of Jewish Students (EA)

EUL .... Euralair International [*France*] [*ICAO designator*] (FAAC)

EULABANK ... Euro-Latin America Bank Ltd. [*British*] (EY)

EULAR...... European League Against Rheumatism (EAIO)

EULEP ...... European Late Effects Project Group (PDAA)

Eu M .... Egeszsegugyi Miniszterium/Miniszter [*Ministry/Minister of Health*] (HU)

EUM.......... Electronic Control Machine (RU)

EUM.......... Entraide Universitaire Mondiale [*World University Service - WUS*] (EAIO)

EUM.......... Teletypewriter (RU)

EUMABOIS ... Comite Europeen des Constructeurs de Machines a Bois [*European Committee of Woodworking Machinery Manufacturers*] (EAIO)

EUM-AFTN ... European Mediterranean Aeronautical Fixed Telecommunications Network (PDAA)

EUMAPRINT ... European Committee of Associations of Printing and Paper Converting Machinery (EA)

EUMETSAT ... European Meteorological Satellite (MCD)

EUMETSAT ... European Organization for the Exploitation of Meteorological Satellites

EUMOTIV ... European Association for the Study of Economic, Commercial, and Industrial Motivation [*Belgium*] (PDAA)

EUMS .... European Union of Music Schools [*See also EMU*] (EA)

EUMT .... Europaeische Union Gegen den Missbrauch der Tiere [*European Union for the Prevention of Cruelty to Animals*] [*Switzerland*] (EAIO)

EUN........... Laayoune [*Morocco*] [*Airport symbol*] (OAG)

EUNC .... Eritrean Unified National Council [*Ethiopia*]

EUNED ..... Editorial de la Universidad Estatal a Distancia [*Publishing house*] [*Costa Rica*] (EY)

EUNMWSCM ... European Union of Natural Mineral Water Sources of the Common Market (EAIO)

EUP .... Electrical Turn Indicator (RU)

EUPA .... European Union for the Protection of Animals (PDAA)

EuPC......... European Plastics Converters [*Belgium*] (EAIO)

EUPE........ European Union for Packaging and the Environment [*EEC*] (PDAA)

euph .... Euphemique [*French*] (TPFD)

euph .... Euphemistic (TPFD)

EUPREN... European Primate Resources Network

EUPSA ..... European Union of Paediatric Surgical Associations (PDAA)

EUR.......... Esposizione Universale di Roma [*Universal Exposition of Rome*] [*Also suburb of Rome*] [*Italian*] (WER)

Eur .... Eurochord [*Record label*] [*France*]

EUR.......... Eurojet SA [*Spain*] [*ICAO designator*] (FAAC)

EUR.......... Europa [*Europe*] [*Afrikaans*]

EURA .... Europa-Afrika-Union

EURA .... European Renderers Association (EAIO)

EurACS .... European Association of Classification Societies (EAIO)

EURAFREP ... Societe de Recherches et d'Exploitation du Petrole [*French*]

EURAG ..... Federation Europeenne des Personnes Agees [*European Federation for the Welfare of the Elderly*] (EAIO)

EURAGRIS ... European Agricultural Research Information System

EURALARM ... Association des Constructeurs Europeens de Systemes d'Alarme Incendie et Vol [*Association of European Manufacturers of Fire and Intruder Alarm Systems*] (EAIO)

EURAM .... European Research on Advanced Materials

EURANP ... European Air Navigation Plan [*ICAO*] (DA)

EURAS...... Association Europeenne l'Anodisation [*European Anodisers' Association*] (EA)

EURASAP ... European Association for the Science of Air Pollution (EAIO)

EURASEP ... European Association of Scientists for Experiments with Pollution (ASF)

EURASIP ... European Association for Signal Processing (EAIO)

EURATEX ... Societe Eurafricaine Textiles

EURATOM ... European Atomic Energy Community [*Also, EAEC*]

EURCO ..... European Composite Unit [*European Economic Community*]

EUREAU .. Union des Associations des Distributeurs d'Eau de Pays Membres des Communautes Europeennes [*Union of the Water Supply Associations from Countries of the European Communities*] (EAIO)

EuReDatA ... European Reliability Data Association

EUREKA... European Research Cooperation Agency [*Non-defense research study group including eighteen European countries*]

EUREL...... Association Europeenne des Reserves Naturelles Libres [*European Association for Free Nature Reserves*] [*Inactive*] (EAIO)

EUREL...... Convention of National Societies of Electrical Engineers of Western Europe (EAIO)

EURES...... European Reticulo-Endothelial Society [*Switzerland*] (SLS)

EUR FCB .. European Frequency Coordinating Body [*ICAO*] (DA)

EURIM...... European Conference on Research into the Management of Information Systems and Libraries (PDAA)

EURIMA... European Insulation Manufacturers Association (PDAA)

EURIPA .... European Information Industry Association [*Formerly, European Information Providers Association*] [*Information retrieval*]   (IID)

EUROAVIA ... Association of European Aeronautical and Astronautical Students   (PDAA)

EUROBA .. European Professional Fair for Industry and Handicraft of Bakery, Confectionery, Pastry, Biscuits, Chocolate, and Ice Cream Making

EUROBANK ... Common designation and telegraphic address of the BCEN [*Banque Commerciale pour l'Europe du Nord*] [*French*]   (WER)

EUROBAT ... Association of European Battery Manufacturers   (EA)

EUROBIT ... European Association of Manufacturers of Business Machines and Data Processing Equipment [*Frankfurt, Federal Republic of Germany*]   (EAIO)

EUROBITUME ... European Bitumen Association   (EA)

EUROBOIS ... Entreprise Europeenne de Courtage des Bois

EUROBUILD ... European Organization for the Promotion of New Techniques and Methods in Building   (EA)

EUROCAE ... European Organization for Civil Aviation Electronics [*France*]   (PDAA)

EUROCAM ... Societe Europ-Cameroun

EUROCEAN ... European Oceanic Association [*Monaco, Monaco*]   (EAIO)

EUROCENTRES ... Foundation for European Language and Educational Centres   (EA)

EUROCHEMIC ... European Company for the Chemical Processing of Irradiated Fuels   (DS)

Eurochemic ... Europese Maatschappij voor de Chemische Bewerking van Bestraalte Reactor Splijtstoffen [*European Company for the Chemical Processing of Irradiated Fuels*] [*Netherlands*]   (WEN)

EUROCHOR ... Arbeitsgemeinschaft Europaeischer Chorverbaende [*European Choral Association - ECA*]   (EA)

EUROCLAMP ... European Clamping Tools Association [*EC*]   (ECED)

EUROCOM ... European Communications

EUROCOMP ... European Computing Congress

EUROCONTROL ... European Organization for the Safety of Air Navigation

EUROCOOP ... European Commmunity of Cooperative Societies   (PDAA)

EUROCOPI ... European Computer Program Information Centre

EUROCOR ... European Congress on Metallic Corrosion   (PDAA)

EUROCORD ... Federation des Industries de Ficellerie et Corderie de l'Europe Occidentale [*Federation of Western European Rope and Twine Industries*]   (EA)

EUROCOTON ... Comite des Industries du Coton et des Fibres Connexes de la CEE [*Committee of the Cotton Industries of the European Economic Community*]   (PDAA)

EURODIDAC ... European Association of Manufacturers and Distributors of Education Materials   (PDAA)

EURODIF ... European Diffusion Agency [*France, Spain, Italy, Belgium*]   (WER)

EUROFAR ... European Future Advanced Rotocraft   (MCD)

EUROFEDOP ... European Federation of Employees in Public Services   (EAIO)

EUROFER ... Association of European Steel Producers   (PDAA)

EUROFER ... European Confederation of Iron and Steel Industries [*EC*]   (ECED)

EUROFEU ... Comite Europeen des Constructeurs de Materiels d'Incendie et de Secours [*European Committee of the Manufacturers of Fire Protection and Safety Equipment and Fire Fighting Vehicles*]   (EAIO)

EURO-FIET ... Organisation Regionale Europeenne de la Federation Internationale des Employes, Techniciens et Cadres [*European Regional Organization of the International Federation of Commercial, Clerical, Professional and Technical Employees*] [*EC*]   (ECED)

EUROFIMA ... Societe Europeenne pour le Financement de Materiel Ferroviaire [*European Society for the Financing of Railway Material*] [*French*]

Eurofina ..... Societe Europeenne pour le Financement du Materiel Ferroviaire   (FLAF)

EUROFINAS ... European Federation of Finance Houses Association [*Belgium*]   (PDAA)

EUROFORGE ... European Committee of Forging and Stamping Industries   (EAIO)

EUROFUEL ... Societe Europeene de Fabrication de Combustibles a Base d'Eranium pour Reacteurs a Eau Legere [*France*]   (PDAA)

EUROGRAM ... Societe Europeenne d'Etudes, de Calcul et de Programmation

EUROGROPA ... Union des Distributeurs de Papiers et Cartons [*European Union of Paper, Board, and Packaging Wholesalers*]   (PDAA)

EUROGYPSUM ... Working Community of the European Gypsum Industry   (EAIO)

EURO-HKG ... European High Temperature Nuclear Power Stations Society   (EAIO)

EuroISDN ... European Integrated Services Digital Network [*Telecommunications*]   (ECON)

EURO-LABO ... European Association for Comparative Testing [*Belgium*]   (SLS)

EUROM .... European Federation of Optical and Precision Instruments Industry [*EC*]   (ECED)

EUROMAISIERS ... Groupement des Associations des Maisiers des Pays de la CEE [*Group of the Maize Processors Associations in the European Economic Community Countries*] [*Brussels, Belgium*]

EUROMAP ... European Committee of Machinery Manufacturers for Plastics and Rubber Industries [*EC*]   (ECED)

EUROMAT ... Federation of European Coin Machine Associations [*EC*]   (ECED)

EUROMECH ... European Mechanics Colloquia   (PDAA)

EUROMICRO ... European Association for Microprocessing and Microprogramming   (PDAA)

EUROMIL ... Europaeische Organisation der Militarverbande [*European Organization of Military Associations*]   (EAIO)

EUROMOT ... European Committee of Associations of Manufacturers of Internal Combustion Engines   (EA)

EUROMPAP ... European Committee of Machinery Manufacturers for the Plastics and Rubber Industries   (PDAA)

EURONAD ... Eurogroup Committee of National Armaments Directors

EURONEM ... European Association of Netting Manufacturers   (EA)

EURONET ... European On-Line Information Network [*Commission of the European Communities*] [*Information service or system*]   (IID)

EuroPACE ... European Programme of Advanced Continuing Education

EUROPEC ... European Offshore Petroleum Conference and Exhibition   (PDAA)

EUROPECHE ... Association des Organisations Nationales d'Entreprises de Peche de la CEE [*Association of National Organizations of Fishing Enterprises in the European Economic Community*]

EUROPLANT ... European Plantmakers Committee   (EA)

EUROPLATE ... European Registration Plate Association   (EA)

EUROPMAISERS ... Groupement des Associations des Maisiers des Pays de la CEE [*Group of Associations of Maize Processors of EEC Countries*]   (EAIO)

EUROPMI ... Comite de Liaison des Petites et Moyennes Entreprises Industrielles des Pays de la CEE [*Liaison Committee for Small and Medium-Sized Industrial Enterprises in the EEC*] [*Brussels, Belgium*]   (EAIO)

EUROPREFAB ... European Organization for the Promotion of Prefabrication and other Industralized Building   (PDAA)

EUROPUMP ... European Committee of Pump Manufacturers   (EA)

EUROPUR ... Association Europeenne des Fabricants de Blocs de Mousse Souple de Polyurethane [*European Association of Flexible Foam Block Manufacturers*]   (EAIO)

EURORAD ... European Association of Manufacturers of Radiators   (EA)

EUROSAC ... European Federation of Manufacturers of Multi-wall Paper Sacks [*France*]   (PDAA)

EUROSAC ... Federation Europeenne des Fabricants de Sacs en Papier a Grande Contenance [*European Federation of Multiwall Paper Sacks Manufacturers*]   (EAIO)

EUROSAM ... European Surface-to-Air Missile [*NATO*]

EUROSID ... European Side Impact Dummy [*Automotive engineering*]

Eurospace .. Groupement Europeen d'Etudes Spatiales [*European Space Study Group*] [*Paris, France*] [*Research center*]   (ERC)

EUROSTAT ... Statistical Office of the European Communities [*Commission of the European Communities*]   (EAIO)

EUROSTEST ... European Association of Testing Institutions   (PDAA)

EUROTALC ... Association Scientifique de l'Industrie Europeenne du Talc [*Scientific Association of European Talc Industry*]   (EAIO)

EUROTECNET ... European Technical Network [*EC*]   (ECED)

EUROTELCAB ... European Conference of Associations of Telecommunications Cables Industries [*EC*]   (ECED)

EUROTEST ... European Association of Testing Institutions [*Belgium*]   (PDAA)

EUROTRANS ... European Committee of Associations of Manufacturers of Gears and Transmission Parts [*EC*]   (ECED)

EUROVALUTA ... European Foreign Exchange   (WEN)

EUROVENT ... European Committee of Ventilating Equipment Manufacturers   (PDAA)

EURPISO ... European Union of Public Relations - International Service Organization [*Hungary*]   (EA)

EURTRAG ... Groupement Europeen d'Entreprises pour le Transgabonais

EURYDICE ... Education Information Network in the European Community [*Commission of the European Communities*] [*Belgium*] [*Information service or system*]   (IID)

EUS .... European User Service

EUSA .... Evangelical Union of South Africa

EUSAMA ... European Shock Absorber Manufacturers Association   (PDAA)

EUSIDIC ... European Association of Scientific Information Dissemination Centres ['s-*Gravenhage*] [*ICSU*]

EUSIREF .. European Scientific Information Referral [*EUSIDIC*] [*Information service or system*]   (IID)

EUSJA ...... European Union of Science Journalists Associations   (EAIO)

EUSM .... European Union of Social Medicine   (EA)
EUSSG ...... European Union for the Scientific Study of Glass   (EA)
EUTB .... Ege Universitesi Talebe Birligi [*Aegean University Student Union*]   (TU)
EUTECA ... European Technical Caramel Association [*EC*]   (ECED)
EUTELSAT ... European Telecommunications Satellite [*Agency*]   (BARN)
EUTELSAT ... European Telecommunications Satellite Organization [*France*] [*Telecommunications*]
EUTO .... European Union of Tourist Officers   (EAIO)
EUTOR ..... Union Europeenne pour la Technopedie, l'Orthopedie, et la Readaptation [*French*]   (SLS)
EUU .... Optimalizing Control Device   (RU)
EUUG .... European UNIX User Group [*Computer science*]
EUVEPRO ... European Vegetable Protein Federation   (EAIO)
EUW .... Euroflight Sweden, AB [*ICAO designator*]   (FAAC)
EUW .... European Union of Women [*Stockholm, Sweden*]
EUWEP ..... European Union of Wholesale Eggs, Egg-Products, Poultry and Game [*EC*]   (ECED)
EUWG .... Energy Use Working Group [*Australia*]
EUWS .... Egyptian University Students' Welfare Society
EUX .... European Expidite [*Belgium*] [*ICAO designator*]   (FAAC)
EUX .... Saint Eustatius [*Antilles*] [*Airport symbol*]   (OAG)
EUYCD ..... European Union of Young Christian Democrats [*Belgium*]   (EY)
EV .... Eccellenza Vostra [*Your Excellency*] [*Italian*]
EV .... Economische Voorlichting [*Benelux*]   (BAS)
ev .... Eerstvolgende [*The Following*] [*Netherlands*]   (GPO)
EV .... Eersvolgende [*Next*] [*Afrikaans*]
ev .... Egeszvaszonkotes [*Cloth Binding*] [*Publishing*] [*Hungary*]
EV .... Eingang Vorbehalten [*Rights reserved, i.e., copyrighted*] [*German*]
eV .... Eingetragener Verein [*Registered Association*] [*German*]   (WEN)
EV .... Electric Fan   (RU)
EV .... Electromagnetic Valve   (RU)
EV .... Electronic Calculator   (RU)
ev .... Electron Volt   (RU)
eV .... Elektronenvolt [*Electron Volt*] [*German*]   (WEN)
eV .... Elektronowolt [*Electron Volt*] [*Poland*]
EV .... Elektrovojvodina [*Establishment for production, transport, and distribution of electric power*] [*Novi Sad*]   (YU)
eV .... Emotionelle Verarbeitung [*Emotional Working Up*] [*German*]
EV .... Empfangsverstaerker [*Receiving Amplifier (RAD)*]   (EG)
EV .... Endverzweiger [*Distribution Terminal (Telephone cables)*]   (EG)
EV .... Energy Victoria [*Australia*]
EV .... Enosis Viotekhnon [*Union of Craftsmen*] [*Greek*]   (GC)
EV .... Enterprise Value [*Finance*]   (ECON)
EV .... En Ville [*Local*] [*French*]
ev .... En Volgende [*And the Following*] [*Afrikaans*]
EV .... Equatorial Air   (RU)
EV .... Equivalent de Vitesse [*Equivalent Airspeed*] [*Aviation*] [*French*]
EV .... Erdelyi Vilagszovetseg [*Transylvanian World Federation - TWF*]   (EAIO)
EV .... Erdoel-Vereinigung [*Switzerland*]
Ev .... Ev Adresi [*Home Address*]   (TU)
ev .... Evangelicky [*Protestant*]   (CZ)
Ev .... Evangelie [*Gospel*] [*Afrikaans*]
ev .... Evangelisch [*Protestant*] [*German*]   (GPO)
Ev .... Evangelium [*Gospel*] [*German*]
ev .... Evente [*Yearly*]   (HU)
EV .... Eventueel [*Possible*] [*Afrikaans*]
ev .... Eventuell [*Eventual*] [*German*]
ev .... Eversti [*Finland*]
EV .... Oriental Epigraphy   (RU)
EVA .... Einkaufs- und Verkaufsabteilung [*Purchasing and Sales Department*]   (EG)
EVA .... Eisenbahn-Verkehrsmittel-Aktiengesellschaft [*Railroad Transportation Joint Stock Company*]
EVA .... Elliniki Vasiliki Aeroporia [*Royal Greek Air Force*]   (GC)
EVA .... Empresa de Viacao e Comercio de Angola, SARL
EVA .... English Vineyards Association
eva .... En Vele Anderen [*And Many Others*] [*Netherlands*]
EVA .... Esperantlingva Verkista Asocio [*Esperanto Writers Association - EWA*] [*Netherlands*]   (EA)
EVA .... Europaeische Vereinigung der Allgemeinarzte [*European Union of General Practitioners*]   (EAIO)
EVA .... Europese Vrijhandels Associatie [*Benelux*]   (BAS)
EVACWP .. Exotic Vertebrate Animals Control Working Party [*Australia*]
EVAF .... International Association for Business Research and Corporate Development [*West Wickham, Kent, England*]   (EAIO)
evak .... Evacuation, Clearing   (RU)
Evakkom .... Evacuation Commission   (RU)
Evakom ...... Evacuation Commission   (RU)
Evakopunkt ... Evacuation Center   (BU)
Evakpriyemnik ... Clearing Station   (RU)
evang .... Evangelikus [*Lutheran*]   (HU)
evang .... Evangelisch [*Protestant*] [*German*]
EVATMI ... European Vinyl Asbestos Tile Manufacturers Institute   (PDAA)

EVAY .... Ethniki Viomikhania Aeroporikou Ylikou [*National Aircraft Equipment Industry*] [*Greek*]   (GC)
EVB .... Energieversorgungsbetrieb [*Energy Supply Plant*]   (EG)
EVC .... Eenheidsvakcentrale [*Unity Trade Union Federation*] [*Netherlands*]   (WEN)
EVCA......... European Venture Capital Association
EVCh .... Sympathetic Electric Clock   (RU)
evcis........... Evidencni Cislo [*Registration Number*]   (CZ)
EVD .... Economische Voorlichtingsdienst [*Economic Information Service*] [*Information service or system*]   (IID)
EVDA .... Engage Volontaire par Devancement d'Appel [*Person who volunteers prior to induction*] [*French*]
EVD/DFEP ... Eidgenoessisches Volkswirtschaftsdepartement/Departement Federal de l'Economie Publique [*Switzerland*]
EVDR .... Entwurfs- und Vermessungsbueros der Deutschen Reichsbahn [*GDR Railroad Design and Surveying Office*]   (EG)
EVE .... Air Evex GmbH [*Germany*] [*ICAO designator*]   (FAAC)
EVE .... Elliniki Vasiliki Enosis [*Greek Royalist Union*]   (GC)
EVE .... Emborikon kai Viomikhanikon Epimelitirion [*Chamber of Commerce and Industry*] [*Followed by initial letter of city name*]   (GC)
EVE .... Evenes [*Norway*] [*Airport symbol*]   (OAG)
EVEA......... Estonian Small Business Association   (EE)
EVED .... Eidgenoessisches Verkehrs- und Energiewirtschafts-Department [*Transportation, Communications, and Energy Department*] [*Switzerland*]   (WEN)
event........... Eventuell [*Eventual*] [*German*]
EVEV........ Ethniki Vasiliki Enosi Voreioelladiton [*National Royalist Union of Northern Greeks*]   (GC)
evf.............. Euphemistic   (RU)
evf.............. Evfolyam [*Year of Publication*] [*Hungary*]   (GPO)
EVG .... Egyesult Villamosgepgyar [*United Electrical Machine Factory*]   (HU)
EVG .... Europaeische Verteidigungsgemeinschaft [*European Defense Community (EDC)*] [*German*]   (EG)
EVG .... Europaische Verteidigungsgemeinschaft [*European Defense Community*] [*German*]   (BARN)
Evg .... Evangel [*Gospel*] [*German*]
EVG .... Stripping Caterpillar Excavator   (RU)
EVGY .... Epito-Vegyianyagokat Gyarto Vallalat [*Construction Chemical Materials Manufacturing Enterprise*]   (HU)
EVHA .... Europese Vereniging voor Haveninformatica [*European Port Data Processing Association*] [*Belgium*]   (EA)
EVI............ Estudios Venezolanos Indigenas [*Venezuelan Indian Studies*] [*Caracas, Venezuela*]   (LAA)
Evidst .... Evidencna Stevilka [*Registration Number*]   (YU)
EVIG......... Egyesult Villamosgepgyar [*United Electrical Machine Factory*]   (HU)
EVITERV ... Elektromos es Villanyhalozatokat Tervezo Vallalat [*Electric Networks Designing Enterprise*]   (HU)
EVITERV ... Szereloipari Tervezo Vallalat [*Fixture Installation Planning Enterprise*]   (HU)
E VIVDISC ... E Vivis Discessit [*Departed from Life*] [*Latin*]   (BARN)
EVK .... Eisenbahnverkehrskasse [*Railroad Cashier's Office*]   (EG)
EVK .... Europai Vedelmi Kozosseg [*European Defense Community*]   (HU)
evk............ Evkonyv [*Yearbook*]   (HU)
EVK .... Large-Panel Interior Structures   (BU)
Evkaf......... Evkaf Idaresi [*Religious Foundations (Trusts) Administration*] [*Turkish Cypriot*]   (TU)
EVKh........ Elliniki Vasiliki Khorofylaki [*Greek Royal Gendarmery*]   (GC)
EVKI........ Europaische Vereinigung der Keramik-Industrie [*Europeean Federation of the Electro-Ceramic Industry*]   (PDAA)
EVKOM .... Elektrisiteitsvoorsieningskommissie [*Electricity Supply Commission*] [*Use ESCOM*]   (AF)
EVKXV...... Enosis Viotekhnon Katergasias Xylou Volou [*Volos Union of Wood Craftsmen*]   (GC)
evltn .... Everstiluutnantti [*Finland*]
evlut........... Evankelis-Luterilainen [*Finland*]
Ev-Luth...... Evangelisch-Lutherisch [*Protestant Lutheran*] [*German*]
evluutn .... Everstiluutnantti [*Finland*]
EVM .... Egyesult Vegyimuvek [*United Chemical Works*]   (HU)
EVM .... Electronic Computer   (RU)
EVM .... Epitesugyi es Varosfejlesztesi Miniszterium [*Ministry of Construction and Urban Development*]   (HU)
EVMCC..... Escuela Vocacional Militar Camilo Cienfuegos [*Camilo Cienfuegos Military Vocational School*] [*Cuba*]   (LA)
EVN.......... Energie Verbrauchsnorm(en) [*Energy Consumption Norm(s)*]   (EG)
EVN.......... Erevan [*Former USSR*] [*Airport symbol*]   (OAG)
EVO.......... Algemene Verladers- en Eigen Vervoerders Organisatie [*Benelux*]   (BAS)
EVO.......... Eisenbahnverkehrsordnung [*Railroad Traffic Regulations*]   (EG)
EVO.......... Elliniki Viotekhnia Oplon [*Greek Arms Industry*]   (GC)
EVON........ Ethniki Vasiliki Organosi Neon [*National Royalist Youth Organization*] [*Greek*]   (GC)
EVOP .... European Volcanological Project

EVP............ Einzelhandelsverkaufspreis [*Retail Selling Price*] (EG)
EVP............ Electron Device, Vacuum Tube (RU)
evp............ Erossa Vakinaisesta Palveluksesta [*Finland*]
EVP............ Evangelische Volkspartei der Schweiz [*Swiss Evangelical People's Party*] [*Political party*] (PPW)
EVP............ Evangelische Volkspartij [*Evangelical People's Party*] [*Netherlands*] [*Political party*] (EY)
EVPE......... Epitropi Voitheias Prosfygon en Elladi [*Refugees Service Committee for Greece*] (GC)
EVPHI...... Europese Vereniging voor Pediatrische Hematologie en Immunologie [*European Society for Paediatric Haematology and Immunology - ESPHI*] (EAIO)
EVPU .... Ethiopian Veterinary Professionals' Union (EAIO)
evr .... Jewish (BU)
evrop .... European (BU)
Evr Tur....... European Turkey (BU)
EVS............ Elektronisches Vertriebssystem [*German*] (ADPT)
EVS............ Elliniki Viomikhania Sakkhareos [*Greek Sugar Industry*] [*Greek*] (GC)
EVS............ Energie-Versorgung Schwaben [*Germany*] (PDAA)
EVS............ Epitropi gia tin Valkanikin Synennoisin [*Committee for a Balkan Understanding*] [*Greek*] (GC)
EVS............ Epitropi Viomikhanikon Skheseon [*Industrial Relations Committee*] [*Cyprus*] (GC)
EVS............ Etaireia Vyzandinon Spoudon [*Society of Byzantine Studies*] [*Greek*] (GC)
EVS............ Europese Vakbeweging Secretariaat [*Benelux*] (BAS)
EVSA......... Enosis Viotekhnikon Somateion Athinon [*Union of Craft Associations of Athens*] (GC)
EVSA......... Entomologiese Vereniging van Suidelike Afrika [*Entomologie Society of South Africa*] (EAIO)
EVSA......... Epidemiologiese Vereniging van Suidelike Afrika [*Epidemiological Society of Southern Africa*] (AA)
EVSz.......... Erdelyi Vilagszovetseg [*Transylvanian World Federation*] (EAIO)
evsz............. Evszam [*Date*] (HU)
EVTC........ Early Vehicle Touring Club [*Australia*]
evtl............. Eventuell [*Perhaps, Possibly*] [*German*] (GPO)
EVTsM...... Electronic Digital Computer (RU)
EVU .... Energeticky Vyzkumny Ustav [*Power Research Institute*] (CZ)
EVV .... En Volgends [*And the Following*] [*Afrikaans*]
EVVA .... Ente per la Valorizzazione dei Vini Astigiani [*Italian*] (SLS)
EVVA .... Europaeische Vereinigung der Veterinaranatomen [*European Association of Veterinary Anatomists - EAVA*] (EAIO)
EVW .... Erdoelverarbeitungswerk [*Crude Oil Processing Plant*] [*German*]
EVW .... Erdoelverarbeitungswerk Schwedt [*Schwedt Oil Refinery*] (EG)
EW .... Eenvormige Wet Betreffende het Internationaal Privaatrecht [*Benelux*] (BAS)
Ew .... Eigenschaftswort [*Adjective*] [*German*]
EW .... Eingetragenes Warenzeichen [*Registered Trademark*] [*German*]
EW .... Einheitswert [*Standard Value*] (EG)
Ew .... Einwohner [*Resident*] [*German*]
EW .... Eisenwerke West [*West Iron Works*] [*See also EKW*] [*German*] (EG)
EW .... Electronic Warfare [*Royal Australian Navy*]
EW .... Elektrowaerme [*Electrical Heating Equipment Plant*] (EG)
Ew .... Euer [*Your*] [*German*]
EW .... Europaeische Wandervereinigung [*European Ramblers' Association - ERA*] [*German*] (EAIO)
ew .... Ewentualnie [*Or, Otherwise*] [*Poland*]
EWA .... East-West Airlines Ltd. [*Australia*] [*ICAO designator*] (FAAC)
EWA .... Esperanto Writers Association (EA)
EWA .... Europaeische Wahrungsabkommen [*European Monetary Agreement*] [*German*] (DCTA)
EWA .... European Wax Association (EAIO)
EWA .... European Welding Association (EAIO)
EWAV .... Electrical Wholesalers' Association, Victoria [*Australia*]
EWB .... Elektrizitatswerk der Stadt Bern [*Slang*] (PDAA)
EWBS........ Exportwarenbegleitschein [*Export Bill of Lading*] [*German*] (EG)
EWCB........ Electrical Workers and Contractors' Board [*Queensland, Australia*]
EWE .... East West European [*Bulgaria*] [*ICAO designator*] (FAAC)
EWEA .... European Wind Energy Association (EAIO)
ewent......... Ewentualnie [*Or, Otherwise*] [*Poland*]
EWF .... Education Without Frontiers [*An association*] (EAIO)
EWF .... European Wax Federation [*Belgium*] (EAIO)
EWF .... European Weightlifting Federation (EA)
EWG .... Ernaehrungswissenschaften Giessen [*Nutrition Sciences - Giessen University*] [*Database*]
EWG .... Europaeische Wirtschaftsgemeinschaft [*European Economic Community (EEC)*] [*German*] (WEN)
EWG .... European Work Group
EWG .... Europejska Wspolnota Gospodarcza [*European Economic Community*] (POL)
EWG .... Executive Working Group [*NATO*]

EWI .... Enarotali [*Indonesia*] [*Airport symbol*] (OAG)
EWk .... Elektrizitaetswerk [*German*]
EWL .... European Women's Lobby [*Belgium*] (EAIO)
EWL &NHS ... Ethiopian Wildlife and Natural History Society (EAIO)
EWMD...... European Women's Management Development Network (EAIO)
EWO.......... Ewo [*Congo*] [*Airport symbol*] (OAG)
EWP .... Electronic Warfare Plans [*NATO*] (NATG)
EWP .... Electronic White Pages [*Australia*]
EWPCA...... European Water Pollution Control Association (EAIO)
EWPHE .... European Working Party on Hypertension in the Elderly [*An association*]
EWRC .... European Weed Research Council [*Portugal*] (DSCA)
EWRIS ...... European Wire Rope Information Service [*EC*] (ECED)
EWRS........ European Weed Research Society [*See also EGH*] [*Research center Germany*] (IRC)
EWS.......... Elektronisches Waehlssystem [*German*] (ADPT)
EWS.......... Engineering Work-Station [*Yokogawa Hewlett Packard Ltd.*] [*Japan*]
EWS.......... European Wings [*Czechoslovakia*] [*ICAO designator*] (FAAC)
EWSA........ EEC Wheat Starch Manufacturers Association [*Defunct*] (EAIO)
EWSD....... Engineering and Water Supply Department [*South Australia*]
EWSLA ..... East-West Sign Language Association [*Japan*] (SLS)
EWT .... Elektrizitaetswerkstelefonie [*Power Plant Telephone System*] [*German*] (EG)
EWT .... Endangered Wildlife Trust [*South Africa*] (AA)
EWTMI..... European Wideband Transmission Media Improvement Program
e Wu.......... Emotionelles Werturteil [*Emotional Evaluation*] [*German*]
EWW .... Eisenwerke West (VEB) [*West Ironworks (VEB)*] [*German*] (EG)
EWWA ..... Ethiopian Women's Welfare Association (AF)
EWWCA ... Ethiopian Water Works Construction Authority [*National Water Resources Commission*] [*Research center*] (EAS)
EWZ .... Elektrizitatswerk der Stadt Zurich [*Switzerland*] (PDAA)
EX .... Excise (DSUE)
ex.............. Exempel [*Example*] [*Sweden*] (GPO)
ex.............. Exemplaar [*Copy*] [*Netherlands*]
ex.............. Exemplaire [*Copy*] [*French*]
Ex.............. Exemplar [*Copy*] [*German*]
ex.............. Exemplar [*Copy*] [*Swedish*]
ex.............. Exemplar [*Copy*] [*Portuguese*]
ex.............. Exemplar [*Copy*] [*Romanian*]
ex.............. Exemple [*Example*] [*French*]
ex.............. Exercice [*Financial Year*] [*French*]
Ex.............. Exodus [*Exodus*] [*Afrikaans*]
Exa .... Excelencia [*Excellency*] [*Portuguese*]
EXACT...... International Exchange of Authenticated Electronic Component Performance Tests Data (PDAA)
EXANDIS ... Exotic Animal Disease Preparedness Consultative Committee [*Australia*]
Ex Att........ Exercice Attache [*Cum Dividend*] [*Finance*] [*French*]
ex-bon .... Ex-Bonification [*Ex-Bonus*] [*Finance*] [*French*]
Exc .... Excelencia [*Excellence*] [*Spanish*]
Exc .... Excellence [*Excellency*] [*French*]
exc............. Excluding (EECI)
ex c .... Ex-Coupon [*Ex-Coupon*] [*Finance*] [*French*]
Ex C .... L'Expert Comptable [*Benelux*] (BAS)
Exca .... Excelencia [*Excellence*] [*Spanish*]
EXCAF ...... Expo Carrefour Afrique
EXCARBON ... Explotaciones Carboniferas SA [*Colombia*] (COL)
ExceptIncomp ... Exception d'Incompetence [*French*] (FLAF)
EXCHEM ... West African Explosives and Chemicals Ltd. [*Liberia*]
Excia .... Excelencia [*Excellency*] [*Portuguese*]
excl........... Excluding (SCAC)
Excma .... Excelentisima [*Most Excellent*] [*Spanish*]
Excmo .... Excelentisimo [*Most Excellent*] [*Spanish*]
Exco .... Executive Council [*Hong Kong*]
EXCOMEX ... Explotaciones. Comercio Exterior Ltda. [*Colombia*] (COL)
ExcPrv .... Excurrendoprovisor [*German*]
EXCUARSO ... Explotaciones de Cuarso Ltda. [*Colombia*] (COL)
ex d .... Ex-Dividende [*Ex-Dividend*] [*Finance*] [*French*]
EXD .... Export Air del Peru SA Cargo Air Lines [*ICAO designator*] (FAAC)
EXDOC ..... Electronic Export Documentation [*Australia*]
ex dr .... Ex-Droits [*Ex-Rights*] [*Finance*] [*French*]
EXE .... Enosis Xenodokheion Ellados [*Hotel Union of Greece*] (GC)
Exec .... Executive (PWGL)
EXEC........ Executive Appointments [*Database*] [*Australia*]
EXECO..... Societe d'Expansion Economique et Commerciale
exemp........ Exemplaire [*Copy*] [*French*]
exempl....... Exemplaar [*Copy*] [*Netherlands*]
exempl....... Exemplaire [*Copy*] [*French*]
Exempl....... Exemplar [*Copy*] [*German*]
EXFORKA ... Exploitation Forestiere du Kiangi
EXGO........ Export Guarantee Office [*Export credit agency*] [*New Zealand*]

EXh .... Mixture of Tetraethyl-Lead and Organic Chlorides and Bromides (RU)
exhdb .... Railroad Operation Battalion (RU)
exhdp .... Railroad Operation Regiment (RU)
EXIM .... Expor Impor [*Export-Import*] (IN)
EXIM .... Export-Import Bank
EXIMAR ... Exportaciones e Importaciones Marinas [*Colombia*] (COL)
EXIMBANK ... Export-Import Bank
EXIMBK ... Export-Import Bank
EXIMCOOP ... Intreprindere de Comert Exterior a Cooperativei de Consum [*Foreign Trade Enterprise of the Consumer Cooperatives*] (RO)
EXIMPO ... Export- und Importgesellschaft [*Export and Import Company*] (EG)
EXJ .... Executive Jet Italiana SRL [*Italy*] [*ICAO designator*] (FAAC)
Exkl .... Exklusiv [*Except(ed), Not Included*] [*German*] (EG)
Exma .... Excelentissima [*Most Excellent*] [*Portuguese*]
EXMIBAL ... Exploraciones y Explotaciones Mineras Izabal SA [*Izabal Mining Exploration and Exploitation, Inc.*] [*Guatemala*] (LA)
Exmo .... Excelentissimo [*or Excellentissimo*] [*Excellency*] [*Portuguese*] (GPO)
ExMun .... Exerziermunition [*Dummy Ammunition, Blank Ammunition*] (EG)
EXN .... Europeaero Service National [*France*] [*ICAO designator*] (FAAC)
EXN .... Exin [*Poland*] [*ICAO designator*] (FAAC)
EXO .... European X-Ray Observatory
EXOBOIS ... Bois Exotiques Ouvrages
Exp .... Expedie [*Shipped*] [*Business term*] [*French*]
Exp .... Experiment [*German*] (GCA)
exp .... Experimentell [*Experimental*] [*German*]
Exp .... Expositur [*German*]
EXPASA .... Compania Exportadora Panamericana Sociedad Anonima [*Colombia*] (COL)
ExPatr .... Exerzierpatrone [*Dummy Cartridge, Blank*] (EG)
Exped .... Expedition [*German*] (GCA)
EXPEDICUBA ... Empresa Cubana Expedidora de Mercancias de Importacion y Exportacion [*Cuban Import and Export Merchandise Expediting Enterprise*] (LA)
EXPEDIPORT ... Empresa Expedidora Portuaria [*Port Expediting Enterprise*] [*Cuba*] (LA)
EXPERTA ... Estacion Experimental del Tabaco [*Venezuela*] (DSCA)
expl .... Exemplaar [*Copy*] [*Netherlands*]
Expl .... Exemplar [*Copy*] [*German*] (EG)
expl .... Exemplar [*Copy*] [*Swedish*]
expl .... Exemplar [*Copy*] [*Portuguese*]
EXPLACO ... Explanaciones Colombia Ltda. [*Colombia*] (COL)
EXPLANICAS ... Explanaciones Mecanicas SA [*Colombia*] (COL)
EXPLANOBRAS ... Explanaciones y Obras Ltda. [*Colombia*] (COL)
explic .... Explication [*Explanation*] [*Publishing*] [*French*]
Explos .... Explosion [*German*] (GCA)
expn .... Expedition [*Dispatching*] [*French*]
EXPORTADORA DEL CARIBE ... Empresa Exportadora de Pescados y Mariscos [*Cuban Enterprise for the Export of Seafood*] (LA)
EXPORTDRVO ... Poduzece za Izvoz Drva i Drvnih Proizvoda [*Enterprise for the Export of Wood and Wood Products*] [*Zagreb*] (YU)
Expos .... Expositur [*German*]
Ex-POWAA ... Ex-Prisoners of War Association of Australia
expr .... Expressao [*Expression*] [*Portuguese*]
EXPRECOL ... Expreso Terrestre Colombiano [*Colombia*] (COL)
EXQUISFORM ... Exquisite Form Brassiere de Colombia Ltda. [*Colombia*] (COL)
ex rep .... Ex-Repartition [*French*]
Exs .... Exsikator [*Desiccator*] [*German*] (GCA)
EXSA .... Exhibition Association of South Africa (EAIO)
EXSA .... Export Sanayi Mamulleri, Satis, ve Arastirma AS [*Export Industry Products, Sales, and Research Corp.*] (TU)
EXSPEC .... Exercise Specification [*NATO*] (NATG)
Ext .... Extension (IDIG)
ext .... Exterieur [*Exterior*] [*French*]
ext .... Externo [*External*] [*Portuguese*]
EXT .... Extra Executive Transport [*Germany*] [*ICAO designator*] (FAAC)
EXTEL ...... Exchange Telegraph [*Press agency*] [*British*] (DCTA)
EXTELCOMS ... East African Telecommunications Co. [*Kenya*] (PDAA)
extr .... Extrait [*Extract*] [*Publishing*] [*French*]
Extr .... Extrakt [*Extract*] [*German*]
EXTRACAR ... Expendedores y Transportadores de Carne [*Colombia*] (COL)
Extrakt ...... Extraktion [*Extraction*] [*German*] (GCA)
EXTRAMAD ... Express Transports Madagascar
EXU .... Executive Transports [*France*] [*ICAO designator*] (FAAC)
EXV .... Executive Air Transport Ltd. [*Switzerland*] [*ICAO designator*] (FAAC)

exx .... Exemplaires [*Copies*] [*French*]
Exx .... Exemplar [*Copy*] [*German*]
exx .... Exemplaren [*Copies*] [*Netherlands*]
EXZ .... Exzellenz [*Excellency*] [*German*]
EY .... Ekriktikai Ylai [*Explosives*] (GC)
EY .... Endoli Ypourgou [*By Direction of the Minister*] [*Appears on public documents over the official signature*] (GC)
EY .... Epiteliki Ypiresia [*Staff Service*] (GC)
EYA .... Ethniki Ypiresia Aimodosias [*National Blood Donation Service*] (GC)
EYAIK ...... Enosis Ypallilon Arkhis Ilektrismou Kyprou [*Union of Cyprus Electricity Authority Personnel*] (GC)
EYAP .... Etaireia Ydrevseos kai Apokhetevseos Protevousis [*Capital Area Water Supply and Drainage Company*] (GC)
EYAT .... Enosis Ypallilon Athinaikou Typou [*Union of Athens Press Employees*] (GC)
EYB .... Europa Year Book [*A publication*] (MHDB)
EYC .... European Youth Centre [*Council of Europe*] (EY)
EYCD .... European Young Christian Democrats [*Formerly, European Union of Young Christian Democrats*] (EA)
EYCE........ Ecumenical Youth Council in Europe (EAIO)
eye .... Electrostatic Unit (RU)
EYE .... European Year of the Environment [*Beginning March 23, 1987*]
EYEO .... Eidiki Ypiresia Ethnikon Odon [*Special National Roads Service*] [*Greek*] (GC)
EYF .... European Youth Foundation (EA)
EYIAA ...... Ellinikon Ydroviologikon Institouton Akadimias Athinon [*Greek Hydrobiological Institute of the Academy of Athens*] (GC)
EYKhOP ... Eidiki Ypiresia Khorotaxias Oikismou kai Perivallondos [*Special Zoning, Housing, and Environment Service*] (GC)
EYOL .... Estudiantes y Obreros Libres [*Free Students and Workers*] [*Mexico*] (LA)
EYOP .... European Year of Older People and Solidarity Between Generations
EYP........... El Yopal [*Colombia*] [*Airport symbol*] (OAG)
EYPT .... Enosis Ypallilikou Prosopikou Typou [*Union of Press Employees*] [*Greek*] (GC)
EYRIK ...... Enosis Ypallilon Radiofonikou Idrymatos Kyprou [*Union of Cyprus Broadcasting Company Employees*] [*Cyprus*] (GC)
EYS........... Eidiki Ypiresia Stegaseos [*Special Service for Housing*] [*Social Services Ministry*] (GC)
EYS........... Ethiopian Youth Service (AF)
EYT .... Europe Aero Service [*France*] [*ICAO designator*] (FAAC)
EYYE........ Eidiki Ypiresia Ydravlikon Ergon [*Special Service for Water and Sewer Projects*] [*Followed by initial letter of district name*] (GC)
EZ .... Delay Element (RU)
EZ .... Economische Zaken [*Netherlands*]
EZ .... Electrolytic Zinc Co. of Australasia (ADA)
EZ .... Electron Capture (RU)
EZ .... Elektromontazni Zavody [*Electrical Machinery Assembly Plant*] (CZ)
EZ .... Elektrotehniski Zbornik [*Collected Papers on Electrical Engineering*] [*Ljubljana A periodical*] (YU)
EZ .... Esterzahl [*Ester Number*] [*German*]
ez .... Lake (BU)
ez .... Language, Linguistics (BU)
EZA .... Stichting Evangelische Zendings Alliante [*Missionary association*] [*Netherlands*]
EZC .... European Zone Charge (DS)
ezd .... Ezred [*Regiment*] (HU)
ezds .... Ezredes [*Colonel*] (HU)
EZE........... Buenos Aires [*Argentina*] Ezeiza [*Airport symbol*] (OAG)
EZES .... Evropaiki Zoni Elevtheron Synallagon [*European Free Trade Area*] (GC)
ezhpb.......... Railway Operation Battalion (BU)
ezhpp.......... Railway Operation Regiment (BU)
ezhpr.......... Railway Operation Company (BU)
EZI........... European Zinc Institute (EA)
EZLP .... Elevthera Zoni Limenos Peiraios [*Piraeus Port Free Zone*] (GC)
EZLTh....... Elevthera Zoni Limenos Thessalonikis [*Salonica Port Free Zone*] [*See also EZTh*] (GC)
EZM .... Elblaskie Zaklady Miesne [*Elblag (Elbing) Meat Establishments*] (POL)
eZn .... And Son [*Correspondence*] [*Netherlands*]
EZN .... Erfinderzentrum Niedersachsen
EZN .... Estacao Zootecnica Nacional [*National Animal Production Station*] [*Research center*] [*Portugal*] (IRC)
EZO .... Eisenbahnzollordnung [*Railroad Customs Regulations*] (EG)
EZO .... Ethylcellulose Protective Coating (RU)
EZOPA ...... Equipe de Zoopatologia [*Brazil*] (DSCA)
EZOSh ...... Electric Time Fuze (RU)
EZOTE....... Equipe de Zootecnia [*Brazil*] (DSCA)
EZP........... Electric Incendiary Cartridge (RU)
EZR .... Eingabezielregister [*German*] (ADPT)
ezr............. Ezrelek [*Thousandth*] (HU)

EZRI.......... Experimental Plant for Cutting Tools   (RU)
EZS............ Elazig [*Turkey*] [*Airport symbol*]   (OAG)
EZS............ Energeticke Zavody na Slovensku, Narodny Podnik [*Power Plants in Slovakia, National Enterprise*]   (CZ)
EZT............ Electric Fuze   (RU)
EZTh .... Elevthera Zoni Thessalonikis [*Salonica Free Zone*]   (GC)
EZTM........ Elektrostal' Heavy Machinery Plant   (RU)
EZU .... Elektronische Zahlungsueberweisung [*German*]   (ADPT)
EZU .... Elektrotechnicky Zkusebni Ustav [*Electrical Engineering Testing Institute*]   (CZ)
EZU .... Europaeische Zahlungsunion [*European Payments Union*]   (EG)
EZUC .... Evropska Zajednica za Ugljen i Celik [*European Coal and Steel Community*]   (YU)
E-Zug......... Eilzug [*Express Train*] [*German*]
EZV .... Elekronischer Zahlungsverkehr [*German*]   (ADPT)
EZW .... Elektryczne Zaklady Wytworcze [*Electric Equipment Plant*]   (POL)
EZWiS....... Europejskie Zjednoczenie Wegla i Stali [*European Coal and Steel Community*]   (POL)

F

/F .... A Titre Fictif [*Brevet*]   (CL)
F .... Fach [*Compartment*] [*German*]
F .... Fahrenheit [*German*]   (EG)
F .... Fahrenheit Degree   (RU)
F .... Fahrenheitia [*Finland*]
F .... Faillissementswet [*Benelux*]   (BAS)
F .... Fall [*Case*] [*German*]
f .... Farad [*Russian*]   (RU)
F .... Faradio [*Farad*] [*Portuguese*]
f .... Fardo [*Package*] [*Spanish*]
F .... Farm [*Topography*]   (RU)
F .... Farthing [*Monetary unit*] [*British*]
f .... Fast [*Almost*] [*German*]
f .... Faux [*Imitation*] [*French*]
f .... Fecha [*Date*] [*Spanish*]
F .... Federative   (RU)
f .... Fehlen [*Lack*] [*German*]
f .... Fein [*Fine*] [*German*]
F .... Feinste Sorte [*Finest Grade*] [*German*]   (GCA)
f .... Femenino [*Feminine*] [*Spanish*]
f .... Feminin [*Feminine*] [*French*]
f .... Feminine   (TPFD)
f .... Feminino [*Feminine*] [*Portuguese*]
f .... Femminile [*Feminine*] [*Italian*]
f .... Femto [*German*]   (ADPT)
F .... Fen [*Monetary unit*] [*China*]
F .... Fener [*Lighthouse*]   (TU)
f .... Fent [*or Fenti*] [*Above or From Above*]   (HU)
f .... Ferrovia [*Railroad*] [*Italian*]   (GPO)
f .... Fest [*Solid*] [*German*]
f .... Feuille [*Sheet*] [*Publishing*] [*French*]
F .... Fiji   (BARN)
f .... Filets [*Fillets*] [*Publishing*] [*French*]
f .... Filler [*Penny*] [*Hungary*]   (GPO)
f .... First Sergeant   (BU)
F .... Fiume [*River*] [*Italian*]   (NAU)
F .... Florin [*Monetary unit*] [*Netherlands*]
F .... Floryn [*Florin*] [*Monetary unit*] [*Afrikaans*]
F .... Fluor [*Fluorine*] [*Chemical element*] [*Portuguese*]
F .... Fluor [*Fluorine*] [*Chemical element*] [*German*]
F .... Flyver [*Aviator*] [*Officer's rating Danish Navy*]
f .... Fodd [*Born*] [*Sweden*]   (GPO)
f:a .... Fodt [*Born*] [*Norgwegian*]   (GPO)
f .... Fodt [*Born*] [*Danish*]   (GPO)
F .... Fok [*Degree*]   (HU)
F .... Folge [*Series*] [*Publishing*] [*German*]
f .... Folgende [*The Following*] [*German*]
f .... Folgende Seite [*Next Page*] [*German*]
f .... Folha [*Sheet*] [*Publishing*] [*Portuguese*]
f .... Folio [*Sheet*] [*Publishing*] [*German*]
f .... Folyo [*River*]   (HU)
f .... Foot   (RU)
f .... For [*Before or For*] [*Norway*]   (GPO)
F .... Force [*Force*] [*French*]
F .... Forint [*Monetary unit*] [*Hungary*]
f .... Form [*Grammar*]   (RU)
f .... Forma [*Form*] [*Portuguese*]
F .... Forretningbanken A/S [*Bank*] [*Norway*]
F .... Fort   (RU)
F .... Forte [*Loud*] [*Music*]
f .... Fotografia [*Photograph*] [*Portuguese*]
f .... Fotografo [*Photographer*] [*Portuguese*]
f .... Founded   (EECI)
F .... Fox [*Phonetic alphabet*] [*World War II*]   (DSUE)
F .... Foxtrot [*Phonetic alphabet*] [*International*]   (DSUE)
F .... Foyer [*Focal Length*] [*Photography*] [*French*]
F .... Franc [*Monetary unit*] [*France*]
F .... France [*International automobile identification tag*]

F .... Freddie [*Phonetic alphabet*] [*Pre-World War II*]   (DSUE)
F .... Freddy [*Phonetic alphabet*] [*Royal Navy World War I*]   (DSUE)
F .... Fremskridtspartiet [*Progress Party*] [*Denmark*] [*Political party*]
          (PPE)
F .... Frente [*Front*] [*Portuguese*]
f .... Frequence [*Frequency*] [*French*]
F .... Frequenz [*Frequency*] [*German*]   (GCA)
F .... Frere [*Brother*] [*French*]
f .... Fuer [*For*] [*German*]
F .... Fulano [*Nameless person, i.e., John Doe*] [*Portuguese*]
F .... Fulano [*Nameless person; i.e., John Doe*] [*Spanish*]
F .... Fund   (BU)
F .... Fundo [*Bottom*] [*Portuguese*]
F .... Fusionspunkt [*Melting Point*] [*German*]
f .... Fuzet [*Brochure*] [*Hungary*]
F .... High-Explosive   (RU)
F .... Oeffentliche Fernsprechstelle [*German*]
f .... Phot   (RU)
F .... Photograph   (BU)
F .... Photoreconnaissance   (RU)
f .... Pound   (RU)
F .... Queen [*Chess*]   (RU)
F .... State Pharmacopoeia, USSR [*Followed by a Roman numeral*]
          (RU)
F .... Stopien Fahrenheita [*Degree Fahrenheit*] [*Poland*]
F-18 .... February 18 Movement [*Trinidadian and Tobagan*]   (LA)
FA .... Fabrik [*Factory, Manufacturer*] [*German*]
FA .... Facharzt [*German*]
Fa .... Fachgruppe [*Division*] [*German*]   (GCA)
fa .... Factura [*Bill*] [*Spanish*]
Fa .... Fakulte [*Faculty*]   (TU)
FA .... Fanny Adams [*Canned mutton stew*] [*Slang*]   (DSUE)
FA .... Father   (DSUE)
FA .... Federace Architektu [*Federation of Architects*]   (CZ)
fa .... Felszamolas Alatt [*In Process of Liquidation*]   (HU)
FA .... Ferrocarriles Argentinos [*Railway*] [*Argentina*]   (EY)
FA .... Fiat-Allis [*Fiat-Allis Chalmers (Excavating machinery)*]
          [*EGEMAK*] [*See also*]   (TU)
FA .... Film Australia   (ADA)
FA .... Finance Act [*British*]   (DCTA)
FA .... Finanzamt [*German*]
FA .... Finnaviation Oy [*Finland*]   (EY)
f:a .... Firm [*Sweden*]   (CED)
Fa .... Firma [*Firm*] [*Dutch*]   (CED)
Fa .... Firma [*Firm*] [*German*]   (GPO)
FA .... Fonte Acieree [*Military*] [*French*]   (MTD)
FA .... Forcas Armadas [*Armed Forces*] [*Portuguese*]   (WER)
FA .... Forces Armees [*Armed Forces*] [*French*]   (AF)
fa .... Forgalmi Ado [*Purchase or Turnover Tax, Sales Tax*]   (HU)
fa .... Forrige Ar [*Last Year*] [*Denmark*]   (GPO)
FA .... Frente Amplio [*Broad Front*] [*Uruguay*] [*Political party*]   (PD)
FA .... Frontline Aviation   (RU)
FA .... Frontoviya Aviatsiya [*Frontal Aviation*] [*Former USSR*]
          (PDAA)
FA .... Fundusz Aprowizacyjny [*Food Supply Fund*]   (POL)
FAA .... Federacion Aeronautica Argentina [*Argentina*]
FAA .... Federacion Agraria Argentina [*Argentine Agrarian Federation*]
          (LA)
FAA .... Federation of Australian Accountants
FAA .... Federation of Australian Anarchists   (ADA)
FAA .... Federation of Australian Astrologers   (ADA)
FAA .... Fellow of the Australian Academy of Science   (ADA)
FAA .... Finnish Aeronautical Association   (EAIO)
FAA .... Forschungsgesellschaft fuer Agrarpolitik und Agrarsoziologie
          [*Information retrieval*]
FAA .... Foundation for Aboriginal Affairs [*Australia*]   (ADA)
FAA .... Franchisors Association of Australia
FAA .... French Australian Association of Victoria [*Australia*]

FAA .... Fuerza Aerea Argentina [*Military Air Force*]   (PDAA)
FAA .... Fulbright Alumni Association [*Later, Fulbright Association*] (EAIO)
FAAA........ Flight Attendants' Association of Australia
FAAB........ Alexander Bay [*South Africa*] [*ICAO location identifier*]   (ICLI)
FAABiol..... Fellow of the Australian Academy of Biology
FAAC........ Airspace Control Command [*South Africa*] [*ICAO location identifier*]
FAAC........ Foreign Aid Advisory Committee
FAACB...... Fellow of the Australian Association of Clinical Biochemists (ADA)
FAACE...... Forces Aeriennes Alliees Centre-Europe [*Allied Air Forces Central Europe*] [*NATO*]   (NATG)
FAACS...... Federation of Australian Amateur Cine Societies   (ADA)
FAAD .... Adelaide [*South Africa*] [*ICAO location identifier*]   (ICLI)
FAAD .... Front Algerien d'Action Democratique
FAAE........ Fellow of the Association of Automotive Engineers [*Australia*]
FAAF........ Fiji Amateur Athletic Federation   (EAIO)
FAAG .... Aggeneys [*South Africa*] [*ICAO location identifier*]   (ICLI)
FAAH .... Fellow of the Australian Academy of the Humanities
FAAH .... South African Air Force Headquarters [*ICAO location identifier*] (ICLI)
FAAHT ..... Federated Association of Australian Housewives, Tasmania
FAAI .... Fellow of the Institute of Administrative Accounting and Data Processing [*British*]   (DCTA)
FAAI .... Frente Amplio Anti-Imperialista [*Anti-Imperialist Broad Front*] [*Panama*]   (LA)
FAAMC..... Federation des Associations d'Antiquaires du Marche Commun (EA)
FAAN .... Aliwal North [*South Africa*] [*ICAO location identifier*]   (ICLI)
FAANE...... Forces Aeriennes Alliees Nord-Europe [*Allied Air Forces Northern Europe*] [*NATO*]   (NATG)
FAANQ ..... Filipino-Australian Association of North Queensland [*Australia*]
FAAO .... Fellow of the Australian Academy of Optometry
FAAP .... Fellow of the Australian Academy of Paediatrics
FAAPF ...... Federacion Argentina de Asociaciones de Productores Forestales [*Argentina*]   (DSCA)
FAAPM..... Fellow of the Australian Association of Practice Managers
FAAR .... Arandis [*Namibia*] [*ICAO location identifier*]   (ICLI)
FAAS........ Fellow of the Australian Anthropological Society
FAAS........ French Association for American Studies   (EAIO)
FAASE ...... Forces Aeriennes Alliees Sud-Europe [*Allied Air Forces Southern Europe*] [*NATO*]   (NATG)
FAAT........ French Australian and Antarctic Territories
FAATD...... Fellow of the Australian Association of Teachers of the Deaf
FAATSE.... Fellow of the Australian Academy of Technological Sciences and Engineering
FAAW .... Federation of Arab Agricultural Workers [*Iraq*]   (EAIO)
FAB........... Aerial High-Explosive Bomb   (RU)
FAB........... Aircraft Demolition Bombs   (BU)
fab .... Fabrication [*Manufacture*] [*Business term*] [*French*]
Fab .... Fabrik [*Factory*] [*Business term*] [*German*]
Fab .... Fabrika [*Factory*]   (TU)
fab .... Factory   (RU)
FAB........... Facultad de Agronomia, Balcarce [*Argentina*]
FAB........... Federal Aborigines Board [*Churches of Christ*] [*Australia*]
FAB........... Federation Algerienne de Boules [*Algerian Bocce Federation*] (EAIO)
FAB........... Federation of Arab Banks
FAB........... Federation Royale des Societes d'Architectes de Belgique [*Royal Federation of the Society of Architects of Belgium*]   (SLS)
FAB........... Field Artillery Brigade [*Australia*]
FAB........... Forca Aerea Brasileira [*Brazilian Air Force*]
FAB........... Forces Armees du Burundi [*Burundi Armed Forces*]   (AF)
FAB........... Forschungsinstitut fuer Arbeit und Bildung [*Research Institute for Work and Education*]   (SLS)
fab .... Franco a Bordo [*Free on Board - FOB*] [*Spanish*]
Fab .... Franco de Bord [*Free on Board - FOB*] [*French*]
fab .... Frei an Bord [*Free on Board - FOB*] [*German*]
FAB........... Fuerza Aerea Boliviana [*Military Air Force*] [*Bolivia*]   (PDAA)
FAB........... Fuerza Aerea Brasileira [*Military Air Force*] [*Brazil*]   (PDAA)
FAB........... Societe Franco-Africaine des Bois
FABA........ Fabrica de Baterias Ltda. [*Colombia*]   (COL)
FABA........ Federacion de Bancos Argentinos [*Federation of Argentine Banks*]   (LA)
FABALQ ... Fundo Assistencial e Banco Agronomica "Luiz de Queiroz" [*Brazil*]   (DSCA)
FABAYAL ... Fabricaciones Ayala Ltda. [*Colombia*]   (COL)
FABB........ Brakpan [*South Africa*] [*ICAO location identifier*]   (ICLI)
FABCOS ... Foundation for African Business and Consumer Services [*South Africa*]   (AA)
FABD........ Burgersdorp [*South Africa*] [*ICAO location identifier*]   (ICLI)
Fabe .... Fabrique [*Factory*] [*Military map abbreviation World War I*] [*French*]   (MTD)
FABE........ Fellow of the Association of Business Executives [*British*] (DCTA)

FABET ...... Faculty of Animal Husbandry [*Gadja Mada University*] [*Indonesian*]
FABI......... Federation Royale des Associations Belges d'Ingenieurs [*Belgium*]
FABI......... Federazione Autonoma Bancari Italiana [*Bank Workers Federation*] [*Italy*]   (EY)
FABL........ Bloemfontein/J. B. M. Hertzog [*South Africa*] [*ICAO location identifier*]   (ICLI)
fabl .... Fablea [*Imitation Leather*] [*Publishing Danish/Norwegian*]
FABLAMP ... Fabrica de Lamparas Fluorescentes [*Colombia*]   (COL)
FABM....... Bethlehem [*South Africa*] [*ICAO location identifier*]   (ICLI)
FABN .... Barberton [*South Africa*] [*ICAO location identifier*]   (ICLI)
FABOPLAST ... Fabrica de Bolsas Plasticas [*Colombia*]   (COL)
FABOR...... Fabrica da Borracha Sintetica [*Rio De Janeiro, Brazil*]   (LAA)
FABR........ Bredasdorp [*South Africa*] [*ICAO location identifier*]   (ICLI)
Fabr.......... Fabrik [*Factory*] [*German*]   (GCA)
fabr........... Factory [*Topography*]   (RU)
FABRICATO ... Fabrica de Hilados el Hato SA [*Colombia*]   (COL)
Fabrikat ..... Fabrikation [*Fabrication*] [*German*]   (GCA)
FABRIMET ... Fabricaciones Metalicas, SA [*Peru*]   (LAA)
FABRIMETAL ... Federation des Entreprises de l'Industrie des Fabrications Metalliques [*Federation of Metal Manufacturers*] [*Belgium*]   (WER)
FABRIPAPEL ... Fabrica General de Papeles Ltda. [*Colombia*]   (COL)
FABRITAPCOL ... Fabrica de Tapas Colombianas Ltda. [*Colombia*]   (COL)
fabr-zav ...... Factory-Plant   (BU)
FABS .... Brits [*South Africa*] [*ICAO location identifier*]   (ICLI)
FABV........ Brandvlei [*South Africa*] [*ICAO location identifier*]   (ICLI)
FABW....... Beaufort West [*South Africa*] [*ICAO location identifier*]   (ICLI)
FABX........ Beatrix Mine [*South Africa*] [*ICAO location identifier*]   (ICLI)
FABY........ Beaufort West/Wes Town [*South Africa*] [*ICAO location identifier*]   (ICLI)
fabzavuch ... Factory Training School   (RU)
Fac .... Faculdade [*Faculty*] [*Portuguese*]
FAC........... Faculte [*Faculty*] [*French*]
FAC........... Fakturierungscomputer [*German*]   (ADPT)
FAC........... Federacion Autonoma de la Carne [*Autonomous Meatworkers Federation*] [*Uruguay*]   (LA)
FAC........... Federal Airports Corp. [*Australia*]
FAC........... Fellowship of Australian Composers
FAC........... Feral Animals Committee [*Northern Territory, Australia*]
FAC........... Ferme Agricole Communale [*Communal Agricultural Farm*] [*Guinea*]   (AF)
FAC........... Film Advisory Committee [*Australia*]
FAC........... Financiere et Agricole Cherifienne
FAC........... Flota Atunera de Cuba [*Cuban Tuna Fishing Fleet*]   (LA)
FAC........... Fonds d'Aide et de Cooperation [*Aid and Cooperation Fund*] [*Paris, France*]   (AF)
FAC........... Food Advisory Committee [*New South Wales, Australia*]
FAC........... Force Aerienne Congolaise
FAC........... Forschungsgemeinschaft Arthrologie und Chirotherapie [*Research Association for the Study of Joints and Chiro- Therapy*]   (SLS)
fac............. Franc d'Avarie Commune [*French*]
FAC........... Front d'Action Commune
FAC........... Front d'Alliberament Catala [*Catalan Liberation Front*] [*Spanish*]   (WER)
FAC........... Fuerza Aerea Colombiana [*Colombian Air Force*] [*Colombia*] (COL)
FAC........... Fuerza Aerea de Chile [*Military Air Force of Chile*]   (PDAA)
FAC........... Fuerzas Armadas de Colombia [*Colombian Armed Forces*]   (LA)
FAC........... Fuerzas Armadas de Cooperacion Nacional [*Armed Forces of National Cooperation*] [*Venezuela*]   (LA)
FACA......... Federacion Argentina de Cooperativas Agrarias [*Argentine Federation of Agricultural Cooperatives*]   (LA)
FACA......... Federation Algerienne de la Cooperation Agricole
FACA......... Monte Carlo [*South Africa*] [*ICAO location identifier*]   (ICLI)
FACAA...... Federation of Autistic Children's Associations of Australia
FACACH... Federacion de Asociaciones de Ahorro y Credito de Honduras [*Honduran Federation of Savings and Loan Associations*]   (LA)
FACAM..... Fabrica de Cajas Metalicas [*Colombia*]   (COL)
FACARDA ... Fabrica de Cajas de Carton Ltda. [*Colombia*]   (COL)
FACB........ Colesburg [*South Africa*] [*ICAO location identifier*]   (ICLI)
FACB........ Federation of Australian Commercial Broadcasters   (ADA)
FACB........ Force Aerienne Belge [*Military Air Force*] [*Belgium*]   (PDAA)
FACC........ Federation Africaine des Chambres de Commerce [*Federation of African Chambers of Commerce*] [*Ethiopia*]   (EAIO)
FACCP ...... Frente Africana Contra o Colonialismo Portugues
FACD........ Cradock [*South Africa*] [*ICAO location identifier*]   (ICLI)
FACD........ Fellow of the Australian College of Dermatologists
FACDS...... Fellow of the Australian College of Dental Surgeons   (ADA)
FACE........ Fabbrica Apparecchiature per Communicazione Elettrich SpA
FACE........ Federacion Argentina de Comercio Exterior [*Argentine Foreign Trade Federation*]   (LA)

FACE......... Federation des Associations de Chasseurs de la CEE [*Federation of Hunters' Associations of the European Economic Community*] [*Brussels, Belgium*]
FACE......... Fellow of the Australian College of Education   (ADA)
FACE......... International Federation of Associations of Computer Users in Engineering Architecture and Related Fields   (EAIO)
FACEA...... Fellow of the Australian Council of Educational Administration
FACEJ....... Forges et Ateliers de Constructions Electriques de Jeumont
FACELA.... Fabrica Centroamericana de Lapices, SA [*Pencils of Central America Corp.*] [*El Salvador*]
FACEM..... Fellow of the Australian College of Emergency Medicine
FACH....... Cookhouse [*South Africa*] [*ICAO location identifier*]   (ICLI)
FACh....... Fuerza Aerea de Chile [*Chilean Air Force*]   (LA)
FACHPER ... Fellow of the Australian College of Health, Physical Education, and Recreation
FachS......... Fachschule [*German*]
FACI......... Federacao Angolana de Ciclismo
FACI......... Fellow of the Australian Chemical Institute [*Later, FRACI*]
FACIAA .... Fellow of the Australian Commercial and Industrial Artists' Association   (ADA)
FACIL....... Feira Agro-Cientifica e Industrial de Limeira [*Brazil*]   (DSCA)
FACL......... Carolina [*South Africa*] [*ICAO location identifier*]   (ICLI)
FACMA..... Fellow of the Australian College of Medical Administrators   (ADA)
FACO .... Copperton [*South Africa*] [*ICAO location identifier*]   (ICLI)
FACO .... Fellow of the Australian College of Ophthalmologists
FACOBO... Fabrica Colombiana de Botones [*Colombia*]   (COL)
FACOBOL ... Fabrica Colonial de Borracha Limitada
FACOENVASES ... Fabrica Colombiana de Envases Ltda. [*Barranquilla*]   (COL)
FACOG ..... Fellow of the Australian College of Obstetricians and Gynaecologists
FACOGAZ ... Union des Fabricants Europeens de Compteurs de Gaz [*Union of European Manufacturers of Gas Meters*]   (EAIO)
FACOL...... Fabricas Colombianas [*Colombia*]   (COL)
FACOLAMP ... Fabrica Colombiana de Lamparas [*Colombia*]   (COL)
FACOLTA ... Fabrica Colombiana de Tapas [*Colombia*]   (COL)
FACOM .... Fellow of the Australian College of Occupational Medicine
FACOMEC ... Fabrica Colombiana de Materiales Electricos SA [*Colombia*]   (COL)
FACONOL ... Fabrica de Conos Linero [*Colombia*]   (COL)
FACP........ Fellow of the Australian College of Physiotherapists
FACP........ Front Provisionnel pour Action Commune [*Provisional Front for Joint Action*] [*Chad*]   (AF)
FACPSEM ... Fellow of the Australasian College of Physical Scientists and Engineers in Medicine [*Australia*]
FACR........ Carletonville [*South Africa*] [*ICAO location identifier*]   (ICLI)
FACR........ Force Assessment in the Central Region [*NATO*]   (NATG)
FACREA ... Federacion Argentina de Consorcios Regionales de Experimentacion Agricola [*Asociacion Argentina de Consorcios Regionales de Experimentacion Agricola*] [*Buenos Aires, Argentina*] [*Later,*]   (LAA)
FACRM..... Fellow of the Australian College of Rehabilitation Medicine
FACS .... Department of Family and Community Services [*New South Wales, Australia*]
facs............ Facsimile [*Facsimile*] [*Publishing Dutch*]
facs............ Facsimile [*Facsimile*] [*Publishing*] [*French*]
facs............ Fac-Simile [*Facsimile*] [*Publishing*] [*Portuguese*]
FACS .... Federation des Amis des Chemins de Fer Secondaires [*Federation of the Friends of Light Railways*] [*France*]   (PDAA)
FACS .... Federation of Afrikaans Cultural Societies [*South Africa*]   (EAIO)
facsim........ Facsimil [*Facsimile*] [*Publishing*] [*Spanish*]
facsim........ Facsimile [*Facsimile*] [*Publishing*] [*French*]
facsim........ Facsimile [*Facsimile*] [*Publishing*] [*Italian*]
FACS(SA) ... Fellow of the Association of Certified Secretaries (South Africa)   (AA)
FACST...... Fellow of the Australian College of Speech Therapists   (ADA)
FACT........ Cape Town [*South Africa*] [*ICAO location identifier*]   (ICLI)
fact .... Factice [*Imitation*] [*French*]
FACT........ Faith and Atheism in Communist Territories [*Australia*]
FACT........ Fertilisers and Chemicals Travancore Ltd. [*India*]
FACT........ Foreign Access to Computer Technology [*USIA*]
FACT........ Foundation for the Abolition of Compulsory Treatment [*Australia*]   (EA)
FACT........ Front d'Action Civique du Tchad
facta .... Factura [*Bill*] [*Spanish*]
FACTS...... Federation on Australian Commercial Television Stations   (ADA)
FACUR...... Federacion de Asociaciones y Comunidades Urbanas [*Federation of Urban Associations and Communities*] [*Venezuela*]   (LA)
FACV........ Calvinia [*South Africa*] [*ICAO location identifier*]   (ICLI)
FACVSc..... Fellow of the Australian College of Veterinary Science   (ADA)
FACW....... Clanwilliam [*South Africa*] [*ICAO location identifier*]   (ICLI)
FAD .... Flavine-Adenine Dinucleotide   (RU)

FAD .... Fondo de Ayuda al Desarrollo [*Assistance Development Fund*] [*Spain*]
FAD .... Fonds Africain de Developpement [*African Development Fund*] [*Use ADF*]   (AF)
FAD .... Force Arabe de Dissuasion
FAD .... Foreign Affairs and Defence Committee [*Australia*]
FAD .... Freiwilliger Arbeitsdienst [*Voluntary Service*] [*German*]
FAD .... Front d'Action Democratique [*Democratic Action Front*] [*Benin*]   (AF)
FAD .... Front d'Algerie Democratique
FAD .... Fuerza Aerea Dominicana [*Dominican Air Force*] [*Dominican Republic*]   (LA)
FAD .... Fuerzas Armadas Democraticas [*Democratic Armed Forces*] [*Nicaragua*]   (PD)
FAD .... International Fund for Agricultural Development   (AF)
FADA .... De Aar [*South Africa*] [*ICAO location identifier*]   (ICLI)
FADA .... Friendship Association Denmark-Albania   (EAIO)
FADA .... Fuerzas de Accion Armada [*Armed Action Forces*] [*Guatemala*]   (PD)
FADALTEC ... Fabrica de Alambres Tecnicos [*Colombia*]   (COL)
FADC........ Douglas Colliery [*South Africa*] [*ICAO location identifier*]   (ICLI)
FADD .... Dundee [*South Africa*] [*ICAO location identifier*]   (ICLI)
F a DE........ Fusee a Double Effet [*Military*] [*French*]   (MTD)
FADEAC ... Federacion Argentina de Entidades Empresarias de Autotransporte de Cargas [*Transportation service*] [*Argentina*]   (EY)
FADECH... Federacion Chilena de Automovilismo Deportivo   (EAIO)
FADEEAC ... Federacion Argentina de Entidades Empresarias del Autotransporte de Cargas [*Argentina*]   (LAA)
FADEFA ... Fundacion Argentina de Erradicacion de la Fiebre Aftosa [*Argentine Foundation for the Eradication of Foot-and-Mouth Disease*]   (LA)
FADEM..... Flower of Friendship and Development of Macau [*Political party*]   (EY)
FADEMA ... Fabrica de Articulos de Madera [*Colombia*]   (COL)
FADEMPA ... Fabrica de Bolsas de Papel [*Colombia*]   (COL)
FADEPSA ... Fonds d'Aide au Developpement de l'Education Physique et du Sport en Afrique
FADES ...... Fonds Arabe pour le Developpement Economic et Social [*Arab Economic and Social Development Fund*]   (AF)
FADETEX ... Fabrica de Accesorios Textiles [*Barranquilla*]   (COL)
FADEXCO ... Fiduciaire Africaine d'Expansion Commerciale
FADG .... First Assistant Director General [*Australia*]
FADH........ Durnacol [*South Africa*] [*ICAO location identifier*]   (ICLI)
FADI........ Frente Amplio de la Izquierda [*Broad Front of the Left*] [*Ecuador*]   (LA)
FADL........ Delareyville [*South Africa*] [*ICAO location identifier*]   (ICLI)
FADN .... Durban/Louis Botha [*South Africa*] [*ICAO location identifier*]   (ICLI)
FADP........ Finnish Association for Data Processing
FADP........ Funtua Agricultural Development Project
FADR .... Dunnottar [*South Africa*] [*ICAO location identifier*]   (ICLI)
FADS .... Dordabis [*Namibia*] [*ICAO location identifier*]   (ICLI)
FADS........ Food and Drink Society [*University of Sydney*] [*Australia*]
FADV .... Devon [*South Africa*] [*ICAO location identifier*]   (ICLI)
FAE........... Faroe Islands [*Denmark*] [*Airport symbol*]   (OAG)
FAE........... Federacion Aeronautica Espanola [*Spain*]
FAE........... Federation Autonome de l'Enseignement
FAE........... Federation of Arab Engineers
FAE........... Fondation Archives Europeennes   (EA)
FAE........... Fondo de Acumulacion Estatal [*State Earnings Fund*] [*Nicaragua*]   (GEA)
FAE........... Frei aber Einsam [*Free but Lonely*] [*Motto of Joseph Joachim, 19th century German violinist*]   (ECON)
FAE........... Frente Anti-Comunista Espanol [*Spanish Anti-Communist Front*]   (WER)
FAE........... Fuerza Aerea Ecuatoriana [*Ecuadorean Air Force*]   (LA)
FAE........... Fundacion de Ayuda para la Educacion [*Colombia*]   (DSCA)
FAEA........ Ellisras Control Reporting Point [*South Africa*] [*ICAO location identifier*]   (ICLI)
FAEAB ...... Federacao das Associacoes dos Engenheiros Agronomos do Brasil [*Brazil*]   (DSCA)
FAeB.......... Forca Aerea Brasileira [*Brazilian Air Force*]
FAEB.......... Fuerza Aerea Boliviano [*Military Air Force*] [*Bolivia*]   (PDAA)
FAEC........ Estcourt [*South Africa*] [*ICAO location identifier*]   (ICLI)
FAEC........ Federation Algerienne de l'Education et de la Culture
FAeC......... Force Aerienne Congolaise [*Military Air Force*] [*Congo*]   (PDAA)
FAEC........ France Afrique d'Expertise Comptable
FAEC........ Societe Anonyme Fiduciaire d'Assistance et d'Expertise Comptable
FAECF...... Federation des Associations Europeennes des Constructeurs de Fenetres [*Federation of European Window Manufacturers Associations - FEWMA*]   (EA)

FAEDA...... Federacion Argentina de Entidades Democraticas Anticomunistas [*Argentine Federation of Democratic Anticommunist Organizations*]   (LA)

FAEH .... French Association of Economic Historians   (EAIO)

FAEL......... East London/Ben Schoeman [*South Africa*] [*ICAO location identifier*]   (ICLI)

faellesbd..... Faellesbind [*Bound Together*] [*Publishing Danish/Norwegian*]

faellesomsl ... Faellesomslag [*Wrappers for Series*] [*Publishing Danish/Norwegian*]

FAEM........ Faculdade de Agronomia Eliseu Maciel [*Brazil*]   (DSCA)

FAEM........ Federation des Associations d'Etudiants de Madagascar [*Federation of Malagasy Student Associations*]   (AF)

FAEMG..... Federacao da Agricultura do Estado de Minas Gerais [*Minas Gerais State Agricultural Federation*] [*Brazil*]   (LA)

FAEO .... Ermelo [*South Africa*] [*ICAO location identifier*]   (ICLI)

FAEPA .... Federacao da Agricultura do Estado da Paraiba [*Brazil*]   (DSCA)

FAEPC ...... Federation des Associations d'Editeurs de Periodiques de la CE [*Brussels, Belgium*]   (EAIO)

FAER......... Ellisras [*South Africa*] [*ICAO location identifier*]   (ICLI)

Faer........... Foeroe Islands   (BARN)

FAERJ....... Federacao de Agricultura do Estado do Rio de Janeiro [*Brazil*]   (DSCA)

FAERN...... Federacao de Agricultura do Estado do Rio Grande do Norte [*Brazil*]   (DSCA)

FAERT ...... Fureszaru es Epuletfa Ertekesito Vallalat [*Wood and Lumber Trade Enterprise*]   (HU)

FAES .... Eshowe [*South Africa*] [*ICAO location identifier*]   (ICLI)

FAES .... Fabrica de Equipos Estereofonicos [*Colombia*]   (COL)

FAESP....... Federacao de Agricultura do Estado de Sao Paulo [*Sao Paulo State Agricultural Federation*] [*Brazil*]   (LA)

FAESP....... Fundacao de Amparo a Pesquisa do Estado de Sao Paulo [*Brazil*]   (LAA)

FAET......... Elliot [*South Africa*] [*ICAO location identifier*]   (ICLI)

FAF............ Facile a Fabriquer

FAF............ Facile a Financer

FAF............ Faellesrepraesentationen foer Danske Arbejdsleder-Ogtekniske Funktionaerforeninger [*Joint Representation of Danish Foremen's and Technical Employees' Association*]   (WEN)

FAF............ Families of Australia Foundation

FAF............ Federation Aeronautique de France [*France*]

FAF............ Force Aerienne Francaise [*French Air Force*]   (WER)

FAF............ Forces Aeriennes Francaises [*France*] [*ICAO designator*]   (FAAC)

FAF............ Forum Atomique Francais [*Nuclear energy*] [*French*]   (NRCH)

FAF............ Front de l'Algerie Francaise

FAFA........ Federation des Alliances Francaises en Australie [*Federation of Alliances Francaises (Institutes for the study of French language and culture) in Australia*]

FAFA........ Finnish Albanian Friendship Association   (EAIO)

FAFB......... Ficksburg [*South Africa*] [*ICAO location identifier*]   (ICLI)

FAFER ...... Fabrica de Fertilizantes [*Brazil*]

FAFF .... Frankfort [*South Africa*] [*ICAO location identifier*]   (ICLI)

FAFI .... Federation des Associations de Fonctionnaires Internationaux   (FLAF)

FAFI .... Federation of the Austrian Food Industry   (EAIO)

FAFILE ...... Faculdade de Filosofia e Letras [*Brazil*]

FAFK .... Fisantekraal [*South Africa*] [*ICAO location identifier*]   (ICLI)

FAFMP ..... French Amateur Federation of Mineralogy and Paleontology   (EAIO)

FAFPAS .... Federation des Associations de Fabricants de Produits Alimentaires Surgeles d e la CE [*European Federation of Quick Frozen Food Manufacturers*] [*Belgium*]   (EAIO)

FAFPIC ..... Forestry and Forest Products Industry Council [*Australia*]

FAFR......... Fraserburg [*South Africa*] [*ICAO location identifier*]   (ICLI)

FAFS .... Federation des Associations Feminines

FAFSV...... Franco-Australian Friendly Society of Victoria [*Australia*]

FAG .... Faggot [*Derogatory term for male homosexual*] [*Slang*]   (DSUE)

FAG .... Federacao Angolana de Ginastica

FAG .... Federacion Antioquena de Ganaderos [*Colombia*]   (DSCA)

FAG .... Financial Assistance Grant [*Australia*]

FAG .... Fliegerabwurfgondel (Einsatzmittel) [*(Aerial Drop) Container (Vector)*]   (EG)

FAG .... Floral Art Guild [*Australia*]

FAG .... Flughafen Frankfurt AG [*Germany*]   (PDAA)

FAG .... Fuerza Aerea Argentina [*ICAO designator*]   (FAAC)

FAGA .... Forces Aeriennes Gabonaises [*Gabonese Air Force*]   (AF)

FAGAA...... Fellow of the Art Galleries Association of Australia

FAGANIC ... Federacion de Asociaciones Ganaderas de Nicaragua [*Federation of Nicaraguan Cattlemen's Associations*]   (LA)

FAGB........ Gobabis [*Namibia*] [*ICAO location identifier*]   (ICLI)

FAGC........ Grand Central [*South Africa*] [*ICAO location identifier*]   (ICLI)

FAGE......... Federacion de Agrupaciones Gremiales de Educadores [*Federation of Educators Union Associations*]   (LA)

FAGE......... Gough Island [*South Africa*] [*ICAO location identifier*]   (ICLI)

FAGEC...... Federation d'Associations et Groupements pour les Etudes Corses [*French*]   (SLS)

FAGF......... Grootfontein [*Namibia*] [*ICAO location identifier*]   (ICLI)

FAGG .... Fakultet za Arhitekturo, Gradnjo, in Geodezijo [*Faculty of Architecture, Construction, and Geodesy*] [*Ljubljana*]   (YU)

FAGG .... George/P. W. Botha [*South Africa*] [*ICAO location identifier*]   (ICLI)

FAGI.......... Federazione Anarchica Giovanile Italiana [*Italian Anarchist Youth Federation*]   (WER)

FAGI.......... Fellow of the Australian Grain Institute

FAGI.......... Giyani [*South Africa*] [*ICAO location identifier*]   (ICLI)

FAGICTMAT ... Ferme Agro-Industrielle et Commerciale des Tabacs et du Mais du Togo

FAGIP .... Fabrica de Gazes Industriais [*Brazil*]   (DSCA)

FAGL........ Groblersdal [*South Africa*] [*ICAO location identifier*]   (ICLI)

FAGM .... Johannesburg/Rand [*South Africa*] [*ICAO location identifier*]   (ICLI)

FAGO .... Fellow in Australia of Gynaecology and Obstetrics   (ADA)

FAGR........ Graaff Reinet [*South Africa*] [*ICAO location identifier*]   (ICLI)

FAGRAM ... Fabrika Gradevinskih Masina [*Construction Machinery Works*] [*Smederevo*]   (YU)

FAGRAVE ... Fabrica Unida de Aceites y Grasas Vegetales   (COL)

FAGRIEMA ... Federacao de Agricultura do Estado do Maranhao [*Brazil*]   (DSCA)

FAGRIN.... Fundo de Desenvolvimento Agricola e Industrial [*Agricultural and Industrial Development Fund*] [*Brazil*]   (LA)

FAGS......... Federation of Astronomical and Geophysical Services [*Research center*] [*France*]   (IRC)

FAGS......... Flinders Association of Graduate Students [*Australia*]

FAGT........ Grahamstown [*South Africa*] [*ICAO location identifier*]   (ICLI)

FAGV .... Gravelotte [*South Africa*] [*ICAO location identifier*]   (ICLI)

FAGY .... Greytown [*South Africa*] [*ICAO location identifier*]   (ICLI)

fah .... Faehig [*Capable of*] [*German*]   (GCA)

FAH .... Federal Association of Hornussen [*Switzerland*]   (EAIO)

FAH .... Forest Association of Hungary   (EAIO)

fah .... Frei aus Hier [*Free at Factory, Free from Here*] [*Business term*] [*German*]

FAH .... Fuerza Aerea Hondurena [*Military Air Force*] [*Honduras*]   (PDAA)

FAHA .... Fellow of the Australian Academy of the Humanities   (ADA)

FAHA .... Harmony [*South Africa*] [*ICAO location identifier*]   (ICLI)

FAHB .... Hartebeespoortdam [*South Africa*] [*ICAO location identifier*]   (ICLI)

FAHD....... Humansdorp [*South Africa*] [*ICAO location identifier*]   (ICLI)

FAHE .... Pullenshope (Hendrina) [*South Africa*] [*ICAO location identifier*]   (ICLI)

FAHG .... Heidelberg [*South Africa*] [*ICAO location identifier*]   (ICLI)

FAHI .... Halali [*Namibia*] [*ICAO location identifier*]   (ICLI)

Fahigk........ Faehigkeit [*Capability*] [*German*]   (GCA)

FAHILOS ... Fabrica de Hilos Cordobes y Rey Ltda. [*Colombia*]   (COL)

FAHM....... Hermanus [*South Africa*] [*ICAO location identifier*]   (ICLI)

FAHN....... Henties Bay [*Namibia*] [*ICAO location identifier*]   (ICLI)

FAHO....... Heilbrond [*South Africa*] [*ICAO location identifier*]   (ICLI)

FAHQ....... Pretoria [*South Africa*] [*ICAO location identifier*]   (ICLI)

Fahr .... Fahrenheit [*German*]   (GCA)

FAHR .... Harrismith [*South Africa*] [*ICAO location identifier*]   (ICLI)

FAHS......... Federation of Australian historical Societies

FAHS......... Hoedspruit [*South Africa*] [*ICAO location identifier*]   (ICLI)

FAHT .... Hoedspruit Civil/Burgerlike [*South Africa*] [*ICAO location identifier*]   (ICLI)

FAHUILA ... Fumigacion Aerea del Huila Ltda. [*Neiva*]   (COL)

FAHV .... Hendrik Verwoerddam [*South Africa*] [*ICAO location identifier*]   (ICLI)

FAI............. All-Union Scientific Research Institute of Agricultural Physics   (RU)

FAI............. Federacion Anarquista Iberica [*Iberian Anarchist Federation*] [*Spanish*]   (WER)

FAI............. Federation Abolitionniste Internationale [*International Abolitionist Federation*] [*India*]

FAI............. Federation Acronautique Internationale   (OLYM)

FAI............. Federation Aeronautique Internationale [*International Aeronautical Federation*] [*France*]

FAI............. Federazione Anarchica Italiana [*Italian Anarchist Federation*]   (WER)

FAI............. Federazione Associati Industriali [*Italy*]

FAI............. Federazione Autonoma Indossatrici [*Autonomous Federation of Models*] [*Italy*]

FAI............. Federazione Autotrasportatori Italiani

FAI............. Fertilizer Association of India   (PDAA)

FAI............. Fondo Aiuti Italiani [*Mauritania*]

FAIA......... Federation Arabe des Industries Alimentaires [*Arab Federation for Food Industries*] [*Iraq*]

FAIA......... Federation of Automobile Importers Association [*Japan*]

FAIA......... Fellow of the Advertising Institute of Australia   (ADA)

FAIAS ...... Fellow of the Australian Institute of Agricultural Science   (ADA)

FAIAT .... Federazione delle Associazioni Italiane Alberghi e Turismo [*Hotels and Tourism Federation*] [*Italy*]   (EY)

FAIB......... Fellow of the Australian Institute of Bankers

FAIB.......... Fellow of the Australian Institute of Building   (ADA)

FAIBiol...... Fellow of the Australian Institute of Biology
FAIBM ...... Fellow of the Australian Institute of Building Management
FAIC......... Federation of Australian Investment Clubs (ADA)
FAIC .... Fellow of the Australian Institute of Cartographers
FAICO....... Fabrica Italo Colombiana de Baterias (COL)
FAIE......... Fellow of the Australian Institute of Energy
FAIEE .... Fellow of the Australian Institute of Electrical Engineers
FAIEx .... Fellow of the Australian Institute of Export (ADA)
FAIFST ..... Fellow of the Australian Institute of Food Science and Technology (ADA)
FAIH .... Fellow of the Australian Institute of Horticulture
FAIHA...... Fellow of the Australian Institute of Hospital Administration
FAII .... Fellow of the Australian Insurance Institute (ADA)
FAILA ...... Fellow of the Australian Institute of Landscape Architects
FAILCLEA ... Federazione Autonoma Italiana Lavoratori Cemento Legno, Edilizia, ed Affini [Workers in Cement, Wood, Construction, and Related Industries Federation] [Italy] (EY)
FAILE........ Federazione Autonoma Italiana Lavoratori Elettrici [Electrical Workers Federation] [Italy] (EY)
Faill............ Faillissement [Benelux] (BAS)
FAIM........ Fellow of the Australian Institute of Management (ADA)
FAIMA...... Federacion Argentina de la Industria Maderera y Afines [Argentina]
FAIMLS.... Fellow of the Australian Institute of Medical Laboratory Scientists
FAIMM..... Fellow of the Australasian Institute of Mining and Metallurgy
FAIN........ Fellow of the Australian Institute of Navigation
FAINT....... File of Administrative Interests [Australia]
faip .... Faipari [Lumber, Woodworking (Adjective)] (HU)
FAIP .... Fellow of the Australian Institute of Physics (ADA)
FAIPA .... Fellow of the Australian Institute of Public Administration
FAIPA .... Front for the Independence of the Azores [Portuguese] (WER)
FAIPet ...... Fellow of the Australian Institute of Petroleum (ADA)
FAIPM ...... Fellow of the Australian Institute of Personnel Management (ADA)
FAIPP....... Fellow of the Australian Institute of Professional Photography
FAIPR .... Fellow of the Australian Institute of Parks and Recreation
FAIR......... Federation of Afro-Asian Insurers and Reinsurers
FAIR......... Female Apprenticeship Incentive for Recruitment [New Zealand]
FAIR......... Irene [South Africa] [ICAO location identifier] (ICLI)
FAIRA ...... Foundation for Aboriginal and Islander Research Action [Australia]
FAIRE ...... Fellow of the Australian Institute of Radio Engineers
FAIS .... Isithebe [South Africa] [ICAO location identifier] (ICLI)
FAISA .... Fortaleza Agro Industrial SA [Brazil] (DSCA)
FAISME.... Fellow of the Australian Institute of Sales and Marketing Executives
FAIST....... Fellow of the Australian Institute of Science and Technology
FAIT......... Fellow of the Australian Institute of Travel (ADA)
FAITA ...... Federacion de Asociaciones Industriales Textiles del Algodon [Mexico] (DSCA)
FAITH...... Federation of Agrarian and Industrial Toiling Hands [Trade union] [Philippines] (FEA)
FAITPM.... Fellow of the Australian Institute of Traffic Planning and Management
FAITT ...... Fellow of the Australian Institute of Travel and Tourism
FAIUS ...... Fellow of the Australian Institute of Urban Studies
FAIV......... Fellow of the Australian Institute of Valuers (ADA)
FAJ .... Fabrika Azotnih Jedinjenja [Nitrogen Compounds Factory] [Gorazde] (YU)
FAJ .... Fajardo [Puerto Rico] [Airport symbol] (OAG)
FAJ .... Fiji Air Services Ltd. [ICAO designator] (FAAC)
FAJ .... Fundiciones Artisticas de Joyas [Colombia] (COL)
FAJARCOL ... Fajardo y Compania Ltda. [Colombia] (COL)
FAJB .... Johannesburg [South Africa] [ICAO location identifier] (ICLI)
FAJDA ...... Federation Algerienne de Judo et de Disciplines Assimilees
FAJE .... Federation Algerienne des Jeux d'Echecs [Algeria]
FAJF......... Jagersfontein [South Africa] [ICAO location identifier] (ICLI)
FAJS......... Johannesburg/Jan Smuts [South Africa] [ICAO location identifier] (ICLI)
FAJURE.... Frente de Accion de la Juventud Reformista [Reformist Youth Action Front] [Dominican Republic] (LA)
fak .... Division (RU)
fak .... Fakulta [Faculty] (CZ)
Fak .... Fakultaet [German]
Fak .... Fakultas, Fakultet [Faculty (School, Department)] (IN)
Fak .... Fakulte [Faculty] (TU)
FAK .... Federasie van Afrikaanse Kultuurvereniginge [Federation of Afrikaner Cultural Associations] [South Africa] (AF)
FAK .... Financial AirExpress [ICAO designator] (FAAC)
FAK .... Foersoeksgruppen foer Fiskevardande Atgaerder i Kraftverksmagasin [Research Group for Fishery Management in River Reservoirs] [Sweden] (ARC)
FAK .... Fondation Aga Khan [Aga Khan Foundation] (EAIO)

fak .... University Department [or School] (BU)
FAKA........ Karibib [Namibia] [ICAO location identifier] (ICLI)
FAKB........ Karasburg [Namibia] [ICAO location identifier] (ICLI)
FAKD .... Klerksdorp [South Africa] [ICAO location identifier] (ICLI)
FAKEM..... Fabrique Khmere d'Emballages Metalliques [Cambodian Metal Container Factory] (CL)
FAKF........ Federacja Amatorskich Klubow Filmowych [Federation of Non-Professional Film Clubs] [Poland] (EAIO)
FAKFWSO ... Federation of Australian Kung Fu and Wun Shu Organisations
FAKG .... Komati Power Station/Kragsentrale [South Africa] [ICAO location identifier] (ICLI)
FAKH....... Kenhardt [South Africa] [ICAO location identifier] (ICLI)
FAKJ .... Kamanjab [Namibia] [ICAO location identifier] (ICLI)
FAKK....... Kakamas [South Africa] [ICAO location identifier] (ICLI)
FAKL........ Kriel [South Africa] [ICAO location identifier] (ICLI)
FAKM ...... Kimberley/B. J. Vorster [South Africa] [ICAO location identifier] (ICLI)
FAKN .... Klippan Control Reporting Point [South Africa] [ICAO location identifier] (ICLI)
FAKNLP ... Forces Armees Khmeres Nationales de Liberation Populaire [Cambodian People's National Liberation Armed Forces] [Use CPNLAF] (CL)
FAKO .... Fachkommission [Technical Commission] [FK] [See also] (EG)
FAKO .... Federation of Australian Karate Do Organisations (ADA)
FAKP........ Komatipoort [South Africa] [ICAO location identifier] (ICLI)
FAKR........ Krugersdorp [South Africa] [ICAO location identifier] (ICLI)
faks .... Faksimile [Facsimile] [Publishing Danish/Norwegian]
Faks .... Faksimile [Facsimile] [Publishing] [German]
faks .... Fakszimile [Facsimile] [Publishing] [Hungary]
FAKS........ Kroonstad [South Africa] [ICAO location identifier] (ICLI)
Faksim .... Faksimile [Facsimile] [Publishing] [German]
fak-t........... Division (RU)
Fakt........... Faktura [Invoice] [Business term] [German]
fakt........... Faktuur [Invoice] [Business term] [Afrikaans]
FAKT........ Keetmanshoop/J. G. H. Van Der Wath [Namibia] [ICAO location identifier] (ICLI)
FAKU .... Kuruman [South Africa] [ICAO location identifier] (ICLI)
FAKX .... Khorixas [Namibia] [ICAO location identifier] (ICLI)
FAKZ........ Kleinsee [South Africa] [ICAO location identifier] (ICLI)
Fak zastop i sots nauki ... School of Economic and Social Sciences (BU)
FAL........... Bundesforschungsanstalt fuer Landwirtschaft Braunschweig-Voelkenrode [Federal Research Center for Agriculture Braunschweig-Voelkenrode] [Research center] (ERC)
FAL........... Facilitation du Transport Aerien [Air Transportation Facilities] [Rwanda] (AF)
FAL........... Forces Armees Laotiannes [Federated Army of Laos]
FAL........... France Amerique Latine [France Latin America] [An association] (EAIO)
FAL........... Frente Anti-Imperialista de Liberacion [Peruvian guerrilla group] (EY)
FAL........... Frente Argentino de Liberacion [Argentine Liberation Front] (LA)
FAL........... Fuerzas Armadas de Liberacion [Armed Forces of Liberation] [Colorado] (LA)
FAL........... Fuerzas Armadas de Liberacion [Armed Forces of Liberation] [El Salvador] (LA)
FAL........... Fuerzas Armadas de Liberacion [Armed Forces of Liberation] [Argentina] (LA)
FAL........... Fusil Automatique Leger [Light Automatic Rifle]
fal............. Phenylalanine (RU)
FALA........ Federation Algerienne de Lutte Amateur
FALA........ Federation of Australian Literature and Art (ADA)
FALA........ Forcas Armadas de Libertacao de Angola
FALA........ Fund for Animals Ltd. Australia
FALA........ Lanseria [South Africa] [ICAO location identifier] (ICLI)
FALANGE ... Frente Anticomunista de Liberacion-Guerra de Eliminacion [Anticommunist Front of Liberation-War of Elimination] [El Salvador]
FALANGE ... Fuerzas Armadas de Liberacion Anticomunistas y Guerra de Eliminacion [Armed Forces for Anticommunist Liberation and War of Elimination] [El Salvador] (LA)
FALB......... Ladybrand [South Africa] [ICAO location identifier] (ICLI)
FALC......... Armed Forces for the Liberation of Cabinda [Angola] (PD)
FALC......... French Association of Landscape Contractors (EAIO)
FALC......... Lime Acres [South Africa] [ICAO location identifier] (ICLI)
FALCA ...... Frente Anticomunista para la Liberacion de Centro America [Anticommunist Front for the Liberation of Central America] [El Salvador] (LA)
FALCRI..... Federazione Autonoma Lavoratori Casse di Risparmio Italiane [Savings Banks Workers Federation] [Italy] (EY)
FALH .... Lohathla [South Africa] [ICAO location identifier] (ICLI)
FALI .... Lichtenburg [South Africa] [ICAO location identifier] (ICLI)
FALIA .... Fellow of the Australian Library and Information Association
FALK........ Foreningen Arkivverksamma i Landsting och Kommun [Association of Employees in Archive Service of County Councils and Local Authorities] [Sweden] (EAIO)
FALK IS .... Falkland Islands (WDAA)

Fall............. Faellung [*Precipitation*] [*German*]   (GCA)
FALL......... Lydenburg [*South Africa*] [*ICAO location identifier*]   (ICLI)
Fallbark.... Faellbarkeit [*Precipitability*] [*German*]   (GCA)
FALLEX..... Fall [*Autumn*] Exercise [*Military*] [*NATO*]   (NATG)
Fallsch...... Fallschirm [*Parachute*]   (EG)
FALM........ Loraine Mine [*South Africa*] [*ICAO location identifier*]   (ICLI)
FALN........ Fuerzas Armadas de Liberacion Nacional [*Armed Forces of National Liberation*] [*Venezuela*]   (PD)
FALN........ Fuerzas Armadas de Liberacion Nacional [*Armed Forces of National Liberation*] [*Mexico*]   (LA)
FALO........ Louis Trichardt [*South Africa*] [*ICAO location identifier*]   (ICLI)
FALT......... Louis Trichardt [*South Africa*] [*ICAO location identifier*]   (ICLI)
Faltkupf..... Faltkupfer [*Folding Copperplate*] [*Publishing*] [*German*]
Falttaf....... Falttafel [*Folding Plate*] [*Publishing*] [*German*]
Falttfln...... Falttaffeln [*Folding Plates*] [*Publishing*] [*German*]
FALW........ Langebaanweg [*South Africa*] [*ICAO location identifier*]   (ICLI)
FALY......... Ladysmith [*South Africa*] [*ICAO location identifier*]   (ICLI)
FALZ......... Luderitz [*Namibia*] [*ICAO location identifier*]   (ICLI)
FAM .... Fabricas de Artefatos Metalicos SA [*Metallic Devices Manufacturing Ltd.*] [*Brazil*]   (LA)
FAM .... Fabrika Masina [*Machinery Works*] [*Novi Sad*]   (YU)
FAM .... Fabrique Africaine de Meubles
fam .... Familiare [*Familiar*] [*Italian*]
Fam .... Familie [*Family*] [*German*]
FAM .... Familie [*Family*] [*Afrikaans*]
FAM .... Federation of Australian Motorcyclists   (ADA)
FAM .... Football Association of Malaya   (ML)
FAM .... Frente Amplio de Masas [*Broad Front of the Masses*] [*Honduras*]   (LA)
FAM .... Frente Anti-Macias [*Anti-Macias Front*] [*Equatorial Guinea*]   (AF)
FAM .... Fuerza Aerea Mexicana [*Military Air Force*] [*Mexico*]   (PDAA)
FAM .... Fumigacion Aerea Andalusa SA [*Spain*] [*ICAO designator*]   (FAAC)
FAMA .... Fabrica Argentina de Material Aerospacial [*Argentine aerospace material manufacturer*]
FAMA .... Federal Agricultural Marketing Authority [*Malaysia*]   (FEA)
FAMA .... Fellow of the Australian Medical Association
FAMA .... Finnish Amateur Musicians' Association   (EAIO)
FAMA .... Fondation pour l'Assistance Mutuelle en Afrique au Sud du Sahara [*Foundation for Mutual Aid in Africa South of the Sahara*]   (AF)
FAMA .... Matatiele [*South Africa*] [*ICAO location identifier*]   (ICLI)
FAMAC..... Fabrica Maquinaria Centroamericana Ltd. [*Costa Rica*]   (DSCA)
FAMAE..... Fabricas y Maestranzas del Ejercito [*Army Ordnance*] [*Chile*]   (LA)
Fa Ma L..... Fabryka Maszyn Lniarskich [*Flax Machine Factory*]   (POL)
FAMAQUIN ... Fabrica de Maquinaria Industrial [*Colombia*]   (COL)
FAMAR...... Federacion Maritima Argentina [*Argentine Maritime Federation*]   (LA)
FAMAS..... Fellow of the Australian Medical Acupuncture Society
FAMB....... Middelburg [*South Africa*] [*ICAO location identifier*]   (ICLI)
FAMBEL .. Fabrica de Malas de Beira Limitada
FAMC....... Middelburg [*South Africa*] [*ICAO location identifier*]   (ICLI)
FAMCO .... Federal Arab Maritime Co. [*Egypt*]
Fam C ofA ... Family Court of Australia
Fam Ct .... Family Court [*Australia*]
FAMD .... Malamala [*South Africa*] [*ICAO location identifier*]   (ICLI)
FAMDEC ... Family Court of Australia Decisions [*Database*]
FAME....... Federation of Australian Mandolin Ensembles
FAME....... Marion Island [*South Africa*] [*ICAO location identifier*]   (ICLI)
FAMECHAS ... Fabrica de Mechas Ltda. [*Manizales*]   (COL)
FAMECOL ... Fabrica de Articulos Metalicos de Colombia [*Colombia*]   (COL)
FAMESA .. Financial and Administrative Management of Research Projects in Eastern and Southern Africa
FAMETAL ... Fabrica de Muebles Metalicos [*Colombia*]   (COL)
FAMG .... Margate [*South Africa*] [*ICAO location identifier*]   (ICLI)
FAMH .... Finnish Association for Mental Health   (EAIO)
FAMH .... Maltahohe [*Namibia*] [*ICAO location identifier*]   (ICLI)
FAMI........ Fellow of the Australian Marketing Institute   (ADA)
FAMI........ Fundacion Africana de Medicina e Investigacion [*Spanish*]
FAMI........ Marble Hall [*South Africa*] [*ICAO location identifier*]   (ICLI)
FamIS........ Family Impact Seminar [*Australia*]
FAMK .... Mafikeng [*South Africa*] [*ICAO location identifier*]   (ICLI)
FAML........ Mariental [*Namibia*] [*ICAO location identifier*]   (ICLI)
FAMM ...... Mmabatho International [*South Africa*] [*ICAO location identifier*]   (ICLI)
FAMN .... Malalane [*South Africa*] [*ICAO location identifier*]   (ICLI)
FAMO .... Mossel Bay/Baai [*South Africa*] [*ICAO location identifier*]   (ICLI)
FAMOLAC ... Fabrica de Molinos y Accesorios [*Colombia*]   (COL)
FAMOS..... Fabrika Motora, Sarajevo [*Motor Works, Sarajevo*]   (YU)
FAMOS..... Fantasias Modernas [*Colombia*]   (COL)
FAMOUS ... French-American Mid-Oceanic Underseas Survey   (WER)
FAMP........ Frontier Armed and Mounted Police [*of the Cape Colony*]

FAMP....... Mpacha [*Namibia*] [*ICAO location identifier*]   (ICLI)
FAMR....... Mariepskop [*South Africa*] [*ICAO location identifier*]   (ICLI)
FAMS....... Messina [*South Africa*] [*ICAO location identifier*]   (ICLI)
FAMSA .... Family and Marriage Society of South Africa   (AA)
FAMSA .... Federation of African Medical Students Associations
FAMSCO .. Farm Services Company
FAMSY ..... Federation of Australian Muslim Students and Youth
FAMT....... Meyerton [*South Africa*] [*ICAO location identifier*]   (ICLI)
FAMTA..... Federation of Australian Music Teachers Associations   (ADA)
FAMY....... Malmesbury [*South Africa*] [*ICAO location identifier*]   (ICLI)
FAMZ....... Msauli [*South Africa*] [*ICAO location identifier*]   (ICLI)
FAN .... Branch of the Academy of Sciences, USSR   (RU)
FAN .... Fabrica de Aparatura Nucleara [*Nuclear Instrumentation Plant*]   (RO)
FAN .... Farsund [*Norway*] [*Airport symbol*]   (OAG)
FAN .... Federacion Agraria Nacional [*National Farmer's Federation*] [*San Jose, Costa Rica*]   (LAA)
FAN .... Fiduciaire de l'Afrique Noire
FAN .... Fondo Aeronautico Nacional [*National Aeronautics Fund*] [*Colorado*]   (LA)
FAN .... Forces Armees du Nord [*Northern Armed Forces*] [*Chad*]   (AF)
FAN .... Forces Armees Neutralistes [*Neutralist Armed Forces*] [*Laos*]
FAN .... Forces Armees Nigeriennes [*Niger Armed Forces*]   (AF)
FAN .... Frente Amplio Nacional [*Broad National Front*] [*El Salvador*]   (LA)
FAN .... Frente Anticomunista Nacional [*National Anticommunist Front*] [*El Salvador*]   (LA)
FAN .... Frente de Avance Nacional [*National Advancement Front*] [*Guatemala*] [*Political party*]
FAN .... Fuerzas Armadas Nacionales [*National Armed Forces*] [*Venezuela*]   (LA)
fan .... Plywood   (RU)
FAN .... Tauern Air Gesellschaft GmbH [*Austria*] [*ICAO designator*]   (FAAC)
FANA .... Federation of Australian Nurserymen's Associations   (ADA)
FANA .... Namatoni [*Namibia*] [*ICAO location identifier*]   (ICLI)
FANABRA ... Fabrica Nacional de Abrasivos [*Colombia*]   (COL)
FANABRO ... Fabrica Nacional de Brochas [*Colombia*]   (COL)
FANAC..... Fabrica Nacional de Accesorios [*Colombia*]   (COL)
FANAF...... Federation des Societes d'Assurances de Droit National Africains [*Federation of African National Insurance Companies*] [*Dakar, Senegal*]   (EAIO)
FANAL...... Federacion Agraria Nacional [*National Farmers Federation*] [*Colorado*]   (LA)
FANALRES ... Fabrica Nacional de Resortes [*Colombia*]   (COL)
FANALSO ... Fabrica Nacional de Sombreros [*Colombia*]   (COL)
FANASYCOA ... Federation Nationale des Syndicats du Commerce Ouest Africain
FANATRAM ... Fabrica Nacional de Tractores y Motores [*National Factory for the Manufacture of Tractors and Motors*] [*Bolivia*]   (LA)
FANAVE ... Fabrica Nacional de Carrocerias para Vehiculos [*Colombia*]   (COL)
FANC .... Newcastle [*South Africa*] [*ICAO location identifier*]   (ICLI)
FANCI....... Forces Armees Nationales de la Cote-D'Ivoire [*National Armed Forces School of the Ivory Coast*]   (AF)
FANCIF ... Fondo Autarquico Nacional para la Capacitacion e Investigacion Forestal [*Argentina*]   (LAA)
F & F .... Finanza & Futuro [*Finance & the Future*] [*Commercial firm*] [*Italy*]
F & G.......... Felten & Guilleaume Carlswerk AG [*Felten and Guilleaume Carlswork Joint Stock Company*]
F & GP....... Finance and General Purposes Committee [*British*]   (DCTA)
F & L.......... Aviation Fuels, Lubricants, and Associated Products [*NATO*]   (NATG)
F & N .... Fraser & Neave [*Soft-drinks manufacturer and bottler*] [*Singapore*]
F & WU ..... Foute en Weglatings Uitgesonderd [*Errors and Omissions Excepted*] [*Afrikaans*]
FANE .... Federation d'Action Nationale et Europeene [*Federation of National and European Action*] [*France*] [*Political party*]   (PPE)
FANEL...... Federacion de Asociaciones Nacionales de Estudiantes Latinoamericanos [*Federation of National Associations of Latin American Students*]   (LA)
FANEON .. Fabrica de Avisos de Gas Neon Ltda. [*Manizales*]   (COL)
fanern......... Plywood Factory [*Topography*]   (RU)
FANF........ Flota Argentina de Navegacion Fluvial [*Argentina*]   (LAA)
FANH........ New Hanover [*South Africa*] [*ICAO location identifier*]   (ICLI)
FANK .... Automatic Circuit Phase Adjustment   (RU)
FANK .... Forces Armees Nationales Khmeres [*Cambodian National Armed Forces*] [*Replaced Royal Cambodian Armed Forces*]
FANL........ New Largo [*South Africa*] [*ICAO location identifier*]   (ICLI)
FANO .... Fabrica Nacional de Oxigeno [*Colombia*]   (COL)
FANO........ Frente Anticomunista del Nororiente [*Northeastern Anticommunist Front*] [*Guatemala*]   (PD)

FANO........ Frente Aranista Nacional Obrero [*National Pro-Arana Workers Front*] [*Guatemala*]   (LA)
FANS........ Nelspruit [*South Africa*] [*ICAO location identifier*]   (ICLI)
FANSW..... Financiers' Association of New South Wales [*Australia*]
fant............ Fantaisie [*Imagination*] [*French*]
FANT........ Forces Armees Nationales Tchadiennes [*Chad*]   (PD)
FANU........ Flota Argentina Navegacion Ultramar [*Argentine Ship Line*]
FANUL...... Friends of the Australian National University Library
FANUS...... Federazione fra le Associazioni Nazionali Ufficiali e Sottufficiali in Congedo Provenienti dal Servizio Effettivo [*Federation of National Associations for Discharged Career Officers and Petty Officers*] [*Italian*]
FANV........ Nieuwoudtville [*South Africa*] [*ICAO location identifier*]   (ICLI)
FANY........ Nylstroom [*South Africa*] [*ICAO location identifier*]   (ICLI)
FANZAAS ... Fellow of the Australian and New Zealand Association for the Advancement of Science   (ADA)
FANZCP ... Fellow of the Australian and New Zealand College of Psychiatrists   (ADA)
FAO............ Compagnie Francaise de l'Afrique Occidentale-Mali
FAO............ Faro [*Portugal*] [*Airport symbol*]   (OAG)
FAO............ Food and Agriculture Organization [*United Nations Italy Information service or system*]   (IID)
FAO............ Forces Armees Occidentales [*Western Armed Forces*] [*Chad*]   (AF)
FAO............ Frente Amplio de Oposicion [*Broad Opposition Front*] [*Nicaragua*]   (LA)
FAOA........ Ondangua [*Namibia*] [*ICAO location identifier*]   (ICLI)
FAO/APS ... FAO [*Food and Agriculture Organization of the United Nations*] Association of Professional Staff [*Rome, Italy*]   (EAIO)
FAOB........ Federation of Australian and Oceanian Biochemists [*ICSU*]
FAOD........ Odendaalsrus [*South Africa*] [*ICAO location identifier*]   (ICLI)
FAOE........ Federation of African Organisations of Engineers   (PDAA)
FAOE........ Omega [*Namibia*] [*ICAO location identifier*]   (ICLI)
FAOFOG... Fellow of the Asia-Oceania Federation of Obstetricians and Gynaecologists
FAOG........ Oranjemund [*Namibia*] [*ICAO location identifier*]   (ICLI)
FAOGIS ... Food and Agriculture Organization Geographic Information System [*United Nations*]   (DUND)
FAOH........ Oudtshoorn [*South Africa*] [*ICAO location identifier*]   (ICLI)
FAOIP...... French Association Online Information Providers   (EAIO)
FAOJ........ Outjo [*Namibia*] [*ICAO location identifier*]   (ICLI)
FAOK........ Okakarara [*Namibia*] [*ICAO location identifier*]   (ICLI)
FAON........ Okahandja [*Namibia*] [*ICAO location identifier*]   (ICLI)
FAOO........ Okaukuejo [*Namibia*] [*ICAO location identifier*]   (ICLI)
FAOP........ Opuwa [*Namibia*] [*ICAO location identifier*]   (ICLI)
FAOR........ Olifants River Bridge [*South Africa*] [*ICAO location identifier*]   (ICLI)
FAORFVF ... Federal Austrian Organisation of Resistance Fighters and Victims of Fascism   (EAIO)
FAOS........ Oshakati [*Namibia*] [*ICAO location identifier*]   (ICLI)
FAOV........ Otavi [*Namibia*] [*ICAO location identifier*]   (ICLI)
FAOW....... Otjiwarongo [*Namibia*] [*ICAO location identifier*]   (ICLI)
FAOY........ Orkney [*South Africa*] [*ICAO location identifier*]   (ICLI)
FAP............ Fabrika Automobila Pionir [*"Pioneer" Automobile Factory*]   (YU)
FAP............ Fabrika Automobila, Priboj [*Automobile Factory, Priboj*]   (YU)
FAP............ Fabrique d'Articles en Plastique
FAP............ Federacion Argentina de Periodistas [*Argentine Newsmen's Federation*]   (LA)
FAP............ Fe y Alegria del Peru [*An association*]   (EAIO)
FAP............ Financial Assistance Policy [*Botswana*]
FAP............ Flanders Agro Processing [*Commercial firm*] [*Belgium*]
FAP........ Forca Aerea Portuguesa [*Portuguese Air Force*]   (WER)
FAP............ Forces Armees Populaires [*People's Armed Forces*] [*Malagasy*]   (AF)
FAP............ Forces Armees Populaires [*People's Armed Forces*] [*Zaire*]   (AF)
FAP............ Forces Armees Populaires [*People's Armed Forces*] [*Chad*]   (AF)
FAP............ Forces Armees Populaires [*People's Armed Forces*] [*Benin*]   (AF)
FAP............ Foreign Assistance Program   (WDAA)
FAP............ Foros Akinitou Periousias [*Real Estate Tax*]   (GC)
FAP............ Forschungsausschuss fur Planungsfragen [*Research Committee on Planning*] [*Switzerland*]   (PDAA)
FAP............ Franc d'Avarie Particuliere [*Free of Particular Average*] [*Business term*] [*French*]
FAP............ Franco d'Avaria Particolare [*Free of Particular Average*] [*Business term*] [*Italian*]
FAP............ Frente Accion Progresista [*Progressive Action Front*] [*Honduras*]
FAP............ Frente de Accao Popular [*Popular Action Front*] [*Portuguese*]   (WER)
FAP............ Front d'Action Patriotique
FAP............ Fuerza Aerea del Peru [*Peruvian Air Force*]   (LA)
FAP............ Fuerza Armada de la Paz [*Inter-American Peace Force*] [*Use IAPF Dominican Republic*]   (LA)
FAP............ Fuerzas Armadas Peruanas [*Peruvian Armed Forces*]   (LA)
FAP............ Fundacao Acucareira de Pernambuco [*Brazil*]   (DSCA)

FAP............ Fundacao Antonio Prudente [*Brazil*]   (SLS)
FAPA........ Family Aide Projects Association [*Australia*]
FAPA........ Federacion Aeronautica Pan-Americana
FAPA........ Fermes Agro-Pastorales d'Arrondissement [*Agro-Pastoral District Farms*] [*Guinea*]   (AF)
FAPA........ Ferro Alloys Producers Association
FAPA........ Force Aerienne Populaire d'Angola
FAPA........ Port Alfred [*South Africa*] [*ICAO location identifier*]   (ICLI)
FAPB........ Pietersburg [*South Africa*] [*ICAO location identifier*]   (ICLI)
FAPC........ Food and Agriculture Planning Committee [*NATO*]   (NATG)
FAPC........ Prince Albert [*South Africa*] [*ICAO location identifier*]   (ICLI)
FAPCO...... Fayoum Petroleum Company
FAPD........ Fundacion Alemana para los Paises en Desarrollo [*Germany*]   (DSCA)
FAPE........ Federacion de Asociaciones de la Prensa de Espana [*Press association*] [*Spain*]   (EY)
FAPE........ Port Elizabeth/H. F. Verwoerd [*South Africa*] [*ICAO location identifier*]   (ICLI)
FAPEL...... Fabrieken van Aktieve en Passieve Electronische Bouwelementen in Nederland [*Netherlands*]   (PDAA)
FAPESP.... Fundacao de Amparo a Pesquisa do Estado de Sao Paulo [*Brazil*]   (LAA)
FAPF........ Piet Retief [*South Africa*] [*ICAO location identifier*]   (ICLI)
FAPG........ Plettenberg Bay [*South Africa*] [*ICAO location identifier*]   (ICLI)
FAPH........ Phalaborwa/Hendrik Van Eck [*South Africa*] [*ICAO location identifier*]   (ICLI)
FAPHA...... Fellow of the Australian Psychology and Hypnotherapy Association
FAPHS...... Fellow of the Australian Psychology and Hypnotherapy Society   (ADA)
FAPI......... Federazione Artisti e Professionisti Italiani [*Italian Federation of the Arts and Professions*]
FAPI......... Fellow of the Australian Planning Institute   (ADA)
FAPI......... Fonds Allemand pour les Perimetres Irrigues [*Tunisia*]
FAPI......... Pietersburg [*South Africa*] [*ICAO location identifier*]   (ICLI)
FAPIG....... [*The*] First Atomic Power Industry Group
FAPIS........ Feira Agropecuaria Industrial de Sorocaba [*Brazil*]   (DSCA)
FAPJ........ Port St. Johns [*South Africa*] [*ICAO location identifier*]   (ICLI)
FAPL........ Forces Armees Populaires de Liberation [*People's Liberation Armed Forces*] [*Use PLAF South Vietnamese*]   (CL)
FAPL........ Pongola [*South Africa*] [*ICAO location identifier*]   (ICLI)
FAPLA...... Forcas Armadas Populares da Liberacao de Angola [*People's Armed Forces for the Liberation of Angola*]   (AF)
FAPLE....... Frente Anti-Totalitario dos Portugueses Libres Exiliados
FAPLK...... Forces Armees Populaires de Liberation Khmere [*Cambodian People's National Liberation Armed Forces*] [*Use CPNLAF*]   (CL)
FAPLNC ... Forces Armees Populaires de Liberation Nationale du Cambodge [*Cambodian People's National Liberation Armed Forces*] [*Use CPNLAF*]   (CL)
FAPM........ Pietermaritzburg [*South Africa*] [*ICAO location identifier*]   (ICLI)
FAPN........ Pilansberg [*South Africa*] [*ICAO location identifier*]   (ICLI)
FAPP........ Potgietersrus [*South Africa*] [*ICAO location identifier*]   (ICLI)
FAPPEC.... Federation of Associations of Periodical Publishers in the EC   (EAIO)
FAPR........ Pretoria [*South Africa*] [*ICAO location identifier*]   (ICLI)
FAPRA...... Federation of African Public Relations Association
FAPS......... Fakulta Architektury a Pozemniho Stavitelstvi [*Department of Architecture and Civil Engineering (of the Czech Institute of Technology in Prague)*]   (CZ)
FAPS......... Potchefstroom [*South Africa*] [*ICAO location identifier*]   (ICLI)
FAPsS....... Fellow of the Australian Psychological Society   (ADA)
FAPT........ Postmasburg [*South Africa*] [*ICAO location identifier*]   (ICLI)
FAPU........ Federacion de Asociaciones de Profesores Universitarios [*Federation of Associations of University Professors*] [*Venezuela*]   (LA)
FAPU........ Frente de Accion Popular Unida [*United Popular Action Front*] [*El Salvador*]   (LA)
FAPV........ Petrusville [*South Africa*] [*ICAO location identifier*]   (ICLI)
FAPY........ Parys [*South Africa*] [*ICAO location identifier*]   (ICLI)
FAPZ........ Progress [*South Africa*] [*ICAO location identifier*]   (ICLI)
FAQT........ Queenstown [*South Africa*] [*ICAO location identifier*]   (ICLI)
FAR........... Fabrica Adesivi Resine [*Italy*]
Far.............. Farsca [*Persian*]   (TU)
FAR........... Federal Department of Agricultural Research
FAR........... Federation of Arab Republics
FAR........... Fontenay-aux-Roses Nuclear Research Center [*Nuclear energy*] [*French*]   (NRCH)
FAR........... Football Association of Rhodesia
FAR........... Force d'Action Rapide [*Rapid Action Force*] [*French*]
FAR........... Forces Armees Royales [*Royal Armed Forces*] [*Morocco*]   (AF)
FAR........... Forces Armees Royales [*Royal Armed Forces*] [*Laos*]
FAR........... Foreign Affairs Research Documentation Center
FAR........... Forum Africain pour la Reconstruction [*Gabon*] [*Political party*]   (EY)
FAR........... Foundation for Australian Resources   (ADA)

FAR .... Fuerza Armada Revolucionaria Peruana [*Peruvian Revolutionary Armed Forces*]   (LA)

FAR .... Fuerzas Armadas Rebeldes [*Rebel Armed Forces*] [*Guatemala*]   (PD)

FAR .... Fuerzas Armadas Revolucionarias [*Revolutionary Armed Forces*] [*Mexico*]   (LA)

FAR .... Fuerzas Armadas Revolucionarias [*Revolutionary Armed Forces*] [*El Salvador*]   (LA)

FAR .... Fuerzas Armadas Revolucionarias [*Revolutionary Armed Forces*] [*Bolivia*]   (LA)

FAR .... Fuerzas Armadas Revolucionarias [*Revolutionary Armed Forces*] [*Argentina*]   (LA)

FAR .... Fuerzas Armadas Revolucionarias [*Revolutionary Armed Forces*] [*Cuba*]   (LA)

FAR .... Societe Franco-Africaine de Raffinage

FARA .... Fundo de Apoio a Reforma Agraria [*Agrarian Reform Assistance Fund*] [*Portuguese*]   (WER)

FARAC ...... Fuerzas Armadas Anticomunistas [*Anti-Communist Armed Forces*] [*Nicaragua*]   (PD)

FARACS .... Faculty of Anaesthetists, Royal Australasian College of Surgeons   (ADA)

FARAPAL ... Fertilizantes, Adubos, e Racoes Paulista Ltd. [*Brazil*]   (DSCA)

Farb............ Faerberei [*Dyeing*] [*German*]   (GCA)

Farb............ Farben [*Colors*] [*German*]

farb............ Farbig [*Colored*] [*Publishing*] [*German*]

FARB .... Federation of Australian Radio Broadcasters   (ADA)

FARB .... Richard's Bay [*South Africa*] [*ICAO location identifier*]   (ICLI)

Farbendr .... Farbendruck [*Color Print*] [*Publishing*] [*German*]

Farbentafln ... Farbentafeln [*Colored Plates*] [*Publishing*] [*German*]

Farbeverf.... Faerbeverfahren [*Dyeing Process*] [*German*]   (GCA)

farbl............ Farblos [*Colorless*] [*German*]

Farbochem ... Baltycka Skladnica Farb i Chemikalii [*Baltic Paint and Chemical Store*]   (POL)

Farbtaf .... Farbtafel [*Colored Plate*] [*Publishing*] [*German*]

Farbw .... Farbwerke [*Dyeworks*] [*German*]

FARC........ Family Advancement Resources Cooperative [*Australia*]

FARC........ Fijian-Australian Resource Centre

FARC........ Fuerzas Armadas Revolucionarias de Colombia [*Revolutionary Armed Forces of Colombia*]   (LA)

FARD .... Riversdale [*South Africa*] [*ICAO location identifier*]   (ICLI)

FARDENTAL ... Union Farmaceutica y Dental [*Colombia*]   (COL)

FAREA ...... Federacao da Agricultura do Estado do Amazonas [*Brazil*]   (DSCA)

FAREB ...... Federacao da Agricultura do Estado da Bahia [*Brazil*]   (DSCA)

FAREC ...... Federacao da Agricultura do Estado do Ceara [*Brazil*]   (DSCA)

FAREG ...... Federacao da Agricultura do Estado de Goias [*Brazil*]   (DSCA)

FAREGAZ ... Union des Fabricants Europeens de Regulateurs de Pression du Gaz [*Union of European Manufacturers of Gas Pressure Controllers*]   (EAIO)

FARELF .... Far East Land Forces   (ML)

FAREM ..... Federacao da Agricultura do Estado de Minas Gerais [*Brazil*]   (DSCA)

FAREMO ... Fabrica de Rebucados de Mocambique

FAREPE.... Federacao da Agricultura do Estado de Pernambuco [*Brazil*]   (DSCA)

FAREPI..... Federacao da Agricultura do Estado do Piaui [*Brazil*]   (DSCA)

FARES ...... Federacao da Agricultura do Estado do Espirito Santo [*Brazil*]   (DSCA)

FARESA..... Fazendas Reunidas SA [*Brazil*]   (DSCA)

FARESC.... Federacao da Agricultura do Estado de Santa Catarina [*Brazil*]   (DSCA)

FARESE.... Federacao da Agricultura do Estado de Sergipe [*Brazil*]   (DSCA)

fareskb .... Faareskindbind [*Bound in Sheepskin*] [*Publishing Danish/Norwegian*]

FARESP.... Federacao da Agricultura do Estado de Sao Paulo [*Brazil*]   (DSCA)

farf............. China Plant [*Topography*]   (RU)

farf-fayans ... China and Faience Plant [*Topography*]   (RU)

FARG........ Rustenburg [*South Africa*] [*ICAO location identifier*]   (ICLI)

FARGOAS ... Federacao da Agricultura do Estado de Alagoas [*Brazil*]   (DSCA)

fargtryckspl ... Faergtrycksplansch [*Color Plate*] [*Publishing*] [*Sweden*]

FARH .... Rehoboth [*Namibia*] [*ICAO location identifier*]   (ICLI)

FARIMA ... Fibreglass and Rockwool Insulation Manufacturers Association [*Australia*]

FARIMBONA ... Alliance of Protestant Youth Movements [*Malagasy*]   (AF)

FARK........ Forces Armees Royales Khmeres [*Royal Cambodian Armed Forces*] [*Replaced by FANK*]

FARK........ Rooikop [*South Africa*] [*ICAO location identifier*]   (ICLI)

FarkhIM-BAN ... Folklore Archives in the Institute of Music of the Bulgarian Academy of Sciences   (BU)

FARL .... Forces Armees Royales Libyennes

FARL........ Fractions Armees Revolutionnaires Libanaise [*Lebanese Armed Revolutionary Faction*]

FARL........ Lebanese Armed Revolutionary Factions

farm............ Farmaceutico [*Pharmacist, Chemist*] [*Portuguese*]

farm............ Farmacia [*Pharmacy*] [*Portuguese*]

farm........... Farmasia [*Pharmacology*] [*Finland*]

FARM....... Foundation for Agricultural and Research Management Systems [*South Africa*]   (AA)

farm........... Pharmaceutical   (RU)

farm........... Pharmacology, Pharmacologist   (BU)

FARMAD ... Laboratoires Pharmaceutiques Malgaches

farmak....... Pharmacology   (RU)

Farmakhim ... Pharmaceutical Chemistry   (BU)

FARMATO ... Federacao da Agricultura do Estado de Mato Grosso [*Brazil*]   (DSCA)

Farmatrest ... Pharmaceutical Industry Trust   (RU)

FARMIN... Pharmaceutical Institute   (RU)

FARMINDUSTRIA ... Associazione Nazionale delle Industrie Farmaceutiche [*Italy*]

Farmupravleniye ... Administration of United Chemical and Pharmaceutical Plants   (RU)

farmzavod .. Pharmaceutical Plant   (RU)

FARN .... Fuerzas Armadas de Resistencia Nacional [*Armed Forces of National Resistance*] [*El Salvador*]   (PD)

FARN .... Fuerzas Armadas Revolucionarias Nicaraguenses [*Nicaraguan Armed Revolutionary Forces*]   (PD)

FARO .... Frente Agropecuario de la Region Oriental [*Agricultural Front of the Eastern Region*] [*El Salvador*]   (LA)

FARO .... Frente de Accion Revolucionaria Obrera [*Revolutionary Workers Action Front*] [*Bolivia*]   (LA)

FARP........ Federacao da Agricultura do Estado do Parana [*Brazil*]   (DSCA)

FARP........ Forcas Armadas da Revolucao Popular [*People's Revolutionary Armed Forces*] [*Guinea*]   (AF)

FARP........ Forcas Armadas Revolucionarias do Povo

FARP........ Forces Armees Revolutionnaires du Peuple

FARP........ Frente Accion Revolucionaria del Pueblo [*People's Revolutionary Action Front*] [*El Salvador*]   (LA)

FARP........ Frente de Accion de la Resistencia Popular [*Popular Resistance Action Front*] [*El Salvador*]   (LA)

FARP........ Rosh Pinah [*Namibia*] [*ICAO location identifier*]   (ICLI)

FAR-PGT .. Fuerzas Armadas Revolucionarias - Partido Guatemalteco de Trabajo [*Revolutionary Armed Forces - Guatemalan Labor Party*]   (LA)

FARR........ Federatia Aeronautica Regala a Romaniei [*Romania*]

FARR........ Fortalor Aerieni Regale ale Romanei [*Royal Air Forces of Romania*]

FARRETOR ... Fabrica de Repuestos y Tornillos Ltda. [*Colombia*]   (COL)

FARS .... Federal Agricultural Research Stations [*Switzerland*]   (DSCA)

FARS .... Robertson [*South Africa*] [*ICAO location identifier*]   (ICLI)

FARSUL.... Federacao de Agricultura do Rio Grande Do Sul [*Rio Grande Do Sul Agricultural Federation*] [*Brazil*]   (LA)

FARTAC ... Federacion Agraria Revolucionaria Tupac Amaru del Cuzco [*Tupac Amaru Revolutionary Agrarian Federation of Cuzco*] [*Peru*]   (LA)

FARU .... Rundu [*Namibia*] [*ICAO location identifier*]   (ICLI)

farv .... Channel, Fairway [*Topography*]   (RU)

FARV........ Riverview [*South Africa*] [*ICAO location identifier*]   (ICLI)

farvefot....... Farvefotografi [*Color Photography*] [*Publishing Danish/Norwegian*]

farveillustr ... Farveillustration [*Color Illustration*] [*Publishing Danish/Norwegian*]

farvetr .... Farvetryk [*Color Print*] [*Publishing Danish/Norwegian*]

farvetvl .... Farvetavle [*Colored Plate*] [*Publishing Danish/Norwegian*]

FARVN...... Forces Armees de la Republique du Viet-Nam [*Armed Forces of the Republic of Vietnam*] [*Use ARVN or South Vietnamese Army*]   (CL)

FAS........... Associazione Nazionale Filosofia Arti Scienze [*Italian*]   (SLS)

FAS .... Family Allowance Supplement [*Australia*]

fas.............. Fasciculo [*Fascicle*] [*Portuguese*]

FAS........... Federacion Autonoma Sindical   (DSCA)

FAS........... Federation des Architectes Suisses [*Federation of Swiss Architects*]   (PDAA)

FAS........... Federation of African Societies

FAS........... Finnish Astronautical Society   (EAIO)

FAS........... Fonds Autonome de Soutien [*Autonomous Support Fund*] [*Benin*]   (AF)

FAS........... Football Association of Selangor   (ML)

FAS........... Football Association of Singapore   (ML)

FAS........... Forces Aeriennes Strategiques [*Strategic Air Force*] [*French*]   (WER)

FAS........... Foreign Area Studies

FAS........... Forschungsgemeinschaft fuer Altersfragen in der Schweiz [*Switzerland*]   (SLS)

FAS........... French Association for Standardization   (EAIO)

FAS........... French Atherosclerosis Society   (EAIO)

FAS........... Frente Autonomo Sindical [*Autonomous Trade Union Front*] [*Uruguay*]   (LA)

FAS........... Frontline Ammunition Depot   (RU)

FAS........... Fuerza Aerea Sandinista [*Sandinist Air Force*] [*Nicaragua*]   (LA)

FASA .... Automobile Manufacturing Plant, Inc. [*Spanish*]   (WER)

FASA .... Federacion Argentina de Sindicatos Agrarios [*Buenos Aires, Argentina*]   (LAA)

FASA......... Federation of ASEAN [*Association of South East Asian Nations*] Shipowners' Associations [*Kuala Lumpur, Malaysia*] (EAIO)
FASA......... Fellow of the Australian Society of Accountants (ADA)
FASA......... Filipino Association of South Australia
FASA......... Fonds Arabe Special pour l'Afrique [*Special Arab Fund for Africa*] (AF)
FASA......... Football Association of South Africa
FASA......... Frigorificos Argentinos Societe Anonima [*Argentine Meatpackers, Inc.*] (LA)
FASA......... Sani Pass [*South Africa*] [*ICAO location identifier*] (ICLI)
FASAB...... Front Autonomiste et Socialiste Autogestionnaire Bretonne [*Breton Autonomist and Socialist Self-Rule Front*] [*France*] [*Political party*] (PPE)
FASACO ... Fabrica de Sacos y Cordeleria [*Sacking and Rope Factory*] [*Dominican Republic*] (LA)
FASANOC ... Fiji Amateur Sports Association and National Olympic Committee (EAIO)
FASAP ...... Federacion de Asociaciones y Sindicatos Autonomos de Paysandu [*Federation of Autonomous Unions and Associations of Paysandu*] [*Uruguay*] (LA)
FASAP ...... Fellow of the Australian Society of Animal Production (ADA)
FASAS...... Federation of Asian Scientific Academies and Societies [*India*] (EY)
FASASA.... Fonds d'Action Sociale pour l'Amenagement des Structures Agricoles [*France*] (FLAF)
FASB........ Fellow of the Asiatic Society of Bengal
FASB........ Springbok [*South Africa*] [*ICAO location identifier*] (ICLI)
fasc........... Fascicolo [*Fascicle*] [*Italian*] (GPO)
fasc........... Fascicule [*Fascicle*] [*French*]
fasc........... Fasciculo [*Fascicle*] [*Portuguese*]
fasc........... Fascykul [*Fascicle*] [*Poland*]
FASC........ Secunda [*South Africa*] [*ICAO location identifier*] (ICLI)
FASCEAC ... Federation Algerienne des Syndicats du Commerce et de l'Industrie de l'Automobile et du Cycle
fascic......... Fascicule [*Part*] [*Publishing*] [*French*]
FASD........ Saldanha [*South Africa*] [*ICAO location identifier*] (ICLI)
FASE........ Federation Europeenne des Societes d'Acoustique [*Federation of Acoustical Societies of Europe*] (EAIO)
FASE........ Federation of Acoustical Societies of Europe (EAIO)
FASE........ Sanae [*South Africa*] [*ICAO location identifier*] (ICLI)
FASECOLDA ... Union de Aseguradores Colombianos [*Colombian Insurance Companies Union*] (LA)
faserform.... Faserfoermig [*Fibrous*] [*German*] (GCA)
FASF .... Southern Air Command [*South Africa*] [*ICAO location identifier*] (ICLI)
FASFID..... Federation des Associations et Societes Francaises d'Ingenieurs Diplomes [*Federation of French Associations and Societies of Chartered Engineers*] (PDAA)
FASG........ Schweizer Reneke [*South Africa*] [*ICAO location identifier*] (ICLI)
FASGUA ... Federacion Autonoma Sindical de Guatemala [*Autonomous Labor Federation of Guatemala*] (LA)
FASH........ Federacion Autentica Sindical Hondurena [*Authentic Trade Union Federation of Honduras*] (LA)
FASH........ Stellenbosch [*South Africa*] [*ICAO location identifier*] (ICLI)
fash dor ...... Fascine Road [*Topography*] (RU)
fash plot ..... Fascine Dam [*Topography*] (RU)
FASI .... Federacion Asturiana de Sindicatos Independientes [*Asturian Federation of Independent Trade Unions*] [*Spanish*] (WER)
FASI .... Springs [*South Africa*] [*ICAO location identifier*] (ICLI)
FASII........ Federation of Associations of Small Industries in India (PDAA)
Fask .... Fasikul [*Fascicule*] [*Section of a book*] (TU)
FASK........ Swartkop [*South Africa*] [*ICAO location identifier*] (ICLI)
FASL........ Sutherland [*South Africa*] [*ICAO location identifier*] (ICLI)
FASM........ Federation Algerienne des Sports Mecaniques (EAIO)
FASM....... Swakopmund [*Namibia*] [*ICAO location identifier*] (ICLI)
FASMEDICO ... Federacion de Asociaciones Medicas de Colombia [*Colombia*] (COL)
FASMF ..... Fellow of the Australian Sports Medicine Federation
FASN........ Senekal [*South Africa*] [*ICAO location identifier*] (ICLI)
FASOL...... Fabricas Associadas de Oleos Limitada
FASP .... Sir Lowry's Pass [*South Africa*] [*ICAO location identifier*] (ICLI)
FASPA ...... Federation Africaine des Syndicats du Petrole et Assimiles [*African Federation of Trade Unions of Oil and Petrochemicals*] [*Tripoli, Libya*] (EAIO)
FASR .... Standerton [*South Africa*] [*ICAO location identifier*] (ICLI)
FASRA ...... Foundation to Assist Scientific Research in Africa (EAIO)
FASS .... Federation Algerienne des Sports Scolaires
FASS .... Sishen [*South Africa*] [*ICAO location identifier*] (ICLI)
FASSA....... Fabrica de Acido Sulfurico, Sociedad Anonima [*Chile*] (LAA)
FASSA....... Fellow of the Academy of Social Sciences in Australia (ADA)
FASSA....... Fellow of the Australian Society of Sports Administrators
FASSU ...... Federation Algerienne des Sports Scolaires et Universitaires
FAST .... Falcon and SOPAC Air Transport [*Australia*]
FAST .... Federation Against Software Theft [*Australia*]

FAST .... Federazione delle Associazioni Scientifiche e Techniche [*Federation of Scientific and Technical Associations*] [*Italian*] (WER)
FAST .... Forecasting and Assessment in Science and Technology [*Commission of the European Communities program, 1978-1983*]
FAST .... Somerset East [*South Africa*] [*ICAO location identifier*] (ICLI)
FASTAR.... Fabrica de Espejos Star [*Colombia*] (COL)
FASTAS.... Fabrikasyon Ayakkabi Sanayi ve Ticaret Anonim Sirketi [*Shoe Manufacturing Industry and Corporation*] (TU)
FASTI........ Federation des Associations de Solidarite avec les Travailleurs Immigres [*France*]
FASTS....... Federation of Australian Scientific and Technological Societies
FASU......... Sace [*South Africa*] [*ICAO location identifier*] (ICLI)
FASV .... Floral Art Society of Victoria [*Australia*]
FASV .... Silvermine [*South Africa*] [*ICAO location identifier*] (ICLI)
FASW........ South West Africa Air Force Headquarters [*Namibia*] [*ICAO location identifier*] (ICLI)
FASX .... Swellendam [*South Africa*] [*ICAO location identifier*] (ICLI)
FASY .... Syferfontein [*South Africa*] [*ICAO location identifier*] (ICLI)
FASZ .... Skukuza [*South Africa*] [*ICAO location identifier*] (ICLI)
FAT........... Far Eastern Air Transportation Corp. [*Taiwan*] (IMH)
FAT........... Farner Air Transport AG [*Switzerland*] [*ICAO designator*] (FAAC)
fat.............. Fatigue [*Worn*] [*French*]
FAT........... Federation of Arab Teachers [*Iraq*] (EAIO)
FAT........... Foereningen Auktoriserade Translatorer [*Association of Authorized Translators*] [*Sweden*]
FAT........... Football Association of Tanzania
FAT........... Forces Armees Tchadiennes [*Chad Armed Forces*] (PD)
FAT........... Forces Armees Togolaises [*Togolese Armed Forces*] (AF)
FAT........... Forschungsvereinigung Automobiltechnik [*Automobile Research Association*] [*Germany*] (IRC)
FAT........... Frappe a Tort [*French*] (ADPT)
FAT........... Frente Autentico del Trabajo [*Authentic Labor Front*] [*Mexico*] (LA)
FAT........... Friends of Appropriate Technology [*Switzerland*]
FAT........... Societe Forestiere Africaine de Transports
FAT........... Swiss Federal Research Station for Farm Management and Agricultural Engineering
FATA .... Federation Arabe des Transports Aeriens [*North African*]
FATA........ Fondo Assicurativo Tra Agricoltori SpA [*Insurance*] [*Italy*] (EY)
FATA .... Foreign Acquisitions and Takeovers Act [*Australia*]
FATAA ...... Federation of Arab Travel Agents' Associations
FATAC...... Force Aerienne Tactique [*French tactical air command*]
FATACONES ... Fabrica Unida de Tacones de Madera Ltda. [*Colombia*] (COL)
FATAGA ... Federacion Argentina de Trabajadores de Aguas Gaseosas y Afines [*Soft Drink Workers Federation*] (LA)
FATAH ..... Palestine Liberation Movement (ME)
FATALCOS ... Fabrica de Talcos [*Colombia*] (COL)
FAT &VTC ... French Airedale Terrier and Various Terriers Club (EAIO)
FATAP ...... Federacion Argentina de Transportadores por Automotor de Pasajeros [*Argentine Federation of Automotive Passenger Carriers*] (LA)
FATC......... Federal Advanced Teachers College
FATC......... Tristan De Cunha [*South Africa*] [*ICAO location identifier*] (ICLI)
FATD........ Federal Association of Teachers of Dancing [*Australia*]
FATD(A)... Federal Association of Teachers of Dancing (Australia)
FATE........ Faipari Tudomanyos Egyesulet [*Scientific Association of the Lumber Industry*] (HU)
FATEIMA ... Fabrication Automatique de Tissus Elastiques Italo-Marocaine
FATELARES ... Fabrica Textil de Los Andes SA [*Colombia*] (COL)
FATH .... Thohoyandou [*South Africa*] [*ICAO location identifier*] (ICLI)
FATI .... Federacion Argentina de Trabajadores de la Imprenta [*Argentine Printers Federation*] (LA)
FATIA .... Federacion Argentina de Trabajadores de la Industria Alimentaria [*Food Industry Workers Federation*] (LA)
FATICA .... Federacion Argentina de Trabajadores de la Industria de Cuero y Afines [*Argentine Leather Workers Federation*] (LA)
FATIFA..... Federacion Argentina de Trabajadores de la Industria Fidera [*Argentine Federation of Alimentary Paste Workers*] (LA)
fatig........... Fatigue [*Worn*] [*French*]
FATIPEC .. Federation d'Associations de Techniciens des Industries de Peintures, Vernis, Emaux, et Encres d'Imprimerie de l'Europe [*Federation of the Associations of Technicians of the Paint, Varnish, and Ink Industries of Continental Europe*] (EAIO)
FATIPEC .. Federation des Associations des Techniciens des Industries des Peintures, Vernis, Emaux, et d'Encres d'Imprimerie de l'Europe Continentale [*Continental European Federation of Associations of Paint, Varnish, Enamel, and Printing Industry Technicians*] [*French*] (WER)

FATIQA .... Federacion Argentina de Trabajadores de la Industria Quimica y Afines [*Argentine Chemical Industry Workers Federation*] (LA)
FATIS .... Food and Agriculture Technical Information Service [*OECD*]
FATK .... Tsumkwe [*Namibia*] [*ICAO location identifier*] (ICLI)
FATLyF ..... Federacion Argentina de Trabajadores de Luz y Fuerza [*Argentine Federation of Light and Power Workers*] (LA)
FATM .... Forca Aerea de Transporte Militar [*Military Air Transport Force*] [*Brazil*] (LA)
FATM .... Tsumeb [*Namibia*] [*ICAO location identifier*] (ICLI)
FATME ..... Fabbrica Apparecchiature Telefoniche e Materiale Electtrico [*Italy*] (PDAA)
FATP .... Bloemfontein/New Tempe [*South Africa*] [*ICAO location identifier*] (ICLI)
FATPAC .... Fishing/Tourist Port Advisory Committee [*New South Wales, Australia*]
FATPREN ... Federacion Argentina de Trabajadores de la Prensa [*Argentine Press Workers Federation*] (LA)
FATR .... Fundacao de Assistencia ao Trabalhador Rural [*Brazil*] (DSCA)
FATRADANCA ... Fako Traditional and Cultural Association
FATRE ...... Federacion Argentina de Trabajadores Rurales y Estibadores [*Argentine Federation of Rural Workers and Stevedores*] (LA)
FATS .... South African Air Force Tactical Support Command [*ICAO location identifier*] (ICLI)
FATSA ...... Federacion de Asociaciones de Trabajadores de la Sanidad Argentina [*Argentine Federation of Associations of Sanitation Workers*] (LA)
FATSA ...... Federation of Amateur Theatrical Societies of South Africa
FATT .... Tutuka [*South Africa*] [*ICAO location identifier*] (ICLI)
FATUN ..... Federacion Argentina de Trabajadores de las Universidades Nacionales [*Argentine Federation of National University Workers*] (LA)
FATUREC ... Federation of Air Transport User Representatives in the European Community (DA)
FATW .... Foundation Against Trafficking in Women [*Netherlands*] (EAIO)
FATZ .... Tzaneen [*South Africa*] [*ICAO location identifier*] (ICLI)
FAU .... Faucher Aviation [*France*] [*ICAO designator*] (FAAC)
FAU .... Frente Antiimperialista Universitario [*University Anti-Imperialist Front*] [*Panama*] (LA)
FAU .... Frente de Accion Universitario [*University Action Front*] [*Costa Rica*] (LA)
FAU .... Fundacion Arte por Uruguay [*Formerly, Relatives Committee for Uruguay*] [*Sweden*] (EAIO)
FAUC .... Ulco [*South Africa*] [*ICAO location identifier*] (ICLI)
FAUH .... Uitenhage [*South Africa*] [*ICAO location identifier*] (ICLI)
FAUI .... Federacion de Agrupaciones Universitarias Integralistas [*Federation of Integralist University Groups*] [*Argentina*] (LA)
FAUI .... Federation of Australian Underwater Instructors (ADA)
FAUK .... Usakos [*Namibia*] [*ICAO location identifier*] (ICLI)
FAUL .... Ulundi [*South Africa*] [*ICAO location identifier*] (ICLI)
FAULT ...... Families Against Legal Trauma [*Australia*]
FAUP .... Upington/Pierre Van Ryneveld [*South Africa*] [*ICAO location identifier*] (ICLI)
FAUS .... Uis [*Namibia*] [*ICAO location identifier*] (ICLI)
FAUSA ...... Federation of Australian University Staff Associations (ADA)
FAusPr .... First Australia Prime Income Fund [*Associated Press*]
FAustCOG ... Fellow of the Australian College of Obstetricians and Gynaecologists
FAUT .... Umtata (K. D. Matanzima) [*South Africa*] [*ICAO location identifier*] (ICLI)
FAV .... Division of Aircraft Armament [*Air Force Academy*] (RU)
FAV .... Facultad de Agronomia y Veterinaria [*Buenos Aires, Argentina*] (LAA)
FAV .... Facultad de Agronomia y Veterinaria [*Paraguay*] (LAA)
FAV .... Fakarava [*French Polynesia*] [*Airport symbol*] (OAG)
FAV .... Finnaviation OY [*Finland*] [*ICAO designator*] (FAAC)
FAV .... Foldalatti Vasut [*Subway, Metro*] (HU)
FAV .... Fuerza Aerea Venezolana [*Air Force of Venezuela*]
FAVB .... Fabrica de Ventilatoare Bucuresti [*Bucharest Ventilator Factory*] (RO)
FAVB .... Vryburg [*South Africa*] [*ICAO location identifier*] (ICLI)
FAVD .... Vrede [*South Africa*] [*ICAO location identifier*] (ICLI)
Favda .... Favor [*Correspondence*] [*Spanish*]
FAVDO ..... Forum of African Voluntary Development Organizations
FAVE .... Ventersdorp [*South Africa*] [*ICAO location identifier*] (ICLI)
FAVF .... Federation des Associations Viticoles de France [*France*] (DSCA)
FAVG .... Durban/Virginia [*South Africa*] [*ICAO location identifier*] (ICLI)
FAVP .... Vanderbijlpark [*South Africa*] [*ICAO location identifier*] (ICLI)
FAVR .... Vredendal [*South Africa*] [*ICAO location identifier*] (ICLI)
FAVSO ...... French Association of Variable Star Observers (EAIO)
FAVU .... Volksrust [*South Africa*] [*ICAO location identifier*] (ICLI)
FAVV .... Vereeniging [*South Africa*] [*ICAO location identifier*] (ICLI)

FAVW .... Victoria West [*South Africa*] [*ICAO location identifier*] (ICLI)
FAVY .... Vryheid [*South Africa*] [*ICAO location identifier*] (ICLI)
FAW .... Fellowship of Australian Writers (ADA)
FAW .... Filmowa Agencja Wydawnicza [*Motion Picture Publication Agency*] (POL)
FAW .... First Automotive Works [*Chinese manufacturer*]
FAWA .... Federation of Asian Women's Associations [*San Marcelino, Philippines*]
FAWA .... Federation of Australian Winemaker Associations
FAWA .... Warmbaths [*South Africa*] [*ICAO location identifier*] (ICLI)
FAWAW ... Federation of Associates of West African Writers
FAWB .... Pretoria/Wonderboom [*South Africa*] [*ICAO location identifier*] (ICLI)
FAWC .... Federation of African Women's Clubs
FAWC .... Worcester [*South Africa*] [*ICAO location identifier*] (ICLI)
FAWD .... Warden [*South Africa*] [*ICAO location identifier*] (ICLI)
FAWE .... Windhoek/Eros [*Namibia*] [*ICAO location identifier*] (ICLI)
FAWH .... Windhoek/J. G. Strijdom [*Namibia*] [*ICAO location identifier*] (ICLI)
FAWI .... Witbank [*South Africa*] [*ICAO location identifier*] (ICLI)
FAWK .... Waterkloof [*South Africa*] [*ICAO location identifier*] (ICLI)
FAWL .... Williston [*South Africa*] [*ICAO location identifier*] (ICLI)
FAWM .... Welkom [*South Africa*] [*ICAO location identifier*] (ICLI)
FAWNA ..... Fostering and Assistance for Wildlife Needing Aid [*Australia*]
FAWNT .... Fellowship of Australian Writers, Northern Territory Chapter
FAWO ...... Willowmore [*South Africa*] [*ICAO location identifier*] (ICLI)
FAWP .... Wepener [*South Africa*] [*ICAO location identifier*] (ICLI)
FAWT .... Kingwilliamstown [*South Africa*] [*ICAO location identifier*] (ICLI)
FAWW ...... Windhoek [*South Africa*] [*ICAO location identifier*] (ICLI)
FAWY .... Wolseley [*South Africa*] [*ICAO location identifier*] (ICLI)
fax .... Facsimile (EECI)
fayans .... Faience Plant [*Topography*] (RU)
FAYP .... Ysterplaat [*South Africa*] [*ICAO location identifier*] (ICLI)
FAYTA .... Fumigadora Agricola y Transportes Aereos [*Ecuador*] (DSCA)
FAZ .... Football Association of Zambia
FAZ .... Forces Armees Zairoises [*Zairian Armed Forces*] (AF)
FAZA .... Force Aerienne Zairoise [*Zairian Air Force*] (AF)
FAZA .... Zastron [*South Africa*] [*ICAO location identifier*] (ICLI)
FAZR .... Zeerust [*South Africa*] [*ICAO location identifier*] (ICLI)
FB .... Bursa Airlines, Inc. [*Turkey*] [*ICAO designator*] (ICDA)
fb .... Felbor [*Half Leather*] [*Publishing*] [*Hungary*]
FB .... Felugyelo Bizottsag [*Supervisory Committee*] (HU)
FB .... Fener Bahce Spor Kulubu [*Fenerbahce Sports Club*] [*Istanbul*] (TU)
F/B .... Fert Basina [*Per Capita*] (TU)
FB .... Fertiliser Board [*Tasmania, Australia*]
FB .... Foiskolai Bajnoksag [*College Championships*] (HU)
FB .... Fondation de Bellerive [*Bellerive Foundation - BF*] (EAIO)
Fb .... Formenbau [*Mold Construction*] [*German*] (GCA)
FB .... Forschungsgemeinschaft Bekleidungsindustrie [*Research Association of the German Apparel Industry*] (EAIO)
FB .... Forskningsberedningen [*Sweden*] (SLS)
FB .... Found Brothers Aviation Ltd. [*Canada ICAO aircraft manufacturer identifier*] (ICAO)
FB .... Frab-Bank International [*Bank*] [*Switzerland*]
FB .... Franc Belge [*Belgian Franc*] [*Monetary unit*]
FB .... Frontline Base (RU)
FB .... High-Explosive Bomb (RU)
fb .... Paper Size (RU)
FB .... Promair Australia [*Airline code*]
FBA .... Fernmeldebauamt [*Signal Communications Construction Office*] (EG)
FBA .... Finnish Badminton Association (EAIO)
FBA .... Finnish Biathlon Association (EAIO)
FBA .... Frontline Bombardment Aviation (RU)
FBAA .... Federation of Bloodstock Agents Australia
FBAF .... Federation Belge des Alliances Francaises [*Belgium*] (SLS)
FBAJ .... Federation of Bankers Associations of Japan (EAIO)
FBAN .... Main Library of the Academy of Sciences (RU)
FBB .... Federation Belge de Boules [*Belgian Bocce Federation*] (EAIO)
FBB .... Fire Brigades Board [*Queensland, Australia*]
FBC .... Federal Bank for Co-Operatives [*Pakistan*] (GEA)
FBC .... Fourah Bay College [*Sierra Leone*]
FBCCI .... Federation of Bangladesh Chambers of Commerce and Industry (EAIO)
FBCE .... Federation Bancaire de la Communaute Europeenne [*Banking Federation of the European Community*] (EAIO)
FBCE .... Federation de Bourses de la Communaute Europeenne [*Federation of Stock Exchanges in the European Community*] (EAIO)
FBCF .... Formation Brute de Capital Fixe [*North African*]
FBCN .... Fundacao Brasileira para a Conservacao da Natureza [*Brazil*] (DSCA)
FBCO .... Camp Okavango [*Botswana*] [*ICAO location identifier*] (ICLI)

FBCSM ..... Federation Belge des Chambres Syndicales de Medecins
[*Belgium*] (SLS)
FBD .... Statens Trafikkflygerskole [*Norway*] [*ICAO designator*] (FAAC)
Fbdr .... Farbendruck [*Color Print*] [*Publishing*] [*German*]
FBE........... Federacao Brasileira de Escoteiros [*Portuguese*]
FBE........... Federation of Bank Employers [*British*] (DCTA)
FBE........... Fernbetriebseinheit [*German*] (ADPT)
FBEA........ Funeral and Bereavement Educators Association
FBEI .... Fonds du Bien-Etre Indigene
FBEP .... Federation Belge d'Education Physique [*Belgium*] (SLS)
FBF .... Folkbildningsforbundet [*National Swedish Federation of Adult
Education*] (EAIO)
FBFA .... Field Battery Federation Artillery (ML)
FBFC .... Societe Franco-Belge de Fabrication de Combustible [*Nuclear
energy*] [*French*] (NRCH)
FBFT .... Francistown [*Botswana*] [*ICAO location identifier*] (ICLI)
Fbg............ Faubourg [*Suburb*] [*Military map abbreviation World War I*]
[*French*] (MTD)
FBG .... Fosters Brewing Group [*Australia*] [*Commercial firm*]
FBGM....... Gomare [*Botswana*] [*ICAO location identifier*] (ICLI)
FBGZ......... Ghanzi [*Botswana*] [*ICAO location identifier*] (ICLI)
FBHA .... Free the Battery Hen Association [*Australia*]
FBHC .... Franciscan Brothers of the Holy Cross [*See also FFSC*]
[*Germany*] (EAIO)
FBHQ .... Gaborone Civil Aviation Headquarters [*Botswana*] [*ICAO
location identifier*] (ICLI)
FBI............ Fish Breeders' Association in Israel (EAIO)
FBI............ Fonds du Bien-Etre Indigene
FBI............ Forets et Bois d'Industrie
FBI............ Friends of the Brain Injured [*Australia*]
FBIA .... Fellow of the Bankers Institute of Australasia (ADA)
FBIA .... Food and Beverage Importers' Association [*Australia*]
FBICNSW ... Friends of Brain Injured Children of New South Wales
[*Australia*]
FBII .... Federasi Buruh Islam Indonesia [*Indonesian Moslem Workers
Federation*] (IN)
FBIL .... Foreign Business and Investments Law [*1973*] [*Oman*] (IMH)
FBIS......... Foreign Broadcast Information Service [*Paraguay*]
FBJW .... Jwaneng [*Botswana*] [*ICAO location identifier*] (ICLI)
Fbk............ Fabrik [*Factory, Manufacturer*] [*German*]
FBKE........ Kasane [*Botswana*] [*ICAO location identifier*] (ICLI)
FBKG........ Kang [*Botswana*] [*ICAO location identifier*] (ICLI)
FBKR........ Khwai River Lodge [*Botswana*] [*ICAO location identifier*]
(ICLI)
Fbksb .... Fabriksbesitzer [*German*]
Fbkt.......... Fabrikant [*German*]
FBKY........ Kanye [*Botswana*] [*ICAO location identifier*] (ICLI)
fbl .... Farblos [*Colorless*] [*German*] (GCA)
fbl .... Friblad [*Flyleaf*] [*Publishing Danish/Norwegian*]
FBLO........ Lobatse [*Botswana*] [*ICAO location identifier*] (ICLI)
fbls .... Farblos [*Colorless*] [*German*] (GCA)
FBM .... Federacao de Badminton de Mexico [*Badminton Federation of
Mexico*] (EAIO)
FBM .... Franco-Belge Monegasque
FBM .... Lubumbashi [*Zaire*] [*Airport symbol*] (OAG)
FBMG....... Machaneng [*Botswana*] [*ICAO location identifier*] (ICLI)
FBML....... Molepolole [*Botswana*] [*ICAO location identifier*] (ICLI)
FBMM...... Makalamabedi [*Botswana*] [*ICAO location identifier*] (ICLI)
FBMN ...... Maun [*Botswana*] [*ICAO location identifier*] (ICLI)
FBMS .... Mosetse [*Botswana*] [*ICAO location identifier*] (ICLI)
FBMV....... Federacion Boliviana de Medicos Veterinarios [*Bolivia*] (DSCA)
FBN .... Fabrique de Batteries Nico
FBNN .... Nokaneng [*Botswana*] [*ICAO location identifier*] (ICLI)
FBNT........ Nata [*Botswana*] [*ICAO location identifier*] (ICLI)
FBNW ...... Gaborone Notwane [*Botswana*] [*ICAO location identifier*]
(ICLI)
FBOK........ Okwa [*Botswana*] [*ICAO location identifier*] (ICLI)
FBON .... Main Library of Social Sciences (of the Academy of Sciences,
USSR) (RU)
FBOR........ Orapa [*Botswana*] [*ICAO location identifier*] (ICLI)
FBP........... Fabrika Bicikla "Partizan" [*"Partisan" Bicycle Factory*]
[*Subotica*] (YU)
FBP........... Formularbeschreibungsprogramm [*German*] (ADPT)
FBP........... Fortschrittliche Buergerpartei [*Progressive Citizens' Party*]
[*Liechtenstein*] (PPW)
FBPA .... Pandamatenga [*Botswana*] [*ICAO location identifier*] (ICLI)
FBPY .... Palapye [*Botswana*] [*ICAO location identifier*] (ICLI)
FBR........... Federal Bureau of Investigation [*FBI*] (RU)
FBR........... Forschungsberichte Bundesrepublik Deutschland
[*Fachinformationszentrum Karlsruhe GmbH*] [*Germany*]
[*Information service or system*] (CRD)
FBR........... Forskningsbiblioteksradet [*Sweden*] (SLS)
FBR........... Foundation for Basic Research [*Russia*]
FBRAIP..... Fellow of the British and Royal Australian Institute of Physics
FBRK........ Rakops [*Botswana*] [*ICAO location identifier*] (ICLI)
FBRO........ Foreign Bank Representative Office

FBS........... Fernbetriebssystem [*German*] (ADPT)
FBS........... Finnish Biochemical Society (EAIO)
FBS........... Fisheries Board of Sweden (MSC)
FBS........... Franco Belgian Services (DS)
FBS........... Fundusz Budowy Szkol [*School-Building Fund*] [*Poland*]
FBSB .... Finance Brokers Supervisory Board [*Western Australia*]
FBSD........ Serondela [*Botswana*] [*ICAO location identifier*] (ICLI)
FBSI......... All Indonesian Labor Federation (IMH)
FBSiOK..... Fundusz Budowy Szkol i Osrodkow Kulturalnych [*Fund for the
Construction of Schools and Cultural Centers*] (POL)
FBSK .... Gaborone/Sir Seretse Khama [*Botswana*] [*ICAO location
identifier*] (ICLI)
FBSNSW... French Benevolent Society of New South Wales [*Australia*]
FBSP......... Selebi-Phikwe [*Botswana*] [*ICAO location identifier*] (ICLI)
FBSR .... Serowe [*Botswana*] [*ICAO location identifier*] (ICLI)
FBSV .... Savuti [*Botswana*] [*ICAO location identifier*] (ICLI)
FBSW .... Shakawe [*Botswana*] [*ICAO location identifier*] (ICLI)
FBSWA ..... Federation of Building Societies of Western Australia
FBT........... Football Thai Factory Ltd. [*Thailand*]
FBT........... Fringe Benefit Tax [*New Zealand*]
FBTE .... Tshane [*Botswana*] [*ICAO location identifier*] (ICLI)
FBTL .... Tuli Lodge [*Botswana*] [*ICAO location identifier*] (ICLI)
FBTPIU..... Federated Brick, Tile, and Pottery Industrial Union of Australia
FBTS .... Tshabong [*Botswana*] [*ICAO location identifier*] (ICLI)
FBU .... Franc Burundaise [*Burundi Franc*] [*Monetary unit*] (AF)
FBU .... Fraternite Blanche Universelle [*Universal White Brotherhood*]
[*France*] (EAIO)
FBU .... Freie-Buerger-Union [*Free Citizens' Union*] [*Germany*] (PPW)
FBVA........ Forstliche Bundesversuchsanstalt [*Federal Forest Research
Station*] [*Austria*] (ARC)
FBVAVT ... Main Library of Foreign Literature of the All-Union Academy of
Foreign Trade (RU)
FBVS .... Federation Belge des Vins et Spiritueux [*Belgium*] (EAIO)
FBW.......... Federation of Black Women
FBW.......... Filmbewertungsstelle Wiesbaden (SLS)
FBW.......... Forschungsgemeinschaft Bauen und Wohnen, Zentrale
Forschungsstelle Baden-Wurttemberg fuer Bauwesen,
Stadtebau und Raumplanung [*Baden-Wurttemberg Central
Agency for Building, Urban Development, and Regional and
Country Planning*] [*Research center*] (IRC)
FBXG........ Xugana [*Botswana*] [*ICAO location identifier*] (ICLI)
FBXX........ Xaxaba [*Botswana*] [*ICAO location identifier*] (ICLI)
FC .... Federacion Campesina [*Venezuela*] (EY)
FC .... Federacion de Comunistas [*Federation of Communists*]
[*Spanish*] (WER)
FC .... Federal Cabinet [*Australia*]
FC .... Fehmi and Co. [*Uganda*]
FC .... Feiten & Ceifers [*Benelux*] (BAS)
FC .... Ferrocarril [*Railroad*] [*Spanish*]
fc................ Fin Courant [*At the End of the Present Month*] [*French*]
FC .... Fire Control [*Royal Australian Navy*]
FC .... Fluoridation Committee [*Tasmania, Australia*]
FC .... Formal Conference on Weights and Measures [*Australia*]
FC .... Foundation for Children [*Thailand*] (EAIO)
FC .... Fournitures Courantes (FLAF)
fc................ Franco [*Shipping Costs Paid*] [*French*]
FC .... Francs Congolais [*Benelux*] (BAS)
FC .... Freres de la Charite [*Brothers of Charity*] (EAIO)
FC .... Front Commun
fc................ Fuori Commercio [*Not for Sale*] [*Publishing*] [*Italian*]
FCA........... Family Court of Australia
FCA........... Federated Council of Academics [*Australia*]
FCA........... Federation Camerounaise d'Athletisme
FCA........... Federation of Central Africa
FCA........... Federation of Commodity Associations (EAIO)
FCA........... Fellow of the Institute of Chartered Accountants in Australia
(ADA)
FCA........... Filipino Cultural Association [*Australia*]
FCA........... Finance Corporation of Australia Ltd. (ADA)
FCA........... Financial Corporations Act [*Australia*]
FCA........... Fishing Clubs of Australia
FCA........... Fonciere de la Cote d'Afrique
FCA........... Fondo de Credito Agropecuario [*Agriculture and Livestock Credit
Fund*] [*Venezuela*] (LA)
FCA........... Foreign Correspondents Association
FCA........... France Cote d'Afrique Assurances
FCA........... Fur Council of Australia
FCAA........ Federacion de Cooperativas Arroceras Argentinas [*Argentina*]
(DSCA)
FCAA........ Federal Council for Aboriginal Advancement [*Australia*] (ADA)
FCAA........ Federated Confectioners' Association of Australia
FCAA........ Fellow of the Australasian Institute of Cost Accountants (ADA)
FCAA........ Foreign Correspondents' Association of Australia
FCAAA...... Federal Council of Australian Apiarists' Associations (ADA)
FCAATSI .. Federal Council for the Advancement of Aborigines and Torres
Strait Islanders [*Australia*] (ADA)

FCA(Aust) ... Fellow of the Institute of Chartered Accountants in Australia (ADA)
FCAC......... Field Crop Advisory Committee [*Western Australia*]
FCACV...... Federacion de Cooperativas de Ahorro y Credito de Venezuela [*Venezuela*] (DSCA)
FCAI.......... Federal Chamber of Automotive Industries [*Australia*] (PDAA)
FCAIA ...... Fellow of the Customs Agents Institute of Australia (ADA)
FCAM........ Federation Cotonniere d'Afrique Francophone et de Madagascar
FCANSW .. Floor Coverings Association of New South Wales [*Australia*]
FCap .... French Capitol [*Record label*]
FCAS......... Federation of Commercial Agents of Sweden (EAIO)
FCAT......... Societe Franco-Centrafricaine des Tabacs
FCB............ Federacion Chilena de Bochas [*Chilean Bocce Federation*] (EAIO)
FCB............ Federation Camerounaise de Boxe
FCB............ Film Censorship Board [*Australia*]
FCB............ First Commercial Bank [*Taiwan*]
FCB............ Food Corporation of Bhutan (GEA)
FCB............ Fundacao do Cinema Brasileiro [*Brazilian Film Foundation*] (EAIO)
FCBA......... Foreign Currency Borrowers' Association [*Australia*]
FCBA......... Friesland Cattle Breeders' Association of South Africa (AA)
FCBA......... Lalouila [*Congo*] [*ICAO location identifier*] (ICLI)
FCBASA.... Friesland Cattle Breeders' Association of South Africa (EAIO)
FCBB .... Brazzaville/Maya Maya [*Congo*] [*ICAO location identifier*] (ICLI)
FCBB .... Federation Camerounaise de Basket-Ball
FCBD .... Djambala [*Congo*] [*ICAO location identifier*] (ICLI)
FCBG......... Madingou [*Congo*] [*ICAO location identifier*] (ICLI)
FCBGH ..... French Committee for Big Game Hunting (EAIO)
FCBK......... Kindamba [*Congo*] [*ICAO location identifier*] (ICLI)
FCBL .... Lague [*Congo*] [*ICAO location identifier*] (ICLI)
FCBM........ Mouyondzi [*Congo*] [*ICAO location identifier*] (ICLI)
FCBO........ M'Pouya [*Congo*] [*ICAO location identifier*] (ICLI)
FCBP .... M'Passa [*Congo*] [*ICAO location identifier*] (ICLI)
FCBS .... Sibiti [*Congo*] [*ICAO location identifier*] (ICLI)
FCBT .... Loutete [*Congo*] [*ICAO location identifier*] (ICLI)
FCBU......... Aubeville [*Congo*] [*ICAO location identifier*] (ICLI)
FCBV .... Brazzaville [*Congo*] [*ICAO location identifier*] (ICLI)
FCBY .... N'Kay/Yokangassi [*Congo*] [*ICAO location identifier*] (ICLI)
FCBZ .... Zanaga [*Congo*] [*ICAO location identifier*] (ICLI)
FCC............ Federation Camerounaise de Cyclisme
FCC............ Fight Crime Committee [*Hong Kong*]
FCC............ Filipino Community Cooperative [*Australia*]
FCC............ Firearms Consultative Committee [*Australia*]
FCC............ First Capital Corp. [*Singapore*]
FCC............ Flota Camaronera de Cuba [*Cuban Shrimp Fleet*] (LA)
FCC............ Foreign Correspondents Club of Japan (NTCM)
FCC............ Franchising Counselling Centre [*Australia*]
FCC............ French Chamber of Commerce (DCTA)
FCCAE ...... Fellow of Canberra College of Advanced Education [*Australia*]
FCCBE ...... Federation des Chambres de Commerce Belges a l'Etranger (EAIO)
FCCC........ Brazzaville [*Congo*] [*ICAO location identifier*] (ICLI)
FCCC......... Federacion de Camaras de Comercio del Istmo Centroamericano [*El Salvador*] (DSCA)
FCCf.......... Flota Camaronera de Cienfuegos [*Cienfuegos Shrimp Fleet*] [*Cuba*] (LA)
FCCI.......... Federation des Chambres de Commerce et d'Industrie [*Federation of Chambers of Commerce and Industry*] [*Morocco*] (AF)
FCCIA ...... French Chamber of Commerce and Industry in Australia
FCCMAR .. Federation Centrale du Credit Mutuel Agricole et Rural [*France*] (EAIO)
FCCN........ Fellowship of Churches of Christian Nigeria
FCCS .... Federation of Chambers of Commerce of Spain (EAIO)
FCCV .... Feline Control Council of Victoria [*Australia*]
FCD .... Fonds Communautaire de Developpement [*Community Development Fund*] (AF)
FCD .... Frente Civico Democratico [*Civilian Democratic Front*] [*Guatemala*] [*Political party*] (PPW)
FCD .... Frente de Cabo Delgado
FCD .... Front Congolais pour le Restauration de la Democratie [*Belgium*] [*Political party*] (EY)
FCD .... Front Congolais pour le Retablissement de la Democratie [*Zaire*] [*Political party*] (EY)
FCDA........ Federal Capital Development Authority [*Abuja, Nigeria*]
FCDC........ Fertilizer and Chemical Development Council [*Israel*]
FCDD .... Fraternidade Crista de Doentes e Deficientes [*Brazil*] (EAIO)
FCE........... Fianarantsoa-Cote Est
FCE........... Fondo de Cultura Economica [*Economic Culture Fund*] [*Mexico*] (LA)
FCE........... Furnas Centrais Electricas SA [*Furnas Electric Power Plants, Inc.*] [*Brazil*] (LA)
FCEA......... Fellow, Association of Cost and Executive Accountants

FCEGAC ... Federacion de Centros y Entidades Gremiales de Acopiadores de Cereales [*Argentina*] (DSCA)
FCEI .... Fraternidad Cristiana de Enfermos e Impedidos [*Bolivia*] (EAIO)
FCEM....... Federatia Comunitatilor Evreiesti Mozaice [*Federation of Jewish Communities*] (RO)
FCEM........ Femmes Chefs d'Entreprises Mondiales [*World Association of Women Entrepreneurs*] (EAIO)
FCEM........ Foreign Capital Export Manufacturing
FCES .... Fellow of the Commercial Education Society of Australia (ADA)
FCES(Aust) ... Fellow of the Commercial Education Society of Australia
FC et S .... Franc de Capture, Saisie, Arret, Contrainte ou Detention [*Clause d'Assurance*] (FLAF)
FCFA .... El Faisal Clearing & Forwarding Agency [*Bahrain*]
FCG .... Federacion Campesina de Guatemala [*Guatemalan Peasant Federation*] (LA)
FCGI.......... Federazione Comunista della Gioventu Italiana [*Italian Communist Youth Federation*] (WER)
FCGOG ..... Fraktion Christlicher Gewerkschafter im Osterreichischen Gewerkschaftsbund [*Austrian Trade Union Federation - Christian Faction*] (EAIO)
FCGU .... Film-und Computer-Unterstuetzter Gruppenunterricht [*German*] (ADPT)
FCH .... Flight-Chernobyl Association [*Russian Federation*] [*ICAO designator*] (FAAC)
FCH .... Fortune Communications Holdings Ltd. [*Australia*]
FCH .... Foundation for Cooperative Housing
FCH .... Freightlines and Construction Holdings [*Australia*]
FCH .... Fundacion Chile [*Chile Foundation*] [*Research center*] (IRC)
f-ch .... Phot-Hour (RU)
FCHB .... Federation Camerounaise de Hand-Ball
FChD .... Phase-Sensitive Discriminator (RU)
FCHP........ Federacion de Choferes del Peru [*Peruvian Federation of Drivers*] (LA)
FChV .... Phase-Sensitive Rectifier (RU)
FCI............ Factors Chain International [*Netherlands*]
FCI............ Fan Circle International (EA)
FCI............ Federacion de Campesinos de Ica [*Federation of Ica Farmers*] [*Peru*] (LA)
FCI............ Federated Chamber of Industries [*South Africa*] (IMH)
FCI............ Federation Colombophile Internationale [*International Pigeon Federation - IPF*] (EAIO)
FCI............ Federation Cynologique Internationale [*International Federation of Kennel Clubs*] [*Thuin, Belgium*] (EA)
FCI............ Fertiliser Corp. of India (PDAA)
FCI............ Fondo de Credito Industrial [*Industrial Credit Fund*] [*Venezuela*] (LA)
FCI............ Food Corp. of India
FCI............ Framatome Connectors International [*Commercial firm*] (ECON)
FCI............ Freedom Communications International News Agency (EAIO)
FCI............ Fysisch Chemisch Instituut [*Institute for Physical Chemistry*] [*Netherlands Central Organization for Applied Natural Scientific Research*] (WED)
FCI............ International Federation of Kennel Clubs [*Belgium*] (EAIO)
FCI............ South African Federated Chamber of Industries
FCIA .... Fellow of the Catering Institute of Australia (ADA)
FCIA .... Foreign Credit Insurance Association [*New York, NY*] (EA)
FCIAS........ Fundacion Centro de Investigacion y Accion Social [*Argentina*] (EAIO)
FCIB .... Fellow of the Confederation of Insurance Brokers of Australia
FCID .... Federal Court Industrial Division [*Australia*]
FCIE .... Fondo Centroamericano de Integracion Economica (LAA)
FCIM........ Federation des Concours Internationaux de Musique [*Federation of International Music Competitions - FIMC*] (EAIO)
FCISA .... Fellow of the Institute of Chartered Secretaries and Administrators [*Australia*]
FCIT .... Fellow of the Chartered Institute of Transport [*South Africa*] (AA)
FCIV .... Fellow of the Commonwealth Institute of Valuers [*Australia*] (ADA)
FCJ .... Federation Camerounaise de Judo [*Cameroonian Federation of Judo*]
FCJDA ...... Federation Cambodgienne de Judo et des Disciplines Assimilees [*Cambodian Federation of Judo and Related Skills*] (CL)
FCJNA ...... Front Commun de la Jeunesse Nationaliste de l'Angola
FCJP......... Flemish Commission for Justice and Peace [*Belgium*] (EAIO)
FCL............ Federacion Campesina Latinoamericana [*Latin American Peasant Federation*] (LA)
FCL............ Federation Camerounaise de Lutte
FCL............ Femme Couleur Libre [*French*] (DLA)
FCL............ Fletcher Challenger Ltd. [*New Zealand*]
FCLAVP.... Flammable and Combustible Liquids Appeal and Variations Panel [*Queensland, Australia*]
FCLN......... Frente Civico de Liberacion Nacional [*Civic Front for National Liberation*] [*FRECILNA*] [*Also,*] [*Argentina*] (LA)

FCLT .... Federation Camerounaise de Lawn-Tennis [*Cameroonian Federation of Lawn-Tennis*]
FCM .... Federation of Muslim Councillors   (MENA)
FCM .... Fellowship of Christian Motorcyclists [*Welwyn Garden City, England*]   (EAIO)
FCM .... Flota Camaronera del Mariel [*Mariel Shrimp Fleet*] [*Cuba*]   (LA)
FCM .... Flying Cargo Private Ltd. [*Maldives*] [*ICAO designator*]   (FAAC)
FCMA........ Mavinza [*Congo*] [*ICAO location identifier*]   (ICLI)
FCMB........ N'Ziba [*Congo*] [*ICAO location identifier*]   (ICLI)
FCMD .... Vouka/Sidetra [*Congo*] [*ICAO location identifier*]   (ICLI)
FCME........ Fabrica de Cabluri si Materiale Electroizolante [*Factory for Cables and Electrical Insulation Materials*]   (RO)
FCMF .... Loufoula [*Congo*] [*ICAO location identifier*]   (ICLI)
FCMG .... Gokango [*Congo*] [*ICAO location identifier*]   (ICLI)
FCMI........ Irogo [*Congo*] [*ICAO location identifier*]   (ICLI)
FCMK........ Kele/Kibangou [*Congo*] [*ICAO location identifier*]   (ICLI)
FCML........ Leboulou [*Congo*] [*ICAO location identifier*]   (ICLI)
FCMM ...... Mossendjo [*Congo*] [*ICAO location identifier*]   (ICLI)
FCMN .... N'Gongo [*Congo*] [*ICAO location identifier*]   (ICLI)
FCMO........ Vouka/Mandoro [*Congo*] [*ICAO location identifier*]   (ICLI)
FCMR........ Marala [*Congo*] [*ICAO location identifier*]   (ICLI)
FCMS........ Foreign Christian Missionary Society
FCMS........ Nyanga [*Congo*] [*ICAO location identifier*]   (ICLI)
FCMT........ Bekol/Thomas [*Congo*] [*ICAO location identifier*]   (ICLI)
FCMY........ Mayoko/Legala [*Congo*] [*ICAO location identifier*]   (ICLI)
FCMZ........ N'Zabi [*Congo*] [*ICAO location identifier*]   (ICLI)
FCN .... Fairfax Community Newspapers Proprietary Ltd. [*Australia*]
FCN .... Falcon Aviation AB [*Sweden*] [*ICAO designator*]   (FAAC)
FCN .... Treaty of Friendship, Commerce, and Navigation [*Indonesia*]   (IMH)
FCNA .... Fellow of the College of Nursing, Australia   (ADA)
FCN(Aust) ... Fellow of the College of Nursing (Australia)
FCN(NSW) ... Fellow of the College of Nursing, New South Wales [*Australia*]
FCNSW ..... Forestry Commission of New South Wales [*Australia*]
FCO .... Aerofrisco [*Mexico*] [*ICAO designator*]   (FAAC)
FCO .... Facklig Central-Organisation [*Trade Union Central Organization on the Local Level*] [*Sweden*]   (WEN)
FCO .... Federal Cartel Office
FCO .... Franco [*Free of Charge*] [*Shipping*] [*Spanish*]
FCO .... Franco [*Free of Charge*] [*Shipping*] [*Italian*]
fco .... Franco [*Free of Charge*] [*Shipping*] [*French*]
fco............ Fuori Commercio Originale [*Originally Not for Sale*] [*Publishing*] [*Italian*]
FCO .... Rome [*Italy*] Leonardo Da Vinci (Fium) Airport [*Airport symbol*]   (OAG)
FCOB........ Boundji [*Congo*] [*ICAO location identifier*]   (ICLI)
FCOCB ..... Fabrica de Carton Ondulat si Confectii Bucuresti [*Corrugated Cardboard and Clothing Factory in Bucharest*]   (RO)
FCOE........ Ewo [*Congo*] [*ICAO location identifier*]   (ICLI)
FCOG .... Gamboma [*Congo*] [*ICAO location identifier*]   (ICLI)
FCOI.......... Impfondo [*Congo*] [*ICAO location identifier*]   (ICLI)
FCOK .... Kelle [*Congo*] [*ICAO location identifier*]   (ICLI)
FCOL........ Loukolela [*Congo*] [*ICAO location identifier*]   (ICLI)
FCOM ...... Makoua [*Congo*] [*ICAO location identifier*]   (ICLI)
FCOO .... Owando [*Congo*] [*ICAO location identifier*]   (ICLI)
fcos .... Francos [*Franks*] [*Spanish*]
FCOS........ Souanke [*Congo*] [*ICAO location identifier*]   (ICLI)
FCOT........ Betou [*Congo*] [*ICAO location identifier*]   (ICLI)
FCOU .... Ouesso [*Congo*] [*ICAO location identifier*]   (ICLI)
FCP .... Fabrika Celuloze Prijedor [*Cellulose Factory, Prijedor*]   (YU)
FCP .... Federal Country Party [*Australia*]   (ADA)
FCP........... Federazione dei Chimici e Petrolieri [*Federation of Chemical and Petroleum Workers*] [*Italian*]
FCP........... Flight Corp. [*New Zealand*] [*ICAO designator*]   (FAAC)
FCP........... Flota Cubana de Pesca [*Cuban Fishing Fleet*]   (LA)
FCP........... Fonds Commun de Placement [*Mutual Fund*] [*French*]
FCPA .... Foreign Corrupt Practices Act [*1977*]
FCPA .... Makabana [*Congo*] [*ICAO location identifier*]   (ICLI)
FCPAG ...... Federacion de Comunicacion, Papel y Artes Graficos [*Spain*]   (EAIO)
FCPAL ...... Ferrocarril Presidente Carlos Antonio Lopez [*Paraguayan railway*]   (IMH)
FCPB .... Bangamba [*Congo*] [*ICAO location identifier*]   (ICLI)
FCPB .... Fremantle Class Patrol Boat [*Australia*]
FCPD........ Loudima [*Congo*] [*ICAO location identifier*]   (ICLI)
FCPE .... Leganda [*Congo*] [*ICAO location identifier*]   (ICLI)
FCPG........ Kibangou [*Congo*] [*ICAO location identifier*]   (ICLI)
FCPI .... Vounda/Loubetsi [*Congo*] [*ICAO location identifier*]   (ICLI)
FCPK .... N'Komo [*Congo*] [*ICAO location identifier*]   (ICLI)
FCPL .... Loubomo [*Congo*] [*ICAO location identifier*]   (ICLI)
FCPM .... M'Baya [*Congo*] [*ICAO location identifier*]   (ICLI)
FCPMA ..... Federacao das Cooperativas de Produtores de Mate Amambai Ltd. [*Brazil*]   (DSCA)
FCPMH..... Foundation Care of People with a Mental Handicap [*Netherlands Antilles*]   (EAIO)

FCPN........ Ferrocarril del Pacifico de Nicaragua [*Nicaragua*]   (LAA)
FCPN........ Noumbi [*Congo*] [*ICAO location identifier*]   (ICLI)
FCPO........ Pemo [*Congo*] [*ICAO location identifier*]   (ICLI)
FCPP .... Federal Colored Peoples Party [*South Africa*]   (AF)
FCPP........ Pointe-Noire [*Congo*] [*ICAO location identifier*]   (ICLI)
FCPPA ..... Front Commun des Partis Politiques de l'Angola
FCPV .... Federacion de Contadores Publicos de Venezuela [*Federation of Public Accountants of Venezuela*]   (LA)
FCPY .... Loukanyi [*Congo*] [*ICAO location identifier*]   (ICLI)
FCR........... France Cables & Radio Co. [*France*] [*Telecommunications*]
FCR........... Front Communiste Revolutionnaire [*Revolutionary Communist Front*] [*French*]   (WER)
FCRA........ Fellow of the College of Radiologists of Australasia   (ADA)
FCRA........ Fellow of the College of Radiologists of Australia
FCRAP ..... Federation of Cattle Raisers Association of the Philippines   (DS)
FCRIM...... Freight Committee of the Rubber Industry of Malaysia   (PDAA)
FCR-PGT .. Frente Central de Resistencia-Partido Guatemalteco del Trabajo [*Political party*]   (EY)
FCRT .... Fabrica de Casete Radio si Televizoare [*Factory for Radio and Television Cabinets*]   (RO)
FCRVC ...... Federacion de Cooperativas Regionales de Venta en Comun Cacaoteros de Tabasco [*Mexico*]   (DSCA)
fcs.............. Facsimile [*Facsimile*] [*Publishing*] [*Italian*]
FCS .... Federation of Catholic Scouts [*Belgium*]   (EAIO)
FCS .... Fiji Computer Society   (EAIO)
FCS .... Financial Computing Services of Australia Proprietary Ltd.
FCS .... Finnish Cardiac Society   (EAIO)
FCS .... Foreign Commercial Service [*International Trade Administration*]
FCS .... Frederic Chopin Society [*Later, IFCF*]   (EA)
FCS .... Free Church of Scotland
FCS .... French Chemical Society [*See also SFC*]   (EAIO)
FCSA .... Family and Children's Services Agency [*New South Wales, Australia*]
FCSC .... Flowers Cove Shipping Co. [*Bahrain*]
FCSC .... Foreign Claims Settlement Committee
FCSCJ ...... Filles de la Charite du Sacre-Coeur de Jesus [*Daughters of Charity of the Sacred Heart of Jesus*] [*France*]   (EAIO)
FCSF........ Festival Ceskoslovenskeho Filmu [*or Filmovy Ceskoslovensky Festival*] [*Czechoslovak Film Festival*]   (CZ)
FCSF........ Finnish Central Sports Federation   (EAIO)
FCSFB .... Financiere Credit Suisse First Boston [*Switzerland*]
FCSMPEUA ... Federated Cold Storage and Meat Preserving Employees' Union of Australia
FCSMPUA ... Federated Cold Storage and Meat Preserving Union of Australia
FCSMR ..... Fonds Commun des Societes Mutuelles Rurals
FCSN........ Federation Camerounaise de Sports Nautiques
FCSP .... Fonds Commun des Societes de Prevoyance
FCSPP....... French Committee for the Study of Paranormal Phenomena   (EAIO)
FCSU .... Federation of Civil Service Unions [*Mauritius*] [*FSCC*] [*See also*]   (AF)
FCSWC ..... Federation of Community Sporting and Workers' Clubs [*Australia*]
FCT........... Federal Capital Territory [*Later, ACT*] [*Australia*]
F ct .... Fin Courant [*At the End of the Present Month*] [*French*]
FCT........... Foreign Currency Translation
FCT........... Forestry Commission of Tasmania [*Australia*]
FCT........... Front Commun de Transport [*Common Transportation Front*] [*Mauritius*]   (AF)
FCTCA ...... Federal Capital Territory Cricket Association [*Australia*]
FCTV .... Federacion de Cooperativas de Transporte de Venezuela [*Venezuela*]   (DSCA)
FCTW .... Federation of Cairo Transport Workers
FCU .... Federacion de Centros Universitarios [*Federation of University Centers*] [*Venezuela*]   (LA)
FCUA .... Federated Clerks' Union of Australia
FCUSAA .... Federated Council of University Staff Associations of Australia   (ADA)
FCV........... Federacion Campesina de Venezuela [*Peasant Federation of Venezuela*]   (LA)
FCVB .... Federation Camerounaise de Volley-Ball [*Cameroonian Federation of Volleyball*]
FCVE........ Foundation for Continuing Veterinary Education [*Murdoch University, Australia*]
FCWA........ Family Court, Western Australia
FCWA........ Freemasons' Club of Western Australia
FCWC....... French Christian Workers Confederation   (EAIO)
FCWV....... Federatie van de Katholieke en Protestant-Christelijke Werkgeversverbonden [*Federation of Catholic and Protestant Employers' Associations*] [*Netherlands*]   (WEN)
FCWVA..... French Committee of the World Veterinary Association   (EAIO)
FD .... Crane Air [*Airline code*] [*Australia*]
FD .... Director's Fund   (BU)
FD .... Fabrika Duvana [*Tobacco Factory*]   (YU)

FD .... Feliks Dzerzhinskiy [*Locomotive type*] (RU)
FD .... Fernschnellzug [*Long-Distance Express Passenger Train (Including Sleepers)*] (EG)
FD .... Fire District [*Australia*]
FD .... Fisheries Department [*Western Australia*]
FD .... Fiskulturno Drustvo [*Physical Culture Society*] (YU)
FD .... Flussdiagramm [*German*] [*Flow Chart*] (ADPT)
fd .... For Detta [*Formerly*] [*Sweden*] (GPO)
FD .... Ford of Europe, Inc. [*British*] [*ICAO designator*] (ICDA)
FD .... Formulardrucker [*German*] (ADPT)
FD .... Fovgh-e Diplome [*Academic qualification*] [*Iran*]
FD .... Franc [*Monetary unit*] [*French Somaliland*]
FD .... Franc Djibouti [*Monetary unit*]
FD .... Frente Democratica [*Democratic Front*] [*Guinea-Bissau*] [*Political party*] (EY)
FD .... Frente Democratico [*Democratic Front*] [*El Salvador*] (LA)
FD .... Front Democratique [*Democratic Front*] [*The Comoros*] [*Political party*] (EY)
FD .... Phase Deflector (RU)
FD .... Phase Discriminator (RU)
FD .... Photodiode (RU)
FDA .... Fondo de Desarrollo Algodonero [*Venezuela*] (DSCA)
FDA .... Fondo de Desarrollo del Ajonjoli [*Venezuela*] (DSCA)
FDA .... Force Development and Analysis Division [*Ministry of Defence*] [*Australia*] (PDAA)
FDA .... Forestry Development Authority [*Liberia*]
FDA .... Forum Democratico Angolana [*Political party*] (EY)
FDA .... Freier Deutscher Autorenverband (SLS)
FDA .... French Diabetes Association (EAIO)
FDA .... Fundacja Domow Akademickich [*Students' House Fund*] (POL)
FDA .... Funeral Directors Association [*Australia*]
FDA .... Phenylenediamine (RU)
FDAE .... Fundo de Desenvolvimento de Areas Estrategicas [*Strategic Areas Development Fund*] [*Brazil*] (LA)
FDAF .... Ford Dealers Advertisers Fund [*Australia*]
FDAF .... Forologikon Dikastirion Amesou Forologias [*Tax Court for Direct Taxes*] [*Greek*] (GC)
FDANSW ... Funeral Directors Association of New South Wales [*Australia*]
FDAR .... Federal Department of Agricultural Research [*Nigeria*] (PDAA)
FDAR .... Fonds de Developpement et d'Action Rurale
FDB .... Faellesforeninger foer Danmarks Brugsforeninger [*Danish Cooperative Wholesale Society*] (WEN)
FDB .... Fiji Development Bank (GEA)
FDBR .... Fachverband Dampfkessel-, Behaelter- and Rohrleitungsbau ev
FDC .... Faculdade de Ciencias Domesticas [*Brazil*] (DSCA)
FDC .... Federacion Democrata Cristiana [*Christian Democratic Federation*] [*Spain*] [*Political party*] (PPE)
FDC .... Federation for a Democratic China [*Australia*]
FDC .... Fisheries Development Corporation
FDC .... Fonds de Developpement Communal [*Communal Development Fund*] [*Rwanda*] (AF)
FDC .... Foodcrop Development Committee [*Mauritius*] (AF)
FDC .... Food Distribution Corporation
FDC .... Foreningen af Danske Civiloekonomer [*Denmark*] (SLS)
FDC .... Frente Democratico de Chile [*Democratic Front of Chile*] (LAA)
FDC .... Friends of Democratic Cuba
FDC .... Front Democratique Camerounais [*Cameroon*] [*Political party*] (EY)
FDC .... Front Democratique Congolais
FDCC .... Family Day Care Centre [*Australia*]
FDCDS ..... Family Day Care Development Service [*Australia*]
FDCL .... Forschungsund Dokumentationszentrum Chile-Lateinamerika [*Germany*]
FDCLF ...... Friends of Dromkeen Children's Literature Foundation [*Australia*]
FDCP .... Family Day Care Program [*Australia*]
FDCR .... Frente Democratico contra la Represion [*Guatemala*] [*Political party*] (EY)
FDCSB ..... Federation for a Democratic China, Sydney Branch [*Australia*]
FDD .... Federacion Dominicana de Desarrollo [*Dominican Development Federation*] [*Dominican Republic*] (LA)
FDD .... Fondation Documentaire Dentaire
FDD .... Franc de Droits [*Free of Charge*] [*Shipping*] [*French*]
FDD .... Frente Democrata Docente [*Teachers Democratic Front*] [*Bolivia*] (LA)
FDD .... Front for Democracy and Development [*Surinam*] [*Political party*]
FdD .... Fuer den Dienstgebrauch [*For the Military Custom*] [*German*]
FDD .... Fundacion Dominicana de Desarrollo [*Dominican Republic*] (DSCA)
FDE .... Fondo Dominicano de Educacion [*Dominican Education Fund*] [*Dominican Republic*] (LA)
FDE .... Forde [*Norway*] [*Airport symbol*] (OAG)
FDE .... Frente Democratico Eleitoral [*Democratic Electoral Front*] [*Portugal*] [*Political party*] (PPE)
FDEF .... Front, Democratique pour une Europe Federale (FLAF)

FDES .... Fonds de Developpement Economique et Sociale [*Economic and Social Development Funds*] [*Guadeloupe*] (LA)
FDES .... Framework for the Development of Environmental Statistics [*Australia*]
FDES .... Fruende inner der Erde - Switzerland [*Friends of the Earth - Switzerland*] (EAIO)
F de T .... Fulano de Tal [*Nameless person; i.e., John Doe*] [*Spanish*]
FDF .... Fondo de Desarrollo Fruticola [*Venezuela*] (DSCA)
FDF .... Fort-De-France [*Martinique*] [*Airport symbol*] (OAG)
FDF .... Front Democratique des Bruxellois Francophones [*French-Speaking Democratic Front*] [*Belgium*] [*Political party*] (PPW)
FDF .... Fructose Diphosphate (RU)
FDFB .... Fiji Development Fund Board (GEA)
FDFM .... Flight Data and Flow Management Group [*ICAO*] (DA)
FDFR .... Federal Department of Forestry Research [*Nigeria*] (PDAA)
FDG .... Fly Dressers Guild [*Pinner, Middlesex, England*] (EAIO)
FDG .... Frente Democratico Guatemalteco [*Guatemalan Democratic Front*] (LA)
FDG .... Gas Filter-Throttle (RU)
FDGB .... Freier Deutscher Gewerkschaftsbund [*Free German Trade Union Federation*] [*Germany*] [*Political party*] (PPE)
FDGD .... Nhlangano [*Swaziland*] [*ICAO location identifier*] (ICLI)
FDGL .... Lavumisa [*Swaziland*] [*ICAO location identifier*] (ICLI)
FDGP .... Front Democratique de la Gauche Progressiste [*Democratic Front of the Progressive Left*] [*Malagasy*] (AF)
FDH .... Friedrichshafen [*Germany*] [*Airport symbol*] (OAG)
FDHKC ..... Filistin Demokratik Halk Kurtulus Cephesi [*Palestine Democratic Peoples Liberation Front*] (TU)
FDI .... Comite Nacional de la Federacion Dental Internacional [*National Committee of the International Dental Federation*] [*Peru*] (SLS)
FDI .... Consejo Peruano de la Federacion Dental Internacional [*Peruvian Council of the International Dental Federation*] [*Peru*] (SLS)
FDI .... Federation Dentaire Internationale [*International Dental Federation*] [*British*] (EA)
FDI .... Federation of Danish Industries
FDI .... Food and Disarmament International [*Belgium*] (EAIO)
FDI .... Frente Democratico de Izquierdas [*Democratic Front of Leftist Forces*] [*Spanish*] (WER)
f/di .... Frondidi [*Care Of*] (GC)
FDI .... Fundacion para el Desarrollo Industrial [*Colombia*] (COL)
FDI .... Fundacion para el Desarrollo Integral del Valle del Cauca [*Colorado*] (EY)
FDIA .... Fellow of the Design Institute of Australia
FDIC .... Front pour la Defense des Institutions Constitutionnelles
FDID .... Federazione Democratica Internazionale delle Donne [*Women's International Democratic Federation - WIDF*] (WER)
FDIF .... Federation Democratique Internationale des Femmes [*Women's International Democratic Federation - WIDF*] [*Germany*] (EAIO)
FDIM .... Federacion Democratica Internacional de Mujeres [*Women's International Democratic Federation - WIDF*] (LA)
FDj .... Franc Djibouti [*Monetary unit*]
FDJ .... Freie Deutsche Jugend [*Free German Youth*] [*Germany*] [*Political party*] (PPE)
FDK .... Filelevtheron Dimokratikon Kendron [*Liberal Democratic Center*] [*Greek*] (GC)
FDK .... Long-Term Credit Fund (RU)
FDKI .... Foreningen af Danske Kemiske Industrier [*Association of Danish Chemical Industries*] (EAIO)
Fdl .... Fahrdienstleiter [*Dispatcher*] (EG)
f dl .... Fale Dlugie [*Long Waves*] [*Poland*]
FDL .... Ferndauerlinie [*Permanent Long-Distance Telephone Line*] (EG)
FDLA .... Frente Democratica para a Libertacao de Angola [*Democratic Front for the Liberation of Angola*]
FDLA .... Front Democratique pour la Liberation de l'Angola [*Democratic Front for the Liberation of Angola*] (AF)
FDLD .... Front Democratique pour la Liberation de Djibouti [*Democratic Front for the Liberation of Djibouti*]
FDLUQ ..... Fronte Democratica Liberale dell'Uomo Qualunque [*Liberal Democratic Front of the Common Man*] [*Italy*] [*Political party*] (PPE)
FDM .... Phenyldimethylurea (RU)
FDMA .... Finnish Direct Marketing Association (EAIO)
FDMB .... Mbabane [*Swaziland*] [*ICAO location identifier*] (ICLI)
FDMH .... Mhlume [*Swaziland*] [*ICAO location identifier*] (ICLI)
FDMM .... Democratic Association of Students of Madagascar (AF)
FDMP .... Foundation for the Development of Medical Psychotherapy [*Switzerland*] (EAIO)
FDMS .... Additional Material Incentive Fund (BU)
FDMS .... Manzini/Matsapa [*Swaziland*] [*ICAO location identifier*] (ICLI)
Fdn .... Fonodan [*Record label*] [*Denmark*]
FDN .... Frende Democratico Nacional [*National Democratic Front*] [*Venezuela*] (LAA)

FDN .... Frente Democratica Nacional [*National Democratic Front*] [*Portuguese*] (WER)

FDN .... Frente Democratico Nacional [*Electoral Alliance*] [*Mexico*] (EY)

FDN .... Frente Democratico Nacionalista [*Nationalist Democratic Front*] [*El Salvador*] (LA)

FDN .... Front Democratique National [*National Democratic Front*] [*Senegal*] (AF)

FDN .... Fuerza Democratica Nicaraguense [*Nicaraguan Democratic Force*] (PD)

FDN .... Fundacion Defensores de la Naturaleza [*Defenders of Nature Foundation*] [*Guatemala*] (EAIO)

FDNB .... Fluorodinitrobenzene (RU)

FDNR .... Frente Democratico Nacional Revolucionario [*National Revolutionary Democratic Front*] [*Spanish*] (WER)

FDOMEZ ... Frente Democratico Oriental de Mexico Emiliano Zapata [*Political party*] (EY)

FDP........... Federal Dominion Party

FDP........... Free Democrat Party [*Turkey*] [*Political party*]

FDP........... Freie Demokratische Partei [*Free Democratic Party*] [*Germany*] [*Political party*] (EAIO)

FDP........... Freisinnig-Demokratische Partei der Schweiz [*Radical Democratic Party of Switzerland*] (PPW)

FDP........... Frente Democratico Popular [*Popular Democratic Front*] [*Peru*] (LA)

FDP........... Front Democratique de la Patrie

FDP........... Frontul Democratic Popular [*Democratic Popular Front*] [*Romania*] [*Political party*] (PPE)

FDP........... Fuerza Democratica Popular [*Popular Democratic Force*] [*Venezuela*] (LA)

FDPA........ Fiji Disabled Persons Association (EAIO)

FDPC........ Federation of Danish Painting Contractors (EAIO)

FDPI......... Finland Disabled Peoples International (EAIO)

FDPM........ Fondation pour le Developpement de la Psychotherapie Medicale [*Foundation for t he Development of Medical Psychotherapy*] [*Switzerland*] (EAIO)

FDPM........ Front Democratique des Patriotes Maliens [*Mali*] [*Political party*] (EY)

FDR .... Federation of Democratic Republicans [*Australia*] (ADA)

FDR .... Frente Democratico Contra la Represion [*Democratic Front Against Repression*] [*Guatemala*] [*Political party*] (PD)

FDR .... Frente Democratico Revolucionario [*Revolutionary Democratic Front*] [*El Salvador*] (LA)

fdR .... Fuer die Richtigkeit [*Approved By*] [*German*] (GCA)

F-Draht...... Fe-Ni Wire [*Iron-nickel alloy*] (RU)

F-DRAKE ... First Dynamic Response and Kinematic Experiment in the Drake Passage [*Project of International Southern Ocean Studies*] (MSC)

FDRE......... Fondation Denis de Rougemont pour l'Europe [.*Switzerland*] (EAIO)

FDR-FMLN ... Frente Democratico Revolucionario - Farabundo Marti de Liberacion Nacional [*Democratic Revolutionary Front/ Farabundo Marti National Liberation Front*] [*El Salvador*] [*Political party*] (EY)

FDR/FMLN ... Frente Democratico Revolucionario / Farabundo Marti para la Liberacion Nacional [*Democratic Revolutionary Front/ Farabundo Marti National Liberation Front*] [*Guatemala*] [*Political party*]

FDRP......... Frente de Defensa de la Revolucion Peruana [*Front for the Defense of the Peruvian Revolution*] (LA)

FDS........... Falusi Dolgozok Spartakiadja [*Village "Spartakiads"*] (HU)

FDS........... Finnish Dental Society (EAIO)

FDS........... Finnish Dermatological Society (EAIO)

FDS........... Flying Doctor Service [*Australia*]

FDS........... Forschungszentrum des Deutschen Schiffbaus [*Shilpbuilding Industry Research Organization*] [*Germany*] (PDAA)

FDS........... Frente Democratica Social [*Democratic Social Front*] [*Guinea-Bissau*] [*Political party*] (EY)

FDSA........ Front Democratique et Social Algerien [*Algerian Democratic and Social Front*] (AF)

FDST .... Siteki [*Swaziland*] [*ICAO location identifier*] (ICLI)

FDT .... Forca Democratica do Trabalho [*Labor Democratic Force*] [*Portuguese*] (WER)

FDT .... Foreningen af Danske Turistchefer [*Danish Union of Tourist Officers*] (EAIO)

FDT .... Frente Democratico de Trabajadores [*Democratic Workers Front*] [*Costa Rica*] (LA)

FDT .... Frente Democratico de Trabajadores [*Democratic Workers Front*] [*Ecuador*] (LA)

FDT .... Front Democratique Tchadien [*Political party*] [*Chad*]

FDTA........ Federacion Departamental de Trabajadores de Arequipa [*Arequipa Departmental Workers Federation*] [*Peru*] (LA)

FDTA........ Fisheries Development Trust Account [*Australia*]

FDTAA...... Federation of Democratic Turkish Associations of Australia

FDTCI .... Federation of Danish Textile and Clothing Industries (EAIO)

FDTh .... Foros Dimosion Theamaton [*Public Entertainment Tax*] [*Greek*] (GC)

FDTJ .... Federace Delnickych Telocvicnych Jednot [*Federation of Workers' Athletic and Gymnastic Organizations*] (CZ)

FDTM .... Tambankulu [*Swaziland*] [*ICAO location identifier*] (ICLI)

FDTN .... Fabrication et Diffusion des Textiles du Nord

FDTS .... Tshaneni [*Swaziland*] [*ICAO location identifier*] (ICLI)

FDU .... Bandundu [*Zaire*] [*Airport symbol*] (OAG)

FDU .... Fernando Democratic Union

FDU .... Finnish Dramatists' Union (EAIO)

FDU .... Frente Democratica Unida [*United Democratic Front*] [*Portuguese*] (WER)

FDUB .... Ubombo [*Swaziland*] [*ICAO location identifier*] (ICLI)

FDUNSW ... Firemen and Deckhands' Union of New South Wales [*Australia*]

FDUR .... Free Democratic Union of Roma [*Political party*]

FDUV .... Forbundet de Utvecklingsstordas Val [*Organization for Swedish-Speaking Mentally Retarded Persons in Finland*] (EAIO)

FDVR........ Federal Department of Veterinary Research

FDYa .... Ferrodiode Cell (RU)

FD(-ZUG) ... Fernschnellzug [*Long-Distance Express Train*] [*German*] (EG)

FE .... Falange Espanola [*Spanish Phalange*] (WER)

FE .... Far Eastern Electric Industry Co. Ltd. [*Taiwan*]

FE .... Far East Knitting Co. Ltd. [*Thailand*]

Fe .... Ferme [*Farm*] [*Military map abbreviation World War I*] [*French*] (MTD)

FE .... Ferrara [*Car registration plates*] [*Italy*]

Fe .... Ferro [*Iron*] [*Chemical element*] [*Portuguese*]

FE .... Filiki Etaireia [*Society of Friends*] [*Greek*] (GC)

fe .... Folyo Evi [*Of the Current Year*] [*Hungary*] (GPO)

fe .... Forward Enterprises Corp. [*Taiwan*]

FE .... Friedensengel [*Angel of Peace*] [*Torpedo auxiliary equipment*] [*German military - World War II*]

FE .... Fuerza Emancipadora [*Emancipating Force*] [*Venezuela*] (LA)

FE .... Photoelectric Cell (RU)

FE .... Physical Electrotonus (RU)

FEA........... Fabrica de Elemente pentru Automatizare [*Factory for Automation Elements*] (RO)

FEA........... Falange Espanola Autentica [*Authentic Spanish Phalange*] (WER)

FEA........... Far Eastern Air Transport Corp. [*Taiwan*] [*ICAO designator*] (FAAC)

FEA........... Federal Electoral [*or Electorate*] Assembly [*Australia*]

FEA........... Federation Europeenne des Associations Aerosols [*Federation of European Aerosol Associations*] (EA)

FEA........... Fetlar [*Shetland Islands*] [*Airport symbol*] (OAG)

FEA........... Filodasiki Enosi Athinon [*Athens Friends of the Forest Association*] (GC)

FEA........... Financiere d'Equipements Automobiles [*Automobile Equipment Finance Company*] [*France*]

FEA........... Fratsuzskaia Ekvatorialnaia Afrika

FEA........... Fraud Enforcement Agency [*Australia*]

FEA........... French Equatorial Africa

FEA........... Further Education Association [*South Australia*]

FEAAF ...... Federation Europeenne des Associations d'Analystes Financiers [*European Federation of Financial Analysts' Societies - EFFAS*] (EAIO)

FEAB........ Federacion Espanola de Industrias de la Alimentacion y Bebidas [*Industrial association*] [*Spain*] (EY)

FEAC........ Foreign Exchange Auction Committee [*Ghana*]

FEACO...... Federation Europeenne des Associations de Conseils en Organisation [*European Federation of Management Consultants Associations*] [*France*]

FEAD........ Federation Europeenne des Associations de Dieteticiens [*European Federation of the Associations of Dietitians - EFAD*] (EAIO)

FEAD......... Fondo Especial de Asistencia para el Desarrollo (de la OEA) [*Organizacion de Estados Americanos*] [*Washington, DC*]

FEAE......... Federation des Etablissements et Arsenaux de l'Etat [*France*]

FEAF .... Far East Air Force (ML)

FEAICSMT ... Federation Europeenne des Associations d'Ingenieurs et Chefs de Services de Securite et des Medecins du Travail [*European Federation of Associations of Enginee rs and Heads of Industrial Safety and Medical Services*] (PDAA)

FEAIE .... Federation Europeenne des Associations d'Instruments a Ecrire [*Federation of European Writing Instruments Associations*] (EAIO)

FEAK........ Foititiki Epitropi Allilengyis pros tous Kyprious [*Student Committee of Solidarity for the Cypriots*] [*Greek*] (GC)

FEAKA...... Foititiki Epitropi Allilengyis dia ton Kypriakon Agona [*Student Solidarity Committee for the Cypriot Struggle*] [*Greek*] (GC)

FEALC ...... Federacion Espeleologica de America Latina y el Caribe [*Speleological Federation of Latin America and the Caribbean*] (LA)

FEAMAR.. Fundacao de Estudos do Mar [*Sea Studies Foundation*] [*Brazil*] (LA)

FEAMIS.... Foreign Exchange Accounting and Management Information System (PDAA)

FEAN .... Federation des Enseignants de l'Afrique Noire [*Federation of Teachers of Black Africa*] (AF)

FEANF ...... Federation des Etudiants de l'Afrique Noire en France [*Federation of Students from Black Africa in France*] (AF)

FEANI .... Federation Europeenne d'Associations Nationales d'Ingenieurs [*European Federation of National Engineering Associations*] (EAIO)

FEAO .... Federation of European American Organizations [*Germany*] (DSCA)

FEAP .... Far East/Pacific

FEAP .... Federation Europeenne des Associations des Psychologues [*European Federation of Professional Psychologists Associations - EFPPA*] (EA)

FEAP .... Fundo de Equipamento Agropecuario [*Brazil*] (DSCA)

FEAPA ...... Federacion Espanola de Agrupaciones de Productores Agrarios (EY)

FEAPS .... Confederacion Espanola de Federaciones y Asociaciones pro Personas Deficientes Mentales [*Spain*] (EAIO)

FEAPTh .... Foititiki Enosis Aristoteleiou Panepistimiou Thessalonikis [*University of Salonica Student Union*] (GC)

FEARALAT ... Federacion Arabe de America Latina [*Arab Federation of Latin America*] (LA)

FEATS .... Festival of European Anglophone Theatrical Societies

Feb .... Febrero [*February*] [*Spanish*]

Feb .... Februar [*February*] [*German*] (GPO)

feb .... Februar [*February*] [*Hungarian*] (GPO)

feb .... Februar [*February*] [*Danish*] (GPO)

feb .... Februari [*February*] [*Netherlands*] (GPO)

Feb .... February (SCAC)

FEB .... Federacion de Empleados Bancarios del Peru [*Peruvian Bank Employees Federation*] (LA)

FEB .... Federation des Entreprises de Belgique [*Federation of Belgian Enterprises*] (WER)

FEB .... Finance and Economics Office (RU)

FEB .... Forca Expedicionaria Brasileira [*Brazilian Expeditionary Force, 1944-1955*]

FEB .... Sanfebagar [*Nepal*] [*Airport symbol*] (OAG)

FEBAB ...... Federacao Brasileira de Associaeoes DeBibliotecarios [*Brazil*] (SLS)

FEBAC ...... Federal Education Broadcasts Advisory Committee [*Australia*]

FEBACAM ... Federation Bananiere du Cameroun

FEBANCOOP ... Federacion de Bancos Cooperativos de la Republica Argentina [*Bankers' association*] [*Argentina*] (EY)

febb .... Febbraio [*February*] [*Italian*]

FEBC .... Far East Broadcasting Co. [*Australia, New Zealand*]

FeBe .... Federation de l'Industrie du Beton [*Precast Concrete Federation*] [*Belgium*] (EY)

FEBEC ...... Federation Belge de l'Industrie du Coton et des Fibres Chimiques [*Belgian Federation of the Cotton and Man-Made Fibre Industry*] (EAIO)

FEBECA .... Federation Belge du Commerce Alimentaire [*Foodstuffs Trade Federation*] [*Belgium*] (EY)

FEBEL .... Ferrageira da Beira Lda.

FEBELBOIS ... Federation Belge des Entreprises de la Transformation du Bois [*An association*] [*Belgium*] (EY)

FEBELBOIS ... Federation Belge des Industriels du Bois [*Belgian Federation of the Timber Industry*] (PDAA)

FEBELGRA ... Federation Belge des Industries Graphiques [*Graphic Industries Federation*] [*Belgium*] (EY)

FEBELTEX ... Federation de l'Industrie Textile Belge [*Federation of the Belgian Textile Industry*] (PDAA)

FEBEM ..... Federacao Estadual do Bem Estar do Menor [*State Child Welfare Foundation*] [*Brazil*] (LA)

FEBI .... Federations Europeennes des Branches d'Industries (DCTA)

FEBIAS ..... Far East Bible Institute and Seminary [*Philippines*]

FEBIC .... Federation Belge de l'Industrie de la Chaussure [*Footwear Federation*] [*Belgium*] (EY)

FEBMA ..... Federation of European Bearing Manufacturers Associations (EAIO)

febo .... Febrero [*February*] [*Spanish*]

febr .... Februar [*February*] (HU)

Febr .... Februarie [*February*] [*Afrikaans*]

FEBRAS .... Federation Belge de Recherches et d'Activitees Subaquantiques [*Belgium*] (PDAA)

FEBS .... Federation of European Biochemical Societies [*ICSU*] [*Bulgarian*] (SLS)

FEBS .... Federation of European Biochemical Societies [*France*]

FEC .... Fabrica de Elementos Combustiveis [*Fuel Elements Factory*] [*Brazil*] (LA)

FEC .... Far East Command (ML)

FEC .... Federal Economic Chamber [*Austria*] (EAIO)

FEC .... Federal Electoral College [*or Commission*]

FEC .... Federation des Entreprises au Congo [*Merger of AIIB and AICB*]

FEC .... Federation Europeenne de Climatotherapie [*European Society of Climatotherapy - ESC*] [*French*] (EAIO)

FEC .... Federation of the European Cutlery and Flatware Industries (EA)

FEC .... Fianarantsoa-East Coast

FEC .... Finnish Export Credit

FEC .... Fondation Europeenne de la Culture [*European Cultural Foundation - ECF*] [*Netherlands*]

FEC .... Fonds d'Equipement Communal

FEC .... Foreign Exchange Certificate [*Special currency notes sold to foreigners*] [*People's Republic of China*] (ECON)

FEC .... Forestiere Equatoriale du Cameroun

FEC .... Free Europe Committee [*Later, RFE/RL*] (EA)

FECABA ... Federation of East and Central African Amateur Boxing Associations

FECAFOOT ... Federation Camerounaise de Football [*Cameroon Football Federation*]

FECAICA ... Federacion de Camaras y Asociaciones Industriales Centroamericanas [*Federation of Central American Industrial Chambers and Associations*] [*Guatemala*] (LA)

FECAMCO ... Federacion de Camaras de Comercio del Istmo Centroamericano [*Federation of Chambers of Commerce of the Central American Isthmus*] [*El Salvador*] (LA)

FECAMU ... Federacion Centroamericana de Mujeres Universitarias [*Central American Federation of University Women*] (LA)

FECANAT ... Federations Camerounaises de Natation

FECANIC ... Federacion de Cooperativas de Ahorro y Credito [*Federation of Savings and Loan Cooperatives*] [*Nicaragua*] (LA)

FECARIBE ... Corporacion Financiera del Caribe [*Colombia*] (COL)

FECC .... Federacion Campesina Crisriana Costarricences [*Costa Rica*] (DSCA)

FECC .... Federation Europeenne du Commerce Chimique [*Federation of European Chemical Merchants - FECM*] (EAIO)

FECCA ...... Federation of Ethnic Community Councils of Australia

FECCAS.... Federacion de Campesinos Cristianos Salvadorenos [*Salvadoran Christian Peasants' Federation*] (LA)

FECCES .... Federacao das Cooperativas de Cafeicultores do Espirito Santo [*Brazil*] (DSCA)

FECCI .... Frente Estudiantil Critico, Combativo, e Independente [*Critical, Combative, and Independent Student Front*] [*Panama*] (LA)

FECCOO... Federacion de Ensenanza de Comisiones Obreras [*Spain*] (EAIO)

FECEE ...... Federacio d'Entitats Catalanes a l'Exilo i a l'Emigracio [*Federation of Catalan Exile and Emigre Organizations*] [*Spanish*] (WER)

FECEGC ... Federation Europeenne des Constructeurs d'Equipement de Grandes Cuisines [*European Federation of Catering Equipment Manufacturers - EFCEM*] (EA)

FECESITLIH ... Federacion Central de Sindicatos de Trabajadores Libres de Honduras [*Central Federation of Unions of Free Honduran Workers*] (LA)

FECETRAG ... Federacion Central de Trabajadores de Guatemala [*Central Federation of Guatemalan Workers*] (LA)

FECEU ...... Federacion Centroamericana de Estudiantes Universitarios [*Central American Federation of University Students*] (LA)

FECh.......... Federacion de Estudiantes de Chile [*Student Federation of Chile*] (LA)

FECHIMIE ... Federation des Industries Chimiques de Belgique [*Federation of the Belgian Chemical Industries*] (PDAA)

FECI .... Fellowship of Evangelical Churches of India

FECIA .... Federacion de Empleados de Comercio e Industria de Arequipa [*Federation of Commercial and Industrial Employees of Arequipa*] [*Peru*] (LA)

FECIT........ Federacion Espanola de Exportadores de Frutos Citricos (EY)

FECM........ Federation of European Chemical Merchants (EA)

FECMA ..... Federation of European Coin-Machine Associations (EAIO)

FEC/ML.... Frente Eleitoral de Comunistas/Marxista-Leninista [*Electoral Front of Communists/Marxist-Leninist*] [*Portuguese*] (WER)

FECN........ Fabrica de Elementos Combustibles Nucleares [*Nuclear Fuel Elements Enterprise*] [*Argentina*] (LA)

FECO......... Fundacion de Estudios para la Comunidad Organizada [*Studies Foundation for the Organized Community*] [*Argentina*] (LA)

FECOAC ... Federacion Nacional de Cooperativas de Ahorro y Credito [*National Federation of Savings and Loan Cooperatives*] [*Ecuador*] (LA)

FECODE... Federacion Colombiana de Educadores [*Colombian Teachers Federation*] (LA)

FeCoFoot ... Federation Congolaise de Football

FECOLAN ... Federacao das Cooperativas de Las do Rio Grande do Sul Ltd. [*Brazil*] (DSCA)

FECOLDROGAS ... Federacion Colombiana de Droguistas [*Colombia*] (COL)

FECOMERCIO ... Federacao do Comercio de Estado do Rio Grande Do Norte [*Natal, Brazil*] (LAA)

FECOONIC ... Federacion de Cooperativas de Nicaragua [*Federation of Nicaraguan Cooperatives*] (LA)

FECOPAM ... Federacion Nacional de Cooperativas de Produccion Agricola y Mercadeo [*National Federation of Cooperatives for Agricultural Production and Marketing*] [*Ecuador*]   (LA)

FECOPESCA ... Federacao das Cooperativas dos Pescadores de Santa Catarina [*Brazil*]   (DSCA)

FECORAH ... Federacion de Cooperativas de Reforma Agraria de Honduras [*Federation of Honduran Agrarian Reform Cooperatives*]   (LA)

FECOSA ... Ferrocarriles de Costa Rica [*Costa Rican Railways*]   (LA)

FECOTRIGO ... Federacao das Cooperativas Brasileiras de Trigo e Soja [*Federation of Brazilian Wheat and Soybean Cooperatives*]   (LA)

FECOVE ... Federacion de Cooperativas de Consumo de Venezuela [*Venezuela*]   (DSCA)

FECS .... Federation Europeenne des Fabricants de Ceramiques Sanitaires [*European Federation of Ceramic Sanitaryware Manufacturers - EFCSM*]   (EAIO)

FECS .... Federation of European Chemical Societies   (EAIO)

FECSA .... Fuerzas Electricas de Cataluna, Sociedad Anonima [*Electric Power of Catalonia, Incorporated*] [*Spanish*]   (WER)

FECSITLIH ... Federacion Central de Sindicatos de Trabajadores Libres de Honduras [*Central Federation of Unions of Free Honduran Workers*]   (LA)

FECT .... Federation of European Chemical Trade   (EAIO)

FECUIMPORT ... Empresa Cubana Importadora de Ferrocarriles [*Cuban Enterprise for Import of Rolling Stock*]   (LA)

FED .... Federacion de Estudiantes Dominicanos [*Federation of Dominican Students*] [*Dominican Republic*]   (LA)

Fed .... Federal   (IDIG)

fed .... Federatie [*Benelux*]   (BAS)

Fed .... Federation   (SCAC)

FED .... Federation des Editevrs Europeens [*Federation of European Publishers*] [*Belgium*]   (EAIO)

FED .... F. E. Dzerzhinskiy [*Camera type*]   (RU)

FED .... Fondo Especial de Desarrollo [*Special Development Fund*] [*Nicaragua*]   (FED)

FED .... Fondo Europeo de Desarrollo [*European Development Fund - EDF*] [*Spanish*]

FED .... Fonds Europeen de Developpement [*European Development Fund*] [*Use EDF*] [*French*]   (AF)

FED .... Fundacion Ecuatoriana de Desarrollo [*Ecuadorian Development Foundation*]   (WED)

FED .... Linea Federal Argentina SEM [*ICAO designator*]   (FAAC)

FED .... Losbladig Fiscaal Weekblad [*Formerly, Fiscaal Economische Documentatie*] [*Benelux*]   (BAS)

FEDA .... Federated Engine Drivers' Association [*Australia*]

FEDA .... Foundation for Ecological Development Alternatives [*Netherlands*]   (EAIO)

FEDAAS ... Federacion Espanola de Asociaciones de Asistentes Sociales [*Spanish*]   (SLS)

FEDAGRI ... Federacion Agricola de Chile [*Chilean Agricultural Federation*]   (LA)

FEDAI .... Foreign Exhcange Dealers Assocation of India   (PDAA)

FEDAN ..... Federacion Educativa para el Desarrollo Agricola [*Educational Federation for Agricultural Development*] [*Colorado*]   (LA)

FEDAN ..... Frente Estudiantil de Accion Nacional [*Student National Action Front*] [*Ecuador*]   (LA)

FEDAP ...... Federacion de Asociaciones de Padres y Apoderados [*Federation of Parents and Guardians Associations*] [*Chile*]   (LA)

FEDAS ...... Federacion Espanola de Actividades Subacuaticas [*Spanish*]   (ASF)

FEDAS ...... Federation of European Delegation Associations of Scientific Equipment Manufacturers, Importers, and Dealers in the Laboratory, Industrial and Medical Fields   (PDAA)

FEDASEC ... Federation Dahomeene des Syndicats de l'Education et de la Culture

FEDCO ...... Federmann Entreprises Overseas Ltd.

Fed C ofA ... Federal Court of Australia

FEDCON .. Federation of Consumers' Co-Operatives in Negros Oriental [*Philippines*]   (EY)

Fed Ct .... Federal Court of Australia

FEDDEC ... Federal Court of Australia Decisions [*Database*]

FEDE .... Federacion Estudiantil [*Student Federation*] [*Argentina*]   (LA)

FEDE .... Federation Europeenne des Ecoles [*Later, European Schools Federation*]   (EAIO)

FEDE .... Frente Estudiantil de Economia [*Economy Students Front*] [*Panama*]   (LA)

FEDEACh ... Federacion de Estudiantes Agricolas de Chile [*Federation of Chilean Agricultural Students*]   (LA)

FEDEAGRO ... Federacion Nacional de Productores Agropecuarios [*National Federation of Agricultural and Livestock Producers*] [*Venezuela*]   (LA)

FEDEARROZ ... Federacion Nacional de Arroceros [*Colombia*]   (COL)

FEDEAU ... Federation pour le Developpement de l'Artisanat Utilitaire [*Federation for the Development of Utilitarian Crafts*] [*Defunct*] [*France*]   (EAIO)

FEDEBAT ... Federation des Bateke

FEDEBATE ... Federation des Batetela

FEDEBOL ... Federacion del Futbol Colombiano [*Colombia*]   (COL)

FEDEBON ... Federacion Boneriana di Trabao [*Bonaire Labor Federation*] [*Netherlands Antilles*]

FEDEC ...... Federacion Democratica de Estudiantes Colombianos [*Democratic Federation of Colombian Students*]   (LA)

FEDECACES ... Federacion de Cooperativas de Ahorro y Credito de El Salvador [*Federation of Savings and Loan Cooperatives of El Salvador*]   (LA)

FEDECAFE ... Federacion Nacional de Cafeteros [*National Federation of Coffee Growers*] [*Colorado*]   (LA)

FEDECAMARA ... Federacion de Camaras de Comercio e Industrias de Honduras [*Federation of the Chambers of Congress*] [*Honduras*]   (EY)

FEDECAMARAS ... Federacion Venezolana de Camaras y Asociaciones de Comercio y Produccion [*Association of the Chambers of Commerce and Industry*] [*Venezuela*]   (LA)

FEDECAME ... Federacao Cafeeira de America [*Federation of Coffee Growers of America*]   (LA)

FEDECAME ... Federacion Cafetalera de America [*Federation of Coffee Growers of America*]   (LA)

FEDECAP ... Federacion Centroamericana de Periodistas [*Central American Federation of Journalists*] [*Honduras*]   (LA)

FEDECARAFE ... Federacion Nacional de Cafeteros [*National Federation of Coffee Growers*] [*Colorado*]   (LAA)

FEDECARBON ... Federacion Nacional de Carboneros [*National Federation of Coal Miners*] [*Colorado*]   (LA)

FEDECh .... Federacion de Educadores de Chile [*Chilean Teachers Federation*]   (LA)

FEDECHAR ... Federation Charbonniere de Belgique [*Belgium*]   (BAS)

FEDECINE ... Federacion Nacional de Exhibidores de Cine [*Colombia*]   (COL)

FEDECO ... Federacion de Comunidades Judias de Centroamerica y Panama [*Federation of Jewish Communities of Central America and Panama*]   (EAIO)

FEDECO ... Federal Electoral Commission [*Nigeria*]

FEDECOCAGUA ... Federacion de Cooperativas Cafetaleras de Guatemala [*Guatemalan Federation of Coffee Cooperatives*]

FEDECONTA ... Federacion de Contadores de Antioquia [*Colombia*]   (COL)

FEDEFAM ... Federacion Latinoamericana de Asociaciones de Familiares de Detenidos-Desaparecidos [*Federation of Associations of Families of Disappeared-Detainees*]   (EAIO)

FEDEGAN ... Federacion Colombiana de Ganaderos [*Colombian Cattlemen's Association*]   (LA)

FEDEGAS ... Federacion Colombiana de Gas [*Colombia*]   (COL)

FEDEIEC ... Federacion Unitaria de Trabajadores de la Industria Electrica del Ecuador [*Single Federation of the Ecuadorean Workers of the Electrical Industry*]   (LA)

FEDEKA ... Federation des Associations Tribales des Originaires du Kasai [*Federation of Associations of Kasai Tribes*]

FEDELAC ... Federacion Dominicana de Ligas Agrarias Cristianas [*Dominican Federation of Christian Agrarian Leagues*] [*Dominican Republic*]   (LA)

FE de lasJONS ... Falange Espanola de las Juntas de Ofensiva Nacional Sindicalista [*Spanish Phalange of the Syndicalist Juntas of the National Offensive*] [*Political party*]   (PPE)

FEDELCO ... Federacion de Loterias de Colombia [*Colombia*]   (COL)

FEDEM ..... Federacion de Estudiantes Democratas de Ensenanza Media [*Federation of Democratic Secondary School Students*] [*Spanish*]   (WER)

FEDEMETAL ... Federacion Metalurgica Colombiana [*Colombian Metallurgical Federation*] [*Colombia*]   (LA)

FEDEMI ... Federacion de Mineros de Cundinamarca [*Cundinamarca Miners Federation*] [*Colorado*]   (LA)

FEDEMO ... Federal Democratic Movement [*Uganda*] [*Political party*]

FEDEMOL ... Federacion Nacional de Molineros de Trigo [*Colombia*]   (COL)

FEDEMRIFAS ... Federacion Nacional de Empresarios de Rifas Autorizadas [*Colombia*]   (COL)

FEDENAGA ... Federacion Nacional de Ganaderos [*Venezuela*]   (DSCA)

FEDENAGRIC ... Federacion Nacional de Trabajadores Agricolas de Colombia [*National Federation of Agricultural Workers of Colombia*]   (LA)

FEDEPALMA ... Federacion Nacional de Cultivadores de Palma Africana [*Colombia*]   (DSCA)

FEDEPAS ... Federacion Nacional de Fabricantes de Pastas Alimenticias [*Colombia*]   (COL)

FEDEPETROL ... Federacion Colombiana de Petroleos [*Colombian Petroleum Federation*] [*Colombia*]   (COL)

FEDEPETROL ... Federacion de Trabajadores Petroleros [*Petroleum Workers Federation*] [*Venezuela*]   (LA)

FEDEPROCOL ... Federacion de Profesionales Colombianos [*Colombian Professionals Federation*]   (LA)

FEDER ...... Fonds Europeen de Developpement Regional [*European Regional Development Fund - ERDF*] [*Belgium*]   (EAIO)

FEDERACAFE ... Federacion Nacional de Cafeteros [*Colombia*]   (DSCA)

FEDERADIO ... Federacion Colombiana de Radiodifusion [*Colombia*] (COL)

FEDERAGRONOMI ... Federazione Nazionale Dottori in Scienze Agrarie e Forestali [*Italian*] (SLS)

FEDERAL ... Federacion de Alimentos Concentrados para Animales [*Colombia*] (COL)

FEDERALGODON ... Federacion Nacional de Algodoneros [*Colombia*] (DSCA)

FEDERBAN ... Federation Bananiere et Fruitiere de la Cote-D'Ivoire

FEDERCHIMICA ... Federazione Nazionale dell'Industria Chimica [*Italian Federation of the Chemical Industry*]

FEDERMAR ... Federation Maritime de la Cote-D'Ivoire

FEDERPESCA ... Federazione Nazionale delle Imprese di Pesca [*Italy*]

FEDERSINDAN ... Federazione dei Sindacati Dipendenti Aziende di Navigazione [*Italy*] (EY)

FEDERTERME ... Federazione Italiana delle Industrie delle Acque Minerali, delle Terme e delle Bevande Analcooliche

FEDERVINI ... Federazione Italiana Industriali Produttori Esportatori ed Importatori di Vini, Acquaviti, Liquori, Sciroppi, Aceti ed Affini [*Producers, Importers and Exporters of Wines, Brandies, Liquers, Syrups, Vinegars, and Allied Products*] [*Italy*] (EY)

FEDES ...... Federation Europeenne de l'Emballage Souple (EAIO)

FEDESA .... Federation Europeenne de la Sante Animale [*European Federation of Animal Health*] [*Belgium*] (ECED)

FEDESARROLLO ... Federacion para el Desarrollo [*Federation for Development*] [*Ecuador*] (LA)

FEDESARROLLO ... Federacion para el Desarrollo [*Federation for Development*] [*Colorado*] (LA)

FEDESEMOLA ... Federacion de Molineros de Semola [*Colombia*] (COL)

FEDETA ... Federacion de Trabajadores de Antioquia [*Federation of Workers of Antioquia*] [*Colorado*] (LA)

FEDETAB ... Federation Belgo-Luxembourgeoise des Industries du Tabac [*An association*] [*Belgium*] (EY)

FEDETAV ... Federacion de Trabajadores del Valle [*Federation of Workers of Valle*] [*Colorado*] (LA)

FEDETEX ... Federacion de Trabajadores Textiles [*Textile Workers Federation*] [*Colorado*] (LA)

FEDETRAN ... Federacion Nacional del Transporte [*National Transport Federation*] [*Colombia*] (COL)

FEDETRAR ... Federacion de Trabajadores de Risaralda [*Risaralda Workers Federation*] [*Colorado*] (LA)

FEDETTOL ... Federacion Departamental de Trabajadores de Tolima [*Departmental Federation of Workers of Tolima*] [*Colorado*] (LA)

FEDEU ...... Federacion Colombiana de Entidades de Ensenanza Universitaria [*Colombia*] (COL)

FEDE-UNEP ... Federacion Unitaria Nacional de Empleados Publicos [*National Single Federation of Public Employees*] [*Venezuela*] (LA)

FEDEXCO ... Federacion de Exportadores Colombianos [*Federation of Colombian Exporters*] (LA)

FEDHASA ... Federated Hotel Associations of Southern Africa

FEDIAF ..... Federation Europeenne de l'Industrie des Aliments pour Animaux Familiers [*European Petfood Industry Federation*] (EAIO)

FED IC ...... Federazione Italiana dei Cineclub [*Italian*] (SLS)

FEDICER ... Federation des Industries Ceramiques de Belgique et du Luxembourg [*Ceramics Federation*] [*Belgium*] (EY)

FEDIL .... Federation des Industriels Luxembourgeois [*Luxembourg*] (EAIO)

FEDINBANA ... Federacion Internacional de Bananeros [*International Federation of Banana Producers*] (LA)

FEDIOL .... Federation de l'Industrie de l'Huilerie de la CEE [*EEC Seed Crushers and Oil Processors' Federation*] [*Belgium*] (EAIO)

FEDIP .... Frentes de Defensa de los Intereses del Pueblo [*Fronts for the Defense of the People's Interests*] [*Peru*] (LA)

FEDIS .... Federation Belge des Entreprises de Distribution [*Belgium*] (EY)

FEDISA ..... Federacion de Estudios Independientes, Sociedad Anonima [*Federation of Independent Studies, Incorporated*] [*Spanish*] (WER)

FEDIVER ... Federation de l'Industrie du Verre [*Benelux*] (BAS)

FEDNACOMA ... Federation Nationale des Cooperatives Malgaches [*National Federation of Malagasy Cooperatives*] (AF)

FEDO .... Fact Engineering and Design Organization [*India*]

FEDOCEF ... Fundo Especial de Desenvolvimento das Operacoes das Caixas Economicas Federais [*Special Fund for Development of Federal Savings Banks Operations*] [*Brazil*] (LA)

FEDOM .... Fonds de Developpement pour les Pays et Territoires d'Outre-Mer

FEDR .... Fondo Europeo de Desarrollo Regional [*European Regional Development Fund - ERDF*] [*Spanish*]

FEDR .... Fonds Europeen de Developpement Regional [*European Regional Development Fund - ERDF*] [*French*]

FEDRABAN ... Federacao Brasileira de Associacoes de Bancos [*Brazilian Federation of Bank Associations*] (LA)

FEDSA ...... Federation of European Direct Selling Associations [*Belgium*] (EAIO)

FEDSEA.... Federal South East Asia Line [*Steamship*] (MHDW)

FEDUNA .. Federacion de Estudiantes de la Universidad Nacional [*Federation of National University Students*] [*Costa Rica*] (LA)

FEDUNEQ ... Federation du Nord de l'Equateur

FEE .... Federation des Experts Comptables Europeens [*Belgium*]

FEE .... Federation of Employers of Ethiopia (AF)

FEE .... Federation of Exiles in Europe [*Switzerland*]

FEE(A) ...... Foundation for Economic Education (Australia)

FEEAL ...... Facultades y Escuelas de Economia de America Latina [*Latin American Faculties and Schools of Economics*] (LA)

FEEBF ...... Federation des Eglises Evangeliques Baptistes de France (EAIO)

FEECA ...... Federation Europeenne pour l'Education Catholique des Adultes [*European Associaton for Catholic Adult Education*] (EAIO)

FEEDBAC ... Foreign Exchange, Eurodollar, and Branch Accounting (PDAA)

FEEDM ..... Federation Europeenne des Emballeurs et Distributeurs de Miel [*European Federation of Honey Packers and Distributors*] [*British*] (EAIO)

FEEM .... Federacion de Estudiantes de Educacion Media [*Federation of Secondary School Students*] [*Venezuela*] (LA)

FEEM .... Federacion de Estudiantes de la Ensenanza Media [*Federation of Middle School Students*] [*Cuba*] (LA)

FEEMA .... Fundacao Estadual de Engenharia do Meio-Ambiente [*State Environmental Engineering Foundation*] [*Brazil*] (LA)

FEF .... Far East Fleet (ML)

FEF .... Photoelectric Fluxmeter (RU)

FEFA .... Alindao [*Central African Republic*] [*ICAO location identifier*] (ICLI)

FEFA .... Fondo Especial para Financiamientos Agropecuarios [*Mexico*] (EY)

FEFA .... Future European Fighter Aircraft (PDAA)

FEFAC ...... Federation Europeenne des Fabricants d'Aliments Composes [*European Federation of Compound Animal Feedingstuff Manufacturers*] (EAIO)

FEFANA ... Federation Europeenne des Fabricants d'Adjuvants pour la Nutrition Animale [*European Federation of Manufacturers of Feed Additives*] (EAIO)

FEFB .... Obo [*Central African Republic*] [*ICAO location identifier*] (ICLI)

FEFC .... Far Eastern Freight Conference (ML)

FEFCEB .... Federation Europeene des Fabricants de Caisses et Emballages en Bois [*European Federation of Manufacturers of Timber Crates and Packing Cases*] (PDAA)

FEFCO ...... Federation Europeenne des Fabricants de Carton Ondule [*European Federation of Manufacturers of Corrugated Board*] [*France*]

FEFEME... Federacion Feminina Metodista [*Federation of Methodist Women*] [*Bolivia*] (EAIO)

FEFF.......... Bangui/M'Poko [*Central African Republic*] [*ICAO location identifier*] (ICLI)

FEFG .... Bangassou [*Central African Republic*] [*ICAO location identifier*] (ICLI)

FEFI .... Birao [*Central African Republic*] [*ICAO location identifier*] (ICLI)

FEFL.......... Bossembele [*Central African Republic*] [*ICAO location identifier*] (ICLI)

FEFLAS .... Frente Estudiantil Flavio Suero [*Flavio Suero Student Front*] [*Dominican Republic*] (LA)

FEFM .... Bambari [*Central African Republic*] [*ICAO location identifier*] (ICLI)

FEFM .... Federazione Europea Fabbricanti Matite [*Federation of Eraser Pencil Manufacturers Associations*] (EAIO)

FEFN .... N'Dele [*Central African Republic*] [*ICAO location identifier*] (ICLI)

FEFO .... Bouar [*Central African Republic*] [*ICAO location identifier*] (ICLI)

FEFPEB .... Federation Europeenne des Fabricants de Palettes et Emballages en Bois [*European Federation of Pallet and Wooden Crate Manufacturers - EFPWCM*] (EAIO)

FEFR .... Bria [*Central African Republic*] [*ICAO location identifier*] (ICLI)

FEFS.......... Bossangoa [*Central African Republic*] [*ICAO location identifier*] (ICLI)

FEFT .... Berberati [*Central African Republic*] [*ICAO location identifier*] (ICLI)

FEFV .... Bangui [*Central African Republic*] [*ICAO location identifier*] (ICLI)

FeFv .... Fernsprech-Fernvermittlung [*Long-Distance Telephone Exchange*] (EG)

FEFY .... Yalinga [*Central African Republic*] [*ICAO location identifier*] (ICLI)

FEFZ .... Zemio [*Central African Republic*] [*ICAO location identifier*] (ICLI)

FEG .... Federacion de Educadores de Guatemala [*Federation of Guatemalan Educators*]   (LA)

FEG .... Federacion de Estudiantes de Guadalajara [*Guadalajara Student Federation*] [*Mexico*]   (LA)

FEG .... Fegyver es Gazkeszulekgyar [*Firearm and Gas Equipment Factory*]   (HU)

FEG .... Flug-Elektronik-Gesellschaft [*Germany*]   (PDAA)

FEG .... Foederation Europaeischer Gewaesserschutz [*Switzerland*]   (DSCA)

FEG .... Frente Estudiantil Guadalupano [*Guadalupano Student Front*] [*Peru*]   (LA)

FEGA........ Film Editors' Guild of Australia   (ADA)

FEGA........ Fondo Especial de Asistencia Tecnica y Garantia para Creditos Agropecuarios [*Mexico*]   (EY)

FEGAP ...... Federation Europeenne de la Ganterie de Peau [*European Federation of Leather Glove-Making*] [*EC*]   (ECED)

FEGECE.... Fonds d'Entr'aide et de Garantie des Emprunts du Conseil de l'Entente [*Mutual Aid and Secured Loans Fund of the Entente Council*]   (AF)

FEGEMARE ... Federazione della Gente del Mare [*Federation of Seamen*] [*Italian*]

FEGPI .... Federasi Gerakan Pemuda Indonesia [*Federation of Indonesian Youth Movements*]   (IN)

FEGUA...... Ferrocarriles Nacionales de Guatemala [*Guatemalan National Railways*]   (LA)

FEGZ........ Bozoum [*Central African Republic*] [*ICAO location identifier*]   (ICLI)

FEH .... Federation Europeenne Halterophile [*European Weightlifting Federation - EWF*]   (EA)

Fehcocal..... Federacion Hondurena de Cooperativas Cafetaleras [*Federation of Coffee Co-operatives of Honduras*]   (EY)

FEHCOVIL ... Federacion Hondurena de Cooperativas de Vivienda [*Honduras*]   (DSCA)

FEHO........ Federation of European Helicopter Operators   (PDAA)

FEHSTRAL ... Federacion Hondurena de Sindicatos de Trabajadores de la Alimentacion [*Honduran Federation of Food Workers Unions*]   (LA)

FEHVA...... Federation of European Heating and Ventilating Associations   (EA)

FEI............ Corporacion de Ferias y Exposiciones, SA [*Colombia*]   (COL)

FEI............ Fakulta Ekonomicko-Inzenyrska [*Department of Engineering Economics*]   (CZ)

FEI............ Falange Espanola Independiente [*Independent Spanish Phalange*]   (WER)

FEI............ Federacion de Estudiantes del Interior [*Federation of Students of the Interior*] [*Uruguay*]   (LA)

FEI............ Federacion Ecuatoriana de Indios [*Ecuadorean Federation of Indians*]   (LA)

FEI............ Federation Equestre Internationale [*International Equestrian Federation*] [*Berne, Switzerland*]   (EAIO)

FEI............ Federation Equestrian Internationale   (OLYM)

FEI............ Federation of Egyptian Industries   (EAIO)

FEI............ Foundation Europalia International   (EAIO)

FEI............ France-Europe International [*An association*]   (EAIO)

FEI............ Free Europe, Inc. [*Later, RFE/RL*]

FEIA .... Financial Executives Institute of Australia

FEIBP........ Federation Europeenne de l'Industrie de la Brosserie et de la Pinceuterie [*European Federation of the Brush and Paint Brush Industries - EFBPBI*]   (EAIO)

FEIC .... Federation Europeenne de l'Industrie du Contreplaque [*European Federation of the Plywood Industry - EFPI*]   (EA)

FEICA .... Federation Europeenne des Industries de Colles et Adhesifs [*Association of European Adhesives Manufacturers*]   (EA)

FEICOM ... Fonds d'Equipement et d'Intervention Intercommunal

FEICRO .... Federation of European Industrial Co-Operative Research Organizations   (EA)

feilpag .... Feilpagina [*Page Wrongly Numbered*] [*Publishing Danish/Norwegian*]

FEIM........ Federation Europeenne des Importateurs de Machines et d'Equipements de Bureau [*European Federation of Importers of Business Equipment*]   (EAIO)

FEIPP........ Fantastic Entertainment in Public Places [*Melbourne, Victoria, Australia*]

FEIQUE .... Federacion Empresarial de la Industria Quimica Espanola [*Spanish chemical association*] [*Madrid, Spain*]

FEIR .... Fonds pour Etudes Industrielles Remboursables

fej .... Fejezet [*Chapter*]   (HU)

FEJ .... France Europe Avia Jet [*ICAO designator*]   (FAAC)

FEJBT .... Federation Europeenne des Jeunesse Bons Templiers [*European Good Templar Youth Federation*] [*Norway*]   (EAIO)

FEJI........... Far East Job International [*Former USSR*]   (ECON)

FEK........... Fahrzeugelektrik [*Plant for the Manufacture of Electrical Equipment for Vehicles*]   (EG)

FEK........... Filelevtheri Enosis Kendrou [*Liberal Union of the Center*] [*Cyprus*]   (GC)

FEK........... Francuski Ekspedicioni Korpus [*French Expeditionary Corps*] [*World War II*]   (YU)

FEK........... Fyllon Efimeridos Kyverniseos [*Government Gazette Issue (Number)*]   (GC)

FEK........... Photoelastic Coefficient   (RU)

FEK........... Photoelectric Colorimeter   (RU)

F/E-Kapazitaeten ... Forschungs- und Entwicklungs-Kapazitaeten [*Research and Development Capacities*]   (EG)

FE KAWE ... Federatie der Katholieke Werkgevers van Belgie [*Belgium*]   (BAS)

FEKI .... Felag Enskukennara a Islandi [*Icelandic*]   (SLS)

FEKI .... Femipari Kutatointezet [*Metallurgical Research Institute*]   (HU)

FEKN........ Photoelectric Colorimeter for the Color Determination of Petroleum Products   (RU)

FEKO........ Federatie van Kleinhandelsorganisaties [*Benelux*]   (BAS)

FEKOSZ ... Foldmunkasok es Kisbirtokosok Orszagos Szovetsege [*National Association of Agricultural Laborers and Small Farmers (1946-47)*]   (HU)

feks............ For Eksempel [*For Example*] [*Danish/Norwegian*]   (GPO)

fel .... Felelos [*Responsible*]   (HU)

fel .... Felieton [*Column*] [*Poland*]

Fel .... Felsefe [*Philosophy*]   (TU)

Fel .... Felsted [*Record label*] [*Great Britain, etc.*]

fel .... Felugyelo [*Supervisor, Inspector*]   (HU)

fel .... Felugyeloseg [*Inspectorate*]   (HU)

FEL........... Front Erythreen de Liberation [*Eritrean Liberation Front*] [*Use ELF Ethiopia*]   (AF)

FELABAN ... Federacion Latinoamericana de Bancos [*Latin American Banking Federation - LABF*] [*Bogota, Colombia*]   (EAIO)

FELACEX ... Federacion Latinoamericana y del Caribe de Exportadores [*Latin American and Caribbean Federation of Exporters*]   (LA)

FELACUTI ... Federacion Latinoamericana de Usuarios del Transporte [*Latin American Federation of Shippers' Councils*]   (EAIO)

FELAP...... Federacion Latinoamericana de Periodistas [*Latin American Journalists Federation*]   (LA)

FELATRAP ... Federacion Latinoamericana de Trajabadores de la Prensa [*Latin American Federation of Press Workers*]   (EAIO)

FELCRA.... Federal Land Consolidation and Rehabilitation Authority [*Malaysia*]   (ML)

FELD........ Federation des Etudiants Libres de Dakar [*Dakar Federation of Free Students*] [*Senegal*]   (AF)

feld .... Felderites [*Reconnaissance, Scouting*]   (HU)

FELDA ..... Federal Land Development Authority [*Malaysia*]   (FEA)

FELDA ...... Foto Electra Analizado [*Colombia*]   (COL)

feldolg .... Feldolgozas [*or Feldolgozo*] [*Arrangement or Arranger Music*]   (HU)

FELN........ Frente Espanol de Liberacion Nacional [*Spanish National Liberation Front*]   (WER)

FELS......... Far East Levingston, Singapore [*Shipyard*]

felsookt ...... Felsooktatas [*Higher Education*]   (HU)

felszer......... Felszereles [*Equipment, Mountings, Fittings*]   (HU)

fel szerk...... Felelos Szerkeszto [*Responsible Editor*]   (HU)

felt .... Felteteles [*Conditional*]   (HU)

FELUBA ... Federation Luxembourgeoise de Badminton [*Luxembourg Badminton Federation*]   (EAIO)

felv............. Felvetel [*Registration, Enrollment, Record (Produced by photography, sound recording of film)*]   (HU)

felv............. Felvonas [*Act (of a play)*]   (HU)

FELVALL ... Felvonojavito Vallalat [*Elevator Repair Enterprise*]   (HU)

FEM .... Fabrica de Metalicas [*Brazil*]   (PDAA)

FEM .... Federation Europeenne de la Manutention [*European Federation of Handling Industries*]   (EAIO)

FEM .... Federation Europeenne des Metallurgistes dans la Communaute [*European Metalworkers' Federation in the Community*] [*EC*]   (ECED)

fem .... Feminiini [*Finland*]

fem .... Feminiinimuoto [*Feminine*] [*Finland*]

fem .... Feminino [*Feminine*] [*Portuguese*]

FEM .... Fondation Europeenne pour le Management [*European Foundation for Management Development*] [*Belgium*]   (EAIO)

Fem .... Force Electro-Motrice [*Electromotive Force*] [*French*]   (MTD)

FEM .... Friends of the Earth - Malaysia   (EAIO)

FEM .... Fuerza Electromotriz [*Electromotive Force*] [*Spanish*]

FEM .... Photoelectric Micrometer   (RU)

FEMA....... Fonds pour l'Enseignement du Management en Afrique

FEMAA..... Food Equipment Manufacturers' Association of Australia

FEMAD.... Federation of European Meteor Astronomers, Denmark   (EAIO)

FEMAR..... Fundacao de Estudos do Mar [*Ocean Studies Foundation*] [*Brazil*]   (LA)

FEMB........ Federation Europeenne du Mobilier de Bureau [*European Federation of Office Furniture*] [*EC*]   (ECED)

FEME....... Federacion de Empleados Municipales de Ecuador [*Ecuadorean Federation of Municipal Employees*]   (LA)

FEMEC..... Federation des Eglises et Missions Evangeliques du Cameroun   (EY)

FEMEPCAP ... Federacion de Medios Publicitarios de Centroamericana y Panama [*Advertising Federation of Central America and Panama*] (LA)

FEMESCTO ... Federation des Mouvements des Etudiants de la Savane et du Centre du Togo

FEMET ..... Federacion Nacional de Trabajadores del Metal [*National Federation of Metalworkers*] [*Chile*] (LA)

FEMFM .... Federation of European Manufacturers of Friction Materials (EA)

FEMGED ... Federation Internationale des Grandes et Moyennes Entreprises de Distribution [*International Federation of Retail Distributors*] [*Belgium*] (EAIO)

FEMI .... Fabrica de Aparate Electronice de Masura si Industriale [*Factory for Electronic Measurement and Industrial Instruments*] (RO)

FEMI .... Fundo Especial de Manutencao e Investimentos [*Special Maintenance and Investment Fund*] [*Brazil*] (LA)

FEMIB ...... Federation Europeenne des Syndicats de Fabricants de Menuiseries Industrielles de Batiment [*European Federation of Building Joinery Manufacturers*] (EAIO)

FEMIDE ... Federacion Mundial de Instituciones Financieras de Desarrollo [*World Federation of Development Financing Institutions - WFDFI*] [*Madrid, Spain*] (EAIO)

FEMIPI ..... Federation Europeenne des Mandataires de l'Industrie en Propriete Industrielle [*European Federation of Agents of Industry in Industrial Property*] (EAIO)

FEMKSF ... Frauendienst der Evangelisch-Methodistischen Kirche in der Schwiez und in Frankreich [*United Methodist Women in Switzerland and in France*] (EAIO)

FEML .... Federacao dos Estudantes Marxistas-Leninistas [*Federation of Marxist-Leninist Students*] [*Portuguese*] (WER)

FEMO .... Federation de l'Enseignement Moyen Officiel du Degre Superieur de Belgique (EAIO)

FEMP .... Federacion Espanola de Municipios Provincias [*Federation of Spanish Municipalities and Provinces*]

FEMP .... Federation des Etudiants Militants du Parti [*Federation of Party Militant Students*] [*Algeria*] (AF)

FEMS .... Federation of the European Microbiological Societies (EAIO)

FEMSA ..... Fabrica Espanola de Magnetos, Sociedad Anonima [*Chile*] (LAA)

FEN .... Far East Network [*US Armed Forces radio station*] [*Japan*]

FEN .... Federacion de Estudiantes Nacionales [*National Student Federation*] [*Argentina*] (LA)

FEN .... Federation de l'Education Nationale [*Federation of National Education*] [*Reunionese*] (AF)

FEN .... Federation de l'Education Nationale [*Federation of National Education*] [*France*] (WER)

FEN .... Free-Net Erlangen Nurnberg [*Information service or system*] (IID)

FEN .... Frente Estudiantil Nacional [*National Student Front*] [*Argentina*] (LA)

FENABAN ... Federacao Nacional dos Bancos [*National Bank Federation*] [*Brazil*] (LA)

FENABEF ... Federation Nationale des Banques et Etablissements Financiers [*National Federation of Banks and Financial Establishments*] [*Senegal*] (AF)

FENAC ...... Federacion Nacional Campesina [*National Federation of Peasants*] [*Costa Rica*] (LA)

FENAC ...... Federacion Nacional de Asociaciones Comerciales [*National Federation of Business Associations*] [*Argentina*] (LA)

FENAC ...... Federacion Nacional de Cafeteros de Colombia [*Colombian Coffee Growers Federation*]

FENACA ... Federacion Nacional de Campesinos [*National Federation of Peasants*] [*Dominican Republic*] (LA)

FENACA ... Federacion Nacional de Cultivadores de Arroz [*National Federation of Rice Growers*] [*Ecuador*] (LA)

FENACAR ... Federacion Nacional de Comerciantes de Bares y Cafes [*Colombia*] (COL)

FENACH .. Federacion Nacional de Campesinos Hondurenos [*National Federation of Honduran Peasants*]

FENACLE ... Federacion Nacional de Campesinos Libres del Ecuador [*National Federation of Free Peasants of Ecuador*] (LA)

FENACOA ... Federacion Nacional de Cooperativas Agropecuarias [*National Federation of Agricultural and Livestock Cooperatives*] [*Uruguay*] (LA)

FENACOBA ... Federacion Nacional de Cooperativas Bananeras [*National Federation of Banana Cooperatives*] [*Ecuador*] (LA)

FENACOCAL ... Federacion Nacional de Cooperativas Caneras Limitada [*National Federation of Sugar Cooperatives Limited*] [*Honduras*] (LA)

FENADESAL ... Ferrocarriles Nacionales de El Salvador [*Railway*] [*El Salvador*] (EY)

FENADIP ... Federacion Nacional de Impedidos del Peru (EAIO)

FENADUBE ... Federacion Nacional de la Alimentacion, Dulces, y Bebidas [*National Federation of Food, Sweets, and Drinks*] [*Dominican Republic*] (LA)

FENAFCO ... Federation Nationale des Femmes Congolaises

FENAGH .. Federacion Nacional de Agricultores y Ganaderos de Honduras [*National Federation of Farmers and Cattlemen of Honduras*] (LA)

FENAJ ...... Federacao Nacional dos Journalistas [*National Federation of Jounalists*] [*Brazil*] (EAIO)

FENAL ...... Federacion Nacional Agraria [*Colorado*] (LAA)

FENALCE ... Federacion Nacional de Cultivadores de Cereales [*National Federation of Cereal Growers*] [*Colorado*] (LA)

FENALCHOL ... Federacion Nacional de Choferes Asalariados del Transporte [*National Federation of Salaried Public Transport Drivers*] [*Colorado*] (LA)

FENALCLUBEX ... Federacion Nacional de Clubes y Loterias Extraordinarias [*Colombia*] (COL)

FENALCO ... Federacion Nacional de Comerciantes [*National Federation of Businessmen*] [*Bogota, Colombia*] (LA)

FENALPORTI ... Federazione Nazionale dei Lavoratori Portuali [*National Federation of Port Workers*] [*Italian*] (LA)

FENALTHYS ... Federacion Nacional de Trabajadores de la Industria Gastronomica y Hotelera [*Colombia*] (COL)

FENALTRACAR ... Federacion Nacional de Trabajadores de Carreteras [*Colombia*] (COL)

FENALTRASE ... Federacion Nacional de Trabajadores al Servicio del Estado [*Colombia*] (COL)

FENALVI ... Federacion Nacional de Agentes Viajeros [*Colombia*] (COL)

FENAMA ... Federacion Nacional de Maestros [*National Teachers Federation*] [*Dominican Republic*] (LA)

FENA-MAPOR ... Federacion Nacional de Trabajadores Maritimos y Portuarios del Peru [*National Federation of Maritime and Port Workers of Peru*] (LA)

FENAME ... Fundacao Nacional de Material Escolar [*Publisher*] [*Brazil*] (EY)

FENAMICO ... Federation Nationale des Travailleurs de Mines du Congo

FENAMIN ... Federacion Nacional Minera y Metalurgica [*National Miners and Metalworkers Federation*] [*Dominican Republic*] (LA)

FENAMU ... Federacion Nacional de Musicos [*Chile*] (EAIO)

FENAMUDE ... Federacion Nacional de Mujeres Democraticas [*National Federation of Democratic Women*] [*Panama*] (LA)

FENAPA ... Federacion Nacional Panelera Ltda. [*Colombia*] (COL)

FENAPES ... Federacion Nacional de la Pequena Empresa Salvadorena [*National Federation of Salvadoran Small Businesses*] (LA)

FENASATREV ... Federacion Nacional de Sindicatos Autonomos de Trabajadores de la Educacion de Venezuela (EY)

FENASEP ... Federacion Nacional de Asociaciones de Empleados Publicos [*National Federation of Associations of Public Employees*] [*Panama*] (EY)

FENASETE ... Federacion de Servidores Telefonicos del Ecuador [*Ecuadorean Federation of Telephone Workers*] (LA)

FENASTRAS ... Federacion Nacional Sindical de Trabajadores Salvadorenos [*Salvadoran Workers National Union Federation*] (LA)

FENASYCOA ... Federation Nationale des Syndicats du Commerce Ouest-Africain [*National Federation of West African Business Associations*] [*French*] (AF)

FENATA ... Federacion Nacional de Trabajadores Azucareros [*National Federation of Sugar Workers*] [*Dominican Republic*] (LA)

FENATI .... Federacion Nacional de Trabajadores Industriales [*National Federation of Industrial Workers*] [*Costa Rica*] (LA)

FENATOP ... Federacion Nacional de Trabajadores de Obras Publicas [*National Federation of Public Works Employees*] [*Dominican Republic*] (LA)

FENATRACA ... Federacion Nacional de Trabajadores de la Cana [*National Federation of Sugarcane Workers*] [*Dominican Republic*] (LA)

FENATRADO ... Federacion Nacional de Trabajadores [*National Federation of Workers*] [*Dominican Republic*] (LA)

FENATRAFINES ... Federacion Nacional del Transporte y sus Afines [*National Federation of Transportation and Related Industries*] [*Dominican Republic*] (LA)

FENATRAICA ... Federacion Nacional de Trabajadores de la Construccion [*National Federation of Construction Workers*] [*Dominican Republic*] (LA)

FENATRAP ... Federacion Nacional de Trabajadores Publicos [*National Federation of Public Workers*] [*Costa Rica*] (LA)

FENATS ... Federacion Nacional de Trabajadores de la Salud [*National Health Workers Federation*] [*Chile*] (LA)

FENATSSP ... Federacion Nacional de Trabajadores Asistenciales de los Seguros Sociales del Peru [*National Federation of Social Welfare Workers of Peru*] (LA)

FENAVES ... Federacion Nacional de Avicultores [*National Federation of Poultry Raisers*] [*Venezuela*] (COL)

FENAVI .... Federacion Nacional de Avicultores [*National Federation of Poultry Raisers*] [*Venezuela*] (LA)

FENAVIVERES ... Federacion Nacional de Viveres [*Colombia*] (COL)

FENAZUCAR ... Federacion Nacional Azucarera [*National Sugar Federation*] [*Dominican Republic*] (LA)

FENCOA ... Federacion Nacional de Cooperativas [*National Cooperatives Federation*] [*Uruguay*] (LA)

FENCOL... Compania de Seguros la Fenix de Colombia SA [*Colombia*] (COL)
fend .... Fendu [*Split*] [*French*]
FENDIPETROLEOS ... Federacion de Distribuidores de Petroleos [*Federation of Petroleum Distributors*] [*Colorado*] (LA)
FENDUP... Federacion Nacional de Docentes Universitarios del Peru [*National Federation of Peruvian University Teachers*] (LA)
FENEAL ... Federazione Nazionale Edili, Affini e del Legno [*National Federation of Building and Construction Workers*] [*Rome, Italy*]
FENEC...... Federacion Nacional de Educadores Catolicos [*National Federation of Catholic Teachers*] [*Nicaragua*] (LA)
FENEC...... Federation Nationale des Etudiants du Cameroun [*National Federation of Students of Cameroon*] (AF)
FENECAFE ... Federacion Nacional de Cooperativas Cafetaleras [*Ecuador*] (DSCA)
FENECEP ... Federacion Nacional de Empleados de Comunicaciones Electrico-Postales [*Trade union*] [*Costa Rica*]
FENECO... Federation Nationale des Enseignants du Congo
FENEGAS ... Federacion Nacional de Estaciones de Servicio y Expendios de Gasolina [*National Federation of Gasoline Service Stations*] [*Venezuela*] (LA)
FENEP...... Federacion Nacional de Educadores del Peru [*National Teachers Federation of Peru*] (LA)
FENEPIA ... Federacion Nacional de Empleados Publicos y de Instituciones Autonomas [*National Federation of Public and Autonomous Institutions Employees*] [*Dominican Republic*] (LA)
FENES...... Federation Nationale des Educateurs Sociaux
FENETEL ... Federacion Nacional de Telecomunicaciones del Ecuador [*Ecuadorean National Telecommunications Federation*] (LA)
FENETEL ... Federacion Nacional de Trabajadores de Telecomunicaciones [*Colombia*] (COL)
FENETEX ... Federacion Nacional Textil, y Trabajadores Textiles, y del Vestuario [*National Federation of Textile and Garment Workers*] [*Chile*] (LA)
FENEU...... Federacion Nacional de Empleados Universitarios [*National Federation of University Employees*] [*Venezuela*] (LA)
FENEX...... Federatie van Nederlandse Expediteursorganisaties [*Netherlands*] (BAS)
FENFA...... Federation des Enseignants de Nationalite Francaise en Algerie [*Federation of Teachers of French Nationality in Algeria*] (AF)
FENIB....... Federation des Entreprises Non Industrielles de Belgique [*Belgium*] (BAS)
FENIT....... Federazione Nazionale Imprese Trasporti [*Transport Undertakings Federation*] [*Italy*] (EY)
FENK........ Filoproodevtiki Enosis Neon Kaisarianis [*Progressive Union of Kaisariani Youth*] [*Greek*] (GC)
FENLAI .... Federazione Nazionale Lavoratori Auto-Ferrotramvieri e Internavigatori [*Transportation industry*] [*Italy*] (EY)
FENNTRAP ... Federacion Nacional de Trabajadores de Plantaciones [*National Federation of Plantation Workers*] [*Costa Rica*] (LA)
FENODE... Federacion Nacional de Obreros Dependientes del Estado [*Venezuela*] (DSCA)
FENOEM ... Federacion Nacional de Obreros y Empleados Municipales [*National Federation of Municipal Workers and Employees*] [*Costa Rica*] (LA)
FENOSA... Fuerzas Electricas del Noroeste, Societe Anonima [*Electric Power of the Northwest, Inc.*] [*Spanish*] (WER)
FENS........ Frente Espanol Nacional Sindicalista [*National Spanish Trade Union Front*] (WER)
FENSA...... Fabrica de Enlosados [*Tile Factory*] [*Chile*] (LA)
FENSIL..... Federacion Nacional Sindical Libre [*Guatemala*] (DSCA)
FENTEMA ... Federacion Nacional de Trabajadores Electromecanicos y Automotrices [*National Federation of Electromechanical and Automotive Workers*] [*Chile*] (LA)
FENTEP.... Federacion Nacional de Trabajadores de la Educacion Peruana [*National Federation of Peruvian Educational Workers*] [*World Federation of Teachers*] (LA)
FENTEVECU ... Federacion Nacional de Textil, Vestido, y Cueros [*National Textile, Clothing, and Leather Federation*] [*Dominican Republic*] (LA)
FeNTO ...... Federation of the Scientific and Technical Organizations of the Socialist Countries [*Formerly, Permanent Council of Scientific and Technical Organizations of Socialist Countries*] (EA)
FENTRACA ... Federacion Nacional de Trabajadores de la Cana [*National Federation of Sugarcane Workers*] [*Dominican Republic*] (LA)
FENTRATEX ... Federacion Nacional de Trabajadores Textiles [*National Federation of Textile Workers*] [*Dominican Republic*] (LA)

FENTUP ... Federacion Nacional de Trabajadores No Docentes de las Universidades del Peru [*National Federation of Peruvian Non-Teaching University Employees*] (LA)
FENU .... Fondo Especial de las Naciones Unidas [*United Nations Special Fund - UNSF*] [*Spanish*]
FENU .... Fonds d'Equipement des Nations Unies [*United Nations Capital Development Fund - UNCDF*] [*French*]
FENUSE ... Federation of Nigerian Unions of Students in Europe (AF)
FENUSIVAL ... Federacion de Sindicatos Unidos del Valle [*Colombia*] (COL)
fenyk .... Fenykep [*or Fenykepesz*] [*Photograph or Photographer*] (HU)
FENYSZOV ... Fenykepesz KSZ [*Cooperative of Photographers*] (HU)
fenyt .... Fenytan [*Optics*] (HU)
FEO .... Fishmeal Exporters Organization [*French*] (ASF)
feod............ Feudal (BU)
FEODET ... Federacion de Empleados y Obreros de Telecomunicaciones [*Federation of Telecommunications Employees and Workers*] [*Uruguay*] (LA)
FEODT...... Federation Europeenne des Organisations des Detaillants en Tabacs [*European Federation of Tobacco Retail Organizations*] (EAIO)
FEOF........ Foreign Exchange Operations Fund [*Laotian*] (CL)
feog............ Felderitoosztag [*Reconnaissance Group, Detachment*] (HU)
FEOGA ..... Fonds European d'Orientation et de Garantie Agriculturel [*European Agricultural Guidance and Guarantee Fund*] (LA)
FEOGA ..... Fonds Europeen d'Orientation et de Garantie Agricole [*European Agricultural Guidance and Guarantee Fund*] [*French*]
FEOIC....... Federacion de Estudiantes de Odontologia del Istmo Centroamericano [*Dentistry Students Federation of the Central American Isthmus*] (LA)
FEOP........ Foititiki Epitropi Organotikis Protovoulias [*Student Committee for Organizational Initiative*] [*Greek*] (GC)
FEOR........ Foglalkozasok Egyseges Osztalyozasi Rendszere [*Unified Classification System for Occupations*] (HU)
FEOU .... Photoelectrooptic Amplifier (RU)
FeOv .... Fernsprech-Ortsverkehr [*Local Telephone Traffic*] (EG)
FEP........... Federacion de Estudiantes del Peru [*Peruvian Students Federation*] (LA)
FEP........... Federacion de Estudiantes Panamenos [*Federation of Panamanian Students*] (LA)
FEP........... Federacion Espanola de Pesca [*Spain*] (DSCA)
FEP........... Federation de l'Enseignement Prive [*Federation of Private Education*] [*France*]
FEP........... Federation Europeenne de Psychanalyse [*European Psycho-Analytical Federation - EPF*] (EAIO)
FEP........... Federation of European Publishers [*Belgium*] (EAIO)
FEP........... Ferrocarril Electrico al Pacifico [*Costa Rica*] (LAA)
FEP........... Foderation der Europaischen Parkettindustrieverbande [*European Federation of the Parquet Floor Industry Associations*] [*EC*] (ECED)
FEP........... Forward Medical and Evacuation Facility (BU)
FEP........... Foundation for Education with Production (EA)
FEP........... Front des Etudiants Progressistes [*Progressive Students Front*] [*Morocco*] (AF)
FEP........... Frontline Evacuation Station (RU)
FEP........... Photoelectric Pyrometer (RU)
FEPA .... Federation Europeenne des Fabricants de Produits Abrasifs [*European Federation of the Manufacturers of Abrasive Products*] [*France*]
FEPA .... Fonds fuer Entwicklung und Partnerschaft in Afrika [*Germany*]
FEPA .... Frente Patriotico Antifascista [*Patriotic Antifascist Front*] [*Chile*] (LA)
FEPAC ...... Federation des Patrons Catholiques [*Federation of Catholic Employers*] [*Belgium*] (WER)
FEPACE.... Federation Europeenne des Producteurs Autonomes et des Consommateurs Industriels d'Energie [*European Federation of Autoproducers and Industrial Consumers of Energy*] (EAIO)
FEPACI..... Federation Panafricaine de Cineastes [*Pan-African Motion Picture Federation*] (AF)
FEPAFEM ... Federacion Panamericana de Asociacions de Facultades de Medicina [*Pan American Federation of Associations of Medical Schools - PAFAMS*] [*Caracas, Venezuela*] (EAIO)
FEPAP...... Federation of European Producers of Abrasives (PDAA)
FEPASA.... Ferrovia Paulista, Sociedade Anonima [*Sao Paulo Railroad, Incorporated*] [*Brazil*] (LA)
FEPC .... Federation of Electric Power Companies [*Japan*] (EAIO)
FEPD........ Federation Europeenne des Parfumeurs Detaillants [*European Federation of Perfumery Retailers*] (EAIO)
FEPE .... Europaeische Vereinigung der Briefumschlagfabrikanten [*European Association of Envelope Manufacturers*] (EAIO)
FEPE .... Federation Europeenne de la Publicite Exterieure [*European Federation of Outdoor Advertising*] [*France*]
FEPE .... Federation Europeenne pour la Protection des Eaux [*European Federation for the Protection of Waters - EFPW*] [*French*] (ASF)

FEPEM ..... Federation of European Petroleum Equipment Manufacturers [*Netherlands*]
FEPEX....... Federacion Espanola de Asociaciones de Productores Exportadores de Frutas y Hortalizas   (EY)
FEPF.......... European Federation of Earthenware, China and Tableware, and Ornamental Ware   (EAIO)
FEPI .... Fideicomiso para la Educacion Pesquera Integral [*Mexico*] (MSC)
FEPICOL.. Federacion de Pequenos Industriales Colombianos [*Colombia*] (COL)
FEPICOL.. Federacion Propulsora de Industrias Colombianas [*Federation for the Promotion of Colombian Industries*]   (LA)
FEPLAS .... Fabrica de Estuches Plasticos [*Colombia*]   (COL)
FEPMA ..... Federation of European Pencil Manufacturers Associations [*See also FEFM*]   (EA)
FEPMB ..... Federacion Espanola de Petanca-Modalidad Bochas [*Spain*] (EAIO)
FEPNS ...... Fabrika Elektroporcelana Novi Sad [*Insulating Porcelain Factory, Novi Sad*]   (YU)
FEPOW..... Far East Prisoner of War
FEPPR....... Federacion de Enfermeria Practica de Puerto Rico   (EAIO)
FEPRABEL ... Federation des Producteurs d'Assurances de Belgique [*Insurance association*] [*Belgium*]   (EY)
FEPRANAL ... Federacion Nacional del Sector Privado para la Accion Comunal [*Colombia*]   (COL)
FEPRINCO ... Federacion de la Produccion, la Industria, y el Comercio [*Federation of Production, Industry, and Commerce*] [*Paraguay*]   (LAA)
FEPRO ...... Federacion de Asociaciones de Profesionales [*Federation of Associations of Professionals*] [*El Salvador*]
FEPRODEI ... Foro Permanente para la Promocion y Defensa de las Exportaciones Militares [*Permanent Body for the Defense and Promotion of Military Exports*] [*Argentina*]   (LA)
FEPROSICS ... Federacion Provincial de Sindicatos Cristianos de Santiago [*Santiago Provincial Federation of Christian Trade Unions*] [*Dominican Republic*]   (LA)
FEPU .... Frente Eleitoral do Povo Unido [*United People's Electoral Front*] [*Portugal*] [*Political party*]   (PPE)
Fer.............. Farm [*Topography*]   (RU)
FER........... Federacion de Estudiantes Revolucionarios [*Federation of Revolutionary Students*] [*Panama*]   (LA)
FER........... Federacion de Estudiantes Revolucionarios [*Federation of Revolutionary Students*] [*Uruguay*]   (PD)
FER........... Federation des Etudiants Revolutionnaires [*Federation of Revolutionary Students*] [*France*]
FER........... Federation of Engine Re-Manufacturers [*Chigwell, Essex, England*]   (EAIO)
FER........... Feria Aviacion [*Spain*] [*ICAO designator*]   (FAAC)
Fer.............. Fermanagh County [*Ireland*]   (BARN)
FER........... Fondo Educativo Regional [*Colombia*]   (COL)
FER........... Fonds d'Entretien Routier
FER........... Fonds d'Extension et de Renouvellement pour le Developpement de la Culture du Palmier a Huile
FER........... Frente Estudiantil Revolucionario [*Revolutionary Student Front*] [*Peru*]   (LA)
FER........... Frente Estudiantil Revolucionario [*Revolutionary Student Front*] [*Uruguay*]   (LA)
FER........... Frente Estudiantil Revolucionario [*Revolutionary Student Front*] [*Panama*]   (LA)
FER........... Frente Estudiantil Revolucionario [*Revolutionary Student Front*] [*Nicaragua*]   (LA)
FER........... Frente Estudiantil Revolucionario [*Revolutionary Student Front*] [*Mexico*]   (LA)
FER........... Fusion Engineering Reactor [*Japan*]
FER........... Roentgen Equivalent Physical   (RU)
FERA........ Federacion Ecuatoriana de Radioaficionados [*Ecuadorean Federation of Radio Hams*]   (LA)
FERA........ Foereningen foer Elektricitetens Rationella Anvaendning [*Sweden*]   (SLS)
FERBUBLANC ... Fernandinos-Bubi-Blancos
FERCAL.... Sociedade de Fertilizantes e Calcareos Ltd. [*Brazil*]   (DSCA)
FERCAMPANA ... Ferreteria la Campana [*Colombia*]   (COL)
FERD........ Foreign Economic Relations Department [*Myanmar*]   (DS)
FERDES.... Fonds d'Equipements Ruraux et de Developpement Economique et Social
FERE......... Federacion Espanola de Religiosos de Ensenanza [*Spanish*] (SLS)
FERE......... Fondation Egyptologique Reine Elisabeth
FEREP....... Federation Executive Recruitment and Education Program
FERIAUTO ... Sociedad de Ferias de Automotores [*Colombia*]   (COL)
ferj............. Ferjezett [*Married Woman*]   (HU)
Ferm.......... Farm [*Topography*]   (RU)
ferm........... Fermoirs [*Clasps*] [*Publishing*] [*French*]
FERMAC.... Ferramentas, Maquinas, e Acessorios Lda.
Fermentat .. Fermentation [*German*]   (GCA)
FernU......... Fernuniversitaet

FEROPA ... Federation Europeenne des Fabricants de Panneaux de Fibres [*European Federation of Fireboard Manufacturers*] [*EC*] (ECED)
FEROPA ... Federation Europeenne des Synicats de Panneaux de Fibres [*European Federation of Manufacturers Associations of Fiber Panels*]   (PDAA)
FERPHOS ... Entreprise Nationale du Fer et du Phosphate [*Nationalized industry*] [*Algeria*]   (EY)
ferr .... Ferrovia [*Railroad*] [*Italian*]   (GPO)
FERRAL.... Ferragens e Acessorios Limitada
FERRANGOL ... Empresa Nacional de Ferro de Angola [*Iron production enterprise*] [*Luanda, Angola*]
FERRIL..... Companhia de Ferrocarriles de Cucuta SA [*Cucuta*]   (COL)
FERRIMPORT ... Empresa Cubana Importadora de Articulos de Ferreteria [*Cuban Enterprise for Hardware Import*]   (LA)
FERROCOL ... Ferrometalurgica de Colombia Ltda. [*Colombia*]   (COL)
FERROMET ... Podnik Zahranicniho Obchodu pro Vyvoz a Dovoz Hutnickych Vyrobku [*Foreign Trade Enterprise for the Export and Import of Metallurgical Products*]   (CZ)
FERRONAL ... Ferrocarriles Nacionales [*Santa Marta*]   (COL)
FERSICRISPP ... Federacion Regional de Sindicatos Cristianos de Puerto Plata [*Puerto Plata Regional Federation of Christian Trade Unions*] [*Dominican Republic*]   (LA)
fert............. Fertotlenito [*Antiseptic*]   (HU)
fert............. Fertozo [*Contagious*]   (HU)
FERTIBERIA ... Fertilizantes de Iberia SA
FERTICA ... Fertilizantes de Centro America, SA [*Central American Fertilizers, Inc.*] [*Mexican, Salvadoran*]   (LA)
FERTIL..... Ruwais Fertilizers Industries Ltd. [*United Arab Emirates*] (MENA)
FERTILBA ... Fertilizantes e Inseticidas da Bahia Ltd. [*Brazil*]   (DSCA)
FERTIMA ... Societe Marocaine des Fertilisants
FERTIMINAS ... Companhia Mineira de Fertilizantes [*Brazil*]   (DSCA)
FERTIPERU ... Empresa de Fertilizantes [*State Fertilizer Enterprise*] [*Peru*] (LA)
FERTISA .. Fertilazantes Ecuatorianos SA [*Ecuador*]   (DSCA)
FERTISM ... Fertilizantes del Itsmo SA [*Mexico*]   (DSCA)
FERTIZA .. Fertilizantes del Ecuador [*Ecuadorean Fertilizer Enterprise*] (LA)
FERTRAM ... Federacion Regional de Trabajadores de Morales [*Guatemala*] (DSCA)
FERTRIN ... Fertilizers of Trinidad and Tobago Ltd.   (LA)
FERTS....... Federacion del Sur [*Guatemala*]   (DSCA)
FERU......... Franco-Ethiopian Railway Union
FES .... Falange Espanola Sindicalista [*Spanish Trade Union Phalange*] (WER)
FES .... Federacion de Estudiantes de Secundaria [*Federation of Secondary School Students*] [*Bolivia*]   (LA)
FES .... Federacion de Estudiantes de Secundaria [*Federation of Secondary School Students*] [*Honduras*]   (LA)
FES .... Federation Europeenne de la Salmoniculture [*Federation of the European Trout and Salmon Industry*] [*Formerly, European Salmon Breeding Federation*]   (EA)
FES .... Federation Francaise de Speleologie [*French*]   (SLS)
FES .... Ferrocarril de El Salvador [*El Salvador*]   (LAA)
FES .... Finnish Egyptological Society   (EAIO)
FES .... Frente de Estudiantes Secundarios [*Secondary School Students Front*] [*Peru*]   (LA)
FES .... Frente de Estudios Sociales [*Social Studies Front*] [*Colorado*] (LA)
FES .... Friedrich Ebert Stiftung [*Trade union*]
FES .... Fuel and Electricity Survey [*Australia*]
FES .... Fundacion para la Educacion Superior. Universidad del Valle [*Colombia*]   (COL)
FESA .... Farmaco Especialidades SA [*Venezuela*]   (DSCA)
FESAC....... Fondation pour l'Enseignement Superieur en Afrique Centrale [*Foundation for Higher Education in Central Africa*]   (AF)
FESC .... Federation Europeenne des Sports Corporatifs [*European Federation for Company Sports - EFCS*]   (EAIO)
FESC .... Frente Estudiantil Social Cristiano [*Social Christian Student Front*] [*Guatemala*]   (LA)
FESCID..... Federation Europeenne des Syndicats de la Chimie et des Industries Diverses [*European Federation of Chemical and General Workers Unions*]   (EAIO)
FESCO ...... Foreign Enterprise Service Corp. [*China*]
FESCRIDINA ... Federacion de Sindicatos Cristianos del Distrito Nacional [*National District Federation of Christian Trade Unions*] [*Dominican Republic*]   (LA)
FESE .... Federacion de Estudiantes Secundarios del Ecuador [*Ecuadorean Federation of Secondary Students*]   (LA)
FESEB....... Federacion Sindical de Empleados Bancarios de Guatemala [*Trade Union Federation of Bank Employees of Guatemala*] (LA)
FESECh..... Federacion de Estudiantes Secundarios de Chile [*Chilean Federation of Secondary Students*]   (LA)
FESES .... Federacion de Estudiantes Secundarios de Santiago [*Santiago Federation of Secondary Students*] [*Chile*]   (LA)

FESGAS.... Fuerzas Especiales de Guerillas Anticomunistas [*Special Forces of Anticommunist Guerrellas*] [*Nicaragua*]   (LA)

FESI.......... Federation Europeenne des Syndicats d'Entreprises d'Isolation [*European Federation of Associations of Insulation Contractors*]   (EA)

FESIAN..... Federacion Sindical Agraria Nacional [*National Agrarian Trade Union Federation*] [*Costa Rica*]

FESIATHONEMB ... Federation des Syndicats des Industries Alimentaires, Tourisme, Hotellerie, Employees de Maison du Benin [*Federation of Unions of Food Industries, Tourism, Hotel, and Housework Employees of Benin*]   (AF)

FESINCONSTRANS ... Federacion de Sindicatos de la Industria de la Construccion, Transporte, y Similares [*Federation of Labor Unions of the Construction, Transportation, and Allied Industries*]   (LA)

FESINOVAL ... Federacion de Sindicatos de Obreros del Valle del Cauca [*Colombia*]   (COL)

FESINTEXIS ... Federacion de Sindicatos Textiles, Similares, y Conexos [*Federation of Textile, Similar, and Related Unions*] [*El Salvador*]   (LA)

FESINTRABS ... Federacion de Sindicatos de Trabajadores de Alimentos, Bebidas, y Similares [*Federation of Labor Unions of the Food, Beverage, and Allied Industries*] [*El Salvador*]   (LA)

FESINTRAH ... Federacion Sindical de Trabajadores Nacionales de Honduras [*Union Federation of National Honduras Workers*]   (LAA)

FESINTRANH ... Federacion Sindical de Trabajadores Nortenos de Honduras [*Union Federation of Northern Honduras Workers*]   (LA)

FESITRANH ... Federacion de Sindicatos de Tranajadores Nortenos de Honduras [*Northern Trade Union Federation of Honduran Workers*]

FESITRISEVA ... Federacion de Sindicatos de Trabajadores en Industrias y Servicios Varios [*Federation of Workers of Unions in Various Industries and Services*] [*El Salvador*]   (LA)

FESNATEP ... Federacion Sindical Nacional de Telecomunicaciones y Postales [*National Labor Federation of Telecommunication and Postal Workers*] [*Bolivia*]   (LA)

FESNESCUB ... Federation des Syndicats Nationaux des Enseignants de la Science et de la Culture du Benin [*Federation of National Unions of Teachers of Science and Culture of Benin*]   (AF)

FESOMENIC ... Federacion de Sociedades Medicas de Nicaragua [*Federation of Nicaragua Medical Societies*]   (LA)

FESPA....... Federation of European Screen Printers Associations   (PDAA)

FESPACO ... Festival Pan-Africain du Cinema de Ouagadougou [*Ouagadougou Pan-African Cinema Festival*]   (AF)

FESPIC ..... Far East and South Pacific

FESR......... Fundo de Estabilidade do Seguro Rural [*Brazil*]   (DSCA)

F es Ralapok ... Fejlesztesi es Reszesedesi Alapok [*Development and Profit Sharing Fund*]   (HU)

FESS.......... Photoelectric Monitoring System [*Chemical engineering*]   (RU)

FESSP....... Fundacion Especial del Servicio de Salud Publica [*Special Foundation of the Public Health Service*] [*Rio De Janeiro, Brazil*]   (LAA)

FEST .... Forschungsstatte de Evangelischen Studiengemeinschaft [*Protestant Institute for Interdisciplinary Research*] [*Research center*]   (IRC)

FEST .... Foundation for Education, Science, and Technology

FEST .... Funkempfangsstelle [*Radio Receiving Station*]   (EG)

FESTAC....... Festival of Arts and Culture [*Nigeria*]   (AF)

Festb .... Festband [*Special Issue*] [*German*]   (GCA)

FESTBRA ... Federacion Departamental de Trabajadores Bancarios y Ramas Afines de La Paz [*La Paz Departmental Federation of Bank Employees and Related Branches*] [*Bolivia*]   (LA)

FestF .... Festival (France) [*Record label*]

FESTIAVTSCES ... Federacion Nacional de Sindicatos de Trabajadores de la Industria del Alimento, Vestido, Textil, Similares y Conexos de El Salvador [*Salvadoran National Trade Union Federation of Workers of the Food, Clothing, Textile, and Related Industries*]   (LA)

Festigk .... Festigkeit [*Strength*] [*German*]   (GCA)

Festktsl ...... Festigkeitlehre [*Strength of Materials*] [*German*]   (GCA)

FESTRA.... Federacion de Trabajadores de Santander [*Federation of Workers of Santander*] [*Colorado*]   (LA)

FESTRAC ... Federacion Sindical de Cundinamarca [*Trade Union Federation of Cundinamarca*] [*Colorado*]   (LA)

FESTRACOL ... Federacion Sindical de Trabajadores Agrarios de Colombia [*Trade Union Federation of Colombian Agricultural Workers*]   (LA)

FESTRAL ... Federacion Sindical de Trabajadores del Atlantico [*Trade Union Federation of Atlantico Workers*] [*Colorado*]   (LA)

FESTRALVA ... Federacion Sindical de Trabajadores Libres del Valle [*Colombia*]   (COL)

FESTRAN ... Federacion Sindical de Trabajadores de Antioquia [*Trade Union Federation of Antioquia Workers*] [*Colorado*]   (LA)

FESTRAS ... Federacion Sindical de Trabajadores Salvadorenos [*Trade Union Federation of Salvadoran Workers*]   (LA)

Festschr ..... Festschrift [*Special Publication*] [*German*]   (GCA)

Feststell ..... Feststellung [*Determination*] [*German*]   (GCA)

FESU .... Farm Economic Survey Unit

FESV .... Federazione Europea per il Diritto alla Sterilizzazione Volontaria [*Italian*]   (SLS)

FESYGA.... Federation Syndicale Gabonaise [*Gabonese Trade Union Federation*]   (AF)

FESYP....... Federation Europeenne des Syndicats de Fabricants de Panneaux de Particules [*European Federation of Associations of Particleboard Manufacturers*]   (EAIO)

FESYSFEB ... Federation des Syndicats des Services Financiers et Economiques du Benin [*Federation of Unions of Financial and Economic Services of Benin*]   (AF)

FESYTRAF ... Federation Syndicale des Travailleurs de l'Agriculture et des Forets [*Trade union*] [*Congo*]

FET........... Division of Electrical Engineering   (RU)

FET........... Falange Espanola Tradicionalista [*Traditionalist Spanish Phalange*]   (WER)

FET........... Fiainana Eokaristian' ny Tanora

FETAC ...... Foreign Economic and Trade Arbitration Commission [*Chinese*]   (GEA)

FETAG ...... Federacao dos Trabalhadores na Agricultura [*Farm Workers Federation*] [*Brazil*]   (LA)

FETAG ...... Feira da Tecnica Agricola [*Brazil*]   (DSCA)

FETAL ...... Federacion de Trabajadores Agricolas del Litoral [*Federation of Coastal Farm Workers*] [*Ecuador*]   (LA)

FETAP...... Federacion de Trabajadores de la Administracion Publica [*Federation of Workers of Public Administration of the UGT*] [*Spanish*]   (WER)

FETBB....... Federation Europeenne des Travailleurs du Batiment et du Bois [*European Federation of Building and Woodworkers - EFBWW*]   (EAIO)

FET delas JONS ... Falange Espanola Tradicionalista y de las Juntas de Ofensiva Nacional Sindicalista [*Traditionalist Spanish Phalange of the Syndicalist Juntas of the National Offensive*] [*Political party*]   (PPE)

FETE .... Department of Further Education, Training and Employment [*New South Wales, Australia*]

FETE .... Federacion de Trabajadores de Ensenanza [*Federation of Educational Workers*] [*Spanish*]   (WER)

FETIBAL .. Federacion de Trabajadores de la Industria del Banano en America Latina y El Caribe [*Honduras*]   (DSCA)

FETICEV .. Federacion de Trabajadores de la Industria Cervecera [*Brewery Workers Federation*] [*Peru*]   (LA)

FETIE........ Federacion Ecuatoriana de Trabajadores de la Industria Electrica [*Ecuadorean Federation of Workers of the Electric Power Industry*]   (LA)

FETIM ...... Societe N. V. Fijnhout en Triplex Import

FETIMP.... Federacion de Trabajadores de la Industria Metalurgica [*Metallurgical Industry Workers Federation*] [*Peru*]   (LA)

FETLIG..... Federacion Ecuatoriana de Trabajadores Libres del Guayas [*Ecuadorean Federation of Free Workers of Guayas*]   (LA)

FETO .... Federation Togolaise des Orchestres

FETPAL.... Federacion de Trabajadores Limonenses [*Federation of Limon Workers*] [*Costa Rica*]   (LA)

FETPQS.... Federacion Ecuatoriana de Trabajadores del Petroleo, Quimicos, y Similares [*Ecuadorean Federation of Workers of the Petroleum, Chemical, and Allied Industries*]   (LA)

FETRA ...... Federation des Industries Transformatrices de Papier et Carton [*Paper and Board Federation*] [*Belgium*]   (EY)

FETRABA ... Federacion de Trabajadores Bananeros [*Federation of Banana Workers*] [*Costa Rica*]   (LAA)

FETRABARINAS ... Federacion de Trabajadores del Estado Barinas [*Barinas State Workers Federation*] [*Venezuela*]   (LA)

FETRACADE ... Federacion de Trabajadores de la Cana de Azucar y sus Derivados [*Venezuela*]   (DSCA)

FETRACID ... Federation des Travailleurs du Commerce et de l'Industrie du Dahomey

FETRACUN ... Federacion de Trabajo de Cundinamarca [*Labor Federation of Cundinamarca*] [*Colorado*]   (LA)

FETRAELEC ... Federacion de Trabajadores de la Industria Electrica [*Federation of Electrical Industry Workers*] [*Venezuela*]   (LA)

FETRAES ... Federacion de Trabajadores de la Educacion Superior [*Federation of Higher Education Workers*] [*Costa Rica*]   (LA)

Fetrahidrocarburos ... Federacion de Trabajadores de la Industria de Hidrocarburos y Sus Derivados [*Federation of Workers of the Industry of Hydrocarbons and Derivatives*] [*Venezuela*]   (LA)

FETRAL.... Federacao dos Trabalhadores Rurais do Estado de Alagoas [*Brazil*]   (DSCA)

FETRAMECOL ... Federacion de Trabajadores de las Industrias Metalurgicas [*Colombia*]   (COL)

FETRAMETAL ... Federacion de Trabajadores Metalurgicos [*Federation of Metalworkers*] [*Venezuela*]   (LA)

FETRANJAS ... Federacion Nacional de Trabajadores Agropecuarios, Recursos Naturales Renovables, Jardineros y Similares [*Venezuela*]   (DSCA)

FETRAPEP ... Federacion de Trabajadores Pesqueros del Peru [*Federation of Fishery Workers of Peru*]   (LA)

FETRASUR ... Federacion de Trabajadores del Sur [*Federation of Southern Workers*] [*Honduras*]   (EY)

FETRICH ... Federacion de Tripulantes de Chile [*Chile*]   (LAA)

FETRIKAT ... Federation Generale des Tribes du Haut Katanga [*General Federation of Tribes of North Katanga*]

FETS .... Far East Trade Service Inc. [*Ivory Coast*]

FETS .... Fellowship of Evangelical Theological Schools [*Indonesia*]

FETSALUD ... Federacion de Trabajadores de la Salud [*Federation of Health Workers*] [*Nicaragua*]   (LA)

FETT .... Feldeffekt Transistor Technologie [*Field Effect Transistor Technology*] [*German*]   (ADPT)

fetthalt .... Fetthaltig [*Fat-Containing*] [*German*]   (GCA)

Fetthart...... Fetthaertung [*Hardening of Fat*] [*German*]   (GCA)

FEU .... Amplifier for Photoelectric Cell   (RU)

FEU .... Compagnie Aeronautique Europeene [*France*] [*ICAO designator*]   (FAAC)

FEU .... Family Education Unit [*Australia*]

FEU .... Federacion de Estudiantes Universitarios [*Federation of University Students*] [*Costa Rica*]   (LA)

FEU .... Federacion de Estudiantes Universitarios [*Federation of University Students*] [*Cuba*]   (LA)

FEU .... Federacion Estudiantil Universitario [*University Student Federation*] [*Dominican Republic*]   (LA)

FEU .... Frente Estudiantil Universitario [*University Student Front*] [*Venezuela*]   (LA)

FEU .... Photomultiplier   (RU)

FEUB........ Federacao dos Estudantes da Universidade de Brasilia [*Brasilia University Students Federation*] [*Brazil*]   (LA)

FEUC........ Federacion de Estudiantes de la Universidad Catolica [*Catholic University Student Federation*] [*Chile*]   (LA)

FEUC........ Federacion de Estudiantes Universitarios de Cuba [*Federation of University Students of Cuba*]   (LA)

FEUCA...... Federacion Estudiantil Universitaria Centroamericana [*Federation of Central American University Students*]   (LA)

FEUCE...... Federacion de Estudiantes de Universidades Catolicas del Ecuador [*Federation of Students of Catholic Universities of Ecuador*]   (LA)

Feuchtigk... Feuchtigkeit [*Moisture*] [*German*]   (GCA)

FEUCP...... Federacion de Estudiantes de la Universidad Catolica del Paraguay [*Federation of Students of the Catholic University of Paraguay*]   (LA)

FEUCR...... Federacion de Estudiantes Universitarios de Costa Rica [*Federation of University Students of Costa Rica*]   (LA)

FEUE........ Federacion de Estudiantes Universitarios del Ecuador [*Federation of Ecuadorean University Students*]   (LA)

Feuer .... Feuerung [*Furnace*] [*German*]   (GCA)

FEUGRES ... Federation Europeenne des Fabricants de Tuyaux en Gre [*European Federation of Manufacturers of Salt Glazed Pipes*]   (PDAA)

FEUH .... Federacion de Estudiantes Universitarios de Honduras [*Honduran University Students Federation*]   (LA)

FEUNA ..... Federacion de Estudiantes de la Universidad Nacional [*Federation of National University Students*] [*Costa Rica*]   (LA)

FEUPF ...... European Federation of Professional Florists' Unions [*Italy*]   (EAIO)

FEUPF ...... Federation Europeenne des Unions Professionelles de Fleuristes [*European Federation of Professional Florists' Unions*]   (EAIO)

FEUTE ..... Federacion de Estudiantes de la Universidad Tecnica del Estado [*Student Federation of the State Technical University*] [*Chile*]   (LA)

FEUTH ..... Federacion Unitaria de Trabajadores de Honduras [*United Federation of Honduran Workers*]   (LA)

FEUU .... Federacion de Estudiantes Universitarios de Uruguay [*Federation of University Students of Uruguay*]   (LA)

FEUV........ Federacion de Estudiantes Universitarios del Valle [*Federation of University Students of Valle*] [*Colorado*]   (LA)

FEV .... Far East Vertical Shaft System [*Mining*] [*South Africa*]

FEV .... Federacion de Estudiantes Venezolanos [*Federation of Venezuelan Students*]   (LA)

fev............. Fevereiro [*February*] [*Portuguese*]   (GPO)

fev............. Fevrier [*February*] [*French*]

FEV .... Forschungs- und Entwicklungswerk des Verkehrswesens [*Research and Development Works for Transportation*]   (EG)

FEV .... Fuszer- es Edessegkereskedelmi Vallalat [*Spices and Confectionery Enterprise*]   (HU)

FEVBE ...... Fovarosi es Videki Belyeggyujtok Egyesulete [*Philatelists' Association*]   (HU)

FEVE .... Federation Europeenne du Verre d'Emballage [*European Container Glass Federation - ECGF*]   (EA)

FEVE........ Ferrocarriles Espanoles de Via Estrecha [*Spanish Narrow-Gauge Railroads*] [*Madrid*]   (WER)

FEVECI..... Federacion Venezolana de Cooperacion Intermunicipal [*Venezuela*]   (LAA)

FEVINAL ... Federacion Avicola Nacional [*Colombia*]   (COL)

FEVIR .... Federation of European Veterinarians in Industry and Research   (EA)

fevo............. Fevereiro [*February*] [*Portuguese*]

fevr .... February   (RU)

FEVSD .... Federation Europeenne pour la Vente et le Service a Domicile [*European Direct Selling Federation*] [*Brussels, Belgium*]   (EA)

FEW.......... Forschungs- und Entwicklungswerk [*Research and Development Works*]   (EG)

FEWAC ..... Far East West African Conference

FEWIA ...... Federation of European Writing Instruments Associations [*See also FEAIE*]   (EA)

FEWITA ... Federation of European Wholesale and International Trade Associations [*Common Market*] [*Belgium*]

FEWMA.... Federation of European Window Manufacturers Associations   (EA)

FEWO .... Federatie van Werknemers Organisaties [*Federation of Employee Organizations*] [*Netherlands*]   (WEN)

FEX........... Ceskoslovensky Filmexport [*Czechoslovak Film Export*]   (CZ)

FEZ........... Federacion Europea de Zootecnia [*European Association for Animal Production - EAAP*] [*Spanish*]   (ASF)

FEZ........... Federation d'Entreprises du Zaire

FEZ........... Federation Europeenne de Zootechnie [*European Association for Animal Production - EAAP*] [*France*]   (ASF)

FEZ........... Federazione Europea di Zootecnia [*European Association for Animal Production - EAAP*] [*Italian*]   (SLS)

FEZ........... Fez [*Morocco*] [*Airport symbol*]   (OAG)

FeZaFA ..... Federation Zairoise de Football Association

FF .... Department of Philology   (BU)

FF .... Department of Philosophy   (BU)

FF .... Faisant Fonction   (FLAF)

FF .... Federation Francaise [*French Federation*]

FF .... Fehlerfreies Arbeiten [*Error-Free Work*]   (EG)

FF .... Feuille Federale [*Switzerland*]   (FLAF)

ff................ Feuillets [*Sheets*] [*Publishing*] [*French*]

FF .... Fianna Fail [*Warriors of Destiny*] [*Irish political party*]

FF .... Filozofski Fakultet [*Faculty of Philosophy*]   (YU)

FF .... Firefighter [*Royal Australian Navy*]

ff................ Folgende [*The Following*] [*Danish*]   (GPO)

FF .... Folgende [*And the Following Pages, Verses, etc.*] [*German*]   (ROG)

ff................ Folhas [*Sheets*] [*Publishing*] [*Portuguese*]

FF .... Foreningen for Familieplanlaegning [*Family Planning Association*] [*Denmark*]   (EAIO)

FF .... Fortissimo [*Very Loud*] [*Music*]

Ff............... Fortsetzung Folgt [*To Be Continued*] [*German*]   (GPO)

FF .... Francs Francais [*French Francs*] [*Monetary unit*]

FF .... Frauen fur den Frieden [*Women for Peace*] [*Switzerland*]   (EAIO)

FF .... Fredspolitisk Folkeparti [*People's Peace Policy Party*] [*Denmark*]   (PPE)

FF .... Freiwillige Feuerwehr [*Volunteer Fire Department*]   (EG)

FF .... Freres [*Brothers*] [*French*]

FF .... Frie Folkevalgte [*Freely Elected Representatives*] [*Norway*]   (PPE)

FF .... Friendship Force [*Australia*]

FF .... Frontline Fellowship [*South Africa*]

ff................ Funds   (RU)

FF .... Phenolphthalein   (RU)

Ff .... Sehr Fein [*Very Fine*]   (EG)

FFA........... Financial Form Asset [*Asset Privatization Trust*] [*Philippines*]

FFA........... Flug und Fahrzeugwerke Altenrhein [*Switzerland*]   (PDAA)

FFA........... Flygtekniska Foersoeksanstalten [*Aeronautical Research Institute of Sweden*] [*Research center*]   (SLS)

FFA........... Forces Francaises en Allemagne [*French Forces in Germany*]

FFA........... Forum Fisheries Agency [*South Pacific Forum*] [*Solomon Islands*]   (EY)

FFA........... Future Farmers of Australia

FFAA......... Flavour and Fragrance Association of Australia

FF AA ...... Forze Armate [*Armed Forces*] [*Italian*]   (WER)

FFAA........ Fuerzas Armadas [*Armed Forces*] [*Colombia*]   (COL)

FFAB .... Funk- und Fernmelde-Anlagenbau (VEB) [*Construction of Radio and Telecommunication Installations (VEB)*]   (EG)

FFAC .... Societe Fiduciaire France-Afrique-Cameroun

FFAC .... Societe Fiduciaire France-Afrique-Congo

FFA-CI ...... Societe Fiduciaire France-Afrique-Cote-D'Ivoire

FFAG......... Societe Fiduciaire France-Afrique-Gabon

FFAHV....... Societe Fiduciaire France-Afrique-Haute-Volta

FFAJ.......... Federation Francaise des Auberges de Jeunesse

FFALA ...... Fund For Animals Ltd. Australia [*Commercial firm*]

FFAMP ..... Federation Francaise Amateur de Mineralogie et Paleontologie [*French Amateur Federation of Mineralogy and Paleontoloy*] (EAIO)

FFAO........ Federation Francaise des Amateurs d'Orchidees [*France*] (EAIO)

FFAP .... Fundo Federal Agropecuario [*Brazil*] (DSCA)

FFARACS ... Fellow of the Faculty of Anaesthetists of the Royal Australian College of Surgeons

FFARACS ... Fellow of the Faculty of Anaesthetists, Royal Australasian College of Surgeons (ADA)

FFAS .... Finnish Automobile Sport Federation (EAIO)

FFAS .... Societe Fiduciaire France-Afrique-Senegal

FFAW....... Fellow of the Fellowship of Australian Writers

FFB .... Africair Service [*Senegal*] [*ICAO designator*] (FAAC)

FFB .... Federation Francaise de la Brosserie [*France*] (EAIO)

FFB .... Fellow of the Faculty of Building [*Australia*]

FFBA .... Federation Francaise de Badminton [*French Badminton Federation*] (EAIO)

FFC .... Film Finance Corp. [*Australia*]

FFC .... Forces Francaises Combattantes (FLAF)

FFC .... Forum Fisheries Committee [*Australia*]

FFCAT ...... Federation Francaise des Commissionaires et Auxiliares de Transport [*France*] (EAIO)

FFCC .... Ford Four Car Club [*Australia*]

FFCCNNde M ... Ferrocarriles Nacionales de Mexico [*National Railways of Mexico*] (LA)

FFCEA ...... Federation of Filipino Civilian Employees Association (EY)

FFCI .... French Federation for the Concrete Industry (EAIO)

FFCM .... Fellow of the Faculty of Community Medicine [*Australia*]

FFCT .... Federation of Finnish Commerce and Trade (EAIO)

FFD........... Phenol Formaldehyde Dicyandiamide (RU)

FFDCP ...... Fondo Financiero para el Desarrollo de la Cuenca del Plata [*River Plate Basin Development Fund*] (LA)

FFE .... Fire Fighting Enterprises (Australia) Ltd.

FFE .... Fundo de Fomento da Exportacao [*Export Promotion Fund*] [*Portuguese*] (WER)

FFE(A)....... Fire Fighting Enterprises (Australia) Ltd. [*Commercial firm*]

FFEE .... Ferrocarriles del Estado [*Chile*] (LAA)

FFEMA ...... Federacion Femenina Evangelica Metodista Argentina (EAIO)

FFEP......... Finlands Folks Enhetsparti [*Finnish People's Unity Party*] (PPE)

FFEPGV.... Federation Francaise d'Education Physique et de Gymnastique Volontaire [*French*] (SLS)

FFESSM ... Federation Francaise d'Etudes et des Sports Sous-Marins [*French*] (MSC)

FFETA...... Fire-Fighting Equipment Traders Association [*South Africa*] (AA)

FFF .... Federal Fighting Fund

FFF .... Federation of Free Farmers [*Philippines*] (FEA)

FFF .... First Foundation Fellow [*Australia*]

fff............. Folgende [*And the Following*] [*German*] (GCA)

fff............. Sehr Fein [*Very Fine*] [*German*]

FFFU .... Federal Fire Fighters' Union [*Australia*]

FFG .... Flugdienst Fehlhaber GmbH [*Germany*] [*ICAO designator*] (FAAC)

FFH .... Forschungsstelle fuer den Handel Berlin eV (SLS)

FFH .... Fovarosi Foldhivatal [*Capital Land Office*] (HU)

FFHC........ Freedom from Hunger Campaign [*FAO*]

FFHC/AD ... Freedom from Hunger Campaign/Action for Development [*FAO*] (ASF)

FFHMP..... Fellow of the Faculty of History of Medicine and Pharmacy [*Australia*]

FFHNCK.... Freedom from Hunger National Committee of Kenya

FFHS .... Federation of Family History Societies (EA)

FFHSA ...... Finnish Folk High School Association (EAIO)

FFI .... Faisal Finance Institution [*Turkey*]

FFI .... Flying Fifteen International (EA)

FFI .... Forces Francaises de l'Interieur [*French Forces of the Interior*] [*World War II*]

FFI .... Fovarosi Fertotlenito Intezet [*Capital Immunization Institute*] (HU)

FFIA .... Fellow of the Federal Institute of Accountants [*Australia*]

FFIIG........ Federation Francaise de l'Imprimerie et des Industries Graphiques [*France*] (EY)

FfIK .... Forschungsstelle fuer Insel- und Kustenschutz [*Research Department for Island and Coastal Protection*] (MSC)

FFIPC........ Federation Francaise des Industries Photo et Cinema [*French Association of Photo, Cinema, and Video Materials*] (EAIO)

FFITP........ Federation Francaise d'Instituts Techniques du Petrole [*French Federation of Petroleum Technical Instututes*] (PDAA)

FFIU .... Forsvarets Forskningsinstitutt Avdeling for Unternvannskrigsforskning [*Norway*] (MSC)

FFK .... Freund-Feind-Kenngeraet [*Friend-Foe Identification Device (IFF)*] (EG)

FFKG........ Freund-Feind-Kenngeraet [*Friend-Foe Identification Device (IFF)*] (EG)

FFKU......... Filozoficka Fakulta Komenskeho Univerzity [*Department of Philosophy of Comenius University*] (CZ)

FFL........... Forces Francaises Libres [*Free French Forces*]

fflo............. Fofelugyelo [*Inspector General*] (HU)

ffls............. Folhas [*Sheets*] [*Publishing*] [*Portuguese*]

FFLT......... Federation Francaise de Lawn-Tennis [*French*]

FFM........... Federation Francaise de la Montagne [*Mountaineering association*]

FFM........... Fleisch, Fette, und Molkereierzeugnisse [*Meats, Fats, and Dairy Products*] (EG)

FFMA....... Friends' Foreign Mission Association

FFMKR ..... Federation Francaise des Masseurs Kinesitherapeutes Reeducateurs [*French*] (SLS)

FFMSPAC ... Farm Financial Management Skills Program Advisory Committee [*Australia*]

FFNSW ..... Filipino Forum in New South Wales [*Australia*]

FFO........... Forces Francaises de l'Ouest

Ffo........... Frankfurt/Oder (EG)

FFO........... Funksjonshemmeds Fellesorganisasjon [*League of Handicap Organizations*] [*Norway*] (EAIO)

ffon........... Faisant Fonction [*French*] (MTD)

ffons........... Faisant Fonctions [*French*] (MTD)

FFP .... Fileleftheri Foititiki Parataxi [*Liberal Student Faction*] (GC)

FFP .... Filmovy Festival Pracujicich [*Workers' Film Festival*] (CZ)

FFP .... Fonciere Financiere et de Participation [*Real Estate Finance and Participation*] [*Commercial firm*] [*France*]

FFPE........ Federation de la Fonction Publique Europeenne [*European Civil Service Federation*] (EAIO)

FFPIC....... Forestry and Forest Products Industry Council [*Australia*]

FFPN........ Variable Ferrite Filter (RU)

FFPRI....... Forestry and Forest Products Research Institute [*Research center*] [*Japan*] (IRC)

FFR .... Factorul Final de Recuperare [*Final Recovery Factor*] (RO)

FFR .... Forsvarets Forskningsrad [*Defense Board*] [*Denmark*]

FFR .... Fosterlaendska Folkroerelsen [*Patriotic People's Movement*] [*Finland*] (PPE)

FFR .... Frente Falangista Revolucionario [*Revolutionary Falangist Front*] [*Spanish*] (WER)

FFRM .... Foundation for Fundamental Research on Matter [*Netherlands*] (EAIO)

FFRSA...... Fondation pour Favoriser les Recherches Scientifiques en Afrique [*Foundation to Assist Scientific Research in Africa*] [*Belgium*] (EAIO)

FFS .... French Sailing Federation (EAIO)

FFS .... Frente Federativo Sindical [*Federated Labor Front*] [*Guatemala*] (LA)

FFS .... Front des Forces Socialistes [*Front of Socialist Forces*] [*Algeria*] [*Political party*] (PD)

FFSA .... Federation Francaise du Sport Automobile [*French Federation of Motorsport*]

FFSAM ..... Federation Francaise des Societies d'Amis de Musees [*French*] (SLS)

FFSB.......... Federation des Foires et Salons du Benelux [*Federation of Fairs and Trade Shows of BENELUX - FFTSB*] (EA)

FFSB.......... Federation Francaise du Sport Boules [*France*] (EAIO)

FFSC.......... Franziskanerbruder vom Heiligen Kreuz [*Franciscan Brothers of the Holy Cross*] [*Germany*] (EAIO)

FFSF .... Federation des Foires et Salons de France (EAIO)

FFSG .... Federation Francaise des Sports de Glace [*France*] (EAIO)

FFSM .... Federation des Fondations pour la Sante Mondiale [*Federation of World Health Foundations - FWHF*] [*Geneva, Switzerland*] (EA)

FFSPN....... Federation Francaise des Societes de Protection de la Nature [*French*] (SLS)

FFSS.......... Ferrovie dello Stato [*State Railroads*] [*Italian*]

FFSTA....... Federated Furnishing Trades Society [*Australia*]

FFSU .... Filozoficka Fakulta Slovenskej Univerzity [*Department of Philosophy of the Slovak University*] [*Bratislava*] (CZ)

FFT .... Foremost Friesland Thailand [*Commercial firm*]

FFTA .... Finnish Foreign Trade Association

FFTC .... Functionnaires Francais Titulaires des Cadres Locaux [*North African*]

FFTC/ASPAC ... Food and Fertilizer Technology Center for the Asian and Pacific Region (EAIO)

FFTRI....... Fruit and Fruit Technology Research Institute [*South Africa*] [*Research center*] (IRC)

FFTS.......... Federated Furnishing Trades Society of Australasia

FFTS.......... Federation Francaise des Travailleurs Sociaux [*French*] (SLS)

FFTSB....... Federation of Fairs and Trade Shows of BENELUX [*Formerly, Federation of Fairs and Exhibitions in BENELUX - FFSB*] (EA)

FFU........... Federated Fire Fighters Union [*Australia*]

FFU........... Federation du Francais Universel [*Federation for Universal French*] (EAIO)

FFU........... Forskningens Faellesudvalg [*Science Advisory Council*] [*Danish*]

FFU........... Forskningsradenes Fellesutsvag [*Joint Committee of the Norwegian Research Councils*]

FFV............ Federation des Femmes Voltaiques
FFV............ Federation Francaise de Voile [*French Sailing Federation*] (EAIO)
FFV............ Foersvarets Fabriksverk [*Sweden*] (PDAA)
FFV............ Forenade Fabricksverken [*Sweden*] (PDAA)
FFV............ Fovarosi Fotovallalat [*Capital Photography Enterprise*] (HU)
FFVM........ Fiezahana Fivoaran'ny Vehivavy Malagasy [*Effort and Advancement of the Malagasy Woman*] (AF)
FFVV .... Federation Francaise de Vol a Voile [*French Federation of Gliding*] (PDAA)
FFW.......... Federation of Free Workers [*Trade union*] [*Philippines*] (FEA)
FFZ............ Forzatissimo [*Extremely Loud*] [*Music*] (ROG)
fg .... Figura [*Illustration*] [*Spanish*]
FG .... Finanzgericht [*Tax Court*] [*German*] (ILCA)
FG .... Fine Gael [*Race of the Irish*] [*Political party*]
FG .... Flota del Golfo [*Gulf Fishing Fleet*] [*Cuba*] (LA)
FG .... Foggia [*Car registration plates*] [*Italy*]
FG .... Frais Generaux [*French*]
FG .... Franc Guineen [*Monetary unit*]
FG .... Freedom Group [*Uganda*] (AF)
FG .... Hydrographic Channel (RU)
FG .... Phenylhydrazine (RU)
FGA .... Federation Generale Agro-Alimentaire [*France*]
FGA .... Fellow of the Art Galleries Association of Australia (ADA)
FGA .... Fondazione Giovanni Agnelli [*Italy*] (EAIO)
FGA .... Fuerzas Guerrilleras de Araguaia [*Guerrilla Forces of Araguaia*] [*Brazil*] (LA)
FGA .... Phosphoglyceraldehyde (RU)
FGA .... Phytohemagglutinin (RU)
FGAA .... Fellow of the Gemmological Association of Australia (ADA)
FGAF........ Fraunhofer-Gessellschaft zur Forderung der Angewandten Forschung [*Fraunhofer Society for the Promotion of Applied Research*] [*Germany*] (PDAA)
FGAKuyb obl ... Branch of the State Archives of the Kuybyshev Oblast (RU)
FGAM .... World Atlas of Physical Geography (RU)
FGANSW .. Flower Growers' Association of New South Wales [*Australia*]
FGATE ...... Fundacion Guatemalteco-Americana de Television Educativa [*Guatemalan-American Educational Television Foundation*] (LA)
FGB .... Familiengesetzbuch [*Family Code*] (EG)
FGB .... Federacion Grafica Bonaerense [*Buenos Aires Printers Federation*] [*Argentina*] (LA)
FGB .... Federation Guineenne de Boules [*Guinea Bocce Federation*] (EAIO)
fgbatr.......... Photogrammetric Battery [*Military term*] (RU)
FGBT........ Bata [*Equatorial Guinea*] [*ICAO location identifier*] (ICLI)
FGC .... Departamento de Agricultura de la Generalitat de Cataluna [*Spain*] [*ICAO designator*] (FAAC)
FGC .... Federation Generale du Congo
FGC .... Federation Genevoise de Cooperation [*Geneva Federation for Cooperation and Development*] [*Switzerland*] (EAIO)
FGC .... Futures Guarantee Corp. [*Hong Kong*] (ECON)
FGCEI ...... Fremantle Gas & Coke Company [*Australia*]
FGCEI ...... Fonds de Garantie des Credits aux Entreprises Ivoiriennes
FGCL .... Federation Generale des Cooperatives Laitieres [*General Federation of Milk Cooperatives*] [*Belgium*] (EAIO)
FGCSP....... Fifth Generation Computer Systems Project [*Japan*] (PDAA)
FGCT........ Fonds de Garantie des Credits aux Entreprises Togolaises
FGCY........ Federation of German Catholic Youth (EAIO)
FGD .... Fondo de Garantia de Depositos [*Banking association*] [*Spain*] (EY)
FGD .... Forschungsgesellschaft Druckmaschinen eV (SLS)
FGDS........ Federation de la Gauche Democratique et Socialiste [*Federation of the Democratic and Socialist Left*] [*French*] (WER)
FGE .... Federation du Gaz et de l'Electricite [*France*]
FGE .... Federation of Greek Employers (EAIO)
Fge .... Forge [*Smithy, Forge*] [*Military map abbreviation World War I*] [*French*] (MTD)
FGEE........ Federacion de Gremios de Editores de Espana [*Federation of Spanish Editors' Unions*] [*Spain*]
FGEI .... Federation Royale des Geometres Experts Independants [*Belgium*] (SLS)
FGEIU .... Federated Gas Employees' Industrial Union [*Australia*]
FGF........... Federation Generale des Fonctionnaires [*France*] (FLAF)
FGF........... Fuerzas Guardafronteras [*Border Patrol Forces*] [*Cuba*] (LA)
FGFA........ Field and Game Federation of Australia
FGFAF ...... Fraunhofer-Gesellschaft zur Forderung der Angewandten Forschung [*Fraunhofer Society for the Advancement of Applied Research*] [*Germany*] (EAIO)
FGG .... Frankfurter Geographische Gesellschaft (SLS)
FGG .... Fruit Growers' Group [*Australia*]
FGGE........ First GARP [*Global Atmospheric Research Program*] Global Experiment [*ICSU*]
FGH.......... Forschungsgemeinschaft fuer Hochspannungs- und Hochstromtechnik eV (SLS)
FGH.......... Friesch-Groningsche Hypotheekbank [*Bank*] [*Netherlands*]

FGI............. Fashion Group International (EAIO)
FGI............. Federation Graphique Internationale [*International Graphical Federation - IGF*] [*Berne, Switzerland*] (EAIO)
FGI............. Federation of Greek Industries [*Belgium*] (EAIO)
FGI............. Fonds Gabonais d'Investissement
FGIFPI ...... Finnish Group of International Federation of the Phonographic Industry (EAIO)
FGIL.......... Federation Generale des Instituteurs Luxembourgeois [*Luxembourg*] (EAIO)
FGK .... Phosphoglyceric Acid (RU)
FGL........... Firestone Ghana Limited
FGL........... Fondazione Giovanni Lorenzini [*Italian*] (SLS)
FGLA.......... Federation of German Library Associations (EAIO)
FGLR......... Frontline Hospital for the Slightly Wounded (RU)
FGM .... Fovarosi Gazmuvek [*Capital Gas Works*] (HU)
FGM .... Freunde Guter Musik Club [*Record label*] [*Germany*]
FGM .... Fundusz Gospodarki Mieszkaniowej [*Housing Management Fund*] (POL)
FGMLI ...... Federazione dei Gruppi Marxisti-Leninisti d'Italia [*Federation of Marxist-Leninist Groups of Italy*] (WER)
FGMM ...... Federation Generale des Mines et de la Metallurgie [*France*]
FGMRI...... Forestry and Game Management Research Institute [*Czechoslovakia*] (DSCA)
FGN .... Gendarmerie Nationale [*France*] [*ICAO designator*] (FAAC)
FGO .... Farmers' Growers Organization [*Philippines*] (EY)
FGOLF ...... Federation des Gynecologues et Obstetriciens de Langue Francaise [*Federation of French-Language Gynaecologists and Obstetricians*] [*Paris, France*] (EAIO)
FGP........... Federacion Grafica del Peru [*Printers Federation of Peru*] (LA)
FGP........... Fuerza de Guerrilleros de los Pobres [*Guerrilla group*] [*Guatemala*] (EY)
FGPE......... Federation Generale du Personnel Enseignant [*Belgium*] (SLS)
Fgr............. Fedorov Symmetry Group (RU)
FGS........... Federation Gymnastique et Sportive [*French*]
FGS........... Federazione Giovanile Socialista [*Italian*]
FGS........... Fikir Iscisi Gazeteciler Sendikasi [*Intellectual Worker Journalists' Union*] (TU)
FGS........... Fischereifahrzeuge und -Geraete-Station [*Fishing Vessel and Equipment Station*] (EG)
FGS........... Friends of Georges Sadoul (EAIO)
FGSI......... Italian Socialist Youth Federation (WER)
FGSL......... Malabo, Isla De Macias, Nguema Biyoga [*Equatorial Guinea*] [*ICAO location identifier*] (ICLI)
FGSMIM .. National Association of German Musical Instrument Manufacturers [*Germany*] (EAIO)
FGSNSW .. Fellow of the Geological Society of New South Wales [*Australia*]
FGSS .... Federazione Generale dei Sindacati Somali
FGTB......... Federation Generale du Travail de Belgique [*Belgian General Federation of Labour*] [*Belgium*] (WER)
FGTE......... Federation Generale des Transports-Equipement [*France*]
FGTK........ Federation Generale du Travail du Kongo [*General Federation of Labor of the Congo*] [*Leopoldville*]
FGTO .... French Government Tourist Office
FGTS .... Fundo de Garantia do Tempo de Servico [*Service Time Surety Fund*] [*Brazil*] (LA)
FGU .... Fangatau [*French Polynesia*] [*Airport symbol*] (OAG)
FGU .... Headgear Factory (RU)
FGV .... Fundacao Getulio Vargas [*Getulio Vargas Foundation*] [*Brazil*] (LA)
FGVT........ Forschungs-Gesellschaft Verfahrens-Technik [*Germany*]
FGW .... Forschungsgemeinschaft Werkzeuge eV (SLS)
FGW .... Forschungsgesellschaft fuer Wohnen, Bauen, und Planen [*Austria*] (SLS)
FH.............. Fachhochschule
FH.............. Feldhaubitze [*Field Howitzer*] (EG)
FH.............. Fen Heyti [*Scientific (or Technical) Committee*] [*As of a ministry*] (TU)
FH.............. Foldhivatal [*Land Office*] (HU)
FH.............. Forum Hotel [*Hungary*]
FH.............. Freedom House
FH.............. Fuji Heavy Industries Ltd. [*Japan*] [*ICAO aircraft manufacturer identifier*] (ICAO)
fha .... Fecha [*Date, Enacted*] [*Spanish*]
FHA .... Fellow of the Australian Institute of Hospital Administrators (ADA)
FHA .... Fiji Hotel Association (EY)
FHA .... Foundation for Humanities Adulthood [*Australia*]
FHA .... Instituto de Fomento de Hipotecas Aseguradas [*Insured Mortgage Development Institute*] [*Guatemala*] (EY)
FHAA .... Field Hockey Association of America (OLYM)
FHAC........ Fellow of the Hawkesbury Agricultural College [*Australia*]
FHAW ...... Wideawake [*Ascension Island*] [*ICAO location identifier*] (ICLI)
FHB .... Fremantle Harbour Board [*Australia*]
FHC .... Fondo Hospitalario de Cundinamarca [*Colombia*] (COL)
FHCP........ Footscray Home Care Project for Elderly People [*Australia*]
FHD.......... Foundation for Human Development [*Australia*]

FHD.......... FrauenhifsDienst [*Women's Auxilliary Service*] [*Army*] [*Switzerland*]

fhdgy .... Fohadnagy [*First Lieutenant*] (HU)

FHEAA ..... Fellow of the Home Economics Association of Australia

FHF .... Federation of Health Funds - International [*British*] (EAIO)

FHF .... F. H. Faulding Proprietary Ltd. [*Australia*]

FHFAI ...... Family Health Guidance Association of Iran (ME)

fhg .... Foherceg [*Archduke*] (HU)

FhG .... Fraunhofer-Gesellschaft zur Foerderung der Angewandten Forschung eV [*Fraunhofer Society for the Advancement of Applied Research*] [*Research center*] (IRC)

FHGA .... Fellow of the Horological Guild of Australia

FHI .... Federation Halterophile Internationale [*International Weightlifting Federation - IWF*] (EAIO)

FHI .... Felag Husgagna- og Innanhussarkitekta [*Association of Furniture Designers and Interior Designers*] [*Iceland*] (EAIO)

FHI .... Fiskeridirektoratet Havforskningsinstitutt [*Norway*] (MSC)

FHI .... Forest Herbarium, Ibadan [*Nigeria*]

FHI .... Fuji Heavy Industries Ltd. [*Japan*]

FHIA .... Fundacion Hondurena de Investigacion Agricola [*Honduran Foundation for Agricultural Research*] [*Research center*] (IRC)

FHKC .... Filistin Halk Kurtulus Cephesi [*Palestine People's Liberation Front*] (TU)

FHKI .... Federation of Hong Kong Industries

FHKLA...... Fellow of the Hong Kong Library Association

FHKO .... Filistin Halk Kurtulus Ordusu [*Palestine People's Liberation Army*] (TU)

FHM.......... Fargo House Movement [*Trinidad and Tobago*] [*Political party*] (PPW)

fho .... Fecho [*Spanish*]

FHO........... Fremde Heere Ost [*German military intelligence*] [*World War II*]

FHP .... Family History Project [*University of Melbourne Archives*] [*Australia*]

FHQ.......... Fleet Headquarters [*Australia*]

Fhr .... Faehnrich [*Troop, Squad*] [*Military*] [*German*]

FHR .... Federal Housing Representative [*Australia*]

FHR .... Focus on Human Rights [*Norway*] (EAIO)

FHRDC ..... Foundation for Human Rights and Democracy in China (EAIO)

Fhrz........... Fahrzeug [*Vehicle*] [*German*] (GCA)

FHS .... Farm Household Support Scheme [*Australia*]

FHS .... Federation Horlogere Suisse [*Swiss watchmakers' trade association*]

FHSV........ Federation of Housing Societies of Victoria [*Australia*]

FHT .... Francs Hoc Tempore [*Francs at the Current Value*] [*Business term*] [*French*]

fhv .... Forhenvaerende [*Former*] [*Denmark*] (GPO)

FHW.......... Fachhochschule fuer Wirtschaft [*Advanced Professional Business School*] [*Berlin, West Germany*] (WEN)

FI............... Fieseler [*Germany*] [*ICAO aircraft manufacturer identifier*] (ICAO)

FI............... Finansiski Inspektorat [*Financial Inspectorate*] (YU)

FI............... Finland [*ANSI two-letter standard code*] (CNC)

FI............... Firenze [*Car registration plates*] [*Italy*]

fi................ Foods & Inns Ltd. [*India*]

FI............... Form Island - Icelandic Association for Design Promotion (EAIO)

FI............... Formula Internationale [*Agreement of Unification of Formulae*] [*Medicine*] (ROG)

FI............... France Info [*Radio France*]

FI............... Front Independantiste [*Independence Front*] [*New Caledonia*] [*Political party*] (PPW)

FI............... Fundacion Invica [*Chile*] (EAIO)

FI............... Institute of Physics (BU)

FI............... Phase Inverter [*Computers*] (RU)

FI............... Photoinclinometer (RU)

FIA .... Faridabad Industries Association [*India*] (PDAA)

FIA .... Fashion Industries of Australia

FIA .... Fasteners Institute of Australia

FIA .... Federacion Interamericana de Abogados [*Washington, DC*]

FIA .... Federated Ironworkers' Association [*Australia*]

FIA .... Federation des Industries Agricoles et Alimentaires [*Benelux*] (BAS)

FIA .... Federation Internationale de l'Automobile [*International Automobile Federation*] (EAIO)

FIA .... Federation Internationale des Acteurs [*International Federation of Actors*] (EAIO)

FIA .... Fellow of the Institute of Actuaries of Australia and New Zealand (ADA)

FIA .... Foire Internationale d'Alger [*Algiers International Fair*] [*Algeria*] (AF)

FIA .... Foreign Investment Application [*Taiwan*] (IMH)

FIA .... Four Island Air Ltd. [*Antigua and Barbuda*] [*ICAO designator*] (FAAC)

FIA .... Fraser Island Association [*Australia*]

FIAA......... Federation Internationale d'Athletisme Amateur [*International Amateur Athletic Federation - IAAF*] [*British*] (EAIO)

FIAA......... Federation of Indian Automobile Associations (EAIO)

FIAA......... Fellow of the Institute of Actuaries of Australia

FIAA......... Fellow of the Institute of Affiliate Accountants [*Australia*]

FIAA......... Fellow of the Institute of Arbitrators of Australia

FIAA......... Fencing Industry Association of Australia

FIAAS........ Fellow of the Institute of Australian Agricultural Science

FIAB......... Federacion Espanola de Industrias de la Alimentacion y Bebidas (EY)

FIAB......... Federacion Internacional de Asociaciones de Bibliotecarios [*International Federation of Library Associations - IFLA*] [*Spanish*]

FIAB......... Federation Internationale des Associations de Bibliothecaires [*International Federation of Library Associations - IFLA*] [*French*]

FIAB......... Fellow of the International Association of Bookkeepers [*British*] (DCTA)

FIABCI...... Federation Internationale des Professions Immobilieres [*International Real Estate Federation*] (EAIO)

FIABGRAL ... Federacao Internacional de Associacoes de Bibliotecarios- Grupo Regional America Latina [*Brazil*] (SLS)

FIAC.......... Federation Internationale Amateur de Cyclisme [*International Amateur Cycling Federation*] [*Rome, Italy*] (EA)

FIAC......... Federation of International American Clubs [*Oslo, Norway*] (EAIO)

FIAC......... Fishing Industry Advisory Committee [*Australia*]

FIAC......... Fnterntional Amateur Cycling Federation (OLYM)

FIAC......... Foire Internationale d'Art Contemporain [*Annual Paris art fair*] [*French*]

FIAC......... Foreign Investment Approvals Committee [*Sri Lanka*] (FEA)

FIAC......... Foreign Investments Assistance Center [*Philippines*] [*Board of Investment*] (DS)

FIACAT .... Federation Internationale de l'Action des Chretiens pour l'Abolition de la Torture [*International Federation of Action of Christians for the Abolition of Torture*] (EAIO)

FIACC .... Five International Associations Coordinating Committee [*Hungary*] (EAIO)

FIAD......... Federation Internationale des Associations de Distributeurs de Films [*International Federation of Associations of Film Distributors*] (EAIO)

FIAEM ...... Federation Internationale des Associations d'Etudiants en Medecine [*International Federation of Medical Students Associations - IFMSA*] [*Vienna, Austria*] (EAIO)

FIAEP........ Federation Internationale des Associations d'Entrepots Publics [*International Federation of Public Warehousing Associations - IFPWA*] (EAIO)

FIAF .... Federation Internationale des Archives du Film [*International Federation of Film Archives*] (EAIO)

FIAGLA .... Forest Industries Advisory Group in Latin America [*Formerly, Latin American Forest Industries Development Group*] (LAA)

FIAI .... Federacion Internacional de las Asociaciones de Institutores [*International Federation of Teachers' Associations - IFTA*] (LA)

FIAI .... Federation Internationale des Associations d'Instituteurs [*International Federation of Teachers' Associations - IFTA*] (EAIO)

FIAI .... Federazione delle Istituzioni Antropologiche Italiana [*Italian*] (SLS)

FIAI .... Federazione Italiana Autoferrotramvieri e Internavigatori [*National Federation of Busdrivers and Streetcar Conductors*] [*Italian*]

FIAII......... Fellow of the Incorporated Australian Insurance Institute (ADA)

FIAIZA...... Federazione Italiana Addetti Industrie Zucchero e Alcole [*Italian Federation of Workers in the Sugar and Alcohol Industry*]

FIAJ .... Federation Internationale des Auberges de la Jeunesse [*International Youth Hostel Federation - IYHF*] [*Welwyn Garden City, Hertfordshire, England*] (EAIO)

FIAL .... Frente Independiente de Accion Laboral [*Independent Labor Action Front*] [*Peru*] (LA)

FIALS........ Federazione Italiana Autonoma Lavoratori dello Spettacolo [*Italian Autonomous Federation of Entertainment Workers*]

FIAMC ...... Federation Internationale des Associations Medicales Catholiques [*International Federation of Catholic Medical Associations*] (EA)

FIAMS ...... Flinders Institute for Atmospheric and Marine Sciences [*Flinders University of South Australia*] (PDAA)

FIAN......... Physics Institute Imeni P. N. Lebedev of the Academy of Sciences, USSR (RU)

FIANATM ... Federation Internationale des Associations Nationales de Negociants en Aciers, Tubes, et Metaux [*International Federation of Associations of Steel, Tube, and Metal Merchants*] (EAIO)

FIAP .... Federation Internationale de l'Art Photographique [*International Federation of Photographic Art*] (EAIO)

FIAP .... Fellow of the Institute of Australian Photographers
FIAPA .... Fraccion de Ingenieros, Arquitectos, y Profesionales Afines del Partido Socialcristiano [*Engineers, Architects, and Professionals for the Social Christian Party*] [*Venezuela*] (LA)
FIAPS .... Federation Internationale des Associations de Professeurs de Sciences [*International Council of Associations for Science Education - ICASE*] (EAIO)
FIAR .... Fabbrica Italiana Apparecchiature Radioelettriche SpA [*General Electric Co.*] [*Italy*] (EAS)
FIArbA ...... Fellow of the Institute of Arbitrators, Australia (ADA)
FIARP .... Federacion Interamericana de Asociaciones de Relaciones Publicas [*Inter-American Federation of Public Relations Associations*] (LA)
FIARVEP .. Federazione Italiana Agenti Rappresentanti Viaggiatorie e Paizzisti [*Italian Federation of Commercial Agents and Travelers*]
FIAS .... Federacion Interamericana de Asociaciones de Secretarias [*Inter-American Federation of Secretaries*] [*San Salvador, El Salvador*] (EAIO)
FIAS .... Federation Internationale Amateur de Sambo [*Anglet, France*] (EAIO)
FIAS .... Federation Internationale des Assistantes Sociales [*International Federation of Social Workers*] [*Switzerland*] (EAIO)
FIAS .... Financiadores Asociados [*Barranquilla*] (COL)
FIAS .... Flinders Institute for Atomic Studies [*Research center*] [*Australia*] (IRC)
FIAS .... Formation Internationale Aeronautique et Spatiale [*France*] (PDAA)
FIASA .... Financiera Industrial y Agropecuaria, SA [*Guatemala*]
FIASTAMA ... Fivondronan'ny Mpanao Asa Tananasy Mpanao Taozavatra Malagasy [*Union of Malagasy Craftsmen and Small Industrial Firms*] (AF)
FIAT .... Fabbrica Italiana Automobile, Torino [*Italian automobile manufacturer*] [*Facetious translations: "Fix It Again, Tony"; "Futile Italian Attempt at Transportation"*]
FIAT .... Federation Internationale des Archives de Television [*International Federation of Television Archives - IFTA*] (EAIO)
FIAT .... Federation Internationale des Associations de Thanatologues [*French*] (SLS)
FIAT .... First Installed Article, Tests [*NATO*] (NATG)
FIAT .... Fishing Industry Appeals Tribunal [*Australia*]
FIAT .... Fonds d'Intervention pour l'Amenagement du Territoire [*French*]
FIAT .... Food Industry Association of Tasmania [*Australia*]
FIATA .... Federation Internationale des Associations de Transitaires et Assimilies [*International Federation of Freight Forwarders Associations*] [*Zurich, Switzerland*] (EAIO)
FIATC .... Federation Internationale des Associations Touristiques de Cheminots [*International Federation of Railwaymen's Travel Associations - IFRTA*] [*France*]
FIAV .... Federation Internationale des Artistes de Varietes (FLAF)
FIA(V) .... Forum of Information Associations (Victoria) [*Australia*]
FIB .... Federation des Industries Belges [*Federation of Belgian Industries*] (WER)
FIB .... Federation Francaise de l'Industrie du Beton (EAIO)
FIB .... Federation Internationale de Badminton [*International Badminton Federation - IBF*] (EA)
FIB .... Federation Internationale de Boules [*International Bocce Federation*] [*Turin, Italy*] (EAIO)
FIB .... Federazione Italiana Badminton [*Italian Badminton Federation*] (EAIO)
FIB .... Federazione Italiana Bancari [*Italian Federation of Bank Employees*]
FIB .... Felag Islenzkra Bifreidaeigenda [*Icelandic Automobile Association*] (EAIO)
FIB .... Foreign Investment Board [*Honiara, Solomon Islands*] (GEA)
FIB .... Franco-Ivoirienne des Bois
FIB .... Freeway Iberica SA [*Spain*] [*ICAO designator*] (FAAC)
FIBA .... Federation International Amatuer de Basketball (OLYM)
FIBA .... Federation Internationale de Basketball Amateur [*International Amateur Basketball Federation*] [*Germany*] (EA)
FIBA .... Federazione Italiana Bancari e Assicuratori [*Italy*] (EY)
FIBAKO .... Ficelleries de Bouake
FIBAN .... Fiscalizacao Bancaria [*Brazil*] (LAA)
FIBAT .... Federation Independente des Batetelas [*Independent Federation of Batetelas*]
FIBATA ..... Fitateram-Bahoakan'ny Tananan' Antananarivo [*Antananarivo City Common Carrier Organization*] [*Malagasy*] (AF)
FIBD .... Ford International Business Development [*Ford Motor Co.*]
FIBEP .... Federation Internationale des Bureaux d'Extraits de Presse [*International Federation of Press Cutting Agencies - IFPCA*] (EAIO)
FIBEP .... Fundo de Financiamento de Importacao de Bens de Producao [*Fund for Financing Capital Goods Imports*] [*Brazil*] (LA)
FIBEX .... First International BIOMASS Experiment [*ICSU*] (MSC)

FIBRA .... Federacao das Industrias de Brasilia [*Brasilia Federation of Industries*] [*Brazil*] (LA)
FIBRACOL ... Fibras de Colombia Ltda. [*Colombia*] (COL)
FIBROMADERA ... Industria Nacional de Maderas Laminadas [*Venezuela*] (DSCA)
FIBT .... Federation Internationale de Bobsleigh et de Tobogganing [*International Bobsledding and Tobogganing Federation*] [*Milan, Italy*] (EAIO)
FIBU .... Finanzbuchhaltungssystem [*Financial Book Keeping System*] [*German*] (ADPT)
FIBV .... Federation Internationale des Bourses de Valeurs [*International Federation of Stock Exchanges*] (EAIO)
FIC .... Congregatio Fratrum Immaculatae Conceptionis Beatae Mariae Virginis [*Brothers of the Immaculate Conception of the Blessed Virgin Mary*] (EAIO)
FIC .... Family Information Centre [*Australian Institute of Family Studies*] [*Information service or system*] (IID)
FIC .... Family Integration Center [*Guatemala*] (EAIO)
FIC .... Federation des Industries Chimiques de Belgique [*Federation of Chemical Industries of Belgium*] (EAIO)
FIC .... Federation Internationale de Canoe [*International Canoe Federation - ICF*] [*Florence, Italy*] (EAIO)
FIC .... Federation Internationale de Cremation [*International Cremation Federation*] (EAIO)
FIC .... Federation Internationale des Chronometreurs [*Rome, Italy*] (EAIO)
FIC .... Federazione Italiana dei Cineforum [*Italian*] (SLS)
FIC .... Foodstuff Industries Corp. [*Myanmar*] (DS)
FIC .... Foreign Investment Committee [*Malaysia*] (IMH)
FIC .... Societe Anonyme Foret Industrie Commerce
FICA .... Federation Internationale de Controle Automatique [*French*] (ADPT)
FICA .... Fellow of the Commonwealth Institute of Accountancy [*Australia*]
FICA .... Ferrocarril Internacional Centroamericano (LAA)
FICA .... Food Industry Council of Australia
FICA .... Forest Industries Campaign Association [*Australia*]
FICAC .... Federation Internationale des Corps et Associations Consulaires [*Federation of International Consular Corps and Associations*] (EAIO)
FICAE .... Federacion Latinoamericana del Caribe de Asociaciones de Exportadores [*Venezuela*] (DSCA)
FICAM ...... Fiscalizacao Cambial [*Brazil*] (LAA)
FICB .... Federation des Instituteurs Chretiens de Belgique [*Christian Teachers Federation of Belgium*] (EAIO)
FICB .... Federation Internationale de la Croix-Bleue [*International Federation of the Blue Cross*] [*Switzerland*] (EAIO)
FICC .... Federation Internationale de Camping et de Caravanning [*International Federation of Camping and Caravanning*] [*Brussels, Belgium*] (EA)
FICCC .... Federation Internationale des Clubs de Camping-Cars [*Montreuil, France*] (EAIO)
FICCI .... Federation of Indian Chambers of Commerce and Industries
FICE .... Federacion de Industriales del Calzado Espanol [*Industrial association*] [*Spain*] (EY)
FICE .... Federation Internationale des Communautes Educatives [*International Federation of Educative Communities*] [*Zurich, Switzerland*] (EAIO)
FICEM ...... Federcion Interamericana del Cemento [*Inter American Cement Federation*] [*Colombia*] (EAIO)
FICEMEA ... Federation Internationale des Centres d'Entrainement aux Methodes d'Education Active [*International Federation of Training Centres in Methods of Active Education*] (EAIO)
FICENSA ... Financiera Centroamericana Sociedad Anonima [*Honduras*] (EY)
FICEP .... Federation Internationale Catholique d'Education Physique et Sportive [*Catholic International Federation for Physical and Sports Education - CIFPSE*] [*Paris, France*] (EAIO)
FICF .... Federation Internationale Culturelle Feminine [*Women's International Cultural Federation - WICF*] (EAIO)
FICF .... Fonds d'Investissement du Chemin de Fer
FICG .... Federation Internationale des Choeurs de Garcons (EAIO)
Fich Prat .... Fiches Pratiques de Documentation Fiscale [*Benelux*] (BAS)
FICICA ...... Federation Internationale du Personnel d'Encadrement des Industries et Commerces Agricoles et Alimentaires [*International Federation of Managerial Staff of Agricultural and Alimentary Industry and Commerce*] (EAIO)
FICITEC ... Fundacion para el Fomento de la Investigacion Cientifica y Tecnologica [*Colorado*] (ASF)
FICJF .... Federation Internationale des Conseils Juridiques et Fiscaux (FLAF)
FICM .... Federation Internationale des Clubs de Motorhomes [*International Federation of Motorhome Clubs*] [*Belgium*] (EAIO)
FICM .... Federation of International Music Competitions (EA)
FICM .... Fellow of the Institute of Credit Management [*British*] (DCTA)

FICOB....... Federation de l'Informatique, de la Communication et de l'Organisation de Bureau [*German*]   (ADPT)

FICOMER ... Fournitures Industrielles et Commerciales [*Morocco*]

FICP.......... Federation Internationale des Clubs de Publicite [*International Federation of Advertising Clubs*] [*Lille, France*]   (EAIO)

FICP.......... Freres de l'Instruction Chretienne de Ploermel [*Brothers of Christian Instruction of Ploermel*] [*Rome, Italy*]   (EAIO)

FICPI........ Federation Internationale des Conseils en Propriete Industrielle [*International Federation of Industrial Property Attorneys*]   (EAIO)

FICR.......... Federazione Internazionale dei Combattenti della Resistenza [*International Federation of Resistance Fighters*] [*Use FIR*] [*Italian*]   (WER)

FICS.......... Federation Internationale des Chasseurs de Son [*International Federation of Sound Hunters - IFSH*]   (EAIO)

FICS.......... Fellow of the South African Institute of Computer Scientists   (AA)

FICSA....... Federation of International Civil Servants' Associations [*Geneva, Switzerland*]   (EA)

FICSAS..... Federation of Institutions Concerned with the Study of the Adriatic Sea [*Former Yugoslavia*]   (SLS)

FICSC....... Federation Intelligence and Counter-Subversive Committee   (ML)

FICSETT... Foundation Member of the Institute of Civil Service Engineering Technicians and Technologists [*South Africa*]   (AA)

FICT.......... Federation Internationale de Centres Touristiques [*International Federation of Tourist Centres*]   (EAIO)

FICTAS..... Federacion Internacional de Campesinos, Trabajadores Agricolas, y Similares [*International Federation of Peasants, Farm Workers, and Related Workers*] [*El Salvador*]   (LA)

FICTS....... Federation Internationale du Cinema et de la Television Sports ifs   (OLYM)

FICU.......... Fonds Internationale de Cooperation Universitaire [*International Fund for University Cooperation*] [*Canada*]   (EAIO)

FICWA...... Floricultural Industry Council of Western Australia

FICZ.......... Falkland Islands Interi, Conservation, and Management Zone

F i D.......... Faden in Dampf [*Thread in Vapor*] [*German*]

FID............. Federacion de Independientes Democratas [*Federation of Independent Democrats*] [*Spanish*]   (WER)

FID............. Federacion Internacional de Documentacion [*International Federation for Documentation - IFD*] [*Spanish*] [*Information service or system*]   (ASF)

FID............. Federation Internationale de Documentation [*International Federation for Documentation - IFD*] [*ICSU*] [*French*]

FID............. Federation Internationale d'Information et de Documentation [*International Federation for Information and Documentation*] [*Netherlands*] [*Information service or system*]   (IID)

FID............. Federation Internationale du Diabete [*International Diabetes Federation - IDF*] [*Brussels, Belgium*]   (EAIO)

FID............. Foire Internationale de Dakar

FIDA.......... Federacion Internacional de Abogadas [*Chile*]   (SLS)

FIDA.......... Federal Independent Democratic Alliance [*South Africa*] [*Political party*]   (EY)

FIDA.......... Federal Industrial Development Authority   (ML)

FIDA.......... Federation of Independent Doctors of Australia

FIDA.......... Fellow of the Institute of Directors in Australia

FIDA.......... Fondo Internacional de Desarrollo Agricola [*International Fund for Agricultural Development*] [*Spanish United Nations*]   (DUND)

FIDA.......... Fonds International de Developpement Agricole [*International Fund for Agricultural Development*] [*French United Nations*]   (DUND)

FIDAC....... Federation Interalliee des Anciens Combattants [*World War I*] [*French*]

FIDAC....... Federazione Italiana Dipendenti da Aziende di Credito [*Italian Federation of Credit Institution Employees*]

FIDAE....... Federazione Italiana Dipendenti Aziende Elettriche [*Italian Federation of Electrical Workers*] [*Rome*]

FIDAG...... Federazione Italiana Dipendenti Aziende Gas [*Italian Federation of Gas Workers*]

FIDAL....... Federacion Interamericana del Algodon [*Mexico*]   (LAA)

FIDAM...... Fundo de Investimentos Privados no Desenvolvimento da Amazonia [*Fund for Private Investments in the Development of Amazonia*] [*Brazil*]   (LA)

FIDAP....... Federacion Interamericana de Administracion de Personal   (LAA)

FIDAP....... Fondo Interamericano de Desarrollo de la Alianza para el Progreso   (LAA)

FIDAQ....... Federation Internationale des Associations de Quincailliers et Marchands de Fer [*International Federation of Ironmongers and Iron Merchants Associations - IFIA*]   (EAIO)

FIDAS .... Formularorientiertes Interaktives Datenbanksystem [*Forms-Oriented Interactive Database System*] [*Germany*]

FIDASA .... Financiera del Asutro Sociedad Anonima [*Ecuador*]   (IMH)

FIDASE..... Falkland Islands and Dependencies Aerial Survey Expedition   (PDAA)

FIDAT....... Federazione Italiana Dipendenti Aziende Telecomunicazioni [*Italian Federation of Communications Workers*] [*Rome*]

FIDC.......... Faculte Internationale de Droit Compare [*Benelux*]   (BAS)

FIDC.......... Falkland Islands Development Corp.   (EY)

FIDC.......... Fishery Industry Development Council [*Philippines*]   (ASF)

FIDC.......... Food Industry Development Centre [*University of New South Wales*] [*Australia*]

FIDC.......... Forestry Industry Development Corporation [*Dominican Republic*]   (GEA)

FID/CAO .. Federation Internationale de Documentation/Commission for Asia and Oceania

FID/CCC... Federation Internationale de Documentation/Central Classification Committee

FID/CLA... Federation Internationale de Documentation/Latin American Commission

FID/CR ..... Federation Internationale de Documentation/Classification Research

FID/DC ..... Federation Internationale de Documentation/Developing Countries

FID/DT ..... Federation Internationale de Documentation/Terminology of Information and Documentation

FIDE.......... Federacion de Institutos de Educacion [*Federation of Educational Institutes*] [*Chile*]   (LA)

FIDE.......... Federation Internationale des Echecs [*International Chess Federation*] [*Switzerland*]

FIDE.......... Federation Internationale pour le Droit Europeen [*International Federation for European Law*] [*Benelux*]   (EAIO)

FIDE.......... Fondo de Inversion para Desarrollo Economico [*Investment Fund for Economic Development*] [*Dominican Republic*]   (LA)

FIDE.......... Foundation for Investment and Development of Exports [*Honduras*]   (EAIO)

FIDE.......... Fundacion de Investigacion para el Desarrollo [*Research and Development Foundation*] [*Argentina*]   (LA)

FIDECO .... Fishing Development Company [*Seychelles*]

FIDEF ...... Federal Almanya Isci Dernekleri Federasyonu [*Federation of West German Worker Associations*]   (TU)

FIDEFA..... Fideicomiso para el Desarrollo de la Fauna Acuatica [*Mexico*]   (MSC)

FIDEL ...... Federazione Italiana Dipendenti Enti Local [*Italian Federation of Local Government Employees*]

FIDEL ...... Frente Izquierda de Libertad [*Leftist Liberty Front*] [*Uruguay*]   (LA)

FIDEM...... Federation Internationale d'Etudes Medievales   (EAIO)

FIDENE .... Fundo de Investimentos para o Desenvolvimento do Nordeste [*Investment Fund for Development of the Northeast*] [*Brazil*]   (LA)

FIDEP .... Federazione Italiana Dipendenti da Enti Parastatali e di Diritto Pubblico [*Italian Federation of Employees of Quasi-Governmental and State-Controlled Agencies*]

FIDES........ Fonds d'Investissement pour le Developpement Economique et Social [*Investment Fund for Economic and Social Development*] [*United Nations*]   (AF)

FIDES........ Fonds d'Investissement pour le Developpement Economique et Social des Territoires d'Outre-Mer   (FLAF)

FIDE-SKE ... Filelevthera Dimokratiki Enosis - Sosialistiko Komma Ellados [*Liberal Democratic Union - Socialist Party of Greece*]   (GC)

FIDESZ..... Federation of Young Democrats [*Hungary*] [*Political party*] [*Acronym is based on foreign phrase*]   (ECON)

FID/ET...... Federation Internationale de Documentation/Education and Training

FIDGA....... Federazione Italiana della Gente dell'Aria [*Italian Federation of Airline Workers*]

FIDH .... Federation Internationale des Droits de l'Homme [*International Federation for Human Rights*] [*Paris, France*]   (EA)

FIDI.......... Federation Internationale des Demenageurs Internationaux [*International Federation of International Furniture Removers - IFIFR*]   (EAIO)

FIDIA .... Fellow of the Industrial Design Institute of Australia

FIDIC .... Federation Internationale des Ingenieurs Conseils [*International Federation of Consulting Engineers*]   (EAIO)

FIDIC .... Fonds d'Investissement pour le Developpement de l'Indochine   (FLAF)

FID/II........ Federation Internationale de Documentation/Information for Industry

FID/LD ..... Federation Internationale de Documentation/Linguistics in Documentation

FIDLIC...... Federacion Interamericana de la Industria de la Construccion [*Mexico*]   (LAA)

FIDOAO ... Federation Internationale des Diffuseurs d'Oeuvres d'Art Originales [*International Federation of Original Art Diffusors*] [*France*]   (EAIO)

FIDOF .... Federation Internationale des Organisateurs de Festivals [*International Federation of Festival Organizations*] (EAIO)

FID/OM .... Federation Internationale de Documentation/Operating Machine Systems

FIDOM ..... Fonds d'Investissements pour les Departements d'Outre-Mer [*Overseas Departments Investment Fund*] [*French*] (AF)

FID/RI .... Federation Internationale de Documentation/Research on Theoretical Basis of Information

FIDS .... Fast Interbroker Delivery Service [*Australian Stock Exchange*]

FIDS .... Flight Information Display System [*Information service or system*] (IID)

FID/SRC ... Federation Internationale de Documentation/Subject-Field Reference Code

FID/TM .... Federation Internationale de Documentation/Theory of Machine Techniques and Systems

FIDU .... Federacion Internacional Deportiva Universitaria [*International University Sports Federation*] (LA)

FIDUCOM ... Fiduciaire Marocaine Comptable et Fiscale

FIDUJID ... Fiduciaire Marocaine Juridique et Fiscale

FIDUMAC ... Fiduciaire Marocaine de Controle

FIDUROP ... Federacion de Fabricantes de Bramantes, Cordeles, y Cabos de Europa Occidental [*Federation of Twine, Cordage, and Rope Manufacturers of Western Europe*] [*Spanish*] (ASF)

FIDUROP ... Federation des Fabricants de Ficelles et Cordages de l'Europe Occidentale [*Federation of Twine, Cordage, and Rope Manufacturers of Western Europe*] [*French*] (ASF)

FIDUSEN ... Fiduciaire Senegalaise

FIDUTEC ... Fiduciaire Marocaine d'Editions Techniques

FIE .... Federation des Industries Egyptiennes [*Federation of Egyptian Industries*] (EAIO)

FIE .... Federation Internationale d'Escrime (OLYM)

FIE .... Field Aviation GmbH & Co. [*Germany*] [*ICAO designator*] (FAAC)

FIE .... Frente Izquierdista Ecuatoriano [*Ecuadorean Leftist Front*] (LA)

FIEA .... Federation Internationale des Experts en Automobiles [*International Federation of Automobile Experts*] [*Rhode St. Genese, Belgium*] (EAIO)

FIEAust ..... Fellow of the Institution of Engineers, Australia (ADA)

FIEB .... Federacao das Industrias do Estado da Bahia [*Brazil*] (DSCA)

FIEC .... Federation de l'Industrie Europeenne de la Construction [*European Construction Industry Federation*] (EAIO)

FIEC .... Federation Internationale des Associations d'Etudes Classiques [*International Federation of the Societies of Classical Studies*] (EAIO)

FIED .... Federation Internationale des Etudiants en Droit (FLAF)

FIEE .... Federation des Industries Electriques et Electroniques [*France*] (EY)

FIEF .... Federation Internationale pour l'Economie Familiale [*International Federation for Home Economics - IFHE*] (EAIO)

FIEG .... Federazione Italiana Editori Giornali [*Italian Federation of Newspaper Publishing*] (EY)

FIEGA .... Federacao das Industrias do Estado da Guanabara [*Guanabara State Federation of Industries*] [*Brazil*] (LA)

FIEGA .... Federation Internationale d'Eutonie Gerda Alexander [*International Federation for Gerda Alexander Eutony*] [*Belgium*] (EAIO)

FIEI .... Fraser Island Environmental Inquiry [*Australia*]

FIEJ .... Federation Internationale des Editeurs de Journaux [*International Federation of Newspaper Publishers*] [*Paris, France*] (EAIO)

FIEL .... Fundacion de Investigaciones Economicas Latinoamericanas [*Latin American Economic Research Foundation*] [*Argentina*] (LA)

FIELTROSA ... Fabrica de Sombreros de Fieltro Ltda. [*Colombia*] (COL)

FIEM .... Federation Internationale de l'Enseignement Manager [*France*] (DSCA)

FIEMC ...... Federacion Industrial de la Construccion [*Industrial Construction Federation*] [*Chile*] (LA)

FIEMG ...... Federacao das Industrias do Estado de Minas Gerais [*Minas Gerais Federation of Industries*] [*Brazil*] (LA)

FIEN .... Forum Italiano dell'Energia Nucleare [*Italian Nuclear Energy Forum*] [*Rome, Italy*]

FIEO .... Federation of Indian Export Organizations (EAIO)

FIEP .... Federacao das Industrias de Pernambuco [*Pernambuco Federation of Industries*] [*Brazil*] (LA)

FIEP .... Federation Internationale d'Education Physique [*International Federation for Physical Education*] (EAIO)

FIEP .... Federation Internationale pour l'Education des Parents [*International Federation for Parent Education - IFPE*] [*Sevres, France*] (EAIO)

FIER .... Federation Internationale des Enseignants de Rythmique [*International Federation of Teachers of Rhythmics - IFTR*] (EA)

FIER .... Fieramente [*Boldly*] [*Music*] (ROG)

FIERGS ..... Federacao das Industrias do Estado de Rio Grande Do Sul [*Rio Grande Do Sul Federation of Industries*] [*Brazil*] (LA)

FIESP .... Federacao das Industrias do Estado de Sao Paulo [*Sao Paulo State Federation of Industries*] [*Brazil*] (LA)

FIET .... Facultad de Ingenieria Electrica y Telecomunicaciones. Universidad del Cauca [*Popayan*] (COL)

FIET .... Federacion Internacional de Empleados y Tecnicos [*International Federation of Employees and Technicians*] (LA)

FIET .... Federation Internationale des Employes, Techniciens, et Cadres [*International Federation of Commercial, Clerical, Professional, and Technical Employees*] [*Geneva, Switzerland*] (EAIO)

FIEU .... Fonds International d'Echanges Universitaires

FIEU .... Forschungsinstitut fuer Energie- und Umweltplanung [*Research Institute for Energy and Environment Planning*] [*Austria*]

FIEV .... Federation des Industries des Equipements pour Vehicules [*France*] (EAIO)

FIEWS .... Food Information and Early Warning System [*FAO*] [*United Nations*]

FIEx .... Fellow of the Institute of Export [*British*] (DCTA)

FIF .... Department of Philosophy and History (BU)

FIF .... Federation Internationale de la Filterie [*International Thread Federation*] [*EC*] (ECED)

FIF .... Federation Ivoirienne de Football

FIF .... Feria Internacional de la Frontera [*Cucuta*] (COL)

FIF .... Forest Industries Federation [*Australia*]

FIF .... Friends of Irish Freedom

FIF .... Frifly SpA [*Italy*] [*ICAO designator*] (FAAC)

FIF .... Fuji International Finance [*Japan*]

FIF .... Fundacion Institucional Federalista [*Federalist Institutional Center*] [*Argentina*] (LA)

FIFA .... Federacao Internacional de Futebol e Atletismo [*Portuguese*]

FIFA .... Federacion International del Futbol Aficionado [*Bogota-Filial*] (COL)

FIFA .... Federation Internationale de Football Association [*International Federation of Association Football*] [*Zurich, Switzerland*] (EA)

FIFA .... Fellow of the Institute of Foresters of Australia (ADA)

FIFARMA ... Federacion Interamericana de la Industria Quimica Farmaceutica [*Colombia*] (COL)

FIFARMA ... Federacion Latinoamericana de la Industria Farmaceutica [*Latin American Pharmaceutical Industry Federation*] [*Argentina*]

FiFAS .... Federation Francaise des Industries du Sport et des Loisirs [*French Federation of the Sporting Goods Industry*] (EAIO)

FIFATO .... Fikambanana Fampandrosoana an'i Toliara [*Development Company of Tulear Region*] [*Malagasy*] (AF)

FIFCh .... Federacion Industrial Ferroviaria de Chile [*Chilean Industrial Railways Federation*] (LA)

FIFCJ .... Federation Internationale des Femmes des Carrieres Juridiques [*France*]

FIFD .... Federatia Internationala a Femeilor Democratice [*International Federation of Democratic Women*] (LA)

FIFDU .... Federation Internationale des Femmes Diplomees des Universites [*International Federation of University Women - IFUW*] (EAIO)

FIFE .... Federation Internationale des Associations de Fabricants de Produits d'Entretien [*International Federation of Associations of Manufacturers of Household Products*] (EAIO)

FIFE .... First ISLSCP [*International Satellite Land Surface Climatology Project*] Field Experiment [*NASA*]

FIFirE .... Fellow of the Institution of Fire Engineers [*British*] (DCTA)

FIFSP .... Federation Internationale des Fonctionnaires Superieurs de Police [*International Federation of Senior Police Officers*] [*France*]

FIF(WA) .... Forest Industries Federation, Western Australia

FIG .... Federation Internationale de Genetique [*International Genetics Federation*] (EAIO)

FIG .... Federation Internationale de Gymnastique [*International Gymnastic Federation - IGF*] [*Lyss, Switzerland*] (EAIO)

FIG .... Federation Internationale des Geometres [*International Federation of Surveyors - IFS*] [*Edmonton, AB*] (EAIO)

fig .... Figur [*Figure*] [*Danish*] (GPO)

fig .... Figur [*Figure*] [*Swedish*]

Fig .... Figur [*Figure*] [*German*]

fig .... Figura [*Figure*] [*Hungarian*]

fig .... Figura [*Figure*] [*Portuguese*]

fig .... Figura [*Figure*] [*Italian*]

fig .... Figura [*Figure*] [*Publishing*] [*Poland*]

fig .... Figuradamente [*Figuratively*] [*Portuguese*]

fig .... figurative (TPFD)

fig .... Figure [*Figure*] [*French*]

fig .... Figure, Illustration, Diagram [*Bibliography*] (RU)

fig .... Figures (BU)

fig .... Figuur [*Figure*] [*Publishing*] [*Netherlands*]

fig .... Figuur(lik) [*Figure*] [*Afrikaans*]
FIG .... Forestiere Ivoirienne du GO
FIGA .... Iberian Federation of Anarchist Groups [*Spain*]   (PD)
FIGADI ..... Financiere Gabonaise de Developpement Immobilier
FIGAPE ..... Fondo de Financiamiento y Garantia para la Pequena Empresa
  [*El Salvador*]   (EY)
FIGAS .... Falkland Islands Government Air Service   (EY)
FIGAWA ... Technische Vereinigung der Firmen im Gas- and Wasserfach eV
FIGAZ .... Federation de l'Industrie du Gaz [*Gas Industry Federation*]
  [*Belgium*]   (EY)
FIGE .... Federation de l'Industrie Granitiere Europeenne [*Federation of
  the European Granite Industry*]   (EAIO)
FIGED .... Federation Internationale des Grandes et Moyennes Entreprises
  de Distribution [*International Federation of Retail
  Distributors*]   (EAIO)
FIGEU .... Falkland Islands General Employees' Union
figg .... Figure [*Figures*] [*Italian*]
figg .... Figures [*Illustrations*] [*Publishing*] [*French*]
FIGIEFA ... Federation Internationale des Grossistes, Importateurs, et
  Exporteurs Fournitures Automobiles [*International
  Federation of Wholesalers, Importers, and Exporters in
  Automobile Fittings*]   (EAIO)
FIGIJ .... Federation Internationale de Gynecologie Infantile et Juvenile
  [*International Federation of Infantile and Juvenile
  Gynecology - IFIJG*] [*Sierre, Switzerland*]   (EAIO)
FIGO .... Federation Internationale de Gynecologie et d'Obstetrique
  [*International Federation of Gynecology and Obstetrics*]
  [*British*]   (EAIO)
FIGSA .... Financiera Guatemalteca Sociedad Anonima [*Guatemala*]   (EY)
figur .... Figurato [*Decorated with Designs*] [*Publishing*] [*Italian*]
figurl .... Figuerlich [*Figured*] [*Publishing*] [*German*]
FIH .... Federation Internationale de Hockey [*International Hockey
  Federation*] [*Brussels, Belgium*]   (EA)
FIH .... Kinshasa [*Zaire*] [*Airport symbol*]   (OAG)
FIHBJO .... Federation Internationale des Horlogers, Bijoutiers, Joailliers,
  Orfevres Detaillants de la CE [*International Federation of
  Retailers in Horology, Jewellery, Gold and Silverware of the
  EC*]   (ECED)
FiHBWE ... National Board of Water and the Environment, Urho Kekkosen
  Katu, Helsinki, Finland [*Library symbol*] [*Library of
  Congress*]   (LCLS)
FIHC .... Federation Internationale des Hommes Catholiques
  [*International Council of Catholic Men - ICCM*] [*Vatican
  City, Vatican City State*]   (EAIO)
FiHCRN .... Finnish Center for Radiation and Nuclear Safety
  [*Sateilyturvakeskus*], Helsinki, Finland [*Library symbol*]
  [*Library of Congress*]   (LCLS)
FiHMR ...... Institute of Marine Research, Helsinki, Finland [*Library symbol*]
  [*Library of Congress*]   (LCLS)
FIHU .... Federation Internationale de l'Habitation et de l'Urbanisme
  [*Benelux*]   (BAS)
FiHU-A ..... Helsinki University, Library of Agriculture, Viikki, Helsinki,
  Finland [*Library symbol*] [*Library of Congress*]   (LCLS)
FIHUAT .... Federation Internationale pour l'Habitation, l'Urbanisme et
  l'Amenagement des Territoires [*International Federation
  for Housing and Planning - IFHP*] [*The Hague,
  Netherlands*]   (EA)
FiHU-F ...... Helsinki University Library of Forestry [*Helsingin Yliopiston
  Metsakirjaston*], Helsinki, Finland [*Library symbol*]
  [*Library of Congress*]   (LCLS)
FII .... Felag Islenskra Idnrekenda [*Iceland*]   (EAIO)
FIIA .... Fellow of the International Institute of Accountants [*Australia*]
FIIC .... Federacion Interamericana de la Industria de la Construccion
  [*Inter-American Federation of the Construction Industry -
  IAFCI*]   (EAIO)
FIID .... Federation Internationale d'Information et de Documentation
  [*International Federation for Information and
  Documentation - IFID*]   (EAIO)
FIIE .... Fellow of the South African Institute of Industrial Engineers
  (AA)
FIIG .... Federation des Institutions Internationales Semi-Officielles et
  Privees Etablies a Geneve [*Federation of Semi-Official and
  Private International Institutions Established in Geneva*]
  [*Switzerland*]   (EA)
FIIHE .... Federation Internationale des Instituts de Hautes Etudes
  [*International Federation of Institutes for Advanced Study*]
  (EAIO)
FIIM .... Federation Internationale de l'Industrie du Medicament
  [*International Federation of Pharmaceutical Manufacturers
  Associations - IFPMA*]   (EAIO)
FIIM .... Federation Internationale des Ingenieurs Municipaux
  [*International Federation of Municipal Engineers - IFME*]
  (EAIO)
FIIM .... Fellow of the Institution of Industrial Managers [*British*]
  (DCTA)
FIIR .... Federal Institute of Industrial Research [*Nigeria*]

FIIRO .... Federal Institute of Industrial Research, Oshodi [*Nigeria*]
  (ARC)
FIISM .... Federation of Indonesian Iron and Steel Manufacturers   (EAIO)
FIJ .... Federation Internationale des Journalistes [*International
  Federation of Journalists - IFJ*] [*Brussels, Belgium*]   (EAIO)
FIJ .... Frente Independiente de Juventudes [*Independent Youth Front*]
  [*Peru*]   (LA)
FIJB .... Fondation Internationale Jacques Brel [*International Jacques
  Brel Foundation - IJBF*]   (EA)
FIJBT .... Federation Internationale des Jeunesse Bons Templiers
  [*International Good Templar Youth Federation*]   (EAIO)
FIJC .... Federacion Internacional de la Juventud Catolica [*International
  Federation of Catholic Youth*] [*Argentina*]   (LAA)
FIJDA ...... Federation Ivoirienne de Judo et Disciplines Associees
FIJET .... Federation Internationale des Journalistes et Ecrivains du
  Tourisme [*World Federation of Travel Journalists and
  Writers*] [*Paris, France*]   (EA)
FIJL .... Federacion Iberica de Juventudes Libertarias [*Iberian Federation
  of Anarchist Youth*] [*Spanish*]   (WER)
FIJM .... Federation Internationale des Jeunesses Musicales [*International
  Federation of Jeunesses Musicales*]   (EAIO)
fijor .... Figyelojaror [*Patrol*]   (HU)
FIJPA .... Federation Internationale des Journalistes Professionels de
  l'Aeronautique [*International Federation of Writers on
  Aeronautics*]   (PDAA)
FIJU .... Federation Internationale des Producteurs de Jus de Fruits
  [*International Federation of Fruit Juice Producers - IFFJP*]
  (EAIO)
FIK .... Fakultas Ilmu Kedokteran [*School of Medicine*]   (IN)
FIK .... Fovarosi Ingatlanforgalmi Kozpont [*Capital Real Estate Center*]
  (HU)
FIKI .... Faipari Kutato Intezet [*Lumber Industrial Research Institute*]
  (HU)
FIKIE .... Fakultas Ilmu Keguruan Ilmu Eksakta [*School of Education and
  Exact Sciences*]   (IN)
FIKIN .... Foire Internationale de Kinshasa [*International Fair in
  Kinshasa*] [*Zaire*]   (AF)
FiKP .... Finn Kommunista Part [*Finnish Communist Party*]   (HU)
fikt zagl ...... Fictitious Title   (BU)
FIL .... Avia Filipines International, Inc. [*Philippines*] [*ICAO designator*]
  (FAAC)
fil .... Branch   (RU)
FIL .... Federation Generale des Instituteurs Luxembourgeois
  [*Luxembourg*]   (BAS)
FIL .... Federation Internationale de Laiterie [*International Dairy
  Federation - IDF*]   (EAIO)
FIL .... Federation Internationale de Luge de Course [*International Luge
  Federation - ILF*] [*Rottenmann, Austria*]   (EA)
FIL .... Federazione Italiana del Lavoro [*Italian Federation of Labor*]
FIL .... Feira Internacional de Lisboa [*Lisbon International Fair*]
  [*Portuguese*]   (WER)
Fil .... Filemon [*Philemon*] [*Afrikaans*]
fil .... Filete [*Fillet*] [*Publishing*] [*Spanish*]
fil .... Fileten [*Fillets*] [*Publishing*] [*German*]
fil .... Filets [*Fillets*] [*Publishing*] [*French*]
fil .... Filetto [*Fillet*] [*Publishing*] [*Italian*]
Fil .... Filiale [*Branch Office*] [*German*]
fil .... Filialka [*Branch*]   (CZ)
Fil .... Filippense [*Philippians*] [*Afrikaans*]
Fil .... Filologia [*Philology*] [*Portuguese*]
fil .... Filosofia [*Philosophy*] [*Finland*]
Fil .... Filosofia [*Philosophy*] [*Portuguese*]
FIL .... Fish Industries Limited [*Sierra Leone*]
FIL .... Frente de Integracion Liberal [*Liberal Integration Front*]
  [*Colorado*]   (LA)
fil .... Philosophy   (BU)
FIL .... Pulse Phototube   (RU)
FILA .... Federation Internationale de Lutte Amateur [*International
  Amateur Wrestling Federation*] [*Lausanne, Switzerland*]
  (EAIO)
FILA .... Federation Internationale des Luttes Associees   (OLYM)
FILA .... Federation of Indian Library Associations   (PDAA)
FILA .... Federazione Italiana Lavoratori Abbigliamento [*Italian
  Federation of Garment Workers*]
FILAI .... Federazione Italiana Lavoratori Ausiliari dell'Impiego [*Italian
  Federation of Auxiliary Services*]
FILAM ...... Federazione Italiana Lavoratori Albergo Mensa e Termali
  [*National Union of Hotel and Restaurant Workers*]
  [*Italian*]
FILAS .... Filialbetriebe Abrechnungssystem [*GRM*]   (ADPT)
filat .... Filatelia [*Philately*] [*Finland*]
FIL-BA ...... Club Filatelico de Barranquilla   (COL)
FILBAS ..... Philippine Base [*Army*] [*World War II*]
FILBDLP .. Fondation Internationale Lelio Basso pour le Droit et la
  Liberation des Peuples [*International Lelio Basso
  Foundation for the Rights and Liberation of Peoples -
  ILBFRLP*]   (EA)

FILC .... Federazione Italiana Lavoratori Chimici [*Italian Federation of Chemical Workers*]
FILCA .... Federazione Italiana Lavoratori Costruzioni e Affini [*Italian Federation of Construction and Related Workers*] [*Rome*]
FILCAM ... Nylon Fils Cameroun
FILCAMS ... Federazione Italiana Lavoratori Commercio Albergo Mensa e Servizi [*Italian Federation of Hotel and Catering Workers*] [*Rome*]
FILCEA ..... Federazione Italiana Lavoratori Commercio e Aggregati [*Italian Federation of Commercial and Associated Workers*]
FILCOTEX ... Societe Industrielle de Filature, Confection, et Textiles
FILDA .... Federazione Italiana Lavoratori degli Acquedotti [*Italian Federation of Aqueduct Workers*]
FILEF .... Federazione Italiana Lavorati Emigrati Famiglie
FILEF .... Federazione Italiana Lavoratori Emigrati e Famiglie [*Italian Federation of Italian Emigrants and Their Families*] (WER)
filfak .... Division of Philology (RU)
FILFP .... Forum International de Liaison des Forces de la Paix [*International Liaison Forum of Peace Forces - ILF*] [*Moscow, USSR*] (EAIO)
FILIA .... Federazione Italiana Lavoratori Industrie Alimentari [*Italian Federation of Food Processing Workers*]
FILIE .... Federazione Italiana Lavoratori Industrie Estrattive [*Italian Federation of Workers in Mining Industries*]
Filintern ..... Philatelic International (RU)
FILIP .... Filippense [*Philippians*] [*Afrikaans*]
FILIS .... Federazione Italiana Lavoratori Informazione Spettacolo [*Italian Federation of Theatre Workers*] [*Italy*] (EY)
FilK .... Filosofian Kandidaatti [*Master's Degree in Philosophy*] [*Finland*]
filkand .... Filosofian Kandidaatti [*Master's Degree in Philosophy*] [*Finland*]
fill .... Filler [*Filler*] (HU)
FILLBAV .. Federazione Italiana Lavoratori Legno-Boschivi - Artistiche e Varie [*National Federation of Carpenters, Lumbermen, and Cabinetmakers*] [*Italian*]
FILLEA ..... Federazione Italiana Lavoratori del Legno, dell'Edilizia e Industrie Affini [*Italian Federation of Workers in Carpentry, Construction, and Related Industries*] [*Rome*]
fillis .... Filosofian Lisensiaatti [*Finland*]
FILLM .... Federation Internationale des Langues et Litteratures Modernes [*International Federation for Modern Languages and Literatures*] (EAIO)
FILM .... Federazione Italiana Lavoratori del Mare [*Italian Federation of Merchant Seamen*] [*Rome*]
FilM .... Filosofian Maisteri [*Finland*]
filmaist .... Filosofian Maisteri [*Finland*]
FILM-IS.... Turkiye Film Iscileri Sendikasi [*Turkish Film Workers Union*] [*Istanbul*] (TU)
Filol .... Filologia [*Philology*] [*Portuguese*]
filol .... Philologic, Philology (RU)
Filol fak...... Department of Philology (BU)
Filos .... Filosofia [*Philosophy*] [*Portuguese*]
filos .... Filosofia [*Philosophy*] [*Finland*]
FILOS .... Filosofie [*Philosophy*] [*Afrikaans*]
filos .... Philosophical, Philosophy (RU)
Filos-istfak ... Department of Philosophy and History (BU)
filosof .... Philosophical (RU)
FILP .... Federazione Italiana Lavoratori dei Porti [*Italian Federation of Longshoremen*]
FILP .... Fiscal Investment and Loan Programme [*Ministry of Posts and Telecommunications*] [*Japan*]
FILPC........ Federazione Italiana Lavoratori Poligrafici e Cartai [*Italian Federation of Printers and Paperworkers*]
FILS .... Federazione Italiana Lavoratori dello Spettacolo [*Italian Federation of Entertainment Workers*]
FILS .... Federazione Italiana Lavoratori Statali [*Italian Federation of Government Employees*]
FILSA .... Federazione Italiana Lavoratori Sanatoriali [*Italian Federation of Public Health Workers - Hospital and Sanatorium Employees*]
FILSTA ..... Federazione Italiana Lavoratori Servizi Tributari e Assicuratori [*Italian Federation of Tax Workers*]
FILT .... Federazione Italiana Sindacati dei Trasporti [*Transportation industry*] [*Italy*] (EY)
FILTA....... Filature et Teinturerie de l'Atlas [*Morocco*]
FILTAT..... Federazione Italiana Trasporti ed Ausiliari del Traffico [*Italian Federation of Transportation and Auxiliary Services*] [*Rome*]
FILTISAC ... Filature, Tissages, Sacs, Cote-D'Ivoire
FILTISAF ... Filatures et Tissages Africains [*Zaire*] (IMH)
filtri .... Filosofian Tohtori [*Finland*]
FIM........... Federation Internationale des Mineurs [*Miners' International Federation - MIF*] [*Brussels, Belgium*] (EAIO)
FIM........... Federation Internationale des Musiciens [*International Federation of Musicians*] [*Zurich, Switzerland*] (EAIO)
FIM........... Federation Internationale Motocycliste [*International Motorcycle Federation*] [*Geneva, Switzerland*] (EAIO)

FIM........... Federazione Italiana Metalmeccanici [*Italian Metal Mechanic Workers' Federation*] [*Rome*]
FIM........... Finnmark [*Finnish Mark*] [*Monetary unit*]
FIM........... Fond Industriel de Modernisation [*Loan agency*] [*French*]
FIM........... Pulse-Phase Modulation (RU)
FIMA........ Fellow of the Institute of Municipal Administration [*Australia*] (ADA)
FIMA........ Fibreglass Insulation Manufacturers' Association of Australia
FIMA........ Food Industries of Malaysia (ML)
FIMACO... Financiamiento de Materiales de Construccion (Programa del BNH) [*Banco Nacional de Habitacion*] [*Construction Material Financing Rio De Janeiro, Brazil*] (LAA)
FIMADOMIA ... Pro-Military Government Peasant's Association [*Malagasy*] (AF)
FIMCAP ... Federation Internationale de Communautes de Jeunesse Catholique Paroissiales [*International Federation of Catholic Parochial Youth Communities*] [*Antwerp, Belgium*] (EAIO)
FIMCEE.... Federation de l'Industrie Marbriere de la Communaute Economique Europeenne [*Federation of the Marble Industry of the European Economic Community*] (EAIO)
FIME........ Factoria e Industrias Metalicas [*Colombia*] (COL)
FIME........ Federation Internationale des Maisons de l'Europe [*International Federation of Europe Houses - IFEH*] (EAIO)
FIME........ Federation of Industrial Manufacturing Employees [*Australia*]
FIME........ Fellow of the Institute of Marine Engineers [*British*] (DCTA)
FIMEE ...... Federation of Industrial Manufacturing and Engineering Employees [*Australia*]
FIMEM ..... Federation Internationale des Mouvements d'Ecole Moderne (EAIO)
FIMH .... Fellow of the Institute of Materials Handling [*South Africa*] (AA)
FIMI .... Fellow of the Institute of the Motor Industry [*South Africa*] (AA)
FIMIG-CEE ... Federation of the Marble Industry of the European Economic Community (EAIO)
FIMISCO ... Financial Mining Industrial and Shipping Corporation [*Greek*]
FIMITIC ... Federation Internationale des Mutiles, des Invalides du Travail, et des Invalides Civils [*International Federation of Disabled Workmen and Civilian Handicapped*] (EAIO)
FIMM....... Federation Internationale de Medecine Manuelle [*International Federation of Manual Medicine*] [*Zurich, Switzerland*] (EAIO)
FIMM....... Fellow of the Institute of Municipal Management [*Australia*]
FIMM....... Mauritius Flight Information Center [*ICAO location identifier*] (ICLI)
FIMMEMA ... Fikambanan' Ny Mpanoratra Sy Mpamoron-Kira Ary Editora Malagasy [*Malagasy Republic*]
FIMP......... Mauritius/Sir Seewoosagur Ramgoolam International [*ICAO location identifier*] (ICLI)
FIMPAMA ... Fivondronan'ny Mpandraharaha Malagasy [*Association of Malagasy Businessmen*] (AF)
FIMPATEMA ... Association des Enseignants de la Langue Malagasy [*Malagasy Language Teachers Association*] (AF)
FIMPS....... Federation Internationale de Medecine Preventive et Sociale [*International Federation for Preventive and Social Medicine*] (EAIO)
FIMR........ Rodriguez Island/Plaine Corail [*Mauritius*] [*ICAO location identifier*] (ICLI)
FIMS .... Federation Internationale de Medecine Sportive (OLYM)
FIMSA ...... Fabricaciones, Ingenieria, y Montajes, Sociedad Anonima [*Mexico*] (LAA)
FIMTM ..... Federation des Industries Mecaniques et Transformatrices des Metaux
FIMunESA ... Fellow of the Institute of Municipal Engineers of South Africa (AA)
FIMUR...... Fideerias y Molinos del Uruguay [*Uruguay*] (DSCA)
Fin............. Finance (PWGL)
Fin............. Financial (PWGL)
Fin............. Finanz [*Finance*] [*German*]
Fin............. Fine [*The End*] [*Music*]
FIN .... Finland [*ANSI three-letter standard code*] (CNC)
FIN .... Finnair OY [*Finland*] [*ICAO designator*] (FAAC)
fin.............. Finnish (RU)
FIN .... Finschhafen [*Papua New Guinea*] [*Airport symbol*] (OAG)
FIN .... Fraternidad Independiente Nacionalista [*Nationalist Independent Fraternity*] [*Honduras*] (LA)
FIN .... Frente de Integracion Nacional [*Front for National Integration*] [*Guatemala*]
FIN .... Future Information Network [*Australia*]
FIN .... Physiological Institute (RU)
FINA......... Federacion de la Industria Naval Argentina [*Argentina*] (LAA)
FINA......... Federation Internationale de Natation Amateur [*International Amateur Swimming Federation*] [*Vancouver, BC*]
FINABEL ... France, Italy, Netherlands, Allemagne, Belgium, Luxembourg [*Army Chiefs of Staff Joint Committee*] (PDAA)
FINADEICO ... Finanzas Administracion y Contabilidad [*Colombia*] (COL)

Finafrica .... Financial Assistance to African Countries

final .... Finalino [*Tailpiece*] [*Publishing*] [*Italian*]

FINAME ... Fundo de Financiamento de Maquinas e Equipamentos [*Fund for the Financing of Machinery and Equipment*] [*Brazil*] (LA)

FINANSA ... Financiamiento para el Saneamiento (Programa del BNH) [*Banco Nacional de Habitacion*] [*Sanitation Financing Rio De Janeiro, Brazil*] (LAA)

FINANSA ... Financiera Nacional Sociedad Anonima [*Ecuador*] (IMH)

FINAPRI... Financiera de Preinversion [*Preinvestment Financing Enterprise*] [*Nicaragua*] (LA)

FINAREP ... Societe Financiere des Petroles [*Petroleum Finance Company*] [*Algeria*] (AF)

FINART .... Feria Internacional de Artesania

FINARTOIS ... Societe Financiere et Industrielle de l'Artois

FINASA ..... Financiera Nacional Azucarera, SNC [*Mexico*] (EY)

FINAT .... Federation Internationale des Fabricants et Transformateurs d'Adhesifs et Thermocollants sur Papiers et Autres Supports [*International Federation of Manufacturers and Converters of Pressure-Sensitive and Heatseals on Paper and Other Base Materials*] (EAIO)

FINATA .... Financiera Nacional de Tierras Agricolas [*El Salvador*] (EY)

FINAUTOS ... Financiadora de Autos [*Colombia*] (COL)

FINAVI ..... Financiera Nacional de Viviendas [*National Housing Finance Company*] [*Honduras*] (LA)

FINCA .... Fabrica Industrial de Concentrados Alimenticios [*Colombia*] (COL)

FINCh .... Low-Pass Measuring Filter (RU)

FINCO .... Finance Corp. of the Bahamas Ltd. (EY)

FINCOL .... Compania Colombiana de Financiamientos [*Colombia*] (COL)

FIND .... Family Information Network for Defence [*Australia*]

FIND .... Festival International de Nouvelle Danse

FINDECO ... Financial Development Corporation [*Zambia*] (AF)

FINDES ..... Fedetracao das Industrias do Estado do Espirito Santo

FINDEX ..... Facettenartiges Indexierungssystem

FINEFTA ... Finland-European Free Trade Association Treaty

FINEK .... Finansiil dan Ekonomi [*Financial and Economic Affairs*] (IN)

FINEK .... Preduzece za Finansiske i Ekonomske Usluge [*Financial and Economic Services Enterprise*] (YU)

finem .... Finemente [*Beautifully*] [*Italian*]

FINEP .... Financiadora de Estudos e Projetos [*Funding Authority for Studies and Projects*] [*Brazil*] (LA)

FINEPI ..... Fondo de Financiamiento de Elaboracion de Proyectos de Inversion [*Peru*] (LAA)

FINEX .... Fundo de Financiamento e Exportacao [*Financing and Export Fund*] [*Brazil*] (LA)

FINF .... Firmen- und Marktinformationen [*Company and Market Information Data Base*] [*Society for Business Information*] [*Information service or system*] (IID)

fingerfl ...... Fingerfleckig [*Finger-Marked*] [*Publishing*] [*German*]

FINGUINEA ... Sociedad Financiera de Guinea

FINIWAX ... Societe de Finition de Tissus Wax

FINK .... Finanzbuchhaltung im Krankenhaus [*Financial Book Keeping in the Hospital*] [*German*] (ADPT)

finl .... Finnish (RU)

FINMECCANICA ... Societa Finanziaria Meccanica [*Italy*] (ERC)

FINN .... Finnish

FINNPAP ... Finnish Paper Mills Association

Finn Pat ..... Finnisches Patent [*Finnish Patent*] [*German*] (GCA)

FINOR .... Fundo de Investimentos do Nordeste [*Northeast Investments Fund*] [*Brazil*] (LA)

finotdel .... Financial Department (BU)

FINPRO .... Finnish Committee in Trade Procedures (DS)

FINPRO .... Finnish Committee on Trade Producers (PDAA)

Fin Publ .... Finances Publiques [*Benelux*] (BAS)

Fin Rev .... Australian Financial Review [*A publication*]

FINSAP ..... Financial Sector Adjustment Program [*West Africa*]

FINSIDER ... Societa Finanziaria Siderurgica [*Italian*]

F Inst CM .. Fellow of the Institute of Commercial Management [*British*] (DCTA)

FInstDA ..... Fellow of the Institute of Directors in Australia (ADA)

FInstE .... Fellow of the Institute of Energy [*South Africa*] (AA)

F Inst LEx ... Fellow of the Institute of Legal Executives [*British*] (DCTA)

FInstRE(Aust) ... Fellow of the Institution of Radio Engineers (Australia)

F Inst TA ... Fellow of the Institute of Transport Administration [*British*] (DCTA)

FINSZ .... Fakutato Intezetek Nemzetkozi Szovetsege [*International Union of Forestry Research Organizations*] (HU)

FINUL .... Force des Nations Unies au Liban

FINUMA... Fabrique Ivoirienne de Nuoc-Mam [*Ivorian Nuoc-Mam Plant*] (AF)

Finupr .... Finance Administration (RU)

FIO .... Federacion Internacional de Oleicultura [*International Olive Oil Federation*] [*Rome, Italy*] [*Defunct*] (EA)

FIO .... Forest Industry Organization [*Thai*] (GEA)

FIO .... Last Name, First Name, and Patronymic (RU)

FIOC .... Flanders Investment Opportunity Council [*Belgium*]

FIOCES..... Federation Internationale des Organisations de Correspondances et d'Echanges Scolaires [*International Federation of Organizations for School Correspondence and Exchange*] [*Paris, France*] (EA)

FIOD .... Fiscale Inlichtingen- en Opsporingsdienst [*Benelux*] (BAS)

FIODS....... Federation Internationale des Organisations de Donneurs de Sang Benevoles [*International Federation of Blood Donor Organizations - IFBDO*] [*Dole, France*] (EAIO)

FIOM .... Federation Internationale des Organisations de Travailleurs de la Metallurgie [*International Metalworkers Federation - IMF*] [*Geneva, Switzerland*] (EAIO)

FIOM .... Federazione Impiegati e Operai Metallurgici [*Federation of Those Employed in Metallurgical Industries*] [*Italian*] (WER)

FIOPM...... Federation Internationale des Organismes de Psychologie Medicale [*International Federation of the Psychological-Medical Organizations - IFPMO*] (EAIO)

FIOPP .... Federacion Interamericana de Organizaciones de Periodistas Profesionales [*Inter-American Federation of Working Newspapermen's Organizations*] [*Use IAFWNO*] (LA)

fior .... Fioriture [*Flowered Designs*] [*Publishing*] [*Italian*]

fiorit .... Fioriture [*Flowered Designs*] [*Publishing*] [*Italian*]

FIOSH....... Fellow of the Institution of Occupational Safety and Health [*British*] (DCTA)

FIOSS........ Federation Internationale des Organisations de Sciences Sociales [*International Federation of Social Science Organizations - IFSSO*] (EAIO)

FIOST .... Federation Internationale des Organisations Syndicales du Personnel des Transporte [*International Federation of Trade Unions of Transport Workers - IFTUTW*] (EAIO)

FIOT .... Federazione Impiegati Operai Tessili [*Federation of Textile Workers*] [*Italian*]

FiOTV .... Tuula Vauhkonen [*Regional Institute of Occupational Health*], Oulv, Finland [*Library symbol*] [*Library of Congress*] (LCLS)

FIP .... Fabrica de Implementos, SA [*Mexico*]

FIP .... Federacion Internacional de Periodistas [*International Federation of Journalists*] [*Use IFJ*] (LA)

FIP .... Federation Internationale de la Precontrainte [*International Federation of Prestressed Concrete*] (EAIO)

FIP .... Federation Internationale de Philatelie [*International Federation of Philately*] (EAIO)

FIP .... Federation Internationale de Podologie [*French*] (SLS)

FIP .... Federation Internationale des Pietons [*International Federation of Pedestrians*] [*Netherlands*]

FIP .... Federation Internationale Pharmaceutique [*International Pharmaceutical Federation*] [*The Hague, Netherlands*] (EAIO)

FIP .... Federation of Indian Publishers

FIP .... Federazione Italiana della Pubblicita [*Italian Federation of Advertisers*] [*Italy*] (EY)

FIP .... Federazione Italiana Pensionati [*Italian Federation of Pensioners*]

FIP .... Federazione Italiana Postelegrafonici [*Italian Federation of Postal, Telegraph, and Telephone Workers*]

FIP .... Finanziaria Italiana di Partecipipazioni [*Italian Finance Bank of Participation*]

FIP .... Fondo de Inversiones Privadas (COL)

FIP .... Formatura Iniezione Polineri [*Injection polymer manufacturing company*] [*Italy*]

FIP .... Frente de Izquierda Popular [*Popular Left Front*] [*Argentina*] [*Political party*] (PPW)

FIP .... Frente Independiente Parlamentario [*Independent Parliamentary Front*] [*Venezuela*] (LA)

FIP .... Fuerzas Interamericanas de la Paz [*Inter-American Peace Force*] [*Use IAPF*] (LA)

FIPA .... Federacion Internacional de Productores Agricolas [*International Federation of Agricultural Producers - IFAP*] [*Spanish*] (ASF)

FIPA .... Federation Internationale des Producteurs Agricoles [*International Federation of Agricultural Producers - IFAP*] [*French*] (ASF)

FIPA .... Fellow of the Institute of Patent Attorneys [*Australia*]

FIPA .... Festival International de Programmes Audiovisuels

FIPAA .... Fellow of the Institute of Patent Attorneys of Australia (ADA)

FIPAAust .. Fellow of the Institute of Park Administration, Australia (ADA)

FIPAD .... Fondation Internationale pour un Autre Developpement [*International Foundation for Development Alternatives - IFDA*] [*Nyon, Switzerland*] (EAIO)

FIPAGO .... Federation Internationale des Fabricants de Papiers Gommes [*International Federation of Manufacturers of Gummed Paper*] (EAIO)

FIPAH....... Federation des Importateurs et Producteurs d'Adjuvants et Additifs pour Coulis Mortier et Beton de Ciment [*Association of Importers and Producers of Admixtures*] (EAIO)

FIPAN .... Federacion de Instituciones Privadas de Asistencia al Nino [*Venezuela*] (LAA)

FIPC .... Federation Internationale des Pharmaciens Catholiques [*International Federation of Catholic Pharmacists*] [*Eupen, Belgium*]   (EAIO)

FIPC .... Fishing Industry Policy Council [*Australia*]

FIPEME.... Fundo de Financiamento as Pequenas e Medias Empresas [*Fund for Financing Small and Medium-Size Businesses*] [*Brazil*]   (LA)

FIPESO..... Federation Internationale des Professeurs de l'Enseignement Secondaire Officiel [*International Federation of Secondary Teachers*]   (EAIO)

FIPF.......... Federation Internationale des Professeurs de Francais [*International Federation of Teachers of French - IFTF*]   (EAIO)

FIPF.......... Federation Internationale pour la Planification Familiale

FIPFP....... Federation Internationale des Petits Freres des Pauvres [*International Federation of the Little Brothers of the Poor - IFLBP*]   (EAIO)

FIPIA........ Fakultas Ilmu Pasti dan Ilmu Alam [*Department of Mathematics and Physics*]   (IN)

FIPIMA..... Fivondronam-Pirenena Malagasy [*Malagasy National Union*]   (AF)

FIPIS........ Fishery Project Information System [*FAO*] [*United Nations*]   (DUND)

FIPJP....... Federation Internationale de Petanque et Jeu Provencal [*Marseille, France*]   (EAIO)

FIPL .... Federacion Internacional de Periodistas Libres [*International Federation of Free Journalists*] [*Use IFFJ*]   (LA)

FIPLF....... Federation Internationale de la Presse de Langue Francaise   (EA)

FIPLV....... Federation Internationale des Professeurs de Langues Vivantes [*International Federation of Modern Language Teachers*] [*Switzerland*]

FIPM .... Federation Internationale de la Philatelie Maritime [*International Federation of Maritime Philately - IFMP*]   (EA)

FIPMA ...... Fellow of the Institute of Personnel Management (Australia)   (ADA)

FIPP .... Federation Internationale de la Presse Periodique [*International Federation of the Periodical Press*]   (EAIO)

FIPP .... Fondation Internationale Penale et Penitentiaire [*International Penal and Penitentiary Foundation - IPPF*] [*Bonn, Federal Republic of Germany*]   (EAIO)

FIPRESCI ... Federation Internationale de la Presse Cinematographique [*International Federation of the Cinematographic Press - IFCP*]   (EAIO)

FIP (SA) .... Fellow of the Institute of Printing (South Africa)   (AA)

FIPSA........ Fellow of the Institute of Private Secretaries (Australia)

FIPSG....... Falkland Islands Philatelic Study Group [*of the American Philatelic Society*] [*Fordingbridge, Hampshire, England*]   (EAIO)

FIPTP....... Federation Internationale de la Presse Technique et Periodique [*International Federation of the Technical and Periodical Press*]

FIPU .... True Track Angle   (RU)

FIPV .... Federacion Internacional de Pelota Vasca [*International Federation of Pelota Vasca - IFPV*]   (EA)

FIPV .... Federation Internationale de Pelolta Vasca   (OLYM)

FIPZ .... Falkland Islands Protection Zone

FIQ .... Federation Internationale des Quillieurs [*International Federation of Bowlers*] [*Espoo, Finland*]   (EA)

FIQ .... Federation Internationale des Quilluers   (OLYM)

FIQSA .... Fellow of the Institute of Quantity Surveyors of Australia   (ADA)

FIR............. Federation Internationale des Resistants

FIR............. Fellow of the Australasian Institute of Radiography   (ADA)

FIR............. Flight Information Region   (TU)

FIR............. Fondo Internacional para la Reconstruccion [*International Reconstruction Fund*] [*Nicaragua*]   (LA)

FIR............. Forschungsinstitut fuer Rationalisierung [*Research Institute for Operations Management*] [*Research center*]   (IRC)

FIR............. Frente de Izquierda Revolucionaria [*Revolutionary Left Front*] [*Peru*]   (LA)

FIR............. Frente Independiente Reformista [*Reformist Independent Front*] [*Venezuela*]   (LA)

FIR............. Freshwater Institute Report [*United Nations*]

FIR............. Fuerza Independiente Revolucionaria [*Independent Revolutionary Force*] [*Venezuela*]   (LA)

FIR............. Photoelectronic Radiation Meter   (RU)

FIRA .... Federation Internationale de Football-Rugby Amateur [*International Amateur Rugby Foundation*]   (EA)

FIRA .... Fideicomisos Instituidos en Relacion con la Agricultura [*Mexico*]   (EY)

FIRB .... Foreign Investment Review Board [*Australia*]

FIRDC ...... Fishing Industry Research and Development Council [*Australia*]

FIRDC ...... Forest Industry Research and Development Corp. [*Commercial firm*] [*Australia*]

FIRE(Aust) ... Fellow of the Institution of Radio Engineers (Australia) [*Later, FIREE (Aust)*]

FIREE(Aust) ... Fellow of the Institution of Radio and Electronics Engineers (Australia) [*Formerly, FIRE (Aust)*]

FIRI .... Fishing Industry Research Institute

FIRM........ Federation Internationale des Reconstructeurs de Moteurs [*International Federation of Engine Reconditioners - IFER*]   (EAIO)

FIR(ML).... Frente de Izquierda Revolucionaria (Marxista-Leninista) [*Revolutionary Left Front (Marxist-Leninist)*] [*Peru*]   (LA)

firn............. Neve Field   (RU)

FIRP .... Foreign Inward Remittance Payment Scheme [*Reserve Bank of India*]   (PDAA)

FIRR......... Federal Institute for Reactor Research [*Switzerland*] [*Nuclear energy*]   (NRCH)

FIRS .... Federation Internationale de Roller-Skating [*International Roller Skating Federation*]   (EAIO)

FIRS .... Fonds d'Intervention et de Regularisation du Marche du Sucre [*France*]

FIRSA....... Fomento de Inversiones Rentables SA [*Nicaragua*]   (DSCA)

FIRST....... Fleurs Interferometric Radio Synthesis Telescope [*Univeristy of Sydney*] [*Australia*]   (PDAA)

FIRST....... Funding for Innovation Research and State Technology [*Australia*]

FIRST....... Furniture Industry Retirement aand Superannuation Trust [*Australia*]

FIRT .... Federation Internationale pour la Recherche Theatrale [*International Federation for Theatre Research - IFTR*]   (EAIO)

FIRTA ...... Fishing Industry Research Trust Account [*Australia*]

FiRUL-A ... University of Lapland, Lapland Artic Center, Rovaniemi, Lapland [*Library symbol*] [*Library of Congress*]   (LCLS)

FIS .... Fakulta Inzenyrskeho Stavitelstvi [*Department of Construction Engineering*]   (CZ)

FIS .... Family Income Support [*Australia*]

FIS .... Federation Internationale de Sauvetage Aquatique [*Germany*]

FIS .... Federation Internationale de Ski [*International Ski Federation*] [*Gumlingen, Switzerland*]   (EA)

FIS .... Federation Internationale du Commerce des Semences [*Netherlands*]   (DSCA)

FIS .... Federation Internationale pour la Sante [*International Federation for Health*] [*France*]   (EAIO)

FIS .... Federazione Informazione Spettacolo [*Tourism industry*] [*Italy*]   (EY)

FIS .... Felag Islenskra Simamanna [*Iceland*]   (EAIO)

FIS .... FINSAP Implementation Secretariat [*West Africa*]

Fis .... Fisica [*Physics*] [*Portuguese*]

FIS .... Fondation Internationale pour la Science [*International Foundation for Science - IFS*]   (EAIO)

FIS .... Fondo de Investigaciones Sanitarias [*Spain*]

FIS .... Fonds d'Intervention Siderurgique [*Steel Intervention Fund*] [*French*]   (GEA)

FIS .... Forces of Islamic Solidarity [*Sudan*]

FIS .... Foreign Investment Secretariat [*Queensland, Australia*]

FIS .... Front Islamique de Salut [*Algeria*] [*Political party*]

FIS .... Fukuoka International School [*Japan*]

FIS .... Islamic Salvation Front [*Algeria*] [*Political party*]   (ECON)

FiS .... Physical Culture and Sport [*Publishing house*]   (RU)

FISA .... Federation Internationale des Societes Aerophilateliques [*International Federation of Aero-Philatelic Societies*] [*Zurich Airport, Switzerland*]   (EAIO)

FISA .... Federation Internationale des Societes d'Aviron [*International Rowing Federation*] [*Neuchatel, Switzerland*]   (EAIO)

FISA .... Federation Internationale du Sport Automobile [*Paris, France*]   (EAIO)

FISA .... Federation Ivoirienne de Sports Automobiles

FISA .... Feria Industrial de Santiago [*Santiago Industrial Fair*] [*Chile*]   (LA)

FISA .... Financiera Industrial Sociedad Anonima [*Guatemala*]   (EY)

FISA .... Fondazione Italiana per la Storia Amministrativa [*Italian Foundation for Administrative History*]

FISA .... Footwear Institute of South Africa   (EY)

FISA .... Fotografia Industrial, Sociedad Anonima

FISAE....... Federation Internationale des Societes d'Amateurs d'Exlibris [*British*]   (EAIO)

FISAJ .... Fiskulturni Savez Jugoslavije [*Physical Culture Federation of Yugoslavia*]   (YU)

FISAM ...... Federazione Italiana delle Scienze e delle Attivita Motorie [*Italian*]   (SLS)

FISAMA ... Firaisana Sendikaly Malagasy

FISANE..... Fondo de Financiacion Sanitaria [*Sanitation Finance Fund*] [*Brazil*]   (LAA)

FISASCA .. Federazione Italiana Sindacati Addetti Servizi Commerciali ed Affini [*Italian Federation of Commercial and Related Workers' Unions*]

FIS(Aust)... Fellow of the Institution of Surveyors, Australia   (ADA)

FISB.......... Federation Internationale de Skibob [*Germany*]   (EAIO)

FISBA........ Federazione Italiana Salariati Braccianti Agricoli e Maestranze Specializzate Agricole e Forestali [*Italian Federation of Permanent Unskilled and Skilled Agricultural Workers*] [*Rome*]

FISBTA..... Federazione Italiana Salariati, Braccianti, e Tecnici Agricoli [*Italian Federation of Permanent, Daily, and Technical Agricultural Workers*]

FISC.......... Federazione Internazionale Sindacati Cristiani [*International Federation of Christian Trade Unions*] [*Italian*]   (WER)

FISC.......... Foundation for International Scientific Co-Ordination [*Paris, France*]   (EAIO)

FISCETCV ... Federation Internationale des Syndicats Chretiens d'Employes, Techniciens, Cadres et Voyageurs de Commerce   (FLAF)

FISCM...... Federation Internationale des Syndicats Chretiens de la Metallurgie   (FLAF)

Fisc Not..... Fiscale Notities [*Benelux*]   (BAS)

FISCO....... Omnium Fiscal et Comptable de Madagascar

FISCOA .... Federation Internationale des Syndicats Chretiens d'Ouvriers Agricoles   (FLAF)

FISCOBB.. Federation Internationale des Syndicats Chretiens d'Ouvriers du Batiment et du Bois   (FLAF)

FISCOR..... Fisheries Development Corporation [*South Africa*]   (MSC)

FISCTTH ... Federation Internationale des Syndicats Chretiens des Travailleurs du Textile et de l'Habillement   (FLAF)

FISE.......... Federacion Internacional Sindical de la Ensenanza [*World Federation of Teachers' Unions*]   (LA)

FISE.......... Federation Internationale Syndicale de l'Enseignement [*World Federation of Teachers' Unions*] [*Berlin, Federal Republic of Germany*]   (EAIO)

FISE.......... Fonds International de Secours a l'Enfance [*United Nations Children's Fund*] [*Use UNICEF*]   (AF)

FIS-ELF .... German Information System on Food, Agriculture, and Forestry [*Bonn*] [*Information service or system*]   (IID)

FISEMA.... Firaisan'ny Sendika Eran'i Madagaskara [*Confederation of All Unions in Madagascar*]

FISEMARE ... Federation des Travailleurs Malagasy Revolutionnaires [*Federation of Revolutionary Trade Unions of Madagascar*]

FISH.......... Feronia International Shipping [*France*]   (EY)

FISHC....... Federation Internationale des Societes d'Histochimie et de Cytochimie [*International Federation of Societies for Histochemistry and Cytochemistry*]   (EAIO)

FISIBA...... Fibras Sinteticas do Bahia SA [*Brazil*]

Fisiol.......... Fisiologia [*Physiology*] [*Portuguese*]

FISIOL...... Fisiologie [*Physiology*] [*Afrikaans*]

FISITA ...... Federation International des Societes d'Ingenieurs des Techniques de l'Automobile

FISKOBIRLIK ... Findik Tarim Satis Kooperatifleri Birligi [*Hazel Nut Agricultural Sales Cooperatives Union*] [*FKB*] [*See also*]   (TU)

FISL.......... Federazione Internazionale dei Sindacati Liberi [*International Federation of Free Trade Unions*] [*Italian*]   (WER)

FISM .... Federation Internationale des Societes Magiques [*International Federation of Magical Societies - IFSM*] [*Paris, France*]   (EAIO)

FISM .... Fellow of the Australian Institute of Sales and Marketing Executives   (ADA)

FISMA ...... Federazione Italiana Strumenti Musicali ed Accessori [*Italian Federation of Manufacturers of Musical Instruments and Parts*]   (EY)

FISMARC ... Federation Internationale du Sport Medical pour l'Aide a la Recherche Cancerologique [*International Medical Sports Federation for Aid to Cancer Research*] [*Beziers, France*]   (EAIO)

Fis Nucl...... Fisica Nuclear [*Nuclear Physics*] [*Portuguese*]

FISOS........ Federazione Italiana Sindacati Ospedalieri [*Italian Federation of Hospital Workers' Unions*] [*Rome, Italy*]   (EY)

FISP.......... Federation Internationale des Societes de Philosophie [*International Federation of Philosophical Societies - IFPS*]   (EAIO)

FISP.......... Federazione Italiana Servizi Pubblici [*Italian Federation of Public Services*]

FISP.......... Financial Information Service for Pensioners [*Department of Social Security*] [*Australia*]

FISRO .... Federation Internationale des Societes de Recherche Operationelle [*International Federation of Operational Research Societies*] [*Denmark*]   (EAIO)

FISSHH .... First International Saturation Study of Herring and Hydroacoustics   (MSC)

FIST.......... Free Indian Socially-Traditionally [*India*] [*Political party*]

FISTA........ Federation Internationale des Syndicats des Travailleurs Audiovisuel [*International Federation of Audio-Visual Workers Unions - IFAVWU*]   (EAIO)

FIST-AV.... Federation Internationale des Syndicats des Travailleurs de l'Audio-Visuel [*Trade union*] [*French*]

FISTEL ..... Fundo de Fiscalizacao das Telecomunicacoes [*Telecommunications Inspection Fund*] [*Brazil*]   (LA)

FISTU .... Federation of Indian School Teachers' Union [*Malaysia*]

FISU.......... Confederacion Internacional Deportiva Universitaria [*International University Sports Federation*] [*Spanish*]   (LA)

FISU.......... Federation Internationale de Sport Universitaire   (OLYM)

FISU.......... Federation Internationale du Sport Universitaire [*International University Sports Federation*] [*Brussels, Belgium*]   (EAIO)

FISYO .... Filmovy Symfonicky Orchestr [*Film Symphony Orchestra*]   (CZ)

FISYS........ Fairplay Information Systems Ltd.   (IID)

FIT............ Federation Internationale des Traducteurs [*International Federation of Translators - IFT*]   (EAIO)

FIT............ Federation Internationale de Trampoline [*International Trampoline Federation*]   (EA)

FIT............ Federazione Italiana di Tribologia

FIT............ Federazione Italiana Trasporti [*Italian Federation of Transport*] [*Italy*]   (EY)

FIT............ Felag Islenskra Tryggingastaerdfraedinga [*Icelandic*]   (SLS)

FIT............ Fiji Institute of Technology

FIT............ Foundations for International Training [*Ghana*]

FIT............ Front Inter-Tropical

FIT............ Interntonal Trampoline Federation   (OLYM)

fit.............. Phytopathology   (RU)

FITA......... Federacion de Industrias Textiles Argentinas [*Federation of Argentine Textile Industries*]   (LA)

FITA......... Federal Interpreter and Translators Association [*Australia*]

FITA......... Federation Internationale de Tir a l'Arc [*International Archery Federation*] [*Milan, Italy*]   (EA)

FITA .... Federazione Italiana Transportatori Artigiani

FITAC .... Federacion Interamericana de Touring y Automovil Clubes [*Inter-American Federation of Touring and Automobile Clubs - IFTAC*]   (EAIO)

FITAM ...... Federation de l'Industrie Textile Africaine et Malgache

FITAP....... Federation Internationale des Transports Aeriens Prives   (FLAF)

FITASC.... Federation Internationale de Tir aux Arms Sportives de Chasse [*International Federation for Sport Shooting*] [*Paris, France*]   (EAIO)

FITB .... Federation Internationale des Techniciens de la Bonneterie [*International Federation of Knitting Technologists - IFKT*]   (EAIO)

FITB .... Fluorospar International Technical Bureau   (EAIO)

FITBB....... Federation Internationale des Travailleurs du Batiment et du Bois   (FLAF)

FITBT....... Fishing Industry Training Board of Tasmania [*Australia*]

FITC .... Fellow of the Institute of Town Clerks of Southern Africa   (AA)

FITC .... Frente Independiente de Trabajadores y Campesinos [*Independent Front of Workers and Peasants*] [*Peru*]   (LA)

FITCE........ Federation des Ingenieurs des Telecommunications de la Communaute Europeenne [*Federation of Telecommunications Engineers in the European Community*]

FITEI......... Festival Internacional de Teatro de Expressao Iberica

FITES........ Svaz Ceskoslovenckych Filmovych a Televiznich Umelcu [*Union of Czechoslovak Film and Television Artists*]   (CZ)

FITH......... Federation Internationale des Travailleurs de l'Abillement   (FLAF)

FITIM .... Federacion Internacional de Trabajadores de las Industrias Metalurgicas [*International Metalworkers' Federation*] [*Mexico*]   (LAA)

FITIM .... Societe de la Filature et de Tissage de Madagascar

FITITHC... Federation Internationale des Travailleurs des Industries du Textile, de l'Habillement, et du Cuir [*International Textile, Garment, and Leather Workers' Federation*] [*Brussels, Belgium*]

FITITV...... Federacion Interamericana de Trabajadores de la Industria Textil y del Vestuario [*Mexico*]   (LAA)

FITITVCC ... Federacion Interamericana de Trabajadores de la Industria Textil, Vestuario, Cuero, y Calzado [*Interamerican Textile, Leather, Garment, and Shoe Workers Federation - ITLGSWF*]   (EA)

FITM......... Federacion Interamericana de Trabajadores Mineros [*Inter-American Federation of Miners*]   (LA)

fitofarm ...... Phytopharmacology   (RU)

fitoklim ...... Phytoclimatology   (RU)

FITP......... Federacion Internacional de Trabajadores Petroleros (Oficina Regional) [*International Federation of Petroleum Workers*] [*Bogota, Colombia*]   (LAA)

FITP......... Federation Internationale des Travailleurs des Plantations   (FLAF)

FITP......... Federation Internationale des Travailleurs du Petrole   (FLAF)

FITPAS ..... Federacion Internacional de los Trabajadores de las Plantaciones Agricolas y Similares [*Switzerland*]   (DSCA)

FITPASC .. Federation Internationale des Travailleurs des Plantations, de l'Agriculture et des Secteurs Connexes   (FLAF)

FITPO....... Federacion Internacional de Petroleros y Quimicos [*Colombia*]   (COL)

FITS.......... Federation Internationale du Tourisme Social [*International Social Travel Federation - ISTF*]   (EAIO)

FITT .... Federation Internationale des Travailleurs de la Terre   (FLAF) fitt.............. Fittizio [*Artificial*] [*Italian*]

FITTHC .... Federation Internationale des Travailleurs des Industries du Textile, de l'Habillement, et du Cuir [*International Textile, Garment, and Leather Workers' Federation - ITGLWF*] (EAIO)

FITUG....... Federation of Independent Trade Unions in Guyana   (EY)

FIU .... Frente de Izquierda Universitaria [*Leftist University Front*] [*Ecuador*]   (LA)

Fiu.............. Pulse Shaper   (RU)

FIUC......... Federation Internationale des Universites Catholiques [*International Federation of Catholic Universities - IFCU*] (EAIO)

FIUL.......... Fundo de Investimentos Ultramarinos

FIUR......... Frente Independiente de Unificacion Revolucionaria [*Independent Front for Revolutionary Unity*] [*Venezuela*] (LA)

FIUS .... Filmove Ustredi [*Motion Picture Center*]   (CZ)

FIUS .... Filmovy Umelecky Sbor [*Film Artists' Ensemble*]   (CZ)

FIUV......... Federation Internationale Una Voce   (EA)

FIV............. Fecundacion in Vitro [*Spanish*]

FIV............. Federation de l'Industrie du Verre [*Federation of the Glass Industry*] [*Belgium*]   (PDAA)

FIV............. Federation Internationale de la Vieillesse [*International Federation on Ageing - IFA*]   (EAIO)

FIV............. Fitness Institute of Victoria [*Australia*]

FIV............. Fondo de Inversiones de Venezuela [*Venezuelan Investment Fund*]   (LA)

FIVA......... Federation Internationale des Vehicules Anciens   (EA)

FIVAG....... Federazione Italiana Venditori Ambulanti e Giornalai [*Italian Federation of Street Vendors and Newspaper Sellers*]

FIVB.......... Federation Internationale de Volleyball [*International Volleyball Federation*] [*Switzerland*]

FIVECA..... Frigorifico Industrial Vencedor CA [*Venezuela*]   (DSCA)

FIVF .... Federazione Italiana Vigili del Fuoco [*Italian Federation of Firemen*]

FIVP .... Economic Incentive and Assistance Fund   (BU)

FIVR .... Federation Internationale de Volleyball   (OLYM)

FIVS .... Federation Internationale des Vins et Spiritueux [*International Federation of Wines and Spirits - IFWS*]   (EAIO)

FiVTRC ..... Technical Research Centre of Finland, Information Service, Espoo, Vuorimiehentie, Finland [*Library symbol*] [*Library of Congress*]   (LCLS)

FIVV .... Federation Internationale de Vo Viet Nam [*An association*] (EAIO)

FIVZ......... Federacion Internacional Veterinaria de Zootecnia [*Spain*] (DSCA)

FIW............ Farmaceutyczny Instytut Wydawniczy [*Pharmaceutical Publishing Institute*]   (POL)

FIW............ Forschungsinstitut fuer Waermeschutz [*Thermal Insulation Research Institute*] [*Germany*]   (WED)

FIWM(SA) ... Fellow of the Institute of Waste Management (South Africa) (AA)

Fixier.......... Fixierung [*Fixation*] [*German*]   (GCA)

f-iya........... Function   (RU)

FIYTO .... Federation of International Youth Travel Organizations [*Copenhagen, Denmark*]   (EAIO)

FIZ............. Dritte Welt Frauensinformationszentrum [*Information Center for Third World Women*] [*Zurich, Switzerland*]   (EAIO)

FIZ............. Fachinformationszentrum [*ICSU*] [*Information retrieval*] [*German*]

fiz .... Fizetes [*Wages, Salary*]   (HU)

Fiz .... Fizik [*Physics or Physical*]   (TU)

fiz .... Fizika [*Physics*]   (HU)

FIZ............. Individual Orders Factory   (RU)

fiz .... Physical, Physics   (RU)

fiz .... Physics   (BU)

FIZATIF ... Progressive Youth League [*Malagasy*]   (AF)

Fizelektropribor ... Physics Electrical Instruments Plant   (RU)

fizfak .... Division of Physics   (RU)

fiziol .... Physiological, Physiology   (RU)

fiziotsentr ... Physiotherapy Center   (RU)

fizk .... Physical Culture   (BU)

fiz-khim..... Physicochemical   (RU)

Fizkultura .. Physical Culture   (RU)

fizmat .... Division of Physics and Mathematics   (RU)

fiz-matem ... Physics and Mathematics   (BU)

Fiz-matfak ... Department of Mathematics and Physics   (BU)

Fizmatgiz ... State Publishing House of Literature on Physics and Mathematics   (RU)

fiz p l .... Actual Printer's Sheet   (RU)

Fizpribor .... Physics Instruments Plant   (RU)

fizruk......... Physical Culture Instructor   (RU)

Fiz sl.......... Dictionary of Physics   (RU)

fiz-tekh....... Physicotechnical   (RU)

FIZ-W........ Fachinformationszentrum Werkstoffe [*Information Center for Materials*] [*Information service or system*]   (IID)

FJ .... Fiji [*ANSI two-letter standard code*]   (CNC)

FJ.............. Filles de Jesus de Kermaria [*Daughters of Jesus of Kermaria - DJK*] [*Paris, France*]   (EAIO)

Fj.............. Fjard [*or Fjord*] [*Fjord*] [*Sweden*]   (NAU)

Fj.............. Fjell, [*or Fjellet, Fjeld, Fjeldet*] [*Mountain*] [*Norway*]   (NAU)

Fj.............. Fjord [*or Fjorden*] [*Fjord Danish/Norwegian*]   (NAU)

FJ.............. Foro Juvenil [*Uruguay*]   (EAIO)

FJ.............. Foyers de Jeunesse [*Algeria*]

FJ.............. Fuerza Joven [*Youth Force*] [*Spanish*]   (WER)

FJA............ Centres de Formation de Jeunes Agriculteurs [*Agricultural education*] [*Burkina Faso*]

FJAR........ Front de la Jeunesse Autonomiste de la Reunion [*Autonomist Youth Front of Reunion*]   (AF)

FJBAC....... Fundacion Javier Barros Associacion Comercial [*Mexico*]

FJBB......... Fabrique de Jouets, de Balles, et Ballons

FJC.......... Federacion Juvenil Comunista [*Communist Youth Federation*] [*Argentina*]   (LA)

FJCA .... Federal Japan Communication Association   (ADPT)

FJCC......... Federation of Jordanian Chambers of Commerce   (EAIO)

FJCE.......... Forum Jeunesse des Communautes Europeennes [*Youth Forum of the European Communities - YFEC*]   (EAIO)

FJCEAOI .. Federation des Jeunes Chambres Economiques d'Afrique et de l'Ocean Indien [*Federation of African and Indian Ocean Junior Chambers of Commerce*] [*Use JAYCEES*]   (AF)

FJDG........ Diego Garcia [*British Indian Ocean Territory*] [*ICAO location identifier*]   (ICLI)

FJDM....... Federation de la Jeunesse Democratique de Madagascar [*Federation of the Democratic Youth of Madagascar*]   (AF)

FJDM....... Frente Jose Dolores Moscote [*Jose Dolores Moscote Front*] [*Panama*]   (LA)

FJI .... Air Pacific Ltd. [*Fiji*] [*ICAO designator*]   (FAAC)

FJI .... Fiji [*ANSI three-letter standard code*]   (CNC)

FJK .... Foldmuvesszovetkezetek Jarasi Kozpontja [*District Center of Agricultural Cooperatives*]   (HU)

FJKM .... Fiangonan'i Jesoa-Kristy eto Madagasikara [*Church of Jesus Christ in Madagascar*]   (AF)

FJL .... Frente de Juventud Liberal [*Liberal Youth Front*] [*Honduras*] (LA)

FJL .... Frente Juvenil Lautaro [*Chile*] [*Political party*]   (EY)

FJN........... Front Jednosci Narodu [*National Unity Front*]   (POL)

FJO........... Fondo de Jubilacion Obrero [*Workers Pension Fund*] [*Peru*] (LA)

FJPC........ French Justice and Peace Commission   (EAIO)

Fjr .... Fjordhur [*Fjord*] [*Icelandic*]   (NAU)

FJSB......... Federation Japonaise du Sport Boules   (EAIO)

FJT .... Foyers de Jeunes Travailleurs [*Youth Workers Centers*] [*French*] (WER)

FJUN........ Frente Juvenil de Unidad Nacional [*Youth Front of National Unity*] [*Chile*]   (LA)

FJV.......... Felsooktatasi Jegyzetellato Vallalat [*Publishing Enterprise of University Textbooks*]   (HU)

FK .... Camera   (RU)

FK .... Fabrika Kablova [*Cable Works*] [*Svetozarevo*]   (YU)

FK .... Fachkommission [*Technical Commission*] [*FAKO*] [*See also*] (EG)

FK .... Falkland Islands [*ANSI two-letter standard code*]   (CNC)

FK .... Federative Committee of the RSDRP [*1905*]   (RU)

FK .... Felderito Kutatas [*Basic Research*]   (HU)

FK .... Feldkanone [*Field Piece, Field Gun*]   (EG)

fk .... Felelos Kiado [*Responsible Publisher, Published By*]   (HU)

FK .... Felleskjopet [*Farmers Cooperative Agricultural, Experimental, and Seed Growing Station*] [*Norway*]   (ARC)

FK .... Festkomma [*German*]   (ADPT)

FK .... Filmovy Klub [*Film Club*]   (CZ)

FK .... Filosofian Kandidaatti [*Finland*]

FK .... Financiele Koerier [*Benelux*]   (BAS)

FK .... Flagship   (RU)

FK .... Flugkoerper [*Missile*]   (EG)

FK .... Focusing Coil   (RU)

FK .... Fokker-VFW BV [*Netherlands*] [*ICAO aircraft manufacturer identifier*]   (ICAO)

FK .... Folic Acid   (RU)

fK .... For Kristus [*Before Christ*] [*Norway*]   (GPO)

FK .... Fotokemika [*Film and Photographic Paper Factory*] [*Zagreb*] (YU)

Fk.............. Funker [*Radio Operator*]   (EG)

FK .... Phenol Red (Indicator)   (RU)

FK .... Physical Culture   (RU)

FK .... Physical Culture Collective   (BU)

FK .... Shaping Stage   (RU)

F-ka........... Fabryka [*Factory*] [*Poland*]

Fka .... Fahrkartenausgabe [*Ticket Counter*]   (EG)

FKAB........ Banyo [*Cameroon*] [*ICAO location identifier*]   (ICLI)

FKAF........ Bafia [*Cameroon*] [*ICAO location identifier*]   (ICLI)

FKAG .... Abong-M'Bang [*Cameroon*] [*ICAO location identifier*]   (ICLI)

FKAL........ Lomie [*Cameroon*] [*ICAO location identifier*]   (ICLI)

FKAM .... Meiganga [*Cameroon*] [*ICAO location identifier*]   (ICLI)

FKAN .... N'Kongsamba [*Cameroon*] [*ICAO location identifier*] (ICLI)
FKAO .... Betare-Oya [*Cameroon*] [*ICAO location identifier*] (ICLI)
FKAV........ Free Kindergarten Association of Victoria [*Australia*]
FKAY........ Yoko [*Cameroon*] [*ICAO location identifier*] (ICLI)
FKB........... Findik Kooperatifleri Birligi [*Hazel Nut Cooperatives Union*] [*FISKOBIRLIK*] [*See also*] (TU)
FKC........... Finnish Kennel Club (EAIO)
FKE........... Federation of Kenya Employees
FKE........... Foros Kyklou Ergasion [*Business Turnover Tax*] [*Greek*] (GC)
FKF........... Fikir Kulupleri Federasyonu [*Federal of Idea (or Intellectual) Clubs*] (TU)
FKF........... Finlands Kristliga Foerbund [*Finnish Christian League*] (PPE)
FKG........... Phonocardiograph (RU)
FKgP......... Fueggetlen Kisgazda-, Foeldmunkas- es Polgari Part [*Independent Smallholders' Party*] [*Hungary*] [*Political party*] (EY)
FKGP........ Fuggetlen Kisgazda, Foldmuves es Polgari Part [*Independent Smallholders' Party*] (HU)
FKH........... Forschungs Kommission fuer Hochspannungsfragen [*Switzerland*]
FKHC .... Filistin Kurtulus Halk Cephesi [*People's Front for the Liberation of Palestine*] . (TU)
FKhNII...... Physicochemical Scientific Research Institute (of the State University Imeni A. A. Zhdanov) (RU)
FKhZ .... Financial and Economic Legislation (RU)
FKI........... Fachverband Klebstoffindustrie [*Association of European Adhesives Manufacturers*] (EAIO)
FKI........... Federation of Korean Industries [*South Korea*]
FKI........... Femipari Kutato Intezet [*Metal Industry Research Institute (Aluminum industry from bauxite to finished aluminum products)*] (HU)
FKI........... Kisangani [*Zaire*] [*Airport symbol*] (OAG)
f ki........... Konstantin Irechek [*or Jirecek*] Fund (BU)
FKIP .... Fakultas Keguruan dan Ilmu Pendidikan [*School of Education*] (IN)
FKK........... Fovarosi Koranyi Kozkorhaz [*Koranyi General City Hospital*] (HU)
FKK........... Freie-Koerper-Kultur [*Nudism, a pre-NAZI fad in Germany*]
FKKA........ Maroua/Ville [*Cameroon*] [*ICAO location identifier*] (ICLI)
FKKB........ Kribi [*Cameroon*] [*ICAO location identifier*] (ICLI)
FKKC........ Tiko [*Cameroon*] [*ICAO location identifier*] (ICLI)
FKKD........ Douala [*Cameroon*] [*ICAO location identifier*] (ICLI)
FKKE........ Eseka [*Cameroon*] [*ICAO location identifier*] (ICLI)
FKKF........ Mamfe [*Cameroon*] [*ICAO location identifier*] (ICLI)
FKKG........ Bali [*Cameroon*] [*ICAO location identifier*] (ICLI)
FKKH .... Kaele [*Cameroon*] [*ICAO location identifier*] (ICLI)
FKKhT....... French Confederation of Christian Workers (RU)
FKKI .... Batouri [*Cameroon*] [*ICAO location identifier*] (ICLI)
FKKJ .... Yagoua [*Cameroon*] [*ICAO location identifier*] (ICLI)
FKKK........ Douala [*Cameroon*] [*ICAO location identifier*] (ICLI)
FKKL........ Maroua/Salak [*Cameroon*] [*ICAO location identifier*] (ICLI)
FKKM....... Foumban/Nkounja [*Cameroon*] [*ICAO location identifier*] (ICLI)
FKKN .... N'Gaoundere [*Cameroon*] [*ICAO location identifier*] (ICLI)
FKKO .... Bertoua [*Cameroon*] [*ICAO location identifier*] (ICLI)
FKKR .... Garoua [*Cameroon*] [*ICAO location identifier*] (ICLI)
FKKS........ Dschang [*Cameroon*] [*ICAO location identifier*] (ICLI)
FKKT........ Tibati [*Cameroon*] [*ICAO location identifier*] (ICLI)
FKKU .... Bafoussam [*Cameroon*] [*ICAO location identifier*] (ICLI)
FKKV .... Bamenda [*Cameroon*] [*ICAO location identifier*] (ICLI)
FKKW....... Ebolowa [*Cameroon*] [*ICAO location identifier*] (ICLI)
FKKY........ Yaounde [*Cameroon*] [*ICAO location identifier*] (ICLI)
FKM .... Fegyveres Erok es Kozbiztonsagi Ugyek Minisztere [*Minister of the Armed Forces and Public Security*] (HU)
FKM .... Finanzkurzmeldung [*Short Financial Report*] [*German*] (EG)
FKNO .... Francuzski Komitet Natsionalnovo Osvobozhdeniia
FKNO .... French Committee of National Liberation [*1943-1944*] (RU)
FKO .... Filistin Kurtulus Orgutu [*Palestine Liberation Organization*] [*Under Yasar Arafat*] (TU)
fko .... Franko [*Freight Prepaid*] (CZ)
FKP........... Finlands Kommunistiska Parti [*Finnish Communist Party*] (PPE)
FKP........... Flag Command Post, Flag Bridge (RU)
FKP........... Foros Katharas Prosodou [*Tax on Net Income*] [*Greek*] (GC)
FKP........... Francia Kommunista Part [*French Communist Party*] [*Political party*]
FKP........... Fratsuzskaia Kommunisticheskaia Partiia [*Political party*]
FKP........... French Communist Party [*Political party*]
FKP........... Fueggetlen Kisgazda Part [*Independent Smallholders' Party*] [*Hungary*] (PPE)
FKP........... Machine-Gun Camera (RU)
FKPU......... Actual Compass Track Angle (RU)
FKQ .... Fak-Fak [*Indonesia*] [*Airport symbol*] (OAG)
f kr........... Fale Krotkie [*Short Waves*] [*Radio*] [*Poland*]
FKS........... Federace Krestanskych Studentu [*Federation of Christian Students*] (CZ)

FKSZ .... Basic Catalog of Weak Stars (RU)
FKT........... Filistin Kurtulus Teskilati [*Palestine Liberation Organization*] (TU)
FKT........... Finance and Credit Technicum (RU)
FKT........... Fovarosi Kozmunkak Tanacsa [*Council of Public Works of the Capital City*] (HU)
FKTGO..... Physical Culture Program "Ready for Labor and Defense" (BU)
f-ktsiya....... Function (RU)
FKTU........ Federation of Korean Trade Unions [*South Korea*]
f kv d .... Pounds per Square Inch (RU)
FL............. Feeder Line (RU)
Fl............... Fernleitung [*Station-to-Station Telephone Line (Germany), Inter-City Telephone Line (Germany)*] (EG)
FL............. Filmove Laboratore [*Film Laboratories*] (CZ)
FL............. Filosofian Lisensiaatti [*Finland*]
f-l............. First Sergeant (BU)
fl............... Flaeckad [*Spotted, Stained*] [*Sweden*]
FL............. Flanders [*Belgium*] (WDAA)
Fl............... Fleck [*or Fleckig*] [*Spot, Stain, or Stained*] [*German*]
fl............... Fleet (RU)
fl............... Flera [*Several*] [*Sweden*]
Fl............... Fleuve [*Large River*] [*French*] (NAU)
fl............... Floren [*or Floreny*] [*Florin or Florins Monetary unit*] [*Poland*]
FL............. Florida (IDIG)
fl............... Floriini [*or Floriinia*] [*Finland*]
fl............... Florim [*Florin*] [*Monetary unit*] [*Portugal*]
FL............. Florin [*Monetary unit*] [*Netherlands*]
fl............... Floryn [*Monetary unit*] [*Afrikaans*]
Fl............... Flu [*or Flua, Fluen*] [*Sunken Rock*] [*Norway*] (NAU)
Fl............... Fluessig [*Liquid*] [*German*] (GCA)
Fl............... Fluessigkeit [*Liquid, Fluid*] [*German*]
Fl............... Fluss [*River*] [*German*] (GCA)
fl............... Folgende [*Following*] [*German*]
fl............... Folha [*Sheet*] [*Publishing*] [*Portuguese*]
FL............. Foreningen af Licentiater [*Denmark*] (SLS)
FL............. Fovgh-e Lesans [*Academic degree*] [*Iran*]
FL............. France-Louisiane [*Later, FLFADDFA*] [*France*] (EAIO)
FL............. Freie Liste [*Free List*] [*Liechtenstein*] [*Political party*] (EY)
F/L............ Freight Liner [*British Railways Board*] (DS)
FL............. Frontove Letectvo [*Frontal Aviation*] (CZ)
FL............. Guilder [*Florin*] [*Monetary unit Netherlands*]
fl............... Gulden [*Florin*] [*Monetary unit*] [*Netherlands*]
Fl a .... Aide-de-Camp of the King (BU)
FLA .... Fabrica de Licores de Antioquia [*Colombia*] (COL)
FLA .... Fachlehranstalt [*German*]
FLA .... Federacion Lanera Argentina [*Argentina*] (SLS)
FLA........... Federazione Lavoratori dell'Agricoltura [*Agriculture Workers Federation*] [*San Marino*] (EAIO)
FLA .... Fiji Library Association (PDAA)
FLA .... Finnish Library Association (EAIO)
FLA .... Florencia [*Colombia*] [*Airport symbol*] (OAG)
Fla .... Flugabwehr [*Antiaircraft Defense*] (EG)
f-la............ Formula (RU)
FLA .... France Latin America [*An association*] (EAIO)
FLA........... Freie Letzeburger Arbechterverband [*Free Luxembourg Workers' Federation*]
FLA........... Frente de Liberacion Americano [*American Liberation Front*] [*Argentina*] (LA)
FLA .... Frente de Libertacao de Angola [*Angolan Liberation Front*]
FLA .... Frente de Libertacao dos Acores [*Azorean Liberation Front*] [*Portuguese*] (WER)
FLA .... Front de Liberation de l'Angola [*Angolan Liberation Front*]
FLA .... Future Large Aircraft [*Cooperative manufacturing effort of France, Germany, Britain, Italy, Portugal, Spain and Turkey*] (ECON)
FLAA........ Federacion Latino Americana de Agrimensores [*Uruguay*] (DSCA)
FLAA........ Fellow of the Library Association of Australia (ADA)
FLABA ...... Societe Fromagere, Laitiere, et Beurriere d'Antsirabe
flack .... Flaeckad [*Spotted, Stained*] [*Publishing*] [*Sweden*]
FLACSO ... Federacion Latinoamericana de Ciencias Sociales [*Latin American School of Social Sciences*] (LA)
FLAEI....... Federazione Lavoratori Aziende Elettriche Italiane [*Federation of Workers for Italian Electrical Firms*] [*Rome*]
FLAER ...... Foundation for Latino-American Economic Research [*Argentina*] (EAIO)
FLAG........ Federation of Leisure Activity Groups [*Australia*]
FLAG........ Feminist Legal Action Group [*Australia*]
FLAG........ Free Legal Assistance Group [*Philippines*]
FLAI .... Federated Liquor and Allied Industries Employees Union [*Australia*]
FLAIA .... Federated Liquor and Allied Industries Association [*Australia*]
FLAIEU..... Federated Liquor and Allied Industries Employees' Union of Australia
FLAIEUA ... Federated Liquor and Allied Industries Employees Union of Australia

FLAIR .... Food-Linked Agricultural Industrial Research [*EC*]   (ECED)
FLAK........ Aviation Construction Sheet Fiber   (RU)
Flak............ Flugzeugabwehrkanone [*Antiaircraft*] [*German*]
flam........... Flemish   (RU)
FLAM........ Forces de Liberation Africaine de Mauritanie [*Political party*]   (EY)
FLAMA..... Frente de Libertacao do Arquipelago da Madeira [*Front for Liberation of the Madeira Islands*] [*Portuguese*]   (WER)
FLAME..... Facts and Logic about the Middle East [*An association*]
FLAMK..... Flugzeugabwehrmaschinenkanone [*Antiaircraft Machine Gun*]   (EG)
FLAP........ Federacion Latinoamericana de Parasitologia [*Latin American Federation of Parasitology*] [*Mexico*]   (SLS)
FLAP......... Federacion Latinoamericana de Periodistas [*Latin American Federation of Journalists*]   (LA)
FLASA ...... Fundacion La Salle de Ciencias Naturales [*La Salle Foundation for Natural Sciences*] [*Research center*] [*Venezuela*]   (IRC)
FLASCO ... Facultad Latinoamericana de Ciencias Sociales [*Latin American School of Social Sciences*]   (LA)
FLASOG ... Federacion Latinoamericana de Sociedades de Obstetricia y Ginecologia [*Latin American Federation of Obstetrics and Gynecology Societies*]   (LA)
FLAT .... Katete [*Zambia*] [*ICAO location identifier*]   (ICLI)
FLAWP ..... French-Language Association of Work Psychology [*Viroflay, France*]   (EAIO)
FLB............ Front de Liberation de la Bretagne [*Brittany Liberation Front*] [*French*]   (WER)
FLB-ARB .. Front de Liberation de la Bretagne - Armee Republicaine Bretonne [*Liberation Front of Brittany - Breton Republican Army*] [*France*]   (PD)
FLB-LNS... Front de Liberation de la Bretagne pour la Liberation Nationale et le Socialisme [*Liberation Front of Brittany for National Liberation and Socialism*] [*France*]   (PD)
FLBPSP..... Federation Luxembourgeoise de Boules et Petanque [*Luxembourg*]   (EAIO)
FLBR .... Film and Literature Board of Review [*Australia*]
FLC........... Federazione Lavoratori delle Costruzioni [*Italy*]   (EY)
FLC........... Fives Lille Cail [*North African*]
FLC........... Front de Liberation Centrafrique [*Central African Liberation Front*]
FLCA .... Folk Lore Council of Australia
FLCB .... Front de Liberation du Congo-Brazzaville [*Congo-Brazzaville Liberation Front*]
FLCH........ Choma [*Zambia*] [*ICAO location identifier*]   (ICLI)
flch .... Fluechtig [*Volatile*] [*German*]   (GCA)
FLCO........ Chocha [*Zambia*] [*ICAO location identifier*]   (ICLI)
FLCP......... Chipata [*Zambia*] [*ICAO location identifier*]   (ICLI)
FLCPN ...... French Language Congress of Psychiatry and Neurology [*France*]   (EAIO)
FLCS .... Chinsali [*Zambia*] [*ICAO location identifier*]   (ICLI)
FLCS .... Front de Liberation de la Cote des Somalis [*Somali Coast Liberation Front*] [*Djibouti*]   (AF)
FLCVNP ... Federation Luxembourgeoise des Cineastes et Videastes Non-Professionnels [*Luxembourg*]   (EAIO)
FLD........... Family Law Division (New South Wales Supreme Court) [*Australia*]
Fld.............. Feld [*Field*] [*German*]   (GCA)
FLD........... Fieldair Freight Ltd. [*New Zealand*] [*ICAO designator*]   (FAAC)
FLDA........ Federal Land Development Agency   (ML)
FLDE........ Delkin (Lusiwasi) [*Zambia*] [*ICAO location identifier*]   (ICLI)
FLDP......... Federation of Liberal and Democratic Parties   (PPE)
FLDRTA ... Federated Long Distance Road Transport Association of Australia
FLE........... Front de Liberation Erythreenne [*Eritrean Liberation Front*] [*Use ELF Ethiopia*]   (AF)
FLE........... Fronte di Liberazione Eritreo
FLEA .... East One [*Zambia*] [*ICAO location identifier*]   (ICLI)
FLEB .... East Two [*Zambia*] [*ICAO location identifier*]   (ICLI)
FLEC .... East Three [*Zambia*] [*ICAO location identifier*]   (ICLI)
FLEC .... Frente de Libertacao do Enclave de Cabinda [*Front for the Liberation of the Cabinda Enclave*] [*Angola*]   (PD)
FLEC .... Front de Liberation de l'Enclave de Cabinda [*Front for the Liberation of the Cabinda Enclave*] [*Angola*]   (AF)
fleck .... Fleckig [*Spotted*] [*Publishing*] [*German*]
Fleckigk .... Fleckigkeit [*Spottiness*] [*German*]   (GCA)
FLED........ East Four [*Zambia*] [*ICAO location identifier*]   (ICLI)
FLEE .... East Five [*Zambia*] [*ICAO location identifier*]   (ICLI)
FLEF......... East Six [*Zambia*] [*ICAO location identifier*]   (ICLI)
FLEG........ East Seven [*Zambia*] [*ICAO location identifier*]   (ICLI)
FLEH........ East Eight [*Zambia*] [*ICAO location identifier*]   (ICLI)
flek .... Fleet Crew   (RU)
FLEPSA .... Fabrica de Ladrillos el Progreso Societe Anonima [*Colombia*]   (COL)
FLERD ...... Front de Liberation et de Rehabilitation de Dahomey
fless........... Flessibile [*Flexible*] [*Italian*]
fleur........... Fleurons [*Large Floral Design*] [*Publishing*] [*French*]
FLEWEACEN ... Fleet Weather Center [*or Central*] [*NATO*]   (NATG)

FLEWEAFAC ... Fleet Weather Facility [*NATO*]   (NATG)
flex .... Flexao [*Flexion*] [*Portuguese*]
flex .... Flexibel [*Flexible*] [*German*]
flex .... Flexoes [*Portuguese*]
flexibl .... Flexibel [*Flexible*] [*German*]
FLFADDFA ... France-Louisiane/Franco-Americaine - Defense et Developpement de la Francophonie Americaine   (EAIO)
FLFI........... Lusaka [*Zambia*] [*ICAO location identifier*]   (ICLI)
FLFW........ Fiwila [*Zambia*] [*ICAO location identifier*]   (ICLI)
FLG........... Federal Libyan Government
Fl G .... Flanc Garde [*Flank Guard*] [*French*]   (MTD)
flg .... Foelgende [*Following*] [*Danish/Norwegian*]
FLG........... Frente de Libertacao da Guine
FLGC........ Frente de Libertacao da Guine Portuguesa e Cabo Verde
FLGE........ Mukinge [*Zambia*] [*ICAO location identifier*]   (ICLI)
Flg Off .... Flying Officer [*Australia*]
FLGPAA ... Federation of Local Government Planners Associations of Australia
FLGW........ Mpongwe [*Zambia*] [*ICAO location identifier*]   (ICLI)
Fl h............. Dutch Florin [*or Guilder*] [*Monetary unit*] [*German*]
FLH .... Federacion Latinoamericana de Hospitales [*Latin American Hospital Federation*]   (EAIO)
FLHQ .... Lusaka [*Zambia*] [*ICAO location identifier*]   (ICLI)
flht.............. Folheto [*Pamphlet*] [*Publishing*] [*Portuguese*]
FLI .... Atlantic Airways, PF (Faroe Islands) [*Denmark*] [*ICAO designator*]   (FAAC)
FLI .... Federation Lainiere Internationale [*International Wool Textile Organization - IWTO*]   (EAIO)
FLI .... Federazione Lavoratori Industria [*Industry Workers Federation*] [*San Marino*]   (EAIO)
FLI .... Flateyri [*Iceland*] [*Airport symbol*]   (OAG)
FLIC .... Financial Low-Intensity Conflict [*Africa*] [*An association*]
FLID .... Front de la Lutte pour l'Independence du Dahomey
FLIK .... Isoka [*Zambia*] [*ICAO location identifier*]   (ICLI)
Flin............ Flinders University of South Australia   (ADA)
FLIN......... Frente de Liberacion Nacional [*National Liberation Front*] [*Bolivia*]   (LA)
Flind.......... Flinders University of South Australia
FLING .... Frente da Luta pela Independencia Nacional da Guine "Portuguesa" [*Front for the Fight for Guinea-Bissau's National Independence*]   (PD)
FLINKS..... Front de Liberation Nationale Kanake Socialiste [*National Liberation Front of Socialist Kanakes*] [*New Caledonia*] [*Political party*]
FLIN-NSW ... Federal Libraries Information Network - New South Wales [*Australia*]
FLIN-NT ... Federal Libraries Information Network - Northern Territory [*Australia*]
FLIN-QLD ... Federal Libraries Information Network - Queensland [*Australia*]
FLIN-VIC ... Federal Libraries Information Network - Victoria [*Australia*]
FLIN-WA ... Federal Libraries Information Network - Western Australia
FLIPG....... Front for the Liberation and Independence of Portuguese Guinea
FLIPPG..... French-Language Infant Pneumology and Phthisiology Group [*Yerres, France*]   (EAIO)
FLIRT........ Free Language Information Retrieval Tool [*IWIS/TNO*] [*'s-Gravenhage*]
Fl J .... La Flandre Judiciaire [*Benelux*]   (BAS)
Fl Jud........ La Flandre Judiciaire [*Benelux*]   (BAS)
FLK........... Falcks Redningskorps Beldringe AS [*Denmark*] [*ICAO designator*]   (FAAC)
FLK........... Falkland Islands [*ANSI three-letter standard code*]   (CNC)
FLKB .... Kawambwa [*Zambia*] [*ICAO location identifier*]   (ICLI)
FLKD........ Kalundu [*Zambia*] [*ICAO location identifier*]   (ICLI)
FLKE........ Kasompe [*Zambia*] [*ICAO location identifier*]   (ICLI)
FLKG........ Kalengwa [*Zambia*] [*ICAO location identifier*]   (ICLI)
FLKJ......... Kanja [*Zambia*] [*ICAO location identifier*]   (ICLI)
FLKK........ Front du Lutte des Khmers du Kampuchea Krom [*Front for the Struggle of the Khmer Krom*] [*Cambodia*]   (CL)
FLKK........ Kakumbi [*Zambia*] [*ICAO location identifier*]   (ICLI)
FLKL .... Kalabo [*Zambia*] [*ICAO location identifier*]   (ICLI)
FLKM........ Kapiri Mposhi [*Zambia*] [*ICAO location identifier*]   (ICLI)
FLKO........ Kaoma [*Zambia*] [*ICAO location identifier*]   (ICLI)
FLKS .... Kasama [*Zambia*] [*ICAO location identifier*]   (ICLI)
FLKU........ Kanyau [*Zambia*] [*ICAO location identifier*]   (ICLI)
FLKW........ Kabwe/Milliken [*Zambia*] [*ICAO location identifier*]   (ICLI)
FLKY .... Kasaba Bay [*Zambia*] [*ICAO location identifier*]   (ICLI)
FLKZ......... Lukuzi [*Zambia*] [*ICAO location identifier*]   (ICLI)
FLL............ Federal Liberal League [*Australia*]   (ADA)
Fll.............. Fluessigkeiten [*Liquids, Fluids*] [*German*]
FLLA .... Front for the Liberation of Lebanon from Aliens
FLLA .... Luanshya [*Zambia*] [*ICAO location identifier*]   (ICLI)
FLLC .... Lusaka [*Zambia*] [*ICAO location identifier*]   (ICLI)
FLLD........ Lundazi [*Zambia*] [*ICAO location identifier*]   (ICLI)
Flli............. Fratelli [*Brothers*] [*Italian*]   (GPO)
FLLI .... Livingstone [*Zambia*] [*ICAO location identifier*]   (ICLI)

FLLK .... Lukulu [*Zambia*] [*ICAO location identifier*]   (ICLI)

FLLO .... Kalomo [*Zambia*] [*ICAO location identifier*]   (ICLI)

FLLS .... Lusaka/International [*Zambia*] [*ICAO location identifier*] (ICLI)

FLLU .... Luampa [*Zambia*] [*ICAO location identifier*]   (ICLI)

FLLY .... Lilayi [*Zambia*] [*ICAO location identifier*]   (ICLI)

FLM .... Family Life Mission [*An association*]   (EAIO)

FLM .... Federation Lutherienne Mondiale [*Lutheran World Foundation - LWF*] [*Geneva, Switzerland*]   (EAIO)

FLM .... Federazione dei Lavoratori Metalmeccanici [*Federation of Metalworkers*] [*Italian*]   (WER)

FLM .... Fiangonana Loterana Malagasy

FLM .... Fotometrischer Leistungsmesser [*Photometric Capacity Meter*] (EG)

FLM .... Friends of the Louvre Museum [*France*]   (EAIO)

FLMA .... Family Life Movement of Australia

FLMA .... Mansa [*Zambia*] [*ICAO location identifier*]   (ICLI)

FLMB .... Maamba [*Zambia*] [*ICAO location identifier*]   (ICLI)

FLMD .... Musonda Falls [*Zambia*] [*ICAO location identifier*]   (ICLI)

FLMF .... Mfuwe [*Zambia*] [*ICAO location identifier*]   (ICLI)

FLMG .... Mongu [*Zambia*] [*ICAO location identifier*]   (ICLI)

FLMI .... Mukonchi [*Zambia*] [*ICAO location identifier*]   (ICLI)

FLMK .... Mkushi [*Zambia*] [*ICAO location identifier*]   (ICLI)

FLML .... Mufulira [*Zambia*] [*ICAO location identifier*]   (ICLI)

FLMM ...... Mwami [*Zambia*] [*ICAO location identifier*]   (ICLI)

FLMO ...... Monze [*Zambia*] [*ICAO location identifier*]   (ICLI)

FLMP .... Mpika [*Zambia*] [*ICAO location identifier*]   (ICLI)

FLMT .... Mutanda [*Zambia*] [*ICAO location identifier*]   (ICLI)

FLMU .... Mulobezi [*Zambia*] [*ICAO location identifier*]   (ICLI)

FLMW ...... Mwinilunga [*Zambia*] [*ICAO location identifier*]   (ICLI)

FLMZ .... Family Life Movement of Zambia   (EAIO)

FLMZ .... Mazabuka [*Zambia*] [*ICAO location identifier*]   (ICLI)

FLN .... Flanders Airlines [*Belgium*] [*ICAO designator*]   (FAAC)

FLN .... Florianopolis [*Brazil*] [*Airport symbol*]   (OAG)

FLN .... Frente de Liberacion Nacional [*National Liberation Front*] [*Peru*] [*Political party*]

FLN .... Frente de Liberacion Nacional [*National Liberation Front*] [*Venezuela*] [*Political party*]   (PD)

FLN .... Frente de Liberacion Nacional [*National Liberation Front*] [*El Salvador*] [*Political party*]

FLN .... Frente de Liberacion Nacional [*National Liberation Front*] [*Chile*] [*Political party*]

FLN .... Frente de Libertacao Nacional [*National Liberation Front*] [*Portuguese*]   (WER)

FLN .... Frente de Libertacao Nacional [*National Liberation Front*] [*Brazil*]   (LA)

FLN .... Front de Liberation Nationale [*National Liberation Front*] [*Algeria*] [*Political party*]   (PPW)

FLN .... Front de Liberation Nationale [*National Liberation Front*] [*South Vietnam Use NFLSV*] [*Political party*]

FLN .... Front de Liberation Nationale [*National Liberation Front*] [*France*] [*Political party*]

FLNA .... Front de Liberation Nationale de l'Angola

FLNA .... Ngoma [*Zambia*] [*ICAO location identifier*]   (ICLI)

FLNC .... Front de Liberation Nationale Congolais [*Congolese National Liberation Front*] [*Zaire*] [*Political party*]   (PD)

FLNC .... Front de Liberation Nationale de la Corse [*Corsican National Liberation Front*] [*Political party*]   (PD)

FLND .... Ndola [*Zambia*] [*ICAO location identifier*]   (ICLI)

Flne .... Fluane [*or Fluene*] [*Sunken Rocks*] [*Norway*]   (NAU)

FLNF .... Front de Liberation Nationale Francaise [*French National Liberation Front*]   (PD)

FLNG .... Front de Liberation Nationale de Guinee [*Guinean National Liberation Front*]   (AF)

FLNK .... Force de Liberation Nationale Kamerunaise [*National Cameroonian Liberation Force*] [*Political party*]

FLNKS ...... Front de Liberation Nationale Kanak Socialiste [*Kanak Socialist National Liberation Front*] [*New Caledonian*]

FLNL .... Namwala [*Zambia*] [*ICAO location identifier*]   (ICLI)

FLNR .... Front de Liberation Nationale de la Reunion [*National Liberation Front of Reunion*]   (AF)

FLNY .... Nyimba [*Zambia*] [*ICAO location identifier*]   (ICLI)

FLO .... Falcon Airlines [*Yugoslavia*] [*ICAO designator*]   (FAAC)

flo .... Felugyelo [*Inspector, Supervisor*]   (HU)

Flo .... Florilege [*Record label*] [*France*]

FLO .... Florin [*Monetary unit*] [*Netherlands*]   (ROG)

FLO .... Front de Liberation des Oubanguiens [*Ubangi People's Liberation Front*] [*Central African Republic*]   (AF)

FLOARCA ... Flotilla y Arrendamientos Compania Anonima [*Venezuela*]

Flock .... Flockung [*Flocculation*] [*German*]   (GCA)

FLOMERCA ... Flota Mercante Gran Centroamericana [*Greater Central American Merchant Fleet*] [*Guatemala*]   (LA)

FLOMERES ... Flota Mercante del Estado [*Paraguay*]   (LAA)

FLOPEC .... Flota Petrolera Ecuatoriana [*Ecuadorean Oil Tanker Fleet*]   (LA)

FLOPETROL ... Societe Auxiliaire des Producteurs de Petrole

Flor .... Floreal [*Eighth month of the "calendrier republicain", from April 20 to May 19*]   (FLAF)

flor .... Floren [*or Floreny*] [*Florin or Florins*] [*Poland*]

FLOREX ... Technical Exhibition for Florists [*Brussels International Trade Fair*]

FLOSY ...... Front for the Liberation of Occupied South Yemen   (PD)

FLOV .... Federation of Latvian Organisations of Victoria [*Australia*]

FLP .... Bristol & Wessex Aeroplane Club Ltd. [*British*] [*ICAO designator*]   (FAAC)

FLP .... Federacion Latinoamericana de Periodistas [*Latin American Federation of Journalists*]   (LA)

Fl P .... Festlegepunkt [*Reference Point*] [*German*]   (GCA)

FLP .... Fiji Labour Party [*Political party*]   (FEA)

FLP .... Finlands Landsbygdsparti [*Finnish Rural Party*] [*Political party*]   (PPE)

FLP .... Fisheries Licensing Panel [*Victoria, Australia*]

FLP .... Frente de Liberacion de los Pobres [*Liberation Front of the Poor*] [*Ecuador*] [*Political party*]   (PD)

FLP .... Frente de Liberacion Popular [*Peoples' Liberation Front*] [*Spanish*]   (WER)

FLP .... Friends of Luna Park [*Sydney, New South Wales, Australia*]

FLP .... Front de Liberation de la Polynesie [*Political party*]   (EY)

FLP .... Front-Line President [*African*]

FLP .... Phytolipopolysaccharide   (RU)

FLPA .... Family Law Practitioners' Association [*of Queensland*] [*Australia*]

FLPA .... Kasempa [*Zambia*] [*ICAO location identifier*]   (ICLI)

FLPAQ ...... Family Law Practitioners' Association of Queensland [*Australia*]

FLPC .... Front de Liberation du Peuple Centrafricain [*Central African People's Liberation Front*]   (AF)

FLPE .... Petauke [*Zambia*] [*ICAO location identifier*]   (ICLI)

FLPK .... Mporokoso [*Zambia*] [*ICAO location identifier*]   (ICLI)

Flpkt .... Flammpunkt [*Flash Point*]   (EG)

FLPO .... Kabompo [*Zambia*] [*ICAO location identifier*]   (ICLI)

FLPP .... Front de Lutte Populaire Palestinien

FLQX .... Juvancourt [*France*] [*ICAO location identifier*]   (ICLI)

FLR .... Family Law Reform Party [*Political party*] [*Australia*]

FLR .... Florence [*Italy*] [*Airport symbol*]   (OAG)

FLR .... Florin [*Monetary unit*] [*Netherlands*]

FLRA .... Family Law Reform Association [*Australia*]

FLRANSW ... Family Law Reform Association of New South Wales [*Australia*]

FLRD .... Front de Liberation et de Rehabilitation du Dahomey [*Dahomey Liberation and Rehabilitation Front*] [*Benin*] [*Political party*]   (PD)

FLRev .... Federal Law Review [*A publication*]

FLRG .... Rusangu [*Zambia*] [*ICAO location identifier*]   (ICLI)

FLRJ .... Federacyjna Ludowa Republika Jugoslowianska [*Federated People's Republic of Yugoslavia*]   (POL)

FLRJ .... Federativna Ljudska Republika Jugoslavija [*Federated People's Republic of Yugoslavia*]   (YU)

FLRJ .... Federativni Lidova Republika Jihoslovenska [*Federated People's Republic of Yugoslavia*]   (CZ)

FLRO .... Rosa [*Zambia*] [*ICAO location identifier*]   (ICLI)

FLRS .... Federativna Ljudska Republika Slovenija [*Federated People's Republic of Slovenia*]   (YU)

FLRS .... Federativna Ljudska Republika Srbija [*Federated People's Republic of Serbia*]   (YU)

FLRU .... Rufansa [*Zambia*] [*ICAO location identifier*]   (ICLI)

FLS .... Federazione Lavoratori dei Servizi [*Service Workers Federation*] [*San Marino*]   (EAIO)

FLS .... Federazione Lavoratori Somali [*Somali Labor Federation*]

FLS .... Flinders Island [*Australia*] [*Airport symbol*]   (OAG)

FLS .... Foundation for Life Sciences [*Australia*]

FLS .... Fremde Legion Suedtirol [*South Tyrolean Foreign Legion*] [*Austria*]   (WEN)

FLS .... Frente de Liberacion Social [*Social Liberation Front*] [*Panama*]   (LA)

FLS .... Front de Liberation de Seguia [*Seguia Liberation Front*] [*Saharan*]   (AF)

FLS .... Fundacion La Salle de Ciencias Naturales [*Venezuela*]   (PDAA)

FLSA .... St. Anthony [*Zambia*] [*ICAO location identifier*]   (ICLI)

FLSC .... Front for the Liberation of the Somali Coast [*Djibouti*]   (AF)

FLSCN ...... French-Language Society for Clinical Neurophysiology   (EAIO)

FLSCN ...... Fundacion La Salle de Ciencias Naturales [*La Salle Foundation for Natural Sciences*] [*Research center*] [*Venezuela*]   (MSC)

FLSE .... Serenje [*Zambia*] [*ICAO location identifier*]   (ICLI)

FLSH .... Shiwan'Gandu [*Zambia*] [*ICAO location identifier*]   (ICLI)

FLSJ .... Sakeji [*Zambia*] [*ICAO location identifier*]   (ICLI)

FLSM .... St. Mary's [*Zambia*] [*ICAO location identifier*]   (ICLI)

FLSMP ...... French-Language Society of Medical Psychology   (EA)

FLSN .... Senanga [*Zambia*] [*ICAO location identifier*]   (ICLI)

FLSND ...... French-Language Society of Nutrition and Dietetics [*France*]   (EAIO)

FLSO .... Front de Liberation de Somalie Occidentale [*Western Somalia Liberation Front*] [*Use WSLF*]   (AF)

FLSO .... Southdowns [*Zambia*] [*ICAO location identifier*]   (ICLI)

FLSR .... French-Language Society for Reanimation   (EAIO)
FLSS .... Sesheke [*Zambia*] [*ICAO location identifier*]   (ICLI)
FLSW .... Solwezi [*Zambia*] [*ICAO location identifier*]   (ICLI)
FLT .... Federacion Latinoamericana de Termalismo [*Latin American Federation of Thermalism and Climatism - LAFTC*] [*Buenos Aires, Argentina*]   (EAIO)
FLT .... Forschungsvereinigung fuer Luft- und Trocknungstechnik eV [*Research Association for Air and Drying Technology*] (SLS)
FLT .... Front de Liberation Tchadien [*Chadian Liberation Front*]   (AF)
Flt Cmdr .... Flight Commander [*Australia*]
Flt Lt .... Flight Lieutenant [*Australia*]
Flt Off........ Flight Officer [*Australia*]
FLTP .... Federacion Latinoamericana de Trabajadores de Plantaciones [*Latin American Federation of Plantation Workers*]   (LA)
Flt Sgt .... Flight Sergeant [*Australia*]
FLU .... Federation of Labor Unions [*Lebanon*]
FLU .... Field Laborers Union [*Mauritius*]   (AF)
FLU .... Frente de Libertacao e da Unidade [*Front for Liberation and Unity*] [*Portuguese*]   (WER)
FLU .... Front de Liberation et d'Union [*Front for Liberation and Unity*] [*Saharan*]   (AF)
FLU .... Front pour la Liberation et l'Unite [*Front for Liberation and Unity*] [*Morocco*]   (AF)
FLUA........ Fellow of the Life Underwriters of Australia
flucht......... Fluechtig [*Volatile*] [*German*]   (GCA)
Fluchtigk..... Fluechtigkeit [*Volatility*] [*German*]   (GCA)
Flugschr..... Flugschrift [*Pamphlet*] [*German*]
FLUNA...... Front de Liberation Unifie de la Nouvelle Algerie [*United Liberation Front for a New Algeria*]   (AF)
Fluorier ...... Fluorierung [*Fluorination*] [*German*]   (GCA)
fluss........... Fluessig [*Liquid*] [*German*]   (GCA)
FLUT........ Festival Lidove Umelecke Tvorivosti [*Folk Arts Festival*]   (CZ)
FLW.......... Santa Cruz, Flores [*Azores*] [*Airport symbol*]   (OAG)
FLWA........ West One [*Zambia*] [*ICAO location identifier*]   (ICLI)
FLWB........ West Two [*Zambia*] [*ICAO location identifier*]   (ICLI)
FLWC........ West Three [*Zambia*] [*ICAO location identifier*]   (ICLI)
FLWD........ West Four [*Zambia*] [*ICAO location identifier*]   (ICLI)
FLWE........ West Five [*Zambia*] [*ICAO location identifier*]   (ICLI)
FLWF .... West Six [*Zambia*] [*ICAO location identifier*]   (ICLI)
FLWG....... West Seven [*Zambia*] [*ICAO location identifier*]   (ICLI)
FLWW....... Waka Waka [*Zambia*] [*ICAO location identifier*]   (ICLI)
FLYA........ Samfya [*Zambia*] [*ICAO location identifier*]   (ICLI)
flybl........... Flyblad [*Flyleaf*] [*Publishing Danish/Norwegian*]
FLZB .... Zambezi [*Zambia*] [*ICAO location identifier*]   (ICLI)
FM .... Federated States of Micronesia [*ANSI two-letter standard code*] (CNC)
FM .... Federation of Malaya   (ML)
FM .... Felag Menntaskolakennara [*Icelandic*]   (SLS)
FM .... Feld Marechal [*Field Marshal*] [*French*]   (MTD)
FM .... Feldmarschall [*German*]
FM .... Ferdinand Marcos [*Former Philippine president*]
Fm .... Fermio [*Chemical element*] [*Portuguese*]
Fm .... Fernmelde [*German*]
FM .... Ferranti Ltd. [*German*]   (ADPT)
FM .... Ferromanganese   (RU)
Fm .... Festmeter [*Cubic Meter*]   (EG)
fm .... Field Marshal   (BU)
FM .... Filosofian Maisteri [*Finland*]
fm .... Finn Marka [*Finnish Mark*]   (HU)
FM .... Fluorometer   (RU)
fm .... Foldmuveles [*Agriculture*]   (HU)
FM .... Foldmuvelesugyi Miniszterium/Miniszter [*Ministry/Minister of Agriculture*]   (HU)
fm .... Foldmuves [*Farmer*]   (HU)
FM .... Fonction Manuelle [*Facility*]   (ADPT)
Fm .... Forstmeister [*German*]
FM .... Franchise Militaire [*French*]
FM .... Franc Mali [*Monetary unit*] [*Mali*]
FM .... Franc Malien
FM .... Free Morocco
FM .... Frekwensiemodulasie [*Frequency Modulation*] [*Afrikaans*]
FM .... Frequence Modulee [*Frequency Modulation*] [*French*]
FM .... Frequency Modulation   (IDIG)
FM .... Fusil Mitrailleur [*Military*] [*French*]   (MTD)
FM .... Invoice Machine   (RU)
FM .... Phase Modulation   (RU)
FM .... Photomagnetic Amplifier   (RU)
FM .... Photometer   (RU)
FM .... Physics and Mathematics   (BU)
FM .... Physics and Mathematics (Division)   (RU)
FMA .... Ammonium Phosphomolybdate   (RU)
FMA .... Fabrica Militar de Aviones [*Military Aircraft Factory*] [*Argentina*]   (PDAA)
FMA .... Federation Mondiale des Annonceurs [*World Federation of Advertisers - WFA*] [*Brussels, Belgium*]   (EAIO)

FMA .... Fernmeldeamt [*Telephone and Telegraph Office*]   (EG)
FMA .... Finnish Museums Association   (EAIO)
F-Ma......... Firma [*Firm*] [*German*]   (GCA)
FMA .... Fish Marketing Authority [*New South Wales, Australia*]
FMA .... Fonds Monetaire Andin [*Andean Monetary Fund*]   (PDAA)
FMA .... Fonds Monetaire Arabe
FMA .... Foremost Aviation Ltd. [*Nigeria*] [*ICAO designator*]   (FAAC)
FMA .... Formosa [*Argentina*] [*Airport symbol*]   (OAG)
FMA .... Frederik Muller Akademie [*Netherlands*]
FMA .... French Military Administration
FMA .... Phenylmercuric Acetate   (RU)
FMAA .... Fellow of the Museums Association of Australia
FMAA .... Footwear Manufacturers' Association of Australia
FMAA .... Furniture Manufacturers Association of Australia
FMAC....... Federation Mondiale des Anciens Combattants [*World Veterans Federation - WVF*] [*Paris, France*]   (EAIO)
FMACCU ... Federation Mondiale des Associations, Centres, et Clubs UNESCO [*World Federation of UNESCO Clubs and Associations*] [*France*]   (EAIO)
FMAM ...... Federation Mondiale des Amis de Musees [*World Federation of Friends of Museums - WFFM*]   (EAIO)
FMANU .... Federatia Mondiala a Asociatiilor pentru Natiunile Unite [*World Federation of United Nations Associations - WFUNA*] (RO)
FMANU .... Federation Mondiale des Associations pour les Nations Unies [*World Federation of United Nations Associations - WFUNA*] [*Geneva, Switzerland*]   (EA)
FMAP"DM" ... Fabrica Militar de Armas Portatiles "Domingo Matheu"
FMATH .... Federation Mondiale de Travailleurs des Industries Alimentaires, du Tabac, et de l'Hotellerie [*World Federation of Workers in Food, Tobacco, and Hotel Industries - WFFTH*]   (EAIO)
FMB .... Fast Missile Boat
FMB .... Federacao Mozambicana de Badminton [*Mozambique Badminton Federation*]   (EAIO)
FMB .... Federal Mortgage Bank [*Nigeria*]
FMB .... Federation Monegasque de Boules [*Monaco Bocce Federation*] (EAIO)
FMBI........ Engineer's Library of Physics and Mathematics   (RU)
FMBN .... Federal Mortgage Bank of Nigeria
FMC .... Family Mediation Centre [*Australia*]
FMC .... Federacion de Mujeres Cubanas [*Federation of Cuban Women*] (LA)
FMC .... Fire Mark Circle [*Liverpool, England*]   (EAIO)
FMC .... Fisheries Management Committee [*Victoria, Australia*]
FMC .... Fish Marketing Corp. [*Papua New Guinea*]
FMC .... Flinders Medical Centre [*Australia*]
FMC .... Flotte Marchande Centrafricaine
FMC .... Fondo Monetario Centroamericano [*Central American Monetary Fund*]   (LA)
FMC .... Food Media Club [*Australia*]
FMC .... La Fiscalite du Marche Commun [*Benelux*]   (BAS)
FMCA....... Federated Music Clubs of Australia
FMCA....... Fermetures Mischler du Cameroun
FMCA....... Flotte Marchande Centrafricaine
FMCA....... Flour Millers Council of Australia
FMCE....... Federation of Malaya Certificate of Education   (ML)
FMCH ...... Moroni/Hahaia [*Comoros*] [*ICAO location identifier*]   (ICLI)
FMCI........ Fermetures Mischler de la Cote-D'Ivoire
FMCI........ Moheli/Bandaressalam [*Comoros*] [*ICAO location identifier*] (ICLI)
FMCIM..... Federation Mondiale des Concours Internationaux de Musique [*World Federation of International Music Competitions - WFIMC*]   (EAIO)
FMCN .... Moroni/Iconi [*Comoros*] [*ICAO location identifier*]   (ICLI)
FMCV........ Anjouan/Ouani [*Comoros*] [*ICAO location identifier*]   (ICLI)
FMCVC..... Federation Mondiale des Communautes de Vie Chretienne [*World Federation of Christian Life Communities - WFCLC*] [*Rome, Italy*]   (EAIO)
FMCZ........ Dzaoudzi/Pamanzi [*Mayotte*] [*ICAO location identifier*]   (ICLI)
FMD .... Feinmess, Dresden [*Dresden Precision Measuring Equipment Plant*]   (EG)
FMD .... Fermetures Mischler Dakar
FMD .... Fiji Marine Department   (MSC)
FMD .... Front Militant Departementaliste [*Militant Departmentalist Front*] [*Reunion*]   (PD)
FMDAA .... Farm Machinery Dealers' Association of Australia
FMDO .... Firmado [*Signed*] [*Spanish*]
FMDP........ Fuggetlen Magyar Demokrata Part [*Independent Hungarian Democratic Party*]   (HU)
FMDR .... Federacion de Mujeres Dominicanas Revolucionarias [*Federation of Revolutionary Dominican Women*] [*Dominican Republic*]   (LA)
FMDR .... Fonds Mutualiste de Developpement Rural
FMDR .... Fundacion Mexicana para el Desarrollo Rural [*Mexican Foundation for Rural Development*]   (EAIO)
FME .... Federatie Metaal- en Elektrotechnische Industrie [*Benelux*] (BAS)

Fme .... Ferme [*Farm*] [*Military map abbreviation World War I*] [*French*] (MTD)
FME .... Fonds de Modernisation et d'Equipement [*France*] (FLAF)
FME .... Photoelectromagnetic Effect (RU)
FMEE........ Saint-Denis/Gillot [*Reunion*] [*ICAO location identifier*] (ICLI)
FMEF........ Federation des Missions Evangeliques Francophones [*Switzerland*]
FMEM...... Federation Mondiale pour l'Enseignement Medical [*World Federation for Medical Education - WFME*] (EA)
FMEP........ Saint-Pierre-Pierrefonds [*Reunion*] [*ICAO location identifier*] (ICLI)
FMer.......... French Mercury [*Record label*]
FMF.......... Fachverband Moderne Fremdsprachen [*Modern Foreign Language Department*] (SLS)
FMF.......... Federalni Ministerstvo Financi [*Federal Finance Ministry*] (CZ)
FMF.......... Federation des Medecins de France [*French*] (SLS)
FMF.......... Financial Markets Foundation
FMF.......... First Malaysia Finance
FMF.......... Footwear Manufacturers Federation of South Africa (EAIO)
FMF.......... Free Market Foundation [*South Africa*] (EAIO)
FMfakultet ... Department of Physics and Mathematics (BU)
FMFC........ Francisco Morazan Frente Constitucional [*Honduras*] [*Political party*] (EY)
FMG .... Federacion Magisterial Guatemalteca [*Federation of Guatemalan Teachers*] (LA)
FMG .... Federal Military Government
FMG .... Fermetures Mischler du Golfe de Guinee
FMG .... Flakmessgerat [*Antiaircraft, gun-laying RADAR*] [*German*]
FMG .... Franc [*Monetary unit*] [*Malagasy Republic*]
FMG .... Franc Malgache [*Malagasy Franc*] (AF)
FMG .... Francs Malgaches (FLAF)
FMGC .... Flota Mercante Gran Colombiana [*Colombian-Ecuadorean*] (LAA)
FMGD .... Federazione Mondiale della Gioventu Democratica [*World Federation of Democratic Youth - WFDY*] [*Italian*] (WER)
FMGM ...... French MGM [*Record label*]
FMH.......... Federation Mondiale de l'Hemophilie [*World Federation of Hemophilia*] (EAIO)
fmh .... Felteteles Megallohely [*Stops on Signal*] (HU)
FMH.......... Foederatio Medicorum Helveticorum [*Association of Swiss Medical Specialists*]
FMHS(NSW) ... Fellow of the Military History Society of (New South Wales) [*Australia*]
FMHSU ...... Federated Miscellaneous and Hospital Service Union [*Australia*]
FMI............ Family Misery Index
FMI............ Fils de Marie Immaculee [*Sons of Mary Immaculate*] [*Saint Fulgent, France*] (EAIO)
FMI............ Flugmalafelag Islands [*Icelandic Aero Club*] (EAIO)
FMI............ Fondo Monetario Internacional [*International Monetary Fund*] [*Spanish United Nations*] (DUND)
FMI............ Fonds Monetaire International [*International Monetary Fund - IMF*] [*French*] (WER)
FMI............ Fondul Monetar International [*International Monetary Fund - IMF*] (RO)
FMI............ Freight Management International [*Australia*]
FMI............ Friedrich Miescher Institute [*Research center*] [*Switzerland*]
FMI............ Institute of Physics and Mathematics (of the Academy of Sciences, USSR) (RU)
FMI............ Kalemi [*Zaire*] [*Airport symbol*] (OAG)
FMI............ Societe France Media International (EY)
FMIC........ Front Malaysian Islamic Council [*Political party*] (FEA)
FMIFD ...... Federacion Mundial de Instituciones Financieras de Desarrollo [*World Federation of Development Financing Institutions*] [*Spain*]
FMIP-P..... Financial Management Improvement Program - Procurement [*Australia*]
FMIS .... Fleet Management Information System [*Australia*]
FMJB .... Federation Mauritanienne de Jeu de Boules [*Mauritania Bocce Federation*] (EAIO)
FMJC .... Federation Mondiale de Jeunesse Catholique [*World Federation of Catholic Youth*] [*Use WFCY*] (AF)
FMJC .... Front de Mouvements des Jeunesse du Congo
FMJD........ Federacion Mundial de la Juventud Democratica [*World Federation of Democratic Youth - WFDY*] (LA)
FMJD........ Federation Mondiale de la Jeunesse Democratique [*World Federation of Democratic Youth - WFDY*] [*Budapest, Hungary*] (EAIO)
FMJD........ Federation Mondiale du Jeu de Dames [*World Draughts (Checkers) Federation - WDF*] [*Dordrecht, Netherlands*] (EAIO)
FMK .... Ferromagnetic Compensator (RU)
FMK .... Flugmedizinische Kommission [*Commission for Flight Medicine (A GST pilot training unit)*] (EG)
F MK .... Markka [*Monetary unit*] [*Finland*]
FMKT........ Fiatal Muszakiak es Kozgazdaszok Tanacsa [*Council of Young Technologists and Economists*] (HU)
FML.......... Feldmarschalleutnant [*German*]

FML........... Ferguson Memorial Library [*Presbyterian Church, Sydney, New South Wales, Australia*]
FMLH .... Frente Morazanista para la Liberacion de Honduras [*Guerrilla forces*] (EY)
FMLN ...... Farabundo Marti National Liberation Front [*Brazil*] [*Political party*] (ECON)
FMLN ...... Frente Farabundo Marti de Liberacion Nacional [*Farabundo Marti National Liberation Front*] [*El Salvador*] (ECON)
FMLN ...... Frente Morazanista de Liberacion Nacional [*Morazanista National Liberation Front*] [*Honduras*] [*Political party*] (PD)
FMLNH .... Frente Morazanista de Liberacion Nacional de Honduras [*Honduran Morazanist National Front*] [*Political party*]
FMLS .... Federazione Mondiale dei Lavoratori Scientifici [*World Federation of Scientific Workers - WFSW*] [*Italian*] (WER)
FMM .... Federation of Malaysian Manufacturers (DS)
FMM .... Fivondronamben'ny Mpiasa Malagasy [*Malagasy Workers Federation*] (AF)
FMM .... French Military Mission (CL)
FMM .... Physics of Metals and Metal Science (RU)
FMMA ...... Antananarivo/Arivonimamo [*Madagascar*] [*ICAO location identifier*] (ICLI)
FMMAA ... Federated Mining Mechanics Association of Australia
FMMC ...... Malaimbandy [*Madagascar*] [*ICAO location identifier*] (ICLI)
FMMD ...... Antananarivo [*Madagascar*] [*ICAO location identifier*] (ICLI)
FMME....... Antsirabe [*Madagascar*] [*ICAO location identifier*] (ICLI)
FMMG ...... Fund for Multinational Management Education (AF)
FMMG ...... Antsalova [*Madagascar*] [*ICAO location identifier*] (ICLI)
FMMGEUA ... Federated Millers and Manufacturing Grocers' Employees' Union of Australia
FMMH...... Fraternite Mauricienne des Malades et Handicapes [*Mauritius*] (EAIO)
FMMH...... Mahanoro [*Madagascar*] [*ICAO location identifier*] (ICLI)
FMMI....... Antananarivo/Ivato [*Madagascar*] [*ICAO location identifier*] (ICLI)
FMMJ....... Ambohijanahary [*Madagascar*] [*ICAO location identifier*] (ICLI)
FMMK ...... Ankavandra [*Madagascar*] [*ICAO location identifier*] (ICLI)
FMML....... Belo-Sur-Tsiribihina [*Madagascar*] [*ICAO location identifier*] (ICLI)
FMMM ...... Antananarivo [*Madagascar*] [*ICAO location identifier*] (ICLI)
FMMN ...... Miandrivazo [*Madagascar*] [*ICAO location identifier*] (ICLI)
FMMO ...... Maintirano [*Madagascar*] [*ICAO location identifier*] (ICLI)
FMMP....... Amparafaravola [*Madagascar*] [*ICAO location identifier*] (ICLI)
FMMQ ...... Ilaka-Est [*Madagascar*] [*ICAO location identifier*] (ICLI)
FMMR ...... Morafenobe [*Madagascar*] [*ICAO location identifier*] (ICLI)
FMMS ...... Sainte-Marie [*Madagascar*] [*ICAO location identifier*] (ICLI)
FMMT....... Toamasina [*Madagascar*] [*ICAO location identifier*] (ICLI)
FMMTP..... Federacion de Mineros y Trabajadores Metalurgicos del Peru [*Federation of Miners and Metalworkers of Peru*] (LA)
FMMU ...... Federated Moulders' (Metal) Union of Australia
FMMU ...... Tambohorano [*Madagascar*] [*ICAO location identifier*] (ICLI)
FMMUA ... Federated Moulders' (Metal) Union of Australia
FMMV ...... Morondava [*Madagascar*] [*ICAO location identifier*] (ICLI)
FMMX ...... Tsiroanomandidy [*Madagascar*] [*ICAO location identifier*] (ICLI)
FMMY ...... Vatomandry [*Madagascar*] [*ICAO location identifier*] (ICLI)
FMMZ ...... Ambatondrazaka [*Madagascar*] [*ICAO location identifier*] (ICLI)
FMN .... Flavine Mononucleotide (RU)
FMN .... France Marine Nationale [*ICAO designator*] (FAAC)
FMN .... Frente Nacional Magisterial [*National Teachers Front*] [*Guatemala*] (LA)
FMNA .... Antsiranana/Arrachart [*Madagascar*] [*ICAO location identifier*] (ICLI)
FMNC .... Mananara-Nord [*Madagascar*] [*ICAO location identifier*] (ICLI)
FMND....... Andapa [*Madagascar*] [*ICAO location identifier*] (ICLI)
FMNE .... Ambilobe [*Madagascar*] [*ICAO location identifier*] (ICLI)
FMNF....... Befandriana Nord [*Madagascar*] [*ICAO location identifier*] (ICLI)
FMNG....... Port Berge [*Madagascar*] [*ICAO location identifier*] (ICLI)
FMNH....... Antalaha [*Madagascar*] [*ICAO location identifier*] (ICLI)
FMNJ........ Ambanja [*Madagascar*] [*ICAO location identifier*] (ICLI)
FMNL .... Analalava [*Madagascar*] [*ICAO location identifier*] (ICLI)
FMNM ...... Mahajanga/Amborovy [*Madagascar*] [*ICAO location identifier*] (ICLI)
FMNN....... Nosy-Be/Fascene [*Madagascar*] [*ICAO location identifier*] (ICLI)
FMNO....... Soalala [*Madagascar*] [*ICAO location identifier*] (ICLI)
FMNP .... Mampikony [*Madagascar*] [*ICAO location identifier*] (ICLI)
FMNQ ...... Besalampy [*Madagascar*] [*ICAO location identifier*] (ICLI)
FMNR .... Maroantsetra [*Madagascar*] [*ICAO location identifier*] (ICLI)
FMNS....... Sambava [*Madagascar*] [*ICAO location identifier*] (ICLI)
FMNT ...... Tsaratanana [*Madagascar*] [*ICAO location identifier*] (ICLI)
FMNV .... Vohemar [*Madagascar*] [*ICAO location identifier*] (ICLI)

FMNW ...... Antsohihy/Ambalabe [*Madagascar*] [*ICAO location identifier*] (ICLI)

FMNX .... Mandritsara [*Madagascar*] [*ICAO location identifier*] (ICLI)

FMO .... Department of Physics and Mathematics (RU)

FMO .... Fabryka Maszyn Odlewniczych [*Foundry Machinery Factory*] (POL)

FMO .... Nederlandse Financiering Maatschappij voor Ontwikkelingslanden

FMP .... Fabryka Maszyn Papierniczych [*Paper Machinery Factory*] (POL)

FMP .... Federalni Ministerstvo Planovani [*Federal Ministry of Planning*] (CZ)

FMP .... Flow Management Position [*ICAO*] (DA)

FMP .... Fonds des Maladies Professionnelles [*Benelux*] (BAS)

FMPA .... Federated Master Plumbers of Australia

FMPA .... Federation Mondiale pour la Protection des Animaux [*World Federation for the Protection of Animals*] [*Use WFPA*] [*French*] (AF)

FMPA .... Forschungs- und Materialpruefungsanstalt Baden-Wuerttemberg [*Research and Material Testing Center Baden-Wuerttemberg*] [*Germany*] (EAS)

FMPB .... Friends Missionary Prayer Band [*India*]

FMPO .... Photometer for Measuring Underwater Light Intensity (RU)

FMPSA ..... Federation of Master Painters and Signwriters of Australia

FMPSV ..... Federalni Ministerstvo Prace a Socialnich Veci [*Federal Ministry of Labor and Social Affairs*] (CZ)

FMPU .... Actual Magnetic Track Angle (RU)

FMRA .... Fertilizer Manufacturers Research Association [*New Zealand*] (ARC)

FMRC .... Financial Management Research Centre [*Research center*] [*Australia*] (IRC)

FMRI .... Fondo de Modernizacao e Reorganizacao Industrial [*Industrial Modernization and Reorganization Fund*] [*Brazil*] (LA)

fmrly .... Formerly (EECI)

FMS .... Federacion Magisterial Salvadorena [*Salvadoran Teachers Federation*] (LA)

FMS .... Federated Malay States (ML)

FMS .... Federatia Mondiala a Sindicatelor [*World Federation of Trade Unions*] (RO)

FMS .... Federation Mondiale des Sourds [*World Federation of the Deaf - WFD*] [*Rome, Italy*] (EA)

FMS .... Foreign Military Sales

FMS .... Franko-Malagasiiskii Soiuz

FMS .... Fratres Maristae Scholarum [*Marist Brothers of the Schools*] [*Also known as Little Brothers of Mary*] (EAIO)

FMS .... Frequency Management System [*ITU*] [*United Nations*] (DUND)

FMS .... Frontline Medical Depot (RU)

FMS .... Funkmessstation [*RADAR Station*] (EG)

FMS .... Future Management Services [*A Lebanese arms company*] (ECON)

FMS .... Hadison Aviation [*Sudan*] [*ICAO designator*] (FAAC)

FMS .... Machine-Calculating Center (RU)

FMS .... Phenazine Methyl Sulfate (RU)

FMSA .... Ambalavao [*Madagascar*] [*ICAO location identifier*] (ICLI)

FMSB .... Beroroha/Antsoa [*Madagascar*] [*ICAO location identifier*] (ICLI)

FMSC .... Federation Mondiale des Societes de Cuisiniers [*World Association of Cooks Societies - WACS*] (EA)

FMSC .... Mandabe [*Madagascar*] [*ICAO location identifier*] (ICLI)

FMSCEUA ... Federated Municipal and Shire Council Employees' Union of Australia

FMSCI ...... Federation of Motor Sports Clubs of India (EAIO)

FMSD .... Tolagnaro [*Madagascar*] [*ICAO location identifier*] (ICLI)

FMSE .... Betroka [*Madagascar*] [*ICAO location identifier*] (ICLI)

FMSF .... Fianarantsoa [*Madagascar*] [*ICAO location identifier*] (ICLI)

FMSG .... Farafangana [*Madagascar*] [*ICAO location identifier*] (ICLI)

FMSI .... Federazione Medico-Sportiva Italiana [*Sports Medicine Federation of Italy*] (SLS)

FMSI .... Ihosy [*Madagascar*] [*ICAO location identifier*] (ICLI)

FMSJ .... Manja [*Madagascar*] [*ICAO location identifier*] (ICLI)

FMSK .... Manakara [*Madagascar*] [*ICAO location identifier*] (ICLI)

FMSL .... Bekily [*Madagascar*] [*ICAO location identifier*] (ICLI)

FMSM .... Federation Mondiale pour la Sante Mentale [*World Federation for Mental Health*] [*Use WFMH*] (AF)

FMSM .... Mananjary [*Madagascar*] [*ICAO location identifier*] (ICLI)

FMSN .... Tanandava-Samangoky [*Madagascar*] [*ICAO location identifier*] (ICLI)

FMSNP ..... Fysiolatrikos Morfotikos Syllogos Neon Peramatos Peiraios [*The Perama, Piraeus Nature Lovers and Cultural Youth Club*] (GC)

FMSO .... Ranohira [*Madagascar*] [*ICAO location identifier*] (ICLI)

FMSR .... Federation des Mouvements Socialistes Regionalistes de la Reunion [*Federation of Socialist Regionalist Movements of Reunion*] [*Political party*] (PPW)

FMSR .... Morombe [*Madagascar*] [*ICAO location identifier*] (ICLI)

FMST .... Federal Ministry of Science and Technology [*Rubber Research Institute of Nigeria*]

FMST .... Toliara [*Madagascar*] [*ICAO location identifier*] (ICLI)

FMSV .... Betioky [*Madagascar*] [*ICAO location identifier*] (ICLI)

FMSVR ..... Federated Malay States Volunteer Reserve (ML)

FMSY .... Ampanihy [*Madagascar*] [*ICAO location identifier*] (ICLI)

FMSZ .... Ankazoabo [*Madagascar*] [*ICAO location identifier*] (ICLI)

fmsz............ Foldmuves Szovetkezet [*Farmers' Cooperative*] (HU)

FMT .... Fabryka Maszyn Tytoniowych [*Tobacco Processing Machine Factory*] (POL)

FMT .... Farrer Memorial Trust [*Australia*]

FMTA .... Federation Mondiale de Travailleurs Agricoles [*World Federation of Agricultural Workers - WFAW*] (EAIO)

FMTC .... Federacion Mundial de Trabajadores Cientificos [*World Federation of Scientific Workers - WFSW*] (LA)

FMTC .... Fellow of Melbourne Technical College [*Australia*] (ADA)

FMTD .... Federatia Mondiala a Tineretului Democrat [*World Federation of Democratic Youth*] (RO)

FMTNM ... Federation Mondiale des Travailleurs Non-Manuels [*World Federation of Trade Unions of Non-Manual Workers - WFNMW*] [*Antwerp, Belgium*] (EAIO)

FMTS .... Federation Mondiale des Travailleurs Scientifiques [*World Federation of Scientific Workers - WFSW*] (EAIO)

FMTZ .... Association for the Youth Liberation Struggle [*Malagasy*] (AF)

FMU .... Fachvereinigung Metallhutten und Umschmelzwerke [*Germany*] (EAIO)

FMU .... Federation of Mining Unions [*South Africa*] (AF)

FMU .... Finnish Musicians Union (EAIO)

FMU .... Frente Militar Unica [*Single Military Front*] [*Portuguese*] (WER)

FMU .... Frequence Maximum Utilisable [*Maximum Usable Frequency*] [*French*]

FMU .... Machine Accounting and Computing Office (RU)

FMUA .... Fabrica de Masini Unelte si Agregate [*Factory for Machine Tools and Aggregates*] (RO)

FMV .... Fakulta Mezinarodnich Vztahu [*Department of International Relations*] [*Charles University*] (CZ)

FMV .... Federacion Medica de Venezuela [*Medical Federation of Venezuela*] (LA)

FMV .... Federalni Ministerstvo Vnitra [*Federal Ministry of the Interior*] (CZ)

FMV .... Fellow of the Museum of Victoria [*Australia*]

FMV .... Finommechanikai Vallalat [*Precision Mechanics Enterprise*] (HU)

FMV .... Foersvarets Materielverk [*Defense Material Administration*] [*Sweden*] (PDAA)

FMV .... Fredrikstad Mekaniske Verksted [*Norway*]

FMVA .... Faculdade de Medicina Veterinaria e Agronomia [*Brazil*] (DSCA)

FMVJ .... Federation Mondiale des Villes Jumelees-Cites Unies [*United Towns Organisation - UTO*] (EA)

FMW .... Fernmeldewerk [*Telecommunications Equipment Plant*] (EG)

FMWA ...... Farm Machineries West Africa Ltd.

FMWB .... Federation of Methodist Women in Bolivia (EAIO)

FMWN ...... Federation of Methodist Women Norway (EAIO)

FMWU ...... Federated Miscellaneous Workers' Union of Australia

FMWUA ..... Federated Miscellaneous Workers Union of Australia

FMY .... Foreign Missons of Yarumal [*Colorado*] (EAIO)

FMYO .... Fiji Muslim Youth Organisation (EAIO)

FMZ .... Fabryka Maszyn Zniwnych [*Harvesting Machine Factory*] (POL)

FMZE .... Fondo Monetario de Zona do Escudo

FN .... Corporacion Financiera Nacional [*Ecuador*] (IMH)

FN .... Fabrique Nationale [*Belgium*]

FN .... Fabrique Nationale d'Armes de Guerre, Societe Anonyme [*Belgium*]

FN .... Fabrique Nationale Herstal SA [*Belgium*]

FN .... Filharmonia Narodowa [*National Philharmonic Society*] [*Poland*]

FN .... Filmske Novosti [*Newsreel*] (YU)

FN .... Forenta Nationerna [*United Nations - UN*] [*Sweden*] (WEN)

FN .... Frente Nacional [*Colombia*] (COL)

FN .... Front Narodowy [*People's Front*] (POL)

FN .... Front Nasional [*National Front*] (IN)

FN .... Front National [*France*] [*Political party*] (PPW)

FN .... Front National [*Belgium*] [*Political party*] (EY)

FN .... Front National [*Gabon*] [*Political party*] (EY)

FN .... Fuerza Nueva [*New Force*] [*Spanish*] (WER)

Fn .... Fusant [*Military*] [*French*] (MTD)

FN .... Futures Network [*Ormskirk, Lancashire, England*] [*Defunct*] (EA)

Fn .... Smokeless Powder [*Symbol*] [*French*] (MTD)

FN .... Territorio de Fernando Noronha [*Portuguese*]

FNA .... Fachnormenausschuss [*Committee on Technical Standards and Specifications*] (EG)

FNA .... Federacion Nacional Agraria [*National Agrarian Federation*] [*Peru*] (LA)

FNA......... Federacion Nacional de Arroceros [*Bogota, Colombia*] (LAA)
FNA......... Federation Nationale Aeronautique [*France*]
FNA......... Federation Nationale de l'Automation [*French*] (ADPT)
FNA......... Federation Nationale des Abattoirs et des Ateliers de Decoupe [*Belgium*] (EAIO)
FNA......... Filature Nord Africaine [*North African*]
FNA......... Flugfelag Nordurlands [*Iceland*] [*ICAO designator*] (FAAC)
FNA......... Fondo Nacional de Ahorro [*National Savings Fund*] [*Colorado*] (LA)
FNA......... Fonds National de l'Assainissement
FNA......... Freetown [*Sierra Leone*] [*Airport symbol*] (OAG)
FNAC........ Field Naturalists Association of Canberra [*Australia*]
FNACE..... Federation Nationale des Agents sous Contract de l'Etat
FNACEM ... Federation Nationale des Associations de Culture et de Musique [*National Federation of Cultural and Musical Associations*] [*French Guiana*] (LA)
FNAET..... Fonds National d'Achat et d'Equipement de Terrain [*Morocco*]
FNAF........ Farvandsdirektoratet Nautisk Afdeling [*Denmark*] (MSC)
FNAF........ Federal Nigerian Air Force (PDAA)
FNAF........ Front National pour l'Algerie Francaise [*National Front for French Algeria*] [*Political party*]
FNAFU..... Fonds National d'Amenagement Foncier et d'Urbanism [*France*] (FLAF)
FNAGE...... Federation Nationale d'Association des Eleves des Grandes Ecoles [*National Federation of the "Grandes Ecoles" Student Association*] [*French*] (WER)
FNAH........ Fonds National d'Amelioration de l'Habitat [*France*] (FLAF)
FNAI........ Federazione Nazionale Autoferrotranvieri Internavigatori [*National Federation of Bus, Railway, and Tram Workers*] [*Italy*] (EY)
FNAIM...... Federation Nationale des Agents Immobiliers et Mandataires en Vente de Fonds de Commerce [*France*] (FLAF)
FNAL........ Frente Nacional de Alianza Libre [*National Front of Free Alliance*] [*Spanish*] (WER)
FNAM....... Ambriz [*Angola*] [*ICAO location identifier*] (ICLI)
FNAMCI... Federation Nationale des Associations des Movements des Jeunes de Cote-D'Ivoire [*National Federation of Ivorian Youth Movement Associations*] (AF)
FNAMI...... Fonds National d'Assurance Maladie-Invalidite [*Belgium*] (BAS)
FNAN........ Luanda [*Angola*] [*ICAO location identifier*] (ICLI)
FNAOE ..... Federation of National AFS Organizations in Europe [*Brussels, Belgium*] (EAIO)
FNAT .... Fonds National d'Amenagement du Territoire [*France*] (FLAF)
FNAT .... Fundacao Nacional para Alegria no Trabalho [*National Foundation of Joy through Work*] [*Portuguese*] (WER)
FNAV .... Federation Nationale des Abattoirs de Volailles [*Belgium*] (EAIO)
FNB .... Federacion Nacional de Badminton [*National Badminton Federation*] [*Guatemala*] (EAIO)
FNB .... Federacion Nacional de Bananeros [*National Federation of Banana Growers*] [*Ecuador*] (LA)
FNB .... Federation Nationale des Boissons [*France*] (EAIO)
FNB .... Forum Nucleaire Belge [*Nuclear energy*] [*Belgium*] (NRCH)
FNBC........ M'Banza-Congo [*Angola*] [*ICAO location identifier*] (ICLI)
FNBG .... Benguela [*Angola*] [*ICAO location identifier*] (ICLI)
FNBIV .... Poor Harvest, Natural Calamities, and Economic Assistance Fund (BU)
FNC .... Federacion Nacional de Cacaoteros [*Colombia*] (DSCA)
FNC .... Federacion Nacional de Cafeteros [*Bogota, Colombia*] (LAA)
FNC .... Federacion Nacional del Campesino [*Bolivia*] (DSCA)
FNC .... Ferrocarriles Nacionales de Colombia [*National Railways of Colombia*] (EY)
FNC .... Frente Nacional Constitucionalista [*National Constitutionalist Front*] [*Ecuador*] [*Political party*] (PPW)
FNC .... Frente Nacional Constitucionalista [*National Constitutionalist Front*] [*Dominican Republic*] (LA)
FNC .... Frente Nacional Opositora [*National Opposition Front*] [*Panama*] [*Political party*] (PPW)
FNC .... Front Nacional Catala [*Catalan National Front*] [*Spanish*] (WER)
FNC .... Front National de Concertation [*Haiti*] [*Political party*] (EY)
FNC .... Front National des Combattants [*Algeria*]
FNC .... Funchal [*Portugal*] [*Airport symbol*] (OAG)
FNCA .... Cabinda [*Angola*] [*ICAO location identifier*] (ICLI)
FNCA .... Federation of Nordic Commercial Agents [*Stockholm, Sweden*] (EA)
FNCA .... Fonds National de Credit Agricole et Artisanal [*National Farming and Crafts Credit Fund*] [*Zaire*] (AF)
FNCAA...... Federation Nationale du Commerce et de l'Artisanat de l'Automobile et du Syndicat General des Garagistes-Motoristes [*France*] (FLAF)
FNCAO ..... Federation Nationale des Comites d'Alliance Ouvriere [*National Federation of the Committees of Workers' Alliance*] [*French*] (WER)
FNCATS ... Federation Nationale de la Cooperation Agricole Technique et Scientifique [*France*] (DSCA)

FNCB........ Camembe [*Angola*] [*ICAO location identifier*] (ICLI)
FNCB........ Federation Nationale de la Construction-Bois [*France*]
FNCBF ...... Federation Nationale des Commercants en Bestiaux de France (EAIO)
FNCC......... Cacolo [*Angola*] [*ICAO location identifier*] (ICLI)
FNCC......... Federacion Nacional de Cafeteros de Colombia [*National Federation of Coffee Growers of Colombia*] (EAIO)
FNCC......... Federation Nationale des Cheminots du Cameroun [*National Federation of Railroad Employees of Cameroon*] (AF)
FNCC......... Federation Nationale des Cooperatives Chretiennes [*Benelux*] (BAS)
FNCC......... Federation of Norwegian Chambers of Commerce (EAIO)
FNCC......... Fondo Nacional del Cafe y del Cacao [*Venezuela*] (LAA)
FNCD .... Front National pour le Changement et la Democratie [*Haiti*] [*Political party*] (EY)
FNCE......... Fabricacion Nacional de Colorantes, SA
FNCETA ... Federation Nationale des Centres d'Etudes Techniques Agricoles [*French*] (SLS)
FNCH........ Chitato [*Angola*] [*ICAO location identifier*] (ICLI)
FNCh......... Low-Pass Filter (RU)
FNCI......... Fondo Nacional de Credito Industrial [*National Industrial Credit Fund*] [*Venezuela*] (LA)
FNCIAWPRC ... Finnish National Committee of the International Association on Water Pollution Research and Control (EAIO)
FNCL......... Federation Nationale des Cooperatives Laitieres [*National Federation of Milk Cooperatives*] [*France*] (EAIO)
FNCM .... Camabatela [*Angola*] [*ICAO location identifier*] (ICLI)
FNCM .... Finnish National Committee for Mathematics (EAIO)
FNCP........ Federacion Nacional de Cooperativas de Produccion [*Venezuela*] (DSCA)
FNCPME .. Federation Nationale des Chefs des Petites et Moyennes Entreprises [*National Federation of Heads of Small and Medium Sized Enterprises*] [*Ivory Coast*] (AF)
FNCR .... Frente Nacional Contra la Represion [*National Front Against Repression*] [*Mexico*] (LA)
FNCS......... Federation Nationale des Cheminots du Senegal [*National Federation of Railroad Workers of Senegal*] (AF)
FNCTL ...... Federatin Nationale des Chaminots et des Travailleurs de Transport Luxembourgeois [*Benelux*] (BAS)
FNCV .... Cuito Cuanavale [*Angola*] [*ICAO location identifier*] (ICLI)
FNCV .... Federacion Nacional de Cooperativas de Vivienda [*Venezuela*] (DSCA)
FNCX........ Camaxilo [*Angola*] [*ICAO location identifier*] (ICLI)
FNCZ........ Cazombo [*Angola*] [*ICAO location identifier*] (ICLI)
FND.......... Flinders Naval Depot [*Australia*] (ADA)
FND.......... Fonds National de Developpement [*Mauritania*] (EY)
FND.......... Frente Nacional Democratico [*Democratic National Front*] [*Venezuela*] (LA)
FND.......... Frente Nacional Democratico [*Democratic National Front*] [*Guatemala*] (LA)
FND.......... Front National Democratique [*Democratic National Front*] [*Central African Republic*] (AF)
FND.......... Frontul National Democratic [*National Democratic Front*] [*Romania*] [*Political party*] (PPE)
FND.......... Fundo Nacional de Desenvolvimento [*National Development Fund*] [*Brazil*] (LA)
FNDB .... Damba [*Angola*] [*ICAO location identifier*] (ICLI)
FNDCT...... Fundo Nacional de Desenvolvimento Cientifico e Tecnologico [*National Scientific and Technological Development Fund*] [*Brazil*] (LA)
FNDE .... Fondo Nacional de Desarrollo Economico [*National Fund for Economic Development*] [*Peru*] (LA)
FNDE .... Fonds National de Developpement et d'Equipement [*National Development and Equipment Fund*] [*Malagasy*] (AF)
FNDE .... Fundo Nacional de Desenvolvimento da Educacao [*National Educational Development Fund*] [*Brazil*] (LA)
FNDEL...... Federazione Nazionale Dipendenti Enti Locali [*National Federation of Local Government*] [*Italian*]
FNDF........ Federal National Democratic Front [*Myanmar*] [*Political party*] (PD)
FNDIRP .... Federation Nationale des Deportes, Internes, Resistants, et Patriotes
FNDP .... First National Development Plan
FNDP .... Frente Nacional Democratico Popular [*Popular National Democratic Front*] [*Mexico*] (PD)
FNDR .... Front National pour la Defense de la Revolution [*National Front for the Defense of the Revolution*] [*Malagasy*] (AF)
FNDRESS ... Federation Nationale des Deportes, Refugies, Expulses, Sinistres, et Spolies
FNDS........ Federazione Nazionale degli Statali [*Italian Federation of Government Employees*]
FNDSCAC ... Frente Nacional de Defensa del Salario y Contra la Austeridad y la Carestia [*National Front for Defense of Salaries and Against Austerity and the High Cost of Living*] [*Mexico*] (LA)

FNE .... Faisceaux Nationalistes Europeens [*European Nationalist Alliances*] [*France*] (PD)

FNE .... Fane [*Papua New Guinea*] [*Airport symbol*] (OAG)

FNE .... Federation National de l'Enseignement [*National Front for the Defense of the Revolution*] [*Morocco*] (AF)

FNE .... Federation of National Education [*France*] (EAIO)

Fne .... Fontaine [*Fountain, Spring*] [*Military map abbreviation World War I*] [*French*] (MTD)

FNE .... Frente Nacional Espanol [*Spanish National Front*] (WER)

FNEB .... Fovarosi Nepi Ellenorzo Bizottsag [*Capital City People's Control Committee*] (HU)

FNEC .... Federacion Nacional de Estudiantes Catalanes [*National Federation of Catalan Students*] [*Spanish*] (WER)

FNECC ...... Federation Nationale des Employes Commerciaux et Cadres

FNED .... Federation Nationale des Etudiants Destouriens [*National Federation of Destourian Students*] [*Tunisia*] (AF)

FNEEGA ... Federation Nationale de l'Energie Electrique et du Gaz d'Algerie [*Algerian National Electric Power and Gas Federation*] (AF)

FNEF .... Federation Nationale des Etudiants de France [*National Federation of Students of France*] (WER)

FNEL .... Federation Nationale des Etudiants au Laos [*National Federation of Students in Laos*] (CL)

FNEM .... Fondo Nacional de Exploracion Minera [*National Mining Exploration Fund*] [*Bolivia*] (GEA)

FNEN .... Federacion Nacional de Empresarios Nacionalistas [*National Federation of Nationalist Entrepreneurs*] [*Mexico*] (LA)

FNES .... Federation Nationale des Enseignants du Senegal [*National Federation of Teachers of Senegal*] (AF)

FNET .... Federacion Nacional de Empleados y Tecnicos [*National Federation of Office Workers and Technicians*] [*Uruguay*] (LA)

FNF .... Federacao Nacional dos Ferroviarios [*National Federation of Railway Workers*] [*Brazil*] (LA)

FNF .... Finnish Air Force Headquarters [*ICAO designator*] (FAAC)

FNF .... Foreningarna Norden's Forbund [*League of Norden Associations*] [*Norway*] (EAIO)

FNF .... Normenausschuss Farbe im DIN [*Deutsches Institut fuer Normung*] eV [*Paint Standards Committee of the German Institute for Standardization*] (SLS)

FNFA .... Fundo Nacional de Financiamento para Abastecimento de Agua [*National Fund for the Financing of Water Supply*] [*Brazil*] (LA)

FNFL .... Forces Navales Francaises Libres [*Free French Naval Forces*] [*World War II*]

FNFPM ..... Federation National de la Fonction Publique de Madagascar [*National Civil Service Federation of Madagascar*] (AF)

FNFPZ ...... Federation Nationale des Femmes Protestantes du Zaire [*Zairian National Federation of Protestant Women*] (AF)

FNFTCC.... Federation of Netherlands Foreign Trade Chambers of Commerce (EAIO)

FNFW .... Normenausschuss Feuerwehrwesen im DIN [*Deutsches Institut fuer Normung*] eV [*Fire Department Standards Committee of the German Institute for Standardization*] (SLS)

FNG .... Fada N'Gourma [*Burkina Faso*] [*Airport symbol*] (OAG)

FNG .... Federacion Nacional de Ganaderos [*National Cattlemen's Federation*] [*Venezuela*] (LA)

FNGA .... Fruit Nurseries Growers' Association [*Israel*] (EAIO)

FNGI .... N'Giva [*Angola*] [*ICAO location identifier*] (ICLI)

FNGIREA ... First National Group of Independent Real Estate Agents Ltd. [*Australia*]

FNGO .... Fachverband der Nahrungs- und Genussmittelindustrie Osterreichs [*Federation of the Austrian Food Industry*] (EAIO)

FNGO .... Federation Nationale des Grossistes en Oeufs [*Belgium*] (EAIO)

FNGP .... Federation Nationale des Gaullistes de Progres [*National Federation of Progressive Gaullists*] [*France*] [*Political party*] (PPW)

FNGRA ..... Federation Nationale des Groupements Agricoles d'Approvisionnement [*France*] (DSCA)

FNGTA...... Fellow of the New South Wales Geography Teachers Association [*Australia*]

FNGU .... N'Gunza [*Angola*] [*ICAO location identifier*] (ICLI)

FNH........... Fonds National de l'Hydraulique

FNHET ..... Federation Nationale de l'Habitat des Equipements et Transports [*French*]

FNHI .... Federation Nationale des Hebdomadaires d'Information [*Belgium*] (EAIO)

FNHU........ Huambo [*Angola*] [*ICAO location identifier*] (ICLI)

FNI .... Fachnormenausschuss Informations-Verarbeitung [*German*] (ADPT)

FNI .... Federation of Netherlands Industry (EAIO)

FNI .... Fonds National d'Investissement [*National Investment Fund*] [*Morocco*] (AF)

FNI .... Fonds National d'Investissement [*National Investment Fund*] [*Niger*]

FNI .... Fonds National d'Investissement [*National Investment Fund*] [*Ivory Coast*] (IMH)

FNI .... Nimes [*France*] [*Airport symbol*] (OAG)

FNIA......... Fondo Nacional de Investigaciones Agropecuarias [*Venezuela*] (DSCA)

FNIC......... Federazione Nazionale dell'Industria Chimica [*Italian Federation of the Chemical Industry*] (EAIO)

FNICGV .... Federation Nationale de l'Industrie et des Commerces en Gros des Viandes [*France*] (EAIO)

FNIE......... Federation Nationale des Industries Electroniques Francaises [*National Federation of French Electronics Manufacturers*]

FNIEF .... Federazione Nazionale Insegnanti Educazione Fisica [*Italian*] (SLS)

FNIF......... Florence Nightingale International Foundation [*Defunct*] (EA)

FNIH .... Federation Nationale de l'Industrie Hoteliere [*National Federation of the Hotel Industry*] [*France*] (EY)

FNIL......... Federation Nationale de l'Industrie Laitiere [*National Federation of the Milk Industry*] [*France*] (EAIO)

FNJ........... Federatie van Nederlandse Journalisten [*Netherlands Journalists' Union*] (WEN)

FNJ........... Frente Nacional de la Juventud [*National Youth Front*] [*Spanish*] (WER)

FNJ........... Front National de la Jeunesse [*National Youth Front*] [*France*] (PD)

FNJ........... Pyongyang [*North Korea*] [*Airport symbol*] (OAG)

FNK .... Fovarosi Nepmuvelesi Kozpont [*Capital Center of Popular Education*] (HU)

FNKE........ Fachnormenausschuss Kerntechnik [*Nuclear Technology Standards Committee*] [*Germany*] (PDAA)

FNKh .... Phosphonitril Chloride (RU)

FNKKHB .. Federatie van Nederlandsche Kamers van Koophandel voor den Handel met het Buit enland [*Federation of Netherlands Foreign Trade Chambers of Commerce*] (EAIO)

FNKU .... Kuito/Bie [*Angola*] [*ICAO location identifier*] (ICLI)

FNL .... Five New Laender [*Lands*] [*Name given to former East German territory after unification*]

FNL .... Front National de Liberation [*National Front for the Liberation of South Vietnam*] [*Use NFLSV*] (CL)

FNL .... Normenausschuss Lichttechnik [*Light Technology Standards Committee*] (SLS)

FNLA........ Frente Nacional de Libertacao de Angola [*Angolan National Liberation Front*] (AF)

FNLA........ Friends of the National Library of Australia

FNLA........ Front National de Liberation de l'Angola [*Angolan National Liberation Front*] (PD)

FNLB........ Front National de Liberation de Bretagne [*National Liberation Front of Brittany*] [*France*] (PD)

FNLB........ Lobito [*Angola*] [*ICAO location identifier*] (ICLI)

FNLC........ Front Nationale de Liberation Congolaise [*Congolese National Liberation Front*] [*Zaire*] (AF)

FNLG .... Front National de Liberation Guyanais [*Guiana National Liberation Front*] [*French Guiana*] (PD)

FNLO .... Front National de Liberation d'Ouganda [*Ugandan National Liberation Front*] [*Use UNLF*] (AF)

FNLU .... Luanda/4 De Fevereiro [*Angola*] [*ICAO location identifier*] (ICLI)

FNM .... Fachnormenausschuss Materialpruefung [*Special Standards Committee Material Test ing*] [*Germany*] (GCA)

FNM .... Fachnormenausschuss Materialpruefung im Deutschen Normenausschuss

FNM .... Ferrocarriles Nacionales de Mexico [*National Railways of Mexico*]

FNM .... Florence Nightingale Medal [*Australia*]

FNM .... Free National Movement [*Bahamas*] [*Political party*] (PPW)

FNM .... Frente Nacional Magisterial [*National Teachers Front*] [*Guatemala*] (LA)

FNMA .... Front National Martiniquais pour l'Autonomie [*Martinique National Front for Autonomy*] [*Political party*] (PPW)

FNMA .... Malanje [*Angola*] [*ICAO location identifier*] (ICLI)

FNMAJ ..... Federation Nationale des Mouvements et Associations de Jeunesse [*National Federation of Youth Movements and Associations*] [*Ivory Coast*] (AF)

FNMAJCI ... Federation Nationale des Mouvements et Associations de Jeunesse de Cote-D'Ivoire [*National Federation of Youth Movements and Associations of the Ivory Coast*]

FNMAL..... Fabrica Nacional de Municoes de Armas Ligeiras [*National Light Weapons Ammunition Factory*] [*Portuguese*] (WER)

FNMC .... French National Music Committee

FNME .... Menongue [*Angola*] [*ICAO location identifier*] (ICLI)

FNMM ...... Federacion Nacional de Mineros y Metalurgicos [*National Miners and Metalworkers Federation*] [*Peru*] (LA)

FNMO....... Mooamedes/Yuri Gagarin [*Angola*] [*ICAO location identifier*] (ICLI)

FNMQ....... Maquela [*Angola*] [*ICAO location identifier*] (ICLI)

FNMT .... Finca Nacional de Moneda y Timbre [*Branch of treasury issuing bank notes and stamps*] [*Spanish*]

FNNG........ Negage [*Angola*] [*ICAO location identifier*] (ICLI)

FNO.......... Fond Narodni Obnovy [*National Reconstruction Fund*] (CZ)
FNO.......... Frente Nacional de Oposicion [*National Opposition Front*] [*Venezuela*] [*Political party*]
FNO.......... Frente Nacional de Oposicion [*National Opposition Front*] [*Guatemala*] [*Political party*]
FNO.......... Front Natsional'novo Osvobozhdeniia
FNO.......... People's Liberation Front (RU)
FNOA........ Federation Nationale des Ouvriers Angolais [*National Federation of Angolan Workers*] (AF)
FNOGF ..... Federazione Nazionale Orafi Gioiellierei Fabbricanti [*Jewellers and Goldsmiths Federation*] [*Italy*] (EY)
FNOI .... Frente Nacional Obrero Intelectual [*National Front of Workers and Intellectuals*] [*Colorado*] (LA)
FNOM....... Federazione Nazionale degli Ordini dei Medici [*Italian*] (SLS)
FNOP .... Federatie van Nederlandse Organisaties voor het Personenvervoer [*Netherlands*] (BAS)
FNOS .... Fundo Nacional de Obras de Saneamento [*National Sanitation Works Fund*] [*Brazil*] (LA)
FNOSS...... Federation Nationale des Organismes de Securite Sociale [*National Federation of Social Security Agencies*] [*Malagasy*] (AF)
FNOVI ...... Federazione Nazionale degli Ordini dei Veterinari Italiani [*Italian*] (SLS)
FNP .... Federation Nationale des Patronages de Belgique
FNP .... Federazione Nazionale Pensionati [*National Federation of Pensioners' Union*] [*Italy*] (EY)
FNP .... Fijian Nationalist Party [*Political party*] (PPW)
FNP .... Frente Nacional de Panama [*Panamanian National Front*] [*Political party*] (PD)
FNP .... Fuerza Nacional Progresista [*Progressive National Force*] [*Bolivia*] (LA)
FNP .... Regional Training Program on Food and Nutrition Planning [*University of the Philippines at Los Banos*] [*Research center*] (IRC)
FNPA........ Porto Amboim [*Angola*] [*ICAO location identifier*] (ICLI)
FNPB........ Sanza Pombo [*Angola*] [*ICAO location identifier*] (ICLI)
FNPC........ Federacion Nacional de Partidos del Centro [*Argentina*] (LAA)
FNPC........ Federacion Nacional de Patronatos Comunales [*National Federation of Community Boards*] [*Honduras*] (LA)
FNPFCP.... Federation of Non-Professional Film Clubs in Poland (EAIO)
FNPG .... Fashoda National Provisional Government [*Sudan*]
FNPG .... Federation Nationale du Petrole et du Gaz [*National Petroleum and Gas Federation*] [*Algeria*] (AF)
FNPH .... Foreningen Nordiska Pappershistoriker [*Association of Nordic Paper Historians - NPH*] [*Stockholm, Sweden*] (EAIO)
FNPHP...... National Association for Periodical Press [*France*] (EAIO)
FNPIS....... National Federation of Specialized Press [*France*] (EAIO)
FNPL .... Federation Nationale des Producteurs de Lait [*France*] (DSCA)
FNPL .... Forces Neutralistes Patriotiques Laotiennes [*Lao Patriotic Neutralist Forces*] (CL)
FNPLT ...... Front Nationaliste Progressiste pour la Liberation de la Tunisie [*Progressive Nationalist Front for the Liberation of Tunisia*] [*Political party*] (PD)
FNPR........ Federation of Independent Trade Unions of Russia (ECON)
FNPS........ Federation Nationale du Personnel de la Sante
FNPS........ Fonds National de Promotion et de Service Social [*National Fund for Social Advancement and Service*] [*Zaire*] (AF)
FNPT........ Fondo Nacional de Proteccion al Trabajo [*National Fund for the Protection of Labor*] [*Spanish*] (WER)
FNQ.......... Far North Queensland [*Australia*] (ADA)
FNQPB...... Far North Queensland Promotion Board [*Australia*]
FNQR....... Far North Queensland Regiment [*Australia*]
FNR .... Federative People's Republic
FNR .... Frente Nacional de Redemocratizacao [*National Redemocratization Front*] [*Brazil*] (LA)
FNR .... Frente Nacional Revolucionario [*National Revolutionary Front*] [*Argentina*] (LA)
FNR .... Front National de Renouvellement [*Algeria*] [*Political party*] (EY)
FNR .... Fundo Nacional de Refinanciamento [*National Refinancing Fund*] [*Brazil*] (LA)
FNRBiH ... Federativna Narodna Republika Bosna i Hercegovina [*Federated People's Republic of Bosnia and Hercegovina*] (YU)
FNRCG...... Federativna Narodna Republika Crna Gora [*Federated People's Republic of Montenegro*] (YU)
FNRH........ Federativna Narodna Republika Hrvatska [*Federated People's Republic of Croatia*] (YU)
FNRI.......... Federation Nationale des Republicains Independants [*National Federation of Independent Republicans*] [*France*] [*Political party*] (PPW)
FNRI.......... Food and Nutrition Research Institute [*Philippines*] (ARC)
FNRJ .... Federativna Narodna Republika Jugoslavija [*Federal People's Republic of Yugoslavia*] (YU)
FNRM .... Federativna Narodna Republika Makedonija [*Federated People's Republic of Macedonia*] (YU)
FNROM .... Fonds National de Retraite des Ouvriers Mineurs [*Benelux*] (BAS)

FNRS......... Federativna Narodna Republika Slovenija [*Federated People's Republic of Slovenia*] (YU)
FNRS......... Federativna Narodna Republika Srbija [*Federated People's Republic of Serbia*] (YU)
FNRS......... Fonds National de la Recherche Scientifique [*Belgium*]
FNRS/NFWO ... Fonds National de la Recherche Scientifique/National Fonds voor Wetenschappelijk Onderzoek [*National Foundation for Scientific Research*] [*Research center*] [*Belgium*] (IRC)
FNRT........ First National Resource Trust [*Australia*]
FNRYu ..... Federal People's Republic of Yugoslavia (BU)
FNS........... Federation of Netherlands Societies [*Australia*]
FNS........... Forces Nucleaires Strategiques [*Strategic Nuclear Forces*] [*French*] (WER)
FNS........... Frente Nacional Sindical [*National Trade Union Front*] [*Guatemala*] (LA)
FNS........... Front National Senegalais
FNSA........ Federation Nationale des Societes d'Assurances [*France*] (FLAF)
FNSA........ Federation Nationale des Syndicats Agricoles [*National Federation of Farmers Unions*] [*French*] (WER)
FNSA........ French National Shipowners Association (EAIO)
FNSA........ Frente Nacional Socialista Argentino [*Argentinian National Socialist Front*] [*Political party*] (PD)
FNSA........ Saurimo [*Angola*] [*ICAO location identifier*] (ICLI)
FNSBS....... Fondo Nacional de Salud y Bienestar Social [*Peru*] (DSCA)
FNSC........ Federation pour une Nouvelle Societe Caledonienne [*Federation for a New Caledonian Society*] [*Political party*] (PPW)
FNSEA ..... Federation Nationale des Syndicats d'Exploitants Agricoles [*National Federation of Unions of Farm Operators*] [*Paris, France*] (WER)
FNSI .... Federacion Nacional de Sindicatos Independientes [*National Federation of Independent Trade Unions*] [*Mexico*] (LA)
FNSI .... Federation Nationale des Syndicats d'Ingenieurs et Cadres [*France*] (FLAF)
FNSI .... Federazione Nazionale della Stampa Italiana [*National Federation of the Italian Press*] (WER)
FNSO .... Soyo [*Angola*] [*ICAO location identifier*] (ICLI)
FNSP .... Federation Nationale des Services Publics
FNSP .... Fondation Nationale des Sciences Politiques [*France*] (FLAF)
FNSP-CERI ... Fondation Nationale des Sciences Politiques Centre d'Etudes des Relations Internationales
FNSRA ...... Fonds National de Solidarite de la Revolution Agraire [*National Fund for Solidarity with the Agrarian Revolution*] [*Algeria*] (AF)
FNSSCE.... Federation Nationale des Syndicats de Societes de Commerce Exterieur [*France*] (EAIO)
fn st .... Pound Sterling (RU)
FNSWIA ... Fellow of the New South Wales Institute of the Arts [*Australia*]
FNSWIT ... Fellow of the New South Wales Institute of Technology [*Australia*]
FNT .... Federacion Nacional de Trabajadores [*National Federation of Workers*] [*Dominican Republic*] (LA)
FNT .... Federation Nationale du Theatre
Fnt............. Fonit [*Record label*] [*Italy*]
FNTA .... Federacion Nacional de Trabajadores Azucareros [*National Federation of Sugar Workers*] [*Uruguay*] (LA)
FNTAL...... Federation Nationale du Teillage Agricole du Lin [*France*] (DSCA)
FNTBB ...... Federation Nordique des Travailleurs du Batiment et du Bois [*Nordic Federation of Building and Wood Workers - NFBWW*] (EAIO)
FNTC........ Fiji National Training Council
FNTC........ Frente Nacional de Trabajadores y Campesinos [*National Workers' and Peasants' Front*] [*Peru*] [*Political party*] (PPW)
FNTM .... Federation Nationale des Travailleurs de la Metallurgie [*National Metallurgy Workers Federation*] [*Algeria*] (AF)
FNTME..... Federacion Nacional de Trabajadores Municipales del Ecuador [*National Federation of Municipal Workers of Ecuador*] (LA)
FNTMMS ... Federacion Nacional de Trabajadores Mineros, Metalurgicos, y Siderurgicos [*Federation of Peruvian Mine-Workers*] (EY)
FNTO .... Toto [*Angola*] [*ICAO location identifier*] (ICLI)
FNTP........ Federacao Nacional dos Productores de Trigo [*Portugal*] (DSCA)
FNTPGA ... Federation Nationale des Travailleurs du Petrole, Gas, et Assimiles [*National Federation of Petroleum, Gas, and Related Industry Workers*] [*Algeria*] (AF)
FNTR........ Federation Nationale des Transports Routiers [*France*] (FLAF)
FNTR........ Federation Nationale des Travailleurs du Rail [*National Federation of Railroad Workers*] [*Morocco*] (AF)
FNTT........ Federation Nationale des Travailleurs de Terre [*National Federation of Farm Workers*] [*Algeria*] (AF)
FNTTR...... Federacion Nacional de Trabajadores Textiles Revolucionarios [*National Federation of Revolutionary Textile Workers*] [*Peru*] (LA)

FNTU .... Federation of Norwegian Transport Users (EAIO)
FNTUP........ Federacion Nacional de Trabajadores de la Universidad Peruana [*National Federation of Peruvian University Workers*] (LA)
FNU .... Front National Uni [*National United Front*] [*Comoros*] (AF)
FNUA .... Luau [*Angola*] [*ICAO location identifier*] (ICLI)
FNUAP...... Fondo de las Naciones Unidas para Actividades de Poblacion [*United Nations Fund for Population Activities*] [*Use UNFPA*] [*Spanish*] (LA)
FNUAP...... Fondo de Poblacion de las Naciones Unidas [*United Nations Population Fund*] [*Spanish*] (DUND)
FNUAP...... Fonds des Nations Unies pour la Population [*United Nations Population Fund*] [*French*] (DUND)
FNUAP...... Fonds des Nations Unies pour les Activites en Matiere de Population [*United Nations Fund for Population Activities*] [*Use UNFPA*] [*French*] (AF)
FNUB .... Lubango [*Angola*] [*ICAO location identifier*] (ICLI)
FNUDC ..... Fondo de las Naciones Unidas para el Desarrollo de la Capitalizacion [*United Nations Capital Development Fund - UNCDF*] [*Spanish*]
FNUDI ...... Fonds des Nations Unies pour le Developpement Industriel
FNUE .... Luena [*Angola*] [*ICAO location identifier*] (ICLI)
FNUFUID ... Fondo de las Naciones Unidas para la Fiscalizacion del Uso Indebido de Drogas [*United Nations Fund for Drug Abuse Control - UNFDAC*] [*Spanish*]
FNUG .... Uige/Vige [*Angola*] [*ICAO location identifier*] (ICLI)
FNUI .... Fondo de las Naciones Unidas para la Infancia [*United Nations Children's Fund*] [*Use UNICEF*] (LA)
FNUJA...... Federation Nationale des Unions des Jeunes Avocats [*Benelux*] (BAS)
FNUK .... Front National Uni des Komores [*National United Front of the Comoros*] [*Political party*] (PD)
FNUK-UNIKOM ... Front National Uni des Komores - Union des Komoriens [*National United Front of the Comoros*]
FNULAD... Fonds des Nations Unies pour la Lutte Contre l'Abus des Drogues [*United Nations Fund for Drug Abuse Control - UNFDAC*] [*French*]
FNUOD..... Force de Desengagement de l'ONU entre Syriens et Israeliens
FNUPA...... Federation Nationale des Unions Professionnelles Agricoles [*Benelux*] (BAS)
FNUR .... Fonds des Nations Unies pour les Refugies [*United Nations Funds for Refugees*]
FNV .... Fabrica Nacional de Vagoes [*National Railway Car Factory*] [*Brazil*] (LA)
FNV .... Federatie Nederlandse Vakbeweging [*Netherlands Trade Union Confederation*] [*Netherlands*] (WEN)
FNV .... Financiera Nacional de la Vivienda [*National Housing Finance Bank*] [*El Salvador*]
FNV .... Partido Federacion Nacional Velasquista [*National Velasquista Federation*] [*Ecuador*] [*Political party*] (PPW)
FNVCA...... Federazione Nazionale Vetro e Ceramica [*National Federation of Glass and Pottery Workers*] [*Italian*]
FNWK .... Wako-Kungo [*Angola*] [*ICAO location identifier*] (ICLI)
FNXA .... Xangongo [*Angola*] [*ICAO location identifier*] (ICLI)
FNZ .... NZ Fasteners Ltd. [*New Zealand*]
FNZE........ N'Zeto/N'Zeto [*Angola*] [*ICAO location identifier*] (ICLI)
FO .... Alon, Inc. [*ICAO aircraft manufacturer identifier*] (ICAO)
FO .... Faroe Islands [*ANSI two-letter standard code*] (CNC)
FO .... Fasistiki Organosis [*Fascist Organization*] (GC)
FO .... Felddienstordnung [*Field Order*] [*German*]
Fo .... Filho [*Son*] [*Portuguese*]
FO .... Finance Department (RU)
FO .... Financieel Overheidsbeheer [*Benelux*] (BAS)
FO .... Fizicki Odgoj [*Physical Education*] (YU)
fo .... Folio [*Folio*] [*Spanish*]
fo .... Folio [*Folio*] [*Portuguese*]
fo .... Folio [*Folio*] [*French*]
FO .... Force Ouvriere [*Workers Force*] [*Trade union*] [*France*] (WER)
FO .... Force Ouvriere [*Workers Force*] [*Trade union Reunion*]
FO .... Foreign Office
FO .... Forli [*Car registration plates*] [*Italy*]
fo .... For Ovrigt [*Besides*] [*Sweden*] (GPO)
FO .... Frente Obrero [*Workers' Front*] [*Nicaragua*] [*Political party*] (PD)
FO .... Frente Obrero [*Workers' Front*] [*of the Carlists in the Workers Commissions*] [*Spain*] [*Political party*]
FO .... Fucikuv Odznak [*Fucik Badge*] (CZ)
FOA .... Filipinas Orient Airways, Inc. [*Philippines*] [*ICAO designator*] (FAAC)
FOA .... Foersvarets Forskningsanstalt [*Defense Research Institute*] [*Sweden*] [*Research center*] (WEN)
FOA .... Forest Owners' Association [*South Africa*] (AA)
FOA .... Forsvarets Forskningsanstalt [*Research Institute of National Defense*] [*Information service or system*] (IID)
FOA-A....... Fackorgan foer Offentliga Arbetsomraden pa Aland [*Joint Organization of Civil Servants and Workers in Aland*] (EY)

FOABC...... Friends of the Australian Broadcasting Commission (ADA)
FOAPH ..... Federation Ouest Africaine des Associations pour la Promotion des Personnes Handicapees [*West African Federation of Associations for the Advancement of Handicapped Persons - WAFAH*] [*Bamako, Mali*] (EAIO)
FOB .... Filmugyek Orszagos Bizottsaga [*National Committee on Motion Pictures*] (HU)
FOB .... Ford Motor Co. Ltd. [*ICAO designator*] (FAAC)
FOB .... Franco Bord [*Free on board*] [*French*] (FLAF)
fob .... Free on Board (OMWE)
FOBA .... Force Obote Back Again [*Political organization*] [*Uganda*]
FOBER...... Fovarosi Epitoipari Beruhazasi Vallalat [*Investment Enterprise of the Capital City Construction Industry*] (HU)
FOBID....... Federatie van Organisaties van Bibliotheek-, Informatie-, Dokumentatiewezen [*Netherlands*] (SLS)
FOBID....... Foundation Federation for the Organizations in the Field of Library, Information, and Documentation Services [*Netherlands*] (EAIO)
Fobiz .... Fobizottsag [*Main Committee*] (HU)
FOC .... Facultad Obrera y Campesina [*Workers and Peasants Faculty*] [*Cuba*] (LA)
FOC .... Federacion Obrera Capitalina [*Capital Labor Federation*] [*Costa Rica*] (LA)
FOC .... Flag of Convenience
FOC .... Fonds des Operations de Changes [*Foreign Exchange Operations Fund*] [*Use FEOF Laotian*] (CL)
FOC .... Force Ouvriere du Congo
FOC .... Front Obrer Catala [*Catalan Workers Front*] [*Spanish*] (WER)
FOC .... Fuzhou [*China*] [*Airport symbol*] (OAG)
FOC .... Office Federal de l'Aviation Civile [*Sweden*] [*ICAO designator*] (FAAC)
FOCA .... Formula One Constructors' Association [*Australia*]
FOCAF...... Flag Officer, Commander, Her Majesty's Australian Fleet
FOCAP...... Federacion Odontologica de Centroamerica y Panama [*Odontological Federation of Central America and Panama*] [*Panama*] (LAA)
FOCAPE ... Fonds d'Aide et de Garantie de Credits aux Petites et Moyennes Entreprises
FOCAS...... Fuji Juken, Ogisaka, Kawabe, Asahi Juken and Sueno Kosan [*Group of Japanese development companies located in Osaka, Japan*] (ECON)
FOCCC...... Federacion de Obreros y Campesinos Cristianos Costarricense [*Trade union*] [*Costa Rica*]
FOCCO ..... Fomento y Cooperacion Comunal con Esfuerzo Propio y Ayuda Mutua [*Self-Help and Mutual Aid Communal Development and Cooperation Program*] [*El Salvador*] (LA)
FOCE........ Frente Obrero Campesino Estudiantil [*Worker-Peasant Student Front*] [*Ecuador*] (LA)
FOCEP...... Frente Obrero Campesino Estudiantil Popular [*Worker-Peasant-Student Popular Front*] [*Peru*] (LA)
FOCH........ Federacion Obrera de Chile [*Trade union*] [*Chile*]
FOC/LAN ... International Fiber Optics and Communications Exposition and Show on Local Area Networks
FOCOBANK ... Foreign Commerce Bank [*Switzerland*]
FOCSAT ... Fovarosi Csatornazasi Muvek [*Capital Sewage Plant*] (HU)
FOCSIV..... Federazione Organismi Cristiani di Servizio
FOD .... Filmowy Osrodek Doswiadczalny [*Film Experimental Center*] (POL)
FOD .... Foersoeks- och Demonstrationsskolan [*Sweden*]
FOD .... Friends of Darl'mat [*An association*] [*France*] (EAIO)
FOD .... Front de l'Opposition Democratique [*Togo*] [*Political party*] (EY)
FOD .... Frydlant nad Ostravici-Bila Draha [*Frydlant nad Ostravici-Bila Railroad*] (CZ)
FOdD......... Fabryka Obrabiarek do Drewna (Bydgoszcz) [*Woodworking Machine Tool Plant (Bydgoszcz)*] (POL)
FODECO .. Frente de Organizaciones Democratas Constitucionalistas [*Constitutionalist Democratic Organizations Front*] [*Dominican Republic*] (LA)
FODELICO ... Forces Democratiques de Liberation du Congo
foder .... Foderato [*Lined*] [*Publishing*] [*Italian*]
FODERCO ... Front de Resistance Congolais [*Congolese Resistance Front*] (AF)
FODERUMA ... Fondo de Desarrollo Rural Marginal [*Marginal Rural Area Development Fund*] [*Ecuador*] (LA)
FODIC....... Fonds pour le Developpement de l'Industrie Cinematographique
FODOK ..... Nederlandse Federatie van Organisaties van Ouders van Dove Kinderen [*Netherlands*] (EAIO)
FoDokAB... Forschungsdokumentation zur Arbeitsmarkt- und Berufsforschung [*Deutsche Bundesanstalt fuer Arbeit*] [*Germany*] [*Information service or system*] (CRD)
foea............. Foeloado [*Chief Consultant*] (HU)
FOEA .... Friends of the Earth - Argentina (EAIO)
FOEB........ Federacion de Obreros y Empleados de la Bebida [*Beverage Workers Federation*] [*Uruguay*] (LA)
FOEB........ Friends of the Earth - Brazil (EAIO)

FOECYT ... Federacion de Obreros y Empleados de Correos y Telecomunicaciones [*Federation of Postal and Telecommunications Workers*] [*Argentina*] (LA)

FOEF .... Friends of the Earth - France (EAIO)

FOEG .... Friends of the Earth - Ghana (EAIO)

FOEHK ..... Friends of the Earth - Hong Kong (EAIO)

FOEI .... Friends of the Earth International

FOEI .... Friends of the Earth - Italy (EAIO)

FOEIMYA ... Federacion de Obreros y Empleados Molineros y Afines [*Flour Mill Workers Federation*] [*Uruguay*] (LA)

FOeJ .... Freie Oesterreichische Jugend [*Free Austrian Youth*] (WEN)

foell .... Foellenor [*General Inspector*]

FOEN .... Friends of the Earth - Netherlands (EAIO)

FOEP .... Friends of the Earth - Portugal (EAIO)

FOES .... Friends of the Earth - Switzerland (EAIO)

FOETRA ... Federacion de Obreros y Empleados Telefonicos de la Republica Argentina [*Federation of Telephone Workers and Employees of the Argentine Republic*] (LA)

FOEVA ..... Federacion de Obreros y Empleados Vitivinicolas y Afines [*Federation of Vineyard and Wine Industry Workers and Employees*] [*Argentina*] (LA)

FOFATUSA ... Federation of Free African Trade Unions of South Africa

F of I .... Fruit of Islam

FOFIPA..... Foibe Filankevitry ny Mpampianatra

foflo .... Fofelugyelo [*General Inspector*] (HU)

FOFTA ...... Federation Odontologique de France et des Territoires Associes [*French*] (SLS)

FOG .... Feinoptisches Werk, Goerlitz [*Goerlitz Precision Optics Plant*] (EG)

fog .... Fogaszat [*Dentistry*] (HU)

FOG .... Fougasse Flamethrower (RU)

FOGA .... Akieni [*Gabon*] [*ICAO location identifier*] (ICLI)

FOGA .... Fondo de Garantia y Apoyo a los Creditos y la Vivienda (del Banco Mexico) (LAA)

FOGA .... Fondo de Orientacion y Garantia Agricola (LAA)

FOGAGA .. Fondo de Garantia y Fomento para la Agricultura, Ganaderia, y Avicultura [*Mexico*] (EY)

FOGAMM ... Friends of the Geological and Mining Museum [*Australia*]

FOGAPE... Fonds d'Aide et de Garantie des Credits aux Petites et Moyennes Entreprises (Cameroonaises) [*Fund for Aid and Loan Guarantees for (Cameroonian) Small and Medium-Size Businesses*] (AF)

FOGB .... Booue [*Gabon*] [*ICAO location identifier*] (ICLI)

FOGE .... N'Dende [*Gabon*] [*ICAO location identifier*] (ICLI)

FOGEBA ... Fournitures Generales pour le Batiment

FOGF........ Fougamou [*Gabon*] [*ICAO location identifier*] (ICLI)

FOGG .... Mbigou [*Gabon*] [*ICAO location identifier*] (ICLI)

FOGI .... Moabi [*Gabon*] [*ICAO location identifier*] (ICLI)

FOGJ......... Ndjole [*Gabon*] [*ICAO location identifier*] (ICLI)

FOGK .... Koula-Moutou/Mabimbi [*Gabon*] [*ICAO location identifier*] (ICLI)

fogl .... Foglalkozas [*Occupation, Profession*] (HU)

FOGL .... Leconi [*Gabon*] [*ICAO location identifier*] (ICLI)

FOGM ...... Mouila [*Gabon*] [*ICAO location identifier*] (ICLI)

FOGO....... Oyem [*Gabon*] [*ICAO location identifier*] (ICLI)

FOGQ....... Okondja [*Gabon*] [*ICAO location identifier*] (ICLI)

FOGR .... Lambarene [*Gabon*] [*ICAO location identifier*] (ICLI)

FOGRA ..... Deutsche Forschungsgesellschaft fuer Druck- und Reproduktionstechnik eV [*German Research Association for Printing and Reproduction Technology*] (SLS)

FOGS........ Functioning of the GATT [*General Agreement on Tariffs and Trade*] System

FOGU....... Federacion Obrera Gastronomica de Uruguay [*Federation of Food Workers of Uruguay*] (LA)

FOGU....... Moupoupa [*Gabon*] [*ICAO location identifier*] (ICLI)

FOGV .... Minvoul [*Gabon*] [*ICAO location identifier*] (ICLI)

FOGW ...... Wonga-Wongue [*Gabon*] [*ICAO location identifier*] (ICLI)

fogy .... Fogyasztas [*Consumption*] (HU)

fohdgy ...... Fohadnagy [*First Lieutenant*] (HU)

fohg .... Foherceg [*Archduke*] (HU)

FOI .... Fruit of Islam

foig .... Foigazgato [*Inspector of Schools, Director*] (HU)

FOINSA .... Fomenta de Inversiones, Sociedad Anonima [*Investments Promotion Corp.*] [*El Salvador*]

foint.......... Fointezo [*General Manager*] (HU)

FOIQ .... Federacion Obrera de la Industria Quimica [*Chemical Workers Federation*] [*Uruguay*] (LA)

FOIS .... First Overseas Investment Services Ltd. [*Belgium*]

foisk .... Foiskola [*College, Academy*] (HU)

FOIST ...... Fondazione per lo Sviluppo e la Diffusione della Istruzione e della Cultura Scientifica e Tecnica [*Foundation for the Development and Diffusion of Instruction and Scientific and Technical Culture*] [*Italian*]

FOITAF .... Federacion Obrera de la Industria Tabaquera de Filipinas [*Workers' Federation of the Tobacco Industry of the Philippines*]

FOITAF .... Federacion Obrera de la Industria Tabaquera y Otros Trabajadores de Filipinas [*Trade union*] [*Philippines*] (EY)

FOK .... Cutting Trench Digger (RU)

fok .... Fokonyvelo [*Head Bookkeeper*] (HU)

FOK .... Foldmivesszovetkezetek Orszagos Kozpontja [*National Center of Farmers' Cooperatives*] (HU)

FOK .... Photocolorimeter (RU)

FOK .... Prague Film and Concert Orchestra

FOK .... Symfonicky Orchestr Hlavni Mesta Prahy FOK [*Prague Symphony Orchestra FOK (Film, Opera, Concert)*] (CZ)

FOKA .... Folyamszabalyozo es Kavicskotro Vallalat [*River Control and Dredging Enterprise*] (HU)

FOL .... Federacion de Obreros en Lana [*Wool Workers Federation*] [*Uruguay*] (LA)

fol .... Folha [*Sheet*] [*Publishing*] [*Portuguese*]

fol .... Folio [*Publishing*] [*French*]

fol .... Folio [*Publishing*] [*Danish/Norwegian*]

fol .... Folio [*Publishing*] [*German*]

fol .... Folio [*Publishing*] [*Afrikaans*]

fol .... Folio [*Publishing*] [*Dutch*]

fol .... Folio [*Publishing*] [*Spanish*]

FOL .... Forest Airline South Africa [*ICAO designator*] (FAAC)

FOL .... Frente Obrero de Liberacion [*Workers' Liberation Front*] [*Netherlands Antilles*] [*Political party*] (PPW)

FOLA........ Federacion Odontologica Latinoamericana [*Latin American Odontological Federation*] [*Buenos Aires*] (LAA)

FOLA........ Friends of Libraries Australia

FOL-CSO ... Australian Festivals of Light - Community Standards Organisation

foldgazd...... Foldgazdasag [*Agricultural Economics*] (HU)

foldr............ Foldrajz [*Geography*] (HU)

FOLDSZOV ... Foldmuvesszovetkezet [*Farmers' Cooperative*] (HU)

FOLDSZOVARU ... Foldmuvesszovetkezetek Arubeszerzo es Ertekesito Vallalata [*Buying and Selling Enterprise of Farmers' Cooperatives*] (HU)

foldt .... Foldtan [*Geology*] (HU)

FOLG .... Federation des Oeuvres Laiques de La Guyane [*Federation of Lay Works of Guiana*] [*French Guiana*] (LA)

folg .... Folgend [*Following*] [*German*]

Folger........ Folgerung [*Conclusion*] [*German*] (GCA)

folh .... Folheto [*Booklet*] [*Portuguese*]

follic .... Follicule [*Follicle*] [*Pharmacy*]

folyt .... Folytatas [*Continuation, Continued*] (HU)

folyt kov .... Folytatasa Kovetkezik [*To Be Continued*] (HU)

FOM .... Federation of Malaya (ML)

FoM .... Felsooktatasi Miniszterium/Miniszter [*Ministry/Minister of Higher Education*] (HU)

FOM .... Filterie et Ouate du Maroc

FOM .... Force Ouvriere Mauricienne [*Mauritian Labor Force*] (AF)

FOM .... Forces Ouvrieres Marocaines [*Moroccan Labor Forces*] (AF)

FOM .... Formation d'Officier-Marinier

FOM .... Foundation for Fundamental Research on Matter [*Netherlands*]

FOM .... France d'Outre-Mer (FLAF)

fom .... Fra Og Med [*From and With*] [*Norway*] (GPO)

FOM .... Free Officers' Movement [*Egypt*]

FOM .... Stichting voor Fundamenteel Onderzoek de Materie [*Foundation of Fundamental Research on Matter*] [*Netherlands*] (WEN)

FOMAV .... Foldmuvelesugyi Miniszterium Anyagellato Vallalata [*Supply Enterprise of the Ministry of Agriculture*] (HU)

FOMETRO ... Fonds Medical Tropical [*Tropical Medicine Fund*] (AF)

FOMEX..... Fondo para el Fomento de Exportaciones de Productos Manufacturados [*Fund for the Promotion of Exports of Manufactured Products*] [*Mexico*] (LA)

FOMGOMIAM ... Pro-Military Government Community Economic Advancement Association of Ambandrika [*Malagasy*] (AF)

FOMI .... Foldmeresi Intezet [*Institute of Geodesy*] (HU)

FOMIZ...... Federation des Ouvriers des Mines du Zaire

FOMO....... Direccion de Formacion de Mano de Obra [*Directorate for the Training of Labor*] [*Bolivia*] (LA)

FOMODA ... Fonds de Modernisation et de Developpement de l'Artisanat [*French*]

FoMRHI.... Fellowship of Makers and Researchers of Historical Instruments [*Formerly, Fellowship of Makers and Restorers of Historical Instruments*] (EA)

FOMTI...... Budapest Fovarosi Tanacs Melyepito Tervezo Vallalat [*Budapest City Council, Designing Unit in Structural Engineering*] (HU)

FOMULAC ... Fondation Medicale de l'Universite de Louvain au Congo

FON.......... Division of Social Sciences (RU)

fon .... Fonetiikka [*Phonetics*] [*Finland*]

fon .... Fonok [*Manager, Head*] (HU)

FON.......... Frente Opositor Nacional [*National Opposition Front*] [*Nicaragua*] (LA)

fon .... Phonetic, Phonetics (RU)

fon .... Phonetics (BU)
FON .... Special Division (RU)
FONADE .. Fondo Nacional de Proyectos de Desarrollo [*National Development Projects Fund*] [*Colorado*] (LA)
FONADER ... Fonds National de Developpement Rural [*National Rural Development Fund*] [*Cameroon*] (AF)
FONAFE... Fondo Nacional de Fomento Ejidal [*National Ejido Development Fund*] [*Mexico*] (LA)
FONAIAP ... Fondo Nacional de Investigaciones Agropecuarias [*National Foundation of Agricultural and Livestock Research*] [*Research center*] [*Venezuela*] (IRC)
FONALI.... Fondo para el Desarrollo del Ajonjoli [*Venezuela*] (DSCA)
FONAMES ... Fonds National Medico-Social [*National Medical and Social Fund*] [*Zaire*] (AF)
FONAPRE ... Fondo Nacional de Preinversion [*National Investment Feasibility Study Fund*] [*Ecuador*] (LA)
FONASA... Forrajera Nacional SA [*Mexico*] (DSCA)
FONASBA ... Federation of National Associations of Shipbrokers and Agents [*British*] (EAIO)
FONATUR ... Fondo Nacional de Fomento al Turismo [*Mexico*] (EY)
FONAVI.... Fondo Nacional de la Vivienda [*National Housing Fund*] [*Argentina*] (LA)
Fond .... Fondeadero [*Anchorage*] [*Spanish*] (NAU)
fond .... Foundation (BU)
fond .... Part de Fondateur [*French*]
FONDILAC ... Fondo de Desarrollo de la Industria Lactea [*Dairy Industry Development Fund*] [*Nicaragua*] (LA)
fondkom ..... Fund Committee (RU)
FONDOUTCHAD ... Fondation de l'Ouvrier Tchadien [*Chadian Worker Foundation*] (AF)
Fondre........ Fondriere [*Quagmire, Slough*] [*Military map abbreviation World War I*] [*French*] (MTD)
FONDUR .. Fondo Nacional de Desarrollo Urbano [*National Urban Development Fund*] [*Venezuela*] (LA)
FONE .... Fondo de Equipamiento Industrial [*Mexico*] (EY)
FONET...... Fonetiek [*Phonetics*] [*Afrikaans*]
FONIAP.... Fondo Nacional de Investigaciones Agropecuarias [*Venezuela*] (DSCA)
FONINVES ... Fondo de Investigaciones Petroleras [*Petroleum Research Fund*] [*Venezuela*] (LA)
FONIVA.... Federacion Obrera Nacional de la Industria del Vestido y Afines [*National Garment Workers Federation*] [*Argentina*] (LA)
FONOL..... Fonologie [*Phonology*] [*Afrikaans*]
FONPLATA ... Fondo Financiero para el Desarrollo de la Cuenca del Plata [*Financial Fund for the Development of the Plata Basin*] (EAIO)
Fontne .... Fontaine [*Fountain, Spring*] [*Military map abbreviation World War I*] [*French*] (MTD)
FONTTCYV ... Federacion Obrera Nacional de Trabajadores Textiles, del Cuero, y del Vestuario [*National Textile, Leather, and Garment Workers Federation*] [*Uruguay*] (LA)
FONUBEL ... Forum Nucleaire Belge [*Nuclear energy*] [*Belgium*] (NRCH)
FONY .... Federation of Nigerian Youth (AF)
FOO........... Numfor [*Indonesia*] [*Airport symbol*] (OAG)
FOOA .... Mouila [*Gabon*] [*ICAO location identifier*] (ICLI)
FOOB .... Bitam [*Gabon*] [*ICAO location identifier*] (ICLI)
FOOC .... Cocobeach [*Gabon*] [*ICAO location identifier*] (ICLI)
FOOD........ Moanda [*Gabon*] [*ICAO location identifier*] (ICLI)
FOOE .... Mekambo [*Gabon*] [*ICAO location identifier*] (ICLI)
FOOF .... Federacion Obrera de Organizaciones Femeniles [*Workers' Federation of Women's Organizations*] [*Mexico*] (EY)
FOOG .... Port Gentil [*Gabon*] [*ICAO location identifier*] (ICLI)
FOOH .... Omboue [*Gabon*] [*ICAO location identifier*] (ICLI)
FOOI .... Iguela [*Gabon*] [*ICAO location identifier*] (ICLI)
FOOK .... Makokou/Epassengue [*Gabon*] [*ICAO location identifier*] (ICLI)
FOOL .... Libreville/Leon M'Ba [*Gabon*] [*ICAO location identifier*] (ICLI)
FOOM .... Mitzic [*Gabon*] [*ICAO location identifier*] (ICLI)
FOON....... Franceville/Mvengue [*Gabon*] [*ICAO location identifier*] (ICLI)
FOOO....... Libreville [*Gabon*] [*ICAO location identifier*] (ICLI)
FOOR .... Lastourville [*Gabon*] [*ICAO location identifier*] (ICLI)
foorv .... Foorvos [*Chief Surgeon*] (HU)
FOOS .... Sette-Cama [*Gabon*] [*ICAO location identifier*] (ICLI)
fooszt......... Foosztaly [*Main Department*] (HU)
FOOT .... Tchibanga [*Gabon*] [*ICAO location identifier*] (ICLI)
FootscrayIT ... Footscray Institute of Technology [*Australia*]
FOOV .... Libreville [*Gabon*] [*ICAO location identifier*] (ICLI)
FOOY .... Mayumba [*Gabon*] [*ICAO location identifier*] (ICLI)
FOP .... Fokker Flight Operations [*Netherlands*] [*ICAO designator*] (FAAC)
FOP .... Friendship Oil Pipeline [*Eastern Europe*]
FOPA........ Families of Prisoners Association [*Australia*]
FOPADESC ... Pan-African Trade Union Foundation for Economic, Social, and Cultural Development
FOPERDA ... Fondation Pere Damien pour la Lutte Contre la Lepre
FOPERPIC ... Association for the Development of Further Professional Training in the Foundry and Related Industries [*France*] (PDAA)

FOPEX...... Fondo de Promocion de Exportaciones No Tradicionales [*Fund for the Promotion of Non-Traditional Exports*] [*Lima, Peru*]
FOPH .... Force Ouvriere et Paysanne d'Haiti [*Trade union*] [*Haiti*]
FOP-PT ..... Front Oubangais Patriotique - Parti du Travail [*Oubangian Patriotic Front - Party of Labor*] [*Central Africa*] (PD)
FOPRODI ... Fonds de Promotion et de Decentralisation Industrielles
FOPS .... Fair Organ Preservation Society [*British*]
FOR .... Federacion Obrera Regional [*Trade union*] [*Puerto Rican*]
FOR .... Federacion Obrera Revolucionaria [*Mexico*] (LAA)
FOR .... Fortaleza [*Brazil*] [*Airport symbol*] (OAG)
FOR .... Fortune SRL [*Italy*] [*ICAO designator*] (FAAC)
FOR .... Fundusz Oszczednosci [*or Oszczednosciowy*] Rolnictwa [*Agricultural Savings Fund*] (POL)
FORA .... Federacion Obrera Regional Argentina [*Argentine Regional Workers Federation*] (LA)
FORANGA ... Societe Forestiere de la Nyanga
FORASSOCRSSA ... Foreign Associate of the Royal Society of South Africa (AA)
FORATOM ... Forum Atomique Europeen [*Association of European Atomic Forums*] (EAIO)
FORCES ... Societe des Forces Hydroelectriques du Bas-Congo
ford............. Forditas [*Translation*] (HU)
ford............. fordito [*Translator*] (HU)
ford............. Forditotta [*Translated By*] [*Hungary*] (GPO)
ford............. Fordits [*Please Turn Page*] (HU)
FORD .... Forum for the Restoration of Democracy [*Kenya*] [*Political party*] (ECON)
fordekl........ Fordekkel [*Front Cover*] [*Publishing Danish/Norwegian*]
Forder .... Foerderung [*Production*] [*German*] (GCA)
FOREAMI ... Fonds Reine Elisabeth pour l'Assistance Medicale aux Indigenes [*Queen Elisabeth Funds for Medical Assistance to the Natives*] [*Belgium*]
foreg .... Foeregaende [*Preceding*] [*Sweden*]
FOREMAIZ ... Comite de Fomento Regional del Maiz [*Venezuela*] (DSCA)
FORENCO ... Compagnie Nouvelle de Forages Petroliers
FORESA ... Industrias Quimicas del Noroeste SA [*Spain*]
FOREX...... Forages et Exploitations Petrolieres [*Petroleum Drilling and Exploitation Company*] [*French*] (AF)
FOREX...... Foreign Exchange [*Investment term*]
FOREXI .... Societe pour la Realisation des Forages d'Exploitation en Cote-D'Ivoire
forf............. Forfattar [*or Forfattarinna*] [*Author or Authoress*] [*Sweden*] (GPO)
forf............. Forfatter [*Author*] [*Denmark*] (GPO)
FORINDI ... Societe Forestiere d'Irindi
FORIS .... Forest Resources Information System [*Global Environmental Monitoring System*]
FORIS .... Forschungs Informations System
fork............. Forkortet [*Abridged*] [*Publishing Danish/Norwegian*]
forkort .... Forkortelse [*Abbreviation*] [*Danish/Norwegian*]
forl............. Foerlag [*Publishing Firm*] [*Sweden*]
forl............. Forlag [*Publishing Firm*] [*Danish/Norwegian*]
FORLAF ... Societe Force et Lumiere Afrique
form........... Foermig [*Formed*] [*German*] (GCA)
form........... Formacao [*Formation*] [*Portuguese*]
form........... Format [*Size*] (POL)
form........... Formato [*Format*] [*Italian*]
FORMA .... Fonds d'Orientation et de Regularisation des Marches Agricoles [*Fund for the Organization and Regulation of Agricultural Markets*] [*French*] (WER)
FORMEZ ... Centro di Formazione e Studi per il Mezzogiorno [*Italian*] (SLS)
Formier ...... Formierung [*Formation*] [*German*] (GCA)
FORMINIERE ... Societe Internationale Forestiere et Miniere du Congo [*International Forestry and Mining Company of the Congo*]
FORMINIERE ... Societe Internationale Forestiere et Miniere du Zaire [*International Forestry and Mining Company of Zaire*] (AF)
Formulier ... Formulierung [*Formulation*] [*German*] (GCA)
forok.......... Foroeket [*Enlarged*] [*Publishing Danish/Norwegian*]
foromsl....... Foromslag [*Front Wrapper*] [*Publishing Danish/Norwegian*]
forp............. Outpost (RU)
FORPPA ... Fondo de Ordenacion y Regulacion de Productos y Precios Agrarios [*Spain*] (DSCA)
FORPRIDECOM ... Forest Products Research and Industries Development Commission [*Philippines*] (ARC)
FORRAD... Societa per la Formazione la Ricerca e l'Addestramento per le Aziende e le Organizzazioni SpA [*Italian*] (SLS)
FORS........ Federal Office of Road Safety [*Australia*]
fors .... Forsats [*Flyleaf*] [*Publishing Danish/Norwegian*]
FORS........ Forschungsprojekte, Raumordnung, Stadtebau, Wohnungswesen [*Regional Planning, Town Planning, Housing, Research Projects Database*] [*Fraunhofer Society*] (IID)
forsatsbl ...... Forsatsblad [*Flyleaf*] [*Publishing Danish/Norwegian*]
Forsch .... Forschung [*Research*] [*German*] (GCA)
Forschg ...... Forschung [*Research*] [*German*] (GCA)
forsk.......... Forskellig [*Different, Various*] [*Danish/Norwegian*]

forskell....... Forskellig [*Different, Various*] [*Danish/Norwegian*]
FORSZ...... Forgacsolo Szerszamok Gyara [*Cutting Tools Factory*]   (HU)
fort............. Fortepian [*Piano*] [*Poland*]
fort............. Fortitel [*Half Title*] [*Publishing Danish/Norwegian*]
FORTA...... Federacion de Organismos de Radio y Television Autonomicos [*Spain*]   (EY)
forteckn...... Foerteckning [*List*] [*Sweden*]
fortegn........ Fortegnelse [*Catalog*] [*Publishing Danish/Norwegian*]
fortgef........ Fortgefuehrt [*Continued*] [*German*]
fortges........ Fortgesetzt [*Continued*] [*German*]
FORTH ..... [*The*] Foundation for Research and Technology Hellas [*Greece*]
Fortif.......... Fortification [*Fortification*] [*Military map abbreviation World War I*] [*French*]   (MTD)
Fortpflanz .. Fortpflanzung [*Reproduction*] [*German*]   (GCA)
Forts........... Fortsetzung [*Continuation*] [*German*]   (GPO)
Fortschr ..... Fortschritt [*Progress*] [*German*]   (GCA)
FORU .... Federacion Obrera Regional Uruguaya [*Uruguayan Regional Workers Federation*]   (LA)
FORWAARD ... Foundation of Rehabilitation with Aboriginal Alcohol Related Difficulties [*Australia*]
FORWARD ... Foundation for Women's Health, Research and Development [*Ghana*]
FOS........... Federal Office of Statistics [*Nigeria*]
FOS........... Federation des Ouvriers Syndiques [*Haiti*]   (EY)
FOS........... Festival of Sydney [*Australia*]
FOS........... Focusing-Deflecting System   (RU)
FOS........... Frauenoberschule [*German*]
FOS........... French Orchid Society   (EAIO)
FOS........... Fuel Oil Surcharge
FOS........... Fundusz Odbudowy Szkol [*School Reconstruction Fund*]   (POL)
FOS........... Organophosphorus Compound   (RU)
FOSAGAMS ... Federation of South African Gem and Mineralogical Societies   (EAIO)
FOSAP-HD ... Forestiere de San Pedro-HD
FOSATU... Federation of South African Trade Unions   (AF)
FOSDA...... Fonds Special de Developpement Agricole [*Special Agricultural Development Fund*] [*Tunisia*]   (AF)
fosf .... Phosphorite Factory [*Topography*]   (RU)
fosf .... Phosphorite Mine [*Topography*]   (RU)
FOSFATOTUK ... Association of Plants and Mines of the Phosphate Fertilizers Industry   (RU)
FOSIDEC ... Fonds de Solidarite et d'Intervention pour le Developpement de la Communaute Economique de l'Afrique de l'Ouest
FOSKh....... Federation of Soviet Artists' Associations [*1930-1932*]   (RU)
FOSKOR... Fosfaatontginningskorporasie Beperk [*Phosphate Development Corporation*]
FOSONAM ... Foyer de la Solidarite Nationale Mobutu [*Mobutu National Solidarity Center*] [*Zaire*]   (AF)
FOSP........ Federation of Soviet Writers' Associations [*1926-1932*]   (RU)
FOSPED ... Fovarosi Szallitasi Vallalat [*Capital Transport Enterprise*]   (HU)
FOSS .... Federaties van Ouders van Slechthorende-en Spraakgestoorde [*Dutch Parents Organization of Hearing and Speech Impaired Children*]   (EAIO)
FOST........ Force Oceanique Strategique [*Strategic Naval Force*] [*French*]   (WER)
FOSTIS..... Food Science and Technology Information Service [*Central Food Technological Research Institute*] [*India*]
FOSVDA... Federation des Organisations et des Services Volontaires pour le Developpement en Afrique [*Zaire*]   (EAIO)
FOT......... Federacion Obrera del Transporte [*Transport Workers Federation*] [*Uruguay*]   (LA)
FOT......... Forster [*Airport symbol*]
fot .... Fotografi [*Photograph*] [*Danish/Norwegian*]
Fot............ Fotografia [*Photograph*] [*Portuguese*]
FOT.......... Fotografie [*Photography*] [*Afrikaans*]
fot .... Fotografo [*Photographer*] [*Portuguese*]
fot .... Fotografowal [*Photoghraphed By*]   (POL)
FOTAB..... Fotografske Aviobombe [*Photoflash Bomb*]   (YU)
fotan .... Fotanacsos [*Chief Councilor (of a council) or Chief Counselor*]   (HU)
FOTAV...... Fovarosi Tavfuto Muvek [*Capital City District Heating Works*]   (HU)
FOTEM..... Folklor Temsilcilik [*Folklore Presentation Organization*]   (TU)
FOTI......... Fovarosi Tervezo Intezet [*Capital Planning Institute*]   (HU)
FOTIA...... Federacion Obrera Tucumana de la Industria del Azucar [*Tucuman Sugar Industry Workers Federation*] [*Argentina*]   (LA)
fotisztv....... Fotisztviselo [*Senior Civil Servant*]   (HU)
fotitk.......... Fotitkar [*General Secretary*]   (HU)
fotobatr...... Photogrammetric Battery [*Military term*]   (BU)
FOTOCOL ... Industria Fotografica Colombiana Ltda. [*Colombia*]   (COL)
fotogr......... Fotografi [*Photograph*] [*Danish/Norwegian*]
fotogr......... Fotografia [*Photography*] [*Italian*]
fotogr......... Fotografie [*Photograph*] [*Dutch*]
Fotogr........ Fotografie [*Photograph*] [*German*]
fotokhromolitogr ... Photochromolithography   (RU)

foto kop ..... Photographic Copy   (BU)
fotokor........ Press Photographer   (RU)
fotom .... Fotomontaz [*Trick Picture*] [*Poland*]
fotooffs........ Fotooffset [*Photo-Offset*] [*Publishing*] [*Poland*]
fotorep........ Fotoreportaz [*Camera-Report*] [*Poland*]
fotoriprod ... Fotoriproduzione [*Photoreproduction*] [*Publishing*] [*Italian*]
fototip......... Phototype   (RU)
FOTP......... Friends of the Prisoners [*Australia*]
fot pl .... Photographic Plate   (RU)
FOTRA...... Federacion de Obreros del Tabaco de la Republica Argentina [*Federation of Tobacco Workers of the Argentine Republic*]   (LA)
FOTS........ Freeman Overseas Testing Services [*Australia*]
FOU.......... Fougamou [*Gabon*] [*Airport symbol*]   (OAG)
FOU.......... Frente Obrero Unido [*United Workers Front*] [*In Alicante*] [*Spanish*]   (WER)
FOUNDEX ... International Foundry Exhibition
FOUPSA ... Frente Obrero Unificado Pro-Sindicatos Autonomos [*Autonomous United Pro-Union Workers Front*] [*Dominican Republic*]   (LA)
FOV .... Federacion Obrera de Venezuela [*Trade union*] [*Venezuela*]
fov............. Fovaros [*or Fovarosi*] [*Metropolis, Capital or Metropolitan, Of the Capital*]   (HU)
fov............. Fovezerseg [*Supreme Command, General Headquarters*]   (HU)
FOV .... Friends of Opera in Victoria [*Australia*]
FOV .... Phosphoric Chemical Agent   (BU)
FOV .... Phosphororganic War Gas   (RU)
FOVI........ Fondo de Operacion y Descuento Bancario para la Vivienda (del Banco de Mexico) [*Mexico*]   (LAA)
FOVIZ...... Fovarosi Vizmuvek [*Capital Water Works*]   (HU)
Fov K........ Fovarosi Kiado [*Capital Publishing Company*]   (HU)
Fov Kvtar ... Fovarosi Konyvtar [*Metropolitan Library, Municipal Library of Budapest*]   (HU)
FOWCIS ... Forest and Wildlands Conservation Information System [*FAO*] [*United Nations*]   (DUND)
FOWU .... Foreign Organisations Workers' Union [*South Korean*]
FOX .... Jetair APS [*Denmark*] [*ICAO designator*]   (FAAC)
FOY .... Foya [*Liberia*] [*Airport symbol*]   (OAG)
FOZ .... Fucikuv Odznak Zdatnosti [*Fucik Badge of Bravery*]   (CZ)
FOZA .... Nabavljacka Zadruga Fotografskih Obrtnika [*Supply Cooperative for Photographers*]   (YU)
FP.............. Absorption Filter   (RU)
FP.............. Family Planning
FP.............. Federacion Progresista [*Spain*] [*Political party*]   (EY)
FP.............. Federal Party [*Namibia*]   (PPW)
FP.............. Federal Party [*South Africa*]   (AF)
FP.............. Federazione della Funzione Pubblica [*Italy*]   (EY)
FP.............. Ferrite Storage, Ferrite Memory   (RU)
FP.............. Festpunkt [*Reference Point*] [*German*]   (GCA)
FP.............. Filharmonie Pracujicich [*Workers' Philharmonic Orchestra*]   (CZ)
FP.............. Filmovy Prumysl [*Film Industry*]   (CZ)
FP.............. Film Polski [*Polish Motion Pictures*]   (POL)
fp .... Fin Prochain [*At the End of Next Month*] [*Business term*] [*French*]
FP.............. First Pacific Special Assets Ltd. [*Hong Kong*]
FP.............. Fiskulturno Popodne [*Physical Culture Afternoons*] [*Military*]   (YU)
FP.............. Flavoprotein   (RU)
FP.............. Flota de la Plataforma [*Insular Shelf Fishing Fleet*] [*Cuba*]   (LA)
FP.............. Folkpartiet [*Liberal Party*] [*Sweden*]   (WEN)
FP.............. Fonction de Production
FP.............. Fonction Publique [*North African*]
FP.............. Forte Piano [*Loud and Then Soft*] [*Music*]
FP.............. Franzoesisches Patent [*French Patent*] [*German*]
FP.............. Fremskridtspartiet [*Progressive Party*] [*Denmark*]   (WEN)
FP.............. Fremskrittspartiet [*Progress Party*] [*Norway*] [*Political party*]   (PPE)
FP.............. Front Populaire [*Burkina Faso*] [*Political party*]   (EY)
FP.............. Fuerzas Populares [*Popular Forces*] [*Peru*]   (LA)
FP.............. Function Converter   (RU)
FP.............. Fundacio per la Pau [*Foundation for Peace*] [*Spain*]   (EAIO)
FP.............. Fundusz Posmiertny [*Death Benefit Fund*]   (POL)
Fp.............. Fusee Percutante [*Percussion-Fuse*] [*French*]   (MTD)
Fp.............. Fusionspunkt [*Melting Point*] [*German*]   (GCA)
FP.............. Petryanov Filter   (RU)
FP.............. Phosphoprotein   (RU)
FP.............. Photopyrometer   (RU)
f-p.............. Piano   (RU)
FP-25 .... People's Forces of 25 April [*Portugal*]   (PD)
FP-31 .... Frente Popular 31 de Enero [*31st January Popular Front*] [*Guatemala*]   (PD)
FPA........... Fabrique de Peintures en Afrique
FPA........... Feature Protection Area [*Conservation*] [*Australia*]
FPA........... Federal Party of Australia [*Political party*]
FPA........... Federation de la Propriete Agricole [*France*]   (DSCA)

FPA............ Fertilizer and Pesticide Authority [*Ministry of Agriculture*] [*Philippines*]
FPA............ Fire Protection Association [*Australia*]
FPA............ Forest Products Association [*Guyana*]   (LA)
FPA............ Forests Production Association [*Australia*]
FPA............ Formacion Professional Acelerada [*Center for the Accelerated Training of Craftsmen*] [*Spain*]   (PDAA)
FPA............ Formation Professionnelle des Adultes [*Adult Vocational Training*] [*French*]   (AF)
FPA............ Fovarosi Penzalap [*Capital Monetary Fund*]   (HU)
FPA............ France-Palestine Association   (EAIO)
FPA............ Frente Politico Anticomunista [*Anticommunist Political Front*] [*El Salvador*]   (LA)
FPA............ Petryanov Analytical Filter   (RU)
FPAA........ Family Planning Association of Australia   (ADA)
FPAA........ Federacion Panamericana de Asociaciones de Arquitectos [*Panamerican Federation of Architects' Associations*]   (EA)
FPAACT.... Family Planning Association of the Australian Capital Territory
FPAB........ Family Planning Association of Bangladesh   (EAIO)
FPAD........ Fret Payable a Destination [*Freight Payable at Destination*] [*French*] [*Business term*]
FPAK........ Family Planning Association of Kenya
FPAL......... Family Planning Association of Liberia   (EAIO)
FPANSW .. Family Planning Association of New South Wales [*Australia*]
f paral........ Forma Paralela [*Portuguese*]
FPASA ...... Fire Protection Association of Southern Africa   (EAIO)
FPB........... Federacao Portuguesa de Badminton [*Portuguese Badminton Federation*]   (EAIO)
FPB........... Federacion Peruana de Bochas [*Peru Bocce Federation*]   (EAIO)
FPBAI....... Federation of Publishers and Booksellers Association in India   (PDAA)
FPBAI....... Federation of Publishers and Booksellers Associations of India
FPBS.......... Fundacion Pro-Bienestar Social [*Colombia*]   (DSCA)
FPC........... Farsi Petroleum Company [*Iran*]   (ME)
FPC........... Federal Pacifist Council [*Australia*]
FPC........... Federal Power Commission   (OMWE)
FPC........... First Pacific Co. [*Asia*]
FPC........... Food Production Corporation [*Accra, Ghana*]
FPC........... Forest Products Council [*Western Australia*]
FPC........... Frente Popular Costarricense [*Costa Rican Popular Front*] [*Political party*]   (PPW)
FPCA .... Federation of Parents and Citizens Associations [*Australia*]
FPCANSW ... Federation of Parents and Citizens' Associations of New South Wales [*Australia*]
FPCC .... Federal Potato Co-ordinating Committee [*Australia*]
FPCCB...... Fabrica de Preparate si Conserve de Carne Bucuresti [*Bucharest Factory for Canned and Preserved Meat*]   (RO)
FPCCI....... Federation of Pakistan Chambers of Commerce and Industry   (ECON)
FPCR .... Fronte Popolare Comunista Rivoluzionario [*Revolutionary Communist Popular Front*] [*Italian*]   (WER)
FPD........... Federacion Popular Democratica [*Popular Democratic Federation*] [*Spain*] [*Political party*]   (PPE)
FPDA........ Five Power Defense Arrangement [*Singapore, Malaysia, Britain, Australia, and New Zealand*]   (ML)
FPDC........ Food Products Development Centre [*Bangladesh*] [*Research center*]   (IRC)
FPDL........ Federacion de Partidos Democraticas y Liberales [*Federation of Democratic and Liberal Parties*] [*Spain*] [*Political party*]   (PPE)
FPDMA...... [*The*] Flush Panel Door Manufacturers Association of Southern Africa   (AA)
FPDT........ Federal Police Disciplinary Tribunal [*Australia*]
FPE........... Federation of Professional Employees [*Proposed*] [*Australia*]
FPE........... Federation Professionnelle des Producteurs et Distributeurs d'Electricite de Belgique [*Belgium*]   (BAS)
FPEP .... Foititiki Pnevmatiki Estia Peiraios [*Piraeus Spiritual Home for Students*]   (GC)
FPF .... Federacion Peruana de Futbol [*Peruvian Soccer Federation*]   (LA)
FPFWF...... Finnish Population and Family Welfare Federation   (EAIO)
FPG........... Absorption Filter   (RU)
FPG........... Aeroleasing SA [*Switzerland*] [*ICAO designator*]   (FAAC)
FPG........... Fabrique de Peintures au Gabon
FPG........... Fischerei-Produktionsgenossenschaft [*Fishing Production Cooperative*]   (EG)
FPG........... Fundusz Pomocy Gospodarczej [*Economic Aid Fund*]   (POL)
FPH .... First Pacific Holdings [*Bank*] [*Hong Kong*]
FPH .... Frente Patriotico Hondureno [*Honduran Patriotic Front*] [*Political party*]   (PD)
FPHC........ First Philippine Holdings Corp.
FPHNH..... Federation of Private Hospitals and Nursing Homes [*Australia*]
FPI .... Federazione Pubblico Impiego [*Civil Service Federation*] [*San Marino*]   (EAIO)
FPI .... Financement du Plan Informatique [*French*]   (ADPT)
FPI .... Forest Products Institute

FPI .... Fraccion Popular Independiente [*People's Independent Faction*] [*Venezuela*]   (LA)
FPI .... Front Populaire Ivoirien [*Ivorian Popular Front*] [*The Ivory Coast*] [*Political party*]   (EY)
FPIA .... Family Planning International Assistance
FPIA .... Fellow of the Plastics Institute of Australia   (ADA)
FPIAA ...... Fire Protection Industry Association of Australia
FPIB .... Forest Products Inspection Bureau [*Ghana*]
FPIC .... Fuel and Power Industries Committee [*British*]   (DCTA)
FPIKP....... Frente Patriotica para a Independencia do Kongo Portugues
FPIKP....... Front Patriotique pour l'Independance du Kongo Dit Portugais
FPIP .... Federation Professionnelle Independant de la Police Nationale [*French*]
FPITC....... Food Processing Industry Training Council [*Australia*]
FPiU .... Fabryka Przyrzadow i Uchwytow [*Tool and Fixture Factory*]   (POL)
FPJ .... Front Patriotique de la Jeunesse
FPJU .... Fonds Special pour la Jeunesse de l'UNESCO [*UNESCO Special Fund for Youth*]   (EAIO)
FPK........... Francuska Partia Komunistyczna [*French Communist Party*]   (POL)
FPK........... Phosphopyruvic Acid   (RU)
FPL........... Fatherland Party of Labor [*Bulgaria*] [*Political party*]
FPL........... Forces Populaires de Liberation [*People's Liberation Forces*] [*Chad*]   (AF)
FPL........... Frente Popular de Liberacion, Nueve de Mayo [*Honduras*] [*Political party*]   (EY)
FPL........... Frente Portugal Livre
FPL........... Fuerzas Populares de Liberacion [*Popular Liberation Forces*] [*El Salvador*]   (LA)
FPL........... Fuerzas Populares de Liberacion Farabundo Marti [*Farabundo Marti Popular Liberation Forces*] [*El Salvador*]   (PD)
FPLD........ Popular Front for the Liberation of Djibouti   (AF)
FPLE .... Fronte Popolare di Liberazione Eritreo [*Eritrean People's Liberation Front*] [*Use EPLF Ethiopia*]
FPLE .... Front Populaire de Liberation de l'Erythree [*Eritrean People's Liberation Front*] [*Use EPLF Ethiopia*]   (AF)
FPL-FMLN ... Popular Liberation Forces - Farabundo Marti National Liberation Front [*El Salvador*]
FPLGAO ... Front Populaire pour la Liberation du Golfe Arabe Occupe
FPLM .... Forcas Populares para a Libertacao do Mocambique [*Popular Forces for the Liberation of Mozambique*]   (AF)
FPLN........ Frente Patriotica de Libertacao Nacional [*National Liberation Patriotic Front*] [*Portuguese*]   (WER)
FPLN........ Frente Patriotico de Liberacion Nacional [*National Liberation Patriotic Front*] [*Colorado*]   (LA)
FPLN........ Frente Portuguesa de Libertacao Nacional
Fplo........... Fahrplananordnungen [*Train Schedule Orders*]   (EG)
FPLP......... Federal Parliamentary Labour Party [*Australia*]
FPLP......... Frente Patriotico de Libertacao de Portugal [*Patriotic Front for the Liberation of Portugal*] [*Political party*]   (PPE)
FPLP......... Front Populaire pour la Liberation de la Palestine [*Popular Front for the Liberation of Palestine*] [*French*]   (WER)
FPLT .... Front Populaire de Liberation du Tchad [*Popular Front for the Liberation of Chad*]   (AF)
FPLT .... Front Populaire de Liberation du Tigre [*Tigre People's Liberation Front*] [*Use TPLF*]   (AF)
Fpm............ Fachverband Pulvermetallurgie [*Powder Metallurgy Department*]   (SLS)
FPM.......... Federation Patronale Monegasque [*Employers' Federation of Monaco*]   (EY)
FPM....... First Pacific Mortgage Ltd. [*Australia*]
FPM.......... Fratres Presentationis Mariae [*Presentation Brothers - PB*]   (EAIO)
FPM.......... Free Papau Movement [*Indonesia*] [*Political party*]
FPM.......... Photo- and Transparency Meter   (RU)
FPMA........ Fiangonana Protestanta Malagasy aty Andafy [*Malagasy Protestant Church in France*]   (AF)
FPMF .... Foundation for the Promotion of Music in Finland   (EAIO)
FPMPI....... French Education Museum in Plovdiv   (BU)
FPMR........ Frente Patriotico Manuel Rodriguez [*Manuel Rodriguez Patriotic Front*] [*Chile*] [*Political party*]
FPMT .... Fund for the Preservation of the Mahyana Tradition [*An association*]
FPN .... Falange Patria Nova [*New Fatherland Phalange*] [*Brazil*]   (PD)
FPN .... Forces de Police Nationale
FPN .... Frente Patriotico Nacional [*National Patriotic Front*] [*Nicaragua*] [*Political party*]   (PPW)
FPN .... Frente Popular Nacionalista [*Nationalist Popular Front*] [*Bolivia*]   (LA)
FPNCD...... Federation Patronale de Nouvelle-Caledonie et Dependances [*New Caledonia*]   (EAIO)
FPNR........ Photosynthetic Pyridine Nucleotide Reductase   (RU)
FPO........... Financne Planovaci Odbor [*Budget Planning Branch*]   (CZ)
FPO .... Freeport [*Bahamas*] [*Airport symbol*]   (OAG)
FPO .... Freiheitliche Partei Oesterreichs [*Liberal Party of Austria (or Austrian Freedom Party)*] [*Political party*]   (PPW)

FPO .... Front Patriotique Oubanguien [*Ubangi People's Patriotic Front*] [*Central African Republic*]   (AF)

FPO .... Fuerza Popular Organizada [*Organized Popular Force*] [*Guatemala*] [*Political party*]   (PPW)

FPOe .... Freiheitliche Partei Oesterreichs [*Liberal Party of Austria (or Austrian Freedom Party)*]   (WEN)

FPOLISARIO ... Frente Popular para la Liberacion de Saguia El Hamra y Rio De Oro [*Popular Front for the Liberation of Saguia El Hamra and Rio De Oro*] [*Use POLISARIO Front*]   (AF)

FPO-PT ..... Front Patriotique Oubanguien-Parti du Travail [*Political party*] [*Central African Republic*]

FPOS .... Federacja Polskich Organizacji Studenckich [*Federation of Polish Students' Organizations*]   (POL)

FPP .... Federacion de Periodistas de Peru [*Peruvian Federation of Journalists*]   (LA)

FPP .... Panama Public Forces

FPPA .... Finnish Power Plant Association   (EAIO)

FPPA .... Foster Parents Plan of Australia

FPPA .... Porto Alegre [*Sao Tome*] [*ICAO location identifier*]   (ICLI)

FPPB .... Federatie van de Periodieke pers van Belgie [*Press association*] [*Belgium*]   (EY)

FPPB .... Federation de la Presse Periodique de Belgique [*Press association*] [*Belgium*]   (EY)

FPPR .... Principe [*Principe*] [*ICAO location identifier*]   (ICLI)

FPPS .... Front Progressiste du Peuple Seychellois [*Seychelles People's Progressive Front*] [*Use SPPF*]   (AF)

FPPTE ...... Federation of Public Passenger Transport Employees [*British*]   (DCTA)

FPr .... Filosofski Pregled [*Philosophy Review*] [*A periodical*]   (BU)

FPR .... Fonds Projets Ruraux

FPR .... Frente Patriotico para la Revolucion [*Patriotic Front for the Revolution*] [*Nicaragua*] [*Political party*]   (PPW)

FPR .... Frente Popular Contra la Represion [*Popular Front Against Repression*] [*Honduras*] [*Political party*]   (PD)

FPR .... Fuerza Aerea del Peru [*ICAO designator*]   (FAAC)

FPR .... Fuerzas Populares Revolucionarias Lorenzo Zelaya [*Lorenzo Zelaya Popular Revolutionary Forces*] [*Honduras*] [*Political party*]   (PD)

FPR .... Nordic Science Policy Council [*Denmark*]   (EAIO)

FPRD .... Forest Products Research Division [*Thai*] [*Research center*]   (IRC)

FPRDI .... Forest Products Research and Development Institute [*Philippines*] [*Research center*]   (IRC)

FPRI .... Forest Products Research Institute [*Ghana*]   (AF)

FPRI(Aust) ... Fellow of the Public Relations Institute of Australia   (ADA)

FPRISA ..... Fellow of the Public Relations Institute of Southern Africa   (AA)

FPS .... Factor de Proteccion Contra el Sol [*Spanish*]

FPS .... Federacion de Partidos Socialistas [*Federation of Socialist Parties*] [*Spanish*]   (WER)

FPS .... Filmovy Poradni Sbor [*Motion Picture Advisory Board*]   (CZ)

FPS .... Floor Price Scheme [*Wool sales*] [*Australia*]

FPS .... Forests Protection Society [*Australia*]

FPS .... Francophone Primatological Society [*See also SFDP*] [*Plelan Le Grand, France*]   (EAIO)

FPS .... Front Populaire Soudanais

FPS .... Photoelectric Device for the Measuring of Scattering of Light   (RU)

FPS .... Underwater Sports Federation   (RU)

FPSB .... Federation of Performance Sheep Breeders [*Australia*]

FPSC .... Federal Public Service Commission

FPSC .... Forum Public Speaking Clubs [*Australia*]

FPSG .... Food Processors and Suppliers Group [*Ireland*]   (EAIO)

F(PS)G ...... Forum (Public Speaking) Group [*Australia*]

FPSP .... Food Production Support Programme [*Gambia*]

FPSSA .... Fellow of the Pharmaceutical Society of South Africa   (AA)

FPST .... Sao Tome [*Sao Tome*] [*ICAO location identifier*]   (ICLI)

FPSTR ...... Fund to Promote Scientific and Technical Research [*Burkina Faso*]   (EAIO)

FPSZ .... Fovarosi Pedagogiai Szeminarium [*Capital Seminary for Advanced Teacher Training*]   (HU)

FPT .... Federacao Portuguesa de Tenis [*Portuguese Tennis Federation*]   (EAIO)

FPT .... Federace Proletarske Telovychovy [*Proletarian Physical Education Federation*]   (CZ)

FPT .... Federazione Poste e Telecomunicazioni [*Italy*]   (EY)

FPT .... Fondo de Promocion Turistica [*Tourism Promotion Fund*] [*Peru*]   (LA)

FPT .... Fundusz Postepu Technicznego [*Fund for the Advancement of Technology*] [*Poland*]

FPTG .... Federacion Provincial de Trabajadores de Guayas [*Guayas Provincial Workers Federation*] [*Ecuador*]   (LA)

FPTM .... Federatsiia Profsoiuzov Trudiashchikhsia Madagaskara

FPTU .... Federation of Progressive Trade Unions [*Tanzania*]   (AF)

FPTUL ...... Federation of Petroleum Trade Unions in Lebanon   (ME)

FPU .... Actual Track Angle   (RU)

FPU .... Finnish Painters' Union   (EAIO)

FPU .... Folkepartiets Ungdomsforbund [*Liberal Youth*] [*Political party*]   (EAIO)

FPU .... Folkpartiets Ungdomsforbund [*Liberal Youth Association*] [*Sweden*]   (WEN)

FPU .... Food Preservers' Union of Australia

FPU .... Frente del Pueblo Unido [*Bolivia*] [*Political party*]   (EY)

FPU .... Small Size Absorption Filter   (RU)

FPUA .... Food Preservers' Union of Australia

FPUP .... Front Populaire pour l'Unite et la Paix

FPUWA ...... Food Preservers' Union of Western Australia

FPV .... Federation of Vietnamese Trade Unions [*North Vietnamese*]   (RU)

FPV .... French Polydor Variable Micrograde [*Record label*]

FPV .... Front Progressiste Voltaique [*Upper Volta Progressive Front*] [*Political party*]   (PPW)

FPVN .... Vila Das Neves [*Sao Tome*] [*ICAO location identifier*]   (ICLI)

FPWSAC... Fluoridation of Public Water Supplies Advisory Committee [*New South Wales, Australia*]

FQAG .... Angoche [*Mozambique*] [*ICAO location identifier*]   (ICLI)

FQBE .... Beira [*Mozambique*] [*ICAO location identifier*]   (ICLI)

FQBI .... Bilene [*Mozambique*] [*ICAO location identifier*]   (ICLI)

FQBR .... Beira [*Mozambique*] [*ICAO location identifier*]   (ICLI)

FQCB .... Cuamba [*Mozambique*] [*ICAO location identifier*]   (ICLI)

FQCH .... Chimoio [*Mozambique*] [*ICAO location identifier*]   (ICLI)

FQES .... Estima [*Mozambique*] [*ICAO location identifier*]   (ICLI)

FQFU .... Furancungo [*Mozambique*] [*ICAO location identifier*]   (ICLI)

FQIA .... Inhaca [*Mozambique*] [*ICAO location identifier*]   (ICLI)

FQIN .... Inhambane [*Mozambique*] [*ICAO location identifier*]   (ICLI)

FQLC .... Lichinga [*Mozambique*] [*ICAO location identifier*]   (ICLI)

FQLU .... Lumbo [*Mozambique*] [*ICAO location identifier*]   (ICLI)

FQMA ...... Maputo [*Mozambique*] [*ICAO location identifier*]   (ICLI)

FQMD .... Mueda [*Mozambique*] [*ICAO location identifier*]   (ICLI)

FQMP .... Mocimboa Da Praia [*Mozambique*] [*ICAO location identifier*]   (ICLI)

FQMR ...... Marrupa [*Mozambique*] [*ICAO location identifier*]   (ICLI)

FQMU ...... Mutarara [*Mozambique*] [*ICAO location identifier*]   (ICLI)

FQNC ...... Nacala [*Mozambique*] [*ICAO location identifier*]   (ICLI)

FQNP .... Nampula [*Mozambique*] [*ICAO location identifier*]   (ICLI)

FQPB .... Pemba [*Mozambique*] [*ICAO location identifier*]   (ICLI)

FQPO .... Ponta Do Ouro [*Mozambique*] [*ICAO location identifier*]   (ICLI)

FQQL .... Quelimane [*Mozambique*] [*ICAO location identifier*]   (ICLI)

FQSG .... Songo [*Mozambique*] [*ICAO location identifier*]   (ICLI)

FQTE .... Tete [*Mozambique*] [*ICAO location identifier*]   (ICLI)

FQTT .... Tete/Chingozi [*Mozambique*] [*ICAO location identifier*]   (ICLI)

Fque .... Fabrique [*Factory*] [*Business term*] [*French*]

FQUG .... Ulongwe [*Mozambique*] [*ICAO location identifier*]   (ICLI)

FQVL .... Vilanculos [*Mozambique*] [*ICAO location identifier*]   (ICLI)

FQXA ...... Xai-Xai [*Mozambique*] [*ICAO location identifier*]   (ICLI)

fr .... Faire Reporter [*Carry Over*] [*Stock exchange term*] [*French*]

Fr .... Father   (EECI)

fr .... Forager   (BU)

FR .... Forstrat [*Forest*] [*German*]

Fr .... Four [*Furnace*] [*Military map abbreviation World War I*] [*French*]   (MTD)

fr .... Fraai [*Handsome*] [*Netherlands*]

fr .... Fraemre [*Front*] [*Publishing*] [*Sweden*]

fr .... Fraesch [*Clean*] [*Sweden*]

fr .... Fran [*From*] [*Sweden*]

fr .... Franc [*French*]   (GPO)

Fr .... Francais [*French*]   (TPFD)

FR .... Franc du Ruanda

FR .... France [*ANSI two-letter standard code*]   (CNC)

fr .... Frances [*French*] [*Spanish*]

fr .... Frances [*French*] [*Portuguese*]

fr .... Francese [*French*] [*Italian*]

fr .... Francia [*French*]   (HU)

Fr .... Francio [*Francium*] [*Chemical element*] [*Portuguese*]

fr .... Franco [*Frank*] [*Portuguese*]

fr .... Frangi [*or Frangia*] [*Finland*]

Fr .... Frank [*or Franki*] [*Franc or Francs*] [*Poland*]

fr .... Frank [*Franc*] [*Monetary unit*] [*Afrikaans*]

fr .... Franko [*Postpaid*] [*German*]

Fr .... Frankryk [*France*] [*Afrikaans*]

Fr .... Frans [*French*] [*Afrikaans*]

fr .... Fransizca [*French*]   (TU)

Fr .... Frau [*Madam*] [*German*]

Fr .... Fray [*or Frey*] [*Friar*] [*Spanish*]

fr .... Fregi [*Decorations, Ornaments*] [*Publishing*] [*Italian*]

Fr .... Frei [*Friar*] [*Portuguese*]

fr .... Frei [*Free*] [*German*]

Fr .... French   (TPFD)

Fr .... Frere [*Brother*] [*French*]

fr .... Friblad [*Flyleaf*] [*Publishing Danish/Norwegian*]

fr .... Frontispizio [*Frontispiece*] [*Publishing*] [*Italian*]

FR .... Frosinone [*Car registration plates*] [*Italy*]

FR .... Fuerza Republicana [*Argentina*] [*Political party*]   (EY)

FR .... Hovedorganisation for Arbejdsleder och Tekniske Funktionaerforeninge r i Danm ark [*Confederation of Supervisors and Technicians in Denmark*]   (EAIO)

f-r .... Medical Assistant   (RU)

FR .... Physical Workers   (BU)

FR₃ .... France Regions₃ [*French*]

FRA .... Fabrika Rezanog Alata [*Cutting Tools Factory*] [*Cacak*]   (YU)

fra .... Factura [*Invoice of Merchandise*] [*Spanish*]

FRA .... Faculte de Resiliation Annuelle [*French*]

FRA .... Federation des Republiques Arabes [*North African*]

FRA .... Fondo de Refinanciamiento Agropecuario [*Agricultural and Livestock Refinancing Fund*] [*Bolivia*]   (LA)

FRA .... Forces Royales Air

FRA .... France [*ANSI three-letter standard code*]   (CNC)

FRA .... France-Reunion-Avenir [*Political party*]   (EY)

FRA .... Frankfurt [*Germany*] [*Airport symbol*]   (OAG)

FRA .... Frente Radical Alfarista [*Radical Alfarista Front*] [*Ecuador*] [*Political party*]   (PPW)

FRA .... Front de Resistance d'Angola [*Angola Resistance Front*]   (AF)

FRAB .... Banque Franco-Arabe d'Investissements Internationaux [*Inter-Arab*]   (ME)

FRAC .... Formation Rationnelle Acceleree de Chauffeurs [*Algeria*]

FRAC .... Frente Revolucionario de Afirmacion Civil [*Mexico*]   (LAA)

FRACDS ... Fellow of the Royal Australian College of Dental Surgeons   (ADA)

FRACGP ... Fellow of the Royal Australian College of General Practitioners   (ADA)

FRACI .... Fellow of the Royal Australian Chemical Institute [*Formerly, FACI*]

FRACMA ... Fellow of the Royal Australian College of Medical Administrators

FRACOG... Fellow of the Royal Australian College of Obstetricians and Gynaecologists

FRACP ...... Fellow of the Royal Australasian College of Physicians   (ADA)

FRACS ...... Fellow of the Royal Australasian College of Surgeons   (ADA)

FRADE ...... Frigorifico Avicola de Descalvado SA [*Brazil*]   (DSCA)

FRAE .... Istituto di Fotochimica e Radiazioni d'Alta Energia [*Institute of Photochemistry and High Energy Radiation*] [*Italy*]   (IRC)

FRAES ...... Fellow of the Royal Aeronautical Society [*South Africa*]   (AA)

FRAFH ...... Magyar Ellenallok Antifasisztak Szovetsege/Measz [*Hungarian Federation of Resisters and Anti-Fascists*]   (EAIO)

fragm .... Fragment [*Fragment*] [*Poland*]

FRAHS ...... Fellow of the Royal Australian Historical Society   (ADA)

FRAIA .... Fellow of the Royal Australian Institute of Architects   (ADA)

FRAIN .... Front Revolutionnaire Africain pour l'Independance Nationale des Colonies Portugaises [*African Revolutionary Front for the National Independence of the Portuguese Colonies*]   (AF)

FRAIPA ..... Fellow of the Royal Australian Institute of Public Administration

FRAIPR ..... Fellow of the Royal Australian Institute of Parks and Recreation

Frakt .... Fraktion [*Fraction*] [*German*]   (GCA)

frakt .... Fraktionieren [*To Fractionate*] [*German*]   (GCA)

frakt .... Fraktioniert [*Fractionated*] [*German*]

Fraktionier ... Fraktionierung [*Fractionation*] [*German*]   (GCA)

FRAM .... Fraternite Franco-Africaine et Malgache

FRAMATOME ... Societe Franco Americaine de Constructions Atomiques [*Franco-American Atomic Construction Co.*] [*French*]   (WER)

FRAMPO ... Frente Amplio Popular [*Broad Popular Front*] [*Panama*] [*Political party*]   (PPW)

FRAN .... Frente Renovador de Accion Nacional [*National Action Renovating Front*] [*Ecuador*]   (LA)

franc .... Francuski [*French*]   (POL)

FRANCAREP ... Compagnie Franco-Africaine de Recherches Petrolieres

FRANCEVIN ... Societe les Bons Vins de France

FRANCIS ... Fichier de Recherches Automatisees sur les Nouvautes, la Communication et l'Information en Sciences Sociales et Humaines [*French Retrieval Automated Network for Current Information in Social and Human Sciences*] [*Database*]

FRANS ...... Family Resource and Network Support [*Australia*]

FRANSW .. Food Retailers' Association of New South Wales [*Australia*]

FRANSW .. Footwear Repairers' Association of New South Wales [*Australia*]

FRANTIR ... France Explosifs

Franz .... Franzoesisch [*French*] [*German*]

FRANZCP ... Fellow of the Royal Australian and New Zealand College of Psychiatrists   (ADA)

FRAP .... Frente de Accion Popular [*Chile*]   (LAA)

FRAP .... Frente Revolucionaria Anti-Facista e Patriota [*Revolutionary Antifascist and Patriotic Front*] [*Portuguese*]   (WER)

FRAP .... Frente Revolucionario Antifascista y Patriota [*Revolutionary Antifascist and Patriotic Front*] [*Spanish*]   (WER)

FRAP .... Frente Revolucionario de Accion Popular [*People's Action Revolutionary Front*] [*Spanish*]   (WER)

FRAP .... Front Revolutionnaire d'Action Proletarienne [*Terrorist organization*] [*Belgium*]   (EY)

FRAP .... Fuerzas Revolucionarias Armadas Populares [*People's Revolutionary Armed Forces*] [*Mexico*]   (PD)

FRAP .... Fuerzas Revolucionarias Armadas Populares [*People's Revolutionary Armed Forces*] [*El Salvador*]   (LA)

FRAPAR ... Front Anticolonialiste pour l'Autodetermination de la Reunion [*Anti-Colonialist Front for the Self-Determination of Reunion*]   (AF)

FRAPH ...... Front for the Advancement and Progress of Haiti [*Political party*]

FRAPI .... Fellow of the Royal Australian Planning Institute   (ADA)

FRAQ .... Footwear Repairers' Association of Queensland [*Australia*]

FRAR .... Fonds Regional d'Amenagement Rural [*Regional Rural Development Fund*]   (AF)

FRAS .... Fuerzas Revolucionarias Antiimperialistas por el Socialismo [*Anti-Imperialist Revolutionary Forces for Socialism*] [*Peru*]   (LA)

FRASA ...... Footwear Repairers' Association of South Australia

Frat .... Fratello [*Brother*] [*Italian*]

FRAT .... Fraternize   (DSUE)

FRAT .... Tanzania Football Referee Association

FRAUL ...... Movimento Nacional de Fraternidade Ultramarina [*National Movement of Overseas Fraternity*] [*Portuguese*]   (WER)

FRAV .... Footwear Repairers' Association of Victoria [*Australia*]

FRAWA ..... Footwear Repairers' Association of Western Australia

FRAWUA ... Federated Rubber and Allied Workers Union of Australia

fraz .... Frazione [*Ward*] [*In addresses*] [*Italian*]   (CED)

fr b .... Belga Frank [*Belgian Franc*]   (HU)

FRB .... Fair Rents Board [*New South Wales, Australia*]

FRB .... Federation Routiere Belge [*Belgium*]   (SLS)

FRB .... Forbes [*Australia*] [*Airport symbol*]   (OAG)

FRB .... Forschungs-Reaktor Berlin [*Nuclear energy*]   (NRCH)

FRB .... Fuerza Revolucionaria Barrientista [*Barrientist Revolutionary Force*] [*Bolivia*]   (LA)

frbl .... Farblos [*Colorless*] [*German*]

frbl .... Friblad [*Flyleaf*] [*Publishing Danish/Norwegian*]

FRC .... Fatah Revolutionary Council [*Libyan-based terrorist organization*]

FRC .... Folk Research Centre [*Saint Lucia*]   (EAIO)

FRC .... Forest Resources Committee [*Australia*]

FRC .... Forestry Research Center [*Malaysia*]   (IRC)

FRC .... Franca [*Brazil*] [*Airport symbol*]   (OAG)

FR CAN .... French-Canadian   (WDAA)

FRCF .... Fonds de la Recherche Fondamentale Collective [*Fund for Collective Fundamental Research*] [*Fonds National de la Recherche Scientifique*] [*Belgium*] [*Research center*]   (EAS)

FRCN .... Federal Radio Corporation of Nigeria [*Kaduna*]

FRCNA ...... Fellow of the Royal College of Nursing, Australia

FRCPA ...... Fellow of the Royal College of Pathologists of Australia   (ADA)

FRCPsych ... Fellow of the Royal College of Psychiatrists [*Australia*]

FRCSA ...... Furniture Retailers Council of South Australia

FRCV .... Furniture Retailers' Council of Victoria [*Australia*]

FRClwthS .. Fellow of the Royal Commonwealth Society

FRD .... Foundation for Research Development [*South Africa*]

FRD .... Frente de Resistencia Democratica [*Democratic Resistance Front*] [*Costa Rica*]   (LA)

FRD .... Frente Revolucionario Democratico [*Democratic Revolutionary Front*] [*El Salvador*]   (LA)

FRD .... Photon Jet Engine   (RU)

FRD .... Record of All Workers' Activities during a Working Day   (RU)

FRDA .... Fisheries Research and Development Agency [*Korean*]   (MSC)

FRDC .... Forest Research and Development Center [*Indonesia*] [*Research center*]   (IRC)

FrDF .... Fructose Diphosphate   (RU)

Frdl .... Freundlich [*Kind, Kindly*] [*German*]   (EG)

FRDMO .... Federalni Rada Detskych a Mladeznickych Organizaci [*Federal Council of Children's and Youth Organizations*]   (CZ)

FRE .... Aviation Services Ltd. [*Guam*] [*ICAO designator*]   (FAAC)

FRE .... Facture [*Invoice*] [*Business term*] [*French*]

FRE .... Fera Island [*Solomon Islands*] [*Airport symbol*]   (OAG)

FRE .... Folkecenter for Renewable Energy [*Denmark*]   (EAIO)

FRE .... Frente Revolucionario Estudiantil [*Revolutionary Student Front*] [*Guatemala*]   (LA)

FREB .... Finnish Real Estate Bank Ltd.

FREC .... Forestry Research and Education Centre [*Sudan*]

FRECILINA ... Frente Civico de Liberacion Nacional [*Civic Front for National Liberation*] [*FCLN*] [*Also,*] [*Argentina*]   (LA)

FRECOMO ... Frente Comun de Mocambique

FRECSA ..... Frigorifica Ecuatoriana [*Ecuadorean Packing Plant*]   (LA)

FRED .... Frente Revolucionario Estudiantil Democratico [*Democratic Student Revolutionary Front*] [*Venezuela*]   (LA)

FREDEMO ... Frente Democratico [*Peru*] [*Political party*]   (EY)

FREE .... Fondation Republicaine pour les Etudes a l'Etranger [*Republican Foundation for Study Abroad*] [*Cambodia*]   (CL)

FREE .... Friends of Refugees of Eastern Europe [*Australia*]

FREEGOLD ... Free State Consolidated Gold Mines [*South Africa*]

FREI .... Fellow of the Real Estate and Stock Institute of Australia   (ADA)

FREI .... Fellow of the Real Estate Institute [*Australia*]

FREI......... Forest Research and Education Institute [*Sudan*]   (PDAA)

FREIA .... Fellow of the Real Estate Institute of Australia

Freibl......... Freibleibend [*Optional*] [*Business term*] [*German*]

Freisetz...... Freisetzung [*Liberation*] [*German*]   (GCA)

Freiw.......... Freiwilliger [*Volunteer*] [*German*]   (GCA)

FREJULI .. Frente Justicialista de Liberacion [*Justicialista Liberation Front*] [*Argentina*]   (LA)

FRELIFER ... Front de Liberation de Fernando Poo [*Fernando Poo Liberation Front*] [*Equatorial Guinea*]   (AF)

FRELIGE.. Frente de Liberacion de Guinea Ecuatorial

FRELIMO ... Frente da Libertacao de Mocambique [*Mozambique Liberation Front*] [*Political party*]   (PPW)

FRELINA ... Frente de Liberacion Nacional [*National Liberation Front*] [*Bolivia*]   (LA)

FRELINAGE ... Front for the Liberation of the Equatorial Guinean People   (AF)

FRELIP..... Frente de Libertacao de Portugal [*Liberation Front of Portugal*]   (WER)

Fremess...... Frequenzmesser [*Frequency Meter*] [*German*]   (GCA)

FREN........ Frente Revolucionario Estudiantil [*Student Revolutionary Front*] [*Dominican Republic*]   (LA)

FREN........ Frente Revolucionario Nacionalista [*Chile*] [*Political party*]   (EY)

FRENA...... Frente de Reivindicacion Nacionalista [*Nationalist Revindication Front*] [*Honduras*]   (LA)

FRENACAIN ... Frente Nacional de Campesinos Independientes [*National Front of Independent Peasants*] [*Honduras*]   (LA)

FRENACAINH ... Frente Nacional de Campesinos Independientes de Honduras [*National Front of Honduran Independent Peasants*]   (LA)

FRENACHODEP ... Frente Nacional de Choferes Revolucionarios, Democraticos, y Progresistas [*National Front of Revolutionary, Democratic, and Progressive Drivers*] [*Dominican Republic*]   (LA)

FRENAO... Frente Nacional de Organizaciones Autonomas [*Trade union*] [*Chile*]   (EY)

FRENAP ... Frente Nacional del Area Privada [*Private Sector National Front*] [*Chile*]   (LA)

FRENAPO ... Frente Nacional y Popular de Liberacion de Guinea Ecuatorial

FRENATRACA ... Frente Nacional de Trabajadores y Campesinos [*National Workers' and Peasants' Front*] [*Peru*] [*Political party*]   (PD)

Freno......... Frente Nacional Opositora [*National Opposition Front*] [*Panama*] [*Political party*]   (PPW)

FRENU...... Frente Nacional de Unidad [*National Unity Front*] [*Guatemala*] [*Political party*]   (PPW)

FREP........ Federacao Revolucionaria dos Estudantes Portugueses [*Revolutionary Federation of Portuguese Students*]   (WER)

FREP........ Frente Reformista de Educadores Panamenos [*Reformist Front of Panamanian Educators*] [*World Federation of Teachers*]   (LA)

FREPA...... Frente Patriotico Anticomunista [*Anticommunist Patriotic Front*] [*Guatemala*]   (LA)

FRES........ Frente Revolucionario Estudiantil [*Student Revolutionary Front*] [*Colorado*]   (LA)

FRES........ Freres [*Brothers*] [*French*]

FRESC....... Frente Revolucionario Estudiantil Social Cristiano [*Christian Social Student Revolutionary Front*] [*Honduras*]   (LA)

FRESCA..... Frigorificos Ecuatorianos CA [*Ecuador*]   (DSCA)

FRESCO ... Frankston Environmental, Social, and Conservation Organisation [*Australia*]   (ADA)

FRESERH ... Fondation pour la Recherche en Endocrinologie Sexuelle et l'Etude de la Reproduction Humaine

FRETILIN ... Frente Revolucionaria de Timor Leste Independente [*Revolutionary Front for East Timor Independence*] [*Indonesian*]   (AF)

FRETRASC ... Frente de Trabajadores Socialcristiano [*Social-Christian Workers' Front*] [*Nica ragua*]   (EY)

FREU........ Frente Revolucionario Estudiantil Universitario [*University Student Revolutionary Front*] [*Guatemala*]   (LA)

FREUCV ... Frente de Reorganizacion Estudiantil de la Universidad Central de Venezuela [*Student Reorganization Front of the Central University of Venezuela*]   (LA)

fr ez .... French Language   (BU)

FRF............ Fernando Rielo Foundation [*Spain*]   (EAIO)

FRF........... Fundusz Rozbudowy Floty [*Fund for the Development of the Fleet*] [*Poland*]

FRFOURRA ... French Fourragere [*Military decoration*]

frfr.............. Francia Frank [*French Franc*]   (HU)

FRG........... Federal Republic of Germany   (RU)

FRG .... Fonds de Reconstitution des Gisements [*North African*]

FRG .... Frente Republicano Guatemalteco [*Political party*]   (EY)

FRGF........ Friedensausschuss der Religiosen Gesellschaft der Freunde [*Peace Committee of the Religious Society of Friends*] [*Germany*]

FrGrALP ... Bibliotheque Americaine, Universite de Grenoble III, Domaine Universitaire, Grenoble, France [*Library symbol*] [*Library of Congress*]   (LCLS)

FRGSA ...... Fellow of the Royal Geographical Society of Australasia   (ADA)

FRGSQ...... Fellow of the Royal Geographical Society, Queensland [*Australia*]

FRH.......... Federation for Respect for Man and Humanity

Frh .... Freiherr [*Baron*] [*German*]

FRHistSQ ... Fellow of the Royal Historical Society of Queensland [*Australia*]   (ADA)

FRHistSV ... Fellow of the Royal Historical Society of Victoria [*Australia*]

Frhr........... Freiherr [*Baron*] [*German*]

FRHSV...... Fellow of the Royal Historical Society of Victoria [*Australia*]   (ADA)

FRHSWA ... Fellow of the Royal Historical Society, Western Australia

FRI............ Family Relationships Institute [*Australia*]

FRI............ Federation Routiere Internationale [*France*]   (FLAF)

FRI........... Fisheries Research Institute [*Australia*]

FRI............ Flandre Air International [*France*] [*ICAO designator*]   (FAAC)

FRI............ Fondo de Refinanciamento Industrial [*Industrial Refinancing Fund*] [*Bolivia*]   (LA)

FRI............ Fondo de Rehabilitacion Industrial [*Industrial Rehabilitation Fund*] [*Bolivia*]   (LA)

FRI............ Food Research Institute [*Australia*]

FRI............ Forest Research Institute [*New Zealand*]

FRI............ Forest Research Institute [*India*]

FRI............ Forestry Research Institute [*South Korea*]   (IRC)

FRI............ Forestry Resources Institute [*Ethiopia*]   (ARC)

FRI............ Frente Revolucionaria de Izquierda [*Left Revolutionary Front*] [*Bolivia*] [*Political party*]   (PPW)

Fri .... Fries [*Frisian*] [*Afrikaans*]

FRIA .... Compagnie Internationale pour la Fabrication de l'Aluminium

FRIB .... Frontline Repair Engineer Base   (RU)

FRIBAL..... Frigorifik Balik Ihracat ve Ticaret AS [*Refrigerated Fish Export and Trade Corp*]   (TU)

fribl .... Friblad [*Flyleaf*] [*Publishing Danish/Norwegian*]

FRIDA ...... Fonds de Recherche d'Investissement pour le Developpement de l'Afrique [*Fund for Research and Investment for the Development of Africa*]   (AF)

Frie............ Fonderie [*Foundry*] [*Military map abbreviation World War I*] [*French*]   (MTD)

FRIE .... Fondo Rotazione Iniziative Economiche [*Revolving Fund for Economic Initiatives*] [*Italian*]   (WER)

FRIGOCA ... Frigorifico de Cartagena [*Colombia*]   (COL)

FRIGOMA ... Societe d'Etudes de Frigorifiques de Mauritanie

FRIM......... Forest Research Institute of Malaysia   (FEA)

FRIM........ Forestry Research Institute of Malawi   (ARC)

Frim .... Frimaire [*Third month of the "Calendrier Republicain", from November 21 to December 20*]   (FLAF)

FRIMISA .. Frigorificos Minas Gerais SA [*Brazil*]   (DSCA)

FRIN......... Forestry Research Institute of Nigeria   (ARC)

FRINLIB.. Forestry Research Institute of Nigeria Library

FRIPUR .... Frigorifico Pesquero Uruguayo [*Uruguayan Fish Cold Storage Company*]   (LA)

Frischhalt .. Frischhaltung [*Keeping fresh*] [*German*]   (GCA)

FRISIC...... Food Research Institute Scientific Information Centre [*CSIR*] [*Ghana*]

FRIU......... Frente Revolucionario de la Izquierda Universitaria [*University Leftist Revolutionary Front*] [*Ecuador*]   (LA)

FRIVOLS ... Frivolities [*Slang*]   (DSUE)

Frk .... Frankies [*Frankish*] [*Afrikaans*]

FRK........... Fregate Island [*Seychelles Islands*] [*Airport symbol*]   (OAG)

frk.............. Froken [*Miss*] [*Danish*]   (GPO)

Frk .... Froken [*Miss*] [*Norwegian*]   (GPO)

frk.............. Froken [*Miss*] [*Swedish*]   (GPO)

FRL........... Fraeulein [*Miss*] [*German*]

FRL........... Fundamental Research Laboratory [*Japan*]

FRLA........ Federation of Right to Life Associations [*Australia*]

FRLA .... Finnish Research Library Association   (EAIO)

fr lux.......... Luxemburgi Frank [*Luxembourg Franc*]   (HU)

FRM .... Fondation pour la Recherche Medicale [*Foundation for Medical Research*] [*France*]

FRMAA.... Fellow of the Records Management Association of Australia

FRMAJ .... Federation Royale Marocaine des Auberges de la Jeunesse

FRMAP..... Foreign Rights Marketing Assistance Program [*Australia*]

FRMF........ Federation Royale Marocaine de Football [*Morocco*]

FRMG .... Fundusz Remontow Mlynow Gospodarczych [*Repair Fund for State Mills*]   (POL)

FRMIA...... Fellow of the Retail Management Institute of Australia

FRMIT ...... Fellow of the Royal Melbourne Institute of Technology [*Australia*]   (ADA)

FrMpALP ... Bibliotheque Americaine, Universite Paul-Valery, Montpellier, France [*Library symbol*] [*Library of Congress*]   (LCLS)

FRMSP ..... Federation Royale Marocaine du Sport Boules [*Morocco*]   (EAIO)

FRMWG ... Floodplain and River Management Working Group [*Australia*]

FRN .... Federation of Rhodesia and Nyasaland
FRN .... Federativnaia Respublika Nigeriia
FRN .... Foreign-Rate Note
FRN .... Forskningsradsnaemnden [*Sweden*]   (SLS)
FRN .... Frente de Reconstruccion Nacional [*Ecuador*] [*Political party*]   (EY)
FRN .... Frontul Renasterii Nationala [*Front of National Rebirth*] [*Romania*] [*Political party*]   (PPE)
FrNALP..... Bibliotheque Americaine de Nantes, Universite de Nantes Chemin du Tertre, Nantes, France [*Library symbol*] [*Library of Congress*]   (LCLS)
FrNanALP ... Bibliotheque Americaine, Universite de Nancy II, Nancy, France [*Library symbol*] [*Library of Congress*]   (LCLS)
FRNS........ Family Respite and Network Support [*Australia*]
FRO .... Faroe Islands [*ANSI three-letter standard code*]   (CNC)
FRO .... Floro [*Norway*] [*Airport symbol*]   (OAG)
FRO .... Forestry Research Office [*Philippines*] [*Research center*]   (IRC)
fro.............. Franco [*Shipping Cost Paid*] [*Business term*] [*French*]
FRO .... Frobisher NV (European Airlines) [*Belgium*] [*ICAO designator*]   (FAAC)
FROE........ Fractional Investigation of the Precipitation Test of Erythrocites   (RU)
FROLINAT ... Front de Liberation Nationale Tchadienne [*Chadian National Liberation Front*]   (AF)
FROLIZI... Front for the Liberation of Zimbabwe [*Political party*] [*Rhodesian*]   (AF)
FROMAC ... Federacion Dominicana de Cooperativas Agropecuarias y del Tabaco, Inc. [*Dominican Republic*]   (DSCA)
FROMAC ... Frota Mecanizada, Agricola, e Construtora SA [*Brazil*]   (DSCA)
FRONAPE ... Fronta Nacional de Petroleiros [*National Tanker Fleet*] [*Brazil*]   (LA)
FRONASA ... Front for National Salvation [*Uganda*]   (AF)
front .... Frontispice [*Frontispiece*] [*Publishing*] [*French*]
front .... Frontispice [*Frontispiece*] [*Publishing Danish/Norwegian*]
front .... Frontispicio [*Frontispiece*] [*Publishing*] [*Portuguese*]
front .... Frontispicio [*Frontispiece*] [*Publishing*] [*Spanish*]
front .... Frontispiece   (RU)
front .... Frontispies [*Frontispiece*] [*Publishing*] [*Netherlands*]
Front .... Frontispiz [*Frontispiece*] [*Publishing*] [*German*]
front .... Frontispizio [*Frontispiece*] [*Publishing*] [*Italian*]
frontis........ Frontispicio [*Frontispiece*] [*Publishing*] [*Spanish*]
frontisp...... Frontispice [*Frontispiece*] [*Publishing*] [*French*]
frontisp...... Frontispice [*Frontispiece*] [*Publishing Danish/Norwegian*]
frontisp...... Frontispicio [*Frontispiece*] [*Publishing*] [*Portuguese*]
frontisp...... Frontispies [*Frontispiece*] [*Publishing*] [*Netherlands*]
frott .... Frotte [*Scraped*] [*Publishing*] [*French*]
FRP........... F-Air AS [*Denmark*] [*ICAO designator*]   (FAAC)
FRP........... Federation des Republicains de Progres [*Federation of Progressive Republicans*] [*France*] [*Political party*]   (PPW)
FRP........... Fracture Research Programme [*University of the Witwatersrand*] [*South Africa*]   (AA)
FrP............. Franzoesisches Patent [*French Patent*] [*German*]
FRP........... Fuerzas Populares Revolucionarias [*Guerrilla forces*] [*Honduras*]   (EY)
FrPALP ..... American Library in Paris, Paris, France [*Library symbol*] [*Library of Congress*]   (LCLS)
FrPAUP..... American University in Paris, Paris, France [*Library symbol*] [*Library of Congress*]   (LCLS)
FrPCF........ College de France, Paris, France [*Library symbol*] [*Library of Congress*]   (LCLS)
FrPJO........ Direction des Journaux Officiels Service de Microfiches, Paris, France [*Library symbol*] [*Library of Congress*]   (LCLS)
FRPL .... Fuerzas Rebeldes y Populares Lautaro [*Chile*] [*Political party*]   (EY)
FRR........... Fundusz Rozwoju Rolnictwa [*Agricultural Development Fund*]   (POL)
FR-RSR ..... Fortele Aerience ale Republicii Populare Romanian [*Air Force of the Romanian People's Republic*]   (PDAA)
FRS........... Flandre Air Service [*France*] [*ICAO designator*]   (FAAC)
FRS........... Flores [*Guatemala*] [*Airport symbol*]   (OAG)
FRS........... Forces Republicaines de Securite [*Republican Security Forces*] [*Malagasy*]   (AF)
FRS........... Forest Resource Survey [*Australia*]
frs.............. Francs [*French*]   (GPO)
FRS........... Frente Republicana e Socialista [*Republican and Socialist Front*] [*Portugal*] [*Political party*]   (PPW)
FRS........... Frente Revolucionaria Sandinista [*Nicaragua*] [*Political party*]   (EY)
FRS........... Frente Revolucionario Sandino [*Sandino Revolutionary Front*] [*Nicaragua*]   (LA)
FRS........... Fries Rundveestamboek [*Benelux*]   (BAS)
FRS........... Frisian [*or Frisic*] [*Language, etc.*]
fr s .... Svajci Frank [*Swiss Franc*]   (HU)
FRSASA.... Fellow of the Royal Society of Arts of South Australia
FRSCh....... Fellow of the Royal Society of Chemists [*Australia*]
Frsch......... Freischnitt [*Shears*] [*German*]   (GCA)
FRSKGD ... Fauna Research Section of the Kenya Game Department

FRSM........ Fonds de la Recherche Scientifique Medicale [*Belgium*]
FRSNZ ...... Fellow of the Royal Society of New Zealand   (ADA)
frsp........... Frontespis [*Frontispiece*] [*Publishing*] [*Sweden*]
FRSSA...... Fellow of the Royal Society of South Australia
FRSSAf ..... Fellow of the Royal Society of South Africa   (AA)
FrSU .... Bibliotheque Nationale et Universitaire, Affaires Generales, Strasbourg, France [*Library symbol*] [*Library of Congress*]   (LCLS)
FRT........... Federacion Revolucionaria de Trabajadores [*Revolutionary Workers Federation*] [*Uruguay*]   (LA)
FRTC .... Friends Rural Training Center [*Zimbabwe*]   (EAIO)
FRTJ.......... Federovane Robotnicke Telocyicne Jednotky [*Federated Workers' Athletic and Gymnastic Organizations*]   (CZ)
FrTlALP.... Bibliotheque Americaine, Universite de Toulouse-Le Mirail, Toulouse, France [*Library symbol*] [*Library of Congress*]   (LCLS)
FRTM........ Filim-Radyo-Televisyon ile Egitim Merkezi [*Film, Radio, Television Training Center*] [*of Education Ministry*]   (TU)
FRTP .... Frente Revolucionario de Trabajadores de la Educacion [*Revolutionary Front of Education Workers*] [*Panama*]   (LA)
FRTU........ Development and Technical Advancement Fund   (BU)
FRTU........ Federation of Revolutionary Trade Unions [*Tanzania*]   (AF)
FRU .... Fire and Rescue Unit [*Australia*]
FRU .... Frente de Reforma Universitaria [*University Reform Front*] [*Honduras*]   (LA)
FRU .... Frente de Reforma Universitaria [*University Reform Front*] [*Panama*]   (LA)
FRU .... Frente Revolucionario Universitario [*University Revolutionary Front*] [*Guatemala*]   (LA)
FRU .... Frunze [*Former USSR*] [*Airport symbol*]   (OAG)
FRUCO ...... Frutera Colombiana Ltda. [*Colombia*]   (COL)
FRUCOM ... Federation Europeenne des Importateurs de Fruits Secs, Conserves, Epices et Miels [*European Federation of Importers of Dried Fruits, Preserves, Spices, and Honey*]
Fruct........... Fructidor [*Twelfth Month of the "Calendrier Republicain", from August 19 to September 17*]   (FLAF)
FRUD .... Front pour la Restauration de l'Unite et de la Democratie [*Djibouti*] [*Political party*]   (EY)
FRUMF ...... Ministry of Finance Financial Auditing Administration   (BU)
FRUN .... Frente Revolucionario Universitario Nacionalista [*Nationalist University Revolutionary Front*] [*Dominican Republic*]   (LA)
FRUS........ Frente Universitario de Estudiantes Socialistas [*Socialist Students University Front*] [*Dominican Republic*]   (LA)
FRVIA .... Fellow of the Royal Victorian Institute of Architects [*Australia*]   (ADA)
FRW .... Francistown [*Botswana*] [*Airport symbol*]   (OAG)
Frw............. Franc Rwandais
Frw............. Freiwilliger [*Volunteer*] [*German*]   (GCA)
FrWAfr ...... French West Africa
FRY .... Federal Republic of Yugoslavia   (EECI)
fr-yag......... Fruit and Berry Orchard [*Topography*]   (RU)
FRYI .... Fairfield Refugee Youth Inter-Agency [*Australia*]
Frz............. Franzoesisch [*French*] [*German*]   (EG)
FRZ........... Wage Fund   (BU)
Frzbd.......... Franzband [*Leather Binding*] [*Publishing*] [*German*]
FRZS .... Fellow of the Royal Zoological Society of New South Wales [*Australia*]   (ADA)
FS.............. Aircraft Landing Light   (RU)
FS.............. Faire Suivre [*Please Forward*] [*French*]
fs................. Fajsuly [*Specific Gravity*]   (HU)
FS.............. Fallschirm [*Parachute*] [*German military*]
FS.............. Federalni Shromazdeni [*Federal Assembly*]   (CZ)
FS.............. Federation des Services [*France*]
FS.............. Feng-Shui [*Earth Magic*] [*Ancient Chinese classics*]
FS.............. Fernschreiben [*or Fernschreiber*] [*Teletype Message or Teletype*] [*German military - World War II*]
FS.............. Ferrovie dello Stato [*Italian State Railways*]
FS.............. Fichtel & Sachs [*Auto industry supplier*] [*German*]
FS.............. Filoproodos Syllogos Anthoupoleos - Neas Ionias [*Anthoupolis - Nea Ionia Progressive Association*] [*Greek*]   (GC)
FS.............. Filtration Society   (EA)
FS.............. Financni Sprava [*Finance Directorate*]   (CZ)
FS.............. Financni Straz [*Customs Guards*]   (CZ)
fs................. Fois [*Once*] [*Knitting*] [*French*]
FS.............. Folio Society [*British*]   (EAIO)
FS.............. Forskningsstiftelsen Skogsarbeten [*Forest Operations Institute of Sweden*]   (EAIO)
FS.............. Foyers Sportifs
FS.............. Franc Suisse [*Swiss Franc*] [*Monetary unit*]
FS.............. Fraunhofer Society [*Germany*]   (EAIO)
FS.............. Fundacion Servivienda [*Colombia*]   (EAIO)
FS.............. Funkstelle [*Radio Station, Wireless Station, Sending Station (Radio)*]   (EG)
FS.............. Glass Light Filter, Violet   (RU)
FS.............. Resistance Photocell   (RU)

FS............... Violet Glass   (RU)
FS3............. Foundation Studio 3 [*Netherlands*]   (EAIO)
fsa.............. Fac Secundum Artem [*Prepare According to Formula*]
　　　　　　[*Pharmacy*]
FSA........... Fellesradet for det Sorlige Afrika [*Norway*]
FSA........... Fernsehamt [*Television Office*]   (EG)
FSA........... Fertility Society of Australia
FSA........... Filipino Shipowners Association   (EAIO)
FSA........... Finnish Society of Adelaide [*South Australia*]
FSA........... Finnish Society of Automation   (EAIO)
FSA........... Firearms Sports Association [*Australia*]
FSA........... Fire Surveyors Association of Southern Africa   (AA)
FSA........... Fonds de Solidarite Africain
FSA........... Forbundet Sveriges Arbetsterapeuter [*Swedish Association of
　　　　　　Occupational Therapists*]   (EAIO)
FSA........... Force Syndicale Africaine [*African Trade Union Force*] [*Zaire*]
　　　　　　(AF)
FSA........... Foster Aviation [*ICAO designator*]   (FAAC)
FSA........... French Society of Acoustics [*Formerly, Group of French-
　　　　　　Speaking Acousticians*]   (EA)
FSA........... Friendly Societies Association New South Wales [*Australia*]
FSA........... Fristelersvereniging van Suid-Afrika [*Friesland Cattle Breeders'
　　　　　　Association of South Africa*]   (EAIO)
FSA........... Front Socialiste Africain
FSAA......... Federation Syndicale Africaine Autonome [*Trade union*]
　　　　　　[*African*]
FSAA......... Fellow of the Society of Incorporated Accountants and Auditors
　　　　　　[*Australia*]
FSAA......... Flight Stewards Association of Australia   (ADA)
FSAAIE..... Fellow of the South African Association of Industrial Editors
　　　　　　(AA)
FSAAR ..... Fraunhofer Society for the Advancement of Applied Research
　　　　　　[*Germany*]   (EAIO)
FS(Abteilung) ... Fernseh-Abteilung [*Television Department*]   (EG)
FSAC........ Firearms Safety Awareness Council [*Australia*]
FSAC........ Folia Scientifica Africae Centralis
FSACORRI ... Fellow of the South African Corrosion Institute   (AA)
FSADS ...... Flight Services Aircraft Display System [*Australia*]
FSAE........ French Society of Agricultural Economics   (EAIO)
FSAE........ French Society of Automotive Engineers   (EAIO)
FSAG........ Fellow of the Society of Australian Genealogists   (ADA)
FSAICE..... Fellow of the South African Institution of Civil Engineers   (AA)
FSAICHE ... Fellow of the South African Institution of Chemical Engineers
　　　　　　(AA)
FSAIEE..... Fellow of the South African Institute of Electrical Engineers
　　　　　　(AA)
FSAIETE .. Fellow of the South African Institute of Electrical Technician
　　　　　　Engineers   (AA)
FSAIM ...... Fellow of the South African Institute of Management   (AA)
FSAIMARENA ... Fellow of the South African Institute of Marine Engineers
　　　　　　and Naval Architects   (AA)
FSAIMECHE ... Fellow of the South African Institute of Mechanical
　　　　　　Engineers   (AA)
FSAIT....... Fellow of the South Australian Institute of Technology
FSAIW ...... Fellow of the South African Institute of Welding   (AA)
FSAN........ Federation Suisse des Amis de la Nature [*Swiss Federation of
　　　　　　Friends of Nature*]   (EAIO)
FSANSW .. Family Support Association of New South Wales [*Australia*]
FSAPH...... Federation des Syndicats d'Armateurs a la Peche Hauturiere
　　　　　　[*France*]   (EAIO)
FSAR .... Fonds Special d'Action Rural
FSAS .... Food Security Assistance Scheme
FSASM...... Fellow of the South Australian School of Mines   (ADA)
FSASM(Met) ... Fellow of the South Australian School of Mines (Metallurgy)
FSASP...... Federation of South African Societies of Pathology   (AA)
FSASQ ...... Fellow of the South African Society for Quality   (AA)
FSASR...... Federation des Societes d'Agriculture de la Suisse Romande
　　　　　　[*Switzerland*]   (SLS)
FSAT .... Finnish Society of Analytical Trilogy   (EAIO)
FSAVP...... Federasie van Suid-Afrikaanse Verenigings van Patologie [*South
　　　　　　Africa*]   (AA)
FSB .... Falange Socialista Boliviana [*Bolivian Socialist Phalange*]
　　　　　　[*Political party*]   (PPW)
FSB .... Family Services Branch [*Australian Capital Territory*]
FSB .... Federation Suisse de Boules [*Swiss Association of Boules*]
　　　　　　(EAIO)
FSB .... Filmove Studio Barrandov [*Barrandov Film Studios*]   (CZ)
FSBA .... Federation Suisse de Basketball Amateur [*Swiss Federation of
　　　　　　Amateur Basketball*]   (EAIO)
FSBI.......... Falange Socialista Boliviana de Izquierda [*Bolivian Socialist
　　　　　　Phalange of the Left*] [*Political party*]   (PPW)
FSBKM ..... Social Services and Cultural Measures Fund   (BU)
FSBTI........ Frontline Armored Equipment Depot   (RU)
FSC .... Fabryka Samochodow Ciezarowych [*Truck Factory*]   (POL)
FSC .... Faculte des Sciences Commerciales [*Faculty of Commercial
　　　　　　Sciences*] [*Cambodia*]   (CL)

FSC........... Federacion Socialista de Cataluna [*Socialist Federation of
　　　　　　Catalonia*] [*Spanish*]   (WER)
FSC........... Federal Sports Club [*Australia*]
FSC........... Federation Socialiste Caledonienne [*Caledonian Socialist
　　　　　　Federation*] [*Political party*]   (PPW)
FSC........... Federation Syndicale du Cameroun [*Trade Union Federation of
　　　　　　Cameroon*]   (AF)
FSC........... Figari [*Corsica*] [*Airport symbol*]   (OAG)
FSC........... Fiji Sugar Corporation   (GEA)
FSC........... Finnish Shippers Council   (DS)
FSC........... First State Computing [*Australia*]
FSC........... Fonds de Soutien des Changes [*Exchange Support Fund*] [*Use
　　　　　　ESF Cambodia*]   (CL)
FSC........... Food Standards Code [*Australia*]
FSC........... Foreign Service Corporation [*China*]
FSC........... Foundation Studies Certificate [*University of New South Wales*]
　　　　　　[*Australia*]
FSC........... Four Star Aviation, Inc. [*Virgin Islands*] [*ICAO designator*]
　　　　　　(FAAC)
FSC........... Fratres Scholarum Christianarum [*Institute of the Brothers of the
　　　　　　Christian Schools*] [*Also known as Christian Brothers*]
　　　　　　(EAIO)
FSC........... French Shippers Council   (DS)
FSC........... Kampuchea Federation of Trade Unions
FSCA .... Federation Suisse des Clubs d'Auteurs de Film et Video
　　　　　　[*Federation of the Swiss Film and Video Authors Clubs*]
　　　　　　(EAIO)
FSCA .... Fellow of the Society of Company and Commercial Accountants
　　　　　　[*British*]   (DCTA)
FSCAI....... Fonds Special de Credit Agricole Indigene
FSCC .... Faisal Siddiq Cricket Club
FSCC .... Federation des Syndicats des Corps Constitues [*Federation of
　　　　　　Civil Service Unions - FCSU*] [*Mauritius*]
FSCEA....... French-Speaking Comparative Education Association [*See also
　　　　　　AFEC*] [*Sevres, France*]   (EAIO)
FSCGC...... Fiji Sugar Cane Growers' Council   (EAIO)
FSCM....... Fellow of the State Conservatorium of Music [*Australia*]
FSCN....... Finnish Society of Clinical Neurophysiology   (EAIO)
FSCS......... Foundation of Socio-Cultural Services [*Sri Lanka*]   (EAIO)
FSD........... Efs-Flugservice GmbH [*Germany*] [*ICAO designator*]   (FAAC)
FSD........... Federacion Social-Democrata [*Social Democratic Federation*]
　　　　　　[*Spanish*]   (WER)
FSD........... Federation des Socialistes Democrates [*Federation of Democratic
　　　　　　Socialists*] [*France*] [*Political party*]   (PPE)
FSD........... Finnish Society for Dermatopathology   (EAIO)
FSD........... Foreningen af Suppeindustri i Danmark [*Denmark*]   (EAIO)
FSD........... Frente Sindical Democratica [*Trade union*] [*Colorado*]   (EY)
FSD........... Frente Sindical Democratico [*Peru*]   (EY)
FSD........... Mixed Action Filter [*Nuclear energy*]   (BU)
FSDH .... Fondation de la Sante et des Droits de l'Homme [*Foundation for
　　　　　　Health and Human Rights*]   (EA)
FSDLWG .. Fundamental Standard Data Link Working Group [*NATO*]
　　　　　　(NATG)
FSDPANSW ... Friendly Societies', Dispensaries, and Pharmacies Association
　　　　　　of New South Wales [*Australia*]
FSDVP ...... Freiheitlich Soziale Deutsche Volkspartei [*Liberal Social German
　　　　　　People's Party*] [*Germany*] [*Political party*]   (PPW)
FSE .... Fellow of the Society of Executives [*Australia*]
FSE .... Fondo Social Europeo [*European Social Fund - ESF*] [*Spanish*]
FSE .... Fonds Social Europeen [*European Social Fund - ESF*] [*French*]
FSE .... Formerly Socialist Economy   (ECON)
FSE .... Forward Security Element [*Soviet military force*]
Fse............. Fosse [*Ditch*] [*Military map abbreviation World War I*] [*French*]
　　　　　　(MTD)
FSEEEC .... Federation of Stock Exchanges in the European Community
　　　　　　[*Belgium*]   (EAIO)
f-sek .... Phot-Second   (RU)
FSEL......... Frontline Sanitary and Epidemiological Laboratory   (RU)
FSESP .... Fundacao Servico Especial de Saude Publica [*Foundation for
　　　　　　Special Public Health Service*] [*Rio De Janeiro, Brazil*]
　　　　　　(LAA)
FSF .... Federation Senegalaise de Football
FSF .... Finlands Svenska Foerfattarefoerening [*Finland*]   (SLS)
FSF .... Foereningen Svensk Form [*Sweden*]   (SLS)
FSF .... French Squash Federation   (EAIO)
FSFRL....... Far Seas Fisheries Research Laboratory [*Japan*]   (ASF)
FSFS.......... Family Security Friendly Society [*Australia*]
FSG........... Federacion Socialista Gallega [*Socialist Federation of Galicia*]
　　　　　　[*Spanish*]   (WER)
FSG........... Federation Syndicale du Gabon [*Gabonese Trade Union
　　　　　　Federation*]   (AF)
FSG........... Follicle-Stimulating Hormone   (RU)
FSG........... Fortress Study Group   (EAIO)
FSG........... Freres de Saint Gabriel [*Brothers of Christian Instruction of St.
　　　　　　Gabriel*] [*Rome, Italy*]   (EAIO)
FSG........... Frontline Fuel Depot   (RU)
FSGD........ Federation of Sports Goods Distributors [*British*]   (DCTA)

FSGN......... Fazenda de Selecao do Gado Nacional [*Brazil*]   (DSCA)
FSH .... Federacion Sindical Hondurena [*Honduran Union Federation*]
FSH .... Flash Airline Ltd. [*Nigeria*] [*ICAO designator*]   (FAAC)
fsh .... Medical Practitioner   (BU)
FShM........ Youth Soccer School   (RU)
FSHP........ Fellow of the Society of Hospital Pharmacists [*Australia*]
FSI .... Federacion Social Independiente [*Independent Social
            Federation*] [*Spanish*]   (WER)
FSI .... Federation of Swedish Industries   (EAIO)
FSI .... Federation Syndicale Internationale [*French*]
FSI .... Forces de Securite Interieures [*Internal Security Forces*]
            [*Lebanon*]
FSI .... Foreign Services Institute [*Australia*]
FSIA .... Fellow of the Safety Institute of Australia
FSIA .... Fellow of the Securities Institute of Australia   (ADA)
FSIL.......... French Society for International Law   (EAIO)
FSIS.......... Finnish Society for Information Services   (EAIO)
FSJ............ Federation Suisse des Journalistes   (EAIO)
FSJ............ Fiskulturni Savez Jugoslavije [*Physical Culture Union of
            Yugoslavia*]   (YU)
FSK........... Fabrika Sinteticog Kaucuka u Osnvanju
FSK........... Farming Systems Kenya   (EAIO)
FSK........... Folgeschlusskarte [*French*]   (ADPT)
FSKZ .... Foerdergemeinschaft fuer das Sueddeutsche Kunststoff-Zentrum
            eV [*Association for the Promotion of the South German
            Plastics Center*]   (SLS)
FSL .... Finlands Svenska Lararforbund [*Finland*]   (EAIO)
FSL .... Fleet Services Ltd. [*New Zealand*]
FSL .... Forskningscentret for Skov and Landskab [*Danish Forest and
            Landscape Research Institute*]   (EAIO)
FSL .... Shaped Castings Shop   (RU)
FSLC .... First School Leaving Certificate Examination [*Africa*]
FSLN .... Frente Sandinista de Liberacion Nacional [*Sandinista National
            Liberation Front*] [*Nicaragua*] [*Political party*]   (PPW)
FSLUS...... Federazione dei Sindacati Lavoratori Uniti della Somalia
            [*Somali Federation of United Trade Unions*]
FSM.......... Fabryka Samochodow Malolotia [*Polish affiliate of Fiat Motors*]
FSM.......... Federacion Sindical de Managua [*Trade Union Federation of
            Managua*] [*Nicaragua*]   (LA)
FSM.......... Federacion Sindical Mundial [*World Federation of Trade Unions
            - WFTU*] [*Spanish*]   (LA)
FSM.......... Federacion Socialista Madrilena [*Spain*] [*Political party*]   (EY)
FSM.......... Federated States of Micronesia [*ANSI three-letter standard code*]
            (CNC)
FSM.......... Federatia Sindicala Mondiala [*World Federation of Trade Unions
            - WFTU*]   (RO)
FSM.......... Federation Sephardite Mondiale [*World Sephardi Federation -
            WSF*] [*Geneva, Switzerland*]   (EAIO)
FSM.......... Federation Socialiste de la Martinique [*Socialist Federation of
            Martinique*] [*Political party*]   (PPW)
FSM.......... Federation Syndicale Mondiale [*World Federation of Trade
            Unions - WFTU*] [*French*]   (EAIO)
FSM.......... Federazione Sindacale Mondiale [*World Federation of Trade
            Unions - WFTU*] [*Italian*]   (WER)
FSM.......... Fiskulturni Sojuz na Makedonija [*Physical Culture Union of
            Macedonia*]   (YU)
FSM.......... French Society of Musicology   (EAIO)
FSMA........ Fashion Sales and Marketing Association [*Australia*]
FSMAWA ... Fashion Sales and Marketing Association of Western Australia
FSME....... Federation of State and Municipal Employees [*Iceland*]   (EAIO)
FSMF .... Federation des Syndicats des Travailleurs de la Sante [*Federation
            of Health Workers' Unions*] [*Malagasy*]   (AF)
FSN........... Family Support Networks Project [*Australia*]
FSN........... Forestiere et Scierie du Nord
FSN........... French-Speaking Nations [*NATO*]
FSN........... Front Syndical National [*National Trade Union Front*]
            [*Mauritius*]
FSN........... Funksjonaersambandet i Norge [*Confederation of Salaried
            Employees of Norway*]   (WEN)
FSN........... National Salvation Front [*Romania*] [*Political party*]
FSNP........ Foititikos Syllogos Nikaias Peiraios [*Nikaia, Piraeus Student
            Club*]   (GC)
FSNS .... French-Speaking Neuropsychological Society [*Paris, France*]
            (EAIO)
FSNU......... Fonds Special des Nations Unies [*United Nations Special Fund -
            UNSF*] [*French*]
FSO........... Fabryka Samochodow Osbowych [*Automobile Factory*]   (POL)
FSO........... Fabryka Samochodow Osobowych [*Polish automobile
            manufacturer*]
FSO........... Finance and Bookkeeping Department   (BU)
FSO........... Funksjonaerenes Sentralorganisasjoh [*Central Organization of
            Salaried Employees*] [*Norwegian*]
FSOC........ Free Serbian Orthodox Church [*Australia*]
FSOD........ Fakultetsko Sumsko Ogledno Dobro [*College Forestry
            Experimental Station*] [*Igman*]   (YU)

FSODC...... Federacion de Sindicatos de Obreros Democraticos de Colon
            [*Federation of Unions of Democratic Workers of Colon*]
            [*Panama*]   (LA)
FSor .... French Cetra-Soria [*Record label*]
FSP .... Family Support Program [*Australia*]
FSP .... Festspeicher [*French*]   (ADPT)
FSP .... Figlie de San Paolo [*Pious Society of the Daughters of Saint Paul -
            PSDSP*] [*Rome, Italy*]   (EAIO)
FSP .... Free Socialist Party [*Egypt*]
FSP .... Freie Sozialistische Partei [*Free Socialist Party (Pro-Chicom)*]
            (WEN)
FSP .... Frente Socialista Popular [*Popular Socialist Front*] [*Portuguese*]
            (WER)
FSP .... Frente Social Progresista [*Progressive Social Front*] [*Ecuador*]
            [*Political party*]   (PPW)
FSPDU ..... Federated Ship Painters' and Dockers' Union of Australia
FSPDUA ... Federated Ship Painters and Dockers' Union of Australia
FSPE........ Federation of Societies of Professional Engineers [*South Africa*]
FSPQ .... Family Support Program (Queensland) [*Australia*]
FSPS .... Foundation for the Study of Plural Societies   (EA)
FSPS .... French Society of Pediatric Surgery   (EAIO)
FSPU .... Federated Storemen and Packers' Union of Australia
FSR........... Falange Social Revolucionaria [*Revolutionary Social Phalange*]
            [*Spanish*]   (WER)
f sr .... Fale Srednie [*Medium Waves*] [*Radio*] [*Poland*]
FSR........... Farming Systems Research [*West Africa*]
FSR........... Federacion Sindical Revolucionaria [*Revolutionary Trade Union
            Federation*] [*El Salvador*]   (LA)
FSR........... Federation Suisse de Rugby [*Swiss Rugby Federation*]   (EAIO)
FSR........... Fotografske Svetlece Rakete [*Photographic Illuminating Rockets*]
            (YU)
FSR........... Fraccion Socialista Revolucionaria [*Revolutionary Socialist
            Faction*] [*Panama*]   (LA)
FSR........... Frente Socialista Revolucionario [*Revolutionary Socialist Front*]
            [*Venezuela*]   (LA)
FSRA .... Fonds de Soutien de la Revolution Agraire [*Agrarian Revolution
            Support Fund*]   (AF)
FSRC .... Financial Systems Research Council [*Japan*]
FSS .... Fabrique Suisse d'Explosifs
FSS .... Family Support Service [*Australia*]
FSS .... Finnish Society of Sydney [*New South Wales, Australia*]
FSS .... Forensic Science Service [*British*]
FSS .... Forensic Science Society   (EAIO)
FSS .... Front Sotsialisticheskikh Sil
FSSA .... Fern Society of Southern Africa   (AA)
FSSA .... Fertilizer Society of South Africa   (EAIO)
FSSANSW ... Family Support Services Association of New South Wales
            [*Australia*]
FSSC.......... Federal Sea Safety Centre [*Australia*]
FSSC.......... Federation des Syndicats du Service Civile [*Federation of Civil
            Service Unions*] [*Use FCSU Mauritius*]   (AF)
FSSC.......... Federation of Serbian Sisters Circle [*Australia*]
FSSC.......... Federazione Svizzera dei Sindicati Cristiani [*Swiss Federation of
            National-Christian Trade Unions*]
FSSCN....... Federation Suisse des Syndicats Chretiens-Nationaux [*Swiss
            Federation of National-Christian Trade Unions*]
FSSE.......... Fellow of the Society of Senior Executives [*Australia*]
FSSH .... Forschungsstelle fuer die Seeschiffahrt zu Hamburg [*Hamburg
            Maritime Research*] [*Research center*]   (ERC)
FSSL .... Finnish Society of Sciences and Letters   (EAIO)
FSSP.......... Federation des Salaries du Secteur Prive [*South Vietnamese*]
FSSF .... Fraternite Sacerdotale Saint Pie X [*International Sacerdotal
            Society Saint Pius X - ISSSP*]   (EAIO)
FSSPX....... International Sacerdotal Society Saint Pius X [*Switzerland*]
            (EAIO)
FSSS.......... Family Support Services Scheme [*Australia*]
FSSS.......... Mahe/Seychelles International   (ICLI)
FST .... Fast Air Ltda. [*Chile*] [*ICAO designator*]   (FAAC)
FST .... Federacion Sindical de Trabajadores [*Workers Trade Union
            Federation*] [*Spanish*]   (WER)
FST .... Federation of Swedish Tailors   (EAIO)
FST .... Fertigungssteuerung [*German*]   (ADPT)
FST .... Foereningen Svenska Tonsaettare [*Sweden*]   (SLS)
Fst .... Forst [*German*]
FST .... Funkstelle [*Radio Station*] [*German military - World War II*]
f st .... Pound Sterling   (RU)
FSTC .... Fellow of Sydney Technical College [*Australia*]   (ADA)
FSTIV........ Frente de Sindicalistas y Trabajadores Independientes de
            Venezuela [*Venezuelan Independent Workers and Trade
            Unionists Front*]   (LA)
FSTMB ..... Federacion de Sindicatos de Trabajadores Mineros de Bolivia
            [*Trade Union Federation of Bolivian Mine Workers*]
FSTR .... Fallschirmtruppen [*Parachute Troops*] [*German military*]
Fstr........... Foerster [*Forester*] [*German*]
FSTSE........ Federacion de Sindicatos de Trabajadores al Servicio del Estado
            [*Federation of Government Workers Unions*] [*Mexico*]
            (LA)

FSTT .... Federation Senegalaise des Travailleurs du Transport [*Senegalese Federation of Transportation Workers*] (AF)

FSTU .... Federacion Sindical de Trabajadores Universitarios [*Federation of University Workers*] [*Mexico*] (LA)

FstW .... Forstwirtschaft [*Forestry*] [*German*]

FSU .... Federalni Statisticky Urad [*Federal Office of Statistics*] (CZ)

FSU .... Finance Sector Union [*Australia*] (EAIO)

FSU .... Freisoziale Union - Demokratische Mitte [*Free Social Union - Democratic Center*] [*Germany*] [*Political party*] (PPW)

FSU .... Photoelectric Reader (RU)

FSUA .... Finance Sector Union of Australia

FSUJ .... Friedrich-Schiller-Universitaet Jena [*Friedrich Schiller University, Jena*] (EG)

FSV .... Aircraft Telescopic Landing Light (RU)

FSV .... Fondo Social para la Vivienda [*El Salvador*] (EY)

FSVCI .... Federation Voltaique du Commerce et de l'Industrie

FSVV .... Frontline Engineer Ammunition and Explosives Depot (RU)

FSW .... Faith in the Second World [*An association*] [*Switzerland See also G2W*] (EAIO)

FSWC .... Foundry Sector Working Circle [*Australia*]

FSWCE .... Federation of Swiss White-Collar Employees (EAIO)

FSWI .... Federation of Swedish Wholesalers and Importers (EAIO)

FSWU .... Federation of Sudanese Workers' Unions

fsz .... Foldszint [*Ground Floor*] (HU)

f sz .... Folyo Szam [*Consecutive Number*] (HU)

FSzEK .... Fovarosi Szabo Ervin Konyvtar [*Ervin Szabo Municipal Library (Budapest)*] (HU)

f szla .... Folyo Szamla [*Current Account*] [*Hungarian*] (HU)

fszmstr ...... Foszallasmester [*Quartermaster General*] (HU)

fszt .... Foldszint [*Ground Floor*] (HU)

f szt .... Funt Szterling [*or Funty Szterlingi*] [*Pound Sterling*] [*Poland*]

FT .... Family Team [*Australia*]

f-t .... Faux-titre [*Half or Bastard Title*] [*Publishing*] [*French*]

FT .... Federal Territory [*Australia*]

ft .... Feet (SCAC)

FT .... Fiat SpA [*Italy*] [*ICAO aircraft manufacturer identifier*] (ICAO)

FT .... Filosofian Tohtori [*Finland*]

F-T .... Fischer-Tropsch [*German*] (GCA)

FT .... Fondstraeger [*Authorized Funds Investor*] (EG)

ft .... Foot (EECI)

Ft .... Foret [*Forest*] [*Military map abbreviation World War I*] [*French*] (MTD)

Ft .... Forint [*Florin*] [*Monetary unit*] [*Hungary*] (GPO)

Ft .... Fort [*Fort*] [*French*] (NAU)

ft .... Fotanacsos [*Chief Councilor (of a council) or Chief Counselor*] (HU)

ft .... Fotisztelendo [*Right Reverend (Catholic)*] (HU)

ft .... Fountain [*Topography*] (RU)

FT .... Fovarosi Tanacs [*Capital City Council*] (HU)

FT .... French Telefunken [*Record label*]

FT .... Funkentelegraphie [*Radio-Telegraphy*] [*German*] (EG)

ft .... Fuori Testo [*Not in the Text*] [*Publishing*] [*Italian*]

FT .... Technical Photographic Film (RU)

f-t .... University Department or School (BU)

FTA .... European Throwsters Association [*Italy*] (EAIO)

FTA .... Facsimile Equipment, Phototelegraphic Apparatus (RU)

FTA .... Federacion de Trabajadores Arubanos [*Aruban Workers' Federation*]

FTA .... Federated Tanners' Association of Australia

FTA .... Fiches Typologiques Africaines

FTA .... Finnish Tennis Association (EAIO)

FTA .... Foerdergesellschaft Technischer Ausbau eV [*Society for the Promotion of Technical Improvement*] (SLS)

FTA .... Forces Terrestres Antiaeriennes [*French*]

FTA .... Foreign Trade Association [*Cologne, Federal Republic of Germany*] (EAIO)

FTA .... Formal Training Allowance [*Australia*]

FTA .... Free Trade Area

FTA .... Phenyltrifluoroacetone (RU)

FTAA .... Federated Tanners' Association of Australia

FTACU ...... Federation Togolaise des Associations et Clubs UNESCO [*Togolese National Federation of UNESCO Clubs and Associations*] (EAIO)

FTAE .... Fonds Territorial d'Action Economique

FTAI .... French Territory of Afars and Issas [*Djibouti*] (AF)

FtAust .... First Australia Fund, Inc. [*Associated Press*]

FTAWA .... Food Technology Association of Western Australia

FTB .... Fabrica de Tigari Bucuresti [*Bucharest Cigarette Factory*] (RO)

FTB .... Fast Torpedo Boat [*NATO*]

FTB .... Federation des Travailleurs Burundi [*Federation of Burundi Workers*] (AF)

FTB .... Federation Tunisienne de Boxe

FTB .... Finnish Tourist Board (EAIO)

FTBB .... Federation Tunisienne de Basketball

FTBP .... Federation Tunisienne de Boules et Petanque [*Tunisian Bocce Federation*] (EAIO)

FTC .... Fair Trade Commission [*Japan*] (ECON)

FTC .... Federacion de Trabajadores del Campo [*Federation of Farm Workers*] [*El Salvador*] (LA)

FTC .... Ferencvarosi Torna Club [*Athletic Club of Ferencvaros*] (HU)

FTC .... Foreign Tax Credits [*Australia*]

FTC .... Foreign Transactions Company [*Iran*] (ME)

FTC .... Frente de Trabajadores Copeyanos [*Social Christian Workers Front*] [*Venezuela*] (LA)

FTC .... Frente de Trabajadores de la Cultura [*Cultural Workers Front*] [*Panama*] (LA)

FTCCP ...... Federacion de Trabajadores en Construccion Civil del Peru [*Peruvian Federation of Civil Construction Workers*] (LA)

FTCV .... Federacion de Trabajadores de Comunicaciones de Venezuela [*Federation of Venezuelan Communication Workers*] (LA)

FTCWU ..... Federated Tobacco and Cigarette Workers' Union [*Australia*]

FTD .... Ferrite-Transistor Levels (RU)

FTD .... Fobeo Timoien Domini [*Fomento el Temor de Dios*] (COL)

FTD .... Foreign Trade Department

FTD .... Freve Theofan Diogene [*Hermano Teofano Diogenes*] (COL)

FTD .... Front de Travailleurs du Dahomey

FTDC .... Federacion de Trabajadores Democrata Cristiana [*Chile*] (EY)

FTDF .... Federacion de Trabajadores del Distrito Federal [*Federation of Federal District Workers*] [*Mexico*] (LA)

FTDM .... Fikambanany Tanora Demokratikan' i Madagasikara [*Association of Malagasy Democratic Youth*] (AF)

Fte .... Forte [*Fort*] [*Portuguese*] (NAU)

Fte .... Forte [*Fort*] [*Italian*] (NAU)

FTE .... Fotografia F3 SA [*Spain*] [*ICAO designator*] (FAAC)

Fte .... Fuerte [*Fort*] [*Spanish*] (NAU)

FTEC .... Federation des Travailleurs de l'Enseignement et de la Culture [*Federation of Educational and Cultural Workers*] [*Algeria*] (AF)

FTEC .... Federation des Travailleurs des Mines et Carrieres [*Algeria*]

FTF .... Faeliesradet for Danske Tjenestemands- og Funktionaerorganisationer [*Joint Council of Civil Servants' and Salaried Employees' Organizations*] [*Denmark*] (WEN)

FTF .... Faellesradet for Danske Tjenestemends- og Funktonaerorganisationer [*A union*] [*Denmark*] (DCTA)

FTF .... Federation Tunisienne de Football

FTF .... Flygtekniska Foereningen [*Sweden*] (SLS)

FTF .... Funksjonser og Tjeneste Mannsorganisasjonenes Fellesutvalg [*Central Committee of Salaried Employees and Public Servants*] [*Norway*] (WEN)

FTF .... Funktionaerernes og Tjenestemaendenes Faellesrad [*Federation of Civil Servants' and Salaried Employees' Organizations*] [*Denmark*]

FTFI .... Fiskeriteknologisk Forskningsinstitutt [*Institute of Fishery Technology Research*] [*Research center*] [*Norway*] (IRC)

FTG .... Federacion de Trabajadores de Guatemala [*Guatemalan Workers' Federation*]

FtG .... Forschungsgemeinschaft fuer Technisches Glas eV (SLS)

FTHB .... Federation Togolaise de Handball

FTHB .... Federation Tunisienne de Handball

FThS .... Foititikos Theologikos Syndesmos [*Theological Association of Students*] [*Greek*] (GC)

FTI .... Dansk Fiskeriteknologisk Institut [*Danish Institute of Fisheries Technology*] [*Information service or system*] (IID)

FTI .... Film and Television Group [*Western Australia*]

FTI .... Flanders Technology International [*European technology fair*]

FTI .... Foldmero es Talajvizsgalo Iroda [*Surveying and Soil Testing Office*] (HU)

FTI .... Foreningen Teknisk Information [*Swedish Society on Technical Communication*]

FTI .... Fundacao de Tecnologia Industrial [*Foundation for Industrial Technology*] [*Rio de Janeiro, Brazil*]

FTI .... Institute of Physiotherapy (RU)

FTI .... Physicotechnical Institute (RU)

FTIA .... Family Therapy Institute of Australia

FTIA .... Fellow of the Taxation Institute of Australia (ADA)

FTIB .... Fiji Trade and Investment Board (EAIO)

FtIber .... First Iberian Fund, Inc. [*Associated Press*]

FTII .... Film & Television Institute of India

FTILAC .... Federation des Travailleurs de l'Information, du Livre, de l'Audiovisuel, et de la Culture [*France*]

FTIM .... Federacion de Trabajadores de la Industria Metalurgica [*Federation of Metallurgical Industry Workers*] [*Peru*] (LA)

FTIP .... Federacion de Trabajadores de la Industria Pesquera [*Federation of Fishing Industry Workers*] [*Venezuela*] (LA)

FTIT .... Fellow of the Institute of Taxation [*British*] (DCTA)

FTIWA ...... Film and Television Institute (Western Australia)

FTK .... Filmova Tiskova Korespondence [*Motion Picture Information Bureau*] (CZ)

FTL .... Federal Territory of Lagos

FTL .... Forsvarets Teletekniska Laboratorium [*Sweden*] (PDAA)

FTM .... Federacion de Trabajadores del Metal [*Metalworkers Federation*] [*Venezuela*] (LA)

FTM .... Federacion de Trabajadores de Managua [*Managua Workers Federation*] [*Nicaragua*] (LA)

FTM .... Foiben-Taosarintanin'i Madagasikara [*National Institute of Geodesy and Cartography*] [*Madagascar*]

FTM .... Fondations et Travaux Miniers

FTM .... Front des Technicians Malgaches [*Malagasy Technicians Front*] (AF)

FTMA....... Fellow of the Australian Institute of Taxation and Management Accountants

FTMMC.... Federacion de Trabajadores Mineros y Metalurgicos del Centro [*Federation of Miners and Metalworkers of the Central Zone*] [*Peru*] (LA)

FTMP........ Federacion de Trabajadores Maritimos de Panama [*Federation of Maritime Workers of Panama*] (LA)

FTMTK ..... Fivondronan'ny Tanora Malagasy Tantsaha Katolika [*Movement of Malagasy Catholic Rural Youth*] (AF)

FTN .... Federacion de Trabajadores Nicaraguenses [*Political party*] (EY)

FTN .... Federation Tunisienne de Natation

FTN .... Forces Terrestres et Navales

FTN .... Franja Transversal del Norte [*Northern Transversal Strip*] [*Guatemala*]

FTN .... Frente de Transformacion Nacional [*Colombia*] (COL)

FTNS........ Frente de Trabajadores Nacional Sindicalista [*National Trade Union Workers Front*] [*Spanish*] (WER)

FTO .... Film and Television Office New South Wales [*Australia*]

FTO .... Foreign Trade Organization (IMH)

FToMM..... International Federation for the Theory of Machines and Mechanisms (SLS)

FTOO .... Fovarosi Tanacs Oktatasi Osztalya [*Education Department of the Capital City Council*] (HU)

ftorm .... Fotorzsormester [*Master Sergeant*] (HU)

FTP............ Faraday Dark Space (RU)

FTP............ Federacion de Trabajadores de Pichincha [*Pichincha Workers Federation*] [*Ecuador*] (LA)

FTP............ Federacion de Trabajadores Pesqueros [*Fishing Industry Workers Federation*] [*Venezuela*] (LA)

FTP............ Federacion de Trabajadores Petroleros [*Oil Workers Federation*] [*Venezuela*] (LA)

FTP............ Francs-Tireurs et Partisans [*Guerrillas and Partisans*] [*French*]

FTPAA ...... Film and Television Producers' [*or Production*] Association of Australia

FTPB .... Federacion de Trabajadores de la Prensa [*Bolivian Press Federation of Newspaper Workers*] (LA)

FTPC .... Francs-Tireurs et Partisans Corses [*Corsican Guerrillas and Partisans*] (PD)

FTPF......... Francs-Tireurs et Partisans Francais [*French Guerrillas and Partisans*]

FTPP .... Festiwal Teatrow Polski Polnocnej [*North Poland Theatre Festival*] (POL)

FTR........... Federacion de Trabajadores Revolucionarios [*Revolutionary Workers' Federation*] [*El Salvador*] (PD)

FTR........... Finist' Air [*France*] [*ICAO designator*] (FAAC)

FTR........... Frente de Trabajadores Revolucionarios [*Revolutionary Workers Front*] [*Chile*] (LA)

F Tr .... Fusion Treaty [*European Communities*] [*1965*] (ILCA)

FTRP .... Federacion de Trabajadores de la Revolucion Peruana [*Federation of Workers of the Peruvian Revolution*] (LA)

FTS .... Fellow of the Australian Academy of Technological Sciences (ADA)

FTS .... Funds Transfer Services (Australia) Ltd.

FTs............ (Pulse-) Shaping Circuit (RU)

FTSC .... Fako Transport Shipping Lines [*Joint venture between Cameroon and the US*] [*Shipping line*] (EY)

FTsGIA ..... Branch of the Central State Historical Archives (RU)

FTsGVIA... Branch of the Central State Archives of Military History (RU)

f-tsiya .... Function [*Mathematics*] (RU)

FTSKB...... Findik Tarim Satis Kooperatifleri Birligi [*Hazel Nut Agricultural Sales Cooperatives Union*] (TU)

FTSNSW... Furnishing Trades Society of New South Wales [*Australia*]

ft solut .... Fiat Solutio [*Let a Solution Be Made*] [*Pharmacy*] [*Latin*] (MAE)

FTsTA .... Branch of Central Technical Archives (RU)

FTT........... Federation Tunisienne de Tennis

FTT........... Solid State Physics (RU)

FTTA .... Sarh [*Chad*] [*ICAO location identifier*] (ICLI)

FTTB .... Bongor [*Chad*] [*ICAO location identifier*] (ICLI)

FTTC .... Abeche [*Chad*] [*ICAO location identifier*] (ICLI)

FTTD........ Moundou [*Chad*] [*ICAO location identifier*] (ICLI)

FTTE .... Biltine [*Chad*] [*ICAO location identifier*] (ICLI)

FTTF .... Fada [*Chad*] [*ICAO location identifier*] (ICLI)

FTTG .... Goz-Beida [*Chad*] [*ICAO location identifier*] (ICLI)

FTTH........ Lai [*Chad*] [*ICAO location identifier*] (ICLI)

FTTI .... Ati [*Chad*] [*ICAO location identifier*] (ICLI)

FTTJ......... N'Djamena [*Chad*] [*ICAO location identifier*]

FTTK........ Bokoro [*Chad*] [*ICAO location identifier*] (ICLI)

FTTL .... Bol [*Chad*] [*ICAO location identifier*] (ICLI)

FTTM....... Mongo [*Chad*] [*ICAO location identifier*] (ICLI)

FTTN........ Am-Timan [*Chad*] [*ICAO location identifier*] (ICLI)

FTTP .... Pala [*Chad*] [*ICAO location identifier*] (ICLI)

FTTR........ Zouar [*Chad*] [*ICAO location identifier*] (ICLI)

FTTS .... Bousso [*Chad*] [*ICAO location identifier*] (ICLI)

FTTT .... N'Djamena [*Chad*] [*ICAO location identifier*] (ICLI)

FTTU........ Mao [*Chad*] [*ICAO location identifier*] (ICLI)

FTTV........ N'Djamena [*Chad*] [*ICAO location identifier*] (ICLI)

FTTY .... Faya-Largeau [*Chad*] [*ICAO location identifier*] (ICLI)

FTTZ .... Bardai-Zougra [*Chad*] [*ICAO location identifier*] (ICLI)

FTU .... Federation des Travailleurs Unis [*United Workers Federation*] [*Mauritius*] (AF)

FTU .... Fishery Technical Unit [*Israel*] (MSC)

FTU .... Fort Dauphin [*Madagascar*] [*Airport symbol*] (OAG)

ftu.............. Fotiszteletu [*Right Reverend*] (HU)

FTU .... Hong Kong Federation of Trade Unions

FTU-B .... Free Trades Unions of Burma

FTUC .... Fiji Trades Union Congress

FTUN .... Federacion de Transportadores Unidos Nicaraguense [*United Transport Workers' Federation of Nicaragua*] (EY)

FTUV........ Federated Teachers' Union of Victoria [*Australia*]

FTV .... Federacion de Trabajadores Venezolanos [*Federation of Venezuelan Workers*] [*Caracas*] (LAA)

FTV .... Filmtechnikai Vallalat [*Phototechnical Enterprise*] (HU)

FTV .... Fovarosi Takarito Vallalat [*Capital Cleaning Enterprise*] (HU)

FTV........... Friestelers van Suid-Afrika [*South Africa*] (AA)

FTV........... Masvingo [*Zimbabwe*] [*Airport symbol*] (OAG)

FTV .... Wage Fund (BU)

FTWUA...... Federated Tobacco Workers' Union of Australia

FTX.......... Owando [*Congo*] [*Airport symbol*] (OAG)

FTYa........ Ferrite-Transistor Cell (RU)

FTYa........ Ferrite-Triode Cell (RU)

FTZ............ Fernmeldtechnisches Zentralamt [*Telecommunications Central Exchange*] (EG)

FTZ........... Free Trade Zone (IMH)

Ftza .... Fortaleza [*Fortress*] [*Portuguese*] (NAU)

FU .... Faglige Ungdom [*Trade Union Youth*] [*Denmark*] (WEN)

FU .... Filmovy Ustav [*Film Institute*] (CZ)

FU .... Finance Administration (RU)

FU .... Firat Universitei [*Euphrates University*] (TU)

FU .... Flinders University [*Australia*]

FU .... Foederalistische Union [*Federal Union*] [*Germany*] [*Political party*] (PPE)

FU .... Freie Union in Niedersachsen [*Free Union in Lower Saxony*] [*Germany*] [*Political party*] (PPW)

FU .... Freie Universitaet (Berlin) [*Free University (Berlin)*] [*Information retrieval*] [*Germany*]

Fu .... Funk [*Radio*] [*German*] (GCA)

Fu .... Funker [*Radio Operator*] (EG)

FU .... Fysikalni Ustav [*Institute of Physics (of the Czechoslovak Academy of Sciences)*] (CZ)

FU .... Shaping Device (RU)

FUA .... Compania Hispano Irlandesa de Aviacion [*Spain*] [*ICAO designator*] (FAAC)

FUA .... Federacion Universitaria Argentina [*Argentine University Federation*] (LA)

FUA .... Frente Unida Angolana [*Angolan United Front*] (AF)

FUAAV...... Federation Universelle des Associations d'Agences de Voyages [*Universal Federation of Travel Agents' Associations - UFTAA*] (EAIO)

FUACE...... Federation Universelle des Associations Chretiennes d'Etudiants [*World Student Christian Federation*] [*Use WSCF*] (AF)

FUAF........ Federation of Uganda African Farmers

FUAI......... Front Uni pour l'Autonomie Interne [*United Front for Internal Autonomy*] [*French Polynesia*] [*Political party*] (PPW)

FUAJ .... Federation Unie des Auberges de Jeunesse [*United Federation of Youth Hostels*] [*French*] (WER)

FUAM .... Freie und Angenommene Maurer [*Free and Accepted Mason*] [*Freemasonry*] [*German*]

FUAN .... Fronte Universitario di Azione Nazionale [*University Front of National Action*] [*Italian*] (WER)

FUAR .... Frente Unido de Accion Revolucionaria [*United Front for Revolutionary Action*] [*Colorado*] (LA)

FUAS........ Fundacion de Viviendas y Asistencia Social [*Chile*] (LAA)

FUB .... Federacion Universitaria Boliviana [*Bolivian University Students Federation*] (LA)

FUB .... Federacion Uruguaya de Bochas [*Uruguayan Bocce Federation*] (EAIO)

FUB .... Federalist Union of Brittany [*France See also UKB*] (EAIO)

FUB .... Fondazione Ugo Bordoni [*Italy*] (PDAA)

FUB .... Front de l'Unite Bangala

FUB .... Fulleborn [*Papua New Guinea*] [*Airport symbol*] (OAG)

FUBA......... Federacion Universitaria de Buenos Aires [*Buenos Aires University Federation*] [*Argentina*] (LA)

FUC .... Federacion Universitaria de Cordoba [*Cordoba University Federation*] [*Argentina*] (LA)

FUC .... Federation Unie Chimie [*France*]

FUC .... Frente de Unidad Campesina [*Peasant Unity Front*] [*Honduras*] (LA)

FUC .... Frente de Unidad Clasista [*Class Unity Front*] [*Ecuador*] (LA)

FUC .... Frente Unico Constitucionalista [*Single Constitutionalist Front*] [*Ecuador*] (LA)

FUCA .... Federacion Uruguaya de Cooperativas Agropecuarias [*Uruguayan Federation of Farm Cooperatives*] (LA)

FUCAC.... Federacion Uruguaya de Cooperativas de Ahorro y Credito [*Uruguayan Federation of Savings and Loan Cooperatives*] (LA)

FUCODES ... Fundacion Costarricense de Desarrollo [*Costa Rican Development Foundation*] (LA)

FUCREA ... Federacion Uruguaya de Centros Regionales de Experimentacion Agropecuaria [*Uruguayan Federation of Regional Agricultural and Livestock Experimentation Centers*] (LA)

FUCU .... Fundacion Cultural Universal [*Colombia*] (COL)

FUD .... Frente Voluntario de Defensa [*Voluntary Defense Front*] [*Guatemala*] (PD)

FUDA .... Frente Unido de Agronomia [*United Front of Agronomy*] [*Panama*] (LA)

FUDC .... Frente Universitario Democrata Cristiano [*Christian Democratic University Front*] [*Bolivia*] (LA)

FUDE .... Federacion Universitaria Democratica Espanola [*Spanish Democratic University Federation*] (WER)

FUDECO... Fundacion para el Desarrollo de la Region Centro Occidental [*Foundation for the Development of the Middle Western Region*] [*Venezuela*] (LA)

FUDEM .... Federacion Uruguaya de Musicos [*Uruguayan Federation of Musicians*] (LA)

FUDEPA ... Frente Unico de Defensa de la Economia Popular de Arequipa [*United Front for the Defense of the People's Economy of Arequipa*] [*Peru*] (LA)

FUDFYFA ... Fideicomiso Unico para el Desarrollo de la Flora y Fauna Acuaticas [*Mexico*] (MSC)

FUDI .... Frente Unido Democratico Independiente [*United Independent Democratic Front*] [*El Salvador*] (LA)

FUDIC....... Frente Unico de Defensa de los Intereses del Departamento de Cuzco [*United Front for the Defense of the Interests of Cuzco Department*] [*Peru*] (LA)

FUDM .... Frente Unida Democratica de Mocambique [*United Democratic Front of Mozambique*] (AF)

FUDP .... Frente de Union Democratica Popular [*Popular Democratic Union Front*] [*Bolivia*] (LA)

FUDUT ..... Federacion Uruguaya de Docentes de la Universidad de Trabajo [*Uruguayan Teachers Federation of the Labor University*] (LA)

FUE .... Fuerteventura [*Canary Islands*] [*Airport symbol*] (OAG)

FUEA........ Frente de Unidad Estudiantil Abelista [*Abelista Student Unity Front*] [*Panama*] (LA)

FUECI .... Federacion Uruguaya de Empleados de Comercio e Industria [*Uruguayan Federation of Employees of Commerce and Industry*] (LA)

FUEGO ..... Frente Unido del Estudiantado Guatemalteco [*United Front of Guatemalan Students*] (LA)

FUEL-GAS ... Federated Union of Energy Leaders - General Allied Services [*Philippines*] (EY)

FUEMSSO ... Federation of United Kingdom and Eire Malaysian and Singaporean Students [*British*]

FUEN .... Federal Union of European Nationalities [*Political party*] (PPW)

FUEP........ Frente Universitario Estudiantil Progresista [*Progressive University Student Front*] [*Guatemala*] (LA)

FUER........ Federacion Universitaria de Estudiantes Revolucionarios [*Federation of Revolutionary University Students*] [*Dominican Republic*] (LA)

FUEV........ Foederalistische Union Europaeischer Volksgruppen [*Federal Union of European Nationalities*]

FUF.......... Federation for Universal French (EAIO)

FUF.......... French Union Forces (VNW)

FUFEPO .. Fuerzas Federalistas Populares [*Popular Federalist Forces*] [*Argentina*] (LA)

FUG .... Felderito Uszo Gepkocsi [*Amphibious Reconnaissance Vehicle*] [*Military*] (HU)

FUG .... Fuyang [*China*] [*Airport symbol*] (OAG)

fugg .... Fuggelek [*Appendix*] [*Publishing*] [*Hungary*]

FUGIT....... First Union General Investment Trust Ltd. [*South Africa*]

fugtpl........ Fugtplettet [*Damp-Stained*] [*Publishing Danish/Norwegian*]

fugtsk .... Fugtskjold [*Damp Stain*] [*Publishing Danish/Norwegian*]

FUH.......... Fondazione Universale Hallesint [*Italian*]

Fuhr.......... Fuehrung [*Conduct*] [*German*] (GCA)

FUI .... Division for the Advanced Training of Engineers (RU)

FUI .... Fisherman's Union in Israel (EAIO)

FUI .... Foresters Union of Italy (EAIO)

FUIAL....... Fabrica Uberlandense de Implementos Agricolas Ltd. [*Brazil*] (DSCA)

FUICO...... Frente Unida para a Independencia dentro la Comunidade

FUILA ...... Federazione Unitaria Italiana Lavoratori Abbigliamento [*Italian Amalgamated Federation of Garment Workers*]

FUINCA.... Fundacion para el Fomento de la Informacion Automatizada [*Foundation for the Promotion of Automated Information*] [*Information service or system*] (IID)

FUJ .... Fujairah Aviation Centre [*United Arab Emirates*] [*ICAO designator*] (FAAC)

FUJ .... Fukue [*Japan*] [*Airport symbol*] (OAG)

FUJA......... Frente Unida da Juventude de Angola

FUK .... Fabryka Urzadzen Kuziennych [*Forge Equipment Factory*] (POL)

FUK .... Fachunterkommission [*Technical Subcommittee*] (EG)

FUK .... Fukuoka [*Japan*] [*Airport symbol*] (OAG)

fuktfl .... Fuktflaeckad [*Damp-Stained*] [*Publishing*] [*Sweden*]

FUL .... Federacion Universitaria Local [*Local University Federation*] [*Bolivia*] (LA)

FUL .... Frente de Unidad Liberal [*Honduras*] [*Political party*] (EY)

FUL .... Frente Unido de Liberacion [*United Liberation Front*] [*Colorado*] (LA)

FUL .... Frente Universitario Laboral [*University Labor Front*] [*Chile*]

FUL .... Front Uni de Liberation de la Guinee et du Cap Vert

FUL .... Front Uni Liberateur de la Guinee Portuguesa et des Isles du Cap Vert [*United Liberation Front of Portuguese Guinea and Cape Verde*] [*Political party*]

FULA........ Frente Unida para a Libertacao de Angola

FULC........ Federazione Unitaria Lavoratori Chimici [*Federation of Chemical and Allied Workers*] [*Rome, Italy*]

fuldst.......... Fuldstaendig [*Complete*] [*Publishing Danish/Norwegian*]

FULK........ Front Uni de Liberation Kanake [*New Caledonia*] [*Political party*] (FEA)

Full............ Fuelling [*Filling*] [*German*] (GCA)

FULN .... Frente Unido de Liberacion Nacional [*United Front of National Liberation*] [*Dominican Republic*] (LA)

FULNA...... Frente Unido de Liberacion Nacional [*United Front of National Liberation*] [*Paraguay*] (LA)

FULPARA ... Frente Unitario de Lucha para la Aplicacion de la Reforma Agraria [*Single Front of Struggle for the Enforcement of the Agrarian Reform*] [*Ecuador*] (LA)

FULPIA..... Federazione Unitaria Lavoratori Prodotti Industrie Alimentari e dello Zucchero e dell'Alcool [*Amalgamated Federation of Food Processing, Sugar, and Liquor Industries' Workers*] [*Italian*]

FULREAC ... Fondation de l'Universite de Liege pour les Recherches Scientifiques en Afrique Centrale [*Foundation of Liege University for Scientific Research in Central Africa*] [*Belgium*] (AF)

FULREC ... Fuel and Leather Research Center [*Government of Pakistan*] (WED)

FULRO...... Front Unifie de Lutte des Races Opprimees [*United Front of the Battle for Oppressed Races*] (CL)

FULS .... Federazione Unitaria Lavoratori dello Spettacolo [*Amalgamated Federation of Entertainment Workers*] [*Italian*]

FULZ........ Federacion Universitaria de Lomas De Zamora [*University Federation of Lomas De Zamora*] [*Argentina*] (LA)

FUM .... Fabryka Urzadzen Mechanicznych [*Mechanical Equipment Factory*] (POL)

FUM .... Federacion Uruguaya del Magisterio [*Uruguayan Federation of Primary Teachers*] (LA)

FuM .... Foldmuvelesugyi Miniszterium/Miniszter [*Ministry/Minister of Agriculture*] (HU)

FUM .... Frente de Unidad Magisterial [*Teachers Unity Front*] [*Honduras*] (LA)

FUM .... Frontul Unic Muncitoresc [*United Workers Front*] (RO)

fum .... Fumaroid [*German*] (GCA)

FUME .... Frente Unido de Mujeres del Ecuador [*United Front of Ecuadorean Women*] (LA)

FUMICOL ... Fumigaciones Colombia Ltda. [*Colombia*] (COL)

FUMISA ... Fumigaciones y Servicios Agricolas, SA [*Ecuador*] (DSCA)

FUMN....... Frente Unido del Magisterio Nacional [*National Teachers United Front*] [*Guatemala*] (LA)

FUMO .... Frente Unida de Mocambique [*Mozambique United Front*] (AF)

FUMOA .... Societe des Futs Metalliques de l'Ouest Africain

FUN .... Federacion Universitaria Nacional [*National University Federation*] [*Colorado*] (LA)

FUN .... Feminist Uniting Women [*Australia*]

FUN .... Fondo Universitario Nacional [*ICFES*] [*Colombia*] [*Later,*] (COL)

FUN .... Frente de Unidad Nacional [*National Unity Front*] [*Guatemala*] [*Political party*] (PPW)

FUN .... Frente de Universitarios Nacionalistas [*National University Students Front*] [*Bolivia*] (LA)

FUN .... Frente Unido Nacionalista [*Nationalist United Front*] [*Venezuela*] [*Political party*] (PPW)

FUN .... Funafuti Atol [*Tuvalu*] [*Airport symbol*] (OAG)

FUN .... Fundament [*Slang*] [*British*] (DSUE)

FUN .... Funtshi Aviation Service [*Zaire*] [*ICAO designator*] (FAAC)

FUNA .... Finnish United Nations Association (EAIO)

FUNA .... Frente Unido Nacional Anticomunista [*Anticommunist National United Front*] [*Guatemala*] (LA)

FUNA .... Front d'Union Nationale de l'Angola [*National Union Front of Angola*] (AF)

FUNABEM ... Fundacao Nacional do Bienestar do Menor [*National Child Welfare Foundation*] [*Brazil*] (LA)

FUNACAMH ... Frente de Unidad Nacional Campesino de Honduras (EY)

FUNACAMH ... Frente de Unidad Nacional de Campesinos de Honduras [*National Unity Front of Honduran Peasants*] (LA)

FUNAGRI ... Fundo Geral para Agricultura e Industria [*General Fund for Agriculture and Industry*] [*Brazil*] (LA)

FUNAI ...... Fundacao Nacional do Indio [*National Indian Foundation*] [*Brazil*] (LA)

FUNAI ...... Fundo Nacional de Investimentos [*National Investment Fund*] [*Brazil*] (LA)

FUNAPER ... Fundicion Andina del Peru, SA [*Peruvian Andean Foundry Enterprise, Inc.*] (LA)

FUNC .... Force de l'Union National Cambodge [*Cambodia*] [*Political party*]

FUNC .... Frente de Unidad Campesina [*Peasant Unity Front*] [*Honduras*]

FUNCINPEC ... Front Uni National pour Cambodge Independant, Neutre, Pacifique et Cooperatif [*National United Front for an Independent National, Peaceful, and Cooperative Cambodia*] [*Political party*] (PD)

FUNCOD .. Fundacion Nicaraguense para la Conservacion y el Desarrollo [*Nicaraguan Foundation for Conservation and Development*] (EAIO)

fund .... Fundador [*Spanish*]

Fund .... Fundeadouro [*Anchorage*] [*Portuguese*] (NAU)

FUNDACOMUN ... Fundacion para el Desarrollo de la Comunidad y Fomento Municipal [*Foundation for Community and Municipal Development*] [*Venezuela*] (LA)

FUNDAEC ... Fundacion para la Aplicacion y Ensenanza de las Ciencias [*Colombia*]

FUNDAG .. Fundo de Desenvolvimento Agricola [*Agricultural Development Fund*] [*Brazil*] (LA)

FUNDAGRO ... Fundo de Desenvolvimento Agropecuario [*Fund for Agriculture and Livestock Development*] [*Brazil*] (LA)

FUNDAGUARICO ... Fundacion para el Desarrollo y Fomento Municipal del Estado Guarico [*Venezuela*] (LAA)

Fundamentproyekt ... State Institute for the Planning of Foundations and Substructures (RU)

FUNDAP... Fundacion para el Desarrollo Integral de Programas Socio-Economicos [*Foundation for the Integrated Development of Socio-Economic Programmes*] [*Guatemala*]

FUNDAPOL ... Fundacion para la Asistencia Social del Policia [*Venezuela*]

FUNDAR .. Fundacion para el Desarrollo Regional [*Foundation for Regional Development*] [*Argentina*] (ASF)

FUNDASE ... Fundo Especial para o Desenvolvimento do Programa Habitacional do Instituto de Previdencia e Assistencia dos Servidores do Estado [*Special Fund for the Development of a Housing Program for the State Employees Social Welfare and Assistance Institute*] [*Brazil*] (LA)

FUNDASOL ... Fundacion Uruguaya de Cooperacion y Desarrollo Solidarios [*Uruguayan Foundation of Joint Cooperation and Development*] (EAIO)

FUNDAVAC ... Fundacion Venezolana para el Avance de la Ciencia [*Venezuela*] (LAA)

FUNDAVICO ... Fundacion Panamena de Vivienda Cooperativa [*Panamanian Cooperative Housing Foundation*] (LAA)

FUNDE ..... Fundacion Nicaraguense de Desarrollo [*Nicaraguan Development Foundation*] (LA)

FUNDEA .. Fundacion para la Extension Agropecuaria [*Agriculture and Livestock Extension Service*] [*Argentina*] (LA)

FUNDECA ... Fundacion para el Desarrollo Rural y la Educacion Campesina [*Venezuela*] (DSCA)

FUNDECE ... Fundo de Democratizacao do Capital das Empresas [*Fund for the Democratization of Enterprise Capital*] [*Brazil*] (LA)

FUNDEFE ... Fundo de Desenvolvimento do Distrito Federal [*Fund for Development of the Federal District*] [*Brazil*] (LA)

FUNDEMOS ... Fundacion para el Desarrollo de Monagas [*Venezuela*] (DSCA)

FUNDEPRO ... Fundo de Desenvolvimento da Produtividade [*Fund for Productivity Development*] [*Brazil*] (LA)

FUNDES... Fundacion Nacional para el Desarrollo Social [*National Foundation for Social Development*] [*Colorado*] (LA)

FUNDESCO ... Fundacion para el Desarrollo de la Funcion Social de las Comunicaciones (IID)

FUNDINOR ... Fundo de Desenvolvimento do Nordeste [*Northeast Development Fund*] [*Brazil*] (LA)

FUNDIPRA ... Fundo de Desenvolvimento da Industrializacao de Produtos Agropecuarios e de Pesca [*Brazil*] (DSCA)

FUNDWI .. United Nations Fund for West Irian (IN)

FUNET...... [*The*] Finnish University Network [*Finland*] [*Computer science*] (TNIG)

FUNFERTIL ... Fundo de Estimulo Financeiro ao Uso de Fertilizantes e Suplementos Minerais [*Fund for Financially Encouraging the Use of Fertilizers and Mineral Supplements*] [*Brazil*] (LA)

FUNGIRO ... Fundo Especial para o Financiamento de Capital de Giro [*Special Fund to Finance Working Capital*] [*Brazil*] (LA)

FUNILS .... Flinders University of South Australia, National Institute of Labour Studies

FUNIMAQ ... Fundiciones y Maquinaria SA [*Bucaramanga*] (COL)

FUNINSO ... Fundo de Investimentos Sociais [*Social Investments Fund*] [*Brazil*] (LA)

FUNIPAMO ... Frente Unida Anti-Imperialista Popular Africana de Mocambique

FUNK .... Front Uni National du Kampuchea [*National United Front of Cambodia*] (CL)

FUNKSN... Frente de Union Nacional de Kampuchea para la Salvacion Nacional [*Kampuchean National Union Front for National Salvation*] [*Use KNUFNS*] (LA)

Funkt.......... Funktion [*Function*] [*German*] (GCA)

FUNOF ..... Fundacion para la Orientacion Familiar [*Colombia*] (COL)

FUNPROCOP ... Fundacion Promotora de Cooperativas [*Cooperatives Promotion Foundation*] [*El Salvador*] (LA)

FUNRES ... Fundo de Recuperacao Economica do Espirito Santo [*Espirito Santo Economic Recovery Fund*] [*Brazil*] (LA)

FUNRURAL ... Fundo de Assistencia e Previdencia ao Trabalhador Rural [*Fund for Social Assistance and Welfare for the Rural Worker*] [*Brazil*] (LA)

FUNSA...... Fabrica Uruguaya de Neumaticos, Societe Anonima [*Uruguayan Tire Plant, Inc.*] (LA)

FUNTAC... Federacion Unitaria Nacional de Trabajadores Agricolas y Campesinos [*United Agricultural Workers and Peasants Federation*] [*Costa Rica*] (LA)

FUNTEC... Fundo de Desenvolvimento Tecnico-Cientifico [*Scientific-Technical Development Fund*] [*Brazil*] (LA)

FUNTEL... Fundo Nacional de Telecomunicacoes [*National Telecommunications Fund*] [*Brazil*] (LA)

FUNTEVE ... Fundo de Financiamento da Televisao Educativa [*Fund for Financing Educational Television*] [*Brazil*] (LA)

FUNTP...... Frente Unico Nacional de Trabajadores de Prensa del Peru [*Single National Front of Peruvian Press Workers*] (LA)

FUNTRAC ... Federacion Unitaria Nacional de Trabajadores Agricolas y Campesinos [*National Unified Federation of Agricultural Workers and Peasants*] [*Costa Rica*] (LA)

FUNU........ Forces d'Urgence des Nations-Unies

FUNVAL... Fundacion de Desarrollo de Valencia [*Venezuela*] (LAA)

FUNVICA ... Fundacion de la Vivienda del Caroni [*Venezuela*] (LAA)

FUNVISIS ... Fundacion Venezolana de Investigaciones Sismologicas [*Venezuelan Foundation for Seismological Research*] [*Research center*] (IRC)

FUP .... Federacion Universitaria del Paraguay [*University Federation of Paraguay*] (LA)

FUP .... Forca de Unidade Popular [*Terrorist group*] [*Portugal*] (EY)

FUP .... Frente de Unidad Popular [*People's Unity Front*] [*Honduras*] (LA)

FUP .... Frente por la Unidad del Pueblo [*United Popular Front*] [*Colorado*] [*Political party*] (PPW)

FUP .... Front de l'Union Populaire [*Peoples Union Front*] [*Morocco*] (AF)

FUPAC...... Federacion de Universidades Privadas de America Central (SLS)

FUPCAAB ... Federation des Unions Professionnelles des Courtiers et Agents d'Assurances de Belgique [*Belgium*] (BAS)

FUPCD...... Fonds un Pour Cent pour le Developpement [*One Percent for Development Fund*] (EAIO)

FUPI......... Federacion Universitaria Pro-Independencia de Puerto Rico [*University Federation for Puerto Rican Independence*]

FUPIT .... Fundo de Pesquisas Industriais e Tecnicas [*Industrial and Technical Research Fund*] [*Brazil*] (LA)

FUPS .... Fabrica de Utilaje si Piese de Schimb [*Factory for Equipment and Spare Parts*] (RO)

FUR .... Federation of Unions of Rizal [*Philippines*] (EY)

FUR .... Fehlerunterbrechungs-routine [*German*] (ADPT)

FUR .... Frente de Unidade Revolucionaria [*Front of Revolutionary Unity*] [*Portuguese*] (WER)

FUR .... Frente Unico de Resistencia [*Single Resistance Front*] [*Chile*] (LA)

FUR .... Frente Unico Revolucionario [*Single Revolutionary Front*] [*Bolivia*] (LA)

FUR .... Frente Unido de la Revolucion [*United Revolutionary Front*] [*Guatemala*] [*Political party*] (PPW)

FUR .... Frente Universitario Revolucionario [*Revolutionary University Front*] [*Honduras*]   (LA)

FUR-30 ...... Frente Universitario Revolucionario 30 de Julio [*30th July Revolutionary University Front*] [*El Salvador*]

FUra .... French Urania [*Record label*]

FURAGRO ... Fundo de Racionalizacao da Agroindustria Canavieira do Nordeste [*Brazil*]   (DSCA)

FURD .... Frente Unido Revolucionario Democratico [*United Revolutionary Democratic Front*] [*Guatemala*]   (LA)

FURE .... Frente Universitario Reformista Ecuatoriano [*Ecuadorean University Reformist Front*]   (LA)

FURENE ... Fundo de Pesquisas e Recursos Naturais do Nordeste [*Brazil*]   (DSCA)

FURF .... Federation des Unions Royalistes de France [*Federation of Royalist Unions of France*]   (PPW)

FURFA ...... Fureszaru es Faanyag Nagykereskedelmi Vallalat [*Wood and Lumber Wholesale Trade Enterprise*]   (HU)

FURG .... Fundacao Universidade do Rio Grande [*University Foundation of Rio Grande*] [*Brazil*]   (MSC)

FURNAS ... Central Electrica de Furnas [*Brazil*]   (PDAA)

FURNIDEC ... International Fair of Furniture, Decoration, Lighting Fixtures, Machinery, and Equipment [*Hellexpo*]

FURO .... Furioso [*Furiously*] [*Music*]   (ROG)

FURR .... Frente Universitario Radical Revolucionario [*Revolutionary Radical University Front*] [*Dominican Republic*]   (LA)

FUS .... Fakultni Umelecky Soubor [*Faculty Art Ensemble*]   (CZ)

FUS .... Federacion Uruguaya de Sanitarios [*Federation of Uruguayan Sanitary Workers*]   (LA)

FUS .... Filmovy Umelecky Sbor [*Motion Picture Artistic Ensemble*]   (CZ)

FUS .... Fondo Unido de Solidaridad [*United Solidarity Front*] [*Spanish*]   (WER)

FUS .... Frente de Unidad Sindical [*United Labor Front*] [*Bolivia*]   (LA)

FUS .... Frontul Unitatii Socialiste [*Front of Socialist Unity*] [*Romania*] [*Political party*]   (PPE)

FUS .... Front Uni du Sud [*Southern United Front*] [*Chad*]   (AF)

FUSA .... Flinders University of South Australia   (ADA)

FUSAGRI ... Fundacion Servicio para el Agricultor [*Farmers' Service Foundation*] [*Venezuela*]   (ARC)

FUSD .... Frente Universitario Socialista Democratico [*Socialist Democratic University Front*] [*Dominican Republic*]   (LA)

FUSE .... Frente Unido Socialista Espanol [*Spanish Socialist United Front*]   (WER)

FUSEP ...... Fuerza de Seguridad Publica [*Public Security Force*] [*Honduras*]   (LA)

FuSf .... Fortsetzung und Schluss Folgen [*To Be Continued and Concluded*] [*German*]

FUSM .... Federacion Universitaria de San Marcos [*San Marcos University Students Federation*] [*Peru*]   (LA)

FUSNA .... Fusileros Navales [*Naval Riflemen Corps*] [*Uruguay*]   (LA)

FUSS .... Federacion Unitaria Sindical Salvadorena [*United Trade Union Federation of El Salvador*]

FUSZERT ... Fuszer Ertekesito Allami Vallalat [*State Retail Grocery Enterprise*]   (HU)

FUT .... Fabryka Urzadzen Technicznych [*Technical Equipment Factory*]   (POL)

FUT .... Federacion Unificada de Trabajadores [*Unified Federation of Workers*] [*Venezuela*]   (LA)

FUT .... Frente Unitario de Trabajadores [*United Workers' Front*] [*Chile*]

FUT .... Frente Unitario de Trabajadores [*Single Workers Front*] [*Ecuador*]   (LA)

fut .... Futeral [*Case*] [*For a Book*]   (POL)

fut .... Futur [*French*]   (TPFD)

fut .... Future   (TPFD)

fut .... Futuro [*Future*] [*Portuguese*]

FUT .... Futurum [*Future*] [*Afrikaans*]

FUTB .... Futbol Internacional [*Ministerio de Cultura*] [*Spain*] [*Information service or system*]   (CRD)

FUTC .... Federacion Unica de Trabajadores Campesinos [*Single Federation of Peasant Workers*] [*Bolivia*]   (PD)

FUTE .... Frente Unico de Trabajadores y Estudiantes [*Single Front of Workers and Students*] [*Peru*]   (LA)

FUTEUNI ... Frente Unico de Trabajadores y Estudiantes de la Universidad Nacional de Ingenieria [*Single Front of UNI Workers and Students*] [*Peru*]   (LA)

FUTH .... Federacion Unitaria de Trabajadores de Honduras [*United Workers' Front of Honduras*]

FUTI .... Fovarosi Epitoipari Uzemgazdasagi es Ugyviteli Iroda [*Capital Construction Industry Business Administration and Management Office*]   (HU)

Futt .... Futteral [*Case*] [*German*]

Futter .... Fuetterung [*Wedge*] [*German*]   (GCA)

FUTU .... Federation of Uganda Trade Unions   (AF)

FUTU .... Futures Information Service [*Institute for Futures Studies*] [*Information service or system*] [*Defunct*]

FUU .... Federacion de Universitarios de Uruguay [*Federation of University Students of Uruguay*]   (PD)

FUUD .... Frente Unido Universitario Democratico [*United University Students Democratic Front*] [*Honduras*]   (LA)

fuv .... Fuvarozas [*Transport*]   (HU)

FUVA .... Federacion Unica de Viajantes de la Republica Argentina [*Single Federation of Traveling Salesmen of Argentina*]   (LA)

FuW .... Funkwerk [*Radio Communications Equipment Plant*]   (EG)

FUWG .... Forest Use Working Group [*Australia*]

fuz .... Fuzet [*Issue, Number (Periodicals), or Fascicle*]   (HU)

fuz .... Fuzott [*or Fuzve*] [*Paperbound*]   (HU)

FUZ .... Street Public Address System Feeder Lines   (RU)

FV .... Fahrdienstvorschriften [*Train Service Regulations*]   (EG)

FV .... Farmacevtski Vestnik [*Pharmaceutical Review*] [*Ljubljana*]   (YU)

Fv .... Farni Vestnik [*Parish Bulletin*]   (CZ)

fv .... Felelos Vezeto [*Chief, Manager*]   (HU)

fv .... Felvaszonkotes [*Half-Cloth Binding*] [*Publishing*] [*Hungary*]

FV .... Fiskale Vraagstukken [*Benelux*]   (BAS)

fv .... Fjala Vjen [*Albanian*]

FV .... Freie Vereinigung von Fachleuten Oeffentlicher Verkehrsbetriebe   (SLS)

FV .... French RCA (Victor) [*Record label*]

FV .... Phase Equalizer   (RU)

FVA .... Filter-Ventilation System   (BU)

FVA .... Filtration and Ventilation Unit   (RU)

FVB .... Federale Volksbeleggings [*Federal People's Investment*] [*South Africa*]   (AF)

FVB .... Fiji Visitors' Bureau   (GEA)

FVB .... Foiskolai Vilagbajnoksag [*World Championships of University Students*]   (HU)

FVBB .... Beit Bridge [*Zimbabwe*] [*ICAO location identifier*]   (ICLI)

FVBD .... Bindura [*Zimbabwe*] [*ICAO location identifier*]   (ICLI)

FVBU .... Bulawayo/Bulawayo [*Zimbabwe*] [*ICAO location identifier*]   (ICLI)

FVCH .... Chipinge [*Zimbabwe*] [*ICAO location identifier*]   (ICLI)

FVCh .... High-Pass Filter   (RU)

FVCP .... Harare/Charles Prince [*Zimbabwe*] [*ICAO location identifier*]   (ICLI)

FVCV .... Chiredzi/Buffalo Range [*Zimbabwe*] [*ICAO location identifier*]   (ICLI)

FVD .... Federalni Vybor pro Dopravu [*Federal Committee for Transportation*]   (CZ)

fvda .... Favorecida [*Esteemed*] [*Spanish*]

FVE .... Federation of Veterinarians of the EEC   (EAIO)

fve .... Fuzve [*Stitched*] [*Publishing*] [*Hungary*]

FVerfO ...... Familienrechtsverfahrensordnung [*Code of Family Law Procedure*]   (EG)

FVFA .... Victoria Falls/Victoria Falls [*Zimbabwe*] [*ICAO location identifier*]   (ICLI)

FVG .... Frevag Airlines [*Belgium*] [*ICAO designator*]   (FAAC)

FVGO .... Gokwe [*Zimbabwe*] [*ICAO location identifier*]   (ICLI)

FVGR........ Mutare/Grand Reef [*Zimbabwe*] [*ICAO location identifier*]   (ICLI)

FVGW ...... Gweru/Gweru [*Zimbabwe*] [*ICAO location identifier*]   (ICLI)

FVH .... Foereningen foer Vattenhygien [*Sweden*]   (SLS)

FVHA .... Harare/Harare [*Zimbabwe*] [*ICAO location identifier*]   (ICLI)

FVHC .... Fundacion de Viviendas Hogar de Cristo [*Hogar de Cristo Housing Foundation*] [*Chile*]   (EAIO)

FVHQ .... Harare [*Zimbabwe*] [*ICAO location identifier*]   (ICLI)

FVIN......... Bulawayo/Induna [*Zimbabwe*] [*ICAO location identifier*]   (ICLI)

FVJ .... Federation Mondiale des Villes Jumelees [*North African*]

FVK .... Fabrika Vagona-Kraljevo [*Former Yugoslavia*]   (EE)

FVK .... Filter-Ventilation Chamber [*Air-raid shelter*]   (BU)

FVK .... Filter-Ventilation Set   (BU)

FVK .... Filtration and Ventilation Chamber   (RU)

Fvk .... Flugverkehr [*German*]

FVK .... Photographic Vertical Circle   (RU)

FVK .... Searched Channel [*Navy*]   (RU)

FVKA .... Karoi [*Zimbabwe*] [*ICAO location identifier*]   (ICLI)

FVKB .... Kariba/Kariba [*Zimbabwe*] [*ICAO location identifier*]   (ICLI)

FVKK .... Kwekwe [*Zimbabwe*] [*ICAO location identifier*]   (ICLI)

FVL .... Frontline Veterinary Hospital   (RU)

FVM .... Farm for Raising Young Animals   (RU)

FVM .... Federacion Venezolana de Maestros [*Venezuelan Teachers Federation*]   (LA)

FVM .... Foreningen Svenska Verktygs-och Verktygsmaskintillverkare [*Swedish Machine Tool and Cutting Tool Manufacturers Association*]   (EAIO)

FVM .... Fovarosi Vizmuvek [*Capital Water Works*]   (HU)

FVM .... Viet-Nam Youth Federation [*North Vietnamese*]   (RU)

FVMA .... Marondera [*Zimbabwe*] [*ICAO location identifier*]   (ICLI)

FVMT........ Mutoko [*Zimbabwe*] [*ICAO location identifier*]   (ICLI)

FVMU .... Mutare/Mutare [*Zimbabwe*] [*ICAO location identifier*]   (ICLI)

FVMV........ Masvingo/Masvingo [*Zimbabwe*] [*ICAO location identifier*]   (ICLI)

FVOZ .... Forschungsinstitut der Vereinigung der Osterreichischen Zementindustrie [*Research Institute of the Association of the Austrian Cement Industry*]   (EAIO)

FVP .... Federalni Vybor pro Prumysl [*Federal Committee for Industry*]   (CZ)

FVP .... Freie Volkspartei [*Free People's Party*] [*Germany*] [*Political party*]   (PPE)

FVPT .... Federalni Vybor pro Posty a Telekomunikace [*Federal Committee for Postal Affairs and Telecommunications*]   (CZ)

FVPTIP ..... Federacion Venezolana de Pescadores y Trabajadores de la Industria Pesquera [*Venezuelan Federation of Fisherman and Fishing Industry Workers*]   (EAIO)

FVR .... Federal Department of Veterinary Research

FVRU .... Rusape [*Zimbabwe*] [*ICAO location identifier*]   (ICLI)

FVS .... Federation of Film Societies   (EAIO)

FVS .... Forschungsgesellschaft fuer das Verkehrs- und Strassenwesen im OIAV [*Austria*]   (SLS)

FVS .... Frontline Clothing and Equipment Depot   (RU)

FVSA .... Federation of Victorian School Administrators [*Australia*]

FVSA .... Fotografiese Vereniging van Suider Afrika [*South Africa*]   (AA)

FVSH .... Zvishavane [*Zimbabwe*] [*ICAO location identifier*]   (ICLI)

FVSSSF .... Finska Vetenskaps-Societeten-Societas Scientiarum Fennica [*Finnish Society of Sciences and Letters*]   (EAIO)

FVSV .... Victoria Falls/Spray View [*Zimbabwe*] [*ICAO location identifier*]   (ICLI)

FVTIR .... Federalni Vybor pro Technicky a Investicni Rozvoj [*Federal Committee for Technical and Investment Development*]   (CZ)

FVTL .... Gweru/Thornhill [*Zimbabwe*] [*ICAO location identifier*]   (ICLI)

FVV .... Forschungsvereiningung Verbrennungskraftmaschine eV   (SLS)

FVV .... Fovarosi Vasutepito Vallalat [*Capital Railway Construction Enterprise*]   (HU)

FVV .... Fovarosi Villamos Vasut [*Capital Electric Railways*]   (HU)

FVVA .... Femmes, Voiture, Villa, Argent

FVWC .... Federation of Victorian Walking Clubs [*Australia*]

FVWN .... Hwange/Hwange National Park [*Zimbabwe*] [*ICAO location identifier*]   (ICLI)

FVWT .... Hiwange Town [*Zimbabwe*] [*ICAO location identifier*]   (ICLI)

FVYa .... Division of Oriental Languages   (RU)

FVZC .... Zisco [*Zimbabwe*] [*ICAO location identifier*]   (ICLI)

FVZV .... Federalni Vybor pro Zemedelstvi a Vyzivu [*Federal Committee for Agriculture and Food*]   (CZ)

Fw .... Faillissementswet [*Benelux*]   (BAS)

Fw .... Feldwebel [*Sergeant*] [*Air Corps rank*]

Fw .... Fermeldewerkstatt [*Communications Shop*]   (EG)

FW .... Festwertspeicher [*German*]   (ADPT)

FW .... Focke-Wulf GmbH [*Germany*] [*ICAO aircraft manufacturer identifier*]   (ICAO)

FW .... Front Walfougui [*Walfougui Front*] [*Mauritania*]   (AF)

Fw .... Fuerwort [*Pronoun*] [*German*]

FW .... Le Point Air [*France*] [*ICAO designator*]   (ICDA)

FWA .... Flemish Watersports Association [*Belgium*]   (EAIO)

FWA .... French Water Study Association   (EAIO)

FWAA .... Fiji-West Australian Association

FWACC.... Federation of West African Chambers of Commerce

FWACP .... Fellowship Examinations of the West African College of Physicians

FWAT .... Free Workmen's Association of Thailand

FWB .... Fresh Water Ballasting

FWBG .... Bangula [*Malawi*] [*ICAO location identifier*]   (ICLI)

FWBPC ..... Federal Wine and Brandy Producers' Council of Australia   (ADA)

FWBS .... Farm Writers and Broadcasters' Society [*Australia*]

FWC .... Filipino Women's Council [*Australia*]

FWC .... Freeway Air BV [*Netherlands*] [*ICAO designator*]   (FAAC)

FWCC....... Chintheche [*Malawi*] [*ICAO location identifier*]   (ICLI)

FWCC....... Federation of West African Chambers of Commerce

FWCC....... Friends World Committee for Consultation [*British*]   (EAIO)

FWCCANZ ... Federation of Wall and Ceiling Contractors of Australia and New Zealand

FWCD ...... Chelinda [*Malawi*] [*ICAO location identifier*]   (ICLI)

FWCL........ Blantyre/Chileka [*Malawi*] [*ICAO location identifier*]   (ICLI)

FWCM ...... Makokola Club [*Malawi*] [*ICAO location identifier*]   (ICLI)

FWCS .... Ntchisi [*Malawi*] [*ICAO location identifier*]   (ICLI)

FWCT....... Chitipa [*Malawi*] [*ICAO location identifier*]   (ICLI)

FWDC ...... Flemings in the World Development Cooperation [*Belgium*]   (EAIO)

FWDP........ Family Worker Development Program [*Australia*]

FWDW ...... Dwanga [*Malawi*] [*ICAO location identifier*]   (ICLI)

FWDZ .... Dedza [*Malawi*] [*ICAO location identifier*]   (ICLI)

FWERAT .. Fourth World Educational and Research Association Trust   (EA)

FWERI ..... Finnish Water and Environment Research Institute   (IRC)

FWG .... Forschungsanstalt der Bundeswehr fuer Wasserschall und Geophysik [*Research Institute of the Federation for Water Resonance and Geophysics*]   (MSC)

FWHQ....... Lilongwe [*Malawi*] [*ICAO location identifier*]   (ICLI)

FWI............ Fachverband Werkzeugindustrie [*Germany*]   (EAIO)

FWI............ Federatie Wijn/Importgedistilleerd [*Federation of Wine and Spirit Importers*] [*Netherlands*]   (EAIO)

FWI............ Federation of Women's Institutes

FWISA ...... Fellow of the Water Institute of Southern Africa   (AA)

FWK .... Funkwerk Koepenick VEB [*Koepenick Radio Factory VEB*]   (EG)

FWKA........ Karonga [*Malawi*] [*ICAO location identifier*]   (ICLI)

FWKB........ Katumbi [*Malawi*] [*ICAO location identifier*]   (ICLI)

FWKG .... Kasungu/Kasungu [*Malawi*] [*ICAO location identifier*]   (ICLI)

FWKI......... Kamuzu International [*Malawi*] [*ICAO location identifier*]   (ICLI)

FWKK........ Nkhotakota [*Malawi*] [*ICAO location identifier*]   (ICLI)

FWLK........ Likoma [*Malawi*] [*ICAO location identifier*]   (ICLI)

FWLL........ Lilongwe [*Malawi*] [*ICAO location identifier*]   (ICLI)

FWLP........ Kasungu/Lifupa [*Malawi*] [*ICAO location identifier*]   (ICLI)

FWMC ...... Mchinji [*Malawi*] [*ICAO location identifier*]   (ICLI)

FWMG ...... Mangochi [*Malawi*] [*ICAO location identifier*]   (ICLI)

FWMY ...... Monkey Bay [*Malawi*] [*ICAO location identifier*]   (ICLI)

FWMZ....... Mzimba [*Malawi*] [*ICAO location identifier*]   (ICLI)

FWN .... Fernwirknetz [*German*]   (ADPT)

FWP........... Fundusz Wczasow Pracowniczych [*Workers' Vacation Fund*]   (POL)

FWQ .... Flight West Airlines [*Australia*] [*ICAO designator*]   (FAAC)

FWR .... Fehlerwortregister [*German*]   (ADPT)

FWRAP .... Federal Water Resources Assistance Program [*Australia*]

FWSI .... Federation of Wine and Spirit Importers [*Netherlands*]   (EAIO)

FWSJ .... Nsanje [*Malawi*] [*ICAO location identifier*]   (ICLI)

FWSM ...... Salima [*Malawi*] [*ICAO location identifier*]   (ICLI)

FWSU .... Nchalo/Sucoma [*Malawi*] [*ICAO location identifier*]   (ICLI)

FWUU ...... Mzuzu [*Malawi*] [*ICAO location identifier*]   (ICLI)

FWVO .... Finanzwirtschafts-Verordnung [*Fiscal Regulations*]   (EG)

FXBB .... Bobete [*Lesotho*] [*ICAO location identifier*]   (ICLI)

FXKB .... Kolberg [*Lesotho*] [*ICAO location identifier*]   (ICLI)

FXLK .... Lebakeng [*Lesotho*] [*ICAO location identifier*]   (ICLI)

FXLR .... Leribe [*Lesotho*] [*ICAO location identifier*]   (ICLI)

FXLS .... Lesobeng [*Lesotho*] [*ICAO location identifier*]   (ICLI)

FXLT .... Letseng [*Lesotho*] [*ICAO location identifier*]   (ICLI)

FXMA .... Matsaile [*Lesotho*] [*ICAO location identifier*]   (ICLI)

FXMF .... Mafeteng [*Lesotho*] [*ICAO location identifier*]   (ICLI)

FXMH .... Mohales'Hoek [*Lesotho*] [*ICAO location identifier*]   (ICLI)

FXMK .... Mokhotlong [*Lesotho*] [*ICAO location identifier*]   (ICLI)

FXML .... Malefiloane [*Lesotho*] [*ICAO location identifier*]   (ICLI)

FXMM ...... Maseru Moshoeshoe International [*Lesotho*] [*ICAO location identifier*]   (ICLI)

FXMN .... Mantsonyane [*Lesotho*] [*ICAO location identifier*]   (ICLI)

FXMP .... Mohlanapeng [*Lesotho*] [*ICAO location identifier*]   (ICLI)

FXMS .... Mashai Store [*Lesotho*] [*ICAO location identifier*]   (ICLI)

FXMT........ Matabeng Store [*Lesotho*] [*ICAO location identifier*]   (ICLI)

FXMU .... Maseru/Leabua Jonathan [*Lesotho*] [*ICAO location identifier*]   (ICLI)

FXMV........ Matabeng Village [*Lesotho*] [*ICAO location identifier*]   (ICLI)

FXNH .... Nohanas [*Lesotho*] [*ICAO location identifier*]   (ICLI)

FXNK .... Nkaus [*Lesotho*] [*ICAO location identifier*]   (ICLI)

FXPG .... Pelaneng [*Lesotho*] [*ICAO location identifier*]   (ICLI)

FXQG .... Quthing [*Lesotho*] [*ICAO location identifier*]   (ICLI)

FXQN .... Qachas' Nek [*Lesotho*] [*ICAO location identifier*]   (ICLI)

FXSE .... Sehlabathebe [*Lesotho*] [*ICAO location identifier*]   (ICLI)

FXSH .... Sehonghong [*Lesotho*] [*ICAO location identifier*]   (ICLI)

FXSK .... Sekake [*Lesotho*] [*ICAO location identifier*]   (ICLI)

FXSM .... Semongkong [*Lesotho*] [*ICAO location identifier*]   (ICLI)

FXSS .... Seshote [*Lesotho*] [*ICAO location identifier*]   (ICLI)

FXST .... St. Theresa [*Lesotho*] [*ICAO location identifier*]   (ICLI)

FXTA .... Thaba Tseka [*Lesotho*] [*ICAO location identifier*]   (ICLI)

FXTB .... Tebellong [*Lesotho*] [*ICAO location identifier*]   (ICLI)

FXTK .... Tlokoeng [*Lesotho*] [*ICAO location identifier*]   (ICLI)

FXY .... Flexair BV [*Netherlands*] [*ICAO designator*]   (FAAC)

FYa .... Formalized Language   (RU)

FYCOCI .... Federation of Yemen Chambers of Commerce and Industry   (EAIO)

FYD .... Federation of Young Democrats [*Hungary*] [*Political party*]   (EY)

FYDEP ...... Empresa Nacional de Fomento y Desarrollo Economico del Peten [*National Agency for the Economic Promotion and Development of El Peten*] [*Guatemala*]   (LA)

FYeBO....... Federation of European Biochemical Societies   (RU)

FYN .... Fuyun [*China*] [*Airport symbol*]   (OAG)

FYROM .... Former Yugoslav Republic of Macedonia [*Temporary name*]   (ECON)

fys.............. Fysiikka [*Physics*] [*Finland*]

fysiol .... Fysiologia [*Physiology*] [*Finland*]

f-z .... Factory   (RU)

FZ .... Farbzahl [*Color Number*] [*German*]   (GCA)

FZ .... Filmove Zpravodajstvi [*Motion Picture Information Service*]   (CZ)

Fz	Forzando [*or Forzato*] [*Strongly Accented Music*]
FZ	Fundusz Ziemi [*Land Fund*] (POL)
FZA	Fratsuzkaia Zapadnaia Afrika
FZAA	Kinshasa/N'Djili [*Zaire*] [*ICAO location identifier*] (ICLI)
FZAB	Kinshasa/N'Dolo [*Zaire*] [*ICAO location identifier*] (ICLI)
FZAD	Celo-Zongo [*Zaire*] [*ICAO location identifier*] (ICLI)
FZAE	Kimpoko [*Zaire*] [*ICAO location identifier*] (ICLI)
FZAF	Nsangi [*Zaire*] [*ICAO location identifier*] (ICLI)
FZAG	Frontline Antiaircraft Artillery Group (RU)
FZAG	Muanda [*Zaire*] [*ICAO location identifier*] (ICLI)
FZAH	Tshela [*Zaire*] [*ICAO location identifier*] (ICLI)
FZAI	Kitona-Base [*Zaire*] [*ICAO location identifier*] (ICLI)
FZAJ	Boma [*Zaire*] [*ICAO location identifier*] (ICLI)
FZAL	Luozi [*Zaire*] [*ICAO location identifier*] (ICLI)
FZAM	Matadi [*Zaire*] [*ICAO location identifier*] (ICLI)
FZAN	Inga [*Zaire*] [*ICAO location identifier*] (ICLI)
FZAP	Lukala [*Zaire*] [*ICAO location identifier*] (ICLI)
FZAR	Nkolo-Fuma [*Zaire*] [*ICAO location identifier*] (ICLI)
FZAS	Inkisi [*Zaire*] [*ICAO location identifier*] (ICLI)
FZAU	Konde [*Zaire*] [*ICAO location identifier*] (ICLI)
FZAW	Kwilu-Gongo [*Zaire*] [*ICAO location identifier*] (ICLI)
FZAX	Luheki [*Zaire*] [*ICAO location identifier*] (ICLI)
FZAY	Mvula-Sanda [*Zaire*] [*ICAO location identifier*] (ICLI)
FZAZ	Kinshasa [*Zaire*] [*ICAO location identifier*] (ICLI)
FZB	Fundacao Zoobotanica do Rio Grande Do Sul [*Zoobotanical Foundation of Rio Grande Do Sul*] [*Brazil*] (ARC)
FZBA	Inongo [*Zaire*] [*ICAO location identifier*] (ICLI)
FZBB	Bongimba [*Zaire*] [*ICAO location identifier*] (ICLI)
FZBC	Bikoro [*Zaire*] [*ICAO location identifier*] (ICLI)
FZBD	Oshwe [*Zaire*] [*ICAO location identifier*] (ICLI)
FZBE	Beno [*Zaire*] [*ICAO location identifier*] (ICLI)
FZBF	Bontika [*Zaire*] [*ICAO location identifier*] (ICLI)
FZBG	Kempa [*Zaire*] [*ICAO location identifier*] (ICLI)
FZBI	Nioki [*Zaire*] [*ICAO location identifier*] (ICLI)
FZBJ	Mushie [*Zaire*] [*ICAO location identifier*] (ICLI)
FZBK	Bosobe-Boshwe [*Zaire*] [*ICAO location identifier*] (ICLI)
FZBL	Djokele [*Zaire*] [*ICAO location identifier*] (ICLI)
FZBN	Malebo [*Zaire*] [*ICAO location identifier*] (ICLI)
FZBO	Bandundu [*Zaire*] [*ICAO location identifier*] (ICLI)
FZBP	Ngebolobo [*Zaire*] [*ICAO location identifier*] (ICLI)
FZBQ	Bindja [*Zaire*] [*ICAO location identifier*] (ICLI)
FZBS	Semendua [*Zaire*] [*ICAO location identifier*] (ICLI)
FZBT	Kiri [*Zaire*] [*ICAO location identifier*] (ICLI)
FZBU	Ibeke [*Zaire*] [*ICAO location identifier*] (ICLI)
FZBV	Kempili [*Zaire*] [*ICAO location identifier*] (ICLI)
FZBW	Bokote/Basengele [*Zaire*] [*ICAO location identifier*] (ICLI)
FZCA	Kikwit [*Zaire*] [*ICAO location identifier*] (ICLI)
FZCB	Idiofa [*Zaire*] [*ICAO location identifier*] (ICLI)
FZCD	Vanga [*Zaire*] [*ICAO location identifier*] (ICLI)
FZCE	Lusanga [*Zaire*] [*ICAO location identifier*] (ICLI)
FZCF	Kahemba [*Zaire*] [*ICAO location identifier*] (ICLI)
FZCI	Banga [*Zaire*] [*ICAO location identifier*] (ICLI)
FZCK	Kajiji [*Zaire*] [*ICAO location identifier*] (ICLI)
FZCL	Banza-Lute [*Zaire*] [*ICAO location identifier*] (ICLI)
FZCO	Boko [*Zaire*] [*ICAO location identifier*] (ICLI)
FZCP	Popokabaka [*Zaire*] [*ICAO location identifier*] (ICLI)
FZCR	Busala [*Zaire*] [*ICAO location identifier*] (ICLI)
FZCS	Kenge [*Zaire*] [*ICAO location identifier*] (ICLI)
FZCT	Fatundu [*Zaire*] [*ICAO location identifier*] (ICLI)
FZCU	Ito [*Zaire*] [*ICAO location identifier*] (ICLI)
FZCV	Masi-Manimba [*Zaire*] [*ICAO location identifier*] (ICLI)
FZCW	Kikongo Sur Wamba [*Zaire*] [*ICAO location identifier*] (ICLI)
FZCX	Kimafu [*Zaire*] [*ICAO location identifier*] (ICLI)
FZCY	Yuki [*Zaire*] [*ICAO location identifier*] (ICLI)
FZDA	Malanga [*Zaire*] [*ICAO location identifier*] (ICLI)
FZDB	Kimbau [*Zaire*] [*ICAO location identifier*] (ICLI)
FZDC	Lukuni [*Zaire*] [*ICAO location identifier*] (ICLI)
FZDD	Wamba-Luadi [*Zaire*] [*ICAO location identifier*] (ICLI)
FZDE	Tono [*Zaire*] [*ICAO location identifier*] (ICLI)
FZDF	Fundacao Zoobotanica do Distrito Federal [*Brazil*] (DSCA)
FZDF	Nzamba [*Zaire*] [*ICAO location identifier*] (ICLI)
FZDG	Nyanga [*Zaire*] [*ICAO location identifier*] (ICLI)
FZDH	Ngi [*Zaire*] [*ICAO location identifier*] (ICLI)
FZDJ	Mutena [*Zaire*] [*ICAO location identifier*] (ICLI)
FZDK	Kipata' Katika [*Zaire*] [*ICAO location identifier*] (ICLI)
FZDL	Kolokoso [*Zaire*] [*ICAO location identifier*] (ICLI)
FZDM	Masamuna [*Zaire*] [*ICAO location identifier*] (ICLI)
FZDN	Mongo Wa Kenda [*Zaire*] [*ICAO location identifier*] (ICLI)
FZDO	Moanda [*Zaire*] [*ICAO location identifier*] (ICLI)
FZDP	Mukedi [*Zaire*] [*ICAO location identifier*] (ICLI)
FZDS	Yasa-Bonga [*Zaire*] [*ICAO location identifier*] (ICLI)
FZDT	Matari [*Zaire*] [*ICAO location identifier*] (ICLI)
FZDU	Kimpangu [*Zaire*] [*ICAO location identifier*] (ICLI)
FZDY	Misay [*Zaire*] [*ICAO location identifier*] (ICLI)
FZEA	Mbandaka [*Zaire*] [*ICAO location identifier*] (ICLI)
FZEB	Monieka [*Zaire*] [*ICAO location identifier*] (ICLI)
FZEG	Lokolela [*Zaire*] [*ICAO location identifier*] (ICLI)
FZEI	Ingende [*Zaire*] [*ICAO location identifier*] (ICLI)
FZEM	Yembe-Moke [*Zaire*] [*ICAO location identifier*] (ICLI)
FZEN	Basankusu [*Zaire*] [*ICAO location identifier*] (ICLI)
FZEO	Beongo [*Zaire*] [*ICAO location identifier*] (ICLI)
FZEP	Mentole [*Zaire*] [*ICAO location identifier*] (ICLI)
FZER	Kodoro [*Zaire*] [*ICAO location identifier*] (ICLI)
FZFA	Libenge [*Zaire*] [*ICAO location identifier*] (ICLI)
FZFB	Imasse [*Zaire*] [*ICAO location identifier*] (ICLI)
FZFD	Gbadolite [*Zaire*] [*ICAO location identifier*] (ICLI)
FZFE	Abumumbazi [*Zaire*] [*ICAO location identifier*] (ICLI)
FZFF	Bau [*Zaire*] [*ICAO location identifier*] (ICLI)
FZFG	Bokada [*Zaire*] [*ICAO location identifier*] (ICLI)
FZFH	Mokaria-Yamoleta [*Zaire*] [*ICAO location identifier*] (ICLI)
FZFJ	Goyongo [*Zaire*] [*ICAO location identifier*] (ICLI)
FZFK	Gemena [*Zaire*] [*ICAO location identifier*] (ICLI)
FZFL	Kala [*Zaire*] [*ICAO location identifier*] (ICLI)
FZFN	Lombo [*Zaire*] [*ICAO location identifier*] (ICLI)
FZFP	Kotakoli [*Zaire*] [*ICAO location identifier*] (ICLI)
FZFQ	Mpaka [*Zaire*] [*ICAO location identifier*] (ICLI)
FZFS	Karawa [*Zaire*] [*ICAO location identifier*] (ICLI)
FZFT	Tandala [*Zaire*] [*ICAO location identifier*] (ICLI)
FZFU	Bumba [*Zaire*] [*ICAO location identifier*] (ICLI)
FZFV	Gbado [*Zaire*] [*ICAO location identifier*] (ICLI)
FZFW	Gwaka [*Zaire*] [*ICAO location identifier*] (ICLI)
FZG	Forschungstelle fuer Zahnrader and Getriebau
FZGA	Lisala [*Zaire*] [*ICAO location identifier*] (ICLI)
FZGB	Bosondjo [*Zaire*] [*ICAO location identifier*] (ICLI)
FZGD	Bokenge [*Zaire*] [*ICAO location identifier*] (ICLI)
FZGF	Bokungu [*Zaire*] [*ICAO location identifier*] (ICLI)
FZGG	Mondombe [*Zaire*] [*ICAO location identifier*] (ICLI)
FZGH	Wema [*Zaire*] [*ICAO location identifier*] (ICLI)
FZGI	Yalingimba [*Zaire*] [*ICAO location identifier*] (ICLI)
FZGN	Boende [*Zaire*] [*ICAO location identifier*] (ICLI)
FZGT	Boteka [*Zaire*] [*ICAO location identifier*] (ICLI)
FZGV	Ikela [*Zaire*] [*ICAO location identifier*] (ICLI)
FZGY	Yemo [*Zaire*] [*ICAO location identifier*] (ICLI)
FZH	Fond Znarodneneho Hospodarstvi [*Fund of the Nationalized Economy*] (CZ)
FZhP	Animal Protein Factor (BU)
FZhYeL	Forced Vital Capacity (RU)
FZIA	Kisangani [*Zaire*] [*ICAO location identifier*] (ICLI)
FZIC	Kisangani/Bangoka [*Zaire*] [*ICAO location identifier*] (ICLI)
FZIF	Ubundu [*Zaire*] [*ICAO location identifier*] (ICLI)
FZIK	Katende [*Zaire*] [*ICAO location identifier*] (ICLI)
FZIR	Yangambi [*Zaire*] [*ICAO location identifier*] (ICLI)
FZIZ	Lokutu [*Zaire*] [*ICAO location identifier*] (ICLI)
FZj	Farbzahl Gegen Jod [*Iodine Number*] [*German*] (GCA)
FZJA	Isiro [*Zaire*] [*ICAO location identifier*] (ICLI)
FZJB	Doko [*Zaire*] [*ICAO location identifier*] (ICLI)
FZJF	Aba [*Zaire*] [*ICAO location identifier*] (ICLI)
FZJH	Isiro/Matari [*Zaire*] [*ICAO location identifier*] (ICLI)
FZJI	Watsha [*Zaire*] [*ICAO location identifier*] (ICLI)
FZJK	Faradje [*Zaire*] [*ICAO location identifier*] (ICLI)
FZJR	Kerekere [*Zaire*] [*ICAO location identifier*] (ICLI)
FZK	Factory Committee (RU)
FZKA	Bunia [*Zaire*] [*ICAO location identifier*] (ICLI)
FZKB	Bambili-Dingila [*Zaire*] [*ICAO location identifier*] (ICLI)
FZKC	Mahagi [*Zaire*] [*ICAO location identifier*] (ICLI)
FZKF	Kilomines [*Zaire*] [*ICAO location identifier*] (ICLI)
FZKI	Front Zashchity Konstitutsionnykh-Institutov
FZKI	Yedi [*Zaire*] [*ICAO location identifier*] (ICLI)
FZKJ	Buta Zega [*Zaire*] [*ICAO location identifier*] (ICLI)
FZKN	Aketi [*Zaire*] [*ICAO location identifier*] (ICLI)
FZKO	Ango [*Zaire*] [*ICAO location identifier*] (ICLI)
FZKP	Bondo [*Zaire*] [*ICAO location identifier*] (ICLI)
FZM	Feldzeugmeister [*German*]
FZMA	Bukavu/Kavumu [*Zaire*] [*ICAO location identifier*] (ICLI)
FZMB	Butembo [*Zaire*] [*ICAO location identifier*] (ICLI)
FZMC	Mulungu [*Zaire*] [*ICAO location identifier*] (ICLI)
FZMK	Bulonge-Kigogo [*Zaire*] [*ICAO location identifier*] (ICLI)
FZMP	Kimano II [*Zaire*] [*ICAO location identifier*] (ICLI)
FZMW	Shabunda [*Zaire*] [*ICAO location identifier*] (ICLI)
FZNA	Goma [*Zaire*] [*ICAO location identifier*] (ICLI)
FZNC	Rutshuru [*Zaire*] [*ICAO location identifier*] (ICLI)
FZNF	Lubero [*Zaire*] [*ICAO location identifier*] (ICLI)
FZNI	Ishasha [*Zaire*] [*ICAO location identifier*] (ICLI)
FZNK	Katanda Sur Rutshuru [*Zaire*] [*ICAO location identifier*] (ICLI)
FZNM	Mweso [*Zaire*] [*ICAO location identifier*] (ICLI)
FZNP	Beni [*Zaire*] [*ICAO location identifier*] (ICLI)
FZNR	Ruindi [*Zaire*] [*ICAO location identifier*] (ICLI)
FZNT	Mutwanga [*Zaire*] [*ICAO location identifier*] (ICLI)
FZO	Fabrichno-Zavodske Obuchenie [*Factory School*] [*Former USSR*]
FZO	Factory Training (RU)
FZOA	Kindu [*Zaire*] [*ICAO location identifier*] (ICLI)

FZOB......... Tingi-Tingi [*Zaire*] [*ICAO location identifier*]   (ICLI)
FZOC......... Kalima-Kamisuku [*Zaire*] [*ICAO location identifier*]   (ICLI)
FZOD .... Kalima [*Zaire*] [*ICAO location identifier*]   (ICLI)
FZOE......... Kampene [*Zaire*] [*ICAO location identifier*]   (ICLI)
FZOF .... Kiapupe [*Zaire*] [*ICAO location identifier*]   (ICLI)
FZOG .... Lulingu-Tshioka [*Zaire*] [*ICAO location identifier*]   (ICLI)
FZOH .... Moga [*Zaire*] [*ICAO location identifier*]   (ICLI)
FZOJ .... Obokote [*Zaire*] [*ICAO location identifier*]   (ICLI)
FZOK .... Kasongo [*Zaire*] [*ICAO location identifier*]   (ICLI)
FZOO .... Kailo [*Zaire*] [*ICAO location identifier*]   (ICLI)
FZOP......... Punia [*Zaire*] [*ICAO location identifier*]   (ICLI)
FZOS......... Kasese [*Zaire*] [*ICAO location identifier*]   (ICLI)
FZPB .... Kamituga [*Zaire*] [*ICAO location identifier*]   (ICLI)
FZQA .... Lubumbashi/Luano [*Zaire*] [*ICAO location identifier*]   (ICLI)
FZQC......... Pweto [*Zaire*] [*ICAO location identifier*]   (ICLI)
FZQD .... Mulungwishi [*Zaire*] [*ICAO location identifier*]   (ICLI)
FZQF......... Fungurume [*Zaire*] [*ICAO location identifier*]   (ICLI)
FZQG .... Kasenga [*Zaire*] [*ICAO location identifier*]   (ICLI)
FZQH......... Katwe [*Zaire*] [*ICAO location identifier*]   (ICLI)
FZQI......... Kamatanda [*Zaire*] [*ICAO location identifier*]   (ICLI)
FZQJ .... Mwadingusha [*Zaire*] [*ICAO location identifier*]   (ICLI)
FZQM........ Kolwezi [*Zaire*] [*ICAO location identifier*]   (ICLI)
FZQN......... Mutshatsha [*Zaire*] [*ICAO location identifier*]   (ICLI)
FZQO .... Lubumbashi/Karavia [*Zaire*] [*ICAO location identifier*]   (ICLI)
FZQP......... Kisenge [*Zaire*] [*ICAO location identifier*]   (ICLI)
FZQU .... Lubudi [*Zaire*] [*ICAO location identifier*]   (ICLI)
FZQV......... Mitwaba [*Zaire*] [*ICAO location identifier*]   (ICLI)
FZQW .... Luishi [*Zaire*] [*ICAO location identifier*]   (ICLI)
FZR............ Fundusz Zasilkow Rodzinnych [*Family Allowance Fund*]   (POL)
FZR............ Funktionszustands-register [*German*]   (ADPT)
FZRA......... Manono [*Zaire*] [*ICAO location identifier*]   (ICLI)
FZRB .... Moba [*Zaire*] [*ICAO location identifier*]   (ICLI)
FZRC........ Mukoy [*Zaire*] [*ICAO location identifier*]   (ICLI)
FZRD........ Kabombo [*Zaire*] [*ICAO location identifier*]   (ICLI)
FZRF .... Kalemie [*Zaire*] [*ICAO location identifier*]   (ICLI)
FZRG......... Kania-Sominka [*Zaire*] [*ICAO location identifier*]   (ICLI)
FZRJ .... Pepa [*Zaire*] [*ICAO location identifier*]   (ICLI)
FZRK .... Kansimba [*Zaire*] [*ICAO location identifier*]   (ICLI)
FZRL......... Lusinga [*Zaire*] [*ICAO location identifier*]   (ICLI)
FZRM....... Kabalo [*Zaire*] [*ICAO location identifier*]   (ICLI)
FZRN........ Nyunzu [*Zaire*] [*ICAO location identifier*]   (ICLI)
FZRO........ Luvua [*Zaire*] [*ICAO location identifier*]   (ICLI)
FZRQ......... Kongolo [*Zaire*] [*ICAO location identifier*]   (ICLI)
FZS............ Factory-Plant Construction   (BU)
FZS............ Factory Seven-Year (School)   (RU)
FZS............ Oesterreichisches Forschungszentrum Seibersdorf GmbH
     [*Austrian Research Center Seibersdorf*] [*Research center*]
     (ARC)
FZSA .... Kamina-Base [*Zaire*] [*ICAO location identifier*]   (ICLI)
FZSB .... Kamina-Ville [*Zaire*] [*ICAO location identifier*]   (ICLI)
FZSC .... Songa [*Zaire*] [*ICAO location identifier*]   (ICLI)
FZSD........ Sandoa [*Zaire*] [*ICAO location identifier*]   (ICLI)
FZSE .... Kanene [*Zaire*] [*ICAO location identifier*]   (ICLI)
FZSh.......... Factory-Plant Course   (BU)
FZSI .... Dilolo [*Zaire*] [*ICAO location identifier*]   (ICLI)
FZSJ .... Kasaji [*Zaire*] [*ICAO location identifier*]   (ICLI)
FZSK .... Kapanga [*Zaire*] [*ICAO location identifier*]   (ICLI)
FZSZ .... Fovarosi Zeneiskola Szervezet [*Capital Music Education
     Institute*]   (HU)
FZT............ Photographic Zenith Telescope   (RU)
FZTK .... Kaniama [*Zaire*] [*ICAO location identifier*]   (ICLI)
FZTL .... Luena [*Zaire*] [*ICAO location identifier*]   (ICLI)
FZTs .... Factory-Plant Prices   (BU)
FZTS .... Kasese/Kaniama [*Zaire*] [*ICAO location identifier*]   (ICLI)
FZU .... Factory-Plant School   (BU)
FZU .... Factory Training School   (RU)
FZUA .... Kananga [*Zaire*] [*ICAO location identifier*]   (ICLI)
FZUE........ Lubondaie [*Zaire*] [*ICAO location identifier*]   (ICLI)
FZUF......... Kasongo [*Zaire*] [*ICAO location identifier*]   (ICLI)
FZUG .... Luisa [*Zaire*] [*ICAO location identifier*]   (ICLI)
FZUH....... Moma [*Zaire*] [*ICAO location identifier*]   (ICLI)
FZUI.......... Mboi [*Zaire*] [*ICAO location identifier*]   (ICLI)
FZUJ .... Muambi [*Zaire*] [*ICAO location identifier*]   (ICLI)
FZUK........ Tshikapa [*Zaire*] [*ICAO location identifier*]   (ICLI)
FZUL......... Bulape [*Zaire*] [*ICAO location identifier*]   (ICLI)
FZUM .... Mutoto [*Zaire*] [*ICAO location identifier*]   (ICLI)
FZUN........ Luebo [*Zaire*] [*ICAO location identifier*]   (ICLI)
FZUO .... Musese [*Zaire*] [*ICAO location identifier*]   (ICLI)
FZUR........ Tshibala [*Zaire*] [*ICAO location identifier*]   (ICLI)
FZUS .... Tshikaji [*Zaire*] [*ICAO location identifier*]   (ICLI)
FZUT......... Katubwe [*Zaire*] [*ICAO location identifier*]   (ICLI)
FZUU .... Lutshatsha [*Zaire*] [*ICAO location identifier*]   (ICLI)
FZUV........ Kalonda [*Zaire*] [*ICAO location identifier*]   (ICLI)
FZVA......... Lodja [*Zaire*] [*ICAO location identifier*]   (ICLI)
FZVC........ Kole Sur Lukenie [*Zaire*] [*ICAO location identifier*]   (ICLI)
FZVD......... Dingele [*Zaire*] [*ICAO location identifier*]   (ICLI)

FZVE......... Lomela [*Zaire*] [*ICAO location identifier*]   (ICLI)
FZVF......... Kutusongo [*Zaire*] [*ICAO location identifier*]   (ICLI)
FZVG........ Katako, Kombe [*Zaire*] [*ICAO location identifier*]   (ICLI)
FZVH .... Shongamba [*Zaire*] [*ICAO location identifier*]   (ICLI)
FZVI.......... Lusambo [*Zaire*] [*ICAO location identifier*]   (ICLI)
FZVJ.......... Tshumbe [*Zaire*] [*ICAO location identifier*]   (ICLI)
FZVK......... Lukombe-Batwa [*Zaire*] [*ICAO location identifier*]   (ICLI)
FZVL......... Wasolo [*Zaire*] [*ICAO location identifier*]   (ICLI)
FZVM....... Mweka [*Zaire*] [*ICAO location identifier*]   (ICLI)
FZVN........ Wembo-Nyama [*Zaire*] [*ICAO location identifier*]   (ICLI)
FZVO .... Bena-Dibele [*Zaire*] [*ICAO location identifier*]   (ICLI)
FZVP......... Dikungu [*Zaire*] [*ICAO location identifier*]   (ICLI)
FZVR......... Basongo [*Zaire*] [*ICAO location identifier*]   (ICLI)
FZVS .... Ilebo [*Zaire*] [*ICAO location identifier*]   (ICLI)
FZVT........ Dekese [*Zaire*] [*ICAO location identifier*]   (ICLI)
FZVU........ Idumbe [*Zaire*] [*ICAO location identifier*]   (ICLI)
FZWA........ Mbuji-Mayi [*Zaire*] [*ICAO location identifier*]   (ICLI)
FZWB........ Bibanga [*Zaire*] [*ICAO location identifier*]   (ICLI)
FZWC....... Gandajika [*Zaire*] [*ICAO location identifier*]   (ICLI)
FZWE........ Mwene-Ditu [*Zaire*] [*ICAO location identifier*]   (ICLI)
FZWF........ Kipushia [*Zaire*] [*ICAO location identifier*]   (ICLI)
FZWI......... Kashia [*Zaire*] [*ICAO location identifier*]   (ICLI)
FZWR........ Kisengwa [*Zaire*] [*ICAO location identifier*]   (ICLI)
FZWS .... Lubao [*Zaire*] [*ICAO location identifier*]   (ICLI)
FZWT......... Kabinda/Tunta [*Zaire*] [*ICAO location identifier*]   (ICLI)
FZZ............ Health Insurance Fund   (BU)
FZZA......... Zaire Fir [*Zaire*] [*ICAO location identifier*]   (ICLI)

G

g .... Annual Issue [*Periodicals and newspapers*]   (BU)
G .... Bitter Water [*Topography*]   (RU)
G .... De Gids [*Benelux*]   (BAS)
G .... Gakushi [*Japan*]
G .... Gallon [*Gallon*] [*Afrikaans*]
G .... Gambia [*Country in West Africa*]   (ROG)
g .... Gaseous, Gasiform   (RU)
G .... Gasse [*Lane, Alley*] [*German*]
g .... Gatan [*Street*] [*Sweden*]   (CED)
g .... Gate [*Street*] [*Norway*]   (CED)
G .... Gauche [*Left*] [*French*]
G .... Gavan' [*Harbour, Basin*] [*Russian*]   (NAU)
G .... Gebel [*Mountain, Hill*] [*Geb Arab*] [*See also*]   (NAU)
G .... Gedeckter Gueterwagen [*Covered Freight Car (Usually a boxcar)*]   (EG)
G .... Gegensatz [*German*]
g .... Geglueht [*Annealed*] [*German*]   (GCA)
g .... Gelb [*Yellow*] [*German*]   (GCA)
G .... Geld [*Monetary unit*] [*German*]
G .... Gendarm [*or Gendarmerie*] [*Constable or Constabulary*] [*German*]
G .... General Duties [*Ranking title*] [*British Women's Royal Naval Service*]
G .... Genie [*French*]   (MTD)
G .... George [*Phonetic alphabet*] [*Royal Navy World War I Pre-World War II*] [*World War II*]   (DSUE)
G .... Gericht [*Court*] [*German*]   (ILCA)
G .... Germany   (WDAA)
G .... Geschichte [*History*] [*German*]   (ILCA)
G .... Gesellschaft [*Company*] [*German*]
G .... Gesetz [*Law*] [*German*]   (ILCA)
G .... Gewicht [*Weight*] [*German*]   (GCA)
G .... Giga [*German*]   (GCA)
G .... Giorno [*Day*] [*Italian*]
G .... Giro [*Money Order*] [*Spanish*]
g .... Godina [*Year*]   (YU)
g .... Godzina [*or Godziny*] [*Hour or Hours*] [*Poland*]
g .... Goetu [*Gate, Street*] [*Icelandic*]   (CED)
G .... Gol [*Lake*]   (TU)
G .... Goldschnitt [*Gilt Edge*] [*Publishing*] [*German*]
G .... Golf [*Gulf*] [*Netherlands*]   (NAU)
G .... Golf [*Phonetic alphabet*] [*International*]   (DSUE)
G .... Golfe [*Gulf*] [*French*]   (NAU)
G .... Golfo [*Gulf*] [*Italian*]   (NAU)
G .... Golfo [*Gulf*] [*Portuguese*]   (NAU)
G .... Golfo [*Gulf*] [*Spanish*]   (NAU)
G .... Gora [*Mountain*] [*Poland*]
G .... Gora [*Mountain*] [*Russian*]   (NAU)
G .... Gourde [*Monetary unit*] [*Haiti*]
G .... Gracia [*Favor*] [*Spanish*]
g .... Grado [*Grade*] [*Portuguese*]
G .... Grado [*Academic degree*] [*Spanish*]
G .... Graduat [*French*]
g .... Gram   (EECI)
g .... Grama [*Gram*] [*Portuguese*]
g .... Gramme [*Gram*] [*French*]
g .... Gramo [*Gram*] [*Spanish*]
g .... Grande [*Large*] [*Portuguese*]
G .... Grandeur [*Highness*] [*French*]
G .... Grand-Orgue [*Great Organ*] [*Music*]
G .... Grani [*Grains*] [*Italian*]
g .... Grau [*Degree*] [*Portuguese*]
g .... Grave [*Engraved*] [*Publishing*] [*French*]
g .... Gravite [*Gravity*] [*French*]
G .... Grondwet [*Constitution*] [*Netherlands*]   (ILCA)
G .... Grondwet voor het Koninkrijk der Nederlanden [*Netherlands*]   (BAS)
G .... Groschen [*Monetary unit*] [*Austria*]

G .... Groszy [*Monetary unit*] [*Poland*]
g .... Group   (BU)
G .... Grumman American Aviation [*ICAO aircraft manufacturer identifier*]   (ICAO)
G .... Guarani [*Monetary unit*] [*Paraguay*]
g .... Guberniya [*1708-1929*]   (RU)
G .... Gueterzuglokomotive [*Freight Train Locomotive*]   (EG)
G .... Guilder [*Modification of gulden*] [*Monetary unit*] [*Netherlands*]
G .... Guinea [*Monetary unit*] [*Obsolete*] [*British*]
G .... Guirsh [*Monetary unit*] [*Saudi Arabia*]
G .... Gulden [*Monetary unit*] [*Netherlands*]
G .... Guney [*South*]   (TU)
G .... Gusslegierung [*Casting Alloy*] [*German*]   (GCA)
G .... Gwatemala [*Guatemala*] [*Poland*]
g .... Mister   (RU)
G .... Mountain [*Topography*]   (RU)
g .... Mrs., Madame   (RU)
G .... Town, City   (RU)
g .... Year   (BU)
G2W .... Glaube in der 2. Welt [*Faith in the Second World - FSW*] [*An association*] [*Switzerland*]   (EAIO)
G5 .... Group of Five [*United States, Japan, West Germany, France, and Britain*]
G10 .... Group of Ten [*United States, Japan, West Germany, France, Britain, Italy, Canada, Sweden, Holland, Belgium, and Switzerland*] [*There are actually eleven member countries*]
G24 .... Group of 24 [*A clearinghouse for monetary aid to Eastern Europe*]   (ECON)
G-30-S .... Gerakan 30 September [*30 September Movement (1965)*]   (IN)
G77 .... Group of Seventy Seven [*Developing nations*]
GA .... City Archives   (BU)
GA .... Civil Aviation   (RU)
GA .... Gabon [*ANSI two-letter standard code*]   (CNC)
Ga .... Galio [*Gallium*] [*Chemical element*] [*Portuguese*]
Ga .... Gawa [*River*] [*Ka*] [*See also*] [*Japan*]   (NAU)
GA .... Gemeinschaftsanlage [*German*]   (ADPT)
GA .... General Aircraft Ltd.
GA .... General Assembly of the United Nations
GA .... General Avia SpA [*Italy*] [*ICAO aircraft manufacturer identifier*]   (ICAO)
GA .... Geomagnetism and Aeronomy   (RU)
ga .... Gepagyu [*Automatic Gun*]   (HU)
GA .... Gesamt-Ausgabe [*German*]
GA .... Gesellschaft fuer Arzneipflanzenforschung [*Society for Medicinal Plant Research*]   (EA)
GA .... Gewijzigde Aansprakelijkheid [*Benelux*]   (BAS)
GA .... Giunta Amministrativa [*Municipal Council*] [*Italian*]
GA .... Glucosamine   (RU)
GA .... Gnomes Anonymous [*New Malden, Surrey, England*]   (EA)
GA .... Government Actuary [*Australia*]
GA .... Great African Insurance Co. Ltd. [*Ghana*]
GA .... Green Alliance Senate - New South Wales [*Political party*] [*Australia*]
GA .... Greening Australia
GA .... Groupe d'Armees [*Army Division*] [*Military*] [*French*]   (MTD)
GA .... Grundaufbauplan [*Basic Development Plan*]   (EG)
GA .... Grupo Andino [*Andean Group*]   (LA)
Ga .... Guba [*Bay, Inlet, Creek*] [*Russian*]   (NAU)
Ga .... Gueterabfertigung [*Freight Office*]   (EG)
GA .... Gulf Air [*Middle East regional air carrier*]
GA .... Gyro Assembly   (RU)
ga .... Hectare   (RU)
GA .... Howitzer Artillery   (RU)
GA .... Les Grands Arrets de la Jurisprudence Administrative [*France*]   (FLAF)
GA .... Mountain Artillery   (RU)
GA .... State Archives   (RU)
GAA .... Gaelic Athletic Association of Australia

519

GAA.......... Galvanizers Association of Australia (ADA)
GAA.......... Gemmological Association of Australia (ADA)
GAA.......... General Aviation Association [*Australia*]
GAA.......... Government Advertising Agency [*New South Wales, Australia*]
GAA.......... Graduate Administrative Assistant [*Australia*]
GAA.......... Grants for Aboriginal Advancement [*Australia*]
GAA.......... Greening Australia Action
GAA.......... Groupement Aeronautique et Automobile
GAA.......... Groupement Atomique Alsacienne Atlantique [*French*]
GAA.......... Les Grands Arrets de la Jurisprudence Administrative [*France*] (FLAF)
GAAA....... General Aviation Association Australia
GAAA....... Groupement Atomique Alsacienne Atlantique [*French*] (PDAA)
GAAA....... Groupement pour les Activites Atomiques et Avancees [*Nuclear energy*] [*French*] (NRCH)
GAAAU..... Ghana Association of Alumni of American Universities
GAAEF..... Grupo de Abogados Argentinos en el Exilio en Francia
GAAF........ Grupo de Accao Antifascista [*Antifascist Action Group*] [*Portuguese*] (WER)
GAAO....... Ansongo [*Mali*] [*ICAO location identifier*] (ICLI)
GAAO....... Gorno-Altay Autonomous Oblast (RU)
GAAP........ General Agreement on Prices and Production [*Australia*]
GAArkhobl ... State Archives of the Arkhangel'sk Oblast (RU)
GAAS......... German Association for American Studies (EAIO)
GAAstrobl ... State Archives of the Astrakhan' Oblast (RU)
GAB.......... Gabon [*ANSI three-letter standard code*] (CNC)
GAB.......... Gabungan [*Association, Group, Joint (Staff), Combined (Operations)*] (IN)
GAB.......... Gaestelijk Arbeidsbureau [*Regional Labor Bureau*] [*Netherlands*] (WEN)
GAB.......... General Arrangements to Borrow [*United Nations*] (EY)
GAB.......... Gepipari Allando Bizottsag [*Standing Committee for the Machine Industry (CEMA)*] (HU)
GAB.......... Gesellschaft fuer Ausland Beteiligungen
GAB.......... Gewestelijk Arbeids Bureau [*Netherlands*]
GAB.......... Great Artesian Basin [*Australia*]
GAB.......... Grievance and Appeals Board [*Australia*]
GAB.......... Guardianship and Administration Board [*Victoria, Australia*]
GABCC....... Great Australian Bight Consultative Committee
GABD....... Bandiagara [*Mali*] [*ICAO location identifier*] (ICLI)
GABELEC ... Gabonaise d'Electricite
GABEXFO ... Gabonaise d'Exploitation Forestiere
GABF........ Bafoulabe [*Mali*] [*ICAO location identifier*] (ICLI)
GABG....... Bougouni [*Mali*] [*ICAO location identifier*] (ICLI)
GABHOTELS ... Grands Hotels du Gabon
GABIDOC ... Gespreksgroep Archief, Bibliotheek, Documentatie [*Netherlands*]
GABIM...... La Gabonaise Immobiliere
GABMIT... Gabungan Minjak Tanah [*Petroleum Association*] (IN)
GABOA..... Societe Gabonaise d'Oxygene et d'Acetylene [*Grabon*]
GABOMA ... Societe Gabonaise de Grands Magasins
GABONAP ... Societe Gabonaise de Diffusion d'Appareils Electriques
GABONEX ... Societe Gabonaise d'Exploitation Vinicole
GABOREP ... Societe Gabonaise de Recherches Petrolieres (EY)
GABOSEP ... Societe Gabonaise de Sepulture
GABR........ Bourem [*Mali*] [*ICAO location identifier*] (ICLI)
GABr........ Howitzer Artillery Brigade (RU)
GABS........ Bamako/Senou [*Mali*] [*ICAO location identifier*] (ICLI)
GABT .... State Academic Large Theater of the USSR [*The Bol'shoy*] (RU)
GABTRANS ... Societe Gabonaise de Transports Internationaux
GABTU ..... Main Directorate of the Armored Troops (RU)
GABV .... Bamako [*Mali*] [*ICAO location identifier*] (ICLI)
GAC.......... General Air Cargo [*Venezuela*] [*ICAO designator*] (FAAC)
GAC.......... Ghana Airways Corp.
GAC.......... Gippsland Agriculture Centre [*Australia*]
GAC.......... Glenormiston Agricultural College [*Australia*]
GAC.......... Green Australian Committee
GAC.......... Groupe d'Armees du Centre [*Military*] [*French*] (MTD)
GAC.......... Grupo Aereo de Combate [*Combat Air Group*] [*Bolivia*]
GAC.......... Grupo Anti-Comunista [*Anticommunist Group*] [*Brazil*] (LA)
GAC.......... Grupo de Accion Catala [*Catalan Action Group*] [*Spanish*] (WER)
GAC.......... Gulf Agency Co.
GAC.......... Guyana Airways Corporation (LA)
GACIC....... German Australian Chamber of Industry and Commerce [*Australia*]
GACIFAL ... Grupo Asesor para la Capacitacion e Investigaciones Forestales de America Latina [*Brazil*] (DSCA)
GACO........ La Gabonaise de Construction
GAD.......... Gadabout (DSUE)
GAD.......... Grand Alliance for Democracy [*Philippines*] [*Political party*]
GAD.......... Groupes d'Auto Defense [*Algeria*]
GADA........ Dioila [*Mali*] [*ICAO location identifier*] (ICLI)
GADASE... Gazete Dagiticilari Sendikasi [*Newspaper Distributors Union*] (TU)
GADC....... Gulf Agriculture Development Company

GADE........ Gulf Authority for the Development of Egypt
GADEF...... Groupement des Associations Dentaires Francophones [*Group of Francophone Dentists' Associations*] [*Paris, France*] (EAIO)
GADIP....... Greater Achievement for Disadvantaged Ipswich People [*Australia*]
GAD-IS ..... Gaziantep Dikim Isciler Sendikasi [*Gaziantep Millinery (Thread) Workers Union*] (TU)
GADIS....... Societe Gabonaise de Distribution
GADIT ...... Groupement Algerien des Industries Textiles
GADNA..... Youth Battalions [*Israel*] (ME)
GADP........ Gongola Agricultural Development Project [*Nigeria*] (ECON)
GADZ........ Douentza [*Mali*] [*ICAO location identifier*] (ICLI)
GAE.......... Grupo Anticomunista Espanol [*Spanish Anti-Communist Group*] (WER)
GAE.......... Grupos Armados Espanoles [*Armed Spanish Groups*] [*Political party*] (PD)
GAEC .... Ghana Atomic Energy Commission
GAEC .... Greek Atomic Energy Commission [*Ministry of Industry, Energy, and Technology*] [*Research center*] (WED)
GAEC .... Groupement Agricole d'Exploitation en Commun [*French*]
GAEL........ Gaelies [*Gaelic*] [*Afrikaans*]
GAES........ Pumped-Storage Electric Power Plant (RU)
GAESRE ... Genealogical Association of English-Speaking Researchers in Europe (EAIO)
GAETAN .. Gestion Automatique de l'Enregistrement a Traitement Alphanumerique [*French*] (ADPT)
GAF.......... German Air Force [*ICAO designator*] (FAAC)
GAF.......... Gesellschaft fuer Aerosolforschung [*Association for Aerosol Research*] [*Germany*] (PDAA)
GAF.......... Giovanni Agnelli Foundation [*Italy*] (EAIO)
GAF.......... Government Aircraft Factories [*Department of Supply*] [*Australia*] (PDAA)
GAF.......... Government Aircraft Factory [*Australia*] (ADA)
GAF.......... State Archives Fund (RU)
GAFCICO ... Societe Generale Africaine de Genie Civil et de Constructions
GAFCOR... Gas and Fuel Corp. [*Victoria, Australia*] [*Commercial firm*]
GAFD .... Faladie [*Mali*] [*ICAO location identifier*] (ICLI)
G-AFGO.... Grafia - Association of Finnish Graphic Design (EAIO)
GAFI......... State Astrophysical Institute (RU)
GAFIC...... Ghana All Forces Inner Council
GAFICA .... Grupo Asesor de la FAO en Integracion Economica Centroamericana [*FAO Advisory Group for Central American Economic Integration*] (LAA)
GAFKE...... State Archives of the Age of Feudalism and Serfdom (RU)
GAFOR ..... Societe Gabonaise de Forage
GAFS........ Civilian Aerial Photography (RU)
GAFS........ German Albanian Friendship Society (EAIO)
GAG.......... Azimuth Gyro Horizon (RU)
GAG.......... Ganzzug [*Through-Freight Train with Specific Load with One or Few Points of Origin and One or Few Points of Destination*] (EG)
GAGI .... State Institute of Obstetrics and Gynecology (RU)
GAGL .... Aguelhoc [*Mali*] [*ICAO location identifier*] (ICLI)
GAGM .... Goundam [*Mali*] [*ICAO location identifier*] (ICLI)
GAGMI ..... Groupement d'Achats des Grands Magasins Independants [*Purchasing agency*] [*France*] (IMH)
GAGO........ Gao [*Mali*] [*ICAO location identifier*] (ICLI)
GAGO........ Gor'kiy Astronomical and Geodetic Society (RU)
GAG obl.... State Archives of the Gor'kiy Oblast (RU)
GAGP .... Generale Africaine du Genie et de la Promotion
GAGR....... Courma-Rharous [*Mali*] [*ICAO location identifier*] (ICLI)
GAH.......... Gayndah [*Australia*] [*Airport symbol*] (OAG)
GAHAL..... Right-Wing Combination of Herut Movement and Liberal Party [*Israel*] (ME)
GAHB....... Hombori [*Mali*] [*ICAO location identifier*] (ICLI)
GAI .... City Automobile Inspection (RU)
GAI .... Gesellschaft fuer Angewandte Informatik (SLS)
GAI .... Grupos Autonomos de Intervencion [*Autonomous Interventionist Groups*] [*Spanish*] (WER)
GAI .... Gruppi Archeologici d'Italia [*Italian*] (SLS)
GAI .... State Automobile Inspection (RU)
GAIBANK ... Guyana Agricultural and Industrial Development Bank (LA)
GAID .... Ghana Agricultural and Industrial Development Ltd.
GAIF......... General Arab Insurance Federation
GAIFZ....... General Authority for Arab and Foreign Investment and Free Zones [*Egypt*] (IMH)
GAIGC ...... Guizhou Aviation Industry Group Corp. [*China*]
GAIL......... Gas Authority of India Ltd. (ECON)
GAIL......... Guyana Agricultural Industries Limited (LA)
GAILL .... Groupement des Allergologistes et Immunologistes de Langues Latines [*Latin Languages Speaking Allergists - LLSA*] (EAIO)
GAIM .... Greek-Arab Investment Meeting
GAIMK ..... State Academy of the History of Material Culture (RU)

GAIN .... Federal and State Governments Assistance Programs [*Database*] [*Australia*]
GAIP .... Graduate of the Australian Institute of Physics (ADA)
GAIRLAC ... Groupement d'Achat, d'Importation, et de Repartition des Laits de Conserves
GAIS .... State Academy for the Study of Art (RU)
GAISF .... General Association of International Sports Federations [*Formerly, GAIF*] (EA)
GAISh .... State Astronomical Institute Imeni P. K. Shternberg (RU)
GAIT .... Guatemalan Association of Interpreters and Translators
GAIZ .... State Antireligious Publishing House (RU)
GAIZ .... State Astronomical Publishing House (RU)
GAJ .... Yamagata [*Japan*] [*Airport symbol*] (OAG)
GAK .... Astatic Quartz Gravimeter (RU)
GAK .... Gemeenschappelijk Administratiekantoor [*Benelux*] (BAS)
GAK .... Gendarmerieabteilungskommando [*German*]
GAKA .... Kenieba [*Mali*] [*ICAO location identifier*] (ICLI)
GAKalinin obl ... State Archives of the Kalinin Oblast (RU)
GAKAS ...... Gabungan Kepala Staf [*Joint Chiefs of Staff*] (IN)
GAKhN ...... State Academy of Arts (RU)
GAKhO ...... State Archives of Khar'kov Oblast (RU)
GAKK .... Genshiryoku Anzen Kenkyu Kyokai [*Nuclear Safety Research Association*] [*Japan*] (EAIO)
GAKK .... State Archives of Krasnodar Kray (RU)
GAKL .... Kidal [*Mali*] [*ICAO location identifier*] ' (ICLI)
GAKM ...... Ke-Macina [*Mali*] [*ICAO location identifier*] (ICLI)
GAKN ...... Kolokani [*Mali*] [*ICAO location identifier*] (ICLI)
GAKO .... Koutiala [*Mali*] [*ICAO location identifier*] (ICLI)
GAKT .... Kita [*Mali*] [*ICAO location identifier*] (ICLI)
GAKurskobl ... State Archives of the Kursk Oblast (RU)
GAKuybobl ... State Archives of the Kuybyshev Oblast (RU)
GAKY .... Kayes [*Mali*] [*ICAO location identifier*] (ICLI)
GAL .... Anti-Terrorist Liberation Group [*Undercover anti-Basque terrorist interior-ministry network*] [*Acronym is based on foreign phrase*] [*Spain*] (ECON)
GAL .... Galasiers [*Galatians*] [*Afrikaans*]
Gal .... Galate [*Afrikaans*]
gal .... Galerie [*French*] (CED)
gal .... Galicismo [*Gallicism*] [*Portuguese*]
gal .... Galon [*Gallon*] [*Poland*]
GAL .... Gdynia-Ameryka Linia [*Gdynia-America Line*] (POL)
GAL .... Gemini Airlines Ltd. [*Ghana*] [*ICAO designator*] (FAAC)
Gal .... General [*General*] [*French*] (MTD)
Gal .... General [*General*] [*Portuguese*]
GAL .... General Aircraft Ltd. [*Australia*]
GAL .... German Atlantic Line [*Steamship*] (MHDB)
GAL .... Gesellschaft fuer Arbeitswissenschaft im Landbau eV (SLS)
GAL .... Gibraltar Airways Limited
GAL .... Gioventu Araba del Littorio
GAL .... Gravimeter of the Aerogravimetric Laboratory (RU)
GAL .... Grupos Armados Libertarios [*Armed Libertarian Groups*] [*Spain*] [*Political party*] (PD)
gal .... Notions Industry Factory [*Topography*] (RU)
GALA .... Gaming and Liquor Authority [*Australian Capital Territory*]
GALA .... Gay and Lesbian Association [*University of Sydney*] [*Australia*]
GALA .... Grupo de Artistas Latino Americanos [*An association*]
GALA .... Guyana Association of Local Authorities (LA)
GALACER ... Ganado, Lanas, Cereales [*Argentina*] (DSCA)
GAlBz .... Aluminiumgussbronze [*Cast Aluminum Bronze*] [*German*] (GCA)
GALC .... Groupement des Associations de Librairies de la CEE [*Group of Booksellers Associations in the EEC*] (ECED)
GALE .... Galerias de Arte y Salas de Exposiciones [*Ministerio de Cultura*] [*Spain*] [*Information service or system*] (CRD)
GALF .... Groupement des Acousticiens de Langue Francaise [*Group of French-Speaking Acousticians*] (EA)
GALIAF .... Societe Gaz Liquefies de l'Afrique
Galie .... Galerie [*Gallery*] [*Military map abbreviation World War I*] [*French*] (MTD)
galkul'tpromsoyuz ... Union of Producers' Cooperatives of the Notions Industry and Goods for Cultural Purposes (RU)
gall .... Galleria [*Italian*] (CED)
Gall .... Gallies [*Gaelic*] [*Afrikaans*]
gall .... Gallon [*Gallon*] [*Afrikaans*]
gallert .... Gallertartig [*Colloidal*] [*German*] (GCA)
gallert .... Gallertig [*Slimy*] [*German*] (GCA)
Galligrassevil ... Gallimard, Grasset, and Le Sevil [*French publishers*]
Gall Prak ... Gallikon Praktoreion [*French Press Agency*] (GC)
GaLTaS ... Gay and Lesbian Teachers and Students [*Australia*]
Galv .... Galvanik [*Galvanotechnics*] [*German*] (GCA)
GAM .... Gambia
GAM .... Garnizonowa Administracja Mieszkaniowa [*Garrison Housing Administration*] (POL)
GAM .... German Army [*ICAO designator*] (FAAC)
GAM .... Groupe d'Action Municipale [*French*]

GAM .... Groupement des Associations Meunieres des Pays de la CEE [*Flour Milling Associations Group of the EEC Countries*] (EAIO)
GAM .... Grupo de Apoyo Mutuo [*Group for Mutual Support*] [*Mexico*] [*Political party*]
GAM .... Grupo de Apoyo Mutuo [*Group for Mutual Support*] [*Guatemala*] [*Political party*]
GAM .... Guyana Association of Musicians (LA)
GAM .... State Antireligious Museum [*Leningrad*] (RU)
GAMA .... Gadjah Mada [*University in Jogjakarta*] (IN)
Gama .... Gdanska Agencja Morska i Asekuracyjna [*Gdansk (Danzig) Maritime and Insurance Agency*] (POL)
GAMA ...... General Arabian Medical & Allied Services [*Saudi Arabia*]
GAMA .... Groupe d'Analyse Macroeconomique Appliquee [*Group for Applied Macroeconomic Analysis*] [*University of Paris - Nanterre*] [*Information service or system*] (IID)
GAMA ...... Markala [*Mali*] [*ICAO location identifier*] (ICLI)
GAMAA ..... Graphic Arts Merchants' Association of Australia
GAMagobl ... State Archives of the Magadan Oblast (RU)
GAMB ...... Mopti/Barbe [*Mali*] [*ICAO location identifier*] (ICLI)
GAMCO .... Gulf Aircraft Maintenance Company (IMH)
GAMD .... Generale Aeronautique Marcel Dassault [*Switzerland*] [*AMD/BA*] [*Later,*]
GAMEDA ... Gazete-Mecmua Dagitim Ltd. Sti. [*Newspaper and Periodicals Distribution Corp.*] (TU)
GAMEFA ... Ghana-American Friendship Association
GAMESA ... Grupo Auxiliar Metalurgico Sociedad Anonima [*Auxiliary Metallurgical Group*] [*Weapons exporter*] [*Spain*]
GAMF .... Gepipari es Automatizalasi Muszaki Foiskola [*Mechanical Engineering and Automation College*] [*Hungary*] [*Research center*] (ERC)
GAMHTE ... General Association of Municipal Health and Technical Experts (EA)
GAMI .... Groupement pour l'Avancement de la Mecanique Industrielle [*France*] (PDAA)
GAMIC ..... Gamma Incomplet [*German*] (ADPT)
GAMK ...... Gamma-Aminobutyric Acid (RU)
GAMK ...... Menaka [*Mali*] [*ICAO location identifier*] (ICLI)
GAMKI .... Gerakan Angkatan Muda Keristen Indonesia [*Indonesian Christian Youth Movement*] (IN)
GAML .... City Model Aircraft Laboratory (RU)
GAMM ...... Gesellschaft fuer Angewandte Mathematik und Mechanik [*Association for Applied Mathematics and Mechanics*]
GAMM ...... Gestion Administrative et Medicale du Malade [*French*] (ADPT)
GAMMA ..... Gay and Married Men's Association of Victoria [*Australia*]
GAMNA ..... Gambia News Agency (EY)
GAMO ...... Groupement Administratif Mobile [*Mobile Administrative Unit*] [*Cambodia*] (CL)
GAMPS .... Gander Automated Message Processing System [*ICAO*] (DA)
GAMS .... Civil Air Weather Station (RU)
GAMS .... Groupement pour l'Avancement des Methodes Spectroscopiques et Physicochimiques d'Analyse [*Group for the Advancement of Spectroscopic and Physicochemical Analysis Methods*] [*ICSU*]
GAMS .... Groupement pour l'Avancement des Methodes Spectroscopiques et Physio-Chimiques d'Analyse [*Group for the Advancement of Spectroscopic Methods and Physicochemical Analysis*] [*Information service or system*] (IID)
GAMS .... Groupe pour l'Avancement des Sciences Analytique [*Group for Advanced Analytical Sciences*] [*France*] (EAIO)
GAMS .... Main Air Weather Station (RU)
GAMSEN ... Turkiye Garanti Bankasi AS Mensuplari Sendikasi [*Turkish Guarantee Bank Corp. Employees Union*] (TU)
GAMSI ...... Groupe d'Application des Methodes et des Systemes d'Information [*French*] (ADPT)
GAMT .... German Association of Medical Technologists (EAIO)
GAMT .... State Academic Small Theater (RU)
GAMTs ...... Main Air Weather Center (RU)
GAN .... Generalauftragnehmer [*General Contractor*] (EG)
GAN .... Georgian Academy of Sciences (RU)
GAN .... German Academy of Sciences [*Germany*] (BU)
GAN .... Gleitpunkt-Addition Normalisiert [*German*] (ADPT)
GAN .... Goldfields Air Navigation [*Australia*]
GAN .... Groupe d'Armees du Nord [*Military*] [*French*] (MTD)
GAN .... Groupe des Assurances Nationales [*France*] (EY)
GANABARALT ... Asociacion Regional de Ganaderos del Departamento Baralt Mene Grande [*Venezuela*] (DSCA)
GANAGRINCO ... Ganaderia, Agricultura, Industria, y Comercio [*Venezuela*] (DSCA)
GANBEO .. Gas-Netz-Beobachtung [*German*]
GANC .... Groupe d'Action Nationale Camerounaise [*Cameroonian National Action Group*]
Gand .... Arret de la Cour d'Appel de Gand [*Benelux*] (BAS)
G and D. ...... Guts and Determination (DSUE)
G & EI .... Gilbert and Ellice Islands (ILCA)
G & G .... Gordon and Gotch [*Australia*]

G & J .... Gruner & Jahr AG & Co. [*Magazine publisher*] [*Germany*]
G & SS .... Gilbert and Sullivan Society [*Australia*]
G & U .... Grafe & Unzer [*Publisher*] [*German*]
GANEFO .. Games of the New Emerging Forces   (CL)
GANESI .... Gas-Netz-Simulation [*German*]
GANF .... Niafunke [*Mali*] [*ICAO location identifier*]   (ICLI)
GANGQ .... Gas-Netz-Simulation for Gas Quality [*German*]
GANIDE ... Gestion-Animation-Developpement
GANIL ...... Grand Accelerateur National d'Ions Lourds [*Facility for heavy-ion physics*] [*French*]
GANK .... Nara/Keibane [*Mali*] [*ICAO location identifier*]   (ICLI)
GANO .... Grupos de Accion Nacionalista Oriental [*Groups for Uruguayan Nationalist Action*]   (LA)
GANPRODA ... Gas-Netz-Simulation mit Prozess-Daten [*German*]
GANR .... Nioro [*Mali*] [*ICAO location identifier*]   (ICLI)
GANUPT .. Groupe d'Assistance Militaire et Civile des Nations Unies pour la Periode de Transition
ganz .... Ganzlich [*Complete*] [*German*]   (BARN)
Ganzl .... Ganzleinen [*Full Cloth*] [*Publishing*] [*German*]
ganzs .... Ganzseitig [*Full-Page*] [*Publishing*] [*German*]
ganzseit ..... Ganzseitig [*Full-Page*] [*Publishing*] [*German*]
GAO .... Glavnaya Astronomicheskaya Observatoriya [*Main Astronomical Observatory*] [*Ukrainian SSR Academy of Sciences*] [*Former USSR*]   (IRC)
GAO .... Golden Air Commuter AB [*Sweden*] [*ICAO designator*]   (FAAC)
GAO .... Guantanamo [*Cuba*] [*Airport symbol*]   (OAG)
GAOCMAO ... Gulf Area Oil Company Mutual Aid Organization
GAOR .... General Assembly Official Records
GAOR .... State Archives of the October Revolution   (RU)
GAOrenoobl ... State Archives of the Orenburg Oblast   (RU)
GAORLO ... State Archives of the October Revolution and of the Building of Socialism of the Leningrad Oblast   (RU)
GAORMO ... State Archives of the October Revolution and of the Building of Socialism of the Moscow Oblast   (RU)
GAORSS ... State Archives of the October Revolution and of the Building of Socialism   (RU)
GAP .... Gemeinsamer Ausbildung Plan [*Training plan*] [*German*]
GAP .... German Academy for Psychoanalysis   (EAIO)
GAP .... Grand Anatolia Project [*Dam system*] [*Turkey*]   (ECON)
GAP .... Great Australian Permanent Building Society   (ADA)
GAP .... Grosshandelsabgabepreis [*Wholesale Price*]   (EG)
GAP .... Groupement Associe de Producteurs
GAP .... Groupement d'Action Populaire [*People's Action Group*] [*Burkina Faso*]   (AF)
GAP .... Groupement d'Action Progressiste [*Progressive Action Group*] [*Belgium*]   (WER)
GAP .... Groupement des Aides Privees
GAP .... Group for Aquatic Primary Productivity [*ICSU*]
GAP .... Grupo de Amigos Personales [*Group of Personal Friends*] [*Chile*]   (LA)
GAP .... Grupo de Auto-Defensa [*Self-Defense Group*] [*Uruguay*] [*Political party*]   (PD)
GAP .... Gruppo d'Azione Partigiana [*Partisan Action Group*] [*Italian*]   (WER)
GAP .... Guards Air Regiment   (RU)
GAP .... Gusap [*Papua New Guinea*] [*Airport symbol*] [*Obsolete*]   (OAG)
GAP .... Howitzer Artillery Regiment   (BU)
GAP .... Main Administration of the Aniline Dye Industry   (RU)
GAP .... "Pravda" Newspaper Plant   (RU)
GAPA .... Guyana Agricultural Producers Association   (LA)
GAPBM ..... Heavy Howitzer Artillery Regiment   (RU)
GAPD .... Gambia Association of Physically Disabled   (EAIO)
GAPE .... Guyana Association of Professional Engineers   (LA)
GAPEFA ... Graphic Arts Platemaking Employers Federation of Australia   (ADA)
GAPEI .... Gabungan Pengusaha Ekspor Indonesia [*Association of Indonesian Exporters*]   (IN)
GAPENA ... Gabungan Persatuan Penulis Nasional Malaysia [*Federation of National Writers' Associations of Malaysia*]   (EAIO)
GAPENI .... Gabungan Pengusaha Nasional Indonesia [*Indonesian National Businessmen's Association*]   (IN)
GAPEX ..... General Agricultural Products Export Corporation [*Tanzania*]   (AF)
GAPHI ...... Guyana Association of Public Health Inspectors   (LA)
GAPI .... Societe Gabonaise d'Armement et de Peche Industrielle
gapl .... Haploid   (RU)
GAPMB ..... Ghana Agricultural Produce Marketing Board   (DSCA)
GAPPINDO ... Indonesian Fisheries Federation   (EAIO)
GAPS .... Grupo Autonomo do Partido Socialista [*Autonomous Group of the Socialist Party*] [*Portuguese*]   (WER)
GAPU .... Main Architectural and Planning Administration   (RU)
GAPU .... Main Pharmaceutical Administration   (RU)
GAQ .... Gao [*Mali*] [*Airport symbol*]   (OAG)
GAR .... Commodore Aviation [*Australia*] [*ICAO designator*]   (FAAC)
Gar .... Gaerung [*Fermentation*] [*German*]   (GCA)
gar .... Garage [*Topography*]   (RU)

GAR .... Garaina [*Papua New Guinea*] [*Airport symbol*]   (OAG)
gar .... General [*Artillery*]   (BU)
GAR .... Grand Axe Routier
GAR .... Grupos de Accion Revolucionaria [*Revolutionary Action Groups*] [*Venezuela*]   (LA)
GAR .... Grupos de Accion Revolucionaria [*Revolutionary Action Groups*] [*Spain*]   (WER)
GAR .... Gruppi Armati Radicali per il Comunismo [*Armed Radical Groups for Communism*] [*Italy*]   (PD)
Gar .... Gueteraussenring [*Outer Freight Ring*] [*Berlin, East Germany*]   (EG)
GARI .... Groupe d'Action Revolutionnaire Internationaliste [*International Revolutionary Action Group*] [*France*] [*Political party*]   (PD)
GARI .... Grupo de Accion Revolucionaria Internacional [*International Revolutionary Action Group*] [*Spain*] [*Political party*]
GARIM ..... Groupe Militaire Aerien de la Republique Islamique de Mauritanie [*Military Air Group of the Islamic Republic of Mauritania*]   (AF)
GARKI .... Gabungan Remilling Karet Indonesia [*Indonesian Rubber Remilling Association*]   (IN)
Garkreba .... Garantie- und Kreditbank [*Guaranty and Credit Bank*] [*Germany*]   (EG)
GARMCO ... Gulf Aluminium Rolling Mill Company [*Bahrain, Saudi Arabia, Kuwait, Iraq, Oman, and Qatar*]   (MENA)
GARNOCI ... Groupement d'Amenagement des Routes du Nord-Ouest de la Cote-D'Ivoire
GARO .... Garage Equipment Plant   (RU)
GARostobl ... State Archives of the Rostov Oblast   (RU)
GAROZ ..... State Artillery Weapons Factory   (RU)
GARP .... Global Atmospheric Research Program [*ICSU*]   (AF)
GARS .... Main Ammunition Depot   (RU)
GARyazobl ... State Archives of the Ryazan' Oblast   (RU)
GARZ .... State Automobile Repair Plant   (RU)
GAS .... Advanced Air Depot   (RU)
GAS .... Advanced Ammunition Depot   (RU)
GAS .... Autonomous Anarchist Groups [*Spanish*]   (PD)
GAS .... Gabinete da Area de Sines [*Sines Area Council*] [*Lisbon, Portugal*]   (WER)
GAS .... Garissa [*Kenya*] [*Airport symbol*]   (OAG)
Gas .... Gegensatz [*Opposite*] [*German*]
GAS .... Geological Association of Students
GAS .... Ghana Academy of Sciences
GAS .... Global Analysis Systems [*Information service or system*]   (IID)
GAS .... Goilala Air Services [*Australia*]
GAS .... Great Attractions of Sydney [*Australia*]
GAS .... Groupement Aerien Senegalais
GAS .... Groupement des Aviculteurs du Senegal
GAS .... Grupo de Accion Sindicalista [*Trade Union Action Group*] [*Spanish*]   (WER)
GAS .... Hydroxylamine Sulfate   (RU)
GAS .... Main Air Depot   (RU)
GAS .... Main Ammunition Depot   (RU)
GAS .... State Administrative Council [*China*]   (RU)
GASA .... Geostatistical Association of South Africa   (AA)
GASA .... German Australian Society of Australia
GASAA ...... Graphic Arts Services Association of Australia
GASANSW ... Graphic Arts Services Association of New South Wales [*Australia*]
Gasaufkohl ... Gasaufkohlung [*Gas Carburization*] [*German*]   (GCA)
GASAV ...... Graphic Arts Services Association of Victoria [*Australia*]
GASBIINDO ... Gabungan Serikat Buruh Islam Indonesia [*Indonesian Moslem Labor Union Federation*]   (IN)
GASC .... German-American Securities Corp.   (BARN)
GASC .... Grupo al Servicio de Cataluna [*Catalan Service Group*] [*Spanish*]   (WER)
GASCARB ... Productora de Gas Carbonico [*Venezuela*]
GASCO ..... Abu Dhabi Gas Industries Ltd. [*United Arab Emirates*]   (MENA)
GASCO ..... Gasolinera Colombiana [*Colombia*]   (COL)
GASCOL ... Gaseosas Colombianas SA [*Colombia*]   (COL)
Gasentw ..... Gasentwicklung [*Evolution of Gas*] [*German*]
GASEQ .... Graziers' Association of South East Queensland [*Australia*]
gasf .... Gasfoermig [*Gaseous*] [*German*]   (GCA)
GASF .... Guaranteed Australian Sharemarket Fund [*Legal and General Insurance*]
gasform ...... Gasfoermig [*Gaseous*] [*German*]   (GCA)
GASG .... Segou [*Mali*] [*ICAO location identifier*]   (ICLI)
GASGA ..... Group for Assistance in Systems Relating to Grain After-Harvest [*Germany*]
GASHDH ... General Association of Secondary Heads and Deputy-Heads [*Netherlands*]   (EAIO)
GASINT .... Gesellschaft fuer Gasinteressen mgH
GASK .... Sikasso [*Mali*] [*ICAO location identifier*]   (ICLI)
GASK .... State Architectural and Construction Control   (RU)
GASKhN ... Georgian Academy of Agricultural Sciences   (RU)
GASN .... San [*Mali*] [*ICAO location identifier*]   (ICLI)

GASNTI .... Gosudarstevannayasistema Nauchno-Teknicheskoi Informatsii [*State Scientific and Technical Information System*] [*Former USSR*] (PDAA)
GASP........ Gas and Oil Separation Plant [*Arab*]
GASP........ German Association of Suicide Prevention (EAIO)
GASP........ Goldfields Against Serious Pollution [*Australia*]
GASP........ Groups Against Sewage Pollution [*Australia*]
GASPEKRI ... Gabungan Serikat Pekerdja Keristen [*Federation of Christian Labor Unions*] (IN)
GASPI .... Gabungan Semkat Sekerdja Partikulis Indonesia [*Federation of Workers in Private Industry*] [*Indonesian*]
GASPS ...... General Aviation Strategic Plan - Sydney [*Australia*]
GASSOMEL ... Groupement des Associations Mutuelles de l'Empire Lunda
GASSR ...... Mountain Autonomous Soviet Socialist Republic [*1921-1924*] (RU)
GAST........ Gastronomia Espanola [*Ministerio de Cultura*] [*Spain*] [*Information service or system*] (CRD)
GAST........ Grenzaufsichtsstelle [*Border Control Point*] (EG)
Gastdoz...... Gastdozent [*Guest Lecturer*] [*German*] (GCA)
Gastrol'byuro ... Theatrical Tour Office (RU)
GAT .... Address-Current Generator [*Computers*] (RU)
gat .... Gatunek [*Sort*] [*Poland*]
GAT.......... Gefechtsaufklaerungstruppe [*Combat Reconnaissance Unit*] (EG)
g-at .... Gram Atom (RU)
GAT.......... Groupe des Assurances de Tunisie
GAT.......... Groupement Africain de Travaux
GAT.......... Guinea Air Traders [*Australia*]
GAT.......... Guyane Air Transport [*Airline*] [*French Guiana*]
GAT.......... Hypersonic Wind Tunnel (RU)
GAT.......... State Academic Theater (RU)
GATA .... Gabinete de Agencias e Trabalhos de Agrimensura
GATA .... Gulhane Askeri Tip Akademisi [*Gulhane Academy of Military Medicine*] [*Ankara*] (TU)
GATASWA ... Gestalt and Transactional Analysis Seminar, Western Australia
GATB .... Tombouctou [*Mali*] [*ICAO location identifier*] (ICLI)
GATE .... Gambia Association of Teachers of English
GATE .... German Appropriate Technology Exchange
GATE .... Global Atlantic Experiment (AF)
GATE .... Godolloi Agrartudomanyi Egyetem [*Godollo University of Agricultural Sciences*] [*Hungary*] (ARC)
GAT-ELS .. Gas Turbine Electric Power Plant (RU)
GATIY....... General Association of Tourist Industry of Yugoslavia (EAIO)
GATKh ...... Trucking Establishment (RU)
GATL .... Group Aerien de Transport et de Liaison [*Air Force*] (PDAA)
GATN .... Taoudenni [*Mali*] [*ICAO location identifier*] (ICLI)
GATOB ..... Leningrad State Academic Theater of Opera and Ballet Imeni S. M. Kirov (RU)
g-atom ...... Gram Atom (RU)
g-atom .... Gramoatom [*Gram Atom*] [*Poland*]
GATRA ..... Gabungan Sasterawan Sedar [*Association of Enlightened Writers*] (ML)
GATRAC... Garages et Transports Commerciaux
GATRAMAR ... Societe Gabonaise de Transports Maritimes
GATs .... Automatic Centralized Switching Control [*Railroads*] (RU)
GATS........ City Automatic Telephone Exchange (RU)
GATS........ General Agreement on Trade in Services
GATS........ Tessalit [*Mali*] [*ICAO location identifier*] (ICLI)
GATT .... General Agreement on Tariffs and Trade [*Organization, and the concept it represents, concerned with adjustment of tariffs among 73 member nations*] [*See also AGTDC*] [*Switzerland*] [*Also, an information service or system*]
GATTA...... Ghana Association of Travel and Tourist Agents
GAU......... Gauhati [*India*] [*Airport symbol*] (OAG)
GAU......... Geriatric Assessment Unit [*Australia*]
GAU......... Groesster Anzunehmender Unfall [*Worst Conceivable (Nuclear) Accident*] (WEN)
GAU......... Groupement d'Architecture et d'Urbanisme
GAU......... Grupos de Accion Unificadora [*Groups for Unified Action*] [*Uruguay*] (PD)
GAU......... Gujarat Agricultural University [*India*] (ARC)
GAU......... Main Archives Administration (RU)
GAU......... Main Artillery Directorate (RU)
gaub........... Howitzer (RU)
gauf .... Gaufre [*Goffered*] [*Publishing*] [*French*]
Gaul .... Gaulish [*Language*] (BARN)
Gaux......... Generaux [*Generals*] [*French*]
GAV......... Gabor Aron Vasontode es Gepgyar [*Aron Gabor Iron Foundry and Machine Factory*] (HU)
GAV......... Gemeinschaftsausschuss Verzinken eV (SLS)
GAV......... Granada Aviacion [*Spain*] [*ICAO designator*] (FAAC)
gav .... Harbor [*Topography*] (RU)
GAVB .... Main Air Base (RU)
GAVladobl ... State Archives of the Vladimir Oblast (RU)
GAVologobl ... State Archives of the Vologda Oblast (RU)
GAVTU ..... Main Automobile Administration (RU)

GAW......... Gambia Airways [*ICAO designator*] (FAAC)
GAW......... Gangaw [*Myanmar*] [*Airport symbol*] (OAG)
GAWA....... Geographical Association of Western Australia
GAWF .... General Arab Women Federation (EA)
GAWI .... Deutsche Foerderungsgesellschaft fuer Entwicklungslaender
GAWU....... Guyana Agricultural and General Workers Union (LA)
GAX......... Gamba [*Gabon*] [*Airport symbol*] (OAG)
GAY......... Guyana Assembly of Youth (LA)
GAYaPEY ... Group of Algorithmic Languages for the Processing of Economic Information (RU)
GAYE .... Gemicilik, Armatorluk, ve Yapim Endustrisi Sanayi ve Ticaret Limited Sirketi [*Shipbuilding, Shipowner, and Construction Industry and Trade Corporation*] (TU)
GAYE .... Yelimane [*Mali*] [*ICAO location identifier*] (ICLI)
GAZ........... Automobile Made by the Gor'kiy Automobile Plant (RU)
Gaz............ Gas Plant [*Topography*] (RU)
gaz............. Gas Well [*Topography*] (RU)
GAZ........... Geographical Association of Zimbabwe (EAIO)
GAZ........... Gor'kiy Automobile Plant (RU)
GAZ........... Gruene Aktion Zukunft [*Green Action for the Future*] [*Germany*] (PPW)
gaz............. Newspaper (RU)
GAZ........... State Aircraft Plant (RU)
gazd............ Gazdasag [*Agriculture, Economy*] (HU)
gazd............ Gazdasagi [*Agricultural, Economic*] (HU)
GAZDEP... Kozepmagyarorszagi Epitesi Vallalat [*Central Hungarian Construction Enterprise*] (HU)
Gazete .... Gazetesi [*Newspaper*] (TU)
gazg .... Gasholder, Gas Tank [*Topography*] (RU)
gazoobr........ Gaseous, Gasiform (RU)
Gazoochistka ... All-Union Trust of Electrical, Chemical, and Mechanical Gas Purification (RU)
gazopr......... Gas Pipeline [*Topography*] (RU)
GAZT .... Gemeinsamer Aussenzolltarif [*Common External Tariff*] (EG)
GB............. Estado da Guanabara [*State of Guanabara*] [*Brazil*]
GB............. Ganzer Bogen [*Full Bow*] [*Music*]
GB............. Garanti Bankasi [*Guarantee Bank*] [*Turkey*]
GB............. Gazdasagi Bizottsag [*Economic Committee*] (HU)
GB............. Gencler Birligi [*Youth Union*] [*Soccer team Cyprus*] (TU)
GB............. Genossenschaftlicher Betrieb [*Cooperative Enterprise*] (EG)
GB............. Geschaeftsbereich [*German*] (ADPT)
gb.............. Gilbert (RU)
GB............. Girls' Brigade [*Australia*]
GB............. Gouvernementsblad van Suriname [*Benelux*] (BAS)
GB............. Gran Bretagna [*Great Britain*] [*Italian*]
GB............. Great Barrier Airlines [*Airline code*] [*Australia*]
GB............. Great Britain [*International automobile identification tag*]
GB............. Grondbelasting [*Benelux*] (BAS)
GB............. Groot-Brittanje [*Great Britain*] [*Afrikaans*]
GB............. Grosses Balles [*Boite a mitraille*] [*Military*] [*French*] (MTD)
GB............. Grundbuch [*Land Register*] [*German*] (ILCA)
GB............. Guardianship Board [*Tasmania, Australia*]
gb.............. Gulf, Bay (RU)
GB............. Main Base (RU)
GB............. State Library (RU)
GB............. State Security (RU)
GB............. United Kingdom [*ANSI two-letter standard code*] (CNC)
GB............. Weekblad voor Gemeente-Belangen [*Benelux*] (BAS)
GB............. Wet op de Grondbelasting [*Benelux*] (BAS)
GBA .... Army Hospital Base (RU)
GBA .... Generalbundesanwalt [*Chief Federal Prosecutor*] (WEN)
GBA .... Geologische Bundesanstalt [*Geological Survey of Austria*] (EAS)
GBA .... Gesetzbuch der Arbeit [*Labor Code*] (EG)
GBA .... Girls' Brigade Australia
GBA .... Grundbuchamt [*Land Registry*] [*German*] (ILCA)
GBAA .... German Business Aviation Association (EAIO)
GBAAC ...... Gambian Black African Arts Club
GBAEV...... Gesellschaft fuer Biologische Anthropologie, Eugenik und Verhaltensforschung [*Germany*] (EAIO)
GBAF........ Gemeentebedrijf en Administratie en de Gemeente-Financien [*Benelux*] (BAS)
GBAO........ Gorno-Badakhshan Autonomous Oblast (RU)
GBAP........ Garment Business Association of the Philippines
gbar .... Howitzer Artillery (BU)
GBB .... Gerakan Buruh Bahari [*Maritime Workers Movement*] (IN)
GBB .... Groupement Belge du Beton [*Belgian Concrete Society*] (EAIO)
GBB .... Guild of British Butlers [*British*] (EAIO)
GB/BHE.... Gesamtdeutscher Block/Bund der Heimatvertriebenen und Entrechteten [*All-German Bloc/Association of Homeless and Disenfranchised*] (PPE)
GBC .... Gebrueder Boehler & Co. AG [*Boehler Brothers and Company*] [*Austria*]
GBC .... General Border Committee (Thai-Malaysian) (ML)
GBC .... Ghana Broadcasting Corporation
GBC .... Gibraltar Broadcasting Corp. (EY)

GBC .... Globe Air Cargo [*Antigua and Barbuda*] [*ICAO designator*] (FAAC)
GBC .... Groupe de Brancardiers de Corps [*Military*] [*French*] (MTD)
GBC .... Gulf Boycott Coalition
GBC .... Guyana Broadcasting Corporation (LA)
GBC .... NV [*Naamloze Vennootschap*] General Biscuit Company SA [*Belgium*]
GBCh .... Gesellschaft fuer Biologische Chemie e V (SLS)
GBCP........ General Baptist Church of the Philippines (EAIO)
Gbd .... Gebaeude [*Building*] [*German*] (GCA)
GbD .... Gradska Biblioteka u Dubrovniku [*City Library in Dubrovnik*] (YU)
GBD .... Groupe de Brancardiers Divisionnaires [*Military*] [*French*] (MTD)
GBDL .... Gesellschaft fuer Bibliothekswesen und Dokumentation des Landbaues (SLS)
gbdn .... Gebunden [*Bound*] [*German*]
GBDT .... Leningrad State Large Dramatic Theater Imeni M. Gor'kiy (RU)
GBE .... Gaborone [*Botswana*] [*Airport symbol*] (OAG)
GBE .... Government Business Enterprise [*Australia*]
GBE .... Groupement Belge des Banques d'Epargne [*Banking association*] [*Belgium*] (EY)
G Best .... Het Gemeentebestuur [*Benelux*] (BAS)
GBF .... Frontline Hospital Base (RU)
GBF .... Gesellschaft fuer Biotechnologische Forschung mbH [*Institute for Biotechnical Research Ltd.*]
Gbf .... Gueterbahnhof [*Railroad Freight Station*] [*German*] (WEN)
GBG .... Grande Boulangerie du Gabon
GBGPGS ... Groupe Bakounine-Gdansk-Paris-Guatemala-Salvador [*Bakunin-Gdansk-Paris-Guatemala-Salvador Group*] [*French*] (PD)
Gbh .... Geburtshilfe [*Midwifery, Obstetrics*] [*German*]
GBH.......... Gesellschaft fuer Betriebsberatung des Handels [*Society for Commercial Management Consultants*] (EG)
GBHRS ..... Granite Belt Horticultural Research Station [*Australia*]
GBI .... Gesellschaft fur Betriebswirtschaftliche Information [*Society for Business Information*] [*Germany*] (EAIO)
GBI .... Godisnjak Balkanoloskog Instituta [*Yearbook of the Balkan Institute*] [*Sarajevo*] (YU)
GBI .... Gridlays Bank International Zambia Ltd.
GBI .... Groupement Brigade d'Infanterie [*Infantry Brigade Group*] [*Cambodia*] (CL)
GBI .... Groupement des Bois Ivoiriens
GBI .... State Library Institute (RU)
GBIL......... State Library of the USSR Imeni V. I. Lenin (RU)
GBJ........... Marie Galante [*French Antilles*] [*Airport symbol*] (OAG)
GBK .... Gbangbatok [*Sierra Leone*] [*Airport symbol*] (OAG)
GBK .... Gesellschaft Bildender Kuenstler Oesterreichs [*Austria*] (SLS)
GBK .... Grenzbrigade Kueste [*Coastal Border Brigade (Part of border command)*] (EG)
GBl............ Gesetzblatt [*Gazette*] [*German*] (DLA)
GBL .... Goulburn Island [*Australia*] [*Airport symbol*] [*Obsolete*] (OAG)
GBL .... Groupe Bruxelles Lambert [*Brussels Lambert Group*] [*Belgium*]
GBL .... State Library Imeni V. I. Lenin (RU)
GBM .... Green Belt Movement [*Kenya*] (EAIO)
GBM .... Gulf Building Materials Co. Ltd. [*United Arab Emirates*] (MENA)
GBMM ...... State Library-Museum of V. V. Mayakovskiy (RU)
GBNO........ State Library for Public Education Imeni K. D. Ushinskiy (RU)
GBO.......... Groupement Belge des Omnipraticiens [*Belgium*] (SLS)
GBO.......... Ogooue Air Cargo [*Gabon*] [*ICAO designator*] (FAAC)
gbor .... Howitzer (BU)
GBP .... Baltic State Steamship Line (RU)
GBP .... Groupement Brigade Parachutiste [*Parachute Brigade Group*] [*Cambodia*] (CL)
GBP .... Guinea-Bissau Peso [*Monetary unit*]
GBP .... Ponomarev Hydraulic Swab [*Artillery*] (RU)
GBPA........ Grand Bahama Port Authority (LA)
GBPDP...... Garrison Bath, Laundry, and Disinfection Station (RU)
gbr .... Gebraeuchlich [*Used Commonly*] [*German*]
gbr .... Gebraeunt [*Burned*] [*German*]
GBR .... Gibberellin (RU)
GBR .... Godolloi Buzatermelesi Rendszer [*Godollo Wheat Growing System*] (HU)
GBR .... Great Barrier Reef [*Australia*] (ADA)
GBR .... Groupement Belge du Remorquage [*Belgium*] (BAS)
GBR .... Grupo Bandera Roja [*Red Flag Group*] [*Dominican Republic*] (LA)
GBR .... United Kingdom [*ANSI three-letter standard code*] (CNC)
GBRA .... Gas-Cooled Breeder Reactor Association [*Nuclear energy*] [*Belgium*] (NRCH)
GBRCC...... Great Barrier Reef Consultative Committee [*Australia*]
GBRMP..... Great Barrier Reef Marine Park [*Australia*]
GBRMPA ... Great Barrier Reef Marine Park Authority [*Australia*] (ADA)
GBRS........ Groupe Belge de Recherche Sous-Marine (ASF)

GBS........... Gesellschaft fuer Biologische Sicherheit (SLS)
GBS........... Gokkusagi Boya Sanayii [*Gokkusagi Paint Industry*] [*A subsidiary of Sanayi Holding Turkish Cypriot*] (GC)
GbS .... Gradska Biblioteka u Splitu [*City Library in Split*] (YU)
GBS........... Groupement des Unions Professionnelles Belges de Medecins Specialistes [*Belgium*] (SLS)
GBS........... Grundbetriebssystem [*German*] (ADPT)
GBS........... Guyana Broadcasting Service (LA)
GBS........... Main Botanical Garden (of the Academy of Sciences, USSR) (RU)
GBS........... Sofia City Library (BU)
GBSN .... Gibson [*Botanical region*] [*Australia*]
Gbsp.......... Gebrauchsspuren [*Marks of Use*] [*Publishing*] [*German*]
GBSU .... Guyana Bauxite Supervisors Union (LA)
GBTA .... Guild of Business Travel Agents [*Australia*]
GBTI........ Gnowangerup Bible Training Institute [*Australia*] (ADA)
GBTU .... Main Directorate of Armored Forces (RU)
GBU .... Transports Aeriens de la Guinee-Bissau [*Guinea-Bissau*] [*ICAO designator*] (FAAC)
GBV .... Gibb River [*Australia*] [*Airport symbol*] [*Obsolete*] (OAG)
GBV .... Gueter-Befoerderungs-Vorschriften [*Freight Transportation Regulations*] (EG)
GBYD .... Banjul [*Gambia*] [*ICAO location identifier*] (ICLI)
GBZ .... Great Barrier Island [*Australia*] [*Airport symbol*] (OAG)
GBz .... Gussbronze [*Casting Bronze*] [*German*] (GCA)
GC .... General Command
GC .... Gesu Cristo [*Jesus Christ*] [*Italian*]
GC .... Gloria Combativa [*Combat Glory (Cuban military units)*] (LA)
GC .... Gold Corp. [*Western Australia*] [*Commercial firm*]
GC .... Gran Croce [*Grand Cross*] [*Decoration*] [*Italian*]
GC .... Grand Champ [*Broad Field*] [*French*] (WER)
GC .... Grand-Croix [*Awarded by the Legion of Honor*] [*French*] (MTD)
GC .... Green Currency [*EEC*]
GC .... Greenhouse Corps [*Australia*]
GC .... Guarda Civil [*Civil Guard*] [*Portuguese*]
GC .... Guardia Civil [*Civil Guard*] [*Peru*] (LA)
GCA .... Garden Centres of Australia
GCA .... Garden Club of Australia
GCA .... Georgist Council of Australia (EAIO)
GCA .... Global Citizens Association [*Quebec, PQ*] (EAIO)
GCA .... Government Coastal Agency [*Nigeria*]
GCA .... Grains Council of Australia
GCA .... Great China Airlines [*Taiwan*] [*ICAO designator*] (FAAC)
GCA .... Grenada Cocoa Association (LA)
GCA .... Groupe des Confiseurs Africains
GCJ .... Guacamayas [*Colombia*] [*Airport symbol*] (OAG)
GCA .... Gun Control Australia
GCA .... Guyana Consumers Association (LA)
GCADC ..... Grupo Coheteril Antiaereo de la Defensa de la Capital [*Antiaircraft Missile Group for the Defense of the Capital*] [*Cuba*] (LA)
GCAL .... General Councillor at Large [*Library Association of Australia*]
Gcal.......... Gigakalorien [*Gigacalories*] (EG)
GCAM ...... Groupement de la Caisse des Depots Automatisation pour le Management [*Bank Group for Automation in Management*] [*Information service or system*] (IID)
GCB .... Ghana Commercial Bank
GCB .... Lignes Nationales Aeriennes - Linacongo [*Congo*] [*ICAO designator*] (FAAC)
GCBA .... General Council of Burmese Associations (FEA)
GCBW ...... Global Cooperation for a Better World [*Australia*]
GCC .... Galaxy Collection Center Co. Ltd. [*Thailand*]
GCC .... General Contracting Co. [*Saudi Arabia*] (PDAA)
GCC .... Georgetown Chamber of Commerce [*Guyana*]
GCC .... Great Council of Chiefs [*Fiji*]
GCC .... Greek Community Centre [*Australia*]
GCC .... Guatemala Chamber of Commerce (EAIO)
GCC .... Gulf Cooperation Council [*Arabian*]
GCCA .... Graduate Careers Council of Australia (ADA)
GCCC .... Canarias [*Canary Islands*] [*ICAO location identifier*] (ICLI)
GCCD .... Guyana Coalition of Citizens with Disability (EAIO)
GCCEA...... General Committee of the Comite Europeen des Assurances [*France*] (EAIO)
GCD.......... Ghana Consolidated Diamonds Ltd.
GCD.......... Global Cultural Diversity
GCDP........ Grupo Coordenador do Desenvolvimento da Pesca [*Brazil*] (DSCA)
GCDU....... Grupo de Convergencia Democratica en Uruguay [*Group of Democratic Convergence in Uruguay*] (EA)
GCE .... Commission Geographical Education [*Germany*] (EAIO)
GCE .... General Certificate Examination
GCEC .... Greater Colombo Economic Commission [*Sri Lanka*] (GEA)
GCEI........ Gemeentelijk Centrum voor Elektronische Informatieverwerking [*Netherlands*]
GCEP........ Governing Council for Environmental Programs [*United Nations*]

GCertClinInstr ... Graduate Certificate in Clinical Instruction [*Australia*]
GCertEd..... Graduate Certificate in Education [*Australia*]
GCertEdStudies ... Graduate Certificate in Educational Studies [*Australia*]
GCertMaths & MathEd ... Graduate Certificate in Mathematics and Mathematics Education [*Australia*]
GCertMusMgmt ... Graduate Certificate of Museum Management [*Australia*]
GCertSc& TechWriting ... Graduate Certificate of Scientific and Technical Writing [*Australia*]
GCertSocAdmin ... Graduate Certificate in Social Administration [*Australia*]
GCFA........ Groupement Commercial Franco-Africain
GCFA........ Guyana Cane Farmers Association   (LA)
GCFI......... Comptoir d'Exportation du Groupement des Commercants Francais Independants
GCFL........ Garde Cotiere, Fluviale, et Lacustre [*Coast, River, and Lake Guard*] [*Zaire*]   (AF)
GCFT........ General Corp. for Foreign Trade [*Yemen*]
GCFV........ Puerto Del Rosario/Fuerteventura [*Canary Islands*] [*ICAO location identifier*]   (ICLI)
GCG.......... Greenhouse Coordinating Group [*Australia*]
GCHC....... Ghana Cargo Handling Company
GCHI........ Hierro [*Canary Islands*] [*ICAO location identifier*]   (ICLI)
GChZ......... State Clock Plant   (RU)
GCI.......... Genie Climatique International   (EA)
GCI .... Guernsey [*Channel Islands*] [*Airport symbol*]   (OAG)
GCIA .... General Confederation of Italian Agriculture   (EAIO)
GCIB......... Grenada Cocoa Industry Board   (LA)
GCIC......... German Chamber of Industry and Commerce   (DS)
GCIC......... Grenada Chamber of Industry and Commerce   (EAIO)
GCIC......... Groupement Cinematographique International de Conciliation   (EA)
GCICGP .... Gold Coast Indy Car Grand Prix [*Australia*]
GCIEA....... Grupo Coordenador das Importacoes e Exportacoes de Animais [*Brazil*]   (DSCA)
GCIP........ GEWEX [*Global Energy and Water Cycle Experiment*] Continental-Scale International Project [*World Climate Research Program*] [*Geoscience*]
GCIRC....... Groupe Consultatif International de Recherche sur le Colza [*International Consultative Research Group on Rape Seed*]   (EAIO)
GCL .... General Confederation of Labor in Lebanon
GCL .... General Credits Corp. Limited [*Australia*]   (ADA)
GCL .... Golden Circle Ltd. [*Australia*] [*Commercial firm*]
GCL .... Government Chemical Laboratories [*Western Australia*]
GCL .... Government Chemical Laboratory (Queensland) [*Australia*]
GCLA .... La Palma [*Canary Islands*] [*ICAO location identifier*]   (ICLI)
GCLP........ Gran Canaria [*Canary Islands*] [*ICAO location identifier*]   (ICLI)
GCLW .... General Confederation of Lebanese Workers
GCM......... Good Company Man [*Theater term*]   (DSUE)
GCM......... Grand Cayman [*West Indies*] [*Airport symbol*]   (OAG)
GCM......... Grande Confiserie du Mali
GCM......... Great Central Mines [*Australia*]
GCMB ...... Ghana Cocoa Marketing Board
GCN.......... General Computer Environment [*Civil Aviation Authority*] [*Australia*]
GCNA....... Grenada Cooperative Nutmeg Association   (LA)
GCNSW .... Gas Council of New South Wales [*Australia*]
GCP .... Gambia Congress Party
GCP .... Ghana Congress Party [*Political party*]
GCP .... Gift Coupon Programme [*Later, Co-Action*] [*UNESCO*]
GCR .... General Competition Rules [*Motorcycle racing*] [*Australia*]
GCR .... Gruppi Comunisti Rivoluzionari [*Communist Revolutionary Groups*] [*Italian*]   (WER)
GCR .... Guerrilleros de Cristo Rey [*Guerrillas of Christ the King*] [*Spanish*]   (WER)
GCRAI...... Groupe Consultatif de la Recherche Agricole Internationale
GCRG .... Groupe de Compagnies de Reserve du Genie [*Algeria*]
GCRI......... German Carpet Research Institute [*See also TFI*]   (EAIO)
GCRI......... Grain Crops Research Institute [*South Africa*] [*Research center*]   (IRC)
GCRR .... Arrecife/Lanzarote [*Canary Islands*] [*ICAO location identifier*]   (ICLI)
GCS .... German Ceramic Society   (EAIO)
GCS .... Government Cleaning Service [*New South Wales, Australia*]
GCSA........ Government Clerical Service Association [*Mauritius*]   (AF)
GCSE........ General Certificate of Secondary Education [*British*]
GCSF........ German Civil Servants Federation   (EAIO)
GCSI......... Societe d'Importation-Exportation du Groupement des Commercants Senegalais Independants
GCSV........ Gurson Cocuk Sagligi Vakfi [*Gurson Foundation for Child Health*] [*Turkey*]   (EAIO)
GCT .... Groupe Chimique Tunisienne [*Tunisian Chemical Group*]
GCT .... Groupe de Coordination Technique [*Group for Technical Coordination - GTC*]   (MSC)
GCTA .... Groupe de Canevas de Tir des Armees [*Military*] [*French*]   (MTD)
GCTOA ..... Greek Cultural and Theatrical Organisation of Australia

GCTS......... Tenerife-Reina Sofia [*Canary Islands*] [*ICAO location identifier*]   (ICLI)
GCU.......... Guyana Cooperative Union   (LA)
GCV .... Glavni Centar Veze [*Chief Communications Center*] [*Military*]   (YU)
GCVO .... Dame [*or Knight*] Grand Cross of the Royal Victorian Order [*Australia*]   (ADA)
GCWA .... German Cement Works Association   (EAIO)
GCXO........ Tenerife [*Canary Islands*] [*ICAO location identifier*]   (ICLI)
GD.............. Advance Party Point   (RU)
GD.............. Air Antilles [*Airline*]   (MHDB)
GD.............. Airtight Door   (RU)
GD.............. Dynamic Loudspeaker   (RU)
GD.............. Freight Yard   (RU)
Gd .... Gadolinio [*Chemical element*] [*Portuguese*]
GD.............. Gambia Dalasi
gd.............. Gazdasagi (Hivatal) [*Paymaster's Office*] [*Military*]   (HU)
Gd .... General Der [*General Of*] [*German*]
GD.............. Generaldirektion [*General Directorate, General Manager's Office*]   (EG)
GD.............. Geografsko Drustvo [*Geographic Society*] [*Belgrade*]   (YU)
GD.............. Germanium Diode   (RU)
GD.............. Gordulocsapagygyar, Debrecen [*Roller Bearing Plant, Debrecen*]   (HU)
Gd .... Grand [*Large*] [*Military map abbreviation World War I*] [*French*]   (MTD)
gd.............. Grand-Ducal [*Benelux*]   (BAS)
GD.............. Granduca [*Grand Duke*] [*Italian*]
GD.............. Greenwich Date
GD.............. Grenada [*ANSI two-letter standard code*]   (CNC)
GD.............. Grossdimension [*Large Size, Oversize*]   (EG)
Gd .... Grund [*Shoal*] [*Grd Swedish*] [*See also*]   (NAU)
Gd .... Grund [*Shoal*] [*Grd Danish*] [*See also*]   (NAU)
Gd .... Grund [*Shoal*] [*Grd*] [*See also*] [*German*]   (NAU)
GD.............. Horizontal Range   (RU)
GD.............. Main Marine Engine   (RU)
GD.............. Motor-Generator Set   (RU)
gda.............. Garda [*Guards, Bodyguard*]   (HU)
GDA........... Gas Distribution Administration [*Iraq*]   (PDAA)
G-da .... Gentlemen   (BU)
GDA........... German Dairy Association   (EAIO)
GDA........... Goat Dairymen's Association [*Australia*]
g-da .... Gospoda [*Madam*]   (RU)
GDA........... Grafik-Design Austria [*Graphic-Design Austria*]   (EAIO)
g-da .... Messieurs [*Plural of Mister*]   (RU)
GDAC....... Goldfields Dust Abatement Committee [*Australia*]   (PDAA)
GDACI ..... Grupo de Deteccao, Alerta, e Conduta de Intercepcao [*Detection, Alert, and Interception Group*] [*Portuguese*]   (WER)
GDB........... Gabonskii Demokraticheskii Blok
GdB........... Gesellschaft des Bauwesens eV   (SLS)
GDB........... Glavna Direkcija Brodogradnje [*General Administration of Shipbuilding*]   (YU)
GDB........... Government Development Bank of Puerto Rico
Gdb .... Grundbesitzer [*Landed Proprietor*] [*German*]
GDBH....... Gesellschaft Deutscher Berg- und Huettenleute [*Society of German Miners and Metallurgists*]   (EG)
GDC........... Gesellschaft Deutscher Chemiker [*Society of German Chemists*]   (PDAA)
GDC........... Gesellschaft fuer Datensysteme und Computer mbH [*German*]   (ADPT)
GDC........... Groupe des Democrates Camerounais [*Cameroonian Democratic Group*]
GDCh........ Gesellschaft Deutscher Chemiker [*German Chemical Society*]
GDCI .... Gaz de Cote-D'Ivoire
GDCP .... Glavna Direkcija Cestnega Prometa [*General Administration of Road Transport*]   (YU)
GDD........... General Distribution Depot [*Australia*]
GDD........... Geniki Dioikisis Dodekanisou [*General Administration of the Dodecanese*]   (GC)
GDD........... Gesellschaft fuer Datenschutz und Datensicherung eV   (SLS)
GDD........... Gocmen Dayanisma Dernegi [*Immigrant's Solidarity Association*]   (TU)
GDDA....... General Desert Development Authority [*Egypt*]
GDDD....... Geniki Dievthynsis Dimosias Dioikiseos [*General Directorate of Public Administration*] [*Greek*]   (GC)
GDDM....... Graphische Daten-Darstellung und Management [*German*]   (ADPT)
GDE........... Gabinete de Dinamizacao do Exercito [*Army Morale Office*] [*Portuguese*]   (WER)
Gde .... Gemeinde [*Community*] [*German*]
GDE........... Gode [*Ethiopia*] [*Airport symbol*]   (OAG)
GDE........... Gourde [*Monetary unit*] [*Haiti*]
gde .... Grande [*Large*] [*Portuguese*]
gde .... Guarde [*Guard*] [*Spanish*]
GDE........... Main Directorate of Electrification   (BU)

GDE........... Servicios Aereos Gadel SA de CV [*Mexico*] [*ICAO designator*] (FAAC)
GDEA........ Geniki Dievthynsis Ethnikis Asfaleias [*YPEA*] [*General Directorate of National Security*] [*Later,*] [*Greek*]   (GC)
GDELRS ... Generalna Direkcija za Elektrogospodarstvo Ljudska Republika Slovenija [*General Administration of the Electrical Industries of Slovenia*] (YU)
GDEZ........ Generalna Direkcija za Eksploatacijo Zeleznic [*General Administration for the Utilization of Railroads*]   (YU)
GDEZ........ Glavna Direkcija Eksploatacije Zeleznica [*General Administration for the Utilization of Railroads*]   (YU)
GDF........... Gaz de France [*French Gas Company*]   (WER)
GDF........... Geniki Dievthynsis Forologias [*General Directorate of Taxation*] [*Greek*]   (GC)
GDF........... Guanosine Diphosphate   (RU)
GdF........... Guardia di Finanza [*Revenue Guard*] [*Italian*]
GDF........... Guyana Defense Force   (LA)
GDF-DETN ... Gaz de France, Direction des Etudes et Techniques Nouvelles [*French Gas, Department of Research and Development*] (WED)
GDFG........ Guanosine Diphosphate Glucose   (RU)
GdF(S)....... Gesellschaft der Freunde der Sowjetunion [*Society of Friends of the Soviet Union*]   (EG)
Gdg............. Grossgueterwagenzug [*Train Consisting of Large Freight Cars*] (EG)
GDH.......... Gesellschaft Deutscher Huettenleute [*Society of German Metallurgists*]   (EG)
GDI........... Gemeinschaft der Ikonenfreunde [*Society of Friends of Icons*] [*Germany*]   (EAIO)
GDIM........ Graduate Diploma in Industrial Management [*Australia*]
GDIPPTPP ... Main Directorate of Publishing Houses, the Printing Industry, and Trade in Printed Matter   (BU)
GDJDRS ... Glavna Direkcija Jugoslovenskog Drzavnog Recnog Saobracaja [*General Administration of Yugoslav State River Traffic*] (YU)
GDJZ......... Generalna Direkcija Jugoslovanskih Zeleznic [*General Administration of Yugoslav Railroads*]   (YU)
Gdk .... Gdansk [*Poland*]   (BARN)
GDK.......... Group Decontamination Kit   (RU)
GDKh........ Main Food Supply Directorate   (BU)
GDKP........ Geniki Dievthynsis Kyvernitikis Politikis [*General Directorate of Government Policy*] [*Greek*]   (GC)
GDL........... Gas Dynamics Laboratory [*1928-1934*]   (RU)
GDL........... Gemeinschaft Deutscher Lehrerverbaende   (SLS)
GDL........... Gleichrichterdioden fuer Leistungselektronik [*German*]   (ADPT)
GDL........... Guadalajara [*Mexico*] [*Airport symbol*]   (OAG)
GDLP........ Grenada Democratic Labour Party [*Political party*]   (EY)
GDM.......... Gdanska Dzielnica Mieszkaniowa [*Gdansk (Danzig) Residential District*]   (POL)
GDM.......... Gesamtverband Deutscher Musikfachgeschafte [*Association of German Music Dealers*]   (EAIO)
GdM........... Gesellschaft der Musikfreunde in Wien [*Austria*]   (SLS)
GDM.......... Ghana Democratic Movement [*Political party*]   (EY)
GDM.......... Gibraltar Democratic Movement [*Political party*]   (PPE)
GDM.......... Grenada Democratic Movement [*Political party*]   (EAIO)
GDM.......... Grunwaldzka Dzielnica Mieszkaniowa [*Grunwald Residential District*]   (POL)
GDM.......... Lead Vehicle of an Advance Party   (RU)
GDMB....... Gesellschaft Deutscher Metallhuetten- und Bergleute   (SLS)
GDN .... Gdansk [*Poland*] [*Airport symbol*]   (OAG)
GDN .... Gleichstrom-Datenuebertragungseinrichtung fueniedrige Sendespannung [*German*]   (ADPT)
GDN .... Gleichstrom-Datenuebertragungsgeraet fuer Niederpegel [*German*]   (ADPT)
GDNA........ Gesellschaft Deutscher Naturforscher und Aerzte   (SLS)
GDO .... Gdanska Dyrekcja Odbudowy [*Gdansk (Danzig) Administration of Reconstruction*]   (POL)
GDO .... Government Diamond Office
GDO .... Guasdualito [*Venezuela*] [*Airport symbol*]   (OAG)
GDO .... Guild of Dispensing Opticians Ltd. [*Australia*]   (ADA)
GDO(A)..... Guild of Dispensing Opticians (Australia)
GDOFA ..... Guide Dog Owners and Friends' Association [*Australia*]
GDOIFK.... State Twice Decorated Institute of Physical Culture Imeni P. F. Lesgaft   (RU)
GDP........... General Defense Plan [*Formerly, EDP*] [*NATO*]   (NATG)
GDP........... Generalna Direkcija Posta [*General Administration of the Postal Service*]   (YU)
GDP........... Geniki Dievthynsis Programmatismou [*General Directorate of Planning*] [*Greek*]   (GC)
GDP........... Gesamtdeutsche Partei [*All-German Party*] [*Political party*] (PPE)
GDP........... Ghana Democratic Party   (AF)
GDP........... Grafeion Dimosion Pliroforion [*Public Information Office*] [*Greek*]   (GC)
GDP........... Gross Domestic Product   (EECI)
GDP........... Groupe des Democrates Patriotes [*Burkina Faso*] [*Political party*]   (EY)

GDP........... Main Dispatcher's Station   (RU)
GDPA........ Geniki Dievthynsis Politikis Amynis [*Civil Defense General Directorate*] [*Greek*]   (GC)
GDPB .... General Department of Publications and Broadcasting
GDPTT...... Generalna Direkcija Posta, Telegrafa, i Telefona [*General Administration of Postal, Telegraph, and Telephone Service*]   (YU)
GDQ .... Gondar [*Ethiopia*] [*Airport symbol*]   (OAG)
GDR........... Generaldirektion der Reichsbahn [*General Directorate of the GDR Railroad*]   (EG)
GDR........... German Democratic Republic   (RU)
GDR........... Groupement des Democrates Revolutionnaires [*Burkina Faso*] [*Political party*]   (EY)
GDRI .... Main Directorate of Radio Information   (BU)
GDRS .... Glavna Direkcija Recnog Saobracaja [*General Administration of River Traffic*]   (YU)
GDRZ........ State House of Broadcasting and Sound Recording   (RU)
GDS .... City Disinfection Station   (RU)
GdS .... Garde des Sceaux [*French*]   (FLAF)
GDS .... Generaldirektion Schiffahrt [*General Directorate for Navigation*] (EG)
GDS .... General Disposal Schedule [*Australia*]
GDS .... Geografsko Drustvo Slovenije [*Former Yugoslavia*]   (SLS)
GD'=s .... Grupas Dinamizadores
GDS .... Main Directorate of Construction   (BU)
GDS .... Main Statistical Directorate   (BU)
GDSF......... Gesellschaft fuer Deutsch-Sowjetische Freundschaft [*German-Soviet Friendship Society*]   (EG)
GDSh......... Large Smoke Pot [*Military*]   (BU)
GDSN........ Global Digital Seismic Network
GDSP........ Guardia Distrital de Seguridad Publica [*District Police Force*] [*Bolivia*]   (LA)
GDSS......... Gabonskii Demokraticheskii i Sotsialnyi Soiuz
GDSS......... General Dutch Singing Society [*Belgium*]   (EAIO)
GDSSI .... General Department for State Security Investigations [*Egypt*] (ME)
GDT.......... Gemeenschappelijk Douanetarief [*Benelux*]   (BAS)
GdT........... Gemeinschaftsausschuss der Technik   (SLS)
GDT.......... Geniki Dievthynsis Takhydromeion [*General Directorate of Post Offices*] [*Greek*]   (GC)
GDT.......... Golden Diamond Travel and Tourism Agency [*Saudi Arabia*]
GDT.......... Grand Turk [*British West Indies*] [*Airport symbol*]   (OAG)
GDTA........ Groupement pour le Developpement de la Teledetection Aerospatiale [*Group for Development of Aerospace Teledetection*] [*French*]   (WER)
GDTP .... Geniki Dievthynsis Typou kai Pliroforion [*General Directorate of Press and Information*] [*Greek*]   (GC)
GDU .... Gas-Arc Unit   (RU)
GDU .... Grupos de Delegados de Unidade [*Unit Delegates' Group*] [*Portuguese*]   (WER)
GDU .... State Far Eastern University   (RU)
GDUP........ Generalna Direkcija Unutrasnje Plovidbe [*General Administration of Inland Navigation*]   (YU)
GDUP........ Grupos de Dinamizacao e Unidade Popular [*Popular Unity Activation Groups*] [*Portuguese*]   (WER)
Gduz.......... Geografska Duzina [*Geographic Longitude*]   (YU)
GDV.......... Gasdynamische Versuchsanstalt [*Gas Dynamic Laboratory*] [*German*]   (GCA)
GDV.......... Gesamtverband der Deutschen Versicherungswirtschaft eV [*Insurance association*]   (EY)
GDV.......... Grafische Datenverarbeitung [*German*]   (ADPT)
GDVE .... Geniki Dioikisis Voreiou Ellados [*General Administration of Northern Greece*]   (GC)
GdVP .... Grossdeutsche Volkspartei [*Pan-German People's Party*] [*Austria*] [*Political party*]   (PPE)
Gdw........... De Gerechtsdeurwaarder [*Benelux*]   (BAS)
GDZ........... Hydrodynamic Component   (RU)
GDZ........... State House of Sound Recording   (RU)
Gdzh.......... Gigajoule   (RU)
GE............. Federal Republic of Germany [*NATO*]
GE............. Genova [*Car registration plates*] [*Italian*]
GE............. Geraeteanschlusseinheit [*German*]   (ADPT)
Ge............. Germanio [*Chemical element*] [*Portuguese*]
GE............. Getreideeinheit [*Grain Unit*]   (EG)
GE............. Gewichtseinheit [*Unit of Weight*] [*German*]
GE............. Gilbert Islands [*ANSI two-letter standard code*] [*Obsolete*] (CNC)
GE............. Grafeio Eparkhion [*Office of the Provinces*] [*Greek*]   (GC)
GE............. Grupo Especial [*Special Group*] [*Mozambique*]   (AF)
GE............. Mining Electromechanics
GE............. Publishing House of the State Hermitage   (RU)
GE............. State Hermitage   (RU)
GEA .... Gambia Employers' Association
GEA .... Genikon Epiteleion Aeroporias [*Air Force General Staff*] [*Greek*] (GC)
GEA .... Georgia Air [*Czechoslovakia*] [*ICAO designator*]   (FAAC)

GEA .... Ghana Employers' Association [*Trade union*]

GEA .... Greek Ecologists Association (EAIO)

GEA .... Grupo de Economistas y Asociados [*Provides economic analysis in Mexico and abroad*] (CROSS)

GEA .... Noumea [*New Caledonia*] Magenta Airport [*Airport symbol*] (OAG)

GEAAE..... Groupement Europeen des Artistes des Ardennes et de l'Eifel [*European Group of Artists of the Ardennes and the Eifel*] (EAIO)

GEAC .... German East Africa Company

GEACAM ... General and Equitable Assurance Cameroon Ltd. (EY)

GEACAP.... Grupo Especial para Assuntos de Calamidade Publica [*Special Group for Handling Public Disasters*] [*Brazil*] (LA)

geadr .... Geadresseer [*Addressee*] [*Afrikaans*]

GEAMPE ... Grupo Facultativo de Assistencia a Media e Pequena Empresa [*Brazil*] (LAA)

GEAMR .... Groupement Europeen des Associations des Maisons de Reforme [*EC*] (ECED)

GEAP........ Groupe Europeen d'Administration Publique [*European Group of Public Administration - EGPA*] [*Brussels, Belgium*] (EAIO)

GEAR .... Generacion de Empleo en el Ambito Rural [*Generation of Employment in Rural Areas*] [*Peru*] (LA)

GEAR .... Government Employees' Association for Reforms [*Philippines*] (EY)

GEAR .... Great Eastern Australian Rally [*Cycling*]

GEAST ...... Groupe d'Etude et d'Action Socialiste Tunisien

GEAT .... Groote Eylandt Aboriginal Trust [*Australia*]

Geb............ Gebel [*Mountain, Hill*] [*G Arab*] [*See also*] (NAU)

geb............. Gebied [*Subject*] [*Publishing*] [*Netherlands*]

geb............. Gebildet [*Educated*] [*German*]

geb............. Gebonden [*Bound*] [*Netherlands*] (GPO)

GEB .... Gebore [*Born*] [*Afrikaans*]

geb............. Geboren [*Born*] [*Dutch*] (GPO)

GEB .... Geboren [*Born*] [*German*]

GEB .... Gebou [*Building*] [*Afrikaans*]

GEB .... Gebrueder [*Brothers*] [*German*]

GEB .... Gebunden [*Bound*] [*Publishing*] [*German*]

GEB .... Gemeente Energiebedrijf van Hilversum [*Benelux*] (BAS)

GEB .... Hemato-Encephalic Barrier, Blood-Brain Barrier (RU)

gebd........... Gebunden [*Bound*] [*German*] (GCA)

gebdn......... Gebunden [*Bound*] [*Publishing*] [*German*]

GEBECOMA ... Groupement Belge des Constructeurs de Materiel Aerospatial [*Belgium*] (PDAA)

Gebr .... Gebraeuchlich [*Customary*] [*German*]

gebr .... Gebrannt [*Burned*] [*German*] (GCA)

Gebr .... Gebrauch [*Usage*] [*German*] (GCA)

gebr .... Gebraucht [*Used, Secondhand*] [*German*]

gebr .... Gebrochen [*Broken*] [*German*]

GEBR. .... Gebroeders [*Brothers*] [*Afrikaans*]

Gebr .... Gebroeders [*Brothers*] [*Dutch*] (GPO)

Gebr .... Gebrueder [*Brothers*] [*German*] (GPO)

gebr .... Gebruikt [*Worn*] [*Netherlands*]

Gebr Anw... Gebrauchsanweisung [*Directions*] [*German*] (GCA)

Gebrauchsanweis ... Gebrauchsanweisung [*Directions*] [*German*] (GCA)

gebrs.......... Gebroeders [*Brothers*] [*Afrikaans*]

Gebrsp .... Gebrauchsspuren [*Marks of Use*] [*Publishing*] [*German*]

GEBWYS .. Gebiedende Wys [*Imperative*] [*Afrikaans*]

GEC .... Gabonese Employers' Conference (EAIO)

gec .... Gecartonneerd [*Bound in Boards*] [*Publishing*] [*Netherlands*]

Gec .... Gecici [*Temporary*] (TU)

GEC .... German Cargo Services [*ICAO designator*] (FAAC)

GEC .... Gradska Elektricna Centrala [*City Electric Power Plant*] (YU)

GEC .... Groupement d'Etudes pour la Construction [*French*] (SLS)

GEC .... Groupes d'Etudes Communistes

GEC .... Guyana Electricity Corporation (LA)

GECACI .... Generale Cafeiere et Cacaoyere de Cote-D'Ivoire

GECAM .... Gerencia de Operacoes de Cambio (do Banco Central) [*Exchange Operations Directorate*] [*Brazil*] (LA)

GECAMINES ... Generale des Carrieres et des Mines [*General Quarries and Mines Company*] [*Zaire*] (AF)

GECAN ..... Grupo Executivo do Carvao Nacional [*National Coal Executive Group*] [*Brazil*] (LA)

gecart .... Gecartonneerd [*Bound in Boards*] [*Publishing*] [*Netherlands*]

gecarton ..... Gecartonneerd [*Bound in Boards*] [*Publishing*] [*Netherlands*]

gecass......... Gecasseerd [*Benelux*] (BAS)

GECE......... Groupement Europeen des Caisses d'Epargne [*European Savings Bank Group*] [*EC*] (ECED)

GECh .... Standard-Frequency Pulse Generator (RU)

GECICAM ... Entreprise de Genie Civil et Construction au Cameroun [*Cameroon Civil Engineering and Construction Company*] (AF)

GECO .... General Enterprises Co. [*Oman*]

GECOMA ... Groupement d'Action Economique Malgache [*Malagasy Economic Action Group*] (AF)

GECOMIN ... Generale Congolaise des Minerais [*Congo*]

Gecomines ... La Generale des Carriers et des Mines du Congolaise des Mines [*Cobalt-producing mine*]

GECOPHAM ... General Organization for Phosphate and Mines [*Syria*] (EY)

GECRI....... Gerencia de Coordenacao do Credito Rural e Industrial [*Management of Rural and Industrial Credit Coordination*] [*Brazil*] (LA)

gecycl .... Gecyclostileerd [*Multigraphed*] [*Publishing*] [*Netherlands*]

GED.......... Electric Paddle-Wheel Engine (RU)

Ged........... Gedaagde [*Defendant*] [*Netherlands*] (ILCA)

GED.......... Gedagteken [*Afrikaans*]

ged........... Gedateer [*Dated*] [*Afrikaans*]

ged........... Gedeckt [*Concealed*] [*German*] (GCA)

ged........... Gedeelte [*Section*] [*Publishing*] [*Netherlands*]

ged........... Gedurende [*During*] [*Netherlands*]

GED.......... Guanidoethyldisulfide (RU)

GEDA .... Goldfields Esperance Development Authority [*Australia*]

GEDA .... Guam Economic Development Authority (GEA)

gedat......... Gedateerd [*Dated*] [*Publishing*] [*Netherlands*]

GEDC .... Ghanaian Enterprises Development Commission (GEA)

GEDC .... Groupement d'Etudes pour le Developpement du Cameroun

GEDEC..... Grupo de Estudos para o Desenvolvimento Communitario de Macau [*Macau*] [*Political party*] (FEA)

GEDEO ..... Groupement d'Equipement et d'Outillage [*Central African Republic*]

GEDIP....... Grupo Executivo do Desenvolvimento da Industria de Pesca [*Brazil*] (ASF)

GEDIS ...... Geological, Exploration and Development Information System [*Australia*]

GEDIS ...... Groupement Europeen des Enterprises de Distribution Integrees [*European Multiple Retailers Association*] [*Belgium*] [*EC*] (ECED)

GEDM ...... Groupement d'Etude pour le Developpement de la Mauritanie

GEDOK..... Verband der Gemeinschaften der Kuenstlerinnen und Kunstfreunde eV (SLS)

GEDPA...... Genikon Epiteleion Dioikiseos Politikis Amynis [*Civil Defense General Administrative Staff*] [*Cyprus*] (GC)

GeDPA/Khoras ... Geniki Dievthynsis Politikis Amynis tis Khoras [*General Directorate of National Civil Defense*] [*Greek*] (GC)

gedr .... Gedruckt [*Printed*] [*Publishing*] [*German*]

gedr .... Gedrukt [*Printed*] [*Publishing*] [*Netherlands*]

GEDRT...... Group European d'Echange d'Experience sur la Direction de la Recherche Textil e [*European Group for the Exchange of Information on Textile Research*] (PDAA)

GEE .... Gaziantep Egitim Enstitusu [*Gaziantep Training Institute*] (TU)

GEE .... Gazi Egitim Enstitusu [*The Gazi Training Institute*] [*Ankara*] (TU)

GEE .... Geotekhnikon Epimelitirion Ellados [*Geotechnical Chamber of Greece*] (GC)

GEE .... Gesellschaft fuer Energiewissenschaft and Energiepolitik eV

GEE .... Grafeion Evreseos Ergasias [*Employment Office*] (GC)

GEEC........ General Egyptian Electricity Corp. (PDAA)

GEEDA ..... Groundnut Extractions Export Development Association [*India*] (PDAA)

GEEF .... Genikon Epiteleion Ethnikis Frouras [*National Guard General Staff*] [*Cyprus*] (GC)

GEEI......... State Experimental Electrotechnical Institute (RU)

GEEMA .... German Electrical and Electronic Manufacturers Association (EAIO)

GEERS ...... Groupe d'Etudes Europeen des Recherches Spatiales

GEES........ Gulf Energy and Environmental Systems

GEEThA... Genikon Epiteleion Ethnikis Amynis [*National Defense General Staff*] [*Greek*] (GC)

GEF .... Air GEFCO [*France*] [*ICAO designator*] (FAAC)

gef............. Gefaellig [*Obliging*] [*German*] (GCA)

gef............. Gefaelligst [*Kindly*] [*German*] (GPO)

Gef............. Gefaells [*Revenue*] [*German*]

Gef............. Gefechts [*Fighting, Engagement, Combat, Battle*] (EG)

gef............. Gefunden [*Found*] [*German*]

GEF .... Global Environment Facility [*Implemented jointly by the World Bank, the United Nations Environment Program, and the United Nations Development Program*]

GEF .... Grenada Employers' Federation (EAIO)

GEFACS.... Groupement des Fabricants d'Appareils Sanitaires en Ceramique de la CEE [*Group of Manufacturers of Ceramic Sanitary Ware of the European Economic Community*] (PDAA)

gefahrl........ Gefaehrlich [*Dangerous*] [*German*] (GCA)

gefalt .... Gefaltet [*Folded*] [*Publishing*] [*German*]

GEFAP ...... Groupement Europeen des Associations Nationales des Fabricants de Pesticides [*European Group of National Pesticide Manufacturer' Associations*] [*Common Market*]

GEFAR...... Groupement d'Interets Economiques d'Exportateurs

GEFDU ..... Groupe Europeen des Femmes Diplomees des Universites [*University Women of Europe - UWE*] (EA)

GE FE BI .. Gesellschaft fuer Vergleichende Felsbildforschung [*Airport symbol*] (SLS)

GEFFA ...... Gesellschaft fuer Forstliche Arbeitswissenschaft

GEFIU .... Gesellschaft fuer Finanzwirtschaft in der Unternehmensfuehrung eV   (SLS)

gefl .... Gefalligst [*Kindly, Please*] [*Correspondence*] [*German*]

GEFLI .... Groupement d'Etudes Francais en Libye

geflt .... Gefaltet [*Folded*] [*Publishing*] [*German*]

GEFO .... Gesellschaft fuer die Foerderung des Ost-West Handels [*Society for the Advancement of East-West Trade*]   (EG)

GEFOSAT ... Groupement pour l'Etude des Fours et Outils Solaires et l'Assistance en Technologies Appropriees [*Association for Studies of Solar Furnaces and Tools and Assistance in Appropriate Technology*] [*France*]   (WED)

Gef P .... Gefrierpunkt [*Freezing Point*] [*German*]

GEFS .... General Electric Financial Services [*Australia*] [*Commercial firm*]

geg .... Gegen [*Against*] [*German*]

GEG .... Geographisch-Ethnologische Gesellschaft Basel [*Switzerland*]   (SLS)

GEG .... Grosseinkaufsgesellschaft Deutscher Konsamgenossenschaften [*Germany*]   (DSCA)

gegenseit .... Gegenseitig [*Mutual*] [*German*]   (GCA)

Gegenstromverteil ... Gegenstromverteilung [*Counter Current Separation*] [*German*]   (GCA)

gegenu .... Gegenueber [*Opposite*] [*German*]   (GCA)

gegenub ...... Gegenueber [*Opposite*] [*German*]   (GCA)

gegenubergest ... Gegenuebergestellt [*Facing*] [*Publishing*] [*German*]   (GCA)

gegenw .... Gegenwaertig [*Presently*] [*German*]   (GCA)

Gegenw ...... Gegenwart [*Presence*] [*German*]

gegl .... Geglueht [*Annealed*] [*German*]   (GCA)

gegr .... Gegraveerd [*Engraved*] [*Publishing*] [*Netherlands*]

gegr .... Gegruendet [*Founded*] [*German*]   (GPO)

gegrav .... Gegraveerd [*Engraved*] [*Publishing*] [*Netherlands*]

Gegw .... Gegenwart [*Presence*] [*German*]   (GCA)

GEGZ .... Geographisch-Ethnographische Gesellschaft Zuerich [*Switzerland*]   (SLS)

Geh. .... Gehalt [*Contents*] [*German*]   (ILCA)

geh .... Geheel [*Whole*] [*Publishing*] [*Netherlands*]

geh .... Geheftet [*Stitched*] [*German*]   (EG)

geh .... Geheim [*Secret*] [*German*]   (GCA)

Geh. .... Geheimrat [*Privy Councillor*] [*German*]   (ILCA)

GEHF .... Government Employees Health Fund [*Australia*]

GEHI .... Guangzhou Environmental Health Institute [*China*]   (IRC)

GehKaem ... Geheimkaemmerer [*Safe Deposit Boxes*] [*German*]

Geh Rat ...... Geheimrat [*Privy Councillor*] [*German*]

GEI .... Gender Equality Indicator [*Australia*]

GEI .... General Electric Information Services Proprietary Ltd. [*Australia*]   (ADA)

GEI .... Gesellschaft fuer Elektronische Informationsverarbeitung [*German*]   (ADPT)

GEI .... Giovani Esploratori Italiani [*Italian Boy Scouts*]

GEI .... Gosudorstvenuse Energeticheskoe Izdatel'stvo

GEI .... State Economic Publishing House   (RU)

GEI .... State Scientific and Technical Power Engineering Publishing House   (RU)

GEIA .... Grupo Executivo da Industria Automobilistica [*Executive Group of the Automobile Industry*] [*Brazil*]   (LAA)

GEICINE .. Grupo Executivo da Industria Cinematografica [*Executive Group of the Motion-Picture Industry*] [*Brazil*]   (LA)

GEIDA ...... Grupo Executivo de Irrigacao para o Desenvolvimento Agricola [*Brazil*]   (DSCA)

GEIFAR .... Grupo Executivo da Industria Farmaceutica [*Brazil*]   (DSCA)

GEIFERC ... Grupo Executivo de Industria de Fertilizantes e Corretivos [*Brazil*]   (DSCA)

GEII .... Geographic and Economic Research Institute   (RU)

geill .... Geillustreer [*Illustrated*] [*Publishing*] [*Afrikaans*]

geill .... Geillustreerd [*Illustrated*] [*Publishing*] [*Netherlands*]

geills .... Geillustreerd [*Illustrated*] [*Publishing*] [*Netherlands*]

geillustr ...... Geillustreerd [*Illustrated*] [*Publishing*] [*Netherlands*]

GEIMA ...... Grupo Executivo da Industria da Mecanica Aeronautica [*Executive Group of the Aviation Mechanics Industry*] [*Brazil*]   (LA)

GEIMAC ... Grupo Executivo da Industria de Materias de Construcao Civil [*Executive Group of the Building Materials Industry*] [*Brazil*]   (LA)

GEIME ...... Grupo Executivo da Industria de Mineracao [*Executive Group of the Mining Industry*] [*Brazil*]   (LA)

GEIMEC ... Grupo Executivo das Industrias Mecanicas [*Executive Group of the Mechanical Industries*] [*Brazil*]   (LA)

GEIMET ... Grupo Executivo da Industria Metalurgica [*Executive Group of the Metallurgical Industry*] [*Brazil*]   (LA)

GEIMOT ... Grupo Executivo da Industria Automotora [*Executive Group of the Automotive Industry*] [*Brazil*]   (LA)

GEINEE .... Grupo Executivo das Industrias Eletrica e Eletronica [*Executive Group of the Electrical and Electronics Industry*] [*Brazil*]   (LA)

GEIPAG .... Grupo Executivo da Industria do Papel e Artes Graficas [*Executive Group of Paper and Graphic Arts Industry*] [*Brazil*]   (LA)

GEIPAL .... Grupo Executivo da Industria de Produtos Alimentares [*Executive Group of the Food Industry*] [*Brazil*]   (LA)

GEIPOT .... Grupo Executivo de Estudos de Integracao da Politica de Transportes [*Executive Group for Study of Transportation Integration Policy*] [*Brazil*]   (LA)

GEIPS .... General Electric Industrial and Power Systems [*Australia*] [*Commercial firm*]

GEIQUIM ... Grupo Executivo da Industria Quimica [*Executive Group of the Chemical Industry*] [*Brazil*]   (LA)

GEIS .... State Experimental Institute of Silicates   (RU)

Geistl .... Geistlich [*Religious*] [*German*]

GEITEX .... Grupo Executivo das Industrias de Fiacao e Tecelagem [*Executive Group of the Spinning and Textile Industries*] [*Brazil*]   (LA)

GEITs .... Main Computer Center   (BU)

gek .... Gekennzeichnet [*Characterized*] [*German*]   (GCA)

gek .... Gekocht [*Boiled*] [*German*]

gek .... Gekuerzt [*Abridged, Abbreviated*] [*German*]   (EG)

GEK .... Geniki Epitropi Katanomon [*General Apportionment Committee*]   (GC)

gekl .... Geklebt [*Pasted*] [*Publishing*] [*German*]

gekl .... Gekleurd [*Colored*] [*Publishing*] [*Netherlands*]

GEKMOA ... Grafeion Elengkhou Kataskevon Monimon Odostromaton Athinon [*Office for the Control of Construction of Athens Permanent Road Pavement*]   (GC)

GEKO .... Grafeion Elengkhou Kataskevis Odon [*Road Construction Control Office*] [*Followed by initial letter of district name*] [*Greek*]   (GC)

GEKON ..... Gesellschaft fuer Konsumgueter mgH

gekr .... Gekroent [*Prize-Winning*] [*German*]

geksag .... Hexagonal   (RU)

geksagon .... Hexagonal   (RU)

geksag s. ..... Hexagonal Syngony   (RU)

geksatetraedr ... Hexatetrahedral   (RU)

geksoktaedr ... Hexoctahedral   (RU)

GEKTEMAS ... State Experimental Theatrical Workshops   (RU)

g-ekv .... Gram Equivalent   (RU)

GEL .... Gabinete Electrotecnico Lda.

GEL .... Gambcrest Enterprises Ltd. [*Gambia*] [*ICAO designator*]   (FAAC)

gel .... Gelag [*Laughter*] [*Afrikaans*]

gel .... Gelegenheid [*Opportunity*] [*Netherlands*]

gel .... Geloest [*Dissolved*] [*German*]

GEL .... General Electric Lighting [*Australia*] [*Commercial firm*]

GEL .... General Enterprise Limited

GEL .... Gilbert Islands [*ANSI three-letter standard code*] [*Obsolete*]   (CNC)

GEL .... Grafeion Ergasias Limenos [*Labor Office of the Port Of*] [*Followed by district name*]   (GC)

GEL .... Groupement Europeen de Lymphologie [*European Lymphology Group - ELG*] [*Brussels, Belgium*]   (EAIO)

GEL .... Guerrilla del Ejercito Libertador [*Liberation Army Guerrillas*] [*Argentina*]   (LA)

GEL .... Santo Angelo [*Brazil*] [*Airport symbol*]   (OAG)

GELAN ..... Laboratory of Helminthology of the Academy of Sciences, USSR   (RU)

gelat .... Gelatinoes [*Gelatinous*] [*German*]

Gelatinier ... Gelatinierung [*Gelation*] [*German*]   (GCA)

gelb .... Gelblich [*Yellowish*] [*German*]   (GCA)

GELC .... Groupe des Editeurs de Livres de la CEE [*Book Publishers Group of EEC*]   (EAIO)

Gelier .... Gelierung [*Gelation*] [*German*]   (GCA)

GELKA ...... Gepipari Elektromos Karbantarto Vallalat [*Electrical Maintenance Enterprise of the Machine Industry*]   (HU)

gell .... Gelling [*Gallon*] [*Afrikaans*]

GELNA ..... Groupe d'Etudes sur la Litterature Neo-Africaine

GELP .... Groupement d'Exploitation de Laboratoire Photo-Cinema

Gelre .... Vereniging tot Beoefening van Geldersche Geschiedenis [*Netherlands*]   (SLS)

GELS .... Group Employment Liaison Scheme [*New Zealand*]

Gem .... De Gemeente [*Benelux*]   (BAS)

gem .... Gemachtgde [*Benelux*]   (BAS)

gem .... Gemaess [*According To*] [*German*]   (GCA)

gem .... Gemahlen [*Powdered*] [*German*]

gem .... Gemalt [*Hand-Colored*] [*Publishing*] [*German*]

Gem .... Gemeentewet [*Benelux*]   (BAS)

gem .... Gemein [*Common*] [*German*]   (GCA)

Gem .... Gemeinde [*Municipality*] [*German*]

GEM .... Gemiddeld(e) [*Average*] [*Afrikaans*]

Gem .... Gemisch [*Mixture*] [*German*]   (GCA)

gem .... Gemischt [*Mixed*] [*German*]

GEM .... General Electric Motors [*Australia*] [*Commercial firm*]

GEM .... Giotto Extended Mission [*European Space Agency*]

GEM .... Gnomodotiki Epitropi Meleton [*Advisory Committee on Studies*]   (GC)

GEM .... Groupe d'Etudes Meroitiques de Paris

GEM.......... Groupes Evangile et Mission [*Institute of the Heart of Jesus - IHJ*] [*France*]   (EA)

GEM.......... Groupeurs d'Export du Maroc

GEM.......... Growth Equities Mutual Properties Trust [*Australia*]

GEM.......... Growth with Equity in Mindano [*A USAID backed organization*] [*Philippines*]

GEMA....... Gerakan Mahasiswa [*College Student Movement*]   (IN)

GEMA....... Gesellschaft fuer Musikalische Auffuehrungs- und Mechanische Vervielfaeltigungsrechte [*Society for Musical Performance Rights and Rights of Mechanical Reproduction*]   (EG)

GEMA....... Gikuyu-Emba-Meru Association [*Kenya*]   (AF)

GEMADA ... Groupement des Entreprises de Manutention du Dahomey

GEMAS..... Genel Muhendislik ve Mimarlik Anonim Sirketi [*General Engineering and Architecture Corporation*] [*Ankara*]   (TU)

GEMAS..... Groupement Europeen des Maisons d'Alimentation et d'Approvisionnement a Succursales [*European Group of Food and Provision Chain Stores*] [*Common Market Brussels, Belgium*]

Gembest..... Gemeentebestuur [*Benelux*]   (BAS)

GEMCO.... Groote Eylandt Mining Co. [*Australia*] [*Commercial firm*]

GEME....... Geniki Etaireia Meleton kai Ekmetallevseon [*General Research and Mining Company*]   (GC)

GEMEE..... Geniki Etaireia Metallevtikon Erevnon kai Ekmetallevseon [*General Company for Mineral Prospecting and Exploitation*] [*Greek*]   (GC)

gemeinverst ... Gemeinverstaendlich [*Popular*] [*German*]

Gem-Geb.... Gemeindegebiet [*Municipal, Area*] [*German*]

GEMI .... Global Environmental Management Initiative [*Environmental science*]

GEMICO... Societe Geologique et Miniere du Congo

GEML .... Melilla [*Spain*] [*ICAO location identifier*]   (ICLI)

GEMMKA ... Grammateia tis Gnomodotikis Epitropis Mitroou Meletiton kai Kanonismou Anatheseos [*Advisory Committee Secretariat of the Researcher Registry and (Contract) Assignment Regulations*] [*Greek*]   (GC)

GEMP .... Government Energy Management Program [*Australia*]

GEMPPS... Groupe d'Etudes Mathematiques de Problemes Politiques et Strategiques [*French*]

GEMS....... General Electric Medical Systems [*Australia*] [*Commercial firm*]

GEMS....... Gilevi Exploration and Mining Syndicate

GEMS....... Global Environment Monitoring System [*ICSU*] [*United Nations (already exists in GUS II database)*]

GEMS....... Government Expenditure Management System [*Australia*]

GEMSA..... Gemmological Association of South Africa   (EAIO)

Gemst........ Gemeentestem [*Benelux*]   (BAS)

GEMU ...... German Economic and Monetary Union

Gem W ...... Gemeente Wet [*Benelux*]   (BAS)

GEMZ .... Harmonic Electromagnetic Sounding   (RU)

GEMZ .... State Experimental Machine Plant   (RU)

gen............. Genannt [*Alias*] [*German*]   (EG)

Gen............ Geneigt [*Inclined To*] [*German*]

Gen............ General [*French*]   (MTD)

Gen............ General [*German*]

Gen............ General [*Spanish*]

gen............. General [*Portuguese*]

Gen............ Generale [*General*] [*Italian*]

gen............. Generalny [*General*]   (POL)

Gen............ Genero [*Genus*] [*Portuguese*]

Gen............ Genesis [*Genesis*] [*Afrikaans*]

gen............. Genetic [*Genetics*]   (RU)

gen............. Genetiivi [*Genitive*] [*Finland*]

GEN.......... Genie [*Engineering*] [*French*]   (CL)

GEN.......... Genikon Epiteleion Navtikou [*Naval General Staff*] [*Greek*]   (GC)

gen............. Genitief [*Genitive*] [*Afrikaans*]

Gen............ Genitiv [*Genitive*] [*German*]

Gen............ Genossenschaft [*Association, Society*] [*German*]

Ge N.......... Geographischer Nord [*Geographical North*] [*German*]

GEN.......... Oslo [*Norway*] Ardermoen Airport [*Airport symbol*]   (OAG)

GENA........ Gepufferte Nachrichtensteurung [*German*]   (ADPT)

GENA........ Gepufferte Nachrichtenverarbeitung [*German*]   (ADPT)

gen-ad ...... Adjutant General   (RU)

GENAREP ... Compagnie Generale de Recherches Petrolieres [*General Petroleum Prospecting Company*] [*Algeria*]   (AF)

GENAVIR ... Groupement d'Interet Economique pour la Gestion des Navires Oceanologiques [*French*]   (MSC)

gen bryg ..... General Brygady [*Brigadier-General*] [*Poland*]

GENCO..... Societe Generale de Construction au Cameroun

Gencor........ General Mining Corporation [*South Africa*]

Gend.......... Gendarmerie [*Gendarmery*] [*Military*] [*French*]   (MTD)

gendir .... General Manager, General Director   (RU)

gen dyw ..... General Dywizji [*Lieutenant-General*] [*Poland*]

GENE .... Grafeion Evreseos Navtikis Ergasias [*Merchant Seamen Employment Office*] [*Greek*]   (GC)

Geneal........ Genealogia [*Genealogy*] [*Portuguese*]

geneal......... Genealogie [*French*]   (TPFD)

geneal......... Genealogy   (TPFD)

GeNeCo ..... Genootschap van Nederlandse Componisten [*Netherlands*]   (EAIO)

geneesk ...... Geneeskunde [*Medicine*] [*Afrikaans*]

GENELEC ... Generale Electronique SA

Genel-Is ..... Turkiye Genel Hizmetler Iscileri Sendikasi [*Public Services Employees Union of Turkey*]   (TU)

gen g........... General of the Army   (RU)

GenG.......... GenossenschaftGesetz [*Law on Cooperative Societies*] [*Germany*]

gengazmotor ... Gas Engine Fueled by Producer Gas   (RU)

GENICIAT ... Genie Civil en Afrique Tropicale

GENII........ Scientific Research Institute of Economic Geography   (RU)

genisl.......... Genisletilmis [*Expanded*]   (TU)

genl............ Generaal [*General*] [*Afrikaans*]

Genl........... General [*General*] [*Spanish*]

gen-l .... Lieutenant General   (RU)

gen-leyt ...... Lieutenant General   (RU)

genl-maj .... Generaal-Majoor [*Major General*] [*Afrikaans*]

gen-m .... Major General   (RU)

genmaj........ General Major [*Major General*]   (CZ)

Genmor...... Naval General Staff   (RU)

genn........... Gennaio [*January*] [*Italian*]

gennemillustr ... Gennemillustreret [*Illustrated Throughout*] [*Publishing Danish/Norwegian*]

gennemsk.... Gennemskudt [*Interleaved*] [*Publishing Danish/Norwegian*]

GENOTO ... General Otomotiv Sanayi ve Ticaret AS [*General Automotive Industry and Trading Corp.*]   (TU)

gen-p .... Colonel General   (RU)

genplk .... General Plukovnik [*Colonel General*]   (CZ)

genpor .... General Porucik [*Lieutenant General*]   (CZ)

Genred .... Generalni Reditel [*Director General*]   (CZ)

gensek........ Secretary General   (RU)

Gen-Sekr.... Generalsekretaer [*Secretary General*] [*German*]

gen shtab.... General Staff   (RU)

GENSI....... Gabungan Etjeran Indonesia [*Indonesian Retailers Association*]   (IN)

GENSORU ... Genel Soru [*General Questioning, Interpellation*]   (TU)

Genst.......... Generalni Stab [*General Staff*]   (CZ)

Gen T .... Genie Territorial [*French*]   (MTD)

GENTAS... Genel Metal Sanayii ve Ticaret Anonim Sirketi [*General Metal Industry and Trading Corporation*]   (TU)

GentmaDottssa ... Gentilissima Dottoressa [*Honorable Doctor*] [*Title used to address a woman who has a doctorate*] [*Italian*]

genumm....... Genummerd [*Numbered*] [*Publishing*] [*Netherlands*]

geo............. Geographie [*French*]   (TPFD)

GEO.......... Georgetown [*Guyana*] [*Airport symbol*]   (OAG)

GEOALP... Instituto di Geografia Umana Alpina [*Italian*]   (SLS)

GEOAR...... General Egyptian Organization for Aquatic Resources   (ASF)

GEOBIRO ... Biro za Geodetske Radove u Zagrebu [*Geodetic Operations Bureau in Zagreb*]   (YU)

GEOBOL .. Servicio Geologico de Bolivia [*Bolivian Geological Service*]   (LA)

GEOCOME ... Geological Congress of the Middle East [*Geological Society of Turkey*]

Geod.......... Geodesia [*Geodesy*] [*Portuguese*]

geod........... Geodesic, Geodesy, Geodetic   (RU)

GEOD........ Geodesie [*Geodesy*] [*Afrikaans*]

geod........... Geodezia [*Geodesy*]   (HU)

GEODEZIZDAT ... Publishing House of Geodetic and Cartographic Literature   (RU)

geofak......... Division of Geography   (RU)

GEOFIAN ... Geophysical Institute of the Academy of Sciences, USSR   (RU)

geofiz.......... Geophysical, Geophysics   (RU)

GEOFIZ .... Geosciences Information Center [*Federal Institute for Geosciences and Natural Resources*] [*Information service or system*]   (IID)

geog........... Geografia [*Geography*] [*Italian*]

geog........... Geography   (TPFD)

Geogr .... Geografia [*Geography*] [*Portuguese*]

geogr .... Geografico [*Geographic*] [*Italian*]

geogr .... Geografie [*Geography*] [*Afrikaans*]

geogr .... Geographic   (BU)

geogr .... Geographic, Geographical, Geography   (RU)

Geografgiz ... State Publishing House of Geographical Literature   (RU)

Geografizdat ... State Publishing House of Geographical Literature   (RU)

Geogrduz... Geografska Duzina [*Geographic Longitude*]   (YU)

GEOIMPRO ... Geological and Mining Surveys   (BU)

GEOISTRAGE ... Preduzece za Geoloske Istrazne Radove [*Geological Research Establishment*] [*Sarajevo*]   (YU)

GEOKARTA ... Geographic Maps Institute [*Belgrade*]   (YU)

Geokartproekt ... Geological Cartographic Design Organization   (BU)

GEOKhI .... Institute of Geochemistry and Analytical Chemistry Imeni V. I. Vernadskiy (of the Academy of Sciences, USSR)   (RU)

geokhim ..... Geochemical, Geochemistry   (RU)

geol............ Geologia [*Geology*] [*Finland*]

Geol............ Geologia [*Geology*] [*Portuguese*]
geol............ Geologie [*Geology*] [*Afrikaans*]
geol............ Geologisch [*Geological*] [*German*]   (GCA)
geol............ Geology   (TPFD)
GeolGeograf i Khim I-t pri BAN ... Institute of Geology, Geography, and Chemistry of the Bulgarian Academy of Sciences   (BU)
Geolgiz....... Geological State Publishing House   (RU)
Geol i min... Geological and Mineralogical   (BU)
Geoli-tutnaBAN ... Geological Institute of the Bulgarian Academy of Sciences   (BU)
Geolkom..... Geological Committee   (RU)
Geolnerudstrom ... Trust for Exploration for Nonmetallic Minerals and Building Materials of the Central Regions (of the Main Administration of Geology and Conservation of Mineral Resources of the Council of Ministers, RSFSR)   (RU)
geolog........ Geologisch [*Geological*] [*German*]
GEOLOGI ... Geological Society of Thailand
geol-razv..... Geological-Exploration   (RU)
geol-razved ... Geological-Exploration   (RU)
Geolstromtrest ... Republic Geological Exploration Trust of the Ministry of the Building Materials Industry, RSFSR   (RU)
Geom......... Geometer [*Surveyor*] [*German*]
Geom......... Geometri [*Geometry*]   (TU)
Geom......... Geometria [*Geometry*] [*Portuguese*]
geom.......... Geometria [*Geometry*] [*Finland*]
GEOM........ Geometrie [*Geometry*] [*Afrikaans*]
geom.......... Geometry   (TPFD)
GEOMANCHE ... English-French Geological Mapping of the Seabed beneath the English Channel   (MSC)
GEOMAR ... Programa Plurianual de Geologia e Geofisica Marinha   (MSC)
GEOMIN .. Company for Mining and Geological Cooperation [*Romania*]   (IMH)
GEOMIN .. Institute of Geology and Mineralogy   (RU)
GEOMINCO ... GEOMINCO Reszvenytarsasag [*GEOMINCO Company (Handles export of geological and mining know-how)*]   (HU)
GEOMINES ... Compagnie Geologique et Miniere des Ingenieurs Industriels Belges [*Geological and Mining Company of Belgian Industrial Engineers*] [*Zaire*]   (AF)
GEOPETROLE ... Societe Geotechnique pour la Production Petrole
Geoplanproekt ... Geological Planning and Designing Organization   (BU)
Geopp........ Geopposserde [*Defendant*] [*Netherlands*] [*Legal term*]   (DLA)
GEOS .... Study of Sedimentary Layer of Oceans [*Russian*]   (MSC)
GEO-TOC ... Geophysical and Oceanographical Trans-Ocean Cable [*Japanese seismic project*]
GEP .... Advanced Evacuation Station   (RU)
GEP .... Advance Echelon of Motor Park   (RU)
GEP .... General Electric Plastics [*Australia*] [*Commercial firm*]
gep.............. Gepulvert [*Powdered*] [*German*]   (GCA)
GEP .... Grosshandels-Einkaufspreis [*Wholesale Purchasing Price*] [*German*]   (EG)
GEP .... Groupement des Exploitants Petroliers
GEP .... Grupo Especial Paraquedista [*Special Paratroop Group*] [*Portuguese*]   (WER)
GEP .... Main Evacuation Station   (RU)
Gepa........... Gepaeckabfertigung [*Baggage Dispatching Room*]   (EG)
GEPA........ Groupement d'Etude de Phenomenes Aeriens [*French*]
GEPA........ Grupo Executivo da Producao Animal [*Brazil*]   (DSCA)
gepagin...... Gepagineerd [*Paged*] [*Publishing*] [*Netherlands*]
gepalkr....... Gepalkatresz [*Machine Part*]   (HU)
GEPAN ..... Groupe d'Etude des Phenomenes Aerospatiaux Non-Identifies [*French*]
GEPATA ... Groupe d'Etude des Problemes de l'Automatisme dans les Travaux Administratifs
GEPC........ Ghana Export Promotion Council   (EAIO)
GEPE........ Groupe d'Etudes Politiques Europeennes   (EA)
GEPEXI .... Koho es Gepipari Miniszterium Gepipari Export Irodaja [*Machine Industry Export Office of the Ministry of Metallurgy and Machine Industry*]   (HU)
GEPI......... Grupo de Estudos de Productividade Industrial [*Brazil*]   (LAA)
GEPI......... Societa Gestione e Partecipazioni Industriali [*Industrial Participations and Management Company*] [*Italian*]   (WER)
gepk........... Gepkocsi [*Motor Vehicle*]   (HU)
gepl............ Geplant [*Planned*] [*German*]
gepl............ Geplatzt [*Burst*] [*German*]
GEPLACEA ... Grupo de Paises Latinoamericanos y del Caribe Exportadores de Azucar [*Group of Latin American and Caribbean Sugar Exporting Countries - GLACSEC*]   (EAIO)
GEPLAN... Grupo de Estudos e Planejamentos para o Nordeste [*Brazil*]   (DSCA)
gepr .... Gepraegt [*Embossed*] [*Publishing*] [*German*]
gepr .... Gepresst [*Stamped*] [*Publishing*] [*German*]
GEPS .... Groupe d'Etudes des Proteines de Soja [*Research Group on Oleaginois Proteins*]   (PDAA)
GEPSA ...... Empresa Guineano-Espanola de Petroleos [*Petroleum production enterprise*] [*Equatorial Guinea*]

gept .... Geptan [*Mechanics*]   (HU)
GEPV........ Groupe d'Etude des Proteines Vegetals [*French*]
GEPVP ...... Groupement Europeen des Producteurs de Verre Plat [*European Group of Flat Glass Manufacturers*]   (EAIO)
Ger .... Geraet [*Equipment*] [*German*]   (GCA)
Ger .... Gericht [*Court*] [*German*]
ger .... Gering [*Cheap*] [*German*]
GER .... Gerisen [*Garrison*]   (ML)
ger .... Gerundio [*Gerund*] [*Portuguese*]
GER .... Grups d'Estudiants Revolucionaris [*Revolutionary Student Groups*] [*Spanish*]   (WER)
GER .... Guilde Europeenne du Raid [*European Expedition Guild - EEG*]   (EAIO)
GER .... Nueva Gerona [*Cuba*] [*Airport symbol*]   (OAG)
GERA .... General Engineering Research and Applications [*Nuclear energy*] [*Belgium*]   (NRCH)
GERA .... Geological Exploration and Resources Appraisal
GERA .... Grupo Executivo da Reforma Agraria [*Executive Group for Land Reform*] [*Brazil*]   (LA)
GERAKAN ... Parti Gerakan Rakyat Malaysia [*People's Action Party of Malaysia*]   (ML)
GERAL...... Gerland Algerie
GERALCO ... Geral de Comercio e Industria Lda.
GERAN ..... Grupo Executivo de Racionalizacao da Agro-Industria Canavieira do Nordeste [*Executive Group for Rationalizing the Northeast Sugarcane Industry*] [*Brazil*]   (LA)
Gerb .... Gerberei [*Tanning*] [*German*]   (GCA)
GERBUMI ... Gerakan Buruh Muslimin Indonesia [*Indonesian Moslem Workers Movement*]   (IN)
GERC .... General Egyptian Refrigeration Company   (ASF)
GERC .... Groupe d'Etudes sur les Ressources du Cambodge [*Cambodian Resources Study Group*]   (CL)
GERCA...... Grupo Executivo de Racionalizacao de Cafeicultura [*Brazil*]   (LAA)
GERCOS... Groupement d'Etudes et de Realizations des Compresseurs Speciaux [*France*]   (PDAA)
GERDAT... Groupement d'Etudes et de Recherche pour le Developpement de l'Agronomie Tropicale [*Group for the Study and Research of Tropical Agronomy*] [*International Cooperation Center of Agricultural Research for Development*] [*Information service or system*]   (IID)
GERDAT... Groupement d'Etudes et de Recherches pour le Developpement de l'Agronomie Tropicale [*Studies and Research Group for Tropical Agriculture Development*] [*French*]   (AF)
GERDEM REP ... German Democratic Republic   (WDAA)
GERDOC .. Groupe d'Etudes, Recherches, et Developpement des Oleagineux et Corps Gras [*France*]
GERE........ Gewerkschaft Erdoel-Raffinerie Emsland [*Germany*]
GEREC...... Groupe d'Etudes et de Recherches en Espace Creolophone [*Study and Research Group in Creole-Speaking Areas*]   (LA)
GEREF...... Gereformeerd [*Reformed*] [*Afrikaans*]
Geref .... Gereformeerde [*Reformed*] [*Calvinist*] [*Netherlands*]   (GPO)
GEREG..... Geregistreerd [*Registered*] [*Afrikaans*]
gerep .... Gerepareerd [*Repaired*] [*Netherlands*]
Gereq......... Gerequireerde [*Defendant*] [*Netherlands*]   (ILCA)
GERES ...... Groupe Energies Renouvelables [*Renewable Energy Group*] [*France*]   (IRC)
GERES ...... Groupement pour l'Exploitation Rationnelle de l'Energie Solaire [*Universite de Provence, Departement d'Heliophysique*] [*France*]
GERES ...... Grupo Executivo de Recuperacao Economica do Espirito Santo [*Executive Group for Espirito Santo Economic Recovery*] [*Brazil*]   (LA)
GERG .... Groupe Europeen de Recherches Gazieres [*European Gas Research Group*]   (EAIO)
GERGU ..... Grupo de Exploracion y Reconocimiento Geografico del Uruguay [*Exploration and Geographical Survey Group of Uruguay*]   (LA)
GERI......... Groupement d'Etude des Routes et de l'Infrastructure [*Road and Infrastructure Study Group*] [*Gabon*]   (AF)
gerichtl....... Gerichtlich [*Judicial*] [*German*]   (GCA)
germ .... Germaaninen [*Finland*]
Germ .... Germaans [*Teutonic*] [*Language, etc.*] [*Afrikaans*]
germ .... German   (BU)
Germ .... Germinal [*Seventh Month of the "Calendrier Republicain," from March 21 to April 19*]   (FLAF)
GERMAE ... Groupe d'Etudes et de Recherches des Methodes Actives de l'Education [*French*]   (SLS)
GERMAHII ... Gerakan Mahasiswa Islam Indonesia [*Indonesian Moslem College Students Movement*]   (IN)
GERME..... Groupe d'Etudes et de Recherches en Microscopie Electronique
GERMINDO ... Gerakan Mahasiswa Indonesia [*Indonesian College Students Movement*]   (IN)
germ p .... German Patent   (RU)
GERNORSEA ... German Naval Forces, North Sea Subarea [*NATO*]   (NATG)

GEROVE... Gesellschaft fuer Rohstoffgewinnung und Verfahrenstechnik [*Raw Material Extraction and Processing Technology Company*] (EG)

GERPII...... Gerakan Pemuda Islam Indonesia [*Indonesian Moslem Youth Movement*] (IN)

GERPOL... Gerilja Politik [*Guerrilla Politics (Subversive political activity)*] (IN)

GERS........ Groupe d'Etude et Recherches Sous-Marin

GERSO...... Groupement Europeen de Recherche Scientifique en Stomato-Odontologie [*Belgium*] (SLS)

geruchl .... Geruchlos [*Odorless*] [*German*] (GCA)

GERWASI ... Gerakan Wanita Sosialis Indonesia [*Indonesian Socialist Women's Movement*] (IN)

GERWASII ... Gerakan Wanita Serikat Islam Indonesia [*Indonesian Islamic Alliance Women's Movement*] (IN)

GES............ Gamma European Systems (ADPT)

GES........... Gaz, Elektrik, ve Su Tesisleri [*Gas, Electric Power, and Hydraulic Installations*] (TU)

GES........... Gemi Kaptanlari Sendikasi [*Ship Captains' Union*] (TU)

GES........... General Electric Silicones [*Australia*] [*Commercial firm*]

GES........... General Santos [*Philippines*] [*Airport symbol*] (OAG)

GES........... Genikon Epiteleion Stratou [*Army General Staff*] [*Greek*] (GC)

GES........... Genikos Epitheoritis Stratou [*Army Inspector General*] [*Greek*] (GC)

GES........... German Ecological Society (EAIO)

ges .... Gesaettigt [*Saturated*] [*German*]

ges .... Gesammelt [*Collected, Compiled*] [*German*]

ges .... Gesamt [*Complete, Total*] [*German*]

Ges .... Gesandter [*Envoy*] [*German*]

Ges .... Gesang [*Song*] [*Afrikaans*]

Ges .... Gesang [*Song*] [*German*]

Ges .... Gesellschaft [*Association, Company, Society*] [*German*] (EG)

GES........... Gesellschaft fuer Elektronische Systemforschung [*Corporation for Electronic System Research*] [*German*] (ADPT)

Ges .... Gesetzlich [*Registered (Trademark)*] [*German*]

GES........... Gestair Executive Jet [*Spain*] [*ICAO designator*] (FAAC)

ges .... Gesucht [*In Demand*] [*German*]

GES........... Ghana Education Service

GES........... Gold Exchange of Singapore (DS)

GES........... Groupe d'Etudes Sartriennes (EAIO)

GES........... Groupements Economiques du Senegal [*Economic Groups of Senegal*] (AF)

GES........... Hydroelectric Power Plant (RU)

GES........... State Electric Power Plant (RU)

GESA........ Gas y Electricidad Sociedad Anonima [*Utilities company*] [*Spain*]

GESAMP .. Group of Experts on the Scientific Aspects of Marine Pollution [*ICSU*] (EAIO)

Ges-Amt..... Gesundheitsamt [*Department of Public Health*] [*German*] (GCA)

Gesamtaufl ... Gesamtauflage [*Entire Edition*] [*Publishing*] [*German*]

Gesamtreg ... Gesamtregister [*General Index*] [*Publishing*] [*German*]

GESAMTTEXTIL ... Gesamtverband der Textilindustrie in der Bundesrepublik Deutschland [*Central Confederation of the Textile Industry in Germany*] (EAIO)

GESASA ... Greek Ex-Servicemen's Association of South Australia

GESASE... Geniki Synomospondia Agrotikon Syllogon Ellados [*General Confederation of Greek Agricultural Unions*] [*GSAS*] [*See also*] (GC)

gesatt.......... Gesaettigt [*Saturated*] [*German*]

GESB........ Government Employees Superannuation Board [*Western Australia*]

gesch .... Geschept [*Handmade*] [*Netherlands*]

GESCH...... Geschichte [*History*] [*German*]

gesch .... Geschieden [*Divorced*] (EG)

gesch .... Geschuetzt [*Protected*] [*German*] (GCA)

geschichtl... Geschichtlich [*Historical*] [*Publishing*] [*German*]

geschl .... Geschlossen [*Closed*] [*German*]

Geschlw...... Geschlechtswort [*Article (Grammar)*] [*German*]

geschm ...... Geschmolzen [*Molten, Melted*] [*German*]

geschn .... Geschnitten [*Engraved*] [*Publishing*] [*German*]

Geschr .... Geschrieben [*Written*] [*German*]

Geschrift .... Geschriften van de Vereniging voor Belastings-Wetenschap [*Benelux*] (BAS)

Geschw....... Geschwindigkeit [*Speed*] [*German*] (EG)

Geschw....... Geschwister [*Brother(s) and Sister(s)*] [*German*] (EG)

Geschwindigk ... Geschwindigkeit [*Speed*] [*German*] (GCA)

gesch Wm .. Geschuetzte Warenmarke [*Patented Trademark*] [*German*]

GESCO...... Groupement d'Entreprises Suisses de Construction

GESCO...... Grupo Executivo de Estatistica e Estudos Economicos [*Brazil*] (DSCA)

GESEM ..... Groupement Europeen des Sources d'Eaux Minerales Naturelles [*European Group of Natural Mineral Water Sources*] (EAIO)

gesetzmass ... Gesetzmaessig [*Legal*] [*German*] (GCA)

ges gesch .... Gesetzlich Geschuetzt [*Registered Trademark, Patented*] [*German*] (GPO)

gesign........ Gesigneerd [*Signed*] [*Publishing*] [*Netherlands*]

Ges-Is......... Turkiye DSI Enerji, Su, ve Gaz Iscileri Sendikasi [*State Irrigation, Energy, Water, and Gas Workers Union*] (TU)

gesk .... Geskiedenis [*History*] [*Afrikaans*]

geslte.......... Gesammelte [*Collected*] [*German*] (GCA)

GESM....... Groupement des Ecoles Superieures Militaires [*Advanced Military Training Schools Group*] [*Zaire*] (AF)

GESMA..... Gesellschaft fuer software und Marketing [*German*] (ADPT)

GESP........ German Socialist Unity Party (BU)

Gespr........ Gesprochen [*Spoken*] [*German*]

Ges St .... Gesamtstaerke [*Total Strength*] [*German*] (GCA)

gest............ Gestempelt [*Stamped*] [*Publishing*] [*German*]

gest............ Gestochen [*Engraved*] [*German*]

Gest........... Gestorben [*Deceased*] [*German*] (EG)

gest............ Gestorwe [*Died*] [*Afrikaans*]

GESTAPU ... Gerakan September Tiga Puluh [*30 September Movement (G-30-S)*] (IN)

GESTAS.... Genel Sinai Tesisleri ve Ticaret Anonim Sirketi [*General Industrial Installations and Trade Corporation*] [*Ankara*] (TU)

gestenc .... Gestencild [*Mimeographed*] [*Publishing*] [*Netherlands*]

GESTOK... Gerakan Satu Oktober [*1 October Movement (Another name for G-30-S)*] (IN)

GESY........ Geniki Ekklisiastiki Synelevsis [*General Ecclesiastical Assembly*] [*Greek*] (GC)

GESyN ...... Groupement d'Etude du Synchrotron National [*French*]

GET .... Geraldton [*Australia*] [*Airport symbol*] (OAG)

get............. Getauft [*Baptized*] [*German*]

Get............ Geteilt [*Divided*] [*Music*]

GET .... Getekend [*Signed*] [*Afrikaans*]

get............. Getuie [*Witness*] [*Afrikaans*]

GET .... Great Eastland Television [*Australia*]

GET .... State Electrotechnical Trust (RU)

GETAX..... Intreprinderea de Transport Bucuresti, Gospodaria Camioane Taximetre [*Bucharest Transportation Enterprise, Truck and Taxi Management*] (RO)

GETEPE ... Grupo Executivo de Trabalhos, Estudos, e Projetos Espaciais [*Executive Group for Space Projects, Studies, and Work*] [*Brazil*] (LA)

geterog .... Heterogeneous (RU)

GETF......... Hexaethyl Tetraphosphate (RU)

GETI......... Gepipari Tervezo Intezet [*Design Institute of the Machine Industry*] (HU)

GETIS .... Ground Environment Technical Installation System [*NATO*] (NATG)

getr .... Getrennt [*Separated*] [*German*]

GETS........ General Electric Transportation Systems [*Australia*] [*Commercial firm*]

GETSC ...... General Electric Technical Services Company

GETSOP ... Grupo Executivo para as Terras do Sudoeste do Parana [*Brazil*] (DSCA)

GEU.......... Electrical Propeller Drive [*Nautical term*] (RU)

GEU.......... Electronically Controlled Generator (RU)

GEU.......... General Employees' Union [*Falkland Islands*]

GEU.......... Main Economic Administration (RU)

GEV.......... Gallivare [*Sweden*] [*Airport symbol*] (OAG)

gev .... Gevang [*Caught*] [*Afrikaans*]

Gev .... Gigaelectron-Volt (RU)

GeV .... Giga-Elektronenvolt [*Giga Electron Volts (One billion electron volts)*] (EG)

GEVEV...... Geniki Etaireia Viomikhanikon Epikheiriseon Volou [*General Association of Volos Industrial Enterprises*] (GC)

GEVF........ Gesellschaft fuer Wirtschafts- und Verkehrswissenschaftliche Forschung eV (SLS)

gevl............ Gevlekt [*Spotted*] [*Publishing*] [*Netherlands*]

GEVL........ Groupement International d'Etude pour l'Exploitation des Voitures-Lits en Europe [*Belgium*] (SLS)

GeW.......... Gemeentewet [*Benelux*] (BAS)

Gew .... Gewerbe [*or Gewerblich*] [*Profession (or Professional)*] [*German*]

GEW .... Gewerkschaft Erziehung und Wissenschaft [*Education and Science Labor Union*] (WEN)

GEW .... Gewestelik(e) [*Dialectal*] [*Afrikaans*]

Gew .... Gewicht [*Weight, Gravity*] [*German*]

gew .... Gewig [*Weight*] [*Afrikaans*]

gew .... Gewijzigde [*Benelux*] (BAS)

Gew .... Gewinnung [*Production*] [*German*] (GCA)

gew .... Gewoehnlich [*Usual, Ordinary*] [*German*]

gew .... Gewonnen [*Obtained*] [*German*] (GCA)

GEW .... Gewoonlik [*Usual*] [*Afrikaans*]

GEW .... Gewoya [*Papua New Guinea*] [*Airport symbol*] (OAG)

gewerbehygien ... Gewerbehygienisch [*Industrial Hygiene*] [*German*] (GCA)

gewerbl....... Gewerblich [*Industrial*] [*German*] (GCA)

GEWEX.... Global Energy and Water Cycle Experiment [*World Climate Research Program*] [*Geo science*]

gewijz .... Gewijzigd [*Altered*] [*Netherlands*]

Gewinn....... Gewinnung [*Production*] [*German*] (GCA)

GewO .... Gewerbeordnung [*Trade Regulations*] [*German*]
Gewohn ...... Gewoehnung [*Habitation*] [*German*]   (GCA)
gewohnl ...... Gewoehnlich [*Usual*] [*German*]   (GCA)
GewS .... Gewerbeschule [*Trade School*] [*German*]
Gew-T .... Gewichtsteil [*Part by Weight*] [*German*]
gew Temp... Gewoehnliche Temperatur [*General Temperature*] [*German*]
GEY .... Geuserland Airways Ltd. [*New Zealand*] [*ICAO designator*]   (FAAC)
Gez .... Gezeichnet [*Signed (Before signatures)*] [*German*]   (EG)
gez .... Gezogen [*Drawn*] [*German*]   (GCA)
GEZAMINES ... Societe Generale Zairoise des Minerais [*Zaire Ores Company*]   (AF)
GF .... Comb Filter   (RU)
GF .... French Guiana [*ANSI two-letter standard code*]   (CNC)
gf .... Gasfoermig [*Gaseous*] [*German*]   (GCA)
GF .... Gaudeamus Foundation [*Netherlands*]   (EAIO)
GF .... Gazdasagi Fotanacs [*Supreme Economic Council*]   (HU)
GF .... Gemeente Financien [*Benelux*]   (BAS)
GF .... Geografiska Foerbundet [*Sweden*]   (SLS)
GF .... Geologiska Foreningen [*Geological Society of Sweden*]   (EAIO)
GF .... Glucose Phosphate   (RU)
gf .... Grama-Forca [*Grams of Force*] [*Portuguese*]
GF .... Great Food (Dehydration) Co. Ltd. [*Thailand*]
gf .... Grobfaserig [*Coarse-Fibered*] [*German*]   (GCA)
GF .... Grumes Flottees
GF .... Guarda Fiscal [*Customs Guard*] [*Portuguese*]   (WER)
GF .... Guardia di Finanza [*Fiscal Guards*] [*Financial fraud investigators*] [*Italy*]
GF .... Gubernium Fiuminense [*Province of Fiume*] [*Rijeka*]   (YU)
GF .... Gustav Fischer Verlag (VEB) [*Gustav Fischer Publishing House (VEB)*]   (EG)
GF .... State Pharmacopoeia   (RU)
GFA .... General Football Association [*Sudan*]
GfA .... Gesellschaft fuer Arbeitswissenschaft eV   (SLS)
GfA .... Gesellschaft fuer Arzneipflanzenforschung eV   (SLS)
GfA .... Gesellschaft fuer Aussenhandelsinformation mbH [*Foreign Trade Information Company Ltd.*]
GfA .... Gesellschaft fuer Forschungen zur Auffuehrungspraxis [*Austria*]   (SLS)
GFA .... Ghana Football Association
GFA .... Gliding Federation of Australia   (ADA)
GFA .... Groupement Foncier Africain
GFA .... Groupement Francais d'Assurances [*Paris, France*]
GFA .... Gulf Air [*United Arab Emirates*] [*ICAO designator*]   (FAAC)
GFAA .... Game Fishing Association of Australia
GFAC........ Groupement des Femmes d'Affaires du Cameroun [*Employers' associations*]   (EY)
GFAVO ..... Grossfeuerungsanlagen Verordnung [*Regulations for Large Boilers*]
G-f-aza .... Glucose Phosphatase   (RU)
GFB .... Gemeinschaft Fachaerztlicher Berufsverbaende   (SLS)
GFB .... Hexafluorobutadiene   (RU)
GFBG........ Gesellschaft fuer Forschung auf Biophysikalischen Grenzgebieten [*Switzerland*]   (SLS)
GFBN .... Bonthe [*Sierra Leone*] [*ICAO location identifier*]   (ICLI)
GfBV .... Gesellschaft fuer Bedrohte Voelker [*Society for Threatened Peoples*]   (EAIO)
GFC .... Gas and Fuel Corporation [*Australia*]
GFC .... General Fertilizers Co. [*Syria*]
GFC .... German Film Centre
GFCD .... Geneva Federation for Cooperation and Development [*Switzerland*]   (EAIO)
GFCh .... Fixed-Frequency Generator   (RU)
GFCH .... Gurson Foundation for Child Health [*Turkey*]   (EAIO)
GFCI........ Groupement Foncier de Cote-D'Ivoire [*Ivory Coast Real Estate Group*]   (AF)
GFCM ...... General Fisheries Council for the Mediterranean [*ICSU*]
GFCV........ Gas and Fuel Corp. of Victoria [*Australia*]
GfD .... Gesellschaft fuer Deutschlandforschung [*Association for Research on Germany*]   (EAIO)
GFD .... Gesellschaft fur Flugzieldarstellung GmbH [*Germany*] [*ICAO designator*]   (FAAC)
GFD .... Groupement Foncier Dakar
GFDC .... Ghana Food Distribution Corporation
GfdS .... Gesellschaft fuer Deutsche Sprache eV   (SLS)
GFDS .... Goldfields Flying Doctor Service [*Australia*]
GfdWd .... Gesellschaft fuer die Wiedervereinigung Deutschlands [*Society for the Reunification of Germany*]   (EG)
GFE .... Gesellschaft fuer Erdkunde Berlin   (SLS)
GFE .... Grossforschungseinrichtungen [*Large Research Establishments*] [*German*]
GfEdH .... Gesellschaft fuer Ernaehrungsphysiologie der Haustiere   (SLS)

GFF........... Gesellschaft zur Foerderung der Industrieorientierten Forschung/ Arbeitsgemeinschaft fuer Industrielle Forschung [*Advancement of Industrial Research Society/Industrial Research Group*] [*Swiss Federal Institute of Technology, Zuerich*] [*Research center*]   (ERC)
GFF........... Griffith [*Australia*] [*Airport symbol*]   (OAG)
GFFIL....... Groupement Francais des Fournisseurs d'Information en Ligne [*French Association of Online Information Providers*] [*Paris*] [*Information service or system*]   (IID)
GfG .... Gesellschaft fuer Ganzheitsforschung [*Austria*]   (SLS)
GfG .... Gesellschaft fuer Gerontologie der Deutschen Demokratischen Republik   (SLS)
GFGA .... Gippsland Fruit Growers' Association [*Australia*]
GFGCA...... Gympie Fruit Growers' Cooperative Association [*Australia*]
GFGK .... Gbangbatok [*Sierra Leone*] [*ICAO location identifier*]   (ICLI)
GFH .... Group Financial Holdings Proprietary Ltd. [*Australia*]
GFHA .... Gaelic Football and Hurling Association [*Australia*]
GFHA .... Hastings [*Sierra Leone*] [*ICAO location identifier*]   (ICLI)
GFHG....... Georg-Friedrich-Haendel-Gesellschaft   (SLS)
gfi .... Geographic Institute   (BU)
GFI........... Geophysical Institute (of the Academy of Sciences, USSR)   (RU)
GFI........... Glas Forsknings Institutet [*Glass Research Institute*] [*Sweden*]   (PDAA)
GFI........... Gmelin Formula Index [*Gmelin-Institut fuer Anorganische Chemie und Grenzgebiete*] [*Germany*] [*Information service or system*]   (CRD)
GFI........... Groupe Francais d'Informatique
GFI........... Groupement Francais d'Informatique [*French*]   (SLS)
GFI........... State Financial Publishing House   (RU)
GFIC........ Ghanaian Film Industry Corp.
GFID......... German Foundation for International Development   (EAIO)
G Fin........ Gemeente Financien [*Benelux*]   (BAS)
GFJTU ..... General Federation of Jordanian Trade Unions
GfK .... Gesellschaft fuer Kernforschung
GfK .... Gesellschaft fuer Konsum-, Markt-, und Absatzforschung   (SLS)
GFK .... Gesellschaft zur Foerderung der Inneren Kolonisation eV   (SLS)
GFK .... Gewerkschaftsgruppe fuer Kleinbetriebe [*Small-Plant Trade Union Group*]   (EG)
GFK .... Glycerophosphoric Acid   (RU)
GFK .... Main Philatelic Office   (RU)
GFKB .... Kabala [*Sierra Leone*] [*ICAO location identifier*]   (ICLI)
GFKE .... Kenema [*Sierra Leone*] [*ICAO location identifier*]   (ICLI)
GFKT........ Gesellschaft zur Foerderung der Kunststofftechnik [*Austrian Society for Plastics Engineering*] [*Research center*]   (IRC)
GFKWE ..... General Federation of Kuwait Workers and Employees   (IMH)
GFLAAL ... Gesellschaft zur Foerderung der Literatur aus Afrika, Asien, und Lateinamerika   (EAIO)
GFLL........ Freetown/Lungi [*Sierra Leone*] [*ICAO location identifier*]   (ICLI)
GflS .... Gesellschaft fuer Linksextremistische Systemanalytiker   (SLS)
GFLU........ General Federation of Labour Unions [*Iraq*]
GFM .... Gesellschaft fuer Marktforschung   (SLS)
GfM .... Gesellschaft fuer Musikforschung eV   (SLS)
GFMC ...... General Federation of Milk Cooperatives [*Belgium*]   (EAIO)
GFMP....... Marampa [*Sierra Leone*] [*ICAO location identifier*]   (ICLI)
GFN .... Global Futures Network [*India*] [*India*]   (EAIO)
GFN .... Gold Fields Namibia [*Commercial firm*]
GFN .... Grafton [*Australia*] [*Airport symbol*]   (OAG)
GFO .... Bartica [*Guyana*] [*Airport symbol*]   (OAG)
GFO .... Gesellschaft fuer Organisation eV [*German*]   (ADPT)
GFO .... Main Physical Observatory   (RU)
GFP........... Geheime Feldpolizei [*Secret Police*] [*German*]
GfP............ Gesellschaft fuer Fuehrungspraxis und Personalentwicklung   (SLS)
GFP........... Gesellschaft zur Foerderung der Privaten Deutschen Wirtschaftlichen Pflanzenzuechtung eV   (SLS)
GFP........... Glasfaserverstaerkte Plaste [*Glass-Fiber-Reinforced Plastics*]   (EG)
GFPA .... Gambia Family Planning Association
GFPA .... Ghana Furniture Producers' Association
GFPBBD ... Groupement Francais des Producteurs de Bases et Banques de Donnees [*French Federation of Data Base Producers*] [*Information service or system*]   (IID)
GFPD........ Groupement Forestier de la Pointe-Denis
GFPE .... Gesellschaft fuer Praktische Energiekunde eV   (SLS)
GFPF .... Gesellschaft zur Foerderung Paedagogischer Forschung eV [*Association for Advancement of Educational Research*] [*Research center*]   (IRC)
GfPhDDR ... Gesellschaft fuer Photogrammetrie in der Deutschen Demokratischen Republik   (SLS)
GFPO .... Port Loko [*Sierra Leone*] [*ICAO location identifier*]   (ICLI)
GFPS .... General Federation of Peasant Societies [*Iraq*]
GFPTU...... General Federation of Producers' Trade Unions [*Libya*]
GFR .... Federal Republic of Germany   (BU)
GFR .... German Federal Republic   (RU)
GFS........... General Fund Services

GfS............ Gesellschaft fuer Sicherheits-Wissenschaft eV (SLS)
GFSA........ Gold Fields of South Africa
GFSTU...... General Federation of Somali Trade Unions (AF)
GFT .... Gazdasagi Fotanacs [*Supreme Economic Council*] (HU)
GfT .... Gesellschaft fuer Tribologie eV (SLS)
GFT .... Glasfaserverstaerkte Thermoplasten [*Glass-Fiber-Reinforced Thermoplastics*] (EG)
GFTANSW ... Grain and Feed Trade Association of New South Wales [*Australia*]
GFTI......... Gor'kiy Physicotechnical Institute (RU)
GFTO .... Tongo [*Sierra Leone*] [*ICAO location identifier*] (ICLI)
GFTRI ...... State Physicotechnical Institute of Roentgenology (RU)
GFTU .... General Federation of Trade Unions [*Iraq*] (ME)
GFTU .... General Federation of Trade Unions [*Syria*]
GFTUL...... General Federation of Trade Unions - Libya
GfU .... Geofysikalni Ustav [*Institute of Geophysics (of the Czechoslovak Academy of Sciences)*] (CZ)
GFU .... Gesellschaft zur Foerderung des Unternehmernachwuchses eV [*Association for the Advancement of the Rising Generation of Entrepreneurs*] (SLS)
GFU .... Gronlands Fiskeri Undersogelser [*Greenland Fisheries Research Institute*] [*Denmark*] (EAS)
G fuer O ..... Gesellschaft fuer Organisation eV [*Association for Organization*]
GfV .... Gueterfernverkehr [*Carriage of Goods*] [*German*] [*Business term*] (ILCA)
GFV .... Gyori Festekipari Vallalat [*Paint Manufacturing Enterprise of Gyor*] (HU)
GfW .... Gesellschaft fuer Wehrkunde eV [*Association for Defence Intelligence*] (SLS)
GfW .... Gesellschaft fuer Weltraumforschung [*Space Research Society*] (EG)
GFW .... Goodman Fielder Wattie Ltd. [*Australia*]
GFY .... Grootfontein [*South-West Africa*] [*Airport symbol*] (OAG)
GFYE........ Yengema [*Sierra Leone*] [*ICAO location identifier*] (ICLI)
GFZ .... Geoforschungszentrum [*Germany*] (EAIO)
gg.............. Cities (RU)
GG............. Deep-Water Hydrostat (RU)
GG............. Gas Generator (RU)
GG............. Gasgewinde [*Gas Thread*] [*German*]
GG............. Gedeckter Gueterwagen [*Boxcar*] (EG)
gg.............. Gegen [*Against*] [*German*]
gg.............. Gelijkgesteldern [*Benelux*] (BAS)
GG............. Genclik Gucu [*Youth Strength Soccer Team*] [*Turkish Cypriot*] (GC)
GG............. Genikos Grammatevs [*Secretary General*] (GC)
GG............. Gesundheitstechnische Gesellschaft eV [*Technical Health Association*] (SLS)
GG............. Gewehrgranate [*Rifle Grenade*] [*German military - World War II*]
GG............. Giorni [*Days*] [*Italian*]
GG............. Goewerneur-Generaal [*Governor-General*] [*Afrikaans*]
Gg.............. Gosong [*or Gosung, Gusong*] [*Shoal, Reef, Islet Malay*] (NAU)
gg.............. Gospoda [*Plural of Mister*] (YU)
GG............. Gouvernement General [*North African*]
GG............. Gouverneur-Generaal [*Benelux*] (BAS)
GG............. Gozdno Gospodarstvo [*Forestry Management*] (YU)
gg.............. Grand'garde [*Outpost*] [*French*]
GG............. Grundgesetz [*Statute*] [*German*]
GG............. Guinea Gulf Line [*Steamship*] (MHDB)
Gg.............. Gunong [*Mountain*] [*Malaysia*] (NAU)
GG............. Gutenberg-Gesellschaft [*Gutenberg Association*] (SLS)
GG............. Gyro Horizon (RU)
GG............. Harmonic Oscillator (RU)
gg.............. Hectogram (RU)
GG............. Main Generator (RU)
gg.............. Messieurs [*Plural of Mister*] (RU)
GG............. Producer Gas (RU)
gg.............. Years (RU)
GGA.......... Gas-Hydraulic Analogy (RU)
GGA.......... Geniki Grammateia Athlitismou [*General Secretariat of Athletics*] (GC)
GGA.......... Ghana Geographical Association (SLS)
GGAA....... Girl Guides Association of Australia
GGAM....... Girl Guides Association Malaysia (EAIO)
GGAO....... Main State Astronomical Observatory (RU)
GGAWA .... Grape Growers' Association of Western Australia
GGB.......... Histohematic Barrier (RU)
GGBB .... Bambadinca [*Guinea-Bissau*] [*ICAO location identifier*] (ICLI)
GGBE........ Bedanda [*Guinea-Bissau*] [*ICAO location identifier*] (ICLI)
GGBF........ Bafata [*Guinea-Bissau*] [*ICAO location identifier*] (ICLI)
GGBI .... Bissora [*Guinea-Bissau*] [*ICAO location identifier*] (ICLI)
GGBO........ Bolama [*Guinea-Bissau*] [*ICAO location identifier*] (ICLI)
GGBU........ Bubaque [*Guinea-Bissau*] [*ICAO location identifier*] (ICLI)
GGC.......... Graduates' General Congress
GGC.......... Grand Garage du Chari

GGCC .... Cacine [*Guinea-Bissau*] [*ICAO location identifier*] (ICLI)
GGCF .... Cufar [*Guinea-Bissau*] [*ICAO location identifier*] (ICLI)
GGCG .... Cantchungo [*Guinea-Bissau*] [*ICAO location identifier*] (ICLI)
GGCT .... Catio [*Guinea-Bissau*] [*ICAO location identifier*] (ICLI)
GGCV .... Caravela [*Guinea-Bissau*] [*ICAO location identifier*] (ICLI)
GGD.......... Gregory Downs [*Australia*] [*Airport symbol*] [*Obsolete*] (OAG)
GGD.......... Grootste Gemene Deler [*Highest Common Factor*] [*Afrikaans*]
GGDO .... Government Gold and Diamond Office [*Sierra Leone*]
Gge............ Gorge [*Pass, Gorge*] [*Military map abbreviation World War I*] [*French*] (MTD)
Gge............ Grange [*Barn*] [*Military map abbreviation World War I*] [*French*] (MTD)
GGEA .... Geniki Grammateia Exoskholikou Athlitismou [*General Secretariat of Extracurricular Athletics*] [*Greek*] (GC)
GGEP .... Empada [*Guinea-Bissau*] [*ICAO location identifier*] (ICLI)
GGES........ Gas Generator Electric Power Plant (RU)
ggf .... Gegebenenfalls [*If Necessary, If the Occasion Arises*] [*German*] (EG)
GGf .... Geology and Geophysics (RU)
GGFI......... State Geophysical Institute (RU)
GGFO .... Formosa [*Guinea-Bissau*] [*ICAO location identifier*] (ICLI)
GGFR .... Farim [*Guinea-Bissau*] [*ICAO location identifier*] (ICLI)
GGFU .... Fulacunda [*Guinea-Bissau*] [*ICAO location identifier*] (ICLI)
GGG.......... Gesetz ueber die Gesellschaftlichen Gerichte [*Law on Social Courts*] (EG)
GGGA........ Galinhas [*Guinea-Bissau*] [*ICAO location identifier*] (ICLI)
GGGB........ Gabu [*Guinea-Bissau*] [*ICAO location identifier*] (ICLI)
GGGTTH .. Ghaqda Ghall-Genituri Tat-Tfal Handikappati [*Society for Parents of Handicapped Children*] [*Malta*] (EAIO)
GGH .... Geographische Gesellschaft zu Hannover [*Geographical Association of Hannover*] (SLS)
GGH .... Gran Guarnicion de La Habana [*Main Havana Garrison*] [*Cuba*] (LA)
GGHP........ Governor-General's Honorary Physician [*Australia*]
GGI........... Main Pulse Generator (RU)
GGI........... Mining and Geological Institute (RU)
GGI........... State Hydrological Institute (RU)
GGIUFAN ... Mining and Geological Institute of the Ural Branch of the Academy of Sciences, USSR (RU)
GGK.......... Gamma-Gamma Logging (RU)
GGK.......... Gehaltsgruppenkatalog [*Salary Grade Schedule*] (EG)
ggk .... Goedgekeurd [*Benelux*] (BAS)
GGK.......... Horizontal Gyrocompass [*Nautical term*] (RU)
GGK.......... State Geodetic Committee (RU)
GGLF........ Gewerkschaft Gartenbau, Land- und Fortswirtschaft [*Trade Union for Horticultural, Agricultural, and Forestry Workers in the German Trade Union Federation*] (EAIO)
GGM.......... Gamma-Gamma Method (RU)
GGMC....... Guyana Geology and Mines Commission [*Research center*] (IRC)
GGMI........ Gor'kiy State Medical Institute Imeni S. M. Kirov (RU)
GGMS ...... Mansoa [*Guinea-Bissau*] [*ICAO location identifier*] (ICLI)
GGN .... Department of the State Geological Inspection (RU)
GGN .... Gagnoa [*Ivory Coast*] [*Airport symbol*] (OAG)
GGNA........ Georgina [*Botanical region*] [*Australia*]
GGO .... Gamma-Gamma Testing (RU)
GGO .... Guiglo [*Ivory Coast*] [*Airport symbol*] (OAG)
GGO .... Main Geophysical Observatory Imeni A. I. Voyeykov (RU)
GGOV........ Bissau/Oswaldo Vieira International [*Guinea-Bissau*] [*ICAO location identifier*] (ICLI)
GGP........... Gas Gathering Pipelines
GGPA .... Greater Glider Productions Australia
GGPC .... Pecixe [*Guinea-Bissau*] [*ICAO location identifier*] (ICLI)
GGPR .... Pirada [*Guinea-Bissau*] [*ICAO location identifier*] (ICLI)
GGPS........ German Group Psychotherapeutic Society (EAIO)
ggr .... Ganger [*Times*] [*Sweden*]
GGR.......... Gas-Cooled Graphite-Moderated Reactor (RU)
GGRU........ Main Administration of Geological Exploration (RU)
GGR-Up .... Gas-Cooled Graphite-Moderated Natural Uranium Reactor (RU)
Ggs............ Gegensatz [*Distinction*] [*German*] (GCA)
GGS .... Gobernador Gregores [*Argentina*] [*Airport symbol*] (OAG)
GGSD .... Sao Domingos [*Guinea-Bissau*] [*ICAO location identifier*] (ICLI)
GGSI......... Main State Sanitary Inspection, USSR (RU)
GGT.......... George Town [*Bahamas*] [*Airport symbol*] (OAG)
GGT.......... Hydrostatic Ground Pipe (RU)
GGT.......... State Geophysical Trust (RU)
GGTT........ Tite [*Guinea-Bissau*] [*ICAO location identifier*] (ICLI)
GGU .... Geodetska Glavna Uprava [*Central Geodetic Administration*] (YU)
GGU .... Gor'kiy State University Imeni N. I. Lobachevskiy (RU)
GGU .... Main Geodetic Administration (RU)
GGUN........ Uno [*Guinea-Bissau*] [*ICAO location identifier*] (ICLI)
GGV.......... Grootste Gemene Veelvoud [*Greatest Common Multiple*] [*Afrikaans*]

GGV............ Ground-Water Level   (RU)
GGVR.......... Varela [*Guinea-Bissau*] [*ICAO location identifier*]   (ICLI)
Ggw............ Gegenwart [*Presence*] [*German*]
GGW.......... Gesellschaft fuer Geologische Wissenschaften der Deutschen Demokratischen Republik [*Association for Geological Sciences of the German Democratic Republic*]   (SLS)
Gh .... Gasthaus [*Inn, Restaurant*] [*German*]
GH .... Gazdasagi Hivatal [*Accounting Office*]   (HU)
GH .... George Horne [*Refers to old news*] [*Slang*]   (DSUE)
GH .... Gerakan Hutan [*Jungle Operation*]   (ML)
GH .... Gesamthochschule
GH .... Ghana [*ANSI two-letter standard code*]   (CNC)
GHA .... German Hospital Association   (EAIO)
GHA .... Ghana [*ANSI three-letter standard code*]   (CNC)
GHA .... Ghana Airways Corp. [*ICAO designator*]   (FAAC)
GHA .... Ghardaia [*Algeria*] [*Airport symbol*]   (OAG)
GHA .... Societe du Grand Hotel Restaurant d'Abidjan
GHAC........ Groupement des Hommes d'Affaires Camerounais
GHACIMS ... Ghana Co-Operative of Indigenous Musicians
GHAFACOOPS ... Ghana Federation of Agricultural Cooperatives
GHAFES... Ghana Fellowship of Evangelical Students
Ghaip .... Ghanaian-Italian Petroleum Co.
GHANABATT ... Ghana Battalion [*Military*]
GHANASO ... Ghana National Student Organization   (AF)
GHANCEM ... Ghana Cement Works
GHASEL... Ghana Sugar Estates Limited
GhB............ Ghaqda Bibljotekarji [*Malta Library Association*]   (EAIO)
GHB........... Governor's Harbour [*Bahamas*] [*Airport symbol*]   (OAG)
GHC........... Great Harbour Cay [*Bahamas*] [*Airport symbol*]   (OAG)
GHD .... Genc Hukukcular Dernegi [*Young Jurists Association*]   (TU)
GHE........... Garachine [*Panama*] [*Airport symbol*]   (OAG)
GHE........... Girne Halk Evi [*Kyrenia Peoples' House*]   (TU)
GHG .... Grosshandelsgenossenschaft [*Wholesale Trade Cooperative*]   (EG)
GHG .... Grosshandelsgesellschaft [*Wholesale Business Establishment*] [*German*]
GHGPD..... Gewerkschaft Hotel, Gastgewerbe, Personlicher Dienst [*Hotel and Restaurant Workers*] [*Austria*]   (EAIO)
GHH.......... Gutehoffnungshuette Aktienverein [*West German engineering group*] [*MAN*] [*Later,*]
GHK .... Gesamthochschule Kassel [*Kassel Comprehensive University*] [*Germany*]   (ARC)
GHK .... Grosshandelskontor [*Wholesale Business Office*] [*German*]
GHL........... Good Harvest Line   (DS)
GHM .... Aero Service Bolivia [*ICAO designator*]   (FAAC)
GHM .... Groupe de Haute Montagne [*Mountaineering association*]
ghm .... Quadrathektometer [*German*]   (ADPT)
GHME....... Gott Hilf Mir Elenden [*God Help Miserable Me*] [*Motto of Eleonore, Electress of Brandenburg (1583-1607)*] [*German*]
GHN .... Ghana Navy
ghn .... Ghienie [*Guinea*] [*Afrikaans*]
GHN .... Groupe Hygiene Naturelle [*European Natural Hygiene Society - ENHS*]   (EAIO)
GHS.......... Gatari Hutama Air Services PT [*Indonesia*] [*ICAO designator*]   (FAAC)
GHS.......... Gesamthochschule [*General High School*] [*Information retrieval*] [*German*]
GHS.......... Grosshandelsspanne [*Wholesale Markup*]   (EG)
GHT........... Gesellschaft fur Hochtemperatur-Reaktor-Technik [*Germany*]   (PDAA)
GHT.......... Ghat [*Libya*] [*Airport symbol*]   (OAG)
GHU .... Gualeguaychu [*Argentina*] [*Airport symbol*]   (OAG)
GHU .... Guyana Headmen's Union   (LA)
GI.............. Gamatronic Electronic Industries Ltd. [*Israel*]
GI.............. Garden Island [*Australia*]   (ADA)
GI.............. Gemeinschaft der Ikonenfreunde [*Society of Friends of Icons - SFI*]   (EAIO)
GI.............. General Intelligence [*Egypt*]   (ME)
GI.............. Geografski Institut [*Geographic Institute*]   (YU)
GI.............. Gesellschaft fuer Informatik eV [*Association for Information*]   (SLS)
GI.............. Gibraltar [*ANSI two-letter standard code*]   (CNC)
GI.............. Goethe Institute   (EA)
GI.............. Gradevinski Inspektorat [*Building Inspectorate*]   (YU)
GI.............. Greenpeace International   (EA)
GI.............. Group Selector   (RU)
GI.............. Guia de Importacao [*Import Licence*] [*Portuguese*]
GI.............. Institute of Geology   (BU)
GI.............. Main Pulse   (RU)
GI.............. Pulse Generator, Impulse Generator   (RU)
gi .... Year of Publication   (RU)
GIA .... Armed Islamic Group [*Anti-government faction*] [*Algeria*] [*Acronym is based on foreign phrase*]   (ECON)
GIA .... Garuda Indonesian Airways   (IN)
GIA .... Garuda Indonesia PT [*ICAO designator*]   (FAAC)
GIA .... General International Agreement [*Legal term*]   (DLA)

GIA .... General Investments Australia
GIA .... Ghana Institute of Architects
GIA .... Government Information and Advertising [*New South Wales, Australia*]
GIA .... Groupement des Independants Africains [*Independent Africans Group*]
GIA .... Groupement Interprofessionnel de l'Automobile
GIA .... Groupement Ivoirien d'Assurances
GIA .... Grupo de Investigaciones Agrarias [*Chile*]
GIA .... Main Historical Archives   (RU)
GIA .... State Scientific Research Institute of Nitrogen   (RU)
GIAA .... German Interior Architects Association   (EAIO)
GIAB .... Grupo Independente de Aviacao de Bombardeamento [*Portuguese*]
GIAC .... Gioventu Italiana di Azione Cattolica [*Catholic Youth Association*] [*Italian*]
GIAC .... Groupement d'Importation Algerien de la Chaussure
GIAD .... Independent Group of Dance Artists [*Spanish*]
GIAE .... Gippsland Institute of Advanced Education [*Australia*]   (ADA)
GIALO ...... Leningrad Oblast State Historical Archives   (RU)
GIAM .... Global Implications of Applied Microbiology [*ICSU*]
GIAM .... Graphischer Interaktiver Anwendungs-Monitor [*German*]   (ADPT)
GIAMO ..... Moscow Oblast State Historical Archives   (RU)
GIAN .... Gruppo Italiano Arricchimento Uranio [*Italian Uranium Enrichment Group*]   (PDAA)
GIAN .... Institute of Geology (of the Academy of Sciences, USSR)   (RU)
GIAP......... Guards Fighter Air Regiment   (RU)
GIAP......... State Scientific Research and Planning Institute of the Nitrogen Industry and Products of Organic Synthesis   (RU)
GIAT .... Groupement d'Industries Atomiques [*France*]   (PDAA)
GIAT .... Groupement Industriel des Armements Terrestres [*Industrial Land Forces Group*] [*France*]
GIAT .... Groupement Interprofessionnel de l'Afrique Tropicale [*Interprofessional Group of Tropical Africa*]   (AF)
GIATO ...... Tambov Oblast State Historical Archives   (RU)
GIAWA ..... Gas Industry Association of Western Australia
GIB .... Air Guinea [*Guinea*] [*ICAO designator*]   (FAAC)
GIB .... Gibraltar [*Airport symbol*]   (OAG)
GIB .... Gibraltar [*ANSI three-letter standard code*]   (CNC)
GIB .... Gulf International Bank [*Bahrain*]   (EY)
GIBA .... Groupement Interprofessionnel des Entreprises du Benin [*Employers' organization*] [*Cotonou, Benin*]
GIBAIR .... Gibraltar Airways Ltd.
GIBAT....... Groupement pour l'Industrialisation du Batiment [*Algeria*]   (EY)
GIBCA....... General International Business Contracting Associates [*Arab*]
GIBER....... Giraschi, Bernadi, et Compagnie
GIBMED... Gibraltar Mediterranean Command [*NATO*]   (NATG)
Gibr........... Gibraltar
gibr............ Hybridization   (RU)
GIBUS....... Groupe Informatiste de Bibliotheque Universitaire et Specialisee [*French*]   (ADPT)
GIC .... Compagnie de Bauxites de Guinee [*Guinea*] [*ICAO designator*]   (FAAC)
GIC .... Gabonaise Industrielle de Construction
GIC .... General Industries Corp. [*Myanmar*]   (DS)
GIC .... General Industry Corporation [*Abu Dhabi*]   (MENA)
GIC .... General Insurance Co. Ltd. [*Jordan*]
GIC .... General Insurance Corp. of India   (EY)
GIC .... Ghana Investment Centre   (GEA)
GIC .... Government Information Centre [*Australia*]   (ADA)
GIC .... Graduate Induction Campaign [*Australia*]
GIC .... Grains Industry Council [*Australia*]
GIC .... Groupement de l'Industrie Chimique [*French*]
GIC .... Groupement d'Impregnateurs Camerounais
GIC .... Grupos Pro-Independencia de Cataluna [*Pro-Independence Groups of Catalonia*] [*Spanish*]   (WER)
GIC .... Guilde Internationale des Cooperatrices
GIC .... Gulf International Company [*Sudan*]
GICA .... Goat Industry Council of Australia
GICA .... Groupement Intersyndical de la Communication Audiovisuelle
GICAF ...... Groupement des Industries de la Conserve Africaine
GICAM ..... Groupement Interprofessionnel pour l'Etude et la Coordination des Interets Economiques au Cameroun [*Interoccupational Group for the Study and Coordination of Cameroon's Economic Interests*]   (AF)
GICAMA... Groupe Interministeriel de Coordination de l'Action en Mer des Administrations [*French*]   (MSC)
GICE.......... Groupement d'Ingenieurs Conseils en Expertise Interessant le Batiment et les Travaux Publics
GICEX....... Groupement Interbancaire pour les Operations de Credits a l'Exportation [*French*]
GICP......... Groupement Professionnel d'Importation des Cuires et Peaux [*Algeria*]

GID .... Gesellschaft fuer Industrielle Datenverarbeitung mbH [*German*] (ADPT)

GID .... Gesellschaft fuer Information und Dokumentation [*Society for Information and Documentation*] [*Database producer*]

GID .... Gesellschaft fuer Information und Dokumentation mbH [*Society for Information and Documentation*] [*Information service or system*]   (IID)

GID .... Gitega [*Burundi*] [*Airport symbol*]   (OAG)

GID .... Grande Imprimerie Dahomeenne

GID .... Guilde International du Disque [*Record label*] [*France*]

GID .... Hydroacoustic Bottom Indicator   (RU)

GID .... Sud Air Transport SA [*Guinea*] [*ICAO designator*]   (FAAC)

GIDA .... Groupe Interministeriel pour le Developpement de l'Aquaculture   (ASF)

GIDA .... Groupement Interprofessionnel des Entreprises du Dahomey

Gida Is .... Turkiye Gida Sanayii Iscileri Sendikasi [*Turkish Food Industry Workers' Union*]   (TU)

GIDAS ...... Association for Hydraulics, Hydraulic Engineering, and Wind Power   (RU)

GIDA-SEN ... Kibris Turk Gida, Tutun, ve Muskirat Iscileri Sendikasi [*Turkish Cypriot Foodstuffs, Tobacco, and Intoxicants Workers' Union*]   (TU)

GIDC .... Gujarat Industrial Development Corp. [*India*]   (PDAA)

GIDC .... Guyana Industrial Development Corporation [*Georgetown, Guyana*]   (LAA)

GIDEC .... Grupo de Informacion y Documentacion Economica [*Colombia*]   (COL)

GIDEP .... All-Union State Planning Institute Gidroenergoproyekt [*Planning hydroelectric power plants*]   (RU)

GIDET .... Groupement International pour le Developpement Economique et Technique

GID-IZ ...... Gesellschaft fuer Information und Dokumentation - Informationszentrum fuer Informationswissenschaft und - Praxis [*Information Center for Information Science and Information Work*] [*Society for Information and Documentation*]   (IID)

GIDLH ...... Government Industrial Development Laboratory, Hokkaido [*Agency for Industrial Science and Technology*] [*Research center*] [*Japan*]   (ERC)

GIDNT ...... Glowny Instytut Dokumentacji Naukowo-Technicznej [*Main Institute of Scientific and Technical Documentation*]   (POL)

GIDOR ...... Gemeenschappelijk Informatie- en Documentatiecentrum voor Organisatiewerk in Rijksdienst [*'s-Gravenhage*]

gidr k-t' ...... Hydrolytic Acidity   (RU)

gidroizol ..... Waterproofing Material   (RU)

gidrokhim .. Hydrochemical, Hydrochemistry   (RU)

Gidromashkomplekt ... Trust for the Supply of Complete Sets of Compressor Pumps and Fittings of the Glavkomplektooborudovaniye   (RU)

Gidromekhanizatsiya ... State All-Union Trust for the Planning and Execution of Hydraulic Excavation Work   (RU)

gidromet ..... Hydrometeorological, Hydrometeorology   (RU)

GIDROMETEOIZDAT ... State Scientific and Technical Hydrometeorological Publishing House   (RU)

Gidrometsluzhba ... Main Administration of the Hydrometeorological Service at the Council of Ministers, USSR   (RU)

Gidromontazh ... State All-Union Construction and Installation Trust of Glavgidroenergostroy   (RU)

Gidropostavka ... Technical Office for the Supply of Hydroelectric-Power and Hydromechanical Equipment   (RU)

gidro-p/p.... Seaplane Landing Area   (RU)

Gidroproyekt ... All-Union Planning, Surveying, and Scientific Research Institute Imeni S. Ya. Zhuk   (RU)

gidrorazryv ... Hydraulic Fracturing   (RU)

Gidrorybproyekt ... State Institute for the Planning of Hydraulic-Engineering, Fishery-Improvement, and Pond Structures   (RU)

Gidrospetsstroy ... State All-Union Trust for the Reinforcement of Foundations and Structures of the Glavgidroenergostroy   (RU)

gidrotekh.... Hydraulic Engineering   (RU)

Gidr st .... Hydrological Station [*Topography*]   (RU)

GIDS.......... Giri Institute of Development Studies [*India*]

GIDUV ...... State Institute for the Advanced Training of Physicians   (RU)

Gi E .... Gite d'Etapes [*Road-Post*] [*Military*] [*French*]   (MTD)

GIE .... Glowny Instytut Elektrotechniki [*Main Institute of Electric Engineering*] [*POL*]

GIE .... Groupement d'Interet Economique [*Economic Interest Group*] [*Western European*]   (WER)

GIE .... Grupo de Interesse Economico [*Economic Interest Group*]

GIE .... Gruppo Industrie Elettromeccaniche per Impianti all'Estero SpA [*Industrial Electromechanical Group for the Foreign Trade Establishment*] [*Milan, Italy*]

GIE .... Guinee Inter Air [*Guinea*] [*ICAO designator*]   (FAAC)

GIEA .... General Industrial Employers' Association [*Netherlands*]   (EAIO)

GIEC.......... Guangzhou Institute of Energy Conversion [*China*]   (PDAA)

GIEFCA .... Groupement d'Interet Economique pour Favoriser le Developpement du Credit Automobile et Industriel en Afrique

GIEK.......... Guarantee Institute for Export Credits [*Norway*]

GIEKI .... State Scientific Research Electroceramic Institute   (RU)

GI El .... Glowny Instytut Elektrotechniki [*Main Institute of Electric Engineering*]   (POL)

GIEM .... Groupement des Importateurs et Exportateurs Mauritaniens

GIES .... Hydraulic Engineering Surveys of Electric Power Plants   (RU)

GIEV......... State Institute of Experimental Veterinary Science   (RU)

GIE VI .... Groupe International Postal d'Echanges d'Information et d'Experience [*International Group for the Exchange of Information and Experience Among Postal Savings Institutions*]   (EAIO)

GIEWS ...... Global Information and Early Warning System [*FAO*] [*United Nations*]   (DUND)

GIF............ German-Israeli Foundation [*US and Israel*]

GIF............ Gesellschaft fuer Informationsmarkt-Forschung [*Society for Information-Market Research*] [*Database producer*]   (IID)

GIF............ Guinee Air Lines SA [*Guinea*] [*ICAO designator*]   (FAAC)

GIF............ Guy in the Front Seat [*Pilot*] [*Slang*]   (DSUE)

GIF............ State Scientific Research Institute of Physiotherapy   (RU)

GIFA.......... Geneva Infant Feeding Association

GIFA.......... Governing International Fisheries Agreements

GIFA.......... Governing International Fishing Agreement   (MSC)

GIFAP .... Groupement International des Associations Nationales de Fabricants de Produits Agrochimiques [*International Group of National Associations of Manufacturers of Agrochemical Products*]   (EAIO)

GIFAS .... Groupement des Industries Francaises Aeronautiques et Spatiales [*French Aerospace Industry Association*]   (PDAA)

GIFATOME ... Groupement pour l'Industrie Nucleaire [*Nuclear Industries Group*] [*French*]   (WER)

GIFF .... State Institute of Physiotherapy and Physical Culture   (RU)

GIFK......... State Institute of Physical Culture Imeni P. F. Lesgaft   (RU)

GIFML...... State Publishing House of Physical and Mathematical Literature   (RU)

GIFO .... State Institute of Physiatrics and Orthopedics   (RU)

GIFON ...... Belorussian State Institute of Physiatrics, Orthopedics, and Neurology   (RU)

GIFS .... Gospel-in-Film Service [*Australia*]

gift .... Giftig [*Poisonous*] [*German*]   (GCA)

GIFTI .... Gor'kiy Research Physicotechnical Institute   (RU)

Giftigk........ Giftigkeit [*Toxicity*] [*German*]   (GCA)

GIFTPOOL ... Datenbank ueber Gifte und Vergiftungen [*Databank for Poisons and Poisoning*] [*German*]

GIFZA .... Ghana Industrial Free Zones Authority

GIG .... Gesellschaft fuer Internationale Geldgeschichte   (EAIO)

GIG .... Glowny Instytut Gornictwa [*Main Institute of Mining*]   (POL)

GIG .... Hydroacoustic Depth Indicator   (RU)

GIG .... Rio De Janeiro [*Brazil*] [*Airport symbol*]   (OAG)

GIGAB...... Goeteborgs Intecknings Garanti AB [*Sweden*]

GIGC .... Grupul Intreprinderlor de Gospodarie Comunala [*Group of Communal Economy Enterprises*]   (RO)

GIGK .... State Scientific Research Institute of Geodesy and Cartography   (RU)

GIGKhS..... State Scientific Research Institute of Chemical Raw Materials Obtained by Mining   (RU)

GIGMS...... Chief Engineer of the Hydrometeorological Service   (RU)

gigrosk .... Hygroscopic, Hygroscopy   (RU)

GIH........... Genel Idari Hizmetleri [*General Administrative Duties*]   (TU)

GIH........... Growth Industrial Holdings [*Malaysia*]

GIHOC ...... Ghana Industrial Holding Company   (AF)

GII .... Georgian Industrial Institute Imeni S. M. Kirov   (RU)

GII .... Gor'kiy Industrial Institute   (RU)

GIIGNL...... Groupe Internationale des Importateur du Gaz Natural Liquefie

GIII........... State Institute of Art History   (RU)

GIIL........... Grupul Intreprinderlor de Industrie Locala [*Group of Local Industry Enterprises*]   (RO)

GIIL.......... State Publishing House of Foreign Literature   (RU)

GIIN .... Groupe Intersyndical de l'Industrie Nucleaire [*Nuclear energy*] [*French*]   (NRCH)

GIINS........ State Publishing House of Foreign and National Dictionaries   (RU)

GIIS .... State Institute of Art Studies   (RU)

GIIVT .... Gor'kiy Institute of Water Transportation Engineers   (RU)

GIJ .... Geoloski Institut Jugoslavije [*Yugoslav Geological Institute*] [*Belgrade*]   (YU)

GIJ .... Ghana Institute of Journalism

GIJNA .... Geografski Institut Jugoslovenske Narodne Armije [*Geographic Institute of the Yugoslav People's Army*]   (YU)

GIK .... Check Pulse Generator   (RU)

GIK .... City Executive Committee   (RU)

GIK .... Gyro Induction Compass   (RU)

GIK .... State Institute of Cinematography   (RU)

GIK .... State Quality Inspection   (RU)

GIKhL .... State Publishing House of Belles Lettres   (RU)

GIKI............ State Scientific Research Institute of Ceramics (RU)
GIKTorf..... State Quality Inspection of Peat (RU)
GIL .... General Instrument Lusitana [*Portuguese*] (WER)
GIL .... Genting International Ltd. [*Australia and the Bahamas*]
GIL .... Glowny Instytut Lotnictwa [*Main Institute of Aeronautics*] (POL)
GiL.............. Gore in Ljudje [*Mountains and Men*] [*Ljubljana A periodical*] (YU)
GIL .... Groupement Interprofessionnel de Legumes [*North African*]
GILA.......... Gruppo Italiano di Linguistica Applicata [*Italian*] (SLS)
GILDH ...... Government Industrial Development Laboratory, Hokkaido [*Agency of Industrial Science and Technology*] [*Japan*]
GILEP .... Groupement Interprofessionel de Logistique et d'Equipements Petroliers [*France*] (PDAA)
GILN .... Glosa International Language Network (EAIO)
GILS i A .... State Publishing House of Literature on Construction and Architecture (RU)
GIM .... Generale Industrie Metallurgiche SpA [*Italian*]
GIM .... Glowny Instytut Mechaniki [*Main Institute of Mechanical Engineering*] (POL)
GIM .... Glowny Instytut Metalurgii [*Main Institute of Metallurgy*] (POL)
GIM .... Grupo de Intervencao Militar [*Military Intervention Group*] [*Portuguese*] (WER)
GIM .... Gruppe Internationale Marxisten [*International Marxist Group*] [*Germany*] [*Political party*] (PPW)
gim .... High School (BU)
GIM .... Hydraulic Servomotor, Hydraulic Control Motor (RU)
GIM .... Long-Distance Group Selector (RU)
GIM .... State Historical Museum [*Moscow*] (RU)
GIM .... State Institute of Makhorka Culture (RU)
GIMA .... Gida ve Ihtiyac Maddeleri TAS [*Foodstuffs and Necessary Articles Corporation*] [*Chain store*] (TU)
GIMA .... Groupement des Importateurs de Mauritanie
Gima .... Grupo Independente de Macau [*Independent Group of Macao*] [*Political party*] (PPW)
GIMAS...... Gida ve Ihtiyac Maddeleri Subesi [*Foodstuff and Necessities Branch*] [*A subsidiary of Industry, Commerce, and Manufacturing Enterprises Ltd. Turkish Cypriot*] (GC)
GIMCI...... Groupement des Industries de la Metallurgie en Cote-D'Ivoire
GIME .... Georgian Scientific Research Institute of Rural Mechanization and Electrification (RU)
GIMEE...... Groupement Syndical des Industries de Materiel d'Equipement Electrique
GIMEIN.... Hydrometeorological Scientific Research Institute (RU)
GIMet........ Glowny Instytut Metalurgii [*Main Institute of Metallurgy*] (POL)
GIMIZ....... Hydrometeorological Publishing House (RU)
GIMMOM ... Groupement des Industries Minieres et Metallurgiques d'Outre-Mer [*Overseas Mining and Metal Industries Group*] (AF)
GIMN........ Gimnasium [*Gymnasium*] [*Afrikaans*]
gimn .... Gimnastiek [*Gymnasium*] [*Afrikaans*]
gimn .... Gimnazium [*High School, Secondary School*] (HU)
GIMN........ State Institute of Musical Science (RU)
gimn u-l .... High School Teacher (BU)
GIMOI ...... Groupe d'Information Madagascar Ocean Indien [*Madagascar-Indian Ocean Information Group*] (AF)
GIM-OPI .. State Historical Museum, Department of Written Sources (RU)
Gimp........ State Institute of Musical Education (RU)
GIMPA...... Ghana Institute of Management and Public Administration (AF)
GIMPEX.... Guyana Import-Export Company Ltd. (LA)
GIMR .... Garvan Institute of Medical Research [*Australia*]
GIM RO .... State Historical Museum, Manuscript and Incunabula Department (RU)
GIMT .... Gott Ist Mein Teil [*God Is My Portion*] [*Motto of Friedrich IV, Duke of Liegnitz (1552-96)*] [*German*]
GIMT .... Gott Ist Mein Trost [*God Is My Comfort*] [*Motto for a number of 16th and 17th century German and Bavarian rulers*]
GIMZ .... State Institute of Medical Sciences [*1919-1930*] (RU)
GIN............ Association de Recherche et d'Exploitation de Diamant et de l'Or [*Guinea*] [*ICAO designator*] (FAAC)
GIN .... Global Information Network [*Proposed*]
GIN .... Glowny Instytut Naftowy [*Main Petroleum Institute*] (POL)
GIN .... Guinea [*ANSI three-letter standard code*] (CNC)
gin .... Gynecology, Gynecologist (BU)
GIN............ Individual Carrier Generator (RU)
GIN............ Institute of Geology (of the Academy of Sciences, USSR) (RU)
GIN............ Last Name Unknown (BU)
GIN............ Pulse Voltage Generator (RU)
GINA .... Gaufretterie Industrielle Africaine
GINAN...... Institute of Geology (of the Academy of Sciences, USSR) (RU)
GINB .... Geodezyjny Instytut Naukowo-Badawczy [*Geodetic Scientific Research Institute*] (POL)
GINETEX ... Groupement International d'Etiquetage pour l'Entretien des Textiles [*International Association for Textile Care Labelling*] [*Barcelona, Spain*] (EA)

GINFIS...... Gemeindliches Integriertes Finanz-Informations-System [*German*] (ADPT)
GINI .... State Scientific Research Institute of Petroleum (RU)
GINK......... Isonicotinic Acid Hydrazide, Isoniazid (RU)
GINMASh ... State Scientific Research Institute of Petroleum Equipment and Machinery (RU)
GINMP ..... Gansu Institute of New Medicine and Pharmacology [*China*] (IRC)
GINP .... State Institute of Scientific Pedagogy (RU)
Ginplastmass ... State Scientific Research Institute of Plastics and Synthetic Resins (RU)
GINS .... Gambia Information News Service
GINSI........ Gabungan Importir Nasional Seluruh Indonesia [*All-Indonesia National Importers Association*] (IN)
GINTRAP ... European Guide to Industrial Trading Regulations and Practice [*EC*] (ECED)
GINTsVETMET ... State Scientific Research Institute of Nonferrous Metals (RU)
GINZ .... State Scientific Institute of Public Health [*1918-1930*] (RU)
Ginzoloto.... State Scientific Research Institute of Gold (RU)
GIO............ City Election District (RU)
GIO............ Glavni Izvrsni Odbor [*Central Executive Committee*] (YU)
GIO............ Government Information Office [*Taiwan*]
GIO............ Government Insurance Office [*Australia*]
GIO............ Operations Research Group (RU)
GIOA .... State Institute of Experimental Agronomy (RU)
GIOAPV.... Gradski Izvrsni Odbor Autonomne Pokrajine Vojvodine [*City Executive Committee of the Autonomous Province of Vojvodina*] (YU)
g-ion .... Gram Ion (RU)
GIONSAPV ... Glavni Izvrsni Odbor Narodne Skupstine Autonomne Provincije Vojvodine [*Central Executive Committee of the People's Assembly of Vojvodina*] (YU)
GIOP .... Glowny Inspektorat Ochrony Pracy [*Chief Inspectorate for the Protection of Labor*] [*Poland*]
giorn........... Giornale [*Journal*] [*Italian*]
GIOV .... Hospital for Veterans of World War II (RU)
GIP .... Forestry Industrial Enterprise (BU)
GIP .... Garden Island Prison [*Australia*] [*World War II*] (DSUE)
GIP .... Geneva Initiative on Psychiatry [*Netherlands*] (EAIO)
GIP .... Gestion Integree du Personnel [*French*] (ADPT)
GIP .... Glowny Instytut Pracy [*Main Institute of Labor*] (POL)
GIP .... Greenhouse Information Program [*Australia*]
GIP .... State Scientific Research Institute of Psychiatry (RU)
GIPA.......... Groupement Interprofessionnel de l'Automobile [*Employers' association*] [*Ivory Coast*]
GIPEC .... Groupe d'Etudes International pour l'Utilization de Profils Creux dans la Construction [*International Study Group on the Use of Hollow Sections in Construction*] [*Switzerland*] (PDAA)
GIPEIE...... Groupe International Postal d'Echanges d'Information et d'Experience [*International Group for the Exchange of Information and Experience among Postal Savings Institutions - IGEIEPSI*] (EAIO)
GIPI.......... Garantie Integrale des Proprietaires d'Immeubles [*Insurance*] [*France*] (FLAF)
GIPI........... State Research and Planning Institute (RU)
GIPKh .... State Institute of Applied Chemistry (RU)
GIPKKh..... Gor'kiy Institute for Improving the Qualifications of Managerial Personnel (RU)
GIPL.......... State Publishing House of Political Literature (RU)
GIPMA...... Main Testing Range for Naval Artillery (RU)
GIPME...... Global Investigation of Pollution in the Marine Environment [*ICSU*]
GIPN .... Glowny Instytut Paliw Naturalnych [*Main Institute of Natural Fuels*] (POL)
GIPOA(SA) ... Genootlede Instituut Parke en Ontspanningsadministrasie (Suid-Afrika) [*South Africa*] (AA)
GIPPSDOC ... Gippsland Database [*Australia*]
GIPPSLD.. Gippsland [*Australia*] (ROG)
Gipredmet ... State Scientific Research and Planning Institute of the Rare Metals Industry (RU)
GIPRiS ...... Glowny Instytut Przemyslu Rolnego i Spozywczego [*Main Institute of the Agriculture and Food Industries*] (POL)
Giproalyuminiy ... State Institute for the Planning of Aluminum, Magnesium, and Electrode Plants (RU)
Giproanilkraska ... State Planning Institute of the Aniline Dye Industry (RU)
Giproarktika ... State Institute for Planning and Exploration in the Arctic and the Far North (RU)
Giproaviaprom ... State Institute for the Planning of Aircraft Industry Plants (RU)
Giproavtoprom ... State Institute for the Planning of Automobile Industry Plants (RU)
Giproavtotraktoroprom ... State Institute for the Planning of Establishments of the Automobile and Tractor Industry (RU)
Giproavtotraktorprom ... State Institute for the Planning of Automobile and Tractor Industry Plants (RU)

Giproavtotrans ... State Institute for the Planning of Automobile Repair and Transportation Establishments and Structures   (RU)

Giproazotmash ... State Institute for the Planning of Nitrogen Machinery Manufacture   (RU)

Giprobum... State Institute for the Planning of Establishments of the Pulp, Paper, and Hydrolysis Industries   (RU)

GIPROBYTPROM ... State Institute for the Planning of Personal-Service Establishments, Bakeries, Local Industries in the Rayons, and of Art Craft Industries   (RU)

Giprodor .... State Institute of Road Planning   (RU)

Giprodortrans ... State Institute for the Planning of Roads, Transportation Establishments, and Structures   (RU)

Giprodrev... State Institute for the Planning of Sawmilling, Woodworking, and Lumber-Hauling Establishments of the Lumber Industry   (RU)

Giprodrevprom ... State Institute for the Planning of Establishments of the Woodworking Industry   (RU)

Giproenergoprom ... State Institute for the Planning of the Power Industry [*Khar'kov*]   (RU)

Giproenergoprom ... State Planning Institute of the Electrotechnical Industry [*Moscow*]   (RU)

Giproesprom ... State Institute for the Planning of Plants of the Electrical Communications Industry   (RU)

Giprogazoochistka ... State Institute for the Planning of Gas-Purifying Installations   (RU)

Giprogaztopprom ... State All-Union Institute for the Planning of Synthetic Liquid Fuel and Gas Plants   (RU)

Giprogidroliz ... State Institute for the Planning of Hydrolysis Industry Establishments   (RU)

Giprogor..... State Institute for the Planning of Cities   (RU)

Giprograd... State Institute for the Planning of Cities   (RU)

Giprogrozneft' ... State Institute for the Planning of Establishments of the Petroleum Industry [*in the Groznyy Region*]   (RU)

Giproiv....... State Institute for the Planning of Synthetic Fiber Establishments   (RU)

Giprokauchuk ... State Planning and Scientific Research Institute of the Synthetic Rubber Industry   (RU)

Giprokhim ... State Institute for the Planning of Plants of the Basic Chemical Industry   (RU)

GIPROKhIMMASh ... State Institute for the Planning of Chemical Machinery Plants   (RU)

Giprokholod ... State Institute for the Planning of Cold Storage Plants, Ice-Cream Factories, and Dry Ice, Ice, and Liquid Carbon Dioxide Plants   (RU)

Giprokinopoligraf ... State Planning Institute (for the Planning of Motion-Picture and Printing-Industry Establishments)   (RU)

Giprokislorod ... State Institute for the Planning of Oxygen Industry Establishments   (RU)

Giprokoks.. State Institute for the Planning of Establishments of the By-Product Coke Industry   (RU)

Giprokommundortrans ... State Institute for the Planning of Municipal Road Transportation Structures   (RU)

Giprokommunenergo ... State [*RSFSR*] Republic Planning Institute of the Municipal Power System Management   (RU)

Giprokommunstroy ... State [*RSFSR*] Republic Institute for the Planning of Municipal Construction   (RU)

Giprokommunvodokanal ... State Republic Institute for the Planning and Surveying of the Municipal Water Supply and Sewer System   (RU)

GIPROLEGPROM ... State Institute for the Planning of Light Industry Establishments   (RU)

Giproleskhim ... State Institute for the Planning of Establishments of the Wood-Chemistry Industry   (RU)

Giprolesmash ... State Institute for the Planning of New Machines for Logging and Rafting   (RU)

Giprolesprom ... State Institute for the Planning of Establishments of the Woodworking Industry   (RU)

Giprolestrans ... State Institute for the Planning of Logging, Rafting, and Woodworking Establishments and Lumber Transportation   (RU)

Gipromash ... State Institute for the Planning of Machinery Plants   (RU)

Gipromashpribor ... State Institute for the Planning of Machinery and Instrument Plants   (RU)

Gipromedprom ... State Planning Institute for the Planning of the Medical Equipment Industry   (RU)

Gipromesttop ... State Institute for the Exploration of Coal and Peat Deposits and the Planning of Fuel Industry Establishments   (RU)

Giprometiz ... State Institute for the Planning of Metalware Plants   (RU)

Gipromez ... State All-Union Institute for the Planning of Metallurgical Plants   (RU)

Gipromoloko ... State Institute for the Planning of Dairy Industry Establishments   (RU)

Gipromolprom ... State Institute for the Planning of Dairy Industry Establishments   (RU)

Gipromorneft' ... State Scientific Research and Planning Institute of Offshore Oil   (RU)

Gipromyaso ... State Institute for the Planning of Meat Industry Establishments   (RU)

Gipromyasomolprom ... State Institute for the Planning of Establishments of the Meat and Dairy Industry   (RU)

Giproneftemash ... State Scientific Research and Planning Institute of Petroleum Machinery Manufacture   (RU)

Gironeftezavod ... State Institute for the Planning of Petroleum-Processing Plants   (RU)

Gipronemetrud ... State Institute for the Planning of Establishments Extracting and Processing Nonmetallic Building Materials   (RU)

GIPRONII ... All-Union State Institute for the Planning of Scientific Research Institutes and Laboratories of the Academy of Sciences, USSR, and the Academies of Sciences of the Union Republics   (RU)

Gipronikel' ... State Institute for the Planning of Nickel Industry Establishments   (RU)

GIPRONISEL'KhOZ ... All-Union Planning and Scientific Research Institute for the Planning of Standard and Experimental Agricultural Production Centers and Establishments for Storing and Processing of Grain   (RU)

Gipronisslyuda ... State Scientific Research and Planning Institute of Mica   (RU)

Giproobshchmash ... State Institute for the Planning of General Machinery Plants   (RU)

Giproogneupor ... All-Union State Institute for the Planning of Plants and Quarries of the Refractory Industry   (RU)

Giproorgkhim ... State Institute for the Planning of Establishments Producing Organic Intermediates, Dyestuffs, and Reagents   (RU)

GIPROORGSEL'STROY ... State Planning Institute for the Organization of Rural Construction and the Rendering of Technical Assistance   (RU)

Giproorgstroy ... State Institute for Planning the Organization and the Carrying-Out of Construction Work   (RU)

Gipropishcheprom ... State Planning Institute for the Planning of Food Industry Establishments   (RU)

Giproplast ... State Institute for the Planning of Establishments Producing Plastics and Semifinished Products   (RU)

Gipropribor ... State Institute for the Planning of Instrument Plants   (RU)

GIPROPROM ... State Planning Institute for the Planning of Industrial Establishments   (RU)

Gipropromtransstroy ... State Planning and Surveying Institute of the State Industrial Committee for Transportation Construction, USSR   (RU)

Gipropros... Republic Planning Institute of the Ministry of Education, RSFSR   (RU)

Giproraszhirmaslo ... All-Union State Institute for the Planning of Establishments of the Vegetable Oils and Fats Industry   (RU)

Giprorechtrans ... State Institute for Planning in River Transportation   (RU)

Giproruda .. State All-Union Institute for the Planning of Establishments of the Ore-Mining Industry   (RU)

Giprorybflot ... State Planning Institute of the Fishing Fleet   (RU)

Giprorybprom ... State Institute for the Planning of Fish Industry Establishments   (RU)

Giprosakhar ... State Institute for the Planning of Sugar Industry Establishments   (RU)

Giprosel'elektro ... All-Union State Institute for the Planning of Rural Electrification   (RU)

Giprosel'khoz ... All-Union State Institute for the Planning of Industrial Buildings and Structures for Agriculture   (RU)

Giprosel'stroy ... State Planning Institute for Rural Housing and Civil Engineering Construction   (RU)

Giproshakht ... State Institute for the Planning of Mines   (RU)

Giproshaktostroymash ... State Planning, Design, and Scientific Research Institute for the Development of New Machines and Mechanisms for Shaft-Sinking Operations   (RU)

Giprosovkhozstroy ... All-Union State Institute for the Planning of Sovkhoz Construction   (RU)

Giprosovkhozvodstroy ... All-Union State Institute for the Planning of Water-Management Construction of the Ministry of Sovkhozes, USSR   (RU)

Giprospetsneft' ... State Institute for the Planning of Special Structures in the Petroleum Industry   (RU)

Giprospetspromstroy ... State Institute for the Planning of Special Structures in Industrial Construction   (RU)

GIPROSPIRTVINO ... State Institute for the Planning of Establishments of Wine-Making, Beer, Soft Drink, Alcohol, Liquor, and Vodka, Tobacco, Enzyme, Starch, and Syrup Industries   (RU)

Giprosport ... State Institute for the Planning of Sports Structures   (RU)

Giprostal'... State Scientific Research and Planning Institute of the Metallurgical Industry   (RU)

Giprostandartdom ... State Institute for the Planning of Three-Four Story Prefabricated Houses   (RU)

Giprostanok ... State Institute for the Planning of Machine Tool, Tool, and Abrasives Plants and Forging-and-Pressing Machinery Plants [*Moscow*]   (RU)

Giprostanok ... State Planning Institute of the Machine Tool Industry [*Kiev*] (RU)

GIPROSTROM ... State All-Union Institute for the Planning of Establishments of the Building Materials Industry (RU)

Giprostrommash ... All-Union State Planning and Design Institute of the Giprostroyindustriya (RU)

Giprostrommekhanizatsiya ... State All-Union Planning Institute for the Mechanization of Production of Building Materials (RU)

Giprostroydormash ... State Institute for the Planning of Construction and Road Machinery Plants (RU)

Giprostroyindustriya ... All-Union State Planning and Design Institute for the Planning of Establishments of the Construction Industry (RU)

Giprostroymaterialy ... State Institute for the Planning of Establishments of the Building Materials Industry (RU)

Giprosvyaz' ... State Institute for the Surveying and Planning of Communications Installations (RU)

Giproteatr .. State Institute for the Planning of Theatrical and Entertainment Establishments (RU)

GIPROTIS ... State Institute for Standard Experimental Planning and Technical Research (RU)

Giprotopprom ... State Institute for the Exploration of Coal and Peat Deposits and Wood Raw-Material Bases and for the Planning of Fuel Industry Establishments (RU)

Giprotorf .... State Planning Institute for the Multipurpose Use of Peat in the National Economy (RU)

Giprotorfrazvedka ... State Planning and Surveying Institute for the Exploration of Peat (RU)

Giprotorg ... State All-Union Institute for the Planning of Trade Establishments and Public Eating Facilities (RU)

Giprotraktorosel'khozmash ... State Institute for the Planning of the Tractor Industry and Agricultural Machinery Manufacture (RU)

Giprotranskar'yer ... State Institute for Geological Exploration and the Planning of Gravel Plants and Quarries of the State Industrial Committee for Transportation Construction, USSR (RU)

Giprotransmost ... State Planning and Surveying Institute for the Survey and Planning of Large Bridges (RU)

Giprotransneft' ... State Institute for the Planning of Transportation Structures and Storage for Petroleum Products (RU)

Giprotranssignalsvyaz' ... State Planning and Surveying Institute for the Planning of Signalization, Centralization, Communications, and Radio in Railroad Transportation (RU)

Giprotranstei ... State Institute for the Technical and Economic Investigation and Planning of Railroad Transportation (RU)

Giprotruboprovod ... State Institute for the Planning of Main Pipelines (RU)

Giprotsement ... All-Union State Scientific Research and Planning Institute of the Cement Industry (RU)

GIPROTsMO ... State Scientific Research and Planning Institute of Alloys and the Working of Nonferrous Metals (RU)

Giprotsvetmet ... State Institute for the Planning of Establishments of Nonferrous Metallurgy (RU)

Giprotsvetmetobrabotka ... State Scientific Research and Planning Institute of Alloys and Nonferrous Metal Processing (RU)

Giprotsvetmetzoloto ... Institute for the Planning of Establishments of Nonferrous Metallurgy and Gold (RU)

Giprotyazhmash ... State Institute for the Planning of Heavy Machinery Plants (RU)

Giprougleavtomatizatsiya ... State Planning and Design, and Scientific Research Institute for the Automation of Operations in the Coal Industry (RU)

Giprouglemash ... State Planning, Design, and Experimental Institute of Coal Machinery Manufacture (RU)

Giprovino ... State Scientific Research Institute for the Planning of the Wine-Making Industry (RU)

Giprovodkhoz ... All-Union State Planning, Surveying, and Scientific Research Institute of Water Management Construction (RU)

Giprovodokanalproyekt ... State Institute for the Planning and Surveying of the Urban Water Supply and Sewer Systems (RU)

Giprovodtrans ... State Institute for Planning and Research in Water Transportation (RU)

Giprovostokneft' ... State Institute for Planning and Research in the Petroleum Production Industry (RU)

Giprovuz .... State All-Union Institute for the Planning of Higher Educational Institutions with Scientific Research and Exploration Departments (RU)

Giprozdrav ... State Planning Institute for the Planning of Establishments for Medical and Preventive Treatment (RU)

Giprozhir ... State Institute for the Planning of the Oil-Extracting, Fats, Soap-Making, Perfumery, and Margarine Industries (RU)

GIPS .... Groupement Industriel des Plastiques Senegalais

Gipzoloto .... State Scientific Research Institute for Gold and Its Accessory Minerals (RU)

gir .... Giria [*Slang*] [*Portuguese*]

GIR .... Groupement Independant de Reflexion et d'Action Politique, Economique, Culturelle, et Sociale

GIR .... State Scientific Research Institute of Rheumatism (RU)

GIRA .... Groupe d'Information Revolution Africaine [*African Revolution Information Group*] [*French*] (WER)

GIRA .... Groupement Independant de Reflexion et d'Action [*Independent Grouping of Reflection and Action*] [*Central Africa*] (PD)

GIRC .... Groupement d'Importation et de Repartition du Coton

GIRCA ...... Groupement Interprofessionnel pour l'Etude et le Developpement de l'Economie Centrafricaine [*Interprofessional Group for the Study and Development of the Central African Economy*] (AF)

GIRCUIL .. Grupul de Intreprinderi de Reparatii si Constructii Utilaje pentru Industria Lemnului [*Group of Enterprises for the Repair and Construction of Equipment for the Wood Industry*] (RO)

GIRD .... Grants for Industry Research and Development [*Australia*]

GIRD .... Group for the Study of Jet Propulsion [*1932-1934*] (RU)

GIRedmet .. State Scientific Research and Planning Institute of the Rare Metals Industry (RU)

GIRGV ...... Groupe International des Ressources Genetiques Vegetales [*International Board for Plant Genetic Resources - IBPGR*] (EA)

GIRI .... Government Industrial Research Institute [*Japan*] (PDAA)

GIRIC .... Government Industrial Research Institute, Chugoku [*Japan*]

GIRIK .... Government Industrial Research Institute, Kyushu [*Japan*]

GIRIN .... Government Industrial Research Institute, Nagoya [*Japan*]

GIRIO .... Government Industrial Research Institute, Osaka [*Japan*]

GIRIT .... Government Industrial Research Institute, Tohoku [*Japan*]

GIRK .... State Institute of Cultivation of Speech (RU)

GIRPB ...... Groupe International de Recherches sur la Preservation du Bois [*Sweden*] (EAIO)

GIRSO ...... Groupement International pour la Recherche Scientifique en Stomatologie et Odontologie [*International Group for Scientific Research on Stomato-Odontology*] (EA)

GIRT .... Groupe des Independants Ruraux Tchadiens [*Chadian Independent Rural Group*]

GIS .... City Statistical Inspectorate (BU)

GIS .... Geographical Information System [*Department of Lands*] [*New South Wales, Australia*]

GIS .... Gisborne [*New Zealand*] [*Airport symbol*] (OAG)

GIS .... Glowny Inspektorat Sanitarny [*Chief Sanitary Inspectorate*] [*Poland*]

GIS .... Government Information Service [*Dominican Republic*] (LA)

GIS .... Government Information Service [*Belize*]

GIS .... Government Information Service [*Australia*] (ADA)

GIS .... Government Information Services [*Hong Kong*]

GIS .... Gozdarski Institut Slovenije [*Forestry Institute of Slovenia*] (YU)

GIS .... Grupo de Intervencao Socialista [*Socialist Intervention Group*] [*Portuguese*] (WER)

GIS .... Guinee Air Service [*Guinea*] [*ICAO designator*] (FAAC)

gis .... Histidine (RU)

GIS .... Hospital Inhalator Station (RU)

GIS .... Main Pulse Shifted by Half-Period (RU)

GIS .... State Institute of Literary Readings (RU)

GIS .... State Publishing House of Foreign and National Dictionaries (RU)

GIS .... State Scientific Research Institute of Glass (RU)

GISAN ...... Geografski Institut Srpska Akademija Nauka [*Geographic Institute of the Serbian Academy of Sciences*] (YU)

GISC .... Government Information and Sales Centre [*Australia*] (ADA)

GISE .... "Soviet Encyclopedia" State Institute (RU)

GISECA .... Groupement Ivoirien des Societes d'Exportation et Cooperatives Agricoles

GISF .... Grupo de Irrigacao do Sao Francisco [*Brazil*] (DSCA)

GISh .... Master-Pulse Bus (RU)

GISI .... Gor'kiy Construction Engineering Institute Imeni V. P. Chkalov (RU)

GISM .... State Planning, Design, and Experimental Institute of Glass Machinery (RU)

GISMER .... Groupe d'Intervention sous la Mer [*French*] (MSC)

GISO .... State Institute of Stomatology and Odontology (RU)

GISOF ...... Gas Industry Salaried Officers' Federation [*Australia*]

Gisogneupor ... State Quality and Service Life Inspection of Refractories (RU)

GISSI .... Gruppo Italiano per lo Studio della Streptochinasi nell'Infarto [*Italy*]

gist .... Histological (RU)

GISTI .... Groupe d'Information et de Soutien des Travailleurs Immigres [*Information and Support Group for Immigrant Workers*] [*France*] (EAIO)

GISU .... Hydrographic Ship (RU)

GIT .... Gesellschaft fuer Informationsvermittlung und Technologieberatung [*Association for Information Brokerage and Technological Consultancy*] (EAIO)

GIT .... Gordon Institute of Technology [*Australia*]

GIT .... Group Inclusive Tour

GIT .... Grupo Independiente de Trabajo [*Independent Labor Group*] [*Spanish*] (WER)

GIT .... Pulse Current Generator (RU)
GITA .... Gremio dos Industriais de Transportes em Automoveis [*Association of Automobile Transportation Industrialists*] [*Portuguese*] (WER)
GITC.......... Government Information Technology Conditions [*Australia*]
GITEXAL ... Groupement d'Importation des Textiles en Algerie [*Algerian Textile Imports Group*] (AF)
GITI .... Global Information and Telecommunications Industries
GITIC........ Guangdong International Trust & Investment Corp. [*Japan*]
GITIS .... State Institute of Theatrical Art Imeni A. V. Lunacharskiy (RU)
GITL......... Government/Industry Technical Liaison Committee [*Australia*]
GITO .... Groupement Interprofessionnel des Entreprises du Togo
GIU .... Gamma-Ray Level Gauge (RU)
GIU .... Geotechnical Information Unit [*Hong Kong*]
GIU .... Main Engineer Directorate (RU)
GIU .... State Publishing House of the Ukraine (RU)
GIU .... Union Guineene de Transports [*Guinea*] [*ICAO designator*] (FAAC)
GIU .... Universal Group Selector (RU)
Giugn .... Giugno [*June*] [*Italian*]
Giun .... Giuniore [*Junior*] [*Italian*] (GPO)
giur .... Giurisprudenza [*Jurisprudence*] [*Italian*]
GIV .... Hydraulic Weight Indicator (RU)
GIV .... Pulse Generator (RU)
GIV .... State Veterinary Inspection (RU)
GIVA .... Chief Engineer of an Air Army (RU)
GIVD .... State Chemical Scientific Research Institute of High Pressures (RU)
GIVD .... State Institute of Veterinary Dermatology (RU)
GIVT......... Gor'kiy Institute of Water Transportation Engineers (RU)
GiW .... Gebethner i Wolff [*Gebethner and Wolff*] [*Publisher*] (POL)
GIWB .... Glowny Inspektorat Wyszkolenia Bojowego [*Main Inspectorate of Combat Training*] (POL)
GIWSA ...... Genoot Instituut Waardeerders Suid-Afrika [*South Africa*] (AA)
Giy-Sen ...... Giyim Iscileri Sendikasi [*Wearing Apparel Workers Union*] [*Turkish Cypriot*] (GC)
GIZ .... Genossenschaftliche Informationszentrale [*German*] (ADPT)
GIZ .... Gizan [*Saudi Arabia*] [*Airport symbol*] (OAG)
GIZ .... State Institute of Dentistry (RU)
GIZ .... State Publishing House (RU)
GIZBel....... State Publishing House of Belorussia (RU)
GIZh......... State Institute of Journalism (RU)
Gizlegprom ... State Scientific and Technical Publishing House of Light Industry (RU)
Gizmestprom ... State Publishing House of Local Industry (RU)
GIZO .... State Institute for the Study of Arid Regions (RU)
GIZU .... State Publishing House of Ukrainian SSR (RU)
GJA .... Ghana Journalists Association (AF)
gjetskbd...... Gjetskindbind [*Sheepskin Binding*] [*Publishing Danish/Norwegian*]
GJK........... Grupa Jurisnih Korpusa [*Group of Assault Corps*] [*Military*] (YU)
GJL........... Jijel [*Algeria*] [*Airport symbol*] (OAG)
gjmu .... Gepjarmu [*Motor Vehicle*] (HU)
GJR........... Gjogur [*Iceland*] [*Airport symbol*] (OAG)
GK............ Calcium Hypochlorite (RU)
GK............ Citizens Committee (BU)
GK............ City Committee (RU)
GK............ Civil Code (RU)
GK............ Compensating Signal Generator (RU)
GK............ Foam Rubber (RU)
GK............ Gallic Acid (RU)
GK............ Gamma-Ray Logging (RU)
GK............ Gas-Engine Compressor (RU)
GK............ Gekose Komittee [*Select Committee*] [*Afrikaans*]
GK............ Genclik Kol [*Youth Auxiliary*] [*As of a political party*] (TU)
gk .... General [*Cavalry*] (BU)
GK............ Geological Committee (RU)
gk .... Gepkocsi [*Motor Vehicle*] (HU)
GK............ Gereformeerde Kerk [*Reformed Church*] [*South Africa*] (AF)
GK............ Geschnittene Kanten [*Edges Cut*] [*German*] (GCA)
GK............ Giant Cell (RU)
GK............ Gibberellic Acid (RU)
GK............ Glavni Kolodvor [*Central Railroad Station*] [*Croatian*] (YU)
GK............ Gleitkomma [*German*] (ADPT)
GK............ Glowna Kwatera [*Headquarters*] [*Poland*]
GK............ Glowny Komitet [*Chief Committee*] [*Poland*]
GK............ Glutamic Acid (RU)
GK............ Goewermentskennisgewing [*Government Notice*] [*Afrikaans*]
GK............ Gondolat Kiado [*Gondolat Publishing House*] (HU)
GK............ Gottwaldovy Knihovny [*Gottwald Libraries*] (CZ)
GK............ Gradska Klanica [*City Slaughterhouse*] (YU)
GK............ Grondkamer [*Benelux*] (BAS)
GK............ Guvenlik Konseyi [*Security Council*] [*United Nations (already exists in GUS II database)*] (TU)
GK............ Gyrocompass (RU)

GK............. Hexokinase (RU)
GK............. High Command (RU)
GK............. Hydrolized Blood (RU)
GK............. Hypophyseal Cell (RU)
Gk .... Pebble and Crushed Stone [*Topography*] (RU)
GK............. Pressurized Cabin (RU)
GK............. Primary Caliber [*Artillery*] (RU)
GK............. Quartz-Crystal Oscillator (RU)
GKA........... Annular Astatic Gravimeter (RU)
GKA........... Gebrauchswert-Kostenanalyse [*Utility Value Cost Analysis*] (EG)
GKA........... Glowna Komisja Arbitrazowa [*Main Arbitration Commission*] (POL)
GKA........... Goroka [*Papua New Guinea*] [*Airport symbol*] (OAG)
GKA........... US Army Aeronautical Services [*ICAO designator*] (FAAC)
GKAE........ State Committee for the Use of Atomic Energy (RU)
Gkal.......... Gigacalorie (RU)
g kat .... Gorog Katolikus [*Greek Catholic, Uniate*] (HU)
GKB .... Chief Design Office (RU)
GKB .... Garantie- und Kreditbank [*Guaranty and Credit Bank*] [*Germany*] (EG)
GKBP........ Gruppe der Kernkraftwerkbetreiber und Projektanten [*Group of Swiss Utilities Operating and Planning Nuclear Power Stations*] (WND)
GKBS........ Urgent [*Military code*] (YU)
GKBZHwP ... Glowna Komisja Badania Zbrodni Hitlerowskich w Polsce [*Main Commission for the Investigation of NAZI Crimes in Poland*] (POL)
GKCh........ Pilot-Frequency Generator (RU)
GKCh........ Wobbulator, Sweep Generator, Frequency-Sweep Generator (RU)
GKCS........ G. K. Chesterton Society (EA)
GKD.......... Ghaqda Kontra d-Dijabete [*Malta*] (EAIO)
GKD.......... Gonyeli Kultur Dernegi [*Gonyeli (or Geunyeli) Cultural Association*] [*Turkish Cypriot*] (GC)
GKD.......... Gornoslaska Kolej Dojazdowa [*Upper Silesia Suburban Railroad*] (POL)
GKDH .... Gubernur/Kepala Daerah [*Governor/Chief of Region*] (IN)
GKDP .... Main Control Tower [*Aviation*] (RU)
GKE.......... Geodeziai es Kartografiai Egyesulet [*Association of Geodesy and Cartography*] (HU)
GKEI......... Gesellschaft fur Klinische und Experimentelle Immunologie [*Germany*] (EAIO)
g kel.......... Gorog Keleti [*Greek Orthodox*] (HU)
GKES........ State Committee of the Council of Ministers, USSR, on Foreign Economic Relations (RU)
GKFN .... Gminny Komitet Frontu Narodowego [*Rural Commune Committee of the People's Front*] (POL)
GKFS........ City Committee for Physical Culture and Sports (BU)
gkg .... Goed Koopmansgebruik [*Benelux*] (BAS)
g/kh.......... Gas-Powered Boat (RU)
GKhA........ Hexachloroacetone (RU)
GKhB........ Hexachlorobenzene (RU)
GKhCh...... Human Chorionic Gonadotrophin (RU)
GKhI .... State Grain Inspection (RU)
GKhI .... State Scientific and Technical Publishing House of Chemical Literature (RU)
GKhK........ Genikon Khimeion Kratous [*State General Chemical Laboratory*] [*Greek*] (GC)
GKhK........ Main Cotton Committee [*1921-1931*] (RU)
GKhP........ Main Administration of the Basic Chemical Industry (RU)
g khr......... Mountain Chain (RU)
GKhTsG .... Hexachlorocyclohexane (RU)
GKhTsPD ... Hexachlorocyclopentadiene (RU)
GKI .... Channel Pulse Generator (RU)
GKI .... Code Pulse Generator (RU)
GKI .... Gazdasagkutato Intezet [*Economic Research Institute*] [*Hungary*] (IRC)
GKI .... Geodeziai es Kartografiai Intezet [*Institute of Geodesy and Cartography*] (HU)
GKI .... Standard-Pulse Generator (RU)
GKI .... State Control Institute of Medical Biological Preparations Imeni L. A. Tarasevich (RU)
GKI .... State Quarantine Inspection (RU)
GKIAE....... Gosudarstvennyy Komitet po Ispolzovaniyu Atomnoi Energi [*State Committee for the Utilization of Atomic Energy*] [*Former USSR*] (PDAA)
GKISV ...... State Control Institute of Serums and Vaccines Imeni L. A. Tarasevich (RU)
GKK.......... City Control Commission (RU)
GKK.......... Civil Board of Appeals of the Supreme Court (RU)
GKK.......... Glowna Komisja Kontrolna [*Main Control Commission*] (POL)
GKK.......... Glowna Komisja Ksiezy [*Main Commission of the Clergy*] (POL)
GKK.......... Main Committee on Concessions (RU)
GKK.......... Pilot-Channel Generator (RU)

GKKF......... Glowny Komitet Kultury Fizycznej [*Main Committee on Physical Culture*]   (POL)

GKKFiT..... Glowny Komitet Kultury Fizycznej i Turystyki [*Main Committee for Physical Culture and Tourism*]   (POL)

GKKh........ City Municipal Services   (RU)

GKL .... Great Keppel Island [*Australia*] [*Airport symbol*]   (OAG)

GKL .... Guzelyurt Kurtulus Lisesi [*Guzelyurt Liberation Lycee*] [*Turkish Cypriot*]

GKL .... State Control Laboratory   (RU)

GKM......... Glavno Komandno Mesto [*Central Command Post*]   (YU)

GKM......... Horizontal Forging Machine   (RU)

GKMTAP ... Guards Red Banner Mine and Torpedo Air Regiment   (RU)

GKN......... Gemeenschappelijke Kernenergiecentrale Nederland NV [*Nuclear energy*] [*Netherlands*]   (NRCH)

GKN.......... Gemeinschaftskernkraftwerk Neckar, GmbH [*Nuclear energy*]   (NRCH)

GKN.......... Gorlickie Kopalnictwo Naftowe [*Gorlice Oil Wells*]   (POL)

GKN.......... Guest, Keen & Nettlefolds Ltd. [*Australia*]   (ADA)

GKN.......... Helium Condensation Pump   (RU)

GK naBKP ... City Committee of the Bulgarian Communist Party   (BU)

GK NIIVVS ... State Red Banner Scientific Testing Institute of the Air Force   (RU)

GKNT .... Gosudarstvennyy Komitet po Nauki i Teknologii [*State Committee for Science and Technology*] [*Former USSR*]   (LAIN)

GKO.......... Garnizonowy Klub Oficerski [*Garrison Officers Club*]   (POL)

GKO.......... State Defense Committee [*1941-1945*]   (RU)

GkOd .... Greek Odeon [*Record label*]

GKOE .... Grafeio Kommatikon Organoseon Exoterikou [*Office of Party Organization Abroad*] [*Greek Communist Party*] [*Greek*]   (GC)

GKOPI....... Glowna Komisja Opiniowania Projektow Inwestycyjnych [*Main Commission on the Evaluation of Investment Plans*]   (POL)

GKP .... Commanding Officer's Battle Station [*Navy*], Main Command Post, Primary Command Post   (RU)

GKP .... Disastrous Flood Level   (RU)

GKP .... German Communist Party   (BU)

GKP .... Glowny Komitet Przeciwpowodziowy [*Main Committee on Flood Control*]   (POL)

GKP .... Gradsko Komunalno Preduzece [*City Communal Establishment*]   (YU)

GKP .... Greek Communist Party   (BU)

GKP .... Main Administration of the Oxygen Industry   (RU)

GKP .... Main Control Post, Primary Control Post   (RU)

GK poKNIR ... State Committee of the Council of Ministers, USSR, for Coordination of Scientific Research   (RU)

GKpoM...... State Committee on Machinery Manufacture   (RU)

GKR.......... Geheimer Kommerzienrat [*German*]

GKR.......... Generalna Konfederacija Rada [*General Confederation of Labor*]   (YU)

GKR.......... Government of the Khmer Republic [*Anticommunist government of Cambodia during the early seventies*]   (VNW)

GKRAM .... Group of Cambodian Residents in America   (CL)

GKRE .... State Committee of the Council of Ministers, USSR, for Radio Electronics   (RU)

GKrS......... Glavna Kurirska Stanica [*Central Courier Station*] [*Military*]   (YU)

GKRT .... State Committee of the Council of Ministers, USSR, on Radio Broadcasting and Television   (RU)

GKS .... City Cooperative Union   (BU)

GKS .... Gabungan Kepala Staf [*Joint Chiefs of Staff*]   (IN)

GKS .... Gas-Logging Station   (RU)

GKS .... Gminna Kasa Spoldzielcza [*Rural Commune Cooperative Bank*]   (POL)

GKS .... Gorniczy Klub Sportowy [*Miners' Sports and Athletics Club*] [*Poland*]

GKS .... Graphisches Kern-System [*German*]   (ADPT)

GKs........... Hypoxanthine   (RU)

GKSNRM ... Glaven Kooperativen Sojuz na Narodnata Republika Makedonija [*Central Cooperative Union of Macedonia*]   (YU)

GKSS........ Gesellschaft fuer Kernenergieverwertung in Schiffbau und Schiffahrt [*Nuclear energy*] [*German*]

GKT .... Annual Temperature Fluctuation   (RU)

GKT .... Gemeinschaftskernkraftwerk Tullnerfeld, GmbH [*Nuclear energy*] [*Austria*]   (NRCH)

GKT .... Gesellschaft Kohle Technologie

GKT .... Gueter-Kraftverkehrs-Tarif [*Truck Freight Rate Schedule*]   (EG)

GKTP........ Main Administration of the Boiler and Turbine Industry   (RU)

GKTSz .... Gepszakmai Kisipari Termelo Szovetkezet [*Cooperative for Machine Production*]   (HU)

GKU.......... Main Health Resort Administration   (RU)

GKV.......... Gesamtverband Kunststoffverarbeitende Industrie eV   (EY)

gkvez .... Gepkocsivezeto [*Chauffeur*]   (HU)

GKW.......... Gemeinschaftkraftwerk Weser, GmbH [*Nuclear energy*]   (NRCH)

GKW.......... Geraer Kompressorenwerk (VEB) [*Gera Compressor Factory (VEB)*]   (EG)

GKW.......... Gesamtkatalog der Wiegendrucke [*Bibliography of Incunabula*] [*German*]

GKW.......... Gesellschaft fuer Klaranlagen und Wasserversorgung [*Mannheim*]

GKW.......... Gminny Komitet Wykonawczy [*Rural Commune Executive Committee*]   (POL)

GKWP .... Glowny Komitet Wspolzawodnictwa Pracy [*Main Committee on Labor Competition*]   (POL)

GKWR .... Glowna Komisja Wynalazczosci i Racjonalizacji [*Chief Committee for Inventiveness and Rationalization*]   (POL)

GKWW...... Gespraechskreis Wissenschaft und Wirtschaft [*Scientific and Economic Discussion Circle*]   (SLS)

GKWZSL .. Glowny Komitet Wykonawczy Zjednoczonego Stronnictwa Ludowego [*Main Executive Committee of the United Peasant Party*]   (POL)

GKZ.......... State Commission on Mineral Resources   (RU)

GKZ.......... State Stud Farm   (RU)

GKZh........ Sealed Cabin for an Animal   (RU)

GKZh........ Waterproofing Organo-Silicon Fluid   (RU)

GK ZSL ..... Gromadzki Komitet Zjednoczonego Stronnictwa Ludowego [*Village Committee of the United Peasants' Party*] [*Poland*]

gl .... Chapter   (RU)

Gl .... Clay, Clay Pit [*Topography*]   (RU)

gl .... Depth   (RU)

GL .... Galeries Lafayette [*Department store*] [*Paris, France*]

gl .... Gammel [*Old*] [*Denmark*]   (GPO)

GL .... Gas Discharge Lamp   (RU)

gl .... General   (BU)

GL .... General Licence to Officiate [*Church of England in Australia*]

GL .... Germanischer Lloyd [*German ship classification society*]   (DS)

GL .... Giustizia e Liberta [*Italy*] [*Political party*]

gl .... Glat [*Smooth*] [*Publishing Danish/Norwegian*]

gl .... Glava [*Chapter*]   (YU)

gl .... Glebokosc [*Depth*] [*Poland*]

Gl .... Gleichung [*Equation*] [*German*]

gl .... Glittet [*Polished*] [*Publishing Danish/Norwegian*]

gl .... Glowny [*Main, Chief*]   (POL)

Gl .... Gluehen [*Annealing*] [*German*]   (GCA)

GL .... Glutamine   (RU)

gl .... Grand Livre [*Ledger*] [*French*]

GL .... Greenland [*ANSI two-letter standard code*]   (CNC)

GL .... Green Library [*See also BVM*] [*France*]   (EAIO)

GL .... Guyana Legion   (EAIO)

GL .... Gwardia Ludowa [*People's Guard (1942-1943)*]   (POL)

GL .... Gymnasieskolernes Laererforening [*Denmark*]   (EAIO)

gl .... Hectoliter   (RU)

gl .... Lieutenant General   (BU)

Gl .... Main, Chief, Primary   (RU)

gl .... See   (BU)

gl .... Verb   (BU)

GLA .... General Library Assistant [*Australia*]

GLA .... Geologische Landesaufnahme [*Research center*] [*Switzerland*]   (EAS)

GLA .... Grain Legume Association [*Australia*]

GLA .... Groupe de Liberation Armee [*Armed Liberation Group*] [*Guadeloupe*]   (PD)

GLA .... Guyana Library Association   (SLS)

GLA &MVST ... Gruenlandlehranstalt und Marschversuchsstation fuer Niedersachsen, Infeld [*Grassland Educational Establishment and Marsh Research Station for Lower Saxony*]   (ARC)

GLA B-W .. Geologisches Landesamt Baden-Wuerttemberg [*Geological Survey of Baden-Wuerttemberg*] [*Ministry of Economic Affairs*] [*Research center*] [*Germany*]   (EAS)

GLAC .... Grain Legume Advisory Committee [*Australia*]

GLACSEC ... Group of Latin American and Caribbean Sugar Exporting Countries [*See also GEPLACEA*] [*Mexico City, Mexico*]   (EAIO)

GLAD .... Gladiator Fighter Aircraft [*British*]   (DSUE)

GLAFAM ... Grand Lodge of Antient Free and Accepted Masons of Scotland [*Founded in 1736*]

GLAG .... Groupe de Liberation Armee de la Guadeloupe [*Armed Liberation Group of Guadeloupe*]   (LA)

Glag........... Verb   (RU)

Glam .... Glamorgan   (IDIG)

GLA NW ... Geologisches Landesamt Nordrhein-Westfalen [*Geological Survey of North Rhine-Westphalia*] [*Research center*] [*Germany*]   (EAS)

glanz.......... Glaenzend [*Brilliant*] [*German*]   (GCA)

Gl AO .... Main Astronomical Observatory   (RU)

GLAR .... Grupo Latinoamericano de RILEM [*Argentina*]   (SLS)

GLARP ...... Grupo Latinoamericano de Rehabilitacion Profesional [*Latin American Vocational Rehabilitation Group*] [*Bogata, Colombia*]   (EAIO)

Glas........... Glashuettenwesen [*Glass Manufacture*] [*German*]   (GCA)

glasahnl ..... Glasaehnlich [*Glassy*] [*German*] (GCA)
Glasf........... Glasfaser [*Glass Fiber*] [*German*] (GCA)
GLASS ...... Generalised Language and Speech System [*Australia*]
Glasw .... Glaswaren [*Glassware*] [*German*] (GCA)
Glasw .... Glaswerk [*Glass Factory*] [*German*] (GCA)
Glav............ Glaven [*Chief, Main*] (YU)
glav............. Main, Chief, Primary (RU)
Glavabraziv ... Main Administration of the Abrasives Industry (RU)
Glavalyuminiy ... Main Administration of the Aluminum Industry (RU)
Glavanilkraska ... Main Administration of the Aniline Dye Industry (RU)
Glavanilprom ... Main Administration of the Aniline Dye Industry (RU)
Glavantibioprom ... Main Administration of the Antibiotics Industry (RU)
GlavAPU ... Main Architectural Planning Administration of the City of Moscow (RU)
Glavarkhiv ... Main Administration of Archives (RU)
Glavasbest ... Main Administration of the Asbestos Industry (RU)
Glavasboshifer ... Main Administration of the Asbestos and Shale Industry (RU)
Glavatom.... Main Administration for the Use of Atomic Energy (RU)
Glavatomenergo ... Main Administration for the Use of Atomic Energy (RU)
Glavaviaprom ... Main Administration of the Aircraft Industry (RU)
Glavaviastroy ... Main Administration of Aircraft Construction (RU)
Glavavtoagregat ... Main Administration of Plants for Automobile Assemblies (RU)
Glavavtogen ... Main Administration of the Gas-Welding Industry (RU)
Glavavtopribor ... Main Administration for the Manufacture of Automobile Instruments and Equipment (RU)
Glavavtoprom ... Main Administration of the Automobile Industry (RU)
Glavavtoremont ... Main Administration of Automobile Repair Plants and Stations (RU)
Glavavtotraktorosbyt ... Main Administration for the Marketing of Tractors, Agricultural Machinery, and Spare Parts for Automobiles and Tractors (RU)
Glavavtozavodov ... Main Administration of Automobile Plants (RU)
Glavazcherrybprom ... Main Administration of the Fish Industry of the Azov - Black Sea Basin (RU)
Glavazot..... Main Administration of the Nitrogen Industry (RU)
Glavbakaleya ... Main Administration of Wholesale Trade in Sugar, Confectionery, Canned Goods, Tobacco, Salt, and Other Groceries (RU)
Glavblagoustroystva ... Main Administration of Urban Improvement and Municipal Services Establishments (RU)
GLAVBUM ... Main Administration of State Establishments of the Paper Industry (RU)
Glavbumdrevstroy ... Main Administration for the Construction of Establishments of the Pulp, Paper, and Woodworking Industries (RU)
Glavbumprom ... Main Administration of the Paper Industry (RU)
Glavbumsbyt ... Main Administration for Marketing Paper Industry Products (RU)
Glavchasprom ... Main Administration of the Watch Industry (RU)
Glavchay .... Main Administration of the Tea Industry (RU)
Glavdal'stroy ... Main Administration for the Construction of Industrial Establishments in the Regions of the Far East (RU)
Glavdal'vostokrybprom ... Main Administration of the Fish Industry of the Far East (RU)
Glavdizel' ... Main Administration of Diesel Building (RU)
Glavdormash ... Main Administration of Road Machinery Manufacture (RU)
Glavdorrestoran ... Main Administration po Railroad Restaurants (RU)
Glavdorstroy ... Main Administration for the Construction of All-Union Highways (RU)
Glavdortrans ... Main Administration of Highways, Dirt Roads, and Automobile Transportation (RU)
Glavdorupr ... Main Administration of Construction and Operation of Republic and Local Roads (RU)
Glavdrevlitmash ... Main Administration of Woodworking and Foundry Machinery (RU)
Glavekskavator ... Main Administration for the Manufacture of Excavators and Cranes (RU)
Glavelektro ... Main Administration of the Electrotechnical Industry (RU)
Glavelektromontazh ... Main Administration for Installation of Electrical Equipment of Electric Power Plants and Substations (USSR) (RU)
Glavelektrosbyt ... Main Administration for the Marketing of Electrotechnical Products (RU)
Glavelektroset'stroy ... Main Administration for the Construction of Substations and Electric Power Networks (RU)
Glavelektrotochpribor ... Main Administration of Electrical Precision Instruments (RU)
Glavelevator ... Main Administration of Elevators (RU)
Glavelevatorspetsstroy ... Main Administration for the Construction of Elevators and Other Specialized Reinforced Concrete Structures (RU)
Glavenergo ... Main Power Supply Administration (RU)
Glavenergoizdat ... Main State Publishing House of Literature on Power Engineering (RU)

Glavenergokomplekt ... Main Administration for Ensuring the Supply of Complete Sets of Power Engineering Equipment of Electric Power Plants, Substations, and Networks (RU)
Glavenergoproyekt ... Main Administration for the Planning of Electric Power Plants, Substations, and Networks (RU)
Glavenergoremont ... Main Administration for the Repair of Electric Power Plant Equipment (RU)
Glavenergostroy ... Main Administration for Construction and Installation of Thermal Electric Power Plants (RU)
Glavenergostroymekhanizatsiya ... Main Administration for Construction Mechanization of the State Industrial Committee for Power Engineering and Electrification, USSR (RU)
Glavenergostroymontazh ... Main Administration for Construction and Installation of Hydroelectric Power Plants (RU)
Glavenergostroyprom ... Main Administration of Establishments for the Manufacture of Structural Parts and Building Materials of the Ministry of Electric Power Plant Construction, USSR (RU)
Glavesprom ... Main Administration of the Electrical Communications Industry (RU)
Glavfanerspichprom ... Main Administration of the Plywood and Match Industries (RU)
Glavfanspichprom ... Main Administration of the Plywood and Match Industries (RU)
Glavfarfor .. Main Administration of the Porcelain and Faience Industry (RU)
Glavflot ...... Main Administration of Shipping and of Ship-Repair Establishments (of the Ministry of the River Fleet, RSFSR) (RU)
Glavgalantereya ... Main Administration of the Wholesale Trade in Notions, Perfume, Cosmetics, and Toilet Soap (RU)
Glavgastronom ... Main Administration of Delicatessen and Grocery Stores (RU)
Glavgaz ...... Main Administration of the Gas Industry [*Former USSR*] (RU)
Glavgeologiya ... Main Geological Exploration Administration (of the Ministry of the Building Materials Industry, USSR) (RU)
Glavgidroenergostroy ... Main Administration for the Construction and Installation of Hydroelectric Power Plants in the Central and Southern Regions (RU)
Glavgidrolizprom ... Main Administration of the Hydrolysis Industry (RU)
Glavgidromash ... Main Administration for the Manufacture of Pumps, Fittings, and Hydraulic Turbines of the Ministry of Machinery Manufacture, USSR (RU)
Glavgidrostroy ... Main Administration of Hydraulic Engineering Construction (RU)
Glavgimet... Main Administration of the Hydrometeorological Service (RU)
Glavgips..... Main Administration of the Gypsum Industry (RU)
Glavgorkhimprom ... Main Administration of the Chemical Raw Materials Mining Industry (RU)
Glavgormash ... Main Administration of Mining and Fuel Machinery Manufacture (RU)
Glavgortop ... Main Mineral Fuel Administration (RU)
Glavgosrybvod ... Main State Inspection for Fish Conservation (RU)
Glavgramplastprom ... Main Administration of the Phonograph Record Industry (RU)
Glavinstrument ... Main Administration of the Tool Industry (RU)
glavinzh...... Chief Engineer (RU)
Glaviskozh ... Main Administration of the Artificial Leather and Industrial Fabric Industry (RU)
Glaviskusstvo ... Glavnoye Upravleniye po Delam Iskusstva [*Main Administration of Art*] [*Russian*] (RU)
Glavizdat.... Main Administration of Publishing Houses, the Printing Industry, and the Book Trade [*Former USSR*] (RU)
Glavizo .... Main Administration of Fine Arts (RU)
glavk.......... Main Administration, Main Directorate [*Military term*] (RU)
Glavkabel' .. Main Administration of the Cable Industry (RU)
Glavkauchuk ... Main Administration of the Synthetic Rubber Industry (RU)
Glavkhimfarmprom ... Main Administration of the Chemical and Pharmaceutical Industry (RU)
Glavkhimmash ... Main Administration of Chemical Machinery Manufacture (RU)
Glavkhimprom ... Main Administration of the Basic Chemical Industry (RU)
Glavkhimpromstroy ... Main Administration for Construction and Installation of Chemical Industry Establishments (RU)
Glavkhimsbyt ... Main Administration of Marketing of Chemical Industry Products (RU)
Glavkhimsnab ... Main Administration of Supply of the Chemical Industry (RU)
Glavkholod ... Main Administration of Cold Storage Plants (RU)
Glavkhoztorg ... Main Administration of Wholesale Trade in Household Goods (RU)
Glavkinofikatsiya ... Main Administration for the Development of Motion-Picture Facilities and for Motion-Picture Distribution (RU)
Glavkinoprokat ... Main Administration of Motion-Picture Distribution (RU)
Glavkinosnab ... Main Supply Administration of the Ministry of Cinematography, USSR (RU)

Glavkirpich ... Main Administration of the Brick Industry   (RU)

Glavkislorod ... Main Administration of the Oxygen Industry   (RU)

Glavkislorodmash ... Main Administration of Oxygen Machinery   (RU)

Glavkiyevstroy ... Main Administration for Housing and Civil Engineering Construction of the Kiev Gorispolkom   (RU)

Glavknigtorg ... Main Administration of the Book Trade   (RU)

Glavknizhtorg ... Main Administration of the Book Trade   (RU)

Glavkoks.... Main Administration of the By-Product Coke Industry   (RU)

Glavkolkhozstroy ... Main Administration for Construction in Kolkhozes   (RU)

Glavkombaynprom ... Main Administration of the Combine Industry and Harvesting Machines   (RU)

Glavkomplekt ... Main Administration of Supply of Equipment in Complete Sets   (RU)

Glavkomplektoooborudovaniye ... Main Administration of Supply of Metallurgical, Power-Engineering, and Petrochemical Equipment in Complete Sets   (RU)

Glavkonditer ... Main Administration of the Confectionery Industry   (RU)

Glavkonserv ... Main Administration of the Canning and Food Concentrates Industry   (RU)

Glavkontsesskom ... Glavny Kontsessionny Komitet [*Main Committee on Concessions*] [*Russian*]   (RU)

Glavkoopbakaleytorg ... Main Administration for the Grocery Trade (of the Tsentrosoyuz)   (RU)

Glavkoopgalantereytorg ... Main Administration for the Notions and Perfumery Trade (of the Tsentrosoyuz)   (RU)

Glavkoopkhoztorg ... Main Administration for Trade in Metalware and Household Goods (of the Tsentrosoyuz)   (RU)

Glavkoopkul'ttorg ... Main Administration for Trade in Goods for Cultural Purposes (of the Tsentrosoyuz)   (RU)

Glavkooplektekhsyr'ye ... Main Administration for the Procurement, Processing, and Marketing of Raw Materials for the Drug Industry, Wild Plants and Berries, and Beekeeping Products (of the Tsentrosoyuz)   (RU)

Glavkoopmetiztorg ... Main Administration for Trade in Metalware and Silicate Products (of the Tsentrosoyuz)   (RU)

Glavkoopplodoovoshch ... Main Administration for the Procurement, Processing, and Marketing of Produce (of the Tsentrosoyuz)   (RU)

Glavkoopsnab ... Main Administration for Equipment Manufacture and Materials and Equipment Supply (of the Tsentrosoyuz)   (RU)

Glavkoopsyr'ye ... Main Administration for Procurement, Processing, and Marketing of Raw Materials, Scrap Metal, and Utility Waste (of the Tsentrosoyuz)   (RU)

Glavkoopzhivsyr'ye ... Main Administration for the Procurement, Processing, and Marketing of Livestock Products, Raw Materials, and Fur (of the Tsentrosoyuz)   (RU)

Glavkord .... Main Administration of the Cord Industry   (RU)

Glavkotloprom ... Main Administration of the Boiler Industry   (RU)

Glavkozh.... Main Administration of the Leather and Tanning Extract Industry   (RU)

Glavkozhsyr'ye ... Main Administration for the Primary Processing of Leather and Fur Raw Materials and the Manufacture of Tanning Extracts   (RU)

Glavkraska ... Main Administration of the Paint Industry   (RU)

Glavkul'tprosvet ... Main Administration of Cultural and Educational Institutions   (RU)

Glavkul'tsnabsbyt ... Main Supply and Marketing Administration of the Ministry of Culture, USSR   (RU)

Glavkul'ttorg ... Main Administration of Wholesale Trade in Goods for Cultural Purposes and Sports   (RU)

Glavkurorttorg ... Main Administration for Trade in Health Resorts   (RU)

Glavkursanupr ... Main Administration of Health Resorts, Sanatoriums, and Rest Homes   (RU)

Glavkurupr ... Main Administration of Health Resorts   (RU)

Glavkustprom ... Main Administration of Cottage Industry   (RU)

Glavlegmash ... Main Administration of Light Machinery Manufacture   (RU)

Glavlegsbytsyr'ye ... Main Administration for the Marketing of Raw Materials of Textile and Light Industries   (RU)

Glavleningradstroy ... Main Administration for the Housing, Civil Engineering, and Industrial Construction of the Leningrad Gorispolkom   (RU)

Glavlenstroymaterialy ... Main Leningrad Administration of the Building Materials and Parts Industry   (RU)

Glavles .... Main Administration for Logging and Woodworking   (RU)

Glavleskhim ... Main Administration of the Wood-Chemistry Industry   (RU)

Glavleskhoz ... Main Administration of Forestry and Forest Conservation   (RU)

Glavleskom ... Main Committee of the Lumber Industry   (RU)

Glavlesosbyt ... Main Administration for the Marketing of Products of the Logging, Sawmilling, and Woodworking Industry   (RU)

Glavlesosplav ... Main Administration for Log Rafting   (RU)

Glavlesstroytorg ... Main Administration of the Lumber and Building Materials Trade   (RU)

Glavleszapchast' ... Main Administration for the Manufacture of Spare Parts, the Repair of Equipment, and the Manufacture of Mechanical Devices for the Lumber Industry   (RU)

Glavleszheldorstroy ... Main Administration for the Construction of Lumber-Hauling Railroads   (RU)

Glavlit .... Main Administration for the Safeguarding of Military and State Secrets in the Press   (RU)

Glavl'nopen'koprom ... Main Administration of the Flax and Hemp Industry   (RU)

Glavl'noprom ... Main Administration of the Flax Industry   (RU)

Glavlokomibil'dizel' ... Main Administration of Locomobile and Diesel Machinery Manufacture   (RU)

Glavmashdetal' ... Main Administration of Machine Parts Manufacture   (RU)

Glavmashfurnitura ... Main Administration of Machine Parts Manufacture and Accessories   (RU)

Glavmashmet ... Main Administration of Machinery Plants of the Ministry of Ferrous Metallurgy, USSR   (RU)

Glavmashsbyt ... Main Administration for the Marketing of Machinery   (RU)

Glavmaslosyrprom ... Main Administration of the Butter and Cheese Industry   (RU)

Glavmebel'prom ... Main Administration of the Furniture Industry   (RU)

Glavmedinstrumentprom ... Main Administration of the Medical Instrument Industry   (RU)

Glavmedsnabsbyt ... Main Administration of Interrepublic Medical Supply and Marketing   (RU)

Glavmekh .. Main Administration of the Fur Industry   (RU)

Glavmekhanomontazh ... Main Administration of Machine-Assembling Operations   (RU)

Glavmekhprom ... Main Administration of the Fur Industry   (RU)

Glavmerves ... Main Administration of Measures and Weights   (RU)

Glavmestpromsbyt ... Main Marketing Administration of the Ministry of Local Industry, RSFSR   (RU)

Glavmestpromsnab ... Main Administration of Materials and Equipment Supply of the Ministry of Local Industry, RSFSR   (RU)

GLAVMETALL ... Main Administration of the Metals Industry   (RU)

Glavmetalloizdeliy ... Main Administration of the Metalware Industry   (RU)

Glavmetallosbyt ... Main Administration for the Marketing of Ferrous Metals and Metalware (of the Ministry of Ferrous Metallurgy, USSR)   (RU)

Glavmetallurgmontazh ... Main Administration for the Installation of Metallurgical Establishments   (RU)

Glavmetiz... Main Administration of the Metalware Industry   (RU)

Glavmezhavtotrans ... Main Administration of Intercity and International Automobile Transportation   (RU)

Glavmoloko ... Main Administration of the Dairy Industry   (RU)

Glavmolprom ... Main Administration of the Dairy Industry   (RU)

Glavmontazhstroy ... Main Administration for Installation Work   (RU)

Glavmorrechstroy ... Main Administration for the Construction of Maritime and River Structures   (RU)

Glavmorrevizor ... Administration of the Chief Inspector for Safety at Sea   (RU)

Glavmorstroy ... Main Administration for the Construction of Maritime Structures   (RU)

Glavmosavtotrans ... Main Administration of Automobile Transportation of the Mosgorispolkom   (RU)

Glavmoskhlopprom ... Main Administration of the Cotton Industry of Moscow Oblast   (RU)

Glavmosoblmestprom ... Main Administration of Local Industry of the Mosoblispolkom   (RU)

Glavmosoblstroy ... Main Administration for Construction in Moscow Oblast   (RU)

Glavmosoblstroymaterialy ... Main Administration of the Building Materials and Structural Parts Industry of the Mosoblispolkom   (RU)

Glavmossovkhozov ... Main Administration of Sovkhozes of the Moscow Area   (RU)

Glavmosstroy ... Main Administration for Housing and Civil Engineering Construction in Moscow City   (RU)

Glavmosstroymaterialy ... Main Administration of the Building Materials Industry of the Mosgorispolkom   (RU)

Glavmostostroy ... Main Administration for Bridge Construction   (RU)

Glavmoszhelezobeton ... Main Administration of Establishments of Reinforced Concrete Structures and Large Building Blocks of the Mosgorispolkom   (RU)

Glavmotoveloprom ... Main Administration of the Motorcycle and Bicycle Industry   (RU)

GlavMRS... Main Administration of Motorized Fishing Stations   (RU)

Glavmuzinstrument ... Main Administration of the Musical Instruments Industry   (RU)

Glavmyasomolmash ... Main Administration for the Manufacture of Machinery and of Packing Materials of the Ministry of the Meat and Dairy Products Industry, USSR   (RU)

Glavmyasomolsnab ... Main Administration of Materials and Equipment Supply of the Ministry of the Meat and Dairy Products Industry, USSR   (RU)

Glavmyasorybtorg ... Main Administration of Cold Storage Plants and Wholesale Meat, Butter, and Fish Trade   (RU)

Glavnauka ... Main Administration of Scientific Institutions, Museums, and Science and Art Establishments (RU)

Glavneft' .... Main Administration of the Petroleum Industry (RU)

Glavneftedorvodstroy ... Main Administration of Hydraulic-Engineering, Water-Supply, Sewer-System, and Road Construction of the Ministry of Construction of Petroleum Industry Establishments, USSR (RU)

Glavneftegaz ... Main Administration of the Petroleum and Gas Industry (RU)

Glavneftemash ... Main Administration of Petroleum Machinery Manufacture (RU)

Glavneftemontazh ... Main Administration of Installation Operations of the Ministry of Construction of Petroleum Industry Establishments, USSR (RU)

Glavneftepererabotka ... Main Administration for Petroleum Processing (RU)

Glavneftepromstroy ... Main Administration of Oil Field Construction (RU)

Glavnefteprovodstroy ... Main Administration for Pipeline Construction of the Ministry of Construction of Petroleum Industry Establishments, USSR (RU)

Glavnefteproyekt ... Main Planning Administration of the Ministry of the Petroleum Industry, USSR (RU)

Glavneftesbyt ... Main Administration for the Marketing and Transportation of Petroleum and Petroleum Products (RU)

Glavneftesnab ... Main Administration for the Transportation and Supply of Petroleum and Petroleum Products (RU)

Glavneftestroymekhanizatsiya ... Main Administration for the Mechanization of Construction of the Ministry of Construction of Petroleum Industry Establishments, USSR (RU)

Glavneftestroysnab ... Main Administration of Materials and Equipment Supply of the Ministry of Construction of Petroleum Industry Establishments, USSR (RU)

Glavnefteurs ... Main Administration of Workers' Supply of the Ministry of the Petroleum Industry, USSR (RU)

Glavneftezavodstroy ... Main Administration of Petroleum Plant Construction (RU)

Glavnerud .. Main Administration of the Nonmetallic Mineral Industry (of the Ministry of the Building Materials Industry, USSR) (RU)

Glavniiproyekt SSSR ... Main Administration of Scientific Research and Planning Organizations, USSR (RU)

Glavnit .... Main Administration for Petroleum Processing and the Manufacture of Synthetic Liquid Fuel (RU)

Glavoboz .... Main Administration of Cart and Sledge Making (RU)

Glavobuv'torg ... Main Administration of the Wholesale Footwear Trade (RU)

Glavogneupor ... Main Administration of the Refractory Industry (RU)

Glavokhota ... Main Administration of Hunting and Game Preserves (RU)

Glavparovoz ... Main Administration of Locomotive Building (RU)

Glavpereselenorgnabor ... Main Administration of Resettlement and Organized Recruitment of Workers (RU)

Glavpochvomash ... Main Administration of Cultivators and Seeding Machines (RU)

Glavpodshipnik ... Main Administration of the Bearing Industry (RU)

Glavpodzemgaz ... Main Administration of Underground Coal Gasification (RU)

Glavpogruztransupr ... Main Freight and Transportation Administration (RU)

Glavpoligrafizdat ... Main Administration of Publishing Houses, the Printing Industry, and the Book Trade (RU)

Glavpoligrafprom ... Main Administration of the Printing Industry (RU)

GLAVPOLITPROSVET ... Main Political Education Committee of the Narkompros RSFSR [1920-1930] (RU)

Glav politupravlenie ... Main Political Administration (BU)

Glavport..... Main Administration of Port Management and Sea Routes (RU)

Glavpribor ... Main Administration of Instrument Making (RU)

Glavpriborsbyt ... Main Administration for the Marketing of Instruments (RU)

Glavprimorrybprom ... Main Administration of the Primor'ye Fish Industry (RU)

Glavprodmash ... Main Administration of Food Machinery Manufacture (RU)

Glavproekt ... Main Designing Organization (BU)

Glavproizvodfil'm ... Main Administration for the Production of Films (RU)

Glavpromenergomontazh ... Main Administration for the Installation of Power Engineering Equipment of Industrial Electric Power Plants (RU)

Glavpromstrom ... Main Administration of the Building Materials Industry (RU)

Glavpromtekhsnab ... Main Administration of Materials and Equipment Supply of the Rospromsovet (RU)

Glavprotez ... Main Administration of the Prosthetics Industry (RU)

Glavproyekt ... Main Administration of Planning Organizations (RU)

Glavproyektmontazhvatomatika ... Main Administration for the Planning and Installation of Automation Systems (RU)

GlavPU ...... Main Political Directorate of the Soviet Army and the Navy (RU)

GlavPURKKA ... Main Political Directorate of the Workers' and Peasants' Red Army (RU)

GlavPUSA i VMF ... Main Political Directorate of the Soviet Army and the Navy (RU)

Glavradiosbyt ... Main Administration for the Marketing of Radiotechnical Products (RU)

Glavraszhirmaslo ... Main Administration of the Vegetable Oils and Fats Industry (RU)

Glavrechstroy ... Main Administration for the Construction of River Structures (RU)

Glavrechtrans ... Main Administration for the Transportation Development and Use of Small Rivers (RU)

Glavredmet ... Main Administration of the Rare Metals Industry (RU)

Glavrepertkom ... Main Committee for Control of Entertainment and Repertoires (RU)

Glavrestoran ... Main Administration of Restaurants (RU)

glavrezh...... Chief Director, Chief Producer (RU)

Glavrezina ... Main Administration of the Rubber, Asbestos, and Industrial Fabric Industries (RU)

Glavrezinprom ... Main Administration of the Industrial Rubber Goods and Rubber Footwear Industry (RU)

Glavrosgosstrakh ... Main Administration of State Insurance, RSFSR (RU)

Glavrossovkhozsnab ... Main Administration of Materials and Equipment Supply of the Ministry of Sovkhozes, RSFSR (RU)

Glavruda .... Main Administration of the Ore Industry (RU)

Glavsakhalinbumprom ... Main Administration of the Sakhalin Paper Industry (RU)

Glavsakhalinlesprom ... Main Administration of the Sakhalin Lumber Industry (RU)

Glavsakhar ... Main Administration of the Sugar Industry (RU)

Glavsantekhmontazh ... Main Administration for Sanitary Engineering and Installation (of the Ministry of Construction of Establishments of the Metallurgical and Chemical Industries, USSR) (RU)

Glavsantekhprom ... Main Administration of the Sanitary Engineering Industry (RU)

Glavsanupr ... Main Medical and Sanitary Administration (RU)

Glavsel'elektro ... Main Administration of Rural Electrification (RU)

Glavsel'elektrostroy ... Main Administration for the Construction of Rural Electric Power Plants and Electric Power Networks (RU)

Glavsel'khoztrans ... Main Administration for the Organization of Transportation of Agricultural Freight (RU)

Glavsel'mash ... Main Administration of Agricultural Machinery Manufacture (RU)

Glavsel'stroy ... Main Administration of Rural Construction (RU)

Glavsel'stroyproyekt ... Main Administration for the Planning of Rural Buildings and Structures at the State Committee for Construction, USSR (RU)

Glavseverotorg ... Main Administration for Planning and for Ahead-of-Time Delivery of Goods to the Far Northern Regions and Similar Remote Areas (RU)

Glavsevlesprom ... Main Administration of the Lumber Industry in the Northern Regions (RU)

Glavsevmorputi ... Main Administration of the Northern Sea Route (RU)

Glavsevuralstroy ... Main Administration of Construction of Industrial Establishments in the Northern Ural Regions (RU)

Glavsevzapenergo ... Main Administration of Electric Power Plants and Networks of the North and West (RU)

Glavsevzapstroy ... Main Administration of Construction of the Northwestern Regions (RU)

Glavshakhtoles ... Main Administration for Supplying Mines with Lumber (RU)

Glavshakhtoproyekt ... Main Administration for the Planning of Mines (RU)

Glavshakhtostroymash ... Main Administration of Mine Construction Machinery Manufacture (RU)

Glavshelk... Main Administration of the Silk Industry (of the Ministry of the Textile Industry) (RU)

Glavshelkprom ... Main Administration of the Silk Industry (RU)

Glavsherst' ... Main Administration of the Wool Industry (RU)

Glavshinprom ... Main Administration of the Tire Industry (RU)

Glavshveyprom ... Main Administration of the Garment Industry (RU)

Glavsibdal'stroy ... Main Administration for the Construction of Industrial Establishments in Siberian and Far Eastern Regions (RU)

Glavsibstroy ... Main Administration for the Construction of Industrial Establishments in Siberian Regions (RU)

Glavsilikatvyazhprom ... Main Administration of the Silicate and Binding-Material Industries (RU)

Glavslanets ... Main Administration of the Shale Industry (RU)

Glavsnab.... Main Supply Administration (RU)

Glavsnabpros ... Main Administration for Supply of and Trade in Educational Visual Aids, Equipment, Materials, and Other Educational and Housekeeping Requirements (of the Ministry of Education, RSFSR) (RU)

Glavsnabsbyt ... Main Administration of Supply and Marketing (RU)

Glavsnabsvyaz' ... Main Administration of Materials and Equipment Supply (of the Ministry of Communications, USSR) (RU)

GLAVSOTsSTRAKH ... Main Administration of Social Insurance (RU)

GLAVSOTsVOS ... Main Administration of Children's Social Upbringing and Polytechnic Education of the Narkompros RSFSR [*1921-1933*] (RU)

GLAVSOVKhOZ ... Main Administration of Sovkhozes (RU)

Glavspetspromstroy ... Main Administration for Special Types of Construction and Installation (RU)

Glavspetsstroy ... Main Administration of Specialized Trusts of the Ministry of Urban and Rural Construction, RSFSR (RU)

Glavsporttorg ... Main Administration for Trade in Sport Goods (RU)

Glavstal'konstruksiya ... Main Administration for the Manufacture and Installation of Steel and Complex Reinforced Concrete Structures (RU)

Glavstandartdom ... Main Administration of Standard Housing Construction (RU)

Glavstankoinstrumentsbyt ... Main Marketing Administration of the Machine Tool and Tool Industry (RU)

Glavstankoprom ... Main Administration of the Machine Tool Industry (RU)

Glavsteklo ... Main Administration of the Glass Industry (RU)

Glavstrommashina ... Main Administration for the Manufacture of Machinery for the Building Materials Industry (RU)

Glavstromsnab ... Main Administration of Materials and Equipment Supply of the Ministry of the Building Materials Industry, RSFSR (RU)

Glavstrotsnab ... Main Administration of Materials and Equipment Supply (of the Ministry of Urban and Rural Construction, RSFSR) (RU)

Glavstroy ... Main Construction Administration (RU)

Glavstroykeramika ... Main Administration of Building Ceramics (RU)

Glavstroyleszag ... Main Administration for Logging of the Ministry of Construction, USSR (RU)

Glavstroymash ... Main Administration for the Manufacture of Construction Machinery (RU)

Glavstroymekhanizatsiya ... Main Administration of Mechanization of Construction Work (RU)

Glavstroyprom ... Main Administration of the Construction Industry (RU)

Glavstroyproyekt ... Main Administration of Planning Organizations at the State Committee for Construction, USSR (RU)

Glavstroysbyt ... Main Administration for the Marketing of Building Materials (RU)

Glavstroysnab ... Main Administration of Materials and Equipment Supply (of the Ministry of Construction, RSFSR) (RU)

Glavstroysteklo ... Main Administration of Structural Glass (RU)

Glavsudkhoz ... Main Administration of the Shipping Industry and Ship Repair Yards (RU)

Glavsudomekh ... Main Administration of the Technical Operation of the Fleet and of Ship Repair Yards (RU)

Glavsvyaz'stroy ... Main Administration for the Construction of Communications Installations (RU)

Glavtekhmontazh ... Main Administration for the Assembly of Technological Equipment and for Installation Operations [*Former USSR*] (RU)

Glavtekhremont ... Main Administration for the Organization of Maintenance and Repair of Machines and Mechanical Devices (RU)

Glavtekstil'torg ... Main Administration of the Wholesale Textile Trade (RU)

Glavteploenergomontazh ... Main Administration for the Installation of Heat and Power Engineering Equipment in Electric Power Plants (RU)

Glavteplomontazh ... Main Administration of Heat Engineering and Heat Insulation (RU)

Glavteplostroy ... Main Administration of Heat Engineering and Heat Insulation of the Ministry of Construction of Establishments of the Metallurgical and Chemical Industries, USSR (RU)

Glavtochmash ... Main Administration of Precision Machinery Manufacture (RU)

Glavtonnel'metrostroy ... Main Administration for the Construction of Tunnels and Subways (RU)

Glavtop ...... Main Administration of the Fuel Industry (RU)

Glavtorf...... Main Administration of the Peat Industry (RU)

Glavtorffond ... Main Administration of Peat Reserves (RU)

Glavtorg ..... Main Administration of Trade (RU)

Glavtorgmash ... Main Administration for Trade in Automobiles, Tractors, Agricultural Machinery, and Other Producer Goods (RU)

Glavtorgmortrans ... Main Administration of Trade and Provisioning of the Fleet (of the Ministry of the Maritime Fleet, USSR) (RU)

Glavtorgoborudovaniye ... Main Administration of Commercial Equipment (RU)

Glavtorgodezhda ... Main Administration of the Wholesale Clothing Trade (RU)

Glavtraktoroprom ... Main Administration of the Tractor Industry (RU)

Glavtramnay ... Main Administration of Streetcars and Trolleybuses (RU)

Glavtranselektromontazh ... Main Administration for the Electrification of Railroads of the Ministry of Transportation Construction, USSR (RU)

Glavtransproyekt ... Main Administration of Planning and Surveying of the State Industrial Committee for Transportation Construction, USSR (RU)

Glavtsellyuloza ... Main Administration of the Pulp Industry (RU)

Glavtsentrelektroset'stroy ... Main Administration for the Construction of High-Voltage Electric Power Networks and Substations of the Central and Southern Regions (RU)

Glavtsentrenergo ... Main Administration of Electric Power Plants and Networks of the Central Region (RU)

Glavtsentroelektroset'stroy ... Main Administration for the Construction and Installation of High-Voltage Electric Power Networks and Substations of the Central and Southern Regions (RU)

Glavtsentroenergostroy ... Main Administration for the Construction and Installation of Thermal Electric Power Plants of the Central and Southern Regions (RU)

Glavtsentrokhloprom ... Main Administration of the Cotton Industry of the Central Regions (RU)

Glavtsentroshakhtostroy ... Main Administration for Construction of Coal Mines and Establishments of the Central Region (RU)

Glavtsentrostroy ... Main Administration for Construction in the Moscow Economic Region (RU)

Glavtsvetmetsbyt ... Main Administration for the Marketing of Products of Nonferrous Metallurgy (RU)

Glavturboprom ... Main Administration of the Turbine Industry (RU)

Glavuborochkhlopkomash ... Main Administration for the Manufacture of Cotton-Picking Machinery (RU)

Glavuchtekhprom ... Main Administration of Technical Education Aids Industry (RU)

Glavuglemash ... Main Administration of Coal Machinery Manufacture (RU)

Glavuglesbyt ... Main Administration for the Marketing of Coal (RU)

Glavuglesnab ... Main Administration of Materials and Equipment Supply of the Ministry of the Coal Industry, USSR (RU)

Glavunivermag ... Main Administration of Department Stores Selling Manufactured Goods (RU)

glavupr .... Chief Director, Head Manager (RU)

glavupr .... Main Administration, Main Directorate (RU)

Glavuralenergo ... Main Administration of Electric Power Plants and Electric Power Networks of the Urals (RU)

Glavurallesprom ... Main Administration of the Ural Lumber Industry (RU)

Glavuralshakhtostroy ... Main Administration for the Construction of Mines in the Urals and Central Asia (RU)

Glavuralstroy ... Main Administration for the Construction of Industrial Establishments in the Ural Regions (RU)

Glavurs ...... Main Administration of Workers' Supply (RU)

Glavurstorg ... Main Administration of Workers' Supply and Trade (RU)

Glavvagon .. Main Administration of Railroad-Car Building (RU)

Glavvetupr ... Main Veterinary Administration (RU)

Glavvino..... Main Administration of the Wine Industry (RU)

Glavvitaminprom ... Main Administration of the Vitamin Industry (RU)

Glavvodkhoz ... Main Administration of Water Management (RU)

Glavvodokanal ... Main Administration of the Water Supply and Sewer Systems (RU)

Glavvodput' ... Main Administration of Waterways and Hydraulic Engineering Structures (RU)

Glavvostbumprom ... Main Administration of the Paper Industry of the Eastern Regions (RU)

Glavvostdrev ... Main Administration for Sawmilling and Woodworking in the Eastern Regions (RU)

Glavvostok ... Main Administration of the Industry of the Regions of Siberia and the Far East (RU)

Glavvostokelektroset'stroy ... Main Administration for Construction and Installation of High-Voltage Electric Power Networks and Substation in the Urals and Siberia (RU)

Glavvostokenergo ... Main Administration of Electric Power Plants and Networks of the East (RU)

Glavvostokenergostroy ... Main Administration for Construction and Installation of Thermal Electric Power Plants in the Urals and Siberia (RU)

Glavvostokgidroenergostroy ... Main Administration for Construction and Installation of Hydroelectric Power Plants of the East (RU)

Glavvostokneftedobycha ... Main Administration for Petroleum Production in the Eastern Regions (RU)

Glavvostokrybosudostroy ... Main Administration of Shipbuilding and Ship Repair in the East of the Ministry of the Fish Industry, USSR (RU)

Glavvostokrybprom ... Main Administration of the Fish Industry of the East (RU)

Glavvostokshakhtstroy ... Main Administration for the Construction of Mines in Eastern Siberia, the Far East, and the Pechora Basin (RU)

Glavvostoktsement ... Main Administration of the Cement Industry of the Eastern Regions (RU)

Glavvostokzoloto ... Main Administration of the Gold and Platinum Industry of the Far East and Eastern Siberia (RU)

Glavvoyenprom ... Main Administration of War Industry (RU)

Glavvoyenpromstroy ... Main Administration of War Industry Construction (RU)

Glavvoyentorg ... Main Administration of Trade Establishments for Military Personnel (RU)

Glavvtorchermet ... Main Administration for the Procurement, Processing, and Marketing of Secondary Ferrous Metals   (RU)

Glavvtormet ... Main Administration for the Procurement, Processing, and Marketing of Secondary Ferrous and Nonferrous Metals   (RU)

Glavvtorsyr'ye ... Main Administration for the Procurement and Processing of Secondary Raw Material   (RU)

Glavvtortsvetmet ... Main Administration for the Procurement, Processing, and Marketing of Secondary Nonferrous Metals   (RU)

Glavyugstroy ... Main Administration for the Construction of Industrial Establishments in the Southern Regions (of the Ministry of Construction, USSR)   (RU)

Glavyuvelirtorg ... Main Administration of the Jewelry Trade   (RU)

Glavyuzhenergo ... Main Administration of Southern Power Systems   (RU)

Glavyuzhenergostroy ... Main Administration for Construction and Installation of Thermal Electric Power Plants of the Central and Southern Regions   (RU)

Glavyuzhgrazhdanstroy ... Main Construction Administration of the Southern Regions of the Ministry of Housing and Civil-Engineering Construction, RSFSR   (RU)

Glavyuzhuralstroy ... Main Administration for Construction in the South Ural Economic Region   (RU)

Glavzagotkhlopprom ... Main Administration of Cotton Procurement and the Ginning Industry   (RU)

Glavzagotstroy ... Main Construction Administration of the Ministry of Procurement, USSR   (RU)

Glavzapadneftedobycha ... Main Administration for Petroleum Production in the Southern and Western Regions   (RU)

Glavzapadneftestroy ... Main Administration for Construction in the Western Regions of the Ministry of the Petroleum Industry, USSR   (RU)

Glavzapadtsement ... Main Administration of the Cement Industry of the Western Regions   (RU)

Glavzapadzoloto ... Main Administration of the Gold and Platinum Industry of Western Siberia, the Urals, and Kazakhstan   (RU)

Glavzapdrev ... Main Administration of Sawmilling and Woodworking in the Western Regions   (RU)

Glavzarubezhkomplekt ... Main Administration for Supplying in Complete Sets Equipment and Materials for Establishments Being Built Abroad   (RU)

Glavzheldorstroy ... Main Administration of Railroad Construction   (RU)

Glavzheldorstroymekhanizatsiya ... Main Administration for the Mechanization of Construction Work in Railroad Transportation   (RU)

Glavzhelezobeton ... Main Administration for the Manufacture of Reinforced Concrete Parts and Structures   (RU)

Glavzhilupr ... Main Housing Administration   (RU)

Glavzhilupravleniye ... Main Housing Administration   (RU)

Glavzhivupr ... Main Administration of Livestock Breeding   (RU)

Glavzverovod ... Main Administration of Fur-Farming Sovkhozes   (RU)

GLB .... Depth Charge   (RU)

GLB .... Global Air [Bulgaria] [ICAO designator]   (FAAC)

GLBI .... State Publishing House of the Lumber and Paper Industries   (RU)

glbp .... Pigeon Communication Service   (BU)

GLBU .... Buchanan [Liberia] [ICAO location identifier]   (ICLI)

GLC .... Gambia Labour Congress

GLC .... Guyana Liquor Corporation   (LA)

GLCG .... Groupe de Liaison sur la Conservation des Grains [Service de la Protection des Vegetaux] [France]

GLCM .... Robertsport/Cape Mount [Liberia] [ICAO location identifier]   (ICLI)

GLCNSW ... Gem and Lapidary Council of New South Wales [Australia]

GLCP........ Harper/Cape Palmas [Liberia] [ICAO location identifier]   (ICLI)

GLCSNSW ... Gay and Lesbian Counselling Service of New South Wales [Australia]

GLCSSA.... Gay and Lesbian Counselling Service of South Australia

GLD .... Germaniki Laiki Dimokratia [German Democratic Republic]   (GC)

GLD .... Golden Star Air Cargo Co. Ltd. [Sudan] [ICAO designator]   (FAAC)

Gld .... Guilder [Modification of gulden] [Monetary unit] [Netherlands]

Gldir.......... Main Directorate   (BU)

GlDirGeolMProuchv ... Main Directorate of Geological and Mining Surveys   (BU)

Gl dir kin.... Main Directorate of Cinematography   (BU)

Gl dir ptt .... Main Directorate of Post, Telegraph, and Telephone   (BU)

Gl dirradio ... Main Directorate of Radio Broadcasting   (BU)

Gl dirstatist ... Main Statistical Directorate   (BU)

Gl dirzzhel i prist ... Main Directorate of Railways and Harbors   (BU)

Gldr............ Ganzleder [All Leather] [German]

GLDR .... Groupe Liberal, Democratique, et Reformateur   (EAIO)

gldsn........... Guldsnitt [Gilt Edge] [Publishing] [Sweden]

GLECS ...... Groupe Linguistique d'Etudes Chamito-Semitiques

gleichbd...... Gleichbedeutend [Synonymous] [German]   (GCA)

gleichgew.... Gleichgewicht [Equilibrium] [German]   (GCA)

gleichh .... Gleichhaltung [Keeping Constant] [German]   (GCA)

gleichmass ... Gleichmaessig [Equal] [German]   (GCA)

gleichzeit.... Gleichzeitig [Simultaneous] [German]   (GCA)

Gleit .... Gleitung [Sliding] [German]   (GCA)

Gler .... Glacier [Glacier] [Military map abbreviation World War I] [French]   (MTD)

GLF........... Golfito [Costa Rica] [Airport symbol]   (OAG)

GLG .... Gewerkschaft Agrar-Nahrung-Genuss [Austria]   (EAIO)

GLG .... Glengyle [Australia] [Airport symbol]   (OAG)

GLGA .... Guyana Local Government Association   (LA)

GLGE .... Greenville/Sinoe [Liberia] [ICAO location identifier]   (ICLI)

GLI .... Gallic Aviation [France] [ICAO designator]   (FAAC)

GLI .... Garp Linyitler Isletmesi [Western Lignites Operation]   (TU)

GLI .... Gioventu Liberale Italia   (EAIO)

GLI .... Glen Innes [Australia] [Airport symbol]   (OAG)

GLI .... State Meadow Institute   (RU)

GLIB......... Government Libraries in Belconnen [Australia]

Glin .... Clay Pit [Topography]   (RU)

gl in .... Quartermaster General, Quartermaster General's Department   (BU)

GLINN ...... Government Libraries Information Network in New South Wales [Australia]

glinoz......... Alumina, Aluminum Oxide [Topography]   (RU)

Gl IPN .... Glowny Instytut Paliw Naturalnych [Main Institute of Natural Fuels]   (POL)

GLIS .... Government Library and Information Service [Tasmania, Australia]

GLISCAC ... Government Library and Information Service Computer Applications Committee [Australia]

Gliss........... Glissando [Gliding] [Music]

GLITF .... Gay and Lesbian Immigration Task Force [Australia]

glits .... Glycine   (RU)

GLJ .... Global Getra Ltd. [Bulgaria] [ICAO designator]   (FAAC)

glk .... Commander in Chief   (BU)

GLK .... Genikon Logistirion Kratous [General State Accounting Office] [Greek]   (GC)

GLK .... Gleitkomma [German]   (ADPT)

GLK .... Glucokinase   (RU)

GLK .... Main Lumber Industry Committee   (RU)

gl kpl .... Eye Drops   (RU)

GLLB........ Buchanan [Liberia] [ICAO location identifier]   (ICLI)

GLM .... Gesellschaft fuer Lehr- und Lernmethoden [Association for Teaching and Learning Methods] [Switzerland]   (SLS)

GLM .... State Literary Museum   (RU)

GLMC....... Monrovia City [Liberia] [ICAO location identifier]   (ICLI)

GLMMS.... Groupement Latin et Mediterraneen de Medecine du Sport [Latin and Mediterranean Group for Sport Medicine - LMGSM]   (EAIO)

GLMR .... Monrovia/Spriggs Payne [Liberia] [ICAO location identifier]   (ICLI)

Gln .... Gleichungen [Equations] [German]   (GCA)

GLN .... Lennox Airways, Gambia Ltd. [ICAO designator]   (FAAC)

GLN .... Linear-Buildup Voltage Generator   (RU)

GLNA .... Nimba [Liberia] [ICAO location identifier]   (ICLI)

GLNSW..... Gould League of New South Wales [Australia]

GLO .... Gospel literature Outreach [Australia]

GLO .... Greens in Love [Political party] [Australia]

GLOAS...... German Liaison Office for the Armament Sector [Military]

gl obr .... Chiefly, Mostly, For the Most Part   (RU)

GLORIA.... Geological Long-Range Inclined ASDIC

GLOS .... Glossarium [Glossary] [Afrikaans]

Glos........... Gloucestershire   (IDIG)

gloss .... Glossario [Glossary] [Portuguese]

Glot........... Glotica [Linguistic] [Portuguese]

GLP .... Gasolina Liquido de Petroleo [Liquefied Petroleum Gas] [Use LPG]   (LA)

GLP .... Gor'kiy Steamship Line   (RU)

GLP .... Guadeloupe [ANSI three-letter standard code]   (CNC)

GLP .... Guyana Labour Party [Political party]   (EY)

GLP .... Linear Sawtooth Generator   (RU)

GLP .... State Forest Nursery   (RU)

GLP-AACR ... Gibraltar Labour Party - Association for the Advancement of Civil Rights [Political party]   (PPW)

GLPN .... Generator of Linearly Decreasing Voltage   (RU)

GLR .... Group Line Relay   (RU)

GLR .... Hospital for the Slightly Wounded   (RU)

GLRB........ Monrovia/Roberts International [Liberia] [ICAO location identifier]   (ICLI)

GLRC........ Grain Legumes Research Council [Australia]

GLRE......... Geniki Laiki Rizospastiki Enosis [General Union of Populists and Radicals] [Greek]   (PPE)

GLRL........ Gay and Lesbian Rights Lobby [Australia]

GLRN........ Generator of Linearly Increasing Voltage   (RU)

GLS........... Global International Ltd. [Bulgaria] [ICAO designator]   (FAAC)

GLS........... Sonar   (RU)

gl sch .... Main Accounting Office   (BU)

gl schet .... Chief Accountant   (BU)

GLSF .... Societe Georges Lesieur & Ses Fils
GLSFNRJ ... Glavni Lovacki Savez Federativna Narodna Republika Jugoslavija [*Central Association of Yugoslav Riflemen*] (YU)
GLSK .... Sanniquellie [*Liberia*] [*ICAO location identifier*] (ICLI)
gls-ka .... Main Account (BU)
GLSS .... Ghana Living Standards Survey
GLST .... Sasstown [*Liberia*] [*ICAO location identifier*] (ICLI)
GlStHrv ..... Glavni Stab Hrvatske [*Supreme Headquarters of Croatia*] [*World War II*] (YU)
GLT .... General Corporation for Light Air Transport & Technical Sevices [*Libya*] [*ICAO designator*] (FAAC)
GLT .... German Large Telescope [*Proposed, 1989*]
GLT .... Gladstone [*Australia*] [*Airport symbol*] (OAG)
GLTN .... Tchien [*Liberia*] [*ICAO location identifier*] (ICLI)
glts .... Glycerol, Glycerin (RU)
GLU .... Gambia Labour Union
GLU .... General Labor Unions [*Malaysia*]
GLU .... Grand Labor Union [*Philippines*] (EY)
GLU .... Gruene Liste Umweltschutz [*Green List Ecology*] [*Germany*] (PPE)
GLU .... Guyana Labor Union (LA)
Gl upr .... Main Administration, Main Directorate (RU)
GLV .... Gould League of Victoria [*Australia*]
GLVA .... Voinjama [*Liberia*] [*ICAO location identifier*] (ICLI)
glvp .... Judge Advocate General (BU)
Glwd .... Ganzleinwand [*Full Cloth*] [*Publishing*] [*German*]
GLX .... Galela [*Indonesia*] [*Airport symbol*] (OAG)
Glyz .... Glyzerin [*Glycerin*] [*German*] (GCA)
Glz .... Gleichzeitig [*Contemporary*] [*German*]
GLZ .... Grubenlampenwerk, Zwickau (VEB) [*Zwickau Mine Lamp Plant (VEB)*] (EG)
GLZ .... Lyubertsy State Agricultural Machinery Plant (RU)
GM .... Cigarette-Wrapping Machine (RU)
GM .... Gambia [*ANSI two-letter standard code*] (CNC)
GM .... Gamma Method (RU)
GM .... Geheimer Mitarbeiter [*Secret Collaborator*] (EG)
G-M .... Geiger-Mueller Counter (RU)
GM .... Genel Muduru [*Director General*] (TU)
GM .... General Major [*Major General*] (YU)
GM .... General Motor [*Bogota-Otras Ciudades*] (COL)
GM .... Genie Mobilier [*Military*] [*French*] (MTD)
GM .... Genio Militare [*Corps of Engineers*] [*Italian*] (WER)
GM .... Gentil Membre [*Guest of Club Mediterranee, a vacation cooperative*]
GM .... Geographic Position (RU)
gm .... Gmina [*Rural Commune*] (POL)
GM .... Goldmark [*Gold Marks*] [*German*]
GM .... Graafiset Muotoilijat [*Graphic Designers*] [*Finland*] (EAIO)
G-M .... Grand-Maitre [*Grand Master*] [*Freemasonry*] [*French*]
GM .... Gran Maestro [*Grand Master*] [*Freemasonry*] [*Italian*]
gm .... Guarda-Marinha [*Midshipman*] [*Portuguese*]
GM .... Gummifaden [*Rubber Thread*] [*German*] (GCA)
GM .... Guvenlik Mahkemesi [*Security Court*] (TU)
GM .... Gyro Pendulum (RU)
gm .... Hectometer (RU)
Gm .... Homogeneous [*Nuclear physics and engineering*] (RU)
gm .... Major General (BU)
GM .... Maleic Acid Hydrazide (RU)
GM .... Mining Machinery (RU)
GM100 .... Groupement Mobile 100 [*Elite French armed forces stationed in Vietnam*] (VNM)
GMA .... Garment Manufacturers' Association [*Australia*]
GMA .... Gazdasagi es Muszaki Akademia [*Academy of Economics and Technology*] (HU)
GMA .... Gemena [*Zaire*] [*Airport symbol*] (OAG)
GMA .... Generale de Mecanique Aeronautique [*French*]
GMA .... German Mathematical Association (EAIO)
GMA .... Gesamtverband der Metallindustriellen Arbeitgeberverbande [*Germany*] (EAIO)
GMA .... Ghana Manufacturers Association
GMA .... Good Morning Australia [*Television program*]
GMA .... Gospel Music Association
GMA .... Graduate Management Association [*Australia*]
GMA .... Grail Movement of Australia
GMA .... Grands Moulins d'Abidjan [*Ivory Coast*]
GMA .... Grocery Manufacturers of Australia (ADA)
GMA .... Groupe Mobile d'Alsace [*Alsace Mobile Group*] [*French Resistance Group*] [*World War II*]
GMA .... Guyana Manufacturers Association (LA)
GMAA .... Agadir/Inezgane [*Morocco*] [*ICAO location identifier*] (ICLI)
GMAA .... Graduate Management Association of Australia
GMAC .... Genetic Manipulation Advisory Committee [*Australia*]
GMAP .... Generelles Makro-Assemblierungsprogramm [*German*] (ADPT)
GMAT .... Tan-Tan/Plage Blanche [*Morocco*] [*ICAO location identifier*] (ICLI)

GMAWA ... Glass Merchants' Association of Western Australia
GMAZ .... Zagora [*Morocco*] [*ICAO location identifier*] (ICLI)
GMB .... Gambela [*Ethiopia*] [*Airport symbol*] (OAG)
GMB .... Gambia [*ANSI three-letter standard code*] (CNC)
GMB .... Goerlitzer Maschinenbau (VEB) [*Goerlitz Machine Construction Plant (VEB)*] (EG)
GMB .... Grain Marketing Board [*Rhodesian*] (AF)
GMB .... Grands Moulins du Benin
GMB .... Hydrometeorological Office (RU)
GMBF .... Gesellschaft fur Molekularbiologische Forschung [*Society for Molecular Biology Research*] [*Germany*] (PDAA)
GmbH .... Gesellschaft mit Beschraenkter Haftung [*Limited Liability Company*] [*German*]
GmbH &CoKG ... Gesellschaft mit Beschraenkter Haftung und Kommanditgesellschaft [*Combined Limited Partnership and Limited Liability Company*] [*German*]
GmbHG ..... Gesetz Betreffend die Gesellschaft mit Beschraenkter Haftung [*Law Governing Limited Liability Company*] [*German*] (ILCA)
GMC .... Gambia Muslim Congress
GMC .... Generale des Matieres Colorantes
GMC .... Gerner-Mathisen Chartering AS [*Norway*] (DS)
GMC .... Grands Moulins du Cameroun [*Great Mills of Cameroon*]
GMC .... Grands Moulins du Congo [*Great Mills of the Congo*] (AF)
GMC .... Guyana Marketing Corporation (LA)
GMCC .... General MISR Car Co. SAE [*General Motors and Egyptian joint venture*]
GMCh .... Guards Mortar Unit (RU)
GMCh .... Motorized Howitzer Unit (RU)
GMCM ...... Guided Missile Countermeasure [*NATO*]
GMCR .... Globe Mackay Cable and Radio Corp. [*Philippines*] [*Telecommunications*]
GMD .... Gemeenschappelijke Medische Dienst [*Community Medical Service*] [*Netherlands*] (WEN)
GMD .... Geologisch Mijnbouwkundige Dienst [*Geological and Mining Service*] [*Suriname*] [*Research center*] (EAS)
GMD .... Gesellschaft fuer Mathematik und Datenverarbeitung [*Society for Mathematics and Data Processing*] [*Germany*] [*Information service or system*] (IID)
GMD .... Grands Moulins de Dakar [*Great Mills of Dakar*]
GMD .... Guards Mortar Division (RU)
GMDITs ..... Hexamethylene Diisocyanate (RU)
GMD-IZ .... GMD-Informationszentrum fuer Informationswissenschaft und - Praxis [*GMD Information Center for Information Science and Information Work*] [*Information service or system*] (IID)
GMDOA .... Government Medical and Dental Officers Association [*Mauritius*] (AF)
GMDS .... Deutsche Gesellschaft fuer Medizinische Dokumentation, Informatik, und Statistik eV [*German Association for Medical Documentation, Information, and Statistics*] (SLS)
GMDTC .... Guyana Management Development and Training Centre
GME .... Gelatine Manufacturers of Europe (EAIO)
GME .... General Modern Enterprises [*Cameroon*]
GME .... State Museum of Ethnography (RU)
GMEA .... Groupement Medical d'Etudes sur l'Alcoolisme [*Medical Association for the Study of Alcoholism*] [*French*] (SLS)
GMEL .... Groupement des Mathematiciens d'Expression Latine [*Group of Mathematicians of Romance Languages - GMRL*] (EAIO)
GME-PC ... General Motors Europe - Passenger Cars [*Switzerland*]
GMF .... Ghorfet el Monchekat el Fondokia [*Egypt*] (EAIO)
GMF .... Groupement Mutuelle des Fonctionnaires [*Mutual Group of Officials*] [*France*]
GMF .... Guanosine Monophosphoric Acid (RU)
GMF .... State Museum Fund (RU)
GMF .... Vereinigung Getreide-, Markt-, und Ernaehrungsforschung eV [*Association of Grain, Market, and Food Research, Inc.*] (SLS)
GMFA .... Ouezzane [*Morocco*] [*ICAO location identifier*] (ICLI)
GMFF .... Fes/Saiss [*Morocco*] [*ICAO location identifier*] (ICLI)
GMFI .... Ifrane [*Morocco*] [*ICAO location identifier*] (ICLI)
GMFJ .... Ghana Movement of Freedom and Justice [*Political party*]
GMFK .... Er-Rachidia [*Morocco*] [*ICAO location identifier*] (ICLI)
GMFM .... Meknes/Bassatine [*Morocco*] [*ICAO location identifier*] (ICLI)
GMFMC ... Gulf of Mexico Fishery Management Council (MSC)
GMFN .... Nador/Taouima [*Morocco*] [*ICAO location identifier*] (ICLI)
GMFN .... Sodium Hexametaphosphate (RU)
GMFO .... Oujda/Angads [*Morocco*] [*ICAO location identifier*] (ICLI)
GMFT .... Touahar [*Morocco*] [*ICAO location identifier*] (ICLI)
GMFU .... Fes/Sefrou [*Morocco*] [*ICAO location identifier*] (ICLI)
GMFZ .... Taza [*Morocco*] [*ICAO location identifier*] (ICLI)
GMG .... Gott Mein Gut [*God Is My Good*] [*Motto of Karl, Margrave of Baden-Durlach (1529-77); Ernst Friedrich, (1560-1604)*] [*German*]
GMG .... State Museum of Georgia [*Former USSR*] (RU)
GMH .... General Motors-Holden's Ltd. [*Australia*] (ADA)

GMHA ...... General Motors Holden's Automotive [*Australia*]

GMI .... Gasmata [*Papua New Guinea*] [*Airport symbol*] (OAG)

GMI .... Germania Fluggesellschaft Koln [*Germany*] [*ICAO designator*] (FAAC)

GMI .... Gor'kiy Medical Institute Imeni S. M. Kirov (RU)

GMI .... State Meat Inspection (RU)

GMII .... State Museum of Fine Arts Imeni A. S. Pushkin (RU)

GMIL .... State Museum of the History of Leningrad (RU)

GMIP .... Depth Manometer Recording Absorption Intensity (RU)

GMIZ .... Gor'kiy Medical Instrument Plant Imeni M. Gor'kiy (RU)

GMK.......... Generator of Mechanical Oscillations (RU)

GMK.......... Gold Mines of Kalgoorlie [*Australia*] (ADA)

GMK.......... Guards Mechanized Corps (RU)

GMK.......... Gyro Magnetic Compass (RU)

GMK.......... Hydrometeorological Committee (RU)

GMK.......... International Geological Congress (RU)

GMK.......... Maleic Hydrazide (RU)

GMKI .... Gerakan Mahasiswa Keristen Indonesia [*Indonesian Christian College Students Movement*] (IN)

GML .... Gemial [*Slovakia*] [*ICAO designator*] (FAAC)

GML .... Goldrich Maritime Line (DS)

GMM.......... Gerakan Mahasiswa Marhaen [*Marhaenist College Students Movement*] (IN)

GMMB ...... Ben Slimane [*Morocco*] [*ICAO location identifier*] (ICLI)

GMMC....... Casablanca/ANFA [*Morocco*] [*ICAO location identifier*] (ICLI)

GMMD...... Beni-Mellal [*Morocco*] [*ICAO location identifier*] (ICLI)

GMME...... Rabat/Sale [*Morocco*] [*ICAO location identifier*] (ICLI)

GMMF ...... Sidi Ifni [*Morocco*] [*ICAO location identifier*] (ICLI)

GMMI .... Essaouira [*Morocco*] [*ICAO location identifier*] (ICLI)

GMMJ ...... El Jadida [*Morocco*] [*ICAO location identifier*] (ICLI)

GMMK...... Khouribga [*Morocco*] [*ICAO location identifier*] (ICLI)

GMMM..... Casablanca [*Morocco*] [*ICAO location identifier*] (ICLI)

GMMN ..... Casablanca/Mohamed V [*Morocco*] [*ICAO location identifier*] (ICLI)

GMMO ..... Taroudant [*Morocco*] [*ICAO location identifier*] (ICLI)

GMMS ...... Safi [*Morocco*] [*ICAO location identifier*] (ICLI)

GMMT ...... Casablanca/Tit-Mellil [*Morocco*] [*ICAO location identifier*] (ICLI)

GMMTA ... Groupement des Moyens Militaires de Transport Aerien [*French*]

GMMX...... Marrakech/Menara [*Morocco*] [*ICAO location identifier*] (ICLI)

GMMY...... Kenitra/Tourisme [*Morocco*] [*ICAO location identifier*] (ICLI)

GMMZ...... Quarzazate [*Morocco*] [*ICAO location identifier*] (ICLI)

GMN .... Grands Moulins de Nouakchott [*Great Mills of Nouakchott*]

GMN .... Monitor, Hydraulic Excavator (RU)

GMNI........ Gerakan Mahasiswa Nasional Indonesia [*Indonesian National College Students Movement*] (IN)

GMNII ...... Mining and Metallurgical Scientific Research Institute (RU)

GMO .... Dead Storage Level [*of a reservoir*] (RU)

GMO .... Hydrometeorological Observatory (RU)

GMOChAM ... Hydrometeorological Observatory of the Black and Azov Seas (RU)

g-mol' .... Gram Molecule (RU)

g-Mol .... Grammolekuel [*Gram Molecule*] [*German*]

GmOR........ Homogeneous Research Reactor (RU)

GMP.......... Grands Moulins de Paris [*Great Mills of Paris*]

GMP.......... Groupements Mutualistes du Progres

GMP.......... Groupe Motopropulseur [*Military*] [*French*] (MTD)

GMP.......... Guards Mortar Regiment (RU)

Gmp .... Gueterzug mit Personenbefoerderung [*Freight Train with Passenger Transportation Facilities*] (EG)

GMP.......... Hydromechanical Gear, Hydromechanical Transmission (RU)

GMP.......... Hydrometeorological Station (RU)

GMP.......... Main Medical Aid Station (RU)

GMPA .... Game Meat Processors of Australia

GMPCA ..... Groupe des Methodes Physiques et Chimiques de l'Archeologie [*Association of Physical and Chemical Methods of Archeology*] [*French*] (SLS)

GMPCS..... Global Mobile Personal Communications System [*International Telecommunications Union*] [*Geneva, Switzerland*] (ECON)

GMPI .... Groupe Mobile de Premiere Intervention [*Mobile First Intervention Group*] [*Algeria*] (AF)

GMPI .... State Music Pedagogical Institute Imeni Gnesiny (RU)

GMPR .... Groupes Mobiles de Protection Rurale [*Algeria*]

GMQ .... Graduate Management Qualification [*University of Tasmania*] [*Australia*]

GMR.......... Gambier Island [*French Polynesia*] [*Airport symbol*] (OAG)

GMR.......... Gouvernement Militaire Revolutionnaire [*Military Revolutionary Government*] [*Benin*] (AF)

GMR.......... Great Man-Made River Authority [*Libya*] (EY)

GMR.......... Grupo Marxista Revolucionario [*Marxist Revolutionary Group*] [*Portuguese*] [*Political party*] (PPE)

GMRD....... Geological and Mineral Resources Department [*Sudan*] [*Research center*] (WED)

GMRITI .... Guangzhou Municipal Research Institute of the Textile Industry [*China*] (IRC)

GMRL .... Group of Mathematicians of Romance Languages [*See also GMEL*] [*Coimbra, Portugal*] (EAIO)

GMRT .... Giant Meterwave Radio Telescope [*India*]

GMRWS.... Geology, Mines, and Rural Water Supplies [*Department of*] [*Vanuatu*] [*Research center*] (EAS)

GMS .... Erasing Magnetic Head (RU)

GMS .... Geographic Position of a Heavenly Body (RU)

GMS .... George MacDonald Society [*Lincoln, England*] (EAIO)

GMS .... Geostationary Meteorological Satellite [*Japan*]

GMS .... German Mozart Society (EAIO)

GMS .... Government Motor Services [*New South Wales, Australia*]

GMS .... Groupement de Missiles Strategiques [*Strategic Missiles Group*] [*French*] (WER)

GMs .... Gussmessing [*Cast Brass*] [*German*] (GCA)

GMS .... Hydrometeorological Service [*or Station*] (RU)

GMSA .... General Motors South African

GMSL....... Sidi Slimane [*Morocco*] [*ICAO location identifier*] (ICLI)

GMSOS..... Gerakan Mahasiswa Sosialis [*Socialist College Students Movement*] (IN)

gm st.......... Hydrometeorological Station [*Topography*] (RU)

GMT .... Gornja Mrtva Tacka [*Upper Dead Center*] [*Engine*] (YU)

GMT .... Governor Macquarie Tower [*Sydney, New South Wales, Australia*]

GMT .... Grands Moulins du Tchad [*Great Mills of Chad*]

GMT .... Greenwich Mean Time (SCAC)

GMT .... Hexamethylenetetramine (RU)

GMT .... Locus, Geometric Locus of Points (RU)

GMT .... Methane Gas Detector (RU)

GMT .... Societe des Generale des Moulins du Togo

GMT .... Societe Generale du Mecanique et Thermique [*Tunisia*]

gmt .... Top Dead Center [*Military*] (BU)

GMTA .... Al Hoceima/Cote Du Rif [*Morocco*] [*ICAO location identifier*] (ICLI)

Gmtebest.... Gemeentebestuur, Maandschrift der Vereeniging van Nederlandsche Gemeenten [*Netherlands*] (BAS)

GMTN....... Tetouan/Sania R'Mel [*Morocco*] [*ICAO location identifier*] (ICLI)

GMTs .... Gidrometeorologicheskyy Nauchno Issledovatelskiy Tsenter [*Scientific Research Research Center for Hydrometeorology*] [*Former USSR*] (PDAA)

GMTT .... Tanger/Boukhalf [*Morocco*] [*ICAO location identifier*] (ICLI)

GMU .... Gadjah Mada University [*Indonesian*]

GMU .... Gospel Missionary Union

GMV.......... Grands Moulins Voltaiques

GMV.......... Grimaldi Mekaniska Verkstaf [*Steel finishing company*] [*Sweden*]

GMV.......... Low-Water Line, Low-Water Level (RU)

GMV.......... Meter-Wave Generator (RU)

GMV.......... Reproducing Magnetic Head (RU)

GMVO...... Royal Grand Master of the Order of Victoria [*Australia*]

Gmw .... Gemeentewet [*Benelux*] (BAS)

GMWOAM ... German Medical Welfare Organisation, Action Medeor (EAIO)

GMWU...... Guyana Mine Workers Union (LA)

GMZ.......... Gor'kiy Metallurgical Plant (RU)

GMZ.......... Gor'kiy Motorcycle Plant (RU)

GMZ.......... Gorlovka Machinery Plant (RU)

GMZ.......... Gur'yev Machine Plant (RU)

GMZ.......... Hydromechanical Lock (RU)

GMZ.......... Mine-Laying and Obstacle Group (RU)

GMZ.......... Vereniging voor den Graan-, Meel- en Zaadhandel [*Benelux*] (BAS)

GN .... Directional Gyro (RU)

GN .... Gas Detector for Command Personnel (RU)

GN .... Gas Heat Exchanger [*Nuclear physics and engineering*] (RU)

GN .... Gendarmerie Nationale [*National Gendarmerie*] [*Replaced GRK Cambodia*] (CL)

Gn .... Genel [*General*] [*Turkey*] (GPO)

GN .... Genio Navale [*Engineer branch of Italian navy*]

Gn .... Gradevinarstvo [*Building Industry*] (YU)

GN .... Gradevinske Norme [*Building Standards*] (YU)

gn .... Grenade (BU)

GN .... Guinea [*ANSI two-letter standard code*] (CNC)

gn .... Henry (RU)

GN .... Hydraulic Pump (RU)

gn .... Mister (RU)

GNA.......... Ghana National Archives

GNA.......... Ghana News Agency

GNA.......... Gnangara [*Australia*] [*Geomagnetic observatory code*]

GNA.......... Grand National Assembly [*Bulgaria*] (EE)

GNA.......... Grupos No-Alineados [*Non-Aligned Groups*] [*Spanish*] (WER)

GNA.......... Gulf News Agency

GNA.......... Guyana News Agency (LA)

GNA.......... Guyana Nurses Association (LA)

GNAC....... Groupement National d'Achat des Cafes [*France*]   (FLAF)
GNAPO..... Groupement National d'Achat des Produits Oleagineux [*France*]
     (FLAF)
GNAR....... Groupement National d'Achat du Riz [*France*]   (FLAF)
GNASII ..... Gruppo Nazionale di Sistemistica e di Informatica
     dell'Ingegneria [*National Research Group for Computer and
     Systems Engineering Sciences*] [*Consiglio Nazionale delle
     Ricerche Rome, Italy*] [*Research center*]   (ERC)
GNASOC .. Ghana National Society of the Crippled   (EAIO)
GNAT....... Ghana National Association of Teachers
GNAT....... Groupement National d'Achat des Tourteaux [*France*]   (FLAF)
GNB.......... Gambia News Bulletin
GNB.......... Global Air Link [*Nigeria*] [*ICAO designator*]   (FAAC)
GNB.......... Grenoble [*France*] [*Airport symbol*]   (OAG)
GNB.......... Guinea-Bissau [*ANSI three-letter standard code*]   (CNC)
GNB.......... State Scientific and Technical Library   (RU)
GNC.......... Gambia National Congress
GNC.......... Godisnjak Nikole Cupica [*Nikola Cupic Yearbook*] [*Belgrade A
     periodical*]   (YU)
GNCB .... Guyana National Cooperative Bank   (LA)
GNCC .... Ghana National Chamber of Commerce
GNCD....... Grenada National Council of the Disabled   (EAIO)
GNCh....... Carrier-Frequency Generator, Low-Frequency Generator   (RU)
GNCSA ..... Good Neighbour Council of South Australia
GNCT .... Good Neighbour Council of Tasmania [*Australia*]
GND .... Grenada [*Windward Islands*] [*Airport symbol*]   (OAG)
GNDE....... Ghana National Dance Ensemble
GNE.......... Gross National Expenditure
GNEC .... Guyana National Engineering Corporation   (LA)
GNERI ...... Gansu Natural Energy Research Institute [*China*]   (WED)
GNFPP...... Ghana National Family Planning Programme
GNFU .... Ghana National Farmers Union
GNG .... Grupe za Neposredno Gadanje [*Groups for Direct Firing*]
     [*Military*]   (YU)
GNI........... Gross National Income
GNI........... Groznyy Petroleum Institute   (RU)
GNIC .... Guangdong Nuclear Investment Company [*Hong Kong*]
GNIGI ...... State Scientific Research Institute of Geophysics   (RU)
GNIGK ...... State Scientific Research Institute of Geodesy and Cartography
     (RU)
GNII .... State Scientific Research Institute   (RU)
GNIIGlaz... State Scientific Research Institute of Eye Diseases Imeni
     Gel'mgol'ts   (RU)
GNIIKhP ... State Scientific Research Institute of the Chemical Industry
     (RU)
GNIIS........ State Scientific Research Institute of Glass   (RU)
GNIISM .... State Scientific Research Institute of Forensic Medicine   (RU)
GNIIT....... State Scientific Research Institute of Tuberculosis   (RU)
GNIIVitamin ... State Scientific Research Institute of Vitaminology   (RU)
GNILICOM ... Le Comptoir de Gnilil [*Senegal*]
GNIOM...... State Scientific Institute of Mother and Child Welfare   (RU)
GNIOMM ... State Scientific Institute of Mother and Child Welfare   (RU)
GNIRRI..... State Scientific Research Institute of Roentgenology and
     Radiology   (RU)
GNIS .... Groupement National Interprofessionnel des Semences, Graines
     et Plants [*France*]   (FLAF)
GNISE....... "Soviet Encyclopedia" State Scientific Institute   (RU)
GNISI........ State Scientific Research Institute of Sanitation Imeni F. F.
     Erisman   (RU)
GNIU .... State Scientific Institute of Coal   (RU)
GNK.......... Gamma-Neutron Logging   (RU)
GnKh .... Genel Karargah [*General Headquarters*]   (TU)
GNKI .... State Control Scientific Research Institute of Veterinary
     Preparations   (RU)
GNKUR..... Genel Kurmay [*General Staff*]   (TU)
GNKURB .. Genel Kurmay Baskanligi [*Chief of the General Staff*]   (TU)
GNL........ Gaz Naturel Liquefie [*Liquified Natural Gas*] [*Use LNG*]   (AF)
Gnl .... General [*General*]   (TU)
GNL......... Low Ice-Floe Level   (RU)
GNLF .... Gurkha National Liberation Front [*Political party*] [*India*]
Gnlk .... Gunluk [*Daily*]   (TU)
GNM .... Gamma-Neutron Method   (RU)
GNM .... Guanambi [*Brazil*] [*Airport symbol*]   (OAG)
GNMB....... State Scientific Medical Library   (RU)
GNMC...... Ghana National Manganese Corporation
GNNCh ..... Low-Frequency Voltage Generator   (RU)
GNNE....... Guild of Nigerian Newspaper Editors   (AF)
GNO .... Gradski Narodni Odbor [*City People's Committee*]   (YU)
GNOE....... Gabinete Nacionale de Organizacao de Eleicoes [*National
     Election Office*] [*Mozambique*]   (AF)
GNOI........ General National Organization for Industrialization [*Libya*]
     (GEA)
GNOT....... Grand National Open Teams [*Bridge*] [*Australia*]
GNP.......... Close Support Party [*Military*]   (BU)
GNP.......... Geonuclear Nobel Paso [*France*]   (PDAA)
GNP.......... Good Neighbour Program [*Australia*]

GNP.......... Grenada National Party [*Political party*]   (PPW)
GNP.......... Gross National Product   (OMWE)
GNPA........ Ghana National Procurement Agency
GNPL .... Groupement National d'Achat des Produits Laitiers [*France*]
     (FLAF)
GNPP .... Great Nigeria People's Party [*Political party*]   (PPW)
GNQ .... Equatorial Guinea [*ANSI three-letter standard code*]   (CNC)
GNR.......... General Roca [*Argentina*] [*Airport symbol*]   (OAG)
GNR.......... Geographical Names Register [*Department of Lands*] [*New South
     Wales, Australia*]
GNR.......... Guarda Nacional Republicana [*Republican National Guard*]
     [*Portuguese*]   (WER)
GNR.......... Sodium-Graphite Reactor   (RU)
GNRA........ Guyana Natural Resources Agency   (EY)
GNRC .... Ghana National Reconstruction Corps
GNRC .... Guyana National Relief Committee   (LA)
GNRR........ Guineiskaia Narodnaia Revoliutsionnaia Respublika
GNS.......... City People's Council   (BU)
GNS.......... Gas Filling Station   (RU)
GNS.......... General Naval Staff [*NATO*]   (NATG)
GNS.......... Gesellschaft fuer Nuklear-Service, mbH [*Nuclear energy*]
     (NRCH)
GNS.......... Group of Negotiations on Services [*European Community*]
GNS.......... Guyana National Service   (LA)
GNS.......... Gyro Navigation System   (RU)
GNSDT ..... City People's Council of Workers' Deputies   (BU)
GNSM .... Gruppo Nazionale di Struttura della Materia [*National Research
     Group for the Structure of Matter*] [*Research center*] [*Italy*]
     (IRC)
GNSP........ Guardia Nacional de Seguridad Publica [*National Guard for
     Public Security*] [*Bolivia*]   (LA)
GNSW .... Governor of New South Wales [*Australia*]
GNSWBR ... Great New South Wales Bike Ride [*Australia*]
GNT.......... Gesellschaft fur Nuklear-Transporte [*Germany*]   (PDAA)
GNT.......... Great Northern Tanning Co. Ltd. [*Nigeria*]
GNTB .... State Scientific and Technical Library   (RU)
GNTC .... Ghana National Trading Corporation
gnte .... Gerente [*Manager*] [*Spanish*]
GNTI .... State Scientific and Technical Publishing House   (RU)
GNTIU ...... State Scientific and Technical Publishing House of the Ukraine
     (RU)
GNTK .... State Scientific and Technical Committee   (RU)
GNTO....... National Tourist Organization of Greece   (EAIO)
GNU .... Underground Heaters [*Pet.*]   (RU)
GNUTSEARCH ... National Research Centre for Groundnuts [*India*]   (IRC)
GNV.......... Downstream Water Line, Downstream Water Level, Level of
     Tail Water, Low-Water Level   (RU)
GNV.......... Gesellschaft fuer Nukleare Verfahrenstechnik [*Commercial firm*]
GNV.......... Grupos de No-Violentos [*Non-Violent Groups*] [*Spanish*]
     (WER)
GNWA....... Gwelo Native Welfare Association
GNY .... German Navy [*ICAO designator*]   (FAAC)
GNYC........ Ghana National Youth Council
GO .... Advance Detachment   (RU)
GO .... Canada - Transport Canada [*Canada ICAO designator*]   (ICDA)
GO .... City Branch Office [*Communications*]   (RU)
GO .... Civil Defense   (RU)
GO .... Course Reading   (RU)
GO .... Estado de Goias [*State of Goias*] [*Brazil*]
GO .... Gemeenschappelijke Opleiding voor Archief, Bibliotheek,
     Documentatie- en Informatiebewerking ['*s-Gravenhage*]
GO .... Generale Occidental [*Compagnie Generale d'Electricite*]
     [*Commercial firm*] [*France*]
GO .... Generalni Oprava [*General Repair*]   (CZ)
GO .... Generaloberst [*Full General*] [*German military - World War II*]
GO .... Gentil Organisateur [*Genial Host*] [*Employee of Club
     Mediterranee, a vacation cooperative*]
GO .... Geographic Society
GO .... Gerilski Odredi [*Guerrilla Detachments*] [*World War II*]   (YU)
GO .... Gesellschaft fur Okologie [*Germany*]   (EAIO)
GO .... Gewerbeordnung [*Trade Regulation*] [*German*]   (GCA)
GO .... Glavni Odbor [*Central Committee*]   (YU)
GO .... Gorizia [*Car registration plates*] [*Italian*]
GO .... Grandes Ondes [*Long Waves*] [*Radio*] [*French*]
GO .... Grand-Officier [*Grand Officer of the Legion of Honor*]
     [*Freemasonry*] [*French*]   (MTD)
GO .... Groepsgemeenschap-Ordonnantie [*Benelux*]   (BAS)
GO .... Grundorganisation [*Basic Organization*]   (EG)
GO .... Main Winding   (RU)
GOA.......... Gebuehrenordnung fuer Architekten [*Scale of Fees for Architects*]
     (EG)
GOA.......... Genoa [*Italy*] [*Airport symbol*]   (OAG)
GOA.......... Government of Australia
GOA.......... Grupos Obreros Autonomos [*Autonomous Workers Groups*]
     [*Spanish*]   (WER)
GOA.......... Optical and Acoustical Gas Analyzer   (RU)

GOAC........ Graduate Office and Alumni Centre [*University of New South Wales*] [*Australia*]

GOAFZM ... Glaven Odbor na Antifasistickiot Front na Zenite od Makedonija [*Central Committee of the Women's Anti-Fascist Front of Macedonia*] (YU)

GOB........... Gobble (DSUE)

GOB........... Government of Botswana

GoB............ Grundsaetze Ordnungsmassiger Buchfuehrung [*Proper Accounting Principles*] [*Germany*]

GOB........... Hemato-Ophthalmic Barrier (RU)

GOBI........ Growth Monitoring, Oral Rehydration, Breastfeeding, and Immunization [*Program*] [*UNICEF plan to reduce child mortality in Third World countries*]

GOBLL...... Glowny Osrodek Badan Lotniczo-Lekarskich [*Main Center of Aviation Medicine Research*] (POL)

Gobno........ Gobierno [*Government*] [*Spanish*]

gobo........... Gobierno [*Government*] [*Spanish*]

g-obr........... Gaseous, Gasiform (RU)

Gobr........... Gobernador [*Governor*] [*Spanish*]

GOBSI........ Gerakan Organisasi Buruh Syarikat Islam Indonesia (EAIO)

GOBSII..... Gabungan Organisasi Buruh Serikat Islam Indonesia [*Federation of Indonesian Moslem Trade and Labor Unions*]

GOBSIINDO ... Gabungan Organisasi Buruh Serikat Islam Indonesia [*Federation of Indonesian Islamic Alliance Labor Organizations*] [*Also known as GOBSII*] (IN)

GOC........... Gora [*Papua New Guinea*] [*Airport symbol*] (OAG)

GOC........... Government of Cyprus

GOC........... Grosseinkaufsgesellschaft Osterreichischer Cunsumvereine [*Austria*] (PDAA)

GOC........... Guatemalan Olympic Committee (EAIO)

GOCA........ Groupement des Organismes de Controle Automobiles [*Association of Automobile Inspection Organizations*] [*Belgium*] (PDAA)

GOCC........ Government-Controlled Corporation [*Philippines*]

GOCM........ Groupe Ophtalmologique Chirurgical Mobile

GOCMV .... Greek Orthodox Community of Melbourne and Victoria [*Australia*]

GOCNAE .. Grupo de Organizacao da Comissao Nacional de Atividades Espaciais [*Organizing Group of the National Commission on Space Activities*] [*Brazil*] (LA)

GOCR........ Groupe Operationnel de la Croix-Rouge pour l'Indochine [*Red Cross Operational Group for Indochina*] (CL)

GOCS .... Gordulocsapagy Gyar, Debrecen [*Roller Bearing Plant of Debrecen*] (HU)

God............. Annals [*Annual Publication*] (BU)

god............. Anniversary (BU)

god............. Godina [*Year*] (YU)

GoD........... Grundsaetze Ordnungsgemaesser [*German*] (ADPT)

god............. Year (BU)

GODCA..... Gabinete de Organizacao e Desenvolvimento das Cooperativas Agricolas [*Department for the Organization and Development of Agricultural Cooperatives*] [*Mozambique*] (AF)

GODE........ Gulf Organisation for the Development of Egypt

GODE........ Gulf Organization for Development in Egypt

GodisnikSNOI ... Godisnik. Sumarsko Naucno Opiten Institut [*Yearbook of the Forestry Research Institute*] [*Skopje*] (YU)

GodisnjakBI ... Godisnjak Bioloskog Instituta u Sarajevu [*Yearbook of the Biological Institute in Sarajevo*] (YU)

GODOS..... Geniki Dievthinsis Diethnon Oikonomikon Skheseon [*General Directorate of International Economic Relations*] (GC)

GODR........ Government of the Dominican Republic (IMH)

GODSA..... Gabinete de Orientacion y Documentacion, SA [*Documentation and Orientation Office, Inc.*] [*Spanish*] (WER)

GodSAN .... Godisnjak Srpske Kraljevske Akademije Nauka [*Yearbook of the Serbian Royal Academy of Sciences*] [*Belgrade*] (YU)

godz........... Godzina [*O'Clock, Hour*] (POL)

GODZS..... Godisnjak Zaduzbine Save i Vase Stojanovica Mostarca [*Yearbook of the Foundation of Sava i Vasa Stojanovic of Mostar*] [*Belgrade*] (YU)

GOE........... Gare Origine d'Etapes [*Military*] [*French*] (MTD)

GOE........... Gonalia [*Papua New Guinea*] [*Airport symbol*] (OAG)

GOEDEB .. General Organization for the Exploitation and Development of the Euphrates Basin [*Syria*] (EY)

GOELRO .. State Commission for the Electrification of Russia [*1920*] (RU)

GOES .... Grupo de Operaciones Especiales [*Special Operations Group*] [*Colorado*] (LA)

GOEV .... Genikos Organismos Engeion Veltioseon [*General Organization for Land Reclamation*] [*Greek*] (GC)

GoeV .... Gesetz ueber die Oertlichen Volksvertretungen [*Law on Local People's Representations*] (EG)

GOEW .... Goewerneur [*Governor*] [*Afrikaans*]

goewt.......... Goewerment [*Government*] [*Afrikaans*]

GOFAT ..... Groupe des Officiers des Forces Armees Tchadiennes [*Officers Group of the Chadian Armed Forces*] (AF)

GOFI .... General Organization for Industrialization [*Egypt*] (IMH)

GOFSM..... Glaven Odbor na Fiskulturniot Savez na Makedonija [*Central Committee of the Physical Culture Union of Macedonia*] (YU)

GOGECA .. Comite Generale de la Cooperation Agricole de la CEE [*General Committee of Agricultural Cooperation of the European Economic Community*] (PDAA)

GOGG .... Ziguinchor [*Senegal*] [*ICAO location identifier*] (ICLI)

GOGK........ Kolda [*Senegal*] [*ICAO location identifier*] (ICLI)

GOGRES... Gor'kiy State Regional Electric Power Plant (RU)

GOGS........ Cap Skirring [*Senegal*] [*ICAO location identifier*] (ICLI)

GOH .... Godthaab [*Denmark*] [*Airport symbol*]

GOH .... Government of Honduras

GOH .... Nuuk [*Greenland*] [*Airport symbol*] (OAG)

GOHBPR .. General Organization for Housing, Building, and Planning Research [*Egypt*] [*Research center*] (IRC)

GOI........... Gebuehrenordnung fuer Ingenieure [*Scale of Fees for Engineers*] (EG)

GOI........... Goa [*India*] [*Airport symbol*] (OAG)

GOI........... Government of India

GOI........... Government of Indonesia (IMH)

GOI........... Government of Iran

GOI........... Government of Israel

GOI........... Single-Pulse Generator (RU)

GOI........... State Institute of Optics Imeni S. I. Vavilov (RU)

GOI........... State Scientific Research Institute of Oncology Imeni P. A. Gertsen (RU)

GOIC .... Government of Ivory Coast

GOIC .... Gulf Organization for Industrial Consulting [*Doha, Qatar*] (EAIO)

GOICEM... General Officer in Command East Malaysia (ML)

GOICWM ... General Officer in Command West Malaysia (ML)

GOIFE .... Government of Israel Furnished Equipment

GOIL .... Ghana Oil Co.

GOIN......... Gosudarstvennyy Okeanografichesky Institut [*State Oceanographic Institute*] [*Russian*] (MSC)

GOIN......... Government of India Nominees [*Nonresident students*]

GOK.......... Genikos Oikodomikos Kanonismos Kratous [*General State Building Regulations*] [*Greek*] (GC)

GOK.......... Government of Kuwait (IMH)

GOK.......... Mining and Concentration Kombinat (RU)

Gokaroren ... Goseikagaku-Sangyo Rodokumiai Rengo [*Japanese Federation of Synthetic Chemical Workers' Union*]

GOKhI....... State Agricultural Publishing House (RU)

GOKhP...... Main Administration of the Basic Chemical Industry (RU)

GOkhR...... Gas-Cooled Reactor (RU)

Gokhran..... State Repository for Precious Metals (RU)

GOKO .... State Defense Committee [*1941-1945*] (RU)

GOL .... Deepwater Oceanographic Winch (RU)

gol.............. Dutch (RU)

GOL........... Government of Liberia

GOL........... Grundorganisationsleitung [*Management of Basic Organizations*] (EG)

gold .... Golden [*German*] (GCA)

GoldCoast CAE ... Gold Coast College of Advanced Education [*Australia*]

Goldfil........ Goldfileten [*Gold Fillets*] [*Publishing*] [*German*]

goldgedr ..... Goldgedruckt [*Printed with Gold*] [*Publishing*] [*German*]

Goldpr........ Goldpraegung [*Gold Stamping*] [*Publishing*] [*German*]

Goldschn.... Goldschnitt [*Gilt Edges*] [*Bookbinding*] [*German*]

goldverz...... Goldverziert [*Decorated with Gold*] [*Publishing*] [*German*]

GOLE .... Groupement Operationnel de la Legion Etrangere [*Operational Group of the Foreign Legion*] [*French*] (WER)

GOLEM .... Grossspeicherorientierte Listenorganisierte Ermittlungsmethode [*Information retrieval*]

golf .... Golfpeli [*Golf*] [*Finland*]

GOLKAR .. Sekber Golongan Karya [*Joint Secretariat of Functional Groups*] [*Indonesia*] [*Political party*] (PPW)

goll .... Dutch (RU)

GOLPOL... Golongan Politik [*Political group (The members of Parliament who represent political parties, as opposed to GOLKAR)*] (IN)

GOLS .... Carrier Pigeon Station (RU)

GOM .... City Militia Station (RU)

GOM .... Gemeenschappelijk Overleg Medefinanciering [*Netherlands*]

GOM .... Gminny Osrodek Maszynowy [*Rural Commune Machinery Station*] (POL)

GOM .... Goma [*Zaire*] [*Airport symbol*] (OAG)

GOM .... Government of Malawi

GOM .... Government of Mauritania

GOM .... Government of Mauritius

GOMAC.... Groupement des Opticiens du Marche Commun [*Common Market Opticians' Group*] [*Paris, France*]

GOMB........ Gambia Oilseeds Marketing Board (AF)

GOMB-TEX ... Gomb- es Textilfeldolgozo Haziipari Termelo Szovetkezet [*Cooperative for Home Production of Buttons and Clothing Accessories*] (HU)

Gomel'sel'mash ... Gomel' Agricultural Machinery Plant (RU)

GOMETs .. State Music, Stage, and Circus Association   (RU)
gomog......... Homogeneous   (RU)
GOMP...... Groupement d'Outre-Mer Pharmaceutique
GOMPCI... Groupement Pharmaceutique de Cote-D'Ivoire
GOMPLA ... Industria Gomez Plata Ltda. [*Barranquilla*]   (COL)
Gomsel'mash ... Gomel' Agricultural Machinery Plant   (RU)
GOMT....... General Organisation for Maritime Transport [*Libya*]
GOMZ....... State Optical Instrument Plant   (RU)
GOMZ....... State United Machinery Plants   (RU)
GOMZA ..... State United Machinery Plants   (RU)
GOMZY .... State United Machinery Plants   (RU)
Gon............ Gonderen [*Sender*] [*of a letter*]   (TU)
GON .... Gonni Air Services Ltd. [*Suriname*] [*ICAO designator*]   (FAAC)
GON .... Gorska Odznaka Narciarska [*Mountain Ski Badge*]   (POL)
GON .... Government of Niger
gon............. Pottery Plant [*Topography*]   (RU)
GON .... Reference Voltage Generator   (RU)
gonch.......... Pottery Plant [*Topography*]   (RU)
gond............ Gondozo [*Caretaker*]   (HU)
gondn .... Gondnok [*Guardian, Curator*]   (HU)
GONFM .... Glaven Odbor na Narodniot Front na Makedonija [*Central Committee of the National Front of Macedonia*]   (YU)
GONG .... Groupe d'Organisation Nationale Guadeloupeenne [*Guadeloupe*]   (PD)
GONMM .. Glaven Odbor na Narodnata Mladina na Makedonija [*Central Committee of the People's Youth of Macedonia*]   (YU)
GONTI ...... State Joint Scientific and Technical Publishing House   (RU)
GOO .... Goondiwindi [*Australia*] [*Airport symbol*]   (OAG)
GOOD ...... Diourbel [*Senegal*] [*ICAO location identifier*]   (ICLI)
GOOG ...... Linguere [*Senegal*] [*ICAO location identifier*]   (ICLI)
GOOK ...... Kaolack [*Senegal*] [*ICAO location identifier*]   (ICLI)
GOOO ...... Dakar [*Senegal*] [*ICAO location identifier*]   (ICLI)
GOOS........ Global Ocean Observation System   (ECON)
GOOV ...... Dakar [*Senegal*] [*ICAO location identifier*]   (ICLI)
GOOY ...... Dakar/Yoff [*Senegal*] [*ICAO location identifier*]   (ICLI)
GOP.......... Gabinet Ochrony Pracy [*Office of Labor Safety*]   (POL)
GOP.......... Genetically Homogeneous Surface   (RU)
GOP.......... Gorakhpur [*India*] [*Airport symbol*]   (OAG)
GOP.......... Gornoslaski Okreg Przemyslowy [*Upper Silesia Industrial District*]   (POL)
GOP.......... Gorski Okreg Przemyslowy [*Mountain Industrial District*]   (POL)
GOP.......... Government of Pakistan   (ECON)
GOP.......... Government of Peru   (IMH)
GOP.......... Government of the Philippines   (IMH)
GOP.......... Gromadzka Organizacja Partyjna [*Gromada Party Organization*]   (POL)
GOPA .... Gesellschaft fuer Organisation, Planning, und Ausbildung
GOPAC ..... Government Offsets and Procurement Advisory Committee [*Australia*]
GOPDEI.... Geniki Omospondia Prosopikou Dimosias Epikheiriseos Ilektrismou [*General Federation of Public Power Corporation Personnel*]   (GC)
GOPEC..... Group Operationnel d'Etudes et de Concertation
GOPEP..... Advanced Section of a Field Evacuation Station   (RU)
GOPERNAS ... Gabungan Organisasi Perusahaan Nasional Swasta [*Federation of Private National Business Firms*]   (IN)
GOPR .... Gorskie Ochotnicze Pogotowie Ratunkowe [*Volunteer Mountain Rescue Service*]   (POL)
GOPRINT ... Government Printer [*Queensland, Australia*]
GOQ .... Golmud [*China*] [*Airport symbol*]   (OAG)
gor .... City, Municipal, Town, Urban   (RU)
GOR.......... Gas-Cooled Reactor   (RU)
GOR.......... Gordo [*Race of maize*] [*Mexico*]
GOR......... Gore [*Ethiopia*] [*Airport symbol*]   (OAG)
GOR.......... Gor'kiy Railroad   (RU)
gor .... Gorog [*Greek*]   (HU)
GOR.......... Groupe Ouvrier Revolutionnaire [*Revolutionary Workers Group*] [*Senegal*]   (AF)
GOR......... Gulf Olympic Ranges
gor .... Horizon   (RU)
gor .... Hot   (RU)
gor .... Hot Spring [*Topography*]   (RU)
gor .... Mountainous, Mining   (RU)
gor ad .... Mountain Artillery Battalion   (RU)
gor ap .... Mountain Artillery Regiment   (RU)
Gorbytpromsoyuz ... City General Services Producers' Union   (RU)
GORCO..... Guam Oil and Refining Co. Inc.
Gordezbyuro ... City Disinfection and Deratization Office   (RU)
Gordorekspluatatsiya ... Moscow City Trust for the Operation of Roads and Drainage Systems of the Administration of the Operation of the Road and Bridge System of the Ispolkom of the Mosgorsovet   (RU)
Gordormekhanizatsiya ... City Trust for Road Operation and Mechanization   (RU)

Gordorremont ... Trust of the Administration for the Operation of the Road and Bridge System of the Mosgorispolkom   (RU)
gorekskursbyuro ... City Excursion Office   (RU)
gorem .... Advance Repair Train   (RU)
Gorenergo .. City Power System Administration Management   (RU)
gorfo .... City Finance Department   (RU)
G Org........... Grand-Orgue [*Great Organ*] [*Music*]
Gorgeonefteizdat ... State Scientific and Technical Publishing House of Mining, Geological, and Petroleum Literature   (RU)
Gorgeos'yemka ... State Trust for the Geodetic Survey of Cities   (RU)
GORINKhU ... City Inspection of the Statistical Survey of the National Economy   (RU)
gor inzh ...... Mining Engineer   (RU)
Gorkhimpromsoyuz ... City Chemical Producers' Union   (RU)
Gorkhimpromstroy ... All-Union Trust for the Construction of Chemical Raw Materials Mining Establishments   (RU)
Gorkhudozhpromsoyuz ... City Producers' Union of Artels of Art Crafts   (RU)
gorkomkhoz ... City Department of Municipal Services   (RU)
gorkommunotdel ... City Department of Municipal Services   (RU)
Gorkoopinsoyuz ... City Union of Disabled Persons' Cooperative Artels   (RU)
gorkooptorg ... City Cooperative Trade Organization   (RU)
Gorkozhpromsoyuz ... City Union of Leather Producers' Cooperatives   (RU)
GORKTEK ... City Office for Container Shipments and Transportation and Forwarding Operations   (RU)
Gormashuchet ... State Office for the Rationalization and Mechanization of Accounting   (RU)
Gormebpromsoyuz ... City Furniture Producers' Union   (RU)
Gormesttopprom ... City Administration of Local and Fuel Industries   (RU)
gormetallopromsoyuz ... City Metal Producers' Union   (RU)
Gormetpromsoyuz ... City Metal Producers' Union   (RU)
Gormnogopromsoyuz ... City Multitrade Producers' Union   (RU)
gorn .... Mountain, Mountainous, Mining   (RU)
gornadompromsoyuz ... City Home-Working Producers' Union   (RU)
gornarobraz ... City Department of Public Education   (RU)
GorONO.... City Department of Public Education   (RU)
Gorpechat'promsoyuz ... City Union of Producers' Cooperatives of the Printing Industry   (RU)
gorpishchetorg ... City Trade Organization for Trade in Food Products   (RU)
gorplan....... City Planning Commission   (RU)
gorpo .... City Consumers' Society   (RU)
gorpotrebsoyuz ... City Union of Consumers' Societies   (RU)
gor prkh ...... Mountain Pass [*Topography*]   (RU)
Gorprom..... Forestry Industrial Enterprise   (BU)
gorpromsovet ... City Council of Producers' Cooperatives   (RU)
gorpromtorg ... City Establishment for Trade in Manufactured Goods   (RU)
gorpromuch ... School of Mining Apprenticeship   (RU)
gorproyekt ... City Soviet Planning Department   (RU)
gorraykom ... City Rayon Committee of the KPSS   (RU)
gorremstroytrest ... City Repair and Construction Trust   (RU)
Gorrybkoop ... City Union of Fisheries Consumers' Cooperatives   (RU)
gorsanepidstantsiya ... City Sanitary and Epidemiological Station   (RU)
Gor-Sen... Kamu Gorevlileri Sendikasi [*Civil Servants' Union*]   (TU)
GOR-SEN ... Kibris Turk Kamu Gorevlileri Sendikasi [*Turkish Cypriot Civil Servants' Union*] [*KAMU-SEN*] [*Later,*]   (TU)
gorSES....... City Sanitary and Epidemiological Station   (RU)
Gorshveypromsoyuz ... City Garment Producers' Union   (RU)
gorsobes....... City Department of Social Security   (RU)
gor solen...... Bitter Salt Mud [*Topography*]   (RU)
gorsportsoyuz ... City Council of the Union of Sports Societies and Organizations   (RU)
GorSt .... Gorsko Stopanstvo [*Forestry Resources*] [*A periodical*]   (BU)
gorstroy...... Administration of Urban Construction   (RU)
Gorstroy...... Forestry Construction Administration   (RU)
Gorstroyproyekt ... State Planning Institute of Urban Construction   (RU)
GORTEK... City Transportation and Forwarding Office   (RU)
gortekhnadzor ... Mining Engineering Inspection   (RU)
Gortekstil'promsoyuz ... City Textile Producers' Union   (RU)
gortop......... City Fuel Department   (RU)
Gortorg...... City Trade Administration   (RU)
GORUBSO ... Bulgarian-Soviet Ore Mining Company   (BU)
goruprmestprom ... City Administration of Local Industry   (RU)
Gorvodkanalstroy ... State Trust for the Survey and Planning of Urban Water Supply and Sewer Systems   (RU)
gorVTEK ... City Medical Commission for Determination of Disability   (RU)
gorzags....... City Civil Registry Office   (RU)
gorzdrav...... City Department of Public Health   (RU)
Gorzelenkhoz ... City Landscape Management Trust   (RU)
Gor zh d ..... Gor'kiy Railroad   (RU)
gorzo.......... City Land Department   (RU)
GOS........... Goldfields Air Services [*Australia*] [*ICAO designator*]   (FAAC)
GOS.......... Gosford [*Australia*] [*Airport symbol*] [*Obsolete*]   (OAG)
GOS.......... Government of Senegal
GOS.......... Government of Sudan
GOS.......... Hospital Ship
GOS.......... Variable Feedback   (RU)
Gosakteatr ... State Academic Theater   (RU)

GOSAP...... Grupo de Organizacao de Sessoes da Assembleia Popular [*Group for the Organization of People's Assembly Sessions*] [*Mozambique*] (AF)

Gosarbitrazh ... State Arbitration Commission (RU)

Gosarkhstroykontrol' ... State Architectural and Construction Control (RU)

Gosatomizdat ... State Publishing House of Literature in the Field of Atomic Science and Technology (RU)

Gosavtoinspektsiya ... State Automobile Inspection (RU)

GOSBEZ ... State Security (RU)

Gosbumizdat ... State Scientific and Technical Publishing House of the Ministry of the Pulp and Paper Industry, USSR (RU)

gosdepartament ... US Department of State (RU)

GOSEK...... State Economic Commission of the Council of Ministers, USSR, for Current Planning of the National Economy (RU)

Gosekonomkomissiya ... State Economic Commission of the Council of Ministers, USSR, for Current Planning of the National Economy (RU)

Gosekonomsovet ... State Scientific and Economic Council of the Council of Ministers, USSR (RU)

GOSENERGOIZDAT ... State Scientific and Technical Power-Engineering Publishing House (RU)

Gosenergonadzor ... State Inspection for Industrial Power Engineering and for Power Engineering Supervision (RU)

GOSET...... State Jewish Theater (RU)

Gosfil .... State Philharmonic (RU)

GOSFINIZDAT ... State Financial Publishing House (RU)

GOSFIZKhIM ... State Physicochemical Institute Imeni L. Ya. Karpov (RU)

Gosgeolizdat ... State Publishing House of Geological Literature (RU)

GOSGEOLTEKHIZDAT ... State Scientific and Technical Publishing House of Literature on Geology, Geodesy, and Conservation of Mineral Resources (RU)

Gosgeonadzor ... Department of the State Geological Inspection (RU)

Gosgeotekhizdat ... State Publishing House of Geological and Technical Literature (RU)

Gosgorgeolnefteizdat ... State Scientific and Technical Publishing House for Petroleum Mining and Geology (RU)

Gosgorizdat ... State Mining Publishing House (RU)

Gosgorkhimproyekt ... State All-Union Institute for the Planning of Establishments of the Chemical Raw Materials Mining Industry (RU)

GOSGORTEKhIZDAT ... State Scientific and Technical Publishing House of Literature on Mining (RU)

GOSGORTEKHNADZOR ... State Committee of the Council of Ministers for Supervision of Industrial Safety and for Mining Inspection [*RSFSR*] [*Established, 1969*] (RU)

GOSI .... General Organization for Social Insurance [*Established, 1969*] [*Saudi Arabia*]

Gosinoizdat ... State Publishing House of Foreign Literature (RU)

Gosinsilikat ... State Experimental Institute of Silicates (RU)

GOSINTI .. State Scientific Research Institute of Scientific and Technical Information (RU)

Gosinzhgorproyekt ... State Trust for the Planning of Units of Municipal Housing Construction (RU)

GOSIP...... Government Open System Interconnect Profile [*Australia*]

GOSISA .... Genoot van Openbare Skakelinstituut van Suidelike Afrika [*South Africa*] (AA)

GOSIZDAT ... State Publishing House (RU)

GOSKAP... Caspian State Steamship Line (RU)

GOSKhIMIZDAT ... State Scientific and Technical Publishing House of Chemical Literature (RU)

Goskhimproyekt ... State All-Union Institute for the Planning of Special Structures, Buildings, and Sanitary-Engineering and Power Installations for Chemical Industry Establishments (RU)

Goskhimtekhizdat ... State Scientific and Technical Publishing House of Chemical Literature (RU)

GOSKINO ... Central State Photography and Motion-Picture Establishment of the Narkompros (RU)

Goskinoizdat ... State Publishing House of Cinematographic Literature (RU)

Goskontrol' ... State Control Commission of the Council of Ministers (RU)

Goskontsert ... State Concert Association of the USSR (RU)

Goskul'tprosvetizdat ... State Publishing House of Cultural and Educational Literature (RU)

Goslegpromizdat ... State Scientific and Technical Publishing House of the Ministry of the Consumers' Goods Industry, USSR (RU)

Goslesbumizdat ... State Publishing House of the Lumber, Paper, and Woodworking Industries (RU)

Goslestekhizdat ... State Publishing House of Forestry Engineering (RU)

GOSLITIZDAT ... State Publishing House of Belles Lettres (RU)

GOSM .... Matam/Ouro Sogui [*Senegal*] [*ICAO location identifier*] (ICLI)

Gosmanopo ... State Visual Aids Workshops (RU)

Gosmashmetizdat ... State Publishing House for Machinery Manufacture, Metalworking, and Ferrous Metallurgy (RU)

Gosmedizdat ... State Publishing House of Medical Literature (of the UkrSSR) (RU)

Gosmestprom ... State Committee of the Council of Ministers, RSFSR, for Local Industry and Art Crafts (RU)

Gosmestpromizdat ... State Publishing House of Local Industry and Art Crafts, RSFSR (RU)

Gosmetallurgizdat ... State Publishing House of Metallurgical Literature (RU)

Gosmontazhspetsstroy ... State Industrial Committee for the Installation and Specialized Construction Operations, USSR (RU)

Gosmuzizdat ... State Music Publishing House (RU)

Gosnardom ... State People's House Imeni Karl Liebknecht and Rosa Luxemburg (RU)

Gosnauchtekhizdat ... State Scientific and Technical Publishing House (RU)

GosNII...... State Scientific Research Institute (RU)

GosNIIGA ... State Scientific Research Institute of Civil Aviation (RU)

GosNIIGVF ... State Scientific Research Institute of the Civil Air Fleet, USSR (RU)

GosNIORKh ... State Scientific Research Institute of Lake and River Fisheries (RU)

GOSNITI .. State All-Union Scientific Research Technological Institute for Repair and Operation of Machine and Tractor Fleets (RU)

Gosp.......... Hospital [*Topography*] (RU)

GOSP .... Podor [*Senegal*] [*ICAO location identifier*] (ICLI)

GOSPLAN ... State Planning Commission (RU)

GOSPLANIZDAT ... State Publishing House of Literature on Economic Planning (RU)

Gospolitizdat ... State Publishing House of Political Literature (RU)

Gospolitnauchizdat ... State Publishing House of Political and Scientific Literature (RU)

Gospozhnadzor ... State Fire Inspection (RU)

Gosprodsnab ... State Committee of the Council of Ministers, USSR, for the Supply of Foodstuffs and Industrial Goods (RU)

GOSR .... Richard-Toll [*Senegal*] [*ICAO location identifier*] (ICLI)

Gosradioizdat ... State Radio Publishing House (RU)

Gosrybflotinspektsiya ... State Inspection for Safety at Sea and Port Supervision of the Fish Industry Fleet (RU)

gosrybnadzor ... State Fishing Inspection (RU)

GOSS......... Saint Louis [*Senegal*] [*ICAO location identifier*] (ICLI)

Gossaninspektsiya ... State Sanitary Inspection (RU)

GOSSEL'KHOZIZDAT ... State Publishing House of Agricultural Literature [*UkrSSR*] (RU)

Gossel'sindikat ... State Russian Agricultural Syndicate (RU)

GOSSH ..... Glavni Odbor Saveza Sindikata Hrvatske [*Central Committee, Council of Trade-Unions of Croatia*] (YU)

GOSSIP..... Government Open Systems Inter-Connection Procurement Policy [*Australia*]

gossortouchastok ... State Crop-Testing Station, State Strain Trial Station (RU)

gossortsemfond ... State Fund of Selected Seeds (RU)

GOSSTATIZDAT ... State Statistical Publishing House (RU)

Gosstrakh .. Main Administration of State Insurance (RU)

Gosstroy..... State Committee for Construction [*Former USSR*] (RU)

GOSSTROYIZDAT ... State Publishing House of Literature on Construction, Architecture, and Building Materials (RU)

GOSSTROYIZDAT USSR ... State Publishing House of Literature on Construction and Architecture, UkrSSR (RU)

GOSSTROY SSSR ... State Committee of the Council of Ministers, USSR, for Construction (RU)

Gosstroytrest ... State Construction Trust of the Glavmosstroy (RU)

GOST .... All-Union State Standard (RU)

Gost........... Hotel [*Topography*] (RU)

Gosteasvet ... State Electromechanical Plant for the Manufacture of Theatrical Equipment (RU)

Gostekhgornadzor ... State Inspection for Technical and Mining Supervision (RU)

Gostekhizdat ... State Publishing House of Technical and Theoretical Literature (RU)

Gostekhnika ... State Committee of the Council of Ministers, USSR, for New Technology (RU)

Gostekhteoretizdat ... State Publishing House of Technical and Theoretical Literature (RU)

GosTIM..... State Theater Imeni V. E. Meyerkhol'd (RU)

Gostopizdat ... State Publishing House of Literature on the Fuel Industry (RU)

GOSTOPTEKhIZDAT ... State Scientific and Technical Publishing House of Petroleum and Mineral Fuel Literature (RU)

GOSTORG ... State Import-Export Trade Office (RU)

Gostorginspektsiya ... Main Administration of State Quality Inspection of Goods and State Trade Inspection (RU)

GOSTORGIZDAT ... State Publishing House of Literature on Trade (RU)

Gostransizdat ... State Transportation Publishing House (RU)

Gostrudizdat ... State Publishing House for Labor Problems (RU)

gostrudsberkassa ... State Workers' Savings Bank (RU)

Gostsentyuz ... State Central Theater for the Young Spectator (RU)

gos-vo......... State (RU)

Gosvodkhoz ... State Committee of the Council of Ministers for Water Management (RU)

Gosvoyenizdat ... State Military Publishing House (RU)

GOSYuRIZDAT ... State Publishing House of Legal Literature (RU)

GOSZ .... Gepeszek Orszagos Szovetsege [*National Association of Mechanics*] (HU)

Goszdravproyekt ... State Planning Office of the Ministry of Public Health, USSR (RU)

Goszelenkhoz ... State Landscape Management Trust (RU)

Goszemvodkhoz SSSR ... State Industrial Committee for the Irrigation Farming and Water Management, USSR (RU)

GOSZHELDORIZDAT ... State Railroad Publishing House (RU)

GOT............ Air Express in Norrkoping AB [*Sweden*] [*ICAO designator*] (FAAC)

GOT............ Gorska Odznaka Turystyczna [*Mountain-Climbing Tourist Badge*] (POL)

GOT............ Gothenburg [*Sweden*] [*Airport symbol*] (OAG)

got............... Gotico [*Gothic*] [*Publishing*] [*Italian*]

Got............... Goties [*Gothic*] [*Afrikaans*]

got............... Gotisch [*Gothic*] [*German*]

GOT............ Government of Tanzania

GOT............ Government of Tunisia (MCD)

GOT............ Reference Current Generator (RU)

GOTA......... Gasdotti Oleodotti Transcontinentali Afro-Europi SPA

GOTA......... Gotabanken [*Bank*] [*Sweden*]

GOTB......... Bakel [*Senegal*] [*ICAO location identifier*] (ICLI)

GOTEDR .. State Dramatic Theater (RU)

goth............ Gothique [*Gothic*] [*Publishing*] [*French*]

GOTK......... Kedougou [*Senegal*] [*ICAO location identifier*] (ICLI)

GOTN......... Niokolo Koba [*Senegal*] [*ICAO location identifier*] (ICLI)

GOTOB..... State Theater of Opera and Ballet (RU)

GOTS......... Simenti [*Senegal*] [*ICAO location identifier*] (ICLI)

GOTT......... Tambacounda [*Senegal*] [*ICAO location identifier*] (ICLI)

GOU............ Garoua [*Cameroon*] [*Airport symbol*] (OAG)

GOU............ Government of Uganda (ECON)

GOU............ Grupo de Oficiales Unidos [*Group of United Officers*] [*Argentina*] (LA)

goudst........ Goudstempel [*Gold Stamping*] [*Publishing*] [*Netherlands*]

GOULB....... Goulburn [*Australia*] (ROG)

Gouv Gen .. Gouverneur General [*France*] (FLAF)

Gouville..... Gouvernement de la Ville [*City or Municipal Government*] (CL)

GOV............ Gove [*Australia*] [*Airport symbol*] (OAG)

Gov.............. Governor (EECI)

GOVPF...... Groupement Obligatoire des Viticulteurs et Producteurs de Fruits [*Tunisia*]

Govt............ Government (EECI)

GOWA........ Guild of Watchmen of Australia (ADA)

GoWG........ Gesellschaft fuer Oeffentliche Wirtschaft und Gemeinwirtschaft eV [*Association for Public Management and Collective Farming*] (SLS)

GOWS........ Government of Western Samoa

GOYA......... Greek Organisation of Young Australians

GOYS......... General Organization for Youth and Sports [*Bahrain*] (EAIO)

GOZ............ Gelders-Overijselse Zuivelbond [*Dairy Federation (Dutch provinces)*] (ARC)

GOZ............ Gorna Orjachovica [*Bulgaria*] [*Airport symbol*] (OAG)

GOZ............ State Optical Plant (RU)

GOZB......... Glavni Odbor Zveze Borcev [*Central Committee of the Union of Veterans*] (YU)

GOZBNOV Slovenije ... Glavni Odbor Zveze Borcev Narodnoosvobodilne Vojske Slovenije [*Central Committee of the Slovenian Union of Veterans of the National Liberation War*] (YU)

GOZNAK ... State Bank Notes, Coins, and Medals Administration (RU)

GOZZD..... Glavni Odbor Zveze Zenskih Drustev [*Central Committee of the Federation of Women's Clubs*] (YU)

GP............... Breakthrough Group (RU)

GP............... Caterpillar Trailer (RU)

GP............... City Enterprise (BU)

GP............... Civilian Gas Mask (RU)

G/P............. Ganhos e Perdas [*Profit and Loss*] [*Business term*] [*Portuguese*]

GP............... Gas Main, Gas Pipeline (RU)

GP............... Generalni Prokurator [*Prosecutor General*] (CZ)

gp................ General of the Infantry (BU)

GP............... General Porucnik [*Lieutenant General*] (YU)

GP............... Geologicky Pruzkum [*Geological Research*] (CZ)

gp................ Geppuska [*Heavy Machine Gun*] (HU)

GP............... Gesellschaft fuer Psychologie der Deutschen Demokratischen Republik [*Association for Psychology of the German Democratic Republic*] (SLS)

GP............... Government Publications [*Northern Territory, Australia*]

GP............... Gozo Party [*Malta*] [*Political party*] (PPE)

GP............... Gradevinsko Preduzece [*Building Establishment*] (YU)

GP............... Gradska Plinara [*City Gas Plant*] (YU)

GP............... Grafeion Periokhis [*Regional Office*] [*Greek*] (GC)

GP............... Grafeion Programmatismou [*Planning Office*] (GC)

GP............... Gran Premio [*Grand Prix*] [*Italian*]

GP............... Great Portland Street [*London*] (DSUE)

GP............... Greenpeace

GP............... Group Converter (RU)

GP............... Groupe de Paris [*France*] (EAIO)

GP............... Grupos Profesionales [*Professional Groups*] [*Spanish*] (WER)

GP............... Guadeloupe [*ANSI two-letter standard code*] (CNC)

GP............... Guard Regiment (BU)

GP............... Guven Partisi [*Reliance Party - RP*] (TU)

GP............... Heterodyne Conversion Transducer (RU)

GP............... Hexagonal Close-Packed (Lattice) (RU)

GP............... Hyaloplasm (RU)

g/p............. Load-Carrying Capacity, Tonnage (RU)

GP............... Pulse-Train Generator (RU)

GP............... Sawtooth Voltage Generator (RU)

GPA............ Genealogical Publications of Australia (ADA)

GPA............ Gerakan Pemuda Ansor [*Ansor Youth Movement*] (IN)

GPA............ Giunta Provinciale Amministrativa [*County Council*] [*Italian*]

GPA............ Global Program on AIDS [*Acquired Immune Deficiency Syndrome*] [*WHO*]

GPA............ Gold Producers' Association [*Australia*]

GPA............ Grafeion Poleodomias Athinon [*Athens City Planning Office*] (GC)

G PA.......... Grand Parc d'Armee [*Military*] [*French*] (MTD)

G PA.......... Grand Parc d'Artillerie [*Military*] [*French*] (MTD)

GPA............ Green Party of Australia [*Political party*]

GPA............ Greenpeace Australia

GPA............ Groupement des Pharmaciens d'Afrique

GPA............ Groupe Professionnel des Architectes UTS [*French*] (SLS)

GPA............ Guyana Press Association (LA)

GPAA........ Hydrolyzed Polyacrylamide (RU)

GPAE........ Gouvernement Provisoire Algerien en Exil [*Algerian Provisional Government in Exile*] (AF)

GPB............ Gazdasagpolitikai Bizottsag [*Economic Policy Committee (of the MSZMP CC)*] (HU)

GPB............ State Public Library Imeni M. Ye. Saltykov-Shchedrin (RU)

GPBA........ General Produce Brokers Association [*Benelux*] (BAS)

GPBN........ Groupement Pharmaceutique Benin-Niger

GPBS......... Grupo de Planejamento de Baixada Sul-Rio-Grandense [*Brazil*] (DSCA)

GPBSShch ... State Public Library Imeni M. Ye. Saltykov-Shchedrin (RU)

GPC............ Compagnie Generale de la Petite Cote

GPC............ General People's Congress [*Yemen*] [*Political party*] (EY)

GPC............ General People's Congress [*or Committee*] [*Libya*] [*Political party*] (PPW)

GPC............ General Petroleum Company [*Cairo, Egypt*]

GPC............ General Poultry Company [*Egypt*] (IMH)

GPC............ Ghana Publishing Corporation

GPC............ Government Paint Committee [*Australia*]

GPC............ Grenada Peace Council (LA)

GPC............ Groupe des Progressistes du Cameroun

GPC............ Groupements de Producteurs de Ciment [*Belgium*] (PDAA)

GPC............ Guyana Petroleum Corporation (LA)

GPC............ Guyana Pharmaceutical Corporation (LA)

GPCE........ Groupement Pharmaceutique de la CE [*Pharmaceutical Group of the EC*] (ECED)

GPCO........ Global Perspective Country Outlooks [*Global Perspective, Inc.*] [*Information service or system*] (CRD)

GPD............ General Political Department [*China*] [*Military*]

GPD............ Generals for Peace and Disarmament [*Ittervoort, Netherlands*] (EAIO)

GPD............ Grupe Podvodnih Diverzanata [*Groups of Underwater Saboteurs*] [*Military*] (YU)

GPECC........ Groupement Professionnel des Exportateurs de Cafe et de Cacao

GPEG........ Advanced Field Evacuation Hospital (RU)

GPEIS........ Gabungan Pengusaha Ekspor Indonesia Sementara [*Provisional Association of Indonesian Exporters*] (IN)

GPEP......... Advanced Field Evacuation Station (RU)

GPEP......... Gabinete para a Pesquisa and Explorocao de Petroleo

GPF............ Gandhi Peace Foundation [*India*] (EAIO)

GPF............ Gibraltar Police Force

GPF............ Greater Pacific Finance Ltd. [*Australia*] (ADA)

GPF............ Group Band Filter (RU)

GPFA........ General Poultry Farmers Association [*Trinidad and Tobago*] (EAIO)

GPFS......... Greater Pacific Financial Services [*Australia*]

GPG............ Gaertnerische Produktions-Genossenschaft [*Horticultural Producer Cooperative*] (EG)

GPGUSMP ... Hydrographic Establishment of the Glavsevmorput' (RU)

GPH............ Green Party of Hungary [*Political party*] (EAIO)

GPH............ Grenzpolizeihaelfer [*Border Police Assistant*] (EG)

GPI............. Geologisch-Paleontologisches Institut [*Geological Paleontological Institute*] (MSC)

GPI............. Georgian Polytechnic Institute Imeni V. I. Lenin (RU)

gpi.............. Geppisztoly [*Machine Pistol, Submachine Gun*] (HU)

GPI............. Gesellschaft fuer Programmierte Instruktion

GPI............. Gor'kiy Polytechnic Institute Imeni A. A. Zhdanov (RU)

GPI............. Graphique et Papeterie Ivoirienne

GPI............. Greenpeace International [*Netherlands*] (EAIO)

GPI............. Grupe za Podvodno Izvidanje [*Groups for Underwater Reconnaissance*] [*Military*] (YU)

GPI............. Grupo Parlamentario Independiente [*Independent Parliamentary Group*] [*Spanish*] (WER)

GPI .... Guapi [*Colombia*] [*Airport symbol*]   (OAG)

GPI .... Guinnes Peat International [*Sudan*]

GPI .... Hydraulic Soil Evaporator   (RU)

GPI .... State Pedagogical Institute   (RU)

GPI .... State Planning Institute   (RU)

GPI .... Underwater Exploration Group   (RU)

GPIA.......... Glass Packaging Institute of Australia

GPIB.......... State Public Historical Library, RSFSR   (RU)

GPIC .... Gulf Petrochemical Industries Company [*Bahrain, Kuwait, and Saudi Arabia*]   (MENA)

GPII .... Gabungan Pengusaha Impor Indonesia [*Indonesia Importers Association*]   (IN)

GPIIYa ...... Gor'kiy Pedagogical Institute of Foreign Languages   (RU)

GPIN .... Groupement Professionnel de l'Industrie Nucleaire [*Also known as NIC*] [*Belgium*]

GPIPOA(SA) ... Gewese President Instituut Parke en Ontspanningsadministrasie [*South Africa*]   (AA)

GPJ............ Great Peace Journey [*Sweden*]   (EAIO)

GPK .... City Consumers' Cooperative   (BU)

GPK .... City Fire Brigade   (RU)

GPK .... City Industrial Kombinat   (RU)

GPK .... City Party Committee   (RU)

GPK .... City Post Office   (RU)

GPK .... Cumene Hydroperoxide   (RU)

GPK .... Direction Indicator   (RU)

GPK .... Geological Survey Branch   (BU)

GPK .... Gradanski Procesualni Kodeks [*Civil Procedure Code*]   (YU)

GPK .... Main Check Point   (RU)

GPK .... Main Compass [*Aviation*]   (RU)

GPK .... State Pedigree Stock Book, State Breeding Register   (RU)

GPK .... State Pedigree Stud Farm   (RU)

GPKhO...... Ready for Chemical Defense   (RU)

GPL .... Gabonaise de Peintures et de Laques [*Paint and varnish manufacturing plant*] [*Gabon*]   (IMH)

GPL .... Gaz et Petrole Liquefies [*Algeria*]

GPL .... Greater Pacific Life [*Australia*]

GPL .... Guapiles [*Costa Rica*] [*Airport symbol*]   (OAG)

GPL .... Societe Gabonaise de Peintures et Laques

GPLS .... Groupement Professionnel des Commercants et Industriels Libanais du Senegal

GPM .... Gepanzerte Pioniermaschine [*Armored Engineer Vehicle*] [*General Electric Co.*] [*German*]   (MCD)

GPM .... Gerakan Papua Merdeka [*Free Papua Movement*]   (IN)

GPM .... Grey Power Movement [*Australia*]

GPM .... Grupe za Podvodno Miniranje [*Groups for Underwater Mine-Laying*] [*Military*]   (YU)

GPM .... Guyana People's Militia   (LA)

GPM .... Main Medical Aid Station   (RU)

GPMA .... German Productivity and Management Association   (EAIO)

GPMB .... Gambia Produce Marketing Board

GPMI .... Grupo Permanente de Mobilizacao Industrial [*Permanent Industrial Mobilization Group*] [*Brazil*]   (LA)

GPMM ...... Guild of Professional Model Makers [*Australia*]

GPMS........ Gabongan Pelajar Melayu Semenanjong [*Malay Peninsula Students Association*]   (ML)

GPMV .... Groupements Pre-Cooperatifs de Mise en Valeur

GPN .... Constant-Potential Generator   (RU)

GPN .... Garden Point [*Australia*] [*Airport symbol*]   (OAG)

GPN .... Grey Power News [*Australia*] [*A publication*]

GPN .... Sawtooth Voltage Generator   (RU)

GPN .... State Fire Inspection   (RU)

GPNCO ..... Great Pacific Navigation Co. Ltd.   (DS)

GPNI .... Groupement Professionnel National de l'Informatique [*French*]   (ADPT)

GPNRB...... Prosecutor General's Office of the Bulgarian People's Republic   (BU)

GPNS........ Advanced Observation and Communication Post   (RU)

GPNTB...... State Public Scientific and Technical Library, USSR   (RU)

GPO .... General Pico [*Argentina*] [*Airport symbol*]   (OAG)

GPO .... Government Pharmaceutical Organization [*Thailand*]   (DS)

GPO .... La Grande Pecherie de l'Ouest

GPO .... Main Defense Zone   (BU)

GPO .... State Border Guard   (RU)

GPP .... Border Guard Infantry Regiment   (BU)

GPP .... City Industrial Enterprise   (BU)

GPP .... Forestry Industrial Enterprise   (BU)

GPP .... Gambia People's Party [*Political party*]   (EY)

GPP .... Geological Surveys Enterprise   (BU)

GPP .... Grafeion Pliforion kai Paraponon [*Information and Complaints Office*] [*Greek*]   (GC)

GPP .... Groupement Professionnel du Petrole

GPP .... Main Dressing Station   (RU)

GPP .... Main Political Education Committee of the Narkompros, RSFSR   (RU)

GPP .... Main Step-Down Sub-Station   (RU)

GPP .... Mountain Infantry Regiment   (RU)

GPP .... Production Preparation Group   (RU)

GPP .... State Fruit Nursery   (RU)

GPPIPCEE ... Groupement Professionel des Pharmaciens de l'Industrie Pharmaceutique de la CEE [*Professional Grouping of Pharmacists of the Pharmaceuticals Industry of the EEC*]   (ECED)

GPPL......... Gdanskie Przedsiebiorstwo Produkcji Lesnej "LAS" [*Gdansk Forest Production Enterprise "LAS"*]   (POL)

GPPP........ Hydrologic Receiving-Sending Post   (RU)

GPr .... Geografski Pregled [*Geographic Review*] [*A periodical*]   (BU)

GPR .... Gran Premio Romeo [*Alfa Romeo race car*] [*Italian*]

GPR .... Grupe za Podvodno Rusenje [*Groups for Underwater Demolition*] [*Military*]   (YU)

GPR .... Main Starting Relay   (RU)

GPR .... Mountain Infantry Company   (RU)

g pr .... Mountain Pass [*Topography*]   (RU)

GPR .... State Pedigree Cattle Breeding Farm   (RU)

GPRA .... Gouvernement Provisoire de la Republique Algerienne [*Provisional Government of the Algerian Republic*]   (AF)

GPRB........ Government of the People's Republic of Benin   (AF)

GPRF........ Gouvernement Provisoire de la Republique Francaise   (FLAF)

GPRFE ..... Gouvernement Provisoire des Revolutionnaires Fiotes en Exil

GPRL........ Gulf Puerto Rico Lines [*Steamship*]   (MHDB)

GPRMC..... Groupement des Plastiques Renforces et Materiaux Composites [*Organization of Reinforced Plastics and Composite Materials*]   (EAIO)

GPrO .... Gesellschaft fuer die Geschichte des Protestantismus in Oesterreich [*Society for the History of Protestantism in Austria*]   (SLS)

GPRz......... Grupe za Podvodno Razminiranje [*Groups for Underwater Mine Removal*] [*Military*]   (YU)

GPS........... Bandwidth Shift Generator   (RU)

GPS........... Forestry Industrial Farm   (BU)

GPS........... Galapagos Islands [*Ecuador*] [*Airport symbol*]   (OAG)

GPS........... Government Printing Service [*New South Wales, Australia*]

GPS........... Grand Prix Sailing [*Australia*]

GPS........... Group Property Services [*Australia*]

GPSA........ Gava Property & Sales Agencies Ltd.

GPSA........ General Practitioners' Society of Australia   (ADA)

GPSD........ Main Message Center   (RU)

GPSH .... Governor Phillip Special Hospital [*Australia*]

GPSU........ Guyana Public Service Union   (LA)

GPS-UWR ... German Peace Society - United War Resisters   (EAIO)

GPSYF ..... Grand Port-Savanne Youth Federation [*Mauritius*]   (AF)

GPT .... Amphibian Tracked Personnel Carrier   (RU)

GPT .... Direct-Current Generator   (RU)

GPT .... General Property Trust [*Australia*]   (ADA)

GPT .... Glutamic Pyruvic Transaminase   (RU)

GPT .... Governor Phillip Tower [*Sydney, New South Wales, Australia*]

GPT .... Graduated Personal Tax

GPT .... Labor Party of Guatemala   (RU)

GPTC........ Groupe Politique des Travailleurs Chretiens [*Christian Workers' Political Group*] [*Belgium*]   (WER)

GPTI......... Georgian Polytechnic Institute   (RU)

GPTU .... Gas and Steam Turbine Power Plant   (RU)

GPU .... Gosudarstvennoe Politicheskoe Upravlenie [*Government Political Administration*] [*Soviet secret service organization, also known as OGPU Later, KGB*]

GPU .... State Political Administration [*1922*]   (RU)

gpuaz......... Hectopoise   (RU)

GPV .... Gereformeerd Politiek Verbond [*Reformed Political League*] [*Netherlands*] [*Political party*]   (PPE)

GPVNaR ... Main Air Observation and Reconnaissance Post   (RU)

GPVNOS... Main Aircraft-Warning Service Post   (RU)

GPVO .... Ready for Antiaircraft Defense   (RU)

GPWA .... Grain Pool of Western Australia

GPZ .... Advance Party   (RU)

gpz............ Hectopieze   (RU)

gpz............ Hectopoise   (RU)

GPZ .... State Bearing Plant   (RU)

GPZB........ Gdanskie Przemyslowe Zjednoczenie Budowlane [*Gdansk (Danzig) Industrial Construction Association*]   (POL)

GPZU .... Hump Program-Setting Device [*Railroads*]   (RU)

GQ .... Equatorial Guinea [*ANSI two-letter standard code*]   (CNC)

GQ .... Governor of Queensland [*Australia*]

GQG .... Grand Quartier General [*General Headquarters*] [*Military*] [*French*]

GQNA .... Aioun El Atrouss [*Mauritania*] [*ICAO location identifier*]   (ICLI)

GQNB........ Boutilimit [*Mauritania*] [*ICAO location identifier*]   (ICLI)

GQNC....... Tichitt [*Mauritania*] [*ICAO location identifier*]   (ICLI)

GQND .... Tidjikja [*Mauritania*] [*ICAO location identifier*]   (ICLI)

GQNE .... Bogue [*Mauritania*] [*ICAO location identifier*]   (ICLI)

GQNF........ Kiffa [*Mauritania*] [*ICAO location identifier*]   (ICLI)

GQNH....... Timbedra [*Mauritania*] [*ICAO location identifier*]   (ICLI)

GQNI......... Nema [*Mauritania*] [*ICAO location identifier*]   (ICLI)

GQNJ........ Akjout [*Mauritania*] [*ICAO location identifier*]   (ICLI)

GQNK........ Kaedi [*Mauritania*] [*ICAO location identifier*] (ICLI)
GQNL........ Moudjeria/Letfotar [*Mauritania*] [*ICAO location identifier*] (ICLI)
GQNM ...... Timbedra/Dahara [*Mauritania*] [*ICAO location identifier*] (ICLI)
GQNN .... Nouakchott [*Mauritania*] [*ICAO location identifier*] (ICLI)
GQNR........ Rosso [*Mauritania*] [*ICAO location identifier*] (ICLI)
GQNS........ Selibabi [*Mauritania*] [*ICAO location identifier*] (ICLI)
GQNT........ Tamchakett [*Mauritania*] [*ICAO location identifier*] (ICLI)
GQNU .... M'Bout [*Mauritania*] [*ICAO location identifier*] (ICLI)
GQNV........ Nouakchott [*Mauritania*] [*ICAO location identifier*] (ICLI)
GQPA........ Atar [*Mauritania*] [*ICAO location identifier*] (ICLI)
GQPF........ F'Derick [*Mauritania*] [*ICAO location identifier*] (ICLI)
GQPP........ Nouadhibou [*Mauritania*] [*ICAO location identifier*] (ICLI)
GQPT .... Bir Moghrein [*Mauritania*] [*ICAO location identifier*] (ICLI)
GQPZ........ Zouerate [*Mauritania*] [*ICAO location identifier*] (ICLI)
gr.............. Citizen, Civic, Civil, Civilian (RU)
gr.............. City (BU)
gr.............. Column (BU)
GR............. De Gemeenteraad [*Benelux*] (BAS)
gr.............. Degree (RU)
GR............. Gamma Relay (RU)
GR............. Gare Regulatrice [*Military*] [*French*] (MTD)
GR............. Gemeinderat [*Alderman, Town Councillor*] [*German*]
GR............. Gendarmerie Royale [*Royal Gendarmerie*] [*Use GRK Cambodia*] (CL)
GR............. Generalne Riaditelstvo [*General Directorate*] (CZ)
GR............. Generalreparaturplan [*General Overhaul Plan*] (EG)
g-r............. Generator, Oscillator (RU)
GR............. Geoktrooieerde Rekenmeester [*Chartered Accountant*] [*Afrikaans*]
GR............. Gospodarsko Razstavisce [*Economic Exhibit*] [*Ljubljana*] (YU)
GR............. Gotong Rojong [*Mutual Cooperation*] (IN)
Gr .... Graben [*Ditch, Trench*] (EG)
gr.............. Gracht [*Canal*] [*Netherlands*] (CED)
gr.............. Grain [*Grain*] [*French*]
gr.............. Graines [*Seeds*] [*Pharmacy*]
gr.............. Gram [*Albanian*]
gr.............. Gramm [*Gram*] (HU)
gr.............. Grammar (RU)
Gr .... Gramme [*Gram*] [*French*] (MTD)
gr.............. Gramo [*Gram*] [*Spanish*]
g-r............. Gram Roentgen (RU)
gr.............. Granat [*or Granatos*] [*Grenade, Shell, Grenade Thrower*] (HU)
Gr .... Granate [*Shell, Grenade*] (EG)
gr.............. Grand [*Large*] [*French*]
gr.............. Grande [*Large*] [*Portuguese*]
gr.............. Grande [*Large*] [*Italian*]
gr.............. Grano [*Grain*] [*Spanish*]
gr.............. Granuliert [*Granulated*] [*German*] (GCA)
gr.............. Grao [*Grain*] [*Portuguese*]
gr.............. Gratis [*Gratis*] [*Portuguese*]
gr.............. Grau [*Degree*] [*Portuguese*]
Gr .... Grave [*Engraved*] [*Publishing*] [*French*]
Gr .... Gravel [*Topography*] (RU)
gr.............. Gravure [*Engraving*] [*Publishing*] [*Netherlands*]
Gr .... Greben [*or Grebeni*] [*Rock, Reef, Cliff, Ridge Former Yugoslavia*] (NAU)
GR............. Grecia [*Greece*] [*Poland*]
GR............. Greece [*ANSI two-letter standard code*] (CNC)
gr.............. Greek (BU)
gr.............. Greek, Grecian (RU)
GR............. Green Revolution
Gr .... Greenwichista [*Finland*]
gr.............. Greenwich Time (RU)
gr.............. Grego [*Greek*] [*Portuguese*]
gr.............. Grein [*Grain*] [*Afrikaans*]
Gr .... Grenz [*Border*] [*German*]
Gr .... Grieks [*Greeks*] [*Afrikaans*]
Gr .... Grondwet [*Benelux*] (BAS)
Gr .... Gros [*Gross*] [*Business term*] [*German*]
gr.............. Grosa [*Gross*] [*Business term*] [*Portuguese*]
gr.............. Grosha [*Old monetary unit*] (BU)
Gr .... Gross [*Big*] [*German*]
GR............. Grosseto [*Car registration plates*] [*Italian*]
GR............. Grossrechner [*German*] (ADPT)
gr.............. Grosz [*A coin, Hundredth part of a zloty*] (POL)
gr.............. Group (RU)
Gr .... Groupe [*Group, Division, Unit*] [*Military*] [*French*] (MTD)
GR............. Groupe Revolution [*Revolution Group*] [*French*] (WER)
GR............. Growth Hormone (RU)
Gr .... Grubu [*Group*] (TU)
gr.............. Gruen [*Green*] [*German*] (GCA)
Gr .... Grunn [*or Grunnen, Grunnane*] [*Shoal or Shoals Norwegian*] (NAU)
Gr .... Grunn [*Shoal*] [*Icelandic*] (NAU)

Gr .... Gruppe [*Group*] [*German*]
GR.............. Guardia Republicana del Peru [*Republican Guard of Peru*] (LA)
GR.............. Gulf Rijad Bank [*Bahrain*]
GR.............. Gurkha Rifles (ML)
G-R .... Hertzsprung-Russell (Diagram) (RU)
Gr .... Load Capacity, Load-Lifting Capacity, Carrying Capacity (RU)
Gr .... Loudspeaker (RU)
GR.............. Mercury Fulminate (RU)
GR.............. Sweep Generator (RU)
Gr .... Tomb [*Topography*] (RU)
gr .... Urban (BU)
gr .... Year of Birth (RU)
GRA .... Genootskap van Regte Afrikaners [*Afrikaans*]
GRA .... German Research Association (EA)
GRA .... Gesellschaft fur Rechnergeteurte Analagen [*Germany*] (PDAA)
GRA .... Government Reservation Area [*Nigeria*]
Gr A .... Groene Amsterdammer [*Benelux*] (BAS)
GRA .... Groupement Francais pour le Developpement des Recherches Aeronautiques [*France*]
grab .... Grabado [*Illustration*] [*Spanish*]
GRACETALES ... Grasas y Aceites Vegetales Ltda. [*Barranquilla*] (COL)
grad .... Degree (RU)
Grad .... Gradevinarstvo [*Building Industry*] (YU)
GRAD .... Groupe Europeen de Realisations Audiovisuelles pour le Developpement [*France*]
GradAIP .... Graduate of the Australian Institute of Physics (ADA)
GRADAPROMET ... Poduzece za Promet Gradevinskim Materijalom [*Enterprise for Trade in Building Materials*] (YU)
GradCert.... Graduate Certificate
GradCertBus ... Graduate Certificate in Business [*Australia*]
GradCertCommunic ... Graduate Certificate in Communication [*Australia*]
GradCertFin ... Graduate Certificate in Finance [*Australia*]
GradCertHelpSkills ... Graduate Certificate in Helping Skills [*Australia*]
GradCertHRD ... Graduate Certificate in Human Resource Development [*Australia*]
GradCertIndRels ... Graduate Certificate in Industrial Relations [*Australia*]
GradCertLitEd ... Graduate Certificate in Literacy Education [*Australia*]
GradCertMarkt ... Graduate Certificate in Marketing [*Australia*]
GradCertMngt ... Graduate Certificate in Management [*Australia*]
GradCertTESOL ... Graduate Certificate in Teaching of English to Speakers of Other Languages [*Australia*]
GradDIndDes ... Graduate Diploma in Industrial Design [*Australia*]
GradDipA .. Graduate Diploma of Arts [*Australia*]
GradDipAbIsEd ... Graduate Diploma in Aboriginal and Islander Education [*Australia*]
GradDipAcc ... Graduate Diploma in Accounting [*Australia*]
GradDipAccom ... Graduate Diploma in Accompaniment [*Australia*]
GradDipAdultEd & Train ... Graduate Diploma in Adult Education and Training [*Australia*]
GradDipAltDispRes ... Graduate Diploma in Alternative Dispute Resolution [*Australia*]
GradDipAppEc ... Graduate Diploma in Applied Economics [*Australia*]
GradDipAppSc ... Graduate Diploma in Applied Science [*Australia*]
GradDipAppScGenStud ... Graduate Diploma in Applied Science, General Studies [*Australia*]
GradDipArts(ChLit) ... Graduate Diploma in Arts (Children's Literature) [*Australia*]
GradDipArts(WelfAdmin) ... Graduate Diploma in Arts (Welfare Administration) [*Australia*]
GradDipAsianLaw ... Graduate Diploma in Asian Law [*Australia*]
GradDipASOS ... Graduate Diploma in Antarctic and Southern Ocean Studies [*Australia*]
GradDipAud ... Graduate Diploma in Audiology [*Australia*]
GradDipBus ... Graduate Diploma in Business [*Australia*]
GradDipCCC ... Graduate Diploma of Computer Control and Communications [*Australia*]
GradDipClinDent ... Graduate Diploma in Clinical Dentistry [*Australia*]
GradDipComEd ... Graduate Diploma in Commercial Education [*Australia*]
GradDipComLaw ... Graduate Diploma of Commercial Law [*Australia*]
GradDipComMus ... Graduate Diploma of Community Music [*Australia*]
GradDipComMusMgmt ... Graduate Diploma of Community Museum Management [*Australia*]
GradDipCompEd ... Graduate Diploma in Computers in Education [*Australia*]
GradDipCompSc ... Graduate Diploma of Computer Science [*Australia*]
GradDipConfRes ... Graduate Diploma in Conflict Resolution [*Australia*]
GradDipCurric ... Graduate Diploma in Curriculum [*Australia*]
GradDipDiplSt ... Graduate Diploma in Diplomatic Studies [*Australia*]
GradDipDramaEd ... Graduate Diploma in Drama in Education [*Australia*]
GradDipE .. Graduate Diploma in Engineering [*Australia*]
GradDipEarlyChildSt ... Graduate Diploma in Early Childhood Studies [*Australia*]
GradDipEconDev ... Graduate Diploma in Economic Development [*Australia*]
GradDipEconGeol ... Graduate Diploma in Economic Geology [*Australia*]
GradDipEconHist ... Graduate Diploma in Economic History [*Australia*]
GradDipEconom ... Graduate Diploma in Econometrics [*Australia*]

GradDipEdAdmin ... Graduate Diploma in Educational Administration [*Australia*]

GradDipEdCouns ... Graduate Diploma in Educational Counseling [*Australia*]

GradDipEdStSptTchg ... Graduate Diploma in Educational Studies Support Teaching [*Australia*]

GradDipEdTrain ... Graduate Diploma in Education and Training [*Australia*]

GradDipEng ... Graduate Diploma in Engineering [*Australia*]

GradDipEnvSt ... Graduate Diploma in Environmental Studies [*Australia*]

GradDipEpi ... Graduate Diploma in Epidemiology [*Australia*]

GradDipFA ... Graduate Diploma of Fine Arts [*Australia*]

GradDipFamLaw ... Graduate Diploma of Family Law [*Australia*]

GradDipForOdont ... Graduate Diploma in Forensic Odontology [*Australia*]

GradDipGalSt ... Graduate Diploma in Gallery Studies [*Australia*]

GradDipGraphCommEd ... Graduate Diploma in Graphic Communication Education [*Australia*]

GradDipHumanPhysiol & Pharmacol ... Graduate Diploma in Human Physiology and Pharmacology [*Australia*]

GradDipImmunolMicrobiol ... Graduate Diploma in Immunology and Microbiology [*Australia*]

GradDipInfoMgt ... Graduate Diploma in Information Management [*Australia*]

GradDipInfTech ... Graduate Diploma in Information Technology [*Australia*]

GradDipIntComLaw ... Graduate Diploma in International and Commercial Law [*Australia*]

GradDipIntPropLaw ... Graduate Diploma in Intellectual Property Law [*Australia*]

GradDipLabRelLaw ... Graduate Diploma in Labour Relations Law [*Australia*]

GradDipLangTchg ... Graduate Diploma in Language Teaching [*Australia*]

GradDipLegSt ... Graduate Diploma of Legal Studies [*Australia*]

GradDipMatAnth ... Graduate Diploma of Material Anthropology [*Australia*]

GradDipMatEng ... Graduate Diploma in Materials Engineering [*Australia*]

GradDipMathSc ... Graduate Diploma in Mathematics Science [*Australia*]

GradDipMathsEd ... Graduate Diploma in Mathematics Education [*Australia*]

GradDipMediaComm & TechLaw ... Graduate Diploma in Media Communications and Technology Law [*Australia*]

GradDipMelSt ... Graduate Diploma of Melanesian Studies [*Australia*]

GradDipMentHlthSc ... Graduate Diploma in Mental Health Science [*Australia*]

GradDipMidwif ... Graduate Diploma in Midwifery [*Australia*]

GradDipMolBiol ... Graduate Diploma in Molecular Biology [*Australia*]

GradDipMovement & Dance ... Graduate Diploma in Movement and Dance [*Australia*]

GradDipMultiStudies ... Graduate Diploma in Multicultural Studies [*Australia*]

GradDipMunEng ... Graduate Diploma in Municipal Engineering [*Australia*]

GradDipMus ... Graduate Diploma in Music [*Australia*]

GradDipMusCur ... Graduate Diploma of Museum Curatorship [*Australia*]

GradDipMusMgmt ... Graduate Diploma in Museum Management [*Australia*]

GradDipMus(Op) ... Graduate Diploma in Music (Opera) [*Australia*]

GradDipMus(Perf) ... Graduate Diploma in Music (Performance) [*Australia*]

GradDipMus(Rep) ... Graduate Diploma in Music (Repetiteur) [*Australia*]

GradDipNatResourcesLaw ... Graduate Diploma in Natural Resources Law [*Australia*]

GradDipOffshEng ... Graduate Diploma in Offshore Engineering [*Australia*]

GradDipPPT ... Graduate Diploma in Pulp and Paper Technology [*Australia*]

GradDipProjMgt ... Graduate Diploma in Project Management [*Australia*]

GradDipPsych ... Graduate Diploma of Psychology [*Australia*]

GradDipScSoc ... Graduate Diploma of Science and Society [*Australia*]

GradDipSocAdmin ... Graduate Diploma in Social Administration [*Australia*]

GradDipSocEcol ... Graduate Diploma in Social Ecology [*Australia*]

GradDipSpecEd ... Graduate Diploma in Special Education [*Australia*]

GradDipStratSt ... Graduate Diploma in Strategic Studies [*Australia*]

GradDipStrucEng ... Graduate Diploma in Structural Engineering [*Australia*]

GradDipStudWel ... Graduate Diploma in Student Welfare [*Australia*]

GradDipTeach ... Graduate Diploma in Teaching [*Australia*]

GradDipTourism ... Graduate Diploma of Tourism [*Australia*]

GradDipWaterEng ... Graduate Diploma in Water Engineering [*Australia*]

GradDipWelfAdmin ... Graduate Diploma in Welfare Administration [*Australia*]

GradDipWomen'sStudies ... Graduate Diploma in Women's Studies [*Australia*]

GradDipWomHlth ... Graduate Diploma in Women's Health [*Australia*]

grad ekv ... Degree of Equator (RU)

GRADEP ... Gradevinsko Preduzece [*Building Establishment*] (YU)

GradIEAust ... Graduate of the Institution of Engineers, Australia (ADA)

GradIEE ... Graduate Member of the South African Institute of Electrical Engineers (AA)

grad mer ... Degree of Meridian (RU)

GradRAES ... Graduate Member of the Royal Aeronautical Society [*South Africa*] (AA)

GradSAIEE ... Graduate Member of the South African Institute of Electrical Engineers (AA)

GradSAIETE ... Graduate Member of the South African Institute of Electrical Technician Engineers (AA)

GRADSPED ... Gradsko Preduzece za Transport i Spediciju [*City Establishment for Transport and Shipment*] [*Rijeka*] (YU)

GRAE ... Gouvernement Revolutionnaire de l'Angola en Exil [*Revolutionary Angolan Government-in-Exile*] [*French*]

GRAE ... Governo Revolucionario de Angola no Exilio [*Revolutionary Angolan Government-in-Exile*] [*Portuguese*] (PD)

graf ... Grafico [*Illustration*] [*Portuguese*]

graf ... Grafico [*Illustration*] [*Spanish*]

graf ... Grafico [*Illustration*] [*Italian*]

graf ... Graficzny [*Printing*] (POL)

graf ... Grafieken [*Benelux*] (BAS)

graf ... Graphite [*Topography*] (RU)

GRAFCET ... Graphe de Commande Etape-Transition [*State transition command graph*] [*Computer language*] (CDE)

Grafol ... Grafologia [*Graphology*] [*Portuguese*]

GRAIL ... Genoa Resources and Investment Ltd. [*Australia*]

GRAINCORP ... New South Wales Grain Corp. [*Australia*] [*Commercial firm*]

Gral ... General [*General*] [*Spanish*] (GPO)

Gram ... Gramatica [*Grammar*] [*Portuguese*]

gram ... Grammar, Grammatical (BU)

Gram ... Grammateia [*Secretariat*] (GC)

gram ... Grammatika [*Grammar*] [*Afrikaans*]

GRAMACOP ... Grain Marketing Cooperative of the Philippines (DSCA)

GRAMAG ... Gradski Magacin [*City Department Store*] (YU)

GRAMAR ... Granitos y Marmoles SA [*Colombia*] (COL)

GRAMAT ... Poduzece za Promet Gradevinskim Materijalom i Tehnickom Robom [*Establishment for Trade in Building and Technical Materials*] [*Zagreb*] (YU)

Gramcheka ... Extraordinary Commission for the Elimination of Illiteracy (RU)

GRAMETAL ... Metalurgica Grancolombiana [*Pacho-Cundinamarca*] (COL)

gramm ... Grammaire [*French*] (TPFD)

gramm ... Grammar (RU)

Gramo ... Gramola [*Record label*] [*Belgium*]

GRAMOA ... Grands Magasins de l'Ouest Africain

GRAN ... Grupo Regional Andino [*Andean Regional Group*] [*Peru*] (LA)

GRANAP ... Gradsko Narodno Preduzece [*City Department Store*] (YU)

GRANAT ... Great Annihilator [*Commonwealth - French satellite*] (ECON)

granetsentrir ... Face-Centered (RU)

GRANIL ... Grand Accelerateur National d'Ions Lourds [*National Heavy Ion Accelerator*] [*France*] (IRC)

granit ... Granite [*Colored to Resemble Granite*] [*Publishing*] [*French*]

GRANUBRAS ... Adubos Granulados SA [*Brazil*] (DSCA)

GRANUPHOS ... Tunisian Granular Phosphate Co. (AF)

GRANVIVIENDA ... Grancolombiana de Vivienda [*Colombia*] (COL)

grapappersomsl ... Grapappersomslag [*Plain Wrapper*] [*Bookbinding*] [*Sweden*]

graph ... Graphiek [*Graph*] [*Publishing*] [*Netherlands*]

graph ... Graphique [*French*] (FLAF)

graph ... Graphisch [*Graphic*] [*Publishing*] [*German*]

Graphitier ... Graphitierung [*Graphitization*] [*German*] (GCA)

GRAPHOR ... Graphes d'Ordonnancement [*French*] (ADPT)

GRAPO ... Grupos de Resistencia Anti-Fascista Primero de Octubre [*October First Antifascist Resistance Groups*] [*Spain*] [*Political party*] (PPE)

GRAPPA ... Grafisches Projektplanungs-Analysesystem [*German*] (ADPT)

GRARRMADGAR ... Goddard Range and Range Rate Station, Madagascar

GRAS ... General Remote Acquisition System [*Weapons Research Establishment*] [*Australia*]

GRASCO ... Grasas y Aceites Vegetales [*Colombia*] (COL)

GRASS ... Grassland Research and Serengeti Systems [*Model for simulation*]

GRATEKS ... Gradsko Trgovinsko Preduzece za Promet Tekstilom [*City Establishment for Trade in Textiles*] (YU)

GRATIS ... Ghana Regional Appropriate Technology Industrial Service

GRATPRED ... Gradsko Trgovinsko Preduzece [*City Commercial Establishment*] (YU)

grav ... Cut, Engraved, Engraving, Print (RU)

grav ... Engraved [*or Engraving*] (BU)

G Rav ... Gare de Ravitaillement [*Military*] [*French*] (MTD)

grav ... Grave [*Engraved*] [*Publishing*] [*French*]

grav ... Gravel Pit [*Topography*] (RU)

grav ... Graverad [*Engraved*] [*Publishing*] [*Sweden*]

grav ... Graveret [*Engraved*] [*Publishing Danish/Norwegian*]

grav ... Gravite [*Seriousness*] [*French*]

Grav ... Gravuere [*Engraving*] [*Publishing*] [*German*]

grav ... Gravura [*Engraving*] [*Publishing*] [*Portuguese*]

grav ... Gravure [*Engraving*] [*Publishing*] [*French*]

GRAVETAL ... Grasas Vegetales de Antioquia Ltda. (COL)

gravitats ... Gravitational, Gravity (RU)

Graz ... Grazioso [*Flowing*] [*Music*]

grazh ... Civilian, Civil, Civic (RU)

grazhd ... Citizen, Civic, Civil, Civilian (RU)

GRB ... Advance Repair Crew (RU)

GrB ... City Library (BU)

GRB .... Glavna Recna Baza [*Main River Base*] [*Navy*]   (YU)
GRB .... Guyana Rice Board   (LA)
grbs .... Grabados [*Illustrations*] [*Spanish*]
GRBS........ Groupe de Recherche en Biologie Spatiale [*Space Biology Research Group*] [*France*]   (PDAA)
GRC .... Grand Cess [*Liberia*] [*Airport symbol*]   (OAG)
Gr C .... Grand'Croix [*Grand Cross (Awarded by the Legion of Honor)*] [*Freemasonry*] [*French*]
GRC .... Greece [*ANSI three-letter standard code*]   (CNC)
GRC .... Greenlandair Charter AS [*Denmark*] [*ICAO designator*]   (FAAC)
GRC .... Group Representation Constituency [*Singapore*]
GRCB .... Greyhound Racing Control Board [*Australia*]
grch .... Griechisch [*Greek*] [*German*]   (GCA)
GRCOP ..... Groupe de Recherche Choregraphique de l'Opera de Paris [*French*]
gr coup....... Grosses Coupures [*Large Denominations (of Currency)*] [*Business term*] [*French*]
GRCS........ Ghana Red Cross Society
GrCu .... University of Crete, Crete, Greece [*Library symbol*] [*Library of Congress*]   (LCLS)
GRCWA .... Grain Research Committee of Western Australia
gr d .... Dirt Road [*Topography*]   (RU)
Grd .... Grand [*Large*] [*Military map abbreviation World War I*] [*French*]   (MTD)
Gr D .... Grand-Duche [*Benelux*]   (BAS)
GRD .... Grenada [*ANSI three-letter standard code*]   (CNC)
GRD .... Groupe de Recherche pour le Developpement [*Haiti*]   (EAIO)
Grd .... Grund [*Shoal*] [*Gd Swedish*] [*See also*]   (NAU)
Grd .... Grund [*Shoal*] [*Gd Danish*] [*See also*]   (NAU)
Grd .... Grund [*Shoal*] [*Gd*] [*See also*] [*German*]   (NAU)
GRD .... Gruppe fur Rustungsdienst [*Defense Procurement Agency of the Federal Defense Department*] [*Switzerland*]   (PDAA)
GRD .... Hybrid Rocket Engine, Hydrojet   (RU)
gr dal .... Grade Decalitri [*Degrees Decaliters*]   (RO)
GRDC .... Geological Research and Development Center [*Ministry of Mines and Energy*] [*Indonesia*] [*Research center*]   (IRC)
GRDC .... Grains Research and Development Corp. [*Australia*]
GRDCh...... Harmonic Relaxation Frequency Divider   (RU)
Grdl .... Grundlage [*Basis*] [*German*]   (GCA)
GRDO....... Gambia River Development Organisation
gr dor.......... Dirt Road [*Topography*]   (RU)
GRDR .... Groupe de Recherche et de Realisations pour le Developpement Rural dans la Tiers Monde [*Research and Development Group for Rural Development in the Third World*] [*France*]   (PDAA)
Grdr .... Grundriss [*Outline*] [*German*]
Grdw .... Grondwet [*Benelux*]   (BAS)
GRE .... Generalreparatur [*General Overhaul*]   (EG)
GRE .... Grant-Related Expenditure [*British*]
GRE .... Greece   (WDAA)
GRE .... [*The*] Greens [*Australia*] [*Political party*]
Gre .... National Library of Greenland [*Nunatta Atuagaategarfi*], Nuuk, Greenland [*Library symbol*] [*Library of Congress*]   (LCLS)
GRE .... SEEA-Southeast European Airlines [*Greece*] [*ICAO designator*]   (FAAC)
GREA .... Groupements pour la Recherche et l'Exploitation Aurifere [*Groups for Gold Prospecting and Exploitation*] [*Malagasy*]   (AF)
GREACAM ... Guardian Royal Exchange Assurance du Cameroun
GREAEM ... Gabinete Regional de Estudos das Associacoes Economicas de Mocambique
GRECAS ... Groupement d'Etudes et de Courtages d'Assurances [*French*]   (SLS)
GRECE...... Groupement de Recherche et d'Etudes pour la Civilisation Europeenne [*Research and Study Group for European Civilization*] [*France*]   (PD)
grech .... Greek, Grecian   (RU)
GREDES ... Grupo de Estudios para el Desarrollo [*Development Studies Group*] [*Peru*] [*Research center*]   (IRC)
Greenl .... Greenland   (BARN)
GREI......... Grupo para la Racionalizacion de la Energia Industrial [*Group for Industrial Energy Efficiency*] [*Uruguay*]   (LA)
GREL........ Ghana Rubber Estates Limited
GREM .... Gremlin [*Refers to a person unskilled in skateboarding*] [*Slang*] [*British*]   (DSUE)
GREO .... Mining Electrical Equipment   (RU)
GREP......... Groupe de Recherche et d'Education pour la Promotion [*French*]   (SLS)
GREPOS ... Grenzpolizei [*Border Guards*]   (EG)
GRES........ Gippsland Regional Environmental Study [*Australia*]
GRES........ State Regional Electric Power Plant   (RU)
GRESEL.... Groupement pour l'Exportation des Systemes Electroniques
GREST ...... Gruppo Estivo [*Church organization which arranges games, etc., for children during summer holidays*] [*Italian*]
GRET........ Groupe de Recherches et des Sciences Technologiques [*France*]
GRETA...... Gestion Rationnelle et Elaboree pour le Traitement de l'Adresse [*French*]   (ADPT)

GRETAL ... Grupo Regional de Telecomunicaciones para America Latina   (LAA)
GRETI .... Groupe Romand pour l'Etude des Techniques d'Instruction [*Switzerland*]
GRF .... Grain Research Foundation [*Australia*]
GRG.......... Green Revolution Gospels [*Liberia*]
GRG.......... Groupe de Reflexion des Guineens [*France-based Guinean political organization*]
GRGDB ..... Gryehound Racing Grounds Development Board [*Victoria, Australia*]
Grge .... Gorge [*Pass, Gorge*] [*Military map abbreviation World War I*] [*French*]   (MTD)
GRGS .... Groupe de Recherche de Goedesie Spatiale [*Space Geodesy Research Group*] [*France*]   (PDAA)
GRH .... Garuahi [*Papua New Guinea*] [*Airport symbol*]   (OAG)
GRI .... Geophysical Research Institute [*University of New England, Australia*]
GRI .... State Radium Institute   (RU)
GRIB........ Gippsland Region Information Bank [*Australia*]
GRIE......... Grupo Regional sobre Interconexion Electrica [*Central American*]   (LAA)
Griff .... Griffith University [*Australia*]   (ADA)
GRII.......... Trust for Geodetic Operations and Engineering Surveys   (RU)
GRIMM .... Groupe de Recherche Interdisciplinaire sur les Materiaux Moleculaires [*Interdisciplinary Research Group for Molecular Materials*] [*France*]   (IRC)
GRINACO ... Grupo de Investigaciones Nacional Aplicadas a la Construccion [*Group for Applied Research in Construction*] [*Cuba*]   (LA)
GRINCOR ... Grindrod Unicorn [*Shipping and transport company*] [*South Africa*]
GRINM ..... General Research Institute for Non-Ferrous Metals [*China*]   (WED)
GRIP........ International Grouping of Pharmaceuticals Distributors in the EEC   (ECED)
GRIS......... Grisons [*Canton in Switzerland*]   (ROG)
GRISUR..... Grupo de Informacion y Solidaridad Uruguay [*Switzerland*]
GRITC...... Graduate Member of the Institute of Town Clerks of Southern Africa   (AA)
GRJ........... George [*South Africa*] [*Airport symbol*]   (OAG)
Gr k .... Civil Code   (RU)
GRK .... Gendarmerie Royale Khmere [*Royal Cambodian Gendarmerie*] [*Replaced by National Gendarmerie*]   (CL)
GRK .... Main Committee for Control of Entertainment and Repertoires   (RU)
gr k .... Pile of Stones, Cairn [*Topography*]   (RU)
gr-ka.......... Citizen   (RU)
gr-kath ...... Griechisch-Katholisch [*German*]
Gr Kod .... Civil Code   (RU)
gr k-t .... City Committee   (BU)
GRKU .... Gerilja Rakjat Kalimantan Utara [*North Kalimantan People's Guerrilla Force*]   (IN)
GRL .... Gendarmerie Royale Lao [*Royal Lao Gendarmerie*]   (CL)
GRL .... Greenland [*ANSI three-letter standard code*]   (CNC)
GRL .... Gronlandsfly Ltd. [*Denmark*] [*ICAO designator*]   (FAAC)
GRM........ Geology of Ore Deposits   (RU)
GRM........ Glide Beacon   (RU)
Grm.......... Gramm [*Gram*] [*German*]   (GCA)
GRM........ Gramme [*Gram*] [*French*]   (ROG)
GRM........ Gruppe Revolutionaerer Marxisten [*Group of Revolutionary Marxists*] [*Austria*] [*Political party*]   (PPE)
GRM........ State Russian Museum   (RU)
gr-n........... Citizen   (RU)
GRN .... Gminna Rada Narodowa [*Rural Commune People's Council*]   (POL)
GRN........ Gouvernement de Redressement National
GRN........ Gouvernement de Renouveau National [*National Renewal Government*] [*Burkina Faso*]   (AF)
GRN........ Greenair Hava Tasimaciligi AS [*Turkey*] [*ICAO designator*]   (FAAC)
GRN........ Greens [*Political party*] [*Australia*]
GRN........ Gromadzka Rada Narodowa [*Gromada People's Council*]   (POL)
gr-ne.......... Citizens   (RU)
Grne .... Grunn [*or Grunnen, Grunnane*] [*Shoal or Shoals*] [*Norway*]   (NAU)
grn lz .... Station Hospital   (BU)
Gr NR .... Sodium-Graphite Reactor   (RU)
GRNSK...... Grafeion Nomikou Symvoulou Kratous [*State Legal Council Office*] [*Greek*]   (GC)
GRNV........ Gesamentlike Raad van Natuurwetenskaplike Verenigings [*South Africa*]
GRO.......... Gerona [*Spain*] [*Airport symbol*]   (OAG)
Gr O .... Grand-Officier [*Grand Officer of the Legion of Honor*] [*Freemasonry*] [*French*]
gro .... Gromada [*Village, Group of Villages*]   (POL)
GRO.......... Lineas Aereas Allegro SA de CV [*Mexico*] [*ICAO designator*]   (FAAC)

GROCOMAF ... Groupement Commercial Africain
GROKO ..... Groupement Commercial de Kossi
GronCond ... Condities van de Bond van Groninger Graanhandelaren [*Benelux*] (BAS)
Gron Exp ... Exportcontract van de Bond van Groninger Graanhandelaren [*Benelux*] (BAS)
gr-or .... Griechisch-Orientalisch [*Greek-Oriental*] [*German*]
Gros .... Generos [*Goods*] [*Business term*] [*Spanish*]
gros .... Grossus [*Coarse*] [*Latin*] (MAE)
grossis .... Grossissimo [*Thick*] [*Publishing*] [*Italian*]
grossiss ...... Grossissimo [*Thick*] [*Publishing*] [*Italian*]
grossoberflach ... Grossoberflaechig [*Large Surfaced*] [*German*] (GCA)
GROUPAGRI ... Groupement des Syndicats et Enterprises Agricoles de Madagascar
GROW .... Group Recovery Organizations of the World (ADA)
GROWIAN ... Grosse Windkraftanlage [*Large Wind-Power Plant*]
GROZNII ... Groznyy Petroleum Scientific Research Institute (RU)
GRP .... Design Flood Level (RU)
GRP .... Gambia and the Rio Pongas
GRP .... Gas-Distributing Point (RU)
GRP .... Gas-Pickup Point (RU)
GRP .... Gas-Regulating Point (RU)
GRP .... Glass Reinforced Plastic Pipes
GRP .... Gouvernement Revolutionnaire Provisoire (de la Republique du Sud Viet Nam) [*Provisional Revolutionary Government (of the Republic of South Vietnam)*] [*Use PGRSV*] (CL)
GRP .... Hydraulic Fracturing [*Pet.*] (RU)
GRP .... Project Starting Management Group (BU)
GRPA .... Groupe de Rapporteurs sur la Pollution Atmospherique [*France*]
GRPA .... Guyana Rice Producers Association [*Guyana*] (DSCA)
GRPE .... Group of Rapporteurs on Pollution and Energy
GRPENT ... Grouped Enterprises Data Base [*Australian Bureau of Statistics*] [*Information service or system*] (CRD)
GRPL .... Grupo Revolucionario Portugues de Libertacao [*Portuguese Revolutionary Liberation Group*] (WER)
Gr Pl B .... Groot Placaetboek [*Benelux*] (BAS)
GRPP .... Advance Company Small Arms Ammunition Point (RU)
GRPP .... Gradanski Parnicni Postupak [*Civil Code of Procedure*] (YU)
Gr protskod ... Code of Civil Procedure (RU)
GRPSM ..... Groupement Rural de Production et de Secours Mutuel
GRQ .... Groningen [*Netherlands*] [*Airport symbol*] (OAG)
GRR .... Government Records Repository [*New South Wales, Australia*]
GRR .... Greek Research Reactor [*Nuclear energy*] (NRCH)
GRRC .... Government Regulations Review Committee [*Western Australia*]
GRRRI ...... State Roentgenology, Radiology, and Cancer Institute (RU)
GRRTSN ... Groupement de Realisation de la Route Transsaharienne du Service National [*North African*]
GRS .... Gas-Distributing Station (RU)
GRS .... German Dermatological Society (EAIO)
GRS .... Gesellschaft fuer Reaktorsicherheit, mbH [*Society for Reactor Safety*] [*Nuclear energy*] (NRCH)
GRS .... Glavni Radnicki Savez [*Central Workers' Council*] (YU)
GRS .... Gminna Rada Spoldzielcza [*Rural Commune Cooperative Council*] (POL)
GRS .... Gorska Resevalna Sluzba [*Mountain Rescue Service*] (YU)
grs .... Gramos [*Grams*] [*Spanish*]
GRS .... Grassland Research Station [*Kenya*] (DSCA)
grs .... Grosa [*Gross*] [*Portuguese*]
GrS .... Grosser Senat (DLA)
GRS .... Groupe Revolutionnaire Socialiste [*Socialist Revolution Group*] [*Martinique*] [*Political party*] (PPW)
GRSA .... General Radioquimica, SA [*Nuclear energy*] [*Spanish*] (NRCH)
GR (SA) ..... Geoktrooieerde Rekenmeester (Suid-Afrika) [*South Africa*] (AA)
GRShch ..... Main Switchboard (RU)
Grssgdb ...... Grossgrundbesitzer [*Landed Proprietor*] [*German*]
Grsshdlr ..... Grosshaendler [*Wholesale Dealer or Merchant*] [*German*]
Grssind ...... Grossindustrieller [*Wholesale Manufacturer or Industrial Magnate*] [*German*]
GRT .... Gabon-Air-Transport [*ICAO designator*] (FAAC)
GRT .... Gambia River Transport (AF)
GRT .... Geriatric Rehabilitation Team [*Australia*]
grt .... Gross Registered Tons (EECI)
Grte .... Grotte [*Grotto*] [*Military map abbreviation World War I*] [*French*] (MTD)
GRTE .... Grupo Regional sobre Tarifas Electricas [*Central American*] (LAA)
GRTOP ..... Groupe de Recherche Theatrale de l'Opera de Paris [*French*]
GRTS .... City Manual Telephone Exchange (RU)
GRTS .... City Radio Wire Broadcasting Network (RU)
GRTs .... Generator of Equally Probable Digits (RU)
grts .... Greek (BU)
GRU .... Glavnoye Razvedyvatelnoye Upravlenie [*Soviet Military Intelligence Service*]
GrU .... Grosshandelsumsatz [*Wholesale Turnover*] (EG)

GRU .... Main Distributing Installation (RU)
GRU .... Main Radio Administration (RU)
GRU .... Regional Administration of Geological Exploration (RU)
GRUAS ..... Grupo Universitario Artistico Surcolombiano [*Neiva*] (COL)
grub .... Grubosc [*Thickness*] [*Poland*]
Gr Uff .... Grande Ufficiale [*Decoration*] [*Italian*]
GRULA ..... Grupo Regional Latinoamericano [*Latin American Regional Group*] (LA)
GRUMCAM ... Grumes du Cameroun
grundl .... Gruendlich [*Entirely, Thorough*] [*German*]
Grundr ...... Grundriss [*Outline*] [*Publishing*] [*German*]
Grunds ...... Grundsatz [*Principle*] [*German*]
GRUNK ..... Gouvernement Royal d'Union Nationale du Kampuchea [*Royal Government of National Union of Cambodia*] (CL)
Gruporg ...... Group Organizer (BU)
GRUR .... Gewerblicher Rechtsschutz und Urheberrecht [*Germany*] (FLAF)
gruz .... Georgian (RU)
Gruzenergo ... Georgian Power System (RU)
GruzFAN ... Georgian Branch of the Academy of Sciences, USSR (RU)
Gruzgiprovodkhoz ... Georgian State Institute for the Planning of Water Management (RU)
Gruzgosplan ... State Planning Commission at the Council of Ministers, Georgian SSR (RU)
Gruzmedgiz ... Georgian State Publishing House of Medical Literature (RU)
Gruzneft' .... Georgian Oil Field Administration (RU)
GruzNIIGiM ... Georgian Scientific Research Institute of Hydraulic Engineering and Reclamation (RU)
GruzNIIGM ... Georgian Scientific Research Institute of Hydraulic Engineering and Reclamation (RU)
GruzNIIVKh ... Georgian Scientific Research Institute of Water Management (RU)
GruzNITO ... Georgian Scientific Research and Technical Society (RU)
GruzNITOLes ... Georgian Scientific and Technical Society of the Lumber Industry and Forestry (RU)
GruzSSR ..... Georgian Soviet Socialist Republic (RU)
GruzTAG ... Georgian News Agency (RU)
GRV .... Gesellschaft fuer Rationale Verkehrspolitik eV [*Society for Rational Business Policy*] (SLS)
Grv .... Gorev [*Duty, Mission*] (TU)
grv .... Granatveto [*Grenade Thrower*] (HU)
Gr v .... Grande Vitesse [*High Speed, Express*] [*French*]
GRVC .... Groupement Revolutionnaire a Vocation Cooperative [*Revolutionary Cooperative Group*] [*Benin*] (AF)
GRV-K ...... Graficheski Vestnik [*Graphics Newspaper*] [*A periodical*] (BU)
Gr VR .... Water-Cooled Graphite Reactor (RU)
Gr VRD ..... Pressurized-Tube Water-Cooled Graphite Reactor (RU)
Gr VRK ..... Boiling-Water Graphite Reactor (RU)
Gr VRK-P .. Boiling-Water Graphite Reactor with Nuclear Superheat (RU)
GRVSA ...... Genoot Rekenaarvereniging van Suid-Afrika [*South Africa*] (AA)
GRW .... Garden Reach Workshops Ltd. [*India*]
GRW .... Geraete- und Reglerwerke (VEB) [*Appliance and Regulator Works (VEB)*] [*Teltow*] (EG)
GRW .... Graciosa Island [*Azores*] [*Airport symbol*] (OAG)
Grw .... Grondwet [*Benelux*] (BAS)
GRX .... Granada [*Spain*] [*Airport symbol*] (OAG)
GRY .... Grey Power [*Political party*] [*Australia*]
GRY .... Grimsey [*Iceland*] [*Airport symbol*] (OAG)
gryaz .... Mud Volcano, Muddy Spring [*Topography*] (RU)
gryaz lech ... Mud-Bath Clinic [*Topography*] (RU)
GRYCC ..... Geraldton Region Youth Co-Ordinating Committee [*Australia*]
GRZ .... Government of the Republic of Zambia
GRZ .... Graz [*Austria*] [*Airport symbol*] (OAG)
Grz .... Grenze [*Frontier*] [*German*] (GCA)
g/s .... Advanced Station (RU)
GS .... Aircraft Generator (RU)
GS .... Chief Referee [*Sports*] (RU)
GS .... City Council (BU)
GS .... Civil Procedure [*Law*] (BU)
GS .... Draw-Off Level (RU)
GS .... Erase Head, Erasing Head (RU)
GS .... Galatasaray Lisesi [*Galatasaray Lycee*] [*Istanbul*] (TU)
Gs .... Gaus [*Gauss*] [*Poland*]
gs .... Gauss (RU)
GS .... Gedeputeerde Staten [*Benelux*] (BAS)
GS .... Gefechtsstand [*Headquarters, Command Post*] (EG)
GS .... Gefechtsstation [*Battle Station*] (EG)
GS .... Generale Staf [*General Staff*] [*Afrikaans*]
GS .... Genikon Symvoulion [*General Council*] (GC)
GS .... Geschaeftsstelle [*German*] (ADPT)
GS .... Gesetzsammlung [*Collection of Statutes, Gazette*] [*German*] (ILCA)
GS .... Glavni Stab [*General Headquarters*] [*Military*] (YU)
GS .... Gminna Spoldzielnia [*Rural Commune Cooperative*] (POL)
GS .... Goldstar Co. Ltd. [*South Korea*]

GS .... Gorsko Stopanstvo [*Forestry Resources*] [*A periodical*]   (BU)
GS .... Gradska Stamparija [*City Printing Office*]   (YU)
gs .... Gram Force   (RU)
GS .... Gran Sport [*Automobile model designation*]
GS .... Gravimetric Station   (RU)
GS .... Group for Support [*to border troops*]   (BU)
GS .... Grupo Socialista [*Socialist Group*] [*Portugal*] [*Political party*]   (PPE)
GS .... Guild of Surveyors [*Middlesex, England*]   (EAIO)
GS .... Guinea Syli
GS .... Gymnastikos Syllogos [*Gymnastics Club*]   (GC)
GS .... Gyro Stabilizer   (RU)
GS .... Hospital Ship   (RU)
GS .... Hydraulic Engineering Construction   (RU)
GS .... Main Forces, Main Body   (RU)
GS .... Second Goniometer   (RU)
GS .... Self-Defense Group   (RU)
GS .... Signal Generator   (RU)
GS .... Signal Oscillator   (BU)
GSA .... Gastroenterological Society of Australia
GSA .... General Series in Anthropology
GSA .... Genetics Society of Australia   (ADA)
GSA .... Geological Society of Africa [*ICSU*]
GSA .... Geological Society of Australia   (ADA)
GSA .... Geranium Society of Australia   (ADA)
GSA .... Gesinsbeplanningsvereniging van Suid-Afrika [*South Africa*]   (EAIO)
GSA .... Government Servants' Association [*Mauritius*]   (EAIO)
GSA .... Government Service Agency [*Liberia*]
GSA .... Government Shareholding Agency [*Honiara, Solomon Islands*]   (GEA)
GSA .... Governor of South Australia
GSA .... [*The*] Green Party South Australia [*Political party*]
GSA .... Groupe Scolaire d'Astrida
GSA .... Grupo di Studio delle Acque [*Water Study Group*] [*FAST*] [*Italian*]   (ASF)
GSA .... Gulf & South American Steamship Co.   (MHDB)
GSA .... Guyana School of Agriculture   (ARC)
GSA .... Guzel Sanatlar Akademisi [*Fine Arts Academy*] [*DGSA, IDGSA*] [*See also*]   (TU)
GSAA .... German State Archaeologists' Association   (EAIO)
GSACH ..... Guides and Scouts Association of Chile   (EAIO)
GSAE........ Geniki Synomospondia Avtokiniston Ellados [*General Confederation of Motorists of Greece*]   (GC)
GSAI......... El Aaiun [*Western Sahara*] [*ICAO location identifier*]   (ICLI)
GSAIDP .... Groupe Suisse de l'Association Internationale de Droit Penal [*Switzerland*]   (EAIO)
GSAIM...... German Society of Anaesthesiology and Intensive Medicine   (EAIO)
GSAIMECHE ... Graduate Member of the South African Institute of Mechanical Engineers   (AA)
GSAL........ Grupo de Solidariedade com America Latina [*Portugal*]
GS &MCOCAI ... General Supply & Marketing Corp. of Chinese Astronautic Industry   (TCC)
GSAP........ General Supported Accommodation Program [*New South Wales, Australia*]
GSAS........ Geniki Synomospondia Agrotikon Syllogon Ellados [*General Confederation of Greek Agricultural Unions*] [*GESASE*] [*See also*]   (GC)
GSAThP.... Geniki Synomospondia Anapiron kai Thymaton [*General Confederation of Handicapped and Victims*] [*Greek*]   (GC)
GSAVE...... Geniki Synomospondia Avtokiniston Voreiou Ellados [*General Confederation of Drivers of Northern Greece*]   (GC)
GSAWHO ... Geneva Staff Association World Health Organization [*Switzerland*]   (EAIO)
GSB........... Genclik ve Spor Bakanligi [*Youth and Sports Ministry*]   (TU)
GSB........... Genc Sosyal Devrimciler Birligi [*Young Socialists' Organization*]   (TU)
GSB........... Ghana Standards Board   (GEA)
GSB........... Government Savings Bank [*Australia*]
GSB........... Graduate School of Business [*University of Chicago*]   (ECON)
GSB........... Grumes et Sciages du Bini
GSB........... Guyana Society for the Blind   (EAIO)
GSBA........ German Society for Baths Activities   (EAIO)
GSBH .... German Society of Business History   (EAIO)
GSBI.......... Gabungan Serikat Buruh Indonesia [*Indonesian Labor Union Federation*]   (IN)
GSC .... Gascoyne Junction [*Australia*] [*Airport symbol*] [*Obsolete*]   (OAG)
GSC .... [*The*] Geological Society of China   (SLS)
GSC .... German Shippers Council   (DS)
GSC .... Gezira Sporting Club [*Egypt*]
GSC .... Ghana Students' Congress
GSCC........ General Staff Consultative Committee [*Australia*]
GSCC......... German Society of Concert Choirs   (EAIO)

GSCCMF .. Gujarat State Cooperative Cotton Marketing Federation [*India*]   (PDAA)
GSCh .... Stable-Frequency Generator   (RU)
gschr........... Geschrieben [*Written*] [*German*]   (GCA)
GSCI.......... Grupul de Santiere Constructii Instalatii [*Group of Construction and Installation Worksites*]   (RO)
GSCR........ Grupul de Santiere Constructii si Reparatii [*Group of Construction and Repair Worksites*]   (RO)
GSD .... Genc Sosyalistler Dernegi [*Young Socialists' Organization*]   (TU)
GSD .... Geological Survey Department [*Ministry of Mines*] [*Zambia*] [*Research center*]   (EAS)
GSD .... Geological Survey Department [*Ministry of Agriculture and Natural Resources*] [*Cyprus*]   (EAS)
GSD .... Geological Survey Division [*Ministry of Mining and Energy*] [*Jamaica*] [*Research center*]   (EAS)
GSD .... German Society for Documentation   (EAIO)
GSD .... Gesellschaft fuer Systemforschung und Dienstleistungen im Gesundheitswesen
GSD .... Government Services Division [*Victoria, Australia*]
GSD .... Mountain Rifle Division   (RU)
GSDA .... Great Southern Development Authority [*Western Australia*]
GSDF .... Ground Self Defense Force
GSDL........ German Shepherd Dog League [*Australia*]
GSDP........ German Social Democratic Party   (BU)
Gsdtr .... Gesandter [*Ambassador*] [*German*]
Gsdtsch ...... Gesandtschaft [*Embassy*] [*German*]
GSE........... Gestion Socialiste des Entreprises [*Socialist Management of Businesses*] [*Algeria*]   (AF)
GSE........... Gross Subsidy Equivalent [*Tariffs*] [*Australia*]
GSE........... Guias y Scouts de Europa [*Spain*]   (EAIO)
GSEAE ...... Geniki Synomospondia Epangelmation Avtokiniston Ellados [*General Confederation of Professional Drivers of Greece*]   (GC)
GSEE .... Geniki Synomospondia Ergaton Ellados [*General Confederation of Greek Labor*]   (GC)
GSEF .... Guides et Scouts d'Europe - France   (EAIO)
GSEI .... "Soviet Encyclopedia" State Dictionary and Encyclopedia Publishing House   (RU)
GSEL .... Great South East Lines Pty. Ltd.   (DS)
GSEL .... Guides et Scouts Europeens du Luxembourg   (EAIO)
GSEM........ Grupul de Santiere Electromontaj [*Group of Electroassembly Worksites*]   (RO)
GSES .... Graduate School of Environmental Science [*Monash University*] [*Australia*]
GSES .... Guides et Scouts d'Europe - Geneve [*Switzerland*]   (EAIO)
GSEU .... Main Sanitary and Epidemiological Administration   (RU)
GSEVE ...... Geniki Synomospondia Epangelmation kai Viotekhnon Ellados [*General Confederation of Tradesmen and Craftsmen of Greece*]   (GC)
GSF........... Geological Survey of Finland
GSF........... German Ski Federation   (EAIO)
GSF........... Gesellschaft fuer Strahlen- und Umweltforschung mbH [*Radiation and Environmental Research Society*]   (ARC)
GSF........... Group of Soviet Forces in Germany   (MCD)
GSF........... Institut fuer Gesundheits-System-Forschung [*Institute for Health Systems Research*]   (SLS)
GSF........... State Strain Seed Fund   (RU)
GSFC .... Ghana State Farm Corporation
GSFC .... Gujarat State Fertiliser Co. [*India*]   (PDAA)
GSFC .... Gujarat State Financial Corp. [*India*]   (PDAA)
GSFK .... City Council of Physical Culture   (RU)
GSFMO..... Grain Silos and Flour Mills Organization [*Saudi Arabia*]
GSG .... Advanced Fuel Depot   (RU)
GSG .... Gay Solidarity Group [*Australia*]
GSG 9 .... Grenzschutzgruppe Neun [*Border Protection Group 9*] [*Antiterrorist commandos*]
GSGCM..... General Secretary of Government and the Council of Ministers [*Burkina Faso*]
GSGM .... Guzel Sanatlar Genel Mudurlugu [*Fine Arts Directorate General*] [*Under Ministry of Culture*]   (TU)
GSGS........ Geographical Section, General Staff
GSh........... Flapping Hinge   (RU)
GSH .... Gambia Air Shuttle Ltd. [*ICAO designator*]   (FAAC)
GSh........... General Staff   (RU)
GSH .... Gesellschaft fur Schwerionenforschung [*Heavy Ion Research Corp.*] [*Germany*]   (PDAA)
GSH .... Glavni Stab Hrvatske [*General Headquarters of Croatia*] [*World War II*]   (YU)
GSH .... Glowna Szkola Handlowa [*Poland*]
GShchT ..... Glutamic Oxaloacetic Transaminase   (RU)
GShchU ..... Main Control Board, Main Control Panel   (RU)
GShl .... Wide Pulse Generator   (RU)
GShK .... State Permanent Staff Commission   (RU)
GShN........ Low-Frequency Noise Generator   (RU)
GSHR .... Generalni Sekretariat Hospodarske Rady [*Office of the Secretary General of the Economic Council*]   (CZ)

GSHR .... Gremium Statni Hospodarske Rady [*Board of the State Economic Council*] (CZ)
GShS.......... Noise-Spectrum Generator (RU)
GShSA ...... General Staff of the Soviet Army (RU)
GShSI .... Wide Strobe-Pulse Generator (RU)
gsht .... General Staff (BU)
GSI............ Gate Generator, Strobe-Pulse Generator (RU)
GSI............ General de Service Informatique [*French*] (ADPT)
GSI............ General Service Industrials
GSI............ Geographical Survey Institute [*Research center*] [*Japan*] (EAS)
GSI............ Geological Society of Israel (SLS)
GSI............ Geological Survey of India
GSI............ Gerdau Servicos de Informatica [*Computer science*] [*Brazil*]
GSI............ Gesellschaft fuer Schwerionenforschung [*Center for Heavy Ion Research*] [*Germany*]
GSI............ Groupe de Strategie Industrielle [*France*]
GSI............ Groupement de Services Informatiques [*French*] (ADPT)
GSI............ Grupul de Supraveghere a Investitiilor [*Investments Supervision Group*] (RO)
GSI............ Main Sanitary Inspection (RU)
GSI............ Standard-Pulse Generator (RU)
GSI............ State Sanitary Inspection (RU)
GSI............ Timing-Pulse Generator [*Computers*] (RU)
GSIC......... Government of Singapore Investment Corporation (GEA)
GSIC......... Gujarat Small Industries Corp. [*India*] (PDAA)
GSICO...... Glaucoma Society of the International Congress of Ophthalmology [*Japan*] (EAIO)
GSIDC....... Arab Gulf States Information Documentation Center [*Information service or system*] (IID)
GSIEN...... Groupement de Scientifiques pour l'Information sur l'Energie Nucleaire [*France*]
GSIK......... Interstitial Cell Stimulating Hormone (RU)
GSIS .... Government Service Insurance System [*Philippines*]
GSJ .... Geological Survey of Japan (MSC)
GSJ .... Gimnasticki Savez Jugoslavije [*Yugoslav Gymnastic Federation*] (YU)
GSJ .... Girl Scouts of Japan (EAIO)
GSK .... Combined-Signal Generator (RU)
GSK .... Gesellschaft fuer Schweizerische Kunstgeschichte [*Swiss Art History Society*] (SLS)
GSK .... Main Board of Referees [*Sports*] (RU)
GSKB........ State Special Design Office (RU)
GSKBD...... State Special Design Office for Engines (RU)
GSKD .... Genclik, Spor, ve Kultur Isleri Dairesi [*Youth, Sports, and Cultural Affairs Office*] [*Turkish Cypriot*] (TU)
GSKhOS.... State Agricultural Experimental Station (RU)
GSL........... Geographic Society of Lima [*Peru*] (EAIO)
GSL........... Georgikos Syllogos Lysis [*Agricultural Society of Lysi*] [*Cyprus*] (GC)
GSL........... German Society for Logistics (EAIO)
GSL........... Greater Somalia League
GSLA........ Graduate School of Librarianship Alumni [*Monash University*] [*Australia*]
GSLA........ Grupul de Santiere Lucrari Hidrotehnice Galati [*Group of Hydrotechnical Projects Worksites in Galati*] (RO)
GSLG........ German Studies Library Group (EAIO)
GSLK........ Gesellschaft fuer Salzburger Landeskunde [*National Custom Society of Salzburg*] [*Austria*] (SLS)
GSLP......... Gibraltar Socialist Labour Party [*Political party*] (PPW)
GSLV........ Geostationary Launch Vehicle [*Indian Space Research Organization*]
GSLV........ Geostationary Satellite Launch Vehicle
GSM .... Fuel and Lubricants (RU)
GSM .... Geological Society of Malaysia (EAIO)
GSM .... Global System for Mobiles [*European mobile-phone network*] (ECON)
GSM .... Groupe Speciale Mobile [*European digital cellular radio standard*]
GSMB........ Grain Sorghum Marketing Board [*New South Wales, Australia*]
GSMBA..... Gesellschaft Schweizerischer Maler, Bildhauer, und Architekten [*Society of Swiss Artists, Sculptors, and Architects*] (SLS)
GSMH....... Gayri Safi Milli Hasili [*Gross National Product*] [*Turkish*] (TU)
GSMP........ Glowna Skladnica Materialow Pocztowych [*Main Warehouse for Postal Materials*] (POL)
GSMP........ Specialized Medical Aid Group (RU)
GSMPP..... Graduate School of Management and Public Policy [*University of Sydney*] [*Australia*]
GSMT........ Glowna Skladnica Materialow Teletechnicznych [*Main Warehouse for Communications Materials*] (POL)
GSN .... Genikon Stratiotikon Nosokomeion [*Army General Hospital*] (GC)
GSN .... Groupement des Soufflantes Nucleaires [*France*] (PDAA)
GSN .... House Supplies Generator [*Power plant*] (BU)
GSN .... Mount Gunson [*Australia*] [*Airport symbol*] (OAG)
GS naBChK ... City Council of the Bulgarian Red Cross (BU)
GSnBz........ Gussbronze [*Cast Bronze*] [*German*] (GCA)

GSNI .... Gerakan Siswa Nasional Indonesia [*Indonesian National Student Movement*] (IN)
GSNOPOJ ... Glavni Stab Narodnooslobodilackih Partizanskih Odreda Jugoslavije [*General Headquarters of the National Liberation Partisan Detachments of Yugoslavia*] [*World War II*] (YU)
GSNOV ..... Glavni Stab Narodnooslobodilacke Vojske [*General Headquarters of the National Liberation Army*] [*World War II*] (YU)
GSNOVM ... Glavni Stab Narodnooslobodilacke Vojske Makedonije [*General Headquarters of the National Liberation Army of Macedonia*] [*World War II*] (YU)
GSNOVPOM ... Glavni Stab na Narodnoosloboditelnata Vojna i Partizanskite Odredi na Makedonija [*General Headquarters of the National Liberation Army and Partisan Detachments of Macedonia*] (YU)
GSNSW..... Geographical Society of New South Wales [*Australia*]
GSNT .... Genealogical Society of the Northern Territory [*Australia*]
GSNZ .... Geological Society of New Zealand (SLS)
GSO .... City Economic Enterprise (BU)
GSO .... Government Solicitor's Office [*Australian Capital Territory*]
GSO .... Government Statistician's Office [*Queensland, Australia*]
GSO .... Government Superannuation Office [*Queensland, Australia*]
GSO .... Government Supply Office [*New South Wales, Australia*]
GSO .... Ready for Medical Defense (BU)
GSO .... Ready for Sanitary Defense (RU)
GSOEA...... Government Servants and Other Employees Association [*Mauritius*] (AF)
g-sol........... Bitter-Salt Water [*Topography*] (RU)
GSOON..... Generalno Sobranie na Organizacijata na Obedinenite Narodi [*General Assembly of the United Nations Organization*] (YU)
GS/OPS .... Generalni Stab, Operacni Planovaci Sprava [*Operations Planning Directorate, General Staff*] (CZ)
GSORB...... Glavni Stab Omladinskih Radnih Brigada [*General Headquarters of Youth Work Brigades*] (YU)
GSOS........ Generalni Sekretariat Obrany Statu [*National Defense General Secretariat*] (CZ)
GS/OS .... Generalni Stab, Operacni Sprava [*Operations Directorate, General Staff*] (CZ)
GSOV .... Group of Soviet Occupation Troops (RU)
GSOVG ..... Group of Soviet Occupation Troops in Germany (RU)
GSP........... Generalised System of Preferences [*Foreign trade*]
GSP........... Geological Survey of Pakistan [*Ministry of Petroleum and Natural Resources, Islamabad*] [*Research center*] (EAS)
GSP........... Global Social Product (SCAC)
GSP........... Government Selling Price [*Oil industry*] [*Kuwait*] (MENA)
GSP........... Grafeion Skhediou Poleos [*City Plan Office*] [*Greek*] (GC)
GSP........... Grossraumspeicher [*German*] (ADPT)
GSP........... Gross State Product [*Australia*]
GSP........... Gyro-Stabilized Platform (RU)
GSP........... Hospital (RU)
GSP........... Mountain Rifle Regiment (RU)
GSP........... Special City Postal Service [*Bulk mail*] (RU)
GSP........... State Instrument System (RU)
GSP........... Tracked Self-Propelled Ferry (RU)
GSPE .... Geniki Synomospondia Polemiston Ellados [*General Confederation of Greek Combatants*] (GC)
GSPE .... Groupe Socialiste du Parlement Europeen [*Socialist Group in the European Parliament - SGEP*] (EAIO)
GSPEU...... Main Epidemic Control Administration (RU)
GSPI .... State All-Union Planning Institute (RU)
GSPKB ..... State Special Planning and Design Office (RU)
GSPKI .... State Special Planning and Design Institute (RU)
GSPM........ Groupement des Sapeurs Pompiers Militaires
GSPNG...... Geological Survey of Papua New Guinea [*Department of Minerals and Energy*] [*Research center*] (EAS)
GSPPE ...... Geniki Synomospondia Palaion Polemiston Ellados [*General Confederation of Greek Veterans*] (GC)
GSPS .... Guberniya Council of Trade Unions (RU)
GSPST....... Grosspeichersteuerung [*German*] (ADPT)
GSPZNRH ... Glavni Savez Poljoprivrednih Zadruga Narodne Republike Hrvatske [*Central Union of Agricultural Cooperatives of Croatia*] (YU)
GSPZNRS ... Glavni Savez Poljoprivrednih Zadruga Narodne Republike Srbije [*Central Union of Agricultural Cooperatives of Serbia*] (YU)
GSQ .... Geological Survey of Queensland [*Australia*]
GSR .... Gardo [*Somalia*] [*Airport symbol*] (OAG)
GSR .... German Sanchez Ruiperez [*Founder and chairman of Anaya, a Spanish publishing enterprise*]
GSR .... German Shipowners' Association (EAIO)
GSRP......... Gambian Socialist Revolutionary Party [*Political party*] (PD)
GSS........... Advance Signal Depot (RU)
GSS........... General Superintendence Society
GSS........... Geological Society of Sweden (EAIO)

GSS............ Glavni Stab Slovenije [*General Headquarters of Slovenia*] [*World War II*] (YU)

GSS............ Glavni Stab Srbije [*General Headquarters of Serbia*] [*World War II*] (YU)

GSS............ Good Shepherd Sisters [*Australia*]

GSS............ Gradovi Van Sastava Sreza [*Towns Outside District Limits*] (YU)

GSS............ Hero of the Soviet Union (RU)

GSS............ Random-Signal Generator, Standard-Signal Generator (RU)

GSS............ Standard Signal Oscillator (BU)

GSS............ State Selection Station [*Agriculture*] (RU)

GSSA........ General Society of Spanish Authors (EAIO)

GSSA........ Geological Society of South Africa (SLS)

GSSA........ Grassland Society of Southern Africa [*See also WVSA*] (EAIO)

GSSD........ Gruppe Sowjetischer Streitkraefte in Deutschland [*Group of Soviet Forces in Germany (GSFG)*] (EG)

GSSEE....... Geniki Synomospondia Syndaxioukhon Ergatoypallilon Ellados [*General Confederation of Pensioned Workers of Greece*] (GC)

GSSFPS .... General Council of the World Federation of Trade Unions (BU)

GSSL........ Genoa, Savona, Spezia, or Leghorn [*Italian ports*] (DS)

GSSl........ Glavni Stab Slovenije [*General Headquarters of Slovenia*] (YU)

GSSLNCV ... Genoa, Savona, Spezia, Leghorn, Naples, or Civita Vecchia [*Italian ports*] (DS)

GSSME..... German Society of School Music Educators (EAIO)

GS/SP........ Generalni Stab, Souhrnny Plan [*Master Plan, General Staff*] (CZ)

GSSR........ Georgian Soviet Socialist Republic (RU)

GSSR........ German Society for Sex Research (EAIO)

GSSSD....... State Service for Standard Information Data (RU)

GST........... City Telephone Exchange (RU)

GST........... Erasing-Current Oscillator (RU)

GSt............ Gefechtsstand [*Command Post*] (EG)

GST........... Genealogical Society of Tasmania [*Australia*]

Gst............ Generalni Stab [*General Staff*] (CZ)

GST........... Gesellschaft fuer Sport und Technik [*Society for Sport and Technology*] (EG)

GST........... Gesellschaft Schweizerischer Tieraerzte [*Swiss Veterinarian Society*] (SLS)

GST........... Goods and Service Tax [*New Zealand*]

GSTANSW ... General Studies Teachers' Association of New South Wales [*Australia*]

GSTB........ Geographic Reference and Transcription Office (RU)

GStbOffz.... Generalstabsoffizier [*Staff Officer*] [*German*]

GSTC........ Gambia Tourist and Shipping Company

GSTC........ Ghana State Tourist Corporation

GSTD........ Gruppe Sowjetischer Truppen in Deutschland [*Group of Soviet Forces in Germany (GSFG)*] (EG)

Gstl .... Geistlich [*Religious*] [*German*]

Gstozer....... Glavni Stozer [*General Headquarters*] [*Croatian*] [*World War II*] (YU)

GSTP........ Global System of Trade Preferences [*United Nations Conference on Trade and Development*] [*Proposed*]

GS/TS .... Generalni Stab, Technicka Sprava [*Technical Directorate, General Staff*] (CZ)

GSTS......... Geodetska Srednja Tehnicka Skola [*Geodetic Technical Secondary School*] (YU)

GSTS .... Stair-Step Generator (RU)

GSTT......... General Agreement on Tariffs and Trade [*GATT*] (RU)

Gstw.......... Gastwirt [*Innkeeper, Landlord*] [*German*]

GSU .... General Sports Union [*Syria*] (EAIO)

GSU .... German Social Union (EAIO)

GSU .... Main Construction Administration (RU)

GSU .... Main Statistical Administration (RU)

GSU .... State Strain-Testing Plot, State Strain-Testing Station (RU)

GSUalf....... GSU [*Annals of Sofia University*] School of Agronomy and Forestry (BU)

GSUBF ...... GSU [*Annals of Sofia University*] School of Theology (BU)

GSUbogf..... GSU [*Annals of Sofia University*] School of Theology (BU)

GSUFF ...... GSU [*Annals of Sofia University*] Department of Philology (BU)

GSUFIF..... GSU [*Annals of Sofia University*] Department of Philosophy and History (BU)

GSUFMF .. GSU [*Annals of Sofia University*] School of Physics and Mathematics (BU)

GSUIFF..... GSU [*Annals of Sofia University*] Department of History and Philology (BU)

GSUmedf.... GSU [*Annals of Sofia University*] School of Medicine (BU)

GSUPrMF ... GSU [*Annals of Sofia University*] School of Mathematics and Natural Science (BU)

GSUvmedf... GSU [*Annals of Sofia University*] School of Veterinary Medicine (BU)

GSUVMF ... GSU [*Annals of Sofia University*] School of Veterinary Medicine (BU)

GSUYuF .... GSU [*Annals of Sofia University*] School of Law (BU)

GSV .... Army General Staff (BU)

GSV .... Genealogical Society of Victoria [*Australia*]

GSv .... Geodisnjak Hrvatskog Sveucilista [*Yearbook of the Croatian University*] (YU)

GSV .... Greenwich Mean Time (RU)

GSVCh ...... Super-High-Frequency Generator (RU)

GSVG .... Group of Soviet Troops in Germany (RU)

GSVO .... Villa Cisneros [*Western Sahara*] [*ICAO location identifier*] (ICLI)

GS/VSV..... Generalni Stab, Velitelstvi Spojovaciho Vojska [*Communications Troop Headquarters, General Staff*] (CZ)

GSW .... Gemeentelijke Sociale Werkvoorziening [*Benelux*] (BAS)

GSYIH....... Gayrisafi Yurtici Hasila [*Gross Domestic Revenue*] [*Turkish*] (TU)

GSYIM...... Gayrisafi Yurtici Mamulati [*Gross Domestic Product*] [*Turkish*] (TU)

GSZ .... Deep Seismic Sounding (RU)

GSZ .... Geological Society of Zimbabwe (EAIO)

gsz .... Golyoszoro [*Light Machine Gun*] (HU)

GSZT........ Gazdaszati Szakoktatasi Tanacs [*National Council of Agricultural Education*] (HU)

GSZZNRM ... Glaven Sojuz na Zemjodelskite Zadrugi na Narodnata Republika Makedonija [*Central Union of Agricultural Cooperatives of Macedonia*] (YU)

GSZZNRS ... Glavni Savez Zemljoradnickih Zadruga Narodne Republike Srbije [*Central Union of Agricultural Cooperatives of Serbia*] (YU)

GT.............. Gas Turbine (RU)

gt .... Gazdaszati (Tiszt) [*Paymaster*] [*Military*] (HU)

GT.............. General Tours [*Jordan*] [*Commercial firm*]

gt .... Generator, Oscillator (RU)

G/T .... Georgtown [*Penang, Malaysia*] (ML)

GT.............. German Growth Trust [*Lloyds Bank International*]

GT.............. Gewichtsteil [*Part By Weight*] [*German*] (GCA)

GT.............. Gibraltar Airways Ltd. [*British*] [*ICAO designator*] (ICDA)

GT.............. Goldberger Textil Muvek [*Goldberger Textile Mills*] (HU)

gt .... Goutte [*Drop*] [*Pharmacy*]

GT.............. Governor of Tasmania [*Australia*]

GT.............. Gradska Tiskarna [*City Printers*] (YU)

GT.............. Greenwich-Tyd [*Greenwich Mean Time*] [*Afrikaans*]

GT.............. Guatemala [*ANSI two-letter standard code*] (CNC)

Gt .... Gueterzugtenderlokomotive [*Freight Train Tender Locomotive*] (EG)

GT.............. Gugus Tugas [*Task Force*] (IN)

GT.............. Gutta-Percha (RU)

GT.............. Gyroscopic Tachometer (RU)

Gt .... Heterogeneous [*Nuclear physics and engineering*] (RU)

GT.............. Hydraulic Turbine (RU)

GT.............. Industrial Hygiene (RU)

GT.............. Trinitrotoluene Nose Fuze (RU)

GTA .... Ghana Timber Association (EY)

GTA .... Gibraltar Teachers' Association (SLS)

GTA .... Gitanair [*Italy*] [*ICAO designator*] (FAAC)

GTA .... Globe Travel Agency

GTA .... Gospel Truth Association

GTA .... Gran Turismo Automatico [*Automobile model designation*]

GTA .... Groupement Technique des Assurances [*France*] (FLAF)

GTA .... Groupement Togolais d'Assurance

GTA .... Groupo de Tecnologia Apropiada [*Panama*]

GTA .... Group Training Association [*British*] (DCTA)

GTA .... Guyana Teachers Association (LA)

GTA .... Gyrotachoaccelerometer (RU)

GTAP........ Heavy Howitzer Artillery Regiment (RU)

GTASA...... Geography Teachers' Association of South Australia

GTB .... Gran Turismo Berlinetta [*Automobile model designation*]

GTB .... Gumruk ve Tekel Bakanligi [*Ministry of Customs and Monopolies*] (TU)

GTBTP ...... Groupement Tchadien des Entreprises du Batiment, Travaux Publics, et Industries Connexes

GTC .... Ghana Tobacco Company Ltd.

GTC .... Gordon Technical College [*Australia*]

GTC .... Government Travel Centre [*Australia*] (ADA)

GTC .... Guild Teachers College [*Australia*] (ADA)

GTCC .... German Touring Car Championship

GTCS........ Groupe de Travail Intergouvernemental du Controle ou de la Surveillance [*Intergovernmental Working Group on Monitoring or Surveillance - IWGM*] [*French*] (ASF)

GTD.......... Gas Turbine Engine (RU)

GTD.......... Grands Travaux de Distribution

GTDC .... Ghana Tourist Development Company Ltd.

GTDD........ Double-Action Turbojet Engine (RU)

GTDN....... Grupo de Trabalho para o Desenvolvimento do Nordeste [*Working Group for Development of the Northeast*] [*Brazil*] (LA)

GTE .... Gepipari Tudomanyos Egyesulet [*Scientific Association for Machine Building*] (HU)

Gte............. Gerente [*Manager*] [*Spanish*] [*Business term*]

GTE .... Government Technology Event [*Australia*]
GTE .... Government Trading Enterprises [*Australia*]
GTE .... Grands Travaux de l'Est [*Algeria*]
GTE .... Gran Turismo Europa [*Automobile model designation*]
GTE .... Groote Island [*Australia*] [*Airport symbol*] (OAG)
GTE .... State Technical Examination (RU)
GTEB .... Guyana Timber and Export Board (LA)
GTES .... Geothermal Electric Power Station (RU)
GTF .... German Territorial Forces (MCD)
GTF .... Gesellschaft fuer Technologiefolgenforschung eV [*Society for Technological Research*] (SLS)
GTF .... Guanosine Triphosphate (RU)
GTF .... Hydraulic Engineering Division (RU)
GTFT .... Groupement du Theatre et du Folklore Togolais
GTG .... Gas Turbogenerator (RU)
GTG .... Gonadotrophic Hormone (RU)
GTG .... Ground Training Group
GTG .... State Tret'yakov Gallery (RU)
GTHB .... Gida-Tarim ve Hayvancilik Bakanligi [*Ministry of Food, Agriculture, and Animal Husbandry*] (TU)
GTI .... Gepipari Technologiai Intezet [*Technological Institute of the Machine Industries*] (HU)
GTI .... Halogen Leak Detector (RU)
GTI .... Mining Engineering Inspection (RU)
GTI .... State Scientific Institute of Tuberculosis (RU)
GTI .... State Technical Publishing House (RU)
GTIV .... Grupo de Trabajo Intergubernamental sobre Vigilancia o Supervision [*Intergovernmental Working Group on Monitoring or Surveillance - IWGM*] [*Spanish*] (ASF)
GTIZ .... State Trust of Construction Engineering Surveying (RU)
GTJ .... Gran Turismo Junior [*Automobile model designation*]
GTK .... Geologian Tutkimuskeskus [*Geological Survey of Finland*] [*Ministry of Trade and Industry*] [*Research center*] (EAS)
GTK .... Geological and Technical Commission (RU)
GTK .... Grand Turk [*British West Indies*]
GTK .... Grosser Touren Kombiwagen [*Grand Touring Station Wagon*] [*German*]
GTL .... Grosstanklager [*Tank Farm*] (EG)
GTL .... Rubber Conveyor Belts (BU)
GTM .... Grands Travaux de Marseille [*French*]
GTM .... Guatemala [*ANSI three-letter standard code*] (CNC)
GTM .... State Theatrical Museum Imeni A. A. Bakhrushin (RU)
GTMB ...... Ghana Timber Marketing Board
GTML ...... State Theatrical Museum in Leningrad (RU)
GTN .... Gdanskie Towarzystwo Naukowe [*Poland*] (SLS)
GTN .... Technical Standardization Group (RU)
GTN .... Voice-Frequency Dialing Generator (RU)
GTNM ...... Grupo Tortura Nunca Mais [*Brazil*] (EAIO)
GTO .... General Telecommunications Organization [*Oman*] [*Telecommunications service*]
GTO .... Gorontalo [*Indonesia*] [*Airport symbol*] (OAG)
GTO .... Grands Travaux de l'Ouest
GTO .... Gran Turismo Omologato [*Grand Touring, Homologated*] [*Automotive engineering*] [*Italian*]
GTO .... Group Technological Operations (RU)
GTO .... "Ready for Labor and the Defense of the USSR" [*Slogan and badge*] (RU)
GTO .... Ready for Work and Defense [*Program*] (BU)
GTODA ..... Grenada Taxi Owners and Drivers Association (EAIO)
GTP .... City Trade Enterprise (BU)
GTP .... Ghana Textiles Printing
GTP .... Glutamine-Pyruvic Transaminase (RU)
GTP .... Grands Travaux Petroliers [*Algeria*]
GTP .... Magnetizing Current Oscillator (RU)
GTP .... Retarding-Field Oscillator (RU)
GTPE .... Technical Assistance and Recovery Group (RU)
GTPI .... Grupo de Trabajo para los Pueblos Indigenas [*Indigenous Peoples Working Group*] [*Netherlands*] (EAIO)
GTRD .... Gas Turbine Jet Engine (RU)
GTRE .... Gas Turbine Research Establishment [*India*]
GTS .... City Telephone Communications (RU)
GTS .... City Telephone Exchange (RU)
GTS .... City Telephone Network (RU)
GTS .... City Trust of Eating Places (RU)
GTS .... City Wire Broadcasting Network (RU)
GTS .... Gesellschaft Tribologie and Schmiertechnik eV
GTS .... Gezira Trade and Services Co. Ltd. [*Sudan*]
GTS .... Gicen Technical Services Ltd. [*Nigeria*]
GTS .... Global Telecommunication System [*World Meteorological Organization*] (IID)
GT's .... Globetrotters' Club (EAIO)
GTS .... Government Tender Service [*Australia*]
GTS .... Gran Turismo Spider [*Automobile model designation*]
GTS .... Groupement des Transporteurs du Senegal
GTS .... Groupement Technique et Financier pour le Sahara
GTS .... Group Training Scheme [*Australia*]

G/Ts .... Guanine-Cytosine Ratio (RU)
GTS .... Guinean Trawling Survey [*United Nations*]
gts .... Hertz, Cycle per Second (RU)
GTSA .... German Telecommunications Statistics Agency
g-tsa .... Hotel (RU)
g-tsa .... Miss [*Title*] (BU)
Gtsb .... Gutsbesitzer [*Landowner*] [*German*]
GTSC .... German Territorial Southern Command [*NATO*] (NATG)
GTsD .... Hepatocerebral Dystrophy (RU)
GTsK .... Face-Centered Cubic [*Lattice*] (RU)
GTSKiGK ... Administration of State Workers' Savings Banks and State Credit (RU)
GTsKP .... State Central Book Chamber (RU)
GTsN .... Primary Circulating Pump, Main Circulating Pump [*Nuclear physics and engineering*] (RU)
GTsNMB... State Central Scientific Medical Library (RU)
GTsNPK.... Primary-Loop Circulating Pump (RU)
GTsOLIFK ... State Central "Order of Lenin" Institute of Physical Culture (RU)
GTsP .... Bar Generator, Color Bar Generator (RU)
GTsP .... Main Circulation Pump (BU)
GT-SPGG ... Free-Piston Gas Turbine (RU)
GTsTB .... State Central Theatrical Library (RU)
GTsTK .... State Central Puppet Theater (RU)
Gtsvwltr ..... Gutsverwalter [*Manager of an Estate*] [*German*]
GTT .... Georgetown [*Australia*] [*Airport symbol*] (OAG)
Gtt .... Gitter [*Grid*] [*German*] (GCA)
GTTA .... General Table Tennis Association [*Sudan*]
GTTA .... Ghana Table Tennis Association
gtte .... Goutte [*Drop*] [*Pharmacy*]
GTTI .... State Publishing House of Technical and Theoretical Literature (RU)
GTTM ...... Grupo de Trabajo sobre Transporte Maritimo y Desarrollo Portuario (del CCE) [*Central American*] (LAA)
GTU .... Gas Turbine Engine, Gas Turbine Power Plant (RU)
GTU .... Government Teachers Union [*Mauritius*] (AF)
GTU .... Main Customs Administration (RU)
GTUA .... Government Technology Users Association [*Australia*]
GTUC .... Gambia Trades Union Congress (EAIO)
GTUC .... Ghana Trade Union Congress (AF)
GTUC .... Grenada Trade Union Council
GTUC .... Guyana Trades Union Congress
GTUCR ..... General Trade Union Confederation of Romania (EAIO)
GTUG .... Gay Trade Unionists Group [*Australia*]
GTU-SPGG ... Free-Piston Gas Turbine Power Plant (RU)
GTV .... Gran Turismo Veloce [*Automobile model designation*]
GTV .... Voice-Frequency Ringing Generator (RU)
GTVD .... Turboprop Engine (RU)
GTVU .... Voice-Frequency-Ringing and Control Generator (RU)
GTW .... Gesellschaft fuer Technik und Wirtschaft [*German*] (ADPT)
GTW .... Gottwaldov [*Former Czechoslovakia*] [*Airport symbol*] (OAG)
GTY .... National Aviation Co. [*Egypt*] [*ICAO designator*] (FAAC)
GTYD .... Girne Taksiciler Yardimlasma Dernegi [*Kyrenia Taxi Drivers' Mutual Aid Association*] (GC)
GTZ .... Deutsche Gesellschaft fuer Technische Zusammenarbeit [*German Agency for Technical Cooperation*]
GTZ .... Gran Turismo Zagato [*Automobile model designation*]
GTZ .... Inhibitor-Current Generator [*Computers*] (RU)
GU .... Dating-Pulse Generator, Ultrasonic Generator (RU)
GU .... Galvanometric Amplifier (RU)
GU .... Gasschutzunteroffizier [*Gas Noncommissioned Officer*] [*German military - World War II*]
GU .... Gazzetta Ufficiale [*Official Gazette*] [*Italian*]
GU .... Gemeentelijke Universiteit [*Benelux*] (BAS)
GU .... Genri Undo [*Unification Church*] [*Japan*]
GU .... Geodetska Uprava [*Geodetic Administration*] (YU)
GU .... Goteborgs Universitet [*Sweden*] (MSC)
GU .... Grand United Friendly Society [*Australia*]
GU .... Greater Union Organisation [*Australia*]
GU .... Griffith University [*Australia*]
GU .... Group Amplifier (RU)
GU .... Guam [*Postal code*] [*ANSI two-letter standard code*] (CNC)
GU .... Gyro Device (RU)
GU .... Hydraulic Amplifier (RU)
GU .... Hydraulic Shock (RU)
GU .... Hydroelectric Development (RU)
GU .... Hydrographic Administration (RU)
GU .... Main Administration (BU)
GU .... Main Center [*Telephony*] (RU)
GU .... Reinforcement Group [*Military term*] (RU)
GU .... State University (RU)
GU .... Unpaved Section of Road (RU)
GUA .... Aerotaxis de Aguascalientes SA de CV [*Mexico*] [*ICAO designator*] (FAAC)
GUA .... Ghana Union Assurance Co. Ltd.

GUA........... Guam [*Mariana Islands*] [*Seismograph station code, US Geological Survey*]

GUA.......... Guatemala City [*Guatemala*] [*Airport symbol*]   (OAG)

GUA.......... Guinea [*Monetary unit*] [*Obsolete*] [*British*]   (ROG)

GUAD....... Main Administration of Archives   (RU)

GUADS..... Main Administration of the Automobile Transportation and Road Service   (RU)

GUALO..... General Union of Associations of Loom Overlookers [*British*]   (DCTA)

GUAME.... Grupul de Uzine pentru Aparataj si Masini Electrice [*Group of Plants for Electrical Machinery and Instruments*]   (RO)

GUAP....... Main Administration of the Aircraft Industry   (RU)

GUAP....... Main Administration of the Nitrogen Industry   (RU)

Guard........ Guardian [*Prior (in a convent)*] [*German*]

GUASS...... Main Administration of Special Machine Tool Units   (RU)

GUATEL... Empresa Guatemalteca de Telecomunicaciones [*Guatemalan Telecommunications Enterprise*]   (LA)

GUATP ..... Main Administration of the Automobile and Tractor Industry   (RU)

GUAU....... Grupo de Unificacion de Admisiones Universitarias. Universidad del Valle [*Colombia*]   (COL)

gub.............. Governor [*1708-1917*]   (RU)

gub.............. Guberniya [*1708-1929*]   (RU)

GUB.......... Gubernur [*Governor*]   (IN)

GUB.......... Guerrero Negro [*Mexico*] [*Airport symbol*]

GUBKOM ... Gubernsky Komitet [*Province Committee*] [*Russian*]

GUBL........ Beyla [*Guinea*] [*ICAO location identifier*]   (ICLI)

GUC.......... Gambia Utilities Corporation

GUC.......... Glowny Urzad Cel [*Head Office of Tariffs*] [*Poland*]

GUC.......... Groupe d'Union Camerounaise

GUCCIAAC ... General Union of Chamber of Commerce, Industry and Agriculture for Arab Countries [*Lebanon*]   (EAIO)

GUCh........ Controlled-Frequency Generator   (RU)

GUCY....... Conakry/Gbessia [*Guinea*] [*ICAO location identifier*]   (ICLI)

GUD .... Goundam [*Mali*] [*Airport symbol*]   (OAG)

GUD .... Main Administration of Traffic   (RU)

GUDD .... Didi [*Guinea*] [*ICAO location identifier*]   (ICLI)

GUDS........ Geologicky Ustav Dionyza Stura [*Dionyz Stur Geological Institute*]   (CZ)

GUE.......... Group for the European Unitarian Left [*EC*]   (ECED)

gue.............. Guarde [*Guard*] [*Spanish*]

GUES........ State Administration of Electric Power Plants   (RU)

GUF.......... French Guiana [*ANSI three-letter standard code*]   (CNC)

GUFA....... Fria [*Guinea*] [*ICAO location identifier*]   (ICLI)

GUFH....... Faranah/Badala [*Guinea*] [*ICAO location identifier*]   (ICLI)

GUFS........ Grand United Friendly Society [*Australia*]

GUFSA...... Griffith University Faculty Staff Association [*Australia*]

GUG .... Empresa Guatemalteca de Aviacion [*Guatemala*] [*ICAO designator*]   (FAAC)

GUG .... Gesellschaft fuer Unternehmensgeschichte [*Germany*]   (EAIO)

GUG .... Guari [*Papua New Guinea*] [*Airport symbol*]   (OAG)

GUGB....... Main Administration of State Security   (RU)

GUGGN .... Main Administration of State Mining Inspection   (RU)

GUGiK....... Glowny Urzad Geodezji i Kartografii [*Head Office of Land-Surveying and Cartography*] [*Poland*]

GuGIN....... Instituto Centro Americano de Investigacion y Tecnologia Industrial, Guatemala City, Guatemala [*Library symbol*] [*Library of Congress*]   (LCLS)

GUGK....... Main Administration of Geodesy and Cartography   (BU)

GUGL....... Gaoual [*Guinea*] [*ICAO location identifier*]   (ICLI)

GUGMP.... Main Administration for Geological and Mining Surveys   (BU)

GUGMR.... Main Administration of State Material Reserves   (RU)

GUGMS.... Main Administration of the Hydrometeorological Service   (RU)

GUGO....... Banankoro/Gbenko [*Guinea*] [*ICAO location identifier*]   (ICLI)

GUGSh...... Main Directorate of the General Staff   (RU)

GUGSK..... Main Administration of State Surveying and Cartography   (RU)

GUGSO..... Main Administration of Civil Legal Bodies   (RU)

GUGVF .... Main Administration of the Civil Air Fleet   (RU)

GUH .... Gunnedah [*Australia*] [*Airport symbol*]   (OAG)

GUI........... Gay Union International [*Paris, France*]   (EAIO)

GUI........... Graphics User Interface [*Australia*]

GUI........... Guiria [*Venezuela*] [*Airport symbol*]   (OAG)

GUI........... Master Oscillator, Pilot Oscillator   (RU)

GUIAS...... Main Directorate of the Aviation Engineering Service   (RU)

GUID........ Kindia [*Guinea*] [*ICAO location identifier*]   (ICLI)

GuideFisc ... Guide Fiscal Permanent [*Benelux*]   (BAS)

GUIMAG .. Societe Guineenne de Grands Magasins

GUIN........ Guinea [*Monetary unit*] [*Obsolete*] [*British*]   (ROG)

GUINELEC ... Societe Guineenne d'Installations Electriques

GUINEMAR ... Guinea-Bissau Empresa Nacional de Agencias e Transportes Maritimos [*National shipping enterprise*]

GUINEXPORT ... Enterprise Nationale d'Exportation de Produits Guineens

guirl........... Guirlande [*Garland*] [*Publishing*] [*French*]

GUITK ...... Main Administration of Corrective Labor Colonies   (RU)

GUIV .... Main Administration of Synthetic Fiber   (RU)

GUJ .... Guaratingueta [*Brazil*] [*Airport symbol*]   (OAG)

Guj Ind....... Gujarat, India   (ILCA)

GUK.......... Grey-Universiteitskollege [*Afrikaans*]

GUKE....... Kerouane [*Guinea*] [*ICAO location identifier*]   (ICLI)

GUKES...... Main Administration for Ensuring the Supply of Complete Sets of Power Engineering Equipment to Electric Power Plants, Substations, and Networks   (RU)

GUKF .... Glowny Urzad Kultury Fizycznej [*Main Office of Physical Culture*]   (POL)

GUKF .... Main Administration of the Motion-Picture and Photography Industry   (RU)

GUKKh...... Main Administration of the Municipal Economy   (RU)

GUKMASh ... Main Administration of Forging and Pressing Machinery Manufacture   (RU)

GUKO....... Main Administration of Municipal Equipment   (RU)

GUKOP..... Main Administration of the Leather and Footwear Industry   (RU)

GUK(PP)... Glowny Urzad Kontroli Prasy, Publikacji, i Widowisk [*Main Office of the Control of the Press, Publishing, and Public Performances*] [*Poland*]

GUKPPiW ... Glowny Urzad Kontroli Prasy, Publikacji, i Widowisk [*Main Office of the Control of the Press, Publishing, and Public Performances*]   (POL)

GUKR....... Kamsar/Kawass [*Guinea*] [*ICAO location identifier*]   (ICLI)

GUKR....... Main Directorate of Counterintelligence   (RU)

GUKS........ Main Administration of Capital Construction   (RU)

GUKU....... Kissidougou [*Guinea*] [*ICAO location identifier*]   (ICLI)

GUKV....... Main Directorate of Convoy Troops   (RU)

GULAG..... Glavnoe Upravlenie Ispravitel'no-Trudovykh Lagerei [*Main Administration of Corrective Labor Camps*] [*Former USSR*]

GULB .... Labe/Tata [*Guinea*] [*ICAO location identifier*]   (ICLI)

gulddek....... Gulddekoration [*Gold Decoration*] [*Danish/Norwegian*]

guldorn....... Guldornerad [*Decorated in Gold*] [*Publishing*] [*Sweden*]

guldpress.... Guldpressad [*Gilt-Stamped*] [*Publishing*] [*Sweden*]

guldsn......... Guldsnit [*Gilt Edges*] [*Publishing Danish/Norwegian*]

gulltoppsn .. Gulltoppsnitt [*Gilt Top Edge*] [*Publishing Danish/Norwegian*]

GULP .... Grenada United Labour Party [*Political party*]   (PPW)

GULP .... Main Administration of Light Industry   (RU)

GULP .... Main Administration of the Lumber Industry   (RU)

Gultigk....... Gueltigkeit [*Validity*] [*German*]   (GCA)

GULZhDS ... Main Administration of Railroad Construction Camps   (RU)

GUM .... City Administration of Militia   (RU)

GUM .... Gdanski Urzad Morski [*Gdansk (Danzig) Maritime Office*]   (POL)

GUM .... Gewaesser- und Meliorationsbetriebe, Frankfurt-Oder (VEB) [*Frankfurt-Oder Waterways and Amelioration Enterprises (VEB)*]   (EG)

GUM .... Glavnoye Upravleniye Militsii [*Main Administration of Militia*] [*Former USSR*]   (LAIN)

GUM .... Glowny Urzad Miar [*Main Office of Measures*]   (POL)

GUM .... Glowny Urzad Morski [*Main Maritime Office*]   (POL)

GUM .... Gosudarstvennyi Universal'nyi Magazin [*Government Department Store*] [*Moscow*]

GUM .... Guam [*ANSI three-letter standard code*]   (CNC)

Gum .... Gumruk [*Customs*]   (TU)

GUM .... Main Administration of Militia   (RU)

GUm .... Umschalter fuer Gemeinschaftsanschluesse [*Commutator Switch for (Telephone) Party Lines*]   (EG)

GUM .... United Mozambique Group

GUMA...... Macenta [*Guinea*] [*ICAO location identifier*]   (ICLI)

GUMD ...... Main Administration of Machine Parts Manufacture   (RU)

GUMMASh ... Main Administration of Metallurgical Machinery Manufacture   (RU)

GUMO ...... Grupo Unido de Mocambique [*United Group of Mozambique*]   (AF)

GUMP....... Glavna Uprava Medicinske Proizvodnje [*Central Administration of Pharmaceutical Production*]   (YU)

GUMP....... Main Administration of the Metallurgical Industry   (RU)

GUMR....... Groupment des Utilisateurs de Materiaux Refractaires [*Group of Refractory Material Users*]   (PDAA)

GUMTO..... Main Administration of Materials and Equipment Supply   (RU)

GUMTTS ... Main Administration of Long-Distance Telegraph and Telephone Communications   (RU)

GUMUZ.... Main Administration of Medical Educational Institutions   (RU)

GUMZ....... Glavnoye Upravleniye Mestami Zaklyucheniya [*Main Administration of Places of Detention*] [*Former USSR*]   (LAIN)

GUMZ....... Main Administration of Prisons   (RU)

GUNA ...... Ghana United Nations Association   (AF)

GUNA ...... Guatemalan United Nations Association   (EAIO)

GUNEYDOGUBIRLIK ... Guneydogu Uzum ve Mamulleri Tarim Satis Kooperatifleri Birligi [*Southeastern Grape and Products' Agricultural Sales Cooperatives' Union*]   (TU)

GUNMOLL ... Gonif's Molly [*Thief's Girl*] [*Yiddish*]

GUNRAL .. Glavna Uprava za Nabavku i Raspodelu Lekova [*Central Administration for Supply and Distribution of Medicines*]   (YU)

GUNRBiH ... Geodetska Uprava Narodne Republike Bosne i Hercegovine [*Geodetic Administration of Bosnia and Hercegovina*] (YU)

GUNRS ..... Geodetska Uprava Narodna Republike Srbije [*Geodetic Administration of Serbia*] (YU)

GUNSSA... Genootskap van Universiteit Natuurwetenskapstudente van Suidelike [*South Africa*] (AA)

GUNT .... Gouvernement d'Union Nationale Transitionnel [*Transitional National Union Government*] [*Chad*] (AF)

GUNZ .... N,Zerekore/Konia [*Guinea*] [*ICAO location identifier*] (ICLI)

GUO .... Gespreksgroep Universitair Onderzoek [*Netherlands*]

GUO .... Greater Union Organisation [*Australia*]

GUOFG ..... Grand United Order of Free Gardeners of Australasia (ADA)

GUOK .... Boke/Baralande [*Guinea*] [*ICAO location identifier*] (ICLI)

GUOO .... Grand United Order of Oddfellows [*Australia*]

GUOS .... Main Directorate of Defense Construction (RU)

GUP .... Glavna Uprava Prometa [*Central Administration of Transportation*] (YU)

GUP .... Industrial Gamma-Ray Source, Mobile Gamma-Ray Source (RU)

GUP .... Main Administration of Roads (BU)

GUPAC ..... Gulf Permanent Assistance Committee

GUPCO ..... Gulf of Suez Petroleum Company [*Cairo, Egypt*] (ME)

GUPer .... Group Repeater (RU)

GUPK .... Glowny Urzad Pomiarow Kraju [*Main Office of Country-Wide Surveying*] (POL)

GUPKO iBG ... Main Administration of Municipal Services Establishments and Urban Improvement (RU)

GUP-LRS .. Glavna Uprava Prometa Ljudske Republike Slovenije [*Central Administration of Transportation of the People's Republic of Slovenia*] (YU)

GUPO .... Main Administration of Fire Prevention (RU)

GUPP .... Glowny Urzad Planowania Przestrzennego [*Main Administration of Area Planning*] (POL)

GUPP .... Main Administration of Industrial Establishments (RU)

GUPS .... Glavna Uprava za Promet Slovenije [*Central Administration of Transportation of Slovenia*] (YU)

GUPS .... Main Postal Administration (RU)

GUPSM ..... Main Administration of the Building Materials Industry (RU)

GUPTMASh ... Main Administration of Hoisting and Conveying Machinery Manufacture (RU)

GUPU .... Main Administration of Teacher Training (RU)

GUPV .... Main Directorate of Border Troops (RU)

GUQ .... Guanare [*Venezuela*] [*Airport symbol*] (OAG)

GUR .... Alotau [*Papua New Guinea*] [*Airport symbol*] (OAG)

GURETS ... Main Administration for Development of Radio Facilities, for Intrarayon Telecommunications, and for the Television Receiving Network (RU)

GURP .... Main Administration for the Distribution of Publications (RU)

GURS .... Glavna Uprava Recnog Saobracaja [*Central Administration of River Traffic*] (YU)

GURS .... Kouroussa [*Guinea*] [*ICAO location identifier*] (ICLI)

GUS .... Gesellschaft fur Umweltsmulation [*Society for the Environment*] [*Germany*] (PDAA)

GUS .... Glavni Ustaski Stan [*Ustashi General Headquarters*] [*World War II*] (YU)

GUS .... Glowny Urzad Statystyczny [*Central Office of Statistics*] (POL)

GUS .... Gosudarstvenny Uchony Soviet [*State Academic Council*] [*Russian*]

GUS .... Guss- und Schmiedeerzeugnisse [*Cast and Forged Products*] (EG)

GUS .... State Scientific Council [*1919-1933*] (RU)

GUSA .... Sangaredi [*Guinea*] [*ICAO location identifier*] (ICLI)

GUSB .... Sambailo [*Guinea*] [*ICAO location identifier*] (ICLI)

GUSH .... Bloc [*Israel*] (ME)

Gushosdor ... Main Administration of Highways (RU)

GUShP ...... Main Administration of the Silk Industry (RU)

GUSI .... Narrow Strobe-Pulse Generator (RU)

GUSI .... Siguiri [*Guinea*] [*ICAO location identifier*] (ICLI)

GUSKO .... Gida Maddeleri Uretim ve Satis Kooperatifi [*Foodstuff Articles Production and Sales Cooperative*] (TU)

GUSMP ..... Main Administration of the Northern Sea Route (RU)

GUSP .... Main Administration of the Shipbuilding Industry (RU)

GUSRIC .... Grupul de Utilaje Speciale si Reparatii in Industria Chimica [*Group for Special Equipment and Repairs in the Chemical Industry*] (RO)

GUSS .... Gradovi u Sastavu Sreza [*Towns within District Limits*] (YU)

GUSV .... Main Administration of Construction Troops (BU)

GUT .... Genc Ulkuculer Teskilati [*Young Idealists Organization*] (TU)

GUT .... Grenada Union of Teachers (EY)

GUT .... Main Administration for Fuel (RU)

GUT .... Main Directorate of the Rear Area (RU)

GUT .... Therapeutic Gamma-Ray Source (RU)

GUTEL ...... Guatemalteca de Telecomunicaciones [*Guatemala Telecommunications*]

GUTM .... Glowny Urzad Telekomunikacji Miedzymiastowei [*Head Office of Interurban Telecommunication*] [*Poland*]

GUT MO... Main Directorate of Trade of the Ministry of Defense, USSR (RU)

GUTP .... Main Administration of the Compulsory Labor Service (BU)

GUTR .... Main Administration of Labor Reserves (RU)

GUTS .... General Understanding on Trade in Services [*International trade*]

GUTsI .... State School of Circus Art (RU)

GUTSK ...... Main Administration of State Workers' Savings Banks and State Credit (RU)

GUTSKiGK ... Main Administration of State Workers' Savings Banks and State Credit, USSR (RU)

GUU .... Grundarfjordur [*Iceland*] [*Airport symbol*] (OAG)

GUUM ...... Grupul de Uzine pentru Utilajul Minier [*Group of Mining Equipment Plants*] (RO)

GUUZ .... Main Administration of Educational Institutions (RU)

GUVECO .. Platerias Colombianas de E. Gutierrez Vega SA [*Colombia*] (COL)

GUVP .... Main Administration of War Industry (RU)

GUVPS ...... Main Administration of War Industry Construction (RU)

GuV-Rechnung ... Gewinn-und-Verlust-Rechnung [*Profit and Loss Statement*] [*German*] (EG)

GUVS .... Main Directorate of Military Supply (RU)

GUVT .... Main Directorate of Military Tribunals (RU)

GUVU .... Gesellschaft fuer Ursachenforschung bei Verkehrsunfaellen eV [*Society for Research into the Causes of Traffic Accidents*] (SLS)

Guvuz .... Main Administration of Higher Educational and Secondary Pedagogical Institutions [*RSFSR*] (RU)

GUVUZ ..... Main Administration of Military Educational Institutions (RU)

GUVV .... Main Directorate of Internal Troops (RU)

GUVVO ..... Main Directorate of Universal Military Training (RU)

GUWiM .... Glowny Urzad Wag i Miar [*Main Office of Weights and Measures*] (POL)

GUXD .... Kankan/Diankana [*Guinea*] [*ICAO location identifier*] (ICLI)

GUY .... Air Guyane [*France*] [*ICAO designator*] (FAAC)

GUY .... Guyana [*ANSI three-letter standard code*] (CNC)

GUYBAU .. Guyana Bauxite Co. (LA)

GUYINTEL ... Guyana International Telecommunications Corp. (LA)

GUYMINE ... Guyana Mining Enterprises Ltd. (LA)

GUYNEC .. Guyana National Engineering Corporation (LA)

GUYOIL ... Guyana Oil Co. (LA)

GUYSTAC ... Guyana State Corporation (LA)

GUYSUCO ... Guyana Sugar Corporation (LA)

GUYWA .... Guyana Water Authority (LA)

GUZ .... Glavna Uprava Zeleznica [*Central Administration of Railroads*] (YU)

GUZh........ Main Administration of Railways (BU)

GV .... Disturbance Function Generator (RU)

GV .... Gasverteilung [*Gas Distribution*] (EG)

GV .... Gazdasagi Vasutak [*or Gazdasagi Vasut*] [*Narrow Gauge Rail Carrier System*] (HU)

GV .... Geografski Vestnik [*Geographic Review*] [*Ljubljana*] (YU)

GV .... Gesellschaft fuer Versuchstierkunde [*Society for Experimental Zoology*] [*Switzerland*] (SLS)

GV .... Girls Volunteers [*Australia*]

GV .... Governor of Victoria [*Australia*]

GV .... Gozdarski Vestnik [*Forestry Review*] (YU)

GV .... Grande Vecchio [*Grand Master*] [*Italian*]

GV .... Grande Velocita [*Express goods service*] [*Italian*]

GV .... Grande Vitesse [*High-speed passenger train*] [*France*]

GV .... Gravimeter-Altimeter (RU)

GV .... Greenwich Time (RU)

GV .... Grow Victoria [*Mental health organisation*] [*Australia*]

GV .... Guard, Guards (RU)

Gv .... Guverte [*Deck*] [*Navy rating*] (TU)

GV .... Reproducing Head (RU)

GV .... Vertical-Flight Gyroscope (RU)

GV .... Water Level (RU)

GVA .... Geneva [*Switzerland*] [*Airport symbol*] (OAG)

GVA .... Genootschap voor Automatisering [*Netherlands*]

GVA .... Gesamtverband Autoteile-Handel [*Germany*] (EAIO)

GVA .... Goetaverken Arendal [*Offshore marine construction yard*] [*Sweden*]

GVA .... Goulburn Valley Airlines [*Australia*]

GVA .... Grupos de Vulgarizacion Agricola [*Argentina*] (LAA)

GVAC .... Amilcar Cabral International/Sal Island [*Cape Verde*] [*ICAO location identifier*] (ICLI)

gvamp........ Guards Artillery Mortar Regiment (RU)

gv ap .... Guards Artillery Regiment (RU)

GVB .... Geschriften van de Vereniging voor Belastingswetenschap [*Benelux*] (BAS)

GVB .... Upper-Water Level, Upstream Water Level (RU)

GVBA .... Boavista, Boavista Island [*Cape Verde*] [*ICAO location identifier*] (ICLI)

GVC .... Garcon, Vallve & Contreras [*Commercial firm*] [*Spain*]

GVC .... Garde des Voies et Communication [*Military*] [*French*] (MTD)

GVC .... Goulburn Valley Canners Proprietary Ltd. [*Australia*] (ADA)
GVC .... Groupements a Vocation Cooperative
GVC .... Gruppo di Volontariato Civile [*Italy*]
GVCh .... High-Frequency Oscillator (RU)
GVChM ..... Main Administration for the Procurement, Processing, and
               Marketing of Secondary Ferrous Metals (RU)
gvdbr .... Guards Airborne Brigade (RU)
gvdp .... Guards Airborne Regiment (RU)
GVDSN ..... Gott Verlaeszt die Seinen Nicht [*God Forsakes Not His Own*]
               [*Motto of Dorothee, Duchess of Braunschweig-Wolfenbuttel
               (1607-34)*] [*German*]
GVE .... Grossvieh-Einheiten [*Live Weight Unit of Cattle*] [*Equal to 500
               kilograms*] (RU)
GVF .... Civil Air Fleet, USSR (RU)
GVF .... Experimental Water-Cooled Graphite (Reactor) (RU)
GVF .... Garnisonsverwendungsfaehig Feld [*Fit for Garrison Duty in the
               Field*] [*German military - World War II*]
GVFM .... Francisco Mendes, Santiago Island [*Cape Verde*] [*ICAO location
               identifier*] (ICLI)
GVFU .... Main Military Finance Directorate (RU)
GVG .... Garrison Hospital (RU)
GVG .... Gerichtsverfassungsgesetz [*Judiciary Act*] [*German*] (EG)
gvgabr .... Guards Howitzer Artillery Brigade (RU)
GVGGU ..... Ganz Vagon es Gepgyar [*Ganz Railroad Car and Machine
               Factory*] (HU)
GVH .... Garnisonsverwendungsfaehig Heimat [*Fit for Garrison Duty in
               Zone of Interior*] [*German military - World War II*]
GVI .... Green River [*Papua New Guinea*] [*Airport symbol*] (OAG)
GVI .... State Institute of Venereal Diseases (RU)
GVI .... Time Interval Generator (RU)
GVII .... Main Military Engineering Inspection (RU)
GVIS .... Main Military Engineer Depot (RU)
GVIU .... Main Military Engineering Directorate (RU)
GVIZ .... State Military Publishing House (RU)
GVJ .... Grupo de Valorizacao do Jaguaribe [*Brazil*] (DSCA)
GVK .... City Military Commissariat (RU)
GVK .... Gesellschaft fuer Vergleichende Kunstforschung [*Austria*]
               (EAIO)
GVK .... Mountain Pack Kitchen (RU)
GVKhU ...... Main Directorate of Logistics (RU)
GVL .... High Ice-Floe Level (RU)
GVL .... Load Line, Load Waterline (RU)
GVL .... Main Waterline (RU)
GVMA .... Maio, Maio Island [*Cape Verde*] [*ICAO location identifier*]
               (ICLI)
GVMB .... Main Naval Base (RU)
GVMT .... Mosteiros, Fogo Island [*Cape Verde*] [*ICAO location identifier*]
               (ICLI)
GVMU .... Main Military Medical Directorate (RU)
GVO .... Graeber-Verwaltungsoffizier [*Graves Registration Officer*]
               [*German military - World War II*]
gvozd .... Nail Plant [*Topography*] (RU)
GVP .... Auxiliary Industries Group (RU)
GVP .... Besluit Geneeskundige Verzorging Politie [*Benelux*] (BAS)
GVP .... Generalni Vojensky Prokurator [*Judge Advocate General*] (CZ)
GVP .... Gesamtdeutsche Volkspartei [*All-German People's Party*]
               [*Germany*] [*Political party*] (PPE)
GVP .... Glasfaserverstaerkte Plasten [*Glass-Fiber Reinforced Plastics*]
               (EG)
GVP .... Government Vehicle Pool [*Victoria, Australia*]
GVP .... Grupos de Vigilancia Popular [*People's Vigilance Groups*]
               [*Mozambique*] (AF)
GVP .... Main Naval Port (RU)
GVP .... Veterinary Aid Group [*Civil defense*] (RU)
GVPM .... Mountain Pack Regimental Mortar (RU)
GVPR .... Praia/Praia, Santiago Island [*Cape Verde*] [*ICAO location
               identifier*] (ICLI)
GVR .... Governador Valadares [*Brazil*] [*Airport symbol*] (OAG)
GVR .... Groupement Vigilance et Reconciliation
GVR .... Water-Cooled Graphite Reactor (RU)
GVRS .... Glenfield Veterinary Research Station [*Australia*] (DSCA)
GVS .... Geheime Verschlusssache [*Secret Material (to be locked in safe)*]
               (EG)
GVS .... German Volunteer Service
GVSA .... Grondkundevereniging van Suid-Afrika [*South Africa*] (EAIO)
GVSC .... Sal Oceanic Area Control Center [*Cape Verde*] [*ICAO location
               identifier*] (ICLI)
GVSF .... Sao Felipe, Fogo Island [*Cape Verde*] [*ICAO location identifier*]
               (ICLI)
GVSI .... Gruppo Volontari della Svizzera Italiana [*Switzerland*] (EAIO)
GVSN .... Sao Nicolau, Sao Nicolau Island [*Cape Verde*] [*ICAO location
               identifier*] (ICLI)
GV-SOLAS ... Gesellschaft fuer Versuchstierkunde - Society of Labortory
               Animal Science [*Switzerland*] (EAIO)
GVSU .... Main Court-Martial Directorate (RU)
GVSU .... Main Medical and Sanitary Administration (RU)

GVSU .... Main Military Construction Directorate (RU)
GVSU .... Main Military Medical Directorate (RU)
GVSV .... Sao Vicente, Sao Vicente Island [*Cape Verde*] [*ICAO location
               identifier*] (ICLI)
Gvt .... Gigawatt (RU)
gvt .... Hectowatt (RU)
gvt-ch .... Hectowatt-Hour (RU)
GVTU .... Main Military Technical Directorate (RU)
GVU .... Main Veterinary Administration (RU)
GVV .... High-Water Level (RU)
GVVA .... Goulburn Valley Viticultural Association [*Australia*]
gvvdd .... Guards Airborne Division (RU)
GVVG .... Gebietsvereinigung Volkseigener Gueter [*Regional Federation of
               State Farms*] (EG)
GVX .... Gavle [*Sweden*] [*Airport symbol*] (OAG)
GVYRM .... State Higher Theatrical Directors' Workshops (RU)
GVYTM .... State Higher Theatrical Workshops (RU)
Gw .... Gegenwart [*Present (time)*] [*German*]
GW .... Geldwissel [*Afrikaans*]
GW .... Griekwaland-Wes [*Griqualand West*] [*Afrikaans*]
Gw .... Grondwet [*Benelux*] (BAS)
GW .... Guinea-Bissau [*ANSI two-letter standard code*] (CNC)
GWA .... Governor of Western Australia
GWA .... Great Wall Airlines [*China*] [*ICAO designator*] (FAAC)
GW & TV... Geassosieerde Wetenskaplike en Tegniese Vereinigings van Suid-
               Afrika [*South Africa*] (AA)
GWAZB .... Gott Wende Alles zum Besten [*May God Turn Everything to the
               Best*] [*Motto of Amoene Amalie, Princess of Anhalt (d.
               1626)*] [*German*]
GWB .... Gesetz Gegen Wettbewerbsbeschrankungen [*German Law
               Against Restraint of Competition*] (DLA)
GWCSA .... Greater World Christian Spiritualist Association (EA)
Gwd .... Greifswald [*Railroad abbreviation*] (EG)
GWD .... Gwadar [*Pakistan*] [*Airport symbol*] (OAG)
GWDB .... Ground-Water Development Bureau [*Taiwan*] (PDAA)
GWDG...... Gesellschaft fuer Wissenschaftliche Datenverarbeitung mbH
               Goettingen [*Society for Scientific Data Processing,
               Goettingen*] [*Research center*] (IRC)
GWDU ...... General Workers' Development Union [*United General Workers
               Union*] [*Belize*] [*Later,*]
GWE .... Gwelo [*Zimbabwe*] [*Airport symbol*] (OAG)
GWESF ..... Guided Weapons and Electronics Support Facility [*Australia*]
GWF .... Gambia Women Federation
GWF .... General Workers Federation [*Mauritius*] (AF)
Gwf............ Geraetewerk Friedrichshagen [*Friedrichshagen Equipment Plant*]
               (EG)
GWF .... Gesellschaft fur Werkzeugmaschinenbau und Fertigungstechnik
               [*Switzerland*] (PDAA)
GWG .... Gemeinnuetzige Wohnungsbaugenossenschaft [*Nonprofit
               Housing Construction Cooperative*] (EG)
GwG .... Gesellschaft fuer Wissenschaftliche Gespraechspsychotherapie
               eV [*Society for Scientific Speech Psychotherapy*] (SLS)
GWG .... Gottes Wille Geschehe [*God's Will Be Done*] [*Motto of Juliane
               Ursula, Margravine of Baden (d. 1614)*] [*German*]
GWG .... Groundwater Working Group [*Australia*]
GWG .... Guided Weapons Group [*Department of Defence*] [*Australia*]
gWh .... Gigawatt Hours (SCAC)
GWh .... Gigawattstunden [*Gigawatt Hours*] [*German*] (WEN)
GWIC .... Great Wall Industry Corporation [*Chinese*]
GWK .... Gesellschaft zur Wiederaufarbeitung von Kernbrennstoffen
               [*Germany*] (PDAA)
GWL .... Gesellschaft fuer Wissenschaft und Leben im Rheinisch-
               Westfaelischen Industriegebiet eV [*Society for Science and
               Life in the Rhineland-Westphalia Industrial Area*] (SLS)
Gwl............ Gueterwagenleitstelle [*Freight Car Routing Office*] (EG)
GWL .... Gwalior [*India*] [*Airport symbol*] (OAG)
GWMU...... Government Workforce Management Unit [*Victoria, Australia*]
GWN .... Golden West Network [*Australia*]
GWN .... Grosswaehlnebenstellenanlage [*Large Extension Switchboard
               Equipped for Dial System*] (EG)
GwN.......... Gruppenwaehler-Nebenanschluss [*Extension Switchboard*]
               (EG)
GWO .... General Workers' Union [*Portugal*] (EAIO)
GWOA....... Guerilla Warfare Operational Area
GWOAFC ... German Women's Organization for Alcohol Free Culture
               (EAIO)
GWP .... Gesellschaft fuer Wirtschaftspublizistik GmbH [*Society for
               Public Economics*] [*Germany*] (IID)
GWRDC .... Grape and Wine Research and Development Council [*Australia*]
GWR/DDR ... Gesellschaft fuer Weltraumforschung und Raumfahrt der
               Deutschen Demokratischen Republik [*Society for Space
               and Space Travel of the German Democratic Republic*]
               (SLS)
GWSC....... Ghana Water and Sewerage Corporation
GWSC....... Greater World Spiritual Centre [*British*] (EAIO)
GWT .... Westerland [*Germany*] [*Airport symbol*] (OAG)
GWTUF .... Government Workers' Trade Union Federation [*Sri Lanka*]

GWU......... Gambia Workers' Union
GWU......... General Workers' Union [*St. Helena*]
GWU......... General Workers' Union [*Malta*]
GWUP....... Gesellschaft zur Wissenschaftlichen Untersuchung von Parawissenschaften [*Society for the Scientific Investigation of Para-Science*] [*Germany*] (EAIO)
GWV......... Gueterwagenvorschriften [*Freight Car Regulations*] (EG)
GWW........ Gesellschaftswissenschaftliche Weiterbildung [*Advanced Social Science Training*] (EG)
GWWS ...... Gott Wirds Wohl Schaffen [*God Will Arrange*] [*Motto of Dorothee Auguste, Duchess of Braunschweig (1577-1625)*] [*German*]
GXAPI....... Guangxi Applied Physics Institute [*China*] (IRC)
GXBI......... Guangxi Botanical Institute [*China*] (IRC)
GXCC .... Guangxi Computer Center [*China*] (IRC)
GXG.......... Negage [*Angola*] [*Airport symbol*] (OAG)
GXQ.......... Coyhaique [*Chile*] [*Airport symbol*]
GXY .... Galaxy Airways Ltd. [*Nigeria*] [*ICAO designator*] (FAAC)
GY............. Gardan [*France*] [*ICAO aircraft manufacturer identifier*] (ICAO)
GY............. Genikai Ypiresiai [*General Services*] (GC)
GY............ Guyana [*ANSI two-letter standard code*] (CNC)
gy.............. Gyalogos [*Infantryman*] (HU)
gy............... Gyalogsag [*Infantry*] (HU)
gy............... Gyar [*Factory*] (HU)
GYA.......... Guayaramerin [*Bolivia*] [*Airport symbol*] (OAG)
GYA.......... Guyana Airways Corp. [*ICAO designator*] (FAAC)
gyak........... Gyakorlati [*Practical*] (HU)
gyak........... Gyakorlo [*Practicing*] (HU)
gyal........... Gyalogos [*Infantryman*] (HU)
GyAR .... Rhein-Westfalische Technische Hochschule, Aachen, Germany [*Library symbol*] [*Library of Congress*] (LCLS)
gyartm....... Gyartmany [*Product*] (HU)
GyAsH....... Hofbibliothek, Aschaffenburg, Germany [*Library symbol*] [*Library of Congress*] (LCLS)
GyBIAI...... Ibero-Amerikanisches Institu Preussicher Kulturbesitz, Berlin, Germany [*Library symbol*] [*Library of Congress*] (LCLS)
GYC .... Gibraltar Yacht Club
GYCSE .... Gyori Csonakazo Egyesulet [*Boating Club of Gyor*] (HU)
GYE .... Guayaquil [*Ecuador*] [*Airport symbol*] (OAG)
GYES......... Gyermekgondozasi Segely [*Childcare Benefits*] (HU)
GYeSS .... State Unified System of Stenography (RU)
GYHA........ German Youth Hostel Association (EAIO)
GyHeU-SS ... Universitat Heidelberg Sinologisches Seminar de Universitat Heidelberg, Heidelberg, Germany [*Library symbol*] [*Library of Congress*] (LCLS)
GyKoB .... Bundesanzeiger Verlagsgesellschaft, mbH, Koln, Germany [*Library symbol*] [*Library of Congress*] (LCLS)
GYM.......... Gelisme Yolundaki Memleketler [*Underdeveloped Countries*] (TU)
GYM.......... Guaymas [*Mexico*] [*Airport symbol*] (OAG)
GYMGV .... Gyori Mezogazdasagi Gepjavito Vallalat [*Agricultural Machine Repair Shop of Gyor*] (HU)
Gymn .... Gymnasium [*Secondary School*] [*German*]
GYN........... Goiania [*Brazil*] [*Airport symbol*] (OAG)
Gyn............ Gynaekologie [*or Gynaekologisch*] [*Gynecology (or Gynecological)*] [*German*]
GYNI .... Gyogypedagogiai Nevelo Intezet [*Institute for Retarded Children*] (HU)
GYO.......... Gandhi Youth Organization [*Guyana*] (LA)
gyogysz....... Gyogyszer [*Medicine, Drug*] (HU)
gyogysz....... Gyogyszeresz [*Druggist*] (HU)
GYOSZ...... Gyariparosok Orszagos Szovetsege [*National Association of Manufacturers*] (HU)
GYP .... Ghana Young Pioneers
GYP .... Gympie [*Australia*] [*Airport symbol*]
GYR .... Gyrafrance [*France*] [*ICAO designator*] (FAAC)
GYS .... Geografiki Ypiresia Stratou [*Army Geographic Service*] [*Greek*] (GC)
GYSEV ...... Gyor- Sopron- Eberfurthi Vasut [*Gyor-Sopron-Eberfurth Railroad*] (HU)
GyT........... Gyori Textilmuvek [*Textile Mill of Gyor*] (HU)
GYUBER... Kulonleges Villamos Gyujtoberendezesek KTSz [*Production Cooperative for Special Ignition Equipment Enterprise*] (HU)
gyujt .... Gyujtemeny [*Collection*] (HU)
gyujt .... Gyujtotte [*Collected By*] (HU)
GYUMERT ... Zoldseg- es Gyumolcs Ertekesito Vallalat [*Vegetable and Fruit Marketing Enterprise*] (HU)
gyv............. Gyorsvonat [*Express Train*] (HU)
GYVGY ..... Gyori Vagongyar [*Railroad Car Factories of Gyor*] (HU)
GZ............. Blocking Party [*Military term*] (RU)
GZ............. Ganzfeld [*Whole Field*] [*ESP test*] [*German*]
Gz............. Gazete [*Newspaper*] (TU)
Gz............. Gefuehlszustand [*Disposition*] [*German*]
GZ............. Geodetska Zveza [*Geodetic Association*] (YU)

GZ............. Geoloski Zavod [*Geological Institute*] [*Zagreb*] (YU)
GZ............. Geschaeftszeichen [*(Business) Reference Number*] (EG)
GZ............. Gesellschaft fuer Zukunftsfragen eV [*Society for Questions of Life Hereafter*] (SLS)
GZ............. Girozentrale und Bank der Oesterreichischen Sparkassen Aktiengesellschaft [*Bank*] [*Vienna, Austria*]
GZ............. Gostinska Zbornica [*Chamber of Hotel and Restaurant Trade*] (YU)
GZ............. Gottlieb-Zair [*Israel*] [*Commercial firm*]
GZ............. Gradanski Zakonik [*Civil Code*] (YU)
GZ............. Grain Boundary (RU)
GZ............. Gramofonove Zavody [*Phonograph Enterprises*] (CZ)
GZ............. Recording Head [*Computers*] (RU)
GZ............. Sound Generator (RU)
GZB .... Gemerske Zelezorudne Bane [*Gemer Iron Ore Mines*] (CZ)
GZB .... Genossenschaftliche Zentralbank AG [*Bank*] [*Austria*]
GZbFF .... Godisen Zbornik na Filozofskiot Fakultet vo Skopje [*Yearbook of the Faculty of Philosophy in Skopje*] (YU)
GZbZSF(S) ... Godisen Zbornik na Zemjodelsko-Sumarskiot Fakultet na Univerzitetot - Skopje [*Yearbook of the Faculty of Agriculture and Forestry, Skopje University. Forestry*] (YU)
GZCh .... Audio-Frequency Oscillator (RU)
gzd............. Chemical Depot (BU)
GZFFUS.... Godisen Zbornik na Filozofskiot Fakultet - Univerzitet Skopje [*Yearbook of the Faculty of Philosophy, University of Skopje*] (YU)
GZFS .... Gor'kiy Milling-Machine Plant (RU)
GZG .... Gdanskie Zaklady Gastronomiczne [*Gdansk (Danzig) Restaurant Enterprises*] (POL)
GZG .... Gutegemeinschaft Zinngerat [*Pewter Quality Association*] [*Germany*] (PDAA)
GZH.......... Gornoslaskie Zaklady Hutnicze [*Upper Silesia Metallurgical Plant*] (POL)
GZH.......... Graficki Zavod Hrvatske [*Graphic Institute of Croatia*] (YU)
g-zha .... Madam (RU)
GZhD........ City Railroad (RU)
GZhK........ Gas-Liquid Contact (RU)
GZI .... Glowny Zarzad Informacji [*Main Information Directorate*] (POL)
GZI .... State Land Holdings (RU)
GZIP......... Gdanskie Zjednoczenie Instalacji Przemyslowych [*Gdansk (Danzig) Industrial Installation Association*] (POL)
GZK .... State Stud Farm (RU)
GZL .... Geoloski Zawod Ljubljana [*Geological Survey of Ljubljana*] [*Former Yugoslavia*] [*Research center*] (IRC)
Gzld........... Ganzleder [*Full Leather*] [*Publishing*] [*German*]
Gzln........... Ganzleinen [*Full Cloth*] [*Publishing*] [*German*]
GZME .... Gdanskie Zaklady Maszyn Elektrycznych [*Gdansk (Danzig) Electric Machinery Plant*] (POL)
GZO.......... City Land Department (RU)
gzo............. Gas Officer (BU)
GZO.......... Gizo [*Solomon Islands*] [*Airport symbol*] (OAG)
GZOS .... Central State Correspondence Courses in Stenography (RU)
GZP .... Glowny Zarzad Polityczny [*Main Political Directorate*] (POL)
GZPB......... Giebultowskie Zaklady Przemyslu Bawelnianego [*Giebultow (Gebhardsdorf) Cotton Mill*] (POL)
GZPG .... Grudziadzkie Zaklady Przemyslu Gumowego [*Grudziadz Rubber Works*] (POL)
GZPI......... State Correspondence Pedagogical Institute (RU)
gzpo........... Gas Sergeant (BU)
GZPT........ Gubinskie Zaklady Przemyslu Terenowego [*Gubin (Guben) Local Industry Plant*] (POL)
GZP WP .... Glowny Zarzad Polityczny Wojska Polskiego [*Main Political Directorate, Polish Army*] (POL)
GZR .... Gdanskie Zaklady Rybne [*Gdansk Fish Industry Enterprise*] (POL)
GZRW .... Gdynskie Zjednoczenie Robot Wiertniczych [*Gdynia Drilling Work Association*] (POL)
GZS .... Geoloski Zavod Slovenije [*Geological Institute of Slovenia*] (YU)
GZS .... Gesellschaft fuer Zahlungssysteme [*International banking*] [*Germany*]
GZS .... Glavni Zdravstveni Savet (SIV) [*General Health Council*] (YU)
GZSFNRJ ... Glaven Zadruzen Sojuz na Federativna Narodna Republika Jugoslavija [*Central Cooperative Union of Yugoslavia*] (YU)
gzsl .... Chemical Warfare Service (BU)
gzsn .... Gas Projectile (BU)
GZSnaNRM ... Glaven Zadruzen Sojuz na Narodna Republika Makedonija [*Central Cooperative Union of Macedonia*] (YU)
GZSNRBiH ... Glavni Zadruzni Savez Narodne Republike Bosne i Hercegovine [*Central Cooperative Union of Bosnia and Hercegovina*] (YU)
GZSNRCG ... Glavni Zadruzni Savez Narodne Republike Crne Gore [*Central Cooperative Union of Montenegro*] (YU)
gzstg .... Ganzseitig [*Full-Page*] [*Publishing*] [*German*]

GZT .... Gaziantep [*Turkey*] [*Airport symbol*]   (OAG)
GZTrst .... Gregorciceva Zalozba, Trst [*Gregorcic Publishing House, Trieste*]
          (YU)
GZU .... City Land Administration   (RU)
GZU .... Hydraulic Ash Removal   (RU)
GZU .... Lightning Protector, Lightning Arrester   (RU)
GZUT .... Gliwickie Zaklady Urzadzen Technicznych [*Gliwice (Gleiwitz)
          Technical Equipment Plant*]   (POL)
GZV .... Glavna Zaprecna Vatra [*Main Barrage Fire*]   (YU)
GZV .... Gueterzugbildungsvorschriften [*Regulations for Freight Train
          Formation*]   (EG)
GZZ .... Gradska Zeljeznica Zagreb [*Zagreb City Railroad*]   (YU)
GZZ .... Main Blocking Valve   (BU)
GZZLRS.... Glavna Zadruzna Zveza Ljudske Republike Slovenije [*Central
          Cooperative Union of Slovenia*]   (YU)
GZZS .... Glavna Zadruzna Zveza Slovenije [*Central Cooperative Union of
          Slovenia*]   (YU)

H

H .... Einzelhaus [*Single Home*] [*German*]
H .... Haben [*Have*] [*German*]
H .... Haber [*Credit*] [*Business term*] [*Spanish*]
h .... Habitantes [*Population*] [*Spanish*]
h .... Hacia [*Around*] [*Spanish*]
h .... Haefte [*Issue*] [*Publishing*] [*Sweden*]
H .... Haelfte [*Half Volume*] [*Publishing*] [*German*]
H .... Haerte [*Hardness*] [*German*]
H .... Hagelkorn [*Hailstone*] [*Bomb*] [*German military - World War II*]
H .... Hakkinda [*Concerning, Regarding*] [*In legal documents*]   (TU)
H .... Hakushi [*Japan*]
H .... Haler [*Monetary unit*] [*Former Czechoslovakia*]
h .... Half [*Half*] [*Netherlands*]
h .... Halv [*Half*] [*Danish/Norwegian*]
h .... Han [*Commercial Building*] [*Turkey*]   (CED)
H .... Han Koot Belt Industrial Co. Ltd. [*South Korea*]
H .... Harry [*Phonetic alphabet*] [*Royal Navy World War I Pre-World War II*]   (DSUE)
h .... Hasab [*Column*] [*Hungary*]
H .... Haupt [*Head*] [*German*]
H .... Haus [*House*] [*German*]
H .... Hauteur [*Height*] [*French*]   (MTD)
H .... Haver [*Credit*] [*Business term*] [*Portuguese*]
H .... Heft [*Number or Part*] [*Publishing*] [*German*]
h .... Hefte [*Issue*] [*Publishing Danish/Norwegian*]
H .... Heilige [*Saint*] [*Afrikaans*]
H .... Heimat [*Home*] [*German*]   (GCA)
h .... Heiss [*Hot*] [*German*]
H .... Heizwert [*Calorific Value*] [*German*]
H .... Helicopteros do Brasil SA [*Brazil*] [*ICAO aircraft manufacturer identifier*]   (ICAO)
h .... Hely [*Place of Publication*] [*Hungary*]
h .... Helyett [*Instead, For*]   (HU)
h .... Helyettes [*Deputy*]   (HU)
H .... Helyi Ipar [*Local Industry*]   (HU)
H .... Henry [*Henry (Symbol for unit of inductance)*] [*Portuguese*]
H .... Henry [*Henry (Symbol for unit of inductance)*] [*German*]
H .... Hermes [*Collection dirigee par J. Hemard*]   (FLAF)
H .... Hetfo [*Monday*]   (HU)
h .... Heure [*Hour*] [*French*]   (GPO)
H .... Hicri [*The Hejira Era*]   (TU)
H .... Hidrogenio [*Hydrogen*] [*Chemical element*] [*Portuguese*]
h .... Hier [*Yesterday*] [*French*]
H .... Highveld Steel and Vanadium Corp. Ltd. [*South Africa*]
h .... Hoch [*High*] [*German*]
H .... Hoehe [*Altitude*] [*German*]
h .... Hoeherer [*Higher*] [*German*]
H .... Hoek [*Cape, Hook*] [*Netherlands*]   (NAU)
H .... Hof [*Court or Farm*] [*German*]
h .... Hoja [*Leaf*] [*Publishing*] [*Spanish*]
(H).............. Holzknechthuette [*Lumberjack Hut*] [*German*]
H .... Hommes [*Men*] [*Military*] [*French*]   (MTD)
h .... Honap [*Month*]   (HU)
H .... Hoofdartikel [*Benelux*]   (BAS)
H .... Hopper-Tainer [*A form of container*] [*British*]   (DCTA)
H .... Horizon Tours [*Egypt*] [*Commercial firm*]
h .... Hors [*Outside*] [*Publishing*] [*French*]
H .... How [*Phonetic alphabet*] [*World War II*]   (DSUE)
H .... Hoyre [*Conservative Party*] [*Norway*] [*Political party*]   (PPE)
H .... Huette [*Cottage*] [*German*]
h .... Hus [*House*] [*Norway*]   (CED)
h .... Hypotheque [*Mortgage*] [*French*]
h .... Tunti [*Finland*]
H .... Turkiye Halk Bankasi [*Bank*] [*Turkey*]
H .... Wegry [*Hungary*] [*Poland*]
H4 .... Solomon Islands [*Aircraft nationality and registration mark*]   (FAAC)

HA .... CASA [*Construcciones Aeronauticas Sociedad Anonima*] [*Spain*] [*ICAO aircraft manufacturer identifier*]   (ICAO)
HA .... De Handelsagent [*Benelux*]   (BAS)
HA .... Haber Ajansi [*Haber Agency*] [*News agency HHA*] [*See also*]   (TU)
HA .... Haiti [*or Haitian*]   (WDAA)
ha .... Hajoallomas [*Quay, Pier*]   (HU)
Ha .... Hana [*Cape, Point*] [*Ba*] [*See also*] [*Japan*]   (NAU)
HA .... Handelsabgabe [*Commercial Tax*] [*German*]   (EG)
HA .... Harb Akademileri [*Military Academies*]   (TU)
Ha .... Haupt [*Chief*] [*German*]   (GCA)
HA .... Hauptabteilung [*Main Department*] [*German*]   (WEN)
HA .... Hauptanschluesse [*German*]   (ADPT)
HA .... Haute Autorite [*Television regulatory agency*] [*French*]
H-A .... Hautes-Alpes [*Department of France*]
HA .... Hawaii [*or Hawaiian*]   (WDAA)
HA .... Hawaiian Airlines, Inc. [*ICAO designator*]   (ICDA)
ha .... Hectare [*Portuguese*]
ha .... Hectare [*French*]
ha .... Hehtaari [*or Hehtaaria*] [*Finland*]
Ha .... Hektaar [*Hectare*] [*Afrikaans*]
ha .... Hektar [*Hectare*] [*Albanian*]
ha .... Hektar [*Hectare*] [*German*]   (EG)
HA .... High Authority of the ECSC [*European Coal and Steel Community*]   (ILCA)
HA .... Historical Association [*British*]   (EAIO)
HA .... Hlas Ameriky [*Voice of America*]   (CZ)
HA .... Hoge Autoriteit [*Benelux*]   (BAS)
HA .... Horse Artillery [*Australia*]
HA .... House of Assembly [*Australia*]   (ADA)
HA .... Housewives Association [*Australia*]
HA .... Hungarian Association [*Australia*]
HA .... Hypoglycemic Association [*Australia*]
HAA .... Hasvik [*Norway*] [*Airport symbol*]   (OAG)
HAA .... Helicopter Association of Australia
HAA .... Herpetological Association of Africa [*South Africa*]   (SLS)
HAA .... Hungarian Society of Angiology   (EAIO)
HAAA .... Addis Ababa [*Ethiopia*] [*ICAO location identifier*]   (ICLI)
HAAB .... Addis Ababa/Bole International [*Ethiopia*] [*ICAO location identifier*]   (ICLI)
HAAD .... Adaba [*Ethiopia*] [*ICAO location identifier*]   (ICLI)
HAAFCE... Headquarters, Allied Air Force, Central Europe [*NATO*]
HAAG .... Agordat [*Ethiopia*] [*ICAO location identifier*]   (ICLI)
HAAL .... Addis Ababa/Liddetta [*Ethiopia*] [*ICAO location identifier*]   (ICLI)
HAAM .... Arba Minch [*Ethiopia*] [*ICAO location identifier*]   (ICLI)
HAAS .... Asmara App [*Ethiopia*] [*ICAO location identifier*]   (ICLI)
HAASA .... Hearing Aid Audiometrists Society of Australia
HAAW .... Awash [*Ethiopia*] [*ICAO location identifier*]   (ICLI)
HAAX .... Axum [*Ethiopia*] [*ICAO location identifier*]   (ICLI)
HAAY .... Asmara/Yohannes IV [*Ethiopia*] [*ICAO location identifier*]   (ICLI)
HAAZ .... Hoofden Automatisering Academische Ziekenhuizen [*Netherlands*]
Hab .... Habakuk [*Habakkuk*] [*Afrikaans*]
hab .... Habitantes [*Inhabitant*] [*Portuguese*]
Hab .... Habitants [*French*]   (FLAF)
HAB......... Hamburg Afrika Bank [*Hamburg Africa Bank*]   (AF)
HAB......... Hauptbuch [*German*]   (ADPT)
HAB......... Hear a Book Service [*Australia*]
HAB........ Hessische Akademie fuer Buerowirtschaft eV   (SLS)
HABACT.. Hear a Book Service, Australian Capital Territory Branch
Habaemfa .. Hallesche Baeckereimaschinenfabrik [*Halle Bakery Machine Plant*]   (EG)
HABB .... Bunno Bedele [*Ethiopia*] [*ICAO location identifier*]   (ICLI)
HABC....... Baco [*Ethiopia*] [*ICAO location identifier*]   (ICLI)
HABD....... Bahar Dar [*Ethiopia*] [*ICAO location identifier*]   (ICLI)
HABE........ Beica [*Ethiopia*] [*ICAO location identifier*]   (ICLI)

567

Haber-Is .... Turkiye Posta, Telgraf, Telefon, Radyo, ve Televizyon Iscileri Sendikasi [*Turkish Postal, Telegraph, Telephone, Radio, and Television Workers Union*] (TU)

HABITAT ... Human Settlements Information System [*Nairobi, Kenya*]

Habt .... Habert [*Cowhouse*] [*Military map abbreviation World War I*] [*French*] (MTD)

HABU .... Bulchi [*Ethiopia*] [*ICAO location identifier*] (ICLI)

HABY .... Haberdashery (DSUE)

HAC .... Hachijojima Island [*Japan*] [*Airport symbol*] (OAG)

HAC .... Hawkesbury Agricultural College [*Australia*] (ADA)

HAC .... Health Administration Corp. [*New South Wales, Australia*]

HAC .... Health Advisory Council [*New South Wales, Australia*]

HAC .... Hellenic Advancement Council [*Australia*]

HAC .... Henebury Aviation Co. [*Australia*] [*ICAO designator*] (FAAC)

HAC .... Hlavni Armadni Cesta [*Main Army Route*] (CZ)

HAC .... Holland Australia Club [*Australia*]

HAC .... Homebush Abattoir Corporation [*Australia*] (ADA)

HAC .... Hospitals Accreditation Committee [*Australia*]

HAC .... Housing Advisory Council [*South Australia*]

HACA .... Hearing Aid Council of Australia

HACB .... Hibernian Australian Catholic Benefit Society (ADA)

HACBS ..... Hibernian Australian Catholic Benefit Society

HACBSS ... Homestead and Community Broadcasting Satellite Service [*Australia*]

HACC .... Help and Action Coordinating Committee [*Defunct*] [*France*] (EAIO)

HACC .... Home and Community Care Program [*Australia*]

HACI .... Hellenic Association of Clothing Industry [*Greece*] (EAIO)

HACOBU ... Hawkesbury Agricultural College Old Boys Union [*Australia*]

HACTL ..... Hong Kong Air Cargo Terminal Ltd.

Hac U .... Hacettepe Universitesi [*Hacettepe University*] [*Ankara*] (TU)

HACU .... Health Advancement Campaign Unit [*Australia*]

HACUITEX ... Habillement, Cuir, et Textile [*France*] (EY)

HAD .... Halmstad [*Sweden*] [*Airport symbol*] (OAG)

HAD .... Hanseatische Afrika-Dienst

HAD .... Helicopteros Andes [*Chile*] [*ICAO designator*] (FAAC)

HAD .... Hrvatsko Arheolosko Drustvo [*Croatian Archaeological Society*] (YU)

HADB .... Dagabour [*Ethiopia*] [*ICAO location identifier*] (ICLI)

HADC .... Dessie/Combolcha [*Ethiopia*] [*ICAO location identifier*] (ICLI)

HADCO .... Hail Agricultural Development Co. [*Saudi Arabia*]

HADD ...... Dembidollo [*Ethiopia*] [*ICAO location identifier*] (ICLI)

HADL ...... Dallol [*Ethiopia*] [*ICAO location identifier*] (ICLI)

HADM ...... Debre Marcos [*Ethiopia*] [*ICAO location identifier*] (ICLI)

hadmtk ...... Hadmernok Torzskar [*Engineer Corps*] (HU)

HADN ...... Danguilla [*Ethiopia*] [*ICAO location identifier*] (ICLI)

HADO ...... Dodola [*Ethiopia*] [*ICAO location identifier*] (ICLI)

HADOSS .. HWWA-Dossiers [*Society for Business Information*] [*Information service or system*] (IID)

hadoszt ...... Hadosztaly [*Division*] [*Military*] (HU)

HADR .... Dire Dawa/Aba Tenna Dejazmatch Yilma [*Ethiopia*] [*ICAO location identifier*] (ICLI)

HADS .... Head of the Australian Defence Staff

HADT .... Debre Tabor [*Ethiopia*] [*ICAO location identifier*] (ICLI)

HAECO ..... Hongkong Aircraft Engineering Co.

HAECO ..... Hong Kong Aircraft Engineering Company

haeors .... Harci Eloors [*Tactical Outpost*] (HU)

HAER .... Hydraulique et de l'Amenagement de l'Espace Rural

HAF .... Hellenic Air Force [*Greece*] [*ICAO designator*] (FAAC)

HAFE .... Hajtomu- es Felvonogyar [*Driving Mechanism and Elevator Factory*] (HU)

HAFMED ... Headquarters, Allied Forces Mediterranean

HAFN .... Fincha [*Ethiopia*] [*ICAO location identifier*] (ICLI)

HAFS .... Heilungkiang Academy of Forestry Sciences [*Chinese*] (SLS)

hafteomsl ... Haefteomslag [*Issue Cover*] [*Publishing*] [*Sweden*]

Hag .... Haggai [*Haggai*] [*Afrikaans*]

HAG .... Hamburger Action Group [*Australia*]

HAG .... Historische und Antiquarische Gesellschaft zu Basel [*Switzerland*] (SLS)

HAGAR ..... Historical and Genealogical Australian Research Index (ADA)

HAGB .... Goba [*Ethiopia*] [*ICAO location identifier*] (ICLI)

HAGE .... Hajdusagi Agroipari Egyesules [*Agro-Industrial Association of Hajdusag*] (HU)

HAGH .... Ghinnir [*Ethiopia*] [*ICAO location identifier*] (ICLI)

HAGL .... Galadi [*Ethiopia*] [*ICAO location identifier*] (ICLI)

HAGM ...... Gambella [*Ethiopia*] [*ICAO location identifier*] (ICLI)

HAGN ...... Gondar [*Ethiopia*] [*ICAO location identifier*] (ICLI)

HAGO ...... Gode [*Ethiopia*] [*ICAO location identifier*] (ICLI)

HAGR ...... Direction de l'Hydraulique Agricole et du Genie Rural [*Vietnam*] (DSCA)

HAGR .... Gore [*Ethiopia*] [*ICAO location identifier*] (ICLI)

HAGSOC .. Heraldry and Genealogy Society of Canberra [*Australia*]

HAGU .... Gura [*Ethiopia*] [*ICAO location identifier*] (ICLI)

HAGY .... Hiradastechnikai Anyagok Gyara [*Telecommunication Materials Factory*] (HU)

HAH .... Hotel Association of Hungary (EAIO)

HAH .... Moroni [*Comoro Islands*] Hahaia Airport [*Airport symbol*] (OAG)

HAHM ...... Debre Zeit/Harar Meda [*Ethiopia*] [*ICAO location identifier*] (ICLI)

HAHS .... Hossana [*Ethiopia*] [*ICAO location identifier*] (ICLI)

HAHU ...... Humera [*Ethiopia*] [*ICAO location identifier*] (ICLI)

HAI .... Haiti (ABBR)

HAI .... Health Action International (EA)

HAI .... Hellenic Aerospace Industry [*Greek*]

HAI .... Hellenic Arms Industry [*Greek*]

HAIB .... Hukumet ve Askeri Isci Birlikleri [*Government and Military Worker Unions*] [*Turkish Cypriot*] (GC)

HAIL .... Hague Academy of International Law [*Netherlands*] (SLS)

HAIT .... Haiti

HAJ .... Hajvairy Airlines [*Pakistan*] [*ICAO designator*] (FAAC)

HAJ .... Hanover [*Germany*] [*Airport symbol*] (OAG)

HAJJ .... Jijiga [*Ethiopia*] [*ICAO location identifier*] (ICLI)

HAJM ...... Jimma [*Ethiopia*] [*ICAO location identifier*] (ICLI)

HAK .... Haikou [*China*] [*Airport symbol*] (OAG)

HAK .... Handelsakademie [*Commerce Academy*] [*German*]

HAK .... Historical Association of Kenya

H Akcja ...... (Akcja) Hodowli [*Pedigree Breeding Drive*] (POL)

HAKD ...... Kabre Dare [*Ethiopia*] [*ICAO location identifier*] (ICLI)

Hak-Is .... Turkiye Hak-Iscileri Ozyol-Is [*Turkish Moral Rights Workers' Trade Union*] [*Konya*] (TU)

HAKK .... Hing Ah Kee Kwa [*Aid Asia Flourishing Association*] [*Hong Kong*]

HAKL .... Kelafo [*Ethiopia*] [*ICAO location identifier*] (ICLI)

HAKS .... Hopital de l'Amitie Khmero-Sovietique [*Cambodian-Soviet Friendship Hospital*] (CL)

hakus .... Hakusana [*Catchword*] [*Finland*]

HAL .... Haftarbeitslager [*Penal Labor Camp*] (EG)

Hal .... Halogen [*Halogen*] [*German*]

hal .... Halozat [*Network, System*] (HU)

HAL .... Handarbeitslehrerin [*Needlework Teacher*] [*German*]

HAL .... Handbook of African Languages

HAL .... Hardboards Australia Limited (ADA)

HAL .... Hindustan-Aeronautics Ltd. [*India*]

HAL .... Hindustan Antibiotics Ltd. [*India*]

HAL .... Hoechst Australia Ltd. [*Commercial firm*]

Hal .... Hopital [*Hospital*] [*Military map abbreviation World War I*] [*French*] (MTD)

HALA .... Awash [*Ethiopia*] [*ICAO location identifier*] (ICLI)

Halbperg .... Halbpergament [*Half Vellum*] [*Publishing*] [*German*]

halbst .... Halbstaatlich [*Semistate*] (EG)

HALERT ... Halertekesito Vallalat [*Fish Market*] (HU)

Halk-Is ...... Halk ve Isci Sirketleri Sendikasi [*Peoples and Workers Companies Labor Union*] [*Related to labor in West Germany*] (TU)

HALL .... Lalibela [*Ethiopia*] [*ICAO location identifier*] (ICLI)

hallg .... Hallgato [*Student, Listener*] (HU)

HALPAS ... Halberg Programm-Ablauf-Steuerung [*German*] (ADPT)

Haltbark .... Haltbarkeit [*Preservability*] [*German*] (GCA)

halv .... Halventavasti [*Disparagingly*] [*Finland*]

halvb .... Halvbind [*Half Volume*] [*Publishing Danish/Norwegian*]

halvfr .... Halvfranskt [*Half-Leather*] [*Publishing*] [*Sweden*]

halvfrbd ..... Halvfranskt Band [*Half-Calf Binding*] [*Publishing*] [*Sweden*]

halvklotbd ... Halvklot Band [*Half-Cloth Binding*] [*Publishing*] [*Sweden*]

halvmarokgbd ... Halvmarokaengband [*Half-Morocco Binding*] [*Publishing*] [*Sweden*]

halvpergmtbd ... Halvpergamentband [*Half-Vellum Binding*] [*Publishing*] [*Sweden*]

halvsh .... Halvshirting [*Half-Cloth*] [*Publishing Danish/Norwegian*]

HAM .... Hamburg [*Germany*] [*Airport symbol*] (OAG)

HAM .... Heart of Africa Mission

HAM .... Holandsche Aanneming Maatschappij [*Netherlands*] (PDAA)

HAMAL-IS ... Turkiye Hamallari ve Yukculeri Sendikasi [*Turkish Porters and Freight Carriers Union*] [*Istanbul*] (TU)

HAME .... Mieso [*Ethiopia*] [*ICAO location identifier*] (ICLI)

HAMIM .... Hizbul Muslimin [*Islamic Front*] [*Malaysia*] [*Political party*] (FEA)

HAMJ .... Maji [*Ethiopia*] [*ICAO location identifier*] (ICLI)

HAMK ...... Makale [*Ethiopia*] [*ICAO location identifier*] (ICLI)

HAML ...... Masslo [*Ethiopia*] [*ICAO location identifier*] (ICLI)

HAMM .... Metema [*Ethiopia*] [*ICAO location identifier*] (ICLI)

hammasl ...... Hammaslaaketiede [*Dentistry*] [*Finland*]

hammaslkand ... Hammaslaaketieteen Kandidaatti [*Finland*]

hammasllis ... Hammaslaaketieteen Lisensiaatti [*Finland*]

hammasltri ... Hammaslaaketieteen Tohtori [*Finland*]

HAMN ...... Mendi [*Ethiopia*] [*ICAO location identifier*] (ICLI)

HAMO ...... Motta [*Ethiopia*] [*ICAO location identifier*] (ICLI)

HAMR ...... Mui River [*Ethiopia*] [*ICAO location identifier*] (ICLI)

HAMS ...... Massawa [*Ethiopia*] [*ICAO location identifier*] (ICLI)

HAMT ...... Mizan Teferi [*Ethiopia*] [*ICAO location identifier*] (ICLI)

HAN .... Hanoi [*Vietnam*] [*Airport symbol*] (OAG)

HAN .... Hauptauftragnehmer [*Main Contractor*] (EG)

HANA .... Haveeru News Agency [*Maldives*] (FEA)
HANAO .... Hrvatska Nacionalisticka Omladina [*Croatian Nationalist Youth*] (YU)
hand .... Haandinbundet [*Hand-Bound*] [*Publishing Danish/Norwegian*]
Hand .... Handelinge [*Acts*] [*Afrikaans*]
Hand .... Handelingen van de Staten-Generaal [*Benelux*] (BAS)
handb .... Haandbog [*Handbook*] [*Publishing Danish/Norwegian*]
Handb .... Handbuch [*Handbook*] [*German*] (GCA)
H & C........ Hoffmann & Campe [*Publisher*] [*Germany*]
H & C........ Ministry of Housing and Construction [*Victoria, Australia*]
H & Cie...... Hentsch & Compagnie [*Bank*] [*Switzerland*]
HANDD .... Holistic Aid and Nurture of the Deaf and Disabled [*Australia*]
handelsubl ... Handelsueblich [*Commercial*] [*German*] (GCA)
handg .... Haandgjort [*Handmade*] [*Danish/Norwegian*]
handgeb...... Handgebunden [*Hand-Bound*] [*Publishing*] [*German*]
handgj .... Haandgjort [*Handmade*] [*Danish/Norwegian*]
Handhab .... Handhabung [*Handling*] [*German*] (GCA)
Hand-I .... Handelingen van de Eerste Kamer [*Benelux*] (BAS)
HANDICO ... Tanzania Handicrafts Corporation
Hand-II...... Handelingen van de Tweede Kamer [*Benelux*] (BAS)
handingekl ... Handingekleurd [*Hand-Colored*] [*Publishing*] [*Netherlands*]
HANDITAL ... Association of Italian Families and Friends of Handicapped Children [*Australia*]
handkol ...... Handkoloriert [*Hand-Colored*] [*Publishing*] [*German*]
HandNJV ... Handelingen van de Nederlandse Juristenvereniging [*Netherlands*] (BAS)
handschr .... Handschrift [*Manuscript*] [*Publishing Dutch*]
Handschr .... Handschrift [*Manuscript, Autograph*] [*Publishing*] [*German*]
handschriftl ... Handschriftlich [*Handwritten*] [*Publishing*] [*German*]
handt .... Handtekening [*Hand Drawing, Signature*] [*Publishing*] [*Netherlands*]
Hand TwK ... Handelingen Tweede Kamer [*Benelux*] (BAS)
H & W....... Holm & Wonsild [*Steamship*] (MHDB)
Hand-Wiss ... Handelswissenschaft [*Science of Commerce and Business Administration*] [*Germany*] (GCA)
HANG .... Neghelle [*Ethiopia*] [*ICAO location identifier*] (ICLI)
hangj .... Hangjegy [*Note*] [*Publishing*] [*Hungary*]
HANJ .... Nejjo [*Ethiopia*] [*ICAO location identifier*] (ICLI)
HANK ...... Nekemte [*Ethiopia*] [*ICAO location identifier*] (ICLI)
HANKAM ... Departemen Pertahanan dan Keamanan [*Department of Defense and Security*] (IN)
HANKAMNAS ... Pertahanan dan Keamanan Nasional [*National Defense and Security*] (IN)
HANKAMRATA ... Pertahanan dan Keamanan Rakjat Semesta [*Total People's Defense and Security*] (IN)
HANNOVER PAPIER ... Hannoversche Papierfabriken Alfred-Gronau [*Alfred-Gronau Hannover Paper Mill*]
HANS........ Hansard [*Database*] [*Australia*]
HANSA..... Herramientas Nacionales, Compania Ltd. [*Ecuador*] (DSCA)
HANSIP.... Pertahanan Sipil [*Civil Defense Organization*] (IN)
HANTOBI ... Hangug Toyang Biryo Haghoe [*South Korea*] (EAIO)
Hants .... Hampshire (IDIG)
HANUDAD ... Pertahanan Udara Angkatan Darat [*Army Air Defense*] (IN)
HAO .... Handelns Arbetsgivare-Organisation [*Commercial Employers Association*] [*Sweden*] (WEN)
hao .... Hataror [*Border Guard*] (HU)
HAP.......... Habourside Amusement Park Proprietary Ltd. [*Australia*]
HAP.......... Happy Bay [*Australia*] [*Airport symbol*] (OAG)
hap .... Harcallaspont [*Command Post, Command Observation Post*] (HU)
HAP.......... Hersteller-Abgabepreis [*Producer Sales Price*] [*German*] (EG)
HAP.......... Whitsunday Resort (Long Island) [*Australia*] [*Airport symbol*]
Hapeko ...... Hutnicze Przedsiebiorstwo Kompletacji Dostaw Maszyn i Urzadzen [*Enterprise for the Supplementing of Deliveries of Metallurgical Machinery and Equipment*] (POL)
HAPS .... Historic Aircraft Preservation Society [*Australia*]
Har............ Harabe [*Ruins*] (TU)
har............. Harant [*Oblong*] [*Hungary*]
Har............. Harici [*Long Distance (Telephone call)*] (GC)
Har............. Harita [*Map, Chart*] (TU)
Har............. Harradine Group [*Australia*] [*Political party*]
HAR.......... Host-Anpassungsrechner [*German*] (ADPT)
HARB-IS... Turk Harb Sanayii ve Yardimci Isci Sendikalari Federasyonu [*Turkish War Industry and Allied Workers Unions Federation*] (TU)
HARF .... Holland Australia Retirement Foundation of Victoria [*Australia*]
HARF .... Honduran Agricultural Research Foundation (EAIO)
HARNET .. [*The*] Hong Kong Academic and Research Network [*Computer science*] (TNIG)
HARP .... Home Renovation Advisory and Referral Project [*Victoria, Australia*]
HARS .... Historic Aircraft Restoration Society [*Australia*]
Hart .... Haerte [*Hardness*] [*German*]
HAR/TAR ... Host- und Terminal-Anpassungsrechner [*German*] (ADPT)
HartRAO... Hartebeesthoek Radio Astronomy Observatory [*Foundation for Research Development*] [*South Africa*] (EAS)

harv .... Harvinainen [*or Havoin*] [*Rare*] [*Finland*]
HAS.......... Hail [*Saudi Arabia*] [*Airport symbol*] (OAG)
HAS.......... Hamburg Airlines, GmbH [*Germany*] [*ICAO designator*] (FAAC)
HAS.......... Head Teachers' Association of Scotland (SLS)
HAS.......... Hellenic Acoustical Society [*Greece*] (EAIO)
HAS.......... Hellenic Astronautical Society [*Greek*] (PDAA)
HASA .... Editorial Hispanoamericana SA [*Argentina*] (DSCA)
HASA .... Harina y Almidones SA [*Ecuador*] (DSCA)
HASAS...... Hali Sanayii ve Pazarlama Anonim Sirketi [*Rug Industry and Marketing Corporation*] (TU)
HASB........ Assab [*Ethiopia*] [*ICAO location identifier*] (ICLI)
HASD........ Sodo [*Ethiopia*] [*ICAO location identifier*] (ICLI)
HASH........ Sheik Hussein [*Ethiopia*] [*ICAO location identifier*] (ICLI)
HASIDA.... Handicrafts and Small-Scale Industries Development Agency [*Ethiopia*] (AF)
HAS-IS...... Turkiye Hastane Iscileri Sendikasi [*Turkish Hospital Workers' Union*] (TU)
HASO....... Assosa [*Ethiopia*] [*ICAO location identifier*] (ICLI)
Hast .... Hastahane [*Hospital*]
HASTAS... Halk Sektoru Turk Anonim Sirketleri [*Turkish Public Sector Corporations*] [*A community of sixteen companies*] (TU)
HASTP...... Hauptsteuerprogramm [*German*] (ADPT)
HASYLAB ... Hamburg Synchrotron Laboratory [*Germany*]
hat .... Hatarozat [*Decision, Resolution, Provision*] (HU)
hat .... Hatosag [*Public Authority*] (HU)
HAT.......... Heathlands [*Australia*] [*Airport symbol*] [*Obsolete*] (OAG)
HAT.......... Hospitals of Australia Trust
HATA .... Hellenic Atlantic Treaty Association [*Greece*] (EAIO)
hatabl .... Harcallomanytabla [*Listing of the Active Military Strength*] (HU)
HATAS ..... Hastahane Tesisleri Ticaret ve Sanayii Anonim Sirketi [*Hospital Equipment Trade and Industry, Incorporated*] (TU)
HATERV... Villamos Halozati Fejleszto es Tervezo Vallalat [*Electric Power Network Development and Designing Enterprise*] (HU)
HATMIS... Housing Applications and Tenancies Management Information Service [*Hong Kong*]
HATO....... Tendaho [*Ethiopia*] [*ICAO location identifier*] (ICLI)
HATP....... Tippi [*Ethiopia*] [*ICAO location identifier*] (ICLI)
HATS .... Holden's Air Transport Services [*Australia*]
HATS .... Tessenei [*Ethiopia*] [*ICAO location identifier*] (ICLI)
HATT .... Hambros Advanced Technology Trust [*Hambros Bank of Britain*]
Hau .... Hameau [*Small Village, Hamlet*] [*Military map abbreviation World War I*] [*French*] (MTD)
HAU .... Haryana Agricultural University [*India*] (PDAA)
HAU .... Haugesund [*Norway*] [*Airport symbol*] (OAG)
HAU .... Hebrew Actors Union
HAU .... Hudebni a Artisticka Ustredna [*Center of Music Performers and Entertainers*] [*CZ*]
Haufigk...... Haeufigkeit [*Frequency*] [*German*] (GCA)
Hauptwrk... Hauptwirkung [*Main Action*] [*German*]
HauswS..... Hauswirtschaftsschule [*Housekeeping School*] [*German*]
haut .... Hauteur [*Height*] [*French*]
HAV.......... Havana [*Cuba*] [*Airport symbol*] (OAG)
hav............. Havonkent [*Monthly*] (HU)
Hav .... Havuz [*Basin, Pond*] (TU)
Hava-Is...... Turkiye Sivil Havacilik Sendikasi [*Turkish Civil Aviation Workers Union*] (TU)
HAVO .... Hoger Algemeen Vormend Onderwijs [*Netherlands*]
HAVOC.... Heritage and Videotex Over the Country [*Australia*]
HAW .... Hochspannungsarmaturenwerk, Radebeul (VEB) [*Radebeul High Voltage Armature Factory (VEB)*] (EG)
HAWC...... Wacca [*Ethiopia*] [*ICAO location identifier*] (ICLI)
HAWS ...... Harcerska Akademia Wiedzy Spolecznej [*Scouting Academy of Social Sciences*] (POL)
Hawthornl Ed ... Hawthorn Institute of Education [*Australia*]
Haz............ Hazirlayan [*The Individual Who Prepared (article or work)*] (TU)
HAZ.......... Historical Association of Zambia
HAZ.......... Historical Association of Zimbabwe (EAIO)
HAZAL ..... Hahameinu Zikhronam Livrakha [*Our Sages of Blessed Memory*] [*Hebrew*]
hazt .... Haztartas [*or Haztartasi*] [*Household or Of the Household*] (HU)
hazt .... Haztartasbeli [*Housekeeper, Servant*] (HU)
HAZU........ Hrvatska Akademija Znanosti i Umjetnosti [*Croatian Academy of Sciences and Arts*] [*JAZU*] (YU)
HB.............. Bell Helicopter Co., Brantly Helicopter Corp., Brditschka [*Heinrich Brditschka Flugzeugbau*] [*ICAO aircraft manufacturer identifier*] (ICAO)
HB.............. Brinellhaerte [*Brinell Hardness*] [*German*] (GCA)
hb.............. Halb [*Half*] [*German*] (GCA)
HB.............. Halk Bankasi [*Peoples Bank of Turkey*] [*See also THB*]
HB.............. Handelsbeziehungen [*Trade Relations*] [*German*] (EG)
Hb.............. Harabe [*Ruins*] (TU)

HB............ Haztartasi Bolt [*Household Goods Stores*]   (HU)

HB............ Helvetisches Bekenntnis [*Helvetian Confession*] [*German*]

HB............ Herbarium Bradeanum [*Brazil*]

HB............ Herri Batazuna [*Union of the People*] [*Spain*] [*Political party*]   (PPE)

HB............ Hesap Birimi [*Unit of Calculation*] [*As kg, liters, etc.*]   (TU)

hb .... Hierboven [*Benelux*]   (BAS)

HB............ Honvedelmi Bizottmany [*Defense Committee*]   (HU)

HB............ Hrazeni Bystrin [*Flood Control*]   (CZ)

HBA.......... Hobart [*Tasmania*] [*Airport symbol*]   (OAG)

HBA.......... Hospital Benefits Association [*Australia*]

HBANZ..... Health Boards New Zealand   (EAIO)

HBBA .... Bujumbura [*Burundi*] [*ICAO location identifier*]   (ICLI)

HBBE .... Gitega [*Burundi*] [*ICAO location identifier*]   (ICLI)

HBBK .... Kiofi-Mosso [*Burundi*] [*ICAO location identifier*]   (ICLI)

HBBL .... Nyanza-Lac [*Burundi*] [*ICAO location identifier*]   (ICLI)

HBBM .... Mugera [*Burundi*] [*ICAO location identifier*]   (ICLI)

HBBN........ Nyakagunda [*Burundi*] [*ICAO location identifier*]   (ICLI)

HBBS........ Hammond Bay Biological Station   (ASF)

HBC.......... Haitian Aviation Line SA [*ICAO designator*]   (FAAC)

HBC.......... Heliopolis Bridge Club [*Egypt*]

HBC.......... Hong Kong Bank of Canada   (ECON)

HBD.......... Haupteisenbahndirektion [*Main Railroad Directorate*]   (EG)

Hbd .... Holzboden-Flaeche [*Lumber-Producing Area*]   (EG)

HBD.......... Hrvatsko Biolosko Drustvo   (EAIO)

Hbf .... Hauptbahnhof [*Main Railroad Station*] [*German*]   (WEN)

Hbg .... Hamburg [*Hamburg*]   (EG)

HBG.......... Hans-Bockler-Stiftung   (SLS)

HBG.......... Hollandsche Beton Groep NV [*Netherlands*]

HBIA .... Hairdressing and Beauty Industry Association [*Australia*]

HBJ .... Hazira-Bijapur-Jagdishpur [*Gas pipeline*] [*India*]

HBK .... Hochschule fuer Bildende Kuenste

HBKL .... Hayvan Besleyicileri Kooperatif Limited [*Animal Raisers' Cooperative Limited*] [*Turkish Cypriot*]   (GC)

HBM.......... Habitations Bon Marche [*North African*]

Hbm .... Hochbaumeisterei [*Office (Section or Shop) for Above-Ground Structures*]   (EG)

HBM.......... Mali-Tinbouctou Air Service [*ICAO designator*]   (FAAC)

HBMA ...... Habitations a Bon Marche Ameliorees [*French*]   (FLAF)

HBMC....... Homebush Bay Ministerial Council [*New South Wales, Australia*]

HBMO ...... Habitations a Bon Marche Ordinaires [*French*]   (FLAF)

HBNC....... Houilleres du Bassin Nord Pas de Calais [*Tunisia*]

HBO .... Hoger Beroeps Onderwijs [*Netherlands*]

HBR .... Herbario Barbosa Rodrigues [*Barbosa Rodrigues Herbarium*] [*Research center*] [*Brazil*]   (IRC)

HBRDC ..... Honey Bee Research and Development Council [*Australia*]

hbs........... Hadbiztos [*Quartermaster Officer*]   (HU)

HBS .... Havergal Brian Society   (EAIO)

HBS .... Hemiska Borbena Sredstva [*Chemical Combat Equipment*]   (YU)

HBS .... Hogere Burgerschool [*Afrikaans*]

HBS .... Hungarian Biophysical Society   (EAIO)

HBSA .... Health and Building Surveyors Association [*Australia*]

HBSANSW ... Health and Building Surveyors' Association of New South Wales [*Australia*]

HBSG .... Home Birth Support Group [*Australia*]

HBU .... Hollandsche Bank-Unie [*Netherlands*]

HBUB....... Hayvan Yetistirici ve Besleyicileri Birligi [*Livestock Raisers and Breeders' Union*]   (TU)

HBV.......... Handel, Banken, und Versicherungen [*Trade, Banks, and Insurance (Trade Union)*]   (WEN)

HBV.......... Hromadna Bytova Vystavba [*Mass Housing Construction*]   (CZ)

HBWR....... Halden Boiling Water Reactor [*Norway*] [*Nuclear energy*]

HC .... Haagse Condities [*Benelux*]   (BAS)

HC .... Heritage Committee [*Australian Capital Territory*]

HC .... Herverkavelingscommissie [*Benelux*]   (BAS)

HC .... Hidroelektricna Centrala [*Hydroelectric Power Station*]   (YU)

HC .... High Commission

HC .... Hodoninske Cihelny [*Hodonin Brick Works*]   (CZ)

HC .... Honoris Crux

HC .... Horng-Chung Productions Industrial Trading Co. Ltd. [*Taiwan*]

HC .... Hors Cadre [*French*]   (MTD)

hc............. Hors Commerce [*Not for Sale*] [*French*]

HC .... Hors Concours [*Not Competing*] [*French*]

HC .... Housing Commission [*Australia*]

HC .... Hydrocentrala [*Hydroelectric Plant*]   (CZ)

HC .... Societe Hatton & Cookson

HCA.......... Handicapped Children's Allowance [*Australia*]

HCA.......... Helsinki Citizens Assembly [*Former Czechoslovakia*]   (EAIO)

HCA.......... High Court of Australia

HCA.......... Historic Cost Accounts [*London Stock Exchange*]

HCA.......... Hospital Corporation Australia   (ADA)

HCA.......... Hunting-Clan Air Transport Ltd.

HCA.......... Lake Havasu Air Service [*ICAO designator*]   (FAAC)

HCAC....... Hazardous Chemicals Advisory Committee [*New South Wales, Australia*]

HCAI .... Haut Comite Administratif pour l'Ivoirisation

HC & C...... Harvard Capital & Consulting [*An investment fund*] [*Czechoslovakia*]   (ECON)

HCAR....... Higher Committee for Agrarian Reform [*Egypt*]

HCAV....... Hunt Clubs Association of Victoria [*Australia*]

HCAV....... Hyperactive Children's Association of Victoria [*Australia*]

HCB........... Hidroelectrica de Cabora Bassa [*Mozambique*]

HCB........... Huileries du Congo Belge

HCB........... Hungarian Credit Bank

HCC........... Hobart Chamber of Commerce [*Australia*]

HCCA .... Health Care Consumers Association [*Australia*]

HCCA .... Hellenic Chamber of Commerce in Australia

HCCAACT ... Health Care Consumers' Association of the Australian Capital Territory

HCCC .... Health Care Complaints Commission [*Australia*]

HCD .... Honoris Crux Diamond

HCEA .... Hairdressers and Cosmetologists Employers' Association [*Australia*]

HCG........... Honoris Crux Gold

HCHF....... Hogar de Cristo Housing Foundation [*Chile*]   (EAIO)

H CH F...... Homme Cherche Femme [*Man Looking for Woman*] [*French*]

HCI .... Hyderabad Contingent Infantry [*India*] [*Army*]

HCIC .... Health Care in Christ [*Australia*]

HCIDE ...... Hungarian Council of Industrial Design and Ergonomics   (EAIO)

HCIS.......... Health Care Interpreter Service [*Department of Health*] [*New South Wales, Australia*]

HCISA ...... Headmasters Conference of the Independent Schools of Australia

HCK.......... Handikappforbundens Centralkommitte [*Sweden*]   (EAIO)

HCL.......... Hindustan Cables Ltd. [*India*]   (IMH)

HCL.......... Hindustan Copper Ltd. [*India*]   (PDAA)

HCL.......... Hospitais Civis de Lisboa [*Lisbon Civilian Hospitals*] [*Portuguese*]   (WER)

HCM.......... Hejocsabai Cement Muvek [*Hejocsaba Cement Works*]   (HU)

HCM.......... Hotarirea Consiliului de Ministri [*Decision of the Council of Ministers*]   (RO)

HCMA...... Alula [*Somalia*] [*ICAO location identifier*]   (ICLI)

HCMA...... Western Australian Health Care Museums Association [*Australia*]

HCMB....... Baidoa [*Somalia*] [*ICAO location identifier*]   (ICLI)

HCMC....... Candala [*Somalia*] [*ICAO location identifier*]   (ICLI)

HCMC....... Ho Chi Minh City [*Vietnam*]

HCMD....... Bardera [*Somalia*] [*ICAO location identifier*]   (ICLI)

HCME....... Eil [*Somalia*] [*ICAO location identifier*]   (ICLI)

HCMF....... Bosaso [*Somalia*] [*ICAO location identifier*]   (ICLI)

HCMG....... Gardo [*Somalia*] [*ICAO location identifier*]   (ICLI)

HCMH ...... Hargeisa [*Somalia*] [*ICAO location identifier*]   (ICLI)

HCMI ...... Berbera [*Somalia*] [*ICAO location identifier*]   (ICLI)

HCMJ .... Lugh Ferrandi [*Somalia*] [*ICAO location identifier*]   (ICLI)

HCMK .... Kisimayu [*Somalia*] [*ICAO location identifier*]   (ICLI)

HCML .... El Bur [*Somalia*] [*ICAO location identifier*]   (ICLI)

HCMM...... Mogadishu [*Somalia*] [*ICAO location identifier*]   (ICLI)

HCMN ..... Belet Uen [*Somalia*] [*ICAO location identifier*]   (ICLI)

HCMO ...... Obbia [*Somalia*] [*ICAO location identifier*]   (ICLI)

HCMP....... Las Anod [*Somalia*] [*ICAO location identifier*]   (ICLI)

HCMR...... Galcaio [*Somalia*] [*ICAO location identifier*]   (ICLI)

HCMS....... Scusciuban [*Somalia*] [*ICAO location identifier*]   (ICLI)

HCMU ...... Erigavo [*Somalia*] [*ICAO location identifier*]   (ICLI)

HCMV...... Burao [*Somalia*] [*ICAO location identifier*]   (ICLI)

h cn........... Hier, Cours Nul [*French*]

HCNSW .... Heritage Council of New South Wales [*Australia*]

HCNUR..... Haut Commissariat des Nations Unies pour les Refugies [*UN High Commission for Refugees*] [*French*]   (BAS)

HCO .... Harco Air Services [*Nigeria*] [*ICAO designator*]   (FAAC)

HCOA ...... Health Care of Australia

HC of A..... High Court of Australia

HCP.......... Handicapped Programs Review [*Australia*]

HCP.......... H. Cegielski, Poznan [*H. Cegielski Works, Poznan*]   (POL)

HCPRN .... Haut-Commissariat au Plan et a la Reconstruction Nationale [*Zaire*]

HCPRU ..... Hot Climate Physiological Research Unit

HCQ .... Halls Creek [*Australia*] [*Airport symbol*] [*Obsolete*]   (OAG)

HCQ .... Harbours Corp. of Queensland [*Australia*]

HCR.......... Haut-Commissaire des Nations Unies pour les Refugies   (FLAF)

HCR.......... Haut Commissariat des Nations Unies pour les Refugies [*United Nations High Commission for Refugees - UNHCR*] [*Switzerland*]

HCRF .... Health Care Research Foundation [*Australia*]

HCRI .... Health Care Research Institution [*Australia*]

HCRI .... Horticulture and Coffee Research Institute [*Zimbabwe*]   (ARC)

HCS.......... Hazardous Chemicals Secretariat [*Victoria, Australia*]

HCS.......... Health Computing Services [*Australia*]

HCS.......... Healthy Cities Secretariat [*Australia*]

HCS.......... Home Care Service [*New South Wales, Australia*]

HCS.......... Honoris Crux Silver

HCS .... Hungarian Chemical Society   (EAIO)

HCS .... Hurtownia Centrali Spozywczych [*Wholesale House for Central Food Stores*]   (POL)

HCSA .... Holland Committee on Southern Africa   (EAIO)

HCSM ...... Mogadishu [*Somalia*] [*ICAO location identifier*]   (ICLI)

HCSNSW ... Home Care Service of New South Wales [*Australia*]

HCSRDG .. Health and Community Services Research and Development Grants [*Australia*]

HCT .... Huilerie Centrale de Tananarive

HCTR .... Heki Cukorrepa Termelesi Rendszer [*Sugar Beet Production System of Hek*]   (HU)

HCTT .... Horticultural Club of Trinidad and Tobago   (DSCA)

HCUSA ..... High Commissioner for the Union of South Africa

HCV .... Home Consumption Value [*Importation*] [*Philippines*]   (IMH)

HCV .... Hutchinson Cable Vision [*Hong Kong*] [*Commercial firm*]

HCVA .... Historic Commercial Vehicle Association of Australia   (ADA)

HCVCS..... Historic Commercial Vehicle Cooperative Society [*Australia*]

HCW .... Health Care Worker [*Australia*]

HCWG...... Heritage Collections Working Group [*Australia*]

HCWU ...... Hotel and Catering Workers Union

hd .... Halk Dili [*Peoples' Language, Vulgarism*]   (TU)

HD .... Handelsvidenskabelig Diplomprove [*Denmark*]

HD .... Hnedouhelne Doly [*Lignite (Brown Coal) Mines*]   (CZ)

Hd .... Hochdeutsch [*High German*] [*Language, etc.*] [*German*]

HD .... Hochdruck [*High Pressure*] [*German*]

HD .... Hochleistungsdrucker [*German*]   (ADPT)

Hd .... Hoogduits [*High German*] [*Language, etc.*] [*Afrikaans*]

HD .... Hospodarske Druzstvo [*Agricultural Cooperative*]   (CZ)

Hd .... Hoved [*Headland*] [*Denmark*]   (NAU)

HD .... Hrvatsko Domobranstvo [*Croatian Home-Guard*] [*World War II*]   (YU)

HD .... Hudebni Soubor [*Music Ensemble*]   (CZ)

Hd .... Hudut [*Border, Boundary*]   (TU)

HD .... Hurel Dubois [*Societe de Construction des Avions Hurel Dubois*] [*France*] [*ICAO aircraft manufacturer identifier*]   (ICAO)

Hd .... Huvud [*Headland*] [*Sweden*]   (NAU)

HDA .... Diploma of the Hawkesbury Agricultural College [*Australia*]   (ADA)

HDA .... Hawkesbury Diploma in Agriculture [*Australia*]

HDA .... Hong Kong Dragon Airlines Ltd. [*ICAO designator*]   (FAAC)

HDA .... Huntington's Disease Association [*Australia*]

HDAS....... Home Deposit Assistance Scheme [*Australia*]

HDATA..... Hydrogene Data [*National College of Chemistry of Paris*] [*France*] [*Information service or system*]   (IID)

hdb .... Hadbiro [*Judge Advocate, Military Prosecutor*]   (HU)

Hdb .... Handbuch [*Handbook, Manual*] [*German*]

HdB........... Handwerkskammer des Bezirks [*District Artisan Chamber*]   (EG)

HDB........... Housing Development Board [*Singapore*]

HDB........... Hunter Development Board [*Australia*]

HDBS .... Hnedouhelne Doly a Briketarny v Sokolove [*Lignite (Brown Coal) Mines and Briquette Plants in Sokolov*]   (CZ)

hdc............. Hier Dernier Cours

HDD .... Diploma of Dairying, Hawkesbury Agricultural College [*Australia*]   (ADA)

HDD .... Halkci Devrimci Dernegi [*Populist Revolutionary Organization*]   (TU)

HDD .... Handlowy Dom Dziecka [*Children's Articles Trade Center*]   (POL)

HDD ... Hyderabad [*Pakistan*] [*Airport symbol*]   (OAG)

HDDS....... Hunter Developmental Disabilities Service [*Australia*]

HDE........... Hora del Este [*Eastern Time*] [*Spanish*]

HDEG....... Union List of Higher Degree Theses [*AUSINET database*]   (ADA)

HDEG....... Union List of Higher Degree Theses in Australian Libraries [*University of Tasmania Library*] [*Australia*] [*Information service or system*]   (CRD)

HDeH .... Hawker De Havilland [*Australia*]

HDeHV ..... Hawker De Havilland Victoria [*Australia*]

HDF........... Hungarian Democratic Forum [*Political party*]   (EY)

HDG .... Hauptverwaltung Deutsche Grenzpolizei [*Main Administration of the German Border Police*]   (EG)

HDG .... Hochdruck-Windkanal Goettingen

HDGB........ Halk Devrimci Genclik Birligi [*Peoples' Revolutionary Youth Union*]   (TU)

HDGF........ Halkci Devrimci Genclik Federasyonu [*Populist Revolutionary Youth Federation*]   (TU)

HDGO .... Halkci Devrimci Genclik Orgutu [*Populist Revolutionary Youth Organization*]   (TU)

hdgs........... Headings [*Australia*]

hdgy........... Hadnagy [*Lieutenant*]   (HU)

HDH .... Hauptverband der Deutschen Holz und Kunststoffe Verarbeitenden Industrie und Verwandter Industriezweige eV [*Germany*]   (EY)

HDHD....... Hilf Du Heilige Dreifaltigkeit [*Help Thou Holy Trinity*] [*Motto of Johann Georg I, Prince of Anhalt-Dessau (1567-1618)*] [*German*]

HDHS........ Hastings District Historical Society [*Australia*]

HDHS........ Hills District Historical Society [*Australia*]

HDI........... Hoteles Dinamicos SA de CV [*Mexico*] [*ICAO designator*]   (FAAC)

HDI........... Human Development Index [*Human Development Report*] [*United Nations Development Program*]

HDIEO...... Histoire du Droit et des Institutions de l'Eglise en Occident [*Publie sous la Direction de Gabriel de Bras*]   (FLAF)

HDII .... Himpunan Disainer Interior Indonesia   (EAIO)

HDIP .... Hydrocarbon Development Institute of Pakistan [*Ministry of Petroleum and Natural Resources*] [*Research center*]   (EAS)

HdK .... Hochschule der Kuenste

Hdl............. Handel [*Trade*] [*German*]

Hdl............. Hauptdispatcherleitung [*Main Dispatcher Office*]   (EG)

HDL........... Heil die Leser [*To the Reader, Greeting*] [*Afrikaans*]

Hdlg .... Handlung [*Store, Trading*] [*Business term*] [*German*]

Hdlr .... Haendler [*Merchant*] [*German*]

hdm .... Hadmuvelet [*or Hadmuveleti*] [*Military Operation or Operational*]   (HU)

HDM .... Hermandad del Maestrazgo [*Brotherhood of Teachers*] [*Spanish*]   (WER)

HDML....... Harbor Defense Motor Launch [*NATO*]   (NATG)

HDMS....... Hisbia Dastouri Mustaquil

HDMS....... Hizbia Digil-Mirifle Somali

HDMSA .... Hydrographic Department of the Maritime Safety Agency [*Japan*]   (MSC)

HDog .... Directive on Contracts   (BU)

HDP........... Hankyore Democratic Party [*South Korea*] [*Political party*]   (EY)

HDP........... Hora del Pacifico [*Pacific Time*] [*Spanish*]

HDP........... Houfnicovy Delostrelecky Pluk [*Howitzer Artillery Regiment*]   (CZ)

HDP........... Huer Demokrat Parti [*Free Democrat Party*] [*Turkish Cyprus*] [*Political party*]   (EY)

HDP........... Human Dimension of Global Environmental Change Programme [*The International Social Science Council*]   (ECON)

HDP........... Statni Ustav pro Projektovani Vodohospodarskych Staveb - Hydroprojekt [*State Planning Institute for Water Construction*]   (CZ)

HDPPA ..... Housing Development and Public Participation Administration [*Turkey*]   (ECON)

HDr............ Doktor der Handelswissenschaften [*German*]

HDRA....... Henry Doubleday Research Association [*Coventry, England*]   (EAIO)

HDRAA..... Henry Doubleday Research Association of Australia

HDRBG..... Heissdampfreaktor Betriebsgesellschaft [*Germany*]   (PDAA)

HDRU .... Human Development and Research Unit

hds............. Hadsereg [*Army*]   (HU)

Hds .... Handschrift [*Manuscript*] [*German*]

HDS........... Hnedouhelne Doly, Sokolov [*Lignite (Brown Coal) Mines in Sokolov*]   (CZ)

HDS........... Hospodarske Dokumentacni Stredisko [*Economic Documentation Center*]   (CZ)

HDS........... Hospodarske Druzstvo Skladistni [*Warehouse Cooperative*]   (CZ)

HDS........... Hrvatski Demokratski Stranka [*Croatian Democratic Party*] [*Political party*]   (EY)

HDS........... Hrvatski Drzavni Sabor [*Croatian Diet*]   (YU)

HDS........... Hungarian Dermatological Society   (EAIO)

Hds M .... Hendes Majestaet [*Her Majesty*] [*Denmark*]   (GPO)

Hds Maj.... Hennes Majestet [*Her Majesty*] [*Norway*]   (GPO)

HDSV .... Hospodarske Druzstvo Skladistni a Vyrobni [*Warehouse and Production Cooperative*]   (CZ)

hdt .... Hadtest [*Army Corps*]   (HU)

HDTC....... Heavy Duty Truck Corp. [*China*]   (TCC)

HDUR .... Hungarian Democratic Union of Romania [*Political party*]   (EY)

HDV .... Health Department Victoria [*Australia*]

HDW .... Hebdrehwaehler [*Two-Motion Selector, Vertical Selector Switch*]   (EG)

HDW .... Howaldtswerke Deutsche Werft [*Howald Shipbuilding Manufacturer of Germany*]

HDWA ...... Health Department of Western Australia

HdwStDB .. Handwerkssteuer-Durchfuehrungsbestimmung [*Implementing Regulation to the Artisan Tax*]   (EG)

HdWStVo ... Handwerkssteuerverordnung [*Artisan Tax Decree*]   (EG)

HDY .... Haadyai [*Thailand*] [*Airport symbol*]   (OAG)

HDZ........... Hrvatska Demokratska Zajednica [*Croatian Democratic Union*] [*Political party*]   (EY)

HDZ........... Hrvatski Dijalektoloski Zbornik [*Croatian Dialect Papers*]   (YU)

HE.............. Halk Evleri [*Peoples' Houses Organization*] [*A very old educational institution, mostly in rural areas*]   (TU)

He .... Halte [*Halt*] [*Military map abbreviation World War I*] [*French*] (MTD)
He .... Helio [*Helium*] [*Chemical element*] [*Portuguese*]
HE............... Helio Aircraft Co. [*ICAO aircraft manufacturer identifier*] (ICAO)
HE............... Her [*or His*] Eminence (IDIG)
HE............... Her [*or His*] Excellency (IDIG)
HE............... Hidroelektrana [*Hydroelectric Power Plant*] (YU)
HE............... Hidro Elektrik [*Hydroelectric*] (TU)
HE............... His Eminence (SCAC)
HE............... His [*or Her*] Excellence [*or Eminence*] (EECI)
HE............... His Excellency (PWGL)
HE............... His Exellency (SCAC)
HE............... Huon Electrical Ltd. [*Papua New Guinea*]
HEA........... Heliavia-Transporte Aereo Lda. [*Portugal*] [*ICAO designator*] (FAAC)
HEA........... Herat [*Afghanistan*] [*Airport symbol*] [*Obsolete*] (OAG)
HEA........... Hungarian Economic Association (EAIO)
HEAA........ Home Economics Association of Australia (ADA)
HEAC........ Higher Education Administration Charge [*Australia*]
HEANET .. Higher Education Authority Network [*Irish*] [*Computer science*] (TNIG)
HEAPS...... Health Education and Promotion Information System [*Australia*]
HEAR........ El Arish/El Arish [*Egypt*] [*ICAO location identifier*] (ICLI)
HEAS........ Home Energy Advisory Service [*Victoria, Australia*]
HEASA ..... Home Economics Association of Southern Africa (AA)
HEAT .... Asyut [*Egypt*] [*ICAO location identifier*] (ICLI)
HEAV........ Health Education Association of Victoria
HEAX........ Alexandria [*Egypt*] [*ICAO location identifier*] (ICLI)
heb............. Heber [*Hebrew*] (HU)
HEBERMA ... Societe Anonyme d'Hebergement en Mauritanie
HEBIS-BIB ... Hessische Bibliographie [*Hessian Bibliography*] [*Database*] [*Information retrieval*]
HEBL .... Abu Simbel [*Egypt*] [*ICAO location identifier*] (ICLI)
hebr............ Hebraico [*Hebrew*] [*Portuguese*]
Hebr........... Hebreeers [*Hebrews*] [*Afrikaans*]
HEC........... Hautes Etudes Commerciales [*School for Advanced Business Studies*] [*French*] (WER)
HEC........... Heliservicio Campeche SA de CV [*Mexico*] [*ICAO designator*] (FAAC)
HEC........... Hidroelectrica de Cataluna SA [*Spanish*]
HEC........... Hidroelektricna Centrala [*Hydroelectric Power Station*] (YU)
HEC........... Hidro-Elektro Central [*Albanian*]
HEC........... Higher Education Contribution [*Scheme*] [*Australia*]
HEC........... High Executive Council [*Sudan*]
HEC........... Hydro-Electric Commission [*Australia*]
HEC........... Hyundai Engineering & Construction [*Commercial firm*] [*South Korea*]
HECA .... Cairo/International [*Egypt*] [*ICAO location identifier*] (ICLI)
HECA .... Cepillos Heca Lda. [*Barranquilla*] (COL)
HECC .... Cairo [*Egypt*] [*ICAO location identifier*] (ICLI)
HECLINET ... Health Care Literature Information Network [*Institut fuer Krankenhausbau*] [*Germany*] [*Information service or system*] (IID)
HECS .... Higher Education Contribution Scheme [*Australia*]
HECSA...... Hidroelectrica de Cataluna SA [*Spain*] (WED)
hect............ Hectare [*Portuguese*] (GPO)
hect............ Hectare [*French*]
hect............ Hectarea [*Hectare*] [*Spanish*]
hectogr....... Hectogramme [*Hectogram*] [*French*]
hectol......... Hectolitre [*Hectoliter*] [*French*]
hectom....... Hectometre [*Hectometer*] [*French*]
HEd........... HoogEdele [*Honorable*] [*Afrikaans*]
HEDC........ Hunter Economic Development Council [*Australia*]
HEDE........ Heavy Engineering Development Establishment [*Australia*]
HEdGestr ... HoogEdel-Gestrenge [*Right Honorable*] [*Afrikaans*]
HEE........... Heli Europe [*Belgium*] [*ICAO designator*] (FAAC)
HEE........... Hydro-Electric Energy
heelk .... Heelkunde [*or Heelkundig*] [*Surgery or Surgical*] [*Afrikaans*]
HEEM ...... Embaba [*Egypt*] [*ICAO location identifier*] (ICLI)
HEerw....... HoogEerwaarde [*Right Reverend*] [*Afrikaans*]
HEF .... Centre Stephanois de Recherches Mecaniques Hydromecanique et Frottement [*Andrezieux-Boutheon, France*]
HEF .... Health Employees' Federation [*Australia*]
HEF .... Hospital Employees' Federation of Australia
HEFA .... Higher Education Funding Act [*Australia*]
HEFA .... Hospital Employees' Federation of Australia
Hefegar ...... Hefegaerung [*Yeast Fermentation*] [*German*] (GCA)
heftn........... Heftning [*Stitching*] [*Publishing Danish/Norwegian*]
HEGN........ Hurghada [*Egypt*] [*ICAO location identifier*] (ICLI)
HEGR........ El-Gora [*Egypt*] [*ICAO location identifier*] (ICLI)
HEGSS....... Higher Education General and Salaried Staff Award [*Australia*]
HEH .... Heho [*Myanmar*] [*Airport symbol*] (OAG)
HeH .... Her (or His) Exalted Highness [*Australia*]

HEI............ Ecole des Hautes Etudes Industrielles [*College of Advanced Industrial Studies*] [*Research center*] [*French*] (ERC)
HEI............ Hammer Exploration Israel [*Commercial firm*]
HEI............ Higher Education Institute [*Australia*]
Heil............ Heilung [*Healing*] [*German*] (GCA)
Heim .... Heimat [*Home*] [*German*] (GCA)
heim .... Heimisch [*Native*] [*German*] (GCA)
Heiz........... Heizung [*Heating*] [*German*] (GCA)
Hek .... Hekimlik [*Medical Science, Medicine*] (TU)
HEKB .... El Nakab/El Nakab [*Egypt*] [*ICAO location identifier*] (ICLI)
hekn .... Hely Ev es Kiado Nelkul [*Without Place of Publication, Date, and Publisher*] [*Hungary*]
HEks.......... Haar Eksellensie [*Her Excellency*] [*Afrikaans*]
HEKS .... Hilfswerk der Evangelischen Kirchen der Schweiz [*Swiss Interchurch Aid*] (EAIO)
Hekt .... Hektoliter [*Hectoliter*] [*German*]
hektogr....... Hektografiert [*Hectographed*] [*German*]
HEL........... Helicol Helicopteros Nacionales de Colombia [*ICAO designator*] (FAAC)
HEL........... Helsinki [*Finland*] [*Airport symbol*] (OAG)
Hel .... Hotel [*Hotel*] [*Military map abbreviation World War I*] [*French*] (MTD)
HELABA... Hessische Landesbank-Girozentrale [*Hessian National Bank*]
helbalycronbd ... Helbalycronbind [*Full-Balycron Binding*] [*Publishing Danish/Norwegian*]
helbuckrambd ... Helbuckrambind [*Full-Buckram Binding*] [*Publishing Danish/Norwegian*]
HELCOM ... Baltic Marine Environment Protection Commission - Helsinki Commission (EAIO)
helfabl .... Helfabrikoidlaederbind [*Imitation Leather Binding*] [*Publishing Danish/Norwegian*]
helgranitolbd ... Helgranitolbind [*Imitation Leather Binding*] [*Publishing Danish/Norwegian*]
HELIBRAS ... Helicopteros de Brasil, SA [*Brazilian Helicopters, Inc.*] (LA)
HELICOL ... Helicopteros Nacionales de Colombia SA [*Buga*] (COL)
helio .... Heliogravure [*Photoengraving*] [*Publishing*] [*French*]
heliogr .... Heliogravure [*Photoengraving*] [*Publishing*] [*French*]
Heliograv .. Heliogravuere [*Photoengraving*] [*German*]
heliograv ... Heliogravure [*Photoengraving*] [*Publishing*] [*French*]
Helios........ Helios - Joies de la Musique [*Record label*] [*France*]
HELIP .... HAWK [*Homing All the Way Killer*] European Limited Improvement Program [*NATO*]
helkbd .... Helklotband [*Full-Cloth Binding*] [*Publishing*] [*Sweden*]
helldr.......... Hellaeder [*Full Leather*] [*Publishing Danish/Norwegian*]
HELLP...... Help the Estonian, Latvian, and Lithuanian Peoples Association (ADA)
hellrd.......... Hellaerred [*Full Cloth*] [*Publishing Danish/Norwegian*]
HELMEPA ... Hellenic Marine Environment Protection Association
HELN .... Hubungan Ekonomi Luar Negeri [*Foreign Economic Relations*] [*Indonesian*] (IN)
HELORS... Hellenic Operational Research Society [*Greek*] (PDAA)
HELP........ Health Education, Liaison, and Promotion [*South Australian Health Commission*]
HELP........ Helping Early Leavers Program [*Australia*]
helplastb .... Helplastikbind [*Full-Plastic Binding*] [*Publishing Danish/Norwegian*]
helpluv ...... Helpluviusin [*Full Leatherette*] [*Publishing Danish/Norwegian*]
helsaffianbd ... Helsaffianbind [*Full-Morocco Binding*] [*Publishing Danish/Norwegian*]
helsh........... Helshirting [*Full Cloth*] [*Publishing Danish/Norwegian*]
helsjirtb....... Helsjirtingsband [*Full-Cloth Binding*] [*Publishing Danish/Norwegian*]
helskb......... Helskindbind [*Full-Leather Binding*] [*Publishing Danish/Norwegian*]
helskind...... Helskindbind [*Full-Leather Binding*] [*Publishing Danish/Norwegian*]
helstrieb ..... Helstriebind [*Full-Buckram Binding*] [*Publishing Danish/Norwegian*]
HELX .... Luxor [*Egypt*] [*ICAO location identifier*] (ICLI)
helyk .... Helyi Kirendeltseg [*Local Branch Office*] (HU)
HEMA...... Hidrolik Makina Sanayii ve Ticaret AS [*Hydraulic Machinery Industry and Trade Corp.*] (TU)
HEMLOC ... Health and Medical Libraries On-Line Catalogue [*Australian Commonwealth Department of Health*] [*Information service or system*]
Hemm .... Hemmung [*Inhibition*] [*German*] (GCA)
HEMM...... Mersa-Matruh [*Egypt*] [*ICAO location identifier*] (ICLI)
HEMPRO ... Hemizacija Poljoprivrede [*Agricultural Chemistry*] (YU)
hen .... Hely es Ev Nelkul [*Without Place and Date of Publication*] [*Hungary*]
HEN .... Hotel, Echo, November [*Russian submarine*]
h en b......... Hoja en Blanco [*Blank Leaf*] [*Publishing*] [*Spanish*]
henk.......... Henkilosta [*About a Person*] [*Finland*]
H Entw...... H-Entwicklung [*Hydrogen*] [*German*]
HENV........ New Valley [*Egypt*] [*ICAO location identifier*] (ICLI)
heo............ Helyorseg [*Garrison*] (HU)

HEO .... Hirurski Epidemoloski Odred [*Surgical Epidemic Detachment*] [*Military*] (YU)

HEP .... Halkin Emek Partisi [*People's Labor Party*] [*Turkey*] [*Political party*] (EY)

HEPAL...... Helicopteros Portugal Africa Limitada

HEPCA ..... Heavy Engineering Projects Corp. of Australia

HEPND..... Hnuti Exulantu pro Navrat Domu [*Exiles' Movement for the Return Home*] (CZ)

HEPnet...... High Energy Physics Network [*Computer science*] (TNIG)

hepr .... Hepreaa [*or Hepreaksi*] [*Finland*]

hepr........... Heprealainen [*Finland*]

HEPS......... Port Said [*Egypt*] [*ICAO location identifier*] (ICLI)

Her .... Haver [*Credit*] [*Business term*] [*Portuguese*]

HER.......... Heraklion [*Greece*] [*Airport symbol*] (OAG)

HER.......... Heraldiek [*Heraldry*] [*Afrikaans*]

her .... Heraldiika [*Heraldry*] [*Finland*]

her .... Heraldique [*French*] (TPFD)

her .... Heraldry (TPFD)

HER.......... Hex'air [*France*] [*ICAO designator*] (FAAC)

HER.......... Hydraulique et Equipement Rural

HERA........ Hadron-Elektron-Ring Anlage [*Hadron-Electron Ring Accelerator*] [*Germany*]

HERA........ Heavy Engineering Research Association, Inc. [*New Zealand*] (ARC)

HERA........ Heritage Australia Information System [*Australian Heritage Commission*] [*Information service or system*] (IID)

Herabsetz... Herabsetzung [*Decrease*] [*German*] (GCA)

Herald .... Heraldica [*Heraldry*] [*Portuguese*]

Herb.......... Herbege [*Hostel*] [*German*]

HERCEGKOOPERATIVA ... Hercegovina Cooperative Establishment [*Mostar*] (YU)

herdr .... Herdruk [*Reprint*] [*Publishing*] [*Netherlands*]

HERDSA... Higher Education Research and Development Society of Australasia [*or Australia*]

herg .... Hergestellt [*Produced*] [*German*]

hergest .... Hergestellt [*Produced*] [*German*] (GCA)

HERL .... Hyderabad Engineering Research Laboratories [*India*]

Hermge...... Hermitage [*Hermitage*] [*Military map abbreviation World War I*] [*French*] (MTD)

HERN........ Ras-Nasrani [*Egypt*] [*ICAO location identifier*] (ICLI)

HERO........ Hydrothermal Environment Research Observatory [*US-French Marine collaboration*]

HERRAGRO ... Herramientas Agricolas SA [*Manizales*] (COL)

Herst.......... Herstellung [*Production*] [*German*]

Herst-Verf ... Herstellungsverfahren [*Production Process*] [*German*] (GCA)

Herts.......... Hertfordshire (IDIG)

Herv .... Hervormd [*Reformed*] [*Afrikaans*]

hervorrag ... Hervorragend [*Outstanding*] [*German*]

herz .... Herzien [*Revised*] [*Publishing*] [*Netherlands*]

HES .... Heli Services [*France*] [*ICAO designator*] (FAAC)

HES .... Hidro-Elektrik Santral [*Hydroelectric Power Plant*] (TU)

HES .... Hidro-Elektrik Sema [*Hydroelectric (Power) Diagram or Plan*] (TU)

HES .... Horticultural Experiment Station [*South Korean*] [*Research center*] (IRC)

HES .... Hygienicko-Epidemicke Stanice [*Public Health and Epidemiology Stations*] (CZ)

HESC .... St. Catherine/St. Catherine [*Egypt*] [*ICAO location identifier*] (ICLI)

HESDC ..... Higher Education Student Data Collection [*Australia*]

HESESCO ... China Health and Sanitation Equipment and Supplies Corp. (TCC)

HESN .... Aswan [*Egypt*] [*ICAO location identifier*] (ICLI)

HESP......... Japanese High Energy Solar Physics

HESSAD... Household Expenditure Survey - Small Area Data [*Australian Bureau of Statistics*]

HESTA...... Health Employees' Superannuation Trust Australia

HET .... Hohhot [*China*] [*Airport symbol*] (OAG)

HET .... Hudson-Essex Terraplane [*Australia*]

HET .... TAF Helicopters SA [*Spain*] [*ICAO designator*] (FAAC)

HETR .... El-Tor [*Egypt*] [*ICAO location identifier*] (ICLI)

hetz............ Hetzelve [*The Same*] [*Netherlands*]

heut .... Heutig [*Modern*] [*German*] (GCA)

HEV.......... Budapesti Helyierdeku Vasut [*Budapest Suburban Railway System*] (HU)

HeV........... Hermlin Verlag [*Hermlin Publishing House*] (EG)

HEVECAM ... Hevea Camerounais [*Cameroonian Rubber Company*] (AF)

HEW.......... Hamburgische Elektrizitaets-Werke Aktiengesellschaft [*Electrical Joint Stock Company of Hamburg*]

HEX.......... Santo Domingo [*Dominican Republic*] [*Airport symbol*] (OAG)

Hey............ Heyet [*Committee, Board*] (TU)

Heyk .... Heykeltraslik [*Sculpture*] (TU)

HEZ.......... Higijensko Epidemoloski Zavod [*Institute of Hygiene and Epidemiology*] (YU)

HEZOBOLLAH ... Hezb Allah [*Party of God*] [*Arabic*] [*An Irananian terrorist organization*]

Hf.............. Einzelhof [*Single-Family Home*] [*German*]

HF.............. Habsburgh, Feldman SA [*Switzerland*]

Hf.............. Hafnio [*Chemical element*] [*Portuguese*]

HF.............. Haute Frequence [*High Frequency*] [*French*]

hf.............. Hefte [*Issue*] [*Publishing Danish/Norwegian*]

hf.............. Heftet [*Stitched*] [*Publishing Danish/Norwegian*]

HF.............. Himma Freight Ltd. [*Nigeria*]

HF.............. Hlutafelag [*Joint-Stock Company*] [*Icelandic*] (CED)

hf.............. Hochfest [*High Strength*] [*German*] (GCA)

HF.............. Hochfrequenz [*High Frequency*] (EG)

HF.............. Hojere Forberedelseseksamen [*Educational examination*] [*Denmark*]

hf.............. Holland Forint [*Dutch Guilder*] (HU)

HF.............. Huna Forschunggesellschaft [*Huna Research Association - HRA*] [*Switzerland*] (EAIO)

HF.............. Hungarofilm [*Film-producing firm*] [*Hungarian*]

Hf.............. Meierhof [*Farmhouse*] [*German*]

HF.............. Messerschmitt-Boelkow-Blohm [*Germany*] [*ICAO aircraft manufacturer identifier*] (ICAO)

HFA .... Haemophilia Foundation of Australia

HFA .... Haifa [*Israel*] [*Airport symbol*] (OAG)

HFA .... Hardware Federation of Australia

HfA .... Hauptverwaltung fuer Aufklaerung [*Main Administration for Intelligence Collection (within Ministry of State Security)*] (EG)

HFA .... Housing for Aboriginal People [*Australia*]

HfB .... Hochschule fuer Berufstaetige

HfBL.......... Hochschule fuer Bauwesen Leipzig [*Leipzig Advanced School for Architecture*] (EG)

HFC .... Hope Foundation Communicators [*Australia*]

HFCK .... Housing Finance Company of Kenya

HfD .... Hauptanschluss fuer Direktruf [*German*] (ADPT)

HFD .... Hrvatsko Filolosko Drustvo [*Croatian Philological Society*] (YU)

hfdst .... Hoofdstuk [*Benelux*] (BAS)

HFE .... Hefei [*China*] [*Airport symbol*] (OAG)

HFEAA ..... Historic Fire Engine Association of Australia

HFF .... Hannoversches Forschungsinstitut fuer Fertigungsfragen eV (SLS)

HFF .... Hazai Fesusfono Reszvenytarsasag [*Domestic Worsted Mills Ltd.*] (HU)

HFF .... Hochschule fuer Fernsehen und Film

HFFF .... Djibouti/Ambouli [*Djibouti*] [*ICAO location identifier*] (ICLI)

HFHKLA .. Honorary Fellow of the Hong Kong Library Association

HFI .... Health Facilities Information File [*Australia*]

HFI .... Home for Incurables [*Australia*]

HFIA .... Home Furnishings International Association (EA)

HFL .... Heliflyg AG [*Sweden*] [*ICAO designator*] (FAAC)

Hfl............. Hollannin Floriini [*or Hollannin Floriinia*] [*Finland*]

HFM.......... Hochschule fuer Musik [*High School for Music*] [*German*]

hfn............. Haefte [*Issue*] [*Publishing*] [*Sweden*]

HFN........... Hofn [*Iceland*] [*Airport symbol*] (OAG)

HFP .... Hamdard Foundation Pakistan (EAIO)

HFP .... Hochschule fuer Politik [*High School for Politics*] [*German*]

HFP .... Huon Forest Products [*Australia*]

HFPP........ Habe Fulami People's Party

hfr.............. Halvfranskt [*Half-Leather Binding*] [*Publishing*] [*Sweden*]

HFR .... Heli France [*ICAO designator*] (FAAC)

HfR .... Horselskadades Riksforbund [*Sweden*] (EAIO)

HFRAF..... Hungarian Federation of Resisters and Antifascists (EAIO)

Hfranzbd.... Halbfranzband [*Half-Calf Binding*] [*Publishing*] [*German*]

hfrbd .... Halvfranskt Band [*Half-Calf Binding*] [*Publishing*] [*Sweden*]

HFRZ......... Halbfranzband [*Half-Calf Binding*] [*Publishing*] [*German*]

Hfrzbd........ Halbfranzband [*Half-Calf Binding*] [*Publishing*] [*German*]

HFS .... Household Financial Services [*Australia*]

HFSP .... Human Frontier Science Program [*An international effort, proposed by Japan in 1987*]

HFSSA ...... Historical Firearms Society of South Africa

Hfst............ Hoofdstuk [*Chapter*] [*Netherlands*] (GPO)

HFST.......... Hoofstuk [*Chapter*] [*Afrikaans*]

HFT .... Hammerfest [*Norway*] [*Airport symbol*] (OAG)

Hft............. Heft [*Part*] [*German*]

hft.............. Hefte [*Issue*] [*Publishing Danish/Norwegian*]

hft.............. Heftet [*Stitched*] [*Publishing Danish/Norwegian*]

HFT .... Hollyfordair Travel Ltd. [*New Zealand*] [*ICAO designator*] (FAAC)

Hftn........... Heften [*Issues*] [*Publishing*] [*German*]

hftr............ Hefter [*Issues*] [*Publishing Danish/Norwegian*]

HfU .... Horselframjandets Riksforbund Ungdomskopsulenten [*Sweden*] (EAIO)

HFV .... Helicopter Flight Vietnam [*Australia*]

HFV .... Hessische Forstliche Versuchsanstalt [*Hessian Forest Research Station*] (ARC)

HfV .... Hochschule fuer Verkehrswesen "Friedrich List" [*"Friedrich List" Advanced School for Transportation*] (EG)

HFVO........ Hochfrequenzverordnung [*High Frequency Regulations*] (EG)

Hfz .... Halbfranzband [*Half-Calf Binding*] [*Publishing*] [*German*]
Hfzbd .... Halbfranzband [*Half-Calf Binding*] [*Publishing*] [*German*]
HG .... Centreline Air Services Ltd. [*British*] [*ICAO designator*]   (ICDA)
hg .... Hectograma [*Hectogram*] [*Portuguese*]
hg .... Hectogramme [*Hectogram*] [*French*]
Hg .... Hectogramo [*Hectogram*] [*Spanish*]
H G .... Hegyseg [*Mountain, Mountain Range*]   (HU)
hg .... Hehtogramma [*or Hehtogrammaa*] [*Finland*]
Hg .... Hektogram [*Hectogram*] [*Afrikaans*]
hg .... Hektogram [*Hectogram*] [*Poland*]
Hg .... Herausgeber [*or Herausgegeben*] [*Editor, Publisher or Edit,
                    Publish*] [*German*]
HG .... Her (or His) Grace [*Australia*]
HG .... Hidrogradnija [*General hydraulic contracting company*] [*Former
                    Yugoslavia*]
HG .... Hlinkova Garda [*Hlinka Guards*]   (CZ)
HGA .... Hargeisa [*Somalia*] [*Airport symbol*]   (OAG)
HGA .... Horological Guild of Australia   (ADA)
HGAPSPA ... Hands of Gold, Association for the Promotion of Sculpture and
                    Plastic Arts [*France*]   (EAIO)
HGB .... Handelsgesetzbuch [*Commercial Code*] [*German*] [*Legal term*]
                    (DLA)
HGD .... Hangard Aviation Ltd. [*Mongolia*] [*ICAO designator*]   (FAAC)
HGD .... Hughenden [*Australia*] [*Airport symbol*]   (OAG)
HG derDDR ... Historiker Gesellschaft der Deutschen Demokratischen
                    Republik   (SLS)
HGer .... Handelsgericht [*Arbitration Tribunal*] [*German*]
HGF .... Helmholtz-Gemeinschaft Deutscher Forschungs-zentren
                    [*Helmholtz association of German research centres*]
HGFA .... Hang Gliding Federation of Australia   (ADA)
HGH .... Arrest van het Hooggerechtshof [*Benelux*]   (BAS)
HGH .... Hangzhou [*China*] [*Airport symbol*]   (OAG)
HGH .... Hoog Gerechts Hof van Nederlands-Indie [*Benelux*]   (BAS)
HGHGHG ... Hilf Gott, Hilf Gott, Hilf Gott [*God Help, God Help, God Help*]
                    [*Motto of Sophie Elisabeth, Countess of Schwarzenburg
                    (1565-1621)*]
HGJP .... Henry George Justice Party [*Australia*]   (ADA)
HGL .... Hauptgesellschaftsleitung [*Main Company Management*]
                    [*German*]   (EG)
HGL .... Hausgemeinschaftsleitung [*Housing Community Leadership*]
                    (EG)
HGL .... Helgoland [*Germany*] [*Airport symbol*]   (OAG)
HGL .... Hochschulgewerkschaftsleitung [*Advanced School Labor Union
                    Leadership*]   (EG)
HGM .... Harita Genel Mudurlugu [*Cartography Directorate General*]
                    [*Under Defense Ministry*]   (TU)
HGM .... Hoog Militair Gerechtshof [*Benelux*]   (BAS)
HGN .... Mae Hong Son [*Thailand*] [*Airport symbol*]   (OAG)
HGO .... Halsgerichtsordnung [*German*]
HGO .... Hoofdgroep Gezondheidsonderzoek [*Division for Health
                    Research*] [*Netherlands Central Organization for Applied
                    Natural Scientific Research*]   (WND)
HGO .... Korhogo [*Ivory Coast*] [*Airport symbol*]   (OAG)
HGP .... Hidrogradevinsko Preduzece [*Hydraulic Construction
                    Establishment*]   (YU)
HGr .... Haeusergruppe [*Group Houses*] [*German*]
HGS .... Freetown [*Sierra Leone*] Hastings Airport [*Airport symbol*]
                    (OAG)
HGS .... Hauptgefechtsstand [*Main Battle Station*] [*Navy*]   (EG)
HGS .... Hoof van die Generale Staf [*Chief of General Staff*] [*Afrikaans*]
HGSC .... Institut Geologique National de Hongrie [*Hungary*]   (EAIO)
HGSC .... Heraldry and Genealogy Society of Canberra [*Australia*]
HGU .... Mount Hagen [*Papua New Guinea*] [*Airport symbol*]   (OAG)
HGUB .... Historisch Genootschap te Utrecht, Bijdragen en Mededeelingen
HGUO .... Hauptverband der Graphischen Unternehmungen Osterreichs
                    [*Austria*]   (EAIO)
hgv .... Hangverseny [*Concert*]   (HU)
hgvkozv ...... Hangversenykozvetites [*Concert Broadcast*]   (HU)
hgy .... Hegyi [*Mountain (Adjective)*]   (HU)
HGZ .... Hrvatska Gradanska Zastita [*Croatian Civil Defense*]   (YU)
Hgz .... Hrvatski Glazbeni Zavod [*Croatian Music Institute*]   (YU)
HGZG .... Hilf Gott zu Glueck [*May God Help Us to Fortune*] [*Motto of
                    Magdalene, Princess of Anhalt (1585-1657)*] [*German*]
HH .... Fairchild/Republic [*ICAO aircraft manufacturer identifier*]
                    (ICAO)
HH .... Haar Hoogheid [*Her Highness*] [*Afrikaans*]
HH .... Hamersley Holdings [*Australia*]
HH .... Handelshochschule [*Commercial College*] [*German*]
HH .... Harmony and Health [*An association*] [*France*]   (EAIO)
HH .... Hashim Hago Group of Companies [*Sudan*]
HH .... Heim und Handwerk [*Handicrafts display*]
HH .... Hemmets Haerold [*Record label*] [*Sweden*]
HH .... Her Highness   (PWGL)
HH .... His Highness   (PWGL)
hh .... Hojas [*Leaves*] [*Spanish*]
HH .... Hojere Handelseksamen [*Educational qualification*] [*Denmark*]

HH .... Hyperactive Help [*Australia*]
HHA .... Haushaltsaufschlaege [*Budget Surtaxes*]   (EG)
HHA .... Hurriyet Haber Ajansi [*Hurriyet News Agency*] [*HA*] [*Formerly,*]
                    (TU)
HHE .... Heli-Holland BV [*Netherlands*] [*ICAO designator*]   (FAAC)
HHEE .... Hulle Eksellensies [*Their Excellencies*] [*Afrikaans*]
HHF .... Hungarian Hospital Association   (EAIO)
HHHHH ... Hilf, Himmlischer Herr, Hoechster Hort [*Help, Heavenly Father,
                    Highest Treasure*] [*Motto of Elisabeth, Duchess of Saxony-
                    Coburg (1540-94)*] [*German*]
HHI .... Ha-Hevra ha-Historit ha-Israelit [*Historical Society of Israel*]
                    (EAIO)
HHKKHH ... Hulle Koninklike Hooghede [*Their Royal Highnesses*]
                    [*Afrikaans*]
HHIU-W ... University of Hawaii at Hilo, West Hawaii Library, Kealakekua,
                    HI [*Library symbol*] [*Library of Congress*]   (LCLS)
HHMM ..... Hulle Majesteite [*Their Majesties*] [*Afrikaans*]
HHO .... Hevrat Ha'Ovdim [*Workers' Company*] [*Israel*]
HHP .... Hunan Hydro and Power Design Institute [*Ministry of Water
                    Conservancy and Power*] [*China*] [*Research center*]   (WED)
HHREA ..... Health and Human Relations Education Association [*Australia*]
HHS .... Hungarian Historical Society [*Australia*]
HHSF .... Habitat and Human Settlements Foundation [*United Nations*]
                    (EY)
HHSG .... Herpes Help Support Group [*Australia*]
HHTNSW ... Historic Houses Trust of New South Wales [*Australia*]
HI .... Hindi   (WDAA)
HI .... Hirth KG [*Germany*] [*ICAO aircraft manufacturer identifier*]
                    (ICAO)
HIAC .... Health Insurance Advisory Committee [*Australia*]
HIB .... Hibiscus Air Services Ltd. [*New Zealand*] [*ICAO designator*]
                    (FAAC)
HIC .... Habitat International Council [*The Hague, Netherlands*]   (EAIO)
HIC .... Hydrographic Information Committee [*NATO*]   (NATG)
HICOA ...... Head Injury Council of Australia
HICOM ...... Heavy Industries Corp. of Malaysia   (ECON)
HIDC .... Housing Industry Development Council [*Australia*]
HIF .... International Helsinki Federation for Human Rights [*Austria*]
                    (EAIO)
HIFRENSA ... Sociedad Hispano-Francesa de Energia Nuclear SA [*Nuclear
                    energy*] [*Spanish*]   (NRCH)
HIG .... Heli-Inter Guyane [*France*] [*ICAO designator*]   (FAAC)
HIHE .... Hunter Institute of Higher Education [*Australia*]
HIJ .... Hiroshima [*Japan*] [*Airport symbol*]   (OAG)
HIM .... Hotel Institute Montreux [*Switzerland*]   (ECON)
HIMAC ..... Heavy-Ion Medical Accelerator in Chiba [*Japan*]
HIN .... Heli Inter [*France*] [*ICAO designator*]   (FAAC)
HIND .... Hindi   (WDAA)
HIND .... Hindu   (WDAA)
Hind .... Hindustan
HIR .... Hammersley Iron Proprietary Ltd. Railway [*Australia*]   (DCTA)
HIR .... Honiara [*Guadalcanal*] [*Airport symbol*]   (OAG)
HIRS .... Harker's Information Retrieval Systems [*Harker's Specialist
                    Book Importers*] [*Information service or system*]   (IID)
HIS .... Hayman Island [*Australia*] [*Airport symbol*]   (OAG)
HIS .... Health Information Services [*Australia*]
HIS .... Hispaniola Airways [*Dominican Republic*] [*ICAO designator*]
                    (FAAC)
HISI .... Honeywell Information System Italia   (ADPT)
HISP .... Hilfsspeicher [*German*]   (ADPT)
Hispa .... Hispavox [*Record label*] [*Spain*]
HISPA .... International Association for the History of Physical Education
                    and Sport [*Belgium*]
HISPID ..... Herbarium Information Standards and Protocols for Interchange
                    of Data [*Australia*]
HIST .... Histoire [*History*] [*French*]   (ROG)
hist .... Historical   (TPFD)
hist .... History   (TPFD)
HISWA ...... Herd Improvement Service of Western Australia [*Animal
                    husbandry*]
HIT .... Hawthorn Institute of Technology [*Australia*]
HIT .... Hunter Institute of Technology [*Australia*]
HITT .... Hittite
HIV .... History Institute Victoria [*Australia*]
HIVOS ...... Humanistisch Instituut voor Ontwikkelings Samenwerking
                    [*Humanistic Institute for Co-Operation with Developing
                    Countries*] [*Hague, Netherlands*]   (EAIO)
HIZA .... Informationsdienst-AUSTAUSCH [*Information Service-
                    EXCHANGE*] [*NOMOS Datapool Database*]   (IID)
HJ .... Heilige Johannes [*Saint John*] [*Freemasonry*] [*German*]
HJA .... Air Haiti [*ICAO designator*]   (FAAC)
HJAS .... Harry James Appreciation Society   (EAIO)
HJR .... Khajuraho [*India*] [*Airport symbol*]   (OAG)
HJS .... Helijet [*Spain*] [*ICAO designator*]   (FAAC)
HK .... Handelskammer [*Chamber of Commerce*] [*German*]

HK .... Hawker De Havilland Australia Pty. Ltd., Kaman Aircraft Corp. [*ICAO aircraft manufacturer identifier*] (ICAO)

HK .... Hong Kong [*ANSI two-letter standard code*] (CNC)

HK .... People's Liberation [*Revolutionary group*] [*Turkey*]

HKAB .... Hong Kong Association of Banks (ECON)

HKAM .... Amboseli [*Kenya*] [*ICAO location identifier*] (ICLI)

HKamCF ... Canada-France-Hawaii Telescope Corp. Kamuela, HI [*Library symbol*] [*Library of Congress*] (LCLS)

HKBA .... Busia [*Kenya*] [*ICAO location identifier*] (ICLI)

HKBA .... Hong Kong Bank Australia

HKBC .... Hong Kong Bank of Canada

HKBR .... Bura [*Kenya*] [*ICAO location identifier*] (ICLI)

HKBU .... Bungoma [*Kenya*] [*ICAO location identifier*] (ICLI)

HKCC .... Hong Kong Cable Communications

HKCE .... Hong Kong Commodities Exchange

HKCS .... Hong Kong Chemical Society

HKD .... Hakodate [*Japan*] [*Airport symbol*] (OAG)

HKDS .... Croatian Christian Democratic Party [*Political party*]

HKEL .... Eldoret [*Kenya*] [*ICAO location identifier*] (ICLI)

HKEM .... Embu [*Kenya*] [*ICAO location identifier*] (ICLI)

HKES .... Eliye Springs [*Kenya*] [*ICAO location identifier*] (ICLI)

HKFE .... Hong Kong Futures Exchange

HKFG .... Kalokol [*Kenya*] [*ICAO location identifier*] (ICLI)

HKG .... Hong Kong [*ANSI three-letter standard code*] (CNC)

HKG .... Hong Kong [*Airport symbol*] (OAG)

HKGA .... Garissa [*Kenya*] [*ICAO location identifier*] (ICLI)

HKGT .... Garba Tula [*Kenya*] [*ICAO location identifier*] (ICLI)

HKHB .... Homa Bay [*Kenya*] [*ICAO location identifier*] (ICLI)

HKHO ...... Hola [*Kenya*] [*ICAO location identifier*] (ICLI)

HKIBOR ... Hong Kong Inter-Bank Offered Rate (MHDW)

HKIS .... Isiolo [*Kenya*] [*ICAO location identifier*] (ICLI)

HKJ .... Hashemite Kingdom of Jordan (BARN)

HKK .... Hokitika [*New Zealand*] [*Airport symbol*] (OAG)

HKKA .... Kabarak [*Kenya*] [*ICAO location identifier*] (ICLI)

HKKE .... Keekorok [*Kenya*] [*ICAO location identifier*] (ICLI)

HKKG .... Kakamega [*Kenya*] [*ICAO location identifier*] (ICLI)

HKKI .... Kisumu [*Kenya*] [*ICAO location identifier*] (ICLI)

HKKK .... Helsingin Kauppakorkeakoulun Kirjasto [*Helsinki School of Economics Library*] [*Finland*] [*Information service or system*] (IID)

HKKL .... Kilaguni [*Kenya*] [*ICAO location identifier*] (ICLI)

HKKR .... Kericho [*Kenya*] [*ICAO location identifier*] (ICLI)

HKKS .... Kisii [*Kenya*] [*ICAO location identifier*] (ICLI)

HKKT .... Kitale [*Kenya*] [*ICAO location identifier*] (ICLI)

HKL .... Hoyrekvinners Landsforbund [*Women's Organization of the Conservative Party*] [*Norway*] [*Political party*] (EAIO)

HKLG .... Lokitaung [*Kenya*] [*ICAO location identifier*] (ICLI)

HKLK .... Lokichoggio [*Kenya*] [*ICAO location identifier*] (ICLI)

HKLO .... Lodwar [*Kenya*] [*ICAO location identifier*] (ICLI)

HKLT .... Loitokitok [*Kenya*] [*ICAO location identifier*] (ICLI)

HKLU .... Lamu [*Kenya*] [*ICAO location identifier*] (ICLI)

HKLY .... Loyengalani [*Kenya*] [*ICAO location identifier*] (ICLI)

HKMA .... Mandera [*Kenya*] [*ICAO location identifier*] (ICLI)

HKMB .... Marsabit [*Kenya*] [*ICAO location identifier*] (ICLI)

HKMG .... Magadi [*Kenya*] [*ICAO location identifier*] (ICLI)

HKMI .... Maralal [*Kenya*] [*ICAO location identifier*] (ICLI)

HKMK .... Mulika [*Kenya*] [*ICAO location identifier*] (ICLI)

HKML .... Malindi [*Kenya*] [*ICAO location identifier*] (ICLI)

HKMO ...... Mombasa/Moi International [*Kenya*] [*ICAO location identifier*] (ICLI)

HKMR .... Mackinnon Road [*Kenya*] [*ICAO location identifier*] (ICLI)

HKMU .... Makindu [*Kenya*] [*ICAO location identifier*] (ICLI)

HKMY .... Moyale [*Kenya*] [*ICAO location identifier*] (ICLI)

HKN .... Hoskins [*Papua New Guinea*] [*Airport symbol*] (OAG)

HKNA .... Nairobi/Jomo Kenyatta International [*Kenya*] [*ICAO location identifier*] (ICLI)

HKNC .... Nairobi [*Kenya*] [*ICAO location identifier*] (ICLI)

HKNI .... Nyeri [*Kenya*] [*ICAO location identifier*] (ICLI)

HKNK .... Nakuru [*Kenya*] [*ICAO location identifier*] (ICLI)

HKNO .... Narok [*Kenya*] [*ICAO location identifier*] (ICLI)

HKNV .... Naivasha [*Kenya*] [*ICAO location identifier*] (ICLI)

HKNW ...... Nairobi/Wilson [*Kenya*] [*ICAO location identifier*] (ICLI)

HKNY .... Nanyuki [*Kenya*] [*ICAO location identifier*] (ICLI)

HKRE .... Nairobi/Eastleigh [*Kenya*] [*ICAO location identifier*] (ICLI)

HKS .... Helikopter Service AS [*Norway*] [*ICAO designator*] (FAAC)

HKSA .... East African School of Aviation [*Kenya*] [*ICAO location identifier*] (ICLI)

HKSB .... Samburu [*Kenya*] [*ICAO location identifier*] (ICLI)

HKSC .... Hong Kong Study Circle (EA)

HKT .... Phuket [*Thailand*] [*Airport symbol*] (OAG)

HKU .... Hong Kong University

HKUST ...... Hong Kong University of Science and Technology (ECON)

HKVO .... Voi [*Kenya*] [*ICAO location identifier*] (ICLI)

HKWJ .... Wajir [*Kenya*] [*ICAO location identifier*] (ICLI)

HL .... Heilig [*Holy, Saint*] [*German*]

HLAHWG ... High Level Ad Hoc Working Group [*NATO*] (NATG)

HLC .... Helicap [*France*] [*ICAO designator*] (FAAC)

HLD.......... Hailar [*China*] [*Airport symbol*] (OAG)

HLF .... Hapag Lloyd Fluggesellschaft GmbH [*Germany*] [*ICAO designator*] (FAAC)

HLF .... Hultsfred [*Sweden*] [*Airport symbol*] (OAG)

HLFL........ Buattifel [*Libya*] [*ICAO location identifier*] (ICLI)

HLG.......... High-Level Group [*NATO*]

HLGL .... Giallo/Warehouse 59 E [*Libya*] [*ICAO location identifier*] (ICLI)

HLGT .... Ghat [*Libya*] [*ICAO location identifier*] (ICLI)

HLH .... Ulanhot [*China*] [*Airport symbol*] (OAG)

HLK .... Heli-Link [*Switzerland*] [*ICAO designator*] (FAAC)

HLKF .... Kufra [*Libya*] [*ICAO location identifier*] (ICLI)

HLLB........ Benghazi/Benina [*Libya*] [*ICAO location identifier*] (ICLI)

HLLL......... Tripoli [*Libya*] [*ICAO location identifier*] (ICLI)

HLLO........ Metega [*Libya*] [*ICAO location identifier*] (ICLI)

HLLQ........ El Beida/Labraq [*Libya*] [*ICAO location identifier*] (ICLI)

HLLS........ Sebha [*Libya*] [*ICAO location identifier*] (ICLI)

HLLT......... Tripoli/International [*Libya*] [*ICAO location identifier*] (ICLI)

HLMB........ Marsa Brega [*Libya*] [*ICAO location identifier*] (ICLI)

HLN .... Hellenic Air SA [*Greece*] [*ICAO designator*] (FAAC)

HLNF........ Ras Lanouf V 40 [*Libya*] [*ICAO location identifier*] (ICLI)

HLON .... Hon [*Libya*] [*ICAO location identifier*] (ICLI)

HLP .... Jakarta [*Indonesia*] [*Airport symbol*] (OAG)

HLPS........ Human Life Protection Society [*Australia*]

HLR .... Heli Air Services [*Bulgaria*] [*ICAO designator*] (FAAC)

HLRA .... Dahra/Warehouse 32 [*Libya*] [*ICAO location identifier*] (ICLI)

HLRF........ Jaref/Sirte [*ICAO location identifier*] (ICLI)

HLS .... Haiti Air Freight [*ICAO designator*] (FAAC)

HLSD........ Essider [*Libya*] [*ICAO location identifier*] (ICLI)

HLT .... Hamilton [*Australia*] [*Airport symbol*] (OAG)

HLT .... Heli Transport [*France*] [*ICAO designator*] (FAAC)

HLTD........ Ghadames [*Libya*] [*ICAO location identifier*] (ICLI)

HLU .... Heli Union Heli Prestations [*France*] [*ICAO designator*] (FAAC)

HLU.......... Houailou [*New Caledonia*] [*Airport symbol*] (OAG)

HLV.......... Heliserv SA de CV [*Mexico*] [*ICAO designator*] (FAAC)

HLW.......... Halbleinwand [*Half-Bound Cloth*] [*Bookbinding, publishing*] [*German*]

HLZ.......... Hamilton [*New Zealand*] [*Airport symbol*] (OAG)

HLZA .... Zella 74 [*Libya*] [*ICAO location identifier*] (ICLI)

HLZBL...... Holzblaeser [*Woodwind Instrument*] [*Music*]

HM .... Hamarein Air [*United Arab Emirates*] [*ICAO designator*] (ICDA)

HM .... Heard and McDonald Islands [*ANSI two-letter standard code*] (CNC)

HM .... Her Majesty (PWGL)

hM .... Herrschende Meinung [*Prevailing Opinion*] [*German*] (ILCA)

HM .... His Majesty (SCAC)

Hma .... Harmona [*Record label*] [*Austria*]

HMAC....... Horticultural Market Access Committee [*Australia*]

H MAJ:T... Hans Majestaet [*His Majesty*] [*Swedish*]

HM & M.... Home Maintenance and Modification Program [*Australia*]

HMB.......... Holderbank Management und Beratung AG [*Switzerland*]

HMC.......... Healing Ministry Centre [*Australia*]

HMC.......... His [*or Her*] Majesty's Council (ROG)

HMD.......... Heard Island and McDonald Islands [*ANSI three-letter standard code*] (CNC)

HME.......... Hassi Messaoud [*Algeria*] [*Airport symbol*] (OAG)

HMH.......... Home Hill [*Australia*] [*Airport symbol*]

HMO.......... Hermosillo [*Mexico*] [*Airport symbol*] (OAG)

HMP.......... Papair Terminal SA [*Haiti*] [*ICAO designator*] (FAAC)

HMS.......... Hemus Air [*Bulgaria*] [*ICAO designator*] (FAAC)

HMS.......... Historical Metallurgy Society [*British*] (EAIO)

HMZ.......... Nigerian International Air Services Ltd. [*ICAO designator*] (FAAC)

HN .... Hindustan-Aeronautics Ltd. [*India*] [*ICAO aircraft manufacturer identifier*] (ICAO)

HN .... Honduras [*ANSI two-letter standard code*] (CNC)

HNA .... Hanamaki [*Japan*] [*Airport symbol*] [*Obsolete*] (OAG)

HNAA .... Holistic Nurses Association of Australia

HNB .... Hrvatska Narodna Banka [*Croatian National Bank*]

HNCMT.... Hawkesbury Nepean Catchment Management Trust [*Resource management*] [*Australia*]

HND.......... Honduras [*ANSI three-letter standard code*] (CNC)

HND.......... Tokyo [*Japan*] Haneda Airport [*Airport symbol*] (OAG)

HNG.......... Hienghene [*New Caledonia*] [*Airport symbol*] [*Obsolete*] (OAG)

HNK .... Hinchinbrook Island [*Australia*] [*Airport symbol*]

HNO.......... Hrvatski Narodni Odbor [*Croatian National Resistance*] [*Former Yugoslavia*] (PD)

HNP.......... Herstigte Nasionale Partye [*Reconstituted National Party*] [*South Africa*] [*Political party*] (PPW)

HNR .... Haiti National Airlines [*ICAO designator*] (FAAC)

HNS........... Haveeru News Service [*Maldives*] (EY)

HNS........... Hazardous and Noxious Substance

HNS........... Hrvatska Narodna Stranka [*Croatian People's Party*] [*Political party*]

HOA .... House of Assembly [*South Australia*]

HOAL........ Homes on Aboriginal Land [*Australia*]

HOANSW ... Hospital Officers' Association of New South Wales [*Australia*]

HOBA........ [4] History of the Book in Australia [*Project*]

HOBIS ...... Home Ownership Building Industry Scheme [*Australia*]

HOBITS.... Haifa On-line Bibliographic Text System [*University of Haifa Library*] [*Information service or system*] (IID)

HOC .... Greek Olympic Committee (OLYM)

HOC .... Hillman Owners Club [*Lancing, Sussex, England*] (EAIO)

HOCOLEA ... Heads of Commonwealth Operational Law Enforcement Agencies [*Australia*]

HOD .... Hodeidah [*Yemen Arab Republic*] [*Airport symbol*] (OAG)

HOF .... Hafuf [*Saudi Arabia*] [*Airport symbol*] (OAG)

HOG .... Holguin [*Cuba*] [*Airport symbol*] (OAG)

HOH .... Help Our Headaches Group [*Australia*]

HOI .... Hao Island [*French Polynesia*] [*Airport symbol*] (OAG)

HOK .... Hooker Creek [*Airport symbol*]

HOLS .... Home Opportunity Loans Scheme [*Australia*]

HOMESWEST ... Western Australian State Housing Commission

HOMS....... Hydrological Operational Multipurpose Subprogramme [*World Meteorological Organization*] [*Information service or system*] (IID)

HON .... Honduras

Hon .... Honorable (PWGL)

Hon .... Honorary (EECI)

Hon .... Honourable (IDIG)

HOPH .... Home of Peace Hospitals [*Australia*]

HOQ......... Hof [*Germany*] [*Airport symbol*] (OAG)

HOR .... Horizon Air-Taxi Ltd. [*Switzerland*] [*ICAO designator*] (FAAC)

HOR .... Horta [*Azores*] [*Airport symbol*] (OAG)

HO-RE-CA ... Federation Internationale des Organisations d'Hoteliers, Restaurateurs, et Cafetiers [*International Organization of Hotel and Restaurant Associations*] (EAIO)

HORECOM ... International Exhibition for the Hotel and Restaurant Trades Communities

HOREST... Handelsorientiertes Einkaufsdispositionssystem mit Trendberuecksichtigung [*German*] (ADPT)

hort............ Horticulture [*French*] (TPFD)

HOS........... Croatian Defense Association [*Political party*]

HOT .... Baltic Airlines Ltd. [*ICAO designator*] (FAAC)

HOTREC .. Confederation of the National Hotel and Restaurant Associations in the EC (ECED)

HOV .... Orsta/Volda [*Norway*] [*Airport symbol*] (OAG)

HOVSA ..... Horizontale Oder Vertikale Struktur-Aufloesung [*German*] (ADPT)

HP............. ALAS, SA [*Uruguay*] [*ICAO designator*] (ICDA)

HP............. Hawker Siddeley Aviation Ltd. [*British*] [*ICAO aircraft manufacturer identifier*] (ICAO)

HP............. Henderson & Pollard Ltd. [*New Zealand*]

hp .... Horsepower (EECI)

HP............. Humanist Party [*Australia*] [*Political party*]

HPA........... House Plants Australia

HPA........... Lifuka [*Tonga Islands*] [*Airport symbol*] (OAG)

HPA........... Pearl Airways Compagne Haitienne [*Haiti*] [*ICAO designator*] (FAAC)

HPC........... Hobart Peace Centre [*Australia*]

HPE........... Inomeni Parataksis Ethnikofronon [*United Front of Nationalists*] [*Political party*] (PPE)

HPG.......... Horticultural Postharvest Group [*Queensland, Australia*]

HPGMI ..... Hunter Postgraduate Medical Institute [*Australia*]

HPL........... Heliportugal-Trabalhos e Transporte Aereo, Representacoes, Importacao e Exportacao Lda. [*Portugal*] [*ICAO designator*] (FAAC)

HPL........... Hotel Properties Ltd. [*Singapore*] (ECON)

HPMAA..... Honey Packers and Marketers' Association of Australia

HPP .... Hernieuwde Progressieve Partij [*Renewed Progressive Party*] [*Surinam*] [*Political party*] (PPW)

HPPP........ High-Priority Production Program [*NATO*] (NATG)

HPSS......... Hrvatska Pucka Seljacka Stranka [*Croatian People's Peasant Party*] [*Former Yugoslavia*] [*Political party*] (PPE)

HPTDC .... Himachal Pradesh Tourist Development Corp. [*India*]

HQ .... Hawker Siddeley Aviation Ltd. [*British*] [*ICAO designator*] (ICDA)

HQ .... Headquarters (EECI)

HQ .... Hong Qi [*Red Flag*] [*China*]

HQASC .... Headquarters, Air Support Command [*NATO*] (NATG)

HQFC....... Headquarters, Fighter Command [*NATO*] (NATG)

HQOC .... Headquarters Operational Command [*Australia*]

HR .... Hessischer Rundfunk [*Hessian Radio Network*] [*Germany*]

HR .... Hoge Raad [*Dutch Supreme Court*] (DLA)

HR .... Hojesteret [*Supreme Court*] [*Netherlands*] (ILCA)

HR .... Human Rights Convention [*Council of Europe*] (DLA)

HR .... Humber Register [*St. Albans, Hertfordshire, England*] (EAIO)

HR .... Hybridrechner [*Hybred Computer*] [*German*] (ADPT)

HR .... Robin Avions [*Pierre Robin*] [*France*] [*ICAO aircraft manufacturer identifier*] (ICAO)

HRA......... Heli-Iberica [*Spain*] [*ICAO designator*] (FAAC)

HRA......... Huna Research Association [*See also HF*] [*Switzerland*] (EAIO)

HRAA....... Hire and Rental Association of Australia

HRAG....... International Human Rights Advisory Group [*Switzerland*]

HRANSW .. Harness Racing Authority of New South Wales [*Australia*]

HRB.......... Croatian Revolutionary Brotherhood [*Former Yugoslavia*] (PD)

HRB.......... Harbin [*Manchuria*] [*Airport symbol*] (OAG)

HRB.......... Hardship Relief Board [*Victoria, Australia*]

HRC.......... Honey Research Council [*Australia*]

HRC/CCPR ... Human Rights Committee (EA)

HRDC .... Honeybee Research and Development Committee [*Australia*]

HRE.......... Aerosucre SA [*Colombia*] [*ICAO designator*] (FAAC)

HRE.......... Harare [*Zimbabwe*] [*Airport symbol*] (OAG)

HREAA..... Health and Research Employees' Association of Australia

HRG .... Human Rights Group [*Edinburgh, Scotland*] [*Defunct*] (EAIO)

HRG .... Hurghada [*Egypt*] [*Airport symbol*] (OAG)

HRH .... Her Royal Highness (IDIG)

HRH .... His Royal Highness (IDIG)

HRH .... Royal Tongan Airlines [*Tonga*] [*ICAO designator*] (FAAC)

HRI .... Hard Rock International [*Restaurant chain*]

HRI .... Heart Research Institute [*Australia*]

HRK.......... Kharkov [*Former USSR*] [*Airport symbol*] (OAG)

HRMDDHG ... Herr, Regiere Mich durch Deinen Heiligen Geist [*Lord, Rule Me through Thy Holy Spirit*] [*Motto for a number of 16th and 17th century German and Bavarian rulers*]

HRMS .... Health Risk Management Service [*Australian Capital Territory*]

HRN .... Herrn [*Sirs, Gentlemen*] [*German*] (ROG)

HRPP........ Human Rights Protection Party [*Western Samoa*] [*Political party*] (PPW)

HRR.......... Heiliges Roemisches Reich [*Holy Roman Empire*] [*German*] (ROG)

HRRC .... Human Rights Resource Center (EAIO)

HRS .... Horticultural Research Station [*Kenya*] (DSCA)

HRS .... Hybrides Rechensystem [*German*] (ADPT)

HRSA .... Historical Radio Society of Australia

hrsg .... Herausgegeben [*Edited, Published*] [*German*]

HRSS......... Hrvatska Republikanska Seljacka Stranka [*Croatian Republican Peasant Party*] [*Former Yugoslavia*] [*Political party*] (PPE)

HRT.......... Hospitals Remuneration Tribunal [*Australia*]

HRT.......... Transporte Aereo Rioplatense [*Argentina*] [*ICAO designator*] (FAAC)

HRYG....... Gisenyi [*Rwanda*] [*ICAO location identifier*] (ICLI)

HRYI .... Butare [*Rwanda*] [*ICAO location identifier*] (ICLI)

HRYO....... Gabiro [*Rwanda*] [*ICAO location identifier*] (ICLI)

HRYR....... Kigali [*Rwanda*] [*ICAO location identifier*] (ICLI)

HRYU....... Ruhengeri [*Rwanda*] [*ICAO location identifier*] (ICLI)

HRZA....... Kamembe [*Rwanda*] [*ICAO location identifier*] (ICLI)

HS............. Aeronoleggi e Lavoro Aereo (AERAL) [*Italy*] [*ICAO designator*] (ICDA)

HS............. Hakluyt Society (EA)

HS............. Hauptsatz [*Leading Theme*] [*Music*]

HS............. Hawker Siddeley Aviation Ltd. [*British*] [*ICAO aircraft manufacturer identifier*] (ICAO)

HS............. Heather Society (EA)

HS............. Heraldisk Selskab [*Denmark*] [*An association*] (EAIO)

HS............. Heraldry Society (EA)

HS............. Housman Society (EA)

HSA .... CHS Aviation Ltd. [*Kenya*] [*ICAO designator*] (FAAC)

HSA .... Heraldry Society of Australia

HSA .... Humane Society of Australia

HSA .... Hunt Saboteurs Association (EAIO)

HSAC .... Historic Shipwrecks Advisory Committee [*Victoria, Australia*]

HSAK .... Akobo [*Sudan*] [*ICAO location identifier*] (ICLI)

HSANSW ... Health Services Association of New South Wales [*Australia*]

HSAT .... Atbara [*Sudan*] [*ICAO location identifier*] (ICLI)

HSAW .... Aweil [*Sudan*] [*ICAO location identifier*] (ICLI)

HSB .... Hospitals Superannuation Board [*Victoria, Australia*]

HSBR .... Bor [*Sudan*] [*ICAO location identifier*] (ICLI)

HSBT........ Bentu [*Sudan*] [*ICAO location identifier*] (ICLI)

HSCG .... Erkowit/Carthago [*Sudan*] [*ICAO location identifier*] (ICLI)

HSDB .... Debba [*Sudan*] [*ICAO location identifier*] (ICLI)

HSDL .... Dilling [*Sudan*] [*ICAO location identifier*] (ICLI)

HSDM....... Dueim [*Sudan*] [*ICAO location identifier*] (ICLI)

HSDN....... Dongola [*Sudan*] [*ICAO location identifier*] (ICLI)

HSDP .... Hungarian Social Democratic Party [*Political party*] (EY)

HSDZ....... Damazin [*Sudan*] [*ICAO location identifier*] (ICLI)

HSE .... Compania Helicopteros del Sureste SA [*Spain*] [*ICAO designator*] (FAAC)

HSE .... Helsinki Stock Exchange [*Finland*]

HSE .... Historically Socialist Economy (ECON)

HSFS......... El Fasher [*Sudan*] [*ICAO location identifier*] (ICLI)

HSGF .... Gedaref/Azaza [*Sudan*] [*ICAO location identifier*]   (ICLI)
HSGG........ Dinder/Galegu [*Sudan*] [*ICAO location identifier*]   (ICLI)
HSGN........ Geneina [*Sudan*] [*ICAO location identifier*]   (ICLI)
HSGO........ Gogerial [*Sudan*] [*ICAO location identifier*]   (ICLI)
HSI .... Hang Seng Index [*Hong Kong Futures Exchange Index*]
HSIP .... Hsinchu Science-Based Industrial Park [*Taiwan*]   (ECON)
HSKA .... Kassala [*Sudan*] [*ICAO location identifier*]   (ICLI)
HSKG........ Khashm El Girba [*Sudan*] [*ICAO location identifier*]   (ICLI)
HSKI .... Kosti/Rabak [*Sudan*] [*ICAO location identifier*]   (ICLI)
HSKJ .... Kago Kaju [*Sudan*] [*ICAO location identifier*]   (ICLI)
HSKP .... Kapoeta [*Sudan*] [*ICAO location identifier*]   (ICLI)
HSL .... Hispania Lineas Aereas SL [*Spain*] [*ICAO designator*]   (FAAC)
HSLI .... Kadugli [*Sudan*] [*ICAO location identifier*]   (ICLI)
HSLR .... Lirangu [*Sudan*] [*ICAO location identifier*]   (ICLI)
HSL'S .... Hlinkova Slovenska l'Udova Strana [*Hlinka's Slovak People's Party*] [*Also, SL'S*] [*Political party*]   (PPE)
HSM .... Horsham [*Australia*] [*Airport symbol*] [*Obsolete*]   (OAG)
HSMAI-EO ... Hotel Sales and Marketing Association International - European Office [*Utrecht, Netherlands*]   (EAIO)
HSMD....... Maridi [*Sudan*] [*ICAO location identifier*]   (ICLI)
HSMK .... Rumbek [*Sudan*] [*ICAO location identifier*]   (ICLI)
HSMO....... Hospital Senior Medical Officer [*Australia*]
HSMR .... Merowe [*Sudan*] [*ICAO location identifier*]   (ICLI)
HSNA .... Nasir [*Sudan*] [*ICAO location identifier*]   (ICLI)
HSND....... Shendi [*Sudan*] [*ICAO location identifier*]   (ICLI)
HSNH .... Nahud [*Sudan*] [*ICAO location identifier*]   (ICLI)
HSNL .... Nyala [*Sudan*] [*ICAO location identifier*]   (ICLI)
HSNM .... Nimule/Nimule [*Sudan*] [*ICAO location identifier*]   (ICLI)
HSNPP...... Hlinka Slovak National People's Party [*Political party*]
HSNR .... Sennar [*Sudan*] [*ICAO location identifier*]   (ICLI)
HSNSW .... Haemophilia Society of New South Wales [*Australia*]
HSNT .... Historical Society of the Northern Territory [*Australia*]
HSNW .... New Halfa [*Sudan*] [*ICAO location identifier*]   (ICLI)
HSO........... Compania Helicopteros de Transporte SA [*Spain*] [*ICAO designator*]   (FAAC)
HSOB .... El Obeid [*Sudan*] [*ICAO location identifier*]   (ICLI)
HSP .... Hauptspeicher [*German*]   (ADPT)
HSP .... Home Services Program [*Australia*]
HSP .... Hrvatska Stranka Prava [*Croatian Party of Rights*] [*Former Yugoslavia*] [*Political party*]   (PPE)
HSP .... Hungarian Socialist Party [*Political party*]   (EY)
HSPA .... Pachella [*Sudan*] [*ICAO location identifier*]   (ICLI)
HSPDP...... Hill State People's Democratic Party [*India*] [*Political party*]   (PPW)
HSPI......... Pibor [*Sudan*] [*ICAO location identifier*]   (ICLI)
HSPU .... Householders for Safe Pesticide Use [*Australia*]
HSRJ......... Raga [*Sudan*] [*ICAO location identifier*]   (ICLI)
HSRN .... Renk [*Sudan*] [*ICAO location identifier*]   (ICLI)
HSS .... Hrvatska Seljacka Stranka [*Croatian Peasant Party*] [*Former Yugoslavia*] [*Political party*]   (PPE)
HSSJ .... Juba [*Sudan*] [*ICAO location identifier*]   (ICLI)
HSSM .... Malakal [*Sudan*] [*ICAO location identifier*]   (ICLI)
HSSP........ Port Sudan [*Sudan*] [*ICAO location identifier*]   (ICLI)
HSSS .... Khartoum [*Sudan*] [*ICAO location identifier*]   (ICLI)
HSSW....... Wadi Halfa/Nuba Lake [*Sudan*] [*ICAO location identifier*]   (ICLI)
HSTO .... Tong [*Sudan*] [*ICAO location identifier*]   (ICLI)
HSTP........ Hauptsteuerprogramm [*German*]   (ADPT)
HSTR .... Torit [*Sudan*] [*ICAO location identifier*]   (ICLI)
HSTU .... Tumbura [*Sudan*] [*ICAO location identifier*]   (ICLI)
HSU.......... Hero of the Soviet Union [*Award*]   (DOMA)
HSUA .... Health Services Union of Australia
HSV .... Haemophilia society of Victoria [*Australia*]
HSV .... Heliservico-Sociedade Portuguesa de Exploracao de Meios Aeros Lda. [*Portugal*] [*ICAO designator*]   (FAAC)
HSW .... Aerocombi SA [*Spain*] [*ICAO designator*]   (FAAC)
HSWP .... Hungarian Socialist Workers' Party [*Political party*]   (PPW)
HSWW....... Wau [*Sudan*] [*ICAO location identifier*]   (ICLI)
HSYA .... Yambio [*Sudan*] [*ICAO location identifier*]   (ICLI)
HSYE .... Yei [*Sudan*] [*ICAO location identifier*]   (ICLI)
HSYL......... Yirol [*Sudan*] [*ICAO location identifier*]   (ICLI)
HSZA .... Zalingei [*Sudan*] [*ICAO location identifier*]   (ICLI)
HT .... Haiti [*ANSI two-letter standard code*]   (CNC)
HTANSW ... History Teachers' Association of New South Wales [*Australia*]
HTAR....... Arusha [*Tanzania*] [*ICAO location identifier*]   (ICLI)
HTB .... Hungarian Tourist Board   (EAIO)
HTBU .... Bukoba [*Tanzania*] [*ICAO location identifier*]   (ICLI)
HTC.......... Haiti Trans Air SA [*ICAO designator*]   (FAAC)
HTCH....... Chunya [*Tanzania*] [*ICAO location identifier*]   (ICLI)
HTDA........ Dar Es-Salaam/Dar Es-Salaam [*Tanzania*] [*ICAO location identifier*]   (ICLI)
HTDC........ Dar Es-Salaam [*Tanzania*] [*ICAO location identifier*]   (ICLI)
HTDO .... Dodoma [*Tanzania*] [*ICAO location identifier*]   (ICLI)
HTDQ .... Dar Es-Salaam [*Tanzania*] [*ICAO location identifier*]   (ICLI)
HTF .... Societe Helitrans France [*ICAO designator*]   (FAAC)
HTFI.......... Fort Ikoma [*Tanzania*] [*ICAO location identifier*]   (ICLI)

HTI .... Haiti [*ANSI three-letter standard code*]   (CNC)
HTI .... Haiti International Air SA [*ICAO designator*]   (FAAC)
HTI .... Hamilton Island [*Australia*] [*Airport symbol*]   (OAG)
HTIR .... Iringa [*Tanzania*] [*ICAO location identifier*]   (ICLI)
HTKA .... Kigoma [*Tanzania*] [*ICAO location identifier*]   (ICLI)
HTKI .... Kilwa Masoko [*Tanzania*] [*ICAO location identifier*]   (ICLI)
HTKJ .... Kilimanjaro [*Tanzania*] [*ICAO location identifier*]   (ICLI)
HTKO....... Kongwa [*Tanzania*] [*ICAO location identifier*]   (ICLI)
HTKT....... Kilimatinde [*Tanzania*] [*ICAO location identifier*]   (ICLI)
HTLI .... Lindi [*Tanzania*] [*ICAO location identifier*]   (ICLI)
HTLM .... Lake Manyara [*Tanzania*] [*ICAO location identifier*]   (ICLI)
HTLO........ Lobo Wildlife Lodge [*Tanzania*] [*ICAO location identifier*]   (ICLI)
HTMA....... Mafia [*Tanzania*] [*ICAO location identifier*]   (ICLI)
HTMB....... Mbeya [*Tanzania*] [*ICAO location identifier*]   (ICLI)
HTMD...... Mwadui [*Tanzania*] [*ICAO location identifier*]   (ICLI)
HTM-DB... High Temperature Materials Data Bank [*Commission of the European Communities*] [*Information service or system*]   (IID)
HTMG....... Morgororo [*Tanzania*] [*ICAO location identifier*]   (ICLI)
HTMI .... Masasi [*Tanzania*] [*ICAO location identifier*]   (ICLI)
HTMK .... Mikumi [*Tanzania*] [*ICAO location identifier*]   (ICLI)
HTMO ...... Mombo [*Tanzania*] [*ICAO location identifier*]   (ICLI)
HTMP .... Mpanda [*Tanzania*] [*ICAO location identifier*]   (ICLI)
HTMR....... Msembe-Ruaha National Park [*Tanzania*] [*ICAO location identifier*]   (ICLI)
HTMS .... Moshi [*Tanzania*] [*ICAO location identifier*]   (ICLI)
HTMT .... Mtwara [*Tanzania*] [*ICAO location identifier*]   (ICLI)
HTMU....... Musoma [*Tanzania*] [*ICAO location identifier*]   (ICLI)
HTMW....... Mwanza [*Tanzania*] [*ICAO location identifier*]   (ICLI)
HTMX....... Mpwapwa [*Tanzania*] [*ICAO location identifier*]   (ICLI)
HTN .... Haiti North Airline [*ICAO designator*]   (FAAC)
HTN .... Hotan [*China*] [*Airport symbol*]   (OAG)
HTNA....... Nachingwea [*Tanzania*] [*ICAO location identifier*]   (ICLI)
HTNG .... Ngerengere [*Tanzania*] [*ICAO location identifier*]   (ICLI)
HTNJ .... Njombe [*Tanzania*] [*ICAO location identifier*]   (ICLI)
HTPE .... Pemba [*Tanzania*] [*ICAO location identifier*]   (ICLI)
HTR.......... Hateruma [*Japan*] [*Airport symbol*]   (OAG)
HTR........... Holstenair Lubeck, Luftverkehrsservice GmbH [*Germany*] [*ICAO designator*]   (FAAC)
HTRP .... Humid Tropics Research Programme [*France*]   (DSCA)
HTSA .... History Trust of South Australia
HTSD .... Singida [*Tanzania*] [*ICAO location identifier*]   (ICLI)
HTSE .... Same [*Tanzania*] [*ICAO location identifier*]   (ICLI)
HTSH .... Mafinga [*Tanzania*] [*ICAO location identifier*]   (ICLI)
HTSN .... Seronera [*Tanzania*] [*ICAO location identifier*]   (ICLI)
HTSO .... Songea [*Tanzania*] [*ICAO location identifier*]   (ICLI)
HTSU .... Sumbawanga [*Tanzania*] [*ICAO location identifier*]   (ICLI)
HTSY .... Shinyanga [*Tanzania*] [*ICAO location identifier*]   (ICLI)
HTT.......... Air Tchad, Societe de Transport Aeriens [*Chad*] [*ICAO designator*]   (FAAC)
HTT........... High Technology Transfer Co. [*Czechoslovakia*]   (ECON)
HTTB .... Tabora [*Tanzania*] [*ICAO location identifier*]   (ICLI)
HTTG .... Tanga [*Tanzania*] [*ICAO location identifier*]   (ICLI)
HTTU .... Tunduru [*Tanzania*] [*ICAO location identifier*]   (ICLI)
HTUR....... Urambo [*Tanzania*] [*ICAO location identifier*]   (ICLI)
HTWH....... Wazo Hill [*Tanzania*] [*ICAO location identifier*]   (ICLI)
HTWK....... Ngare Nairobi [*Tanzania*] [*ICAO location identifier*]   (ICLI)
HTZ.......... Hato Corozal [*Colombia*] [*Airport symbol*]   (OAG)
HTZA .... Zanzibar [*Tanzania*] [*ICAO location identifier*]   (ICLI)
HU .... Central Airlines Ltd. [*Nigeria*] [*ICAO designator*]   (ICDA)
HU .... Hughes Tool Co. [*Aircraft Division*] [*ICAO aircraft manufacturer identifier*]   (ICAO)
HU .... Hungary [*ANSI two-letter standard code*]   (CNC)
HUAR....... Arua [*Uganda*] [*ICAO location identifier*]   (ICLI)
HUC .... Humacao [*Puerto Rico*] [*Airport symbol*]   (OAG)
HUE .... Humera [*Ethiopia*] [*Airport symbol*]   (OAG)
HUEC........ Entebbe Area Control Center [*Uganda*] [*ICAO location identifier*]   (ICLI)
HUEN .... Entebbe/International [*Uganda*] [*ICAO location identifier*]   (ICLI)
HUFP .... Fort Portal [*Uganda*] [*ICAO location identifier*]   (ICLI)
HUGA .... Human Genome Analyzer [*System for analysis of DNA*] [*Institute of Physical and Chemical Research, Japan Genetics*]
HUGU....... Gulu [*Uganda*] [*ICAO location identifier*]   (ICLI)
HUH .... Huahine [*French Polynesia*] [*Airport symbol*]   (OAG)
HUJI .... Jinja [*Uganda*] [*ICAO location identifier*]   (ICLI)
HUK .... Hungarian-Ukranian Heavy Lift Ltd. [*Hungary*] [*ICAO designator*]   (FAAC)
HUKB .... Kabale [*Uganda*] [*ICAO location identifier*]   (ICLI)
HUKF .... Kabalega Falls [*Uganda*] [*ICAO location identifier*]   (ICLI)
HUKS .... Kasese [*Uganda*] [*ICAO location identifier*]   (ICLI)
HULA .... Lake George [*Uganda*] [*ICAO location identifier*]   (ICLI)
HULI .... Lira [*Uganda*] [*ICAO location identifier*]   (ICLI)
HUM .... Hummingbird Helicopters Maldives (Pvt) Ltd. [*ICAO designator*]   (FAAC)

HUMA ...... Mbarara/Obote [*Uganda*] [*ICAO location identifier*]   (ICLI)
HUMI........ Masindi [*Uganda*] [*ICAO location identifier*]   (ICLI)
HUMO ...... Moroto [*Uganda*] [*ICAO location identifier*]   (ICLI)
HUN .... Hualien [*Taiwan*] [*Airport symbol*]   (OAG)
HUN .... Hungary [*ANSI three-letter standard code*]   (CNC)
HUNA .... Namulonge Agrometeorology Station [*Uganda*] [*ICAO location
              identifier*]   (ICLI)
HUQ .... Houn [*Libya*] [*Airport symbol*]   (OAG)
HURIDOCS ... Human Rights Information and Documentation System
              (EA)
HUSO........ Soroti [*Uganda*] [*ICAO location identifier*]   (ICLI)
HUTO .... Tororo [*Uganda*] [*ICAO location identifier*]   (ICLI)
HUU .... Huanuco [*Peru*] [*Airport symbol*]   (OAG)
HUV .... Hudiksvall [*Sweden*] [*Airport symbol*]   (OAG)
HV .... Boeing-Vertol Division [*The Boeing Co.*] [*ICAO aircraft
              manufacturer identifier*]   (ICAO)
HV .... Haricots Verts [*Green Beans*] [*French*]
HVA........... Analalava [*Madagascar*] [*Airport symbol*]   (OAG)
HVB........... Hervey Bay [*Australia*] [*Airport symbol*]   (OAG)
HVG .... Honningsvag [*Norway*] [*Airport symbol*]   (OAG)
HVK........... Holmavik [*Iceland*] [*Airport symbol*]   (OAG)
HVN .... Hang Khong Viet Nam [*ICAO designator*]   (FAAC)
HVRF .... The Hunter Valley Research Foundation [*Australia*]   (DSCA)
HVST .... Hauptvermittlungsstelle [*German*]   (ADPT)
HW .... Hauptwerk [*Masterpiece*] [*German*]
HW .... Howard Aero Manufacturing [*ICAO aircraft manufacturer
              identifier*]   (ICAO)
HWA .... Hawa-Air [*Belgium*] [*ICAO designator*]   (FAAC)
HWAL....... Holland West-Afrika Line [*Steamship*]   (MHDB)
HWB.......... Handwoerterbuch [*Pocket Dictionary*] [*German*]
HWK .... Hawker [*Australia*] [*Airport symbol*]   (OAG)
HWK .... Swazi Air Charter (Pty) Ltd. [*Swaziland*] [*ICAO designator*]
              (FAAC)
HWP.......... Hungarian Workers' Party [*Political party*]   (PPW)
HXX........... Hay [*Australia*] [*Airport symbol*]   (OAG)
HYD .... Hyderabad [*India*] [*Airport symbol*]   (OAG)
HYE........... Hyeres Aero Service [*France*] [*ICAO designator*]   (FAAC)
HYF........... Hayfields [*Papua New Guinea*] [*Airport symbol*]   (OAG)
HYPOCON ... Hypochondria   (DSUE)
HZA........... Hauptzollamt [*Chief Customs Office*] [*German*]   (DLA)
HZBL .... Holzblaeser [*Woodwind Instrument*] [*Music*]
HZD........... Hessische Zentrale fuer Datenverarbeitung [*German*]   (ADPT)
HZG........... Hanzhong [*China*] [*Airport symbol*]   (OAG)
HZK........... Husavik [*Iceland*] [*Airport symbol*]   (OAG)
HZL........... Hazelton Airlines [*Australia*] [*ICAO designator*]   (FAAC)

I

I .... Ihr [*Your*] [*German*]
I .... India [*Phonetic alphabet*] [*International*]   (DSUE)
I .... Ink [*Phonetic alphabet*] [*Royal Navy World War I Pre-World War II*]   (DSUE)
I .... Item [*Phonetic alphabet*] [*World War II*]   (DSUE)
I2S .... Imagerie, Industrie, Systeme [*Machine vision manufacturer*] [*France*]
IA .... Comando de Material - Fabrica Militar de Aviones [*Argentina*] [*ICAO aircraft manufacturer identifier*]   (ICAO)
IA .... IATA [*International Air Transport Association*] Containers [*Shipping*]   (DCTA)
IA .... Im Auftrage [*By Order Of*] [*German*]
IA .... Indian Airlines   (PDAA)
IA .... Indicateur d'Appel [*French*]   (ADPT)
IA .... Institut de l'Amiante [*Asbestos Institute - AI*]   (EA)
IA .... Institute of Architects [*Australia*]
IA .... Interciencia Association [*Caracas, Venezuela*]   (EAIO)
IA .... Intercity Airways [*Australia*]
IA .... Interflora Australia
IA .... International Alert   (EA)
IA .... International Alliance of Theatrical Stage Employees   (NTCM)
IAA .... Inex Adria Aviopromet [*Yugoslavia*] [*ICAO designator*]   (FAAC)
IAA .... Institute of Administrative Accountants [*Sevenoaks, Kent, England*]   (EAIO)
IAA .... Institute of Arbitrators Australia
IAA .... Interamerican Accounting Association [*Mexico City, Mexico*]   (EA)
IAA .... International Academy of Astronautics [*Paris, France*]   (EA)
IAA .... International Aerosol Association [*Zurich, Switzerland*]   (EAIO)
IAA .... International Association of Art [*See also AIAP*]   (EA)
IAA .... Israel Antiquities Authority
IAAB .... Inter-American Association of Broadcasters [*Later, IAB-AIR*]
IAAC .... International Association of Art Critics [*Australia*]
IAACA .... Industria Aerea Agricola, CA [*Venezuela*]   (DSCA)
IAACC .... Ibero-American Association of Chambers of Commerce [*See also AICO*] [*Bogota, Colombia*]   (EAIO)
IAAEM ...... International Association of Aquaculture Economics and Management
IAAF .... International Amateur Athletic Federation [*See also FIAA*] [*British*]   (EAIO)
IAAF .... International Association of Art for the Future [*Indonesia*]   (EAIO)
IAAFE .... Instituto de Aprovechamiento de Aguas y Fomento Electrico [*Colombia*]   (DSCA)
IAAG .... Inter-American Association of Gastroenterology   (EA)
IAAH .... International Action Against Hunger   (EAIO)
IAAIP .... Inter-American Association of Industrial Property [*See also ASIPA*] [*Buenos Aires, Argentina*]   (EAIO)
IAALD .... International Association of Agricultural Librarians and Documentalists   (EA)
IAAMRH .. International Association of Agricultural Medicine and Rural Health   (EA)
IAAOPA .... International Association of Aircraft Owners and Pilots Association   (BARN)
IAAP .... International Association of Applied Psychology [*Nijmegen, Netherlands*]   (EA)
IAAPEA .... International Association Against Painful Experiments on Animals   (EA)
IAAS .... International Association of Agricultural Students [*See also AIEA*] [*Uppsala, Sweden*]   (EAIO)
IAASA .... Indian Australian Association of South Australia
IAASEES .. Inter-American Association of Sanitary Engineering and Environmental Sciences   (EAIO)
IAASM ...... International Academy of Aviation and Space Medicine   (EAIO)
IAASP .... International Association of Airport and Seaport Police [*Canada*]   (EAIO)
IAAT .... International Association Against Torture   (EAIO)

IAATM ...... International Association for Accident and Traffic Medicine   (EA)
IAB .... Institut fuer Arbeitsmarkt- und Berufsforschung [*Institute for Employment Research*] [*Federal Employment Institute*] [*Germany*]   (IID)
IAB .... Internal Audit Bureau [*New South Wales*]
IAB .... International Association of Bibliophiles [*See also AIB*] [*Paris, France*]   (EAIO)
IAB .... International Association of Bookkeepers [*British*]   (EAIO)
IAB .... International Association of Broadcasting   (NTCM)
IAB .... Internationale Akademie fuer Bader-, Sport-, und Freizeitheitbau [*International Board for Aquatic, Sports, and Recreation Facilities*] [*Bad Neustadt/Saale, Federal Republic of Germany*]   (EAIO)
IABA .... International Association of Aircraft Brokers and Agents [*Norway*]   (EAIO)
IAB-AIR .... International Association of Broadcasting - Asociacion Internacional de Radiodifusion [*Formerly, Inter-American Association of Broadcasters*]   (EA)
IABC .... International Association of Building Companions [*See also IBO*] [*Marche-En-Famenne, Belgium*]   (EAIO)
IABE .... Ibero-American Bureau of Education [*See also OEI*] [*Madrid, Spain*]   (EAIO)
IABG .... International Association of Botanic Gardens [*Australia*]   (EA)
IABG .... International Association of Buying Groups [*See also IVE*]   (EAIO)
IABK .... International Association of Book-Keepers [*Sevenoaks, Kent, England*]   (EA)
IABLA .... Inter-American Bank for Latin America   (WDAA)
IABM .... International Association of Broadcasting Manufacturers [*Hayes, Middlesex, England*]   (EAIO)
IABO .... Internacia Asocio de Bibliistoj kaj Orientalistoj [*International Association of Biblicists and Orientalists - IABO*]   (EA)
IABO .... International Association for Biological Oceanography [*Aberdeen, Scotland*]   (EAIO)
IABS .... International Association for Byzantine Studies [*See also AIEB*] [*Thessaloniki, Greece*]   (EAIO)
IABS .... International Association of Biological Standardization [*See also AISB*] [*ICSU Geneva, Switzerland*]   (EAIO)
IABSE .... International Association for Bridge and Structural Engineering [*ICSU*] [*Zurich, Switzerland*] [*Research center*]   (EA)
IABSIW ..... International Association of Bridge, Structural, and Ornamental Iron Workers   (BARN)
IAC .... Indian Airlines Corp. [*ICAO designator*]   (FAAC)
IAC .... International Academy of Ceramics [*See also AIC*] [*Geneva, Switzerland*]   (EAIO)
IAC .... International Academy of Cytology [*Quebec, PQ*]   (EA)
IAC .... International Artists' Cooperation   (EAIO)
IAC .... International Association for Cybernetics [*See also AIC*] [*Namur, Belgium*]   (EAIO)
IAC .... International Association of Charities [*See also AIC*]   (EAIO)
IAC .... Island Advisory Council [*Australia*]
IAC .... Italian Aircraft Corp.
IACA .... International Air Carrier Association [*Zaventhem, Belgium*]   (EAIO)
IACA .... International Association for Classical Archaeology [*See also AIAC*] [*Rome, Italy*]   (EAIO)
IACAAC .... International Artists' Cooperation Audio Art Center [*Defunct*]   (EA)
IACAPAP ... International Association for Child and Adolescent Psychiatry and Allied Professions [*Copenhagen, Denmark*]   (EA)
IACB .... International Advisory Committee on Bibliography [*UNESCO*]   (WDAA)
IACC .... Indo-American Chamber of Commerce   (PDAA)
IACC .... Instituto Argentino de Control de la Calidad [*Argentina*]   (DSCA)
IACC .... International Air Cargo Corp. [*Egypt*] [*ICAO designator*]   (FAAC)
IACC .... International Americas Cup Class [*Yachting*]

IACC.......... International Art Cinemas Confederation (EAIO)

IACC.......... Israel-America Chamber of Commerce and Industry (EAIO)

IACCE....... Inter-American Confederation for Catholic Education [*Bogota, Colombia*] (EAIO)

IACCP....... International Association for Cross-Cultural Psychology [*Canada*] (EA)

IACF.......... Inter-American Cement Federation [*Colombia*] (EAIO)

IACI.......... Inter-American Children's Institute [*Uruguay*] [*Research center*] (IRC)

IACITC ..... International Advisory Committee of the International Teletraffic Congress (EAIO)

IACJ .... Inter-American Council of Jurists [*Organization of American States*] [*Washington, DC*]

IACL.......... International Association of Constitutional Law [*See also AIDC*] [*Belgrade, Yugoslavia*] (EAIO)

IACLE .... International Association of Contact Lens Educators

IACM .... International Association for Computational Mechanics [*International Council of Scientific Unions*]

IACME...... International Association of Crafts and Small- and Medium-Sized Enterprises [*Switzerland*] (EY)

IACNRE.... International Association for Conservation of Natural Resources and Energy

IACO .... Inter-African Coffee Organization (EAIO)

IACOMS... International Advisory Committee on Marine Sciences [*UNESCO*] (ASF)

IACR.......... International Association of Cancer Registries [*Lyon, France*] (EAIO)

IACRD...... Inter-American Center for Regional Development (EAIO)

IACRDVT ... Inter-American Centre for Research and Documentation on Vocational Training [*See also CINTERFOR*] [*Montevideo, Uruguay*] (EAIO)

IACS .... International Academy of Cosmetic Surgery [*Rome, Italy*] (EA)

IACS .... International Association of Classification Societies (EAIO)

IACSM...... International Association of Computer Service Managers

IACSS....... Inter-American Conference on Social Security [*See also CISS*] [*Mexico City, Mexico*] (EAIO)

IACST .... International Association for Commodity Science and Technology (EAIO)

IACT......... Inter-Association Commission on Tsunami [*Brussels, Belgium*] (EAIO)

IACT.......... International Association of Counselors and Therapists (EA)

IACW .... Inter-American Commission of Women [*Organization of American States*] [*Washington, DC*]

IACW .... International Association of Crime Writers (EAIO)

IAD .... International Association of Documentalists and Information Officers [*France*] (EY)

IAD .... Internationale Arbeitsgemeinschaft Donauforschung [*International Working Association for Danube Research*] (EAIO)

IADA .... Internationale Arbeitsgemeinschaft der Archiv-, Bibliotheks-, und Graphikrestauratoren [*International Association for Conservation of Books, Paper, and Archival Material*] (EAIO)

IADB .... Inter-American Development Bank [*Also, IDB*]

IADC .... International Alliance for Distribution by Cable [*Formerly, International Alliance for Distribution by Wire*] (EA)

IADC .... International Association of Dentistry for Children [*British*] (EAIO)

IADC .... International Association of Dredging Companies [*The Hague, Netherlands*] (EA)

IADC .... International Association of Drilling Contractors

IAdEM ...... Internacia Asocio de Esperantistaj Matematikistoj [*International Association of Esperantist Mathematicians*] (EAIO)

IADH......... International Association of Dentistry for the Handicapped [*Toronto, ON*] (EAIO)

IADIWU.... International Association for the Development of International and World Universities [*See also AIDUIM*] [*Aulnay-Sous-Bois, France*] (EAIO)

IADL......... International Association of Democratic Lawyers [*Brussels, Belgium*] (EA)

IADMFR... International Association of Dento-Maxillo-Facial Radiology (EAIO)

IADP......... INTELSAT Assistance and Development Program

IADS......... International Association of Department Stores [*See also AIGM*] (EAIO)

IAE .... Institut d'Administration des Entreprises [*Institute of Company Management*] [*Information service or system*] (IID)

IAE .... Interstate Airlines Ltd. [*Nigeria*] [*ICAO designator*] (FAAC)

IAEA......... International Advertising Executives' Association (NTCM)

IAEA......... International Agricultural Exchange Association [*British*] (EA)

IAEA......... International Association of Empirical Aesthetics [*Paris, France*] (EAIO)

IAEA......... International Atomic Energy Agency [*Database originator and operator*] [*United Nations Austria*]

IAEAC....... International Association of Environmental Analytical Chemistry [*Therwil, Switzerland*] (EAIO)

IAEC.......... International Association of Electrical Contractors [*See also AIE*] (EAIO)

IAEC.......... International Association of Environmental Coordinators [*Belgium*] (DCTA)

IAECOSOC ... Inter-American Economic and Social Council [*United Nations*]

IAED .... International Association of Exchange Dealers [*British*] (EA)

IAEDT...... International Association of Equine Dental Technicians (EA)

IAEE.......... International Association for Earthquake Engineering [*ICSU*] [*Tokyo, Japan*] (EAIO)

IAEG .... International Association of Engineering Geology [*International Union of Geological Sciences*] [*ICSU Paris, France*] (EA)

IAEI .... Institut d'Automatique et d'Electronique Industrielle [*French*] (ADPT)

IAEL......... International Association for Esperanto in Libraries [*See also TEBA*] (EAIO)

IAEL......... International Association of Entertainment Lawyers [*Amsterdam, Netherlands*] (EAIO)

IAEMS...... International Association of Environmental Mutagen Societies [*Helsinki, Finland*] (EAIO)

IAEP......... International Academy of Eclectic Psychotherapists [*St. Ives, NSW, Australia*] (EAIO)

IAES .... International Academy for Environmental Safety

IAESC....... Inter-American Economic and Social Council [*United Nations*]

IAESTE.... International Association for the Exchange of Students for Technical Experience [*Lisbon, Portugal*] (EAIO)

IAEVG...... International Association for Educational and Vocational Guidance [*See also AIOSP*] [*Belfast, Northern Ireland*] (EAIO)

IAEVI .... International Association for Educational and Vocational Information [*See also AIISUP*] [*Paris, France*] (EAIO)

IAF............ EPAG - Group Air France [*ICAO designator*] (FAAC)

IAF............ Interallied Force [*NATO*] (NATG)

IAF............ International Abolitionist Federation [*India*]

IAF............ International Aikido Federation [*Tokyo, Japan*] (EAIO)

IAF............ International Apparel Federation [*Berlin, Federal Republic of Germany*] (EAIO)

IAF............ International Association for Falconry and Conservation of Birds of Prey (EAIO)

IAF............ International Astronautical Federation [*ICSU*] [*Research center*] [*France*]

IAF............ International Athletic Footwear and Apparel Manufacturers Association [*Zurich, Switzerland Defunct*] (EAIO)

IAF............ Israel Air Force (BJA)

IAF............ Israeli Air-Force [*ICAO designator*] (FAAC)

IAFAW...... International Association of Friends of Angkor Wat (EAIO)

IAFC......... Inter-American Freight Conference - Section C (EA)

IAFC......... International Association of Financial Consultants (BARN)

IAFCI .... Inter-American Federation of the Construction Industry [*See also FIIC*] [*Mexico City, Mexico*] (EAIO)

IAFCT....... International Association of French-Speaking Congress Towns [*See also AIVFC*] [*France*] (EAIO)

IAFES....... International Association for the Economics of Self-Management [*Belgrade, Yugoslavia*] (EAIO)

IAFLUP..... International Association of French-Language University Presses [*Defunct*] (EA)

IAFS .... International Association for Food Self-Sufficiency (EA)

IAFS .... International Association of Forensic Sciences [*Defunct*] (EA)

IAFSA....... International Association of French-Speaking Aircrews (EAIO)

IAFSDEI ... International Association of French-Speaking Directors of Educational Institutions (EAIO)

IAG .... Institute for Australasian Geodynamics [*Flinders University*] [*Australia*]

IAG .... International Art Guild (EA)

IAG .... International Association of Geodesy [*ICSU*] [*Paris, France*] (EAIO)

IAG .... International Auditing Guideline

IAGA .... International Association of Geomagnetism and Aeronomy [*ICSU*] [*Scotland*] (ASF)

IAGAE...... International Association for Gerda Alexander Eutony [*See also AIEGA*] [*Switzerland*] (EAIO)

IAGC .... International Association of Geochemistry and Cosmochemistry [*Edmonton, AB*] (EA)

IAGLL ...... International Association of Germanic Languages and Literatures [*See also IVG*] (EAIO)

IAGMA ..... International Assembly of Grocery Manufacturers Associations (EAIO)

IAGOD...... International Association of the Genesis of Ore Deposits [*ICSU*] [*Prague, Czechoslovakia*] (EAIO)

IAGRO ...... Instituto Agropecuario Universidad Federal do Rio Grande do Norte [*Brazil*] (DSCA)

IAGS......... International Association for Germanic Studies (EAIO)

IAH........... International Association of Hydrogeologists [*Arnhem, Netherlands*] (EA)

IAH........... Internationales Arbeiter-Hilfswerk [*International Workers Aid*] [*Bonn, Federal Republic of Germany*] (EAIO)

IAHA......... International Association of Historians of Asia [*Quezon City, Philippines*] (EA)

IAHB .... International Association of Human Biologists [*ICSU*] [*Newcastle-Upon-Tyne, England*] (EAIO)

IAHI .... International Association of Hail Insurers (EA)

IAHM .... International Academy of the History of Medicine [*Defunct*] (EA)

IAHMS ..... International Association of Hotel Management Schools (EA)

IAHR .... International Association for Hydraulic Research [*ICSU*] [*Delft, Netherlands*] (EA)

IAHR .... International Association for the History of Religions [*Marburg, Federal Republic of Germany*] (EAIO)

IAHRONA ... International Arabian Horse Registry of North America (EA)

IAHS .... International Academy of the History of Science [*Paris, France*] (EA)

IAHS .... International Association of Hydrological Sciences

IAHSSP ..... International Association of Home Safety and Security Professionals (EA)

IAI .... Independent Accountants International (EAIO)

IAI .... Indo-Africa, Inc. (ECON)

IAI .... International African Institute [*British*]

IAI .... Israel Aircraft Industries Ltd. [*ICAO designator*] (FAAC)

IAIALAR ... Ibero-American Institute of Agrarian Law and Agrarian Reform [*See also IIDARA*] [*Mexida, Venezuela*] (EAIO)

IAIB .... International Association of Islamic Banks

IAIC .... International Academy of Indian Culture (EAIO)

IAIDEC ..... Instituto Argentino de la Industria y Exportacion de Carnes [*Argentina*] (DSCA)

IAIDPA ..... International Association for Information and Documentation in Public Administration (EAIO)

IAIE .... International Association for Integrative Education [*Versoix, Switzerland*] (EAIO)

IAII .... Inter-American Indian Institute [*OAS*] [*Mexico City, Mexico*] (EA)

IAIN .... International Association of Institutes of Navigation [*British*] (EAIO)

IAIR .... International Association of Industrial Radiation [*France*] (PDAA)

IAIRI .... International Association of Insurance and Reinsurance Intermediaries [*See also BIPAR*] [*Paris, France*] (EAIO)

IAITO .... International Association of Independent Tanker Owners

IAJ .... International Association of Judges [*Rome, Italy*] (EAIO)

IAJA .... International Association of Jazz Appreciation (EA)

IAJFCM .... International Association of Juvenile and Family Court Magistrates [*Paris, France*] (EA)

IAK .... International Air Cargo Corp. [*Egypt*] [*ICAO designator*] (FAAC)

IAK .... Internationales Auschwitz-Komitee [*International Auschwitz Committee*] [*Warsaw, Poland*] (EAIO)

IAKS .... Groupe International de Travail pour les Equipements de Sport et de Loisirs (OLYM)

IAKS .... Internationaler Arbeitskreis Sport- und Freizeiteninrichtungen [*International Working Group for the Construction of Sports and Leisure Facilities*] (EAIO)

IAL .... Indian Airlines (PDAA)

IAL .... Institut fuer Auslaendische Landwirtschaft [*Germany*] (DSCA)

IAL .... Instituto Agronomico do Leste [*Brazil*] (DSCA)

IAL .... International Algebraic Language (ADPT)

IAL .... International Association of Limnology (PDAA)

IALA .... International Association of Lighthouse Authorities [*Paris, France*] (EA)

IALA .... Islamic Alliance for the Liberation of Afghanistan (PD)

IALACS ..... International Association of Latin American and Caribbean Studies (EAIO)

IALHI .... International Association of Labour History Institutions [*Zurich, Switzerland*] (EAIO)

IALP .... International Association of Logopedics and Phoniatrics [*Dublin, Republic of Ireland*] (EA)

IALS .... Institute of Applied Language Studies [*Edith Cowan University*] [*Australia*]

IALS .... International Association of Legal Science [*See also AISJ*] [*Paris, France*] (EAIO)

IAM .... In Amenas [*Algeria*] [*Airport symbol*] (OAG)

IAM .... Instituto do Algodao de Mocamgique [*Mozambique*] (DSCA)

IAM .... International Academy of Myodontics, Oceanic Chapter [*Sydney, NSW, Australia*] (EAIO)

IAM .... International Association of Metaphysicians

IAMA .... Independent Agricultural Merchants' Association [*Australia*]

IAMA .... International Abstaining Motorists' Association [*Hagersten, Sweden*] (EAIO)

IAMA .... International Academy of Myodontics, Asian Chapter [*Tokyo, Japan*] (EAIO)

IAMAM .... International Association of Museums of Arms and Military History [*Ingolstadt, Federal Republic of Germany*] (EA)

IAMANEH ... International Association for Maternal and Neonatal Health [*Zurich, Switzerland*] (EAIO)

IAMB .... International Association for the Protection of Monuments and Restoration of Buildings (EAIO)

IAMBE ...... International Association of Medicine and Biology of Environment [*See also AIMBE*] [*Paris, France*] (EAIO)

IAMC .... Inter-American Markets Corp. [*Latin America*]

IAMC .... Inter-American Music Council (EAIO)

IAMCR ...... International Association for Mass Communication Research [*British*]

IAMFE ...... International Association on Mechanization of Field Experiments [*Aas, Norway*] (EA)

IAMFS ...... International Association for Maxillo-Facial Surgery (EA)

IAMHIST ... International Association of Audio-Visual Media in Historical Research and Education [*Bologna, Italy*] (EAIO)

IAMIC .... International Association of Mutual Insurance Companies [*See also AISAM*] (EAIO)

IAML .... International Association of Music Libraries, Archives, and Documentation Centers (EA)

IAMLADP ... Inter-Agency Meeting on Language Arrangements, Documentation, and Publications [*United Nations*]

IAMLO ..... International African Migratory Locust Organization [*See also OICMA*] (EA)

IAMLT ...... International Association of Medical Laboratory Technologists [*Bootle, Merseyside, England*] (EA)

IAMM .... Institute Agronomique Mediterraneen de Montpellier [*France*] (DSCA)

IAMMM ... International Association of Margaret Morris Method [*Glasgow, Scotland*] (EAIO)

IAMP .... International Academy of Medicine and Psychology [*Australia*] (EA)

IAMP .... International Association of Mathematical Physics (EA)

IAMRC ...... International Antarctic Meteorological Research Center (PDAA)

IAMRC ...... International Antarctic Meteorological Research Centre (PDAA)

IAMS .... International Association for Mission Studies [*Hamburg, Federal Republic of Germany*] (EAIO)

IAMTS ...... International Association of Model and Talent Scouts (EAIO)

IAMWMW ... International Association of Ministers' Wives and Ministers' Widows (EAIO)

IAN .... Compania Internadia de Aviacion [*Colombia*] [*ICAO designator*] (FAAC)

IAN .... Informatsionnoye Agentstvo Novosti [*Novosti Press Agency*] [*Russian Federation*]

IANC .... International Air Navigation Convention

IANC .... International Anatomical Nomenclature Committee [*British*] (EAIO)

IA/NLP ..... International Association for Neuro-Linguistic Programming (EAIO)

IANLS .... International Association for Neo-Latin Studies [*St. Andrews, Scotland*] (EAIO)

IANOS ...... International Assembly of National Organizations Sports (OLYM)

IANSW ...... Ileostomy Association of New South Wales [*Australia*]

IANVS .... International Association for Non-Violent Sport [*See also AICVS*] [*Monte Carlo, Monaco*] (EAIO)

IAO .... Institute of Ambulance Officers [*Australia*]

IAOAD ...... International Association of Original Art Diffusors (EAIO)

IAOD .... International Association of Opera Directors (EAIO)

IAOMO ..... International Association of Olympic Medical Officers [*Rugby, Warwickshire, England*] (EAIO)

IAOMS ...... International Association of Oral and Maxillofacial Surgeons (EA)

IAOMT ..... International Academy of Oral Medicine and Toxicology

IAOP .... International Association of Oral Pathologists (EA)

IAOS .... International Association for Official Statistics [*International Statistical Institute*] [*Voorburg, Netherlands*] (EAIO)

IAOS .... International Association of Oral Surgeons (EAIO)

IAOT .... International Association for Oxygen Therapy

IAP .... Industria Agro Pecuaria [*Brazil*] (DSCA)

IAP .... International Association of Planetology [*Brussels, Belgium*] (EA)

IAPA .... International Association of Physicians in Audiology (EAIO)

IAPAC .... Injection Assistee par Air Comprise [*Pneumatic Direct Fuel Injection*] [*French*]

IAPBPPV .. International Association of Plant Breeders for the Protection of Plant Varieties (EAIO)

IAPC .... International Association of Political Consultants (EA)

IAPCO .... International Association of Professional Congress Organizers [*Brussels, Belgium*] (EAIO)

IAPD .... International Association of Paediatric Dentistry [*British*] (EAIO)

IAPG .... International Association of Physical Geography (BARN)

IAPG .... International Association of Psychoanalytic Gerontology [*Paris, France*] (EAIO)

IAPH .... International Association of Paper Historians (DGA)

IAPH .... International Association of Ports and Harbors [*Japan*]

IAPL .... International Association of Penal Law [*Freiburg, Federal Republic of Germany*] (EAIO)

IAPM .... International Association of Photoplate Makers (DGA)

IAPMA ...... International Association of Hand Papermakers and Paper Artists (EAIO)

IAPN .... International Association of Professional Numismatists [*See also AINP*] [*Zurich, Switzerland*] (EAIO)
IAPO .... International Association of Printers' Overseers (DGA)
IAPP .... Indian Association for Plant Physiology [*India*] (DSCA)
IAPP .... International Association for Plant Physiology [*Australia*] (EAIO)
IAPPHAP ... International Association for Past and Present History of the Art of Printing (EA)
IAPPI .... International Association of Public Pawnbroking Institutions [*Milan, Italy*] (EA)
IAPPP .... International Amateur-Professional Photoelectric Photometry [*An association*]
IAPR .... International Association for Pattern Recognition [*British*] (EA)
IAPR .... International Association for Psychotronic Research [*Prague, Czechoslovakia*] (EA)
IAPRI .... International Association of Packaging Research Institutes [*British*] (EAIO)
IAPT .... International Association for Plant Taxonomy [*Utrecht, Netherlands*] (EA)
IAPTE .... International Academy of Pediatric Transdisciplinary Education [*British*] (EAIO)
IAPUP .... International Association on the Political Use of Psychiatry [*Amsterdam, Netherlands*] (EAIO)
IAQ .... International Academy for Quality [*Grobenzell, Federal Republic of Germany*] (EAIO)
IAR .... Iliamna Air Taxi, Inc. [*ICAO designator*] (FAAC)
IAR .... International Association of Radiopharmacology (EA)
IARA .... Industrial Arbitration Registrars' Association [*Australia*]
IARC .... International Action for the Rights of the Child [*See also AIDE*] [*Paris, France*] (EAIO)
IARC .... International Agency for Research on Cancer [*World Health Organization*] [*Lyon, France*] [*Research center*] (EAIO)
IARCA .... International Association Residential and Community Alternatives (EAIO)
IARF .... International Association for Religious Freedom [*Germany*] (EY)
IARIGAI ... International Association of Research Institutes for the Graphic Arts Industry [*St. Gallen, Switzerland*]
IARIL .... International Association of Rural and Isolated Libraries [*Australia*]
IARMCLRS ... International Agreement Regarding the Maintenance of Certain Lights in the Red Sea (EA)
IARN .... International Amateur Radio Network
IARP .... International Association for Religion and Parapsychology [*Tokyo, Japan*] (EA)
IARR .... International Association for Radiation Research [*Rijswijk, Netherlands*] (EAIO)
IARSB .... International Association of Rolling Stock Builders [*See also AICMR*] (EAIO)
IARUS .... International Association for Regional and Urban Statistics [*Voorburg, Netherlands*] (EA)
IAS .... Iasi [*Romania*] [*Airport symbol*] (OAG)
IAS .... Institute of Aviation Studies [*University of Newcastle*] [*Australia*]
IAS .... International Academy of Sciences (EAIO)
IAS .... International AIDS Society (EAIO)
IAS .... International Air Service Co. [*ICAO designator*] (FAAC)
IAS .... International Association of Sedimentologists [*Liege, Belgium*] (EA)
IAS .... International Aviation Services [*Belgium*]
IASA .... Ileostomy Association of South Australia
IASA .... Implementos Avicolas SA [*Mexico*] (DSCA)
IASA .... Importers' Association of South Australia
IASA .... Industrias de Aceite SA [*Bolivia*] (DSCA)
IASA .... Institute for Atomic Sciences in Agriculture [*Netherlands*] (DSCA)
IASA .... Institute of Agricultural Secretaries of Australasia
IASA .... International Alliance for Sustainable Agriculture (GNE)
IASA .... International Association of Sound Archives [*Milton, Keynes, England*] (EAIO)
IASAIL ...... International Association for the Study of Anglo-Irish Literature [*Maynooth, Republic of Ireland*] (EAIO)
IASAJ .... International Association of Supreme Administration Jurisdictions GG2 [*See also AIHJA*] (EAIO)
IASC .... Inter-American Scout Committee [*See also CIE*] [*San Jose, Costa Rica*] (EAIO)
IASC .... International Accounting Standards Committee [*of the International Federation of Accountants*] [*British*] (EAIO)
IASC .... International Arctic Science Committee
IASC .... International Association for Statistical Computing (EA)
IASC .... International Association of Seed Crushers [*British*] (EAIO)
IASC .... International Association of Skal Clubs [*Spain*] (EAIO)
IASCB .... Ibero-American Society for Cell Biology [*See also SIABC*] (EAIO)
IASCP .... International Association for the Study of Common Property (EA)
IASEES ..... International Association of South-East European Studies [*See also AIESEE*] [*Bucharest, Romania*] (EAIO)

IASI .... International Association for Sports Information [*The Hague, Netherlands*] (EA)
IASILL ...... International Association for the Study of the Italian Language and Literature [*See also AISLLI*] [*Padua, Italy*] (EAIO)
IASL .... International Association for the Study of the Liver [*Gottingen, Federal Republic of Germany*] (EAIO)
IASL .... International Association of School Librarianship (PDAA)
IASM .... Istituto per l'Assistenza allo Sviluppo del Mezzogiorno [*Italy*] (EY)
IASMIRT ... International Association for Structural Mechanics in Reactor Technology (EAIO)
IASMW ..... International Association of Sheet Metal Workers (BARN)
IASP .... International Association for Social Progress [*Belgium*] (DSCA)
IASP .... International Association of Scholarly Publishers [*Norway*]
IASPEI ...... International Association of Seismology and Physics of the Earth's Interior [*ICSU*] [*Newbury, Berkshire, England*] (EAIO)
IASPM ...... International Association for the Study of Popular Music [*Berlin, German Democratic Republic*] (EAIO)
IASPPV ..... International Association of Former Soviet Political Prisoners and Victims of Communist Regime
IASPS .... International Association for Statistics in Physical Sciences [*Netherlands*] (DSCA)
IASS .... International Association for Scandinavian Studies [*Norwich, England*] (EAIO)
IASS .... International Association for Shell and Spatial Structures [*Madrid, Spain*] (EA)
IASS .... International Association of Sanskrit Studies (EA)
IASS .... International Association of Semiotic Studies [*Palermo, Italy*] (EA)
IASS .... International Association of Survey Statisticians [*See also AISE*] [*France*] (EA)
IASSIST .... International Association for Social Science Information Service and Technology (EA)
IASSMD ... International Association for the Scientific Study of Mental Deficiency [*Dublin, Republic of Ireland*] (EA)
IASSRF ..... International Amateur Snowshoe Racing Federation (EA)
IASSW ...... International Association of Schools of Social Work [*Austria*]
IASTED .... International Association of Science and Technology for Development [*Calgary, AB*] (EAIO)
IASTWL .... International Association for Social Tourism and Workers' Leisure (EAIO)
IAT .... International Air Transport Association [*ICAO designator*] (FAAC)
IATA .... International Air Transport [*formerly, Traffic*] Association [*Canada*]
IATA .... International Amateur Theatre Association [*Denmark*]
IATDP .... International Association of Textile Dyers and Printers [*See also AITIT*] (EAIO)
IATE .... International Association for Temperance Education [*Later, IVES*] (EA)
IATEFL ..... International Association of Teachers of English as a Foreign Language [*Whitstable, Kent, England*] (EAIO)
IATG .... International Association of Teachers of German [*See also IDV*] [*Copenhagen, Denmark*] (EAIO)
IATI .... International Association of Teachers of Italian [*Belgium*] (EAIO)
IATM .... International Association of Transport Museums [*See also AIMT*] [*Berne, Switzerland*] (EAIO)
IATP .... International Airlines Technical Pool (PDAA)
IATROS .... Organisation Mondiale des Medicins Independants [*International Organization of Private and Independent Doctors*] (EAIO)
IATSIS ...... Institute of Aboriginal and Torres Strait Islander Studies [*Australia*]
IATSS .... International Association of Traffic and Safety Sciences [*Tokyo, Japan*] (EAIO)
IATU .... Inter-American Telecommunications Union [*US*]
IATUL .... International Association of Technological University Libraries [*Goteborg, Sweden*]
IAU .... International Academic Union (EA)
IAU .... International Association of Universities [*France*]
IAU .... International Astronomical Union [*ICSU*] [*Paris, France*] [*Research center*] (IRC)
IAU .... Internationale Armbrustschutzen Union [*International Crossbow Shooting Union*] (EAIO)
IAUP .... International Association of University Presidents
IAUPE .... International Association of University Professors of English [*British*]
IAUPL .... International Association of University Professors and Lecturers (EAIO)
IAV .... Airavia [*France*] [*ICAO designator*] (FAAC)
IA(V) .... Ileostomy Association (Victoria) [*Australia*]
IAVCEI ..... International Association of Volcanology and Chemistry of the Earth's Interior [*Germany*]
IAVE .... International Association of Volunteer Effort (EA)

IAVFH....... International Association of Veterinary Food Hygienists [*Netherlands*] (DSCA)

IAVRT....... Independent Association of Victorian Registered Teachers [*Australia*]

IAVS......... International Association for Vegetation Science [*See also IVV*] [*Gottingen, Federal Republic of Germany*] (EAIO)

IAVSD....... International Association for Vehicle Systems Dynamics [*ICSU*] [*Delft, Netherlands*] (EAIO)

IAVTC....... International Audio-Visual Technical Centre [*Netherlands*]

IAW .... International Alliance of Women [*See also AIF*] [*Valetta, Malta*] (EAIO)

IAW .... Iraqi Airways [*ICAO designator*] (FAAC)

IAWA .... International Association of Wood Anatomists [*Utrecht, Netherlands*] (EA)

IAWE........ International Association for Wind Engineering [*Aachen, Federal Republic of Germany*] (EAIO)

IAWL........ International Association for Water Law [*See also AIDA*] [*Rome, Italy*] (EAIO)

IAWMC .... International Association of Workers for Troubled Children and Youth [*See also AIEJI*] (EAIO)

IAWP........ International Association of Women Philosophers [*Zurich, Switzerland*] (EAIO)

IAWPR...... International Association of Water Polo Referees (EA)

IAWPRC ... International Association on Water Pollution Research and Control [*British*] (EA)

IAWR .... Internationale Arbeitsgemeinschaft der Wasserwerke im Rheineinzugsgebiet [*International Association of Waterworks in the Rhine Basin Area - IAWRBA*] (EAIO)

IAWRBA... International Association of Waterworks in the Rhine Basin Area (EAIO)

IAWRT...... International Association of Women in Radio and Television (NTCM)

IAYMC...... International Association of Y's Men's Clubs [*Geneva, Switzerland*] (EA)

IAZ .... Industrie Air Charter [*France*] [*ICAO designator*] (FAAC)

IB .... International Baccalaureate

IB .... International Bank for Reconstruction and Development [*Also known as World Bank*]

IB .... Investigation Branch [*British*] [*Australia*] (DCTA)

IBA .... Ibadan [*Nigeria*] [*Airport symbol*] (OAG)

IBA .... Indian Banks Association (PDAA)

IBA .... Indonesian-British Association (DS)

IBA .... Industria Beneficiadora do Algodao Ltd. [*Brazil*] (DSCA)

IBA .... Instituto de Biologia Animal [*Brazil*] (DSCA)

IBA .... Instituto de Botanica Agricola [*Argentina*] (DSCA)

IBA .... International Bar Association [*British*] (EA)

IBA .... International Bartenders Association [*Paris, France*] (EAIO)

IBA .... International Baseball Association (OLYM)

IBA .... International Bauxite Association [*Kingston, Jamaica*]

IBA .... International Biliary Association [*Later, IHBPA*] (EAIO)

IBA .... International Bodyguard Association (EA)

IBA .... International Bridge Academy [*The Hague, Netherlands*] (EA)

IBA .... International Bryozoology Association [*See also AIB*] [*Paris, France*] (EAIO)

IBAA......... International Business Aircraft Association (DA)

IBAG .... Ich Bau auf Gott [*I Build on God*] [*Motto of Heinrich Posthumus, Count Reuss (1572-1635)*] [*German*]

IBAR......... Inter-African Bureau of Animal Resources [*Kenya*]

IBB............. Binter Canarais [*Spain*] [*ICAO designator*] (FAAC)

IBB............. Instituto Biologico da Bahia [*Brazil*] (DSCA)

IBBC......... International Business Communications Council [*Japan*] (ECON)

IBBL .... Islamic Bank of Bangladesh [*Commercial bank*] (EY)

IBBY .... International Board on Books for Young People [*Basel, Switzerland*] (EA)

IBC............. Informatica Bulgarien Corp. [*Bulgaria*] [*ICAO designator*] (FAAC)

IBC............. Institute for Biomedical Communication [*South African Medical Research Council*] [*Information service or system*] (IID)

IBC............. International Biotoxicological Center [*World Life Research Institute*] [*US*] (ASF)

IBC............. International Board of Cytopathology [*International Academy of Cytology*] [*Quebec, PQ*] (EAIO)

IBC............. International BRCA [*Breast Cancer*] Consortium

IBC............. International Broadcasting Convention [*Legal term*] (DLA)

IBC............. International Federation of the Blue Cross [*Formerly, International Federation of the Temperance Blue Cross Societies*] (EA)

IBCA......... Instituto Boliviano de Cultivos Andinos [*Bolivia*] (DSCA)

IBCA......... International Braille Chess Association [*Abcoude, Netherlands*] (EA)

IBCASA..... International Banking Campaign Against South Africa [*Later, ICABA*] (EA)

IBCC .... International Business Communications Council (ECON)

IBCE......... Indo-British Cultural Exchange

IBCSVP..... International Breeding Consortium for St. Vincent Parrot (EAIO)

IBD .... Instituto de Botanica Darwnion [*Argentina*] (DSCA)

IBD .... Internationale Bildungs- und Informations- Datenbank [*International Education and Information Data Bank*] [*Thiede & Thiede Mittelstandische Systemberatung GmbH*] [*Information service or system*] (IID)

IBDB........ Internationaal Belasting Documentatie Bureau [*International Bureau of Fiscal Documentation*] (EAIO)

IBE............ Ibague [*Colombia*] [*Airport symbol*] (OAG)

IBE............ Iberia-Lineas Aereas de Espana SA [*Spain*] [*ICAO designator*] (FAAC)

IBE............ International Bureau for Epilepsy [*Alderley Edge, Cheshire, England*] (EAIO)

IBE............ International Bureau of Education [*See also BIE*] [*UNESCO*] (EAIO)

IBE(A) ...... Institution of Biomedical Engineering (Australia)

IBEC......... International Bank for Economic Cooperation [*Moscow, USSR*] (EY)

IBED......... Inter-African Bureau for Epizootic Diseases [*Later, IBAR*]

IBERLANT ... Iberian Atlantic Area [*NATO*] (NATG)

IBEX .... International Building Exposition

IBF............ Instituto Bahiano do Fumo [*Brazil*] (DSCA)

IBF............ International Badminton Federation [*Cheltenham, Gloustershire, England*] (EAIO)

IBF............ International Balint Federation [*Brussels, Belgium*] (EAIO)

IBF............ International Balut Federation [*Bangkok, Thailand*] (EAIO)

IBF............ International Bandy Federation [*Lulea, Sweden*] (EAIO)

IBF............ International Booksellers Federation [*Formerly, ICBA*] [*Austria*] (EA)

IBF............ Internationales Begegnungszentrum Friedenshaus [*Germany*] (EAIO)

IBFD......... International Bureau of Fiscal Documentation (EAIO)

IBFEG ...... Internationaler Bund Freier Evangelischer Gemeinden [*International Federation of Free Evangelical Churches - IFFEC*] (EA)

IBFR......... Institute for Biological Field Research [*Netherlands*] (DSCA)

IBFRBTWB ... International Book Fair of Radical Black and Third World Books

IBG .... Internationale Begegnung in Gemeinschaftsdiensten [*Germany*] (EAIO)

IBG .... Internationale Brecht Gesellschaft [*International Brecht Society*] (EAIO)

IBG .... Internationale Bruckner Gesellschaft [*Vienna, Austria*] (EAIO)

IBG .... Internationales Buro fuer Gebirgsmechanik [*International Bureau of Strato-Mechanics - IBSM*] (EAIO)

IBI............. Intergovernmental Bureau for Informatics [*Telecommunications*] (EA)

IBI............. International Bankers, Inc.

IBI............. Internationales Burgen-Institut [*International Castles Institute*] [*Rozendaal, Netherlands*] (EA)

IBI............. Islamic Bank International

IBICT .... Instituto Brasileiro de Informacao em Ciencia e Tecnologia [*Brazilian Institute for Information in Science and Technology*] [*National Council of Scientific and Technological Development*] [*Information service or system*] (IID)

ibid .... Ibidem [*In the same place*] (SCAC)

IBiS........... Initiative in Biomolecular Structures [*University of New South Wales*] [*Australia*]

IBIS .... Integrated Botanical Information System [*Computer database*]

IBISL........ Integriertes Bestandsbearbeitungs und Informationssystem fuer Lebensversicherungen [*German*] (ADPT)

IBJ............ Industrial Bank of Japan

IBJI........... Industrial Bank of Japan International Ltd. (ECON)

IBMNSW ... Independent Bread Manufacturers of New South Wales [*Australia*]

IBMP........ International Board of Medicine and Psychology [*Later, IAMP*] (EA)

IBN .... Institut Belge de Normalisation [*Belgian Institute for Standardization*] [*Information service or system*] (IID)

IBO .... International Baccalaureate Office [*See also OBI*] [*Later, International Baccalaureate Organization Grand-Saconnex, Switzerland*] (EAIO)

IBO .... Internationale Bouworde [*International Association of Building Companions - IABC*] [*Marche-En-Famenne, Belgium*] (EAIO)

IBOS......... International Business Opportunities Service [*World Bank*] [*United Nations*] (DUND)

IBPA .... International Business Press Associates (PDAA)

IBPCA .... International Bureau of the Permanent Court of Arbitration (EAIO)

IBP/CT...... International Biological Programme/Conservation of Terrestrial Biological Communities [*London, England*]

IBPCT .... International Customs Tariffs Bureau [*International Bureau for the Publication of Customs Tariffs*] [*Acronym is based on former name,*] (EA)

IBPGR .... International Board for Plant Genetic Resources [*FAO*] [*Italy*]

IBPT .... International Bureau for Plant Taxonomy and Nomenclature [*Netherlands*] (DSCA)
IBQ .... Instituto de Biologia e Quimica [*Brazil*] (DSCA)
IBQA .... Institute of Building Quality Australia
IBR .... Index-Barrikaden-Register [*German*] (ADPT)
IBRA .... International Bee Research Association [*Cardiff, Wales*] (EA)
IBRA .... International Bible Reading Association [*Redhill, Surrey, England*] (EAIO)
IBRAR ...... Instituto Brasileiro de Reforma Agraria Regional [*Brazil*] (DSCA)
IBRD .... International Bank for Reconstruction and Development [*Also known as World Bank*]
IBRG .... International Biodeterioration Research Group (EA)
IBRO .... International Brain Research Organization [*Paris, France*] (EA)
IBS .... Ibis [*Belgium*] [*ICAO designator*] (FAAC)
IBS .... Institute of Behavioural Studies [*University of Newcastle*] [*Australia*]
IBS .... Integriertes Buchhaltungssystem [*Integrated Book Keeping System*] [*German*] (ADPT)
IBS .... International Bank for Settlements (MHDW)
IBS .... International Bentham Society (EAIO)
IBS .... International Bookbinders Secretariat (DGA)
IBS .... International Bulb Society (EAIO)
IBS .... International Business Services [*Switzerland*] (ECON)
IBSA .... International Blind Sports Association [*See also AISA*] [*Farsta, Sweden*] (EAIO)
IBSD .... Information-Based School Development
IBSFC .... International Baltic Sea Fishery Commission [*Warsaw, Poland*] (ASF)
IBSH .... Institute of the Brothers of the Sacred Heart [*See also IFSC*] [*Rome, Italy*] (EAIO)
IBSM .... International Bureau of Strata Mechanics [*See also IBG*] (EAIO)
IBSRAM ... International Board for Soil Research and Management [*Thailand*]
IBST .... International Bureau of Social Tourism [*See also BITS*] [*Brussels, Belgium*] (EAIO)
IBST .... International Bureau of Software Test
IBSWU ...... International Boot and Shoe Workers' Union
IBT .... Instituto de Botanica [*Brazil*] (DSCA)
IBTF .... Investment Bank for Trade and Finance [*United Arab Emirates*]
IBTO .... International Broadcasting and Television Organization (NTCM)
IBU .... International Broadcasting Union [*Defunct*] (NTCM)
IBV .... Internationale Buchhandler-Vereinigung [*International Booksellers Federation - IBF*] (EAIO)
IBW .... International Business Week
IBWM .... International Bureau of Weights and Measures [*France*] (DSCA)
IBY .... International Bank of Yemen
IBZ .... Ibiza [*Spain*] [*Airport symbol*] (OAG)
IBZ .... International Business Air [*Sweden*] [*ICAO designator*] (FAAC)
IC .... Iceland [*NATO*]
IC .... Incrementation Memoire [*French*] (ADPT)
IC .... Infrastructure Committee of the North Atlantic Council [*NATO*]
IC .... Ingenieur Commercial [*French*] (ADPT)
IC .... Iniciativia per Catalunya [*Spain*] [*Political party*] (EY)
IC .... Intelligence Committee [*NATO*] (NATG)
IC .... Izquierda Cristiana [*Christian Left*] [*Chile*] [*Political party*] (EY)
ICA .... Icabaru [*Venezuela*] [*Airport symbol*] (OAG)
ICA .... Institut Culturel Africain [*African Cultural Institute*] (EAIO)
ICA .... International Cartographic Association [*Australia*] (EA)
ICA .... International Chianina Association (EAIO)
ICA .... International Coffee Agreement [*Signed September, 1962*]
ICA .... International Commercial Arbitration (BARN)
ICA .... International Commission on Acoustics [*Aachen, Federal Republic of Germany*] (EAIO)
ICA .... International Commodity Agreement
ICA .... International Communication Association (ADPT)
ICA .... International Computer Association
ICA .... International Confederation of Accordionists [*Vienna, Austria*] (EA)
ICA .... International Congress of Africanists [*Lagos, Nigeria*] (EAIO)
ICA .... International Congress of African Studies (EAIO)
ICA .... International Congress of Americanists [*Manchester, England*] (EA)
ICA .... International Co-Operative Alliance [*Grand-Saconnex, Switzerland*] (EA)
ICA .... International Copper Association [*British*] (IRC)
ICA .... International Council on Archives [*UNESCO*] (EA)
ICAA .... International Civil Airports Association [*Orly, France*] (EAIO)
ICAA .... International Council of Accrediting Agencies [*Australia*] (EAIO)
ICAA .... International Council on Alcohol and Addictions [*Switzerland*]
ICAC .... International Confederation for Agricultural Credit [*Switzerland*] (DSCA)
ICAC .... International Cotton Advisory Committee (EA)

ICACCP .... International Commission Against Concentration Camp Practices [*Brussels, Belgium*] [*Defunct*] (EAIO)
ICADIS ..... Instituto Centroamericano de Documentacion y Investigacion Social (EA)
ICADTS .... International Committee on Alcohol, Drugs, and Traffic Safety [*Linkoping, Sweden*] (EA)
ICAE .... International Centre for Art Education (EAIO)
ICAE .... International Commission on Atmospheric Electricity (EA)
ICAE .... International Council for Adult Education [*Toronto, ON*] (EAIO)
ICAEC .... International Confederation of Associations of Experts and Consultants [*Paris, France*] (EA)
ICAF .... International Committee on Aeronautical Fatigue [*Delft University of Technology*] [*Netherlands*] (EAIO)
ICAI .... Institute of Cultural Affairs International (EA)
ICAITI .... Instituto Centroamericano de Investigacion y Tecnologia Industrial [*Central American Institute of Research and Industrial Technology*] [*Guatemala*] [*Research center*] (IRC)
ICAK .... International College of Applied Kinesiology (EA)
ICAL .... Industria e Comercio de Cafe e Amendoim Ltd. [*Brazil*] (DSCA)
ICAL .... Industria e Comercio do Acucar e Alcool Ltd. [*Brazil*] (DSCA)
ICALEO .... International Congress on Applications of Lasers and Electro-Optics [*Laser Institute of America*]
ICAM .... International Confederation of Architectural Museums [*Montreal, PQ*] (EAIO)
ICAMAS ... International Center for Advanced Mediterranean Agronomic Studies [*FAO*]
ICAME ...... International Conference on the Applications of the Mossbauer Effect
ICAMQ ..... International Committee of Automation of Mines and Quarries [*Budapest, Hungary*] (EAIO)
ICAN .... Iniciativa Canaria [*Spain*] [*Political party*] (EY)
ICAO .... International Civil Aviation Organization [*Montreal, PQ*] [*United Nations*]
ICAP .... International Congress of Applied Psychology (PDAA)
ICAPF .... Instituto Centroamericano de Poblacion y Familia [*Guatemala*] (DSCA)
ICARA ...... International Conference on Assistance for Refugees in Africa [*See also CIARA*] [*United Nations Geneva, Switzerland*] (EAIO)
ICARDA .... International Center for Agricultural Research in Dry Areas [*Syria*]
ICARE .... International Christian Aid Relief Enterprises [*Australia*]
ICAS .... Institute of Contemporary Asian Studies [*Monash University*] [*Australia*]
ICAS .... Isolated Children's Assistance Scheme
ICASC .... International Contraception, Abortion, and Sterilization Campaign [*Later, WGNRR*] (EAIO)
ICASE .... International Council of Associations for Science Education [*See also FIAPS*] (EAIO)
ICASIS ...... International Conference of African States on Insurance Supervision [*See also CICA*] [*Gabon*] (EAIO)
ICAT .... International Committee for the Coordination of Clinical Application and Teaching of Autogenic Therapy [*North Vancouver, BC*] (EAIO)
ICATL .... International Council of Associations of Theological Libraries (EA)
ICAWA ...... Indo-Chinese Australian Women's Association [*Australia*]
ICB .... Icebird Airline Ltd. [*Iceland*] [*ICAO designator*] (FAAC)
ICB .... Industrial and Commercial Bank [*China*]
ICB .... Instituto Central de Biologia [*Chile*] (DSCA)
ICB .... Instituto de Cacau da Bahia [*Brazil*] (DSCA)
ICB .... Ivory Coast Basin [*Geology*]
ICBB .... International Commission for Bee Botany [*Later, ICPBR*] (EA)
ICBD .... International Children's Book Day [*Australia*]
ICBD .... International Council of Ballroom Dancing [*British*] (EAIO)
ICBK .... International Centrum voor Beurzen en Kongressen [*Belgium*] (EAIO)
ICBN .... International Commission on the Biological Effects of Noise (GNE)
ICBP .... International Council for Bird Preservation [*Cambridge, England*] (EAIO)
ICBP(AS) .. International Council for Bird Protection (Australian Section)
ICC .... Instituto Cartografico de Cataluna [*Spain*] [*ICAO designator*] (FAAC)
ICC .... Intensive Care Certificate [*Medicine*]
ICC .... International Association for Cereal Science and Technology [*Formerly, International Association of Cereal Chemists*] [*Acronym represents association's former name*] [*Austria*]
ICC .... International Cello Centre [*Duns, Scotland*] (EAIO)
ICC .... International Chamber of Commerce [*See also CCI*] [*Paris, France*] (EAIO)
ICC .... International Children's Centre [*Paris, France*]
ICC .... International Color Consortium
ICC .... International Committee of ICOM [*International Council of Museums*] for Conservation [*Later, ICOM-CC*] (EAIO)

ICC............ International Computing Centre [*United Nations*]   (ECON)
ICC............ International Coordinating Committee for the Presentation of Science and the Development of Out-of-School Scientific Activities [*See also CIC*]   (EAIO)
ICC............ International Coordinating Committee of World Sports Organizations for the Disabed   (OLYM)
ICC............ International Corrosion Council [*Orsay, France*]   (EAIO)
ICC............ International Cricket Conference   (EA)
ICC............ Inuit Circumpolar Conference [*Godthaab, Greenland, Denmark*]   (EAIO)
ICCA........ International Commission on Commercial Activities   (EAIO)
ICCA........ International Congress and Convention Association [*Amsterdam, Netherlands*]   (EA)
ICCA........ International Conventions and Congresses Association [*Australia*]
ICCA........ International Corrugated Case Association [*Paris, France*]   (EAIO)
ICCA........ International Council for Commercial Arbitration [*Vienna, Austria*]   (EAIO)
ICCA........ International Council of Chemical Associations
ICCAD...... International Centre for Computer Aided Design   (PDAA)
ICCARD.... International Commission for Central American Recovery and Development
ICCAT...... International Commission for the Conservation of Atlantic Tunas [*Spain*]
ICCATCI... International Committee to Coordinate Activities of Technical Groups in Coatings Industry [*Paris, France*]   (EAIO)
ICCB........ International Catholic Child Bureau [*Geneva, Switzerland*]   (EAIO)
ICCC........ International Center for Comparative Criminology   (EA)
ICCC........ International Concentration Camp Committee [*Vienna, Austria*]   (EAIO)
ICCC........ International Conference on Circuits and Computers   (MCD)
ICCD........ Intergovernmental Commission for Chagas Disease   (ECON)
ICCE........ International Council for Correspondence Education [*Later, ICDE*]
ICCEA....... International Committee for the Study and Conservation of Earthen Architecture   (EAIO)
ICCFM...... International Confederation of Christian Family Movements   (EAIO)
ICCG........ International Catholic Conference of Guiding   (EAIO)
ICCG........ International Conference on Crystal Growth   (PDAA)
ICCHRLA ... Inter-Church Committee on Human Rights in Latin America [*Canada*]   (EAIO)
ICCIA .... Italian Chamber of Commerce and Industry in Australia
ICCICE...... Islamic Chamber of Commerce, Industry and Commodity Exchange [*See also CICIEM*] [*Karachi, Pakistan*]   (EAIO)
ICCILMB ... Interim Committee for Coordination of Investigations of the Lower Mekong Basin   (EA)
ICCIR .... International Coordination Committee for Immunology of Reproduction [*Bulgaria*] [*Research center*]   (IRC)
ICCJ .... International Council of Christians and Jews [*Heppenheim, Federal Republic of Germany*]   (EAIO)
ICCLA .... International Center for Coordination of Legal Assistance [*Switzerland*]   (PDAA)
ICCM........ International Committee for the Conservation of Mosaics [*Hungerford, Berkshire, England*]   (EAIO)
ICCM........ International Council of Catholic Men [*See also FIHC*] [*Vatican City, Vatican City State*]   (EAIO)
ICCMB...... International Committee for the Conservation of Mud-Brick   (EAIO)
ICCN .... International Committee of Catholic Nurses [*See also CICIAMS*] [*Vatican City, Vatican City State*]   (EAIO)
ICCO .... International Carpet Classification Organization [*Brussels, Belgium*]   (EAIO)
ICCO .... International Cocoa Organization [*London, England*]   (EAIO)
ICCO .... International Council of Containership Operators [*British*]   (DCTA)
ICCP .... International Committee for Coal Petrology [*Liege, Belgium*]   (EAIO)
ICCP .... International Council for Children's Play [*Groningen, Netherlands*]   (EAIO)
ICCR .... International Committee for Coal Research [*Brussels, Belgium*]   (EAIO)
ICCROM... International Centre for the Study of the Preservation and the Restoration of Cultural Property [*Rome, Italy*]   (EAIO)
ICCS .... Institutului de Cercetari Pentru Cultura Cartofului si Sfeclei de Zahar-Cartoful [*Romania*]   (DSCA)
ICCS .... International Center for Criminological Studies   (BARN)
ICCS .... International Centre for Chemical Studies [*See also CIEC*]   (EAIO)
ICCS .... International Commission on Civil Status [*See also CIEC*] [*Strasbourg, France*]   (EAIO)
ICCS .... International Committee of Creole Studies [*Aix-En-Provence, France*]   (EAIO)
ICCS .... International Committee on Clinical Sociology [*See also CISC*] [*Later, International Group on Clinical Sociology*]   (EAIO)

ICCS .... International Conference on Composite Structures [*Paisley, Scotland*]   (EAIO)
ICCS .... International Cork Cutters' Society [*A union*]
ICCS .... International Group on Clinical Sociology [*Formerly, International Committee on Clinical Sociology*]   (EA)
ICD .... Informal Clearance Document [*Customs*]
ICD .... Institute of Civil Defence [*British*]   (EAIO)
ICD .... International Code Designator [*Telecommunications*]   (OSI)
ICD .... Intracommunity Directive [*Meat-shipping plants*] [*European Community*]
ICDA .... International Coalition for Development Action [*See also CIAD*]   (EAIO)
ICDBL ...... International Committee for the Defense of the Breton Language [*See also CISLB*] [*Brussels, Belgium*]   (EAIO)
ICDCR....... Instituto de Colonizacion y Desarrollo de Comunidades Rurales [*Bolivia*]   (DSCA)
ICDDR ..... International Center for Diarrhoeal Diseases Research   (PDAA)
ICDDR ..... International Centre for Diarrhoeal Disease Research [*Bangladesh*]
ICDDRB.... International Centre for Diarrhoeal Disease Research, Bangladesh   (ECON)
ICDE........ International Council for Distance Education [*Australia*]   (EAIO)
ICDF........ International Christian Dance Fellowship   (EAIO)
ICDL........ International Centre for Distance Learning [*United Nations University*]   (DUND)
ICDO .... International Civil Defence Organization [*Switzerland*]
ICDP........ International Confederation for Disarmament and Peace [*British*]
ICDP.......... International Continental Scientific Drilling Program [*Originated by the US, China, and Germany*]
ICDSRHP ... International Committee for the Defense of Salman Rushdie and His Publishers   (EAIO)
ICDT.......... Islamic Centre for Development of Trade [*See also CIDC*] [*Casablanca, Morocco*]   (EAIO)
ICE............ Icelandair [*ICAO designator*]   (FAAC)
ICE............ Institute for Christian Education [*Australia*]
ICE............ Inter City Express [*Electric train*] [*Germany*]
ICE............ International Congress of Entomology [*Later, CICE*]   (EA)
ICE............ International Council on Electrocardiology [*Glasgow, Scotland*]   (EAIO)
ICEA........ Institution of Chemical Engineers in Australia
ICEA........ Instituto Campineiro de Ensino Agricola [*Brazil*]   (DSCA)
ICEA........ International Commission for Environmental Assessment   (GNE)
ICEAM..... International Committee on Economic and Applied Microbiology [*ICSU*]   (EAIO)
ICEAP .... Instituto de Cooperativismo de Extensao Agro Pecuaria [*Brazil*]   (DSCA)
ICEB........ Indonesian Commodity Exchange Board [*Badan Pelaksana Bursa Komoditi*] [*Indonesia*]   (FEA)
ICEC .... International Committee of Enamelling Creators   (EAIO)
ICEC .... International Cryogenic Engineering Committee   (EAIO)
ICECA .... Indochina Ethnic Chinese Association of Victoria [*Australia*]
ICED......... International Coalition on Energy for Development
ICED......... International Congress on the Education of the Deaf
ICEED .... International Center for Energy and Economic Development
ICEF .... International Children's Emergency Fund [*United Nations*]   (DLA)
ICEL......... International Committee for Ethnic Liberty [*See also IKEL*]   (EAIO)
ICEL......... International Council of Environmental Law [*Bonn, Federal Republic of Germany*]   (EA)
ICEM........ International Confederation for Electroacoustic Music   (EA)
ICEP.......... Instituto do Comercio Externo (Lisbon, Portugal) [*Institute of Commercial Exports*]   (EY)
ICEPF........ International Commission for the Eriksson Prize Fund   (EAIO)
ICERA-VIC ... Indo-Chinese Elderly Refugee Association of Victoria [*Australia*]
ICES .... International Centre for Ethnic Studies   (EA)
ICES .... International Civil Engineering System   (ADPT)
ICES .... International Council for the Exploration of the Sea [*Denmark*]
ICESC....... International Committee for European Security and Co-Operation [*See also CISCE*]   (EAIO)
ICET.......... International Centre for Earth Tides [*See also CIMT*] [*Belgium*]   (EAIO)
ICEVH....... International Council for Education of the Visually Handicapped [*Bensheim, Federal Republic of Germany*]   (EAIO)
ICF............ International Canoe Federation [*See also FIC*] [*Florence, Italy*]   (EAIO)
ICF............ International Carpet Fair
ICF............ International Casting Federation   (EAIO)
ICF............ International Congregational Fellowship   (EA)
ICF............ International Congress on Fracture [*ICSU*] [*Sendai, Japan*]   (EAIO)
ICF............ International Cremation Federation   (EAIO)
ICF............ Societe des Ingenieurs Civils de France [*French*]   (ADPT)

ICFA .... International Computer Facsimile Association   (PS)
ICFCYP ..... International Centre of Films for Children and Young People [*France*]   (EY)
ICFFO .... International Council of Folklore Festival Organizations and Folk Art   (EA)
ICFG .... International Commission on Fungal Genetics [*International Council of Scientific Unions*]
ICFL .... International Council of the French Language [*See also CILF*] [*Paris, France*]   (EAIO)
ICFMH ...... International Committee on Food Microbiology and Hygiene [*ICSU*] [*Frederiksberg, Denmark*]   (EAIO)
ICFSHG .... International Committee of French-Speaking Historians and Geographers   (EAIO)
ICFSRT ..... International Council of French-Speaking Radio and Television   (EAIO)
ICFTU .... International Confederation of Free Trade Unions [*Belgium*]
ICFTU-ARO ... International Confederation of Free Trade Unions-Asian Regional Organisation [*India*]
ICFTUE .... International Center of Free Trade Unionists in Exile [*France*] [*Defunct*]
ICG .... Icelandic Coast Guard [*ICAO designator*]   (FAAC)
ICG .... Industria Conservera del Guayas [*Ecuador*]   (DSCA)
ICG .... International Commission on Glass [*See also CIV*] [*Prague, Czechoslovakia*]   (EAIO)
ICGEB .... International Centre for Genetic Engineering and Biotechnology [*United Nations Development Organization*]   (EAIO)
ICGEBNET ... International Centre for Genetic Engineering and Biotechnology Network [*United Nations Development Organization*]   (DUND)
ICGGI .... Internationale Coronelli-Gesellschaft fuer Globen- und Instrumentkunde [*International Coronelli Society - ICS*]   (EAIO)
ICGH .... International Confederation of Genealogy and Heraldry [*See also CIGH*] [*Paris, France*]   (EAIO)
ICGM .... International Colloquium about Gas Marketing   (EA)
ICGR .... Ivory Coast - Ghana Ridge [*Geology*]
ICHFST ..... International Council of Health Fitness and Sports Therapists [*British*]
ICHG .... International Conference on the Holocaust and Genocide   (EAIO)
ICHLM ..... International Conference of Historians of the Labour Movement [*Vienna, Austria*]   (EAIO)
ICHM .... International College of Hotel Management
ICHMT ...... International Centre for Heat and Mass Transfer   (EAIO)
ICHOHYP ... International Committee of Hard of Hearing Young People [*Frederiksberg, Denmark*]   (EAIO)
ICHP .... International Commission of Health Professionals for Health and Human Rights   (EA)
ICHR .... Inter-American Commission on Human Rights [*OAS*]   (PD)
ICHRPI ..... International Commission for the History of Representative and Parliamentary Institutions [*Rome, Italy*]   (EAIO)
ICHRT ...... International Committee for Human Rights in Taiwan   (EA)
ICHS .... Inter-African Committee for Hydraulic Studies [*See also CIEH*] [*Ouagadougou, Burkina Faso*]   (EAIO)
ICHS .... International Committee for Historical Sciences [*Paris, France*]   (EA)
ICHS .... International Council of Homehelp Services [*See also CISAF*] [*Driebergen-Rijsenburg, Netherlands*]   (EAIO)
ICHSMSS ... International Commission for the History of Social Movements and Social Structures [*Paris, France*]   (EAIO)
ICHSWW ... International Committee for the History of the Second World War   (EAIO)
ICHT .... International Council of Holistic Therapists [*British*]
ICHTSP .... International Conference on the Hydraulic Transport of Solids in Pipes   (PDAA)
ICHY .... International Council of Hindoo Youth   (EAIO)
ICI .... Cicia [*Fiji*] [*Airport symbol*]   (OAG)
ICI .... Imperial Chemical Industries Ltd. [*New Zealand*]   (DSCA)
ICI .... Instituto de Colonizacion e Inmigracion [*Colombia*]   (DSCA)
ICIA .... International Center of Information on Antibiotics   (EA)
ICIA .... International Credit Insurance Association [*Zurich, Switzerland*]   (EAIO)
ICIC .... International Copyright Information Centre [*UNESCO*]   (PDAA)
ICIC .... International Copyrights Information Center   (WDAA)
ICICI .... Industrial Credit & Investment Corp. of India Ltd.
ICID .... International Commission on Irrigation and Drainage [*See also CIID*] [*ICSU New Delhi, India*]   (EAIO)
ICIE .... International Center for Industry and the Environment   (DCTA)
ICIF .... International Cooperative Insurance Federation [*Manchester, England*]   (EAIO)
ICIFP .... Institutul de Cercetari Pentru Imbunatatiri Funciare si Pedologie [*Romania*]   (DSCA)
ICII .... International Culture Institute [*Japan*]   (EAIO)
ICIMOD .... International Centre for Integrated Mountain Development [*Kathmandu*]   (ECON)

ICIP .... Instituto Colombiano de Investigacion Pedagogica [*Colombia*]   (DSCA)
ICIP .... International Conference on Information Processing   (ADPT)
ICIPE .... International Centre of Insect Physiology and Ecology [*ICSU*] [*Nairobi, Kenya*]   (EAIO)
ICIS .... International Centre for Industrial Studies [*United Nations*]
ICJ .... International Commission of Jurists [*Switzerland*]
ICJ .... International Court of Justice [*United Nations*]
ICJAS .... International Commission of Jurists Australian Section
ICJC .... International Council of Jews from Czechoslovakia [*British*] [*Defunct*]   (EAIO)
ICK .... Interdepartmental Committee on Nuclear Energy [*Netherlands*]   (EY)
ICK .... Nieuw Nickerie [*Surinam*] [*Airport symbol*]   (OAG)
ICL .... Cavei Avir Lemitanim [*Israel*] [*ICAO designator*]   (FAAC)
ICL .... Instituto Cientifico de Lebu [*Chile*]   (DSCA)
ICL .... Interactive Computer Learning
ICL .... International Computer Ltd.   (ADPT)
ICL .... Inter-Union Commission on the Lithosphere [*NASA*]
ICLA .... Investigadores de Cafe de Latino America [*Costa Rica*]   (DSCA)
ICLAM ...... International Committee for Life Assurance Medicine [*Zurich, Switzerland*]   (EAIO)
ICLARM ... International Center for Living Aquatic Resources Management [*Makati, Metro Manila, Philippines*]   (EAIO)
ICLC .... International Centre for Local Credit [*The Hague, Netherlands*]   (EAIO)
ICLC .... International Congress on Lightweight Concrete   (PDAA)
ICLCP .... International Conference on Large Chemical Plants [*Antwerp, Belgium*]   (EAIO)
ICLR .... International Committee for Lift Regulations [*See also CIRA*] [*Saint-Yvelines, France*]   (EAIO)
ICLRSQ .... Incorporated Council of Law Reporting for the State of Queensland [*Australia*]
ICLT .... International Committee of Lawyers for Tibet
ICM .... Independent Citizens' Movement [*US Virgin Islands*]   (PPW)
ICM .... Integrated Catchment Management [*Water resources*]
ICM .... International Confederation of Midwives [*British*]   (EAIO)
ICM .... International Congress on Mechanical Behaviour of Materials   (EAIO)
ICM .... Soeurs Missionnaires du Coeur Immacule de Marie [*Missionary Sisters of the Immaculate Heart of Mary*] [*Italy*]   (EAIO)
ICMA .... International Christian Maritime Association [*Felixstone, Suffolk, England*]   (EAIO)
ICMA .... International Cigarette Makers' Association [*A union*]
ICMB .... International Center for Monetary and Banking Studies [*Switzerland*]   (ECON)
ICMC .... International Catholic Migration Commission [*See also CICM*] [*Geneva, Switzerland*]   (EAIO)
ICME .... International Clearinghouse on the Military and the Environment   (EA)
ICME .... International Congress on Mathematical Education [*International Council of Scientific Unions*]
ICME .... International Council on Metals and the Environment
ICMEDC ... International Council of Masonry Engineering for Developing Countries [*Formerly, International Symposium on Reinforced and Prestressed Masonry*]   (EA)
ICMG .... International Commission for Microbial Genetics [*International Council of Scientific Unions*]
ICMH .... International Commission of Military History
ICMI .... Indonesian Muslim Intellectuals Association [*Political party*]   (EY)
ICMI .... International Commission on Mathematical Instruction [*British*]
ICMICA .... Pax Romana, International Catholic Movement for Intellectual and Cultural Affairs [*See also MIIC*] [*Geneva, Switzerland*]   (EAIO)
ICMID ...... International Committee for Microbiological and Immunological Documentation [*International Council of Scientific Unions*]
ICMM .... International Committee of Military Medicine [*Belgium*]   (EAIO)
ICMMP ..... International Committee of Military Medicine and Pharmacy [*Belgium*]
ICMP .... International Confederation of Music Publishers [*British*]   (EAIO)
ICMP .... International Conference on Marine Pollution   (ILCA)
ICMPD ..... International Centre for Migration Policy Development [*Austria*]   (ECON)
ICMPH ..... International Center of Medical and Psychological Hypnosis [*Milan, Italy*]   (EA)
ICMR .... Indian Council of Medical Research
ICMS .... Institute of Club Managers and Secretaries [*Australia*]
ICMS .... International Centre for Mathematical Sciences [*Heriot-Watt University*]   (ECON)
ICMSA ...... Institute of Corporate Managers, Secretaries and Administrators [*Australia*]
ICMT .... International Commission on Mycotoxicology [*International Council of Scientific Unions*]
ICN .... International Communes Network   (EAIO)

ICN .... International Conference on Nutrition [*United Nations*]
ICN .... International Council of Nurses [*Switzerland*]   (EY)
ICNAF ...... International Committee of North American Federation
ICNCP ...... International Commission for the Nomenclature of Cultivated Plants [*Wageningen, Netherlands*]   (EA)
ICNDT ...... International Committee on NDT [*Nondestructive Testing*] [*Brazil*]   (EAIO)
ICNDT ...... International Conference on Non-Destructive Testing   (PDAA)
ICNEM ...... Internacia Centro de la Neutrala Esperanto-Movado [*International Center of the Neutral Esperanto Movement*] [*Defunct*]   (EAIO)
IC(NSW) ... Industrial Court New South Wales [*Australia*]
ICNV .... International Committee on Nomenclature of Viruses [*Later, ICTV*]
ICO .... Interim Conservation Order
ICO .... International Carbohydrate Organization [*Aberdeen, Scotland*]   (EAIO)
ICO .... International Catholic Organizations
ICO .... International Civil Aviation Organization [*ICAO designator*]   (FAAC)
ICO .... International Coffee Organization   (EAIO)
ICO .... International Commission for Optics [*See also CIO*] [*ICSU Delft, Netherlands*]   (EAIO)
ICO .... International Council of Ophthalmology   (EA)
ICOC .... International Commission for Orders of Chivalry   (EA)
ICOGRADA ... International Council of Graphic Design Associations [*British*]   (EA)
ICOH .... International Commission of Occupational Health   (EA)
ICOHTEC ... International Committee for the History of Technology   (EA)
ICOLD .... International Commission on Large Dams [*See also CIGB*] [*ICSU Paris, France*]   (EAIO)
ICOLP .... Industry Cooperative for Ozone Layer Protection
ICOM .... International Church of Metaphysics   (EA)
ICOM .... International Council of Museums [*France*]
ICOM-CC ... ICOM [*International Council of Museums*] Committee for Conservation   (EAIO)
ICOME ..... International Committee on Microbial Ecology [*ICSU*]   (EAIO)
ICOMIA .... International Council of Marine Industry Associations [*Weybridge, Surrey, England*]   (EA)
IComm(SA) ... Industrial Commission (South Australia)
ICOMOS ... International Council of Monuments and Sites [*France*]   (EA)
ICOMP ...... International Council on Management of Population Programmes [*Kuala Lumpur, Malaysia*]   (EAIO)
ICONMIG ... International Conference on Numerical Methods in Geomechanics
ICOS .... International Committee of Onomastic Sciences [*Belgium*]
ICOSI .... International Committee on Smoking Issues [*Brussels, Belgium*]   (EAIO)
ICP .... Indo-Chinese Communist Party [*Vietnam*] [*Political party*]   (VNW)
ICP .... Industry Cooperative Program [*United Nations*]
ICP .... Integrated Chemists of the Philippines
ICP .... International Classification of Patents [*Council of Europe*]   (PDAA)
ICP .... International Computer Programs   (ADPT)
ICP .... International Institute of Cellular and Molecular Pathology [*Belgium*]   (IRC)
ICP .... Inter-University Cooperation Program [*EC*]   (ECED)
ICP .... Iraqi Communist Party [*Political party*]   (PPW)
ICPAM ...... International Centre for Pure and Applied Mathematics [*United Nations*]   (EA)
ICPBR .... International Commission for Plant-Bee Relationships   (EAIO)
ICPC .... International Cable Protection Committee [*British*]   (EAIO)
ICPC .... International Commission of Catholic Prison Chaplains   (EA)
ICPC .... International Confederation of Popular Credit [*See also CICP*] [*Paris, France*]   (EAIO)
ICPCI .... International Conference on the Performance of Computer Installations   (PDAA)
ICPE .... International Center for Public Enterprises in Developing Countries [*Ljubljana, Yugoslavia*]   (EAIO)
ICPE .... International Conference on Public Education [*International Bureau of Education*] [*Switzerland*]
ICPEMC ... International Commission for Protection Against Environmental Mutagens and Carcinogens [*Rijswijk, Netherlands*]   (EAIO)
ICPES .... Intergovernmental Committee for Physical Education and Sport [*United Nations France*]   (EY)
ICPFR .... International Council for Physical Fitness Research [*Research center Canada*]   (IRC)
ICPHS .... International Council for Philosophy and Humanistic Studies [*Paris, France*]
ICPI .... Instituto Colombiano de Planeacion Integral [*Colombia*]   (DSCA)
ICPIC .... International Cleaner Production Information Clearinghouse   (GNE)
ICPIC .... International Conference on Phenomena in Ionised Gases   (PDAA)

ICPIC .... International Council for Philosophical Inquiry with Children [*Iceland*]   (EAIO)
ICPICH ..... International Commission for the Preservation of Islamic Cultural Heritage   (EA)
ICPIG .... International Conference on Phenomena in Ionised Gases   (PDAA)
ICPL .... International Committee of Passenger Lines   (PDAA)
ICPM .... International Congress of Physical Medicine   (PDAA)
ICPME ...... International Center for Peace in the Middle East   (EA)
ICPMP ...... International Commission for the Protection of the Moselle Against Pollution   (EA)
ICPMS ...... International Council of Prison Medical Services [*Vancouver, BC*]   (EAIO)
ICPO .... International Criminal Police Organization [*France*]
ICPRAP ..... International Commission for the Protection of the Rhine Against Pollution [*See also ICPRP, IKSR*] [*Germany*]   (EAIO)
ICPRCPCO ... Intergovernmental Committee for Promoting the Return of Cultural Property to Its Countries of Origin or Its Restitution in Case of Illicit Appropriation   (EA)
ICPS .... Institute for Cultural Policy Studies [*Griffith University*] [*Australia*]
ICPS .... International Cerebral Palsy Society [*British*]   (EAIO)
ICPTUR .... International Conference for Promoting Technical Uniformity on Railways [*Berne, Switzerland*]   (EAIO)
ICQC .... International Conference on Quality Control   (PDAA)
IC(Qld) ...... Industrial Court (Queensland) [*Australia*]
ICR .... Institute of Coal Research [*University of Newcastle*] [*Australia*]
ICR .... International Consumer Reports [*Consumers' Association*] [*British*] [*Information service or system*]   (IID)
ICR .... Nicaro [*Cuba*] [*Airport symbol*] [*Obsolete*]   (OAG)
ICRAF .... International Council for Research in Agroforestry [*See also ICRAF*] [*Kenya*]   (EAIO)
ICRA(V) .... Indo-Chinese Refugee Association (Victoria) [*Australia*]
ICRB .... International Co-Operative Reinsurance Bureau [*Manchester, England*]   (EAIO)
ICRC .... International Committee to the Red Cross [*Geneva, Switzerland*]   (EAIO)
ICRDD ...... Institute for Community Resource Development [*Australia*]
ICRGR .... International Consultative Research Group on Rape [*See also GCIRC*]   (EAIO)
ICRM .... International Cliff Richard Movement   (EAIO)
ICRO .... Interallied Confederation of Reserve Officers [*See also CIOR*]   (EAIO)
ICRO .... International Cell Research Organization [*ICSU*] [*Paris, France*]   (EAIO)
ICRP .... International Commission on Radiological Protection [*International Society of Radiology*] [*British*]
ICRPMA ... International Committee for Recording the Productivity of Milk Animals [*See also CICPLB*] [*Rome, Italy*]   (EAIO)
ICRW .... International Convention for the Regulation of Whaling   (ASF)
ICS .... Institute of Caribbean Science [*Puerto Rico*]   (DSCA)
ICS .... Intensive Care Society [*British*]   (EAIO)
ICS .... Inter-Celtic Society   (EAIO)
ICS .... Intercontinental Church Society [*British*]   (EAIO)
ICS .... Interlinked Computerized Storage and Processing System of Food and Agricultural Data [*Databank*] [*United Nations Information service or system*]   (IID)
ICS .... International Camellia Society [*Worcester, England*]   (EAIO)
ICS .... International Chamber of Shipping [*British*]   (EAIO)
ICS .... International Chemometrics Society [*Brussels, Belgium*]   (EAIO)
ICS .... International College of Scientists [*See also ISK*] [*International Academy of Sciences*] [*Paderborn, Federal Republic of Germany*]   (EAIO)
ICS .... International Committee of Slavists [*Sofia, Bulgaria*]   (EAIO)
ICS .... International Committee on Sarcoidosis [*British*]   (EAIO)
ICS .... International Communications System
ICS .... International Coronelli Society [*See also ICGGI*]   (EAIO)
ICSA .... Indian Council of South America [*See also CISA*] [*Lima, Peru*]   (EAIO)
IC(SA) .... Industrial Court (South Australia)
ICSA .... International Council Against Apartheid, Racism, and Colonialism in Southern Africa [*British*] [*Defunct*]   (EAIO)
ICSAF .... International Commission for the Southeast Atlantic Fisheries [*See also CIPASE*]   (EAIO)
ICSB .... International Committee on Systematic Bacteriology [*London, ON*]   (EA)
ICSC .... International Council of Shopping Centres [*Australia*]
ICSD .... Inorganic Crystal Structure Database [*University of Bonn*] [*Germany*]
ICSEAF .... International Commission for the Southeast Atlantic Fisheries
ICSEES ..... International Committee for Soviet and East European Studies   (EAIO)
ICSEM ...... International Commission for the Scientific Exploration of the Mediterranean Sea   (EAIO)
ICSG .... International Center for Social Gerontology [*Later, TCSG*] [*Defunct*]   (EA)

ICSH......... International Committee for Standardization in Haematology [*Louvain, Belgium*] [*Research center*] (EAIO)

ICSID .... International Council of Societies of Industrial Design [*Helsinki, Finland*] (EA)

ICSK .... International Cultural Society of Korea [*Seoul, Republic of Korea*] (EAIO)

ICSLS .... International Convention for Safety of Life at Sea (BARN)

ICSM........ International Confederation of Societies of Music (EA)

ICSOBA .... International Congress on Bauxite-Alumina-Aluminium (PDAA)

ICSPRDC ... International Committee on Social Psychological Research in Developing Countries (EA)

ICSR .... International Conference of Sociology of Religion [*Paris, France*] (EA)

ICSRE .... International Centre for Studies in Religious Education [*Brussels, Belgium*] (EAIO)

ICSS .... International Conference on Solid Surfaces

ICSSD .... International Committee for Social Science Information and Documentation [*Information service or system*] (IID)

ICSSEA ..... Integrated Communications System South-East Asia [*Australia*]

ICSSPE ..... International Council of Sport Science and Physical Education (EA)

ICSSVM.... International Commission for Small Scale Vegetation Maps [*Pondicherry, India*] (EAIO)

ICSTI........ International Center for Scientific and Technical Information [*Moscow, USSR*] (EAIO)

ICSTI........ International Council for Scientific and Technical Information [*Information service or system*] (IID)

ICSTND .... Information Center of Science and Technology for National Defense [*Chinese library*]

ICSU......... International Council of Scientific Unions [*Research center*] [*France*]

ICSU AB ... International Council of Scientific Unions Abstracting Board [*Also, IAB*] [*Later, ICSTI*] (EA)

ICSU-CTS ... Committee on the Teaching of Science of the International Council of Scientific Unions [*York, England*] (EAIO)

ICSUIA ..... Instituto de Ciencias Sociales de la Universidad Iberoamericana [*Mexico*] (DSCA)

ICSW........ International Committee on Seafarer's Welfare Office (EAIO)

ICSW........ International Council on Social Welfare (EA)

ICT............ Institute of Circuit Technology [*Oxford, England*] [*Defunct*] (EAIO)

ICT............ Instituto de Ciencias da Terra [*Brazil*] (DSCA)

ICT............ Intercontinental de Aviacion Ltd. [*Colombia*] [*ICAO designator*] (FAAC)

ICT............ International Campaign for Tibet (EA)

ICT............ International Commission on Trichinellosis (EA)

ICT............ International Computers and Tabulators Ltd. (ADPT)

ICT............ International Council of Tanners [*See also CIT*] [*Lewes, East Sussex, England*] (EAIO)

ICTA......... International Confederation for Thermal Analysis [*Jerusalem, Israel*] (EA)

ICTAM...... International Congress of Theoretical and Applied Mechanics (PDAA)

IC(Tas) ...... Industrial Commission (Tasmania) [*Australia*]

ICTB......... International Customs Tariffs Bureau (DLA)

ICTC......... Indian Central Tobacco Committee (DSCA)

ICTED....... International Cooperation in the Field of Transport Economics Documentation [*European Conference of Ministers of Transport*] [*Information service or system*] (IID)

ICTF .... International Cocoa Trades Federation [*British*]

ICTF .... International Conference on Thin Films (PDAA)

ICTH .... International Commission for the Teaching of History [*Brussels, Belgium*] (EA)

ICTME...... International Conference on Tribo-Terotechnology and Maintenance Engineering (PDAA)

ICTP .... International Center for Theoretical Physics [*Trieste, Italy*] (EA)

ICTR......... International Center of Theatre Research (EA)

ICTV......... International Committee on Taxonomy of Viruses [*ICSU*] [*Rennes, France*] (EAIO)

ICU .... International Code Use (BARN)

ICUAE...... International Congress of University Adult Education [*Fredericton, NB*] (EAIO)

ICUAER.... International Committee on Urgent Anthropological and Ethnological Research [*Vienna, Austria*] (EAIO)

ICUMSA... International Commission for Uniform Methods of Sugar Analysis [*Mackay, QLD, Australia*] (EAIO)

ICUS......... International Committee on Urgent Surgery [*Milan, Italy*] (EAIO)

ICV .... Indoor Cricket Victoria [*Australia*] [*An association*]

ICVA......... International Council of Voluntary Agencies (GNE)

ICVAN ...... International Committee on Veterinary Anatomical Nomenclature [*See also CINAV*] [*Zurich, Switzerland*] (EAIO)

ICVGAN.... International Committee on Veterinary Gross Anatomical Nomenclature [*Cornell University*] [*Ithaca, NY*] (EY)

ICW .... International Council of Women [*France*]

IC(WA)...... Industrial Appeal Court (Western Australia)

ICX .... International Charter Xpress Limited Liability Co. [*ICAO designator*] (FAAC)

ICX .... International Computer Exchange (ADPT)

ICY .... International Commission on Yeasts and Yeast-Like Microorganisms [*ICSU*] [*France*] (EAIO)

ICYO .... International Committee of Youth Organizations (EAIO)

ICYT......... Instituto de Informacion y Documentacion en Ciencia y Tecnologia [*Institute for Information and Documentation in Science and Technology*] [*Database originator and host*] [*Information service or system*] [*Spain*] (IID)

ICZN .... International Commission on Zoological Nomenclature [*British*] (EAIO)

ID.............. Indonesia [*ANSI two-letter standard code*] (CNC)

ID.............. Information and Documentation [*Royal Tropical Institute*] [*Information service or system*] (IID)

ID.............. Instituto de Investigaciones de las Naciones Unidas para el Desarrollo Social [*Switzerland*] (DSCA)

ID.............. Intelligence Division [*NATO*] (NATG)

ID.............. Iraqi Dinar [*Monetary unit*] (BJA)

ID.............. Islamic Dinar [*Monetary unit*] (EY)

ID.............. Izquierda Democratica [*Democratic Left*] [*Ecuador*] [*Political party*] (PPW)

IDA .... Indonesia Air Transport PT [*ICAO designator*] (FAAC)

IDA .... Industrial Development Abstracts [*Database*] [*UNIDO*] (CRD)

IDA .... International Desalination Association (EA)

IDA .... International Development Agency [*United Nations*] (NUCP)

IDA .... International Development Association (DSCA)

IDA .... International Dispensary Association [*Acronym is used as association name*] (EAIO)

IDA .... Islamic Democratic Alliance [*Pakistan*] [*Political party*]

IDAC .... International Disaster Advisory Committee

IDAF........ International Defence and Aid Fund for Southern Africa [*British*] (EAIO)

IDAGO ..... Instituto de Desenvolvimento Agrario de Goias [*Brazil*] (DSCA)

IDAK .... Integriertes Datenverarbeitungs-und Auskunfssystem [*German*] (ADPT)

IDAS......... International Database Access Service [*Bahrain Telecommunications Co.*] [*Information service or system*] (IID)

IDB .... Industrial Data Bank Department [*Gulf Organization for Industrial Consulting*] [*Qatar*] [*Information service or system*] (IID)

IDB .... Industrial Development Bank [*Jordan*]

IDB .... Industrial Development Bank [*Kenya*] (IMH)

IDB .... Insurance Development Bureau [*Guelph, ON*] (EAIO)

IDB .... Inter-American Development Bank [*Also, IADB*]

IDB .... Islamic Development Bank [*Saudi Arabia*]

IDB .... Israel Discount Bank

IDBI .... Industrial Development Bank of India (ECON)

IDBI .... Industrial Development Bank of Israel (IMH)

IDBRA...... International Drivers' Behaviour Research Association [*Paris, France*] (EAIO)

IDBT......... Industrial Development Bank of Turkey (PDAA)

IDC .... Industries Development Committee

IDC .... Information and Documentation Center [*Royal Institute of Technology Library*] [*Information service or system*] (IID)

IDC .... International Dance Council [*See also CIDD*] (EAIO)

IDC .... International Data Connector

IDC .... International Data Corp. (ADPT)

IDC .... International Diamond Council [*Antwerp, Belgium*] (EAIO)

IDC .... Internationale Democrate Chretienne [*Christian Democrat International*] [*Belgium*] (EAIO)

IDCA .... International Dolphin Conservation Act [*1993*]

IDCA .... International Dragon Class Association (EAIO)

IDCAS...... Industrial Development Center for Arab States [*Later, AIDO*]

IDCC......... Inter-Departmental Consultative Committee

IDCCC ...... International Dredging Conference Coordinating Committee (EAIO)

IDCFC ...... International David Cassidy Fan Club (EAIO)

IDD........... Institute for Drafting and Design [*Australia*]

IDDP .... International Dairy Development Programme [*FAO/DANIDA Dairy Development Programme and International Scheme for the Coordination of Dairy Development*] [*Formed by a merger of United Nations*]

IDDRG ...... International Deep Drawing Research Group [*British*]

IDEA .... Instituto para el Desarrollo de Antioquia [*Colombia*] (DSCA)

IDEA .... Interaktive Daten-Eingabe und -Abfrage [*German*] (ADPT)

IDEA .... International Desalination and Environmental Association [*Later, IDA*] (EA)

IDEAS ...... International Data Exchange for Aviation Safety [*ICAO*] (DA)

IDEB........ Interessenvereinigung der EDV Benutzer [*German*] (ADPT)

IDECA...... Industria e Comercio do Cafe Ltd. [*Brazil*] (DSCA)

IDEF .... Institut International de Droit d'Expression Francaise [*International Institute of Law of the French Speaking Countries - IILFSC*] [*Paris, France*] (EAIO)

IDEP......... Institut Africain de Developpement Economique et de Planification [*African Institute for Economic Development and Planning*] [*Dakar, Senegal*] (AF)
IDER......... Instituto Dominicano de Educacion Rural [*Dominican Republic*] (DSCA)
IDESP....... Instituto de Desenvolvimento Economico e Social do Para [*Brazil*] (DSCA)
IDF............ Industrial Diesel Fuel
IDF............ International Dairy Federation [*See also FIL*] [*Brussels, Belgium*] (EAIO)
IDF............ International Diabetes Federation [*See also FID*] (EAIO)
IDF............ International Drilling Fluids [*Singapore*]
IDF............ Iron Dragon-Fly Ltd. [*Russian Federation*] [*ICAO designator*] (FAAC)
IDFA......... International Dairy Foods Association (EA)
IDFB......... Internationales Daunen- und Federn-Bureau [*International Down and Feather Bure au*] (EAIO)
IDH........... International Data Highways Ltd. (ADPT)
IDHIDH.... In dem Herrn Ist das Heil [*In the Lord Is Salvation*] [*Motto of Dorothee, Princess of Anhalt (1580-1618)*] [*German*]
IDI .... International Diabetes Institute [*Australia*] (IRC)
IDIA.......... Informativo de Investigacions Agricolas [*Argentina*] (DSCA)
IDIC.......... International Drought Information Center
IDII........... Institut za Drvno-Industriska Istrazivanja [*Research Institute on Industrial Utilization of Wood*] (YU)
IDIK.......... Integrierte Datenverarbeitung l.c. Krankenhaus [*German*] (ADPT)
idiopath...... Idiopathisch [*Idiopathic*] [*German*] (GCA)
IDIR.......... Institute for Development and International Relations [*Canton and Enderbury Islands*] (EAIO)
IDIS........... Industrial Drip Irrigation System
IDIS........... Institut fuer Dokumentation und Information ueber Sozialmedizin und Oeffentliches Gesundheitswesen [*Institute for Documentation and Information in Social Medicine and Public Health*] [*Information retrieval*] [*Germany*]
idJ .... In Diesem Jahr [*In This Year*] [*Correspondence*] [*German*]
IDJEN....... Inspektur Djenderal [*Inspector General*] (IN)
IDK .... Iktisadi Devlet Kurulus [*Economic State Enterprise*] (TU)
IDK .... Individual Decontamination Kit (RU)
IDK .... Integrierte Datenverarbeitung fuer Kommunalverwaltungen [*German*] (ADPT)
IdK .... Internationale der Kriegsdienstgegner [*Conscientious Objectors' International*] [*Switzerland*] (WEN)
IDK .... Irodalomtorteneti Dokumentacios Kozpont [*Documentation Center for Literary History*] (HU)
IDKD .... Istanbul Demokratik Kultur Dernegi [*Istanbul Democratic Cultural Organization*] (TU)
IDM .... Institute of Defence Management [*India*] (PDAA)
IDM .... Institute of Development Management [*Ministry of Manpower Development*] [*Tanzania*]
IDM .... Instituto de Desarrollo Municipal [*Municipal Development Institute*] [*Paraguay*] (GEA)
IDM .... International Data Management [*India*] (PDAA)
IDMA .... Indian Drug Manufacturers Association (PDAA)
IDMA .... International Dancing Masters Association (BARN)
IDMA .... International Destination Management Association (EAIO)
IDMMA .... Istanbul Devlet Mimarlik ve Muhendislik Akademisi [*Istanbul State Academy of Architecture and Engineering*] [*DMMA*] [*See also*] (TU)
IDMS........ Industrie de Matieres Synthetiques
IDMS........ Intreprinderea de Difuzare a Materialelor Sportive [*Enterprise for the Dissemination of Sports Equipment*] (RO)
IDN........... Indagen [*Papua New Guinea*] [*Airport symbol*] (OAG)
IDN........... Indonesia [*ANSI three-letter standard code*] (CNC)
IDN........... Integriertes Daten-Netz [*German*] (ADPT)
IDN........... Integriertes Fernschreib-und Datennetz [*German*] (ADPT)
IDN........... Integriertes Text-und Datennetz [*German*] (ADPT)
IDNDR ...... International Decade for Natural Disaster Reduction [*1990's*] [*United Nations*]
IDO........... Degradation Failure Rate (RU)
IDO........... Industrial Development Organization [*United Nations*]
IDO........... International Disarmament Organization
IDO........... Santa Isabel Do Morro [*Brazil*] [*Airport symbol*] (OAG)
IDO........... Societe Industrie des Oleagineux
IDOC........ International Documentation and Communication Center [*Formerly, Council for Development of Religious Information and Documentation - IDOC International*] [*Rome, Italy*] (SLS)
IDOC........ International Documentation on the Contemporary Church [*Later, International Documentation and Communication Center*] (EA)
IDOCO...... Internationale des Organisations Culturelles Ouvrieres [*Austria*] (EAIO)
idorb.......... Engineer Road Battalion (RU)
idorbr .... Engineer Road Brigade (RU)
idorp.......... Engineer Road Regiment (RU)

idorr .... Engineer Road Company (RU)
IDORT ...... Instituto de Organizacao Racional do Trabalho [*Institute for the Efficient Organization of Labor*] [*Brazil*] (LA)
idorv .... Engineer Road Platoon (RU)
IDP .... Independent Democratic Party [*Liberia*] [*Political party*] (EY)
IDP .... Independent Democratic Party [*Gibraltar*] [*Political party*]
IDP .... Individual Decontamination Kit (RU)
IDP .... Institut pour le Developpement et le Progres [*Institute for Development and Progress*] [*Mauritius*] (AF)
IDP .... Italian Democratic Party (RU)
IDPB......... Intreprinderea de Drumuri si Poduri Bucuresti [*Bucharest Enterprise for Roads and Bridges*] (RO)
IDPC......... Intreprinderea de Desfacere a Produselor Chimice [*Enterprise for the Sale of Chemical Products*] (RO)
IDPD .... Institut du Droit de la Paix et du Developpement [*Institute for Peace Law and Development*] [*France*] (IRC)
IDPJI......... Intreprinderea de Drumuri si Poduri a Judetului Ilfov [*Ilfov County Enterprise for Roads and Bridges*] (RO)
IDPL......... Indian Drugs and Pharmaceuticals Ltd. (PDAA)
IDPM .... Institute of Data Processing Management [*DPMA and Institute of Data Processing - IDP*] [*Formed by a merger of*] (EAIO)
IDPT......... International Donkey Protection Trust (EAIO)
i dr............ And Others (BU)
i dr............. And Others, The Rest (RU)
IDR .... Indore [*India*] [*Airport symbol*] (OAG)
IDR .... Institut du Developpement Rural [*Rural Development Institute*] [*Congo*]
IDR .... Institute for Development Research [*Denmark*]
IDR .... Institute of Development Research [*Ethiopia*] (IRC)
IDR .... International Drawing Rights
IDRAS....... Institute of Desert Research, Academia Sinica [*China*] [*Research center*] (IRC)
IDRC .... International Development Research Centre [*ICSU*] [*Research center Canada*]
IDREM...... Institut de Documentation de Recherches et d'Etudes Maritimes
IDRF......... International Development and Refugee Foundation
Idr IlmFak ... Idare Ilimler Fakultesi [*Administrative Science Faculty (of METU)*] [*Ankara*] (TU)
IDRO......... Industrial Development and Renovation Organization [*Iran*] (ME)
IDRP......... Intellectual Disability Review Panel
IDRP......... Irrigation and Drainage Research Project
i dr pod .... Et Cetera (BU)
IDRS......... Intellectual Disability Rights Service [*Australia*] (EAIO)
i dr t........... Et Cetera (BU)
IDS............ Dispersing Power Index (RU)
IDS............ Identifikacni Skupina [*Identification Group*] (CZ)
IDS............ Income Distribution Survey
IDS............ Institute for Development Studies of the University of Nairobi
IDS............ Institut fuer Deutsche Sprache [*Institute for German Language*] [*Information service or system*] (IID)
IDS............ Instituto de Desarrollo de Salud [*Institute for Health Development*] [*Cuba*] (LA)
IDS............ Integrierte Datenspeicherung [*German*] (ADPT)
IDS............ Intellectual Disability Services [*Australian Capital Territory, Queensland*]
IDS............ International Dealer Systems (ADPT)
IDS............ International Development Services, Inc.
IDS............ International Development Strategy [*United Nations*]
IDS............ Israel Dermatological Society (EAIO)
IDSA......... Indian Dairy Science Association (SLS)
IDSA......... Instituto Dominicano de Servicios Agrarios [*Dominican Institute of Agrarian Services*] [*Dominican Republic*] (LA)
IDSC......... Interior Designer Spanish Council (EAIO)
IDSC......... International Distributed Systems Centre [*German*] (ADPT)
ID(SM)...... In Diens van Sy Majesteit [*In Service of His Majesty*] [*Afrikaans*]
IDSO .... International Diamond Security Organization (BARN)
IDSO .... Istanbul Devlet Senfoni Orkestrasi [*Istanbul State Symphony Orchestra*] (TU)
IDSS .... Instituto Dominicana de Seguros Sociales [*Dominican Social Security Institute*] [*Dominican Republic*] (LA)
IDSS .... International Development Support Services Pty. Ltd. [*Australia*] (ECON)
IDSSA ...... Infectious Diseases Society of Southern Africa (EAIO)
IDT .... Corrective Labor Home (RU)
IDT .... Iktisadi Devlet Tesekkulleri [*Economic State Enterprises*] (TU)
IDT .... Imprimerie du Tchad
idt .... In de Tekst [*In the Text*] [*Publishing*] [*Netherlands*]
IDT .... Institute of Drug Technology Ltd. [*Australia*]
IDT .... Institutul de Documentare Tehnica [*Institute for Technical Documentation*] (RO)
IDT .... Integriertes, Dialogorientiertes Testsystem [*German*] (ADPT)
IDT .... International Discount Telecommunications (ECON)
IDT .... Island's Dawn for Trading [*Saudi Arabia*] [*Commercial firm*]
IDTA .... Institute of Drug Technology Australia

IDTC.......... Industrial Development Technical Centre [*Doha, Qatar*] (MENA)

IDTC.......... Industrial Studies and Development Centre [*Riyadh, Saudi Arabia*] (MENA)

IDTF....... International Documents Task Force

IDTs.......... Radar Moving-Target Indicator (RU)

IDU............ Instituto de Desarrollo Urbano [*Urban Development Institute*] [*Colorado*] (LA)

IDU............ International Democrat Union (EA)

iDurchschn ... Im Durchschnitt [*On the Average*] [*German*] (EG)

IDUSCOA ... Societe Industrielle de Conservation Agricole [*Morocco*]

IDV............ Institut fuer Datenverwaltung [*German*] (ADPT)

IDV............ Integrierte Datenverarbeitung [*Integrated Data Processing*] (EG)

IDV............ Internationaler Deutschlehrerverband [*International Association of Teachers of German - IATG*] [*Copenhagen, Denmark*] (EAIO)

IDV............ Istorisko Drustvo Vojvodine [*Historical Society of Vojvodina*] (YU)

IdV Bank ... Innerdeutsche Verrechnungsbank [*Inner-German Clearing Bank*] (EG)

IDVC .... Import and Delivery Verification Certificate [*Singapore*]

IdW............ Institut Der Wirtschaftspruefer [*Institute of Accountants*] [*Germany*]

IDW.......... Institut fuer Dokumentationswesen [*German*]

IDWSSD ... International Drinking Water Supply and Sanitation Decade

Id Yp.......... Idiaitera Ypiresia [*Special Service*] [*In datelines*] (GC)

IDZA .... Interdepartementale Documentatiezaken [*Ministerie Binnenlandse Zaken, 's-Gravenhage*]

IDZ-B .... Internationales Design Zentrum Berlin [*International Design Center Berlin*] [*Germany*] (EAIO)

IE .... Electric Welding Institute (RU)

IE .... Fighter Squadron (RU)

IE .... Idees pour l'Europe [*Paris, France*] (EAIO)

ie................. Id Est [*That is to say*] [*Latin*] (EECI)

ie................. Idoszamitasunk Elott [*Before Christ*] (HU)

IE .... Industrie-Entwurf [*Industrial Designing Office*] (EG)

IE .... Industriele Eigendom [*Benelux*] (BAS)

IE .... Information Express [*Australia*]

IE .... Informations Economiques [*Benelux*] (BAS)

IE .... Institut Egyptien

IE .... Institute of Economics (of the Academy of Sciences, USSR) (RU)

IE .... Institute of Ethnography Imeni N. N. Miklukho-Maklay (of the Academy of Sciences, USSR) (RU)

IE .... Institution of Engineers [*India*] (PDAA)

IE .... Instructor Education [*Diving*] [*Australia*]

IE .... International Units (BU)

IE .... Ireland [*ANSI two-letter standard code*] (CNC)

IE .... Measuring Element (RU)

IE .... Pulse Element (RU)

ie................. That Is (TPFD)

IEA .... Import Entitlement Agreement [*United Arab Republic*]

IEA .... Industrias Electricas Asociadas [*Colombia*] (COL)

IEA .... Ingenieria Electronica Aplicada [*Colombia*] (COL)

IEA .... Institut de l'Enseignement pour Adultes

IEA .... Institut Economique Agricole [*Institute of Agricultural Economics*] [*Research center*] [*Belgium*] (IRC)

IEA .... Institution of Engineers, Australia (ADA)

IEA .... Instituto de Economia Agricola [*Agricultural Economy Institute*] [*Brazil*] (LA)

IEA .... Instituto de Energia Atomica [*Atomic Energy Institute*] [*Brazil*] (LA)

IEA .... Instituto de Experimentaciones Agropecuarias [*Institute for Experimental Dairy Farming*] [*Sante Fe, Argentina*] (LAA)

IEA .... Instytut Energii Atomowej [*Institute of Atomic Energy*] [*Poland*] (WND)

IEA .... Intereuropean Airways Ltd. [*British*] [*ICAO designator*] (FAAC)

IEA .... InterExchanges Assistance [*An association*] [*France*] (EAIO)

IEA .... International Association for the Evaluation of Educational Achievement [*See also AIERS*] [*University of Stockholm*] [*Sweden*] (EAIO)

IEA .... International Economic Association [*See also AISE*] [*Paris, France*] (EAIO)

IEA .... Internationale Energieagentur [*International Energy Agency*] (WEN)

IEA .... International Emergency Action [*See also AUI*] [*Paris, France*] (EAIO)

IEA .... International Energy Agency [*OECD*] [*Research center*] [*France*] (IRC)

IEA .... International Ergonomics Association (EA)

IEA .... Intreprinderea de Elemente pentru Automatizari [*Enterprise for Automation Elements*] (RO)

IEAA.......... Institut d'Etudes Administratives Africaines [*Institute of African Administrative Studies*] (AF)

IEAB.......... Internacia Esperanto-Asocio de Bibliotekistoj [*International Association of Esperanto-Speaking Librarians*] [*Later, IAEL*] (EA)

IEABS .... Intreprinderea Economica de Administrare a Bazelor Sportive [*Economic Enterprise for the Administraton of Sports Installations*] (RO)

IEACS .... Institut Europeen des Armes de Chasse et de Sport [*European Institute of Hunting and Sporting Weapons - EIHSW*] (EAIO)

IEAF.......... Imperial Ethiopian Air Force (AF)

IEAG .... Instituto Ecuatoriano de Antropologia y Geografia [*Ecuador*] (DSCA)

IEAJ .... Internacia Esperanto - Asocio de Juristoj [*International Esperanto - Association of Jurists*] [*Graz, Austria*] (EAIO)

IEAP.......... Ilektriki Etaireia Athinon-Peiraios [*Athens-Piraeus Electric Company*] (GC)

IEAP......... Institut Europeen d'Administration Publique [*European Institute of Public Administration - EIPA*] (EAIO)

IEAR.......... Instituto de Energia Atomica Reactor [*Brazil*] (NRCH)

IEAR.......... Internacia Esperanto-Amikaro de Rotarianoj [*International Esperanto Fellowship of Rotarians*] [*British*] (EAIO)

IEAS.......... Instituto de Estudios Agro-Sociales [*Spain*] (DSCA)

IEAS.......... International Economic Appraisal Service [*The Economist Publications Ltd.*] [*British*] [*Information service or system*]

IEAT.......... Importers and Exporters Association of Taipei [*Taiwan*] (EAIO)

IEAT.......... Industrial Estates Authority of Thailand (GEA)

IEAT.......... Institute of Electronics, Automation, and Remote Control (of the Academy of Sciences, Georgian SSR) (RU)

IEAust....... Institution of Engineers of Australia

IEAv.......... Instituto de Estudos Avancados [*Institute of Advanced Studies*] [*Research center*] [*Brazil*] (IRC)

IEAZ.......... Instituto Experimental de Agricultura Zootecnica [*Experimental Institute of Agriculture and Animal Husbandry*] (LAA)

IE B........... Industriele Eigendom, Bijblad [*Benelux*] (BAS)

IEB........... Institute of Experimental Biology (RU)

IEB........... Instituto de Estudos Brasileiros [*Institute of Brazilian Studies*] [*Rio De Janeiro*] (LAA)

IEB........... Integrierte Elektronische Baugruppe [*German*] (ADPT)

IEB........... Intreprinderea Electrocentrale Bucuresti [*Bucharest Electric Power Enterprise*] (RO)

IEBiM....... Institute of Experimental Biology and Medicine (of the Siberian Department of the Academy of Sciences, USSR) (RU)

IEBS .... Institut d'Ecologie du Bassin de la Somme [*French*] (ASF)

IEBS .... Intreprinderea de Exploatare a Bazelor Sportive [*Enterprise for the Utilization of Sports Installations*] (RO)

IEC............ Institut d'Etudes Centrafricaines

IEC............ Institute of Early Childhood [*Macquarie University*] [*Australia*]

IEC............ Institut Europeen de la Communication [*European Institute for the Media - EIM*] (EAIO)

IEC............ Instituto de Electronica de Comunicaciones [*Electronic Communications Institute*] [*Madrid, Spain*] [*Research center*] (ERC)

IEC............ Instituto Evandro Chagas [*Brazil*]

IEC............ Intensive English Centre [*Australia*]

IEC............ Interface Efficiency Council [*Computer science*]

IEC............ International Egg Commission [*British*] (EAIO)

IEC............ International Electrotechnical Commission [*See also CEI*] [*Standards body Geneva, Switzerland*] (EAIO)

IEC............ Internationales Electronic Comitee (ADPT)

IEC............ International Exchange Center [*Latvia*] (EAIO)

IEC............ Israel Electric Corp. (PDAA)

IECA.......... Imperial Ethiopian College of Agriculture [*Ethiopia*] (DSCA)

IECA.......... Instituto Espanol del Cemento y sus Aplicaciones [*Spanish Institute of Cement and Its Applications*] (EAIO)

IECAMA... Imperial Ethiopian College of Agriculture and Mechanical Arts

IECCF .... Intreprinderea de Electrificare si Centralizare Cai Ferate [*Enterprise for the Electrification and Centralization of Railways*] (RO)

IECD.......... Institute of Early Childhood Development [*Melbourne College of Advanced Education*] [*Australia*]

IECE.......... Instituto Ecuatoriano de Credito Educativo [*Ecuadorean Institute of Educational Credit*] (LA)

IECEE .... International Electrotechnical Commission System for Conformity Testing to Standards for Safety of Electrical Equipment [*Switzerland*] (EA)

IECES....... Instituto de Investigaciones Escuela de Ciencias Economicas y Sociales [*Costa Rica*] (DSCA)

IECI.......... Institute for Esperanto in Commerce and Industry [*Netherlands*] (SLS)

IECIC .... International Engineering and Construction Industries Council (PDAA)

IECL.......... International Esperantist Chess League [*See also ESLI*] (EAIO)

IECLB .... Igreia Evangelica de Confissao Luterana do Brasil [*Protestant church*] [*Brazil*] (EY)

IECMGM ... Intreprinderea de Exploatare a Conductelor Magistrale de Gaz Metan [*Enterprise for the Exploitation of Main Pipelines for Methane Gas*] (RO)

IECN .... Instituto Ecuatoriano de Ciencias Naturales [*Ecuadorean Institute for Natural Sciences*] [*Quito*] (LAA)
IED .... Ilektroenergetiki Dynamis [*Electromotive Force*] (GC)
IED .... Information Engineering Directorate [*Japan*]
IEDA .... Institut d'Etudes du Developpement Africain
IEDC .... Illawarra Economic Development Council [*Australia*]
IEDC .... International Energy Development Corporation
IEDES .... Institut d'Etude du Developpement Economique et Social [*Institute for the Study of Economic and Social Development*] [*French*] (WER)
IEDI .... Instituto Ecuatoriano de Derecho Internacional [*Ecuadorean Institute of International Law*] (LA)
IeDLIP....... Lembaga Ilmu Pengetahuan Indonesia, Pusat Dokumentasi Ilmiah Nasional, Jakarta, Indonesia [*Library symbol*] [*Library of Congress*] (LCLS)
IEDOM ..... Institut d'Emissions des Departements d'Outre-Mer [*Overseas Departements Institute for Broadcasting*] [*French Guiana*] (LA)
IEDS.......... Income Equalization Deposits Scheme
IEDS.......... International Environmental Data Service [*European Commodities Exchange*] [*United Nations*] (DUND)
IEE .... Institut des Etudes Ethiopiennes [*Institute for Ethiopian Studies*] (EAIO)
IEE .... International Institute for Hydraulic and Environmental Engineering [*Netherlands*] (IRC)
IEEA .... Instituto de Ecologia e Experimentacao Agricola [*Brazil*] (LAA)
IEEE .... Institute of Electrical and Electronics Engineers
IEEE .... Instituto Espanol del Envase y Embalaje [*Spain*] (EAIO)
IEEE .... Istoriki kai Ethnologiki Etaireia tis Ellados [*Greek Historical and Ethnological Society*] (GC)
IEEFI........ Institut Europeen pour l'Etude des Fibres Industrielles [*French*] (SLS)
IEENSW ... Institution of Electrical Engineers New South Wales [*Australia*]
IEEP .... Institute for European Environmental Policy [*Germany*] (EAIO)
IEER .... Institute of Energy and Earth Resources [*CSIRO*]
IEEU......... Instituto de Estudios de Estados Unidos [*Studies Mexico/US relations, US domestic politics, US economy, and US foreign policy*] [*Mexico*] (CROSS)
IEEV .... Institution of Electrical Engineers Victoria [*Australia*]
IEF .... Institute of Evolutionary Physiology Imeni I. M. Sechenov (of the Academy of Sciences, USSR) (RU)
IEF .... Instituto de Economia y Finanzas (de la Universidad Nacional de Cordoba) [*Argentina*] (LAA)
IEF .... Instituto Estadual de Florestas [*Brazil*] (DSCA)
IEF .... International Equestrian Federation (EAIO)
IEF .... Izmir Enternasyonal Fuari
IEFAEP..... Instituto de Ejecutivos Financieros y Administrativos de Empresas Publicas [*Public Enterprise Executives Institute*] [*Peru*] (LA)
IEF-Chile... Instituto de Estudios del Futuro - Chile (SLS)
IEFE .... Istituto di Economia delle Fonti di Energia [*Italian*] (SLS)
IEFM........ Intreprinderea de Exploatare a Flotei Maritime [*Enterprise for the Operation of the Maritime Fleet*] (RO)
IEFR .... International Emergency Food Reserve
IEFR .... International Esperanto Fellowship of Rotarians [*See also IEAR*] (EAIO)
IEFS.......... Institutul de Educatie Fizica si Sport [*Institute for Physical Education and Sports*] (RO)
IEG .... Zielona Gora [*Poland*] [*Airport symbol*] (OAG)
IEGA .... Instituto de Economia y Geografia Aplicadas [*Institute of Applied Economics and Geography*] [*Spain*] (IRC)
IEGF......... Imperial Ethiopian Ground Forces (AF)
IEGR......... Imperial Ethiopian Government Railways (AF)
IEH .... Instituto de Edafologia e Hidrologia [*Argentina*] (DSCA)
IEHA .... International Economic History Association [*Paris, France*] (EA)
IE-HAS ..... Institute of Economics - Hungarian Academy of Sciences (EAIO)
IEI .... Institut d'Etudes Islamiques [*Institute for Islamic Studies*] (AF)
IEI .... Institute of Engineering Economics Imeni Sergo Ordzhonikidze (RU)
IEI .... Institution of Engineers of Ireland (SLS)
IEI .... Internacia Esperanto Instituto [*International Esperanto Institute*] [*Netherlands*] (EAIO)
IEI .... International Enamellers Institute [*Derby, England*] (EAIO)
IEI .... Istituto Ecologico Internazionale [*Italian*] (SLS)
IEI .... Istituto Erpetologico Italiano [*Italian*] (SLS)
IEI .... Ivanovo Power Engineering Institute Imeni V. I. Lenin (RU)
IEIA .... Insurance Employers' Industrial Association [*Australia*]
IEIAS........ Institut Europeen Interuniversitaire de l'Action Sociale [*Inter-University European Institute on Social Welfare - IEISW*] (EAIO)
IEICE .... Institute of Electronics, Information, and Communication Engineers [*Japan*] (EAIO)

IEILIFGA ... Intreprinderea de Exploatare si Intretinere a Lucrarilor de Imbunatatiri Funciare si Gospodarirea Apelor [*Enterprise for the Exploitation and Maintenance of Land Improvement Projects and Water Management*] (RO)
IEiOP........ Instytut Ekonomiki i Organizacji Przemyslu [*Institute of Industrial Economics and Organizations*] (POL)
IEISW .... Inter-University European Institute on Social Welfare (EA)
IEJ .... Institut Europeen du Jouet [*European Toy Institute - ETI*] (EAIO)
IEJE .... Institut d'Etudes Juridiques Europeennes [*Benelux*]
IEJE .... Institut Economique et Juridique de l'Energie [*Energy Economic and Legal Insitute*] [*France*] (PDAA)
IEKA......... Internacia Esperanto Klubo Automobilista [*International Automobile Esperanto Club*] (EAIO)
IEL............ Industrial Engineering Limited [*Australia*] (ADA)
IEL............ Industrial Equity Ltd. [*Australia*]
IEL............ International Electrochemical Commission
IEL............ Istanbul Erkek Lisesi [*Istanbul Men's Lycee*] (TU)
IELA .... International Exhibition Logistics Associates [*Geneva, Switzerland*] (EAIO)
IELAN....... Institute of Electrochemistry of the Academy of Sciences, USSR (RU)
IELC .... International Environmental Law Centre [*Australia*]
IELG .... International Esperantist League for Go (EA)
IELTS .... International English Language Testing Service [*Australia*]
iem............. Iemand [*Somebody*] [*Afrikaans*]
IEM .... Ilektriki Etaireia Metaforon [*Electric Transport Company Ltd.*] [*Greek*] (GC)
IEM .... Infectious Encephalomyelitis (of Horses) (RU)
IEM .... Institut de l'Enseignement Medical [*Medical Teaching Institute*] [*Zaire*] (AF)
IEM .... Institute of Electromechanics (RU)
IEM .... Institute of Epidemiology and Microbiology (RU)
IEM .... Institute of Evolutionary Morphology Imeni Academician A. N. Severtsov (RU)
IEM .... Institute of Experimental Medicine (of the Academy of Medical Sciences, USSR) (RU)
IEM .... Institute of Experimental Mineralogy [*Commonwealth of Independent States*]
IEM .... Institute of Experimental Morphogenesis (RU)
IEM .... Institution of Engineers, Malaysia (EAIO)
IEM .... Instituto Emissor de Macau [*Issuing Authority of Macao*] (GEA)
IEM .... Instituut vir Elektronmikroskopie [*Institute for Electron Microscopy*] [*South African Medical Research Council*] (AA)
IEMA .... Indian Electrical Manufacturers Association (PDAA)
IEMAC..... Israeli-Egyptian Mixed Armistice Commission
IEMAE...... Institute of Evolutionary Morphology and Animal Ecology [*Commonwealth of Independent States*]
IEMBAL ... Instituto de Envase y Embalaje [*Canning and Packing Institute*] [*Ecuador*] (LA)
IEMC........ Imperial Ethiopian Marine Corps (AF)
IEMF........ Imperial Ethiopian Military Forces (AF)
IEMG .... Scientific Research Institute of Epidemiology, Microbiology, and Hygiene (RU)
IEMI.......... Intreprinderea de Aparate Electronice de Masura si Industriale [*Enterprise for Electronic Measurement and Industrial Instruments*] (RO)
IEMMI...... Instituto de Estudios de la Marina Mercante Iberoamericana [*Argentina*] (LAA)
IEMS........ Institute of Extra-Mural Studies [*Lesotho*]
IEMSA...... Institution of Engineering and Mining Surveyors, Australia
IEMSS....... Institute of Economics of the World Socialist System (of the Academy of Sciences, USSR) (RU)
IEON........ International Esperantist Organization of Naturists [*See also INOE*] [*Frankfurt, Federal Republic of Germany*] (EAIO)
IEP............ Institut fuer Europaeische Politik [*Institute of European Politics*] (EAIO)
IEP............ Instituto de Educacion Popular [*Chile*] (DSCA)
IEPA.......... Istituto di Economia e Politica di Agraria [*Italy*] (DSCA)
IEPALA..... Instituto de Estudios Politicos para America Latina y Africa [*Spain*]
IEPAP .... Instituto de Experimentacao e Pesquisas Agropecuarias [*Brazil*] (DSCA)
IEPE......... Instituto de Estudos e Pesquisas Economicas [*Brazil*] (DSCA)
IEPFCHK ... International Elvis Presley Fan Club, Hong Kong (EAIO)
IEPG......... Independent European Program Group [*NATO*]
IER............ Impression/Enregistrement de Resultats [*French*] (ADPT)
IER............ Organization for International Economic Relations [*Vienna, Austria*] (EAIO)
IERA......... Institut d'Etudes et de Recherches pour l'Arabisation [*French*] (ADPT)
IERE .... Institute of Electronics and Radio Engineers [*British*]
IERESM.... Institut Europeen de Recherches et d'Etudes Superieures en Management [*European Institute for Advanced Studies in Management - EIASM*] [*Brussels, Belgium*] (EA)

IERH .... Instituto Ecuatoriano de Recursos Hidraulicos [*Ecuador*] (DSCA)
IERP .... Instituto de Educacion Rural de Panama [*Panama*] (DSCA)
IERS .... International Earth Rotation Services
IERS .... International Educational Reporting Service [*International Bureau of Education*] [*United Nations*] (EY)
IERTA ...... Implementos e Equipamentos Rurais para Trabalho Agricola Ltd. [*Brazil*] (DSCA)
IES .... Institution of Environmental Sciences (EAIO)
IES .... Inter-Island Air Services Ltd. [*Grenada*] [*ICAO designator*] (FAAC)
IES .... International Education Exchange Service [*Department of State*]
IES-DC ...... IES [*Information Exchange System*] Data Collections [*Commission of the European Communities*] [*Information service or system*] (CRD)
IESRA ...... Interim Employment Services Regulatory Authority
IET .... Institute of Engineers and Technicians [*British*] (EAIO)
IETA .... International Electrical Testing Association (EAIO)
IETC .... International Environmental Technology Centre [*United Nations*] (ECON)
I-ETS .... Interim European Telecommunication Standard (OSI)
IEU .... Independent Education Union [*Australia*]
IEUP .... Institut fuer Europaeische Umweltpolitik [*Institute for European Environmental Policy - IEEP*] (EAIO)
IEV .... Kiev [*Former USSR*] [*Airport symbol*] (OAG)
IEZ .... Institut Europeen du Zinc [*European Zinc Institute - EZI*] (EA)
IF .... Instrument Flying [*Aviation*]
IF .... International Federations (OLYM)
IF .... International Foundation (EAIO)
IF .... Isotta-Fraschini [*Italian luxury auto maker*]
IFA .... Association Internationale de l'Industrie des Engrais [*International Fertilizer Industry Association - IFA*] (EAIO)
IFA .... Institut Fuer Automation [*German*] (ADPT)
IFA .... Instituto de Fiebre Aftosa [*Argentina*] (DSCA)
IFA .... International Federation of Accountants (ADA)
IFA .... International Federation of Airworthiness [*Middlesex, England*] (EAIO)
IFA .... International Fertilizer Industry Association [*Paris, France*] (EAIO)
IFA .... International Fiction Association (EAIO)
IFA .... International Filariasis Association (EA)
IFA .... International Finn Association [*Madrid, Spain*] (EAIO)
IFA .... International Fiscal Association [*Rotterdam, Netherlands*] (EAIO)
IFA .... International Freight Apron
IFA .... Majma'a al-Fiqh al-Islami [*Islamic Jurisprudence Academy - IJA*] (EAIO)
IFAAB ...... International Fiscal Association, Australian Branch
IFAB .... Integrated Fire Direction System for the Artillery Battery [*German*]
IFABC ...... International Federation of Audit Bureaux of Circulations (EAIO)
IFAC .... International Federation of Automatic Control [*Laxenburg, Austria*]
IFAD .... International Fund for Agricultural Development [*United Nations*]
IFALPA ..... International Federation of Air Line Pilots Associations [*Egham, England*] (EAIO)
IFAMAP ... Industria de Farinha de Mandioca Piratininga [*Brazil*] (DSCA)
IFAN .... Internationale Foederation der Ausschusse Normenpraxis [*International Federation for the Application of Standards*] (EAIO)
IFANC ...... International Free Academy of New Cosmology (EA)
IFAP .... International Federation of Agricultural Producers (BARN)
IFAP .... International Foundation for Airline Passengers (EAIO)
IFAPA ...... International Foundation of Airline Passengers Associations (EAIO)
IFAPAO .... International Federation of Asian and Pacific Associations of Optometrists [*Australia*] (EAIO)
IFAPP .... International Federation of Associations of Pharmaceutical Physicians [*Italy*] (EAIO)
IFAPWE.... Institute of Ferro-Alloy Producers in Western Europe [*Defunct*] (EA)
IFAR .... International Forum for AIDS Research [*Institute of Medicine*]
IFARD ...... International Federation of Agricultural Research Systems for Development [*Netherlands*]
IFAS .... International Federation for the Application of Standards (PDAA)
IFAT .... Institut Francais d'Amerique Tropicale [*French Guyana*] (DSCA)
IFATCA .... International Federation of Air Traffic Controllers' Associations [*Dublin, Republic of Ireland*] (EAIO)
IFATE .... International Federation of Airworthiness Technology and Engineering [*Later, IFA*]
IFATSEA .. International Federation of Air Traffic Safety Electronic Associations [*British*] (EAIO)

IFAVWU... International Federation of Audio-Visual Workers Unions [*See also FISTA*] (EAIO)
IFAWPCA ... International Federation of Asian and Western Pacific Contractors' Associations [*Pasig, Metro Manila, Philippines*] (EAIO)
IFB .... Integrierte Finanzbuchhaltung [*Integrated Financial Book Keeping*] [*German*] (ADPT)
IFB .... Internationales Federn-Bureau [*International Feather Bureau - IFB*] (EAIO)
IFB .... International Federation of the Blind [*Later, WBU*]
IFB .... Investment Finance Bank Ltd. [*Malta*]
IFBB .... International Federation of Bodybuilders [*Montreal, PQ*] (EA)
IFBC .... International Federation of the Blue Cross (EA)
IFBDO...... International Federation of Blood Donor Organizations [*See also FIODS*] [*Dole, France*] (EAIO)
IFBPW ...... International Federation of Business and Professional Women (EA)
IFBWW ..... International Federation of Building and Wood Workers [*Sweden*]
IFC .... Cefi Aviation SRL [*Italy*] [*ICAO designator*] (FAAC)
IFC .... Interfirm Comparison (ADA)
IFC .... International Federation of Master-Craftsmen [*See also IFH*] (EAIO)
IFC .... International Finance Corp. [*Affiliate of International Bank for Reconstruction and Development*]
IFCAA ...... International Fire Chiefs' Association of Asia (EAIO)
IFCATI..... International Federation of Cotton and Allied Textile Industries [*Switzerland*] (DSCA)
IFCB .... International Federation of Cell Biology [*Toronto, ON*] (EAIO)
IFCC .... International Federation of Children's Communities [*Later, FICE*]
IFCC .... International Federation of Clinical Chemistry [*Vienna, Austria*] (EA)
IFCE .... International Federation of Consulting Engineers (NUCP)
IFCF .... International Frederic Chopin Foundation [*Poland*] (EAIO)
IFCGWU... International Federation of Chemical and General Workers Union
IFCMI ...... International Federation of Children of Mary Immaculate [*Paris, France*] (EAIO)
IFCN......... International Federation of Clinical Neurophysiology (EAIO)
IFCO......... International Fisheries Cooperative Organization (BARN)
IFCP .... International Federation of the Cinematographic Press [*See also FIPRESCI*] (EAIO)
IFCPC....... International Federation of Cervical Pathology and Colposcopy [*Dundee, Scotland*] (EAIO)
IFCRM ...... International Federation of Catholic Rural Movements (EAIO)
IFCU .... International Federation of Catholic Universities [*See also FIUC*] [*Paris, France*] (EAIO)
IFD .... Internationale Foderation des Dachdeckerhandwerks [*International Federation of Roofing Contractors*] (EAIO)
IFD .... International Federation for Documentation [*Also, FID*] [*Later, IFID*]
IFDA .... International Foundation for Development Alternatives [*See also FIPAD*] [*Nyon, Switzerland*] (EAIO)
IFDAS ...... International Federation of Dental Anesthesiology Societies [*British*] (EAIO)
IFDCO....... International Flying Dutchmen Class Organization [*Berlin, Federal Republic of Germany*] (EAIO)
IFDO .... International Federation of Data Organizations for the Social Sciences [*Amsterdam, Netherlands*] (EAIO)
IFE .... Institut Francais de l'Energie [*French Institute of Energy*] [*Paris*] [*Information service or system*] (IID)
IFEA .... Institute of Fire Engineers in Australia
IFEAT ...... International Federation of Essential Oils and Aroma Trades [*British*] (EAIO)
IFEF .... Internacia Fervojista Esperanto Federacio [*International Federation of Esperantist Railwaymen*] (EAIO)
IFEPT....... International Federation for Enteric Phage Typing [*International Council of Scientific Unions*]
IFER .... Internationale Foederation der Eisenbahn-Reklame-Gesellschaften [*International Federation of Railway Advertising Companies*] [*British*] (EAIO)
IFER .... International Federation of Engine Reconditioners [*See also FIRM*] [*Paris, France*] (EAIO)
IFES.......... International Fellowship of Evangelical Students (EA)
IFF .... Iffley [*Australia*] [*Airport symbol*] [*Obsolete*] (OAG)
IFF .... Interfreight Forwarding Ltd. [*Sudan*] [*ICAO designator*] (FAAC)
IFF .... International Fencing Federation [*Paris, France*] (EA)
IFFA .... Institut fuer Forstliche Arbeitswissenschaft an der Bundesforschungsanstalt [*Germany*] (DSCA)
IFFAA ...... Inland Fish Farming Association of Australia
IFFE .... Inspeccion de Frutos Frescos y Elaborados [*Puerto Rico*] (DSCA)
IFFEC....... International Federation of Free Evangelical Churches (EA)
IFFEX....... International Frozen Food Exhibition and Congress

IFFH.......... International Federation for Family Health [*Bandung, Indonesia*] (EA)

IFFIT......... International Facility for Food Irradiation Technology [*Netherlands*] (WND)

IFFJ.......... International Federation of Free Journalists [*British*]

IFFJP........ International Federation of Fruit Juice Producers [*See also FIJU*] [*Paris, France*] (EAIO)

IFFS........... International Federation of Fertility Societies (EAIO)

IFFTU .... International Federation of Free Teachers' Unions [*See also SPIE*] [*Amsterdam, Netherlands*] (EAIO)

IFGA.......... International Federation of Grocers' Associations [*See also IVLD*] [*Bern, Switzerland*] (EAIO)

IFGAE .... International Federation for Gerda Alexander Eutony [*Belgium*] (EAIO)

IFH .... Internationale Foderation des Handwerks [*International Federation of Master-Craftsmen - IFMC*] [*Vienna, Austria*] (EAIO)

IFHBT....... International Federation of Health and Beauty Therapists

IFHE.......... International Federation for Home Economics [*See also FIEF*] [*Paris, France*] (EAIO)

IFHE.......... International Federation of Hospital Engineering (PDAA)

IFHOH...... International Federation of the Hard of Hearing [*Kampen, Netherlands*] (EAIO)

IFHP.......... International Federation for Housing and Planning [*Netherlands*]

IFHPM...... International Federation of Hydraulic Platform Manufacturers [*Later, IPAF*] (EAIO)

IFHPSM ... International Federation for Hygiene, Preventive, and Social Medicine [*France*] (EAIO)

IFHRO ...... International Federation of Health Records Organizations [*Munich, Federal Republic of Germany*] (EAIO)

IFHTM...... International Federation for the Heat Treatment of Materials (PDAA)

IFI .... Inter-Freight International [*Steamship*] (MHDB)

IFI .... Internationales Fernlehrinstitut [*German*] (ADPT)

IFI .... International Federation of Interior Architects/Interior Designers [*Amsterdam, Netherlands*] (EAIO)

IFI .... International Fund for Ireland [*United States, Canada, and New Zealand*]

IFIA .... International Federation of Inventors' Associations [*Stockholm, Sweden*] (EAIO)

IFIA .... International Federation of Ironmongers and Iron Merchants Associations [*See also FIDAQ*] [*Zurich, Switzerland*] (EAIO)

IFIAS........ International Federation of Institutes for Advanced Study [*ICSU*] [*Toronto, ON*] (EAIO)

IFIC .... International Ferrocement Information Center [*Asian Institute of Technology*] (IID)

IFICB........ International Finance Investment and Commerce Bank Ltd. [*Bangladesh*] (EY)

IFID .... International Federation for Information and Documentation [*See also FIID*] (EAIO)

IFIEC........ International Federation of Industrial Energy Consumers [*Geneva, Switzerland*] (EA)

IFIFR........ International Federation of International Furniture Removers [*See also FIDI*] [*Brussels, Belgium*] (EAIO)

IFIJG........ International Federation of Infantile and Juvenile Gynecology [*See also FIGIJ*] [*Sierre, Switzerland*] (EAIO)

IFIP .... International Federation of Information Processing (ADPT)

IFIP .... International Food Irradiation Project [*Food and Agricultural Organization*] (PDAA)

IFIPS .... International Federation of Information Processing Societies (ADPT)

IFIRA .... Information Facility for Indigenous Resources for Australia

IFIS........... International Food Information Service [*Database producer*] [*Germany*]

IFISRR ...... International Federation of Institutes for Socio-Religious Research [*Louvain, Belgium*] (EA)

IFIWA .... International Federation of Importers and Wholesale Grocers Associations [*The Hague, Netherlands*] (EAIO)

IFJ .... International Federation of Journalists [*See also FIJ*] [*Brussels, Belgium*] (EAIO)

IFJ .... Isafjordur [*Iceland*] [*Airport symbol*] (OAG)

IFK............ Interfunk & Co. [*Yugoslavia*] [*ICAO designator*] (FAAC)

IFKT .... International Federation of Knitting Technologists [*See also FITB*] [*Frauenfeld, Switzerland*] (EAIO)

IFL............. Innisfail [*Australia*] [*Airport symbol*]

IFLA .... International Federation of Landscape Architects [*Versailles, France*] (EAIO)

IFLA .... International Finance and Leasing Association (MHDB)

IFLAIC...... Instituto Forestal Latinoamericano de Investigacion y Capacitacion [*Venezuela*] (DSCA)

IFLASC ..... International Federation of Latin American Study Centers [*Mexico City, Mexico*] (EAIO)

IFLB .... Islamic Front for the Liberation of Bahrain [*Political party*] (PD)

IFLBP........ International Federation of the Little Brothers of the Poor [*See also FIPFP*] (EAIO)

IFLO .... Islamic Front for Liberation of Oromo [*Ethiopia*] [*Political party*] (EY)

IFLRY........ International Federation of Liberal and Radical Youth (EAIO)

IFLS........... International Federation of Law Students (DLA)

IFLS........... International Federation of Little Singers (EAIO)

IFLWU ...... International Fur and Leather Workers Union (MHDB)

IFM............ International Financial Markets Trading Ltd.

IFMA........ International Farm Management Association [*Reading, Berkshire, England*] (EAIO)

IFMA........ International Federation of Margarine Associations [*Brussels, Belgium*] (EAIO)

IFMBE ...... International Federation for Medical and Biological Engineering [*ICSU*] [*Ottawa, ON*] (EA)

IFMC........ International Federation of Master-Craftsmen (EA)

IFMC........ International Federation of Motorhome Clubs [*Belgium*] (EAIO)

IFME........ International Federation of Municipal Engineers [*See also FIIM*] [*British*] (EAIO)

IFML........ International Film Management Ltd. [*Australia*]

IFMM........ International Federation of Manual Medicine (EA)

IFMP........ International Federation for Medical Psychotherapy [*See also IGAP*] [*Oslo, Norway*] (EAIO)

IFMP......... International Federation of Maritime Philately [*Livorno, Italy*] (EAIO)

IFMP......... International Federation of Married Priests (EAIO)

IFMS .... International Federation of Magical Societies [*See also FISM*] (EAIO)

IFMSA ...... International Federation of Medical Students Associations [*See also FIAEM*] [*Vienna, Austria*] (EAIO)

IFMSS....... International Federation of Multiple Sclerosis Societies [*British*] (EAIO)

IFN .... International Feminist Network

IFN .... International Friends of Nature [*See also NFI*] [*Zurich, Switzerland*] (EAIO)

IFN .... Isfahan [*Iran*] [*Airport symbol*] (OAG)

IFNA........ International Federation of Netball Associations [*Glasgow, Scotland*] (EAIO)

IFNP......... International Federation of Newspaper Publishers (NTCM)

IFO .... Integriertes Finanzbuchhaltungs-Online-System [*German*] (ADPT)

IFOAD...... International Federation of Original Art Diffusors [*France*] (EAIO)

IFOAM...... International Federation of Organic Agriculture Movements [*Witzenhausen, Federal Republic of Germany*] (EA)

IFOFSAG ... International Fellowship of Former Scouts and Guides [*Brussels, Belgium*]

IFOPA .... International Fibrodysplasia Ossificans Progressiva Association (EA)

IFOR......... International Federation of Operation Research Societies (BARN)

IFOR......... International Fellowship of Reconciliation [*Alkmaar, Netherlands*] (EA)

IFORD...... Institut de Formation et de Recherche Demographiques [*Institute for Training and Demographic Research - ITDR*] (EAIO)

IFORS ...... International Federation of Operational Research Societies [*ICSU*] [*Lyngby, Denmark*] (EAIO)

IFOS .... International Federation of Ophthalmological Societies [*Nijmegen, Netherlands*] (EA)

IFOS .... International Federation of Oto-Rhino-Laryngological Societies [*Berchem, Belgium*] (EAIO)

IFOS .... Ion Formation from Organic Solids [*International conference*]

IFOTES..... International Federation of Telephonic Emergency Services [*Jorn, Sweden*] (EA)

IFP .... Inkatha Freedom Party [*Afrikaans*] [*Political party*] (ECON)

IFP .... Institut Francais du Petroles [*French Institute of Petroleum*] [*Paris*]

IFP .... International Federation of Pedestrians (EA)

IFPA .... International Federation of Psoriasis Associations [*Stockholm, Sweden*] (EAIO)

IFPA .... International Fighter Pilots Academy [*Slovak Air Force*]

IFPAAW ... International Federation of Plantation, Agricultural, and Allied Workers [*Switzerland*]

IFPCA .... International Federation of Press Cutting Agencies (EA)

IFPDA ...... International Fine Print Dealers Association

IFPE .... International Federation for Parent Education [*See also FIEP*] [*Sevres, France*] (EAIO)

IFPLVB ..... Internationale Foederation der Plantagen und Landarbeiter und Vermandter Berufsgruppen [*Switzerland*] (DSCA)

IFPMA ...... International Federation of Pharmaceutical Manufacturers Associations [*See also FIIM*] [*Geneva, Switzerland*] (EAIO)

IFPMM ..... International Federation of Purchasing and Materials Management [*Aarau, Switzerland*] (EAIO)

IFPMO ..... International Federation of Psychological-Medical Organizations [*See also FIOPM*] [*Lausanne, Switzerland*] (EAIO)

IFPRA .... International Federation of Park and Recreation Administration [*Reading, England*] (EAIO)

IFPRI........ International Fine Particle Research Institute

IFPS........... International Federation of Palynological Societies   (EAIO)

IFPS........... International Federation of Philosophical Societies [*See also FISP*] [*Fribourg, Switzerland*]   (EAIO)

IFPSM....... International Federation for Preventive and Social Medicine   (EAIO)

IFPTO .... International Federation of Popular Travel Organisations [*Paris, France*]   (EAIO)

IFPV .... International Federation of Pelota Vasca   (EA)

IFPVP........ International Federation of Phonogram and Videogram Producers   (EA)

IFPWA ...... International Federation of Public Warehousing Associations [*Formerly, IFPWKA*]   (EAIO)

IFPWKA ... International Federation of Public Warehouse Keepers Associations [*Later, IFPWA*]   (EAIO)

IFR............. Instituts Federatifs de Recherche [*France*]

IFRA........... INCA [*International Newspaper Color Association*]-FIEJ Research Association [*Federation Internationale des Editeurs de Journaux*] [*Research center*] [*Germany*]   (IRC)

IFRA........... International Fragrance Association [*Geneva, Switzerland*]   (EAIO)

IFRAC .... Imported Food Risks Advisory Committee [*Australia*]

IFRAC .... International Federation of Railway Advertising Companies [*British*]   (EA)

IFRB .... International Frequency Registration Board [*ITU*] [*United Nations*]

IFRC .... International Federation of Roofing Contractors [*See also IFD*]   (EAIO)

IFRC .... International Futures Research Conference   (PDAA)

IFRD.......... International Federation of Retail Distributors   (EAIO)

IFREMER ... Institut Francais de Recherche pour l'Exploitation de la Mer [*French Research Institute for Ocean Utilization*] [*Research center*]   (IID)

IFRF .... International Federation of Resistance Fighters   (BJA)

IFRFOM ... Institut Francais de Recherches Fruitieres outre Mer [*France*]   (DSCA)

IFRIP......... Institut Francais de Recherche et de Technologie Polaires [*Public interest group*] [*French Southern and Antarctic Territories*]   (EY)

IFRM......... International Federation of Resistance Movements [*Vienna, Austria*]   (EA)

IFRS .... Inland Fisheries Research Station [*Australia*]   (DSCA)

IFRTA .... International Federation of Railwaymen's Travel Associations   (EA)

IFS .... Institute of Financial Services [*Australia*]

IFS .... Interaktives Finanzsystem [*Interactive Finance System*] [*German*]   (ADPT)

IFS .... International Federation of Settlements and Neighbourhood Centers   (EAIO)

IFS .... International Federation of Surveyors [*See also FIG*]   (EAIO)

IFS .... International Flying Services SRL [*Italy*] [*ICAO designator*]   (FAAC)

IFS .... International Foundation for Science [*See also FIS*] [*ICSU Stockholm, Sweden*]   (EAIO)

IFS .... Internationella Forsurningssekretariatet [*International Secretariat on Acid Rain*] [*Sweden*]   (EAIO)

IFSA .... International Federation of Sports Acrobatics [*Sofia, Bulgaria*]   (EAIO)

IFSA .... International Fuzzy Systems Association   (EA)

IFSB........... International Flying Saucer Bureau [*Defunct*]

IFSC .... International Federation of Surgical Colleges [*Dublin, Republic of Ireland*]   (EAIO)

IFSCC........ International Federation of Societies of Cosmetic Chemists [*Luton, England*]   (EAIO)

IFSDA .... International Federation of Stamp Dealers' Associations   (EA)

IFSDP........ International Federation of the Socialist and Democratic Press [*Milan, Italy*]   (EAIO)

IFSECN..... International Federation of Societies for Electroencephalography and Clinical Neurophysiology [*Amsterdam, Netherlands*]   (EA)

IFSF........... Investment Feasibility Study Facility [*United Nations Development Programme*] [*Ghana*]

IFSH.......... International Federation of Sound Hunters   (EA)

IFSHC .... International Federation of Societies for Histochemistry and Cytochemistry   (EAIO)

IFSMA ...... International Federation of Shipmasters Associations [*See also FIAPN*]   (EAIO)

IFSPO .... International Federation of Senior Police Officers   (EA)

IFSR .... International Federation for Systems Research   (EAIO)

IFSRC........ International Financial Services Research Center [*Massachusetts Institute of Technology*] [*Research center*]   (RCD)

IFSS........... International Fertilizer Supply Scheme [*FAO*] [*United Nations*]

IFSSEC ..... International Fire, Security and Safety Exhibition and Conference   (PDAA)

IFSSO........ International Federation of Social Science Organizations [*See also FIOSS*] [*Copenhagen, Denmark*]   (EAIO)

IFSTAD..... Islamic Foundation for Science, Technology, and Development [*BARN*]

IFSTD....... Interim Fund for Science and Technology for Development [*International Council of Scientific Unions*]

IFSTD....... Islamic Foundation for Science, Technology and Development [*Saudi Arabia*]   (PDAA)

IFSTM....... International Federation of Sewing Thread Manufacturers   (EA)

IFSW .... International Federation of Social Workers [*Switzerland*]

IFT............. International Federation of Translators [*See also FIT*] [*Ghent, Belgium*]   (EAIO)

IFT............. Italian Federation of Labor   (RU)

IFTA .... Institut Francais du Transport Aerien   (FLAF)

IFTA .... International Federation of Teachers' Associations [*Later, WCOTP*]   (EAIO)

IFTA .... International Federation of Television Archives [*See also FIAT*] [*Madrid, Spain*]   (EAIO)

IFTA .... International Federation of Thanatologists Associations [*Saint-Ouen, France*]   (EA)

IFTAC ...... Inter-American Federation of Touring and Automobile Clubs [*See also FITAC*]   (EAIO)

IFTAR ...... Institutul de Fizica si Tehnologia Aparatelor cu Radiatii [*Institute for the Physics and Technology of Radiation Instruments*]   (RO)

IFTBCS ..... International Federation of the Temperance Blue Cross Societies [*Later, IBC*]   (EA)

IFTC .... International Federation of Thermalism and Climatism [*Bad Ragaz, Switzerland*]   (EA)

IFTF .... International Federation of Teachers of French [*See also FIPF*] [*Sevres, France*]   (EAIO)

IFTF .... International Fur Trade Federation [*British*]   (EAIO)

IFTM......... Institutul de Fizica si Tehnologia Materialelor [*Institute for the Physics and Technology of Materials*]   (RO)

IFTN.......... Information for the Nation [*Program*] [*Australia*]

IFTO......... International Federation of Tour Operators [*Lewes, East Sussex, England*]   (EAIO)

IFToMM ... International Federation for the Theory of Machines and Mechanisms [*Warsaw, Poland*]   (EAIO)

IFTR .... Institute of Fundamental Technological Research [*Research center*] [*Poland*]   (IRC)

IFTR .... International Federation for Theatre Research [*British*]   (EAIO)

IFTR .... International Federation of Teachers of Rhythmics   (EA)

IFTs .... Price Equalization Fund   (BU)

IFTU .... International Federation of Trade Unions

IFTUTW ... International Federation of Trade Unions of Transport Workers [*See also FIOST*] [*Brussels, Belgium*]   (EAIO)

IFU .... Industrialiseringsfonden for Udviklingslandene [*Industrialization Fund for Developing Countries*] [*Denmark*]

IFU .... Inter-Democracy Federal Union [*Australia*]

IFUW........ International Federation of University Women   (EA)

IfV............. Institut fuer Verkehrsforschung [*Institute for Transport Research*] [*EG*]

IFV............. Internationaler Faustball-Verband   (EAIO)

IFVC......... International Federation for Victory over Communism

IFVD......... Institute of Physics of High Pressures   (RU)

IFVHSF.... Federation of Health Funds - International [*International Federation of Voluntary Health Service Funds*] [*Later, FHF*] [*Acronym is based on former name,*]

IFVTCC..... Internationale Foderation der Vereine der Textilchemiker und Coloristen [*International Federation of Associations of Textile Chemists and Colorists*]   (EAIO)

IFVUKh.... Institute for Physical Education and School Hygiene   (BU)

IFW........... Institut fuer Nationale und Internationale Fleischwirtschaft [*Heidelberg*] [*Information retrieval*]

IfW........... Institut fuer Werkzeugmaschinen [*Machine Tool Institute*]   (EG)

IFW........... Institut fur Fertigungstechnik und Spanende Werkzeugmaschinen [*Institute for Production Engineering and Machine Tools*] [*Germany*]   (IRC)

IFWEA ...... International Federation of Workers' Educational Associations [*See also IVB*] [*Tel Aviv, Israel*]   (EAIO)

IFWS .... Internationale Foederation von Wirkerei- und Strickerei-Fachleuten [*International Federation of Knitting Technologists*] [*Switzerland*]

IFWS .... International Federation of Wines and Spirits [*See also FIVS*]   (EAIO)

IFWSTI ..... International Federation of Wines and Spirits, Trade, and Industry   (EA)

IFWTWA .. International Food, Wine, and Travel Writers Association   (EAIO)

IFY............. Indian Fiscal Year   (IMH)

IFYE........... International Farm Youth Exchange

IFZ............. Institute of Physics of the Earth Imeni O. Yu. Shmidt (of the Academy of Sciences, USSR)   (RU)

IG............... ALISARDA SpA [*Italy*] [*ICAO designator*]   (ICDA)

IG............... Hospital for Contagious Diseases   (RU)

ig .... Igazgatas [*or Igazgatasi*] [*Administration or Administrative*]   (HU)

ig .... Igazgato [or Igazgatosag] [Director or Directorate]   (HU)
IG .... Illawarra Greens [Political party] [Australia]
iG .... Im Generalstab [Attached to the General Staff (appended to, or preceding army rank)]   (EG)
IG .... Indische Gids [Benelux]   (BAS)
IG .... Industriegewerkschaft [Industrial Labor Union]   (WEN)
IG .... Institute of Geography (of the Academy of Sciences, USSR)   (RU)
IG .... Instituto Geologico [Geological Institute] [Secretaria de Agricultura e Abastecimento] [Brazil] [Research center]   (EAS)
IG .... Institutul de Geriatrie [Geriatrics Institute]   (RO)
IG .... Institut za Geoloska Istrazivanja [Geological Research Institute]   (YU)
IG .... Instruction Generale [Benelux]   (BAS)
IG .... Instytut Geografii [Institute of Geography]   (POL)
IG .... Instytut Geologiczny [Institute of Geology] [Poland] [Research center]
IG .... Interessengemeinschaft [Business Pool, Trust]   (WEN)
IG .... Interessengemeinschaft Deutschsprachiger Suedwester [Interest Society of German-Speaking Southwesterners] [Namibia]   (AF)
IG .... Interessengruppe [Interest Group (Society for the protection of interests of the German-speaking population)] [Namibia]   (AF)
IG .... Internationaal Gerechtshof [Benelux]   (BAS)
IG .... Internationale Kunstgilde [International Art Guild - IAG]   (EAIO)
IG .... International Guides' Club   (EAIO)
IG .... Izmenyaemaya Geometriya [Variable Geometry] [Suffix letters on Soviet combat aircraft]
IG .... Izvidacka Grupa [Reconnaissance Group] [Military]   (YU)
IG .... Measuring Head   (RU)
IG .... Signal Generator   (RU)
IG .... Spark Generator   (RU)
IGA .... Inagua [Bahamas] [Airport symbol]   (OAG)
IGA .... Industrie-Gemeinschaft Aerosole eV [Aerosol Industry Society]   (SLS)
IGA .... Innsbrucker Germanistische Arbeitsgemeinschaft [German Teachers Society of Innsbruck] [Austria]   (SLS)
IGA .... Instituto de Geofisica y Astronomia [Institute of Geophysics and Astronomy] [Cuba]   (LA)
IGA .... Instituto Guatemalteco-Americano [Guatemala]   (SLS)
IGA .... International Association of Geomagnetism and Aeronomy [University of Tokyo] [Research center]   (EAS)
IGA .... International Gartenbauausstellung [International Horticultural Exhibition]   (EG)
IGA .... International Gay Association - International Association of Lesbians/Gay Women and Gay Men   (EAIO)
IGA .... Ipoh Garden Australia Ltd.
IGAC .... Instituto Geofisico de los Andes Colombianos [Colombia]   (DSCA)
IGAC .... Instituto Geografico "Agustin Codazzi" [Agustin Codazzi Geographic Institute] [Colorado]   (LA)
IGACC ...... Inspection Generale de l'Aviation Civile et Commerciale [French]
IGACSM ... Inter-Governmental Advisory Committee on Surveying and Mapping [Australia]
IGADD ...... Intergovernmental Authority on Drought and Development [Djibouti]   (EY)
IGAE .... Intergovernmental Agreement on the Environment [Australia]
IGAeM ...... Internationale Gesellschaft fuer Aerosole in der Medizin [International Society for Aerosols in Medicine - ISAeM]   (EAIO)
IGAME...... Inspecteur General de l'Administration en Mission Extraordinaire [Inspector General of Administration on Extraordinary Mission] [Algeria]   (AF)
IGAN .... Institute of Geography (of the Academy of Sciences, USSR)   (RU)
IGAP......... Internationale Gesellschaft fuer Arztliche Psychotherapie [International Federation for Medical Psychotherapy - IFMP] [Oslo, Norway]   (EAIO)
IGAS......... Inspection Generale des Affaires Sociales [France]
IGASK ...... Inspection of the State Architectural and Construction Control [RU]
IGAT .... Iranian Gas Trunkline   (ME)
IGB .... Ihtilalci Gencler Birligi [Revolutionary Youth Union]   (TU)
IGB .... International Gravimetric Bureau [Toulouse, France]   (EAIO)
IGB .... Ipargazdasagi Bizottsag [Committee of Industrial Economy] [HU]
IGBA .... Institute de Geologie du Bassin d'Aquitaine [French]   (MSC)
IGBE......... Industriegewerkschaft Bergbau und Energie [Mining and Energy Workers Union] [Germany]   (EAIO)
IGBE......... Institute of State Certified Accountants   (RU)
ig biz......... Igazolo Bizottsag [Screening Committee]   (HU)
IGBP......... International Geosphere-Biosphere Programme [Australia]
IGBS .... International Gas Bearings Symposium   (PDAA)

IGC .... Institut du Genie Chimique [Chemical Engineering Institute] [France]   (WED)
IGC .... Institute for Graphic Communication [Defunct]   (EA)
IGC .... Instituto Geografico e Cadastral [Geographic and Cadastral Institute] [Research center] [Portugal]   (EAS)
IGC .... Inter-Governmental Committee [National Crime Authority] [Australia]
IGC .... Intergovernmental Committee on Refugees [Post-World War II]   (DLA)
IGC .... Inter-Governmental Conference [European Union]   (ECON)
IGC .... Inter-Governmental Conferences [European Community]
IGC .... Intergovernmental Copyright Committee [See also CIDA] [Paris, France]   (EAIO)
IGC .... International Geological Congress [ICSU]
IGC .... International Geophysical Committee [ICSU]   (ASF)
IGC .... International Grassland Congress   (DSCA)
IGC .... International Gravity Commission   (MSC)
IGC .... International Guides' Club   (EAIO)
IGCAR...... Indira Gandhi Centre for Atomic Research [India]
IGCAS....... Institute of Geochemistry, Academia Sinica [China] [Research center]   (IRC)
IGCB.......... Institut Geographique du Congo Belge
IGCC......... Intergovernmental Panel on Climate Change [World Meteorological Organization]
IGCI.......... Institut Geographique de Cote d'Ivoire [Geographic Institute of the Ivory Coast] [Research center]   (EAS)
IGCI.......... Internationale Gesellschaft fuer Chemo- und Immuntherapie [Austria]   (SLS)
IGCMC...... Israel Government Coins and Medals Corporation
IGCP......... International Geological Correlation Programme [See also PICG] [ICSU Paris, France]   (EAIO)
IGCPK...... Industriegewerkschaft Chemie Papier Keramik [Chemical, Paper, and Ceramic Workers' Industrial Union] [Germany]   (EAIO)
IGCR......... Instituto Geografico de Costa Rica [San Jose, Costa Rica]   (LAA)
IGCRN ...... Instituto de Geografia y Conservacion de Recursos Naturales [Institute of Geography and Conservation of Natural Resources] [Research center] [Venezuela]   (EAS)
IGD........... Ilerici Gencler Dernegi [Progressive Youth Association]   (TU)
IGD........... Institute of Hydrodynamics (of the Siberian Department of the Academy of Sciences, USSR)   (RU)
IGD........... Mining Institute   (RU)
IGDO........ International Guild of Opticians [International Guild of Dispensing Opticians] [Acronym is based on former name,]   (EAIO)
IGDZ .... Inspecteur van de Geneeskundige Dienst Zeemacht [Benelux]   (BAS)
IGE .... Iguela [Gabon] [Airport symbol] [Obsolete]   (OAG)
IGE .... Imposta Generale sull'Entrata [Income Tax] [Italian]   (WER)
IGE .... Institouton Geoponikon Epistimon [Agricultural Sciences Institute] [VIGE] [See also]   (GC)
IGEA .... Institution of Gas Engineers (Australia)   (ADA)
IGECO ...... Inspection Generale pour la Cooperation Hors Metropole [General Inspectorate for Overseas Cooperation] [French]   (WER)
IGEGM ..... Internationale Gesellschaft zur Erforschung von Grenzgebieten der Medizin [Austria]   (SLS)
IGEIEPSI ... International Group for the Exchange of Information and Experience Among Postal Savings Institutions [Geneva, Switzerland]   (EAIO)
IGEM .... Ihracat Gelistirme Etud Merkezi [Export Development Studies Center] [IGEME] [See also]   (TU)
IGEM .... Institute of Geology of Ore Deposits, Petrography, Mineralogy, and Geochemistry (of the Academy of Sciences, USSR)   (RU)
IGEME...... Ihracati Gelistirme Etud Merkezi [Center for Export Development Studies] [IGEM] [See also]   (TU)
IGEN .... Inspecteur General de l'Education Nationale [French]
IGEN .... Institute of Genetics (of the Academy of Sciences, USSR)   (RU)
IGER......... Institut National de Gestion et d'Economie Rurale [National Institute of Rural Management and Economy] [France]   (PDAA)
IGERGI ..... Institute of Geology and Development of Mineral Fuels   (RU)
IGESUCO ... International Ground Environment Subcommittee [NATO]
IGEX......... Intreprinderea Geologica de Explorari [Geological Enterprise for Explorations]   (RO)
IGEY......... Institouton Geologias kai Erevnon Ypedafous [Geology and Subsoil Research Institute] [EthIGME is preferred]   (GC)
IGF............ Fondation Internationale pour la Sauvegarde du Gibier [International Foundation for the Conservation of Game]   (EAIO)
IGF............ Institut za Geodeziju i Fotogrametriju [Institute of Geodesy and Photogrammetry]   (YU)
IGF............ International Genetics Federation [See also FIG] [England]   (EA)

IGF............ International Graphical Federation [*See also FGI*] [*Berne, Switzerland*] (EAIO)

IGF............ International Gymnastic Federation [*See also FIG*] (EAIO)

IGF............ Island Games Foundation (EAIO)

I GFarben ... Interessengemeinschaft der Farbenindustrie [*German Dye Trust*]

IGFCOT .... Institutul de Geodezie, Fotogrametrie, Cartografie, si Organizarea Teritoriului [*Institute for Geodesy, Photogrammetry, Cartography, and Territorial Organization*] (RO)

IGFFA .... Immobiliere Gabonaise Fiduciaire France Afrique

IGFM........ Internationale Gesellschaft fuer Menschenrechte [*International Society for Human Rights - ISHR*] (EA)

IGfP .... Internationale Gemeinschaft fuer Psychologie [*Switzerland*] (SLS)

IGFRC ...... International Game Fish Research Conference (MSC)

IGFRI .... Indian Grassland and Fodder Research Institute (DSCA)

IGG .... Innsbrucker Gesellschaft zur Pflege der Geisteswissenschaften [*Austria*] (SLS)

IGG .... Institute of Geodesy and Geophysics [*Chinese Academy of Sciences*] [*Research center*] (EAS)

IGG .... Institute of Geology and Geophysics (of the Siberian Department of the Academy of Sciences, USSR) (RU)

IGG .... Institute of Hydrology and Hydraulic Engineering (of the Academy of Sciences, Ukrainian SSR) (RU)

IGG .... Institutul de Geologie si Geofizica [*Institute for Geology and Geophysics*] (RO)

IGG .... Internationale Gesellschaft fuer Geschichtsdidaktik [*International Society for History Didactics*] (EAIO)

IGGCI....... International Geological/Geophysical Cruise Inventory (MSC)

IGGI .... Inter-Governmental Group on Indonesia (IN)

IGH........... Ingham [*Australia*] [*Airport symbol*]

IGH........... Instituto Geofisico de Huancayo [*Peru*] (DSCA)

IGH........... Interessengemeinschaft fuer Halonversuche [*Community of Interests in Halon Experiments*] [*Switzerland*] (PDAA)

IGH........... Internationaal Gerechtshof [*Benelux*] (BAS)

IGI .... Institute of Civil Engineers (RU)

IGI .... Institute of Mineral Fuels (RU)

IGI .... International Wallcovering Manufacturers Association [*Belgium*] (EAIO)

IGI .... Italiana Gas Industriali

IGIF .... International Geographic Information Foundation

IGiG......... Institute of Geology and Geophysics (of the Siberian Department of the Academy of Sciences, USSR) (RU)

IGiG......... Institute of Hydrology and Hydraulic Engineering (of the Academy of Sciences, Ukrainian SSR) (RU)

IGiK .... Institute of Geodesy and Cartography (RU)

IGiK .... Instytut Geodezji i Kartografji [*Institute of Land-Surveying and Cartography*] [*Poland*]

IGiO.......... Instytut Gluchoniemych i Ociemnialych [*Institute for the Deaf-Mute and the Blind*] [*Poland*]

IGIP .... Internationale Gesellschaft fuer Ingenieurpaedagogik [*International Society for Engineering Education*] (EAIO)

IGiRGI...... Institute of Geology and Development of Mineral Fuels (RU)

IGIS .... International Group of Users of Information Systems [*Netherlands*] (EY)

IGJ .... Internationale Gesellschaft fuer Jazzforschung [*Austria*] (SLS)

IGK .... Il [*or Ilce*] Genclik Kolu [*Provincial (or District) Youth Branch*] [*of a political organization*] (TU)

IGK .... Ingeboude Kaste [*Built-In Cupboards*] [*Afrikaans*]

IGK .... Ingenieurgemeinschaft Kernverfahrenstechnik [*Germany*] (PDAA)

IGK .... Institute of Geodesy and Cartography (RU)

IGK .... Instytut Gospodarki Komunalnej [*Institute of Municipal Economy*] (POL)

IGKB........ Internationale Gewasserschutz Kommission fur den Bodensee [*International Commission for the Protection of Lake Constance*] (EA)

IGKG .... Internationale Gesellschaft fuer Kiefer- und Gesichtschirurgie [*International Association for Maxillo-Facial Surgery*] (EAIO)

IGL .... Internationale Gesellschaft fuer Lymphologie [*International Society of Lymphology*] (EAIO)

IGL .... Intreprinderile Gospodariei Locale [*Enterprises of the Local Economy*] (RO)

IGL .... Izmir [*Turkey*] Cigli Airport [*Airport symbol*] (OAG)

igla .... Iglesia [*Church*] [*Spanish*]

IGLHRC.... International Gay and Lesbian Human Rights Commission (EA)

IGLL......... Inspectia Generala de Locuinte si Locale [*General Inspectorate for Housing and Public Buildings*] (RO)

IGLL......... Intermediate General Leadership Level [*Philippines*]

IGLM .... Limnos [*Greece*] [*ICAO location identifier*] (ICLI)

IGLOSS.... Integrated Global Ocean Station System [*Surrey, England*] [*See also IGOSS UNESCO*]

IGM .... Institouton Georgikis Mikhanologias [*Agricultural Engineering Institute*] (GC)

IGM .... Institute of Mining Mechanics (RU)

IGM .... Instituto Geografico Militar [*Chile*] (LAA)

IGM .... Instituto Geografico Militar [*Peru*] (LAA)

IGM .... Instituto Geografico Militar [*Argentina*] (EAS)

IGM .... Instituut van Gevorderde Motoriste van Suid-Afrika [*Institute of Advanced Motorists of South Africa*] (AA)

IGM .... Internationale Gesellschaft fuer Menschenrechte [*International Society for Human Rights - ISHR*] (EAIO)

IGM .... Internationale Gesellschaft fuer Moorforschung [*International Society for Research on Moors*]

IGM .... Istituto Geografico Militare (Florence) [*Military Geographic Institute*] [*Italian*] (WER)

IGM .... Izcilik Genel Mudurlugu [*Scouting Directorate General*] (TU)

IGMB-TNO ... Instituut voor Graan, Meel, en Brood Nederlands Centrale Organisatie voor Toegepast-Natuurwetenschappelijk Onderzoek [*Institute for Cereals, Flour, and Bread Netherlands Central Organization for Applied Natural Scientific Research*] (ARC)

IGME .... Idryma Geologikon kai Metallevtikon Epevnon [*Institute for Geological and Mineral Research*] (GC)

IGME .... Institute of Geological and Mining Research [*Greek*] (IMH)

IG Metall... Industriegewerkschaft Metall [*Metalworkers Union*] (EG)

IG/MG ...... Inspecteur General/Mobilisation Generale [*or Inspection Generale/Mobilisation Generale*] [*Inspector General, General Mobilization or Inspectorate General, General Mobilization Cambodia*] (CL)

IGMG........ Internationale Gustav Mahler Gesellschaft [*International Gustav Mahler Society*] (EA)

IGMI .... Irkutsk State Medical Institute (RU)

IGMI .... Istituto Geografico Militare [*Italian*] (SLS)

IGMI .... Ivanovo State Medical Institute (RU)

Ig Min........ Igazsagugyminiszterium/Miniszter [*Ministry/Minister of Justice*] (HU)

IGMR .... Institut de Recherches Geologiques et Minieres [*Institute for Geological and Mining Research*] [*Cameroon*] (WED)

IGMR .... Institute for Geological and Mining Research [*Cameroon*] [*Research center*] (EAS)

IGMW ...... Internationale Gesellschaft fuer Musikwissenschaft [*Switzerland*] (SLS)

IGN............ Iligan [*Philippines*] [*Airport symbol*] (OAG)

IGN............ Institute of Geological Sciences (RU)

IGN............ Institut Geographique National [*National Geographic Institute*] [*French*] (WER)

IGN............ Instituto Geografico Nacional [*National Geographic Institute*] [*Panama*] (MSC)

IGN............ Instituto Geografico Nacional [*National Geographic Institute*] [*Guatemala*] (MSC)

IGN............ Instituto Geografico Nacional [*National Geographic Institute*] [*Honduras*] (MSC)

IGN............ Instituto Geografico Nacional [*National Geographic Institute*] [*El Salvador*] (MSC)

IGN............ Instituut vir Geskiedenisnavorsing [*Institute for Historical Research*] [*Human Sciences Research Council*] [*South Africa*] (AA)

IGN............ Instytut Gospodarki Narodowej [*Institute of the National Economy*] (POL)

IGN............ Societe de l'Imprimerie Generale du Niger

IGNC........ International Good Neighbor Council [*See also CIBV*] [*Monterrey, Mexico*] (EAIO)

IGNM........ Internationale Gesellschaft fuer Neue Musik [*Austria*] (SLS)

IGO............ Chigorodo [*Colombia*] [*Airport symbol*] (OAG)

IGO............ Hospital for Highly Contagious Diseases (RU)

IGO............ International Governmental Organisation

IGOSS....... Integrated Global Ocean Station System [*See also IGLOSS*] [*UNESCO*] [*British*]

IGP .... Indice Geral de Precos [*General Price Index*] [*Brazil*] (LA)

IGP .... Inspector-General of Police

IGP .... Institut de Gestion du Portefeuille

IGP .... Instituto Geofisico del Peru [*Peru*] (DSCA)

IGP .... Istituto Geografico Polare [*Italian*] (SLS)

IGPAI........ Inspeccao-Geral dos Produtos Agricolas e Industriais [*Inspectorate of Agricultural Products and Manufactured Goods*] [*Portugal*] (PDAA)

IGPAN ...... Institute of Government and Law of the Academy of Sciences, USSR (RU)

IG PAN..... Instytut Geografii Polskiej Akademii Nauk [*Polish Academy of Sciences Institute of Geography*] (POL)

IGPSMS.... Intreprinderea Geologica de Prospectiuni pentru Substante Minerale Solide [*Geologic Prospecting Enterprise for Solid Mineral Substances*] (RO)

IGR .... Graphite Pulse Reactor (RU)

IGR .... Iguazu [*Argentina*] [*Airport symbol*] (OAG)

IGR .... Impot General sur le Revenu [*General Income Tax*] [*Belgian, French*] (WER)

IGR .... Institute of Geomantic Research (EAIO)

IGR .... Instytut Genetyki Roslin [*Institute of Plant Genetics*] [*Poland*]

IGRA .... Instituto Gaucho de Reforma Agraria [*Rio Grande Do Sul Institute of Agrarian Reform*] [*Brazil*]   (LA)
IGRDC....... Institute for Genome Research for Developing Countries [*Tunisia*] [*Proposed for 1996*]
IGS............ Impot General sur les Salaires
IGS............ Instytut Gospodarstwa Spolecznego [*Institute of the Nation's Economy*]   (POL)
IGS............ International Glaciological Society [*Cambridge, England*]
IGS............ Irish Georgian Society   (SLS)
IGS............ Isla Grande Flying School [*Puerto Rico*] [*ICAO designator*] (FAAC)
IGS............ Israel Geographical Society   (SLS)
IGS............ Israel Geological Society   (EAIO)
IGS............ Israel Gerontological Society   (SLS)
IGS............ Istanbul Giyim Sanayii ve Ticaret AS [*Istanbul Wearing Apparel Industry and Trade Corp.*]   (TU)
IGSA .... Istanbul Devlet Guzel Sanatlar Akademisi [*Istanbul State Fine Arts Academy*]   (TU)
IGSAS .... Istanbul Gubre Sanayii Anonim Sirketi [*Istanbul Fertilizer Industry Corporation*]   (TU)
IGSC......... International Group for Scientific Coordination   (MSC)
IGSCCP..... Inspectoratul General de Stat pentru Controlul Calitatii Produselor [*State General Inspectorate for Product Quality Control*]   (RO)
IGSCCPE.. Inspectoratul General de Stat pentru Controlul Calitatii Produselor de Export [*State General Inspectorate for Quality Control of Exported Products*]   (RO)
IGSN .... International Gravity Standardization Net   (PDAA)
IGSP......... Inspection Generale des Services de la Police Nationale [*Inspectorate General for National Police Services*] [*Cambodia*]   (CL)
IGSS .... Instituto Guatemalteco de Seguridad Social [*Guatemalan Social Security Institute*]   (LA)
IGSSS....... Indo-German Social Service Society [*India*]   (EAIO)
IGST......... Intergovernmental Committee on Science and Technology (BARN)
IGT .... Igala Tribal Union
IGT .... Imprimerie Graphique Tananarive
IGTPZ....... Institute of Labor Hygiene and Occupational Diseases   (RU)
IGTYF ...... International Good Templar Youth Federation [*Oslo, Norway*] (EAIO)
IGU.......... Iguassu Falls [*Brazil*] [*Airport symbol*]   (OAG)
IGU.......... Internationale Gewerbeunion [*International Association of Crafts and Small and Medium Sized Enterprises - IACME*] [*Berne, Switzerland*]   (EAIO)
IGU.......... International Gas Union [*See also UIIG*]   (EAIO)
IGU.......... International Geographical Union [*ICSU*] [*Edmonton, AB*] (EA)
IGU.......... Irkutsk State University Imeni A. A. Zhdanov   (RU)
IGU.......... Schweizerischer Gewerbeverband [*Swiss Association of Crafts and Small and Medium-Sized Enterprises*]   (EAIO)
IGUCC ...... International Geographical Union Commission on Climatology [*Switzerland*]   (EAIO)
IGUCH...... Instituto de Geografia de la Universidad de Chile [*Santiago, Chile*]   (LAA)
IGUD........ Antifascistim We'Kurbanot Ha'Nazism in Israel   (EAIO)
IGUL .... Instytut Geograficzny Uniwersytetu Lodzkiego [*Lodz University Institute of Geography*]   (POL)
IGUR .... Instituto de Geologia da Universidade do Recife [*Brazil*] (DSCA)
IGUSZI ..... Ipargazdasagi es Uzemszervezesi Intezet [*Institute of Industrial Economy and Business Organization (of the Ministry of Heavy Industry)*]   (HU)
IGUW .... Instytut Geograficzny Uniwersytetu Warszawskiego [*Warsaw University Institute of Geography*]   (POL)
IGV .... Irodagepipari es Finommechanikai Vallalat [*Business Machine and Precision Mechanics Enterprise*]   (HU)
IGVF........ Institute of the Civil Air Fleet   (RU)
IGW .... Instytut Gospodarki Wodnej [*Institute for Water Control and Exploitation*] [*Poland*]
IGW .... Interessengemeinschaft fuer Weltraumforschung [*Austria*]   (SLS)
IGWEISA ... Instituut vir Gedplomeerde Werktuigkundige en Elektegniese Ingeniurs, Suid -Afrika [*Institute of Certified Mechanical and Electrical Engineers, South Africa*]   (EAIO)
IGWT .... Internationale Gesellschaft fuer Warenkunde und Technologie [*International Association for Commodity Science and Technology*]   (EA)
IGWUA ..... International Glove Workers Union of America   (MHDB)
IGX .... Institute of Geology and Exploration [*China*]   (IRC)
IGY .... International Geophysical Year [*1958-1959*] [*ICSU*]
IGZ........... Is Guclugu Zammi [*Labor Hardship Increase*]   (TU)
IGZa .... Institut Geographique du Zaire [*Geographic Institute of Zaire*] [*Research center*]   (IRC)
IH............. Idegenforgalmi Hivatal [*Tourist Bureau*]   (HU)
IH............. Influential Hotel Ltd. [*Nigeria*]
iH .... In Heften [*In Parts*] [*Publishing*] [*German*]
ih .... In Het [*Benelux*]   (BAS)

IH............. Instituto Hidrografico [*Hydrographic Institute*] [*Portuguese*] (MSC)
IH............. Instituto Hidrografico de la Armada [*Chile*]   (MSC)
IH............. Instytut Historii [*Institute of History*] [*Poland*]
IH............. Internationale Horngesellschaft [*International Horn Society*] (EAIO)
IHA........... Imperial Highway Authority [*Ethiopia*]   (AF)
IHA........... Indian Hospital Association   (EAIO)
iha .... In Het Algemeen [*Benelux*]   (BAS)
IHA........... International Harvester Australia Ltd.
IHA........... International Hotel Association [*Paris, France*]   (EA)
IHA........... Irish Hardware Association   (SLS)
IHAR........ Instytut Hodowli i Aklimatyzacji Roslin [*Institute of Plant Cultivation and Acclimatization*] [*Warsaw, Poland*] [*Research center*]   (POL)
IHAS .... Institute for the History of Arabic Science [*Syria*] [*Research center*]   (IRC)
IHB........... Industrie- und Handelsbank [*Industry and Commerce Bank*] (EG)
ihb .... In Het Bijzonder [*Benelux*]   (BAS)
ihb .... In het Boek [*In the Book*] [*Publishing*] [*Netherlands*]
IHB........... International Hydrographic Bureau [*Monaco*]
IHBC........ International Health and Beauty Council [*British*]
IHBR .... Institut Historique Belge de Rome [*Belgium*]   (SLS)
IHC........... Institute of Hospital Catering [*Australia*]
IHC........... Instituto de Humanismo Cristiano [*Santiago, Chile*]   (LAA)
IHC........... Intercontinental Hotels Corporation
IHC........... International Hydrochemical Commission   (MSC)
IHC........... Israel Histadrut Campaign
IHCA .... International Hebrew Christian Alliance [*Ramsgate, Kent, England*]   (EA)
IHCAFE .... Instituto Hondureno del Cafe   (EY)
IHCAI....... Institut Haitien de Credit Agricole et Industriel [*Port-Au-Prince, Haiti*]   (LAA)
IHCF......... International Hospital Christian Fellowship [*Australia, Netherlands*]
IHCSERS ... International Health Centre of Socio-Economics Researches and Studies [*See also CIERSES*] [*Lailly En Val, France*] (EAIO)
IHD........... Institut Henry-Dunant [*Henry Dunant Institute*] [*Geneva, Switzerland*]   (EAIO)
IHD........... International Hydrological Decade [*UNESCO*] [*Later, IHP*]
IHDP .... Independent Hungarian Democratic Party [*Political party*] [*Hungary*]   (EAIO)
IHE........... Institute of Hospital Engineers [*Australia*]
IHE........... International Institute for Hydraulic and Environmental Engineering [*Netherlands Universities Foundation for International Cooperation*] [*Research center*]
IHEDN...... Institut des Hautes Etudes de Defense Nationale [*Institute for High National Defense Studies*] [*French*]   (WER)
IHEDREA ... Institut des Hautes Etudes de Droit Rural et d'Economie Agricole [*France*]   (DSCA)
IHEI .... Institut des Hautes Etudes Internationales de la Faculte de Droit de Paris [*France*]   (FLAF)
IHEOM..... Institut des Hautes Etudes d'Outre-Mer [*Overseas Institute of Higher Learning*] [*French*]   (AF)
IHEP .... Institute for High-Energy Physics [*China*]
IHEP .... Institute of High Energy Physics [*Chinese Academy of Sciences*] [*Research center*]   (WND)
IHES .... Institut des Hautes Etudes Scientifiques [*France*]
IHEU .... International Humanist and Ethical Union [*Utrecht, Netherlands*]   (EA)
IHF .... Federation Internationale de Handball   (OLYM)
IHF .... International Handball Federation [*Basel, Switzerland*]   (EA)
IHF .... International Health Foundation [*Brussels, Belgium*]   (EAIO)
IHF .... International Helsinki Federation for Human Rights   (ECON)
IHF .... International Hockey Federation   (BARN)
IHF .... Internazionale Holding Fiat SA [*Italy*]
IHFHR ...... International Helsinki Federation for Human Rights   (EA)
IHFPA....... Instituto de Higiene y Fomento de la Produccion Animal [*Chile*] (DSCA)
IHFR .... Institut Hydrometeorologique de Formation et de Recherche [*Hydrometeorology Research Institute*] [*Algeria*]   (EAS)
IHG........... Institute on the Holocaust and Genocide [*Israel*]   (EAIO)
IHG........... Internationale Hegel Gesellschaft   (EA)
IHGB .... Instituto Historico e Geografico Brasileiro [*Brazilian Historical and Geographical Institute*] [*Rio De Janeiro*]   (LAA)
IHGC........ International Hop Growers Convention [*See also CICH*] [*Zalec, Yugoslavia*]   (EAIO)
IHI .... Ishikawajima-Harima Heavy Industries [*Japan*]   (ECON)
IHI .... Ishkawajima Harima Heavy Industries [*Japan*]   (PDAA)
IHJ .... Institute of the Heart of Jesus [*France*]   (EAIO)
IHK........... Industrie- und Handelskammer [*Chamber of Industry and Commerce*]   (EG)
IHKM........ Instytut Historii Kultury Materialnej [*Institute of the History of Material Culture*]   (POL)
IHL........... Independent Holdings Ltd. [*Australia*]

IHLADI..... Instituto Hispano-Luso-Americano de Derecho Internacional [*Hispano-Luso-American Institute of International Law*] [*Madrid, Spain*]   (LAA)

IHM.......... Instituto Hidrografico de la Marina [*Spanish*]   (MSC)

IHMA....... Instituto Hondureno de Mercadeo Agricola [*Honduran Agricultural Marketing Institute*]   (LA)

IHMA....... International House Members Association [*University of Sydney*] [*Australia*]

IHMAT ..... Instituto de Hidrologia, Meteorologia, y Adecuacion de Tierras [*Hydrology, Meteorology, and Soil Preparation Institute*] [*Colorado*]   (LA)

IHMB....... Industrie des Huiles Minerales de Belgique [*Industry of Mineral Oils of Belgium*]   (EY)

IHM-SBF ... Insan Haklari Merkezi, Siyasal Bilgiler Fakueltesi [*Turkey*]

IHO .... International Hydrographic Organisation [*Monacon*] [*ICSU*]

IHO .... International Hydrographic Organization [*See also BHI*] [*Monaco*]

IHP .... International Hydrological Program [*UNESCO*] [*France*]

IHP .... International Hydrological Programme [*ICSU*] [*Research center*] [*France*]

IHPB .... Institute of Horticultural Plant Breeding [*Netherlands*]   (DSCA)

IHPCADE ... Institut Haitien de Promotion du Cafe et des Denrees d'Exportation [*Haitian Institute for the Promotion of Coffee and Export Commodities*]   (LA)

IHPCDE.... Institut Haitien de Promotion du Cafe et des Dendrees d'Exportation [*Haiti*]   (DSCA)

IHPMI...... International Health Policy and Management Institute   (EAIO)

IHR........... Institute for Historical Research, Bellville [*South Africa*] [*Research center*]   (IRC)

IHR........... Intreprinderile de Hoteluri si Restaurante [*Hotel and Restaurant Enterprises*]   (RO)

IHRA .... Icelandic Hotel and Restaurant Association   (EAIO)

IHS .... Iesous Hemeteros Soter [*Jesus, Our Savior*] [*Greek*]

IHS .... Iesus Heiland Seligmacher [*Jesus, Savior, Sanctifier*] [*German*]

IHS .... International Heritage Site [*UNESCO*]

IHS .... International Hurling Society

IHS .... International Hydrofoil Society   (EAIO)

IHSA .... International Headquarters of the Salvation Army   (EA)

IHSG .... Internationale Heinrich Schutz-Gesellschaft [*International Heinrich Schutz Society*]   (EAIO)

IHSRC...... International Heat Stress Research Center [*Sudan*]   (IRC)

IHSS .... Instituto Hondureno de Seguridad Social [*Honduran Social Security Institute*]   (LA)

IHSS .... International Heinrich Schutz Society [*See also IHSG*] [*Germany*]   (EA)

IHSSA ...... Industrie Horlogere Suisse [*Swiss watch manufacturer*]

IHT .... International Association of Health and Therapy Instruments [*Japan*]   (EAIO)

IHT .... Istanbul Halk Tiyatrosu [*Istanbul Peoples' Theatre*]   (TU)

IHTP .... Institut d'Histoire du Temps Present [*Institute of Contemporary History*] [*Research center*] [*France*]   (IRC)

IHU........... Ihu [*Papua New Guinea*] [*Airport symbol*]   (OAG)

IHV .... Internationale Hegel-Vereinigung [*Munich, Federal Republic of Germany*]   (EAIO)

IHVE .... Institution of Heating and Ventilating Engineers [*Later, CIBSE*]

IHW .... Instytut Handlu Wewnetrznego [*Institute of Domestic Trade*] (POL)

IHWG....... Internationale Hugo Wolf Gesellschaft [*Vienna, Austria*]   (EAIO)

IHZ........... Instytut Handlu i Zywienia [*Institute of Trade and Catering*] (POL)

IHZZ .... Instytut Handlu i Zywienia Zbiorowego [*Institute of Trade and Communal Catering*]   (POL)

II .... Aer Arann Teoranta [*Ireland*] [*ICAO designator*]   (ICDA)

i i .... I Inni [*And Others*]   (POL)

II .... Ikebana International [*Japan*]

II .... Insol International   (EA)

II .... Institute of Economics   (BU)

II .... Institute of History (of the Academy of Sciences, USSR)   (RU)

II .... Instituto de la Infancia [*Children's Institute*] [*Cuba*]   (LA)

II .... Istoriski Institut [*Historical Institute*]   (YU)

IIA............. Institute of Inter-American Affairs [*Washington, DC*]

IIA............. Institute of International Affairs

IIA............. Institut International Africain [*International African Institute*] [*Use IAI*]   (AF)

IIA............. Institut International d'Anthropologie [*International Institute of Anthropology*]   (EAIO)

IIA............. Instituto de Ingenieros Agronomos [*Argentina*]   (DSCA)

IIA............. Instituto de Investigaciones Agroindustriales [*Institute of Agroindustrial Research*] [*Peru*]   (LA)

IIA............. Instituto de Investigaciones Agronomicas [*Institute of Agronomic Research*] [*Guatemala*]   (IRC)

IIA............. Instituto de Investigaciones Agropecuarias [*Agricultural Research Institute*] [*Chile*]   (LAA)

IIA............. Interamericana de Aviacion Ltda. [*Colombia*] [*ICAO designator*] (FAAC)

IIA............. Internatioal Internet Association

IIA............. International Institute of Andragogy [*See also INSTIA*]   (EAIO)

IIA............. Israel Interfaith Association   (EAIO)

IIA............. Istituto Internazionale per l'Africa [*Italian*]   (SLS)

IIA............. Istituto Italiano degli Attuari [*Italian Institute of Actuaries*] [*Italy*]   (EAIO)

IIA............. Istituto Italo-Africano [*Italian*]   (SLS)

IIAA........... Imperial Iranian Army Aviation Corps   (ME)

IIAA........... Institute of Industrial Arts of Australia

IIAA........... Institute of Inter-American Affairs [*United Nations*]

IIAA........... Instituto de Investigacao Agronomica de Angola

IIAA........... Instituto Internacional de Asuntos Ambientales [*International Institute of Environmental Affairs - IIEA*] [*Spanish*]   (ASF)

IIAE .... Instituto de Investigaciones Aeronauticas y Espaciales [*Aeronautics and Space Research Institute*] [*Argentina*] (LA)

IIAF .... Imperial Iranian Air Force   (ME)

IIAL........... International Institute of African Languages and Culture (BARN)

IIALC .... International Institute of African Languages and Culture

IIALM .... International Institute for Adult Literacy Methods [*Tehran, Iran*] (EAIO)

IIAM......... Institut de la Recherche Agronomique Mozambique

IIAN .... Institute of History (of the Academy of Sciences, USSR)   (RU)

IIAP .... Institut International d'Administration Publique [*International Institute of Public Administration*] [*French*]   (AF)

IIAP .... Insurance Institute for Asia and the Pacific   (DS)

IIAPCO ..... Independent Indonesian American Petroleum Co.

IIAS .... Indian Institute of Asian Studies   (IRC)

IIAS .... Inter-Island Air Services   (LA)

IIAS .... International Institute for the Administrative Sciences [*Brussels, Belgium*] [*Research center*]

IIAS .... Istituto Italiano Alimento Surgelati [*Italian*]   (SLS)

IIASA .... International Institute for Applied Systems Analysis [*Research center*] [*Austria*]   (IRC)

IIB............. Ic Isleri Bakanligi [*Interior Ministry*]   (TU)

IIB............. Imar ve Iskan Bakanligi [*Reconstruction and Settlement Ministry*]   (TU)

IIB............. Institut International des Brevets [*Rijswijk*]

IIB............. Instituto de Investigaciones Bibliograficas [*Mexico*]

IIB............. Instituto Indigenista Boliviano [*Bolivia*]   (DSCA)

IIB............. International Investment Bank [*Moscow, USSR*]

IIB............. Intreprinderea Instalatii Bucuresti [*Bucharest Enterprise for Installations*]   (RO)

IIB............. Ionospharen-Institut Breisach [*Germany*]

IIB............. Irish Intercontinental Bank Ltd.

IIB............. Island Industries Board [*Australia*]

IIB............. Italian International Bank

IIBCE .... Instituto de Investigaciones Biologicas "Clemente Estable" [*Clemente Estable Institute of Biological Research*] [*Uruguay*]   (IRC)

IIBH .... International Institute of Biological Husbandry [*Ipswich, Suffolk, England*] [*Defunct*]   (EAIO)

IIBK .... Is ve Isci Bulma Kurumu Genel Mudurlugu [*Labor and Employment Organization Directorate General*]   (TU)

IIBM......... Instituto Interuniversitario de Biologia Marina [*Argentina*] (ASF)

IIBR .... Israel Institute for Biological Research   (IRC)

IIBSA .... Instituut van Inligtingsbestuur vir Suider-Afrika [*Institute of Information Management of Southernn Africa*]   (AA)

IIBT .... International Institute of Business and Technology [*Australia*]

IIC............ India International Centre   (EAIO)

IIC............ Industrial Information Centre [*Federal Institute of Industrial Research, Oshodi*] [*Nigeria*]

IIC............ Insearch Institute of Commerce [*University of Technology, Sydney, Australia*]

IIC............ Institut International des Communications [*International Institute of Communications*]   (EA)

IIC............ Instituto de Ingenieros de Chile [*Santiago, Chile*]   (LAA)

IIC............ Instituto de Integracion Cultural [*Colombia*]   (DSCA)

IIC............ Instituto de Investigacion Cientifica [*Scientific Research Institute*] [*Research center*] [*Mexico*]   (IRC)

IIC............ Instituto Interamericano da Crianca [*Montevideo, Uruguay*] (LAA)

IIC............ Inter-Institutional Committee [*Guatemala*]

IIC............ International Institute for Conservation of Historic and Artistic Works [*British*]   (EAIO)

IIC............ International Institute for Cotton [*Belgium*]   (FEA)

IIC............ Intreprinderea pentru Industrializarea Carnii [*Enterprise for the Industrialization of Meat*]   (RO)

IIC............ Iran Investment Company   (ME)

IIC............ Islamic Investment Company

IIC............ Istituto Internazionale delle Comunicazioni [*Italian*]   (SLS)

IICA.......... Institute of Instrumentation and Control, Australia   (ADA)

IICA.......... Instituto de Investigacao Cientifica de Angola

IICA.......... Instituto Interamericano de Ciencias Agricolas (de la OEA) [*Inter-American Institute of Agricultural Sciences (of the Organization of American States)*] [*Costa Rica*]   (LA)

IICA.......... Instituto Interamericano de Cooperacion para la Agricultura [*Inter-American Institute of Cooperation in Agriculture*] [*Costa Rica*]   (SLS)

IICA.......... Instituto Internacional de Ciencias Administrativas [*International Institute of Administrative Sciences*] [*Use IIAS*]   (LA)

IICA.......... Interamerican Institute for Cooperation on Agriculture [*Formerly, IAIAS*]   (EA)

IICA-CTEI ... Instituto Interamericano de Ciencias Agricolas. Centro Tropical de Ensenanza e Investigacion [*Costa Rica*]   (DSCA)

IICA-DG.... Instituto Interamericano de Ciencias Agricolas [*Costa Rica*]   (DSCA)

IICAT .... Investigacion Internacional Cooperativa del Atlantico Tropical [*International Cooperative Investigation of the Tropical Atlantic - ICITA*] [*Spanish*]   (ASF)

IICATS...... Integrated Instrumentation, Control, Automation, and Telemetry System [*Australia*]

IICA-ZA .... Instituto Interamericano de Ciencias Agricolas. Zonqa Andina [*Peru*]   (DSCA)

IICA-ZN.... Instituto Interamericano de Ciencias Agricolas, Zona Norte [*Guatemala*]   (DSCA)

IICA-ZS .... Instituto Interamericano de Ciencias Agricolas. Zone Sur [*Uruguay*]   (DSCA)

IICC.......... Industrial Investment Credit Corporation

IICC.......... Institut International d'Etude et de Documentation en Matiere de Concurrence Commerciale [*International Institute for Commercial Competition*] [*Belgium*]   (EA)

IICE .... Institut International des Caisses d'Epargne [*International Savings Banks Institute - ISBI*] [*Geneva, Switzerland*]   (EAIO)

IICE .... Instituto de Investigaciones en Ciencias Economicas [*Economic Science Research Institute*] [*Costa Rica*]   (LA)

IICG.......... Istoriski Institut Crne Gore [*Historical Institute of Montenegro*]   (YU)

IICLRR...... International Institute for Children's Literature and Reading Research [*Vienna, Austria*]   (EA)

IICM.......... Instituto de Investigacao Cientifica de Mocambique

IICM.......... Intreprinderea pentru Intretinerea Cladirii Ministerului Transporturilor si Telecomunicatiilor [*Building Maintenance Enterprise for the Ministry of Transportation and Telecommunications*]   (RO)

IICMRPS .. Intreprindere Intercooperatista de Constructii, Montaj, Reparatii, si Prestari de Servicii [*Intercooperative Enterprise for Constructions, Installations, Repairs, and Services*]   (RO)

IICMSD .... International Institute for Comparative Music Studies and Documentation [*Berlin, Federal Republic of Germany*]   (EA)

IICT .... Instituto de Investigacao Cientifica Tropical [*Institute for Tropical Scientific Research*] [*Ministry of Education*] [*Portugal*]   (EAS)

IICT .... Instituto de Investigaciones Cientificas y Tecnologicas [*Institute for Scientific and Technological Research*] [*Santa Fe, Argentina*]   (LAA)

IICY.......... International Independent Christian Youth [*See also JICI*] [*Paris, France*]   (EAIO)

IICY.......... International Investment Corp. for Yugoslavia   (IMH)

IID .... Institute of Industrial Design [*Former Czechoslovakia*]   (EAIO)

IID .... Institut International de Documentation

IID .... True Motion Indicator   (RU)

IIDA.......... Instituto Interamericano de Direito de Autor [*Interamerican Copyright Institute*]   (EAIO)

IIDARA..... Instituto Iberoamericano de Derecho Agrario y Reforma Agraria [*Ibero-American Institute of Agrarian Law and Agrarian Reform - IAIALAR*]   (EAIO)

IIDB.......... Illawarra Industry Development Board [*Australia*]

IIDC.......... Industrial Information and Documentation Centre [*Ministry of Industry*] [*People's Democratic Republic of Yemen*]

IIDES .... Instituto de Investigaciones para el Desarrollo de la Salud [*Research Institute for Health Development*] [*Ecuador*]   (IRC)

IIDET .... International Institute of Dental Ergonomics and Technology [*Germany*]   (EAIO)

IIDH .... Institut International de Droit Humanitaire [*International Institute of Humanitarian Law - IIHL*]   (EAIO)

IIDH .... Instituto Interamericano de Derechos Humanos [*Inter-American Institute of Human Rights - IIHR*]   (EA)

IIDU .... Istituto Internazionale di Diritto Umanitario [*Italian*]   (SLS)

IIe............. Deuxieme [*Second*] [*French*]   (GPO)

IIE............. Institute for International Economics

IIE............. Institute of Industrial Economics [*University of Newcastle*] [*Australia*]

IIE............. Institute of Industrial Engineers [*Irish*]   (SLS)

IIE............. Institute of International Education   (CL)

IIE............. Institut International de L'Environnement [*International Institute of Environmental Affairs - IIEA*] [*French*]   (ASF)

IIE............. Instituto de Investigaciones Economicas (Universidad de Los Andes) [*Merida, Venezuela*]   (LAA)

IIE............. Instituto de Investigaciones Electricas [*Institute of Electrical Research*] [*Research center*] [*Mexico*]   (IRC)

IIE............. Instituto do Investimento Estrangeiro [*Overseas Investment Institute*] [*Lisbon, Portugal*]   (GEA)

IIE............. Instituto Interamericano de Estadistica [*Inter-American Statistical Institute - IASI*] [*Washington, DC*]

IIEC.......... International Institute for Energy Conservation   (EA)

IIED.......... Institut International pour l'Environnement et le Developpement [*International Institute for Environment and Development - IIED*] [*French*]   (ASF)

IIED.......... International Institute for Environment and Development [*Research center*] [*British*]   (IRC)

IIEF .... Instituto de Investigaciones Economicas y Financieras [*Ecuador*]   (DSCA)

IIEFC........ Iran International Exhibitions and Fairs Corporation   (ME)

IIEJI .... Instituto Interamericano de Estudios Juridicos Internacionales   (LAA)

IIEL .... Institut International d'Etudes Ligures [*International Institute for Ligurian Studies - IILS*]   (EAIO)

IIEL .... Instituto Internacional de Estudios Laborales [*International Institute for Labor Studies - IILS*] [*Spanish*]

IIEM .... Indian Institute of Experimental Medicine   (PDAA)

IIEO.......... International Islamic Economic Organization

IIEP .... International Institute for Educational Planning [*Paris, France*] [*United Nations*]   (EA)

IIES .... Institute of Immigration and Ethnic Studies [*La Trobe University*] [*Australia*]

IIES .... Institut International d'Etudes Sociales [*International Institute for Social Studies*] [*Geneva, Switzerland*]

IIES .... Instituto de Investigaciones Economicas y Sociales [*Institute of Economic and Social Research*] [*Guatemala*]   (LA)

IIES .... International Institute for Environmental Studies   (ASF)

IIESES ...... Instituto de Investigaciones y Estudios Superiores Economicos y Sociales [*Institute for Advanced Economic and Social Research*] [*Research center*] [*Mexico*]   (IRC)

IIETF........ Information Industries Education and Training Foundation [*Australia*]

IIE-UCAB ... Instituto de Investigaciones Economicas (Universidad Catolica Andres Bello) [*Caracas, Venezuela*]   (LAA)

IIF .... Institute of History and Philosophy   (RU)

IIF .... Institut International du Froid [*International Institute of Refrigeration - IIR*] [*French*]   (ASF)

IIF .... Instituto Internacional del Frio [*International Institute of Refrigeration - IIR*] [*Spanish*]   (ASF)

IIF .... Internationales Institut fuer den Frieden [*International Peace Institute*]   (EG)

IIFCOOP .. Instituto Interamericano de Financiamiento Cooperativo [*Inter-American Institute of Cooperative Financing*] [*Santiago*]   (LAA)

IIF-IMC .... Institut des Industries de Fermentation - Institut Meurice Chimie [*CERIA Institute of the Fermentation Industry - Meurice Chemistry Institute*] [*Research center*] [*Belgium*]   (IRC)

IIFMC .... Istanbul Iktisat Fakultesi Mezunlar Cemiyeti [*Istanbul Faculty of Economics' Alumni Society*]   (TU)

IIFP .... Institut International de Finances Publiques [*International Institute of Public Finance*]   (EAIO)

IIFSO .... International Islamic Federation of Student Organizations [*Salimiyan, Kuwait*]   (EAIO)

IIFT .... Indian Institute of Foreign Trade   (PDAA)

IIG .... Indian Institute of Geomagnetism [*Ministry of Tourism and Civil Aviation*] [*Research center*]   (EAS)

IIG .... Institute of Gas Utilization   (RU)

IIG .... Instituto de Investigaciones Geologicas [*Geological Research Institute*] [*Santiago, Chile*]   (LAA)

IIGB.......... International Institute of Genetics and Biophysics [*Italy*]

IIGBM....... Institut International de Genie Biomedical [*French*]   (SLS)

IIGEAG ..... Instituto de Investigaciones Geologicas, Edafologicas y Agrobiologicas de Galic ia [*Spain*]   (DSCA)

IIGF .... Imperial Iranian Ground Forces   (ME)

IIH .... Italthai International Hotel [*Thailand*]

IIHF.......... International Ice Hockey Federation   (EAIO)

IIHHT .... International Institute of Health and Holistic Therapies [*British*]

IIHK .... Insurance Institute of Hong Kong   (EAIO)

IIHL.......... International Institute for Home Literature [*See also MIKK*] [*Belgrade, Yugoslavia*]   (EAIO)

IIHL.......... International Institute of Humanitarian Law [*See also IIDH*] [*San Remo, Italy*]   (EAIO)

IIHR .... Indian Institute of Horticultural Research   (IRC)

IIHR .... Inter-American Institute of Human Rights [*See also IIDS*] [*San Jose, Costa Rica*]   (EAIO)

IIHR .... International Institute of Human Rights   (EA)

III .... Institute for Information Industry [*Information service or system*]   (IID)

III .... Institute of Art History (of the Academy of Sciences, USSR)   (RU)

III............. Instituto de Investigaciones Industriales [*Institute of Industrial Research*] [*Mexico*]   (LAA)

III............. Instituto Indigenista Interamericano [*Indigenous Inter-American Institute*] [*Mexico*]   (EAIO)

III............. International Institute of Interpreters [*United Nations*]   (BARN)

IIIAN........ Institute of Art History (of the Academy of Sciences, USSR)   (RU)

IIIC .... International Institute for Intellectual Cooperation [*UNESCO*]

IIIE .... Indian Institute of Industrial Engineers   (PDAA)

IIIHS .... International Institute of Integral Human Sciences [*See also IISHI*]   (EAIO)

IIIT .... International Institute of Instructional Technology [*British*]

IIJ .... Inspecteur d'Identite Judiciaire [*France*]   (FLAF)

IIJM .... Institut International Jacques Maritain [*International Jacques Maritain Institute - IJMI*]   (EAIO)

IIJP........... Instituto de Investigaciones Juridico-Politicas [*Institute for Juridical and Political Research*] [*Argentina*]   (LAA)

IIK............. Icra ve Iflas Kanunu [*Executor and Bankruptcy Law*]   (TU)

IIkonSS ..... Institute of Agricultural Economics

IIL............. India International Airways (P) Ltd. [*ICAO designator*]   (FAAC)

IIL............. Institute of International Law [*Geneva, Switzerland*]   (EA)

IIL............. Intreprinderea de Industrie Locala [*Local Industry Enterprise*]   (RO)

IIL............. Publishing House of Foreign Literature   (RU)

IILA .... Instituto Italo Latino Americano [*Italo-Latin American Institute*]   (EAIO)

IILA .... Istituto Italo-Latino-Americano [*Italian-Latin American Institute*] [*Rome, Italy*]

IILFSC ...... International Institute of Law of the French Speaking Countries [*See also IDEF*] [*Paris, France*]   (EAIO)

IILRI......... International Institute for Land Reclamation and Improvement [*Netherlands*]   (DSCA)

IILS .... International Institute for Labor Studies [*Switzerland*]

IILS .... International Institute for Ligurian Studies   (EA)

IIM .... File Computer   (BU)

IIM .... Indian Institute of Metals   (SLS)

IIM .... Institut International des Meteorologists [*International Institute of Forecasters*]   (EAIO)

IIM .... Institut International du Manganese [*International Insitute of Manganese*] [*France*]   (EAIO)

IIM .... Instituto de Investigaciones en Materiales [*Institute for Materials Research*] [*Research center*] [*Mexico*]   (IRC)

IIM .... Instituto de Investigaciones Microquimicas [*Institute for Microchemical Research*] [*Rosario, Argentina*]   (LAA)

IIM .... Intreprindere de Instalatii si Montaje [*Enterprise for Installations and Assemblies*]   (RO)

IIM .... Istituto Idrografico della Marina [*Italian*]   (MSC)

IIMA......... Indian Institute of Management   (PDAA)

IIMA......... Instituto de Investigacao Medica de Angola

IIMAS .... Instituto de Investigacion en Matematicas Aplicadas y en Sistemas [*Institute of Applied Mathematics and Systems Research*] [*Research center*] [*Mexico*]   (IRC)

IIMB......... Indian Institute of Management Bagalore

IIMC......... International Institute of Maritime Culture [*Irish*]   (SLS)

IIMC......... Istituto Internazionale di Musica Comparativa [*Italian*]   (SLS)

IIME......... Instituto de Investigaciones de Mejoramiento Educativo [*Guatemala*]   (DSCA)

IIMF .... Odessa Institute of Engineers of the Maritime Fleet   (RU)

IIMI.......... International Irrigation Management Institute [*Sri Lanka*] [*Research center*]   (IRC)

IIMI.......... Intreprinderea Instalatii, Montaj, si Izolatii [*Enterprise for Installation, Assembly, and Insulation*]   (RO)

IIMK......... Institute of the History of Material Culture [*1937-1959*]   (RU)

IIMLIF...... Intreprinderea de Instalatii si Montaje pentru Lucrari de Imbunatatiri Funciare [*Enterprise for Installations and Assembly for Land Improvement Projects*]   (RO)

IIMM .... Instituto de Investigacao Medica de Mocambique

IIMM .... Instituto de Investigaciones Minero-Metalurgicas [*Mining and Metallurgical Research Institute*] [*Bolivia*]   (LA)

IIMO .... Istanbul Insaat Muhendisleri Odasi [*Istanbul Chamber of Construction Engineers*]   (TU)

IIMP......... Instituto de Investigaciones de Materias Primas [*Institute for Research on Raw Materials*] [*Santiago, Chile*]   (LAA)

IIMS .... Istituto Italiano de Medicina Sociale [*Italian*]   (SLS)

IIMSA ...... Institute of Information Management for Southern Africa   (AA)

i in .... I Inni [*And Others*]   (POL)

IIN .... Imperial Iranian Navy   (ME)

IIN .... Instituto Indigenista Nacional [*National Institute for Indian Affairs*] [*Guatemala*]   (LAA)

IIN .... Instituto Interamericano del Nino [*Inter-American Children's Institute - IACI*] [*Montevideo, Uruguay*]   (LAA)

IIN .... Istituto Italiano di Navigazione [*Italian*]   (SLS)

IIN .... Istituto Italiano di Numismatica [*Italian*]   (SLS)

IINA .... International Islamic News Agency [*Jeddah, Saudi Arabia*]   (EAIO)

IINC........ International Institute of Novel Computing [*Japan*]

IiNI .... Indian National Scientific Documentation Center, Hillside Road, New Delhi, India [*Library symbol*] [*Library of Congress*]   (LCLS)

IINIT .... Institute of the History of Science and Technology (of the Academy of Sciences, USSR)   (RU)

IINITAN ... Institute of the History of Science and Technology (of the Academy of Sciences, USSR)   (RU)

IINTE........ Instytut Informacji Naukowej, Technicznej, i Ekonomicznej [*Institute of Scientific, Technical, and Economic Information*] [*Information service or system*]   (IID)

i inzh v........ Inspector General of Engineering Troops   (BU)

IIO .... Instituto de Investigaciones Oceanologicas [*Mexico*]   (MSC)

IIO .... Inter-Allied Insurance Organization [*NATO*]   (NATG)

IIODRFES ... International Information Office of the Democratic Revolutionary Front of El Salvador [*See also OIIFDRES*] [*San Jose, Costa Rica*]   (EAIO)

IIOP........... Institut Ivoirien d'Opinion Publique [*Ivorian Institute of Public Opinion*]   (AF)

IIP............. Indian Institute of Packaging [*Research center*]   (IRC)

IIP............. Indian Institute of Petroleum [*Council of Scientific and Industrial Research*]   (EAS)

IIP............. Industria Italiana Petroli SpA

IIP............. Institute of the History of the Party   (RU)

IIP............. Institut International de la Potasse [*International Potash Institute*]   (EAIO)

IIP............. Institut International de la Presse [*International Press Institute*] [*Use IPI*]   (CL)

IIP............. Institut International de Philosophie [*International Institute of Philosophy*]   (EAIO)

IIP............. Instituto de Investigaciones Pesqueras [*Spanish*]   (MSC)

IIP............. Instituto Internacional de la Prensa [*International Press Institute*] [*Use IPI*]   (LA)

IIP............. Intergovernmental Informatics Programme [*UNESCO*]

IIP............. International Institute for Peace [*Vienna, Austria*]   (EA)

IIP............. Irish Independence Party [*Political party*]   (PPW)

IIP............. [*The*] Israel Institute of Productivity   (SLS)

IIP............. Istituto di Indagini Psicologiche   (SLS)

IIP............. Istituto Internazionale per la Pace [*International Institute for Peace*] [*Italian*]   (WER)

IIP............. Istituto Italiano dei Plastici

IIP............. Istituto Italiano di Pubblicismo [*Italian*]   (SLS)

IIPA........... India Institute of Public Administration

IIPA........... Instituto das Industrias de Pesca em Angola

IIPA........... International Intellectual Property Association   (EA)

IIPC........... Intreprinderea Industriala de Produse pentru Constructii [*Industrial Enterprise for Construction Products*]   (RO)

IIPCCPMR ... Institutul de Istorie al Partidului pe Linga Comitetul Central al Partidului Muncitoresc Roman [*Institute for Party History of the Central Committee of the Romanian Workers' Party*]   (RO)

IIPE .... India Institute of Production Engineers   (PDAA)

IIPE .... Institut International de Planification de l'Education [*French*]   (SLS)

IIPER .... International Institute for Production Engineering Research   (EAIO)

IIPF .... International Institute of Public Finance [*Saarbrucken, Federal Republic of Germany*]   (EAIO)

IIPFM .... Instituto de Investigaciones y Proyectos Forestales y Madereros [*Colombia*]   (DSCA)

IIPG.......... International Institute of Practical Geomancy [*Formerly, Society for Symbolic Studies*]   (EA)

IIPM.......... Institutul de Igiena si Protectia Muncii [*Institute for Hygiene and Labor Safety*]   (RO)

IIPO.......... International Institute of Physical Oceanography   (MSC)

IIPP .... International Institute for Promotion and Prestige [*Geneva, Switzerland*]   (EAIO)

IIPP .... Istituto Italiano di Preistoria e Protostoria [*Italian*]   (SLS)

IIPR .... Istituto Internazionale di Psicologia della Reliosita' [*International Institute for the Psychology of Religion*] [*Italy*]   (IRC)

IIPS .... Institute of Transportation Engineers   (RU)

IIPU.......... Istituto Italiano di Paleontologia Umana [*Italian*]   (SLS)

IIR............. Institute for International Research [*Australia*]

IIR............. Institute of International Relations [*Former Czechoslovakia*] [*Research center*]   (IRC)

IIR............. Institute of International Relations for Advanced Studies on Peace and Development in Asia [*Japan*]   (IRC)

IIR............. Institut International du Froid [*International Institute of Refrigeration*] [*France*]   (EA)

IIR............. Interdisciplinary Institute for Urban and Regional Studies [*Research center*] [*Austria*]   (IRC)

IIRA .... International Industrial Relations Association [*Geneva, Switzerland*]   (EA)

IIRB .... Institut International de Recherches Betteravieres [*International Institute for Sugar Beet Research*] [*Brussels, Belgium*]   (EA)

IIRB .... Israel Institute for Biological Research

IIRD..........	International Institute for Resource Development [*Austria*]
IIRG..........	Institut International de Recherches Graphologiques [*French*] (SLS)
IIRG..........	Istituto Internazionale per le Ricerche Geotermiche [*International Institute for Geothermal Research*] [*Research center*] [*Italy*] (IRC)
IIRM.........	Instituto de Investigacion de los Recursos Marinos [*Peru*] (DSCA)
IIRP..........	Institut za Izucavanje Radnickog Pokreta [*Institute for the Study of the Labor Movement*] (YU)
IIRR	International Institute of Rural Reconstruction
IIRS	Institute for Industrial Research and Standards [*Irish*] (SLS)
IIRSA	Institut International de Recherche Scientifique d'Adiopodoume
IIRUC.......	Intreprinderea pentru Intretinerea si Repararea Utilajelor de Calcul [*Enterprise for Maintenance and Repair of Computer Equipment*] (RO)
IIS	Industrial Information Service [*Industrial Development Board*] [*Sri Lanka*]
IIS	Industrial Information Services [*Council of Scientific and Industrial Research*] [*India*]
IIS	Information Industries Strategy [*Australia*]
IIS	Institute of Industrial Science [*University of Tokyo*] [*Japan*] (WED)
IIS	Institute of Information Science [*Taiwan*] (IRC)
IIS	Institute of Information Scientists [*British*] (EAIO)
IIS	Institut International de la Soudure [*International Institute of Welding - IIW*] (EAIO)
IIS	Institut International de Statistique [*International Statistical Institute - ISI*] [*French*] (ASF)
IIS	International Information Service Ltd. [*Information service or system*] (IID)
IIS	International Institute of Stress (EA)
IIS	International Insurance Society (EAIO)
IIS	Intreprinderea Industriala de Stat [*State Industrial Enterprise*] (RO)
IIS	Istituto Italiano di Speleologia [*Italian*] (SLS)
IIS	Measuring Information System (RU)
IIS	Nissan Island [*Papua New Guinea*] [*Airport symbol*] (OAG)
IISA	Institut International des Sciences Administratives [*Belgium*] (SLS)
IISc	Indian Institute of Science [*Research center*] (ERC)
IISCO	Indian Iron and Steel Company
IISE	International Institute of Social Economics [*Hull, England*] (EAIO)
IISEC........	Instituto de Investigaciones Socioeconomicas [*Socioeconomic Research Institute*] [*Bolivia*] (LA)
IISEE........	International Institute of Seismology and Earthquake Engineering [*Research center*] [*Japan*] (IRC)
IISG	Internationaal Instituut voor Sociale Geschiedenis [*International Institute for Social History*] (EA)
IISHI	Institut International des Sciences Humaines Integrales [*International Institute of Integral Human Sciences - IIIHS*] (EAIO)
IISI	International Iron and Steel Institute [*Brussels, Belgium*] [*Research center*] (EA)
IISI	Istituto Internazionale per gli Studi e le Informazioni [*Italian*] (SLS)
IISK	Institute of Art History (RU)
IISKDOO ...	Instruction for the Election of Councils and Commissions on State Social Insurance (BU)
IISL	IIS [*Intelligent Information Systems*] Ltd. [*NASDAQ symbol*]
IISL	International Institute of Space Law [*Baarn, Netherlands*] (EAIO)
IISL	Istituto Internazionale di Studi Liguri [*Italian*] (SLS)
IISM	Istituto Italiano per la Storia della Musica [*Italian*] (SLS)
IISN	Institut Interuniversitaire des Sciences Nucleaires [*Interuniversity Institute of Nuclear Sciences*] [*IUINS*] [*See also*] [*Belgium*] (WER)
IISP	Institutul de Igiena si Sanatate Publica [*Institute for Hygiene and Public Health*] (RO)
IISR	Indian Institute of Sugarcane Research (ARC)
IISR	International Institution of Submarine Research (ASF)
IISS	Institute of Agricultural Economics (BU)
IISS	International Institute for Strategic Studies (EA)
IISS	International Institute for the Science of Sintering [*Belgrade, Yugoslavia*] (EAIO)
IISSM........	Istituto Internazionale Suore di Santa Marcellina [*Milan, Italy*] (EAIO)
IIST	International Institute of Sports Therapy [*British*]
IISV	Instituto de Investigaciones de Sanidad Vegetal [*Plant Health Research Institute*] [*Cuba*] (LA)
IIT	Indian Institute of Technology [*Research center*] (ERC)
IIT	Institute of Information Technology [*University of New South Wales*] [*Australia*]
IIT	Institut Interafricain du Travail
IIT	Institut International de Transport [*International Transport Institute*] [*Research center*] [*French*] (ERC)

IIT	Institut Internationale du Theatre [*International Theatre Institute - ITI*] (EAIO)
IIT	Instituto de Investigaciones Tecnologicas [*Technological Research Institute*] [*Bogota, Colombia*] (LAA)
IIT	Instituto de Investigaciones Tecnologicas [*Institute of Technological Research*] [*Ecuador*] [*Research center*] (IRC)
IIT	Technicum of Industrial Instructors (RU)
IIT	Technion Israel Institute of Technology
IITA	International Institute of Tropical Agriculture [*Ibadan, Nigeria*] [*Research center*] (EAIO)
IITF	Imperial Iranian Task Force (ME)
IITF	India International Trade Fair
IITF	Information Industries Training Foundation [*Australia*]
IITIA	Istanbul Iktisadi ve Ticari Ilimler Akademisi [*Istanbul Academy of Economy and Commercial Science*] [*ITIA*] [*See also*] (TU)
IITM.........	Indian Institute of Tropical Meteorology
IITM.........	International Institute for Traditional Music [*Germany*] (EAIO)
IITR	Inspection of Corrective Labor (RU)
IITT-IITW ...	Institut International du Travail Temporaire - International Institute for Temporary Work (EAIO)
IIUDP.......	Institut International pour l'Unification du Droit Prive (FLAF)
IIUG	Internationales Institut fuer Umwelt und Gesellschaft [*International Institute for Environment and Society*] [*Research center*] (IRC)
IIV	Instituto de Investigaciones Veterinarias [*Chile*] (DSCA)
IIVKh.......	Institute of Hydraulic Engineers Imeni V. R. Vil'yams (RU)
IIW	Indian Institute of Welders (PDAA)
IIW	International Institute of Welding [*See also IIS*] [*British*] (EAIO)
IIWC.........	Indian Institute of World Culture (EAIO)
IIWG	International Industry Working Group [*of the Air Transport Association of America*] (EAIO)
IIYeSTEKh ...	Institute of History of Natural Sciences and Technology (of the Academy of Sciences, USSR) (RU)
IIYeT	Institute of History of Natural Sciences and Technology (RU)
IIZhT........	Institute of Railroad Transporation Engineers (RU)
ij	Idojaras Jelentes [*Weather Forecast*] (HU)
iJ	Im Jahre [*In the Year*] [*German*]
IJ	Inadana Jati [*Banque*] [*National Commerce (Bank) Cambodia*] (CL)
IJA............	Institut des Jeunes Aveugles de Faladie
IJA............	International Jute Agreement [*1982*] (FEA)
IJA............	Islamic Jurisprudence Academy [*See also IFA*] (EAIO)
IJB	Internationale Jugendbibliothek [*International Youth Library - IYL*] [*Munich, Federal Republic of Germany*] (EAIO)
IJBF..........	International Jacques Brel Foundation (EA)
iJdW	Im Jahre der Welt [*In the Year of the World*] [*German*]
IJE	Avijet SA de CV [*Mexico*] [*ICAO designator*] (FAAC)
IJF	Internationale Judo Foederation [*International Judo Federation*] [*Germany*] (EA)
IJF	International Judo Federation (OLYM)
IJGM........	Irian Jaya Geological Mapping Project [*Indonesia-Australia*]
IJI	Internationaal Juridisch Instituut [*International Juridical Institute*] [*BENELUX*]
IJI	Islamic Jamhoori Ittedad [*Islamic Democratic Alliance*] [*Pakistan*] [*Political party*]
IJI	Istok Jugo-Istok [*East South-East*] (YU)
IJIRA........	Indian Jute Industries' Research Association
IJK	Internationale Juristen-Kommission [*International Commission of Jurists*]
IJLFI	Intreprinderea Judeteana pentru Legume si Fructe Ilfov [*Ilfov County Enterprise for Vegetables and Fruit*] (RO)
IJM	Institusi Jurutera, Malaysia [*Institution of Engineers, Malaysia*] (EAIO)
IJMA........	Indian Jute Mills Association (PDAA)
IJMB.........	Interim Joint Matriculation Board
IJMI	International Jacques Maritain Institute [*See also IIJM*] (EAIO)
IJNPS.......	Instituto Joaquim Nabuco de Pesquisas Sociais [*Brazil*] (DSCA)
IJO...........	International Juridical Organization [*Later, IJOED*] (EAIO)
IJO...........	International Jute Organization [*Bangladesh*] (FEA)
IJOED	International Juridical Organization for Environment and Development (EAIO)
IJP	Israel Jewish Press (BJA)
IJPC..........	Iran-Japan Petrochemical Company (ME)
IJU	Ijui [*Brazil*] [*Airport symbol*] (OAG)
IK	Artificial Leather (RU)
IK	Executive Committee (RU)
Ik	Iktisat [*Economy*] (TU)
IK	Indeks Kupovne Snage [*Purchasing Power Index*] [*Yugoslavian*] (YU)
IK	Infrared (RU)
IK	Initiatwkreis Freiheit fuer Angola, Guinea-Bissau, und Mocambique
i k	Inspector General of Cavalry (BU)
IK	Inspekter Kanan [*Senior Inspector*] (ML)

IK .... Institute of Crystallography (of the Academy of Sciences, USSR) (RU)
IK .... Institute of Sinology (RU)
IK .... Instytut Kultury [*Cultural Institute*] [*Poland*] (EAIO)
IK .... Integrating Circuit (RU)
IK .... Intelligensiekwosient [*Intelligence Quotient*] [*Afrikaans*]
IK .... Invalidska Komisija [*Commission for the Disabled*] (YU)
IK .... Ionization Chamber (RU)
IK .... Izvrsni Komitet [*Executive Committee*] (YU)
IK .... Publishing Commission (RU)
IK .... Test Set (RU)
IK .... Tool Stock Room (RU)
IK .... True Course (RU)
IKA .... Idryma Koinonikon Asfaliseon [*Social Insurance Foundation*] [*Greek*] (GC)
IKA .... Publishing House of the Communist Academy (RU)
IKA .... Social Security [*Greek*]
IKA .... Vereinigung Internationaler Kulturaustausch
IKAG .... Internationale Konfoederation Arabischer Gewerkschaften [*International Confederation of Arab Trade Unions*] (EG)
IKAHI .... Ikatan Hakim Indonesia [*Indonesian Jurists Association*] (IN)
IKAPEL..... Ikatan Pelaut [*Seamen's Association*] (IN)
IKAPI .... Ikatan Penerbit Indonesia [*Indonesian Publishers Association*] (IN)
IKAR........ Internationale Kommission fuer Alpines Rettungswesen [*International Commission for Alpine Rescue*] [*Birchwil, Switzerland*] (EAIO)
IKB............ Industriekreditbank AG [*Bank*]
IKB............ Information Knowledge Base [*Department of Trade Development*] [*Western Australia*]
IKB............ Internationale Kommunistenbond [*International Communist League*] [*Netherlands*] (PPW)
IKB............ Isolierstoff- und Kondensatorenwerk, Berlin (VEB) [*Berlin Insulator and Condenser Plant (VEB)*] (EG)
IKC .... Ilustrowany Kurier Codzienny [*Poland*]
IKCh .... Pilot-Frequency Indicator (RU)
IKD .... All Pacific and Asian Dockworkers' Corresponding Committee [*DCC*] (RU)
IKD .... Ilerici Kadinlar Dernegi [*Progressive Women's Organization*] (TU)
IKDP......... Institute of Books, Documents, and Letters (RU)
IKE............ Institut fuer Kerntechnik und Energiewandlung [*Nuclear Technology and Energy Conversion Institute*] [*University of Stuttgart*] [*Germany*] (WND)
IKE............ United Nations Economic Commission for Europe (BU)
IKEI .... Ikerketarako Euskal Institutoa [*Instituto Vasco de Estudios e Investigacion*] [*Spain*]
IKEL.......... Internacia Komitato por Etnaj Liberecoj [*International Committee for Ethnic Liberty - ICEL*] [*Eschweiler, Federal Republic of Germany*] (EAIO)
IKF............ Etablissements I. Karim Freres
IKF............ Institouton Kalliterevseos Fyton [*Plant Improvement Institute*] [*Greek*] (GC)
IKF............ Institut fuer Kraftfahrwesen
IKF............ Instituti i Kultures Fizike [*Albanian*]
IKF............ International Korfball Federation (EA)
IKFF .... Internationella Kvinnoforbundet For Fred Och Frihet [*Women's International League for Peace and Freedom*] [*Sweden*]
IKFM........ Italian Communist Youth Federation (RU)
IKG .... Institute of Kinetics and Combustion (of the Siberian Department of the Academy of Sciences, USSR) (RU)
IKh .... Idiotikis Khriseos [*(For) Private Use*] [*Automobile license plate designation*] (GC)
IKH........... Ihre Koenigliche Hoheit [*Her Royal Highness*] [*German*]
IKhF.......... Institute of Chemical Physics (of the Academy of Sciences, USSR) (RU)
IKhFK....... Isopropylchlorophenyl Carbamate (RU)
IKhFK....... Isopropyl Ester of Trichlorophenylcarbamic Acid (RU)
IKhN......... Scientific Research Institute of Surgical Neuropathology (RU)
IKhPS .... Institute of the Chemistry of Naturally Occuring Compounds (of the Academy of Sciences, USSR) (RU)
IKhR .... Institute of Chemical Reagents (RU)
IKhS.......... Institute of the Chemistry of Silicates (of the Academy of Sciences, USSR) (RU)
IKhTI........ Ivanovo Institute of Chemical Technology (RU)
IKI............. Cosmic Radiation Intensity (RU)
IKI............. Iki [*Japan*] [*Airport symbol*] (OAG)
IKI............. Industrija Kovinskih Izdelkov [*Metal Products Industry*] [*Maribor*] (YU)
IKI............. Institute of Space Research [*Former USSR*] [*Acronym is based on foreign phrase*]
IKIM......... Institute of Islamic Understanding [*Think-tank*] [*Malaysia*] (ECON)
IKINDO .... Association of Indonesian Consultants (IMH)
IKIP .... Institut Keguruan dan Ilmu Pendidikan [*Teacher Training Institute*] (IN)

IKJ .... Internationales Kuratorium fuer das Jugendbuch [*International Board on Books for Young People*]
IKK .... Informationen zu Kernforschung und Kerntechnik
IKK .... International Control Commission (RU)
IKKA......... Kulfoldi Kereskedelmi Akcio [*Foreign Trade Enterprise*] (HU)
IKKh .... Institute of Potato Growing (RU)
IKKI......... Executive Committee of the Communist International [*1919-1943*] (BU)
IKKI......... Ispolnitelny Komitet Kommunisticheskogo Internatsionale [*Executive Committee of the Communist International*] [*1919-1943*] [*Russian*] (RU)
IKKIM...... Executive Committee of the Communist Youth International (RU)
IKKN .... Instytut Ksztalcenia Kadr Naukowych [*Institute for Training Scientific Personnel*] (POL)
IKKP......... Indochinese Communist Party (RU)
IKL............ Industrija Kotrljajucih Lezaja [*Roller Bearing Industry*] [*Belgrade*] (YU)
IKL............ Infrared Rays (RU)
IKL............ Ingenieurkontor Lubeck [*Lubeck Engineering Office*] [*Submarine design firm*]
IKL............ Isaenmaallinen Kansanliike [*Patriotic People's Movement*] [*Finland*] [*Political party*] (PPE)
IKM .... Ikatan Karyawan Muhammadijah [*Muhammadijah Workers Association*] (IN)
Ikm............ Ikmal [*Completion (of a project or job), Supplies*] (TU)
IKM .... Institut Kimia Malaysia
IKM .... Pulse-Code Modulation (RU)
IKMVO .... Electoral Committee of Moscow Military District (RU)
IKN .... Internationale Kommission fuer Numismatik [*International Numismatic Commission*]
IKNPT....... Italian Confederation of National Trade Unions (RU)
IKO .... Catastrophic Failure Rate (RU)
IKO .... Instituut voor Kernphysisch Onderzoek [*Institute for Research in Nuclear Physics*] [*Netherlands*] (WEN)
IKO .... Plan Position Indicator (RU)
IKOA .... Institouton Koinonikis kai Oikonomikis Anasyngrotiseos [*Social and Economic Reconstruction Institute*] (GC)
IKOKD ...... Istanbul Kibrislilar Ogrenim ve Kultur Dernegi [*Istanbul Cypriots' Educational and Cultural Association*] (GC)
IKOM .... Industriska Kovnica "Oreskovic Marko" [*"Marko Oreskovic" Industrial Plant*] [*Zagreb*] (YU)
IKOMM .... Instituut vir Kommunikasienavorsing [*Institute for Communication Research*] [*Human Sciences Research Council*] [*South Africa*] (AA)
IKOM priBAN ... Institute of Clinical and Social Medicine of the Bulgarian Academy of Sciences (BU)
ikon .... Economic [*Bulgarian*] (BU)
IKOPZ....... Testing Commission of the Okhta Gunpowder Plant (RU)
IKOS.......... Institut fuer Kommunikations- und Organisationssoziologische Forschung eV (SLS)
IKOSZ....... Informaciofeldolgozasi, Kibernetikai, es Operaciokutatasi Kozponti Szakosztaly [*Central Department for Information Processing, Cybernetics, and Operations Research*] (HU)
IKP............ Indiai Kommunista Part [*Communist Party of India*] [*Political party*]
IKP............ Indian Communist Party [*Political party*]
IKP............ Indonesian Communist Party [*Political party*]
IKP............ Institute of the Red Professoriat (RU)
IKP............ International Karahoram Project [*Pakistan*]
IKP............ Irakskaia Kommunisticheskaia Partiia [*Iraqi Communist Party*] [*Political party*]
IKP............ Iranian Communist Party [*Political party*]
IKP............ Iraqi Communist Party [*Political party*]
IKP............ Israeli Communist Party [*Political party*]
IKP............ Italian Communist Party [*Political party*]
IKPK......... International Kriminal-Polizei-Kommission [*International Criminal Police Commission*]
IKPT......... Italian Confederation of Trade Unions (RU)
IKR .... Ikaros DK [*Denmark*] [*ICAO designator*] (FAAC)
IKR .... Iparszeru Kukoricatermelesi Rendszer [*Industry-Type Corn Production System*] (HU)
IKR .... Izba Kontroli Rachunkowej [*Account Auditing Bureau*] (POL)
IKRPiT ...... Izba Kontroli Rachunkowej Poczty i Telekomunikacji [*Account Auditing Bureau of Posts and Telecommunications*] (POL)
IKrS .... Istaknuta Kurirska Stanica [*Advanced Courier Station*] [*Military*] (YU)
IKS............ Indicirana Konjska Snaga [*Indicated Horsepower*] (YU)
IKS............ Infrared Glass (RU)
IKS............ Inspektorat Kontroli Skarbowej [*Poland*]
IKS............ Institute of Kolkhoz Construction (RU)
IKS............ Institut fuer Kirchliche Sozialforschung [*Institute for the Sociology of Religion*] [*Research center*] [*Austria*] (IRC)
IKS............ Instituut vir Kleinsake [*University of the Western Cape*] [*South Africa*] (AA)
IKS............ International Kodaly Society (EAIO)

IKS............. International Kolping Society [*See also IKW*] [*Cologne, Federal Republic of Germany*]   (EAIO)

IKSA......... Measuring, Checking, and Counting Equipment   (RU)

IKSM........ Institute of Clinical and Social Medicine   (BU)

IKSR .... Internationale Kommission zum Schutze des Rheins Gegen Verunreinigung [*International Commission for the Protection of the Rhine Against Pollution - ICPRAP*]   (EAIO)

IKT............ Iakutaviatrans [*Russian Federation*] [*ICAO designator*]   (FAAC)

Ikt .... Iktisadi [*Economy, Economic*] [*Turkish*]   (TU)

IKT............ Infrared Engineering   (RU)

IKT............ Irkutsk [*Former USSR*] [*Airport symbol*]   (OAG)

IKT............ Isolier- und Kaeltetechnik [*Insulation and Refrigeration Equipment Works*]   (EG)

IKTC......... Ingiltere Kibris Turk Cemiyeti [*Turkish Cypriot Society of Great Britain*]   (GC)

IKTP......... Institute of Complex Transportation Problems   (RU)

IKTTC .... Istanbul Kibris Turkler Talebe Cemiyeti [*Istanbul Turkish Cypriot Student Society*]   (GC)

IKU .... Institutt for Kontinentalsokkelundersokelser og Petroleumsteknologi A/S [*Continental Shelf and Petroleum Technology Research Institute*] [*Research center*] [*Norway*]   (IRC)

IKU .... Ivanovo Communist University   (RU)

IKV .... Boiler Water Evaporator   (RU)

IKV .... Iktisadi Kalkinma Vakfi [*Economic Development Fund Directorate General*]   (TU)

IKV .... Ingatlankezelo Vallalat [*Real Estate Management Enterprise*]   (HU)

IKV .... Institute of Communist Education   (RU)

IKV .... Institut fuer Kunststoffverarbeitung [*Plastic Processing Institute*] [*Rheinisch-Westfaelische Technische Hochschule Aachen*] [*Research center*]   (ERC)

IKV .... InterKerkelijk Vredesberaad [*Interchurch Peace Council*] [*Netherlands*]

IKW .... Internationales Kolpingwerk [*International Kolping Society - IKS*] [*Cologne, Federal Republic of Germany*]   (EAIO)

IKWN .... Instytut Krajowych Wlokien Naturalnych [*Institute of Natural Fibers*] [*Research center*] [*Poland*]   (IRC)

IKY .... Idryma Kratikon Ypotrofion [*State Scholarships Institute*] [*Greek*]   (GC)

IKZh .... All-Union Scientific Research Institute of Farm Animal Feeding   (RU)

IL .... Aircraft Designed by S. V. Il'yushin   (RU)

IL .... Foreign Literature   (RU)

Il................ Ilinio [*Portuguese*]

Il................ Illinois   (IDIG)

il................. Illustrated By, Illustrated   (BU)

il................. Ilman Lisamaksuvelvollisuutta [*Finland*]

il................. Ilustrace [*or Ilustrator*] [*Illustration or Illustrator*]   (CZ)

il................. Ilustracja [*Illustration*] [*Publishing*] [*Poland*]

il................. Ilustrado [*Illustrated*] [*Publishing*] [*Portuguese*]

Il................ Ilustre [*Illustrious*] [*Correspondence*] [*Spanish*]

IL .... Ilyushin [*Former USSR*] [*ICAO aircraft manufacturer identifier*]   (ICAO)

IL .... Indicator Lamp   (RU)

IL .... Industrielaeden [*Industrial Sales Outlets (in production enterprises)*]   (EG)

iL .... In Liquidation [*In Liquidation*]   (EG)

IL .... Institut fur Leichte Flachentragwerke [*Institute for Lightweight Structures*] [*Germany*]   (IRC)

IL .... Instituto del Libro [*Book Institute*] [*Cuba*]   (LA)

IL .... Instytut Lacznosci [*Communication Institute*]   (POL)

IL .... Invoerend Land [*Benelux*]   (BAS)

IL .... Israel [*ANSI two-letter standard code*]   (CNC)

IL .... Israel Lira   (BJA)

IL .... Italian Lira [*Monetary unit*]

IL .... Izrael [*Israel*] [*Poland*]

IL .... Lenin Institute   (RU)

IL .... Measuring Line   (RU)

IL .... Publishing House of Foreign Literature   (RU)

ILA............ Illaga [*Indonesia*] [*Airport symbol*]   (OAG)

ILA............ Impresa Libica Asfalti

ILA............ Indian Library Association   (SLS)

ILA............ Informationsstelle Lateinamerika [*Germany*]

ILA............ Institute of Latin American Studies   (RU)

ILA............ International Landbouw Instituut [*Benelux*]   (BAS)

ILA............ International Law Association [*British*]   (EA)

ILA............ International Leprosy Association [*India*]

ILA............ Iranian Library Association   (SLS)

ILA............ Israel Library Association   (SLS)

ILA............ Italo Libica Agricola

ILAB.......... International League of Antiquarian Booksellers [*See also LILA*] [*Bonn, Federal Republic of Germany*]   (EAIO)

ILACC....... Indo-Latin American Chamber of Commerce [*India*]

ILACD....... Ibero Latin American College of Dermatology   (EA)

ILACDE .... Instituto Latinoamericano de Cooperacion y Desarrollo [*Latin American Institute for Cooperation and Development*]   (EAIO)

ILACIF...... Instituto Latinoamericano de Ciencias Fiscalizadoras [*Caracas, Venezuela*]   (LAA)

ILADES..,.. Instituto Latinoamericano de Doctrina y Estudios Sociales [*Latin American Institute of Social Doctrine and Social Studies*] [*Chile*]   (EAIO)

ILADT....... Instituto Latinoamericano de Derecho Tributario [*Latin American Tax Law Institute*]   (EAIO)

ILAFA ...... Instituto Latinoamericano del Fierro y el Acero [*Latin American Iron and Steel Institute*]   (EAIO)

ILAI.......... Italo-Latin American Institute   (EA)

ILAM........ International Library of African Music [*Rhodes University*] [*South Africa*]   (AA)

ILAMA..... International Life-Saving Appliance Manufacturers Association   (PDAA)

ILAN .... Forest Institute of the Academy of Sciences, USSR   (RU)

ILANET .... Information and Libraries Access Network [*Australia*]

ILANUD ... Instituto Latinoamericano de las Naciones Unidas para la Prevencion del Delito y Tratamiento del Delincuente [*United Nations Latin American Institute for the Prevention of Crime and the Treatment of Offenders*] [*Costa Rica*] [*Research center*]   (IRC)

ILAP......... Instituto Latinoamericano del Plastico [*Latin American Plastics Institute*] [*Buenos Aires, Argentina*]

ILAP......... Integrated Local Area Planning

ILAR......... Ilmi Istisare ve Arastirmalar Kurulu [*Council of Scientific Consultation and Research*] [*National Defense Ministry*]   (TU)

ILAR......... International League Against Rheumatism [*Switzerland*]   (SLS)

ILAR......... International League for Animal Rights   (EA)

ILARI .... Instituto Latinoamericano de Relaciones Internacionales [*Latin American Institute of International Relations*]   (LA)

ILAS......... Institute of Latin American Studies [*China*]   (IRC)

ILASA ...... Institute of Landscape Architects of Southern Africa   (AA)

ILASA ...... Instituut van Landskapargitekte van Suidelike Afrika [*Institute of Landscape Architects of Southern Africa*]   (AA)

ILASE-Esperantisto Internacia Ligo de Agrikulturaj Specialistoj-Esperantistoj [*International League of Agricultural Specialists-Esperantists - ILASE*]   (EAIO)

ILATES..... Instituto Latinoamericano de Estudios Sindicales   (LAA)

ilb.............. Engineer Airdrome Battalion   (BU)

ILB............ Institut fuer Landmaschinenbau [*Institute for Agricultural Machine Production*]   (EG)

ILBANK .... Iller Bankasi [*Provinces Bank*]   (TU)

ILBE .... International League of Blind Esperantists [*See also LIBE*] [*Belgrade, Yugoslavia*]   (EAIO)

ILBFRLP... International Lelio Basso Foundation for the Rights and Liberation of Peoples   (EA)

ILC............ Independent Living Centre [*Australia*]

ILC............ Insearch Language Centre [*Australia*]

ILC............ International Labor Conference [*A section of the International Labor Organization*] [*United Nations*]

ILC............ International Law Commission [*United Nations*]

ILCA......... Industria Lechera de Caldas [*Armenia*]   (COL)

ILCA......... Instituto Linguistico Colombo Americano [*Colombia*]   (COL)

ILCA......... International Livestock Center for Africa [*Addis Ababa, Ethiopia*] [*Research center*]   (AF)

ILCA......... International Livestock Centre for Africa [*Addis Ababa, Ethiopia*]

ILCC......... Italian Language and Culture Center [*Australia*]

ILCCG....... International Laity and Christian Community Group [*See also LAEEC*] [*Sion, Switzerland*] [*Defunct*]   (EAIO)

ILCCTC..... International Liaison Committee on Co-Operative Thrift and Credit [*Paris, France*]   (EA)

ILCE......... Instituto Latinoamericano de Cinematografia Educativa [*Latin American Educational Film Institute*] [*Mexico*]   (LAA)

ILCE......... Instituto Latinoamericano de la Comunicacion Educativa [*Latin American Institute for Educational Communication*] [*Mexico*] [*Research center*]   (IRC)

ILCO......... Infrastructural, Logistics, Council Operations [*NATO*]

ILCRPK..... International Liaison Committee for Reunification and Peace in Korea   (EAIO)

ILCT......... Instituto de Laticinios Candido Tostes [*Brazil*]   (DSCA)

ILCTA .... International League of Commercial Travelers and Agents   (EA)

ILCV......... Inscriptiones Latinae Christianae Veteres

ILD .... I Love Dance [*Competition in US and Canada*]

ILDA......... Industrial Lands Development Authority [*Australia*]

ILDA......... International LASER Display Association   (EA)

ILDES .... Instituto Latinoamericano de Desenvolvimento Economico e Social [*Latin American Institute for Social and Economic Research*] [*Research center*] [*Brazil*]   (IRC)

ILDIS .... Instituto Latinoamericano de Investigaciones Sociales [*Latin American Social Research Institute*]   (LA)

ILDP......... Industrial Land Development Program [*Australia*]

ILDS .... International League of Dermatological Societies [*Vancouver, BC*] (EAIO)

ILDSC .... Industrial Land Development Subcommittee [*New South Wales, Australia*]

ILDU .... Industrias Laneras del Uruguay [*Wool Industries of Uruguay*] (LA)

ILDV .... Instituto Libertad y Democracia de Venezuela [*Institute for Liberty and Democracy of Venezuela*] [*Research center*] (IRC)

Ile .... Ilustre [*Illustrious*] [*Correspondence*] [*Spanish*]

ILE .... Institute of Language Education [*Hong Kong*]

ILE .... Institute of Legal Executives [*Australia*]

ILE .... Institut fuer Lateinamerikaforschung und Entwicklungszusammenarbeit [*Institute for Cooperation in Latin American Research and Development*] [*Switzerland*] (SLS)

ILEC .... Institut de Liaisons et d'Etudes Commerciales [*France*] (FLAF)

ILEF .... Internacia Ligo de Esperantistaj Foto-Kino-Magnetofon-Amatoroj [*International League of Esperantist Amateur Photographers, Cinephotographers, and Tape-Recording*] (EAIO)

ILEI .... Internacia Ligo de Esperantistaj Instruistoj [*International League of Esperantist Teachers*] (EAIO)

ILEI .... Ligue Internationale des Enseignants Esperantistes [*International League of Teachers of Esperanto*] (AF)

ILek .... Instytut Lekow [*Institute of Pharmacy*] [*Poland*]

ILEP .... Federation Internationale des Associations Contre la Lepre [*International Federation of Anti-Leprosy Associations - ILEP*] (EAIO)

ILESA .... Institute of Lighting Engineers of South Africa (AA)

ILET .... Instituto Latinoamericano de Estudios Transnacionales [*Latin American Institute for Transnational Studies - LAITS*] (EAIO)

ILE(V) .... Institute of Legal Executives (Victoria) [*Australia*]

ILEXIM ..... Intreprinderea de Stat pentru Comert Exterior [*State Enterprise for Foreign Trade*] (RO)

Il F .... Ilahiyet Fakultesi [*School of Divinity*] [*Ankara University*] (TU)

ILF .... Industrie Lainiere Francaise (FLAF)

ILF .... Institut de la Langue Francaise [*France*]

ILF .... International Liaison Forum of Peace Forces [*See also FILFP*] [*Moscow, USSR*] (EAIO)

ILF .... International Lifeboat Federation [*England*] (EAIO)

ILF .... International Lotto Fund

ILF .... International Luge Federation [*Austria*]

ILFF .... International Liga for Fred og Frihed [*International League for Peace and Freedom*] [*Denmark*] (EAIO)

ILFJIMB... Intreprinderea Legume Fructe Judet Ilfov Municipiul Bucuresti [*Ilfov County Bucharest Municipality Enterprise for Vegetables and Fruits*] (RO)

ILFMB ...... Intreprinderea pentru Legume si Fructe Municipiul Bucuresti [*Bucharest Municipality Enterprise for Vegetables and Fruits*] (RO)

ILFP .... Forum International de Liaison des Forces de la Paix [*International Liaison Forum of Peace Forces - ILF*] (EA)

ILGA .... International Lesbian and Gay Association [*Formerly, International Gay Association*] (EA)

ILGA .... Israel Landscape Gardeners' Association (EAIO)

ILGAZ .... Institute of Local Government Association of Zambia

ILGU .... Publishing House of the Leningrad State University (RU)

Ilh .... Ilahiri [*Etcetera*] (TU)

ILHA .... International Labor History Association

ILHS .... Intreprinderea de Lucrari Hidrotehnice Speciale [*Enterprise for Special Hydrotechnical Projects*] (RO)

ILI .... Institute of Flight-Testing (RU)

ILI .... Institute of History and Linguistics (RU)

ILIAD .... Inter-Library Image Access and Delivery [*Australia*]

ILIC .... Intreprinderile Locale Industriale din Cluj [*Local Industrial Enterprises of Cluj*] (RO)

ILID .... Institut fuer Landwirtschaftliche Information und Dokumentation [*Germany*] (DSCA)

ILID .... Integrated Land Information Database [*Australia*]

ILIS .... Integriertes Leitungs- und Informationssystem [*Integrated Control and Data System*] (EG)

ILIS .... International Labour Information System [*Proposed*]

ILIXCO .... International Liquid Xtal Corp. (ADPT)

ILIYaZV.... Institute of Literature, Art, and Language of the East (RU)

ILJAK .... Il Jandarma Alay Komutani [*Provincial Gendarmery Regimental Command*] (TU)

Ilk-Der ...... Ilkokul Ogretmenleri Dernegi [*Elementary School Teachers' Association*] (TU)

ILKE .... Internacia Libro-Klubo Esperantista (EA)

Ilk Sen........ Istanbul Ilkokul Ogretmenleri Sendikasi [*Istanbul Elementary School Teachers' Union*] (TU)

ill .... Illatiivi [*Finland*]

ill .... Illetekes [*Authoritative*] (HU)

ill .... Illustrasjon [*Illustration*] [*Publishing Danish/Norwegian*]

ill .... Illustrated, Illustration, Illustrator (RU)

ill .... Illustratie [*Illustration*] [*Publishing*] [*Netherlands*]

ill .... Illustration [*Illustration*] [*Publishing*] [*French*]

ill .... Illustrazione [*Illustration*] [*Publishing*] [*Italian*]

ill .... Illustrerad [*Illustrated*] [*Publishing*] [*Sweden*]

ill .... Illustriert [*Illustrated*] [*Publishing*] [*German*]

ill .... Illusztracio [*Illustration*] (HU)

ILL .... Institut Laue-Langevin [*Grenoble, France*] (ECON)

ILL .... Institut Max Von Laue/Paul Langevin [*Max Von Laue/Paul Langevin Institute*] [*Grenoble, France*] [*Research center*] (IRC)

ILL .... Intreprinderea de Locuinte si Locale [*Housing and Public Buildings Enterprise*] (RO)

Illmo........... Illustrissimo [*Most Illustrious*] [*Italian*] (GPO)

Il(l)mo .... Il(l)ustrissimo [*Most Illustrious*] [*Portuguese*] (GPO)

ILLS .... Institutul de Limbi si Literaturi Straine [*Institute for Foreign Languages and Literatures*] (RO)

illum .... Illuminerede [*Illuminated*] [*Publishing Danish/Norwegian*]

illust .... Illustratie [*Illustration*] [*Publishing*] [*Netherlands*]

illust .... Illustriert [*Illustrated*] [*Publishing*] [*German*]

illustr.......... Illustrasjon [*Illustration*] [*Publishing Danish/Norwegian*]

illustr.......... Illustratie [*Illustration*] [*Publishing*] [*Netherlands*]

illustr.......... Illustrazione [*Illustration*] [*Publishing*] [*Italian*]

illustr.......... Illustre [*Illustrated*] [*Publishing*] [*French*]

illustr.......... Illustrerad [*Illustrated*] [*Publishing*] [*Sweden*]

Illustr .... Illustrissime [*Most Illustrious*] [*French*] (MTD)

Illustrat ...... Illustration [*Illustration*] [*Publishing*] [*German*]

illusztr........ Illusztralt [*Illustrated*] [*Publishing*] [*Hungary*]

ilm .... Ilmailu [*Aeronautics*] [*Finland*]

ilm .... Ilmaisee [*or Ilmauksessa*] [*Express or Expression*] [*Finland*]

ilm .... Ilmaista [*Finland*]

ilm .... Ilmestynyt [*Finland*]

ilm .... Ilmoittaa [*Finland*]

ilm .... Ilmoitus [*Finland*]

ILM .... Immeubles a Loyer Moyen [*French*] (FLAF)

ILM .... Information Logical Machine (RU)

ILM .... International Legal Materials [*Ethiopia*]

Ilma .... Ilustrisima [*Most Illustrious*] [*Spanish*]

Ilma .... Ilustrissima [*Illustrious*] [*Portuguese*]

ILMA........ Instituto Latinoamericano de Mercadeo Agricola [*Colombia*] (COL)

ILMAC ...... Israeli-Lebanese Mixed Armistice Commission (ME)

Ilmo........... Ilustrisimo [*Most Illustrious*] [*Spanish*]

Ilmo........... Ilustrissimo [*Most Illustrious*] [*Portuguese*]

ILMR........ International Laboratory of Marine Radioactivity (MSC)

ILN .... Immeubles a Loyer Normal [*French*] (FLAF)

ILN .... Interne Leitungsnummer [*German*] (ADPT)

ILO .... Iloilo [*Philippines*] [*Airport symbol*] (OAG)

ILO .... International Labor Office (CL)

ILO .... International Labor Organization [*ICSU*] (LA)

ILO .... International Labour Organisation [*Geneva, Switzerland*] [*United Nations*] (EA)

ILO .... Islamic Liberation Organization

ILOB......... Institute of Animal Nutrition and Physiology [*TNO*] [*Research center*] [*Netherlands*] (IRC)

ILOB......... Instituut voor Landbouwkundig Onderzoek van Industriele Biologische, Biochemische, en Chemische Producten [*Institute for Agricultural Research of Industrial Biological, Biochemical, and Chemical Products*] [*Netherlands*] (ARC)

ILO MIZ ... International Latitude Observatory of Mizusawa [*Research center*] [*Japan*] (EAS)

ILOR......... Local Tax on Income [*Italian*] (IMH)

ILOSU....... International Labor Organization Staff Union [*Geneva, Switzerland*] (EAIO)

ILot .... Instytut Lotnictwa [*Institute of Aircraft*] [*Poland*]

ILOTES..... Innovative Languages Other than English in Schools [*Australia*]

ILP .... Ile Des Pins [*New Caledonia*] [*Airport symbol*] (OAG)

ILP .... Ilpo Aruba Cargo NV [*ICAO designator*] (FAAC)

ILP .... Independent Labor Party [*Trinidadian and Tobagan*] (LA)

ILP .... Independent Liberal Party [*Israel*] [*Political party*] (BJA)

ILP .... Industria Lopez Pallomaro [*Colombia*] (COL)

ILP .... Institut Libyen du Petrole

ILP .... International Links Program [*Overseas aid*] [*Australia*]

ILP .... Islamic Liberation Party [*Tunisia*] [*Political party*] (MENA)

ILP .... Israel Labor Party [*Political party*]

ILPA .... Industria e Laboracao de Produtos Agricolas [*Labor and Industry of Agricultural Products*] [*Portuguese*] (WER)

ILPAP........ Ilektrokinita Leoforeia Periokhis Athinon-Peiraios [*Electric-Powered Buses of the Athens-Piraeus Area*] (GC)

ILPE .... Industria Lobera y Pesquera del Estado [*National Seal and Fishing Industry*] [*Uruguay*] (LA)

ILPES........ Instituto Latinoamericano de Planificacion Economica y Social [*Latin American Institute for Economic and Social Planning*] [*Santiago, Chile*] [*United Nations*]

ILPiKhD.... Institute of Forestry Problems and Wood Chemistry (of the Academy of Sciences, Latvian SSR) (RU)

ILPNR....... International League for the Protection of Native Races

ILR............. Air Iliria [*Yugoslovia*] [*ICAO designator*]   (FAAC)

ILR............. Ilorin [*Nigeria*] [*Airport symbol*]   (OAG)

ILRAD....... International Laboratory for Research on Animal Diseases [*Nairobi, Kenya*]

ILRC......... International LASER RADAR Conference   (PDAA)

ILRES........ Istituto Ligure di Ricerche Economiche e Sociali [*Italian*]   (SLS)

ILRI........... International Institute for Land Reclamation and Improvement [*Research center*] [*Netherlands*]   (ARC)

ILRLP........ International League for the Rights and Liberation of Peoples [*Rome, Italy*]   (EAIO)

ILRS .... Interlibrary Resource Sharing Section [*National Library of Australia*]

ILRS .... International League of Religious Socialists [*Aerdenhout, Netherlands*]   (EAIO)

ILRZeleznik ... Ivo Lola Ribar Zeleznik [*Ivo Lola Ribar Machine Factory in Zeleznik*]   (YU)

ILS............. Icelandic Literary Society   (EAIO)

ils............... Indicated Horsepower   (RU)

ILS............. Information Logical System   (RU)

ILS............. Institute of Labor Studies [*Lesotho*]   (IRC)

ILS............. Institut fuer Landes- und Stadtentwicklungsforschung [*Dortmund, West Germany*] [*Information retrieval*]

ILS............. Institut fuer Lichtempfindliche Stoffe [*Institute for Light-Sensitive Materials*]   (EG)

ILS............. Instrument Landing System   (AF)

ILS............. International Limnological Society [*See also SIL*]   (ASF)

ILS............. International Lunar Society [*Spain*]

ILS............. Inzenyrsko Letecka Sluzba [*Aviation Engineer Service*]   (CZ)

ILS............. Societe Ivoirienne Leroy-Somer

ILSA......... International Law Students Association   (EAIO)

ILSAM ..... International Language for Servicing and Maintenance   (PDAA)

ILSAN .... Ilac ve Ham Maddeleri Sanayii AS [*Medicine and Raw Materials Industry Corporation*]   (TU)

ILSMH...... International League of Societies for Persons with Mental Handicap [*Brussels, Belgium*]   (EA)

ILSSA-VIOLA ... Industria Lamiere Speciali Soc. Az.-Carlo Viola [*Italian*]

ILS-TNO... Institute for Leather and Shoe Research - Netherlands Central Organization for Applied Natural Scientific Research [*Netherlands*]

ILTAS........ Ilac Sanayii ve Ticaret Anonim Sirketi [*Medicinal Industry and Trade Corporation*]   (TU)

ILTC.......... International Leadership Training Conference

ILTE .... Industria Libraria Tipografica Editrice

ILTE .... Ioniki kai Laiki Trapeza tis Ellados [*Ionian and People's Bank of Greece*]   (GC)

ILTL .... Israel Lung and Tuberculosis League   (EAIO)

ILTS .... Institute of Low Temperature Science [*Hokkaido University*] [*Japan*]   (EAS)

ilus........... Ilustracion [*Illustration*] [*Publishing*] [*Spanish*]

ilust .... Ilustracion [*Illustration*] [*Publishing*] [*Spanish*]

ilustr......... Ilustracao [*Illustration*] [*Publishing*] [*Portuguese*]

ilustr.......... Ilustracja [*Figure, Illustration*]   (POL)

ilustr.......... Ilustrowal [*Illustrated By*]   (POL)

ILUVM...... I Love You Very Much [*Correspondence*]   (DSUE)

ILV............ Fraunhofer-Institut fuer Lebensmitteltechnologie und Verpackung [*Fraunhofer Institute for Food Technology and Packaging*] [*Munich, West Germany*] [*Information retrieval*]   (ARC)

ilv .... Ilave [*Supplement*] [*Turkey*]   (GPO)

ILV............ Instituto Linguistico de Verano [*Summer Institute of Linguistics*]   (LA)

ILVBIDT... In Liebe Vereint bis in dem Tod [*United in Love until Death*] [*German*]

Ilv Rev....... Ilaveler ve Revisyonlar [*Additions and Revisions, as to a document*]   (TU)

ILY............ International Literacy Year

ILY............ Italian Liberal Youth [*Political party*]   (EAIO)

ILYa......... Information Logical Language   (RU)

ILYaZV ..... Scientific Research Institute of Comparative History of Literatures and Languages of the West and East   (RU)

ILZIC .... Indian Lead Zinc Information Centre   (PDAA)

ILZSG .... International Lead and Zinc Study Group [*British*]   (EA)

IM .... Actuating Mechanism   (RU)

IM .... Data Processor, Data-Processing Machine   (RU)

im .... Idezett Mu [*Opus Citatum*]   (HU)

IM .... Igazsagugyminiszter [*Minister of Justice*]   (HU)

IM .... Ihre Majestaet [*Her Majesty*] [*German*]

im .... Imeni [*Named For*]   (RU)

im .... Imienia [*Named For*]   (POL)

IM .... Immanuel Mission

IM .... Im Mittel [*On an Average*] [*German*]

IM .... Imperia [*Car registration plates*] [*Italian*]

IM .... Indische Mercuur [*Benelux*]   (BAS)

IM .... Industrial Magistrate [*Australia*]

IM .... Industriemeldung [*Industrial Statistics*]   (EG)

IM .... Information for Mariners   (RU)

IM .... Institute of Mathematics (of the Siberian Department of the Academy of Sciences, USSR)   (RU)

IM .... Institute of Microelectronics [*Sweden*]   (IRC)

IM .... Institutet for Metalforskning [*Institute for Metals Research*] [*Sweden*]   (PDAA)

IM .... Instituto de la Mujer [*Women's Insitute*] [*Spain*]   (EAIO)

IM .... Instruction Ministerielle [*Benelux*]   (BAS)

IM .... Instytut Metalurgii [*Institute of Metallurgy*]   (POL)

IM .... Instytut Morski [*Marine Institute*] [*Poland*]   (MSC)

im .... Intramuskulaer [*Intramuscular*] [*German*]   (GCA)

IM .... Intreprinderea Miniera [*Mining Enterprise*]   (RO)

IM .... Iraq Museum   (BJA)

IM .... Israel Museum   (BJA)

IM .... Measuring Device   (RU)

IM .... Multiseater Fighter   (RU)

im .... Nominal   (BU)

im .... Nominative [*Case*]   (RU)

IM .... Performing Mechanism   (BU)

IM .... Power Meter   (RU)

IM .... Pulse Modulation   (RU)

IM .... Research Method   (RU)

Im .... Testing Machine   (RU)

IMA .... Iamalele [*Papua New Guinea*] [*Airport symbol*]   (OAG)

IMA .... Independent Music Association   (EAIO)

IMA .... India Missions Association

IMA .... [*The*] Indian Medical Association   (SLS)

IMA .... Indonesische Maatschappij op Aandelen [*Indonesia*]   (BAS)

IMA .... Industria de Articulos de Madera [*Colombia*]   (COL)

IMA .... Industria Metalica para Automotores [*Colombia*]   (COL)

IMA .... Industria Mocambicana de Aco   (EY)

IMA .... Information Medicale Automatisee [*Automated Medical Information*] [*INSERM*] [*Information service or system*]   (IID)

IMA .... Institute of Marine Affairs [*Trinidadian and Tobagan*]   (ASF)

IMA .... Institute of Mediterranean Affairs

IMA .... Institute of Mercantile Agents [*Australia*]

IMA .... Institute of Modern Art [*Brisbane*] [*Australia*]

IMA .... Institute of the Science of Machines and Automation (of the Academy of Sciences, Ukrainian SSR)   (RU)

IMA .... Instituto de Matematica Aplicadas [*Institute of Applied Mathematics*] [*Rosario, Argentina*]   (LAA)

IMA .... Instituto de Mecanica Aplicada [*Applied Mechanics Institute*] [*Argentina*] [*Research center*]   (ERC)

IMA .... Instituto Magdalena Aulina [*Magdalena Aulina Institute*] [*Barcelona, Spain*]   (EY)

IMA .... Inter-Mountain Airways [*ICAO designator*]   (FAAC)

IMA .... International Milling Association [*See also AIM*] [*Brussels, Belgium*]   (EAIO)

IMA .... International Mineralogical Association [*ICSU*] [*Marburg, Federal Republic of Germany*]   (EA)

IMA .... International Mycological Association [*See also AIM*] [*England*]   (EAIO)

IMA .... Intreprinderea pentru Mecanizarea Agriculturii [*Enterprise for the Mechanization of Agriculture*]   (RO)

IMA .... Irish Medical Association   (SLS)

IMA .... Israel Medical Association   (SLS)

IMA .... Itinerant Medicine Association [*Ivory Coast*]

IMA .... Tagged-Atom Rate Meter   (RU)

IMABRA... Implementos Agricola Brasil, Industria, e Comercio Ltd. [*Brazil*]   (DSCA)

IMAC .... International Movement of Apostolate of Children [*Paris, France*]   (EA)

Imaca .... Imaculada [*Immaculate*] [*Portuguese*]

IMACASA ... Implementos Agricolas Centroamericanos, SA [*Agricultural Implements Corp.*] [*El Salvador*]

IMACC...... Instituto de Matematica, Cibernetica, y Computacion [*Institute of Mathematics, Cybernetics, and Computation*] [*Cuba*]   (LA)

IMACE...... Association des Industries Margarinieres des Pays de la CEE [*Association of Margarine Industries of the EEC Countries*] [*Belgium*]

IMACOL... Importadora Agricola e Comercial Ltd. [*Brazil*]   (DSCA)

IMACS...... Association Internationale des Mathematiques et Calculateurs en Simulation [*International Association for Mathematics and Computers in Simulation*] [*ICSU*] [*Belgium*]   (SLS)

IMACY...... Industrie Malienne de Cycles et Cyclomoteurs

IMADA ..... Ikatan Mahasiswa Djakarta [*Djakarta College Student Association*]   (IN)

IMADE ..... Instituto Madrileno de Desarrollo [*Spain*]   (EY)

Imadefolk... Institut Malgache des Arts Dramatiques et Folkloriques [*Malagasy*]   (SLS)

IMADUNI ... Impuesto Aduanero Unico a las Importaciones [*Single Import Customs Tax*] [*Uruguay*]   (LA)

IMAF........ Instituto de Matematicas, Astronomia, y Fisica de Cordoba [*Argentina*]   (LAA)

IMAF........ International Martial Arts Federation   (EAIO)

IMAG .... Implementos e Maquinas Agricolas Ltd. [*Brazil*] (DSCA)
IMAG .... Institut de Mathematiques Appliquees de Grenoble [*Institute of Applied Mathmatics in Grenoble*] [*French*] (ADPT)
IMAG .... Instituut voor Mechanisatie, Arbeid, en Gebouwen [*Institute of Agricultural Engineering, Labor, and Buildings*] [*Research center*] [*Netherlands*] (IRC)
IMAGE ...... Institut de Mathematiques de Grenoble [*Grenoble Institute of Mathematics*] [*France*] (PDAA)
IMAGIS .... Igazsagugyi Muszaki-Gazdasagi Szakertok (Kozponti Bizottsag) [*(Central Committee of) Judicial Scientific-Economic Experts*] (HU)
IMAI .... Instituto Mexicano de Asistencia a la Industria [*Centro de Informacion Sobre Envase y Embalaje*] [*Mexico*]
IMAIA ...... Intreprinderea Mecanica a Agriculturii si Industriei Alimentare [*Machine Enterprise for Agriculture and the Food Industry*] (RO)
IMAJ .... International Management Association of Japan (PDAA)
IMAL .... Industrias Metalicas Asociadas Limitada [*Colombia*] (COL)
IMAL .... Industries Maghrebines de l'Aluminium [*Manufacturer and distributor of aluminum products*] [*Tunis, Tunisia*] (MENA)
IMALCO ... Muebles Metalicos de Aluminio [*Colombia*] (COL)
IMAM .... Instituto Mexicano de Administracion [*Mexican Institute of Management*] (PDAA)
IMAM .... Intercessory Ministry among Muslims [*India*]
IMAN .... Institucion Mexicana de Asistencia a la Ninez [*Mexican Child Welfare Institution*] (LAA)
IMAN .... Instituut vir Mannekragnavorsing [*Institute for Manpower Research*] [*Human Sciences Research Council*] [*South Africa*] (AA)
IMANF ...... Institute of Manufacturing [*Royal Leamington Spa, Warwickshire, England*] (EAIO)
IMAPEC ... Industries Mauritaniennes de Peche [*Mauritanian Fishing Industries*] (AF)
IMARC ...... Israeli Movement Against Religious Coercion (EAIO)
IMARPE ... Instituto del Mar de Peru [*The Sea Institute of Peru*] (LA)
IMART ...... International Medical Association for Radio and Television [*Brussels, Belgium*] (EAIO)
IMAS .... Industrial and Management Services Ltd.
IMAS .... Industrie Marbriere Senegalaise [*Senegalese Marble Industry*] (AF)
IMAS .... Institute of Microbiology, Academia Sinica [*China*] (IRC)
IMAS .... Instituto Mixto de Ayuda Social [*Mixed Institute for Social Aid*] [*Costa Rica*] (LA)
IMASA ...... Industria de Maquinas Agricolas Fuchs SA [*Brazil*] (DSCA)
IMASh .... Institute of the Science of Machines (RU)
imaskb .... Engineer Camouflage Battalion (RU)
imaskr .... Engineer Camouflage Company (RU)
IMASLA ... International Muslim Academy of Sciences, Letters, and Arts
IMASOIE ... Industrie Marocaine de Soieries [*Moroccan Silk Industry*] (AF)
IMATDFW ... International Movement ATD Fourth World [*France*] (EAIO)
IMAU .... Instituto Metropolitano de Aseo Urbano [*Urban Agency for Solid Wastes Handling*] [*Venezuela*] (IMH)
IMAUS ...... Integriertes Marketing-Analyse-und Ueberwachungssystem [*German*] (ADPT)
IMB .... Illawarra Mutual Building Society Ltd. [*Australia*]
IMB .... Imbaimadai [*Guyana*] [*Airport symbol*] (OAG)
IMB .... Industria Metalurgica Banateana [*Banat Metallurgical Industry*] (RO)
IMB .... Institute of Marine Biology [*Puerto Rico*] (DSCA)
IMB .... Institute of Molecular Biotechnology [*Germany*]
IMB .... Instituto Municipal de Botanica [*Argentina*] (DSCA)
IMB .... Institutul Meteorologic Bucuresti [*Bucharest Meteorological Institute*] (RO)
IMB .... International Marine Board
IMB .... International Maritime Bureau [*Research center*] [*British*] (IRC)
IMB .... International Merchant Bank Ltd. [*Nigeria*]
IMB .... Intreprinderea de Montaje Bucuresti [*Bucharest Assembly Enterprise*] (RO)
IMBASA ... Industria de Mamona da Bahia SA [*Brazil*] (DSCA)
IMBB .... Institute of Molecular Biology and Biotechnology [*Greece*] (IRC)
IMBC .... Independent Multicultural Broadcasting Corporation
IMBEC ...... Importadora de Bens de Consumo [*Importer of consumer goods*] [*Mozambique*]
IMBEL ...... Industria de Material Belico [*Ordnance Industry*] [*Brazil*] (LA)
IMBiGS ..... Instytut Mechanizacji Budownictwa i Gornictwa Skalnego [*Institute for the Mechanization of Building and Rock Mining*] [*Poland*] (IRC)
IMC .... Industria de Materiales de la Construccion [*Construction Materials Industry*] [*Cuba*] (LA)
IMC .... Industria Materialelor de Constructii [*Construction Materials Industry*] (RO)
IMC .... Ingenieria Mecanica Colombiana [*Colombia*] (COL)
IMC .... Institute for Mass Communication [*Norway*] (EAIO)
IMC .... Instituto Mexicano del Cafe [*Mexican Coffee Institute*] (LA)
IMC .... International Management Center [*Hungary*] (ECON)

IMC .... International Maritime Committee (ASF)
IMC .... International Marketing Commission [*See also CIM*] [*Brixham, Devonshire, England*] (EAIO)
IMC .... International Materials Conference (DCTA)
IMC .... International Medical Commission for Health and Human Rights [*Switzerland*]
IMC .... International Meeting Center [*Germany*] (EAIO)
IMC .... International Meteorological Center [*India*] [*WMO*] (MSC)
IMC .... International Micrographic Congress
IMC .... International Mineral & Chemical Corp. (DSCA)
IMC .... International Monetary Conference (ECON)
IMC .... International Music Council [*Paris, France*] (EA)
IMC .... Intreprinderea de Materiale de Constructie [*Construction Materials Enterprise*] (RO)
IMC .... Irish Manuscripts Commission (SLS)
IMC .... Preparatory Committee for the International Medical Commission for Health and Human Rights (EAIO)
IMCA .... Information Management and Consulting Association [*Information service or system*] (IID)
IMCA .... Institute of Management Consultants in Australia
IMCAR ..... International Movement of Catholic Agricultural and Rural Youth [*Belgium*] (DSCA)
IMCARY ... International Movement of Catholic Agricultural and Rural Youth [*See also MIJARC*] [*Louvain, Belgium*] (EAIO)
IMCC .... International Medical Co-Operation Committee
IMCE .... Instituto Mexicano de Comercio Exterior [*Mexican Foreign Trade Institute*] (LA)
IMCE .... International Meeting of Cataloguing Experts
IMCES ...... Industrias Mecanicas Colombo Espanolas [*Colombia*] (COL)
IMCh .... Testing Machine for Pig Iron (RU)
IMCI .... Industries Metallurgiques de la Cote-D'Ivoire
IMCIC .... Instituto Mexicano-Cubano de Intercambio Cultural [*Mexican-Cuban Cultural Exchange Institute*] (LA)
IMCJ .... International Movement of Catholic Jurists (EAIO)
IMCJ .... International Music Competition of Japan
IMCL .... International Movement of Catholic Lawyers [*France*]
IMCM .... Intreprinderea de Montaje Conducte Magistrale [*Enterprise for the Installation of Main Pipelines*] (RO)
IMCO .... Industrial Merchandising Company
IMCO .... Intergovernmental Maritime Consultative Organization [*Later, IMO*] (WEN)
IMCOLEMN ... Intreprinderea de Stat pentru Constructii si Montaje Lemn [*State Enterprise for Wood Constructions and Assemblies*]
IMCOMA ... Immobiliere Construction du Maroc
IMCoS .... International Map Collectors' Society (EAIO)
IMCS .... Industrias Metalicas Colombo Espanolas [*Colombia*] (COL)
IMCS .... International Meeting in Community Service [*Germany*] (EAIO)
IMCS .... International Movement of Catholic Students [*France*]
IMCS .... Pax Romana, International Movement of Catholic Students [*See also MIEC*] [*Fribourg, Switzerland Paris, France*] (EAIO)
IMCSAC ... International Movement of Catholic Students - African Secretariat [*An association*] (EAIO)
IMCWR ..... International Movement of Conscientious War Resisters [*Tel Aviv, Israel*] (EAIO)
IMCYC ...... Instituto Mexicano del Cemento y del Concreto [*Mexican Institute for Cement and Concrete*] (PDAA)
IMCyP .... Instituto de Madera, Celulosa, y Papel [*Institute of Wood, Cellulose, and Paper*] [*Research center*] [*Mexico*] (IRC)
IMD .... Imonda [*Papua New Guinea*] [*Airport symbol*] (OAG)
IMD .... Indian Meteorological Department (MSC)
IMD .... Institute of Music and Drama [*Sudan*]
IMD .... Institut fur Maschinelle Dokumentation (NITA)
IMD .... Instytut Medycyny Doswiadczalnej [*Institute for Experimental Medicine*] [*Poland*]
IMD .... International MTM [*Methods-Time-Measurement*] Directorate (EA)
IMD .... Intreprinderea de Material Didactic [*Teaching Materials Enterprise*] (RO)
IMD .... Intreprinderile Metalurgice Dunariene [*Danube Metallurgical Enterprises*] (RO)
IMD .... Introduction Manuelle des Donnees [*French*] (ADPT)
IMD .... Iron and Minerals Development
IMD .... Istituto di Mutagenesi e Differenziamento [*Mutagenesis and Differentiation Institute*] [*Italian*] (ARC)
IMDB .... Intreprinderea de Material Didactic Bucuresti [*Bucharest Teaching Materials Enterprise*] (RO)
IMDBI .... Industrial and Mining Development Bank of Iran (ME)
IMDEQUI ... Industrias Mecanicas del Quindio [*Armenia*] (COL)
IMDER ...... Investigaciones Multidisciplinarias para el Desarrollo Rural. Universidad del Valle [*Colombia*] (COL)
IMDIA .... Italian Milk and Dairy Industries Association (EAIO)
IMDICOL ... Importadora y Distribuidora Colombiana de Licores [*Colombia*] (COL)
IMDP .... Integrated Management Development Program [*Australia*]

IMDS........ International Meat Development Scheme [*United Nations Defunct*] (EAIO)
IMDT .... International Institute for Music, Dance, and Theatre in the Audio-Visual Media [*Later, Mediacult International Institute for Audio-Visual Communication and Cultural Development*]
IME .... Ideiglenes Muszaki Eloirasok [*Temporary Technical Directives*] (HU)
IME .... Industrias Mecanicas del Estado [*State Mechanical Industries*] [*Argentina*] (LA)
IME .... Institute of Mathematics Education [*La Trobe University*] [*Australia*]
IME .... Institut Mondial de l'Environnement [*World Environment Institute - WEI*] [*French*] (ASF)
IME .... Instituto de Medicos Especialistas [*Institute of Medical Specialists*] [*Rio De Janeiro, Brazil*] (LAA)
IME .... Instituto Militar de Engenharia [*Military Engineering Institute*] [*Brazil*] (LA)
IME .... Manual for Assembly and Operation (RU)
IME .... Marx and Engels Institute [*1920-1931*] (RU)
IME(AB) ... Institution of Mechanical Engineers (Australian Branch)
IMEB........ Institute of Microbiology, Epidemiology, and Bacteriophage (RU)
IMEB........ International Movement of Esperantist Bicyclists [*See also BEMI*] [*The Hague, Netherlands*] (EAIO)
IMEB........ Intreprinderea pentru Mecanizarea Evidentei Bucuresti [*Bucharest Enterprise for the Mechanization of Records*] (RO)
IMEC........ Industria de Materiales Electricos Colombianos [*Colombia*] (COL)
IMEC........ Institut Marocain de l'Emballage et du Conditonnement [*Morocco*]
IMEC........ Institut Mondial d'Ecologie et de Cancerologie [*World Institute of Ecology and Cancer*] [*Belgium*] (FLAF)
IMEC........ Interuniversity Microelectronics Center [*Belgium*] (IRC)
IMEC........ Intreprinderea de Microproductie si Lucrari Experimentale de Constructii [*Enterprise for Microproduction and Experimental Construction Projects*] (RO)
IMECO ..... Intreprinderea de Comert Exterior [*Foreign Trade Enterprise*] [*Romanian*] (RO)
IMEDE...... Institut pour l'Etude des Methodes de Direction de l'Enterprise [*A management development institute*] [*Lausanne, Switzerland*]
IMEG .... Iranian Management Engineering Group
IMEI.......... Ipari Minoseg Ellenorzo Intezet [*Quality Control Institute for Industry*] (HU)
IMEKh ...... Institute of Mechanics (of the Academy of Sciences, USSR) (RU)
IMEKO ..... Internationale Messtechnische Konfoderation [*International Measurement Confederation*] [*ICSU Budapest, Hungary*] (EAIO)
IMEKO ..... Miedzynarodowa Federacja Pomiarow i Budowy Przyrzadow Precyzyjnych [*International Measurement and Precision Instrument Construction Federation*] (POL)
IMEL........ Marx-Engels-Lenin Institute at the TsK KPSS (RU)
IMELCA ... Ingenieria Electrica y Mecanica Ltda. [*Barranquilla*] (COL)
IMELPA ... Industrias Metalicas de Palmira [*Colombia*] (COL)
IMELS ...... Marx-Engels-Lenin-Stalin Institute (RU)
IMEMO .... Institute of World Economics and International Affairs [*Russian*] (BARN)
IMEMO .... Institute of World Economics and International Relations (of the Academy of Sciences, USSR) (RU)
IMENUR .. Institut Mondial des Cites Unies pour l'Environnement et l'Urbanisme [*French*] (SLS)
IMEO .... Istituto Italiano per il Medio ed Estremo Oriente [*Italian Near and Far East Association*]
IMEPLAN ... Institut Mexicain pour l'Etude des Plantes Medicinales [*Mexico*]
IMER........ Instytut Mechanizacji i Elektryfikacji Rolnictwa [*Institute for Mechanization and Electrification of Agriculture*] (POL)
IMER........ Instytut Mechanizacji i Elektrypikacji Rolnictwa [*Institute for Mechanization and Electrification of Agriculture*] [*Poland*] (PDAA)
IMERUC... Istituto Meridionale di Urbanistica Commerciale [*Italian*] (SLS)
IMES........ Industrias Metalicas Escobar [*Colombia*] (COL)
IMES........ Instituto Militar de Estudios Superiores [*Military Institute of Advanced Studies*] [*Uruguay*] (LA)
IMESA ...... Institution of Municipal Engineers of Southern Africa (AA)
IMESCO ... Industrias Metalicas y Esmaltes de Colombia Ltda. [*Colombia*] (COL)
IMESKO ... Izmir Madeni Esya Sanayii Anonim Sirketi [*Izmir Metal Products Industry Corporation*] (TU)
IMESS....... Institute for the Mechanization and Electrification of Agriculture (BU)
IMET........ Institute of Metallurgy Imeni A. A. Baykov (RU)
IMETAL ... Industria de Metales [*Colombia*] (COL)

IMETRA ... Institut de Medecine Tropicale Reine Astrid
IMEUDC ... International Medium Edition of the Universele Decimale Classificatie
IMEVALLE ... Industrias Metalicas del Valle [*Colombia*] (COL)
IMEWACO ... Industrias Metalicas Waco [*Barranquilla*] (COL)
IMEX........ Importadora e Exportadora de Produtos Regionais e Mercantis Ltd. [*Brazil*] (DSCA)
IMEX........ International Marine Expedition (MSC)
IMEX........ Procedure d'Importation et d'Exportation [*France*] (FLAF)
IMEXCO... Importaciones Exportaciones Comerciales [*Colombia*] (COL)
IMEX-GAL ... Sociedade Importadora e Exportadora de Generos Alimenticios [*Brazil*] (DSCA)
IMEXIN.... Empresa Importadora y Exportadora de Infraestructura [*Enterprise for Import and Export of Infrastructure*] [*Cuba*] (LA)
IMEXPAL ... Empresa Importadora y Exportadora de Plantas Alimentarias, Sus Implementos, y Derivados [*Import and Exports Enterprise for Food Processing Plants and Related Accessories*] [*Cuba*] (LA)
IMF............ Imphal [*India*] [*Airport symbol*] (OAG)
IMF............ Indonesian Missionary Fellowship
IMF............ Inosinemonophosphoric Acid, Inosinic Acid (RU)
IMF............ Institute of Physics of Metals (RU)
IMF............ Institutul de Medicina si Farmacie [*Institute for Medicine and Pharmacy*] (RO)
IMF............ Institutul Medico-Farmaceutic [*Medico-Pharmaceutical Institute*] (RO)
IMF............ Interim Minesweeping Force [*Military*]
IMF............ Internasionale Monetere Fonds [*International Monetary Fund*] [*Afrikaans*]
IMF............ International Marketing Federation [*Paris, France*] (EAIO)
IMF............ International Metalworkers Federation [*See also FIOM*] [*Geneva, Switzerland*] (EAIO)
IMF............ International Monetary Fund [*United Nations*] (EA)
IMFBRM .. Institutul de Medicina Fizica, Balneoclimatologie, si Recuperare Medicala [*Institute for Physical Medicine, Balneo-Climatology, and Medical Recovery*] (RO)
IMFC........ Investment and Merchant Finance Corporation Ltd. [*Australia*] (ADA)
IMFC........ Iron Maiden Fan Club [*British*] (EAIO)
IMFCA ...... Institutul de Mecanica Fluidelor si Constructii Aerospatiale [*Institute for Fluid Mechanics and Aerospace Constructions*] (RO)
IMF-JC ..... International Metal Workers' Federation Japan Council
IMFL........ Institut de Mecanique de Fluides de Lille
IMFU .... Imperial Military Foul-Up [*Bowdlerized version*] (DSUE)
IMG........... Imperial Cargo Airlines Ltd. [*Ghana*] [*ICAO designator*] (FAAC)
IMG .... Institut de Mecanique de Grenoble [*Grenoble Institute of Mechanics*] [*National Scientific Research Center*] [*France*] (ERC)
IMG .... Institute of Marketing [*Ghana*] (EY)
IMG .... Instytut Mechanizacji Gornictwa [*Institute of Mining Mechanization*] (POL)
IMG .... International Mail Gram (MHDB)
IMG .... International Marxist Group (EY)
IMG .... Ivoirienne du Marbre et du Granit
IMG .... Societe Commerciale d'Importation de Marchandises Generales
IMGB .... Intreprinderea de Masini Grele din Bucuresti [*Bucharest Heavy Machinery Enterprise*] (RO)
IMGC .... Istituto di Metrologia "Gustavo Colonetti" [*Colonetti (Gustavo) Institute of Metrology*] [*Italian*] [*Research center*] (IRC)
IMGCSA ... Islamic Missionaries Guild of the Caribbean and South America (EAIO)
IMGD .... Inspecteur Militair Geneeskundige Dienst [*Benelux*] (BAS)
IMGE .... Idryma Metallevtikon kai Geologikon Epevnon [*Institute for Mineral and Geological Research*] [*IGME*] [*See also*] (GC)
IMGE .... Initiation aux Mecanismes Generaux de l'Economie [*Collection dirigee par Jean Marchal*] (FLAF)
IMGO .... Sailing Instructions of Fleet Hydrographic Departments (RU)
IMGRE...... Institut Mineralogii Geokhimii i Kristallokhimii Redkikh Elementov [*Institute of Mineralogy, Geochemistry, and Crystallochemistry of Rare Elements*] [*Former USSR*] (IRC)
IMGSAC ... Islamic Missionaries' Guild of South America and the Caribbean [*Trinidad and Tobago*]
IMG-TNO ... Instituut voor Milieuhygiene en Gezondheidstechniek TNO [*Research Institute for Environmental Hygiene TNO*] [*Netherlands Organization for Applied Scientific Research (TNO)*] [*Research center*] [*Netherlands*] (ERC)
IMGU .... Publishing House of the Moscow State University Imeni M. V. Lomonosov (RU)
IMGW/OM ... Instytut Meteorologii i Gospodarki Wodnej, Oddzial Morski [*Institute of Meteorology and Water Economy, Marine Division*] [*Poland*] (MSC)
IMH.......... Institute of Materials Handling [*South Africa*] (SLS)

IMH......... Institutul de Meteorologie si Hidrologie [*Institute of Meteorology and Hydrology*] [*Consiliul National al Apelor Romania*] (EAS)

IMH.......... Instytut Ministerstwa Hutnictwa [*Institute of the Ministry of Metallurgy*] (POL)

IMH.......... Island Maternity Hospital

IMH.......... Suid-Afrikaanse Instituut van Materiaalhantering [*South African Institute of Materials Handling*] (AA)

IMHE........ Programme on Institutional Management in Higher Education [*Research center*] [*French*] (IRC)

IMI .... Ine [*Marshall Islands*] [*Airport symbol*] (OAG)

IMI .... Institute of the Motor Industry [*South Africa*] (AA)

IMI .... Institut Metapsychique International [*International Metaphysics Institute*] [*France*] (EAIO)

IMI .... Instituto de Medicina Industrial Ltda. [*Colombia*] (COL)

IMI .... Institut pour le Management de l'Information [*Information Management Institute*] [*Ministere de l'Industrie; Universite de Compiegne*] [*Research center*] [*French*] (ERC)

IMI .... International Manganese Institute [*France*] (EAIO)

IMI .... International Marketing Institute

IMI .... Irkutsk Medical Institute (RU)

IMI .... Israeli Military Industry

IMI .... Istituto Mobiliare Italiana [*Italian state-owned bank*] (ECON)

IMI .... Istituto Mobiliare Italiano [*Italian Public Law Credit Institute*]

IMI .... Izhevsk Mechanical Engineering Institute (RU)

IMIA......... International Machinery Insurers Association [*Munich, Federal Republic of Germany*] (EAIO)

IMIA......... International Marketing Institute of Australia (ADA)

IMIA......... International Medical Informatics Association [*IFIP special interest group*] [*Richmond Hill, ON*] (EAIO)

IMIA......... Intreprinderea Montaj Instalatii Automatizare [*Enterprise for Automation Assemblies and Installations*] (RO)

IMIC......... Iceland Music Information Centre (EAIO)

IMIC......... Industria Mecanica Italo-Colombiana [*Colombia*] (COL)

IMIC......... International Medical Information Center, Inc. [*Tokyo, Japan*]

IMIC......... International Music Industry Conference

IMiD......... Instytut Matki i Dziecka [*Mother and Child Institute*] [*Poland*]

IMIF......... International Maritime Industries Forum [*British*] (EAIO)

IMII........... Industrial Manufacturers' Inspection Institute [*Ministry of International Trade and Industry*] [*Japan*]

IMINOCO ... Iranian Marine International Oil Company (ME)

Iminoco ... Iran Marine International Company (OMWE)

IMIO........ Marine Research and Oceanographic Institute (BU)

IMIQ .... Instituto Mexicano de Ingenieros Quimicos [*Mexican Institute of Chemical Engineers*] (LA)

IMIS......... Instituto Mexicano de Investigaciones Siderurgicas [*Mexico*]

IMISA .... Instituut van Munisipale Ingenieurs van Suidelike Afrika [*Institution of Municipal Engineers of Southern Africa*] (AA)

Imit .... Imitation [*Imitation*] [*German*]

imit............ Imiteret [*Imitated*] [*Danish/Norwegian*]

imit............ Imitiert [*Artificial*] [*German*]

IMIT......... Instituto Mexicano de Investigaciones Tecnologicas [*Mexican Institute of Technological Research*] [*Mexico*] (LAA)

IMJ .... Institut za Makedonski Jezik [*Macedonian Language Institute*] (YU)

IMJHCA ... International Messianic Jewish Hebrew Christian Alliance [*British*] (EAIO)

IMK .... Institute of Material Culture (RU)

IMK .... Institut Makanda Kabobi [*Makanda Kabobi Institute*] [*Zaire*] (AF)

IMK .... Institutt for Masse Kommunikasjon [*Institute for Mass Communications*] [*Norway*] (EAIO)

IMK .... Simikot [*Nepal*] [*Airport symbol*] (OAG)

IMKh .... Institute of World Economy and World Politics [*1925-1947*] (RU)

IMKhA ...... Idryma Meleton tis Khersonisou tou Aimou [*Aimos Peninsula Studies Foundation*] [*A Macedonian studies society in Salonica*] (GC)

IMKhiMP ... Institute of World Economy and World Politics (RU)

IML .... Industrias Metalicas Lisasa [*Colombia*] (COL)

IML .... Institute of Marxism-Leninism at the TsK KPSS (RU)

IML .... Institut fuer Marxismus-Leninismus (Beim ZK der SED) [*Institute for Marxism-Leninism (A part of the SED Central Committee)*] (EG)

IML .... Institut Monetaire Luxembourgeois [*Luxembourg Monetary Institute*] (GEA)

IML .... Instituto Medico Legal [*Institute of Medical Law*] [*Portuguese*]

IML .... Institutul de Medicina Legala [*Institute of Legal Medicine*] (RO)

IML .... Instituut vir Mediese Literatuur [*Institute for Medical Literature*] [*South African Medical Research Council*] (AA)

IML .... Island Air Ltd. [*Fiji*] [*ICAO designator*] (FAAC)

IMLE........ Industria Maderera Laminada Ecuatoriana [*Ecuador*] (DSCA)

IMLI......... Institute of World Literature Imeni A. M. Gor'kiy (of the Academy of Sciences, USSR) (RU)

IMM .... Ilektromagnitikai Monades [*Electromagnetic Units*] (GC)

Imm........... Immeuble [*French*]

imm .... Immune (RU)

IMM .... Institute of Marketing Management [*South Africa*] (AA)

IMM .... Institute of Materia Medica [*Chinese Academy of Medical Sciences*] (IRC)

IMM .... Institute of Metal Science and Metallurgy (RU)

IMM .... Institute of Municipal Management [*Australia*]

IMM .... Instytut Maszyn Matematycznych [*Computer Institute*] [*Poland*]

IMM .... Instytut Medycyny Morskiej [*Institute for Marine Medicine*] [*Poland*]

IMM .... International Maritime Mobile [*Telecommunications*]

IMM .... Intreprinderea Metalurgica de Morarit [*Metallurgical Milling Enterprise*] (RO)

IMMA ...... Institute of Metals and Minerals Australasia

IMMA ...... Institute of Muslim Minority Affairs (EAIO)

IMMA ...... International Motorcycle Manufacturers Association (EAIO)

IMMB ...... Inspectoratul de Militie a Municipiului Bucuresti [*Militia Inspectorate of the Bucharest Municipality*] (RO)

IMME .... Instituto de Materiales y Modelos Estructurales [*Universidad Central de Venezuela*] [*Venezuela*]

IMMI .... International Irrigation Management Institute (GNE)

IMMI .... International Mass Media Institute (EA)

IMMOAF ... Societe Immobiliere et Hypothecaire Africaine [*African Real Estate and Mortgage Company*] [*Zaire*] (AF)

IMMOAFRIC ... Societe Immobiliere Afrique

IMMP .... Institute of Malaria and Medical Parasitology (BU)

IMMPC.... International Marine Meteorological Punch Card (MSC)

IMMT .... Institute for Manufacturing Management and Technology [*University of New South Wales*] [*Australia*]

IMN........... Instituto Meteorologico Nacional [*Costa Rica*] (SLS)

i mn dr........ And Many Others (BU)

IMNL .... International Messengers Nigerian Limited

IMNR .... Institutul de Proiectari si Cercetari pentru Industria Metalelor Neferoase si Rare [*Design and Research Institute for the Nonferrous and Rare Metals Industry*] (RO)

IMO.......... Insaat Muhendisleri Odasi [*Chamber of Construction Engineers*] (TU)

IMO.......... Institute of International Relations (RU)

IMO.......... Institute of Teaching Methods (of the Academy of Pedagogical Sciences, RSFSR) (RU)

IMO.......... Instytut Materialow Ogniotrwalych [*Institute of Fireproof Materials*] [*Poland*]

IMO.......... Inter-American Municipal Organization [*Tegucigalpa, Honduras*] (LAA)

IMO.......... International Maritime Organization [*See also OMI*] [*ICSU London, England*] (EAIO)

IMO.......... International Meteorological Organization [*Replaced by World Meteorological Organization in December 1951*]

IMO.......... International Money Order [*Business term*] (DS)

IMO.......... Young People's Art (RU)

IMOA .... International Mercury Owners Association (EA)

IMOP .... Instituto Mexicano de Opinion Publica [*Mexican Public Opinion Institute*] (LA)

IMOPI...... Institute for the Mechanical Processing of Minerals (RU)

imostb....... Engineer Bridge-Building Battalion (BU)

imostb....... Engineer Bridge Construction Battalion (RU)

imostr........ Engineer Bridge-Building Company (BU)

imostr........ Engineer Bridge Construction Company (RU)

imostv....... Engineer Bridge Construction Platoon (RU)

imp .... Emperor (RU)

imp .... Impaye [*Unpaid*] [*French*]

imp .... Imperatief [*Imperative*] [*Afrikaans*]

IMP .... Imperatriz [*Brazil*] [*Airport symbol*] (OAG)

Imp............ Imperial [*Record label*]

IMP .... Imperial Air [*Peru*] [*ICAO designator*] (FAAC)

Imp............ Imprenta [*Printers*] [*Spanish*]

imp .... Impressioni [*Stamping*] [*Publishing*] [*Italian*]

imp .... Impresso [*Pamphlet*] [*Publishing*] [*Portuguese*]

Imp............ Imprime [*Printed*] [*French*] (ILCA)

Imp............ Imprimeur [*Printer*] [*French*] (ILCA)

IMP .... Independence of Malaya Party (ML)

IMP .... Independent Magazine Publishers [*Australia*]

IMP .... Industrias Metalicas de Palmira (COL)

IMP .... Institute for Molecular Pathology [*Austria*]

IMP .... Institute of Modern Physics [*Chinese Academy of Sciences*] [*Research center*] (WND)

IMP .... Instituto Mexicano del Petroleo [*Mexican Petroleum Institute*] (LA)

IMP .... Instituts Medico-Pedagogiques [*France*] (FLAF)

IMP .... Institut za Mehanizaciju Poljoprivrede [*Institute for Agricultural Mechanization*] [*Former Yugoslavia*] [*Research center*] (IRC)

IMP .... Instytut Mechaniki Precyzyjnej [*Institute of Precision Mechanics*] (POL)

IMP .... Instytut Medycyny Pracy [*Institute of Industrial Medicine*] (POL)

IMP .... Intermeccanica-Puch [*Italian-Austrian specialty car maker*]

imp .... Pulse, Impulse (RU)
IMPA........ Industrias Metalurgicas del Pacifico Ltda. [*Palmira*] (COL)
Impa........... Industrija Metalnih Proizvoda [*Metal Products Industry*] [*Zemun*] (YU)
IMPA........ Instituto de Matematica Pura e Aplicada [*Institute of Pure and Applied Mathematics*] [*Brazil*] (LA)
IMPA........ International Maritime Pilots Association (EAIO)
IMPA........ International Master Printers Association [*Brussels, Belgium*]
imp a........ Pulse Analyzer (RU)
IMPADOC ... Impalpables de Occidente Ltda. [*Colombia*] (COL)
impag .... Impaginazione [*Layout*] [*Publishing*] [*Italian*]
IMPALA ... Industria Mineira e Paulistana de Lacticinios SA [*Brazil*] (DSCA)
IMPAS ...... Insaat Malzemeleri Pazarlama Subesi [*Construction Materials' Marketing Branch*] [*A subsidiary of Industry, Commerce, and Manufacturing Enterprises Ltd. Turkish Cypriot*] (GC)
IMPBI .... International Modern Pentathlon and Biathlon Union (OLYM)
IMPCO...... Iran Milk Producers Cooperative Organization (ME)
impe .... Imperatif [*French*] (TPFD)
IMPE .... Institutul de Microbiologie, Parazitologie, si Epidemiologie [*Institute for Microbiology, Parasitology, and Epidemiology*] (RO)
imper.......... Imperative (TPFD)
imper .... Imperativo [*Imperative*] [*Portuguese*]
imperat....... Imperatiivi [*Imperative*] [*Finland*]
IMPERCOL ... Impermeabilizaciones Colombia [*Colombia*] (COL)
imperf........ Imperfeito [*Imperfect*] [*Portuguese*]
impers .... Impersonal (TPFD)
impers .... Impersonale [*Impersonal*] [*Italian*]
impers .... Impersonnel [*French*] (TPFD)
IMPEX ...... Comercial, Importadora, e Exportadora Agropecuaria Ltd. [*Brazil*] (DSCA)
impf........... Imperfekti [*Past Tense*] [*Finland*]
IMPF .... Imperfektum [*Imperfect*] [*Afrikaans*]
IMPG .... Institut de Meteorologie et de Physique du Globe [*Algeria*]
IMPGA...... Institut de Meteorologie et de Physique du Globe d'Algerie
IMPHOS... Institut Mondial du Phosphate [*World Phosphate Institute*] [*Paris, France*] (SLS)
IMPI .... Societe Independante Maritime de Peche Ivoirienne
IMPICS..... Integriertes Management Planungs-Informations-und Kontrollsystem [*Integrated Management Planning, Information and Controll System*] [*German*] (ADPT)
IMPiHW ... Instytut Medycyny Pracy i Higieny Wsi [*Institute of Industrial Medicine and Rural Hygiene*] [*Poland*]
IMPITM ... Institute of Medical Parasitology and Tropical Medicine Imeni Ye. I. Martsinovskiy (RU)
impl .... Implicite [*French*] (FLAF)
IMPL........ International Microwave Power Institute (PDAA)
IMPLEMAQ ... Implementos e Maquinas Agricolas Ltd. [*Brazil*] (DSCA)
IMPM .... Institut de Recherches Medicales et d'Etudes des Plantes Medicinales [*Institute of Medical Research and Medicinal Plant Studies*] [*Cameroon*] (IRC)
IMPOD ..... Importkontoret foer U-Landsprodukter [*Import Promotion Office for Products from Developing Countries*] [*Sweden*]
IMPOREXCO ... Importaciones, Exportaciones, Representaciones Comerciales [*San Andres*] (COL)
IMPORGA ... Societe Gabonaise pour l'Importation et l'Exportation
IMPORTTEX ... Textilbehozatali Vallalat [*Textile Import Enterprise*] (HU)
IMPOS...... Instituto Mexicano de Planeacion y Operacion de Sistemas
IMPP .... Institut za Medunarodnu Politiku i Privredu [*Institute for International Politics and Economics*] (YU)
impr........... Impressioni [*Stamping*] [*Publishing*] [*Italian*]
impr........... Impresso [*Pamphlet*] [*Publishing*] [*Portuguese*]
Impr .... Impressum [*Imprint*] [*Publishing*] [*German*]
impr........... Imprimeur [*Printer*] [*Publishing*] [*French*]
IMPR........ International of Seamen and Port Workers (RU)
Impragnier ... Impraegnierung [*Impregnation*] [*German*] (GCA)
Impragnierbark ... Impraegnierbarkeit [*Impregnatibility*] [*German*] (GCA)
IMPRE ...... Instituto de Medicina Preventiva para Ejecutivos [*Colombia*] (COL)
IMPRECO ... Societe Impression de Textiles de la Republique Populaire du Congo
impress....... Impressioni [*Stamping*] [*Publishing*] [*Italian*]
IMPRIGA ... Imprimerie Centrale d'Afrique [*Publisher*] [*Gabon*] (EY)
IMPRIGA ... Imprimerie Gabonaise
IMPRIKIN ... Imprimeries de Kinshasa [*Kinshasa Press*] [*Zaire*] (AF)
imprim....... Imprimerie [*Printing Firm*] [*French*]
IMPRIM ... Imprimerie Mauritanienne
IMPROME ... Impuesto a la Produccion Minima de las Explotaciones Agro [*Tax on Minimum Crop Yields*] [*Spanish*] (LA)
IMPROME ... Impuesto Minimo a la Produccion Media [*Minimum Tax on Average Production*] [*Spanish*] (LA)
IMPROMER ... Societe Ivoirienne d'Importation des Produits de la Mer
IMPS........ International Medical Placement Services [*Australia*]
IMQ........... Istituto Italiano del Marchio di Qualita [*Italian Institution for Quality Branding*] (PDAA)

IMR .... Impulse-Aero [*Russian Federation*] [*ICAO designator*] (FAAC)
IMR .... Industrija Motora Rakovica [*Rakovica Motor Industry*] (YU)
IMR .... Institute for Medical Research [*Malaysia*] (SLS)
IMR .... Institute for Mideast Research
IMR .... Institute of Marine Research [*Finland*] (MSC)
IMR .... Institute of Marxist Research [*France*] (EAIO)
IMR .... Institute of Metal Research, Academia Sinica [*China*] (IRC)
IMR .... Institute of Mining Research [*University of Zimbabwe*]
IMR .... Institut fuer Metallphysik und Reinstmetalle [*Institute for Metal Physics and High-Purity Metals*] (EG)
IMRA .... Inner Metropolitan Regional Association [*Australia*]
IMRI......... International Marian Research Institute [*University of Dayton*] [*Research center*] (RCD)
IMRNR ..... Instituto Mexicano de Recursos Naturales Renovables [*Mexico*] (LAA)
IMRO .... Internal Macedonian Revolutionary Organization [*Bulgaria*] [*Political party*] (PPE)
IMRO-DPMNU ... Internal Macedonian Revolutionary Organization - Democratic Party for Macedonian [*Bulgaria*] National Unity [*Political party*] (EY)
IMRP .... International Meeting on Radiation Processing (EA)
IMRS........ Industrial Market Research Service [*Thailand*] (DS)
IMS........... Industrias Mecanicas Sistematizadas [*Mechanical Systems Industry*] [*Brazil*] (LA)
IMS........... Ingenieria Mecanica Sanitaria [*Colombia*] (COL)
IMS........... Inspectia Metrologiei de Stat [*State Inspectorate for Metrology*] (RO)
IMS........... Institute for Molecular Science [*China*] (PDAA)
IMS........... Institute of Management Specialists [*Royal Leamington Spa, Warwickshire, England*] (EAIO)
IMS........... Institute of Mineral Raw Materials (RU)
IMS........... Instituto de Materiales de Servia [*Serbian Materials Institute*] [*Cuba*] (LA)
IMS........... Institut za Ispitivanje Materijala SR Srbije [*Testing Materials Institute, Serbia*] [*Former Yugoslavia*] [*Research center*] (ERC)
IMS........... [*The*] Intelligent Manufacturing System [*Japanese project*]
IMS........... Intelligent Manufacturing Systems (Program) [*Australia*]
IMS........... International Magnetic System
IMS........... International Magnetospheric Study [*ICSU*]
IMS........... International Marine Services [*Salvage company*] [*United Arab Emirates*]
IMS........... International Meditation Society (ADA)
IMS........... International Military Staff [*NATO*]
IMS........... International Montessori Society
IMS........... International Multihull Society [*Formerly, International Hydrofoil and Multihull Society*] [*Defunct*] (EA)
IMS........... International Musicological Society [*Basel, Switzerland*] (EA)
IMS........... Intreprinderea Metalurgica de Stat [*State Metallurgical Enterprise*] (RO)
IMS........... Irish Mathematics Society
IMS........... Irish Meteorological Service (MSC)
IMS........... Israel Musicological Society (EAIO)
IMSA........ Industrias Metalicas Sudamericanas Ltda. [*Colombia*] (COL)
IMSA........ Ingenieros Mecanicos Siderurgicos Asociados [*Colombia*] (COL)
IMSA........ Istanbul Mesrubat Sanayii Anonim Sirketi [*Istanbul Non-Alcoholic Drink Industry Corporation*] (TU)
IMSAC ...... Institut Mecanographique de Statistiques et d'Applications Comptables [*French*] (ADPT)
IMSAP ...... International Marine Science Affairs Policy (MSC)
IMSCOM ... International Military Staff Communication [*NATO*] (NATG)
IMSDD...... Institut fuer Medizinische Statistik, Dokumentation, und Datenverarbeitung der Universitaet Bonn [*Information retrieval*]
IMShR....... Institute of School Work Methods (RU)
IMSKh....... Institute of Agricultural Mechanization (RU)
IMSM....... International Military Staff Memorandum [*NATO*] (NATG)
ImSND ...... Imikiniton Nosokomeion Diakomidis [*Semimobile Evacuation Hospital*] (GC)
IMSS .... Institute of Powder Metallurgy and Special Alloys (of the Academy of Sciences, Ukrainian SSR) (RU)
IMSS........ Instituto Mexicano de Seguridad Social [*Mexican Social Security Institute*] (LA)
IMSS .... Iron Man Super Series Proprietary Ltd. [*Australia*]
IMSSA ...... Institute of Mine Surveyors of South Africa (AA)
IMST........ Institut de Mecanique Statistique de la Turbulence [*Institute for the Study of Statistical Mechanics of Turbulence*] [*French*]
IMST .... International Mushroom Society for the Tropics (EAIO)
IMSUM.... International Military Staff Summary [*NATO*] (NATG)
IMSUT...... Institute of Medical Science, University of Tokyo [*Japan*] (PDAA)
IMSWM.... International Military Staff Working Memorandum [*NATO*] (NATG)
IMT .... Industrija Masina i Traktora [*Former Yugoslavia*] (EE)
IMT .... Institute of Management and Training
IMT .... Institute of Materials Technicians [*South Africa*] (AA)

IMT .... Institut fuer Molekularbiologie und Tumorforschung [*Germany*]
IMTA .... Institut de Medicine Tropicale Appliquee [*Institute of Applied Tropical Medicine*]   (AF)
IMTACO... Impermeabilizacion Tecnica Colombiana [*Colombia*]   (COL)
IMTAS ...... Ittihadi Milli Turk Anonim Sigorta Sirketi [*United National Turkish Insurance Corporation*]   (TU)
IMTEC ..... International Marine Trades Exhibit and Convention [*National Marine Manufacturers Association*]
IMTEC ..... International Movements toward Educational Change [*Later, IMTEC-The International Learning Cooperative*]   (EAIO)
IMTFC ..... International Movement for Therapeutic Free Choice [*France*]   (EAIO)
IMTG .... Internationale Moor und Torf-Gesellschaft [*International Peat Society - IPS*]   (EAIO)
IMTI .... Instituto del Minifundio y de las Tierras Indivisas [*Argentina*]   (LAA)
IMTMA..... Indian Machine Tool Manufacturers Association   (PDAA)
IMTP .... International Musa Testing Program [*United Nations*]   (ECON)
IMTP .... Itim Mizrah News Agency. Teleprinter Service   (BJA)
IMTP .... Mining Research Institute   (BU)
IMTPA ...... Institut de Medecine Tropicale Princesse Astrid
IMU .... Internacionalna Matematicka Unija [*International Mathematical Union*]   (YU)
IMU .... Internationale Metall Union [*International Metal Union*]   (EA)
IMU .... International Mathematical Union [*See also UMI*] [*ICSU Helsinki, Finland*]   (EAIO)
IMU .... Intreprinderea Metalurgica de Utilaj [*Metallurgical Equipment Enterprise*]   (RO)
IMU .... Istituto Sperimentale per le Macchine Utensili [*Machine Tools Experimental Institute*] [*Consiglio Nazionale delle Ricerche*] [*Research center*] [*Italian*]   (ERC)
IMU .... Italian Mathematical Union   (EAIO)
IMUA .... Intreprinderea de Masini Unelte si Agregate [*Machine Tools and Aggregates Enterprise*]   (RO)
IMUAB ..... Intreprinderea de Masini Unelte si Agregate Bucuresti [*Bucharest Machine Tool and Aggregates Enterprise*]   (RO)
IMUC .... Intreprinderea Mecanica de Utilaj Chimic [*Machine Enterprise for Chemical Equipment*]   (RO)
IMUDel ..... Control Pulse from Local Division Control [*Computers*]   (RU)
IMUFP ...... Instituto de Micologia. Universidad de Federal de Pernambuco [*Brazil*]   (DSCA)
IMUGFLEI ... Israel Musicians Union General Federation of Labour in Eretz-Israel   (EAIO)
IMUJ .... Instytut Matematyczny Uniwersytetu Jagiellonskiego [*Jagiellonian University Institute of Mathematics*]   (POL)
IMUM .... Industriile Metalurgice de Unelte si Masini [*Metallurgical Tools and Machines Industries*]   (RO)
IMUSA ...... Industrias Metalurgicas Unidas Sociedad Anonima [*Colombia*]   (COL)
IMUZ .... Instytut Melioracji i Uzytkow Zielonych [*Land Reclamation and Grassland Farming Institute*] [*Poland*]   (ARC)
IMV .... Internationaler Metzgermeisterverband [*International Federation of Meat Traders' Associations*]   (EAIO)
IMVIC ...... International Motor Vehicle Inspection Committee [*Belgium*]   (EAIO)
IMVR .... Institute of Extra-Scholastic Work Methods   (RU)
IMVS .... Institute of Medical and Veterinary Science [*Australia*]   (ADA)
IMVTs ...... Institute of Mathematics with Computation Center (of the Academy of Sciences, Moldavian SSR)   (RU)
IMWA ...... International Mine Water Association [*Madrid, Spain*]   (EAIO)
im wl .... Imie Wlasne [*Proper Name*] [*Poland*]
IMwO .... Instytut Mazurski w Olsztynie [*Masurian Institute in Olsztyn (Allenstein)*] [*POL*]
IMWOO.... Instituut voor Maatschappij-Wetenschappelijk Onderzoek in Ontwikkelingslanden [*Netherlands*]   (SLS)
IMX .... Zimex Aviation Ltd. [*Switzerland*] [*ICAO designator*]   (FAAC)
IMZ .... Instytut Metalurgii Zelaza [*Institute for Metallurgy of the Ferrous Metals*] [*Poland*]
IMZ .... Internationales Musikzentrum [*International Music Center*] [*Vienna, Austria*]   (EAIO)
IMZ .... Irbit Motorcycle Plant   (RU)
IMZh .... Institute of Animal Morphology Imeni A. N. Severtsov (of the Academy of Sciences, USSR)   (RU)
IMZO .... Institute for Mass Correspondence Training of Party Activists at the TsK VKP(b)   (RU)
In .... Commissariat   (BU)
IN .... Direction Finder   (RU)
in .... Foreign   (RU)
IN .... Imprensa Nacional [*National Printing House*] [*Portuguese*]
in .... Inaczej [*Or, Also*] [*Poland*]
in .... Inch   (SCAC)
IN .... India [*ANSI two-letter standard code*]   (CNC)
IN .... Indicator Lamp   (RU)
In .... Indio [*Indium*] [*Chemical element*] [*Portuguese*]
in .... Inny [*or Inni*] [*Other or Others*] [*Poland*]
in .... Inspector   (RU)
IN .... Institute of Nationalities   (RU)

IN .... Institut National [*National Institute*] [*French*]
IN .... Instytut Naftowy [*Petroleum Institute*] [*POL*]
IN .... Petroleum Institute (of the Academy of Sciences, USSR)   (RU)
in .... Quartermaster, Supply Officer   (BU)
IN .... Voltage Source   (RU)
IN2P3 .... Institute National de Physique Nucleaire et de Physique des Particules [*National Institute of Nuclear and Particle Physics*] [*France*]   (PDAA)
in-4 .... In-Quarto [*Quarto*] [*French*]
in-8 .... In-Octavo [*Octavo*] [*French*]
INA .... Industria Nacional de Armas [*National Weapons Industry*] [*Brazil*]   (LA)
INA .... Industrias Nacionales Agricolas [*Nicaragua*]   (DSCA)
INA .... Industrija Nafte [*State Oil Agency*] [*Former Yugoslavia*] [*France*]   (PDAA)
INA .... Informationssystem fuer den Niedergelassenen Arzt [*German*]   (ADPT)
INA .... Institute of National Affairs [*Papua New Guinea*] [*Research center*]   (IRC)
INA .... Institute of Nuclear Agriculture [*Bangladesh*]   (ARC)
INA .... Institute of the Peoples of Asia (of the Academy of Sciences, USSR)   (RU)
INA .... Institut National Agronomique [*National Agronomic Institute*] [*French*]   (AF)
INA .... Institut National des Arts [*National Art Institute*] [*Zaire*]   (AF)
INA .... Instituto Nacional Agrario [*National Agrarian Institute*] [*Honduras*]   (LA)
INA .... Instituto Nacional Agropecuario [*Guatemala*]   (LAA)
INA .... Instituto Nacional de Abastecimentos [*National Supply Institute*] [*IDEMA Bogota, Colombia*] [*Later,*]   (LA)
INA .... Instituto Nacional de Administracao [*National Institute of Administration*] [*Research center*] [*Portuguese*]   (IRC)
INA .... Instituto Nacional de Agricultura [*Venezuela*]   (LAA)
INA .... Instituto Nacional de Aprendizaje [*National Apprenticeship Institute*] [*Costa Rica*]   (LAA)
INA .... International Newsreel and News Film Association [*Later, INANEWS*]   (EAIO)
INA .... Iraqi News Agency   (ME)
INA .... Irish National Association [*Australia*]
INA .... Isolants Nord Africain [*North African*]
INA .... Istituto Nazionale delle Assicurazioni [*National Insurance Institute*] [*Rome, Italy*]   (WER)
INAA .... Institut National d'Art et d'Archeologie [*National Institute of Art and Archaeology*] [*Tunisia*]   (EAIO)
INAA .... Instituto Nicaraguense de Acueductos y Alcantarillados [*Nicaraguan Water and Sewage Institute*]   (LA)
INAA .... Irish National Association of Australasia
INABU ...... Imprimerie Nationale du Burundi [*Government publishing house*] [*Burundi*]   (EY)
INAC .... Instituto Nacional de Cultura [*National Culture Institute*] [*Panama*]   (LA)
INAC .... Instituto Nacional de la Carne [*National Meat Institute*] [*Uruguay*]   (LA)
INAC .... Instituto Nazionale per le Applicazioni del Calco [*National Institute for Computer Applications*] [*Italy*]   (PDAA)
INACAP.... Instituto Nacional de Capacitacion Profesional [*National Professional Training Institute*] [*Chile*]   (LA)
INACESA ... Industria Nacional de Cemento Sociedad Anonima [*National Cement Industry, Incorporated*] [*Chile*]   (LA)
INACH ...... Instituto Antartico Chileno [*Chilean Antarctic Institute*]   (LA)
INACOL.... Institut National pour l'Amelioration des Conserves des Legumes [*National Institute for the Improvement of Vegetable Preserves*] [*Belgium*]   (PDAA)
INACOP.... Instituto Nacional de Cooperativas [*National Institute of Cooperatives*] [*El Salvador*]   (LA)
INACRE.... Industria Nacional de Cremalleras [*Colombia*]   (COL)
INAD .... Instituto Nacional de Administracion para el Desarrollo [*National Institute of Administration for Development*] [*Guatemala*]   (LA)
INADEPAL ... Instituto Americano de Eficiencia Personal [*Colombia*]   (COL)
INADES.... Institut Africain pour le Developpement Economique et Social [*African Institute for Economic and Social Development*] [*Ivory Coast*]   (AF)
INAE .... Instituto de Altos Estudios [*Institute for Higher Studies*] [*Peru*]   (LA)
INAFOR.... Instituto Nacional Forestal [*National Forestry Service*] [*Guatemala*]   (LA)
INAG .... Institut National d'Astronomie et de Geophysique [*National Institute of Astronomy and Geophysics*] [*Research center*] [*French*]   (IRC)
INAGEC.... Industrial, Agricultural, Engineering Consultants [*Nigeria*]
INAGEO ... Instituto Nacional de Geologia [*Angola*] [*Research center*]   (EAS)
INAGOR ... Industrias Agricolas Organizadas [*Nicaragua*]   (DSCA)
INAGRARIO ... Almacenes Generales de Deposito Organizado por INA y por la Caja de Credito Agrario [*Colombia*]   (COL)
INAGRICO ... Industria Agricultura e Comercio Lda.

INAGRO ... Investimentos Agricolas e Industriais SA [*Brazil*]   (DSCA)
INAH......... Instituto Nacional de Antropologia e Historia [*Mexico*]
INAIL........ Istituto Nazionale Assicurazione Contro gli Infortuni sul Lavoro [*National Work Accident Insurance Institute*] [*Italian*]   (WER)
inakt........... Inaktiv [*Inactive*] [*German*]
INAL .... Indian National Agricultural Library   (DSCA)
INALI .... Instituto Nacional de Limnologia [*Argentina*]   (ASF)
INALPRE ... Instituto Nacional de Preinversion [*National Investment Feasibility Studies Institute*] [*La Paz, Bolivia*]   (LA)
INALPRO ... Instituto Nacional de Provisiones [*Colombia*]   (COL)
INALS....... Indian National Agricultural Library System   (DSCA)
INALTRA ... Industria Nacional de Troqueles Ltda. [*Colombia*]   (COL)
Inalum........ Indonesia Asahan Aluminium [*Commercial firm*]
INALWA... International Airlift West Africa
INAM .... Istituto Nazionale Assicurazione Contro le Malattie [*National Health Insurance Institute*] [*Italian*]   (WER)
INAMHI ... Instituto Nacional de Meteorologia e Hidrologia [*National Meteorology and Hydrology Institute*] [*Ecuador*]   (LA)
INAMI ...... Institut National d'Assurance Maladie-Invalidite [*National Institute for Illness and Disability Insurance*] [*Belgium*]   (WER)
INAMM .... Institut National des Mass Media [*National Institute of Mass Media*] [*Zaire*]   (AF)
INAMPS ... Instituto Nacional de Assistencia Medica da Previdencia Social [*National Institute for Social Security Medical Assistance*] [*Brazil*]   (LA)
INAN......... Infectious Anemia of Horses   (RU)
INAN......... Instituto Nacional de Alimentacao e Nutricao [*National Food and Nutrition Institute*] [*Brazil*]   (LA)
INANDINA ... Industria Quimica Andina Ltda. [*Colombia*]   (COL)
INANEWS ... International Newsreel Association   (EAIO)
INANK...... Petroleum Institute of the Chinese Academy of Sciences   (RU)
INANTIC ... Instituto Nacional de Normas Tecnicas y Certificacion [*National Institute of Technical Standards and Certification*] [*Peru*]   (LA)
INAOE ...... Instituto Nacional de Astrofisica, Optica y Electronica [*National Insitute for Astrophysics, Optics and Electronics*] [*Research center*] [*Mexico*]   (EAS)
INAP .... Instituto Nacional de Accion Poblacional e Investigacion [*Santiago, Chile*]   (LAA)
INAP .... Instituto Nacional de Administracion Publica [*National Public Administration Institute*] [*Guatemala*]   (IRC)
INAP .... Instituto Nacional de Administracion Publica [*National Public Administration Institute*] [*Peru*]   (LA)
INAP .... Instituto Nacional de Aprendizaje [*National Apprenticeship Institute*] [*Managua, Nicaragua*]   (LAA)
INAP .... Instituto Nicaraguense de Administracion Publica [*Nicaraguan Public Administration Institute*]   (LA)
INAPA...... Instituto Nacional de Aguas Potables y Alcantarillados [*National Institute of Waterworks and Sewage*] [*Dominican Republic*]   (LA)
INAPE....... Instituto Nacional de Pesca [*National Fishing Institute*] [*Uruguay*]   (LA)
INAPET .... Instituto de Adiestramiento Petrolero y Petroquimico [*Petroleum and Petrochemical Training Institute*] [*Venezuela*]   (LA)
INAPI....... Institut Algerien de Normalisation et de Propriete Industrielle [*Algeria*]   (IMH)
INAPI........ Instituto Nacional de Prevencion Contra Incendios [*National Institute of Fire Prevention*] [*Nicaragua*]   (LA)
INAPROMEF ... Instituto Nacional de Promocion del Menor y la Familia [*National Institute for the Aid and Advancement of Minors and the Family*] [*Peru*]   (LA)
INAR .... Comercial de Ingenieros y Arquitectos de Caldas [*Manizales*]   (COL)
INARC...... Institut Nord-Africain de Recherches Cottonieres
IN/ARCH ... Istituto Nazionale di Architettura [*Italian*]   (SLS)
INARCON ... Ingenieria, Arquitectura, Construcciones [*Colombia*]   (COL)
INARS....... Istituto Nazionale per le Regioni Storiche [*Italian*]   (SLS)
INAS......... Institut National d'Animation Sociale [*National Institute for Social Promotion*] [*Zaire*]   (AF)
INAS......... Institut National des Assurances Sociales [*North African*]
INAS......... Istituto Nazionale Assistenza Sociale [*Italian*]
INASA...... Industrias Nacionales Agricolas SA [*Nicaragua*]   (DSCA)
IN-ASA ..... Istituto Nazionale Arredo Urbano e Strutture Ambientali [*Italian*]   (SLS)
INASEN.... International Assembly of Non-Governmental Organizations Concerned with Environment
INAS-FMH ... International Sports Federation for Persons with Mental Handicap   (OLYM)
INASOL.... Instituto Aleman de Soldadura [*Colombia*]   (COL)
INAT .... Institut National Agronomique de Tunisie [*National Agronomic Institute of Tunisia*] [*Research center*]   (IRC)
InaugDiss ... Inauguraldissertation [*Inaugural Dissertation*] [*German*]   (GCA)
INAUM ..... Istituto Nazionale di Architettura e Urbanistica Montana [*Italian*]   (SLS)

INAV .... Informationsverarbeitung fuer die Angebotsverfolgung [*German*]   (ADPT)
INAVI....... Instituto Nacional de Vivienda [*National Housing Institute*] [*Venezuela*]   (LA)
INAZUCAR ... Instituto Azucarero Dominicano [*Dominican Republic*]   (EY)
inb .... Inbunden [*Bound*] [*Publishing*] [*Sweden*]
INB .... Independence [*Belize*] [*Airport symbol*]   (OAG)
INB .... Inspekcja Nadzoru Budowlanego [*Inspectorate of Construction Control*] (POL)
INB .... Instalbud [*Poland*] [*ICAO designator*]   (FAAC)
INB .... Instytut Naukowo-Badawczy [*Scientific Research Institute*] (POL)
INB .... Internationale Natrium-Brutreaktor-Bau, GmbH [*Nuclear energy*]   (NRCH)
INBA .... Instituto Nacional de Biologia Animal [*Bolivia*]   (DSCA)
INBEC....... Instituto Nacional de Becas y Credito Educativo [*National Scholarship and Educational Credit Institute*] [*Peru*]   (LA)
INBEL....... Institut Belge d'Information et de Documentation [*Belgian Institute of Information and Documentation*]   (WER)
INBELSA ... Industria Brasileira de Eletricidade Sociedade Anonima [*Brazilian Electric Power Industry, Incorporated*]   (LA)
INBF......... Imprimerie Nationale du Burkina Faso [*Government publishing house*]
INBI......... Institute of Biochemistry Imeni A. N. Bakh (of the Academy of Sciences, USSR)   (RU)
INBio .... Biodiversity Institute [*Center established to inventory wildlife*]   (PS)
INBIS .... INBIS [*Industrial and Business Information Services*] Australia
INBK .... Instytut Naukowo-Badawczy Kolejnictwa [*Railroad Scientific Research Institute*]   (POL)
INBOLCA ... Instituto Boliviano del Cafe [*Bolivia*]   (DSCA)
INBOLPEX ... Instituto Boliviano de Promocion a las Exportaciones [*Bolivian Institute for the Promotion of Exports*]   (LA)
INBPW...... Instytut Naukowo-Badawczy Przemyslu Weglowego [*Coal Industry Scientific Research Institute*]   (POL)
INBTP....... Institut National du Batiment et des Travaux Publics [*National Institute of the Building Trades and Public Works*] [*Zaire*]   (AF)
INBWL...... Instytut Naukowo-Badawczy Wojsk Lotniczych [*Air Force Scientific Research Institute*]   (POL)
inc............... Incidenteel [*Benelux*]   (BAS)
inc............... Incisione [*Engraving*] [*Publishing*] [*Italian*]
Inc .... Incorporated   (EECI)
INC .... Indian National Congress
INC .... Institut National de Cartographie [*National Cartography Institute*] [*Algeria*]   (AF)
INC .... Institut National de Cartographie [*National Cartography Institute*] [*Benin*]   (AF)
INC .... Instituto Nacional de Canalizaciones [*Venezuela*]
INC .... Instituto Nacional de Cinema [*National Motion-Picture Institute*] [*Brazil*]   (LA)
INC .... Instituto Nacional de Colonizacion [*National Settlement Institute*] [*Uruguay*]   (LA)
INC .... Instituto Nacional de Colonizacion [*National Settlement Institute*] [*Ecuador*]   (LAA)
INC .... Instituto Nacional de Colonizacion [*National Settlement Institute*] [*Bolivia*]   (LA)
INC .... Instituto Nicaraguense del Cafe [*Nicaragua*]   (DSCA)
INC .... International Numismatic Commission [*Denmark*]   (SLS)
INC .... International Nut Council   (EAIO)
INC .... Iraqi National Congress [*Political party*]   (ECON)
INC .... Jet Air Internacional Charters CA [*Venezuela*] [*ICAO designator*]   (FAAC)
INC .... Yinchuan [*China*] [*Airport symbol*]   (OAG)
INCA .... Implementation of New Carrier Arrangements [*Telecommunications*]
INCA .... Institut National de Credit Agricole [*Benelux*]   (BAS)
INCA .... Instituto Centroamericano de Ciencias Agricolas [*Costa Rica*]   (LAA)
INCA .... Instituto de Ciencia Agricola [*Institute of Agricultural Sciences*] [*Cuba*]   (LA)
INCA .... Instituto Nacional de Cirugia y Anestesiologia [*National Institute of Surgery and Anesthesiology*] [*Cuba*]   (LA)
INCA .... International Newspaper and Colour Association [*Later, IFRA*]   (EA)
INCA .... Istituto Nazionale Confederale di Assistenza [*Italian*]
INCADELMA ... Instituto de Capacitacion y Perfeccionamiento del Magisterio [*Colombia*]   (COL)
INCAE....... Instituto Centroamericano de Administracion de Empresas [*Central American Institute of Business Administration*] [*Nicaragua*]
INCAFE .... Instituto Nacional del Cafe [*National Coffee Institute*] [*El Salvador*]   (EY)
INCAISE... Instituto Universitario Centroamericano de Investigaciones Sociales y Economicas [*San Jose, Costa Rica*]   (LAA)
Incalz .... Incalzando [*Music*]
INCAME... Industria Nacional de Repuestos [*Colombia*]   (COL)

INCAP....... Instituto de Nutricion de Centro America y Panama [*Institute of Nutrition of Central America and Panama*] [*Guatemala, Guatemala*]   (EAIO)

INCAPE.... Instituto de Investigaciones en Catalisis y Petroquimica [*Argentina*]

INCAR...... Industrias Metalicas Carbonell [*Ibague*]   (COL)

INCAR...... Instituto Nacional del Carbon y Sus Derivados "Francisco Pintado Fe" [*Francisco Pintado Fe National Institute of Coal and Its Derivatives*] [*Research center*] [*Spain*]   (IRC)

INCARE.... Instituto Chileno de Administracion Racional de Empresas [*Chile*]   (DSCA)

INCARIBE ... Ingenieria del Caribe Ltda. [*Barranquilla*]   (COL)

INCAS....... Ingenieros Constructores Arquitectos Asociados Ltda. [*Colombia*]   (COL)

INCASA.... Industria de Cafe SA [*Guatemala*]   (DSCA)

INCASIS... Instituto de Capacitacion Sindical y Social [*Santiago, Chile*]   (LAA)

INCATEL ... Instituto Centroamericano de Telecomunicaciones [*Central American Telecommunications Institute*]   (LA)

INCAUCA ... Ingenio del Cauca SA [*Colombia*]   (COL)

INCAUCHO ... Industria de Caucho de Medellin   (COL)

INCB .... International Narcotics Control Board [*Vienna, Austria*]   (CL)

INCBE .... Israel National Committee on the Biosphere and Environment

incc............ Incisioni [*Engravings*] [*Publishing*] [*Italian*]

INCC .... Interim National Coordinating Committee [*Ghana*]   (PPW)

INCC .... International Nuclear Credit Corporation

INCCA....... Instituto Colombiano de Ciencias Administrativas [*Colombian Institute of Administrative Sciences*]   (LA)

Incd .... Incorporated   (EECI)

INCE .... Industria Nacional de Conductores Electricos [*Colombia*]   (COL)

INCE .... Instituto Nacional de Cooperacion Educativa [*National Institute of Cooperative Education*] [*Colombia*]   (COL)

INCE .... Instituto Nacional de Cooperacion Educativa [*National Institute of Cooperative Education*] [*Venezuela*]   (LA)

INCE .... International Network for Chemical Education [*Samoa*]   (EAIO)

INCEF....... Institutul de Cercetari Forestiere [*Forestry Research Institute*]   (RO)

INCEI........ Instituto Nacional de Comercio Exterior e Interior [*National Institute of Foreign and Domestic Trade*] [*Nicaragua*]   (LA)

INCERC.... Institutul de Cercetari in Constructii si Economia Constructoriilor [*Research Institute for Constructions and the Construction Economy*] [*Research center*]   (RO)

INCERDA ... Industria Colombiana de Cerdas [*Colombia*]   (COL)

INCERG.... Institutul de Cercetari Electroenergetice si pentru Termoficare [*Electrical and Thermal Power Research Institute*]   (RO)

INCH........ Institute for Contemporary History

INCI.......... Instituto Nacional de Ciegos [*Colombia*]   (COL)

INCIBA ..... Instituto Nacional de Cultura y Bellas Artes [*National Institute of Culture and Fine Arts*] [*Venezuela*]   (LA)

INCIDI ...... Institut International des Civilisations Differentes [*International Institute of Differing Civilizations*]

INCINATUR ... Instituto de Ciencias Naturales [*Colombia*]   (DSCA)

INCIRS ..... International Communication Information Retrieval System [*University of Florida*]   (PDAA)

incis........... Inciso [*Engraved*] [*Publishing*] [*Italian*]

INCIS .... Istituto Nazionale Case per gli Impiegati di Stato [*Institute for Providing Houses for Civil Servants*] [*Italian*]

INCITEMI ... Instituto Cientifico y Tecnologico Minero [*Scientific and Technological Mining Institute*] [*Peru*]   (LA)

INCIVA..... Institute of the Cauca Valley [*Scientific Research*] [*Colombia*]

incl .... Including   (TPFD)

incl .... Incluyendo [*Including*] [*Spanish*]

INCLAS .... Ingenieros Civiles Asociados Ltda. [*Colombia*]   (COL)

INCLINIC ... Instituto Clinico Ltda. [*Colombia*]   (COL)

INCN .... Institut National pour la Conservation de la Nature

INCO .... Industria de Congreto Centrifugado Ltda. [*Colombia*]   (COL)

INCO .... Industrias Consolidadas, SA [*Consolidated Industries Corp.*] [*El Salvador*]

INCOA ...... Ingenieros Constructores Asociados [*Colombia*]   (COL)

INCOAGRO ... Inversiones Comerciales y Agropecuarios Ltda. [*Barranquilla*]   (COL)

INCOAL.... Industria de Cobre y Aluminio Ltda. [*Colombia*]   (COL)

INCOATE ... Instituto de Cooperacion y Ayuda Tecnica a los Consejos Municipales del Estado de Merida [*Venezuela*]   (LAA)

INCOBOL ... Industria Colombiana de Bolos Ltda. [*Palmira*]   (COL)

INCOBRA ... Instituto Cientifico Colombo Brasilero Ltda. [*Barranquilla*]   (COL)

INCOCEGA ... Industrie et Commerce General Gabonais [*Gabonese Industry and General Trade*]   (AF)

INCOCOL ... Internacional Colombiana [*Colombia*]   (COL)

INCODENTAL ... Industrias Colombianas Dentales [*Colombia*]   (COL)

INCODES ... Instituto de Colonizacion y Desarrollo de Comunidades Rurales [*Bolivia*]   (DSCA)

INCOFER ... Instituto Costarricense de Ferrocarriles [*Costa Rica*]   (EY)

INCOFRAN ... Ingenieria Colombo Francesa [*Colombia*]   (COL)

INCOGEGA ... Industrie et Commerce General Gabonais

INCOHORMAS ... Industria Colombiana de Hormas Ltda. [*Colombia*]   (COL)

INCOIN .... Ingenieros Constructores Industriales [*Colombia*]   (COL)

INCOLANA (EPS) ... Empresa de Explotacion de Lana de Vicuna [*Vicuna Wool Production Enterprise*] [*Peru*]   (LA)

INCOLCA ... Industria Colombiana de Cauchos [*Colombia*]   (COL)

INCOLDA ... Instituto Colombiano de Administracion [*Colombian Institute of Administration*] [*Colombia*]   (LA)

INCOLDER ... Industria Colombiana de Troqueles [*Colombia*]   (COL)

INCOLDEX ... Industria Colombiana de Extinguidores [*Colombia*]   (COL)

INCOLFRENOS ... Industria Colombiana de Liquidos para Frenos Gardiol [*Colombia*]   (COL)

INCOLGRASOS ... Industria Colombiana de Derivados Grasos SA [*Colombia*]   (COL)

incoll .... Incollato [*Mounted*] [*Publishing*] [*Italian*]

INCOLMA ... Industria Colombo Alemana de Machetes [*Manizales*]   (COL)

INCOLQUIPO ... Industria Colombiana de Equipos de Oficina [*Colombia*]   (COL)

INCOLTRA ... Industria Colombiana de Transformadores Ltda. [*Colombia*]   (COL)

INCOM..... Internacional Comercial Lda.

INCOMAL ... Industria Comercial y de Alimentos [*Colombia*]   (COL)

INCOMEX ... Instituto de Comercio Exterior [*Foreign Trade Institute*] [*Colorado*]   (LA)

INCOMEX ... Instituto Mexicano de Comercio Exterior [*Mexican Foreign Trade Institute*]   (LA)

INCOMIC ... China Industry-Commerce-Economic Development Corporation   (FEA)

INCOMINDIOS ... International Committee for the Indians of the Americas [*Kaiseraugst, Switzerland*]   (EAIO)

INCOMME ... Integrated Communication Effects [*Australia*]

INCON...... Industrias Consolidadas Ltda. [*Barranquilla*]   (COL)

INCONAV ... Industria e Comercio Naval [*Shipbuilding Industry and Commerce*] [*Brazil*]   (LA)

INCONAVE ... Industria de Construcao Naval [*Shipbuilding Industry*] [*Brazil*]   (LA)

INCONCRYO-ISC ... International Conference on Cryogenics - International Steering Committee   (EAIO)

INCOOP ... Instituto Nacional de Cooperativas [*Peru*]   (DSCA)

INCOP ...... Instituto Costarricense de Puertos del Pacifico [*Costa Rica*]   (EY)

INCOPE.... Industria Colombiana de Productos Electricos [*Colombia*]   (COL)

INCOPLAN ... Instituto Colombiano de Planeacion Integral [*Colombia*]   (COL)

INCOPLAS ... Industria Colombiana de Plastico [*Colombia*]   (COL)

INCOPORE ... Internationales Kommittee der Politischen Fluechtlinge und Verschleppten Personen in Deutschland [*International Committee for Political Refugees and Displaced Persons in Germany*]   (EG)

INCOPP.... Instituto Costarricense de Puertos del Pacifico [*Costa Rican Pacific Ports Institute*]   (LA)

INCOR ...... Indian National Committee on Oceanic Research   (PDAA)

INCOR ...... Israeli National Committee for Oceanographic Research

INCORA ... Instituto Colombiano de Reforma Agraria [*Colombian Agrarian Reform Institute*]   (LA)

incorn .... Incorniciato [*Framed*] [*Publishing*] [*Italian*]

incornic ...... Incorniciato [*Framed*] [*Publishing*] [*Italian*]

Incorp........ Incorporated   (EECI)

INCORSA ... Industria Colombiana de Refrigeracion SA [*Manizales*]   (COL)

INCOSAR ... Ingenieros Constructores Arquitectos Ltda. [*Colombia*]   (COL)

INCOSEM ... Instituto Costarricense del Sector Empresarial [*Costa Rican Institute of the Business Sector*]   (LA)

INCOSPAR ... Indian National Committee for Space Research   (PDAA)

INCOSUR ... Industria del Cono Sur [*Southern Cone Industries*] [*Peru*]   (LA)

INCOVIAS ... Ingenieria de Construcciones y Vias [*Colombia*]   (COL)

INCP......... Instituto Nacional de Ciencia Politica [*National Institute of Political Science*] [*Brazil*]   (LAA)

INCP......... Instituto Nacional de Contadores Publicos [*Colombia*]   (COL)

INCRA....... Instituto Nacional de Colonizacao e Reforma Agraria [*National Land Reform and Settlement Institute*] [*Brasilia, Brazil*]   (LA)

INCRA....... International Copper Research Association [*Research center*] [*British*]   (IRC)

INCREDIAL ... Instituto de Credito Territorial [*Territorial Credit Institute*] [*Colorado*]   (LA)

INCREST ... Institutul pentru Creatie Stiintifica si Tehnica [*Institute for Scientific and Technical Creativity*]   (RO)

INCRET .... Instituto para Capacitacion y Recreacion de los Trabajadores [*Workers Training and Recreation Institute*] [*Venezuela*]   (LA)

INCS.......... Iran National Cancer Society   (ME)

INCSAS..... Ingenieros Civiles y Sanitarios Asociados Ltda. [*Colombia*]   (COL)

INCUBAR ... Asociacion Colombiana de Incubadoras [*Colombia*]   (COL)

INCURSABA ... Industria de Curtidos Sabaneta Ltda. [*Colombia*]   (COL)

INCUSA.... Industria del Cuero SA [*Uruguay*] (DSCA)
INCYTH ... Instituto Nacional de Ciencia y Tecnica Hidricas [*Argentina*] (ASF)
Ind............. De Industrie [*Benelux*] (BAS)
ind............. Indecatif [*French*] (TPFD)
ind............. Indefinido [*Indefinite*] [*Portuguese*]
IND........... Indeks [*Index*] [*Afrikaans*]
Ind............. Independent (EECI)
Ind............. Independents [*Pakistan*] [*Political party*]
ind............. Index [*Index*] [*Hungary*]
ind............. Index, Indicator (BU)
IND........... India [*IYRU nationality code*] [*ANSI three-letter standard code*] (CNC)
ind............. Indian (RU)
ind............. Indicacao [*Indication*] [*Portuguese*]
ind............. Indicative (TPFD)
ind............. Indicativo [*Indicative*] [*Portuguese*]
ind............. Indice [*Index*] [*Spanish*]
ind............. Indice [*Index*] [*Portuguese*]
IND........... Indie [*India*] [*Afrikaans*]
ind............. Indikatief [*Indicative*] [*Afrikaans*]
ind............. Indikatiivi [*Indicative Mood*] [*Finland*]
Ind............. Indikativ [*Indicative*] [*German*]
Ind............. Indirme [*Debarkation*] (TU)
ind............. Indisch [*India*] [*German*] (GCA)
ind............. Indulas [*Departure*] (HU)
Ind............. Industrie [*Industry*] [*German*]
IND........... Inligtings-en Navorsingsdienste [*Council for Scientific and Industrial Research*] [*South Africa*] (AA)
IND........... Instituto Nacional de Deportes [*National Institute of Sports*]
IND........... Instituto Nacional de Desarrollo [*National Development Institute*] [*Peru*] (GEA)
ind............. Megindult [*First Published*] (HU)
INDA........ Industrias de Aluminio [*Colombia*] (COL)
INDA........ Instituto Nacional de Alimentacion [*National Nutrition Institute*] [*Uruguay*] (LA)
INDA........ Instituto Nacional de Desenvolvimento Agricola [*National Institute of Agricultural Development*] [*Brazil*] (LA)
INDA........ Istituto Nazionale del Dramma Antico [*Italian*] (SLS)
INDACOM ... Bureau d'Etudes Industrielles Agricoles et Commerciales
INDACY.... Industrie Dahomeenne du Cycle
INDAER-PERU ... Empresa Publica de la Industria Aeronautica [*Aeronautics Industry State Enterprise*] [*Peru*] (LA)
INDAF....... Instituto Nacional de Desarrollo y Aprovechamiento Forestales [*National Institute of Forestry Development and Exploitation*] [*Cuba*] (LA)
Ind-AFD .... Independent-Anti Franklin Dam Party [*Australia*]
INDAG...... Industrial and Agricultural Co. Ltd.
INDAGRO ... Industrias Agropecuarias SA [*Uruguay*] (DSCA)
INDAL ...... Fabrica Nacional de Aluminio [*Colombia*] (COL)
INdAM...... Istituto Nazionale di Alta Matematica Francesco Severi [*Italian*] (SLS)
INDAP ...... Instituto de Desarrollo Agropecuario [*Agriculture and Livestock Development Institute*] [*Chile*] (LA)
INDAR ...... Industria Artesanal Colombiana [*Colombia*] (COL)
INDASA.... Maquinas Agricolas e Industriais SA [*Brazil*] (DSCA)
INDBCY.... Industrie Beninoise du Cycle
INDC .... Indian National Democratic Congress (BARN)
INDCA ...... Industria de Caucho [*Colombia*] (COL)
INDCAM .. Societe Indocamerounaise
INDDA...... Instituto Nacional de Desarrollo Agro-Industrial [*National Institute of Agroindustrial Development*] [*Peru*] [*Research center*] (IRC)
IndDem...... Independent Democrat [*Australia*] (ADA)
INDE........ Instituto Nacional de Electrificacion [*National Electrification Institute*] [*Guatemala*] (LA)
INDE........ Instituto Nicaraguense de Desarrollo [*Nicaraguan Institute of Development*] (LA)
INDEA ...... Industria Nacional de Ingenieria Automotriz [*Colombia*] (COL)
INDEASE ... Industria de Acero Ltda. [*Colombia*] (COL)
INDEBANK ... Investment and Development Bank [*Malawi*]
INDEC ...... Instituto Nacional de Estadisticas y Censo [*National Statistics and Census Industry*] [*Argentina*] (LA)
INDECA.... Instituto Nacional de Comercializacion Agricola [*National Institute of Agricultural Marketing*] [*Guatemala*] (LA)
INDECAM ... Independants Camerounais
INDECO .. Industrial Development Corporation [*Zambia*] (AF)
INDECO ... Instituto Nacional para el Desarrollo de la Comunidad Rural y la Vivienda Popular [*National Institute for the Development of the Rural Community and Low-Cost Housing*] [*Mexico*] (LA)
INDECON ... Inspectores de Construccion Ltda. [*Colombia*] (COL)
INDECS .... Immigration and Nationality Department Electronic Computer System (BARN)
indef .... Indefini [*French*] (TPFD)
indef .... Indefinido [*Indefinite*] [*Portuguese*]

indef .... Indefiniittinen [*Finland*]
indef .... Indefinite (TPFD)
indef .... Indefinito [*Indefinite*] [*Italian*]
INDEF....... Instituto de Financiamiento [*Financing Institute*] [*Bolivia*] (LA)
indef pron... Indefiniittipronomini [*Indefinite Pronoun*] [*Finland*]
INDEGA ... Industria de Gaseosas SA [*Colombia*] (COL)
INDEHI .... Instituto de Investigacion y Desarrollo Hidrobiologico [*Hydrobiological Research and Development Institute*] [*Peru*] (IRC)
INDEICOOP ... Instituto Nacional de Estudios e Investigaciones Cooperativas [*National Institute of Studies and Cooperative Research*] [*Peru*] (LA)
INDELCAR ... Industrias Electronicas del Caribe Ltda. [*Colombia*] (COL)
INDELCO ... Industrias Electrometalicas Colombia Ltda. [*Colombia*] (COL)
INDELVA ... Industrias Electronicas del Valle [*Colombia*] (COL)
INDEMA .. Instituto de Mercado Agropecuario [*Agricultural and Livestock Marketing Institute*] [*Colorado*] (LA)
INDENG ... Industrial Engineering Ltd. [*Australia*]
Ind Enreg... Indicateur de l'Enregistrement des Domaines et du Timbre [*France*] (FLAF)
INDEP....... Industrias Nacionais de Defesa [*National Defence Industries*] [*Portugal*] (PDAA)
INDEP....... Instituto Nacional de Desenvolvimento da Educacao e Pesquisa [*National Institute for Promoting Education and Research*] [*Brazil*] (LA)
INDEPAC ... Industria de Papel Carbon y Cintas para Maquina [*Colombia*] (COL)
INDEPORT ... Industria Deportiva [*Colombia*] (COL)
INDEPTH ... International Deep Profiling of Tibet and the Himalaya [*Geology*] [*China*]
INDER ...... Instituto Nacional de Deportes, Educacion Fisica, y Recreacion [*National Institute for Sports, Physical Education, and Recreation*] [*Cuba*] (LA)
INDER ...... Instituto Nacional de Reaseguros [*National Institute of Reinsurance*] [*Argentina*] (LA)
INDERENA ... Instituto de Desarrollo de los Recursos Naturales Renovables [*Institute for Development of Renewable Natural Resources*] [*Colorado*] (LA)
inders .... Inderside [*Inner Side*] [*Danish/Norwegian*]
INDES....... Instituto Nacional de los Deportes de El Salvador [*National Sports Institute of El Salvador*] (LA)
INDESA.... Inversiones Nicaraguenses de Desarrollo SA [*Nicaragua*] (DSCA)
INDESCO ... Instituto de Economia Social y Cooperativismo [*Bogota, Colombia*] (LAA)
INDETRO ... Industria Nacional de Troqueles Ltda. [*Colombia*] (COL)
Ind-Eur ...... Indo-European
INDEVA .... Industrias Fotograficas Eva y Compania Ltda. [*Barranquilla*] (COL)
INDEVCO ... Industrial Development Company SARL [*Beirut, Lebanon*] (MENA)
Ind-GP....... Independent Green Party [*Australia*]
indholdsfortgn ... Indholdsfortegnelse [*Index*] [*Publishing Danish/Norwegian*]
India LC..... Law Commission of India (DLA)
indik.......... Indicator (RU)
INDIMARI ... Istituto Nazionale per il Diabete e le Malattie del Ricambio [*Italian*] (SLS)
INDISA .... Indega de Inversiones SA [*Colombia*] (COL)
INDITECNOR ... Instituto Nacional de Investigaciones Tecnicas y Normalizacion [*National Institute of Technical Research and Standards*] [*Chile*] (LA)
indl .... Indlagt [*Enclosed*] [*Danish/Norwegian*]
indl .... Indledning [*Introduction*] [*Publishing Danish/Norwegian*]
IndLab .... Independent Labor [*Australia*] (ADA)
IndLib .... Independent Liberal [*Australia*] (ADA)
IndMR .... Independent Moderate Realist [*Australia*]
INDNAGA ... Industrias Naga [*Colombia*] (COL)
IndNat....... Independent Nationalist [*Australia*]
IndO.......... Indian Ocean
INDOC...... Indochina [*or Indochinese*] (WDAA)
INDOC...... Indonesian Documentation and Information Centre [*Leiden, Netherlands*] (EAIO)
INDOCAS ... Instituto Dominicano de Capacitacion Sindical [*Dominican Institute of Trade Union Training*] [*Dominican Republic*] (LA)
INDOCHEM ... Indian Ocean GEOSECS Program (MSC)
INDOELECTRA ... Industrias Electromecanicas [*Colombia*] (COL)
INDOGEN ... Intetgriertes Dokumentations-und Generatorsystem [*German*] (ADPT)
INDOL ...... Industrias Oleiferas SA [*Colombia*] (COL)
Indon.......... Indonesia (BARN)
INDON....... Indonesie [*Indonesia*] [*Afrikaans*]
indonez....... Indonesian (RU)
INDOS ...... Industrija Obdelovalnih Strojev [*Agricultural Machinery Industry*] [*Ljubljana*] (YU)
INDOTEC ... Instituto Dominicano de Tecnologia Industrial [*Dominican Republic*]

Ind P .... Indisches Patent [*Indian Patent*] [*German*]   (GCA)
INDPRO ... Indian Committee for Simplifications of External Trade
     Documents   (PDAA)
Indproekt ... Industrial Design   (BU)
IndProt...... Independent Protectionist [*Australia*]
INDRAP.... Institut National de Recherches et Application Pedagogique
INDRHI .... Instituto Nacional de Recursos Hidraulicos [*National Institute of
     Water Resources*] [*Dominican Republic*]   (LA)
Ind S........... Staatsblad van Indonesie [*Benelux*]   (BAS)
INDSL......... Indian National Dairy Science Library   (DSCA)
Ind Stbl ...... Staatsblad van Nederlandsch-Indie [*Benelux*]   (BAS)
indstr......... Indstreget [*Underlined*] [*Publishing Danish/Norwegian*]
INDUACERO ... Industrias Centrales de Acero [*Colombia*]   (COL)
INDUACOPLES ... Industria de Acoples Flexibles [*Colombia*]   (COL)
INDUAGRO ... Industrias Agricolas Ltda. [*Colombia*]   (COL)
IndUAP ..... Independent United Australia Party [*Political party*]
INDUARROZ ... Federacion de Industriales del Arroz [*Colombia*]   (DSCA)
INDUBOLCES ... Industria Nacional de Boceles [*Colombia*]   (COL)
INDUCARTON ... Cartoneria Industrial Ltda. [*Colombia*]   (COL)
INDUCERAMICA ... Ceramica Industrial Pegaso Ltda. [*Colombia*]   (COL)
INDUCERRA ... Industria de Cerraduras Metalicas [*Colombia*]   (COL)
INDUCO ... Industrial de Confecciones Carlos Restrepo Olano & Compania
     Ltda. [*Colombia*]   (COL)
INDUCON ... Industria de Concreto Ltda. [*Colombia*]   (COL)
INDUCOR ... Industria Cordelera Ltda. [*Manizales*]   (COL)
INDUCUIR ... Societe Industrielle du Cuir
INDUDECOL ... Industria Colombiana de Colas [*Colombia*]   (COL)
INDUFARMA ... Industria de Farmacia Franco-Colombiana Ltda.
     [*Colombia*]   (COL)
INDUFULL ... Industrias Full Ltda. [*Colombia*]   (COL)
INDUGAN ... Industria Ganadera Colombiana SA [*Colombia*]   (COL)
INDUGAS ... Industria Colombiana de Gas   (COL)
INDULAC ... Industria Lactea Venezolana CA [*Venezuela*]   (DSCA)
INDULAMP ... Industria de Lamparas Ltda. [*Barranquilla*]   (COL)
INDULECHE ... Industrial de Leches [*Colombia*]   (COL)
Indulgplen ... Indulgencia Plenaria [*Plenary Indulgence*] [*Spanish*]
INDULLERA ... Industrial Hullera SA [*Colombia*]   (COL)
INDUMA ... Industrias Manizales   (COL)
INDUMALLAS ... Industria de Mallas [*Colombia*]   (COL)
INDUMEC ... Industrias Mecanicas Ltda. [*Colombia*]   (COL)
INDUMEL ... Industrias Mel Ltda. [*Colombia*]   (COL)
INDUMII ... Industria Militar [*Military Industry*] [*Colorado*]   (IMH)
INDUMIL-PERU ... Industrias Militares del Peru [*Military Industries of
     Peru*]   (LA)
INDUMINERA ... Corporacion Induminera de Desarrollo SA [*Colombia*]
     (DSCA)
INDUMODE ... Industrias Modernas [*Colombia*]   (COL)
INDUMOL ... Industrias Molineras Ltda. [*Colombia*]   (COL)
INDUPAL ... Industria Paulista de Laminados [*Sao Paulo, Brazil*]   (LAA)
INDUPALMA ... Industrial Agraria la Palma SA [*Colombia*]   (COL)
INDUPAN ... Industria Panificadora Nacional [*Colombia*]   (COL)
INDUPERU ... Industrias del Peru [*Peruvian State Industries*]   (LA)
INDUPLANO ... Industrial de Vidrio Plano [*Colombia*]   (COL)
INDUPLAS ... Industrias Plasticas Ltda.   (COL)
INDUPLATI ... Industrija Platnenih Izdelkov [*Linen Products Industry*]
     [*Jarse*]   (YU)
INDUPOL ... Industria Nacional de Poleas [*Manizales*]   (COL)
INDUPOMO ... Industria de Pomos Ltda. [*Colombia*]   (COL)
INDURACE ... Industria Purace SA [*Cauca*]   (COL)
INDURRAJES ... Industria de Herrajes Ltda. [*Colombia*]   (COL)
INDUS ...... Industrias Quimicas Basicas SA [*Peru*]   (DSCA)
IndusCt ...... Industrial Court [*Australia*]   (ADA)
INDUSFIBRA ... Associacao de Industria de Extracao de Fibras Vegetais e
     Descarocamento do Algodao no Estado do Parana [*Brazil*]
     (DSCA)
INDUSGUAN ... Industrias de Guantes de Cuero [*Barranquilla*]   (COL)
INDUSPANAM ... Industrializacion Panamericana Ltda. [*Colombia*]   (COL)
IndusRelations Commn ... Industrial Relations Commission [*Australia*]
Industroy.... All-Union Construction and Installation Trust of the Ministry of
     Construction of the Metallurgical and Chemical Industries,
     USSR   (RU)
Industroyproyekt ... Planning and Design Office of the State Committee for the
     Building Materials Industry of the Gosstroy SSSR   (RU)
INDUTEC ... Industrias Tecnoquimicas de la Costa [*Barranquilla*]   (COL)
INDUTRENZ ... Industria Colombiana de Trenzados Ltda. [*Barranquilla*]
     (COL)
INDUVAR ... Industrias Varias [*Colombia*]   (COL)
INDUVIC ... Industrias Victoria [*Colombia*]   (COL)
INE .... Institut National d'Education [*National Education Institute*]
     [*Burkina Faso*]   (AF)
INE .... Instituto Nacional de Energia [*National Energy Institute*]
     [*Ecuador*]   (LA)
INE .... Instituto Nacional de Estadisticas [*National Statistics Institute*]
     [*Spanish*]   (LA)
INE .... Instituto Nacional de Estatistica [*National Statistics Institute*]
     [*Portuguese*]   (WER)

INE .... Instituto Nicaraguense de Energia [*Nicaraguan Institute of
     Energy*]   (LA)
INE .... Istituto Nazionale di Ecologia [*Italian*]   (SLS)
INE .... Istituto Nazionale Esportazioni [*National Institute for the
     Promotion of Export Trade*] [*Italian*]   (WER)
INEA .... Institut National pour l'Enseignement pour Adultes [*National
     Institute for Adult Education*] [*Tunisia*]   (AF)
INEA .... Instituto Nacional para la Educacion de los Adultos [*Mexico*]
INEA .... Istituto Nazionale di Economia Agraria [*National Institute of
     Agricultural Economics*] [*Italian*]   (ARC)
INEAC...... Institut National pour l'Etude Agronomique au Congo Belge
INEC .... Institut Europeen d'Ecologie et de Cancerologie [*European
     Institute of Ecology and Cancer - EIEC*]   (EA)
INEC .... Institut Europeen des Industries de la Gomme de Caroube
     [*European Institute of Carob Gum Industries*] [*EC*]
     (ECED)
INEC .... Instituto Nacional de Estadistica y Censos [*Ecuador*]   (SLS)
INEC .... Instituto Nacional para el Mejoramiento de la Ensenanza de las
     Ciencias [*Argentina*]   (LAA)
INEC .... Instituto Nicaraguense de Estadistica y Censos [*Nicaraguan
     Institute of Statistics and Census*]   (LA)
INECA...... Industrial Energy Conservation Abstracts [*UNIDO*] [*United
     Nations*]   (DUND)
INECAFE ... Instituto Ecuatoriano del Cafe [*Ecuador*]   (LAA)
INECEL .... Instituto Ecuatoriano de Electrificacion [*Ecuadorean
     Electrification Institute*]   (LA)
INECOOP ... Istituto Nazionale per l'Educazione Cooperativa [*Italian*]
     (SLS)
ined........... Inedit [*Unpublished*] [*Publishing*] [*French*]
ined........... Inedito [*Unpublished*] [*Publishing*] [*Italian*]
INED .... Institute for New Enterprise Development   (EAIO)
INED .... Institut National d'Etudes Demographiques [*French*]
INED .... International Network for Educational Information   (EAIO)
INEDECA ... Industria Ecuatoriana Elaboradora de Cacao [*Ecuador*]   (DSCA)
INEDES .... Instituto Ecuatoriano de Planificacion para el Desarrollo Social
     [*Ecuador*]   (LAA)
INEEP....... Institut National d'Education et d'Etudes Politiques [*National
     Institute for Political Education and Studies*] [*Mauritania*]
     (AF)
INEF......... Instituto Nacional de Educacao Fisica [*National Physical
     Education Institute*] [*Portuguese*]   (WER)
INEFIP...... Integriertes Erfolgs-und Finanzplanungsmodell [*German*]
     (ADPT)
INEFTI...... Petroleum Institute   (RU)
InEG .... Institute of Power Engineering and Hydraulics (of the Academy
     of Sciences, Armenian SSR)   (RU)
INEGI....... Instituto Nacional de Estadistica, Geografia e Informatica [*Main
     government clearinghouse for statistical information*]
     [*Mexico*]   (CROSS)
Ineksbio ..... Institute of Experimental Biology   (RU)
INEL......... Instituto Nacional de Estudios Linguisticos [*National Institute of
     Linguistic Studies*] [*Bolivia*] [*Research center*]   (IRC)
INELCA .... Industrias Electronicas Colombo Alemanas Ltda. [*Colombia*]
     (COL)
INELGO.... Institut za Elektrisko Gospodarstvo [*Institute of Electrical Power*]
     [*Ljubljana*]   (YU)
INEM .... Instituto Nacional de Ensenanza Media Diversificada [*National
     Institute for Diversified Medium-Level Education*]
     [*Colorado*]   (LA)
INEM .... Institutos Nacionales de Educacion Media [*Colombia*]   (COL)
INEMET... Instituto Nacional de Meteorologia [*National Meteorological
     Institute*] [*Brazil*] [*Research center*]   (EAS)
INEMO ..... Istituto Nazionale di Economia Montana [*Italian*]   (SLS)
INEN .... Instituto Ecuatoriano de Normalizacion [*Ecuadorean Standards
     Institute*]   (GEA)
INEN .... Instituto Nacional de Energia Nuclear [*National Nuclear Energy
     Institute*] [*Spanish*]   (LA)
INENCO ... Instituto de Investigaciones en Energia no Convencional
     [*Argentina*]
INEOS...... Institute of Hetero-Organic Compounds (of the Academy of
     Sciences, USSR)   (RU)
INEP.......... Institut National d'Etudes Politiques [*National Institute for
     Political Studies*] [*Zaire*]   (AF)
INEP.......... Instituto Nacional de Estabilizacion de Precios [*National Price
     Stabilization Institute*] [*Venezuela*]   (LA)
INEP.......... Instituto Nacional de Estudos Pedagogicos [*National Institute of
     Educational Research*] [*Brazil*]   (LA)
INEP.......... Institut Primenu Nuklearne Energije u Poljoprivredi,
     Veterinarstru, i Sumarstvu [*Institute for the Application of
     Nuclear Energy in Agriculture, Veterinary Medicine, and
     Forestry*] [*Former Yugoslavia*]   (ARC)
INEPS .... Institut National de l'Education Physique et Sportive [*National
     Institute of Physical and Sports Education*] [*Cambodia*]
     (CL)
INER .... Institute of Nuclear Energy Research [*Taiwanese*] [*Research
     center*]   (IRC)

INER .... Instituto Nacional de Electrificacion Rural [*National Rural Electrification Institute*] [*Bolivia*] (IMH)

INERA .... Institut National pour les Etudes et des Recherches Agronomiques [*National Institute for Agronomic Study and Research*] [*Zaire*] (AF)

INERBA .... Institut National d'Etudes et de Recherches, Ministere de l'Habitat et de l'Urbanisme [*Algeria*]

INERGON ... Industrial Electrica Ergon Ltda. [*Colombia*] (COL)

INERHI ..... Instituto Ecuatoriano de Recursos Hidraulicos [*Ecuadorean Institute for Water Resources*] (LA)

INERIS ...... Institut National de l'Environnement Industriel et des Risques [*National Laboratory of Industrial Environment and Risks Analysis*] [*France*] (IRC)

INERYCT ... Instituto Nacional de Enfermedades Respiratorias y Cirugia Toracica [*National Institute of Respiratory Diseases and Thoracic Surgery*] [*Chile*] [*Research center*] (IRC)

INES .... Instituto Nacional de Estudios Sindicales [*National Labor Studies Institute*] [*Venezuela*] (LA)

INESCO .... Ingenieria Estudios Construcciones [*Colombia*] (COL)

INESPAL ... Industria Espanol del Aluminio [*Spanish Aluminium Industry*] [*Commercial firm*]

INESPRE ... Instituto Nacional de Estabilizacion de Precios [*National Price Stabilization Institute*] [*Dominican Republic*] (LA)

iness .... Inessiivi [*Finland*]

INET .... Instituto Nacional de Estudios del Teatro [*National Institute for the Study of the Theater*] [*Buenos Aires, Argentina*] (LAA)

INETER .... Instituto Nicaraguense de Estudios Territoriales [*Nicaraguan Institute of Territorial Studies*] (LA)

INEUM ..... Institute of Electronic Control Machines (of the Academy of Sciences, USSR) (RU)

INEUT ...... Istituto Nazionale di Economia Urbana e Territoriale [*Italian*] (SLS)

INEX .... Industrieanlagen-Export (VEB) [*Industrial Facilities Exports (VEB)*] (EG)

INEXTRA ... Industrias Extractivas [*Colombia*] (COL)

inf .... Faites Infuser [*Infuse*] [*Pharmacy*]

inf .... Infantaria [*Infantry*] [*Portuguese*]

INF .... Infanterie [*Infantry*] [*Afrikaans*]

Inf............ Infanterie [*Infantry*] [*French*] (MTD)

inf .... Inferieur [*Lower*] [*French*]

inf .... Inferiore [*Bottom*] [*Publishing*] [*Italian*]

inf .... Infime [*Very Small*] [*French*]

inf .... Infinitief [*Infinitive*] [*Afrikaans*]

inf .... Infinitiivi [*Infinitive*] [*Finland*]

inf .... Infinitive (RU)

inf .... Infinitivo [*Infinitive*] [*Portuguese*]

inf .... Infinito [*Infinite*] [*Portuguese*]

INF .... Influence (WDAA)

in-f.............. In-Folio [*Folio*] [*French*]

INF .... Informaatiopalvelulaitos [*Information Service*] [*Technical Research Center of Finland Espoo*] [*Information service or system*] (IID)

inf .... Informacio [*Information*] (HU)

INF .... Institute of Physiology Imeni I. P. Pavlov (RU)

INF .... Instituto Nacional de Farmacologia [*National Institute of Pharmacology*] [*Brazil*] (LAA)

INF .... Intermediate-Range Nuclear Forces (EECI)

INF .... International Naturist Federation [*Antwerp, Belgium*] (EA)

INF .... International Nepal Fellowship

INF .... Inventario Nacional Forestal [*Mexico*] (DSCA)

INF .... Iranian National Front (PPW)

INF .... Islamic National Front [*Sudan*] (MENA)

INFA......... India News Feature Alliance

INFA......... Informationsausgabe [*Information Output*] [*German*] (ADPT)

INFA......... International Federation of Aestheticians [*Brussels, Belgium*] (EAIO)

INFACON ... International Ferro-Alloys Congress

INFACT .... Infant Formula Action Coalition

infak .... Division of Foreign Languages (RU)

INFAS .... Institute for Applied Social Science [*Bad Godesberg, West Germany*] (WEN)

INFAS .... Institut fuer Angewandte Sozialwissenschaft [*Institute of Applied Social Science*] (SLS)

INFAS .... Instituto Nacional de Formacion Agraria y Sindical [*National Institute of Agrarian and Labor Training*] [*Dominican Republic*] (LA)

INFAVA .... Industria Farmaceutica del Valle [*Colombia*] (COL)

Infbl .... Informatieblad van het Economisch en Sociaal Instituut voor de Middenstand [*Benelux*] (BAS)

INFC......... Institut National de Formation de Cadres [*National Institute for the Training of Cadres*] [*Zaire*] (AF)

INFCE .... International Nuclear Fuel Cycle Evaluation

Inf ChEnt ... Informateur du Chef d'Entreprise [*France*] (FLAF)

Inf Constet Parl ... Informations Constitutionnelles et Parlementaires [*France*] (FLAF)

INFE.......... Instituto Nacional de Fomento de la Exportacion [*National Institute of Export Development*] [*Spain*] (EY)

INFEDOP ... International Federation of Employees in Public Service [*Brussels, Belgium*] (EAIO)

Infekt .... Infektion [*Infection*] [*German*] (GCA)

INFELOR ... Informacio Feldolgozo Laboratorium [*Information Processing Laboratory*] (HU)

infer............ Inferieur [*Lower*] [*French*]

infer............ Inferiore [*Bottom*] [*Publishing*] [*Italian*]

INFESA..... Industria Farmaceutica Ecuatoriana SA [*Ecuador*] (DSCA)

INFI.......... Investment and Finance Bank SAL [*Beirut, Lebanon*] (MENA)

INFIC .... International Network of Feed Information Centers (EA)

INFICO..... Industria Fiquera de la Costa Ltda. [*Barranquilla*] (COL)

infin............ Infinitif [*French*] (TPFD)

INFIND..... Bureau de l'Information pour l'Indigenes

INFISA..... Inversiones Financieras, Sociedad Anonima [*Managua, Nicaragua*] (LAA)

INFIZKUL'T ... Institute of Physical Culture (RU)

INFLI .... Institut pour la Formation Litteraire [*Institute of Literary Training*] [*Cambodia*] (CL)

Inflot .... Maritime Agency for Servicing Foreign Ships in Soviet Ports (RU)

INFLTEC ... Instalaciones Electricas Tecnicas [*Colombia*] (COL)

INFN .... Istituto Nazionale di Fisica Nucleare [*National Institute for Nuclear Physics*] [*Italian*] (WER)

INFNET .... Istituto Nazionale Fisica Nucleare Network [*National Institute for Nuclear Physics Network*] [*Italian*] [*Computer science*] (TNIG)

INFO .... Information Department (RU)

INFOBANK ... [*The*] Information Bank [*Computer Sciences of Australia Pty. Ltd.*] [*Information service or system*]

INFOCLIMA ... World Climate Data Information Referral Service [*World Meteorological Organization*] [*Information service or system*] (IID)

INFOCO ... Industrial Forestal Colombiana Ltda. [*Tumaco*] (COL)

INFOCOOP ... Instituto Nacional de Fomento Cooperativo [*National Cooperatives Development Institute*] [*Costa Rica*] (LA)

INFODATA ... Datenbank Informationswissenschaft und -Praxis [*Database Information Science and Practice*] [*Database*] [*Information retrieval*]

INFODEMA ... Industria Foliadora de Maderas, SA [*Chile*] (LAA)

INFOGAN ... Instituto de Fomento Ganadero [*Colorado*] (LAA)

INFOGE.... Instituto de Fomento de Guinea Ecuatorial

INFOKOM ... Gesellschaft fuer Informations-und Kommunikationstechnik [*German*] (ADPT)

INFOM ..... Instituto de Fomento Municipal [*Municipal Development Institute*] [*Guatemala*] (LA)

INFOMARK ... Information Market News [*Database*] [*EC*] (ECED)

INFONAC ... Instituto de Fomento Nacional [*National Development Institute*] [*Nicaragua*] (LA)

INFONAVIT ... Instituto del Fondo Nacional de la Vivienda para los Trabajadores [*Institute of the National Fund for Workers Housing*] [*Mexico*] (LA)

INFOP....... Instituto de Fomento de la Produccion [*Production Development Institute*] [*Guatemala*] (LA)

INFOP....... Instituto Nacional de Formacion Profesional [*National Institute of Professional Training*] [*Honduras*] (LA)

INFOPE.... Instituto de Fomento Pesquero [*Chile*] (DSCA)

INFOPLAN ... Latin American Planning Information Network [*Santiago, Chile*]

INFOR....... Instituto Forestal [*Chile*]

INFORAMA ... Information et Radiodiffusion de Mauritius

INFORAV ... Istituto per lo Sviluppo e la Gestione Avanzata dell'Informazione [*Italian*] (SLS)

INFORBW ... Information on Research in Baden-Wurttemberg [*Fachinformationszentrum Karlsruhe GmbH*] [*Germany*] [*Information service or system*] (CRD)

INFORCONGO ... Office de l'Information et des Relations Publiques pour le Congo Belge et le Ruanda-Urundi

inform........ Information (RU)

inform........ Informational (BU)

Informbyuro ... Information Bureau (BU)

Informbyuro ... Information Office of Communist and Workers' Parties [*1947-1956*] (RU)

InformChef Entrep ... Informateur du Chef d'Entreprise [*France*] (FLAF)

informot ..... Information Department (RU)

informupr ... Information Administration (RU)

INFORSA ... Industrias Forestales, SA [*Forestry Industries, Inc.*] [*Chile*] (LA)

INFOS....... Informatik-Organisationssystem [*German*] (ADPT)

INFOS....... Information Network for Official Statistics [*Department of Statistics*] [*Information service or system*] (IID)

INFOS....... Informationszentrum fuer Schnittwerte [*Cutting Data Information Center*] [*Germany*] [*Information service or system*] (IID)

INFOSEC ... Institut de Formation Sociale, Economique, et Civique [*Institute for Social, Economic, and Civic Training*] [*Benin*] (AF)

Infospecs.... Information Specialists Ltd. [*Information service or system*] (IID)

INFOTEC ... Servicio de Informacion Tecnica [*Technical Information Service*] [*Mexico*]   (LA)

INFOTEP ... Instituto Nacional de Formacion Tecnico-Profesional [*National Institute of Technical-Professional Training*] [*Dominican Republic*]

INFOTERM ... International Information Centre for Terminology [*UNESCO*]   (IID)

INFOTERRA ... International Referral System for Sources of Environmental Information [*Formerly, IRS*] [*United Nations Environment Program*]   (ASF)

INFP .... Institut National de Formation Professionnelle [*France*]   (FLAF)

INFRA .... Industrias el Fraile [*Colombia*]   (COL)

INFRAERO ... Empresa Brasileira de Infraestrutura Aeroportuaria [*Brazilian Airport Support Enterprise*]   (LA)

INFREMER ... Institut Francais de Recherche pour l'Exploitation de la Mer [*France*]   (PDAA)

Inf Soc .... Informateur Social [*France*]   (FLAF)

Inf SocBIT ... Informations Sociales du Bureau International du Travail   (FLAF)

Inf T .... Infanterie Territoriale [*Military*] [*French*]   (MTD)

INFT .... Instituto Nacional de Fomento Tabacalero [*Colombia*]   (DSCA)

Ing .... Engineer [*Former Czechoslovakia*]

ing .... Ingebonden [*Bound In*] [*Publishing*] [*Netherlands*]

ING .... Ingegnere [*Engineer*] [*Italian*]

ING .... Ingeniero [*Engineer*] [*Spanish*]

Ing .... Ingenieur [*Engineer*] [*German*]   (GPO)

ING .... Ingenieur [*Engineer*] [*French*]

ing .... Ingiallito [*Yellowed*] [*Publishing*] [*Italian*]

Ing .... Ingilizce [*English*]   (TU)

ing .... Ingles [*English*] [*Portuguese*]

ING .... Institut National de Gestion [*National Management Institute*] [*Niger*]   (AF)

Ing .... Inzenyr [*Engineer (Academic degree)*]   (CZ)

ING .... Lago Argentino [*Argentina*] [*Airport symbol*]   (OAG)

INGACOL ... Industria Galvanotecnica Colombiana Ltda. [*Colombia*]   (COL)

INGAS .... Integriertes Grosshandels-Abrechnungssystem [*Integrated Wholesale Calculation System*] [*German*] [*Integrated Wholesale Calculation System*]   (ADPT)

ingatl .... Ingatlan [*Real Estate*]   (HU)

INGC .... Istituto Nazionale di Genetica per la Cerelicoltura [*Italy*]   (DSCA)

IngC .... Kandidat Inzenyrstvi [*Candidate for Engineering Degree*]   (CZ)

IngCom ...... Komercni Inzenyr [*Business School Graduate*]   (CZ)

Ing Cons ..... Ingenieur-Conseil [*Benelux*]   (BAS)

ingekl .... Ingekleurd [*Colored*] [*Publishing*] [*Netherlands*]

ingel .... Ingeleid [*Introduced*] [*Publishing*] [*Netherlands*]

INGELCO ... Ingenieros Electricistas Contratistas Ltda. [*Colombia*]   (COL)

INGELCO ... Instalaciones Electricas [*Colombia*]   (COL)

INGEMAR ... Cooperativa de Ingenieros y Oficiales Marinos Ltda. [*Colombia*]   (COL)

INGEMETAL ... Industria General de Metales [*Colombia*]   (COL)

INGEMMET ... Instituto Geologico, Minero, y Metalurgico [*Geological, Mining, and Metallurgical Institute*] [*Peru*] [*Research center*]   (EAS)

ingen .... Ingenaaid [*Sewed*] [*Publishing*] [*Netherlands*]

INGEN ...... Ingenieria para el Ahorro de Energia [*Argentina*]   (WED)

INGENAGRO ... Oficina de Ingenieria Agronomica [*Venezuela*]   (DSCA)

INGEOMINAS ... Instituto Nacional de Investigaciones Geologico-Mineras [*National Institute of Geological and Mining Research*] [*Colombia*]   (LA)

INGER ...... International Network on Genetic Evaluation in Rice   (ECON)

INGESCOL ... Ingenieros Civiles [*Colombia*]   (COL)

INGESISTEMAS ... Ingenieria de Sistemas Ltda. [*Colombia*]   (COL)

INGETEC ... Ingenieros Consultores Civiles y Electricos Ltda. [*Colombia*]   (COL)

ingetr .... Ingetrokken Bij [*Benelux*]   (BAS)

ingev .... Ingevoegd Bij [*Benelux*]   (BAS)

Ingh .... Inghilterra [*England*] [*Italian*]

INGI .... Institute of Civil Engineers   (RU)

ingial .... Ingiallito [*Yellowed*] [*Publishing*] [*Italian*]

ingl .... Inglese [*English*] [*Italian*]

INGM .... Instituto Nacional de Geologia y Mineria [*National Institute of Geology and Mines*] [*Buenos Aires, Argentina*]   (LAA)

INGOMPLA ... Industria Gomez Plata de Oriente Ltda. [*Bucaramanga*]   (COL)

INGRA ...... Industrisko Gradevna Exportna Zajednica [*Industrial Building Export Association*]   (YU)

INGROS .... Integriertes Grosshandelssystem [*Integrated Wholesale System*] [*German*]   (ADPT)

INGROSS ... Integrierte Programmkreise fuer den Grosshandel [*German*]   (ADPT)

INGUAT ... Instituto Guatemalteco de Turismo [*Guatemalan Institute of Tourism*]   (LA)

INGY .... Ideiglenes Nemzetgyules [*Temporary National Assembly*]   (HU)

INGYO ...... International Nongovernmental Youth Organization   (PDAA)

Inh .... Inhaber [*Proprietor*] [*German*]   (EG)

Inh .... Inhalt [*Contents*] [*German*]   (EG)

inh .... Inheemsch [*Benelux*]   (BAS)

inh .... Inhoud [*Contents*] [*Publishing*] [*Netherlands*]

INH .... Instituto Nacional de Hidrocarburos [*National Institute of Hydrocarbons*] [*State holding company Madrid, Spain*]   (EY)

INH .... Instituto Nacional de Higiene [*National Institute of Health*] [*Guayaquil, Ecuador*]   (LAA)

INH .... Instituto Nacional de Hipodromos [*Venezuela*]

INHELIOS ... Industrias Graficas Helios Ltda. [*Colombia*]   (COL)

INHIGEO ... International Commission on the History of the Geological Sciences [*ICSU*] [*Paris, France*]   (EAIO)

InhRechtspr ... Regeling van de Inheemse Rechtspraak in Rechtsstreeks Bestuurd Gebied [*Benelux*]   (BAS)

Inh-Verz ..... Inhaltsverzeichnis [*Table of Contents*] [*German*]

INI .... Institute of Scientific Information   (RU)

INI .... Institut National de l'Industrie [*National Industry Institute*]

INI .... Instituto Nacional de Identificacao [*National Identification Institute*] [*Brazil*]   (LA)

INI .... Instituto Nacional de Industria [*National Institute of Industry*] [*Madrid, Spain*]   (WER)

INI .... Instituto Nacional de Inversiones [*National Investment Institute*] [*La Paz, Bolivia*]   (LA)

INI .... Instituto Nacional Indigenista [*Mexico*]   (DSCA)

INI .... Institut za Nacionalnu Istoriju [*National History Institute*]   (YU)

INI .... Istituto Nazionale dell'Informazione [*Italian*]   (SLS)

INI .... Nonlinear Distortion Meter   (RU)

INIA .... Instituto de Investigaciones Agropecuarias [*Agricultural Research Institute*] [*Chile*] [*Research center*]   (IRC)

INIA .... Instituto Nacional de Investigacao Agraria [*National Institute for Agrarian Studies*] [*Portuguese*]   (WER)

INIA .... Instituto Nacional de Investigacion Agraria [*National Institute for Agrarian Research*] [*Peru*]   (LA)

INIA .... Instituto Nacional de Investigaciones Agrarias [*National Institute for Agricultural Research*] [*Spanish*]   (ARC)

INIA .... Instituto Nacional de Investigaciones Agricolas [*National Institute for Agricultural Research*] [*Mexico*]   (LA)

INIAG ...... Instituto de Investigaciones Agrarias [*Agricultural Research Institute*] [*Colorado*]   (ARC)

INIAP .... Instituto Nacional de Investigaciones Agropecuarias [*Ecuador*]   (DSCA)

INIBAP ..... International Network for the Improvement of Banana and Plantain [*Affiliated with the Consultative Group on International Agricultural Research*] [*France*]

INIBP .... Instituto Nacional de Investigaciones Biologico Pesqueras [*Spanish*]   (ASF)

inic .... Iniciale [*Initial Letter*] [*Hungary*]

INIC .... Instituto Nacional de Imigracao e Colonizacao [*National Immigration and Settlement Institute*] [*Brazil*]   (LA)

INIC .... Instituto Nacional de Investigaciones Cientificas [*National Institute for Scientific Research*] [*Mexico*]   (LA)

INIC .... Instituto Nacional de Investigacion y Capacitacion [*National Research and Training Institute*] [*Peru*]   (LA)

INICA .... Insecticidas Internacionales CA [*Venezuela*]   (DSCA)

INICHAR ... Institut National de l'Industrie Charbonniere [*National Institute of the Coal Industry*] [*Belgium*]   (PDAA)

INID .... Institutul National de Informare si Documentare [*National Institute for Information and Documentation*] [*National Council for Science and Technology*] [*Information service or system*]   (IID)

INID .... Institutul National de Informare si Documentare Stiintifica si Tehnica [*National Institute for Scientific and Technical Information and Documentation*]   (RO)

INIDCYA ... Institute for the Intellectual Development of Children and Young Adults [*Iran*]   (PDAA)

INIDEP ..... Instituto Nacional de Investigacion y Desarrollo de la Industria Pesquera [*National Institute for the Development and Research of the Fishing Industry*] [*Argentina*]   (LA)

INIE .... Instituto Nacional de Investigaciones Energeticas [*National Energy Research Institute*] [*Peru*]   (LA)

INIES .... Instituto Nacional de Investigaciones y Estudios Sociales [*National Social Studies Research Institute*] [*Tegucigalpa, Honduras*]   (LAA)

INIEX .... Institut National des Industries Extractives [*National Institute of Mining Industries*] [*Belgium*]

INIF .... Instituto Nacional de Investigaciones Forestales [*National Forestry Research Institute*] [*Research center*] [*Mexico*]   (IRC)

INIFAT ..... Instituto de Investigaciones Fundamentales en Agricultura Tropical [*Institute for Basic Research in Tropical Agriculture*] [*Cuba*]   (LA)

INIFT .... Italian National Institute for Foreign Trade   (EAIO)

INIFTA ..... Instituto de Investigaciones Fisicoquimicas Teoricas y Aplicadas [*Argentina*]

INIG .... International Nutritional Immunology Group   (EA)

INII .... Instituto Nacional de Investigacao Industrial [*Portugal*]   (DSCA)

INIL .... Institut National des Industries Legeres [*Algeria*]

ININ .... Instituto Nacional de Investigaciones Nucleares [*National Institute for Nuclear Research*] [*Mexico*]   (LA)

ININ .... Instituto Nacional de Investigaciones Nucleares [*National Institute for Nuclear Research*] [*Cuba*]   (LA)

ININMS.... Instituto Nacional de Investigaciones Nutricionales y Medico-Sociales [*National Institute for Nutritional and Socio-Medical Research*] [*Ecuador*] [*Research center*]   (IRC)

ININTEC .. Instituto de Investigacion Tecnologica Industrial y de Normas Tecnicas [*Industrial Technology and Standards Research Institute*] [*Peru*]   (LA)

ININTEF .. Instituto de Investigacion Tecnica Fundamental [*Institute for Basic Technical Research*] [*Cuba*]   (LA)

INIP........... Instituto Nacional de Investigacao das Pescas [*National Institute for Fisheries Research*] [*Portugal*]   (EAS)

INIP........... Istituto Nazionale per l'Incremento della Produttivita [*National Institute for Increased Productivity*] [*Spanish*]   (ASF)

INIPA........ Instituto Nacional de Investigacion y Promocion Agropecuaria [*National Research Institute of Agricultural and Livestock Development*] [*Peru*] [*Research center*]   (IRC)

INIREB ..... Instituto Nacional de Investigaciones sobre Recursos Bioticos [*National Institute of Research on Biological Resources*] [*Mexico*]   (ARC)

INIRO .... Indonesish Institut voor Rubberonderzoek

INIS........... International Nuclear Information System [*International Atomic Energy Agency*]   (IID)

INISER...... Instituto Nicaraguense de Seguros y Reaseguros [*Nicaraguan Institute of Insurance and Reinsurance*]   (LA)

INISM....... Istituto Nazionale Italiano per lo Studio del Microclima [*Italian*]   (SLS)

INIST .... Institute de l'Information Scientifique et Technique [*Institute of Scientific and Technical Information*] [*Information service or system*]   (IID)

init.............. Initiaal [*Initial Letter*] [*Publishing*] [*Netherlands*]

init.............. Initial [*Initial Letter*] [*Publishing Danish/Norwegian*]

init.............. Initiale [*Initial Letter*] [*Publishing*] [*French*]

Init .... Initialen [*Initial Letters*] [*German*]

INIT........... Instituto Nacional de la Industria Turistica [*National Institute of the Tourist Industry*] [*Cuba*]   (LAA)

INITDI ...... Institute of Scientific and Technical Documentation and Information   (RU)

INITEC ..... Empresa Nacional de Ingenieria y Tecnologia, SA [*Nuclear energy*] [*Spanish*]   (NRCH)

Initiier .... Initiierung [*Initiation*] [*German*]   (GCA)

INITO .... Societe Initiative Togolaise

iniz.............. Iniziale [*Initial Letter*] [*Publishing*] [*Italian*]

inj................ Injection [*Injection*] [*Pharmacy*]

Inja............. Inadana Jati [*National Commerce (Bank)*] [*Cambodia*]   (CL)

INJM......... Instituto Nacional de la Juventud Mexicana [*National Institute of Mexican Youth*]   (LA)

INJS .... Institut National de la Jeunesse et des Sports

INJUPEM ... Instituto de Jubilaciones y Pensiones del Magisterio [*Teachers Retirement and Pension Institute*] [*Honduras*]   (LA)

INJUVE .... Instituto Nacional de la Juventud Mexicana [*National Institute of Mexican Youth*]   (LA)

INK............ Ideiglenes Nemzeti Kormany [*Temporary National Government*]   (HU)

INK............ Indian National Congress   (RU)

INKA .... Informationssystem Karlsruhe [*Karlsruhe Information System*] [*Information service or system*] [*Germany*]

INKA .... Institouton Prostasias Katanaloton [*Consumer Protection Institute*] [*Greek*]   (GC)

Ink Bel .... Inkomstenbelasting [*Benelux*]   (BAS)

INKh.......... Institute of Inorganic Chemistry (of the Siberian Department of the Academy of Sciences, USSR)   (RU)

INKh.......... Moscow Institute of National Economy Imeni G. V. Plekhanov   (RU)

INKhP .... Institute of New Chemical Problems   (RU)

INKhP .... Institute of Petrochemical Processes   (RU)

INKhS .... Institute of Petrochemical Synthesis Imeni A. V. Topchiyev (of the Academy of Sciences, USSR)   (RU)

INKhUK.... Institute of Art Culture   (RU)

inkl............. Inkluderad [*Included*] [*Sweden*]

inkl............. Inklusief [*Inclusive*] [*Afrikaans*]

inkl............. Inklusive [*Inclusive, Included*] [*German*]   (GPO)

inklistr .... Inklistrad [*Pasted In*] [*Publishing*] [*Sweden*]

INKOM..... Interdissiplinere Komitee van Omgewingsbeplanningsprofessies [*South Africa*]   (AA)

INKOPAD ... Induk Koperasi Angkatan Darat [*Main Army Cooperative*]   (IN)

INKP.......... Indian National Trade Union Congress   (RU)

Inkun.......... Inkunabel [*Incunabulum*] [*German*]

inl .... Inlander [*or Inlandsch*] [*Benelux*]   (BAS)

inl .... Inledning [*Introduction*] [*Sweden*]

inl .... Inleiding [*Introduction*] [*Publishing*] [*Netherlands*]

INL .... Instituto Nacional do Livro [*National Book Institute*] [*Brazil*]   (LA)

INLA .... International Nuclear Law Association [*See also AIDN*] [*Brussels, Belgium*]   (EAIO)

INLACA.... Industria Lactea de Carabobo CA [*Venezuela*]   (DSCA)

INLASA ... Industria Nacional Laminadora Sociedad Anonima [*National Sheet Steel Industry, Incorporated*] [*Uruguay*]   (LA)

INLC......... Instituto Nacional de Lucha Contra el Cancer [*Spanish*]

INLE......... Instituto Nacional del Libro Espanol [*Spanish*]   (SLS)

inledn .... Inledning [*Introduction*] [*Sweden*]

inleid .... Inleiding [*Introduction*] [*Publishing*] [*Netherlands*]

INLES ...... Forest Institute (of the Academy of Sciences, USSR)   (RU)

INLI.......... Institute of Literature   (RU)

INLICO.... Industrias Livinas de Colombia [*Colombia*]   (COL)

In Liq .... In Liquidation [*Australia*]

Inlit .... Moulding and Casting Equipment Plant   (RU)

INM.......... Imbokodvo National Movement [*Swaziland*] [*Political party*]   (PPW)

INM.......... Imprimerie Nationale du Mali

INM.......... Institut National de Musique [*National Institute of Music*] [*Algeria*]   (EAIO)

INM.......... Institut National des Mines [*National Mines Institute*] [*Zaire*]   (AF)

INM.......... Instituto Nacional de Mate [*Rio De Janeiro, Brazil*]   (LAA)

INM.......... International Narcotics Matters [*Department of State*]

INMA........ Quarry Materials   (BU)

INMALLAS ... Industria de Mallas Ltda. [*Colombia*]   (COL)

INMARCO ... Industria de Marmoles y Cementos del Nare SA [*Colombia*]   (COL)

INMARSAT ... International Maritime Satellite Organization

INMAS...... Intensifikasi Massa [*Mass Intensification (Name of government-supported agricultural production projects)*] [*Indonesia*]   (FEA)

INMB .... Institutul National de Metrologie Bucuresti [*National Institute for Metrology in Bucharest*]   (RO)

INMC .... Iraq National Minerals Company   (ME)

INME......... Industrias Metalicas Ltda. [*Colombia*]   (COL)

INMEC...... Industrias Metalicas Ltda. [*Colombia*]   (COL)

INMECA... Industria Metalurgica [*Colombia*]   (COL)

INMECAFE ... Instituto Mexicano del Cafe [*Mexican Coffee Institute*]   (LA)

INMECOL ... Ingenieria Metalurgica Colombiana [*Colombia*]   (COL)

INMEP....... Institute for a New Middle East Policy

INMERO .. Institute of Permafrost Study Imeni V. A. Obruchev   (RU)

INMES...... Institut National Medico-Social [*National Medical-Social Institute*] [*Benin*]   (AF)

INMETAL ... Industria de Metales Preciosos Ltda. [*Colombia*]   (COL)

INMETRO ... Instituto Nacional de Metrologia, Normalizacao e Qualidade Industrial [*Government advisory body*] [*Brazil*]   (EY)

INMG........ Instituto Nacional de Meteorologia e Geofisica [*National Institute of Meteorology and Geophysics*] [*Portuguese*]   (SLS)

INMI .... Institute of Microbiology (of the Academy of Sciences, USSR)

INMINEH ... Instituto Nicaraguense de Minas e Hidrocarburos [*Nicaraguan Institute of Mines and Hydrocarbons*]   (LA)

INMV .... Instituto Nacional de Medicina Veterinaria [*National Institute of Veterinary Medicine*] [*Cuba*]   (LA)

inn .... Innerlich [*Internal*] [*German*]   (GCA)

INN.......... Innsbruck [*Austria*] [*Airport symbol*]   (OAG)

INN.......... Instituto Nacional de Normalizacion [*Chile*]   (SLS)

INN........... Instituto Nacional de Nutricion [*National Nutrition Institute*] [*Venezuela*]   (LA)

INN........... Instituto Nacional de Nutricion [*National Nutrition Institute*] [*Colombia*]   (COL)

INN........... L'Imprimerie Nationale du Niger [*Government publishing house*]   (EY)

INN........... Low-Voltage Indicator   (RU)

INNA .... International Newsreel and News Film Association [*Belgium*]   (EAIO)

innb .... Innbundet [*Bound*] [*Publishing Danish/Norwegian*]

inneh .... Inneholder [*Contains*] [*Danish/Norwegian*]

INNERTAP ... Information Network on New and Renewable Energy Resources and Technologies for Asia and the Pacific [*UNESCO*]   (DUND)

INNICA..... Instituto Nicaraguense de la Costa Atlantica [*Nicaraguan Institute of the Atlantic Coast*]   (LA)

INNK........ Iranian National Petroleum Company   (RU)

INNK........ Pulsed Neutron-Neutron Logging   (RU)

INNK-t ...... Pulsed Neutron-Neutron Logging with Thermal Neutron Recording   (RU)

innl .... Innledning [*Introduction*] [*Publishing Danish/Norwegian*]

innledn .... Innledning [*Introduction*] [*Publishing Danish/Norwegian*]

INNO-BM ... SA Innovation-Bon Marche NV [*Belgium*]

INNOTECH ... Innovation et Technologie de l'Education [*Educational Innovation and Technology*]   (CL)

INNOTECH ... Regional Center for Educational Innovation and Technology [*SEAMEO*] [*Philippines*]

InNPl........ Instruction for Applying the Directive on Payments   (BU)

INNRLNT ... Instruction for Applying the Directive on the Work of the Bureaus of Registration and Direction of Manpower and for Job Placement of People with Reduced Working Capacity (BU)

INNS .... International Neural Network Society (EA)

INO .... Foreign Department (RU)

INO .... Inongo [*Zaire*] [*Airport symbol*] (OAG)

INO .... Institute of Public Education (RU)

INO .... Instruction for the Application of the Directive on Workers' and Employees' Leaves (BU)

INO .... Istituto Nazionale d'Ottica [*Italian*] (SLS)

INOC .... Intergovernmental Oceanographic Commission [*ICSU*]

INOC .... Iraq National Oil Company [*Baghdad*] (ME)

INOCAR ... Instituto Oceanografico de la Armada [*Ecuador*] (MSC)

INOCO ...... Compagnie Nationale des Petroles

INOCO ...... Indonesia Nippon Oil Cooperative Co.

INODEP .... Institut Oecumenique pour le Developpement des Peuples [*Ecumenical Institute for the Development of Peoples*] [*Paris, France*] (EAIO)

INOE .... Internacia Naturista Organizo Esperantista [*International Esperantist Organization of Naturists - IEON*] (EAIO)

INOGIZ .... State Publishing House of Foreign Language Literature (RU)

INOiK .... Instytut Naukowy Organizacji i Kierownictwa [*Scientific Institute of Organization and Management*] (POL)

INOIZDAT ... Publishing House of Foreign Literature (RU)

INOMGA ... L'Industrie des Objets Moule's au Gabon

INORCA ... Industrias Nortecaucanas [*Colombia*] (COL)

INORCOL ... Instituto de Normas Colombiana [*Standards Institute*] [*Colombia*] (PDAA)

INORFE .... Industria e Comercio de Algodao Ltd. [*Brazil*] (DSCA)

INORFE .... Industria Nordestina de Feculas Ltd. [*Brazil*] (DSCA)

INOROSTA ... Foreign Department of the Russian News Agency (RU)

INOS .... Instituto Nacional de Obras Sanitarias [*National Institute of Sanitation Works*] [*Venezuela*] (LA)

INOS .... Instituto Nacional de Obras Sociales [*National Institute for Social Works*] [*Argentina*] (LA)

INOSHAC ... Indian Ocean and Southern Hemisphere Analysis Center (BARN)

INOSHAC ... Indian Ocean and Southern Hemisphere Analysis Centre (PDAA)

Inoslovizdat ... State Publishing House of Foreign Dictionaries (RU)

INOT .... Institute of Scientific Organization of Labor (RU)

INOTEX .... Industrie Nouvelle Textile

INOUT ...... North Sea In and Out Flow Experiment (MSC)

INOV .... Association Internationale du Nouvel Objet Visuel [*International Association for New Visual Objects*] [*Paris, France*] (EAIO)

INOX .... Industrias Inoxidables [*Colombia*] (COL)

INP .... Engineer Observation Point (BU)

INP .... Engineer Observation Post (RU)

INP .... FA Naval del Peru [*ICAO designator*] (FAAC)

INP .... Field-Strength Meter (RU)

INP .... Institut de Neurophysiologie et Psychophysiologie [*Institute of Neurophysiology and Psychophysiology*] [*Research center*] [*French*] (IRC)

INP .... Institute of National Planning [*Egypt*]

INP .... Institut National des Prix [*National Price Institute*] [*Algeria*] (AF)

INP .... Instituto Nacional de la Productividad [*National Institute of Productivity*] [*Argentina*] (LAA)

INP .... Instituto Nacional de Pesca [*National Fishing Institute*] [*Cuba*] (LA)

INP .... Instituto Nacional de Pesca [*National Fishing Institute*] [*Mexico*] (MSC)

INP .... Instituto Nacional de Planificacion [*National Planning Institute*] [*Peru*] (LA)

INP .... Instituto Nacional de Prevision [*National Institute of Social Security*] [*Spanish*] (WER)

INP .... Instituto Nacional de Puertos [*National Institute of Ports*] [*Venezuela*] (LA)

INP .... Instituto Nacional do Pinho [*Brazil*] (DSCA)

INP .... Israeli National Police (ME)

INPA .... Industria Nacional de Productos Alimenticios [*Colombia*] (COL)

INPA .... Instituto Nacional de Pesquisas da Amazonia [*National Institute for Amazon Region Research*] [*Brazil*] (LA)

INPABO ... Instituto Paranaense de Botanica [*Brazil*] (DSCA)

INPADE .... Instituto Panameno de Desarrollo [*Panama*] (LAA)

INPADOC ... International Patent Documentation Center [*Information service or system*] (IID)

INPADOC ... International Patent Documentation Centre [*Vienna, Austria*]

INPAP ...... Instituto Pro-Alimentacion Popular [*Venezuela*] (DSCA)

INPAR ...... Institut National de Promotion Agricole de Rennes [*France*] (DSCA)

INPB .... Irish National Pipe Band

INPC .... Indice Nacional de Precos ao Consumidor [*National Consumer Price Index*] [*Brazil*] (LA)

INPC .... Iran-Nippon Petrochemical Company (ME)

INPE .... Instituto Nacional de Perfeccionamiento Estomatologico [*National Dental Training Institute*] [*Cuba*] (LA)

INPE .... Instituto Nacional de Pesca del Ecuador (ASF)

INPE .... Instituto Nacional de Pesquisas Espaciais [*National Space Research Institute*] [*Brazil*] (LA)

INPE .... Instituto Nacional Pastoral Ecuatoriano [*Ecuadorean National Pastoral Institute*] (LA)

INPED ...... Institut National de la Productivite et du Developpement Industriel [*National Productivity and Industrial Development Institute*] [*Algeria*] (AF)

INPELCA ... Industria de Productos Electricos Centroamericana, SA [*Electric Products Corp.*] [*El Salvador*]

INPEP .... Instituto Nacional de Pensiones de los Empleados Publicos [*National Government Employee Pension Institute*] [*El Salvador*] (LA)

INPES .... Instituto Nacional de Pesquisa [*National Research Institute*] [*Brazil*] (LA)

INPES .... Instituto Nacional para Programas Especiales de Salud [*Colombia*] (COL)

INPESCA ... Instituto Nicaraguense de Pesca [*Nicaraguan Institute of Fisheries*] (LA)

INPFL .... Independent National Patriotic Front of Liberia [*Political party*] (EY)

INPGE .... Institut National de Productivite et de Gestion des Entreprises [*National Institute for Enterprises Productivity and Management*] [*Tunisia*] (AF)

INPI .... Institute of Proletarian Fine Arts (RU)

INPI .... Institut National de la Propriete Industrielle [*National Institute for Industrial Property*] [*France*] [*Information service or system*] (IID)

INPI .... Instituto Nacional da Propriedade Industrial [*National Institute of Industrial Property*] [*Rio De Janeiro, Brazil*] (LA)

INPI .... Instituto Nacional de Promocion Industrial [*National Industrial Promotion Institute*] [*Peru*] (LA)

INPI .... Instituto Nacional de Proteccion de la Infancia [*National Institute for Infant Protection*] [*Mexico*] (LA)

INPI .... Istituto Nazionale per la Prevenzione degli Infortuni [*National Institution for the Prevention of Accidents*] [*Italian*]

INPIBOL ... Instituto Promotor de Inversiones en Bolivia

in-pl .... In-Plano [*Full Sheet*] [*French*]

INPM .... Institute of Normal and Pathological Morphology (of the Academy of Medical Sciences, USSR) (RU)

INPM .... Instituto Nacional de Pesos e Medidas [*National Institute of Weights and Measures*] [*Brazil*] (LA)

Inposhiv ..... Custom Sewing and Repair of Clothing (RU)

INPP .... Institut National de Preparation Professionnelle [*National Institute for Vocational Preparation*] [*Zaire*] (AF)

INPP .... Institut National du Perfectionnement Permanent

INPRAV .... Institute of Government and Law (RU)

INPRECC ... Industria de Prefabricados de Concreto [*Colombia*] (COL)

INPRES ..... Instituto Nacional para Prevenciones Sismicas [*National Institute for Seismic Prevention*] [*Argentina*] (LA)

INPRHU ... Instituto de Promocion Humana [*Institute for Human Development*] [*Nicaragua*] (LA)

INPRIS ...... Investment Promotion Information System [*UNIDO*] [*United Nations*] (DUND)

INPRO ...... Instituto Nacional de la Productividad [*National Institute of Productivity*] [*Venezuela*] (LAA)

IN-PRO ..... Instituto Salvadoreno de Productividad [*Salvadoran Institute of Productivity*] (LA)

INPROA .... Instituto de Promocion Agraria [*Santiago, Chile*] (LAA)

inprs .... Inspector of Wire Communications (RU)

INPS .... Instituto Nacional de Previdencia Social [*National Social Security Institute*] [*Brazil*] (LA)

INPS .... Istituto Nazionale della Previdenza Sociale [*National Social Security Institute*] [*Italian*] (WER)

INPT .... Institut National des Postes et Telecommunications [*National Institute of Posts and Telecommunications*] [*Malagasy*] (AF)

INPUD ...... Industrias Nacionales de Productos y Utensilios Domesticos [*National Industries for Domestic Products and Utensils*] [*Cuba*] (LA)

INPUT ...... International Public Television [*An association*] (NTCM)

INPZ .... Irkutsk Petroleum-Processing Plant (RU)

inqor .... Inquisidor [*Examiner*] [*Spanish*]

inqr .... Inquisidor [*Examiner*] [*Spanish*]

INQUA ..... International Union for Quaternary Research [*Research center*] [*France*] (IRC)

INQUA ...... Union Internationale pour l'Etude du Quaternaire [*International Association for Quaternary Research*] [*Zurich, Switzerland*] ICSU]

INQUIFAR ... Instituto Quimico Farmaceutico [*Barranquilla*] (COL)

INQUINAL ... Industria Quimica Nacional Ltda. [*Yumbo-Valle*] (COL)

INR .... Impot des Non-Redidents [*Benelux*] (BAS)

INR .... Institute of Natural Resources [*University of Natal*] [*South Africa*] (EAS)

INR.......... Institute of Natural Resources [*Fijian*]

INR.......... Institut National de Radiodiffusion [*Belgium*]

INR.......... Inter Air AB [*Sweden*] [*ICAO designator*] (FAAC)

INRA........ Indian Nationals Residing Abroad

INRA........ Industria Nacional de Repuestos y Accesorios SA [*Colombia*] (COL)

INRA........ Institute of Rationalizations (BU)

INRA........ Institut National de la Recherche Agronomique [*National Institute of Agricultural Research*] [*Research center*] [*France*] (IRC)

INRA........ Instituto Nacional de la Reforma Agraria [*National Institute for Agrarian Reform*] [*Nicaragua*] (LA)

INRA........ Instituto Nacional de la Reforma Agraria [*National Institute for Agrarian Reform*] [*Cuba*] (LA)

INRA........ International Natural Rubber Agreement [*1982*] (FEA)

INRA........ International Research Associates [*Thailand*] (DS)

INRAA...... Institut National de la Recherche Agronomique de l'Algerie [*National Institute of Agronomic Research for Algeria*]

INRAF....... Institut National de la Recherche Agronomique Francaise [*North African*]

INRAF....... Institut National de Recherches Agronomiques de Foulaya [*Foulaya National Agricultural Research Institute*] [*Guinea*] (ARC)

INRAM ..... Institut de Recherches Agronomiques a Madagascar [*Madagascar Agronomic Research Institute*] (AF)

INRAN ...... Institut National de Recherches Agronomiques du Niger [*Niger National Institute for Agronomic Research*] [*Research center*] (IRC)

INRAT....... Institut National de la Recherche Agronomique de Tunisie

INRAVISION ... Instituto Nacional de Radio y Television [*National Radio and Television Institute*] [*Colombia*] (LA)

INRC .... International Natural Rubber Council [*Established in January, 1978*]

INRCA...... Istituto Nazionale di Ricovero e Cura Anziani [*Italy*] (PDAA)

INRDG ...... Institut National de Recherches et Documentation de la Guinee [*Guinean National Institute of Research and Documentation*] (AF)

INRE .... Institute of Natural Resources and Environment [*Australia*] (EAIO)

INRED ...... Instituto Nacional de Recreacion, Educacion Fisica, y Deportes [*National Institute for Recreation, Physical Education, and Sports*] [*Peru*] (LA)

INRENA ... Instituto Nacional de Recursos Naturales [*National Institute of Natural Resources*] [*Nicaragua*] (LA)

INRESA .... Industrias Reunidas, Sociedad Anonima [*United Industries, Incorporated*] [*Peru*] (LA)

INRES/TCDC ... Information Referral System for Technical Cooperation among Developing Countries [*United Nations (already exists in GUS II database)*] [*Information service or system*] (IID)

INRETS .... Institut National de Recherche sur les Transports et leur Securite [*National Institute for Research on Transportation and Transport Safety*] [*Research center*] [*France*] (ERC)

INRF......... Institut National de Recherches Forestieres [*National Institute for Forestry Research*] [*Tunisia*] (ARC)

INRH........ Instituto Nacional de Recursos Hidraulicos [*National Institute of Water Resources*] [*Cuba*] (LA)

INRIA....... Institut National de Recherche en Informatique et en Automatique [*National Institute for Research in Informatics and Automation*] [*Research center and database originator*] [*France*] [*Information service or system*] (IID)

INRO........ International Natural Rubber Organization [*Kuala Lumpur, Malaysia*] (EAIO)

INROADS ... Information on Roads [*Australian Road Research Board*] [*Information service or system*] (IID)

INRPR....... Institut National de Recherche sur les Plantes-Racines [*Nigeria*]

INRS........ Institut National de la Recherche Scientifique [*National Institute of Scientific Research*] [*French*] (WER)

INRS......... Institut National de Recherche et de Securite pour la prevention des accidents du travail et des maladies professionelles [*National Institute for Occupational Safety and Health*] [*France*] (PDAA)

INRST....... Institut National de Recherche Scientifique et Technique [*National Institute for Scientific and Technical Research*] [*Tunisia*] (WND)

INRT .... Instituto Nacional de Racionalizacion del Trabajo [*National Institute for Business Management*] [*Spain*] (PDAA)

INRV .... Institut National de Recherches Veterinaires [*National Institute of Veterinary Research*] [*Belgium*] (ARC)

INS .... Indian Nuclear Society

Ins .... Insaat [*Construction*] (TU)

ins........... Insegna [*Mark*] [*Publishing*] [*Italian*]

ins........... Insinoori [*Finland*]

ins........... Insonderheid [*Especially*] [*Afrikaans*]

INS .... Inspector of Communications (RU)

INS .... Institute for Nuclear Study [*University of Tokyo*] [*Japan*] (WND)

INS .... Institute of the North (RU)

INS .... Institut National de la Sante [*North African*]

INS .... Institut National de la Statistique [*Tunisia*]

INS .... Institut National de Securite [*France*] (FLAF)

INS .... Institut National des Sports [*French*]

INS .... Institut National de Statistique [*Belgium*]

INS .... Instituto Nacional de Salud [*National Institute of Health*] [*Lima, Peru*] (LAA)

INS .... Instituto Nacional de Seguros [*National Insurance Institute*] [*Portuguese*] (WER)

INS .... Instytut Nauk Spolecznych [*Institute of Social Sciences*] (POL)

INS .... International Network for Self-Reliance (EA)

INS .... International Numismatic Society (EAIO)

INS .... Inter-Nation Simulation (ADPT)

INS .... Israel Naval Ship (BJA)

INS .... Israel News Service (BJA)

INS .... Italian Nuclear Society (EAIO)

INSA......... Indian National Science Academy [*Research center*] (IRC)

INSA......... Indian National Shipowners' Association

INSA......... Indonesian National Ship Owners' Association (FEA)

INSA......... Industria Nacional de Neumaticos [*National Tire Industry*] [*Chile*] (LA)

INSA......... Industrija Satova [*Watch Industry*] [*Zemun*] (YU)

INSA......... Institut National des Sciences Appliquees de Lyon [*National Institute of Applied Sciences of Lyon*] [*French*] (ARC)

INSA......... Instituts Nationaux de Sciences Appliquees [*National Institutes of Applied Sciences*] [*French*]

INSA......... International Shipowners' Association [*See also MAS*] [*Gdynia, Poland*] (EAIO)

INSA......... Istanbul Naylon Sanayii Anonim Sirketi [*Istanbul Nylon Industry Corporation*] (TU)

INSAC...... Instituto Nacional de Sistemas Automatizados y Tecnicas de Computacion [*National Institute of Automated Systems and Computer Technology*] [*Cuba*] (LA)

INSACS..... Information Network in Social and Community Services [*Australia*]

INSAE....... Institut National de la Statistique et de l'Analyse Economique [*National Institute of Statistics and Economic Analysis*] [*Benin*] (GEA)

INSAFI...... Instituto Salvadoreno de Fomento Industrial [*Salvadoran Institute for Industrial Development*] (LA)

INSAFOCOOP ... Instituto Salvadoreno de Fomento Cooperativo [*Salvadoran Institute of Cooperative Development*] (LA)

INSAFOP ... Instituto Salvadoreno de Fomento de la Produccion [*Salvadoran Production Promotion Institute*] (LA)

INSAG...... International Nuclear Safety Advisory Group [*United Nations*] (EY)

INSAT .... Indian National Satellite System [*Bangalore, India*] [*Telecommunications*]

INSATC .... Instituto Nacional de Sistemas Automatizados y Tecnicas de Computacion [*National Institute of Automated Systems and Computer Technology*] [*Cuba*] (LA)

INSATEC ... Instalaciones Sanitarias y Tecnicas [*Colombia*] (COL)

insb............. Insbesondere [*In Particular*] [*German*] (GPO)

insbes .... Insbesondere [*In Particular*] [*German*] (GCA)

INSCIN ..... Institutul pentru Studierea Conjuncturii Economice Internationale [*Institute for the Study of the International Economic Situation*] (RO)

INSCOL.... Instituto Psicologico Colombiano [*Colombia*] (COL)

INSCOMO ... Instituto Comercial Moderno [*Colombia*] (COL)

inscr .... Inscription [*Inscription*] [*Publishing*] [*French*]

INSCREDIAL ... Instituto de Credito Territorial [*Territorial Credit Institute*] [*Colombia*] (LA)

INSDOC.... Indian National Scientific Documentation Centre [*Council of Scientific and Industrial Research*]

INSE.......... Institut National des Sciences de l'Education

INSE.......... Instituto Superior de Educacion [*Colombia*] (COL)

INSE.......... National Institute for Education [*French*]

INSEA .... Institut National de Statistique et d'Economie Applique [*National Institute of Statistics and Applied Economics*] [*Morocco*] (AF)

INSEA .... International Society for Education through Art [*Corsham, England*]

INSEA .... International Society for Education through the Arts

INSEAD.... Institut Europeen d'Administration des Affaires [*European Business Management Institute*] [*France*] (PDAA)

INSEAN.... Istituto Nazionale per Studi ed Esperienze di Architettura Navale [*National Naval Architecture Research and Testing Institute*] [*Rome, Italy*] [*Research center*] (ERC)

INSEE .... Institut National de la Statistique et des Etudes Economiques [*National Institute of Statistics and Economic Research*] [*Paris, France*]

INSEH........ Instituto de Investigaciones Socio-Economicas de Honduras [*Institute of Honduran Socio-Economic Research*] [*Mexico*] (EAIO)

insepar .... Inseparabili [*Not Sold Separately*] [*Publishing*] [*Italian*]
INSERE .... Institut National de la Statistique et des Recherches Economiques [*National Economic Research and Statistics Institute*] [*Cambodia*] (CL)
INSERM ... Institut National de la Sante et de la Recherche Medicale [*National Institute for Health and Medical Research*] [*France*] [*Information service or system*] (IID)
INSESO .... Instituto Nacional de Seguridad Social
INSET .... In-service Education for Teachers [*Australia*]
INSET .... Institut National Superieur de l'Enseignement Technique [*Ivory Coast*]
INSFOPAL ... Instituto de Fomento Municipal [*Municipal Development Institute*] [*Colombia*] (LA)
insges .... Insgesamt [*All Together*] [*Publishing*] [*German*]
INSH .... Institut National des Sciences Humaines
INSI .... Institut za Naucna Sumarska Istrazivanja [*Forestry Research Institute*] (YU)
insign......... Insignifiant [*Insignificant*] [*French*]
insignif ...... Insignifiant [*Insignificant*] [*French*]
INSINCA .. Industrias Sinteticas de Centro America, SA [*Synthetic Industries of Central America Corp.*] [*El Salvador*]
INSIVUMEH ... Instituto Nacional de Sismologia, Vulcanologia, Meteorologia, e Hidrologia [*National Institute of Seismology, Vulcanology, Meteorology, and Hydrology*] [*Guatemala*] (LA)
INSJ .... Institute for Nuclear Study [*Tokyo University*] [*Japan*] (PDAA)
inskapoch... Postal Service Inspector Attached to the Chief Signal Officer of the Red Army (RU)
Inskoksugol' ... Coking Coal Inspection (RU)
insl .... Insluitend [*Enclose*] [*Afrikaans*]
INSMAK... Yol ve Insaat Makinalari Sanayii AS [*Highway and Construction Machinery Industry Corp.*] [*Izmir*] (TU)
INSMET ... Instituto de Meteorologia [*Institute of Meteorology*] [*Cuba*] (LA)
INSNA ...... International Network for Social Network Analysis [*University of Toronto*] [*Toronto, ON*] (EAIO)
insolv.......... Insolvency [*Australia*]
INSONA ... Indian Society of Naturalists (PDAA)
INSOR....... Istituto Nazionale di Sociologia Rurale [*National Institute of Rural Sociology*] [*Italian*] (SLS)
INSORA.... Instituto de Organizacion y Administracion de Empresas [*Institute for Company Organization and Administration*] [*Chile*] (LA)
insp............ Inspecteur [*or Inspectie*] [*Benelux*] (BAS)
Insp .... Inspector (EECI)
insp........... Inspekteur [*Inspector*] [*Afrikaans*]
Insp .... Inspektion [*German*]
Insp .... Inspektor [*Inspector*] (CZ)
INSP........ Inspektur [*Inspector*] (IN)
INSP........ Institut National de Sante Publique
INSP........ Internet Name Server Protocol (TNIG)
insparm...... Inspector of the Army (RU)
INSPART ... Inspector of Artillery (RU)
inspartarm ... Inspector of Army Artillery (RU)
INSPAT ... Institute of Comparative Pathology (RU)
INSPE ...... Istituto Nazionale di Studi Politici ed Economici [*Italian*] (SLS)
INSPECT ... Integrated Nationwide System for Processing Entries from Customs Terminals [*Australia*]
inspekh ...... Inspector of Infantry (RU)
inspets....... Foreign Specialist (RU)
INSPEX..... International Measurement and Inspection Technology Exposition
Insp gen...... Inspecteur General [*Inspector General*] [*French*]
Inspiz .... Inspizient [*German*]
insposvedupr ... Inspection and Information Department of the Political Administration of a Republic (RU)
Inspred....... State Enterprise for International Transport (BU)
inspvozdukh ... Inspector of the Air Force (RU)
INSRE .... Institut National de la Statistique et de la Recherche Economique [*National Institute for Statistics and Economic Research*] [*Malagasy*] (AF)
INSRFP..... Institut National Superieur de Recherches et de Formation Pedagogique
INSS .... Institut National de Securite Sociale [*National Social Security Institute*] [*Zaire*] (AF)
INSS .... Instituto Nicaraguense de Seguridad Social [*Nicaraguan Institute of Social Security*] (LA)
INSSED .... Institut Superieur des Sciences de l'Education [*Congo*] (SLS)
INSSEJAG ... Institut Superieur des Sciences Economiques, Juridiques, Administratives, et de Gestion [*Congo*] (SLS)
INSSSA..... Institut des Sciences de la Sante [*Congo*] (SLS)
Inst............ Instandesetzung [*Repair*] [*German*] (GCA)
Inst............ Institut [*Institute*] [*German*]
Inst............ Institute (PWGL)
Inst............ Institution (PWGL)
Inst............ Instituto (SCAC)
inst .... Institutt [*Institute*] [*Danish/Norwegian*]

INST......... Instituut [*Institute*] [*Afrikaans*]
Inst............. Instytut [*Institute*] [*Poland*]
INST......... International Numbering System for Tides (MSC)
insta .... Instancia [*Spanish*]
Inst AdmEnreg ... Instruction de l'Administration de l'Enregistrement [*France*] (FLAF)
in stat pup .. In Statu Pupillari [*Subject to the Rule of the Institution*] [*Latin*] (BARN)
INSTEAD ... Information Service on Technological Alternatives for Development [*ILO*] [*United Nations*] (DUND)
Inst GenFin ... Instruction Generale du Ministre des Finances [*France*] (FLAF)
Inst HEI..... Institut des Hautes Etudes Internationales de l'Universite de Paris (FLAF)
INSTIA ..... Instituto Internacional de Andragogia [*International Institute of Andragogy - IIA*] (EAIO)
INSTISOJA ... Instituto Privado de Fomento a Soja [*Brazil*] (DSCA)
INSTMC .. Institute of Measurement and Control [*British*] (EAIO)
Inst Min .... Instruction Ministerielle [*France*] (FLAF)
INSTN....... Institut National des Sciences et Techniques Nucleaires [*French*]
INSTOP .... Institut National Scientifique et Technique d'Oceanographie et de Peche [*Tunisia*]
InstOP .... Instruction for the Application of the Directive for Payment for Responsible Care of Property (BU)
Instorf .... Scientific Experimental Institute of Peat (RU)
instr........... Instruction [*French*] (FLAF)
instr........... Instructor (RU)
INSTR ...... Instruksie [*Instruction*] [*Afrikaans*]
instr........... Instruktiivi [*Finland*]
INSTR ...... Instrumentalis [*Instrumental*] [*Afrikaans*]
instr........... Orchestrated (BU)
InstrAdmin Enreg ... Instruction de l'Administration de l'Enregistrement [*France*] (FLAF)
INSTRAW ... International Research and Training Institute for the Advancement of Women [*Dominican Republic*] [*United Nations Research center*] (IRC)
INSTRIMPEX ... China National Instruments Import & Export Corp. [*China*] (IMH)
Instr Min ... Instruction Ministerielle [*Benelux*] (BAS)
Instr Pub.... Instruction Publique [*French*] (FLAF)
Instr Reg .... Instruction de la Regie [*France*] (FLAF)
INSTRUEQUIPO ... Instrumental y Equipos Cientificos [*Colombia*] (COL)
Instr Wsk... Instructie voor de Weeskamer in Indonesie [*Benelux*] (BAS)
INSU .... Institut National des Sciences de l'Univers [*French*]
INSUMAR ... Instituto Superior del Mar [*Brazil*] (ASF)
INSUPAV ... Ingenieria de Suelos y Pavimentos [*Colombia*] (COL)
INSUS .... Intensifikasi Khusus [*Name of government-supported agricultural production projects*] [*Indonesia*] (FEA)
INSz.......... Instytut Nawozow Sztucznych [*Institute of Artificial Fertilizers*] [*Poland*]
INT .... Fraunhofer-Institut fuer Naturwissenschaftlich-Technische Trendanalysen [*Fraunhofer Institute for Scientific-Technical Trend Analysis*] [*Research center*] [*Germany*] (WND)
in-t........... Institute (BU)
INT .... Institut fuer Nachrichtentechnik [*Communications Engineering Institute (in Berlin-Oberschoeneweide)*] (EG)
INT .... Institut Nikola Tesla [*Nikola Tesla Institute*] (YU)
INT .... Instituto Nacional del Trabajo [*National Labor Institute*] [*Uruguay*] (LA)
INT .... Instituto Nacional del Trigo [*National Wheat Institute*] [*Bolivia*] (IMH)
INT .... Instituto Nacional de Tecnologia [*National Institute of Technology*] [*Rio De Janeiro, Brazil*] (LA)
INT .... Instituto Nacional de Turismo [*National Institute of Tourism*] [*Cuba*] (LA)
int .... Integral (RU)
int .... Inteiro [*Entire*] [*Portuguese*]
Int............. Intendant [*Administrative Officer*] [*Military*] [*French*] (MTD)
Int............. Intendant [*or Intendent*] [*German*]
INT .... Interes [*Interest*] [*Afrikaans*]
Int............. Interessi [*Interest*] [*Italian*] [*Business term*]
int .... Interet [*Interest*] [*French*]
INT .... Intergovernmental Negotiating Team
int .... Interieur [*Interior*] [*French*]
int .... Interior [*Inside*] [*Publishing*] [*Spanish*]
int .... Intern [*Internal*] [*German*]
Int............. International (SCAC)
int .... Interno [*Internal*] [*Portuguese*]
int .... Interno [*Internal*] [*Italian*]
int .... Intezet [*Institute*] (HU)
int .... Intezo [*Manager, Steward*] (HU)
int .... Intialainen [*India*] [*Finland*]
int .... Intonso [*Untrimmed*] [*Publishing*] [*Italian*]
int .... Intransitivo [*Intransitive*] [*Portuguese*]

INT .... Istituto Nazionale Trasporti [*National Transport Institute*] [*Italian*]
int .... Quartermaster (RU)
int .... Quartermaster Section (RU)
Int .... Quartermaster Service (RU)
INTA .... Institut National de Techniques Administratives [*National Institute for Administrative Procedures*] [*Burundi*] (AF)
INTA .... Instituto Nacional de Tecnica Aeroespacial [*National Institute for Aerospace Research*] [*Spain*] (WER)
INTA .... Instituto Nacional de Tecnologia Agropecuaria [*National Institute of Agricultural and Livestock Technology*] [*Argentina*] (LA)
INTA .... Instituto Nacional de Tecnologia Agropecuaria [*National Institute of Agricultural and Livestock Technology*] [*Nicaragua*] (LA)
INTA .... Instituto Nacional de Transformacion Agraria [*National Agrarian Transformation Institute*] [*Guatemala*] (LA)
INTA .... International Association for the Development and Management of Existing and New Towns (EAIO)
INTABACO ... Instituto de Fomento Tabacalero [*Colombia*] (DSCA)
INTACH ... Indian National Trust for Art and Cultural Heritage
INTAD ...... Intendans Angkatan Darat [*Army Quartermaster*] (IN)
INTAE....... Instituto Tecnologico de Administracion de Empresas [*Technological Institute for Enterprise Administration*] [*Honduras*]
INTAGRO ... Instituto Agrario de Estudios Economicos [*Agrarian Institute of Economic Studies*] [*Chile*] (ARC)
INTAK....... Instituut vir Taal- en Kunstenavorsing [*Human Sciences Research Council*] [*South Africa*] (AA)
INTAL....... Instituto para la Integracion de America Latina [*Institute for Latin American Integration*] (EAIO)
INTALPEL ... Fabrica de Bolsas y Rollos de Papel [*Colombia*] (COL)
INTAMEL ... International Association of Metropolitan City Libraries [*The Hague, Netherlands*] (EA)
INTAMIC ... International Microcircuit Card Association [*Paris, France*] [*Defunct*] (EAIO)
INTAPUC ... International Association of Public Cleansing [*Later, ISWA*]
INTAS....... Insaatcilar Sosyal Sehircilik Sanayi ve Ticaret Anonim Sirketi [*Constructors Social City Planning Industry and Trade Corporation*] (TU)
INTASAFCON ... International Tanker Safety Conference (DS)
INTASAT ... Instituto Nacional de Tecnica Aeroespacial Satelite [*Spain*]
INTASGRO ... Interallied Tactical Study Group [*NATO*] (NATG)
Int Aut....... Inter-Auteur [*France*] (FLAF)
Int Brig....... Internationale Brigade [*International Brigade*] (EG)
INTC .... Isfahan Nuclear Technology Centre [*Isfahan, Iran*] (MENA)
INTD .... Institut National des Techniques de la Documentation [*National Institute for Information Science*] [*France*] [*Information service or system*] (IID)
INTE.......... Incorporacion de Nuevas Tecnologias en la Empresa [*Spanish*]
INTE.......... Instituto de Tecnicas Energeticas [*Institute of Energetics*] [*Spain*] (WED)
INTE.......... Instituto Nacional de Teleducacion [*National Television Education Institute*] [*Peru*] (LA)
INTEBIS... Industrias Texteis de Beiriz
INTEC....... Industrie Textile Centrafricaine
INTEC....... Instituto de Investigaciones Tecnologicas [*Technological Research Institute*] [*Chile*] [*Research center*] (IRC)
INTEC....... Instituto des Desarrollo Tecnologico para la Industria Quimica [*Argentina*]
INTEC....... Instituto Tecnologico de Santo Domingo [*Technological Institute of Santo Domingo*] [*Dominican Republic*] (LA)
INTECAP ... Instituto Tecnico de Capacitacion y Productividad [*Technical Institute for Training and Productivity*] [*Guatemala*] (LA)
INTECMAR ... Instituto de Tecnologia y Ciencias Marinas [*Marine Sciences and Technology Institute*] [*Venezuela*] (LA)
INTECNOR ... Instituto Nacional de Tecnologia y Normalizacion [*National Institute of Technology and Standardization*] [*Paraguay*] (PDAA)
INTECO.... Industrias Tecnicas Colombianas Ltda. [*Barranquilla*] (COL)
INTECOL ... International Association for Ecology [*University of Georgia*] [*Athens, GA*] (EAIO)
INTECOM ... International Council for Technical Communication (SLS)
INTECOM ... International Society of Technical Communication [*Denmark*] (EAIO)
INTECON ... Ingenieria y Tecnica de Construccion Ltda. [*Colombia*] (COL)
integr.......... Integral (RU)
inteken .... Intekenaar [*Subscriber*] [*Publishing*] [*Netherlands*]
INTEL....... Instituto Nacional de Telecomunicaciones [*National Telecommunications Institute*] [*Panama*] (LA)
INTELCAM ... Societe des Telecommunications Internationales du Cameroun [*International Telecommunications Company of Cameroon*] (AF)
INTELCI... Telecommunications Internationales de la Cote-D'Ivoire [*International Telecommunications of the Ivory Coast*] (AF)

INTELCO ... Office des Telecommunications Internationales du Congo [*International Telecommunications Office of the Congo*] (AF)
INTELCUBA ... Telecomunicaciones Internacionales [*International Telecommunications*] [*Cuba*] (LA)
INTELEC ... Instalaciones Electricas Ltda. [*Colombia*] (COL)
INTEMA... Industrielle Textile du Maroc
intendte ...... Intendente [*Spanish*]
intenokr...... Quartermaster Directorate of a Military District (RU)
INTEQUIM ... Quimica Integrada CA [*Venezuela*]
INTEQUIP ... Intequip Nuclear [*Netherlands*] (WND)
inter........... Interieur [*Interior*] [*French*]
inter........... Interiezione [*Interjection*] [*Italian*]
inter........... Interjeicao [*Interjection*] [*Portuguese*]
inter........... Interrogatif [*French*] (TPFD)
inter........... Interrogative (TPFD)
INTERALUMINA ... Interamericana de Alumina CA [*Venezuela*] (IMH)
INTERALUMINIO ... Internacional de Aluminio Ltda. [*Colombia*] (COL)
INTERAMA ... Centro Comercial y Cultural Interamericano (LAA)
INTERASMA ... International Association of Asthmology [*Lisbon, Portugal*] (EAIO)
INTERATOM ... Internationale Atomreactorbau [*German*]
INTERBASE ... Empresa Cabo-Verdiana das Infraestruturas de Pesca [*Cape Verdean Fishing Infrastructures Company*] (AF)
INTERBEV ... International Beverage Industry Exhibition and Congress [*National Soft Drink Association*]
INTERBRABANT ... Union Intercommunale des Centrales Electriques du Brabant SA [*Business and Trade*] [*Belgium*]
INTERBRANT ... Union Intercommunale des Centrales Electriques du Brabant SA [*Business and Trade*] [*Belgium*] (PDAA)
INTERBRAS ... PETROBRAS Comercio Internacional SA [*PETROBRAS International Trade, Inc.*] [*Brazil*] (LA)
INTERBRIGHT ... International Literary and Information Centre in Science Extension (IID)
interc.......... Intercalado [*Intercalated*] [*Publishing*] [*Spanish*]
interc.......... Intercalato [*Inserted*] [*Publishing*] [*Italian*]
interc.......... Intercale [*Intercalated*] [*Publishing*] [*French*]
INTERCA ... Societe Commerciale Intercamerounaise
INTERCAFE ... Compania Interamericana de Cafe [*Guatemala*] (DSCA)
intercal....... Intercalado [*Intercalated*] [*Publishing*] [*Spanish*]
INTERCAM ... Internacional de Caucho Manufacturado [*Colombia*] (COL)
INTERCARGO ... International Association of Dry Cargo Shipowners (EAIO)
INTERCENTRE ... International Centre for the Terminology of the Social Sciences [*Grand-Saconnex, Switzerland*] (EA)
INTERCERAMIC ... Internacional de Ceramica [*International Ceramic*] [*Commercial firm*] [*Mexico*]
INTERCO ... Federation des Personnels du Ministere de l'Interieur et des Collectivites Locales [*France*]
INTERCO ... International Code of Signals (PDAA)
INTERCO ... International Council on Jewish Social and Welfare Services [*Geneva, Switzerland*] (EAIO)
INTERCOL ... International Petroleum Colombia Limited [*Dorada-Caldas*] (COL)
INTERCOM ... Societe Intercommunale Belge de Gaz et d'Electricite SA [*Belgium*]
INTERCOMEX ... Intermediaria en las Operaciones de Compensaciones y Trueques [*Export Trade Handling Enterprise*] [*Cuba*] (LA)
INTERCOMSA ... Intercontinental de Comunicaciones por Satelite, SA [*Intercontinental of Communications via Satellite, Inc.*] [*Panama*] (LA)
INTERCON ... Interventoria de Construcciones Ltda. [*Colombia*] (COL)
INTERCOOP ... International Organization for Consumer Co-Operative Distributive Trade (EAIO)
INTERCOSMOS ... Council on International Cooperation in the Study and Utilization of Outer Space
INTEREDEC ... International Research & Development Corporation [*Saudi Arabia*]
INTEREG ... Internationales Institut fuer Nationalitatenrecht und Regionalismus [*International Institute for Ethnic Group Rights and Regionalism*] (EA)
INTERELECTRA ... Empresa Distribuidora de Equipamento Electrico e Electronico e Componentes [*Electrical equipment trade enterprise*] [*Mozambique*]
interess....... Interessante [*Interesting*] [*Italian*]
interf.......... Interfolert [*Interleaved*] [*Publishing Danish/Norwegian*]
INTERFACE ... Internationally Recognized Format for Automatic Commercial Exchange (PDAA)
INTERFAIS ... International Food Aid Information System [*World Food Program*] [*United Nations*] (DUND)
INTERFILM ... International Inter-Church Film Center [*Hilversum, Netherlands*]
INTERFLUG ... Internationale Fluggesellschaft mbH [*Name of GDR airline*] (EG)
interfol .... Interfoliad [*Interleaved*] [*Publishing*] [*Sweden*]

INTERFOOD ... International Exhibition of Foodstuffs, Fast Food, and Traditional and Mass Catering

INTERFORM ... Societe Internationale de Formation

INTERFRANCA ... Lojas Francas de Mocambique [*Trading company*] [*Mozambique*]

INTERFRIGO ... International Railway-Owned Company for Refrigerated Transport   (EAIO)

INTERGEO ... Laboratoire d'Information et de Documentation en Geographie [*Geographical Information and Documentation Laboratory*] [*Centre National de la Recherche Scientifique*] [*France*]   (EAS)

INTERGU ... Internationale Gesellschaft fuer Urheberrecht [*International Copyright Society*]   (EAIO)

interj.......... Interjection [*French*]   (TPFD)

interj.......... Interjektio [*Interjection*] [*Finland*]

INTERKAMA ... Internationaler Kongress mit Ausstellung fuer Mess- and Automatisierungstechnik [*Germany*]

INTERLAINE ... Comite des Industries Lainieres de la CEE [*Committee of the Wool Textile Industry in the EEC*]   (EAIO)

InterlVonn ... Interlocutoir Vonnis [*Benelux*]   (BAS)

INTERMAQUINA ... Empresa de Comercio Externo de Equipamentos Industriais [*Industrial equipment trade enterprise*] [*Mozambique*]

INTERMARC ... International Machine Readable Cataloguing

INTERMEC ... Industria Termico Mecanica [*Colombia*]   (COL)

INTERMECANO ... Empresa Nacional de Importacao e Exportacao de Veiculos Motorizadas [*Machinery trade enterprise*] [*Mozambique*]

INTERMETAL ... Empresa Distribuidora e Importadora de Metais [*Metals trade enterprise*] [*Mozambique*]

INTERMETAL ... Internal Trade Corporation for Metals and Construction Materials [*Syria*]   (ME)

Intermex .... International Mexican Bank Ltd. [*British*]   (EY)

INTERMILPOL ... International Military Police [*NATO*]

INTERMORGEO ... International Organization for Marine Geology [*Council for Mutual Economic Assistance*] [*Riga, Union of Soviet Socialist Republics Defunct*]   (EAIO)

intern.......... International [*German*]

INTERNACO ... Representaciones Internacionales Ltda. [*Colombia*]   (COL)

internam..... Internamente [*Internally*] [*Italian*]

InternatBar Assoc ... International Bar Association   (DLA)

INTEROM ... L'Intermediaire Outre-Mer

INTERPAG ... International Problem Area Group

INTERPEX ... International Philatelic Exhibition [*American Stamp Dealers Association*]

INTERPHIL ... International Standing Conference on Philanthropy [*Yalding, Kent, England*]   (EAIO)

INTERPLAX ... Industria Tecnica de Plasticos [*Colombia*]   (COL)

INTERPOL ... International Criminal Police Organization   (CL)

INTERPUBLIC ... Izdavacki Institut i Agencija za Unutrasnju i Spoljnu Trgovacku Propagandu, Publicitet, i Organizaciju [*Publishing Institute and Agency for Domestic and Foreign Commercial Propaganda, Publicity, and Organization*]   (YU)

INTERQUIMICA ... Empresa Mocambicana de Importacao e Exportacao de Produtos Quimicos e Plasticos [*Chemical trade enterprise*] [*Mozambique*]

interr .... Interrogativo [*Interrogative*] [*Portuguese*]

interrog ...... Interrogativo [*Interogative*] [*Italian*]

interrpron ... Interrogatiivipronomini [*Interrogative Pronoun*] [*Finland*]

INTERSAPA ... Inter-Southern African Philatelic Agency

INTERSPUTNIK ... International Organization of Space Communications [*Moscow, USSR*]   (EAIO)

INTERSTENO ... Federation Internationale de Stenographie et de Dactylographie [*International Federation of Shorthand and Typewriting*] [*Bonn, Federal Republic of Germany*]   (EAIO)

INTERTANKO ... International Association of Independent Tanker Owners [*Oslo, Norway*]   (EAIO)

INTERTEX ... International Textile and Fabrics Trade Fair

INTERWOOLABS ... International Association of Wool and Textile Laboratories   (EAIO)

INTESCA ... Internacional de Ingenieria y Estudios Tecnicos SA [*Spain*]   (PDAA)

INTEVEP ... Instituto de Tecnologia Venezolana del Petroleo [*Venezuelan Institute of Petroleum Technology*]   (LA)

INTEX....... Industria Textil de Mocambique Lda.

INTEXTIL ... Industria Nacional de Textiles [*Colombia*]   (COL)

INTEYCO ... Ingenieria Tecnica y Comercial Ltda. [*Colombia*]   (COL)

intezm......... Intezmeny [*Institution*]   (HU)

inth ed .... Intihap Eden [*Selected, Chosen*]   (TU)

INTI.......... Institute of Scientific and Technical Information   (RU)

INTI.......... Instituto Nacional de Tecnologia Industrial [*National Institute of Industrial Technology*] [*Argentina*]   (LA)

INTIB .... Industrial and Technological Information Bank [*UNIDO*]   (IID)

INTIiP .... Institute of Scientific and Technical Information and Propaganda   (RU)

INTIS .... International Transport Information System [*Netherlands*]

intk............ Intezkedes [*Order, Command, Arrangement, Directive*]   (HU)

Int'l .... International   (PWGL)

INTL.......... International Movement of Catholic Students [*France*]

Int'l LComm'n ... International Law Commission [*United Nations*]   (DLA)

Int'l RevCrim Policy ... International Review of Criminal Policy [*United Nations*]   (DLA)

INTN .... Instituto Nacional de Tecnologia y Normalizacion del Paraguay [*Asuncion, Paraguay*]   (LAA)

INTOC ...... Industria Tornillera Colombiana [*Colombia*]   (COL)

INTOPLAN ... Ingenieria Topografica-Planeacion [*Colombia*]   (COL)

INTOSAI .. International Organization of Supreme Audit Institutions [*Vienna, Austria*]   (EA)

Intourist ..... Sowjetisches Reiseburo Internationale Touristik [*Soviet Travel Bureau for International Tourism*]   (EG)

INTP.......... Institut National des Telecommunications et des Postes [*National Institute of Telecommunications and Postal Services*] [*Malagasy*]   (AF)

INTP.......... Instituto Nacional do Trabalho e Previdencia [*National Institute of Labor and Social Welfare*] [*Portuguese*]   (WER)

INTR .... Intransitief [*Intransitive*] [*Afrikaans*]

intr............. Intransitiivinen [*Finland*]

intr............. Intransitiv [*Intransitive*] [*German*]   (GCA)

intr............. Intransitivo [*Intransitive*] [*Italian*]

intr............. Intrekking [*Benelux*]   (BAS)

intr............. Introduction [*Introduction*] [*Publishing*] [*French*]

INTRA...... Instituto Nacional de Transporte [*National Transport Institute*] [*Colorado*]   (LA)

INTRACO ... International Trading Corporation [*Singapore State trading company*]   (ML)

INTRADEP ... Cabinet Interafricain d'Etudes, de Pilotage, et de Promotion de Travaux

INTRAMETAL ... Industrie et Travaux Metalliques [*Metallurgical Industry and Works*] [*Congo*]   (AF)

INTRAMETALES ... Industria Transformadora de Metales Ltda. [*Colombia*]   (COL)

INTRANST ... International Transportation Tracking System [*Department of Transportation*]

INTRATA ... International Trading and Credit Company of Tanganyika Ltd.

INTRATEX ... Industria de Transformacion Textil Ltda. [*Colombia*]   (COL)

Int RevCrim Pol ... International Review of Criminal Policy [*United Nations*]

intro........... Introduccion [*Introduction*] [*Spanish*]

introd......... Introduccion [*Introduction*] [*Spanish*]

introd......... Introduzione [*Introduction*] [*Italian*]

INTROMARC ... International Tropical Marine Resource Centre [*Australia*]

INTROPLAS ... Industria de Troqueles y Moldes para Plasticos [*Colombia*]   (COL)

INTRUSCO ... International Trust Company of Liberia

INTs........... Cycle-Start Pulse   (RU)

INTSH...... Institut National Tchadien pour les Sciences Humaines

INTSHU ... Institut Togolais des Sciences Humaines

INTSOY...... International Soybean Program

Int Tit ...... Inleidende Titel [*Benelux*]   (BAS)

INTUC ...... Indian National Trade Union Congress   (PDAA)

INTUG ...... International Telecommunications Users Group [*Telecommunications*] [*Information service or system*]   (IID)

INTUMEL ... Industria de Tubos Metalicos [*Colombia*]   (COL)

INTUR ...... Instituto Nacional de Turismo [*National Institute of Tourism*] [*Cuba*]   (LA)

INTURISMO ... Instituto Nicaraguense de Turismo   (EY)

Inturist....... All-Union Joint-Stock Company for Foreign Tourism in the USSR   (RU)

INTUSA.... Industrias Turisticas, Sociedad Anonima [*Tourist Industries, Incorporated*] [*Spanish*]   (WER)

INU........... Foreign Directorate [*MVD*]   (RU)

INU........... History of the Peoples of Uzbekistan   (RU)

INU........... Initial Setting Pulse [*Of converter*]   (RU)

INU........... Inonu Universitesi [*Inonu University*]   (TU)

INU........... Institut za Narodnu Umjetnost [*Institute of Folk Arts*] [*Zagreb*]   (YU)

INU........... Institut za Nuklearne Nauke [*Institute of Nuclear Sciences*] [*Vinca*]   (YU)

INU........... Istituto Nazionale di Urbanistica [*Italian*]   (SLS)

INU........... Nauru [*Nauru*] [*Airport symbol*]   (OAG)

INUA........ Istituto Nazionale di Ultracustica [*National Institute of Ultrasonics*] [*Italy*]   (PDAA)

inum .... Inumerado [*Unnumbered*] [*Publishing*] [*Portuguese*]

inums.......... Inumerados [*Unnumbered*] [*Publishing*] [*Portuguese*]

INUR .... Instituto Nacional de Urbanismo [*National Institute of City Planning*] [*Spanish*]   (WER)

INUTOM .. Institut Universitaire des Territoires d'Outre-Mer

INV .... Institut National de Verre [*National Institute of Glass*] [*Belgium*]   (PDAA)

INV .... Instituto Nacional de Vitivinicultura [*National Institute of Viti-Viniculture*] [*Research center*] [*Argentina*]   (IRC)

INV .... Instituto Nacional de Vivienda [*National Housing Institute*] [*Mexico*] (LAA)

inv............... Inventorial (BU)

INV .... Inversia [*Latvia*] [*ICAO designator*] (FAAC)

Inv .... Invoeringswet Militair Straf- en Tuchtrecht [*Benelux*] (BAS)

INVA .... Instituto Nacional de Vivienda [*National Housing Institute*] [*Honduras*] (LAA)

INVAP....... Instituto de Investigacion Aplicada [*Applied Research Institute*] [*Argentina*] (LA)

invar .... Invariable [*French*] (TPFD)

INVARSA ... Inversiones Industriales y Comerciales [*Colombia*] (COL)

INVARSAL ... Administracion e Inversiones Ltda. [*Colombia*] (COL)

INVASA .... Industrias Varias, Sociedad Anonima [*Miscellaneous Industries, Incorporated*] [*Chile*] (LA)

INVATEX ... Industria de Derivados Textiles Ltda. [*Colombia*] (COL)

Inv Besl...... Invoeringsbesluit [*Benelux*] (BAS)

INVE .... Instituto Nacional de Viviendas Economicas [*National Institute of Low-Cost Housing*] [*Uruguay*] (LA)

INVE .... Investitionen [*Investments*] (EG)

INVED ...... Instituto de Investigacion y Desarrollo Industrial [*Industrial Research and Development Institute*] [*Venezuela*] (ERC)

INVEDI..... Instituto de Investigacion y Desarrollo Industrial [*Industrial Research and Development Institute*] [*Venezuela*] (ERC)

INVEMAR ... Instituto de Investigaciones Marinas de Punta De Betin [*Punta De Betin Institute for Marine Research*] [*Research center*] [*Colorado*] (IRC)

INVEPET ... Instituto Venezolano de Petroquimica [*Venezuelan Petrochemical Institute*] (LA)

INVERCOL ... Inversiones Colombia [*Colombia*] (COL)

INVES....... Integriertes Verkaufsabrechnungs-System [*German*] (ADPT)

INVESCO ... Investigaciones Comerciales Ltda. [*Colombia*] (COL)

INVESGE ... Instituto de Investigaciones Geologicas [*Geological Research Institute*] [*Santiago, Chile*] (LAA)

INVESTA ... Akciova Spolecnost pro Dovoz a Vyvoz Vyrobku Tezkeho Strojirenstvi [*Import and Export Joint-Stock Company for Heavy Machinery*] (CZ)

INVESTCORP ... Arabian Investment Banking Corporation [*Bahrain*]

INVESTI... Instituto Venezolano de Investigaciones Tecnologicas e Industriales [*Caracas, Venezuela*] (LAA)

INVI .... Instituto de Vivienda [*Institute of Housing*] [*Lima, Peru*] (LAA)

INVI .... Instituto Nacional de Vivienda [*National Housing Institute*] [*Guatemala*] (LA)

INVI .... Instituto Nacional de Vivienda [*National Housing Institute*] [*Dominican Republic*] (LA)

INVI .... Instituto Nicaraguense de la Vivienda [*Nicaraguan Housing Institute*] [*Managua, Nicaragua*] (LAA)

INVICA..... Instituto de Viviendas Populares [*Santiago, Chile*] (LA.A)

INVICALI ... Instituto de Vivienda de Cali (COL)

inv kniga .... Inventory Book (BU)

inv op.......... Inventory (RU)

Invord........ Wet op de Invordering van 's Rijks Directe Belastingen [*Benelux*] (BAS)

INVSL....... Indian National Veterinary Science Library (DSCA)

Inv Sw .... Invoeringsverordening van het Wetboek van Strafrecht [*Benelux*] (BAS)

INVU .... Instituto Nacional de Vivienda y Urbanismo [*National Institute of Housing and City Planning*] [*Costa Rica*] (LA)

INWACOL ... Industria Wayne de Colombia [*Colombia*] (COL)

INWRL...... Instytut Naukowy Wydawnictw Rolniczych i Lesnych [*Scientific Publishing Institute for Agriculture and Forestry*] (POL)

Inxh............ Inxhinier [*Albanian*]

IN-YaZ .... Institute of Foreign Languages (RU)

INYC .... Indonesian National Youth Council (EAIO)

Inyurkollegiya ... College of Foreign Law at the Moscow City Bar Association (RU)

INZ .... Industrija Nafte Zagreb [*Former Yugoslavia*]

INZ .... In Salah [*Algeria*] [*Airport symbol*] (OAG)

inz............... Inzake [*Benelux*] (BAS)

Inz .... Inzenyr [*Engineer (Academic degree)*] (CZ)

inz................ Inzynier [*Engineer (Academic degree)*] (POL)

INZ .... Public Health Institute (BU)

inza............ Tool Plant (RU)

inz agr .... Inzynier Agronomii [*Agricultural Engineer*] [*Poland*]

inz arch ...... Inzynier Architektury [*Architectural Engineer*] [*Poland*]

INZAV........ Investicni Zavod [*Investment Enterprise*] (CZ)

inz chem..... Inzynier Chemii [*Chemical Engineer*] [*Poland*]

INZEL....... Industrias Zeus de Elementos Electronicos Ltda. [*Colombia*] (COL)

inz elektr .... Inzynier Elektrotechnik [*Electrical Engineer*] [*Poland*]

inz gor .... Inzynier Gornik [*Mining Engineer*] [*Poland*]

inzh .... Engineer, Engineering (RU)

Inzh .... Engineer Troops (RU)

inzhb .... Engineer Battalion (RU)

inzhbat .... Engineer Battalion (RU)

inzhbr......... Engineer Brigade (RU)

INZhEKIN ... Leningrad Institute of Engineering Economics (RU)

inzh-mekh ... Mechanical Engineer (RU)

inzh ob........ Engineer Train (BU)

inzh p.......... Engineer Mobile Depot (BU)

inzhp .... Engineer Park (RU)

inzhp .... Engineer Regiment (RU)

Inzhrez .... Engineer Reserve (RU)

inzh s .... Engineer Depot (BU)

Inzhstroy.... Engineering Construction Administration (BU)

inzh-tekhnol ... Engineer-Technologist (RU)

inzhtekhot ... Engineering and Technical Department (RU)

inzhtr.......... Engineer Tank Company (RU)

inz hut .... Inzynier Hutnik [*Metallurgic Engineer*] [*Poland*]

inzh v .... Corps of Engineers (BU)

inz inz......... Inzynierowie [*Engineers*] [*Poland*]

inz lesn .... Inzynier Lesnik [*Forestry Engineer*] [*Poland*]

inz mech ..... Inzynier Mechanik [*Mechanical Engineer*] [*Poland*]

IO............... Acting (RU)

IO............... Actuating Element (RU)

IO............... British Indian Ocean Territory [*ANSI two-letter standard code*] (CNC)

IO............... Election District (RU)

IO............... Institute of Oceanology (of the Academy of Sciences, USSR) (RU)

IO............... Institut Oceanographique [*Oceanographic Institute*] [*Research center*] [*France*] (EAS)

IO............... Instituto Oceanografico [*Oceanographic Institute*] [*Oriente University*] [*Venezuela*] (EAS)

Io................ Ionio [*Ions*] [*Portuguese*]

IO................ Isa'dan Once [*Before Christ*] (TU)

IO............... Izvidacki Organi [*Reconnaissance Units*] (YU)

IO............... Izvrsilni Odbor [*Executive Committee*] (YU)

IO............... Quartermaster Section (RU)

IO............... Test Sample (RU)

IO............... Tools Section (BU)

IOA............ Impact Office Automation [*Australia*]

IOA............ Indian Ocean Arts Association [*Australia*]

IOA............ Indian Optometric Association (PDAA)

IoA .... Institute of Administration [*University of New South Wales*] [*Australia*]

IOA .... International Office for Audiophonology [*Belgium*] (SLS)

IOA .... International Olympic Academy (OLYM)

IOA .... International Orthoptic Association [*British*] (EAIO)

IOA .... Ioannina [*Greece*] [*Airport symbol*] (OAG)

IOA .... Israel Orienteering Association (EAIO)

IOAKMO .. Izvrsni Odbor Autonomne Kosovo-Metohija Oblasti [*Executive Committee of the Autonomous Region of Kosovo-Metohija*] (YU)

IOAN........ Institut Okeanologii Akademii Nauk [*Institute of Oceanology of the Academy of Sciences USSR*] (RU)

IOAT .... International Organization Against Trachoma [*Creteil, France*] (EA)

IOATO ...... Instituto de Orientacion y Asistencia Tecnica del Oeste [*Spain*] (DSCA)

IOB .... Institute of Bankers [*Later, CIB*] [*British*] (EAIO)

IOB .... Inter-Organization Board for Information Systems [*United Nations*] (IID)

IOB .... Inter-Organization Board for Information Systems and Related Activities [*Switzerland*]

IOBB.......... International Organization of Biotechnology and Bioengineering [*Guatemala, Guatemala*]

IOBC .... Indian Ocean Biological Center (BARN)

IOBC .... Indian Ocean Biological Centre (ASF)

IOBC .... International Organization for Biological Control of Noxious Animals and Plants [*See also OILB*] [*ICSU Montpellier, France*] [*Research center*] (EAIO)

IOBE.......... Institute of Economic and Industrial Research [*Greece*]

IOC .... Indian Ocean Commission [*Port Louis, Mauritius*] (EAIO)

IOC .... Intergovernmental Oceanographic Commission [*See also COI*] [*ICSU Paris, France*] (EAIO)

IOC .... Internationaal Ontmoetings Centrum [*International Network for Self-Reliance - INS*] (EA)

IOC .... Internationales Olympisches Komitee [*International Olympic Committee*] (EG)

IOC .... International Olympic Committee

IOC .... International Ornithological Congress [*New Zealand*]

IOC .... Iran Ocean Company (ME)

IOC .... Iraq Olympic Committee

IOCARIBE ... Intergovernmental Oceanographic Commission Association for the Caribbean and Adjacent Regions (ASF)

IOCC .... International Office of Cocoa and Chocolate [*Later, IOCCSC*] (EAIO)

IOCCC....... International Office of Cocoa, Chocolate, and Sugar Confectionary [*Belgium*] (EAIO)

IOCCSC .... International Office of Cocoa, Chocolate, and Sugar Confectionary [*IOCC and International Sugar Confectionary Manufacturers Association*] [*Formed by a merger of*] (EAIO)

IOCD .... International Organization for Chemical Sciences in Development [*Brussels, Belgium*] (EA)
IOC/EC ..... Intergovernmental Oceanographic Commission/Executive Council (MSC)
IOCG .... International Organization on Crystal Growth [*ICSU*]
IOCHC ...... International Organization for Cooperation in Health Care [*See also MMI*] [*Nijmegen, Netherlands*] (EAIO)
IOCO .... Izvrsni Odbor Centralnog Odbora [*Executive Committee of the Central Committee*] (YU)
IOCOL ...... Industria Ortopedica Colombiana [*Colombia*] (COL)
IOCS......... Institute of Overseas Chinese Studies
IOCU .... International Organization of Consumers Unions [*The Hague, Netherlands*] (EA)
IOCV .... International Organization of Citrus Virologists (LAA)
IOC/VAP .. Intergovernmental Oceanographic Commission/Voluntary Assistance Program (MSC)
IOD........... International Institute for Organizational and Social Development [*Belgium*] (SLS)
IOD .... Open Door International [*For the Economic Emancipation of the Woman Worker*] (RU)
IODC .... Interchurch Organization for Development Cooperation [*Netherlands*] (EAIO)
IODMM .... International Office of Documentation on Military Medicine (EA)
IOE .... Institut d'Observation Economique [*France*] (FLAF)
IOE .... Institute of Offshore Engineering [*Heriot-Watt University*] [*Information service or system*] (IID)
IOE .... International Organization of Employers [*Geneva, Switzerland*]
IOE .... International Organization of Experts (EAIO)
IOEI.......... Indian Ocean Export-Import [*Somalia*] [*Commercial firm*]
IOEPCO.... Iranian Oil Exploration and Producing Company (ME)
IOF .... Imposto sobre Operacoes Financeiras [*Financial Operations Tax*] [*Brazil*] (LA)
IOF .... Internationale Orientierungslauf Foderation [*International Orienteering Federation*] (EA)
IOF .... International Oceanographic Foundation (ASF)
IOF .... International Orienteering Federation (OLYM)
IOF .... Ion-Exchange Filter (RU)
IOFC........ Indian Ocean Fisheries Commission [*FAO*]
IOFC........ Indian Ocean Fishery Commission [*FAO*] [*Italy United Nations*]
IOFI.......... International Organization of the Flavor Industry [*Geneva, Switzerland*] (EAIO)
IOFOS ...... International Organization for Forensic Odonto-Stomatology [*Formerly, International Society of Forensic Odonto-Stomatology*] (EA)
IOFS......... International Organ Festival Society (EA)
IOFSG ...... International Orienteering Federation, Scientific Group [*See also IOFWA*] (EAIO)
IOFWA...... Internationale Orientierungslauf Foderation, Wissenschaftliche Arbeitsgruppe [*International Orienteering Federation, Scientific Group - IOFSG*] (EAIO)
IOGM .... Ilk Ogretim Genel Mudurlugu [*Elementary Education Directorate General*] (TU)
IOGT .... International Order of Good Templars (ADA)
IOGT .... International Organization of Good Templars [*Oslo, Norway*] (EAIO)
IOHE........ International Organization for Human Ecology (EAIO)
IOI .... International Ocean Institute [*Valetta, Malta*] (EAIO)
IOI .... International Ombudsman Institute [*University of Alberta*] [*Edmonton, AB*] [*Research center*] (EAIO)
IOJ........... Internationale Journalistenorganisation [*International Organization of Journalists*] (EG)
IOJ........... International Organization of Journalists [*See also OIJ*] [*Prague, Czechoslovakia*] (EAIO)
IOJD......... International Organization for Justice and Development (EAIO)
IOK.......... Internasionale Olimpiese Komitee [*International Olympic Committee - IOC*] [*Afrikaans*]
IOK.......... Internationales Olympisches Komitee [*International Olympic Committee*] [*German*]
IOK.......... International Order of Kabbalists (EA)
IOK.......... Iokea [*Papua New Guinea*] [*Airport symbol*] (OAG)
IOK.......... Ipartestuletek Orszagos Kozpontja [*National Center of Craftsmen's Associations*] (HU)
IOKAE...... Institouton Okeanografikon kai Alievtikon Meleton [*Institute of Oceanographic and Fishing Studies*] [*Greek*] (GC)
IOKG .... Institute of General and Municipal Hygiene (RU)
IOKh......... Institute of Organic Chemistry Imeni N. D. Zelinskiy (of the Academy of Sciences, USSR) (RU)
IOKSZ ...... Iparosok Orszagos Kozponti Szovetkezete [*Central Handicraft Cooperative*] (HU)
IOL .... Footwear-Testing Laboratory (RU)
IOL .... Indian Oxygen Limited
IOL .... India Office Library and Records (PDAA)
IOL .... Institute of Librarians [*India*]
IOLI.......... Israel Oceanographic and Limnological Institute (MSC)
IOLO .... Izvrsni Odbor Ljudskega Odbora [*Executive Committee of the People's Committee*] (YU)

IOLPS .... Izvrsni Odbor Ljudske Prosvete Slovenije [*Executive Committee, People's Education of Slovenia*] (YU)
IOLR......... Israel Oceanographic and Limnological Research Ltd. (ASF)
IOM.......... Independants d'Outre-Mer [*Overseas Independents*] [*Burkina Faso*] (AF)
IOM.......... Index Octane Moteur [*French*]
IOM.......... Institute of Metals [*Institution of Metallurgists - IM and Metals Society - MS*] [*Formed by a merger of*] (EAIO)
IOM.......... Instituto de Organizacion y Metodos [*Colombia*] (COL)
IOM.......... International Options Market [*Australian Options Market, European Options Exchange in Amsterdam, Montreal Exchange, and Vancouver Stock Exchange*]
IOM.......... International Organization for Migration (EAIO)
IOMACI.... Indian Ocean Marine Affairs Cooperation Conference
IOMB .... Instytut Organizacji i Mechanizacji Budownictwa [*Institute of Organization and Mechanization of Construction*] (POL)
IOML .... International Organization of Legal Metrology [*France*]
IOMP .... International Organization for Medical Physics [*ICSU*]
IOMTR ..... International Organization for Motor Trades and Repairs [*Rijswljk, Netherlands*] (EAIO)
IOMVM .... International Organization of Motor Vehicle Manufacturers (EAIO)
ION .... Impfondo [*Congo*] [*Airport symbol*] (OAG)
ION .... Indicator of Dangerous Voltages (RU)
ION .... Instelling van Openbaar Nut [*Benelux*] (BAS)
ion .... Ionisiert [*Ionized*] [*German*] (GCA)
IOnk......... Instytut Onkologii [*Institute of Oncology*] [*Poland*]
ion k .... Ionization Chamber (RU)
IONKh....... Institute of General and Inorganic Chemistry Imeni N. S. Kurnakov (of the Academy of Sciences, USSR) (RU)
IONO........ Izvrsni Odbor Narodnog Odbora [*Executive Committee of the People's Committee*] (YU)
IOO........... Social Insurance Institute (BU)
IOOC .... International Conference on Integrated Optics and Optical Fiber Communication (PDAA)
IOOC .... International Olive Oil Council [*See also COI*] [*Madrid, Spain*] (EAIO)
IOOC .... Iranian Offshore Oil Company (MENA)
IOOF .... Izvrsni Odbor Osvobodilne Fronte [*Executive Committee of the Liberation Front*] (YU)
IOOL .... International Optometric and Optical League [*British*] (EAIO)
IOOS .... Instytut Obrabiarek i Obrobki Skrawaniem [*Institute of Machine Tools and Machining by Cutting*] (POL)
IOP .... Caliop [*France*] [*ICAO designator*] (FAAC)
IOP .... Ibero-American Organization of Pilots [*See also OIP*] [*Mexico City, Mexico*] (EAIO)
IOP .... Institute of Pyramidology [*Harpenden, Hertfordshire, England*] (EA)
IOP .... Institut Oceanographique de Paris [*Oceanographic Institute of Paris*] [*French*] (MSC)
IOP .... International Organization of Palaeobotany [*British*]
IOP .... International Organization of Psychophysiology [*See also IPO*] [*Montreal, PQ*] (EAIO)
IOP .... Ioma [*Papua New Guinea*] [*Airport symbol*] (OAG)
IOP .... Iran Oil Participants (ME)
IOP .... Istioploikos Omilos Peiraios [*Piraeus Sailing Club*] [*Greek*] (GC)
IOP .... True Reciprocal Bearing (RU)
IOPB......... International Organization of Plant Biosystematists [*St. Anne De Bellevue, PQ*] (EA)
IOPC......... Institute of Paper Conservation (EA)
IOPEC .... International Oil Pollution Exhibition and Conference (PDAA)
IOPEC ...... Iranian Oil Exploration and Production Company (PDAA)
IOPM .... Instytut Organizacji Przemyslu Maszynowego [*Machinery Industry Institute on Organization*] (POL)
IOPP......... International Oil Pollution Prevention
IOPS......... Relative Network [*Load*] Increase Meter (RU)
IOP (SA).... Institute of Plumbing (South Africa) (AA)
IOR .... Index Octane Recherche [*French*]
IOR .... Instituto per le Opere di Religione [*Institute for Religious Works*] [*The Vatican bank*]
IOR .... Institut za Oceanografiju i Ribarstivo [*Institute of Oceanography and Fisheries*] [*Split, Yugoslavia*] (MSC)
IOR .... Instytut Ochrony Roslin [*Institute of Plant Protection*] (POL)
IOR .... Inter-Organizacoes dos Refugiados [*Interorganizations of Refugees*] [*Portuguese*] (WER)
IORD .... International Organization for Rural Development
IORLO ..... Izvrsni Odbor, Rajonski Ljudski Odbor [*Executive Committee, District People's Committee*] (YU)
IORN .... Instruction for Annulling Decisions of Conciliation Commissions by Central Committees of Trade Unions through Supervision (BU)
IORR .... It's Only Rock 'n' Roll: Rolling Stones Fan Club [*Norway*] (EAIO)
IOS .... Ilheus [*Brazil*] [*Airport symbol*] (OAG)
IOS .... Instituto de Organizacion y Sistemas [*Colombia*] (COL)

IOS .... Instituut vir Ontwikkelingstudies [*Rand Afrikaans University*] [*South Africa*] (AA)

IOS .... Instytut Obrobki Skrawanien [*Metal Cutting Institute*] [*Poland*] (PDAA)

IOS .... Instytut Ochrony Srodowiska [*Institute of Environmental Protection*] [*Poland*] (EE)

IOS .... Internationale Organisation fuer Sukkulentenforschung [*International Organization for Succulent Plant Study - IOS*] (EAIO)

IOS .... Investor Overseas Service [*Barranquilla*] (COL)

IOS .... Iraqi Organisation for Standardization (PDAA)

IOS .... [*The*] Israel Oriental Society (SLS)

IOSA .... Incorporated Oil Seed Association [*Benelux*] (BAS)

IOSCS .... International Organization for Septuagint and Cognate Studies [*Canadian*] (SLS)

IOSE .... Instituto de Obra Social del Ejercito [*Army Social Benefits Institute*] [*Argentina*] (LA)

IOSEWR ... International Organization for the Study of the Endurance of Wire Ropes [*Paris, France*] (EAIO)

IOSMTS ... Instruction for Organizing Machine-Tractor Stations Accounting (BU)

IOSOT ...... International Organisation for the Study of the Old Testament

IOSOT ...... International Organization for the Study of the Old Testament [*British*]

IOSS .... Imperial Organization for Social Services [*Iran*] (ME)

IOSTA .... Comission Internationale de l'Organisation Scientifique du Travail [*International Committee of Work Study and Labour Management in Agriculture*] (EAIO)

IOSZ .... Ifjumunkasok Orszagos Szovetsege [*National Federation of Working Youth*] (HU)

IOT .... British Indian Ocean Territory [*ANSI three-letter standard code*] (CNC)

IOT .... Institute of Technology [*Australia*] (ADA)

IOT .... Institute of Work Safety (RU)

IOTA .... Inbound Tourism Organisation of Australia

IOTA .... Institut d'Ophthalmologie Tropicale de l'Afrique [*Tropical Ophthalmological Institute of Africa*] (AF)

IOTA .... Institute of Transport Administration [*British*] (DCTA)

IOTA/ES... International Occultation Timing Association - European Section [*Germany*] (EAIO)

IOTC .... Iraqi Oil Tankers Company (ME)

IOTCG ...... International Organization for Technical Cooperation in Geology (EAIO)

IOTER....... Interim Optical Target Engagement Recorder [*Australia*]

IOTO .... Industrie des Oleagineux du Togo [*Cottonseed oil processing company*] [*Togo*]

IOTPD....... International Organization for the Transition of Professionals Dancers [*Switzerland*]

IOTTSG .... International Oil Tanker Terminal Safety Group (PDAA)

IOUO........ Instituto Oceanografico Universidad de Oriente [*Venezuela*] (MSC)

IOUSP....... Instituto Oceanografico do Universidad de Sao Paulo [*Oceanography Institute of the University of San Paulo*] [*Brazil*] (MSC)

IOV .... Disabled Veterans of World War II (RU)

IOV .... Instituto Oceanografico de Valparaiso [*Oceanographic Institute of Valparaiso*] [*Chile*] (LAA)

IOVE .... Institouto Oikonomikon kai Viomikhanikon Erevnon [*Institute of Economic and Industrial Research*] (GC)

IOVIF....... Instituto de Ordenacion de Vertientes e Ingenieria Forestal [*Argentina*] (DSCA)

IOW.......... Interdepartementaal Overleg Wetenschapsbeleid [*Netherlands*]

IOZPK....... Institute for Improving the Qualifications of Engineering and Technical Personnel through Resident and Correspondence Training (RU)

IP .... Actuating Station (RU)

ip .... And the Like (BU)

IP .... Cannon-Armed Fighter (RU)

IP .... Empresa AVIAIMPORT [*Cuba*] [*ICAO designator*] (ICDA)

IP .... Iles de Paix [*Islands of Peace*] [*An association*] [*Belgium*] (EAIO)

ip .... Iltapaivalla [*Afternoon*] [*Finland*] (GPO)

IP .... Independence Party

IP .... Indian Police

IP .... Induction Electric Furnace (RU)

IP .... Indulgencia Plenaria [*Plenary Indulgence*] [*Spanish*]

IP .... Industrias Pallomaro [*Colombia*] (COL)

IP .... Information a la Presse [*French*]

IP .... Information Packets [*or Packages*] (GNE)

IP .... Information Publications [*Singapore, Hong Kong, Australia*]

IP .... Initial Point (RU)

IP .... Initial Position, Assault Position, Forming-Up Place (RU)

IP .... Injector Preheater (RU)

IP .... In Preussen [*In Prussia*] [*German*]

IP .... Inspecteur de Police [*France*] (FLAF)

IP .... Inspector Polis [*Police Inspector*] (ML)

IP .... Inspektur Polisi [*Police Inspector*] (IN)

IP .... Institute of Nutrition (RU)

IP .... Institute of Physics [*British*] (EAIO)

IP .... Institute of Semiconductors (of the Academy of Sciences, USSR) (RU)

IP .... Institute of Soil Science Imeni V. V. Dokuchayev (RU)

IP .... Instituto de Pesca [*Sao Paulo Fishery Institute*] [*Brazil*] (ARC)

IP .... Institut Poluprovodnikov [*Institute of Semiconductors*] [*Former USSR*] (PDAA)

IP .... Instruccion Programada (COL)

IP .... Instruction Station (RU)

IP .... Instytut Pracy [*Institute of Labor*] [*Poland*]

IP .... Inter-Plama (Thailand) Co. Ltd.

IP .... Interpretative Routine (RU)

IP .... Invalid Pension

ip .... Ipar [*Industry*] (HU)

ip .... Iparos [*Craftsman*] (HU)

IP .... Islam-Pasand [*Islam-Loving*] [*Pakistan*] [*An association*]

IP .... Isomeric Transition (RU)

IP .... Israeli Pound (BJA)

IP .... Istoricheski Pregled [*Historical Review*] [*A periodical*] (BU)

IP .... Izquierda de los Pueblos [*Spain*] [*Political party*] (ECED)

IP .... Izvidacka Patrola [*Reconnaissance Patrol*] (YU)

IP .... Izvrsni Postupak [*Executive Procedure*] (YU)

IP .... Law Institute (of the Academy of Sciences, USSR) (RU)

IP .... Measuring Plate (RU)

IP .... Needle Bearing (RU)

IP .... Oxygen-Breathing Gas Mask (BU)

IP .... Portable Inhaler (RU)

IP .... Power Supply (RU)

IP .... Predicate Calculus (RU)

IP .... Roads Institute (BU)

IP .... Spark Gap (RU)

IP .... Stratum Tester (RU)

IP .... Summary Puncher (RU)

IP .... True Bearing (RU)

IPA............ Empresa Pernambucana de Pesquisa Agropecuraria [*Brazil*] (SLS)

IPA............ Fraunhofer-Institut fuer Produktionstechnik und Automatisierung [*Fraunhofer Institute for Production Engineering and Automation*] [*Stuttgart, West Germany*] [*Research center*] (ERC)

IPA............ Idrocarburi Policiclici Aromatici [*Italian*]

IPA............ Independent Peace Association (EAIO)

IPA............ Independent Psychiatrists' Association [*Commonwealth of Independent States*]

IPA............ Independent Publishers of Australia (ADA)

IPA............ [*The*] Indian Pharmaceutical Association (SLS)

IPA............ Indice de Precos no Atacado [*Wholesale Price Index*] [*Brazil*] (LA)

IPA............ Industrie des Peches Algeriennes [*Algeria*] (ASF)

IPA............ Information Processing Association [*Israel*]

IPA............ Inomenai Politeiai Amerikis [*United States of America*] (GC)

IPA............ Institouto Perifereiakis Anaptyxeos [*Regional Development Institute*] (GC)

IPA............ Institute of Patent Attorneys [*Australia*]

IPA............ Instituto de Pesquisas Agronomicas [*Institute of Agronomic Research*] [*Brazil*] (LAA)

IPA............ Instituto Petroquimico Argentino

IPA............ Instituto Provincial Agropecuario [*Mendoza, Argentina*] (LAA)

IPA............ Institut Pedagogique Africain [*African Pedagogical Institute*] [*French*] (AF)

IPA............ Institut Pochvovedeniya i Agrokhimii [*Institute of Soil Science and Agrochemistry, Baku*] [*Research center*] [*Former USSR*] (IRC)

IPA............ International Association for the Child's Right to Play [*International Playground Association*] [*Acronym is based on former name,*] (EA)

IPA............ Internationale Paediatrie-Gesellschaft [*France*] (SLS)

IPA............ International Packaging Abstracts [*Database*] [*Information retrieval*]

IPA............ International Palaeontological Association [*ICSU*]

IPA............ International Patent Agreement

IPA............ International Pediatric Association [*See also AIP*] [*Paris, France*] (EAIO)

IPA............ International Phonetic Association [*University College*] [*Leeds, England*] (EA)

IPA............ International Police Association [*Maidstone, Kent, England*] (EAIO)

IPA............ International Press Agency

IPA............ International Psycho-Analytical Association [*British*] (EAIO)

IPA............ International Psychogeriatric Association (EA)

IPA............ International Publishers Association [*See also UIE*] [*Geneva, Switzerland*] (EAIO)

IPA............ Ipec Aviation Pty Ltd. [*Australia*] [*ICAO designator*] (FAAC)

IPA............ Ipota [*Vanuatu*] [*Airport symbol*] (OAG)

IPA............ Israel Psychological Association (EAIO)

IPA............. Istituto di Psicoterapia Analitica-Esistenziale [*Italian*] (SLS)
IPAA........ Independent Petroleum Association of Africa
IPAA........ Insolvency Practitioners Association of Australia
IPAA......... Institute of Patent Attorneys of Australia (ADA)
IPAAC....... Instituto Provincial de Asuntos Agrarios y Colonizacion [*Cordoba, Argentina*] (LAA)
IPAB.......... Istituto di Psicoterapia Analitica Biopsicoesistenziale [*Italian*] (SLS)
IPAC........ Industria Papelera Andina Colombiana [*Colombia*] (COL)
IPAC......... Industria Pecuaria, Agricultura, e Comercio Lda.
IPAC......... Institut Polytechnique de l'Afrique Centrale
IPAC......... Ipac Pan American Oil Company (OMWE)
IPAC......... Iran Pan American Oil Company (ME)
IPACE .... International Professional and Continuing Education [*Australia*]
IPACH....... Institutul Pentru Planuri de Amenajare si Constructii Hidrotehnice [*Romania*] (DSCA)
IPACK...... International Packaging Material Suppliers Association (PDAA)
IPAD......... International Plastics Association Directors
IPADE....... Instituto Panamericano de Alta Direccion de Empresa [*Panamerican Institute for Business Management*] [*Mexico*] (PDAA)
IPAE......... Instituto Peruano de Administracion de Empresas [*Peruvian Institute of Business Administration*] (LA)
IPAFI........ Importadora Paulista de Fertilizantes e Inseticidas Ltd. [*Brazil*] (DSCA)
IPAFRIC ... Inter-Peches-Afrique
IPAG.......... Electronics Commission - Information, Planning, and Analysis Group [*New Delhi, India*] [*Research center*] (ERC)
IPAG......... Instituto de Pedagogia Autoactiva de Grupo [*Colombia*] (COL)
IPAGRO.... Instituto de Pesquisas Agronomicas [*Institute of Agronomic Research*] [*Brazil*]
IPAI.......... International Primary Aluminium Institute [*British*] (EAIO)
IPAIC .... Istituto di Psicoterapia Analitica e di Integrazione Corporea [*Italian*] (SLS)
IPAKO...... Industrias Petroquimicas Argentinas SA
IPAL.......... Instituto de Planificacion para America Latina [*Santiago, Chile*] (LAA)
IPALMO ... Istituto per le Relazioni tra l'Italia e i Paesi dell' Africa, America Latina, e Medio Oriente [*Institute for Italy's Relations with Africa, Latin America, and the Middle East*] (WER)
IPAM........ Institut Pedagogique Africain et Malgache
IPAN .... Institute of Semiconductors (of the Academy of Sciences, USSR) (RU)
IPAP.......... Idryma Prostasias Aprosarmoston Paidon [*Institute for the Protection of Handicapped Children*] (GC)
IPAP .... Instituto de Pesquisas Agronomicas de Pernambuco [*Brazil*] (DSCA)
IPAP .... Instituto Peruano de Administracion Publica [*Lima, Peru*] (LAA)
IPAR......... Institute of Policy Analysis and Research [*Nairobi, Kenya*] [*Research center*] (ECON)
IPAR......... Instituto de Planejamento Agricola Regional [*Brazil*] (DSCA)
IPARDES ... Instituto Paranaense de Desenvolvimento Economico e Social [*Parana Economic and Social Development Institute*] [*Brazil*] (LA)
IPARSA..... Industria de Produtos Alimenticios Racoes e Sacaria SA [*Brazil*] (DSCA)
IPARTERV ... Ipari es Mezogazdasagi Tervezo Vallalat [*Architectural Designing Enterprise for Industry and Agriculture*] (HU)
IPAS .... Independants et Paysans d'Action Sociale [*Independents and Peasants of Social Action*] [*French*] (PPE)
IPAS .... Informatives Personalabrechnungssystem [*German*] (ADPT)
IPAS .... Istituto di Patronato per l'Assistenza Sociale [*Italian*]
IPASA .... Inversiones, Promociones, y Administracion [*Colombia*] (COL)
IPASE........ Instituto de Previdencia e Assistencia aos Servidores do Estado [*Welfare and Aid Institute for Civil Servants*] [*Brazil*] (LA)
IPASME.... Instituto de Prevision y Asistencia Social del Ministerio de Educacion [*Institute of Social Welfare and Aid of the Ministry of Education*] [*Venezuela*] (LA)
IPAT......... Instituto Panameno de Turismo [*Panamanian Tourist Institute*] (LA)
IPAT......... Interdisziplinaere Projektgruppe fuer Angepasste Technologie [*Interdisciplinary Project Group of Appropriate Technology*]
IPAT......... Inventario del Patrimonio Historico Artistico Espanol [*Ministerio de Cultura*] [*Spain*] [*Information service or system*] (CRD)
ipb .... Engineer Road Battalion (BU)
IPB............. Institut Pasteur de Brazzaville
IPB............. Institut Pasteur of Brabant [*Belgium*]
IPB............. Institutul Politehnic Bucuresti [*Bucharest Polytechnic Institute*] [*Romanian*] (ARC)
IPB............. Instituut vir Personeelbestuur [*Institute of Personnel Management*] [*South Africa*] (AA)
IPB............. Interna Poljska Bolnica [*Field Hospital for Internal Medicine*] [*Military*] (YU)
IPB............. International Peace Bureau [*Geneva, Switzerland*] (EA)
IPB............. Investment Promotion Bureau [*Pakistan*] (IMH)

IPBA .... India, Pakistan, and Bangladesh Association (PDAA)
IPBC .... India, Pakistan, Bangladesh Conference (DS)
IPBMM ..... International Permanent Bureau of Motor Manufacturers (BARN)
ipbr............. Engineer Pontoon Brigade (RU)
ipbr............. Engineer Road Brigade (BU)
IPC............. Easter Island [*Chile*] [*Airport symbol*] (OAG)
IPC............. Indice de Precios al Consumidor [*Consumer Price Index*] [*Use CPI*] (LA)
IPC............. Industrial Planning Committee [*NATO*] (NATG)
IPC............. Industrial Production Corporation [*Sudan*] (GEA)
IPC............. Industrie des Papiers et Carbones
IPC............. Institut de Promotion Commerciale [*Institute for Trade Promotion*] [*Guadeloupe*] (LA)
IPC............. Institute of Paper Conservation [*Formerly, International Institute for Conservation of Historic and Artistic Works Paper Group*] (EA)
IPC............. Institute Pierre de Coubertin (OLYM)
IPC............. Instituto de Promocion Civica [*Santiago, Chile*] (LAA)
IPC............. Institut Politique Congolais [*Congolese Political Institute*]
IPC............. Instructor Preparatory Course [*Diving*] [*Australia*]
IPC............. Instytut Przemyslu Cukrowniczego [*Institute of Sugar Industry*] [*Poland*]
IPC............. Integrated Programme for Commodities [*UNCTAD*] (EY)
IPC............. Inter-African Phytosanitary Commission
IPC............. International Pacific Corporation [*Australia*]
IPC............. International Paralympic Committee (OLYM)
IPC............. International Peace Camp [*Italy*]
IPC............. International Peace Campaign
IPC............. International Penpal Club (EAIO)
IPC............. International People's College [*Denmark*]
IPC............. International Pepper Community [*Indonesia*] [*Research center*] (IRC)
IPC............. International Petroleum Company [*Peru*] (LA)
IPC............. International Photosynthesis Committee [*Stockholm, Sweden*] (EAIO)
IPC............. International Poplar Commission [*FAO*] [*Rome, Italy*] [*United Nations*] (EA)
IPC............. Iraq Petroleum Company (ME)
IPCA .... Isolated Parents Children's Association [*Australia*]
IPCAIL..... International Pacific Corporation Australian Investments Limited (ADA)
IPCC .... Intergovernmental Panel on Climate Change [*World Meteorological Organization*]
IPCCB .... Inter-Parliamentary Consultative Council of Benelux (EA)
IPCCC .... International Peace, Communication, and Coordination Center [*The Hague, Netherlands*] (EAIO)
IPCE .... Instituto de Promocion del Comercio Exterior [*Peru*] (LAA)
IPCE .... Instituto Panameno de Comercio Exterior (EY)
IPCE .... International Parliamentary Conference on the Environment (ASF)
IPCh.......... Gas Tube Frequency Converter (RU)
IPCL .... Indian Petrochemical Ltd.
IPCL .... Indian Petro-Chemicals Corp. (PDAA)
IPCL .... Iraq Petroleum Co. Ltd.
IPCORN.... Industrial Promotion Corporation of Rhodesia and Nyasaland Ltd.
IPCPA ...... Institute of Private Clinical Psychologists of Australia
IPCR......... Institute of Physical and Chemical Research [*Japan*] (ARC)
IPCS .... Institutul de Proiectari de Constructii Speciale [*Design Institute for Special Constructions*] (RO)
IPCS .... International Playing-Card Society (EA)
IPCS .... International Programme on Chemical Safety (EA)
IPCS .... International Program on Chemical Safety (GNE)
IPCSJ .... Israeli Public Council for Soviet Jewry (EAIO)
IPCT .... Institutul de Proiectari a Constructiilor Tip [*Design Institute for Model Constructions*] (RO)
IPCUP ...... Institutul de Proiectari si Cercetari pentru Utilaj Petrolier [*Design and Research Institute for Petroleum Equipment*] (RO)
IPD .... Industrial Planning Department [*Myanmar*] (DS)
IPD .... Industrial Processing Division [*Department of Scientific and Industrial Research*] [*New Zealand*] (ERC)
IPD .... Industrial Promotion Department [*Ministry of Commerce and Industry*] [*Kenya*]
I pd .... In Podobno [*And the Like*] (YU)
IPD .... Institute for Planning and Development [*Israel*]
IPD .... Instituto de Pesquisas e Desenvolvimento [*Research and Development Institute*] [*Brazil*] (LA)
IPD .... Institut Panafricain pour le Developpement [*Pan-African Institute for Development*] (AF)
IPD .... Institut Prumysloveho Designu [*Former Czechoslovakia*] (EAIO)
IPD .... Intermediate Peritoneal Dialysis [*Medicine*] (BARN)
IPD .... Interuniversity Program in Demography [*Free University of Brussels*] [*Research center*] [*Belgium*] (IRC)

IPD/AC ..... Institut Panafricain pour le Developpement, Afrique Centrale [*Pan African Institute for Development, Central Africa*] [*Cameroun*] (PDAA)

IPDC.......... Instituto Puertorriqueno de Derechos Civiles [*Puerto Rican Cival Rights Institute*] (EAIO)

IPDC.......... International Program for the Development of Communications [*UNESCO*]

IPDE.......... Investissements Prives Directs Etrangers

IPDI.......... Implicit Price Deflator Index [*Economics*]

IPDiR........ Instytut Przemyslu Drobnego i Rzemiosla [*Institute of Light Industries and Handicraft*] [*Poland*]

IPDiRz....... Instytut Przemyslu Drobnego i Rzemiosla [*Institute of Light Industries and Handicraft*] [*Poland*]

IPDR.......... Institut Pratique de Developpement Rural

IPD-TNO .. Hoofdgroep Industriele Produkten en Diensten TNO [*Division for Industrial Products and Services TNO*] [*Netherlands Organization for Applied Scientific Research (TNO)*] [*Research center*] [*Netherlands*] (ERC)

IPE............ Asociacion de Investigacion Tecnica de la Industria Papelera Espanola [*Spanish Paper Industry Research Association*] (ARC)

IPE............ Associacion de Investigation Tecnica de la Industrial Paperlera Espanola [*Spanish Paper Industry Technical Research Association*] (EAIO)

IPE............ Informacion de Prensa Especial [*Special Press Information*] [*Bolivia*] (LA)

IPE............ Institute of Public Enterprise [*India*] [*Research center*] (IRC)

IPE............ Instituto de Investigaciones y Planeacion Educacionales. Universidad del Valle [*Colombia*] (COL)

IPE............ International Partners Facility

IPE............ International Petroleum Exchange [*British*]

IPE............ Inter-Pacific Equity [*Australia*]

IPE............ Investimentos e Participacoes do Estado, SARL [*Nationalized industry*] [*Portugal*] (EY)

IPEA.......... Instituto de Pesquisa Economico-Social Aplicada [*Institute of Applied Economic-Social Research*] [*Brazil*] (LA)

IPEAAD .... Instituto de Pesquisas e Experimentacao Agropecuarias da Amazonia Ocidental [*Brazil*] (DSCA)

IPEAC........ Instituto de Pesquisas, Estudos, e Assessoria do Congresso [*Congressional Research, Study, and Advisory Institute*] [*Brazil*] (LA)

IPEACO .... Instituto de Pesquisas e Experimentacao Agropecuarias do Centro-Oeste [*Brazil*] (DSCA)

IPEACS..... Instituto de Pesquisas e Experimentacao Agropecuaria do Centro-Sul [*Brazil*] (LAA)

IPEAL .... Instituto de Pesquisas e Experimentacao Agropecuaria do Leste [*Cruz Das Almas, Brazil*] (LAA)

IPEAME ... Instituto de Pesquisas e Experimentacao Agropecuarias do Meridional [*Brazil*] (DSCA)

IPEAN....... Instituto de Pesquisas e Experimentacao Agropecuaria do Norte [*Northern Institute for Agricultural and Livestock Research and Experiment*] [*Brazil*] (LA)

IPEANE .... Instituto de Pesquisas e Experimentacao Agropecuaria do Nordeste [*Recife, Brazil*] (LAA)

IPEAO....... Instituto de Pesquisas e Experimentacao Agropecuaria do Oeste [*Sete Lagos, Brazil*] (LAA)

IPEAS....... Instituto de Pesquisas e Experimentacao Agropecuario do Sul [*Rio Grande Do Sul, Brazil*] (LAA)

IPEC .... Instituto de Pesquisas Economicas [*Brazil*] (DSCA)

IPEC .... International Patient Education Council (EAIO)

IPEDA....... Iuran Pembangunan Daerah [*Regional Development Tax*] (IN)

IPEDEHP ... Instituto Peruano de Educacion para los Derechos Humanos y la Paz [*Peruvian Institute of Education through Human Rights and Peace*] (EAIO)

IPEE .... Instituto de Pesquisas e Estudos Economicos [*Brazil*]

IPEE .... International Peace, Economy, and Ecology (EA)

IPEF .... Instituto de Pesquisas e Estudos Florestais [*Forest Research and Studies Institute*] [*Brazil*] (ARC)

IPEG .... Internationale Pharmako-EEG-Gesellschaft (SLS)

IPEI .... Institute of Industrial and Economic Research (RU)

IPEIL........ Intreprinderile pentru Exploatarea si Industrializarea Lemnului [*Enterprises for the Exploitation and Industrialization of Wood*] (RO)

IPEM........ Institute for Psycho-Acoustics and Electronic Music [*Belgium*]

IPEN......... Instituto de Pesquisas Energeticas e Nucleares [*Nuclear and Energy Research Institute*] [*Brazil*] (LA)

IPEN......... Instituto Peruano de Energia Nuclear [*Peruvian Nuclear Energy Institute*] (LA)

IPEN......... Pan American Institute of Naval Engineering (EAIO)

IPENB....... International PEN - Bangladesh (EAIO)

IPENB....... International PEN - Belgium (EAIO)

IPENC....... International PEN - Chile (EAIO)

IPENC....... International PEN- Colombia (EAIO)

IPENC....... International PEN - Czechoslovakia (EAIO)

IPEND....... International PEN - Denmark (EAIO)

IPENE....... International PEN - Egypt (EAIO)

IPENF....... International PEN - Finland (EAIO)

IPENHKC ... International PEN - Hong Kong Chinese (EAIO)

IPENHKE ... International PEN - Hong Kong English (EAIO)

IPENI....... International PEN - Iceland (EAIO)

IPENI....... International PEN - Indonesia (EAIO)

IPENI....... International PEN - Israel (EAIO)

IPENI....... International PEN - Italy (EAIO)

IPENJ .... International PEN - Jordan (EAIO)

IPENKWA ... International PEN - Kurdish Center [*Germany*] (EAIO)

IPENL....... International PEN - Latvian (EAIO)

IPENL....... International PEN - Lebanese (EAIO)

IPENLAWS ... International PEN - Latin American Writers in Spain (EAIO)

IPENM...... International PEN - Mexico (EAIO)

IPENM...... International PEN - Monaco (EAIO)

IPENN...... International PEN - Netherlands (EAIO)

IPENN...... International PEN - Nicaragua (EAIO)

IPENP....... International PEN Club - Poland (EAIO)

IPENP....... International PEN - Pakistan (EAIO)

IPENP....... International PEN - Perth [*Australia*] (EAIO)

IPENPH.... International PEN - Philippines (EAIO)

IPENS .... International PEN - Switzerland (EAIO)

IPENSACT ... International PEN - South Africa (EAIO)

IPENSP...... International PEN - Spain (EAIO)

IPENSR..... International PEN - Suisse Romande [*Switzerland*] (EAIO)

IPENVWA ... International PEN - Vietnamese Writers Abroad [*France*] (EAIO)

IPENWIE ... International PEN - Writers in Exile [*Germany*] (EAIO)

IPENYC .... International PEN - Croatia (EAIO)

IPEPO .... Instituto para la Propaganda Espanola de los Productos del Olivar [*Industrial association*] [*Spain*] (EY)

IPER .... Institute for Psychological and Edumetric Research [*South Africa*] [*Research center*] (IRC)

IPERA .... Indian Psychometric and Educational Research Association (EAIO)

IPES .... Institut de Preparation aux Enseignements du Second Degre [*French*]

IPES .... Institutions Publiques d'Education Surveillee [*France*] (FLAF)

IPES .... Instituto de Pesquisas e Estudos Sociais [*Research and Social Studies Institute*] [*Brazil*] (LA)

IPES .... Instituto de Planejamento Economico e Social [*Institute of Economic and Social Planning*] [*Brazil*] (LA)

IPES .... Instituts Preparatoires aux Enseignements Secondaires [*France*] (FLAF)

IPESA....... Instituto de Pesquisa Economico-Social Aplicada [*Institute of Applied Economic-Social Research*] [*Brazil*] (LA)

IPESAN .... Institut de Promotion Economique et Sociale de l'Afrique Noire [*Institute for the Economic and Social Promotion of Black Africa*] (AF)

IPETAC..... Interim Police Education and Training Advisory Council [*New South Wales, Australia*]

IPETB........ Institutul de Proiectare a Uzinelor si Instalatiilor pentru Industria Electrotehnica Bucuresti [*Bucharest Institute for the Design of Plants and Installations for the Electrotechnical Industry*] (RO)

IPETE........ Instituto de Promocion del Trabajo [*Chile*] (DSCA)

IPF .... Indicative Planning Figures

IPF .... Institute of Applied Physics (RU)

IPF .... Institut Francaise du Petrole, des Carburants et Lubrifiants [*French Institute of Petrol, Motor Fuels and Lubricants*] (PDAA)

IPF .... Institut fuer Post und Fernmeldewesen [*Institute for Postal Affairs and Telecommunications*] (EG)

IPF .... Institutul de Proiectari Forestiere [*Forestry Design Institute*] (RO)

IPF .... Institut za Proucavanje Folklora [*Institute of Folklore Research*] [*Sarajevo*] (YU)

IPF .... International Pharmaceutical Federation [*Netherlands*] (EAIO)

IPF .... International Pigeon Federation [*See also FCI*] (EAIO)

IPF .... International Podrabinek Fund [*Defunct*] (EA)

IPF .... International Powerlifting Federation [*Hagersten, Sweden*] (EAIO)

IPF .... Polarizing Interference Filter (RU)

IPFC .... Indo-Pacific Fisheries Commission [*or Council*] [*FAO ICSU Bangkok, Thailand*] [*United Nations*] (ASF)

IPFC .... Indo-Pacific Fishery Commission (EAIO)

IPFE .... Institutul de Proiectare pentru Forajul Sondelor si Extragerea Titeiului si Gazelor [*Design Institute for Well Drilling and Extraction of Crude Oil and Gas*] (RO)

Ip Fel.......... Iparfelugyeloseg [*Industrial Inspectorate*] (HU)

IPFEO .... Institut des Producteurs de Ferro-Alliages d'Europe Occidentale [*Institute of Ferro-Alloy Producers in Western Europe - IFAPWE*] [*Defunct*] (EA)

IPFK .... Isopropyl Phenyl Carbamate (RU)

IPFS........... Instituto Privado de Fomento a Soja [*Brazil*] (DSCA)

IPFS........... International Pen Friend Service (EAIO)

IPG .... Industrial Performance Group [*Australia*]

IPG .... Information Policy Group [*OECD*]

IPG .... INPADOC Patent Gazette

IPG .... Institut de Physique du Globe [*France*]

IPG .... Institut de Physique du Globe de Paris [*Paris Institute of Earth Physics*] [*Research center*] [*France*] (EAS)

IPG .... Institute of Applied Geophysics (of the Academy of Sciences, USSR) (RU)

IPG .... Institutul de Petrol si Gaze [*Petroleum and Gas Institute*] (RO)

IPG .... Instytut Przemyslu Gumowego [*Institute of Rubber Industry*] [*Poland*]

IPG .... Internationale Paracelsus-Gesellschaft [*Austria*] (SLS)

IPG .... Interparlamentarische Gruppe [*Interparliamentary Group*] (EG)

IPGAN ...... Institut Polytechnique Gamal Abdel Nasser [*Gamal Abdel Nasser Polytechnic Institute*] [*Guinea*] (AF)

IPGC.......... Institutul de Proiectare a Constructiilor si Instalatiilor de Gospodarie Comunala [*Design Institute for Communal Economy Constructions and Installations*] (RO)

IPGC.......... Institutul de Proiectari de Geniu Civil [*Civil Engineering Design Institute*] (RO)

IPGE.......... Idea Popular de la Guinea Ecuatorial [*Nationalistic movement*] [*Equatorial Guinea*]

IPGG .... Institutul de Petrol, Gaze, si Geologie [*Institute for Petroleum, Gases, and Geology*] (RO)

IPGGH ...... Intreprinderea de Prospectiuni Geologice si Geofizice pentru Hidrocarburi [*Enterprise for Geological and Geophysical Prospecting for Hydrocarbons*] (RO)

IPGH .... Instituto Panamericano de Geografia e Historia [*Pan American Institute of Geography and History - PAIGH*] [*Mexico*] (LAA)

IPGH .... Instituto Panamericano de Geografia e Historia [*Panamerican Institute of Geography and History*] [*Peru*]

IPGH .... Institut Panamericain de Geographie et d'Histoire [*Pan American Institute of Geography and History - PAIGH*] [*French*] (MSC)

IPGM .... Institut Penyelidikan Getah Malaysia [*Rubber Research Institute of Malaysia*] (ARC)

IPGMR...... Institute of Postgraduate Medicine and Research [*Bangladesh*] [*Research center*] (IRC)

IPGP .... Institut de Productivite et de Gestion Previsionnelle [*Mali*]

IPGRI .... International Plant Genetic Resources Institute [*Consultative Group on International Agricultural Research*] (ECON)

IPGRI .... International Plant Genetic Resources Institute [*Italy*]

IPGS .... Internationale Paracelsus-Gesellschaft zu Salzburg (EAIO)

IPGum ...... Instytut Przemyslu Gumowego [*Institute of Rubber Industry*] [*Poland*]

IPH .... Institute of Public Health [*Japan*] (IRC)

IPH .... International Association of Paper Historians (EA)

IPH .... International Pacific Holdings

IPH .... Ipoh [*Malaysia*] [*Airport symbol*] (OAG)

IPH .... Izba Przemyslowo-Handlowa [*Chamber of Industry and Trade*] (POL)

IPHA .... Instituto Peruano del Hierro y del Acero [*Peruvian Iron and Steel Institute*] (LA)

IPHA .... Interior Plantscaping and Hire Association [*Australia*]

IPHAMETRA ... Institut de Pharmacopee et de Medecine Traditionnelles [*Institute of Pharmacopoeia and Traditional Medicine*] [*Gabon*] [*Research center*] (IRC)

IPHAN ...... Instituto do Patrimonio Historico e Artistico Nacional [*National Historic and Artistic Heritage Institute*] [*Brazil*] (LA)

IPHT .... Institute of Physical High Technology [*Germany*]

IPI .... Imposto sobre Produtos Industrializados [*Finished Goods Tax*] [*Brazil*] (LA)

IPI .... Institute of Production Innovation

IPI .... Institute of Professional Investigators (EA)

IPI .... Institutul de Proiectari Ilfov [*Ilfov Design Institute*] (RO)

IPI .... Institutul de Proiectari Industriale [*Industrial Design Institute*] (RO)

IPI .... International Patent Institute [*Later, EPO*]

IPI .... International Potash Institute [*See also IIP*] (EAIO)

IPI .... International Press Institute [*Switzerland*] (PDAA)

IPI .... Investment Publications Information Services Pty. Ltd. [*Australia*]

IPI .... Ipiales [*Colombia*] [*Airport symbol*] (OAG)

IPIA .... Instituto para la Promocion Industrial en Andalucia [*Spain*] (EY)

IPIA .... Institutul de Patologie si Igiena Animala [*Institute for Animal Pathology and Hygiene*] [*Romanian*] (RO)

IPIA .... Institutul de Proiectari al Industriei Alimentare [*Design Institute for the Food Industry*] (RO)

IPIAPS ...... Intreprinderea de Productie Industriala Autoutilare si Prestari Servicii [*Enterprise for Industrial Production, Self-Equipping, and Services*] (RO)

IPIB .... Industrial Projects Implementation Bureau [*Arab*]

IPIBC........ Institutul de Proiectari al Industriei Bunurilor de Consum [*Design Institute for the Consumer Goods Industry*] (RO)

IPIC .... International Petroleum Investment Company [*Abu Dhabi*] (MENA)

IPIE .... Institut de Politique Internationale et Europeenne [*Institute of International and European Politics*] [*Research center*] [*France*] (IRC)

IPIECA...... International Petroleum Industry Environmental Conservation Association [*British*] (EAIO)

IPIF .... Institutul de Proiectari Pentru Lucrari de Imbunatatiri Funciare [*Romania*] (DSCA)

IPIK .... Institute for the Training of Party Cadres (RU)

IPIL .... Institutul de Proiectari al Industriei Lemnului [*Design Institute for the Wood Industry*] (RO)

IPILF .... Intreprinderea pentru Producerea si Industrializarea Legumelor si Fructelor [*Enterprise for the Production and Industrialization of Vegetables and Fruit*] (RO)

IPIMC ...... Institutul de Proiectari pentru Industria Materialelor de Constructii [*Design Institute for the Construction Materials Industry*] (RO)

IPIMIGEO ... Instituto Panamericano de Ingenieria de Minas y Geologia [*Santiago, Chile*] (LAA)

IPI/MIS .... International Press Institute/Management and Information System [*Switzerland*]

IPIN .... Institute for the Study of Nationalities of the USSR (RU)

IPIN .... Instituto Pan-Americano de Ingenieria Naval [*Pan American Institute of Naval Engineering*] (LAA)

IPIP .... Institutul de Proiectari pentru Instalatii Petroliere [*Design Institute for Petroleum Installations*] (RO)

IPIRA .... Indian Plywood Industries Research Association (PDAA)

IPIRI......... Indian Plywood Industries Research Institute [*Research center*] (IRC)

IPIS .... International Peace Information Service [*Belgium*]

IPIU .... Institutul de Proiectari al Industriei Usoare [*Design Institute for Light Industry*] (RO)

IPIW .... Independent Panel on Intractable Waste [*Australia*]

IPK............ Fraunhofer-Institut fuer Produktionsanlagen und Konstruktionstechnik [*Fraunhofer Institute for Manufacturing Systems and Design Technology*] [*Research center*] [*Germany*] (ERC)

IPK............ Ilektroniko Pliroforiako Kentro [*Computerized Information Center*] (GC)

IPK............ Industrijsko Poljoprivredni Kombinat [*Croatia*] (EE)

IPK............ Inspektorat Parnih Kotlova [*Steam Boilers Inspectorate*] (YU)

IPK............ Institute for the Improvement of Qualifications (RU)

IPK............ Institute of Blood Transfusion (RU)

IPK............ Institute of Consumers' Cooperatives (RU)

IPK............ Institut Polytechnique de Kankan [*Kankan Polytechnic Institute*] [*Guinea*] (AF)

IPK............ Institut za Proucavanje Knjizevnost [*Institute of Literary Studies*] (YU)

IPKF .... Indian Peace-Keeping Force [*Army*]

ipkh........... Inspector General of Infantry (BU)

IPKh .... Transfer-Characteristic Meter (RU)

IPKI .... Ikatan Pendukung Kemerdekaan Indonesia [*Association of Supporters of Indonesian Independence*] (IN)

IPKIR .... Institut Povysheniya Kvalifikkatsii Informatsionnykh Rabotnikov [*Institute for the Advancement of Qualifications of Information Workers*] [*Former USSR*] (PDAA)

IPKITR...... Institute for Improving the Qualifications of Engineering and Technical Personnel (RU)

IPKKNO.... Institute for Improving the Qualifications of Public Education Personnel (RU)

IPKP .... Institute for Improving the Qualifications of Teachers (RU)

IPKPON.... Institute for Improving the Qualifications of Instructors in Social Sciences (RU)

IPKRK ...... Institute for Improving the Qualifications of Supervisory Personnel (RU)

IPKVOD.... Institute for Improving the Qualifications of Water Transportation Workers (RU)

IPL............ Air Charter Services (Pty) Ltd. South Africa [*ICAO designator*] (FAAC)

IPL............ Ibu Pejabat Laut [*Navy Headquarters*] (ML)

IPL............ Inchcape Pacific Ltd. [*Asian and Pacific trading*] [*Hong Kong*]

IPL............ Institutul pentru Proiectari de Laminoare [*Institute for Rolling Mill Design*] (RO)

IPL............ International Photographic Library Proprietary Ltd. [*Australia*]

IPL............ Ivoirienne de Peinture et Laques

IPLA .... Instituto Pastoral Latino Americano [*Latin American Pastoral Institute*] (LA)

IPLA .... Instituto Petroquimico Latinoamericano [*Argentina*]

IPLA .... Istituto per le Piante da Legno e l'Ambiente SpA [*Italian*] (SLS)

IPLAN...... Instituto de Planejamento Economico e Social [*Institute for Social and Economic Planning*] [*Brazil*]

IPLC .... Intreprinderea de Produse din Lemn pentru Constructii [*Enterprise for Wood Products for Constructions*] (RO)

IPLCA .... International Pipe Line Contractors Association [*Later, IPOCA*] (EA)

IPLM .... Intreprinderea Produse Lemn Mobila [*Enterprise for Furniture Wood Products*] (RO)

IPLOCA .... International Pipe Line and Offshore Contractors Association [*Belgium*] (EAIO)
IPLT .... Iuran Pembangunan Lima Tahun [*5-Year Development Tax*] (IN)
IPM .... Flight Departure Point (BU)
IPM .... Impot des Personnes Morales [*Benelux*] (BAS)
IPM .... Independent Peace Movement [*Greece*] (EAIO)
IPM .... Inquerito Policial-Militar [*Police-Military Inquiry*] [*Brazil*] (LA)
IPM .... Institut de Physique Meteorologique [*Institute of Physical Meteorology*] [*Senegal*] (PDAA)
IPM .... Institute of Applied Mineralogy (RU)
IPM .... Institute of Personnel Management [*South Africa*] (AA)
IPM .... Institute of Personnel Management [*Australia*] (ADA)
IPM .... Institute of the Problems of Mechanics (RU)
IPM .... Institute Pasteur du Maroc [*Pasteur Institute of Morocco*] (PDAA)
IPM .... Institut fuer Polygraphische Maschinen [*Institute for Printing Machines*] (EG)
IPM .... Instituto de Prevision Militar [*Military Social Welfare Institute*] [*Guatemala*]
IPM .... Institutul de Proiectari Metalurgice [*Metallurgical Design Institute*] (RO)
IPM .... Institutul de Proiectari Miniere [*Institute for Mining Design*] (RO)
IPM .... Institutul de Protectie a Muncii [*Labor Safety Institute*] (RO)
IPM .... Instytut Prawa Miedzynarodowego [*Institute of the International Law*] [*Poland*]
IPM .... Instytut Przemyslu Miesnego [*Institute of the Meat Industry*] [*Poland*]
IPM .... Instytut Przemyslu Mleczarskiego [*Institute of the Dairy Industry*] [*Poland*]
IPM .... Interpersonal Messaging Service
Ip M .... Iparugyi Miniszterium/Miniszter [*Ministry/Minister of Industry*] (HU)
IPM .... Point of Departure [*Aviation*] (RU)
IPM .... Statens Institut foer Psykosocial Miljoemedicin [*National Institute for Psychosocial Factors and Health*] [*Research center*] [*Sweden*] (IRC)
IPMA .... Institute of Personnel Management (Australia) (ADA)
IPMA .... International Primary Market Association
IPMA .... Intreprinderea de Proiectari si Prototipuri pentru Masini Agricole [*Enterprise for Agricultural Machine Design and Prototypes*] (RO)
IPMM .... Institute of Applied Mineralogy and Metallurgy (RU)
IPMP .... Institut za Proucavanje Medunarodnih Pitanja [*Institute of International Studies*] [*Belgrade*] (YU)
IPMP .... Intreprinderea de Prelucrarea Mase Plastice [*Enterprise for Processing Plastics*] (RO)
IPMPB ...... Intreprinderea de Poduri Metalice si Prefabricate din Beton [*Enterprise for Metallic and Prefabricated Concrete Bridges*] (RO)
IPMS .... Institution of Professionals, Managers, and Specialists [*British*]
IPMS .... International Plastic Modelers Society (EA)
IPMS .... International Polar Motion Service [*ICSU*] [*Research center*] [*Japan*]
IPMS .... Izdavacko Preduzece Matice Srpske [*"Matica Srpska" Publishing House*] [*Novi Sad*] (YU)
IPMUPaFNRJ ... Izdavacko Preduzece Ministarstva Unutrasnjih Poslova Federativna Narodna Republika Jugoslavija [*Publishing House of the Yugoslav Ministry of Internal Affairs*] (YU)
IPN .... Industri Pesawat Terbang Nusantara PT [*Indonesia*] [*ICAO designator*] (FAAC)
IPN .... Initial Aiming Point [*Artillery*], Initial Guidance Point [*To an objective*] (BU)
IPN .... Instituto Politecnico Nacional [*National Polytechnic Institute*] [*Mexico*] (LA)
IPN .... Institut Pedagogique National [*National Pedagogic Institute*] [*French*]
IPN .... Instytut Pamieci Narodowej [*Institute of National Memorabilia*] (POL)
IPN .... Ipatinga [*Brazil*] [*Airport symbol*] (OAG)
IPNC .... International Council of Plant Nutrition [*Australia*] (EAIO)
IPNCB ...... Institut des Parcs Nationaux du Congo Belge
IPNETP ..... Institut Pedagogique National de l'Enseignement Technique et Professionnel
IPNRK ...... Institut des Parcs Nationaux et des Reserves Naturelles de Katanga
IPO .... Instituut voor Perceptie Onderzoek [*Institute for Perception Research*] [*Netherlands*] (PDAA)
IPO .... Instituut voor Plantenziektenkundig Onderzoek [*Research Institute for Plant Protection*] [*Research center*] [*Netherlands*] (IRC)
IPO .... International Payment Order (DCTA)
IPO .... International Progress Organization [*Vienna, Austria*] (EAIO)
IPO .... Inter-Provinciaal Overleg [*Netherlands*]
IPO .... Istituto per l'Oriente

IPO .... Ivanovo Industrial Region (RU)
IPO .... True Check Point Bearing (RU)
IPOA .... Instituut van Parke- en Ontspanningsadministrasie Suid-Afrika [*South Africa*] (AA)
IPOCA ...... International Pipe Line and Offshore Contractors Association [*Belgium*] (EAIO)
ipod .... And So Forth (BU)
i pod .... Et Cetera, And So Forth (RU)
IPOD .... International Phase of Ocean Drilling
IPOFAC .... International Project on Family and Community [*Australia*]
IPOL .... Institute of Semiconductors (of the Academy of Sciences, USSR) (RU)
IPOL .... Point of Departure of Return Flight (RU)
IPOP .... Instruction for the Procedure for Granting, Paying, and Accounting Financial Indemnities and Aids (BU)
ipozb .... Engineer Positional Battalion (BU)
ipozb .... Fortification Battalion (RU)
ipozbr .... Engineer Positional Brigade (BU)
ipozbr .... Fortification Brigade (RU)
ipozr .... Engineer Positional Company (BU)
ipozr .... Fortification Company (RU)
IPP .... Flight Instructions (RU)
IPP .... Gas Casualty First Aid Kit (RU)
IPP .... Impot des Personnes Physiques [*Benelux*] (BAS)
IPP .... Incapacite Permanente Partielle [*France*] (FLAF)
IPP .... Independent People's Party [*Political party*] [*Germany*] (EAIO)
IPP .... Indice de Precos do Produtor [*Producer Price Index*] [*Brazil*] (LA)
IPP .... Institute for Study and Design (BU)
IPP .... Institute of Plasma Physics [*Nagoya University*] [*Japan*] (PDAA)
IPP .... Institut fuer Plasmaphysik [*Institute for Plasma Physics*] [*Max-Planck Institute*]
IPP .... Quarantine Clearing Station (RU)
IPP .... Surgical Dressing Kit (RU)
IPPA .... Indo-Pacific Prehistory Association [*Australia*] (EA)
IPPA .... Intensive Pig Producers of Australia
IPPA .... International Pectin Producers Association [*Switzerland*] (EAIO)
Ippandomei ... Zenkoku Ippan Rodokumiai Domei [*National Federation of General Workers' Unions*] [*Japan*]
IPPB .... Interna Pukovska Poljska Bolnica [*Regimental Field Hospital for Internal Medicine*] (YU)
IPPB .... Mobile Communicable Diseases Hospital (BU)
IPPC .... Infrastructure Payments and Progress Committee [*NATO*] (NATG)
IPPC .... International Penal and Penitentiary Commission [*Later, IPPF*]
IPPC .... International Plant Protection Convention
IPPEC ...... Inventaire Permanent des Periodiques Etrangers en Cours
IPPF .... International Penal and Penitentiary Foundation [*See also FIPP*] [*Bonn, Federal Republic of Germany*] (EAIO)
IPPF .... International Planned Parenthood Federation (EA)
IPPG .... Mobile Communicable Diseases Hospital (BU)
IPPG .... Mobile Field Hospital for Contagious Diseases (RU)
IPPI .... Institute of Information Transmission Problems (of the Academy of Sciences, USSR) (RU)
IPPI .... Instituto Nacional para el Progreso [*Colombia*] (COL)
IPPJ .... Institute of Plasma Physics, Japan
IPPK .... Infectious Pleuropneumonia of Goats (RU)
IPPL .... Industrial Preparedness Planning List
IPPLM ...... Institute of Plasma Physics and Laser Microfusion [*Poland*] (IRC)
IPPNP .... Inpatient Pain Management Programme [*Australia*]
IPPP .... Institute of Plant Production and Processing [*Commonwealth Scientific and Industrial Research Organization*] [*Australia*] (EAS)
IPPP .... Institute of Private Practicing Psychologists [*Australia*]
IPPS .... International Philippine Philatelic Society (EAIO)
IPPTA .... Indian Pulp and Paper Technical Association (EAIO)
IPQ .... Instituto Portugues da Qualidade [*Portugal*]
IPQI .... Intermediate Personality Questionnaire for Indian Pupils [*Personality development test*] [*Psychology*]
IPqM .... Instituto de Pesquisas da Marinha [*Brazil*] (MSC)
ipr .... And So On (BU)
i pr .... Et Cetera, And So Forth (RU)
IPR .... Industrial Public Relations Service of Australia (ADA)
IPR .... Industriepreisreform [*Industrial Price Reform*] (EG)
IPR .... Institute for Planning Research [*University of Port Elizabeth*] [*South Africa*] (AA)
IPR .... Institute of Peace Research [*La Trobe University*] [*Australia*]
IPR .... Institute of Public Relations [*Geneva, Switzerland*] (SLS)
IPR .... Instituto de Pesquisas Radioativas [*Radioactive Research Institute*] [*Brazil*] (LA)
IPR .... Instituto de Pesquisas Rodoviarias [*Highway Research Institute*] [*Brazil*] (LA)

ipr .... Internationaal Privaatrecht [*Private International Law*] [*Benelux*] (BAS)

IPR .... International Public Relations (ADA)

IPR .... Investerings Premie Regeling [*Investment Premium Law*] [*Netherlands*] (IMH)

IPR .... Istituto per le Pubbliche Relazioni [*Italian Public Relations Institute*]

IPr .... Istoricheski Pregled [*Historical Review*] [*A periodical*] (BU)

IPR .... True Bearing of a Radio Station (RU)

IPRA .... Institute of Park and Recreation Administration South Africa (AA)

IPRA .... International Peace Research Association [*Research center*] [*Japan*] (IRC)

IPrA .... International Pragmatics Association [*Belgium*] (EAIO)

IPRA .... International Public Relations Associations [*Switzerland*]

IPRA .... Ivoirienne Pieces de Rechange Automobile

IPRALCOOP ... Intreprinderea de Produse Alimentare a Cooperatiei de Consum [*Consumer Cooperative Food Products Enterprise*] (RO)

IPRAN .... Institutul de Proiectari Tehnologica pentru Industria Chimica Anorganica si Ingrasaminte [*Technological Design Institute for the Inorganic Chemicals and Fertilizer Industry*] (RO)

IPRAO .... Institution de Prevoyance et de Retraites de l'Afrique Occidentale [*West African Institute of Welfare and Retirement*] [*Togo*] (AF)

IPRAS .... Istanbul Petrol Rafinerisi Anonim Sirketi [*Istanbul Petroleum Refinery Corporation*] (TU)

IPRE .... International Professional Association for Environmental Affairs (EA)

IPREC .... Intreprinderea de Prestatii, Reclama, si Expozitii [*Enterprise for Services, Advertising, and Exhibits*] (RO)

IPREIG...... Institute Professionnel de Recherches et d'Etudes des Industries Graphiques [*Professional Research Institute for the Printing Industry*] [*France*] (PDAA)

IPRES........ Istituto Pugliese di Ricerche Economiche e Sociali [*Italian*] (SLS)

IPRG......... Industry Policy Reference Group [*Technical and Further Education Commission*] [*New South Wales, Australia*] (EA)

IPRI .... Industrial Products Research Institute [*Agency for Industrial Science and Technology*] [*Research center*] [*Japan*] (ERC)

IPRI .... Instituto Peruano de Relaciones Internacionales [*Peruvian International Relations Institute*] (LA)

IPRI .... International Plant Research Institute (PDAA)

IPRI .... Italian Peace Research Institute [*Research center*] (IRC)

IPRiS .... Instytut Przemyslu Rolnego i Spozywczego [*Institute of the Agriculture and Food Industry*] (POL)

IPRO......... International Pallet Recycling Organization (PDAA)

IPROC....... Institutul de Proiectari Carbonifere [*Institute for Coal Design*] (RO)

IPROCHIM ... Institutul de Proiectari pentru Industria Chimica Organica de Baza si Petrochimica [*Design Institute for the Basic Organic Chemical and Petrochemical Industry*] (RO)

IPROCIL... Institutul de Proiectari Cercetari Stiintifice pentru Industria Lemnului [*Scientific Research and Design Institute for the Wood Industry*] (RO)

IPROCOM ... Institutul de Cercetari si Proiectari pentru Comert [*Research and Design Institute for Trade*] (RO)

IPROED.... Institutul de Proiectari Edilitare [*Municipal Design Institute*] (RO)

IPROFIL... Institutul de Proiectari Forestiere si pentru Industria Lemnului [*Design Institute for Forestry and the Wood Industry*] (RO)

IPROFIL... Intreprinderile de Produse Finite din Lemn [*Enterprises for Finished Wood Products*] (RO)

IPROIL ..... Institutul de Proiectari din Industria Lemnului [*Design Institute for the Wood Industry*] (RO)

IPROLAM ... Institutul de Proiectare Tehnologica pentru Laminoare [*Technological Design Institute for Rolling Mills*] (RO)

IPROM...... Institutul de Proiectari de Masini [*Machinery Design Institute*] (RO)

IPROMET ... Institutul de Proiectari de Uzine si Instalatii Metalurgice [*Design Institute for Metallurgical Plants and Installations*] (RO)

IPROMIN ... Institutul de Proiectari si Tehnica Miniera [*Institute for Mining Design and Technology*] (RO)

IPRONAV ... Institutul pentru Proiectarea Constructiilor Navale [*Naval Construction Design Institute*] (RO)

IPROSCO ... Instituto de Promocion Industrial Suizo-Colombiano [*Swiss-Colombian Institute for Industrial Promotion*] (LA)

IPROSIN .. Institutul de Proiectari pentru Industria Chimica Organica de Sinteza Medicamente si Fibre Sintetice [*Design Institute for the Organic Chemical Industry for Drug Syntheses and Synthetic Fibers*] (RO)

IPROUP.... Institutul de Proiectari Utilaj Petrolifer [*Design Institute for Petroleum Equipment*] (RO)

IPROYAZ ... Instituto de Projectos de la Industria Azucarera [*Sugar Industry Planning Institute*] [*Cuba*] (LA)

IPRS .... International Confederation for Plastic and Reconstructive Surgery [*Montreal, PQ*] (EAIO)

IPRS .... Intreprinderea de Piese Radio si Semiconductori Baneasa [*Baneasa Enterprise for Radio Parts and Semiconductors*] (RO)

IPRU......... Instituto de Planamiento Regional y Urbano [*Regional and Urban Planning Institute*] [*Research center*] [*Argentina*] (IRC)

IPS .... Ibero-American Philosophical Society [*Madrid, Spain*] (EAIO)

IPS .... Inaltimea Prea Sfinta [*Most High Holiness*] (RO)

IPS .... Incubator Poultry-Raising Station (RU)

IPS .... Indian Phytopathological Society (SLS)

IPS .... Indizierte Pferdestaerke [*Indicated Horsepower*] [*German*] (GCA)

IPS .... Industrial Program Services [*Australia*]

IPS .... Industrial Promotion Services [*Kenya*] Ltd.

IPS .... Information Retrieval System (RU)

IPS .... Institute for Palestine Studies [*Lebanon*] (SLS)

IPS .... Institute for Planetary Synthesis [*Switzerland*] (EAIO)

IPS .... Institute for Planned Economy (BU)

IPS .... Institute of Plant Science [*Australia*]

IPS .... Institute of Population Studies [*Peru*] (IRC)

IPS .... Instituto de Prevision Social [*Paraguay*] (LAA)

IPS .... Institutul de Proiectari Schele [*Derrick Design Institute*] (RO)

IPS .... International of Proletarian Freethinkers (RU)

IPS .... International Paracelsus Society [*Salzburg, Austria*] (EA)

IPS .... International Peat Society [*See also IMTG*] [*Helsinki, Finland*] (EAIO)

IPS .... International Perimetric Society (EA)

IPS .... International Phycological Society [*IUBS*] (ASF)

IPS .... International Primatological Society (EA)

IPS .... International Publishing Service [*Australia*]

IPS .... Inter/Press Service - Third World News Agency (EA)

IPS .... Intreprinderea Prestari Servicii [*Services Enterprise*] (RO)

IPS .... Isopropyl Alcohol (RU)

IPS .... Israel Physical Society (EAIO)

IPS .... Israel Prehistoric Society (EAIO)

IPS .... Istituto di Psicosociologia [*Italian*] (SLS)

IPS .... Italian Physical Society (EAIO)

IPS .... Office of Information Programmes and Services [*UNESCO*] (IID)

IPS .... True Bearing of an Aircraft (RU)

IPSA .... Infirmiers Pilotes Secouristes de l'Air [*France*] (FLAF)

IPSA .... Institute of Private Secretaries, Australia (ADA)

IPSA .... International Political Science Association (EA)

IPSA .... International Press Service Association (ADA)

IPSA .... International Professional Security Association [*Paignton, Devonshire, England*] (EAIO)

IPSA .... Iraq Pipeline across Saudi Arabia

IPSA .... Israel Political Science Association (EAIO)

IPSC .... Instytut Przemyslu Skla i Ceramiki [*Glass and Ceramics Industries Institute*] [*Poland*] (PDAA)

IPSCAM.... International Program for Study of Climate and Man

IPSCI........ Industrial Promotion Services Cote-D'Ivoire

IPSEJES ... Institut de Planification, de Statistique et d'Etudes Juridiques, Economiques, et Sociales [*Tunisia*]

IPSF .... International Pharmaceutical Students' Federation [*Jerusalem, Israel*] (EAIO)

IPSFA....... Instituto de Prevision Social de las Fuerzas Armadas [*Armed Forces Social Insurance Institute*] [*Venezuela*]

IPSFAN..... Instituto de Prevision Social de las Fuerzas Armadas Nacionales [*National Armed Forces Social Insurance Institute*] [*Venezuela*] (LA)

IPSHU...... Institute for Peace Science, Hiroshima University [*Japan*]

IPSI .... Institut de Presse et des Sciences de l'Information [*Tunisia*]

IPSI .... Institut de Presse et des Sciences de l'Information [*Algeria*]

IPSiC .... Instytut Przemyslu Szkla i Ceramiki [*Institute of the Glass and Ceramics Industry*] (POL)

IPSICM..... International PSI Committee of Magicians [*See also CIEPP*] (EAIO)

IPSJ .... Information Processing Society of Japan [*Information service or system*] (IID)

IPSM .... Institute of Purchasing and Supply Management [*Australia*] (PDAA)

IPSMF....... Institutul de Perfectionare si Specializare a Medicilor si Farmacistilor [*Institute for the Advanced Training and Specialization of Physicians and Pharmacists*] (RO)

IPSN .... Inspecteur de Police de la Surete Nationale [*France*] (FLAF)

IPSN .... Institut de Protection et Surete Nucleaire [*Protection and Nuclear Safety Institute*] [*France*] [*Research center*] (EAS)

IPSO .... Institut de Physique Spatiale d'Orsay [*French*]

IPSO .... Instituut voor Politiek en Sociaal Onderzoek [*Institute for Political and Social Research*] [*Netherlands*] (WEN)

IPSOA .... Istituto per lo Studio dell'Organizzazione Aziendale [*Italian*] (SLS)

IPSS.......... Instituto Peruano de Seguridad Social [*Peruvian Institute of Social Security*] (LA)

IPST .... Institut de Promotion Superieure du Travail [*Institute for the Advancement of Labor*] [*Algeria*] (AF)
IPST .... International Practical Scale of Temperature (PDAA)
IPSTAS ..... Izmir Plastik Sunger Sanayi ve Ticaret Anonim Sirketi [*Izmir Plastic Sponge Industry and Trading Corporation*] (TU)
IPSTsIChM ... Institute of Precision Alloys of the Central Institute of Ferrous Metallurgy (RU)
IPT .... Fraunhofer-Institut fuer Produktionstechnologie [*Fraunhofer Institute for Production Technology*] [*Research center*] (ERC)
IPT .... Instituto de Pesquisas Tecnologicas [*Technological Research Institute*] [*Brazil*] (LA)
IPT .... Instituto de Promocao Turistica [*Portugal*] (EY)
IPT .... Instituto de Promocion de Trabajo [*Santiago, Chile*] (LAA)
IPT .... Instituto Postal Telegrafico [*Telegraph and Postal Institute*] [*Venezuela*] (LA)
IPT .... International Planning Team [*NATO*] (NATG)
IPT .... Interport Corp. [*ICAO designator*] (FAAC)
IPT .... Ipelske Tehelne [*Ipel Brick Works*] (CZ)
IPTA .... Antitank Artillery (RU)
IPTA .... Indian People's Theatre Association
IPTAAS ..... Isolated Patients Travel and Accommodation Assistance Scheme [*Australia*]
iptab .... Antitank Artillery Battery (RU)
iptabr .... Antitank Artillery Brigade (RU)
iptabr .... Tank-Destroyer Artillery Brigade (BU)
IPTAD ...... Antitank Artillery Battalion (RU)
iptadn .... Tank-Destroyer Artillery Battalion (BU)
IPTAP .... Antitank Artillery Regiment (RU)
iptap .... Tank-Destroyer Regiment (BU)
iptb .... Antitank Battery (RU)
iptbat .... Antitank Battery (RU)
iptbatr .... Antitank Battery (RU)
IPTC .... Institutul de Proiectari Telecomunicatii [*Telecommunications Design Institute*] (RO)
IPTC .... International Polar Transportation Conference
IPTC .... International Press Telecommunications Council [*See also CIPT*] [*Telecommunications An association Defunct*] (EA)
IPTD .... Antitank Battalion (RU)
iptd .... Tank-Destroyer Battalion (BU)
IPTEA .... Internacia Postista kaj Telekomunikista Esperanto-Asocio [*International Esperanto Association of Post and Telecommunication Workers*] (EAIO)
IPTF .... Indo-Pacific Theosophical Federation (EAIO)
IPTIC .... International Pulse Trade and Industry Confederation [*FAO*]
IPTN .... Industri Pesawat Terbang Nusantara [*Indonesia*]
IPTO .... International Pet Trade Organization [*Defunct*] (EAIO)
IPTP .... Antitank Regiment (RU)
IPTPA .... International Professional Tennis Players Association (BARN)
IPTs .... Moving-Target Indicator (RU)
IPTT .... Internationale du Personnel des Postes, Telegraphes, et Telephones [*Postal, Telegraph, and Telephone International - PTTI*] [*Geneva, Switzerland*] (EAIO)
IPTTc .... Institutul de Proiectari Transporturi si Telecomunicatii [*Institute for Transportation and Telecommunications Design*] (RO)
IPU .... Igala Progressive Union
IPU .... Igbirra Progressive Union
IPU .... Igreja Presbiteriana Unida do Brasil [*Brazil*] (EAIO)
IPU .... Industrial Promotion Unit [*Tongan*] (GEA)
IPU .... International Population Union [*France*] (DSCA)
IPU .... Interparlamentarische Union [*Interparliamentary Union*] [*German*] (EG)
IPU .... Inter-Parliamentary Union [*See also UI*] [*Switzerland*]
IPU .... Sparking Prevention Device (RU)
IPU .... True Track Angle (RU)
IPUC .... Institutul de Proiectari de Uzine Chimice [*Institute for Chemical Plant Design*] (RO)
IPUEC .... Instituto Preuniversitario en el Campo [*Pre-University Farming and Academic Institute*] [*Cuba*] (LAA)
IPUP .... Intreprinderea de Plase si Unelte Pescaresti [*Enterprise for Fishing Nets and Equipment*] (RO)
ipv .... In Plaats Van [*Instead Of*] [*Netherlands*] (GPO)
IPV .... Instituut vir Persoonsvoorligting [*University of the Western Cape*] [*South Africa*] (AA)
IPV .... Italian Polydor Variable Microgroove [*Record label*]
IPVD .... Instituto de Pesquisa Veterinaria "Desiderio Finamor" [*Brazil*] (DSCA)
IPVDF .... Instituto de Pesquisas Veterinarias "Desiderio Finamor" [*Desiderio Finamor Veterinary Research Institute*] [*Brazil*] (IRC)
IPVP .... Support for Military Reasons (BU)
IPVR .... Institute for Plant Virus Research [*Japan*] (ARC)
IPVS .... International Pig Veterinary Society [*Amer, Spain*] (EAIO)
IPVU .... Instituto Paraguayo de Vivienda y Urbanismo [*Paraguayan Housing and Urban Institute*] (LAA)
IPWF .... International Public Works Federation (EA)

IPWL .... Instytut Przemyslu Wlokien Lykowych [*Institute of the Bast Fiber Industry*] (POL)
IPYa .... Information Retrieval Language (RU)
IPZ .... Crosstalk Attenuation Meter (RU)
IPZ .... Instytut Przemyslu Zielarskiego [*Institute of the Herbal Industry*] [*Poland*]
IPZ .... Integrata Programmierzentrum [*German*] (ADPT)
IPZ .... Inzinjersko Projektni Zavod [*Engineering Planning Institute*] (YU)
IQ .... Import Quota System [*Japan*] (IMH)
IQ .... Institute of Quarrying [*South Africa*] (SLS)
IQ .... Interne Quittung [*German*] (ADPT)
IQ .... Iraq [*ANSI two-letter standard code*] (CNC)
IQA .... Industrias Quimicas Asociadas SA
IQA .... Instituto de Quimica Agricola [*Institute of Agricultural Chemistry*] [*Rio De Janeiro, Brazil*] (LAA)
IQAD .... Institute of Quarrying - Australian Division (EAIO)
IQB .... Instituto Quimico Biologico [*Institute of Chemistry and Biology*] [*Belo Horizonte, Brazil*] (LAA)
IQHKB ..... Institute of Quarrying - Hong Kong Branch (EAIO)
IQISA .... Interest Questionnaire for Indian South Africans [*Vocational guidance test*]
IQM .... Qiemo [*China*] [*Airport symbol*] (OAG)
IQN .... Qingyang [*China*] [*Airport symbol*] (OAG)
IQNZB ...... Institute of Quarrying - New Zealand Branch (EAIO)
IQPR .... Institute of Qualified Personnel Resources [*China*] (IRC)
IQQ .... Caribbean Airways [*Barbados*] [*ICAO designator*] (FAAC)
IQQ .... Iquique [*Chile*] [*Airport symbol*] (OAG)
IQS .... Instituto Quimico de Sarria [*Sarria Institute of Chemistry*] [*Universidad Autonoma de Barcelona*] [*Research center*] [*Spanish*] (ERC)
IQSA .... Industrias Quimicas, Sociedad Anonima [*Chemical Industries Corporation*] [*Salvadorean*]
IQSAB ...... Institute of Quarrying - South African Branch (EAIO)
IQSY .... International Years of the Quiet Sun [*ICSU*]
IQT .... Iquitos [*Peru*] [*Airport symbol*] (OAG)
IQW .... Individuelle Quantitative Wert [*Mean Total Ridge Count*] [*Anatomy*]
IR .... Engineer Reconnaissance (RU)
ir .... Idezett Resz [*Section Cited*] (HU)
IR .... Imperiale Regio [*Imperial and Royal*] [*Italian*]
IR .... Impulse Relay (RU)
iR .... Im Ruhestand [*Retired*] [*German*] (EG)
IR .... Indian Railways (IMH)
IR .... Induction Flow Meter (RU)
IR .... Industrial Registry [*New South Wales, Australia*]
IR .... Infanterieregiment [*Infantry Regiment*] [*German*]
IR .... Infrarot [*Infrared*] [*German*] (GCA)
Ir .... Ingenieur [*Engineer*] [*Netherlands*]
Ir .... Ingenieur [*Engineer*] [*French*]
IR .... Inlandsch Reglement [*Benelux*] (BAS)
iR .... In Ruhe [*In Peace*] [*German*]
IR .... Insinjur [*Engineer*] (IN)
i-r .... Inspector (BU)
IR .... Inspektorat Rada [*Labor Inspectorate*] (YU)
IR .... Inspektur [*Inspector*] (IN)
IR .... Institut de Recherches [*CERIA Research Institute*] [*Research center*] [*Belgium*] (IRC)
IR .... Institute of Rationalizations (BU)
IR .... Institut fur Raumfahrttecknik [*Institute for Space Technology*] [*Technical University*] [*Germany*] (PDAA)
IR .... Institut Rizeni [*Management Institute*] (CZ)
IR .... Internationale de la Resistance [*Resistance International - RI*] (EAIO)
IR .... International Registration (BARN)
IR .... Iran [*ANSI two-letter standard code*] (CNC)
IR .... Iran [*Poland*]
ir .... Iranyito [*Leading*] [*Military*] (HU)
Ir .... Iridio [*Iridium*] [*Chemical element*] [*Portuguese*]
Ir .... Irmak [*River, Large Stream*] (TU)
ir .... Iroda [*Office*] (HU)
ir .... Ivret [*Folio*] (HU)
IR .... Izquierda Republicana [*Republican Left*] [*Spain*] [*Political party*] (PPE)
IR .... Lockout Relay (RU)
IR .... Manual Injector (RU)
IR .... Proportional-Plus-Integral Controller (RU)
IRA .... Industrial Relations Act [*Mauritius*] (AF)
IRA .... Industrial Relations Authority [*New South Wales, Australia*]
IRA .... Industries et Representations en Afrique
IRA .... Institut de la Recherche Agronomique [*Institute of Agronomic Research*] [*Cameroon*] [*Research center*] (IRC)
IRA .... Instituto de Reforma Agraria [*Asuncion, Paraguay*] (LAA)
IRA .... Instituto de Reorganizacao Agraria [*Agrarian Reorganization Institute*] [*Portuguese*] (WER)

IRA .... Instituto Regulador de Abastecimientos [*Supply Regulation Institute*] [*El Salvador*] (LA)
IRA .... International Reading Association (ADA)
IRA .... International Registration Authority [*Botany*] (PDAA)
IRA .... International Rubber Association [*Kuala Lumpur, Malaysia*] (EAIO)
IRA .... Intreprinderile de Reparatie Auto [*Automotive Repair Enterprises*] (RO)
IRA .... Iran National Airlines Corp. [*ICAO designator*] (FAAC)
IRA .... Islamic Research Association
IRA .... Istituto di Ricerca sulle Acque [*Water Research Institute*] [*Italian*] (MSC)
IRA .... Istituto di Ricerche Ambientali [*Italian*] (SLS)
IRA .... Kira Kira [*Solomon Islands*] [*Airport symbol*] (OAG)
IRABA .... Institut de Recherche Appliquee du Beton Arme [*Applied Research Institute for Reinforced Concrete*] [*France*] (PDAA)
IRAC......... Industrial Relations Advisory Council [*Australia*]
IRAC......... Instituto de Reforma Agraria y Colonizacion [*Peru*] (LAA)
IRAC......... Institut pour le Redressement des Arts Classiques [*Belgium*] (SLS)
IRAD .... Institut de Recherches Appliquees du Dahomey [*Dahomey*] (DSCA)
IRADES .... Istituto Ricerche Applicate Documentazione e Studi [*Italian*] (SLS)
IRAF......... Institut de Recherches Agronomiques et Forestieres [*Institute for Research in Agronomy and Forestry*] [*Gabon*] [*Research center*] (IRC)
IRALCOOP ... Intreprinderea de Produse Alimentare a Cooperativei de Consum [*Food Products Enterprise for the Consumer Cooperatives*] (RO)
IRAM .... Institut de Recherches Agronomiques a Madagascar [*Madagascar Agronomic Research Institute*] (AF)
IRAM .... Institut de Recherches et d'Applications des Methodes de Developpement [*Institute of Research and Application of Development Methods - IRAM*] (EAIO)
IRAM .... Institute for Research in Alternative Medicines [*France*] (EAIO)
IRAM .... Institut fuer Radioastronomie im Millimeterwellenbereich [*French*] (SLS)
IRAM .... Instituto Argentino de Racionalizacion de Materiales [*Buenos Aires, Argentina*] (SLS)
IRAM .... Instituto de Radioastronomia Millimetrica [*Institute for Radioastronomy in the Millimeter Range*] [*Spain*]
IRAN .... Industries Reunies de l'Afrique Noire
IRANDOC ... Iranian Documentation Centre [*Ministry of Culture and Higher Education*] [*Tehran*]
IRANOR ... Instituto Espanol de Normalizacion [*Spanish*] (SLS)
IRANSENCO ... Iran-Senegal Company (ME)
IRAP......... Institut de Recherches Appliquees Anti-Pollution
IRAS......... Institute on Religion in an Age of Science
IRASENCO ... Societe Irano-Senegalaise des Petroles et des Mines
IRAT......... Institut de Recherches Agronomiques Tropicales [*Institute for Tropical Agricultural Research*] [*Martinique*] (ARC)
IRAT......... Institut de Recherches Agronomiques Tropicales [*Institute for Tropical Agricultural Research*] [*French Guiana*] (ARC)
IRAT......... Institut de Recherches Agronomiques Tropicales et des Cultures Vivrieres [*Institute of Tropical Agronomic Research and Food Crops*] [*Comoros*] (AF)
IRAT......... Institut de Recherches Agronomiques Tropicales et des Cultures Vivrieres [*Institute for Tropical Agricultural Research and Food Crops*] [*Research center*] [*France*] (IRC)
IRAT/HV ... Institut de Recherches Agronomiques Tropicales et des Cultures Vivieres en Haute-Volta [*Institute for Tropical Agricultural Research and Food Crops - Upper Volta*] (ARC)
IRB............ Informationszentrum Raum und Bau [*Information Center for Regional Planning and Building Construction*] [*Germany*] [*Information service or system*] (IID)
IRB............ Instituto de Resseguros do Brasil [*Brazilian Reinsurance Institute*] [*Rio De Janeiro*] (LA)
IRB............ International Rugby Board [*Australia*]
IRB............ Iranair Tours Co. [*Iran*] [*ICAO designator*] (FAAC)
IRB............ Istituto Ricerche Breda, SpA [*Breda Research Institute*] [*Nuclear energy*] [*Italian*] (NRCH)
IRBAA .... Institute of Rural Business Administration of Australasia
IRBAR .... Irian Barat [*West Irian*] (IN)
IRBM......... Istituto di Ricerche di Biologia Molecolaire [*Italy*]
IRC .... Indian Roads Congress (PDAA)
IRC .... Industrial Relations Centre [*New Zealand*] (IRC)
IRC .... Industrial Relations Commission [*Australia*]
IRC .... Industrial Research Center [*Philippines*] (ERC)
IRC .... Industrial Research Centre [*Libya*]
IRC .... Institut de Recherches Chimiques [*Chemical Research Institute*] [*Belgium*] (ARC)
IRC .... Institutul Roman de Consulting [*Romanian Consulting Institute*] (RO)
IRC .... Integrated Research Center [*De La Salle University*] [*Philippines*]

IRC .... International Radiation Commission [*of the International Association of Meteorology and Atmospheric Physics*] (EAIO)
IRC .... International Radio Carrier (NTCM)
IRC .... International Record Carriers (ADPT)
IRC .... International Red Cross
IRC .... International Relations Committee [*American Library Association*]
IRC .... International Relations Committee [*Library Association of Australia*]
IRC .... International Rescue Committee
IRC .... International Rice Commission
IRC .... Inter-Regional Capital Account [*Inter-American Development Bank*]
IRC .... Iran Asseman Airline [*ICAO designator*] (FAAC)
IRC .... Iraqi Communist Party [*Also, ICP*] [*Political party*] (MENA)
IRC .... IRC International Water and Sanitation Centre [*International Reference Centre for Community Water Supply and Sanitation*] [*Acronym is based on former name,*] (EAIO)
IRC .... Islamic Revival Committee [*Sudan*]
IRC .... Istituto Internazionale Ricerca Camping Caravanning [*Italian*] (SLS)
IRCA......... Institut de Recherches sur le Cafe
IRCA......... Institut de Recherches sur le Caoutchouc [*Rubber Research Institute*] [*French*] (ARC)
IRCA......... Institut de Recherches sur le Caoutchouc en Afrique [*Institute for Rubber Research in Africa*] [*French*] (AF)
IRCA......... International Railway Congress Association [*Belgium*]
IRCACIM ... Institution de Retraites des Chefs d'Atelier, Contre-Maitres et Assimiles des Industries des Metaux [*France*] (FLAF)
IRCAFEX ... Institution de Retraites des Cadres et Assimiles de France et de l'Exterieur
IRCAM..... Institut de Recherche et de Coordination Acoustique/Musique [*Institute for Research and Coordination Acoustics/Music*] [*French*]
IRCAM..... Institut de Recherches Scientifiques du Cameroun
IRCAU...... Instituto de Relaciones Culturales entre Argentina y la URSS [*Argentine-USSR Cultural Relations Institute*] (LA)
IRCB......... Institut Royal Colonial Belge
IRCC......... Institut de Recherches sur le Caoutchouc au Cambodge [*Cambodian Rubber Research Institute*] (CL)
IRCC......... Institute de Recherches du Cafe et du Cacao [*Coffee and Cocoa Research Institute*] [*Research center*] [*French*] (IRC)
IRCE......... Istituto per le Relazioni Culturali con l'Estero [*Institute for Cultural Relations with Foreign Countries*] [*Italian*] (WER)
IRCh .... Frequency-Difference Relay (RU)
IRCHA ...... Institut National de Recherche Chimique Appliquee [*National Institute of Applied Chemical Research*] [*French*] (ARC)
IRCI.......... Industrial Reconstruction Corp. of India Ltd. (PDAA)
IRCI.......... Industrial Research and Consultancy Institute [*Sudan*]
IRCICA ..... Research Centre for Islamic History, Art, and Culture [*of the Organization of the Islamic Conference*] (EAIO)
IRCIHE..... International Referral Center for Information Handling Equipment [*Former Yugoslavia*] [*UNESCO*] (IID)
IRCIS........ Istituto Romano di Coordinamento e d'Intervento Sociale [*Italian*] (SLS)
IRC-L........ Instituto Regional Castellano-Leones [*Castille-Leon Regional Institute*] [*Spanish*] (WER)
IRCL......... International Research Centre on Lindane [*See also CIEL*] [*Brussels, Belgium*] (EAIO)
IRCM........ Impot sur les Revenues de Capitaux Mobilier [*French*] (IMH)
IRCM........ Institutul Romanesc de Cercetari Marine [*Romanian Institute for Marine Research*] (RO)
IRCNSW ... Industrial Relations Commission of New South Wales [*Australia*]
IRCO .... International Rubber Conference Organization (EAIO)
IRCOBI ..... International Research Committee on the Biokinetics of Impacts [*Later, International Research Council on the Biokinetics of Impacts*] (EAIO)
IRC of A..... Industrial Relations Court of Australia
IRCOL....... Institute for Information Retrieval and Computational Linguistics [*Bar Ilam University*] [*Isreal*] (PDAA)
IRCON ...... Indian Rail Construction Co.
IRCOSA .... International Radio Corporation Societe Anonyme
IRCOTEX ... Institut de Recherches du Coton et des Textiles Exotiques [*Research Institute for Cotton and Exotic Textile Plants*] [*Research center*] [*French*]
IRCPAL..... International Research Council on Pure and Applied Linguistics (EA)
IRCQ .... Industrial Relations Commission of Queensland [*Australia*]
IRC(Qld).... Industrial Relations Commission (Queensland) [*Australia*]
IRCS......... Interdisciplinary Research Center on Suicide [*Italy*] (EAIO)
IRCT......... Institut de Recherches du Coton et des Textiles Exotiques [*Research Institute for Cotton and Exotic Textile Plants*] [*Benin*] [*Research center*] (ARC)

IRCT......... Institut de Recherches du Coton et des Textiles Exotiques [*Research Institute for Cotton and Exotic Textile Plants*] [*Burkina Faso*] [*Research center*]   (ARC)

IRCT......... Institut de Recherches du Coton et des Textiles Exotiques [*Research Institute for Cotton and Exotic Textile Plants*] [*Research center*] [*French*]   (IRC)

IRCT......... Institut Recherche Coloniale Tropicale

IRCV......... Industrial Relations Commission of Victoria [*Australia*]

IRD .... Engineer Reconnaissance Patrol   (RU)

IRD .... Institute for Research Development [*South Africa*] [*Research center*]   (IRC)

IRD .... Institute of Radiation Dosimetry [*Former Czechoslovakia*]   (IRC)

IRD .... Instituto de Radioprotecao e Dosimetria [*Radio-Protection and Dosimetry Institute*] [*Brazil*]   (LA)

IRD .... International Resource Development   (ADPT)

IRD .... Ishurdi [*Bangladesh*] [*Airport symbol*]   (OAG)

IRDA .... Institute Regional do Desenvolvimento do Amapa [*Brazil*]   (DSCA)

IRDA .... Institut Royal de Droit et l'Administration [*Royal Institute of Law and Administration*] [*Laotian*]   (CL)

IRDABI ..... Institute for Research and Development of Agro-Based Industry [*Department of Industry*] [*Indonesia*] [*Research center*]   (IRC)

IRDB......... Industry Research and Development Board [*Australia*]

IRDC .... International Development Research Centre   (GNE)

IRDC .... Istituto Regionale di Documentazione e Comunicazione [*Italian*]   (SLS)

IRDCLI ..... Institute for Research and Development of Cellulose Industries [*Agency for Industrial Research and Development*] [*Indonesia*] [*Research center*]   (IRC)

IRDE......... Instruments Research and Development Establishment [*India*]   (PDAA)

IRDEB....... Instituto Radiodifusao Educacional de Bahia [*Brazil*]

IRDG .... Industrial Research and Development Grants [*Australia*]   (ADA)

IRDHBI..... Institute for Research and Development of Handicraft and Batik Industries [*Indonesia*] [*Research center*]   (IRC)

IRDJENAU ... Inspektur Djemderal Angkat Udara [*Air Force Inspector General*]   (IN)

IRDP......... Icelandic Research Drilling Project

IRDP......... Institut Romand de Recherches et de Documentation Pedagogiques [*Institute for Educational Research and Documentation for French-Speaking Cantons of Switzerland*] [*Research center*]   (IRC)

IRDTI .... Institute for Research and Development of Textile Industry [*Agency for Industrial Research and Development*] [*Indonesia*]

IRE............ Indian Rare Earths Ltd.   (PDAA)

IRE............ Institut des Reviseurs d'Entreprises [*Belgium*]   (EAIO)

IRE............ Institute of Radio Engineering and Electronics (of the Academy of Sciences, USSR)   (RU)

IRE............ Institute of Road Engineering [*Indonesia*] [*Research center*]   (ERC)

IRE............ Institut National des Radioelements [*National Institute for Radioelements*] [*Research center*] [*Belgium*]   (IRC)

IRE............ Intreprinderea Regionala de Electricitate [*Regional Electricity Enterprise*]   (RO)

IREA......... All-Union Scientific Research Institute of Chemical Reagents and Ultrapure Chemical Substances   (RU)

IREB......... Intreprinderea de Retele Electrice Bucuresti [*Bucharest Enterprise for Electricity Networks*]   (RO)

IREB......... Intreprinderea Regionala de Electricitate Bucuresti [*Bucharest Regional Electricity Enterprise*]   (RO)

IRED......... Innovations et Reseaux pour le Developpement [*Development Innovations and Networks*] [*Geneva, Switzerland*]   (EAIO)

IREDA....... Iuran Rehabilitasi Daerah [*Regional Rehabilitation Tax*]   (IN)

IreDNCA... National College of Art and Design, Dublin, Ireland [*Library symbol*] [*Library of Congress*]   (LCLS)

IREDS .... Illawarra Regional Economic Development Strategy [*Australia*]

IREE......... Institut de Recherches et d'Etudes Europeennes [*Institute of European Research and Studies*]   (EAIO)

IREE......... Institution of Radio and Electronics Engineers, Australia

IREEA ...... Institution of Radio and Electronics Engineers, Australia   (ADA)

IREEAust ... Institution of Radio and Electronics Engineers, Australia   (ADA)

IREF .... Istituto di Ricerche Educative e Formative [*Italian*]   (SLS)

IREFAC..... International Real Estate Federation Australian Chapter

IREG......... Industriradets Industriregister [*Federation of Danish Industries' Register of Industries*]   (EY)

IREL......... Australian Industrial Relations Database [*Brisbane College of Advanced Education*] [*Information service or system*]   (IID)

IREL......... Industrial Relations [*AUSINET database*]

IREM........ Institut de Recherche pour l'Enseignement des Mathematiques [*Institute for Research in the Teaching of Mathematics*] [*Malagasy*]   (AF)

IREMAM ... Institut de Recherches et d'Etudes sur le Monde Arabe et Musulman [*Institute for Research and Studies on the Arab and Muslim World*] [*France*] [*Information service or system*]   (IID)

iremb......... Engineer Maintenance Battalion   (RU)

IREMIL..... Impresa Rappresentanze e Mediazioni in Libia

IREMOAS ... Intreprinderea de Radiatoare, Echipament Metalic, Obiecte, si Armaturi Sanitare [*Enterprise for Radiators, Metal Equipment, and Sanitary Articles and Fittings*]   (RO)

iremr.......... Engineer Maintenance Company   (RU)

iremvb .... Engineer Maintenance and Recovery Battalion   (RU)

IREN .... Institut de Recherche sur les Energies Nouvelles [*Alternative Energies Research Institute*] [*Ivory Coast*]

IRENA...... Instituto de Recursos Naturales [*Institute of Natural Resources*] [*Nicaragua*]   (LA)

IRENE....... Industrial Restructuring and Education Network Europe

irer............ Engineer Maintenance and Recovery Company   (RU)

IReR.......... Istituto Regionale di Ricerca della Lombardia [*Regional Institute of Research for the Lombardy Region*]   (SLS)

IRES .... Institut de Recherches Economiques et Sociales [*Institute of Economic and Social Research*] [*Belgium*]   (IRC)

IRES .... Institut de Recherches Economiques et Sociales [*Institute of Economic and Social Research*] [*Zaire*]   (AF)

IRES .... Intreprinderea Regionala de Electricitate din Sibiu [*Sibiu Regional Electricity Enterprise*]   (RO)

IRES .... Istituto Ricerche Economico-Sociali del Piemonte [*Italian*]   (SLS)

IRESA ...... Institut de Recherches Economiques et Sociales [*Institute of Economic and Social Research*] [*Algeria*]

IRESCO .... Institut de Recherche sur les Societes Contemporaines [*Institute for Research on Contemporary Societies*] [*Research center*] [*France*]   (IRC)

IRESCO .... Instituto de Reforma de las Estructuras Comerciales [*Spain*]

IRESS....... Istituto Regionale Emiliano Romagnolo per il Servizio Sociale [*Italian*]   (SLS)

IRET......... Institut de Recherches en Ecologie Tropicale [*Institute for Research in Tropical Ecology*] [*Gabon*] [*Research center*]   (IRC)

IRETIJ ...... Institut de Recherches et d'Etudes pour le Traitement de l'Information Juridique [*Institute of Research and Study for the Treatment of Legal Information*] [*University of Montpellier*] [*Information service or system*]   (IID)

IRF............ Institut de Recherches Fruitieres

IRF............ Institutet foer Rymdfysik [*Swedish Institute of Space Physics*] [*Research center*] [*Sweden*]   (IRC)

IRF............ International Racquetball Federation   (EAIO)

IRF............ International Religious Fellowship   (EA)

IRF............ International Road Federation   (EECI)

IRFA......... Imprimerie Reliure Franco Africaine

IRFA......... Institut de Recherches sur les Fruits et Agrumes [*Fruit and Citrus Research Institute*] [*Research center*] [*French*]   (IRC)

IRFA......... Istituto di Ricerche e Formazione in Agricoltura [*Italian*]   (SLS)

IRFE.......... Ispettorato Generale per i Rapporti Finanziari con l'Estero [*General Inspectorate for Financial Relations with Foreign Countries*] [*Italian*]   (WER)

IRFED .... Institut International de Recherches et de Formation en Vue du Developpement Harmonise [*International Institute for Research and Training for Standardized Development*] [*French*]   (AF)

IRFIS........ Istituto Regionale per il Finanziamento alle Industrie in Sicilia [*Regional Institute for Financing Sicilian Industry*] [*Palermo, Italy*]   (GEA)

IRFKhB ..... Institute of Radiation and Physicochemical Biology (of the Academy of Sciences, USSR)   (RU)

IRFRH....... Institut de Recherche et de Formation aux Relations Humaines [*Institute for Research and Training in Human Relations*] [*Research center*] [*France*]   (IRC)

IRG .... Engineer Reconnaissance Group   (RU)

IRG .... Immigration Reform Group [*Australia*]

IRG .... Institut de Reescompte et de Garantie [*Development bank*] [*Belgium*]   (EY)

IRG .... Internationale des Resistants a la Guerre [*War Resisters International - WRI*] [*British*]   (EA)

IReR........... International Research Group on Wear of Engineering Materials   (PDAA)

IRG .... International Research Group on Wood Preservation [*Stockholm, Sweden*]   (EAIO)

IRG .... Intreprinderea Regionala de Constructii [*Regional Constructions Enterprise*]   (RO)

IRG .... Ipari Robbanoanyaggyar [*Industrial Explosives Factory*]   (HU)

IRG .... Lockhart Rivers [*Australia*] [*Airport symbol*]   (OAG)

IRGA .... Instituto Riograndense do Arroz [*Rio Grande Do Sul Rice Institute*] [*Brazil*]   (LA)

IRGC......... Islamic Revolution Guards Corps [*Iran*]

IRGCVD.... International Research Group on Colour Vision Deficiencies [*Ghent, Belgium*]   (EAIO)

IRGIREDMET ... Irkutsk Scientific Research Institute of Rare Metals   (RU)

IRGK .... Engineer Reserve of the High Command   (RU)
IRGM .... Institut de Recherches Geologiques et Minieres [*Institute for Geological and Mining Research*] [*Cameroon*] [*Research center*]   (IRC)
IRGRD ...... International Research Group on Refuse Disposal [*Later, ISWA*]
IRH .... Illawarra Regional Hospital [*Australia*]
IRH .... Instituto de Recursos Hidraylicos [*Ecuador*]   (DSCA)
IRH .... Service de l'Inventaire des Recherches Hydrauliques [*Alto Volta*]   (DSCA)
IRHE .... Instituto de Recursos Hidraulicos y Electrificacion [*Panama*]   (EY)
IRHO........ Institut de Recherches pour les Huiles et Oleagineux [*Research Institute for Oils and Oil Crops*] [*French*]   (AF)
IRHOHV ... Institut de Recherches pour les Huiles et Oleagineux - Haute Volta [*Research Institute for Oils and Oil Crops - Upper Volta Section*]   (ARC)
IRHT .... Institut de Recherche et d'Histoire des Textes [*Institute for the Study of Ancient Manuscripts*] [*Research center*] [*France*]   (IRC)
IRI............. Industrial Research Institute [*Research center*] [*Japan*]   (IRC)
IRI............. Industrial Research Institute [*Council for Scientific and Industrial Research*] [*Ghana*]
IRI............. Information Researchers, Inc. [*Information service or system*]   (IID)
IRI............. Institut des Relations Internationales [*Institute of International Relations*] [*Zaire*]   (AF)
IRI............. Institut fuer Rationalisterung und Informatik GmbH [*German*]   (ADPT)
IRI............. Instituto de Relacoes Internacionais [*Institute of International Relations*] [*Research center*] [*Brazil*]   (IRC)
IRI............. International Republican Institute   (ECON)
IRI............. Interuniversitair Reactor Instituut [*Interuniversity Reactor Institute*] [*Research center*] [*Netherlands*]   (IRC)
IRI............. Investment Research Institute [*China*]   (IRC)
IRI............. Iringa [*Tanzania*] [*Airport symbol*]   (OAG)
IRI............. Istituto per la Ricostruzione Industriale [*Industrial Reconstruction Institute*] [*Rome, Italy*]   (WER)
IRIA.......... Indian Rubber Industries Association   (PDAA)
IRIA.......... Institut de Recherche d'Informatique et d'Automatique [*French*] [*Research center*]
IRIA.......... Instituto Regional de Investigaciones del Algodon [*El Salvador*]   (DSCA)
IRIB.......... Islamic Republic of Iran Broadcasting [*Teheran*]   (MENA)
IRIC.......... Institut des Relations Internationales du Cameroun [*Cameroon Institute of International Relations*]
IRICASE... Institution de Retraite Interprofessionnelle des Cadres Superieurs d'Enterprises
IRICS........ Israel Research Institute of Contemporary Society
IRIDE .... Istituto per le Ricerche e le Iniziative Demografiche [*Italian*]   (SLS)
IRIIPP ...... Instituto de Relaciones Internacionales e Investigaciones para la Paz [*Institute of International Relations and Peace Research*] [*Guatemala*]   (EAIO)
IRIP .... Indonesian Resources and Information Programme [*Australia*]
IRIRC .... International Refugee Integration Resource Centre [*Later, CDR*]   (EAIO)
IRIS .... Immigration Record Information System [*Australia*]
IRIS .... Independent Research and Information Services Proprietary Ltd. [*Australia*]
IRIS .... Industrial Relations Information System [*Western Australia*]
IRIS .... Institut de Recherches de l'Industrie Sucriere [*France*]
IRIS .... International Relations Information System [*Forschungsinstitut fuer Internationale Politik und Sicherheit*] [*Germany*]   (IID)
IRIS .... Italian Research Interim Stage
IRISA .... Institut de Recherche en Informatique et Systemes Aleatoires [*Research Institute on Computing Science, Automatics, Robotics, and Statistics*] [*Research center*] [*French*]   (ERC)
IRISL........ Islamic Republic of Iran Shipping Lines [*Ministry of Commerce*] [*Teheran*]   (MENA)
IRITUN..... Instituto Regional de Investigaciones Tecnologicas de la Universidad del Norte [*Regional Institute for Technological Research of the University of the North*] [*Chile*]   (LA)
IRJ .... La Rioja [*Argentina*] [*Airport symbol*]   (OAG)
IRJC .... Institut de Recherches Juridiques Comparatives [*Centre National de la Recherche Scientifique*] [*French*]
IRK .... Institute of Kiswahili Research [*Tanzania*]   (IRC)
IRK .... Internationales Rotes Kreuz [*International Red Cross*] [*German*]
IRK .... Kirksville [*Missouri*] [*Airport symbol*]   (OAG)
IRK .... Kish Air [*Iran*] [*ICAO designator*]   (FAAC)
IRK .... Tool-Distributing Stock Room   (RU)
IRKAZ....... Irkutsk Aluminum Plant   (RU)
IRKTD....... Instruction for the Registration of Collective Labor Contracts   (BU)
IRL............ Independent Resources Ltd. [*Australia*]
IRL............ Indexed Repayment Loan

IRL............ Internationaler Ring fuer Landarbeit am Kauzenberg [*Germany*]   (DSCA)
IRL............ Ireland [*ANSI three-letter standard code*]   (CNC)
irl............. Irish   (RU)
Irl .... Irland [*Ireland*] [*German*]   (GCA)
irl .... Irlantilainen [*Irish*] [*Finland*]
IRLA.......... Institute for Research into Language and the Arts [*Human Sciences Research Council*] [*South Africa*]   (AA)
IRLA......... International Religious Liberty Association
irland......... Irish   (RU)
IRLCO-CSA ... International Red Locust Control Organization for Central and Southern Africa   (EAIO)
IRLCOSA ... International Red Locust Control Organisation for Central and Southern Africa
IRLCS........ International Red Locust Control Service
IRLI .... Institute of Russian Literature (of the Academy of Sciences, USSR)   (RU)
IRLOC ...... Illawarra Region Libraries Operations Centres [*Australia*]   (ADA)
IRM .... Industrial Workers of the World [*IWW*]   (RU)
IRM .... Institut de Recherches Marxistes [*Institute of Marxist Research*] [*France*]   (EAIO)
IRM .... Islamskaia Respublika Mauritaniia
IRMA .... Immissionsratenmessapparatur [*Immission Rate Measuring Apparatus*] [*Analytical chemistry*] [*German*]
IRMA .... Institut de Recherche les Medecines Alternatives [*Institute of Alternative Medicine Research*] [*France*]   (EAIO)
IRMA .... Intreprinderea de Reparat Material Aeronautic [*Enterprise for the Repair of Aeronautical Material*]   (RO)
IRMASA ... Industrial Rubber Manufacturers of South Africa   (AA)
IRMC........ Information Resource Management Unit [*Health Department*] [*New South Wales, Australia*]
IRME........ Intreprinderea pentru Rationalizarea si Modernizarea Instalatiilor Energetice [*Enterprise for the Rationalization and Modernization of Power Installations*]   (RO)
IRMO .... Institut za Razvoj i Medjunarodne Odnose [*Institute for Development and International Relations*] [*Canton and Enderbury Islands*]   (EAIO)
IRMOSAL ... Industria de Racoes e Moaqem de Sal SA [*Brazil*]   (DSCA)
IRMPC ...... Industrial Raw Materials Planning Committee [*NATO*]   (NATG)
IRMRA...... Indian Rubber Manufacturers Research Association   (SLS)
IRMS........ Institute of Rationalization of the Council of Ministers   (BU)
IRMS........ International Robert Musil Society [*See also SIRM*] [*Saarbrucken, Federal Republic of Germany*]   (EAIO)
IRN .... Import Release Note   (DS)
IRN .... Iran [*ANSI three-letter standard code*]   (CNC)
IRN .... Source of Regulated Voltage   (RU)
IRNA .... Iranian [*or Islamic Republic*] News Agency
IRNA .... Islamic Republic News Agency [*Teheran, Iran*]   (MENA)
IRNE .... Institutul de Reactori Nucleari Energetici [*Institute for Nuclear Power Reactors*]   (RO)
IRNR .... Instituto de Recursos Naturales Renovables [*Institute for Renewable Natural Resources*] [*Ecuador*]   (LA)
IRNRTR.... Instruction for Assignment and Job Placement of Labor Reserves   (BU)
IRNU .... Institut de Recherche des Nations Unies pour le Developpement Social Switzerland [*Switzerland*]   (DSCA)
IRO .... Institut de Recherches sur l'Onchocerose [*Institute for Research on Onchocerosis*]   (AF)
IRO .... Intensity of X-Ray Reflections   (RU)
IRO .... International Refugee Organization [*Later, UNHCR*]
IROC .... Illawarra Regional Organisation of Councils [*Australia*]
irod .... Irodalom [*Literature*]   (HU)
IROFA .... International Robotics and Factory Automation Center [*Japan*]
IRO-FIET ... Interamerican Regional Organization of the International Federation of Commercial, Clerical, Professional, and Technical Employees [*Willemstad, Netherlands Antilles*]   (EAIO)
Irokyo........ Nihon Iryo Rodohumiai Kyogikai [*Japanese Council of Medical Workers' Unions*]
IROM .... Industria Raffinazione Oli Minerali [*Italy*]   (PDAA)
iron............ Ironic   (RU)
iron............ Ironical   (TPFD)
iron............ Ironique [*French*]   (TPFD)
iron............ Ironisesti [*Ironically*] [*Finland*]
IROPCO..... Iranian Offshore Petroleum Company   (ME)
IROS .... Iranian Oil Services [*NIOC*]   (MENA)
IRP............ Indian Reform Party [*South Africa*]   (AF)
IRP............ Individual Jet Exhaust Nozzle   (RU)
IRP............ Institutional Revolutionary Party [*Mexico*] [*Political party*]
IRP............ International Education Workers [*1920-1939*]   (RU)
IRP............ International Rostrum of Young Performers [*See also TIJE*]   (EAIO)
IRP............ Isiro [*Zaire*] [*Airport symbol*]   (OAG)
IRP............ Islahat Refah Partisi [*Reformation and Welfare Party*] [*Turkish Cypriot*]   (PPE)

IRP............. Islamic Renaissance Party [*Commonwealth of Independent States*] (ECON)
IRP............. Islamic Republican Party [*Iran*] [*Political party*] (PPW)
IRP............. Italian Republican Party (RU)
IRP............. True Radio Bearing (RU)
IRPA.......... All-Union Scientific Research Institute of Radio Broadcasting, Reception, and Acoustics (RU)
IRPA.......... Instituto de la Reforma y Promocion Agrarias [*Agrarian Reform and Development Institute*] [*Peru*] (LA)
IRPA.......... International Radiation Protection Association [*Vienna, Austria*] (EAIO)
IRPA.......... Istituto Regionale di Psicopedagogia dell'Apprendimento [*Italian*] (SLS)
IRPEF....... Personal Income Tax [*Italian*] (IMH)
IRPEG....... Tax on Legal Entities [*Italian*] (IMH)
IRPEM...... Istituto di Ricerche sulla Pesca Marittima [*Marine Fisheries Research Institute*] [*Italy*] (IRC)
IRPEN....... Instituto Regional de Pesquisas de Recursos Naturais (LAA)
IRPET .... Istituto Regionale per la Programmazione Economica della Toscana [*Regional Institute for economic Planning of Tuscany*] [*Italian*] (SLS)
IRPF .... Independent Racing Pigeon Federation [*Australia*]
IRPGR .... Inspektorat Rejonowy Panstwowych Gospodarstw Rybackich [*District Inspectorate of State Fish Farms*] (POL)
IRPI .... Istituto di Ricerca per la Protezione Idrogeologica nell' Italia Meridionale ed Insulare [*Research Institute for Hydrogeological Protection in Southern Italy and the Islands*] [*Research center*] (ERC)
IRPM........ Impot sur le Revenue des Personnes Morales
IRPP .... Impot sur le Revenue des Personnes Physiques
IRPRI .... International Relations and Peace Research Institute [*Guatemala*] (EAIO)
IRPTC ...... International Register of Potentially Toxic Chemicals [*United Nations Environment Program*] [*Geneva, Switzerland*]
irpu............ Engineer Company for Preparation of Command Posts (BU)
IRPVRP..... Institution de Retraite et de Prevoyance des Voyageur Representant Placier [*France*] (FLAF)
IRQ .... Irak [*Iraq*] [*Poland*]
IRQ .... Iraq [*ANSI three-letter standard code*] (CNC)
irr .... Engineer Reconnaissance Company (RU)
IRR .... Institute for Research in Reproduction [*Bombay*]
IRR .... Institute of Race Relations [*British*] (EAIO)
IRR .... Interest Rates Revolt [*Australia*]
IRR .... International Rate of Return [*Finance*]
IRR .... Isreal Research Reactor (PDAA)
IRRA........ Industrial Relations Reform Act [*Australia*]
IRRC........ Investor Responsibility Research Center
IRRCS ...... Institutul Romanesc pentru Relatii Culturale cu Strainatatea [*Romanian Institute for Cultural Relations with Foreign Countries*] (RO)
IRRD .... International Road Research Documentation [*AUSINET database*] (ADA)
IRRDB...... International Rubber Research and Development Board [*Brickendonbury, Hertford, England*] (EAIO)
irreg.......... Irregular [*Irregular*] [*Portuguese*]
IRREP .... Institut de Retraites des Representants [*France*] (FLAF)
IRRI.......... Institut Royal des Relations Internationales [*Belgium*] (SLS)
IRRI.......... International Rice Research Institute [*Manila, Philippines*] [*Research center*] (IRC)
Irrig.......... Irrigation [*Irrigation*] [*Military map abbreviation World War I*] [*French*] (MTD)
IRRIPLAN ... Irrigaciones Planificadas Ltd. [*Colombia*] (DSCA)
IRRMA...... Institut Romand de Recherche Numerique en Physique des Materiaux
IRS............ Indian Register of Shipping (DS)
IRS............ Indian Remote-Sensing Satellite
IRS............ Indonesian Radiological Society (EAIO)
IRS............ Industrial Rehabilitation Service [*Australia*]
IRS............ Industrial Rubber Sales Ltd. [*Australia*] (ADA)
IRS............ Information and Research Services [*Council for Scientific and Industrial Research*] [*South Africa*] (AA)
IRS............ Information Retrieval Service [*European Space Agency*] (IID)
IRS............ Institut de Recherche Scientifique [*Scientific Research Institute*] [*Zaire*] [*Research center*] (AF)
IRS............ Institut de Recherches Sahariennes
IRS............ Institute of Religious Studies [*Australia*]
IRS............ Institut fuer Reaktorsicherheit der Technischen Ueberwachungs-Vereine, eV [*Nuclear energy*] (NRCH)
IRS............ Institutul Romanesc de Standarde [*Romanian Institute of Standards*] (RO)
IRS............ Instytut Rybactwa Srodladowego (Olsztyn) [*Institute of Inland Fisheries (Olsztyn)*] (POL)
IRS............ International Referral System [*United Nations Environment Programme*]
IRS............ International Rorschach Society [*Strasbourg, France*] (EA)
IRS............ Israel Rehabilitation Society (EAIO)
IRS............ Reactivity Index (RU)

IRSA......... Industrial Relations Society of Australia (ADA)
IRSA......... Istituto di Ricerca sulle Acque [*Water Research Institute*] [*Research center*] [*Italian*] (IRC)
IRSAC .... Institut pour la Recherche Scientifique en Afrique Centrale [*Institute for Scientific Research in Central Africa*] [*Zaire*] (AF)
IRSB .... Istituto per la Ricerca Sociale di Bergamo [*Italian*] (SLS)
IRSC .... Institut de Recherches Scientifiques au Congo
IRSCC .... International Relief Service of Caritas Catholica [*Belgium*] (EAIO)
IRSCL........ International Research Society for Children's Literature [*Cadaujac, France*] (EA)
IRSE .... Istituto Regionale di Studi Europei del Friuli-Venezia Giulia [*Italian*] (SLS)
IRSES....... Istituto Ricerche Sindacali Economiche Sociali [*Italian*] (SLS)
IRSES....... Istituto Ricerche Studi Economici e Sociali [*Italian*] (SLS)
IRSET........ Istituto Romano di Studi Economici e Tributari [*Italian*] (SLS)
IRSEV .... Istituto Regionale di Studi e Ricerche Economico-Sociali del Veneto [*Italian*] (SLS)
IRSFC....... International Rayon and Synthetic Fibres Committee [*See also CIRFS*] [*Paris, France*] (EAIO)
IRSG .... Internationale Richard Strauss Gesellschaft [*An association*] (EAIO)
IRSG .... International Rubber Study Group [*London, England*] (EAIO)
IRSH........ Institut de Recherche en Sciences Humaines [*Institute for Research in Human Sciences*] [*Niger*] (AF)
IRSI .... Istituto Ricerca Sicurezza Industriale [*Italian*] (SLS)
IRSIA .... Institut pour l'Encouragement de la Recherche Scientifique dans l'Industrie et l'Agriculture [*Institute for the Promotion of Scientific Research in Industry and Agriculture*] [*Belgium*] (WER)
IRSID .... Institut de Recherches de la Siderurgie [*Institute of Siderurgical Research*] [*French*] (WER)
IRSIS........ Istituto di Ricerche e Studi sull'Informazione per la Sardegna [*Italian*] (SLS)
IRSL .... Istituto di Ricerche e Studi Legislativi [*Italian*] (SLS)
IRSM........ Institut de Recherches Scientifiques de Madagascar
IRSM........ Institut de Recherches Scientifiques du Mali
IRSO......... International Rope Skipping Organization
IRSPME.... Institution de Retraite des Salaries des Petites et Moyennes Entreprises [*France*] (FLAF)
IRSS .... Infrared Search System [*Institut za Nuklearne Nauke Boris Kidric*] [*Former Yugoslavia*] [*Information service or system*] (CRD)
IRSTA .... Istituto di Ricerche sullo Stato e l'Amministrazione [*Italian*] (SLS)
Irstroypromsoyuz ... Irkutsk Special Producers' Union for the Manufacture of Building Materials (RU)
IRT............ Immigration Review Tribunal [*Australia*]
IRT............ Institut de Recherche des Transports [*Transportation Research Institute*] [*French*] (WER)
IRT............ Institut de Recherches Agronomiques Tropicales et des Cultures Vivrieres [*Institute of Tropical Agronomic Research and Food Crops*] [*Gabon*] (SLS)
IRT............ Institut de Recherches Technologiques [*Institute of Technological Research*] [*Gabon*] [*Research center*] (IRC)
IRT............ Instituto Nacional de Radio y Television [*National Radio and Television Institute*] [*Colombia*] (COL)
IRT............ Interot Air Service [*Germany*] [*ICAO designator*] (FAAC)
Irt............. Irtibat [*Liaison, Communication*] (TU)
IRTA........ Intreprinderile Regionale Transport Auto [*Regional Automotive Transportation Enterprises*] (RO)
IRTAC....... International Round Table for the Advancement of Counseling [*British*]
IRTCES..... International Research and Training Center on Erosion and Sedimentation [*China*] (EAIO)
IRTDA....... Indian Roads and Transport Development Association (PDAA)
IRTE........ Institute of Road Transport Engineers (EAIO)
IRTF......... Industry Restructuring Task Force
IRTF......... International Radio and Television Foundation, Inc. [*International Radio and Television Society*] (NTCM)
Irtf............ Irtifa [*Altitude*] (TU)
IRTIS........ Inter-Regional Training Information System [*International Labor Organization*] [*United Nations*] (DUND)
IRTO .... Institut de Recherches Scientifiques du Togo
IRTRA....... Instituto de Recreacion de los Trabajadores de Guatemala [*Guatemala*] (DSCA)
IRU .... Information Resources Unit [*CSIRO*] [*Australia*] [*Information service or system*] (IID)
IRU .... Institute de Recherche d'Urbanisme [*Urban Planning Research Institute*] [*France*] (PDAA)
IRU .... Internationale Raiffeisen-Union [*International Raiffeisen Union*] (EAIO)
IRU .... Internationale Rijnvaart Unie [*Benelux*] (BAS)
IRU .... International Raiffeisen Union (EA)
IRU .... International Road Transport Union [*Geneva, Switzerland*] (EAIO)

IRU .... International Romani Union (EAIO)
IRUC .... Intreprinderea de Reparatii Utilajelor de Calcul [*Enterprise for the Repair of Computer Equipment*] (RO)
IRUM .... Intreprinderea de Reparatii, Utilaje, si Montaj [*Enterprise for Repairs, Equipment, and Assembly*] (RO)
IRUSTAT ... Institut Rundi des Statistiques
irv .... Engineer Reconnaissance Platoon (RU)
IRV .... International Reference Version (OSI)
IRVM .... Impot sur le Revenu des Valeurs Mobilieres [*Tunisia*]
IRW .... International Rehabilitation Week [*Trade show*]
IRWEP ...... International Register for the White Eared Pheasant (EAIO)
IRYa .... Institute of Russian Language (of the Academy of Sciences, USSR) (RU)
IRYaZ .... Institute of Russian Language (of the Academy of Sciences, USSR)
IRYDA .... Instituto Nacional de Reforma y Desarrollo Agrario [*National Institute for Agrarian Reform and Development*] [*Spain*] (EY)
IRZ .... Institut de Recherches Zootechniques [*Institute of Animal Research*] [*Cameroon*] [*Research center*] (IRC)
IRZ .... Is Riski Zammi [*Labor Risk Premium*] (TU)
IS .... Artificial Satellite (RU)
IS .... Banque Indosuez [*France*]
IS .... Extraordinary Session (BU)
Is .... Iasi [*Iasi*] (RO)
IS .... Iceland [*ANSI two-letter standard code*] (CNC)
IS .... IDS Aircraft Ltd. [*British*] [*ICAO designator*] (ICDA)
IS .... Impot des Societes [*Benelux*] (BAS)
iS .... Im Sinne [*In the Meaning*] (EG)
IS .... Indische Staatsregeling [*Benelux*] (BAS)
IS .... Informacni Sluzba [*Information Service*] (CZ)
IS .... Ingenior-Sammenslutningen [*Denmark*]
IS .... Insake [*Regarding*] [*Afrikaans*]
IS .... Inspektorat za Sumarstvo [*Forestry Inspectorate*] (YU)
IS .... Institute of Slavic Studies (of the Academy of Sciences, USSR) (RU)
IS .... Institute of Speech (RU)
IS .... Institute of Statisticians [*British*]
IS .... Instituto de Soldadura [*Welding Institute*] [*Research center*] [*Portuguese*] (IRC)
IS .... Institut za Stocarstvo [*Livestock Institute*] [*Former Yugoslavia*] (ARC)
IS .... Instructie Schepen [*Benelux*] (BAS)
IS .... Instytut Sztuki [*Institute of Fine Arts*] [*Poland*]
IS .... Integrierter Schaltkreis [*GRM*] (ADPT)
IS .... Integrierte Schaltung [*German*] (ADPT)
IS .... Interdiction de Sejour [*France*] (FLAF)
IS .... Internationaler Suchdienst [*International Tracing Service*] (EAIO)
IS .... Internationale Schutzenunion [*International Shooting Union*] (EAIO)
IS .... International Socialists (ADA)
IS .... International Standard [*ISO*]
IS .... Internazionale Socialista [*Socialist International*] [*Italian*] (WER)
IS .... Interpretive System (RU)
IS .... Intreprindere de Stat [*State Enterprise*] (RO)
IS .... Isa'dan Sonra [*After Christ*] (TU)
Is .... Is Adresi [*Business Address*] (TU)
Is .... Isernia [*Car registration plates*] [*Italy*]
IS .... Iskrcne Stanice [*Unloading Stations*] [*Military*] (YU)
Is .... Islam (BJA)
IS .... Islandia [*Iceland*] [*Poland*]
Is .... Islands (SCAC)
is .... Islenmis [*Processed, Fabricated, Made Up*] (TU)
Is .... Israel [*IYRU nationality code*] (BJA)
IS .... Izvrsni Svet [*Executive Council*] (YU)
IS .... Pulse Counter (RU)
IS .... Quartermaster Service (RU)
IS .... Reset Pulse (RU)
IS .... Staatsblad van Indonesie [*Benelux*] (BAS)
Is .... Turkiye Is Bankasi [*Turkish Business Bank*]
ISA .... Association des Ecoles Internationales [*Switzerland*] (SLS)
ISA .... Associazione per Imola Storico-Artistica [*Italian*] (SLS)
ISA .... Iatrikos Syllogos Athinon [*Athens Medical Association*] (GC)
ISA .... Incest Survivors' Association [*Australia*]
ISA .... Independent Schools Association [*Australia*]
ISA .... Indian Society of Advertisers (EAIO)
ISA .... Indonesian Sawmill Association (DS)
ISA .... Industrie Siderurgiche Associate [*Associated Iron and Steel Industries*] [*Italy*] (EY)
ISA .... Ingenieros Sanitarios Asociados Ltda. [*Colombia*] (COL)
ISA .... Ingenieursvereniging van Suid-Afrika [*South Africa*] (AA)
ISa .... In Sachsen [*In Saxony*] [*German*]
ISA .... Institut de Selection Animale [*Institute of Animal Selection*] [*France*]

ISA .... Institute for Sustainable Agriculture [*Australia*]
ISA .... Institution of Surveyors, Australia (ADA)
ISA .... Instituto de Investigaciones de Arquitectura y Sistemas Ambientales [*Research Institute in Architecture and Environmental Systems*] [*Venezuela*] (IRC)
ISA .... Instituto Social Agrario [*Argentina*] (DSCA)
ISA .... Instituto Superior de Agricultura [*Dominican Republic*]
ISA .... Institut Superieur des Affaires [*Chamber de Commerce et d'Industrie de Paris*] (ECON)
ISA .... Institut Superieur des Arts Plastiques
ISA .... Insurance Surveyors Association [*South Africa*] (EAIO)
ISA .... Interconexion Electrica SA [*Colombian Electrical Grid Interconnection Agency*] [*Colombia*] (COL)
ISA .... Internal Security Act [*Singapore*]
ISA .... International Schools Association [*Geneva, Switzerland*] (EA)
ISA .... International Seaweed Association [*Norway*] (SLS)
ISA .... International Security Affairs
ISA .... International Service Association
ISA .... International Shakespeare Association (EA)
ISA .... International Shipping Agency Ltd. [*Kuwait*]
ISA .... International Soling Association [*Bordon, Hampshire, England*] (EAIO)
ISA .... International Songwriters' Association (EAIO)
ISA .... International Strabismological Association (EAIO)
ISA .... International Students Association
ISA .... International Studies Association
ISA .... International Subscription Agencies Pty. Ltd. [*Australia*]
ISA .... International Sugar Agreement [*1958*]
ISA .... International Surfing Association [*Swansea, England*] (EAIO)
ISA .... Iron and Steel Authority [*Philippines*] (DS)
ISA .... Israel Sheepbreeders' Association (EAIO)
ISA .... Israel Society of Allergology (EAIO)
ISA .... Israel Society of Anesthesiologists (SLS)
ISA .... Israel Space Agency [*Israel*]
ISA .... Istituto Sperimentale Agronomico [*Agronomy Experimental Institute*] [*Italian*] (ARC)
ISA .... Italian Society of Anatomy (EAIO)
ISA .... Mount Isa [*Australia*] [*Airport symbol*] (OAG)
ISA .... UNRWA [*United Nations Relief and Works Agency*] International Staff Association (EAIO)
ISAA .... Institute of South African Architects (AA)
ISAA .... Instituut van Suid-Afrikaanse Argitekte [*Die*] [*Institute of South African Arch itects*]
ISAA .... Intreprinderile de Stat pentru Gospodarirea Apelor din Agricultura [*State Enterprises for Water Management in Agriculture*] (RO)
ISAA .... Israel Society of Aeronautics and Astronautics (SLS)
ISAAA .... International Service for the Acquisition of Agri-Biotech Applications
ISAAC .... International Society for Alternative and Augmentative Communication (EA)
ISABA .... Instituto Solar Arquitectura Buenos Aires [*Solar Architecture Institute of Buenos Aires*] [*Argentina*] (WED)
ISABC .... International Society Against Breast Cancer (EAIO)
ISABR .... International Society for Animal Blood Group Research [*Australia*] (EAIO)
ISABR .... International Society for Animal Genetics [*Australia*] (EAIO)
ISABU .... Institut des Sciences Agronomiques du Burundi [*Institute of Agronomic Studies of Burundi*] [*Bujumbura*] (AF)
ISAC .... Industrial Sector Adjustment Credit [*Ministry of Industries, Science, and Technology*] [*Ghana*]
ISAC .... Information Systems Advisory Committee
ISAC .... International Society for Analytical Cytology (EAIO)
ISAC .... ISRO [*Indian Space Research Organization*] Satellite Centre [*Research center*] (ERC)
ISAC .... Istituto di Studi delle Antichita Classiche [*Italian*] (SLS)
ISACC ...... Instituto de Suelos, Academia de Ciencias de Cuba [*Soils Institute*] [*Cuba*] (ARC)
ISAC-EEO ... Interdepartmental Standing Advisory Committee on Equal Employment Opportunities [*New Zealand*]
ISACMETU ... International Secretariat of Arts, Communications Media, and Entertainment Trade Unions (EAIO)
ISADA ...... Industries et Savonneries du Dahomey
ISAE .... [*The*] Indian Society of Agricultural Economics (SLS)
ISAE .... Internacia Scienca Asocio Esperantista [*International Association of Esperanto-Speaking Scientists*] [*Oslo, Norway*] (EA)
ISAE .... Italian Society of Anthropology and Ethnology (EAIO)
ISAeM ...... International Society for Aerosols in Medicine [*See also IGAeM*] (EAIO)
ISAF .... Intreprinderea de Semnalizari si Automatizari Feroviare [*Enterprise for Railways Signals and Automation*] (RO)
ISAI .... Immeubles sans Affectation Individuelle [*France*] (FLAF)
ISAIV .... Integriertes System der Automatisierten Informationsverarbeitung [*Integrated System of Automated Information Processing*] (EG)
ISAL .... Icelandic Aluminum Co. (IMH)
ISAL .... Istituto per la Storia dell'Arte Lombarda [*Italian*] (SLS)

ISAL-Bolivia ... Iglesia y Sociedad para America Latina - Seccion Boliviana [*Church and Society for Latin America - Bolivian Section*] (LA)

ISAM........ International Society for Aerosols in Medicine (EAIO)

ISAMEPS ... Istituto di Scienze Amministrative e di Promozione Sociale [*Italian*] (SLS)

ISAO......... Istituto Superiore Internazionale per gli Studi Sociali Amministrativi e dell'Organizzazione [*Italian*] (SLS)

ISAP .... Ilektriki Sidirodromi Athinon-Pireos [*Athens-Piraeus Electric Railways*] [*Greece*] (EY)

ISAP .... Ilektrikoi Sidirodromoi Athinon-Peiraias Anonymos Etaireia [*Athens-Piraeus Electric Railways*] (GC)

ISAP .... Instituto Sudamericano de Petroleo [*South American Petroleum Institute*] (LA)

ISAP .... Instituto Superior de Administracion Publica [*Advanced Institute for Public Administration*] [*Bolivia*] (LA)

ISAP .... Instituto Superior de Capacitacion Azucarera [*Higher Institute for Sugar Technology Training*] [*Cuba*] (LA)

ISAP .... Institut Superieur des Arts Plastiques

ISAP .... International Society of Art and Psychopathology [*Paris, France*] (EA)

isapb........ Engineer Battalion (RU)

isapp........ Engineer Regiment (RU)

isapr .... Engineer Company (RU)

isapv......... Engineer Platoon (RU)

ISAPVS ..... Intreprinderea de Stat pentru Asigurarea Producerii si Valorificarii Semintelor [*State Enterprise to Ensure the Production and Utilization of Seeds*] (RO)

ISAR......... Institut des Sciences Agronomiques du Rwanda [*Institute of Agronomic Sciences of Rwanda*] (AF)

ISAR......... Instituto Superior de Agronomia Regional [*Argentina*] (DSCA)

ISART .... Institutul de Studii, Cercetari, si Proiectari pentru Sistematizare, Arhitectura, si Tipizare [*Studies, Research, and Design Institute for Systematization, Architecture, and Standardization*] (RO)

ISAS .... Industrial Sales and Service Ltd. [*Queensland, Australia*] (ADA)

ISAS .... Institute of Space and Aeronautical Science [*Under Tokyo University*]

ISAS .... Institut fuer Spektrochemie und Angewandte Spektroskopie [*Institute for Spectrochemistry and Applied Spectroscopy*] [*Research center*] (IRC)

ISAS .... Istituto di Scienze Amministrative e Socio-Economiche [*Italian*] (SLS)

ISAT .... International Society of Analytical Trilogy [*See also SITA*] [*Sao Paulo, Brazil*] (EAIO)

ISATA .... Israel-South Africa Trade Association

IS Aust....... Institution of Surveyors, Australia (ADA)

ISAVVT..... International Symposium on the Aerodynamics and Ventilation of Vehicle Tunnels (PDAA)

isb.............. Combat Engineer Battalion (BU)

ISB............. Engineer Battalion (RU)

isb.............. Engineer Construction Battalion (RU)

ISB............. Information Services Branch [*SHAPE Technical Center*] [*The Hague, Netherlands*]

ISB............ Institute for Small Business [*University of the Western Cape*] [*South Africa*] (AA)

ISB............. Institut Sumarstva - Beograd [*Belgrade Forestry Institute*] (YU)

ISB............. Internationaler Studentenbund [*International Union of Students, IUS*] (EG)

ISB............. International Society of Biometeorology [*See also SIB*] [*Zurich, Switzerland*] (EAIO)

ISB............. International Society of Biorheology [*Germany*] (EAIO)

ISB............. Intreprinderea de Salubritate Bucuresti [*Bucharest Sanitation Enterprise*] (RO)

ISB............. Islamabad/Rawalpindi [*Pakistan*] [*Airport symbol*] (OAG)

ISB............. Istituto per la Storia di Bologna [*Italian*] (SLS)

ISBA .... International Seabed Area (MSC)

ISBA .... International Seabed Authority [*Proposed*] [*UNCLOS*] (ASF)

ISBC .... Intreprinderile de Statiuni Balneo-Climaterice [*Health Spa Enterprises*] (RO)

ISBD......... International Standard Bibliographic Description (ADA)

ISBD(CP).. International Standard Bibliographic Description (Component Parts)

ISBD (G).... International Standard Bibliographic Description (General) (ADA)

ISBD(M) ... International Standard Bibliographic Description (Monographs) (ADA)

ISBD(NBM) ... International Standard Bibliographic Description (Nonbook Materials) (ADA)

ISBD(S)..... International Standard Bibliographic Description (Serials) (ADA)

ISBI .... International Savings Banks Institute [*See also IICE*] [*Geneva, Switzerland*]

ISBI .... International Society for Burn Injuries (EAIO)

ISBN......... Internasionale Standaard-Boeknommer [*International Standard Book Number*] [*Afrikaans*]

ISBN......... International Standard Book Number

ISBO.......... Instituto de Sociologia Boliviana [*Institute of Bolivian Sociology*] (IRC)

ISBO.......... Islamic States Broadcasting Organization [*Jeddah, Saudi Arabia*] (EAIO)

isbr .... Combat Engineer Brigade (BU)

ISBr .... Engineer Brigade (RU)

ISBRA .... International Society Biomedical Research on Alcoholism (EAIO)

ISC............. Independent Schools Council [*South Africa*] (AA)

ISC............. Industrial Services Centre [*Nepal*]

ISC............. Infrastructure Special Committee [*NATO*] (NATG)

ISC............. Instituto de Solos e Cultura [*Brazil*] (DSCA)

ISC............. Institut Scientifique Cherifien [*Morocco*]

ISC............. Insurance and Superannuation Commission [*Australia*]

ISC............. Inter-American Society of Cardiology [*Mexico City, Mexico*] (EAIO)

ISC............. International Seismological Centre [*ICSU*] [*Newbury, Berkshire, England*] (EAIO)

ISC............. International Sericultural Commission [*See also CSI*] [*La Mulatiere, France*] (EAIO)

ISC............. International Society of Cardiology [*Later, ISFC*]

ISC............. International Society of Chemotherapy [*Bad Heilbrunn, Federal Republic of Germany*] (EAIO)

ISC............. International Society of Copoclephologists [*British*] (EAIO)

ISC............. International Society of Cryosurgery [*Turin, Italy*] (EAIO)

ISC............. International Study Center [*State Council*] [*China*]

ISC............. International Sugar Council [*London*] [*Later, ISO*]

ISC............. Inter-State Commission [*Australia*]

ISC............. Investment Service Center [*Thailand*] (IMH)

ISC............. Israeli Shippers Council (DS)

ISC............. Israel Society of Criminology (EAIO)

ISC............. Istituto di Studi Corporativi [*Italian*] (SLS)

ISC............. Italian Shippers Council (DS)

ISCA .... Indian Science Congress Association (SLS)

ISCA .... Instituto Superior de Ciencias Agropecuarias [*Higher Institute of Agricultural and Animal Sciences*] [*Cuba*] (LA)

ISCA .... International Sailing Craft Association [*Exeter, Devonshire, England*] (EAIO)

ISCA .... Istituto per lo Studio e le Diffusione del Cinema d'Animazione [*Italian*] (SLS)

ISCAB .... Instituto Superior de Ciencias Agropecuarias de Bayamo [*Bayamo Higher Institute of Agricultural-Livestock Sciences*] [*Cuba*] (LA)

ISCAE .... Institut Superieur de Commerce et Administration des Entreprises a Casablanca [*Morocco*]

ISCAH....... Instituto Superior de Ciencias Agropecuarias de La Habana [*Higher Institute of Agricultural and Animal Sciences of Havana*] [*Cuba*] (LA)

ISCAM ...... Institut Superieur des Cadres Militaires [*Higher Institute for Military Cadres*] [*Burundi*] (AF)

ISCAS....... Institutul Central de Studii, Cercetari Stiintifice, si Proiectari in Constructii, Arhitectura, si Sistematizare [*Central Institute for Studies, Scientific Research, and Design in Constructions, Architecture, and Systematization*] (RO)

ISCAS....... Institutul de Studii si Proiectare pentru Constructii, Arhitectura, si Sistematizare [*Studies and Design Institute for Constructions, Architecture, and Systematization*] (RO)

ISCAY .... International Solidarity Committee with Algerian Youth

ISCB .... International Society for Cell Biology [*Later, IFCB*] (ASF)

ISCB .... International Society for Classical Bibliography [*Paris, France*] (EAIO)

ISCC .... International Somali Cat Club

ISCC .... International Standard Commodity Classification of All Goods and Services

ISCC .... International Supervisory and Control Commission (CL)

ISCC .... International System and Control Corporation

ISCD .... International Society for Community Development

ISCE .... Instituto Salvadoreno de Comercio Exterior [*Salvadoran Foreign Trade Institute*] (LA)

ISCE .... International Society for Clinical Enzymology [*Hanover, Federal Republic of Germany*] (EAIO)

ISCE .... Intreprinderile de Stat pentru Comertul Exterior [*State Enterprises for Foreign Trade*] (RO)

ISCED .... International Society of Continuing Education in Dentistry [*See also SIECD*] [*Brussels, Belgium*] (EAIO)

ISCED .... International Standard Classification of Education

ISCEI........ Institutul pentru Studierea Conjuncturii Economice Internationale [*Institute for the Study of the International Economic Situation*] (RO)

ISCF .... Inter-School Christian Fellowship [*Australia*]

ISCF .... Istituto Sperimentale per le Colture Foraggere [*Fodder Crops Experimental Research Institute*] [*Italian*] (ARC)

ISCFD .... Instituto Superior de Cultura Fisica y Deportes [*Higher Institute for Physical Education and Sports*] [*Cuba*] (LA)

ISCH......... Institutul de Studii si Cercetari Hidrotehnice [*Institute for Hydrotechnical Studies and Research*] (RO)

ISCI .... Istituto Sperimentale per le Colture Industriali [*Industrial Crops Experimental Institute*] [*Italian*] (ARC)

ISCIF .... Institutul de Studii si Cercetari pentru Imbunatatiri Funciare [*Studies and Research Institute for Land Improvement*] (RO)

ISCIFGA ... Institutul de Studii si Cercetari pentru Imbunatatiri Funciare si Gospodarirea Apelor [*Studies and Research Institute for Land Improvement and Water Management*] (RO)

ISCIP .... Intreprindere de Stat pentru Cresterea si Ingrasarea Porcilor [*State Enterprise for the Raising and Fattening of Hogs*] (RO)

ISCIR .... Inspectoratul de Stat pentru Cazane si Instalatii de Ridicat [*State Inspectorate for Pressure Vessels and Hoisting Installations*] (RO)

ISCJ .... International Ski Club of Journalists (EAIO)

ISCM .... Instituto Superior de Ciencias Medicas [*Higher Institute of Medical Sciences*] [*Cuba*] (LA)

ISCM .... International Society for Contemporary Music (ADA)

ISCM .... International Society of Cybernetic Medicine [*Italian*] (SLS)

ISCM .... Intreprinderea de Stat pentru Materiale de Constructii [*State Enterprise for Construction Materials*] (RO)

ISCN .... International System for Human Cytogenetic Nomenclature

ISCO .... International Society of Corvette Owners

ISCO .... International Standard Classification of Occupations (WDAA)

ISCO .... Istituto Nazionale per lo Studio della Congiuntura [*Data Resources, Inc.*] [*Database*]

ISCO .... Istituto per la Congiuntura [*Institute for the Study of Economic Trends*] [*Italian*] (WER)

ISCOM ...... Istituto per gli Studi e la Documentazione sul Commercio e sul Turismo [*Italian*] (SLS)

ISCOR ...... South African Iron and Steel Corporation (AF)

ISCOS .... Inter-Governmental Standing Committee on Shipping (AF)

ISCOTT .... Iron and Steel Company of Trinidad and Tobago (LA)

ISCP .... Institutul de Studii si Cercetari Pedologice [*Pedological Studies and Research Institute*] (RO)

ISCPA .... Institutul de Studii, Cercetari, si Proiectari pentru Constructii si pentru Organizarea Productiei Agricole [*Studies, Research, and Design Institute for Constructions and for the Organization of Agricultural Production*] (RO)

ISCPCH .... Institutul de Studii, Cercetari, si Proiectari pentru Constructii Hortiviticole [*Studies, Research, and Design Institute for Horticultural and Viticultural Constructions*] (RO)

ISCPCZ ..... Institutul de Studii, Cercetari, si Proiectari pentru Constructii Zootehnice [*Studies, Research, and Design Institute for Zootechnical Constructions*] (RO)

ISCPGA ..... Institutul de Studii, Cercetari, si Proiectari pentru Gospodarirea Apelor [*Studies, Research, and Design Institute for Water Management*] (RO)

ISCPP .... International Society of Crime Prevention Practitioners (EAIO)

ISCPVS ..... Istituto Sindacale per la Cooperazione con i Paesi in Via di Sviluppo [*Trade Union Institute for Cooperation with Developing Countries*] [*Italy*] (EAIO)

ISCR .... Institut Superieur de Culture Religieuse

iscr. .... Iscrizione [*Inscription*] [*Publishing*] [*Italian*]

ISCRT .... Institut Superieur de Cinema, Radio, et Television [*Television and video school*] [*French*]

ISCS .... International Symposium on Cooling Systems (PDAA)

ISCSP .... Instituto Superior de Ciencias Sociais e Politicas [*Institute of Higher Social and Political Studies*] [*Portuguese*] (WER)

ISCSPU ..... Instituto Superior de Ciencias Sociais e Politicas Ultramarina

ISCSS .... Illawarra & South Coast Steam Ship Co. [*Australia*]

ISCT .... Institute of Science Technology (PDAA)

ISCTI .... Insitut Syndical de Cooperation Technique Internationale

ISCTP .... International Study Commission for Traffic Police (SLS)

ISCTR .... International Scientific Committee for Trypanosomiasis Research

ISD .... Innovative Software Design [*South Africa*] [*ICAO designator*] (FAAC)

ISD .... Institute for Social Development [*University of the Western Cape*] [*South Africa*] (AA)

ISD .... Institute of the Building Industry (RU)

ISD .... Internal Security Department [*Singapore*] (ML)

ISD .... Internal Security Division [*Bahamas*] (LA)

ISD .... International Subscriber Dialling (ADA)

ISD .... Investors Services and Discounts (Australia) Proprietary Ltd.

ISDA .... International Sculpteurs et Designers Associes [*Paris, France*] (EAIO)

ISDA .... International Swap Dealers' Association

ISDA .... International Swaps and Derivatives Association (ECON)

ISDAIC ..... International Staff Disaster Assistance Information Coordinator [*NATO*] (NATG)

ISDB .... International Society of Development Biologists [*Formerly, IIE*] [*Nogent-Sur-Marne, France*]

IsDB .... Islamic Development Bank [*Arab-African*]

ISDC .... Industrial Studies and Development Centre [*Saudi Arabia*]

ISDE .... International Seismic Data Exchange [*Geology*]

ISDE .... International Society for Diseases of the Esophagus [*Tokyo, Japan*] (EAIO)

ISDE .... Izquierda Social Democrata Espanola [*Spanish Social Democratic Left*] (WER)

ISDEE .... Istituto di Studi e Documentazione sull'Est Europeo [*Italian*] (SLS)

ISDEMIR ... Iskenderun Demir-Celik Isletmeleri Muessese [*Iskenderun Iron and Steel Works Enterprise*] (TU)

ISDGM ...... Istituto per lo Studio della Dinamica delle Grandi Masse [*Institute for the Study of the Dynamics of Large Masses*] [*Research center*] [*Italy*] (EAS)

ISDI .... International Society of Dietetic Including All Infant and Young Children Food Industries (EAIO)

ISDI .... International Special Dietary Foods Industries [*France*] (EAIO)

ISDM .... International Society for Disaster Medicine (EA)

ISDN .... Integrated Services Digital Network [*Australia*]

ISDN .... International Society for Developmental Neuroscience (EA)

ISDO .... International Staff Duty Officer [*NATO*] (NATG)

ISDP .... Italian Social Democratic Party (RU)

ISDPG ...... Independent Social Democratic Party of Germany [*Political party*] (EAIO)

ISDR .... Institut Superieur du l'Developpment Rural [*Higher Institute for Rural Development*] [*Zaire*] (PDAA)

ISDRE .... Istituto per la Documentazione e gli Studi Regionali [*Italian*] (SLS)

ISDS .... International Serials Data System [*Database*] (EA)

ISDS .... International Sheep Dog Society [*Bedford, England*] (EAIO)

ISDS/IC .... International Center of the International Serials Data System [*UNESCO*] (PDAA)

ISDT .... International Symposium on Dredging Technology (PDAA)

ISDU .... International Standard Density Unit (DGA)

ISE .... Fraunhofer-Institut fuer Solare Energiesysteme [*Fraunhofer Institute for Solar Energy Systems*] [*Germany*] (WED)

ISE .... India Society of Engineers (PDAA)

ISE .... Institute of Information Sciences and Electronics [*University of Tsukuba*] [*Research center*] [*Japan*] (ERC)

ISE .... Institution of Structural Engineers [*British*] (EAIO)

ISE .... Instituto de Seguros del Estado [*Chile*] (EY)

ISE .... Instituto de Superacion Educacional [*Educational Advancement Institute*] [*Cuba*] (LA)

ISE .... Institutos Superiores de Educacion [*Higher Institutes of Education*] [*Spanish*]

ISE .... International Society of Electrochemistry [*Graz, Austria*] (EA)

ISE .... International Society of Endocrinology (EA)

ISE .... International Software Enterprise (ADPT)

ISE .... International Stock Exchange

ISE .... Italian Society of Ecology (EAIO)

ISEA .... Institut de Science Economique Appliquee [*French*]

ISEA .... Institut Superieur d'Etudes Agronomiques [*Higher Institute of Agronomic Studies*] [*Zaire*] (AF)

ISEA .... Istituto per lo Sviluppo Economico dell'Appennino Centro-Settentrionale [*Italian*] (SLS)

ISEAAN .... Institut de Science Economique Appliquee. Centre d'Afrique du Nord [*North African*]

ISEANSW ... Institute of Senior Educational Administrators of New South Wales [*Australia*]

ISEAS .... Institute of Southeast Asian Studies [*Singapore*] [*Research center*] (IRC)

ISEB .... Instituto Superior de Estudos Brasileiros [*Advanced Institute of Brazilian Studies*] (LA)

ISEC .... Iran Solar Energy Company (ME)

ISECAAN ... Institut des Sciences Economiques et Commerciales Appliquees a l'Afrique Noire

ISECS .... International Society for Eighteenth-Century Studies [*See also SIEDS*] [*Oxford, England*] (EAIO)

ISEDET ..... Instituto Superior Evangelico de Estudios Teologicos [*Superior Evangelical Institute and Theological School*] [*Argentina*]

ISEE .... International Society for Engineering Education [*Austria*] (EAIO)

ISEF .... Institut fur Sozio-Okonomische Entwicklungsforschung [*Institute of Socioeconomic Development Research*] [*Austria*] (IRC)

ISEI .... Jyoti Solar Energy Institute [*BVM Engineering College, Vallabh Vidyanagar*] [*India*] (WED)

ISEK .... International Society of Electrophysiological Kinesiology [*Montreal, PQ*] (EA)

ISEL .... Institute of Shipping Economics and Logistics [*See also ISL*] [*Bremen, Federal Republic of Germany*] (EAIO)

ISEM .... International Society for Ecological Modelling [*Vaerloese, Denmark*] (EAIO)

ISEM .... Intreprinderile de Servicii Edilitare si Montaj [*Municipal Services and Installations Enterprises*] (RO)

ISEN .... Institut Superieur d'Electronique du Nord, Laboratoires [*Higher Electronics Institute of the North, Laboratories*] [*Research center*] [*French*] (ERC)

ISEN .... Instituut vir Sosiale en Ekonomiese Navorsing [*Institute for Social and Economic Research*] [*University of the Orange Free State*] [*South Africa*] (AA)

ISENCY .... Industrie Senegalaise du Cycle
ISEP .... Instituto Superior de Estudios Policiales [*Higher Institute for Police Studies*] [*Costa Rica*]   (LA)
ISEP .... Institutul de Stiinte Economice si Planificare [*Institute for Economic Sciences and Planning*]   (RO)
ISEP .... International Society of Esperantist-Philologists [*See also IUEFI*]   (EAIO)
ISEP .... International Standard Equipment Practice   (ADPT)
ISEPS .... Institut Superieur d'Education Physique et Sportive [*Congo*]   (SLS)
ISER .... Institute of Social and Economic Research [*Barbados*] [*Research center*]   (IRC)
ISER .... Institute of Social and Economic Research [*South Africa*] [*Research center*]   (IRC)
ISER .... Institute of Social and Economic Research [*Trinidad and Tobago*]   (IRC)
ISER .... Instituto Superior de Educacion Rural [*Pamplona*]   (COL)
ISER .... Instituto Superior de Ensino Rural [*Brazil*]   (DSCA)
ISERI .... Institut Superieur d'Etude et de Recherche Islamiques [*Superior Institute of Islamic Research and Studies*] [*Mauritania*]   (IRC)
ISERP .... Istituto di Studi e Ricerche sulla Pubblicita [*Italian*]   (SLS)
ISERST ..... Institut Superieur d'Etudes et de Recherches Scientifiques et Techniques [*Advanced Institute for Scientific and Technical Research and Study*] [*Djibouti*]   (AF)
ISES .... International Ship Electric Service Association [*British*]   (EAIO)
ISES .... International Solar Energy Society [*Australia*]   (EAIO)
ISESANZ Section ... International Solar Energy Society, Australian and New Zealand Section   (SLS)
ISESCO ..... Islamic Educational, Scientific, and Cultural Organization [*United Nations*]
ISESP .... Istituto Superiore Europeo di Studi Politici [*Italian*]   (SLS)
ISET .... Institut fuer Sozio-Oekonomische Entwicklungsforschung und Technikbewertung [*Institute of Socioeconomic Development and Technology Assessment*] [*Research center*] [*Austria*]   (IRC)
ISETC .... International Society for Environmental Toxicology and Cancer   (EAIO)
ISETI .... Institut Superieur de l'Etat de Traducteurs et Interpretes [*State Higher Institute of Translators and Interpreters*] [*Belgium*]
ISETU .... International Secretariat of Entertainment Trade Unions [*Geneva, Switzerland*]
ISF .... Internationale Schulsport Foderation [*International School Sport Federation*]   (EAIO)
ISF .... International School Sport Federation   (EAIO)
ISF .... International Science Foundation [*ICSU*]
ISF .... International Shipping Federation [*British*]   (EAIO)
ISF .... International Society for Fat Research [*Sweden*]   (SLS)
ISF .... International Softball Federation   (OLYM)
ISF .... International Spiritualist Federation [*British*]
ISF .... Istituto di Studi Friulani [*Italian*]   (SLS)
ISFA .... International Scientific Film Association [*ICSU*]
ISFC .... International Short Film Conference   (EAIO)
ISFC .... International Society and Federation of Cardiology [*International Cardiology Federation and International Society of Cardiology - ISC*] [*Formed by a merger of*]   (EAIO)
ISFI .... Institute of Students and Faculty on Israel
ISFIS .... Selective Fisheries Information Service   (IID)
ISFL .... International Society of Family Law [*Cambridge, England*]   (EAIO)
ISFNR .... International Society for Folk-Narrative Research [*Turku, Finland*]   (EA)
ISFP .... Institut Superieur de Formation Pedagogique
ISFR .... International Society for Fluoride Research
ISG .... Innsbrucker Sprachwissenschaftliche Gesellschaft [*Austria*]   (SLS)
ISG .... Institut fuer Sozialforschung und Gesellschaftspolitik [*Institute for Social Research and Social Policy*] [*Research center*]   (IRC)
ISG .... Integrated Survey Grid
ISG .... Internationale Heinrich Schuetz Gesellschaft eV   (SLS)
ISG .... International SYSOP [*System Operator*] Guild
ISG .... Ishigaki [*Japan*] [*Airport symbol*]   (OAG)
ISGD .... International Study Group of Diabetes in Children and Adolescents [*Linkoping, Sweden*]   (EAIO)
ISGE .... Institut Superieur de Gestion des Entreprises [*Higher Business Management Institute*] [*Tunisia*]   (AF)
ISGE .... International Society for Group Activity in Education   (SLS)
ISGEA .... Istituto di Studi Giurdici Economici, e dell'Ambiente [*Italian*]   (SLS)
ISGI .... International Service of Geomagnetic Indices [*Research center*] [*Netherlands*]   (IRC)
ISGO .... International Society of Geographic Ophthalmology [*Montreal, PQ*]   (EAIO)
ISGO .... Istituto di Studi per la Gestione e l'Organizzazione [*Italian*]   (SLS)

ISGP .... International Society of General Practice [*Germany*]   (PDAA)
ISGP .... International Society of Geographical Pathology [*Australia*]   (EY)
ISGPB .... Indian Society of Genetics and Plant Breeding   (DSCA)
ISGR .... Inzinierske Stavitelstvo, Generalne Riaditelstvo [*Engineering Construction, General Directorate*]   (CZ)
ISGRA ...... International Study Group on Risk Analysis
ISGRe .... Istituto di Studi Giurdici Regionali [*Italian*]   (SLS)
ISGSH ...... International Study Group for Steroid Hormones [*Rome, Italy*]   (EAIO)
ISH .... Institut fuer Seefischerei [*Institute for Marine Fisheries*]   (ASF)
ISH .... Institut fuer Strahlenhygiene [*Institute for Radiation Hygiene*] [*Bundesgesundheitsamt*] [*Research center*] [*Germany*]   (WND)
ISH .... Integrated Securities House [*Taiwan*] [*Commercial firm*]
ISH .... International Society of Hematology [*Argentina*]   (SLS)
ISh .... Measuring Disk   (RU)
ISHA .... Israel Secular Humanist Association   (EAIO)
ISHAKS .... Instituti Shteteror i Arkave te Kursimit dhe i Sigurimeve [*Albanian*]
ISHAM ..... Internationale Gesellschaft fuer Human- und Veterinaermedizinische Mykologie [*International society for Human and Animal Mycology*] [*Switzerland*]   (SLS)
ISHAM ..... International Society for Human and Animal Mycology [*London School of Hygiene and Tropical Medicine*] [*British*]
ISHASH .... Lidhja e Shkrimtareve dhe Artisteve te Shqiperise [*Union of Writers and Artists of Albania*]   (EAIO)
ISHIBRAS ... Ishikawajima do Brasil Estaleiros SA [*Ishikawajima Shipyards of Brazil, Inc.*]   (LA)
Ishimbayneft' ... Ishimbay Petroleum Industry Trust   (RU)
IShK .... Outgoing Cord Assembly   (RU)
ISHL .... International Society for Historical Linguistics   (EAIO)
ISHLT .... International Society for Heart and Lung Transplantation   (EAIO)
ISHM .... Institut des Sciences Humaines du Mali
ISHP .... Instituti Shteteror i Projektimeve [*Albanian*]
ISHPES ..... International Society for the History of Physical Education and Sport [*Belgium*]   (EAIO)
ISHR .... International Society for Heart Research [*Winnipeg, MB*]   (EA)
ISHR .... International Society for Human Rights [*See also IGM*] [*Frankfurt, Federal Republic of Germany*]   (EAIO)
ISHS .... International Society for Horticultural Science [*See also SISH*] [*ICSU Wageningen, Netherlands*]   (EAIO)
ISI .... Construction Engineering Institute   (RU)
ISI .... Engineering Construction Institute   (BU)
ISI .... Fraunhofer-Institut fuer Systemtechnik und Innovationsforschung [*Fraunhofer Institute for Systems and Innovation Research*] [*Research center*]   (IRC)
ISI .... Iera Synodos tis Ierarkhias [*Holy Synod of the Hierarchy*] [*Greek*]   (GC)
ISI .... Ikatan Sardjana Indonesia [*Indonesian College Graduates Association*]   (IN)
ISI .... Indian Social Institute [*Research center*]   (IRC)
ISI .... Indian Standards Institution [*Netherlands*]   (SLS)
ISI .... Industrial Security International
ISI .... Industrial Service Institute [*Department of Industrial Promotion*] [*Thailand*]
ISI .... Information Services International [*Information service or system*]   (IID)
ISI .... Institute for Economic Research   (BU)
ISI .... Institut za Sumarska Istrazivanja [*Forestry Research Institute*]   (YU)
ISI .... International Statistical Institute [*ICSU*] [*Voorburg, Netherlands*]   (EA)
ISI .... Inter-Services Intelligence [*Pakistan*]   (ECON)
ISI .... Isisford [*Australia*] [*Airport symbol*]   (OAG)
ISI .... Istanbul Sular Idaresi [*Istanbul Water Works Administration*]   (TU)
ISI .... Istok Severo-Istok [*East North-East*]   (YU)
ISIA .... International Ski Instructors' Association   (ECON)
Is IA .... Istituto Italiano per l'Asia [*Italian*]   (SLS)
ISIAME ..... International Symposium on the Industrial Applications of the Mossbauer Effect
ISIAP .... Intreprinderea de Stat pentru Imprimate si Administratia Publicatiilor [*State Enterprise for Printing and Administration of Publications*]   (RO)
ISIC .... Instituto Salvadoreno de Investigaciones del Cafe [*Salvadoran Institute of Coffee Research*]   (LA)
ISIC .... International Standard Industrial Classification
ISIC .... International Student Identity Card   (BARN)
ISI/CID ..... Institute for Scientific Information/Chemical Information Division
ISID .... Indonesian Society of Interior Designers   (EAIO)
ISID .... Inter-Services Intelligence Division [*Pakistan*] [*Military*]
ISIF .... Instituto Superior de Idiomas y Finanzas [*Colombia*]   (COL)
ISIG .... Institute of Standards and Industrial Research [*Ghana*]
ISIG .... Istituto di Sociologia Internazionale di Gorizia [*Italian*]   (SLS)

ISIJ............ Iron and Steel Institute of Japan
ISIL .... International Society for Individual Liberty (EAIO)
ISIM .... Institutul de Sudura si Incercari de Materiale [*Institute for Welding and Testing Materials*] (RO)
ISIM .... [*The*] International School of Inforamtion Management, Inc. [*Denver, CO*] (ECON)
ISIM .... [*The*] International School of Information Management, Inc. [*Denver, CO*] (ECON)
ISIM .... International Society of Internal Medicine [*Langenthal, Switzerland*] (EA)
ISIMA .... Industrie Sisaliere du Maroc [*North African*]
ISIMC .... International Study Institution of the Middle Classes [*Brussels, Belgium*] (EAIO)
ISIMEP..... International Symposium on Identification and Measurement of Environmental Pollutants (PDAA)
ISIPP........ Information System for Improved Plant Protection [*FAO*] [*United Nations*] (DUND)
ISIR .... International Society of Invertebrate Reproduction (EA)
ISIR .... International Symposium on Industrial Robots (PDAA)
ISIRC....... International Statistical Institute Research Center [*Research center*] [*Netherlands*] (IRC)
ISIRI........ Institute of Standards and Industrial Research of Iran (ME)
ISIRS........ International Sorption Information Retrieval System [*Nuclear Energy Agency*] (EY)
ISIS........... Institute of Strategic and International Studies [*Malaysia*] (ECON)
ISIS........... Institutul de Studii Istorice si Social-Politice [*Institute for Historical and Sociopolitical Studies*] (RO)
ISIS........... Integriertes Statistisches Informationssystem [*Integrated Statistical Information System*] [*Central Statistical Office Vienna, Austria*] [*Information service or system*] (IID)
ISIS........... Internationale de Services Industriels and Scientifiques
ISIS........... International Science Information Service (PDAA)
ISIS........... International Space Information System [*United Nations*] (DUND)
ISIS........... Intratest Software Informationssystem (ADPT)
ISIS........... Istituto di Studi per l'Informatica e i Sistemi [*Italian*] (SLS)
ISIS........... Istituto Internazionale per gli Studi e l'Informazione Sanitaria [*Italian*] (SLS)
ISIS........... Women's International Information and Communication Service [*Italy and Switzerland*]
ISISA........ Individual Scale for Indian South Africans [*Intelligence test*]
ISISC........ Istituto Superiore Internazionale di Scienze Criminali [*Italy*]
ISISP........ Instituto Superior de Investigaciones Sociales y Politicas [*Advanced Institute for Social and Political Research*] [*Ecuador*] (LA)
ISISSAPORCI ... International Section of ISSA [*International Social Security Association*] on the Prevention of Occupational Risks in the Construction Industry [*Boulogne-Billancourt, France*] (EAIO)
ISIS-WICCE ... ISIS [*Women's International Information Communication Service*] - Women's International Cross-Cultural Exchange (EAIO)
ISITA......... Instructions sur le Service International des Telecommunications de l'Aeronautique [*French*]
ISITT........ Instituut vir Staatsdiensingenieurswesetegnici en -Tegnoloe [*South Africa*] (AA)
ISIUP .... Islamic Society for International Unity and Peace [*Pakistan*] (EAIO)
ISJ .... Inspectoratul Scolar Judetean [*County School Inspectorate*] (RO)
ISJCT .... International Symposium on Jet Cutting Technology (PDAA)
ISK............ Historical Commission (RU)
ISK............ Institute for Construction Cybernetics (BU)
ISK............ Instituut van Stadsklerke van Suidelike Afrika [*South Africa*] (AA)
ISK............ Internacia Scienca Kolegio [*International College of Scientists - ICS*] [*Paderborn, Federal Republic of Germany*] (EAIO)
ISK............ Ishihara Sangyo Kaisha Ltd. [*Japan*]
Isk .... Iskele [*Landing Place, Wharf*] (TU)
isk............. Iskola [*School*] (HU)
ISK............ Nasik [*India*] [*Airport symbol*] (OAG)
ISKD.......... Izmir Sinema Kultur Dernegi [*Izmir Cinema Cultural Association*] (TU)
ISKh.......... Institute of Agriculture (RU)
ISKhI........ Irkutsk Agricultural Institute (RU)
ISKhI........ Izhevsk Agricultural Institute (RU)
iskh r-zh..... Line of Departure (RU)
ISKI.......... International Secretariat of the Knitting Industries [*Paris, France*] (EAIO)
ISKLP........ Institute for Medical Treatment and Rest at Health Resorts (BU)
ISKNG....... Instituti i Studimeve dhe i Kerkimeve te Naftes dhe te Gazit [*Albanian*]
ISKO......... International Society for Knowledge Organization [*Germany*] (EAIO)
Iskolastrel ... Executive Committee of Latvian Riflemen (RU)

Iskolat....... Executive Committee of the Soviet of Workers', Soldiers', and Peasants' Deputies of Latvia (RU)
ISKOMOF ... Executive Committee of the Soviet of Officers' Deputies (RU)
ISKOMZAP ... Executive Committee of the Soviet of Soldiers' Deputies of the Western Front (RU)
ISKORAD ... Executive Committee of the Soviet of Workers' Deputies (RU)
ISKORASOL ... Executive Committee of the Soviet of Workers' and Soldiers' Deputies (RU)
ISKOSOL ... Executive Committee of the Soviet of Soldiers' Deputies (RU)
ISKOSOVDEP ... Executive Committee of the Soviet of Deputies (RU)
Iskozh .... Artificial Leather Factory (RU)
ISKUR .... Isci, Isadami, Kimya Sanayii Kuruluslari AS [*Worker, Businessmen, Chemical Industry Organizations, Corporation*] [*Bandirma fertilizer factory*] (TU)
iskusstv ...... Artificial, Synthetic (RU)
ISL............ Artificial Moon Satellite (RU)
ISL............ Eagle Air Ltd. [*Iceland*] [*ICAO designator*] (FAAC)
ISL............ Iceland [*ANSI three-letter standard code*] (CNC)
isl............. Icelandic (RU)
ISL............ Institut Franco-Allemand de Recherches de Saint-Louis [*Franco-German Research Institute at Saint-Louis*] [*French*] (WER)
ISL............ Institut fuer Seeverkehrwirtschaft und Logistik [*Institute of Shipping Economics and Logistics - ISEL*] [*Bremen, Federal Republic of Germany*] (EAIO)
ISL............ Institut fuer Stahlbau und Leichtmetallbau [*Institute for Steel and Light-Metal Construction*] (EG)
ISL............ Instrumental Services Laboratory [*Australia*]
ISl............ Instytut Slaski [*Silesian Institute*] (POL)
ISL............ International Society of Literature [*Ilkley, Yorkshire, England*] (EAIO)
Isl............ Island [*Iceland*] [*German*] (GCA)
isl............ Islantia [*or Islanniksi*] [*Finland*]
Isl............ Islantilainen [*Finland*]
Isl............ Islavca [*Slavic*] (TU)
isl............ I Slicno [*And the Like*] (YU)
ISL............ Istituto di Studi sul Lavoro [*Italian*] (SLS)
ISL............ Istituto Storico Lucchese [*Italian*] (SLS)
island........ Icelandic (RU)
ISLAR ...... International Symposium on Laboratory Automation and Robotics
ISLD......... Institute for the Study of Learning Difficulties [*Flinders University*] [*Australia*]
ISLE .... Istituto per la Documentazione e gli Studi Legislativi [*Italian*] (SLS)
ISLGC ...... Institutul de Cercetari si Proiectari pentru Sistematizare Locuinte si Gospodarie Comunala [*Research and Design Institute for Systematization of Housing and Communal Administration*] (RO)
ISLIC........ Israel Society of Special Libraries and Information Centers (SLS)
ISLIF .... Intreprinderea de Stat pentru Lucrari si Imbunatatiri Funciare [*State Enterprise for Land Projects and Improvements*] (RO)
ISLIMA..... Industrie Senegalaise de Linge de Maison
ISLLSS...... International Society for Labor Law and Social Security [*International Congresses of Labour Law and International Society for Social Law*] [*Formed by a merger of*] (EAIO)
ISLR .... International Symposium on Laboratory Robotics
ISLRS........ Izvrsni Svet Ljudska Republika Slovenija [*Executive Council of Slovenia*] (YU)
ISLSCB ..... Intreprinderea Santier de Lucrari Speciale in Constructii Bucuresti [*Bucharest Worksite Enterprise for Special Construction Projects*] (RO)
ISLT .... International Snow Leopard Trust (EA)
ISLWG ...... Working Group on International Shipping Legislation [*UNCTAD*] (DS)
ISM........... Artificial and Synthetic Materials (RU)
ISM........... Ilektrostatikai Monades [*Electrostatic Units*] (GC)
ISM........... Institute of Sports Medicine [*Australia*]
ISM........... Institute of Structural Mechanics (of the Academy of Sciences, USSR) (RU)
ISM........... Institut Scientifique de Madagascar
ISM........... Internationaal Bodenkundig Museum [*International Soil Museum*] (ARC)
ISM........... International Sweets Market [*Trade fair*] [*Cologne, West Germany 1982*]
ISM........... International Symposium on Microchemistry
ism............ Ismeretlen [*Unknown*] (HU)
ism............ Ismertetes [*or Ismerteti*] [*Review or Reviewed By*] (HU)
ism............ Ismetles [*Repeat*] (HU)
ISM........... Istituto di Struttura della Materia [*Institute for the Structure of Matter*] [*Research center*] [*Italy*] (IRC)
ISM........... Istituto di Studi nel Mezzogiorno e nelle Aree Depresse [*Italian*] (SLS)
ISM........... Istituto Internazionale Suore di Santa Marcellina [*Also, Instituto Marcelline*] [*Italy*] (EAIO)

ISM............ Istituto Sieroterapico Milanese [*Italy*]
ISMA......... Indian Sugar Mills Association (PDAA)
ISMA........ Industrie Senegalaise des Marbres et Agglomeres
ISMA......... Institute for the Study of Man in Africa
ISMA........ Institute of Sisters of Mercy of Australia
ISMA........ Institutul de Cercetari Pentru Mecanizarea Agriculturii [*Romania*] (DSCA)
ISMA........ International Superphosphate Manufacturers' Association [*Later, IFA*]
ISMA......... Istituto Sperimentale per la Meccanizzazione Agricola [*Agricultural Mechanization Experimental Institute*] [*Italian*] (ARC)
ISMAC...... Israeli-Syrian Mixed Armistice Commission (ME)
ISMAK...... Istif Makinalari Sanayi ve Ticaret AS [*Loading and Unloading Machinery Industry and Trade Corp.*] (TU)
ISMAL...... Institut National des Sciences de la Mer et de l'Amenagement du Littoral [*National Institute of Ocean and Sciences and Coastal Management*] [*Algeria*] (IRC)
ISMAR...... International Society of Magnetic Resonance
ISMB........ Information System Management Board [*NATO*] (NATG)
ISMB........ International Society of Mathematical Biology [*See also SIBM*] [*Antony, France*] (EAIO)
ISMCM..... Institut Superieur des Materiaux et de la Construction Mecanique [*Advanced Institute of Materials and Construction Mechanics*] [*France*] (PDAA)
ISME........ International Society for Music Education (EA)
ISME........ International Society of Marine Engineers
ISME........ International Society of Mechanical Engineers
ISME........ International Sysmposium on Marine Engineering (PDAA)
IsMeDin .... Istituto di Medicina Dinamica SpA [*Italian*] (SLS)
ISMEO...... Istituto Italiano per il Medio ed Estremo Oriente [*Italian Institute for the Middle and Far East*] [*Rome*] (WER)
ISMES...... Experimental Institute for Models and Structures [*Italy*]
ISMEX ...... Indo-Soviet Monsoon Experiment (MSC)
ISMG........ International Scientific and Management Group (MSC)
ISMGF ..... International Stoke Mandeville Games Federation [*Aylesbury, Buckinghamshire, England*] (EA)
ISMHC...... International Society of Medical Hydrology and Climatology (EA)
ISMiS .... Institute of Building Materials and Structures (RU)
ISMIT .... International Society for Mental Imagery Techniques [*France*] (EAIO)
ISML........ Instituto Sperimentale dei Metalli Leggeri
ISML........ Istituto per la Storia del Movimento Liberale [*Italian*] (SLS)
ISMM....... International Society for Music in Medicine (EAIO)
ISMM....... International Society of Mini- and Micro-Computers [*Calgary, AB*] (EAIO)
ISMN .... International Standard Music Number
ISMS .... International Society for Mushroom Science [*Braunschweig, Federal Republic of Germany*] (EA)
ISMSD ...... Istituto delle Suore Maestre di Santa Dorotea [*Rome, Italy*] (EAIO)
ISMUN ..... International Youth and Student Movement for the United Nations [*Geneva, Switzerland*] (EA)
ISN .... Instituto Social Nicaraguense [*Nicaraguan Social Institute*] (LA)
ISN .... Instituut vir Statistiese Navorsing [*Institute for Statistical Research*] [*Human Sciences Research Council*] [*South Africa*] (AA)
ISN .... International Society for Neurochemistry [*Kjeller, Norway*] (EA)
ISNA........ Indian Science News Association (DSCA)
ISNA......... Istituto di Studi Nucleari per l'Agricoltura [*Italian*] (SLS)
ISNAR...... International Service for National Agricultural Research [*The Hague, Netherlands*]
ISNN .... Measurement of Night Sky Luminescence (RU)
ISNSE ...... International School for Nuclear Science and Engineering
ISO .... Engineer Construction Section (RU)
ISO .... Engineering Economic Organization (BU)
ISO .... Instituut voor Scheikundig Onderzoek [*Chemical Research Institute*] [*Belgium*] (ARC)
ISO .... International Organization for Standardization [*Geneva, Switzerland*] [*United Nations*]
ISO .... International Shopfitting Organization [*Zurich, Switzerland*] (EAIO)
ISO .... International Society of Organbuilders [*Levallois-Perret, France*] (EAIO)
ISO .... International Sugar Organization [*See also OIA*] [*British*]
ISO .... Istanbul Sanayi Odasi [*Istanbul Chamber of Industry*] (TU)
ISO .... Lime-Sulfur Solution (RU)
ISOA......... Indian Society of Oriental Art (SLS)
I Soc .... Impot des Societes [*Benelux*] (BAS)

ISOC.......... Instituto de Informacion y Documentacion en Ciencias Sociales y Humanidades [*Institute for Information and Documentation in the Social Sciences and Humanities*] [*Higher Council for Scientific Research*] [*Information service or system*] (IID)
ISOCAR .... ISO Colombiana Ltda. [*Colombia*] (COL)
ISoCaRP.... International Society of City and Regional Planners [*See also AIU*] [*The Hague, Netherlands*] (EAIO)
ISOD .... International Society for Orbital Disorders (EAIO)
ISOD .... International Sports Organization for the Disabled [*Farstn, Sweden*] (EA)
ISODARCO ... International School of Disarmament and Research on Conflicts
ISODEM... Instituut vir Sosiologiese en Demografiese Navorsing [*Institute for Sociological and Demographic Research*] [*Human Sciences Research Council*] [*South Africa*] (AA)
ISODOC.... International Information Centre for Standards in Information and Documentation (ADA)
ISOE......... International Society for Optical Engineering (EA)
ISOF .... International Society for Ocular Fluorophotometry (EAIO)
Isolier......... Isolierung [*Isolation*] [*German*] (GCA)
Isomerisier ... Isomerisierung [*Isometrization*] [*German*] (GCA)
ISONET .... International Organization for Standardization Information Network [*United Nations*] [*Geneva, Switzerland*] (IID)
ISOO .... International Symposium on Opthalmological Optics (PDAA)
ISOP......... Instituto de Selecao e Orientacao Professional [*Institute for Professional Selection and Guidance*] [*Rio De Janeiro, Brazil*] (LAA)
ISORID ..... International Information System on Research in Documentation [*UNESCO*]
ISOS .... Interplanetare Sonnensonde
ISOSC .... International Society for Soilless Culture [*Wageningen, Netherlands*] (EAIO)
ISOTAL .... Isolamentos Termicos e Acusticos Lda.
ISOU .... Israel Sea-Officers' Union (EAIO)
isp............. Combat Engineer Regiment (BU)
isp............. Engineer Regiment (RU)
ISP .... Ilektrikoi Sidirodromoi Protevousis [*Capital Electrical Railways*] [*EIS*] [*Formerly,*] [*Greek*] (GC)
ISP........... Independent Smallholders' Party [*Hungary*] [*Political party*] (EY)
ISP........... Industrija Stakla, Pancevo [*Glass Industry, Pancevo*] (YU)
ISP........... Information Systems Plan [*USAID*] (ECON)
ISP........... Institute of Hygiene Education (RU)
ISP........... Instituto de Seguros de Portugal [*Insurance regulatory agency*] [*Portugal*] (EY)
ISP........... Instituto Superior Pedagogico [*Advanced Institute of Teaching*] [*Cuba*] (LA)
ISP........... Institut pour une Synthese Planetaire [*Institute for Planetary Synthesis - IPS*] [*Geneva, Switzerland*] (EAIO)
ISP........... Institut Superieur Pedagogique
ISP........... Institut Superieur Polytechnique
ISP........... Institutul de Stiinte Pedagogice [*Institute for Pedagogical Sciences*] (RO)
ISP........... Institutul de Studii si Proiectari [*Institute for Studies and Design*] (RO)
ISP........... Internacional de Servidores Publicos [*Public Services International*] [*Use PSI*] (LA)
ISP........... Internationale des Services Publics [*Public Service International - PSI*] [*Ferney Voltaire, France*] (EAIO)
ISP........... International Society for Photogrammetry
ISP........... International Society for Plastination (EA)
ISP........... International Society of Postmasters [*Montreal, PQ*] (EAIO)
ISP........... International Study Program
Isp .... Ispanyolca [*Spanish*] (TU)
ISP........... Istituto di Sperimentazione per la Pioppicoltura [*Poplar Research Institute*] [*Italian*] (ARC)
ISP........... Italian Socialist Party (RU)
ISP........... Izdavacko Stamparsko Preduzece [*Publishing and Printing Establishment*] (YU)
ISP........... Network Power Supply (RU)
isp............. Spanish (RU)
ISPA .... Institut de Studii si Proiectari i Agricole Institut d'Etudes et de Projections Agricoles [*Romania*] (DSCA)
I/SPA........ International Spa and Fitness Association
ISPA .... International Squash Players Association [*Cardiff, Wales*] (EAIO)
ISPA .... Istituto di Studi Politici e Amministrativi [*Italian*] (SLS)
ISPACAIA ... Institutul de Studii si Proiectari de Constructii pentru Agricultura si Industrie Alimentara [*Institute for Studies and Designs of Constructions for Agriculture and the Food Industry*] (RO)
ISPAN .... Instytut Sztuki Polskiej Akademii Nauk [*Art Institute of the Polish Academy of Sciences*] (EAIO)
ispan........... Spanish (RU)
ISPASA ..... Istituto Siciliano di Psicologia Applicata e di Scienze Antropologiche [*Italian*] (SLS)

ISPC .... Industrial Survey and Promotion Center

ISPC .... Institut Superieur de Pastorale Catechetique de Paris

ISPCMCF ... Institutul de Stat pentru Controlul Medicamentelor si Cercetari Farmaceutice [*State Institute for Drug Control and Pharmaceutical Research*]　(RO)

ISPE .... Institutul de Studii si Proiectari Energetice [*Institute for Power Studies and Design*]　(RO)

ISPE .... Istituto per lo Studio dei Problemi dell'Emigrazione [*Italian*]　(SLS)

ISPE .... Istituto Studi Programmazione Economica [*Institute for Studies in Economic Planning*] [*Italian*]　(WER)

ISPEA .... Institut de Statistique, de Planification, et d'Economie Appliquee

ISPECO ..... Instituto Superior de Pesquisas e Estudos de Cooperativismo [*Brazil*]　(DSCA)

ISPEM ...... Istituto Studi per i Problemi Economici del Mediterraneo [*Italy*]　(DSCA)

ISPER .... Istituto per la Direzione del Personale [*Italian*]　(SLS)

ISPES .... Istituto per la Promozione dello Sviluppo Economico e Sociale [*Italian*]　(SLS)

ISPF .... Institutul de Studii si Proiectari al Ministerului Economiei Forestiere [*Studies and Design Institute of the Ministry of the Forestry Economy*]　(RO)

ISPF .... International Science Policy Foundation　(EAIO)

ISPGC .... Institutul de Studii si Proiectari pentru Constructii si Instalatii de Gospodarie Comunala [*Studies and Design Institute for Constructions and Installations of the Communal Economy*]　(RO)

ISPH .... Institut Superieur de Pedagogie du Hainaut [*Belgium*]

ISPH .... Institutul de Studii si Proiectari Hidroenergetice [*Hydroelectric Power Studies and Design Institute*]　(RO)

ISPH .... International Society of Psychology of Handwriting [*Milan, Italy*]　(EA)

ISPI .... International Society for Prevention of Infertility　(EAIO)

ISPI .... Istituto per gli Studi di Politica Internazionale [*Institute for International Policy Studies*] [*Italian*]　(WER)

ISPIF .... Institutul de Studii si Proiectari pentru Imbunatatiri Funciare [*Studies and Design Institute for Land Improvements*]　(RO)

ISPIFGA ... Institutul de Studii si Proiectari pentru Imbunatatiri Funciare si Gospodarirea Apelor [*Studies and Design Institute for Land Improvements and Water Management*]　(RO)

ISPJAE ..... Instituto Superior Politecnico Jose Antonio Echeverria [*Jose Antonio Echeverria Higher Polytechnic Institute*] [*Cuba*]　(LA)

ISPL .... Intreprinderea de Stat pentru Produse Lactate [*State Enterprise for Dairy Products*]　(RO)

ISPM .... Instituti i Studimeve dhe i Projektimeve Mekanike [*Albanian*]

ISPM .... Institut Scientifique des Peches Maritimes [*Morocco*]　(ASF)

ISPM .... International Society of Plant Morphologists [*Delhi, India*]　(EAIO)

ISPM .... International Staff Planners Message [*NATO*]　(NATG)

ISPMEMO ... International Staff Planners Memo [*NATO*]　(NATG)

ISPO .... International Sports Equipment Fair [*Germany*]

ISPOG .... International Society of Psychosomatic Obstetrics and Gynaecology　(PDAA)

ISPOLKOM ... Ispolnietelny Komitet [*Executive Committee*] [*Russian*]

ISPORT ..... Istituto Sperimentale per l'Orticoltura [*Vegetable Crops Experimental Research Institute*] [*Italian*]　(ARC)

ISPOTA .... Institutul de Studii si Proiectari pentru Organizarea Teritoriului Agricol [*Studies and Design Institute for the Organization of Agricultural Land*]　(RO)

ISPP .... Internationale Studiengemeinschaft fuer Pranatale Psychologie [*International Society for the Study of Prenatal Psychology - ISPP*]　(EAIO)

ISPP .... International Society for Plant Pathology　(EAIO)

ISPP .... International Society for the Study of Prenatal Psychology　(EAIO)

ISPP .... International Society of Prenatal and Perinatal Psychology and Medicine　(EAIO)

ispr .... Corrected, Correction, Revised, Revision　(RU)

ispravdom .. Corrective Labor Home　(RU)

ISPROM ... Istituto di Studi e Programmi per il Mediterraneo [*Institute of Studies for the Mediterranean Area*] [*Italian*]　(ASF)

ISPRS .... International Society for Photogrammetry and Remote Sensing [*Royal Institute of Technology*] [*Research center*] [*Sweden*]　(IRC)

ISPS .... Intreprinderea de Sirma si Produse de Sirma [*Enterprise for Wire and Wire Products*]　(RO)

ISPSPN ..... Institutul de Stiinte Politice si de Studiere a Problemei Nationale [*Institute for Political Sciences and for the Study of the National Question*]　(RO)

ISPT .... Industry Superannuation Property Trust

ISPT .... Istituto San Paolo di Torino [*San Paolo Institute of Turin*] [*Italian bank*]

ISPU .... Investment Servicing and Promotion Unit

ISPW .... International Society for the Psychology of Writing [*Italian*]　(SLS)

ISPWP ...... International Society for the Prevention of Water Pollution [*Alton, Hampshire, England*]　(EAIO)

ISPX .... Secular Institute of Pius X　(EA)

ISQ .... Instituto de Soldadura e Qualidade [*Welding and Quality Institute*] [*Portugal*]　(IRC)

ISQA .... Israel Socity for Quality Assurance　(PDAA)

isr .... Engineer Company　(RU)

ISR .... Institute for Statistical Research [*Human Sciences Research Council*] [*South Africa*]　(AA)

ISR .... Institut fur Stadt und Regionalforschung [*Institute for Urban and Regional Research*] [*Austria*]　(EAIO)

ISR .... Internationale Syndicale Rouge　(FLAF)

ISR .... International Society of Radiology [*Berne, Switzerland*]　(EA)

ISR .... Israel [*ANSI three-letter standard code*]　(CNC)

ISR .... Istituto di Scienze Religiose [*Italian*]　(SLS)

ISR .... Istra Air [*Slovakia*] [*ICAO designator*]　(FAAC)

ISRA .... Institut Senegalais de Recherches Agricoles [*Senegal Institute of Agricultural Research*]　(ARC)

ISRA .... International Seabed Resource Authority　(AF)

ISRALPA .. Israel AirLine Pilots Association　(EAIO)

ISRC .... International Standard Recording Code

ISRCA .... Institute for Scientific Research in Central Africa

ISRCDVS ... International Society for Research on Civilization Diseases and Vital Substances　(PDAA)

ISRD .... International Society for Rehabilitation of the Disabled

ISRDS .... Istituto di Studi sulla Ricerca e Documentazione Scientifica [*Institute for Study of Scientific Research and Documentation*] [*National Research Council*] [*Information service or system*]　(IID)

ISRE .... Istituto di Studi e Ricerche Ecologiche [*Italian*]　(SLS)

ISRE .... Istituto Superiore Regionale Etnografico [*Italian*]　(SLS)

ISREC .... Institut Suisse de Recherches Experimentales sur le Cancer [*Swiss Institute for Experimental Cancer Research*] [*Research center*] [*Switzerland*]　(IRC)

ISRER .... Istituto Regionale per la Storia della Resistenza e della Guerra di Liberazione in Emilia-Romagna [*Italian*]　(SLS)

ISRF .... International Squash Rackets Federation [*Cardiff, Wales*]　(EAIO)

ISRF .... International Sugar Research Foundation [*Later, WSRO*]　(EA)

ISRHAI ..... International Secretariat for Research on the History of Agricultural Implements [*Lyngby, Denmark*]　(EAIO)

ISRI .... Istituto di Studi sulle Relazioni Industriali [*Italian*]　(SLS)

ISRIC .... International Soil Reference and Information Centre [*Research center*] [*Netherlands*]　(IRC)

ISRIL .... Istituto di Studi sulle Relazioni Industriali e di Lavoro [*Italian*]　(SLS)

ISRIN .... Istituto per le Ricerche sull'Informatica [*Italian*]　(SLS)

ISRM .... International Society for Rock Mechanics [*Lisbon, Portugal*]　(EA)

ISRN .... International Standard Record Number

ISRO .... Indian Space Research Organization

ISRP .... Spanish Socialist Workers' Party　(RU)

ISRRT .... International Society of Radiographers and Radiological Technicians [*Don Mills, ON*]　(EA)

ISRS .... Institutul de Studii Roman-Sovietic [*Romanian-Soviet Institute for Studies*]　(RO)

ISRT .... Istituto di Scienze Religiose in Trento [*Italian*]　(SLS)

ISRT .... Istituto Storico della Resistenza in Toscana [*Italian*]

ISRU .... International Scientific Radio Union [*Also, URSI*]

ISS .... Economic and Social Council　(BU)

ISS .... Indian Secular Society　(EAIO)

ISS .... Industrial Security Section [*NATO*]　(NATG)

ISS .... Information Reference System　(RU)

ISS .... Information Science Section [*Australia*]

ISS .... Institute of Social Studies [*Research center*] [*Netherlands*]　(IRC)

ISS .... Instituto de Seguros Sociales [*Social security*] [*Colorado*]　(IMH)

ISS .... Instituto Superiore di Sanita [*Italian*]

ISS .... Intercommunication Service System Inc. [*Information service or system*]　(IID)

ISS .... Internationale Gesellschaft fuer Stereologie [*International Society for Stereology*]　(EAIO)

ISS .... International Institute of Sociology [*Cordoba, Argentina*]　(LAA)

ISS .... International Scotist Society [*See also SIS*] [*Rome, Italy*]　(EAIO)

ISS .... International Seaweed Association　(EAIO)

ISS .... International Seaweed Symposium [*Trondheim, Norway*]　(MSC)

ISS .... International Self-Service Organization [*Cologne, Federal Republic of Germany*]　(EAIO)

ISS .... International Social Service [*See also SSI*] [*Geneva, Switzerland*]　(EAIO)

ISS .... International Society of Surgery　(EA)

ISS .... International Space Station

ISS .... Ionospheric Sounding Satellite [*Japan*]

ISS .... Iraqi Intelligence Service

ISS .... Ishmaelites Salvation Society [*India*]

ISS .... Israel Surgical Society　(SLS)

ISS .... Meridiana SpA [*Italy*] [*ICAO designator*] (FAAC)

ISSA .... Association Internationale des Ecoles de Voile [*International Sailing Schools Association*] [*France*] (EAIO)

ISSA .... Independent Schools Staff Association [*Australia*]

ISSA .... Informationsstelle Sudliches Afrika e V

ISSA .... International Sailing Schools Association (EA)

ISSA .... International Ship Suppliers Association [*Wimbledon, England*] (EA)

ISSA .... International Slurry Surfacing Association (EAIO)

ISSA .... International Social Security Association [*Geneva, Switzerland*] (EA)

ISSA-ACT ... Independent Schools Staff Association - Australian Capital Territory

ISSAB .... International Social Service, Australian Branch [*An association*]

ISSARA ..... Instituto de Servicios Sociales para las Actividades Rurales y Afines [*Institute of Social Services for Rural and Related Activities*] [*Argentina*] (LA)

ISSBD .... International Society for the Study of Behavioural Development [*Nijmegen, Netherlands*] (EAIO)

ISSBI .... Istituto Siciliano di Studi Bizantini e Neoellenici [*Italian*] (SLS)

ISSC .... International Ship Structure Congress (MSC)

ISSC .... International Social Science Council [*See also CISS*] [*Paris, France*] [*Research center*] (EAIO)

ISSCA .... Institute of Steel Service Centres of Australia (ADA)

ISSCM .... International Society for the Study of Church Monuments [*Later, CMS*] (EA)

ISSCT .... International Society of Sugar Cane Technologists [*Piracicaoa, Brazil*] (EA)

ISSD .... International Society for Social Defence [*See also SIDS*] [*Paris, France*] (EAIO)

ISSDS .... Istituto Sperimentale per lo Studio e la Difesa del Suolo [*Italy*] (DSCA)

ISSE .... Instituto Superior del Servicio en el Extranjero [*Higher Institute of the Foreign Service*] [*Cuba*] (LA)

ISSE .... Istituto di Studi Storici ed Ecologici "Giustiniano Nicolucci" [*Italian*] (SLS)

ISSEP .... Institute Scientifique de Service Public [*Scientific Insitute of Public Service*] [*Belgium*] (IRC)

ISSEP .... International Soros Science Education Program [*Privately-funded program for former Soviet Republics*]

ISSER .... Institute of Statistical Social and Economic Research [*Legon*]

ISSES .... International Stationary Steam Engine Society (EAIO)

ISSGA .... International Society for the Study of Ghosts and Apparitions

ISSI .... Institute for Small-Scale Industries [*University of the Philippines*]

ISSICO ...... Istituto Siciliano per la Storia dell'Italia Contemporanea [*Italian*] (SLS)

ISSID .... International Society for the Study of Individual Differences (EAIO)

ISSK .... International Society for the Sociology of Knowledge [*St. John's, NF*] [*Defunct*] (EAIO)

issl .... Research, Investigation, Analysis (RU)

issled .... Research, Investigation, Analysis (RU)

ISSMB .... Inspectoratul Sanitar de Stat al Municipiului Bucuresti [*State Health Inspectorate of Bucharest Municipality*] (RO)

ISSMFE .... International Society for Soil Mechanics and Foundation Engineering [*See also SIMSTF*] (EA)

ISSN .... International Standard Serial Number

ISSOA-WA ... Independent Schools Salaried Officers Association of Western Australia

ISSP .... Indian Society for the Study of Pain [*India*] (EAIO)

ISSP .... International Society of Sports Psychology [*Italian*] (SLS)

ISSP .... International Solar Systems Program [*ICSU*]

ISSR .... International Society for the Sociology of Religion [*Italy*] (EAIO)

ISSRU .... Information Science and Scientometrics Research Unit [*Hungarian Academy of Sciences Library*] [*Budapest*] [*Information service or system*] (IID)

ISSS .... Instituto Salvadoreno de Seguro Social [*Salvadoran Institute of Social Security*] (LA)

ISSS .... International Society of Soil Science [*See also AISS*] [*ICSU Wageningen, Netherlands*] (EAIO)

ISSSA .... International Society for Strategic Studies (Africa) [*Formerly, Africa Society for Strategic Studies*] (EA)

ISSSP .... International Sacerdotal Society Saint Pius X (EA)

ISSSTE ...... Instituto de Seguridad y Servicios Sociales de Trabajadores Estatales [*Institute of Social Security and Services for Government Workers*] [*Mexico*] (LA)

ISSTDR ..... International Society for STD [*Sexually Transmitted Diseases*] Research (EA)

ISSUP .... Instituut vir Strategiese Studies, Universiteit van Pretoria [*Institute for Strategic Studies, University of Pretoria*] [*South Africa*] (AA)

ISSX .... International Society for the Study of Xenobiotics

ist .... Historical (RU)

IST .... Information Scientifique et Technique

IST .... Institut fuer Softwaretechnik [*German*] (ADPT)

IST .... Instituto Superior Tecnico [*Higher Technical Institute*] [*Portuguese*] (WER)

IST .... Institut Superieur de Theologie [*Zaire*]

IST .... Institut za Spoljnu Trgovinu [*Institute of Foreign Trade*] (YU)

IST .... Istanbul [*Turkey*] [*Airport symbol*] (OAG)

IST .... Istanbul Airlines [*Turkey*] [*ICAO designator*] (FAAC)

Ist .... Istasyon [*Station*] (TU)

ISt .... Iststaerke [*Actual Strength*] [*Military*] (EG)

IST .... Italian Labor Union (RU)

ist .... Spring [*Topography*] (RU)

ISTA .... Indian Scientific Translators Association

ISTA .... Instituto Salvadoreno de Transformacion Agraria [*Salvadoran Institute of Agrarian Transformation*] (LA)

ISTA .... Instituto Superior Tecnico Azucarero [*Higher Institute of Sugar Technology*] [*Cuba*] (LA)

ISTA .... Institut Superieur des Techniques Appliques [*Advanced Institute of Applied Techniques*] [*Zaire*] (AF)

ISTA .... International Seed Testing Association [*Switzerland*]

ISTA .... International Special Tooling Association [*Frankfurt, Federal Republic of Germany*] (EA)

ISTA .... Istanbul Ajansi [*Istanbul Agency*] [*News agency*] (TU)

IStA .... Istituto di Studi per l'Alto Adige [*Italian*] (SLS)

ISTAC .... International Science and Technology Advisory Committee [*Australia*]

ISTAM ...... Israel Society for Theoretical and Applied Mechanics (SLS)

ISTAM ...... Istituto di Tecniche Aziendali e di Mercato [*Italian*] (SLS)

ISTAO ...... Istituto Adriano Olivetti [*For business/industrial studies*] [*Italian*]

ISTARKh .. Historical Archives (RU)

ISTAT .... Istituto Centrale di Statistica [*Central Statistics Institute*] [*Italian*] (WER)

ISTC .... Indo-Swiss Training Centre [*India*] (PDAA)

ISTC .... International Student Travel Confederation [*Switzerland*] (EAIO)

ISTE .... International Society for Technology in Education (EAIO)

ISTE .... International Society for Tropical Ecology (EA)

ISTEC .... International Superconductivity Technology Center [*Japan*]

ISTEI .... Intreprinderea de Stat pentru Transporturi si Expedieri Internationale [*State Enterprise for International Transportation and Shipments*] (RO)

Istekhkozh ... Leningrad Industrial Artificial Leather Plant (RU)

ISTF .... International Social Travel Federation [*See also FITS*] [*Brussels, Belgium*] (EAIO)

i st f .... I Stallet For [*In Place Of*] [*Sweden*] (GPO)

istfak .... History Division (RU)

Ist-fil fak .... Department of History and Philosophy (BU)

ISTI .... Institut des Sciences et Techniques de l'Information [*Institute of Media Sciences and Techniques*] [*Zaire*] (AF)

ISTIC .... Institute of Scientific and Technical Information of China [*INFOTERM*] [*Beijing*]

ISTIC .... Instituto de Servicios Sociales para Trabajadores de la Industria de la Construccion [*Argentina*] (LAA)

Istih .... Istihsal [*Production*] [*Ur*] [*See also*] (TU)

ISTIMARBIRKO ... Istanbul ve Marmara Bolge Koy Kalkinma ve Diger Tarimsal Amacli Kooperatifler Birligi [*Union of Istanbul and Marmara Region Village Development Cooperatives and Other Agriculturally Inclined Cooperatives*] (TU)

ISTIS .... International Scientific and Technical Information System (EAIO)

ISTISSS .... Istituto per gli Studi di Servizio Sociale [*Italian*] (SLS)

ISTIUAPS ... Intreprinderea de Servicii Tehnice pentru Instalatii, Utilaje, Aparate, si Piese de Schimb [*Technical Services Enterprise for Installations, Equipment, Instruments, and Spare Parts*] (RO)

ISTL .... Inner Sydney Transport Link [*Australia*]

ISTLC .... Intreprinderea de Servicii Tehnice pentru Lucrari Capitale si Livrari de Instalatii Complexe in Industria Materialelor de Constructii [*Technical Services Enterprise for Capital Projects and Deliveries of Complex Installations in the Construction Materials Industry*] (RO)

ISTM .... Institute of Strata Title Management [*Australia*]

ISTM .... Instituto Superior Tecnico-Militar [*Advanced Institute of Military Technology*] [*Cuba*] (LA)

Istmat .... Historical Materialism (RU)

Istmol .... Commission for the Study of the History of the Komsomol (RU)

ISTNET ..... Industry, Science and Technology Overseas Counsellor Network [*Australia*]

ISTOR .... Istituto per la Storia del Risorgimento Italiano [*Italian*] (SLS)

ISTORA .... Istana Olah Raga [*Sports Stadium*] (IN)

ISTP .... Interagency Solar Terrestrial Programme [*European Space Agency*]

ISTP .... International Society of Tropical Pediatrics [*Philippines*] (EAIO)

Istpart .... Commission for Collection and Study of Materials on the History of the October Revolution and the History of the Communist Party (RU)

ISTPM ...... Institut Scientifique et Technique des Peches Maritimes [*Scientific and Technical Institute of Ocean Fishing*] [*French*]

IstPr .... Istoricheski Pregled [*Historical Review*] [*A periodical*]   (BU)

ISTPROF .. Commission for the Study of the History of Trade Unionism   (RU)

ISTPROFLOSPS ... Department for the Study of the History of Trade Unionism of the Leningrad Oblast Council of Trade Unions   (RU)

ISTRA .... Istituto di Studi per la Transizione [*Italian*]   (SLS)

ISTRACEMENT ... Istrian Cement Factory   (YU)

ISTRATEKSTIL ... Istrian Textile Trade [*Rijeka*]   (YU)

istraviaotryad ... Fighter Detachment   (RU)

ISTRAVINO ... Istrian Wine and Alcoholic Beverage Trade [*Rijeka*]   (YU)

istrb .... Engineer Construction Battalion   (BU)

istrbr .... Engineer Construction Brigade   (BU)

ISTRO .... International Soil Tillage Research Organization [*Netherlands*] (EAIO)

ISTS .... International Simultaneous Translation Service

ISTS .... International Society for Twin Studies [*Rome, Italy*]   (EA)

ISTU .... Instituto Salvadoreno de Turismo [*Salvadoran Institute of Tourism*]   (LA)

ISTUD ...... Istituto Italiano di Studi Legislativi [*Italian*]   (SLS)

ISTUD ...... Istituto Studi Direzionali SpA [*Italian*]   (SLS)

ist vr .... Apparent Time, True Time   (RU)

ISU .... Idoma State Union

ISU .... Information Service Unit [*International Potato Center*] [*Information service or system*]   (IID)

ISU .... Internal Security Unit

ISU .... Internationale Skating Union   (OLYM)

ISU .... International Salvage Union   (PDAA)

ISU .... International Skating Union [*See also UIP*] [*Davos-Platz, Switzerland*]   (EAIO)

ISU .... International Society of Urology [*See also SIU*] [*Lille, France*] (EAIO)

ISU .... International Space University [*Strasbourg, France*]

ISU .... International Stereoscopic Union   (PDAA)

ISU .... Isabela State University [*Philippines*]   (ARC)

ISU .... Israel Seamen's Union   (EAIO)

ISU-ERI .... Iowa State University - Engineering Research Institute   (PDAA)

ISUL .... Institute for Specialization and Advanced Study of Physicians (BU)

ISUPTTS .. International Sports Union of Post, Telephone, and Telecommunications Service   (EA)

ISUS .... International Society for Utilitarian Studies [*British*]   (EAIO)

ISV .... Informacni Sluzba Vystrizkova [*Clipping Information Service*] (CZ)

ISV .... Innerschweizer Schriftstellerverein Luzern [*Swiss Authors Association of Lucerne*]   (SLS)

ISV .... International Society for Vaccines [*Gaithersburg, MD*]

ISV .... Iparszeru Sertestarto Termeloszovetkezetek [*Cooperatives for Hog Raising on an Industrial Scale*]   (HU)

ISV .... Islena de Inversiones SA [*Honduras*] [*ICAO designator*]   (FAAC)

ISV .... Istituto Sperimentale per la Viticoltura [*Viticulture Research Institute*] [*Italian*]   (ARC)

ISVA .... Instituttet for Stromningsmekanik og Vandbygning [*Institute of Hydrodynamics and Hydraulic Engineering*] [*Research center*] [*Denmark*]   (IRC)

ISVA .... International Society for Vibroacoustics   (EAIO)

ISVBM ..... International Society of Violin and Bow Makers [*Basel, Switzerland*]   (EAIO)

ISVE .... Istituto di Studi per lo Sviluppo Economico [*Institute for Studies on Economic Development*] [*Research center*] [*Italy*]   (IRC)

ISVEIMER ... Istituto per lo Sviluppo Economico dell'Italia Meridionale [*Institute for the Economic Development of Southern Italy*] (WER)

ISVI .... Istituto di Formazione e Ricerca sui Problemi Sociali dello Sviluppo [*Italian*]   (SLS)

ISVNA ...... Istituto per lo Studio e la Valorizzazione di Noto Antica [*Italian*] (SLS)

ISW .... Institut fuer Schiffbautechnik Wolgast [*Wolgast Institute for Naval Engineering*]   (EG)

ISW .... Institut fuer Steuerungstechnik der Werkzeugmaschinen

ISW .... Serib Wings [*Italy*] [*ICAO designator*]   (FAAC)

ISWA .... Association Internationale pour les Residus Solides et le Nettoiement des Vil les [*International Solid Wastes and Public Cleansing Association*] [*INTAPUC and IRGRD*] [*Formed by a merger of*] [*Denmark*]   (EAIO)

ISWA .... International Science Writers Association [*ICSU*]

ISWA .... International Ski Writers Association [*Riehen, Switzerland*] (EA)

ISWG .... Item Selection Working Group [*NATO*]   (NATG)

ISWM .... Institute of Solid Waste Management [*South Africa*]   (AA)

ISY .... International Space Year [*1992*]

ISYa .... Information Reference Language   (RU)

ISYVC .... International Sivananda Yoga Vedanta Center   (EAIO)

ISYVO .... International Sivananda Yoga Vedanta Organization [*Val Morin, PQ*]   (EAIO)

ISZ .... Artificial Earth Satellite   (RU)

isz .... Idoszamitasunk Szerinti [*In the Year of Our Lord*] [*Hungary*] (GPO)

ISz .... Instytut Sztuki [*Institute of Fine Arts*] [*Poland*]

ISZM .... Indeziert Sequentielle Zugriffsmethode [*German*]   (ADPT)

ISZOT .... Ipari Szovetkezetek Orszagos Tanacsa [*National Council of Industrial Cooperatives*]   (HU)

ISZP .... Indiai Szocialista Part [*Socialist Party of India*]   (HU)

ISZSZI ...... Ipargazdasagi, Szervezesi, es Szamitastechnikai Intezet [*Institute of Industrial Management, Organization, and Computer Technology*]   (HU)

IT .... Air Inter, Societe [*France*] [*ICAO designator*]   (ICDA)

IT .... Current Source   (RU)

IT .... Inalta Tensiune [*High Voltage*]   (RO)

IT .... Indeks Troskova Zivota [*Cost of Living Index*] [*Yugoslavian*] (YU)

iT .... In der Trockenmasse [*In the Dry Measure*] [*German*]

iT .... Indonesia Timur [*East Indonesia (Sulawesi, Maluku, Nusatenggara, Irian Barat)*]   (IN)

IT .... Informationstraeger [*German*]   (ADPT)

IT .... Ingenieur de Travaux [*French*]

IT .... Inspektorat [*Inspectorate*]   (IN)

IT .... Inspektorat na Trudot [*Labor Inspectorate*]   (YU)

IT .... Institut de Technologie [*North African*]

i-t .... Institute   (BU)

IT .... Institute of Trichologists   (EAIO)

IT .... Institute of Tuberculosis (of the Academy of Medical Sciences, USSR)   (RU)

IT .... Instituto de Texteis [*Textile Institute*] [*Portuguese*]   (WER)

IT .... Instytut Torfowy [*Peat Institute*]   (POL)

IT .... Integrity Team [*Australia*]

IT .... Inzenjeri i Tehnicari [*Engineers and Technicians*]   (YU)

it .... Itainen [*Finland*]

it .... Italian   (RU)

it .... Italiano [*Italian*] [*Portuguese*]

IT .... Italie [*Italy*] [*Afrikaans*]

it .... Italienisch [*Italian*] [*German*]   (GCA)

IT .... Italy [*ANSI two-letter standard code*]   (CNC)

it .... Item [*Spanish*]

IT .... Pulse Transformer   (RU)

IT .... Technical School of Economics   (BU)

IT .... Testing Telephone   (RU)

IT .... Thickness Gauge   (RU)

IT .... Three-Phase Induction Meter   (RU)

ITA .... Indian Tea Association   (DSCA)

ITA .... Individual Telephone   (RU)

ITA .... Industrie Technologique Alimentaire de Dakar

ita .... Initial Teaching Alphabet

ITA .... Institut de Technologie Agricole [*Institute of Agricultural Technology*] [*Algeria*]   (AF)

ITA .... Institut de Technologie Alimentaire de Dakar

ITA .... Institut du Transport Aerien [*Institute of Air Transport*] [*Research center*] [*France*]   (IRC)

ITA .... Institute of the Arts [*Australian National University*]

ITA .... Institute of Theoretical Astronomy (of the Academy of Sciences, USSR)   (RU)

ITA .... Institute of Transport Administration [*Later, IoTA*]   (EAIO)

ITA .... Instituto de Tecnologia Agricola e Alimentar [*Brazil*]   (DSCA)

ITA .... Instituto Tecnico Americano [*Colombia*]   (COL)

ITA .... Instituto Tecnologico Agricola. Universidad de Narino [*Pasto*] (COL)

ITA .... Instituto Tecnologico de Aeronautica [*Technical Aeronautics Institute*] [*Brazil*]   (LA)

ITA .... International Alphabet

ITA .... International Tea Agreement [*Signed in 1933*]

ITA .... International Tin Agreement   (FEA)

ITA .... International Tornado Association [*Germany*]   (EAIO)

ITA .... International Touring Alliance [*Belgium*]   (EAIO)

ITA .... International Trans-Aerea [*Colombia*]   (COL)

ITA .... International Tube Association [*Leamington Spa, Warwickshire, England*]   (EAIO)

ITA .... International Tunnelling Association

ITA .... Intreprinderea de Transport Auto [*Automotive Transportation Enterprise*]   (RO)

ITA .... Israel Translators' Association   (EAIO)

ITA .... Italy [*ANSI three-letter standard code*]   (CNC)

Ita .... Italyanca [*Italian*]   (TU)

ITA .... Itapemirim Transportes Aereos SA [*Brazil*] [*ICAO designator*] (FAAC)

ITA .... Technical Institutes of Agriculture [*Spanish*]

ITAA .... Income Tax Assessment Act [*Australia*]   (ADA)

ITAB .... Institut Technique Agricole du Burundi

ITABC .... Istituto per le Tecnologie Applicate al Beni Culturali [*Institute for Applied Technologies to Cultural Properties*] [*Research center*] [*Italy*] (IRC)

ITABRASCO ... Companhia Italo-Brasileira de Mineracao [*Italian-Brazilian Mining Company*] (LA)

ITAC .... Independent Trade Unions Action Council [*Jamaica*]

ITAC .... Intreprinderea de Transporturi Auto Comerciale [*Enterprise for Automotive Transportation in Trade*] (RO)

ITADE .... Italconsult Argentina [*Argentina*]

ITAE .... Institut de Technologie d'Agriculture et d'Elevage [*Algeria*]

ITAE .... Instituto Tecnologico de Administracion y Economia [*Technological Institute of Administration and Economy*] [*Colorado*] (LA)

ITAER .... Instituto Tecnologico de la Alimentacion "Ejercito Rebelde" [*Ejercito Rebelde Food Technology Institute*] [*Cuba*] (LA)

ITAI(Aust) ... Institute of Technical Authors and Illustrators of Australia (PDAA)

ITAISA ...... Itabuna Industrial Sociedade Anonima [*Brazil*]

ITAK .... Illankai Tamil Arasu Kadchi [*Federal Party*] [*Sri Lanka*] [*Political party*] (PPW)

ITAL .... Instituto de Tecnologia de Alimentos [*Institute of Food Technology*] [*Research center*] [*Brazil*] (IRC)

ITAL .... Instituto Tecnico Agricola de Lorica (COL)

ITAL .... Instituut voor Toepassing van Atoomenergie in de Landbouw [*Institute for the Application of Nuclear Energy to Agriculture*] [*Netherlands*] (WEN)

ital .... Italiaa [*or Italiaksi*] [*Finland*]

ital .... Italialainen [*Finland*]

ital .... Italian (RU)

ital .... Italiano [*Italian*] [*Portuguese*]

ITALCEL .. Industria Italo-Colombiana de Conductores Electricos Ltda. [*Colombia*] (COL)

ITALJUG ... Italijansko-Jugoslovenska Komora u Rimu [*Italo-Yugoslav Chamber in Rome*] (YU)

ITALPIANTI ... Societa Italiana Impianti [*Italian Industrial Plant Company*] (WER)

ITALSIEL ... Societa Italiana Sistemi Informativ Elettronica [*Italy*] (PDAA)

ITALTEL .. Italia Telecommunications [*Italy*]

ITALTEL .. Societa Italiana Telecomunicazioni [*Italy*] (PDAA)

ITALTOGO ... Societe Italo-Togolaise

ITAM .... Instituto Tecnologico Autonomo de Mexico [*Economic research*] [*Mexico*] (CROSS)

ITAN .... Instituto Tecnico de Administracion de Negocios [*Costa Rica*]

ITAS .... Istituto Trentino-Alto Adige per Assicurazioni [*Insurance*] [*Italy*] (EY)

ITATE .... Institute of Technical and Adult Teacher Education [*Sydney College of Advanced Education*] [*Australia*]

ITB .... Industrial Training Board [*Iran*] (ME)

ITB .... Industry Training Body [*Australia*]

ITB .... Innovations- und Technologieberatungsstelle

ITB .... Instituto Tecnologico Boliviano [*Bolivia*] (DSCA)

ITB .... Institut Technique du Batiment [*Technical Institute for Building*] [*France*] [*Information service or system*] (IID)

ITB .... Institut Teknologi Bandung [*Bandung Technological Institute*] (IN)

ITB .... Instytut Techniki Budowlanej [*or Budownictwa*] [*Institute of Civil Engineering*] (POL)

ITB .... International Terminal Building [*Australia*]

ITB .... Intreprinderea de Transport Bucuresti [*Bucharest Transportation Enterprise*] (RO)

ITBA .... Industries Tunisiennes de Broderie Automatique

ITBA .... Istituto di Tecnologie Biomediche Avanzate [*Institute of Advanced Biomedical Technology*] [*Italy*] (IRC)

ITBF .... Iktisadi ve Ticari Bilimler Fakultesi [*Faculty of Economy and Commercial Science*] [*Aegean University*] (TU)

ITBM .... Institut du Batiment et des Travaux Publics [*Morocco*]

ITBON ...... Instituut voor Toegepast Biologisch Onderzoek in der Natuur Field [*Institute for Biological Field Research*] [*Netherlands*] (DSCA)

ITBTP .... Institut Technique du Batiment et des Travaux Publics [*Technical Institute for Building and Public Works*] [*Information service or system*] (IID)

ITC .... Compagnia Italiana dei Cavi Telegrafici Sottomarini [*Italian Underwater Telegraph Cable Company*] (WER)

ITC .... Ilangai Thozilazar Congress [*Sri Lanka*] (EAIO)

ITC .... Illawarra Technology Corp. [*Australia*]

ITC .... Industrial Technology Centre [*Royal Melbourne Institute of Technology*] [*Australia*]

ITC .... Industrial Technology Centre [*Singapore*]

ITC .... Industrial Tribology Centre [*Chisholm Institute of Technology*] [*Australia*]

ITC .... Ingenieurs, Techniciens, et Cadres [*Engineers, Technicians, and Middle Management People*] [*French*] (WER)

ITC .... Ingenieur Technico-Commercial [*French*] (ADPT)

ITC .... Inland Transport Committee [*United Nations*]

ITC .... Institute of Town Clerks of Southern Africa (AA)

ITC .... Institutul de Cercetari pentru Tehnica de Calcul [*Research Institute for Computer Technology*] (RO)

ITC .... Instytut Techniki Cieplnej [*Institute of Thermal Technics*] [*Poland*]

ITC .... Integrated LCD Technology Corp. [*Taiwan*]

ITC .... Internationaal Instituut voor Lucht-en Ruimtekaartering an Aardkunde [*International Institute for Aerospace Survey and Earth Sciences*] [*Netherlands*] (EAIO)

ITC .... International Air Carrier Association [*ICAO designator*] (FAAC)

ITC .... International Tar Conference [*See also CIG*] [*Paris, France*] (EAIO)

ITC .... International Tea Committee (EAIO)

ITC .... International Technology Center [*Singapore*]

ITC .... International Tin Council [*See also CIE*] [*Defunct*] (EAIO)

ITC .... International Trade Centre [*Switzerland United Nations*] (MCD)

ITC .... International Trading Certificate (DS)

ITC .... International Trading Company [*Thailand*] (IMH)

ITC .... International Translations Centre [*Formerly, ETC*] (EA)

ITC .... International Transport Co. (Cyprus) Ltd.

ITC .... International Trypanotolerance Centre [*Gambia*]

ITC .... Intreprinderile de Transporturi Comerciale [*Enterprises for Commercial Transportation*] (RO)

ITC .... Israel Tennis Center

ITC .... Ivoirienne de Transactions Commerciales

ITCABIC ... Inter-Territorial Catholic Bishops' Conference (EAIO)

ITCF .... Institut Technique des Cereales et des Fourrages [*Technical Insitute for Cereals and Fodder*] [*France*] (PDAA)

ITCME ...... Institutul de Studii si Cercetari Tehnologice pentru Industria Constructiilor de Masini si Electrotehnica [*Technological Studies and Research Institute for the Electrotechnical and Machine Building Industry*] (RO)

ITCO .... Instituto de Tierras y Colonizacion [*Institute of Lands and Settlement*] [*Costa Rica*] (LA)

ITCOM ..... Information Technology and Communications Bureau [*United Nations*] (ECON)

ITCR .... Instituto Tecnologico de Costa Rica [*Technological Institute of Costa Rica*] (LA)

ITCRA ...... International Textile Care and Rental Association [*Netherlands*] (EY)

ITCS .... International Telephone Card Society [*Australia*]

ITCSA .... Institute of Technical Communicators of Southern Africa (EAIO)

ITCV .... Industrial Training Commission of Victoria [*Australia*]

ITCWRM ... International Training Centre for Water Resources Management [*France*]

ITCZ .... Intertropical Convergence Zone

ITD .... Corrective Labor House (RU)

ITD .... Individual'naya Trudovaya Deyatel'nost' [*Individual Labor Activity*] [*Government program designed to foster private enterprise*] [*Russian*]

ITD .... Industry Training Division [*Technical and Further Education*] [*New South Wales, Australia*]

ITD .... Information et Traitement des Donnees [*Information and Data Processing*] (AF)

ITD .... Institute of Training and Development (EAIO)

ITD .... Instytut Technologii Drewna [*Institute of Lumber Technology*] (POL)

i td .... I Tak Dalee [*And So Forth*] (RU)

itd .... I Tak Dalej [*And So Forth*] (POL)

itd .... I Tako Dalje [*And So Forth*] (YU)

ITDC .... International Trade Development Centre [*Australia*]

ITdelT .... Instituto Tecnologico del Tabaco [*Technological Institute for Tobacco*] [*Cuba*] (LA)

ITDG .... Intermediate Technology Development Group [*Rugby, Warwickshire, England*] (EAIO)

ITDI .... Industrial Technology Development Institute [*Philippines*] (IRC)

ITDJEN .... Inspektorat Djenderal [*Inspectorate General*] (IN)

ITDR .... Institute for Training and Demographic Research (EA)

ITDT .... Instituto Torcuato di Tella [*Buenos Aires, Argentina*] (LAA)

ITE .... Institiuid Teangeolaiochta Eireann [*Semigovernmental agency responsible for linguistic research*] [*Irish*]

ITE .... Interestatal de Aviacion SA de CV [*Mexico*] [*ICAO designator*] (FAAC)

ITEA .... Infraestructura Teatral [*Ministerio de Cultura*] [*Spain*] [*Information service or system*] (CRD)

ITEA .... Instituto Tecnico Administrativo [*Administrative Technical Institute*] [*Colorado*] (LA)

ITEAA ...... Interpreter Translator Education Association of Australia

ITEBA .... Institut Technique du Batiment et des Travaux Publics d'Algerie [*Technical Institute for Building Trade and Public Works of Algeria*] (AF)

ITeC .... Information Technology Centre [*Australia*]

ITEC .... Ingenieria Termodinamica Ltda. [*Colombia*] (COL)

ITEC .... Institute of Building Technology of Catalonia [*Spain*]

ITEC .... International Total Energy Congress

ITEC......... International Total Engineering Corporation [*Japan*]
ITEC......... International Transport Exhibition
ITEC......... International Transport Exposition and Conference
ITECA...... International Educational and Cultural Association [*Belgium*] (SLS)
ITECIF...... Institut de Technologie des Cultures Industrielles et Fourrageres [*Algeria*]
ITECMO... Instituto Tecnico Comercial [*Colombia*] (COL)
ITECS....... Instituto Tecnologico de Educacion Superior [*Colombia*] (COL)
ITEF......... Institut de Technologie Forestiere [*Forest Technology Institute*] [*Algeria*] (AF)
ITEF......... Institute of Theoretical and Experimental Physics (RU)
ITEGA...... Industrie Textile Gabonaise
ITEIN....... Institute of Technical and Economic Information (RU)
itekhr........ Engineer Equipment Company (RU)
ITEM........ Heating Technology and Power Generation Machinebuilding Institute [*Bulgarian*] (SLS)
ITEM........ Instituto Tecnologico y de Estudios Superiores de Monterrey [*Technological Institute of Higher Studies of Monterrey*] [*Mexico*] (LAA)
ITEM........ Internationale Technische Messe [*German*] (ADPT)
ITEMCOP ... Industrial Textile Manufacturing Company of the Philippines (FEA)
ITEMS ...... INCOTERM [*International Commerce Term*] Transaction Entry Management System
ITEP.......... Fundacao Instituto Tecnologico do Estado de Pernambuco [*Technological Institute of the State of Pernambuco*] [*Research center*] [*Brazil*] (AF)
ITEP.......... Impressions Techniques et Publicitaires [*French*]
ITERCG.... Institut Technique d'Etudes et des Recherches des Corps Gras
ITERG....... Institut des Corps Gras [*France*]
ITERS........ Instituto Tecnologico de Rio Grande do Sul [*Brazil*] (DSCA)
ITES.......... International Trade Enhancement Scheme [*Australia*]
ITESM ...... Instituto Tecnologico de Estudios Superiores de Monterrey [*Research institute onMexico/US relations*] [*Mexico*] (CROSS)
ITESM ...... Instituto Tecnologico y de Estudios Superiores de Monterrey [*Technological Institute of Higher Studies of Monterrey*] [*Mexico*] (LAA)
ITESNIC... Instituto Tecnologico Nicaraguense [*Nicaraguan Technological Institute*] (LA)
ITESSA ..... Institute of Topographical and Engineering Surveyors of South Africa (AA)
ITF............ Air Inter, Societe [*France*] [*ICAO designator*] (FAAC)
ITF............ Independent Teachers Federation [*Australia*]
ITF............ Industrial Training Fund [*Nigeria*] (AF)
ITF............ Inosinetriphosphoric Acid (RU)
ITF............ Institute of Theoretical Physics (RU)
ITF............ Institute of Thermophysics (of the Siberian Department of the Academy of Sciences, USSR) (RU)
ITF............ Institute of Tropical Forestry [*Puerto Rican*] (ARC)
ITF............ Institut Textile de France [*French Textile Institute*] [*Boulogne-Billancourt*] [*Information service or system*] (IID)
ITF............ Instrumenttekniska Foereningen [*Sweden*] (SLS)
ITF............ International Teaching Fellowship
ITF............ International Tennis Federation [*Formerly, ILTF*] (EA)
ITF............ International Trade and Finance Division
ITF............ International Trade Fair [*New Zealand*]
ITF............ International Transport Workers' Federation [*London, England*] (EAIO)
ITF............ Islamic Thought Foundation [*Iran*] (EAIO)
ITF............ Istituto di Terapia Familiare SRL [*Italian*] (SLS)
ITFA......... Independent Teachers Federation of Australia
ITFCA....... International Track and Field Coaches Association [*Athens, Greece*] (EAIO)
ITFW........ Industry Training Fund for Women [*Australia*]
ITG........... Institute of Theoretical Geophysics (of the Academy of Sciences, USSR)
ITGLWF ... International Textile, Garment, and Leather Workers' Federation [*See also FITTHC*] [*Brussels, Belgium*] (EAIO)
ITGWU ..... Irish Transport and General Workers' Union (DCTA)
ITGY......... Iskolai Taneszkozok Gyara [*School Epuipment Manufacturers*] (HU)
ITH........... Institut des Techniques Hotelieres [*North African*]
ITHE .... International Travel Host Exchange
ITHR .... Intreprinderea de Turism, Hoteluri, si Restaurante [*Enterprise for Tourism, Hotels, and Restaurants*] (RO)
ITHRPB .... Institute for Teaching of Human Rights - Paris Bar [*France*] (EAIO)
ITHT .... Institut des Techniques Hotelieres et Touristiques [*North African*]
ITI............ Iceberg Transport International Ltd. [*Saudi Arabia*] (PDAA)
ITI............ Indian Telephone Industries Ltd. (IMH)
ITI............ Institut de Technologie Industrielle [*Ivory Coast*]
ITI............ Institute of Technical Information (RU)

ITI............ Institut TNO voor Toegepaste Informatica [*TNO Institute of Applied Computer Science*] [*Information service or system*] (IID)
ITI............ International Theatre Institute [*Paris, France*] (EAIO)
ITI............ International Trade & Investment [*Investment consortium*] [*Hong Kong*]
ITI............ International Tungsten Indicator [*Industry price index*] (FEA)
ITIA .... Iktisat ve Ticari Ilimler Akademisi [*The Academy of Economics and Commercial Science*] [*Eskisehir IITIA*] [*See also*] (TU)
ITIA .... Intreprinderea pentru Turism International Automobilistic [*Enterprise for International Automobile Tourism*] (RO)
ITIC .... Industrial Technical Information Centre [*Australia*]
ITIC .... Instituto Tecnico de Inmigracion y Colonizacion [*Venezuela*] (DSCA)
ITIC .... Instituto Tropical de Investigaciones Cientificas [*San Salvador, El Salvador*] (LAA)
ITIC .... International Tsunami Information Center [*IOC*] (ASF)
ITIEINEFTEGAZ ... Institute of Technical Information and Economic Research (of the State Committee of the Council of Ministers, USSR, for the Fuel Industry) (RU)
ITIM .... Institutul de Tehnologie Isotopica si Moleculara [*Institute for Isotopic and Molecular Technology*] (RO)
ITIM .... News Agency of Associated Israel Press Limited (ME)
ITINTEC... Instituto de Investigacion Tecnologica Industrial y de Normas Tecnicas [*Institute of Technological Research and Technical Standards*] [*Peru*]
ITiOP........ Institute of Trade and Public Eating Facilities (RU)
ITIP .... International Technical Integration Panel
ITIPAT...... Institut pour la Technologie et l'Industrialisation des Produits Agricoles Tropicaux [*Ivory Coast*]
ITIS .... Industrial Technical Information Service [*Singapore*] (IID)
ITIS .... Institute for Standard Designing and Industrialization of Construction (BU)
ITIS .... Intermediate Technology Industrial Services
ITJ .... Instytut Techniki Jadrowej [*Institute of Nuclear Technics*] [*Poland*]
ITJ .... International Telecom Japan
ITJ .... Inzenjeri i Tehnicari Jugoslavije [*Engineers and Technicians of Yugoslavia*] (YU)
ITJ .... Ipari Termekek Jegyzeke [*Industrial Products Register*] (HU)
ITJ .... Societa' Italjet [*Italy*] [*ICAO designator*] (FAAC)
ITK............ Corrective Labor Code (RU)
ITK............ Corrective Labor Colony (RU)
ITK............ Idegennyelvu Tovabbkepzo Kozpont [*Center for Continuing Education in Foreign Languages*] (HU)
ITK............ Instytut Technologii Krzemianow [*Institute of Silicate Technology*] (POL)
ITK............ Itokama [*Papua New Guinea*] [*Airport symbol*] (OAG)
ITK............ Technical Control Inspection (RU)
ITK............ True Boiling Point (RU)
ITKSA ...... Instituut vir Tegniese Kommunikators van Suidelike Afrika [*Institute of Technical Communicators of Southern Africa*] (EAIO)
ITKUM ..... Inspektorat Hukum [*Inspectorate of Legal Affairs*] (IN)
ITL............ Corrective Labor Camp (RU)
ITL............ Isotopotekniska Laboratoriet [*Isotopes Techniques Laboratory*] [*Sweden*] (PDAA)
Itl................ Italian (BARN)
ITLB .... International Trade Law Branch [*United Nations*] (DUND)
ITLGSWF ... Interamerican Textile, Leather, Garment, and Shoe Workers Federation (EA)
ITLPP........ Intreprinderea Transpoarte si Livrari Produse Petroliere [*Enterprise for the Transportation and Delivery of Petroleum Products*] (RO)
ITLR......... Institut fur Thermodynamik der Luft- und Raumfahrt [*Institute of Aerospace Thermodynamics*] [*Germany*] (IRC)
ITLS .... International Thomson Library Services
ITM .... Industria Tehnico-Medicala [*Medical Technology Industry*] (RO)
ITM .... Industrija Traktora i Masina [*Tractors and Machines Industry*] [*Belgrade*] (YU)
ITM .... Industry and Trade Ministry
ITM .... Information Technology Month [*Australia*]
ITM .... Ingenieur Technique de Maintenance [*French*] (ADPT)
ITM .... Inspection du Travail et des Mines [*Luxembourg*]
ITM .... Institute of Transportation Machinery (RU)
ITM .... Instituto Tecnico Militar [*Institute of Military Technology*] [*Cuba*] (LA)
ITM .... Institut Teknoloji MARA [*MARA Technology Institute*] (ML)
ITM .... International Tourism Management [*Australia*]
ITM .... ITA [*Itapemirim Transportes Aereos SA*] [*Brazil*] [*ICAO designator*] (FAAC)
ITMA .... Institut de Technologie Moyens Agricoles [*Agricultural Implements Institute of Technology*] [*Algeria*] (AF)
ITMA .... International Textile Machinery Association

ITMF .... International Textile Manufacturers Federation [*Zurich, Switzerland*]   (EA)

ItMGM ...... Italian MGM [*Record label*]

ITM i VT ... Institute of Precision Mechanics and Computer Engineering (RU)

itn .... And So On   (BU)

ITN .... Independent Television Network [*Sri Lanka*]   (FEA)

ITN .... Industrias Titan SA [*Spain*] [*ICAO designator*]   (FAAC)

ITN .... Initial Aiming Point [*Artillery*], Initial Guidance Point [*To an objective*]   (BU)

ITN .... Institutul de Tehnologie Nucleara [*Nuclear Technology Institute*] (RO)

ITN .... Itabuna [*Brazil*] [*Airport symbol*]   (OAG)

itn .... I Taka Natamu [*Et Cetera*]   (YU)

ITO .... Icelandic Teachers Organization   (EAIO)

ITO .... Income Tax Order

ITO .... Information Technology Officer [*Australia*]

ITO .... Institut der Technologie und Organisation [*Institute of Technology and Organization*]   (EG)

ITO .... Institute of Technical Training   (RU)

ITO .... Instituto de Tecnologia de Oleos [*Brazil*]   (DSCA)

ITO .... International Trade Organization

ITO .... Istanbul Tabibler Odasi [*Istanbul Chamber of Physicians*]   (TU)

ITO .... Istanbul Ticaret Odasi [*Istanbul Chamber of Commerce*]   (TU)

ITOA .... Inbound Tourism Organisation of Australia

ITOChMEKh ... Institute of Precision Mechanics and Computer Engineering (RU)

ITOCY ...... Industrie Togolaise du Cycle et du Cyclomoteur

ITOF .... Ingiltere Turk Ogrenci Federasyonu [*Turkish Student Federation of Great Britain*] [*Turkish Cypriot*]   (GC)

ITOMKKh ... Institute of Technical Training of the Ministry of the Municipal Economy, RSFSR   (RU)

ITO of SA .. Institute of Traffic Officers of Southern Africa   (AA)

ITOPF .... International Tanker Owners Pollution Federation

ITOSA .... Institute of Traffic Officers of Southern Africa   (EAIO)

ITOV .... Ipari Tanfolyamok Orszagos Vezetosege [*National Headquarters of Industrial Training Courses*]   (HU)

ITOV .... Ipartestuletek Orszagos Vezetosege [*National Office of Craftsmen's Associations*]   (HU)

ITP .... Engineering and Technical Personnel   (RU)

i tp .... Et Cetera, And So Forth   (RU)

ITP .... Impozitele si Taxele ale Populatie [*Public Taxes and Fees*] (RO)

ITP .... Index to Proceedings [*Information service or system United Nations*]   (DUND)

ITP .... Industrie Togolaise des Plastiques [*Manufacturer of plastics*] [*Togo*]

ITP .... Industrija Tepiha "Proleter" [*The "Proleter" Rug Factory*] [*Zrenjanin*]   (YU)

ITP .... Ingenieurtechnisches Personal [*Engineering and Technical Personnel*]   (EG)

ITP .... Institute of Tropical Pisciculture [*Colorado*]   (ASF)

ITP .... Instituto Tecnologico Pesquero del Peru [*Peru*]

ITP .... Institut Technique du Port [*France*]

ITP .... International Test Pilot School [*British*] [*ICAO designator*] (FAAC)

ITP .... Inzenyrsko-Technicti Pracovnici [*Engineering and Technical Specialists*]   (CZ)

itp .... Itaista Pituutta [*Finland*]

It P .... Italienisches Patent [*Italian Patent*] [*German*]   (GCA)

ITP .... Ittihat ve Terakki Partisi [*Union and Progress Party*] [*Historic*] (TU)

itp .... I Tym Podobne [*And the Like*]   (POL)

ITPA .... International Tea Promotion Association [*Defunct*]   (EAIO)

ITPAS .... Instituto do Trabalho, Previdencia, e Accao Social [*Institute of Labor, Welfare, and Social Security*] [*Mozambique*]   (AF)

itpbatr .... Tank-Destroyer Battery   (BU)

ITPEA .... Institut des Techniques de Planification et d'Economie Appliquee [*Algeria*]

ITPM .... Institute of Theoretical and Applied Mechanics (of the Siberian Department of the Academy of Sciences, USSR)   (RU)

ITPO .... International TOGA [*Tropical Ocean Global Atmosphere*] Project Office [*Geneva, Switzerland*]   (EAIO)

ITPP .... Ilorin Talaka Parapo Party

i-tr .... Corrective Labor   (RU)

itr .... Engineer Equipment Company   (RU)

ITR .... Engineering and Technical Personnel   (RU)

ITR .... Engineering and Technical Workers   (BU)

ITR .... Institut Technique Roubaisien [*Roubaix Technical Institute*] [*French*] [*Research center*]   (ERC)

ITR .... Instytut Tele- i Radiotechniczny [*Institute of Telecommunications*]   (POL)

itralb .... Engineer Mine-Sweeping Battalion   (RU)

itralr .... Engineer Mine-Sweeping Company   (RU)

ITRC .... Indian Toxicology Research Centre

ITRC .... International Tin Research Council [*Middlesex, England*] (EAIO)

ITRI .... Industrial Technology Research Institute [*Taiwanese*] [*Research center*]   (IRC)

ItRI .... Institute Centrale Catalogo Unico delle Bibliotheche Italiane e per le Informazioni Bibliografiche, Rome, Italy [*Library symbol*] [*Library of Congress*]   (LCLS)

ITRMLM .. Institut Territorial de Recherches Medicales Louis Malarde [*Louis Malarde Territorial Institute of Medical Research*] [*Tahiti*] [*Research center*]   (IRC)

ITRPF .... International Tyre, Rubber, and Plastic Federation   (EAIO)

ItRUN .... Centro di Documentazione Umberto Nobile, Museo Storico, Rome, Italy [*Library symbol*] [*Library of Congress*] (LCLS)

ITS .... Aeronautica Interespacial SA de CV [*Mexico*] [*ICAO designator*] (FAAC)

ITS .... Engineering and Technical Convention   (RU)

ITS .... Engineering and Technical Council   (RU)

ITS .... Engineering and Technical Section   (RU)

ITS .... Engineering and Technical Service   (RU)

its .... Engineering and Technical Staff   (RU)

ITS .... Engineering and Technical Union   (RU)

ITS .... Impot sur les Traitements et Salaires

ITS .... Independent Tyre Service [*Australia*]

ITS .... Index to Speeches [*Information service or system United Nations*] (DUND)

ITS .... Indo-Thai Synthetics [*Thailand*] [*Commercial firm*]

ITS .... Industrial Training Service

ITS .... Instalaciones Tecnicas Sanitarias Hidraulicas y Mecanicas [*Colombia*]   (COL)

ITS .... Institute Technical Supervision [*Ghana*]

ITS .... Institut Teknologi Sepuluh Nopember [*Surabaya Institute of Technology*] [*Indonesia*]   (ERC)

ITS .... Instytut Transportu Samochodowego [*Institute of Motor Transport*]   (POL)

ITS .... Instytut Tworzyw Sztucznych [*Institute of Plastics*] [*Poland*]

ITS .... Integriertes Transportstererungs System [*German*]   (ADPT)

ITS .... Integrierte Transportsteurung [*German*]   (ADPT)

ITS .... International Teleconference Symposium [*Australia*]

ITS .... International Tracing Service [*Arolsen, Germany*]   (EAIO)

ITS .... International Trade Secretariats [*ICFTU*]

ITS .... Inzenjerska Tehnicka Sluzba [*Engineering Technical Service*] [*Military*]   (YU)

ITS .... Inzenjerstvo Tehnicko Snabdevanje [*Engineering and Technical Supplying*] [*Military*]   (YU)

ITS .... Irish Texts Society   (EAIO)

ITS .... Technical Information Collection   (RU)

ITSA .... Insolvency and Trustee Service Australia

ITSAC .... International Thermal Storage Advisory Council   (EAIO)

ITSAKS ..... Institut Technique Superieur de l'Amitie Khmero-Sovietique [*Cambodian-Soviet Friendship Higher Technological Institute*]   (CL)

ITSB .... Information Technology Service Bureau [*Department of Primary Industries and Energy*] [*Australia*]

ITSC .... Information Technology Steering Committee [*Australia*]

ITSC .... International Television Studies Conference

ITSC .... Interpreting and Translating Services Committee [*New South Wales, Australia*]

itsen........... Itsenainen [*Used as a Noun, Substantively*] [*Finland*]

ITsG........... Institute of Cytology and Genetics (of the Siberian Department of the Academy of Sciences, USSR)   (RU)

itsl .... I Tome Slicno [*And the Like*]   (YU)

ITSM .... Institut fur Thermische Stromungsmaschinen und Maschinenlaboratorium [*Thermal Turbomachines Institute and Machines Laboratory*] [*Germany*]   (IRC)

ITSR .... Indo-Pacific Fisheries Council [*IPFC*]   (RU)

ITSTC....... International Telecommunictaions Standards Technical Council (OSI)

ITSU .... Tsunami Warning System in the Pacific   (MSC)

ITsYeZhD ... Information Center of the European Railways [*ICER*]   (RU)

ITT............ Industrie Textile Togolaise

ITT............ Instituto Tecnologico del Tabaco [*Technological Institute for Tobacco*] [*Cuba*]   (LA)

ITT............ Instituut voor Tuinbouwtechniek Institute of Horticultural Engineering [*Netherlands*]   (DSCA)

ITTA......... International Tropical Timber Agreement   (ECON)

ITTA......... Intreprinderea de Transporturi Turistice Auto [*Enterprise for Tourism Automotive Transportation*]   (RO)

ITTC......... International Tropical Timber Council [*Australia*]

ITTE......... Information Technology for Training and Education [*Australia*]

ITTF......... International Table Tennis Federation [*British*]

ittiol............ Ittiologia [*Ichthyology*] [*Italian*]

ITTO......... International Tropical Timber Organization [*Yokohama, Japan*] [*United Nations*]

ITTTA...... International Technical Tropical Timber Association

ITTU......... Intermediate Technology Transfer Unit [*Ghana*]

ITU .... Corrective Labor Establishment   (RU)

ITU .... Igbirra Tribal Union

ITU .... Individual Telephone Amplifier   (RU)

ITU .... Institute of Managerial Techniques   (RU)
ITU .... Institutul Teologic Universitar [*University Theological Institute*] (RO)
ITU .... Intendanska Uprava [*Quartermaster Administration*]   (YU)
ITU .... Intensive Therapy Unit [*Australia*]
ITU .... International Telecommunication Union [*Formerly, International Telegraphic Union*] [*A specialized agency of the United Nations*] [*Switzerland*] [*Research center*]
ITU .... International Triathlon Union   (OLYM)
ITU .... Israel Teachers Union   (EAIO)
ITU .... Istanbul Teknik Universitesi [*Istanbul Technical University*] (TU)
ITUCNW .. International Trade Union Committee of Negro Workers
ITUCSTL.. International Trade Unions Committee of Social Tourism and Leisure [*See also CSITSL*] [*Prague, Czechoslovakia*] (EAIO)
ITUEHB.... Istanbul Teknik Universitesi Elektronik Hesap Bilimleri Enstitusu [*Electronic Accounting Science Institute of Istanbul Technical University*] [*EHB*] [*See also*]   (TU)
ITUMMF ... Istanbul Teknik Universitesi Mimarlik ve Muhendislik Fakultesi [*Istanbul Technical University Faculty of Architecture and Engineering*]   (TU)
ITUOB ...... Istanbul Teknik Universitesi Ogrenci Birligi [*Istanbul Technical University Student Union*] [*ITUTB*] [*See also*]   (TU)
ITUSCO .... Instituto Universitario Surcolombiano [*Neiva*]   (COL)
ITUTB .... Istanbul Teknik Universitesi Talebe Birligi [*Istanbul Technical University Student Union*] [*ITUOB*] [*See also*]   (TU)
ITUTOTB ... Istanbul Teknik Universitesi Teknik Okulu Talebe Birligi [*Istanbul Technical University's Technical School Student Union*]   (TU)
ITV............. Industrijska Televizija [*Industrial Television*]   (YU)
ITV............. Intervuelo SA [*Mexico*] [*ICAO designator*]   (FAAC)
ITV............. Irodagepteknika Vallalat [*Enterprise of Business Machine Technology*]   (HU)
ITV............. Israel Television   (BJA)
ItV............. Italian RCA [*Victor*] [*Record label*]
ITVA......... International Industrial Television Association   (NTCM)
ITVICOOP ... Instituto de Vivienda Cooperativa [*Panama*]   (DSCA)
ItVox......... Italian Vox [*Record label*]
ITVS .... Institut Telesne Vychovy a Sportu [*Institute of Physical Education and Sports*]   (CZ)
ITW............ Independent True Whig Party [*Liberia*] [*Political party*]
ITW .... Information Technology Week   (ADA)
ITW .... Institut fuer Technische Weiterbildung   (SLS)
ITWL........ Instytut Techniczny Wojsk Lotniczych [*Air Force Institute of Technology*]   (POL)
ITX............. Individual Tour Excursion
ITZN......... International Trust for Zoological Nomenclature   (DSCA)
ITZU......... Installation of Technical Establishments and Equipment   (BU)
IU .... Actuating Amplifier   (RU)
IU .... Actuating Device   (RU)
IU .... Engineering Administration   (RU)
iu .... Idoszamitasunk Kezdete Utan [*Of Our Era, Anno Domini*] (HU)
iu .... Igazsagugy [*Justice, Judiciary*]   (HU)
IU.............. In- en Uitvoer [*Benelux*]   (BAS)
IU.............. Integrating Amplifier   (RU)
iU.............. Intellektuelle Unterlage [*Intellectual Base*] [*German*]
IU.............. Izquierda Unida [*United Left*] [*Spain*] [*Political party*]   (ECED)
IU.............. Izquierda Unida [*United Left*] [*Bolivia*] [*Political party*]   (EY)
IU.............. Izquierda Unida [*United Left*] [*Peru*] [*Political party*]
IU.............. Level Gauge   (RU)
IU.............. Measuring Device   (RU)
IU.............. Needle Filter Installation   (RU)
IU.............. Quartermaster Directorate   (RU)
IUA .... Instytut Urbanistyki i Architektury [*Institute of City Planning and Architecture*]   (POL)
IUAA .... International Union of Advertisers Associations [*Later, WFA*] (EAIO)
IUAA .... International Union of Amateur Astronomers [*Italian*]   (SLS)
IUAB .... Internal Unity Advisory Body [*Revolutionary Council*] [*Myanmar*]   (FEA)
IUAES .... International Union of Anthropological and Ethnological Sciences [*See also UISAE*] [*ICSU Gwynedd, Wales*] (EAIO)
IUAI .... International Union of Aviation Insurers [*British*]   (EAIO)
IUAJ .... International Union of Agricultural Journalists   (DSCA)
IUAKP...... Iuzhno-Afrikanskaia Kommunisticheskaia Partiia
IUAM .... Islamic Unity of Afghan Mujahadeen [*Afghanistan*] [*Political party*]
IUAO........ Internationalen Union fuer Angewandte Ornithologie [*International Union for Applied Orthithology*]   (EAIO)
IUAPPA .... International Union of Air Pollution Prevention Associations [*See also UIAPPA*] [*England*]   (EAIO)
IUAR .... Iuzhno-Afrikanskaia Respublika
IUAS......... International Union of Agricultural Sciences [*France*]   (DSCA)
IUAS.......... Iuzhno-Afrikanskii Soiuz

IUAT .... International Union Against Tuberculosis [*Later, IUATLD*] (EAIO)
IUATLD.... International Union Against Tuberculosis and Lung Disease [*See also UICTMR*]   (EAIO)
IUB .... International Union of Biochemistry [*ICSU*]   (ASF)
IUBCTW ... International Union of Bakery, Confectionery, and Tobacco Workers   (BARN)
IUBMB...... International Union of Biochemistry and Molecular Biology [*Germany*]   (EAIO)
IUBS......... International Union of Biological Sciences [*Paris, France*]
IUBSSA..... International Union of Building Societies and Savings Associations [*Later, IOHFI*] [*Chicago, IL*]   (EA)
IUC .... Inter-University Council
IUC .... Intreprinderea de Utilaj Chimic [*Chemical Equipment Enterprise*]   (RO)
IUCAA ...... Inter-University Center for Astronomy and Astrophysic [*India*]
IUCAB...... International Union of Commercial Agents and Brokers [*EC*] (ECED)
IUCADC.... Inter-Union Commission of Advice to Developing Countries [*of the International Union of Geodesy and Geophysics*] [*Mississauga, ON*]   (EAIO)
IUCED....... Inter-Union Commission of European Dehydrators [*See also CIDE*] [*Paris, France*]   (EAIO)
IUCN .... International Union for Conservation of Nature and Natural Resources [*Research Center*] [*ICSU*] [*Switzerland*]   (EA)
IUCNNR ... International Union for Conservation of Nature and Natural Resources [*ICSU*] [*Research center*] [*Switzerland*]
IUCNPSG ... International Union for the Conservation of Nature's Primate Specialist Group   (EA)
IU Cr......... International Union of Crystallography [*See also UIC*]   (EA)
IUCRM ..... Inter-Union Commission on Radio Meteorology [*International Council of Scientific Unions*] [*Research center*]
IUCS.......... Inter-Union Commission on Spectroscopy [*International Council of Scientific Unions*]
IUCST .... Inter-Union Commission on Science Teaching [*Italy*]   (DSCA)
IUCT......... Intreprinderea de Utilaje Constructii Transport [*Enterprise for Transportation Equipment and Constructions*]   (RO)
IUCW .... International Union for Child Welfare [*Geneva, Switzerland*] [*Defunct*]
IUD........... Information und Dokumentation [*Information and Documentation*] [*German*] [*Information retrieval*]
IUDOP ...... Instituto Uruguayo de la Opinion Publica [*Public Opinion Institute of Uruguay*]   (LA)
IUDP .... Intreprinderea Utilaje Drumuri si Poduri [*Enterprise for Road and Bridge Equipment*]   (RO)
IuD-Programm ... Information und Dokumentation Programm
IUDSE....... Internationale Union Demokratischer Sozialistischer [*Switzerland*] (SLS)
IUDZG ...... International Union of Directors of Zoological Gardens [*Canada*]   (EAIO)
IUE .... Niue Island [*Niue*] [*Airport symbol*]   (OAG)
IUED .... Institut Universitaire d'Etudes du Developpement [*France*]
IUED .... Institut Universitaire d'Etudes du Developpement [*Switzerland*] (PDAA)
IUEF......... Internacia Unuigo de la Esperantistoj-Filologoj [*International Union of Esperantist-Philologists - IUEP*] [*Sofia, Bulgaria*] (EAIO)
IUEF......... International University Exchange Fund
IUEFI........ Internacia Unuigo de la Esperantistoj-Filologoj [*International Union of Esperantist-Philologists - IUEP*] [*Sofia, Bulgaria*] (EA)
IUEGS....... International Union of European Guides and Scouts [*See also UIGSE*] [*Chateau Landon, France*]   (EAIO)
IUEP......... International Union of Esperantist-Philologists [*Sofia, Bulgaria*] (EAIO)
IUES.......... Instituto Uruguayo de Educacion Sindical [*Uruguayan Institute for Labor Union Education*]   (LA)
IUF .... International Union of Food and Allied Workers' Associations [*See also IUL*] [*Petit-Lancy, Switzerland*]   (EAIO)
IUFLJP...... International Union of French-Language Journalists and Press [*See also UIJPLF*] [*Paris, France*]   (EAIO)
IUFO .... International Union of Family Organizations [*Paris, France*]
IUFoST...... International Union of Food Science and Technology [*ICSU*] [*Dublin, Republic of Ireland*]   (EAIO)
IUFRO....... International Union of Forestry Research Organizations [*Vienna, Austria*] [*Research center*]   (EAIO)
IUG .... Intreprinderea de Utilaj Greu [*Heavy Equipment Enterprise*] (RO)
IUGB .... International Union of Game Biologists [*Canada*]   (EAIO)
IUGG .... International Union of Geodesy and Geophysics [*Brussels, Belgium*]
IUGRI........ International Union of Graphic Reproduction Industries [*Later, IUI*]   (EAIO)
IUGS.......... International Union of Geological Sciences [*ICSU*] [*Trondheim, Norway*]   (EA)
IUHE......... International Union of Health Education [*See also UIES*] [*Paris, France*]   (EAIO)

IUHF .... Istanbul Universitesi Hukuk Fakultesi [*Istanbul University Faculty of Law*] (TU)

IUHFI .... International Union of Housing Finance Institutions (EAIO)

IUHPS ...... International Union of the History and Philosophy of Science [*ICSU*] [*Uppsala, Sweden*] (EAIO)

IUiA .... Instytut Urbanistyki i Architektury [*Institute of City Planning and Architecture*] (POL)

IUIkF .... Istanbul Universitesi Iktisat Fakultesi [*Istanbul University Faculty of Economics*] (TU)

IUIN .... International Union for Inland Navigation [*Strasbourg, France*] (EA)

IUINS .... Interuniversity Institute of Nuclear Sciences [*See also IISN*] [*Nuclear energy*] [*Belgium*] (NRCH)

IUIP .... Instituto Nacional de Investigacao das Pescas [*Portuguese*] (ASF)

IUIS .... International Union of Immunological Societies [*ICSU*]

IUJ .... International University of Japan (ECON)

IUK .... Indolylacetic Acid (RU)

IUL .... Institute of Ukrainian Literature Imeni T. G. Shevchenko (RU)

IUL .... Internationale Union der Lebens- und Genussmittelarbeiter-Gewerkschaften [*International Union of Food and Allied Workers Associations - IUF*] [*Petit-Lancy, Switzerland*] (EAIO)

IUL .... Italian Union of Labour (EAIO)

IULA .... International Union of Local Authorities [*The Hague, Netherlands*] (EA)

IULCLG .... Imposto Unico sobre Lubrificantes e Combustiveis Liquidos e Gasosos [*Single Tax on Lubricants and Liquid or Gaseous Fuels*] [*Brazil*] (LA)

IULD .... International Union of Lorry Drivers [*See also UICR*] [*Munich, Germany*] (EAIO)

IULTCS ..... International Union of Leather Technologists and Chemists Societies [*Spain*]

IULVTFT ... International Union for Land Value Taxation and Free Trade [*British*] (EAIO)

IUM .... Internationale Unie van Magistraten [*Benelux*] (BAS)

IUMDA ..... Information Unit on Militarisation and Demilitarisation in Asia [*India*]

IUMI .... International Union of Marine Insurance [*Basel, Switzerland*]

IUMP .... International Union of Master Painters [*See also UNIEP*] [*Brussels, Belgium*] (EAIO)

IUMP .... International Upper Mantle Program (MSC)

IUMS .... International Union of Marine Sciences [*Proposed*] (MSC)

IUMS .... International Union of Microbiological Sciences [*ICSU*]

IUMSBD ... International Union of Microbiological Societies Bacteriology Division [*Beckenham, Kent, England*] (EAIO)

IUNG .... Instytut Uprawy, Nawozenia, i Gleboznawstwa [*Institute of Cultivation, Fertilization, and Soil Science*] (POL)

IUNS .... International Union of Nutritional Sciences [*Wageningen, Netherlands*]

IUNT .... Instituto Uruguayo de Normas Tecnicas [*Uruguay*] (DSCA)

IUOTO ..... International Union of Official Travel Organizations (CL)

IUP .... International Union of Phlebology [*Paris, France*] (EA)

IUP .... Sociedade Unificada Paulista de Ensino Renovada Objectivo [*Brazil*] (SLS)

IUP .... University Polytechnical Institute [*Spanish*]

IUPAB .... International Union of Pure and Applied Biophysics [*ICSU*] [*Pecs, Hungary*] [*Research center*] (EA)

IUPAC ...... International Union of Pure and Applied Chemistry [*Research center*] [*British*] (IRC)

IUPAP .... International Union of Pure and Applied Physics [*ICSU*] [*Goteborg, Sweden*] (EA)

IUPERJ ..... Instituto Universitario de Pesquisas do Rio De Janeiro [*Brazil*] (LAA)

IUPESM ... International Union for Physical and Engineering Sciences in Medicine [*ICSU*] [*Ottawa, ON*] (EAIO)

IUPHAR ... International Union of Pharmacology [*ICSU*] [*Buckingham, England*] (MSC)

IUPIP .... International Union for the Protection of Industrial Property

IUPN .... International Union for the Protection of Nature [*Later, IUCN*]

IUPOV ...... International Union for the Protection of New Varieties of Plants (GNE)

IUPPS .... International Union of Prehistoric and Protohistoric Sciences [*Ghent, Belgium*] (EAIO)

IUPS .... International Union of Physiological Sciences [*ICSU*] [*Gif-sur-Yvette, France*] (ASF)

IUPS .... Intreprinderea de Utilaje si Piese de Schimb [*Enterprise for Equipment and Spare Parts*] (RO)

IUPSMB ... Intreprinderea de Utilaje si Piese de Schimb a Municipiului Bucuresti [*Bucharest Municipality Enterprise for Equipment and Spare Parts*] (RO)

IUPsyS ...... International Union of Psychological Science (EA)

IUR .... International Union of Radioecologists (EA)

IUR .... Level Indicator (RU)

IURAP ...... International Users Resource Allocation Panel

IURC .... International Union for Research of Communication [*Berne, Switzerland*] (EAIO)

IURMS ...... International Union of Railway Medical Services (EA)

IURN .... Institut Unifie de Recherches Nucleaires

IURP .... International Union of Roofing and Plumbing (EAIO)

IURR .... Institute for Urban and Regional Research [*Austria*] (EAIO)

IURS .... International Union of Radio Science (MSC)

IUS .... Information Index of Standards (RU)

IUS .... International Union of Speleology [*See also UIS*] [*Vienna, Austria*] (EAIO)

IUS .... International Union of Students [*See also UIE*] [*Prague, Czechoslovakia*] (EAIO)

IUS .... Istituto Internazionale per l'Unificazione del Diritto [*Italian*] (SLS)

IUSA .... Industrias Unidas, Sociedad Anonima [*United Industries Corporation*] [*El Salvador*]

IUSAMH .. International Union of Societies for the Aid of Mental Health [*Bordeaux, France*] (EAIO)

IUSDT ...... International Union of Socialist Democratic Teachers (EAIO)

IUSE .... Institut Universitaire des Sciences de l'Education

IUSE .... Istituto Universitario di Studi Europei [*Italian*] (SLS)

IUSF .... International Union for Surface Finishing (EAIO)

IUSF .... International Union of Societies of Foresters [*See also UISIF*] [*Ottawa, ON*] (EAIO)

IUSIT .... Institute for the Advanced Training of Specialists, Engineers, and Technicians (BU)

IUSP .... Internationale Union fuer Wissenschaftliche Psychologie [*International Union for Scientific Psychology*] (EG)

IUSSI .... International Union for the Study of Social Insects [*Utrecht, Netherlands*]

IUSSP .... International Union for the Scientific Study of Population [*Liege, Belgium*]

IUSTI .... Institut Universitaire des Sciences et Techniques de l'Information [*University Institute for Information Sciences and Techniques*] [*Zaire*] (AF)

IUSUHM .. International Union of School and University Health and Medicine [*See also UIHMSU*] [*Brussels, Belgium*] (EAIO)

IUSY .... International Union of Socialist Youth (AF)

IUT .... Instituto Universitario de Tecnologia [*University Technological Institute*] [*Colombia*] (COL)

IUT .... Institut Universitaire de Technologie [*University Institute of Technology*] [*French*] (WER)

IUT .... International Union of Tenants [*Stockholm, Sweden*] (EAIO)

IUT .... Intreprinderea de Utilaje Transport [*Enterprise for Transportation Equipment*] (RO)

IUTAM ..... International Union of Theoretical and Applied Mechanics [*Germany*]

IUTAO ...... International Union of Technical Associations and Organizations [*France*] (EAIO)

IUTB .... Istanbul Universitesi Talebe Birligi [*Istanbul University Student Union*] (TU)

IUTCA ...... International Union of Technical Cinematograph Associations [*See also UNIATEC*] [*Paris, France*] (EAIO)

IUTS .... Instituts Universitaires de Technologie [*France*]

IUU .... Institute for the Advanced Training of Teachers (RU)

IUV .... Industrija Usnja, Vrhnika [*Vrhnika Leather Industry*] (YU)

IUV .... Institute for the Advanced Training of Physicians (RU)

IUVDT ...... International Union Against Venereal Diseases and Treponematoses (EAIO)

IUVSTA .... International Union for Vacuum Science, Technique, and Applications [*See also UISTAV*] (EAIO)

IUWA .... International Union of Women Architects [*See also UIFA*] [*Paris, France*] (EAIO)

IUWDS ...... International Ursigram and World Days Service [*ICSU*]

IUYCD ...... International Union of Young Christian Democrats [*Rome, Italy*]

IUZA .... Iugo-Zapadnaia Afrika

IUZSSKh .. Institute for the Advanced Training of Agricultural Specialists Imeni Academician V. R. Vil'yams (RU)

IV .... Call Finder (RU)

IV .... Gas Tube Rectifier (RU)

iV............. Im Vakuum [*In a Vacuum*] [*German*]

iV............. Im Vorjahre [*Last Year*] [*German*] (EG)

IV .... Informationsverarbeitung [*Information Processing*] [*German*] (ADPT)

IV .... Information Victoria [*Australia*] [*An association*]

IV .... Inspecteur de Ville [*City Inspector*] [*French*] (ADPT)

IV .... Institute of Oriental Studies (of the Academy of Sciences, USSR) (RU)

iv............. Intravenoes [*Intravenous*] [*German*] (GCA)

iV............. In Vertretung [*By Proxy, By Order, On Behalf Of*] [*German*] (EG)

iV............. In Vollmacht [*In Proxy*] [*German*]

IV .... Izvrsno Vece [*Executive Council*] [*YU*] (YU)

IV .... Output Meter (RU)

IV .... Propositional Calculus (RU)

IV .... Viscosity Index (RU)

IV .... Visibility Meter (RU)

IVA .... Ambanja [*Madagascar*] [*Airport symbol*] (OAG)

IVA .... Imposta sul Valore Aggiunto [*Value-Added Tax*] [*Italian*]
IVA .... Impuesto al Valor Agregado [*Value-Added Tax*] [*Spanish*]   (LA)
IVA .... Impuesto sobre el Valor Anadido [*Value-Added Tax*] [*Spanish*]
IVA .... Indian Veterinary Association   (DSCA)
IVA .... Ingeniorsveten-Skapsakademien [*Academy of Engineering Sciences*] [*Sweden*]   (WEN)
IVA .... Instituto de Vacuna Antivariolica, Sucre [*Smallpox Vaccination Institute*] [*La Paz, Bolivia*]   (LAA)
IVA .... Instituut voor Automatisering [*Rotterdam*]
IVA .... Intendanska Vojna Akademija [*Quartermaster Military Academy*]   (YU)
IVA .... Internationaler Verband fuer Arbeiterbildung [*International Federation of Workers' Educational Associations - IFWEA*]   (EAIO)
IVAAP .... International Veterinary Association for Animal Production [*See also AIVPA*] [*Brussels, Belgium*] [*Research center*]   (EAIO)
IVAB .... Instituut vir Vasteafvalbestuur [*South Africa*]   (AA)
IVAC .... Instituto Venezolano de Accion Comunitaria [*Venezuelan Institute for Community Action*]   (LA)
IVAN .... Institute of Oriental Studies (of the Academy of Sciences, USSR)   (RU)
IVANK ...... Internationale Veterinaer-Anatomische Nomenklatur-Kommission [*Switzerland*]   (SLS)
IVB .... Internationaal Motorrijtuigverzekeringsbewijs [*Benelux*]   (BAS)
IVB .... Internationaler Verband fuer Arbeiterbildung [*International Federation of Workers' Educational Associations - IFWEA*]   (EAIO)
IVBF .... International Volleyball Federation   (EA)
IVBiH .... Izvrsno Vijece Bosne i Hercegovine [*Executive Council of Bosnia and Hercegovina*]   (YU)
IVBS .... Industriele Vereniging tot Bevordering van de Stralingsveiligheid [*Industrial Association to Promote Security from Radiation*] [*Netherlands*]   (PDAA)
IVB vanSA ... Instituut van Verkeersbeamptes van Suider-Afrika [*South Africa*]   (AA)
IVC .... Industrial Vigilance Council [*Australia*]
IVC .... Industrievereinigung Chemiefasern [*Germany*]
IVC .... Instituto Venezolano del Consumo [*Venezuelan Consumer Institute*]   (LA)
IVC .... Invercargill [*New Zealand*] [*Airport symbol*]   (OAG)
IVCA .... Instituto Venezolano-Cubano de Amistad [*Venezuelan-Cuban Friendship Institute*]   (LA)
IVCLG .... Internatinnaler Verband Christlicher Landarbeiteroewerkschaften [*Belgium*]   (DSCA)
IVCPT .... Intreprinderea de Valorificare a Cerealelor si Plantelor Tehnice [*Enterprise for the Utilization of Grains and Technical Crops*]   (RO)
Iv Cst .... Ivory Coast
IVD .... Height-Range Indicator   (RU)
IVD .... Indemnite Viagere de Depart [*France*]   (FLAF)
IVDA .... Indonesia Veterinary Drug Association   (EAIO)
iv Dei .... Institut Voluntas Dei   (EA)
IVDJ .... Internationale Vereinigung Demokratischer Juristen [*International Union of Democratic Jurists*]   (EG)
IVDZ .... Institouton Veltioseos kai Diatrofis Zoon [*Animal Husbandry Institute*] [*Greek*]   (GC)
IVE .... Institut fur Virologie und Epidemiologie [*Institute for Virology and Epidemiology*] [*Germany*]   (IRC)
IVE .... Instituto Vallecaucano de Estadistica [*Colombia*]   (COL)
IVE .... Instituto Veterinario Ecuatoriano [*Quito, Ecuador*]   (LAA)
IVE .... Internationale Vereinigung von Einkaufsverbanden [*International Association of Buying Groups - IABG*]   (EAIO)
IVECOM... Ivoirienne d'Echanges Commerciaux
IVEL .... Instituto Veterinario Ecuatoriano del Litoral [*Guayaquil, Ecuador*]   (LAA)
IVEPO .... Venezuelan Institute of Popular Education
IVES .... Internationaler Verband fuer Erziehung zu Suchtmittelfreiem Leben [*International Association for Education to a Life without Drugs*]   (EAIO)
IVES .... International Teachers Temperance Association [*Denmark*]   (EAIO)
IVF .... Institutet foer Verkstadsteknisk Forskning [*Institute for Production Engineering Research*] [*Sweden*] [*Research center*]
IVF .... Internationale Viola Forschunggesellschaft [*International Viola Society*] [*Germany*]   (EAIO)
IVfgR .... Internationale Vereinigung fuer Gewerblichen Rechtsschutz [*Switzerland*]   (SLS)
IVFZ .... International Veterinary Federation of Zootechnics [*Later, IVAAP*]
IVG .... Industrieverwaltungsgesellschaft
IVG .... Instituto Venezolano de Genealogia [*Venezuelan Institute of Genealogy*]   (EAIO)
IVG .... Internationale Vereinigung der Gewerkschaften [*International Union of Trade Unions*]   (EG)

IVG .... Internationale Vereinigung fuer Germanische Sprach - und Literaturwissenschaft [*International Association of Germanic Studies - IAGS*] [*Tokyo, Japan*]   (EAIO)
IVGG .... Institute of Volcanic Geology and Geochemistry [*Commonwealth of Independent States*]
IVGGD ...... Internationale Vereinigung fuer Geschichte und Gegenwart der Druckkunst [*International Association for Past and Present History of the Art of Printing*]   (EAIO)
Ivgiz .... Ivanovo State Publishing House   (RU)
IVGO .... Israel Vegetable Growers' Organization   (EAIO)
Ivgres .... Ivanovo State Regional Electric Power Plant   (RU)
IVHA .... Instituto Venezolano del Hierro y del Acero [*Venezuela*]   (LAA)
IVHESM ... International Voluntary Historical Enlightenment Society Memorial   (EAIO)
IVIA .... Instituto Valenciano de Investigaciones Agrarias [*Valencian Institute of Agricultural Research*] [*Research center*] [*Spain*]   (IRC)
IVIC .... Instituto Venezolano de Investigaciones Cientificas [*Venezuelan Institute of Scientific Research*] [*Research center*]   (LA)
IVIETA ..... Instituto de Vuelo por Instrumentos y Escuela de Tierra [*Colombia*]   (COL)
IvIOT .... All-Union Scientific Research Institute of Work Safety of the VTsSPS [*Ivanovo*]   (RU)
IVITA .... Instituto Veterinario de Investigaciones Tropicales y de Altura [*The Veterinary Institute for Tropical and Altitude Research*] [*Peru*]   (LA)
IVIZ .... Institutionenverzeichnis fuer Internationale Zusammenarbeit [*Institutions for International Cooperation*] [*NOMOS Datapool Database*]   (IID)
IVJS .... International Jewish Vegetarian Society [*Formerly, Jewish Vegetarian Society*]   (EA)
IVK .... Institute of Medical Cosmetology   (RU)
IVK .... Institutet for Vaeutforskning och Kyllagring [*Institute for Plant Research and Cold Storage*]   (DSCA)
IVK .... Invalidska Vrhovna Komisija [*Supreme Commission for the Disabled*]   (YU)
IVKh .... Institute of Restorative Surgery   (RU)
IVKh .... Institute of Water Management   (RU)
IVKT .... Italian General Confederation of Labor   (RU)
IVL .... Institutet foer Vatten - och Luftvardsforskning [*Swedish Water and Air Pollution Research Institute*] [*Research center*]   (IRC)
IVL .... Ivalo [*Finland*] [*Airport symbol*]   (OAG)
IVL .... Publishing House of Oriental Literature   (RU)
IVLD .... Internationale Vereinigung der Organisationen von Lebensmittel-Detail-Listen [*International Federation of Grocers' Associations - IFGA*]   (EAIO)
IVLV .... Industrievereinigung fuer Lebensmitteltechnologie und Verpackung [*Information retrieval*]
IVM .... Institut fuer Verbrennungsmotoren und Kraftfahrwesen [*Institute for Internal Combustion Engines and Motor Vehicles*]   (EG)
ivm .... In Verband Met [*Benelux*]   (BAS)
iVm .... In Verbindung Mit [*In Conjunction With, In Association With*]   (EG)
IVMA .... Israel Veterinary Medical Association   (EAIO)
IVMB .... Internationale Vereinigung der Musikbibliotheken, Musikarchive, und Dokumentationszentren [*International Association of Music Libraries, Archives, and Documentation Centers*]
IVN .... High-Voltage Source   (RU)
IVN .... Institute of High Voltages (of the Siberian Department of the Academy of Sciences, USSR)   (RU)
IVN .... Internationale Vereniging voor Neerlandistiek [*International Association of Dutch Studies*]   (EAIO)
IVND .... Institute of Higher Nervous Activity   (RU)
IVNDiNF .. Institute of Higher Nervous Activity and Neurophysiology (of the Academy of Sciences, USSR)   (RU)
IVNIOT ..... Ivanovo Scientific Research Institute of Work Safety and Occupational Diseases   (RU)
IVNITI ...... Ivanovo Scientific Research Textile Institute   (RU)
IVO .... Imatran Voima Osakeyhtio [*A nuclear power company*] [*Finland*]   (NRCH)
IVO .... Imatran Voima Oy [*Finland*]   (WED)
IVO .... Instituut voor Ontwikkelingsvraagstukken [*Development Research Institute*] [*Research center*] [*Netherlands*]   (IRC)
IVOBRA .... Ivoirienne de Brasserie
IVOIRAGRI ... Societe Ivoirienne d'Exploitation Agricole, Industrielle, Commerciale et de Transports
IVOIRAL ... Compagnie Ivoirienne de l'Aluminium
IVOIRAUTO ... Cote-D'Ivoire Automobile
IVOIRLAIT ... Societe Ivoirienne de Produits Laitiers
IVOLCY .... Industrie Voltaique du Cycle et Cyclomoteur
ivoorperk.... Ivoorperkament [*Ivory Vellum*] [*Publishing*] [*Netherlands*]
IVOSEP .... Societe Ivoirienne de Sepultures et Transports Speciaux
IVOSEPSASEP ... Societe Ivoirienne de Sepultures et Transports Speciaux
IVOTEX .... Societe Ivoirienne de Textiles

IVP............ Institute of Water Problems   (RU)
IVP............ Instituto Venezolano de Petroquimica [*Venezuelan Petrochemical Institute*]   (LA)
IVP............ Instituut voor Visserijproducten [*Institute for Fishery Products*] [*Netherlands*]   (MSC)
IVP............ Internationaler Verband der Pektinproduzenten [*International Pectin Producers Association*] [*Switzerland*]   (EAIO)
IVP............ Soil Moisture Meter   (RU)
IVPA......... Indian Vanaspati Producers' Association
IVPI........... Ivanovo-Voznesensk Polytechnic Institute Imeni M. V. Frunze   (RU)
IVPP......... Institute of Vertebrate Palaeontology and Palaeoanthropology [*China*]
IVPP......... Surfaced Runway   (RU)
IVP-TNO .. Instituut voor Visserijproducten Nederlands Centrale Organisatie voor Toegepast-Natuurwetenschappelijk Onderzoek [*Institute for Fishery Products Netherlands Central Organization for Applied Natural Scientific Research*]   (ARC)
IVR........... International Association for the Rhine Vessels Register [*Netherlands*]   (EY)
IVR........... Internationale Vereinigung fuer Rechts- und Sozialphilosophie [*International Association for Philosophy of Law and Social Philosophy*]   (EAIO)
IVR........... Inverell [*Australia*] [*Airport symbol*]   (OAG)
IVRG........ International Verticillium Research Group   (EAIO)
IVRI.......... Indian Veterinary Research Institute   (IRC)
IVRO........ Instituut voor Rassenonderzoek van Landbouwgewassen [*Institute for Research on Varieties of Field Corps*] [*Netherlands*]   (DSCA)
IVS............ Air Evasion [*France*] [*ICAO designator*]   (FAAC)
IVS............ Informationsverarbeitungssystem [*Information Processing System*] [*German*]   (ADPT)
IVS............ Informationsvermittlungsstelle [*Telephone Information Exchange*] [*Information retrieval*] [*German*]
IVS............ Institute of Macromolecular Compounds (of the Academy of Sciences, USSR)   (RU)
IVS............ Institute of Vaccines and Serums   (RU)
IVS............ International Visitor Survey [*Australia*]
IVS............ International Voluntary Service   (CL)
IVS............ Isturena Veterinarska Stanica [*Advanced Veterinary Station*] [*Military*]   (YU)
IVSA......... Instituut van Verkeersbeamptes van Suider-Afrika [*Institute of Traffic Officers of Southern Africa*]   (EAIO)
IVSA......... International Veterinary Students Association [*Utrecht, Netherlands*]   (EAIO)
IVSS .... Instituto Venezolano de Seguros Sociales [*Venezuelan Social Security Institute*]   (LA)
IVSS .... Internationale Vereinigung fuer Soziale Sicherheit [*International Social Security Association*]
IVSU........ International Veterinary Students Union [*Later, IVSA*]
IVSZ......... Szakszervezeti Iskolat Vegzettek Szovetsege [*Association of Graduates of Trade Union Schools*]   (HU)
IVT............ Industrieverband Textil [*Switzerland*]   (EY)
IVT............ Informationsvermittlung Technik
IVT............ Institute of Air Transport   (RU)
IVT............ Institute of Foreign Trade   (RU)
IVT............ Instituut voor de Veredeling van Tuinbouwgewassen [*Horticultural Plant Breeding Institute*] [*Netherlands*]   (ARC)
IVT............ Internationale Vereinigung der Textileinkaufsverbande [*International Association of Textile Purchasing Societies*]
IVTAN...... Institut Vysokikh Temperatur [*Institute of High Temperatures*] [*Former USSR*]   (IRC)
IVTE......... Institute for Medical Determination of Disability   (RU)
Ivtekmash .. Ivanovo Textile Machinery Plant   (RU)
IVTN .... Internasionale Vereniging vir Tandheelkundige Navorsing [*South Africa*]   (AA)
Ivtorfmash ... Ivanovo Peat Machinery Plant   (RU)
IVTPA .... Istituto Sperimentale per la Valorizzazione Tecnologica dei Prodotti Agricoli [*Technical Improvement of Agricultural Products Research Institute*] [*Italian*]   (ARC)
IVTs.......... Information and Computation Center   (RU)
IVU .... Instituto de Vivienda Urbana [*Urban Housing Institute*] [*Guatemala*]   (LAA)
IVU .... Instituto de Vivienda Urbana [*Urban Housing Institute*] [*El Salvador*]   (LA)
IVU .... Instituto de Vivienda y Urbanismo [*Institute of Housing and City Planning*] [*Panama*]   (LA)
IVU .... International Vegetarian Union [*Stockport, Cheshire, England*]
IVUz .... Institute of Oriental Studies (of the Academy of Sciences, Uzbek SSR)   (RU)
IVV .... Initiator [*Expl.*]   (RU)
IVV .... Internationaal Verbond van Vakverenigingen [*Benelux*]   (BAS)
IVV .... Internationaler Verband fuer Verkehrsschulung und Verkehrserziehung   (SLS)

IVV .... Internationaler Volkssportverband [*International Federation of Popular Sports - IFPS*]   (EAIO)
IVV .... Internationale Vereinigung fuer Vegetationskunde [*International Association for Vegetation Science - IAVS*]   (EAIO)
IVVO .... Instituut voor Veevoedingsonderzoek "Hoorn" [*Institute for Livestock Feeding and Nutrition Research Hoorn*] [*Netherlands*]   (ARC)
IVVS .... Air Force Inspection   (RU)
IvV-TNO ... Instituut Nederland Centrale Organisatie voor Toegepast-Natuurwetenschappelijk Onderzoek voor Verpakking [*Institute Netherlands Central Organization for Applied Natural Scientific Research for Packaging Research*]   (ARC)
IVVV......... Internationaal Verbond van Vrije Vakverenigingen [*Benelux*]   (BAS)
IVW .... Informationsgemeinschaft zur Feststellung der Verbreitung von Werbetraegern eV   (IMH)
IVWSR ...... Internationaler Verband fuer Wohnungswesen, Staedtebau und Raumordnung [*International Federation for Housing and Planning*]
IVYa .... Institute of Oriental Languages   (RU)
IVYa .... Institut Vostochnykh Yazykov
IVZ .... Islamska Vjerska Zajednica [*Islamic Religious Community*] [*Bosnia and Hercegovina*]   (YU)
IW .... Industriewerk [*Industrial Plant*] [*German*]   (EG)
IW .... Innere Weite [*Inside Diameter*] [*German*]
IW .... Instituut voor Wegtransportmiddelen [*Research Institute for Road Vehicles*] [*Netherlands Central Organization for Applied Natural Scientific Research*]   (WED)
IW .... Instytut Weglowy [*Coal Institute*]   (POL)
IW .... Instytut Wlokiennictwa [*Textile Institute*]   (POL)
IW .... Invaliditeitswet [*Benelux*]   (BAS)
IW .... In Westfalen [*In Westphalia*] [*German*]
iW .... In Worten [*In Words*] [*German*]   (EG)
IW .... Israelitische Wochenschrift, Breslau/Magdeburg
IWA .... International Waterproofing Association [*See also AIE*] [*Brussels, Belgium*]   (EAIO)
IWA .... International Wheat Agreement   (ADA)
IWA .... International Workers of Africa
IWBP......... Integration with Britain Party [*Gibraltar*]   (PPE)
IWBS........ Importwarenbegleitschein [*Import Bill of Lading*] [*Legal term*] [*German*]   (EG)
IWC .... Infant Welfare Certificate [*Australia*]
IWC .... Interim Wilderness Committee [*Australia*]
IWC .... International Whaling Commission [*Cambridge, England*]
IWC .... International Wheat Council [*See also CIB*] [*British*]   (EAIO)
IWCC........ International Women's Cricket Council [*Australia*]   (EAIO)
IWCC........ International Wrought Copper Council [*British*]   (EAIO)
IWD .... Inland Waterways Department
IWDA .... International Women's Day Association [*Sierra Leone*]
IWECO-TNO ... Instituut TNO voor Werktuigkundige Constructies [*Institute TNO for Mechanical Constructions*] [*Netherlands Organization for Applied Scientific Research (TNO)*] [*Research center*]   (ERC)
IWEM .... Institution of Water and Environmental Management   (EAIO)
IWEP........ Institute of Water and Ecological Problems [*Russian Federation*]   (EE)
IWEVO ..... Informatiespecialisten Werkgroep voor Voedingsmiddelen [*Netherlands*]
IWF........... Industry Workers Federation [*San Marino*]   (EAIO)
IWF........... Institut fur Werkzeugmaschinen und Fertigungstechnik [*Institute of Machine Tool and Processing Technology*] [*Germany*]   (IRC)
IWF........... Internationale Wahrungsfond
IWF........... International Weightlifting Federation [*See also FHI*] [*Budapest, Hungary*]   (EAIO)
IWFA .... International Window Film Association   (EA)
IWFS .... International Wine and Food Society [*British*]   (EAIO)
IWG .... Institut fuer Wirtschaft- und Gesellschaft Bonn eV [*Bonn Institute for Economic and Social Research*] [*Research center*]   (IRC)
IWG .... Intergovernmental Working Group [*United Nations*]
IWG .... International Working Group [*NATO*]   (NATG)
IWGA........ International World Games Association   (EA)
IWGC .... Imperial War Graves Commission [*Australia*]   (ADA)
IWGCS...... International Working Group in Clinical Sociology   (EAIO)
IWGGDM ... International Working Group on Graminaceous Downy Mildews [*Defunct*]   (EAIO)
IWGIA...... International Work Group for Indigenous Affairs [*Copenhagen, Denmark*]   (EAIO)
IWGM .... Intergovernmental Working Group on Monitoring or Surveillance [*United Nations*]   (ASF)
IWGMS..... Intergovernmental Working Group on Monitoring or Surveillance [*United Nations*]   (MSC)
IWHR .... Institute of Water Conservation and Hydroelectric Power Research [*China*]   (IRC)
IWI .... Interimwet Invaliditeitsrentetrekkers [*Benelux*]   (BAS)

IWIPC .... Interim Wool Industry Policy Council [*Australia*]
IWIS/TNO ... Instituut voor Wiskunde, Informatieverwerking, en Statistiek/ Toegepast Natuurwetenschappelijk Onderzoek [*'s-Gravenhage*] [*Institute for Mathematics, Information Processing, and Statistics - TNO Netherlands Organization for Applied Scientific Research*]
IWK .... Institut fuer Wissenschaft und Kunst [*Austria*] (SLS)
IWM .... Fraunhofer-Institut fuer Werkstoffmechanik [*Fraunhofer Institute for Materials and Mechanics*] [*Freiburg, West Germany*] [*Research center*] (ERC)
IWM .... Institut fuer Angewandte Wirtschaftsforschung im Mittelstand GmbH (SLS)
IWMA .... International Wire and Machinery Association [*Leamington Spa, Warwickshire, England*] (EAIO)
IWME .... Indian Woollen Mills Federation [*India*]
IWM(SA) ... Institute of Waste Management (South Africa) (AA)
IWN .... Indigenous Women's Network (EAIO)
IWO .... International Wine Office [*France*] (DSCA)
IWO .... Iran Women's Organization (ME)
IWO .... Iran Workers' Organization (ME)
IWONL ..... Instituut tot Aanmoediging van het Wettenschappelijk Onderzoek in Nijverheid en Landbouw [*Benelux*] (BAS)
IWP .... Illawarra Workers Party [*Political party*] [*Australia*]
IWP .... Indicative World Plan
IWP .... Indicative World Plan for Agricultural Development [*United Nations*]
IWP .... Instytut Wzornictwa Przemyslowego [*Industrial Pattern Institute*] (POL)
IWP .... Internationale Weltfriedens Partei [*International World Peace Party*] [*Germany*] [*Political party*] (PPW)
IWP .... International Word Processing Association (ADA)
IWP .... Irish Workers' Party [*Political party*] (PPW)
IWPC .... Institute of Water Pollution Control [*Later, IWEM*] (EAIO)
IWRAW .... International Women's Rights Action Watch (EAIO)
IWRB .... International Waterfowl and Wetlands Research Bureau (EAIO)
IWS .... Internasionale Wolsekretariaat [*International Wool Secretariat*] [*Afrikaans*]
IWS .... International Wool Secretariat [*British*]
IWSA .... International Water Supply Association [*British*] (EAIO)
IWSAW .... Institute for Women's Studies in the Arab World [*Beirut, Lebanon*] (EAIO)
IWSF .... International Water Ski Federation (OLYM)
IWSF .... Italian Winter Sport Federation (EAIO)
IWSG .... International Wool Study Group [*British*] [*Defunct*] (EAIO)
IWSS .... Instytut Wlokien Sztucznych i Syntetycznych [*Institute of Artificial and Synthetic Fibers*] [*Poland*]
IWT .... Informationssystem Wissenschaft und Technik [*German*] (ADPT)
IWT .... Internationaal Watertribunaal [*International Water Tribunal*] [*Netherlands*] (EAIO)
IWT .... International Working Team [*NATO*] (NATG)
IWTC .... Inland Water Transport Corporation [*Myanmar*] (DS)
IWTF .... International Water Tribunal Foundation [*Netherlands*] (EAIO)
IWTO .... International Wool Testing Organisation [*Australia*]
IWTO .... International Wool Textile Organization [*See also FLI*] [*Brussels, Belgium*] (EAIO)
IWUAW .... Institut fur Wirtschaftswissenshaften Ungarische Akademie der Wissenshaften [*Institute of Economics-Hungarian Academy of Sciences*] (EAIO)
IWUL .... Irrigators and Water Users' League [*Australia*]
IWv .... Im Werte Von [*Amounting To*] [*German*]
IWW .... Industrial Workers of the World (ADA)
IWWA ...... Israel Water Works Association (EAIO)
IWWRB .... International Waterfowl and Wetlands Research Bureau (EAIO)
IWY .... International Women's Year (ADA)
IXA .... Agartala [*India*] [*Airport symbol*] (OAG)
IXAE .... International X-Ray Astrophysics Explorer
IXB .... Bagdogra [*India*] [*Airport symbol*] (OAG)
IXbre .... Novembre [*November*] [*French*]
IXbre .... Noviembre [*November*] [*Spanish*]
IXC .... Chandigarh [*India*] [*Airport symbol*] (OAG)
IXD .... Allahabad [*India*] [*Airport symbol*] (OAG)
IXE .... Mangalore [*India*] [*Airport symbol*] (OAG)
IXEE .... International X-Ray and Extreme Ultraviolet Explorer
IXG .... Belgaum [*India*] [*Airport symbol*] (OAG)
IXI .... Lilabari [*India*] [*Airport symbol*] (OAG)
IXJ .... Jammu [*India*] [*Airport symbol*] (OAG)
IXK .... Keshod [*India*] [*Airport symbol*] (OAG)
IXL .... Leh [*India*] [*Airport symbol*] (OAG)
IXM .... Madurai [*India*] [*Airport symbol*] (OAG)
IXR .... Ranchi [*India*] [*Airport symbol*] (OAG)
IXS .... Silchar [*India*] [*Airport symbol*] (OAG)
IXT .... Lineas Aereas de Ixtlan SA de CV [*Mexico*] [*ICAO designator*] (FAAC)
IXU .... Aurangabad [*India*] [*Airport symbol*] (OAG)
IXZ .... Port Blair [*Andaman Islands*] [*Airport symbol*] (OAG)

IYa .... Information Language (RU)
IYA .... Ismailia Youth Association [*North African*]
IYA .... Israel Yachting Association (EAIO)
IYaIMK ..... Institute of Language, History, and Material Culture (RU)
IYaIYaE .... Institute for Nuclear Research and Nuclear Power Industry (BU)
IYAK .... Isci Yardimlasma Kurumu [*Workers Mutual Aid Organization*] [*IYK*] [*See also*] (TU)
IYaL .... Institute of Language and Literature (RU)
IYaLI .... Institute of Language, Literature, and History (RU)
IYaM .... Institute of Language and Thought Imeni N. Ya. Marr (Academy of Sciences, USSR) (RU)
IYaP .... Institute of Nuclear Problems (RU)
IYaSh .... Foreign Languages in the School (RU)
IYaZ .... Institute of Linguistics (of the Academy of Sciences, USSR) (RU)
IYC .... International Year of the Child [*United Nations*] (AEE)
IYC .... International Youth Conference (EG)
IYCW .... International Young Christian Workers [*See also JOCI*] (EAIO)
IYD .... Institute for Youth and Development [*India*] (EAIO)
IYDP .... International Year for Disabled Persons
IYDU .... International Young Democratic Union [*Defunct*] (EAIO)
IYe .... Immunizing Unit (RU)
IYE .... Institouto Ypotropikon kai Elaias [*Institute for Sub-Tropical Plants and Olive Trees*] (GC)
IYe .... International Unit (RU)
IYE .... Yemenia, Yemen Airways [*ICAO designator*] (FAAC)
IYEP .... International Youth Exchange Program [*Australia*]
IYeSTEKh ... Institute of History of Natural Sciences and Technology (of the Academy of Sciences, USSR) (RU)
IYF .... International Youth Federation for Environmental Studies and Conservation (EAIO)
IYFS .... International Young Friends Society [*Pakistan*] (EAIO)
IYHA .... Israel Youth Hostels Association (EAIO)
IYHF .... International Youth Hostel Federation [*See also FAIJ*] [*Welwyn Garden City, Hertfordshire, England*] (EAIO)
IYK .... Isci Yardimlasma Kurumu [*Workers Mutual Aid Organization*] [*IYAK*] [*See also*] (TU)
IYL .... International Youth Library [*See also IJB*] [*Munich, Federal Republic of Germany*] (EAIO)
IYOD .... Istanbul Yuksek Ogrenim Dernegi [*Istanbul Higher Education Association*] (TU)
IYOKD ...... Istanbul Yuksek Ogrenim Kultur Dernegi [*Istanbul Higher Education Cultural Association*] (TU)
IYOKD ...... Izmir Yuksek Ogrenim Kultur Dernegi [*Izmir Higher Education Cultural Association*] (TU)
IYOTB .... Istanbul Yuksek Okullar Talebe Birligi [*Istanbul Advanced Schools Student Union*] (TU)
IYRU .... International Yacht Racing Union [*British*]
IYSH .... International Year of Shelter for the Homeless [*1987*]
IYTA .... International Yoga Teachers Association (ADA)
IYTOTB .... Istanbul Yuksek Teknik Okulu Talebe Birligi [*Istanbul Advanced Technical School Student Union*] (TU)
IYWIP ...... International Year of the World's Indigenous People
IYY .... International Youth Year [*1985*] [*United Nations (already exists in GUS II database)*]
IZ .... East, West (BU)
IZ .... Electoral Law (BU)
IZ .... Industriezweig [*Industrial Branch*] (EG)
IZ .... Informationszentrum [*Information Center*] [*Information retrieval*] [*German*]
IZ .... Informationszentrum Sozialwissenschaften [*Social Sciences Information Center*] [*Information service or system*] (IID)
IZ .... Instalacni Zavody [*Installation Enterprises*] [*Prague*] (CZ)
IZ .... Instruments Plant (BU)
IZ .... Instytut Zachodni [*Institute of the Western Territories*] (POL)
IZ .... Instytut Zootechniki [*Institute of Animal Husbandry*] (POL)
i-z .... Istok-Zapad [*East-West*] (YU)
iz .... Izquierda, Izquierdo [*Left*] [*Spanish*]
IZ .... Trigger Pulse (RU)
IZA .... International Zen Association [*Formerly, European Zen Association*] (EA)
IZA .... International Zeolite Association
IZB .... Industries Zairoises des Bois [*State forestry enterprise*] [*Zaire*]
IZB .... Informationszentrum fuer Biologie [*Forschungsinstitut Senckenberg*] [*Frankfurt*] [*Information retrieval*]
IZB .... Ingenieurtechnisches Zentralbuero Boehlen VEB
IZB .... Inspektorat za Zastitu Bilja [*Plant Protection Inspectorate*] (YU)
izbr .... Elected (BU)
izd .... Edition, Publication, Issue (RU)
izd .... Izdanje [*Edition*] (YU)
izd .... Publication, Publisher, Publishing House (BU)
izd .... Publisher (RU)
izd .... Publishing House (RU)
Izdatinlit ... Publishing House of Foreign Literature (RU)
izd avt .... Published by the Author (BU)

izdinlit....... Publishing House of Foreign Literature (RU)
izd-vo......... Publishing House (RU)
IzfP .... Fraunhofer-Institut fuer Zerstoerungsfreie Pruefverfahren [*Fraunhofer Institute for Non-Destructive Test Methods*] [*Research center*] [*Germany*] (WND)
IZGRADNJA ... Gradevinsko Preduzece [*Building Establishment*] (YU)
izh.............. Izhaja [*Published*] (YU)
IZh .... Izhevsk Motorcycle Plant (RU)
IZh .... Motorcycle Made by the Izhevsk Motorcycle Plant (RU)
IZhB .... Izhevsk Hammerless Gun (RU)
IZhS........... Housing Constructions Institute (BU)
IZhSA .... Institute of Painting, Sculpture, and Architecture Imeni I. Ye. Repin (of the Academy of Arts, USSR) (RU)
IZhT .... Synthetic Liquid Fuel (RU)
IZI .... Interdisziplinaeres Zentrum fuer Forschung und Entwicklung in der Intensivmedizin [*Austria*] (SLS)
IZIGIZ....... State Publishing House of Fine Arts (RU)
IZIP .... Instituto de Zoonosis e Investigacion Pecuaria [*Institute of Zoonosis and Research of Animal Diseases*] [*Peru*] (ARC)
IZIPEFC ... Instituto de Zootecnia e Industrias Pecuarias "Fernando Costa" [*Brazil*] (DSCA)
IZiZ .... Instytut Zywnosci i Zywienia [*Institute of Food and Feeding*] [*Poland*]
IZJA .... Izdavacki Zavod Jugoslavenske Akademije [*Publishing Institute of the Yugoslav Academy*] [*Zagreb*] (YU)
izk.............. Art (BU)
izkh .... Output [*Electricity*] (BU)
izl.............. Exposition, Statement (BU)
izl.............. Fracture, Fissure (RU)
IZL............. Industriezweigleitung [*Industrial Branch Management*] (EG)
IZL............. Irgun Zevai Leumi [*Israeli underground paramilitary group, 1940's*]
IZLC .... Izvestaj Zaduzbine Luke Celovica [*Report of the Luka Celovic Foundation*] [*Belgrade*] (YU)
izm.............. Change (RU)
izm.............. Changed, Amended, Modified, Change (BU)
IZM .... Izmir [*Turkey*] [*Airport symbol*] (OAG)
IZM .... Measuring Machine (RU)
izmerit........ Measuring (RU)
IZMIRAN ... Institute of Terrestrial Magnetism, the Ionosphere, and Radio Wave Propagation of the Academy of Sciences, USSR (RU)
IZO .... Fine Arts (RU)
IZO .... Izumo [*Japan*] [*Airport symbol*] (OAG)
IZO .... Quarantine Clearing Station (RU)
Izogiz.......... State Publishing House of Fine Arts (RU)
izokruzhok ... Fine Arts Group (RU)
izol............ Isoleucine (RU)
Izolit........... Moscow Insulation Plant (RU)
Izomuzgiz... State Publishing House of Fine Arts and Music Literature [*UkrSSR*] (RU)
Izoplit........ Insulation Tile Plant (RU)
Izopropunkt ... Quarantine Clearing Station (RU)
IZORAM... Fine Arts Group of Working Youth (RU)
IZOS.......... Inicijativni Zadruzni Odbor za Slovenijo [*Initiatory Cooperative Committee for Slovenia*] (YU)
IZOS.......... Lzyum Optical Glass Plant Imeni F. E. Dzerzhinskiy (RU)
Izostat .... Scientific Research Institute for the Graphic Presentation of Statistics on Soviet Construction and Economy (RU)
IZOTUM .. Izolasyon Maddeleri Sanayii ve Ticaret Ltd. Sirketi [*Insulation Materials Industry and Marketing Corp. Ltd.*] (TU)
Izpulkom.... Executive Committee (BU)
Izq .... Izquierda [*Left*] [*Correspondence*] [*Spanish*]
izqa............ Izquierda [*Left*] [*Spanish*]
izqda........... Izquierda [*Left*] [*Spanish*]
izqdo........... Izquierdo [*Left*] [*Spanish*]
izqo............ Izquierdo [*Left*] [*Spanish*]
IZR............. Institute for the Protection of Plants (RU)
iz-r............. Insulator (RU)
izr .... Israeli (RU)
izr .... Izraelita [*Jew, Jewish*] (HU)
izr .... Sentence [*Grammar*] (BU)
izrab .... Prepared, Completed, Earned (BU)
IZSK .... Institut za Zastitu Spomenika Kulture [*Institute for the Protection of Cultural Monuments*] (YU)
Izsled.......... Research (BU)
izt .... East, Eastern (BU)
izt .... Sources (BU)
iz tekh .... Computer Equipment (BU)
IZTM........ Irkutsk Heavy Machinery Plant Imeni V. V. Kuybyshev (RU)
IZTO .... Correspondence Institute of Technical Education (RU)
IZTO .... Interzonal Trade Office [*NATO*] (NATG)
IZU .... Office of Inventions and Improvements (RU)
IZUL.......... Office of Inventions and Improvements of Transportation Technology (RU)
izumr .... Emerald Mines [*Topography*] (RU)

izv .... Bulletin, Information (BU)
Izv .... Extraordinary (BU)
IZV .... Industriezweigverband [*Industrial Branch Association*] (EG)
izv .... Izvadak [*Excerpts*] (YU)
izv .... Lime Plant [*Topography*] (RU)
izv .... Lime Quarry [*Topography*] (RU)
Izv .... News (RU)
IzvBAI ...... Bulletin of the Bulgarian Archeological Institute (BU)
IzvjescaBIU ... Izvjesca Botanickog Instituta Universiteta u Zagrebu [*Report of the Botanical Institute of the University in Zagreb*] (YU)
izvlech........ Abstract (RU)
izvlech........ Extract, Excerpt (BU)
izv p .... Lime Kiln [*Topography*] (RU)
IZWO .... Instituut voor Zeewetenschappelijk Onderzoek [*Institute for Marine Scientific Research*] [*Belgium*] (ARC)

.

J

J .... Action Variable [*Physics*]   (BARN)
J .... Angular Momentum [*Physics*]   (BARN)
J .... Das Joule [*Joule*]   (EG)
J .... Het Jachtbedrijf [*Benelux*]   (BAS)
J .... Jaar [*Year*] [*Afrikaans*]
J .... Jabal [*or Jabel or Jebel*] [*Jl Mountain, Hill Arab*] [*See also*]
              (NAU)
J .... Jahr [*Year*] [*German*]
J .... Jahrbuch [*Journal, Annual Report*] [*German*]
J .... Jahresbericht [*Journal, Annual Report*] [*German*]
j .... Jalka [*Finland*]
J .... Jameel Holdings (Bermuda) Ltd.
J .... Jandarma [*Gendarme, Gendarmery*]   (TU)
J .... Janvier [*January*] [*French*]
j .... Japon [*Japan Paper*] [*Publishing*] [*French*]
j .... Jaras [*District*]   (HU)
j .... Jarat [*Line, Route (Bus line)*]   (HU)
J .... Jezioro [*Lake*] [*Poland*]
J .... Jig [*Phonetic alphabet*] [*World War II*]   (DSUE)
j .... Jih [*South*]   (CZ)
J .... Jime Shipyards Ltd. [*Nigeria*]
j .... Jobb [*On the Right Side*]   (HU)
J .... Jod [*Iodine*] [*Chemical element*] [*German*]
J .... Jodium [*Iodine*] [*Chemical element*] [*Afrikaans*]
J .... Johnnie [*Phonetic alphabet*] [*Royal Navy World War I*]   (DSUE)
J .... Johnny [*Phonetic alphabet*] [*Pre-World War II*]   (DSUE)
J .... Joule [*French*]
J .... Joule [*German*]   (GCA)
J .... Joule Internacional [*International Joule*] [*Portuguese*]
j .... Jour [*Day*] [*French*]
j .... Journal [*Newspaper*] [*French*]
J .... Journal [*Annual Report*] [*German*]
J .... Judaeo-Persian
J .... Jug [*South*]   (YU)
J .... Jugoagent [*Shipping agent*] [*Former Yugoslavia*]
J .... Juliett [*Phonetic alphabet*] [*International*]   (DSUE)
J .... Jurisprudence [*French*]   (FLAF)
J .... Justitia [*Benelux*]   (BAS)
J .... Justiz [*Justice*] [*German*]
J2 .... Djibouti [*Aircraft nationality and registration mark*]   (FAAC)
J3 .... Grenada [*Aircraft nationality and registration mark*]   (FAAC)
J6 .... St. Lucia [*Aircraft nationality and registration mark*]   (FAAC)
J7 .... Dominica [*Aircraft nationality and registration mark*]   (FAAC)
J8 .... St. Vincent and the Grenadines [*Aircraft nationality and
              registration mark*]   (FAAC)
JA .... Jeux Africains
Ja .... Jima [*Island*] [*Sa*] [*See also*] [*Japan*]   (NAU)
JA .... Judge of Appeal [*Australia*]
JA .... Jugoslavenska Akademija Znanosti i Umjetnosti [*Yugoslav
              Academy of Sciences and Arts*] [*Zagreb*]   (YU)
JA .... Jugoslovenska Armija [*Yugoslav Army*]   (YU)
JA .... Jurisprudence Algerienne [*de 1830 a 1876, par Rob Estoublon*]
              (FLAF)
JAA .... Jamiat Adduwal Alarabia [*League of Arab States - LAS*]   (EAIO)
JAA .... Japan Afghanistan Association   (EAIO)
JAA .... Japan Asia Airways
JAA .... Japan Asia Airways Co. Ltd. [*ICAO designator*]   (FAAC)
JAA .... Jewellers' Association of Australia
JAA .... Jordan Arab Army   (ME)
JAA .... Jugoslovenska Autorska Agencija [*Yugoslav Authors' Agency*]
              (YU)
JAAC .... Juventude Africana Amilcar Cabral
JA(ACT).... Jobless Action (Australian Capital Territory) [*An association*]
JAAOC ..... Joint Antiaircraft Operation Center [*NATO*]   (NATG)
JAAS .... Julian Ashton Art School [*Australia*]
Jab .... Jabal [*Mountain, Hill*] [*J, Jl Arabic*] [*See also*]   (NAU)
JAB .... Jet Business Airlines [*Belgium*] [*ICAO designator*]   (FAAC)
JAB .... Joint Africa Board

JABA .... Japanese Association for Behavior Analysis   (EAIO)
JABF .... Japan Australia Business Foundation
JABLONEX ... Podnik Zahranicniho Obchodu pro Vyvoz Jabloneckeho
              Zbozi [*Foreign Trade Enterprise for the Export of Jablonec
              Glassware*]   (CZ)
JAC .... Jacobean   (WDAA)
JAC .... Jago Art Centre [*Bangladesh*]   (EAIO)
JAC .... Japan Air Commuter Co. Ltd. [*ICAO designator*]   (FAAC)
JAC .... Jeunesse Agricole Catholique [*Catholic Farm Youth*]
              [*Cameroon*]   (AF)
JAC .... Jeunesse Agricole Catholique [*Catholic Farm Youth*] [*Congo*]
              (AF)
JAC .... Jeunesse Agricole Chretienne [*French*]
JAC .... Job and Course Explorer [*Computer program*] [*Australia*]
JAC .... Joint Action Committee [*Nigeria*]
JAC .... Joint Assistance Centre [*India*]   (EAIO)
JAC .... Junta de Aeronautica Civil [*Civil Aeronautics Board*] [*Spanish*]
              (LA)
JAC .... Juventud de Accion Catolica [*Catholic Action Youth*] [*Argentina*]
              (LA)
JACA .... Japan Air Cleaning Association   (PDAA)
JACADS.... Johnston Atoll Chemical Agents Disposal System [*Australia*]
JACC .... Jobless Action Community Campaign [*Australia*]
JACE .... Japan Association of Corporate Executives   (EAIO)
JACFA ...... Jamaican-Cuban Friendship Association   (LA)
JACM .... Japan Association of City Mayors
JACS .... Japan-American Cultural Society   (EAIO)
JACT .... Japanese Association of Casting Technology   (EAIO)
JADDA...... Junee and District Development Association [*Australia*]
JADE........ Japan Area Defense Environment
JADE........ Japan Asian Dance Event
JADMA..... Japan Direct Marketing Association   (EAIO)
JADRANSPORT ... Adriatic Shipbuilding [*Pula*]   (YU)
Jadrolinija ... Jadranska Linijska Plovidba [*The Adriatic Shipping Line*]
              [*Rijeka*]   (YU)
JAE........... Japan Aviation Electronics Industry Ltd.
JAE........... Joint Atomic Exercise [*NATO*]   (NATG)
JAE........... Junta Autonoma de Estradas [*Portugal*]   (EY)
JAEA .... Junta Autonoma de Estradas de Angola
JAEC .... Japan Atomic Energy Commission   (PDAA)
Jaehrl........ Jaehrlich [*Annual*] [*German*] [*Business term*]
JAEIP....... Japan Atomic Energy Insurance Pool   (PDAA)
JAERI....... Japan Atomic Energy Research Institute [*Tokyo*]
JAERO...... Japan Atomic Energy Relations Organization [*Nuclear energy*]
              (NRCH)
JAES .... Japan Atomic Energy Society   (PDAA)
JAF........... Japan-Australia Foundation
JAF........... Japan Automobile Federation
JAF........... Jordanian Air Force
JAF........... Jordanian Armed Forces   (ME)
JAFC .... Jamaica Association for Friendship with China   (LA)
JAFC .... Japan Atomic Fuel Corporation   (PDAA)
JAFCA ...... Japan Fashion Color Association   (EAIO)
JAFI .... Jarmufejlesztesi Intezet [*Institute of Transportation
              Development*]   (HU)
JAFPP .... Jordanian Association for Family Planning and Protection
              (EAIO)
JAFSA....... Japan Foundation for Shipbuilding Advancement
JAFTA....... Japan Forest Technical Association   (EAIO)
JAFZA...... Jebel Ali Free Zone Authority [*United Arab Emirates*]
JAG .... Etablissements Jean Abile Gal, SA [*South Africa*]
JAG .... Jetag AB [*Switzerland*] [*ICAO designator*]   (FAAC)
Jagerspr..... Jaegersprache [*Hunting Jargon*] [*German*]
JAGO........ Jugendarrestgeschaeftsordnung [*Germany*]
JAGPRO ... New Zealand Journalists and Graphic Process Union   (EAIO)
JAH .... Wilajah [*Territory, Region, Area*]   (IN)
Jahrb.......... Jahrbuch [*Yearbook*] [*German*]   (GCA)
Jahresg ...... Jahresgabe [*New Year's Publication*] [*German*]

Jahrg	Jahrgang [*Annual Set*] [*German*]
Jahrh	Jahrhundert [*Century*] [*German*]
jahrl	Jaehrlich [*Annual*] [*German*]
JAI	Jaipur [*India*] [*Airport symbol*] (OAG)
JAI	Japan Analytical Industry Co. Ltd.
JAIA	Japan Aromatic Industry Association (EAIO)
JAIA	Japan Automobile Importers Association
JAIC	Japan ASEAN Investment [*ASEAN-Japan Development Fund*]
JAIC	Joint Arab Investment Company
JAIC	Joint Australian Information Council [*Proposed*]
JAICA	Japan's International Cooperation Agency
JAICI	Japan Association for International Chemical Information
JAICI	Japanese Association for International Chemical Information [*Tokyo*]
JAICORP	Joint Arab Investment Corporation
JAIF	Japan Atomic Industrial Forum
JAIMS	Japan-American Institute of Management Science
JAIS	Japan Aircraft Industry Society (PDAA)
Jak	Jakobus [*James (the Apostle)*] [*Afrikaans*]
JAK	Journalists' Association of Korea [*South Korean*]
JAK	Jugoslovenski Akademski Klub [*Yugoslav Academic Club*] (YU)
JAKIS	Japanese Keyword Indexing Simulator
JAL	Jala [*Race of maize*] [*Mexico*]
JAL	Japan Air Lines
JAL	Japan Air Lines Ltd. [*ICAO designator*] (FAAC)
JAL	Jordanian Air Line (ME)
JALAAO	Joint Anti-Locust and Anti-Avian Organization [*Senegal*]
JALGO	Jamaica Association of Local Government Officers (LA)
jalk	Jalkeen [*After*] [*Finland*]
jalkap	Jalkapallo [*Football*] [*Finland*]
JAM	Jamaica [*ANSI three-letter standard code*] (CNC)
JAM	Japanese Association for Microbiology
JAM	Jednotne Analyticke Metody [*Standard Analytical Processes*] (CZ)
JAMA	Moslem People's Revolutionary Movement [*Iran*] [*Political party*] (PPW)
JAMAL	Jamaican Movement for the Advancement of Literacy (LA)
JAMALCO	Jamaica Alumina Company (LA)
JAMARC	Japan Marine Fishery Resource Research Center (ASF)
JAMB	Joint Admissions and Matriculation Board [*Nigeria*] (AF)
JAMBA	Japan-Australia Migratory Bird Agreement
JAMC	Japan Aircraft Manufacturing Corp. (PDAA)
JAMCO	Japanese Aircraft Maintenance Corp.
JAMDA	Japan Machinery Development Association (PDAA)
JAMGA	Jewellers and Metalsmiths Group of Australia
JAMINTEL	Jamaica International Telecommunications Ltd. [*Kingston*] [*Telecommunications service*]
JamKI-L	Institute of Jamaica, National Library of Jamaica, Kingston, Jamaica [*Library symbol*] [*Library of Congress*] (LCLS)
JAMPO	Joint Allied Military Petroleum Office [*NATO*]
JAMPRO	Jamaica Promotions (EY)
JAMRI	Japan Maritime Research Institute (PDAA)
JAMSAT	Japan Radio Amateur Satellite Corp. (PDAA)
JAMSTEC	Japan Marine Science and Technology Center
JAMTS	Japan Association of Motor Trade and Service (PDAA)
JAMU	Janackova Akademie Musickych Umeni [*Janacek Academy of the Fine Arts*] (CZ)
jan	Janeiro [*January*] [*Portuguese*] (GPO)
jan	Januar [*January*] [*Denmark*] (GPO)
jan	Januar [*January*] [*Hungary*] (GPO)
Jan	Januar [*January*] [*German*] (GPO)
jan	Januari [*January*] [*Netherlands*] (GPO)
Jan	Januarie [*January*] [*Afrikaans*]
Jan	January (SCAC)
Jan	Janus Airways [*Airline call sign*]
JAN	Junta de Asistencia Nacional [*National Assistance Board*] [*Peru*] (LA)
JANA	Jamahiriyah News Agency [*Libya*]
JANAP	Joint Army-Navy-Air Force Procedure [*NATO*] (NATG)
JANGO	Joint Australian Non-Government Organisations
JANGRID	Joint Army-Navy Grid System [*NATO*]
JANHIDROS	Jawatan Hidro-Oseanografi [*Hydro-Oceanographic Office*] [*Indonesia*] [*Research center*] (EAS)
Jano	Janeiro [*January*] [*Portuguese*]
jans	Janseniste [*An unornamented style of binding*] [*Publishing*] [*French*]
jansen	Janseniste [*An unornamented style of binding*] [*Publishing*] [*French*]
JANSTD	Joint Army-Navy Standard [*NATO*] (NATG)
JANU	Jugoslovenska Akademija na Naukite i Umetnosta [*Yugoslav Academy of Sciences and Arts (JAZU)*] [*Zagreb*] (YU)
JANV	Janvier [*January*] [*French*]
JaOS	Jamaica Orchid Society (EAIO)
JAP	Japanese (ROG)
jap	Japania [*or Japaniksi*] [*Finland*]
jap	Japanilainen [*Finland*]
Jap	Japannees [*Japanese*] [*Afrikaans*]
jap	Japones [*Japanese*] [*Portuguese*]
JAP	Jerusalem Academic Press (BJA)
JAP	Junta de Abastecimientos y Precios [*Supply and Price Board*] [*Chile*] (LA)
JAP	Juntas de Accao Patriotica [*Patriotic Action Boards*] [*Portuguese*] [*Political party*] (PPE)
JAP	Juventud Aprista Peruana [*Peruvian Aprista Youth*] (LA)
JAP	Juventudes de Accion Popular [*Spanish*] (PPE)
JAPAC	[*The*] Japan Atomic Power Company
JAPANMEC	Japan International Measuring and Control Industry Show
JAPATIC	Japan Patient Information Center [*Information service or system*] (IID)
JAPC	Japan Association of Parasite Control (EAIO)
JAPC	Japan Atomic Power Company [*Nuclear energy*] (NRCH)
JAPC	Joint Air Photo Center [*NATO*] (NATG)
JAPCO	Japan Atomic Power Co. (PDAA)
JAPDEVA	Junta de Administracion Portuaria para el Desarrollo Economico de la Vertiente Atlantica [*Port Administration Board for the Economic Development of the Atlantic Coast*] [*Costa Rica*] (LA)
JAPEX	Japan Petroleum Exploration Co. Ltd.
JAPI	Jajasan Pensiaran Islam [*Foundation for the Propagation of Islam*] (IN)
JAPIA	Japan Auto Parts Industries Association (PDAA)
JAPIC	Japan Pharmaceutical Information Center [*Tokyo*] [*Information service or system*] (IID)
JAPINDA	Japan-Indonesia Association (IN)
JAPIO	Japan Patent Information Organization [*Database producer*]
JAPIS	Jajasan Pendidikan Islam [*Islamic Educational Institute*] (IN)
JAPIT	Japanese Association for the Promotion of International Trade (EY)
JAQ	Jacquinot Bay [*Papua New Guinea*] [*Airport symbol*] (OAG)
JAR	Airlink Luftverkehrsgesellschaft GmbH [*Austria*] [*ICAO designator*] (FAAC)
JAR	Japanese Association of Refrigeration (EAIO)
jar	Jaras [*District*] (HU)
JAR	Jewish Autonomous Region [*Eastern Siberia*]
JARC	Joint Air Reconnaissance Center [*NATO*] (NATG)
JARE	Japanese Antarctic Research Expedition (PDAA)
JARG	Justice Administration Research Group [*Australia*]
JARI	Japan Automotive Research Institute
JARI	Jiangsu Automation Research Institute [*China*] (IRC)
JARI	Jute Agricultural Research Institute [*India*] (ARC)
JARIB	Joint Air Reconnaissance Intelligence Board [*Australia*]
JARL	Japan Amateur Radio League (PDAA)
JARRP	Japan Association for Radiation Research on Polymers (PDAA)
JARTS	Japan Railway Technical Service (PDAA)
JAS	Jane Austen Society [*Basingstoke, Hampshire, England*] (EAIO)
JAS	Japan Agricultural Standards (PDAA)
JAS	Japan Air System Co. Ltd. [*ICAO designator*] (FAAC)
JAS	Japan Association of Shipbuilders (PDAA)
JAS	Javen Avto-Soobrakaj [*Public Motor Transport*] (YU)
JAS	Juventud Argentina por la Soberania [*Argentine Youth for Sovereignty*] (LA)
JAS	Jysk Arkaelogisk Selskab [*Denmark*] (SLS)
JAS	Narodni Podnik pro Prodej Kozeneho Zbozi a Obuvi [*National Sales Enterprise of Leather Goods and Footwear*] (CZ)
JAS-1	Japan Amateur Satellite-1
JASA	Jewellers' Association of South Africa (AA)
JASDF	Japan Air Self-Defence Force (PDAA)
JASEC	Junta Administrativa del Servicio Electrico de Cartago [*Costa Rica*] (LAA)
JASEMA	Junta Administrativa del Servicio Electrico Municipal de Alajuela [*Costa Rica*] (LAA)
JASEMH	Junta Administrativa del Servicio Electrico Municipal de Heredia [*Costa Rica*] (LAA)
jasp	Jaspe [*Marbled*] [*Publishing*] [*French*]
jasp	Jaspeado [*Marbled*] [*Publishing*] [*Spanish*]
JASPA	Jobs and Skills Programme for Africa
jaspead	Jaspeado [*Marbled*] [*Publishing*] [*Spanish*]
JASRAC	Japanese Society for the Rights of Authors, Composers, and Publishers
JAST	Jamaican Association of Sugar Technologists [*Sugar Industry Research Institute*]
JAST	Jazz Action Society of Tasmania
JASTA	Junta de Assistencia e Trabalho de Angola [*Angolan Labor and Welfare Board*] (AF)
JASTPRO	Japan Association for Simplification of International Trade Procedures (PDAA)
JASZOV	Jarasi Foldmuves Szovetkezet [*District Farmers' Cooperative*] (HU)
JAT	Jabat [*Marshall Islands*] [*Airport symbol*] (OAG)
JAT	Japan Assets Trust [*Commercial firm*]

JAT........... Jugoslovenski Aerotransport [*Yugoslav Air Transport*] [*ICAO designator*]
JAT........... Junta de Asistencia Tecnica [*Joint Technical Support*] [*Spanish*]
JATA........ Japan Association of Travel Agents   (EAIO)
JATAN...... Japan Tropical Rainforest Action Network
JATCHA ... Jamaican Alternative Tourism, Camping, and Hiking Association
JATCO...... Japan Automatic Transmission Co.
JATE......... Jozsef Attila Tudomanyegyetem [*Attila Jozsef University of Sciences*]   (HU)
JATELCO ... Jamaica Telephone Company   (LA)
JATES....... Japan Techno-Economics Society   (SLS)
JATHECCA ... Japan Association for the Training of Home Economists in Clothing Consumer Affairs   (EAIO)
jatk............ Jatketaan [*Finland*]
jatk............ Jatkoa [*Finland*]
jatk............ Jatkuu [*Finland*]
JATMA...... Japan Automobile Tire Manufacturers Association
Jato........... Jahrestonne [*Metric Ton Per Year*] [*German*]   (GCA)
JATVC...... Jewellery and Allied Trades Valuers Council [*Australia*]
JAV........... Java
JAV........... Javaans [*Javanese (Language)*] [*Afrikaans*]
jav............. Javara [*For the Benefit Of, In Favor Of*]   (HU)
jav............. Javitas [*Correction*] [*Hungary*]
jav............. Javitott [*Revised*] [*Hungary*]
JAVCF...... Japan Australia Venture Capital Fund
javit.......... Javitott [*Revised*] [*Hungary*]
JAW.......... Confederation of Japan Automobile Workers' Unions   (EAIO)
JAW.......... Jamahiriya Airways [*Libya*] [*ICAO designator*]   (FAAC)
JAWA....... Janecek-Wanderer, Narodni Podnik [*Janecek-Wanderer, National Enterprise*] [*Automobile works*]   (CZ)
JAZ........... Japan Air Charter Co. Ltd. [*ICAO designator*]   (FAAC)
JAZA........ Jews Against Zionism and Anti-Semitism [*Australia*]
Jazh.......... Jazireh [*Island, Peninsula*] [*Persian*]   (NAU)
Jazt .... Jazirat [*Island, Peninsula*] [*Arab*]   (NAU)
JAZU........ Jugoslavenska Akademija Znanosti i Umjetnosti [*Yugoslav Academy of Sciences and Arts*] [*Zagreb*]   (YU)
JB............. Etablissements Jean Bergounioux
JB.............. IML Air Services Ltd. [*British*] [*ICAO designator*]   (ICDA)
Jb.............. Jaarboek [*Yearbook*] [*Netherlands*]   (BJA)
JB.............. Jahrbuch [*Yearbook*] [*German*]
Jb.............. Jahresbericht [*Journal, Annual Report*] [*German*]
j b .... Jarasi Bizottsag [*District Committee*]   (HU)
JB.............. Johore Bahru [*Refers to Europeans named after Malaysian towns*]   (DSUE)
Jb .... Juristenblad [*Benelux*]   (BAS)
JBA .... Jamaica Badminton Association   (EAIO)
JBA .... Japan Bag Association   (EAIO)
JBA .... Japanese Bankers Association   (EAIO)
JBA .... Japanese Basketball Association
JBAD........ Jervis Bay Armament Depot [*Australia*]
JBC........... Jamaica Broadcasting Corp.
JBC........... Japan Baptist Convention   (EAIO)
JBCE .... Joint Board of Christian Education of Australia and New Zealand
JBD........... Jewish Board of Deputies [*Australia*]
Jber........... Jahresbericht [*Journal, Annual Report*] [*German*]   (BJA)
JBF .... Jeune Ballet de France
JBFC......... James Bond 007 Fan Club [*British*]   (EAIO)
JBH .... Jarasi Begyujtesi Hivatal [*District Collection Committee*]   (HU)
JBI .... Jamaica Bauxite Institute   (LA)
JBIA .... Japan Book Importers Association   (EAIO)
JBJ .... James Bond Journalism [*Term coined by leader Sinnathamby Bajaratman of Singapore and referring to Western journalism*]
JBLS......... James Bennett Library Services [*Australia*]
JBLU .... Japan Broadcasting Labour Union   (EAIO)
JBMA....... Japan Bag Manufacturers Association   (EAIO)
JBMMA.... Japanese Business Machine Makers' Association
JBNB........ Jardin Botanique National de Belgique [*National Botanic Garden of Belgium*] [*Belgium*]   (ARC)
JBPA .... Japan Book Publishers Association   (PDAA)
JBS .... Jamaica Bureau of Standards
JBS .... Jewish Burial Society [*Australia*]
JBST......... Jugoslovenska Banka za Spoljnu Trgovinu [*Yugoslav Foreign Trade Bank*]   (YU)
JBU........... Japan Baptist Union   (EAIO)
JBWA....... Japan Bag Wholesalers Association   (EAIO)
JC.............. Jesucristo [*Jesus Christ*] [*Spanish*]
J-C............ Jesus-Christ [*Jesus Christ*] [*French*]   (GPO)
JC.............. Jesus Cristo [*Jesus Christ*] [*Portuguese*]
JC.............. Jeunesse Communiste [*Communist Youth*] [*French*]   (WER)
JC.............. Journalists' Club [*Australia*]
JC.............. Judicial Committee [*Australia*]
JC.............. Junta de Comandantes [*Junta of Commanders*] [*Spanish*]   (WER)

JC.............. Juventud Comunista [*Communist Youth*] [*Spanish*]   (WER)
JC.............. Juventudes Carlistas [*Carlist Youth*] [*Spanish*]   (WER)
JCA........... Jetcom SA [*Switzerland*] [*ICAO designator*]   (FAAC)
JCA........... Jewish Colonization Association [*British*]
JCA........... Jewish Communal Appeal [*Australia*]
JCA........... Johnson Corp. Australia Proprietary Ltd.
JCA........... Judo Club d'Abidjan
JCA........... Jurisclasseur Administratif [*France*]   (FLAF)
JCA........... Juventude Crista de Angola
JCAAHB... Japan Council Against A and H Bombs   (EAIO)
JCAB........ Japan Civil Aeronautics Board   (PDAA)
JCAFU ...... Joint Committee of the Autonomous Federations and Unions [*Comite d'Entente des Federations et Syndicats Autonomes d'Algerie*] [*Algeria*]
JCALM ..... Joint Committee on Aboriginal Lands and Mining [*Australia*]
JCAN........ Junta Coordinadora de Afirmacion Nacional [*Coordinating Junta of National Affirmation*] [*Spanish*]   (WER)
J can Dr ..... Doktor des Kanonischen Rechtes [*German*]
JCAP........ Junta Central de Accao Patriotica
JCB........... Japan Credit Bureau
JCB........... Jeunesse Communiste de Belgique [*Communist Youth of Belgium*]   (WER)
JCB........... Joint Consultative Board [*NATO*]   (NATG)
JCB........... Jurisprudence Commerciale de Bruxelles [*Belgium*] [*A publication*]   (FLAF)
JCB........... Juventud Comunista de Bolivia [*Bolivian Communist Youth*]   (LA)
JCC........... Japan Cultural Centre (Sydney) [*Australia*]
JCC........... Jeunesse Cotiere Cabindienne
JCC........... Jharkhand Coordination Committee [*Jharkhand Samanvaya Samiti*] [*India*] [*Political party*]
JCC........... Jihoceske Cihelny [*South Bohemian Brick Works*]   (CZ)
JCC........... Johannesburg Construction Corp. [*South Africa*]   (AA)
JCC........... Joint Consultative Committee [*Australia*]
JCC........... Jowett Car Club   (EA)
JCC........... Judo Club de Cocody
JCC........... Juventud Comunista de Colombia [*Communist Youth of Colombia*]   (LA)
JCC-BI ..... Jurisclasseur Commercial-Brevets d'Invention [*France*]   (FLAF)
JCC-CBI.... Jurisclasseur Commercial-Contrefacon des Brevets d'Inventions [*France*]   (FLAF)
JCCE .... Joint Consultative Committee on Education [*Nigeria*]
JCCEM ..... Joint Committee of Cultural and Education Ministers [*Australia*]
JCCI .... Johannesburg Chamber of Commerce and Industry [*South Africa*]   (AA)
JCCIS....... Japan Chamber of Commerce and Industry, Sydney [*Australia*]
JCCIUK .... Japanese Chamber of Commerce and Industry in the United Kingdom   (DS)
JCC-MF .... Jurisclasseur Commercial-Marques de Fabrique [*France*]   (FLAF)
JC Comm ... Jurisclasseur Commercial [*France*]   (FLAF)
JCD........... Juventud Costarricense Democratica [*Democratic Costa Rican Youth*]   (LA)
JCDI .... Jurisclasseur de Droit International   (FLAF)
JCE........... Jeunes Chambres Economiques [*Youth Economic Chambers*]   (LA)
JCE........... Jihoceske Elektrarny, Narodni Podnik [*South Bohemian Electric Power Plants, National Enterprise*]   (CZ)
JCE........... Jockey Club of Egypt
jce............. Jouissance [*Payable Interest*] [*French*] [*Business term*]
JCE........... Judo Club Eburneen
JCE........... Junta Central Electoral [*Central Electoral Board*] [*Dominican Republic*]   (LA)
JCE........... Juventud Comunista Ecuatoriana [*Ecuadorean Communist Youth*]   (LA)
JCEA .... Joint Committee for European Affairs [*Defunct*]   (EA)
JCEA .... Junta de Control de Energia Atomica [*Atomic Energy Control Board*] [*Peru*]   (LA)
JCEHV...... Jeune Chambre Economique de Haute Volta [*Junior Economic Chamber of Upper Volta*]   (AF)
JCEM .... Jeune Chambre Economique Marocaine
JCE (M-L) ... Juventud Comunista de Espana (Marxista-Leninista) [*Communist Youth of Spain (Marxist-Leninist)*]   (WER)
JCEWG ..... Joint Communications and Electronics Working Group [*NATO*]   (NATG)
JCF .... Jamaica Constabulary Force   (LA)
JCF .... Japanese Federation of Chemical and General Workers' Unions   (EAIO)
JCF .... Jaycees Community Foundation [*Australia*]
JCF .... Jet Center Flight Training SA [*Spain*] [*ICAO designator*]   (FAAC)
JCF .... Jeunesse Communiste Francaise [*French Communist Youth*]   (WER)
JCFA .... Japan Chemical Fibers Association
JCFC........ Japan-China Joint Fisheries Commission   (ASF)
JCFC........ Jordan Cement Factory Company
JCFOM ..... Jurisclasseur de la France d'Outre-Mer [*France*]   (FLAF)

JCG............ Joint Conservation Group
JCH............ Joint Control Headquarters [*Singapore*] (ML)
Jchtbd........ Juchtenband [*Russia Leather Binding*] [*German*]
Jchtn......... Juchtenband [*Russia Leather Binding*] [*German*]
Jchtnb........ Juchtenband [*Russia Leather Binding*] [*German*]
JCI............. Johannesburg Consolidated Investment Co. Ltd. [*South Africa*]
JCI............. Junior Chamber International (EAIO)
JCI............. Jute Corp. of India
JCIA.......... Japan Chemical Industry Association
JCIC.......... Jewish Community Information Center [*Australia*]
JCIE.......... Japan Center for International Exchange (EAIO)
JC InstrCrim ... Jurisclasseur d'Instruction Criminelle [*France*] (FLAF)
JCIPP........ Jewish Committee for Israeli-Palestinian Peace (EA)
JCIT.......... Joint Committee on Information Technology [*Australia*]
JCK........... Jugoslovenski Crveni Krst [*Yugoslav Red Cross*] (YU)
JCK........... Julia Creek [*Australia*] [*Airport symbol*] (OAG)
JCKGOM ... Jugoslovenski Crven Krst, Glaven Odbor za Makedonija [*Yugoslav Red Cross, Central Committee of Macedonia*] (YU)
JCL............ Jet Cargo-Liberia [*ICAO designator*] (FAAC)
JCl Civil..... Jurisclasseur Civil [*France*] (FLAF)
J Cl FormProc ... Jurisclasseur-Formulaire Analytique de Procedure [*France*] (FLAF)
J Cl ProcCiv ... Jurisclasseur de Procedure Civile [*France*] (FLAF)
JCM.......... Jacobina [*Brazil*] [*Airport symbol*] (OAG)
JCM.......... Jego Cesarska Mosc [*His Imperial Majesty*] [*Poland*]
JCM.......... Jeunesse Chretienne Malgache [*Malagasy Christian Youth*] (AF)
JCM.......... John Chard Medal
JCM.......... Juventud Comunista de Mexico [*Mexican Communist Youth*] (LA)
JCMA....... Japan Construction Mechanization Association (EAIO)
JCMED..... Joint Council for Music Education in Denmark (EAIO)
JCMF .... Jednota Ceskych Matematiku a Fysiku [*Association of Czech Mathematicians and Physicists*] (CZ)
JCMWA.... Joint Christian Ministry in West Africa
JCN .... Junta Civica Nacional [*National Civic Board*] [*Ecuador*] (LA)
JCN .... Jurisclasseur Notarial [*France*] (FLAF)
JCNMT..... Joint Committee of Nordic Marine Technology [*See also NSTM*] (EAIO)
JCNMT..... Joint Committee of Nordic Master Tailors (EA)
JCNNSRC ... Joint Committee of the Nordic Natural Science Research Councils (EA)
JCNSW ..... Judicial Commission of New South Wales [*Australia*]
JCO .... Johannesburg Consolidated Investments [*South Africa*]
JCO .... Jordan Co-Operative Organization (GEA)
JCOC........ Joint Command Operations Center [*NATO*] (NATG)
JCODC...... Japan-China Oil Development Co.
JCOMCEN ... Joint Communications Center
JCOME..... Jewish Committee on the Middle East (EA)
JCOS........ Joint Chiefs of Staff [*Military*]
JCOSA ..... Joint Chiefs of Staff in Australia (ADA)
JCP........... Japan Communist Party [*Nikon Kyosanto*] [*Political party*] (PPW)
JCP........... Jetcopter [*Denmark*] [*ICAO designator*] (FAAC)
JCP........... Jewish Communist Party [*Political party*] (BJA)
JCP........... Jordanian Communist Party [*Political party*] (PD)
JCP........... Juventud Comunista Peruana [*Peruvian Communist Youth*] (LA)
JCPA .... Jerusalem Center for Public Affairs [*Israel*] [*Research center*] (IRC)
JCR........... Jesus Cares Refuge Incorporated [*Australia*] [*An association*]
JCR........... Jeunesse Communiste Revolutionnaire [*Revolutionary Communist Youth*] [*Student group*] [*French*] (WER)
JCR........... Junta Coordenativa Revolucionaria [*Revolutionary Coordinating Junta*] [*Portuguese*] (WER)
JCR........... Junta de Coordinacion Revolucionaria [*Revolutionary Coordinating Junta*] [*Argentina*] (LA)
JCS .... Japan Club of Sydney [*Australia*]
JCS .... Joint Commonwealth Societies [*Australia*] (ADA)
JCS .... Juventud Comunista de El Salvador [*Salvadoran Communist Youth*] (LA)
JCSA .... Jamaica Civil Service Association (LA)
JCSAV...... Joint Council of Subject Associations of Victoria [*Australia*]
JC/SCAMEP ... Joint Commonwealth/States Committee on the Adult Migration Education Program [*Australia*]
JCSCCF .... Joint Commission of the Socialist Countries on Cooperation in the Field of Fisheries (PDAA)
JCSMF...... Jednota Ceskoslovenskych Matematiku a Fysiku Praha [*Former Czechoslovakia*] (SLS)
JCSMR...... John Curtin School of Medical Research [*Australia*] (ADA)
JCSP......... Jednota Ceskoslovenskych Pravniku [*Union of Czechoslovak Lawyers*] (CZ)
JCSRE....... Joint Chiefs of Staff Representative, Europe [*NATO*] (NATG)
JCSS......... Jaffee Center for Strategic Studies [*Israel*] [*Research center*] (IRC)

JCSS......... Joint Council of Scientific Societies [*South Africa*] (AA)
JCSZ......... Jednota Ceskoslovenskych Zemedelcu [*Czechoslovak Farmers' Association*] (CZ)
JCT .... Jewish Cemetery Trust [*Australia*]
JCTND...... Jugoslovenski Centar za Tehnicku i Naucnu Dokumentaciju [*Yugoslav Center of Technical and Scientific Documentation*] (YU)
JCU........... James Cook University of North Queensland [*Australia*]
JCUNQ ..... James Cook University of North Queensland [*Australia*] (ADA)
JCV........... Juventud Comunista Venezolana [*Venezuelan Communist Youth*] (LA)
JCW.......... J. C. Williamson Ltd. [*Australia*] (ADA)
JCW.......... Jego Cesarska Wysokosc [*His Imperial Highness*] [*Poland*]
JCWI........ Joint Council for the Welfare of Immigrants
JCWP .... Joint Conservation Working Party [*Australia*] [*Political party*]
JD .... Jandarma [*Gendarme, Gendarmery*] (TU)
JD .... Jeunesse Democratique [*Democratic Youth*] [*Luxembourg*] (WER)
JD .... Jordanian Dinar [*Monetary unit*] (BJA)
j/d............. Jours de Date [*Days after Date*] [*French*]
JD .... Junta Democratica [*Democratic Junta*] [*Spain*] [*Political party*] (PPE)
JD .... Justizdienst [*Legal Service or Judge Advocate's Office*] [*Military*] (EG)
JD .... Juventudes Democraticas [*Democratic Youth*] [*Spanish*] (WER)
JDA .... Japan Defence Agency (PDAA)
JDA .... Japan Domestic Airlines (PDAA)
JDA .... Juventude Democratica de Angola [*Angolan Democratic Youth*] (AF)
JDB........... Japan Development Bank (PDAA)
JDBTHI .... Jajasan Dana Bantuanuntuk Tjalon Hadji Indonesia [*Aid Foundation for Prospective Indonesian Pilgrims to Mecca*] (IN)
JDC........... Deere & Co. [*ICAO designator*] (FAAC)
JDC........... Japan Airlines Development Co.
JDC........... Jeunesse Democratique Camerounaise
JDC........... Jewish Documentation Centre [*See also BJVN*] (EAIO)
JDC........... Juventud Democrata Cristiana [*Christian Democratic Youth*] [*Chile*] (LA)
JDC........... Juventud Democrata Cristiana [*Christian Democratic Youth*] [*Paraguay*] (LA)
JDC........... Juventud Democrata Cristiana [*Christian Democratic Youth*] [*El Salvador*] (LA)
JDCB........ Juventud del Partido Democrata Cristiano [*Christian Democratic Party Youth*] [*Bolivia*] (LA)
JDCE........ Jeunes Democrates Chretiens Europeens [*European Young Christian Democrats - EYCD*] (EA)
JDE........... Air Med Jetoperations [*Austria*] [*ICAO designator*] (FAAC)
JDF........... Jamaica Defence Force (PDAA)
JDF........... Jamaican Defense Forces
JDF........... Juiz De Fora [*Brazil*] [*Airport symbol*] (OAG)
JDFA .... Juvenile Diabetes Foundation Australia
JDFC .... Joint Danube Fishery Commission [*See also ZKRVD*] [*Zilina, Czechoslovakia*] (EAIO)
JDFI .... Juvenile Diabetes Foundation in Israel (EAIO)
JDH........... Jodhpur [*India*] [*Airport symbol*] (OAG)
JDI............ Junta de Defensa del Tabaco [*Costa Rica*] (DSCA)
jdk........... Joidenkuiden [*Finland*]
JDK........... Joodsch-Democratische Kiespartij [*Political party*] (BJA)
JDL........... Jeunesse Democratique Luxembourgeoise [*Democratic Youth of Luxembourg*] (EAIO)
JDP........... Joint Declaration of Principles
JDP........... Paris-Moulineaux [*France*] [*Airport symbol*] (OAG)
JDr............ Doktor der Rechte [*German*]
JDRB........ Jugoslovensko Drzavno Recno Brodarstvo [*Yugoslav State River Transport*] (YU)
JDRMA..... Japanese Digital Road Mapping Association
JDS........... Jamhuuriyadda Dimoqraadiga ee Soomaliya [*Somali Democratic Republic*] [*Use SDR*] (AF)
JDS........... Joint Defense Staff [*NATO*] (NATG)
JDS........... Jugoslovenska Demokratska Stranka [*Yugoslav Democratic Party*] [*Political party*] (PPE)
JDT........... Jednotny Dunajsky Tarif [*Standard Danube Tariff*] (CZ)
JDT........... Jeunesse Democratique du Togo
JDU .... Jednota Duchovnich a Ucitelu Nabozenstvi Cirkve Ceskoslovenske [*Association of Clergyman and Teachers of Religion of the Czechoslovak Church*] (CZ)
JDZ........... Jingdezhen [*China*] [*Airport symbol*] (OAG)
JDZ........... Jugoslovanske Drzavne Zeleznice [*Yugoslav State Railroads*] (YU)
JDZV .... Yugoslav Society for Water Protection (EAIO)
JE .... Informationseinheit [*German*] (ADPT)
JE .... Jego Ekscelencia [*His Excellency*] [*Poland*]
Je............. Jeune [*Junior*] [*French*]
JE .... Jitsuroku Eiga [*True Document Films*] [*Japan*]
JE .... Juge des Enfants [*French*] (FLAF)

JEA............ Jamaica Exporters Association (LA)
JEA............ Jersey European Airways [*British*] [*ICAO designator*] (FAAC)
JEA............ Jordan Electricity Authority
Jeb.............. Jebel [*Mountain, Hill*] [*J, Jl Arab*] [*See also*] (NAU)
JEC............ Jeunesse Etudiante Catholique Internationale [*International Young Catholic Students*] (EAIO)
JEC............ Jeunesse Etudiante Chretienne [*French*]
JEC............ Joint Economic Committee [*Mauritius*] (EAIO)
JEC............ Junta de Exportacao do Cafe
JEC............ Juventud Estudiantes Catolicos [*Catholic Student Youth*] [*Argentina*] (LA)
JEC............ Juventud Estudiantil Catolica [*Catholic Student Youth*] [*Paraguay*] (LA)
JECC........ Japan Electronic Computer Corp. (PDAA)
JECC........ Joint Egyptian Cotton Committee
JECI......... Jeunesse Etudiante Catholique Internationale [*International Young Catholic Students*]
JECMOS .. Joint Electronic Countermeasures Operation Section [*NATO*] (NATG)
JECS........ Job Evaluation and Classification Scheme [*Sudan*]
JED........... Jeddah [*Saudi Arabia*] [*Airport symbol*] (OAG)
JED........... Jugoslovensko Entomolosko Drustvo [*Yugoslav Entomological Society*] [*Belgrade*] (YU)
jedn............ Jednostka [*Unit*] [*Poland*]
JEDPE ...... Joint Emergency Defense Plan Europe [*NATO*] (NATG)
Jee.............. Jetee [*Pier, Jetty, Mole*] [*Military map abbreviation World War I*] [*French*] (MTD)
JEF .... Jamaica Employers Federation (LA)
JEF .... Jetflite OY [*Finland*] [*ICAO designator*] (FAAC)
JEF .... Jeunesses Europeennes Federalistes
JEG........... Joint Exploratory Group [*NATO*] (NATG)
jegyz.......... Jegyzet [*Note, Footnote*] [*Hungary*] (GPO)
JEIA .... Japanese Electronic Industries Association
JEIDA ...... Japanese Electronic Industries Development Association
JEIDA ...... Japanese Electronic Industry Development Association (CDE)
JEIPAC .... JICST [*Japanese Information Center of Science and Technology*] Electronic Information Processing Automatic Computer
JEJ .... Jets Ejecutivos SA [*Mexico*] [*ICAO designator*] (FAAC)
JEK........... Jugoslovenska Elektrotehnicka Komisija [*Yugoslav Electrotechnical Commission*] (YU)
jel............. Jelenet [*Scene (Theater)*] (HU)
jel .... Jelentes [*Report*] (HU)
JEL........... Jeunesses Europeennes Liberales (FLAF)
JELI.......... Junta Revolucionaria de Libertacao Iberica
JEM........... Japan Evangelical Mission
j em........... Jednostka Elektromagnetyczna [*Electromagnetic Unit*] [*Poland*]
JEMIMA .. Japan Electric Measuring Instruments Manufacturers Association (EAIO)
JEN........... Jenair Ltd. [*Cyprus*] [*ICAO designator*] (FAAC)
JEN........... Junta de Energia Nuclear [*Nuclear Energy Board*] [*Madrid, Spain*] (WER)
JENAKAT ... Jeunesse Nationale Katangaise [*Katangan National Youth*]
Jeod.......... Jeodetik [*Geodetic*] (TU)
JEOL........ Japan Electron Optics Laboratory (PDAA)
Jeol........... Jeoloji [*Geology*] (TU)
JEPG........ Joint Exercise Planning Group [*Military*]
JEPIA....... Japan Electronic Parts Industry Association
JEPM .... Junta de Exportacao da Provincia de Mocambique
JEPP......... Japan English Publications in Print [*Japan Publications Guide Service*] [*Japan*] [*Information service or system*] (CRD)
JEPP......... Japanese Earthquake Prediction Plan
JEPPT ...... Jeunesse du Parti Progressiste du Tchad [*Youth of the Progressive Party of Chad*] (AF)
JEPS......... Joint Exercise Planning Staff [*NATO*] (NATG)
JEQ........... Jequie [*Brazil*] [*Airport symbol*] (OAG)
Jer............ Janvier [*January*] [*French*]
Jer............. Jeremia [*Jeremiah*] [*Afrikaans*]
JER........... Jersey [*Channel Islands*] [*Airport symbol*] (OAG)
JERC........ Japan Economic Research Center (PDAA)
JERI......... Japan Economic Research Institute (PDAA)
JERS......... Japan Earth Remote Sensing Satellite
JERS......... Japan Ergonomics Research Society (PDAA)
JES........... Japan Electroplating Society (PDAA)
JES........... Japanese Export Standard
jes............ Jednostka Elektrostatyczna [*Electrostatic Unit*] [*Poland*]
JES........... Jeju Experiment Station [*South Korean*] [*Research center*] (IRC)
JES........... Jes Air [*Bulgaria*] [*ICAO designator*] (FAAC)
Jes............. Jesaja [*Isaiah*] [*Afrikaans*]
JES........... Young European Students' Union [*Pro-OeVP*] [*Austria*] (WEN)
JESA .... Japanese Engineering Standards Association (ADPT)
JESSI .... Joint European Semiconductor Silicon Initiative
JEST......... Joint Entertainment Superannuation Trust [*Australia*]
JET........... Japan Exchange and Teaching Program [*Australia*]
JET........... J. E. Thiebaut & Cie. [*Malagasy*]
Jet............. Juillet [*July*] [*French*]

JET............ Junta de Estudiantes Tradicionalistas [*Junta of Traditionalist Students*] [*Spanish*] (WER)
JETCO ...... Jamaica Export Trading Company (LA)
JETOX ...... Japan Chemical Industry Ecology-Toxicology Information Center (PDAA)
JEUBAKAT ... Jeunesses Balubakat
JEUCAFRA ... Jeunesse Camerounaise Francaise
JEWEL...... Joint Endeavor for Welfare, Education, and Liberation [*Part of Grenadian political party, the New JEWEL Movement*]
JEWEL...... Joint Endeavour for Welfare, Education, and Liberation
JEYESCO ... Justice Eyeson Memorial College
Jez.............. Jezioro [*Lake*] [*Poland*] (NAU)
Jez.............. Jezirat [*Island, Peninsula*] [*Arabic*] (NAU)
jez.............. Jezyk [*Language*] (POL)
jez oryg....... Jezyk Oryginalu [*Original Language*] [*Poland*]
JF.............. Japan Foundation (EAIO)
jf................ Javnfor [*Compare*] [*Denmark*] (GPO)
JF.............. Jeune Fille [*French*]
JF.............. Juznoslovenski Filolog [*South Slavic Philologist*] [*Belgrade A periodical*] (YU)
JF.............. Trehaven Aviation Ltd. [*British*] [*ICAO designator*] (ICDA)
JFA .... Japan Fishery Agency (MSC)
JFA .... Judo Federation of Australia
JFAI .... Joint Formal Acceptance Inspection [*NATO*] (NATG)
JFBA .... Japan Federation of Bar Associations (EAIO)
JFBIA .... Japan Fashion Belts Industries Association (EAIO)
JFC .... Japan Food Corp.
JFC .... Jewish Folk Center [*Australia*]
JFC .... Jungle Force Companies (ML)
JFCC .... Japan Fine Ceramics Center [*Nagoya*]
JFE .... Junta de Fomento de Esmeraldas [*Ecuador*] (DSCA)
JFEA .... Japan Federation of Employers Association
JFFF .... Japan Freight Forwarders Federation (EAIO)
JFHQ........ Joint Force Headquarters [*Military*]
JFIC.......... Japan Fisheries Information Center (ASF)
JFIC.......... Jordan Fertilizer Industries Company (MENA)
JFL .... Jamaica Freedom League (LA)
J Fl .... Jurisprudence Commerciale des Flandres [*Belgium*] (FLAF)
JFLN .... Jeunesse du Front de Liberation Nationale [*National Liberation Front Youth*] [*Algeria*] (AF)
JFM.......... Jeunesses Federalistes Mondiales [*France*] (FLAF)
JFM.......... Junkers Flugzeug-und-Motorenwerk [*Junkers Aircraft and Engines Plant*] (EG)
JFNDR ...... Jeunesse du Front National pour la Defense de la Revolution [*Youth of the National Front for the Defense of the Revolution*] [*Malagasy*] (AF)
JFNLA ...... Juventude da Frente Nacional de Libertacao de Angola [*Youth of the Angolan National Liberation Front*] (AF)
JFP .... Jednotny Fond Pracujicich [*Workers United Fund*] (CZ)
JFPEO .... Junta de Fomento Provincial de El Oro [*Ecuador*] (DSCA)
JFPL......... Junta de Fomento Provincial de Loja [*Ecuador*] (DSCA)
JFPLN....... Juventude da Frente Patriotica de Libertacao Nacional
jfr............... Jamfor [*Compare*] [*Sweden*] (GPO)
jfr............... Jevnfor [*Compare*] [*Denmark*] (GPO)
JFRCS .... Japanese Fisheries Resources Conservation Association (ASF)
JFRO .... Joint Fisheries Research Organization of Northern Rhodesia and Nyassaland
JFS............ Jamaica Freight and Shipping Co. Ltd. (EY)
JFS............ Juanda Flying School [*Indonesia*] [*ICAO designator*] (FAAC)
JFSEO....... Japan Federation of Smaller Enterprise Organizations (EY)
JFSP......... Juventude da Frente Socialista Popular [*Socialist Popular Youth Front*] [*Portuguese*] (WER)
JFSS .... Joint Force Signals Staff [*Military*]
JFT .... Jet Fret [*France*] [*ICAO designator*] (FAAC)
JFTU .... Jordanian Federation of Trade Unions
jg............... Jaargang [*Volume*] [*Afrikaans*]
JG .... Jahrgang [*Year of Publication/Volume*] [*German*]
JG .... Jurisprudence Generale [*Dalloz*] [*France*] (FLAF)
JGA .... Jamnagar [*India*] [*Airport symbol*] (OAG)
JGB........... Japanese Government Bond (ECON)
JGC .... Japan Gasoline Company Ltd. [*Nuclear energy*] (NRCH)
JGCR........ Japan Gas-Cooled Reactor [*Nuclear energy*] (NRCH)
Jgdhbg...... Jugendherberge [*Youth Hostel*] [*German*]
JGE........... Junta de Generales del Ejercito [*Army Council of Generals*] [*Uruguay*] (LA)
JGG .... Jugendgerichtsgesetz [*Juvenile Court Law*] [*German*] (EG)
Jgge........... Jahrgaenge [*Volumes, Years*] [*Publishing*] [*German*]
JGGMA .... Japan Glue and Gelatine Manufacturers Association (EAIO)
JGK........... Jandarma Genel Komutanligi [*Gendarmery General Command*] [*Interior Ministry*] (TU)
JGOFS ...... Joint Global Ocean Flux Study [*International experiment*]
JGR........... Belize Trans Air [*ICAO designator*] (FAAC)
JGR........... Joven Guardia Roja [*Young Red Guard*] [*Spanish*] (WER)
JGRIP....... Japanese Government and Public Research in Progress [*International database*]

JGRN .... Junta de Gobierno de Reconstruccion Nacional [*Junta of the Government of National Reconstruction*] [*Nicaragua*] (LA)

JGS .... Jeunes Gardes Socialistes [*Young Socialist Guards*] [*Belgium*] (WER)

JGS .... Jurisprudence Generale, Supplement [*Dalloz*] [*France*] (FLAF)

jgyz .... Jegyzek [*List, Catalog, Memorandum*] (HU)

Jh .... Jahrhundert [*Century*] [*German*]

JH .... Jeune Homme [*Young Man*] [*French*]

JH .... Joint House [*Commonwealth Parliament*] [*Australia*]

JH .... Jugendherberge [*Youth Hostel*] [*German*]

JHB .... Johore Bahru [*Malaysia*] [*Airport symbol*] (OAG)

Jhdt .... Jahrhundert [*Century*] [*German*]

Jhdte .... Jahrhunderte [*Centuries*] [*German*]

JHDV .... Jewish Historical Documentation Centre, Vienna

JHI .... James Hardie Industries [*Australia*]

JHIA.......... Japan Hide Importers Association (EAIO)

jhk .... Johonkin [*Finland*]

jhk .... Johonkuhun [*Finland*]

JHK .... Jugendhilfekommission [*Youth Aid Commission*] (EG)

JHMA ...... Japan Handbag Manufacturers Association (EAIO)

JHMA ...... Japan Shirts and Underwear Manufacturers Association (EAIO)

JHO .... Junior House Officer [*Military*]

JHQ.......... Shute Harbour [*Australia*] [*Airport symbol*]

JHR........... Jednotlive Hospodarici Rolnici [*Individual Farmers*] (CZ)

Jhr............. Jonkheer [*Baron*] [*Afrikaans*]

JHS .... Jesus Hominum Salvator [*Jesus, Savior of Men*] (ROG)

JHVO .... Jugendhilfeverordnung [*Youth Aid Decree*] (EG)

JHWA ...... Japan Handbag Wholesalers Association (EAIO)

JI .... Air Balear [*ICAO designator*] (ICDA)

JI .... Jaduram Industries Ltd. [*Fiji*]

JI .... Jamaat-i-Islami [*Pakistan*] [*Political party*] (FEA)

JI .... Juge d'Instruction [*French*] (FLAF)

JI .... Jugoistok [*Southeast*] (YU)

JI .... Jurisprudence Immobiliere [*France*] (FLAF)

JIA .... Jordan International Airline

JIB .... Djibouti [*Airport symbol*] (OAG)

JIB .... Djibouti Airport

JIB .... Jos International Breweries [*Nigeria*]

jib .... Jubilee International Business Co. Ltd. [*Thailand*]

JIB .... Jugoslovenska Investiciona Banka [*Yugoslav Investment Bank*] (YU)

JIC .... Joint Industry Council (EAIO)

JIC .... Jugoslovenski Istoriski Casopis [*Yugoslav Historical Journal*] (YU)

JIC .... Juventudes Inconformes de Colombia [*Political party*] (EY)

JICA .... Japan International Cooperation Agency

JICANA .... Joint Intelligence Collecting Agency, North Africa

JICG .... Joint International Coordination Group (MSC)

JICI .... Jeunesse Independante Chretienne Internationale [*International Independent Christian Youth - IICY*] (EA)

JICOA ...... Japan Information and Communication Association [*Information service or system*] (IID)

JICST .... Japan Information Center for Science and Technology

JICST .... Japan Information Center of Science and Technology [*Tokyo*] (IID)

JICST .... Japan Information Centre of Science and Technology [*ICSU*]

JID............ Air Condal SA [*Spain*] [*ICAO designator*] (FAAC)

JID............ Junta Inter-Americana de Defensa [*Inter-American Defense Board*] [*Use IADB*] (LA)

JIDC .... Jamaica Industrial Development Corporation (LA)

JIDC .... Junta Inter-Americana de Defensa Continental [*Inter-American Board for Continental Defense*] (LA)

Jidosharoren ... Nihon Jidoshasangyo Rodokumiai Rengokai [*Federation of Japanese Automobile Workers' Unions*]

Jidoshasoren ... Zen-Nihon Jidosha Sangyo Rodokumiai Sorengokai [*Confederation of Japanese Automobile Workers' Unions*]

JIDPO .... Japan Industrial Design Promotion Organization (EAIO)

JIDR......... Junta Interministerial del Desarrollo Rural [*Bolivia*] (DSCA)

JIEA .... Japan Industrial Explosives Association (PDAA)

JIF .... Journees Ivoiriennes du Froid

JIFMA...... Japan Industrial Furnace Manufacturers Association (EAIO)

JIFS.......... Jerusalem Institute for Federal Studies [*Israel*] [*Research center*] (IRC)

JIH .... Jamaat-e-Islami Hind [*India*] (EAIO)

JIIA .... Japan Institute of International Affairs (IRC)

JIIA .... Journees Internationales de l'Informatique et de l'Automatique [*French*] (ADPT)

JIII........... Japan Institute of Invention and Innovation (PDAA)

JIL .... Japan Institute of Labour (DLA)

JIM .... Jakarta Informal Meeting

JIM .... Jamaica Institute of Management (LA)

JIM .... Jimma [*Ethiopia*] [*Airport symbol*] (OAG)

JIN .... Japanese Institute of Navigation (PDAA)

Jin .... Jardin [*Garden*] [*Military map abbreviation World War I*] [*French*] (MTD)

JIN............ Junta de Inteligencia Nacional [*National Intelligence Board*] [*Colorado*] (LA)

JINR......... Joint Institute of Nuclear Research [*Dubna, USSR*]

JIP/AMD ... JIP/Areal Marketing Database [*Toyo Keizai Shinposha Co. Ltd.*] [*Japan*] [*Information service or system*] (CRD)

JIPDC........ Japan-Iraq Petroleum Development Corporation

JIPID......... Japanese International Protein Information Database

JIR .... Jeunes Instituteurs Revolutionnaires [*Young Revolutionary School Teachers*] [*Benin*] (AF)

JIR .... Jiri [*Nepal*] [*Airport symbol*] (OAG)

JIRA .... Japan Industrial Robot Association

JIRAMA ... Societe Jiro sy Rano Malagasy [*Malagasy Electricity and Water Company*] (AF)

JIS .... Jamaica Information Service [*Formerly, API*] (LA)

JIS .... Japanese Industrial Standards

JIS .... Justice Information System [*Australia*]

JISC.......... Japanese Industrial Standards Committee [*Agency of Industrial Science and Technology, Ministry of International Trade and Industry*]

JISETA ..... Joint Investigation of the Southeastern Tropical Atlantic [*Angola, US*] (MSC)

JISHA .... Japan Industrial Safety and Health Association [*Research center*] (IRC)

JISTEC ..... Japan International Science and Technology Exchange Center

JIT .... Jamiat-i-Talaba [*Pakistan*] [*Political party*] (PD)

JITA .... Japanese Industrial Technology Association

JITK .... Jugoslovensko-Italijanska Trgovinska Komora [*Yugoslav-Italian Chamber of Commerce*] [*Belgrade*] (YU)

JIU........... Joint Inspection Unit [*United Nations*]

JIU........... Junta das Missoes Geograficas e de Investigacoes do Ultramar [*Portugal*] (DSCA)

JIW........... J. Inglis Wright [*Advertising agency*] [*New Zealand*]

JIW........... Jiwani [*Pakistan*] [*Airport symbol*] (OAG)

JIWP .... Joint Interim Working Party

jj .... Juoksujalka(a) [*Finland*]

JJCC........ Juventudes Comunistas [*Communist Youth*] [*Spanish*] (WER)

JJG .... Joachim-Jungius-Gesellschaft der Wissenschaften eV [*Joachim Jungius Society of Learning*] (SLS)

JJI............. Juanjui [*Peru*] [*Airport symbol*] (OAG)

JJI............. Jug Jugo-Istok [*South Southeast*] (YU)

JJLL......... Juventudes Libertarias [*Anarchist Youth*] [*Spanish*] (WER)

JJN........... Jinjiang [*China*] [*Airport symbol*] (OAG)

JJP........... Jatiya Janata Party [*National People's Party*] [*Bangladesh*] [*Political party*] (PPW)

JJSS .... Juventudes Socialistas [*Socialist Youth*] [*Spanish*] (WER)

jjv .... Jiho-Jihovychod [*South-Southeast*] (CZ)

JJV .... Jug Jugovzhod [*South-Southeast*] (YU)

jjz .... Jiho-Jihozapad [*South-Southwest*] (CZ)

JJZ .... Jug Jugo-Zapad [*South-Southwest*] (YU)

JK .... Jalkikirjoitus [*Finland*]

jk .... Jegyzek [*List, Catalog, Memorandum*] (HU)

JK .... Jernkontoret [*Ironmasters' Association*] [*Research center*] [*Sweden*] (IRC)

jk .... Jokin [*Finland*]

jk .... Joku [*Finland*]

JK .... Trabajos Aereos y Enlaces SA [*Spain*] [*ICAO designator*] (ICDA)

JKA........... Jakarta [*Indonesia*] (ABBR)

JKAA........ Japan Karate Association of Australia

JKACI ...... Jeunes Khmers Anti-Communistes Indochinois [*Young Cambodians Against Indochinese Communism*] (CL)

JKFC .... Japan-Korea Joint Fisheries Commission (MSC)

JKG........... Jonkoping [*Sweden*] [*Airport symbol*] (OAG)

JKH .... Chios [*Greece*] [*Airport symbol*] (OAG)

jkh .... Johonkuhun [*Finland*]

JKHN .... Johannesburgse Kamer van Handel en Nywerheid [*South Africa*] (AA)

JKI .... Jugoslovenska Krznarska Industrija [*Yugoslav Fur Industry*] [*Indija*] (YU)

JKIA .... Jajasan Kesedjahteraan Ibu dan Anak [*Welfare Foundation for Mothers and Children*] (IN)

JKLF......... Jammu and Kashmir Liberation Front [*India*] [*Political party*] (ECON)

jklla .... Jollakulla [*Finland*]

jklle .... Jollekulle [*Finland*]

jklta .... Joltakulta [*Finland*]

JKM........... Jego Krolewska Mosc [*His Royal Majesty*] [*Poland*]

JKMci........ Jego Krolewskiej Mosci [*His Royal Majesty's*] [*Poland*]

JKMosci .... Jego Krolewskiej Mosci [*His Royal Majesty's*] [*Poland*]

JKMRC.... Julius Kruttschnitt Mineral Research Centre [*Australia*]

jkn .... Jonkun [*Finland*]

jkna .... Jonakuna [*Finland*]

JKNC........ Jammu and Kashmir National Conference [*India*] [*Political party*] (PPW)

JKol .... Jadranski Koledar [*Adriatic Almanac*] [*A periodical*] (YU)

JKP........... Jawatankuasa Perhubungan [*Public Relations Committee*] (ML)

JKPN......... Jabatan Kuasa Kerja Perang Negeri [State War Executive Committee] (ML)
JKR............. Jabatan Kerja Raya [Public Works Department] (ML)
jKr .... Jalkeen Kristuksen Syntyman [Finland]
JKR............. Janakpur [Nepal] [Airport symbol] (OAG)
jksk............. Joksikin [Finland]
jksk............. Joksikuksi [Finland]
jkssa.......... Jossakussa [Finland]
jksta .... Jostakusta [Finland]
JKT............. Jakarta [Indonesia] [Airport symbol] (OAG)
JKT............. National Development Army [Tanzania] (AF)
jkta .... Jotakuta [Finland]
JKTC........ Japan Key Technology Centre [Research center] (EAS)
JKU .... Jeshi la Kujenga Uchumi
JKU .... Youth Contact for International Solidarity and Exchange [Netherlands] (WEN)
jkv .... Jegyzokonyv [Minutes] (HU)
JKV .... Jonkvrou [Baroness] [Afrikaans]
jkvo............. Jegyzokonyvvezeto [Recording Secretary] (HU)
jkvv............. Jegyzokonyvvezeto [Recording Secretary] (HU)
JKW........... Jego Krolewska Wysokosc [His Royal Highness] [Poland]
JI................. Jabal [Jabel, Jebel] [Mountain, Hill J Arab] [See also] (NAU)
JL................. Jabatan Laut [Navy Department] (ML)
Jl................. Jalan [Street]
jl .... Jongslede [Last] [Afrikaans]
jl .... Jongstleden [Last] [Netherlands] (GPO)
jl .... Journal [Record Book] [French]
JL................ Justice Libre [Benelux] (BAS)
JLA .... Jamaica Livestock Association (LA)
JLA .... Japan Luminaires Association (EAIO)
JLA .... John Lysaght (Australia) Ltd. (ADA)
JLA .... Jugoslovanska Ljudska Armija [Yugoslav People's Army] (YU)
JLC .... Japanese Linear Collider [High energy physics]
JLEM .... Jerusalem (ABBR)
JLG............ Joint Liaison Group [Established in 1984 to facilitate Hong Kong's transition to Chinese sovereignty]
JLIA .... Japan Leather and Leather Goods Industries Association (EAIO)
JLIA .... Japan Leather Importers Association (EAIO)
JLJM........ Jurutera Letrik dan Jentera Malaysia [Malaysian Electrical and Mechanical Engineers] (ML)
Jll .... Juillet [July] [French]
jllak .... Jollakin [Finland]
jllak .... Jollakulla [Finland]
jllek .... Jollekin [Finland]
jllek .... Jollekulle [Finland]
jllk .... Jollekin [Finland]
JLM........... Jesus Lives Ministry [Sri Lanka]
JLM........... Jugoslovenska Liga za Mir, Nezavisnost i Ravnopravnost Naroda [Yugoslav League for Peace, Independence and Equality of Peoples] (EAIO)
JLM........... Junior Legacy Melbourne [Australia] [An association]
JLO............ Jurisprudence du Louage d'Ouvrage [Belgium] (FLAF)
JLOIC .... Joint Logistics, Operations, Intelligence Center [NATO] (NATG)
JLP .... Jamaica Labour Party [Political party] (PPW)
JLR .... Jabalpur [India] [Airport symbol] (OAG)
JLR .... Junta Local de Reconstruccion [Local Reconstruction Board] [Nicaragua] (LA)
JLS .... Jet Alsace [France] [ICAO designator] (FAAC)
JLSIF .... Japan Leather Shoe Industries Federation (EAIO)
JLTA .... Japan Leather Traders Association (EAIO)
jltk.............. Joltakin [Finland]
jltk.............. Joltakulta [Finland]
JM .... Jamaica [ANSI two-letter standard code] (CNC)
JM .... Jang Mulia [The Honorable, His Excellency, Your Excellency] (IN)
j M............. Jednostka Macke'a [Macke Unit] [Poland]
jm .... Jednostka Masy Magnetycznej [Magnetic Unit] [Poland]
JM .... Jego Magnificencja [Rector's title] [Poland]
JM .... Jeho Magnificence [Academic title of the president of a university] (CZ)
JM .... Jeunesse Militante [Militant Youth] [Mauritius] (AF)
JM .... Jiyu-Minshuto [Liberal-Democratic Party] [Japan] [Political party]
jm .... Jmeno [Name] (CZ)
JM .... Journal Militaire [French] (MTD)
JM .... Justice Militaire [France] (FLAF)
JM .... Justizminister [Minister of Justice] [German] (ILCA)
JM .... Justizministerium [Ministry of Justice] [German] (ILCA)
JMA .... Jamaica Manufacturers Association (LA)
JMA .... Japanese Meteorological Agency (ASF)
JMA .... Japan Management Association
JMAE.......... Junta Militar Angolano no Exilio
JMB........... Jeunesse Musulmane de Bardo [Tunisia]
JMB........... Joint Movements Branch [NATO] (NATG)

JMC........... Japan Monopoly Corp. (PDAA)
JMCA.......... Joint Movement Coordination Agency
JMCC.......... Joint Mobile Communications Center [NATO] (NATG)
JMci........... Jego Mosci [The Honorable Gentleman's] [Poland]
jmd .... Jemand [Somebody] [German] (GCA)
JMD .... Jeoloji ve Maden Dairesi [Geology and Mining Department (Office)] [Turkish Cypriot] (GC)
JMD .... Jihomoravske Doly [South Moravian Mines] (CZ)
jmdm .... Jemandem [To Somebody] [German] (GCA)
jmdn .... Jemanden [Somebody] [German] (GCA)
jmds............ Jemandes [Of Somebody] [German] (GCA)
JME........... Jihomoravske Energeticke Zavody [South-Moravian Electrical Power Plants] (CZ)
JME........... Juventudes Musicales de Espana [Spain] (EAIO)
JMF........... Jeunesses Musicales de France [Young People's Musical Association of France] (WER)
jmfr............. Jaemfoer [Compare] [Sweden]
JMGA........ Jewellers and Metalsmiths Group of Australia
JMGK....... Juznomoravska Grupa Korpusa [Southern Moravia Group of Corps] [World War II] (YU)
JMH .... Jardine Matheson Holdings [Hong Kong]
JMH .... Jeunesses Musicales of Hungary (EAIO)
JMI............ Japan Machinery and Metal Inspection Institute (PDAA)
JMI............ Jeunesses Musicales of Israel (EAIO)
JMIA .... Japan Machinery Importers Association (EAIO)
JMIA .... Japan Mining Industry Association (EAIO)
JMIF .... Japan Motor Industrial Federation (PDAA)
JMIP .... Jewish Memories, Inheritance through Photography [France] (EAIO)
J-MIR .... Juventud-Movimiento de la Izquierda Revolucionaria [Youth Movement of the Revolutionary Left] [Venezuela] (LA)
JMJ .... Jesus, Maria, Jose [Jesus, Mary, Joseph] [Portuguese]
JMK........... Mikonos [Greece] [Airport symbol] (OAG)
JML........... Jihomoravske Lignitove Doly [South Moravian Lignite Mines] (CZ)
JML........... Jihomoravsky Lignitovy Revir [South Moravian Lignite Basin] (CZ)
JML........... Taxi Aereo de Jimulco SA de CV [Mexico] [ICAO designator] (FAAC)
JMLA .... Japan Medical Library Association (EAIO)
JMM .... Jamaica Merchant Marine (EY)
JMM .... Jeunesses Musicales of Monaco (EAIO)
JMMA...... Japan Materials Management Association (PDAA)
JMMA...... Japan Microscope Manufacturers Association (PDAA)
JMMS....... Jeunesses Musicales Magyarorszagi Szervezete [Jeunesses Musicales of Hungary] (EAIO)
JMN .... Johan Mangku Negara [Third Grade of the Most Distinguished Order of Pangkuan Negara] [Malaysia] (ML)
JMNA .... Juventude Movimento Nacional de Angola [Youth of the Angolan National Movement] (AF)
JMNCL..... Jeunesse du Mouvement National Congolaise-Lumumba
JMNR .... Jeunesse du Mouvement National de la Revolution [Political party] [Congo]
JMNS........ Jednota Mladych Narodnich Socialistu [Youth Association of the National Socialist Party] (CZ)
JMO .... Jesuit Mission Office [Australia]
JMO .... Jomsom [Nepal] [Airport symbol] (OAG)
JMO .... Jugoslovenska Muslimanska Organizacija [Yugoslav Moslem Organization] [Political party] (PPE)
JMP.......... Jen Min Piao [or Yuan] [Peoples money of China] (BARN)
JMP.......... Juventude Musical Portuguesa [Portuguese Musical Youth] (EAIO)
JMPLA ..... Juventude Movimento Popular de Libertacao de Angola [Youth of the Popular Movement for the Liberation of Angola] (AF)
JMPR .... Jeunesse du Mouvement Populaire de la Revolution [Youth of the Popular Movement of the Revolution] [Zaire] (AF)
JMPS .... Jeunesse Marocaine pour le Progres et le Socialisme [Moroccan Youth for Progress and Socialism] (AF)
JMPSTPW ... Jaworznicko-Mikolowskie Przedsiebiorstwo Spedycyjno-Transportowe Przemyslu Weglowego [Jaworznik-Mikolow Coal Industry Forwarding and Transport Enterprise] (POL)
JMRC....... Joint Microelectronic Research Centre [Australia]
JMRL....... Juventudes del Movimiento Revolucionario Liberal [Youth of the Liberal Revolutionary Movement] [Colorado] (LA)
jms.............. Ja Muuta Sellaista [Finland]
jms.............. Ja Muuta Semmoista [Finland]
JMS.......... Japanese Meteorological Society (MSC)
JMS.......... Jeunesses Musicales de Suisse (EAIO)
JMSA........ Japanese Maritime Safety Agency (MSC)
JMSDF...... Japan Maritime Self Defense Force (MSC)
JMTR...... Japan-Made Material Testing Reactor
jn .... Jak Nizej [As Below] [Poland]
JN .... Jeunesse Nationaliste
JN .... Jugoslavenska Njiva [Zagreb] [A periodical] (YU)
JNA .... Jordanian News Agency (ME)

JNA .... Jugoslovenska Narodna Armija [*Yugoslav People's Army*]   (YU)

JNA .... Junta Nacional del Aloodon [*Argentina*]   (DSCA)

JNA .... Yugoslav People's Army

JNADPI .... Japan National Assembly of Disabled Peoples' International   (EAIO)

JNAEB ...... Junta Nacional de Auxilio Escolar y Becas [*Santiago, Chile*]   (LAA)

JNAF .... Japanese Navy Air Force

JNAF .... Joint Navy-Air Force

jnak .... Jonakin [*Finland*]

jnak .... Jonakuna [*Finland*]

JNB .... Johannesburg [*South Africa*] [*Airport symbol*]   (OAG)

JNB .... Jugoslavenska Narodna Banka [*Yugoslav National Bank*]   (YU)

JNC .... Jeunesse Nationale Camerounaise [*Cameroonian National Youth*]   (AF)

JNC .... Junta Nacional de Carnes [*National Meat Board*] [*Buenos Aires, Argentina*]   (LAA)

JNCC .... Junior Naval Command Course

JNCIMC ... Japanese National Committee of the International Music Council   (EAIO)

JND .... Jihoceske Narodni Divadlo [*South Bohemian National Theater*]   (CZ)

JNDA .... Junta Nacional de Distribucion de los Abastecimientos [*National Board for Distribution of Supplies*] [*Cuba*]   (LA)

jne .... Ja Niin Edelleen [*Et Cetera, And So On*] [*Finland*]

JNE .... Ja Niin Edespain [*And So On*] [*Finnish*]

Jne .... Jeune [*Junior*] [*French*]

JNE .... Jurado Nacional de Elecciones [*National Election Jury*] [*Peru*]   (LA)

JNEC .... Jamaica National Export Corporation   (LA)

Jne Not ...... Jeune Notariat [*Benelux*]   (BAS)

JNF .... Japan Nuclear Fuel Co. Ltd. [*A joint entity set up by Toshiba, Hitachi, and US General Electric*]

JNF .... Jewish National Fund [*Israel*]   (ME)

JNFA .... Jewish National Fund of Australia

JNFI .... Japan Nuclear Fuel Industries [*Power company consortium*]

JNG .... Junta Nacional de Granos [*National Grain Board*] [*Argentina*]   (LA)

jni .... Juoksumetria [*Finland*]

JNIB .... Jamaica National Investment Bank   (GEA)

JNIC .... Jamaica National Investment Company   (LA)

JNIP .... Jamaica National Investment Promotions   (LA)

JNj .... Jugoslavenska Njiva [*Zagreb*] [*A periodical*]   (YU)

JNJGF ...... Jack Newton Junior Golf Foundation [*Australia*]

JNK .... Jeunesse Nationale Katangaise

jnk .... Jonkin [*Finland*]

jnk .... Jonkun [*Finland*]

JNKFAO ... Jugoslovenska Nacionalna Komisija za Saradnju sa FAO [*Yugoslav National Commission for Cooperation with FAO*]   (YU)

JNKMOR ... Jugoslovenska Nacionalna Komisija za Medunarodnu Organizaciju Rada [*Yugoslav National Commission for the International Labor Organization*]   (YU)

JNKUNESKO ... Jugoslovenska Nacionalna Komisija za UNESKO [*Yugoslav National Commission for UNESCO*]   (YU)

JNKVV ...... The Jawaharlal Nehru Krishi Vishwa Vidyalaya [*India*]   (DSCA)

JNL .... Jeunesse Nationale Lumumbiste

jnnk .... Jonnekin [*Finland*]

JNO .... Jugoslovenski Narodni Odbor [*Yugoslav National Committee*]   (YU)

JNOC .... Japan National Oil Corp.   (PDAA)

JNOF .... Jedinstveni Narodno Oslobodilacki Front [*United National Liberation Front*]   (YU)

JNOF .... Jugoslovenski Narodnooslobodilacki Front [*Yugoslav National Liberation Front*]   (YU)

JNP .... Junta Nacional de Planificacion y Coordinacion [*National Planning and Economic Coordination Board*] [*Ecuador*]   (LAA)

JNP .... Juventud Nacionalista Popular [*Nationalist Popular Youth*] [*Colorado*]   (LA)

JNPC .... Junta Nacional de Planificacion y Coordinacion [*Dominican Republic*]   (DSCA)

JNPCE ...... Junta Nacional de Planificacion y Coordinacion Economica [*Ecuador*]   (DSCA)

JNPN .... Jeunesse Nationale Pierre Ngendenduniwe

JNPP .... Junta Nacional dos Produtos Pecuarios [*National Beef Products Board*] [*Portuguese*]   (WER)

JNR .... Japanesae National Railways   (BARN)

JNR .... Japanese National Railways   (FEA)

JNR .... Jeunesse Nationaliste Rwagasore [*Rwagasore Nationalist Youth*] [*Burundi*]   (AF)

JNRC .... Jeunesse Nationaliste Rurale du Congo

JNS .... Japan Nuclear Society   (PDAA)

JNS .... Jugoslovenska Nacionalna Stranka [*Yugoslav National Party*] [*Political party*]   (PPE)

JNSC .... Japan Nuclear Safety Commission   (FEA)

JNSDA ...... Japan Nuclear Ship Development Agency   (PDAA)

JNSRDA ... Japan Nuclear Ship Research and Development   (FEA)

JNTO .... Japan National Tourist Organization   (PDAA)

JNTU .... Jawaharlal Nehru Technological University [*India*]

JNV .... Jednotny Narodni Vybor [*United National Committee*]   (CZ)

JNV .... Junta Nacional de la Vivienda [*National Housing Board*] [*Lima, Peru*]   (LAA)

JNV .... Junta Nacional do Vinho [*National Wine Board*] [*Portuguese*]   (WER)

JO .... Jasnie Oswiecony [*His Highness, His Grace*] [*Poland*]

JO .... Jeux Olympiques [*Olympic Games*] [*French*]   (WER)

JO .... Jilemnickeho Odznak [*Jilemnicky Badge*]   (CZ)

JO .... Jordan [*ANSI two-letter standard code*]   (CNC)

JO .... Journal Officiel [*Official Bulletin*] [*French*]   (WER)

JO .... Jugoslovenski Odbor [*Yugoslav Committee*]   (YU)

jo .... Juncto [*Benelux*]   (BAS)

JOA .... Jawatankuasa Olimpik Antarabangsa [*International Olympic Committee*]   (ML)

JOAC .... Juventud Obrera de Accion Catolica [*Catholic Action Worker Youth*] [*Spanish*]   (WER)

JOB .... Aerojobeni SA de CV [*Mexico*] [*ICAO designator*]   (FAAC)

JOC .... Jeunesse Ouvriere Catholique [*Young Catholic Workers*] [*Rwanda*]   (AF)

JOC .... Jeunesse Ouvriere Catholique [*Young Catholic Workers*] [*Belgium*]   (WER)

JOC .... Jeunesse Ouvriere Chretienne [*Christian Workers Youth Organization*] [*Reunionese*]   (AF)

JOC .... Jeunesse Ouvriere Congolaise [*Congolese Workers Youth Organization*]

joc .... Jocular   (TPFD)

JOC .... Jordan Olympic Committee   (EAIO)

JOC .... Juventude Operaria Catolica [*Catholic Labor Youth*] [*Portuguese*]   (WER)

JOC .... Juventud Obrera Catolica [*Young Catholic Workers*] [*Spanish*]   (WER)

JOCF .... Jeunesse Ouvriere Chretienne Feminine [*Young Christian Female Workers*] [*Belgium*]   (EAIO)

JOCF .... Juventud Obrera Catolica Femenina [*Catholic Young Women Workers*] [*Spanish*]   (WER)

JOCI .... Jeunesse Ouvriere Chretienne Internationale [*International Young Christian Workers - IYCW*]   (EAIO)

JOCI .... Juventud Obrera Catolica Internacional [*International Catholic Worker Youth*]   (LA)

JOCS .... Japan Oil Chemists' Society

JOCT .... Junior Officers Common Training

JOCV .... Japanese Overseas Co-Operation Volunteers

JODAC ...... Johannesburg Democratic Action Committee [*South Africa*]

JODC .... Japan Oceanographic Data Center [*Information service or system*]   (IID)

JODCO ...... Japan Oil Development Co.   (MENA)

Jodco .... Japan Oil Development Company   (OMWE)

Jodier .... Jodeirung [*Iodination*] [*German*]   (GCA)

jodometr .... Jodometrisch [*Iodometric*] [*German*]   (GCA)

JOE .... Joensuu [*Finland*] [*Airport symbol*]   (OAG)

JOESCO .... Jovenes Escritores Colombianos [*Colombia*]   (COL)

JOF .... Juntas de Oposicion Falangistas [*Falangist Opposition Juntas*] [*Spanish*]   (WER)

JOFA .... Jukwa, Okumaning, Fosu, and Akwansrem

JOFIEA .... Japan Oil and Fat Importers and Exporters Association   (EAIO)

JOG .... Jogyakarta [*Indonesia*] [*Airport symbol*]   (OAG)

JOG .... Junior Offshore Group [*Boating*] [*Australia*]

JOG .... Junta de Oficiales Generales [*Council of General Officers*] [*Uruguay*]   (LA)

jogsz .... Jogszabaly [*Legal Provision*]   (HU)

jogtan .... Jogtanacsos [*Legal Counselor*]   (HU)

Joh .... Johannes [*John*] [*Afrikaans*]

JOH .... Johore   (ML)

Johnnies .... Johannesburg Consolidated Investment and Anglovaal Groups [*South Africa*]

joht .... Johtaja [*Finland*]

JOI .... Joinville [*Brazil*] [*Airport symbol*]   (OAG)

JOIDES .... Joint Oceanographic Institute for Deep Earth Sampling

JOIS .... Japan Online Information System [*Database*]

JOK .... Airtaxi Bedarfsluftverkehrsges GmbH [*Austria*] [*ICAO designator*]   (FAAC)

JOKA .... People's Democratic Students of Jyvaskyla [*Finland*]   (WEN)

JOKs .... Jasnie Oswiecony Ksiaze [*His Highness Duke Of ————*] [*Poland*]

JOL .... Jeunesse Ouvriere Luxembourgeoise [*Luxembourg Working Youth*]   (WER)

JOL .... Jolo [*Philippines*] [*Airport symbol*]   (OAG)

JOM .... Japan's Offshore Market

JOM .... Jeunesse Ouvriere Marocaine [*Moroccan Working Youth*]   (AF)

JOME .... Job-Oriented Migrant English [*Australia*]

JON .... Johnston Island [*Airport symbol*]   (OAG)

JONGEHR ... Jongeheer [*Master*] [*Afrikaans*]

JONLINUD ... Bataljon Lintas Udara [*Airborne Battalion*]   (IN)

JONS......... Juntas de Ofensiva Nacional Sindicalista [*Syndicalist Juntas of the National Offensive*] [*Spain*] [*Political party*]   (PPE)

JONSDAP ... Joint North Sea Data Acquisition Project [*An informal group of Belgian, German, British, Dutch, and Swedish scientific institutes*]   (PDAA)

JONSDAP ... Joint Oceanographic North Sea Data Acquisition Program   (MSC)

JONSIS..... Joint North Sea Information Systems   (PDAA)

JONSWAP ... Joint North Sea Wave Project [*An informal group of Belgian, German, British, Dutch, and Swedish scientific institutes*]   (PDAA)

JOPA......... Juventud Organizada del Pueblo en Armas [*Armed People's Organized Youth*] [*Guatemala*]   (PD)

JOPEFIN ... Journalists' Peace Committee in Finland

JOPP......... Jednotna Organisace Podnikoveho Pocetnictvi [*Standard Organization of Management Accounting*]   (CZ)

jor.............. Jaror [*Patrol*]   (HU)

JOR .... Jordan [*ANSI three-letter standard code*]   (CNC)

JORC........ Jeddah Oil Refinery Company [*Jeddah, Saudi Arabia*]   (MENA)

JORD .... Jordan   (ABBR)

JORN .... Jindalee Operational RADAR Network [*Australia*]

jorn............. Jornalismo [*Journalism*] [*Portuguese*]

JOS............ Jeunesse Ouvriere du Senegal

JOS............ Joint Operations Staff [*Military*]

JOS............ Jos [*Nigeria*] [*Airport symbol*]   (OAG)

Jos.............. Josua [*Joshua*] [*Afrikaans*]

josk............. Joskus [*Sometimes*] [*Finland*]

JOSP .... Jezdecky Odbor Sokola Prazskeho [*Equestrian Division of the Sokol (Athletic and Gymnastic Association) in Prague*]   (CZ)

JOT............ Journalists' Organisation of Tanzania   (EAIO)

JOTU .... Joint Organization of Trade Unions [*Finland*]

jou .... Jouissance [*Payable Interest*] [*French*] [*Business term*]

jov............... Jovedelem [*Income*]   (HU)

JOVD .... Jongeren Organisatie Vrijheid en Democratie [*Youth Organization Freedom and Democracy*] [*Netherlands*]   (EAIO)

JOY .... Joy [*Poland*] [*ICAO designator*]   (FAAC)

JOZ .... Jugoslovanska Orlovska Zveza [*Yugoslav Union of Eagles*] [*Slovenia*]   (YU)

JP.............. Die Juedische Presse [*The Jewish Press*] [*German*]   (BJA)

JP.............. Jabatan Polis [*Police Department*]   (ML)

JP.............. Janata Party [*India*] [*Political party*]   (PPW)

JP.............. Japan [*ANSI two-letter standard code*]   (CNC)

JP.............. Jasnie Pan [*His Lordship*] [*Poland*]

JP.............. Jasnie Pani [*Her Ladyship*] [*Poland*]

JP.............. Jatiya Party [*Bangladesh*] [*Political party*]

JP.............. Javno Paravobranilstvo [*Body of Government Attorneys*]   (YU)

JP.............. Jones Party [*Malta*] [*Political party*]   (PPE)

JP.............. Juge de Paix [*France*]   (FLAF)

JP.............. Jugoplastika [*Manufacturer of plastic articles*] [*Split*]   (YU)

JP.............. Junge Pioniere [*Young Pioneers*]   (EG)

JP.............. Junta de Planeamento [*Planning Council*] [*Portuguese*]   (WER)

jp............... Jurisprudence [*French*]   (FLAF)

JP.............. Justice de Paix [*Benelux*]   (BAS)

JP.............. Justice Party [*Turkey*] [*Political party*]

JP.............. Kim Jong Pil [*South Korean politician*]

JPA .... Japan Petroleum Association   (PDAA)

JPA .... Japan Psychological Association   (PDAA)

JPA .... Jeunesse Pionniere Agricole [*Young Agricultural Pioneers*] [*Togo*]   (AF)

JPA .... Joao Pessoa [*Brazil*] [*Airport symbol*]   (OAG)

JPA .... Jurisprudence du Port d'Anvers   (FLAF)

JPA .... Justices of the Peace Association [*Australia*]

J Paix........ Juge de Paix [*France*]   (FLAF)

JPAT .... Jeunesse Pionniere Agricole Togolaise [*Togolese Agricultural Pioneer Youth*]   (AF)

JpC............ Japanese Columbia [*Record label*]

JPC .... [*The*] Japan Productivity Center

JPC .... Jeunesse Pionniere Camerounaise [*Cameroonian Pioneer Youth*]   (AF)

JPC .... Jeunesse pour Christ [*Youth for Christ International - YFCI*]   (EA)

JPC .... Jeunesse Progressiste Casamancaise

JPC .... Joint Planning Center

JPC .... Jordan Plastics Co.

JPC .... Junior Police Call [*Police/youth organization*] [*Hong Kong*]

JPC .... Polar Air Co. [*Russian Federation*] [*ICAO designator*]   (FAAC)

JPCA .... Japan Petrochemical Industry Association   (EAIO)

JPCC .... Joint Petroleum Coordination Center/Committee [*NATO*]   (NATG)

JPCSA .... Japan Personal Computer Software Association

JPD........... Japan Publishers Directory [*Japan Publications Guide Service*] [*Japan*] [*Information service or system*]   (CRD)

JPD........... Jednotne Polnohospodarske Druzstvo [*United Agricultural Cooperative*]   (CZ)

JPD........... Jeunesse Progressiste Dahomeenne

JPD........... Jugoslovensko Profesorsko Drustvo [*Yugoslav Professors' Society*]   (YU)

JPDA .... Japan Petroleum Development Association   (EAIO)

JPDA .... Juventude do Partido Democratico Angolano [*Youth of the Angolan Democratic Party*]   (AF)

JPDC .... Japan Petroleum Development Corp.   (PDAA)

JPDC .... Jeunesse du Parti Democrate Congolais

JPDP .... Juventud del Partido del Pueblo [*People's Party Youth*] [*Panama*]   (LA)

JPDR .... Japan Power Development Reactor

JPENC ...... Japan PEN Club   (EAIO)

JPET......... Job Placement and Employment Training

JPFE......... Junta Provincial de Fomento de Esmeraldas [*Ecuador*]   (LAA)

JPFNRJ .... Javno Pravobraniostvo Federativna Narodna Republika Jugoslavija [*Body of Government Attorneys of Yugoslavia*]   (YU)

JPG........... Joint Planning Group [*NATO*]   (NATG)

JPGS .... Japan Publications Guide Service [*Information service or system*]   (IID)

JPIA .... Japan Petroleum Industry Association

JPJ............ Jabatan Penyiasatan Jenayat [*Criminal Investigation Department*]   (ML)

JPK .... Jabatan Pemereksa Kapal [*Shipping Survey Department*]   (ML)

JPK .... Jednolity Plan Kont [*Unified Accountancy Scheme*] [*Poland*]

JPL .... Jeunesse Progressiste Luxembourgeoise [*Luxembourg Progressive Youth*]   (WER)

JPMA .... Japan Plywood Manufacturers' Association   (EAIO)

JPMAP ..... Jednota Pratel Masarykovy Akademie Prace [*Association of Friends of the Masaryk Academy of Labor*]   (CZ)

JPMC .... Jordan Phosphate Mines Company Ltd.   (MENA)

JPN .... Japan [*ANSI three-letter standard code*]   (CNC)

JPN .... Jeunesse Pionniere Nationale [*National Pioneer Youth*] [*Zaire*]   (AF)

JPN .... Jeunesse Pionniere Nigerienne [*Nigerien Pioneer Youth*] [*Niger*]   (AF)

JPN .... Junta Patriotica Nacional [*National Patriotic Board*] [*Ecuador*]   (LA)

JPNT .... Junta Permanente Nacional de Telecomunicaciones [*Peru*]   (LAA)

JPO........... Japanese Patent Office

JPO........... Junior Professional Officer [*United Nations*]

JPO-SS..... Jugoslavanski Pomozni Odbor, Slovenska Sekcija [*Yugoslav Welfare Committee, Slovenian Section*]   (YU)

JPP .... Jalkeen Puolenpaiuan [*Afternoon*] [*Finland*]

JPP .... Jasa Perkasa Persekutuan [*Federation Gallantry Decorations*] [*Malaysia*]   (ML)

JPP .... Jasnie Panowie [*The Honourables*] [*Poland*]

JPPA .... Junta Provincial de Povoamento de Angola

JPPAC...... Joint Project Policy Advisory Committee [*Australia*]

JPPM .... Jeunesse du Parti du Peuple Mauritanien [*Youth of the Mauritanian People's Party*]   (AF)

JPPM .... Junta Provincial de Povoamento de Mocambique

JPR .... Jeunes Professeurs Revolutionnaires [*Young Revolutionary Professors*] [*Benin*]   (AF)

JPRA .... Japan Phonograph Record Association

JPS .... Jamaica Public Service Co.   (LA)

JPS .... Jeunesse Populaire Senegalaise

JPS .... Jordan Pediatric Society   (EAIO)

JPS .... Juventud Popular Socialista [*Socialist Popular Youth*] [*Mexico*]   (LA)

JPSA......... Japanese Plating Supplier's Association [*Environmetal science*]

JPSA......... Junior Philatelic Society of Australia   (ADA)

JPT .... Jednota Proletarske Telovychovy [*Proletarian Physical Education Association*]   (CZ)

JPT .... Juventud del Partido de Trabajo [*Labor Party Youth*] [*Guatemala*]   (LA)

JPTT......... Jugoslovenske Poste, Telegrafi, i Telefoni [*Yugoslav Post, Telegraph, and Telephone Services*]   (YU)

JpV........... Japanese Victor [*Record label*]

JQA .... Trans Jamaican Airlines Ltd. [*ICAO designator*]   (FAAC)

JQE .... Jaque [*Panama*] [*Airport symbol*]   (OAG)

jr............... Jaar [*Year*] [*Netherlands*]   (GPO)

JR............. Jonkheer [*Netherlands*]   (EY)

JR............. Jouet Rationnel [*French*]   (ADPT)

JR............. Jour [*Day*] [*French*]

JR............. Jugoslav Register [*Yugoslavian ship classification society*]   (DS)

JR............. Jugoslovenski Radio [*Yugoslav Radio*]   (YU)

jr............... Jungere [*Junior*] [*German*]

Jr.............. Junior [*Netherlands*]   (GPO)

Jr.............. Junior [*Portuguese*]

jr............... Junior [*Finland*]

JR............. Junta Revolucionaria [*Revolutionary Junta*] [*Peru*]   (LA)

jr............... Juridico [*Juridical*] [*Portuguese*]

JR.............. Juventud Radical [*Radical Youth*] [*Chile*]   (LA)
JRA........... Jaguar Rover Australia
JRA........... Japan Racing Association   (ECON)
JRAPAD ... Japan Research Association for Petroleum Alternatives
           Development
JRB........... Jugoslovenski Registar Brodova [*Yugoslav Ship Register*]   (YU)
JRB........... Jugoslovensko Recno Brodarstvo [*Yugoslav River Shipping*]
           (YU)
JRC........... Jamaica Railway Corporation   (LA)
JRC........... Japan Radio Co.
JRC........... Jeunesse Rurale Catholique [*Catholic Rural Youth*] [*Belgium*]
           (WER)
JRC........... Joint Research Center [*Commission of the European
           Communities*]
JRC........... Juventudes Revolucionarias Catalanas [*Catalan Revolutionary
           Youth*] [*Spanish*]   (WER)
JRC........... Juventud Revolucionaria Copeyana [*COPEI Revolutionary
           Youth*] [*Venezuela*]   (LA)
JRC........... Juventud Revolucionaria Cristiana [*Christian Revolutionary
           Youth*] [*Dominican Republic*]   (LA)
JRCC......... Japan Railway Construction Corp.
JRD........... Jednotne Riadeni Dopravy [*Unified Control Over
           Transportation*]   (CZ)
JRD........... Jednotne Rolnicke Druzstvo [*United Agricultural Cooperative in
           Slovakia*]   (CZ)
JRDA........ Jeunesse de la Revolution Democratique Africaine [*Youth of the
           African Democratic Revolution*] [*Guinea*]   (AF)
JRDACI .... Jeunesse de RDA de la Cote-D'Ivoire [*Youth of the RDA in Ivory
           Coast*]   (AF)
JRDC......... Japan Research Development Corp.
JRDS........ Jugoslovenska Republikanska Demokratska Stranka [*Yugoslav
           Republican Democratic Party*]   (YU)
JRF........... Janssen Research Foundation [*Belgium*]   (IRC)
JRF........... Juventud Revolucionaria Febrerista [*Revolutionary Febrerist
           Youth*] [*Paraguay*]   (LA)
jrg.............. Jaargang [*Year*] [*Publishing*] [*Netherlands*]
JRG........... Junta Revolucionaria de Gobierno [*Revolutionary Governing
           Junta*] [*El Salvador*]   (LA)
JRH .... Jorhat [*India*] [*Airport symbol*]   (OAG)
JRI .... Joint Research Institute [*ICL, Compagnie Machine Bull,
           Siemens AG*] [*Munich, West Germany*] [*Research center*]
           (ERC)
JRIA .... Japan Radioisotope Association
JRIA .... Japan Rocket Industry Association   (PDAA)
JRIA .... Japan Rubber Industry Association   (PDAA)
JRK .... Jeunesse de la Republique Khmere [*Cambodian Republic Youth*]
           (CL)
JRK .... Jugoslvanski Rdeci Kriz [*Yugoslav Red Cross*]   (YU)
JRLI .... Junta Revolucionaria de Libertacao Iberica
JRLZ .... Junta de Recuperacion Economica de Loja y Zamora Chinchipe
           [*Ecuador*]   (DSCA)
JRM.......... Jugoslovenska Ratna Mornarica [*Yugoslav Navy*]   (YU)
JRMP .... Jugoslavenska Revija za Medunarodno Pravo [*Former
           Yugoslavia*]   (FLAF)
JRN .... Jet Rent SA [*Mexico*] [*ICAO designator*]   (FAAC)
JRN .... Junta de Reconstruccion Nacional [*Junta of National
           Reconstruction*] [*Nicaragua*]   (LA)
JRO .... Jicamarca Radar Observatory [*Peru*]
JRO .... Jugoslovenska Ravnogorska Omladina [*Yugoslav Ravna Gora
           Youth*] [*World War II*]   (YU)
JRO .... Kilimanjaro [*Tanzania*] [*Airport symbol*]   (OAG)
JRP .... Juventud Revolucionaria del Peru [*Peruvian Revolutionary
           Youth*]   (LA)
Jrprok .... Jednaci Rad Prokuratur [*Regulations for Public Prosecutors*]
           (CZ)
JRPT .... Jeunesse du Rassemblement du Peuple Togolais [*Youth of the
           Rally of the Togolese People*]   (AF)
JRR .... Japan Research Reactor
JRR .... Jeunesse Revolutionnaire Rwagasore [*Rwagasore Revolutionary
           Youth*] [*Burundi*]   (AF)
JRRC .... Joint Regional Reconnaissance Center [*NATO*]   (NATG)
JRRP .... Junta Reguladora de Remuneraciones y Precios [*Wage and Price
           Control Board*] [*Chile*]   (LA)
Jrs .... Jednaci Rad Soudni [*Court Rules*]   (CZ)
JRS .... Jerusalem [*Israel*] [*Airport symbol*]   (OAG)
JRS .... Jugoslovenska Radnicka Stranka [*Yugoslav Workers' Party*]
           (YU)
JRSMA ..... Japan Rolling Stock Manufacturers Association   (PDAA)
JRSY .... Jersey   (ABBR)
JRT........... Jugoslovenska Radiotelevizija [*Association of Yugoslav Radio
           and Television Organizations*]   (EY)
JRUV........ Juventud Revolucionaria. Universidad del Valle [*Colombia*]
           (COL)
JRV........... Jugoslovensko Ratno Vazduhoplovstvo [*Yugoslav Air Force*]
           (YU)
JRZ........... Jugoslovenska Radikalna Zajednica [*Yugoslav Radical Union*]
           [*Political party*]   (PPE)

JS.............. Japan Society   (EAIO)
JS.............. Jeunesse de Sauvetage [*Salvation Youth*] [*Cambodia*]   (CL)
JS.............. Jeunes Socialistes [*Young Socialists*] [*Belgium*]   (WER)
JS.............. Johnson Society   (EA)
j/s............. Joule por Segundo [*Joules per Second*] [*Portuguese*]
JS.............. Jugoslavenska Suma [*Yugoslav Forest*] [*Belgrade, Zagreb A
           periodical*]   (YU)
JS.............. Jugoslovanski Sokol [*The Yugoslav Hawk*] [*An organization for
           physical culture and sport*]   (YU)
JS.............. Junior Sertifikaat [*Junior Certificate*] [*Afrikaans*]
JS.............. Juventude Socialista [*Socialist Youth*] [*Portuguese*]   (WER)
JS.............. Juventud Socialista [*Socialist Youth*] [*Chile*]   (LA)
JS.............. Juventud Socialista [*Socialist Youth*] [*Nicaragua*]   (LA)
JS.............. Juzna Sirina [*Southern Latitude*]   (YU)
JS.............. Sea of Japan
JS 19 J .... Juventud Sandinista 19 de Julio [*19 July Sandinist Youth*]
           [*Nicaragua*]   (LA)
JSA .... Japanese Standards Association   (NTCM)
JSA .... Japan Spinners' Association   (EAIO)
JSA .... Jeunesse pour la Solidarite Africaine
JSAE......... Japanese Society of Automotive Engineers
JSAIS .... Junior South African Individual Scales [*Intelligence test*]
JSAP......... Japan Society of Animal Psychology   (PDAA)
JSAP......... Japan Society of Applied Physics   (PDAA)
JSASS .... Japan Society for Aeronautical and Space Sciences [*Tokyo*]
           [*Research center*]   (ERC)
JSB .... Japanese Society in Brisbane [*Australia*]
JSC .... Jamaica School Certificate   (LA)
JSC .... Japanese Studies Center [*Monash University*] [*Australia*]
JSC .... Japan Science Council   (PDAA)
JSC .... Japan Shippers' Council   (EAIO)
JSC .... Joint Scientific Committee [*Commonwealth and New South
           Wales governments*] [*Australia*]
JSC .... Junior Soccer Club [*Australia*]
JSC .... Juventud Socialista Costarricense [*Costa Rican Socialist Youth*]
           (LA)
JSCBT .... Joint Steering Committee of the Book Trade [*Australia*]
JSCC........ Japanese Securities Clearing Corp.
JSCF......... Jamaica Special Constabulary Force   (LA)
JSCM .... Japan Society of Composite Materials   (PDAA)
JSCs.......... Jezdecky Svaz Ceskoslovensky [*Czechoslovak Equestrian
           Association*]   (CZ)
JSCZ......... Jednotny Svaz Ceskych Zemedelcu [*Central Union of Czech
           Farmers*]   (CZ)
JSD........... Jatiya Samajtantrik Dal [*National Socialist Party*] [*Bangladesh*]
           [*Political party*]   (PPW)
JSD........... Jeunesse Sociale Democrate [*Social Democratic Youth*]
           [*Malagasy*]   (AF)
JSD........... Johan Setia Di-Raja [*Second Grade of the Most Honorable Order
           of Setia Di-Raja*] [*Malaysia*]   (ML)
JSD........... Jugoslovensko Statisticko Drustvo [*Yugoslav Statistical Society*]
           (YU)
JSD........... Juventude Social-Democratica [*Social Democratic Youth*]
           [*Portuguese*]   (WER)
JSDA......... Japanese Securities Dealers Association   (ECON)
JSDP .... Jewish Social Democratic Party [*Political party*]   (BJA)
JSE .... Johannesburg Stock Exchange
JSE .... Juventudes Socialistas Espanolas [*Spanish*]
JSEA .... Japan Ship Exporters Association   (DS)
JSEA .... Junior Secondary Education Assessment [*Hong Kong*]
JSEDC....... Johore State Economic Development Council [*Malaysia*]
JSEM .... Japan Society for Electron Microscopy   (PDAA)
JSEM .... Japan Society of Electrical Discharge Machining   (PDAA)
JSeTU ...... Tohoku University, Sendai, Japan [*Library symbol*] [*Library of
           Congress*]   (LCLS)
JSF........... Junior Sports Federation [*Australia*]
JSFA......... Japanese Standards of Food Additives
JSFC.......... Japanese-Soviet Fisheries Commission for the Northwest Pacific
           [*FAO*]   (ASF)
JSFK......... Jydsk Selskab for Fysik og Kemi [*Denmark*]   (SLS)
JSH........... Jetstream Ltd. [*Hungary*] [*ICAO designator*]   (FAAC)
JSHA........ Japan Skin and Hide Association   (EAIO)
JSHAA ...... Junior School Heads' Association of Australia
JSI .... Skiathos [*Greece*] [*Airport symbol*]   (OAG)
JSIA .... Japan Software Industry Association   (PDAA)
JSICI .... Japan Society for International Chemical Information   (PDAA)
JSIM .... Japan Society of Industrial Machinery Manufacturers   (EAIO)
JS/IWAL .. Jeco Shipping/Interwave West Africa Line
JSJ........... Jabatan Siasatan Jenayat [*Criminal Investigation Department*]
           (ML)
JSK .... Jeunesse du Sud-Kasai
JSK .... Jeunesse Sportive Kairouanaise
JSL .... Jeunesse Socialiste Luxembourgeoise [*Luxembourg Socialist
           Youth*]   (WER)
JSL .... Jurong Shipyard Ltd. [*Singapore*]
JSLA......... Japan Special Libraries Association   (EAIO)

JSLPC .... Joint Service Local Planning Committee
JSM .... Jan Sin Mee [*Hong Kong*] [*Commercial firm*]
JSM .... Johan Setia Mahkota [*Third Grade of Darjah Yarg*]   (ML)
JSM .... Jose de San Martin [*Argentina*] [*Airport symbol*]   (OAG)
JSMA .... Japan Shoe Manufacturers Association   (EAIO)
JSME .... Japan Society of Mechanical Engineers
JSMEA ..... Japan Ship Machinery Export Association   (PDAA)
JSMIR....... Juventud Socialista Movimiento de la Izquierda Revolucionaria [*Movement of the Revolutionary Left Socialist Youth*] [*Venezuela*]   (LA)
JSN .... Junta de Salvacao Nacional [*Junta of National Salvation*] [*Portuguese*]   (WER)
JSN .... Juventud Socialista Nicaraguense [*Nicaraguan Socialist Youth*] (LA)
JSNDI .... Japan Society for Non-Destructive Inspection   (PDAA)
JSO .... Jerusalem Symphony Orchestra   (BJA)
JSOI .... Japan Spectacles and Popular Optics Inspection Institute (EAIO)
JSP .... Jackson-Strukturierte Programmierung [*German*]   (ADPT)
JSP .... Japan Socialist Party [*Nikon Shakaito*] [*Political party*]   (PPW)
JSP .... Job Support Program
JSP .... Joint Services Publication
JSP .... Jugoslovensko Stamparsko Preduzece [*Yugoslav Printing Establishment*] [*Belgrade*]   (YU)
JSP .... Juventud Social Progresista [*Progressive Social Youth*] [*Peru*] (LA)
JSPB .... Joint Staff Pension Board [*United Nations*]
JSPF .... Joint Staff Pension Fund [*United Nations*]
JSPME...... Jordan Society for Producing and Marketing Eggs
JSPP .... Joint Council of Swaziland Political Parties
JSPRS .... Japan Society of Plastic and Reconstructive Surgery   (EAIO)
JSPS .... Japanese Society for the Promotion of Science
JSPU .... Joint Sugar Projects Unit [*Indonesia*]
JSQC .... Japan Society for Quality Control   (PDAA)
JSQS .... Japan Shipbuilding Quality Standard   (PDAA)
JSR .... Japan Synthetic Rubber Co. Ltd.
JSR .... Jessore [*Bangladesh*] [*Airport symbol*]   (OAG)
JSR .... Job Seeker Register [*New Zealand*]
JSR .... Juventudes Socialistas Revolucionarias [*Revolutionary Socialist Youth*] [*Spanish*]   (WER)
JSRA .... Japan Shoe Retailers Association   (EAIO)
JSRK .... Jeunesse Socialiste Royale Khmere [*Royal Cambodian Socialist Youth*] [*Political party*]
JSS........... Japanese Society of Sydney [*Australia*]
JSS........... Jathika Sevaka Sangamaya [*National Employees' Union*] [*Sri Lanka*]   (FEA)
JSS........... Jednota Spolecenstev Stavitelu [*Association of Builders' Cooperatives*]   (CZ)
JSS........... Jednotna Stredni Skola [*Uniform Secondary School*]   (CZ)
JSSA .... Japan Student Science Awards   (PDAA)
JSSC........ Joint Services Staff College [*Australia*]
JSSE........ Japanese Software Support Environment
jssk.......... Jossakin [*Finland*]
jssk.......... Jossakussa [*Finland*]
JSSP .... Jednolity System Stenografii Polskiej [*Standardized System of Polish Stenography*]   (POL)
JSSR .... Jednotny Svaz Slovenskych Rolnikov [*Central Association of Slovak Farmers*]   (CZ)
JSST .... Jamaican Society of Scientists and Technologists   (EAIO)
JSST .... Japan Society for Simulation Technology   (PDAA)
JST .... Japanese Standard Time
JST .... Japan Universal System Transport Co. Ltd. [*ICAO designator*] (FAAC)
jstk .... Jostakin [*Finland*]
jstk .... Jostakusta [*Finland*]
JSTU .... Joint Services Trials Unit [*Australia*]
JSU .... Juventudes Socialistas Unificadas [*Unified Socialist Youth*] [*Ecuador*]   (LA)
JSW .... Japan Steel Works Ltd. [*Nuclear energy*]   (NRCH)
JSWA .... Japan Shoe Wholesalers Association   (EAIO)
JSWE .... Japan Society on Water Environment   (EAIO)
JSZ .... Jednota Slovanskych Zen [*Association of Slavic Women*]   (CZ)
JSZ .... Jugoslovenski Savez za Zavarivanje [*Former Yugoslavia*]   (SLS)
jt .... Jaart [*Yard*] [*Afrikaans*]
JT .... Jananayaga Thozhilali [*Democratic Workers' Congress*] [*Sri Lanka*]   (EAIO)
JT .... Japan Times [*A publication*]   (BARN)
jt .... Jarasi Tanacs [*District Council*]   (HU)
JT .... Jatekvezetok Testulete [*Association of Sports Referees*]   (HU)
JT .... Javno Tozilstvo [*Public Prosecutors*]   (YU)
jt .... Joint   (EECI)
JT .... Jurisclasseur du Travail [*France*]   (FLAF)
JTA .... Jabatan Pertahan Awam [*Public (or Civil) Defense Department*] (ML)
JTA .... Jamaica Teachers Association   (LA)
JTA .... Japan Transocean Air Co. Ltd. [*ICAO designator*]   (FAAC)

JTA........... Jewish Telegraphic Agency [*Jerusalem, Israel*]   (MENA)
JTAQ........ Japanese Tourism Association of Queensland [*Australia*]
JTB .... Jamaica Tourist Board   (LA)
JTB .... Japanese Tourist Board
JTC .... Jamaica Telephone Company   (LA)
JTC .... Japan Tobacco Corp.   (PDAA)
JTC .... Jets Corporativos SA de CV [*Mexico*] [*ICAO designator*] (FAAC)
JTC .... Jurong Town Corporation [*Singapore*]   (ML)
JTC .... Juventud Trabajadora Colombiana [*Colombian Worker Youth*] (LA)
JTEC .... Japan Telecommunications Engineering and Consultancy
JTFLRJ..... Javno Tozilstvo Federativna Ljudska Republika Jugoslavija [*Public Prosecutors of Yugoslavia*]   (YU)
JTFNRJ .... Javno Tuziostvo Federativna Narodna Republika Jugoslavija [*Public Prosecutors of Yugoslavia*]   (YU)
JTI .... Japan Tobacco, Incorporated
JTI .... Jordbrukstekniska Institutet [*Institute of Agricultural Engineering*] [*Sweden*]   (IRC)
JTI .... Jutland Technological Institute [*Denmark*]
JTIA .... Japan Tanning Import Association   (EAIO)
jtk .... Jotakin [*Finland*]
jtk .... Jotakuta [*Finland*]
JTK .... Jugoslovenska Trgovinska Komora [*Yugoslav Chamber of Commerce*]   (YU)
JTL .... Juapong Textiles Limited
JTM.......... Jeunes Travailleurs Marocains
JTO .... Jeunesse Travailleuse Oubanguienne
JTR .... Jet-Air Bedarfsflugunternehmen [*Austria*] [*ICAO designator*] (FAAC)
JTR .... Santorini [*Thira Islands*] [*Airport symbol*]   (OAG)
JTRC .... Joint Theatre Reconnaissance Committee [*NATO*]   (NATG)
JTRI .... Jakarta Textile Research Institute [*Indonesia*]
JTRU .... Joint Tropical Research Unit [*Australia*]
JTS .... Japan Tobacco and Salt Public Corp.
JTSG .... Joint Trials Subgroup [*NATO*]   (NATG)
JTT .... Jamiet At-Tanmiah and At-Tatweer [*Association for the Advancement and Development of the Palestinian Community Inside Israel*]   (EAIO)
JTT .... Jednotny Transitni Tarif [*Standard Transit Tariff*]   (CZ)
JTTA .... Japan Table Tennis Association   (EAIO)
JTTRE....... Joint Tropical Trials Research Establishment [*Australia*]
JTURDC ... Joint Trade Unions Research Development Center [*Jamaica*] (LA)
jtv .... Jarasi Tanacs ala Rendelt Varos [*Town Administered by a District Council*]   (HU)
JTW.......... Journey-to-Work Database [*Computer Sciences of Australia Pty. Ltd.*] [*Information service or system*]   (CRD)
JTWS .... Journal of Third World Studies [*A publication*]
JU .... Jeunesse Universelle
Ju .... Jute [*German*]   (GCA)
JUB.......... Juba [*Sudan*] [*Airport symbol*]   (OAG)
Jubil.......... Jubilaeum [*Jubilee*] [*German*]   (GCA)
JUBM....... Jajasan Urusan Bahan Makanan [*Food Affairs Board*]   (IN)
JUBMES... Jugoslovanska Banka Za Medjunarodnu Ekonomsku Saradnju [*Yugoslav Bank for International Economic Coorporation*] (EE)
JUC.......... Jabatan Urusan China [*Chinese Affairs Department*]   (ML)
JUC.......... Juventud Universitaria Catolica [*Catholic University Youth*] [*Argentina*]   (LA)
JUC.......... Kandidat Prav (Iuris Utriusque Candidatus) [*Candidate for a Law Degree*]   (CZ)
JUCEI .... Junta de Coordinacion, Ejecucion, e Inspeccion [*Coordination, Execution, and Inspection Board*] [*Cuba*]   (LA)
JUCEPLAN ... Junta Central de la Planificacion [*Central Planning Board*] [*Cuba*]   (LA)
JUCO .... Juventud Comunista [*Communist Youth*] [*Colorado*]   (LA)
JUCODA... Junta Coordinadora para el Desarrollo Agropecuario [*Colombia*] (DSCA)
JUD .... Jeunesse d'Union Dahomeenne
JUD .... Judas [*Jude*] [*Afrikaans*]
JUDECA ... Juventud Democrata Cristiana de America [*Christian Democratic Youth of America*]   (LA)
JUDr........ Doktor Prav (Iuris Utriusque Doctor) [*Doctor of Law*]   (CZ)
JUDRAL ... Juventudes Democraticas Revolucionarias de America Latina [*Revolutionary Democratic Youth of Latin America*]   (LA)
JUDY .... Jamaica Union of Democratic Youth   (LA)
juev.......... Jueves [*Thursday*] [*Spanish*]
JUF .... Jamaica United Front   (LA)
juf............. Juffrou [*Miss*] [*Afrikaans*]
JUFI .... Jugoslovenska Filatelisticka Izlozba [*Yugoslav Philatelic Exhibit*] (YU)
JUG .... Jugoslav   (DSUE)
Jug .... Jugoton [*Former Yugoslavia*] [*Record label*]
JUGEL...... Jugoslovenska Elektroprivreda [*Yugoslav Electrical Industries*] (YU)

JUGELEKSPORT ... Eksport Electricne Energije iz Jugoslavije [*Electric Power Export from Yugoslavia*] (YU)

JUGOAGENCIJA ... Jugoslovenska Pomorska Agencija [*Yugoslav Maritime Agency*] [*Belgrade*] (YU)

JUGOAGENT ... Jugoslovenska Pomorska Agencija [*Yugoslav Maritime Agency*] [*Belgrade*] (YU)

JUGOALAT ... Fabrika Alata [*Tool Factory*] [*Novi Sad*] (YU)

JUGOALKO ... Proizvodnja Alkoholnih Pijac [*Alcoholic Beverages Production*] [*Maribor*] (YU)

JUGOAUTO ... Yugoslav Automobile Import-Export [*Belgrade*] (YU)

JUGOAZBET ... Industrija Azbesta [*Asbestos Industry*] [*Mladenovac*] (YU)

JUGOBANKA ... Jugoslovenska Banka za Spoljnu Trgovinu [*Yugoslav Foreign Trade Bank*] (YU)

JUGODIJETETIKA ... Tvornica Farmaceutsko Dijetetskih Proizvoda [*Pharmaceutical and Dietetic Products Factory*] [*Zagreb*] (YU)

JUGODRVO ... Preduzece za Prodaju Drveta [*Establishment for the Sale of Lumber*] [*Beograd*] (YU)

JUGOELEKTRO ... Preduzece za Izvoz i Uvoz Elektricnog Materijala [*Electrical Equipment Export and Import Establishment*] (YU)

JUGOFOTO ... Yugoslovenska Foto Agencija [*Yugoslav Photograph Agency*] [*Beograd*] (YU)

JUGOFUND ... Jugoslovensko Preduzece za Fundiranje [*Yugoslav Establishment for Building Foundations*] [*Belgrade*] (YU)

JUGOINVEST ... Zajednica Preduzeca za Investicionu Izgradnju u Inostranstvu [*Union of Establishments for Foreign Investment Development*] [*Belgrade*] (YU)

JUGOKOZA ... Yugoslav Wool and Hide Trade (YU)

JUGOLEK ... Preduzece za Izvoz i Uvoz Lekova [*Yugoslav Pharmaceutical Export-Import Establishment*] (YU)

JUGOLINIJA ... Jugoslovenska Linijska Plovidba [*The Yugoslav Passenger Line*] [*Rijeka*] (YU)

JUGOMETAL ... Preduzece za Uvoz i Izvoz Ruda i Metala [*Yugoslav Ores and Metal Export-Import Establishment*] [*Belgrade*] (YU)

JUGOMINERAL ... Poduzece za Izvoz i Uvoz Ruda, Metala, Legura, i Nemetala [*Establishment for Export and Import of Ores, Metals, Alloys, and Nonmetals*] [*Zagreb*] (YU)

JUGOMONT ... Tvornica Montaznih Kuca [*Factory of Prefabricated Houses*] [*Zagreb*] (YU)

JUGONAFTA ... Preduzece za Uvoz i Izvoz Nafte i Naftinih Derivativa [*Export-Import Establishment for Petroleum and Its Derivatives*] [*Zagreb*] (YU)

JUGOPAPIR ... Preduzece za Spoljnu i Unutrasnju Trgovinu Papirom i Kancelarijskim Materijalom [*Establishment for Domestic and Foreign Trade in Paper and Office Equipment*] (YU)

JUGOPETROL ... Yugoslav Petrol and Petrol Derivatives Trade [*Zagreb*] (YU)

JUGOPLASTIKA ... Tvornica Plasticnih Masa [*Plastics Factory*] [*Kastel Sucurac*] (YU)

JUGOPRES ... Jugoslovenska Novinska Agencija [*Yugoslav News Agency*] [*Belgrade*] (YU)

JUGOPROEKT ... Proektantsko Pretprijatie [*Industrial Design Establishment*] [*Skopje*] (YU)

JUGOPROJEKT ... Preduzece za Izradu Gradevinskih i Elektromasinskih Projekata [*Enterprise for Drafting Construction and Electrical Engineering Designs*] (YU)

JUGORADIO ... Preduzece za Promet Radio Aparatima i Elektromaterijalom [*Radio Apparatus and Electric Materials Establishment*] (YU)

JUGOREGISTAR ... Jugoslovenski Registar Brodova [*Yugoslav Ships' Register*] (YU)

JUGOREKLAM ... Preduzece za Privrednu Reklamu [*Industrial Advertising Establishment*] (YU)

JUGORIBA ... Poduzece za Eksport-Import Ribljih Proizvoda [*Canned Fish Export-Import Establishment*] [*Zagreb*] (YU)

JUGOSANITARIJA ... Poduzece za Uvoz i Izvoz i Raspodelu Lekarskog i Sanitetskog Materijala [*Establishment for Import, Export, and Distribution of Medical Instruments and Apparatus*] (YU)

JUGOSEMEKOOP ... Proizvodnja Svih Vrsti Semena [*Yugoslav Seed Production Cooperative*] (YU)

jugosl .... Jugoslavenski [*Former Yugoslavia*] (YU)

JUGOSPED ... Preduzece za Medunarodnu Spediciju i Javna Skladista [*Agency for International Forwarding and Public Warehouses*] (YU)

JUGOTEKSTIL ... Preduzece za Promet Tekstilom [*Yugoslav Textile Trade Establishment*] (YU)

JUGOTRANSPORT ... Yugoslav Agency for International Forwarding and Warehouses [*Zagreb*] (YU)

JUGOTURBINA ... Tvornica Parnih Turbina i Dizel Motora [*Yugoslav Steam Turbines and Diesel Engines Factory*] [*Karlovac*] (YU)

JUGOTURIST ... Preduzece za Turisticku Stamparsko-Izdavacku Delatnost [*Printing and Publishing Establishment for Tourism*] [*Belgrade*] (YU)

JUGOUGOSTITELJ ... Preduzece za Snabdevanje Ugostiteljstva Opremom [*Hotel and Catering Equipment Establishment*] (YU)

JUGOVINO ... Yugoslav Alcoholic Beverage Trade (YU)

JUGOVISKOZA ... Preduzece za Proizvodnju Viskoze [*Viscose Production Establishment*] [*Loznica*] (YU)

jugozap .... Jugozapadni [*Southwestern*] (YU)

Jug P .... Jugoslawisches Patent [*Yugoslavian Patent*] [*German*] (GCA)

JUI .... Jamiatul Ulama-i-Islam [*Pakistan*] [*Political party*] (FEA)

JUI .... Juist [*Germany*] [*Airport symbol*] [*Obsolete*] (OAG)

Juil .... Juillet [*July*] [*French*]

JUJ .... Jujuy [*Argentina*] [*Airport symbol*] (OAG)

jul .... Julho [*July*] [*Portuguese*] (GPO)

Jul .... Juli [*July*] [*German*] (GPO)

JUL .... Juliaca [*Peru*] [*Airport symbol*] (OAG)

Jul .... Julie [*July*] [*Afrikaans*]

jul .... Julio [*July*] [*Spanish*]

jul .... Julius [*July*] [*Hungary*] (GPO)

JULAC ..... Joint-Use Libraries Advisory Committee [*South Australia*]

julk .... Julkaisija [*Finland*]

julk .... Julkaissut [*Finland*]

JUM .... Jumla [*Nepal*] [*Airport symbol*] (OAG)

JUMEI ...... Business Association of Yugoslav Machine Industry (EE)

JUMP .... Jugoslovensko Udruzenje za Medunarodno Pravo [*Yugoslav International Law Association*] (YU)

jun .... Junho [*June*] [*Portuguese*] (GPO)

Jun .... Juni [*June*] [*German*] (GPO)

Jun .... Junie [*June*] [*Afrikaans*]

jun .... Junio [*June*] [*Spanish*]

jun .... Junior [*Poland*]

jun .... Junior [*German*]

jun .... Junior [*Finland*]

jun .... Juniore [*Junior*] [*Italian*]

jun .... Junius [*June*] [*Hungary*] (GPO)

JUN .... Junta Unificadora Nacional [*National Unifying Board*] [*Chile*] (LA)

JUNA .... Juventude da Uniao Nacional Angolana [*Youth of the Angolan National Union*] (AF)

JUNAC ..... Grupo Andino - Junta del Acuerdo de Cartagena [*Andean Group - Cartagena Agreement Board - ANCOM*] (EAIO)

JUNAC ..... Juventud Nacionalista Costarricense [*Costa Rican Nationalist Youth*] (LA)

JUNAEB ... Junta Nacional de Auxilio Escolar y Becas [*National Board of School Aid and Scholarships*] [*Chile*] (LA)

JUNAL ...... Junta Nacional do Algoao [*Rio De Janeiro, Brazil*] (LAA)

JUNAPLA ... Junta de Planificacion y Coordinacion Economica [*National Planning and Economic Coordination Board*] [*Ecuador*] (LA)

JUNAPRE ... Junta Nacional de Precios de Bienes Esenciales [*National Price Control Board for Essential Commodities*] [*Ecuador*] (LA)

JUNC .... Jeunesse de l'Union Nationale Camerounaise [*Cameroonian National Union Youth*] (AF)

JUNC .... Jeunesse d'Union Nationale Congolaise

JUNCO ..... Junta de la Comunidad de Cochabamba [*Cochabamba Community Board*] [*Bolivia*] (LA)

JUNECH .. Junta Nacional de Empleados de Chile [*Trade union*] [*Chile*]

JUNET ...... Japan UNIX Network [*Japan*] [*Computer science*] (TNIG)

JUNRE ...... Juventud Nacionalista Revolucionaria [*Revolutionary Nationalist Youth*] [*Ecuador*] (LA)

Junta delAcuer ... Grupo Andino - Junta del Acuerdo de Cartagena [*Andean Group - Cartagena Agreement Board - ANCOM*] (EA)

JUP .... Jamiatul Ulama-i-Pakistan [*Political party*] (FEA)

JUP .... Journees Universite de la Paix [*University Days for Peace*] [*Belgium*] (EAIO)

JUP .... Juventud Uruguaya de Pie [*Upstanding Uruguayan Youth*] (PD)

JUPA .... Juventude do Uniao de Populacoes Angolanas [*Youth of the Union of Angolan People*] (AF)

JUPA .... Juventudes Patrioticas [*Patriotic Youth*] [*Colorado*] (LA)

JUPCE ...... Junta Permanente de Coordinacion Educativa [*Educational Permanent Coordination Board*] [*Peru*] (LA)

Jur .... Juridica (FLAF)

Jur .... Jurisprudence [*French*] (FLAF)

Jur .... Jurisprudencia [*Jurisprudence*] [*Portuguese*]

JUR .... Jurisprudensie [*Afrikaans*]

Jur .... Jurist [*German*]

jur .... Juristisch [*Legal*] [*German*] (GCA)

JurAnvers ... Jurisprudence du Port d'Anvers [*Belgium*] (FLAF)

Jur Auto ..... Jurisprudence Automobile [*France*] (FLAF)

Jur ClassAT ... Jurisclasseur Accidents du Travail [*France*] (FLAF)

Jur CommBruxelles ... Jurisprudence Commerciale de Bruxelles [*Belgium*] (FLAF)

JURDC ...... Juventud Universitaria Revolucionaria Democrata Cristiana [*Christian Democratic Revolutionary Youth*] [*Costa Rica*] (LA)

Jur DrUnif ... Jurisprudence de Droit Uniforme [*Uniform Law Cases*] [*Italy*] (FLAF)

JURE........ Junta Revolucionaria Cubana [*Exile action group*]
Jur Gen ...... Jurisprudence Generale Dalloz [*Repertoire alphabetique de legislation, de doctrine et de jurisprudence*] [*France*] (FLAF)
JURIS........ Juristisches Informationssystem [*Judicial Information System*] [*Federal Ministry of Justice Legal database*] [*Germany*] (IID)
JUS............ Jugoslovenski Standard [*Yugoslav Standard*] (YU)
JUSAT ...... Jugoslovensko-Sovjetski Aero-Transport [*Yugoslav-Soviet Air Transport*] (YU)
JUSCIMPC ... Joint United States/Canada Industrial Mobilization Planning Committee [*NATO*] (NATG)
JUSE .... Japan Union of Scientists and Engineers (BARN)
JUSEK ...... Fordundet for Jurister, Samhallsvetare, Ochekomomer [*Federation of Lawyers, Social Scientists and Economists*] [*Sweden*] (EAIO)
JUSPAD ... Jugoslovensko-Sovjetsko Parabrodsko Akcionarsko Drustvo [*Yugoslav-Soviet Joint-Stock Shipping Company*] (YU)
JUSRDA ... Jeunesse Union Soudanaise, Rassemblement Democratique Africain
JUST .... Jordan University of Science and Technology
JUST .... Journalists Unions Superannuation Trust [*Australia*]
JUSTA ...... Jugoslovensko-Sovjetska Mesovita Drustva [*Yugoslav-Soviet Mixed Companies*] (YU)
Justn .... Justinian [*483-565, Byzantine emperor*]
Justsl........ Justicni Sluzba [*Juridical Service*] (CZ)
JUSU........ Juba University Students Union [*Sudan*]
JUT............ Jeunesse de l'Unite Togolaise
JUT............ Jugoslovenski Standard za Tekstil [*Yugoslav Standard for Textiles*] (YU)
JUTA........ Jamaica Union of Travelers Association (LA)
JUTRA ...... Jurutera [*Engineers*] (ML)
JUV .... Jednota Umelcu Vytvarnych [*Creative Artists' Association*] (CZ)
JUVENTO ... Justice-Union-Vigilance-Education-Nationalisme-Tenacite-Optimisme
JUVENTO ... Mouvement de la Jeunesse Togolaise
JUWATA ... Jumuia ya Wafanyakazi wa Tanzania [*Tanzanian Workers Association*] (AF)
juz............ Juzen [*Southern*] (YU)
JV............. Air Charters [*Senegal*] [*ICAO designator*] (ICDA)
jv.............. Janvier [*January*] [*French*]
jv.............. Jihovychod [*Southeast*] (CZ)
j/v............. Jour de Vue [*Days after Sight*] [*French*]
JV............. Jugovzhod [*Southeast*] (YU)
JVA........... Ankavandra [*Madagascar*] [*Airport symbol*] (OAG)
JVA........... Genavia SRL [*Italy*] [*ICAO designator*] (FAAC)
JVA........... Jordan Valley Authority (GEA)
JVC........... Jewelry Valuers' Council [*Australia*]
JVC........... Jules Verne Circle (EA)
JVC........... Juventud de Vanguardia Comunista [*Communist Vanguard Youth*] [*Venezuela*] (LA)
JVC........... Juventud Vanguardista Costarricense [*Costa Rican Vanguardist Youth*] (LA)
JVP........... Janatha Vimukhti Peramuna [*People's Liberation Front*] [*Sri Lanka*] [*Political party*] (PPW)
JVP........... Joint Venture Partners
JVP........... Jongeren Vrijwilligers Programma [*Youth Volunteer Program*] [*Netherlands*] (WEN)
Jvsl........... Jaarverslag Centrale Adoptieraad [*Benelux*] (BAS)
JVSPLNMQNSC ... Je Vous Salue par les Noms Maconniques que Nous Seul Connoissons [*I Salute You by the Masonic Names, Which We Only Know*] [*Freemasonry*] [*French*]
JVU .... Jednota Vytvarnych Umelcu [*Creative Artists' Association*] (CZ)
JVUO .... Jugoslovenska Vojska u Otadzbini [*Yugoslav Army in the Fatherland*] [*World War II*] (YU)
jw............. Jak Wyzej [*As Above*] (POL)
JW .... Jasnie Wielmozny [*The Honorable*] [*Poland*]
JW .... Joint Warfare
JW .... Justizwache [*German*]
JWA.......... Japan Writers' Association (EAIO)
JWA.......... Jetworld Airways Ltd. [*Antigua and Barbuda*] [*ICAO designator*] (FAAC)
JWAALS... Joint Western Australian Academic Library System
JWAC....... Joint West Africa Committee
JWAHK .... Jewish Women's Association of Hong Kong (EAIO)
JWCA....... Japan Watch and Clock Association (PDAA)
JWDS........ Japan Work Design Society (PDAA)
JWG .... Jugendwohlfahrtsgesetz [*Youth Welfare Law*] [*German*] (ILCA)
JWI .... Jehovah's Witnesses Information [*Sweden*] (EAIO)
JWIA .... Japan Wool Importers' Association (EAIO)
JWIC .... Japanese Whaling Information Center (MSC)
JWNS........ Jewish News Service (BJA)
JWP.......... Jamaican Workers' Party [*Political party*] (PPW)
JWP.......... Jasnie Wielmozny Pan [*The Honorable Gentleman*] [*Poland*]
JWP.......... Joint Women's Programme [*India*] (EAIO)
JWS .... Jazz World Society (EAIO)

JWS.......... Jewish Welfare Society [*Australia*]
JWSO....... Joint Wool Selling Organisation [*Australia*]
JWS/TD.... Jungle Warfare School Trial and Development Wing [*Johore Bahru, Malaysia*]
JWT.......... J. Walter Thompson Australia Proprietary Ltd. (ADA)
JWV.......... Junge Welt Verlag [*"Junge Welt" (Young World) Publishing House*] (EG)
JYARRI..... Jiang You Aerial Ropeway Research Institute [*China*] (IRC)
JYEP .... Jubilee Youth Employment Program [*South Australia*]
JYV........... Jyvaskyla [*Finland*] [*Airport symbol*] (OAG)
jz................ Jihozapad [*Southwest*] (CZ)
JZ.............. Jodzahl [*Iodine Number*] [*German*]
JZ.............. Jugoslovenske Zeleznice [*Yugoslav Railroads*] (YU)
JZ.............. Jugozapad [*Southwest*] (YU)
JZ.............. Juristenzeitung [*Germany*] (FLAF)
JZD........... Jednotne Zemedelske Druzstvo [*Unified Agricultural Cooperative*] (CZ)
JZF .... Jeleniogorskie Zaklady Farmaceutyczne [*Jelenia Gora (Hirschberg) Pharmaceutical Plant*] (POL)
jzo............. Jegyzo [*Clerk, Notary*] (HU)
JZP .... Jeleniogorskie Zaklady Papiernicze [*Jelenia Gora (Hirschberg) Paper Mill*] (POL)
JZPT .... Jeleniogorskie Zaklady Porcelany Technicznej [*Jelenia Gora (Hirschberg) Industrial Porcelain Plant*] (POL)
JZS .... Jamarska Zveza Slovenije [*Former Yugoslavia*] (SLS)
JZS .... Jugoslovenski Zavod za Standardizacijas [*Standards Institute*] [*Former Yugoslavia*] (PDAA)
JZT .... Jugoslovenski Zavod za Telekomunikaciju [*Yugoslav Telecommunication Institute*] (YU)

K

k	Acid (RU)
K	Arbetarpartiet Kommunisterna [*Communist Workers' Party*] [*Sweden*] (WEN)
k	Carat (RU)
K	Cathode (BU)
k	Cavalry (BU)
K	Chritiania Bank og Kreditkasse [*Bank*] [*Norway*]
K	Cobalt (RU)
K	Coke (RU)
K	Commandant (RU)
K	Commandant's Post (RU)
k	Coulomb (BU)
K	Crane (RU)
K	Curie (RU)
K	Fortress, Citadel, Stronghold (RU)
K	Helicopter Designed by N. I. Kamov (RU)
K	Kaap [*Cape*] [*Netherlands*] (NAU)
k	Kaart [*Chart, Map*] [*Netherlands*]
k	Kade [*Quay, Wharf*] [*Netherlands*] (CED)
K	Kadenz [*Cadence*] [*Music*]
K	Kadinlar [*Women*] (TU)
k	Kaiserlich [*Imperial*] [*German*]
K	Kalium [*Potassium*] [*Chemical element*] [*German*]
K	Kallio [*Rock*] [*Finland*] (NAU)
K	Kalorie [*Calorie*] [*German*]
k	Kalt [*Cold*] [*German*]
K	Kalt Verformt [*Cold Worked*] [*German*] (GCA)
K	Kammer [*Chamber*] [*German*]
K	Kandidaat [*Academic degree*] [*Netherlands*]
K	Kandidaatti [*Finland*]
K	Kandidat [*Candidate*] [*Denmark*]
K	Kandidat [*Candidate*] [*Russian*]
K	Kandidat na Naukite [*Bulgarian*]
K	Kandidatsprof [*Academic examination*] [*Icelandic*]
K	Kandidatus [*Candidate*] [*Hungary*]
K	Kandidat Ved [*Former Czechoslovakia*]
K	Kantongerecht [*Benelux*] (BAS)
K	Kap [*Cape*] [*Denmark*] (NAU)
K	Kap [*Cape*] [*German*] (NAU)
K	Kap [*Cape*] [*Sweden*] (NAU)
K	Kapitel [*Chapter*] [*German*]
K	Kapp [*Cape*] [*Norway*] (NAU)
K	Kari [*Rock, Reef*] [*Finland*] (NAU)
k	Karton [*Pasteboard*] [*Publishing*] [*Poland*]
k	Kasse [*German*]
k	Katu [*Street*] [*Finland*]
K	Kelet [*East*] [*Hungary*] (GPO)
k	Kelt [*Dated*] (HU)
K	Kelvin [*German*] (GCA)
K	Kelvin Degree (RU)
K	Ker [*House*] [*Military map abbreviation World War I*] [*French*] (MTD)
k	Kerulet [*District*] (HU)
K	Kesko [*Retail trade chain in Finland*]
K	KGB [*Komitet Gossudarstvennoi Bezopasnosti*] Agent
K	Khawr [*Inlet, Channel*] [*Arab*] (NAU)
K	Khowr [*Inlet, Channel*] [*Persian*] (NAU)
K	Kilo [*Phonetic alphabet*] [*International*] (DSUE)
K	Kilogramme [*Kilogram*] [*French*] (MTD)
K	King [*Phonetic alphabet*] [*Royal Navy*] (DSUE)
K	King [*Monetary unit*] [*Papua, New Guinea*] (BARN)
K	Kip [*Monetary unit*] [*Laos*]
k	Kis [*Small*] (HU)
K	Kivi [*Rock*] [*Finland*] (NAU)
K	Knight [*Chess*]
K	Koder [*or Kodra*] [*Hill Albanian*] (NAU)
k	Koeniglich [*Royal*] [*German*]
K	Kollaborateur [*Nickname given Alain Robbe-Grillet*] [*World War II*]
k	Kolo [*Near*] [*Poland*]
k	Konnyu [*Light (such as, light artillery)*] (HU)
k	Konska Sila [*Horsepower*] (CZ)
K	Konstante [*Constant*] [*German*]
K	Kontra [*Contra*] [*Music*]
K	Kopeck [*Monetary unit*] [*Former USSR*]
K	Korrektur [*German*] (ADPT)
K	Koruna [*Monetary unit*] [*Former Czechoslovakia*]
K	Kotet [*Volume*] [*Hungary*] (GPO)
K	Koy [*Village*] (TU)
k	Kozseg [*Village*] (HU)
K	Kray (RU)
K	Krona [*Monetary unit*] [*Iceland, Sweden*]
K	Krone [*Crown*] [*Monetary unit Denmark, Norway*]
K	Kroon [*Monetary unit*] [*Estonia*]
K	Kuala [*Mouth of River (Name of towns, as Kuala Lumpur, Kuala Lupis)*] (ML)
K	Kumanda [*or Kumandan*] [*Command or Commander*] (TU)
k	Kuoli [*Finland*]
k	Kuollut [*Finland*]
K	Kurus [*Monetary unit*] [*Turkey*]
K	Kustode [*Signature Marking*] [*Publishing*] [*German*]
K	Kuzey [*North*] (TU)
K	Kwacha [*Monetary unit*] [*Malawi, Zambia*]
K	Kyat [*Monetary unit*] [*Myanmar*]
K	Kyst [*Coast artillery*] [*Officer's rating Danish Navy*]
K	Large-Caliber, Heavy-Caliber (RU)
K	Map (BU)
K	Master Gauge (RU)
K	Red Banner (RU)
k	Room (RU)
k	Short-Distance [*City transit lines*] (RU)
K	Silicon (RU)
K	Stone [*Road-paving material*] [*Topography*] (RU)
K	Stony [*Nature of bottom of a ford*] [*Topography*] (RU)
K	Stopien Kelvina [*Degree Kelvin*] [*Poland*]
K	Well [*Topography*] (RU)
K	Wetboek van Koophandel [*Commercial Code*] [*Dutch*] (ILCA)
KA	Activity Coefficient (RU)
KA	Address Key (RU)
KA	Alkair [*Denmark*] [*ICAO designator*] (ICDA)
KA	Army Commander (RU)
KA	Catechol Amine (RU)
KA	Cavalry Army (RU)
KA	Communist Academy (RU)
KA	Compass Azimuth (RU)
KA	Corps Artillery (RU)
KA	Helicopter Designed by N. I. Kamov (RU)
Ka	Kaernten [*German*]
KA	Kamov [*Former USSR*] [*ICAO aircraft manufacturer identifier*] (ICAO)
KA	Kapitalistisches Ausland [*Capitalist Countries*] (EG)
Ka	Karaatti(a) [*Finland*]
KA	Kartenart [*German*] (ADPT)
Ka	Kathode [*Cathode*] [*German*]
KA	Katolicka Akce [*Catholic Action*] (CZ)
KA	Katolicka Akcija [*Catholic Action*] (YU)
Ka	Kawa [*River*] [*Japan*] (NAU)
KA	Kenya Airways
K A	Kepzomuveszeti Alap Kiadovallalata [*The Fine Arts Fund-Publishing House*] (HU)
ka	Kiloampere (RU)
KA	Know-All [*Australia*] [*Slang*] (DSUE)
KA	Koini Agora [*Common Market*] (GC)
KA	Koningsadvokaat [*King's Counsel*] [*Afrikaans*]
KA	Krajsky Aeroklub [*Regional Aero Club*] (CZ)

669

KA .... Ksiaznica Atlas ["*Atlas*" *Bookstore and Publishing House*]   (POL)
KA .... Kuenstliche Anforderung [*German*]   (ADPT)
KA .... Kulugyi Akademia [*Foreign Service Academy*]   (HU)
KA .... Kypriakes Aerogrammes [*Cyprus Airlines*]
KA .... Motion-Picture Projector   (RU)
k-a .... Rear Admiral   (RU)
KA .... Red Army [*1918-1946*]   (RU)
KA .... Space Vehicle   (RU)
KAA .... Asia Aero Survey & Consulting Engineers, Inc. [*Korea*] [*ICAO designator*]   (FAAC)
KAA .... Cambodian Alumni Association   (CL)
KAA .... Kasama [*Zambia*] [*Airport symbol*]   (OAG)
KAA .... Kendrikos Aerolimin Athinon [*Ellinikon (Athens) Airport*]   (GC)
KAA .... Kentrikos Apokhetevtikos Agogos [*Central Sewage Pipe*]   (GC)
KAA .... Kenya Automobile Association   (EAIO)
KAA .... Komma Adesmevtis Anexartisias [*Nonaligned Independence Party*] [*Greek*]   (GC)
KAA .... Korean Actuarial Association   (EAIO)
KAAA .... Kenya Amateur Athletics Association
KAAPV ...... Kendron Apokatastaseos Anapiron Paidon Voulas [*Voula Rehabilitation Center for Crippled Children*] [*Greek*]   (GC)
KAAU .... King Abdul-Aziz University [*Saudi Arabia*]
kab .... Cable [*Topography*]   (RU)
KAB .... Kabupaten [*Regency*] [*Replaced by DASWATI-II*]   (IN)
KAB .... Kariba Dam [*Zimbabwe*] [*Airport symbol*]   (OAG)
KAB .... Katholieke Arbeidersbeweging [*Catholic Workers' Movement*] [*Defunct*] [*Netherlands*]   (WEN)
KAB .... Katholische Arbeitnehmerbewegung [*Catholic Employees' Movement*] [*Switzerland*]   (WEN)
KAB .... Kinevezesi es Alkalmazasi Bizottsag [*Personnel Committee*]   (HU)
KAB .... Kontinuierliche Arbeitsplatzbelegung [*Personnel Continuously on Duty*]   (EG)
KAB .... Kozgazdasagi Allando Bizottsag (Kolcsonos Gazdasagi Segitseg Tanacsa) [*Permanent Economic Commission (CEMA)*]   (HU)
KAB .... Kozlekedesi Allando Bizottsag [*Standing Committee for Transportation (CEMA)*]   (HU)
Kaba .... Kaba Konusma [*Coarse, Rough Speech*]   (TU)
KABAG ..... Kepala Bagian [*Division Chief, Section Chief*]   (IN)
kab-balk ..... Kabardino-Balkarian   (RU)
Kabbalkgosizdat ... Kabardino-Balkarian State Publishing House   (RU)
Kabbalkgosnatsizdat ... Kabardino-Balkarian State National Publishing House   (RU)
Kabbalknatsizdat ... Kabardino-Balkarian National Publishing House   (RU)
KABC .... Keep Australia Beautiful Council   (ADA)
KABCC .... Korea Australia Business Cooperation Council
Kabgiz .... Kabardinian State Publishing House   (RU)
KABI .... Kesatuan Aksi Buruh Indonesia [*Indonesian Workers Action Front*]   (IN)
KABr .... Corps Artillery Brigade   (RU)
KAC .... Kameshli [*Syria*] [*Airport symbol*]   (OAG)
KAC .... Kuwait Airways Corp. [*ICAO designator*]   (FAAC)
kach .... Qualitative, Quality, High-Grade   (RU)
kachestv ...... Qualitative, Quality, High-Grade   (RU)
kach-vo .... Quality, Property, Grade   (RU)
KACIA .... Korea Agricultural Chemicals Industrial Association   (EAIO)
KACN .... Korean Association for Conservation of Nature   (EAIO)
KACS .... Korean Agricultural Chemical Society   (EAIO)
KACST ...... King Abdul-Aziz City for Science and Technology [*Saudi Arabia*] [*Research center*]   (IRC)
KAD .... Capacitive Induction Motor   (RU)
KAD .... Commander of Division Artillery   (RU)
KAD .... Division Artillery Commander   (BU)
kad .... Kadet [*Cadet*] [*Poland*]
KAD .... Kaduna [*Nigeria*] [*Airport symbol*]   (OAG)
KAD .... Kendron Amesou Draseos [*Instant Response Center*] [*AD*] [*See also*]   (GC)
KAD .... Korps Auglarrungs Drohn
kad .... Rear Admiral   (BU)
KADA .... Kemubu Agriculture Development Association   (ML)
KADAPOLMETRODJAYA ... Kepala Daerah Kepolisian Metropolitan Djakarta Raya [*Chief of the Metropolitan Djakarta Police Region*]   (IN)
KADEP ...... Kepala Departemen [*Department Head*]   (IN)
kadet .... Member of the Constitutional Democratic Party [*1905-1917*]   (RU)
KADIN ...... Kamar Dagang dan Industri Indonesia [*Indonesian Chamber of Commerce and Industry*]   (FEA)
KADIN ...... Kepala Dinas [*Service Chief*]   (IN)
KADIR ...... Kepala Direktorat [*Directorate Head*]   (IN)
KADIS ...... Kepala Dinas [*Service Chief*]   (IN)
KADIT ...... Kepala Direktorat [*Directorate Head*]   (IN)
KADJATI ... Kepala Kedjaksaan Tinggi [*Chief of the District Attorney's Office*]   (IN)
KADJAWA ... Kepala Djawatan [*Office Chief*]   (IN)

KADKY ..... Klados Asfaliseos Dimotikon kai Koinotikon Ypallilon [*Municipal and Communal Employees Insurance Branch*] [*Greek*]   (GC)
kadm .... Kontradmiral [*Rear-Admiral*] [*Poland*]
k-adm .... Rear Admiral   (RU)
KADP .... Kaduna State Agricultural Development Project [*Nigeria*]   (ECON)
KADS .... Kompatible Anwendungs-und Dialog-Sprache [*German*]   (ADPT)
KADU .... Kenya African Democratic Union [*Political party*]   (PPW)
KADY .... Kanonismos Allilografias Dimosion Ypiresion [*Public Services Correspondence Regulations*] [*Greek*]   (GC)
KAE .... Aerological Observation Record Book   (RU)
KAE .... Atomic Energy Commission   (RU)
KAE .... Commission on Aerology (of the World Meteorological Organization)   (RU)
KAE .... Complex Antarctic Expedition   (RU)
KAE .... Kama Archaeological Expedition   (RU)
KAE .... Komma Agroton kai Ergazomenon [*Agrarian and Workers Party*] [*Greek*]   (GC)
KAE .... Krupp Atlas - Elektronik   (MSC)
KAEF .... Katholisches Arbeitskreises Entwicklung und Frieden
KAERI .... Korea Advanced Energy Research Institute   (WND)
KAERI .... Korea Atomic Energy Research Institute [*Nuclear energy*]   (NRCH)
KAEV .... Konnyuipari Alkatreszgyarto es Ellato Vallalat [*Spare Parts Manufacturing and Supply Enterprise of the Light Industry*]   (HU)
KAF .... Committee of Antifascist Resistance Fighters [*Germany*]   (EAIO)
KAF .... Kafue International Air Services Ltd. [*Zambia*] [*ICAO designator*]   (FAAC)
KAF .... Karato [*Papua New Guinea*] [*Airport symbol*]   (OAG)
KAF .... Kaseinfaser [*Casein Fiber*] [*German*]   (GCA)
KAF .... Kefalaion Apozimioseos Fortoekfortoton [*Stevedores Compensation Fund*] [*Greek*]   (GC)
KAF .... Kenya Air Force
KAF .... Khmer [*Cambodia*] Air Force   (VNW)
KAF .... Kivalo Aruk Foruma [*Forum of Outstanding Goods*]   (HU)
KAF .... Konrad Adenauer Foundation [*Germany*]   (EAIO)
KAF .... "Red Banner" Amur Flotilla   (RU)
KAFCO ...... Karnaphuli Fertilizer Co. [*Bangladesh*]
KAFCO ...... Kuwait Aviation Fueling Company   (ME)
KAFM ...... Catholic Association of French Youth   (RU)
KAFTZ ...... Kandla Free Trade Zone [*India*]   (IMH)
KAFU .... Kenya African Farmers' Union
KAG .... Air Group Commander   (RU)
KAG .... Corps Artillery Group   (BU)
KAG .... Korpusna Artiljeriska Grupa [*Corps Artillery Group*]   (YU)
Kagakudomei ... Kagaku-Sangyo Rodokumiai Domei [*Japanese Federation of Chemical Industry Workers' Unions*]
KAGE .... Kommission fur Alte Geschichte und Epigraphik [*Commission for Ancient History and Epigraphy*] [*Germany*]   (EAIO)
KAGGM .... Koy Arastirma ve Gelistirme Genel Mudurlugu [*Village Research and Development Directorate General*]   (TU)
KAGI .... Kesatuan Aksi Guru Indonesia [*Indonesian Teachers Action Front*]   (IN)
Kagit-Is ...... Paper Workers Union   (TU)
KAI .... Kaieteur [*Guyana*] [*Airport symbol*]   (OAG)
KAI .... Kazan' Aviation Institute   (RU)
KAI .... Kiruna Geofysiska Institut [*Kiruna Geophysical Institute*] [*Swedish Board for Space Activities*]   (EAS)
KAI .... Kuybyshev Aviation Institute   (RU)
KAIF .... Korea Atomic Industrial Forum [*Nuclear energy*]   (NRCH)
Kais .... Kaiserlich [*Imperial*] [*German*]
KAIS .... Kazakhstan Complex Scientific Research Institute of Structures and Building Materials   (RU)
KAIS .... Korea Advanced Institute for Science
KAIST .... Korea Advanced Institute of Science and Technology [*Seoul*] [*Information service or system*]   (IID)
kaivost .... Kaivostyo [*Mining*] [*Finland*]
KAJ .... Kajaani [*Finland*] [*Airport symbol*]   (OAG)
KAJ .... Katholieke Arbeiders Jeugd [*Catholic Labor Youth*] [*Netherlands*]   (WEN)
KAJ .... Kristelijke Arbeidersjeugd [*Belgium*]   (EAIO)
KAJA .... Cambodian Alumni from Japan   (CL)
KAK .... Corps Artillery Commander   (BU)
KAK .... Kommunistisk Arbejdskreds [*Communist Labor Circle*] [*Denmark*]   (WEN)
kal .... Kalastus [*Fishing*] [*Finland*]
kal .... Kalendarz [*Calendar*] [*Poland*]
Kal .... Kalender [*Calendar*] [*German*]   (GCA)
KAL .... Kalgoorlie [*Australia*]   (DSUE)
Kal .... Kaliber [*Caliber*] [*German*]   (GCA)
kal .... Kalori(a) [*Calorie*] [*Finland*]
kal .... Kaloria [*Calorie*]   (HU)

kal .... Kalorie [*Calorie*] [*Afrikaans*]
Kal............. Kalorifer [*or Kaloriferli*] [*Heater or Equipped with Heater*]   (TU)
Kal............. Kilogramm Kalorie [*Kilogram Calorie*] [*German*]
KAL .... Korean Air Lines Co. Ltd. [*ICAO designator*]   (FAAC)
KAL .... Korean Air Lines, Inc.
Kalbdrbd .... Kalblederband [*Full-Calf Binding*] [*Publishing*] [*German*]
kalimag ...... Potassium-Magnesium Sulfate Fertilizer   (RU)
ka li sz .... Kotelezo Altalanos Ipari Szamlarendszer [*Compulsory
            Bookkeeping System (in industry)*]   (HU)
kalligr......... Kalligraphisch [*Calligraphic*] [*German*]
Kalmgosizdat ... Kalmyk State Publishing House   (RU)
Kalmizdat... Kalmyk Publishing House   (RU)
KALP........ Kenya African Liberal Party
KALSEL.... Kalimantan Selatan [*South Kalimantan*]   (IN)
KALTARA ... Kalimantan Utara [*North Kalimantan (Sarawak, Sabah,
            Brunei)*]   (IN)
Kaltbruchigk ... Kaltbruechigkeit [*Cold-Shortness*] [*German*]   (GCA)
KALTENG ... Kalimantan Tengah [*Central Kalimantan*]   (IN)
KALTIM ... Kalimantan Timur [*East Kalimantan*]   (IN)
kalz............. Kalziniert [*Calcined*] [*German*]   (GCA)
kam .... Kamara [*Chamber*]   (HU)
kam .... Kamat [*Interest*]   (HU)
Kam........... Kamen [*Rock*] [*Russian*]   (NAU)
Kam........... Kammer [*Small Unheated Room, Chamber (of a gun)*] [*German*]
KAM .... Kenya African Movement
KAM .... Konserwacja Architektury Monumentalnej [*Administration for
            the Conservation of Historical Buildings*]   (POL)
KAM .... Panstwowe Przedsiebiorstwo Robot Konserwatorskich
            Architektury Monumentalnej [*State Enterprise for
            Conservation Work on Historical Buildings*]   (POL)
kam .... Stone, Stony [*Topography*]   (RU)
KAM .... Study Center for Aviation Medicine   (RU)
KAMA ...... Korea Automobile Manufacturers Association   (EAIO)
KAMAMI ... Komtin'ny Artista Malagasy Mitolona [*National Committee of
            Artists and Musicians*] [*Malagasy*]   (AF)
KAMBRUS ... Industrija Naravnih Brusnih Kamnov [*Natural Grindstones
            Industry*] [*Rogatec*]   (YU)
Kamchatrybprom ... Kamchatka Oblast Fish Industry Administration   (RU)
KAMDE .... Kanonismos Anatheseos Meleton Dimosion Ependyseon
            [*Regulation for the Assignment of Studies for Public
            Investments*] [*Greek*]   (GC)
KamGES.... Kama Hydroelectric Power Plant   (RU)
KAMI .... Kasatuan Aksi Mahasiswa Indonesia [*Political party*]   (BARN)
KAMI .... Kesatuan Aksi Mahasiswa Indonesia [*Indonesian College
            Students Action Front*]   (IN)
Kamiparoren ... Zenkoku Kamiparupu-Sangyo Rodokumiai Rengokai
            [*National Federation of Paper and Pulp Industry Workers'
            Unions*] [*Japan*]
KAMK .... Krajsky Auto-Moto Klub [*Regional Motoring Club*]   (CZ)
KAMPDE ... Kanonismos Anatheseos Meleton Programmatos Dimosion
            Ependyseon [*Regulation for the Assignment of Studies
            under the Public Investments Program*] [*Greek*]   (GC)
KAMTIB ... Keamanan dan Ketertiban [*Security and Order*]   (IN)
kam-ug .... Coal   (RU)
KAMU-SEN ... Kibris Turk Kamu Gorevlileri Sendikasi [*Turkish Cypriot
            Civil Servant's Union*] [*GOR-SEN*] [*Formerly,*]   (TU)
kamv.......... Worsted Mill [*Topography*]   (RU)
Kan............ Kanal [*Canal, Channel*] [*Poland*]   (NAU)
KAN.......... Kano [*Nigeria*] [*Airport symbol*]   (OAG)
kan .... Kanonier [*Gunner, Artilleryman*] [*Poland*]
kan .... Kanonik [*Cannon*] [*Poland*]
Kan............ Kanonikus [*German*]
Kan............ Kantorei [*Record label*] [*Germany*]
KAN.......... Kenya Association Manufacturers   (EAIO)
KAN.......... Klub Angazovanych Nestraniku [*Club of Committed Non-Party
            Persons (organized in 1968)*]   (CZ)
KAN.......... Knight of St. Alexander Nevsky [*Obsolete*] [*Russian*]
KAN.......... Koppelanordnung [*German*]   (ADPT)
KAN.......... Kriegsausruestungsnachweisung [*Table of Basic Allowances*]
            [*German military - World War II*]
Kanaz........ Kanaker Aluminum Plant   (RU)
kanc.......... Kancelaria [*or Kancelaryiny*] [*Office*] [*Poland*]
kanc.......... Kanclerz [*Chancellor*] [*Poland*]
kand .... Candidate   (RU)
kand .... Kandidaatti [*Finland*]
kand .... Kandidatus [*Candidate*]   (HU)
kand .... Kandydat [*Candidate*] [*Poland*]
K & D .... Kitchen and Dining Room [*Real estate terminology*]
kand n .... Kandydat Nauk [*Candidate of Science*] [*Poland*]
K &SEAFA ... Korea and South East Asia Forces Association of Australia
KANI .... Kesatuan Aksi Nelajan Indonesia [*Indonesian Fishermen's
            Action Front*]   (IN)
Kankororen ... Kanko Kamotsusango Rodokumiai Rengokai [*Japan
            Federation of Travel and Aircargo Agency Workers' Unions*]
KANOON ... Institute for the Intellectual Development of Children and
            Young Adults [*Iran*]   (EAIO)

Kan P .... Kanadisches Patent [*Canadian Patent*] [*German*]   (GCA)
KANSAK... Turk Kanser Arastirma ve Savas Kurumu [*Turkish Organization
            for Research and Combating Cancer*]   (TU)
kansakop.... Kansakoulunopettaja [*Finland*]
KANTAFU ... Kenya African National Traders and Farmers Union
KANTL...... Koninklijke Academie voor Nederlandse Taal- en Letterkunde
            [*Belgium*]   (SLS)
Kantong...... Kantongerecht [*Benelux*]   (BAS)
kants .... Office Term   (BU)
KANU........ Kenya African National Union [*Political party*]   (PPW)
KANUPP... Karachi Nuclear Power Plant [*Pakistan*] [*Nuclear energy*]
            (NRCH)
KANZEKO ... Kahama Nzega Co-Operative Union
KANZUS... Korea, Australia, New Zealand, and the United States
KAO......... Crimean Astrophysical Observatory   (RU)
KAO......... Kalmyk Autonomous Oblast   (RU)
KAO......... Kiev Astronomical Observatory   (RU)
KAO......... Knights of Aquarius Order   (EAIO)
KAO......... Kuusamo [*Finland*] [*Airport symbol*]   (OAG)
kaol .... Kaolin Plant [*Topography*]   (RU)
KAP .... Artillery Regiment Commander   (RU)
kap .... Captain   (RU)
KAP .... Combined Automatic Parachute   (RU)
KAP .... Confederation of Arab Trade Unions [*CATU*]   (RU)
KAP .... Corps Air Regiment   (RU)
KAP .... Corps Artillery Regiment   (RU)
KAP .... Horse Artillery Regiment   (RU)
kap .... Kapelan [*Chaplain*] [*Poland*]
kap .... Kapitaal [*Capital*] [*Afrikaans*]
kap .... Kapitael [*Chapter*] [*Norway*]   (GPO)
kap .... Kapitael [*Chapter*] [*Denmark*]   (GPO)
Kap......... Kapitel [*Chapter*] [*German*]   (EG)
kap .... Kapitel [*Chapter*] [*Sweden*]   (GPO)
KAP .... Kapittel [*Chapter*] [*Afrikaans*]
kap .... Kapitula [*Chapter*] [*Poland*]
Kap......... Kapitular [*German*]
Kap......... Kaplica [*Hot Spring*]   (TU)
KAP .... Kapten [*Captain*]   (IN)
KAP .... Kefalaion Asfaliseos Pistoseon [*Credit Insurance Fund*] [*Greek*]
            (GC)
kap .... Klauzula o Autorskom Pravu [*Copyright Clause*]   (YU)
KAP .... Koini Agrotiki Politiki [*Joint Agricultural Policy*]   (GC)
KAP .... Komisija za Agitaciju i Propagandu [*Agitation and Propaganda
            Commission*]   (YU)
KAP .... Kooperative Abteilung Pflanzenproduktion [*Cooperative Crop
            Production Department*]   (EG)
KAP .... Korean Academy of Psychotherapists   (EAIO)
KAP .... Kuwait Action Plan [*Advisory Committee on Pollution of the Sea*]
KAP .... Large-Panel Reinforced Foam Concrete Slab   (RU)
KAP .... "Red Banner" Air Regiment   (RU)
KAP .... "Red Banner" Artillery Regiment   (RU)
KAPAPs ... Kendron Apokatastaseos Politikon Anapiron Psykhikou
            [*Psykhiko Rehabilitation Center for Handicapped Civilians*]
            [*Greek*]   (GC)
KAPBI .... Kesatuan Aksi Pengemudi Betjak Indonesia [*Indonesian Pedicab
            Drivers Action Front*]   (IN)
KAPFER.... Turkiye Kapi ve Kalorifer Iscileri Sendikasi [*Turkish Building,
            Custodial, and Heating Plant Workers Union*]   (TU)
KAPI .... Kasatuan Aksi Peladjar Indonesia [*Political party*]   (BARN)
KAPI .... Kesatuan Aksi Peladjar Indonesia [*Indonesian Students Action
            Front*]   (IN)
kapit.......... Capitalist   (BU)
Kapl.......... Kaplanei [*German*]
KAPNI....... Kesatuan Aksi Pengusaha Nasional Indonesia [*Indonesian
            National Businessmen's Action Front*]   (IN)
KAPOLRI ... Kepala Kepolisian Republik Indonesia [*Chief of the Republic of
            Indonesia Police Force*]
KAPP........ Karelian Association of Proletarian Writers [*1926-1932*]   (RU)
KAPP........ Kenya African People's Party
KAPP........ Korean Association of Proletarian Writers   (RU)
KAPPI .... Kesatuan Aksi Pemuda Peladjar Indonesia [*Indonesian Youth
            and Students Action Front*]   (IN)
KAPSh....... Engineer Shaposhnikov Arctic Frame Tent   (RU)
kap str........ Capital Construction   (BU)
kapt.......... Kapteeni [*Finland*]
kapt........... Kaptein [*Captain*] [*Afrikaans*]
kar............. Carat   (RU)
KAR .... Corps Artillery Reserve   (RU)
kar............. Horse Artillery   (BU)
KAR .... Kamarang [*Guyana*] [*Airport symbol*]   (OAG)
kar............. Karaat [*Carat*] [*Afrikaans*]
KAR .... Kar-Air OY [*Finland*] [*ICAO designator*]   (FAAC)
Kar .... Karakol [*Police Station, Outpost*]   (TU)
KAR .... King's African Rifles
kar............. Quarantine [*Topography*]   (RU)
Karakalpakgiz ... Karakalpak State Publishing House   (RU)

Karakalpakgosizdat ... Karakalpak State Publishing House　(RU)
Karakalpakvodtrans ... Water Transportation Administration at the Council of Ministers, Karakalpak ASSR　(RU)
karakul...... Karakul Sheep-Breeding [*Topography*]　(RU)
karant........ Quarantine [*Topography*]　(RU)
karap.......... Machine-Gun Artillery Regiment　(BU)
Karbat........ Guard Battalion　(RU)
KARD .... Artillery Division Commander　(RU)
kard .... Kardynal [*Cardinal*] [*Poland*]
Kargopol'lag ... Kargopol' Corrective Labor Camp　(RU)
KARIS .... Karadeniz Nisasta-Glikoz-Misirozuyagi Sanayii ve Ticaret AS [*Black Sea Starch, Glucose, Corn Oil Industry and Marketing Corp.*]　(TU)
Karlag .... Karaganda Corrective Labor Camp　(RU)
KARM .... Corps Artillery Repair Shop　(RU)
karn............ Karnagy [*Conductor (Music)*]　(HU)
KARNA ..... Kweekintituut van Aardappelrassen ten Behove van de Nderlandse Aardappelmeelindustrie Breeding Institute of Potato Varieties for the Dutch Potato Flour Industry [*Netherlands*]　(DSCA)
karnach...... Guard Commander　(RU)
Karnt.......... Kaernten [*German*]
KARO .... Kepala Biro [*Bureau Chief*]　(IN)
KARS........ Katumani Agricultural Research Station [*Kenya*]　(DSCA)
kart............ Card　(RU)
kart............ Kartars [*Colleague*]　(HU)
kart............ Karton [*Cartoon*] [*Poland*]
kart............ Kartoniert [*Bound in Boards*] [*Publishing*] [*German*]
kart............ Kartonnerad [*In Paper Boards*] [*Publishing*] [*Sweden*]
kart............ Map [*Bibliography*]　(RU)
kart............ Picture　(BU)
kart............ Scene [*Theater*]　(RU)
kartbl .... Kartblad [*Map*] [*Publishing*] [*Sweden*]
Kartensk .... Kartenskizze [*Sketch Map*] [*Publishing*] [*German*]
KARTGEOFOND ... Kartograficky a Geodeticky Fond [*Cartograhic and Geodetic Fund*]　(CZ)
kartnbd ...... Kartonbundet [*Bound in Boards*] [*Publishing Danish/ Norwegian*]
kartogr .... Cartogram　(RU)
kartogr .... Kartografia [*or Kartograficzny*] [*Cartography or Cartographic*] [*Poland*]
karton......... Kartonert [*Bound in Boards*] [*Publishing Danish/Norwegian*]
kartonbd..... Kartonbind [*Bound in Boards*] [*Publishing Danish/Norwegian*]
Kartontol'... Cardboard and Tar Paper Plant　(RU)
KAS .... Kenya-Australia Society
KAS .... Konrad Adenauer Stiftung [*Germany*] [*Political party*]
KAS .... Korean Astronomical Society　(EAIO)
KAS .... Medical Launch　(RU)
KASAB ...... Kepala Staf Angkatan Bersendjata [*Chief of Staff of the Armed Forces*] [*KSAB*] [*Also,*]　(IN)
KASAD...... Kepala Staf Angkatan Darat [*Army Chief of Staff*] [*KSAD*] [*Also,*]　(IN)
KASAL ...... Kepala Staf Angkatan Laut [*Navy Chief of Staff*] [*KSAL*] [*Also,*]　(IN)
KASAU...... Kepala Staf Angkatan Udara [*Air Force Chief of Staff*] [*KSAU*] [*Also,*]　(IN)
KASCHA... Kastriertes Schach [*German*]　(ADPT)
KASI .... Kepala Seksi [*Section Chief*]　(IN)
KASI .... Kesatuan Aksi Sardjana Indonesia [*Indonesian College Graduates Action Front*]　(IN)
kasit .... Kasityo [*Needlework*] [*Finland*]
KASK........ Kinisi Allagis Synetairistikou Kinimatos [*Movement for Change in the Cooperative Movement*] [*Greek*]　(GC)
KASKA-NHISKA ... Koninklijke Academie en Nationaal Hoger Instituut voor Schone Kunsten [*Belgium*]　(SLS)
KASKhN ... Kazakh Academy of Agricultural Sciences　(RU)
KasNIGMI ... Kazakhnskii Nauchno-Issledovatel'skii Gidrometeorologicheskii Institut [*Kazakh Scientific-Research Hydrometeorological Institute*] [*Former USSR*]　(DSCA)
KASP........ Chamber Ensemble for Free Dance [*Former Yugoslavia*]
KASP........ Commission for Complex Study of the Caspian Sea [*Of the Academy of Sciences, USSR*]　(RU)
Kaspar........ Caspian Sea Steamship Line　(RU)
Kaspflot ..... Caspian Dry-Cargo Steamship Line　(RU)
Kaspmorput' ... Caspian Administration of Sea Routes　(RU)
Kaspnefteflot ... Caspian Administration of Oil Tanker Fleet　(RU)
KASPNIIRKH ... Kaspiyskiy Nauchno-Isseldovatel'skiy Institut Rybnogo Khozyaystva [*Caspian Scientific Research Institute of Fisheries*] [*Russian*]　(MSC)
KaspNIRO ... Kaspijskij Nauchno-Issledovatel'skij Institut Morskogo Rybnogo Khozyajstva i Okeanografii [*Caspian Scientific Research Institute of Sea Fisheries and Oceanography*] [*Russian*]　(RU)
Kasptanker ... Caspian Oil Tanker Steamship Line　(RU)
KASRA...... Kano State Recruitment Agency [*Nigeria*]

KASS .... Kara-Bogas-Gol Salt Station (of the Academy of Sciences, USSR)　(RU)
Kass .... Kassier [*German*]
KASS .... Kulturni a Spolecenska Strediska [*Cultural and Social Centers*]　(CZ)
KASSR ...... Kabardinian Autonomous Soviet Socialist Republic　(RU)
KASSR ...... Karelian Autonomous Soviet Socialist Republic [*1925-1936*]　(RU)
KASSR ...... Kazakh Autonomous Soviet Socialist Republic　(RU)
KASU .... Kenya African Study Union
kasv............ Kasvitiede [*Botany*] [*Finland*]
kasvatustkand ... Kasvatustieteiden Kandidaatti [*Finland*]
KASZ........ Kozalkalmazottak Szakszervezete [*Trade Union of Civil Service Workers*]　(HU)
KAT .... Autotransformer for Motion-Picture Projector　(RU)
kat .... Catalyst, Catalytic　(RU)
Kat............. Catholic Cemetery [*Topography*]　(RU)
KAT .... Control of Automotive Transport　(BU)
KAT .... Kaitaia [*New Zealand*] [*Airport symbol*]　(OAG)
kat .... Katalogus [*Catalog*]　(RU)
kat .... Kataszteri [*Cadastral*]　(HU)
kat .... Katedra [*Chair, Department*] [*Poland*]
kat .... Katedralny [*Cathedral*] [*Poland*]
Kat............. Kategorie [*German*]
kat .... Katolicki [*Catholic*] [*Poland*]
kat .... Katolikus [*Catholic*]　(HU)
kat .... Katolinen [*Finland*]
KAT .... Kattegat Air, AS [*Denmark*] [*ICAO designator*]　(FAAC)
KAT .... Kendron Apokatastaseos Travmation [*Rehabilitation Center for the Injured*] [*Greek*]　(GC)
KATAK..... Kibris Adasi Turk Azinlik Kurumu [*Turkish Minority Organization for the Island of Cyprus*]　(GC)
katal .... Kateisalennus [*Finland*]
katalitich.... Catalytic　(RU)
Katalogizdat ... State Publishing House of Catalogs　(RU)
katalyt........ Katalytisch [*Catalytic*] [*German*]　(GCA)
KATE........ Kendra Anoteras Tekhnikis Ekpaidevseos [*Higher Technical Education Centers*] [*Greek*]　(GC)
KATEE....... Kendra Anoteras Tekhnikis kai Epangelmatikis Ekpaidevseos [*Higher Technical and Vocational Training Centers*] [*KATE*] [*See also*]　(GC)
KATEK...... Kuybyshev Automobile and Tractor Electrical Equipment and Carburetor Plant　(RU)
kat h .... Kataszteri Hold [*Cadastral Yoke*]　(HU)
kath .... Katholisch [*Catholic*] [*German*]　(GPO)
KATH........ Komfo Anokye Teaching Hospital [*Ghana*]
KATI......... Kesatuan Aksi Tani Indonesia [*Indonesian Farmers Action Front*]　(IN)
Katoenhandel ... Vereniging van Katoenhandelaren in Nederland [*Netherlands*]　(BAS)
katol.......... Catholic　(BU)
KATRIN.... Kilombero Agricultural Training and Research Institute
KATS........ Ship Automatic Telephone Exchange　(RU)
KATShch... Mine-Sweeping Boat　(RU)
KAU.......... Kenya African Union [*1944*] [*Political party*]　(PPW)
KAUB .... Kluwer Algemene Uitgeverijen Belgie [*Publisher*] [*Belgium*]　(EY)
kauch.......... Rubber-Bearing　(RU)
Kaucuk-Is .. Turkiye Kaucuk, Lastik ve Plastik Iscileri Sendikasi [*Turkish Rubber and Plastic Workers Union*]　(TU)
KAUFE...... Oxyethylated Phenols from Coal Tar　(RU)
KAUKEVA ... Kaupan Keskusvaliokunta [*Central Board of Finnish Wholesale and Retail Trade*]　(EAIO)
kaup .... Kauppa [*Business, Trade*] [*Finland*]
kaup .... Kaupunki [*Finland*]
kaupp .... Kauppala [*Finland*]
kaupp .... Kauppias [*Finland*]
kauppatkand ... Kauppatieteiden Kandidaatti [*Finland*]
kauppatlis .. Kauppatieteiden Lisensiaatti [*Finland*]
kauppatmaist ... Kauppatieteiden Maisteri [*Finland*]
kauppattri .. Kauppatieteiden Tohtori [*Finland*]
kaust .... Kaustisch [*Caustic*] [*German*]　(GCA)
kav............. Cavalry　(RU)
kAV............ Continental Antarctic Air　(RU)
kAV............ Continental Arctic Air　(RU)
KAV.......... Katholischer Akademikerverband [*Catholic Academy Association*]　(SLS)
KAV.......... Kavaleri [*Cavalry*]　(IN)
KAV.......... Kohaszati Alapanyagellato Vallalat [*Supply Enterprise of Basic Metallurgical Materials*]　(HU)
kav............. Koste, Assuransie, Vrag [*Cost, Insurance, Freight*] [*Afrikaans*] [*Business term*]
KAV.......... Krajsky Akcni Vybor [*Regional Action Committee*]　(CZ)
KAV.......... Kristelijke Arbeiders-Vrouwengilden [*Benelux*]　(BAS)
KAV.......... Nationaal Verbond der Kristelijke Arbeidersvrouwenbeweging [*Belgium*]　(EAIO)

KAVAA	Kenya Audio-Visual Aid Association (EAIO)
kavk	Caucasian (RU)
Kavkaznefterazvedka ... Caucasian Petroleum Exploration Trust (RU)
KAVNF......	Krajsky Akcni Vybor Narodni Fronty [Regional Action Committee of the National Front] (CZ)
KAVZ	Kurgan Bus Plant (RU)
KAW..........	Kawthaung [Myanmar] [Airport symbol] (OAG)
KAW	Krajowa Agencja Wydawnicza [National Publishing Agency] [Poland] (EY)
KAWBBA ... Kenya Amateur Weightlifting and Body-Building Association
KAWC	Kenya African Workers Congress
KAWI	Kesatuan Aksi Wanita Indonesia [Indonesian Women's Action Front] (IN)
KAWU	Kenya African Workers Union
KAX	Kalbarri [Australia] [Airport symbol] (OAG)
Kay...........	Kaynak [Source, Spring] (TU)
KAY	Wakaya [Fiji] [Airport symbol] [Obsolete] (OAG)
KAYA	Young Cambodian Artists Association (CL)
Kaym.........	Kaymakam [District Governor] [Within a province] (TU)
KAYO	Kenya Anglican Youth Organization
kayt	Kaytetaan [Is Used] [Finland]
kaz.............	Barrack [Topography] (RU)
KAZ	Kandalaksha Aluminum Plant (RU)
kaz.............	Kazakh (RU)
KAZ	Kazan' Railroad (RU)
KAZ	Krasnoyarsk Aluminum Plant (RU)
KAZ	Kurgan Bus Plant (RU)
KAZ	Kutaisi Automobile Plant (RU)
KAZAIR	Kazakhstan Airlines [ICAO designator] (FAAC)
Kazakhsel'mash ... Kazakh Agricultural Machinery Plant (RU)
Kazakhstanneft' ... Association of the Kazakhstan Petroleum Industry (RU)
KazFAN.....	Kazakh Branch of the Academy of Sciences, USSR (RU)
Kazgeupr....	Kazakh Geodetic Administration (RU)
Kazgiprogorsel'stroy ... Kazakh State Planning Institute for the Planning of Urban and Rural Construction (RU)
KAZGIPRONIIKhIMMASH ... Kazakh State Planning and Scientific Research Institute of Chemical and Machinery Industries (RU)
Kazgiprotsvetmet ... Kazakh State Institute for the Planning of Establishments of Nonferrous Metallurgy (RU)
KAZGOSIZDAT ... Kazakh State Publishing House (RU)
KAZGOSLITIZDAT ... Kazakh State Publishing House of Belles Lettres (RU)
Kazgres	Kazan' State Regional Electric Power Plant (RU)
KazGU	Kazakh State University Imeni S. M. Kirov (RU)
KazIMS	Kazakh Scientific Research Institute of Mineral Raw Materials (RU)
KazIOT......	All-Union Scientific Research Institute of Work Safety of the VTsSPS [Kazan'] (RU)
Kazkhlopkosoyuz ... Kazakh Kray Union of Cotton-Growing Cooperatives (RU)
Kazkhlopkotsentr ... Kazakh Center of Cotton-Growing Cooperatives (RU)
Kazmetallzavod ... Kazakh Metallurgical Plant (RU)
KazMI........	Kazakh Medical Institute (RU)
KazMZ	Kazakh Metallurgical Plant (RU)
KazNIGMI ... Kazakh Scientific Research Hydrometeorological Institute (RU)
KazNIIAT ... Kazakh Scientific Research Institute of Automobile Transportation (RU)
KazNIIE	Kazakh Scientific Research Institute of Power Engineering (RU)
KazNIIVKh ... Kazakh Scientific Research Institute of Water Management (RU)
KazNIIZh ..	Kazakh Scientific Research Institute of Livestock Breeding (RU)
KazNIPIAT ... Kazakh Scientific Research and Planning Institute of Automobile Transportation (RU)
KazPI........	Kazakh Pedagogical Institute Imeni Abay (RU)
Ka Zrf	Kapali Zarfi [Sealed Envelope Bidding] (TU)
Kazsel'khozgiz ... Kazakh State Publishing House of Agricultural Literature (RU)
Kazsel'mash ... Kazakh Agricultural Machinery Plant (RU)
KazSSR......	Kazakh Soviet Socialist Republic (RU)
KazTAG	Kazakh News Agency (RU)
Kaztsentroarkhiv ... Central Archives Administration, Kazakh ASSR (RU)
KazTsIK	Central Executive Committee, Kazakh SSR (RU)
Kazuchpedgiz ... Kazakh State Publishing House of Textbooks and Pedagogical Literature (RU)
Kazvetinstitut ... Kazakh State Veterinary and Zootechnical Institute (RU)
KB	Battery Commander (BU)
KB	Cable Drum (RU)
kb	Cable Length (RU)
Kb	Cavalry Brigade (BU)
kb	Cubic (RU)
KB	Design Office (RU)
KB	Kadry Bezpieczenstwa [Security Cadres] [Military Battalions] [World War II] (POL)

KB	Kantor Berita [News Agency] (IN)
kb	Karabin Bojowy [Rifle] [Poland]
KB	Karadeniz Bakir [Black Sea Copper Works] [KBI] [See also] (TU)
KB	Kasboek [Cash Book] [Afrikaans] [Business term]
KB	Kazalisna Biblioteka [Theater Library] [Zagreb] (YU)
KB	Kincheng Banking Corp. [Hong Kong]
KB	Kisa Boylu [Short Length] [As of a timber] (TU)
KB	Komercni Banka AS [Czech Republic] [Banking]
KB	Komitet Blokowy [City Block Committee] (POL)
KB	Kommanditbolaget [Limited Partnership] [German] (ILCA)
KB	Kommunistischer Bund [Communist Union (Radical Left)] [Austria] (WEN)
KB	Komunalna Banka [Communal Bank] (YU)
KB	Koninklijk Besluit [Royal Decree] [Dutch] (ILCA)
KB	Koninklijke Bibliotheek ['s-Gravenhage]
KB	Kontrabass [Double Bass] [Music]
KB	Korpusna Baza [Corps Base] (YU)
kb	Korulbelul [About, Approximately] [Hungary] (GPO)
K/B	Kota Bahru [Malaysia] (ML)
K B	Kozponti Bizottsag [Central Committee] (HU)
KB	Kray Library (RU)
KB	Kredietbrief [Letter of Credit] [Afrikaans] [Business term]
KB	Kultur Bakanligi [Ministry of Culture] (TU)
KB	Kulturbund der Deutsche Demokratische Republik [German League of Culture] (EY)
Kb..............	Kunstbastfaser [Synthetic Bast Fiber] [German] (GCA)
KB	Large Alidade (RU)
KB	Monitor Unit (RU)
KB	Paper Capacitor (RU)
KB	Tower Crane (RU)
KBA	Kabala [Sierra Leone] [Airport symbol] (OAG)
KBA	Kenya Badminton Association (EAIO)
kba	Kontant by Aflewering [Cash on Delivery] [Afrikaans] [Business term]
KBA	Korea Badminton Association (EAIO)
KBAC........	Korea Broadcasting Advertising Corporation
KBAO	Kabardino-Balkarian Autonomous Oblast [1922-1936] (RU)
KBAP.......	"Red Banner" Bomber Regiment (RU)
KBASSR....	Kabardino-Balkarian Autonomous Soviet Socialist Republic (RU)
KBAT........	Design Office of Automation and Remote Control Equipment for the Petroleum and Gas Industry (RU)
KBAZ........	Base Commander (RU)
kbb	Counterbattery Fire (RU)
KBB	Kavernen Bau- und Betriebs GmbH
KBB	Kulak, Burun, ve Bogaz (Klinigi or Mutehassis) [Ear, Nose, and Throat (Clinic or Specialist)] (TU)
KBB	NV [Naamloze Vennootschap] Koninklijke Bijenkorf Beheer [Netherlands]
KBC	Kenya Broadcasting Corporation
KBC	Koguna, Babura & Co. [Nigeria]
KBC	Korea Baptist Convention (EAIO)
kbd	Klotband [Cloth Binding] [Publishing] [Sweden]
KBDU	Kom-Bum Development Union
KBE	Katholische Bundesarbeitsgemeinschaft fuer Erwachsenenbildung [Catholic Confederation Study Group for Adult Education] (SLS)
KB(E)A	Kenya Bankers' (Employers') Association (EAIO)
KBF..........	Kaisahang Buhay Foundation [Philippines]
KBF..........	Kandy Bible Fellowship [Sri Lanka]
KBF..........	Katholische Bibelfoderation [Catholic Biblical Federation] [Germany] (EAIO)
KBF..........	Kurzberichte aus der Bauforschung [Information retrieval]
KBF..........	"Red Banner" Baltic Fleet (RU)
KBG	Hermetically Sealed Paper Capacitor (RU)
KBG	Kernkraftwerk-Betriebsgesellschaft, mbH [Nuclear energy] (NRCH)
KBG	Kristelijke Beweging van Gepensioneerden [Belgium] (EAIO)
KBGS........	Design Office of Hydromechanical Structures (RU)
KBGS........	Tower Crane for Hydraulic Engineering Construction (RU)
KBGU	Kabardino-Balkarian State University (RU)
KBI...........	Institute of Criticism and Bibliography (RU)
KBI...........	Karadeniz Bakir Isletmeleri Anonim Sirketi [Black Sea Copper Works Corporation] [KB] [See also] (TU)
KBI...........	Kontrollbericht der Industrie [Industry Control Report] (EG)
KBI...........	Kribi [Cameroon] [Airport symbol] (OAG)
KBI...........	Municipal and Personal Services Inspection (RU)
KBiGK	Komisja Budownictwa i Gospodarki Komunalnej [Commission for Construction and Communal Economy] (POL)
KBIM........	Kongres Buruh Islam Merdeka [Free Islamic Trade Union Congress] [Indonesia]
KBKA	Kongres Buruh Karata Api [Congress of Railway Workers] [Indonesia]
KBKI........	Kesatuan Buruh Kerakjatan Indonesia [Indonesian Democratic Workers Federation] (IN)

KBL............ Kabul [Afghanistan] [Airport symbol]   (OAG)
KBL............ Kenya Breweries Limited
KBL............ Kilusan ng Bangong Lipunan [New Society Movement] [Philippines]   (PD)
KBL............ Kredietbank Luxembourgeoise [Luxembourg]
KBL............ Kumasi Brewery Ltd. [Ghana]
KbLg.......... Kabellaenge [Cable Length (Generally 600 feet)]   (EG)
KBM.......... Kabwum [Papua New Guinea] [Airport symbol]   (OAG)
KBM.......... Karissimo Bene Merenti [To the Most Dear and Well-Deserving] [Correspondence]
KBM.......... Kesatuan Buruh Marhaenis [Marhaenist Workers Federation]   (IN)
kbn............ Candidate of Biological Sciences   (RU)
KBNP........ Design Office for Oil Field Automation and Geophysical Instrument Making   (RU)
KBO.......... Kommunistischer Bund Oesterreichs [Communist League of Austria] [Political party]   (PPW)
KBO.......... Kurs Borbene Obuke [Combat Training Course]   (YU)
KBO.......... Organization for the Management and Development of the Kagera River Basin   (EA)
KBO.......... Personal Services Kombinat   (RU)
KBOt.......... Klasicni Bojni Otrovi [Classic Poison Gases] [Military]   (YU)
KBP.......... Combat Training Course   (RU)
KBP............ Flight Safety Control   (RU)
KBP............ Kapisanan ng mga Brodkaster sa Pilipinas [Association of Broadcasters in the Philippines]   (FEA)
KBP............ Kiev Borispol Airport [Former USSR] [Airport symbol]   (OAG)
KBP............ Komisaris Besar Polisi [Chief Police Commissioner]   (IN)
KBP............ Paper Duct Capacitor   (RU)
KBP............ Pulverulent Concentrate of Spent Sulfite Liquor   (RU)
KBPL........ Communist League Proletarian Left [Netherlands] [Political party]   (PPW)
KBPM........ Kesatuan Buroh Padang Minyak [Oil Field Workers Union]   (ML)
KBR .... Kota Bharu [Malaysia] [Airport symbol]   (OAG)
KBRI.......... Kedutaan Besar Republik Indonesia [Embassy of the Republic of Indonesia]   (IN)
KBS............ Bo [Sierra Leone] [Airport symbol] [Obsolete]   (OAG)
KBS............ Bureau of Standards [Industrial Advancement Administration] [South Korea]
KBS............ Communal Public Services   (BU)
KBS............ Gamair Ltd. [Gambia] [ICAO designator]   (FAAC)
KBS............ Kenya Bus Services Ltd.
KBS............ Kiev Botanical Garden   (RU)
KBS............ Korean Bibliographical Society   (EAIO)
KBS............ Korean Broadcasting System [South Korea]   (FEA)
KBS............ Kreisbuchungsstation [Kreis Accounting Office]   (EG)
KBSA........ Kenya Booksellers and Stationers Association   (EAIO)
KBSh.......... Kuybyshev Railroad   (RU)
KBSI .... Kongres Buruh Seluruh Indonesia [All Indonesia Congress of Workers]
KBSK........ Carboxylated Butadiene-Styrene Rubber   (RU)
kbt............ Cable Length   (RU)
KBT .... Kongres Britanskih Tredjuniona [Congress of British Trade-Unions]   (YU)
KBt............ Kontrabatiranje [Counterbattery Fire]   (YU)
KBT .... Solid Concentrate of Spent Sulfite Liquor   (RU)
KBTsMA ... Design Office of Tsvetmetavtomatika   (RU)
KBUiA .... Komitet Budownictwa, Urbanistyki, i Architektury [Committee for Construction, Urban Development, and Architecture]   (POL)
KBV .... Kamer van Volksvertegenwoordigers-Beknopt Verslag [Benelux]   (BAS)
KBV .... Kassenaerztliche Bundesvereinigung [Panel Doctors' Confederation]   (SLS)
KBV .... Kustbevakningen [Sweden] [ICAO designator]   (FAAC)
KBV .... Traveling-Wave Ratio   (RU)
KBVE........ Koninklijke Belgische Vereniging der Elektrotechnici [Also, Societe Royle Belge des Electriciens] [Belgium]   (EAIO)
KBW .... Kinderbijslagwet [Benelux]   (BAS)
KBW .... Kommunistischer Bund Westdeutschland [Communist League of West Germany] [Political party]   (PPW)
KBW .... Korpus Bezpieczenstwa Wewnetrznego [Internal Security Corps]   (POL)
KBWKZ..... Kinderbijslagwet voor Kleine Zelfstandigen [Benelux]   (BAS)
KBWL..... Kinderbijslagwet voor Loontrekkenden [Benelux]   (BAS)
KBWP........ Kernkraftwerk Baden-Wuerttemberg Planungsgesellschaft [Nuclear energy]   (NRCH)
KBWR .... Kinderbijslagwet voor Rentetrekkers [Benelux]   (BAS)
KBY .... Streaky Bay [Australia] [Airport symbol]   (OAG)
KBZ .... Komise pro Branne Zalezitosti [Commission for Defense Matters]   (CZ)
KBZh .... Liquid Concentrate of Spent Sulfite Liquor   (RU)
KC .... Kenya Coalition
KC .... Kilociclos [Kilocycles] [Spanish]
k/c............ Klub Ctenaru [Readers' Club]   (CZ)

KC .... Knight of the Crescent [Turkey]
KC .... Kodeks Cywilny [Civil Code] [Poland]
KC .... Komandir Cete [Company Commander]   (YU)
KC .... Komitet Centralny [Central Committee]   (POL)
Kc .... Koruna [Czech Coin]   (BARN)
Kc .... Koruna Ceskoslovenska [Czechoslovak Koruna] [Currency]   (CZ)
Kc .... Kucuk [Small, Minor]   (TU)
KCA .... Karting Club d'Abidjan
KCA .... Kikuyu Central Association
KCA .... Kimberley-Clark of Australia Proprietary Ltd.   (ADA)
k-ca .... Knjizarnica [Bookshop]   (YU)
KCAA .... Korean Companies Association of Australia
KCAC .... Korean Civil Action Corps
KCAE........ Kuring-Gai College of Advanced Education [Australia]   (ADA)
KCAF........ Korean Culture and Arts Foundation   (EAIO)
KCAG .... Korean Civic Action Group
kcal............ Kilogramm Kalorie [Kilogram Calorie] [German]
kcal............ Kilokaloria [Kilocalorie] [Poland]
kcal............ Kilo Kaloria [Kilo Calorie]   (HU)
KCB .... Kennel Club Boliviano   (EAIO)
KCB .... Kernwaffen-, Chemische, und Biologische (Aufklaerung) [Nuclear, Chemical, and Biological (Reconnaissance)]   (EG)
KCB-Anlage ... Kern, Chemische, Bakteriologische-Anlage [ABC-Detector]   (EG)
KCC .... Kampala City Council
KCC .... Kembla Coal and Coke [Australia]   (ADA)
KCC .... Kenya Co-Operative Creameries Ltd.
KCC .... Kuwait Cement Co.   (IMH)
KCC .... Kuwait Chamber of Commerce and Industry   (EAIO)
KCCI........ Kuwait Chamber of Commerce and Industry
KCCU .... Kilimanjaro Chagga Citizens' Union
KCDB .... Kaduna Capital Development Board
KCDC .... Kenya Citizens Democratic Congress
KCE .... Collinsville [Australia] [Airport symbol]   (OAG)
KCE .... Kultura Centro Esperantista [Esperanto Cultural Centre] [Switzerland]   (EAIO)
KCFC........ Kenya Chemical and Food Corporation
KCFC........ Kuwait Chemical Fertilizer Company   (ME)
KC FPK .... Komitet Centralny Francuskiej Partii Komunistycznej [Central Committee of the French Communist Party]   (POL)
KCGM ...... Kalgoorlie Consolidated Gold Mines [Australia]
KCh.......... Black Silicon Carbide   (RU)
KCh.......... Commission for the Study of the Quaternary Period (of the Academy of Sciences, USSR)   (RU)
KCh.......... Frequency Corrector   (RU)
KCH .... Kuching [Malaysia] [Airport symbol]   (OAG)
kch .... Locksmith, Doorkeeper, Turnkey   (BU)
KCh.......... Malleable Iron   (RU)
K-Chemie... Kampfstoffchemie [Chemical Warfare Chemistry]   (EG)
kch r .... Machine-Gun Company   (BU)
KChSR...... Kuban'-Black Sea Soviet Republic [1918]   (RU)
kch vd.......... Machine-Gun Platoon   (BU)
KChZhD ... Chinese Ch'ang-Ch'un Railroad [1945-1953]   (RU)
KCIA .... Korea Cement Industrial Association   (EAIO)
KCIA........ South Korean Central Intelligence Agency [Later, Agency for National Security Planning]   (PD)
KCIC .... Kuwait Chemical Industries Co.
KCK .... Ketua Chawangan Khas [Chief Special Branch]   (ML)
KC KPJ...... Komitet Centralny Komunistycznej Partii Japonii [Central Committee of the Communist Party of Japan]   (POL)
KC KPP .... Komitet Centralny Komunistycznej Partii Polski [Central Committee of the Communist Party of Poland]   (POL)
KC KPZR .. Komitet Centralny Komunistycznej Partii Zwiazku Radzieckiego [Central Committee of the Communist Party of the Soviet Union]   (POL)
KCLB........ Katholiek Centrum voor Lectuurinformatie en Bibliotheekvoorziening [NBLC] [Netherlands]
KCM .... Key Center for Mines [University of Wollongong] [Australia]
KCMA .... Klub Cyklistu, Motocyklistu, a Automobilistu [Bicycle, Motorcycle, and Automobile Club]   (CZ)
KCMC ...... Kilimanjaro Christian Medical Centre
KCME ...... Kuznetsk Commodity and Raw Materials Exchange [Russian Federation]   (EY)
KCMU .... Kumba Co-Operative Marketing Union
KCNA .... Korean Central News Agency   (CL)
KCNM........ San Jose, Philippines [AM radio station call letters]
KCNP .... Ku-Ring-Gai Chase National Park [Australia]   (ADA)
KCO.......... Kenya Consumers' Organisation   (EAIO)
KCOS .... Knihovna Ceskoslovenska Obce Sokolske [Library of the Czechoslovak Sokol Organization]   (CZ)
KCP .... Kirghiz Communist Party [Political party]
KCP .... Koala Conservation Program [Australia]
KCP .... Korean Communist Party [Political party] [North Korea]   (FEA)

KC PPR ..... Komitet Centralny Polskiej Partii Robotniczej [*Central Committee of the Polish Workers Party*] (POL)

KC PZPR... Komitet Centralny Polskiej, Zjednoczonej Partii Robotniczej [*Central Committee of the Polish United Workers' Party*] (POL)

KCR .... Kowloon-Canton Railway [*Hong Kong*]

Kcs .... Csehszlovak Korona [*Czechoslovak Crown*] [*Currency*] (HU)

KCS........... Korean Chemical Society

Kcs .... Koruna Ceskoslovenska [*Czechoslovak Koruna*] [*Currency*] (CZ)

KCSN........ Kralovska Ceska Spolecnost Nauk [*Royal Czech Society of Sciences*] (CZ)

KCSP .... Kontrola Cywilna Statkow Powietrznych [*Civil Aircraft Control*] (POL)

KCSR........ Kuwaiti Company for Shipbuilding and Repairs (ME)

KCSS .... Key Center for Statistical Services [*Deakin University*] [*Australia*]

KCST .... Klub Ceskoslovenskych Turistu [*Czechoslovak Tourist Club*] (CZ)

KCT .... Klub Ceskych Turistu [*Czech Tourist Club*] (CZ)

KCT .... Krajsky Cirkevni Tajemnik [*Regional Church Secretary*] (CZ)

KCT .... Krusoe & Co. Transit [*Denmark*]

KCTL......... Klub Ctenaru Technicke Literatury [*Club of Technical Literature Readers*] (CZ)

KCV .... Klub Ceskych Velocipedistu [*Czech Cycling Club*] (CZ)

KCVO .... Knight Commander of the Royal Victorian Order [*Australia*] (ADA)

KCVP........ Konservativ-Christlichsoziale Volkspartei [*Conservative Christian-Social Party*] [*Switzerland*] [*Political party*] (PPE)

KCWKP(b) ... Komitet Centralny Wszechzwiazkowej Komunistycznej Partii (Bolszewikow) [*Central Committee of the All-Union Communist Party (Bolsheviks)*] (POL)

KCWU .... Korea Church Women United

KCZ .... Kochi [*Japan*] [*Airport symbol*] (OAG)

KC ZMS .... Komitet Centralny Zwiazku Mlodziezy Socjalistycznej [*Central Committee of the Socialist Youth Union*] [*Poland*]

KCZZ........ Komisja Centralna [*or Centralny*] Zwiazkow Zawodowych [*Central Commission of Trade Unions*] (POL)

KD............. Battalion Commander (BU)

KD............. Blood Pressure (RU)

Kd .... Cavalry Division (BU)

kd .... Conductor [*Railroad, Trolley, Bus*] (BU)

KD............. Constitutional Democrat (RU)

k-d............. Constitutional Democratic Party [*1905-1917*] (RU)

KD............. Detonating Cap (RU)

KD............. Division Commander (RU)

KD............. Kaini Diathiki [*New Testament*] (GC)

KD............. Kaizai Doyukai [*Association of Corporate Executives*] [*Japan*]

KD............. Kamenouhelne Doly [*Black Coal Mines*] (CZ)

kd .... Kansandemokraatti(nen) [*Finland*]

KD............. Kartographischer Dienst der Nationalen Volksarmee [*National People's Army Cartographic Service*] (EG)

Kd .... Kidemli [*Senior, Seniority in Rank, Rating*] (TU)

KD............. Kisa Dalga [*Short Wave*] (TU)

KD............. Kladenske Doly [*Kladno Mines*] (CZ)

KD............. Klasyfikacja Dziesietna [*Decimal Classification*] [*Poland*]

KD............. Kolektivni Dum [*Communal (Social) Center*] (CZ)

Kd .... Komanda Divisiona [*Headquarters of Artillery Battalion*] (YU)

KD............. Komitet Dzielnicowy [*City Section Committee*] (POL)

KD............. Konvertible Devisen [*Convertible Foreign Exchange*] (EG)

KD............. Kreisdienststelle [*Kreis Agency*] (EG)

KD............. Kriegs Dekoration [*War Decoration*] [*German*]

KD............. Kuwaiti Dinar [*Monetary unit*] (BJA)

kd .... Pack Horse Driver, Horseholder (BU)

KD............. Pressurizer (RU)

KDA........... Karachi Development Authority [*Pakistan*] (EY)

KDA........... Katholischer Deutscher Akademikerinnen Bund [*Union of German Catholic University Women*] [*German*]

KDA........... Kendall Airlines [*Australia*] [*ICAO designator*] (FAAC)

KDA........... Kenya Darts Association

KDA........... Kenya Dental Association (SLS)

KDA........... Klub Demokratickych Akademikov [*Democratic University Students' Club*] (CZ)

k-da........... Komanda [*Command*] [*Military*] (YU)

KDA........... Kongelig Dansk Aeroklub [*Royal Danish Aeroclub*] (EAIO)

KDA........... Kono Development Association

K-daKoV ... Komanda Kopnene Vojske [*Ground Forces Command*] (YU)

KDAS .... Koini Dievthynsis ton Aktoploikon Syngoinonion [*Coastal Communications Joint Directorate*] [*Greek*] (GC)

KDB........... Kambalda [*Australia*] [*Airport symbol*] (OAG)

KDB........... Kenya Dairy Board

KDB........... Kocaeli Devrimciler Birligi [*Kocaeli Revolutionaries' Union*] (TU)

KDB........... Korea Development Bank

KDC........... Katholiek Documentatiecentrum [*Catholic Document Center*] [*Netherlands*] (SLS)

KDC........... Klub Delnickych Cyklistu [*Workers' Cycling Club*] (CZ)

KDC........... Koroshio Data Center [*Japan*] (ASF)

KDCI .... Kepala Daerah Chusus Ibukota [*Head of the Special Capital Region (Governor of Djakarta)*] (IN)

KDD........... Kasarni Dozorci Dustojnik [*Garrison Officer of the Day*] (CZ)

KDD........... Kokusai Denshin Denwa Co. Ltd. [*Telegraph & Telephone Corp.*] [*Tokyo, Japan*] [*Telecommunications*]

KDE........... Kendron Didaskalias Enilikon [*Adult Education Center*] [*Greek*] (GC)

Kde............ Klein-Durchgangseilgueterzug [*Small Express Through Freight Train*] [*German*] (EG)

KDE........... Koroba [*Papua New Guinea*] [*Airport symbol*] [*Obsolete*] (OAG)

KDF........... Kassem Darwish Fakhroo & Sons [*Engineering contractor*] [*Doha, Qatar*] (MENA)

KDF........... Kraft durch Freude [*Strength through Joy Movement*] [*Pre-World War II*] [*German*]

KDFC........ Korea Development Finance Corp.

Kdg............ Kindergarten [*or Kindergaertnerin*] [*Kindergarten or Female Kindergartener*] [*German*]

KDG........... Kinisi Dimokratikon Gynaikon [*Movement of Democratic Women*] [*Greek*] (GC)

Kdg............ Klein-Durchgangsgueterzug [*Small Through Freight Train*] [*German*] (EG)

KDGS .... Kongelige Danske Geografiske Selskab [*Royal Danish Geographical Society*] (EAIO)

KDGTh...... Kinisis Dimokratikon Gynaikon Thessalonikis [*Movement of Salonica's Democratic Women*] (GC)

KDH .... Kandahar [*Afghanistan*] [*Airport symbol*] (OAG)

KDH .... Kepala Daerah [*Chief of Region*] (IN)

KDI .... Kendari [*Indonesia*] [*Airport symbol*] (OAG)

KDI .... Korea Development Institute (ECON)

KDI .... Kuwaiti Dinar [*Monetary unit*] (DS)

KDI .... Stichting Kwaliteitsdienst voor de Industrie [*Society for Industrial Quality Control*] [*Netherlands*] (PDAA)

KDK .... Ceramic Disc Capacitor (RU)

KDK .... Children Book Pool (RU)

KDK .... Commission for the Compilation of a Dialectological Map of the Russian Language (RU)

KDK .... Kozgazdasagtudomanyi Dokumentacios Kozpont [*Economics Documentation Center*] (HU)

KDK .... Kreis-Direktion fuer den Kraftverkehr [*Kreis Directorate for Motor Traffic*] (EG)

KDK .... State Control Commission (BU)

KDKE .... Kommounistiko Diethnistiko Kinima Elladas [*Communist Internationalist Movement of Greece*] (GC)

KDKhVD... Kray House of Children's Art Education (RU)

KDL .... Compagnie des Chemins de Fer Kinshasa-Dilolo-Lubumbashi [*Kinshasa-Dilolo-Lubumbashi Railway Company*] [*Zaire*] (AF)

KDL .... Kraje Demokracji Ludowej [*People's Democracies*] [*Poland*]

KDL .... Smoke and Volatility Coefficient (RU)

KDL .... Societe des Chemins de Fer Katanga-Dilolo-Leopoldville

KDM.......... Democratic Youth Committee (BU)

KDM.......... Kyrgyzstan Democratic Movement [*Political party*]

KDMalaya ... Kapal Di-Raja Malaya [*Royal Malayan Ship*] (ML)

KDMMA... Kadikoy Devlet Muhendislik ve Mimarlik Akademisi [*Kadikoy State Engineering and Architectural Academy*] [*Istanbul*] (TU)

KDMMA... Konya Devlet Muhendislik ve Mimarlik Akademisi [*Konya State Engineering and Architecture Academy*] (TU)

kdmos........ Kodarithmos [*Code Number*] (GC)

KDN.......... Battalion Commander (RU)

KdN........... Koninkrijk der Nederlanden [*Kingdom of the Netherlands*] [*Dutch*] (BARN)

KDN.......... N'Dende [*Gabon*] [*Airport symbol*] (OAG)

KDNK....... Committee for State and People's Control (BU)

KDNK....... Keluaran Dalam Negeri Kasar [*Gross National Product*] (ML)

KDNP .... Keresztenydemokrata Neppart [*Christian Democratic People's Party*] [*Hungary*] [*Political party*] (EY)

KDO.......... Kendrika Dioikitika Organa [*Central Administrative Organs*] [*Greek*] (GC)

KDO.......... Kendriki Dioikitiki Organosis [*Central Administrative Organization*] [*Greek*] (GC)

Kdo............ Kommando [*German*]

KDO.......... Landing Detachment Commander (RU)

KDOSM ... Combine for the Extraction and Processing of Rock-Lining Materials (BU)

KDP.......... Control Tower [*Aviation*] (RU)

KDP.......... Differential Absorption Coefficient (RU)

KDP.......... Dispatcher's Command Post (RU)

KDP.......... Fire-Control Tower, Plotting Room [*Navy*] (RU)

KDP.......... Horse-Drawn Decontamination Wagon (RU)

KDP.......... Kandep [*Papua New Guinea*] [*Airport symbol*] [*Obsolete*] (OAG)

KDP.......... Kanonovy Delostrelecky Pluk [*Gun Artillery Regiment*] (CZ)

KDP .... Korean Democratic Party [*North Korea*] [*Political party*]   (FEA)
KDP .... Krajske Divadlo Pracujicich [*Regional Workers' Theater*]   (CZ)
KDP .... Kurdish Democratic Party [*Iran*] [*Political party*]
KDP .... Peasants' Democratic Party [*German Democratic Republic*]   (RU)
KDPC .... Korea Design and Packaging Centre [*South Korea*]
KDPC .... Korea Institute of Industrial Design and Packaging   (EAIO)
KDPG .... Peasant's Democratic Party of Germany [*German Democratic Republic*]   (RU)
KDPI......... Kurdish Democratic Party of Iran [*Political party*]   (PPW)
KDPS......... Kurdish Democratic Party of Syria [*Political party*]
KDR.......... Code Relay   (RU)
KDR.......... Kandrian [*Papua New Guinea*] [*Airport symbol*]   (OAG)
KDRMB ..... Code Relay with Magnetic Blocking   (RU)
KDRSh ...... Code Relay with Plug Switching   (RU)
KDRShMB ... Code Relay with Magnetic Blocking and Plug Switching   (RU)
KDRSM..... Komity Demokratika Manohana ny Fototra Iorenan' ny Revolisiona Sosialista Malagasy [*Democratic Committee to Support the Malagasy Socialist Revolution*]   (AF)
KDRT .... Code Relay for Jolting Conditions   (RU)
KDS .... K2 Del Aire SA de CV [*Mexico*] [*ICAO designator*]   (FAAC)
KDS .... Kendrika Dioikitika Somata [*Central Administrative Bodies*] [*Greek*]   (GC)
KDS .... Kendrikon Dioikitikon Symvoulion [*Central Administrative Council*] [*Greek*]   (GC)
KDS .... Kendron Dierkhomenon Stratou [*Army Transients Center*] [*Greek*]   (GC)
KDS .... Khusitan Development Service [*Iran*]
KDS .... Komma Dimokratikou Sosialismou [*Party for Democratic Socialism*] [*Greek*] [*Political party*]   (PPE)
KDS .... Kristen Demokratisk Samling [*Christian Democratic Union*] [*Sweden*] [*Political party*]   (PPE)
KDS .... Oxygen-Producing Plant   (RU)
KDSE......... Katholische Deutsche Studenten-Einigung [*German Catholic Student Union*]   (EG)
Kdstg.......... Klein-Dienstgutzug [*Intra-Enterprise Freight Train*]   (EG)
KDSZ......... Kohaszati Dolgozok Szakszervezete [*Trade Union of Metallurgical Workers*]   (HU)
KdT .... Kammer der Technik [*Chamber of Technology*]   (EG)
kdt .... Komandant [*Commander*]   (YU)
Kdt .... Kommandant [*German*]
KDTK .... Kokusai Digital Tsushin Kikaku [*Telecommunications*] [*Japan*]
KDTM .... Democratic Committee of Youth and Students for the Defense of the Malagasy Socialist Revolution   (AF)
KDTTMB ... Kibris Dahili Telekommunikasyon Turk Mustahdemler Birligi [*Union of Turkish Employees of Cyprus Inland Telecommunications*]   (GC)
KDU.......... Remote-Control Device   (RU)
KDV .... Kandavu [*Fiji*] [*Airport symbol*]   (OAG)
KDV .... Kozlekedesi Dokumentacios Vallalat [*Transportation Documentation Enterprise*]   (HU)
KDV .... Kvinnornas Demokratiska Varldsforbund [*Women's International Democratic Federation*] [*Use WIDF*] [*Sweden*]   (WEN)
KDVS........ Det Kongelige Danske Videnskabernes Selskab [*Denmark*]   (SLS)
KDW .... Komitet Drobnej Wytworczosci [*Small-Scale Industries Committee*]   (POL)
Kdz.......... Karadeniz [*Black Sea*]   (TU)
KDZ.......... Kmetijska Delavna Zadruga [*Peasant Working Cooperative*]   (YU)
kdzh .... Kilojoule   (RU)
KDZTU ..... Karadeniz Teknik Universitesi [*Black Sea Technical University*]   (TU)
KE .... Acarid Encephalitis   (RU)
ke................. Cavalry Squadron, Cavalry Troop   (BU)
KE .... Cruiser Squadron   (RU)
KE .... Electrolytic Capacitor   (RU)
KE .... Kalomelelektrode [*Calomel Electrode*] [*German*]   (GCA)
KE .... Karteneinheit [*German*]   (ADPT)
KE .... Kendriki Epitropi [*Central Committee*]   (GC)
KE .... Kenya [*ANSI two-letter standard code*]   (CNC)
KE .... Kern [*Nucleus or Core*] [*German*]   (ADPT)
ke................. Keskiviikko(na) [*Finland*]
KE .... Kinetic Energy   (RU)
KE .... Komma Ellinososialiston [*Greek Socialists Party*]   (GC)
KE .... Kyvernitiki Epitropi [*or Kyvernitikos Epitropos*] [*Government Committee or Government Commissioner*] [*Greek*]   (GC)
KE .... Oxygen Effect   (RU)
ke................. Starch Equivalent   (RU)
KEA .... Kendron Ekpaidevseos Anapiron [*Training Center for the Handicapped*] [*Greek*]   (GC)
KEA .... Kendron Ethnikis Asfaleias [*National Security Center*]   (GC)
KEA .... Kinima Eniaias Aristeras [*United Left Movement*]   (GC)
KEA .... Kinima Epanastatikis Aristeras [*Movement of the Revolutionary Left*] [*Greek*]   (GC)

KEA .... Kinima Ethnikis Anagenniseos [*Movement of National Regeneration*] [*Greek*]   (GC)
KEA .... Kinima Ethnikis Andistaseos [*National Resistance Movement*] [*Greek*]   (GC)
KEA .... Kinisis Ethnikis Anadimiourgias [*National Regeneration Movement*] [*Grivas*] [*Greek*]   (GC)
KEA .... Koini Evropaiki Agora [*European Common Market*]   (GC)
KEA .... Komma Ethnikis Anagenniseos [*National Rebirth Party*] [*Greek*]   (GC)
KEA .... Kratikon Ergostasion Aeroplanon [*State Aircraft Factory*] [*Greek*]   (GC)
KEADEA... Kinima gia Ethniki Anexartisia Diethni Eirini kai Afoplismo [*Movement for National Independence, International Peace, and Disarmament*]   (GC)
KEAE........ Kendron Erevnon Atomikis Energeias (Andidrastir Kholargou) [*Atomic Energy Research Center (Kholargos Reactor)*] [*Greek*]   (GC)
KEAK .... Kendriki Epitropi Apokatastaseos Kratoumenon [*Central Committee for the Rehabilitation of Prisoners*] [*Greek*]   (GC)
KEAK .... Kinima Ethnikis Apokatastaseos Kyprou [*Movement for the National Restoration of Cyprus*]   (GC)
KEAM .... Concentrate of Anthracene-Oil Emulsion   (RU)
KEAP........ Kendron Ekpaidevseos Anorthodoxou Polemou [*Unconventional Warfare Training Center*] [*Greek*]   (GC)
KeATA...... Kendriki Agora Trofimon Athinon [*Athens Central Food Market*]   (GC)
KEB .... Konstruktions- und Entwicklungsbuero [*Design and Development Office*]   (EG)
KEB .... Korea Exchange Bank   (IMH)
KEB .... Kozponti Ellenorzo Bizottsag [*Central Control Committee*]   (HU)
KEB .... Kuwait Engineering Bureau
KEBKOR... Kernbrandstofkorporasie [*Nuclear Fuel Corporation*] [*South Africa*]   (AF)
KEBORA... Kebudajaan dan Olah Raga [*Culture and Sports*]   (IN)
KEBS........ Kenya Bureau of Standards
KEC .... Korean Engineering Company
KEC .... Korean Evangelical College [*South Korea*]
KECh .... Billeting Operation Unit   (RU)
KECME..... Kuzbass Commodity and Raw Materials Exchange [*Russian Federation*]   (EY)
KECO .... Korea Electric Co.   (PDAA)
KED.......... Customs Duty List [*EEC*]   (GC)
KED.......... Erythema Dose   (RU)
KED.......... Kaedi [*Mauritania*] [*Airport symbol*]   (OAG)
KED.......... Kendriki Epitropi Daneion [*Central Loans Committee*] [*Greek*]   (GC)
KED.......... Kendriki Epitropi Diaitisias [*Central Arbitration Committee*] [*Greek*]   (GC)
KED.......... Kendron Ekpaidevseos Diavivaseon [*Communications Training Center*] [*Greek*]   (GC)
KED.......... Kinima Ethnikis Draseos [*Movement for National Action*] [*Greek*]   (GC)
KED.......... Komma Ethnikis Draseos [*National Action Party*] [*Greek*]   (GC)
KED.......... Kratiki Ekmetallevsis Dason [*State Exploitation of Forests*] [*Greek*]   (GC)
KED.......... Ktimatiki Etaireia Dimosiou [*Public Land Company*]   (GC)
KEDI......... Korea Educational Development Institute
KEDJAGUNG ... Kedjaksaan Agung [*Office of the Attorney General*]   (IN)
KEDJARI ... Kedjaksaan Negeri [*Office of the Public Prosecutor*]   (IN)
KEDJATI ... Kedjaksaan Tinggi [*Office of the District Attorney*]   (IN)
KEDKE...... Kendriki Enosis ton Dimon kai Koinotiton tis Ellados [*Central Union of Municipalities and Communes of Greece*]   (GC)
KEDO....... Korea Energy Development Organisation [*A consortium formed by the US, North Korea, and South Korea to finance and build reactors*]   (ECON)
KEDUBES ... Kedutaan Besar [*Embassy*]   (IN)
KEE .... Kallitechnikon Epimelitirion Ellados [*Greek*]   (SLS)
KEE .... Kelle [*Congo*] [*Airport symbol*]   (OAG)
KEE .... Kendriki Elengtiki Epitropi [*Central Control Committee*] [*Cyprus*]   (GC)
KEE .... Kendron Ekpaidevseos Efedron [*Reserves Training Center*] [*Greek*]   (GC)
KEE .... Kendron Englimatologikon Erevnon [*Criminology Research Center*] [*Greek*]   (GC)
KEE .... Koinoniki Enosis Epistimonon [*Social Union of Professionals*] [*Greek*]   (GC)
KEE .... Komma Ergazomenon Ellados [*Greek Workers' Party*]   (GC)
KEEA .... Kypriaki Enosis Epangelmation Avtokinitiston [*Cypriot Union of Professional Drivers*]   (GC)
KEED .... Kinisis Ethnikis Enoseos Dexias [*National Unification Movement of the Right*] [*Cyprus*]   (GC)
KEEE......... Kendriki Eklogiki Epitropi Ethnikofronon [*Central Electoral Committee of Nationalists*] [*Cyprus*]   (GC)
KEEE......... Kiniton Epidimiologikon Ergastirion Erevnon [*Mobile Epidemiological Research Laboratory*] [*Greek*]   (GC)

KEEF......... Kratikon Ergastirion Elengkhou Farmakon [*National Drug Control Laboratory*] [*Greek*] (GC)

KEEK......... Kentriki Epitropi Epilogis kai Kritirion [*Selection and Criteria Central Committee*] (GC)

KEEM....... Kendron Ekpaidevseos Efodiasmou kai Metaforon [*Supply and Transportation Training Center*] [*Greek*] (GC)

KEEP......... Kendron Epikheirimatikis Epikoinonias kai Provolis [*Center for Entrepreneurial Communication and Projection*] (GC)

KEEPTh .... Kendriki Eforevtiki Epitropi Paidopoleon Thessalonikis [*Central Supervisory Committee for Salonica Children's Centers*] (GC)

KEES......... Komma Ethnikis ton Ellinon Sotirias [*Party for the National Salvation of Greeks*] (GC)

KEEThA.... Kendron Erevnon Ethnikis Amynis [*National Defense Research Center*] [*Greek*] (GC)

KEF........... Kabinet pro Etnografii a Folkloristiku [*Ethnography and Folklore Department (of the Czechoslovak Academy of Sciences)*] (CZ)

kef............. Kefalaion [*Chapter (of Document)*] (GC)

KEF........... Reykjavik [*Iceland*] Keflavik Airport [*Airport symbol*] (OAG)

KEFE......... Kendriki Enosis Froutoparagogon Ellados [*Central Fruitgrowers Union of Greece*] (GC)

KEFEM..... Kemenyfemipari Vallalat [*Hard Metal Industry Enterprise*] (HU)

kEFr.......... Kilo Energetische Futtereinheit [*1,000 High Energy Fodder Units for Beef Cattle*] (EG)

KEG.......... Examining and Evacuation Hospital (RU)

KEGE........ Kendron Erevnon kai Georgikis Ekpaidevseos [*Research and Agricultural Training Center*] (GC)

KEGE........ Kendron Georgikis Ekpaidevseos [*Agricultural Training Center*] [*Greek*] (GC)

KEGEPOA ... Kendriki Gnomodotiki Epitropi Programmatos Oikonomikis Politikis [*Central Advisory Committee for Economic Policy Programs*] [*Greek*] (GC)

KEI............ Commission for Expeditionary Research (of the Academy of Sciences, USSR) (RU)

KEI............ Kenoolaj Ellenorzo Intezet [*Quality Control Institute on Lubricating Oils*] (HU)

KEI............ Kepi [*Indonesia*] [*Airport symbol*] (OAG)

KEI............ Kozponti Eloadoi Iroda [*Central Office of Special Consultants*] (HU)

KEI............ Kozponti Elorejelzo Intezet [*Central Forecasting Institute*] (HU)

KEIA......... Kodaly Education Institute of Australia

KEIB......... Chair of Epidemiology and Communicable Diseases (BU)

KEIDANREN ... Keizaidantai Rengo-Kai [*Japan Federation of Economic Organizations*] (EY)

Keikinzokuroren ... Zenkoku Keikinzoku Rodokumiai Rengokai [*National Council of Light Metal Industry Workers' Unions*] [*Japan*]

KEIS......... Kiev Experimental Research Plant [*Of the NIISMI*] (RU)

KEISZ....... Kepzomuveszek es Iparmuveszek Szovetsege [*Association of Artists and Designers*] (HU)

keitt........... Keittotaito [*Culinary Art, Cookery*] [*Finland*]

KEK.......... Kendron Epangelmatikis Katartiseos [*Vocational Training Center*] (GC)

KEK.......... Konferenz Europaeischer Kirchen [*Conference of European Churches - CEC*] (EA)

KEK.......... Konferenz Evangelischer Kirchen Europas [*Conference of European Protestant Churches*] (EG)

KEK.......... Kozepeuropa-Kupa [*Central Europe Cup (Sports)*] (HU)

KEK.......... Kypriakon Ethnikon Komma [*Cypriot National Party (1944-1960)*] [*Greek Cypriot*] [*Political party*] (PPE)

KEK.......... Kyvernitiki Epitropi Kapnou [*Government Tobacco Committee*] [*Greek*] (GC)

KEK.......... Marx Karoly Kozgazdasagi Egyetem Kozponti Konyvtara [*Central Library of the Karl Marx School of Economics*] (HU)

KEKATE ... Kendron Mathiteias kai Takhyrrythmou Epangelmatikis Katartiseos Enilikon [*Apprenticeship and Rapid Vocational Training Center for Adults*] (GC)

KeKE......... Kendriki Kallitekhniki Epitropi [*Central Artistic Committee*] [*Greek*] (GC)

KEKELE.... Jeunesse Ngufu-Madimba-Kinzambi-Kinfunda-Ladi

KEKI........ Kozponti Elelmiszeripari Kutatointezet [*Central Research Institute of the Food Industry*] (HU)

KEKMA .... Kinisi gia Eniaio Komma Marxistikis Aristeras [*Movement for a United Party of the Marxist Left*] [*Greek*] (GC)

KEKN........ Kendron Ergazomenon Koritsion kai Neotiton [*Center for Working Girls and Youths*] [*Greek*] (GC)

k ekv.......... Starch Equivalent (RU)

KEL........... Karntner Einheitsliste [*Carinthian Unity List*] [*Austria*] [*Political party*] (PPE)

KEL........... Koroska Enotna Lista [*Carinthian Unity List*] [*Austria*] [*Political party*] (PPE)

KELI......... Kristaina Esperantista Ligo Internacia [*International Christian Esperanto Association*] [*Netherlands*] (SLS)

KELI......... Kristana Esperantista Ligo Internacia [*International Christian Esperanto Association*] (EAIO)

KELS......... Kendron Ekpaidevseos tou Limenikou Somatos [*Port Corps Training Center*] [*Greek*] (GC)

KELTEX.... Kelenfoldi Textilkombinat [*Kelenfold Textile Concern*] (HU)

KELV......... Kendriki Epitropi Logistikon Vivlion [*Central Accounts Board*] (GC)

KEM .... Electromagnetic Classifier (RU)

KEM .... Kemi [*Finland*] [*Airport symbol*] (OAG)

kem .... Kemia [*Chemistry*] [*Finland*]

KEM .... Kendron Ekpaidevseos Mikhanikou [*Engineers Training Center*] [*Greek*] (GC)

KEM .... Kendron Ekpaidevseos Mikhanokiniton [*Mechanized Forces Training Center*] [*Greek*] (GC)

KEM .... Kontzientzi Eragozpen Mugimendua [*Basque Anti-Militarist and Conscientious Objection Movement*] [*Spain*]

KEM .... Kooperation Evangelischer Kirchen und Missionen [*Switzerland*] (EAIO)

KEM .... Kypriaki Etaireia Metaforon [*Cyprus Transport Company*] (GC)

KEMA .... NV tot Keuring van Elektrotechnische Materialen [*Office for the Inspection of Electrotechnical Material*] [*Netherlands*] (WEN)

KEMAM ... Kesatuan Malaya Merdeka [*Free Malaya Front*] (ML)

KEMAS.... Kelantan Malay Syndicate (ML)

KEMCO .... Korea Energy Management Corp. [*South Korea*]

KEME ...... Kendron Ekpaidevtikon Meleton kai Epimorphosis [*Center for Educational Research and Training (Development)*] (GC)

KEME ...... Kendron Epitheoriseos Mesis Ekpaidevseos [*Secondary Education Supervision Center*] (GC)

KEMEDI... Kendron Metafraston kai Diermineon [*Center for Translators and Interpreters*] (GC)

KEMI........ Kereskedelmi Minosegellenorzo Intezet [*Commercial Quality Control Institute*] (HU)

KEMK ...... Kendron Ekpaidevseos Monadon Katadromon [*Raiding Forces Training Center*] [*Greek*] (GC)

KEML........ Kinisi Ellinon Marxiston-Leniniston [*Movement of Greek Marxist-Leninists*] (GC)

KEMRI...... Kenya Medical Research Institute (IRC)

KEMSA..... Kemik Urunleri Sanayi ve Ticaret AS [*Bone Products Industry and Trade Corp.*] (TU)

KEMZ .... Kaluga Electromechanical Plant (RU)

KEMZ .... Kemerovo Electromechanical Plant (RU)

KEMZ .... Kiev Electromechanical Plant (RU)

KEMZ .... Kurgan Electromechanical Plant (RU)

KEMZ .... Moscow Motion-Picture Electromechanical Equipment Plant (RU)

ken .... Candidate of Economic Sciences (RU)

KEN .... Kendron Ekpaidevseos Neosyllekton [*Recruit Training Center*] [*Greek*] (GC)

KEN .... Kenema [*Sierra Leone*] [*Airport symbol*] (OAG)

KEN .... Kenya [*ANSI three-letter standard code*] (CNC)

KENATCO ... Kenya National Transport Company

KENDACOL ... Industrias Kendall de Colombia Ltda. [*Colombia*] (COL)

KENE .... Kendriki Epitropi Nomothetikis Ergasias [*Central Legislative Processing Committee*] [*Greek*] (GC)

KENEXTEL ... Kenya External Telecommunications Co.

KENPRO... Kenyan Committee on Trade Procedures (PDAA)

kenr........... Kenraali [*Finland*]

kenrluutn ... Kenraaliluutnantti [*Finland*]

kenrmaj..... Kenraalimajuri [*Finland*]

Kensetsurengo ... Nihon Kensetsu Kumiai Rengo [*Japan Construction Workers' Council*]

KENSO ..... Kensington Racecourse [*Australia*] (DSUE)

KENSTA ... Kenya Stationers Ltd.

KENTAS... Kimya Endustrisi ve Ticaret Anonim Sirketi [*Chemical Industry and Trade Corporation*] (TU)

KENYAC... Kenya National Capital Corp. Ltd.

KEO.......... Design and Experimental Department (RU)

KEO.......... Housing Operation Department (RU)

KEO.......... Kray Export Association (RU)

KEO.......... Odienne [*Ivory Coast*] [*Airport symbol*] (OAG)

KEOK....... Kulfoldiekt Ellenorzo Orszagos Kozpont [*National Center of Alien Registration*] (HU)

KEOKH..... Kulfoldieket Ellenorzo Orszagos Kozponti Hatosag [*National Center of Alien Registration*] (HU)

KEOM .... Kendron Ekpaidevseos Oreinon Metaforon [*Mountain Transport Training Center*] [*Greek*] (GC)

KEONICS ... Karnataka State Electronics Development Corporation Ltd. [*India*]

KEP............ Catelectrotonic Potential (RU)

KEP............ Electric Instruction Device (RU)

KEP............ Electropneumatic Instruction Device (RU)

KEP............ Examining and Evacuation Station (RU)

KEP............ Kendriki Epitropi Protathlimatos [*Central Championship Committee (of the Greek Soccer Federation)*] (GC)

KEP........... Kendron Ekpaidevseos Pyrovolikou [*Artillery Training Center*] [*Greek*] (GC)

KEP........... Kendron Epangelmatikou Prosanatolismou [*Occupational Orientation Center*] [*Greek*] (GC)

KEP........... Keputusan [*Directive*] (IN)

KEP........... Nepalganj [*Nepal*] [*Airport symbol*] (OAG)

KEPA........ Kendron Endatikon Programmaton Anaptyxeos [*Center of Intensive Development Planning*] (GC)

KEPA........ Kendron Paragogikotitos [*Productivity Center*] [*Greek*] (GC)

KEPE........ Kendriki Epitropi Prosfygon Ellados [*Central Committee of Greek Refugees*] (GC)

KEPE........ Kendron Programmatismou kai Oikonomikon Erevnon [*Center for Planning and Economic Research or Center for Planning and Research*] [*Greek*] (GC)

KEPEL...... Kynigetiki Enosis Poleos-Eparkhias Lemesou [*Limassol City and District Hunters Union*] [*Cyprus*] (GC)

KEPES...... Kendriki Epitropi Prostasias tis Engkhoriou Sitoparagogis [*Central Committee for the Protection of Domestic Wheat Production*] [*Greek*] (GC)

KEPIP .... Komisja Episkopatu Polski Iustitia et Pax [*Poland*] (EAIO)

KEPOA...... Kendriki Epitropi Programmatos Oikonomikis Anaptyxeos [*Central Committee for the Economic Development Program*] [*Greek*] (GC)

KEPOS...... Koinofelis Epikheirisis Poleodomias, Oikismou, kai Stegaseos [*Town Planning and Housing Public Utility Enterprise*] (GC)

KEPOS...... Kratiki Epikheirisis Poleodomias, Oikismou, Stegaseos [*State Town Planning and Housing Enterprise*] [*Greek*] (GC)

KEPPE ...... Kendriki Epitropi Politikon Prosfygon Ellados [*Central Committee of Greek Political Refugees*] (GC)

KEPPRES ... Keputusan Presiden [*Presidential Directive*] (IN)

KEPRO...... Office for Operation, Rental, and Servicing of Equipment (of the Metrostroy) (RU)

kepsomuv .. Kepzomuveszetek [*or Kepzomuveszeti*] [*Fine Arts or Of Fine Arts*] (HU)

KEPZ........ Karachi Export Processing Zone [*Pakistan*] (EY)

KEQ.......... Kebar [*Indonesia*] [*Airport symbol*] (OAG)

ker............. Keraaminen Teollisuus [*Ceramics*] [*Finland*]

ker............. Kereszteny [*Christian*] [*Hungary*] (GPO)

KER .... Kerman [*Iran*] [*Airport symbol*] (OAG)

ker............. Kerulet [*District*] [*Hungary*] (GPO)

KER .... Kurzfristige Erfolgsrechnung [*German*] (ADPT)

keram........ Ceramics Plant [*Topography*] (RU)

Keram .... Keramik [*Ceramics*] [*German*] (GCA)

Keramik-Is ... Turkish Porcelain, Cement, Brick, and Soils Industries Workers Union (TU)

Keramostroj ... Zavody na Vyrobu Keramickych Stroju [*Plants for the Manufacture of Ceramics Machinery*] (CZ)

KERAVILL ... Kerekpar, Radio, es Villamossagi Kiskereskedelmi Vallalat [*Retail Trade Enterprise for Bicycles, Radios, and Electrical Appliances*] (HU)

KERAZ...... Keramicke Zavody [*Ceramics Works*] (CZ)

Ker es IpKam ... Kereskedelmi es Iparkamara [*Chamber of Commerce and Industry*] (HU)

KERINFORG ... Belkereskedelmi Ugyvitelszervezesi es Informaciofeldolgozasi Intezet [*Management Organization and Information Processing Institute of Domestic Trade*] (HU)

KERIPAR ... Kereskedelmi Asztalos es Lakatosipari Vallalat [*Carpenters and Locksmiths Trade Enterprise*] (HU)

KERM .... Komitet Ekonomiczny Rady Ministrow [*Economic Committee of the Council of Ministers*] (POL)

KERMI...... Kereskedelmi Minosegellenorzo Intezet [*Commercial Quality Control Institute*] (HU)

kers .... Kersantti [*Finland*]

KERTVALL ... Kertgondozo Vallalat [*Park Maintenance Organization*] (HU)

KES........... Kendriki Epitropi Sporoparagogis [*Seed Production Central Committee*] [*Greek*] (GC)

KES........... Kendrikon Ekklisiastikon Symvoulion [*Central Ecclesiastical Council*] [*Greek*] (GC)

KES........... Kendrikon Epoptikon Symvoulion [*Central Supervisory Council*] [*Greek*] (GC)

KES........... Kinima Elevtherou Syndikalismou [*Free Labor Movement*] [*Greek*] (GC)

KES........... Konferencija Evropskih Statisticara [*Conference of European Statisticians*] (YU)

KES........... Kray Economic Conference (RU)

KES........... Kvakera Esperantista Societo [*Quaker Esperanto Society - QES*] (EAIO)

KES........... Motion-Picture Electric Power Unit (RU)

KES........... Space Power Plant (RU)

KESA........ Kendron Ekpaidevseos Stratiotikis Astynomias [*Military Police Training Center*] [*Greek*] (GC)

Kesk .... Keskustapuolue [*Center Party*] [*Finland*]

kesk.......... Keskustapuoluelainen [*Finland*]

KESMA..... Kenya Sugar Manufacturers' Association

KESPEKRI ... Kesatuan Pekerdja Keristen Indonesia [*Indonesian Christian Workers Association*] (IN)

KESSBANEG ... Kesatuan Serikat-Serikat Sekerdja Bank-Bank Negara [*Federation of State Bank Trade Unions*] (IN)

KEST .... Kypriakos Ergodotikos Syndesmos Trapezon [*Cyprus Bankers Employers Association*] (EAIO)

KEST .... Studiengesellschaft fur Forderung der Kernenergieverwertung in Schiffbau und Schiffahrt [*Study Group on the Requirements if Nuclear Energy is Applied to Shipbu ilding and Navigation*] [*Germany*] (PDAA)

kestom....... Kestomuodossa [*Progressive Form*] [*Finland*]

kesz .... Keszitette [*Prepared By*] (HU)

KESZ........ Kutatasi Ellatasi Szolgalat [*Research Supply Service*] (HU)

KET .... Kendron Ekpaidevseos Tethorakismenon [*Armored Forces Training Center*] [*Greek*] (GC)

KET .... Kengtung [*Myanmar*] [*Airport symbol*] (OAG)

KETA........ Kenya External Trade Authority

KETE........ Kendra Epangelmatikis kai Tekhnikis Ekpaidevseos [*Vocational and Technical Education Centers*] [*KATE, KATEE*] [*See also*] (GC)

KETI......... Kisipari Exportra Termelteto Iroda [*Office for Promoting Export Production by Artisans*] (HU)

KETJ .... Ketjamatan [*District*] (IN)

KETRI ...... Kenya Trypanosomiasis Research Institute

KETS .... Kendron Ekpaidevseos Tekhnikou Somatos [*Technical Corps Training Center*] [*Greek*] (GC)

KEU .... Housing Operation Administration (RU)

KEU .... Kommunalekonomiska Utredningen [*Sweden*]

kEV .... Continental Equatorial Air (RU)

KEV .... Enameled High-Voltage Composition [*Resistor*] (RU)

kev .... Kilo Electron Volt (RU)

KeV .... Kiloelektronenvolt [*Kilo Electron Volt*] (EG)

keV .... Kiloelektronovolt [*Kilo Electron Volt*] [*Poland*]

KeV .... Koningin en Vaderland [*Benelux*] (BAS)

KEV .... Kozlekedesi Epito Vallalat [*Construction Enterprise for Transportation Facilities*] (HU)

KEVA .... Kendriki Epitropi Voreioipeirotikou Agonos [*Central Committee of the Northern Ipeiros Struggle*] [*See also KEVIA*] [*Greek*] (GC)

KEVA .... Kendron Ethnikis Viomikhanikis Anaptyxeos [*Center for National Industrial Development*] [*Greek*] (GC)

KEVA .... Kendron Viotekhnikis Anaptyxeos [*Center for Development of Crafts*] [*Greek*] (GC)

KEVE........ Kypriakon Emborikon kai Viomikhanikon Epimelitirion [*Cyprus Chamber of Commerce and Industry*] (GC)

KEVIA ...... Kendriki Epitropi Voreioipeirotikou Agonos [*Central Committee of the Northern Ipeiros Struggle*] [*See also KEVA*] [*Greek*] (GC)

KEVOP...... Kendron Ekpaidevseos Vareon Oplon Pezikou [*Infantry Heavy Weapons Training Center*] [*Greek*] (GC)

KEWA .... Kernbrennstoff-Wiederaufarbeitungs-Gesellschaft mbH [*Nuclear energy*] (NRCH)

KEWIS ...... Kommunales Einwohner-Informationssystem [*German*] (ADPT)

KEX .... Kanabea [*Papua New Guinea*] [*Airport symbol*] (OAG)

KEY .... Kendron Ekpaidevseos Ygeionomikou [*Medical Service Training Center*] [*Greek*] (GC)

KEYP........ Kendron Ekpaidevseos Ylikou Polemou [*Ordnance Training Center*] [*Greek*] (GC)

kez............ Kezelo [*Operator, Attendant*] (HU)

kezb........... Kezbesitve [*Delivered by Hand*] (HU)

kezirat gy ... Kezirat Gyanant [*In Manuscript Form*] (HU)

KF .... Caspian Flotilla (RU)

kf................ Cationite Filter (BU)

KF .... Creatine Phosphate (RU)

KF .... Fale Krotkie [*Short Waves*] [*Poland*]

KF .... Front Commander (RU)

KF .... Kabinet Filosofie [*Department of Philosophy (of the Czechoslovak Academy of Sciences)*] (CZ)

KF .... Kemisk Forening [*Danish Chemical Society*] (EAIO)

KF .... Kepzomuveszeti Foiskola [*Academy of Fine Arts*] (HU)

KF .... Keramidas Freres et Fils

KF .... Komma Fileleftheron [*Liberal or Neo-Liberal Party*] [*Greek*] (GC)

KF .... Kommunistisk Forbund (M-L) [*Communist League (Marxist-Leninist)*] [*Denmark*] (WEN)

KF .... Konservative Folkeparti [*Conservative People's Party (Commonly called the Conservative Party)*] [*Denmark*] [*Political party*] (PPE)

KF .... Kontrafagott [*Double Bassoon*] [*Organ stop Music*]

KF .... Kooperativa Forbundet [*Consumers' Cooperative Union*] [*Sweden*] (WEN)

KF .... Koroski Fuzinar [*Carinthian Ironsmith*] [*Gustanj A periodical*] (YU)

kf................ Kozepfoku [*Secondary (School)*] (HU)

KF .... Kratky Film Praha [*Film Shorts Prague*] (CZ)

KF .... Kuaj Fuqi [*Albanian*]

KF .... Kuebel Foundation [*Germany*] (EAIO)
KF .... Kultura Fizyczna [*Physical Culture*] (POL)
K + F .... Kutatas-Fejlesztes [*Research and Development*] (HU)
KF .... Kvinnor for Fred [*Women for Peace*] [*Sweden*] (EAIO)
k/f .... Motion Picture (RU)
KF .... Rhine Air AG [*Sweden*] [*ICAO designator*] (ICDA)
KfA .... Kammer fuer Aussenhandel [*Chamber for Foreign Trade*] (EG)
KFA .... Kenya Farmers Association Ltd.
KFA .... Kernforschungsanlage Juelich [*Juelich Nuclear Research Center*] [*Research center*] (IRC)
KFA .... Kiffa [*Mauritania*] [*Airport symbol*] (OAG)
KFAED ..... Kuwaiti Fund for Arab Economic Development (ME)
KFAN .... Kazan' Branch of the Academy of Sciences, USSR (RU)
KFAN .... Kola Branch of the Academy of Sciences, USSR (RU)
KFAP .... Krakowska Fabryka Aparatow Pomiarowych [*Krakow Measurement Apparatus Plant*] (POL)
KFAS .... Kuwait Foundation for the Advancement of Sciences [*Research center*] (IRC)
KFB .... Kozsegi Foldigenylo Bizottsag [*Village Committee on Land Claims*] (HU)
KFB .... Kuwait French Bank
KFC .... Kenya Film Corporation
KFC .... Kerala Finance Corp. [*India*] (PDAA)
KFESRAS ... Kuveitskii Fond Ekonomicheskovo i Sotsial'novo Razvitiia Arabskikh Stran
KFF .... Kenya Football Federation
KFF .... Kvinnenes Frie Folkevalgte [*Women's Freely Elected Representatives*] [*Norway*] [*Political party*] (PPE)
KFFHC ...... Kenya Freedom from Hunger Council for National Development (EAIO)
KFH .... Kuwait Finance House
KFIA .... King Fahd International Airport [*Saudi Arabia*]
k fin n .... Candidate of Financial Sciences (BU)
KFK .... Kernforschungszentrum Karlsruhe GmbH [*Nuclear Research Center*] [*Karlsruhe, West Germany*]
KFKI .... Koezponti Fizikai Kutato Intezet [*Central Research Institute of Physics*] [*Budapest, Hungary*] [*Research center*] (HU)
KFKI .... Kuratorium fuer Forschung im Kuesteningenieurwesen [*Coastal Engineering Research Council*] [*Germany*] (EAS)
KFKI .... Kuratorium fuer Forschung im Kusteningenieurwesen [*Coastal Engineering Research Council*] [*Germany*] (ERC)
KFKis .... Committee for Physical Culture and Sports (RU)
KFKP .... Kodix Forologias Katharas Prosodou [*Net Income Tax Code*] [*Greek*] (GC)
kfl .... Kaeuflich [*Commercial Grade*] [*German*] (GCA)
KFL .... Kenya Federation of Labor (AF)
KFL .... Kenya Flamingo Airways Ltd. [*ICAO designator*] (FAAC)
KfL .... Kreisbetrieb fuer Landtechnik [*Kreis Enterprise for Agricultural Equipment*] (EG)
KFL .... Kunngjoring fra Luftfartsstyret [*Norway*]
kfm .... Kaufmaennisch [*Commercial*] (EG)
Kfm .... Kaufmann [*Merchant*] (EG)
KFML .... Kommunistiska Foerbundet Marxist-Leninisterna [*Communist League of Marxist-Leninists*] [*Sweden*] [*Political party*] (PPE)
KFML(r) .... Kommunistiska Foerbundet Marxist-Leninisterna (Revolutionar) [*Communist League of Marxists-Leninists (Revolutionary)*] [*Sweden*] (WEN)
k f-m n .... Candidate of Physical and Mathematical Sciences (RU)
kfn .... Candidate of Philological Sciences (RU)
kfn .... Candidate of Philosophical Sciences (RU)
k f n .... Candidate of Physical Sciences (BU)
KFN .... Komitet Frontu Narodowego [*Committee of the People's Front*] (POL)
KFP .... Komisja Funduszu Posmiertnego [*Commission on the Death Benefit Fund*] (POL)
KFP .... Konstitutionella Folkpartiet [*Constitutional People's Party*] [*Finland*] [*Political party*] (PPE)
KFP .... Korean Fighter Program
KFP .... Kozponti Fejlesztesi Programok [*Central Development Programs*] (HU)
KFP .... Kristelig Folkeparti [*Christian People's Party*] [*Norway*] (WEN)
KFPC .... Kassala Fruit Processing Co. Ltd. [*Sudan*]
KFRD .... Koor Foods' Research and Development [*Israel*] (IRC)
KFRI .... Kerala Forest Research Institute [*India*] (ARC)
KFS .... Committee for Physical Culture and Sports (BU)
KFS .... Kallopistikos kai Filanthropikos Syllogos Aigaleo "I Proodos" [*"The Proodos" Beautification and Charitable Club of Aigaleo*] [*Greek*] (GC)
KFS .... Kodix Forologikon Stoikheion [*Tax Revenue Data Code*] (GC)
KFS .... Kontrollfernschreiber [*German*] (ADPT)
KFSA .... Keep Fit South Australia
KFSB .... Korea Federation of Small Business [*South Korea*] (FEA)
KFSH &RC ... King Faisal Specialist Hospital and Research Center [*Saudi Arabia*]
KFSKh .... Kinisi Foititon Skholis Khimikon [*Movement of Chemistry School Students*] [*Greek*] (GC)

KFSSR ...... Karelo-Finnish Soviet Socialist Republic [*1940-1956*] (RU)
KFST .... Kuestenfunkstelle [*Coastal Radio Station*] (EG)
kft .... Korlatolt Felelossegu Tarsasag [*Limited Liability Company*] (HU)
KFTA .... Korea Foreign Trade Association (EAIO)
KFTCIC .... Kuwait Foreign Trading, Contracting & Investment Co.
KFTD .... Kibris Federe Turk Devleti [*Turkish Federated State of Cyprus*] (GC)
KFTU .... Kampuchean Federation of Trade Unions (FEA)
KFTU .... Korean Federation of Trade Unions [*North Korea*]
KFU .... King Faisal University [*Saudi Arabia*] (PDAA)
KFUK .... Kristelig Forening for Unge Kvinder [*Young Women's Christian Associations - YWCA*] [*Denmark*]
KFUM .... Kristelig Forening for Unge Maend [*Young Men's Christian Associations - YMCA*] [*Denmark*]
KFUPM ..... King Fahd University of Petroleum and Minerals [*Saudi Arabia*]
KFUPM-RI ... King Fahd University of Petroleum and Minerals, Research Institute [*Saudi Arabia*] (EAS)
KFUT .... Klodzka Fabryka Urzadzen Technicznych [*Klodzko (Glatz) Technical Equipment Factory*] (POL)
KFV .... Koolajkutato es Feltaro Vallalat [*Enterprise for Oil Prospecting and Drilling*] (HU)
KfV .... Kuratorium fuer Verkehrssicherheit [*Research center*] [*Austria*] (ERC)
KF VNII .... Krasnodar Branch of the All-Union Scientific Research Institute of Petroleum and Gas (RU)
KFVNIIneft' ... Krasnodar Branch of the All-Union Scientific Research Institute of Petroleum and Gas (RU)
KfW .... Kreditanstalt fuer Wiederaufbau [*Reconstruction Credit Institution, Loan Bank*] (EG)
KfW .... Kreditanstalt fur Wiederaufbau [*Finance*] [*Germany*]
KfW .... Kuratorium fuer Wasserwirtschaft eV [*Water Conservation Board*] (SLS)
KFWM ...... Krasnicka Fabryka Wyrobow Metalowych [*Krasnik Metal Products Plant*] (POL)
KFX .... Korean Foreign Exchange (IMH)
KfZ .... Katalysatorfahrzeugen [*Catalyst-Outfitted Auto*] [*German*]
Kfz .... Kraftfahrzeug [*Motor Vehicle*] [*German*] (EG)
KG .... Coke-Oven Gas (RU)
KG .... Corps Hospital (RU)
KG .... Kabinet pro Geomorfologii [*Department of Geomorphology (of the Czechoslovak Academy of Sciences)*] (CZ)
KG .... Kamara Group Ltd. [*Ghana*]
KG .... Kammergericht [*District Court, Berlin*] [*German*] (DLA)
Kg .... Kampong [*or Kampung*] [*Village, Settlement Malay*] (NAU)
Kg .... Kampong [*or Kampung*] [*Village, Settlement Indonesian*] (NAU)
KG .... Karang [*Coral Reef, Reef*] [*Malay*] (NAU)
KG .... Karta Gornicza [*Miner's Identity Card*] (POL)
KG .... Katastralgemeinde [*German*]
kg .... Kilo [*Finland*]
kg .... Kilogram [*Albanian*]
kg .... Kilogramm [*Kilogram*] [*German*] (EG)
kg .... Kilogramma(a) [*Kilogram*] [*Finland*]
kg .... Kilogramme [*Kilogram*] [*French*]
Kg .... Kilogramo [*Kilogram*] [*Spanish*]
KG .... Kilogram Sily [*Kilogram-Force*] [*Poland*]
KG .... Kmetijsko Gospodarstvo [*Farm Economy*] (YU)
Kg .... Koenig [*German*]
KG .... Komenda Glowna [*Main Headquarters*] (POL)
KG .... Komitet Glowny [*Main Committee*] (POL)
KG .... Komitet Gminny [*Poland*]
KG .... Kommandant-Generaal [*Commandant-General*] [*Afrikaans*]
KG .... Kommanditgesellschaft [*Limited Partnership*] [*German*]
Kg .... Kompong [*Often part of a place name*] [*Cambodia*] (CL)
KG .... Konsumgenossenschaft [*Consumer Cooperative*] (EG)
KG .... Koppelgruppe [*German*] (ADPT)
kg .... Kort Geding [*Benelux*] (BAS)
KG .... Krajska Galeria [*Regional Gallery*] (CZ)
KG .... Main Contactor (RU)
KGA .... Kananga [*Zaire*] [*Airport symbol*] (OAG)
KGA .... Kyrghyzstan Airlines [*ICAO designator*] (FAAC)
KGA .... Mountain Horse Artillery (RU)
KGaA .... Kommanditgesellschaft auf Aktien [*Limited Partnership with Shares*] [*German*]
KGAA .... Kungliga Gustav Adolfs Akademien (SLS)
KGAP .... Kommunistische Gruppe Arbeiter-Politik [*Communist Group for Workers' Policies*] [*Switzerland*] (WEN)
KGB .... Committee of State Security (PWGL)
KGB .... Kampfgruppenbataillon [*Workers Militia Battalion*] (EG)
KGB .... Komitet Gosudarstvennoi Bezopasnosti [*Committee of State Security*] [*Russian Secret Police Also satirically interpreted as Kontora Grubykh Banditov, or "Office of Crude Bandits"*]
KGB .... Konge [*Papua New Guinea*] [*Airport symbol*] (OAG)
KGC .... Kibris Gaziler Cemiyeti [*League of Cypriot Veterans*] [*Turkish Cypriot*] (GC)

KGC .... Kingscote [*Australia*] [*Airport symbol*]   (OAG)
KGCAE...... Kelvin Grove College of Advanced Education [*Australia*]   (ADA)
kgcc .... Kilograme de Combustibil Conventional [*Kilograms of Conventional Fuel*]   (RO)
KGCC .... Korea General Chemical Corp.
KGDB .... Kozponti Gazdasagi Dontobizottsag [*Central Economic Arbitration Committee*]   (HU)
KGE .... Kendron Georgikis Ekpaidevseos [*Agricultural Training Center*] [*Greek*]   (GC)
KGEN .... Kendriko Grafeio tis Ergatikis Neolaias [*Central Office for Working Youth*] [*Cyprus*]   (GC)
k geogr k .... Candidate of Geographic Sciences   (BU)
KGF .... Kriegsgefangener [*Prisoner of War*] [*German*]
KGG.......... Kedougou [*Senegal*] [*Airport symbol*]   (OAG)
KGGA .... Kenya Girl Guides Association   (EAIO)
KGH .... Kommunaler Grosshandel [*Communal Wholesale Enterprise*]   (EG)
KGHM ...... Kombinat Gorniczo-Hutniczy Miedzi [*Poland*]   (EE)
KGI .... Kalgoorlie [*Australia*] [*Airport symbol*]   (OAG)
KGI .... Kano Guest Inn Ltd. [*Nigeria*]
KGI .... Kompleksni Godisnji Izvestaj [*Consolidated Annual Report*]   (YU)
KGJ .... Karonga [*Malawi*] [*Airport symbol*]   (OAG)
KGK .... Hermetically Sealed Ceramic Capacitor   (RU)
KGL .... Kigali [*Rwanda*] [*Airport symbol*]   (OAG)
KGL .... Koeniglich [*Royal*] [*German*]
KGL .... Kombinatsgewerkschaftsleitung [*Combine Trade-Union Headquarters*] [*German*]   (EG)
kgl .... Kongelig [*Royal*] [*Denmark*]   (GPO)
KGM.......... Karayollari Genel Mudurlugu [*Highways Directorate General*]   (TU)
kgm .... Kilogrammametri(a) [*Finland*]
kgm .... Kilogrammeter [*Albanian*]
kGm .... Kilogram Meter   (RU)
kgm .... Kilogrammetre [*Kilogram Meter*] [*French*]
KGM.......... Koho- es Gepipari Miniszterium/Miniszter [*Ministry/Minister of Metallurgical and Machine Industries*]   (HU)
KGM .... Kutuphaneler Genel Mudurlugu [*Libraries Directorate General*] [*Under Ministry of Culture*]   (TU)
KGMI .... Kalinin State Medical Institute   (RU)
KGMI .... Kazakh Mining and Metallurgical Institute   (RU)
KGMI .... Kazan' State Medical Institute   (RU)
KGMI .... Kemerovo State Medical Institute   (RU)
KGMI .... Kishinev State Medical Institute   (RU)
KGMI .... Kursk State Medical Institute   (RU)
KGMI .... Kuybyshev State Medical Institute   (RU)
k g-m n ..... Candidate of Geological and Mineralogical Sciences   (RU)
KGMP ...... Data-Collecting Hydrometeorological Station   (RU)
KGMTI...... Koho- es Gepipari Miniszterium Tervezo Irodai [*Planning Offices of the Ministry of Metallurgy and Machine Industry*]   (HU)
KGMZ ...... Kerch' State Metallurgical Plant Imeni P. L. Voykov   (RU)
kgn .... Candidate of Geographical Sciences   (RU)
KGO.......... Kiruna Geophysical Observatory [*Sweden*]   (PDAA)
KGO.......... Kommunist Genclik Orgutu [*Communist Youth Organization (Network)*]   (TU)
KGO.......... Kozmikus Geodeziai Obszervatorium [*Cosmic Geodesic Observatory*]   (HU)
KGP .... Commandant of Mountain Pass   (RU)
KGP .... Kmetijsko Gozdarsko Posestvo [*Agricultural and Forest Property*] [*YU*]
KGP .... Komma Georgiou Papandreou [*Party of George Papandreou*] [*Greek*] [*Political party*]   (PPE)
KG PAN .... Komitet Geograficzny Polskiej Akademii Nauk [*Polish Academy of Sciences Committee on Geography*]   (POL)
KGPI.......... Kaluga State Pedagogical Institute   (RU)
KGPI.......... Kiev State Pedagogical Institute Imeni A. M. Gor'kiy   (RU)
KGPI.......... Kirgiz State Pedagogical Institute   (RU)
KGPI.......... Kishinev State Pedagogical Institute Imeni I. Kryange   (RU)
KGPI.......... Kuybyshev State Pedagogical Institute Imeni V. V. Kuybyshev   (RU)
KGR .... Galvanic Skin Reflex   (RU)
KGR .... Kierownictwo Grupy Robot [*Management of a Work Unit*]   (POL)
kgr .... Kilogram   (BU)
kgr .... Kizigranat [*Hand Grenade*]   (HU)
Kgr .... Koenigreich [*Kingdom*] [*Correspondence*] [*German*]
Kgr .... Vonnis van het Kantongerecht [*Benelux*]   (BAS)
KGRI .... Krivoy Rog Institute of Ore Mining   (RU)
KGRZ .... Kommunale Gebietsrechenzentren [*German*]   (ADPT)
KGS .... Kant-Gesellschaft [*Kant Society*] [*Germany*]   (EAIO)
kgs .... Kilogram Force   (RU)
KGS .... King George Sound [*Indian Ocean*]   (ADA)
KGS .... Kommando-Geraete-Steuerung [*German*]   (ADPT)
KGS .... Korean Geological Survey   (PDAA)

KGS .... Kos [*Greece*] [*Airport symbol*]   (OAG)
KGS .... Kreisgeschaeftsstelle [*Kreis Business Office*]   (EG)
KGSD .... Kibris Guzel Sanatlar Dernegi [*Cypriot Fine Arts Society*] [*Turkish Cypriot*]   (GC)
KGST......... Kolcsonos Gazdasagi Segitseg Tanacsa [*Council for Mutual Economic Assistance (CEMA)*]   (HU)
KGTF......... Agana, GU [*Television station call letters*]
kḁts .... Kilohertz, Kilocycles per Second   (RU)
KGTY .... Kibris Gecici Turk Yonetimi [*Cyprus Provisional Turkish Administration*]   (GC)
KGU.......... Kampfgruppe Gegen Unmenschlichkeit [*Fighting Group Against Inhumanity*]   (EG)
KGU.......... Kazan' State University Imeni V. I. Ul'yanov (Lenin)   (RU)
KGU.......... Keningau [*Malaysia*] [*Airport symbol*]   (OAG)
KGU.......... Kenya Golf Union
KGU.......... Kiev State University Imeni T. G. Shevchenko   (RU)
KGU.......... Kirgiz State University   (RU)
KGUM....... Agana, GU [*AM radio station call letters*]
KGUP......... Kuwait Gas Utilization Project   (ME)
KGV .... Kleinste Gemene Veelvoud [*Least Common Multiple*] [*Afrikaans*]
KGV .... Konnyuipari Gepalkatresz es Anyagforgalmi Vallalat [*Machine Supply Enterprise for Light Industry*]   (HU)
KGV .... Konsumgenossenschaftsverband [*Union of Consumer Cooperatives*]   (EG)
KGVI .... Kazan' State Veterinary Institute Imeni N. E. Bauman   (RU)
KGvL .... Koninklijk Genootschap voor Landbouwwetenschap [*Netherlands*]   (SLS)
KGW.......... Kagi [*Papua New Guinea*] [*Airport symbol*]   (OAG)
KGW.......... Kenya Glass Works Ltd.
KGW.......... Kolo Gospodyn Wiejskich [*Rural Housewives' Circle*]   (POL)
KGW.......... Komitet Gospodarki Wodnej [*Water Supply Committee*]   (POL)
KGY .... Kingaroy [*Australia*] [*Airport symbol*]   (OAG)
K Gy .... Kobanyai Gyogyszerarugyar [*Pharmaceutical Factory of Kobanya*]   (HU)
KGZ .... Caucasian State Reservation   (RU)
KGZ .... Committee for State Contracts   (RU)
KGZS......... Koziarske a Gumarenske Zavody na Slovensku [*Leather and Rubber Plants in Slovakia*]   (CZ)
Kgzv.......... Kilogram Zive Vahy [*Kilogram of Live Weight*]   (CZ)
KGZVI...... Kazan' State Zootechnical and Veterinary Institute   (RU)
kh .... Administrative (Service of a Ship)   (RU)
KH .... Cambodia [*ANSI two-letter standard code*]   (CNC)
kh .... Farmstead [*Topography*]   (RU)
Kh. .... Karargah [*Headquarters*]   (TU)
KH .... Kawasaki Heavy Industries Ltd. [*Japan*] [*ICAO aircraft manufacturer identifier*]   (ICAO)
Kh. .... Khao [*Hill, Mountain*] [*Thai*]   (NAU)
Kh. .... Khatzi [*Cyprus*]   (GC)
KH .... Kirchliche Hochschule
kH .... Kurzerhand [*Briefly*] [*German*]
kh .... Kylpyhuone [*Finland*]
kh .... Normal Running Fit   (RU)
Kh. .... Surgical Hospital   (RU)
kh .... Thousand   (BU)
Kha .... Hectare   (BU)
KHA .... Kindergarten Headmistresses Association
KHA........... Korean Hospital Association   (EAIO)
KHA........... Kosciusko Huts Association [*Australia*]
KhAAK ..... Adipyl Chloride   (RU)
KhAB .... Aerial Chemical Bomb   (RU)
KhAB .... Chemical Air Bomb   (BU)
KhabIIZhT ... Khabarovsk Institute of Railroad Transportation Engineers   (RU)
KhADI ...... Khar'kov Highway Institute   (RU)
KhAEE ...... Khoresm Archaeological and Ethnographical Expedition   (RU)
KhAF .... Chloroacetophenone   (RU)
KhAI .... Khar'kov Aviation Institute   (RU)
khakas .... Khakass   (RU)
Khakasgiz .. Khakass State Publishing House   (RU)
Khakasoblnatsizdat ... Khakass Oblast National Publishing House   (RU)
Khakgiz...... Khakass State Publishing House   (RU)
Khakizdat .. Khakass Book Publishing House   (RU)
Khakknigizdat ... Khakass Book Publishing House   (RU)
Khakoblgosizdat ... Khakass Oblast State Publishing House   (RU)
khald .... Chaldean   (RU)
KhAN......... Khristianiki Adelfotis Neon [*Young Men's Christian Association*]   (GC)
KhAO........ Khar'kov Astronomical Observatory   (RU)
Khargiprotrans ... Khar'kov State Planning and Surveying Institute   (RU)
KhARZ ...... Khar'kov Apparatus and Radiator Plant   (RU)
Khas .... Hydroacoustic Station   (BU)
KhATK ...... Terephthalyl Chloride   (RU)
KhAZOS .... Khar'kov Plant for Experimental Aircraft Construction   (RU)
KhB .... Chemical Battalion   (RU)
kh/b .... Cotton   (RU)

KHB.......... Korea Housing Bank   (IMH)

KhBR......... Chemical, Bacteriological, and Radiological   (RU)

kh br.......... Thousand Issues   (BU)

KhBS.......... Cold White Light (Fluorescent Lamp)   (RU)

KHCE....... Khabarovsk Commodity Exchange [*Russian Federation*]   (EY)

khch .... Administrative and Supply Department   (RU)

khch .... Chemically Pure   (RU)

KHCME .... Kharkov Commodity and Raw Materials Exchange [*Ukraine*]   (EY)

KHD .... Klockner-Humboldt-Deutz [*Diesel engine manufacturer*]

KhDA......... Khristiansko-Demokraticheskaya Assotsiatsiya Molodezhi Gruzii [*Christian-Democratic Youth Assocaition of Georgia*]   (EAIO)

KhDP......... Chemical Decontamination Station   (RU)

KHE.......... Kenya Horticultural Exporters (1977) Ltd.

KhE............ Khristiano-Koinoniki Enosis [*Christian Socialist Union*] [*Greek*]   (GC)

KhEG........ Chemical Generator of Electrical Energy   (RU)

KhEG........ Hygiene-Epidemiological Group   (BU)

KhEG........ Surgical Evacuation Hospital   (RU)

KhEI .... Hygiene-Epidemiological Institute   (BU)

KhELZ...... Khar'kov Electrotechnical Plant   (RU)

KhEMZ..... Khar'kov Electromechanical Plant   (RU)

KhEN........ Khristianiki Enosis Neanidon [*Young Women's Christian Association*]   (GC)

KhEP .... Khrimatistirion Emborevmaton Peiraios [*Piraeus Commodity Exchange*]   (GC)

KHES .... Krajska Hygienicko-Epidemiologicka Stanice [*Regional Public Health and Epidemiology Station*]   (CZ)

KhETI....... Khar'kov Electrotechnical Institute   (RU)

KhETZ....... Khar'kov Diesel Locomotive Electrical Equipment Plant   (RU)

KhEU......... Hygiene-Epidemiological Administration   (BU)

KhF .... Chemical Mine   (RU)

KhF .... Chromium Phosphate Electrolyte   (RU)

KhFDM..... Chlorophenyldimethylurea   (RU)

KhFI .... Khar'kov Pharmaceutical Institute   (RU)

KhFM .... Chlorophenyldimethylurea   (RU)

KhFZ .... Chemical-Pharmaceutical Plant   (BU)

KHG .... Kabinet pro Historickou Geografii [*Department of Historical Geography (of the Czechoslovak Academy of Sciences)*]   (CZ)

KHG .... Kashi [*China*] [*Airport symbol*]   (OAG)

KHG .... Kommunistische Hochschulgruppe [*Communist Student Organization*]   (WEN)

KhG............ Surgical Hospital   (RU)

KhGBI .... Khar'kov State Library Institute   (RU)

KhGI .... Khar'kov Mining Institute   (RU)

KhGIMIP ... Khar'kov State Institute of Measures and Measuring Instruments   (RU)

KhGNMB ... Khar'kov State Scientific Medical Library   (RU)

kh/gr .... Khiliogrammon [*Kilogram*]   (GC)

KhGSEE .... Khristianiki Geniki Synomospondia Ergazomenon Ellados [*Christian General Confederation of Greek Workers*]   (GC)

KhGU .... Khar'kov State University Imeni A. M. Gor'kiy   (RU)

KhGU .... Surgical Reinforcement Group   (RU)

KHGW....... Kunsthistorische Gesellschaft Wien [*Society of Art History*] [*Austria*]   (EAIO)

KHGYP ..... Kraliyet Hava Gucu Yardimci Polis ve Aylikci Mustahdemler Sendikasi [*Royal Air Force Auxiliary Police and Monthly Salaried Employees Union*] [*Turkish Cypriot*]   (GC)

KHH .... Kaohsiung [*Taiwan*] [*Airport symbol*]   (OAG)

KhI............ Chlorinated Lime   (RU)

KHI .... Karachi [*Pakistan*] [*Airport symbol*]   (OAG)

KHI............ Kawasaki Heavy Industries [*Japan*]

KhI .... Khimiya i Industriya [*Chemistry and Industry*] [*A periodical*]   (BU)

KHIC .... Korea Heavy Industries & Construction

Khidrostroy ... Hydraulic Constructions Organization   (BU)

KhIGS........ Khibiny Mountain Station (of the Academy of Sciences, USSR)   (RU)

KhIIT........ Khar'kov Institute of Railroad Transportation Engineers Imeni S. M. Kirov   (RU)

KhIK .... Chemical Institute Imeni L. Ya. Karpov   (RU)

khil............ Thousand(s)   (BU)

khim.......... Chemical, Chemistry   (BU)

KhIM .... Khar'kov Scientific Research Institute of Metals   (RU)

khimbaklab ... Chemical and Bacteriological Laboratory   (RU)

khimfak...... Division of Chemistry   (RU)

khimfarm ... Chemical and Pharmaceutical   (RU)

Khimfarmprom ... Administration of the Chemical and Pharmaceutical Industry   (RU)

Khimfarmproyekt ... Office for the Planning of Chemical and Pharmaceutical Plants   (RU)

Khimfarmsbyt ... All-Union Trade Office for Chemical and Pharmaceutical Goods and Sanitary Articles   (RU)

khimfugas .. Chemical Mine   (RU)

Khimgaz..... All-Union Scientific Research Institute of the Chemical Processing of Gases   (RU)

Khimimport ... Enterprise for Import and Export of Chemicals and Drugs   (BU)

Khimizdat .. State Publishing House of Scientific and Technical Chemical Literature   (RU)

khimleskhoz ... Wood-Chemistry Establishment   (RU)

Khimlesprom ... All-Union Trust for the Procurement and Processing of Lumber of the Glavkhimpromstroy   (RU)

khimlespromkhoz ... Wood-Chemistry Industrial Establishment   (RU)

Khimleszag ... State Trust for the Procurement of Industrial Raw Materials and Fuel of the Glavleskhim   (RU)

khim mel .... Chemical Soil Improvement   (RU)

khimprom .. Chemical Industry   (RU)

Khimr......... Chemical Company   (RU)

khimrazvedka ... Chemical Reconnaissance   (RU)

Khimsantekhmontazh ... All-Union Trust of the Glavkhimpromstroy   (RU)

KHIMSNARYAD ... Chemical Shell   (RU)

khim sost.... Chemical Composition   (RU)

Khimtekhizdat ... State Publishing House of Chemical and Technical Literature   (RU)

khimtrevoga ... Gas Alarm [*Military term*]   (RU)

khimugolok ... Chemical Study Room   (RU)

khim zn ...... Chemical Symbol   (RU)

KhIn.......... Khimiya i Industriya [*Chemistry and Industry*] [*A periodical*]   (BU)

KhINO....... Khar'kov Institute of Public Education   (RU)

KhIOT .... Khar'kov Institute of Work Safety   (RU)

KhIP.......... Random Pulse Interference   (RU)

khir .... Surgeon, Surgery   (BU)

khir .... Surgery, Surgical   (RU)

KhISI........ Khar'kov Construction Engineering Institute   (RU)

khist.......... Histology, Histologist   (BU)

khizh .... Hut [*Topography*]   (RU)

KHK.......... Khark [*Iran*] [*Airport symbol*] [*Obsolete*]   (OAG)

KHK.......... Kouatsu-Gasu Hoan Kyokai [*High Pressure Gas Safety Institute of Japan*]   (EAIO)

KhK.......... Refrigeration Chamber   (RU)

kh-ka......... Characteristic, Performance   (RU)

khkh.......... No-Load Condition (Electricity)   (RU)

KhKhTI ..... Khar'kov Institute of Chemical Technology Imeni S. M. Kirov   (RU)

KHKO .... Kurt Halk Kurtulus Ordusu [*Kurdish Peoples' Liberation Army*]   (TU)

KhKPV ...... Chemical Combine for Polyester Fibers   (BU)

KhKUKS.... Chemical Courses for the Advanced Training of the Command Personnel of the RKKA   (RU)

KhKZ........ Kherson Combine Plant   (RU)

khl .... Belles Lettres   (RU)

khl .... Chloroform   (RU)

KhL .... Laboratory Chromathermograph   (RU)

Khladpromstroy ... Construction and Installation Trust of the Rosmyasorybtorg of the Ministry of Trade, RSFSR   (RU)

Khladstroy ... Refrigeration and Apparatus Plant   (BU)

khlak.......... Kihlakunta [*Finland*]

khl-bum...... Cotton   (RU)

Khleboizdat ... Publishing House of Technical and Economic Literature on Problems of the Flour-Milling, Groats, and Combined-Fodder Industry and on Elevators and Storage Facilities   (RU)

Khlebsbyt... Moscow Office of the Administration of the Baking Industry of the Mosoblispolkom   (RU)

khlf............. Chloroform   (RU)

khlop .... Cotton   (RU)

Khlor-IFK ... Isopropyl Chlorophenylcarbamate   (RU)

KhLS.......... SONAR Station   (BU)

kh lv .... Thousand Leva   (BU)

KHM .... Cambodia [*ANSI three-letter standard code*]   (CNC)

khM .... Cold (Air) Mass   (RU)

KhM.......... Khamtis [*Myanmar*] [*Airport symbol*]   (OAG)

KhM.......... Magnesium Chlorate   (RU)

KhM.......... Ship's Chemical Service   (RU)

khm .... Thousand Meters   (RU)

KhMA .... Ammonia Refrigeration Unit   (RU)

KhMB .... Chloromercuribenzoate   (RU)

KHMC....... King Hussein Medical Center [*Jordan*]

KhMDMB ... Chloromethyldimethylbenzene   (RU)

KhMG........ Chemical Generator of Mechanical Energy   (RU)

KhMI .... Khar'kov Medical Institute   (RU)

KhMMI ..... Khar'kov Institute of Mechanics and Mechanical Engineering   (RU)

KhMO .... Khar'kov Mathematical Society   (RU)

KhMS .... Hydrometeorological Service   (BU)

KhMU .... Administrative and Materials Supply Management   (RU)

KhN .... Chemical Attack [*Warning*]   (RU)

KHN .... Komitet Historii Nauki [*Committee on the History of Science*] (POL)
KHN .... Nanchang [*China*] [*Airport symbol*] (OAG)
KhNIKhFI ... Khar'kov Scientific Research Chemical and Pharmaceutical Institute (GC)
KhNOS ..... Chemical Observation and Warning Service (RU)
KhNP .... Chemical Observation Post (RU)
KhNSR ..... Khoresm People's Soviet Republic [*1920-1923*] (RU)
KhNV .... Chemistry and Technology of Inorganic Substances (RU)
kho .... Chemical Defense (RU)
KhO .... Chemical Weapon (RU)
KhO .... Chemical Weapons (RU)
KHO .... Korkein Hallinto-Oikeus [*Supreme Administrative Court*] [*Finland*] (WEN)
KhOGES ... Khar'kov Oblast State Electric Power Plant (RU)
khol .... Cold (RU)
khol .... Dutch (BU)
kholod .... Cold Storage Plant [*Topography*] (RU)
khon prep... Paid Instructor (BU)
KhOON ..... United Nations Charter (BU)
khor .... Good (RU)
Khoremag .. State Enterprise for Hotels, Restaurants, and Stores (BU)
KhORGES ... Khar'kov Oblast State Electric Power Plant (RU)
khoz .... Economic, Economy, Establishment, Farm (RU)
Khozakarf .. Logistics Academy of the Red Army and Navy (RU)
khozmag ..... Household Goods Store (RU)
KhOZO ..... Administrative and Supply Department (RU)
khoztorg ..... Specialized Organization for Trade in Household Goods (RU)
KhOZU ..... Administrative and Supply Management (RU)
khozupr ...... Administrative and Supply Management (RU)
khoz-vo ...... Economy, Establishment, Farm (RU)
KhP .... Chemical Industry (RU)
KhP .... Chloroprene (RU)
KhP .... Cold Period [*Meteorology*] (RU)
KHP .... Keban Holding ve Ortaklari Plastik Sanayii AS [*Keban Holding and Partners Plastic Industry Corp.*] (TU)
KhP .... Khamili Piesis [*Low Pressure*] (GC)
KhPI .... Khar'kov Polytechnic Institute Imeni V. I. Lenin (RU)
KHPI .... Khimicheskii Poglotitel Izvestkovyi [*Chemical absorbent*] [*Former USSR*]
KhPI .... Lime Chemical Absorbent (RU)
KhPL .... Chemical Field Laboratory (RU)
KhPO .... Administrative and Production Department (RU)
KhPPG .... Mobile Field Surgical Hospital (BU)
KhPS .... Artistic and Political Council (RU)
KhPZ .... Khar'kov Locomotive Plant (RU)
KhR .... Chemical Company (RU)
KhR .... Chemical Reconnaissance (BU)
khr .... Christian (RU)
khr .... Chronometer (RU)
khr .... Farmstead [*Topography*] (RU)
KHR .... Khazar [*Turkmenistan*] [*ICAO designator*] (FAAC)
khr .... Mountain Range [*Topography*] (RU)
kh-ra .... Farmsteads [*Topography*] (RU)
khra .... Kirkkoherra [*Finland*]
Khramges ... Khrami Hydroelectric Power Plant (RU)
Khraneksport ... State Enterprise for the Export of Food Products (BU)
KhRD .... Chemical Reconnaissance Patrol (BU)
Khr e .... Christian Era [*In historic dates*] (RU)
khreb .... Mountain Range [*Topography*] (RU)
KhRIKE ..... Khristiano-Dimokratikon Koinonikon Komma Ellados [*Greek Christian Democratic Party*] (GC)
KhRISKEL ... Khristiano-Dimokratikon Komma tis Ellados [*Christian Democratic Party of Greece*] (GC)
khrom .... Chromium Mines [*Topography*] (RU)
khromzavod ... Box Calf Plant (RU)
KhRR .... Chemical and Radiation Reconnaissance (RU)
KhRU .... Art Trade School (RU)
khrust .... Cut Glass Factory [*Topography*] (RU)
KhS .... Chemical Service (RU)
khs .... Connecting Trench (RU)
KhS .... Khamili Sykhnotis [*Low Frequency*] (GC)
KHS .... Kniznica Hudobneho Seminara [*Library of the Music Seminary (of the Slovak University)*] (CZ)
KHS .... Krankenhaus-System [*Hospital System*] [*German*] (ADPT)
KHS .... Krosnienskie Huty Szkla [*Krosno Glass Works*] (POL)
KhS .... Sulfuryl Chloride (RU)
KhSh .... Household Refrigerator (RU)
KhSK .... Khristiano-Sosialistiki Kinisi [*Christian Socialist Movement*] [*Greek*] (GC)
KhSKhI ..... Khar'kov Agricultural Institute Imeni V. V. Dokuchayev (RU)
KhSO .... Chemical Fragmentation Shell (BU)
KhSSR .... Khoresm Soviet Socialist Republic [*1923-1924*] (RU)
KhSSRZ ..... Kherson Shipyard Imeni Komintern (RU)
KhSZ .... Khar'kov Machine Tool Plant (RU)
KhSZ .... Use of Chemicals in Socialist Agriculture (RU)

KhT .... Chemical Alarm [*Military term*] (RU)
KhT .... Chromathermograph (RU)
kht .... Cold-Drawn (RU)
KhT .... Gas Alert (BU)
KHT .... Keskuskauppakamarin Hyvaksyma Tilintarkastaja [*Finland*]
KhT .... Khamili Tasis [*Low Voltage*] (GC)
KHT .... Khost [*Afghanistan*] [*Airport symbol*] [*Obsolete*] (OAG)
KhTG .... Chemical Generator of Heat (RU)
KhTG .... Chymotrypsinogen (RU)
KhTGZ ...... Khar'kov Turbogenerator Plant Imeni S. M. Kirov (RU)
KhTI .... Chemical and Technical Institute (BU)
KhTM .... Turbocompressor Refrigeration Unit (RU)
KHTMK ..... Kibris Hukumeti Turk Memurin Kurumu [*Turkish Cypriot Civil Servants Association*] (GC)
KhTs .... Chordal Center (RU)
khts .... Hertz (BU)
KhTSZ .... Khar'kov Tractor Assembly Plant (RU)
KhTZ .... Khar'kov Tractor Plant Imeni Sergo Ordzhonikidze (RU)
KhTZ .... Khar'kov Turbine Plant Imeni S. M. Kirov (RU)
KhTZ .... Tractor Made by the Khar'kov Tractor Plant Imeni Sergo Ordzhonikidze (RU)
KHU .... Kenya Hockey Union
khud .... Artist, Painter (RU)
KhudA .... Academy of Fine Arts (BU)
Khudozh ..... Artistic, Artist (BU)
khudozhpromsoyuz ... Art Crafts Producers' Association (RU)
khudruk ...... Art Adviser (RU)
Khut .... Farmstead [*Topography*] (RU)
Khutemast ... Art and Craft Shops (RU)
KhV .... Chromophil Substance (RU)
KHV .... Khabarovsk [*Former USSR*] [*Airport symbol*] (OAG)
KHV .... Kozuti Hidfenntarto Vallalat [*Highway Bridge Maintenance Enterprise*] (HU)
KhVO .... Chemical Water Purification (BU)
kh-vo .... Economy, Establishment, Farm (RU)
KhVO .... Khar'kov Military District (RU)
KhVP .... Food Industry (BU)
KhVS .... Vertical Spindle Automotive Cotton Picker (RU)
KhVSh .... Vinyl-Perchloride Putty (RU)
KhVT .... Khar'kov Military Court (RU)
KhVZ .... Khar'kov Bicycle Plant (RU)
KHVZ .... Komise pro Hnuti Vynalezcu a Zlepsovatelu [*Commission for the Inventors' and Improvers' Movement*] (CZ)
KhVZD ...... Chemical Delayed-Action Fuze (RU)
KHX .... Hugo Rizzuto [*ICAO designator*] (FAAC)
khyem .... Chemical Mass Unit (RU)
KhZ .... Chemical Defense (RU)
khz .... Chemical Plant (RU)
khz .... Kiloherc [*Kilo-Cycle per Second*] [*Poland*]
KHz .... Kilohertz [*Kilohertz*] [*German*] (EG)
KhZ .... Refrigeration Equipment Plant (BU)
KhZMI ..... Khar'kov Plant of Mine Surveying Instruments (RU)
KhZTM ..... Khar'kov Transportation Machinery Plant (RU)
KhZZM ..... Khar'kov Dental Materials Plant (RU)
KI .... Communist International (RU)
Ki. .... Corps Engineer (RU)
KI .... Fighter Airplane Compass (RU)
Ki. .... Kali [*River*] [*Malaysia*] (NAU)
KI .... Kamer van Inbeschuldigingstelling [*Benelux*] (BAS)
KI .... Kathleen Investments [*Australia*] (ADA)
KI .... Kennarasamband Islands [*Iceland*] (SLS)
KI .... Keramicna Industrija [*Ceramic Industry*] (YU)
KI .... King Island [*Australia*] (ADA)
KI .... Kiribati [*ANSI two-letter standard code*] (CNC)
KI .... Kmetijski Inspektorat [*Inspectorate of Agriculture*] (YU)
KI .... Kodansha International [*Japan*]
KI .... Komitet Informatsii [*Committee of Information*] [*Former USSR*]
KI .... Kommunista Internacionale [*Communist International (COMINTERN)*] (HU)
KI .... Komunisticka Internacionala [*Communist International (COMINTERN)*] (CZ)
KI .... Konjunkturinstitutet [*National Institute of Economic Research*] [*Sweden*] (GEA)
KI .... Krajsky Inspektorat [*Regional Inspectorate*] (CZ)
KI .... Kulturni Informace [*Cultural Information Service (of the Ministry of Information)*] (CZ)
KI .... Kunsmatige Inseminasie [*Artificial Insemination*] [*Afrikaans*]
KI .... Oxygen Inhaler (RU)
KI .... Oxygen Utilization Factor (RU)
KIA .... Cambodian Information Agency [*Use AKI*] (CL)
KIA .... Kachin Independence Army [*Myanmar*] [*Political party*] (EY)
KIA .... Kansai International Airport [*Japan*]
KIA .... Kenya Institute of Administration
KIA .... Kilimanjaro International Airport
KIA .... KIWI International Air Lines, Inc. [*ICAO designator*] (FAAC)
KIA .... Kotoka International Airport [*Ghana*]

KIA .... Kuwait Investment Authority [*Finance Ministry*]

K i A .... Monitoring and Automation [*Equipment*]   (RU)

KIAA .... Kangaroo Industries Association of Australia

KIAC .... Kansai International Airport Co. [*Japan*]

KIACS .... Kenya Independent Armoured Car Squadron

kiad .... Kiadas [*Edition*] [*Publishing*] [*Hungary*]

kiadv .... Kiadvany [*Publication*] [*Hungary*]

KIAI........... Caucasian Historical and Archaeological Institute   (RU)

KIAMC...... Kenya Institute of Administration Motor Club

KIB............ Kikepzo Bazis [*Training Base*]   (HU)

KIB............ Konstruktions- und Ingenieurbuero [*Design and Engineering Office*]   (EG)

KIB............ Koy Isleri Bakanligi [*Village Affairs Ministry*]   (TU)

KIB............ Kozigazgatasi Birosag [*Public Administration Court*]   (HU)

KIB............ Kozigazgatasi Bizottsag [*Committee on Public Administration*]   (HU)

KIB............ Kraftfahrzeuginstandsetzungsbetrieb [*Motor Vehicle Repair Enterprise*]   (EG)

KIB............ Kredit Investasi Besar [*Indonesia*]   (IMH)

KIBI .... Kirjastonhoitajat ja Informaatikot Bibliotekarier och Informatikek [*Research and University Libraries*] [*Finland*]   (EAIO)

KIBIC .... Karolinska Institutets Bibliotek och Informationscentral [*Karolinska Institute Library and Information Center*] [*Sweden*] [*Information service or system*]   (IID)

KIC .... Khonaini International Co. Ltd. [*Saudi Arabia*]

KIC .... Kuwait Insurance Co.   (EY)

KIC .... Kuwait Investment Company [*Kuwait City*]   (ME)

KICC......... Kenyatta International Conference Centre

KIChP....... Commission for the Study of the Quaternary Period   (RU)

KICOMI.... Kisamu Cotton Mills Ltd.

KID .... Collegium of Foreign Affairs   (RU)

KID .... Ion Diffusion Coefficient   (RU)

KID .... Kranjska Industrijska Druzba [*Carniolan Industrial Society*]   (YU)

KID .... Kristianstad [*Sweden*] [*Airport symbol*]   (OAG)

KIDC .... Kenya Industrial Development Corporation

KIDC .... Kiowa Industrial Development Commission

KIDECO.... Kilimanjaro Development Corporation

KiDKP ...... Ksztalcenie i Doskonalenie Kadr Pedagogicznych [*Education and Improvement of Pedagogical Personnel*]   (POL)

KIDO .... Kish Island Development Organisation

kidolg .... Kidolgozta [*Composed By*] [*Hungary*]

KIE............ Kenya Industrial Estates Ltd.

KIE............ Kenya Institute of Education

KIE............ Keresztyen Ifjusagi Egyesulet [*Young Men's Christian Association*]   (HU)

KIE............ Kieta [*Papua New Guinea*] [*Airport symbol*]   (OAG)

Kie............ Kompanjie [*Company*] [*Afrikaans*]

KIEE.......... Korean Institute of Electrical Engineers

kieg............ Kiegeszites [*Supplement*] [*Publishing*] [*Hungary*]

kieg............ Kiegeszitve [*Completed*] [*Hungary*]

kieg psag .... Kiegeszito Parancsnoksag [*Replacement Center*]   (HU)

kiel............ Kielessa [*Finland*]

kielit .... Kielitiede [*Finland*]

Kier .... Kierownik [*Manager*] [*Poland*]

KIER .... Korea Institute of Energy and Resources

KIET......... Korea Institute for Industrial Economics and Trade   (ECON)

KIET......... Korea Institute of Electronics Technology [*South Korea*]

KIFCO....... Kuwait International Finance Company   (ME)

KIG .... Koingnaas [*South Africa*] [*Airport symbol*]   (OAG)

KiG............ Kotar i Grad [*District and City*]   (YU)

KIGAM ..... Korea Research Institute of Geoscience and Mineral Resources [*Korea Institute of Energy and Resources*]

KIGM .... Kultur Isleri Genel Mudurlugu [*Cultural Affairs Directorate General*]   (TU)

KIGST ...... Kirchliche Gemeinschaftsstelle fuer Elektronische Datenverarbeitung [*German*]   (ADPT)

KIGVF ...... Kiev Institute of the Civil Air Fleet   (RU)

KIH........... Kaisar-I-Hind [*Indian medal*]

KIH........... Kish Island [*Iran*] [*Airport symbol*]   (OAG)

KIHASA.... Korea Institute for Health and Social Affairs   (IRC)

KIHUB ...... Kompi Perhubungan [*Signal Company*]   (IN)

KII............ Kiev Industrial Institute   (RU)

KII............ Kuybyshev Industrial Institute Imeni V. V. Kuybyshev   (RU)

KIIC.......... Kuwait International Investment Co.

kiir............ Kiireellinen [*Finland*]

KIIVKh...... Kiev Institute of Hydraulic Engineers   (RU)

kij............. Kijarat [*Exit*]   (HU)

KIJ .... Niigata [*Japan*] [*Airport symbol*]   (OAG)

KIK .... Committee for Art and Culture   (BU)

KIK .... Kamu Iktisadi Kuruluslari [*Public Economic Establishments*]   (TU)

KIK .... Karma Isci Komitesi [*Mixed Workers' Committee*] [*Turkish Cypriot*]   (GC)

KIK .... Keramicka Industrija Kumanovo [*Kumanovo Ceramic Industry*]   (YU)

kik .... Kikepzes [*or Kikepzett*] [*Basic Training or Trained*]   (HU)

KIK .... Kray Executive Committee   (RU)

KIK .... Kredit Investasi Kecil [*Indonesia*]   (IMH)

KIKhL........ Kazakh Institute of Belles Lettres   (RU)

KIKhN .... Kiniton Kheirourgikon Nosokomeion [*Mobile (Army) Surgical Hospital*]   (GC)

KIKI .... Kiev Institute of Motion Picture Engineers   (RU)

KIL............ Caprylolactam   (RU)

KIL............ Control and Measuring Laboratory   (RU)

KIL............ Kapitalistisches Industrieland [*Capitalist Industrial Country*]   (EG)

KIL............ Kontor fuer Import und Lagerung [*Import and Warehousing Agency*]   (EG)

KILA .... Korean Institute of Landscape Architecture   (EAIO)

kildehenvisn ... Kildehenvisning [*Reference to Sources*] [*Publishing Danish/Norwegian*]

Kilo........... Kilogramme [*Kilogram*] [*French*]   (MTD)

kilog .... Kilogramme [*Kilogram*] [*French*]

kilogr.......... Kilogramme [*Kilogram*] [*French*]

Kilom......... Kilometre [*Kilometer*] [*French*]

KILO-MOTO ... Office des Mines d'Or de Kilo-Moto

KIM .... Communist Youth International   (BU)

KIM .... Jacketed Small Composition [*Resistor*]   (RU)

KIM .... Kenya Institute of Management

KIM .... Kimberley [*South Africa*] [*Airport symbol*]   (OAG)

kim .... Kimutatas [*Account, Financial Statement*]   (HU)

Kim........... Kimya [*Chemistry, Chemical*]   (TU)

KIM.......... Koelner Integrationsmodell [*German*]   (ADPT)

KIM .... Kolej Islam Malaya [*Malayan Moslem College*]   (ML)

KIM .... Kombinat Industrieller Mast [*Industrial Fattening Combine*]   (EG)

KIM .... Komity Iobonan'ny Mpitolona [*Joint Struggle Committee*] [*Malagasy*]   (AF)

KIM .... Komunisticka Internacionala Mladeze [*Communist Youth International*]   (CZ)

KIM .... Konnyuipari Miniszterium/Miniszter [*Ministry/Minister of Light Industry*]   (HU)

KIM .... Pulse-Code Modulation   (RU)

KIMA .... Kompi Markas [*Headquarters Company*]   (IN)

KIMB........ Kimberley [*Botanical region*] [*Australia*]

KIMC .... Kenya Institute of Mass Communication

KIMESKh ... Kazakh Institute of Rural Mechanization and Electrification   (RU)

Kimka .... Commission for Operation of Small Mines   (RU)

KIMM .... Korea Institute of Machinery and Metals [*South Korea*]

KIMMA .... Kongres Indian Muslim Malaysia [*Malaysia Indian Moslem Congress*] [*Political party*]   (PPW)

KIMPA...... Hakim Perwira [*Military Judge*]   (IN)

KIMS........ Caucasian Institute of Mineral Raw Materials   (RU)

KIMS........ Checkout Magnetic Station   (RU)

KIMSAT ... Kimyevi Maddeler Ticaret ve Sanayi Ltd. Sti. [*Chemicals Trade and Industry, Inc.*]   (TU)

KIMSZ ...... Kommunista Ifjumunkasok Magyarorszagi Szovetsege [*Federation of Young Communist Workers in Hungary*]   (HU)

KIMTES.... Kimya Tesisleri Sanayin Ticaret AS [*Chemical Equipment Industry and Corporation*]   (TU)

KIMTUA... Hakim Ketua [*Chief Justice*]   (IN)

kimut.......... Kimutatas [*Account, Financial Statement*]   (HU)

Kimya-Is .... Turkiye Kimya Iscileri Sendikasi [*Turkish Chemical Workers Union*] [*Turkimya*] [*See also*]   (TU)

k i n .... Candidate of Economic Sciences   (BU)

kin .... Candidate of Historical Sciences   (RU)

KIN .... Kingston [*Jamaica*] [*Airport symbol*]   (OAG)

kin .... Motion Picture Industry Plant [*Topography*]   (RU)

KINAP....... Motion Picture Equipment Plant   (RU)

KIND .... Kodix Idiotikou Navtikou Dikaiou [*Code of Private Maritime Law*]   (GC)

Kinel'neft' .. Kinel' Petroleum Industry Trust   (RU)

KINET....... Kienzle Netzwerksystem [*German*]   (ADPT)

kinet.......... Kinetisch [*Kinetic*] [*German*]   (GCA)

kinetich ...... Kinetic   (RU)

KINFIS...... Kommunales Integriertes Finanz-Informationssystem [*German*]   (ADPT)

Kinofotoizdat ... All-Union State Publishing House for Cinematography and Photography   (RU)

KIN/OPH ... Kirche in Not/Ostprieterhilfe [*Aid to the Church in Need*] [*Germany*]   (EAIO)

Kinostroymontazh ... Construction and Installation Office of the Ministry of Cinematography, USSR   (RU)

KINS......... Commission for the Study of the National Composition of the Population of the USSR   (RU)

KIO .... Committee for Inventions and Discoveries   (RU)

KIO .... Kachin Independence Organization [*Myanmar*] [*Political party*] (EY)

KIO .... Kenya Information Office

KIO .... Kili [*Marshall Islands*] [*Airport symbol*] (OAG)

KIO .... Kongres Industrijskih Organizacija [*Congress of Industrial Organizations*] (YU)

KIO .... Kraiaero [*Russian Federation*] [*ICAO designator*] (FAAC)

KIO .... Kring Industriele Ontwerpers [*Industrial Designers Association*] [*Netherlands*] (EAIO)

KIO .... Kuwait Investment Office (ECON)

KiO .... Of Culture and Rest (RU)

KIOSZ ...... Kisiparosok Orszagos Szervezete [*National Organization of Artisans*] (HU)

kip .... Boiling (RU)

KIP .... Check-and-Test Apron (RU)

KIP .... Check-and-Test Point (RU)

KIP .... Control and Measuring Instrument (BU)

KIP .... Control and Measuring Instruments (RU)

KIP .... Control and Measuring Instruments Plant (RU)

KIP .... Insulating Oxygen Set (RU)

KIP .... Kenya Industrial Plastics Ltd.

KIP .... Kommission Iustitia et Pax der Deutschen Dominikaner [*Germany*] (EAIO)

KIP .... Konfeksiyon Imalat Pazarlama Sanayi Ticaret AS [*Ready-Made Clothing Manufacture and Marketing Industry Corporation*] (TU)

KIP .... Measuring Instruments Set (RU)

KIP .... Red International of Trade Unions (RU)

KIPH .... Korea Institute for Population and Health [*Research center*] (IRC)

KIPiA .... Control and Measuring Instruments and Automation Equipment (RU)

KIPIC .... Kuwait International Petroleum Investment Company (MENA)

KIPIG .... Kibris Iktisadi Planlama Istisare Grubu [*Cyprus Economic Planning Consultative Group*] [*Turkish Cypriot*] (GC)

KIPLAS .... Chemical, Petroleum, Rubber and Plastic Industries Employers' Association of Turkey (EAIO)

Kip M .... Konnyuipari Miniszterium/Miniszter [*Ministry/Minister of Light Industry*] (HU)

KIPO .... Korea Industrial Property Office

KIPO .... Useful Volume Utilization Factor [*Of a blast furnace*] (RU)

KIPP .... Institute for Comprehensive Study and Design (BU)

KIPP .... Krasnodar Institute of the Food Industry (RU)

KIPS .... Mobile Check-and-Test Station (RU)

KIPS .... Permanent Commission for the Study of the Tribal Compositon of the Population of the USSR (at the Academy of Sciences, USSR) (RU)

KIPSZER .. Konnyuipari Szerelo es Epito Vallalat [*Light Industry Assembling and Construction Enterprise*] (HU)

KIQ .... Kira [*Papua New Guinea*] [*Airport symbol*] (OAG)

KIR .... Khartoum Flight Information Region

kir .... Kiralyi [*Royal*] (HU)

KIR .... Kiribati [*ANSI three-letter standard code*] (CNC)

KIR .... Kirov Railroad (RU)

KIR .... Komisija za Izucavanje Rada i Radnih Uslova Sindikata Gradevinara [*Commission to Study Labor and Labor Conditions, Builders' Trade-Union*] (YU)

KiR .... Natural and Vulcanized Rubber (RU)

kirad .... Kiradirozva [*Erased*] [*Hungary*]

Kira-Kod .... Kisracilari Koruma Dernegi [*Associaton for the Protection of Tenants*] (TU)

KIRAPP.... Kirgiz Association of Proletarian Writers [*1930-1932*] (RU)

KIRBS ...... Korean Institute for Research in the Behavioral Sciences [*South Korean*] [*Research center*] (IRC)

KIRDEP .... Kilimanjaro Regional Integrated Development Programme

KIRDI ...... Kenya Industrial Research and Development Institute

kirend........ Kirendeltseg [*Local Office*] (HU)

kirg........... Kirgiz (RU)

KirgizFAN ... Kirgiz Branch of the Academy of Sciences, USSR (RU)

Kirgizgosizdat ... Kirgiz State Publishing House (RU)

Kirgizneft'.. Kirgiz Oil Field Administration (RU)

Kirgizuchpedgiz ... Kirgiz State Publishing House of Textbooks and Pedagogical Literature (RU)

KirgNIIZh ... Kirgiz Scientific Research Institute of Livestock Breeding (RU)

KirgNIIZhV ... Kirgiz Scientific Research Institute of Livestock Breeding and Veterinary Science (RU)

kirj........... Kirjallisessa Tyylissa [*Literary*] [*Finland*]

kirj........... Kirjataan [*Finland*]

kirj........... Kirjoittanut [*Finland*]

kirjall .... Kirjallisuus [*Literature*] [*Finland*]

kirjanp ...... Kirjanpito [*Bookkeeping*] [*Finland*]

kirjap........ Kirjapaino [*Typography, Printing*] [*Finland*]

kirj sid ...... Kirjansidonta [*Bookbinding*] [*Finland*]

kirk .... Kirkossa [*or Kirkollinen*] [*Ecclesiastic*] [*Finland*]

kirp .... Brickyard [*Topography*] (RU)

KirSSR...... Kirgiz Soviet Socialist Republic (RU)

KirTAG...... Kirgiz News Agency (RU)

KIS............ Check-and-Test Station (RU)

KIS............ Contactair Flugdienst & Co. [*Germany*] [*ICAO designator*] (FAAC)

KIS............ Kendrikon Israilitikon Symvoulion [*Central Jewish Council*] (GC)

KIS............ Keramicka Industrija Skopje [*Skopje Ceramic Industry*] (YU)

KIS............ Key Independent System [*Instant photo development company*] [*France*]

KIS............ Kiepenheur-Institut fuer Sonnenphysik [*Kiepenheuer-Institute for Solar Physics*] [*Research center*] [*Germany*] (EAS)

Kis............. Kisi [*or Kisiler*] [*Individual or Individuals*] (TU)

KIS............ Kisumu [*Kenya*] [*Airport symbol*] (OAG)

KIS............ Klub Inzenyru a Stavitelu [*Engineers' and Builders' Club*] (CZ)

KIS............ Komisia pre Industrializaciu Slovenska [*Commission for the Industrialization of Slovakia*] (CZ)

KIS............ Kontrolna Isturena Stanica [*Advanced Control Station*] [*Military*] (YU)

KIS............ Krankenhaus Informations System [*Hospital Information System*]

KIS............ Oxygen-Inhalation Station (RU)

KISA .... Karaoke International Sing-Along Association (EA)

KISA .... Kikuyu Independent Schools Association

KISA .... Korean International Steel Associates (PDAA)

Kisankyo .... Zenkoku Kikai Sangyo Rodokumiai Kyogikai [*National Council of Machine Industry Workers' Unions*] [*Japan*]

kiserl .... Kiserleti [*Experimental*] (HU)

KISI .... Kiev Construction Engineering Institute (RU)

KISKER..... Kiskereskedelmi Vallalat [*Retail Enterprise*] (HU)

k isk n........ Candidate of Art Studies (RU)

k is n.......... Candidate of Historical Sciences (RU)

KISO......... Commission for Solar Research (of the Academy of Sciences, USSR) (RU)

KISOSZ..... Kiskereskedok Orszagos Szabadszervezete [*National Free Organization of Retailers*] (HU)

KISR......... Kuwait Institute for Scientific Research

KISTEX..... Kispesti Textilgyar [*Kispest Textile Mill*] (HU)

KISZ .... Magyar Kommunista Ifjusagi Szovetseg [*Hungarian Communist Youth League*] [*Budapest*] (HU)

KISZOK .... Kommunista Ifjusagi Szovetseg Orszagos Kozpontja [*National Center of the Hungarian Communist Youth League*] (HU)

KISZOV .... Kisipari Szovetkezetek Szovetsege [*Association of Small Industrial Cooperatives*] (HU)

kit .... Chinese (RU)

KIT........... Committee of Rural Union [*Malagasy*] (AF)

KIT........... Control and Measurement Engineering (RU)

KIT........... Kamu Iktisadi Tesebbusleri [*Public Economic Enterprises*] [*Turkish Cypriot*] (GC)

KIT........... Kanazawa Institute of Technology [*Japan*] (PDAA)

KIT........... Kithira [*Greece*] [*Airport symbol*] (OAG)

KIT........... Koninklijk Instituut voor de Tropen [*Royal Tropical Institute*] [*Netherlands*] [*Research center*]

KITA......... Kesatuan Insaf Tanah Air [*National Consciousness Party*] [*Malaysia*] [*Political party*] (PPW)

KITA......... Korea Industrial Technology Association (EAIO)

KITCO...... Kerala Industrial and Technical Consultancy Organization [*India*]

KITE........ Kukorica es Iparinoveny Termelesi Egyuttmukodes [*Corn and Industrial Crop Growing Cooperation (Located at Nadudver)*] (HU)

KITI......... Kohoipari Tervezo Iroda [*Planning Office for Metallurgical Industry*] (HU)

KITLV ...... Koninklijk Instituut voor Taal-, Land, en Volkenkunde [*Netherlands*] (SLS)

KITSAB..... Kibris Turk Seyahat Acentalari Birligi [*Turksih Cypriot Travel Agents Association*] (TU)

KITSAK-SEN ... Kibris Turk Sanayi Kesimi Memurlar Sendikasi [*Turkish Cypriot Industrial Sector Employees Union*] (GC)

KITT......... Korean International Telephone & Telegraph

KITV......... Konnyuipari Tervezo Vallalat [*Light Industry Designing Enterprise*] (HU)

KIU .... Commission for the Study of the Ukraine (at the VUAN) (RU)

KIUA .... Kazakhstan Institute of Fertilizers and Soil Science (RU)

KIUTA ...... Kiwanda cha Uchapaji cha Taifa

KIUV .... Kiev Institute for the Advanced Training of Physicians (RU)

KIV .... Kishinev [*Former USSR*] [*Airport symbol*] (OAG)

kiv .... Kivitel [*Export*] (HU)

kiv .... Kivonat [*Abstract, Resume*] [*Hungary*]

KIVA........ Workgroup for Indians of North America [*Acronym is based on foreign phrase*] [*Netherlands*]

KIVB......... Kommunista Internacionale Vegrehajto Bizottsaga [*Executive Committee of the Communist International*] (HU)

KIvI......... Koninklijk Instituut van Ingenieurs ['*s-Gravenhage*]

KIVM .... Committee for Permafrost Study (of the Academy of Sciences, USSR)

KIVUMINES ... Compagnie Miniere de Kivu [*Mining Company of Kivu*] [*Zaire*] (AF)

KIW .... Kitwe [Zambia] [Airport symbol]   (OAG)

KiW .... Ksiazka i Wiedza [Book and Knowledge] [Publisher]   (POL)

KIWA .... Keurings Instituut Waterleiding Artikelen [Rijswijk]

KIWZ........ Kupiecki Instytut Wiedzy Zawodowej [Institute of Business Administration]   (POL)

KIY .... Kilwa [Tanzania] [Airport symbol]   (OAG)

KIYa .... Foreign Language Courses   (RU)

KIYaLI ...... Kazan' Institute of Language, Literature, and History (of the Academy of Sciences, USSR)   (RU)

Kiyevmetrostroy ... Construction Administration of the Kiev Subway   (RU)

KiyevZNIIEP ... Kiev Zonal Scientific Research and Planning Institute for Standard and Experimental Planning of Residential and Public Buildings   (RU)

KIYU .... Kibris-Yunanistan Dairesi General Mudurlugu [Cyprus-Greece Office Directorate General] [of Foreign Affairs Ministry]   (TU)

KIZ .... Kanaf-Arkia Airlines Ltd. [Israel] [ICAO designator]   (FAAC)

KIZ .... Kazakh Scientific Research Institute of Agriculture   (RU)

KIZ .... Kemijska Industrijska Zajednica [Chemical Industrial Association] [Zagreb]   (YU)

KIZ .... Komisja dla Spraw Inwalidztwa i Zatrudnienia [Commission on Problems of Disability and Employment]   (POL)

Kizelugol' ... Kizel Coal Basin   (RU)

KIZh .... Communist Institute of Journalism   (RU)

KIZILAY... Turkiye Kizilay Dernegi [Turkish Red Crescent Society] [Similar to Red Cross TKD] [See also]   (TU)

KiZPS .... Kopalnictwo i Zaklady Przetworcze Siarki [Sulphur Mining and Processing Enterprise]   (POL)

KJ .... Kilodzul [Kilojoule] [Poland]

KJ .... Kommenden [or Kuenftigen] Jahres [Coming Year] [German]

KJ .... Kostnicka Jednota [Union of Constance]   (CZ)

KJ .... Scierie Kakou Joseph

KJA .... Avistar (Cyprus) Ltd. [ICAO designator]   (FAAC)

KJB .... Katholieke Jeugdbeweging [Catholic Youth Movement] [Netherlands]   (WEN)

KJB .... Kommunistische Jugendbewegung [Communist Youth Movement] [Austria]   (WEN)

KJF .... Karl-Jaspers Foundation   (EA)

KJG........... Kaerntner Juristische Gesellschaft [Kaerntner Legal Society] [Austria]   (SLS)

KJ K .... Kozlekedesi es Jogi Kiado [Publishers of Economic and Legal Literature]   (HU)

KJO .... Kommunistische Jugend Oesterreich [Communist Youth of Austria]

KJOe......... Kommunistische Jugend Oesterreichs [Communist Youth of Austria]   (EG)

KJP .... Kommissionen Justitia et Pax [Denmark]   (EAIO)

KJR........... Katholieke Jeugdraad voor Nederland [Catholic Youth Council for the Netherlands]   (WEN)

KJS .... Karl-Jaspers Stiftung [Karl-Jaspers Foundation - KJF]   (EA)

KJSE......... Kenya Junior Secondary Education

KJU .... Kamiraba [Papua New Guinea] [Airport symbol] [Obsolete]   (OAG)

KJV .... Kerkjeugvereniging [Afrikaans]

KJV........... Kommunistischer Jugendverband [Communist Youth Federation] [Switzerland]   (WEN)

KJV .... Kraljevska Jugoslovenska Vojska [Royal Yugoslav Army]   (YU)

KJVDM..... Kraljevska Jugoslovenska Vojska Draza Mihailovic [Royal Yugoslav Army of Draza Mihailovic]   (YU)

k/k .... Candidate's Membership Card   (RU)

KK .... Cavalry Corps   (RU)

KK .... Committee for Cinematography   (BU)

KK .... Compass Course   (RU)

KK .... Control Commission   (RU)

KK .... End of Curve [Railroads]   (RU)

KK .... Kabushiki Kaisha [Public Limited Company]

KK .... Kaien Kaisha   (IDIG)

KK .... Kaiser Koenigliche [Imperial and Royal] [Title of Austrian Royalty]

KK .... Kandang Kerbau   (ML)

kk .... Kansakoulu [Finland]

KK .... Kansallinen Kokoomus [National Coalition (Conservative Party)] [Finland]   (WEN)

KK .... Kara Komutani [Ground (Forces) Commander]   (TU)

KK .... Kasvatustieteiden Kandidaatti [Finland]

KK .... Kenneth Kaunda [Zambian president, 1964-]

KK .... Kepala Keluarga [Head of Family]   (IN)

KK .... Kepala Kepolisian [Chief of Police]   (IN)

kk .... Kerskrag [Candle Power] [Afrikaans]

KK .... Khmer Krom [Lower Cambodians] [Cambodians living in South Vietnam]   (CL)

kk .... Kiettokomero [Finland]

kk .... Kihlakunta [Finland]

kk .... Kirkonkyla [Finland]

KK .... Kleinkaliber [Small Caliber] [German military]

KK .... Kodeks Karny [Penal Code] [Poland]

KK............ Koku Kanti [Air Fleet] [Japan]

KK............ Kokusai Koryu [Japan Foundation]   (EAIO)

KK............ Komisija za Katastar [Cadastre Commission]   (YU)

KK............ Komitet Koordynacyjny [Coordinating Committee]   (POL)

KK............ Komitet Kuracjuszy [Health Resort Patients' Committee]   (POL)

KK............ Kommerskollegium [National Board of Trade] [Sweden]

KK............ Kommounistikon Komma [Communist Party]   (GC)

KK............ Kommunista Kialtvany [Communist Manifesto]   (HU)

kk............ Konekivaari [Finland]

KK............ Konfliktkommission [Conflict Commission]   (EG)

KK............ Kongka Knitting Co. Ltd. [Thailand]

K k............ Konyvkiado [Book Publishers]   (HU)

kk............ Konyvtari Kotesben [In Library Binding] [Publishing] [Hungary]

kk............ Korona [Crown]   (HU)

K K............ Kossuth Kiado [Kossuth Publishing House]   (HU)

KK............ Kozepeuropai Kupa [Mid-European Cup]   (HU)

KK............ Krajska Konference [Regional Conference]   (CZ)

KK............ Krasnodar Kray   (RU)

KK............ Kremlin Kommandant

KK............ Kuala Kangsar   (ML)

KK............ Kugelkopf [German]   (ADPT)

KK............ Kulturni Komise [Cultural Commission]   (CZ)

KK............ Kulutusosuuskuntien Keskusliitto [Co-Operative Union] [Finland]   (EY)

Kk............ Kunze-Knorr Bremse [Kunze-Knorr Brake]   (EG)

kk............ Kuukaudet [Finland]

kk............ Kuukausi [or Kuukautta] [Finland]

KK............ Kuvvet Kontrollu [Power Controlled] [As of a tractor for vehicles in tow]   (TU)

KK............ Quality Control   (BU)

KK............ Red Cross   (RU)

KK............ Spaceship   (RU)

kk............ Trooper, Cavalryman   (BU)

KKA .... Caucasian Red Army   (RU)

KKA .... Kinima Kypriakis Andistaseos [Cypriot Resistance Movement]   (GC)

KKA .... Kodix Koinonikis Asfaliseos [Social Insurance Code] [Greek]   (GC)

KKA .... Kommounistikon Komma Alvanias [Albanian Communist Party]   (GC)

kkal .... Kilocalorie   (BU)

k Kal.......... Kleine Kalorie [Small Calorie] [German]   (GCA)

KKASSR..... Karakalpak Autonomous Soviet Socialist Republic   (RU)

KKAZ .... Kuybyshev Carburetor and Fittings Plant   (RU)

KKB .... Kernkraftwerk Brunsbuettel, GmbH [Nuclear energy]   (NRCH)

KKB .... Korespondencyjny Kurs Bibliotekarski [Library Science Correspondence Course]   (POL)

KKB .... Kozlekedesi Konyvesbolt [Transportation Publications Book Shop]   (HU)

KKB .... Kunderkreditbank KGaA [Public Credit Bank]

KKBC........ Korea Kuwait Banking Corp.

KKBK........ Kongres Kesatuan Buroh Kebangsaan [National Trade Union Congress]   (ML)

KKC .... Khon Kaen [Thailand] [Airport symbol]   (OAG)

KKD.......... Kokoda [Papua New Guinea] [Airport symbol]   (OAG)

KKDD........ Katalog Kandidatskikh i Doktorskikh Dissertatsii [A bibliographic publication]

KKDDY ..... Kodix Katastaseos Dimosion Dioikitikon Ypallilon [Public Administrative Employees Schedule Code] [Greek]   (GC)

KKE .... Complex Kenimekh Expedition   (RU)

KKE .... Kerikeri [New Zealand] [Airport symbol]   (OAG)

KKE .... Kommunistiko Komma Ellados [Communist Party of Greece] [Political party]   (PPW)

KKEA .... Kikuyu Karinga Educational Association

KKEes........ Kommunistiko Komma Ellados - Esoterikou [Communist Party of Greece - Interior] [Political party]   (PPE)

KKEex ...... Kommunistiko Komma Ellados - Exoterikou [Communist Party of Greece - Exterior] [Political party]   (PPE)

KKE/ML ... Kommunistiko Komma Elladas/Marxiston-Leniniston [Communist Party of Greece/Marxist-Leninist]   (GC)

KKES........ Kommunistiko Komma Ellados - Esoterikou [Communist Party of Greece - Interior] [Political party]   (PPW)

KKF........... Komitet Kultury Fizycznej [Physical Culture Committee]   (POL)

KKF........... "Red Banner" Caspian Naval Flotilla   (RU)

KKFiT........ Komitet Kultury Fizycznej i Turystyki [Physical Culture and Tourism Committee]   (POL)

KKG .... Kesatuan Kebangsaan Guru [National Union of Teachers]   (ML)

KKG .... Konawaruk [Guyana] [Airport symbol] [Obsolete]   (OAG)

KKG .... Kreiskonsumgenossenschaft [Kreis Consumer Cooperative]   (EG)

Kkgbr .... Kunze-Knorr-Bremse fuer Gueterzuege [Kunze-Knorr Brake for Freight Trains]   (EG)

KKh............ Katastatikos Khartis [Charter]   (GC)

KKh............ Koroi Khorikotitos [Net Tons, Net Tonnage] [See also KKKh]   (GC)

Kkh .... Potassium Chloride (RU)

kkhn .... Candidate of Chemical Sciences (RU)

KKhT .... Ktimatologikon kai Khorometrikon Tmima [*Cadastral and Zoning Department*] [*TPPE*] [*See also*] (GC)

KKhTI .... Kazan' Institute of Chemical Technology Imeni S. M. Kirov (RU)

KKhTs .... Kilohertz (BU)

KKhZ .... By-Product Coke Plant (RU)

KKhZhD .... Kiev-Khar'kov Railroad (RU)

KKI .... Committee for Culture and Art (BU)

KKI .... Krajsky Kulturni Inspektorat [*Office of the Regional Inspector of Cultural Activities*] (CZ)

KKI .... Kulturkapcsolatok Intezete [*Institute for Cultural Relations*] (HU)

KKIK .... Keramicno Kemicna Industrija Kamnik [*Kamnik Ceramic and Chemical Industry*] (YU)

KKiKP .... Red Cross and Red Crescent [*Society*] (RU)

KKIV .... Kiallitasokat Kivitelezo Ipari Vallalat [*Enterprise Affiliated with Industry for Arrangement of Exhibits*] (HU)

KKJ .... Kita Kyushu [*Japan*] [*Airport symbol*] [*Obsolete*] (OAG)

KKK .... End of Belt Line [*Railroads*] (RU)

KKK .... Kara Kuvvetler Komutani [*Ground Forces Commander*] (TU)

KKK .... Kernkraftwerk Kruemmel, GmbH [*Nuclear energy*] (NRCH)

KKK .... Kesunyans Keltek Kernow [*Celtic League in Cornwall*]

KKK .... Khmer du Kampuchea Krom [*Association of Friends of the Khmer Krom*] [*Use AKKK Cambodia*] (CL)

KKK .... Kibris Koordinasyon Komitesi [*Cyprus Coordination Committee*] [*Turkish Cypriot*] (TU)

KKK .... Kommounistikon Komma Kyprou [*Communist Party of Cyprus*] [*See also AKEL*] (GC)

KKK .... Konferenzberichte Kernforschung, Kerntechnik [*Information retrieval*]

KKK .... Kosmofysikon kai Kosmotheikon Kinima [*Cosmophysic and Cosmotheist Movement*] [*Greek*] (GC)

KKK .... Krajsky Kynologicky Klub [*Regional Kennel Club*] (CZ)

KKK .... Kreiskontrollkommission [*Kreis Control Commission*] (EG)

KKK .... Switchboard for Checking Credit Rating (RU)

KKKA .... Caucasian "Red Banner" Red Army (RU)

KKKh .... Koroi Katharas Khorikotitos [*Net Register(ed) Tonnage*] [*KKh*] [*See also*] (GC)

KKKT .... Canadian Catholic Confederation of Labor (RU)

KKL .... Card Hopper Contact (RU)

KKL .... Kaupan Keskusliitto [*Federation of Finnish Commerce and Trade*] (EAIO)

KKL .... Kemian Keskusliitto [*Chemical Industry Federation of Finland*] (EAIO)

KKL .... Kernkraftwerk Leibstadt, AG [*Switzerland*] [*Nuclear energy*] (NRCH)

KKLK .... Krajska Komise Lidove Kontroly [*Regional Commission of People's Control*] (CZ)

KKM .... Kereskedelem- es Kozlekedesugyi Miniszter [*Minister of Trade and Transportation*] (HU)

KkM .... Kulkereskedelmi Miniszterium/Miniszter [*Ministry/Minister of Foreign Trade*] (HU)

KKMP .... Korespondencyjny Klub Mlodych Pisarzy [*Young Writers' Correspondence Club*] (POL)

KKN .... Kaapse Kamer van Nywerhede [*South Africa*] (AA)

KKN .... Kernkraftwerk Niederaichbach, GmbH [*Nuclear energy*] (NRCH)

KKN .... Kirkenes [*Norway*] [*Airport symbol*] (OAG)

KKN .... Krosnienskie Kopalnictwo Naftowe [*Krosno Oil Wells*] (POL)

KKO .... Cockpit Oxygen Equipment (RU)

KKO .... Kaikohe [*New Zealand*] [*Airport symbol*] [*Obsolete*] (OAG)

KKO .... Kibris Kurtulus Ordusu [*Cyprus Liberation Army*] (TU)

kko .... Kirkko [*Finland*]

KKO .... Komunalna Kasa Oszczednosci [*Communal Savings Bank*] (POL)

KKO .... Konflikt-Kommissionsordnung [*Conflict Commission Regulations*] (EG)

KKO .... Korps Komando [*Marine Corps*] (IN)

KKO .... National Citizens' Committee [*Poland*] [*Political party*]

KKON .... Koinonikon Kendron Oikogeneias kai Neotitos [*Family and Youth Social Center*] [*Greek*] (GC)

KKOV .... Cossack Mutual Aid Committee (RU)

KKOV .... Peasants' Public Mutual Aid Committee (RU)

KKP .... Canadian Trade-Union Congress (RU)

KKP .... Chinese Communist Party [*Political party*]

KKP .... Cuban Communist Party [*Political party*]

KKP .... Cypriot Communist Party [*Political party*]

KKP .... Kendron Koinonikis Pronoias [*Social Welfare Center*] (GC)

KKP .... Kernkraftwerk Phillipsburg, GmbH [*Nuclear energy*] (NRCH)

KKP .... Kina Kommunista Partja [*Communist Party of China*] [*Political party*]

KKP .... Konfederatsiia Kongolezskikh Profsoiuzov (RU)

KKP .... Leather and Fur Industry (BU)

Kkpbr .... Kunze-Knorr-Bremse fuer Personenzuege [*Kunze-Knorr Brake for Passenger Trains*] (EG)

KKPT .... Kakitangan Khas Periksaan Tentera [*Special Military Intelligence Staff*] (ML)

KKR .... Kaukura [*French Polynesia*] [*Airport symbol*] (OAG)

KK-RKI ...... Control Commission and Workers' and Peasants' Inspection [*1923-1934*] (RU)

KKS .... Aerial Surveying Compass Course (RU)

k ks .... Cavalry Corps (BU)

KKS .... Courses for Command Personnel (RU)

KKS .... Kolejowy Klub Sportowy [*Railway Workers' Sports and Athletics Club*] [*Poland*]

KKS .... Komisja Kontroli Stronnictwa [*Party Control Commission*] (POL)

KKS .... Kongres Kesatuan Sakerja [*Trade Union Congress (TUC)*] (ML)

Kksbr .... Kunze-Knorr-Bremse fuer Schnellzuege [*Kunze-Knorr Brake for Express Trains*] (EG)

KKSFA ...... Kypros - Koreatikos Syndesmos Filias kai Allilengyis [*Cyprus - Korea Friendship and Solidarity League*] (GC)

kkt .... Kozos Kozsegi Tanacs [*Joint Village Council (of two of more villages)*] (HU)

KKT .... Kulturalis Kapcsolatok Tanacsa [*Council of Cultural Relations*] (HU)

KKTD .... Kanunlar ve Kararlar Tetkik Dairesi [*Laws and Decisions' Investigation Office*] [*Under office of Premier*] (TU)

KKTSK ..... Kucuk Kaymakli Turk Spor Kulubu [*Kucuk Kaimakli Turkish Sports Club*] [*Turkish Cypriot*] (GC)

KKU .... Kniznica Komenskeho Univerzity [*Comenius University Library*] [*Bratislava*] (CZ)

KKUH .... King Khalid University Hospital [*Saudi Arabia*]

K Kuv .... Kara Kuvvetleri [*Ground Forces*] (TU)

KKV .... Kiskereskedelmi Vallalat [*Retail Enterprise*] (HU)

KKv .... Komandir Komandnog Voda Baterije [*Commander of the Command Platoon of a Battery*] (YU)

KKV .... Kommounistikon Komma Voulgarias [*Bulgarian Communist Party*] (GC)

KKVI .... Komisija za Kulturne Veze sa Inostranstvom [*Commission for Cultural Relations with Foreign Countries*] (YU)

KKW .... Kikwit [*Zaire*] [*Airport symbol*] (OAG)

KKX .... Kikaiga Shima [*Japan*] [*Airport symbol*] (OAG)

KKZ .... Kamyshin Crane Plant (RU)

KKZ .... Kinderbijslagwet voor Kleine Zelfstandigen [*Children's Allowance Act for Self-Employed of Small Means*] [*Netherlands*] (WEN)

KKZA .... Heavy Caliber Antiaircraft Artillery (BU)

KKZVV ...... Krajska Komise pro Zemedelskou Vyrobu a Vykup [*Regional Commission for Agricultural Production and Bulk Buying*] (CZ)

kl .... Caliber, Gauge (RU)

KL .... Caprolactam (RU)

kl .... Class [*or Category*] (BU)

kl .... Class, Sort, Grade (RU)

Kl .... Clinker [*Road-paving material*] [*Topography*] (RU)

kl .... Club (RU)

kl .... Cosmic Rays (RU)

kl .... Grade (BU)

KL .... Gunboat (RU)

Kl .... Kale [*Castle, Fortress*] (TU)

KL .... Kansalaisvallen Liitto [*League of Civil Power*] [*Finland*] [*Political party*] (PPW)

KL .... Kartenleser [*German*] (ADPT)

KL .... Kartenlocher [*German*] (ADPT)

KL .... Kaufmaennische Leitung [*Business Management*] [*German*] (EG)

kl .... Kaum Loeslich [*Slightly Soluble*] [*German*] (GCA)

kl .... Kevatlukukausi [*Finland*]

kl .... Kiloliter (RU)

kl .... Kilolitre [*Kiloliter*] [*French*] (GPO)

Kl. .... Kilolitro [*Kiloliter*] [*Spanish*] (GPO)

KL .... Klaeger [*Plaintiff*] [*German*] (ILCA)

kl .... Klang [*Musical Overtone*] [*German*]

kl .... Klapka [*Extension (Telephone)*] (CZ)

kl .... Klasa [*Class*] (POL)

kl .... Klasifikacija [*Classification*] (YU)

KL .... Klasse [*Class*] [*German*]

kl .... Klasse [*Class*] [*Denmark*] (GPO)

kl .... Klein [*Small*] [*German*]

KL .... Klemm Flugzeugbau GmbH & Apparatebau Nabern [*Germany*] [*ICAO aircraft manufacturer identifier*] (ICAO)

kl .... Klockan [*O'Clock*] [*Sweden*] (GPO)

kl .... Klokken [*O'Clock*] [*Denmark*] (GPO)

KL .... Komisija za Lekove [*Pharmaceutical Commission*] (YU)

KL .... Komitet Lodzki

KL .... Kontrola Letenja [*Flight Control*] [*Military*] (YU)

KL .... Konzentrationslager [*Concentration Camp*] [*German*] (BJA)

KL .... Kozponti Laboratorium [*Central Laboratory*] (HU)

KL .... Kuala Lumpur [*Malaysia*]

Kl. .... Kuopion Laani(a) [*Finland*]

KL .... Kurang Lebih [*More or Less, Approximately*] (IN)
KL .... Line Contactor (RU)
KL .... Pilot Lamp, Supervisory Lamp (RU)
k-l .... Some (RU)
kl .... Spring, Source [*Topography*] (RU)
KLA .... Air Lituava [*Lithuania*] [*ICAO designator*] (FAAC)
KLA .... Karachi Library Association [*Pakistan*] (PDAA)
KLA .... Kingdom of Libya Airways [*or Airlines*]
Kla.............. Kuala [*River Mouth*] [*Indonesian*] (NAU)
Kla.............. Kuala [*River Mouth*] [*Malaysia*] (NAU)
KLA .... Kwazulu Legislative Assembly
KLA .... Spacecraft (RU)
KLAAGL... Klaagliedere [*Lamentations*] [*Afrikaans*]
kladb .... Cemetery [*Topography*] (RU)
Klar .... Klaerung [*Clarification*] [*German*] (GCA)
klasich....... Classic (BU)
KLASS....... Klassieke [*Classic*] [*Afrikaans*]
klassich...... Classic (RU)
Klassifikat ... Klassifikation [*Classification*] [*German*] (GCA)
KLB........... Kalabo [*Zambia*] [*Airport symbol*] (OAG)
klb .... Klotband [*Cloth Binding*] [*Publishing*] [*Sweden*]
KLB........... Korea Long Term Credit Bank (GEA)
klbd .... Klotband [*Cloth Binding*] [*Publishing*] [*Sweden*]
Klbldbd ..... Kalblederband [*Full-Calf Binding*] [*Publishing*] [*German*]
KLC .... KLM Cityhopper BV [*Netherlands*] [*ICAO designator*] (FAAC)
KLCC......... Kuala Lumpur City Center [*Malaysia*] (ECON)
KLCE......... Kuala Lumpur Commodities Exchange [*Malaysia*]
KLD .... Kongres Liberalno-Demokratyczny [*Liberal Democratic Congress*] [*Poland*] [*Political party*] (EY)
KLDR .... Korejska Lidove-Demokraticka Republika [*Korean People's Republic*] (CZ)
Kldr .... Kunstleder [*Artificial Leather*] [*Publishing*] [*German*]
KLEG........ Kancelar Legii [*Office of Czechoslovak Legions (Attached to the Ministry of National Defense)*] (CZ)
kleurendr.... Kleurendruk [*Color Print*] [*Publishing*] [*Netherlands*]
Kleytuk ...... Moscow Bone Glue and Fertilizer Plant (RU)
KLF .... Cambodian Liberation Front (CL)
KLFA .... Kenya Land Freedom Army
KLFB .... Knihovna Lekarske Fakulty, Brno [*Library of the School of Medicine in Brno*] (CZ)
KLFI .... Kozponti Legkorfizikai Intezet [*Central Institute of Atmospheric Physics*] (HU)
KLFK .... Kniznica Lekarskej Fakulty, Kosice [*Library of the School of Medicine in Kosice*] (CZ)
KLFOL ...... Knihovna Lekarske Fakulty v Olomouci [*Library of the School of Medicine in Olomouc*] (CZ)
KLFP .... Knihovna Lekarske Fakulty, Praha [*Library of the School of Medicine in Prague*] (CZ)
KLFPl .... Knihovna Lekarske Fakulty, Plzen [*Library of the School of Medicine in Plzen*] (CZ)
KLGC........ Kuala Lumpur Garrison Command (ML)
KLH .... Kingdom of Lesotho Handicrafts
KLH .... KLM Helicopters NV [*Netherlands*] [*ICAO designator*] (FAAC)
KLI .... Kalinin Railroad (RU)
Kli .... Klinik [*Clinic*] (TU)
KLIAU....... Korea Land Improvement Association Union (PDAA)
KLIC......... Korumburra Living for Independence Centre [*Australia*]
klim............ Climatic, Climatology (RU)
Klimakde ... Klimakunde [*Climatology*] [*German*] (GCA)
Klin .... Klinik [*Clinic*] [*German*]
klinich........ Clinical (RU)
KLK .... Card-Tape-Card Machine (RU)
KLK .... Katolicky Literarni Klub [*Catholic Literary Club*] (CZ)
KLK .... Kelas Latehan Kerja [*Work (Job) Training Class*] (ML)
KLK .... Krajska Lidova Knihovna [*Regional People's Library*] (CZ)
klkh............ Kolkhoz [*Topography*] (RU)
klkh dv .... Kolkhoz Yard [*Topography*] (RU)
KLKhTI..... Leningrad "Red Banner" Institute of Chemical Technology Imeni Lensovet (RU)
KLKSNR ... Komise Lidove Kontroly Slovenske Narodni Rady [*Commission of People's Control of Slovakia's National Council*] (CZ)
kl Ldg......... Kleine Ladung [*Small Charge*] [*German*] (GCA)
klm .... Kilolumen (RU)
KLM .... KLM Royal Dutch Airlines [*Netherlands*] [*ICAO designator*] (FAAC)
KLM .... Koninklijke Luchtvaart Maatschappij [*Royal Dutch Airlines*] (WEN)
klm-ch........ Kilolumen-Hour (RU)
KLN .... Kypriaki Leskhi Neolaias [*Cypriot Youth Club*] [*London*] (GC)
klny .... Kulonlenyomat [*Reprint*] [*Hungary*]
KLO .... Kalibo [*Philippines*] [*Airport symbol*] (OAG)
k-lo .... Kello [*Hour, O'Clock*] [*Finland*] (GPO)
KLO .... Krajevni Ljudski Odbor [*District People's Committee*] (YU)
KLOIA ...... Korea Lubricating Oil Industry Association (EAIO)
Klopffestigk ... Klopffestigkeit [*Octane Number*] [*German*] (GCA)
klotb .... Klotband [*Cloth Binding*] [*Publishing*] [*Sweden*]

klotbd .... Klotband [*Cloth Binding*] [*Publishing*] [*Sweden*]
KLP........... Flight Training Course (RU)
klp .... Kai Loipa [*Et Cetera*] (GC)
KLP........... Kendrikon Limenarkheion Peiraios [*Piraeus Central Port Authority*] (GC)
KLP........... Korean Labor Party [*Political party*]
KLP........... Krajowa Loteria Pieniezna [*National Lottery*] (POL)
KLR .... Kalmar [*Sweden*] [*Airport symbol*] (OAG)
KLR .... Kreislandwirtschaftsrat [*Kreis Agricultural Council*] (EG)
KLR .... Linear Expansion Coefficient (RU)
KLRC........ Kimberley Language Resource Centre [*Australia*]
KLRI .... Kainji Lake Research Institute [*Nigeria*] (ARC)
klrn............ Kleuren [*Color*] [*Publishing*] [*Netherlands*]
KLS............ Kommunisten und Linkssozialisten [*German*]
KLS........... Stationary Belt Conveyor (RU)
KLSE .... Kuala Lumpur Stock Exchange
Klstr .... Kloster [*Monastery*] [*German*]
KLTCB ...... Korean Long Term Credit Bank
KLTE .... Kossuth Lajos Tudomanyegyetem [*Lajos Kossuth University of Sciences*] (HU)
KLTM....... Kuala Lumpur Tin Market [*Malaysia*]
KLU .... Klagenfurt [*Austria*] [*Airport symbol*] (OAG)
KLu .... Koninklijk Luchtmacht [*Royal Air Force*] [*Netherlands*]
Klurabis ..... Club of Workers in the Arts (RU)
KLV .... Kalgoorlie Lake View Proprietary Ltd. [*Australia*] (ADA)
KLV .... Karlovy Vary [*Former Czechoslovakia*] [*Airport symbol*] (OAG)
klv .... Kilowatt (BU)
KLW .... Karl-Liebknecht-Werke, Magdeburg [*Karl-Liebknecht Works, Magdeburg*] (EG)
KLX........... Kalamata [*Greece*] [*Airport symbol*] (OAG)
KLZ............ Kleinzee [*South Africa*] [*Airport symbol*] (OAG)
KM............ Acid Mucopolysaccharide (RU)
km .... Commandant (BU)
KM............ Comoros [*ANSI two-letter standard code*] (CNC)
KM............ Contact Mechanism (RU)
KM............ Crystal Modulator (RU)
KM............ Cyril and Methodius (BU)
KM............ De Koninklijke Marechaussee [*Benelux*] (BAS)
KM............ Kabataang Makabayan [*Nationalist Youth*] [*Philippines*]
KM............ Kablovska Mreza [*Cable Network*] [*Military*] (YU)
km .... Karabin Maszynowy [*Machine Gun*] [*Poland*]
Km............. Kilometer [*Afrikaans*]
km .... Kilometer [*Albanian*]
km .... Kilometer [*German*]
km .... Kilometr [*Kilometer*] (POL)
km .... Kilometre [*Kilometer*] [*French*]
km .... Kilometre [*Kilometer*] [*Turkey*] (GPO)
km .... Kilometri(a) [*Kilometer*] [*Finland*]
Km............. Kilometro [*Kilometer*] [*Spanish*]
KM............ Komanda Mesta [*Command of a City*] (YU)
KM............ Komisija za Mehanizaciju [*Mechanization Commission*] (YU)
KM............ Komitet Miejski [*City Committee*] (POL)
kM............. Kommenden Monats [*Of Next Month*] [*German*]
KM............ Koni Maszynowych [*Horsepower*] (POL)
KM............ Kon Mechaniczny [*Horsepower*] [*Poland*]
KM............ Kozellatasi Miniszterium/Miniszter [*Ministry/Minister of Supply*] (HU)
KM............ Kozlekedesugyi Miniszterium/Miniszter [*Ministry/Minister of Transportation*] (HU)
km .... Kozmondas [*Proverb*] (HU)
KM............ Kozoktatasugyi Miniszterium/Miniszter [*Ministry/Minister of Public Education (Since 1951)*] (HU)
KM............ Krajske Muzeum [*Regional Museum*] (CZ)
KM............ Krauss-Maffei [*Weapons manufacturer*]
KM............ Kritisches Muster [*German*] (ADPT)
KM............ Kuenftigen Monats [*Coming Months*] [*German*]
KM............ Kulugyminiszterium/Miniszter [*Ministry/Minister of Foreign Affairs*] (HU)
K M .... Kurucu Meclis [*Organizing Assembly*] (TU)
KM............ Kutahya Manyezit Isletmeleri AS [*Kutahya Magnezite Operations Corp.*] (TU)
km .... Kyvika Metra [*Cubic Meters*] (GC)
KM............ March Route Commandant (RU)
KM............ March Route Commander (BU)
KM............ Marrow (RU)
KM............ Meteorological Observation Record Book (RU)
KM............ Michaelis Constant (RU)
km .... My Italics (BU)
KM............ Naval Fortress (RU)
KM............ Oxygen Mask (RU)
Km............. Potassium Magnesium Sulfate (RU)
KM²........... Stone Bridge (RU)
Km² .... Kilometre Carre [*Square Kilometer*] [*French*] (MTD)
km² .... Kilometr Kwadratowy [*Square Kilometer*] [*Poland*]
km² .... Square Kilometer (BU)
km³ .... Kilometr Szescienny [*Cubic Kilometer*] [*Poland*]

KMA......... Kalgoorlie Mining Associates [*Australia*]   (ADA)

KMA......... Kenya Medical Association

KMA......... Kepzomuveszeti Alap [*Fine Arts Fund*]   (HU)

KMA......... Kerema [*Papua New Guinea*] [*Airport symbol*]   (OAG)

KMA......... Koninklijke Militaire Academie [*Royal Military Academy*] [*Netherlands*]   (WEN)

KMA......... Korea Military Academy

KMA......... Kungliga Musikaliska Akademien [*Sweden*]   (SLS)

KMA......... Kursk Magnetic Anomaly   (RU)

KMAC....... Koztarsasagi Magyar Automobil Club [*Automobile Club of the Hungarian Republic*] [*Formerly Royal Hungarian Automobile Club*]   (HU)

KMAGV.... Korean Military Assistance Group, Vietnam   (VNW)

KMAS........ Kibris Madenler Anonim Sirketi [*Cyprus Mines Corporation*] [*Turkish Cypriot*]   (GC)

KMAU....... Moscow "Red Banner" Aviation School   (RU)

KMB......... Kaspar, Melchior, and Balthazar [*Initials of the three Wise Men placed on Polish homes during the Christmas season*]

KMB......... Koinambe [*Papua New Guinea*] [*Airport symbol*]   (OAG)

KMB......... Konstruktions-Montage-Buero [*Design and Assembly Office*]   (EG)

kmb .... Kontant met Bestelling [*Cash with Order*] [*Business term*] [*Afrikaans*]

KMB......... Public Libraries Pool   (RU)

KMC......... Kenya Meat Commission

KMC......... Klub Mladych Ctenaru [*Club of Young Readers*]   (CZ)

km/ch....... Kilometers per Hour   (BU)

KMD........ Kadikoy Musik Dernegi [*Kadikoy Music Association*] [*Istanbul*]   (TU)

KMD........ Kenya Meteorological Department [*Research center*]   (EAS)

KMDH ...... Dienst Hydrografie der Koninklijke Marine [*Netherlands*]   (MSC)

KM-DK..... Machine-Gun Mortar Decontamination Kit   (BU)

KMDOR.... Kommodoor [*Commodore*] [*Afrikaans*]

kmdr......... Komandor [*Commodore*] [*Poland*]

KMDR...... Kommandeur [*Commander*] [*Afrikaans*]

kmdt......... Komendant [*Commander*] [*Poland*]

kmdt......... Kommandant [*Commandant*] [*Afrikaans*]

KME......... Kypriaki Metallevtiki Etaireia [*Cyprus Mines Corporation*]   (GC)

KME......... Kyushu Matsushita Electric [*Commercial firm*] [*Japan*]

KMEA....... Kinitai Monades Ethnofylakis Amynis [*National Guard Mobile Defense Units*] [*Greek*]   (GC)

KMEIA...... Kodaly Music Education Institute of Australia

KMET .... Committee on Meteorites (of the Academy of Sciences, USSR)   (RU)

KMF .... Kabinet Moderni Filologie [*Department of Modern Philology (of the Czechoslovak Academy of Sciences)*]   (CZ)

KMF .... Kamina [*Papua New Guinea*] [*Airport symbol*]   (OAG)

kmf............ Kelt Mint Fent [*Date as Above*]   (HU)

KMF .... Klub Modernich Filologu [*Modern Philology Club*]   (CZ)

KMF .... Short Film   (RU)

KMFD ...... National Committee for Liberty and Decentralization [*Malagasy*]   (AF)

KMFOAW ... Kommission fur Musikforschung der Osterreichischen Akademie der Wissenschaft en [*Commission for Music Research of the Austrian Academy of Sciences*]   (EAIO)

KMFRI ...... Kenya Marine Fisheries Research Institute   (ASF)

KMFRV..... Committee in Support of the Demand for a New Republic [*Malagasy*]   (AF)

KMG........ Cavalry Motorized and Mechanized Group   (RU)

KMG........ Kendrikon Morfotikon Grafeion [*Central Educational Office*]   (GC)

km/g........ Kilometry na Godzine [*Kilometers per Hour*] [*Poland*]

KMG........ Klynveld Main Goerdeler [*European accounting firm*]

KmG........ Kmecki Glas [*Peasant's Voice*] [*A periodical*]   (YU)

KMG........ Kombinat za Montazne i Opste Gradevinske Radove [*Combine for General Construction Jobs*]   (YU)

KMG........ Kunming [*China*] [*Airport symbol*]   (OAG)

KMGV ...... Pro-Military Government Committee in the Ambatondrazaka Subprefecture [*Malagasy*]   (AF)

Km/h........ Kilometros por Hora [*Kilometers per Hour*] [*Spanish*]

KMh.......... Koniogodzina [*Horse-Power-Hour*] [*Poland*]

KMI .... Kaunas Medical Institute   (RU)

KMI .... Kereskedelmi Minosegellenorzo Intezet [*Commercial Quality Control Institute*]   (HU)

KMI .... Kiev Medical Institute Imeni Academician A. A. Bogomolets   (RU)

KMI .... Kirgiz State Medical Institute   (RU)

KMI .... Klub Mlodej Inteligencji [*Club of Young Intelligentsia*]   (POL)

KMI .... Miyazaki [*Japan*] [*Airport symbol*]   (OAG)

KMIAE..... Committee for the Peaceful Utilization of Atomic Energy   (BU)

KMIDC.... Korea Marine Industry Development Corporation   (MSC)

KMIP .... Committee on Measures and Measuring Instruments   (RU)

KMiP .... Komitet Miejski i Powiatowy [*City and County (Party) Committee*]   (POL)

KMITL...... King Mongkut's Institute of Technology, Ladkrabang [*Ministry of University Affairs*] [*Thailand*]   (ERC)

KMITT...... King Mongkut's Institute of Technology, Thonburi [*Thailand*]   (ERC)

KMIZ........ Correlation Methods in Earthquake Investigation   (RU)

KMJ.......... Kumamoto [*Japan*] [*Airport symbol*]   (OAG)

KMK .... Kibris Maden Kumpanyasi [*Cyprus Mining Company*]   (TU)

KMK .... Konyvtartudomanyi es Modszertani Kozpont [*Center for Library Science and Methodology*] [*Hungary*] [*Information service or system*]   (IID)

KMK .... Krestanska Mirova Konference [*Christian Peace Conference*]   (CZ)

KMK .... Kultusministerkonferenz

KMK .... Kuznetsk Metallurgical Kombinat   (RU)

KMK .... Medical Control Commission   (BU)

kmk/kaemka ... Kozveszelyes Munkakerulo [*Work-Shirking That Endangers Public Order or Vagrancy*]   (HU)

KMKP........ Kredit Modal Kirja Penanaman [*Indonesia*]   (IMH)

KMKS........ Multipurpose Magnetic Logging Station   (RU)

KML .... Kamileroi [*Australia*] [*Airport symbol*] [*Obsolete*]   (OAG)

KML .... Kenya Muslim League

KMM .... Etudiants des Provinces [*Provincial Students*] [*Malagasy*]   (AF)

KMM .... Kesatuan Malaya Merdeka [*Free Malaya Front*]   (ML)

KMM .... Kimam [*Indonesia*] [*Airport symbol*]   (OAG)

KMM........ Mechanized Treadway Bridge   (RU)

KMMC ...... Kangaroo Marketing and Management Committee [*Australia*]

KMMC ...... Kerala Minerals and Metals Corp. [*India*]   (PDAA)

KMME ...... Concentrate of Mineral-Oil Emulsion   (RU)

KMME ...... Kendron Marxistikon Meleton kai Erevnon [*Center for Marxist Studies and Research*] [*Greek*]   (GC)

kmn .... Candidate of Medical Sciences   (RU)

KMN........ Kamina [*Zaire*] [*Airport symbol*]   (OAG)

KMN........ Kasatria Mangku Negara [*Fourth Grade of Most Distinguished Order of Pangkuan Negara*] [*Malaysia*]   (ML)

KMNI .... Komisija za Medicinsko-Naucna Istrazivanja [*Medical Research Commission*]   (YU)

KMNO ...... Kolegium Ministerstva Narodni Obrany [*Ministry of National Defense Advisory Board*]   (CZ)

KMO........ After Engine Room   (RU)

KMO........ Committee of Youth Organizations of the USSR   (RU)

km/o......... Kilometer Ora [*Kilometers per Hour*]   (HU)

KMO........ Kimya Muhendisleri Odasi [*Chamber of (Turkish) Chemical Engineers*]   (TU)

KMO........ Kobe Marine Observatory   (BARN)

KMO........ Music Education Courses   (RU)

KMODD.... Kendron Metekpaidevseos Organon Dimosias Dioikiseos [*Advanced Training Center for Public Administration Officials*] [*Greek*]   (GC)

KMOETs... Carboxymethyl Hydroxyethyl Cellulose   (RU)

KMOJMA ... Kobe Marine Observatory/Japan Meteorological Agency   (MSC)

kmol'......... Kilogram Molecule, Kilomole   (RU)

KMP .... Corps Medical Station   (RU)

KMP .... International Law Commission   (BU)

KMP .... Kabinet Mezinarodniho Prava [*Department of International Law (of the Czechoslovak Academy of Sciences)*]   (CZ)

KMP .... Kangaroo Management Program [*Australia*]

KMP .... Katipunang Manggagawang Pilipino [*Trade Union Congress of the Philippines - TUCP*]

KMP .... Keetmanshoop [*South-West Africa*] [*Airport symbol*]   (OAG)

KMP .... KERAMOPROJEKT - Statni Ustav pro Projektovani Zavodu Prumyslu Stavebnich Hmot a Keramiky [*State Planning Institute of Enterprises for Building Material and Ceramics Industry*]   (CZ)

KMP .... Kilusang Mabubukid ng Pilipnas [*Philippine Peasant Federation*] [*Political party*]

KMP .... Kommunistak Magyarorszagi Partja [*Communist Party of Hungary*] [*Political party*]   (PPE)

KMP .... Koyala Mazdoor Panchayat [*India*]

KMPI........ Kuwait Metal Pipes Industries   (ME)

KMPiK ...... Klub Miedzynarodowej Prasy i Ksiazki [*International Press and Book Club*]   (POL)

KMPP........ Kisan Mazdoor Praja Party [*India*] [*Political party*]

KMP-TUCP ... Katipunang Manggagawang Pilipino [*Trade Union Congress of the Philippines*]   (EY)

KMPV .... Correlation Method of Refracted Waves   (RU)

KMPZPR ... Komitet Miejski Polskiej Zjednoczonej Partii Robotniczej [*City Committee of the Polish United Workers Party*]   (POL)

KMQ......... Komatsu [*Japan*] [*Airport symbol*]   (OAG)

KMR .... Karimui [*Papua New Guinea*] [*Airport symbol*]   (OAG)

KMR .... Kulturno Masovni Rad [*Mass Culture Program*] [*Military*]   (YU)

KMR .... Kyrkomusikernas Riksforbund [*Society of Swedish Church Musicians*]   (EAIO)

KMR .... Low-Speed Code Relay   (RU)

KMRI .... Kunming Metallurgy Research Institute [*China*]   (IRC)

KM RNP.... Correlation Modification of Controlled Directional Reception (RU)
KMS .... Karitane Mothercraft Society [*Australia*]
KMS .... Kenya Museum Society (EAIO)
KMS .... Komunalni Sluzba [*Public Service*] [*Civil defense*] (CZ)
KMS .... Korean Meteorological Society (EAIO)
KMS .... Kumasi [*Ghana*] [*Airport symbol*] (OAG)
KMSB....... Commander of Motorized Rifle Battalion (RU)
KMSB........ Komity Mpanazava ny Saim-Bahoaka [*National Public Information Committee*] [*Malagasy*] (AF)
KMSD .... Commander of Motorized Rifle Division (RU)
km/sek ...... Kilometry na Sekunde [*Kilometers per Second*] [*Poland*]
KMSMRR ... Kapisanan ng mga Manggagawa Sa MRR [*Manila Railroad Workers' Union*] [*Philippines*]
Kmsn......... Kommission [*Commission*] [*German*]
KMSP....... Commander of Motorized Rifle Regiment (RU)
Kmsr......... Kommissaer [*Deputy, Commissioner*] [*German*]
KMST....... Courses of Masters of Socialist Labor (RU)
Kmst.......... Karl-Marx-Stadt [*Karl-Marx-Stadt*] (EG)
km–st........ Kilometerstunden [*Kilometer per Hour*] [*German*] (GCA)
KMSTIBF ... Kibris Maden Sirketi Turk Isciler Birligi Federasyonu [*Federation of Turkish Workers Unions of the Cyprus Mines Corporation*] (GC)
KMSU .... Komsomol Youth Construction Administration (RU)
KMT .... Cobalt-Manganese Thermistor (RU)
KMT .... KiMidar Tours [*Egypt*]
KMT .... Klub Milosnikow Teatru [*Theater Fans' Club*] [*Poland*]
KMT .... Kuomintang [*Nationalist Party of Taiwan*] [*Political party*] (PD)
KMTB .... Kibris Milli Turk Birligi [*Cypriot National Turkish Union*] (PPE)
KMTC .... Kuwait Marine Transportation Co.
KMTP....... Committee for the Defense of the Revolution [*Malagasy*] (AF)
KMTP....... Koninklijke Maatschappij Tuinbouw en Plantkunde [*Netherlands*] (SLS)
KMTs .... Carboxymethylcellulose (RU)
KMTS....... Office of Materials and Equipment Supply (RU)
KMTVE..... Komity Malagasy Momba ny Taonan'ny Vehivary Erantany
KMU......... Karl-Marx-Universitaet [*Karl Marx University*] (EG)
KMU .... Kilusang Mayo Uno [*May First Movement*] [*Philippines*] [*Political party*]
KMU .... Kismayu [*Somalia*] [*Airport symbol*] (OAG)
KMU .... Kurucu Meclis Uyesi [*Organizing Assembly Member*] (TU)
KMUJ .... Kolo Medykow Uniwerstetu Jagiellonskiego [*Medical Students' Circle of Jagiellonian University*] (POL)
KMUL .... Kolo Medykow Uniwersytetu Lodzkiego [*Medical Students' Circle of Lodz University*] (POL)
KMUMCS ... Kolo Medykow Uniwersytetu Marii Curie-Sklodowskiej [*Medical Students' Circle of Maria Curie-Sklodowska University*] (POL)
KMUR....... Komisja Miedzyministerialna Uplynnienia Remanentow [*Inter-Ministerial Commission on the Distribution of Surpluses*] (POL)
KMV .... Caucasian Spas [*Health resort area*] (RU)
KMV .... Kalemyo [*Myanmar*] [*Airport symbol*] (OAG)
KMV .... Kikuya Mission Volunteers
KMW........ Kola Mlodziezy Wojskowej [*Military Youth Circle*] (POL)
KMZ......... Kangaroo Management Zone
KMZ......... Kazakh Metallurgical Plant (RU)
KmZ......... Kmecka Zena [*The Farm Woman*] [*A periodical*] (YU)
KMZ......... Kol'chugino Metal-Rolling Plant Imeni S. Ordzhonikidze (RU)
KMZ......... Komitim-Pirenena Miaro ny Zon' Olombelona [*Standing Committee of the National Congress*] [*Malagasy*] (AF)
KMZ......... Kraftfahrzeug- und Motorenwerk, Zwickau (VEB) [*Zwickau Motor Vehicle and Engine Plant (VEB)*] (EG)
KMZ......... Kuznetsk Metallurgical Plant (RU)
KmzlR .... Kommerzialrat [*German*]
kn .... Book [*or Volume*] (BU)
k-n............. Captain (RU)
KN............. GKN Group Services Ltd. [*British*] [*ICAO designator*] (ICDA)
KN............. Horse Van (RU)
Kn............. Kainite (RU)
KN............. Kaltverformt und Normalgeglueht [*Cold Worked and Normalized Steel*] [*German*] (GCA)
KN............. Katolicke Noviny [*Catholic News*] [*A newspaper*] (CZ)
KN............. Kenya Navy
kn .... Kiado Nelkul [*Without Publisher*] [*Hungary*]
Kn............. Kleiner Nahgueterzug [*Small Local Freight Train*] (EG)
Kn............. Knaben [*Boy*] [*German*]
kn .... Kniga [*Book, Volume*] (YU)
Kn............. Knoten [*Knot*] [*German*]
KN............. Kopalnictwo Naftowe [*Oil Wells*] (POL)
KN............. Kuantan [*Malaysia*] (ML)
KN............. Low-Voltage Cable (RU)
kn .... Our Italics (BU)
KN............. Overall Adjustment (RU)

KN............. Petroleum Coke (RU)
kn .... Prince (BU)
k-n............. Some (RU)
KN............. St. Christopher-Nevis [*ANSI two-letter standard code*] (CNC)
KNA........... Committee on New Alphabet (RU)
KNA.......... Katholische Nachrichten-Agentur [*Catholic Press Agency*] [*Germany*]
KNA.......... Kenya National Archives [*Nairobi*]
KNA.......... Kenya News Agency
KNA.......... Kommounistiki Neolaia Athinon [*Communist Youth of Athens*] (GC)
KNA.......... Korean People's Army [*Korean People's Democratic Republic*] (RU)
KNA.......... Kuki National Assembly [*India*] [*Political party*] (PPW)
KNA........... St. Christopher-Nevis [*ANSI three-letter standard code*] (CNC)
KNAAS...... Kenya National Academy for Advancement of Arts and Sciences
KNAG....... Koninklijk Nederlands Aardrijkskundige Genootschap [*Netherlands*] (SLS)
KNAG....... Koninklijk Nederlands Aardrijkskundig Genootschap [*Royal Dutch Geographical Society*] [*Netherlands*] (EAIO)
KNAP .... Center for Agitation and Propaganda by Visual Means (RU)
KNAW....... Koninklijke Nederlandse Akademie van Wetenschappen [*Royal Netherlands Academy of Arts and Sciences*] (EAIO)
KNB........... Krajowa Narada Budownictwa [*All-Polish Conference on Construction*] (POL)
KNBC .... Kariba North Bank Company
KNBPKN ... Komisja Normalizacyjna Budownictwa Polskiego Komitetu Normalizacyjnego [*Construction Standardization Commission of the Polish Committee on Standardization*] (POL)
KNBT .... Katholieke Nederlandse Boeren en Tuinbouwsbond [*Netherlands Catholic Farmers and Horticultural Workers Union*] (WEN)
KNBTB...... Katholieke Nederlandse Boerenen en Tuin-Bows-Bond [*Netherlands*] (BAS)
KNBTB...... Katholieke Nederlandse Boerenen Tuindersbond [*Netherlands Catholic Farmers' and Growers' Union*] (EAIO)
KNBV .... Koninklijke Nederlandse Botanische Vereniging [*Netherlands*] (SLS)
KNC........... Kamerun National Congress [*or Convention*] [*Cameroon*] (AF)
KNCCI....... Kenya National Chamber of Commerce and Industry (EAIO)
KNCIAWPRC ... Korean National Committee of the International Association on Water Pollution Research and Control (EAIO)
KNCIAWPRC ... Kuwaiti National Committee of the International Association on Water Pollution Research and Control (EAIO)
KNCJ........ Katalog Norm i Cen Jednostkowych [*Catalog of Norms and Unit Prices*] (POL)
KNCSS...... Kenya National Council of Social Services
KNCU .... Kilimanjaro Native Co-Operation Union Ltd.
KNCV .... Koninklijke Nederlandse Chemische Vereniging [*'s-Gravenhage*]
KND.......... Directive Gain [*Antenna*] (RU)
KND.......... Kindu [*Zaire*] [*Airport symbol*] (OAG)
KND.......... Low-Pressure Chamber (RU)
KND.......... Low-Pressure Compressor (RU)
KNDD....... Kendron Neotitos Dimou Athinaion [*Athens Municipality Youth Center*] (GC)
KNDK....... Kodix Nomon Dimon kai Koinotiton [*Law Code for Municipalities and Communes*] [*Greek*] (GC)
KNDK....... Koreai Nepi Demokratikus Koztarsasag [*Democratic People's Republic of Korea*] (HU)
KNDO ...... Karen National Defence Organization [*Myanmar*] (FEA)
KNDP....... Kamerun National Democratic Party [*Cameroon*] (AF)
KNDR....... Korean People's Democratic Republic (RU)
KNDR....... People's Democratic Republic of Korea (BU)
KNDTP...... Kiev House of Scientific and Technical Propaganda (RU)
Kne.......... Kleiner Naheilzug [*Small Local Express Train*] (EG)
KNE.......... Komisija za Nuklearnu Energiju [*Nuclear Energy Commission*] (YU)
KNE.......... Kommounistiki Neolaia Ellados [*Greek Communist Youth*] (GC)
KNEB .... Kozponti Nepi Ellenorzesi Bizottsag [*Central People's Control Committee*] (HU)
KNER .... Keshilli i Ndihmes Ekonomike Reciproke [*Albanian*]
KNF .... Komma Neon Filelevtheron [*Young Liberals' Party*] [*Greek*] (GC)
KNFC .... Kenya National Federation of Cooperatives (EAIO)
KNFDI....... Korea Nuclear Fuel Development Institute [*Nuclear energy*] (NRCH)
KNFK .... Kodix Nomon Forologias Kapnou [*Code of Tobacco Tax Laws*] [*Greek*] (GC)
KNFU .... Kenya National Farmers Union
KNG.......... Kaimana [*Indonesia*] [*Airport symbol*] (OAG)
KNGMG.... Koninklijk Nederlands Geologisch Mijnbouwkundig Genootschap [*Netherlands*] (SLS)

KNHM ...... Koninklijke Nederlandsche Heidemaatschappij [*Royal Netherlands Land Development and Reclamation Society*] [*Netherlands*]   (DSCA)

KNI .... Kalallit Niuerfiat [*Greenland Trade*]   (EY)

KNI .... Kantorberita Nasional Indonesia [*News service*] [*Indonesia*]   (EY)

kni .... Kumppani [*Finland*]

knigoizd .... Knigoizdatelstvo [*Publishing House*]   (YU)

knigotorg.... Book Trade Administration   (RU)

knigotorg.... Book Trade Association   (RU)

knigotorg.... Book Trade Office   (RU)

knigouch .... Book Trade Apprenticeship School   (RU)

KNII .... Complex Scientific Research Institute   (RU)

KNIIKiF .... Kirgiz Scientific Research Institute of Health Resorts and Physiotherapy   (RU)

KNIIOT..... Kazan' Scientific Research Institute of Work Safety   (RU)

KNIIPP ..... Krasnodar Scientific Research Institute of the Food Industry   (RU)

KNIITIM .. Kuban' Scientific Research Institute for Testing Tractors and Agricultural Machinery   (RU)

KNIK .... Committee for Science, Art, and Culture   (BU)

KNIPI........ Complex Scientific Research and Design Institute   (BU)

KNIPITIS ... Complex Scientific Research and Design Institute for Construction Standardization and Industrialization   (BU)

KNIPITUGA ... Complex Scientific Research and Design Institute of Territorial Structure, Urban Planning, and Architecture   (BU)

knipl........... Kniplingsmoenster [*Lacelike Pattern*] [*Danish/Norwegian*]

KNiT .... Komitet Nauki i Techniki [*Committee for Science and Technology*]   (POL)

KNIUI .... Karaganda Scientific Research Institute of Coal   (RU)

KNIUI .... Kusnetsk Scientific Research Institute of Coal   (RU)

KNIVI........ Kazan' Veterinary Scientific Research Institute   (RU)

kn izd .... Book Publishing House   (RU)

knizh .... Bookstore   (BU)

knizh .... Literary   (BU)

KNJ .... Kindamba [*Congo*] [*Airport symbol*]   (OAG)

knj .... Knjiga [*Book, Volume*]   (YU)

KNJJS .... Knjizevnost i Jezik u Skoli [*Literature and Language in the School*] [*Belgrade A periodical*]   (YU)

KnjN .... Knjizevne Novine [*Literary News*] [*Belgrade A periodical*]   (YU)

KNK........... Kinai Nepkoztarsasag [*Chinese People's Republic*]   (HU)

KNK........... People's Youth Chamber   (BU)

KNKP .... Committee for Scientific Consultation and Propaganda (of the Academy of Sciences, USSR)   (RU)

KNKV .... Koninklijk Nederlands Korfbalverbond [*Royal Dutch Korfball Association*]   (EAIO)

KnL .... Kenquip (Nigeria) Ltd.

KNL........... Kokoomuksen Nuorten Liitto [*Youth League of the Coalition Party*] [*Finland*]   (EAIO)

KNL........... Kumi- ja Nahkatyoevaen Liitto [*Rubber and Leather Workers*] [*Finland*]   (EY)

KNLA .... Karen National Liberation Army [*Myanmar*] [*Political party*]

KNLC .... Koninklijk Nederlands Landbouw-Comite [*Royal Dutch Agricultural Committee*]   (EAIO)

KNLF........ Karen National Liberation Front [*Myanmar*] [*Political party*]   (PD)

KNM.......... Kenya National Museum

kn mag .... Bookstore   (RU)

KNMB....... Koninklijke Nederlandse Middenstandsbond [*Netherlands*]   (BAS)

KNMD....... Koninklijke Nederlandse Maatschappij voor Diergeneeskunde [*Royal Netherlands Veterinary Association*]   (EAIO)

KNMG....... Koninklijke Nederlandse Maatschappij tot Bevordering der Geneeskunst [*Netherlands*]   (SLS)

KNMI........ Koninklijk Nederlands Meteorologisch Instituut [*Royal Netherlands Meteorological Institute*] [*Research center*]   (WEN)

KNMP .... Koninklijke Nederlandse Maatschappij ter Bevordering der Pharmacie [*Royal Dutch Society for Advancement of Pharmacy*]   (EAIO)

KNMvD..... Koninklijke Nederlandse Maatschappij voor Diergeneeskunde [*Netherlands*]   (SLS)

KNN .... Khabouan (Kan) Neo Thang Noum [*Youth Front Movement*] [*Same as Parti des Jeunes Laotian*]   (CL)

kn n .... Officer of the Guards   (BU)

KNNV........ Koninklijke Nederlandse Natuurhistorische Vereniging [*Netherlands*]   (SLS)

KNO .... Koch, Neff & Oetinger [*Book wholesaler*]

KNO .... Kotarski Narodni Odbor [*District People's Committee*]   (YU)

kn o .... Truck Transport Squad   (BU)

KNOA....... Chinese People's Liberation Army   (BU)

KNOC....... Kuwait National Oil Company   (ME)

KNOJ .... Korpus Narodnog Oslobodenja Jugoslavije [*National Liberation Corps of Yugoslavia*]   (YU)

KNOPO..... Krajiski Narodnooslobodilacki Partizanski Odred [*Krajina National Liberation Partisan Detachment*] [*Croatia*] [*World War II*]   (YU)

KNOPP ..... Study Center for Scientific Organization of Industrial Establishments (of the Academy of Sciences, USSR)   (RU)

KNOV........ Koninklijke Nederlands Ondernemersverbond [*Royal Dutch Employers' Association*]   (WEN)

KNOV........ Korpus Narodnooslobodilacke Vojske [*National Liberation Army Corps*]   (YU)

KNP .... Catholic People's Party [*Dutch*]   (RU)

KNP .... Command and Observation Post   (RU)

KNP .... Commander's Observation Post   (RU)

KNP .... Command Observation Point   (BU)

KNP .... Compagnie Kouilou Niari Pool

KNP .... Katholieke Nationale Partij [*Catholic National Party*] [*Netherlands*] [*Political party*]   (PPE)

KNP .... Katholisk Nederlands Persbureau [*Catholic Netherlands Press Agency*] [*Netherlands*]

KNP .... Kenya National Properties Ltd.

Kn P .... Knotenpunkt [*Junction*] [*German*]   (GCA)

KNP .... Komise Narodniho Pojisteni [*National Insurance Commission*]   (CZ)

KNP .... Kongres Nauki Polskiej [*Congress of Polish Science*]   (POL)

KNP .... Korea National Party [*South Korea*] [*Political party*]   (PPW)

KNP .... Krajska Nemocenska Pojistovna [*Regional Health Insurance Agency*]   (CZ)

KNPA .... Kilimanjaro Native Planters' Association

KNPC .... Kuwait National Petroleum Company [*Kuwait City*]   (ME)

KNPI........... Komite Nasional Pemuda Indonesia [*Indonesian National Youth Council*]   (EAIO)

KN PN ...... Komisja Nadzorcza Panstw Neutralnych (w Korei) [*Neutral Nations Supervisory Commission (in Korea)*]   (POL)

KNPP........ Karenni National Progressive Party [*Myanmar*] [*Political party*]   (EY)

KNPS........ Kuosheng Nuclear Power Station [*Taiwanese*] [*Nuclear energy*]   (NRCH)

KNQ........... Kone [*New Caledonia*] [*Airport symbol*] [*Obsolete*]   (OAG)

KNR........... Chinese People's Republic   (RU)

KNR........... Kalaallit Nunaata Radioa [*Greenland*]   (EY)

KNR........... Komitet Nauk Rolniczych [*Committee on Agricultural Sciences*]   (POL)

KNR........... Koninklijke Nederlandsche Reedersvereeniging [*Netherlands*]   (BAS)

KNR........... Korean National Railroad   (DCTA)

KNR........... People's Republic of China   (BU)

KNRB .... Constitution of the Bulgarian People's Republic   (BU)

KNRG........ Kwame Nkramah Revolutionary Guards [*Ghana*]

KNRV .... Koninklijke Nederlandse Redersvereniging [*Royal Netherland Shipowners Association*]   (EAIO)

KNRV .... Koninklijke Nederlandse Reder Vereniging [*Royal Netherlands Shipowners' Association*]   (WEN)

KNS .... Kancelar Narodniho Shromazdeni [*The National Assembly Office*]   (CZ)

KNS .... Kara-Bogaz-Gol Scientific Research Station (of the Academy of Sciences, USSR)   (RU)

KNS .... Kenuz Airlines Ltd. [*Nigeria*] [*ICAO designator*]   (FAAC)

KNS .... Kenya News Service   (AF)

KNS .... King Island [*Tasmania*] [*Airport symbol*]   (OAG)

KNS .... Kinisi Neon Sosialiston [*Movement of Young Socialists*] [*Greek*]   (GC)

KNS .... Komise pro Narodni Spotrebu [*National Consumption Commission*]   (CZ)

Kns .... Kumulativni Narodni Sprava [*Joint National Administration*]   (CZ)

KNSC........ Kenya National Sports Council

kn skl .... Book Warehouse   (RU)

KNSM .... Koninklijke Nederlandsche Stoomboot Maatschappij [*Netherlands*]   (BAS)

KnsR .... Konsistorialrat [*German*]

KNT.......... Kereszteny Noi Tabor [*Assembly of Christian Women*]   (HU)

KNTB .... Scientific and Technical Libraries Pool   (RU)

KNTC .... Kenya National Trading Corporation

KNThVE ... Kendron Nosimaton Thorakos Voreiou Ellados [*Northern Greece Center for Thoracic Diseases*]   (GC)

Kntlr........... Kontrollor [*Controller*] [*German*]

KNTM .... Knihovna Narodniho Technickeho Musea [*Library of the National Museum of Technology*] [*Prague*]   (CZ)

KNTPVO... Committee for Science, Technical Progress, and Higher Education   (BU)

KNTT .... Committee on Scientific and Technical Terminology (of the Academy of Sciences, USSR)   (RU)

KNTV .... Koninklijke Nederlandse Toonkunstenaars-Verenining [*Royal Netherlands Association of Musicians*]   (EAIO)

KNU........... Kanpur [*India*] [*Airport symbol*]   (OAG)

KNU........... Karen National Union [*Myanmar*]   (PD)

KNU........... Kolarcev Naroden Univerzitet [*Kolarac People's University*] [*Belgrade*]   (YU)

KNUB....... Koninklijke Nederlandse Uitgeversbond
KNUFNS... Kampuchean National United Front for National Salvation (PD)
KNUST...... Kwame Nkrumah University of Science and Technology
KNUT....... Kenya National Union of Teachers
KNV......... Krajsky Narodni Vybor [Regional National Committee]   (CZ)
KNVD....... Koninklijk Nederlands Verbond van Drukkerijen [Royal Netherlands Printing Association]
KNVK....... Koninklijke Nederlandse Vereniging voor de Koffiehandel [Netherlands]   (EAIO)
KNVKH..... National Farmers and Workers Union [Trinidad and Tobago] (EAIO)
KNVL .... Koninklijke Nederlandse Vereniging voor Luchtvaart [Royal Netherlands Aeronautical Association]   (EAIO)
kn-vo .... Book Publishing House   (RU)
KNVTO..... Koninklijke Nederlandse Vereniging van Transport-Ondernemingen [Netherlands]   (BAS)
KNW......... Kolektyw Norm Wewnetrznych [Collective on Domestic Norms] (POL)
KNX.......... Kununurra [Australia] [Airport symbol]   (OAG)
kny .... Kozlony [Bulletin]   (HU)
kny .... Kulonnyomat [Reprint]   (HU)
knytb .... Kozsegi Nyilvanos Tavbeszelo Allomas [Village Public Telephone]   (HU)
KNZ.......... Kenieba [Mali] [Airport symbol]   (OAG)
KNZHRM ... Koninklijke Noord -en Zuid-Hollandsche Redding-Maatschappij [Royal North and South Holland Lifeboat Institution] [Netherlands]   (PDAA)
KO............. Acid Treatment   (RU)
KO............. Check Point [Aviation]   (RU)
KO............. Compensating Winding   (RU)
KO............. Cooperative Organizations   (BU)
KO............. Design Department   (RU)
KO............. Detachment Commander   (RU)
Ko............. Kaikyo [Strait] [Japan]   (NAU)
KO............. Kandidaat-Offisier [Commanding Officer] [Afrikaans]
KO............. Kassenordnung [Financial Decree (Usually relating to the state budget)]   (EG)
KO............. Kihlakunnanoikeus [Finland]
KO............. Kingsley Ozumba [Nigerian politician]
KO............. Komandantska Osmatracnica [Command Observation Post] (YU)
Ko............. Komisja Okregowa [District Commission]   (POL)
Ko............. Komite [Committee]   (TU)
KO............. Komitet Okregowy [District Committee]   (POL)
KO............. Kommatiki Omas [Party Group, Parliamentary Group]   (GC)
KO............. Kommatiki Organosis [Party Organization] [Plus the initial letter of the district or sector of the organization] [Greek]   (GC)
Ko............. Kompanie [Company] [German]   (GCA)
Ko............. Kompanjie [Company] [Afrikaans]
KO............. Kongo Overzee
KO............. Konkursordnung [Legislation on Bankruptcy] [German]
KO............. Koordinacioni Odbor (SIV) [Coordinating Committee]   (YU)
KO............. Korkein Oikeus [Supreme Court] [Finland]   (WEN)
KO............. Krajevni Odbor [Local Committee]   (YU)
KO............. Kulturalno-Oswiatowa (Prace) [Cultural and Educational (Work)]   (POL)
ko .... Kyseessa Oleva [Under Discussion, In Question] [Finland] (GPO)
ko .... Kysymyksessa Oleva [Finland]
KO............. Opposite of OK [Slang] [German]
KO............. Organosilicon   (RU)
KO............. Turnover Coefficient   (RU)
KO............. Volume Compensator [Nuclear energy]   (BU)
KoA .... Coenzyme A   (RU)
KOA .... Kalinin Oblast Archives   (RU)
KOA .... Kommatiki Organosi Akhtidas [Sector Party Organization] (GC)
KOA .... Kommounistiki Organosis Aeroporias [Communist Organization for the Air Force] [Greek]   (GC)
KOA .... Kommounistiki Organosis Athinon [Communist Organization of Athens]   (GC)
KOA .... Kone Air Ltd. [Finland] [ICAO designator]   (FAAC)
koa .... Kontant op Aflewering [Cash on Delivery] [Business term] [Afrikaans]
KOA .... Kratiki Orkhistra Athinon [Athens State Orchestra]   (GC)
KOA .... Kypriakos Organismos Anaptyxeos [Cypriot Development Organization]   (GC)
KOA .... Kypriakos Organismos Athlitismou [Cypriot Athletic Organization]   (GC)
Koagulat..... Koagulation [Coagulation] [German]   (GCA)
KOALA ..... Knowledge Online and Library Automation [Australia]
KOAM....... Korean-American Oil Co.
KOAP .... Kommounistiki Organosis Astynomias Poleon [Communist Organization for the Cities Police] [Greek]   (GC)
KoASSR .... Komi Autonomous Soviet Socialist Republic   (RU)

Koat........... Kommissariat [Office of Commissioner] [German]
KOB.......... Kob Air Ltd. [Uganda] [ICAO designator]   (FAAC)
KOB.......... Koutaba [Cameroon] [Airport symbol]   (OAG)
KOB.......... Kriegsoffizier-Bewerber [Applicant for Wartime Commission] [German military - World War II]
KOB.......... Public Safety Committee   (RU)
kobb .... Kobber [Copper Engraving] [Publishing Danish/Norwegian]
kobberst .... Kobberstik [Copper Engraving] [Publishing Danish/Norwegian]
kobbertr ..... Kobbertrykt [Copperplate Printing] [Publishing Danish/Norwegian]
KOBIDIC .. Korea Bedding and Interior Decoration Industry Cooperative (EAIO)
KO Biuro.... Kulturalno-Oswiatowe Biuro [Office of Culture and Education] (POL)
KOBP .... Komanda Odeljenja Borbenih Potreba [Headquarters of Department of Combat Supplies]   (YU)
KOBue .... Konstruktionsbuero [Designing Office]   (EG)
KOC.......... Koumac [New Caledonia] [Airport symbol]   (OAG)
KOC.......... Kuwait Oil Company [Ahmadi]   (ME)
KOC.......... Kuwait Olympic Committee   (EAIO)
KOCE .... Komi Commodity Exchange [Russian Federation]   (EY)
KOCGP ..... Kuwait Oil Company Gas Project   (ME)
koch.......... Nomad Camp [Topography]   (RU)
KOD.......... Komisija za Opojne Droge [Intoxicating Drugs Commission] (YU)
KOD.......... Krajske Oblastni Divadlo [Regional Theater]   (CZ)
KOD.......... Kurs pro Osvetove Dustojniky [Instruction Course for Armed Forces Cultural and Education Officers]   (CZ)
KODAERAL ... Komando Daerah Angkatan Laut [Naval Region Command] (IN)
KODAM.... Komando Daerah Militer [Military Region Command (Subordinate commands: KOREM, KODIM, KORAMIL)] (IN)
KODAU..... Komando Daerah Udara [Air Region Command]   (IN)
KODCO..... Korean Overseas Development Co. [Korean government agency]
KODIM ..... Komando Distrik Militer [Military District Command] [See KODAM]   (IN)
KODIS....... Koordinations-, Dokumentations-, und Informationsstelle fuer Berufsbildung in Entwicklungslaendern [Coordination, Documentation, and Information Center for Vocational Training in Developing Countries] [Switzerland]
KODISO ... Komma Dimokratikou Sosialismou [Democratic Socialism Party]   (GC)
KODYA ..... Kotamadya [Municipality]   (IN)
KOE.......... Kapnemboriki Omospondia tis Ellados [Tobacco Merchants' Federation of Greece]   (GC)
KOE.......... Kendron Oikonomikon Erevnon [Center of Economic Research] (GC)
KOE.......... Kendron Okeanologikon Erevnon [Center for Oceanological Research]   (GC)
KOE.......... Kommatiki Organosi Ellados [Party Organization of Greece] (GC)
KOE.......... Kooperative Einrichtung [Cooperative Facility]   (EG)
KOE.......... Kupang [Indonesia] [Airport symbol]   (OAG)
KOEE .... Kulfoldi Osztondijasok Egyetemi Elokeszitoje [University Preparatory School for Foreign Scholarship Students] (HU)
koef .... Coefficient   (RU)
Koeff......... Koeffizient [Coefficient] [German]
Koeffiz........ Koeffizient [Coefficient] [German]
KOEK .... Kallitekhnikos Organismos Ellinikon Kinimatografon [Artistic Organization of the Greek Cinema]   (GC)
KOEM .... Communist Organization of Aegean Macedonia   (BU)
KOEP .... Kendron Oikonomikon Erevnon kai Programmatismou [Economic Research and Programing Center] [Greek] (GC)
KOF .... Fatherland Front Committee   (BU)
KOFEM..... Szekesfehervar Konnyufemmu [Szekesfehervar Light Metal Works]   (HU)
KOFIM...... Common Committee for the Struggle in Majunga [Malagasy] (AF)
KOG.......... Kendrikon Organotikon Grafeion [Central Organizational Office] [Cyprus]   (GC)
KOG.......... Kendrikos Organotikos Grammatevs [Central Organizational Secretary]   (GC)
KOG.......... Koninklijk Oudheidkundig Genootschap [Royal Antiquarian Society] [Netherlands]   (EAIO)
KOG.......... Koninklijk Oudheidkundig Genootschap Amsterdam [Netherlands]   (SLS)
KOGA .... Kalinin Oblast State Archives   (RU)
KOGAB ..... Komando Gabungan [Joint Command]   (IN)
Kogakurokyo ... Zen-Nihon Kogaku Kogyo Rodokumiai Kyogikai [All-Japan Council of Optical Industry Workers' Unions]
KOGE........ Magyar Kozhasznalatu Gepjarmuvallalatok Orszagos Egyesulete [National Association of Public Motor Vehicle Enterprises in Hungary]   (HU)
KOGEC ..... Kuwait Oil, Gas, and Energy Corporation   (ME)

KOGEF...... Kibrislilar Ogrenlik ve Genclik Federasyonu [*Cypriots'*
Education and Youth Federation]   (TU)
koger.......... Coherent   (RU)
KOGF........ Kibrislilar Ogrenlik ve Genclik Federasyonu [*Cypriots'*
Education and Youth Federation] [*Also, KOGEF Turkish*
Cypriot]   (GC)
KOGIZ ...... Book Trade Association of State Publishing Houses   (RU)
KOGV........ Kypriakos Organismos Galaktomikis Viomikhanias [*Cyprus*
Dairy Industry Organization]   (GC)
KOGYOGY ... Kobanyai Gyogyszerarugyar [*Pharmaceutical Factory of*
Kobanya]   (HU)
KOH .... Koolatah [*Australia*] [*Airport symbol*] [*Obsolete*]   (OAG)
KOHANMARNAS ... Komando Pertahanan Maritim Nasional [*National*
Maritime Defense Command]   (IN)
KOHANUDNAS ... Komando Pertahanan Udara Nasional [*National Air*
Defense Command]   (IN)
KOHDOSZ ... Kohaszati Dolgozok Szakszervezete [*Trade Union of*
Metallurgical Workers]   (HU)
KOHERT .. Kohoipari Ertekesito Kozpont [*Marketing Center of the*
Metallurgy Industry]   (HU)
KOHHIKI ... Konzerv-, Hus- es Hutoipari Kutato Intezet [*Industrial Research*
Institute on Food Canning and Refrigeration]   (HU)
Kohlezeich ... Kohlezeichnung [*Charcoal Drawing*] [*German*]
KOHNKI... Kokusai Ongaku Hyogikai Nippon Kokunai Iinkai [*Japanese*
National Committee of the International Music Council]
(EAIO)
KOI .... Kirkwall [*Orkney Islands*] [*Airport symbol*]   (OAG)
KOI .... Komite Olympiade Indonesia [*Olympic Committee of Indonesia*]
(EAIO)
KOI .... Komorka Organizacji Inwestycji [*Investment Organization Unit*]
(POL)
KOI .... Krajsky Osvetovy Inspektorat [*Office of the Regional Inspector of*
Cultural Affairs]   (CZ)
koill .... Koillinen [*Finland*]
KOIP .... Komisija za Odobravanje Investicionih Programa [*Commission*
for Approval of Investment Programs]   (YU)
KOIZ .... All-Union Cooperative Joint Publishing House   (RU)
KOJ .... Kagoshima [*Japan*] [*Airport symbol*]   (OAG)
KOJAL...... Kozegeszsegugyi es Jarvanyugyi Allomas [*Public Health and*
Medical Clinic for Contagious Diseases]   (HU)
kok .... Kai Outo Kathexis [*And So Forth*]   (GC)
KOK.......... Kansallinen Kokoomus [*National Coalition Party*] [*Finland*]
[*Political party*]   (EAIO)
KOK.......... Kodix Odikis Kykloforias [*Traffic Code*]   (GC)
KOK.......... Kokkola [*Finland*] [*Airport symbol*]   (OAG)
kok .... Kokoomuslainen [*Finland*]
KOK.......... Krajsky Odbor Kultury [*Regional Department of Culture*]   (CZ)
KOK.......... Kynigetiki Omospondia Kyprou [*Cyprus Hunting Federation*]
(GC)
KOKARMINDAGRI ... Korps Karyawan Pemerintahan Dalam Negeri
[*Indonesian*]
KOKERT... Kozsegi Kenyergyarak Reszvenytarsasag [*Municipal Bakeries*
Limited (Prewar)]   (HU)
KOKEV ..... Kohaszati Alapanyagokat Keszletezo Vallalat [*Stockpiling*
Enterprise for Metallurgical Primary Materials]   (HU)
KOKh........ Kommounistiki Organosis Khorofylakis [*Communist*
Organization for the Gendarmerie]   (GC)
kokh .... Koroi Olikis Khoritikotitos [*Gross Register Tons*]   (GC)
KOKhIMI ... Department of General Chemistry of the Irkutsk Medical
Institute   (RU)
KOKI .... Kiserleti Orvostudomanyi Kutato Intezet [*Research Institute in*
Experimental Medicine]   (HU)
KO-KO ..... Kommerzielle Koordination [*Former East German political*
party]
koks........... By-Product Coke Plant [*Topography*]   (RU)
KOKSI....... Kesatuan Organisasi Koperasi Seluruh Indonesia [*All-Indonesia*
Federation of Cooperatives]   (IN)
Koksokhimmontazh ... All-Union Trust for the Construction and Installation
of By-Product Coke Plants   (RU)
KOKSZ...... Kereskedok Orszagos Kozponti Szovetsege [*National Central*
Merchants Association]   (HU)
Kokudomei ... Zen-Nihon Koku Sangyo Rodokumiai Sodomei [*Japanese*
Confederation of Aviation Labor]
Kokuro ...... Kokutetsu Rodokumiai [*National Railway Workers' Union*]
[*Japan*]
Kokurokyo ... Koku-Sangyo Rodokumiai Kyogikai [*Council of Aircraft*
Industry Workers' Unions] [*Japan*]
Kokuzeikaigi ... Kokuzei Rodokumiai Zenkokukaigi [*National Federation of*
Inland Revenue Employees' Unions] [*Japan*]
KO KVKSC ... Komise Obrany KV KSC (AV KSS) [*Defense Commission,*
Regional Committee of the Communist Party of
Czechoslovakia (Regional Committee of the Communist
Party of Slovakia)]   (CZ)
kol .... Collection   (BU)
kol .... Colony [*Topography*]   (RU)
kol .... Column   (BU)
kol .... Kolega [*Colleague*] [*Poland*]

kol .... Kolom [*Column*] [*Publishing*] [*Netherlands*]
kol .... Kolonel [*Colonel*] [*Afrikaans*]
Kol............. Kolonne [*Column*] [*German*]   (GCA)
Kol............. Kolophon [*Colophon*] [*German*]
kol .... Koloreret [*Colored*] [*Publishing Danish/Norwegian*]
kol .... Koloriert [*Colored*] [*German*]
Kol............. Kolossense [*Colossians*] [*Afrikaans*]
Kol............. Kolumne [*Column*] [*German*]
KOL .... Kuvaamataidonopettajain Liitto [*Finland*]   (SLS)
kol .... Oscillation   (RU)
kol'chugalyuminiy ... Aluminum Alloy Produced by the Kol'chugino
Nonferrous Metals Plant [*1922*]   (RU)
KOLEYSEN ... Kibris Turk Otel, Lokanta, ve Eglence Yerleri Iscileri
Sendikasi [*Turkish Cypriot Hotel, Restaurant, and*
Amusement Place Workers' Union]   (TU)
kolich .... Quantitative, Quantity, Amount, Number   (RU)
kolichestv... Quantitative   (RU)
KOLK .... Kosten-und Leistungsrechnung in Krankenhaeusern [*German*]
(ADPT)
Kolkhoztsentr ... All-Union Council of Collective Farms   (RU)
koll .... Colloidal, Colloid   (RU)
KOLL........ Kollege [*College*] [*Afrikaans*]
Koll.......... Kollegium [*Corporation*] [*German*]
KOLL........ Kollektief [*Collective*] [*Afrikaans*]
Koll.......... Kolloid [*Colloid*] [*German*]   (GCA)
koll .... Ryhmasana, Kollektiivisesti [*Collective Noun*] [*Finland*]
Kollat .... Kollation [*Collation*] [*German*]
kollig .... Kolligatum [*Work Bound with Another*] [*Publishing*] [*Hungary*]
Koll Srt ...... Kollektif Sirketi [*Corporation*]   (TU)
Kolon....... Colony [*Topography*]   (RU)
kolor........ Kolorerad [*Colored*] [*Sweden*]
kolor........ Koloreret [*Colored*] [*Publishing Danish/Norwegian*]
kolor........... Koloriert [*Colored*] [*German*]
Kol Ort ...... Kollektif Ortakligi [*Collective Partnership*] [*Turkey*]   (CED)
kol red ...... Kolegium Redakcyjne [*Editorial Staff*] [*Poland*]
Kol S .... Kollektif Sirketi [*Collective Company*] [*Turkey*]   (CED)
KOLS........ Kommounistiki Organosis Limenikou Somatos [*Communist*
Organization for the Port Corps] [*Greek*]   (GC)
KOLSS ..... Korean Library Science Society [*South Korean*]   (SLS)
KolSt........ Koloniale Studien [*Benelux*]   (BAS)
Kolstok....... State Commercial Grocery Enterprise   (BU)
kolts .... Koltseg [*Cost, Expenses*]   (HU)
KOLUC ...... Kongolees Leuvens Universitair Centrum
kol-vo........ Quantity, Amount, Number   (RU)
KOM........ Commanding, Command, Command Element   (BU)
kom .... Commissar   (BU)
Kom........... Commissariat   (RU)
kom .... Committee   (BU)
kom .... Communist   (RU)
KOM........ Compressor   (RU)
kom .... Kilohm   (RU)
KOM........ Kiniti Odondoiatriki Monas [*Mobile Dental Unit*] [*Greek*]   (GC)
Ko M .... Kohaszati Miniszterium/Miniszter [*Ministry/Minister of*
Metallurgy]   (HU)
Kom........... Komando [*Commando*]   (TU)
kom .... Komendant [*Commander*] [*Poland*]
Kom........... Komiser [*Commissioner*] [*As of a police department*]   (TU)
kom .... Komitee [*Committee*] [*Afrikaans*]
kom .... Komnata [*Room*] [*Commonwealth of Independent States*]
(EECI)
KOM........ Komodor [*Commodore*]   (IN)
KOM......... Komo-Manda [*Papua New Guinea*] [*Airport symbol*] [*Obsolete*]
(OAG)
KOM......... Kompeni [*Company*]   (ML)
KOM......... Kraftomnibusse [*Motor Buses*]   (EG)
KOMABAL ... Komando Markas Besar Angkatan Laut [*Navy Headquarters*
Command]   (IN)
KOMAFI... Kooperative Malagasy Fitaterana [*Malagasy Transportation*
Cooperative]   (AF)
KOMAK.... Communist Academy   (RU)
Komalyum ... Commission on Aluminum   (RU)
KOMAMAFIMI ... Komity Maharitra Manohana ny Fitondra-Miaramila
[*Permanent Committee to Support the Military*
Government] [*Malagasy*]   (AF)
KOMANDAK ... Komando Antar Daerah Kepolisian [*Police Interregional*
Command]   (IN)
komandarm ... Army Commander   (RU)
KOMAO.... Caucasian Branch of the Moscow Archaeological Society   (RU)
komartbat .. Artillery Battery Commander   (RU)
komartform ... Commissar of Artillery Formations   (RU)
komb .... Kombineret [*Combined*] [*Publishing Danish/Norwegian*]
kombat ...... Battalion Commander   (RU)
kombat ...... Battery Commander   (RU)
kombed...... Committee of the Poor [*1918*]   (RU)
KOMBESPOL ... Komisar Besar Polisi [*Chief Police Commissioner*]   (IN)
kombik .... Combined-Fodder Plant [*Topography*]   (RU)

Kombinat ... Kombination [*Combination*] [*German*]   (GCA)
Kombinier .. Kombinierung [*Combination*] [*German*]   (GCA)
kombizhir ... Mixed Fat   (RU)
kombrig ...... Brigade Commander   (RU)
komchon ..... Commander of Special-Purpose Units   (RU)
KOMDAK ... Komando Daerah Kepolisian [*Police Region Command (Subordinate commands: KOMDIN, KOMRES, KOMDIS, KOMSEK)*] [*See KOMDAPOLMETRODJAYA*]   (IN)
KOMDAPOLMETRODJAYA ... Komando Daerah Kepolisian Metropolitan Djakarta Raya [*Djakarta Metropolitan Police Region Command (Subordinate commands: KOMWIL, KOMSEKKO, KOMDET)*]   (IN)
KOMDE .... Kratikos Organismos Mikhanimaton Dimosion Ergon [*State Organization for Public Works Machinery*] [*Greek*]   (GC)
KOMDET ... Komando Detasemen [*Detachment Command*] [*See KOMDAPOLMETRODJAYA*]   (IN)
KOMDIN ... Komando Daerah Inspeksi [*Inspection Region Command*] [*See KOMDAK*]   (IN)
KOMDIS ... Komando Distrik [*District Command*] [*See KOMDAK*]   (IN)
komdiv .... Division Commander   (RU)
KOMDJEN ... Komisaris Djenderal [*Commissioner General*]   (IN)
Komelprom ... Committee for Small Industry   (RU)
koment .... Commentary   (BU)
KOMENT ... Commentator, Commented   (BU)
koment .... Komentarz [*Commentary*] [*Poland*]
komesk .... Squadron Commander [*Aviation*]   (RU)
komeska ..... Squadron Commander [*Aviation*]   (RU)
KOMGF .... Commission for Soil Mechanics and Foundation Construction   (RU)
KOMGRAP ... Komunalno Gradevinsko Preduzece [*Communal Building Establishment*] [*YU*]
komich .... Comical   (RU)
Komigiz ...... Komi State Publishing House   (RU)
Komiles ...... Kombinat of the Lumber Industry of the Komi ASSR   (RU)
Kominform ... Communist Information Bureau   (BU)
Kominformbyuro ... Communist Information Bureau   (BU)
Komintern ... Communist International [*1919-1943*]   (RU)
komis .... Commission   (RU)
Komisko ..... Committee of the International Socialist Conference   (BU)
komit .... Komitatiivi [*Finland*]
komkhoz .... Department of Municipal Services   (RU)
komkor .... Corps Commander   (RU)
komm .... Commutator, Switchboard   (RU)
Komm .... Kommentar [*Commentary*] [*German*]
komm .... Kommentiert [*Explained*] [*German*]
Komm .... Kommerzial [*Commercial*] [*German*]
komm .... Kommissie [*Commission*] [*Afrikaans*]
Komm .... Kommunal [*Communal*] [*German*]
komm .... Kommunisti(nen) [*Finland*]
KOMMA ... Korea Machine Tool Manufacturers' Association   (EAIO)
kommelprom ... Committee for Small Industry   (RU)
komment .... Commentary   (RU)
Komment .... Kommentar [*Commentary*] [*German*]
kommerch .. Commercial   (RU)
Kommerpribor ... Committee on Measures and Measuring Instruments (at the Council of Ministers, USSR)   (RU)
kommestprom ... Committee of Local Industry   (RU)
KommGes ... Kommanditgesellschaft [*Joint Stock Company*] [*German*]   (GCA)
Kommunenergoproyekt ... Office for the Planning of Municipal Electric Power Plants   (RU)
Kommunenergostroy ... State Municipal Trust for the Installation and Construction of Power Engineering Installations   (RU)
kommunkhoz ... Department of Municipal Services   (RU)
komnachsostav ... Command Personnel   (RU)
KOMNIS ... Komisija za Medicinsko-Naucna Istrazivanja [*Medical Research Commission*] [*YU*]
KOMOB .... Komando Mobil Brigade [*Mobile Brigade Command*]   (IN)
Komones .... Commission for Cases Concerning Minors   (RU)
komp .... Composed, Composer   (BU)
Komp .... Kompanie [*Company*] [*German*]   (EG)
komp .... Komparatief [*Comparative*] [*Afrikaans*]
komp .... Komparatiivi [*Comparative*] [*Finland*]
komp .... Kompenzacio [*Compensation*]   (HU)
komp .... Komplet [*Complete*] [*Publishing Danish/Norwegian*]
komp .... Komplett [*Complete*] [*German*]
komp .... Komponeret [*Composed*] [*Publishing Danish/Norwegian*]
komp .... Komponiert [*or Komponist*] [*Composed or Composer Publishing*] [*German*]
kompar .... Komparatiivi(nen) [*Comparative*] [*Finland*]
Kompartiya ... Communist Party   (BU)
KOMPASS ... Kompaktes Anwendungspaket fuer Kreditinstitute [*German*]   (ADPT)
KOMPERINDRA ... Kompartimen Perindustrian Rakjat [*Indonesian*]
KOMPIPA ... National Synthesis Committee [*Malagasy*]   (AF)
kompl .... Komplett [*Complete*] [*German*]

kompl .... Komplett [*Complete*] [*Sweden*]
KOMPLEX ... KOMPLEX Nagyberendezesek Export-Import Vallalata [*KOMPLEX Export-Import Enterprise for Factory Equipment*]   (HU)
Kompod ...... Komunalni Podnik [*Communal Enterprise*]   (CZ)
KOMPOL ... Komisaris Polisi [*Police Commissioner*]   (IN)
Kompolk .... Regimental Commander   (BU)
Kompomgol ... Famine Relief Committee   (RU)
kompp .... Komppania [*Finland*]
kompr .... Komprimiert [*Compressed*] [*German*]
kom red ...... Komitet Redakcyjny [*Editorial Committee*] [*Poland*]
Komrem ..... All-Russian Commission for Repair of Rolling Stock   (RU)
KOMRES ... Komando Resort [*Area Command*] [*See KOMDAK*]   (IN)
komroty ...... Company Commander   (RU)
KOMS .... Kaliningrad Oblast Experimental Reclamation Station   (RU)
Kom S .... Komandit Sirketi [*Limited Partnership*] [*Turkey*]   (CED)
KOMSEK ... Komando Seksi [*Section Command*] [*See KOMDAK*]   (IN)
KOMSEKKO ... Komando Seksi Kota [*City Section Command*] [*See KOMDAPOLMETRODJAYA*]   (IN)
komsod .... Commission for Assistance   (RU)
Komsomol .. Communist Youth Union   (BU)
Komspol ..... Komanditni Spolecnost [*Limited Partnership Company*] [*Former Czechoslovakia*]   (CZ)
Komstr .... Komunisticka Strana [*Communist Party*]   (CZ)
KOMTA .... Commission on Heavy Aircraft   (RU)
KOMThE .. Kommounistiki Theoritiki Epitheorisi [*Communist Theoretical Review*]   (GC)
Komtrud ..... Committee for Universal Labor Service   (RU)
Komtsvetfond ... Commission for the Establishment of a Special Fund for Financing Nonferrous Metallurgy   (RU)
KOMUCh ... Committee of Members of the Constituent Assembly [*1918*]   (RU)
komukr .... Commander of a Fortified Area   (RU)
komun .... Communist   (BU)
komus .... Commander of a Fortified Sector   (RU)
KOMUS .... Komisija za Ucbenike in Skripta [*Textbooks Commission*] [*Ljubljana*]   (YU)
komvuz .... Commanding Officer of a Military Educational Institution   (RU)
Komvuz ...... Communist Higher Educational Institution   (RU)
komvzvod ... Platoon Commander   (RU)
KOMWIL ... Komando Wilajah [*Territory Command*] [*See KOMDAPOLMETRODJAYA*]   (IN)
Komzag ...... Committee for Procurement of Agricultural Products   (RU)
Komzet .... Land Settlement Committee for Jewish Workers   (RU)
KON .... Convoy [*Navy*]   (RU)
kon .... Horse-Breeding Sovkhoz [*Topography*]   (RU)
KON .... Kendron Oikogeneias kai Neotitos [*Family and Youth Center*] [*Greek*]   (GC)
Kon .... Konak [*Halting Place, Inn*]   (TU)
Kon .... Koninge [*Kings*] [*Afrikaans*]
Kon .... Koninklijke [*Royal*] [*Netherlands*]   (CED)
kon .... Koninklik [*Royal*] [*Afrikaans*]
KON .... Konsole [*German*]   (ADPT)
konarm .... Cavalry Army   (RU)
konart .... Horse Artillery   (RU)
konartbat ..... Horse Artillery Battery   (RU)
konartvzvod ... Horse Artillery Platoon   (RU)
KONB .... Office of Experimental Directed Drilling   (RU)
kond .... Confectionery Factory [*Topography*]   (RU)
kond .... Konditionaali(n) [*Conditional*] [*Finland*]
Kondensat .. Kondensation [*Condensation*] [*German*]   (GCA)
kondit .... Konditionaali [*Conditional*] [*Finland*]
konf .... Konferencia [*Conference*] [*Hungary*]
konfigurats ... Configuration, Configurational   (RU)
KONGKARBU ... Konsentrasi Golongan Karya Buruh [*Indonesia*]
kongl .... Kongelig [*Royal*] [*Danish/Norwegian*]
kongr .... Kongresszus [*Congress*]   (HU)
kongreg .... Kongregacio [*Congregation*]   (HU)
KONI .... Komite Olahraga Nasional Indonesia
KONIIS ..... Kiev Branch of the Central Scientific Research Institute of Communications   (RU)
konj .... Konjunksie [*Conjunctive*] [*Afrikaans*]
konj .... Konjunktiivi [*Subjunctive Mood*] [*Finland*]
konj .... Konjunktio [*Conjunction*] [*Finland*]
Konj .... Konjunktiv [*Subjunctive Mood*] [*German*]
konkr .... Specifically   (BU)
KonnyuipK ... Konnyuipari Kiado [*Light Industry Publishing House*]   (HU)
konopl .... Hemp-Growing Sovkhoz [*Topography*]   (RU)
Kon/polis ... Konstandinoupolis [*Constantinople*] [*Istanbul is preferred*]   (GC)
kons .... Cannery [*Topography*]   (RU)
Kons .... Konservativ [*Conservative*] [*German*]
KONS .... Konserwatief [*Conservative*] [*Afrikaans*]
kons .... Konsonant [*Consonant*] [*Afrikaans*]
kons .... Konsonantti [*Finland*]
Kons .... Konsul [*or Konsulent*] [*Consul or Counsel*] [*German*]

Konservier ... Konservierung [*Canning*] [*German*]   (GCA)
Konservles ... All-Union Trust for Logging and Sawmilling of the Glavkonserv   (RU)
Konservsteklotara ... All-Union Trust for the Manufacture of Glass Containers for the Canning Industry   (RU)
konsp.......... Konspekt [*Synopsis*] [*Poland*]
Konst.......... Constitutional   (BU)
KONST .... Konstabel [*Constable, Policeman*] [*Afrikaans*]
konst .... Konstant [*Constant*] [*German*]
Konst.......... Konstitution [*Constitution*] [*German*]   (GCA)
KONSTAL ... Chorzowska Wytwornia Konstrukcji Stalowych [*Chorzow Steel Construction Plant*]   (POL)
Konstr .... Konstruktion [*Construction*] [*German*]   (GCA)
kontinuierl ... Kontinuierlich [*Continuous*] [*German*]   (GCA)
Kontr .... Kontroll [*or Kontrollor*] [*German*]
Kontrol'pribor ... Moscow Experimental Plant of Control Instruments   (RU)
konts .... Concentrated   (RU)
konts .... Concentration   (BU)
Kontsesskom ... Committee on Concessions   (RU)
konts-iya .... Concentration   (RU)
konts-t........ Concentrate   (RU)
KONV........ Komisia Okresneho Narodneho Vyboru [*Commission of the District National Committee*]   (CZ)
konyvimpex ... Konyvimport-Export [*Book Export and Import Enterprise*]   (HU)
konyvny...... Konyvnyomda [*Book Printer*]   (HU)
konyvt .... Konyvtar [*Library*] [*Hungary*]
konyvizsg ... Konyvvizsgalo [*Auditor, Accountant*] [*Hungarian*]   (HU)
KonZ.......... Kontaminirano Zemljiste [*Contaminated Area*] [*Military*]   (YU)
Konz.......... Konzentration [*Concentration*] [*German*]   (GCA)
konz........... Konzentriert [*Concentrated*] [*German*]
Konz.......... Konzipient [*Draftsman*] [*German*]
KOO .... Kongolo [*Zaire*] [*Airport symbol*]   (OAG)
KOOBIKh ... Cooperative of Bulgarian Engineers and Chemists   (BU)
kookk .... Kookkuns [*Cookery*] [*Afrikaans*]
koop .... Cooperative   (BU)
KOOP........ Kooperasie [*Cooperation*] [*Afrikaans*]
Koop.......... Kooperatifleri [*Cooperative*] [*Turkey*]   (CED)
Koop.......... Kooperator [*German*]
KOOPH..... Koophandel [*Commerce*] [*Afrikaans*]
koopinsoyuz ... Union of Disabled Persons' Cooperative Artels   (RU)
Koop-Is ...... Turkiye Tarim Kredi Kooperatifleri Personeli Sendikasi [*Turkish Agricultural Credit Cooperative Employees Union*]   (TU)
Koopkredit ... Moscow Credit Association   (RU)
KOOP-KUR ... Turk Kooperatifcilik Kurumu [*Turkish Cooperative Association*]   (EAIO)
Kooposyltorg ... Main Administration of Wholesale and Small-Scale Wholesale Mail-Order Trade (of the Tsentrosoyuz)   (RU)
Koopstrakhsoyuz ... All-Russian Cooperative Insurance Union   (RU)
Kooptorgreklama ... All-Union Office of Commercial Advertising   (RU)
Koordinat ... Koordination [*Coordination*] [*German*]   (GCA)
KOOSPOL ... Podnik Zahranicniho Obchodu pro Dovoz a Vyvoz Zemedelskych Vyrobku a Potreb [*Foreign Trade Enterprise for the Import and Export of Agricultural Products and Materials*]   (CZ)
KO OVKSC ... Komise Obrany OV KSC (OV KSS) [*Defense Commission, District Committee of the Communist Party of Czechoslovakia (District Committee of the Communist Party of Slovakia)*]   (CZ)
KOP .... Complex Experimental Station   (BU)
KOP .... Corps Supply Relay Point   (BU)
KOP .... Gunnery Training Course   (RU)
KOP .... Kansallis-Osake-Pankki [*National Capital Stock Bank*] [*Finland*]
KOP .... Klippfontain Organic Product Corp.
KOP .... Komisia Ochrony Pracy [*Labor Protection Board*] [*Poland*]
KOP .... Komisja Oceny Projektow Inwestycyjnych [*Commission on the Evaluation of Investment Plans*]   (POL)
KOP .... Komitet Obroncow Pokoju [*Committee of Partisans of Peace*]   (POL)
KOP .... Kommatiki Organosi Perifereias [*Area Party Organization*]   (GC)
KOP .... Kommatiki Organosi Poleos [*City Party Organization*]   (GC)
KOP .... Kommatiki Organosis Periokhis [*Regional Party Organization*] [*Greek*]   (GC)
KOP .... Kommounistiki Organosis Peiraios [*Communist Organization of Piraeus*]   (GC)
KOP .... Koninski Okreg Przemyslowy [*Industrial Region of Konin*] [*Poland*]
kop .... Kopalnia [*or Kopalnictwo*] [*Mine or Mining*]   (POL)
kop .... Kopeck   (RU)
kop .... Kopeekka(a) [*Finland*]
Kop........... Kopru [*Bridge*]   (TU)
KOP .... Korpus Ochrony Pogranicza [*Poland*]
KOP .... Krakowski Okreg Przemyslowy [*Industrial Region of Cracow*] [*Poland*]

KOP.......... Kypriaki Omospondia Podosfairou [*Cyprus Soccer Federation*]   (GC)
KOP.......... Leather and Footwear Industry   (RU)
KOP.......... Nakhon Phanom [*Thailand*] [*Airport symbol*] [*Obsolete*]   (OAG)
KOP.......... Operation Code   (RU)
KOPart ...... Corps Artillery Supply Relay Point   (RU)
KOPASGAT ... Komando Pasukan Gerak Tjepat [*Strike Troop Command (Air Force paratroops)*]   (IN)
KOPELAPIP ... Komando Pelaksana Persiapan Industri Penerbangan [*Aviation Industry Development Command*]   (IN)
KOPEP...... Kypriakos Organismos Protypon kai Elengkhou Poiotitos [*Cypriot Organization for Quality Control and Standards*]   (GC)
kopergr....... Kopergravure [*Copper Engraving*] [*Publishing*] [*Netherlands*]
kopergrav.... Kopergravure [*Copper Engraving*] [*Publishing*] [*Netherlands*]
KOPEX...... Przedsiebiorstwo Budowy Zakladow Gorniczych Zagranica [*Enterprise for the Construction of Mining Facilities Abroad*]   (POL)
Kopft .... Kopftitel [*Headline, Running Title*] [*Publishing*] [*German*]
KOPI .... Komisja Oceny Projektow Inwestycyjnych [*Commission on the Evaluation of Investment Plans*]   (POL)
KOPKAMTIB ... Komando Operasi Pemulihan Keamanan dan Ketertiban [*Command for the Restoration of Security and Order*] [*India*]   (IN)
KOPLAX ... Compania Colombiana de Plasticos Koplax Ltda. [*Colombia*]   (COL)
koprogen-aza ... Coproporphyrinogen Oxidase   (RU)
KOPROSAN ... Komando Operasi Projek-Projek Sandang [*Indonesian*]
KOPS........ Komando Perjuangan Sarawak [*Sarawak Struggle Command (Chinese Communist)*]   (ML)
KOPTAS ... Kamyon, Otomobil, ve Yedek Parca Ticaret Anonim Sirketi [*Truck, Automobile, and Spare Parts Trade Corporation*] [*Istanbul*]   (TU)
KOR.......... Air Koryo [*North Korea*] [*ICAO designator*]   (FAAC)
kor............. Correspondent   (BU)
kor............. Cover   (BU)
KOR.......... Klub Oficerow Rezerwy [*Reserve Officers Club*]   (POL)
KOR.......... Kokoro [*Papua New Guinea*] [*Airport symbol*]   (OAG)
kor............. Korean
Kor .... Korinthiers [*Corinthians*] [*Afrikaans*]
kor............. Korona [*Crown*]   (HU)
kor............. Korrigiert [*Corrected*] [*German*]
KOR.......... Korzeti Orvosi Rendelo [*District Medical Center*]   (HU)
KOR.......... Kostenrechnung [*German*]   (ADPT)
KOR.......... Krajska Odborova Rada [*Regional Trade Union Council*]   (CZ)
kor............. Mounted Orderly   (BU)
KOR.......... Republic of Korea [*ANSI three-letter standard code*]   (CNC)
kor............. Short [*Film*]   (RU)
KOR.......... Social Self-Defense Committee [*Also, SSDC*] [*Poland*]   (PD)
KOR.......... Workers Defense Committee [*Poland*]
Kora .... Koramiral [*Vice Admiral*]   (TU)
KORAG .... Koloniale Reichsarbeitsgemeinschaft
Koralovag... Ship, Locomotive, and Railroad Car Building Enterprise   (BU)
KORAMIL ... Komando Rayon Militer [*Military Precinct Command*] [*See KODAM*]   (IN)
KORAMO ... Kolinske Rafinerie Mineralnich Oleju [*Kolin Oil Refineries*]   (CZ)
KORANDAK ... Koordinasi Antar Daerah Kepolisian [*Police Interregional Coordinating Command (May have replaced KOMANDAK)*]   (IN)
KORBSO... Bulgarian-Soviet Shipbuilding Company   (BU)
KORDI ...... Korean Ocean Research and Development Institute [*South Korea*]   (PDAA)
KORDSA ... Kord Bezi Sanayi ve Ticaret AS [*Cord Cloth Industry and Trade Corp.*]   (TU)
KOREM .... Komando Resort Militer [*Military Area Command*] [*See KODAM*]   (IN)
koresp .... Korespondent [*or Korespondencyjny*] [*Correspondent or Correspondence*] [*Poland*]
koreysk ...... Korean
Korg .... Korgeneral [*Lieutenant General*]   (TU)
korl............ Korlevel [*Circular Letter*]   (HU)
Korm .... Kormany [*Cabinet*]   (HU)
korm yed .... Feed Unit   (RU)
korn............ Koernig [*Granular*] [*German*]   (GCA)
kor opis ...... Imprint Description   (BU)
korp........... Building [*In addresses*]   (RU)
KORP .... Korporasie [*Corporation*] [*Afrikaans*]
korpr .... Korpraali [*Finland*]
korr .... Correspondent   (RU)
korr .... Korrektura [*Proof Sheet*]   (HU)
korr .... Korrespondensie [*Correspondence*] [*Afrikaans*]
korr .... Korrespondierend [*Corresponding*] [*German*]
korr .... Korrigiert [*Corrected*] [*German*]
Korros .... Korrosion [*Corrosion*] [*German*]   (GCA)

Korsavas .... Kore'de Savasanlar Dernegi [*Association of Korean Veterans*] (TU)
KORSEL ... Korea Selatan [*South Korea*] (IN)
KORSTIC ... Korea Scientific and Technological Information Center [*INSPEC operator*]
kortfatt....... Kortfattet [*Concise*] [*Publishing Danish/Norwegian*]
Kortged ...... Kortgeding [*Benelux*] (BAS)
korttip .... Korttipeli [*Card Games*] [*Finland*]
KORUT .... Korea Utara [*North Korea*] (IN)
kor zagl ...... Cover Title (BU)
KOS .... Communications Section Commander (RU)
KOS .... Correction and Drainage System (BU)
KOS .... Counterintelligence Service (BU)
KOS .... Kendrikon Oikonomikon Symvoulion [*Central Economic Council*] [*Greek*] (GC)
KOS .... Kenya Oilfield Services Ltd.
KOS .... Kolkhoz Experimental Station (RU)
KOS .... Komise Organisace Stavebnictvi [*Organizational Commission for the Construction Industry*] (CZ)
KOS .... Kommounistiki Organosis Stratou [*Communist Organization for the Army*] [*Greek*] (GC)
KOS .... Komunisticka Omladina Srbije [*Communist Youth of Serbia*] (YU)
KOS .... Kosinus [*Cosine*] [*Afrikaans*]
KOS .... Kosovaair [*Yugoslavia*] [*ICAO designator*] (FAAC)
KOS .... Krajske Osvetove Stredisko [*Regional Cultural Center*] (CZ)
KOS .... Kuratorium Okregu Szkolnego [*School District Department*] (POL)
KOS .... Kyvernitikon Oikonomikon Symvoulion [*Government Economic Council*] (GC)
KOSARTOP ... Commission for Special Artillery Experiments (RU)
KOSATGAS ... Komando Satuan Tugas [*Task Force Command*] (IN)
kosc .... Kosciol [*Church*] [*Poland*]
KOSCO ..... Korea Steel Chemical Co. Ltd.
KOSEK...... Coordinating Secretariat of National Unions of Students [*COSEC*] (RU)
KOSEK...... Coordination Secretariat of the National Students Unions (BU)
KOSEK...... Kosekans [*Cosecant*] [*Afrikaans*]
KOSGORO ... Kesatuan Organisasi Serba Guna Gotong Rojong [*Federation of Cooperating Multipurpose Organizations*] (IN)
KOSLO...... Konferenz Schweizerischer Lehrerorganisationen [*Swiss Teacher Organization Confeence*] (SLS)
kosm.......... Cosmic, Space (RU)
kosm.......... Cosmonautics [*or Astronautics*] (BU)
kosmet....... Kosmetisch [*Cosmetic*] [*German*] (GCA)
KOSMS..... Courses for Advanced Training of Officers of the Fleet Medical Service (RU)
KOSOS...... Design Department of the Experimental Land-Based Aircraft Construction (of the TsAGI) (RU)
KOSSA ...... Kommatikos Organismos Stratou-Somaton Asfaleias [*or Kommounistiki Organosis Stratou kai Somaton Asfaleias*] [*Party Organization for the Army and Security Forces*] [*Greek*] (GC)
KOSSU...... Krajska Oddeleni Statniho Statistickeho Uradu [*Regional Departments of the State Office of Statistics*] (CZ)
KOSTRAD ... Komando Strategis Angkatan Darat [*Army Strategic Command*] (IN)
KOSTRANAS ... Komando Strategis Nasional [*National Strategic Command*] (IN)
KOT.......... Committee for Recreation and Tourism (BU)
Ko-T.......... Co-Thiaminase (RU)
KOT.......... Kolarska Odznaka Turystyczna [*Tourist Bicycle Badge*] (POL)
KOT.......... Konyvtarak Orszagos Tanacsa [*National Council of Libraries*] (HU)
KOT.......... Kotangens [*Cotangent*] [*Afrikaans*]
kot.............. Kotet [*Volume*] [*Hungary*]
KOT.......... Kypriakos Organismos Tourismou [*Cyprus Tourism Organization*] (GC)
KOTA .... Confederation Ouvriers Travailleurs Haitiens (EY)
KOTA .... Korusok Orszagos Tanacsa [*National Council of Choruses*] (HU)
KOTC .... Kuwait Oil Tanker Company [*Kuwait City*] (ME)
KOTh......... Kommounistiki Organosis Thessalonikis [*Communist Organization of Salonica*] (GC)
KOTIB...... Commission for Healthier Working and Living Conditions (RU)
KOTINRO ... Kamchatka Branch of the Pacific Ocean Scientific Research Institute of Fisheries and Oceanography (RU)
KOTKA ..... Konfekcija i Tkaonica [*Ready-Made Clothing and Textile Mill*] [*Krapina*] (YU)
kotl............. Hollow (RU)
KOTL .... Koolajbanyaszati Tudomanyos Laboratorium [*Scientific Laboratory of Petroleum Prospecting*] (HU)
Kotlostroy .. Boiler Plant (RU)
Kotlotermomontazh ... Trust for the Installation of Industrial Heating and Boiler Units (RU)
KOTRA ..... Korea Trade Promotion Corporation [*South Korea*]

KOTsM ..... Nonferrous Metals Processing Combine (BU)
Kotsuroren ... Zenkoku Kotsu Unyu Rodokumiai Sorengo [*Japan Federation of Transport Workers' Unions*]
KOTUKI.... Kozuti Kozlekedesi Tudomanyos Kutato Intezet [*Scientific Research Institute for Highway Transport*] (HU)
kotv .... Kotveny [*Bond*] (HU)
KOTY .... Kiz Orta Talebeler Yurdu [*Women's Secondary Student Home*] [*Turkish Cypriot*] (GC)
KOU .... Koula Moutou [*Gabon*] [*Airport symbol*] (OAG)
koul .... Koulussa [*or Koululaiskielessa*] [*School*] [*Finland*]
KOV.......... Firing Platoon Commander (BU)
KOV.......... Kabinet Odborarske Vychovy [*Department of Trade Union Education*] (CZ)
KOV.......... Katholieke Onderwijs Vakorganisatiekov [*Catholic Teachers Union*] [*Netherlands*] (EAIO)
KOV.......... Kommatiki Organosi Vaseos [*Base Party Organization*] (GC)
KOV.......... Kommounistiki Organosis Vaseos [*Communist Organization of the Base*] (GC)
KOV.......... Kooperationsverband [*Production Cooperation Association*] (EG)
KoV .... Kopnena Vojska [*Ground Forces*] (YU)
kov.............. Kovetkezo [*Following*] [*Hungary*] (GPO)
KOV.......... Peasants' Mutual Aid Society (RU)
KOVAC ..... Kobanya Vas es Acelontode [*Kobanya Iron and Steel Foundry*] (HU)
KOVAC ..... Kovacsolt es Ontott Vas- es Acelmuvek [*Wrought Iron, Cast Iron, and Steel Factory*] (HU)
KOVAGO ... Kiev Branch of the All-Union Astronomical and Geodetic Society (RU)
KOVM....... Committee for Permafrost Study (RU)
KOVN....... Kommounistiki Organosis Vasilikou Navtikou [*Communist Organization for the Royal Navy*] [*Greek*] (GC)
KOVO....... Podnik Zahranicniho Obchodu pro Dovoz z Vyvoz Vyrobku Presneho Strojirenstvi [*Foreign Trade Enterprise for the Import and Export of Products of the Precision Engineering Industry*] (CZ)
Kovona ...... Tovarny na Kovovy Nabytek [*Metal Furniture Factories*] (CZ)
KOVOSMALT ... Narodni Podnik pro Prodej Kuchynskeho a Zelezneho Zbozi [*National Enterprise for the Retail Sale of Kitchen Ware and Hardware*] (CZ)
KOVR....... Harbor Defense Commander (RU)
KOW......... Ghanzhou [*China*] [*Airport symbol*] (OAG)
KOWANI.. Kongres Wanita Indonesia
KOWILMAN ... Komando Wilajah Pertahanan [*Defense Territorial Command*] (IN)
KOYHD.... Koy Ogretmenleri ile Haberlesme ve Yardimlasma Dernegi [*Society for the Promotion of Mutual Communication and Mutual Aid re Village Teachers*] (TU)
KOY-KOOP ... Koy Kalkinma ve Diger Tarimsal Amacli Kooperatifleri Birligi [*Union of Cooperatives for Village Development and Other Agricultural Goals*] (TU)
KOZ.......... Kmetijske Obdelovalne Zadruge [*Peasant Working Cooperatives*] [*Collective farms*] (YU)
KOZDOK ... Kozlekedesi Dokumentacios es Nyomtatvanyellato Vallalat [*Transportation Forms and Stationery Printing Enterprise*] (HU)
Kozdok....... Kozlekedesi Dokumentacios Vallalat [*Transportation Documentation Establishment*] (HU)
KOZEPTERV ... Kozlekedesuzemi Epulettervezo Vallalat [*Construction Designing Enterprise of the Transportation Establishments*] (HU)
KOZERT... Kozsegi Elelmiszerkereskedelmi Reszvenytarsasag [*Municipal Food Trade Company Limited (Prewar)*] (HU)
KOZGEP... Kozlekedesepitesi Gepjavito Vallalat [*Highway Construction Machine Repair Shop*] (HU)
kozh............ Tannery [*Topography*] (RU)
KOZhFURNITURA ... Trust of Auxiliary Establishments of the Leather and Footwear Industry (RU)
KOZHIR ... Kozponti Hirlapiroda [*Central Newspaper Office*] (HU)
Kozhsindikat ... All-Union Leather Syndicate (RU)
Kozhsyr'ye ... Moscow Plant for the Processing of Leather Raw Materials (RU)
Kozhtekhzamenitel' ... Moscow Plant for the Production of Industrial Leather Substitutes (RU)
Kozl K .... Kozlekedes- es Melyepitestudomanyi Kiado [*Transport and Civil Engineering Publishing House*] (HU)
Kozokt K ..... Kozoktatasugyi Kiado [*Public Education Publishing House*] (HU)
kozp............ Kozpont [*Center*] [*Hungary*]
Kozp StatHiv ... Kozponti Statisztikai Hivatal [*Central Statistical Office*] (HU)
KO ZSP ..... Komisja Okregowa Zrzeszenia Studentow Polskich [*District Commission of the Polish Student Association*] (POL)
kozv............ Kozvetlen [*Immediate, Close-Range*] (HU)
KP .... Blood-Penicillin Preparation (RU)
KP .... Bridge Crane (RU)
KP .... Cable Appliance (RU)

KP .... Cardan Suspension, Gimbal Suspension (RU)
KP .... Cathode Follower (RU)
KP .... Cavalry Regiment (RU)
KP .... Ceramic Coating [*For aircraft*] (RU)
KP .... Checking Subroutine (RU)
KP .... Check Point (RU)
KP .... Command Device (RU)
KP .... Command Post (RU)
KP .... Communist Party (RU)
KP .... Compass Bearing (RU)
KP .... Control Panel (RU)
KP .... Democratic People's Republic of Korea [*ANSI two-letter standard code*] (CNC)
Kp .... Express Train (RU)
KP .... Gearbox, Gearshift (RU)
KP .... Kaapprovinsie [*Cape Province*] [*Afrikaans*]
KP .... Kazneno-Popravni [*Penal-Reformatory*] (YU)
K/P............ Kedah/Perlis [*Malaysia*] (ML)
kp .... Kerekpar [*or Kerekparos*] [*Bicycle or Cyclist*] (HU)
KP .... Keshilli Popullor [*Albanian*]
KP .... Keskustapuolue [*Center Party of Finland*] [*Political party*] (PPW)
kp .... Keszpenz [*Cash*] (HU)
KP .... Ketua Penguasa [*Chief Superintendent*] (ML)
kp .... Kilopond [*1 kilogram of thrust*] [*Poland*]
Kp .... Kilopond [*1 kilogram of thrust*] [*German*] (HU)
kp .... Kleiner Personenzug [*Small Passenger Train*] (EG)
KP .... Kmetijsko Posestvo [*Agricultural Estate*] (YU)
Kp .... Kochpunkt, Siedepunkt [*Boiling Point*] [*German*]
KP .... Kodi Penal [*Penal Code*] [*Albanian*]
KP .... Komisija za Plate [*Wage Commission*] (YU)
KP .... Komisija za Produktivnost i Norme [*Labor Productivity and Norms Commission*] (YU)
KP .... Komitet Powiatowy [*District Committee*] (POL)
KP .... Komma Panevropis [*Pan-European Party*] [*Greek*] (GC)
KP .... Komma Proodeftikon [*Progressive Party*] [*Greek*] [*Political party*] (PPE)
KP .... Kommunista Part [*Communist Party*] (HU)
KP .... Kommunistesch Partei [*Communist Party*] [*Luxembourg*] [*Political party*] (PPE)
KP .... Kommunistische Partei [*Communist Party*] [*German*] [*Political party*]
Kp .... Kompanie [*Company*] (EG)
kp .... Komunalni Podnik [*Communal Enterprise*] (CZ)
KP .... Komunalno Podjetje [*Communal Establishment*] (YU)
KP .... Komunisticka Partija [*Communist Party*] (YU)
KP .... Komunistyczna Partia [*Communist Party*] [*Poland*]
kp .... Konepistooli [*Finland*]
kP .... Konstanter Preis [*Constant Price*] (EG)
KP .... Kooperativna Praktika [*Cooperative Practice*] [*A periodical*] (BU)
KP .... Koppelpunkt [*German*] (ADPT)
KP .... Kovinsko Podjetje [*Metallurgical Establishment*] (YU)
KP .... Kozos Piac [*Common Market*] (HU)
KP .... Krajska Poradna [*Regional Advisory Bureau (for folk arts activities)*] (CZ)
kp .... Kuollutta Painoa [*Finland*]
KP .... Kutahya Porselen Sanayii AS [*Kutahya Porcelain Industry Corporation*] (TU)
KP .... Loading Crane (RU)
KP .... Oxygen Apparatus (RU)
KP .... Oxygen Potential (RU)
KP .... Oxygen Tent (RU)
KP .... Red Crescent [*Society*] (RU)
KP .... Regimental Commander (RU)
KP .... River Crossing Commandant (RU)
KP .... Start Button (RU)
KP .... Transportation Committee (RU)
Kp 10........ Kochpunkt bei 10mm Quecksilberdruck [*Boiling Point at 10 millimeters of Mercury Pressure*] [*German*]
KPA .... Communist Party of Albania (RU)
KPA .... Communist Party of Algeria (RU)
KPA .... Communist Party of Argentina (RU)
KPA .... Communist Party of Armenia (RU)
KPA .... Communist Party of Australia (RU)
KPA .... Communist Party of Austria (RU)
KPA .... Communist Party of Azerbaydzhan (RU)
KPA .... Cooperative Producers' Artel (RU)
KPA .... Domestic Fuel Laboratory [*Finland*]
KPA .... Kaapse Provinsiale Administrasie [*Cape Provincial Administration*] [*South Africa*] (AA)
KPA .... Kikuyu Provincial Association
KPA .... Kinisis Prosfygon Ammokhostou [*Famagusta Refugees Movements*] [*Cyprus*] (GC)
KPA .... Kodeks Postepowania Administracyjnego [*Code of Administrative Proceedings*] [*Poland*]

KPA .... Komunisticka Partija Albanije [*Communist Party of Albania*] (YU)
KPA .... Komunistyczna Partia Algierii [*Algerian Communist Party*] [*Poland*]
KPA .... Komunistyczna Partia Australii [*Australian Communist Party*] [*Poland*]
KPA .... Komunistyczna Partia Austrii [*Austrian Communist Party*] [*Poland*]
KPA .... Kontrollpostamt [*Control Post Office*] (EG)
KPA .... Kopiago [*Papua New Guinea*] [*Airport symbol*] (OAG)
KPA .... Oblique Cross Reinforcement (RU)
KPAP......... Kendron Prostasias Anapirou Paidiou [*Center for the Protection of the Handicapped Child*] [*Greek*] (GC)
KPaS........ Krajska Poradna a Studovna [*Regional Advisory Bureau and Study Center*] (CZ)
KPB........... Battalion Command Post (RU)
KPB........... Communist Party of Belorussia (RU)
KPB........... Communist Party of Bolivia (RU)
KP(b)........ Communist Party (of Bolsheviks) [*1925-1952*] (RU)
KPB........... Communist Party of Brazil (RU)
KPB........... Communist Party of Burma (RU)
KPB........... Kenya Pyrethrum Board
K-PB .... Kommandeur Panzerbataillon [*Tank Battalion Commander*] (EG)
KPB........... Kommunistische Partij van Belgie [*Communist Party of Belgium*] [*See also PCB*] [*Political party*] (PPE)
KPB........... Komunisticka Partija Bugarske [*Communist Party of Bulgaria*] (YU)
KPB........... Komunisticka Partija Burme [*Communist Party of Burma*] (YU)
KPB........... Komunistyczna Partia Belgii [*Belgian Communist Party*] [*Poland*]
KP(b)........ Komunistyczna Partia (Bolszewikow) [*Communist Party (Bolsheviks)*] (POL)
KPB........... Kuwait Planning Board (ME)
KPB........... Trade-Union Congress of Burma (RU)
KP(b)A...... Communist Party (of Bolsheviks) of Armenia [*1920-1952*] (RU)
KP(b)A...... Communist Party (of Bolsheviks) of Azerbaydzhan (RU)
KP(b)B...... Communist Party (of Bolsheviks) of Belorussia [*1919-1952*] (RU)
KP(b)E...... Communist Party (of Bolsheviks) of Estonia [*1940-1952*] (RU)
KP(b)G...... Communist Party (of Bolsheviks) of Georgia (RU)
KPBiH ...... Komunisticka Partija Bosne i Hercegovine [*Communist Party of Bosnia and Hercegovina*] (YU)
KP(b)K...... Communist Party (of Bolsheviks) of Kazakhstan (RU)
KP(b)K...... Communist Party (of Bolsheviks) of Kirgizia (RU)
KP(b)L...... Communist Party (of Bolsheviks) of Latvia [*1919-1952*] (RU)
KP(b)L...... Communist Party (of Bolsheviks) of Lithuania [*1940-1952*] (RU)
KP(b)M..... Communist Party (of Bolsheviks) of Moldavia [*1940-1952*] (RU)
KP(b)T...... Communist Party (of Bolsheviks) of Tadzhikistan (RU)
KP(b)T...... Communist Party (of Bolsheviks) of Turkmenistan (RU)
KP(b)U ..... Communist Party (of Bolsheviks) of the Ukraine [*1918-1952*] (RU)
KP(b)Uz..... Communist Party (of Bolsheviks) of Uzbekistan [*1924-1952*] (RU)
KPC .... Kangaroo Protection Committee [*Australia*] (ADA)
KPC .... Kenya Power Company
KPC .... Kenya Press Club
KPC .... Kodeks Postepowania Cywilnego [*Code of Civil Procedure*] (POL)
KPC .... Komunisticka Partija Cehoslovacke [*Communist Party of Czechoslovakia*] (YU)
KPC .... Kuwait Petroleum Corp.
KPCA........ Korean Printing Cultural Association (EAIO)
KPCG........ Komunisticka Partija Crne Gore [*Communist Party of Montenegro*] (YU)
KPCh .... Communist Party of Chile (RU)
KPCh .... Communist Party of Czechoslovakia (RU)
KPCh .... Komunistyczna Partia Chin [*Chinese Communist Party*] [*Poland*]
KPCJ .... Kruh Pratel Ceskeho Jazyka [*Circle of Friends of the Czech Language*] (CZ)
KPCSR ...... Komunisticka Partija Cehoslovacke Republike [*Communist Party of the Czechoslovak Republic*] (YU)
KPCU .... Kenya Planters' Cooperative Union (EAIO)
KPCz........ Komunistyczna Partia Czechoslowacji [*Communist Party of Czechoslovakia*] (POL)
KPD .... Battalion Command Post (RU)
KPD .... Carboxypeptidase
KPD .... Communist Party of Denmark (RU)
KPD .... Efficiency Factor (BU)
KPD .... Kazneno-Popravni Dom [*Penal-Reformatory Institution*] (YU)
KPD .... Kodix Poinikis Dikonomias [*Code of Criminal Procedure*] [*Greek*] (GC)

KPD .... Kodix Politikis Dikonomias [*Code of Civil Procedure*] [*Greek*] (GC)
KPD .... Kolejowe Przedsiebiorstwo Dowozowe [*Railroad Forwarding Enterprise*] (POL)
KPD .... Kommunistische Partei Deutschlands [*Communist Party of Germany*] [*Political party*] (PPW)
KPD .... Kratiki Ploti Dexameni [*State Floating Dock*] [*Greek*] (GC)
KPD .... Kulturno-Prosvetno Drustvo [*Cultural and Educational Society*] (YU)
KPD .... Large-Panel Housing Construction (RU)
KPD .... Large-Panel Plant for Housing Construction (RU)
KPD-AO .... Kommunistische Partei Deutschlands - Aufbau-Organisation [*Communist Party of Germany - Party-Building Organization*] (EG)
KPD-ML ... Kommunistische Partei Deutschlands/Marxisten-Leninisten [*Communist Party of Germany/Marxists-Leninists*] [*Political party*] (PPW)
KPDSU...... Kommunistische Partei der Sowjet Union [*Communist Party of the Soviet Union (CPSU)*] (WEN)
KPDU .... Kaffa People's Democratic Union [*Ethiopia*] [*Political party*] (EY)
KPE............ Communist Party of Ecuador (RU)
KPE............ Communist Party of Estonia (RU)
KPE............ Katholische Pfadfinderschaft Europas [*Germany*] (EAIO)
KPE............ Kenya Preliminary Examination
KPE............ Kenya Primary Education
KPE............ Polyethylene for Cables (RU)
KPED........ Kendron Pyrinikon Erevnon Dimokritos [*Dimokritos Nuclear Research Center*] [*Greek*] (GC)
KPEE........ Kendro Politikis Erevnas kai Epimorfosis [*Center for Political Research and Training*] [*Greek*] (GC)
KPENC...... Korean Centre of International PEN (EAIO)
KPEO .... Katholische Pfadfinderschaft Europas - Osterreich [*Austria*] (EAIO)
KPES .... Commission for the Suddenly Deaf and the Profoundly Hearing Impaired [*Netherlands*] (EAIO)
KPF............ Communist Party of Finland (RU)
KPF............ Communist Party of France (RU)
KPF............ Kern Property Fund [*Australia*]
KPF............ Kolkhoz Poultry-Raising Farm (RU)
KPF............ Komisija za Pregled Filmova [*Film Control Commission*] (YU)
KPF............ Komitet Polonii Francuskiej [*Committee of the Poles in France*] (POL)
KPF............ Komunisticka Partija Francuske [*Communist Party of France*] (YU)
KPF............ Komunistyczna Partia Finlandii [*Finland Communist Party*] [*Poland*]
KPF............ Komunistyczna Partia Francji [*Communist Party of France*] [*Poland*]
KPF............ Korea Polio Foundation (EAIO)
KPFA........ Knackery and Pet Food Association [*Australia*]
KPFDSH ... Keshilli i Pergjithshem i Frontit Demokratik te Shqiperise [*Albanian*]
KPFN........ Kefalaion Prostasias Fymatikon Navtikon [*Insurance Fund for Tubercular Seamen*] [*Greek*] (GC)
Kpfr........... Kupfer [*Copper*] [*German*]
Kpfrst........ Kupferstich [*Etching*] [*German*]
Kpfrtaf...... Kupfertafel [*Copper Engraving*] [*German*]
KPFV .... Kancelar Predsednictva Federalni Vlady [*Office of the Presidium of the Federal Government*] (CZ)
KPG .... Communist Party of Georgia (RU)
KPG .... Communist Party of Germany (RU)
KPG .... Communist Party of Greece (RU)
KPG .... Communist Party of Holland (RU)
KPG .... Communist Party of Honduras (RU)
KPG .... Emergency Backwater Level (RU)
KPG .... Komisja Planowania Gospodarczego [*Economic Planning Committee*] (POL)
KPG .... Komunisticka Partija Grcke [*Communist Party of Greece*] (YU)
KPG .... Kurupung [*Guyana*] [*Airport symbol*] (OAG)
KPG .... Load Position Contact (RU)
KPGB........ Kantor Proyek Gula Bersama [*Joint Sugar Projects Unit*] [*Indonesia*]
KPGMPTM ... Kesatuan Persekutuan Guru Melayu, Persekutuan Tanah Melayu [*Federation of Malay Teachers' Unions, Federation of Malaya*]
KPGY .... Kobanyai Porcellangyar [*Porcelain Factory of Kobanya*] (HU)
KPH........... Kingston Public Hospital [*Jamaica*] (LA)
KPH........... Kniznice "Podnikoveho Hospodarstvi" [*Publication Series "Podnikove Hospodarstvi" (Management)*] (CZ)
KPH........... Komunisticka Partija Hrvatske [*Communist Party of Croatia*] [*Political party*]
KPH........... Komunistyczna Partia Hiszpanii [*Spanish Communist Party*] [*Poland*]
KPH........... Komunistyczna Partia Holandii [*Communist Party of Holland*] [*Poland*]
KPI............ Communist Party of India (RU)

KPI............ Communist Party of Indonesia (RU)
KPI............ Communist Party of Iraq (RU)
KPI............ Communist Party of Israel (RU)
KPI............ Communist Party of Italy (RU)
KPI............ Communist Party of Spain (RU)
KPI............ Information Transmission Channel (RU)
KPI............ Kapit [*Malaysia*] [*Airport symbol*] (OAG)
KPI............ Karelian Pedagogical Institute (RU)
KPI............ Kaunas Polytechnic Institute (RU)
KPI............ Kiev Polytechnic Institute (RU)
KPI............ Komunisticna Partija Italije [*Communist Party of Italy*] (YU)
KPI............ Komunistyczna Partia Indonezji [*Communist Party of Indonesia*] (POL)
KPI............ Kuwait Petroleum International (ECON)
KPIA......... Keep Printing in Australia Campaign
KPIC........ Korea Petrochemical Industrial Co. Ltd.
KPIIIMK... Committee for Field Research of the Institute of the History of Material Culture (of the Academy of Sciences, USSR) (RU)
KPJ .... Klub Pomoraca Jugoslavije [*Yugoslav Seamen's Club*] [*USA*] (YU)
KPJ .... Komunisticka Partija Jugoslavije [*Communist Party of Yugoslavia*] [*Political party*] (PPE)
KPJ .... Komunistyczna Partia Japonji [*Communist Party of Japan*] (POL)
k pk .... Cavalry Regiment (BU)
KPK .... Commission of Party Control at the TsK VKP(b) [*1934-1952*] (RU)
KPK .... Commission of Personnel Training (of the Academy of Sciences, USSR) (RU)
KPK .... Committee of Party Control at the TsK KPSS [*1952-1962*] (RU)
KPK .... Communist Party of Canada (RU)
KPK .... Communist Party of Catalonia (RU)
KPK .... Communist Party of China (RU)
KPK .... Communist Party of Colombia (RU)
KPK .... Communist Party of Kazakhstan (RU)
KPK .... Communist Party of Kirgizia (RU)
KPK .... Communist Party of Korea [*1925-1946*] (RU)
KPK .... End of Transition Curve [*Railroads*] (RU)
KPK .... Ketua Pegawai Kechil [*Chief Petty Officer*] (ML)
KPK .... Kodeks Postepowania Karnego [*Code of Criminal Procedure*] (POL)
KPK .... Komunisticka Partija Kine [*Communist Party of China*] (YU)
KPK .... Komunistyczna Parti Kanady [*Communist Party of Canada*] [*Poland*]
KPK .... Krajska Planovacia Komisia [*Regional Planning Commission*] (CZ)
KPK .... Plans and Documents Control (BU)
KPK .... Short-Period Oscillation, Short-Period Vibration (RU)
KPK .... Trade-Union Congress of Canada (RU)
KPKA........ Konstruktion und Projektierung Kerntechnischer Anlagen [*Enterprise for Design and Planning of Nuclear Installations*] (EG)
KPKhZ....... Collective Chemical Defense (RU)
KPKK....... Kreisparteikontrollkommission [*Kreis Party Control Commission*] (EG)
KPKVCh.... Committee for Friendship and Cultural Relations with Foreign Countries (BU)
KPL............ Committee on Applied Linguistics (RU)
KPL............ Communist Party of Latvia (RU)
KPL............ Communist Party of Lithuania (RU)
KPL............ Communist Party of Luxembourg (RU)
kpl .... Drops (RU)
kpl .... Kappale(tta) [*Finland*]
KPL............ Ketua Pegawai Laut [*Chief Naval Officer*] (ML)
KPL............ Khao San Pathet Lao [*News agency*] [*Laos*] (FEA)
KPL............ Kommunisticheskaia Partiia Lesoto
KPL............ Kommunistisch Partei vu Leetzebuerg [*Communist Party of Luxembourg*] [*Political party*] (PPW)
kpl .... Komplet [*Complete*] [*Publishing Danish/Norwegian*]
kpl .... Komplett [*Complete*] [*German*] (GCA)
KPL............ Korporaal [*Corporal*] [*Afrikaans*]
KPlB .... Klein Placaatboek [*Benelux*] (BAS)
KPLiB........ Communist Party of Lithuania and Belorussia (RU)
KPLPH...... Komandan Pusat Latehan Polis Hutan [*Commander Central Training Police Field Force*] (ML)
Kplt .... Komplet [*Complete*] [*Danish/Norwegian*]
kplt .... Komplett [*Complete*] [*German*]
kplt .... Komplett [*Complete*] [*Sweden*]
KPLU........ Kaaplandse Landbou-Unie [*Afrikaans*]
KPM .... Combination Sprinkling and Washing Machine (RU)
KPM .... Communist Party of Mexico (RU)
KPM .... Communist Party of Moldavia (RU)
KPM .... Communist Party of Morocco (RU)
KPM .... Kancelar Prace a Mzdy [*Labor and Wage Office*] (CZ)

KPM .... Kesatuan Pelajar Melayu Melaka [*Malay Students' Union of Malacca*] (ML)

KPM .... Kombinovany Pontonovy Most [*Combined Pontoon Bridge*] (CZ)

KPM .... Komunisticka Partija Madarske [*Communist Party of Hungary*] (YU)

KPM .... Komunisticka Partija Makedonije [*Communist Party of Macedonia*] (YU)

KPM .... Kono Progressive Movement

KPM .... Kontrolni Propousteci Misto [*Traffic Release Point*] (CZ)

KPM .... Kozlekedesi- es Postaugyi Miniszterium [*Ministry of Transportation and Postal Affairs*] (HU)

KPM .... Kumpulan Perubatan Medan [*Field Ambulance Corps*] (ML)

KPM .... Terminal Point [*Aviation*] (RU)

KPM .... Terminal Point of the March Route (BU)

KPMA .... Komitim-Pirenena Miandraikitra ny Anaran-Tany [*National Committee on Geographic Names*] [*Malagasy*] (AF)

KPMG .... Klynveld Peat Marwick Goerdeler

KP MO ...... Komenda Powiatowa Milicji Obywatelskiej [*District Headquarters of the Civic Militia*] [*Poland*]

KPMS........ Medical Service Command Post (RU)

kpn........ Candidate of Pedagogical Sciences (RU)

KPN .... Communist Party of Netherlands (RU)

KPN .... Communist Party of Norway (RU)

KPN .... Confederation for an Independent Poland (PD)

Kpn........ Kepulauan [*Archipelago*] [*Indonesian*] (NAU)

KPN .... Ketua Polis Negara [*Chief National Police*] (ML)

KPN .... Konfederacja Polski Niepodleglej [*Confederation for an Independent Poland*] (EE)

KPN .... Koninklijke PTT Nederland [*Post and telecommunications company*] (ECON)

KPNLF ...... Khmer People's National Liberation Front [*Cambodia*] [*Political party*] (PD)

KPNZ .... Communist Party of New Zealand (RU)

KPO .... Control and Planning Department (RU)

KPO .... Cooperative Producers' Society (RU)

k po .... Junior Sergeant (BU)

KPO .... Kommunistische Partei Oesterreichs [*Communist Party of Austria*] [*Political party*] (PPW)

KPO .... Kulturne-Propagacni Oddeleni [*Cultural and Propaganda Department*] (CZ)

KPO .... Kulturno-Prosvetnite Organizacii [*Cultural and Educational Organizations*] (YU)

KPO .... Kulturno-Prosvjetni Odbor [*Cultural and Educational Committee*] (YU)

KPOE .... Kendron Programmatismou kai Oikonomikon Erevnon [*Center for Programing and Economic Research*] [*Greek*] (GC)

KPOe .... Kommunistische Partei Oesterreichs [*Communist Party of Austria*] (EG)

KPOP........ Komitet Porozumiewawczy Organizacji Podziemnych [*Underground Organizations' Consultative Committee*] [*World War II*] (POL)

KPOWU .... Kenya Petroleum and Oil Workers' Union

KPP............ Check Point for Motor Transport (RU)

KPP............ Communist Party of Pakistan (RU)

KPP............ Communist Party of Poland [*1925-1938*] (RU)

KPP............ Communist Party of Portugal (RU)

KPP............ Congress of Industrial Organizations [*CIO*] (RU)

KPP............ Control and Check Point (RU)

KPP............ Control-Traffic Point/Post (BU)

KPP............ Kamerun People's Party

KPP............ Kano People's Party [*Nigeria*] (AF)

KPP............ Ketua Egawai Polis [*Chief Police Officer*] (ML)

K-pp .... Komandir Pesadiskog Puka [*Infantry Regiment Commander*] (YU)

KPP............ Kombinat of Auxiliary Establishments (RU)

KPP............ Kombinat of Industrial Establishments (RU)

KPP............ Komisija za Plate u Privredi [*Industrial Wage Commission*] (YU)

KPP............ Komunisticka Partija Poljske [*Communist Party of Poland (1925-1938)*] (YU)

KPP............ Komunistyczna Partia Polski [*Communist Party of Poland (1925-1938)*] [*Political party*] (PPE)

KPP............ Kontrollpassierpunkt [*Border Control Point*] (EG)

KPP............ Krajske Plachtarske Preteky [*Regional Glider Contest*] (CZ)

KPP............ Regimental Command Post (RU)

KPPC......... Kuwait Petrochemical Products Co.

KPP iAFT ... Congress of Industrial Organizations and American Federation of Labor (BU)

KPPMS ..... Kesatuan Pelajar-Pelajar Melayu Selangor [*Malayan Students' Association of Selangor*] (ML)

KPPR........ Komunistyczna Partia Polska Robotnicza [*Communist Polish Workers' Party (1918)*] (POL)

KP PZPR... Komitet Powiatowy Polskiej Zjednoczonej Partii Robotniczej [*District Committee of the Polish United Workers' Party*] [*Poland*]

k pr............ Cavalry Escort (BU)

KPR .... Communist Party of Romania [*1921-1948*] (RU)

KPR .... Company Command Post (RU)

KPR .... Control-Marshaling Post (BU)

KPR .... Demolition Set (RU)

KPR .... Kancelar Presidenta Republiky [*Office of the President*] (CZ)

kpr............ Kapral [*Corporal*] [*Poland*]

KPR .... Kenya Police Reserve

KPR .... Kulturne-Propagacni Referat [*Cultural and Propaganda Section*] (CZ)

Kpr .... Kupferstich [*Etching*] [*German*]

KPR .... River Crossing Commandant (RU)

KPRL........ Kolejowe Przedsiebiorstwo Robot Ladunkowych [*Railroad Loading Enterprise*] (POL)

KPRM .... Komitet Planowania przy Radzie Ministrow [*Council of Ministers Planning Committee*] (POL)

KPRP........ Kampuchean [*or Khmer*] People's Revolutionary Party [*Political party*] (PD)

KPRP........ Komunistyczna Partia Robotnicza Polski [*Communist Workers' Party of Poland (1918-1925)*] [*Poland*]

kprst......... Kopparstick [*Copper Engraving*] [*Publishing*] [*Sweden*]

kps........ Capsule (RU)

KPS........... Communist Party of Slovakia (RU)

KPS........... Kempsey [*Australia*] [*Airport symbol*] (OAG)

KPS........... Ketua Penguasa Setor [*Chief Superintendent of Stores*] (ML)

kps........... Kiloparsec (RU)

KPS........... Kobanyai Polgari Serfozo Reszvenytarsasag [*Civic Brewery of Kobanya Limited*] (HU)

KPS........... Komisija za Plati vo Stopanstvo [*Industrial Wage Commission*] (YU)

KPS........... Kommunistische Partei der Schweiz [*Communist Party of Switzerland*] [*Political party*] (PPE)

KPS........... Kommunistische Partij Suriname [*Communist Party of Surinam*] [*Political party*] (PPW)

KPS........... Komunisticka Partija Srbije [*Communist Party of Serbia*] (YU)

KPS........... Komunisticna Partija Slovenije [*Communist Party of Slovenia*] (YU)

KPS........... Kotarska Poljoprivredna Stanica [*District Agricultural Station*] (YU)

KPS........... Krajska Politicka Skola [*Regional Political School*] (CZ)

KPS........... Krajsky Pedagogicky Sbor [*Regional Educational Board*] (CZ)

KPS........... Kurs Politickeho Skoleni [*Political Training Course*] (CZ)

KPSAD ..... Komunisticka Partija Sjedinjenih Americkih Drzava [*Communist Party of the United States of America*] (YU)

KPSh......... Communist Party of Sweden (RU)

KPSh......... Communist Party of Switzerland (RU)

KPSH....... Komisioni i Planit te Shtetit [*Albanian*]

KPSNSW .. Koala Preservation Society of New South Wales [*Australia*]

KPsO .... Kendron Psykhagogias Opliton [*Enlisted Men's Recreation Center*] (GC)

KPSS .... Kommunisticheskaya Partiya Sovetskogo Soyuza [*Communist Party of the Soviet Union*] [*Political party*]

KPSS .... Komunisticka Partija Sovjetskog Saveza [*Communist Party of the Soviet Union*] (YU)

KPSShA .... Communist Party of the United States of America (RU)

KPSTO ..... Komunisticna Partija Svobodnega Trzaskega Ozemlja [*Communist Party of the Free Territory of Trieste*] (YU)

KPsY......... Kendron Psykhikis Ygieinis [*Mental Health Center*] [*Greek*] (GC)

KPT........... Communist Party of Thailand (RU)

KPT........... Communist Party of Transjordan (RU)

KPT........... Communist Party of Tunisia (RU)

KPT........... Communist Party of Turkestan (RU)

KPT........... Communist Party of Turkey (RU)

KPT........... Communist Party of Turkmenia (RU)

kpt............ Kapitan [*Captain*] [*Poland*]

kpt............ Kaptajn [*Captain*] [*Denmark*] (GPO)

KPT........... Karpatair [*Hungary*] [*ICAO designator*] (FAAC)

Kpt .... Kupfertitel [*Engraved Title Page*] [*German*]

KPT........... Tank Regiment Commander (RU)

KPTA........ Korea Pharmaceutical Traders Association (EAIO)

KPTC........ Kuwait Public Transport Co. (EY)

KPTF .... Kolkhoz Poultry Farm (RU)

KPTI .... Kozponti Pedagogus Tovabbkepzo Intezet [*Central Institute for Advanced Teacher Training*] (HU)

KPTP .... Committee for Industry and Technological Progress (BU)

KPTs.......... Communist Party of Ceylon (RU)

KPU .... Communist Party of the Ukraine (RU)

KPU .... Communist Party of Uruguay (RU)

KPU .... Kazneno-Popravne Ustanove [*Penal-Reformatory Institutions*] (YU)

K pu........... Keleti-Palyaudvar [*Keleti (East) Railway Station (Budapest)*] (HU)

KPU .... Kenya People's Union (AF)

KPU .... Kommunisticheskaia Partiia Ukrainy [*Communist Party of the Ukraine*] [*Political party*]

KPU .... Shipboard Intercommunication System (RU)

KPUG .... Hunter-Killer Group [*Navy*]   (RU)
KPUNIA.... Fighter Aviation Ship's Control and Guidance Post   (RU)
KPUV .... Kanony Proti Utocne Vozbe [*Antitank Guns*]   (CZ)
KPUz .... Communist Party of Uzbekistan   (RU)
KPUZ .... Kommunisticheskaia Partiia Uzbekistana [*Communist Party of Uzbekistan*] [*Political party*]   (RU)
KPV .... Communist Party of Great Britain   (RU)
KPV .... Communist Party of Hungary [*1918-1948*]   (RU)
KPV .... Communist Party of Venezuela   (RU)
kPV .... Continental Modified Air   (RU)
kPV .... Continental Polar Air   (RU)
KPV .... [*The*] Culture and Literature of the East [*Bibliography*]   (RU)
KPV .... Kaaplandse Pomologiese Vereniging [*South Africa*]   (AA)
KPV .... Kancelar Predsednictva Vlady [*Office of the Government Presidium*]   (CZ)
KPV .... Searchlight Platoon Commander   (RU)
KPVDOSZ ... Kereskedelmi, Penzugyi, es Vendeglatoipari Dolgozok Szakszervezete [*Trade Union of Workers in Commerce, Finance, and the Catering Industries*]   (HU)
KPVO .... Air Defense Ship, Antiaircraft Ship   (RU)
kPVO .... Antiaircraft Defense Corps   (BU)
KPVRZ ..... Konotop Locomotive and Railroad Car Repair Plant   (RU)
KPVS .... Komise Pomoci Vychodnimu Slovensku [*Relief Commission for Eastern Slovakia*]   (CZ)
KPWB .... Komunistyczna Partia Wielkiej Brytanii [*Communist Party of Great Britain*] [*Poland*]
KPYa .... Communist Party of Japan   (RU)
KPYe .... Variable Capacitor   (RU)
KPYu .... Communist Party of Yugoslavia [*1919-1952*]   (RU)
KPZ .... Kotarska Poljoprivredna Zadruga [*District Agricultural Cooperative*]   (YU)
KPZ .... Kulturno-Prosvetna Zajednica [*Cultural and Educational Association*]   (YU)
KPZ .... Pretrial Detention Cell   (RU)
KPZB .... Communist Party of Western Belorussia   (RU)
KPZB .... Kieleckie Przemyslowe Zjednoczenie Budowlane [*Kielce Industrial Construction Association*]   (POL)
KPZB .... Komunistyczna Partia Zachodniej Bialorusi [*Communist Party of Western Belorussia (Prewar)*]   (POL)
KPZB .... Krakowskie Przemyslowe Zjednoczenie Budowlane [*Krakow Industrial Construction Association*]   (POL)
KPZDA ...... Komunisticna Partija Zdruzenih Drzav Amerike [*Communist Party of the United States of America*]   (YU)
KPZF .... Komisija za Poljoprivredni Zemljisni Fond [*Agricultural Land Fund Commission*]   (YU)
KPZh .... Liquid Cargo Container   (RU)
KP ZMS .... Komitet Powiatowy Zwiazku Mlodziezy Socjalistycznej [*District Committee of the Socialist Youth Union*] [*Poland*]
KPZR .... Komunistyczna Partia Zwiazku Radzieckiego [*Communist Party of the Soviet Union*]   (POL)
KPZRZ ...... Krakowskie Przedsiebiorstwo Zmechanizowanych Robot Ziemnych [*Krakow Mechanized Earthmoving Enterprise*]   (POL)
KPZU .... Communist Party of the Western Ukraine   (RU)
KPZU .... Komunistyczna Partia Zachodniej Ukrainy [*Communist Party of Western Ukraine (Prewar)*]   (POL)
KPZZ .... Krajsky Podnik Zemedelskeho Zasobevani [*Regional Agricultural Supply Enterprise*]   (CZ)
KQA .... Kenya Airways Ltd. [*ICAO designator*]   (FAAC)
KQBPSH ... Keshilli Qendror i Bashkimeve Profesionale te Shqiperise [*Albanian*]
KQL .... Kol [*Papua New Guinea*] [*Airport symbol*]   (OAG)
KQMWU ... Kenya Quarry and Mine Workers' Union
KR .... Area Commandant   (RU)
KR .... Box Car   (RU)
KR .... Code Register   (RU)
kr .... Commander [*or Officer in Charge*]   (BU)
k-r .... Commander, Commanding Officer, Leader   (RU)
KR .... Commander's Reconnaissance   (RU)
KR .... Company Commander   (RU)
k-r .... Condenser, Capacitor   (RU)
KR .... Cosmic Radiation   (RU)
k-r .... Counterrevolutionary   (RU)
Kr .... Criptonio [*Chemical element*] [*Portuguese*]
kr .... Critical   (RU)
Kr .... De Kroniek [*Benelux*]   (BAS)
KR .... (Heavy) Cruiser   (RU)
Kr .... Kantonrechter [*Benelux*]   (BAS)
kr .... Karat [*Carat*] [*Poland*]
KR .... Kenya Railways
KR .... Kenya Regiment
KR .... Kernresonance [*Nuclear Magnetic Resonance*] [*German*]   (GCA)
KR .... Khimji Ramdas [*Oman*] [*Commercial firm*]
KR .... Khmer Rouge [*or Khmers Rouges*] [*Red Cambodian*]   (CL)
KR .... Kinderrechter [*Benelux*]   (BAS)
Kr .... King [*Chess*]   (RU)

KR .... Kjeller Research Establishment [*Norwegian*]
KR .... Kladensky Revir [*Kladno Basin (Coal)*]   (CZ)
KR .... Klasifikacija Robe [*Goods Classification*]   (YU)
KR .... Knihovni Rada [*Library Council (of the Local People's Committee)*]   (CZ)
KR .... Kolko Rolnicze [*Agricultural Cooperative*] [*Poland*]
KR .... Koloniale Rundschau
KR .... Komandni Racunar [*Staff Computer*] [*Military*]   (YU)
KR .... Komisja Rewizyjna [*Board of Control*] [*Poland*]
KR .... Komisja Rozjemcza [*Conciliation Commission*]   (POL)
KR .... Kommerzienrat [*German*]
KR .... Kontenrahmen [*Accounting System*]   (EG)
KR .... Koppelreihe [*German*]   (ADPT)
KR .... Korean Register [*Korean ship classification society*]   (DS)
Kr .... Kran [*Crane*] [*German*]
Kr .... Kranken [*Ill*] [*German*]
kr .... Kray   (RU)
kr .... Krediteur [*Creditor*] [*Business term*] [*Afrikaans*]
Kr .... Kreis [*District*] [*German*]
KR .... Kreuzer [*Monetary unit*] [*German*]
Kr .... Kriminal [*Criminal*] [*German*]
Kr .... Kristall [*Crystal*] [*German*]   (GCA)
kr .... Kristallinisch [*Crystalline*] [*German*]   (GCA)
Kr .... Kristallographie [*Crystallography*] [*German*]   (GCA)
KR .... Krona [*Crown*] [*Monetary unit Iceland, Sweden*]   (EY)
KR .... Krone [*Crown*] [*Monetary unit Denmark, Norway*]   (EY)
KR .... Kroon [*Crown, Top Chandelier*] [*Afrikaans*]
Kr .... Krueng [*River*] [*Indonesian*]   (NAU)
kr .... Kruunu(a) [*Finland*]
Kr .... Krystallographie [*Crystallography*] [*German*]
KR .... Kulon Rendelet [*Special Decree (Legal)*]   (HU)
Kr .... Kurus [*Kurus*] [*Piastre Monetary unit*]   (TU)
kr .... Machine-Gun Company   (BU)
KR .... Major Repair, General Overhaul   (RU)
KR .... Mine-Clearing Set   (RU)
KR .... Oxygen Reducer   (RU)
KR .... Pilot Relay   (RU)
Kr .... Red [*Toponymy*]   (RU)
KR .... Republic of Korea [*ANSI two-letter standard code*]   (CNC)
kr .... Shell Rock [*Topography*]   (RU)
Kr .... Wet op de Krijgstucht [*Benelux*]   (BAS)
KRA .... Karenni Revolutionary Army [*Myanmar*] [*Political party*]   (EY)
KRA .... Kleinrechenanlage [*German*]   (ADPT)
KRA .... Kreis-Registrierabteilung [*Kreis Registration Department*]   (EG)
k-ra .... Office   (RU)
KRA .... Spotter Observation Aviation   (BU)
KRA .... Spotting and Reconnaissance Aviation   (RU)
krae .... Spotter Observation Aviation Squadron   (BU)
krae .... Spotting and Air Reconnaissance Squadron   (RU)
KRAK .... Kato Rossia, Ameriki, Kina [*Down with Russia, America, China (Movement)*] [*Greek*]   (GC)
krakhm ...... Starch Plant [*Topography*]   (RU)
Krankh ...... Krankheit [*Sickness*] [*German*]   (GCA)
Krankzw .... Wet tot Regeling van het Staatstoezicht op Krankzinnigen [*Benelux*]   (BAS)
KrAO .... Crimean Astrophysical Observatory   (RU)
KRAONA .. Kraonita Malagasy
krap .... Spotter Observation Aviation Regiment   (BU)
krap .... Spotting and Air Reconnaissance Regiment   (RU)
KRAS .... Check-and-Repair Aviation Station   (RU)
KRAS .... Krasnoyarsk Railroad   (RU)
Krasges ...... Krasnoyarsk Hydro-Electric Power Plant   (RU)
kraskom ..... Red Commander   (RU)
Kraslag ...... Krasnoyarsk Corrective Labor Camp   (RU)
Krasmash ... Krasnoyarsk Machinery Plant   (RU)
krasnoarm ... Red Army   (RU)
Krasnomash ... Krasnoyarsk Heavy Machinery Plant   (RU)
Krasnoyargiz ... Krasnoyarsk State Publishing House   (RU)
krat .... Kratica [*Abbreviation*]   (YU)
krayekoso... Kray Economic Conference   (RU)
krayeved..... Regional Studies   (RU)
krayfo........ Kray Finance Department   (RU)
krayFU ...... Kray Finance Administration   (RU)
Kraygiz....... Kray State Publishing House   (RU)
krayknigotorg ... Kray Book Trade Office   (RU)
kraykomkhoz ... Kray Department of Municipal Services   (RU)
kraykoopinsoyuz ... Kray Union of Disabled Persons' Cooperative Artels   (RU)
kraykozhpromsoyuz ... Kray Leather Producers' Union   (RU)
krayono...... Kray Department of Public Education   (RU)
krayplan..... Kray Planning Commission   (RU)
kraypoligrafizdat ... Department of Publishing Houses and Printing Industry of a Krayispolkom Cultural Administration   (RU)
kraypotrebsoyuz ... Kray Union of Consumers' Societies   (RU)
kraysobes... Kray Department of Social Security   (RU)
kraysovprof ... Kray Council of Trade Unions   (RU)

KrayTASS ... Khabarovsk Kray Branch of the News Agency of the Soviet Union (RU)
krayVTEK ... Kray Medical Commission for Determination of Disability (RU)
krayzdrav... Kray Department of Public Health (RU)
krayzo .... Kray Land Department (RU)
krayzu .... Kray Land Administration (RU)
KRAZ .... Automobile Made by the Kremenchug Automobile Plant (RU)
KRAZ .... Kremenchug Automobile Plant (RU)
kr b .... Brigade Commander (BU)
KRB .... Karumba [Australia] [Airport symbol] (OAG)
KRB .... Kernkraftwerk RWE-Bayernwerk, GmbH [Nuclear energy] (NRCH)
kr bt .... Battery Commander (BU)
KRCh .... Tuning-Fork Frequency Controller (RU)
KRCS .... Kenya Red Cross Society
KRD .... Collective Workers' Movement [Philippines] (RU)
KRD .... Krajska Rada Druzstev [Regional Council of Cooperatives] (CZ)
KRDA .... Kweneng Rural Development Association
KRDC .... Kenya Rally Drivers' Club
KRDL .... Kommission Reinhaltung der Luft im VDI und DIN [Commission on Air Pollution Prevention VDI-DIN] [Germany] (EAIO)
KRDP .... Karonga Rural Development Project
kr dr .... Battalion Commander (BU)
KRE .... Kreditoren [German] (ADPT)
Kr e .... Krisztus Elott [Before Christ] (HU)
KREI .... Korea Rural Economics Institute [Research center] (IRC)
KREIC .... Koweit Real Estate Investment Consortium
kreik .... Kreikassa [Finland]
kreik .... Kreikkaa [or Kreikaksi] [Finland]
kreikk .... Kreikkalainen [Greek] [Finland]
kreikkal ..... Kreikkalainen [Greek] [Finland]
KREMENCO ... Kuwait Industrial Refinery, Maintenance, and Engineering Company (ME)
KremGES .. Kremenchug Hydroelectric Power Plant (RU)
KREMU .... Kenya Rangeland Ecological Monitoring Unit
KREMZ ..... Kalinin Electromechanical Plant (RU)
KREMZ ..... Kiev Electromechanical Repair Plant (RU)
Krep .... Fortress, Citadel, Stronghold [Topography] (RU)
KRES .... Kiev Regional Electric Power Plant (RU)
KRES .... Krasnodar Regional Electric Power Plant (RU)
kr esk .... Troop Commander (BU)
Krestintern ... Peasants' International (RU)
krestkom .... Peasants' Mutual Aid Committee (RU)
Krestlit .... Lithuanian Red Cross (RU)
krestpom .... Peasants' Mutual Aid Committee (RU)
krest'yan .... Peasant (RU)
KRESZ ...... A Kozuti Kozlekedes Rendjenek Szabalyzata [Traffic Regulations for Public Thoroughfares] (HU)
KREUZ...... Kreuzer [Monetary unit] [German] (ROG)
KREZ........ Konstantinovka Electrical Repair Plant (RU)
KRF........... Kramfors [Sweden] [Airport symbol] (OAG)
KrF............. Kristelig Folkpartiet [Christian People's Party] [Norway] [Political party] (PPE)
KrF............. Kristeligt Folkeparti [Christian People's Party] [Denmark] [Political party] (PPE)
KRG .... Karaganda Railroad (RU)
KRG .... Karasabai [Guyana] [Airport symbol] (OAG)
KrG .... Kriegsgericht [War Tribunal] [German]
KRH........... Komisja Rozbudowy Hutnictwa [Commission for Metallurgical Development] (POL)
KRI .... Kikori [Papua New Guinea] [Airport symbol] (OAG)
KRICT ...... Korea Research Institute of Chemical Technology
KRIHS...... Korea Research Institute for Human Settlements
krik .... Kriketti [Cricket] [Finland]
KRIKASA ... Kristiyani Kamkaru Sahodaratvaya [Christian Workers Fellowship] [Sri Lanka] (EAIO)
Krim.......... Kriminal [Criminal] [German]
KRINGRAMAT ... Krizevacka Industrija Gradevnog Materijala [Krizevci Building Materials Industry] (YU)
KRIPO...... Kriminalpolizei [Ordinary Criminal Police] [German]
KrISK .... Crimean Institute of Special Crops (RU)
KRISP....... Kenya Rift International Seismic Project
krist........... Crystal, Crystalline (RU)
Krist .... Kristallisation [Crystallization] [German]
krist........... Kristallisiert [or Kristallinisch] [Crystallized or Crystalline] [German]
Kristal-Is.... Turkiye Sise, Cam, ve Kristal Sanayii Iscileri Sendikasi [Turkish Bottle, Glass, and Crystal Industry Workers Union] (TU)
kristallich... Crystal, Crystalline (RU)
kristallokhim ... Crystal-Chemistry (RU)
Kristfm....... Kristallform [Crystal Form] [German] (GCA)
krist sp ...... Crystal Spectrometer (RU)
krit .... Critical (RU)
krit .... Kritisch [Critical] [German]

kritich .... Critical (RU)
krit Temp... Kritische Temperatur [Critical Temperature] [German] (GCA)
Krivbass ..... Krivoy Rog Iron Ore Basin (RU)
Krivorozhstal' ... Krivoy Rog Metallurgical Plant (RU)
KRIZTO .... Commission for Fisheries Research in the Western Pacific Ocean (RU)
krj............... Kirja(a) [Finland]
krjm............ Krestni Jmeno [Christian Name] (CZ)
kr k .... Corps Commander (BU)
KRK .... Krakow [Poland] [Airport symbol] (OAG)
KRK .... Kreisrevisionskommission [Kreis Audit Commission] (EG)
krkat .... Kreikkalais-Katolinen [Finland]
kr kdrt .... Blood Count Card (RU)
Krkh........... Krankenhaus [Hospital] [German]
KRKO .... Kibris Rum Kurtulus Ordusu [Greek Cypriot Liberation Army] [EKAS is preferred Turkish Cypriot] (GC)
KRKP........ Krajowa Rada Kobiet Polskich [All-Polish Council of Women] (POL)
Krkw .... Krankenkraftwagen [Motor Ambulance] (EG)
KRL .... Koreanska Republika Ludowa [Korean People's Republic] (POL)
KRL .... Korla [China] [Airport symbol] (OAG)
KRL .... Light Cruiser (RU)
KRLD .... Koreanska Republika Ludowo-Demokratyczna [Korean People's Democratic Republic] [Poland]
KRLS .... Ship Radar (RU)
KRM......... Radio Range Beacon (RU)
KRN........... Kiruna [Sweden] [Airport symbol] (OAG)
KRN........... Krajowa Rada Narodowa [National People's Council (1944-1947)] [Poland]
krn.............. Rhizome (RU)
KRNG....... Kwame Nkrumah Revolutionary Guards
KRNK....... Koordinerende Raad vir Natuurbewaring in Kaapland [South Africa] (AA)
krnpl .... Root Crop (RU)
KRNV....... Komise Rizeni Narodnich Vyboru [Commission for the Direction of People's Committees] (CZ)
KRO.......... Aliblu Airways SpA [Italy] [ICAO designator] (FAAC)
KRO.......... Counterintelligence Section of the OGPU (RU)
KRO.......... Katholieke Radio Omroep [Catholic Broadcasting Association] [Netherlands]
KRO.......... Krajska Rada Odboru [Regional Trade Union Council] (CZ)
KRO.......... Reconnaissance Detachment Commander (RU)
KRO.......... Workers' Education Center (RU)
KRO.......... Workers' Training Courses (RU)
KROAG ..... Committee for the Revolution in Oman and the Arabian Gulf [Denmark]
KROC .... Kids Reading Oz Choice Award [Australia]
Kron .... Kronieke [Chronicles] [Afrikaans]
KROW....... Komitet Rozbudowy Otoczenia Wawelu [Committee for Development of the Wawel Area] (POL)
KRP .... Checking and Clearing Point [At a decontamination station] (RU)
KRP .... Compass Radio Bearing (RU)
KRP .... Kama River Steamship Line (RU)
KRP .... Karup [Denmark] [Airport symbol] (OAG)
KRP .... Keskusrikospoliisi [Central Criminal Police] [Finland] (WEN)
KRP .... Knihovna Rudeho Prava [Library of the "Rude Pravo" Newspaper] (CZ)
KRP .... Komisija za Reviziju Projekata [Design Revision Commission] (YU)
KRP .... Kurdistan Revolutionary Party [Iraq] [Political party] (PPW)
KRPG .... Communist Workers' Party of Germany (RU)
kr pk.......... Regimental Commander (BU)
KRPP........ Communist Workers' Party of Poland [1918-1925] (RU)
KRR .... Kansai Research Reactor [Nuclear energy] [Japan] (NRCH)
KRR .... Krasnodar [Former USSR] [Airport symbol] (OAG)
KRR .... Rat-Reticulocyte Reaction (RU)
KRRL........ Kabinet pro Studia Recka, Rimska, a Latinska [Department of Greek, Roman, and Latin Studies (of the Czechoslovak Academy of Sciences)] (CZ)
KRRS........ Kenya Rugby Referees Society
KRS........... Cosmic Rocket System (RU)
krs .... Kerros [Finland]
KRS........... Korsar [Russian Federation] [ICAO designator] (FAAC)
KRS........... Kristiansand [Norway] [Airport symbol] (OAG)
krs .... Krossi(a) [Finland]
KrS............ Kurirska Stanica [Courier Station] [Military] (YU)
Krs............. Kurus [Piastre] [Monetary unit]
KRSEDE ..... Kendrikos Radiofonikos Stathmos Enoplon Dynameon Ellados [Main Radio Station of the Armed Forces of Greece] (GC)
KRSS .... Krajska Sprava Spoju [Regional Administration Office for Communications] (CZ)
KRT .... Code Relay Transformer (RU)
KRT .... Cretan Airlines SA [Greece] [ICAO designator] (FAAC)
KRT .... Heavy Cruiser (RU)

krt.............. Kaart [*Chart, Map*] [*Publishing*] [*Netherlands*]
Krt.............. Karte [*Map, Chart*] [*German*]
KRT .... Khartoum [*Sudan*] [*Airport symbol*]   (OAG)
KRT .... Khartoum International Airport
krt.............. Korut [*Avenue, Boulevard*]   (HU)
KRTA .... Katoomba Retail Traders Association [*Australia*]
krtjes.......... Kaartjes [*Small Charts, Maps*] [*Publishing*] [*Netherlands*]
krtn .... Kaarten [*Charts, Maps*] [*Publishing*] [*Netherlands*]
kr-ts........... Red Army Soldier   (RU)
KRU .... Category Distribution System [*Nuclear energy*]   (BU)
KRU .... Control and Inspection Administration   (RU)
KRU .... Directorate of Counterintelligence   (RU)
Kr u .... Krisztus Utan [*Anno Domini*]   (HU)
KRUIK...... Kaaplandse Raad vir die Uitvoerende Kunste [*Capetown
                Performing Arts Board - CAPAB*] [*Afrikaans*]
KRV .... Auxiliary Cruiser   (RU)
KRV .... Komanda Ratnog Vazduhoplovstva [*Air Force Command*]
                (YU)
KRV .... Kommissie Rechtvaardigheid en Vrede [*Flemish Commission for
                Justice and Peace*] [*Belgium*]   (EAIO)
KRWRiOP ... Komisja Rzadowa Wyznan Religijnych i Oswiecenia
                Publicznego [*State Commission on Religious
                Denominations and Public Education*] [*Pre-World War II*]
                (POL)
KRX .... Kar Kar [*Papua New Guinea*] [*Airport symbol*]   (OAG)
KRY .... Karamay [*China*] [*Airport symbol*]   (OAG)
kr-yets....... Red Army Soldier   (RU)
krygsk....... Krygskunde [*Military*] [*Afrikaans*]
Krymgosizdat ... Crimean State Publishing House   (RU)
Krymizdat .. Crimean Oblast Book Publishing House   (RU)
KrymTsIK ... Central Executive Committee of the Crimean ASSR   (RU)
kryoskop .... Kryoskopisch [*Cryoscopic*] [*German*]   (GCA)
Kryst .... Krystall [*or Krystallisation or Krystallographie*] [*Crystal or
                Crystallization or Crystallography*] [*German*]
kryst .... Krystallisieren [*Crystallize*] [*German*]   (GCA)
k-ryy.......... Which, That, Who   (RU)
KRZ .... Kiri [*Zaire*] [*Airport symbol*]   (OAG)
KRZh .... Railroads of the Korean People's Democratic Republic   (RU)
KS .... Apparent Resistance   (RU)
KS .... Boilermaking   (RU)
KS .... Cathode Glow   (RU)
KS .... Check Signal   (RU)
KS .... Combustion Chamber   (RU)
KS .... Command Personnel   (RU)
KS .... Communications Channel   (RU)
KS .... Compressor Station   (RU)
ks.............. Control Station   (RU)
ks.............. Corps   (BU)
KS .... Cybernetic Collection [*Bibliography*]   (RU)
KS .... Duty on Board [*Navy*]   (RU)
KS .... Gearbox   (RU)
KS .... Guard Duty   (RU)
KS .... Gunnery Training Course   (RU)
ks.............. Horsepower   (BU)
KS .... Kamerunskii Soiuz
KS .... Kancelarske Stroje [*Office Machinery*]   (CZ)
k-s .... Kantasana [*Finland*]
KS .... Kant Society [*Germany*]   (EAIO)
KS .... Kapitalisticke Staty [*Capitalist States*]   (CZ)
KS .... Kartografiska Sallskapet [*Swedish Cartographic Society*]   (EAIO)
ks.............. Katso [*See, Compare*] [*Finland*]   (GPO)
KS .... Keltic Society and the College of Druidism   (EA)
KS .... Kempense Steenkolenmijnen [*Belgium*]
KS .... Kendrikon Symvoulion [*Central Council*]   (GC)
KS .... Kepala Staf [*Chief of Staff*]   (IN)
KS .... Kilosekonde [*Kilosecond*] [*Afrikaans*]
KS .... Kilosikl [*Kilocycle*]   (TU)
KS .... Kingsford Smith (Airport) [*Australia*]   (ADA)
Ks .... Kisa [*Short*]   (TU)
Ks .... Kisim [*Section*] [*As of a publication*]   (TU)
KS .... Klanje Stoke [*Livestock Slaughter*]   (YU)
KS .... Klub Sportowy [*Sport Club*]   (POL)
KS .... Knjizevni Sever [*Literary North*] [*Subotica A periodical*]   (YU)
KS .... Kollisionsschutzanlage [*Anticollision Device*]   (EG)
KS .... Koloniale Studien [*Benelux*]   (BAS)
Ks .... Kolpos [*Gulf*] [*Greek*]   (NAU)
KS .... Komisija Strucnjaka [*Commission of Specialists*]   (YU)
KS .... Komisija za Standardizaciju [*Standardization Commission*]
                (YU)
KS .... Komitet Stoleczny [*Poland*]
KS .... Komunisticka Strana [*Communist Party*]   (CZ)
KS .... Komunisticka Stranka [*Communist Party*]   (YU)
KS .... Konjska Sila [*Horsepower*]   (YU)
KS .... Konjska Snaga [*Horsepower*]   (YU)
KS .... Kontrolna Stanica [*Control Station*] [*Radio*] [*Military*]   (YU)
KS .... Konungariket Sverige [*Kingdom of Sweden*]   (BARN)

KS .... Krajska Sprava [*Regional Administration*]   (CZ)
KS .... Kreditsaldo [*Credit Balance*] [*Afrikaans*]
KS .... Kritiki Syspirosi [*Critical Thinking Group*] [*Marxist-Leninist-
                Maoist*] [*Greek*]   (GC)
KS .... Krojastvo in Siviljstvo [*Tailoring and Dressmaking*]   (YU)
ks.............. Ksiadz [*Priest, Reverend*]   (POL)
ks.............. Ksiaze [*Duke*] [*Poland*]
KS .... Kuebel Stiftung [*Kuebel Foundation*] [*Germany*]   (EAIO)
KS .... Kuestenschiff [*Coastal Ship*]   (EG)
KS .... Kuestenschutzboot [*Coastal Patrol Boat, Coastal Protection
                Boat*]   (EG)
KS .... Kunstseide [*Rayon*] [*German*]   (GCA)
KS .... Kurze Sicht [*Short Sight*] [*German*]
ks.............. Kus [*Each, Piece, Unit*]   (CZ)
KS .... Oscillating System   (RU)
KS .... Quartz Spectrograph   (RU)
KS .... Resistance Method in Logging   (RU)
KS .... Shim Rod [*Nuclear physics and engineering*]   (RU)
KS .... Spotter   (RU)
KS .... Stop Button   (RU)
KS .... Vitreous-Enamel Capacitor   (RU)
KSA .... Committee on Construction and Architecture   (BU)
KSA .... Eidgenossische Kommission fuer die Sicherheit von Kernanlagen
                [*Federal Commission for the Safety of Nuclear
                Installations*] [*Switzerland*]   (WND)
KSA .... Kenya Shipping Agency Ltd.
KSA .... Krajska Sdruzeni Advokatu [*Regional Associations of Lawyers*]
                (CZ)
KSAC........ Kingston-Saint Andrew Corporate Area [*Jamaica*]   (LA)
KSAK........ Kungliga Svenska Aeroklubbon [*Sweden*]
KSAVU...... Kniznica Slovenskej Akademie Vied a Umeni [*Library of the
                Slovak Academy of Sciences and Arts*]   (CZ)
KSB.......... Communal Economy and Public Works   (BU)
KSB.......... Klein, Schanzlin & Becker Aktiengesellschaft [*Klein, Schanzlin &
                Becker Joint Stock Company*]   (NRCH)
KSB.......... Kombuis, Spens, Badkamer [*Kitchen, Pantry, Bathroom*]
                [*Afrikaans*]
KSB.......... Kozponti Statisztikai Bizottsag [*Central Statistical Committee*]
                (HU)
KSB.......... Kradschuetzen-Bataillon [*Motorcycle Battalion*] [*German
                military - World War II*]
KSB.......... Ksiazka Sprzetu Budowlanego [*Record Book for Building
                Equipment*]   (POL)
K Sb .... Kumandan Subay [*Commanding Officer*]   (TU)
KSB.......... Rifle Battalion Commander   (RU)
KSC.......... Kagoshima Space Center [*Japan*]
KSC.......... Kenana Sugar Company [*Sudan*]
KSC.......... Komandir Streljacke Cete [*Commanding Officer of a Rifle
                Company*]   (YU)
KSC.......... Komunisticka Strana Ceskoslovenska [*Communist Party of
                Czechoslovakia*] [*Political party*]   (PPW)
KSC.......... Korea Shipping Corp.   (DS)
KSC.......... Kosice [*Former Czechoslovakia*] [*Airport symbol*]   (OAG)
KSC.......... Krajsky Soud Civilni [*Regional Civil Court*]   (CZ)
KSC.......... Krajsky Soud Obchodni [*Regional Court of Business Litigation*]
                (CZ)
KSC.......... Kuwait Science Club   (EAIO)
KSCSN...... Klub Svazu Ceskoslovenskych Novinaru [*Czechoslovak
                Journalists' Club*]   (CZ)
KSCSS....... Klub Svazu Ceskoslovenskych Soisovatelu [*Czechoslovak
                Writers' Club (Club of the Czechoslovak Writers' Union)*]
                (CZ)
KSD .... Karlstad [*Sweden*] [*Airport symbol*]   (OAG)
KSD .... Kodix Stratiotikis Dikaiosynis [*Code of Military Justice*] [*Greek*]
                (GC)
KSD .... Kontrollstreifenausdruck [*German*]   (ADPT)
KSD .... Krajove Slovenske Divadlo [*Slovak Regional Theater*]   (CZ)
KSD .... Medium-Pressure Compressor   (RU)
KSD .... Rifle Division Commander   (RU)
KSDA .... Korean Securities Dealers' Association   (ECON)
KSDB........ Kommunal Statistisk DataBank [*Danmarks Statistik*]
                [*Denmark*] [*Information service or system*]   (CRD)
KSDIC ...... Kerala State Industrial Development Corp. [*India*]   (PDAA)
KSE .... Karachi Stock Exchange [*Pakistan*]
KSE .... Kasese [*Uganda*] [*Airport symbol*]   (OAG)
kse............. Kassette [*Slipcase*] [*Publishing Danish/Norwegian*]
KSE .... Kisbee Air Ltd. [*New Zealand*] [*ICAO designator*]   (FAAC)
KSE .... Korea Stock Exchange   (ECON)
KSE .... Kuwait Society of Engineers   (PDAA)
KSEM........ Korean Society of Electron Microscopy   (EAIO)
KSEPL....... Koninklijke/Shell Exploratie en Produktie Laboratorium [*Royal/
                Shell Exploration and Production Laboratory*] [*Research
                center*] [*Netherlands*]   (IRC)
KSES .... Kendriki Synetairistiki Enosis Sykoparagogon (Sykiki) [*Central
                Fig Producers Cooperative Union*] [*Greek*]   (GC)
KSF .... Kassel [*Germany*] [*Airport symbol*]   (OAG)

KSF .... Kungliga Svenska Flygvapnet [*Royal Swedish Air Force*] (PDAA)
KSFC .... Karnataka State Financial Corp. [*India*]   (PDAA)
KSFC .... Keep Stanton Free Committee [*Australia*]
KSG .... Hermetically Sealed Mica Capacitor   (RU)
KSGM .... Kalgoorlie Southern Gold Mines [*Australia*]
KSGR .... Konferenz Schweizerischer Gymnasialrektoren [*Switzerland*] (EAIO)
KSGU .... Knihovna Statniho Ustavu Geologickeho [*Library of the State Geological Institute*]   (CZ)
KSGUCSR ... Knihovna Statniho Ustavu Geologickeho Ceskoslovenske Republiky [*Library of the State Geological Institute of the Czechoslovak Republic*]   (CZ)
KSh .... Code Bus [*Computers*]   (RU)
KSH .... Kaplan Seiner Heiligkeit [*German*]
KSH .... Kenya Shilling [*Monetary unit*]   (IMH)
KSH .... Kernenergie-Gesellschaft Schlesweg-Holstein, mbH [*Nuclear energy*]   (NRCH)
KSH .... Kombinat Seeverkehr und Hafenwirtschaft [*Germany*]   (PDAA)
KSH .... Kozponti Statisztikai Hivatal [*Central Statistical Office*]   (HU)
KSH .... Kuwait Society for the Handicapped   (EAIO)
KShA .... Address Code Bus [*Computers*]   (RU)
KShB .... Children and School Libraries Pool   (RU)
KShCh ...... Number Code Bus   (RU)
KShR .... Telephone Construction Company   (RU)
KSHS.......... Korean Society for Horticultural Science   (EAIO)
ksht a .... Army Commander   (BU)
KShtM....... Command Staff Car   (BU)
ksht o a...... Separate Army Commander   (BU)
KShU .... Command and Staff Exercise, Command Post Exercise   (RU)
KShZ .... Kirov Tire Plant   (RU)
KSI............. Kozponti Sportiskola [*Central Sports School*]   (HU)
KSI............. Red Sports International   (RU)
KSIA .... Brief Communications of the Institute of Archaeology   (RU)
KSIE .... Brief Communications of the Institute of Ethnography   (RU)
ksieg.......... Ksiegarnia [*Bookshop*]   (POL)
KSIIMK .... Brief Communications on Reports and Field Research of the Institute of Material Culture (Academy of Sciences, USSR) (RU)
KSIV .... Brief Communications of the Institute of Oriental Studies [*Academy of Sciences, USSR*]   (RU)
KSJ .... Kasos Island [*Greece*] [*Airport symbol*]   (OAG)
KSK............ Commission of Soviet Control (at the Council of People's Commissars, USSR) [*1934-1940*]   (RU)
KSK............ Committee for Economic Coordination   (BU)
KSK............ Kanser Savas Konseyi [*Council to Combat Cancer*] [*Under Ministry of Health and Social Welfare*]   (TU)
KSK............ Karlskoga [*Sweden*] [*Airport symbol*]
KSK............ Karsiyaka Spor Kulubu [*Karsiyaka Sports Club*] [*Izmir*]   (TU)
KSK............ Klub Socialisticke Kultury [*Socialist Culture Club*]   (CZ)
KSK............ Komise Stranicke Kontroly [*Party Control Commission*]   (CZ)
KsK .... Potassium Sulfate   (RU)
KSKhI........ Kishinev Agricultural Institute Imeni M. V. Frunze   (RU)
KSKhI........ Kuban' Agricultural Institute   (RU)
k s-kh n ...... Candidate of Agricultural Sciences   (RU)
KSKhOS... Complex Agricultural Experimental Station   (RU)
KSKhSh..... Communist Agricultural School   (RU)
KSKO .... Sovkhoz and Kolkhoz Education Center   (RU)
KSKP......... Kumpulan Sekuad Khas Polis [*Police Special Squad Group*] (ML)
ksl .... Kalt Sehr Loeslich [*Very Soluble When Cold*] [*German*]   (GCA)
KSL............ Kassala [*Sudan*] [*Airport symbol*]   (OAG)
Ksl............. Kisla [*Barracks*]   (TU)
KSL............ Krajska Sprava Lesu [*Regional Forest Administration*]   (CZ)
KSL............ Kuala Selangor   (AA)
KSL............ Perforation Solenoid Contact   (RU)
KSLA .... Kungliga Skogs- och Lantbruksakademien [*Sweden*]   (SLS)
KSLS .... Krajska Sprava Inseminacnich Stanic [*Regional Administration of Insemination Stations (Attached to the Regional National Committee)*]   (CZ)
KSM .... Building Materials Kombinat   (RU)
KSM .... Commission on Synoptic Meteorology (of the World Meteorological Organization)   (RU)
ksm............ Cubic Centimeter   (BU)
KSM .... Katholiek Staatskundig Maandschrift [*Benelux*]   (BAS)
KSM .... Keyboard Calculating Machine   (RU)
KSM .... Kooperative Serbaguna Malaysia [*Bank*]
KSM .... Kothagudem School of Mines [*Osmania University*] [*India*] (EAS)
KSM .... Young Communist League   (RU)
KSMA....... Keats-Shelley Memorial Association   (SLS)
KSMB....... Young Communist League of Belorussia   (RU)
KSME........ Young Communist League of Estonia [*1921-1940*]   (RU)
KSMIP ...... Committee of Standards, Measures, and Measuring Instruments (RU)
KSMK........ Young Communist League of China   (RU)

KSML........ Young Communist League of Latvia [*1919-1936*]   (RU)
KSML........ Young Communist League of Lithuania [*1918-1940*]   (RU)
KSMM ...... Katolickie Stowarzyszenie Mlodziezy Meskiej [*Catholic Association of Young Men*]
KSMU .... Young Communist League of the Ukraine [*1919-1923*]   (RU)
KSMW ...... Komitet Studiujacej Mlodziezy Wiejskiej [*Peasant Youth Student Committee*]   (POL)
KSMZO..... Komisija za Saradnju sa Medunarodnim Zdravstvenim Organizacijama [*Commission for Cooperation with International Health Organizations*]   (YU)
KSN .... Command Guidance System   (RU)
KSN .... Kabinet pro Spolecenske Nauky [*Department of Social Sciences*] (CZ)
KSN .... Komunisticka Strana Nemecka [*Communist Party of Germany*] (CZ)
KSNDTC... Kiem Sat Nhan Dan Toi Cao [*People's Supreme Procurate*]
KSNK .... Katalog Scalonych Norm Kosztorysowych [*Catalog of Standard Norms for Cost Estimators*]   (POL)
KSNKh ...... Caucasian Council of the National Economy   (RU)
KSNKh ...... Kazakh Council of the National Economy   (RU)
KSO .... Kaernkraftskommunernas Samarbetsorgan [*Association of Swedish Municipalities with Nuclear Reactors*]   (WND)
KSO .... Karlovarsky Symfonicky Orchestr [*Karlsbad Symphony Orchestra*]   (CZ)
KSO .... Kastoria [*Greece*] [*Airport symbol*]   (OAG)
KSO .... Kendron Symbarastaseos Oikogeneias [*Family Assistance Center*] [*Greek*]   (GC)
KSO .... Pressed Mica Capacitor   (RU)
KSONISFO ... Koordinatsionnyy Sovet po Organizatsii Nauchnykh Issledovanii Filosofskogo Ob shchestva [*Coordinating Council of Scientific Research Associations of the Philosophy Society*] [*Former USSR*]   (EAIO)
KSOS........ Koinopraxia Synetairistikon Organoseon Soultaninas [*Confederation of Sultana Cooperative Organizations*] [*Greek*]   (GC)
KSP........... Braunkohlenkombinat "Schwarze Pumpe" (VEB) [*"Schwarze Pumpe" Brown Coal Combine (VEB)*]   (EG)
KSP........... Instrument-Flight Control Room   (RU)
KSP........... Kendrikos Stathmos Paragogis [*Central Productivity Station*] [*Greek*]   (GC)
KSP........... Kenya Socialist Party
KSP........... Kernspeicher [*German*]   (ADPT)
KSP........... Komisija za Proucavnje Stanbene Problematike i Izgradnje [*Commission for the Study of Housing Problems and Construction*]   (YU)
KSP........... Komma Sosialistikis Protovoulias [*Socialist Initiative Party*] [*Greek*]   (GC)
KSP........... Korean Society of Pharmacology   (EAIO)
KSP........... Kulturni Sluzba Pracujicim [*Cultural Service for the Working People*]   (CZ)
KSP........... Rifle Regiment Commander   (RU)
KSP........... Servicios Aereos Especializados en Transportes Petroleros [*Colombia*] [*ICAO designator*]   (FAAC)
KSPC .... Kuwait-Spanish Petroleum Company   (ME)
KSPCA ...... Kenya Society for the Prevention of Cruelty to Animals
KSPO .... Komitee van Staatspadowerhede [*South Africa*]   (AA)
KSPRS ...... Korean Society of Plastic and Reconstructive Surgery   (EAIO)
KSPS .... Kray Council of Trade Unions   (RU)
KSPU .... Kniznica Statneho Pedagogickeho Ustavu [*Library of the State Pedagogical Institute*] [*Bratislava*]   (CZ)
KSPY .... Kendron Syndonismou Pyron Ypostirixeos [*Fire Support Coordination Center*] [*Greek*]   (GC)
KSPZ .... Kotarski Savez Poljoprivrednih Zadruga [*District Union of Agricultural Cooperatives*]   (YU)
KSPZPR.... Komitet Stoleczny Polskiej Zjednoczonej Partii Robotniczej [*Warsaw Committee of the Polish United Workers Party*] (POL)
KSR........... Association of Swedish Municipalities with Nuclear Reactors (EAIO)
KSR........... Canonical Simplicial Partition   (RU)
KSR........... Kenya-Somalia Relations
KSR........... Kniznica Sovietskych Romanov [*Soviet Fiction Literary Series*] (CZ)
KSR........... Kokusai Shokyo Rengo [*International Federation for Victory Over Communism*] [*Japan*]
KSR........... Konferencja Samorzadu Robotniczego [*Workers' Self-Government Conference*]   (POL)
KSR........... Krajsky Sbor Radioamateru [*Regional Board of Amateur Radio Operators*]   (CZ)
KSR........... Rifle Company Commander   (BU)
KSR(b)....... Komunisticka Strana Ruska (Bolseviku) [*Communist Party of Russia (Bolshevik)*]   (CZ)
KSRC .... Kuwait Shipbuilding & Repairyard Co.
KSRI .... Komandno-Stabne Ratne Igre [*Staff Officers' War Games*]   (YU)
KSRI .... Korea Standards Research Institute [*South Korea*]
KSS .... Kaivalyadhama SMYM Samiti [*India*]   (EAIO)
KSS .... Kenya Soil Survey

KSS........... Knight of the Southern Star [*Brazil*]

KSS........... Knight of the Sword of Sweden

KSS........... Kolo Srpskih Sestara [*Serbian Sisters Society*] [*Libertyville, IL*] (YU)

KSS........... Komunisticka Strane Slovenska [*Communist Party of Slovakia*] [*Former Czechoslovakia*] [*Political party*] (PPW)

KSS........... Krajevni Sindikalni Svet [*Local Council of Trade-Unions*] (YU)

KSS........... Kumpulan Simpan Senggara [*Ordnance Maintenance Group*] (ML)

KSSBI....... Konfederasi Serikat Serikat Buruh Islam [*Confederation of Islamic Trade Unions of Indonesia*]

KSSD........ Krajsky Svaz Spotrebnich Druzstev [*Regional Union of Consumers' Cooperatives*] (CZ)

KSSP........ Kerala Shastra Sahitya Parishad [*India*]

KSSR........ Kazakh Soviet Socialist Republic (RU)

KSSR........ Kirgiz Soviet Socialist Republic (RU)

KSSRZ....... Kiev Shipyard (RU)

KSSS........ Komunisticka Strana Sovetskeho Svazu [*Communist Party of the Soviet Union*] (CZ)

KSSSF....... Korean Society of Soil Science and Fertilizer (EAIO)

KSSZF....... Komisija za Selsko-Stopanskiot Zemjisen Fond [*Agricultural Land Fund Commission*] (YU)

KST........... Compressor Station (RU)

KST........... Concentric Laminar Texture (RU)

Kst............. Kamerstukken [*Benelux*] (BAS)

KST........... Kartenstanzer [*German*] (ADPT)

KST........... Kendriki Synergatiki Trapeza [*Central Cooperative Bank*] [*Cyprus*] (GC)

KST........... Kingsford Smith Transport Proprietary Ltd. [*Australia*]

Kst............. Kohlenstaub [*Powdered Coal*] (EG)

KST........... Kolcsonos Segito Takarekpenztarak [*Mutual Savings Banks*] [*Hungarian*]

KST........... Komitet za Spoljnu Trgovinu (DSPRP) [*Foreign Trade Committee*] (YU)

KST........... Kostenstelle [*German*] (ADPT)

KST........... Krajsky Trestni Soud [*Regional Criminal Court*] (CZ)

KSt............ Railroad Station Commandant (RU)

KSTC........ Kenya Science Teachers College

KstG......... Korperschaftsteuergesetz [*German Corporation Taxation Act*] (DLA)

KSTL........ Klub Slovenskych Turistov Lyziarov [*Slovak Tourist and Skiing Club*] (CZ)

KSTN........ Kriegsstaerke-Nachweisung [*Table of Organization*] [*German military - World War II*]

KSTR........ Kema Suspension Test Reactor [*Netherlands*]

KSU .... Administration of Health Resorts and Sanatoriums (RU)

KSU .... Checking and Reading Device (RU)

KSU .... Commission for Assistance to Scientists (RU)

KSU .... Health Resort Administration (BU)

KSU .... King Saud University [*Saudi Arabia*]

KSU .... Kniznica Slovenskej Univerzity [*Slovak University Library*] [*Bratislava*] (CZ)

KSU .... Kristiansund [*Norway*] [*Airport symbol*] (OAG)

KSU .... Switching-Connecting Device (RU)

KSUP........ Kulturny Svaz Ukrajinskych Pracujucich [*Cultural Association of Ukrainian Workers*] [*Slovakia*] (CZ)

KSV.......... Knight of St. Vladimir [*Obsolete*] [*Russian*]

KSV.......... Komandir Streljackog Voda [*Rifle Platoon Commander*] (YU)

KSV.......... Kommunistischer Studentenverband [*Communist Student Federation*] (WEN)

KSV.......... Kommunistische Studentenvereinigung [*Communist Students Union*] [*Austria*] (WEN)

KSV.......... Kotarsko Sindikalno Vece [*District Trade-Union Council*] (YU)

KSV.......... Standing Wave Ratio (RU)

KSV.......... Viskose-Kunstseide [*Viscose Rayon*] [*German*] (GCA)

ksvb......... Corps Signal Battalion (BU)

KSVB........ Krajska Sprava Verejne Bezpecnosti [*Regional Administration of Public Security*] (CZ)

KSV-Kommission ... Knotenpunkt-Stueckgut-Verkehrs-Kommission [*Railroad Junction Commission for LCL Cargo or for General Cargo*] (EG)

KSVN .... Voltage Standing Wave Ratio (RU)

KSWC....... Khartoum Spinning and Weaving Company

KSWILWPG ... Kolo Studentow Wydzialu Inzynierii Ladowo-Wodnej Politechniki Gdanskiej [*Students' Circle of the Land and Water Engineering Department of the Gdansk (Danzig) Polytechnic Institute*] (POL)

KSWPRC .. Korean Society of Water Pollution Research and Control (EAIO)

KSWST ..... Korean Society of Wood Science and Technology (EAIO)

KSZ........... Catalog of Weak Stars (RU)

KSZ........... Shipyard (BU)

KSZB .... Kereskedelmi Szakoktatasi Bizottsag [*Committee on Specialized Commercial Training*] (HU)

KSZB .... Kozponti Szabvanyositasi Bizottsag [*Central Standardization Committee*] (HU)

KSZDOSZ ... Kozlekedesi es Szallitasi Dolgozok Szakszervezete [*Trade Union of Communication and Transportation Workers*] (HU)

KSZE......... Konferenz fuer Sicherheit und Zusammenarbeit in Europa [*Conference on Security and Cooperation in Europe (CSCE)*] (EG)

KSZE......... Kukoricatermelesi Szocialista Egyuttmukodes [*Socialist Cooperation in Corn Production (Located at Szekszard)*] (HU)

KSZh .... Committee of Soviet Women (RU)

KSZh .... Communist Union of Journalists (RU)

KSZI .... Kozonsegszervezo Iroda [*Office for Organizing People's Cultural Entertainment*] (HU)

KSZ K .... Kisipari Szovetkezetek Kiadovallalata [*Publishing House of the Producers' Cooperative Enterprises*] (HU)

KSZKBI.... Kisipari Szovetkezeti Kolcsonos Biztosito Intezet [*Mutual Insurance Institute for Cooperatives*] (HU)

KSZKV ..... Kisipari Szovetkezeti Kiado Vallalat [*Cooperative Publishing Enterprise*] (HU)

K Sz M ...... Kereskedelem- es Szovetkezetugyi Miniszter [*Minister of Commerce and Cooperatives*] (HU)

KSZS .... Kovorobne a Strojarenske Zavody na Slovensku, Narodny Podnik [*Metallurgical and Machine Building Plants in Slovakia, National Enterprise*] (CZ)

KSZT .... Kereskedelmi Szakoktatasi Tanacs [*Council on Specialized Commercial Training*] (HU)

KSzT .... Kozponti Szallitasi Tanacs [*Central Transportation Council*] (HU)

KSZTB ...... Kozalkalmazottak Szakszervezete Teruleti Bizottsag [*Trade Union of Government Employees, Territorial Committee*] (HU)

KT .... British Airtours Ltd. [*British*] [*ICAO designator*] (ICDA)

kt............... Captain [*Army*] (BU)

KT .... Code Transformer (RU)

k-t............. Committee (BU)

k-t............. Concentrate (RU)

k-t............. Credit (RU)

kt............... Critical Temperature (RU)

Kt .... Kanton [*Canton*] [*Switzerland*]

Kt .... Karte [*Map, Chart*] [*German*]

kt............... Kartoniert [*Bound in Boards*] [*Publishing*] [*German*]

Kt .... Kereskedelmi Torveny [*Commercial Code*] (HU)

KT .... Ketua Turus [*Chief of Staff*] [*Malaysia*] (ML)

KT .... Khaksar Tehrik [*Pakistan*] [*Political party*] (FEA)

kt............... Kiloton (RU)

k-t............. Komandant [*Commander*] (YU)

KT .... Komandni Toranj [*Control Tower*] [*Airport*] (YU)

k-t............. Kombinat (RU)

kT .... Konkreter Tatbestand [*Concrete Fact*] [*German*]

KT .... Kontrola Techniczna [*Technical Control Board*] (POL)

kt............... Korter [*Circle*] (HU)

kt............... Kozsegi Tanacs [*Village Council*] (HU)

KT .... Kratki Talasi [*Short Waves*] (YU)

KT .... Kredit [*Credit*] [*Afrikaans*]

KT .... Ktimatiki Trapeza [*Land Bank*] [*EKTE*] [*See also*] (GC)

KT .... Kungtang [*Labor party*] [*Taiwan*] [*Political party*] (EY)

KT .... Kuroi Tanima [*Dark Valley*] [*1930s decade of political repression*] [*Japan*]

KT .... Kwoh-Ting Li [*Physicist and government official*] [*Taiwan*]

KT .... Labor Code (BU)

k/t .... Motion-Picture Theater (RU)

kt............... Room Temperature (RU)

KT .... Television Camera (RU)

k-ta........... Acid (RU)

KTA .... Commercial News Agency (RU)

KTA .... Karratha [*Australia*] [*Airport symbol*] (OAG)

KTA .... Kendrikon Takhydromeion Athenon [*Athens Main Post Office*] (GC)

KTA .... Kerntechnischer Ausschuss [*Nuclear Safety Standards Commission*] [*Germany*] (EAIO)

KTA .... Kibris Turk Alayi [*Turkish Cypriot Regiment*] (TU)

KTA .... Kim's Tourist & Travel Agency [*Israel*]

KTA .... Korean Traders Association (IMH)

KTA .... Korea Tourist Association (EAIO)

KTA .... Kozuletek Tamogatasi Alapja [*Relief Fund for Public Institutions*] (HU)

KTA .... Kraftfahrzeugtechnische Anstalt [*Motor Vehicle Technical Facility*] (EG)

KTA .... Kreistransportaktiv [*Kreis Transportation Aktiv*] (EG)

KTAC........ Korea Technology Advancement Corp. (PDAA)

KTACYD... Kibris Turk Autistik Cocuklara Yardim Dernegi [*Association for Aid to Turkish Cypriot Autistic Children*] (GC)

KTAD .... Kibris Turk Anneler Dernegi [*Turkish Cypriot Mothers' Organization*] (TU)

KTAD .... Kibris Turk Aydinlar Dernegi [*Turkish Cypriot Intellectuals Association*] (GC)

KTAF........ Kibris Turk Atletizm Federasyonu [*Turkish Cypriot Athletic Federation*] (TU)

KTAMS..... Kibris Turk Amme Memurlari Sendikasi [*Turkish Cypriot Public Service Officials Union*] (GC)

KTAMS..... Kibris Turk Askeri Mustahdemler Sendikasi [*Turkish Cypriot Military Employees' Union*] [*As-Sen*] [*See also*] (TU)

KTAP........ Corps Heavy Artillery Regiment (RU)

KTAS........ Kjobenhavns Telefon Aktieselskab [*Denmark*]

KTB .... Concert and Theatrical Office (RU)

ktb .... Corps Tank Battalion (BU)

KTB .... Design and Technological Office (RU)

KTB .... Kibris Tib Birligi [*Cypriot Medical Union*] [*Turkish Cypriot*] (GC)

KTB .... Kibris Turk Birligi [*Turkish Cypriot Unit*] [*Military*] (TU)

KTB .... Kooperacios Tarcakozi Bizottsag [*Interministerial Committee on Cooperation*] (HU)

KTB .... Tank Battalion Commander (RU)

KTBB........ Kibris Turk Benzinciler Birligi [*Turkish Cypriot Gasoline Dealers' Union*] (TU)

KTBK........ Kibris Turk Baris Kuvvetleri [*Turkish Cypriot Peace Forces*] (TU)

KTBK........ Kibris Turk Birligi Kumandasi [*Turkish Cypriot (Military) Unit Command*] (TU)

KTBKK...... Kibris Turk Birligi Kara Kuvvetleri [*Turkish Cypriot Unit Ground Forces*] (TU)

KTBL........ Kuratorium fuer Technik und Bauwesen in der Landwirtschaft eV [*Board of Technology and Architecture in Agriculture*] (SLS)

KTBMC..... Kibris Turk Birlesmis Milletler Cemiyeti [*Turkish Cypriot United Nations' Society*] (GC)

KTBR........ Tank Brigade Commander (RU)

ktbtk.......... Katonai Bunteto Torvenykonyv [*Military Penal Code, Articles of War*] (HU)

KTC .... Kawambwa Tea Company

KTC .... Kibris Turk Cemiyeti [*Turkish Cypriot Society*] (TU)

KTC .... Kindergarten Teachers' College [*Australia*] (ADA)

KTC .... Koofi Trading Corp. [*Somalia*]

KTC .... Kuwait Transport Company SAK [*Kuwait City*] (MENA)

KTCB........ Kibris Turk Ciftciler Birligi [*Turkish Cypriot Farmers' Union*] (TU)

KTCEK..... Kibris Turk Cocuk Esirgeme Kurumu [*Turkish Cypriot Child Protection Association*] (TU)

KTCh .... Confederation of Workers of Chile (RU)

KTCK........ Kibris Turk Cografya Kurumu [*Turkish Cypriot Geographic Organization*] (TU)

KTCM .... Kibris Turk Cemaat Meclisi [*Turkish Cypriot Communal Assembly*] (GC)

KTCMS..... Kibris Turk Cemaat Meclisi Sendikasi [*Turkish Cypriot Communal Assembly Union*] (GC)

KTD .... Collective Labor Contract (BU)

KTD .... Kemicna Tovarna Domzale [*Chemical Factory in Domzale*] (YU)

KTD .... Kita-Daito [*Japan*] [*Airport symbol*] (OAG)

KTD .... Tank Division Commander (RU)

KTDA........ Kenya Tea Development Authority

KTDC .... Kenya Tourist Development Corporation

KTDD........ Kibris Turk Demokrasi Dernegi [*Turkish Cypriot Democracy Society*] (TU)

KTDI........ Kibris Turk Denizcilik Isletmesi [*Turkish Cypriot Maritime Operations Directorate General*] (TU)

KTDT .... Kibris Turk Devlet Tiyatrolari [*Turkish Cypriot State Theatres*] (GC)

KTDU .... Kabinet pro Theorii a Dejiny Umeni [*Department for the Study of the Theory and History of Art (of the Czechoslovak Academy of Sciences)*] (CZ)

Kte........... Karte [*Map, Chart*] [*German*]

KTE .... Kendron Tekhnologikon Efarmogon [*Applied-Technology Center*] [*Greek*] (GC)

KTE .... Koinonia ton Ethnon [*League of Nations*] (GC)

KTE .... Kozlekedestudomanyi Egyesulet [*Scientific Association of Transportation*] (HU)

KTEB........ Kibris Turk Eczacilar Birligi [*Turkish Cypriot Pharmacists' Union*] (TU)

KTEE........ Kendron Takhyrrythmou Ekpaidevseos Enilikon [*Accelerated Training Center for Adults*] [*Greek*] (GC)

KTEE........ Kendron Takhyrrythmou Epangelmatikis Ekpaidevseos [*Accelerated Vocational Training Center*] [*Greek*] (GC)

KTEFA ...... Koinon Tameion Eispraxeon Fortigon Avtokiniton [*Joint Freight Truck Collection Funds*] [*Greek*] (GC)

KTEK........ Kibris Turk Elektrik Kurumu [*Turkish Cypriot Electric Power Enterprise*] (GC)

KTEK........ Office for Container Shipments and Transportation and Forwarding Operations (RU)

KTEL........ Koinon Tameion Eispraxeon Leoforeion [*Joint Bus Receipts Fund*] [*Greek*] (GC)

KTEMO ..... Kibris Turk Elektrik Muhendisler Odasi [*Chamber of Turkish Cypriot Electrical Engineers*] (TU)

KTEP......... Konstrukcne Technicke a Ekonomicke Pracoviste Investicni Vystavby Zeleznic [*Technical and Economic Development Center for Railroad Investment Construction*] (CZ)

KTEYL ...... Koinon Tameion Eispraxeon Yperastikon Leoforeion [*Joint Urban Bus Receipts Fund*] [*Greek*] (GC)

KTF........... Kolkhoz Commodity Farm (RU)

KTF............ Kommunaltjaenstemannafoerbundet [*Federation of Municipal Officers*] [*Finland*] (EY)

KTF........... Koumiss Farm (RU)

KTFD......... Kibris Turk Federe Devleti [*Turkish Cypriot Federated State*] (GC)

KTFDKM ... Kibris Turk Federe Devleti Kurucu Meclisi [*Constituent Assembly of the Turkish Cypriot Federated State*] (TU)

KTFF .... Kibris Turk Futbol Federasyonu [*Turkish Cypriot Soccer Federation*] (GC)

KTFHB..... Kibris Turk Futbol Hakemler Birligi [*Turkish Cypriot Soccer Referees' Union*] (TU)

Ktg........... Kantongerecht [*Benelux*] (BAS)

KTG .... Kerntechnische Gesellschaft in Deutschen Atomforum, eV [*Nuclear energy*] (NRCH)

KTG .... Ketapang [*Indonesia*] [*Airport symbol*] (OAG)

KTGA .... Kenya Tea Growers Association

KTGC .... Kibris Turk Gazeteciler Cemiyeti [*Turkish Cypriot Journalists Association*] (GC)

KTGD .... Kibris Turk Genclik Dernegi [*Turkish Cypriot Youth Association*] (TU)

KTGKD ..... Kendrikon Tameion Georgias, Ktinotrofias, kai Dason [*Central Fund for Agriculture, Animal Raising, and Forests*] (GC)

KTH .... Krynickie Towarzystwo Hokejowe [*Krynica Hockey Society*] (POL)

KTH .... Kungliga Tekniska Hoegskolan [*Royal Institute of Technology*] [*Stockholm, Sweden*] (ARC)

KTHB .... Kibris Turk Hakemler Birligi [*Turkish Cypriot Referees' Union*] (TU)

KTHB .... Kibris Turk Hastabakicilar Birligi [*Turkish Cypriot Nurses' Union*] (GC)

KTHB .... Kibris Turk Hekimler Birligi [*Turkish Cypriot Physicians' Union*] (TU)

KTHB .... Kungliga Tekniska Hogskolans Bibliotek [*Royal Institute of Technology Library*] [*Information service or system*] (IID)

KTHD....... Kibris Turk Hematoloji Dernegi [*Turkish Cypriot Hematology Society*] (TU)

KTHD....... Kibris Turk Hukukcular Dernegi [*Turkish Cypriot Jurists' Association*] (GC)

KTHHB.... Kibris Turk Hemsire ve Hastabakicilar Birligi [*Turkish Cypriot Union of Nurses and Nurses Aides*] (TU)

KTHKG ..... Kibris Turk Hava Kuvvetlerini Guclendirme Vakfi [*Turkish Cypriot Air Force Strengthening Fund*] (TU)

KTHMK.... Kibris Turk Hukumeti Memurlari Kurumu [*Turkish Cypriot Government Employees' Association*] (GC)

KTHS .... Kibris Turk Hekimler Sendikasi [*Turkish Cypriot Physicians' Union*] (TU)

KThVE ...... Kratikon Theatron Voreiou Ellados [*State Theater of Northern Greece*] (GC)

KTHY .... Kibris Turk Hava Yollari [*Turkish Cypriot Airlines*] (TU)

KTHYB ..... Kibris Turk Hayvan Yetistiricileri ve Besleyicileri Birligi [*Turkish Cypriot Animal Raisers and Stock Feeders' Union*] (TU)

KTHYBB... Kibris Turk Hayvan Yetistiricileri ve Besleyicileri Birligi [*Turkish Cypriot Animal Raisers and Stock Feeders' Union*] (TU)

KTI........... Kalinin Peat Institute (RU)

KTI........... Kano Transport International Ltd. KATI Air [*Nigeria*] [*ICAO designator*] (FAAC)

KTI........... Khartoum Technical Institute

KTI........... Kinetics Technology International BV

KTI........... Kostroma Textile Institute (RU)

KTI........... Krapinska Tekstilna Industrija [*Krapina Textile Industry*] (YU)

KTI........... Kriminaltechnisches Institut [*Criminological Institute*] (EG)

KTIBF .... Kibris Turk Iscileri Birlikleri Federasyonu [*Federation of Turkish Cypriot Worker Unions*] (TU)

KTIC......... Kibris Turk Islam Cemiyeti [*Turkish Cypriot Islamic Society*] (TU)

KTIC......... Kibris Turk Isverenler Cemiyeti [*Turkish Cypriot Employers' Association*] (TU)

KTIC......... Korea Toy Industry Cooperative (EAIO)

KTICA ...... Kibris Turk Ilmi Calismalar Akademisi [*Turkish Cypriot Academy of Science*] (GC)

KTID......... Kibris Turk Isverenler Dernegi [*Turkish Cypriot Employers' Association*] (TU)

kt III r ...... Lieutenant Commander [*Navy*] (BU)

kt II r....... Commander [*Navy*] (BU)

KTIKD...... Kibris Turk Islam Kultur Dernegi [*Turkish Cypriot Islamic Culture Association*] [*Turkish Cypriot*] (GC)

KTIL........ Koinon Tameion Idiotikon Leoforeion [*Joint Fund for Privately Owned Buses*] [*Greek*] (GC)

KTILP ...... Kiev Technological Institute of Light Industry (RU)

KTIOS....... Kibris Turk Ilkokul Ogretmenler Sendikasi [*Turkish Cypriot Elementary School Teachers Union*] [*KTOS*] [*Later,*] (TU)

kt I r .... Captain [*Navy*] (BU)

KTiR .... Klub Techniki i Racjonalizacji [*Technology and Rationalization Club*] (POL)

KTIRP .... Kaliningrad Technical Institute of the Fish Industry and Fisheries (RU)

KTIS .... Kibris Turk Isverenler Sendikasi [*Turkish Cypriot Employers' Union*] (TU)

KTIS .... Standard Design and Technical Research Office (RU)

KTK .... Confederation of Workers of Colombia (RU)

KTK .... Confederation of Workers of Cuba (RU)

KTK .... Kauppatieteiden Kandidaatti [*Finland*]

KtK .... Kommission fuer den Ausbau des Technischen Kommunikationssystems [*German*] (ADPT)

ktk .... Kozos Tanacsu Kozseg [*Village Administrated by a Joint Village Council (of two or more villages)*] (HU)

KTK .... Kozponti Technologiai Konyvtar [*Central Technological Library*] (HU)

KTK .... Krakowskie Towarzystwo Kolarskie [*Krakow Cycling Society*] (POL)

KTK .... Quality Technical Control (BU)

KTK .... Tubular Ceramic Capacitor (RU)

KTKA .... Kibris Turk Kuvvetleri Alayi [*Turkish Cypriot Forces Regiment*] (TU)

KTKB........ Kibris Turk Kadinlar Birligi [*Turkish Cypriot Women's Association*] (GC)

KTKD .... Kibris Turk Kizilay Dernegi [*Turkish Cypriot Red Crescent Organization*] (GC)

KTKD .... Kibris Turk Kultur Dernegi [*Turkish Cypriot Culture Society*] (GC)

KTKK .... Kibris Turk Kadinlar Komitesi [*Turkish Cypriot Women's Committee*] (TU)

KTKK .... Kibris Turk Kooperatifcilik Kurumu [*Turkish Cypriot Cooperatives' Association*] (GC)

KTKL........ Kozponti Technologiai Kutato Laboratorium [*Central Technological Research Laboratory of the Szekesfehervar Light Metal Works (Research on all aluminum semifinished goods)*] (HU)

KTKM .... Kibris Turk Kurucu Meclisi [*Turkish Cypriot Constituent Assembly*] (TU)

KTKMB..... Kibris Turk Kooperatif Merkez Bankasi [*Turkish Cypriot Cooperatives Central Bank*] (TU)

KTKMO .... Kibris Turk Kimye Muhendisleri Odasi [*Chamber of Turkish Cypriot Chemical Engineers*] (GC)

KTKOV ..... Kommatikon Tmima Kommatikis Organosis Vaseos [*Base Party Organization Section*] (GC)

ktl.............. Kai ta Loipa [*And the Rest, And So Forth*]

KTL........... Kauppatieteiden Lisensiaatti [*Finland*]

KTL........... Kuratorium fuer Technik in der Landwirtschaft eV Council of Agricultural Engineering [*Germany*] (DSCA)

KTLA........ Confederation of Workers of Latin America (RU)

KTLIS....... Kibris Turk Liman Iscileri Sirketi [*Turkish Cypriot Harbor Workers Corporation*] (TU)

KTM .... Code of Merchant Marine Navigation of the USSR (RU)

KTM .... Confederation of Workers of Mexico (RU)

KTM .... Katmandu [*Nepal*] [*Airport symbol*] (OAG)

KTM .... Kauppatieteiden Maisteri [*Finland*]

KTM .... Kemicna Tovarna Moste [*Moste Chemical Factory*] (YU)

KTM .... Kenva Taitex Mills

KTM .... Keretapi Tanah Melavu [*Malayan Railways*] (ML)

KTM .... Krajnja Tacka Marsrute [*Final Point of a March*] [*Army*] (YU)

KTM .... Merchant Navigation Code (RU)

KTMB .... Kibris Turk Milli Birligi Partisi [*Turkish Cypriot National Unity Party*] (GC)

KTMC .... Kibris Turk Musiki Cemiyeti [*Turkish Cypriot Music Society*] (GC)

KTMDES .. Kibris Turk Maarif Dairesi Egitimciler Sendikasi [*Turkish Cypriot Education Office Instructors' Union*] (GC)

KTMK .... Kaynak Teknigi Turk Milli Komitesi Yonetmeligi [*Turkish National Committee for Welding Techniques*] (TU)

KTMK .... Kereskedelmi Tovabbkepzo es Modszertani Kozpont [*Center of Refresher Courses and Methodology of Trade*] (HU)

KTMMOB ... Kibris Turk Muhendis ve Mimar Odalari Birligi [*Union of Turkish Cypriot Chambers of Engineers and Architects*] (TU)

KTMPB..... Kibris Turk Memurin ve Polis Birligi [*Union of Turkish Cypriot Workers and Police*] [*On British sovereign bases*] (GC)

KTMSUK ... Kibris Turk Meyva-Sebze Uretim Kooperatifi [*Turkish Cypriot Fruit and Vegetable Production Cooperative*] (GC)

ktn .... Candidate of Technical Sciences (BU)

Ktn .... Kaernten [*or Kaerntner*] [*German*]

Ktn .... Karten [*Maps, Charts*] [*German*]

KTN........... Kelantan [*Malaysia*] (ML)

KTN........... Kieleckie Towarzystwo Naukowe [*Poland*] (SLS)

KTN.......... Kuratorium fuer die Tagungen der Nobelpreistrager [*Standing Committee for Nobel Prize Winners' Congresses - SCNPWC*] [*Germany*] (EA)

k-t nademokr bulg zheni ... Bulgarian Democratic Women's Committee (BU)

KTNB .... Kibris Turk Narenciye Birligi [*Turkish Cypriot Orange Growers' Union*] (GC)

KTNUB ..... Kibris Turk Narenciye Ureticiler Birligi [*Turkish Cypriot Citrus Fruit Producers' Union*] (GC)

KTO .... Coefficient of Heat Emission (RU)

KTO .... Kato [*Guyana*] [*Airport symbol*] (OAG)

KTO .... Kibris Turk Ocagi [*Turkish Cypriot Hearth*] [*Club*] (TU)

KTO .... Konto [*Account on Credit*] [*German*]

KTO .... Technical Inspection, Technical Control (RU)

KTOB .... Kibris Turk Ogretmenler Birligi [*Turkish Cypriot Teachers' Union*] (GC)

KTOEOB... Kibris Turk Orta Egitim Ogretmenler Birligi [*Union of Turkish Cypriot Secondary Education Teachers*] (GC)

KTOEOS... Kibris Turk Orta Egitim Ogretmenler Sendikasi [*Turkish Cypriot Secondary Education Teachers' Union*] (GC)

KTOK .... Kibris Turk Ogretmen Koleji [*Turkish Cypriot Teachers' College*] [*Kyrenia*] (TU)

KTOK .... Kibris Turk Otomobil Kurumu [*Turkish Cypriot Automobile Association*] (TU)

Kto-Nr....... Kontonummer [*Account Number*] (EG)

KTOS......... Kibris Turk Ogretmenler Sendikasi [*Turkish Cypriot Teachers' Union*] [*KTIOS*] [*Formerly,*] (TU)

KTOTSD... Kibris Turk Oto Tamirciler ve Sanatkarlari Dernegi [*Turkish Cypriot Auto Mechanics' and Artisans' Organization*] (GC)

KTOYMO ... Kibris Turk Orman Yuksek Muhendisleri Odasi [*Turkish Cypriot Chamber of Senior Forestry Engineers*] (TU)

KTP........... Coefficient of Heat Transfer (RU)

KTP........... Kingston-Tinson [*Jamaica*] [*Airport symbol*] (OAG)

Ktp .... Kitaplik [*Library, Book Shelves*] (TU)

KTP........... Komisija za Tehnicku Pomoc [*Technical Assistance Commission*] [*United Nations (already exists in GUS II database)*] (YU)

KTP........... Kommunistinen Tyovaenpuolue [*Communist Workers' Party*] [*Finland*] [*Political party*] (EY)

KTP........... Korean Labor Party (BU)

KTP........... Korpus Techniczny Pozarnictwa [*Technical Fire Brigade*] (POL)

KTP........... Krajevno Trgovinsko Podjetje [*Local Commercial Establishment*] (YU)

KTP........... Tank Regiment Commander (RU)

KTP........... Technical Check Point [*Of tank workshops, etc.*] (BU)

KTP........... Technical Control Point (RU)

KTP........... Television Channel (RU)

KTPI .... Kaum-Tani Persatuan Indonesia [*Indonesian Farmers' Party*] [*Surinam*] [*Political party*] (PPW)

KTPR........ Thermal Conductivity Coefficient (RU)

KTPS .... Kibris Turk Petrolleri Sirketi [*Turkish Cypriot Petroleum Corporation*] (TU)

KTR .... Code Transmitter Relay (RU)

KTR .... Coefficient of Thermal Expansion (RU)

KTR .... Helikoptertransport AB [*Sweden*] [*ICAO designator*] (FAAC)

Ktr............. Kantonrechter [*Benelux*] (BAS)

Ktr............. Katorzhane [*Prison compound*] [*Russian*]

KTR .... Klub Techniki i Racjonalizacji [*Technology and Rationalization Club*] (POL)

K/TR .... Kuala Trengganu [*Capital of Trengganu State, Malaysia*] (ML)

ktr............. Tank Company Commander (RU)

KTRI .... Keith Turnbull Research Institute [*Australia*]

KTRI .... Korea Telecommunication Research Institute [*South Korea*]

KTRZ........ Committee for Labor and Wages (BU)

KTs .... Acid-Resistant Cement (RU)

KTS........... Commission on Labor Disputes (RU)

KTS........... Kanoo Terminal Services Ltd. [*Saudi Arabia*]

KTS........... Kerntechnische Sektion der Schweizerischen Vereinigung fuer Atomenergie [*Nuclear energy*] (NRCH)

KTS........... Kriziacke Tazenie za Slobodu [*Crusade for Freedom*] (CZ)

KTS........... Transportation Construction Crane (RU)

KTSA .... Commission for Technical Co-Operation in Africa South of the Sahara (RU)

KTSAB ...... Kibris Turk Seyahat Acentleri Birligi [*Turkish Cypriot Travel Agents' Union*] [*Turkish Cypriot*] (GC)

KTsADA.... Kiev Central Archives of Ancient Documents (RU)

KTSCD...... Kibris Turk Sosyal Calismacilar Dernegi [*Turkish Cypriot Social Workers' Organization*] (TU)

KTSD........ Kibris Turk Sanatcilar Dernegi [*Turkish Cypriot Artists' Organization*] (TU)

KTShCh... Minesweeping Boat (RU)

KTSI .... Kibris Turk Sanayi Isletmeleri Holding Ltd. Sirketi [*Turkish Cypriot Industrial Operations Holding Corporation*] (GC)

k-tsiya........ Concentration (RU)

k-t s/ka ...... Credit Account (BU)

KTsKhFD .. Cellulose, Paper, and Fodder Yeast Combine   (BU)
KTsM .... Nonferrous Metals Combine   (BU)
KTSO .... Kibris Turk Sanatcilar Ocagi [*Turkish Cypriot Artisans' Club*]   (GC)
KTSOK ...... Kibris Turk Devlet Senfoni Orkestra ve Korosu [*Turkish Cypriot State Symphony Orchestra and Chorus*]   (TU)
KTsP .... Paper and Cellulose Industry   (BU)
KTSPO ...... Kibris Turk Sehir Plancilari Odasi [*Turkish Cypriot Chamber of City Planners*]   (TU)
KTsU .... Central-Control Board [*Computers*]   (RU)
KTsV .... Acid-Resistant and Waterproof Cement   (RU)
ktsz .... Kisipari Termeloszovetkezet [*Artisan Cooperative*]   (HU)
KTT .... Committee on Technical Terminology (of the Academy of Sciences, USSR)   (RU)
KTT .... Kauppatieteiden Tohtori [*Finland*]
KTT .... Kittila [*Finland*] [*Airport symbol*]   (OAG)
KTTB .... Kibris Turk Tabibler Birligi [*Turkish Cypriot Physicians' Union*]   (TU)
Kttbd .... Kattunband [*Cloth Binding*] [*German*]
KTTC .... Kenya Technical Teachers College
KTTD .... Kibris Turk Telekomunikasyon Dairesi [*Turkish Cypriot Telecommunications Office*]   (GC)
KTTD .... Kibris Turk Tuccarlar Dernegi [*Turkish Cypriot Merchants' Organization*]   (TU)
KTTE .... Kibris Turk Tutun Endustrisi Limited Sirketi [*Turkish Cypriot Tobacco Industry Corporation*]   (TU)
KTTI .... Kibris Turk Turizm Isletmeleri Ltd Sirketi [*Turkish Cypriot Tourism Operations Limited Liability Company*]   (TU)
KTTILS ..... Kibris Turk Turizm Isletmeleri Limited Sirketi [*Turkish Cypriot Tourism Operations Limited Liability Company*]   (GC)
KTTK .... Kibris Turk Tarih Kurumu [*Turkish Cypriot Historical Society*]   (TU)
KTTL .... Kommunikasjons og Teletilsattes Landsforbund [*Norway*]   (EAIO)
KTTMS ..... Kibris Telekomunikasyon Turk Mustahdemler Sendikasi [*Turkish Cypriot Telecommunications Employees Union*]   (TU)
KTTO .... Kibris Turk Ticaret Odasi [*Turkish Cypriot Chamber of Commerce*]   (TU)
KTTs .... Committee on Labor and Prices   (BU)
KTTs .... Kiev Television Center
KTTTB ...... Kibris Turk Turizm ve Tanitma Birligi [*Turkish Cypriot Tourism and Orientation Union*]   (TU)
KTU .... Karadeniz Teknik Universitesi [*Black Sea Technical University*]   (TU)
KTU .... Kota [*India*] [*Airport symbol*]   (OAG)
KTU .... Remote-Control Key   (RU)
KTU .... School of Office and Trade Apprenticeship   (RU)
KTUC .... Kenya Trades Union Congress
KTUC .... Kiribati Trades Union Congress   (FEA)
KTUF .... Kuwait Trade Union Federation
kTV .... Continental Tropical Air   (RU)
KTV .... Kaffee und Tee Verband [*Coffee and Tea Federation of Austria*]   (EAIO)
KTV .... Kamarata [*Venezuela*] [*Airport symbol*]   (OAG)
KTV .... Kunnallisten Tyontekijain ja Viranhaltijain Liitto [*Municipal Workers' Union*] [*Helsinki, Finland*]   (WEN)
KTV .... Kuwait Television
KTVF .... Kibris Turk Voleybol Federasyonu [*Turkish Cypriot Volleyball Federation*]   (GC)
KTVHB ..... Kibris Turk Veteriner Hekimler Birligi [*Turkish Cypriot Veterinary Physicians' Union*]   (GC)
KTVTL ...... Katedra Telesne Vychovy a Telovychovneho Lekarstvi [*Chair of Physical Education and Medicine Related to Physical Education (at the Comenius University)*]   (CZ)
KTVVSP .... Katedra Telesne Vychovy Vysoke Skoly Pedagogicke [*Chair of Physical Education at the College of Education*]   (CZ)
KTW .... Katowice [*Poland*] [*Airport symbol*]   (OAG)
KTY .... Kibris Turk Yonetimi [*Turkish Cypriot Administration*]   (GC)
KTYe .... Final Thematic Unit [*Lexicography*]   (RU)
KTYMC ..... Kibris Turk Yapi Muteahhitleri Cemiyeti [*Turkish Cypriot Construction Contractors' Association*]   (GC)
KTYOO ..... Kiz Teknik Yusek Ogretmen Okulu [*Women's Advanced Technical Teachers' School*]   (TU)
k tyt .... Karta Tytulowa [*Title Page*]   (POL)
KTYYK ...... Kibris Turk Yonetimi Yurutme Kurulu [*Turkish Cypriot Administration Executive Council*]   (GC)
KTZ .... Kafue Textiles of Zambia
KTZ .... Kaluga Turbine Plant   (RU)
KTZ .... Klin Thermometer Plant   (RU)
KTZ .... Krouzek Techniku-Zlepsovatelu [*Group of Technicians and Innovators*]   (CZ)
KU .... Amplification Factor   (RU)
KU .... Cable Section   (RU)
KU .... Checking Device   (RU)
KU .... Combined Attack   (RU)
KU .... Commandant of a Sector   (RU)

KU .... Conductometric Apparatus   (RU)
KU .... Control Key   (RU)
KU .... Correcting Device   (RU)
KU .... Course Angle   (RU)
KU .... Kagoshima University [*Japan*]   (MSC)
KU .... Karlova Universita [*Charles University*] [*Prague*]   (CZ)
KU .... Katastarska Uprava [*Cadastral Administration*]   (YU)
KU .... Keuangan [*Finance*]   (IN)
KU .... Knightsbridge University [*Denmark*]   (ECON)
KU .... Komitet Uczelniany [*College (or University or Polytechnical School) Committee*]   (POL)
KU .... Kriminalni Ustredna [*Criminal Investigation Bureau*]   (CZ)
KU .... Kuasa Usaha [*Charge d'Affaires*]   (IN)
Ku .... Kucuk [*Small, Little*]   (TU)
KU .... Kunstfaser [*Synthetic Fiber*] [*German*]   (GCA)
Ku .... Kunststoff [*Plastic*] [*German*]   (GCA)
Ku .... Kuyu [*Well, Pit*]   (TU)
Ku .... Reduction Coefficient   (RU)
KU .... Sector Commander   (BU)
KU .... Stability Factor   (RU)
KU .... Univerzita Komenskeho [*Comenius University*] [*Bratislava*]   (CZ)
KUA .... Kuantan [*Malaysia*] [*Airport symbol*]   (OAG)
KuAI .... Kuybyshev Aviation Institute   (RU)
KUAP .... Komisja Usprawnienia Administracji Publicznej [*Commission for Increasing the Efficiency of Public Administration*]   (POL)
kub .... Cubic   (RU)
KUB .... Kubiek [*Cubic*] [*Afrikaans*]
kub .... Kubisch [*Cubic*] [*German*]
KUBA .... Korean United Buddhist Association   (EY)
KUBES ...... Ku-Ring-Gai Bushland and Environmental Society [*Australia*]
Kub Gew .... Kubik Gewicht [*Weight per Cubic Meters in Tons, Density*] [*German*]
kubm .... Cubic Meter   (BU)
KUBP .... Combat Training Course   (RU)
KUBS .... Commission for the Improvement of Students' Living Conditions   (RU)
KUBU .... Commission for the Improvement of Scientists' Living Conditions   (RU)
KUBUCH ... Commission for the Improvement of Students' Living Conditions   (RU)
KUC .... Kenyatta University College
KUC .... Kuria [*Kiribati*] [*Airport symbol*]   (OAG)
KUCE .... Kiev Universal Commodity Exchange [*Ukraine*]   (EY)
KUCP .... Kamerun United Commoners' Party
KUD .... Komisija za Ustedu Drveta [*Commission for Wood Saving*]   (YU)
KUD .... Kudat [*Malaysia*] [*Airport symbol*]   (OAG)
kud .... Kudonta [*or Tekstiiliteollisuus*] [*Weaving, Textiles*] [*Finland*]
KUD .... Kulturno-Umetnicko Drustvo [*Cultural and Artistic Society*]   (YU)
KU'DAMM ... Kurfuerstendamm [*Fashionable shopping district in West Berlin*]
KUER .... Eidgenoessische Kommission zur Ueberwachung der Radioaktivitaet [*Swiss Federal Commission of Radioactivity Surveillance*]   (WND)
KUF .... Kommunistisk Ungdoms Forbund [*Communist Youth League*] [*Denmark*]   (WEN)
KUFNCD .. Kampuchean United Front for National Construction and Defence [*Political party*]   (PPW)
Kufpec .... Kuwait Foreign Exploration Company   (OMWE)
KUFPEC ... Kuwait Foreign Petroleum Explorations Company KSC   (MENA)
KUG .... Ship Striking Force   (RU)
KUH .... Kitab Undang-Undang Hukum [*Code of Laws*]   (IN)
KUH .... Kushiro [*Japan*] [*Airport symbol*]   (OAG)
Kuhl .... Kuehlung [*Cooling*] [*German*]   (GCA)
KUIMB ..... Karachi University Institute of Marine Biology [*Pakistan*]   (MSC)
KUINS .... Committee for Registration and Study of Scientific Manpower (of the Academy of Sciences, USSR)   (RU)
KUINZh ... Courses for Advanced Training of Engineers   (RU)
KUJ .... Kenya Union of Journalists
KUK .... Komitet Upowszechienia Ksiazki [*Committee on the Popularization of Books*]   (POL)
KUK .... Koordinacni Ukrajinsky Komitet [*Ukrainian Coordination Committee*]   (CZ)
KUK .... Krajska Ucitelska Knihovna [*Regional Teachers' Library*]   (CZ)
Ku KM ...... Kulkereskedelmi Miniszterium/Miniszter [*Ministry/Minister of Foreign Trade*]   (HU)
KUKS .... Courses for Advanced Training of Command Personnel   (RU)
KUKS .... Courses for Organizing Communist Personnel   (BU)
kul .... Coulomb   (RU)
KUL .... Katholijke Universiteit te Leuven [*Belgium*]   (BAS)

KUL .... Katolicki Uniwersytet Lubelski [*Lublin Catholic University*] (POL)
KUL .... Kuala Lumpur [*Malaysia*] [*Airport symbol*] (OAG)
KUL .... Post Graduate Centre - Human Settlements [*University of Leuven*] [*Belgium*]
Kulb........... Kulhanbey Agzi [*Coarse Speech, Vulgarity*] (TU)
kulf............ Kulfoldi [*Foreign*] (HU)
KULFORG ... Magyar Kulforgalmi Reszvenytarsasag [*Hungarian Foreign Trade Limited (Prewar)*] (HU)
KulkerMin ... Kulkereskedelmi Miniszterium/Miniszter [*Ministry/Minister of Foreign Trade*] (HU)
Kuloylag..... Kuloy Corrective Labor Camp and Colonies (RU)
KULP........ Flight Training Course (RU)
kul't........... Cultural (RU)
kult............ Culture, Cultural (BU)
kult............ Kultiviert [*Cultivated*] [*German*] (GCA)
Kult .... Kultur Dairesi Genel Mudurlugu [*Cultural Office Directorate General*] [*Of Foreign Affairs Ministry*] (TU)
KULTEX ... Kulonleges Textil- es Divatarukeszito Haziipari Szovetkezet [*Cooperative Enterprise for the Manufacture of Men's and Women's Fashion Wear*] (HU)
KULTINT ... Kulturkapcsolatok Intezete [*Institute for Cultural Relations*] (HU)
kul'tmag..... Store of Goods for Cultural Purposes (RU)
kul'tprop .... Department of Culture and Propaganda (RU)
Kultprop..... Kulturne-Propagacni Referat [*Culture and Propaganda Department (of the Communist Party of Czechoslovakia)*] (CZ)
Kultprop..... Kulturni a Propagacni Oddeleni [*Culture and Propaganda Department (of the Communist Party of Czechoslovakia)*] (CZ)
kult-prosv... Cultural and Educational (BU)
kul'ttorg ..... Organization for Trade in Goods for Cultural Purposes (RU)
KULU .... Kvindernes u Landsudvalg [*Women and Development*] [*Denmark*] (EAIO)
Ku M .... Kulugyminiszterium/Miniszter [*Ministry/Minister of Foreign Affairs*] (HU)
kum .... Small Oriental Temple [*Topography*] (RU)
KUM......... Yaku Shima [*Japan*] [*Airport symbol*] (OAG)
KUMAS .... Kutahya Manyezit Isletmeleri Anonim Sirketi [*Kutahya Magnesite Processing Corporation*] (TU)
KUML....... Kommunistisk Ungdom Marxister-Leninister [*Marxist-Leninist Communist Youth*] [*Denmark*] (WEN)
KUMP .... Kray Administration of the Local Industry (RU)
kumpp....... Kumppani [*Finland*]
KUMS .... Course for Advanced Training of Medical Personnel (RU)
KUMSAN ... Kum Cakil Sanayii ve Ticaret AS [*Sand and Gravel Industry and Commercial Corporation*] (TU)
KUMZ....... Krasnoural'sk Copper-Smelting Plant (RU)
KUNA........ Kuwait News Agency [*Kuwait City*] (MENA)
KUNC....... Kamerun United National Congress
kungl......... Kunglig [*Royal*] [*Sweden*] (GPO)
KUNMV.... Communist University of National Minorities of the East (RU)
KUNMZ.... Komunisticki Univerzitet Nacionalnih Manjina Zapada [*Communist University of National Minorities of the West*] [*Former USSR*] (YU)
KUNS .... Courses for Advanced Training of Command Personnel (RU)
kunstgengiv ... Kunstgengivelse [*Art Reproduction*] [*Publishing Danish/ Norwegian*]
kunstl .... Kuenstlich [*Artificial*] [*German*] (GCA)
kunstled ..... Kunstleder [*Imitation Leather*] [*Publishing*] [*Netherlands*]
kunsttr........ Kunsttryk [*Art Printing*] [*Publishing Danish/Norwegian*]
KUNZ....... Krajsky Ustav Narodniho Zdravi [*Regional Public Health Institute*] (CZ)
KUO .... Kuopio [*Finland*] [*Airport symbol*] (OAG)
KUOMS .... Courses for Advanced Training of Medical Service Officers (RU)
KUOS .... Courses for Advanced Training of Officers (RU)
KUOS .... Krajske Ustredi Osvetovych Sboru [*Regional Center of Boards of Education*] (CZ)
KUP .... Kanalumschalteplatte [*German*] (ADPT)
KUP .... Khartoum University Press [*Sudan*]
KUP .... Kupiano [*Papua New Guinea*] [*Airport symbol*] (OAG)
KUPA .... Amplification Factor of Receiving Antenna (RU)
Kupf.......... Kupferstich [*Etching*] [*German*]
Kupfert....... Kupfertitel [*Engraved Title Page*] [*German*]
KUPON..... Communist University for Social Science Teachers (RU)
Kuppl .... Kupplung [*Coupling*] [*German*] (GCA)
Kupplg .... Kupplung [*Coupling*] [*German*] (GCA)
KUPROD .. Kulturno-Prosvetno Drustvo [*Cultural and Educational Society*] (YU)
KUR.......... Crimean Fortified Region (RU)
KUR.......... Fortified Area Commandant (RU)
kur .... Health Resort [*Topography*] (RU)
Kur .... Kurat [*or Kurator*] [*Curator*] [*German*]
kur .... Kurator [*School Superintendent*] [*Poland*]
Kur .... Kurmay [*Staff*] (TU)

Kur .... Kurum [*Organization, Society*] (TU)
KUR.......... Kyoto University Reactor [*Japan*] (PDAA)
KUR.......... Relative Bearing of Radio Station (RU)
Kur Bak..... Kurmay Baskani [*Chief of Staff*] (TU)
KURDI ...... Kasetsart University Research and Development Institute [*Thailand*] (ARC)
kurg........... Hill, Tumulus [*Topography*] (RU)
Kurgansel'mash ... Kurgan Agricultural Machinery Plant (RU)
KurGPI ...... Kursk State Pedagogical Institute (RU)
kur p........... Health Resort Settlement (RU)
KURRI...... Kyoto University Research Reactor Institute [*Japan*] (PDAA)
KURS........ Kursief [*Italicised*] [*Afrikaans*]
kurs .... Kursiivi(a) [*Finland*]
Kurupr....... Administration of Health Resorts (RU)
kur'yer........ Express [*Train*] (RU)
kurz .... Kurziv [*Italics*] (HU)
kurzleb .... Kurzlebig [*Short-Lived*] [*German*] (GCA)
KUS .... Combined Speed Indicator (RU)
KUSA .... Kennel Union of Southern Africa (AA)
KUSCO ..... Kenya United Steel Company Ltd.
KUSEK...... Kubieke Voet per Sekonde [*Cubic Feet per Second*] [*Afrikaans*]
KUSES ...... Kyoto University Scientific Expedition to the Sahara and the Surrounding Areas
KuS-Fonds ... Kultur- und Sozialfonds [*Cultural and Social Fund*] (EG)
KUSKS ...... Courses for Advanced Training of Senior Command Personnel (RU)
Kust........... Kustode [*Signature Marking*] [*Publishing*] [*German*]
kustprom.... Cottage Industry (RU)
KUSU .... Khartoum University Students' Union [*Sudan*] (AF)
kut............. Kutatas [*Research*] [*Hungary*]
KUTESZ ... Magyar Tudomanyos Akademia Kutatasi Eszkozoket Kivitelezo Vallalata [*Research Equipment Branch of the Hungarian Academy of Sciences*] (HU)
KUTSAN... Kutbi Ogullari Boya ve Vernik Sanayii AS [*Kutbi Sons Paint and Varnish Industry Corp.*] (TU)
Kutup .... Kutuphaneci [*Librarian*] (TU)
KUTV .... Communist University of Workers of the East (RU)
KUUD....... Koperasi Usaha Unit Desa [*Hamlet Enterprise Cooperatives*] [*Indonesia*] (FEA)
KUV.......... Continental Air from Temperate Latitudes (RU)
KUV .... Course Wind Angle (RU)
kuv............. Kuvaannollisesti [*Figuratively*] [*Finland*]
kuv............. Kuvittanut [*Finland*]
KUVNAS.. Advanced Training Courses for Higher Command Personnel (BU)
Kuvv .... Kuvvetler [*Force*] (TU)
KUW......... Kuwait (ABBR)
Kuybyshevgaz ... Trust of the Kuybyshev Gas Industry (RU)
Kuybyshevgidrostroy ... Construction Administration of the Kuybyshev Hydroelectric Power Plant (RU)
Kuybyshevneft' ... Association of the Kuybyshev Petroleum Industry (RU)
Kuybyshevneftegeofizika ... Kuybyshev Administration of Geophysical Exploration (RU)
Kuybyshevugol' ... State Trust of Coal Establishments of the Kuybyshev Region (RU)
Kuzbass...... Kuznetsk Coal Basin (RU)
Kuzbassgiproshakht ... State Institute for the Planning of Mines and Concentration Plants of the Kuznetsk Coal Basin (RU)
KUZhD...... Commission for the Improvement of Children's Living Conditions (RU)
KU ZMP.... Komitet Uczelniany Zwiazku Mlodziezy Polskiej [*College Committee of the Polish Youth Union*] (POL)
KU ZMS.... Komitet Uczelniany Zwiazku Mlodziezy Socjalistycznej [*College Committee of the Socialist Youth Union*] [*Poland*]
KUZNIUI ... Kuznetsk Scientific Research Institute of Coal (RU)
KU ZSP ..... Komitet Uczelniany Zrzeszenia Studentow Polskich [*College Committee of the Polish Students' Association*] (POL)
Kuztekstil'mash ... Kuznetsk Textile Machinery Plant [*Penza oblast*] (RU)
kv............... Apartment (RU)
kv............... Billeting Detail, Quartering Party (BU)
KV .... Bottom Cup [*Ammunition*] (RU)
KV .... Breeding Ratio, Conversion Ratio [*Nuclear physics and engineering*], Reproduction Factor (RU)
KV .... Capillary Soil Moisture Capacity (RU)
kV.............. Continental Air (RU)
KV .... Convalescent Party [*In a hospital*] (RU)
KV .... Cultural and Educational (RU)
kv............... District (BU)
KV .... End Switch (RU)
KV .... High-Voltage Cable (RU)
kv............... Kadervezeto [*Leader of Cadre*] (HU)
KV .... Kalt Verformt und Verguetet [*Cold Worked and Heat-Treated Steel*] [*German*] (GCA)
KV .... Karny Vybor [*Disciplinary Committee*] (CZ)

KV .... Kartellverband der Katholischen Oesterreichischen Studentenverbindungen [*Alliance of Austrian Catholic Student Associations*]   (WEN)

K V .... Kartografiai Kiadovallalat [*The Cartographic Institute Press*]   (HU)

KV .... Kartografiai Vallalat [*Cartographic Enterprise*]   (HU)

kv .... Kilovat [*Kilowatt*] [*Albanian*]

kv .... Kilovatio [*Kilowatt*] [*Spanish*]

kV .... Kilovoltti(a) [*Finland*]

kV .... Kilowolt [*Kilovolt*] [*Poland*]

KV .... Koloniaal Verslag [*Benelux*]   (BAS)

KV .... Komisija za Vodoprivredu [*Commission for Water Management*]   (YU)

KV .... Koncentraciona Vatra [*Concentration of Fire*] [*Military*]   (YU)

KV .... Kongsberg Vaapenfabrikk [*Norwegian*]

kv. .... Konyv [*Book*]   (HU)

KV .... Koordinacni Vybor [*Coordinating Committee (of the Association of Czech and of Slovak Librarians)*]   (CZ)

KV .... Kopnena Vojska [*Ground Forces*]   (YU)

KV .... Koppelvielfach [*German*]   (ADPT)

kv. .... Korte Verklaring [*Benelux*]   (BAS)

KV .... Kozponti Vezetoseg [*Central Committee*]   (HU)

KV .... Kraftverkehr [*Motor Vehicle Traffic*]   (EG)

KV .... Krajsky Vybor [*Regional Committee*]   (CZ)

KV .... Kratka Vlna [*Shortwave*]   (CZ)

KV .... Kriegsverwendungsfaehig [*Fit for Active Service*] [*German military - World War II*]

kv. .... Kuintal [*Albanian*]

kv. .... Kvartal [*Apartment block*]   (IDIG)

kv. .... Kvartira Kvartal [*Apartment*] [*Commonwealth of Independent States*]   (EECI)

KV .... Platoon Commander   (RU)

KV .... Potassium Tartrate   (RU)

kv. .... Quarter [*Of a year*]   (RU)

KV .... Shortwave   (RU)

KV .... Short Waves   (BU)

kv. .... Square   (RU)

KV .... Water-Tube Boiler   (RU)

kv. .... Wilson Cloud Chamber   (RU)

KVA .... Kavala [*Greece*] [*Airport symbol*]   (OAG)

kVa .... Kilovolt-Ampere [*Kilowatt*] [*French*]

kVA .... Kilowoltoamper [*Kilovolt-Ampere*] [*Poland*]

KVA .... Kungliga Svenska Vetenskapsakademien [*Royal Swedish Academy of Sciences*]   (WEN)

kVAr .... Kilowar [*Kilovar*] [*Poland*]

Kvartal .... Apartment Block [*Commonwealth of Independent States*]   (EECI)

KVB .... Komintern Vegrehajto Bizottsaga [*Executive Committee of the COMINTERN*]   (HU)

KVB .... Korpusna Veterinarska Bolnice [*Corps Veterinary Hospital*]   (YU)

KVc .... Kilovat Cas [*Kilowatt-Hour*]   (YU)

KVCh .... Cultural and Educational Section [*In a corrective labor camp*]   (RU)

kvch .... Kilowatt Hour   (BU)

KVCh .... Quartz-Crystal Clock   (RU)

KVD .... High-Pressure Boiler   (RU)

KVD .... High-Pressure Compressor   (RU)

KVD .... Kurz-Vier-Dieselmotor [*Short-Stroke, Four-Cycle Diesel Engine*]   (EG)

KVDP .... Catarrhal Inflammation of Upper Respiratory System   (RU)

KVDR .... Koreanische Volksdemokratische Republik [*Democratic People's Republic of Korea (DPRK)*]   (EG)

kve .... Kotve [*Bound*]   (HU)

Kvergold .... Kantenvergoldung [*Gilding on Edges of Cover*] [*Publishing*] [*German*]

KVF .... Caspian Naval Flotilla   (RU)

KVF .... Red Air Force   (RU)

KVF .... Vacuum Canning Factory   (BU)

KVG .... Kavieng [*Papua New Guinea*] [*Airport symbol*]   (OAG)

KVG .... Kulonleges Villamos Gepgyar [*Special Electrical Machinery Factory*]   (HU)

KVG .... Military Clinic   (RU)

KVH. .... Krajsky Vybor Hornicky [*Regional Mining Committee*]   (CZ)

KVHAA .... Kungliga Vitterhets Historie och Antikvitets Akademien [*Sweden*]   (SLS)

KVHV .... Katholiek Vlaams Hoogstudenten Verbond [*Flemish Catholic Secondary Students Union*] [*Belgium*]   (WEN)

KVI .... Kazan' Veterinary Institute Imeni N. E. Bauman   (RU)

KVI .... Kernfysisch Versneller Instituut [*Nuclear Physics Accelerator Institute*] [*Netherlands*]

KVI .... Koninklijke Vlaamse Ingenieursvereiniging [*Netherlands*]

KVI .... Scientific Research Institute of Dermatology and Venereal Diseases   (RU)

KVIC .... Khadi and Village Industries Commission [*Gobar Gas Scheme*] [*India*]

KVIV .... Royal Flemish Association of Engineers [*Belgium*]   (ASF)

KVK .... Internal Conversion Ratio   (RU)

KvK .... Kamer van Koophandel [*Business information service*] [*Belgium*]

KVK .... Krajska Vodohospodarska Komise [*Regional Water Utilization Committee*]   (CZ)

KVK .... Kriegsverdienstkreuz [*War Service Cross*] [*German military decoration - World War II*]

KVKSC .... Krajsky Vybor Komunisticke Strany Ceskoslovenska [*Regional Committee of the Communist Party of Czechoslovakia*]   (CZ)

KVKSS .... Krajsky Vybor Komunisticke Strany Slovenska [*Regional Committee of the Communist Party of Slovakia*]   (CZ)

KVL .... Corps Veterinary Hospital   (RU)

KVL .... Designer's Waterline   (RU)

KVL .... Kunnallisvirkamiesliitto [*Federation of Municipal Officers*] [*Finland*]   (EY)

KVM .... Driving Course   (RU)

KVM .... Khmer Viet Minh [*Cambodian Viet Minh*] [*Term formerly used by Prince Sihanouk to refer to Cambodian leftists*]   (CL)

kvm .... Square Meter   (BU)

KVMK .... Kronshtadt Naval Fortress   (RU)

kvn .... Candidate of Military Sciences   (RU)

kvn .... Candidate of Veterinary Sciences   (RU)

KVNB .... Komise Vnitrni Narodni Bezpecnosti [*Internal National Security Commission*]   (CZ)

KVNB .... Krajske Velitelstvi Narodni Bezpecnosti [*Regional National Security Corps Headquarters*]   (CZ)

KVO .... Auxiliary Boiler Equipment   (RU)

KVO .... Caucasian Military District   (RU)

KVO .... Cultural and Educational Department [*In a corrective labor camp*]   (RU)

KVO .... Kiev Military District   (RU)

KVO .... Korpusna Vojna Oblast [*Corps Military Territory*]   (YU)

KVO .... Kraftverkehrsordnung fuer den Gueterfernverkehr mit Kraftfahrzeugen [*Regulation for the Carriage of Goods by Motor Vehicles*] [*German*] [*Business term*]   (ILCA)

k-vo .... Publishing House   (BU)

KVOM .... Krajsky Vybor Obrancu Miru [*Regional Committee of Peace Defenders*]   (CZ)

KVOT .... Special Mutual Aid Fund   (RU)

KVP .... Corps Military Prosecutor   (RU)

KVP .... Kasernierte Volkspolizei [*Garrisoned People's Police*]   (EG)

KVP .... Katholieke Volkspartij [*Catholic People's Party*] [*Netherlands*] [*Political party*]   (PPE)

KVP .... Komisija za Verska Pitanja (SIV) [*Commission on the Religious Question*]   (YU)

KVP .... Krajsky Vykupni Podnik [*Regional Purchasing Enterprise (for agricultural products)*]   (CZ)

KVP .... Mutual Aid Fund   (RU)

KVP .... Punched-Card Ejection Contact   (RU)

KVPD .... Constant-Pressure Capillary Viscometer   (RU)

KVPD .... Kasernierte Volkspolizei-Dienststelle [*Garrisoned People's Police Office*]   (EG)

KVPG .... Field Hospital for Dermatology and Venereal Diseases   (RU)

KVPPG .... Mobile Field Hospital for Dermatology and Venereal Diseases   (RU)

KVR .... Boiling-Water Reactor   (RU)

KVR .... Capital Repair, Overhaul   (BU)

KVRZ .... Kiev Railroad Car Repair Plant   (RU)

KVS .... Auxiliary Ship Boiler   (RU)

KVS .... Compressor Diving Station   (RU)

KVS .... Kansanvalistusseura [*Society for Culture and Education*] [*Finland*]   (EAIO)

KVS .... Kotarska Veterinarska Stanica [*District Veterinary Station*]   (YU)

KVS .... Krajska Vodohospodarska Sluzba [*Regional Water Management Service*]   (CZ)

KVS .... Krajska Vojenska Sprava [*Regional Military Directorate*]   (CZ)

KVS .... Oxygen-Air Mixture   (RU)

KVS .... Signal Platoon Commander   (RU)

KVST .... Knihovny Vysokych Skol Technickych [*Libraries of the Institutes of Technology*] [*Prague*]   (CZ)

KVST .... Kniznica Vysokej Skoly Technickej [*Library of the Institute of Technology*] [*Bratislava*]   (CZ)

KVST .... Knotenvermittlungsstelle [*German*]   (ADPT)

KVStB. .... Krajske Velitelstvi Statni Bezpecnosti [*Regional State Security Headquarters*]   (CZ)

KVSZMH ... Krajsky Vybor Svazu Zamestnancu Mistniho Hospodarstvi [*Regional Committee of the Union of Employees in the Local Economy*]   (CZ)

KVT .... Committee for Internal Transportation   (RU)

KVT .... Corps of Military Topographers   (RU)

KvT .... Kamer van Toezicht [*Benelux*]   (BAS)

kvt .... Kilowatt   (BU)

KVT .... Klub Vojskoveho Telesa [*Military Post Club*]   (CZ)

kvt .... Konyvtar [*Library*]   (HU)

kvtar.......... Konyvtar [*Library*] (HU)
kvtch .... Kilowatt-Hour (BU)
KVTs......... Auxiliary-Shop Complex (RU)
KVTs......... Coordinating Computation Center (RU)
KVTVS...... Krajsky Vybor Telesnej Vychovy a Sportu [*Regional Committee for Physical Education and Sports*] (CZ)
KVU.......... Headquarters Platoon Commander (BU)
KVU.......... Klokneruv Vyzkumny Ustav [*Klokner Research Institute*] (CZ)
KVU.......... Klub Vytvarnych Umelcu [*Creative Artists' Club*] (CZ)
KVU.......... Krajsky Vyzkumny Ustav [*Regional Research Institute*] (CZ)
KVU.......... Peripheral Equipment Switching Device (RU)
KVU-CO.... Krajske Vojenske Utvary, Civilni Obrany [*Regional Military Units, Civil Defense*] (CZ)
KVUVV ..... Komplexny Vyskumny Ustav Vinohradnicky a Vinarsky [*Viticulture and Oenology Research Institute*] [*Former Czechoslovakia*] (ARC)
KVUZ........ Krajsky Vyzkumny Ustav Zemedelsky [*Regional Agricultural Research Institute*] (CZ)
KVV .... Koolajvezetek Vallalat [*Oil Pipeline Enterprise*] (HU)
KVV .... Krajske Vojenske Velitelstvi [*Regional Military Headquarters*] (CZ)
KVV .... Krajsky Volebni Vybor [*Regional Election Committee*] (CZ)
KVV .... Krajsky Vykorny Vybor [*Regional Executive Committee*] (CZ)
KVY .... CAI [*Compagnia Aeronautica Italiana SpA*] [*Italy*] [*ICAO designator*] (FAAC)
KVZ .... Committee for Military Contracts (RU)
KVZ .... Kalinin Railroad Car Plant (RU)
KVZ .... Kmetijska Vrtnarska Zadruga [*Horticultural Cooperative*] (YU)
KVZ .... Kryukovo Railroad Car Plant (RU)
KVZhD ...... Chinese Eastern Railroad [*1903-1945*] (RU)
KVZP........ Antiaircraft Machine-Gun Platoon Commander (RU)
KW.............. Het Koloniaal Weekblad [*Benelux*] (BAS)
KW.............. Kaiser Wilhelm [*King William*] [*Name of two Prussian kings and emperor of Germany*] (ROG)
KW.............. Kamera Werke, Niedersedlitz (VEB) [*Niedersedlitz Camera Works (VEB)*] (EG)
KW.............. Katholieke Werkgever [*Benelux*] (BAS)
kW.............. Kilowat [*Kilowatt*] [*Poland*]
kW.............. Kilowatt [*French*]
kW.............. Kilowatti(a) [*Finland*]
KW.............. Knight of Windsor (ROG)
Kw.............. Kohlenwasserstoff [*Hydrocarbon*] [*German*] (GCA)
KW.............. Komenda Wojewodzka [*Province Headquarters*] [*Poland*]
KW.............. Komitet Warszawski [*Warsaw Committee*] [*Poland*]
KW.............. Komitet Wojewodzki [*Province Committee*] [*Poland*]
KW.............. Komitet Wykonawczy [*Executive Committee*] (POL)
KW.............. Kraftwagen [*Motor Vehicle*] [*German*]
KW.............. Krankzinningenwet [*Benelux*] (BAS)
KW.............. Kreditanstalt fuer Wiederaufbau
KW.............. Kurzwelle [*Short Wave*] [*German*] (EG)
KW.............. Kuwait [*ANSI two-letter standard code*] (CNC)
kw.............. Kwadratowy [*Square*] (POL)
KW.............. Kwanza
KW.............. Kwartaal [*Quarter*] [*Afrikaans*]
kw.............. Kwartal [*Three Months*] [*Poland*]
KWA........ Kwajalein [*Marshall Islands*] [*Airport symbol*] (OAG)
KWAIDS... Kids With Acquired Immune Deficiency Syndrome [*Australia*]
KWAL ...... Kwaliteit [*Quality*] [*Afrikaans*]
KWANT ... Kwantiteit [*Quantity*] [*Afrikaans*]
kwart........ Kwartalnik [*or Kwartaly*] [*Quarterly*] [*Poland*]
KWB........ Katholieke Werkliedenbonden [*Benelux*] (BAS)
KWB .... Kristelijke Werknemersbeweging [*Belgium*] (EAIO)
KWBF....... Katholische Welt-Bibelfoderation [*World Catholic Federation for the Biblical Apostolate - WCFBA*] (EAIO)
KWE........ Guiyang [*China*] [*Airport symbol*] (OAG)
KWE .... Knight of the White Eagle [*Poland*]
KWEBBOTU ... Kweneng West Branch of the Botswana Teachers Union
KWF .... Kommission zur Foerderung der Wissenschaftlichen Forschung [*Commission for the Advancement of Scientific Research*] [*Switzerland*] (SLS)
KWF .... Kuratorium fuer Waldarbeit und Forsttechnik [*Federal Center of Forest Operations and Techniques*] (ARC)
KWG........ Kernkraftwerk Graben, AG [*Switzerland*] [*Nuclear energy*] (NRCH)
KwG .... Kesselwagen [*Tank Car*] [*German*] (EG)
KWH .... Keramische Werke, Hermsdorf (VEB) [*Hermsdorf Ceramic Works (VEB)*] (EG)
kWh .... Kilowatogodzina [*Kilowatt-Hour*] [*Poland*]
kWh .... Kilowatt-Heure [*Kilowatt-Hour*] [*French*]
kWh .... Kilowatt-Hour (OMWE)
kWh .... Kilowatt Hours (SCAC)
kWh .... Kilowattitunti [*Finland*]
kWh .... Kilowattstunde [*Kilowatt-Hour*] [*German*] (EG)
KWI .... Komorka Wykonawstwa Inwestycyjnego [*Unit for Investment Operations*] (POL)
KWI .... Kuwait [*Airport symbol*] (OAG)

KWK .... Kabelwerk Koepenick [*Koepenick Cable Works*] (EG)
KWK .... Kampfwagenkanone [*Tank Gun*] (EG)
KWK .... Kolonial-Wirtschaftliche Komitee
KWK .... Kurs Wynikowy Kalkulacyjny [*Calculated Effective Rate*] [*Foreign trade Polish*] (POL)
KWKZ .... Komitet Wspolpracy Kulturalnej z Zagranica [*Committee on Cultural Cooperation with Foreign Countries*] (POL)
KWL .... Guilin [*China*] [*Airport symbol*] (OAG)
KWL .... Kalt Wenig Loeslich [*Not Very Soluble Cold*] [*German*]
KWL .... Kernkraftwerk Lingen, GmbH [*Nuclear energy*] (NRCH)
Kwl .... Kesselwagen Leitstelle [*Tank Car Operations Office*] (EG)
KWL .... Kinderbijslagwet voor Loontrekkenden [*Children's Allowance Act for Employees*] [*Netherlands*] (WEN)
KWM......... Kowanyama [*Australia*] [*Airport symbol*] (OAG)
KW MO..... Komenda Wojewodzka Milicji Obywatelskiej [*Provincial Headquarters of the Civic Militia*] [*Poland*]
KW MZS... Komitet Wykonawczy Miedzynarodowego Zwiazku Studentow [*Executive Committee of the International Union of Students*] (POL)
kwn.......... Kwintal [*Quintal*] [*Poland*]
KWO......... Kabelwerk Oberspree (VEB) [*Oberspree Cable Works (VEB)*] (EG)
KWO......... Kenya Women's Organisation
KWO......... Kernkraftwerk Obrigheim, GmbH [*Nuclear energy*] (NRCH)
kWo .... Kilowatt Ora [*Kilowatt-Hour*] (HU)
KWP......... Kierownictwo Walki Podziemnej [*Command of the Underground Resistance Movement*] [*World War II*] (POL)
KWP .... Korean Workers' Party [*North Korea*] [*Political party*] (PD)
KWPZPR ... Komitet Wojewodzki Polskiej Zjednoczonej Partii Robotniczej [*Provincial Committee of the Polish United Workers' Party*]
KWR......... Krosnienskie Warsztaty Remontowe [*Krosno Repair Shops*] (POL)
KWRNZSP ... Komitet Wykonawczy Rady Naczelnej Zrzeszenia Studentow Polskich [*Executive Committee of the Chief Council of the Polish Students' Association*] [*Poland*]
KWS .... Kernkraftwerk Sud, GmbH [*Nuclear energy*] (NRCH)
KWS .... Kleinwanzlebener Saatzucht AG [*Small Insect Life Cycle Study*]
KWS .... Komisja do Walki ze Spekulacja [*Commission for the Struggle Against Speculation*] (POL)
KWS .... Korean Welfare Society [*Australia*]
KWSA....... Kerkhistoriese Werkgemeenskap van Suider-Afrika [*South Africa*] (AA)
KW SP ...... Komenda Wojewodzka Sluzby Polsce [*Voivodship Headquarters of Service to Poland*] [*Semimilitary youth organization*] (POL)
Kwst .... Kilowattstunde [*Kilowatt-Hour*] [*German*]
KW-stoff .... Kohlenwasserstoff [*Hydrocarbon*] [*German*]
KWT .... Kuwait [*ANSI three-letter standard code*] (CNC)
KW TUR ... Komitet Wykonawczy Towarzystwa Uniwersytetow Robotniczych [*Executive Committee of the Workers' Universities Society*] [*Poland*]
KWU......... Kommunales Wirtschaftsunternehmen [*Local Economic Enterprise*] (EG)
KWU......... Kraftwerk Union [*Construction company*]
KWV......... Kommunale Wohnungsverwaltung [*Municipal Housing Administration*] (EG)
KWV......... Kooperatiewe Wijnbouwers Vereniging van Zuid-Afrika [*Cooperative Winemakers' Association of South Africa*]
KWW........ Kolo Wiedzy Wojskowej [*Military Science Circle*] (POL)
KWWL ...... Kurs Wstepnych Wiadomosci Lotniczych [*Preliminary Aviation Course*] (POL)
KWX .... Kiwai Island [*Papua New Guinea*] [*Airport symbol*] (OAG)
KWZ .... Kinderbijslagwet voor Kleine Zelfstandigen [*Benelux*] (BAS)
KW ZMS... Komitet Wojewodzki Zwiazku Mlodziezy Socjalistycznej [*Provincial Committee of the Socialist Youth Union*] [*Poland*]
KW ZSL ... Komitet Wykonawczy Zjednoczonego Stronnictwa Ludowego [*Executive Committee of the United Peasants' Party*] [*Poland*]
KXF........... Koro [*Fiji*] [*Airport symbol*] (OAG)
KY .... Cayman Islands [*ANSI two-letter standard code*] (CNC)
KY .... Kabaka Yekka [*The King Alone*] [*Uganda Suspended*] [*Political party*]
KY .... Kapustin Yar [*Test Facility*] [*US prefix for Soviet-Russian developmental missiles*] (DOMA)
KY .... Kol Yisroel [*Israeli Broadcasting Service*]
KY .... Koy Yollari [*Village Roads*] (TU)
KY .... Kratiki Ypiresia [*Government (Vehicle), For Government (Official) Use*] (GC)
KYa........... Aiming Box (RU)
KYA .... Yana Air Cargo (Kenya) Ltd. [*ICAO designator*] (FAAC)
KYAE .... Kentron Ygiinis ke Asfalias tis Ergassias [*Center for Occupational Hygiene and Safety*] [*Research center*] [*Greek*] (IRC)
KYBE........ Kentron Hydrobiologikon Ereynon [*Hydrobiological Research Center*] [*Greece*] (IRC)
KYCCA...... Kenya Youth Christian Choirs Association

KYDEP...... Kendriki Ypiresia Diakhoriseos Enkhorion Proiondon [*Central Service for the Separation of Domestic Products*] [*Greek*] (GC)

KYDF........ Istanbul Orta Ogretim Ogrencileri Koruma ve Yardim Dernekleri Federasyonu [*Federation of Organizations for the Protection and Aid to Secondary Students*] (TU)

KYeD......... Cat Unit (RU)

k yed........... Feed Unit (RU)

KYeD......... Rat Unit (RU)

KYEP........ Kendriki Ypiresia Erevnis Paraponon [*Central Service for the Investigation of Complaints*] [*In the Office of the Minister to the Premier*] [*Greek*] (GC)

KYEP........ Koinoniki Ypiresia Ektakton Peristaseon [*Social Service for Special Cases*] [*Greek*] (GC)

KYePS ...... Permanent Commission for the Study of Natural Productive Forces of the USSR (at the Academy of Sciences, USSR) (RU)

KYET........ Kendron Ypodokhis Ekpaidevseos Tekhniton [*Technicians Training Reception Center*] [*Greek*] (GC)

KYF........... Yeelirie [*Australia*] [*Airport symbol*] (OAG)

KYHA....... Kenya Youth Hostels Association (EAIO)

Kyl............ Kymen Laani [*Finland*]

KYN........... Kyrnair [*France*] [*ICAO designator*] (FAAC)

KYP........... Kendriki Ypiresia Pliroforion [*Central Intelligence Service*] [*Greek*] (GC)

KYP .... Kyaukpyu [*Myanmar*] [*Airport symbol*] (OAG)

KYP .... Kypriaki Ypiresia Pliroforion [*Cyprus Information Service*] (GC)

KYPA........ Kendriki Ypiresia Politikis Aeroporias [*State Civil Aviation Administration*] [*Greek*] (GC)

KYPE........ Kendriki Ypiresia Paralavis Ekpombon [*Central Radio Monitoring Service*] [*Greek*] (GC)

KYPE........ Kendriki Ypiresia Pliroforion kai Erevnon [*Central Service of Intelligence and Investigation*] (GC)

KYS........... Kayes [*Mali*] [*Airport symbol*] (OAG)

KYS........... Koinotikos Ygeionomikos Stathmos [*Community Medical Station*] (GC)

KYSE........ Koy Yollar, Sular, ve Elektrik Isciler Sendikasi [*Village Roads, Water, and Electrification Workers Union*] (TU)

KYSEA ...... Kyvernitikon Symvoulion Ethnikis Amynis [*Government Council for National Defense*] (GC)

KYSME..... Kendrikon Ypiresiakon Symvoulion Mesis Ekpaidevseos [*Central Service Council for Secondary Education*] [*Greek*] (GC)

KYSOP...... Kyvernitiko Symvoulio Oikonomikis Politikis [*Government Council of Economic Policy*] (GC)

KYSSE....... Kendrikon Ypiresiakon Symvoulion Stoikheiodous Ekpaidevseos [*Central Service Council for Elementary Education*] [*Greek*] (GC)

KYT .... Kendriki Ypiresia Takhydromeion [*Central Postal Service*] [*Greek*] (GC)

KYT .... Kendron Ypodokhis Tekhniton [*Technicians' Reception Center*] [*Greek*] (GC)

KYT .... Kyauktaw [*Myanmar*] [*Airport symbol*] (OAG)

KYuA .... Club of Young Automobilists (RU)

KYuBZ...... Group of Young Zoo Biologists (RU)

KYuGE ...... Complex Southern Geological Expedition (RU)

KYuLF .... Club of Young Physics Amateurs (RU)

kyun .... Candidate of Laws (RU)

KYuTO ...... South Pacific Commission [*SPC*] (RU)

KYX .... Yalumet [*Papua New Guinea*] [*Airport symbol*] (OAG)

KZ............. Flight Commander (RU)

KZ............. Kerosene Fueler, Kerosene Vehicle (BU)

KZ............. Kerosene Refueling Truck (RU)

KZ............. Kmetijska Zadruga [*Agricultural Cooperative*] (YU)

KZ............. Kodeks Zobowiazan [*Law on Contracts*] (POL)

k-z............. Kolkhoz (RU)

KZ............. Kolomna Locomotive Plant Imeni Kuybyshev (RU)

KZ............. Komitet Zakladowy [*Plant Committee*] (POL)

KZ............. Konzentrationslager [*Concentration Camp*] [*Initials also used in medicine to indicate a psychiatric syndrome found in surviving victims of the World War II camps*] [*German*]

KZ............. Konzervatorski Zavod [*Conservation Institute*] (YU)

KZ............. Koordinationszahl [*Coordination Number*] [*German*] (GCA)

KZ............. Krajsky Zavod [*Regional Plant*] (CZ)

KZ............. Krivicni Zakonik [*Criminal Code*] (YU)

KZ............. Krojacka Zadruga [*Tailoring Cooperative*] (YU)

KZ............. Kulturny Zivot [*Cultural Life*] [*A periodical*] (CZ)

KZ............. Kurszettel [*Stock Exchange List*] [*German*]

kZ............. Kurze Sicht [*Short Sight*] [*German*] [*Business term*]

Kz............. Kwanza [*Monetary Unit*] [*Angola*] (BARN)

KZ............. Shipyard (BU)

KZ............. Short Circuit, Short Circuited (RU)

KZ............. Starch Grain (RU)

KZA .... Heavy Caliber Antiaircraft Artillery (BU)

KZA .... Kazakhstan Airlines [*ICAO designator*] (FAAC)

KZA .... Knihovna Zemedelske Akademie [*Library of the Academy of Agriculture*] (CZ)

KZA .... Komitee Zuidelyk Afrika [*Holland Committee on Southern Africa*] [*Netherlands*] (EAIO)

KZA .... Krajske Zdruzenie Advokatov [*Regional Association of Lawyers*] (CZ)

KZA .... Large-Caliber Antiaircraft Artillery (RU)

KZA .... Sound Control Unit (RU)

KZAG .... Corps Antiaircraft Artillery Group (RU)

KZB .... Concert and Entertainment Office (RU)

KZBP........ Krakowskie Zjednoczenie Budownictwa Przemyslowego [*Krakow Industrial Construction Association*] (POL)

KZBV........ Kassenzahnaerztliche Bundesvereinigung [*Panel Dentists Association*] (SLS)

KZD .... Kurz-Zwei-Dieselmotor [*Short-Stroke, Two-Cycle Diesel Engine*] (EG)

kz dr .... Bicycle Battalion (BU)

KZEMB.... Kibris Zahire Encumeni Mustahdemleri Birligi [*Union of Cypriot Cereals Committee Employees*] [*Turkish Cypriot*] (GC)

KZF........... Kaintiba [*Papua New Guinea*] [*Airport symbol*] (OAG)

KZG .... Katowickie Zaklady Gastronomiczne [*Katowice Catering (or Restaurant) Establishments*] [*Poland*]

KZG .... Kieleckie Zaklady Gastronomiczne [*Kielce Catering (or Restaurant) Establishments*] [*Poland*]

KZG .... Kolejowe Zaklady Gastronomiczne [*Railroad Catering (or Restaurant) Establishments*] (POL)

KZG .... Krakowskie Zaklady Gastronomiczne [*Krakow Catering (or Restaurant) Establishments*] (POL)

kzh .... Treasurer, Cashier (BU)

KZhB .... Kustanay Iron Ore Basin (RU)

KZI .... Kozani [*Greece*] [*Airport symbol*] (OAG)

KZIP......... Katowickie Zjednoczenie Instalacji Przemyslowych [*Katowice Industrial Installation Association*] (POL)

KZIP......... Krakowskie Zjednoczenie Instalacji Przemyslowych [*Krakow Industrial Installation Association*] (POL)

KZK .... Kvalifikacni Zdokonalovaci Kurzy [*Specialty Improvement Courses*] (CZ)

KZK .... Kyautata Zaman Karkara [*Cocin Rural Development Programme*] [*Nigeria*] (EAIO)

KZKh .... Kazakh Railroad (RU)

Kzl............. Kanzlei [*Chancellery*] [*German*]

Kzlr............ Kanzler [*Chancellor*] [*German*]

KZM .... Concentrate of Green-Oil Emulsion (RU)

KZM .... Komunistyczny Zwiazek Mlodziezy [*Communist Union of Youth*] (POL)

KZMA ...... Kiev Medical Equipment Plant (RU)

KZMH...... Krajske Zakladny Mistniho Hospodarstvi [*Regional Centers of the Local Economy*] (CZ)

KZMP........ Komunistyczny Zwiazek Mlodziezy Polskiej [*Communist Union of Polish Youth*] (POL)

KZMR ...... Komunistyczny Zwiazek Mlodziezy Robotniczej [*Communist Union of Working Youth*] (POL)

KZN .... Kabinet Zdenka Nejedleho [*Zdenek Nejedly Department (of the Czechoslovak Academy of Sciences)*] (CZ)

KZN .... Kazan [*Former USSR*] [*Airport symbol*] (OAG)

KZNS........ Kujawskie Zaklady Naprawy Samochodow [*Kujawy Auto Repair Shop*] (POL)

KZO .... Foreign Organization Committee of the RSDRP [*1911-1917*] (RU)

KZO .... Komise pro Zahranicni Obchod [*Foreign Trade Commission*] [*Czechoslovakian*] (CZ)

KZO .... Koninklijke Zout-Organon, NV [*Later, AKZO*] [*Netherlands*]

KZoBSiO... Marriage, Family, and Guardianship Code (RU)

KZoBSO .... Marriage, Family, and Guardianship Code (RU)

KZOMS.... Kursk Zonal Experimental Reclamation Station (RU)

KZOT .... Labor Code (RU)

KZP........... Katowickie Zaklady Piekarnicze [*Katowice Bakeries*] (POL)

KZPG........ Krakowskie Zaklady Przemyslu Gumowego [*Krakow Rubber Works*] (POL)

KZPS........ Kotarski Zadruzni Poslovni Savez [*District Agricultural Cooperative Business Union*] (YU)

KZ PZPR.. Komitet Zakladowy Polskiej Zjednoczonej Partii Robotniczej [*Plant Committee of the Polish United Workers' Party*] (POL)

kz r .... Bicycle Company (BU)

KZS........... Antiaircraft Gunnery Courses (RU)

KZS........... Keramicke a Sklarske Zavody na Slovensku, Narodny Podnik [*Ceramics and Glass Factories in Slovakia, National Enterprise*] (CZ)

KZS........... Kontrolno Zastitna Sluzba [*Control Defense Service*] [*Army*] (YU)

KZS........... Krajowe Zawody Samolotowe [*Country-Wide Airplane Contests*] (POL)

KZSB .... Krakowski Zwiazek Spoldzielni Branzowych [*Krakow Union of Business Cooperatives*] (POL)

KZSO......... Kirov Sports Equipment Plant (RU)

KZSSLP .... Kmetijski Zemljiski Sklad Splosnega Ljudskega Premozenja [*Agricultural Land Fund of the National Property*]   (YU)

KZST .... Krajowy Zwiazek Spoldzielni Transportu [*National Union of Transport Cooperatives*]   (POL)

KZTM .... Kiev Commercial Machinery Plant   (RU)

KZTS .... Kiev Turning Lathe Plant   (RU)

KZTS .... Kolomna Heavy Machine Tool Plant   (RU)

KZWI .... Katowickie Zjednoczenie Wodno-Inzynierskie [*Katowice Hydraulic Engineering Association*]   (POL)

KZWME .... Krakowskie Zaklady Wytworcze Materialow Elektrotechnicznych [*Krakow Electric Engineering Materials Plant*]   (POL)

KZWME .... Krakowskie Zaklady Wytworcze Materialow Elektrycznych [*Krakow Electric Materials Plant*]   (POL)

KZZhBK .... Kurakhovka Reinforced Concrete Structural Parts Plant   (RU)

KZZM .... Klasowy Zwiazek Zawodowy Metalowcow [*Class Trade Union of Metal Workers*]   (POL)

KZ ZMS .... Komitet Zakladowy Zwiazku Mlodziezy Socjalistycznej [*Works Committee of the Socialist Youth Union*] [*Poland*]

L

l	Eli [*Or*] [*Finland*] (GPO)
L	Free Fit, Easy-Running Fit (RU)
l	Laan [*Lane*] [*Netherlands*] (CED)
l	Laani [*Finland*]
L	Lac [*Lake*] [*French*] (NAU)
L	Lac [*Lake*] [*Romanian*] (NAU)
L	Ladung [*Charge*] [*German*] (GCA)
L	Laenge [*Length*] [*German*]
L	Lage [*Quire, Signature*] [*Publishing*] [*German*]
L	Lago [*Lake*] [*Spanish*] (NAU)
L	Lago [*Lake*] [*Italian*] (NAU)
L	Lago [*Lake*] [*Portuguese*] (NAU)
L	Lagoa [*Small Lake, Marsh*] [*Portuguese*] (NAU)
l	Lakos [*Inhabitant*] (HU)
L	Lamp, Tube (RU)
l	Lancado [*Lance*] [*Portuguese*]
L	Land [*Land, Country*] [*German*]
l	Lang [*Long*] [*German*] (GCA)
L	Langwelle [*Long Wave*] [*German*] (GCA)
l	Lap [*Page*] (HU)
l	Largeur [*Width*] [*French*]
L	Largo [*Wide*] [*Portuguese*]
l	Lasd [*See*] [*Hungary*] (GPO)
L	Lassen [*Let*] [*German*] (GCA)
L	Lat [*Monetary unit*] [*Latvia*]
L	Laurea [*Academic degree*] [*Italian*]
L	Left, Left-Hand (RU)
L	Legge [*Law, Act, Statute*] [*Italian*] (ILCA)
L	Legislation [*French*] (FLAF)
L	Lehre [*Instruction*] [*German*] (GCA)
L	Lehrer [*Teacher*] [*German*]
L	Leicanc [*License*] [*Afghanistan*]
l	Leicht [*Slightly*] [*German*]
L	Lek [*Monetary unit*] [*Albania*] (BARN)
L	Lekarz [*Academic qualification*] [*Poland*]
L	Lempira [*Monetary unit*] [*Honduras*]
L	Lengte [*Length*] [*Afrikaans*]
L	Leningrad (RU)
L	Leste [*East*] [*Portuguese*]
l	Letra [*Letter*] [*Portuguese*]
L	Letra [*Letter*] [*Spanish*]
l	Lettre [*Letter*] [*Publishing*] [*French*]
l	Letzt [*Last*] [*German*]
L	Leu [*Monetary unit*] [*Romania*]
l/	Leur [*Their, Your*] [*Business term*] [*French*]
L	Lev [*Monetary unit*] [*Bulgaria*]
l	Lever (BU)
l	Lewy [*Left*] [*Poland*]
l	Ley [*Law*] [*Spanish*]
l	Libro [*Book*] [*Spanish*]
l	Licence [*License*] [*French*]
L	Licenciado [*One Who Is Licensed in a Profession*] [*Spanish*]
L	Licenciado [*One Who is Licensed in a Profession*] [*Portuguese*]
L	Licenciatura [*Academic qualification*] [*Spanish*]
L	Licenciatura [*Academic qualification*] [*Portuguese*]
L	Licenta [*Academic qualification*] [*Romanian*]
L	Licentiat [*Denmark*]
l	Licht [*Slightly*] [*Netherlands*]
l	Liczba [*Number*] (POL)
l	Lid [*Benelux*] (BAS)
l	Lies [*Read*] [*German*]
l	Lieu [*Place*] [*Publishing*] [*French*]
l	Lieue [*League*] [*French*]
L	Light [*Class of river ship*] (RU)
L	Lilangeni [*Monetary unit*] [*Swaziland*] (BARN)
L	Lima [*Phonetic alphabet*] [*International*] (DSUE)
L	Line (RU)
L	Line Contactor (RU)
l	Linha [*Thread*] [*Portuguese*]
l	Links [*Left*] [*German*]
l	Linksdrehend [*Counterclockwise*] [*German*]
l	Linnen [*Cloth*] [*Publishing*] [*Netherlands*]
l	Liquidation [*Liquidation*] [*Business term*] [*French*]
L	Lira [*Monetary unit*] [*Italy*]
L	Lisans [*Turkey*]
L	Lisensiaatti [*Finland*]
l	List [*Sheet*] (CZ)
L	Litas [*Monetary unit*] [*Lithuania*]
L	Liter [*German*] (GCA)
l	Liter [*Albanian*]
l	Litr [*Liter*] (POL)
l	Litra(a) [*Finland*]
l	Litre [*Liter*] [*French*]
l	Litro [*Liter*] [*Portuguese*] (GPO)
l	Litro [*Liter*] [*Spanish*]
L	Livre [*Monetary unit*] [*Obsolete*] [*French*]
l	Livro [*Book*] [*Portuguese*]
L	Lockheed Aircraft Corp. [*ICAO aircraft manufacturer identifier*] (ICAO)
l	Loeslich [*Soluble*] [*German*]
L	Loesung [*Solution*] [*German*]
L	Loi [*Law*] [*French*]
l	Loja [*Shop*] [*Portuguese*]
L	London [*Phonetic alphabet*] [*Royal Navy World War I Pre-World War II*] (DSUE)
L	Long [*Of guns*] [*French*] (MTD)
l	Longueur [*Length*] [*French*]
L	Loti [*Monetary unit*] [*Lesotho*] (BARN)
L	Love [*Phonetic alphabet*] [*World War II*] (DSUE)
l	Lugar [*Place*] [*Spanish*]
l	Lugar [*Place*] [*Portuguese*]
L	Luitingh [*Holland*]
L	Luka [*Harbor, Port*] [*Former Yugoslavia*] (NAU)
L	Luksemburg [*Luxembourg*] [*Poland*]
l	Person [*Grammar*] (RU)
l	Physician (BU)
l	Readily (Soluble) (RU)
L	Rook, Castle [*Chess*] (RU)
L	Selbstinduktionskoeffizient [*Inductivity*] [*German*]
l	Sheet (BU)
l	Sheet, Leaf (RU)
L	Summer [*Automobile and tractor diesel fuel designation*] (RU)
L	Winch (RU)
L123UA	Lotus 1-2-3 Users' Association
LA	Aircraft Designed by S. A. Lavochkin (RU)
LA	Laden Adresse [*German*] (ADPT)
La	Laguna [*Lagoon*] [*Portuguese*] (NAU)
La	Laguna [*Lagoon*] [*Italian*] (NAU)
La	Laguna [*Lagoon*] [*Norway*] (NAU)
La	Laguna [*Lagoon*] [*Spanish*] (NAU)
LA	Lake Aircraft [*ICAO aircraft manufacturer identifier*] (ICAO)
La	Langsamfahrstellen [*Reduced Speed Track Sections*] (EG)
LA	Lanska Akce [*"Lany Action" (Manpower recruitment drive)*] (CZ)
La	Lantanio [*Chemical element*] [*Portuguese*]
La	Lanthan [*Lanthanum*] [*Chemical element*] [*German*]
LA	L'Anthropologie
LA	Laos [*or Lao People's Democratic Republic*] [*ANSI two-letter standard code*] (CNC)
la	Lasd Alabb [*See Below*] (HU)
la	Lauantai(na) [*Finland*]
LA	Lekka Atletyka [*Athletics, Track and Field Events*] [*Poland*]
LA	Letecka Armada [*Air Army*] (CZ)
la	Lettre Autographe [*Autograph Letter*] [*Publishing*] [*French*]
L/A	Lettre d'Avis [*Letter of Advice*] [*French*]
LA	Libertarian Alliance [*British*] (EAIO)

La .... Licenza Accademia di Belli Arti [*Italian*]
LA .... Life Australia
LA .... Liga Africana
LA .... Light Artillery (RU)
LA .... Lovacka Avijacija [*Fighter Aviation*] (YU)
LA .... Motorized Laboratory (RU)
LA .... Vehicle, Aircraft (RU)
LAA .... Amphibious Assault Ship [*Military*]
LAA .... Jamahiriya Libyan Arab Airlines [*ICAO designator*] (FAAC)
LAA .... Laboratoire d'Anthropologie Appliquee [*Laboratory of Applied Anthropology*] [*Research center*] [*France*] (IRC)
LAA .... Laundrette Association of Australia
LAA .... Library Association of Australasia [*or Australia*]
LAA .... Library Association of Australia
LAA .... Library Association of Austria (EAIO)
LAA .... Libyan Arab Airlines
LAA .... Little Athletics Association [*Australia*]
LAAA .... Latin American Association of Archives [*See also ALA*] (EAIO)
LAAAAS ... Latin American Association for Afro-Asian Studies [*Mexico*] (EAIO)
LAABAM ... Latin American Association of Behavior Analysis and Modification [*Uruguay*] (EAIO)
LAACT ...... Legislative Assembly of the Australian Capital Territory
LAAD .... Latin American Agribusiness Development Corp.
LAADIW ... Latin American Association for the Development and Integration of Women [*See also ALADIM*] [*Chile*] (EAIO)
LAAEMCTS ... Latin American Association of Environmental Mutagens, Carcinogens, and Teratogens Societies [*Mexico*] (EAIO)
LAAF .... Libyan Arab Air Force (PDAA)
LAAF .... Ligue Anti-Anemie Falciforme [*Anti-Sickle Cell Anemia League*] [*Haiti*] (EAIO)
laak .... Laaketiede [*Surgery*] [*Finland*]
laaket .... Laaketiede [*Surgery*] [*Finland*]
laaket(jakir)tri ... Laaketieteen (Ja Kirurgian) Tohtori [*Finland*]
laaketkand ... Laaketieteen Kandidaatti [*Finland*]
laaketlis ..... Laaketieteen Lisensiaatti [*Finland*]
LAAMS ..... Legal and Accounting Management Seminars Proprietary Ltd. [*Australia*]
LAAMSF .. Latin American Association of Medical Schools and Faculties [*See also ALAFEM*] [*Ecuador*] (EAIO)
LAANSW ... Little Athletics Association of New South Wales [*Australia*]
L A Ant ...... Latin America Antiquity [*A publication*]
LAAP .... Law Association for Asia and the Pacific [*Australia*]
LAAPI .... Latin American Association of Pharmaceutical Industries [*See also ALIFAR*] (EAIO)
LAARG ..... Library Association of Australia Reform Group (ADA)
LAAS .... Laboratoire d'Automatique et d'Analyse des Systemes
LAAS .... Laboratoire d'Automatique et de ses Applications Spatiales
LAASL ...... Latin American Association for the Study of the Liver [*Mexico*] (EAIO)
LAASP ...... Latin American Association for Social Psychology [*Formerly, Latin American Social Psychology Committee*] (EA)
LAATD ..... Licentiate of the Australian Association of Teachers of the Deaf (ADA)
laatstel .... Laatstelijk [*Benelux*] (BAS)
Lab .... Labil [*Variable*] [*German*]
LAB .... Lablab [*Papua New Guinea*] [*Airport symbol*] (OAG)
lab .... Laborant [*Laboratory Assistant*] [*Poland*]
lab .... Laboratorium [*Laboratory*] [*Poland*]
lab .... Laboratory (RU)
lab .... Laboratory Assistant (RU)
Lab .... Labuan [*or Labuhan*] [*Anchorage or Harbor Malaysia*] (NAU)
Lab .... Labuan [*or Labuhan*] [*Anchorage or Harbor Indonesian*] (NAU)
LAB .... Latin America Bureau [*British*] (EAIO)
LAB .... Library Association of Bermuda (PDAA)
LAB .... Linear Alkyl Benzene (OMWE)
LAB .... Liquor Administration Board [*New South Wales, Australia*]
LAB .... Lloyd Aereo Boliviano SA [*Lloyd Bolivian Air Line*]
LABAN ...... Lakas ng Bayan [*Peoples' Power Movement - Fight*] [*Philippines*] [*Political party*] (PPW)
LABEN ...... Laboratori Elettronici e Nucleari [*Electronic and Nuclear Laboratories*] [*Italy*] (PDAA)
LABF .... Latin American Banking Federation [*Bogota, Colombia*] (EA)
LABFROSST ... Laboratorio Frost de Colombia Ltda. [*Colombia*] (COL)
LAbg .... Landtagsabgeordneter [*German*]
LABIB .... Laboratory for the Study of Protein (of the Academy of Sciences, USSR) (RU)
LABIFR .... Laboratory of Biochemistry and Physiology of Plants (of the Academy of Sciences, USSR) (RU)
LABIOF .... Laboratory of Biophysics (of the Academy of Sciences, USSR) (RU)
LABIZh .... Laboratory of Biochemistry and Physiology of Animals (of the Academy of Sciences, USSR) (RU)
labj .... Labjegyzet [*Footnote*] (HU)
LABM .... Laboratoires d'Analyses Biologiques Medicales
LABMEOZ ... Laboratorio Meoz Ltda. [*Colombia*] (COL)

Labn .... Labuan [*or Labuhan*] [*Anchorage or Harbor Malaysia*] (NAU)
Labn .... Labuan [*or Labuhan*] [*Anchorage or Harbor Indonesian*] (NAU)
Labor .... Laboratorium [*Laboratory*] [*German*] (GCA)
labor .... Laboratory (RU)
labor .... Laboratory Assistant (RU)
LABORELEC ... Laboratoire Belge de l'Industrie Electrique [*Belgian Electricity Industry Laboratory*] (WED)
LABORIA ... Laboratoire de Recherche en Informatique et en Automatique [*Research Laboratory for Data Processing and Automation*] [*France*] (PDAA)
LABORINFO ... Labour Information Database [*International Labour Office*] [*Information service or system*] (IID)
LABOURMIN ... National Institute for Productivity, Ministry of Labour and Social Welfare [*Tanzania*]
LABr .... Light Artillery Brigade (RU)
LABRE ...... Liga de Amadores Brasileiros de Radio Emissao [*Brazilian Amateurs Radio Relay League*] (PDAA)
LABU .... Latin American Blind Union [*See also ULAC*] [*Uruguay*] (EAIO)
lac .... Lacina [*or Lacinski*] [*Poland*]
LAC .... Lae-City [*Papua New Guinea*] [*Airport symbol*] (OAG)
LAC .... Library Association of China (SLS)
LAC .... Liga Antituberculosa Colombiana [*Colombia*] (COL)
LAC .... Lincoln Agricultural College [*New Zealand*] (DSCA)
LAC .... Little Apostles of Charity [*Italy*] (EAIO)
LAC .... Longeranong Agricultural College [*Australia*]
LACAC ...... Latin American Civil Aviation Commission [*See also CLAC*] (EAIO)
LACADEL ... La Casa de Electricidad Ltda. [*Colombia*] (COL)
LACAP ...... Latin American Co-Operative Acquisition Project [*Libraries*] (LAA)
LACAS ...... Lineas Aereas Costarricenses SA [*Costa Rica*] [*ICAO designator*] (FAAC)
LACCB ...... Latin American Confederation of Clinical Biochemistry [*Colombia*] (EAIO)
LACCSM .. Latin American and Caribbean Council for Self-Management (EAIO)
lacer .... Lacerazione [*Tear*] [*Publishing*] [*Italian*]
LACFFP .... Latin American Commission of Forestry and Forestry Products (LAA)
LAChKh .... Logarithmic Frequency Response Characteristic (RU)
LACHSA ... Licentiate of the Australian College of Health Service Administrators
LACIM ...... Latin American and Caribbean International Moving [*Panama*] (EAIO)
LACIMAR ... Laboratorio de Ciencias do Mar [*Brazil*] (MSC)
LACITO .... Laboratoire de Langues et Civilisations a Traditions Orales [*Laboratory for the Study of Languages and Civilizations of Oral Tradition*] [*Research center*] [*French*] (IRC)
LACLA ...... Latin American Constitutional Law Association [*Argentina*] (EAIO)
LACMA ..... Latin American and Caribbean Movers Association (EAIO)
LACNSW .. Legal Aid Commission of New South Wales [*Australia*]
LACNT ...... Legal Aid Commission of the Northern Territory [*Australia*]
LACOED ... Lagos State College of Education [*Nigeria*]
LACOFA ... La Cooperation Franco-Africaine
LACOFACI ... Lacofa Cote-D'Ivoire
LACQLD ... Legal Aid Commission of Queensland [*Australia*]
LACSA ...... Lineas Aereas Costarricenses Sociedad Anonima [*Airline*] [*Costa Rica*]
LACST ...... Licentiate of the Australian College of Speech Therapists (ADA)
LACT .... Legal Aid Commission of Tasmania [*Australia*]
LACV .... Legal Aid Commission of Victoria [*Australia*]
LACVW .... Landelijk Algemeen Christelik Verbond van Werkgevers [*Flemish General Association of Christian Rural Employers*] [*Belgium*] (WEN)
LACWA ..... Legal Aid Commission of Western Australia
LACYMCA ... Latin American Confederation of YMCAs [*See also CLACJ*] (EAIO)
Lad .... Ladung [*Charge*] [*German*] (GCA)
lad .... Laediert [*Slightly Damaged*] [*German*]
LAD .... Lebanon Airport Development Corp. [*ICAO designator*] (FAAC)
LAD .... Les Amis de Delage [*An association*] [*France*] (EAIO)
LAD .... Luanda [*Angola*] [*Airport symbol*] (OAG)
LADB .... Lesotho Agricultural Development Bank
LADDER ... Leisure, Activities, Disadvantaged, Disabled, Elderly Resources [*Australia*]
LADE .... Lineas Aereas del Estado [*State Airlines*] [*Argentina*] (LA)
LADECO ... Linea Aerea del Cobre SA [*Chile*] (EY)
LADEM ..... Laboratorio de Aplicaciones Electronicas en Ciencias del Mar [*Laboratory for Electronic Applications in Ocean Sciences*] [*Chile*] [*Research center*] (IRC)
Ladenpr ..... Ladenpreis [*List Price*] [*German*]
laderbd .... Laederband [*Leather-Bound*] [*Publishing*] [*Sweden*]
LADH .... Liga Argentina por los Derechos del Hombre [*Argentine League for Human Rights*] (LA)

LADI......... Leningrad Highway Institute Imeni V. V. Kuybyshev (RU)
LADO........ Liga Apararii Drepturilor Omului [*League for the Defense of Human Rights in Romania*] (EAIO)
LADT .... Leningrad Highway Technicum (RU)
LAE .... Lae [*Papua New Guinea*] [*Airport symbol*] (OAG)
Lae .... Laengstwelle [*Long Wave*] [*German*] (GCA)
LAE .... Lineas Aereas Colombianas Ltd. [*Colombia*] [*ICAO designator*] (FAAC)
LAEC......... Law and Aboriginal and Ethnic Communities [*Curriculum Development Project*] [*Australia*]
LAECC...... Groupe International Laicat et Communaute Chretienne [*International Laity and Christian Community Group - ILCCG*] [*Defunct*] (EA)
LAECG...... Local Aboriginal Education Consultative Group [*Australia*]
LAeF......... Ligue Aeronautique de France [*France*]
LAEPC...... Local Aboriginal Employment Promotion Committee [*Australia*]
LAER........ Laboratory of Aerial Methods (RU)
laerredsbd .. Laerredsbind [*Cloth Binding*] [*Publishing Danish/Norwegian*]
LAES........ Latin American Economic System
LAF........... Lebanese Armed Forces
LAF........... Libyan Arab Force [*World War II*]
LAFA........ Lao-Australian Friendship Association [*Use AALA*] (CL)
LAFB........ Libyan Arab Foreign Bank
LAFC......... Latin American Forestry Commission [*FAO*] (LAA)
LAFE........ Laboratorio de Fisica Espacial [*Brazil*]
LAFIDG .... Latin American Forest Industries Development Group [*Later, Forest Industries Advisory Group in Latin America*] (LAA)
LAFKhI ..... Laboratory of Physiological Chemistry (RU)
LAFOKI .... Laboratory of Scientific Applied Photography and Cinematography (of the Academy of Sciences, USSR) (RU)
LAFR........ Laboratory for Plant Anatomy and Physiology (of the Academy of Sciences, USSR) (RU)
LAFRANCOL ... Laboratorio Franco Colombiano [*Colombia*] (COL)
LAFTA ...... Latin American Association of Freight and Transport Agents [*Paraguay*] (EAIO)
LAFTA ...... Latin-American Free Trade Association [*Later, LAIA*]
LAFTC ...... Latin American Federation of Thermalism and Climatism [*See also FLT*] [*Argentina*] (EAIO)
LAFTO...... Latin American Confederation of Tourist Organizations [*Argentina*] (EAIO)
LAG .... Aerovias de Lagos SA de CV [*Mexico*] [*ICAO designator*] (FAAC)
LAG .... Arab League (RU)
lag .... Camp (RU)
LAG .... Laboratory of Genetics (of the Academy of Sciences, USSR) (RU)
lag .... Lagoon [*Topography*] (RU)
Lag .... Lagune [*Lagoon*] [*Military map abbreviation World War I*] [*French*] (MTD)
LAG .... Liga Arabskikh Gosudarstv
LAG .... Liga Armada Gallega [*Armed Galician League*] [*Spain*] (PD)
LAGAS...... Laboratoire de Geophysique Appliquee et Structurale de Nancy [*French*]
LAGB........ Linhas Aereas da Guine-Bissau [*Airline*] [*Guinea-Bissau*]
LAGE........ Lineas Aereas de Guinea Ecuatorial [*Airlines of Equatorial Guinea*] (AF)
LAGE........ Location of Australian Government Employment Committee
LAGED...... Laboratory of Precambrian Geology (of the Academy of Sciences, USSR) (RU)
LAGEMAR ... Laboratorio de Geologia Marinha [*Brazil*] (MSC)
Lager......... Lagerung [*Storage*] [*German*] (GCA)
Lagerfahigk ... Lagerfaehigkeit [*Storability*] [*German*] (GCA)
LAGG .... Aircraft Designed by S. A. Lavochkin, V. P. Gorbunov, and M. I. Gudkov (RU)
LAGO .... Laboratorio Argo [*Bucaramanga*] (COL)
LAGOVEN ... Subsidiary of PETROVEN [*A*] [*Venezuela*] (LA)
LAGU .... Laboratory of Coal Geology (of the Academy of Sciences, USSR) (RU)
LAH........... Labuha [*Indonesia*] [*Airport symbol*] (OAG)
lah .... Lahemmin [*Finland*]
lah .... Lahettaja [*Finland*]
LAH.......... Library of Australian History (ADA)
LAHF .... Latin American Hospital Federation [*Mexico*] (EAIO)
lah V.......... Lahin Vastine [*Approximately*] [*Finland*]
LAI............ Lannion [*France*] [*Airport symbol*] (OAG)
LAI............ League Against Imperialism [*Australia*]
LAI............ Lesotho Airways Corp. [*ICAO designator*] (FAAC)
LAI............ Liquor and Allied Industries Employees Union [*Australia*]
LAIA......... Latin American Industrialists Association [*Uruguay*] (EAIO)
LAIA......... Latin American Integration Association [*Formerly, LAFTA*] [*See also ALADI Uruguay*] (EAIO)
LAIC......... Les Argiles Industrielles du Cameroun
LAIC......... London Australia Investment Company Ltd. (ADA)
LAICA .... Lineas Aereas Interiores de Catalina [*Colombia*] (PDAA)
LAICO....... Latinoamerican Investment Consultants [*Colombia*] (COL)

LAICO...... Lineas Aereas Internacionales y Colombianas (COL)
LAIEC ...... Latin American Institute of Educational Communication [*Mexico*] (EAIO)
LAIICS...... Latin American Institute for Information and Computer Sciences [*Chile*] (PDAA)
LAIS .... Latinamerika-Institutet i Stockholm [*Institute of Latin American Studies*] [*Research center*] [*Sweden*] (IRC)
LAISDSS .. Latin American Institute of Social Doctrine and Social Studies [*Chile*] (EAIO)
LAITS....... Latin American Institute for Transnational Studies (EA)
LAJ .... Lajes [*Brazil*] [*Airport symbol*] (OAG)
LAJS........ Libyan American Joint Service for Agriculture and Natural Resources
LAK .... Laboratory of Architectural Ceramics (RU)
lak .... Lakitermi [*Law, Juridical Term*] [*Finland*]
lak .... Lakitiede [*Finland*]
LAK .... Lennox Airways [*Kenya*] [*ICAO designator*] (FAAC)
LAKAM.... Liaison Bureau for Scientific Affairs [*Acronym represents Hebrew phrase*] [*Israel*]
LAKh .... Logarithmic Frequency Response Characteristic (RU)
LAKhU ...... Leningrad Administrative Office (of Institutions of the Academy of Sciences, USSR) (RU)
LAKI......... Lakkipari Kutato Intezet [*Research Institute for the Lacquer Industry*] (HU)
lakokr........ Varnish and Paint Plant [*Topography*] (RU)
LAKORED ... Laboratory for Document Preservation and Restoration (of the Academy of Sciences, USSR) (RU)
LAKOTERV ... Lako- es Kommunalis Epuleteket Tervezo Vallalat [*Planning Enterprise for Residential and Communal Buildings*] (HU)
LAKRIST .. Laboratory of Crystallography (of the Academy of Sciences, USSR) (RU)
LAKSDA ... Laksamana Muda [*Rear Admiral*] (IN)
LAKSDYA ... Laksmana Madya [*Vice Admiral*] (IN)
LAKSUS.... Pelaksana Chusus [*Special Executive Officer*] (IN)
LAKSZER ... Lakatos es Szerszamkeszito Kisipari Termeloszovetkezet [*Small Industrial Producers' Cooperative of Locksmiths and Toolmakers*] (HU)
lakt .... Laktanya [*Barracks*] (RU)
LAKTERV ... Lakoepulettervezo Vallalat [*Designing Enterprise for Residential Dwellings*] (HU)
LAI............ Aluminiumlot [*Aluminum Solder*] [*German*] (GCA)
LAL............ Laboratoire de l'Accelerateur Lineaire [*French*]
LALAT ...... Liga Argentina Contra la Tuberculosis [*Argentine Anti-Tuberculosis League*] [*Buenos Aires*] (SLS)
LALP .... Leningrad Academy of Light Industry Imeni S. M. Kirov (RU)
LAlSi .... Aluminiumlot mit Silizium [*Aluminum Solder with Silicon*] [*German*] (GCA)
LAM .... Laboratory of Aerial Methods (RU)
LAM .... Laboratory of Aviation Medicine (RU)
Lam .... Lamelle [*Lamella*] [*German*] (GCA)
lam .... Lamina [*Plate*] [*Publishing*] [*Spanish*]
lam .... Laminiert [*Laminated*] [*Publishing*] [*German*]
LAM .... Liberalium Artium Magister [*Master of Liberal Arts*] [*French*] (GPO)
LAM .... Library Association of Malaysia (EAIO)
LAM .... Linhas Aereas de Mocambique [*Mozambique*] [*ICAO designator*] (FAAC)
LAM .... Litografia de Arte Moderno [*Colombia*] (COL)
LAM .... Societa Laziale - Abruzzese Marchigiana Molisana di Ostetricia e Ginecologia [*Italian*] (SLS)
LAMCo...... Liberian-American-Swedish Minerals Company [*Liberia*] (AF)
LAMCS..... Latin American-American Communications Systems (PDAA)
LAMINACO ... Laminacion de Colombia Ltda. [*Colombia*] (COL)
LAMOST .. Large Sky Area Multi-Objects Fiber Spectoscopic Telescope [*China*]
LAMP........ Lost and Missing Persons [*Australia*]
lams........... Laminas [*Plates*] [*Publishing*] [*Spanish*]
LAN .... Chronicles of the Bulgarian Academy of Sciences (BU)
LAN .... Laboratorio di Automozione Navale [*Italian*] (MSC)
LAN .... Latin American Newsletters [*British*] [*Information service or system*] (IID)
LAN .... Lembaga Administrasi Negara [*State Administration Institute*] (IN)
LAN .... Lenguaje de Alto Nivel [*High-Level Language*] [*Spanish*]
LAN .... Linea Aerea Nacional [*National Airline*] [*Chile*]
LAN .... Linea Aerea Nacional de Chile [*ICAO designator*] (FAAC)
LAN .... Pengadilan [*Court of Law*] (IN)
LANA .... Lignes Aeriennes Nord-Africaines
LANAPHARM ... Laboratoire National Pharmaceutique
LANC .... Liga Apararii Nationale Crestine [*League of National Christian Defense*] [*Romania*] [*Political party*] (PPE)
Lancs........ Lancashire (IDIG)
LANDB...... Landboukunde [*Agriculture*] [*Afrikaans*]
LANDCENT ... Allied Land Forces Central Europe [*NATO*]
LANDENMARK ... Allied Land Forces Denmark [*NATO*]
LANDJUT ... Allied Land Forces Schleswig-Holstein and Jutland [*NATO*] (NATG)

LANDNON ... Allied Land Forces North Norway [*NATO*] (NATG)
LANDNORTH ... Allied Land Forces Northern Europe [*NATO*] (NATG)
LANDNORWAY ... Allied Land Forces Norway [*NATO*]
L & P......... Lighting and Power
LANDS...... Landsearch [*Database*] [*Australia*]
LANDSONOR ... Allied Land Forces South Norway [*NATO*] (NATG)
LANDSOUTH ... Allied Land Forces Southern Europe [*NATO*]
LANDSOUTHEAST ... Allied Land Forces Southeastern Europe [*NATO*]
Landw .... Landwirtschaft [*Agriculture*] [*German*] (GCA)
landw......... Landwirtschaftlich [*Agricultural*] [*German*] (EG)
landwS....... Landwirtschaftliche Schule [*Agricultural School*] [*German*]
LANDZEALAND ... Allied Land Forces Zealand [*NATO*] (NATG)
LANEFICO ... Lanera del Pacifico Ltda. [*Mengua-Cali*] (COL)
LANFI....... Laboratorio Nacional de Fomento Industrial [*Federal Industrial Development Laboratory*] [*Mexico*] (LAA)
lang .... Langage [*French*] (TPFD)
lang .... Language (TPFD)
langfr......... Langfristig [*Long-Term*] [*German*] (GCA)
langfrist...... Langfristig [*Long-Term*] [*German*] (GCA)
langj .... Langjaehrig [*For Many Years*] [*German*]
Langlei....... Langleitung [*Long Line (Telephones)*] (EG)
langw......... Langwerpig [*Oblong*] [*Netherlands*]
LANICA.... Linea Aerea de Nicaragua [*Nicaraguan Airline*] (LA)
LANMORA ... Landers Mora y Compania Ltda. [*Colombia*] (COL)
LANS......... Land Navigation System
LANS......... Legion Argentina Nacional Sindicalista [*Argentine National Labor Union Legion*] (LA)
LANSA...... Lineas Aereas Nacionales Consolidadas Sociedad Anonima
LANSW..... Laryngectomee Association of New South Wales [*Australia*]
LANSW..... Legislative Assembly of New South Wales [*Australia*]
LANSW..... Lupus Association of New South Wales [*Australia*]
LANT .... Legislative Assembly of the Northern Territory [*Australia*]
LANTAS ... Lalu Lintas [*Traffic*] (IN)
LANTER... Laboratorios y Agencias Internacionales [*Colombia*] (COL)
LANTFAP ... Allied Command Atlantic Frequency Allocation Panel [*Obsolete*] [*NATO*] (NATG)
lantp.......... Lantista Pituutta [*Finland*]
LANU....... Pangkalan Udara [*Air Base*] (IN)
LANZACOL ... Lanzaceras Colombianas SA [*Colombia*] (COL)
LAO .... Laoag [*Philippines*] [*Airport symbol*] (OAG)
LAO .... Lao Aviaton [*Laos*] [*ICAO designator*] (FAAC)
LAO .... Laos [*or Lao People's Democratic Republic*] [*ANSI three-letter standard code*] (CNC)
LAO .... Legal Aid Office
LAO .... Les Amis de l'Orgue [*Friends of the Organ*] [*France*] (EAIO)
LAO .... Ligue pour l'Avenir et l'Ordre [*Somali*]
LAO .... L'vov Astronomical Observatory (RU)
LAOKh...... Laboratory of General Chemistry (of the Academy of Sciences, USSR) (RU)
LAOKO..... Looking After Our Kosciusko Orphans [*Australia*]
LAOS........ Laikai Antistasiakai Omades Sambotaz [*Popular Resistance Sabotage Groups*] [*Greek*] (GC)
Lao-Viet..... Pathet Lao-Viet Cong (CL)
LAP........... La Paz [*Mexico*] [*Airport symbol*] (OAG)
LAP........... Latin American Parliament [*See also PLA*] [*Colombia*] (EAIO)
LAP........... Liberation Action Party [*Trinidad and Tobago*] [*Political party*] (PPW)
LAP........... Lineas Aereas Paraguayas [*Paraguay*] [*ICAO designator*] (FAAC)
LAPAN...... Lembaga Penerbangan dan Antariksa Nasional [*National Aviation and Space Agency*] (IN)
LAPCO...... Laboratoires Pharmaceutiques du Congo
LAPCO...... Lavan Petroleum Company [*Iran*] (ME)
LAPI......... Leningrad Agricultural Pedagogical Institute (RU)
LAPIP........ Lembaga Persiapan Industri Penerbangan [*Aviation Industry Development Foundation*] (IN)
lapk .... Lapkiado [*Newspaper Publisher*] (HU)
lapp .... Lappalainen [*Finland*]
LAPP........ Latvian Association of Proletarian Writers (RU)
LAPP........ Leningrad Association of Proletarian Writers (RU)
LAPRIZ..... Laboratory of Applied Zoology (of the Academy of Sciences, USSR) (RU)
LAPSA ...... Lineas Aereas Paraguayas Sociedad Anonima [*Airline*] [*Paraguay*]
LAQ.......... Beida [*Libya*] [*Airport symbol*] (OAG)
LAQ.......... Leathercrafters' Association of Queensland [*Australia*]
LAQ.......... Lebanese Air Transport [*ICAO designator*] (FAAC)
LAQ.......... Legislative Assembly of Queensland [*Australia*]
LAR .... Libya Arap Cumhuriyeti [*Libyan Arab Republic*] (TU)
LAR .... Ligacoes Aereas Regionais, SA [*Portugal*] (EY)
LAR .... Linhas Aereas Regionais SA [*Portugal*] [*ICAO designator*] (FAAC)
LAR .... Liniile Aeriene Romane [*Romanian Airlines*] (RO)
LAR .... Loita Armada Revolucionaria [*Armed Revolutionary Struggle*] [*Spain*] (PD)
LARA........ Latin American Railways Association (EA)

LArbG....... Landesarbeitsgericht [*Provincial Labor Court of Appeal*] [*German*] (ILCA)
LARC........ Language Acquisition Research Centre [*University of Sydney*] [*Australia*]
LARC....... Legal Aid Review Committee
LARC........ Libyan-American Reconstruction Commission
LARC........ Regional Conference for Latin America [*UN Food and Agriculture Organization*]
LARCAE ... Ligeia Association pour le Renouvellement de la Culture Artistique Europeenne [*France*] (EAIO)
LARCCH... Latin America Resource Center and Clearinghouse [*Defunct*] (EA)
LARCO..... Laminados Metalicos y Aires Acondicionados [*Colombia*] (COL)
LARES ...... Liniile Aeriene Romane Exploatate de Stat [*Bucharest*]
LARF........ Lebanese Armed Revolutionary Faction
larg............ Largeur [*Width*] [*French*]
larg............ Largo [*Large*] [*Spanish*]
largh.......... Larghezza [*Width*] [*Publishing*] [*Italian*]
larghiss ...... Larghissimo [*Very Wide*] [*Publishing*] [*Italian*]
laring........ Laryngology, Laryngologist (BU)
LARK........ Library Access Resource Kit [*Technical and Further Education Library Services*] [*New South Wales, Australia*]
LARMS..... Glacier Automatic Radiometeorological Station (RU)
LARN .... Laboratoire d'Analyses par Reactions Nucleaires [*Laboratory for the Analysis of Nuclear Reactions*] [*Research center*] [*Belgium*] (IRC)
LARO .... Latin American Regional Office [*United Nations Food and Agricultural Organization*] (BARN)
LARP........ Local Approvals Review Program [*Australia*]
LARSA ...... Latin American Rural Sociological Association (EAIO)
LARSA ...... Latino Americana de Reaseguros Sociedad Anonima [*Panama*] (EY)
LARZ........ Leningrad Automobile Repair Plant (RU)
LAS........... Air Rescue Dinghy (RU)
LAS........... Arab League (RU)
LAS........... Laboratoire d'Astronomie Spatiale [*Astronomy Laboratory*] [*Research center*] [*France*] (EAS)
LAS........... Laboratory of Anisotropic Structures (of the Academy of Sciences, USSR) (RU)
LAS........... League of Arab States [*Tunis, Tunisia*]
LAS........... Library Association of Singapore (SLS)
LAS........... Library Association of Slovenija [*Samoa*] (EAIO)
LAS........... Ligne Aerienne Seychelles [*Airlines*] (EY)
LAS........... Lignes Aerienne Seychelles [*ICAO designator*] (FAAC)
LAS........... Luftfracht-Abwicklungs-System [*German*] (ADPT)
LA(SA)...... Latvian Association of South Australia
LASA........ Levantamentos Aerofotogrametricos SA [*Brazil*] (DSCA)
LASA........ Licentiate of the Art of Speech, Australia (ADA)
LASCo....... Larkin Aircraft Supply Co. [*Australia*]
LASCO...... Latin America Science Cooperation Office (MSC)
LASECNA ... L'Agence pour la Securite de la Navigation Aerienne en Afrique et Madagascar
LASH .... Latin American Society of Hepatology [*See also SLH*] (EAIO)
LASH .... Lighter Aboard Ship
LASHIP .... Lighter Aboard Ship
LASIE....... Library Automated Systems Information Exchange [*Australia*] (PDAA)
LASIN .... Laboratory for the Study and Synthesis of Vegetable and Animal Products (of the Academy of Sciences, USSR) (RU)
Lasmo .... London & Scottish Marine Oil plc (OMWE)
LASORS ... Literature Analysis System on Road Safety [*Australia Department of Transport and Communications*] [*Information service or system*] (CRD)
LASRA ...... Leather and Shoe Research Association, Inc. [*New Zealand*] (ARC)
LASSA....... Lastik Sanayi ve Ticaret Anonim Sirketi [*Rubber Industry and Trade Corporation*] [*Istanbul*] (TU)
LASSC....... Latin American Social Sciences Council [*Argentina*] [*Database producer*] (EA)
LASSO ...... Light Air-to-Surface Semiautomatic Optical [*French missile*]
L AssurEmpl ... Loi d'Assurance de Rentes des Employes [*France*] (FLAF)
last .... Lastenkielta [*Baby Talk*] [*Finland*]
LASU........ Lagos State University [*Nigeria*]
LASZ......... Legfobb Allami Szamvevoszek [*Supreme State Auditing Office*] [*Hungary*] (HU)
LAT .... Aviation Legere de l'Armee de Terre [*France*] [*ICAO designator*] (FAAC)
lat.............. Lateinisch [*Latin*] [*German*]
lat.............. Latim [*Latin*] [*Language, etc.*] [*Portuguese*]
lat.............. Latin (RU)
Lat.............. Latince [*Latin*] (TU)
lat.............. Latino [*Latin*] [*Language, etc.*] [*Portuguese*]
lat.............. Latitude [*Portuguese*]
lat.............. Latitude [*French*]
Lat.............. Latitudine [*Latitude*] [*Italian*]

La T............ La Trobe University [*Australia*] (ADA)
lat............... Latvian (RU)
LAT.......... Latvian Railroad (RU)
Lat.............. Latyn [*Latin*] [*Language, etc.*] [*Afrikaans*]
LAT.......... Lebanese Air Transport (Charter) Company SAL (ME)
LATr.......... Leitungsanpassungsteil [*German*] (ADPT)
LAT.......... Licensing Appeals Tribunal [*Australia*]
l at............ Liczba Atomowa [*Atomic Number*] [*Poland*]
LAT.......... Liga Argentina Contra la Tuberculosis [*Argentine Anti-Tuberculosis League*] [*Buenos Aires, Argentina*] (LAA)
LATA........ Laboratoire Africain de Therapeutique Appliquee
LATA........ Labour Adjustment Training Arrangements [*Australia*]
lat-amer..... Latin American (RU)
LATF........ Legal Aid Task Force
Latgiprogorstroy ... Latvian State Institute for the Planning of Urban Construction (RU)
Latgiproprom ... Latvian State Institute for the Planning of Industrial Establishments (RU)
Latgiprosel'stroy ... Latvian State Institute for the Planning of Rural Construction (RU)
Latgiprovodkhoz ... Latvian State Institute for the Planning of Reclamation (RU)
Latgiz........ Latvian State Publishing House (RU)
Latgosizdat ... State Publishing House of the Latvian SSR (RU)
Latgosrybvod ... Latvian State Inspection for Fish Conservation and Reproduction and the Regulation of Fish Breeding (RU)
LatINTI..... Latvian Republic Institute of Scientific and Technical Information and Propaganda (RU)
LaTL.......... La Trobe Library [*Australia*]
LATLI .... Latin American Tax Law Institute [*Uruguay*] (EAIO)
l-atm........ Liter-Atmosphere (RU)
LATMA..... Label and Tag Manufacturers Association [*Australia*]
LATN .... Lineas Aereas de Transporte Nacional [*Paraguay*]
LatNIIGiM ... Latvian Scientific Research Institute of Hydraulic Engineering and Reclamation (RU)
LATOGOLAISE ... Union pour le Commerce et l'Industrie au Togo
Latpotrebsoyuz ... Latvian Republic Union of Consumers' Societies (RU)
Latpromsovet ... Council of Producers' Cooperatives of the Latvian SSR (RU)
LATR......... Laboratory Autotransformer (RU)
LaTr.......... La Trobe University [*Australia*]
LATRA...... Library Association of Transkei [*South Africa*] (EAIO)
LATRA...... Umbutho Wendlu Yeencwadi Wase-Transkei [*Library Association of Transkei*] [*South Africa*] (EAIO)
LATRAF ... Laminoir Trefilerie d'Afrique
LATU .... Laboratorio Tecnologico del Uruguay [*Technological Laboratory of Uruguay*] (LA)
Latv............ Latvian
Latvenergo ... Administration of Power System Management of the Sovnarkhoz of the Latvian SSR (RU)
LatvSSR..... Latvian Soviet Socialist Republic (RU)
latysh .... Latvian (RU)
LAU .... Lamu [*Kenya*] [*Airport symbol*] (OAG)
LAU .... Lineas Aereas Suramericanas Ltd. [*Colombia*] [*ICAO designator*] (FAAC)
LAUDA ..... Laboratorios Unidos de America SA [*Argentina*] (DSCA)
Laug.......... Laugen [*Leaching*] [*German*] (GCA)
laus............ Lauseessa [*In a Sentence*] [*Finland*]
lav.............. Lava [*Field*] [*Topography*] (RU)
lav............. Lavalliere [*Russet-Colored*] [*Publishing*] [*French*]
LAV .... Law Association of Victoria [*Australia*]
LAV .... Legislative Assembly of Victoria [*Australia*]
LAV .... Library Association of Victoria [*Australia*] (ADA)
LAV .... Linea Aeropostal Venezolana [*Venezuela*] [*ICAO designator*] (FAAC)
lavall .... Lavalliere [*Russet-Colored*] [*Publishing*] [*French*]
LAVD .... Laboratory of High Pressures and Temperatures (of the Academy of Sciences, USSR) (RU)
LAVE........ Association Vocanologique Europeenne [*European Volcanological Association*] [*Paris, France*] (EAIO)
lavo........... Lager Algemeen Voortgezet Onderwijs [*Benelux*] (BAS)
LAVOLTAIQUE ... Union pour le Commerce et l'Industrie en Haute-Volta
lavoraz....... Lavorazione [*Craftsmanship*] [*Publishing*] [*Italian*]
law............. Laatst Aangehaaldwerk [*Benelux*] (BAS)
LAW .... Land Authority for Wales (GEA)
LAW .... Leipziger Arzneimittelwerk (VEB) [*Leipzig Pharmaceutical Works (VEB)*] (EG)
LAW .... Liberian Association of Writers (EAIO)
LAW .... Link Airways of Australia [*Australia*] [*ICAO designator*] (FAAC)
LAWA .... Legislative Assembly of Western Australia
LAWAN .... Labour Writers Association of Nigeria
LAWASIA ... Law Association for Asia and the Pacific [*Australia*] (EAIO)
LAWC .... Labor Anti-War Committee [*Australia*]
LAWC .... Land Air Warfare Committee [*Military*]
Lax............ Laxans [*Laxative*] [*German*] (GCA)
LAY .... Ladysmith [*South Africa*] [*Airport symbol*] (OAG)

LAY .... Leningrad Arctic School (RU)
LAYDER ... Laminacion y Derivados Ltda. [*Colombia*] (COL)
LAZ .... Balkan-Bulgarian Airlines [*ICAO designator*] (FAAC)
LAZ .... Bom Jesus Da Lapa [*Brazil*] [*Airport symbol*] (OAG)
LAZ .... Line Equipment Room (RU)
LAZ .... L'vov Bus Plant (RU)
LB .... Besluit op de Loonbelasting [*Benelux*] (BAS)
L/B............. Ladingsbrief [*Bill of Lading*] [*Afrikaans*]
lb .... Lambert (RU)
LB .... Landolt-Boernstein Physikalisch-Chemische Tabellen [*Landolt-Boernstein Tables*] [*German*] (GCA)
LB .... Lastentarhanopettajaliitto Barntradgardslararforbundet [*Association of Kindergarten Teachers*] [*Finland*] (EAIO)
LB .... Lebanon [*ANSI two-letter standard code*] (CNC)
LB .... Lecteur de Bande [*French*] (ADPT)
LB .... Lenin Library [*State Library of the USSR Imeni V. I. Lenin*] (RU)
Lb............... Libelle [*Liquid Level*] [*German*] (GCA)
LB .... Liberalized Imports [*Former Yugoslavia*] (IMH)
LB .... Lichtbild [*Photograph*] [*German*] (GCA)
LB .... Line Battery (RU)
LB .... Ljubljanska Banka [*Bank*] [*Former Yugoslavia*]
LB .... Lochband [*German*] (ADPT)
LB .... Lovci-Bombarderi [*Fighter Bombers*] (YU)
LB .... Pond [*Pound*] [*Afrikaans*]
lb .... Port, Larboard (RU)
lb .... Pound (EECI)
LB .... Ski Battalion (RU)
LBA .... Legiao Brasileira de Assistencia [*Brazilian Welfare Legion*] (LA)
LBA .... Lehrerbildungsanstalt [*Teacher Training College*] [*German*]
LBA .... Liberia Bankers' Association
LBA .... Licensed Buying Agent
LBA .... Light Bombardment Aviation (RU)
LBA .... Limas Bulgarian Airlines [*ICAO designator*] (FAAC)
LBA .... Lovacko-Bombarderska Avijacija [*Fighter-Bomber Aviation*] (YU)
LBA .... Luftfahrt Bundesamt [*German Civil Aviation Authority*] (PDAA)
lbak........... Light Bombardment Aviation Wing (BU)
LBAN .... L'vov Library of the Academy of Sciences, UkrSSR (RU)
LBAP........ Light Bomber Regiment (RU)
LBA-SPSR ... Ludwig Boltzmann Association - Austrian Society for the Promotion of Scientific Research [*Austria*] (EAIO)
LBat.......... Dummy Battery (RU)
LBB........... Light Bomber Brigade (RU)
LBBG........ Burgas [*Bulgaria*] [*ICAO location identifier*] (ICLI)
LBC........... Albanian Airline Co. [*ICAO designator*] (FAAC)
LBC........... Lae Builders & Contractors Ltd. [*Papua New Guinea*]
LBC........... Landelijke Bedienden Centrale [*Benelux*] (BAS)
LBC........... Landelijke Bibliotheek-Centrale [*Netherlands*]
LBC........... Law Book Co. [*Australia*]
LBC........... Les Bois du Cameroun
LBC........... Les Bois du Congo
LBC........... Local Branch Committee [*Mauritius*] (AF)
LB Co........ Law Book Co. [*Australia*]
LBD.......... Les Bois Debites
LBD .... Lidove Bytove Druzstvo [*People's Apartment Cooperative*] (CZ)
LBDI........ Liberian Bank for Development and Investment (GEA)
LBEPO..... Light Armored Train (RU)
LBF.......... Lunds Botaniska Foerening [*Sweden*] (SLS)
LBFC .... Lesotho Building Finance Corp. (EY)
LBGO .... Gorna Orechovitsa [*Bulgaria*] [*ICAO location identifier*] (ICLI)
LBH .... Laker Airways (Bahamas) Ltd. [*ICAO designator*] (FAAC)
LBH .... Land-, Bau-, und Holzbearbeitungsmaschinen [*Agricultural, Construction, and Woodworking Machines*] (EG)
LBH .... Sydney [*Australia*] [*Airport symbol*] (OAG)
LBH .... Yayasan Lembaga Bantuan Hukum Indonesia [*Indonesian Legal Aid Foundation*] (EAIO)
LBI .... Albi [*France*] [*Airport symbol*] (OAG)
LBI .... Lloyds Bank International (ADA)
LBI .... Lysaght Brownbuilt Industries [*Australia*] (ADA)
LBIDI .... Liberian Bank for Industrial Development and Investment (AF)
LBK .... Landbaukombinat [*Rural Construction Combine*] (EG)
LBK .... Line Battery Switch (RU)
LBKM........ Lembaga Beasiswa Kenangan Maulud [*Mohammad's Birth Memorial Scholarship Foundation*] (ML)
LBL........... Limited Broadcasting License [*Australia*]
LBMA....... London Bullion Market Association
LBN .... Lebanon [*ANSI three-letter standard code*] (CNC)
LBN .... Lembaga Biologi Nasional [*National Biological Institute*] [*Indonesian*] (ARC)
LBNM .... Stichting Landbouwkundig Bureau van de Nederlandse Meststoffenindustrie [*Foundation Agricultural Bureau of the Netherlands Fertilizer Industry*] (ARC)
LBO .... Laboratorium voor Bloembollenonderzoek Flower Bulb Research Center [*Netherlands*] (DSCA)

LBP .... Bayerische Landesanstalt fuer Bodenkultur und Pflanzenbau [*Bavarian State Institute for Soil Cultivation and Plant Production*] (ARC)
LBP .... Bomb Run (RU)
LBPD .... Plovdiv [*Bulgaria*] [*ICAO location identifier*] (ICLI)
LBPJ .... Lembaga Bandaran Petaling Jaya [*Petaling Jaya Municipal Institute*] (ML)
LBQ .... Lambarene [*Gabon*] [*Airport symbol*] (OAG)
LBR .... Liberia [*ANSI three-letter standard code*] (CNC)
LBr .... Ski Brigade (RU)
LBRS .... Rousse [*Bulgaria*] [*ICAO location identifier*] (ICLI)
LBS .... Labasa [*Fiji*] [*Airport symbol*] (OAG)
LBS .... Les Bois de Sassandra
lbs .... Libras [*Pounds*] [*Spanish*]
LBS .... Libyan Broadcasting Service
lbs............ Lineman Battalion (RU)
LBS .... Lochstreifenbetriebssystem [*German*] (ADPT)
LBS .... Lopende Betaalstelsel [*Pay as You Earn*] [*Afrikaans*]
LBSA .... Libraries Board of South Australia
LBSF........ Sofia [*Bulgaria*] [*ICAO location identifier*] (ICLI)
LBSV .... Lineman Battalion (RU)
LBSZ .... Stara Zagora [*Bulgaria*] [*ICAO location identifier*] (ICLI)
LBT........... Air Liberte Tunisie [*Tunisia*] [*ICAO designator*] (FAAC)
LBTP .... Laboratoire du Batiment et des Travaux Publics
LBU .... Course-Line Deviation (RU)
LBU .... Labuan [*Malaysia*] [*Airport symbol*] (OAG)
LBV........... Legiao de Boa Vontade [*Legion of Good Will*] [*Brazil*]
LBV........... Libreville [*Gabon*] [*Airport symbol*] (OAG)
LBV........... Traveling-Wave Tube [*Radio*] (BU)
LBVM....... Traveling-Wave Magnetron-Type Tube (RU)
LBVP .... Le Bons Vins Pennone
LBW .... Long Bawan [*Indonesia*] [*Airport symbol*] (OAG)
LBWA .... Library Board of Western Australia
LBWN ...... Varna [*Bulgaria*] [*ICAO location identifier*] (ICLI)
LBY .... Libya [*ANSI three-letter standard code*] (CNC)
LBZ........... Leitstelle fuer Baumaschinenersatzteile und -Zubehoer [*Control Office for Construction Machine Spare Parts and Accessories*] (EG)
LC .... League of Communists [*Former Yugoslavia*]
LC .... Legislative Council
L/C........... Lettera di Credito [*Letter of Credit*] [*Italian*] [*Business term*]
LC .... Letter of Credit
LC .... Lettre de Credit [*Letter of Credit*] [*Business term*] [*French*]
l/c............ Leur Compte [*Their Account*] [*French*]
LC .... Leyland Cars [*Leyland Daf Ltd.*]
LC .... Liberalt Centrum [*Liberal Center*] [*Denmark*] [*Political party*] (PPE)
LC .... Libertarisch Centrum [*Belgium*] (EAIO)
lc.............. Lieue Carree [*Square League*] [*French*]
LC .... Liga Comunista [*Communist League*] [*Spanish*] (WER)
LC .... Loi Communale [*French*] (BAS)
LC .... Lokalisierungscode [*German*] (ADPT)
LC .... Lotta Continua [*Continuous Struggle*] [*Italy*] [*Political party*] (PPE)
LC .... Lumiere Centrale [*On cartridge bags*] [*Military*] [*French*] (MTD)
LC .... St. Lucia [*ANSI two-letter standard code*] (CNC)
LCA .... Laboratoire Central d'Armement [*Central Armament Laboratory*] [*French*]
LCA .... Landscape Contractors Association [*Australia*]
LCA .... Larnaca [*Cyprus*] [*Airport symbol*] (OAG)
LCA .... Law Consumers' Association [*Australia*]
LCA .... Law Council of Australia
LCA .... Les Comptoirs Africains
LCA .... Licensed Clubs Association of Australia
LCA .... Liga Comunista Armada [*Armed Communist League*] [*Mexico*] (LA)
LCA .... Local Coal Authority [*Australia*]
LCA .... Lussazione Congenita dell'Anca [*Congenital Hip Dislocation*] [*Italian*] [*Medicine*]
LCA .... Lutheran Church of Australia
LCA .... St. Lucia [*ANSI three-letter standard code*] (CNC)
LCAA........ Licensed Clubs Association of Australia
LCAACT ... Licensed Clubs Association of the Australian Capital Territory
LCACT ...... Law Council of the Australian Capital Territory
LCAIA ...... Licentiate of the Customs Agents Institute of Australia (ADA)
LCANSW .. Landscape Contractors' Association of New South Wales [*Australia*]
LCANSW .. Licensed Clubs Association of New South Wales [*Australia*]
LC Art........ Lois Coordonnees sur les Societes Commerciales, Article [*French*] (BAS)
LCASA ...... Licensed Clubs Association of South Australia
LCAT........ Licensed Clubs Association of Tasmania [*Australia*]
LCAT........ Lifts and Cranes Appeals Tribunal [*Australia*]
LCATC ...... Livingstonia Central African Trading Company Ltd.

LCAUE...... Liaison Committee of the Architects of United Europe [*EC*] (ECED)
LCAV........ Landscape Contractors Association of Victoria [*Australia*]
LCAV........ Licensed Clubs Association of Victoria [*Australia*]
LCB........... Liefdezusters van de H. Carolus Borromeus [*Sisters of Charity of St. Charles Borromeo - SCSCB*] (EAIO)
LCBC........ Lake Chad Basin Commission (ASF)
LCC........... Lagos City Council
LCC........... Land Conservation Council of New South Wales [*Australia*]
LCC........... Legacy Coordinating Council [*Australia*]
LCC........... Liberia Chamber of Commerce
LCC........... Liberian Council of Churches
LCC........... Libraries Consultative Committee [*Australia*]
LCC........... Libraries Copyright Committee [*Australia*]
LCC........... Logistics Coordination Center [*NATO*]
LCCA........ Light Car Club of Australia
LCCC........ Nicosia [*Cyprus*] [*ICAO location identifier*] (ICLI)
LCCI .... Lagos Chamber of Commerce and Industry [*Nigeria*]
LCCI .... Lusaka Chamber of Commerce and Industry [*Zambia*]
LCCLC ...... Laboratorul Central de Cercetari Lacuri si Cerneluri [*Central Laboratory for Research on Varnishes and Inks*] (RO)
LCCNC...... Lois Coordonnees Relatives a la Contribution Nationale de Crise [*French*] (BAS)
LCCO .... Landing Craft Control Officer [*Military*]
LCCP........ Landing Craft Control Primary [*Military*]
LCC-PDR .. League of Communists of Croatia - Party of Democratic Reform [*Political party*]
LCCS .... Laboratorul Central de Cercetari Stiintifice [*Central Laboratory for Scientific Research*] (RO)
LCD .... Louis Trichardt [*South Africa*] [*Airport symbol*] (OAG)
LCDB........ Lois Coordonnees Relatives a la Taxe d'Ouverture sur les Debits de Boissons [*French*] (BAS)
LCDDH ..... Ligue Congolaise pour la Defense des Droits de l'Homme
Lcdo .... Licenciado [*Licensed*] [*Spanish*]
LCE........... La Ceiba [*Honduras*] [*Airport symbol*] (OAG)
LCE........... Liga Comunista Espartaca [*Spartacus Communist League*] [*Mexico*] (LA)
LCEBM ..... Liaison Committee of European Bicycle Manufacturers [*Belgium*] (EAIO)
LCEECSTI ... Liaison Committee of the European Economic Community Steel Tube Industry [*Defunct*] (EAIO)
LCEMM.... Liaison Committee of European Motorcycle Manufacturers [*Belgium*] (EAIO)
LCFA .... Librarians' Christian Fellowship of Australia
LCFTU ...... Lesotho Congress of Free Trade Unions (EAIO)
LCG .... La Coruna [*Spain*] [*Airport symbol*] (OAG)
LCG .... Lalupate Cultural Group of Nepal
LCG .... Letzeburger Chrestleche Gewerkschaftsbund [*Benelux*] (BAS)
LCH........... Dachverband Schweizer Lehrerinnen und Lehrer [*Swiss Teachers Federtion*] (EAIO)
LCh .... Poor Audibility (BU)
LCHF......... Laboratoire Centrale d'Hydraulique de France
LCHQ........ Local Command Headquarters [*NATO*] (NATG)
LCHS........ Lund Committee on Habitat and Development Studies [*Sweden*] (EAS)
LCI............ Leerplancommissie Cursorisch Informatica-Onderwijs [*Netherlands*]
LCI............ Liga Comunista Internacionalista [*International Communist League*] [*Portugal*] [*Political party*] (PPE)
LCIA .... London Court of International Arbitration
LCIE .... Laboratoire Central des Industries Electriques [*Electrical Industries Central Laboratory*] [*French*]
LCIR .... Lois Coordonnees Relatives aux Impots sur les Revenus [*French*] (BAS)
LCL............ Labor Congress of Liberia
LCL............ Liberal Country League [*Australia*] (BARN)
LCLK .... Larnaca [*Cyprus*] [*ICAO location identifier*] (ICLI)
LCL(SAust) ... Liberal and Country League (South Australia)
LCL(WA) .. Liberal and Country League (Western Australia)
LCM .... Landsbond der Christelijke Mutualiteiten [*Belgium*] (EAIO)
LCM .... Libertarian Center Netherlands [*Belgium*] (EAIO)
LCMCFC .. Liaison Committee for Mediterranean Citrus Fruit Culture [*See also CLAM*] [*Madrid, Spain*] (EAIO)
LCM-PDR ... League of Communists of Macedonia - Party for Democratic Reform [*Political party*]
LC-MY ...... League of Communists - Movement for Yugoslavia [*Political party*]
LCN .... Lineas Aereas Canarias SA [*Spain*] [*ICAO designator*] (FAAC)
LCNC .... Nicosia [*Cyprus*] [*ICAO location identifier*] (ICLI)
LC NGO-EC ... Liaison Committee of Development Non-Governmental Organizations to the European Communities [*Belgium*] (EAIO)
LCNN .... Land Commander, North Norway [*NATO*] (NATG)
LCNS........ Legislative Council for National Security [*South Korea*] (FEA)
LCNSW..... Labor Council of New South Wales [*Australia*]
LCNSW..... Legislative Council of New South Wales [*Australia*]

LCO .... Landbouwcrisis Organisatie [*Benelux*] (BAS)
LCO .... Linea Aerea del Cobre Ltda. [*Chile*] [*ICAO designator*] (FAAC)
LCom .... Lotta Comunista [*Communist Struggle*] [*Italian*] (WER)
L Comm ..... Loi Communale [*French*] (BAS)
L Const...... Loi Constitutionnelle [*France*] (FLAF)
L Coord ...... Lois Coordonnees [*French*] (BAS)
LCP........... League of Coloured Peoples
LCP............ Lesotho Congress Party (AF)
LCP............ Liberal-Country Party [*Australia*] (ADA)
LCP............ Loi de Construction des Programmes [*Program Construction Law*] [*French*] (ADPT)
LCPC .... Laboratoire Central des Ponts et Chaussees [*Main Highway Department Laboratory*] [*French*] (WER)
LCPE .... Leux & Cie. - Plomberie Electricite
LCPH .... Paphos [*Cyprus*] [*ICAO location identifier*] (ICLI)
LCPR .... Liga Comunista Partidaria Reconstrutiva [*Communist League for the Reconstruction of the Communist Party*] [*Portuguese*] (WER)
LCPR .... Liga para a Construcao do Partido Revolucionario [*League for Construction of the Revolutionary Party*] [*Portuguese*] (WER)
LCR........... Laboratoire Central de Recherches [*French*] (MCD)
L/CR.......... Lettre de Credit [*Letter of Credit*] [*French*]
LCR........... Libyan Arab Company for Air Cargo [*ICAO designator*] (FAAC)
LCR........... Liga Comunista Revolucionaria [*Revolutionary Communist League*] [*Spanish*] (WER)
LCR........... Ligue Communiste Revolutionnaire [*Revolutionary Communist League*] [*France*] [*Political party*] (PPW)
LCRA........ Akrotiri [*Cyprus*] [*ICAO location identifier*] (ICLI)
LCRI .... Lake Chad Research Institute [*Nigeria*] (AF)
LCRI .... Lucky Central Research Institute [*South Korean*] [*Research center*] (IRC)
LCRO .... Episkopi [*Cyprus*] [*ICAO location identifier*] (ICLI)
LCRR........ Nicosia [*Cyprus*] [*ICAO location identifier*] (ICLI)
LCRSMEEC ... Liaison Committee of the Rice Starch Manufacturers of the EEC [*Belgium*] (EAIO)
LCS........... Liberian Cartographic Service (PDAA)
LCS........... Library Catalogue System [*Australia*]
LCS........... Logique de Conception des Systemes [*French*] (ADPT)
LCS........... Lois Coordonnees sur les Societes Commerciales [*French*] (BAS)
LCSA .... Legislative Council of South Australia
LCSA .... Lotteries Commission of South Australia
LCsM........ Liga Ceskoslovenskych Motoristu [*Czechoslovak Motoring Club*] (CZ)
LCS-PDR .. League of Communists of Slovenia - Party of Democratic Reform [*Political party*]
LCSS.......... Laboratorio Central del Servicio de Sismologia
LCT........... Laboratoire Central de Telecommunications [*Central Telecommunications Laboratory*] [*French*] (WER)
LCT........... Laboratorio Central de Telecomunicaciones [*Central Telecommunications Laboratory*] [*Cuba*] (LA)
LCT........... Labour Congress of Thailand
LCT........... Legislative Council of Tasmania [*Australia*]
LCT........... Licensing Commission of Tasmania [*Australia*]
LCT........... Ligue Communiste des Travailleurs [*Communist Workers' League*] [*Senegal*] [*Political party*] (PPW)
LCTC......... Lagos City Transport Corporation
LCTES...... Lefke Cengiz Topel Erkek Sanat Enstitusu [*Lefke (Lefka) Cengiz Topel Men's Trade Institute*] [*Turkish Cypriot*] (GC)
LCTS........ Lagos City Transport Service
LCTU........ Libyan Confederation of Trade Unions
LCTU........ Luxembourg Confederation of Christian Trade Unions (EAIO)
LCuP......... Phosphorkupferlot [*Phosphorous-Copper Solder*] [*German*] (GCA)
LCV .... Legislative Council of Victoria [*Australia*]
LCV .... Library Council of Victoria [*Australia*] (ADA)
LCVP........ Landing Craft, Vehicle, Personnel [*Navy symbol*] [*NATO*]
LCW .... Lesotho Council of Workers
LCWA .... Legislative Council of Western Australia
LCWA .... Lotteries Commission of Western Australia
LCWHN.... Latin American and Caribbean Women's Health Network (EAIO)
LCY........... League of Communists of Yugoslavia [*Savez Komunista Jugoslavije*] [*Political party*] (PPW)
ld .... File Sheet, Dossier Sheet (RU)
LD .... Laboratorio de Dosimetria [*Rio De Janeiro, Brazil*] (LAA)
LD .... Lae Druk [*Afrikaans*]
LD .... Laiki Dimokratia [*or Laokratiki Dimokratia*] [*People's Republic*] (GC)
Ld .... Land [*German*] (GCA)
LD .... Landdros [*Magistrate*] [*Afrikaans*]
ld .... Lasd [*See, Refer To*] (HU)
LD .... Leader [*Navy*] (RU)
LD .... Lecteur de Documents [*Document Reader*] [*French*] (ADPT)
LD .... Lekarnicky Dum [*Pharmacists' Building*] (CZ)

LD .... Lethal Dose (RU)
LD .... Libyan Dinar [*Monetary unit*] (BJA)
LD .... Licence de Docteur en Medecine [*French*]
LD .... Licni Dohodak [*Individual Income*] (YU)
LD .... Lidova Demokracie [*People's Democracy (Also name of a newspaper)*] (CZ)
LD .... Literarni Duvernik [*Book Agent*] (CZ)
LD .... Ljubljanski Dnevnik [*Ljubljana Daily*] [*A newspaper*] (YU)
LDA .... Lahore Development Authority [*Pakistan*] (EY)
LDA .... Land Development Authority [*Fijian*] (GEA)
LDA .... Lauda Air [*Austria*] [*ICAO designator*] (FAAC)
LDA .... Lead Development Association [*British*] (EAIO)
Lda .... Licenciada [*Licentiate*] [*Portuguese*]
Lda .... Limitada [*Limited*] [*Spanish*]
lda .... Limitada [*Limited*] [*Portuguese*] (CED)
LDA .... Livestock Development Agency
LDA .... Local Development Association [*or Agency*] [*Yemen Arab Republic*] (IMH)
LDAN .... Engine Laboratory of the Academy of Sciences, USSR (RU)
LDB .... Londrina [*Brazil*] [*Airport symbol*] (OAG)
LDC .... Labor Day Committee [*Australia*]
LDC .... Law Development Centre
LDC .... Less Developed Country
LDC .... Liberian Development Corporation
LDC .... Lindeman Island [*Australia*] [*Airport symbol*]
LDC .... Lus Development Corp. [*Papua New Guinea*]
LDCA .... Land Development Contractors' Association [*Australia*]
LDE .... Laiki Dimokratiki Enotita (Enotis) [*Popular Democratic Unity*] (GC)
Lde .... Lande [*Heath, Moor*] [*Military map abbreviation World War I*] [*French*] (MTD)
LDE .... Lineas Aereas del Estado [*Argentina*] [*ICAO designator*] (FAAC)
LDE .... Locomotive Diesel si Electrice [*Diesel and Electric Locomotives*] (RO)
LDE .... Lourdes/Tarbes [*France*] [*Airport symbol*] (OAG)
LDEC........ Librarians of Distance Education Centres [*Australia*]
L de C .... Lucha de Clases [*Class Struggle*] [*Spanish*] (WER)
L de S .... Latinoamericana de Seguros SA [*Colombia*] (COL)
LDF........... Landesverband der Dolmetscher und Fremdsprachenlehrer [*National Association of Interpreters and Foreign Language Teachers*]
LDFK........ Leningrad House of Physical Culture (RU)
LDFL........ Lusaka and District Football League
Ldg .... Ladung [*Charge*] [*German*] (GCA)
LDG .... Laiki Dimokratia Germanias [*German Democratic Republic*] (GC)
LDH.......... Ligue des Droits de l'Homme [*France*]
LDH.......... Lord Howe Island [*Australia*] [*Airport symbol*] (OAG)
LDHR....... League for the Defense of Human Rights in Romania (EAIO)
LDHRR ..... League for the Defense of Human Rights in Romania [*Paris, France*] (EAIO)
LDI .... Lauda Air [*Italy*] [*ICAO designator*] (FAAC)
LDI .... Lindi [*Tanzania*] [*Airport symbol*] (OAG)
LDK .... Lodzki Dom Kultury [*Lodz Social and Recreation Club*] [*Poland*]
LDK .... Sawmilling and Woodworking Kombinat (RU)
LDKhVD ... Leningrad House of Children's Art Education (RU)
LDLN .... Lumieres dans la Nuit [*Unidentified flying objects*] [*French*]
LDMC .... Livestock Development and Marketing Corporation [*Myanmar*] (DS)
LD-MPT.... Ligue Democratique - Mouvement pour le Parti des Travailleurs [*Democratic League - Movement for the Workers' Party*] [*Senegal*] [*Political party*] (PPW)
LDN .... Lamidanda [*Nepal*] [*Airport symbol*] (OAG)
Ldnpr .... Ladenpreis [*List Price*] [*German*]
LDNTP...... Leningrad House of Scientific and Technical Propaganda (RU)
LDO .... Ladouanie [*Suriname*] [*Airport symbol*] (OAG)
LDO .... Leningrad House of Officers Imeni S. M. Kirov (RU)
LDO .... Lesni Druzstvo Obce [*Communal Forest Cooperative*] (CZ)
Ldo .... Licenciado [*One Who Is Licensed in a Profession*] [*Spanish*]
Ldo .... Licenciado [*Licentiate*] [*Portuguese*]
ldo .... Limitado [*Limited*] [*Portuguese*]
LDOK .... Sawmilling and Woodworking Kombinat (RU)
LDP .... Laban ng Demokratikong Pilipino [*Democratic Filipino's Struggle*] [*Political party*]
LDP .... Landed Duty Paid [*Military*]
LDP .... League for Democracy and Peace [*Myanmar*] [*Political party*] (EY)
LDP .... Leningrad Palace of Pioneers Imeni A. A. Zhdanov (RU)
LDP .... Letecky Dopravni Pluk [*Air Transport Regiment*] (CZ)
LDP .... Liberal Democratic Party [*Slovenia*] [*Political party*] (EY)
LDP .... Liberal-Democratic Party of Japan [*Jiyu-Minshuto*] [*Political party*] (PPW)
LDP .... Liberal Demokratische Partei [*Liberal Democratic Party*] [*Germany*] [*Political party*] (PPE)

LDP .... Liberal'no-Demokraticheskaya Partiya [*Liberal Democratic Party*] [*Political party*] [*Former USSR*]   (EAIO)

LDP .... Lietuviy Demokraty Partija [*Lithuanian Democratic Party*] [*Political party*]   (PPE)

LdP .... Ljudska Pravica [*The People's Rights*] [*A daily Ljubljana*]   (YU)

LdP-B .... Ljudska Pravica - Borba [*The People's Rights - Struggle*] [*A daily Ljubljana*]   (YU)

LDPD .... Liberal-Demokratische Partei Deutschlands [*Liberal Democratic Party of Germany*] [*Political party*]   (PPW)

LDPG .... Liberal Democratic Party of Germany [*German People's Republic*]   (RU)

LdProsv ...... Ljudska Prosveta [*The People's Education*] [*A periodical Ljubljana*]   (YU)

LDR .... Aero Lider SA de CV [*Mexico*] [*ICAO designator*]   (FAAC)

Ldr .... Leder [*Leather*] [*German*]

ldr .... Leder [*Leather*] [*Netherlands*]

LDR .... Liberal, Democratic and Reformist Group [*European Parliament*] [*Belgium*]   (EAIO)

LDR .... Liberal, Democratic, and Reformist Group [*European political movement*]   (ECON)

Ldrb .... Lederband [*Leather Binding*] [*Publishing*] [*German*]

Ldrbd .... Lederband [*Leather Binding*] [*Publishing*] [*German*]

Ldrecke ...... Lederecke [*Leather Corner*] [*Publishing*] [*German*]

LDRG .... Liberal, Democratic and Reformist Group [*See also GLDR*]   (EAIO)

LDRN .... Ligue de Defense de la Race Negre

Ldrr .... Lederruecken [*Leather Back*] [*Publishing*] [*German*]

ldrryg .... Laederryg [*Leather Back*] [*Publishing Danish/Norwegian*]

LDRTA ...... Long Distance Road Transport Association of Australia   (ADA)

ldrtitelfelt ... Laedertitelfelt [*Leather Title Piece*] [*Publishing Danish/Norwegian*]

LDS .... Landesamt fuer Datenverarbeitung und Statistik [*Regional Bureau for Data Processing & Statistics*] [*German*]   (ADPT)

LDS .... Letecke Dispecerske Stanoviste [*Aviation (or Aircraft) Dispatch Center*]   (CZ)

LDS .... Lidove Demokraticke Staty [*The People's Democratic Countries*]   (CZ)

LDS .... Lietuvos Darbininku Sajunga [*Lithuania*]   (EAIO)

LDSA .... Leningrad House of the Soviet Army   (RU)

LDSK .... Sawmilling and House Construction Kombinat   (RU)

LDSOO ..... Leningrad Voluntary Sports Society of Hunters   (RU)

LDSP .... Lietuvos Socialdemokratu Partija [*Social Democratic Party of Lithuania*] [*Political party*]   (EAIO)

LDTM .... Leningrad House of Machinery-Manufacturing Technology   (RU)

LDTU .... Leningrad House of Technical Training   (RU)

LDU .... Lahad Datu [*Malaysia*] [*Airport symbol*]   (OAG)

LdU .... Landesring der Unabhaengigen [*Independent Party*] [*Switzerland*] [*Political party*]   (PPE)

LDU .... Leningrad House of Scientists Imeni A. M. Gor'kiy   (RU)

LDU .... Lenjingradsko Drustvo Univerziteta [*Leningrad Society of Universities*] [*Russian*]   (YU)

LDU .... Liberal and Democratic Union [*Australia*]   (ADA)

LDV .... Linguistische Datenverarbeitung [*Linguistic Data Processing*] [*German*]   (ADPT)

Ldw .... Landwirt [*or Landwirtschaft*] [*Farmer or Farming*] [*German*]

LDY .... Laundry

l dz .... Liczba Dziennika [*Number on the Agenda*] [*Poland*]

LDZ .... Logarithmic Attenuation Ratio   (RU)

LE .... Egyptian Pound   (ME)

LE .... Laborator pro Elektrotechniku [*Electrical Engineering Laboratory (of the Czechoslovak Academy of Sciences)*]   (CZ)

LE .... Laiki Exousia [*Popular Power*] [*Communist organization*] [*Greek*]   (GC)

Le .... Laje [*Flat-Topped Rock*] [*Portuguese*]   (NAU)

LE .... Lecce [*Car registration plates*] [*Italian*]

LE .... Lehreinheit [*German*]   (ADPT)

LE .... Leitungsanschlusseinheit [*German*]   (ADPT)

LE .... Leone [*Monetary unit*] [*Sierra Leone*]

LE .... Licence d'Enseignement [*Academic qualification*] [*French*]

LE .... Lineal Element, Linear Element   (RU)

LE .... Loero [*Horsepower*]   (HU)

LE .... Logarithmic Element   (RU)

LEA .... Laboratorio de Engenharia de Angola   (PDAA)

LEA .... Laiki Epanastatiki Andistasi [*Popular Revolutionary Resistance*] [*Greek*]   (GC)

LEA .... Lead Air Jet Service [*France*] [*ICAO designator*]   (FAAC)

LEA .... Learmonth [*Australia*] [*Airport symbol*]   (OAG)

LEA .... Liga Ecuatoriana Anti-Tuberculosa [*Ecuadorean League Against Tuberculosis*]   (LA)

LEA .... Lucha Espanola Antimarxista [*Spanish Anti-Marxist Struggle*]   (WER)

LEAB .... Albacete [*Spain*] [*ICAO location identifier*]   (ICLI)

LEAC .... Madrid [*Spain*] [*ICAO location identifier*]   (ICLI)

LEAD .... Laboratoire d'Electronique et d'Informatique Dauphinois [*Laboratory of Electronics and Information Techniques*] [*France*]   (IRC)

LEAD .... Laboratoires d'Electronique et d'Automatique Dauphinois [*France*]   (PDAA)

LEAD .... Leadership for Environment and Development Institute [*Non-profit organization*]   (ECON)

LEADR ...... Lawyers Engaged in Alternative Dispute Resolution [*Australia*] [*An association*]

LEAF .... Ladies Environmentally Aware of Forests [*Australia*]

LEAF .... Living Environment Action Front [*South Africa*]   (AA)

LEAL .... Alicante [*Spain*] [*ICAO location identifier*]   (ICLI)

LEAM .... Almeria [*Spain*] [*ICAO location identifier*]   (ICLI)

LEAN .... Law Enforcement Action Network [*Australia*]

LEANORD ... Electronics and Automation Laboratory of Northern France [*Research center*]   (IRC)

LEANORD ... Laboratoire d'Electronique et d'Automatique du Nord de la France [*Electronics and Automation Laboratory of Northern France*]   (IRC)

LEAO .... Almagro [*Spain*] [*ICAO location identifier*]   (ICLI)

leao .... Lager Economisch en Administratief Onderwijs [*Benelux*]   (BAS)

LEAP .... Lifestyles for Elite Athletes Programme [*Australia*]

LEAP .... Loan and Educational Aid Programme

LEAS .... Aviles/Asturias [*Spain*] [*ICAO location identifier*]   (ICLI)

LEAS .... Laikos Ethnikos Apelevtherotikos Syndiasmos [*Popular National Liberation League*] [*Cyprus*]   (GC)

LEB .... Landesarbeitsgemeinschaft fuer Laendliche Erwachsenenbildung eV   (SLS)

LEB .... Lebap [*Turkmenistan*] [*ICAO designator*]   (FAAC)

LEBA .... Cordoba [*Spain*] [*ICAO location identifier*]   (ICLI)

LEBAKA .. Lebowa Bakeries [*South Africa*]

LEBAMA .. Le Batiment Mauritanien

LEBB .... Bilbao [*Spain*] [*ICAO location identifier*]   (ICLI)

LEBEN ...... Large European Bio-Energy Project [*Italy*]

lebensl .... Lebenslaenglich [*For Life*] [*German*]   (GCA)

Lebensl .... Lebenslauf [*Career*] [*German*]

LEBG .... Burgos [*Spain*] [*ICAO location identifier*]   (ICLI)

LEBL .... Barcelona [*Spain*] [*ICAO location identifier*]   (ICLI)

LEBR .... Bardenas Reales [*Spain*] [*ICAO location identifier*]   (ICLI)

LEBT .... Betera [*Spain*] [*ICAO location identifier*]   (ICLI)

LEBZ .... Badajoz/Talavera La Real [*Spain*] [*ICAO location identifier*]   (ICLI)

LEC .... Land and Environment Court [*New South Wales, Australia*]

LEC .... Lesotho Evangelical Church

LEC .... Liberia Electricity Corporation

LEC .... Life Education Centre [*Australia*]

LECA .... Madrid [*Spain*] [*ICAO location identifier*]   (ICLI)

LECB .... Barcelona [*Spain*] [*ICAO location identifier*]   (ICLI)

LECE .... Ligue Europeenne de Cooperation Economique [*European League for Economic Cooperation*]

LECH .... Calamocha [*Spain*] [*ICAO location identifier*]   (ICLI)

lech .... Hospital, Clinic [*Topography*]   (RU)

Lechsanupr ... Medical and Sanitary Administration   (RU)

LECL .... Valencia [*Spain*] [*ICAO location identifier*]   (ICLI)

LECM .... Madrid [*Spain*] [*ICAO location identifier*]   (ICLI)

LEC(NSW) ... Land and Environment Court (New South Wales) [*Australia*]

LECO .... Ferme Experimentale d'Elevage de la Songolo

LECO .... La Coruna [*Spain*] [*ICAO location identifier*]   (ICLI)

LECO .... Librarie Evangelique au Congo

LECP .... Palma [*Spain*] [*ICAO location identifier*]   (ICLI)

LECS .... Sevilla [*Spain*] [*ICAO location identifier*]   (ICLI)

LECT .... League for the Exchange of Commonwealth Teachers   (EA)

Lect y V ..... Lectura y Vida [*A publication*]

LECUSA ... Lesotho Credit Union Scheme for Agriculture

LECV .... Colmenar Viejo [*Spain*] [*ICAO location identifier*]   (ICLI)

LED .... Icebreaker   (RU)

led .... Ice, Glacial   (RU)

led .... Leder [*Leather*] [*Netherlands*]

Led .... Leder [*Leather*] [*German*]

LED .... Leningrad [*Former USSR*] [*Airport symbol*]   (OAG)

LED .... Licht-Emittierende Diode [*German*]   (ADPT)

LED .... Local Employment Development [*Australia*]

LEDA .... Ley de Desarrollo Agropecuario [*Agricultural-Livestock Development Law*] [*Mexico*]   (LA)

LEDAC ...... Long Range Weapons Electronic Digital Computer [*Australia*]

LEDAS ...... Lebensmittel-Dispositions und Abrechnungssystem [*German*]   (ADPT)

LEDB .... Lagos Executive Development Board

Lederschl ... Lederschliesse [*Leather Clasp*] [*Publishing*] [*German*]

Ledflot .... Arctic Ocean Flotilla   (RU)

LEDI .... Local Employment Development Initiative [*Australia*]

LEDM .... Valladolid [*Spain*] [*ICAO location identifier*]   (ICLI)

ledn .... Glacier [*Topography*]   (RU)

LEDU .... Local Enterprise Development Unit [*Northern Ireland*]

LEE .... L'Equatoriale Electronique

LEEC .... Sevilla-El Copero Base [*Spain*] [*ICAO location identifier*]   (ICLI)
LEEE .... Madrid [*Spain*] [*ICAO location identifier*]   (ICLI)
LEEL .... Leningrad Experimental Electrotechnical Laboratory   (RU)
LEF .... Art's Left Front [*Literary group, 1923-1930*]   (RU)
LEF .... Landbouw-Egalisatiefonds [*Benelux*]   (BAS)
LEF .... Licentiate in Economics and Finance
LEF .... Lobby Europeen des Femmes [*European Women's Lobby*] [*Belgium*]   (EAIO)
LEF .... Logements Economiques et Familiaux [*France*]   (FLAF)
LEFI .... Leningrad Institute of Electrophysics   (RU)
leg .... Droit Legal [*French*]   (TPFD)
LEG .... General Lycee [*French*]
leg .... Legal   (TPFD)
Leg .... Legation [*French*]   (MTD)
Leg .... Legation [*German*]
leg .... Legatura [*Binding*] [*Publishing*] [*Italian*]
leg .... Legenyseg [*Enlisted Men, Privates*]   (HU)
leg .... Leger [*Slight*] [*Publishing*] [*French*]
Leg .... Legierung [*Alloy*] [*German*]   (GCA)
Leg .... Legislation [*French*]   (FLAF)
leg .... Legua [*League*] [*Portuguese*]
LEGA .... Granada/Armilla [*Spain*] [*ICAO location identifier*]   (ICLI)
legat .... Legatura [*Binding*] [*Publishing*] [*Italian*]
LEGCO ...... Legislative Council [*Hong Kong*]   (ECON)
LEGCO ...... Legislative Council [*Trade union*] [*Uganda*]
LEGE .... Gerona/Costa Brava [*Spain*] [*ICAO location identifier*]   (ICLI)
legf .... Legfelso [*or Legfobb*] [*Highest or Supreme*]   (HU)
Legf Bir ...... Legfelso Birosag [*Supreme Court*]   (HU)
Legf U ...... Legfobb Ugyeszseg [*Supreme Prosecutor's Office*]   (HU)
legg .... Leggero [*Slight*] [*Italian*]
Legg .... Legierungen [*Alloys*] [*German*]
leggerm ...... Leggermente [*Slightly*] [*Italian*]
Leggo .... Leggiero [*Light and Rapid*] [*Music*]
Legier .... Legierung [*Alloy*] [*German*]   (GCA)
legn .... Legislation
legos .... Legoltalmi [*Officer in Civil Air Defense Work*]   (HU)
LEGr .... Electric Cargo Winch   (RU)
LEGR .... Granada [*Spain*] [*ICAO location identifier*]   (ICLI)
Leg Rat ...... Legationsrat [*Embassy Attache*] [*German*]
legt .... Legerement [*Slightly*] [*Publishing*] [*French*]
LEGT .... Lycee d'Enseignement General et Technologique [*High School for General and Technical Studies*] [*French*]   (BARN)
LEGT .... Madrid/Getafe [*Spain*] [*ICAO location identifier*]   (ICLI)
LEGTIS ..... Lefkosa ve Kazasi Endustri ve Genel Turk Isciler Sendikasi [*Nicosia and District Industrial and Public Turkish Workers' Union*] [*Turkish Cypriot*]   (GC)
LEH .... Le Havre [*France*] [*Airport symbol*]   (OAG)
LEHC .... Huesca [*Spain*] [*ICAO location identifier*]   (ICLI)
LEHI .... Hinojosa Del Duque [*Spain*] [*ICAO location identifier*]   (ICLI)
Lehrauftr.... Lehrauftrag [*Appointment to a Professorship*] [*German*]   (GCA)
Lehrb .... Lehrbeauftragter [*Appointed Professorship*] [*German*]
Lehrb .... Lehrbuch [*Textbook*] [*German*]   (GCA)
Lehrg......... Lehrgang [*Course of Instruction*] [*German*]   (GCA)
Lehrkr .... Lehrkraft [*Teacher, Instructor*] [*German*]   (GCA)
leht .... Lehtori [*Finland*]
LEI .... Almeria [*Spain*] [*Airport symbol*]   (OAG)
LEI .... Landbouweconomisch Instituut [*Agricultural Economics Institute*]   (ARC)
LEI .... Legal Expense Insurance Ltd. [*Australia*]
lei .... Leicht [*Light*] [*German*]   (GCA)
Lei .... Leijona [*Record label*] [*Finland*]
LEI .... Local Employment Initiative [*Australia*]
LEIAC .... Livestock Exports Industry Advisory Committee [*Australia*]
LEIB .... Ibiza [*Spain*] [*ICAO location identifier*]   (ICLI)
leichtl .... Leichtloeslich [*Easily Soluble*] [*German*]
Leig .... Leichter Gueterzug [*Light Freight Train*]   (EG)
leik .... Leikillisesti [*Jocularly*] [*Finland*]
Leinw .... Leinwand [*Cloth*] [*Publishing*] [*German*]
Leinwbd ... Leinwandband [*Cloth Binding*] [*Publishing*] [*German*]
Le Is .... Leeward Islands   (BARN)
LEIS .... LeisureLine [*Footscray Institute of Technology Library*] [*Database*] [*Information service or system*]   (IID)
LEIS .... Leningrad Electrotechnical Institute of Communications Imeni M. A. Bonch-Bruyevich   (RU)
Leistungssteiger ... Leistungssteigerung [*Increase in Efficiency or Production*] [*German*]   (GCA)
Leitfaehigk .. Leitfaehigkeit [*Conductivity*] [*German*]   (GCA)
LEJ .... Leipzig [*Germany*] [*Airport symbol*]   (OAG)
LEJR .... Jerez [*Spain*] [*ICAO location identifier*]   (ICLI)
LEK........... Laiko Enotiko Komma [*Populist Union Party*] [*Greece*] [*Political party*]   (PPE)
lek .... Lecture   (BU)
lek .... Lekarz [*Physician*] [*Poland*]
lekarstv ...... Medicinal   (RU)
Lekoop .... Physicians' Cooperative   (BU)
Lekoopizdat ... Physicians' Cooperative Publishers   (BU)

LekPr .... Lekarski Pregled [*Physicians' Review*] [*A periodical*]   (BU)
LEKRA ...... Lembaga Kebudayaan Rakyat [*People's Institute for Culture*] [*Indonesia*]
Lekrastrest ... State Trust for the Cultivation and Procurement of Medicinal Plant Raw Materials   (RU)
LEKt .... Electric Whaling Winch   (RU)
Lekt........... Lektor [*Lecturer*] [*German*]   (GCA)
LEL........... Labour Educational League [*Australia*]
LEL........... Lake Evella [*Australia*] [*Airport symbol*]   (OAG)
LELC .... Murcia/San Javier [*Spain*] [*ICAO location identifier*]   (ICLI)
LELL .... Sabadell [*Spain*] [*ICAO location identifier*]   (ICLI)
LELM .... Leipzig Evangelical Lutheran Mission
LELN .... Leon [*Spain*] [*ICAO location identifier*]   (ICLI)
LELO .... Logrono [*Spain*] [*ICAO location identifier*]   (ICLI)
LELU........ Lugo [*Spain*] [*ICAO location identifier*]   (ICLI)
LEM .... Laboratory of Evolutionary Morphology (of the Academy of Sciences, USSR)   (RU)
LEM .... Laboratory of Experimental Morphogenesis   (RU)
LEM .... Laiki Etaireia Metaforon [*Popular Transport Company*] [*Cyprus*]   (GC)
LEMAC..... Local Government Ethnic Affairs Ministerial Council [*Australia*]
LEMB........ Laborator pro Elektronovou Mikroskopii v Biologii [*Laboratory of Electron Microscopy in Biology (of the Czechoslovak Academy of Sciences)*]   (CZ)
LEMC........ Local Emergency Management Committee [*New South Wales, Australia*]
LEMD .... Madrid/Barajas [*Spain*] [*ICAO location identifier*]   (ICLI)
LEMG .... Malaga [*Spain*] [*ICAO location identifier*]   (ICLI)
LEMH .... Mahon/Menorca [*Spain*] [*ICAO location identifier*]   (ICLI)
LEMHANNAS ... Lembaga Pertahanan Nasional [*National Defense Institute*]   (IN)
LEMI........ Leningrad Electromechanical Institute   (RU)
LEMIGAS ... Lemigas Documentation and Scientific Information Centre [*Indonesia Petroleum Institute*]
LEMIT ...... Laboratorios de Ensayos de Materiales e Investigaciones Tecnologicas [*Material Testing and Technological Research Laboratory*] [*Argentina*]   (LAA)
LEMM ...... Madrid [*Spain*] [*ICAO location identifier*]   (ICLI)
LEMO .... Local Emergency Management Officer
LEMO .... Sevilla/Moron [*Spain*] [*ICAO location identifier*]   (ICLI)
LEMP........ Lengyel Egyesult Munkaspart [*United Workers' Party of Poland*]   (HU)
LEMT........ Leningrad Electrotechnical Medical Technicum   (RU)
LEMUK..... Leningrad Electromechanical Training Center for Railroad Transportation Engineers   (RU)
LEMZ........ Leningrad Electromechanical Plant   (RU)
LEN .... Legal Electronic Network [*Australia*]
LEN .... Lentini Aviation, Inc. [*ICAO designator*]   (FAAC)
LEN .... Leon [*Mexico*] [*Airport symbol*]   (OAG)
LEN .... Less Expressway Noise Proprietary Ltd. [*Australia*]
LEN .... Liberation et d'Edification Nationale [*Direction Generale de*] [*(Directorate General of) Liberation and National Construction Use LENA Cambodia*]   (CL)
LEN .... Ligue Europeenne de Natation [*European Swimming Federation*] [*Sweden*]   (EAIO)
LEN .... Logements Economiques Normalises [*France*]   (FLAF)
LENA .... Laboratorio Energia Nucleare Applicata [*Applied Nuclear Energy Laboratory*] [*Italy*]   (PDAA)
LENA .... Liberation et d'Edification Nationale [*Direction Generale de*] [*(Directorate General of) Liberation and National Construction Cambodia*]   (CL)
Lenbriketmash ... Leningrad State Briquette Machinery Plant   (RU)
L en D ...... Licencie en Droit [*Licentiate in Law*] [*French*]
Lendorstroy ... Leningrad Road Construction Trust   (RU)
LENDVI.... Leningrad Scientific Research Institute of Dermatology and Venereology   (RU)
Lenenergo .. Leningrad Regional Administration of Power System Management   (RU)
LENFI .... Leningrad Pharmaceutical Scientific Research Institute   (RU)
Lenfil'm...... Leningrad Motion Picture Studio   (RU)
Lengas....... Gas Supply System Administration of Lengorispolkom   (RU)
Lengeolnerud ... Leningrad State All-Union Geological Exploration Trust for Nonmetallic Minerals   (RU)
LenGES ..... Leningrad State Electric Power Plant   (RU)
LENGIDEP ... Leningrad Branch of the All-Union State Planning Institute "Gidroenergoproyekt"   (RU)
LenGIDUV ... Leningrad State Institute for the Advanced Training of Physicians Imeni S. M. Kirov   (RU)
Lengiprogaz ... Leningrad State Institute for the Planning of Synthetic Liquid Fuel and Gas-Producing Establishments   (RU)
Lengiprogor ... Leningrad Branch of the State Institute for the Planning of Cities   (RU)
Lengiprokhim ... Leningrad Branch of the State Institute for the Planning of Plants of the Basic Chemical Industry   (RU)
Lengipromash ... Leningrad State Institute for the Planning of Machinery and Metalworking Plants   (RU)

Lengiprorechtrans ... Leningrad State Institute for Planning in River Transportation (RU)

Lengiprotorf ... Leningrad Branch of the State Planning Institute for the Multipurpose Use of Peat in the National Economy (RU)

Lengiprotrans ... Leningrad State Planning and Surveying Institute of the State Industrial Committee for Transportation Construction, USSR (RU)

Lengiprovodkhoz ... Leningrad State Institute for the Planning of Water-Management and Reclamation Construction (RU)

Lengird....... Leningrad Group for the Study of Jet Propulsion [*1932-1934*] (RU)

Lengiz .... Leningrad Branch of the State Publishing House (RU)

Lengorispolkom ... Executive Committee of the Leningrad City Soviet of Workers' Deputies (RU)

Lengorono ... Leningrad City Department of Public Education (RU)

Lengorpromsovet ... Leningrad City Council of Producers' Cooperatives (RU)

Lengorsovet ... Leningrad City Soviet of Workers' Deputies (RU)

Lengorspravka ... Leningrad City Reference and Information Office (RU)

Lengortel'set' ... Leningrad City Telephone Network (RU)

Lengorvoyenkomat ... Leningrad City Military Commissariat (RU)

Lengoryos .. Leningrad City Branch of the All-Russian Society for the Blind (RU)

Lengorzdravotdel ... Leningrad City Department of Public Health (RU)

Lengosfil ... Leningrad State Philharmonic (RU)

Lengosstroyizdat ... Leningrad Branch of the State Publishing House of Literature on Construction, Architecture, and Building Materials (RU)

Lengostoptekhizdat ... Leningrad Branch of the State Scientific and Technical Publishing House of the Petroleum and Mineral-Fuel Industry (RU)

leningr........ Leningrad (RU)

LenIUU ..... Leningrad City Institute for the Advanced Training of Teachers (RU)

Lenizdat ..... Newspaper, Periodical, and Book Publishing House of the Leningrad Oblast and City Committees of the KPSS (RU)

Lenkarz...... Leningrad Carburetor Plant (RU)

LENKER ... Len- Kender- es Muszaki Textilertekesito Vallalat [*Commercial Enterprise for Industrial Cordage and Textiles*] (HU)

Lenkhimles ... Leningrad State Trust of the Wood-Chemistry Industry (RU)

LenKhIMMASh ... Leningrad Branch of the All-Union Scientific Research and Design Institute of Chemical Machinery (RU)

Lenkhimsektor ... Leningrad Branch of the Chemical Department of the United Scientific and Technical Publishing House (RU)

Lenkhimtekhizdat ... Leningrad Branch of the State Chemical and Technical Publishing House (RU)

Lenkinap.... Leningrad Motion-Picture Equipment Plant (RU)

Lenkogiz .... Leningrad Oblast Branch of the Book Trade Association of State Publishing Houses (RU)

LENKOMBANK ... Leningrad City and Oblast Municipal Bank (RU)

Lenkubu..... Leningrad Commission for the Improvement of Scientists' Living Conditions (RU)

Lenlikvodzavod ... Leningrad Liqueur and Vodka Plant (RU)

Lenmashgiz ... Leningrad State Publishing House of Literature on Machinery Manufacture (RU)

Lenmetrostroy ... Leningrad Subway Construction Administration (RU)

lenn .... Lennatin [*Telegraph*] [*Finland*]

Lennauchfil'm ... Leningrad Motion-Picture Studio of Popular Science Films (RU)

LENNIIKhIMMASH ... Leningrad Scientific Research and Design Institute of Chemical Machinery (RU)

LenNIILKh ... Leningrad Scientific Research Institute of Forestry (RU)

LenNIKhFI ... Leningrad Scientific Research Chemical and Pharmaceutical Institute (RU)

LENNIILKhI ... Leningrad Scientific Research Institute of Wood Chemistry (RU)

LenNITO... Leningrad Scientific, Engineering, and Technical Society (RU)

Lenoblispolkom ... Executive Committee of the Leningrad Oblast Soviet of Workers' Deputies (RU)

Lenoblono .. Leningrad Oblast Department of Public Education (RU)

Lenoblpotrebsoyuz ... Leningrad Oblast Union of Consumers' Societies (RU)

Lenoblproyekt ... Institute for the Planning of Housing, Civil-Engineering, and Municipal Construction of the Lenoblispolkom (RU)

Lenoblsovet ... Leningrad Oblast Soviet of Workers' Deputies (RU)

Lenoblsovprof ... Leningrad Oblast Council of Trade Unions (RU)

Lenoblvetsnab ... Leningrad Oblast Veterinary Supply Office (RU)

Lenogiz....... Leningrad Association of State Publishing Houses (RU)

Lenokogiz .. Leningrad Oblast Branch of the Book Trade Association of State Publishing Houses (RU)

Lenpartizdat ... Leningrad Branch of the Publishing House of the TsK VKP (b) (RU)

Lenpishchepromizdat ... Leningrad Branch of the State Scientific and Technical Publishing House of the Food Industry (RU)

Lenplan...... Planning Commission of the Lengorispolkom (RU)

Lenproyekt ... Institute for the Planning of Housing and Civil Engineering Construction of the Lengorispolkom (RU)

Lenshveymash ... Leningrad State Sewing-Machine Plant (RU)

Lensotsekgiz ... Leningrad Branch of the State Publishing House of Social and Economic Literature (RU)

Lensovet..... Leningrad Soviet of Workers' Deputies (RU)

Lensovnarkhoz ... Council of the National Economy of the Leningrad Economic Region (RU)

Lenstankolit ... Leningrad Machine Tool Castings Plant (RU)

LenTASS... Leningrad Branch of the News Agency of the Soviet Union (RU)

Lentekstil'mash ... Leningrad Textile Machinery Plant (RU)

Lenteplopribor ... Leningrad State Plant of Electronic Heat-Control Instruments (RU)

Lentorfmash ... Leningrad Peat Machinery Plant (RU)

Lentrublit... Leningrad Pipe-Casting Plant (RU)

lenugolok ... Lenin Corner (RU)

LENVAT... Leningrad Oblast Office of the All-Union Gas-Welding Trust (RU)

LENVNIGI ... Leningrad Branch of the All-Union Scientific Research Institute of Gas and Synthetic Liquid Fuel (RU)

LENVNIIPT ... Leningrad Branch of the All-Union Scientific Research Institute of Industrial Transportation (RU)

Lenvodokanalstroy ... Leningrad Water Supply and Sewer System Construction Trust (RU)

Lenvodopribor ... Leningrad Water Supply Equipment Plant (RU)

Lenvodput' ... Administration of Leningrad Waterways (RU)

Lenvoyenport ... Leningrad Naval Port (RU)

Lenzagotmorsnab ... Leningrad Procurement Office of the Maritime Fleet (RU)

Lenzhet ...... Leningrad Fats Trust (RU)

LEO .... Leopair SA [*Switzerland*] [*ICAO designator*] (FAAC)

LEOC .... Local Emergency Operations Controller

LEOC .... Ocana [*Spain*] [*ICAO location identifier*] (ICLI)

LEOK .... Laboratium voor Elekronische Ontwikkelingen voor de Krijsmacht [*Electronic Developement Laboratory for the Armed Forces*] [*Netherlands*] (PDAA)

LEOK-TNO ... Laboratorium Elektronische Ontwikkelingen voor de Krijsmacht TNO [*Laboratory for Electronic Development of the Armed Forces TNO*] (ERC)

LEON .... Leonora [*Botanical region*] [*Australia*]

LEOV .... Oviedo [*Spain*] [*ICAO location identifier*] (ICLI)

LEP........... Air West Airlines, Inc. [*ICAO designator*] (FAAC)

LEP........... Electric Power Transmission Line (RU)

LEP........... Laboratoires d'Electronique et de Physique Appliquee [*Electronics and Applied Physics Laboratory*] [*French*] (WER)

LEP........... Laboratoires d'Electronique Philips [*Philips Electronics Laboratory*] [*France*] (IRC)

LEP........... Local Environment Plan [*Australia*]

LEP........... Lycee d'Enseignement Professionel [*Professional Secondary School for Advanced Studies*] [*French*] (BARN)

LEP........... Lycee d'Enseignement Professionnel [*Professional High School*] [*French*]

LEPA........ Palma De Mallorca [*Spain*] [*ICAO location identifier*] (ICLI)

LEPO........ Pollensa [*Spain*] [*ICAO location identifier*] (ICLI)

LEPP........ Pamplona/Noain-Pamplona [*Spain*] [*ICAO location identifier*] (ICLI)

LEPPU ...... Laboratorio de Estudios Petrologicos e Paleontologicos de Ultramar [*Portugal*] (DSCA)

LEPRA ...... Leprosy Relief Association [*Malawi*] [*Research center*] (AF)

LEPSUK.... Leningrad Track Construction Training Center for Railroad Transportation Engineers (RU)

LER........... Laboratorio de Estudos Radioisotopos [*Portugal*] (DSCA)

LER........... Leinster [*Australia*] [*Airport symbol*] (OAG)

LER........... Liga de Economistas Revolucionarios [*League of Revolutionary Economists*] [*Mexico*] (LA)

LER........... Line Operation Company (RU)

LERC........ Language for Export Research Center [*University of Western Sydney*] [*Australia*]

LERI........ Murcia/Alcantarilla [*Spain*] [*ICAO location identifier*] (ICLI)

LERM....... Line Maintenance and Repair Shop (RU)

LERN .... Library Enquiry into Role and Needs [*State Library of New South Wales*] [*Australia*] (ADA)

LERN .... Literacy and Education Resource Network [*Australia*]

lerretsovertr ... Lerretsovertraekket [*Cloth-Covered*] [*Publishing Danish/ Norwegian*]

LERS .... Reus [*Spain*] [*ICAO location identifier*] (ICLI)

LERSh .... Electrically and Manually Operated Boat Winch (RU)

LERT .... Rota [*Spain*] [*ICAO location identifier*] (ICLI)

LES .... Automotors Salta SACYF [*Argentina*] [*ICAO designator*] (FAAC)

LES .... Laboratoire d'Energetique Solaire [*Solar Energy Laboratory*] [*France*] (WED)

LES .... Laboratorio de Energia Solar [*Solar Energy Laboratory*] [*Brazil*] (WED)

LES .... Legal Electronic System [*Australia*]

LES .... Leipziger Eisen- und Stahlwerke [*Leipzig Iron and Steelworks*] (EG)

les .... Lesione [*Injury*] [*Publishing*] [*Italian*]

LES............ Lesobeng [*Lesotho*] [*Airport symbol*]   (OAG)
LES............ Licensing Executives Society of South Africa   (AA)
LES............ Livestock Experiment Station [*South Korean*] [*Research center*]   (IRC)
LES............ Locomobile Electric Power Station   (RU)
LES............ Telecommunications Line   (RU)
LESA .... Lecheria Higienica Sociedad Anonima [*Colombia*]   (COL)
LESA .... Licensing Executives Society of Australia   (ADA)
LESA .... Salamanca [*Spain*] [*ICAO location identifier*]   (ICLI)
LESANZ ... Licensing Executives Society - Australia and New Zealand
Lesbumizdat ... State Publishing House of Literature of the Lumber and Paper Industries   (RU)
LESC .... Licence es-Sciences Commerciales [*Master's Degree (License) in Commercial Sciences*]   (CL)
Les fak ...... School of Forestry   (BU)
LESJ .... Son San Juan Air Force Base [*Spain*] [*ICAO location identifier*]   (ICLI)
L es L .... Licencie es Lettres [*Licentiate in Letters*] [*French*]
LESM .... Murcia [*Spain*] [*ICAO location identifier*]   (ICLI)
Lesmetprom ... State All-Union Lumber Industry Trust of the Ministry of Ferrous Metallurgy, USSR   (RU)
Lesn .... Forester's House [*Topography*]   (RU)
lesnich........ Forestry Section, Forest Range [*Topography*]   (RU)
LESO......... San Sebastian [*Spain*] [*ICAO location identifier*]   (ICLI)
lesokhoz..... Forest Management   (RU)
LESOMA .. Socialist League of Malawi   (AF)
Lesop.......... Sawmill [*Topography*]   (RU)
LESP .... Madrid [*Spain*] [*ICAO location identifier*]   (ICLI)
lesp............. Sawmill [*Topography*]   (RU)
lesprom ...... Lumber Industry   (RU)
Lespromash ... All-Union Logging and Woodworking Trust of the Ministry of Machinery Manufacture and Instrument Making, USSR   (RU)
Lespromtyazh ... All-Union Lumber Industry Trust of the Ministry of Heavy Machinery Manufacture, USSR   (RU)
LesS .... Licencie es Sciences [*Licentiate in Science*] [*French*]   (BARN)
L es Sc....... Licencie es Sciences [*Licentiate of Sciences*] [*French*]
LEST .... Large Earth-Based [*formerly, European*] Solar Telescope
Lest .... Licencie es Lettres [*Licentiate in Letters*] [*French*]   (BARN)
LEST .... Santiago [*Spain*] [*ICAO location identifier*]   (ICLI)
LESU .... Seo De Urgel [*Spain*] [*ICAO location identifier*]   (ICLI)
LET............ Aerolineas Ejecutivas SA [*Mexico*] [*ICAO designator*]   (FAAC)
LET............ Leningrad Power Engineering Technicum   (RU)
Let.............. Letectvo [*Air Force*]   (CZ)
LET............ Leticia [*Colombia*] [*Airport symbol*]   (OAG)
let .... Letra [*Letter, Typeface*] [*Publishing*] [*Spanish*]
let .... Lettre [*Letter, Draft*] [*Business term*] [*French*]
Leta .... Latvian News Agency   (RU)
LETA......... Latvian Telegraph Agency   (EY)
LETA......... Sevilla/Tablada [*Spain*] [*ICAO location identifier*]   (ICLI)
LETAC...... Lexique Thematique de l'Afrique Centrale
LETDA...... Letnan Dua [*Second Lieutenant*]   (IN)
LETDJEN ... Letnan Djenderal [*Lieutenant General*]   (IN)
LETEKS.... Leskovacka Tekstilna Fabrika [*Textile Factory in Leskovac*]   (YU)
LETG........ Lettergreep [*Syllable*] [*Afrikaans*]
LETI .... Laboratoire d'Electronique et de Technologie de l'Informatique [*France*]   (PDAA)
LETI .... Leningrad Electrotechnical Institute Imeni V. I. Ul'yanov (Lenin)   (RU)
LETIISS.... Leningrad Electrotechnical Institute of Signal and Communications Engineers [*1937-1951*]   (RU)
LETIIZhT ... Leningrad Electrotechnical Institute of Railroad Transportation Engineers   (RU)
LETKOL ... Letnan Kolonel [*Lieutenant Colonel*]   (IN)
letnab......... Aerial Observer   (RU)
LETO........ Madrid/Torrejon [*Spain*] [*ICAO location identifier*]   (ICLI)
LETOV...... Letalska Tovarna [*Airplane Factory*] [*Ljubljana*]   (YU)
Letpl........... Letecky Pluk [*Air Force Regiment*]   (CZ)
LETs........... Airfield Center   (BU)
lett .... Lettera [*Letter*] [*Italian*]
lett .... Lettere [*Letter*] [*Afrikaans*]
lett .... Letterlik [*Literal*] [*Afrikaans*]
Lett............ Lettre [*French*]   (FLAF)
LETTK ..... Letterkunde [*Literature*] [*Afrikaans*]
LETTU ..... Letnan Satu [*First Lieutenant*]   (IN)
LETUL...... Lefkosa Turk Lisesi Musik Toplulugu [*Nicosia Turkish Lycee Musical Society*]   (TU)
LETZ .... Leningrad Electrotechnical Plant   (RU)
LETZ .... Lyskovo Electrotechnical Plant   (RU)
LEU .... Medical and Evacuation Directorate   (RU)
LEU .... Seo De Urgel [*Spain*] [*Airport symbol*]   (OAG)
LEUC........ Leucotomy [*European term for lobotomy*]   (DSUE)
LEV.......... Bureta [*Fiji*] [*Airport symbol*]   (OAG)
LEV.......... Landsforeningen Evnesvages Vel [*National Society for the Mentally Handicapped*] [*Denmark*]   (EAIO)

lev.............. Left, Left-Hand   (RU)
LEV.......... Levant
lev.............. Level [*Leaf*] [*Publishing*] [*Hungary*]
Lev .... Leviticus [*Leviticus*] [*Afrikaans*]
LEVAPAN ... Levaduras y Materias Primas para Panificacion y Biscocheria [*Colombia*]   (COL)
LEVC........ Valencia [*Spain*] [*ICAO location identifier*]   (ICLI)
LEVD........ Valladolid [*Spain*] [*ICAO location identifier*]   (ICLI)
Levensv...... Wet op het Levensverzekeringsbedrijf [*Benelux*]   (BAS)
LEVM....... Valencia [*Spain*] [*ICAO location identifier*]   (ICLI)
LEVS .... Levnedsmiddelselskabet [*Denmark*]   (SLS)
LEVS .... Madrid/Cuatro Vientos [*Spain*] [*ICAO location identifier*]   (ICLI)
LEVSA ...... Landbou-Ekonomievereniging van Suid-Afrika [*South Africa*]   (AA)
LEVT........ Vitoria [*Spain*] [*ICAO location identifier*]   (ICLI)
LEVX........ Vigo [*Spain*] [*ICAO location identifier*]   (ICLI)
LEW .... Lech-Elektrizitaetswerke Aktien-Gesellschaft
LEW .... Lokomotivbau-Elektrotechnische Werke [*Locomotive Construction and Electrotechnical Plant*]   (EG)
Lex .... Lexikon [*Dictionary*] [*German*]
lex-8vo........ Lexikon-Octavo [*Large Octavo*] [*Publishing Danish/Norwegian*]
LEXJ .... Santander [*Spain*] [*ICAO location identifier*]   (ICLI)
leyt .... Lieutenant   (RU)
leyts........... Leucine   (RU)
LEZ........... Electric Winch for the Gangway Ladder   (RU)
LEZ........... Laboratory of Experimental Zoology   (RU)
LEZA .... Zaragoza [*Spain*] [*ICAO location identifier*]   (ICLI)
LEZG........ Zaragoza [*Spain*] [*ICAO location identifier*]   (ICLI)
LEZL .... Sevilla [*Spain*] [*ICAO location identifier*]   (ICLI)
LEZM........ Laboratory of Experimental Zoology and Animal Morphology (of the Academy of Sciences, USSR)   (RU)
LF.............. Front Line, Line of Battle   (BU)
LF.............. Laborator pro Experimentalni a Theoretickou Fysiku [*Laboratory for Experimental and Theoretical Physics (of the Czechoslovak Academy of Sciences)*]   (CZ)
LF.............. La Fraternidad [*Brotherhood of Locomotive Engineers and Firemen*] [*Argentina*]   (LA)
LF.............. Lapp-Finze Eisenwarenfabriken Aktiengesellschaft [*Lapp Finze Iron Foundry Joint Stock Company*]
lf................. Lasd Fent [*See Above*]   (HU)
LF.............. Lebanese Forces
LF.............. Leningrad Branch   (RU)
LF.............. Liberation Front [*Namibia*]   (AF)
LF.............. Ligue de Foyer [*Salvation Army Home League - SAHL*]   (EAIO)
LF.............. Siebelwerke ATG GmbH [*Germany*] [*ICAO aircraft manufacturer identifier*]   (ICAO)
LFA........... Land Force, Airmobility [*NATO*]   (NATG)
LFA........... Land Freedom Army
LFA........... Language Foundation of Australia
LFA........... Local Football Association [*Sudan*]
LFAA........ Ambleteuse [*France*] [*ICAO location identifier*]   (ICLI)
LFAA........ Lone Fathers' Association, Australian Capital Territory
LFAB........ Dieppe/Saint-Aubin [*France*] [*ICAO location identifier*]   (ICLI)
LFAC........ Calais/Dunkerque [*France*] [*ICAO location identifier*]   (ICLI)
LFAD........ Compiegne/Margny [*France*] [*ICAO location identifier*]   (ICLI)
LFAE........ Eu-Mers/Le Treport [*France*] [*ICAO location identifier*]   (ICLI)
LFAF........ Laon/Chambry [*France*] [*ICAO location identifier*]   (ICLI)
LFAG........ Peronne/Saint-Quentin [*France*] [*ICAO location identifier*]   (ICLI)
LFAH........ Soissons/Cuffies [*France*] [*ICAO location identifier*]   (ICLI)
LFAI......... Nangis/Les Loges [*France*] [*ICAO location identifier*]   (ICLI)
LFAJ......... Argentan [*France*] [*ICAO location identifier*]   (ICLI)
LFAK........ Dunkerque-Ghyvelde [*France*] [*ICAO location identifier*]   (ICLI)
LFAL .... La Fleche/Thoree-Les-Pins [*France*] [*ICAO location identifier*]   (ICLI)
LFAM........ Berck-Sur-Mer [*France*] [*ICAO location identifier*]   (ICLI)
LFAN........ Conde-Sur-Noireau [*France*] [*ICAO location identifier*]   (ICLI)
LF & CB.... Legal Fees and Costs Board [*Australia*]
LFAO........ Bagnole-De-L'Orne [*France*] [*ICAO location identifier*]   (ICLI)
LFAP........ Rethel-Perthes [*France*] [*ICAO location identifier*]   (ICLI)
LFAQ........ Albert/Bray [*France*] [*ICAO location identifier*]   (ICLI)
LFAR......... Montdidier [*France*] [*ICAO location identifier*]   (ICLI)
LFAS .... Falaise-Monts-D'Eraines [*France*] [*ICAO location identifier*]   (ICLI)
LFAS .... League of Finnish-American Societies   (EAIO)
LFAT........ Le Touquet/Paris-Plage [*France*] [*ICAO location identifier*]   (ICLI)
LFAU........ Vauville [*France*] [*ICAO location identifier*]   (ICLI)
LFAV........ Valenciennes/Denain [*France*] [*ICAO location identifier*]   (ICLI)
LFAW........ Villerupt [*France*] [*ICAO location identifier*]   (ICLI)
LFAX........ Mortagne-Au-Perche [*France*] [*ICAO location identifier*]   (ICLI)
LFAY........ Amiens/Glisy [*France*] [*ICAO location identifier*]   (ICLI)
LFB........... Licensed Fishing Boat
LFBA........ Agen/La Garenne [*France*] [*ICAO location identifier*]   (ICLI)
LFBB .... Bordeaux [*France*] [*ICAO location identifier*]   (ICLI)

LFBC .... Cazaux [*France*] [*ICAO location identifier*]   (ICLI)
LFBD........ Bordeaux/Merignac [*France*] [*ICAO location identifier*]   (ICLI)
LFBE .... Bergerac/Roumaniere [*France*] [*ICAO location identifier*]
　　　　　　(ICLI)
LFBF......... Toulouse/Francazal [*France*] [*ICAO location identifier*]   (ICLI)
LFBG........ Cognac/Chateau Bernard [*France*] [*ICAO location identifier*]
　　　　　　(ICLI)
LFBH........ La Rochelle/Laleu [*France*] [*ICAO location identifier*]   (ICLI)
LFBI .... Poitiers/Biard [*France*] [*ICAO location identifier*]   (ICLI)
LFBJ.......... Saint-Junien [*France*] [*ICAO location identifier*]   (ICLI)
LFBK........ Montlucon-Gueret [*France*] [*ICAO location identifier*]   (ICLI)
LFBL .... Limoges/Bellegarde [*France*] [*ICAO location identifier*]   (ICLI)
LFBM....... Mont-De-Marsan [*France*] [*ICAO location identifier*]   (ICLI)
LFBN........ Niort/Souche [*France*] [*ICAO location identifier*]   (ICLI)
LFBO........ Toulouse/Blagnac [*France*] [*ICAO location identifier*]   (ICLI)
LFBP .... Pau/Pont-Long-Uzein [*France*] [*ICAO location identifier*]
　　　　　　(ICLI)
LFBQ........ Toulouse [*France*] [*ICAO location identifier*]   (ICLI)
LFBR........ Muret/Lherm [*France*] [*ICAO location identifier*]   (ICLI)
LFBS......... Biscarosse/Parentis [*France*] [*ICAO location identifier*]   (ICLI)
LFBT .... Tarbes/Ossun-Lourdes [*France*] [*ICAO location identifier*]
　　　　　　(ICLI)
LFBU........ Angouleme/Brie-Champniers [*France*] [*ICAO location identifier*]
　　　　　　(ICLI)
LFBV .... Brive/La Roche [*France*] [*ICAO location identifier*]   (ICLI)
LFBW .... Mont-De-Marsan [*France*] [*ICAO location identifier*]   (ICLI)
LFBX........ Perigeux/Bassillac [*France*] [*ICAO location identifier*]   (ICLI)
LFBY .... Dax/Seyresse [*France*] [*ICAO location identifier*]   (ICLI)
LFBZ .... Biarritz-Bayonne/Anglet [*France*] [*ICAO location identifier*]
　　　　　　(ICLI)
LFC............ Lands and Forests Commission [*Australia*]
LFC............ League of Filipino Composers   (EAIO)
LFC............ Libyan Finance Corporation
LFCA .... Chatellerault/Targe [*France*] [*ICAO location identifier*]   (ICLI)
LFCB .... Bagneres De Luchon [*France*] [*ICAO location identifier*]   (ICLI)
LFCB .... Legal Fees and Costs Board [*Australia*]
LFCB .... Ligue Francaise Contre le Bruit [*French*]   (SLS)
LFCC .... Cahors/Lalbenque [*France*] [*ICAO location identifier*]   (ICLI)
LFCD........ Andernos-Les-Bains [*France*] [*ICAO location identifier*]   (ICLI)
LFCE .... Gueret/Saint-Laurent [*France*] [*ICAO location identifier*]   (ICLI)
LFCF .... Figeac/Livernon [*France*] [*ICAO location identifier*]   (ICLI)
LFCG........ Saint-Girons/Antichan [*France*] [*ICAO location identifier*]
　　　　　　(ICLI)
LFCH........ Arcachon/La Teste De Buch [*France*] [*ICAO location identifier*]
　　　　　　(ICLI)
LFCh.......... Laborator Fysikalni Chemie [*Laboratory for Physical Chemistry
　　　　　　(of the Czechoslovak Academy of Sciences)*]   (CZ)
LFChKh..... Logarithmic Phase Frequency Characteristic   (RU)
LFCI .... Albi/Le Sequestre [*France*] [*ICAO location identifier*]   (ICLI)
LFCJ.......... Jonzac/Neulles [*France*] [*ICAO location identifier*]   (ICLI)
LFCK......... Castres/Mazamet [*France*] [*ICAO location identifier*]   (ICLI)
LFCL .... Less Than Full Container Load
LFCL .... Toulouse/Lasbordes [*France*] [*ICAO location identifier*]   (ICLI)
LFCM....... Millau/Larzac [*France*] [*ICAO location identifier*]   (ICLI)
LFCN........ Nogaro [*France*] [*ICAO location identifier*]   (ICLI)
LFCO........ Oloron/Herrere [*France*] [*ICAO location identifier*]   (ICLI)
LFCP .... Pons/Avy [*France*] [*ICAO location identifier*]   (ICLI)
LFCQ........ Graulhet/Mondragon [*France*] [*ICAO location identifier*]   (ICLI)
LFCR........ Rodez/Marcillac [*France*] [*ICAO location identifier*]   (ICLI)
LFCS .... Bordeaux/Saucats [*France*] [*ICAO location identifier*]   (ICLI)
LFCT .... Thouars [*France*] [*ICAO location identifier*]   (ICLI)
LFCU........ Ussel/Thalamy [*France*] [*ICAO location identifier*]   (ICLI)
LFCV .... Villefranche-De-Rouergue [*France*] [*ICAO location identifier*]
　　　　　　(ICLI)
LFCW .... Villeneuve-Sur-Lot [*France*] [*ICAO location identifier*]   (ICLI)
LFCX .... Castelsarrasin/Moissac [*France*] [*ICAO location identifier*]
　　　　　　(ICLI)
LFCY .... Royan/Medis [*France*] [*ICAO location identifier*]   (ICLI)
LFCZ .... Mimizan [*France*] [*ICAO location identifier*]   (ICLI)
lfd .... Laufend [*Consecutive, Current, Running*] [*German*]   (EG)
LFDA........ Aire-Sur-L'Addour [*France*] [*ICAO location identifier*]   (ICLI)
LFDB........ Montauban [*France*] [*ICAO location identifier*]   (ICLI)
LFDC........ Montendre/Marcillac [*France*] [*ICAO location identifier*]   (ICLI)
LFDE......... Egletons [*France*] [*ICAO location identifier*]   (ICLI)
LFDF .... Sainte-Foy-La-Grande [*France*] [*ICAO location identifier*]
　　　　　　(ICLI)
LFDG........ Gaillac/Lisle Sur Tarn [*France*] [*ICAO location identifier*]
　　　　　　(ICLI)
LFDH .... Auch/Lamothe [*France*] [*ICAO location identifier*]   (ICLI)
LFDI .... Libourne/Artiques De Lussac [*France*] [*ICAO location identifier*]
　　　　　　(ICLI)
LFDJ .... Pamiers/Les Pujols [*France*] [*ICAO location identifier*]   (ICLI)
LFDK......... Soulac-Sur-Mer [*France*] [*ICAO location identifier*]   (ICLI)
LFDL .... Loudun [*France*] [*ICAO location identifier*]   (ICLI)
Lfdm........... Laufender Meter [*Linear Meter*] [*German*]   (EG)
LFDM....... Marmande/Virazeil [*France*] [*ICAO location identifier*]   (ICLI)

LFDN .... Rochefort/Saint-Agnant [*France*] [*ICAO location identifier*]
　　　　　　(ICLI)
lfd Nr........ Laufende Nummer [*Serial Number, Running Number*] [*German*]
LFDO .... Bordeaux/Souge [*France*] [*ICAO location identifier*]   (ICLI)
LFDP......... Saint-Pierre D'Oleron [*France*] [*ICAO location identifier*]
　　　　　　(ICLI)
LFDQ .... Castelnau-Magnoac [*France*] [*ICAO location identifier*]   (ICLI)
LFDR......... La Reole/Floudes [*France*] [*ICAO location identifier*]   (ICLI)
LFDS .... Sarlat/Domme [*France*] [*ICAO location identifier*]   (ICLI)
LFDT......... Tarbes/Laloubere [*France*] [*ICAO location identifier*]   (ICLI)
LFDU .... Lesparre/St. Laurent Du Medoc [*France*] [*ICAO location
　　　　　　identifier*]   (ICLI)
LFDV .... Couhe/Verac [*France*] [*ICAO location identifier*]   (ICLI)
LFDW .... Chauvigny [*France*] [*ICAO location identifier*]   (ICLI)
LFDX........ Fumel/Montayral [*France*] [*ICAO location identifier*]   (ICLI)
LFDY .... Bordeaux-Yvrac [*France*] [*ICAO location identifier*]   (ICLI)
LFDZ .... Condat-Sur-Vezere [*France*] [*ICAO location identifier*]   (ICLI)
LFE............ Laboratoriet for Energiforskning [*Energy Research Laboratory*]
　　　　　　[*Denmark*]   (WED)
LFEA .... Delle-Ile [*France*] [*ICAO location identifier*]   (ICLI)
LFEB .... Dinan/Trelivan [*France*] [*ICAO location identifier*]   (ICLI)
LFEC .... Ouessant [*France*] [*ICAO location identifier*]   (ICLI)
LFED........ Pontivy [*France*] [*ICAO location identifier*]   (ICLI)
LFEE .... Reims [*France*] [*ICAO location identifier*]   (ICLI)
LFEF .... Amboise/Dierre [*France*] [*ICAO location identifier*]   (ICLI)
LFEG........ Argenton-Sur-Creuse [*France*] [*ICAO location identifier*]   (ICLI)
LFEH........ Aubigny-Sur-Nere [*France*] [*ICAO location identifier*]   (ICLI)
LFEI .... Briare/Chatillon [*France*] [*ICAO location identifier*]   (ICLI)
LFEI .... Leningrad Institute of Finance and Economics   (RU)
LFEJ.......... Chateauroux/Villers [*France*] [*ICAO location identifier*]   (ICLI)
LFEK........ Issoudun/Le Fay [*France*] [*ICAO location identifier*]   (ICLI)
LFEL .... Le Blanc [*France*] [*ICAO location identifier*]   (ICLI)
LFEM .... Land Forces East Malaysia   (ML)
LFEM .... Montargis/Vimory [*France*] [*ICAO location identifier*]   (ICLI)
LFEN........ Tours/Sorigny [*France*] [*ICAO location identifier*]   (ICLI)
LFEO......... Saint-Malo/Saint-Servan [*France*] [*ICAO location identifier*]
　　　　　　(ICLI)
LFEP .... Pouilly-Maconge [*France*] [*ICAO location identifier*]   (ICLI)
LFEQ......... Quiberon [*France*] [*ICAO location identifier*]   (ICLI)
LFER .... Redon/Bains-Sur-Oust [*France*] [*ICAO location identifier*]
　　　　　　(ICLI)
LFES......... Guiscriff-Scaer [*France*] [*ICAO location identifier*]   (ICLI)
LFET .... Til-Chatel [*France*] [*ICAO location identifier*]   (ICLI)
LFEU .... Bar-Le-Duc [*France*] [*ICAO location identifier*]   (ICLI)
LFEV .... Gray-Saint-Adrien [*France*] [*ICAO location identifier*]   (ICLI)
LFEW .... Saulieu-Liernais [*France*] [*ICAO location identifier*]   (ICLI)
LFEX .... Nancy-Azelot [*France*] [*ICAO location identifier*]   (ICLI)
LFEY .... Ile-D'Yeu/Le Grand Phare [*France*] [*ICAO location identifier*]
　　　　　　(ICLI)
LFEZ .... Nancy-Malzeville [*France*] [*ICAO location identifier*]   (ICLI)
LFF............ Laerere For Fred [*Teachers for Peace*] [*Denmark*]
LFF............ Liberian Frontier Force
LFFA .... CORTA (Orly Ouest) [*France*] [*ICAO location identifier*]   (ICLI)
LFFB......... Buno-Bonnevaux [*France*] [*ICAO location identifier*]   (ICLI)
LFFC......... Mantes-Cherence [*France*] [*ICAO location identifier*]   (ICLI)
LFFD......... Saint-Andre-De L'Eure [*France*] [*ICAO location identifier*]
　　　　　　(ICLI)
LFFE......... Enghien-Moisselles [*France*] [*ICAO location identifier*]   (ICLI)
LFFF......... Paris [*France*] [*ICAO location identifier*]   (ICLI)
LFFG......... La Ferte-Gaucher [*France*] [*ICAO location identifier*]   (ICLI)
LFFH......... Chateau-Thierry-Belleau [*France*] [*ICAO location identifier*]
　　　　　　(ICLI)
LFFI.......... Ancenis [*France*] [*ICAO location identifier*]   (ICLI)
LFFJ.......... Joinville-Mussey [*France*] [*ICAO location identifier*]   (ICLI)
LFFK......... Fontenay-Le-Conte [*France*] [*ICAO location identifier*]   (ICLI)
LFFL......... Bailleau-Armenonville [*France*] [*ICAO location identifier*]
　　　　　　(ICLI)
LFFM .... La Motte-Beuvron [*France*] [*ICAO location identifier*]   (ICLI)
LFFN........ Brienne-Le-Chateau [*France*] [*ICAO location identifier*]   (ICLI)
LFFO......... Tonnerre-Moulins [*France*] [*ICAO location identifier*]   (ICLI)
LFFP......... Pithiviers [*France*] [*ICAO location identifier*]   (ICLI)
LFFQ......... La Ferte-Alais [*France*] [*ICAO location identifier*]   (ICLI)
LFFR......... Bar-Sur-Seine [*France*] [*ICAO location identifier*]   (ICLI)
LFFS......... Suippes [*France*] [*ICAO location identifier*]   (ICLI)
LFFT......... Neufchateau-Roucaux [*France*] [*ICAO location identifier*]
　　　　　　(ICLI)
LFFU......... Chateauneuf-Sur-Cher [*France*] [*ICAO location identifier*]
　　　　　　(ICLI)
LFFV .... Vierzon-Mereau [*France*] [*ICAO location identifier*]   (ICLI)
LFFW .... Montaigu-Saint-Georges [*France*] [*ICAO location identifier*]
　　　　　　(ICLI)
LFFX .... Tournus-Cuisery [*France*] [*ICAO location identifier*]   (ICLI)
LFFY .... Etrepagny [*France*] [*ICAO location identifier*]   (ICLI)
LFFZ .... Sezanne-Saint-Remy [*France*] [*ICAO location identifier*]   (ICLI)
LFG............ Laboratory of Combustion Physics   (RU)
Lfg.............. Lieferung [*Issue*] [*Publishing*] [*German*]

LFGA........ Colmar/Houssen [*France*] [*ICAO location identifier*]   (ICLI)
LFGB........ Mulhouse/Habsheim [*France*] [*ICAO location identifier*]   (ICLI)
LFGC........ Strasbourg/Neuhof [*France*] [*ICAO location identifier*]   (ICLI)
LFGD........ Arbois [*France*] [*ICAO location identifier*]   (ICLI)
LFGE........ Avallon [*France*] [*ICAO location identifier*]   (ICLI)
LFGF........ Beaune/Challanges [*France*] [*ICAO location identifier*]   (ICLI)
LFGG........ Belfort/Chaux [*France*] [*ICAO location identifier*]   (ICLI)
LFGH........ Cosne-Sur-Loire [*France*] [*ICAO location identifier*]   (ICLI)
LFGI........ Dijon/Val Suzon [*France*] [*ICAO location identifier*]   (ICLI)
LFGJ .... Dole/Tavaux [*France*] [*ICAO location identifier*]   (ICLI)
LFGK........ Joigny [*France*] [*ICAO location identifier*]   (ICLI)
LFGL......... Lons Le Saunier/Courlaoux [*France*] [*ICAO location identifier*]   (ICLI)
LFGM....... Montceau Les Mines/Pouilloux [*France*] [*ICAO location identifier*]   (ICLI)
Lfgn........... Lieferung [*Issue*] [*Publishing*] [*German*]
LFGN....... Paray Le Monial [*France*] [*ICAO location identifier*]   (ICLI)
LFGO....... Pont-Sur-Yonne [*France*] [*ICAO location identifier*]   (ICLI)
LFGP........ Saint-Florentin/Cheu [*France*] [*ICAO location identifier*]   (ICLI)
LFGQ........ Semur-En-Auxois [*France*] [*ICAO location identifier*]   (ICLI)
LFGR........ Doncourt-Les-Conflans [*France*] [*ICAO location identifier*]   (ICLI)
LFGS........ Longuyon/Villette [*France*] [*ICAO location identifier*]   (ICLI)
LFGT........ Sarrebourg/Buhl [*France*] [*ICAO location identifier*]   (ICLI)
LFGU........ Sarreguemines/Neunkirch [*France*] [*ICAO location identifier*]   (ICLI)
LFGV .... Thionville/Yutz [*France*] [*ICAO location identifier*]   (ICLI)
LFGW....... Verdun/Rozelier [*France*] [*ICAO location identifier*]   (ICLI)
LFGX........ Champagnole/Crotenay [*France*] [*ICAO location identifier*]   (ICLI)
LFGY........ Saint-Die/Remoneix [*France*] [*ICAO location identifier*]   (ICLI)
LFGZ........ Nuits-Saint-Georges [*France*] [*ICAO location identifier*]   (ICLI)
LFHA .... Issoire/Le Broc [*France*] [*ICAO location identifier*]   (ICLI)
LFHB....... Moulins/Avermes [*France*] [*ICAO location identifier*]   (ICLI)
LFHC........ Perouges/Meximieux [*France*] [*ICAO location identifier*]   (ICLI)
LFHD .... Pierrelatte [*France*] [*ICAO location identifier*]   (ICLI)
LFHE .... Romans/Saint-Paul [*France*] [*ICAO location identifier*]   (ICLI)
LFHF .... Ruoms [*France*] [*ICAO location identifier*]   (ICLI)
LFHG .... Saint-Chamond/L'Horme [*France*] [*ICAO location identifier*]   (ICLI)
LFHH .... Vienne/Reventin [*France*] [*ICAO location identifier*]   (ICLI)
LFHI .... Morestel [*France*] [*ICAO location identifier*]   (ICLI)
LFHJ........ Lyon/Corbas [*France*] [*ICAO location identifier*]   (ICLI)
LFHK .... Camp De Canjuers [*France*] [*ICAO location identifier*]   (ICLI)
LFHL........ Langogne/L'Esperon [*France*] [*ICAO location identifier*]   (ICLI)
LFHM ...... Megeve [*France*] [*ICAO location identifier*]   (ICLI)
LFHN ...... Bellegarde/Vouvray [*France*] [*ICAO location identifier*]   (ICLI)
LFHO .... Aubenas-Vals-Lanas [*France*] [*ICAO location identifier*]   (ICLI)
LFHP .... Le Puy/Loudes [*France*] [*ICAO location identifier*]   (ICLI)
LFHQ .... Saint-Flour/Coltines [*France*] [*ICAO location identifier*]   (ICLI)
LFHR....... Brioude-Beaumont [*France*] [*ICAO location identifier*]   (ICLI)
LFHS........ Bourg/Ceyreziat [*France*] [*ICAO location identifier*]   (ICLI)
LFHT....... Ambert-Le-Poyet [*France*] [*ICAO location identifier*]   (ICLI)
LFHU .... L'Alpe D'Huez [*France*] [*ICAO location identifier*]   (ICLI)
LFHV .... Villefrance/Tarare [*France*] [*ICAO location identifier*]   (ICLI)
LFHW ...... Belleville-Villie-Morgon [*France*] [*ICAO location identifier*]   (ICLI)
LFHX........ Lapalisse-Perigny [*France*] [*ICAO location identifier*]   (ICLI)
LFHY........ Moulins/Montbeugny [*France*] [*ICAO location identifier*]   (ICLI)
LFHZ........ Sallanches-Mont-Blanc [*France*] [*ICAO location identifier*]   (ICLI)
LFI .... Leningrad Pharmaceutical Institute   (RU)
LFI .... Luxembourg Federation of Industry   (EAIO)
LFIB .... Belves-Saint-Pardoux [*France*] [*ICAO location identifier*]   (ICLI)
LFIB .... Liga Feminina Israelita do Brasil [*League of Jewish Women of Brazil*]   (EAIO)
LFIC .... Cross Corsen [*France*] [*ICAO location identifier*]   (ICLI)
LFID .... Condom-Valence-Sur-Baise [*France*] [*ICAO location identifier*]   (ICLI)
LFIE .... Cross Etel [*France*] [*ICAO location identifier*]   (ICLI)
LFIF.......... Saint-Afrique-Belmont [*France*] [*ICAO location identifier*]   (ICLI)
LFIG .... Cassagnes-Begonhes [*France*] [*ICAO location identifier*]   (ICLI)
LFIH......... Chalais [*France*] [*ICAO location identifier*]   (ICLI)
LFIJ.......... Cross Jobourg [*France*] [*ICAO location identifier*]   (ICLI)
LFIK .... Riberac-Saint-Aulaye [*France*] [*ICAO location identifier*]   (ICLI)
LFIL .... Rion-Des-Landes [*France*] [*ICAO location identifier*]   (ICLI)
LFIM .... Saint Gaudens Montrejeau [*France*] [*ICAO location identifier*]   (ICLI)
LFIN .... Cross Gris-Nez [*France*] [*ICAO location identifier*]   (ICLI)
LFIP .... Peyresourde-Balestas [*France*] [*ICAO location identifier*]   (ICLI)
LFIR .... Revel-Montgey [*France*] [*ICAO location identifier*]   (ICLI)
LFIT .... Toulouse-Bourg-Saint-Bernard [*France*] [*ICAO location identifier*]   (ICLI)
LFIV .... Vendays-Montalivet [*France*] [*ICAO location identifier*]   (ICLI)

LFIX .... Itxassou [*France*] [*ICAO location identifier*]   (ICLI)
LFIY .... Saint-Jean-D'Angely [*France*] [*ICAO location identifier*]   (ICLI)
LFJ .... Ljudska Fronta Jugoslavije [*People's Front of Yugoslavia*]   (YU)
LFJG .... Cross La Garde [*France*] [*ICAO location identifier*]   (ICLI)
LFK .... Therapeutic Physical Culture   (RU)
LFKA .... Albertville [*France*] [*ICAO location identifier*]   (ICLI)
LFKB .... Bastia/Poretta, Corse [*France*] [*ICAO location identifier*]   (ICLI)
LFKC .... Calvi/Sainte-Catherine, Corse [*France*] [*ICAO location identifier*]   (ICLI)
LFKD .... Sollieres-Sardieres [*France*] [*ICAO location identifier*]   (ICLI)
LFKE .... Saint-Jean-En-Royans [*France*] [*ICAO location identifier*]   (ICLI)
LFKF .... Figari, Sud-Corse [*France*] [*ICAO location identifier*]   (ICLI)
LFKG .... Ghisonaccia-Alzitone [*France*] [*ICAO location identifier*]   (ICLI)
LFKh......... Logarithmic Phase Frequency Characteristic   (RU)
LFKH .... Saint-Jean-D'Avelanne [*France*] [*ICAO location identifier*]   (ICLI)
LFKJ .... Ajaccio/Campo Dell'Oro, Corse [*France*] [*ICAO location identifier*]   (ICLI)
LFKL .... Lyon-Brindas [*France*] [*ICAO location identifier*]   (ICLI)
LFKM .... Saint-Galmier [*France*] [*ICAO location identifier*]   (ICLI)
LFKO .... Propriano [*France*] [*ICAO location identifier*]   (ICLI)
LFKP .... La Tour-Du-Pin-Cessieu [*France*] [*ICAO location identifier*]   (ICLI)
LFKS .... Solenzara, Corse [*France*] [*ICAO location identifier*]   (ICLI)
LFKT .... Corte [*France*] [*ICAO location identifier*]   (ICLI)
LFKU .... Lekarska Fakulta Komenskeho [*Faculty of Medicine of Comenius University*]   (CZ)
LFKY .... Belley-Peyrieu [*France*] [*ICAO location identifier*]   (ICLI)
LFKZ .... Saint-Claude-Pratz [*France*] [*ICAO location identifier*]   (ICLI)
LFL .... La Forestiere de Lambarene
LFL .... Lithuanian Freedom League   (EAIO)
LFLA .... Auxerre/Moneteau [*France*] [*ICAO location identifier*]   (ICLI)
LFLAP...... Liquid Fuels, Lubricants, and Allied Products Committee [*Australia*]
LFLB .... Chambery/Aix-Les-Bains [*France*] [*ICAO location identifier*]   (ICLI)
LFLC .... Clermont-Ferrand/Aulnat [*France*] [*ICAO location identifier*]   (ICLI)
LFLD .... Bourges [*France*] [*ICAO location identifier*]   (ICLI)
LFLE .... Chambery/Challes-Les-Eaux [*France*] [*ICAO location identifier*]   (ICLI)
LFLF.......... Orleans [*France*] [*ICAO location identifier*]   (ICLI)
LFLG .... Grenoble/Le Versoud [*France*] [*ICAO location identifier*]   (ICLI)
LFLH......... Chalon/Champforgeuil [*France*] [*ICAO location identifier*]   (ICLI)
LFLI .... Annemasse [*France*] [*ICAO location identifier*]   (ICLI)
LFLJ .... Courchevel [*France*] [*ICAO location identifier*]   (ICLI)
LFLK .... Oyonnax/Arbent [*France*] [*ICAO location identifier*]   (ICLI)
LFLL.......... Lyon/Satolas [*France*] [*ICAO location identifier*]   (ICLI)
LFLM .... Macon/Charnay [*France*] [*ICAO location identifier*]   (ICLI)
LFLN......... Saint-Yan [*France*] [*ICAO location identifier*]   (ICLI)
LFLO .... Roanne/Renaison [*France*] [*ICAO location identifier*]   (ICLI)
LFLP......... Annecy/Meythet [*France*] [*ICAO location identifier*]   (ICLI)
LFLPU ...... Libyan Federation of Labour and Professional Unions
LFLQ .... Montelimar/Ancone [*France*] [*ICAO location identifier*]   (ICLI)
LFLR .... Saint-Rambert-D'Albon [*France*] [*ICAO location identifier*]   (ICLI)
LFLS.......... Grenoble/Saint-Geoirs [*France*] [*ICAO location identifier*]   (ICLI)
LFLT .... Montlucon/Domerat [*France*] [*ICAO location identifier*]   (ICLI)
LFLU .... Liberian Federation of Labour Unions
LFLU .... Valence/Chabeuil [*France*] [*ICAO location identifier*]   (ICLI)
LFLV .... Vichy/Charmeil [*France*] [*ICAO location identifier*]   (ICLI)
LFLW .... Aurillac [*France*] [*ICAO location identifier*]   (ICLI)
LFLX .... Chateauroux/Deols [*France*] [*ICAO location identifier*]   (ICLI)
LFLY .... Lyon/Bron [*France*] [*ICAO location identifier*]   (ICLI)
LFLZ .... Feurs/Chambeon [*France*] [*ICAO location identifier*]   (ICLI)
LFM........... La Forestiere de Moloundou
Lfm............ Landforstmeister [*Regional Forester*]   (EG)
lfm.............. Laufender Meter [*Linear Meter*]   (EG)
LFM........... Lieutenant Feld Marechal [*French*]   (MTD)
LFM........... Lodzka Fabryka Mebli [*Lodz Furniture Factory*]   (POL)
LFMA .... Aix-Les-Milles [*France*] [*ICAO location identifier*]   (ICLI)
LFMB .... Aix-En-Provence [*France*] [*ICAO location identifier*]   (ICLI)
LFMC....... Le Luc/Le Cannet [*France*] [*ICAO location identifier*]   (ICLI)
LFMD....... Cannes/Mandelieu [*France*] [*ICAO location identifier*]   (ICLI)
LFME .... Nimes/Courbessac [*France*] [*ICAO location identifier*]   (ICLI)
LFMF .... Fayence [*France*] [*ICAO location identifier*]   (ICLI)
LFMG....... La Montagne Noire [*France*] [*ICAO location identifier*]   (ICLI)
LFMG....... Liquid Fuels Management Group [*Energy Research Consultancy*] [*New Zealand*]   (WED)
LFMH ...... Saint-Etienne/Boutheon [*France*] [*ICAO location identifier*]   (ICLI)
LFMI .... Istres/Le Tube [*France*] [*ICAO location identifier*]   (ICLI)
LFMI......... Laboratory of Physico-Mechanical Tests   (RU)

LFMJ .... Nice/Mont Agel [*France*] [*ICAO location identifier*]   (ICLI)
LFMK........ Carcassonne/Salvaza [*France*] [*ICAO location identifier*]   (ICLI)
LFML......... Marseille/Marignane [*France*] [*ICAO location identifier*]   (ICLI)
LFMM....... Aix-En-Provence [*France*] [*ICAO location identifier*]   (ICLI)
LFMN........ Nice/Cote D'Azur [*France*] [*ICAO location identifier*]   (ICLI)
LFMO .... Orange/Caritat [*France*] [*ICAO location identifier*]   (ICLI)
LFMP........ Perpignan/Rivesaltes [*France*] [*ICAO location identifier*]   (ICLI)
LFMQ........ Le Castellet [*France*] [*ICAO location identifier*]   (ICLI)
LFMR........ Barcelonnette/Saint-Pons [*France*] [*ICAO location identifier*]
                (ICLI)
LFMR........ Lubelska Fabryka Maszyn Rolniczych [*Lublin Agricultural
                Machinery Plant*]   (POL)
LFMS .... Ales/Deaux [*France*] [*ICAO location identifier*]   (ICLI)
LFMT........ Leningrad Physico-Mechanical Technicum   (RU)
LFMT........ Montpellier/Frejorgues [*France*] [*ICAO location identifier*]
                (ICLI)
LFMU........ Beziers/Vias [*France*] [*ICAO location identifier*]   (ICLI)
LFMU........ Leningrad Machine Accounting and Computing Office   (RU)
LFMV........ Avignon/Caumont [*France*] [*ICAO location identifier*]   (ICLI)
LFMW....... Castelnaudary/Villeneuve [*France*] [*ICAO location identifier*]
                (ICLI)
LFMX........ Chateau-Arnoux/Saint-Auban [*France*] [*ICAO location
                identifier*]   (ICLI)
LFMY........ Salon [*France*] [*ICAO location identifier*]   (ICLI)
LFMZ........ Lezignan-Corbieres [*France*] [*ICAO location identifier*]   (ICLI)
LFN .... Lembaga Fisika Nasional [*National Institute for Physics*]
                [*Indonesia*] [*Research center*]   (WED)
LFNA........ Gap/Tallard [*France*] [*ICAO location identifier*]   (ICLI)
LFNB........ Mende/Brenoux [*France*] [*ICAO location identifier*]   (ICLI)
LFNC........ Mont-Dauphin/Saint-Crepin [*France*] [*ICAO location identifier*]
                (ICLI)
LFND .... Pont-Saint-Esprit [*France*] [*ICAO location identifier*]   (ICLI)
LFNE........ Salon/Eyguieres [*France*] [*ICAO location identifier*]   (ICLI)
LFNF........ Vinon [*France*] [*ICAO location identifier*]   (ICLI)
LFNG........ Montpellier/L'Or [*France*] [*ICAO location identifier*]   (ICLI)
LFNH .... Carpentras [*France*] [*ICAO location identifier*]   (ICLI)
LFNI......... Conqueyrac [*France*] [*ICAO location identifier*]   (ICLI)
LFNJ .... Aspres-Sur-Buech [*France*] [*ICAO location identifier*]   (ICLI)
LFNK........ Vars-Les-Crosses-Et-Les-Tronches [*France*] [*ICAO location
                identifier*]   (ICLI)
LFNL......... Saint-Martin-De-Londres [*France*] [*ICAO location identifier*]
                (ICLI)
LFNM .... La Mole [*France*] [*ICAO location identifier*]   (ICLI)
LFNO .... Florac-Sainte-Enimie [*France*] [*ICAO location identifier*]   (ICLI)
LFNP......... Pezenas-Nizas [*France*] [*ICAO location identifier*]   (ICLI)
LFNQ .... Mont-Louis-La-Quillane [*France*] [*ICAO location identifier*]
                (ICLI)
LFNR........ Berre-La-Fare [*France*] [*ICAO location identifier*]   (ICLI)
LFNS .... Sisteron-Theze [*France*] [*ICAO location identifier*]   (ICLI)
LFNT........ Avignon-Pujaut [*France*] [*ICAO location identifier*]   (ICLI)
LFNU .... Uzes [*France*] [*ICAO location identifier*]   (ICLI)
LFNV........ Valreas-Visan [*France*] [*ICAO location identifier*]   (ICLI)
LFNW........ Puivert [*France*] [*ICAO location identifier*]   (ICLI)
LFNX........ Bedarieux-La-Tour-Sur-Orb [*France*] [*ICAO location identifier*]
                (ICLI)
LFNY......... Saint-Etienne-En-Devoluy [*France*] [*ICAO location identifier*]
                (ICLI)
LFNZ........ Le Mazet-De-Romanin [*France*] [*ICAO location identifier*]
                (ICLI)
LFO .... Legal Framework Order [*Pakistan*]
LFO .... Light Infantry Flamethrower   (RU)
LFOA........ Avord [*France*] [*ICAO location identifier*]   (ICLI)
LFOB........ Beauvais/Tille [*France*] [*ICAO location identifier*]   (ICLI)
LFOC........ Crateaudun [*France*] [*ICAO location identifier*]   (ICLI)
LFOC........ Lea-Francis Owners Club [*British*]   (EAIO)
LFOD .... Saumur/Saint-Florent [*France*] [*ICAO location identifier*]
                (ICLI)
LFOE........ Evreux/Fauville [*France*] [*ICAO location identifier*]   (ICLI)
LFOF........ Alencon/Valframbert [*France*] [*ICAO location identifier*]   (ICLI)
LFOG........ Flers/Saint-Paul [*France*] [*ICAO location identifier*]   (ICLI)
LFOH........ Le Havre/Octeville [*France*] [*ICAO location identifier*]   (ICLI)
LFOI......... Abbeville [*France*] [*ICAO location identifier*]   (ICLI)
LFOJ......... Orleans/Bricy [*France*] [*ICAO location identifier*]   (ICLI)
LFOK........ Chalons/Vatry [*France*] [*ICAO location identifier*]   (ICLI)
LFOL........ L'Aigle/Saint-Michel [*France*] [*ICAO location identifier*]   (ICLI)
LFOM .... Lessay [*France*] [*ICAO location identifier*]   (ICLI)
LFON........ Dreux/Vernouillet [*France*] [*ICAO location identifier*]   (ICLI)
LFOO .... Les Sables D'Olonne/Talmont [*France*] [*ICAO location
                identifier*]   (ICLI)
LFOP........ Rouen/Boos [*France*] [*ICAO location identifier*]   (ICLI)
LFOQ........ Blois/Le Breuil [*France*] [*ICAO location identifier*]   (ICLI)
LFOR........ Chartres/Champhol [*France*] [*ICAO location identifier*]   (ICLI)
LFOS........ Saint-Valery/Vittefleur [*France*] [*ICAO location identifier*]
                (ICLI)
LFOT........ Tours/Saint-Symphorien [*France*] [*ICAO location identifier*]
                (ICLI)

LFOU .... Cholet/Le Pontreau [*France*] [*ICAO location identifier*]   (ICLI)
LFOV........ Laval/Entrammes [*France*] [*ICAO location identifier*]   (ICLI)
LFOW .... Saint-Quentin/Roupy [*France*] [*ICAO location identifier*]   (ICLI)
LFOX........ Etampes/Mondesir [*France*] [*ICAO location identifier*]   (ICLI)
LFOY........ Le Havre/Saint-Romain [*France*] [*ICAO location identifier*]
                (ICLI)
LFOZ........ Orleans/Saint-Denis-De-L'Hotel [*France*] [*ICAO location
                identifier*]   (ICLI)
LFP .... Liberala Folkpartiet [*Liberal People's Party*] [*Finland*] [*Political
                party*]   (PPE)
LFP .... Track [*Aviation*]   (RU)
LFPA .... Persan-Beaumont [*France*] [*ICAO location identifier*]   (ICLI)
LFPB........ Paris/Le Bourget [*France*] [*ICAO location identifier*]   (ICLI)
LFPC........ Creil [*France*] [*ICAO location identifier*]   (ICLI)
LFPD........ Bernay/Saint-Martin [*France*] [*ICAO location identifier*]   (ICLI)
LFPE........ Meaux/Esbly [*France*] [*ICAO location identifier*]   (ICLI)
LFPF........ Beynes/Thiverval [*France*] [*ICAO location identifier*]   (ICLI)
LFPG .... Paris/Charles-De-Gaulle [*France*] [*ICAO location identifier*]
                (ICLI)
LFPH........ Chelles/Le Pin [*France*] [*ICAO location identifier*]   (ICLI)
LFPI......... Paris/Issy-Les-Moulineaux [*France*] [*ICAO location identifier*]
                (ICLI)
LFPJ .... Taverny [*France*] [*ICAO location identifier*]   (ICLI)
LFPK .... Coulommiers/Voisins [*France*] [*ICAO location identifier*]
                (ICLI)
LFPL........ Lognes/Emerainville [*France*] [*ICAO location identifier*]   (ICLI)
LFPM .... Melun/Villaroche [*France*] [*ICAO location identifier*]   (ICLI)
LFPN........ Toussus-Le-Noble [*France*] [*ICAO location identifier*]   (ICLI)
LFPO........ Paris/Orly [*France*] [*ICAO location identifier*]   (ICLI)
LFPP........ Le Plessis-Belleville [*France*] [*ICAO location identifier*]   (ICLI)
LFPQ .... Fontenay-Tresigny [*France*] [*ICAO location identifier*]   (ICLI)
LFPR .... Guayancourt [*France*] [*ICAO location identifier*]   (ICLI)
LFPS........ Paris [*France*] [*ICAO location identifier*]   (ICLI)
LFPT .... Pontoise/Cormeilles-En-Vexin [*France*] [*ICAO location
                identifier*]   (ICLI)
LFPU .... Moret/Episy [*France*] [*ICAO location identifier*]   (ICLI)
LFPV .... Villacoublay/Velizy [*France*] [*ICAO location identifier*]   (ICLI)
LFPW .... Paris, Centre Meteorologique [*France*] [*ICAO location identifier*]
                (ICLI)
LFPX .... Chavenay/Villepreux [*France*] [*ICAO location identifier*]   (ICLI)
LFPY .... Bretigny-Sur-Orge [*France*] [*ICAO location identifier*]   (ICLI)
LFPZ .... Lecebny Fond Postovnich Zamestnancu [*Postal Employees'
                Medical Fund*]   (CZ)
LFPZ .... Saint-Cyre-L'Ecole [*France*] [*ICAO location identifier*]   (ICLI)
LFQA........ Reims/Prunay [*France*] [*ICAO location identifier*]   (ICLI)
LFQB........ Troyes/Barberey [*France*] [*ICAO location identifier*]   (ICLI)
LFQC........ Luneville/Croismare [*France*] [*ICAO location identifier*]   (ICLI)
LFQD........ Arras/Roclincourt [*France*] [*ICAO location identifier*]   (ICLI)
LFQE........ Etain/Rouvres [*France*] [*ICAO location identifier*]   (ICLI)
LFQF........ Autun/Bellevue [*France*] [*ICAO location identifier*]   (ICLI)
LFQG........ Nevers/Fourchambault [*France*] [*ICAO location identifier*]
                (ICLI)
LFQH........ Chatillon-Sur-Seine [*France*] [*ICAO location identifier*]   (ICLI)
LFQI......... Cambrai/Epinoy [*France*] [*ICAO location identifier*]   (ICLI)
LFQJ......... Maubeuge/Elesmes [*France*] [*ICAO location identifier*]   (ICLI)
LFQK........ Chalons/Ecury-Sur-Coole [*France*] [*ICAO location identifier*]
                (ICLI)
LFQL......... Lens/Benifontaine [*France*] [*ICAO location identifier*]   (ICLI)
LFQM........ Besancon-La-Veze [*France*] [*ICAO location identifier*]   (ICLI)
LFQN........ Saint-Omer/Wizernes [*France*] [*ICAO location identifier*]   (ICLI)
LFQO........ Lille/Marcq-En-Baroeul [*France*] [*ICAO location identifier*]
                (ICLI)
LFQP .... Phalsbourg/Bourscheid [*France*] [*ICAO location identifier*]
                (ICLI)
LFQQ .... Lille/Lesquin [*France*] [*ICAO location identifier*]   (ICLI)
LFQR........ Romilly-Sur-Seine [*France*] [*ICAO location identifier*]   (ICLI)
LFQS........ Vitry-En-Artois [*France*] [*ICAO location identifier*]   (ICLI)
LFQT........ Merville/Calonne [*France*] [*ICAO location identifier*]   (ICLI)
LFQU .... Sarre-Union [*France*] [*ICAO location identifier*]   (ICLI)
LFQV........ Charleville/Mezieres [*France*] [*ICAO location identifier*]   (ICLI)
LFQW........ Vesoul-Frotey [*France*] [*ICAO location identifier*]   (ICLI)
LFQY........ Saverne-Steinbourg [*France*] [*ICAO location identifier*]   (ICLI)
LFQZ........ Dieuze-Gueblange [*France*] [*ICAO location identifier*]   (ICLI)
L FR .... Franc [*Monetary unit*] [*Luxembourg*]
LFR .... La Fria [*Venezuela*] [*Airport symbol*]   (OAG)
LFRA........ Angers/Avrille [*France*] [*ICAO location identifier*]   (ICLI)
LFRAIA.... Life Fellow of the Royal Australian Institute of Architects
                (ADA)
LFRAPI..... Life Fellow of the Royal Australian Planning Institute
LFRB........ Brest/Guipavas [*France*] [*ICAO location identifier*]   (ICLI)
LFRC .... Cherbourg/Maupertus [*France*] [*ICAO location identifier*]
                (ICLI)
LFRD........ Dinard/Pleurtuit-Saint-Malo [*France*] [*ICAO location identifier*]
                (ICLI)
LFRE........ La Baule/Escoublac [*France*] [*ICAO location identifier*]   (ICLI)
LFRF .... Granville [*France*] [*ICAO location identifier*]   (ICLI)

LFRG......... Deauville/Saint-Gatien [France] [ICAO location identifier] (ICLI)

Lfrg .... Lieferung [Delivery, Installment, Part] (EG)

LFRH......... Lorient/Lann-Bihoue [France] [ICAO location identifier] (ICLI)

LFRI .... La Roche-Sur-Yon/Les Ajoncs [France] [ICAO location identifier] (ICLI)

LFRJ .... Landivisiau [France] [ICAO location identifier] (ICLI)

LFRK .... Caen/Carpiquet [France] [ICAO location identifier] (ICLI)

LFRL .... Lanveoc/Poulmic [France] [ICAO location identifier] (ICLI)

LFRM .... Le Mans/Arnage [France] [ICAO location identifier] (ICLI)

LFRN......... Rennes/Saint-Jacques [France] [ICAO location identifier] (ICLI)

LFRO......... Lannion/Servel [France] [ICAO location identifier] (ICLI)

LFRP .... Ploermel-Loyat [France] [ICAO location identifier] (ICLI)

LFRQ......... Quimper/Pluguffan [France] [ICAO location identifier] (ICLI)

LFRR .... Brest [France] [ICAO location identifier] (ICLI)

LFRS .... Nantes/Chateau Bougon [France] [ICAO location identifier] (ICLI)

LFRT .... Luxembourg Federation of Retail Trade (EAIO)

LFRT .... Saint-Brieuc Armor [France] [ICAO location identifier] (ICLI)

LFRU......... Morlaix/Ploujean [France] [ICAO location identifier] (ICLI)

LFRV .... Vannes/Meucon [France] [ICAO location identifier] (ICLI)

LFRW........ Avranches/Le Val Saint-Pere [France] [ICAO location identifier] (ICLI)

LFRX .... Brest [France] [ICAO location identifier] (ICLI)

LFRY .... Cherbourg [France] [ICAO location identifier] (ICLI)

LFRZ .... Saint-Nazaire/Montoir [France] [ICAO location identifier] (ICLI)

LFS .... Lancucka Fabryka Srub [Lancut Bolt and Nut Factory] (POL)

LFS .... League of Filipino Students

LFS .... Luftfahrzeug Service - Aircraft Service [Austria] [ICAO designator] (FAAC)

LFSA .... Besancon/Thise [France] [ICAO location identifier] (ICLI)

LFSA .... Landesverband Freier Schweizer Arbeiter [Swiss Association of Autonomous Unions]

LFSB......... Bale/Mulhouse [France/Switzerland] [ICAO location identifier] (ICLI)

LFSC .... Colmar/Meyenheim [France] [ICAO location identifier] (ICLI)

LFSD......... Dijon/Longvic [France] [ICAO location identifier] (ICLI)

LFSE......... Epinal/Dogneville [France] [ICAO location identifier] (ICLI)

LFSF......... Metz/Frescaty [France] [ICAO location identifier] (ICLI)

LFSG .... Epinal/Mirecourt [France] [ICAO location identifier] (ICLI)

LFSH......... Haguenau [France] [ICAO location identifier] (ICLI)

LFSI.......... Saint-Dizier/Robinson [France] [ICAO location identifier] (ICLI)

LFSJ .... Sedan/Douzy [France] [ICAO location identifier] (ICLI)

LFSK .... Vitry-Le-Francois/Vauclerc [France] [ICAO location identifier] (ICLI)

LFSL......... Toul/Rosieres [France] [ICAO location identifier] (ICLI)

LFSM .... Montbeliard/Courcelles [France] [ICAO location identifier] (ICLI)

LFSN .... Nancy/Essey [France] [ICAO location identifier] (ICLI)

LFSO .... Nancy/Ochey [France] [ICAO location identifier] (ICLI)

LFSP......... Pontarlier [France] [ICAO location identifier] (ICLI)

LFSQ .... Belfort/Fontaine [France] [ICAO location identifier] (ICLI)

LFSR .... Reims/Champagne [France] [ICAO location identifier] (ICLI)

LFST......... Strasbourg/Entzheim [France] [ICAO location identifier] (ICLI)

LFSU .... Rolampont [France] [ICAO location identifier] (ICLI)

LFSV .... Aircraft Telescopic Headlight (RU)

LFSV .... Pont-Saint-Vincent [France] [ICAO location identifier] (ICLI)

LFSW .... Epernay/Plivot [France] [ICAO location identifier] (ICLI)

LFSX .... Luxeuil/Saint-Sauveur [France] [ICAO location identifier] (ICLI)

LFSY .... Chaumont-La Vendue [France] [ICAO location identifier] (ICLI)

LFSZ......... Vittel/Champ De Courses [France] [ICAO location identifier] (ICLI)

LFT .... Aerolift Philippines Corp. [ICAO designator] (FAAC)

LFT .... Latest Finish Time

LFT .... Law Foundation of Tasmania [Australia]

Lft .... Luft [Air] [German] (GCA)

LFTB .... Liquid Fuel Trust Board [New Zealand]

LFTC .... Toulon [France] [ICAO location identifier] (ICLI)

LFTD......... Stichting Landbouw Fysisch-Technische Dienst [Netherlands] (DSCA)

LFTF......... Cuers/Pierrefeu [France] [ICAO location identifier] (ICLI)

LFTH........ Hyeres/Le Palyvestre [France] [ICAO location identifier] (ICLI)

LFTI .... Leningrad Physico-Technical Institute (RU)

LFTL .... Leningrad Physico-Technical Laboratory (RU)

LFTN........ La Grand'Combe [France] [ICAO location identifier] (ICLI)

LFTR .... Toulon/Saint-Mandrier [France] [ICAO location identifier] (ICLI)

LFTS......... Toulon [France] [ICAO location identifier] (ICLI)

LFTsGVIA ... Leningrad Branch of the Central State Archives of Military History (RU)

LFTU .... Frejus/Saint-Raphael [France] [ICAO location identifier] (ICLI)

LFTU........ Lesotho Federation of Trade Unions

LFTU......... Liberian Federation of Trade Unions (AF)

LFTW....... Nimes/Garons [France] [ICAO location identifier] (ICLI)

LFU .... Leichflugtechnik-Union [Germany] (PDAA)

LFU .... Leonhartsberger Flugunternchmen GmbH [Austria] [ICAO designator] (FAAC)

LfV .... Landesamt fuer Verfassungsschutz [State Office for the Protection of the Constitution] (WEN)

LFVE .... Laboratory of High-Energy Physics (RU)

LFVM........ Miquelon [France] [ICAO location identifier] (ICLI)

LFVP .... Saint-Pierre, Saint-Pierre-Et Miquelon [France] [ICAO location identifier] (ICLI)

LFVZ .... Lecebny Fond Verejnych Zamestnancu [Public Employees' Medical Fund] (CZ)

LFW........... Lome [Togo] [Airport symbol] (OAG)

LFW........... Lubelskie Fabryki Wag [Lublin Scale Factories] (POL)

LFWB........ Sccom Sud-Ouest [France] [ICAO location identifier] (ICLI)

LFWRFA... Life Fellow, Water Resources Foundation of Australia

LFXA .... Amberieu [France] [ICAO location identifier] (ICLI)

LFXB .... Saintes/Thenac [France] [ICAO location identifier] (ICLI)

LFXC .... Contrexeville [France] [ICAO location identifier] (ICLI)

LFXD........ Doullens/Lucheux [France] [ICAO location identifier] (ICLI)

LFXE .... Camp De Mourmelon [France] [ICAO location identifier] (ICLI)

LFXF .... Limoges/Romanet [France] [ICAO location identifier] (ICLI)

LFXG........ Camp De Bitche [France] [ICAO location identifier] (ICLI)

LFXH........ Camp Du Valdahon [France] [ICAO location identifier] (ICLI)

LFXI .... Apt/Saint-Christol [France] [ICAO location identifier] (ICLI)

LFXJ......... Bordeaux [France] [ICAO location identifier] (ICLI)

LFXK .... Camp De Suippes [France] [ICAO location identifier] (ICLI)

LFXL .... Mailly-Le-Camp [France] [ICAO location identifier] (ICLI)

LFXM .... Mourmelon [France] [ICAO location identifier] (ICLI)

LFXN........ Narbonne [France] [ICAO location identifier] (ICLI)

LFXO........ Tours/Cinq-Mars La Pile [France] [ICAO location identifier] (ICLI)

LFXP .... Camp De Sissonne [France] [ICAO location identifier] (ICLI)

LFXQ........ Camp De Coetquidan [France] [ICAO location identifier] (ICLI)

LFXR .... Rochefort/Soubise [France] [ICAO location identifier] (ICLI)

LFXS .... Camp De La Courtine [France] [ICAO location identifier] (ICLI)

LFXT......... Camp De Caylus [France] [ICAO location identifier] (ICLI)

LFXU........ Les Mureaux [France] [ICAO location identifier] (ICLI)

LFXV .... Lyon/Mont-Verdun [France] [ICAO location identifier] (ICLI)

LFXW .... Camp Du Larzac [France] [ICAO location identifier] (ICLI)

LFYA .... Drachenbronn [France] [ICAO location identifier] (ICLI)

LFYD........ Damblain [France] [ICAO location identifier] (ICLI)

LFYF .... Centre Meteorologique de Concentration et de Diffusion, French Air Force [France] [ICAO location identifier] (ICLI)

LFYG........ Cambrai/Niergnies [France] [ICAO location identifier] (ICLI)

LFYH........ Broye-Les-Pesmes [France] [ICAO location identifier] (ICLI)

LFYL......... Lure/Malbouhans [France] [ICAO location identifier] (ICLI)

LFYM....... Marigny-Le-Grand [France] [ICAO location identifier] (ICLI)

LFYO........ Villacoublay [France] [ICAO location identifier] (ICLI)

LFYR .... Romorantin/Pruniers [France] [ICAO location identifier] (ICLI)

LFYS......... Sainte-Leocadie [France] [ICAO location identifier] (ICLI)

LFYT......... Saint-Simon/Clastres [France] [ICAO location identifier] (ICLI)

LFYX .... Paris [France] [ICAO location identifier] (ICLI)

LFZ............ Lubelska Fabryka Zgrzeblarek [Lublin Flax Carding Factory] (POL)

LFZ............ Lucobne a Farmaceuticke Zavody [Chemical and Pharmaceutical Plants] (CZ)

lg .... Laasgenoemde [The Latter] [Afrikaans]

LG .... Laban Guild [Formerly, LAMG] (EA)

Lg.............. Laenge [Length] [German] (GCA)

LG .... Landgericht [Regional Court] [German] (ILCA)

lg .... Lang [Long, In Length] [German]

lg .... Largo [Square] [Portuguese] (CED)

lg .... Largo [Broadway] [Italian] (CED)

Lg.............. Lebendgewichtstatistik fuer Rinder und Schweine [Live-Weight Statistics for Cattle and Hogs] (EG)

Lg.............. Ligroin [Ligroin] [German] (GCA)

LG .... Local Government

lg .... Logarytm [Logarithm] [Poland]

LG .... Lokalno Gospodarstvo [Local Economy] (YU)

LG .... Luteinizing Hormone (RU)

LG .... Vacuum-Tube Generator, Vacuum-Tube Oscillator (RU)

LGA .... Elgaz [Poland] [ICAO designator] (FAAC)

LGA .... Landesgewerbeamt [Nuremburg] [Information retrieval]

LGA .... Liptako-Gourma Authority [Burkina Faso]

LGA .... Local Government Area

LGAANSW ... Local Government Auditors' Association of New South Wales [Australia]

LGAB........ Local Government Advisory Board [Tasmania, Australia]

LGAB........ Local Government Auditors' Board [Queensland, Australia]

LGAC .... Athinai [Greece] [ICAO location identifier] (ICLI)

LGACHP... Local Government and Community Housing Program [*Australia*]
LGAD........ Andravida [*Greece*] [*ICAO location identifier*]   (ICLI)
LGAG........ Agrinion [*Greece*] [*ICAO location identifier*]   (ICLI)
LGAL......... Alexandroupolis [*Greece*] [*ICAO location identifier*]   (ICLI)
LGAM .... Amphiali [*Greece*] [*ICAO location identifier*]   (ICLI)
LGANSW ... Local Government Association of New South Wales [*Australia*]
LGANT ..... Local Government Association of the Northern Territory [*Australia*]
LGAO .... Laboratoire de Geophysique Appliquee a l'Oceanographie [*French*]   (MSC)
LGASA ...... Local Government Association of South Australia
LGAT........ Athinai [*Greece*] [*ICAO location identifier*]   (ICLI)
LGAX .... Alexandria [*Greece*] [*ICAO location identifier*]   (ICLI)
LGBC........ Local Government Boundaries Commission [*New South Wales, Australia*]
LGBI........ Leningrad State Library Institute Imeni N. K. Krupskaya   (RU)
LGBL........ Nea Anghialos [*Greece*] [*ICAO location identifier*]   (ICLI)
LGC .... Launceston Gas Company [*Australia*]
LGC .... Local Government Commission [*Victoria, Australia*]
LGC .... Local Government Council
LGCA .... Local Government Clerks' Association [*Australia*]
LGCANSW ... Local Government Clerks' Association of New South Wales [*Australia*]
LGCB........ Local Government Clerks' Board [*Queensland, Australia*]
LGCC........ Local Government Clerks' Certificate
LGCC........ Local Government Community Council [*Australia*]
LGCSA ...... Local Government Community Services Association [*Australia*]
LGD .... Compagnie Aerienne du Languedoc [*France*] [*ICAO designator*]   (FAAC)
LGDHC ..... Ligue Guineenne des Droits de l'Homme [*Guinea*] [*Political party*]   (EY)
LGDJ........ Librairie Generale de Droit et de Jurisprudence [*North African*]
LGDP .... Local Government Development Program [*Australia*]
LGE .... Laboratoire de Geophysics Extern [*External Geophysics Laboratory*] [*France*]   (PDAA)
LGE .... Local Government Engineer
LGEA........ Australian Council of Local Government Engineers Associations
LGEANSW ... Local Government Electricity Association of New South Wales [*Australia*]
LGEANSW ... Local Government Engineers' Association of New South Wales [*Australia*]
LGEAQ ..... Local Government Engineers Association of Queensland [*Australia*]
Lgebez........ Lagebezeichnung [*Signatures*] [*Publishing*] [*German*]
Lgebzg........ Lagebezeichnung [*Signatures*] [*Publishing*] [*German*]
LGEEQC... Local Government Electrical Engineering Qualifications Committee [*Australia*]
LGEL........ Elefsis [*Greece*] [*ICAO location identifier*]   (ICLI)
LGEME..... Legion of Greeks from Egypt and the Middle East [*Australia*] [*An association*]
LGEMP..... Local Government Energy Management Program
LGEP........ Laboratoire de Genie Electrique de Paris [*Electrical Engineering Laboratory, Paris*] [*France*]   (WED)
LGEQC...... Local Government Engineering Qualifications Committee [*Australia*]
LGES........ Leningrad State Electric Power Plant   (RU)
LGG .... Gueterwagenleerzug aus Gedeckten Wagen [*Empty Freight Train Consisting of Covered Freight Cars*]   (EG)
LGG .... Liege [*Belgium*] [*Airport symbol*]   (OAG)
LGGC .... Local Government Grants Commission
LGGE .... Laboratoire de Glaciologie et de Geophysique de l'Environnement [*Glaciology and Environmental Geophysics Laboratory*] [*Jointly affiliated with the National Center for Scientific Research and the University of Grenoble*] [*France*]   (EAS)
LGGG .... Athinai [*Greece*] [*ICAO location identifier*]   (ICLI)
LGGP........ Laboratory of Hydrogeological Problems Imeni F. P. Savarenskiy   (RU)
LGH .... Leigh Creek [*Australia*] [*Airport symbol*]   (OAG)
LGHI .... Khios [*Greece*] [*ICAO location identifier*]   (ICLI)
LGHL......... Porto Heli [*Greece*] [*ICAO location identifier*]   (ICLI)
LGI .... Deadman's Cay [*Bahamas*] [*Airport symbol*]   (OAG)
LGI .... Leningrad Mining Institute Imeni G. V. Plekhanov   (RU)
LGIFK .... Lithuanian State Institute of Physical Culture   (RU)
LGILI .... Leningrad State Institute of Historical Linguistics   (RU)
LGIO .... Ioannina [*Greece*] [*ICAO location identifier*]   (ICLI)
LGIP......... Local Government Initiative Program [*Australia*]
LGIR .... Iraklion [*Greece*] [*ICAO location identifier*]   (ICLI)
LGIS .... Local Government Information System [*Australia*]
LGITC .... Local Government Industrial Training Committee [*Australia*]
LGIUU ...... Leningrad City Institute for the Advanced Training of Teachers   (RU)
LGK .... Langkawi [*Malaysia*] [*Airport symbol*]   (OAG)
LGk........... Late Greek [*or Low Greek*] [*Language*]   (BARN)
LGK .... Leningrad City Committee   (RU)

LGK .... Leningrad State Conservatory Imeni N. A. Rimskiy-Korsakov   (RU)
LGKA .... Kastoria [*Greece*] [*ICAO location identifier*]   (ICLI)
LGKC......... Kithira [*Greece*] [*ICAO location identifier*]   (ICLI)
LGKF........ Kefallinia [*Greece*] [*ICAO location identifier*]   (ICLI)
LGKJ........ Kastelorizo [*Greece*] [*ICAO location identifier*]   (ICLI)
LGKL........ Kalamata [*Greece*] [*ICAO location identifier*]   (ICLI)
LGKM ...... Kavala/Amigdhaleon [*Greece*] [*ICAO location identifier*]   (ICLI)
LGKO .... Kos [*Greece*] [*ICAO location identifier*]   (ICLI)
LGKP........ Karpathos [*Greece*] [*ICAO location identifier*]   (ICLI)
LGKR .... Kerkira [*Greece*] [*ICAO location identifier*]   (ICLI)
LGKS........ Kasos [*Greece*] [*ICAO location identifier*]   (ICLI)
LGKV........ Kavala/Khrisoupolis [*Greece*] [*ICAO location identifier*]   (ICLI)
LGKZ........ Kozani [*Greece*] [*ICAO location identifier*]   (ICLI)
LGL .... Long Lellang [*Malaysia*] [*Airport symbol*]   (OAG)
LGL .... Luxair-Societe Luxembourgeoise de Navigation Aerienne SA [*Germany*] [*ICAO designator*]   (FAAC)
LGLE........ Leros [*Greece*] [*ICAO location identifier*]   (ICLI)
LGLR........ Larissa [*Greece*] [*ICAO location identifier*]   (ICLI)
LGM .... Laboratorio per la Geologia Marina [*Italian*]   (MSC)
LGM .... Laboratorium voor Grondmechanica [*Soil Mechanics Laboratory*] [*Netherlands*]   (PDAA)
LGMC .... Local Government Ministers' Conference [*Australia*]
LGMG ...... Megara [*Greece*] [*ICAO location identifier*]   (ICLI)
LGMI .... Leningrad Hydrometeorological Institute   (RU)
LGMI .... Leningrad State Milk Inspection   (RU)
LGMK ...... Mikonos [*Greece*] [*ICAO location identifier*]   (ICLI)
LGML........ Milos [*Greece*] [*ICAO location identifier*]   (ICLI)
LGMR ...... Marathon [*Greece*] [*ICAO location identifier*]   (ICLI)
LGMT .... Leningrad Hydrometeorological Technicum   (RU)
LGMT .... Mitilini [*Greece*] [*ICAO location identifier*]   (ICLI)
LGO .... Gueterwagenleerzug aus Offenen Gueterwagen [*Empty Freight Train Consisting of Open Freight Cars*]   (EG)
LGO .... Local Government Office
LGOLU ..... Leningrad State "Order of Lenin" University Imeni A. A. Zhdanov   (RU)
LGP .... Legaspi [*Philippines*] [*Airport symbol*]   (OAG)
LGP .... Libyan Gas Producers
LGPA........ Local Government Planners Association [*Australia*]
LGPA........ Paros [*Greece*] [*ICAO location identifier*]   (ICLI)
LGPANSW ... Livestock and Grain Producers' Association of New South Wales [*Australia*]
LGPAV ..... Local Government Planners Association of Victoria [*Australia*]
LGPF........ Local Government Pension Fund [*Australia*]
LGPI......... Leningrad State Pedagogical Institute Imeni A. I. Gertsen   (RU)
LGPIIYa... Leningrad State Pedagogical Institute of Foreign Languages   (RU)
LGPMI...... Leningrad State Institute of Pediatric Medicine   (RU)
LGPZ........ Preveza [*Greece*] [*ICAO location identifier*]   (ICLI)
LGQ .... Laboratoire de Geologie du Quaternaire [*Quaternary Geology Laboratory*] [*National Center for Scientific Research*] [*France*]   (EAS)
LGQ .... Lago Agrio [*Ecuador*] [*Airport symbol*]   (OAG)
LGQB .... Local Government Qualifications Board [*Victoria, Australia*]
LGR .... Landesgerichtsrat [*Assize Court Counsel*] [*German*]
LGR .... Leitungsgruppe [*German*]   (ADPT)
LGR .... London Grand Rank [*Freemasonry*]
LGRA .... Local Government Recreation Association [*Australia*]
LGRAV...... Local Government Recreation Association of Victoria [*Australia*]
LGRD .... Rodos/Maritsa [*Greece*] [*ICAO location identifier*]   (ICLI)
LGRI .... Leningrad Institute of Geological Exploration   (RU)
LGRI .... Leningrad State Quality Inspection of Fish   (RU)
LGRP........ Rodos/Paradisi [*Greece*] [*ICAO location identifier*]   (ICLI)
LGRS........ Leningrad City Radio Wire Broadcasting Network   (RU)
LGRT........ Leningrad Trust for Geological Exploration   (RU)
LGRT........ Local Government Remuneration Tribunal (New South Wales) [*Australia*]
LGRX........ Araxos [*Greece*] [*ICAO location identifier*]   (ICLI)
LGS........... Lebowa Granite Suite [*Bushveld Complex, South Africa*] [*Geology*]
LGS........... Leningrad City Soviet   (RU)
LGS........... Ligue pour la Grande Somalie
LGSA........ Khania/Souda [*Greece*] [*ICAO location identifier*]   (ICLI)
LGSA........ Local Government and Shires Association [*Australia*]
LGSB .... Local Government Services Bureau [*South Australia*]
LGSB .... Local Government Superannuation Board [*Queensland, Australia*]
LGSBA ...... Lahore Graduate School of Business Administration [*Pakistan*]
LGSC......... [*The*] Liquefied Gas Shipping Company Ltd. [*Abu Dhabi*]   (MENA)
LGSD........ Sedes [*Greece*] [*ICAO location identifier*]   (ICLI)
LGSK........ Skiathos [*Greece*] [*ICAO location identifier*]   (ICLI)
LGSM....... Samos [*Greece*] [*ICAO location identifier*]   (ICLI)
LGSP........ Sparti [*Greece*] [*ICAO location identifier*]   (ICLI)
LGSPS....... Leningrad City Council of Trade Unions   (RU)

LGSR........	Santorini [*Greece*] [*ICAO location identifier*] (ICLI)
LGST........	Sitia [*Greece*] [*ICAO location identifier*] (ICLI)
LGSV........	Stefanovikion [*Greece*] [*ICAO location identifier*] (ICLI)
LGSY........	Skyros [*Greece*] [*ICAO location identifier*] (ICLI)
LGT	Leningrad State Planning and Surveying Institute of the State Industrial Committee for Transportation Construction, USSR (RU)
LGTA........	Liga General dos Trabalhadores Angolanos [*Leopoldville*]
LGTA........	Ligue Generale des Travailleurs de l'Angola [*General League of Angolan Workers*] (AF)
LGTA........	Local Government Training Authority [*Australia*]
LGTC........	National Local Government Training Council [*Australia*]
LGTG........	Tanagra [*Greece*] [*ICAO location identifier*] (ICLI)
LGTL........	Kasteli [*Greece*] [*ICAO location identifier*] (ICLI)
LGTP........	Local Government Town Planner Certificate [*Australia*]
LGTP........	Tripolis [*Greece*] [*ICAO location identifier*] (ICLI)
LGTPB......	Local Government Town Planners' Board [*Queensland, Australia*]
LGTS........	Leningrad City Telephone Network (RU)
LGTS........	Thessaloniki [*Greece*] [*ICAO location identifier*] (ICLI)
LGTT........	Dekeleia/Tatoi [*Greece*] [*ICAO location identifier*] (ICLI)
LGU..........	Latvian State University Imeni P. Stuchka (RU)
LGU..........	Leningrad State University Imeni A. A. Zhdanov (RU)
LGU..........	L'vov State University Imeni Ivan Franko (RU)
LGUMP	Leningrad Branch of the State Administration of the Metallurgical Industry (RU)
LGV	Legvedelem [*or Legvedelmi*] [*Air Defense or Antiaircraft (Gun)*] (HU)
LGV	Ligue Guadeloupeen de Voile [*France*] (EAIO)
LGVC........	Local Government Valuers' Committee [*New South Wales, Australia*]
LGVO	Volos [*Greece*] [*ICAO location identifier*] (ICLI)
LGW	Legion of Good Will [*Brazil*]
LGW	Lufttarhtgesellschaft Walter GmbH [*Germany*] [*ICAO designator*] (FAAC)
LGWF........	Libyan General Workers' Federation
LGWU.......	Libyan General Workers' Union
LGZ	Laboratorij Gradevinarstva - Zagreb [*Construction Laboratory in Zagreb*] (YU)
LGZA	Zakinthos [*Greece*] [*ICAO location identifier*] (ICLI)
LGZhD......	Leningrad City Railways (RU)
LGZU	Leningrad State Correspondence University (RU)
LH..............	Laborator Hutnicka [*Metallurgical Laboratory (of the Czechoslovak Academy of Sciences)*] (CZ)
LH..............	Landbouwhogeschool [*Wageningen*]
LH..............	Landwirtschaftliche Hochschule [*Agricultural College*] [*German*] (GCA)
LH..............	Ledra Hotel [*Cyprus*]
LH..............	Lidova Hvezdarna [*People's Observatory*] (CZ)
LH..............	Light Horse [*Australia*]
LH..............	Lorinci Hengermu [*Rolling Mills of Lorinc*] (HU)
LHA...........	Licentiate of the Australian Institute of Hospital Administrators (ADA)
LHAA........	Budapest [*Hungary*] [*ICAO location identifier*] (ICLI)
LHBP........	Budapest/Ferihegy [*Hungary*] [*ICAO location identifier*] (ICLI)
LHC...........	Large Hadron Collider [*Nuclear physics*] (ECON)
LHCC	Budapest [*Hungary*] [*ICAO location identifier*] (ICLI)
LHCH........	Laboratoires d'Hydrodynamique, d'Hydraulique Appliquee, et de Constructions Hydrauliques [*Hydrodynamics, Applied Hydraulics, and Hydraulic Construction Laboratories*] [*University of Liege*] [*Research center*] [*Belgium*] (IRC)
LHCN........	Laboratoires d'Hydraulique Appliquee et de Constructions Hydrauliques et Navales [*Applied Hydraulics, Hydraulic Construction and Naval Architecture Laboratories*] [*Belgium*] (IRC)
LHCP	Local History Coordination Project [*Australia*]
LHCR	League for Human and Civil Rights (EAIO)
LHDA........	Lesotho Highlands Development Authority (ECON)
LHDC........	Debrecen [*Hungary*] [*ICAO location identifier*] (ICLI)
LHE...........	Lahore [*Pakistan*] [*Airport symbol*] (OAG)
LHFCS	Long Haul Fuel Conservation System
LHH	League of Home Help [*Australia*] [*An association*]
LHI............	Ligue Homeopathique Internationale [*International Homeopathic League*]
LHI............	Lord Howe Island [*Australia*] (ADA)
LHIB	Lord Howe Island Board [*Australia*]
LHK...........	Lebenshaltungskosten [*Cost of Living*] [*German*] (EG)
LHM..........	Landbau- und Holzbearbeitungsmaschinen [*Agricultural and Woodworking Machines*] (EG)
lhno	Lager Huishoud en Nijverheidsonderwijs [*Benelux*] (BAS)
LHP...........	Lehu [*Papua New Guinea*] [*Airport symbol*] (OAG)
LHptm	Landeshauptmann [*Responsible Local Government Official*] [*German*]
LHQ...........	Land Headquarters [*Australia*]
LHRC	Levin Horticultural Research Centre [*New Zealand*] (DSCA)
LHRF........	League for Human Rights and Freedoms [*Finland*] (EAIO)

LHRL	Lucas Heights Research Laboratories [*Australia*]
LHS	Laborator Heterocyklickych Sloucenin [*Laboratory for the Study of Heterocyclic Compounds (of the Czechoslovak Academy of Sciences)*] (CZ)
LHS	Landsforening for Huntingtons Sykdom [*Norway*] (EAIO)
LHTM	Laboratorio de Histologia a Tecnologia de Madeiras [*Portugal*] (DSCA)
LHV	Luchtvaart Historische Vereniging [*Society of Aeronautical Historians*] [*Netherlands Defunct*] (EAIO)
LHW	Lanzhou [*China*] [*Airport symbol*] (OAG)
LHWP	Lesotho Highlands Water Project (ECON)
LI	Aircraft Designed by B. P. Lisunov (RU)
LI	Final Selector (RU)
LI	Lahmeyer International GmbH [*Germany*] (EAS)
LI	Leeward Islands (BARN)
LI	Lesna Industrija [*Lumber Industry*] (YU)
LI	Liberal International [*World Liberal Union*] [*British*] (EAIO)
LI	Liberia (ABBR)
LI	Liechtenstein [*ANSI two-letter standard code*] (CNC)
LI	Ligue Internationale de la Representation Commerciale [*International League of Commercial Travelers and Agents - ILCTA*] (EAIO)
Li	Liman [*or Limani*] [*Harbor, Port Turkish*] (NAU)
LI	Lincoln Institute [*Australia*]
li	Links [*German*]
LI	Literary Institute Imeni A. M. Gor'kiy (RU)
Li	Litio [*Lithium*] [*Portuguese*]
LI	Livorno [*Car registration plates*] [*Italian*]
LI	Loeknafelag Islands [*Icelandic*] (SLS)
LI	Lucka Intendatura [*Harbor Commissariat*] (YU)
LIA............	Land Information Access [*Western Australia*]
LIA............	Landtechnische Industrieanlagen (VEB LIA) [*Industrial Agricultural Technology Installations (VEB)*] (EG)
LIA............	Lebanese International Airways
LIA............	Leeward Islands Air Transport (1974) Ltd. [*Antigua and Barbuda*] [*ICAO designator*] (FAAC)
LIA............	Life Insurance Act [*Australia*]
LIA............	Linhas Aereas da Guine-Bissau [*Airlines*] (EY)
LIA............	Lithographic Institute of Australia
LIAA.........	Library and Information Association of Australia [*Proposed*]
LIAC.........	Legal Information Access Centre [*State Library of New South Wales*] [*Australia*]
LIAC.........	Liberian International American Corporation
LIAC.........	Local Investment Approvals Committee [*Sri Lanka*] (FEA)
LIADA.......	Liga Ibero-Americana de Astronomia [*Ibero-American Astronomy League*] (EAIO)
LIAM........	Liga Intensificadora da Accao Missionaria
LIAP.........	Leningrad Institute of Aviation Instruments (RU)
LIAT.........	Leeward Island Air Transport [*Antigua*] (LA)
LIAZ.........	Automobile Made by the Likino Bus Plant (RU)
LIAZ.........	Liberecke Automobilove Zavody [*Liberec Automobile Works*] (CZ)
LIAZ.........	Likino Bus Plant (RU)
LIB...........	Air Liberte [*France*] [*ICAO designator*] (FAAC)
Lib...........	Libelle [*Liquid Level*] [*German*] (GCA)
LIB...........	Liberaal [*Liberal*] [*Afrikaans*]
lib...........	Liberaali(nen) [*Finland*]
lib...........	Libere [*Discharged, Liberated*] [*French*]
Lib...........	Liberia
lib...........	Libra [*Pound*] [*Spanish*]
lib...........	Librairie [*Bookstore*] [*French*]
lib...........	Libro [*Book*] [*Spanish*]
LIBA.........	Amendola [*Italy*] [*ICAO location identifier*] (ICLI)
LIBA.........	Licentiate of the Institute of Business Administration
LIBAS.......	Libya Insaat ve Yatirim Anonim Sirketi [*Libyan Construction and Investment Corporation*] (TU)
LIBB.........	Brindisi [*Italy*] [*ICAO location identifier*] (ICLI)
LIBC.........	Crotone [*Italy*] [*ICAO location identifier*] (ICLI)
LibCert......	Library Certificate [*Australia*]
LIBCO.......	Liberty Investors Benefit Insurance Co.
LIBD.........	Bari/Palese Macchie [*Italy*] [*ICAO location identifier*] (ICLI)
LIBE.........	Ligo Internacia de Blindaj Esperantistoj [*International League of Blind Esperantists - ILBE*] (EAIO)
LIBE.........	Monte S. Angelo [*Italy*] [*ICAO location identifier*] (ICLI)
LIBECO	Societe Librevilloise de Constructions [*Libreville Construction Company*] [*Gabon*] (AF)
LIBER	Ligue des Bibliotheques Europeennes de Recherche [*League of European Research Libraries*] (EAIO)
LIBERESE ...	La Libertad-Compania de Seguros Generales SA [*Colombia*] (COL)
LIBERTAS ...	Library Board Extendable Real Time Automation System [*Western Australia*]
LIBF.........	Foggia [*Italy*] [*ICAO location identifier*] (ICLI)
LIBF.........	London International Book Fair [*England*]
Lib Forum ..	Liberal Forum Party of Australia (ADA)
LIBG.........	Grottaglie [*Italy*] [*ICAO location identifier*] (ICLI)

LIBH .... Marina Di Ginosa [*Italy*] [*ICAO location identifier*] (ICLI)
LIBI .... Vieste [*Italy*] [*ICAO location identifier*] (ICLI)
LIBID .... London Interbank Bid Rate [*for Eurodollar deposits*] [*London Stock Exchange*]
LIBIDI .... Liberian Bank for Industrial Development and Investment
LIBIS .... Leuvens Integraal Bibliotheek en Informatie Systeem
LIBISAC ... Livres Bibliotheque Saclay Database [*Commissariat a l'Energie Atomique*] [*France*] [*Information service or system*] (CRD)
LIBJ .... Vibo Valentia [*Italy*] [*ICAO location identifier*] (ICLI)
LIBK .... Caraffa Di Catanzaro [*Italy*] [*ICAO location identifier*] (ICLI)
LIBL .... Palascia [*Italy*] [*ICAO location identifier*] (ICLI)
LIBM .... Grottammare [*Italy*] [*ICAO location identifier*] (ICLI)
LIBN .... Lecce [*Italy*] [*ICAO location identifier*] (ICLI)
LIBNOR .... Institut Libanais de Normalisation [*Lebanon*]
LIBO .... Ortanova [*Italy*] [*ICAO location identifier*] (ICLI)
LIBOR .... London Interbank Offered Rate [*Reference point for syndicated bank loans*]
LIBP .... Pescara [*Italy*] [*ICAO location identifier*] (ICLI)
LIBQ .... Monte Scuro [*Italy*] [*ICAO location identifier*] (ICLI)
LIBR .... Brindise/Casale [*Italy*] [*ICAO location identifier*] (ICLI)
libr .... Librairie [*Bookstore*] [*French*]
LIBRA .... Linnas Brasileiras de Navegacao, SA [*Brazilian Steamship Lines*] (LA)
LIBRAPORT ... Entreprise Nationale d'Importation de Librairie
Libri .... Lindenbrink [*Book wholesaler*]
LIBRIS ...... Library Information Service [*or System*] [*The Royal Library Database*] [*Information service or system*] (IID)
LIBRIS ...... Library Realtime Information System [*South Australian College of Advanced Education*]
LIBROCUBA ... Empresa de Comercio Exterior de Publicaciones [*Foreign Trade Enterprise for Periodicals*] [*Cuba*] (LA)
LIBS .... Campobasso [*Italy*] [*ICAO location identifier*] (ICLI)
LIBSUCO ... Liberian Sugar Corporation
LIBT .... Termoli [*Italy*] [*ICAO location identifier*] (ICLI)
LIBTRACO ... Liberia Tractor & Equipment Co.
LIBU .... Latronico [*Italy*] [*ICAO location identifier*] (ICLI)
LIBV .... Gioia Del Colle [*Italy*] [*ICAO location identifier*] (ICLI)
Libvest .... Liberty Investors Benefit Insurance Co. [*South Africa*]
LIBW .... Bonifati [*Italy*] [*ICAO location identifier*] (ICLI)
LIBX .... Martina Franca [*Italy*] [*ICAO location identifier*] (ICLI)
LIBY .... Santa Maria Di Leuca [*Italy*] [*ICAO location identifier*] (ICLI)
LIBZ .... Potenza [*Italy*] [*ICAO location identifier*] (ICLI)
LIC .... Land Information Centre [*New South Wales, Australia*]
LIC .... Landstingens Inkopscentral [*Sweden*] (IMH)
LIC .... Langage Intermediaire Condense [*French*] (ADPT)
LIC .... Large Integrated Circuit [*Electronics*]
LIC .... League International for Creditors (DCTA)
lic. .... Licenciado [*Licentiate*] [*Spanish*]
Lic .... Licentiatus (FLAF)
LIC .... Life Insurance Corp. [*India*] (PDAA)
LIC .... Lineas Aereas del Caribe [*Colombia*] [*ICAO designator*] (FAAC)
lic. .... Lizentiat [*Licentiate*] [*German*]
LIC .... Local Indigenous Civilian [*Military*]
LIC .... Low Income Country
LICA .... Lamezia/Terme [*Italy*] [*ICAO location identifier*] (ICLI)
LICA .... Licentiate of the Institute of Commonwealth Accountants [*Australia*] (ADA)
LICB .... Comiso [*Italy*] [*ICAO location identifier*] (ICLI)
LICB .... Life Insurance Complaints Board [*Australia*]
LICC .... Catania/Fontanarossa [*Italy*] [*ICAO location identifier*] (ICLI)
LICCD .... Ligue Internationale Contre la Concurrence Deloyale [*International League Against Unfair Competition*] (EAIO)
LICD .... Lampedusa [*Italy*] [*ICAO location identifier*] (ICLI)
Licda .... Licenciada (SCAC)
LICE .... Enna [*Italy*] [*ICAO location identifier*] (ICLI)
Lic en Fily Let ... Licenciado en Filosofia y Letras [*Bachelor of Arts*] [*Spanish*]
LICF .... Messina [*Italy*] [*ICAO location identifier*] (ICLI)
LICG .... Pantelleria [*Italy*] [*ICAO location identifier*] (ICLI)
LICH .... Capo Spartivento [*Italy*] [*ICAO location identifier*] (ICLI)
LICh .... Linear Pulse Part (RU)
lich .... Personal [*Pronoun*] (BU)
lichn sost .... Personnel, Staff (RU)
Lichtabhaengigk ... Lichtabhaengigkeit [*Light Dependance*] [*German*] (GCA)
Lichtdr .... Lichtdruck [*Photoengraving*] [*Publishing*] [*German*]
lichtdr .... Lichtdruk [*Photoengraving*] [*Publishing*] [*Netherlands*]
LICI .... Finale [*Italy*] [*ICAO location identifier*] (ICLI)
LICI .... Limonaderie de la Cote-D'Ivoire
LicIP(SA) ... Licentiates Institute of Printing (South Africa) (AA)
LICJ .... Palermo/Punta Raisi [*Italy*] [*ICAO location identifier*] (ICLI)
LICL .... Gela [*Italy*] [*ICAO location identifier*] (ICLI)
LICM .... Calopezzati [*Italy*] [*ICAO location identifier*] (ICLI)
LICO .... Cozzo Spadaro [*Italy*] [*ICAO location identifier*] (ICLI)
LICOTRA ... L'Essor Ivoirien de Construction et de Travaux Publics
LICOVALLE ... Industria de Licores del Valle [*Colombia*] (COL)
LICP .... Palermo/Boccadifalco [*Italy*] [*ICAO location identifier*] (ICLI)

LICR .... Reggio Calabria [*Italy*] [*ICAO location identifier*] (ICLI)
LICRA .... Ligue Internationale Contre le Racisme et l'Antisemitisme [*France*]
LICROSS .. League of International Red Cross Societies
LICS .... Sciacca [*Italy*] [*ICAO location identifier*] (ICLI)
LICT .... Trapani/Birgi [*Italy*] [*ICAO location identifier*] (ICLI)
LICU .... Ustica [*Italy*] [*ICAO location identifier*] (ICLI)
LICX .... Prizzi [*Italy*] [*ICAO location identifier*] (ICLI)
LICZ .... Sigonella [*Italy*] [*ICAO location identifier*] (ICLI)
liczn .... Liczny [*Numerous*] [*Poland*]
LID .... Alidaunia SRL [*Italy*] [*ICAO designator*] (FAAC)
LID .... Lectuur- en Informatie Dienst [*NBLC*] [*Netherlands*]
LID .... Lehr Institut fuer Dokumentation
LID .... Literaturdienst Medizin und Umwelt [*Literature Service in Medicine and Environment*] [*Austrian National Institute for Public Health*] [*Information service or system*] (IID)
LIDA .... Laboratorio de Investigacion y Diagnostico de Avicultura [*Avian Research and Diagnosis Laboratory*] [*Cuba*] (LA)
LIDA .... Ligue Internationale des Droits de l'Animal [*International League for Animal Rights*] (EAIO)
LIDA .... Livestock Development Authority [*Tanzania*] (AF)
LIDC .... Ligue Internationale du Droit de la Concurrence [*International League for Competition Law*] [*Paris, France*] (EA)
LIDE .... Liga de la Activacion de la Region del Delta [*Argentina*] (LAA)
LIDEE .... L'Investissement et la Distribution Economique Eburneenne
LI des AT ... Ligue Internationale des Associations Touristes [*International League of Tourist Associations*] [*French*]
LIDH .... Ligue Internationale des Droits de l'Homme
LIDIA .... Lernen im Dialog [*German*] (ADPT)
LIDIA .... Licentiate of the Industrial Design Institute of Australia
LIDU .... Lega Internazionale dei Diritti dell' Uomo [*International League of Human Rights*] [*Italian*] (WER)
LIDUS .... Liberal-Demokratische Union der Schweiz [*Liberal Democratic Union of Switzerland*] [*Political party*] (PPE)
LIE .... Libenge [*Zaire*] [*Airport symbol*] [*Obsolete*] (OAG)
LIE .... Liechtenstein [*ANSI three-letter standard code*] (CNC)
LIEA .... Alghero [*Italy*] [*ICAO location identifier*] (ICLI)
LIEB .... Capo Bellavista [*Italy*] [*ICAO location identifier*] (ICLI)
Liebhaberausg ... Liebhaberausgabe [*Collector's Edition*] [*German*]
LIEC .... Capo Carbonara [*Italy*] [*ICAO location identifier*] (ICLI)
Liecht .... Liechtenstein
LIED .... Decimomannu [*Italy*] [*ICAO location identifier*] (ICLI)
LIEE .... Cagliari/Elmas [*Italy*] [*ICAO location identifier*] (ICLI)
LIEF .... Capo Frasca [*Italy*] [*ICAO location identifier*] (ICLI)
Lief .... Lieferung [*Number*] [*Publishing*] [*German*]
Lieferg .... Lieferung [*Number*] [*Publishing*] [*German*]
Liefg .... Lieferung [*Number*] [*Publishing*] [*German*]
LIEG .... Guardiavecchia [*Italy*] [*ICAO location identifier*] (ICLI)
LIEH .... Capo Caccia [*Italy*] [*ICAO location identifier*] (ICLI)
LIEI .... Leningrad Institute of Economic Research (RU)
LIEI .... Leningrad Institute of Engineering Economics (RU)
LIEL .... Capo S. Lorenzo [*Italy*] [*ICAO location identifier*] (ICLI)
LIEM .... Leningrad Institute of Experimental Meteorology (RU)
LIEM .... Macomer [*Italy*] [*ICAO location identifier*] (ICLI)
LIEN .... Fonni [*Italy*] [*ICAO location identifier*] (ICLI)
LIEN .... Ligue Internationale pour l'Education Nouvelle [*World Education Fellowship*]
LIENS .... Ligue Europeenne pour une Nouvelle Societe [*European League for a New Society - ELNS*] [*Paris, France*] (EAIO)
LIEO .... Olbia/Costa Smeralda [*Italy*] [*ICAO location identifier*] (ICLI)
LIEP .... Perdasdefogu [*Italy*] [*ICAO location identifier*] (ICLI)
LIES .... Library Information and Enquiry System
LIETIN ..... Leningrad Scientific Research Institute for Determination of Disability and Organization of Work for Disabled Persons (RU)
LIETTIN ... Leningrad Scientific Research Institute for Determination of Disability and Employment of Disabled Persons (RU)
Lieut .... Lieutenant [*Lieutenant*] [*Military*] [*French*] (MTD)
Lieut Col .... Lieutenant-Colonel [*Lieutenant Colonel*] [*Military*] [*French*] (MTD)
liev .... Lievemente [*Slightly*] [*Italian*]
lievem .... Lievemente [*Slightly*] [*Italian*]
lieviss .... Lievissimamente [*Very Slightly*] [*Italian*]
LIF .... Lifu [*Loyalty Islands*] [*Airport symbol*] (OAG)
LIFA .... Life Insurance Federation of Australia
LIFE .... Laboratorios Industriales Farmaceuticos Ecuatorianos [*Ecuadorean Pharmaceutical Industrial Laboratories*] (LA)
LIFEMO ... Liga Feminina de Mocambique [*Mozambique Women's League*] (AF)
LiFHAS ..... Libertarian Foundation for Human Assistance (EAIO)
LiFHAS ..... Libertarische Fonds voor Hulp Acties [*Libertarian Foundation for Human Assistance*] [*Netherlands*] (EAIO)
LIFL .... Laboratoire d'Informatique Fondamentale de Lille [*Laboratory of Information Science*] [*Research center*] [*France*] (IRC)
LIFLI .... Leningrad Institute of History, Philosophy, and Literature (RU)

LIFPL .... Ligue Internationale de Femmes pour la Paix et la Liberte [*Women's International League for Peace and Freedom - WILPF*] (EAIO)

LIFPL/SF ... Ligue Internationale de Femmes pour la Paix et la Liberte, Section Francaise (EAIO)

LIFT .... London International Freight Terminal (DS)

Liftoremont ... Moscow City Trust for the Repair of Elevators in Dwelling Houses (RU)

Liftstroy ..... Administration of Elevator Construction (RU)

LIFZA .... Liberia Industrial Free Zone Authority (GEA)

lig .... Ligacao [*Union*] [*Portuguese*]

LIG .... Limoges [*France*] [*Airport symbol*] (OAG)

ligeir .... Ligeiramente [*Slightly*] [*Portuguese*]

LIGEM ..... Lomonosov Institute of Geochemistry, Crystallography, and Mineralogy (of the Academy of Sciences, USSR) (RU)

LIGENCO ... Liberian General Enterprises Company

LIGI .... Leningrad Institute of Civil Engineers (RU)

LIGNA ...... Podnik Zahranicniho Obchodu pro Dovoz a Vyvoz Dreva a Vyrobku Prumyslu Drevozpracujiciho a Papirenskeho [*Foreign Trade Enterprise for the Import and Export of Wood and Products of the Lumber and Paper Industries*] (CZ)

ligr .... Ligroin (RU)

LIGVF ...... Leningrad Institute of the Civil Air Fleet (RU)

LIHG .... Ligue Internationale de Hockey sur Glace [*International Ice Hockey Federation*]

LII .... Flight Research Institute (RU)

LII .... Leningrad Industrial Institute (RU)

LII .... Mulia [*Indonesia*] [*Airport symbol*] (OAG)

LIIA .... Italy International NOTAM Office [*Italy*] [*ICAO location identifier*] (ICLI)

LIIB .... Roma [*Italy*] [*ICAO location identifier*] (ICLI)

LIIC .... Italy Military International NOTAM Office [*Italy*] [*ICAO location identifier*] (ICLI)

LIIGVF ..... Leningrad Institute of Civil Air Fleet Engineers (RU)

LIII .... Roma [*Italy*] [*ICAO location identifier*] (ICLI)

liik .... Liike-Clama(ssa) [*Finland*]

LIIKP .... Leningrad Institute of Motion-Picture Industry Engineers (RU)

LIIKS .... Leningrad Institute of Municipal Construction Engineers (RU)

LIIMP .... Leningrad Institute of Dairy Industry Engineers (RU)

LIIMSZ ..... Leningrad Institute of Mechanical Engineers of Socialist Agriculture (RU)

LIIOP .... Leningrad State Institute of Engineers for Public Eating Facilities (RU)

LIIPS .... Leningrad Institute of Industrial Construction Engineers (RU)

LIIPT .... Leningrad Institute of Industrial Transportation Engineers (RU)

LIIR .... Italian Agency for Air Navigation Services [*Italy*] [*ICAO location identifier*] (ICLI)

LIIVT .... Leningrad Institute of Water Transportation Engineers (RU)

LIIZhT ...... Leningrad Institute of Railroad Transportation Engineers Imeni Academician V. N. Obraztsov (RU)

LIJJ .... Roma [*Italy*] [*ICAO location identifier*] (ICLI)

LIK .... Artificial Climate Laboratory (RU)

LIK .... Leman Industries Kaduna Ltd.

LIK .... Lesno Industrijski Kombinat [*Industrial Combine in Wood Products*] [*Sostanj*] (YU)

LIK .... Likiep [*Marshall Islands*] [*Airport symbol*] (OAG)

LIK .... Switchboard Final Selector [*Telephony*] (RU)

LIK .... Zadruga Likovnih Umjetnika [*Representational Artists' Cooperative*] [*Sarajevo*] (YU)

LIKAT-IS ... Turkiye Liman ve Kara Tahmil-Tahliye Iscileri Sendikasi [*Turkish Longshoremen's Union*] (TU)

LIKb .... Large Exchange Final Selector [*Telephony*] (RU)

LIKh .... Leningrad Institute for Managerial Personnel (RU)

LIKhF .... Leningrad Institute of Chemical Physics (RU)

LIKhMP .... Leningrad Institute of the Refrigeration and Dairy Industries (RU)

LIKhT .... Leningrad Scientific Research Institute of Surgical Tuberculosis and Bone and Joint Diseases (RU)

LIKI .... Leningrad Institute of Motion-Picture Engineers (RU)

LIKP .... Leningrad Institute of the Confectionery Industry (RU)

likpunkt ..... Center for the Elimination of Illiteracy (RU)

LIKUD .... Political Bloc [*Israel*] (ME)

LIKUM ...... Zadruga Likovnih Umjetnika Hrvatske [*Representational Artists' Cooperative of Croatia*] (YU)

Likvidkom ... Liquidation Commission (RU)

LIL .... Lille [*France*] [*Airport symbol*] (OAG)

LIL .... Lithuanian Airlines [*ICAO designator*] (FAAC)

LILA .... Ligue Internationale de la Librairie Ancienne [*International League of Antiquarian Booksellers - ILAB*] (EAIO)

LILACS ...... Latin American and Caribbean Health Sciences Literature (IID)

LILI .... Leningrad Institute of Historical Linguistics (RU)

lim .... Estuary, Firth [*Topography*] (RU)

LIM .... Final Trunk Selector (RU)

LIM .... Leningrad Institute of Metals (RU)

LIM .... Liberia Inland Mission

LIM .... Lima [*Peru*] [*Airport symbol*] (OAG)

lim .... Liminaire [*Preliminary*] [*Publishing*] [*French*]

lim .... Limitato [*Limited*] [*Publishing*] [*Italian*]

lim .... Limite [*Limited*] [*Publishing*] [*French*]

LIM .... Livingstone Inland Mission

LIM .... Livingstone Interior Mission

LIM .... Materials-Testing Laboratory (RU)

LIMA .... Torino [*Italy*] [*ICAO location identifier*] (ICLI)

LIMAN-SEN ... Kibris Turk Liman ve Tasit Iscileri Sendikasi [*Turkish Cypriot Harbor Workers and Stevedores' Union*] (GC)

LIMB .... Milano/Bresso [*Italy*] [*ICAO location identifier*] (ICLI)

LIMBRAVOD ... Limarsko-Bravarska i Vodoinstalaterska Radionica [*Tinsmiths, Locksmiths, and Plumbers Shop*] [*Titograd*] (YU)

LIMC .... Milano/Malpensa [*Italy*] [*ICAO location identifier*] (ICLI)

LIMD .... Grigna Settentrionale [*Italy*] [*ICAO location identifier*] (ICLI)

LIME .... Bergamo/Orio Al Serio [*Italy*] [*ICAO location identifier*] (ICLI)

LIMES .... Litton-Management-Erfolgssystem [*German*] (ADPT)

LIMF .... Torino/Caselle [*Italy*] [*ICAO location identifier*] (ICLI)

LIMG .... Albenga [*Italy*] [*ICAO location identifier*] (ICLI)

LIMH .... Pian Rosa [*Italy*] [*ICAO location identifier*] (ICLI)

LIMI .... Colle Del Gigante [*Italy*] [*ICAO location identifier*] (ICLI)

LIMI .... Leningrad International Management Institute [*Joint Venture between Bocconi University, Italy and Leningrad University*] (ECON)

LIMIG ...... Ligue Luxembourgeoise des Mutiles et Invalides de Guerre (1940-1945) [*Luxembourg League of WWII Cripples and Invalids*] (WER)

limin .... Liminaire [*Preliminary*] [*Publishing*] [*French*]

LIMINCO ... Liberian Mining Company

limit .... Limitiert [*Limited*] [*German*]

LIMJ .... Genova/Sestri [*Italy*] [*ICAO location identifier*] (ICLI)

LIMK .... Torino/Bric Della Croce [*Italy*] [*ICAO location identifier*] (ICLI)

LIML .... Milano/Linate [*Italy*] [*ICAO location identifier*] (ICLI)

LIMM .... Milano [*Italy*] [*ICAO location identifier*] (ICLI)

LIMN .... Cameri [*Italy*] [*ICAO location identifier*] (ICLI)

LIMO .... Monte Bisbino [*Italy*] [*ICAO location identifier*] (ICLI)

LIMP .... Parma [*Italy*] [*ICAO location identifier*] (ICLI)

LIMQ .... Govone [*Italy*] [*ICAO location identifier*] (ICLI)

LIMR .... Novi Ligure [*Italy*] [*ICAO location identifier*] (ICLI)

LIMS .... Piacenza/San Damiano [*Italy*] [*ICAO location identifier*] (ICLI)

LIMSI .... Laboratoire d'Informatique pour la Mecanique et les Sciences de l'Ingenieur [*French*] (ADPT)

LIMSKh ..... Leningrad Institute of Agricultural Mechanization (RU)

LIMSZ ...... Leningrad Institute for the Mechanization of Socialist Agriculture (RU)

LIMT .... Passo Della Cisa [*Italy*] [*ICAO location identifier*] (ICLI)

LIMU .... Capo Mele [*Italy*] [*ICAO location identifier*] (ICLI)

LIMV .... Passo Dei Giovi [*Italy*] [*ICAO location identifier*] (ICLI)

LIMW .... Aosta [*Italy*] [*ICAO location identifier*] (ICLI)

LIMY .... Monte Malanotte [*Italy*] [*ICAO location identifier*] (ICLI)

LIMZ .... Levaldigi [*Italy*] [*ICAO location identifier*] (ICLI)

LIN .... Institute for Forest Study (of the Academy of Sciences, USSR) (RU)

LIN .... Lembaga Instrumentasi Nasional [*National Institute for Instrumentation*] [*Indonesian*] [*Research center*] (IRC)

lin .... Linea [*Line*] [*Spanish*]

lin .... Liniment [*Liniment*] [*Pharmacy*]

LIN .... Milan [*Italy*] Forlanini-Linate [*Airport symbol*] (OAG)

LINA .... Liberian National News Agency (AF)

LINA .... Liberian News Agency (EY)

LINA .... Literaturnachweise [*Literature Compilations Database*] [*Fraunhofer Society*] (IID)

LINABOL ... Lineas Navieras Bolivianas [*Shipping line*] [*Bolivia*] (EY)

LINACO .... Lignes Nationales Aeriennes Congolaises

LINA-CONGO ... Lignes Nationales Aeriennes Congolaises

LINAR .... Larkana Institute of Nuclear Medicine and Radiotherapy [*Pakistan*] [*Research center*] (IRC)

LINBOV .... Leningrad Institute for Pest and Disease Control in Agriculture (RU)

LINC .... Libraries and Information for the North Coast [*Australia*] (ADA)

lingv .... Linguistics (RU)

LINK .... Lawyers Information Network [*Australia*]

linksdr .... Linksdrehend [*Counterclockwise*] [*German*]

lin metur ..... Linear Meter (BU)

linn .... Linnen [*Cloth*] [*Publishing*] [*Netherlands*]

LINOA ..... Librairie Nouvelle de l'Ouest Africain

LINOCO .... Societe Nationale des Petroles Libyens [*Libyan National Oil Corporation*]

LINOS ...... Learning and Information Needs of Schools [*Australia*]

LINSU .... Liberian National Students Union

LINW .... Lekarski Instytut Naukowo-Wydawniczy [*Medical Scientific Publishing Institute*] (POL)

LIO .... Laboratorio de Investigaciones Oncologicas [*Oncological Research Laboratory*] [*Cuba*] (LA)
LIO .... Laboratorium voor Insekticidenonderzoek [*Laboratory for Research on Insecticides*] [*Netherlands*] (ARC)
LIO .... Laboratory for Artificial Insemination of Animals (RU)
LIO .... Land Information Office [*Australian Capital Territory*]
LIO .... Leiten, Informieren, Organisieren [*German*] (ADPT)
LIO .... Lesno Industrijski Obrat [*Industrial Plant for Wood Products*] (YU)
LIO .... Limon [*Costa Rica*] [*Airport symbol*] (OAG)
LIOK .... Ludowy Instytut Oswiaty i Kultury [*People's Institute for Education and Culture*] (POL)
LION .... Library Information OnLine [*International Atomic Energy Agency*] [*United Nations*] (DUND)
LIOOT ...... Leningrad Scientific Research Institute of Work Organization and Safety (RU)
LIOT .... All-Union Scientific Research Institute of Work Safety of the VTsSPS [*Leningrad*] (RU)
LIP .... Label Integrity Program [*Australia*]
LIP .... Liga Iberista Portuguesa [*Portuguese Iberian League*] (WER)
LIPA .... Aviano [*Italy*] [*ICAO location identifier*] (ICLI)
LIPA .... Liga de Iniciacao e Propaganda Aeronautica [*Portugal*]
LIPA .... L'Industrie de Peche en Afrique [*African Fishing Industry*] [*Congo*] (AF)
LIPAD ...... Ligue Patriotique pour le Developpement [*Burkina Faso*] [*Political party*] (EY)
LIPAP .... Lanzhou Institute of Plateau Atmospheric Physics [*Chinese Academy of Sciences*] [*Research center*] (EAS)
LIPB .... Bolzano [*Italy*] [*ICAO location identifier*] (ICLI)
LIPB .... Lloyd's International Private Banking [*Finance*]
LIPC .... Cervia [*Italy*] [*ICAO location identifier*] (ICLI)
LIPC .... Livestock Industry Promotion Council [*Australia*]
LIPD .... Udine/Campoformido [*Italy*] [*ICAO location identifier*] (ICLI)
LIPE .... Bologna/Borgo Panigale [*Italy*] [*ICAO location identifier*] (ICLI)
LIPETCO ... Compagnie Petroliere Libyenne
LIPF .... Ferrara [*Italy*] [*ICAO location identifier*] (ICLI)
LIPG .... Gorizia [*Italy*] [*ICAO location identifier*] (ICLI)
LIPH .... Treviso/San Angelo [*Italy*] [*ICAO location identifier*] (ICLI)
LIPI .... Lembaga Ilmu Pengetahuan Indonesia [*Indonesian Council of the Sciences*] (IN)
LIPI .... Rivolto [*Italy*] [*ICAO location identifier*] (ICLI)
LIPJ .... Bassano Del Grappa [*Italy*] [*ICAO location identifier*] (ICLI)
LIPK .... Forli [*Italy*] [*ICAO location identifier*] (ICLI)
LIPK .... Leningrad Scientific Research Institute of Blood Transfusion (RU)
LIPKKh ..... Leningrad Institute for Improving the Qualifications of Managerial Personnel (RU)
LIPKRI ..... Leningrad Institute for Improving the Qualifications of Workers in the Arts (RU)
LIPL .... Ghedi [*Italy*] [*ICAO location identifier*] (ICLI)
LIPN .... Verona/Boscomantico [*Italy*] [*ICAO location identifier*] (ICLI)
LIPO .... Local Industry Promotion Organisation [*Australia*]
LIPO .... Montichiari [*Italy*] [*ICAO location identifier*] (ICLI)
LIPOS .... Livnica i Tvornica Poljoprivrednih Sprava [*Foundry and Factory of Agricultural Tools*] [*Tuzla*] (YU)
LIPP .... Padova [*Italy*] [*ICAO location identifier*] (ICLI)
LIPQ .... Ronchi De'Legionari [*Italy*] [*ICAO location identifier*] (ICLI)
LIPR .... Rimini [*Italy*] [*ICAO location identifier*] (ICLI)
LIPS .... Libraries Initiating Promotions [*Australia*]
LIPS .... Treviso/Istrana [*Italy*] [*ICAO location identifier*] (ICLI)
LIPT .... Vicenza [*Italy*] [*ICAO location identifier*] (ICLI)
LIPTOL ..... Lignitorykheia Ptolemaidos [*Ptolemais Lignite Mines*] [*Greek*] (GC)
LIPU .... Padova [*Italy*] [*ICAO location identifier*] (ICLI)
LIPV .... Venezia/San Nicolo [*Italy*] [*ICAO location identifier*] (ICLI)
LIPX .... Villafranca [*Italy*] [*ICAO location identifier*] (ICLI)
LIPY .... Ancona/Falconara [*Italy*] [*ICAO location identifier*] (ICLI)
LIPZ .... Leningrad Scientific Research Institute of Occupational Diseases (RU)
LIPZ .... Venezia/Tessera [*Italy*] [*ICAO location identifier*] (ICLI)
liq .... Liquidacion [*Liquidation*] [*Spanish*]
liq .... Liquidation [*Liquidation, Settlement*] [*French*]
LIQ .... Lisala [*Zaire*] [*Airport symbol*] (OAG)
LIQB .... Arezzo [*Italy*] [*ICAO location identifier*] (ICLI)
LIQC .... Capri [*Italy*] [*ICAO location identifier*] (ICLI)
LIQC .... Laboratorio de Investigaciones sobre la Quimica del Cafe [*Coffee Chemistry Research Laboratory*] [*Research center*] [*Colorado*] (IRC)
LIQD .... Passo Della Porretta [*Italy*] [*ICAO location identifier*] (ICLI)
LIQI .... Gran Sasso [*Italy*] [*ICAO location identifier*] (ICLI)
LIQJ .... Civitavecchia [*Italy*] [*ICAO location identifier*] (ICLI)
LIQK .... Capo Palinuro [*Italy*] [*ICAO location identifier*] (ICLI)
LIQM .... Rifredo Mugello [*Italy*] [*ICAO location identifier*] (ICLI)
liqn .... Liquidacion [*Liquidation*] [*Spanish*]
LIQN .... Rieti [*Italy*] [*ICAO location identifier*] (ICLI)
liqo .... Liquido [*Liquid*] [*Spanish*]

LIQO .... Monte Argentario [*Italy*] [*ICAO location identifier*] (ICLI)
LIQP .... Palmaria [*Italy*] [*ICAO location identifier*] (ICLI)
liq pr .... Liquidation Prochaine [*French*]
LIQQ .... Monte Cavo [*Italy*] [*ICAO location identifier*] (ICLI)
LIQR .... Radicofani [*Italy*] [*ICAO location identifier*] (ICLI)
LIQS .... Siena [*Italy*] [*ICAO location identifier*] (ICLI)
LIQT .... Circeo [*Italy*] [*ICAO location identifier*] (ICLI)
Liqu .... Liquor [*Liquid*] [*German*] (GCA)
LIQV .... Volterra [*Italy*] [*ICAO location identifier*] (ICLI)
LIQW .... Sarzana/Luni [*Italy*] [*ICAO location identifier*] (ICLI)
LIQZ .... Ponza [*Italy*] [*ICAO location identifier*] (ICLI)
LIR .... Liberia [*Costa Rica*] [*Airport symbol*] (OAG)
LIR .... Lionair SA [*Luxembourg*] [*ICAO designator*] (FAAC)
LIRA .... Logging Industry Research Association, Inc. [*New Zealand*] (ARC)
LIRA .... Roma/Ciampino [*Italy*] [*ICAO location identifier*] (ICLI)
LIRB .... Vigna Di Valle [*Italy*] [*ICAO location identifier*] (ICLI)
LIRC .... Centocelle [*Italy*] [*ICAO location identifier*] (ICLI)
LIRC .... Ligue Internationale de la Representation Commerciale [*International League of Commercial Travelers and Agents - ILCTA*] (EAIO)
LIRCI .... Liga Internacional de Reconstruccion de la IV Internacional [*International Reconstruction League of the Fourth International*] [*Spanish*] (WER)
LIRE .... Pratica Di Mare [*Italy*] [*ICAO location identifier*] (ICLI)
LIRF .... Roma/Fiumicino [*Italy*] [*ICAO location identifier*] (ICLI)
LIRG .... Guidonia [*Italy*] [*ICAO location identifier*] (ICLI)
LIRG .... Leningrad Institute of Radiation Hygiene (RU)
LIRH .... Frosinone [*Italy*] [*ICAO location identifier*] (ICLI)
LIRI .... Leather Industries Research Institute [*Council for Scientific and Industrial Research*] [*South Africa*]
LIRI .... Salerno/Pontecagnano [*Italy*] [*ICAO location identifier*] (ICLI)
lirich .... Lyrical (RU)
LIRJ .... Marina Di Campo [*Italy*] [*ICAO location identifier*] (ICLI)
LIRK .... Monte Terminillo [*Italy*] [*ICAO location identifier*] (ICLI)
LIRL .... Latina [*Italy*] [*ICAO location identifier*] (ICLI)
LIRM .... Grazzanise [*Italy*] [*ICAO location identifier*] (ICLI)
LIRN .... Napoli/Capodichino [*Italy*] [*ICAO location identifier*] (ICLI)
LIRP .... Pisa [*Italy*] [*ICAO location identifier*] (ICLI)
LIRQ .... Firenze [*Italy*] [*ICAO location identifier*] (ICLI)
LIRR .... Luoyang Institute of Refractories Research [*China*] (IRC)
LIRR .... Roma [*Italy*] [*ICAO location identifier*] (ICLI)
LIRS .... Grosseto [*Italy*] [*ICAO location identifier*] (ICLI)
LIRT .... Trevico [*Italy*] [*ICAO location identifier*] (ICLI)
LIRTA .... Laboratoire d'Infrarouge Technique et Appliquee [*France*] (PDAA)
LIRU .... Roma/Urbe [*Italy*] [*ICAO location identifier*] (ICLI)
LIRV .... Viterbo [*Italy*] [*ICAO location identifier*] (ICLI)
LIRZ .... Perugia [*Italy*] [*ICAO location identifier*] (ICLI)
LIS .... Airlis SA [*Spain*] [*ICAO designator*] (FAAC)
LIS .... Laboratory Salt-Content Indicator (RU)
LIS .... Land Information System [*New South Wales, Australia*]
LIS .... Land Inquiry Service [*Australia*]
LIS .... Leningrad Scientific Research Institute of Structures and Building Materials (RU)
LIS .... Liberian Information Service (AF)
lis .... Lisays [*Finland*]
LIS .... Lisbon [*Portugal*] [*Airport symbol*] (OAG)
LIS .... Lisensiaat [*or Lisensie*] [*Licentiate or Licence*] [*Afrikaans*]
lis .... Lisensiaatti [*Finland*]
LIS .... Locate in Scotland [*Agency*]
LIS .... Test Flight Station (RU)
LISA .... Licht Sammler [*Light Collector*] [*Fluorescent plastic used in commercial displays*] [*German*]
LISCo .... Liberian Iron and Steel Corporation (AF)
LISDOK .... Literaturinformationssystem [*Literature Information System*] [*North Rhine-Westphalia Institute for Air Pollution Control*] [*Information service or system*] (IID)
Lise-Der ..... Lycee (High School) Students' Organization (TU)
LISH .... Laboratoire d'Informatique pour les Sciences de l'Homme [*French*] (SLS)
LISI .... Leningrad Construction Engineering Institute (RU)
LISP .... Listensprache [*German*] (ADPT)
LIsp .... Special Final Selector [*Telephony*] (RU)
LISPD .... Library and Information Services for People with Disabilities [*Australia*]
LISS .... Leningrad Institute of Soviet Construction Imeni M. I. Kalinin (RU)
LIST .... Leningrad Institute of Soviet Trade Imeni F. Engels (RU)
LIST .... Logisch-Integrative Strukturierung von Texten [*German*] (ADPT)
LISU .... Library and Information Staff Union [*Australia*]
LISWA ...... Library and Information Service of Western Australia
LISWG ...... Land Interface Sub-Working Group [*NATO*] (NATG)
LIT .... Air Littoral [*France*] [*ICAO designator*] (FAAC)
lit .... Foundry [*Topography*] (RU)

LIT............. Leningrad Industrial Technicum   (RU)
Lit............... Lire Italiane [*Italian Lire*] [*Monetary unit*]
lit............... Liten [*Little, Small*] [*Sweden*]
lit............... Liter [*Liter*]   (HU)
lit............... Literary, Literature   (RU)
Lit............. Literatur [*Literature*] [*German*]   (EG)
Lit............. Literatura [*Literature*] [*Portuguese*]
lit............. Literatura [*Former Czechoslovakia*]
lit............. Literature, Literary   (BU)
lit............. Lithographic, Lithography   (RU)
lit............. Lithuanian   (RU)
LIT............. Lithuanian Railroad   (RU)
lit............. Litografi [*Lithography*] [*Publishing Danish/Norwegian*]
lit............. Litografia [*Lithography*] [*Publishing*] [*Italian*]
lit............. Litre [*Liter*] [*French*]
Lit............. Litro [*Liter*] [*Italian*]
lit............. Litteraire [*French*]   (TPFD)
LITBANG ... Penelitian dan Pengembangan [*Research and Development*]   (IN)
LITCA .... Licensing, Innovation, and Technology Consultants' Association [*Italy*]   (EAIO)
LitDokAB .. Literaturdokumentation zur Arbeitsmarkt- und Berufsforschung [*Deutsche Bundesanstalt fuer Arbeit*] [*Germany*] [*Information service or system*]   (CRD)
liter............. Literature, Literary   (BU)
Litf............. Literaturen Front [*Literary Front*] [*A newspaper*]   (BU)
litfak........... Division of Literature (Division of Russian Language and Literature)   (RU)
Litfront....... Literaturen Front [*Literary Front*] [*A newspaper*]   (BU)
Lith............. Lithografie [*Lithography*] [*Publishing*] [*German*]
lith............. Lithografie [*Lithograph*] [*Publishing*] [*French*]
litho............. Lithografie [*Lithography*] [*Publishing*] [*Netherlands*]
litho............. Lithographie [*Lithography*] [*Publishing*] [*French*]
Lithogr....... Lithografie [*Lithography*] [*Publishing*] [*German*]
lithogr........ Lithografie [*Lithography*] [*Publishing*] [*Netherlands*]
lithogr........ Lithographie [*Lithography*] [*Publishing*] [*French*]
Lithograf.... Lithografie [*Lithography*] [*Publishing*] [*German*]
LITIN .... Leningrad Scientific Research Institute for the Study and Organization of Work for Disabled Persons   (RU)
Litinstitut... Moscow Literary Institute Imeni A. M. Gor'kiy   (RU)
Litizdat...... State Publishing House of Belles Lettres   (RU)
LITKhUDGIZ ... State Publishing House of Belles Lettres   (RU)
lit-khudozh ... Belletristic   (RU)
Litkoopinsoyuz ... Republic Union of Disabled Persons' Cooperatives of the Lithuanian SSR   (RU)
Litkruzhok ... Literary Circle   (BU)
LITM........ Leningrad Institute of Precision Mechanics   (RU)
LITMiO..... Leningrad Institute of Precision Mechanics and Optics   (RU)
LITMO...... Leningrad Institute of Precision Mechanics and Optics   (RU)
LitNIIGiM ... Lithuanian Scientific Research Institute of Hydraulic Engineering and Reclamation   (RU)
LITO......... Literary Publishing Division of Narkompros   (RU)
litogr.......... Lithographed   (RU)
litogr.......... Lithography, Lithographed, Lithographic   (BU)
litogr.......... Litografia [*Lithography*] [*Hungary*]
litogr.......... Litografia [*Lithography*] [*Poland*]
Litogr izd.... Lithographic Publication   (BU)
LITOMETAL ... Litografia en Metal SA [*Colombia*]   (COL)
LITOPAN ... Litografia Panamericana Ltda. [*Colombia*]   (COL)
litopg......... Literatuuropgave [*Benelux*]   (BAS)
LITOTAPAS ... Fabrica Tapas Litografiadas Continental Ltda. [*Colombia*]   (COL)
Litovenergo ... Lithuanian Regional Administration of Power System Management   (RU)
Litovtorsyr'ye ... Lithuanian Republic Administration for the Procurement and Processing of Secondary Raw Materials   (RU)
Litpotrebsoyuz ... Lithuanian Republic Union of Consumers' Societies   (RU)
Litpromsovet ... Council of Producers' Cooperatives of the Lithuanian SSR   (RU)
Lit-ra......... Literature   (BU)
Litrybvod ... Lithuanian Administration of Fish Conservation and Fish Culture   (RU)
Litsel'energo ... Lithuanian Republic Office for the Operation of Electric Power Plants   (RU)
LitSSR .... Lithuanian Soviet Socialist Republic   (RU)
LITT .... Leningrad Industrial Peat Technicum   (RU)
litteraturforteckn ... Litteraturfoerteckning [*List of References*] [*Publishing*] [*Sweden*]
LITTT........ Luoyang Institute of Tracking and Telecommunications Technology [*China*]   (IRC)
Liturg .... Liturgia [*Liturgy*] [*Portuguese*]
liturg......... Liturgical   (TPFD)
liturg.......... Liturgique [*French*]   (TPFD)
LIU .... Combination Connector [*Telephony*]   (RU)
LIU .... Library and Information Unit
LIU .... Light Wellpoint Apparatus   (RU)

LIUU .... Leningrad City Institute for the Advanced Training of Teachers (RU)
LIV............. Law Institute of Victoria [*Australia*]   (ADA)
LIV............. Livraison [*Delivery*] [*French*]
liv .... Livraria [*Book Shop*] [*Portuguese*]
LIV............. Livre [*Book or Pound*] [*French*]
Liv .... Livro [*Book*] [*Portuguese*]
LIVB .... Passo Del Brennero [*Italy*] [*ICAO location identifier*]   (ICLI)
LIVC........ Monte Cimone [*Italy*] [*ICAO location identifier*]   (ICLI)
LIVD........ Dobbiaco [*Italy*] [*ICAO location identifier*]   (ICLI)
LIVD........ Leningrad Scientific Research Institute of High Pressures   (RU)
LIVE......... Passo Resia [*Italy*] [*ICAO location identifier*]   (ICLI)
LIVF......... Frontone [*Italy*] [*ICAO location identifier*]   (ICLI)
LIVG........ Monte Grappa [*Italy*] [*ICAO location identifier*]   (ICLI)
LIVM........ Marino Di Ravenna [*Italy*] [*ICAO location identifier*]   (ICLI)
LIVO......... Tarvisio [*Italy*] [*ICAO location identifier*]   (ICLI)
LIVOCI ..... L'Ivoirienne de Confection Industrielle
LIVOTEX ... L'Ivoirienne de Textiles
LIVOTI ..... Leningrad Institute of Instrument Making of the All-Union Precision Industry Association   (RU)
LIVP .... Paganella [*Italy*] [*ICAO location identifier*]   (ICLI)
livr............. Livraison [*Issue*] [*Publishing*] [*French*]
LIVR......... Passo Rolle [*Italy*] [*ICAO location identifier*]   (ICLI)
LIVT......... Leningrad Institute of Water Transportation   (RU)
LIVT......... Trieste [*Italy*] [*ICAO location identifier*]   (ICLI)
LIVV .... Monte Venda [*Italy*] [*ICAO location identifier*]   (ICLI)
LIW .... Landtechnische Instandsetzungswerke [*Agricultural Equipment Maintenance Works*]   (EG)
LIW .... Loikaw [*Myanmar*] [*Airport symbol*]   (OAG)
Liyepaysel'mash ... Liepaja Agricultural Machinery Plant   (RU)
LIYW........ Aviano [*Italy*] [*ICAO location identifier*]   (ICLI)
LIZ............. Leningrad Tool Plant   (RU)
liz.............. Lysine   (RU)
LIZhT....... Leningrad Institute of Railroad Transportation   (RU)
LIZhVYa ... Leningrad Institute of Living Oriental Languages   (RU)
LJ.............. Laufenden Jahres [*Of the Current Year*] [*German*]
Lj............... Ljubljana [*Ljubljana*]   (YU)
LJA .... Lodja [*Zaire*] [*Airport symbol*]   (OAG)
LJCE .... Livre Jubilaire du Conseil d'Etat [*France*]   (FLAF)
LjD .... Ljubljanski Dnevnik [*Ljubljana Daily*] [*A newspaper*]   (YU)
LJEWU ..... Lanka Jathika Estate Workers' Union [*Sri Lanka*]
LJF .... Le Joint Francais [*French*]
LjJA .... Ljetopis Jugoslavenske Akademije Znanosti i Umjetnosti [*Annals of the Yugoslav Academy of Sciences and Arts*] [*Zagreb*]   (YU)
LJM .... Liga da Juventude de Mocambique [*Mozambique Youth League*]   (AF)
LJNA........ Librairie du Journal des Notaires et des Avocats [*France*]   (FLAF)
LjT .... Ljubljanska Tiskarna [*Ljubljana Printing House*]   (YU)
LJU........... Ljubljana [*Slovenia*] [*Airport symbol*]   (OAG)
ljustrycksplchr ... Ljustrycksplanscher [*Heliogravure Plate*] [*Publishing*] [*Sweden*]
LjV .... Ljevaonica Zeljeza Varazdin [*Varazdin Iron Foundry*]   (YU)
LK .... Battleship   (RU)
LK .... Commission for Liquidations   (BU)
LK .... False Combination   (RU)
L/K........... Icebreaker   (RU)
LK .... Laaketieteen Kandidaatti [*Finland*]
LK .... Laaste Kwartier [*Last Quarter*] [*Business term*] [*Afrikaans*]
LK .... Laiko Komma [*Populist Party*] [*Greece*] [*Political party*]   (PPE)
LK .... Landeklappe [*Landing Flap (Airplane)*]   (EG)
L/K........... Las/Koperal [*Lance Corporal*]   (ML)
LK .... Lastensuojelun Keskusliitto [*An association*] [*Finland*]   (EAIO)
LK .... Lebih Kurang [*More or Less, Approximately*]   (IN)
lk .... Lehky Kulomet [*Light Machine Gun*]   (CZ)
LK .... Lek [*Monetary unit*] [*Albania*]
LK .... Lekarska Komora [*Medical Association*]   (CZ)
LK .... Lekarske Knihkupectvi a Nakladatelstvi [*Sales and Publishing Firm for Medical Literature*]   (CZ)
lk .... Lewenskoste [*Cost of Living*] [*Afrikaans*]
LK .... Lidova Knihovna [*People's Library*]   (CZ)
LK .... Liga Kobiet [*League of Women*]   (POL)
LK .... Liman Kontrolu [*Harbor Control*] [*Turkish Cypriot*]   (GC)
LK .... Line Contactor   (RU)
LK .... Line-Switchboard   (RU)
lk .... Linkerkolom [*Benelux*]   (BAS)
LK .... Lochkarte [*German*]   (ADPT)
LK .... Loziskovy Kov [*Bearing Metal*]   (CZ)
lk .... Luokka [*Finland*]
lk .... Lux [*Measures*]   (RU)
LK .... Lyzarsky Klub [*Ski Club*]   (CZ)
LK .... Medical Commission   (BU)
LK .... Pilot Lamp, Supervisory Lamp   (RU)
LK .... Red Light   (RU)
LK .... Sri Lanka [*ANSI two-letter standard code*]   (CNC)

LKA .... Alkair Flight Operations APS [*Denmark*] [*ICAO designator*] (FAAC)

LKA .... Landeskriminalamt [*State Criminal Police Office*] (WEN)

LKA .... Larantuka [*Indonesia*] [*Airport symbol*] (OAG)

LKA .... Lochkartenausgabe [*German*] (ADPT)

LKA .... Sri Lanka [*ANSI three-letter standard code*] (CNC)

LKAA .... Praha [*Former Czechoslovakia*] [*ICAO location identifier*] (ICLI)

LKAB........ Loussavaara-Kiirunavaara Aktiebolag [*The LKAB Mining Co.*] [*Sweden*] (WEN)

LKAO .... Linear Combination of Atomic Orbitals (RU)

LKartB...... Landeskartellbehoerde [*Provincial Cartel Authority*] [*German*] (DLA)

LKB........... Lakeba [*Fiji*] [*Airport symbol*] (OAG)

LKB........... Leistungs- und Kostenermittlungsbogen [*Form for Determination of Work Output and Costs*] (EG)

LKBB........ Bratislava [*Former Czechoslovakia*] [*ICAO location identifier*] (ICLI)

lk bk .... Scout Car (BU)

LKBNAntara ... Lembaga Kantor Berita Nasional Antara [*Antara National News Agency*] (IN)

lkbs .... Cable-Laying Battalion (RU)

LKC .... Lekana [*Congo*] [*Airport symbol*] (OAG)

LKC .... Lekarska Komora pro Zemi Ceskou [*Medical Association of Bohemia*] (CZ)

LKD .... Light Cableway (RU)

LKDP........ Lietuviu Krikscioniu Demokratu Partija [*Lithuanian Christian Democratic Party*] [*Political party*] (PPE)

LKE .... Lochkarteneingabe [*German*] (ADPT)

LKF........... Leningrad Cartographic Factory (RU)

LKFJN ...... Lodzki Komitet Frontu Jednosci Narodu [*Lodz Committee of the National Unity Front*] [*Poland*]

LKG .... Leipziger Kommissions- und Grossbuchhandel [*Leipzig Commission and Wholesale Book Trade*] (EG)

LKG .... Lochkartengeraet [*German*] (ADPT)

lkh .... Logou Kharin [*For Example*] (GC)

LKHO....... Holesov [*Former Czechoslovakia*] [*ICAO location identifier*] (ICLI)

LKhTI....... Leningrad Institute of Chemical Technology (RU)

LKhTIMP ... Leningrad Chemical Technology Institute of the Dairy Industry (RU)

LKI............ Leningrad Shipbuilding Institute (RU)

LKIB......... Bratislava/Ivanka [*Former Czechoslovakia*] [*ICAO location identifier*] (ICLI)

LKIM........ Lembaga Kemajuan Ikan Malaysia

LKIP .... Laboratory of Control and Measuring Instruments (RU)

LKK .... Medical Consultation Commission (BU)

LKK .... Medical Control Commission (RU)

lk kch .... Light Machine-Gun (BU)

LKKFiT ..... Lodzki Komitet Kultury Fizycznej i Turystyki [*Lodz Committee for Physical Culture and Tourism*] [*Poland*]

LKKV........ Karlovy Vary [*Former Czechoslovakia*] [*ICAO location identifier*] (ICLI)

LKKZ........ Kosice [*Former Czechoslovakia*] [*ICAO location identifier*] (ICLI)

LKL............ Lakselv [*Norway*] [*Airport symbol*] (OAG)

LKL............ Lochkartenleser [*German*] (ADPT)

LKM .... Lazna Komanda Mesta [*Fake Command Post*] (YU)

lkm .... Lekki Karabin Maszynowy [*Light Machine Gun*] [*Poland*]

LKM .... Lenin Kohaszati Muvek, Diosgyor [*Lenin Metallurgical Works of Diosgyor*] (HU)

LKM .... Lochkartenmaschine [*German*] (ADPT)

lk mn .... Light Mortar (BU)

LKMT....... Ostrava [*Former Czechoslovakia*] [*ICAO location identifier*] (ICLI)

LKN .... Leknes [*Norway*] [*Airport symbol*] (OAG)

LKN .... Lim Kah Ngam [*Singapore*]

LKO .... Cables-Lines Department (BU)

LKO .... Lucknow [*India*] [*Airport symbol*] (OAG)

LKP........... Lembaga Kemajuan Perusahaan [*Industrial Promotion Board*] (ML)

LKP........... Liberaalinen Kansanpuolue [*Liberal People's Party*] [*Finland*] [*Political party*] (PPE)

LKP........... Lietuvos Komunisty Partija [*Communist Party of Lithuania*] [*Political party*] (PPE)

LKP........... Light Cable Ferry, Light Rope Ferry (RU)

LKPP........ Piestany [*Former Czechoslovakia*] [*ICAO location identifier*] (ICLI)

LKPR........ Praha/Ruzyne [*Former Czechoslovakia*] [*ICAO location identifier*] (ICLI)

LKQCP...... Licentiate of the King and Queen's College of Physicians [*Australia*]

LKR .... Battle Cruiser (RU)

Lkr .... Landkreis [*Rural Kreis*] (EG)

LKR .... Lidove Kurzy Rustiny [*People's Russian Language Courses*] (CZ)

LKRD .... Laboratory of Document Preservation and Restoration (of the Academy of Sciences, USSR) (RU)

lkrs .... Cable-Laying Company (RU)

LKS........... Leningrad Cable Network (RU)

LKS........... Liberation Kanake Socialiste [*Socialist Kanak Liberation*] [*New Caledonia*] (PD)

LKS........... Lochkartenstanzer [*German*] (ADPT)

LKS........... Lodzki Klub Sportowy [*Lodz Sports Club*] (POL)

LKS........... Ludowy Klub Sportowy [*Popular Sports and Athletics Club*] [*Poland*]

lk-sek .... Lux-Second (RU)

LKSL .... Sliac [*Former Czechoslovakia*] [*ICAO location identifier*] (ICLI)

LKSM ...... Lenin Young Communist League (RU)

LKSMA .... Lenin Young Communist League of Armenia (RU)

LKSMB .... Leninski Komunistychny Saiuz Moladzi Belarusi [*Lenin Young Communist League of Belorussia*] [*Russian*]

LKSMD..... Lenin Young Communist League of Dagestan (RU)

LKSME..... Lenin Young Communist League of Estonia (RU)

LKSMG..... Lenin Young Communist League of Georgia (RU)

LKSMK.... Lenin Young Communist League of Kazakhstan (RU)

LKSML .... Lenin Young Communist League of Latvia (RU)

LKSML .... Lenin Young Communist League of Lithuania (RU)

LKSMM ... Lenin Young Communist League of Moldavia (RU)

LKSMT .... Lenin Young Communist League of Turkmenistan (RU)

LKSMU..... Lenin Young Communist League of the Ukraine (RU)

LKSMUz... Lenin Young Communist League of Uzbekistan (RU)

LKT........... Laaketieteen (Ja Kirurgian) Tohtori [*Finland*]

LKT........... Laboratorium fur Kunststofftechnik [*Plastics Technology Laboratory*] [*Austria*] (PDAA)

LKT........... Leningrad Municipal Services Technicum (RU)

LKTP........ Lembaga Kemajuan Tanah Persekutuan [*Federal Land Development Authority - FLDA*] (ML)

l k-tsa .... Light Machine-Gun (BU)

LKTT........ Poprad/Tatry [*Former Czechoslovakia*] [*ICAO location identifier*] (ICLI)

LKU .... Lesnicke Kulturne Ustredie [*Forest Cultural Center*] (CZ)

LKV .... Lochkartenverfahren [*German*] (ADPT)

LKVVA .... Leningrad "Red Banner" Air Force Academy (RU)

LKVVIA .... Leningrad "Red Banner" Air Force Engineering Academy (RU)

LKW......... Lastkraftwagen [*Truck*] [*German*] (EG)

LKZ........... Leningrad Carburetor Plant (RU)

LKZ........... Leningrad Kirov Plant (RU)

LKZ........... Letaba Airways [*South Africa*] [*ICAO designator*] (FAAC)

ll .... Fluorescent Lamp (RU)

LL .... Laaketieten Lisensiaatti [*Finland*]

ll .... Laaslede [*Last*] [*Afrikaans*]

ll .... Laatsleden [*Last*] [*Netherlands*] (GPO)

ll .... Laatste Lid [*Benelux*] (BAS)

Ll .... Lapin Laani [*Finland*]

LL .... Lega Lombarda [*Italy*] [*Political party*] (ECED)

ll .... Leicht Loeslich [*Easily Soluble*] [*German*]

LL .... Liga Lotnicza [*Aeronautical League*] (POL)

LL .... Liga para la Liberacion [*Liberation League*] [*El Salvador*] (LA)

LL .... Liiketyontekijain Liitto [*Retail Shop Clerks Union*] [*Finland*] (WEN)

LL .... Lin Lee Industrial Co. Ltd. [*Taiwan*]

LL .... Lloyd Aviation [*Airline code*] [*Australia*]

LL .... Loyalist League [*Australia*] (ADA)

LL .... Lutlag [*Limited Company*] [*Norwegian*]

ll .... Sheets [*Manuscript*] (BU)

ll .... Sheets, Leaves (RU)

LLA........... Lesotho Liberation Army (PD)

LLA........... Lesotho Library Association (EAIO)

LLA........... Lulea [*Sweden*] [*Airport symbol*] (OAG)

LLA........... Servicio Leo Lopez SA de CV [*Mexico*] [*ICAO designator*] (FAAC)

LLAA........ Israel Airports Authority Headquarters [*Israel*] [*ICAO location identifier*] (ICLI)

LLAA........ Leurs Altesses [*Their Highnesses*] [*French*]

LLAA........ Loro Altezze [*Their Highnesses*] [*Italian*]

LLAAII..... Leurs Altesses Imperiales [*Their Imperial Highnesses*] [*French*]

LLAARR ... Leurs Altesses Royales [*Their Royal Highnesses*] [*French*]

LLAD........ Ben Gurion [*Israel*] [*ICAO location identifier*] (ICLI)

LL & N...... Language, Literacy and Numeracy Skills Taskforce [*Australia*]

LLAOR...... Langues et Langage en Afrique Orientale [*Research Center on East African Languages*] [*Research center*] [*France*] (IRC)

L LB .... Bachelor of Laws (PWGL)

LLB........... Liquor Licensing Board [*Australian Capital Territory*]

LLB........... Lloyd Aereo Boliviano SA [*Bolivia*] [*ICAO designator*] (FAAC)

LLBD........ Meteorological Service [*Israel*] [*ICAO location identifier*] (ICLI)

LLBG........ Tel Aviv/D. Ben Gurion [*Israel*] [*ICAO location identifier*] (ICLI)

LLBS........ Beersheba/Teyman [*Israel*] [*ICAO location identifier*] (ICLI)

LLC........... Lieutenant au Long Cours

LLC........... Liquor Licensing Commission [*Victoria, Australia*]

LLDP........ Lilongwe Land Development Programme [*or Project*]

LLEE .... Leurs Eminences [*Their Eminences*] [*French*]
LLEE .... Leurs Excellences [*Their Excellencies*] [*French*]
LLEE .... Loro Eccellenze [*Their Excellencies*] [*Italian*]
LLES .... Eyn-Shemer [*Israel*] [*ICAO location identifier*]   (ICLI)
LLET .... Elat/J. Hozman [*Israel*] [*ICAO location identifier*]   (ICLI)
LLG .... Chillagoe [*Australia*] [*Airport symbol*] [*Obsolete*]   (OAG)
LLH .... Ladies Left Handed
LLHA .... Haifa/U. Michaeli [*Israel*] [*ICAO location identifier*]   (ICLI)
LLHR .... Libyan League for Human Rights [*Switzerland*]   (EAIO)
LLHZ .... Herzlia [*Israel*] [*ICAO location identifier*]   (ICLI)
LLI .... Lalibella [*Ethiopia*] [*Airport symbol*]   (OAG)
LLI .... Leningrad Forest Institute   (RU)
LLIB .... Rosh Pina/Mahanaim-I. Ben-Yaakov [*Israel*] [*ICAO location identifier*]   (ICLI)
LLIBC .... Lotus Lantern International Buddhist Center [*South Korea*]   (EAIO)
LLJM .... Ministry of Transport [*Israel*] [*ICAO location identifier*]   (ICLI)
LLL .... Lietuvos Laisves Lyga [*An association*] [*Lithuania*]   (EAIO)
LLL .... Logs and Lumber Ltd. [*Ghana*]
LLM .... Librairie de Madagascar "Quartier Latin"
LLMM .... Leurs Majestes [*Their Majesties*] [*French*]
LLMM .... Loro Maesta [*Their Majesties*] [*Italian*]   (GPO)
LLMR .... Mitzpe-Ramon [*Israel*] [*ICAO location identifier*]   (ICLI)
LLMZ .... Metzada/I. Bar Yehuda [*Israel*] [*ICAO location identifier*]   (ICLI)
LLN .... Language, Literacy and Numeracy
LLN .... Lembaga Letrik Negara [*National Electricity Board*]   (ML)
LLO .... Eliadamello SPA [*Italy*] [*ICAO designator*]   (FAAC)
LLO .... Laerlings Landsorganisation [*National Federation of Apprentices*] [*Denmark*]   (WEN)
LLOKh ...... Leningrad Laboratory of General Chemistry   (RU)
LLOV .... Ovda [*Israel*] [*ICAO location identifier*]   (ICLI)
LLP .... Liberian Liberal Party [*Political party*]   (EY)
LLP .... Local Language Program
LLPNO ...... Ligue Luxembourgeoise pour la Protection de la Nature et des Oiseaux [*Luxembourg*]   (SLS)
LLPP(Ministero dei) ... Ministero dei Lavori Pubblici [*Ministry of Public Works*] [*Italian*]   (WER)
LLSA .... Latin Languages Speaking Allergists [*See also GAILL*]   (EAIO)
LLSC .... Israel South Control Area Control Center Unit [*Israel*] [*ICAO location identifier*]   (ICLI)
LLSD .... Tel Aviv/Sde Dov [*Israel*] [*ICAO location identifier*]   (ICLI)
LLTA .... Tel Aviv [*Israel*] [*ICAO location identifier*]   (ICLI)
LLTD .... Leningrad Heat Engine Laboratory   (RU)
LLW .... Lilongwe [*Malawi*] [*Airport symbol*]   (OAG)
LLWP .... Local Liaison Working Party [*Australian Atomic Energy Commission*]
LM .... Laboratory Agitator   (RU)
Lm .... Laem [*Cape, Point*] [*Thai*]   (NAU)
LM .... Laufenden Monats [*Of the Current Month*] [*German*]
LM .... Leipziger Messeamt [*Leipzig Fair Office*]   (EG)
LM .... Leitender Maschinist [*Chief Machinist*] [*Navy*]   (EG)
LM .... Leprosy Mission [*England, Australia, New Zealand*]
LM .... Leprosy Mission [*Australia*] [*An association*]
LM .... Lesotho Maloti
LM .... Letnan Muda [*Ensign*]   (IN)
LM .... Leucocytes   (RU)
LM .... Lidova Milice [*People's Militia*]   (CZ)
LM .... Liga Morska [*Maritime League*]   (POL)
lm .... Linear Meter   (BU)
Lm .... [*Maltese*] Lira [*Monetary Unit*] [*Malta*]   (BARN)
LM .... Ljudska Mladina [*People's Youth*]   (YU)
lm .... Lumen [*Poland*]
LM .... Lumen [*Afrikaans*]
LM .... Slide Balance, Slide-Wire Bridge   (RU)
LMA .... Labanese Management Association   (PDAA)
LMA .... Laboratoire de Mecanique et d'Acoustique [*Mechanics and Acoustics Laboratory*] [*Marseille, France*] [*Research center*]   (ERC)
LMA .... Lebanese Moslem Association [*Australia*]
LMA .... Liquor Merchants' Association [*Australia*]
LMA .... Livestock and Meat Authority [*Queensland, Australia*]
LMA .... Livingstone Motors Assemblers
LMAA .... Lift Manufacturers Association of Australia   (ADA)
LMAA .... Liquor Merchants' Association of Australia
LMAA .... Logistics Management Association of Australia
LMAQ .... Liquor Merchants Association of Queensland [*Australia*]
LMAQ .... Livestock and Meat Authority of Queensland [*Australia*]
LMB .... Landmaschinenbau (VEB) [*Farm Machine Construction Plant (VEB)*]   (EG)
LMB .... Livestock and Meat Board
LMC .... Laborator pro Mereni Casu [*Laboratory of Horology (of the Czechoslovak Academy of Sciences)*]   (CZ)
LMC .... Lamacarena [*Colombia*] [*Airport symbol*] [*Obsolete*]   (OAG)
LMC .... Lancia Motor Club [*Ledbury, Herefordshire, England*]   (EAIO)
LMC .... Languages and Multicultural Centre [*South Australia*] [*Australia*]

LMC .... Liberian Mining Company   (AF)
LMC .... Liga Maritima de Chile [*Chilean Maritime League*] [*Valparaiso*]   (LAA)
lm-ch .... Lumen-Hour   (RU)
LMCS .... Legal Management Consultancy Services [*Australia*]
LMD .... Laboratoire de Meteorologie Dynamique [*Dynamic Meteorology Laboratory*] [*French*]
LMD .... Lamda Airlines [*Greece*] [*ICAO designator*]   (FAAC)
LMD .... Licensed Motor Dealer
LMD .... Liga Municipal Dominicana [*Dominican Municipal League*] [*Dominican Republic*]   (LA)
LMD .... Livestock Marketing Division [*Ministry of Agriculture*] [*Kenya*]   (IMH)
LMDC .... Laboratorie Materiaux et Durabilite des Constructions [*Materials and Construction Durability Laboratory*] [*France*]   (IRC)
LMDM ...... Little Mission for the Deaf [*Italy*]   (EAIO)
LMDM ...... Little Mission for the Deaf-Mute [*See also PMS*] [*Rome, Italy*]   (EAIO)
LME .... L. M. Ericsson [*Swedish telecommunications company*]
LME .... Telefonaktiebolaget L. M. Ericsson [*L. M. Ericsson Telephone Co.*] [*Sweden*]
LMEC .... Laboratorio Nacional de Engenharia Civil [*National Civil Engineering Laboratory*] [*Portugal*]   (PDAA)
LMG .... Galitskiy Flying Bomb   (RU)
LMG .... Labour Monitoring Group [*Witwatersrand University*] [*South Africa*]
LMGKhRM ... Laboratory of Mineralogy and Geochemistry of Rare Metals (of the Academy of Sciences, USSR)   (RU)
LMGR .... Liberation Movement of the German Reich [*An association*]   (EAIO)
LMGSM .... Latin and Mediterranean Group for Sport Medicine   (EA)
lmh .... Lumenogodzina [*Lumen-Hour*] [*Poland*]
LMHI .... Liga Medicorum Homoeopathica Internationalis [*International Homoeopathic Medical League*]   (EA)
LMI .... La Metalli Industriale [*Italian copper company*]
LMI .... Lebensmittelindustrie [*Foodstuffs Industry*]   (EG)
LMI .... Le Magnesium Industriel [*French*]
LMI .... Leningrad Institute of Mechanical Engineering   (RU)
LMI .... Leningrad Mechanical Institute   (RU)
LMI .... Leningrad Medical Institute   (RU)
LMI .... Liga Monarquica Independente
LMI .... Lumi [*Papua New Guinea*] [*Airport symbol*]   (OAG)
LMIM .... Labor Muszeripari Muvek [*Labor Instrument Industry Works*]   (HU)
LMJ .... Ljudska Mladina Jugoslavije [*People's Youth of Yugoslavia*]   (YU)
LMK .... Pusat Penelitian Masalah Kelistrikan [*Electric Power Research Center*] [*Indonesia*]
LML .... Lae [*Marshall Islands*] [*Airport symbol*]   (OAG)
LMM .... Laboratoire de Metallurgie Mecanique [*Laboratory for Mechanical Metallurgy*] [*Research center*] [*Switzerland*]   (IRC)
LMM .... Los Mochis [*Mexico*] [*Airport symbol*]   (OAG)
LMMC ...... Livestock and Meat Marketing Corporation [*Sudan*]
LMML ...... Malta/Luqa [*Malta*] [*ICAO location identifier*]   (ICLI)
LMMM ..... Malta [*Malta*] [*ICAO location identifier*]   (ICLI)
LMMU ...... Latin Mediterranean Medical Union [*See also UMML*] [*Mantua, Italy*]   (EAIO)
LMN .... Lembaga Metallurgi Nasional [*National Institute for Metallurgy*] [*Indonesia*] [*Research center*]   (IRC)
lmn .... Liczba Mnoga [*Plural*]   (POL)
LMN .... Limbang [*Malaysia*] [*Airport symbol*]   (OAG)
LMN .... Small Pneumatic Boat   (RU)
LMO .... Meadow Reclamation Detachment   (RU)
LMP .... Labour Market Programme [*Australia*]
LMP .... Lampedusa [*Italy*] [*Airport symbol*]   (OAG)
LMP .... Lesotho Mounted Police
LMP .... Light Bridge Train   (RU)
LMR .... Licensed Motor Repairer
LMR .... Ligne de Moindre Resistance [*Military*] [*French*]   (MTD)
LMR .... Ligue Marxiste Revolutionnaire [*Revolutionary Marxist League*] [*Switzerland*] [*Political party*]   (PPW)
LMR .... River Boat Motor   (RU)
LMRC .... Labour Market Research Centre [*Australia*]
LMRI .... Laboratoire de Metrologie des Rayonnements Ionisants [*Metrology Laboratory of Raionuclides*] [*France*]   (PDAA)
LMS .... Laborator Matematickych Stroju [*Mathematical Instrument Laboratory (of the Czechoslovak Academy of Sciences)*]   (CZ)
LMS .... Lanka Mahila Samiti [*An association*] [*Sri Lanka*]   (EAIO)
LMS .... Letopis Matice Slovenske [*Annals of Matica Slovenska (Slovenian Cultural Society)*]   (YU)
LMS .... Letopis Matice Srpske [*Annals of Matica Srpska (Serbian Cultural Society)*] [*Novi Sad*]   (YU)
LMS .... Ljudska Milicija Slovenije [*People's Police of Slovenia*]   (YU)
LMS .... Ljudska Mladina Slovenije [*People's Youth of Slovenia*]   (YU)

LMS.......... Lotto Management Services Proprietary Ltd. [*Australia*]
LMS.......... Lumber Machinery Station   (RU)
LMS.......... Meadow Reclamation Station   (RU)
LMs .... Messinglot [*Brass Solder*] [*German*]   (GCA)
LMS.......... Riksfoereningen foer Laerarna i Moderna Sprak [*Sweden*]   (SLS)
LMSACORRI ... Life Member of the South African Corrosion Institute   (AA)
LMsAg....... Silbermessinglot [*Silver-Brass Solder*] [*German*]   (GCA)
lm-sek .... Lumen-Second   (RU)
LMSWA.... Land Management Society of Western Australia
LMT .... Air Limousin TA [*France*] [*ICAO designator*]   (FAAC)
LMT .... Laboratoire de Mecanique et Technologie [*Mechanics and Technology Laboratory*] [*France*]   (IRC)
LMT .... Le Materiel Telephonique SA [*French*]
LMTN .... Labor Market Training Needs
LMU .... Leningrad Nautical School   (RU)
LMU .... Letecke Mimoradne Udalosti [*Air Accidents*]   (CZ)
LMU .... Letnan Muda Udara [*Air Sublieutenant (Warrant officer)*]   (IN)
LMusA ...... Licentiate in Music, Australia
LMusSAA ... Licentiate in Music, Society of Australasian Arts
LMV .... La Mala Vida [*An association*] [*Venezuela*]   (EAIO)
LMX .... Aerolineas Mexicanas JS SA de CV [*Mexico*] [*ICAO designator*]   (FAAC)
LMY .... Lake Murray [*Papua New Guinea*] [*Airport symbol*]   (OAG)
LMY .... League of Malawi Youth   (AF)
lmz............. Foundry and Machine Plant   (RU)
LMZ .... Leningradskii Metallicheskii Zavod [*Leningrad Metal Plant*]
LN .... Landwirtschaftliche Nutzflaeche [*Agricultural Area*]   (EG)
Ln............. Leinen [*or Leinenband*] [*Cloth or Cloth Binding Publishing*] [*German*]
LN .... Lembaran Negara [*State Gazette*]   (IN)
LN .... Les Lois Nouvelles [*France*]   (FLAF)
Ln............. Limin [*Harbor*] [*Greek*]   (NAU)
ln .... Line [*Measures*]   (RU)
ln .... Linnen [*Cloth*] [*Publishing*] [*Netherlands*]
LN .... Lira Nuova [*Monetary unit*] [*Italy*]   (ROG)
LN .... Lyon [*On cartridge bags*] [*Military*] [*French*]   (MTD)
LN .... Neon Lamp   (RU)
LN .... Nickel Brass   (RU)
LN .... Sodium Laurate   (RU)
LNA .... Airlen [*Russian Federation*] [*ICAO designator*]   (FAAC)
LNA .... Laboratorio de Nutricion Animal [*Costa Rica*]   (DSCA)
LNA .... Laboratorio Nacional de Astrofisica [*National Laboratory of Astrophysics*] [*Brazil*]   (IRC)
LNA .... Lahu National Army [*Myanmar*] [*Political party*]   (EY)
LNA .... Laikon Nosokomeion Athinon [*Athens Public Hospital*]   (GC)
LNA .... League for National Advancement [*Papua New Guinea*] [*Political party*]   (EY)
LNA .... League of the Norden Associations   (EA)
LNA .... Liberation Press Agency [*of the NFLSV*] [*Use LPA South Vietnamese*]   (CL)
LNA .... Liberian National Airlines   (AF)
LNA .... Liberian News Agency
LNA .... Libyan News Agency   (AF)
LNA .... Liga Nacional Africana
LNB .... Lamen Bay [*Vanuata*] [*Airport symbol*]   (OAG)
Lnb............ Leinenband [*Cloth Binding*] [*Publishing*] [*German*]
LNBEE...... Laboratoire National Belge d'Electrothermie et d'Electrochime [*Belgian National and Electrochemical Laboratory*]   (PDAA)
LNBS......... Lesotho National Broadcasting Service
LNC .... Lega Nazionale delle Cooperative e Mutue [*National League of Cooperatives*] [*Italian*]   (WER)
LNC .... Local Native Councils
LNCC .... Laboratorio Nacional de Computacao Cientifica [*National Laboratory for Scientific Computing*] [*Research center*] [*Brazil*]   (IRC)
L-NCP ...... Liberal-National Country Party [*Australia*] [*Political party*]   (PPW)
LND.......... Loterie Nationale du Benin [*National Lottery of Benin*]   (AF)
LNDB .... Lesotho National Development Bank   (GEA)
LNDC .... Lake Nasser Development Centre
LNDC .... Lesotho National Development Corporation
LNE .... Lonorore [*Vanuata*] [*Airport symbol*]   (OAG)
LNEC........ Laboratorio Nacional de Engenharia Civil [*National Civil Engineering Laboratory*] [*Portugal*]   (PDAA)
LNERV...... Laboratoire de l'Elevage et de Recherches Veterinaires [*National Laboratory of Animal Health and Production*] [*Senegal*]   (ARC)
LNETI .... Laboratorio Nacional de Engenharia e Tecnologia Industrial [*National Laboratory for Engineering and Industrial Technology*] [*Lisbon, Portugal*]   (ARC)
LNF .... Associazione la Nostra Famiglia [*Italy*]   (EAIO)
LNF .... Laboratoire de Neurosciences Fonctionnelles [*Laboratory of Functional Neurosciences*] [*Research center*] [*France*]   (IRC)
LNF .... Laboratori Nazionali di Frascati [*Italy*]   (PDAA)

LNF .... Landwirtschaftliche Nutzflaeche [*Agricultural Area*]   (EG)
LNF .... Latvian National Foundation [*Stockholm, Sweden*]   (EAIO)
LNFCS ...... Leonard Nimoy Fan Club, Spotlight   (EAIO)
LNG.......... Lese [*Papua New Guinea*] [*Airport symbol*]   (OAG)
LNG.......... Liberian National Guard
LNG.......... Liquefied Natural Gas   (OMWE)
LNG.......... Liquified Natural Gas   (IDIG)
LNGRI....... Leningrad Scientific Research Institute of Petroleum Geological Exploration   (RU)
LNH.......... Lisovny Novych Hmot [*Pressing Plants for New Materials*]   (CZ)
LNI .... Lega Navale Italiana [*Italian*]
LNIIAKKh ... Leningrad Scientific Research Institute of the Academy of Municipal Services Imeni K. D. Pamfilov   (RU)
LNIIFK...... Leningrad Scientific Research Institute of Physical Culture   (RU)
LNIIKKh ... Leningrad Scientific Research Institute of Municipal Services   (RU)
LNIIP .... Leningrad Scientific Research Institute of Prosthetics   (RU)
LNIKhO .... Leningrad Chemical Scientific Research Society   (RU)
LNISI .... Leningrad Shale Scientific Research Institute   (RU)
LNIVI .... Leningrad Veterinary Scientific Research Institute   (RU)
LNIYa....... Leningrad Scientific Research Institute of Linguistics   (RU)
LNJP .... Ligue Nationale de la Jeunesse Patriotique [*National League of Patriotic Youth*] [*Benin*]   (AF)
LNK .... Airlink Airlines (Pty) Ltd. [*South Africa*] [*ICAO designator*]   (FAAC)
LNK .... Lengyel Nepkoztarsasag [*Polish People's Republic*]   (HU)
LNKhMGU ... Laboratory of Inorganic Chemistry of the Moscow State University Imeni M. V. Lomonosov   (RU)
LNM .... Langimar [*Papua New Guinea*] [*Airport symbol*]   (OAG)
LNM .... Lebanese National Movement [*Political party*]   (PPW)
LNMC ...... Monaco [*Monaco*] [*ICAO location identifier*]   (ICLI)
lnn .... Linnen [*Cloth*] [*Publishing*] [*Netherlands*]
LNNK....... Latvijas Nacionala Neatkaribas Kustiba [*Latvian National Independence Movement*] [*Political party*]
LNO.......... Lager Nijverheidsonderwijs [*Benelux*]   (BAS)
LNO.......... Leonora [*Australia*] [*Airport symbol*]   (OAG)
LNOC....... Liberian National Olympic Committee   (EAIO)
LNOC....... Libyan National Oil Corporation
l'novod....... Flax-Growing Sovkhoz [*Topography*]   (RU)
LNP .... Chieftain Aviation PC [*South Africa*] [*ICAO designator*]   (FAAC)
LNP .... Dummy Observation Point   (RU)
LNP .... Liberal/National Party [*Political party*] [*Australia*]
LNP .... Libertarian Party [*Australia*] [*Political party*]
LNPF .... Lebanese National Patriotic Forces [*Political party*]
Lnpl........... Letecky Nahradni Pluk [*Air Force Replacement Regiment*]   (CZ)
LNPPRA ... Laboratoire National de Pathologie des Petits Ruminants, et des Abeilles [*National Laboratory for Pathology of Sheep, Goats, and Bees*] [*French*]   (ARC)
LNR .... Lao National Radio   (CL)
lnr.............. Links na Regs [*Left to Right*] [*Afrikaans*]
LNR .... Sky Liners Air Services Ltd. [*Suriname*] [*ICAO designator*]   (FAAC)
LNRT .... Ministry of Land, Natural Resources, and Tourism [*Zambia*]   (IMH)
LNS .... Laboratoire National Saturne [*Saturne National Laboratory*] [*Research center*] [*France*]   (IRC)
LNS .... League of National Security [*Australia*]   (ADA)
LNS .... Line of Least Resistance   (RU)
LNS .... Luxembourg Naturalist Society   (EAIO)
LNSHS...... Lower North Shore Housing Scheme [*Australia*]
LNSL........ Liberia National Shipping Line   (EY)
LNSU .... Library Network of SIBIL Users   (EAIO)
LNSW .... Library of New South Wales [*Australia*]   (ADA)
LNT .... Loterie Nationale Togolaise
LNTO .... Lento [*Very Slow*] [*Music*]   (ROG)
LNTP........ Laboratoire National des Travaux Publics [*Ministere de l'Equipement, des Transports, et des Telecommunications*] [*Mauritania*]
LNTPB ...... Laboratoire National des Travaux Publics et du Batiment [*National Laboratory of Public Works and Building*] [*Algeria*]   (PDAA)
LNU.......... League of Nations Union
LNUS .... Liberian National Union of Students   (AF)
LNV .... Londolovit [*Papua New Guinea*] [*Airport symbol*] [*Obsolete*]   (OAG)
LNX .... Lenex [*Poland*] [*ICAO designator*]   (FAAC)
L'nyan....... Linen Goods Factory [*Topography*]   (RU)
LNYO....... Liberian National Youth Organization
LNZ .... Linz [*Austria*] [*Airport symbol*]   (OAG)
LO .... Laborator Optiky [*Optical Laboratory (of the Czechoslovak Academy of Sciences)*]   (CZ)
LO .... Laer Onderwys [*Primary Education*] [*Afrikaans*]
LO .... Lager-Onderwijswet [*Benelux*]   (BAS)
LO .... La Legion d'Orient [*Foreign Legion*] [*France*]

LO.............. Landsorganisasjonen i Norge [*Norwegian Federation of Trade Unions*] (WEN)
LO.............. Landsorganisation de Samvirkende Fagforbund [*Danish Federation of Trade Unions*] (WEN)
LO.............. Landsorganisationen i Sverige [*Swedish Federation of Trade Unions*]
lo................ Lasd Ott [*See*] (HU)
LO.............. Leningrad Branch (RU)
LO.............. Leningrad Oblast (RU)
LO.............. Letecky Okrah [*Air Force District*] (CZ)
l/o.............. Leur Ordre [*French*]
LO.............. Liggaamlike Opvoeding [*Physical Education*] [*Afrikaans*]
LO.............. Linija Otkrivanja [*Detection Line*] [*RADAR*] [*Air Force*] (YU)
LO.............. Ljudski Odbor [*People's Committee*] (YU)
LO.............. Lochung [*German*] (ADPT)
LO.............. Lucha Obrera [*Workers' Struggle*] [*Spanish*] (WER)
LO.............. Lutte Ouvriere [*Workers' Struggle*] [*France*] [*Political party*] (PPW)
LOA........... Local Education Authority
LOA........... Lorraine [*Australia*] [*Airport symbol*] [*Obsolete*] (OAG)
LOAC........ Ligne Ouvriere d'Action Catholique [*Workers' League for Catholic Action*] [*Mauritius*] (AF)
LOAD........ Leyte Organization of Associated Drivers [*Philippines*] (EY)
LO & Cie.... Lombard, Odier & Compagnie [*Bank*] [*Switzerland*]
LOAOR..... Leningrad Oblast Archives of the October Revolution (RU)
LOAS........ Liga Oriental Antisemita [*Uruguayan Antisemitic League*] (LA)
LOAT....... Trausdorf [*Austria*] [*ICAO location identifier*] (ICLI)
LOAU....... Leningrad Oblast Archives Administration (RU)
LOAV....... Lift Owners' Association of Victoria [*Australia*]
LOAV....... Voslau [*Austria*] [*ICAO location identifier*] (ICLI)
LOB........... Leningrad Society of Bibliophiles (RU)
LOBE........ Laboratoire d'Optique de Besancon [*France*] (PDAA)
LOBK....... Leningrad Oblast Office of Regional Study (RU)
LOC.......... Ligue Ouvriere Catholique [*France*]
loc............ Localita [*Italian*] (CED)
loc............ Locativo [*Locative*] [*Portuguese*]
LOC.......... Locavia 49 [*France*] [*ICAO designator*] (FAAC)
loc............ Locucao [*Locution*] [*Portuguese*]
LOCABAIL ... Compagnie pour la Location d'Equipements Professionnels SA [*French*]
LOCAUTO ... Societe Senegalaise de Location d'Automobiles
locb............ Hoffd ban Plaatselijk Bestuur [*Benelux*] (BAS)
Loc Cit ...... Locutions Citees [*France*] (FLAF)
Loc GovtCt ... Local Government Court [*Australia*]
LOCH....... London Option Clearing House [*A clearing corporation created in April 1978 by the London Stock Exchange*]
LOCMAT ... Entreprise de Location de Materiel et de Terrassement
Locre.......... Locature [*Farmhouse*] [*Military map abbreviation World War I*] [*French*] (MTD)
LOD........... Landsorganisationen i Danmark (EAIO)
LOD........... Longana [*Vanuata*] [*Airport symbol*] (OAG)
LOE........... Loei [*Thailand*] [*Airport symbol*] [*Obsolete*] (OAG)
LOE........... Loeser, Luftfahrtgesellschaft GmbH [*Germany*] [*ICAO designator*] (FAAC)
LOEL........ Laiki Oinoviomikhaniki Etaireia Lemesou Ltd. [*Popular Distillers Company of Limassol*] [*Cyprus*] (GC)
Loes........... Loesung [*Solution*] [*German*] (GCA)
Loesbark ... Loesbarkeit [*Solubility*] [*German*] (GCA)
Loeslichk ... Loeslichkeit [*Solubility*] [*German*] (GCA)
LOFC........ Ligues Ouvrieres Feminines Chretiennes [*French*] (BAS)
LOFEUK.... Leningrad Oblast Finance and Economics Training Center (RU)
LOFOB...... [*The*] League of Friends of the Blind [*South Africa*] (AA)
LOG........... Laboratory of Distant Hybridization (RU)
LOG........... Labor Old Guard [*Australia*] [*An association*]
Log............. Logarithmus [*Logarithm*] [*German*]
log............. Logaritme [*Logarithm*] [*Afrikaans*]
log............. Logaritmo [*Logarithm*] [*Portuguese*]
log............. Logarytm [*Logarithm*] [*Poland*]
log............. Logic (TPFD)
Log............ Logica [*Logic*] [*Portuguese*]
log............. Logiikka [*Logic*] [*Finland*]
log............. Logika [*Logic*] [*Afrikaans*]
log............. Logique [*French*] (TPFD)
LOG........... Logisch [*Logical*] [*German*] (ADPT)
LOG........... Logistik [*Logistics*] (IN)
LOG........... Lohn und Gehalt [*German*] (ADPT)
LOGAIS .... Leningrad Branch of the State Academy for the Study of Art (RU)
Logecos ...... Logements Economiques et Familiaux [*France*] (FLAF)
LOGIDEP ... Leningrad Branch of the Gidroenergoproyekt (RU)
LOGIPROAVTOTRANS ... Leningrad Branch of the Giproavtotrans (RU)
LOGK .... Kapfenberg [*Austria*] [*ICAO location identifier*] (ICLI)
LOGO........ Logotype [*Advertising*] (DSUE)
LOGS .... Labor's Old Guard Socialists [*Australia*] [*An association*]
LOGTsKP ... Leningrad Branch of the State Central Book Chamber (RU)
LOH........... Loja [*Ecuador*] [*Airport symbol*] (OAG)

LOI .... Leningrad Institute of Optics (RU)
LOI .... Leningrad Oblast Executive Committee (RU)
LOID .... Leningrad Branch of the Institute of Rainmaking (RU)
LOIH........ Hohenems-Dornbirn [*Austria*] [*ICAO location identifier*] (ICLI)
LOII.......... Leningrad Branch of the Institute of History (of the Academy of Sciences, USSR) (RU)
LOIIMK.... Leningrad Branch of the Institute of the History of Material Culture (RU)
LOII RO.... Leningrad Branch of the Institute of History of the Academy of Sciences, USSR. Manuscript Division (RU)
LOIJ .... St. Johann, Tirol [*Austria*] [*ICAO location identifier*] (ICLI)
LOIKFUN ... Leningrad Society of Researchers in the Culture of the Finno-Ugrian Peoples (RU)
LOINA ...... Leningradsk Otdeleni Instituta Narodov Azii
LOIP......... Leningrad Society of Naturalists (RU)
LOIPKKNO ... Leningrad Branch of the Institute for Improving the Qualifications of Public Education Personnel (RU)
Lois Nouv... Les Lois Nouvelles [*France*] (FLAF)
LOIV .... Loyal Orange Institution of Victoria [*Australia*]
LOIZ......... Leningrad Oblast Publishing House (RU)
Loj............. Lojman [*Housing, Quarters*] (TU)
LOK.......... Leningrad Oblast Committee (RU)
LOK.......... Leningrad Oblast Office (RU)
LOK.......... Leningrad Society of Collectors (RU)
LOK.......... Leveltarak Orszagos Kozpontja [*National Archives Center*] (HU)
LOK........... Liga Obrony Kraju [*National Defense League*] [*LPZ*] [*Formerly,*] (POL)
Lok............ Locomotive (EG)
LOK.......... Lokhos Oreinon Katadromon [*Mountain Raider Company*] [*Greek*] (GC)
lok .... Loxodromic (RU)
LOKA .... Leningrad Branch of the Communist Academy (RU)
Lokalisat... Lokalisation [*Localization*] [*German*] (GCA)
Lokalisier... Lokalisierung [*Localization*] [*German*] (GCA)
LOKB........ Leningrad City and Oblast Municipal Bank (RU)
LOKBI....... Leningrad Branch of the Scientific Research Institute of Criticism and Bibliography (RU)
Lokf........... Lokomotivfuehrer [*Locomotive Engineer*] (EG)
Lokh.......... Lokomotivheizer [*Locomotive Fireman*] (EG)
LOKhO...... Leningrad Society of Orthopedic Surgeons (RU)
LOKK .... League of Red Cross Societies (RU)
lokkm......... Lokomotivni Kilometr [*Locomotive Kilometer*] (CZ)
Lokltkm..... Lokomotivleistungs-Tonnenkilometer [*Locomotive Performance Ton-Kilometers (Unit of measurement for locomotive performance)*] (EG)
Lokomotivprojekt ... Locomotive Design Office (RU)
Lok P......... Loxodromic Bearing (RU)
LOKSPEDIT ... Lokalno Transportno Spedietersko Preduzece [*Local Transport and Shipping Establishment*] (YU)
LOKU .... Leningrad Oblast Communist University (RU)
Lokum....... Dinamit Lokumu [*Small Plastic Bomb or Explosive, Dynamite Bomb*] [*Turkish Cypriot*] (GC)
LOKUNMZ ... Leningrad Branch of the Communist University of National Minorities of the West (RU)
LOKZ .... Leningrad Oblast Collegium of Defense Lawyers (RU)
LOLGU ..... Leningrad "Order of Lenin" State University Imeni A. A. Zhdanov (RU)
LOLIS ...... Literature of Librarianship and Information Science [*Australia*]
LOLLTA ... Leningrad "Order of Lenin" Forestry Engineering Academy Imeni S. M. Kirov (RU)
LOLW ...... Wels [*Austria*] [*ICAO location identifier*] (ICLI)
LOM......... Liga Obrera Marxista [*Marxist Labor League*] [*Mexico*] (LA)
lom .... Lomo [*Back*] [*Publishing*] [*Spanish*]
LOM......... SERTEL [*Servicios Telereservacios SA de CV*] [*ICAO designator*] (FAAC)
Lombard .... Loads of Money but a Real Dolt [*Bowdlerized version*] [*Lifestyle classification*] [*Australia*]
LOMI .... Leningrad Branch of the Institute of Mathematics Imeni V. A. Steklov (of the Academy of Sciences, USSR) (RU)
LOMO...... Ljudski Odbor Mestne Obcine [*Municipal People's Committee*] (YU)
LOMZ ...... Leningrad Optical Instrument Plant (RU)
LON.......... Special Assignment Camp [*Corrective labor camps*] (RU)
LONA....... Local News Agency
LONACI.... Loterie Nationale de Cote-D'Ivoire
LONASE.... Loterie Nationale Senegalaise
long .... Longitude [*Portuguese*]
long .... Longitude [*French*]
Long.......... Longitudine [*Longitude*] [*Italian*]
long .... Longueur [*Length*] [*French*]
LONIIS ..... Leningrad Branch of the Scientific Research Institute of Communications (RU)
LONIIV..... Leningrad Branch of the NIIV (RU)
LONITI..... Leningrad Branch of the Textile Scientific Research Institute (RU)

LONITO ... Leningrad Branch of the All-Union Scientific, Engineering, and Technical Society (RU)
LONITOE ... Leningrad Branch of the All-Union Scientific, Engineering, and Technical Society of Power Engineers (RU)
LONITOL ... Leningrad Branch of the All-Union Scientific, Engineering, and Technical Society of Foundry Workers (RU)
LONITOMASh ... Leningrad Branch of the All-Union Scientific, Engineering, and Technical Society of Machine Builders (RU)
LONITOS ... Leningrad Branch of the All-Union Scientific, Engineering, and Technical Society of Welders (RU)
LONITOVT ... Leningrad Branch of the All-Union Scientific, Engineering, and Technical Society of Water Transportation (RU)
LONPI .... Leningrad Institute of Theoretical and Applied Ophthalmology (RU)
LONRHO ... London and Rhodesian Mining and Land Co.
LONTO ..... Leningrad Oblast Administration of the Scientific and Technical Society (RU)
LONTOVT ... Leningrad Branch of the Scientific and Technical Society of Water Transportation (RU)
LOOGAPU ... Leningrad Oblast Department of the Main Pharmaceutical Administration (RU)
LOOKKh ... Leningrad Oblast Department of Municipal Services (RU)
LOOMP .... Leningrad Association of Experimental Machine Establishments (RU)
LOONO .... Leningrad Oblast Department of Public Education (RU)
LOONTI ... Leningrad Branch of the United Scientific and Technical Publishing House (RU)
LOOSVOD ... Leningrad Oblast Society for Assisting the Development of Water Transportation and Safeguarding Human Life on Waterways (RU)
LOOVOG ... Leningrad Oblast Branch of the All-Union Society of Deaf-Mutes (RU)
LOP .... Dummy Firing Position (RU)
LOP .... Laboratoire d'Oceanographie Physique [*French*] (MSC)
LOP .... Liga Ochrony Przyrody [*League for the Preservation of Nature*] [*Poland*]
LOP .... Lodzki Okreg Przemyslowy [*Lodz Industrial Region*] [*Poland*]
LOPI .... Leningrad Oblast Pedagogical Institute (RU)
Lopofa ...... Logements Populaires et Familiaux [*France*] (FLAF)
LOPOZRz ... Lodzkie Okregowe Przedsiebiorstwo Obrotu Zwierzetami Rzeznymi [*Lodz District Establishment for Marketing Animals for Slaughter*] (POL)
LOPP .... Liga Obrony Powietrznej Panstwa [*State Air Defense League*] (POL)
LOPP .... Liga Obrony Przeciwlotniczej i Przeciwgazowej [*Poland*]
LOPPE ...... Ley Federal de Organizaciones Politicas y Procesos Electorales [*Federal Law on Political Organizations and Electoral Processes*] [*Mexico*] (LA)
LOPS .... Limited Offer to Purchase Scheme [*Australia*]
LOPU .... Leningrad District Assay Administration (RU)
LOR .... Laboratory of Finishing Operations (RU)
LOR .... Otalaryngology, Otorhinolaryngology (RU)
LOR .... Otorhinolaryngology (CL)
LORIDS .... Long Range Iranian Detection System (PDAA)
LOS .... Forest Experimental Station (RU)
LOS .... Laboratory of Organic Synthesis (of the Academy of Sciences, USSR) (RU)
LOS .... Lager-und Orangisationssystem [*German*] (ADPT)
LOS .... Lagos [*Nigeria*] [*Airport symbol*] (OAG)
LOS .... Latin Old Style (ADA)
LOS .... Law of the Sea [*United Nations*] (ASF)
LOS .... Leningrad Oblast Soviet (RU)
LOS .... Letecke Obranne Stredisko [*Air Defense Center*] (CZ)
LOSA .... Leningrad Branch of the Union of Architects of the USSR (RU)
LOSC .... Law of the Sea Conference [*United Nations*] (MSC)
LOSC .... Law of the Sea Convention [*Australia*]
loshch .... Ravine, Hollow, Depression [*Topography*] (RU)
LOSISA ..... Lid van Openbare Skaklinstituut van Suidelike Afrika [*South Africa*] (AA)
LOSKh ...... Leningrad Branch of the Union of Artists of the RSFSR (RU)
losl .... Loeslich [*or Loeslichkeit*] [*Soluble or Solubility*] [*German*]
LOSNITO ... Leningrad Oblast Council of Scientific, Engineering, and Technical Societies (RU)
losnr .... Loesnummer [*Separate Number*] [*Publishing*] [*Sweden*]
LOSNTO... Leningrad Oblast Council of Scientific, Engineering, and Technical Societies (RU)
LOSO .... Leningrad Oblast Construction Association (RU)
LOSP .... Leningrad Branch of the Union of Writers of the USSR (RU)
LOSPO ...... Leningrad Oblast Union of Consumers' Societies (RU)
LOSPS .... Leningrad Oblast Council of Trade Unions (RU)
LOSSKh ..... Leningrad Oblast Union of Soviet Artists (RU)
Losungsm... Loesungsmittel [*Solvent*] [*German*]
losz .... Loszer [*Ammunition*] (HU)
LOT .... Dummy Emplacement (RU)
LOT .... Polskie Linie Lotnicze [*National Polish Airlines*]
LOTE .... Languages Other than English
LOTEYCA ... Lote y Casa Constructora [*Colombia*] (COL)

LOTI .... Leningrad Oblast Scientific Research Institute of Heat Engineering (RU)
lotn .... Lotnictwo [*Aircraft*] [*Poland*]
lotn .... Lotniczy [*Air*] [*Poland*]
LOTS .... Land Ownership and Tenure System [*Australia*]
LOTsES ...... Leningrad Branch of the Central Electrotechnical Council (RU)
LOTsF .... Laboratory for the Processing of Color Films (RU)
LOTsGIA .. Leningrad Branch of the Central State Historical Archives (RU)
LOTsIA ...... Leningrad Branch of the Central Historical Archives (RU)
LOTsIYaP ... Leningrad Branch of the Central Scientific Research Institute of Language and Literature of Peoples of the USSR (RU)
LOTsNIIP ... Leningrad Branch of the Central Scientific Research Institute of Pedagogy (RU)
LOTSS ...... Libraries of the Social Sciences [*Australia*] [*An association*]
LOTsT .... Leningrad District Central Printing Office (RU)
LOTU .... Lefkosa Ozel Turk Universitesi [*Nicosia Special (Private) Turkish University*] (GC)
LOUChGIZ ... Leningrad Branch of the Publishing House of Textbooks and Pedagogical Literature (RU)
LOUMP ... Leningrad Oblast Administration of Local Industry (RU)
LOUMS .... Leningrad Oblast Administration of the Ministry of Communications, USSR (RU)
LOUYeGMS ... Leningrad Oblast Administration of United Hydrometeorological Service (RU)
LOV .... Backward-Wave Tube (RU)
lov .... Hunting (BU)
lov .... Lovas [*Mounted, Cavalry*] (HU)
LOVAGO .. Leningrad Branch of the All-Union Astronomical and Geodetic Society (RU)
LOVEK ...... Leningrad Branch of the All-Union Power Engineering Committee (RU)
LOVEO ..... Leningrad Branch of the All-Union Electrotechnical Association (RU)
LOVET ...... Leningrad Branch of the All-Union Electrotechnical Trust (RU)
LOVIShS... Leningrad Joint Military Engineering School of Communications (RU)
LOVIUAA ... Leningrad Branch of the All-Union Institute of Fertilizers, Soil Science, and Agricultural Engineering (RU)
LOVIZh ..... Leningrad Branch of the All-Union Scientific Research Institute of Livestock Breeding (RU)
LOVM .... Magnetron-Type Backward-Wave Tube (RU)
LOVNITOE ... Leningrad Branch of the All-Union Scientific, Engineering, and Technical Society of Power Engineers (RU)
LOVNITOL ... Leningrad Branch of the All-Union Scientific, Engineering, and Technical Society of Foundry Workers (RU)
LOVODGEO ... Leningrad Branch of the All-Union Scientific Research Institute of Water Supply, Sewer Systems, Hydraulic Engineering Structures, and Engineering Hydrogeology (RU)
LOVSU ...... Leningrad District Military Medical Directorate (RU)
LOVV .... Wien [*Austria*] [*ICAO location identifier*] (ICLI)
LOVZITO ... Leningrad Branch of the All-Union Correspondence Institute of Technical Education (RU)
LOW .... Land- en Tuinbouwongevallenwet [*Benelux*] (BAS)
LOWA .... Lokomotiv- und Waggonbau [*Locomotive and Railroad Car Construction Plant*] (EG)
LOWG .... Graz [*Austria*] [*ICAO location identifier*] (ICLI)
LOWI .... Innsbruck [*Austria*] [*ICAO location identifier*] (ICLI)
LOWK .... Klagenfurt [*Austria*] [*ICAO location identifier*] (ICLI)
LOWL .... Linz [*Austria*] [*ICAO location identifier*] (ICLI)
LOWM ...... Wien [*Austria*] [*ICAO location identifier*] (ICLI)
LOWS .... Salzburg [*Austria*] [*ICAO location identifier*] (ICLI)
LOWW ...... Wien/Schwechat [*Austria*] [*ICAO location identifier*] (ICLI)
LOWZ .... Zell Am See [*Austria*] [*ICAO location identifier*] (ICLI)
LOXA .... Aigen/Ennstal [*Austria*] [*ICAO location identifier*] (ICLI)
LOXG .... Graz [*Austria*] [*ICAO location identifier*] (ICLI)
LOXK .... Klagenfurt [*Austria*] [*ICAO location identifier*] (ICLI)
LOXL .... Horsching [*Austria*] [*ICAO location identifier*] (ICLI)
LOXN .... Wiener Neustadt [*Austria*] [*ICAO location identifier*] (ICLI)
LOXS .... Schwaz, Tirol [*Austria*] [*ICAO location identifier*] (ICLI)
LOXT .... Langenlebarn [*Austria*] [*ICAO location identifier*] (ICLI)
LOXZ .... Zeltweg [*Austria*] [*ICAO location identifier*] (ICLI)
LOYe .... Leningrad Society of Naturalists (RU)
LOYePA .... Leningrad Branch of the United Party Archives (RU)
LOZKU ..... Leningrad Oblast Communist Correspondence University (RU)
LP .... Airfield, Flying Field (RU)
LP .... Collating and Gathering Machine (RU)
LP .... Forest Belt, Forest Zone (RU)
LP .... Foundry Production (RU)
LP .... Laboratorni Pristroje [*Laboratory Appliances*] (CZ)
LP .... Laboratory Penetrometer (RU)
LP .... Labour Party [*Namibia*]
LP .... Labour Party of South Africa [*Political party*] (PPW)
LP .... Laburisticka Partija [*Labor Party*] (YU)
LP .... Ladeprogramm [*German*] (ADPT)
LP .... Laiki Paideia [*Popular Education (Group)*] [*Greek*] (GC)

LP .... Lasy Panstwowe [*State Forests*]   (POL)
LP .... Lehrprogramm [*Teaching Program*] [*German*]   (ADPT)
LP .... Leitungspuffer [*German*]   (ADPT)
LP .... Leta Pane [*In the Year of Our Lord*]   (CZ)
LP .... Letni Plan [*Year Plan*] [*Usually preceded by a number*]   (CZ)
LP .... Liberaalinen Kansanpuolue [*Liberal Party*] [*Finland*]   (WEN)
LP .... Liberal Party [*Australia*]   (ADA)
LP .... Liberation Populaire [*People's Liberation*] [*French*]   (WER)
LP .... Liberator Party [*Guyana*] [*Political party*]   (PPW)
l p .... Liczba Pojedyncza [*Singular*]   (POL)
lp .... Liczba Porzadkowa [*Ordinal number*]   (POL)
LP .... Linear Programing   (RU)
LP .... Line of Sight   (RU)
LP .... Ljudski Pravnik [*People's Lawyer*] [*A periodical Ljubljana*]   (YU)
LP .... Loi Provinciale [*French*]   (BAS)
lp .... Petal   (RU)
LP .... Position Line   (RU)
LP .... Steam Winch   (RU)
LP .... Tree-Planting Machine, Tree Planter   (RU)
LP .... Vacuum-Tube Potentiometer   (RU)
LP-28 .... Ligas Populares de 28 de Febrero [*February 28 Popular Leagues*] [*El Salvador*]   (PD)
LPA............. Laboratoires Pharmaceutiques Africains
LPA............. Lagos Plan of Action [*Nigeria*]
LPA............. Las Palmas [*Canary Islands*] [*Airport symbol*]   (OAG)
LPA............. Liberal Party of Australia
LPA............. Liberation Press Agency [*of the NFLSV*] [*South Vietnamese*]   (CL)
LPA............. Librairie-Editions du Peuple Africain
LPA............. Liga Panstw Arabskich [*The Arab League*] [*Poland*]
LPA............. PAL Aerolineas SA de CV [*Mexico*] [*ICAO designator*]   (FAAC)
LPAA............. Laka Protivavionska Artiljerija [*Light Antiaircraft Artillery*]   (YU)
LPAA........ Little People's Association of Australia   (ADA)
LPAB........ Legal Practitioners' Admission Board [*Australia*]
LPAI .... Ligue Populaire Africaine pour l'Independance [*African People's League for Independence*] [*Djibouti*]   (AF)
LPAM........ Lisboa [*Portugal*] [*ICAO location identifier*]   (ICLI)
LPAR........ Alverca [*Portugal*] [*ICAO location identifier*]   (ICLI)
LPAV........ Aveiro [*Portugal*] [*ICAO location identifier*]   (ICLI)
Lpaz .... Lokomotive mit Gepaeckwagen als Zug [*Locomotive with Baggage Car, Operated as a Train*]   (EG)
LPAZ........ Santa Maria, Santa Maria Island [*Portugal*] [*ICAO location identifier*]   (ICLI)
LPb .... Bleilot [*Lead Solder*] [*German*]   (GCA)
LPB............ La Paz [*Bolivia*] [*Airport symbol*]   (OAG)
LPB............ Library Promotion Bureau [*Pakistan*]   (EAIO)
LPBA........ Lime Producers Brazilian Association   (EAIO)
LPBE .... Beja [*Portugal*] [*ICAO location identifier*]   (ICLI)
LPBG........ Braganca [*Portugal*] [*ICAO location identifier*]   (ICLI)
LPBJ........ Beja [*Portugal*] [*ICAO location identifier*]   (ICLI)
LPBR........ Braga [*Portugal*] [*ICAO location identifier*]   (ICLI)
LPC............ Land Protection Council [*Victoria, Australia*]
LPC............ Less Prosperous Country
LPC............ Library Practice Certificate [*Australia*]   (ADA)
LPCC .... Legal Practitioners Complaints Committee [*South Australia*]
LPCC .... Library Practice Certificate Course [*Australia*]
LPCE .... Laboratoire de Physique et Chimie de l'Environnement [*Environmental Physics and Chemistry Laboratory*] [*Research center*] [*France*]   (EAS)
LPCH .... Chaves [*Portugal*] [*ICAO location identifier*]   (ICLI)
LPCO........ Coimbra [*Portugal*] [*ICAO location identifier*]   (ICLI)
LPCS .... Cascais [*Portugal*] [*ICAO location identifier*]   (ICLI)
LPCS .... Laboratoire de Physique des Composants a Semiconducteurs [*Laboratory of Physics of Semiconductor Devices*] [*France*]   (IRC)
LPCV........ Covilha [*Portugal*] [*ICAO location identifier*]   (ICLI)
LPCWA..... Library Promotion Council of Western Australia
LPD .... Laboratoire de Physique des Decharges [*Physics of Discharge Laboratory*] [*France*]   (WED)
LPD .... Labour Party of Dominica [*Political party*]   (EY)
LPD .... La Pedrera [*Colombia*] [*Airport symbol*]   (OAG)
LPD .... Line of Adjusted Ranges   (RU)
LPD .... Line of Range Corrections   (RU)
LPDSA ...... Libyan Public Development and Stabilization Agency
LPDT........ Legal Practitioners Disciplinary Tribunal [*South Australia*]
LPE............ Laboratorul de Proiectari Educationale [*Educational Design Laboratory*]   (RO)
LPE............ Linear Energy Loss   (RU)
LPER .... Lubelskie Przedsiebiorstwo Elektryfikacji Rolnictwa [*Lublin Enterprise for Electrification of Agriculture*]   (POL)
LPEV .... Evora [*Portugal*] [*ICAO location identifier*]   (ICLI)
LPF .... Lao Patriotic Front [*Use NLHS*]   (CL)
LPF .... Latvian Popular Front [*Political party Defunct*]   (EAIO)

LPFEI........ Leningrad Pedagogical Institute of Finance and Economics   (RU)
LPFL.......... Flores, Flores Island [*Portugal*] [*ICAO location identifier*]   (ICLI)
LPFL.......... Lembaga Penjelidikan Fishenes Laut [*Indonesian*]   (MSC)
LPFR.......... Faro [*Portugal*] [*ICAO location identifier*]   (ICLI)
LPFSSB..... Lone Parents' Family Support Service - Birthright [*Australia*]
LPFU .... Funchal, Madeira Island [*Portugal*] [*ICAO location identifier*]   (ICLI)
LPG .... Landwirtschaftliche Produktionsgenossenschaft [*Agricultural Producer Cooperative*] [*German*]   (EG)
LPG .... Langage de Programmation et de Gestion [*French computer language*]
LPG .... La Plata [*Argentina*] [*Airport symbol*]   (OAG)
LPG .... Le Parti de la Guadeloupe [*Political party*]   (EY)
LPG .... Likid Petrol Gaz [*Liquefied Petroleum Gas, Butane Gas*]   (TU)
LPG .... Liquefied Petroleum Gas
LPGR........ Graciosa, Graciosa Island [*Portugal*] [*ICAO location identifier*]   (ICLI)
LPGSASA ... Liquefied Petroleum Gas Safety Association of South Africa   (EAIO)
LPH .... Letecke Pohonne Hmoty [*Aviation Fuels*]   (CZ)
LPHM .... Letecke Pohonne Hmoty a Maziva [*Aviation Fuels and Lubricant*]   (CZ)
LPHR .... Horta, Faial Island [*Portugal*] [*ICAO location identifier*]   (ICLI)
LPI............. Leningrad Polytechnic Institute Imeni M. I. Kalinin   (RU)
LPI............. Liberal Party of Italy   (RU)
LPI............. Linkoeping [*Sweden*] [*Airport symbol*]   (OAG)
LPI............. L'vov Polytechnic Institute   (RU)
LPI............. Societe Librairie Papeterie Ivoirienne
LPIN.......... Espinho [*Portugal*] [*ICAO location identifier*]   (ICLI)
LPIS.......... Lembaga Penelitian Ilmu-Ilmu Sosial [*Indonesian*]   (SLS)
LPJF......... Leiria [*Portugal*] [*ICAO location identifier*]   (ICLI)
LPJO .... Alijo [*Portugal*] [*ICAO location identifier*]   (ICLI)
LPK .... Laikon Proodevtikon Kinima [*People's Progressive Movement*] [*Greek*]   (GC)
LPK .... Lao Pen Kang [*Lao Neutralist (Party)*]   (CL)
LPK .... Lekarska Poradni Komise [*Medical Advisory Committee*]   (CZ)
LPK .... Lumber Industry Complex   (RU)
LPK .... Lumber Producers' Cooperatives   (RU)
LPKh .... Lumber Industry Establishment   (RU)
LPKIS........ Lietuvos Politiniu Khliniu Irtremtiniu Sayunga [*An association*] [*Lithuania*]   (EAIO)
LPL .... Lembaga Penjelidikan Laut [*Indonesian*]   (MSC)
LPL .... Linear Programming Language [*Intertechnique*] [*French*] [*Computer science*]
LPLA .... Lajes, Terceira Island [*Portugal*] [*ICAO location identifier*]   (ICLI)
LPLA .... Lao People's Liberation Army   (CL)
LPLG .... Lagos [*Portugal*] [*ICAO location identifier*]   (ICLI)
LPM .... Labor Party of Malaya   (ML)
LPM .... Lamap [*Vanuatu*] [*Airport symbol*]   (OAG)
LPM .... Librairie Populaire du Mali
LPM .... Tape Feed, Tape Mechanism, Tape-Drive Mechanism [*Computers*]   (RU)
LPMC........ Liberian Produce Marketing Corporation   (AF)
LPMF........ Monfortinho [*Portugal*] [*ICAO location identifier*]   (ICLI)
LPMG........ Lisboa [*Portugal*] [*ICAO location identifier*]   (ICLI)
LPMI........ Leningrad Institute of Pediatric Medicine   (RU)
LPMI......... Mirandela [*Portugal*] [*ICAO location identifier*]   (ICLI)
LPMO .... Laboratoire de Physique et Metrologie des Oscillateurs [*Physics and Metrology of Oscillators Laboratory*] [*Research center*] [*French*]   (ERC)
LPMO .... Livestock Products Management Organization [*South Korea*]
LPMR....... Monte Real [*Portugal*] [*ICAO location identifier*]   (ICLI)
LPMT........ Montijo [*Portugal*] [*ICAO location identifier*]   (ICLI)
LPN .... Alpenair GmbH & Co. KG [*Austria*] [*ICAO designator*]   (FAAC)
LPN .... Lembaga Padi dan Beras Negara [*National Paddy and Rice Institute*]   (ML)
LPN .... Ligue Progressiste des Interets Economiques et Sociaux des Populations du Nord Cameroun
LPN .... Line of Adjusted Deflections   (RU)
LPN .... Line of Deflection Corrections   (RU)
LPN .... Logements de Premiere Necessite [*France*]   (FLAF)
LPO .... Letecky Poradni Organ [*Aviation Advisory Staff*]   (CZ)
LPO .... Liberale Partei Oesterreichs [*Liberal Party of Austria*] [*Political party*]   (PPE)
LPO .... Lique Francaise pour la Protection des Oiseaux [*French*]   (SLS)
l poj .... Liczba Pojedyncza [*Singular*]   (POL)
LPOT........ Ota [*Portugal*] [*ICAO location identifier*]   (ICLI)
LPP........... Lappeenranta [*Finland*] [*Airport symbol*]   (OAG)
LPP........... Lebowa People's Party [*South Africa*] [*Political party*]   (PPW)
LPP........... Lembaga Penelitian Perencanaan Wilayah & Kota [*Center for Urban and Regional Studies*] [*Indonesia*] [*Research center*]   (IRC)
LPP............ Liberian People's Party [*Political party*]   (EY)

LPP .... Liga dos Patriotas Presos [*League of Jailed Patriots*] [*Portuguese*] (WER)

LPP .... Light Bridge Train (RU)

lpp .... Light River-Crossing Fleet (BU)

LPPA .... Licensed Pearl Producers' Association [*Australia*]

LPPC .... Liberian Palm Products Corporation

LPPC .... Lisboa [*Portugal*] [*ICAO location identifier*] (ICLI)

LPPD .... Lembaga Penelitian Perikanan Dalam [*Freshwater Fisheries Research Institute*] [*Indonesian*] (ASF)

LPPD .... Ponta Delgada, Sao Miguel Island [*Portugal*] [*ICAO location identifier*] (ICLI)

LPPG .... Liquid Paperboard Packaging Group of Australia

LPPI .... Pico, Pico Island [*Portugal*] [*ICAO location identifier*] (ICLI)

LPPL .... Lembaga Penelitian Perikanan Laut [*Marine Fisheries Research Institute*] [*Indonesian*] (ASF)

LPPM .... Portimao [*Portugal*] [*ICAO location identifier*] (ICLI)

LPPO .... Santa Maria [*Portugal*] [*ICAO location identifier*] (ICLI)

LPPP .... Lembaga Pemasaran Pertanian Persekutuan [*Federal Agricultural Marketing Association*] (ML)

LPPR .... Porto [*Portugal*] [*ICAO location identifier*] (ICLI)

LPPS .... Porto Santo, Porto Santo Island [*Portugal*] [*ICAO location identifier*] (ICLI)

LPPT .... Lisboa [*Portugal*] [*ICAO location identifier*] (ICLI)

LPPV .... Praia Verde [*Portugal*] [*ICAO location identifier*] (ICLI)

l/pr .... Icing of Road and Slopes (Obstacle) [*Topography*] (RU)

LPR .... Lid van die Provinsiale Raad [*Member of the Provincial Council*] [*Afrikaans*]

LPR .... Linea Aerea Privadas Argentina [*ICAO designator*] (FAAC)

LPRC .... Liberia Petroleum Refining Corporation

l prom .... Light Industry Factory [*Topography*] (RU)

LProv .... Loi Provinciale [*French*] (BAS)

LPRP .... Lao People's Revolutionary Party [*Phak Pasason Pativat Lao*] [*Political party*] (PPW)

LPS .... Aircraft Position Line (RU)

LPS .... Flying Personnel (RU)

LPS .... Lebanese Press Syndicate (EAIO)

LPS .... Les Planteurs du Sassandra

LPS .... Letecka Priprava a Sport [*Aviation Preparedness and Athletics*] (CZ)

LPS .... Liberale Partei der Schweiz [*Liberal Party of Switzerland*] [*Political party*] (PPE)

LPS .... Limenikos Pyrosvestikos Stathmos [*Port Fire Station*] (GC)

LPSC .... Santa Cruz [*Portugal*] [*ICAO location identifier*] (ICLI)

LPSES ...... Laboratoire de Physique du Solide et Energie Solaire [*Solid State Physics and Solar Energy Laboratory*] [*French*] (WED)

LPSI .... Sines [*Portugal*] [*ICAO location identifier*] (ICLI)

LPSJ .... Sao Jorge, Sao Jorge Island [*Portugal*] [*ICAO location identifier*] (ICLI)

LPSP .... Laboratoire de Physique Stellaire et Planetaire [*Laboratory for Stellar and Planetary Physics*] [*Research center*] [*French*] (IRC)

LPST .... Sintra [*Portugal*] [*ICAO location identifier*] (ICLI)

LPT .... Lampang [*Thailand*] [*Airport symbol*] (OAG)

LPT .... Linear Rotary Transformer (RU)

LPTC .... Lower Primary Teaching Certificate [*Australia*]

LPTF .... Laboratoire Primaire du Temps et des Frequences [*French*] (PDAA)

LPTHE ...... Laboratoire de Physique Theorique et Hautes Energies (MCD)

LPTN .... Tancos [*Portugal*] [*ICAO location identifier*] (ICLI)

LPTP .... Lubelska Przetwornia Tytoniu Przemyslowego [*Lublin Tobacco Factory*] (POL)

LPU .... Establishment for Medical Preventive Treatment (RU)

LPU .... Lembaga Pemilihan Umum [*General Election Board*] (IN)

LPU .... Letecke Povetrnostni Ustredi [*Air Weather Center*] (CZ)

LPU .... Line of Adjusted Deflections [*Artillery*] (RU)

LPU .... Low-Pay Unit [*Employment/finance*]

LPU priMNZST ... Medical Prophylactic Administration of the Ministry of Public Health and Social Welfare (BU)

LPV .... Landing Pontoon Vehicle [*Military*]

lpv .... Light Antiaircraft Battery (BU)

LPV .... Listos para Vencer [*Ready-to-Win*] [*Physical fitness program*] [*Cuba*] (LA)

LPVCS ...... Letectvo Protivzdusne Obrany Statu [*Aviation Component of National Air Defense*] (CZ)

LPVR .... Vila Real [*Portugal*] [*ICAO location identifier*] (ICLI)

LPVZ .... Viseu [*Portugal*] [*ICAO location identifier*] (ICLI)

LPW .... Laboratorium Przemyslu Weglowego [*Laboratory of the Coal Industry*] (POL)

LPW .... Laboratorium Przemyslu Welnianego [*Laboratory of the Wool Industry*] (POL)

LPW .... Liberal Party of Wales [*Political party*]

LPW .... Lotnicze Przysposobienie Wojskowe [*Pre-Military Air Training*] (POL)

Lpz .... Leipzig (EG)

LPZ .... Liga Przyjaciol Zolnierza [*League of Soldier's Friends*] (POL)

LPZ .... Lugansk Locomotive Plant (RU)

LPZB .... Lubelskie Przemyslowe Zjednoczenie Budowlane [*Lublin Industrial Construction Association*] (POL)

LQM .... Puerto Leguizamo [*Colombia*] [*Airport symbol*] (OAG)

LQN .... Qala-Nau [*Afghanistan*] [*Airport symbol*] [*Obsolete*] (OAG)

LQS........... Les Quatre Saisons [*Record label*] [*France*]

LQT .... Liverpool Quay Terms (DS)

LR .... Congregation de la Retraite [*France*] (EAIO)

LR .... Hand Winch (RU)

LR .... Laerarnas Riksfoerbund [*Sweden*] (SLS)

Lr .... Landraad [*Benelux*] (BAS)

lr .... Lastno Rocno [*By One's Own Hand*] (YU)

lR .... Laufend Rechnung [*Current Account*] [*German*] [*Business term*]

Lr .... Lavoir [*Wash House*] [*Military map abbreviation World War I*] [*French*] (MTD)

LR .... Lear [*ICAO aircraft manufacturer identifier*] (ICAO)

lr .... Leder [*Leather*] [*Publishing*] [*Netherlands*]

LR .... Left Hand (RU)

LR .... Liberaal Reveil [*Benelux*] (BAS)

LR .... Liberia [*ANSI two-letter standard code*] (CNC)

LR .... Lincoln Red [*Livestock terminology*]

LR .... Lineas Aereas Costarricenses, Sociedad Anonima (LACSA) [*Costa Rica*] [*ICAO designator*] (ICDA)

LR .... Line Distributor (RU)

LR .... Line Relay (RU)

lr .... Lira (RU)

LR .... Ljudska Republika [*People's Republic*] (YU)

LR .... London Rank [*Freemasonry*]

lr .... Lopende Rekening [*Current Account*] [*Business term*] [*Afrikaans*]

LR .... Slightly Wounded (RU)

LRA .... Larissa [*Greece*] [*Airport symbol*] (OAG)

LRA .... Lawyers' Reform Association [*Australia*]

LRA .... Light Rail Association [*Australia*]

LRA .... Light Rocket Artillery (BU)

LRA .... Line of Equal Azimuths (RU)

LR & D ...... Louvain Research and Development [*Research center*] [*Belgium*] (IRC)

LRAR........ Arad [*Romania*] [*ICAO location identifier*] (ICLI)

LRB........... Lidova Republika Bulharska [*Bulgarian People's Republic*] (CZ)

LRBA .... Laboratoire de Recherches Balistiques et Aerodynamiques [*Ballistic and Aerodynamic Research Laboratory*] [*French*] (WER)

LRBB .... Bucuresti [*Romania*] [*ICAO location identifier*] (ICLI)

LRBC......... Bacau [*Romania*] [*ICAO location identifier*] (ICLI)

LRBH .... Ljudska Republika Bosna in Hercegovina [*People's Republic of Bosnia and Hercegovina*] (YU)

LRBM....... Baia Mare/Tauti Magherusi [*Romania*] [*ICAO location identifier*] (ICLI)

LRBS .... Bucuresti/Baneasa [*Romania*] [*ICAO location identifier*] (ICLI)

LRC........... Latrobe Regional Commission [*Victoria, Australia*]

LRC........... Law Reform Commission [*Ghana*] (DLA)

LRC........... Law Reform Committee [*Australia*]

LRC........... Law Revision Committee [*Bahamas*] (DLA)

LRC........... Legal Resources Center [*South Africa*] (EAIO)

LRC........... Liberia Refinery Company

LRC........... Lineas Aereas Costarricenses SA [*Costa Rica*] [*ICAO designator*] (FAAC)

LRC........... Local Referees Committee

LRCC........ Laboratoire de Recherches et de Control du Caoutchouc [*France*] (PDAA)

LRCG........ Ljudska Republika Crna Gora [*People's Republic of Montenegro*] (YU)

LRCK........ Constanta/M. Kogalniceau [*Romania*] [*ICAO location identifier*] (ICLI)

LRCL........ Cluj-Napoca/Someseni [*Romania*] [*ICAO location identifier*] (ICLI)

LRCNSW .. Law Reform Commission of New South Wales [*Australia*]

LRCS .... Caransebes/Caransebes [*Romania*] [*ICAO location identifier*] (ICLI)

LRCS .... League of Red Cross and Red Crescent Societies [*Switzerland*] (EA)

LRCSA ...... Lincoln Red Cattle Society of Australia

LRCV........ Craiova [*Romania*] [*ICAO location identifier*] (ICLI)

LRCWA..... Law Reform Commission of Western Australia

LRD .... Hunting and Fishing Association (BU)

LRD .... Jet Propulsion Laboratory [*California*] (RU)

LRDC........ Land Resources Development Centre [*Somalia*]

LRE........... Laboratoire de Recherches Energetiques [*Institut de Recherches Geologiques et Minieres*] [*Cameroon*]

LRE........... Linear Power Consumption (RU)

LRE........... Longreach [*Australia*] [*Airport symbol*] (OAG)

LRF........... Lantbrukarnas Riksforbund [*Federation of Swedish Farmers*] [*Sweden*] (EAIO)

LRG .... Landscape Research Group [*Lutterworth, Leicestershire, England*] (EAIO)

LRgl .... Landgerechtreglement [*Benelux*]   (BAS)
LRGRU ..... Leningrad Regional Geological Exploration Administration (RU)
LRH .... La Rochelle [*France*] [*Airport symbol*]   (OAG)
LRH .... Linija Radarskog Horizonta [*RADAR Horizon Line*]   (YU)
LRH .... Ljudska Republika Hrvatska [*People's Republic of Croatia*] (YU)
LRI .... Legiforgalmi es Repuloter Igazgatosag [*Air Traffic and Airport Authority*]   (HU)
LRI .... Legiforgalmi Repuloteri Igazgtatosag [*Air Traffic and Airport Administration*] [*Hungary*]   (PDAA)
LRIA .... Iasi [*Romania*] [*ICAO location identifier*]   (ICLI)
LRK .... Readily Soluble Component   (RU)
LRM .... La Romana [*Dominican Republic*] [*Airport symbol*]   (OAG)
LRM .... Ljudska Republika Makedonija [*People's Republic of Macedonia*] (YU)
LRO .... Locale Raden Ordonnantie [*Benelux*]   (BAS)
LROD .... Oradea [*Romania*] [*ICAO location identifier*]   (ICLI)
LROP .... Bucuresti/Otopeni [*Romania*] [*ICAO location identifier*]   (ICLI)
LRP .... Lebanese Revolutionary Party [*Political party*]   (PD)
LRP .... Lena River Steamship Line   (RU)
LRP .... Line of Equal Bearings   (RU)
LRPSSA .... Long-Range Planning Society of Southern Africa   (AA)
LRR .... Land-Rover Register 1947-1951 [*Petersfield, Hampshire, England*]   (EAIO)
LRR .... Letecky Rizena Raketa [*Air Guided Rocket*]   (CZ)
LRR .... Line of Equal Distance   (RU)
LRRA .... Litter and Recycling Research Association [*Australia*]
LRRP .... Line of Equal Radio Bearings   (RU)
LRRSA ...... Light Railway Research Society of Australia
LRS .... Hunting and Fishing Union   (BU)
LRS .... Legislative Research Service [*Commonwealth Parliamentary Library*] [*Australia*]
lrs .... Line Signal Company   (RU)
LRS .... Ljudska Republika Slovenija [*People's Republic of Slovenia*] (YU)
LRS .... Ljudska Republika Srbija [*People's Republic of Serbia*]   (YU)
LRS .... Ludovy Rybarsky Spolok [*People's Fishing Club*]   (CZ)
LRSB .... Sibiu/Turnisor [*Romania*] [*ICAO location identifier*]   (ICLI)
LRSLP .... Lietuvos Revoliuciniu Socialistu Liaudininkai Partija [*Revolutionary Socialist Populists Party of Lithuania*] [*Political party*]   (PPE)
LRSM .... Satu Mare [*Romania*] [*ICAO location identifier*]   (ICLI)
LRSV .... Suceava/Salcea [*Romania*] [*ICAO location identifier*]   (ICLI)
LRT .... Ligue Revolutionnaire des Travailleurs [*Revolutionary Workers' League*] [*Belgium*]   (WER)
LRT .... Lorient [*France*] [*Airport symbol*]   (OAG)
LRTA .... Laboratoire Radio-Television Abidjan
LRTA .... Light Rail Transit Association [*Milton, Keynes, England*] (EAIO)
LRTC .... Law Reform Commission of Tasmania [*Australia*]
LRTC .... Tulcea/Cataloi [*Romania*] [*ICAO location identifier*]   (ICLI)
LRTM .... Tirgu Mures/Vidrasau [*Romania*] [*ICAO location identifier*] (ICLI)
LRTR .... Timisoara/Giarmata [*Romania*] [*ICAO location identifier*] (ICLI)
LRU .... Las Cruces [*New Mexico*] [*Airport symbol*]   (OAG)
LRUK .... Commander's Personal Radio Center   (RU)
LRV .... Light Reconnaissance Vehicle [*Military*]
LRV .... Line of Equal Altitudes   (RU)
LRVSA ...... Lid van Rekenaarvereniging van Suid-Afrika [*South Africa*] (AA)
LRWE .... Long-Range Weapons Establishment [*Australia*]
LRWES ..... Long-Range Weapons Experimental Station [*Australia*]   (ADA)
LRWO .... Long Range Weapons Organisation [*Australia*]
LRWO(A) ... Long-Range Weapons Organisation (Australia)
LRWRE ..... Long-Range Weapons Research Establishment [*Australia*] (ADA)
LS .... Communication Line, Line, Circuit   (RU)
ls .... Horsepower   (RU)
LS .... Labologists Society [*Farnborough, Hampshire, England*]   (EAIO)
LS .... Laborator Strojnicka [*Machine Building Laboratory (of the Czechoslovak Academy of Sciences)*]   (CZ)
LS .... Laboratory of Speleology (of the Academy of Sciences, USSR) (RU)
LS .... Laererskoleeksamen [*Norway*]
LS .... Laikos Synagermos [*People's Rally*]   (GC)
LS .... Lakheion Syndakton [*Editors Lottery*]   (GC)
lS .... Lange Sicht [*Long Sight*] [*German*]
LS .... Lekarz Stomatolog [*Dentist*] [*Poland*]
LS .... Lesni Spolecenstva [*Forestry Corporations*]   (CZ)
LS .... Lesotho [*ANSI two-letter standard code*]   (CNC)
LS .... Lexicographic Collection [*Bibliography*]   (RU)
LS .... Lidove Soudnictvi [*People's Judiciary*] [*A periodical*]   (CZ)
LS .... Lidovy Soudce [*People's Judge*]   (CZ)
LS .... Liga Socialista [*Socialist League*] [*Venezuela*]   (LA)

LS .... Light Forces [*Navy*]   (RU)
LS .... Limenikon Soma [*Port Corps*]   (GC)
LS .... Linear Resistance   (RU)
LS .... Linksozialisten [*Left Socialists*] [*Austria*] [*Political party*]   (PPE)
LS .... Linnean Society [*Australia*]
Ls .... Lise [*High School, Lycee*]   (TU)
LS .... Livre Soudanaise
LS .... Ljudska Skupscina [*People's Assembly*]   (YU)
LS .... Lochstreifen [*German*]   (ADPT)
LS .... Lochstreifensender [*German*]   (ADPT)
LS .... Loutkovy Soubor [*Puppet Theater Ensemble*]   (CZ)
LS .... Luftschutz [*Civil Defense, Passive Air Defense*]   (EG)
LS .... Lugar del Sello [*Place of the Seal*] [*Spanish*]
LS .... Lute Society [*Harrow, England*]   (EAIO)
LS .... Medical Serum   (RU)
LS .... Personnel, Staff   (RU)
LS .... Signal Light   (RU)
LS .... Sudanese Pound   (IMH)
L/sa .... Lefkosa [*Nicosia*] [*Turkish Federated State of Cyprus*]   (GC)
LSA .... Licensed Stores Association of Western Australia
LSA .... Linea Aerea Nacional (Lansa) [*Dominican Republic*] [*ICAO designator*]   (FAAC)
LSA .... Little Sisters of the Assumption [*See also PSA*] [*France*]   (EAIO)
LSA .... Lochstreifenausgabe [*German*]   (ADPT)
LSA .... Losuia [*Papua New Guinea*] [*Airport symbol*]   (OAG)
L-SACA ..... Larkin-Sopwith Aviation Co. of Australasia Ltd.
LSACT ...... Law Society of the Australian Capital Territory
LSAFHI .... Lid van Suid-Afrikaanse Federasie van Hospitaal Ingenieurswese [*South Africa*]   (AA)
LSAG .... Geneve [*Switzerland*] [*ICAO location identifier*]   (ICLI)
LSAIVERT ... Lid van Suid-Afrikaanse Instituut van Vertalers en Tolke [*South Africa*]   (AA)
LSANSW .. Limbless Soldiers' Association of New South Wales [*Australia*]
LSANSW .. Liquor Stores Association of New South Wales [*Australia*]
LSAP .... Letzeburger Sozialistesch Arbechter Partei [*Socialist Workers' Party of Luxembourg*] [*Political party*]   (PPE)
LSAP .... Luxemburgische Sozialistische Arbeiterpartei [*Luxembourg Socialist Workers Party*]   (WEN)
LSAQ .... Limbless Soldiers' Association of Queensland [*Australia*]
LSASA ...... Limbless Soldiers' Association of South Australia
LSASVV .... Lid van Suid-Afrikaanse Steenkoolverwerkingsvereniging [*South Africa*]   (AA)
LSAV .... Limbless Soldiers' Association of Victoria [*Australia*]
LSAV .... Liquor Stores' Association of Victoria [*Aerospace*]
LSAWA ..... Liquor Stores' Association of Western Australia
LSAZ .... Zurich [*Switzerland*] [*ICAO location identifier*]   (ICLI)
LSB .... Belen'kiy's Therapeutic Serum   (RU)
LSB .... Legal Service Bulletin Co-Operative Ltd. [*Australia*]
LSBC .... Lagos State Broadcasting Corporation [*Nigeria*]
LSC .... Labor Socialist Committee [*Australia*]
LSC .... Language and Society Centre [*Monash University*] [*Australia*]
LSC .... Languages Services Centre [*South Australia*]
LSC .... Law of the Sea Conference [*United Nations*]
LSC .... Liberian Shipowners Council   (PDAA)
LSC .... Library Store Catalogue [*Australia*]
LSC .... Little Sisters of Carmel
LSC .... Loehmer Schulcomputer [*German*]   (ADPT)
LSCE .... Licentiate of the Sydney College of Elocution [*Australia*]
lsch .... Horsepower per Hour   (RU)
LSCR .... Ligue des Societes de la Croix-Rouge
LSCSA .... Legal Services Commission of South Australia
LSCSE .... Lady Southern Cross Search Expedition [*Australia*]
LSD .... Langage Simple pour Debutants [*French*]   (ADPT)
LSD .... Lembaga Sosial Desa [*Village Social Agency*]   (IN)
LSD .... Lemnul Stratificat Densificat [*Stratified Densified Wood*]   (RO)
LSD .... Liberaler Studentenbund Deutschlands [*Liberal Student Federation of Germany*]   (WEN)
LSD .... Lidove Spotrebni Druzstvo [*People's Consumer Cooperative*] (CZ)
LSD .... Lisergiensuur-Dietielamide [*Lysergic Acid Diethylamide*] [*Afrikaans*]
LSDGM ..... Laboratorio per lo Studio della Dinamica delle Grandi Masse [*Italian*]   (MSC)
LSDH .... Ligue Suisse des Droits de l'Homme [*Switzerland*]
LSDP .... Lietuvos Socialdemokratu Partija [*Lithuanian Social Democratic Party*] [*Political party*]   (PPE)
LSDPC ...... Lagos State Development and Property Corporation
LSDSP .... Latvijas Socialdemokratiska Stradnieku Partija [*Latvian Social Democratic Workers' Party*] [*Political party*]   (EAIO)
LSE .... Langage Symbolique d'Enseignement [*French*]   (ADPT)
LSE .... Lochkarten-Lese-Stanz-Einheit [*Punch Card Reader-Perforator*] (EG)
LSE .... Lochstreifeneingabe [*German*]   (ADPT)
LSE .... Luxembourg Stock Exchange
LSER .... Raron [*Switzerland*] [*ICAO location identifier*]   (ICLI)
LSEZ .... Zermatt [*Switzerland*] [*ICAO location identifier*]   (ICLI)

LSF .... Logistic Support Force [Military]
LSG .... Lagos State Government
LSG............ Ligo Samseksamaj Geesperantistoj [Richmond, Surrey, England] (EAIO)
Lsg .... Loesung [Solution] [German]
LSGC .... Laboratoire des Sciences du Genie Chimique [Chemical Engineering Science Laboratory] [French] (ARC)
LSGC .... Les Eplatures [Switzerland] [ICAO location identifier] (ICLI)
LSGE .... Ecuvillens [Switzerland] [ICAO location identifier] (ICLI)
LSGG .... Geneve/Cointrin [Switzerland] [ICAO location identifier] (ICLI)
Lsgg .... Loesungen [Solutions] [German]
LSGK .... Saanen [Switzerland] [ICAO location identifier] (ICLI)
LSGL .... Lausanne/Blecherette [Switzerland] [ICAO location identifier] (ICLI)
Lsgm .... Loesungsmittel [Solvent] [German] (GCA)
LSGM....... Long Service and Good Conduct Medal [Australia] [Military decoration]
LSGN........ Neuchatel [Switzerland] [ICAO location identifier] (ICLI)
LSGP .... La Cote [Switzerland] [ICAO location identifier] (ICLI)
LSGS .... Sion [Switzerland] [ICAO location identifier] (ICLI)
Lsgs-Mittel ... Loesungsmittel [Solvent] [German] (GCA)
LSGT .... Gruyeres [Switzerland] [ICAO location identifier] (ICLI)
LSH .... Lashio [Myanmar] [Airport symbol] (OAG)
LSh .... Light Attack Aircraft (RU)
LSHA .... Gstaad-Inn Grund [Switzerland] [ICAO location identifier] (ICLI)
LShchP ...... Line Switchboard (RU)
LSHD .... Luftschutzhilfsdienst [Civil Defense Auxiliary Service] (WEN)
LSHG .... Gampel [Switzerland] [ICAO location identifier] (ICLI)
LSHS......... Sezegnin [Switzerland] [ICAO location identifier] (ICLI)
LSI .... Landesschulinspektor [District School Inspector] [German]
LSJ .... La Societe Jersiaise (EAIO)
LSJ .... Little Sisters of Jesus [See also PSJ] [Italy] (EAIO)
LSK .... Livsmedelsstadgekommitten [Sweden]
LSK .... Lochstreifenkarte [German] (ADPT)
LSK .... Luftschutz Kommando [Civil Air Defense Command] (EG)
LSKhA ...... Latvian Agricultural Academy (RU)
LSKhI .... Leningrad Agricultural Institute (RU)
LSK/LV ..... (Kommando der) Luftstreitkraefte und Luftverteidigung [Air Forces and Air Defense (Command)] (EG)
LSKT .... Leningrad Glass and Ceramics Technicum (RU)
LSL .... Langsame Stoerungssichere Logik [German] (ADPT)
LSL .... Latvijas Sieviesu Liga [Latvia] (EAIO)
LSL .... Lochstreifenleser [German] (ADPT)
LSL .... Los Chiles [Costa Rica] [Airport symbol] (OAG)
LSLB .... Land Surveyors' Licensing Board [Western Australia]
LSLDP....... Lietuvos Socialistu Liaudininku Demokratu Partija [Socialist Populists Democratic Party of Lithuania] [Political party] (PPE)
LSLP.......... Lietuvos Socialistu Liaudininku Partija [Socialist Populists Party of Lithuania] [Political party] (PPE)
LSLRS ...... Ljudska Skupscina Ljudske Republike Slovenije [People's Assembly of the People's Republic of Slovenia] (YU)
LSM.......... Liberation Support Movement
LSM.......... London & Scandinavian Metallurgical Co. Ltd.
LSM.......... Long Semado [Malaysia] [Airport symbol] (OAG)
LSM.......... Lubelska Spoldzielnia Mieszkaniowa [Lublin Housing Cooperative] (POL)
LSMB .... Lint and Seed Marketing Board
LSMD........ Dubendorf [Switzerland] [ICAO location identifier] (ICLI)
LSME........ Emmen [Switzerland] [ICAO location identifier] (ICLI)
LSMGI ...... Leningrad Sanitation and Hygiene Medical Institute (RU)
l/smos .... Logariasmos [Account] [Greek] (GC)
LSMP .... Payerne [Switzerland] [ICAO location identifier] (ICLI)
LSMT .... Land Site Marshalling Team [Military]
LSN .... Lei de Seguranca Nacional [National Security Law] [Brazil] (LA)
LSn............ Zinnlot [Tin Solder] [German] (GCA)
LS/NE .... Laendersektion Nordeuropa [North European Countries Section] (EG)
LSNKh....... Leningrad Council of the National Economy (RU)
LSNSW ..... Law Society of New South Wales [Australia]
LSNT .... Law Society of the Northern Territory [Australia]
LSO .... Lesotho [ANSI three-letter standard code] (CNC)
LSO .... Letecky Spojovaci Oddil [Air Communications Battalion] (CZ)
LSO .... Liberal Socialists Organization [Egypt] (ME)
lsoccomm ... Lois Coordonnees sur les Societes Commerciales [French] (BAS)
LSP .... Las Piedras [Venezuela] [Airport symbol] (OAG)
LSP .... Liberale Staatspartij [Liberal State Party] [Netherlands] [Political party] (PPE)
LSP .... Liberal Socialist Party [Egypt] [Political party] (PPW)
LSP .... Liberal Socialist Party [Singapore] [Political party] (ML)
LSP .... Lochspalte [German] (ADPT)

lsp.............. Sawmill [Topography] (RU)
LSPA .... Amlikon [Switzerland] [ICAO location identifier] (ICLI)
LSPC .... Long Service Payments Corp. [Australia]
LSPD .... Dittingen [Switzerland] [ICAO location identifier] (ICLI)
LSPF .... Schaffhausen [Switzerland] [ICAO location identifier] (ICLI)
LSPH .... Winterthur [Switzerland] [ICAO location identifier] (ICLI)
LSPK .... Hasenstrick [Switzerland] [ICAO location identifier] (ICLI)
LSPL .... Langenthal [Switzerland] [ICAO location identifier] (ICLI)
LSPN .... Triengen [Switzerland] [ICAO location identifier] (ICLI)
LSPO .... Leningrad Union of Consumers' Societies (RU)
LSPP......... Lands, Surveys, and Physical Planning [Department of] [Lesotho] (EAS)
LSPV .... Wangen-Lachen [Switzerland] [ICAO location identifier] (ICLI)
LSPZ .... Luzern-Beromunster [Switzerland] [ICAO location identifier] (ICLI)
LSR .... Alsair Societe [France] [ICAO designator] (FAAC)
LSR .... Landesschulrat [District School Council] [German]
Lsr............. Landschapsrechter [Benelux] (BAS)
LSR .... Legitimerade Sjukgymnasters Riksforbund [Swedish Association of Registered Physical Therapists] (EAIO)
LSR .... Saw Frame, Log Frame (RU)
LSR .... Sectional Saw Frame (RU)
LSRH........ Laboratoire Suisse de Recherches Horlogeres [Swiss Laboratory of the Watch Industry] [Neuchatel] [Research center] (ERC)
LSRI .... Life Science Research Israel Ltd. [Research center] (IRC)
LSS .... Landslaget for Spraklig Samling [Norway] (SLS)
LSS .... Leopold Stokowski Society (EA)
LSS .... Les Saintes [Guadeloupe] [Airport symbol] (OAG)
LSS .... Lochstreifenstanzer [German] (ADPT)
LSS .... Lubelska Spoldzielnia Spozywcow [Lublin Consumers' Cooperative] (POL)
LSSA .... Law Society of South Australia
LSSA .... Limnological Society of Southern Africa (SLS)
LSSB........ Bern Radio [Switzerland] [ICAO location identifier] (ICLI)
LSSE........ Federation of Lawyers, Social Scientists, and Economists [Sweden] (EAIO)
LSSK .... Leningrad Union of Soviet Composers (RU)
LSSKh ...... Leningrad Union of Soviet Artists (RU)
LSSO .... Bern. Office Federal de l'Air [Switzerland] [ICAO location identifier] (ICLI)
LSSP .... Lanka Sama Samaja Party [Sri Lanka Equal Society Party] [Political party] (PPW)
LSSR .... Berne/Radio Suisse SA [Switzerland] [ICAO location identifier] (ICLI)
LSSR .... Latvian Soviet Socialist Republic (RU)
LSSR .... Lithuanian Soviet Socialist Republic (RU)
LSSS .... Geneve [Switzerland] [ICAO location identifier] (ICLI)
LSST .... Lochstreifenstanzer [German] (ADPT)
LSSW .... Zurich [Switzerland] [ICAO location identifier] (ICLI)
LST .... Launceston [Tasmania] [Airport symbol] (OAG)
LST .... Law Society of Tasmania [Australia]
LST .... Leningrad Shipbuilding Technicum (RU)
Lst............. Lire Sterline [Pounds Sterling] [Italian]
LSTB .... Bellechasse [Switzerland] [ICAO location identifier] (ICLI)
LSTO......... Motiers [Switzerland] [ICAO location identifier] (ICLI)
LStR .... Lohnsteuer-Richtlinie [Wages Tax Directives] (EG)
LSTR .... Montricher [Switzerland] [ICAO location identifier] (ICLI)
LSTX .... Bex [Switzerland] [ICAO location identifier] (ICLI)
LSTY .... Yverdon [Switzerland] [ICAO location identifier] (ICLI)
LSU........... Landsradet for Sveriges Ungdomsorganisationer [National Council of Swedish Youth] (EAIO)
LSU........... Liberalsoziale Union [Liberal Social Union] [Germany] [Political party] (PPW)
LSU........... Library Services Unit [Ministry for the Arts] [Victoria, Australia]
LSU........... Long Sukang [Malaysia] [Airport symbol] (OAG)
LSUE......... Lochschriftuebersetzer [German] (ADPT)
LSV .... Alak [Former USSR] [ICAO designator] (FAAC)
LSV .... Landelijke Specialisten Vereniging [Netherlands] (SLS)
LSVS .... Lager-Speditionsversicherungsschein [Warehouse Shipping Insurance Certificate] (EG)
LSW .... Licensed Shorthand Writer
LSW .... Ludowa Spoldzielnia Wydawnicza [People's Publishing House] (POL)
LSWA........ Law Society of Western Australia
LSWF .... Light of Salvation Women's Fellowship [Nigeria] (EAIO)
LSXB .... Balzers/FL [Switzerland] [ICAO location identifier] (ICLI)
LSXD .... Domat-Ems [Switzerland] [ICAO location identifier] (ICLI)
LSXE .... Erstfeld [Switzerland] [ICAO location identifier] (ICLI)
LSXH........ Holzkien [Switzerland] [ICAO location identifier] (ICLI)
LSXL......... Lauterbrunnen [Switzerland] [ICAO location identifier] (ICLI)
LSXM....... St. Moritz [Switzerland] [ICAO location identifier] (ICLI)
LSXO .... Gossau SG [Switzerland] [ICAO location identifier] (ICLI)
LSXS .... Schindellegi [Switzerland] [ICAO location identifier] (ICLI)
LSXT .... Trogen [Switzerland] [ICAO location identifier] (ICLI)
LSXU........ Untervaz [Switzerland] [ICAO location identifier] (ICLI)

LSXV .... San Vittore [*Switzerland*] [*ICAO location identifier*] (ICLI)
LSXW .... Wurenlingen [*Switzerland*] [*ICAO location identifier*] (ICLI)
LSY .... Lismore [*Australia*] [*Airport symbol*] (OAG)
LSYC .... League of Socialist Youth of Croatia [*Political party*]
lsz .... Leltari Szam [*Inventory Number*] (HU)
LSZ .... Leninogorsk Lead Plant (RU)
LSZ .... Lidova Skola Zemedelska [*People's Agricultural School*] (CZ)
LSZA .... Lugano [*Switzerland*] [*ICAO location identifier*] (ICLI)
LSZB .... Bern/Belp [*Switzerland*] [*ICAO location identifier*] (ICLI)
LSZC .... Bad Ragaz [*Switzerland*] [*ICAO location identifier*] (ICLI)
LSZD........ Ascona [*Switzerland*] [*ICAO location identifier*] (ICLI)
LSZE .... Bad Ragaz [*Switzerland*] [*ICAO location identifier*] (ICLI)
LSZF......... Birrfeld [*Switzerland*] [*ICAO location identifier*] (ICLI)
LSZG .... Grenchen [*Switzerland*] [*ICAO location identifier*] (ICLI)
LSZH........ Zurich [*Switzerland*] [*ICAO location identifier*] (ICLI)
LSZI .... Fricktal-Schupfart [*Switzerland*] [*ICAO location identifier*] (ICLI)
LSZJ......... Courtelary [*Switzerland*] [*ICAO location identifier*] (ICLI)
LSZK .... Speck-Fehraltorf [*Switzerland*] [*ICAO location identifier*] (ICLI)
LSZL .... Locarno [*Switzerland*] [*ICAO location identifier*] (ICLI)
LSZM....... Bale [*Switzerland*] [*ICAO location identifier*] (ICLI)
LSZN........ Hausen Am Albis [*Switzerland*] [*ICAO location identifier*] (ICLI)
LSZP .... Biel/Kappelen [*Switzerland*] [*ICAO location identifier*] (ICLI)
LSZR .... Altenrhein [*Switzerland*] [*ICAO location identifier*] (ICLI)
LSZS........ Samedan [*Switzerland*] [*ICAO location identifier*] (ICLI)
LSZT .... Lommis [*Switzerland*] [*ICAO location identifier*] (ICLI)
LSZU .... Buttwil [*Switzerland*] [*ICAO location identifier*] (ICLI)
LSZV .... Sitterdorf [*Switzerland*] [*ICAO location identifier*] (ICLI)
LSZW .... Thun [*Switzerland*] [*ICAO location identifier*] (ICLI)
LSZX .... Schanis [*Switzerland*] [*ICAO location identifier*] (ICLI)
LSZY .... Porrentruy [*Switzerland*] [*ICAO location identifier*] (ICLI)
LSZZ .... Collective address for NOTAM and SNOWTAM [*Switzerland*] [*ICAO location identifier*] (ICLI)
LT .... Beam Tetrode (RU)
LT .... Conveyor Belt (RU)
lt .... Laatikko [*Finland*]
LT .... Larsen and Toubro Ltd. [*India*] [*Commercial firm*]
lt .... Lateinisch [*Latin*] [*German*] (GCA)
LT .... Latina [*Car registration plates*] [*Italian*]
lt .... Laut [*According To*] [*German*] (EG)
Lt.............. Leutnant [*Lieutenant*] [*German*]
Lt.............. Lieutenant [*French*] (MTD)
Lt.............. Lieutenant (EECI)
LT .... Line Transformer (RU)
LT .... Lira Toscana [*Tuscany Pound*] [*Monetary unit*] [*Italian*] (ROG)
LT .... Lira Turca [*Turkish Pound*] [*Monetary unit*] [*Italian*] (ROG)
lt .... Litre [*Liter*] (TU)
LT .... Lords' Taverners [*Australia*]
LT .... Luitenant [*Lieutenant*] [*Afrikaans*]
LT .... Precision Casting (RU)
LT .... Technical Lycee [*French*]
LT .... Telegramme-Lettre [*Telegram-Letter*] (CL)
Lt............... Triebwagen-Leerzug [*Empty Rail Motor Car and Consist*] (EG)
LTA .... Laboratorio de Tecnologia de Alimentos [*Puerto Rico*] (DSCA)
LTA .... Lady Teachers' Association [*Australia*]
LTA .... Land Tenure Act [*Rhodesian*] (AF)
LTA .... Lembaga Tenaga Atom [*Atomic Energy Institute*] (IN)
LTA .... Leningrad Forestry Engineering Academy Imeni S. M. Kirov (RU)
LTA .... Lettera di Transporto Aereo [*Air Waybill*] [*Italian*] [*Business term*]
LTA .... Lettre de Transport Aerien [*Air Waybill*] [*French*] [*Business term*]
LTA .... Linea Aerea Tama [*Chile*] [*ICAO designator*] (FAAC)
LTA .... Tape-Printing Apparatus (RU)
LTA .... Tzaneen [*South Africa*] [*Airport symbol*] (OAG)
LTAA........ Ankara [*Turkey*] [*ICAO location identifier*] (ICLI)
LTAA........ Lawn Tennis Association of Australia (ADA)
LTAB........ Guvercinlik [*Turkey*] [*ICAO location identifier*] (ICLI)
LTAC........ Ankara/Esenboga [*Turkey*] [*ICAO location identifier*] (ICLI)
LTAD .... Ankara/Etimesgut [*Turkey*] [*ICAO location identifier*] (ICLI)
LTAE........ Ankara/Murted [*Turkey*] [*ICAO location identifier*] (ICLI)
LTAF........ Adana/Sakirpasa [*Turkey*] [*ICAO location identifier*] (ICLI)
LTAG........ Adana/Incirlik [*Turkey*] [*ICAO location identifier*] (ICLI)
LTAH .... Afyon [*Turkey*] [*ICAO location identifier*] (ICLI)
LTAI......... Antalya [*Turkey*] [*ICAO location identifier*] (ICLI)
LTAJ .... Gaziantep [*Turkey*] [*ICAO location identifier*] (ICLI)
LTAK........ Iskenderun [*Turkey*] [*ICAO location identifier*] (ICLI)
LTAL........ Kastamonu [*Turkey*] [*ICAO location identifier*] (ICLI)
LTAM....... Kayseri [*Turkey*] [*ICAO location identifier*] (ICLI)
LTAN........ Konya [*Turkey*] [*ICAO location identifier*] (ICLI)
LTAO .... Malatya/Erhac [*Turkey*] [*ICAO location identifier*] (ICLI)
LTAP........ Merzifon [*Turkey*] [*ICAO location identifier*] (ICLI)
LTAQ........ Samsun [*Turkey*] [*ICAO location identifier*] (ICLI)
LTAR........ Sivas [*Turkey*] [*ICAO location identifier*] (ICLI)

LTAS .... Zonguldak [*Turkey*] [*ICAO location identifier*] (ICLI)
LTAT........ Malatya/Erhac [*Turkey*] [*ICAO location identifier*] (ICLI)
LTAU .... Kayseri/Erkilet [*Turkey*] [*ICAO location identifier*] (ICLI)
LTAV........ Sivrihisar [*Turkey*] [*ICAO location identifier*] (ICLI)
LTBA .... Istanbul/Yesilkoy [*Turkey*] [*ICAO location identifier*] (ICLI)
LTBB .... Istanbul [*Turkey*] [*ICAO location identifier*] (ICLI)
LTBB .... Lefkosa Turk Berberler Birligi [*Nicosia Turkish Barbers' Union*] (TU)
LTBC .... Alasehir [*Turkey*] [*ICAO location identifier*] (ICLI)
LTBD........ Aydin [*Turkey*] [*ICAO location identifier*] (ICLI)
LTBE .... Bursa [*Turkey*] [*ICAO location identifier*] (ICLI)
LTBF .... Balikesir [*Turkey*] [*ICAO location identifier*] (ICLI)
LTBG .... Bandirma [*Turkey*] [*ICAO location identifier*] (ICLI)
LTBH .... Canakkale [*Turkey*] [*ICAO location identifier*] (ICLI)
LTBI .... Eskisehir [*Turkey*] [*ICAO location identifier*] (ICLI)
LTBJ......... Izmir/Cumaovasi [*Turkey*] [*ICAO location identifier*] (ICLI)
LTBK........ Izmir/Gaziemir [*Turkey*] [*ICAO location identifier*] (ICLI)
LTBL .... Izmir/Cigli [*Turkey*] [*ICAO location identifier*] (ICLI)
LTBM....... Isparta [*Turkey*] [*ICAO location identifier*] (ICLI)
LTBMMS ... Lefkosa Turk Belediyesi Memur ve Mustahdemleri Sendikasi [*Nicosia Turkish Municipal Officials and Employees' Union*] [*Turkish Cypriot*] (GC)
LTBN........ Kutahya [*Turkey*] [*ICAO location identifier*] (ICLI)
LTBO........ Usak [*Turkey*] [*ICAO location identifier*] (ICLI)
LTBP........ Yalova [*Turkey*] [*ICAO location identifier*] (ICLI)
LTBQ........ Topel [*Turkey*] [*ICAO location identifier*] (ICLI)
LTBr .... Light Tank Brigade (RU)
LTBR .... Yenisehir [*Turkey*] [*ICAO location identifier*] (ICLI)
LTBS .... Dalaman [*Turkey*] [*ICAO location identifier*] (ICLI)
LTBT .... Akhisar [*Turkey*] [*ICAO location identifier*] (ICLI)
LtBz .... Leitbronze [*High Conductivity Bronze*] [*German*] (GCA)
LTC .... Land Tenure Center
LTC........... Language Testing Center [*University of Melbourne*] [*Australia*]
LTC........... Launceston Technical College [*Australia*]
LTC........... Levis Technical Co. (Nigeria) Ltd.
LTC........... Liberia Telecommunications Corp. (IMH)
LTC........... Lubrizol Transarabian Company [*Saudi Arabia*]
LTC........... Lutheran Teachers College [*Australia*] (ADA)
LTCA........ Elazig [*Turkey*] [*ICAO location identifier*] (ICLI)
LTCB........ Agri [*Turkey*] [*ICAO location identifier*] (ICLI)
LTCB........ Long Term Credit Bank [*Japan*] (ECON)
LTCB........ Long-Term Credit Bank of Japan, Ltd. (ECON)
LTCC........ Diyarbakir [*Turkey*] [*ICAO location identifier*] (ICLI)
LTCC........ Language Testing and Curriculum Center [*Griffith University*] [*Australia*]
LTCD........ Erzincan [*Turkey*] [*ICAO location identifier*] (ICLI)
LTCE........ Erzurum [*Turkey*] [*ICAO location identifier*] (ICLI)
LTCF .... Kars [*Turkey*] [*ICAO location identifier*] (ICLI)
LTCG .... Trabzon [*Turkey*] [*ICAO location identifier*] (ICLI)
LTCH .... Urfa [*Turkey*] [*ICAO location identifier*] (ICLI)
LTCI .... Van [*Turkey*] [*ICAO location identifier*] (ICLI)
LTCJ .... Batman [*Turkey*] [*ICAO location identifier*] (ICLI)
Lt Col .... Lieutenant Colonel (PWGL)
LTD .... Ghadames [*Libya*] [*Airport symbol*] (OAG)
LTD .... Land Titles Division [*South Australia*]
ltd .... Leitend [*Chief*] (EG)
LTD .... Letecka Technicka Divize [*Aviation (or Air) Technical Division*] (CZ)
Ltd.............. Limited (PWGL)
Ltda............ Limitada [*Limited*] [*Spanish*]
Ltda............ Limitada [*Limited*] [*Portuguese*]
LTDP......... Long-Term Defense Program [*NATO*] (MCD)
Ltd S .... Limited Sirketi [*Limited Company, Corporation*] [*Sti, TAS Turkish*] [*See also*] (CED)
Ltd Sti .... Limited Sirketi [*Limited Company, Corporation*] [*Sti, TAS Turkish*] [*See also*] (TU)
Lte .... Lette [*Swamp*] [*Military map abbreviation World War I*] [*French*] (MTD)
Ltee .... Limitee [*Limited*] [*French*]
LTEU......... Leningrad Tourist and Excursion Administration (RU)
LTF........... Laboratory of Theoretical Physics (RU)
LTF........... Latvijas Tautas Fronte [*Popular Front of Latvia*] [*Political party*] (EY)
LTF........... Telegramme-Lettre [*Telegram-Letter*] [*Use LT*] (CL)
LTFQMP .. Laboratorio de Tecnicas Fisico-Quimicas Aplicadas a Mineralogia e Petrologia [*Mineralogical and Petrological Applications of Physical and Chemical Tech niques Laboratory*] [*Junta de Investigacoes Cientificas do Ultramar*] [*Research center*] [*Portugal*] (EAS)
Ltg.............. Leitung [*Performance*] [*German*]
LTG .... Lufttransportgeschwader [*Transport Element of the German Military Airforce*] (PDAA)
lt-genl........ Luitenant-Generaal [*Lieutenant-General*] [*Afrikaans*]
LTGH .... Lefkosa Turkiye Genel Hastane [*Nicosia Turkish General Hospital*] (TU)

LTI............ Aerotaxis Latinoamericanos SA de CV [*Mexico*] [*ICAO designator*] (FAAC)
LTI............ Forestry Engineering Institute (RU)
LTI............ Leningrad Technological Institute Imeni Lensovet (RU)
LTI............ Leningrad Textile Institute Imeni S. M. Kirov (RU)
LTI............ Lerotholi Freedom Party
LTI............ Licentiate of the Textile Institute [*South Africa*] (AA)
LTIC......... Library and Technical Information Centre [*Royal Scientific Society*] [*Jordan*]
LTIPP....... Leningrad Technological Institute of the Food Industry (RU)
ltk.............. Laatikko [*Finland*]
LTK........... Latakia [*Syria*] [*Airport symbol*] (OAG)
LTK........... Liiketyonantajain Keskusliitto [*Commercial Employers' Association*] [*Helsinki, Finland*] (WEN)
LTK........... Luonnontieteiden Kandidaatti [*Finland*]
LTKL........ Lefkosa Turk Kiz Lisesi [*Nicosia Turkish Women's Lycee*] (TU)
LT-KMDR ... Luitenant-Kommandeur [*Lieutenant Commander*] [*Afrikaans*]
lt-kol.......... Luitenant-Kolonel [*Lieutenant-Colonel*] [*Afrikaans*]
LTL........... Lastourville [*Gabon*] [*Airport symbol*] (OAG)
LTL........... Latvian Airlines [*ICAO designator*] (FAAC)
LTL........... Lefkosa Turk Lisesi [*Nicosia Turkish Lycee*] [*Cyprus*] (TU)
LTM .... Laici per il Terzo Mondo [*Italy*]
LTM .... Letecky Technicky Material [*Aviation Technical Equipment*] (CZ)
LTM .... Lethem [*Guyana*] [*Airport symbol*] (OAG)
LTM-HB ... Sluzba Lesotechnickych Melioraci a Hrazeni Bystrin [*Forest Engineering and Flood Control Service*] (CZ)
LTN .... Aerolineas Latinas CA [*Venezuela*] [*ICAO designator*] (FAAC)
LTN .... Laboratory for Technical Standarization (RU)
LTN .... Lodzkie Towarzystwo Naukowe [*Lodz Learned Society*] (POL)
ltn.............. Luutnantti [*Finland*]
lto.............. Lager Technisch Onderwijs [*Benelux*] (BAS)
LTO .... Land Titles Office [*Australia*]
LTO .... Lithuanian Theatrical Society (RU)
LTO .... Loreto [*Mexico*] [*Airport symbol*] (OAG)
LTOP........ Lesnicko-Technicka Ochrana Pudy [*Technical Forest Soil Conservation*] (CZ)
LTP........... Laboratoire des Travaux Publics
LTP........... Laboratorio di Technologia della Pesca [*Italian*] (MSC)
LTP........... Letecky Technicky Pluk [*Air Technical Regiment*] (CZ)
LTP........... Local Tourism Plan
LTP........... Lucko Transportno Preduzece [*Port Transport Establishment*] [*YU*]
LTPA........ Lorraine de Travaux Publics Africains
LTQ .... Le Touquet [*France*] [*Airport symbol*] (OAG)
ltq.............. Torok Font [*Turkish Pound*]
LTR........... AS Lufttransport [*Norway*] [*ICAO designator*] (FAAC)
LTR........... LaemThong Rice Co. Ltd. [*Thailand*]
LTR........... Langue Temps Reel [*French*] (ADPT)
Ltr .... Leiter [*Leader, Manager*] (EG)
LTR........... Local Thermodynamic Equilibrium (RU)
LTs............ Flight Center (RU)
LTS............ Leichtes Torpedoschnellboot [*Light Motor Torpedo Boat*] (EG)
LTS............ Lesnicka Technicka Skola [*Technical School of Forestry*] (CZ)
LTS............ Library Technicians Section [*Library Association of Australia*]
LTS............ Loi Toa Soan [*Editorial Comment, Editorial Note*]
LTS............ LTU [*Lufttransport Unternehmen Sud*] GmbH [*Germany*] [*ICAO designator*] (FAAC)
LTS............ Lufttransport-Sud [*Airline*] [*Germany*]
LTS............ Lysteknisk Selskab [*Denmark*] (SLS)
LTSA .... Leningrad Theater of the Soviet Army (RU)
LTSI .... Laboratoire Traitement du Signal et Instrumentation [*Signal Processing and Instrumentation Laboratory*] [*France*] (IRC)
LTsIA .... Leningrad Central Historical Archives (RU)
LTT........... Lignes Telegraphiques et Telephoniques [*Algeria*]
LTTE......... Liberation Tigers of Tamil Eelam [*Sri Lanka*]
LTTs.......... Leningrad Television Center (RU)
LTU .... La Trobe University [*Australia*]
LTU .... Lufttransport Unternehmen GmbH [*Germany*] [*ICAO designator*] (FAAC)
LTU .... Tactical Flight Training (RU)
LTU .... Technical Flight Exercise (BU)
LTUSA...... La Trobe University Staff Association [*Australia*]
LTV........... Cable-Line Connection (BU)
LTV........... Letacko-Takticke Vezbe [*Tactical Flight Exercises*] (YU)
LTV........... Ling-Temco-Vought International NV [*Bank*]
LTW .... League of Tasmanian Wheelmen [*Australia*]
LTW .... NV Luchtvaartmaatschappij Twente [*Netherlands*] [*ICAO designator*] (FAAC)
LTX........... Leo Taxi Aereo SA de CV [*Mexico*] [*ICAO designator*] (FAAC)
LTZ........... Lipetsk Tractor Plant (RU)
LTZhDT.... Leningrad Railroad Transportation Technicum Imeni F. E. Dzerzhinskiy (RU)
LU............. Amplifier Tube (RU)
LU............. Left Unity Group [*European political movement*] (ECON)

LU............. Leningrad University (RU)
LU............. Lidova Universita [*People's University*] (CZ)
LU............. Liga Ultramarina
LU............. Ligue Universelle [*Esperantiste*]
LU............. Linear (Program) Part [*Automation*] (RU)
LU............. Ljudska Uprava [*People's Administration*] [*Ljubljana A periodical*] (YU)
LU............. Logarithmic Amplifier (RU)
LU............. Loi Uniforme Relative au Droit International Prive (Eenvormige Wet) [*Benelux*] (BAS)
LU............. Lucca [*Car registration plates*] [*Italian*]
Lu............. Luglio [*July*] [*Italian*]
Lu............. Luoto [*or Luodet*] [*Rock or Rocks*] [*Finland*] (NAU)
Lu............. Lutecio [*Chemical element*] [*Portuguese*]
Lu............. Lutetium [*Lutetium*] [*Chemical element*] [*German*]
LU............. Luxembourg [*ANSI two-letter standard code*] (CNC)
LUA .... Life Underwriters Association of Australia (ADA)
LUA .... Lukla [*Nepal*] [*Airport symbol*] (OAG)
LUAR .... Liga da Uniao e Accao Revolucionaria [*League for Unity and Revolutionary Action*] [*Portuguese*] (WER)
LUAT .... Leningrad Administration of Automobile Transportation (RU)
lub .... Bast Plant [*Topography*] (RU)
l ub .... Lata Ubiegle [*The Past Years*] [*Poland*]
LUB .... Lusiana [*Czechoslovakia*] [*ICAO designator*] (FAAC)
LUBA .... Parti du Rassemblement des Peuples Luba
LUBAKO .. Association Lumiere du Bas-Congo
LUBREF .... PETROMIN Lubricating Refinery
LUBTEX .... Societe Lubrifiants Texaco
LUC .... Laborator Uzinal de Cercetari [*In-Plant Research Laboratory*] (RO)
LUC .... Laucala Island [*Fiji*] [*Airport symbol*] (OAG)
LUCC .... Land Use and Cover Change [*Environmental studies*] (ECON)
LUCE........ L'Unione Cinematografica Educativa [*Italian*]
luchtv .... Luchtvaart [*Benelux*] (BAS)
LUCT........ Liga Uruguaya Contra la Tuberculosis [*Uruguay*] (SLS)
LUD........... Land Use Division [*Sri Lanka*] (ARC)
LUD........... Luderitz [*South-West Africa*] [*Airport symbol*] (OAG)
ludn .... Ludnosc [*The Population*] [*Poland*]
LUDPP....... Lithuanian Union of Deportees and Political Prisoners (EAIO)
LUDRN .... Ligue Universelle pour la Defense de la Race Noire
LUE .... Linear Electron Accelerator (RU)
Luep .... Laenge ueber Puffer [*Length over Buffers*] (EG)
LUF .... Labor Unity Front [*Nigeria*] (AF)
LUF .... Liberation and Unity Front [*Saharan*] (AF)
LUFO .... Legugyi Foosztaly [*Main Department of Aviation (Part of Kozlekedesi- es Postaugyi Miniszterium)*] (HU)
LUFPT ...... Laktologicky Ustav Fakulty Potravinarske Technologie [*Milk Produce Research Institute of the Faculty of Food Technology*] [*Prague*] (CZ)
Luftf .... Luftfahrt [*Aviation*] [*German*] (GCA)
LUG........... Lohn und Gehalt [*German*] (ADPT)
LUG........... Lugano [*Switzerland*] [*Airport symbol*] (OAG)
lug .... Lugar [*Place*] [*Portuguese*]
LUGMI ...... Leningrad Administration of State Meat Inspection (RU)
LUGMS..... Leningrad Administration of the Hydrometeorological Service (RU)
LUGV .... Lugvaartkunde [*Aeronautics*] [*Afrikaans*]
LUGVSA .. Lugvaartkundige Vereniging van Suid-Afrika [*South Africa*] (AA)
LUI .... La Union [*Honduras*] [*Airport symbol*] [*Obsolete*] (OAG)
LUI .... Leningrad Teachers' Institute (RU)
LUI .... Linear Ion Accelerator (RU)
LUINSA .... Laboratorios Unidos Interamericanos [*Colombia*] (COL)
luit .... Luitenant [*Lieutenant*] [*Afrikaans*]
LUJ .... Lesotho Union of Journalists (EAIO)
LUK .... Laerarutbildningskommitten [*Sweden*]
LUK .... Lamellen und Kupplungsbau
LUK .... Lid van die Uitvoerende Komitee [*Member of the Executive Committee*] [*Afrikaans*]
Luk............ Lukas [*Luke*] [*Afrikaans*]
LuK........... Luonnontiet Kandidaatti [*Finland*]
LUKS........ Leningrad Communications Training Center (RU)
luks .... Luksusowe (Wydanie) [*Deluxe (Edition)*] (POL)
luksusudg... Luksusudgave [*Deluxe Edition*] [*Publishing Danish/Norwegian*]
lukus .... Lukusana [*Numeral*] [*Finland*]
LUL .... Labor Union of Liberia
LUL .... Lease Underwriting Ltd. [*Australia*]
Lum........... Lumen [*Record label*] [*France*]
LUM .... Maputo [*Mozambique*] [*Airport symbol*]
lun .... Lunes [*Monday*] [*Spanish*]
LUN........... Lusaka [*Zambia*] [*Airport symbol*] (OAG)
LUNKhU... Leningrad Administration of the Statistical Survey of the National Economy (RU)
LUO........... Luena [*Angola*] [*Airport symbol*] (OAG)
Luonnontiet Kand ... Bachelor's Degree in Natural Science [*Finland*]
luonnontkand ... Luonnontieteiden Kandidaatti [*Finland*]

LUP .... Liberia Unification Party [*Political party*]
LUP .... Lupenga Air Charters [*Zambia*] [*ICAO designator*]   (FAAC)
LUPRI ...... Lund University Peace Research Institute [*Sweden*]
LUPU .... Leningrad Junction Administration of Freight Loading and Unloading   (RU)
LUQ.......... San Luis [*Argentina*] [*Airport symbol*]   (OAG)
LUR .... Lid van die Uitvoerende Raad [*Member of the Executive Council*] [*Afrikaans*]
LUR .... Linear Turn Lead   (RU)
LUR .... Lineas Aereas Latur SA de CV [*Mexico*] [*ICAO designator*]   (FAAC)
LURE........ Laboratoire d'Utilisation du Rayonnement Electromagnetique [*Laboratory for the Utilization of Electromagnetic Radiation*] [*France*]
LUs .... Line Amplifier, Linear Amplifier   (RU)
LUS........... Lusitanair-Transportes Aereos Comercials SA [*Portugal*] [*ICAO designator*]   (FAAC)
lus.............. Lusitanismo [*or Lusitano*] [*Portuguese idiom*]
LUT .... Laura Station [*Australia*] [*Airport symbol*] [*Obsolete*]   (OAG)
LUT .... Letecke Technicke Uciliste [*Aviation Technical Training Center*]   (CZ)
LUT .... Lidova Umelecka Tvorivost [*Folk Arts Activities*]   (CZ)
LUT .... Loge Unie des Theosophes
lut .... Luteranus [*Lutheran*]   (HU)
LUTH .... Lagos University Teaching Hospital [*Nigeria*]
luth............ Lutherisch [*Lutheran*] [*German*]   (EG)
LUTH .... Luthers [*Lutheran*] [*Afrikaans*]
Lutt .... Luttenberg's Chronologische Verzameling der Wetten, Besluiten, Arresten, Enz., Betrekkelijk het Openbaar Bestuur in de Nederlanden [*Netherlands*]   (BAS)
Lutt (B enZ) ... Luttenberg's Chronologische Verzameling der Wetten, Besluiten, Arresten, Enz., Besluiten en Arresten [*Benelux*]   (BAS)
LuttVerord ... Luttenberg's Chronologische Verzameling der Wetten, Besluiten, Arresten, Enz., Verordeningenblad [*Benelux*]   (BAS)
LUU .... Laura [*Australia*] [*Airport symbol*] [*Obsolete*]   (OAG)
luutn .... Luutnantti [*Finland*]
LUV .... Langgur [*Indonesia*] [*Airport symbol*]   (OAG)
LUVO........ Luftvorwaermer [*Air Preheater*] [*German*]
LUW.......... Luwuk [*Indonesia*] [*Airport symbol*]   (OAG)
LUWN....... Leeuwin [*Botanical region*] [*Australia*]
LUX .... Luxembourg [*Airport symbol*]   (OAG)
LUX .... Luxembourg [*ANSI three-letter standard code*]   (CNC)
LUXATOM ... Syndicat Luxembourgeois pour l'Industrie Nucleaire [*Luxembourg*] [*Nuclear energy*]   (NRCH)
Luxem .... Luxembourg
LUZ .... La Universidad del Zulia [*The University of Zulia*] [*Venezuela*]   (LA)
LV .... De Levensverzekering [*Benelux*]   (BAS)
LV .... Electron Tube Voltmeter, Tube Voltmeter   (RU)
lv................. Influence Line   (RU)
LV .... Lacrosse Victoria [*Australia*] [*An association*]
LV .... Landesverteidigung [*Home Defense*] [*German*]
LV .... Laverda SpA [*Italy*] [*ICAO aircraft manufacturer identifier*]   (ICAO)
lv................. Leiviska [*Finland*]
LV .... Lev [*Monetary unit*] [*Bulgaria*]
LV .... Levazim [*Supplies, Provisions*] [*Military*]   (TU)
lv................. Lev, Leva   (BU)
LV .... Libreria Voluntad [*Colombia*]   (COL)
LV .... Lid Volksraad [*Member of Parliament*] [*South Africa*]   (AF)
LV .... Liechtensteiner Vaterland   (EAIO)
LV .... Lieutenant de Vaisseau [*French*]   (MTD)
LV .... Line Equalizer, Line Compensator   (RU)
LV .... Linschoten Vereeniging, Werke
LV .... Lok Virsa [*An association*] [*Pakistan*]   (EAIO)
LV .... Luftverteidigung [*Air Defense*]   (EG)
L'V .... L'vov Railroad   (RU)
LV .... Lytic Substance   (RU)
LV .... Vacuum-Tube Rectifier   (RU)
LVA .... Letecka Vojenska Akademie [*Air Force Academy*]   (CZ)
LVB .... Livramento [*Brazil*] [*Airport symbol*]   (OAG)
LVBR .... Land Valuation Boards of Review [*Australia*]
LVCC........ Landelijk Verbond der Christelijke Cooperatieven [*Benelux*]   (BAS)
LVCVSA ... Landbou- en Veeartsenykundige Chemikaliee Vereniging van Suid-Afrika [*South Africa*]   (EAIO)
LVD .... Luft-Verteidigungsdivision [*Air Defense Division*]   (EG)
LvervW ...... Wet Houdende Voorzieningen Inzake het Luchtvervoer [*Benelux*]   (BAS)
lv es .... Fighter Squadron   (BU)
LVF............ Ladoga Naval Flotilla   (RU)
LVF............ Legion des Volontaires Francais Contre le Bolchevisme
LVFS .... Lake Victoria Fisheries Service

LVG .... Lehr- und Versuchsanstalt fuer Gartenbau [*Experimental and Training Center for Horticultural Science*] [*German*]   (ARC)
LVG .... Lehr- und Versuchsgut [*Training and Experimental Farm*]   (EG)
L'vGU .... L'vov State University Imeni Ivan Franko   (RU)
LVH .... Laborator pro Vodni Hospodarstvi [*Water Management Laboratory (of the Czechoslovak Academy of Sciences)*]   (CZ)
LVI............. Leningrad Oriental Institute   (RU)
LVI............. Leningrad Veterinary Institute   (RU)
LVI............. Livingstone [*Zambia*] [*Airport symbol*]   (OAG)
LVIA .... Lay Volunteers International Association
LVIMU...... Leningrad Higher Engineering Nautical School Imeni Admiral S. O. Makarov   (RU)
LVIN.......... Low Viscosity Index
LVIPI......... Leningrad Higher Pedagogical Institute of Engineering   (RU)
LVKSKhSh ... Leningrad Higher Communist School of Agriculture Imeni S. M. Kirov   (RU)
LVL............ Lee's Video Library [*Papua New Guinea*]
LVLB .... Land Valuers' Licensing Board [*Western Australia*]
LVM .... Light Suspension Bridge   (RU)
LVMH .... Louis Vuitton Moet-Hennessy [*Commercial firm*] [*Belgium*]
LVMI .... Leningrad Military Mechanical Engineering Institute   (RU)
LVMU .... Leningrad Higher Nautical School   (RU)
LVNC .... Laborator Vyssi Nervove Cinnosti [*Laboratory of Higher Nervous Activity (of the Czechoslovak Academy of Sciences)*]   (CZ)
LVO .... Laverton [*Australia*] [*Airport symbol*]   (OAG)
LVO .... Leningrad Military District   (RU)
LVO .... Lieferverordnung [*Delivery Regulations*]   (EG)
LVO .... Luftverkehrsordnung [*Switzerland*]
L'vovsel'mash ... L'vov Agricultural Machinery Plant   (RU)
LVR .... Luchtverkeersreglement [*Benelux*]   (BAS)
LVRI .... Legiun Veteran Republik Indonesia [*Republic of Indonesia Veterans Legion*]   (IN)
LVRL......... Latrobe Valley Regional Library [*Australia*]
LVRT .... Land and Valuation Review Tribunal [*Northern Territory, Australia*]
LVRZ .... Locomotive and Railroad Car Repair Plant   (RU)
LVS .... Aqualung Diving Station   (RU)
LVS .... Letecke Vycvikove Stredisko (Presov) [*Aviation Training Center (Presov)*]   (CZ)
LVSA .... Limnologiese Vereniging van Suidelike Afrika [*Limnological Society of Southern Africa*]   (AA)
LVSCL...... Letecka Vysetrovaci Stanice Ceskoslovenskeho Letectva [*Czechoslovak Air Force Investigating Station*]   (CZ)
LVShPD .... Leningrad Higher School of Trade Unionism of the VTsSPS   (RU)
LVSt........... Landwirtschaftliche Versuchsstation [*Agricultural Experiment Station*] [*German*]   (GCA)
LVT .... Linear Rotary Transformer   (RU)
LVU .... Letecky Vyzkumny Ustav [*Aeronautic Research Institute*] [*Prague-Letnany*]   (CZ)
lvv.............. Liikevaihtovero [*Finland*]
LVVA......... Leningrad Air Force Academy   (RU)
lvveroineen ... Liikevaihtoveroineen [*Finland*]
LVVIA .... Leningrad Air Force Engineering Academy Imeni A. F. Mozhayskiy   (RU)
lvvineen....... Liikevaihtoveroineen [*Finland*]
LVVS .... Liquidatie Vermogens Verwaltung Sarphatistraat [*Amsterdam, The Netherlands*]
Lvw............ Luchtvaartwet [*Benelux*]   (BAS)
LVZ............ Locomotive and Railroad Cars Plant   (BU)
LVZ............ L'vov Bicycle Plant   (RU)
LVZh .... Inflammable Liquid   (RU)
lw .... Laatste Wijziging [*Benelux*]   (BAS)
LW .... Laden Wort [*German*]   (ADPT)
LW .... Lange Welle [*German*]   (ADPT)
Lw .... Lehnwort [*Loan Word*] [*German*]
Lw .... Leinwand [*Linen, Cloth*] [*German*]
LW .... Leitungswaehler [*Final Selector, Line Selector*]   (EG)
LW .... Lekarz Weterynarii [*Veterinarian*] [*Poland*]
LW .... Let Wel [*Mark Well*] [*Afrikaans*]
lw .... Lichte Weite [*Inside Diameter*] [*German*]
lw .... Lidwoord [*Article*] [*Afrikaans*]
LWA .... Lesotho Workcamps Association   (EAIO)
LWA .... Liberian World Airlines, Inc. [*ICAO designator*]   (FAAC)
Lwb .... Leinwandband [*Cloth Binding*] [*Publishing*] [*German*]
LWB .... Lutherischer Weltbund [*Lutheran World Federation*]   (EG)
LWCU .... Lebanese World Cultural Union
Lwd .... Leinwand [*Linen, Cloth*] [*German*]
LWD.......... Lotnicze Warsztaty Doswiadczalne [*Aeronautical Research Shops*]   (POL)
LWD.......... Louw Wepener Decoration
Lwdb .... Leinwandband [*Cloth Binding*] [*Publishing*] [*German*]
Lwdbd .... Leinwandband [*Cloth Binding*] [*Publishing*] [*German*]

LWF.......... Labor Welfare Fund [*Iran*]　(ME)
LWF.......... Lutheran World Federation [*See also FLM*] [*Geneva, Switzerland*]　(EAIO)
LWF/WS... Lutheran World Federation/World Service
LWG .... Logistic Work Group [*NATO*]　(NATG)
LWH.......... Lawn Hill [*Australia*] [*Airport symbol*] [*Obsolete*]　(OAG)
LWI .... Laden Wort Indirekt [*German*]　(ADPT)
LWL.......... Lichtwellenleiter [*German*]　(ADPT)
LWM .... Louw Wepener Medal
LWO .... Lwow [*Former USSR*] [*Airport symbol*]　(OAG)
LWOST..... Low Water Ordinary Spring Tide
LWP.......... Ludowe Wojsko Polskie [*Polish People's Army*]　(POL)
LWR .... Landwirtschaftsrat (beim Ministerrat) [*Agricultural Council (in the GDR Council of Ministers)*]　(EG)
LWR .... Lid van die Wetgewende Raad [*Member of the Legislative Assembly*] [*Afrikaans*]
LWRRDC ... Land and Water Resources Research and Development Corp. [*Australia*]
LWS.......... Lutheran Welfare Services [*Australia*]
LWS.......... Lutheran World Service
LWSC........ Library Workforce Standing Committee [*Australia*]
LWSiS .... Lubelska Wytwornia Surowic i Szczepionek [*Lublin Serum and Vaccine Manufacturing Plant*]　(POL)
LWTP........ Lubelska Wytwornia Tytoniu Przemyslowego [*Lublin Tobacco Factory*]　(POL)
LWU .... Lithuanian Workers' Union　(EAIO)
LWUA ...... Local Water Utilities Administration [*Philippines*]　(DS)
LWV .... Lid van die Wetgewende Vergadering [*Member of Parliament*] [*Afrikaans*]
LWVPR..... League of Women Voters of Puerto Rico　(EAIO)
LWVV .... League of Women Voters of Victoria [*Australia*]
LWY .... Lawas [*Malaysia*] [*Airport symbol*]　(OAG)
LXA .... Lhasa [*China*] [*Airport symbol*]　(OAG)
LXGB........ Gibraltar/North Front [*Gibraltar*] [*ICAO location identifier*]　(ICLI)
LXR .... Airluxor Ltda. [*Portugal*] [*ICAO designator*]　(FAAC)
LXR .... Luxor [*Egypt*] [*Airport symbol*]　(OAG)
LXS .... Lemnos [*Greece*] [*Airport symbol*]　(OAG)
ly .... Lampoyksikko [*Finland*]
LY .... Liberal Youth [*Sweden*] [*Political party*]　(EAIO)
LY .... Libya [*ANSI two-letter standard code*]　(CNC)
LY .... Lokhos Ygeionomikou [*Medical Company*]　(GC)
LYA .... Lyon Air [*France*] [*ICAO designator*]　(FAAC)
LYaP........ Laboratory of Nuclear Problems　(RU)
LYaPAS..... Logical Language of Synthesis Algorithm Representation　(RU)
LYaR......... Laboratory of Nuclear Reactions　(RU)
LYB........... Little Cayman [*West Indies*] [*Airport symbol*]　(OAG)
LYBA........ Beograd [*Former Yugoslavia*] [*ICAO location identifier*]　(ICLI)
LYBB........ Beograd [*Former Yugoslavia*] [*ICAO location identifier*]　(ICLI)
LYBE........ Beograd [*Former Yugoslavia*] [*ICAO location identifier*]　(ICLI)
LYBK........ Banja Luka [*Former Yugoslavia*] [*ICAO location identifier*]　(ICLI)
LYD .... Lydende [*Passive (Voice)*] [*Afrikaans*]
LYDU .... Dubrovnik [*Former Yugoslavia*] [*ICAO location identifier*]　(ICLI)
LYeD .... Frog Unit [*Biology*]　(RU)
lyh .... Lyhenne [*Finland*]
lyh .... Lyhennetty [*Finland*]
lyh .... Lyhennys [*or Lyhennettyna*] [*Abbreviation*] [*Finland*]
LYLJ......... Ljubljana [*Former Yugoslavia*] [*ICAO location identifier*]　(ICLI)
LYM .... Lagos Youth Movement [*Political party*] [*Nigeria*]
LYMB........ Maribor [*Former Yugoslavia*] [*ICAO location identifier*]　(ICLI)
LYMO ...... Mostar [*Former Yugoslavia*] [*ICAO location identifier*]　(ICLI)
LYOH........ Ohrid [*Former Yugoslavia*] [*ICAO location identifier*]　(ICLI)
LYONS..... Library On-Line System [*Alcoa of Australia*]
LYOS........ Osijek [*Former Yugoslavia*] [*ICAO location identifier*]　(ICLI)
LYP........... Faisalabad [*Pakistan*] [*Airport symbol*]　(OAG)
LYPL........ Pula [*Former Yugoslavia*] [*ICAO location identifier*]　(ICLI)
LYPR........ Pristina [*Former Yugoslavia*] [*ICAO location identifier*]　(ICLI)
LYPZ........ Portoroz [*Former Yugoslavia*] [*ICAO location identifier*]　(ICLI)
LYR .... Longyear [*Norway*] [*Airport symbol*]　(OAG)
LYRI......... Rijeka [*Former Yugoslavia*] [*ICAO location identifier*]　(ICLI)
LYS........... Lyon [*France*] [*Airport symbol*]　(OAG)
LYSA........ Sarajevo [*Former Yugoslavia*] [*ICAO location identifier*]　(ICLI)
LYSK........ Skopje [*Former Yugoslavia*] [*ICAO location identifier*]　(ICLI)
LYSP........ Split [*Former Yugoslavia*] [*ICAO location identifier*]　(ICLI)
LYSSO ...... Libyan Standards and Specifications Office [*Department of Industrial Organization*] [*Libyan Arab Jamahiriya*]
lystryksgengiv ... Lystryksgengivelse [*Reproduction in Photolithography*] [*Publishing Danish/Norwegian*]
LYTI .... Titograd [*Former Yugoslavia*] [*ICAO location identifier*]　(ICLI)
LYTV........ Tivat [*Former Yugoslavia*] [*ICAO location identifier*]　(ICLI)
LYul......... Leningrad Law Institute Imeni M. I. Kalinin　(RU)
lyut............ Lutheran　(RU)
Lyut........... Lutheran Cemetery [*Topography*]　(RU)
Lyut kir ...... Lutheran Church [*Topography*]　(RU)

LYVR........ Vrsac [*Former Yugoslavia*] [*ICAO location identifier*]　(ICLI)
LYYY........ Beograd [*Former Yugoslavia*] [*ICAO location identifier*]　(ICLI)
LYZA........ Zagreb [*Former Yugoslavia*] [*ICAO location identifier*]　(ICLI)
LYZB........ Zagreb [*Former Yugoslavia*] [*ICAO location identifier*]　(ICLI)
LYZD........ Zadar [*Former Yugoslavia*] [*ICAO location identifier*]　(ICLI)
LZ .... Delay Line　(RU)
LZ .... Green Light　(RU)
LZ .... Leksikografski Zavod [*Lexicographic Institute*] [*Zagreb*]　(YU)
LZ .... Letecka Zakladna [*Air Force Base*]　(CZ)
LZ .... Letecke Zavody, Narodni Podnik [*Aircraft Factories, National Enterprise*]　(CZ)
LZ .... Ljubljanski Zvon [*Ljubljana Bell*] [*A periodical*]　(YU)
Lz .... Lokleerfahrt [*Locomotive Run without Cars*]　(EG)
l/z............. Sawmill [*Topography*]　(RU)
LZB........... Literaturen Zbornik Spisanije na Drustvoto za Makedonski Jazik i Literatura [*Literary Collection. Papers of the Society for Macedonian Language and Literature*] [*Skopje*]　(YU)
LZB........... Lubelskie Zjednoczenie Budownictwa [*Lublin Construction Union*]　(POL)
LZCh .... Lubelskie Zaklady Chmielarskie [*Lublin Hops Plant*]　(POL)
LZETD ..... Leninovy Zavody, Elektrotechnicka Tovarna v Plzni-Doudlevcich [*Lenin Works, Electric Machinery Plant in Plzen-Doudlevce*] [*Skoda Works*] [*Formerly,*]　(CZ)
LZG .... Lodzkie Zaklady Gastronomiczne [*Lodz Restaurant Establishments*]　(POL)
LZG .... Lubelskie Zaklady Gastronomiczne [*Lublin Restaurant Establishments*]　(POL)
LZh .... Yellow Light　(RU)
LZI .... Leningrad Zootechnical Institute　(RU)
LZI .... Luminescent Symbol Indicator　(RU)
LZIF .... Lyudmila Zhivkova International Foundation　(EAIO)
LZII .... Leningrad Industrial Correspondence Institute　(RU)
LZIP .... Lubelskie Zjednoczenie Instalacji Przemyslowych [*Lublin Association of Industrial Installations*]　(POL)
LZITO ...... Leningrad Correspondence Institute of Technical Education　(RU)
LZK........... Lodzkie Zaklady Kinotechniczne [*Lodz Motion Picture Establishments*]　(POL)
LZM .... Lodzki Zespol Miejski [*Lodz Metropolitan Area*]　(POL)
LZM .... Lubelskie Zaklady Metalowe [*Lublin Metal Works*]　(POL)
LZM .... Lubelskie Zaklady Miesne [*Lublin Meat Stores*]　(POL)
LZMI........ Leningrad Correspondence Institute of Mechanical Engineering　(RU)
LZn .... Zinklot [*Zinc Solder*] [*German*]　(GCA)
LZnAl .... Aluminium-Zinklot [*Aluminum-Zinc Solder*] [*German*]　(GCA)
LZnCd ...... Aluminium-Zinklot mit Cadmium [*Aluminum-Zinc Solder with Cadmium*] [*German*]　(GCA)
LZnSn .... Aluminium-Zinklot mit Zinn [*Aluminum-Zinc Solder with Tin*] [*German*]　(GCA)
LZO .... Lukowskie Zaklady Obuwia [*Lukow Footwear Factory*]　(POL)
LZP........... Latvian Green Party [*Political party*]　(EY)
LZP........... Lubelskie Zaklady Piekarnicze [*Lublin Bakeries*]　(POL)
LZP........... Planned Course Line, Desired Course Line　(RU)
LZPHAPoPHSiPG ... Ludzkie Zjednoczenie Przedsiebiorstw Handlu Artykulami Przemyslowymi oraz Przedsiebiorstw Handlu Spozywczego i Przemyslu Gastronomicznego [*Lodz Union of Industrial Product Trade Enterprises and of Food Trade and Catering Industry Enterprises*]　(POL)
LZPlzen ..... Leninovy Zavody, Plzen [*Lenin Works, Plzen*] [*Skoda Works*] [*Formerly,*]　(CZ)
LZPO........ Lodzki Zarzad Przemyslu Odziezowego [*Lodz Clothing Industry Administration*]　(POL)
LZPOG...... Lodzkie Zaklady Przemyslu Obuwia Gumowego [*Lodz Rubber Footwear Plant*]　(POL)
LZPP .... Lubelskie Zaklady Przemyslu Piekarniczego [*Lublin Bakeries*]　(POL)
LZPS .... Lubelskie Zaklady Przemyslu Skorzanego [*Lublin Leather Industry Enterprise*]　(POL)
LZPT .... Lodzkie Zaklady Przetworczo-Tluszczowe [*Lodz Fat Processing Plant*]　(POL)
LZPT .... Lubelskie Zaklady Przemyslu Terenowego [*Lublin Local Industry Plants*]　(POL)
LZR........... Lizard Island [*Australia*] [*Airport symbol*]　(OAG)
LZS........... Forest Conservation Station　(RU)
LZS........... Ludowe Zespoly Sportowe [*People's Sports Unions*]　(POL)
LZS........... Ludowe Zrzeszenie Sportowe [*People's Sports Association*]　(POL)
LZS........... Ludowy Zespol Sportowy [*People's Sports Union*]　(POL)
LZSP .... Lodzki Zwiazek Spoldzielczosci Pracy [*Lodz Labor Cooperative Union*]　(POL)
LZT i GT ... Easily Inflammable Fluids and Combustible Fluids　(BU)
LZTM........ Leningrad Commercial Machinery Plant　(RU)
L Zug....... Luxuszug [*Saloon Train*] [*German*]
LZV........... Lovacka Zadruga Vojvodine [*Vojvodina Hunters' Cooperative*]　(YU)
LZWS .... Lodzkie Zaklady Wyrobow Skorzanych [*Lodz Leather Goods Plant*]　(POL)

LZZ............ Lesezwangszyklus [*German*]　(ADPT)

M

M............... Boy [*In questionnaires*] (RU)
m .... Bridge (RU)
m .... Cape, Promontory [*Topography*] (RU)
M............... De Magistratuur [*Benelux*] (BAS)
M............... Emma [*Phonetic alphabet*] [*In use in 1904 and 1914*] (DSUE)
m .... International (RU)
M............... Little [*Toponymy*] (RU)
M............... Maasbode [*Benelux*] (BAS)
M............... Mach Number (RU)
m .... Madde [*Article, Paragraph*] (TU)
M............... Madre [*Mother*] [*Spanish*]
M............... Madrid [*Capital of Spain*]
M............... Maedchen [*Girl*] [*German*]
M............... Maennlich [*Male*] [*German*]
M............... Maestria [*Master's Degree*] [*Spanish*]
M............... Maestro [*Master*] [*Spanish*]
m .... Magan [*Private*] (HU)
M............... Magistar [*Academic qualification*] [*Former Yugoslavia*]
M............... Magistr [*Egypt*]
m .... Magyar [*Hungarian*] (HU)
m .... Mahalle [*Ward, Quarter*] [*Turkey*] (CED)
m .... Maille [*Stitch*] [*Knitting*] [*French*]
M............... Maisteri [*Finland*]
M............... Maitrise [*Master's Degree*] [*French*]
M............... Majestad [*Majesty*] [*Spanish*]
M............... Majeste [*Majesty*] [*French*]
m .... Major [*Rank*] (BU)
M............... Maloti [*Plural of Loti*] [*Monetary Unit*] [*Lesotho*] (BARN)
m .... Man [*Statistics*] (RU)
m .... Manana [*Tomorrow*] [*Spanish*]
m .... Manches [*Sleeves*] [*French*]
M............... Manichaean Middle Persian
m .... Manlik [*Masculine*] [*Afrikaans*]
M............... Mannai Trading Co. Ltd. [*Qatar*]
M............... Mano [*Hand*] [*Spanish*]
M............... Marais [*Swamp*] [*Military map abbreviation World War I*] [*French*] (MTD)
m .... Marbre [*Marbled*] [*Publishing*] [*French*]
M............... Mark [*Monetary unit*] [*German*] (GPO)
M............... Markka [*Monetary unit*] [*Finland*]
M............... Markt [*Market*] [*German*]
m .... Marocchino [*Morocco*] [*Publishing*] [*Italian*]
m .... Maroquin [*Morocco*] [*Publishing*] [*French*]
M............... Marquis [*or Marquess*]
M............... Married (EECI)
m .... Marroqui [*Morocco*] [*Publishing*] [*Spanish*]
M............... Mars [*March*] [*French*]
M............... Martin Co. Division [*Martin-Marietta Corp.*] [*ICAO aircraft manufacturer identifier*] (ICAO)
M............... Mas [*Farm*] [*Military map abbreviation World War I*] [*French*] (MTD)
m .... Maschile [*Masculine*] [*Italian*]
m .... Masculin [*Masculine*] [*French*]
m .... Masculine (TPFD)
m .... Masculine (Gender) (RU)
m .... Masculino [*Masculine*] [*Portuguese*]
m .... Masculino [*Masculine*] [*Spanish*]
M............... Masse [*Mass*] [*German*]
M............... Maxwell [*German*] (GCA)
M............... Mediano [*On an Examination: Fair*] [*Spanish*]
M............... Medio [*Half*] [*Spanish*]
M............... Meile [*League*] [*German*]
m .... Mein [*My*] [*German*]
M............... Meisteraprof [*Academic examination*] [*Icelandic*]
M............... Melantrich [*A publishing and printing firm*] (CZ)
M............... Melbourne [*Mint mark*] [*Australia*]
M............... Memoire [*Memory*] [*French*] (ADPT)
M............... Mensuel [*Monthly*] [*French*]

M............... Merced [*Grace, Mercy*] [*Spanish*]
M............... Mercredi [*Wednesday*] [*French*]
m .... Meret [*Size*] [*Hungary*]
M............... Merke [*Marks*] [*German*]
m .... Mes [*Month*] [*Portuguese*]
m .... Mes [*Month*] [*Spanish*]
m .... Mester [*Master, Chief*] (HU)
M............... Mestre [*Master*] [*Portuguese*]
m .... Met [*With*] [*Netherlands*]
m .... Meta [*Meta*] [*German*]
m .... Meter [*German*] (GCA)
m .... Meter [*Albanian*]
m .... Metr [*Meter*] (POL)
M............... Metre [*Meter*] [*French*] (MTD)
m .... Metri(a) [*Finland*]
M............... Metro [*Meter*] [*Italian*]
m .... Metro [*Meter*] [*Portuguese*] (GPO)
m .... Metro [*Meter*] [*Spanish*]
M............... Metro Travel and Tours [*Cyprus*]
m/............... Meu [*My, Mine*] [*Portuguese*]
M............... Mezzo [*Moderate*] [*Music*]
m .... Mi [*My*] [*Business term*] [*Spanish*]
m .... Miasto [*City, Town*] (POL)
m .... Miesiac [*Month*] [*Poland*]
m .... Mieszkanie [*Apartment*] (POL)
M............... Mike [*Phonetic alphabet*] [*International*] [*World War II*] (DSUE)
M............... Mil [*Monetary unit*] [*Cyprus*]
M............... Miladi [*Anno Domini*] [*In the Year of Our Lord*] (TU)
M............... Mille [*One Thousand*] [*French*]
M............... Millime [*Monetary unit*] [*Tunisia*]
m .... Million (EECI)
m .... Millions (BU)
m .... Mine (BU)
m/............... Minha [*My, Mine*] [*Portuguese*]
M............... Ministre [*France*] (FLAF)
m .... Mint [*As*] (HU)
m .... Minute [*French*] (MTD)
m .... Minute [*German*]
m .... Minuto [*Minute*] [*Portuguese*]
m .... Minuto [*Minute*] [*Spanish*]
M............... Minuut [*Minute*] [*Afrikaans*]
M............... Minuutti [*Minute*] [*Finland*] (GPO)
m .... Mio [*My*] [*Italian*]
M............... MIR [*Peace*] [*A periodical*] (BU)
M............... Miracle Bookhouse Ltd. [*Ghana*]
m .... Mit [*With*] [*German*]
M............... Mitrailleuse [*Machine Gun*] [*Military*] [*French*] (MTD)
M............... Mittelsorte [*Medium Grade*] [*German*] (GCA)
m .... Mittler [*Mean, Average*] [*German*] (GCA)
M............... Mobilization Day (BU)
M............... Modele [*Model*] [*French*] (MTD)
M............... Modell [*Model*] [*German*] (GCA)
M............... Moderata Samlingspartiet [*Moderate Coalition Party*] [*Sweden*] (WEN)
M............... Modernized (RU)
M............... Modifie [*Modified*] [*French*] (MTD)
M............... Modulator (RU)
m .... Mois [*Month*] [*French*]
M............... Molarity of Solution (RU)
M............... Molecular Weight (RU)
M............... Molekulargewicht [*Molecular Weight*] [*German*]
m/............... Mon [*My*] [*French*]
M............... Monat [*Month*] [*German*]
M............... Monkey [*Phonetic alphabet*] [*Royal Navy World War I Pre-World War II*] (DSUE)
M............... Monsieur [*Mister*] [*French*]
M............... Mont [*Monte, etc.*] [*Italy and Sicily only*]

M............... Montagne [*Of guns*] [*French*]   (MTD)
m .... Month   (BU)
M............... Mort [*Dead*] [*French*]   (ROG)
M............... Morto [*Died*] [*Italian*]
M............... Morze [*Sea*] [*Poland*]
M............... Moscow   (BU)
M............... Mosyo [*Mister*] [*Turkey*]   (GPO)
m .... Mozgositas [*Mobilization*]   (HU)
M............... Muerto [*or Muerta*] [*Died*] [*Spanish*]
M............... Muff, Coupling, Clutch   (RU)
m .... Myelocyte   (RU)
m .... Myl [*Mile*] [*Afrikaans*]
m .... Myos [*Also*] [*Finland*]
M............... Mys [*Cape*] [*Russian*]   (NAU)
m .... Oil, Lubricant   (RU)
M............... Scale   (RU)
m .... Sea   (RU)
M............... Shallow [*Ford or river crossing*] [*Topography*]   (RU)
m .... Small Town [*Topography*]   (RU)
M............... Subway [*Sign on stations*]   (RU)
m .... Tomb, Grave [*Topography*]   (RU)
M............... Torpedo Boat   (RU)
m² .... Metre Carre [*Square Meter*] [*French*]   (GPO)
m² .... Metr Kwadratowy [*Square Meter*] [*Poland*]
m² .... Metro Cuadrado [*Square Meter*] [*Spanish*]
m² .... Negyzetmeter [*Square Meter*]   (HU)
m² .... Neliometri(a) [*Finland*]
m² .... Quadratmeter [*Square Meter*]   (EG)
m² .... Square Meter   (BU)
m³ .... Cubic Meter   (BU)
m³ .... Kobmeter [*Cubic Meter*]   (HU)
m³ .... Kubikmeter [*Cubic Meter*]   (EG)
m³ .... Kuutiometri(a) [*Finland*]
M³ .... Mains sur Manche et Manette [*Hands on Stick and Throttle - HOST*] [*Aviation*] [*French*]
m³ .... Metro Cubico [*Cubic Meter*] [*Spanish*]
m³ .... Metr Szescienny [*Cubic Meter*] [*Poland*]
m³d .... Cubic Meters per Day   (BU)
M3G........... Marx, Mao, Marighella, e Guevara [*Marx, Mao, Marighella, and Guevara*] [*Brazil*]   (LA)
M-3V .... Movimiento 3V [*Nicaragua*] [*Political party*]   (EY)
m³vm .... Cubic Meter Capacity   (BU)
M-18-X ...... Movimiento 18 de Octubre de Accion Revolucionaria Astra [*Astra 18th October Movement of Revolutionary Action*] [*Ecuador*] [*Political party*]   (PD)
M-20 .... Movimiento-20 [*Panama*] [*Political party*]   (EY)
MA............ Aanschrijving van het Ministerie van Financien [*Benelux*]   (BAS)
MA............ Artillery Shop   (RU)
MA............ Estado do Maranhao [*State of Maranhao*] [*Brazil*]
MA............ Land-Surveying Archives   (RU)
MA............ Le Petit Moniteur des Assurances [*French*]   (BAS)
ma .... Maanantai(na) [*Finland*]
MA............ Maandag [*Monday*] [*Afrikaans*]
MA............ Maandblad voor Accountancy en Bedrijfshuis-Houdkunde [*Benelux*]   (BAS)
MA............ Magister Artium [*Master of Arts*]   (GPO)
MA............ Magnetic Analyzer   (RU)
MA............ Magnetic Azimuth   (RU)
MA............ Makhitiki Aristera [*Militant Left*] [*Greek*]   (GC)
MA............ Maleic Anhydride   (RU)
MA............ Mangels Annahme [*For Non-Acceptance*] [*Business term*] [*German*]
MA............ Manohan Aluminium Ltd. [*New Zealand*]
MA............ Manufacture d'Armes [*French*]   (MTD)
Ma............. Maria [*Spanish*]
MAL........... Marineamt, Abteilung Geophysik   (MSC)
MA............ Maroko [*Morocco*] [*Poland*]
MA............ Massachusetts   (IDIG)
MA............ Master of Arts   (PWGL)
Ma............. Masurio [*Portuguese*]
Ma............. Matala [*Shoal*] [*Finland*]   (NAU)
MA............ Mature Australia [*An association*]
MA............ Mechanized Army   (BU)
M/A........... Mediterranean/Adriatic [*Shipping*]   (DS)
MA............ Megas Alexandros [*Alexander the Great*] [*Greek*]   (GC)
MA............ Melanesian Alliance [*Papua New Guinea*] [*Political party*]   (FEA)
ma .... Mellekallomas [*Extension (Telephone)*]   (HU)
MA............ Memoire Associative [*Associative Memory*] [*French*]   (ADPT)
MA............ Memoire Auxiliaire [*Auxillary Memory*] [*French*]   (ADPT)
ma .... Mesma [*Like*] [*Portuguese*]
MA............ Messageries Africaines
MA............ Methyl Acetate (Solvent)   (RU)
m/a........... Meu Aceite [*My Acceptance*] [*Portuguese*]
MA............ Microammeter   (RU)

MA............ Middle Assyrian [*Language, etc.*]   (BJA)
mA............ Miliamperio [*Miliampere*] [*Portuguese*]
MA............ Milliammeter   (RU)
ma .... Milliampere   (RU)
ma .... Minha [*My, Mine*] [*Portuguese*]
MA............ Miniaturausgabe [*Miniature Edition*] [*German*]
MA............ Ministerio da Aeronautica [*Aeronautics Agency*] [*Portuguese*]
MA............ Ministerio da Agricultura [*Agricultural Agency*] [*Portuguese*]
MA............ Minister van Arbeid [*Benelux*]   (BAS)
MA............ Mitarbeiter [*Staff Employee*]   (EG)
MA............ Mitotic Activity [*Biology*]   (RU)
MA............ Mittelalter [*or Mittelalterlich*] [*Middle Ages or Medieval*] [*German*]
MA............ Mode d'Adressage [*French*]   (ADPT)
MA............ Mohamed Egypt Aly
MA............ Monimos Andiprosopeia [*Permanent Delegation*]   (GC)
MA............ Morocco [*IYRU nationality code*] [*ANSI two-letter standard code*]   (CNC)
MA............ Morphological Analysis   (RU)
MA............ Movimento Associativo de Estudantes [*Associative Movement of Students*] [*Portuguese*]   (WER)
MA............ Moyen Age [*Middle Ages*] [*French*]
Ma............. Muara [*River Mouth*] [*Malay*]   (NAU)
ma .... Mundartlich [*Dialectal*] [*German*]
MA............ Munitionsanstalt [*Ammunition Depot*] [*German military - World War II*]
MA............ Munitions Australia   (DMA)
Ma............. Mura [*Village*] [*Japan*]   (NAU)
MA............ Muzeum Archeologiczne [*Archeological Museum*]   (POL)
MA............ Myanma Airways   (EY)
MA............ Myria   (ADPT)
MA............ Product Form Algorithm   (RU)
MAA........... Aerotransportes Mas de Carga SA de CV [*Mexico*] [*ICAO designator*]   (FAAC)
MAA........ International Academy of Astronautics   (RU)
MAA........ Madras [*India*] [*Airport symbol*]   (OAG)
MAA........ Maison de l'Agriculture Algerienne
MAA........ Malaysian Assurance Alliance
MAA........ Mallona Association Australia
MAA........ Marineartillerieabteilung [*Naval Coast Artillery Battalion*] [*German military - World War II*]
MAA........ Mastectomy Association of Australia   (ADA)
MAA........ Mature Age Allowance
MAA........ Microfilm Association of Australia   (ADA)
MAA........ Micrographics Association of Australia   (ADA)
MAA........ Ministere des Affaires Africaines
MAA........ Ministerio de Asuntos Agrarios [*Argentina*]   (DSCA)
MAA........ Ministry of Aboriginal Affairs [*Australia*]
MAA........ Motor Accidents Authority [*New South Wales, Australia*]
MAA........ Mouvement Anti-Apartheid [*France*]
MAA........ Multichannel Pulse-Height Analyzer   (RU)
MAA........ Multicultural Arts Alliance [*Australia*]
MAA........ Museums Association of Australia   (ADA)
MAAA....... Malayan Amateur Athletic Association   (ML)
MAACB ..... Member of the Australian Association of Clinical Biochemists   (ADA)
MAACP..... Mediterranean African Airlift Command Post
MAAE .... International Atomic Energy Agency   (BU)
MAAE .... Mezinarodni Agentura pro Atomovou Energii [*International Agency for Atomic Energy*]   (CZ)
MAAF .... Mediterranean Allied Air Forces
MAAFSc ... Member of the Australian Academy of Forensic Science
MAAIF...... Mutuelle Assurance Automobile des Instituteurs de France [*French Teachers Mutual Automobile Insurance Association*]   (WER)
MAAK....... Movement for All-Macedonian Action [*Political party*]
MAAL....... Microfilm Association of Australia Limited   (ADA)
Maan(d)..... Maandag [*Monday*] [*Afrikaans*]
Maandblad ... Maandblad voor Berechting en Reclassering van Volwassenen en Kinderen [*Benelux*]   (BAS)
maanmitt..... Maanmittaus [*Geodesy*] [*Finland*]
maant .... Maantiede [*Geography*] [*Finland*]
MA'ARAKH ... Political Bloc [*Israel*]   (ME)
maar art ..... Maaraava Artikkeli [*Definite Article*] [*Finland*]
maas.......... Maaseudunpuoluelainen [*Finland*]
MAASc....... Member of the Australian Academy of Science
MAASLA .. Movimiento Argentino Antiimperialista de Solidaridad Latinoamericana
maat .... Maatalous [*Agriculture*] [*Finland*]
MAATEC ... Mutuelle Algerienne d'Assurances des Travailleurs de l'Education et de la Culture [*Algerian Mutual Insurance Company for Educational and Cultural Workers*]   (AF)
maatjametsatiettri ... Maatalous-Ja Metsatieteiden Tohtori [*Finland*]
maatjametsatkand ... Maatalous-Ja Metsatieteiden Kandidaatti [*Finland*]
maatjametsatlis ... Maatalous-Ja Metsatieteiden Lisensiaatti [*Finland*]
MAAV .... Maritime Archaeology Association of Victoria [*Australia*]

MAB......... Aerial Antibridge Bomb   (RU)
MAB......... Maandblad voor Accountancy en Bedrijfshuis-Houdkunde [*Benelux*]   (BAS)
MAB......... Magyar Allami Biztosito [*Hungarian State Insurance Enterprise*] (HU)
MAB......... Management Analysis Branch [*Vietnam*]
MAB......... Man and the Biosphere Program [*UNESCO*] [*Paris, France*]
MAB......... Man and the Biosphere Programme [*ICSU*]
MAB......... Manufacture d'Armes Automatiques Bayonne [*Bayonne Automatic Arms Factory*] [*French*]
MAB......... Maraba [*Brazil*] [*Airport symbol*]   (OAG)
MAB......... Militaerische Abnahmebestimmungen [*Acceptance (Purchase) Terms for Military Commodities*]   (EG)
MAB......... Minoterie, Aliments de Betail, Boulangerie [*Congo*]   (EY)
MAB......... Misiles Antibalisticos [*Antiballistic Missiles*] [*Spanish*]
mab........... Motorized Battalion of Submachine Gunners   (BU)
MAB......... Naval Air Base   (RU)
MABAD.... Markas Besar Angkatan Darat [*Army Headquarters*] [*MBAD*] [*Also,*]   (IN)
MABAL..... Markas Besar Angkatan Laut [*Navy Headquarters*] [*MBAL*] [*Also,*]   (IN)
MABAU.... Markas Besar Angkatan Udara [*Air Force Headquarters*] [*MBAU*] [*Also,*]   (IN)
MABCO.... Manufacturing & Building Company Ltd. [*Saudi Arabia*] (MENA)
MABECY... Manufacture Beninoise du Cycle
MABEGOSZ ... Magyarorszagi Bercseplok es Gepkocsitulajdonosok Orszagos Szovetsege [*National Association of Threshing Machine and Automobile Owners*]   (HU)
MABEOSZ ... Magyar Belyeggyujtok Orszagos Szovetsege [*National Association of Hungarian Philatelists*]   (HU)
MABI .... Meganalkalmazottak Biztosito Intezete [*Insurance Institute for Private Employees*]   (HU)
MABINI.... Movement of Attorneys for Brotherhood, Integrity, and Nationalism Inc. [*Philippines*]
MABIS ...... Maschinelle Bilanz-Simulation [*German*]   (ADPT)
MABLA..... Movimento Afro-Brasileiro para a Libertacao de Angola
MABOPA ... Malaysian Book Publishers' Association   (EAIO)
MABOSE ... Manufacture de Bonneterie Senegalaise
MABR .... Inter-American Development Bank   (RU)
MABU .... Maschinengewehr-Eisenbeton-Unterstand [*Machine-Gun-Iron-Reinforced Concrete Emplacement*] [*German "pill box," battlefield redoubts World War I*]
Mac........... Macarca [*Hungarian*]   (TU)
MAC......... Macau [*ANSI three-letter standard code*]   (CNC)
MAC......... Mackintosh   (DSUE)
mac........... Macule [*Soiled*] [*Publishing*] [*French*]
MAC......... Magyar Atletikai Club [*Hungarian Athletic Club*]   (HU)
MAC......... Malta Air Charter Co. Ltd. [*ICAO designator*]   (FAAC)
MAC......... Manual Assistance Centre [*Australia*]
MAC......... Manufacture Africaine de Cycle
MAC......... Manufacture d'Allumettes et Cigarettes [*Cigarette and Match Manufacturing Company*] [*Cambodia*]   (CL)
MAC......... Maritime Air Command [*Canada NATO*]   (NATG)
MAC......... Maritime Arbitration Commission [*Chinese*]   (GEA)
MAC......... Memoire Adressable par son Contenu [*French*]   (ADPT)
MAC......... Microcomputer Applications Centre [*Australia*]
MAC......... Ministerio de Agricultura y Cria [*Ministry of Agriculture and Livestock*] [*Venezuela*]   (LA)
MAC......... Misir Arap Cumhuriyeti [*Arab Republic of Egypt*]   (TU)
MAC......... Mission Agricole Chinoise [*Chinese Agricultural Mission*] [*Zaire*] (AF)
MAC......... Mixed Armistice Commission [*Arab-Israel borders*]   (BJA)
MAC......... Moniteur Africain du Commerce et de l'Industrie
MAC......... Moscow Art Center   (EAIO)
MAC......... Moslem Action Committee [*Mauritius*]   (AF)
MAC......... Mouvement Anti-Colonialiste [*Anti-Colonialist Movement*] (AF)
MAC......... Mouvement Autonomiste Canarien
MAC......... Mouvement d'Action Civique [*Civil Action Movement*] [*Belgium*]   (WER)
MAC......... Movimento Anti-Colonialista [*Anti-Colonialist Movement*]
MAC......... Movimento Anticomunista [*Anticommunist Movement*] [*Brazil*] (LA)
MAC......... Movimiento Amplio Colombiano [*Broad-Based Movement of Colombia*] [*Political party*]   (PPW)
MAC......... Movimiento Autentico Cristiano [*El Salvador*] [*Political party*] (EY)
MAC......... Movimiento de Autenticidad Colorada [*Paraguay*] [*Political party*]   (EY)
MAC......... Mudiad Amdyffyn Cymru [*Welsh Defense Movement*]
MAC......... Multicultural Access Centre [*Technical and Further Education*] [*New South Wales, Australia*]
MAC......... Museu de Arte Contemporanea [*Museum of Contemporary Art*] [*Brazil*]
MAC......... Museum Association of the Caribbean   (EAIO)

MAC......... Musiciens Amateurs du Canada [*Canadian Amateur Musicians*] (EAIO)
MACA .... Malaysian Agricultural Chemicals Association
MACA .... Maritime Air Control Authority [*NATO*]   (NATG)
MACA .... Mazda Automobile Club of Australia
MACA .... Ministerial Advisory Committee on AIDS [*Australia*]
MACAC .... Anti-Communist Commando Movement [*Portugal*]   (WER)
MACACI... Manufacture de Caoutchouc de la Cote-D'Ivoire
MA(C)AT ... Motor Accidents (Compensation) Appeal Tribunal [*Northern Territory, Australia*]
MACB .... Martial Arts Control Board [*Victoria, Australia*]
MACBAA ... Maine/Anjou Cattle Breeders' Association of Australia
macc .... Macchia [*Stain*] [*Publishing*] [*Italian*]
MACC .... Malaysian-American Chamber of Commerce [*Later, AAACC*]
MACC .... Manufacture d'Armes et de Cartouches Congolaises [*Congolese Weapons and Cartridges Manufacturing Company*]   (AF)
MACC .... Military Assistant to the Civil Community
MACC .... Ministerial Advisory Committee on Co-Operation [*Victoria, Australia*]
macch .... Macchia [*Stain*] [*Publishing*] [*Italian*]
MACD....... Macdonnell [*Botanical region*] [*Australia*]
MACD....... Member of the Australasian College of Dermatologists   (ADA)
MACD....... Member of the Australian College of Dentistry   (ADA)
MACE .... Measuring and Control Equipment Company Proprietary Ltd. [*Australia*]
MACE .... Mechanical & Civil Engineering Contractors Ltd. [*United Arab Emirates*]   (MENA)
MACE .... Member of the Australian College of Education   (ADA)
MACEA .... Member of the Australian Council for Educational Administration
Maced .... Macedonia
MACEL..... Manufacturas de Cuero Ltda. [*Colombia*]   (COL)
MAC/FD... Ministry of Agriculture and Cooperation/Fishery Department [*Thai*]   (MSC)
MACGP .... Member of the Australian College of General Practitioners (ADA)
MAChA ..... Member of the Australian Chiropody Association   (ADA)
MACHIMPEX ... China National Machinery Import & Export Corp. [*China*] (IMH)
MACHO.... Machismo [*Spanish*]   (DSUE)
Macho........ Movimiento Anticomunista Hondureno [*Honduran Anti-Communist Movement*] [*Political party*]   (PD)
MACI .... Ministerio de Agricultura, Comercio, e Industria [*Panama*] (LAA)
MACI .... Mutuelle Agricole de Cote-D'Ivoire
MACIMEA ... Materiel Automobiles, Carrieres, Industries, Mines, Entreprises Agricoles [*Morocco*]
MACIMO ... Compagnie Malgache des Ciments de Moramanga
MAC(K).... Military Armistice Commission (Korea)
MACL .... Maison Assuree Contre l'Incendie [*House Insured Against Fire*] [*French*]
MACMME ... Ministerial Advisory Committee on Multicultural and Migrant Education [*Victoria, Australia*]
MACN....... Museo Argentino de Ciencias Naturales "Bernardino Rivadavia" [*Argentina*]   (DSCA)
MACO....... Member of the Australian College of Ophthalmologists   (ADA)
MACODEX ... Compagnie Malgache d'Elevage et d'Exportation
MACODI .. Manufacture de Confection de Cote-D'Ivoire
MACOMA ... Materiaux de Construction de Madagascar
MACON.... Manufactura Colombiana de Carton [*Colombia*]   (COL)
MACP .... Macroprocesseur [*French*]   (ADPT)
MACP .... Member of the Australian College of Paediatrics
MACPCP .. Member, Australian College of Private Consulting Psychologists
Macq........ Macquarie University [*Australia*]   (ADA)
MACRO.... Monopole, Astrophysics and Cosmic Ray Observatory [*Italy*]
MACS........ Maharashtra Association for the Cultivation of Science [*India*] (EAS)
MACS........ Member of the Australian Computer Society   (ADA)
MACS........ Multiple Access Communications System [*West German and Dutch*]
MACTIS ... Marine and Coastal Technology Information Service [*United Nations (already exists in GUS II database)*]   (IID)
MACVSc ... Member of the Australian College of Veterinary Scientists
MACWUSA ... Motor Assemblies and Components Union of South Africa
Mad............ Madagascar
Mad........... Madame [*Madam*] [*French*]   (MTD)
Mad........... Madde [*Article*]   (TU)
MAD......... Madrid [*Spain*] [*Airport symbol*]   (OAG)
MAD......... Mexican Academy of Dermatology   (EAIO)
MAD......... Mikta Apospasmata Dioxeos [*Joint Pursuit Detachments*] [*Greek*]   (GC)
MAD......... Militaerischer Abschirmdienst [*Military Security Service*] (WEN)
MAD......... Militarischer Abschirmdienst [*Military counterintelligence*] [*Germany*]
MAD......... Military Action Dockers

MAD......... Mittlere Absolute Abweichung [*German*]   (ADPT)
MAD......... Moscow Playwrights' Association   (RU)
MADA....... Malaysian Agriculture Development Association   (ML)
MADA....... Muda Agricultural Development Authority [*Malaysia*]   (EY)
MADAIR... Societe Nationale Malgache de Transports Aeriens
MADAL... Implementos Agricolas e Rodoviarios Ltd. [*Brazil*]   (DSCA)
MADALI... Manufacture Dakardse de Literie [*Senegal*]
MADAUTO ... Madagascar-Automobile
MADCAP ... Societe Madecasse de Chapellerie et Autres Industries
MADCONSERVES ... Madagascar-Conserves
MADE....... Master of Agricultural Development Economics
MADE....... Movimento de Apoio aos Desempregados [*Movement for Assistance to the Unemployed*][*Portuguese*]   (WER)
MADECAUCHO ... Manufacturas de Caucho [*Colombia*]   (COL)
MADECO ... Manufacturas de Cobre, SA [*Copper Manufactures, Inc.*] [*Chile*]   (LA)
MADECONCRETO ... Maderas Concreto [*Colombia*]   (COL)
MADEINDECO ... Maderas Industriales de Colombia [*Colombia*]   (COL)
MADEMA ... Manufacturas de Madera [*Colombia*]   (COL)
MADEMSA ... Manufacturas de Metales, SA [*Metal Manufactures, Inc.*] [*Chile*]   (LA)
MadenFederasyonu ... Turkiye Maden Isci Sendikalari Federasyonu [*Turkish Mine Workers Federation*]   (TU)
MADENGRAIS ... Madagascar-Engrais
Maden-Is ... Turkish Mine, Metal, Metal Works, and Machine Industry Workers Union   (TU)
Maden-Is ... Turkiye Maden, Madeni Esya, ve Makina Sanayii Iscileri Sendikasi [*Metal, Metal Goods, and Machine Industry Workers' Union of Turkey*]   (MENA)
MADEPA ... Movimiento Apolitico de Productores Agropecuarios [*Uruguay*]   (LAA)
MADERA ... Mission d'Aide au Developpement des Ecomomics Rurales en Afghanistan [*France*]   (EAIO)
MADESA ... Maderera del Ecuador SA [*Ecuador*]   (DSCA)
MADETACO ... Manufacturas Corona Ltda. [*Barranquilla*]   (COL)
MADEZORZI ... Madeireira De Zorzi SA [*Brazil*]   (DSCA)
MADGE.... Malaysian Air Defense Ground Environment [*RADAR*]
MADGE.... Microwave Aircraft Digital Guidance Equipment
MADI........ Moscow Highway Institute   (RU)
MADIMPORT ... Comptoir Malgache d'Importation [*Malagasy Import Agency*]   (AF)
MADIS...... Burda-MarketingInfoSystem [*Burda GmbH, Marketing Service Department*] [*Information service or system*]   (IID)
MADISCA ... Distribuidora de Madera [*Venezuela*]   (DSCA)
Mad Isls..... Madeira Islands
MADISZ ... Magyar Demokratikus Ifjusagi Szovetseg [*Association of Hungarian Democratic Youth*]   (HU)
MADK....... Monoamino Dicarboxylic Acid   (RU)
MADO....... Mezhregional'naya Assotsiatsiya Demokraticheskikh Organizatsii i Dvizhenii SSS R [*Interregional Association of Democratic Organizations and Movements of the USSR*]   (EAIO)
MADOC.... Magnetband Austauschformat fuer Dokumentationszweck
MADOME ... Magyar Dolgozok Muveszfenykepezo Egyesulete [*Art Photography Association of Hungarian Workers*]   (HU)
MADPRINT ... Madagascar Print and Press Co. [*Publisher*]
MADS....... Macquarie Association of Disabled Students [*Australia*]
MAD-SMS ... Movement for Autonomous Democracy-Society for Moravia and Silesia [*Former Czechoslovakia*] [*Political party*]   (EY)
MADU....... Mombasa African Democratic Union
MAE......... Machine a Ecrire [*Typewriter*] [*French*]   (ADPT)
MAE......... Maersk Commuter IS [*Netherlands*] [*ICAO designator*]   (FAAC)
Mae........... Maestro [*Record label*] [*Belgium, etc.*]
MAE......... Magyar Agrartudomanyi Egyesulet [*Association of Hungarian Agricultural Sciences*]   (HU)
MAE......... Magyar Agrartudomanyi Egyetem [*Hungarian Agricultural University*]   (HU)
MAE......... Migrant Access to Education [*Western Australia*]
MAE......... Ministero degli Affari Esteri [*Ministry of Foreign Affairs*] [*Italian*]   (WER)
MAE......... Ministerul Afacerilor Externe [*Ministry of Foreign Affairs*]   (RO)
MAE......... Mision Andina del Ecuador [*Ecuadorean Andean Mission*]   (LA)
MAE......... Mission Anti-Erosive
MAE......... Movimiento de Accion Estudiantil [*Student Action Movement*] [*Argentina*]   (LA)
MAE......... Museum of Anthropology and Ethnography   (RU)
MAEA....... Miedzynarodowa Agencja Energii Atomowej [*International Atomic Energy Agency*]   (POL)
MAEDY.... Monas Aeporikis Exypiretiseos Dimosion Ypiresion [*Public Services Air Service Unit*] [*Greek*]   (GC)
MAEI........ Malaysian-American Electronics Industry
MAEM...... Missao Antropologica e Etnologica de Mocambique
MAER....... Ministry of Agriculture, Eastern Region
Maes........... Maestoso [*Majestic*] [*Music*]
MAES........ Multicultural Adult Education Service [*Proposed*] [*Australia*]
MAESON ... Marxist All-Ethiopian Socialist Movement [*Political party*]   (PD)

MAET....... Mission Francaise d'Aide Economique et Technique [*French Mission for Economic and Technical Aid*]   (CL)
MAETU..... Medical Air Evacuation Transport Unit [*Australia*]
MAETUR ... Mission d'Amenagement et d'Equipement des Terrains Urbains et Ruraux [*Cameroon*]   (EY)
MAF......... Front Militant Autonome [*Autonomous Militant Front*] [*French*]   (PD)
MAF......... International Astronautical Federation [*IAF*]   (RU)
MAF......... Malaysian Armed Forces   (ML)
MAF......... Maroc, Algerie, France
MAF......... Ministry of Agriculture and Fisheries [*New Zealand*]   (PDAA)
MAF......... Ministry of Agriculture and Fisheries [*Barbados*]   (DSCA)
MAF......... Ministry of Agriculture and Forestry [*Japan*]   (PDAA)
MAF......... Mission Aviation Fellowship [*Indonesia*] [*ICAO designator*]   (FAAC)
MAF......... Moscow Futurists' Association [*Publishing house*]   (RU)
MAF......... Movimento de Arregimentacao Feminina [*Women's Regimentation Movement*] [*Brazil*]   (LA)
MAFA...... Maison des Agriculteurs Francais d'Algerie
Mafa.......... Maschinenfabrik (Halle) [*Halle Machine Building Enterprise*]   (EG)
MAFAS..... Maschinelle Auftragsbearbeitung mit Fabrikate-Stueckliste [*German*]   (ADPT)
MAFCO.... Mauritanian Fishery Company
MAFDAL ... National Religious Party [*Israel*]   (ME)
MAFF....... Ministry of Agriculture, Forestry and Fisheries [*Japan*]   (ECON)
MAFI........ Mafi-Fahrzeugwerke International [*Germany*]   (PDAA)
MAFI........ Magyar Allami Foldtani Intezet [*Hungarian State Geological Institute*]   (HU)
MAFIA...... Morte alla Francia Italia Anelo [*Death to the French is Italy's Cry*] [*When used in reference to the secret society often associated with organized crime, "Mafia" is from the Sicilian word for boldness or lawlessness*]
MAFILM.. Magyar Filmgyarto Vallalat [*Hungarian Film Producing Enterprise*]   (HU)
MAFIRT ... Magyar Filmipari Reszvenytarsasag [*Hungarian Film Industry Limited (Prewar)*]   (HU)
MAFISZ.... Magyar Forradalmi Ifjumunkas Szovetseg [*Hungarian Young Revolutionary Workers' Association*]   (HU)
MAFKI...... Magyar Asvanyolaj es Foldgaz Kiserleti Intezet [*Hungarian Petroleum and Natural Gas Experimental Institute*]   (HU)
MAFL....... Monaro Australian Football League
MAFM-KTMA ... Union of Revolutionary Students [*Malagasy*]   (AF)
MAFPADUM ... Mouvement Algerien des Forces Populaires et de l'Armee pour la Democratie et l'Union Maghrebine [*Algerian Movement of People's Forces and of the Army for Democracy and Maghreb Union*]   (AF)
MAfr....... Society of Missionaries of Africa   (EAIO)
MAFRAM ... Maison de l'Amitie Frano-Africaine et Malgache
MAFREMO ... Malawi Freedom Movement
MAFS........ Mexico-Albania Friendship Society   (EAIO)
MAFW...... Movement ATD Fourth World [*Switzerland*]   (EAIO)
MAG......... Air Margarita [*Venezuela*] [*ICAO designator*]   (FAAC)
MAG......... Ambtenarengerecht te 's-Gravenhage Rechtsprekende in Militaire Ambtenarenzaken [*Benelux*]   (BAS)
Mag........... De Magistratuur [*Benelux*]   (BAS)
MAG......... High-Power Aerosol Generator   (RU)
MAG........ International Association of Geodesy [*IAG*]   (RU)
MAG......... Madang [*Papua New Guinea*] [*Airport symbol*]   (OAG)
Mag........... Magazin [*Magazine*] [*German*]   (GCA)
mag............ Magazine [*Military term*], Shop, Store   (RU)
Mag........... Magister [*Schoolmaster*] [*German*]
mag............ Magistraat [*Magistrate*] [*Afrikaans*]
Mag........... Magistrat von Gross-Berlin [*Greater Berlin Magistrate*]   (EG)
MAG......... Ministerio de Agricultura y Ganaderia [*Ministry of Agriculture and Cattle Breeding*] [*El Salvador*]
MAG......... Ministerio de Agricultura y Ganaderia [*Ministry of Agriculture and Cattle Breeding*] [*Nicaragua*]   (LA)
mag............ Mohammedan Cemetery [*Topography*]   (RU)
MAG......... Morska Agencja w Gdyni [*Maritime Agency in Gdynia*]   (POL)
MAG......... Motorists' Action Group [*Australia*]
MAG......... Mutuello Agricole du Gabon
MAGA....... International Association of Geomagnetism and Aeronomy [*IAGA*]   (RU)
MAGA....... Magnetohydrodynamic Analogy   (RU)
MAGA....... Member of the Australian Gas Association
MAGA....... Music Arrangers' Guild of Australia   (ADA)
MAGAMOD ... Magasins Modernes Gabonais
Mag arch.... Magister der Architektur [*Master of Architecture*] [*German*]
MAGATE ... International Atomic Energy Agency [*IAEA*]   (RU)
MAGBNT ... Museums and Art Galleries Board of the Northern Territory [*Australia*]
MAGD....... Mitteilungen der Afrikanischen Gesellschaft in Deutschland
MAGERWA ... Magasins Generaux du Rwanda
MAGETAT ... Magasin d'Etat d'Alimentation [*State Food Store*] [*Liquidated 1 July 1970 Cambodia*]   (CL)

MAGEV .... Muszaki Anyag- es Gepkereskedelmi Vallalat [*Technical Material and Machinery Trade Enterprise*] (HU)
magg .... Maggio [*May*] [*Italian*]
magg .... Maggiore [*Major*] [*Italian*]
MAGI .... Member of the Australian Grain Institute
MAGIC ..... Mozambique, Angola, Guinea-Bissau Information Center (AF)
Magin .... Magasin [*Shop*] [*Military map abbreviation World War I*] [*French*] (MTD)
MAGMA ... Empresa Nacional de Minas [*Export of precious and semi-precious stones*] [*Mozambique*]
magmat ...... Magmatisch [*Magmatic*] [*German*] (GCA)
magn .... Magnetic (RU)
magn .... Magnetique [*French*] (TPFD)
magn .... Magnetisch [*Magnetic*] [*German*]
magn .... Magnetism (TPFD)
magnet .... Magnetisch [*Magnetic*] [*German*]
magn rez ..... Magnetic Resonance (RU)
MAGNT .... Museums and Art Galleries of the Northern Territory [*Australia*]
MAgrEc ..... Master of Agricultural Economics
MAGRIN .. Maquinaria Agricola e Industrial Ltda. [*Colombia*] (COL)
MAgrSci ..... Master of Agricultural Science
MAgSci ...... Master of Agricultural Science
MAGU .... Moscow City Trucking and Carting Administration (RU)
magy .... Magyar [*Hungarian*] (HU)
Magy .... Magyar Muza [*Record label*] [*Hungary*]
MAGZI ..... Mission d'Amenagement et de Gestion des Zones Industrielles
Mah .... Mahalle [*Quarter, Precinct*] [*of a city*] (TU)
MAH .... Mahkamah [*Court, Tribunal*] (IN)
Mah .... Mahkeme [*Court, Tribunal*] (TU)
MAH .... Mahon [*Spain*] [*Airport symbol*] (OAG)
MAH .... Malev-Hungarian Airlines [*ICAO designator*] (FAAC)
MAH .... Milli Asayis Hizmeti [*Turkish National Security Service*] (TU)
MAHA ...... Member of the Australian Hypnotherapists Association (ADA)
MAHABI .. Magyar Hajozasi Betegsegbiztosito Intezet [*Hungarian Health Insurance Institute for Seamen*] (HU)
MAHART ... Magyar Hajozasi Reszvenytarsasag [*Hungarian Shipping Company Limited*] (HU)
MAHB .... Mobilna Armiska Hirurska Bolnica [*Mobile Army Surgical Hospital*] (YU)
mahd .... Mahdollinen [*Finland*]
mahd .... Mahdollisesti [*Finland*]
MAH enN ... Minister van Arbeid, Handel en Nijverheid [*Benelux*] (BAS)
MAHIR ..... Magyar Hirdeto Vallalat [*Hungarian Advertising Enterprise*] (HU)
MAHMILLUB ... Mahkamah Militer Luar Biasa [*Special Military Tribunal*] [*Indonesia*]
MAHOG ... Mahogany (DSUE)
Mahr .... Maehrchen [*Fairy Tale*] [*German*]
MAI .... Air Moravia [*Czechoslovakia*] [*ICAO designator*] (FAAC)
MAI .... International Institute of Agriculture (RU)
MAI .... Mean Annual Increment
MAI .... Ministerio da Administracao Interna [*Ministry of Interior*] [*Portuguese*] (WER)
MAI .... Ministerium fuer Aussenhandel und Innerdeutschen Handel [*Ministry for Foreign Trade and Domestic German Trade*] [*See also MfAI*]
MAI .... Ministre Attache a l'Interieur [*Minister Assigned to (Ministry of) Interior*] (CL)
MAI .... Ministry of Agriculture and Irrigation [*India*] (PDAA)
MAI .... Monash Asia Institute [*Monash University*] [*Australia*]
MAI .... Moscow Aeronautical Institute
MAI .... Moscow Aviation Institute Imeni Sergo Ordzhonikidze (RU)
MAI .... Moscow Institute of Architecture (RU)
MAI .... Movimento Antimilitarista Italiano [*Italian Anti-Militarist Movement*] (WER)
MAI .... Movimiento de Abogados Independientes [*Movement of Independent Lawyers*] [*Panama*] (LA)
MAI .... Museums Association of India (SLS)
MAIA .... Materiel Automobile Industriel Agricole [*Morocco*]
MAIA .... Member of the Advertising Institute of Australia (ADA)
MAIA .... Ministerul Agriculturii si Industriei Alimentare [*Ministry of Agriculture and the Food Industry*] (RO)
MAIAS ...... Member of the Australian Institute of Agricultural Science (ADA)
MAIB .... Member of the Australian Institute of Biology
MAIB .... Member of the Australian Institute of Building
MAIB .... Motor Accidents Insurance Board [*Tasmania, Australia*]
MAIC .... Member of the Australian Institute of Cartographers
MAIChP .... International Association on Quaternary Research [*INQUA*] (RU)
MAID .... Member of the Australian Institute of Dieticians
MAIEA ...... Member of the Australian Institute of Educational Administration
MAIEx ...... Member of the Australian Institute of Export
MAIG .... Matsushita Atomic Industrial Group [*Japan*] (PDAA)
MAIHR ..... Member of the Australian Institute of Human Relations (ADA)

MAIJA ...... Member of the Australian Institute of Judicial Administration
MAIK .... Maschinelle Anlagenbuchhaltung im Krankenhaus [*German*] (ADPT)
MAIL .... Melbourne Australia Investments Ltd.
MAIM .... International Academy of the History of Medicine (RU)
MAIM .... Member of the Australian Institute of Management
MAIMA .... Manufacturas Maderas Industriales Ltda. [*Barranquilla*] (COL)
MAIME ..... Member of the Australian Institute of Mining Engineers
MAIMM ... Member of the Australasian Institute of Mining and Metallurgy (ADA)
main .... Mainittu [*Finland*]
MAINCOL ... Maquinaria Internacional de Colombia SA [*Colombia*] (COL)
MAIP .... Member of the Australian Institute of Physics
MAIPA ...... Maranhao Industria de Pesca e Produtos Alimenticios [*Maranhao Fishing and Food Products Industry*] [*Brazil*] (LA)
MAIPA ...... Movimiento Anti-Imperialista Patriotico de Alicante [*Anti-Imperialist Patriotic Movement of Alicante*] [*Spanish*] (WER)
MAIRAH .. Member of the Australian Institute of Refrigeration, Air Conditioning, and Heating (ADA)
MAIS .... Mediterranean Association of International Schools (EA)
MAIS .... Multicultural Australia Information System
Maist .... Maisteri [*Master of Arts*] [*Finland*] (GPO)
MAIT .... Member of the Australian Institute of Travel
MAITA ...... Mauritius Association of IATA Travel Agents [*Mauritius*] (EAIO)
MAITT ...... Member of the Australian Institute of Travel and Tourism
MAIW .... Member of the Australian Institute of Welfare Officers
MAIWO .... Member of the Austrlaian Institute of Welfare Officers
maj .... Majoor [*Major*] [*Afrikaans*]
maj .... Major [*Portuguese*]
Maj .... Major [*French*] (MTD)
maj .... Majuri [*Finland*]
MAJ .... Majuro [*Marshall Islands*] [*Airport symbol*] (OAG)
maj .... Majus [*May*] (HU)
maj .... Majuscula [*Capital*] [*Publishing Romanian*]
Maj .... Majuskel [*Uppercase Letter*] [*German*]
MAJ .... Medical Association of Jamaica (SLS)
MAJDJEN ... Majoor Djenderal [*Major General*] (IN)
MAJE .... Movimento Angolano de Juventude Estudante
mak .... Macedonian (RU)
MAK .... Magyar Altalanos Koszenbanya Reszvenytarsasag [*Hungarian General Coal Mines Limited (Prewar)*] (HU)
MAK .... Magyar Autoklub [*Hungary*] (EAIO)
Mak .... Makina [*Machinery, Mechanical*] (TU)
MAK .... Malakal [*Sudan*] [*Airport symbol*] (OAG)
MAK .... Maritime Arbitration Commission (RU)
MAK .... Materialanforderungs-karte [*German*] (ADPT)
MAK .... Materials on the Archaeology of the Caucasus (RU)
MAK .... Maximale Arbeitsplatzkonzentration [*Maximum Workplace Concentration*] [*German*]
MAK .... Moskovskaya Assotsiatsiya Kardiologov (EAIO)
makb .... Camouflage Battalion (RU)
MAKh .... Museum of the Academy of Arts, USSR (RU)
MAKhD .... Moscow Association of Theatrical Scenery Painters (RU)
MAKI .... Israel Communist Party (ME)
MAKI .... Mathitiki Anexartiti Kinisi [*Student Independent Movement*] (GC)
MAKIT ...... Magyar Allergologiai es Klinikai Immunologiai Tarsasag [*Hungary*] (SLS)
Makiz .... Moscow Academic Publishing House (RU)
MakNII ..... Makeyevka Scientific Research Institute for Work Safety in the Mining Industry (RU)
MAKODAM ... Markas Komando Daerah Militer [*Military Region Command Headquarters*] (IN)
MAKPROFIL ... Macedonian Mine Prospecting and Boring Establishment [*Skopje*] (YU)
makroscop ... Makroskopisch [*Macroscopic*] [*German*] (GCA)
MAKS .... Inter-African Committee on Statistics (RU)
MAKS .... International Seed Testing Association [*ISTA*] (RU)
MAKS .... Makina ve Klima Sanayii AS [*Machinery and Air Conditioning Industry Corp.*] (TU)
maks .... Maksanut [*Finland*]
maks .... Maksettu [*Finland*]
maks .... Maksimum [*Maximum*] [*Afrikaans*]
maks .... Maksimum [*or Maksymalny*] [*Maximum*] [*Poland*]
maks .... Maximum (RU)
MAKSA ...... Mainzer Arbeitskreis Sudafrika
maks davl ... Maximum Pressure (RU)
maksim ...... Maximum (RU)
MAKTAS .. Makarnacilik ve Ticaret Turk Anonim Sirketi [*Macaroni Manufacture and Trade Corporation*] (TU)
Mak Tec .... Makina ve Techizat [*Machinery and Equipment*] (TU)
MAKTRANSPORT ... Macedonian Public Transportation Establishment [*Skopje*] (YU)

Mal .... Little, Small   (RU)
MAL .... Malacca [*Malaysia*]   (ML)
MAL .... Malay   (WDAA)
MAL .... Malayan Airways Ltd.
MAL .... Malaysia   (WDAA)
MAL .... Malaysian Air Lines
Mal .... Maleagi [*Malachi*] [*Afrikaans*]
Mal .... Maleis [*Malay*] [*Afrikaans*]
Mal .... Maliye [*Finance*]   (TU)
mal .... Malowal [*Painted By*]   (POL)
MAL .... Malta   (WDAA)
mal .... Malum [*Ill*] [*Latin*]   (MAE)
MAL .... Mandated Airlines [*Australia*]
MAL .... Manufacturera Agricola [*Colombia*]   (COL)
Mal .... Marechal [*Marshal*] [*French*]
mal .... Marechal [*Marshal*] [*Portuguese*]
MAL .... Ministry of Agriculture and Livestock [*Burkina Faso*]
MAL .... Monsanto Australia Limited
MALA ...... Malawi Library Association
MALACA ... Manufacturas de Caucho [*Colombia*]   (COL)
MALAGOC ... Mutual Assistance of the Latin American Government Oil
           Companies G2 [*See also ARPEL*]   (EA)
MalagRep ... Malagasy Republic
MaLAM .... Medical Lobby for Appropriate Marketing [*Australia*]
malaysk...... Malay, Malayan   (RU)
MALB....... Maliye Bakanligi [*Finance Ministry*]   (TU)
Mald Isls.... Maldive Islands
MALEV ..... Magyar Legikozlekedesi Vallalat [*Hungarian Air Transport
           Enterprise*]   (HU)
Malgobekneft' ... Trust of the Malgobek Petroleum Industry   (RU)
MALIAP ... Societe Malienne de Diffusion d'Appareils Electriques
MALIGAZ ... Societe Malienne des Gaz Industriels
MALIMAG ... Societe Malienne de Grands Magasins
MALINET ... Master List of Medical Indexing Terms [*EM*] [*Netherlands*]
MALN ...... Mouvement Africain de Liberation Nationale [*African Movement
           for National Liberation*]
Mal-Port.... Maleis-Portugees [*Malayo-Portuguese*] [*Afrikaans*]
Malre .... Maladrerie [*Hospital for Lepers*] [*Military map abbreviation
           World War I*] [*French*]   (MTD)
MAM........ Madzi a Moyo
MAM........ Matamoros [*Mexico*] [*Airport symbol*]   (OAG)
MAM........ Medical Association of Malta   (SLS)
MAM........ Meta Aviotransport-Macedonia [*Yugoslavia*] [*ICAO designator*]
           (FAAC)
MAM........ Miroiterie Africaine Moderne
MAM........ Mot a Mot [*Word for Word*] [*French*]
MAM........ Museu de Arte Moderna [*Museum of Modern Art*] [*Portuguese*]
mam .... Myriametre [*Myriameter*] [*French*]   (GPO)
MAMA...... Mothers and Midwives Action [*Australia*]
MAMA...... Movement for All-Macedonian Action [*Political party*]
MAMA...... Mutuelle d'Assurances Malagasy [*Insurance*] [*Madagascar*]
MAMBO... Mediterranean Association for Marine Biology and Oceanology
           [*ICSU*]   (EAIO)
MAMC...... Mananga Agricultural Management Center [*Swaziland*]
MAMC...... Mining and Allied Machinery Corporation Ltd. [*India*]
MAMENIC ... Marina Mercante Nicaraguense [*Nicaragua*]   (LAA)
MAMG..... Magyar Allami Mezogazdasagi Gepuzem [*Hungarian State
           Agricultural Machine Factory*]   (HU)
MAMI ...... Moscow Aircraft Engine Institute   (RU)
MAMI ...... Moscow Institute of Automotive Engineering   (RU)
MAMK..... Mistni Auto-Moto Klub [*Local Motoring Club*]   (CZ)
MAMO...... International Association of Microbiological Societies [*IAMS*]
           (RU)
MAMR..... International Association of Marine Radio Interests   (RU)
MAMSER ... Mass Mobilisation for Self-Reliance, Economic Recovery, and
           Social Justice [*Nigeria*]
MAMT...... Moscow Technicum of Automative Engineering   (RU)
MAMYu.... Former Moscow Archives of the Ministry of Justice, Kept at the
           TsGADA   (RU)
Man........... Manager   (EECI)
Man........... Managing   (EECI)
man .... Manana [*Tomorrow*] [*Spanish*]
Man........... Mancando [*Dying Away*] [*Music*]
MAN........ Mandato de Accion y Unidad Nacional [*Mandate of Action and
           National Unity*] [*Bolivia*] [*Political party*]   (PPW)
MAN......... Manege [*Horsemanship*] [*French*]
MAN......... Manitoba [*Canadian province*]
man .... Manovrato [*Handmade*] [*Publishing*] [*Italian*]
MAN........ Mantisse   (ADPT)
MAN......... Manuel Antonio Noriega [*Military commander and de facto ruler
           of Panama*]
MAN......... Manufacturers Association of Nigeria   (AF)
man .... Manuscrit [*Manuscript*] [*Publishing*] [*French*]
MAN......... Marea Adunare Nationala [*Grand National Assembly*]   (RO)
MAN......... Maschinenfabrik Augsburg-Nuernberg AG [*Augsburg-Nuernberg
           Machine Factory, Inc.*]   (EG)

MAN......... Maschinenfabrik Augsburg-Nuernburg [*Manufacturer of diesel
           engines*]
mAn .... Meiner Ansicht Nach [*In My Opinion*] [*German*]   (EG)
MAN......... Metropolitan Area Networking [*Telecommunications*]
           [*Australia*]
MAN......... Ministerul Apararii Nationale [*Ministry of National Defense*]
           (RO)
MAN......... Mouvement pour une Alternative Non-Violente [*Movement for a
           Nonviolent Alternative*] [*France*] [*Political party*]   (PPE)
MAN......... Movement for the Advancement of Nationalism
MAN......... Movementu Antiyas Nobo [*New Antilles Movement*]
           [*Netherlands*] [*Political party*]   (EAIO)
MAN......... Movimentu Antiyas Nobo [*New Antilles Movement*] [*Political
           party*]   (EY)
MAN......... Movimiento Agricola Nacional [*National Agriculture Movement*]
           [*Colorado*]   (LA)
MAN......... Movimiento Anti-Comunista Nacional [*National Anticommunist
           Movement*] [*El Salvador*]   (LA)
MAN......... Movimiento Antilliyana Nobo [*New Antillean Movement*]
           [*Netherlands Antilles*]   (LA)
MAN......... Movimiento de Accion Nacional [*National Action Movement*]
           [*Colorado*]   (LA)
MAN......... Movimiento de Accion Nacional [*National Action Movement*]
           [*Venezuela*]   (LA)
MAN......... Movimiento de Accion Nacionalista [*National Action
           Movement*] [*Uruguay*] [*Political party*]   (EY)
MANA...... Malawi News Agency
MANA...... Mision Aerea Norteamericana [*Chile*]   (LAA)
MANAGRO ... Manufacturas Agroindustriales [*Colombia*]   (COL)
MANAPO ... Makedonski Narodni Pokret [*Macedonian National Movement*]
           (YU)
MANATEX ... Manufacture Nationale Textile [*Textile and furnishings
           manufacturer*] [*Casablanca, Morocco*]   (MENA)
manc........... Mancante [*Lacking*] [*Publishing*] [*Italian*]
MANC...... Mocambique African National Congress
MANC...... Mouvement d'Action Nationale Camerounaise
MANCER ... Manufacturas de Ceramica SA [*Colombia*]   (COL)
Manch....... Manchuria
MANCO..... Mocambique African National Congress
M & Cie ..... Miraband & Compagnie [*Bank*] [*Switzerland*]
MANDFHAB ... Male and Female Homosexual Association of Great Britain
M and L ..... Management and Logistics [*NATO*]   (NATG)
M & M....... Manchester & Milford Railway [*Wales*]
M & R .... Murray en Roberts Beherend Beperk [*Murray and Roberts
           Holdings Ltd.*] [*South Africa*]   (AA)
M & SL...... Mukhi & Sons Ltd. [*Kenya*]
MANE....... Magyar Allami Nepi Egyuttes [*Hungarian State Folk Ensemble*]
           (HU)
MANEX .... Management Experten-Nachweis [*Management Experts Data
           Base*] [*Society for Business Information*] [*Information
           service or system*]   (IID)
mangruppa ... Mobile Group, Maneuver Group   (RU)
MANI....... Ministry of Agriculture for Northern Ireland
MANIPOL ... Manifesto Politik [*Political Manifesto*]   (IN)
MANIT ...... Manitoba [*Canadian province*]
MANK...... International Scientific Film Association [*ISFA*]   (RU)
mannl........ Maennlich [*German*]
MANO ...... Movimiento Anti-Comunista Nacional Organizado [*Organized
           National Anticommunist Movement*] [*Bolivia*]   (LA)
MANO ...... Movimiento Anti-Comunista Nacional Organizado [*Organized
           National Anticommunist Movement*] [*Guatemala*]   (LA)
MANO ...... Movimiento Argentino Nacional Organizado [*Argentine
           National Organized Movement*]   (LA)
MANOPLAS ... Manufacturas Plasticas Ltda. [*Colombia*]   (COL)
MANPA ..... Manufacturas de Papel, CA [*Venezuela*]   (LAA)
manq .... Manquant [*Lacking*] [*Publishing*] [*French*]
MANR....... Ministry of Agriculture and Natural Resources of Western
           Nigeria
MANS .... Makedonsko-Avstraliski Naroden Sojuz [*Macedonian-Australian
           People's League*] [*Melbourne*]   (YU)
Mant .... Mantik [*Logic*]   (TU)
MANTECH ... Manufacturing Technology [*Division of*] [*CSIRO Institute of
           Industrial Technology*] [*Research center*] [*Australia*]
           (ERC)
MANTEP ... Management Training for Education Personnel
MANU ...... Makedonska Akademija na Naukite i Umetnostite [*Former
           Yugoslavia*]   (SLS)
MANU ...... Makonde African National Union
MANU ...... Mozambique African National Union [*Later, FRELIMO*]
MANUCACIG ... Manufacture Centrafricaine de Cigares
MANUCAM ... Manufacture de Toiles et Baches du Cameroun
MANUCONGO ... Societe Congolaise de Manutention
MANUFRANCE ... Manufacture Francaise d'Armes et Cycles de Saint-
           Etienne [*French*]
Manufre..... Manufacture [*Manufactory*] [*Military map abbreviation World
           War I*] [*French*]   (MTD)
MANUGAB ... Manufacture Gabonaise

manus........ Manuscrito [*Manuscript*] [*Publishing*] [*Spanish*]
Manuskr.... Manuskript [*Manuscript*] [*Publishing*] [*German*]
MANVOS ... Manual Visas for Overseas System [*Australia*]
MANZ........ Medical Assoiation of New Zealand   (PDAA)
MANZCP ... Member of the Australian and New Zealand College of
    Psychiatrists
MAO.......... MAC Aviation SL [*Spain*] [*ICAO designator*]   (FAAC)
MAO.......... Manaus [*Brazil*] [*Airport symbol*]   (OAG)
MAO.......... Mari Autonomous Oblast [*1920-1936*]   (RU)
mao............. Med Andra Ord [*In Other Words*] [*Sweden*]   (GPO)
mao............. Med Andre Ord [*In Other Words*] [*Norway*]   (GPO)
MAO.......... Mordvinian Autonomous Oblast [*1930-1934*]   (RU)
MAO.......... Moscow Archaeological Society   (RU)
MAO.......... Moscow Architectural Society [*1867-1930*]   (RU)
MAO.......... Movimiento Armado Obrero [*Workers' Armed Movement*]
    [*Guatemala*]   (LA)
MAO.......... Movimiento de Asociaciones de Obreros [*Workers' Associations
    Movement*] [*Argentina*]   (LA)
MAO.......... Movimiento de Autodefensa de los Obreros [*Workers' Self-
    Defense Movement*] [*Colorado*]   (LA)
MAOGA.... Metropolitan Atlanta Olympic Games Authority   (OLYM)
MAORT.... Magyar-Amerikai Olajipari Reszvenytarsasag [*Hungarian-
    American Oil Company Limited*]   (HU)
MAOT....... Mobile Air Operations Team [*Military*]
MAOTE .... Magyar Altalanos Orvosok Tudomanyos Egyesuelete [*Hungary*]
    (SLS)
MAP .... International Association of Soil Science [*IASS*]   (RU)
MAP .... Maghreb-Arabe Presse [*Maghreb Arab Press Agency*] [*Morocco*]
MAP .... Mamai [*Papua New Guinea*] [*Airport symbol*]   (OAG)
MAP .... Manufacture Abidjanaise de Plastiques
map .... Mapa [*Map*] [*Publishing*] [*Spanish*]
MAP .... Masarykova Akademie Prace [*Masaryk Academy of Labor*]
    (CZ)
MAP .... Mediterranean Action Plan [*UNEP*]   (ASF)
MAP .... Mezhdunarodnaya Assotsiatsiya Pochvovedov International Soil
    Scientists Association [*Former USSR*]   (DSCA)
MAP .... Middle Atmosphere Programme [*International Council of
    Scientific Unions*]
MAP .... Mikhanokinitos Astynomia Poleon [*Motorized Cities Police*]
    (GC)
MAP .... Milicias de Accion Popular [*People's Action Militias*] [*Spanish*]
    (WER)
MAP .... Military Assistance Program
MAP .... Ministerio de Agricultura e Pesca [*Ministry of Agriculture and
    Fisheries*] [*Portuguese*]   (WER)
MAP .... Ministerstwo Administracji Publicznej [*Ministry of Public
    Administration*]   (POL)
MAP .... Ministry of the Aircraft Industry, USSR   (RU)
MAP .... Ministry of the Automobile Industry, USSR   (RU)
MAP .... Mise Au Point [*Tuning*] [*French*]   (ADPT)
MAP .... Moslem Association Party [*Ghana*]
MAP .... Movement of the Assemblies of People [*Grenada*]
MAP .... Movimiento Agrario Panameno [*Panamanian Agrarian
    Movement*]   (LA)
MAP .... Movimiento de Accion Patriotica [*Patriotic Action Movement*]
    [*Uruguay*]   (LA)
MAP .... Movimiento de Accion Popular [*Popular Action Movement*]
    [*Mexico*]   (LA)
MAP .... Mpitolona any Amin'ny Provansa [*Provincial Demonstrators*]
    [*Malagasy*]   (AF)
MAP .... Muscle Adenylic Preparation   (RU)
MAP .... Mutual African Press Agency
MAP .... Portuguese Action Movement   (WER)
MAPA ...... Malaysian Agricultural Producers Association   (ML)
MAPA ...... Member of the Australian Physiotherapy Association   (ADA)
MAPA .... Movimento de Autodeterminacao para os Acores [*Movement for
    the Self-Determination of the Azores*] [*Portuguese*]   (WER)
MAPAI...... Israel Workers Party
MAPAM ... Mifleget Hapoalim Hameuchedet [*An association*] [*Israel*]
    (EAIO)
MAPAM ... United Workers Party   (ME)
MAPAMA ... Manufacture Papetiere du Maroc
MAPANTJAS ... Mahasiswa Pantjasila [*Pantjasila College Students
    Association*]   (IN)
MAPAS..... Malatya Patron Sanayi ve Ticaret Anonim Sirketi [*Malatya
    Pattern Industry and Trade Corporation*]   (TU)
MAPE........ Movimiento de Afirmacion y Progreso de la Educacion
    [*Educational Affirmation and Progress Movement*]
    [*Argentina*]   (LA)
MAPHILINDO ... Malaysia, Philippines, and Indonesia   (IN)
MAPI........ Member of the Australian Planning Institute   (ADA)
MAPI........ Mitsubishi Atomic Power Industries   (IAA)
MAPI........ Mitsubishi Atomic Power Industries, Inc.
MAPI........ Movimiento de Accion Popular Independiente [*Independent
    Popular Action Movement*] [*Colorado*]   (LA)
MAPIS ...... Medicinal and Aromatic Plants Information Service [*Council of
    Scientific and Industrial Research*] [*India*]

MAPLAS .. Plasticos y Maquinaria [*Colombia*]   (COL)
MAPN....... International Political Science Association [*IPSA*]   (RU)
MAPO....... Magazina Popullore [*Albanian*]
MAPodA ... Member of the Australian Podiatry Association
MAPOLEX ... Muanyagfeldolgozo Kisipari Termeloszovetkezet [*Production
    Cooperative of Plastic Materials*]   (HU)
MAPP........ International Association of Proletarian Writers   (RU)
MAPPENAS ... Musjawarah Perentjanaan Pembangunan Indonesia
    [*Indonesia Development Planning Council*]   (IN)
MAppEpidem ... Master of Applied Epidemiology
MAppSci ... Master of Applied Science
MAppSc(SocEcol) ... Master of Applied Science in Social Ecology
MAPRC..... Mediterranean Allied Photographic Reconnaissance Command
MAPRE..... Maquinaria de Precision Ltda. [*Colombia*]   (COL)
MAPRESA ... Madera Prensada SA [*Peru*]   (DSCA)
MAPRIAL ... Mezhdunarodnaja Assotsiatsija Professorov Russkogo Jazyka i
    Literatury [*International Association of Teachers of Russian
    Language and Literature*]   (EAIO)
MAPRINTER ... Empresa Cubana Importadora de Materias Primas y
    Productos Intermedios [*Cuban Enterprise for Import of
    Raw Materials and Intermediate Products*]   (LA)
MAPS........ International Superphosphate Manufacturers' Association
    [*ISMA*]   (RU)
MAPS........ Management and Policy Studies Centre [*Canberra College of
    Advanced Education*] [*Australia*]
MAPS........ Member of the Australian Psychological Society
MAPS........ Migrant Access Projects Scheme [*Australia*]
MAPsS ...... Member of the Australian Psychology Society   (ADA)
MAPU .... Matabeleland African Peoples Union [*Rhodesian*]   (AF)
MAPU .... Movimiento de Accion Popular Unida [*Unified Popular Action
    Movement*] [*Chile*] [*Political party*]   (PD)
MAPU .... Movimiento de Avanzada Popular Universitario [*Advanced
    Popular University Movement*] [*Argentina*]   (LA)
MAPU-OC ... Movimiento de Accion Popular Unitario - Obreros y
    Campesinos [*United Popular Action Movement - Workers
    and Peasants Faction*] [*Chile*]   (LA)
MAPV .... Malaysian Association of Phonogram and Videogram Producers
    and Distributors   (EAIO)
MAPW ...... Medical Association for the Prevention of War [*Australia*]
maq .... Maquinista [*Machinist*] [*Portuguese*]
MAQ-AVI ... Industria e Comercio de Maquinas Avicolas Ltd. [*Brazil*]
    (DSCA)
MAQM...... Mouvement ATD Quart Monde [*Switzerland*]   (EAIO)
MAQS .... Metropolitan Air Quality Study [*Sydney, Australia*]
MAQUIMPORT ... Empresa Cubana Importadora de Maquinaria y Equipos
    [*Cuban Enterprise for Import of Machinery and Equipment*]
    (LA)
MAQUINEGO ... Maquinaria y Negocios [*Colombia*]   (COL)
MAQUIT .. Comercial de Maquinas e Equipamentos [*Machinery and
    Equipment Marketing Company*] [*Brazil*]   (LA)
MAR......... Automatic Recorder   (RU)
MAR......... International Development Association [*IDA*]   (RU)
MAR......... Magyar Allamrendorseg [*Hungarian State Police*]   (HU)
MAR......... Maracaibo [*Venezuela*] [*Airport symbol*]   (OAG)
mar............ Mardi [*Tuesday*] [*French*]
mar............ Mari   (RU)
mar............ Mark [*Currency*]   (RU)
mar............ Marocchino [*Morocco*] [*Publishing*] [*Italian*]
mar............ Marokijn [*Morocco*] [*Publishing*] [*Netherlands*]
Mar............ Maroquin [*Morocco*] [*Publishing*] [*German*]
mar............ Maroquin [*Morocco*] [*Publishing*] [*French*]
mar............ Marroquim [*Morocco*] [*Publishing*] [*Portuguese*]
Mar............ Marshall   (PWGL)
mar............ Marynarz [*Sailor, Mariner*] [*Poland*]
mar............ Marzo [*March*] [*Spanish*]
MAR......... Materials on Russian Archaeology   (RU)
MAR......... Mezhdunarodnaia Assotsiats Razvitiia
MAR......... Morocco [*ANSI three-letter standard code*]   (CNC)
MAR......... Movimento de Acao Revolucionaria [*Revolutionary Action
    Movement*] [*Brazil*]   (LA)
MAR......... Movimiento di Azione Rivoluzionaria [*Revolutionary Action
    Movement*] [*Italian*]   (PD)
MAR......... Movimiento Armada Revolucionaria - Accion [*Armed
    Revolutionary Movement - Action*] [*Mexico*]   (LA)
MAR......... Movimiento de Accion Revolucionaria [*Revolutionary Action
    Movement*] [*Uruguay*]   (LA)
MAR......... Movimiento de Accion Revolucionaria [*Revolutionary Action
    Movement*] [*Panama*]   (LA)
MAR......... Movimiento de Accion Revolucionaria [*Revolutionary Action
    Movement*] [*Guatemala*]   (LA)
MAR......... Movimiento de Accion Revolucionaria [*Revolutionary Action
    Movement*] [*Mexico*]   (PD)
MARA .... Majlis Amanah Rakyat [*Council of Trust for the Indigenous
    People*] [*Malaysia*]   (ML)
MARA .... Ministere de l'Agriculture et de la Reforme Agraire [*Ministry of
    Agriculture and Agrarian Reform*]   (AF)

MARA .... Movimiento Autentico de Recuperacion Argentino [*Argentine Authentic Renewal Movement*] (LA)

MARAGRA ... Marracuene Agricola Acucareira

MARAIRMED ... Maritime Air Forces Mediterranean [*NATO*] (NATG)

MARAS ..... Middle Airspace Radar Advisory Service

MarASSR ... Mari Autonomous Soviet Socialist Republic (RU)

MARAVEN ... Subsidiary of PETROVEN [*A*] [*Venezuela*] (LA)

marb .... Marbre [*Marbled*] [*Publishing*] [*French*]

Marbas ...... Maritsa Basin (BU)

marc .... Marcius [*March*] (HU)

MARC ...... Micro-Analytical Research Centre [*Australia*]

MARC ...... Mouvement d'Action pour la Resurrection du Congo [*Action Movement for the Resurrection of the Congo*] [*Zaire*] (PD)

MARC .... Movimiento Agrario Revolucionario del Campesinado Boliviano [*Revolutionary Movement of Bolivian Indian Peasants*] [*Political party*] (PPW)

MARCHILE ... Chilean Oceanographic Expedition (MSC)

MARCOGAZ ... Union of the Gas Industries of the Common Market Countries [*Defunct*] (EAIO)

MARCOM ... Maritime Command [*Canada, since 1964*]

MARCOMAF ... Societe Commerciale au Service du Marche Commun et de l'Afrique

MARCONFOR ... Maritime Contingency Force [*NATO*] (NATG)

MARCONFORLANT ... Maritime Contingency Forces, Atlantic [*NATO*] (NATG)

MARCS ..... Melcom All Round Adaptive Consolidated Software [*Japan*]

Mardec ...... Malaysian Rubber Development Corporation (GEA)

MARDEC ... Malaysia Rubber Development Corporation (DS)

MARDI ..... Malaysian Agricultural Research and Development Institute (ML)

mare .... Menere [*Gentlemen*] [*Afrikaans*]

MARECS .. Satellite de Communication Maritime [*Maritime Communications Satellite*] (LA)

MARENG ... Marine and Engineering Services Division [*Maritime Services Board*] [*New South Wales, Austrlaia*]

MARETRAC ... Marine Research and Training Center [*Former Yugoslavia*] (ASF)

marg .... Margarine Plant [*Topography*] (RU)

marg .... Marge [*Margin*] [*Publishing*] [*French*]

marg .... Marginal [*Publishing*] [*French*]

marg .... Marginal [*Margin*] [*Publishing*] [*Sweden*]

marg .... Marginoso [*With Wide Margins*] [*Publishing*] [*Italian*]

margants ... Manganese Mines [*Topography*] (RU)

Marge .... Marecage [*Marsh*] [*Military map abbreviation World War I*] [*French*] (MTD)

margin .... Marginal [*Marginal*] [*Publishing*] [*French*]

margin .... Marginale [*Marginal*] [*Publishing*] [*Italian*]

Margosizdat ... Mari State Publishing House (RU)

margr .... Margrabia [*Margrave*] [*Poland*]

MARIA ..... Marine Aquarium Research Institute of Australia (ADA)

MARIF ...... Malang Research Institute for Food Crops [*Indonesia*] [*Research center*] (IRC)

MARIMEX ... Maroc-Import-Export [*Moroccan Import-Export Co.*] (AF)

MARIN ..... Maritiem Research Instituut Nederland [*Netherlands Maritime Research Institute*] (ERC)

MARINCO ... Arabian Marine Petroleum Co. [*Saudi Arabia*] (MENA)

MARINTEK ... Norsk Marineteknisk Forskningsinstitutt AS [*Norwegian Marine Technology Research Institute*] [*Research center*] (IRC)

MARIS ...... Management Research and Information Services [*Development Academy of the Philippines*]

Mark .... Markus [*Mark*] [*Afrikaans*]

MARKFED ... Punjab State Cooperative Supply and Marketing Federation [*India*] (PDAA)

Marknigoizdat ... Mari Book Publishing House (RU)

MARKSTRAT ... Marketing Strategy [*Simulation package developed by Professors Jean-Claude Larreche and Hubert Gatignon*]

MARLIN ... Malaysian Research Libraries Network (PDAA)

marm .... Marmoreret [*Marbled*] [*Publishing Danish/Norwegian*]

marm .... Marmoriert [*Marbled*] [*Publishing*] [*German*]

marm .... Marmorizzato [*Marbled*] [*Publishing*] [*Italian*]

marmor ...... Marmoreret [*Marbled*] [*Publishing Danish/Norwegian*]

marmor ...... Marmoriert [*Marbled*] [*Publishing*] [*German*]

marmor ...... Marmorizzato [*Marbled*] [*Publishing*] [*Italian*]

marmoriz .... Marmorizzato [*Marbled*] [*Publishing*] [*Italian*]

MARN ...... Movimento de Agricultores Rendeiros do Norte [*Northern Tenant Farmers Movement*] [*Portuguese*] (WER)

MARNR .... Ministry of the Environment and Renewable Natural Resources [*Venezuela*] (IMH)

MARO .... Maritime Air Radio Organization [*NATO*] (NATG)

marocch ...... Marocchino [*Morocco*] [*Publishing*] [*Italian*]

maroq .... Maroquin [*Morocco*] [*Publishing*] [*French*]

Maroq .... Maroquin [*Morocco*] [*Publishing*] [*German*]

MARPDIC ... Marine Pollution Documentation and Information Center (MSC)

MARPE ..... Movimiento de Afirmacion y Renovacion Peronista [*Peronist Renewal and Reaffirmation Movement*] [*Argentina*] (LA)

MARPESCA ... Empresa Cubana Importadora de Buques Mercantes y de Pesca [*Cuban Enterprise for the Import of Merchant and Fishing Ships*] (LA)

MARPOL ... International Convention for the Prevention of Pollution from Ships [*1973*]

MARPORT ... Empresa Maritima Portuaria de Importacion [*Maritime and Ports Importation Enterprise*] [*Cuba*] (LA)

MARQ .... Marquis [*or Marquess*]

marr .... Marroqui [*Morocco*] [*Publishing*] [*Spanish*]

MARS .... Migration Agents' Registration Scheme [*Australia*]

MARS .... Movimiento de Accion Revolucionaria Socialista [*Socialist Revolutionary Action Movement*] [*Costa Rica*] (LA)

MARSA ..... Margarin Sanayi AS [*Margarine Industry Corp.*] (TU)

MARSA ..... Microfilm Association of the Republic of South Africa (AA)

MARSAVCO ZAIRE ... Compagnie des Margarines, Savons, et Cosmetiques au Zaire SARL [*Manufacturer of vegetable oil products*] [*Zaire*]

marsh .... Marshal (RU)

MARSIM .. International Conference on Marine Simulation (PDAA)

MARSS ..... Mountains Area Resource Sharing Scheme [*New South Wales libraries*] [*Australia*]

marsz .... Marszalek [*Marshal*] [*Poland*]

mart .... Martes [*Tuesday*] [*Spanish*]

MART .... Martinique [*West Indies*] (WDAA)

MARTD .... Multidisciplinary Association for Research and Teaching in Demography (EAIO)

MARTEKS ... Maras Tekstil Sanayii AS [*Maras Textile Industry Corp.*] (TU)

MARTRANS ... Egyptian Marine Transport Co. (IMH)

marts .... Martires [*Martyrs*] [*Spanish*]

MARU .... Instantaneous Automatic Gain Control (RU)

MARUNET ... Maruzen Online Network [*Maruzen Co. Ltd.*] [*Japan*] [*Telecommunications*]

MARVIL ... Societe de Production Maraichere Vilmorin

Marz .... Marzo [*March*] [*Italian*]

MARZ .... Moscow Automobile Repair Plant (RU)

MAS .... International Astronomical Union [*IAU*] (RU)

MAS .... Interplanetary Automatic Station (RU)

MAS .... Local Automatic System (RU)

MAS .... Madang Air Services [*Australia*]

MAS .... Malaysia Air System (ML)

MAS .... Malaysian Airline System [*ICAO designator*] (FAAC)

MAS .... Manufacture National d'Armes de Saint Etienne [*Groupement Industriel des Armaments Terrestres*] [*France*] (PDAA)

MAS .... Manufacture Nationale d'Armes de la St. Etienne [*France*]

MAS .... Manus [*Papua New Guinea*] [*Airport symbol*] (OAG)

MAS .... Marine Archaeological Society [*Australia*]

MAS .... Maschinenausleihstation [*Machine Rental Station*] (EG)

MAS .... Metals Advisory Service [*Ministry of Industries*] [*Pakistan*]

MAS .... Mezhdunarodnaya Assotsiatsiya Sudovladeltsev [*International Shipowners' Association*] [*Poland*] (EAIO)

MAS .... Military Agency for Standardization [*Brussels, Belgium*] [*NATO*]

MAS .... Ministerio dos Asountos Sociais [*Ministry of Social Affairs*] [*Portuguese*] (WER)

MAS .... Mission d'Amenagement du Fleuve Senegal

MAS .... Missive van den Algemeenen Secretaris [*Benelux*] (BAS)

MAS .... Monetary Authority of Singapore

MAS .... Moravske Akciove Strojirny, Narodni Podnik [*Moravian Machine Building Joint-Stock Company, National Enterprise*] (CZ)

MAS .... Motoscafo Antisommergibile [*Naval*] [*Italian*]

MAS .... Motoscafo Anti-Sommergibile [*Antisubmarine Motor Boat*] [*Italian Navy*]

MAS .... Mouvement d'Action Socialiste [*Socialist Action Movement*] [*Belgium*] (WER)

MAS .... Movimiento al Socialismo [*Movement towards Socialism*] [*Venezuela*] [*Political party*] (PPW)

MAS .... Movimiento al Socialismo [*Movement towards Socialism*] [*Argentina*] [*Political party*] (PPW)

MAS .... Movimiento de Accion Social [*Social Action Movement*] [*Dominican Republic*] (LA)

MAS .... Movimiento de Accion Socialista [*Peru*] [*Political party*] (EY)

MAS .... Movimiento de Afirmacion Social [*Social Affirmation Movement*] [*Argentina*] (LA)

MAS .... Movimiento para Accion y Solidaridad [*Guatemala*] [*Political party*] (EY)

MAS .... Muerte a los Secuestradores [*Death to Kidnappers*] [*Colorado*] (PD)

MAS .... Mujeres en Accion Sindical [*Organizes national and international conferences on women in the economy*] [*Mexico*] (CROSS)

mas .... Oil Mill [*Topography*] (RU)

MASA .... Mathematical Association of South Australia

MASA .... Mathematical Association of Southern Africa (AA)

MASA .... Medical Aid for Southern Africa

MASA .... Medical Association of South Africa

MASA .... Mediterranean Allied Strategic Air Force
MASA .... Member of the Australian Society of Accountants
MASA .... Men Against Sexual Assault [*Australia*]
MASA .... Mines' African Staff Association
MASA .... Montenegrin Academy of Sciences and Arts [*Former Yugoslavia*] (EAIO)
Masc .... Maschile [*Masculine*] [*Italian*]
masc .... Masculino [*Masculine*] [*Portuguese*]
MASC .... Movimiento Agrario Social-Cristiano [*Venezuela*] (EY)
MASCEH ... Member of the Australian Society for Clinical and Experimental Hypnosis
Masch .... Maschine [*Machine*] [*German*] (GCA)
MASCH .... Member of the Australian Society of Clinical Hypnotherapists (ADA)
MASCP ..... Multicultural and Cross-Cultural Supplementation Program [*Australia*]
MASD .... Minimal Absolute Lethal Dose (RU)
MASD .... Movimiento al Socialismo Democratico [*Movement toward Democratic Socialism*] [*Bolivia*] (LA)
MASET ..... Member of the Australian Society for Educational Technology
mash.......... Machinery Plant [*Topography*] (RU)
mash.......... Machine Shop [*Topography*] (RU)
MAShGIZ ... State Scientific and Technical Publishing House of Literature on Machinery Manufacture (RU)
mashin .... Typewritten (BU)
mashinno-trakt ... Machine-and-Tractor (RU)
Mashinoimport ... All-Union Association for the Import of Machinery (RU)
Mashmetizdat ... State Publishing House of the Machinery, Metalworking, and Aircraft Industries (RU)
mash opytst ... Machine Experimental Station [*Topography*] (RU)
Mashpriborstroy ... All-Union Construction and Installation Trust of the Ministry of Machinery Manufacture and Instrument Making, USSR (RU)
mashprom .. Machinery Industry (RU)
MASI .... Inter-American Statistical Institute [*IASI*] (RU)
MASI .... Molinera Argentina Sociedad Industrial [*Argentina*] (DSCA)
MASIS ...... Maruzen Scientific Information Service Center [*Maruzen Co. Ltd.*] [*Japan*] [*Telecommunications*]
mask.......... Camouflage (RU)
MASK....... International Credit Insurance Association [*ICIA*] (RU)
mask.......... Maskuliini [*Finland*]
MASK....... Materials Warehouses and Stock Rooms (RU)
maskinopsk ... Maskinopskaaret [*Machine-Trimmed*] [*Publishing Danish/Norwegian*]
maskinskr .. Maskinskrevet [*Typed*] [*Danish/Norwegian*]
maskkov..... Camouflage Drape (RU)
maskr .... Camouflage Company (RU)
maskv .... Camouflage Platoon (RU)
Masl.......... Oil Mill [*Topography*] (RU)
masloprom ... Oil Industry (RU)
MASLOTsENTR ... Central Union of Dairy Cooperatives (RU)
MASLPI.... Mexican American State Legislators Policy Institute (CROSS)
MASM ...... Member of the Australian Society of Microbiology (ADA)
MASME.... Member of the Australian Society for Music Education
MASMO ... Medical Equipment Workshops (RU)
MASO .... International Social Security Association [*ISSA*] (RU)
MASPEC .. Istituto di Materiale Speciali per Elettronica e Magnetismo [*Institute of Special Materials for Electronics and Magnetism*] [*Research center*] [*Italian*] (IRC)
MASPED .. Magyar Altalanos Szallitmanyozasi Vallalat [*Hungarian General Shipping Enterprise*] (HU)
MASPLA .. Movimiento por la Autodeterminacion y la Solidaridad de los Pueblos LatinoAmericanos [*Movement for the Self-Determination and Solidarity of Latin American Peoples*] [*Argentina*] (LA)
MASPS ..... Moroccan Association for the Support of the Palestinian Struggle (AF)
masr .... Camouflage Company (RU)
mass .... Massimo [*Largest*] [*Publishing*] [*Italian*]
MAss .... Middle Assyrian [*Language, etc.*] (BJA)
MASSA ..... Member of the Academy of the Social Sciences of Australia
Masspartgiz ... State Publishing House of Mass Party Literature (RU)
MASSR ..... Mari Autonomous Soviet Socialist Republic (RU)
MASSR ..... Moldavian Autonomous Soviet Socialist Republic [*1924-1940*] (RU)
MASSR ..... Mordvinian Autonomous Soviet Socialist Republic (RU)
mass yed..... Mass Unit (RU)
mast.......... Ink (BU)
MAST....... Medical Anti-Shock Trousers [*Military*]
mast.......... Workshop, Shop (RU)
MASTA..... Medical Advisory Services for Travellers Abroad [*London School of Hygiene and Tropical Medicine*] [*Information service or system*] (IID)
MASTAS .. Marmara Melamin Sanayi ve Ticaret Anonim Sirketi [*Marmara Melamine (Cyanuramide) Industry and Marketing Corporation*] (TU)

MASTER .. Movimento de Agricultores sem Terras [*Landless Farmers Movement*] [*Brazil*] (LA)
MASYDA ... Materiaux de Synthese de Dakar
MASZ........ Magyar Allami Szenbanyak [*Hungarian State Coal Mines*] (HU)
MASZ........ Magyar Atletikai Szovetseg [*Hungarian Athletic Association*] (HU)
maszek .... Magan Szektor [*Private Sector (of Economy) or Private Merchant or Craftsman, Moonlighter*] (HU)
MASZI ...... Magyar Szabvanyugyi Intezet [*Hungarian Bureau of Standards*] (HU)
MASZOBAL ... Magyar-Szovjet Bauxit-Aluminium Reszvenytarsasag [*Hungarian-Soviet Bauxite Aluminium Company Limited*] (HU)
MASZOLAJ RT ... Magyar-Szovjet Olajipari Reszvenytarsasag [*Hungarian-Soviet Industrial Oil Company Limited*] (HU)
MASZOVAL ... Magyar-Szovjet Bauxit-Aluminium Tarsasagok [*Hungarian-Soviet Bauxite Companies*] (HU)
MASZOVLET ... Magyar-Szovjet Polgari Legiforgalmi Tarsasag [*Hungarian-Soviet Civilian Airline*] (HU)
MASZOVOL ... Magyar-Szovjet Nyersolaj Reszvenytarsasag [*Hungarian-Soviet Crude Oil Company Limited*] (HU)
MAT......... International Automotive Transport (BU)
MAT......... Magyar Aluminiumipari Troszt [*Hungarian Aluminum Industry Trust*] (HU)
MAT......... Magyar Angiologiai Tarsasag [*Hungary*] (EAIO)
MAT......... Magyar Autonom Tartomany [*Hungarian Autonomous Territory (in Romania)*] (HU)
mat .... Mandat [*Authority*] [*French*]
MAT......... Manufacture Alsacienne de Tabacs [*Alsatian Tobacco Manufacturer*] [*Commercial firm*] [*France*]
m at .... Masa Atomowa [*Atomic Mass*] [*Poland*]
MAT......... Matadi [*Zaire*] [*Airport symbol*] [*Obsolete*] (OAG)
mat .... Matematica [*Mathematics*] [*Italian*]
mat .... Matematiikka [*Mathematics*] [*Finland*]
Mat .... Matematik [*Mathematics*] (TU)
mat .... Matematyczny [*or Matematyka*] [*Mathematical or Mathematics*] (POL)
mat .... Matesis [*Mathematics*] [*Afrikaans*]
mat .... Mathematical (BU)
MAT......... Mathematical Association of Tanzania
mat .... Mathematical, Mathematics (RU)
mat .... Matita [*Pencil*] [*Publishing*] [*Italian*]
MAT......... Medical Assessment Tribunal [*Queensland, Australia*]
MAT......... Medical Association of Tanzania
MAT......... Mobile Advisor Team [*Vietnamese team trained by US Army advisors*] (VNW)
MAT......... Monades Andimetopiseos Tarakhon [*Riot Center Units*] [*MMAD, OAT*] [*See also*] (GC)
MAT......... Monades Apokatastaseos Taxeos [*Order Restoration Units*] (GC)
MAT......... Moscow Art Theater
MAT......... Motorlu Araclar Ticaret AS [*Motorized Vehicles Trading Corporation*] (TU)
MAT......... Municipal Association of Tasmania [*Australia*]
MATA ...... Museums Association of Tropical Africa (AF)
MATAF.... Mediterranean Allied Tactical Air Force
MATCO .... Materiales de Construccion Ltda. [*Santa Marta*] (COL)
MATCV..... Mobile Air Traffic Control Vehicle [*Military*]
MATE .... Merestechnikai es Automatizalasi Tudomanyos Egyesulet [*Scientific Association of Measures and Automation*] (HU)
MATE .... Modern Aids to Education
MATEIP ... Magyar Textilipari Vallalat [*Hungarian Textile Mill*] (HU)
MATEL-AFRIC ... Materiel Electrique Africain
MATELCA ... Societe Marocaine de Telecommunications par Cables Sousmarins [*Morocco*]
MATELCO ... Societe de Materiel Electrique du Congo
MATELECS ... Materiales Electricos [*Colombia*] (COL)
MATELO ... Maritime Air Telecommunications Organization [*NATO*] (NATG)
MATELT .. Ministere de l'Amenagement du Territoire, de l'Equipement, du Logement, et du Tourisme [*Ministry of Territorial Development, Equipment, Housing, and Tourism*] [*French*] (WER)
Matem........ Matematica [*Mathematics*] [*Portuguese*]
matem .... Mathematical (BU)
matemat ..... Mathematical, Mathematics (RU)
MATEOSZ ... Magyar Teherfuvarozok Orszagos Kozponti Szovetkezete [*National Central Cooperative of Hungarian Truckers*] (HU)
mater .... Materials (RU)
MATERAUTO ... Materiel Automobile et Industriel
MATERMACO-Congo ... Materiel et Materiaux de Construction - Congo
MA(TESOL) ... Master of Arts in Teaching English to Speakers of Other Languages [*Australia*]
MATESZ .. Magyar Tekezo Szovetseg [*Hungarian Bowling Association*] (HU)
MATESZ .. Magyar Teruleti Szinhaz [*Hungarian Regional Theater*] (HU)

MATFA..... Meat and Allied Trade Federation of Australia
MATFA..... Meat and Allied Trades Federation of Australia (ADA)
math .... Mathematics (TPFD)
Math .... Mathematik [*Mathematics*] [*German*]
math .... Mathematique [*French*] (TPFD)
math .... Mathematisch [*German*]
MATI .... Magasepitesi Tervezo Intezet [*Designing Institute for Building Construction*] (HU)
MATI .... Maldives Association of the Tourism Industry (EY)
MATI .... Ministry of Agriculture Training Institute
MATI .... Moscow Aviation Technological Institute (RU)
MATICOSE ... Manufacture de Tissage et de Confection Senegalaise
MATIF ...... Marche a Terme des Instruments Financiere [*French stock exchange*]
MATIF ...... Marche a Terme des Instruments Financiers [*French Financial Futures Market*]
MATIF ...... Marche a Terme International de France
MATIN ..... Ministry of Agriculture Training Institute at Nyegezi
MATiShD ... Ministry of Automobile Transportation and Highways (RU)
MATLAS .. Melbourne Allied Tertiary Library Automation System [*Australia*]
MATMCGFF ... Ministerul Aprovizionarii Tehnico-Materiale si Controlul Gospodaririi Fondurilor Fixe [*Ministry of Technical-Material Supply and Control of the Management of Fixed Assets*] (RO)
mat med...... Matiere Medicale
MATOBA ... Manufacture de Toiles et Baches
MATP....... Ministry of the Automobile and Tractor Industry (RU)
Matrez .... Uprava Materiajalnih Rezervi [*Administration of Material Reserves*] (YU)
matriek....... Matrikulasie [*Matriculation*] [*Afrikaans*]
MATS........ Long-Distance Automatic Telephone Communication (RU)
MATs .... Methylacetone (RU)
MATS....... Metropolitan Adelaide Transport Study [*Australia*]
MATS....... Middle Africa Transportation Survey
MATShD .. Ministry of Automobile Transportation and Highways (RU)
MATShOSDOR ... Ministry of Automobile Transportation and Highways (RU)
MATSS ..... Marine and Transportation Services (Saudi) Ltd. [*Saudi Arabia*]
Matt .... Mattheus [*Matthew*] [*Afrikaans*]
MATTA..... Malaysian Association of Tour and Travel Agents (EAIO)
MATTRA ... Societe Mauritanienne de Transit, Transport, Representation, Assurances
MATZPEN ... Political Party [*Israel*] (ME)
MAU......... Air Mauritius Ltd. [*ICAO designator*] (FAAC)
MAU......... International Association of Universities [*IAU*] (RU)
MAU......... Malabar Assessment Unit [*Australia*]
MAU......... Maupiti [*French Polynesia*] [*Airport symbol*] (OAG)
MAud........ Master of Audiology
MAUD....... Movimento Academico pela Uniao Democrata [*Academic Movement for Democratic Union*] [*Portugal*] [*Political party*] (PPE)
MAUK....... Moscow Automobile Training Center (RU)
MAUND ... Mouvement Algerien pour l'Unite Nationale et la Democratie [*Algerian Movement for National Unity and Democracy*] (AF)
MAUP....... International Association of Criminal Law (RU)
Maur .... Mauritania
Maur .... Mauritius
MAURELEC ... Societe Mauritanienne d'Electricite [*Mauritanian Electricity Company*] (AF)
MAUREX ... Societe Mauritanienne d'Explosifs
MAURINAP ... Societe Mauritanienne de Diffusion d'Appareils Electriques
MAURIPEX ... Mauritania Import-Export
Maurit........ Mauritania
MAUS .... Markt-Analyse-und Ueberwachungssystem [*German*] (ADPT)
MAUS .... Materialwissenschaftliche Autonomoe Experimente unter Schwerelosigkeit
MAUS .... Movimiento de Accion y Unidad Socialista [*Socialist Movement for Action and Unity*] [*Mexico*] [*Political party*] (PPW)
MAusIMM ... Member of the Australasian Institute of Mining and Metallurgy (ADA)
M AusIMM ... Member of the Australian Institute of Mining and Metallurgy
MAUSS..... Mouvement Anti-Utilitariste dans les Sciences Sociales [*France*] (EAIO)
M AustIM ... Member of the Australian Institute of Mining and Metallurgy
mauv.......... Mauvais [*Bad*] [*French*]
MAV .... Magyar Allamvasutak [*Hungarian State Railways*]
MAV .... Maloelap [*Marshall Islands*] [*Airport symbol*] (OAG)
mAV .... Maritime Antarctic Air (RU)
mAV .... Maritime Arctic Air (RU)
MAV .... Maximum Adsorptive Moisture Capacity (RU)
MAV .... Misti Akcni Vybor [*Local Action Committee*] (CZ)
MA(V) .... Motorcycling Australia (Victoria) [*Australia*] [*An association*]
MAV .... Municipal Association of Victoria [*Australia*]
MAV .... Small Amphibian (RU)

MAVAG .... Magyar Allami Vas, Acel-, es Gepgyarak [*Hungarian State Iron, Steel, and Machine Factories*] (HU)
MAVAS..... Monimos Andiprosopeia Voreio-Atlandikou Symfonou [*Permanent Delegation to NATO*] (GC)
MAVAUT ... Magyar Allamvasutak Autobusz Uzeme [*Autobus Service of the Hungarian State Railways*] (HU)
MAVI .... Metopon Apelevtheroseos Voreiou Ipeirou [*Northern Ipeiros Liberation Front*] [*Greek*] (GC)
MAVIE...... Manufacture Voltaique d'Insecticides et d'Esthetique
MAVJegyny ... Magyar Allamvasutak Jegynyomdaja [*Ticket Printing Office of the Hungarian State Railroads*] (HU)
mavo.......... Middelbaar Algemeen Voortgezet Onderwijs [*Benelux*] (BAS)
MAVOCI ... Manufacture Voltaique de Cigarettes
MAVOSZ ... Magyar Vadaszok Orszagos Szovetsege [*National Association of Hungarian Hunters*] (HU)
MAVTI...... Magyar Allamvasutak Tervezo Intezet [*Planning Institute of Hungarian State Railways*] (HU)
MAVTRANS ... Magyar Allamvasutak Szallitmanyozasi Szolgalata [*Transfer Service of the Hungarian State Railroads*] (HU)
MAW........ Mauritius Alliance of Women (AF)
MAW........ Messegeraete- und Armaturenwerk, Magdeburg (VEB) [*Magdeburg Measuring Instrument and Fittings Plant (VEB)*] (EG)
maw.......... Met Ander Woorde [*In Other Words*] [*Afrikaans*]
MAW........ Militare Ambtenarenwet [*Benelux*] (BAS)
MAW........ Militant Action Workers
MAW........ Ministry of Agriculture and Works [*Pakistan*] (MSC)
maW......... Mit Anderen Worten [*In Other Words*] [*German*]
MAW........ Mlodziezowa Agencja Wydawnicza [*Youth Publishing Agency*] [*Poland*] (EY)
MAW........ Mustique Airways [*Barbados*] [*ICAO designator*] (FAAC)
MAWA..... Maltese Australian Women's Association
MAWA..... Mathemehatical Association of Western Australia
MAW &F ... Movement Against War and Fascism [*Australia*]
MAWR..... Ministry of Agriculture, Western Region
MAWU..... Mechanical and Allied Workers Union [*Liberia*] (AF)
MAWU..... Metal and Allied Workers' Union [*South Africa*]
MAWU..... Montserrat Allied Workers' Union (EY)
MAX......... Matam [*Senegal*] [*Airport symbol*] (OAG)
max .... Maxima [*Very Large*] [*Portuguese*]
max .... Maximum [*or Maximum*] [*German*]
Max.......... Maximum [*French*]
MAX......... Mediterranean Airlines SA [*Greece*] [*ICAO designator*] (FAAC)
MAY .... Mangrove Cay [*Bahamas*] [*Airport symbol*] (OAG)
MAY .... Maya Airways Ltd. [*Belize*] [*ICAO designator*] (FAAC)
MAY .... Monades Asfaleias Ypaithrou [*Rural Security Units*] [*Greek*] (GC)
MAYA ...... Moscow Amateur Yachting Association (EAIO)
MAYC ...... Malaysian Association of Youth Clubs (ML)
maymo........ Mayordomo [*Spanish*]
MAYSAN ... Makine ve Yedekparca Sanayi ve Ticaret AS [*Machinery and Spare Parts Industry and Trade Corp.*] (TU)
MAYuD..... International Association of Democratic Lawyers (BU)
MAYuN..... International Association of Legal Science [*IALS*] (RU)
MAZ......... Magistrates Association of Zambia
MAZ......... Magistrates' Association of Zimbabwe (EAIO)
MAZ......... Magnetaufzeichnung [*German*] (ADPT)
MAZ......... Mayaguez [*Puerto Rico*] [*Airport symbol*] (OAG)
MAZ......... Mines Air Service Zambia Ltd. [*ICAO designator*] (FAAC)
MAZh........ Minsk Automobile Plant (RU)
MAZh........ International Alliance of Women [*IAW*] (RU)
MAZhK..... International Railway Congress Association [*IRCA*] (RU)
MAZI .... Movement for the Advancement of the Zionist Idea [*Israel*] [*Political party*] (EY)
MB............ Bridge Battalion (RU)
MB............ Local Battery (RU)
MB............ Local Office (RU)
MB............ Maandblad voor Belastingrecht [*Benelux*] (BAS)
MB............ Maandblad voor het Boekhouden [*Benelux*] (BAS)
MB............ Maatschappij Belangen [*Benelux*] (BAS)
MB............ Magnetbandschreiber [*German*] (ADPT)
MB............ Magnetic Drum (RU)
MB............ Magyar Bajnoksag [*Hungarian Championship*] (HU)
MB............ Majlis Bandar [*City or Town Council*] (ML)
MB............ Makedonska Bibliografija [*Macedonian Bibliography*] (YU)
MB............ Makti Bahini [*Liberation Forces*] [*Pakistan*]
MB............ Malaysia Barat [*West Malaysia*] (ML)
MB............ Manitoba [*Canadian province*] [*Postal code*]
MB............ Marburger Bund [*Marburg Alliance*] (SLS)
MB............ Markas Besar [*Main Headquarters*] (IN)
MB............ MBB-UV, MBB-UD [*Messerschmitt-Boelkow-Blohm*], und Pneuma-Technik [*Germany*] [*ICAO aircraft manufacturer identifier*] (ICAO)
MB............ Medical Base (RU)
mb .... Megyei Birosag [*County Court*] (HU)

MB............ Melbourne Bitter [*Brand of beer*] [*Initialism used by Australians as slang for "inebriated"*]

MB............ Menteri Besar [*Chief Minister*]   (ML)

mb .... Metr Biezacy [*Running Meter*] [*Poland*]

MB............ Middle Babylonian [*Language, etc.*]   (BJA)

mb .... Millibar [*French*]

Mb .... Mineral Bath   (BU)

MB............ Ministerieel Besluit [*Benelux*]   (BAS)

MB............ Ministeriele Beschikking [*Benelux*]   (BAS)

MB............ Ministerstwo Bezpieczenstwa [*Ministry of Security*]   (POL)

MB............ Ministerstwo Budownictwa [*Ministry of Construction*]   (POL)

MB............ Minobacac [*Mine Thrower*]   (YU)

MB............ Mission Biblique [*Switzerland*]

MB............ Mobile Base, Tender [*Navy*]   (RU)

MB............ Mobilienbelasting [*Benelux*]   (BAS)

MB............ Mohandes Bank [*Egypt*]

m/b............ Mon Billet [*My Bill*] [*French*]

MB............ Moniteur Belge [*Belgium*]   (BAS)

mb .... Mortar Battalion   (RU)

mb .... Mortar Battery   (RU)

M/b............ Motorni Brod [*Motor Ship*]   (YU)

MB............ Motorrijtuigenbelastingwet [*Benelux*]   (BAS)

MB............ Muslim Brothers

mb .... Perhaps   (RU)

m-b............ Scale   (RU)

MBA......... Automobilvertriebs Aktiengesellschaft [*Austria*] [*ICAO designator*]   (FAAC)

MBA......... Interlibrary Loan   (RU)

MBA......... Macao Badminton Association   (EAIO)

MBA......... Malaysian Booksellers Association   (EAIO)

MBA......... Malta Broadcasting Authority   (PDAA)

MBA......... Master Bakers' Association [*Australia*]

MBA......... Master of Business Administration   (PWGL)

MBA......... Mauritius Badminton Association   (EAIO)

MBA......... Military Basketball Association [*Sudan*]

MBA......... Mombasa [*Kenya*] [*Airport symbol*]   (OAG)

MBA......... Multiple Birth Association [*Australia*]

MBAA....... Mortgage Brokers' Association of Australia

MBab......... Middle Babylonian [*Language, etc.*]   (BJA)

MBACT..... Medical Board of the Australian Capital Territory

MBAI....... Marine Biological Association of India   (MSC)

MBAM...... Missao Botanica de Angola e Mocambique, Junta de Investigacoes do Ultramar

MBANSW ... Master Butchers' Association of New South Wales [*Australia*]

MBANSW ... Medical Benevolent Association of New South Wales [*Australia*]

MBAPH .... Melbourne, Brisbane, Adelaide, Perth, Hobart [*Australia*]

mbar.......... Milibar [*Millibar*] [*Poland*]

MBAR ...... Millibar [*Millibar*] [*Afrikaans*]

mbarn........ Millibarn   (RU)

MBASA..... Medical Benevolent Association of South Australia

mbatr.......... Meteorological Battery   (BU)

MBAV ...... Master Builders Association of Victoria [*Australia*]

MBB .... Magyar Beruhazasi Bank [*Hungarian Investment Bank*]   (HU)

MBB .... Marble Bar [*Australia*] [*Airport symbol*]   (OAG)

MBB .... Messerschmitt-Boelkow-Blohm

MBB .... Messerschmitt-Boelkow-Blohm GmbH [*West German aircraft company*]

MBBAQ .... Master Boat Builders' Association of Queensland [*Australia*]

MBBB....... Marmara ve Bogazlari Belediyeleri Birligi [*Marmara and Straits (of Bosporus) Municipalities' Union*]   (TU)

Mb Bo .... Mededelingenblad Bedrijfsorganisatie [*Benelux*]   (BAS)

MBBS........ Boy Scouts International Bureau [*BSIB*]   (RU)

MBBS........ Malaya Borneo Building Society Ltd.   (ML)

MBC......... Malawi Broadcasting Corporation   (AF)

MBC......... Malaysia Baptist Convention   (EAIO)

MBC......... Mauritius Broadcasting Corporation   (AF)

MBC......... M'Bigou [*Gabon*] [*Airport symbol*]   (OAG)

MBC......... Metropolitan Business College [*Australia*]   (ADA)

MBC......... Military Budget Committee [*NATO*]   (NATG)

MBC......... Munhwa Broadcasting Corporation [*South Korea*]   (FEA)

MBC......... Myanmar Baptist Convention   (EAIO)

MBCA ...... Merchant Bank of Central Africa Ltd.

MBCC ...... Medical Benefits Consultative Committee

MBCEU ... Mauritius Broadcasting Corporation Employees Union   (AF)

MBCHA ... Master Builders, Construction, and Housing Association [*Australia*]

MB-CHAA ... Master Builders - Construction and Housing Association of Australia

MBCNT .... Multilingual Broadcasting Council of the Northern Territory [*Australia*]

MBCS........ Manufacture de Bonneterie et de Confection Senegalaise

MBCV ...... Manufacturers Bottle Company of Victoria [*Australia*]   (ADA)

MBD........ International Office of Railway Documentation   (RU)

MBD......... Majlis Belia Daerah [*District Youth Council*]   (ML)

MBD......... Millions of Barrels per Day

MBDP .... Ministry of the Paper and Woodworking Industries   (RU)

MB(DP)AC ... Medical Benefits (Dental Practitioners) Advisory Committee

MbDw........ Maandblad der Vereeniging van Deurwaarders bij de Verschillende Rechtscollegien in Nederland [*Netherlands*]   (BAS)

MBE......... Magnetbandeinheit [*German*]   (ADPT)

MBE......... Magyarorszagi Baptista Egyhaz [*An association*] [*Hungary*]   (EAIO)

MBE......... Monbetsu [*Japan*] [*Airport symbol*]   (OAG)

Mbelr........ Maandblad voor Belastingrecht [*Benelux*]   (BAS)

MB en R.... Maandblad voor Berechtiging en Reclassering van Volwassenen en Kinderen [*Benelux*]   (BAS)

MBER....... Inter-American Development Bank   (RU)

mber......... Millirem   (RU)

Mber .... Monatsbericht [*Monthly Report*] [*German*]   (GCA)

MBES....... Mezhdunarodnyi Bank Ekonomicheskovo Sotrudnichestva [*International Bank for Economic Co-Operation - IBEC*] [*Moscow, USSR*]   (EAIO)

MBF .... Master Bibliographic File

MBF .... Medunarodna Bibliotekarska Federacija [*International Federation of Library Associations*]   (YU)

MBF .... Monobutyl Phosphate   (RU)

MBF .... Myanmar Badminton Federation   (EAIO)

MBFA .... Master Builders Federation of Australia

MBFT....... Magyar Biofizikai Tarsasag [*Hungary*]   (SLS)

MBG........ Milli Birligi Grupu [*National Unity Group*] [*MBK*] [*See also*]   (TU)

MBG........ Mission Biologique du Gabon

MBGT ...... Grand Turk [*Turks and Caicos Islands*] [*ICAO location identifier*]   (ICLI)

MBH........ Macquarie Broadcasting Holdings Ltd. [*Australia*]

MBH........ Manning Base Hospital [*Australia*]

MBH........ Maryborough [*Australia*] [*Airport symbol*]   (OAG)

MBH........ Megyei Begyujtesi Hivatal [*County Crop Collection Office*]   (HU)

mbH .... Mit Beschraenkter Haftung [*With Limited Liability*] [*German*]   (EG)

MBH........ Movimiento de Bases Hayistas [*Movement of Hayista Bases*] [*Peru*] [*Political party*]   (PPW)

MBH........ Muzej Bosne i Hercegovine [*Museum of Bosnia and Hercegovina*]   (YU)

MBHB...... Malaysian Batik and Handicrafts Bureau   (ML)

MBI......... Biological Immersion Microscope   (RU)

MBI......... International Institute of Bibliography [*1895-1931*]   (RU)

MBI......... Maritime Bank of Israel   (BJA)

MBI......... Mbeya [*Tanzania*] [*Airport symbol*] [*Obsolete*]   (OAG)

MBI......... Military Board Instruction

MBIA .... Malaysian Book Importers Association   (EAIO)

MBIBTC ... Malting and Brewing Industry Barley Technical Committee [*Australia*]

MBiDP ...... Ministry of the Paper and Woodworking Industries   (RU)

MBIFCT.... Mgahinga and Bwindi Inpenetrable Forest Conservation Trust   (ECON)

MBIS........ International Bank for Economic Cooperation   (BU)

MBIS........ Molecular Biological Information Service [*CSIRO*] [*Australia*]   (PDAA)

MBJ.......... Montego Bay [*Jamaica*] [*Airport symbol*]   (OAG)

MBJT .... Grand Turk [*Turks and Caicos Islands*] [*ICAO location identifier*]   (ICLI)

MBK .... International Congress of Biochemistry   (RU)

MBK .... International Container Bureau [*ICB*]   (RU)

MBK .... Madchen-Bibel-Kreise [*Bible Reading Circles*] [*German*]

MBK .... Maedchen-Bibel-Kreise [*Bible Reading Circles*] [*German*]

MBK .... Magyar Beke-Kongresszus [*Hungarian Peace Congress*]   (HU)

MBK .... Milli Birligi Kurulu [*National Unity Committee*] [*MBG*] [*See also*]   (TU)

Mbl .... Maandblad van de Centrale Raad van Beroep [*Benelux*]   (BAS)

MBL .... Malayan Breweries Ltd. [*Malaysia*]

MBL .... Medical Biological Laboratory [*Netherlands*]

MBL .... Medisch Biologisch Laboratorium [*Medical Biological Laboratory, Netherlands Central Organization for Applied Natural Scientific Research*] [*Research center*]

MBL .... Movimiento Bolivia Libre [*Political party*]   (EY)

MBL .... Steinitz (Heinz) Marine Biology Laboratory at Elat [*Israel*] [*Research center*]   (IRC)

MblBdorg ... Mededelingenblad Bedrijfsorganisatie [*Benelux*]   (BAS)

MblBelrecht ... Maandblad voor Belastingrecht [*Benelux*]   (BAS)

Mb Lbs ...... Mededelingenblad Landbouwschap [*Benelux*]   (BAS)

MBLE........ Manufacture Belge de Lampes et de Materiel Electronique [*Belgium*]   (PDAA)

MBM........ Majlis Belia Malaysia [*Malaysian Youth Council*]   (ML)

MBM........ Miedzykolkowe Bazy Maszynowe [*Inter-Circle Machine Bases*] [*Agriculture*]   (POL)

MBM........ Missao de Biologia Maritima, Junta de Investigacoes do Ultramar

MBMC ...... Middle Caicos [*Turks and Caicos Islands*] [*ICAO location identifier*]   (ICLI)

MBMiO..... Ministerstwo Budownictwa Miast i Osiedli [*Ministry of City and Settlement Construction*] (POL)
MBMU...... Middle Belt Mineworkers' Union [*Nigeria*]
MBNC....... North Caicos [*Turks and Caicos Islands*] [*ICAO location identifier*] (ICLI)
MBO......... Mamburao [*Philippines*] [*Airport symbol*] (OAG)
MBO......... Musterbetriebsordnung [*Model Factory Regulations, Model Shop Rules*] (EG)
MBOG...... International Office of Public Hygiene [*1907-1946*] (RU)
MBOR....... Miedzynarodowy Bank Odbudowy i Rozwoju [*International Bank for Reconstruction and Development*] [*Poland*]
mbp .... Ammunition Supply Workshop (RU)
MBP .... International Biological Program (RU)
MBP .... Mathematischer Beratungs-und Programmierungsdienst [*German*] (ADPT)
MBP .... Miedzynarodowe Biuro Pracy [*International Labor Office*] [*Poland*]
MBP .... Miejska Biblioteka Publiczna [*Municipal Public Library*] [*Poland*]
MBP .... Milli Birlik Partisi [*National Unity Party*] [*UBP Cyprus*] [*See also*] (TU)
MBP .... Ministerstwo Bezpieczenstwa Publicznego [*Ministry of Public Security*] (POL)
MBP .... Ministerstwo Budownictwa Przemyslowego [*Ministry of Industrial Construction*] (POL)
MBP .... Moscow Trade-Union Office (RU)
MBPI........ Pine Cay [*Turks and Caicos Islands*] [*ICAO location identifier*] (ICLI)
MBPM ...... Maurice Bishop Patriotic Movement [*Grenada*]
MBPP....... Middle Belt Peoples' Party
MBPP....... Movimento Brasileiro dos Partidarios da Paz [*Brazilian Movement of Peace Partisans*] (LA)
MBPP....... Movimiento Blanco Popular y Progresista [*National Action Movement*] [*Uruguay*] [*Political party*] (EY)
MBPV....... Providenciales [*Turks and Caicos Islands*] [*ICAO location identifier*] (ICLI)
MBQ......... Marine Board of Queensland [*Australia*]
MBQ......... Mbarara [*Uganda*] [*Airport symbol*] (OAG)
MBQ......... Medical Board of Queensland [*Australia*]
mbr............ Bridge Brigade (RU)
MBR......... Intercontinental Ballistic Missile (BU)
MBR......... International Labor Office [*ILO*] (RU)
MBR......... Maandblad voor Berechtiging en Reclassering van Volwassenen en Kinderen [*Benelux*] (BAS)
Mbr........... Member (PWGL)
MBR......... Mineracoes Brasileiras Reunidas [*Brazilian Mines Association*] (LA)
Mbr........... Mitropolija Broj [*Metropolis Number*] [*Orthodox Eastern Church Serbian*] (YU)
MBR......... Naval Short-Range Reconnaissance Aircraft (RU)
MBRET...... Middle Breton [*Language, etc.*]
MBRKh...... International Office of Revolutionary Artists (RU)
MBRL....... International Office of Revolutionary Literature (RU)
MBRR ...... International Bank for Reconstruction and Development [*IBRD*] (RU)
MBRR ...... Mezhdunarodni Bank Rekonstruktsii i Razvitiia
MBS.......... Biological Stereomicroscope (RU)
MBS.......... Boring and Polesetting Machine (RU)
MBS.......... Intercontinental Ballistic Missile (RU)
MBS.......... International Union of Biochemistry [*IUB*] (RU)
MBS.......... Mano Blanca Salvadorena [*Salvadoran White Hand*] (LA)
MBS.......... Market Basket Survey [*Business term*]
MBS.......... Master Bibliographic System
MBS.......... Medborgerlig Samling [*Citizens Rally*] [*Sweden*] [*Political party*] (PPE)
MBS.......... Medicare Benefits Schedule [*Australia*]
MBS.......... Methodist Boys School (ML)
MBS.......... Ministerio de Bienestar Social [*Ministry of Social Welfare*] [*Nicaragua*] (LA)
MBS.......... Mozambique Bible Society
MBSA....... Medical Board of South Australia
MBSA....... Montserrat Boy Scout Association (EAIO)
MBSA....... Museum Board of South Australia
MBSC....... Major Bricklaying Sub-Contractors Association [*Australia*]
MBSC....... South Caicos [*Turks and Caicos Islands*] [*ICAO location identifier*] (ICLI)
MBSHC..... Mediterranean and Black Sea Hydrographic Commission (MSC)
MBSQ ...... Music Broadcasting Society of Queensland [*Australia*]
MBST....... Magnetbandsteuerung [*German*] (ADPT)
MBSY....... Salt Cay [*Turks and Caicos Islands*] [*ICAO location identifier*] (ICLI)
MBT......... International Labor Bureau (BU)
MBT......... Local Remote-Control Unit (RU)
MBT......... Magyar Beke-Tanacs [*Hungarian Peace Council*] (HU)
MBT......... Magyar Biofizikai Tarsasag [*An association*] [*Hungary*] (EAIO)
MBT......... Magyar Biologiai Tarsasag [*Hungary*] (SLS)

MbT.......... Mariborska Tiskarna [*Maribor Printers*] (YU)
MBT.......... Masbate [*Philippines*] [*Airport symbol*] (OAG)
MBT......... Met Betrekking Tot [*With Reference To*] [*Afrikaans*]
MBTI........ Markaz Buhuth al-Taleen al-Islami [*Saudi Arabia*] (EAIO)
MBTK ...... Mobile Tubular Tower Crane (RU)
MB-TKA ... Motor Torpedo Boat Tender (RU)
MBU......... Mbambanakira [*Solomon Islands*] [*Airport symbol*] (OAG)
MBU......... Medical Reinforcement Brigade (RU)
MBU......... Moscow Basin Administration (RU)
M Buit........ Minister van Buitenlandsche Zaken [*Benelux*] (BAS)
MBV......... International Time Bureau (RU)
MBV......... Marine Board of Victoria [*Australia*]
MBV......... Medical Board of Victoria [*Australia*]
MBV......... Mistni Bezpecnostni Vybor [*Local Security Committee*] (CZ)
MBVR ...... Local Clearinghouse (RU)
MBVV ...... International Wine and Vine Office [*IWO*] (RU)
MBW........ Miedzynarodowe Biuro Wychowania [*International Education Bureau*] [*Poland*]
MBW........ Moorabbin [*Airport symbol*]
MBX......... Maribor [*Former Yugoslavia*] [*Airport symbol*] (OAG)
MC............ Aermacchi SpA [*Italy*] [*ICAO aircraft manufacturer identifier*] (ICAO)
MC............ Alliance Nationale des Mutualites Chretiennes [*French*] (BAS)
MC............ CAA Flying Unit [*British*] [*ICAO designator*] (ICDA)
MC............ Macerata [*Car registration plates*] [*Italian*]
MC............ Maggior Consiglio [*Grand Council*] [*Italian*]
MC............ Magistrates' Court [*Legal term*] [*Australia*]
MC............ Manganese Centre (EA)
MC............ Maps and Charts [*Interservice*] [*NATO*]
MC............ Marche Commun [*France*] (FLAF)
MC............ Marque de Commerce [*Trademark*]
MC............ Maschinencode [*German*] (ADPT)
MC............ Mathematisch Centrum [*Netherlands*] (PDAA)
MC............ McAuley College [*Australia*]
Mc............ Megaciclo [*Megacycle*] [*Portuguese*]
MC............ Memoire Centrale [*French*] (ADPT)
MC............ Mercado Comun [*Common Market*] [*Spanish*]
Mc............ Metre Cube [*Cubic Meter*] [*French*] (MTD)
mc............ Metru Cub [*Cubic Meter*] (RO)
M/c............ Mi Cuenta [*My Account, My Debit*] [*Business term*] [*Spanish*]
m-c............ Miesiac [*Month*] [*Poland*]
MC............ Military Committee [*NATO*]
MC............ Milli Cephesi [*National Front (Government)*] (TU)
m/c............ Minha Carta [*My Respects*] [*Correspondence*] [*Portuguese*]
m/c............ Minha Conta [*My Regards*] [*Correspondence*] [*Portuguese*]
MC............ Mining Corporation
MC............ Ministere des Colonies
MC............ Ministere du Congo Belge et du Ruanda-Urundi
MC............ Minore Conventuale [*Italian*]
MC............ Monaco [*International automobile identification tag*]
MC............ Monaco [*ANSI two-letter standard code*] (CNC)
MC............ Monako [*Monaco*] [*Poland*]
m/c............ Mon Compte [*My Account*] [*French*] [*Business term*]
MC............ Moneda Corriente [*Current Money*] [*Spanish*]
MC............ Moore Theological College [*Australia*]
MC............ Morse Code
M/c............ Motorni Camac [*Motor Boat*] (YU)
M/c............ Motorni Coln [*Motor Boat*] (YU)
MC............ Muan Chon [*Mass Party*] [*Political party*]
MC............ Mycenaean Commission [*Austria*] (EAIO)
MCA......... Malaysian Chinese Association [*Political party*] (PPW)
MCA......... Marketing Confederation of Australia
MCA......... Master of Creative Arts
MCA......... Media Council of Australia (ADA)
MCA......... Medical Consumers Association [*Australia*]
MCA......... Member of Constituent Assembly
mca............ Miesiaca [*Month*] [*Poland*]
MCA......... Mining Corporation of Australia Ltd. (ADA)
MCA......... Monetary Compensation Amount [*European Community*]
MCA......... Motor Coach Australia
MCA......... Mouvement Cooperatif Algerien [*Algerian Cooperative Movement*] (AF)
MCA......... Museum of Contemporary Art [*Sydney, Australia*]
MCA......... Muslim Committee of Action [*Mauritania*]
MCA......... Mutuelle Centrale d'Assurances [*France*] (EY)
MCAA ...... Master Concreters Association of Australia
MCAA ...... Medical Consumers Association of Australia (ADA)
MCAA ...... Military Civil Affairs Administration [*Netherlands*] [*World War II*]
MCAAB .... Moorabbin Citizens' Advice and Aid Bureau [*Australia*]
MCAE .... Mitchell College of Advanced Education [*Australia*] (ADA)
MCAF....... Mauritius Co-Operative Agricultural Federation (EAIO)
McAl......... McEnearny/Alstons [*Trinidad*]
Mcal.......... Megakaloria, Termia [*Megacalorie, Ton Calorie, Therm*] [*Poland*]

MCANSW ... Medical Consumers' Association of New South Wales [*Australia*]

MCASA..... Master Cleaners' Association of South Australia [*Australia*]

MCAT .... Maritime Central Analysis Team [*NATO*]   (NATG)

MCB .... Management Center do Brasil [*Sao Paulo, Brazil*]   (LAA)

MCB .... Metric Conversion Board [*Australia*]   (ADA)

MCB .... Metropolitan Cemeteries Board [*Western Australia*]

MCB .... Music Confederation of Belgium   (EAIO)

MCB .... Muslim Commercial Bank [*Pakistan*]

MCBA .... Malaysian Commercial Banks Association   (ML)

MCBSF ..... Mixed Commission for Black Sea Fisheries [*FAO*]   (ASF)

MCC .... Macquarie Commercial College [*Australia*]

MCC .... Malawi Correspondence College

MCC .... Manufacture Camerounaise de Caoutchouc

MCC .... Manufacture de la Couture Camerounaise

MCC .... Maoist Communist Center [*India*]

MCC .... Melanesian Council of Churches

MCC .... Member of Central Committee

MCC .... Mercado Comun Centroamericano [*Central American Common Market*] [*Use CACM*]   (LA)

MCC .... Military Co-Ordinating Committee

MCC .... Mine Countermeasures Command and Support Ship [*Navy*]

MCC .... Ministerial Council for Corporations [*Australia*]

MCC .... Moslem Construction Company Ltd.

MCC .... Movimiento Civico Cristiano [*Civic Christian Movement*] [*Uruguay*]   (LA)

MCC .... Movimiento Conciencia Catolica [*Catholic Awareness Movement*] [*Mexico*]   (LA)

MCC .... Mozambique Chamber of Commerce   (EAIO)

MCCA .... Conference of the Methodist Church in the Caribbean and the Americas   (EAIO)

MCCA .... Malacca [*Malaysia*]   (ML)

MCCA .... Marche Commun Centramericain [*Central American Common Market - CACM*] [*French*]

MCCA .... Muslim Community Cooperative of Australia

MCCC .... Ministerial Consultative Committee on Curriculum [*Queensland, Australia*]

MCCF........ Mixed Commission for Cooperation in Marine Fishing   (MSC)

MCCI........ Mauritius Chamber of Commerce and Industry   (EAIO)

MCCI........ Moto-Club de Cote-D'Ivoire

MCCM ...... Mohanga Consolidated Copper Mines [*Zimbabwe*]

MCCNSW ... Mini Car Club of New South Wales [*Australia*]

MCCO .... Mercado Comun del Caribe Oriental   (LAA)

MCCOC .... Model Criminal Code Officers' Committee [*Australia*]

MCCOPO ... Mennonite Central Committee Overseas Peace Office   (EAIO)

MCCS........ Magistrates' Court Civil System [*Australia*]

MCCS........ Military Committee in Chiefs of Staff Session [*NATO*]   (NATG)

MCCS........ Ministry of Cooperation, Commerce, and Supply [*Sudan*]

MCCSP ..... Ministerial Council on Common Services Provision [*Australia*]

MCCTU .... Mongolian Central Council of Trade Unions

MCD .... Massimo Comune Divisore [*Highest Common Factor*] [*Italian*]

MCD......... Melbourne College of Divinity [*Australia*]   (ADA)

MCD .... Movimento Contra a Ditadura [*Movement Against Dictatorship*] [*Brazil*]   (LA)

MCD......... Movimiento por el Cambio Democratico [*Mexico*] [*Political party*]   (EY)

MCD......... Municipal Corporation of Delhi [*India*]

MCDAA .... Member of the Company Directors' Association of Australia

MCDN ...... Movimiento Civico Democratico Nacional [*Ecuador*]   (LAA)

MCDS .... Ministerial Council on Drug Strategy [*Australia*]

MCE .... Malayan Certificate of Education   (ML)

MCE .... Management Centre/Europe

MCE .... Melbourne Corn Exchange [*Australia*]

MCE .... Mercado Comun Europeo [*European Common Market*]   (LA)

MCE .... Military Corrective Establishment

MCE .... Ministerio de Comercio Exterior [*Ministry of Foreign Trade*] [*Portuguese*]   (WER)

MCE .... Moscow Commodity Exchange [*Russian Federation*]   (EY)

MCE .... Movimiento Civil Ecuatoriano [*Ecuadorean Civil Movement*] (LA)

MCE .... Movimiento Comunista de Espana [*Communist Movement of Spain*]   (WER)

MCE .... Mwangi Coffee Exporters Co. [*Kenya*]

MCECEI ... Ministerul Comertului Exterior si Cooperarii Economice Internationale [*Ministry of Foreign Trade and International Economic Cooperation*]   (RO)

MCES........ Major City Earth Stations [*Australia*]

MCEWG ... Multinational Communication-Electronics Working Group [*Formerly, SGCEC*] [*NATO*]   (NATG)

MCF .... Medical and Commercial Finance Corp. Ltd. [*Australia*]

MCF .... Missions Church Federation

MCF .... Multilateral Clearing Facility [*Caribbean Community and Common Market*]   (EY)

MCFI........ Mauritius Chemical and Fertilizer Industry   (AF)

MCG......... Movimiento Comunista de Galicia [*Communist Movement of Galicia*] [*Spanish*]   (WER)

MCG .... Movimiento Cooperativista Guatemalteco [*Guatemalan Cooperationist Movement*]   (LA)

MCh.......... Clockwork   (RU)

MCh.......... Interval Frequency   (BU)

MCH......... Machala [*Ecuador*] [*Airport symbol*]   (OAG)

m/ch.......... Machine/Hour   (BU)

MCh.......... Materiel   (RU)

MCH......... Maternal Child Health

MCh.......... Meridional Parts   (RU)

MCH......... Morska Centrala Handlowa [*Maritime Trade Center*]   (POL)

MCHAP .... Maternal and Child Health Association of the Philippines   (EAIO)

m/chas .... Machine/Hour   (BU)

MChE........ Magyar Chemikusok Egyesulete [*Association of Hungarian Chemists*]   (HU)

Mche......... Marche [*Market*] [*Military map abbreviation World War I*] [*French*]   (MTD)

MCHFP..... Maternity and Child Health and Family Planning Project [*Sudan*]

MChK .... Moscow Extraordinary Commission for Combating Counterrevolution and Sabotage [*1917-1922*]   (RU)

MChM....... Ministry of Ferrous Metallurgy   (RU)

MChP........ Ministerstvo Chemickeho Prumyslu [*Ministry of the Chemical Industry*]   (CZ)

MChZ........ Method of Frequency Sounding   (RU)

MChZ........ Moravske Chemicke Zavody [*Moravian Chemical Plants*]   (CZ)

MChZ........ Moscow Watchmaking Plant   (RU)

MCI .... Maya Carga Internacional SA de CV [*Mexico*] [*ICAO designator*]   (FAAC)

MCI .... Ministerio de Comercio Interior [*Ministry of Domestic Commerce*] [*Portuguese*]   (WER)

MCI .... Ministerul Comertului Interior [*Ministry of Domestic Trade*]   (RO)

MCI .... Ministerul Constructiilor Industriale [*Ministry of Industrial Construction*]   (RO)

MCI .... Ministry of Commerce and Industry [*Korea*]

MCI .... Mitsubishi Chemical Industries [*Japan*]

MCI .... Mother and Child International [*Switzerland*]   (EAIO)

MCI .... Movimiento Campesino Independiente [*Independent Peasants Movement*] [*Guatemala*]   (LA)

MCIArb..... Member of the Chartered Institute of Arbitrators [*Australia*]

Mcin.......... Medecin [*Doctor*] [*Military*] [*French*]   (MTD)

MCInd .... Ministerul Constructiilor Industriale [*Ministry of Industrial Construction*]   (RO)

MCIT .... Member of the Chartered Institute of Transport [*South Africa*]   (AA)

MCJ.......... Maicao [*Colombia*] [*Airport symbol*]   (OAG)

MCK .... Mezinarodni Cerveny Kriz [*International Red Cross*]   (CZ)

MCK .... Miedzynarodowy Czerwony Krzyz [*International Red Cross*] [*Poland*]

MCKS........ Makedonski Centralen Kooperativen Sojuz [*Macedonian Central Cooperative Union*]   (YU)

MCKS........ Mednarodni Center za Kemijske Studije [*Samoa*]   (EAIO)

MCL .... Mauritius Confederation of Labor   (AF)

MCL .... Mercantile Credits Limited [*Australia*]   (ADA)

MCL .... Ministering Children's League [*Australia*]

MCL .... Movimiento Comunista Liberatorio [*Liberatory Communist Movement*] [*Mexico*]   (LA)

MCLA .... Mercado Comun Latinoamericano [*Latin American Common Market*]   (LAA)

MCLE........ Mandatory Continuing Legal Education [*Australia*]

MCLN .... Mouvement Centrafricain de Liberation Nationale [*Central African Movement for National Liberation*]   (PD)

MCLN .... Movimiento Civico Latino Nacional [*Colorado*]

MCM......... Heli-Air-Monaco [*ICAO designator*]   (FAAC)

MCM......... Marche Commun Maghrebin

MCM......... Military Committee Memorandum [*NATO*]   (NATG)

mcm........... Million Cubic Metres   (OMWE)

MCM......... Minimo Comune Multiplo [*Lowest Common Multiple*] [*Italian*]

MCM......... Mobile Community Management Team [*Australia*]

MCM......... Monte Carlo [*Monaco*] [*Airport symbol*]   (OAG)

MCM......... Movimiento Catorce de Mayo [*14 May Movement*] [*Paraguay*]   (LA)

MCMCAT ... Mine Countermeasures Catamaran [*Military*]

MCMG....... Military Committee Meteorological Group [*NATO*]   (NATG)

MCN......... Mac Dan Aviation Corp. [*ICAO designator*]   (FAAC)

MCN......... Methanol Chemie Nederland VOF

MCN......... Mouvement Congolais National [*Zaire*] [*Political party*]   (EY)

MCN......... Movimiento de Conciliacion Nacional [*National Conciliation Movement*] [*Dominican Republic*] [*Political party*]   (PPW)

MCn.......... Triturated Gun Powder [*Symbol*] [*French*]   (MTD)

McNAA ..... McNair Anderson Associates Proprietary Ltd. [*Australia*]   (ADA)

MCNL....... Military Committee of National Liberation [*Mali*] [*Political party*]   (PPW)

MCO......... Aerolineas Marcos SA de CV [*Mexico*] [*ICAO designator*]   (FAAC)

mco............ Marco [*March*] [*Portuguese*]   (GPO)
MCO........... Monaco [*ANSI three-letter standard code*]   (CNC)
Mcoletti ..... Maiuscoletti [*Lowercase Letters*] [*Italian*]
Mcoli.......... Maiuscoli [*Capital Letters*] [*Italian*]
MComSc.... Master of Computer Science
mcos .... Marcos [*Marks*] [*Spanish*]
MCoT .... Mass Communication Organization of Thailand
MCP .... Macapa [*Brazil*] [*Airport symbol*]   (OAG)
MCP .... Malaria Control Plan   (ML)
MCP .... Malawi Congress Party [*Nyasaland*] [*Political party*]   (PPW)
MCP .... Malayan Communist Party [*Political party*]
MCP .... Martinique Communist Party [*Political party*]
MCP .... Mision Conjunta de Programacion para Centroamerica [*Guatemala*]   (LAA)
MCP .... Mouvement Chretien pour la Paix [*Christian Movement for Peace - CMP*] [*Brussels, Belgium*]   (EAIO)
MCP .... Movimento de Cultura Popular [*People's Culture Movement*] [*Brazil*]   (LA)
MCP .... Movimiento Civico Popular [*Panama*] [*Political party*]   (EY)
MCPA .... Member of the College of Pathologists of Australia   (ADA)
MCPH....... McPherson [*Botanical region*] [*Australia*]
MCPS....... Military Committee in Permanent Session [*NATO*]   (NATG)
MCPS....... Ministry of Commerce and People's Supply [*Burkina Faso*]
MCPT........ Maritime Central Planning Team [*NATO*]   (NATG)
MCQ......... Macquarie Island [*Australia*] [*Geomagnetic observatory code*]
MCR .... Monacair-Agusta [*Monaco*] [*ICAO designator*]   (FAAC)
MCR .... Movimiento Comunista Revolucionario [*Revolutionary Communist Movement*] [*Brazil*]   (LA)
MCR .... Movimiento Campesino Revolucionario [*Revolutionary Peasant Movement*] [*Chile*]   (LA)
MCR .... Movimiento Cristiano Revolucionario [*Revolutionary Christian Movement*] [*Nicaragua*]   (LA)
MCR .... Mullins, Clarke & Ralph [*Australia*]   (ADA)
MCRA ...... Member of the College of Radiologists of Australasia   (ADA)
MCRL....... Movimiento Costa Rica Libre [*Free Costa Rican Movement*]   (LA)
MCS .... Maandblad Centraal Bureau Statistiek [*Benelux*]   (BAS)
MCS .... Malayan Civil Service
MCS .... Maritime Communication Subsystem [*INTELSAT/ INMARSAT*]
MCS .... Ministerio da Comunicacao Social [*Ministry of Mass Communication*] [*Portuguese*]   (WER)
MCS .... Movimento Convergencia Socialista [*Socialist Convergence Movement*] [*Brazil*]   (LA)
MCS .... Movimiento Cristiano Social [*Ecuador*]   (LAA)
MCSA....... Malaysian Civil Service Association   (ML)
MCSA....... Mountain Club of South Africa
MCSD ...... Member of the Chartered Society of Designers [*Australia*]
MCSP....... Mesic Ceskoslovensko-Sovetskeho Pratelstvi [*Czechoslovak-Soviet Friendship Month*]   (CZ)
MCSS....... Marine Climatological Summaries Scheme [*World Meteorological Organization*] [*United Nations*]   (DUND)
MCSSG .... Military Committee Special Study Group [*NATO*]   (NATG)
MCSZ........ Magyarorszagi Cionista Szovetseg [*Zionist Federation in Hungary*]   (HU)
MCT .... Manufacture de Cigarettes du Tchad
MCT .... Missao de Combate as Tripanosomiases
MCT .... Mission de Controle du Transgabonais
MCT .... Mobile Community Treatment Service [*Australia*]
MCT .... Muscat [*Oman*] [*Airport symbol*]   (OAG)
m/cta......... Mi Cuenta [*My Account, My Debit*] [*Spanish*]
MCTA ...... Mild Coffee Trade Association
MCTBA..... Mercado de Cereales a Termino de Buenos Aires SA [*Argentina*]   (DSCA)
MCTC .... Movimiento Campesino Tupaj Catari [*Bolivia*] [*Political party*]   (PPW)
m/cte .... Mon Compte [*My Account*] [*French*] [*Business term*]
MCTLA..... Motor Car Traders' Licensing Authority [*Victoria, Australia*]
MCTS........ Ministerial Correspondence Tracking System [*Australia*]
MCTU .... Mauritius Confederation of Trade Unions   (AF)
MCU .... Meru Citizens Union
MCU.......... Mikrocomputer-Universalkarte [*German*]   (ADPT)
MCU.......... Mladez Ceskoslovenskych Unitaru [*Czechoslovak Unitarian Youth Group*]   (CZ)
MCU.......... Mountain Club of Uganda   (EAIO)
MCU.......... Movimiento Civico Unitario [*United Civic Movement*] [*Chile*]   (LA)
MCUPA .... Medical Committee Under the Poisons Act [*Australia*]
MCV .... Manufacturing Council of Victoria [*Australia*]
MCV .... Movimiento Comunista Vascongado [*Basque Communist Movement*] [*Spanish*]   (WER)
MCWAP.... Maternity and Child Welfare Association of Pakistan   (EAIO)
MCWCS.... Ministerial Conference of West and Central African States on Maritime Transportation [*See also CMEAOC*] [*Abidjan, Ivory Coast*]   (EAIO)
MCY .... Maroochydore [*Australia*] [*Airport symbol*]   (OAG)

MCYL........ Malayan Communist Youth League [*South Thailand, supporting CTO*]   (ML)
MCZ.......... Maceio [*Brazil*] [*Airport symbol*]   (OAG)
m cz .... Mala Czestotliwosc [*Low Frequency*] [*Poland*]
MD............. Air Madagascar
MD............. Differential Manometer, Differential Pressure Gauge   (RU)
MD............. Doctor of Medicine   (PWGL)
MD............. Dose Rate   (RU)
MD............. Le Monde Diplomatique [*France*]   (FLAF)
md .... Maand [*Month*] [*Afrikaans*]
m/d............ Maande na Datum [*Months after Date*] [*Afrikaans*]
Md .... Madrid [*Capital of Spain*]
MD............. Magnetdrahtspeicher [*German*]   (ADPT)
MD............. Magnetic Disk   (RU)
MD............. Magnetographic Defectoscope   (RU)
MD............. Main Droite [*With the Right Hand*] [*Music*]
M-D........... Maiz Dulce [*Race of maize*] [*Mexico*]
MD............. Marchand [*Merchant, Trader*] [*French*]
MD............. Maryland   (IDIG)
MD............. Masarykovy Domovy v Krci [*Masaryk Homes for the Aged in Krc*]   (CZ)
MD............. Masarykuv Dul [*Masaryk Mine*] [*Tynec*]   (CZ)
MD............. Matica Dalmatinska [*A Dalmatian literary and publishing society*] [*Zadar*]   (YU)
MD............. Maximal-Einzel-Dosis [*Maximum Single Dose*] [*German*]   (GCA)
MD............. Mechanized Division   (RU)
MD............. Medical Documentation   (RU)
Md .... Megadina [*Megadynes*] [*Portuguese*]
MD............. Melayu Di-Raja [*Royal Malay*]   (ML)
m/d............ Meses de Data [*Day of the Month*] [*Portuguese*]
MD............. Mestske Divadlo [*Municipal Theater*]   (CZ)
MD............. Meteorologischer Dienst [*Meteorological Service*]   (EG)
MD............. Mevcut Degil [*Not Available*]   (TU)
MD............. Middle Dutch [*Language, etc.*]
Md .... Milliarde [*Billion*] [*German*]
MD............. Mine Detonator   (RU)
MD............. Mine Surveying   (RU)
MD............. Ministerio de Defesa [*Ministry of Defense*] [*Portuguese*]   (WER)
MD............. Ministerstvo Dopravy [*Ministry of Transportation*]   (CZ)
MD............. Minister van Defense [*Minister of Defense*] [*Benelux*]   (BAS)
MD............. Ministry of Supply [*Obsolete*]   (BU)
MD............. Mitteldruck [*Intermediate Pressure*] [*German*]
md .... Mobilization Documents   (RU)
MD............. Modulator   (RU)
m/d............ Mois de Date [*French*]
MD............. Moroccan Dinar [*Monetary unit*]
md .... Mortar Battalion   (RU)
MD............. Movimiento Desarrollista [*Movement for Development*] [*Venezuela*]   (LA)
Md .... Mudur [*or Mudurlik*] [*Director or Directorate*]   (TU)
Md .... Mudurlugu [*Management*] [*Turkey*]   (CED)
MD............. Muhendis Diplomasi [*Engineering qualification*] [*Turkey*]
MD............. Muito Digno [*Very Worthy*] [*Portuguese*]
MD............. Mujeres Democraticas [*Democratic Women*] [*Spanish*]   (WER)
md .... Placing of Troops   (RU)
Md .... Range Scale [*Artillery*]   (RU)
MD............. Road Mine   (RU)
MDA......... Magen David Adom [*Israel's Red Cross Service*]
MDA......... Maltese Diabetes Association   (EAIO)
MDA......... Mandarian Airlines [*ICAO designator*]   (FAAC)
MDA......... Methyl Diamphetamine
MDA......... Metropolitan Development Agency
MDA.......... Mouvement pour la Democratie en Algerie [*Algeria*] [*Political party*]   (MENA)
MDAN....... Angelina, Cotui [*Dominican Republic*] [*ICAO location identifier*]   (ICLI)
MDANSW ... Muscular Dystrophy Association of New South Wales [*Australia*]
MDASA .... Muscular Dystrophy Association of South Australia
Mdat .... Mandat [*Order*] [*Business term*] [*French*]
MDAV....... Muscular Dystrophy Association of Victoria [*Australia*]
MDB......... Medical Disciplinary Board [*Iran*]   (ME)
MDB......... Mitglied des Deutschen Bundestages [*Member of the German Federal Parliament*]
MDB......... Movimento Democratico Brasileiro [*Brazilian Democratic Movement*] [*Political party*]   (PPW)
MDB......... Murray-Darling Basin [*Australia*]
MDB......... Naval Long-Range Bomber   (RU)
MDBH....... Barahona [*Dominican Republic*] [*ICAO location identifier*]   (ICLI)
MDBI .... Murray Darling Basin Initiative [*Australia*]
MDBMC.... Murray Darling Basin Ministerial Council [*Australia*]
MDBS........ Mikro-Datenbankmanagementsystem [*German*]   (ADPT)
MDC.......... Maison du Cycle
MDC.......... Malawi Development Corporation

MDC......... Malta Development Corporation   (GEA)

MDC......... Management Development Center [*Sudan*]   (IRC)

MDC......... Management Development Centre [*Australia*]

MDC......... Marine Diamond Corporation

MDC......... Menado [*Indonesia*] [*Airport symbol*]   (OAG)

MDC......... Motor Dealers' Council [*New South Wales, Australia*]

MDC......... Movimiento Democrata Cristiano [*Christian Democratic Movement*]   (LA)

MDC......... Movimiento Democratico del Campesinado [*Democratic Movement of Rural Workers*] [*Spanish*]   (WER)

MDC......... Mwananchi Development Corporation

Mdch........ Maedchen [*German*]

MDCO....... Consuelo, San Pedro De Macoris [*Dominican Republic*] [*ICAO location identifier*]   (ICLI)

MDCR....... Cabo Rojo [*Dominican Republic*] [*ICAO location identifier*]   (ICLI)

MDCS....... Magyar Divatcsarnok [*Hungarian Fashion Store*]   (HU)

MDCS....... Santo Domingo [*Dominican Republic*] [*ICAO location identifier*]   (ICLI)

MDCZ....... Constanza [*Dominican Republic*] [*ICAO location identifier*]   (ICLI)

MDD......... Digital Computer   (RU)

MDD......... Mezinarodni Den Deti [*International Children's Day*]   (CZ)

MDD......... Miedzynarodowy Dzien Dziecka [*International Children's Day*]   (POL)

MDD......... Milli Demokratik Devrimciler [*National Democratic Revolutionaries*]   (TU)

MDD......... Ministry of State Supply [*Obsolete*]   (BU)

MDD......... Mouvement Democratique Dahomeen [*Dahomean Democratic Movement*] [*Political party*]

MDDC....... Motor Dealers' Disputes Council [*Australia*]

MDDJ....... Dajabon [*Dominican Republic*] [*ICAO location identifier*]   (ICLI)

MDDSZ .... Magyarorszagi Delszlavok Demokratikus Szovetsege [*The Democratic Association of Southern Slavs in Hungary*]   (HU)

MDE......... Magnetic Diode Element   (RU)

Mde........... Marchande [*Merchant, Trader*] [*French*]   (MTD)

MDE......... Medellin [*Colombia*] [*Airport symbol*]   (OAG)

MDEN....... Enriquillo [*Dominican Republic*] [*ICAO location identifier*]   (ICLI)

M desReq ... Maitre des Requetes [*France*]   (FLAF)

MDesSt ..... Master of Design Studies

MDF .... International Road Federation [*IRF*]   (RU)

MDF .... Les Meubles de France [*Abidjan*]

MDF .... Magyar Demokrata Forum [*Hungarian Democratic Forum*] [*Political party*]   (EY)

MDF .... Mednarodni Denarni Fond [*International Monetary Fund*]   (YU)

MDF .... Micro Defect Free

MDF .... Midtfly Aps [*Denmark*] [*ICAO designator*]   (FAAC)

MDF .... Mid-West Democratic Front

MdF .... Ministerium der Finanzen [*Ministry of Finance*]   (EG)

MDF .... Movement for Democracy in Fiji

MDFKS...... Remote-Control Scale Photoelectric Copying System   (RU)

MDFM ...... Mezinarodni Demokraticka Federace Mladeze [*World Federation of Democratic Youth*]   (CZ)

MDFV .... Magyar Diafilmgyarto Vallalat [*Hungarian Filmstrip Production Enterprise*]   (HU)

MDFZ .... Mezinarodni Demokraticka Federace Zen [*Women's International Democratic Federatin - WIDF*]   (CZ)

MDFZh ..... Women's International Democratic Federation [*WIDF*]   (RU)

MDG......... Air Madagascar, Societe Nationale Malgache de Transports Aeriens [*ICAO designator*]   (FAAC)

MDG......... Madagascar [*ANSI three-letter standard code*]   (CNC)

MDG......... Movimento Democratico da Guine

Mdg........... Muendung [*Mouth*] [*German*]   (GCA)

MDGA....... Guerra [*Dominican Republic*] [*ICAO location identifier*]   (ICLI)

MDH .... Mean Dominant Height

MDHC....... Melbourne Diocesan Historical Commission [*Australia*]

MDHE....... Herrera [*Dominican Republic*] [*ICAO location identifier*]   (ICLI)

MDHY ...... Higuey [*Dominican Republic*] [*ICAO location identifier*]   (ICLI)

MDI.......... Makurdi [*Nigeria*] [*Airport symbol*]   (OAG)

MdI........... Ministerium des Inneren [*Ministry of the Interior*]   (EG)

MDI........... Mouvement pour la Democratie et l'Independance [*Movement for Democracy and Independence*] [*Central Africa*]   (PD)

MDI........... Movimiento Democratico Independiente [*Independent Democratic Movement*] [*Venezuela*]   (LA)

MDIA .... Mouvement pour la Defense des Interets de l'Angola [*Movement for the Defense of Angolan Interests*] [*French*]   (AF)

MDIA .... Movimento para a Defesa dos Intereses de Angola [*Movement for the Defense of Angolan Interests*]

MDIN........ Mouvement de la Defense des Interets Nationaux

MDIO........ Intergovernmental Economic Organizations   (BU)

MDIPO ..... Mezhdunarodnoe Dobrovolnoe Istoriko-Prosvetitel'skoye Obshchestvo Memorial   (EAIO)

MDIS........ Minstere du Development Industriel et Scientifique [*Ministry of Industrial and Scientific Development*] [*France*]   (PDAA)

MDITC...... Mauritius Development Investment Trust Co.   (EY)

MDJ .... Jaro International SA [*Romania*] [*ICAO designator*]   (FAAC)

MdJ .... Ministerium der Justiz [*Ministry of Justice*]   (EG)

MD-jedinica ... Moto-Desantna Jedinica [*Motorized Landing Unit*]   (YU)

MDJM ...... Jainamosa [*Dominican Republic*] [*ICAO location identifier*]   (ICLI)

MDJMA.... Marine Department/Japan Meteorological Agency   (MSC)

MDJO .... Mornaricko-Desantno-Jurisno Odeljenje [*Marine Landing Attack Department*]   (YU)

MDK......... Calcium Molybdate   (RU)

MDK......... Copper Extraction Combine   (BU)

MDK......... International Danube Commission   (RU)

MDK......... Maximum Permissible Concentration   (RU)

MDK......... Mbandaka [*Zaire*] [*Airport symbol*]   (OAG)

MD K........ Medicina Kiado [*Medicina Publishing House*]   (HU)

MDK......... Medunarodna Decimalna Klasifikacija [*International Decimal Classification*]   (YU)

MDK......... Miejski Dom Kultury [*Municipal Social and Recreation Club*] [*Poland*]

MDK......... Mistni Dopravni Komise [*Local Transportation Commission*]   (CZ)

MDK......... Mlodziezowy Dom Kultury [*Youth House of Culture*]   (POL)

MDK......... Moscow Dialectological Commission   (RU)

MDK......... Muszaki Dokumentacios Kozpont [*Technical Documentation Center*]   (HU)

MDKhP .... Ministry of Supply and Food Industry [*Obsolete*]   (BU)

md l .... Doctor of Medicine   (BU)

MDL......... Mandala Airlines PT [*Indonesia*] [*ICAO designator*]   (FAAC)

MDL......... Mandalay [*Myanmar*] [*Airport symbol*]   (OAG)

MDL......... Mauri Development Limited

MDL......... Mineral Deposits Limited [*Australia*]

MdL.......... Mitglied des Landtags [*Member of the Landtag*] [*German*]

MDL.......... Movimiento de Democratizacion Liberal [*Liberal Democratization Movement*] [*Colorado*]   (LA)

mdl .... Muendlich [*Verbal*] [*German*]   (GCA)

MDLN....... Mouvement Democratique de Liberation Nationale

MDLP .... Movimento Democratico para a Libertacao de Portugal [*Democratic Movement for the Liberation of Portugal*]   (WER)

MDLPC..... Movimento Democratico de Libertacao de Portugal e Colonias

MDLR....... La Romana [*Dominican Republic*] [*ICAO location identifier*]   (ICLI)

MDM........ Magnetic Road Mine   (RU)

MDM........ Marszalkowska Dzielnica Mieszkaniowa [*Marszalkowska Residential District*]   (POL)

MDM........ Mass Democratic Movement [*Political coalition*] [*South Africa*]

MDM........ Mestske Divadlo Mladych [*Municipal Young People's Theater*] [*Brno*]   (CZ)

MDM........ Miedzynarodowy Dzien Mlodziezy [*International Youth Day*] [*Poland*]

M-DM .... Modulation-Demodulation   (RU)

MDM........ Movimento Democratico das Mulheres [*Women's Democratic Movement*] [*Portuguese*]   (WER)

MDM........ Movimento Democratico de Mocambique [*Democratic Movement of Mozambique*]   (AF)

MDMAF ... Mekong Delta Mobile Afloat Force [*Vietnam*]

MDMC...... Monte Cristy [*Dominican Republic*] [*ICAO location identifier*]   (ICLI)

MDN .... International Children's Week   (RU)

MDN .... Mark der Deutschen Notenbank [*Mark of the German Bank of Issue*] [*Later, M*]   (EG)

MDN .... Ministere de la Defense Nationale [*National Defense Minister*] [*French*]   (BAS)

MDN .... Mobilisation pour le Developpement National [*Haiti*] [*Political party*]   (EY)

MDN .... Movimiento Democratico Nacional [*National Democratic Movement*] [*Colorado*]   (LA)

MDN .... Movimiento Democratico Nacionalista [*Nationalist Democratic Movement*] [*Guatemala*] [*Political party*]

MDN .... Movimiento Democratico Nicaraguense [*Nicaraguan Democratic Movement*] [*Political party*]   (PPW)

MDN .... Universair [*Spain*] [*ICAO designator*]   (FAAC)

MDNF....... Minimal Disjunctive Normal Form   (RU)

MD(NI)..... Ministry of Development [Northern Ireland]

MDNS....... Ministrstvo za Drzavne Nabave Slovenije [*Ministry of State Supply of Slovenia*]   (YU)

MDNT....... Moscow House of Folk Art   (RU)

MDNTP .... Moscow House of Scientific and Technical Propaganda Imeni F. E. Dzerzhinskiy   (RU)

MDO .... Macedonia AS [*Yugoslavia*] [*ICAO designator*]   (FAAC)

MDO .... Mericsky Delostrelecky Oddil [*Survey Battalion*]   (CZ)

MDO .... Mestsky Dum Osvety [*Municipal Cultural Center*]   (CZ)

MDO .... Milli Devrim Ordusu [*National Revolutionary Army*]   (TU)

MDO .... Mlodziezowy Dom Oswiaty [*Youth Education House*] [*Poland*]

MDO .... Road Machinery Detachment   (RU)

MDOL....... Movimento pela Defesa do Ocidente Livre [*Movement for the Defense of the Free West*] [*Portuguese*]　(WER)

MDP......... Madagascar-Presse　(AF)

MDP......... Magyar Dolgozok Partja [*Hungarian Workers' Party*] [*Political party*]　(PPE)

MDP......... Maximum Dynamic Error　(RU)

MDP......... Milli Duzenlik Partisi [*National Order Party*]　(TU)

MDP......... Milliyetci Demokrasi Partisi [*Nationalist Democracy Party*] [*Turkey*] [*Political party*]　(EY)

MDP......... Mindiptana [*Indonesia*] [*Airport symbol*]　(OAG)

MDP......... Moslem Democratic Party [*Philippines*] [*Political party*]　(PPW)

MDP......... Mouvement Democrate Progressiste

MDP......... Mouvement Democratique et Populaire [*Popular Democratic Movement*] [*Senegal*] [*Political party*]　(PPW)

MDP......... Mouvement Democratique Populaire [*Popular Democratic Party*] [*The Comoros*] [*Political party*]　(EY)

MDP......... Mouvement Democratique Populaire [*Morocco*]

MDP......... Mouvement des Democrates Progressistes [*Burkina Faso*] [*Political party*]　(EY)

MDP......... Movimento Democratico Portugues [*Portuguese Democratic Movement*] [*Political party*]　(PPE)

MDP......... Movimiento Democratico del Pueblo [*Paraguay*] [*Political party*]　(EY)

MDP......... Movimiento Democratico Peruano [*Peruvian Democratic Movement*] [*Political party*]

MDP......... Movimiento Democratico Popular [*Popular Democratic Movement*] [*Ecuador*] [*Political party*]　(PPW)

MDP......... Movimiento Democratico Popular [*Popular Democratic Movement*] [*Chile*] [*Political party*]　(PPW)

MDPA....... Mines Domaniales des Potasses d'Alsace

MDPC....... Punta Cana [*Dominican Republic*] [*ICAO location identifier*]　(ICLI)

MDP/CDE ... Movimento Democratico Portugues/Commissao Democratica Eleitoral [*Portuguese Democratic Movement/Democratic Electoral Commission*]　(WER)

MDPI .... Management Development and Productivity Institute [*Ghana*]

MDPL .... Mouvement pour le Desarmement, la Paix et la Liberte [*Movement for Disarmament, Peace, and Liberty*] [*France*]　(EAIO)

MDPNE .... Ministere de la Protection de la Nature et de l'Environment [*Ministry for the Protection of Nature and the Environment*] [*France*]　(PDAA)

MDPO....... Mission de Developpement du Perimetre d'Ombessa [*Mbam*]

MDPP .... Puerto Plata/La Union [*Dominican Republic*] [*ICAO location identifier*]　(ICLI)

MDPPD .... Movimento Democratico Portugues de Ponta Delgada [*Portuguese Democratic Movement of Ponta Delgada*]　(WER)

MDPPQ .... Mouvement pour la Defense des Prisonniers Politiques du Quebec [*Movement for the Defense of Political Prisoners of Quebec*]

MDPS....... Mouvement pour la Democratie et le Progres Social [*Benin*] [*Political party*]　(EY)

MDPT .... Ministerstvo Dopravy, Post, a Telekomunikacii [*Ministry of Transportation, Posts, and Telecommunications*] [*Slovakia*]　(CZ)

MDQ .... Mar Del Plata [*Argentina*] [*Airport symbol*]　(OAG)

MDR......... Compania Mexicana de Aeroplanos SA [*Mexico*] [*ICAO designator*]　(FAAC)

MdR......... Mitglied des Reichstags [*Member of the Reichstag*] [*German*]

MDR......... Monatsschrift fuer Deutsches Recht [*Germany*]　(FLAF)

MDR......... Naval Long-Range Reconnaissance Aircraft

MDRA....... Mouvement Democratique de Renouveau Algerien [*Democratic Movement for Algerian Renewal*]　(AF)

MDRAF..... Mekong Delta Riverine Assault Force [*Vietnam*]

MDRM...... Mouvement Democratique de Renovation Malgache [*Democratic Movement Malagasy Restoration*]

MDRP .... Movimiento Democratico Reformista Peruano [*Peruvian Democratic Reformist Movement*] [*Political party*]　(PPW)

MDRPARMEHUTU ... Mouvement Democratique Republicain du Parti du Mouvement de l'Emancipation Hutu [*Republican Democratic Movement of the Hutu Emancipation Movement Party*] [*Rwanda*]　(AF)

MDRRA .... Ministere du Developpement Rural et de la Reforme Agraire [*Ministry of Rural Development and Agrarian Reform*] [*Malagasy*]　(AF)

MDRT .... Mouvement Democratique de Renovation Tchadienne [*Democratic Movement for Chadian Renewal*]　(AF)

MDS .... International Falcon Movement [*IFM*]　(RU)

MDS .... Magnetomotive Force　(RU)

MDS .... Mezinarodni Druzstevni Svaz [*International Cooperative Alliance*]　(CZ)

MDS .... Middle Caicos [*British West Indies*] [*Airport symbol*]　(OAG)

MDS .... Miedzynarodowy Dzien Spoldzielczosci [*International Co-Operative Day*] [*Poland*]

MDS .... Mitteilungen aus dem Deutschen Schutzgebieten

MDS .... Montant de Soutien [*Amount of Support*] [*A trade negotiating plan EC*]

MDS .... Mouvement Democrate Socialiste [*Democratic Socialist Movement*] [*France*] [*Political party*]　(PPW)

MDS .... Mouvement Democratique et Social [*Democratic and Social Movement*] [*Reunionese*]　(AF)

MDS .... Mouvement des Democrates Socialistes [*Movement of Socialist Democrats*] [*Tunisia*] [*Political party*]　(PPW)

MDS .... Mouvement pour la Democratie Sociale [*Burkina Faso*] [*Political party*]　(EY)

MDS .... Movement for a Democratic Slovakia [*Former Czechoslovakia*] [*Political party*]　(EY)

MDS .... Road Machinery Station　(RU)

MDSA .... Malayan Democratic Students Alliance [*Selangor*]　(ML)

MDSD .... Santo Domingo/De las Americas Internacional [*Dominican Republic*] [*ICAO location identifier*]　(ICLI)

MDSF .... Mouvement Democrate Socialiste de France [*Democratic Socialist Movement of France*] [*Political party*]　(PPE)

MDSh....... Naval Smoke Pot　(RU)

MDSI........ San Isidro [*Dominican Republic*] [*ICAO location identifier*]　(ICLI)

MDSJ .... San Juan [*Dominican Republic*] [*ICAO location identifier*]　(ICLI)

MDSK ...... International Movement of Catholic Students [*IMCS*]　(RU)

MDSP....... Magnetdrahtspeicher [*German*]　(ADPT)

MDSP........ San Pedro De Macoris [*Dominican Republic*] [*ICAO location identifier*]　(ICLI)

MDST....... Santiago [*Dominican Republic*] [*ICAO location identifier*]　(ICLI)

MDSz .... Mezogazdasagi Dolgozok Szakszervezete [*Trade Union of Agricultural Workers*]　(HU)

MDT......... Compagnie Air Mediterrannee [*France*] [*ICAO designator*]　(FAAC)

MDT......... Magyar Dermatologiai Tarsulat [*Hungary*]　(EAIO)

MDT......... Mezinarodni Desetinne Trideni [*International Decimal Classification System*]　(CZ)

MDT......... Mezinarodni Dopravni Tarif [*International Transportation Tariff*]　(CZ)

MDT......... Miejski Dom Towarowy [*Municipal Department Store*] [*Poland*]

MDT......... Mittlere Datentechnik [*German*]　(ADPT)

MDT......... Moviment de Defensa de la Terra [*Spain*] [*Political party*]　(EY)

MDU .... Malayan Democratic Union [*Singapore*] [*Political party*]　(FEA)

MDU .... Medical Defence Union [*Australia*]

MDU .... Mendi [*Papua New Guinea*] [*Airport symbol*]　(OAG)

MDU .... Middle Dutch [*Language, etc.*]

MDU .... Mobile Development Unit [*Thailand*]

MDU .... Moscow House of Scientists　(RU)

MDU .... Remote-Control Device　(RU)

MDUS....... Medium Data Utilization Station [*Australia*] [*Telecommunications*]

MDV......... Maldives [*ANSI three-letter standard code*]　(CNC)

MDV......... Mannesmann Datenverarbeitung [*German*]　(ADPT)

MDV......... Medizinischer Dienst des Verkehrswesens [*Medical Service for Transportation*]　(EG)

MDV......... Medouneu [*Gabon*] [*Airport symbol*]　(OAG)

MDV......... Miestny Dozorny Vybor [*Local Supervisory Committee*]　(CZ)

MDV......... Mouvement Democratique Voltaique [*Upper Volta Democratic Movement*]

MDX......... Mercedes [*Argentina*] [*Airport symbol*]　(OAG)

MDY......... Mutemerkiz Dingil Yuku [*Concentrated Axial Load*]　(TU)

Mdyn .... Megadyna [*Megadyne*] [*Poland*]

MDZ......... Camouflaging Smoke Screen　(RU)

MDZ......... Melitopol' Diesel Plant　(RU)

MDZ......... Mendoza [*Argentina*] [*Airport symbol*]　(OAG)

MDZ......... Mezinarodni Den Zen [*International Women's Day*]　(CZ)

ME........... International Units　(BU)

ME........... Maailmanennatys [*Finland*]

ME........... Maandschrift Economie [*Benelux*]　(BAS)

ME........... Mache-Einheit [*Mache Unit*] [*German*]

Me............ Madre [*Mother*] [*Portuguese*]

Me............ Madre [*Mother*] [*Spanish*]

ME............ Magnetoelectric Instrument　(RU)

Me............ Maitre [*Master*] [*French*]

ME............ Majority Elements　(RU)

ME............ Malaysian Engineers　(ML)

ME............ Malomipari Egyesules [*Industrial Milling Cooperative*]　(HU)

ME............ Marche de l'Europe [*March of Europe*]　(EAIO)

ME............ Masinstvo i Elektrotehnika [*Machinery and Electrical Engineering*]　(YU)

ME............ Materials on Ethnography　(RU)

ME............ Medio Evo [*Middle Ages*] [*Italian*]

mE............ Meines Erachtens [*In My Opinion*] [*German*]　(EG)

Me............ Memur [*Official, Employee*] [*Government*]　(TU)

ME............ Mengeneinheit [*Unit of Quantity*]　(EG)

ME............ Messerschmitt AG [*Germany*] [*ICAO aircraft manufacturer identifier*]　(ICAO)

ME............ Messina [*Car registration plates*] [*Italian*]
Me............. Metal (RU)
Me............. Metall [*Metal*] [*German*]
Me............. Methyl [*Methyl*] [*German*]
Me............. Middeleeue [*Middle Ages*] [*Afrikaans*]
ME............ Middel-Engels [*Middle English*] [*Language, etc.*] [*Afrikaans*]
ME............ Middle English [*Language, etc.*]
ME............ Mikton Epiteleion [*Joint Staff*] [*Greek*] (GC)
ME............ Milattan Evvel [*Before Christ*] (TU)
ME............ Ministerio da Educacao [*Ministry of Education*] [*Portuguese*]
ME............ Ministerstvo Energetiky [*Ministry of Power Industry*] (CZ)
ME............ Ministerstwo Energetyki [*Ministry of Power*] (POL)
ME............ Ministry of Electrification [*Obsolete*] (BU)
Me............. Molhe [*Mole*] [*Portuguese*] (NAU)
ME............ Monomereneinheit [*Monomer Unit*] [*German*] (GCA)
ME............ Mouvement Europeen [*European Movement*]
Me............. Muelle [*Mole*] [*Spanish*] (NAU)
ME............ Muenze Einheit [*Coinage*] [*German*]
ME............ Muszaki Egyetem [*Technical University*] (HU)
ME............ Muszaki Eloirasok [*Technical Instructions*] (HU)
MEA......... International Economic Association [*IEA*] (RU)
MEA......... Le Materiel Electrique Aeronautique [*French*]
MEA......... Macae [*Brazil*] [*Airport symbol*] (OAG)
MEA......... Macao Exporters Association (EAIO)
MEA......... Metopon Ethnikis Adadimiourgias [*National Regeneration Front*] [*Greece*] [*Political party*] (PPE)
MEA......... Metopon Ethnikis Anasyngrotiseos [*National Reconstruction Front*] [*Greek*] (GC)
MEA......... Metropolitan Electricity Authority [*Thailand*] (PDAA)
MEA......... Middle East Airlines - Air Liban [*Lebanon*]
MEA......... Middle East Association [*British*] (EAIO)
MEA......... Ministry of Economic Affairs [*Taiwan*]
MEA......... Missionary Evangelical Alliance [*See also AME*] [*Switzerland*] (EAIO)
MEA......... Monades Ethnikis Amynis [*National Defense Units*] [*Greek*] (GC)
MEAA....... Museum Education Association of Australia (ADA)
MEAE....... Ministere d'Etat aux Affaires Etrangeres [*Ministry of State for Foreign Affairs*] [*Mauritania*] (AF)
MEAF....... Mediterranean Expeditionary Allied Forces
MEAF....... Middle East Air Force
MEAFOPS ... Middle East Air Force Operations
MEAFSA .. Middle East, Southern Asia, and Africa South of the Sahara
MEAN....... Mission d'Etude et d'Amenagement du Niger
MEANT .... Meat Exporters' Association of the Northern Territory [*Australia*]
MEAO....... Middelbaar Economisch en Administratief Onderwijs [*Benelux*] (BAS)
MEAP....... Mikroviologikon Ergastirion Afthodous Pyretou (Dimosion) [*Foot-and-Mouth Disease Microbiological Laboratory (Public)*] [*Greek*] (GC)
MEAT .... Meat Exporters' Association of Tasmania [*Australia*]
MEAU....... Missao de Estudos Agronomicos do Ultramar [*Portugal*] (DSCA)
MEAUP .... Missao de Estudos Apicolas do Ultramar Portugues, Junta de Investigacoes do Ultramar
MEAV .... Meat Exporters' Association of Victoria [*Australia*]
MEAV .... Museum Education Association of Victoria [*Australia*]
meb............ Furniture Factory [*Topography*] (RU)
MEB .... International Office of Epizootics (RU)
MEB .... Melbourne [*Australia*] [*Airport symbol*] (OAG)
MEB .... Milli Egitim Bakanligi [*National Education Ministry*] (TU)
MEB .... Movimiento de Educacao de Base [*Basic Education Movement*] [*Brazil*] (LA)
MEBAN .... Menkul Degerler Bankerlik ve Finansman AS [*Securities Banking and Finance Corp.*] (TU)
MEBD .... Milchwirtschaftlicher Erzeugerberatungsdienst [*Dairy Producers Advisory Service*] [*German*] (EG)
MEBECO ... Menuiserie et Ebenisterie Congolaise
MEBPA..... Missao de Estudos Broceanologicas e de Pesca de Angola
MEBU .... Maschinengewehr-Eisenbeton-Unterstand [*Machine-Gun-Iron-Concrete-Emplacement*] [*German "pill box," battlefield redoubts World War I*]
MEC .... Major Events Committee [*Victoria, Australia*]
MEC .... Manta [*Ecuador*] [*Airport symbol*] (OAG)
MEC .... Masina Electronica de Calcul [*Electronic Calculator*] (RO)
mec............ Mecazi [*Figurative*] (TU)
Mec........... Meclisi [*Assembly*] (TU)
MEC .... Medicines Evaluation Committee [*Australia*]
MEC .... Member of the Executive Council [*Namibia*] (AF)
MEC .... Mercado Comune Europeo [*European Common Market*] [*Spanish*] (DLA)
MEC .... Mercato Europeo Comune [*European Common Market*] [*Use EEC*] [*Italian*] (WER)
MEC .... Mineral Exploration Co. [*India*] (PDAA)
MEC .... Ministerial Executive Council [*OPEC*] (MENA)

MEC .... Ministerio da Educacao e Cultura [*Ministry of Education and Culture*] [*Brazil*] (LA)
MEC .... Ministry of Education and Culture [*Mozambique*] (AF)
MEC .... Movimiento Emergente de Concordia [*Emerging Movement for Harmony*] [*Guatemala*] [*Political party*] (PPW)
MEC .... Movimiento Estudiantil Cristiano [*Christian Student Movement*] [*Costa Rica*] (LA)
MECA .... Macedonian Educational and Cultural Association [*Australia*]
MECA .... Metal Metalica Colombiana de Accesorios Ltda. [*Colombia*] (COL)
MECA .... Societe Congolaise de Mecanographie Congo
MECAB..... Regional Bureau of the Middle East Committee for the Affairs of the Blind [*Saudi Arabia*] (EAIO)
MECACON ... Middle East Civil Aviation Conference (PDAA)
Mecan....... Mecanica [*Mechanics*] [*Portuguese*]
MECANAGRO ... Empresa de Assistencia Tecnica ao Equipamento Agricola [*Agricultural machinery enterprise*] [*Mozambique*]
MECANEMBAL ... Societe Africaine d'Emballages Metalliques
MECAS..... Middle East Center for Arab Studies
mecc .... Meccanica [*Mechanics*] [*Italian*]
MECC .... Middle East Council of Churches (EA)
mech.......... Mecanique [*French*] (TPFD)
mech.......... Mechanics (TPFD)
Mech......... Mechanik [*Mechanic*] [*German*] (GCA)
mech.......... Mechanika [*or Mechaniczny*] [*Mechanics or Mechanical*] (POL)
mech.......... Mechanisiert [*Mechanized*] [*German*] (GCA)
mechan...... Mechanisch [*Mechanical*] [*German*]
Mechanism ... Mechanismus [*Mechanism*] [*German*] (GCA)
MECHIM ... Societe de Genie Metallurgique et Chimique [*Algeria*]
Mechinstitut ... Institute of Infectious Diseases Imeni I. I. Mechnikov (RU)
MECIPA ... Societe Malgache d'Etudes de Construction et d'Investissements Papetiers
MECM ...... Methodist Episcopal Congo Mission
MECOL..... Metalurgica Colombiana Ltda. [*Colombia*] (COL)
MECOM ... Middle East Electronic Communications Show and Conference [*Arabian Exhibition Management WLL*] [*Manama, Bahrain*]
MECON .... Mideast Constructors [*Commercial firm*] [*Qatar*]
MECOR .... Ministerio Extraordinario da Coordenacao dos Organismos Regionais [*Brazil*] (DSCA)
MECWB.... Middle East Committee for the Welfare of the Blind (EA)
MED......... Medical [*Royal Australian Navy*]
med............ Medical [*French*] (TPFD)
med............ Medical, Medicine (RU)
Med.......... Medicina [*Medicine*] [*Portuguese*]
med............ Medico [*Physician*] [*Portuguese*]
Med.......... Medico [*Doctor*] [*Italian*]
med............ Medies [*Medical*] [*Afrikaans*]
MED......... Medina [*Saudi Arabia*] [*Airport symbol*] (OAG)
MED......... Medisyne [*Medicine*] [*Afrikaans*]
Med.......... Mediterranean
MED......... Mediterranean Pollution Study Pilot Project (MSC)
Med.......... Medizin [*or Medizinisch*] [*Medicine or Medical*] [*German*]
med............ Medycyna [*or Medyczny*] [*Medicine or Medical*] [*Poland*] (POL)
MED......... Ministerio de Educacion [*Ministry of Education*] [*Nicaragua*] (LA)
MedA........ Medical Academy (BU)
MEDA....... Mouvement pour l'Evolution Democratique en Afrique
MedAACSReg ... Mediterranean Airways and Communication Service Region
MedA-AnI ... Medical Academy - Institute of Anatomy (BU)
MedA-BioII ... Medical Academy - Institute of Biology (BU)
MEDAC .... Military Electronic Data Advisory Committee [*NATO*] (NATG)
MEDAC .... Mouvement de l'Evolution Democratique de l'Afrique Centrale [*Central African Democratic Evolution Movement*]
MedA-DetKl ... Medical Academy - Pediatric Clinic (BU)
MedA-FizioII ... Medical Academy - Institute of Physiology (BU)
MedA-GinKl ... Medical Academy - Gynecological Clinic (BU)
medagl........ Medaglione [*Medallion*] [*Italian*]
MedA-IBiolKhim ... Medical Academy - Institute of Biological Chemistry (BU)
MedA-IEpiz ... Medical Academy - Institute of Epizootiology (BU)
MedA-IFar ... Medical Academy - Institute of Pharmacology (BU)
MedA-Ikhig ... Medical Academy - Institute of Hygiene (BU)
MedA-IKhistEmbr ... Medical Academy - Institute of Histology and Embryology (BU)
MedA-IMedfiz ... Medical Academy - Institute of Medical Physics (BU)
MedA-IMedKhim ... Medical Academy - Institute of Medical Chemistry (BU)
MedA-IPatAn ... Medical Academy - Institute of Pathological Anatomy (BU)
MedA-IPatfiziol ... Medical Academy - Institute of Pathological Physiology (BU)
MedA-IRadiolfiziot ... Medical Academy - Institute of Radiology and Physiotherapy (BU)
MedA-ISotsKhig ... Medical Academy - Institute of Social Hygiene (BU)
MedA-ISudMed ... Medical Academy - Institute of Forensic Medicine (BU)
MedA-ITrBol ... Medical Academy - Institute of Occupational Diseases (BU)

MedA-IVoennoMedPod ... Medical Academy - Institute for the Training of Military Physicians (BU)

MedA-IZuboprot ... Medical Academy - Institute of Dentistry (BU)

MedA-KhirPropKl ... Medical Academy - Clinic of Preliminary Medical Instruction (BU)

MedA-KlInfBol ... Medical Academy - Clinic for Communicable Diseases (BU)

MedA-KlOpZub ... Medical Academy - Clinic of Dental Surgery (BU)

MedA-KozhVenKl ... Medical Academy - Clinic for Skin and Venereal Diseases (BU)

medaljbeskr ... Medaljbeskrivning [*Description of Medal*] [*Sweden*]

MEDALSA ... Mediterranean Algeria-Sahara Zone [*NATO*] (NATG)

MedA-MikrobIolSerI ... Medical Academy - Institute of Microbiology and Serology (BU)

MedA-NervPsikhKl ... Medical Academy - Neuropsychiatric Clinic (BU)

MedA-OchKl ... Medical Academy - Ophthalmological Clinic (BU)

MedA-OrtTravKl ... Medical Academy - Clinic of Orthopedics and Traumatology (BU)

MedA Pl .... Medical Academy in Plovdiv (BU)

medarb .... Medarbeider [*Collaborator*] [*Publishing Danish/Norwegian*]

MEDAS ..... Mobilya Ev Dekorasyonu Anonim Sirketi [*Furniture and Home Decoration Corporation*] (TU)

MedA-TerKl ... Medical Academy - Therapeutic Clinic (BU)

MedA-UshNGurKl ... Medical Academy - Clinic for Ear, Nose, and Throat Diseases (BU)

MedA-VutrKl ... Medical Academy - Internal Diseases Clinic (BU)

MedA-VutrPolikl ... Medical Academy - Internal Diseases Polyclinic (BU)

MedA-Yasli ... Medical Academy - Nursery (BU)

Med bibl ..... Medical Library (BU)

MEDC .... Menos Esquerra Democratica de Catalunya [*Catalonian Democratic Left*] [*Menos*] [*Spanish*] (WER)

MEDCENT ... Central Mediterranean Area [*NATO*]

med ch .... Copper Number (RU)

MEDCOMPLAN ... Mediterranean Communications Plans [*NATO*] (NATG)

MEDEA .... Masters Degree in Energy and Environmental Management and Economics (ECON)

MEDEAST ... Eastern Mediterranean Area [*NATO*] (NATG)

MededNVIR ... Mededelingen van de Nederlandse Vereniging voor Internationaal Recht [*Netherlands*] (BAS)

Medepl .... Copper-Smelting Plant [*Topography*] (RU)

MEDERCO ... Mouvement de l'Evolution et de Developpement Rural - Congo [*Movement for the Evolution and Rural Development - Congo*] [*Leopoldville*]

MEDESAN ... Melamin Desen Sanayi [*Melamin Ornamental Design and Metal Working Industry*] (TU)

medew .... Medewerking [*Collaboration*] [*Publishing*] [*Netherlands*]

MEDEX ..... Medecin Extension [*Doctors' Aides, or Medics*] [*French*]

Med fak .... School of Medicine (BU)

Medgiz .... State Publishing House of Medical Literature (RU)

MEd(Guid&Coun) ... Master of Education in Guidance and Counselling

MEDI .... Marine Environmental Data Information Referral System [*UNESCO*] [*Paris, France*]

MEDI .... Movimiento de Empresarios del Interior [*Movement of Managers from the Interior*] [*Argentina*] (LA)

MEDIA ..... Mauritius Export Development and Investment Authority (EY)

MEDIA ..... Measures for Encouraging the Development of the Audiovisual Production Industry [*EC*] (ECED)

MEDICO .. Medical International Cooperation (CL)

MEDICOK ... Rontgen Kulkereskedelmi Vallalat [*Export-Import Enterprise for X-Ray Equipment*] (HU)

MEDICOR ... Orvosi Rontgenkeszulekek Vallalata [*Medical X-Ray Equipment Enterprise*] (HU)

MEDICUBA ... Empresa Cubana Importadora y Exportadora de Productos Medicos [*Cuban Enterprise for the Import and Export of Medical Products*] (LA)

MEDIMPEX ... MEDIMPEX Gyogyszer Kulkereskedelmi Vallalat [*MEDIMPEX Foreign Trade Enterprise for Pharmaceutical Products*] (HU)

medindbd ... Medindbundet [*Bound With*] [*Publishing Danish/Norwegian*]

Mediobanca ... Banca di Credito Finanziario [*Italy*] (IMH)

MEDISTAT ... Banque de Donnees Socio-Economiques des Pays Mediterraneens [*Socioeconomic Data Bank on the Mediterranean Countries*] [*International Center for Advanced Mediterranean Agronomic Studies*] [*Information service or system*] (IID)

Medit .... Mediterranean

MEDITEC ... Dodumentation Medizinische Technik [*Medical Technology Documentation*] [*TechnicalInformation Center*] [*Germany*] [*Information service or system*] (IID)

mediz .... Medizinisch [*Medical*] [*German*] (GCA)

MedL .... Meditsinski Letopis [*Medical Chronicle*] [*A periodical*] (BU)

medl .... Medlem [*Member*] [*Danish/Norwegian*]

medl .... Medlem [*Member*] [*Sweden*]

MedLandEx ... Mediterranean Landing Exercise

MEDLOC ... Mediterranean Lines of Communication

MEDME ... Mediterranean and Middle East

Medn .... Copper Mines [*Topography*] (RU)

Med NedVer Int R ... Mededelingen van de Nederlandse Vereniging voor Internationaal Recht [*Netherlands*] (BAS)

MEDNOREAST ... Northeast Mediterranean Area [*NATO*] (NATG)

Medn-prov ... Copper Wire Plant [*Topography*] (RU)

MEDOC .... Mediterranean Occidental

MEDOC .... Mediterranean Occidental Survey (MSC)

MEDOC .... Western Mediterranean Area [*NATO*] (NATG)

MEDOCHAN ... Mary Ellen, Dorothy, Chuck, Ann [*Famous Canadian resort, named for the owners' children*]

MEDOSZ ... Mezogazdasagi es Erdeszeti Dolgozok Szakszervezete [*Trade Union of Workers in Agriculture and Forestry*] [*Budapest, Hungary*]

med p .... Medical Station [*Topography*] (RU)

MEDPOL ... Mediterranean Pollution Monitoring and Research Program [*UNEP*] (MSC)

MEDRECO ... Mediterranean Refinery Company [*Lebanon*] (ME)

MEd(RuralEd) ... Master of Education in Rural Education

MedS .... Mediterranean Sea

Medsanchast ... Medical Unit (BU)

Medsantrud ... Medical and Sanitary Workers' Trade Union (RU)

medsb .... Medical Battalion (RU)

medsb .... Medical Battalion, Medical Squadron (BU)

MEDSOUEAST ... Southeast Mediterranean Area [*NATO*] (NATG)

MEDSUPPACT ... Mediterranean Support Activity

medsv .... Medical Platoon (RU)

medt .... Medtaget [*Damaged, Worn*] [*Danish/Norwegian*]

MEDTC ..... Military Equipment Delivery Team Cambodia (VNW)

Meduchposobiye ... Republic Trust for Medical Educational Visual Aids (RU)

MEDUNSA ... Mediese Universiteit van Suid-Afrika [*Medical University of South Africa*] [*Research center*]

Med VBN .. Mededelingen van het Verbond der Belgische Nijverheid [*Belgium*] (BAS)

MEDY .... Monas Exypiretiseos Dimosion Ypiresion [*Public Services Support Unit*] [*Greek*] (GC)

MEE .... Machine a Ecrire Electrique [*Electric Typewriter*] [*French*] (ADPT)

MEE .... Magyar Elektronikai Egyesulet [*Hungarian Electronics Association*] (HU)

MEE .... Magyar Elektrotechnikai Egyesulet [*Hungarian Electrotechnical Association*] (EAIO)

MEE .... Mare [*Loyalty Islands*] [*Airport symbol*] (OAG)

MEE .... Mikti Ergatiki Epitropi [*Mixed Labor Committee*] [*Greek*] (GC)

MEE .... Ministerul Energiei Electrice [*Ministry of Electric Power*] (RO)

MEEA .... Mobil Exploration Equatorial Africa, Inc. [*Cameroon*] (AF)

MEEC .... Middle East Emergency Committee (OMWE)

MEECI ...... Mouvement des Etudiants et des Eleves de Cote-D'Ivoire [*Movement of Students and Pupils of the Ivory Coast*] (AF)

MEEI .... Magyar Elektrotechnika Ellenorzo Intezet [*Hungarian Electrotechnical Control Institute*] (HU)

MEEN ...... Ministere d'Etat a l'Economie Nationale [*Ministry of State for National Economy*] [*Mauritania*] (AF)

MEENEN ... Monimos Ektimitiki Epitropi Navtikon Epitaxeon kai Navloseon [*Permanent Committee for Assessing Naval Requisitions and (Ship) Charters*] (GC)

meetk .... Meetkunde [*Geometry*] [*Afrikaans*]

MEETK ..... Meetkundig [*Geometrical*] [*Afrikaans*]

MEEU .... Missao de Estudos Economicos do Ultramar, Junta de Investigacoes do Ultramar

MEF .... Malaysian Employers Federation

MEF .... Material Evaluation Facility [*Civil Aviation Authority*] [*Australia*]

MEF .... Mauritian Employers Federation (AF)

MEF .... Mediterranean Expeditionary Force

MEF .... Methylphosphonic Acid (RU)

MEF .... Middle East Forum [*Lebanon*] (BJA)

MEF .... Mideast File [*Tel-Aviv University*] [*Israel*] [*Information service or system*] (IID)

MEF .... Ministry for Environment and Forests [*India*]

MEFEM .... Mechanikai es Femtomegcikk Kisipari Termeloszovetkezet [*Cooperative Enterprise for Manufacture of Metalware*] (HU)

MEFERT .. Magyar Ertekpapirforgalmi Reszvenytarsasag [*Hungarian Stock Brokerage Limited (Prewar)*] (HU)

MEFESZ ... Magyar Egyetemi es Foiskolai Egyesuletek Szovetsege [*Federation of Hungarian University and College Associations*] (HU)

MEFEX ..... Middle East Food and Equipment Exhibition [*Arabian Exhibition Management*]

MEFI .... Mezogepfejleszto Intezet [*Agricultural Machine Developing Institute*] (HU)

MEFMC .... Ministerul Economiei Forestiere si Materialelor de Constructii [*Ministry of the Forestry Economy and Construction Materials*] (RO)

MEFORI ... Mezogazdasagi Fordito Iroda [*Translation Office for Literature on Agriculture*] (HU)

MEFOS..... Stiftelsen for Metallurgisk Forskning [*Foundation for Metallurgical Research*] (IRC)

MEFTER .. Magyar Folyam- es Tengerhajozasi Reszvenytarsasag [*Hungarian River and Sea Navigation Company Limited*] (HU)

MEG......... Malange [*Angola*] [*Airport symbol*] (OAG)

MEG......... Max-Eyth Gesellschaft zur Forderung der Landtechnik [*Germany*] (DSCA)

MEGA....... Mejoramiento Ganadero (Programa) [*El Salvador*] (LAA)

Me-Ga....... Tvornica Metalne Galanterije i Pisacih Pera [*Factory of Metal Notions and Fountain Pens*] [*Zagreb*] (YU)

megb.......... Megbeszeles [*Conference*] (HU)

megb.......... Megbizott [*Trustee, Representative*] (HU)

MEGEV..... Mezogazdasagi Gepalkatresz Ellato Vallalat [*Agricultural Machinery Spare Parts Supply Enterprise*] (HU)

megh.......... Meghalt [*Deceased*] (HU)

megh.......... Meghatalmazott [*Proxy, Plenipotentiary*] (HU)

megh min ... Meghatalmazott Miniszter [*Minister Plenipotentiary*] (HU)

megj.......... Megjegyzes [*Comment, Footnote*] (HU)

megj.......... Megjelenik [*Appear*] [*Hungary*]

megsz........ Megszallas [*or Megszallo*] [*Occupation or Occupying*] (HU)

MEGVED ... Munkaegeszsegvedelmi es Gepiberendezeseket Keszito KTSZ [*Cooperative Manufacturing Enterprise for Industrial Safety Equipment*] (HU)

MEGY .... Max-Eyth Association of Agricultural Engineering [*Germany*] (EAIO)

MEGYEVILL ... Megyei Villanyszerelo Vallalat [*County Electrical Engineering Enterprise*] (HU)

MEH......... Mehamn [*Norway*] [*Airport symbol*] (OAG)

MEH......... Mellektermek es Hulladekgyujto Troszt [*Trash and Garbage Collection Trust*] (HU)

MEH......... Meres et Enfants d'Haiti [*An association*] (EAIO)

MEHECO ... China National Medicine & Health Import & Export Corp.

MEHECO ... China National Medicines and Health Products Import and Export Corp. (TCC)

MEHECOS ... China National Medicines & Health Import & Export Corp., Shanghai Branch

MEHNG.... Missao de Estudos do Habitat Nativo na Guine, Junta de Investigacoes do Ultramar

MEHNT.... Missao de Estudos do Habitat Nativo em Timor

MeHo........ Medizinische Hochschule

mehr........ Mehrere [*Several*] [*German*]

mehrbas ..... Mehrbasisch [*Polybasic*] [*German*] (GCA)

mehrf......... Mehrfach [*Several Copies*] [*Publishing*] [*German*]

mehrstd...... Mehrstuendig [*For Several Hours*] [*German*] (GCA)

mehrwert.... Mehrwertig [*Multivalent*] [*German*] (GCA)

Mehrz........ Mehrzahl [*Majority*] [*German*]

MEHTAP ... Merkezi Hukumet Teskilati Arastirma Projesi [*Central Government Organization Research Project*] (TU)

MEI .... Maatskappy vir Europese Immigrasie

MEI .... Machine-Electrical Engineering Institute (BU)

MEI .... Madagascar Electro-Industrie

Mei........... Meiji Seika Kaisha Ltd. [*Japan*]

MEI .... Meres et Enfants Internationale [*Switzerland*] (EAIO)

MEI .... Middle East Information Service (BJA)

MEI .... Ministerul Educatiei si Invatamintului [*Ministry of Education and Instruction*] (RO)

MEI .... Moscow Power Engineering Institute (RU)

MEI .... Moscow Power Institute (BU)

MEI .... Movimiento Estudiantil Independiente [*Independent Student Movement*] [*Argentina*] (LA)

MEI .... Mysore Electrical Industries Ltd. [*India*]

MEI .... Societe Marocaine pour l'Entreprise et l'Industrie

MEIA .... Member of the Institution of Engineers Australia

MEIC........ Ministerio de Economia, Industria, y Comercio [*Ministry of the Economy, Industry, and Commerce*] [*Costa Rica*] (LA)

MEIC........ Ministerio de Educacao e Investigacao Cientifica [*Ministry of Education and Scientific Research*] [*Portuguese*] (WER)

MEIC........ Myanma Export-Import Corporation [*Burmese*] (GEA)

MEICO ..... Mecanica Industrial Colombiana [*Colombia*] (COL)

MEIDA ..... Metals and Engineering Industries Development Association [*Tanzania*] (AF)

MEIO .... Malaysian External Intelligence Organization (ML)

MEIR........ Mideast Information Resource (BJA)

MEIS .... Middle East Information Service (BJA)

MEIS .... Moscow Electrotechnical Institute of Communications (RU)

MEISON... Me'ei Sone All Ethiopian Socialist Movement

MEIZ........ Moscow Electrical Insulation Plant (RU)

mej........... Mejuffrou [*Miss*] [*Afrikaans*]

Mej........... Mejuffrouw [*Miss*] [*Netherlands*] (GPO)

mejj .... Mejuffroue [*Misses*] [*Afrikaans*]

MEK .... Budapesti Muszaki Egyetem Konyvtara [*Library of the Technical University of Budapest*] (HU)

MEK .... International Electrical Engineering Commission (BU)

MEK .... International Electrotechnical Commission [*IEC*] (RU)

MEK .... Mathitiko Ethnikistiko Kinima [*Student Nationalist Movement*] [*Greek*] (GC)

MEK .... Medical Education Kit

MEK .... Megyei Mezogazdasagi Termekeket Ertekesito Kozpont [*County Agricultural Products Store and Distribution Center*] (HU)

mek .... Mekaniikka [*Mechanics*] [*Finland*]

MEK .... Mezogazdasagi Termekeket Ertekesito Szovetkezeti Kozpont [*Cooperative Center for Agricultural Marketing*] (HU)

MEK .... Mikhani Esoterikis Kavseos [*Internal Combustion Engine*] (GC)

mekh .... Mechanical, Mechanics, Mechanized (RU)

mekhanich ... Mechanical (RU)

MEKhANOBR ... All-Union Scientific Research and Planning Institute for the Mechanical Processing of Minerals (RU)

mekhfak..... Division of Mechanics (RU)

mekhmat.... Division of Mechanics and Mathematics (RU)

mekh mat ... Mechanico-Mathematical (RU)

mekhom ..... Mechanical Ohm (RU)

Mekhtorg... All-Union State Association for Trade in Fur Goods (RU)

MeKLK..... Mestska Komise Lidove Kontroly [*City Commission of People's Control*] (CZ)

MEKOROT ... National Water Company [*Israel*] (ME)

meks.......... Mexican (RU)

MEKSZ ..... Magyar Epiteszek Kamaraja es Skovetsege [*An association*] [*Hungary*] (EAIO)

mekv.......... Milliequivalent (RU)

mel............. Chalk Pit [*Topography*] (RU)

MEL .... Mantenimientos Electricos [*Colombia*] (COL)

MEL .... Mechanical Engineering Laboratory [*Agency of Industrial Science and Technology*] [*Japan*] (WED)

MEL .... Melbourne [*Australia*] [*Airport symbol*] (OAG)

mel........... Mill [*Topography*] (RU)

MEL .... Minimum Effective Level

MEL .... Ministere de l'Equipement et du Logement [*Ministry of Equipment and Housing*] [*France*] (PDAA)

MEL .... Mitsubishi Electric Corp. [*Nuclear energy*] [*Japan*] (NRCH)

MEL .... Moslem Electoral Lobby [*Australia*]

MEL .... Muzika Esperanto Ligo [*Esperantist Music League*] (EAIO)

mel........... Reclamation (RU)

MELA....... Middle East Librarians Association

MELB....... Melbourne [*Australia*] (ROG)

Melb.......... University of Melbourne [*Australia*] (ADA)

Melb CollDivinity ... Melbourne College of Divinity [*Australia*]

MelbCollTex ... Melbourne College of Textiles [*Australia*]

MELCO..... Mitsubishi Electric Corp. [*Japan*]

MElektr..... Ministry of Electrification [*Obsolete*] (BU)

MELETEX ... Metall-, Lebensmittel, -Textil-GmbH Export und Import [*Metal, Foodstuffs, and Textile Export and Import Co.*] (EG)

melh .... Melhorado [*Improved*] [*Portuguese*]

MELI........ Marx-Engels-Lenin-Institut beim ZK der SED [*Marx-Engels-Lenin Institute of the SED Central Committee*] (EG)

meliorat...... Reclamation (RU)

mell .... Muszaki Ellenor [*Technical Inspector, Supervisor*] (HU)

mell rass..... Moller Scattering (RU)

MELM ..... Middle East Lutheran Ministry [*Lebanon*] (EAIO)

Mel'n.......... Mill [*Topography*] (RU)

MELN ...... Mouvement Egyptien de Liberation Nationale (BJA)

MELS .... Marx-Engels-Lenin-Stalin-Institut beim ZK der SED [*Marx-Engels-Lenin-Stalin Institute of the SED Central Committee*] (EG)

MELSOR.. Marx, Engels, Lenin, Stalin, October Revolution [*Given name popular in Russia after the Bolshevik Revolution*]

MELT....... Mouseion Ellinikis Laikis Tekhnis [*Museum of Greek Folk Art*] (GC)

MELYEPTERV ... Melyepitesi Tervezo Vallalat [*Civil Engineering Designing Enterprise*] (HU)

MELYGEP ... Melyfurasi Szerszamgepgyarto es Gepjavito Vallalat [*Manufacturing and Repair Enterprise for Deep-Drilling Equipment*] (HU)

MELYTERV ... Melyepito Tervezo Iroda [*Civil Engineering Designing Office*] (HU)

MELZ....... Moscow Electric Bulb Plant (RU)

MEM........ Magyar Elet Mozgalma [*Movement of Hungarian Life*] [*Political party*] (PPE)

mem........... Member (EECI)

mem........... Memoire [*Report*] [*French*]

Mem.......... Memorial du Grand-Duche de Luxembourg (BAS)

Mem.......... Memorie [*Memoir*] [*German*] (GCA)

MEM........ Mezogazdasagi es Elelmezesugyi Miniszterium [*Ministry of Agriculture and Food Industry*] [*Hungary*] (HU)

MEM........ Middle East Media [*Cyprus*]

MEM........ Mid East Minerals Ltd. [*Australia*]

MEM........ Ministerio de Energia y Minas [*Ministry of Energy and Mines*] [*Venezuela*] (LA)

MEM........ Ministry of Electrification and Land Reclamation [*Obsolete*] (BU)

MEM........ Mondpaca Esperantista Movado [*Esperantist Movement for World Peace - EMWP*] [*Tours, France*] (EAIO)

MEM......... Moscow State Electrical Installation Trust (RU)
MEM......... Muswellbrook Energy and Minerals Ltd. [*Australia*]
MEM......... Small Electron Microscope (RU)
MEMA...... Missao para o Estudo do Missionologia Africana, Junta de Investigacoes do Ultramar
MEMAA ... Missao de Estudos dos Movimentos Associativos em Africa
MEMACO ... Metal Marketing Corporation [*Zambia*]
MEMATA ... Messageries Malgaches Tamataviennes
MEM-DER ... Memurlar Dernegi [*Civil Servants Association*] (TU)
Mem desPerc ... Memorial des Percepteurs [*France*] (FLAF)
MEME ...... Malaysian Electrical and Mechanical Engineers (ML)
MEME ...... Missao de Estudos das Minorias Etnicas do Ultramar Portugues, Junta de Investigacoes do Ultramar
MEMFHISZ ... Mellektermek es Maradek Feldolgozo Kisipari Termeloszovetkezet [*Domestic Industrial Production Cooperative for Processing Byproducts and Waste*] (HU)
MEMIC..... Medical Microbiology Interdisciplinary Committee [*International Council of Scientific Unions*]
MEMIIT ... Moscow Electromechanical Institute of Railroad Transportation Engineers Imeni F. E. Dzerzhinskiy (RU)
MEMO...... Middle East Money [*London-Beirut*] (BJA)
MEMOSZ ... Magyar Epitomunkasok Orszagos Szakszervezete [*National Union of Hungarian Construction Workers*] (HU)
MEMOSZ ... Magyar Epitomunkasok Orszagos Szovetsege [*National Union of Hungarian Construction Workers*] (HU)
MEMRSZ ... Mezogazdasagi es Elelmezesugyi Miniszterium Repulogepes Szolgalata [*Ministry of Agriculture and Food Industry's Aviation Service*] (HU)
MEMRZ.... Moscow Electromechanical Repair Plant (RU)
MEMSAN ... Mekanik ve Elektrik Muhendislik Sanayii Anonim Sirketi [*Mechanical and Electrical Engineering Industry Corporation*] (TU)
MEMT ...... Moscow Electromechanical Technicum (RU)
MEMZ ...... Moscow Electromechanical Plant (RU)
MEMZ ...... Moscow Experimental Machine Plant (of the Glavgaz, USSR) (RU)
MEN......... Meno [*Slower*] [*Music*]
MEN......... Menteri [*Minister*] (IN)
men............ Menu [*Minor*] [*French*]
MEN......... Ministerio de Educacion Nacional [*National Education Ministry*] [*Venezuela*] (LA)
MEN......... Resimen [*Regiment*] (IN)
MENA...... Middle East News Agency
MENADA ... Menuiserie de l'Adamaoua
MENAG.... Menteri Agama [*Minister of Religious Affairs*] (IN)
m end......... Maille Tricotee a l'Endroit [*Knitting*] [*French*]
MEND...... Metal Workers to Enforce Nuclear Disarmament [*Australia*]
MENDAGRI ... Menteri Dalam Negeri [*Minister of Internal Affairs*] (IN)
MENEBA ... NV [*Naamloze Vennootschap*] Meelfabrieken der Nederlandse Bakkerij [*Netherlands*]
MENEVEN ... Subsidiary of PETROVEN [*A*] [*Venezuela*] (LA)
meng.......... Menguante [*Spanish*]
MEng(NSWIT) ... Master of Engineering (Control Engineering), New South Wales Institute of Technology [*Australia*] (ADA)
MENHANKAM ... Menteri Pertahanan dan Keamanan [*Minister of Defense and Security*] (IN)
MENI .... Movimiento Electoral Nacional Independiente [*Independent National Electoral Movement*] [*Venezuela*] (LA)
MENKES.. Menteri Kesehatan [*Minister of Health*] (IN)
MENKESRA ... Menteri Kesedjahteraan Rakjat [*Minister of People's Welfare*] (IN)
MENKO.... Muszaki Ertelmisegi Nok Kore [*Women's Technical-Intellectual Circle*] (HU)
MENKU.... Menteri Keuangan [*Minister of Finance*] (IN)
MENLU .... Menteri Luar Negeri [*Minister of Foreign Affairs*] (IN)
MENPEN ... Menteri Penerangan [*Minister of Information*] (IN)
MENPERDA ... Menteri Perdagangan [*Minister of Commerce*] (IN)
MENPERHUB ... Menteri Perhubungan [*Minister of Communications*] (IN)
Mens......... Mensucat [*Textile*]
MENS .... Middle East Neurosurgical Society [*Beirut, Lebanon*] [*Research center*]
MENSA..... Mensucat Sanayi ve Ticaret AS [*Textile Industry and Trade Corporation*] [*Adana*] (TU)
menschl...... Menschlich [*Human*] [*German*] (GCA)
MENSOS ... Menteri Sosial [*Minister of Social Affairs*] (IN)
MENSZT.. Magyar Ensz Tarsasag [*An association*] [*Hungary*] (EAIO)
MENTAN ... Menteri Pertanian [*Minister of Agriculture*] (IN)
MENTAS ... Menkul Degerler Ticaret Anonim Sirketi [*Securities Trade Corporation*] (TU)
MENTEKER ... Menteri Tenaga Kerdja [*Minister of Manpower*] (IN)
MENTRANSKOP ... Menteri Transmigrasi dan Koperasi [*Minister of Resettlement and Cooperatives*] (IN)
m env......... Maille Tricotee a l'Envers [*Knitting*] [*French*]
MeNV....... Mestsky Narodni Vybor [*City National Committee*] (CZ)
MEO......... International Economic Organizations [*Reference book*] (RU)
MEO......... Marine Engineering Officer [*Royal Australian Navy*]
MEO.......... Medical Executive Officer [*Australia*]

MEO......... Mikti Ekpaidevtiki Omas [*Joint Training Unit*] [*Military*] [*Greek*] (GC)
MEO......... Mikti Epiteliki Omas [*Joint Staff Group*] (GC)
meo............ Minosegi Ellenorzo Osztaly [*Department of Quality Control*] (HU)
MEO......... Music Hall Association (RU)
MEO......... Muszaki Ellenorzo Osztaly [*Technical Inspection Department*] (HU)
MEO......... Scandinavian Aviation Center AS [*Denmark*] [*ICAO designator*] (FAAC)
MEOA...... Malaysian Estate Owners Association (PDAA)
MEOC...... Marine Emergency Operations Center [*Western Australia*]
MEOC...... Middle East Oil Co. (MENA)
MEOCAM ... Mouvement d'Etudiants de l'Organisation Commune Africaine, Malgache, et Mauricienne [*Student Movement of the Afro-Malagasy-Mauritian Common Organization*] (AF)
MEON...... Ministere d'Etat a l'Orientation Nationale [*Ministry of State for National Orientation*] [*Mauritania*] (AF)
MEOP .... Mathitiki Epitropi Organotikis Protovoulias [*Student Committee for Organizational Initiative*] (GC)
MEOPTA ... Spojene Tovarny pro Jemnou Mechaniku a Optiku, Narodni Podnik [*United Factories for Precision and Optical Instruments, National Enterprise*] (CZ)
MEOS .... Mechanizace Oprav a Sluzeb [*Mechanization of Repairs and Services*] (CZ)
MEOSA..... Mikti Epiteliki Omas Somaton Asfaleias [*Security Corps Joint Staff Unit*] (GC)
MEP .... Electrode Potential Method (RU)
MEP .... Local Evacuation Station (RU)
MEP .... Magnetoelectric Converter (RU)
MEP .... Magyar Elet Partja [*Party of Hungarian Life*] [*Political party*] (PPE)
MEP .... Mahajana Eksath Peramuna [*People's United Front*] [*Sri Lanka*] [*Political party*] (PPW)
MEP .... Member of the European Parliament
MEP .... Mersing [*Malaysia*] [*Airport symbol*] (OAG)
MEP .... Mestske Elektricke Podniky [*Municipal Electric Power Enterprises*] (CZ)
MEP .... Mikti Epitropi Prosopikou [*Mixed Committee of Personnel*] [*Cyprus*] (GC)
MEP .... Ministry of Economic Promotion [*Burkina Faso*]
MEP .... Ministry of the Electrical Equipment Industry, USSR (RU)
MEP .... Ministry of the Electrotechnical Industry, USSR (RU)
MEP .... Mise En Page [*French*] (ADPT)
MEP .... Mouvement d'Ecologie Politique [*Ecology Political Movement*] [*France*] [*Political party*] (PPW)
MEP .... Movimiento Electoral del Pueblo [*People's Electoral Movement*] [*Netherlands Antilles*] [*Political party*] (PPW)
MEP .... Movimiento Electoral del Pueblo [*People's Electoral Movement*] [*Venezuela*] [*Political party*] (PPW)
MEP .... Movimiento Electoral di Pueblo [*Peoples Electoral Movement*] [*Aruba Political party*] (EAIO)
MEPA....... Meteorological and Environmental Protection Agency [*Saudi Arabia*]
MEPA....... Mikti Epitropi Prosopikou Astynomias [*Police Mixed Personnel Committee*] [*Greek*] (GC)
MEPA....... Missao de Estudos de Pesca de Angola (ASF)
MEPAI...... Mouvement Etudiant du Parti Africain de l'Independance [*Student Movement of the African Independence Party*] [*Senegal*] (AF)
MEPC....... Malawi Export Promotion Council (GEA)
MEPC....... Marine Environment Protection Committee [*IMCO*] (ASF)
MEPC....... Middle East Propulsion Centre [*Saudi Arabia*]
MEPEY ..... Mikti Epitropi Prosopikou Ekpaidevtikis Ypiresias [*Mixed Committee of Educational Services Personnel*] [*Cyprus*] (GC)
MEPHISTO ... Material pour l'Etude des Phenomenes Interessant la Solidification sur Terre et en Orbite
MEPLACO ... Fabrica Metales y Plasticos Colombiana Ltda. [*Colombia*] (COL)
MEPLASCO ... Mecanica y Plasticos Colombianos [*Colombia*] (COL)
MEPMPU ... Missao de Estudo dos Problemas Migratorios e do Povoamento no Ultramar, Junta de Investigacoes do Ultramar
MEPO ..... Mejoramiento Porcino (Programa) [*El Salvador*] (LAA)
MEPOD .... (Ustav pre) Mechanizovanie Podohospodarskej Vyroby na Slovensku [(*Institute for*) *Mechanization of Agricultural Production in Slovakia*] (CZ)
MEPP....... Societe Mauritanienne d'Entreposage de Produits Petroliers
MEPR....... Ministere d'Etat a la Promotion Rurale [*Ministry of State for Rural Development*] [*Mauritania*] (AF)
MEPRA..... Mision de Estudios de Patologia Regional Argentina [*Commission for the Study of Regional Pathology in Argentina*] [*Jujuy*] (LAA)
MEPROBA ... Mouvement Progressiste Bahutu [*Progressive Hutu Movement*] [*Burundi*] (AF)
Mepro-Valpro ... Rolled Metal Industry (BU)

MEPS........ Ministere d'Etat a la Promotion Sociale [*Ministry of State for Social Development*] [*Mauritania*] (AF)

MEPSA..... Metalurgica Peruana, Sociedad Anonima [*Peruvian Metalworks, Incorporated*] (LA)

MEPW ...... Ministry of Economic Planning, Western Region

MEPZ........ Mactan Export Processing Zone [*Philippines*]

MEPZ........ Mauritius Export Processing Zone

MEPZA..... Mauritius Export Processing Zones Association [*Mauritania*] (AF)

MEQB .... Migrant Employment and Qualifications Board [*New South Wales, Australia*]

MER .... Maison d'Enfants de Rabat [*Morocco*]

MER .... Management Expense Ratio

MER .... Market Exchange Rates [*Monetary conversion rate*] (ECON)

mer .... Merenkulku [*Seafaring, Nautical Term*] [*Finland*]

Mer .... Merkez [*Administrative Center, Capital*] (TU)

MER .... Ministry of External Relations [*Burkina Faso*]

MER .... Mitteleuropaeisches Reisebuero [*Middle European Travel Bureau*] [*German*]

MERA .... Manufacture Electronique et Mecanique du Rwanda

MERA .... Medical Engineering Research Association [*Australia*]

MERA .... Zjednoczenie Przemyslu Automatyki i Aparatury Pomiarowej [*Automation and Measuring Apparatus Industry Association*] (POL)

MERADO ... Mechanical Engineering Research and Development Organization [*India*] (PDAA)

MERALCO ... Manila Electric Railroad & Light Company [*Still known by acronym, although official name now Manila Electric Company*]

MERB........ Myanmar Education Research Bureau (IRC)

MERC .... Materials and Energy Research Center [*Iran*] (ME)

merc .... Mercaderias [*Spanish*]

MERCAM ... Mercados Campesinos [*Venezuela*] (DSCA)

MERCAPAN ... Corporacion Antioquena de Mercados [*Colombia*] (COL)

MERCATOR ... MERCATOR KFT Export-Import Kereskedelmi Keviseletek [*MERCATOR Limited Liability Company/Export-Import Commercial Agencies*] (HU)

MERCOLA ... Mercantil Colombiana Ltda. [*Colombia*] (COL)

MERCON ... Mercantil de Confecciones [*Colombia*] (COL)

MERECEN ... Movimiento Estable Republicano Centrista [*El Salvador*] [*Political party*] (EY)

merend .... Merendeels [*Greater Part*] [*Netherlands*]

MERGA .... Mathematics Education Research Group of Australia

MERHAI .. Ministere d'Etat aux Ressources Humaines et Affaires Islamiques [*Ministry of State for Human Resources and Islamic Affairs*] [*Mauritania*] (AF)

MERI........ Marine Ecology Research Institute [*Japan*] (ASF)

MERIWA ... Minerals and Energy Research Institute of Western Australia

merk .... Merkita [*Finland*]

merk .... Merkitseva [*Finland*]

merk .... Merkitty [*Finland*]

merk .... Merkitys [*Finland*]

merkl......... Merklich [*Noticeable*] [*German*] (GCA)

merkw .... Merkwuerdig [*Unusual*] [*German*]

merlett....... Merlettatura [*Dentelle Design*] [*Publishing*] [*Italian*]

MERN .... Missao de Estudo do Rendimento Nacional do Ultramar

MERRA..... Middle East Relief and Rehabilitation Administration

MERRC..... Middle Eastern Regional Radioisotope Centre for the Arab Countries [*Cairo, Egypt*] (WND)

MERS....... Movimiento de Estudiantes Revolucionarios Salvadorenos [*Revolutionary Movement of Salvadoran Students*] (PD)

MERSEX .. Merchant Ship Code Systems [*NATO*] (NATG)

MERSIFRICA ... Mercados, Silos, y Frigorificos del Distrito Federal, Compania Anonima [*Caracas, Venezuela*] (LAA)

MERT....... Mechanical and Electrical Redundancy Trust [*Australia*]

mert.......... Mertek [*Measure, Scale*]

MERT....... Minosegi Ellenorzo Reszvenytarsasag [*Quality Control Company*] (HU)

MERU .... Mechanical Engineering Research Unit

MERZONE ... Merchant Shipping Control Zone [*NATO*] (NATG)

MES.......... Excavating Machine Station (RU)

MES.......... International Telecommunications of the USSR (RU)

MES.......... Maharashtra Ekikaran Samithi [*India*] [*Political party*] (PPW)

MES.......... Mainly English-Speaking

MES.......... Malayan Economic Society [*Malaya*] (DSCA)

MES.......... Management Entscheidungssystem [*German*] (ADPT)

MES.......... Medan [*Indonesia*] [*Airport symbol*] (OAG)

MES.......... Mikrocomputer-Entwicklungssystem [*German*] (ADPT)

MES.......... Ministerio de Educacao e Saude [*Rio de Janeiro, Brazil*] (LAA)

MES.......... Ministerio de Educacion Superior [*Ministry of Higher Education*] [*Cuba*] (LA)

MES.......... Ministry of Electric Power Plants, USSR (RU)

MES.......... Mitropolitika Ekklisiastika Symvoulia [*Metropolitan Ecclesiastical Councils*] [*Greek*] (GC)

mes .... Month (RU)

mes .... Monthly (BU)

MES.......... Movimiento de Esquerda Socialista [*Movement of the Socialist Left*] [*Portugal*] [*Political party*] (PPE)

MES.......... Multicultural Education Services [*Victoria, Australia*]

MesA .... Maitre es Arts [*Master of Arts*] [*French*]

MESA........ Marconi Espanola S.A. [*Spain*]

MESA........ Marine Education Society of Australasia

ME-SA ..... Mesken Sanayii AS [*Housing Industry Corporation*] (TU)

MeSA......... Mestske Sdruzeni Advokatu v Praze [*City Association of Lawyers, Prague*] (CZ)

ME/SA ...... Middle East/Southern Asia

MESA........ Ministerio (Ministro) do Equipamento Social e do Ambiente [*Ministry (Minister) of Public Services and the Environment*] [*Portuguese*] (WER)

MESAEP... Mediterranean Scientific Association of Environmental Protection (ASF)

MESAN..... Mouvement de l'Evolution Sociale de l'Afrique Noire [*Black African Social Evolution Movement*]

MESC....... Middle East Supercomputer Centre [*Bahrain Centre for Studies and Research*] (ECON)

MESC....... Ministry of Education, Science, and Culture [*Japan*]

MESC....... Movimiento Estudiantil Social Cristiano [*Social Christian Student Movement*] [*Colorado*] (LA)

MESE....... Morfotikos Ekpolitistikos Syllogos Elevsinos [*Elevsis Educational and Cultural Association*] [*Greek*] (GC)

MESEP ..... Ministry of Electric Power Plants and the Electrical Equipment Industry, USSR (RU)

MESG....... Mediterranean Shipping Group [*NATO*] (NATG)

MESI........ Ministere d'Etat a la Souverainete Interne [*Ministry of State for Internal Sovereignty*] [*Mauritania*] (AF)

MESI........ Moscow Institute of Economics and Statistics (RU)

MESiEP .... Ministry of Electric Power Plants and the Electrical Equipment Industry, USSR (RU)

MESIRES ... Ministere de l'Enseignement Superieur de l'Informatique et de la Recherche Scientifique [*Ministry of Higher Education in Information and Scientific Research*] [*Cameroon*] (IRC)

Mesl.......... Meslek [*Profession or Professional*] (TU)

MESM....... Small Electronic Computer (RU)

MESM....... Small Electrostatic Microscope (RU)

MESRES... Ministere de l'Enseignement Superieur et de la Recherche Scientifique [*Ministry of Higher Education and Scientific Research*] [*Cameroon*] [*Research center*] (IRC)

MESRS ..... Ministere de l'Enseignement Superieur et de la Recherche Scientifique [*Algeria*]

MESRU..... Mission pour Economie Rurale et Sociologie [*Mission for Rural Economy and Sociology*] [*Research center*] [*France*] (IRC)

MESS .... Maden Esya Sanayicileri Sendikasi [*Metal Products Industrialists Union*] (TU)

MESS .... Messerschmitt [*German fighter aircraft*] (DSUE)

Mess .... Messidor [*Tenth month of the "Calendrier Republicain", from June 20 to July 19*] (FLAF)

Mess .... Messung [*Measurement*] [*German*] (GCA)

MESSAGAL ... Messageries du Senegal

MESSRS... Messieurs [*Plural of Mister*] [*French*]

Mest.......... Mestsky [*Municipal, City, Urban*] (CZ)

mest.......... Pronoun (BU)

mestoim...... Pronoun (RU)

Mestprom .. Local Industry (BU)

MESZ....... Magyar Evezos Szovetseg [*Hungarian Rowing Association*] (HU)

MESZHART ... Magyar-Szovjet Hajozasi Reszvenytarsasag [*Hungarian-Soviet Shipping Company Limited*] (HU)

MESZOV ... Mezogazdasagi Termelo Szovetkezet [*Agricultural Production Cooperative*] (HU)

Met.......... Metall [*Metal*] [*German*] (GCA)

met .... Metallisch [*Metallic*] [*German*] (GCA)

met .... Metallurgia [*Metallurgy*] [*Finland*]

met .... Metallurgical, Metallurgy (HU)

met .... Metallurgical Plant [*Topography*] (RU)

Met.......... Metallurgie [*Metallurgy*] [*German*] (GCA)

met .... Metal, Metallic (RU)

met .... Metalware Plant [*Topography*] (RU)

met .... Metalworking Plant [*Topography*] (RU)

met .... Metaphysics (TPFD)

Met........... Metropolitan Transit Authority [*Australia*]

MET .... Ministry of Environment and Tourism [*Burkina Faso*]

MET .... Modern Egitim Tesisleri AS [*Modern Training Facilities Corp.*] (TU)

META .... Mejoramiento de Tierras Agricolas (Programa) [*El Salvador*] (LAA)

META .... Modificacion Experimental del Tiempo Atmosferico [*Chile*] (DSCA)

METADEX ... Metal Abstracts Index Data Base [*Bibliographic database*] [*British*] (IID)

METAF ..... Metafoor [*or Metafories*] [*Metaphor or Metaphorical*] [*Afrikaans*]

METAFRAM ... Metallurgie Francaise des Poudres, SA [*Nuclear energy*] [*French*] (NRCH)

METAG .... Meteorological Advisory Group [*ICAO*] (DA)

metal .... Metallurgie [*French*]   (TPFD)
metal .... Metallurgy, Metallurgical   (BU)
Metal .... Metalurgia [*Metallurgy*] [*Portuguese*]
METALCAR ... Metalurgica el Carmen [*Colombia*]   (COL)
METALCO ... Productos Metalicos de Cartagena Ltda.   (COL)
METALDOM ... Complejo Metalurgico Dominicano [*Dominican Metallurgical Complex*] [*Dominican Republic*]   (LA)
METALFA ... Industrias Metalicas Alfa [*Colombia*]   (COL)
METAL-GABON ... Societe Metallurgique du Gabon
METALIMEX ... Podnik Zahranicniho Obchodu pro Dovoz a Vyvoz Rud, Kovu, a Tuhych Paliv [*Foreign Trade Enterprise for the Import and Export of Ores, Metals, and Solid Fuels*]   (CZ)
METALIMPEX ... METALIMPEX Acel es Fem Kulkereskedelmi Vallalat [*METALIMPEX Foreign Trade Enterprise for Steel and Metal*]   (HU)
Metal-Is ..... Turkiye Metal, Celik, Muhimmat, Makine, Metalden Mamul Esya ve Oto Sanayii Isci Sendikalari Federasyonu [*Turkish Metal and Allied Workers Federation*]   (TU)
METALKAT ... Societe Metallurgique du Katanga
metall .... Metallisch [*Metallic*] [*German*]
metall .... Metallurgia [*Mettalurgy*] [*Italian*]
metallich .... Metal, Metallic   (RU)
Metallk ...... Metallkunde [*Metallurgy*] [*German*]   (GCA)
METALLO ... Societe de Constructions Metalliques
METALLOGLOBUS ... Metalloglobus Femipari es Ertekesito Vallalat [*Trade Enterprise for Metal Products*]   (HU)
metalloizol ... Waterproof Material Made from Metal Foil   (RU)
metallopromsoyuz ... Producers' Union of the Metalworking Industry   (RU)
metallopromsoyuz ... Union of Metal Producers' Cooperatives   (RU)
Metallosbyt ... Administration for the Marketing of Ferrous Metals   (RU)
Metallurgavtomatika ... Trust for the Automation of Metallurgical Establishments   (RU)
METALLURGIZDAT ... State Scientific and Technical Publishing House of Literature on Ferrous and Nonferrous Metallurgy   (RU)
Metallurgprokatmontazh ... Trust for the Installation of Rolling-Mill and Other Metallurgical Equipment   (RU)
METALSEN ... Metal Iscileri Sendikasi [*Metal Workers Union*] [*Cyprus*]   (TU)
METAMAD ... Metale y Maderas, SA [*Colombia*]   (COL)
METAMIG ... Metais Minas Gerais [*Minas Gerais Metals*] [*Brazil*]   (LA)
METAP ..... Meldungs-und Tastatur-Alarme von Prozessen [*German*]   (ADPT)
METAROM ... Romanian Agency for Foreign Trade   (PDAA)
METAS ..... Izmir Metalurji Fabrikasi Turk Anonim Sirketi [*Izmir Metallurgy Factory Corporation*]   (TU)
METAVAL ... Metalurgica del Valle Ltda. [*Colombia*]   (COL)
METAZ ..... Metalurgicke Zavody [*Metallurgical Works*]   (CZ)
METCO ... Middle East Terminal Co. [*Saudi Arabia*]
METCON ... Metropolitan Intersection Control [*Victoria, Australia*]
METE .... Magyar Elektrotechnikai Egyesulet [*Hungarian Electrotechnical Association*]   (HU)
METE .... Magyar Elelmezesipari Tudomanyos Egyesulet [*Scientific Association of the Hungarian Food Industry*]   (HU)
METE .... Mezoegazdasagi es Elelmiszeripari Tudomanyos Egyesulet
METECNA ... Metalotecnica de Mocambique Lda.
Meteo NA .. Meteorologische Dienst Nederlandse Antillen [*Meteorological Service Netherlands Antilles*] [*Research center*]   (EAS)
meteor .... Meteorologia [*Meteorology*] [*Finland*]
meteor .... Meteorological, Meteorology   (RU)
METEOR ... Meteorological Satellite [*Former USSR*]
METEOR ... Meteorologie [*Meteorology*] [*Afrikaans*]
meteor .... Meteorologie [*French*]   (TPFD)
meteor .... Meteorology, Meteorological   (BU)
meteorolog ... Meteorologiai [*Meteorological*]   (HU)
METESZ ... Mernokok es Technikusok Szovetsege [*Federation of Engineers and Technicians*]   (HU)
METESZ ... Muszaki es Termeszettudomanyi Egyesuletek Szovetsege [*Federation of Technological and Scientific Associations*]   (HU)
Meth .... Methode [*Method*] [*German*]
METHAPLAN ... Methodenbank Ablaufsystemfuer Planung und Analyse [*German*]   (ADPT)
met haz .... Metni Hazirlayan [*Prepared Text*]   (TU)
METHODOS ... Methodisches Organisationssystem [*German*]   (ADPT)
METI .... Machine-Electrical Engineering Institute   (BU)
METIISS .. Moscow Electrotechnical Institute of Signalization and Communications Engineers [*1932-1937*]   (RU)
Metizsbyt ... All-Union State Office for the Marketing of Metalware   (RU)
METKA ..... Mehanicna Tkalnica [*Mechanized Textile Mill*] [*Celje*]   (YU)
METO .... Middle East Treaty Organization
metod .... Systematic, Methodic, Methodological   (RU)
METON .... Metonimic [*Metonymy*] [*Afrikaans*]
METOPLASTICAS ... Industrias Metoplasticas Ltda. [*Colombia*]   (COL)
metpromsoyuz ... Union of Metal Producers' Cooperatives   (RU)
Metr .... Metrica [*Metric*] [*Portuguese*]

METRANS ... Podnik pro Mezinarodni Zasilatelstvi [*International Freight Transportation Enterprise*]   (CZ)
metrich .... Metric   (RU)
Metrie .... Metairie [*Small Farm*] [*Military map abbreviation World War I*] [*French*]   (MTD)
METRIMPEX ... METRIMPEX Muszeripari Kulkereskedelmi Vallalat [*METRIMPEX Foreign Trade Enterprise of the Instrument Industry*]   (HU)
METRO .... Meralco Transit Organization [*Philippines*]   (FEA)
METRO .... Metropolitan [*Subway system*]   (DSUE)
METROBER ... Metro Koezlekedesztesi es Beruhazasi Vallalat [*Transportation Engineering and Metro Investments Office*] [*Research center*] [*Hungary*]   (EAS)
Metrogiprotrans ... State Planning and Surveying Institute for the Construction of Subways and Transportation Facilities   (RU)
METROP ... Mesno Trgovinsko Podjetje [*Commercial Meat Establishment*]   (YU)
Metroproyekt ... Technical Office for the Planning of the Moscow Subway   (RU)
Metrostroy ... State Administration of Construction of the Moscow Subway   (RU)
metr t .... Metric Ton   (RU)
mets .... Metsastys [*Hunting*] [*Finland*]
METs .... Motor Electric Power Plant   (BU)
metsh .... Metsanhoito [*Forestry*] [*Finland*]
metsz .... Metszes [*Tooling*] [*Publishing*] [*Hungary*]
metsz .... Metszet [*Engraving*] [*Hungary*]
METU .... Middle East Technical University [*Turkey*]   (PDAA)
METX .... Metadex [*AUSINET database*] [*Australia*]   (ADA)
MEU .... Federated Municipal and Shire Council Employers' Federation of Australia
MEU .... Malabar Emergency Unit [*Australia*]
MEU .... Multicultural Education Unit [*Australia*]
MEU .... Municipal Electricity Undertaking
MEU .... Museu de Etnologia do Ultramar [*Portugal*]   (DSCA)
MEUA ...... Million European Units of Account   (PDAA)
MEUPM ... Mouvement d'Entente et de l'Unite du Peuple Muluba
MEUTU .... Movimiento Estudiantil de la Universidad del Trabajo del Uruguay [*Student Movement of the Labor University of Uruguay*]   (LA)
MEV .... Macro-Economische Verkenning
MEV .... Mega Electron Volts   (EECI)
MeV .... Megaelektronowolt [*Mega-Electron-Volt*] [*Poland*]
mev .... Mevrou [*Madam*] [*Afrikaans*]
Mev .... Million Electronvolts   (RU)
MEV .... Moravske Energeticke Vyrobny [*Moravian Electric Power Plants*]   (CZ)
MEVEA ..... Mesogeiakai Epikheiriseis Viomikhanias-Emboriou-Andiprosopeion [*Mediterranean Industrial, Commercial, and Distribution Enterprises*] [*Greek*]   (GC)
MEVIEP ... Mezogazdasagi Vizi Epito Vallalat [*Agricultural Hydraulic Engineering Enterprise*]   (HU)
MEVIR ...... Movimiento de la Erradicacion de la Vivienda Insalubre [*Movement for Erradication of Substandard Housing*] [*Uruguay*]   (LAA)
mevr .... Mevrou [*Madam*] [*Afrikaans*]
Mevr .... Mevrouw [*Madam*] [*Netherlands*]   (GPO)
MEVRO .... Mezinarodni Vystava Rozhlasu [*International Radio Exposition*]   (CZ)
MEVS .... Ministry of Electrification and Water Resources [*Obsolete*]   (BU)
MEVT .... Moscow Technicum for Electric Vacuum Devices   (RU)
MEW .... Ministry of Electricity and Water [*Kuwait*]
MEWA ...... Metallwaren-Industrie [*Hardware Industry*]   (EG)
MEWA ...... Ministry of Education, Western Australia
MEWAC ... Mediterranean Europe West Africa Conference
MEWU ...... Malayan Estates Workers' Union
MEWU ...... Metal and Engineering Workers' Union [*Australia*]
MEWU ..... Mining and Energy Workers Union [*Germany*]   (EAIO)
MEX .... Meksyk [*Mexico*] [*Poland*]
MEX .... Mexico [*ANSI three-letter standard code*]   (CNC)
MEX .... Mexico City [*Mexico*] [*Airport symbol*]   (OAG)
MEXCONCRETO ... Mezclas de Concreto Ltda. [*Colombia*]   (COL)
MEXPO .... Malaysian Export Trade Center [*Ministry of Trade and Industry*]
MEXSVM ... Mexican Service Medal
MEY .... Meghauli [*Nepal*] [*Airport symbol*]   (OAG)
MEY .... Metallion Evdokimou Ypiresias [*Medal of Honorable Service*] [*Greek*]   (GC)
Mey .... Meydan [*Public Square, Field*]   (TU)
MEYAK ..... Memur Yardimlasma Kurumu [*Government Employees Mutual Aid Society*] [*Under Prime Ministry*]   (TU)
MEYBUZ ... Meyve ve Buzlu Muhafaza ve Enternasyonal Nakliyat AS [*Fruit Refrigeration and International Transport Corp.*]   (TU)
MEYEA ..... Metales y Baterias SA [*Colombia*]   (COL)
MEYSU ..... Meyva Sulari Anonim Sirketi [*Fruit Juices Corporation*]   (TU)
MEZ .... Mezzo [*Moderate*] [*Music*]
MEZ .... Mezzotinto [*Medium Tint, Half Tone*] [*Engraving*]   (ROG)

MEZ .... Ministerie van Economische Zaken [*Ministry of Economic Affairs*] [*Netherlands*]
MEZ .... Mittel Europaeische Zeit [*Central European Time*] [*German*]
MEZ .... Moravske Elektrotechnicke Zavody [*Moravian Electric Appliances Plants*] (CZ)
MEZ .... Moravskoslezske Elektrotechnicke Zavody, Narodni Podnik [*Moravian-Silesian Electric Appliances Plant, National Enterprise*] (CZ)
MEZ .... Oil Extraction Plant (RU)
mezhd .... Interjection [*Grammatical*] (BU)
mezhdunar ... International (BU)
Mezhduved ... Interdepartmental (RU)
Mezhgorsvyaz'stroy ... All-Union State Trust for the Construction of Long-Distance Wire Communications Structures (RU)
Mezhkniga ... International Book [*All-Union Association for the International Book Trade*] (RU)
mezhkolkhozstroy ... Interkolkhoz Construction Organization (RU)
Mezhrabkom ... International Workers' Committee (RU)
Mezhrabpom ... International Workers' Relief (RU)
Mezhsovkhim ... Interdepartmental Conference on Chemical Defense (RU)
mezh st .... Landmark, Boundary Mark [*Topography*] (RU)
MEZOERT ... Mezogazdasagi Termekeket Ertekesito Vallalat [*Agricultural Produce Market·Enterprise*] (HU)
MEZOKER ... Zoldseg- es Gyumolcs Ertekesito Szovetkezeti Kozpont [*Cooperative Center for the Sale of Vegetables and Fruit*] (HU)
MEZOMAG ... Mezogazdasagi Magkereskedelmi Vallalat [*Agricultural Seed-Trade Enterprise*] (HU)
MEZOSZOV ... Mezogazdasagi Eszkozoket Ertekesito Szovetkezet [*Sales Cooperative for Agricultural Epuipment*] (HU)
MEZOVILL ... Mezogazdasagi es Falusi Villanyszerelesi Vallalat [*Agricultural and Village Electrical Repair and Installation Enterprise*] (HU)
MEZU .... Missao de Estudos Zoologicos do Ultramar [*Portugal*] (DSCA)
MF .... Maandblad van Financien [*Benelux*] (BAS)
MF .... Macra na Feirme [*Irish Farm Center at An Cloigin Gorm in Laighin*]
MF .... Mali Franc [*Monetary unit*]
MF .... MAM Aviation Ltd. [*British*] [*ICAO designator*] (ICDA)
MF .... Mechanical Filter (BU)
MF .... Medical Foundation [*Australia*]
MF .... Medicine and Physical Culture Publishing House (BU)
MF .... Mediterranean Fleet
MF .... Medufrekventni [*Intermediate Frequency*] (YU)
MF .... Melomanes Francais [*Record label*] [*France*]
mf .... Merfold [*Mile*] (HU)
MF .... Mezzo Forte [*Moderately Loud*] [*Music*] (ROG)
MF .... Microphotometer (RU)
MF .... Middle French [*Language, etc.*]
MF .... Mi Favor [*My Favor*] [*Spanish*]
mf .... Millifarad (RU)
mf .... Milliphot (RU)
MF .... Miniaturni Filips [*Miniature Phillips*] [*Radio*] (YU)
MF .... Ministere des Finances [*France*] (FLAF)
MF .... Ministerio da Fazenda [*Ministry of Finance*] [*Portuguese*]
MF .... Ministerio das Financas [*Ministry of Finance*] [*Portuguese*] (WER)
MF .... Ministerstvo Financi [*Ministry of Finance*] (CZ)
MF .... Ministerstwo Finansow [*Ministry of Finance*] (POL)
MF .... Ministerul Finantelor [*Ministry of Finance*] (RO)
MF .... Ministry of Finance (RU)
mf .... Mint Fent [*As Above*] (HU)
MF .... Mlada Fronta [*The Youth Front (A newspaper and publishing house)*] (CZ)
MF .... Modulation de Frequence [*Frequency Modulation - FM*] [*French*]
Mf .... Moeglichkeitsform [*Subjunctive Mood*] [*German*]
MF .... Monophosphate (RU)
MF .... Moravska Filharmonie [*Moravian Philharmonic Orchestra*] (CZ)
MF .... Moscow Branch (RU)
MF .... Movimento Federalista [*Federalist Movement*] [*Portuguese*] (WER)
Mf .... Mufettis [*Inspector*] (TU)
MF .... Muszaki Foiskola [*Technical College*] (HU)
MF .... Mzdovy Fond [*Wage Fund*] (CZ)
MF .... SAAB-Scania AB [*Sweden*] [*ICAO aircraft manufacturer identifier*] (ICAO)
MFA .... International Astronautical Federation [*IAF*] (RU)
MFA .... International Phonetic Alphabet (RU)
MFA .... International Phonetic Association [*IPA*] (RU)
MFA .... Mafia Islands [*Tanzania*] [*Airport symbol*] (OAG)
MFA .... Malawi Football Association
MFA .... Manufacture Florence Actualite
MFA .... Menningar- og Fraedslusamband Althydu [*Workers' Educational Association*] [*Iceland*] (EY)

MFA .... Ministry of Foreign Affairs (ML)
MFA .... Motel Federation of Australia (ADA)
MFA .... Movimento das Forcas Armadas [*Armed Forces Movement*] [*Portugal*] [*Political party*] (PPE)
MFA .... Multi-Fiber Arrangement [*International trade*]
MfAA .... Ministerium fuer Auswaertige Angelegenheiten [*Ministry for Foreign Affairs*] (EG)
MfAI .... Ministerium fuer Aussen- und Innerdeutschen Handel [*Ministry for Foreign and Inner-German Trade*] [*MAI*] [*See also*] (EG)
MFAL .... Marginal Farmers' and Labourers' Development Agency [*India*]
MfaL .... Medaille fuer Ausgezeichnete Leistungen [*Medal for Distinguished Achievement*] [*German*] (EG)
MFALP ..... International Federation of Air Line Pilots Associations [*IFALPA*] (RU)
MFAM ...... Missao de Fotogrametria Aerea de Mocambique
MFANS..... Ministry of Family Affairs and National Solidarity [*Burkina Faso*]
MFANSW ... Master Farriers' Association of New South Wales [*Australia*]
MFAR........ Milicias del Frente Armado de Resistencia [*Militia of the Armed Fronts for Resistance*] [*Argentina*] (LA)
MFARACS ... Member of the Faculty of Anaesthetists, Royal Australian College of Surgeons (ADA)
MFASM.... International Federation of Medical Students Associations [*IFMSA*] (RU)
MFAts .... Methyl Fluoroacetate (RU)
MfB........... Ministerium fuer Bauwesen [*Ministry for Construction*] (EG)
MFBA........ International Federation of Library Associations [*IFLA*] (RU)
MFBB........ Metropolitan Fire Brigades Board [*Australia*]
MFBRO....... Miedzynarodowa Federacja Bojownikow Ruchu Oporu [*International Federation of Fighters in the Resistance Movement*] [*Poland*]
MFC .... Messageries Fluviales de la Cuvette
MfC........... Ministerium fuer Chemische Industrie [*Ministry for the Chemical Industry*] (EG)
MFC .... Movimiento Familiar Cristano [*Christian Family Movement*]
MFC .... Movimiento Familiar Cristiano [*Christian Family Movement*] [*Montevideo, Uruguay*] (LAA)
MFCO ...... Melbourne Family Care Organisation [*Australia*]
MFCT....... Ministry for the Federal Capital Territory [*Nigeria*]
MFD .... International Federation for Documentation [*IFD*] (RU)
MFD .... Mezinarodni Federace Dopravy [*International Transportation Federation*] (CZ)
MFDC ...... Mouvement des Forces Democratiques de la Casamance [*Senegal*] [*Political party*]
MFDK ...... Ministry of Finance and State Control [*Obsolete*] (BU)
MFDKhS... Dichloromethylphenylsilane (RU)
MFD-KLA ... Latin-American Committee of the International Federation for Documentation (RU)
MFDO .... International Federation of Children's Communities [*IFCC*] (RU)
MFDP....... Ministry of Finance and Development Planning [*Botswana*]
MFDZ .... Mezinarodni Federace Demokratickych Zen [*International Federation of Democratic Women*] (CZ)
MFDZh ..... International Federation of Democratic Women (BU)
MFE .... Magyar Fogorvosok Egyesulete [*Hungary*] (SLS)
MFE .... Maison de la Fondation Europeenne (EAIO)
MfE........... Ministerium fuer Eisenbahnwesen [*Ministry for Railroads*] [*German*] (EG)
MFE .... Mouvement Federaliste Europeen [*European Federalist Movement*] [*France*]
MFE .... Movimento Federalista Europeo [*European Federalist Movement*] [*Italian*]
MfEE .... Ministerium fuer Elektrotechnik und Elektronik [*Ministry for Electrotechnology and Electronics*] [*German*] (EG)
MFEI........ Moscow Institute of Finance and Economics (RU)
MfEMK..... Ministerium fuer Erzbergbau, Metallurgie, und Kali [*Ministry for Mining, Metalurgy, and Potash*] [*German*] (EG)
MFEP....... Ministry of Finance and Economic Planning [*Ghana*]
MFF .... International Federation of Film Archives [*IFFA*] (RU)
MFF .... Mashonaland Field Force
MFF .... Melbourne Film Festival [*Australia*]
MFF .... Mezinarodni Filmovy Festival [*International Film Festival*] (CZ)
MFF .... Mezzo Fortissimo [*Rather Loud*] [*Music*] (ADA)
MFF .... Moanda [*Gabon*] [*Airport symbol*] (OAG)
MFG .... Miners' International Federation [*MIF*] (RU)
MfG .... Ministerium fuer Gesundheitswesen [*Ministry for Health*] (EG)
MfG .... Ministerium fuer Grundstoffindustrie [*Ministry for the Raw Materials Industry*] [*German*] (EG)
MFGS........ Mittheilungen von Forschungsreisenden und Gelehrten aus den Deutschen Schutzgebieten [*Communication from Traveling Researchers and Educators from the German Protectorates*]
MFH.......... Megyei Foldhivatal [*County Land Office*] (HU)
MFHA .... Medal for Humane Action [*Berlin Airlift, 1948-9*] [*Military decoration*]

MfHV .... Ministerium fuer Handel und Versorgung [*Ministry for Trade and Supply*] [*German*] (EG)

MFI .... Benakeion Fytopathologikon Institouton [*Benakeion Plant Pathology Institute*] [*Initial letters of Benakeion are "mp" in Greek*] (GC)

MFI .... Meralco Foundation Inc. [*Philippines*]

MFI .... Military Financial Instruction

MFI .... Moscow Institute of Finance (RU)

MFI .... Moscow Pharmaceutical Institute (RU)

MFIAJ .... Marine and Fire Insurance Association of Japan (EAIO)

MFinStud .. Master of Financial Studies

MFJ .... Moala [*Fiji*] [*Airport symbol*] (OAG)

MFJ .... Movement for Freedom and Justice [*Ghana*] [*Political party*] (EY)

MFK .... International Finance Corporation [*IFC*] (RU)

MFK .... Mafeking [*South Africa*] [*Airport symbol*] (OAG)

MfK .... Ministerium fuer Kultur [*Ministry for Culture*] [*German*] (EG)

MFKE .... Mehrfunktions-Karteneinheit [*German*] (ADPT)

MFKhP ..... International Federation of Christian Trade Unions [*IFCTU*] (RU)

MFKI .... Muszaki Fizikai Kutato Intezet [*Technical Physics Research Institute*] [*Magyar Tudomanyos Akademia*] [*Research center*] [*Hungary*] (ERC)

MFKM ...... International Catholic Youth Federation [*ICYF*] (RU)

MFKM ...... Mejdunarodna Fondatzia Sveti Sveti Kiril i Metodii [*Bulgaria*] (EAIO)

MFL .... Machines Francaises Lourdes [*French Heavy Machines*] [*Commercial firm*]

MFL .... Mauritius Federation of Labor

m fl .... Med Flera [*With Others*] [*Sweden*] (GPO)

mfl .... Med Flere [*With Others*] [*Denmark*] (GPO)

m fl .... Med Flere [*And Others*] [*Norway*] (GPO)

MFL .... Mindanao Federation of Labor [*Philippines*]

MfL .... Ministerium fuer Leichtindustrie [*Ministry for Light Industry*] [*German*] (EG)

MFLB .... Motor Fuel Licensing Board [*Australia*]

MFlem ...... Middle Flemish [*Language*] (BARN)

MFLU .... Miyako Federation of Labor Unions [*Ryukyu Islands*]

MFLV .... Magyar Filmlaboratorium Vallalat [*Hungarian Film Laboratory*] (HU)

MFLZ .... Mejdunarodna Fondatzia Lyudmila Zhivkova [*Lyudmila Zhivkova International Foundation*] (EAIO)

MFM .... International Metalworkers Federation [*IMF*] (RU)

MfM .... Ministerium fuer Maschinenbau [*Ministry for Machine Building*] [*German*] (EG)

MfM .... Ministerium fuer Materialwirtschaft [*Ministry for Material Management*] [*German*] (EG)

MFM .... Modifiziertes Frequenzmodulationsverfahren [*German*] (ADPT)

MFM .... Mouvement pour le Pouvoir Proletarien [*or aux Petits*] [*Movement for Proletarian Power Malagasy*] [*Political party*] (PPW)

MFM .... Mpitolona Hoan'ny Fanjakan'ny Madinika [*Militants for the Establishment of a Proletarian Regime*] [*Malagasy*] (AF)

MFMANSW ... Master Fish Merchants' Association of New South Wales [*Australia*]

MFMK ...... International Federation of Young Cooperators [*IFYC*] (RU)

MFMM ..... International Federation of Musical Youth (RU)

MFMPK .... Magyar Forradalmi Munkas- Paraszt Kormany [*Hungarian Revolutionary Workers' and Peasants' Government*] (HU)

MFMS ...... Monaro Folk Music Society [*Australia*]

MFMU ...... Moscow Machine Accounting and Computing Office (RU)

MFN .... International Federation of Petroleum Workers [*IFPW*] (RU)

MFN .... Milford Sound [*New Zealand*] [*Airport symbol*] (OAG)

MFN .... Most-Favored-Nation [*Trading status*]

MFNE .... Ministry of Finance and National Economy [*Saudi Arabia*] (ECON)

MFNF .... Magyar Fuggetlensegi Nepfront [*Hungarian Independence People's Front*] (HU)

MFNFOT ... Magyar Fuggetlensegi Nepfront Orszagos Tanacsa [*National Council of the Hungarian Independence People's Front*] (HU)

MFNRM ... Ministarstvo na Financiite na Narodnata Republika Makedonija [*Ministry of Finance of Macedonia*] (YU)

MfNV .... Ministerium fuer Nationale Verteidigung [*Ministry for National Defense*] [*German*] (EG)

MFO .... Interbranch Turnover [*Banking*] (RU)

MFO .... Military Forwarding Organization

MFO .... Moscow Finance Department (RU)

MFO .... Multinational Force and Observers

MFOI .... Malta Federation of Industry (EAIO)

MFP .... International Graphical Federation [*IGF*] (RU)

MFP .... Magyar Fuggetlensegi Part [*Hungarian Independence Party*] (HU)

MFP .... Marematlou Freedom Party [*Basotho*] (AF)

MFP .... Master Force Plan [*Thailand*]

MFP .... Move for Peace [*Australia*]

MFP .... Movimento Federalista Portugues [*Portuguese Federalist Movement*] (WER)

MFPA .... Mauritius Family Planning Association (AF)

MFPROO ... International Federation of Unions of Employees in Public and Civil Services [*IFPCS*] (RU)

MFPRP ..... International Federation of Professional Workers in Education (BU)

MFPRP ..... World Federation of Teachers' Unions (RU)

MFQ .... Maradi [*Niger*] [*Airport symbol*] (OAG)

MFr .... Melomanes Francais [*Record label*] [*France*]

MFR .... Member of the Order of the Federal Republic

MFR .... Middle French [*Language, etc.*]

MFR .... Ministry of Financial Resources [*Burkina Faso*]

MFR .... Mouvement Familial Rural [*Rural Family Movement*]

MFRCT ..... Marine Fisheries Research Center of Tripoli (ASF)

MFRD .... Mexican Foundation for Rural Development (EAIO)

MFRDB ..... Malaysian Forest Research and Development Board (FEA)

MFROK .... International Shoe and Leather Workers' Federation [*ISLWF*] (RU)

MFRP .... International Federation of Workers in Education (BU)

MFRPSKh ... International Federation of Plantation, Agriculture, and Allied Workers [*IFPAAW*] (RU)

mfrs .... Manufacturers (EECI)

MFS .... International Shipping Federation [*ISF*] (RU)

MFS .... Mezinarodni Fond Solidarity [*International Solidarity Fund*] (CZ)

MfS .... Ministerium fuer Staatssicherheit [*Ministry for State Security*] [*See also MISTAI, MSS*] [*Germany*] (EG)

MFS .... Ministrstvo za Finance Slovenije [*Ministry of Finance of Slovenia*] (YU)

MFS .... Miraflores [*Colombia*] [*Airport symbol*] (OAG)

MFS .... Morocco Film Services

MFS .... Mutual Friendly Society [*Australia*]

MFSA .... Maurel Freres Societe Anonyme

MfSAB ...... Ministerium fuer Schwermaschinen- und Anlagenbau [*Ministry for Heavy Machine Construction and Plant Construction*] [*German*] (EG)

MFSD .... International Federation of Building and Woodworkers [*IFBWW*] (RU)

MFSF .... International Pharmaceutical Students' Federation [*IPSF*] (RU)

MFSM ...... Miedzynarodowa Federacja Schronisko Mlodziezowych [*International Youth Hostel Federation*] [*Poland*]

MFSN ...... Medzinarodna Federacia Slobodnych Novinarov [*International Federation of Free Journalists*] (CZ)

MFST .... International Federation of Commercial, Clerical, and Technical Employees [*IFCCTE*] (RU)

MFT .... International Transport Workers' Federation [*ITF*] (RU)

MFT .... Magyar Farmakologiai Tarsasag [*Hungary*] (SLS)

MFT .... Magyar Foldrajzi Tarsasag [*Hungary*] (SLS)

MFT .... Magyarhoni Foldtani Tarsulat [*Geological Society of the Hungarian Fatherland*] (HU)

MFT .... Medizinischer Fakultatentag der Bundesrepublik Deutschland Einschl [*Medical Faculty Day of the Federal Republic of Germany*] (SLS)

MFT .... Megyei Foldbirtokrendezo Tanacs [*County Council on Redistribution of Land*] (HU)

MFT .... Methylphenyltriazene (RU)

MFT .... Militants pour la Concretisation de la Revolution [*Militants for the Realization of the Revolution*] [*Malagasy*] (AF)

MFT .... Ministry of Foreign Trade (IMH)

MFT .... Svenska Foereningen foer Medicinsk Fysik och Teknik [*Sweden*] (SLS)

MFTA .... Mouvement des Femmes Travailleuses de l'Angola [*Angolan Working Women's Movement*] (AF)

MFTB .... Myanma Foreign Trade Bank [*Myanmar*] (DS)

MFTI .... Moscow Physicotechnical Institute (RU)

MFTTShP ... International Textile and Garment Workers' Federation [*ITGWF*] (RU)

MFTU .... Mehrfunktionsmagnet-film-Einheit [*German*] (ADPT)

MFU .... Functional Micromodule Block (RU)

MFU .... Malayan Film Unit (ML)

MFU .... Mfuwe [*Zambia*] [*Airport symbol*] (OAG)

MFU .... Mission Francaise d'Urbanisme

MfV .... Ministerium fuer Verkehrswesen [*Ministry for Transport*] [*German*] (EG)

MfVF .... Ministerium fuer Verarbeitungsmaschinen- und Fahrzeugbau [*Ministry for Processing-Machine and Vehicle Construction*] [*German*] (EG)

MFVNIGRI ... Moscow Branch of the All-Union Scientific Research Institute of Geological Exploration (RU)

MFVNIIZh ... Moscow Branch of the All-Union Scientific Research Institute of Fats (RU)

MFW .... Miedzynarodowy Fundusz Walutowy [*International Monetary Fund*] [*Poland*]

MFZ .... Mezzo Forzando [*Music*]

MFZhUO .. International Federation of University Women [*IFUW*] (RU)

MG .... Estado de Minas Gerais [*State of Minas Gerais*] [*Brazil*]

mg .... Gecici Madde [*Temporary Article*] [*As of a bill*]   (TU)
MG............. Gradient Method   (RU)
mg .... Last Year   (BU)
MG............. Local Oscillator   (RU)
MG............. Madagascar [*ANSI two-letter standard code*]   (CNC)
mg .... Magan [*Private, Privately Owned*]   (HU)
Mg............. Magara [*Cavern, Grotto*]   (TU)
Mg............. Magnesio [*Magnesium*] [*Chemical element*] [*Portuguese*]
MG............. Magnetbandgeraet [*German*]   (ADPT)
MG............. Magnetic Head   (RU)
MG............. Maharashtrawadi Gomantak [*India*] [*Political party*]   (PPW)
MG............. Main Gauche [*With the Left Hand*] [*Music*]
mg .... Mange [*Many*] [*Danish/Norwegian*]
MG............. Maof Airlines [*Israel*] [*ICAO designator*]   (ICDA)
MG............. Maschinengewehr [*Machine Gun*] [*German*]   (EG)
MG............. Maximum Hygroscopicity   (RU)
Mg............. Megagram   (RU)
MG............. Metallgesellschaft [*German commodities and futures contractor*]   (ECON)
MG............. Methylene Blue   (RU)
MG............. MG Car Club   (EA)
mg .... Miligrama [*Milligram*] [*Portuguese*]
mg .... Miligrama-Forca [*Milligrams of Force*] [*Portuguese*]
mg .... Miligramo [*Milligram*] [*Spanish*]
MG............. Militair Gezag [*Benelux*]   (BAS)
mg .... Milligramm [*Milligram*]   (EG)
mg .... Milligramma(a) [*Milligram*] [*Finland*]
mg .... Milligramme [*Milligram*] [*French*]
MG............. Mine-Surveying Gyrocompass   (RU)
MG............. Ministarstvo Gradevina [*Ministry of Building*]   (YU)
MG............. Ministerio da Guerra [*Ministry of War*] [*Portuguese*]
MG............. Ministerstwo Gornictwa [*Ministry of Mining*]   (POL)
MG............. Ministry of Forests [*Obsolete*]   (BU)
MG............. Misioneros de Guadalupe [*Missionaries of Guadelupe*] [*Mexico*]   (EAIO)
mG .... Mit Goldschnitt [*With Gilt Edges*] [*German*]
mg .... Mobile Group, Maneuver Group   (RU)
MG............. Molekulargewicht [*Molecular Weight*] [*German*]
MG............. Mouvement Geographique
MG............. Muvakkat Gol [*Temporary (Seasonal) Lake*]   (TU)
MGA......... International Association of Geodesy [*IAG*]   (RU)
MGA......... Maandblad Gemeente-Administratie [*Benelux*]   (BAS)
MGA......... Malaysian Golf Association   (EAIO)
MGA......... Managua [*Nicaragua*] [*Airport symbol*]   (OAG)
MGA......... Manufacture Generale Alimentaire
MGA......... Ministerio de Ganaderia y Agricultura [*Uruguay*]   (LAA)
MGA......... Ministry of Civil Aviation   (RU)
MGA......... Missao Geografica de Angola [*Angola Geographical Mission*]   (AF)
MGA......... Moscow Mining Academy   (RU)
MGA......... Motor Glass Association [*South Africa*]   (AA)
MGAD...... Machine-Gun Artillery Division [*Former USSR*]
MGAL....... Major General [*Major General*]   (CL)
MGAMID ... Moscow State Archives of the Ministry of Foreign Affairs   (RU)
MGAMTs ... Moscow Main Air Weather Center   (RU)
MGAP .... Mouvement Gabonais d'Action Populaire [*Gabonese Popular Action Movement*]   (AF)
MGAWA... Market Gardeners' Association of Western Australia
mgb .... Megabar   (RU)
MGB......... Ministerstvo Gosudarstvennoi Bezopasnosti [*Former USSR*]
MGB......... Ministerstvo Gosudarstvennoy Bezopasnosti [*Ministry of State Security*] [*Former USSR*]   (LAIN)
MGB......... Ministry of State Security [*1946-1953*]   (RU)
MGB......... Mount Gambier [*Australia*] [*Airport symbol*]   (OAG)
mgbatr........ Weather Battery [*Military*]   (RU)
MGBCS..... Murray Grey Beef Cattle Society [*Australia*]
MGBI .... Moscow State Library Institute   (RU)
MGBN ...... Bananera [*Guatemala*] [*ICAO location identifier*]   (ICLI)
Mgbr......... Ministarstvo Gradevina Broj [*Ministry of Building Number*]   (YU)
MGBT .... Moscow City Library Technicum   (RU)
MGC......... Maadi Golf Club [*Egypt*]
MGC......... Methodist Girls Comradeship [*Australia*]
MGCAE .... Mount Gravatt College of Advanced Education [*Australia*]   (ADA)
MGCB .... Coban [*Guatemala*] [*ICAO location identifier*]   (ICLI)
MGCC .... Mitsubishi Gas Chemical Co. [*Japan*]
MGCR .... Carmelita [*Guatemala*] [*ICAO location identifier*]   (ICLI)
MGCT .... Coatepeque [*Guatemala*] [*ICAO location identifier*]   (ICLI)
MGD......... Hydromagnetic   (RU)
MGD......... Machine for Deep Drainage   (RU)
MGD......... Machine Gaming Division [*Queensland, Australia*]
MGD......... Magnetohydrodynamic   (RU)
MGD......... Militair Geneeskundige Dienst [*Benelux*]   (BAS)
MGD......... Moscow City Administration   (RU)

MGD......... North-East Cargo Airlines [*Russian Federation*] [*ICAO designator*]   (FAAC)
MG/DDR .. Mathematische Gesellschaft der Deutschen Demokratischen Republik [*Mathematical Society of the German Democratic Republic*]   (SLS)
MGDG...... Magnetogas-Dynamic Generator   (RU)
MGDG...... Magnetohydrodynamic Generator   (RU)
MGDNT.... Moscow City House of Folk Art   (RU)
MGDP....... Moscow City House of Pioneers   (RU)
MGDPO.... Moscow City Volunteer Fire Society   (RU)
MGDSP..... Moscow City House of Hygiene Education   (RU)
MGDU ...... Moscow City Teacher's House   (RU)
mgdzh........ Megajoule   (RU)
MGE......... Magyar Geofizikusok Egyesulete [*Association of Hungarian Geophysicists*]   (HU)
Mge........... Mouillage [*Anchorage*] [*French*]   (NAU)
MGEFA..... Manufacturing Grocers Employees Federation of Australia
MGEI .... Moscow State Institute of Economics   (RU)
mg-ekv .... Milligram-Equivalent   (RU)
MGES........ Esquipulas [*Guatemala*] [*ICAO location identifier*]   (ICLI)
MGES........ Moscow State Electric Power Plant   (RU)
MGESA..... Manisa Genclik ve Spor Akademisi [*Manisa Youth and Sports Academy*]   (TU)
mgev .... Million Electron-Volts   (RU)
MGF .... Madagascar Franc
MGF .... Maringa [*Brazil*] [*Airport symbol*]   (OAG)
MGF .... Moscow State Philharmonic   (RU)
MGFHU..... Missao de Geografia Fisica e Humana do Ultramar, Junta de Investigacoes do Ultramar
MGFL....... Flores [*Guatemala*] [*ICAO location identifier*]   (ICLI)
MGFZB..... Mein Gott, Fueg Es zum Besten [*My God, Order It for the Best*] [*Motto of Sophie, consort of Georg Friedrich, Margrave of Brandenburg-Anspach (1563-1639)*] [*German*]
MGG......... Helical Depth Gage   (RU)
MGG......... International Geophysical Year [*IGY*]   (BU)
MGG......... Medunarodna Geofizicka Godina [*International Geophysical Year*] [*1957-1958*]   (YU)
MGGE .... International Greenland Glaciological Expedition   (RU)
MGGS ...... International Union of Geodesy and Geophysics [*IUGG*]   (RU)
MGGT....... Guatemala/La Aurora [*Guatemala*] [*ICAO location identifier*]   (ICLI)
mggts.......... Megahertz, Megacycles per Second   (RU)
MGH .... Margate [*South Africa*] [*Airport symbol*]   (OAG)
MGH .... Mathematische Gesellschaft in Hamburg [*Mathematical Society of Hamburg*]   (SLS)
MGHT....... Huehuetenango [*Guatemala*] [*ICAO location identifier*]   (ICLI)
MGI .... Imperial Ethiopian Mapping and Geographical Institute
MGI .... Long-Distance Selector   (RU)
MGI .... Marine Geological Institute of Indonesia [*Research center*]   (IRC)
MGI .... Marine Hydrophysical Institute   (RU)
MGI .... Mining and Geological Institute   (BU)
MGI .... Moscow Geodetic Institute   (RU)
MGI .... Moscow Mining Institute   (RU)
MGIAI...... Moscow State Institute of Historical Archives   (RU)
MGICA ..... Mortgage Guarantee Insurance Corporation of Australia Ltd.   (ADA)
MGiE......... Ministerstwo Gornictwa i Energetyki [*Ministry of Mining and Power*]   (POL)
MGIMIP... Moscow State Institute of Measures and Measuring Instruments   (RU)
MGIMO.... Moscow State Institute of International Relations   (RU)
MGiON ..... Ministry of Geology and Conservation of Mineral Resources   (RU)
MGiSS...... Ministry of Urban and Rural Construction   (RU)
MGIUU..... Moscow City Institute for the Advanced Training of Teachers   (RU)
MGK........ Interdepartmental Geophysical Committee   (RU)
MGK........ International Convention Concerning the Carriage of Goods by Rail   (RU)
MGK........ International Geological Congress   (RU)
MG K........ Mezogazdasagi Konyv- es Folyoirat Kiado [*Publishers of Agricultural Books and Periodicals*]   (HU)
MGk........ Middle Greek [*Language*]   (BARN)
MGK........ Milli Guvenlik Kurulu [*National Security Council*]   (TU)
MGK........ Ministerstwo Gospodarki Komunalnej [*Ministry of Municipal Economy*]   (POL)
MGK........ Ministry of State Control   (RU)
MGK........ Modern Greek [*Language, etc.*]
MGK........ Moscow City Committee   (RU)
MGK........ Moscow City Office   (RU)
MGK........ Moscow State Conservatory Imeni P. I. Chaykovskiy   (RU)
MGKA....... Moscow City Lawyers' Collegium   (RU)
mgkal........ Megacalorie   (RU)
MGKhI...... Moscow State Art Institute Imeni V. I. Surikov   (RU)
mgkhts .... Megahertz   (BU)

MGKI .... Magyar Gazdasagkutato Intezet [*Hungarian Institute of Economic Research*] (HU)
MGKI .... Mezogazdasagi Gepkiserleti Intezet [*Experimental Institute for Agricultural Machinery*] (HU)
MGKT ...... Moscow State Chamber Theater (RU)
MGKU ...... Mumbai Girni Kamgar Union [*Bombay Mill Workers' Union*] [*India*]
mgl .... Mangler [*Missing*] [*Danish/Norwegian*]
MGL .... Marine Hydrophysical Laboratory (RU)
MGL .... Miniere des Grands Lacs Africains [*African Great Lakes Mining Co.*] [*Zaire*] (AF)
MGL .... Mongolian Airlines [*ICAO designator*] (FAAC)
MGLB .... Moscow City Lecture Bureau (RU)
MGLL .... La Libertad [*Guatemala*] [*ICAO location identifier*] (ICLI)
MGM .... Magasins Gabonais Modernes
MGM .... Magyar Gordulocsapagy Muvek [*Hungarian Ballbearing Works*] (HU)
mgm .... Megameter
MGM .... Meteoroloji Genel Mudurlugu [*Turkey*] (MSC)
MGM .... Missao Geografica de Mocambique, Junta de Investigacoes do Ultramar
MGM .... Muhasebat Genel Mudurlugu [*Directorate General of Accounting*] (TU)
MGMI ...... Magnitogorsk Mining and Metallurgical Institute Imeni G. I. Nosov (RU)
MGMI ...... Moscow Hydrometeorological Institute [*1930-1941*] (RU)
MGMI ...... Moscow Institute of Water Reclamation (RU)
MGMI ...... Second Moscow State Medical Institute Imeni N. I. Pirogov (RU)
MGML ...... Malacatan [*Guatemala*] [*ICAO location identifier*] (ICLI)
MGMM ..... Melchor De Mencos [*Guatemala*] [*ICAO location identifier*] (ICLI)
MGMP ...... Multispeed Hydromechanical Gear (RU)
MGMR ...... Ministry of Geology and Mineral Resources [*China*]
Mgmt .... Management (PWGL)
MGN .... Majlis Gerakan Negara [*National Operations Council*] (ML)
mgn .... Millihenry (RU)
MGN .... Morgan Aviation Services Ltd. [*Nigeria*] [*ICAO designator*] (FAAC)
Mgne .... Montagne [*Mountain*] [*Military map abbreviation World War I*] [*French*] (MTD)
MGNITI .... Moscow City Scientific Research Institute of Tuberculosis (RU)
MGO .... Militaergerichtsordnung [*Rules of Procedure of a Military Court*] (EG)
MGO .... Moscow City Branch, Moscow City Department (RU)
mgom .... Megohm (BU)
MGON ...... Ministry of Geology and Conservation of Mineral Resources, USSR (RU)
MGONI ..... Moscow City Real Estate Department (RU)
MGOPS .... Ministry of Forests and Protection of Environment (BU)
MGOT .... Moscow City Labor Department (RU)
MGOTS .... Long-Distance Oblast Telephone Exchange (RU)
MGOTZK ... Moscow City Association of Theater and Show Ticket Offices (RU)
MGP .... Macarthur Gruen Party [*Political party*] [*Australia*]
MGP .... Magnetic Directional Gyro (RU)
MGP .... Manga [*Papua New Guinea*] [*Airport symbol*] (OAG)
MGP .... Marina de Guerra del Peru [*Peruvian Navy*] (LA)
MGP .... Metal-Film Hermetically Sealed Precision (Resistor) (RU)
MGP .... Milli Guven Partisi [*National Reliance Party*] (TU)
MGP .... Morgan Gallup Poll [*Australia*]
MGP .... Moscow City Administration (RU)
MGP .... Mouvement Gaulliste Populaire [*Popular Gaullist Movement*] [*France*] [*Political party*] (PPW)
MGP .... Piston Depth Gauge (RU)
MGPB .... Puerto Barrios [*Guatemala*] [*ICAO location identifier*] (ICLI)
MGPDI ..... Moscow State Pedagogical Institute of Defectology (RU)
MGPI .... Melekess State Pedagogical Institute (RU)
MGPI .... Moscow City Pedagogical Institute Imeni V. P. Potemkin (RU)
MGPI .... Moscow State Pedagogical Institute Imeni K. Liebknecht (RU)
MGPI .... Moscow State Pedagogical Institute Imeni V. I. Lenin (RU)
MGPIIYa .. First Moscow State Pedagogical Institute of Foreign Languages (RU)
MGP iMR ... Ministry of State Food and Material Reserves, USSR (RU)
MGPP .... Mechanized Hospital Field Laundry (RU)
MGPP .... Poptun [*Guatemala*] [*ICAO location identifier*] (ICLI)
MGQ .... Mogadishu [*Somalia*] [*Airport symbol*] (OAG)
MGQC ...... Quiche [*Guatemala*] [*ICAO location identifier*] (ICLI)
MGQZ ...... Quezaltenango [*Guatemala*] [*ICAO location identifier*] (ICLI)
Mgr .... Manager (PWGL)
MGR .... Marina de Guerra Revolucionaria [*Revolutionary Navy*] [*Cuba*] (LA)
MGR .... Medieval Greek [*Language, etc.*]
MGR .... M. G. Ramachandran [*Indian film actor and political party leader*]
M GR .... Middle Greek [*Language, etc.*] (ROG)

mgr .... Milligramm [*Milligram*] (HU)
Mgr .... Monseigneur [*My Lord*] [*French*] (GPO)
Mgr .... Monsignor (IDIG)
MGR .... Mouvement de la Gauche Reformatrice [*Movement of the Reformist Left*] [*France*] [*Political party*] (PPW)
MGRC .... Melbourne Greyhound Racing Club [*Australia*]
MGRI .... Moscow Institute of Geological Exploration Imeni Sergo Ordzhonikidze (RU)
MGRS .... Moscow City Administration of the Radio Wire Broadcasting Network (RU)
MGRS .... Moscow City Radio Wire Broadcasting Network (RU)
MGRT .... Retalhuleu [*Guatemala*] [*ICAO location identifier*] (ICLI)
MGS .... International Freight Agreement (RU)
MGS .... International Gas Union [*IGU*] (RU)
MGS .... International Geographical Union (RU)
MGS .... International Geophysical Cooperation (RU)
MGS .... Mangaia [*Cook Islands*] [*Airport symbol*] (OAG)
MGS .... Master Gas System [*Saudi Arabia*]
MGS .... Methodist Girls School (ML)
MGS .... Mezhdunarodnoye Gruzovoye Soglasheniye [*Agreement Concerning International Railroad Freight Traffic (Between USSR and Satellites)*] (EG)
mgs .... Milligram Force (RU)
MGS .... Missive van den (als Regel Eersten) Gouvernementssecretaris [*Benelux*] (BAS)
MGS .... Moscow City Soviet (RU)
MGS .... Museum of City Sculpture (RU)
MGSA .... Marriage Guidance South Australia
MGSB .... Local Geodetic Information Office (RU)
MGSC .... Malaysian General Service Corps (ML)
MGSh .... Naval General Staff (RU)
MGSJ .... San Jose [*Guatemala*] [*ICAO location identifier*] (ICLI)
MGSM ...... San Marcos [*Guatemala*] [*ICAO location identifier*] (ICLI)
MGSNKh .. Moscow City Council of the National Economy (RU)
MGSovet .... Interdepartmental Geodetic Council (RU)
MGSPS ..... Moscow City Council of Trade Unions (RU)
MGSS .... International Year of the Quiet Sun [*IQSY*] (RU)
MGSS .... Ministry of Urban and Rural Construction (RU)
MGT .... Margate Air Services [*South Africa*] [*ICAO designator*] (FAAC)
Mgt .... Megaton (RU)
MGT .... Millingimbi [*Airport symbol*]
MGT .... Missao Geografica de Timor, Junta de Investigacoes do Ultramar
MGTAV ... Modern Greek Teachers' Association of Victoria [*Australia*]
MGTE .... Moscow State Music Hall (RU)
MGTI .... Mezogeptervezo Iroda [*Office for the Design of Agricultural Machinery*] (HU)
MGTS .... Long-Distance Telephone Exchange (RU)
Mgts .... Megahertz, Megacycles per Second (RU)
MGTS .... Moscow City Telephone Network (RU)
MGTUA .... Member of the Government Technology Users Association [*Australia*]
MGU .... Marine Geoscience Unit [*University of Cape Town, Geological Survey*] [*South Africa*] (AA)
MGU .... Mezogazdasagi Gepuzem [*Agricultural Machine Factory*] (HU)
MGU .... Moscow City Administration (RU)
MGU .... Moscow State University Imeni M. V. Lomonosov (RU)
MGU .... Moskovskiy Gosudarstvenniy Universitet [*Moscow State University*] [*Former USSR*] (MSC)
MGU .... Powerful Loudspeaker (RU)
MGULP ... Moscow City Administration of Light Industry (RU)
MGUMP .. Moscow City Administration of Local Industry (RU)
MGV .... Maandblad voor de Geestelijke Volksgezondheid [*Benelux*] (BAS)
mgvt .... Megawatt (RU)
mgvt-ch ..... Megawatt-Hour (RU)
MGW .... Messgeraetewerk [*Measuring-Instrument Plant*] (EG)
MGWA ...... Marriage Guidance Western Australia
MGX .... Moabi [*Gabon*] [*Airport symbol*] (OAG)
mgy .... Magangyujtemeny [*Private Collection*] [*Hungary*]
MGYE .... Magyar Gyogypedagogusok Egyesulete [*Association of Hungarian Teachers in Special Education*] (HU)
MGYT .... Magyar Gyogyszertudomanyi Tarsasag [*Hungarian Pharmaceutical Association*] (HU)
MGZ .... Maschinengewehr-Zieleinrichtung [*Machine-Gun Sighting Mechanism*] [*German military - World War II*]
MGZ .... Mergui [*Myanmar*] [*Airport symbol*] (OAG)
MGZF .... Maschinengewehr-Zielfernrohr [*Machine-Gun Telescopic Sight*] [*German military - World War II*]
MGZhD ..... Moscow City Railways [*Trust*] (RU)
MGZPI ...... Moscow State Pedagogical Correspondence Institute (RU)
MH .... Air-Cushion Vehicle built by Mitsubishi [*Japan*] [*Usually used in combination with numerals*]
MH .... Almarhum [*Deceased*] (IN)
MH .... Magyar Helikon [*Hungarian Helicon Publishing House*] (HU)
MH .... Marshall Islands [*ANSI two-letter standard code*] (CNC)

MH .... Matica Hrvatska [*A Croatian literary and publishing society*] [*Zagreb*] (YU)
mh .... Megallohely [*Stop*] (HU)
mH .... Milihenry [*Millihenry*] [*Portuguese*]
MH .... Ministerstvo Hornictvi [*Ministry of Mining*] (CZ)
MH .... Ministerstwo Hutnictwa [*Ministry of Metallurgy*] (POL)
MH .... Misr Hotels Co. [*Egypt*]
MH .... Mitsubishi Heavy Industries Ltd. [*Japan*] [*ICAO aircraft manufacturer identifier*] (ICAO)
MHA .... Madonna House Apostolate [*Combermere, ON*] (EAIO)
MHA .... Mahdia [*Guyana*] [*Airport symbol*] (OAG)
MHA .... Maritime Heritage Association [*Australia*]
MHA .... Meat Hygiene Authority [*Australia*]
MHA .... Medal for Humane Action [*Berlin Airlift, 1948-9*] [*Military decoration*]
MHA .... Mining Houses of Australia
MHaBZCH ... Magnezitove Hute a Bane Zavodu Cervenej Hviezdy [*Red Star Magnetite Works and Mines*] (CZ)
MHAI .... Mott, Hay & Anderson International
MHAM ..... Amapala [*Honduras*] [*ICAO location identifier*] (ICLI)
MHAP ...... Muzeum Historyczne Aptekarstwa Polskiego [*Historical Museum of Polish Pharmacy*] (POL)
MHAS ...... Mental Health Advocacy Service [*Australia*]
MHAST .... Missao Hidrografica de Angola e Sao Tome
MHAT ...... Moskovski Hudozestveni Akademski Teatr [*Moscow Academic Art Theater*] (YU)
MHAWA... Master Hairdressers' Association of Western Australia
MHC......... Mesovita Hemiska Ceta [*Mixed Chemical Company*] [*Military*] (YU)
MHCA...... Catacamas [*Honduras*] [*ICAO location identifier*] (ICLI)
MHCAT .... Minehunter Catamaran [*Military*]
MHCC...... Mental Health Coordinating Council [*Australia*]
MHCG...... Comayagua [*Honduras*] [*ICAO location identifier*] (ICLI)
MHCH ...... Choluteca [*Honduras*] [*ICAO location identifier*] (ICLI)
MHCT ...... Puerto Castilla [*Honduras*] [*ICAO location identifier*] (ICLI)
MHCU ...... Ministere de l'Habitat, de la Construction, et de l'Urbanisme [*Algeria*]
MHD .... Magyar Hajo es Darugyar [*Hungarian Ship and Crane Factory*] (HU)
MHD .... Mashhad [*Iran*] [*Airport symbol*] (OAG)
MHD .... Meteorologischer-Hydrologischer Dienst [*Meteorological and Hydrological Service*] (EG)
Mhd .... Middelhoogduits [*Middle High German*] [*Language, etc.*] [*Afrikaans*]
MHD .... Miejski Handel Detaliczny [*Municipal Retail Trade*] (POL)
MHD .... Ministerstvo Hutniho Prumyslu a Rudnych Dolu [*Ministry of the Metallurgical Industry and Ore Mines*] (CZ)
MHD .... Ministerstwo Handlu Detalicznego [*Ministry of Retail Trade*] (POL)
mhd .... Mittelhochdeutsch [*Middle High German*] [*Language, etc.*] [*German*]
MHDGS.... Ministarstvo Hrvatskog Domobranstva - Glavni Stozer [*Ministry of Croatian Home Defense - General Headquarters*] [*World War II*] (YU)
MHE.......... Magyar Hajozasi Egyesulet [*Hungarian Shipping Association*] (HU)
MHeb .... Middle Hebrew [*Language, etc.*] (BJA)
MHEO ...... Migrant Health Education Officer [*Australia*]
MHESR .... Ministry of Higher Education and Scientific Research [*Burkina Faso*]
MHF.......... Al Maimouni & Al Humaidan Factories [*Saudi Arabia*]
MHF.......... Mezinarodni Hudebni Festival [*International Music Festival*] (CZ)
MHF.......... Microsillon et Haute-Fidelite [*Record label*] [*France*]
MHF(V) .... Mental Health Foundation (Victoria) [*Australia*]
MHG .... Mannheim [*Germany*] [*Airport symbol*] (OAG)
MHG .... Materialhanteringsgruppen [*Swedish Association of Suppliers of Mechanical Handling*] (EAIO)
MHG .... Mauritius Hotels Group
MHG .... Middle High German [*Language, etc.*]
MHG .... Modern High German [*Language, etc.*] (ROG)
MHGA ...... Member, Horological Guild of Australia (ADA)
MHH .... Marsh Harbour [*Bahamas*] [*Airport symbol*] (OAG)
MHH .... Medizinische Hochschule Hannover [*Information retrieval*]
MHI........... Minehunter Inshore [*Royal Australian Navy*]
MHI........... Mitsubishi Heavy Industries Ltd. [*Nuclear energy*] [*Japan*] (NRCH)
MHIC....... Islas Del Cisne O Santanilla [*Honduras*] [*ICAO location identifier*] (ICLI)
MHIDAS .. Major Hazard Incident Data Service [*Atomic Energy Authority*] [*British*] [*Information service or system*] (IID)
MHJ .... Minosegi Hangszerkeszito es Javito Kisipari Termeloszovetkezet [*Cooperative Enterprise for the Production and Repair of Musical Instruments*] (HU)
MHJU .... Juticalpa [*Honduras*] [*ICAO location identifier*] (ICLI)
MHK .... Medunarodna Hidrografska Konferencija [*International Hydrographic Conference*] (YU)

MHK .... Minimale Hemmkonzentration [*Minimum Inhibiting Concentration*] [*German*]
MHK .... Munkara Harcra Kesz [*Ready for Work and Defense*] (HU)
MHKD ...... Matica Hrvatskih Kazalisnih Dobrovoljaca [*Croatian Amateur Theatrical Society*] [*Zagreb*] (YU)
MHKLA .... Member of the Hong Kong Library Association
Mhl .... Mahalli [*Local, Quarter*] [*As of a city*] (TU)
MHL.......... Marrickville Holdings Limited [*Australia*] (ADA)
MHL.......... Marshall Islands [*ANSI three-letter standard code*] (CNC)
Mhlbes....... Muehlenbesitzer [*Mill Owner*] [*German*]
MHLC ...... La Ceiba/Goloson Internacional [*Honduras*] [*ICAO location identifier*] (ICLI)
MHLE .... La Esperanza [*Honduras*] [*ICAO location identifier*] (ICLI)
MHLM...... San Pedro Sula/La Mesa Internacional [*Honduras*] [*ICAO location identifier*] (ICLI)
MHLNS .... Museo de Historia Natural La Salle [*Venezuela*] (DSCA)
MHM .... Miejski Handel Miesny [*Municipal Meat Trade*] (POL)
MHM .... Miejski Handel Mleczarski [*Poland*]
MHM .... Mill Hill Missionaries
MHMA ...... Marcala [*Honduras*] [*ICAO location identifier*] (ICLI)
MHMA ..... Master House Movers' Association [*Australia*]
MHN .... Museo Historico Nacional [*National Historical Museum*] [*Buenos Aires, Argentina*] (LAA)
MHNJ ...... Guanaja [*Honduras*] [*ICAO location identifier*] (ICLI)
Mhno .... Middelbaar Huishoud- en Nijverheidsonderwijs [*Benelux*] (BAS)
MHNV ...... Nuevo Ocotepeque [*Honduras*] [*ICAO location identifier*] (ICLI)
MHO .... Maandblad voor het Handelsonderwijs [*Benelux*] (BAS)
MHO .... Materiel Hospitalier Outre-Mer
MHO .... Metallurgies Hoboken-Overpelt [*Antwerp, Belgium*]
MHOA ...... Olanchito [*Honduras*] [*ICAO location identifier*] (ICLI)
MHP.......... Milli Hedef Partisi [*National Goal Party*] [*Turkish Cyprus*] [*Political party*] (PPE)
MHP.......... Milli Yetci Hareket Partisi [*Nationalist Action Party*] [*CKMP*] [*Formerly,*] (TU)
MHPA ...... Palmerola [*Honduras*] [*ICAO location identifier*] (ICLI)
MHPE .... Progreso [*Honduras*] [*ICAO location identifier*] (ICLI)
MHPL .... Puerto Lempira [*Honduras*] [*ICAO location identifier*] (ICLI)
MHPRD.... Ministerstvo Hutniho Prumyslu a Rudnych Dolu [*Ministry of the Metallurgical Industry and Ore Mines*] (CZ)
MHPU ...... Puerto Cortes [*Honduras*] [*ICAO location identifier*] (ICLI)
MHQ .... Mariehamn [*Finland*] [*Airport symbol*] (OAG)
MHR .... Members of the House of Representatives
MHRA ...... Malta Hotels and Restaurants Association (EAIO)
MHRB ...... Mental Health Review Board [*Victoria, Australia*]
MHRD ...... Ministerstvo Hutniho Prumyslu a Rudnych Dolu [*Ministry of the Metallurgical Industry and Ore Mines*] (CZ)
MHRT....... Magyar Hajozasi Reszvenytarsasag [*Hungarian Shipping Company Limited*] (HU)
MHRU ...... Materials Handling Research Unit [*University of the Witwatersrand*] [*South Africa*] (AA)
MHRU ...... Ruinas De Copan [*Honduras*] [*ICAO location identifier*] (ICLI)
MHS.......... Malta Historical Society [*Maltese*] (SLS)
MHS.......... Matabele Home Society
MHS.......... Mladezne Hnuti za Svobodu [*Youth Freedom Movement*] (CZ)
MHSA .... Military Historical Society of Australia (ADA)
MHSP .... San Pedro Sula [*Honduras*] [*ICAO location identifier*] (ICLI)
MHSR .... Santa Rosa De Copan [*Honduras*] [*ICAO location identifier*] (ICLI)
MHSS(NI) ... Ministry of Health and Social Services (Northern Ireland)
MHSz .... Magyar Helyesiras Szabalyai [*Hungarian Orthographic Rules*] (HU)
MHSZ .... Magyar Honvedelmi Sportszovetseg [*Hungarian Sports Federation for National Defense*] (HU)
MHSZ .... Magyar Honvedelmi Szovetseg [*Hungarian National Defense Association*] (HU)
MHSZ .... Santa Barbara [*Honduras*] [*ICAO location identifier*] (ICLI)
MHT......... Magyar Hidrologiai Tarsasag [*Hungarian Hydrological Association*] (HU)
mht............ Med Hensyn Til [*With Regard To*] [*Norway*] (GPO)
mht............ Med Hensyn Til [*With Regard To*] [*Denmark*] (GPO)
MHTE....... Tela [*Honduras*] [*ICAO location identifier*] (ICLI)
MHTG....... Tegucigalpa/Toncontin Internacional [*Honduras*] [*ICAO location identifier*] (ICLI)
MHTJ .... Trujillo [*Honduras*] [*ICAO location identifier*] (ICLI)
MHU .... Medunarodni Hidrografski Ured [*International Hydrographic Office*] (YU)
MHU .... Ministerio da Habitacao e Urbanismo [*Ministry of Housing and Urbanization*] [*Portuguese*] (WER)
MHV .... Magyar Hanglemezgyarto Vallalat [*Hungarian Sound Recording Enterprise*] (HU)
MHV .... Mellektermek- es Hulladekgyujto Vallalat [*Trash and Garbage Collection Enterprise*] (HU)
MHV .... Minder as Houervrag [*Afrikaans*]
MHW .... Maandblad voor Handelswetenschappen en Administratieve Praktijk [*Benelux*] (BAS)

MHW .... Metallhuetten- und Halbzeugwerke, Berlin (VEB) [*Berlin Metallurgical and Semifinished Product Works (VEB)*] (EG)

MHW .... Ministerstwo Handlu Wewnetrznego [*Ministry of Domestic Trade*] (POL)

MHW .... Ministry of Health and Welfare [*Japan*] (ECON)

MHW .... Mittleres Hochwasser [*Mean High Water Mark*] [*German*] (EG)

MHWU ..... Mauritius Hotel Workers Union (AF)

MHY .... Morehead [*Papua New Guinea*] [*Airport symbol*] (OAG)

MHz........... Megahertz [*Megahertz*] [*German*] (EG)

MHZ.......... Ministerstwo Handlu Zagranicznego [*Ministry of Foreign Trade*] (POL)

MI .... Groupe Musulman-Independent pour la Defense du Federalisme Algerien

MI .... Helicopter Designed by M. L. Mil' (RU)

MI .... Induction Method (RU)

MI .... Institute of Mathematics (BU)

MI .... Institute of Mathematics Imeni V. A. Steklov (RU)

Mi .... Machi [*Town*] [*Japan*] (NAU)

MI .... Magister Inzynier [*Master of Technical Sciences*] [*Poland*]

MI .... Marches Industriels [*France*] (FLAF)

MI .... Marker Pulse (RU)

MI .... Marubeni International Finance [*Trading company*] [*Japan*]

MI .... Masinski Institut [*Mechanical Engineering Institute*] (YU)

MI .... Mensa International [*British*] (EAIO)

MI .... Meridional Index (RU)

MI .... Metalna Industrija [*Metal Industry*] (YU)

MI .... Meteorologisk Institut [*Meteorological Institute*] [*Norway*] (MSC)

mi .... Miedzy Innymi [*Among Others*] (POL)

Mi .... Mijns Inziens [*Benelux*] (BAS)

MI .... Mil [*Former USSR*] [*ICAO aircraft manufacturer identifier*] (ICAO)

MI .... Milano [*Car registration plates*] [*Italian*]

Mi .... Milchzug [*Milk Train*] (EG)

MI .... Militia Mariae Immaculatae [*Militia of the Immaculate*] (EAIO)

MI .... Ministerio da Industria [*Ministry of Industry*] [*Portuguese*] (WER)

MI .... Ministerstvo Informaci [*Ministry of Information*] (CZ)

MI .... Ministerul de Interne [*Ministry of the Interior*] (RO)

MI .... Ministry of Information [*British*] [*World War II*]

Mi .... Misaki [*Cape*] [*Mki*] [*See also*] [*Japan*] (NAU)

MI .... Mischer [*Mixer*] [*German*] (ADPT)

MI .... Mobility International (EA)

MI .... Monitor International (ASF)

MI .... Moose, International (EAIO)

MI .... Multiseater Fighter (RU)

mi .... Myns Insiens [*In My Opinion*] [*Afrikaans*]

MI .... Naval Fighter Airplane (RU)

mi .... Palace of Publication (RU)

MI .... Pulse Modulator (RU)

MI .... Testing Methods (RU)

MIA .... AMI (Air Mercury International) [*Belgium*] [*ICAO designator*] (FAAC)

MIA .... Malaysia Institute of Art (EAIO)

MIA .... Maldives International Airlines (FEA)

MIA .... Manila International Airport

MIA .... Marxista Ifjusagi Akademia [*Marxist Youth Academy*] (HU)

MIA .... Maschinelle Inventur-Auswertung [*German*] (ADPT)

MIA .... Materials and Research on the Archaeology of the USSR (RU)

MIA .... Meat Inspectors' Association [*Australia*]

MIA .... Medical Industry Association [*Bulgaria*] (EAIO)

MIA .... Metal Industries Association [*Australia*]

MIA .... Movimento para a Independencia de Angola

MIA .... Movimiento Industrial Argentino [*Argentine Industrial Movement*] (LA)

MIA .... Murray Irrigation Area [*Australia*]

MIA .... Murrumbidgee Irrigation Area [*Australia*] (BARN)

MIA .... Museum of the History of Architecture (RU)

MIAA .... Medical Industry Association of Australia

MIAA .... Meetings Industry Association of Australia

MIAA .... Missao de Inqueritos Agricolas de Angola

MIAA .... Mortgage Insurers Association of Australia (ADA)

MIA &DMB ... Murray Irrigation Area and Districts Management Board [*Australia*]

MIA(APS) ... Meat Inspectors' Association (Australian Public Service)

MIAC .... Manufacturing Industries Advisory Council [*Australia*] (PDAA)

MIAC .... Meat Industry Advisory Committee [*Australia*]

MIACO ..... Malta International Aviation Co.

MIAESR ... Melbourne Institute of Applied Economic and Social Research [*Australia*]

MIAF........ Mauritanian Islamic Air Force (PDAA)

MIAGE...... Maitrise de Methodes Informatiques Appliquees a la Gestion [*French*]

MIAM .... Manufacture Ivoirienne d'Articles de Menage

MIAMSI ... Mouvement International d'Apostolat des Milieux Sociaux Independants [*International Movement of Apostolate in the Independent Social Milieux*] [*Vatican City*] (EAIO)

MIAN .... Institute of Mathematics Imeni V. A. Steklov of the Academy of Sciences, USSR (RU)

Mian .... Kasa Imienia Mianowskiego [*Mianowski Fund*] [*For the Promotion of Science and Letters in Poland*] (POL)

MIAN .... Medunarodni Institut za Administrativne Nauke [*International Institute on Administration*] (YU)

MIAP........ Movimiento Independiente de Accion Popular [*Independent Movement for Popular Action*] [*Venezuela*] (LA)

MIAQ .... Music Industry Association of Queensland [*Australia*]

MIAS........ Muhyiddin Ibn Arabi Society

MIASA ..... Motorcycle Industry Association of South Australia

MIASS ..... Marble Image Art of SomeTime Slims [*Cigarette brand*] [*Japan*]

MIAT .... Music Industry Association of Tasmania [*Australia*]

MIATA ...... Murrumbidgee Irrigation Area Tourist Association [*Australia*]

MIB .... Battelle Memorial Institute [*US*] (RU)

MIB .... Malaysian Infantry Brigade (ML)

MIB .... Mecanisation Industrielle des Bois

MIB .... Mediterranean Insurance Brokers Ltd.

MIB .... Medium Industry Bank [*South Korea*] (IMH)

MIB .... Mexican Investment Board [*Public relations and investor assistance*] [*Mexico*] (CROSS)

MIB .... Mezhdunarodnyi Investitsionnyi Bank [*International Investment Bank - IIB*] [*Moscow, USSR*] (EAIO)

mib .... Motorized Engineer Battalion (RU)

MIB .... Mouvement d'Insoumission Bretonne [*Breton Insubordination Movement*] [*France*] (PD)

MIBA .... Malta International Business Authority (EY)

MIBA .... Miniere de Bakwanga [*Bakwanga Mining Co.*] [*Zaire*] (AF)

MIBIEN ... Ministerio de Bienestar Social [*Ministry of Social Welfare*] [*Nicaragua*] (LA)

MIBOR ..... Madrid Interbank Offered Rate (MHDW)

MIBRAG... Mitteldeutschen Brunkohle (ECON)

MIC .... Aerolineas de Michoacan [*Mexico*] [*ICAO designator*] (FAAC)

MIC .... Malaysian Indian Congress [*Political party*] (PPW)

MIC .... Management and Investment Company [*Australia*]

MIC .... Marketing Intelligence Corp. [*Information service or system*] (IID)

MIC .... Meat Industry Council [*Australia*]

MIC .... Meteorological Information Committee [*NATO*] (NATG)

MIC .... Metropolitan Industrial Court [*Victoria, Australia*]

MIC .... Mikrocumputer [*German*] [*Micro Computer*] (ADPT)

MIC .... Mining Industry Council of Thailand (EAIO)

MIC .... Ministerio de Industria e Comercio [*Ministry of Industry and Commerce*] [*Brazil*] (LA)

MIC .... Ministerul Industriei Chimice [*Ministry of the Chemical Industry*] (RO)

MIC .... Modulation d'Impulsions Codees [*French*] (ADPT)

MIC .... Modulation par Impulsion et Codage [*French*] (ADPT)

MIC .... Modulation par Impulsions Codees [*French*] (ADPT)

MIC .... Mouvement Chretien des Independents et des Cadres [*Christian Movement of Independents and Professionals*] [*Belgium*] (WER)

MIC .... Movimiento de Integracion Colorada [*Paraguay*] [*Political party*] (EY)

MIC .... Movimiento de Integracion Cristiana [*Christian Integration Movement*] [*Colorado*] (LA)

MIC .... Movimiento de Izquierda Cristiana [*Christian Left Movement*] [*Chile*] (LA)

MICA .... Microwave Information Council of Australia

MICA .... Missile d'Interception et de Combat Aerien [*Aerial Combat and Missile Interception*] [*Military aircraft equipment*] [*French*]

MICAI ...... Mines et Carrieres de l'Imerina

MICC........ Malaysian International Chamber of Commerce (DS)

MICCI ...... Malaysia International Chamber of Commerce and Industry (EAIO)

MICE........ Manufacture Ivoirienne de Confection Enfantine

MICE........ Ministerio de Comercio del Exterior [*Ministry of Foreign Trade*] [*Nicaragua*] (LA)

MICh .... Ministerul Industriei Chimice [*Ministry of the Chemical Industry*] (RO)

MICHFOND ... Christian Michelsens Institutt for Videnskap og Andsfrihet [*Christian Michelsen Institute of Science and Intellectual Freedom*] [*Research center*] [*Norway*] (ARC)

MICI......... Manufacture d'Imprimerie et de Cartonnage Ivoirienne

MICK .... Manufacture Industrielle de Cuirs de Kaedi [*Mauritania*]

MICLB ...... Management and Investment Companies Licensing Board [*Australia*]

MICM .... Ministerul Industriei Constructiilor de Masini [*Ministry of the Machine Building Industry*] (RO)

MICMUE ... Ministerul Industriei Constructiilor de Masini-Unelte si Electrotehnicii [*Ministry of the Machine Tool Building and Electrical Engineering Industry*] (RO)

MICO .... Motor Industries Company Ltd. [*India*]

MICOIN ... Ministerio de Comercio Interior [*Ministry of Domestic Trade*] [*Nicaragua*] (LA)

MICOL...... Manufacturas Industriales Colombianas Ltda. [*Colombia*] (COL)

MICONEX ... Multinational Instrumentation Conference and Exposition [*China Instrument Society*]

MICONS... Ministerio de la Construccion [*Ministry of Construction*] [*Cuba*] (LA)

MICONS... Ministerio de la Construccion [*Ministry of Construction*] [*Nicaragua*] (LA)

MICP........ Management and Investment Companies Program

MICS........ Member of the South African Institute of Computer Scientists (AA)

MICSETT ... Member of the Institute of Civil Service Engineering Technicians and Technologists [*South Africa*] (AA)

MICSIG .... Microprocessor Special Interest Group [*Australian Computer Society, Canberra Branch*]

MICTI....... Ministerio de Industria, Comercio, Turismo, e Integracion [*Ministry of Industry, Commerce, Tourism, and Integration*] [*Peru*] (LA)

MICUM .... Mission Interalliee de Controle des Usines et des Mines [*Inter-Allied Mission to Control Manufacturing and Mining*] [*French*]

MICUMA ... Societe des Mines de Cuivre de Mauritanie

MID.......... International Institute for Documentation (RU)

MID.......... MacCarthy Island Division

MID.......... Mailles Inclinees a Droite [*Knitting*] [*French*]

MID.......... Management Information Division [*Vietnam*]

MID.......... Merida [*Mexico*] [*Airport symbol*] (OAG)

MID.......... Military Intelligence Directorate [*Malaysia*] (ML)

MID.......... Ministerstvo Inostrannykh Del [*Ministry of Foreign Affairs*] [*Former USSR*]

MID.......... Ministry of Interior and Defense [*Singapore*] (ML)

MID.......... Moscow Institute of Declamation (RU)

MID.......... Movimiento de Integracion Democratica [*Democratic Integration Movement*] [*Dominican Republic*] [*Political party*] (PPW)

MID.......... Movimiento de Integracion y Desarrollo [*Integration and Development Movement*] [*Argentina*] [*Political party*] (LA)

MID.......... Movimiento de la Izquierda Democratica [*Movement of the Democratic Left*] [*Honduras*] (LA)

MID.......... Movimiento Independiente Democratico [*Independent Democratic Movement*] [*Panama*] [*Political party*] (PPW)

MID.......... Nederlandse Militaire Inlichtingendienst [*Dutch Military Intelligence Service*] (WEN)

MIDA....... Malaysian Industrial Development Authority (GEA)

MIDA....... Moviemiento de Integracion Democratica [*The Dominican Republic*] [*Political party*] (EY)

MIDA....... Movimiento de Integracion Democratica Anti-Reeleccionista [*Antireelection Democratic Integration Movement*] [*Dominican Republic*] (LA)

MIDADE .. Mouvement International d'Apostolat des Enfants [*International Movement of Apostolate of Children*] [*France*]

MIDAS...... Managed Inputs Delivery Agricultural Services Project

MIDAS...... Marktinformations-Datensystem [*German*] (ADPT)

MIDAS...... Multimode International Data Acquisition Service [*Australia*] [*Information service or system*] (IID)

MIDB....... Misr Iran Development Bank

MIDC........ Market Infrastructure Development Council [*Philippines*] (GEA)

MIDC........ Metal Industries Development Centre [*Taiwan*] [*Research center*] (ERC)

MIDEBOM ... Mission de Developpement de l'Embouche Bovine de Mbandjock

MIDEC...... Middle East Industrial Development Projects Corporation

MIDEM .... Marche Internationale du Disque et de l'Edition Musical

MIDEMA ... Minoteries de Matadi

MIDENO .. Mission de Developpement de la Province du Nord-Ouest [*Cameroon*] (EY)

MIDERIM ... Mission de Developpement de la Riziculture dans la Plaine des Mbo [*Cameroon*]

MIDEST ... Marche International de la Sous-Traitance

MIDEVIV ... Mission de Developpement des Cultures Vivrieres Maraicheres et Fruitieres

MIDF........ Malaysia Industrial Development Finance Berhad [*Corporation*] (ML)

MIDF........ Malaysian Industrial Development Finance (DS)

MIDH....... Mouvement pour l'Instauration de la Democratie en Haiti [*Political party*] (EY)

MIDIA....... Member of the Industrial Design Institute of Australia

MIDINRA ... Ministerio de Desarrollo Agropecuario y Reforma Agraria [*Ministry of Agricultural-Livestock Development and Agrarian Reform*] [*Nicaragua*] (LA)

MIDIST .... Mission Interministerielle de l'Information Scientifique et Technique [*Interministerial Mission for Scientific and Technical Information*] [*France*] [*Information service or system*] (IID)

MIDONAS ... Military Documentation Systems [*Department of Defense*] [*Switzerland*] (PDAA)

MIDS........ Multifunctional Information Distribution System [*NATO*] (MCD)

MIDU........ Mineral Investigation Drilling Unit [*Department of Mines*] [*Malaysia*] (PDAA)

MIDVIV.... Mission de Developpement des Cultures Vivrieres, Maraicheres, et Fruitieres [*Cameroon*]

MIE.......... European Federation for Medical Informatics [*Sweden*] (EAIO)

MIE.......... Magyar Iparjogvedelmi Egyesulet [*Association for the Protection of Hungarian Industrial Rights*] (HU)

MIE.......... Mauritius Institute of Education (AF)

MIE.......... Member of the Institution of Engineers, Australia

MIE Aust... Member of the Institution of Engineers, Australia

MIEAWA ... Meat Industries Employers' Association of Western Australia

MIEC........ Branche Africaine du Mouvement International des Etudiants Catholiques [*African International Movement of Catholic Students - AIMCS*] (EAIO)

MIEC........ Pax Romana, Mouvement International des Etudiants Catholiques [*Pax Romana, International Movement of Catholic Students - IMCS*] [*Paris, France*] (EAIO)

MIEC........ Pax Romana, Movimiento Internacional de Estudiantes Catolicos [*Pax Romana, International Movement of Catholic Students - IMCS*] (LA)

MIEG .... Mineraloel Import- und Export- GmbH [*Mineral-Oil Import and Export Co.*] (EG)

MIEI......... Moscow Institute of Engineering Economics Imeni Sergo Ordzhonikidze (RU)

miejsc........ Miejscowosc [*Place, Locality*] [*Poland*]

miekk........ Miekkailu [*Fencing*] [*Finland*]

MIEL........ Malaysian Industrial Estates Limited (ML)

Miel........... Mielizna [*Shoal*] [*Poland*] (NAU)

miel .... Mieluummin [*Finland*]

MIEM .... Moscow Institute of Electronic Machinery (RU)

MIER........ Malaysian Institute of Economic Research

mierc........... Miercoles [*Wednesday*] [*Spanish*]

mies........... Miesiac [*or Miesiecznie or Miesiecznik*] [*Month or Monthly*] [*Poland*]

mieszk........ Mieszkaniec [*Inhabitant*] [*Poland*]

MIEU .... Miscellaneous Industries Employees' Union [*Aden*]

MIF........... MARC [*Machine-Readable Cataloging*] International Format

MIF........... Marubeni International Finance [*Trading company*] [*Japan*]

MIF........... Melbourne International Festival [*Australia*]

MIF........... Miners' International Federation [*See also FIM*] [*Brussels, Belgium*] (EAIO)

mif............. Mythology (RU)

MIFA........ Member of the Institute of Foresters of Australia (ADA)

MIFERGUI ... Mines de Fer de Guinee [*Iron Mining Co. of Guinea*] (AF)

MIFERMA ... Mines de Fer de Mauritanie [*Iron Mining Co. of Mauritania*]

MIFERSO ... Societe des Mines de Fer du Senegal Oriental

MIFI.......... Moscow Engineering Physics Institute (RU)

MIFLI .... Moscow Institute of Philosophy, Literature, and History (RU)

MIFR........ Materials and Research on the History of the Flora and Vegetation of the USSR (RU)

MIFRIFI ... Mittelfristige Finanzplanung [*Medium-Term Financial Planning*] [*German*] (EG)

MiG .... Aircraft Designed by Artem Ivanovich Mikoyan and M. I. Gurevich (RU)

MIG .... Mailles Inclinees a Gauche [*Knitting*] [*French*]

MIG .... Meat Innovation Grant

MIGA .... Multilateral Investment Guarantee Agency [*World Bank*]

MIGAI........ Moskovskiy Institut Inzhenerov Geodezii, Aerofotosyemki i Kartografi [*Moscow Institute of Geodetic, Aerial Mapping and Cartographic Engineers*] [*Former USSR*] (PDAA)

MIGERT ... Muszer- es Irodagepertekesito Vallalat [*Instrument and Office Machine Marketing Enterprise*] (HU)

Migrat........ Migration [*Germany*] (GCA)

MIGSh ...... International Wool Study Group [*IWSG*] (RU)

MIH.......... Matica Iseljenika Hrvatske [*Society of Emigrants of Croatia*] (YU)

MIH.......... Miedzynarodowa Izba Handlowa [*International Chamber of Commerce*] (POL)

MIHILIST ... Military History Listing [*Australian Defence Force Academy*]

MIHS .... Malian Institute of Human Sciences

MII .... Interference Microscope (RU)

MII .... Madjelis Industri Indonesia [*Indonesian Industrial Council*] (IN)

MII .... Marilia [*Brazil*] [*Airport symbol*] (OAG)

MII .... State Fine Arts Museum Imeni A. S. Pushkin (RU)

MIIC.......... Pax Romana, Mouvement International des Intellectuels Catholiques [*Pax Romana, International Catholic Movement for Intellectual and Cultural Affairs - ICMICA*] [*Geneva, Switzerland*] (EAIO)

MIIC.......... Pax Romana, Movimiento Internacional de Intelectuales Catolicos [*Pax Romana, International Catholic Movement for Intellectual and Cultural Affairs - ICMICA*]   (LA)

MIICA....... Member of the Institute of Instrumentation and Control, Australia   (ADA)

MIIE.......... Member of the South African Institute of Industrial Engineers   (AA)

MIIGAIK .. Moscow Institute of Engineers of Geodesy, Aerial Surveying, and Cartography   (RU)

MIIGS....... Moscow Institute of Urban Construction Engineers   (RU)

MIIMSKh ... Melitopol' Institute of Agricultural Mechanical Engineers   (RU)

MIIOP....... Moscow Institute of Engineers for Public Eating Facilities   (RU)

MIIS.......... Manufacture Ivoirienne d'Isolants Synthetiques

MIIS.......... Moscow Institute of Communications Engineers   (RU)

MIIT.......... Milletlerarasi Iktisadi Isbirligi Teskilati Genel Sekreterligi [*International Economic Cooperation Organization General Secretariat*] [*of Finance Ministry*]   (TU)

MIIT.......... Moscow Institute of Railroad Transportation Engineers   (RU)

MIIVKh..... Moscow Institute of Hydraulic Engineers   (RU)

MIIZ.......... Moscow Institute of Land Use Measures Engineers   (RU)

MIIZhT..... Moscow Institute of Railroad Transportation Engineers   (RU)

MIJ............ Maatschappij [*Joint Stock Company*] [*Netherlands*]

MIJ............ Mili [*Marshall Islands*] [*Airport symbol*]   (OAG)

MIJ............ Movimiento Iglesia Joven [*Young Church Movement*] [*Chile*]   (LA)

MIJARC ... Mouvement International de la Jeunesse Agricole et Rurale Catholique [*International Movement of Catholic Agricultural and Rural Youth - IMCARY*] [*Louvain, Belgium*]   (EAIO)

MIJARC ... Movimiento Internacional de la Juventud Agraria y Rural Catolica [*International Movement of Catholic Agricultural and Rural Youth - IMCARY*]   (LA)

MIJC........ Mouvement International des Juristes Catholiques, Pax Romana [*France*]

MIJE......... Magyar Iparjogvedelmi Egyesulet [*Association for the Protection of Hungarian Industrial Rights*]   (HU)

MIJM....... Mouvement International de Jeunesse Mazdaznan

MIK.......... Maximale Immissionskonzentration [*Maximum Emission Concentration*] [*German*]   (EG)

MIK.......... Mikkeli [*Finland*] [*Airport symbol*]   (OAG)

MI K.......... Minerva Kiado [*Minerva Publishing House*]   (HU)

MIKhM..... Moscow Institute of Chemical Machinery   (RU)

MIKI.......... Muszeripari Kutatointezet [*Research Institute of the Instrument Industry*]   (HU)

MIKK .... Medjunarodni Institut za Kucnu Knjizevnost [*International Institute for Home Literature - IIHL*] [*Belgrade, Yugoslavia*]   (EAIO)

MIKKh ...... Moscow Scientific Research Institute of Municipal Services   (RU)

MIKP........ Moscow Institute of the Leather Industry   (RU)

mikr........... Microbiology   (RU)

mikr........... Microscope   (RU)

Mikrobest.. Mikrobestimmung [*Microdetermination*] [*German*]   (GCA)

mikrobiol.... Microbiological, Microbiology   (RU)

MIKS........ Multichannel Investigation of Vibrations of Structures and Soils   (RU)

MI K YO.... Mikhanografiko Kendron Ypourgeiou Oikonomikon [*Ministry of Finance Computer Center*]   (GC)

MIL.......... Manufacturas Industriales Ltda. [*Colombia*]   (COL)

MIL.......... Manufacturing Investments Limited [*Australia*]   (ADA)

MIL.......... Mensa International [*British*]   (EAIO)

MIL.......... Milan [*Italy*] [*Airport symbol*]   (OAG)

mil............ Milha [*Mile*] [*Portuguese*]

mil............ Militaire [*French*]   (TPFD)

mil............ Militare [*Military*] [*Italian*]

Mil............ Military   (PWGL)

mil............ Militer [*Military*] [*Afrikaans*]

mil............ Militia   (RU)

MIL.......... Millieme [*Monetary unit*] [*Egypt, Sudan*]

Mil............ Millimetre [*Millimeter*] [*French*]   (MTD)

MIL.......... Mobel- og Innredingsprodusentenes Landsforening [*Norway*]   (EAIO)

MIL.......... Movimiento de Integracion Liberal de la Guajira [*Movement for the Liberal Integration of Guajira*] [*Colorado*]   (LA)

MIL.......... Movimiento Iberico de Liberacion [*Iberian Liberation Movement*] [*Spanish*]   (WER)

MIL.......... Movimiento Iberico Libertario [*Spain*] [*Political party*]

MIL.......... Movimiento Independiente Liberal [*Independent Liberal Movement*] [*Colorado*]   (LA)

MILA........ Movimiento pro Integracion Latinoamericana   (LAA)

MILAN ..... Missile d'Infanterie Leger Antichar

MILAS ..... Missile di Lutto Anti-Submarine [*Italy*]

MILASA ... Member of the Institute of Landscape Architects of South Africa   (AA)

Milchz........ Milchzucker [*Milk Sugar*] [*German*]   (GCA)

MILCO...... Movimiento de Integracion Liberal de la Costa [*Movement for the Liberal Integration of the Coast*] [*Colorado*]   (LA)

MILCOM ... Military Committee Communication [*NATO*]

MILCT ...... Mouvement International pour le Libre Choix Therapeutique [*France*]   (EAIO)

miles.......... Milesimas [*Thousandths*] [*Spanish*]

miless......... Milesimas [*Thousandths*] [*Spanish*]

MILF......... Moro Islamic Liberation Front [*Philippines*] [*Political party*]

MILIHOUSE ... Military Housing Establishment [*Syria*]

militaer....... Militaerisch [*Military*] [*German*]   (GCA)

milj............ Miljoona(a) [*Finland*]

mill............ Millieme [*Thousandth*] [*French*]

mill............ Milliliter   (BU)

Mill............ Million [*Million*] [*German*]   (WEN)

MILLE ..... Movimento per l'Italia Libera nella Libera Europa [*Movement for a Free Italy in a Free Europe*]   (WER)

milligr......... Milligramme [*Milligram*] [*French*]

millim......... Millimetre [*Millimeter*] [*French*]

MILOC...... Military Oceanographic Survey [*NATO*]   (MSC)

MILPAS.... Milicias Populares Antisomocistas [*Anti-Somoza People's Militia*] [*Nicaragua*]   (LA)

Mils........... Member of the Institute of Land Surveyors [*South Africa*]   (AA)

MILS .... Minerva Library System [*Australia*]

MILSTAM ... International Military Staff Memorandum [*NATO*]   (NATG)

MILSTAN ... Military Agency for Standardization [*NATO*]

MilSW........ Militair Strafwetboek [*Benelux*]   (BAS)

MILTUR ... Milliyet Turizm Anonim Sirket [*Milliyet Tourism Corporation*] [*Turkish Cypriot*]   (GC)

MILUBA... Societe Miniere du Lualaba

MIM.......... Magnezitipari Muvek [*Magnesite Industry Works*]   (HU)

MIM.......... Malaysian Institute of Management

MIM.......... Marketing Internacional de Mocambique Lda.

MIM.......... Matica na Iselenicite od Makedonija [*Society of Emigrants of Macedonia*]   (YU)

MIM.......... Merimbula [*Australia*] [*Airport symbol*]   (OAG)

MIM.......... Metal-Insulator-Metal [*Thin-film circuits*]   (RU)

MIM.......... Metallographic Microscope   (RU)

MIM.......... Military Iranian Mission [*World War II*]

Mim........... Mimarlik [*Architecture*]   (TU)

MIM.......... Mindanao Independence Movement [*Philippines*] [*Political party*]

MIM.......... Ministerul Industriei Metalurgice [*Ministry of the Metallurgical Industry*]   (RO)

MIM.......... Mount Isa Mines [*Australia*]   (ADA)

MIM.......... Mouvement Independantiste Martiniquais [*Martinique Independence Movement*] [*Political party*]   (PD)

MIM.......... Movimiento Institucionalista Militar [*Military Institutionalist Movement*] [*Paraguay*]   (LA)

MIMA ...... Modern Image Makers Association [*Australia*]

MIMA .... Motor Inn and Motel Association of New South Wales [*Australia*]

MIMAA .... Motor Inn, Motel and Accommodation Association [*Australia*]

MIMCOL ... Malta Investment Management Co. Ltd.   (EY)

MIME .... Ministere de l'Industrie, des Mines, et de l'Energie [*Benin*]

mimeogr...... Mimeographeerd [*Mimeographed*] [*Publishing*] [*Netherlands*]

MIMESKh ... Moscow Institute of Rural Mechanization and Electrification   (RU)

MIMH....... Member of the Institute Materials Handling [*South Africa*]   (AA)

MIMI .... Member of the Institute of the Motor Industry [*South Africa*]   (AA)

MIMKTM ... Member of the Institute of Marketing Management [*South Africa*]   (AA)

MIML .... Macquarie Investment Management Ltd. [*Australia*]

MIMO...... Moscow State Institute of International Relations   (RU)

mimorprof.. Mimoradny Professor [*Associate Professor*]   (CZ)

MIMR .... Ma'anshan Institute of Mining Research [*Ministry of Metallurgical Industry*] [*China*]   (EAS)

MIMT .... Member of the Institute of Materials Technicians [*South Africa*]   (AA)

MIMunESA ... Member of the Institute of Municipal Engineers of South Africa   (AA)

min .... First Name Unknown   (BU)

MIN.......... Institute of Mineralogy (of the Academy of Sciences, USSR)   (RU)

m in .... Miedzy Innymi [*Among Others*] [*Poland*]

min .... Mineral   (RU)

min .... Mineralisch [*Mineral*] [*German*]   (GCA)

min .... Mineralogia [*Mineralogy*] [*Finland*]

Min .... Mineralogie [*Mineralogy*] [*German*]   (GCA)

min .... Mineralogie [*French*]   (TPFD)

min .... Mineralogy   (TPFD)

Min .... Mineral Spring [*Topography*]   (RU)

Min .... Miniatur [*Miniature*] [*German*]

min .... Miniatura [*Miniature*] [*Hungary*]

min .... Minimal [*or Minimum*] [*German*]

min .... Minimum [*Afrikaans*]

Min .... Minimum [*French*]

min .... Mining   (BU)

min .... Minister [*Afrikaans*]
Min .... Minister [*or Ministerial*] [*German*]
min .... Ministeri [*Finland*]
Min .... Ministerium [*Ministry*] [*German*] (GCA)
min .... Minister, Ministry (RU)
Min .... Ministerstwo [*Ministry*] (POL)
Min .... Ministre [*or Ministere*] [*Minister or Ministry*] [*French*] (MTD)
min .... Miniszter [*Minister (In the cabinet)*] [*Hungary*] (GPO)
min .... Minuscoli [*Lowercase Letters*] [*Italian*]
Min .... Minuskel [*Lowercase Letter*] [*German*]
min .... Minut [*Minute*] [*Poland*]
Min .... Minute [*German*] (GCA)
min .... Minuto [*Minute*] [*Portuguese*]
min .... Minuut [*Minute*] [*Afrikaans*]
min .... Minuuttia [*Finland*]
Min .... Moulin [*Mill*] [*Military map abbreviation World War I*] [*French*] (MTD)
MIN .... Movimiento de Integracion Nacional [*National Integration Movement*] [*Dominican Republic*] (LA)
MIN .... Movimiento de Integracion Nacional [*National Integration Movement*] [*Ecuador*] [*Political party*] (PPW)
MIN .... Movimiento de Integracion Nacional [*National Integration Movement*] [*Venezuela*] [*Political party*] (PPW)
MIN .... Movimiento de Integridad Nacional [*National Integrity Movement*] [*Venezuela*] (LA)
MIN .... Movimiento de Intransigencia Nacional [*National Intransigency Movement*] [*Argentina*] (LA)
MIN .... Movimiento de Izquierda Nacional [*National Left-Wing Movement*] [*Bolivia*] [*Political party*] (PPW)
MIN .... Movimiento Industrial Nacional [*National Industrial Movement*] [*Argentina*] (LA)
MINA .... Medical Imaging Nurses Association [*Australia*]
MINA .... Ministry of Information and National Affairs [*Pakistan*]
MINA .... Movimento para la Independencia Nacional de Angola
MINAD..... Mines Administration Proprietary Ltd. [*Australia*]
Minaferes .. Ministre des Affaires Etrangeres [*or Ministere des Affaires Etrangeres*] [*Minister of Foreign Affairs or Ministry of Foreign Affairs Cambodia*] (CL)
MINAG..... Ministerio de Agricultura [*Ministry of Agriculture*] [*Cuba*] (LA)
Minagri...... Ministere de l'Agriculture [*or Ministre de l'Agriculture*] [*Ministry of Agriculture or Minister of Agriculture Cambodia*] (CL)
MINAGRI ... Ministerio de Agricultura [*Ministry of Agriculture*] [*Cuba*] (LA)
MINAGRI ... Ministerio de Agricultura [*Santiago, Chile*] (LAA)
MinAI........ Ministero dell'Africa Italiana
MINAL ..... Ministerio de la Industria Alimenticia [*Ministry of the Food Industry*] [*Cuba*] (LA)
MINAT ..... Ministere de l'Administration Territoriale
Minaviaprom ... Ministry of the Aircraft Industry, USSR (RU)
Minavtoprom ... Ministry of the Automobile Industry, USSR (RU)
Minavtoshosdor ... Ministry of Automobile Transportation and Highways (RU)
MINAZ ..... Ministerio de la Industria Azucarera [*Ministry of the Sugar Industry*] [*Cuba*] (LA)
minb .... Mortar Battalion (RU)
MINBAS... Ministerio de la Industria Basica [*Ministry of Basic Industry*] [*Cuba*] (LA)
minbatr ...... Mortar Battery (RU)
MinBesch .. Ministeriele Beschikking [*Benelux*] (BAS)
MinBl........ Ministerialblatt [*Ministerial Gazette*] (EG)
MinBlZ...... Ministerie van Buitenlandse Zaken [*Benelux*] (BAS)
Minbumdrevprom ... Ministry of the Paper Industry (RU)
Minbumprom ... Ministry of the Paper Industry (RU)
minc........... Minometna Ceta [*Mortar Platoon*] (CZ)
MINCE...... Ministerio do Comercio Externo [*Ministry of Foreign Trade*] [*Portuguese*] (AF)
MINCEX... Ministerio de Comercio Exterior [*Ministry of Foreign Trade*] [*Spanish*] (LA)
Minchermet ... Ministry of Ferrous Metallurgy (RU)
MINCI....... Ministerio do Comercio Interno [*Ministry of Internal Trade*] (AF)
MINCIN ... Ministerio de Comercio Interior [*Ministry of Domestic Trade*] (LA)
MINCOM ... Ministerio de Comunicaciones [*Ministry of Communications*] [*Cuba*] (LA)
MINCONMAR ... Ministerial Conference of West and Central African States on Maritime Transport [*Ivory Coast*] (EAIO)
Mincultes... Ministere des Cultes [*or Ministre des Cultes*] [*Ministry of Religious Affairs or Minister of Religious Affairs Cambodia*] (CL)
MIND........ Ministerio da Industria [*Ministry of Industry*] [*Angola*]
MIND........ Ministerio de Industria [*Ministry of Industry*] [*Nicaragua*] (LA)
mind .... Mortar Battalion (BU)
MINDECO ... Mining Development Corporation [*Zambia*] (AF)
MINDEF... Ministry of Defense [*Singapore*] (ML)
MINDEFOM ... Ministerio de Fomento [*Venezuela*] (DSCA)
Min de laSPP ... Ministre De La Sante Publique et de la Population [*France*] (FLAF)

minderwert ... Minderwertig [*Low-Grade*] [*German*] (GCA)
MINDESARROLLO ... Ministerio de Desarrollo Economico [*Colombia*] (DSCA)
mindeudg ... Mindeudgave [*Commemorative Edition*] [*Publishing Danish/Norwegian*]
Mindeveloppement ... Ministere de Developpement [*or Ministre de Developpement*] [*Ministry of Development or Minister of Development Cambodia*] (CL)
MINDIN ... Ministerio del Desarrollo Industrial [*Ministry of Industrial Development*] [*Cuba*] (LA)
mindn .... Mortar Battalion (BU)
mindr......... Minometne Druzstvo [*Mortar Squad*] (CZ)
MINDS ..... Mental Illness Nervous Disorders Society [*Australia*]
MINDS ..... Movement for the Intellectually Disabled of Singapore (EAIO)
MINE .... Microbial Information Network Europe [*EEC*]
MINED ..... Ministerio de Educacion [*Ministry of Education*] [*Cuba*] (LA)
MINEDUC ... Ministerio de Educacion Publica [*Santiago, Chile*] (LAA)
Mineducanale ... Ministere de l'Education Nationale [*or Ministre de l'Education Nationale*] [*Ministry of National Education or Minister of National Education Cambodia*] (CL)
MINEL...... Ministarstvo Elektroprivrede [*Ministry of Electric Industries*] (YU)
MINEP...... Ministere de l'Economie et du Plan
miner......... Mineral (RU)
Miner........ Mineralogia [*Mineralogy*] [*Portuguese*]
MINER ..... Mineralogie [*Mineralogy*] [*Afrikaans*]
miner......... Mineralogy, Mineralogical (BU)
MINERALIMPEX ... MINERALIMPEX Olaj- es Banyatermek Kulkereskedelmi Vallalat [*MINERALIMPEX Foreign Trade Enterprise for Oil and Mine Products*] (HU)
MINEROPERU ... Peruvian State Mining and Mineral Merchandising Enterprise (LA)
MINERVEN ... Minerias Venezolanas CA [*Venezuela Mining Company, Inc.*] (IMH)
MINESEB ... Ministere de l'Enseignement Secondaire et de l'Education de Base
MINEX ..... Minelaying, Minesweeping, and Mine-Hunting Exercise [*NATO*] (NATG)
MINEXPLORE ... Mineral Exploration Corp. Ltd. [*Department of Mines, and Ministry of Steel and Mines*] [*India*] (EAS)
MINFAR... Ministerio de las Fuerzas Armadas Revolucionarias [*Ministry of the Revolutionary Armed Forces*] [*Cuba*] (LA)
Min Fin...... Ministre des Finances [*France*] (FLAF)
Minfin........ Ministry of Finance (RU)
Minfinances ... Ministre des Finances [*or Ministere des Finances*] [*Minister of Finance or Ministry of Finance Cambodia*] (CL)
MINFOC... Ministere de l'Information et de la Culture
MInfoTech ... Master of Information Technology and Communication
MInfSys..... Master of Information Systems
M Ing .... Magister in die Ingenieurswese [*Master of Engineering*] [*Afrikaans*]
MIng.......... Maitre in Ingenierie [*Master of Engineering*] [*French*]
MING........ Movimento de Independencia Nacional da Guine Portuguesa
Mingechaursel'mash ... Mingechaur Agricultural Machinery Plant (RU)
Mingorsel'stroy ... Ministry of Urban and Rural Construction (RU)
Mingoskontrol' ... Ministry of State Control (RU)
MINIE....... Ministerio de la Industria Electrica [*Ministry of the Electric Power Industry*] [*Cuba*] (LA)
MINIL....... Ministerio de la Industria Ligera [*Ministry of Light Industry*] [*Cuba*] (LA)
minim........ Minimum, Minimal (RU)
Minindel .... Ministry of Foreign Affairs (RU)
Min InstrPub ... Ministre de l'Instruction Publique [*France*] (FLAF)
MININT.... Ministerio del Interior [*Ministry of the Interior*] [*Nicaragua*] (LA)
MININT.... Ministerio del Interior [*Ministry of the Interior*] [*Cuba*] (LA)
Min Int...... Ministre de l'Interieur [*France*] (FLAF)
Min ist .... Mineral Spring [*Topography*] (RU)
minist......... Ministry (BU)
Ministsuv ... Council of Ministers (BU)
MINITRFOP ... Ministere de l'Interieur et de la Fonction Publique
MINJUS ... Ministerio de Justicia [*Ministry of Justice*] [*Cuba*] (LA)
Minjustice ... Ministre de la Justice [*or Ministere de la Justice*] [*Minister of Justice or Ministry of Justice Cambodia*] (CL)
MINKh...... Moscow Institute of the National Economy Imeni G. V. Plekhanov (RU)
MINKhiGP ... Moscow Institute of the Petrochemical and Gas Industry Imeni Academician I. M. Gubkin (RU)
Minkhimprom ... Ministry of the Chemical Industry, USSR (RU)
MINKhU... Moscow Institute for the Statistical Survey of the National Economy (RU)
Minkomkhoz ... Ministry of the Municipal Economy (RU)
Minkomkhozizdat ... Publishing House of the Ministry of the Municipal Economy (RU)
Minkororen ... Nihon Minkan Koku Rodokumiai Rengokai [*Japan Federation of Civil Aviation Workers' Unions*]
Minlegprom ... Ministry of Light Industry (RU)

Minlesbumprom ... Ministry of the Lumber and Paper Industries (RU)
Minlesprom ... Ministry of the Lumber Industry (RU)
Minmash ... Ministry of Machinery Manufacture, USSR (RU)
Minmestprom ... Ministry of Local Industry (RU)
MINMET ... National Minerals & Metals Import/Export Corp. [*China*]
Minmetallurgkhimstroy ... Ministry of Construction of Establishments of the Metallurgical and Chemical Industries (RU)
Minmetallurgprom ... Ministry of the Metallurgical Industry, USSR (RU)
MINMG .... Ministerio de Mineria y Geologia [*Ministry of Mines and Geology*] [*Cuba*] (LA)
MINMINAS ... Ministro/Ministerio de Minas y Energia [*Minister/Ministry of Mines and Energy*] [*Colorado*] (LA)
Minmobigale ... Ministere de la Mobilisation Generale [*or Ministre de la Mobilisation Generale*] [*Ministry of General Mobilization or Minister of General Mobilization Cambodia*] (CL)
Minmorflot ... Ministry of the Maritime Fleet, USSR (RU)
Minmyasomolprom ... Ministry of the Meat and Dairy Industry (RU)
Minnefteprom ... Ministry of the Petroleum Industry (RU)
mino .... Ministro [*Minister*] [*Spanish*]
Minoboronprom ... Ministry of the Defense Industry, USSR (RU)
MINOKA .. Minoteries de Kakontwe
MINORDIA ... Societe Africaine des Mines Or-Diamant
MINOTLRS ... Ministrstvo Notranjih Poslov Ljudske Republike Slovenije [*Ministry of the Interior, People's Republic of Slovenia*] (YU)
minotryad ... Mine Detachment (RU)
minp .... Mortar Regiment (BU)
MINPECO ... Minero Peru Comercial [*Peruvian State Mineral Marketing Company*] (LA)
MINPES ... Ministerio de la Industria Pesquera [*Ministry of the Fishing Industry*] [*Cuba*] (LA)
Min PiT ..... Ministerstwo Poczt i Telegrafow [*Ministry of Posts and Telegraphs*] (POL)
MINPOREN ... National Association of Commercial Broadcasters in Japan (EY)
Minpred ..... Ministersky Predseda [*Prime Minister*] (CZ)
MINPRI .... Metal and Mineral Prices [*Database*] [*Australia*]
MINPROEKT ... Mine Designing Institute (RU)
Minpromprodtovarov ... Ministry of the Foodstuffs Industry (RU)
Minpros ..... Ministry of Education (RU)
Min Pub ..... Ministere Public [*France*] (FLAF)
Min r .... Mine Company (BU)
minr .... Minometna Rota [*Mortar Company*] (CZ)
Min Rat ...... Ministerialrat [*Senior Civil Servant*] [*German*]
Minrechflot ... Ministry of the River Fleet (RU)
Minrefugies ... Ministre des Refugies [*or Ministere des Refugies*] [*Minister of Refugees or Ministry of Refugees Cambodia*] (CL)
Minres .... Ministeriele Resolutie [*Benelux*] (BAS)
MINREX ... Ministerio de Relaciones Exteriores [*Ministry of Foreign Relations*] [*Cuba*] (LA)
MinribNRH ... Ministarstvo Ribolova Narodna Republika Hrvatska [*Croatian Ministry of Fisheries*] (YU)
Minrybprom ... Ministry of the Fish Industry (RU)
MINSA ...... Ministerio de Salud [*Ministry of Health*] [*Nicaragua*] (LA)
Minsante .... Ministre de Sante [*or Ministere de Sante*] [*Minister of Health or Ministry of Health Cambodia*] (CL)
MINSAP ... Ministerio de Salud Publica [*Ministry of Public Health*] [*Cuba*] (LA)
Minsecurinale ... Ministre de la Securite Nationale [*or Ministere de la Securite Nationale*] [*Minister of National Security or Ministry of National Security Cambodia*] (CL)
Minsel'khoz ... Ministry of Agriculture (RU)
MINSIME ... Ministerio de la Industria Sidero-Mecanica [*Ministry of Steelworking Industry*] [*Cuba*] (LA)
MINSK ...... [*A*] Russian digital computer [*Moscow University*]
Minsotsob ... Ministry of Social Security (RU)
Minsovkhoz ... Ministry of Sovkhozes (RU)
Minsredmash ... Ministry of Medium Machinery Manufacture, USSR (RU)
MInstE ...... Member of the Institute of Energy [*South Africa*] (AA)
Minstroy .... Mining Construction Administration (BU)
Minstroy .... Ministry of Construction (RU)
Minstroydormash ... Ministry of Construction and Road Machinery Manufacture, USSR (RU)
Minsudprom ... Ministry of the Shipbuilding Industry, USSR (RU)
Minsvyazi .. Ministry of Communications (RU)
MINSZ ...... Magyar Ifjusagi Nepi Szovetseg Uttoro Mozgalom [*Hungarian People's Youth Federation, Pioneer Movement*] (HU)
MINTECO ... Misr-India Tea Export Co.
MINTEK ... Council for Mineral Technology [*South Africa*] [*Research center*] (IRC)
Mintekstil'prom ... Ministry of the Textile Industry (RU)
MINTER ... Ministerio do Interior [*Ministry of the Interior*] [*Information service or system*] (IID)
Mintorg ...... Ministry of Trade (RU)
MINTRAB ... Ministerio del Trabajo [*Ministry of Labor*] [*Cuba*] (LA)
MINTRANS ... Ministerio del Transporte [*Ministry of Transportation*] [*Cuba*] (LA)

Mintransmash ... Ministry of Transportation Machinery Manufacture, USSR (RU)
Mintransstroy ... Ministry of Transportation Construction, USSR (RU)
Min Trav .... Ministre du Travail [*France*] (FLAF)
Mintravo .... Ministere des Travaux Publics [*or Ministre des Travaux Publics*] [*Ministry of Public Works or Minister of Public Works Cambodia*] (CL)
Min TravPub ... Ministre des Travaux Publics [*France*] (FLAF)
Mintsvetmet ... Ministry of Nonferrous Metallurgy (RU)
Mintsvetmetzoloto ... Moscow Institute of Nonferrous Metals and Gold Imeni M. I. Kalinin (RU)
Mintyazhmash ... Ministry of Heavy Machinery Manufacture, USSR (RU)
Mintyazhstroy ... Ministry of Construction of Heavy Industry Establishments, USSR (RU)
MINU .... Administrasi Umum [*General Administration*] (IN)
Minugleprom ... Ministry of the Coal Industry (RU)
Minuglestroy ... Ministry of Construction of Coal Industry Establishments (RU)
MINUH .... Ministry of Urban Development and Housing [*Cameroon*] (IMH)
Minusinnefterazvedka ... Minusinsk Trust of Petroleum Exploration (RU)
minv .... Mortar Platoon (RU)
MINVAH ... Ministerio de la Vivienda y Asentamientos Humanos [*Ministry of Housing and Human Settlements*] [*Nicaragua*] (LA)
Minville ..... Ministere Charge de la Ville de Phnom Penh [*or Ministre Charge de la Ville de Phnom Penh*] [*Ministry for the City of Phnom Penh or Minister for the City of Phnom Penh Cambodia*] (CL)
Minvneshtorg ... Ministry of Foreign Trade, USSR (RU)
min-vo .... Ministry (RU)
Minvostokugol' ... Ministry of the Coal Industry of the Eastern Regions, USSR (RU)
min vr .... Past Tense (BU)
MINVU ..... Ministerio de Vivienda y Urbanismo [*Ministry of Housing and Urban Affairs*] [*Chile*] (LA)
minzag .... Minelayer (RU)
Minzag .... Ministry of Procurement (RU)
Minzapadugol' ... Ministry of the Coal Industry of the Western Regions, USSR (RU)
Minzdrav .... Ministry of Public Health (RU)
MIO .... Midas Commuter Airlines CA [*Venezuela*] [*ICAO designator*] (FAAC)
Mio. .... Million [*Million*] [*German*]
MIO .... Ministerstvo Informaci a Osvety [*Ministry of Information and Culture*] (CZ)
MIO .... Montaz Instalacji Okretowej [*Assembly of Ship Equipment*] (POL)
MIOG .... Mitteilungen des Instituts fuer Oesterreichische Geschichtsforschung [*German*]
MIOI .... Magyar Izraelitak Orszagos Irodaja [*National Office of Hungarian Jews*] (HU)
MIOK .... Magyar Izraelitak Orszagos Kepviselete [*National Representation of the Hungarian Jews*] (HU)
MIOT .... Magyar Ifjusag Orszagos Tanacsa [*National Council of Hungarian Youth*] (HU)
MIOT .... Moscow Institute of Work Safety (RU)
MIP .... Between Foreign Ports (RU)
MIP .... Maatschappij voor Industrieele Projecten [*Partnership for Industrial Schemes*] [*Netherlands*]
MIP .... Marche International des Programmes de Television International [*International Marketplace for Buyers and Sellers of Television Programs*] (NTCM)
MIP .... Mikroprozessor [*Micro Processor*] [*German*] (ADPT)
MIP .... Milicias de Izquierda Proletaria [*Militias of the Proletarian Left*] [*Spanish*] (WER)
MIP .... Ministarstvo Inostranih Poslova [*Ministry of Foreign Affairs*] [*YU*]
MIP .... Mouvement Independent Populaire [*Popular Independent Movement*] [*Luxembourg*] [*Political party*] (PPE)
MIP .... Mouvement Islamique Progressiste [*Islamic Progressive Movement*] [*Tunisia*] [*Political party*] (PD)
MIP .... Movimento Italiano della Pace [*Italian Peace Movement*] (WER)
MIP .... Movimiento Independiente Peruano [*Peruvian Independent Movement*] [*Political party*]
MIPA .... Manufacture Ivoirienne des Plastiques Africains
MIPC .... Manufacture Ivoirienne des Platres Chimiques
MIPD .... Monoisopropyldiphenyl (RU)
MIPDC ...... Management Improvement Program Design Committee [*Australia*]
MIPDI .... Moscow Institute of Applied and Decorative Art (RU)
MIPE .... Ministerio de Pesqueria [*Peru*]
MIPI .... Madjelis Ilmu Pengetahuan Indonesia [*Council for Sciences of Indonesia*]
MIPLAN ... Ministerio de Planificacion [*Ministry of Planning*] [*Nicaragua*] (LA)

MIPLAN... Ministerio de Planificacion [*Ministry of Planning*] [*Argentina*] (LA)
MIPMA..... Member of the Institute of Personnel Management, Australia
MIPMR..... Muzeul Historic al Partidului Muncitoresc Roman [*Historical Museum of the Romanian Workers Party*] (RO)
MIPRA...... Mouvement Independant PRA [*Independent PRA Movement*] [*Burkina Faso*] (AF)
MIPS........ Martinsreid Institute for Protein Sequence [*Database*] [*Max Planck Institute for Biochemistry*]
MIPS........ Millionen Instruktionen Pro Sekunde [*German*] (ADPT)
MIPTES.... Movimiento Independiente de Profesionales Salvadorenos [*Independent Movement of Salvadoran Professionals*] (LA)
MIPTV ...... Marche International des Programmes de Television [*Cannes Film Festival*] [*France*]
MIQ.......... Ministerio de la Industria Quimica [*Ministry of the Chemical Industry*] [*Cuba*] (RO)
MIR .... Long-Distance Outgoing Register [*Telephony*] (RU)
MIR .... Maintenance Inspection Report
MIR .... Malaysian Infantry Regiment (ML)
MIR .... Medicos Internos y Residentes [*Interns and Resident Doctors*] [*Spanish*] (WER)
MIR .... Member of the Australasian Institute of Radiography (ADA)
MIR .... Middle Irish [*Language, etc.*]
MIR .... Mijnindustrieraad [*Benelux*] (BAS)
MIR .... Ministere de l'Industrie et de la Recherche [*Ministry of Industry and Research*] [*France*] (PDAA)
MIR .... Monastir [*Tunisia*] [*Airport symbol*] (OAG)
MIR .... Monthly Intelligence Report
MIR .... Morski Instytut Rybacki [*Maritime Fisheries Institute*] [*Poland*] (POL)
MIR .... Mouvement International de la Reconciliation [*International Fellowship of Reconciliation*]
MIR .... Mouvement pour l'Independance de la Reunion [*Movement for the Independence of Reunion*] [*Political party*] (PD)
MIR .... Movimiento de Izquierda Revolucionaria [*Movement of the Revolutionary Left*] [*Peru*] (LA)
MIR .... Movimiento de Izquierda Revolucionaria [*Movement of the Revolutionary Left*] [*Chile*] (LA)
MIR .... Movimiento de Izquierda Revolucionaria [*Movement of the Revolutionary Left*] [*Venezuela*] (LA)
MIR .... Movimiento de Izquierda Revolucionario [*Movement of the Revolutionary Left*] [*Venezuela*] [*Political party*]
MIR .... Movimiento de Izquierda Revolucionario [*Movement of the Revolutionary Left*] [*Chile*] [*Political party*]
MIR .... Movimiento de Izquierda Revolucionario [*Movement of the Revolutionary Left*] [*Bolivia*] [*Political party*] (PPW)
MIR .... Movimiento Independiente Revolucionario [*Independent Revolutionary Movement*] [*Ecuador*] (LA)
MIR .... Museum of the History of Religion (RU)
MIR .... Muszer- es Irodagep Ertekesito Vallalat [*Trade Enterprise for Office Equipment*] (HU)
MIR .... Revolutionary Leftist Movement [*Spanish*] (WER)
MIRA .... Movimiento de Independencia Revolucionaria en Armas [*Puerto Rican independence group*] [*Political party*]
MIRA .... Movimiento de Izquierda Revolucionaria Argentina [*Argentine Movement of the Revolutionary Left*] (LA)
MIRA .... Movimiento Independentista Armado [*Armed Pro-Independence Movement*] [*Puerto Rico*] [*Political party*] (PD)
MIRA .... Museum of the History of Religion and Atheism (RU)
MIRAF...... Miroiteries Africaines a Pointe-Noire
MIRAK...... Minimum Rocket [*German*]
MIRCEN... Microbiological Resource Center [*Egypt*] (IRC)
MIRCEN... Microbiological Resources Center [*UNESCO and UNEP program*] [*Research center*] (IRC)
MIRDC...... Metals Industry Research and Development Center [*Ministry of Industry*] [*Philippines*]
MIREAust ... Member of the Institution of Radio Engineers, Australia
MIREE(Aust) ... Member of the Institution of Radio and Electronics Engineers, Australia (ADA)
MIREK...... World Power Conference [*WPC*] (RU)
MIRGEM ... Moscow Institute of Radio Electronics and Mining Electromechanics (RU)
MIRH........ Movimiento Independiente de Humanidades [*Independent Movement of Humanities*] [*Panama*] (LA)
MIRI.......... Meat Industry Research Institute of New Zealand (DSCA)
MIRI.......... Mitsubishi Sogo Kenkyusho [*Mitsubishi Research Institute*] [*Japan*] (IRC)
MIRINZ.... Meat Industry Research Institute of New Zealand, Inc. (ARC)
MIRKOZ... Muszaki Irodai es Kozszuksegleti Cikkeket Gyarto es Javito Kisipari Szovetkezet [*Cooperative Enterprise for Manufacture and Repair of Office Equipment*] (HU)
MIRL........ Mechanical Industry Research Laboratories [*Taiwan*] [*Research center*] (IRC)
MIR-ML ... Movimiento de Izquierda Revolucionaria - Marxista-Leninista [*Movement of the Revolutionary Left - Marxist-Leninist*] [*Peru*] (LA)

MIRN .... Movimento Independente da Reconstrucao Nacional [*Independent Movement of National Reconstruction*] [*Portugal*] (PPE)
MIRN-PDP ... Movimento Independente de Reconstrucao Nacional - Partido da Derecha Portuguesa [*Independent Movement for National Reconstruction - Party of the Portuguese Right*] [*Political party*] (PPW)
Mirongres ... Mironovskiy State Regional Electric Power Plant (RU)
MIR-Peru .. Movimiento de Izquierda Revolucionaria [*Movement of the Revolutionary Left of Peru*] [*Political party*] (PPW)
MIRR .... Mitsubishi Research Reactor [*Japan*]
MIRT........ Meteorological Institute for Research and Training [*Egypt*] (PDAA)
Mir Vr....... Universal Time, Greenwich Time (RU)
MIS........... International Institute of Welding [*IIW*] (RU)
MIS........... Machine-Testing Station (RU)
MIS........... Management Information Systems Proprietary Ltd. [*Australia*] (ADA)
MIS........... Manufacture d'Isolants Synthetiques
Mis........... Marquis [*Marquis*] [*French*]
MIS........... Matica Iseljenika Srbije [*Society of Emigrants of Serbia*] (YU)
MIS........... Media and Information Services [*Queensland, Australia*]
MIS........... Middle-East Intelligence Survey (BJA)
MIS........... Military Intelligence Section [*South Africa*]
MIS........... Miserable (DSUE)
MIS........... Misima [*Papua New Guinea*] [*Airport symbol*] (OAG)
mis........... Misura [*Measure*] [*Italian*]
MIS........... Moscow Institute of Steel (RU)
MIS........... Myer Information Services [*Australia*]
MIS........... Repeated-Use Circuit (RU)
MIS........... (Rotational) Speed Change Mechanism (RU)
MISA........ Motor Iberica SA [*Spanish*]
MISAust.... Member of the Institution of Surveyors, Australia (ADA)
MISC........ Malaysian International Shipping Corp. (DS)
Misch........ Mischung [*Mixture*] [*German*] (GCA)
Mischbark ... Mischbarkeit [*Miscibility*] [*German*] (GCA)
mise........ Marchandise [*Merchandise*] [*French*]
Mise.......... Marquise [*Marchioness*] [*French*]
MISEP ...... Mutual Information System on Employment Policies in Europe (IID)
MISh .... Pitch-Control Mechanism (RU)
MISI.......... Moscow Construction Engineering Institute Imeni V. V. Kuybyshev (RU)
MISIPA..... Minera Siderurgica Patagonica [*Argentina*] (LAA)
MISK........ Milliyetci Isci Sendikalar Konfederasyonu [*Confederation of Nationalist Labor Unions*] [*NAP-associated labor confederation*] (TU)
MISKT...... Moscow Institute of Soviet Cooperative Trade (RU)
MISL........ Mysore Iron and Steel Works Ltd. [*India*] (PDAA)
MISMER .. Mission Interministrielle de la Mer [*France*]
MISO .... Mzumbe Institute Students Organisation
MISPL....... Management Informationssystem fuer die Planung [*Management Planning Information System*] [*German*] (ADPT)
MISR........ Malawi Institute of Social Research
Misrair...... Egyptian Aviation Company (ME)
MISSIO..... Internationales Katholisches Missionswerk [*Pontifical Mission Society*] [*Aachen, Federal Republic of Germany*] (EAIO)
MISTASI .. Ministerium fuer Staatssicherheit [*Ministry for State Security*] [*MfS, MSS*] [*See also*] (EG)
MISTC ...... Men's International Squash Tournament Council [*Cardiff, Wales*] (EAIO)
MISTRAL ... Memorisation d'Informations, Selection, Traitement, et Recherche Automatique [*CII*] [*French*]
MISURA... Miskito, Sumo, and Rama [*Nicaraguan Indian coalition*]
MISURASATA ... Miskito, Sumo, and Rama [*Nicaraguan Indian coalition*]
MISZ........ Magyar Ipari Szabvany [*Hungarian Industrial Standards*] (HU)
MISZ........ Magyar Irok Szovetsege [*Hungarian Writers' Association*] (HU)
MISZB ...... Magyar Ipari Szabvanyosito Bizottsag [*Hungarian Committee of Industrial Standardization*] (HU)
MIT .... Manuel Isidro Tejevor [*Manuel Isidro Fabrics*] [*Commercial firm*] [*Spain*]
MIT .... Middle Italian [*Language, etc.*]
MIT .... Milli Istihbarat Teskilati [*National Intelligence Organization*] (TU)
MIT .... Ministerio de Industria y Turismo [*Ministry of Industry and Tourism*] [*Peru*] (LA)
MIT .... Ministry of Industry and Trade [*Israel*]
Mit............ Mitologia [*or Mitologico*] [*Mythology or Mythological*] [*Portuguese*]
Mit............ Mitoloji [*Mythology*] (TU)
mit............ Mitonimo [*Portuguese*]
Mit............ Mitsubishi Chemical Industries [*Japan*]
MIT .... Mobile Information Team [*Thailand*]
MIT .... Morski Instytut Techniczny [*Maritime Engineering Institute*] (POL)
MIT .... Mythological, Mythology (BU)

Mitarb........ Mitarbeit [*Collaboration*] [*German*]
Mitarb........ Mitarbeiter [*Co-Worker, Colleague*] [*German*]   (GCA)
MITAS ...... Maden Insaat Turk Anonim Sirketi [*Turkish Metal Construction Corporation*]   (TU)
MITAS ...... Modern Iplik Ticaret Anonim Sirketi [*Modern Thread Trade Corporation*] [*Urfa*]   (TU)
Mitch .... Mitchell College of Advanced Education [*Australia*]
MITCSA ... Member of the Institute of Technical Communicators of Southern Africa   (AA)
MITE......... Mezogazdasagi Ipari Tudomanyos Egyesulet [*Scientific Association for Industries Related to Agriculture*]   (HU)
MITEBI..... Manufacture Ivoirienne de Materiaux pour le Batiment et l'Industrie
MITEC ...... Metal Industry Technology Center [*Malaysia*]
MITEP ...... Moscow Institute of Standard and Experimental Planning   (RU)
MITEX ...... Societe Mitidja-Textiles
MITF......... Milletlerarasi Islam Teskilatlari Federasyonu [*Federation of International Islamic Organizations*]   (TU)
Mitfaell...... Mitfaellung [*Coprecipitation*] [*German*]   (GCA)
mitget........ Mitgeteilt [*Contributed*] [*German*]
Mitgl......... Mitglied [*Member*] [*German*]
Mitgl dBR ... Mitglied des Bundesrates [*Member of the Federal Council*] [*German*]
Mitgliedsch ... Mitgliedschaft [*Membership*] [*German*]   (GCA)
Mithrsg...... Mitherausgeber [*Co-Editor*] [*German*]   (GCA)
MITI......... Ministerio de Industria, Turismo, e Integracion [*Peru*]
MITI......... Ministry of International Trade and Industry [*Japan*]
MITI......... Moms in Touch International   (EA)
MITIC ...... Myanmar International Trust and Investment Co.   (ECON)
MITKA...... Movimiento Indio Tupaj Katari [*Tupaj Katari Indian Movement*] [*Bolivia*] [*Political party*]   (PPW)
MITKhT.... Moscow Institute of Fine Chemical Technology Imeni M. V. Lomonosov   (RU)
MI-TNO.... Metaalinstituut TNO [*Metal Research Institute TNO*] [*Netherlands Organization for Applied Scientific Research (TNO)*] [*Research center*]   (ERC)
MITOS...... Khar'kov Plant for Mechanical and Heat Treatment of Glass   (RU)
MIT-P........ Movimiento Intersindical de Trabajadores de Paraguay [*Inter-Trade Union Movement of Paraguayan Workers*]
MITRANS ... Ministerio de Transporte [*Ministry of Transportation*] [*Cuba*]   (LA)
Mitredakt .. Mitredakteur [*Co-Editor*] [*German*]   (GCA)
MITROPA ... Mitteleuropa [*Central Europe*] [*German*]
Mitropa...... Mitteleuropaeische Schlaf- und Speisewagen-Aktiengesellschaft [*Central European Dining- and Sleeping-Car Corporation*] [*German*]   (EG)
mit sang...... Mitte Sanguinem [*Take Away Blood*] [*Latin*]   (MAE)
MITsKE .... International Center of Research and Information on Collective Economy [*ICRICE*]   (RU)
MITsMiZ ... Moscow Institute of Nonferrous Metals and Gold Imeni M. I. Kalinin   (RU)
MITsMZ ... Moscow Institute of Nonferrous Metals and Gold Imeni M. I. Kalinin   (RU)
MITT........ Materials on the History of Turkmenia and the Turkmenians   (RU)
Mitt........... Mitteilung [*Report*] [*German*]
mitt............ Mittels [*By Means Of*] [*German*]
Mitt........... Mittente [*Sender*] [*Italian*]
Mittlg........ Mitteilung [*Report*] [*German*]
Mitw.......... Mitwirkung [*Assistance*] [*German*]
MIU.......... Maiduguri [*Nigeria*] [*Airport symbol*]   (OAG)
MIU.......... Ministerul Industriei Usoare [*Ministry of Light Industry*]   (RO)
MIU.......... Movimiento Izquierdista Universitario [*University Leftist Movement*] [*Ecuador*]   (LA)
MIUK .... Monoiodoacetic Acid   (RU)
MIULP...... Movimiento Indispensable Unido para Liberar al Pueblo [*United Vital Movement for the Liberation of the People*] [*Venezuela*]   (LA)
MIV .... Met Ingang Van [*Commencing With*] [*Afrikaans*]
MIV .... Mi-Avia [*Russian Federation*] [*ICAO designator*]   (FAAC)
MIVA .... Missionary Vehicle Association [*Austria*]
MIVI.......... Manufacture Ivoirienne de Vitrages Isolants
MIVOTI.... Moscow Institute of Instrument Making of the All-Union Precision Industry Association   (RU)
MIW .... Airborne of Sweden AB [*ICAO designator*]   (FAAC)
MIW .... Mijnwerkersinvaliditeitswet [*Benelux*]   (BAS)
MIWAC .... Marine and Inland Waters Advisory Committee [*Australian Environment Council*]
MIWM(SA) ... Member of the Institute of Waste Management (South Africa)   (AA)
MIZ .... Local Industry and Trades   (BU)
MIZ .... Materialinformations-Zentrum der Marine [*Germany*]   (PDAA)
MIZ .... Missile Interception Zone [*Military*]
MIZ .... Moscow Institute of Land Use Measures   (RU)
MIZ .... Moscow Measuring Instruments Plant   (RU)
MIZ .... Moscow Tool Plant   (RU)

MIZ .... Workshop for Individual Orders   (RU)
MIZh .... Moscow Institute of Journalism   (RU)
MJ .... Makedonski Jazik [*Macedonian Language*] [*A periodical Skopje*]   (YU)
Mj .... Megajoule [*Megajoule*] [*Portuguese*]
MJ .... Megajoule Internacional [*International Megajoule*] [*Portuguese*]
mj .... Mezinarodni Jednotka [*International Unit (Pharmaceutical measure)*]   (CZ)
MJ .... Microturbo [*France*] [*ICAO aircraft manufacturer identifier*]   (ICAO)
MJ .... Ministerul Justitiei [*Ministry of Justice*]   (RO)
MJ .... Minister van Justitie [*Benelux*]   (BAS)
MJ .... Mistni Jednota [*Local Unit*]   (CZ)
mj .... Mjesec [*Month, Moon*]   (YU)
mj .... Mjesto [*Place*]   (YU)
MJA .... Manja [*Madagascar*] [*Airport symbol*]   (OAG)
MJA .... Movimiento de la Juventud Agraria [*Uruguay*]   (LAA)
MJAJ .... Maanpuolustuksen ja Turvallisuuden Ammattijaerjestoet [*Defence and Security Employees Union*] [*Finalnd*]   (EY)
MJB .... Mejit [*Marshall Islands*] [*Airport symbol*]   (OAG)
MJC.......... Man [*Ivory Coast*] [*Airport symbol*]   (OAG)
MJC.......... Mouvement de la Jeunesse Communiste [*Communist Youth Movement*] [*French*]   (WER)
MJC.......... Movimento da Juventude Comunista [*Communist Youth Movement*] [*Portuguese*]   (WER)
MJC.......... Movimiento Juvenil Cristiano [*Christian Youth Movement*] [*Costa Rica*]   (LA)
MJCC........ Melbourne Junior Chamber of Commerce [*Australia*]
MJD .... Mohenjo Daro [*Pakistan*] [*Airport symbol*]   (OAG)
MJD .... Mouvement de la Jeunesse Djiboutienne [*Political party*]   (EY)
MJD .... Musikalische Jugend Deutschland [*Germany*]   (EAIO)
MJL .... Mouila [*Gabon*] [*Airport symbol*]   (OAG)
MJL .... Mouvement de la Jeunesse Luxembourgeoise [*Luxembourg Youth Movement*]   (WER)
MJM .... Mbuji-Mayi [*Zaire*] [*Airport symbol*]   (OAG)
MJN .... Majunga [*Madagascar*] [*Airport symbol*]   (OAG)
MJN .... Royal Air Force of Oman (Air Transport) [*ICAO designator*]   (FAAC)
MJNI........ Ministerio da Justica e Negocios Interiores [*Ministry of Justice and Domestic Trade*] [*Portuguese*]
MJOA .... Mouvement de la Jeunesse Ouvriere Angolaise [*Angolan Working Youth Movement*]   (AF)
MJP.......... Moniteur des Juges de Paix [*France*]   (FLAF)
MJP.......... Mouvement de la Jeunesse Panafricaine [*Panafrican Youth Movement*]
MJP.......... Movimiento de la Juventud Panamena [*Panamanian Youth Movement*]   (LA)
MjPD......... Mjesecnik Pravnickog Drustva [*Lawyers' Society Monthly*]   (YU)
MJPP .... Memoires Juives, Patrimoine Photographique [*France*]   (EAIO)
MJPS .... Mouvement des Jeunesses Progressistes Soudanaises [*Sudanese Progressive Youth Movement*] [*Mali*]
Mjr............ Major [*German*]
MJS.......... Mouvement de la Jeunesse Sioniste   (BJA)
MJS.......... Movimiento Juvenil Salesiano [*Salesian Youth Movement - SYM*]   (EAIO)
MJS.......... Movimiento Juventud Sandinista [*Sandinist Youth Movement*] [*Nicaragua*]   (LA)
MJSA .... Mouvement des Jeunesses Socialistes Africaines [*African Socialist Youth Movement*]
MJSz .... Magyar Jogasz Szovetseg [*Association of Hungarian Jurists*]   (HU)
MJT .... Mouvement de la Jeunesse Tchadienne
MJT .... Mytilene [*Greece*] [*Airport symbol*]   (OAG)
MJTA........ McDonald's Junior Tennis Australia
MJU .... Mamuju [*Indonesia*] [*Airport symbol*]   (OAG)
MJUO ...... Mount John University Observatory [*New Zealand*]
MJUPG..... Movimiento da Juventude da Uniao Popular da Guine [*Youth Movement of Guinean People's Union*]
MJUPS ..... Mouvement des Jeunes de l'Union Progressiste Senegalaise [*Youth Movement of the Senegalese Progressive Movement*]
MJur.......... Militaire Jurisprudentie [*Benelux*]   (BAS)
MJV.......... Murcia [*Spain*] [*Airport symbol*]   (OAG)
MK .... Bridge Logging Method   (RU)
MK .... Camouflage Paint   (RU)
MK .... Erection Crane   (RU)
MK .... Intergranular Corrosion   (RU)
MK .... International Book [*All-Union Association for the International Book Trade*]   (RU)
m/k............ Junior Commander   (RU)
Mk .... Lighthouse, Beacon   (RU)
MK .... Local Committee   (RU)
MK .... Long-Distance Switchboard, Toll Switchboard   (RU)
MK .... Magnetic Correction   (RU)
MK .... Magnetic Course, Magnetic Heading   (RU)
MK .... Magnetkarte [*German*]   (ADPT)

MK............ Magnetski Kurs [*Magnetic Course*] [*Aviation*] (YU)
MK............ Magveto Kiado [*Magveto Publishing House*] (HU)
MK............ Magyar Kozlony [*Hungarian Gazette*] (HU)
MK............ Magyar Koztarsasag [*Hungarian Republic*] (HU)
MK............ Magyar Kupa [*Hungarian Cup*] (HU)
MK............ Makedonski Komitet [*Macedonian Committee*] (YU)
MK............ Malawi Kwacha [*Monetary unit*]
MK............ Marinekabel [*Marine Cable*] (EG)
Mk .... Mark [*Mark*] [*German*]
Mk .... Marke [*Stamp, Grade*] [*German*] (GCA)
MK............ Markka [*Monetary unit*] [*Finland*] (GPO)
MK............ Marschkolonne [*March Column*] [*German military - World War II*]
MK............ Maschinen- und Kapazitaetserfassung [*Census of Machinery and Capacity*] (EG)
MK............ Meat Kombinat (RU)
MK............ Mebyon Kernow [*Sons of Cornwall*] [*National liberation party*] [*Political party*]
MK............ Mechanized Corps (RU)
MK............ Mededelingen van het Kadaster [*Benelux*] (BAS)
MK............ Medeni Kanun [*Civil Law*] (TU)
MK............ Mediteranska Komisija [*Mediterranean Commission*] (YU)
mk .... Megakykloi [*Megacycles*] (GC)
MK............ Member of Knesset (ME)
MK............ Mesni Komitet [*Local Committee*] (YU)
MK............ Mestska Knihovna [*Municipal Library*] (CZ)
MK............ Metallurgical Combine (BU)
MK............ Metarrithmistikon Komma [*Reformist Party*] [*Greece*] [*Political party*] (PPE)
MK............ Methyl Red (Indicator) (RU)
MK............ Mezhdunarodnaya Kniga [*Book trade organization*] [*Former USSR*]
mk .... Micron (RU)
MK............ Microphone Inset, Transmitter Inset [*Telephony*] (RU)
mk .... Mikroskopisch [*Microscopic*] [*German*]
mk .... Millicoulomb (RU)
MK............ Milton Keynes [*Russian city*]
MK............ Minel Kotlogradnja [*Steam generator manufacturing company*] [*Former Yugoslavia*]
MK............ Ministerstvo Kultury [*Ministry of Culture*] (CZ)
MK............ Ministerstwo Kolei [*Ministry of Railroads*] (POL)
MK............ Ministerstwo Komunikacji [*Ministry of Transportation*] (POL)
MK............ Mit Kappe [*With Cap*] [*German military - World War II*]
MK............ Mit Kern [*With Core*] [*German military - World War II*]
MK............ Mitotic Index (RU)
M-K .... Monte Carlo Method (RU)
MK............ Moscow Committee (RU)
MK............ Motorboat (RU)
MK............ Motor Ship (BU)
Mk .... Muldenkipper [*Rail-Dump Car*] (EG)
MK............ Multiple-Cut Trench Excavator (RU)
MK............ Pendulum Hammer, Impact Tester (RU)
mk .... Seaman [*or Sailor*] (BU)
m/k .... Small Caliber (BU)
mk .... Small-Caliber, Small-Bore (RU)
Mk .... Torque (RU)
MK............ Verband der Marianischen Studentenkongregationen Oesterreichs [*Federation of Sodalities of Our Lady for Students*] [*Austria*] (WEN)
MK............ Youth Committee (BU)
MKA.......... International Cooperative Alliance [*ICA*] (RU)
MKA.......... Marine-Kuestenartillerie [*Naval Coast Artillery*] [*German military - World War II*]
m-ka .... Marka [*Mark*] [*Poland*]
MKA.......... Mbrojtja Kunderajrore [*Albanian*]
MKA.......... Mezhregional'naya Kinologicheskaya Assotsiatsiya (EAIO)
mka .... Microampere (RU)
MKA.......... Multikonferenzanlage [*German*] (ADPT)
MKAD...... Moscow Belt Highway (RU)
Mkal .... Megacalorie (RU)
MKAP ...... International Confederation of Arab Trade Unions [*ICATU*] (RU)
MKB .... International Cooperative Bank [*ICB*] (RU)
MKB .... Mekambo [*Gabon*] [*Airport symbol*] (OAG)
mkb .... Microbar (RU)
mkbar........ Microbar (RU)
mkber........ Microrem (RU)
MKBK ...... Moscow Motion-Picture Equipment Design Office (RU)
MKBR ...... Intercontinental Ballistic Missile (RU)
MKBS........ Intercontinental Ballistic Missile (RU)
MKC .... Magnetkontencomputer [*German*] (ADPT)
MKCh .... International Tea Committee (RU)
MKChM.... Ferrous Metals Metallurgical Combine (BU)
MKCK ...... Medunarodni Komitet Crvenog Krsta [*International Red Cross Committee*] (YU)

MKCK ...... Miedzynarodowy Komitet Czerwonego Krzyza [*International Red Cross Committee*] [*Poland*]
MKD......... Magnetic Annular Arc (RU)
MKD......... Motorized Cavalry Division (RU)
MKDNRM ... Muzejsko-Konservatorsko Drustvo na Narodnata Republika Makedonija [*Museum and Preservation Society of Macedonia*] (YU)
MKDON ... Moscow-Kursk-Donbass Railroad (RU)
MKE .... A Magyar Koztarsasag Elnoke [*President of the Hungarian Republic*] (HU)
MKE .... Magyar Kemikusok Egyesulete [*Association of Hungarian Chemists*] (HU)
MKE .... Magyar Konyvtarosok Egyesulete [*Hungary*] (SLS)
MKE .... Makina ve Kimya Endustri [*Machine and Chemical Industry*] [*MKEK*] [*See also*] (TU)
MKE .... Miejskie Koleje Elektryczne [*Municipal Electrical Railroads*] (POL)
MKE .... Militaerische Koerpertuechtigung [*Military Physical Training*] [*German*]
MKEA ...... International Conference of Agricultural Economists [*ICAE*] (RU)
MKEK ...... Makina ve Kimya Endustri Kurumu [*The Machine and Chemical Industry Establishment*] [*MKE*] [*See also*] (TU)
MKF .... Magnetischer Kugelfernschalter [*Magnetic Ball Teleswitch*] [*German*] (EG)
mkf............ Microfarad (BU)
MKF .... Monocalcium Phosphate (RU)
MK FJN .... Miejski Komitet Frontu Jednosci Narodu [*National Unity Front City Committee*] (POL)
MKFN ...... Miejski Komitet Frontu Narodowego [*Municipal Committee of the People's Front*] (POL)
MKG......... Crawler Erection Crane (RU)
MKG......... Maurer Kunst Geselle [*Fellowcraft*] [*Freemasonry*] [*German*]
mkg .... Meterkilogramm [*Kilogram-Meter*] [*German*]
mkg .... Microgram (RU)
MKGM..... Milli Kutuphane Genel Mudurlugu [*National Library Directorate General*] (TU)
mkgn .... Microhenry (RU)
MKGR ...... Musjawarah Kekeluargaan Gotong Rojong [*Consultative Council of Cooperative Groups*] (IN)
MKGSS .... Meter-Kilogram Force-Second [*System of units*] (RU)
MKGYa .... International Commission on Large Dams (BU)
MKH .... Magyar Kozponti Hirado [*Hungarian Central News Agency*] (HU)
MKh......... Meta Khristou [*In the Year of Our Lord*] (GC)
MKh.......... Ministry of Grain Products, USSR (RU)
MKH .... Mokhotlong [*Lesotho*] [*Airport symbol*] (OAG)
MKhAT ..... Moscow Academic Art Theater of the USSR Imeni M. Gor'kiy (RU)
mkhg .... Mobile Surgical Group [*Navy*] (RU)
MKhI........ Moscow Art Institute Imeni V. I. Surikov (RU)
MKhIMP... World Economy and World Politics (RU)
MKhORM ... International Young Christian Workers [*YCW*] (RU)
MKhP....... Mechanized Storage and Search (RU)
MKhP....... Ministry of Chemical Industry (BU)
MKhP....... Ministry of the Chemical Industry, USSR (RU)
MKhP....... Polarizing Microscope for Cotton (RU)
m/khs .... Camouflaged Communication Trench [*Topography*] (RU)
MKHS ...... Medunarodna Konferencija Hriscanskih Sindikata [*International Federation of Christian Trade Unions (IFCTU)*] (YU)
MKhT....... Moscow Art Theater [*1898-1920*] (RU)
MKhT........ Moscow State Organization for the Baked Goods and Confectionery Retail Trade
MKhTI ...... Moscow Institute of Chemical Technology Imeni D. I. Mendeleyev (RU)
MKhTIMP ... Moscow Institute of Chemical Technology of the Meat Industry (RU)
MKhTT ..... Moscow Technicum of Chemical Technology (RU)
MKI .... Ministerstvo Kultury a Informaci [*Ministry of Culture and Information*] (CZ)
Mki .... Misaki [*Cape*] [*Japan*] (NAU)
MKI .... Small Control Testing (RU)
MKINKK... International Commission for the Study of Folk Culture in the Carpathians (RU)
MKIOlimp... Miedzynarodowy Komitet Igrzysk Olimpijskich [*International Committee on the Olympic Games*] (POL)
MKiS .... Ministerstwo Kultury i Sztuki [*Ministry of Culture and Art*] (POL)
MKISZ...... Magyar Kommunista Ifjusagi Szovetsg [*Hungarian Communist Youth Association*] (HU)
M-Kiyev..... Moscow-Kiev Railroad (RU)
MKJ.......... Makoua [*Congo*] [*Airport symbol*] (OAG)
MKJK....... Kingston [*Jamaica*] [*ICAO location identifier*] (ICLI)
MKJM....... Montego Bay [*Jamaica*] [*ICAO location identifier*] (ICLI)
MKJP........ Kingston/Norman Manley International [*Jamaica*] [*ICAO location identifier*] (ICLI)

MKJS .... Montego Bay/Sangster International [*Jamaica*] [*ICAO location identifier*] (ICLI)
MKK .... International Advisory Committee on Bibliography, Documentation, and Terminology (RU)
MKK .... International Red Cross [*IRC*] (RU)
MKK .... International Whaling Commission (RU)
MKK .... Magnetkontokarte [*German*] (ADPT)
MKK .... Magyar Kepzomuveszeti Kiallitas [*Hungarian Fine Arts Exhibit*] (HU)
MKK .... Magyar Kereskedelmi Kamara [*Hungarian Chamber of Commerce*] (HU)
MKK .... Marine-Kunststoffkabel [*Plastic Marine Cable*] (EG)
Mkk .... Markka [*Monetary unit*] [*Finland*]
MKK .... Matematiikan Kansallinen Komitea [*Finland*] (EAIO)
mkk .... Microcoulomb (RU)
MKK .... Misubishi Kakoki Kaishi [*Japan*] (PDAA)
MKK .... Muszaki Konyvkiado [*Publishing House for Technical Books*] (HU)
MKK .... Muveszet Kis Konyvtara [*Small Library of Arts*] [*Name of publication series*] (HU)
MKKE .... Marx Karoly Kozgazdasagtudomanyi Egyetem [*Karl Marx University of Economic Sciences*] (HU)
MKKF .... International Telephone Consultative Committee (RU)
MKKF .... Miejski Komitet Kultury Fizycznej [*Municipal Committee on Physical Culture*] (POL)
MKKFiT .... Miejski Komitet Kultury Fizycznej i Turystyki [*City Committee for Physical Culture and Tourism*] (POL)
MKKH .... Magyar Kulkereskedelmi Hivatal [*Hungarian Foreign Trade Office*] (HU)
MKKh .... Ministry of the Municipal Economy (RU)
MKKh .... Moscow Department of Municipal Services (RU)
MKKhP ..... International Federation of Christian Trade Unions [*IFCTU*] (RU)
MKKhU ..... Ministry of the Municipal Economy, Ukrainian SSR (RU)
MKKI .... Magyar Kulkereskedelmi Igazgatosag [*Hungarian Foreign Trade Directorate*] (HU)
MKKK ...... International Committee of the Red Cross [*ICRC*] (RU)
MKKL .... Merestechnikai Kozponti Kutato Laboratorium [*Central Research Laboratory for Measuring Technology*] (HU)
MKKM ...... Mezinarodni Koaxialni Kabelova Magistrala [*International Coaxial Cable Line*] (CZ)
MKKP .... Miejska Komisja Kontroli Partyjnej [*City Party Control Commission*] (POL)
MKKPSS ... Moscow Committee of the KPSS (RU)
MKKR .... International Radio Consultative Committee (RU)
MKKT .... International Telegraph Consultative Committee (RU)
MKKT .... Muszaki Kutatasokat Koordinalo Tanacs [*Council for Coordinating Technical Research*] (HU)
MKKTT ..... International Telegraph and Telephone Consultative Committee (RU)
mkkyuri ..... Microcurie (RU)
mkl .... Microliter (RU)
MKL .... Miejska Komisja Lokalowa [*Municipal Housing Commission*] (POL)
MKL .... Muzeum Kultur Ludowych [*Folk Culture Museum*] (POL)
MKLK .... Mistni Komise Lidove Kontroly [*Local Commission of People's Control*] (CZ)
MKLMS .... Mladinski Komite Ljudske Mladine Slovenije [*Youth Committee of the People's Youth of Slovenia*] (YU)
MKM .... Magyar Kabel Muvek [*Hungarian Cable Works*] (HU)
mkm .... Micron (RU)
MKM .... Mukah [*Malaysia*] [*Airport symbol*] (OAG)
MKMH ..... Mala Knjiznica "Matice Hrvatske" [*The "Mala Knjiznica" Publication Series, issued by the Matica Hrvatska Publishing House*] [*Zagreb*] (YU)
mkmk .... Micromicron (RU)
mkmkf .... Micromicrofarad (RU)
mkmkg .... Micromicrogram (RU)
mkmkv ...... Micromicrovolt (RU)
mkmkvt ...... Micromicrowatt (RU)
MKMMRT ... Magyar Kozlony, Minisztertanacsi es Miniszteri Rendeletek Tara [*Hungarian Gazette, Collection of Cabinet and Departmental Decrees*] (HU)
MKMO ...... Memgyhapoqublie Komnmem Mehgyhapoquorx Optahuzauyie [*International Committee of Youth Organizations*] [*Commonwealth of Independent States*] (EAIO)
mkmol' ...... Micromole (RU)
MKMR .... International Radio-Maritime Committee (RU)
MKMV .... International Committee on Weights and Measures (RU)
MKN .... Malekolon [*Papua New Guinea*] [*Airport symbol*] (OAG)
MKN .... Metodistkirkens Kvinneforbund Norge [*An association*] [*Norway*] (EAIO)
mkn .... Micron (RU)
MKN .... Minimal Controlled Level (BU)
MKN .... Mouvement Cooperatif National [*Haiti*] [*Political party*] (EY)
MKN .... Muzeum Kultur Narodowych [*Poland*]
MKO .... Engine and Boiler Room (RU)

MKO .... International Commission on Illumination (BU)
MKO .... Makung Airlines [*Taiwan*] [*ICAO designator*] (FAAC)
m-ko .... Small Town (RU)
MKOl .... Miedzynarodowy Komitet Olimpijski [*International Olympic Games Committee*] [*Poland*]
MKOM ...... Intergovernmental Maritime Consultative Organization [*IMCO*] (RU)
mkom .... Microhm (RU)
MKOS ...... Manych-Kuma Irrigation System (RU)
MKOSZ ..... Magyar Kozalkalmazottak Orszagos Szovetsege [*National Federation of Hungarian Civil Servants*] (HU)
MKOW ...... Miejski Komitet Odbudowy Warszawy [*Municipal Committee on the Reconstruction of Warsaw*] (POL)
MKOWU ... Madras Kerosene Oil Workers' Union [*India*]
MKozlony ... Magyar Kozlony Kiado [*"Magyar Kozlony" Publishing House*] (HU)
MKP .... International Propaganda Committee (RU)
MKP .... Magyar Kommunista Part [*Hungarian Communist Party*] [*Political party*] (PPE)
MKP .... Makemo [*French Polynesia*] [*Airport symbol*] (OAG)
MKP .... Manggagawa ng Komunikasyon sa Pilipinas [*Trade union*] [*Philippines*] (EY)
MKP .... Maritime Coastal Navigation (BU)
MKP .... Marokanskaia Kommunisticheskaia Partiia [*Moroccan Communist Party*]
MKP .... Masove-Kulturni Prace [*Mass Cultural Work*] (CZ)
MKP .... Mechanical Forging Press (RU)
MKP .... Medunarodna Konvencija o Prevozu Putnika [*International Convention Concerning the Carriage of Passengers and Luggage by Rail (CIV)*] (YU)
MKP .... Ministerstwo Kontroli Panstwowej [*Ministry of State Control*] (POL)
MKP .... Motorkerekpar [*Motorcycle*] (HU)
MKP .... Multiconfigurational Approximation (RU)
MKP .... Pneumatic Riveting Hammer (RU)
MKP .... Pneumatic-Tired Erection Crane (RU)
MK Pasa .... Mustafa Kemal Pasha [*Ataturk*] (TU)
mkpd .... Mechanical Efficiency (RU)
MKPG .... Miejska Komisja Planowania Gospodarczego [*Municipal Commission on Economic Planning*] (POL)
MKPiK ..... Miedzynarodowy Klub Prasy i Ksiazki [*International Press and Book Club*] (POL)
MKQ .... Merauke [*Indonesia*] [*Airport symbol*] (OAG)
MKR .... International Rice Commission [*IRC*] (RU)
MKR .... Medunarodna Konvencija o Prevozu Robe na Zeleznicama [*International Convention Concerning the Carriage of Goods by Rail (CIM)*] (YU)
MKR .... Meekatharra [*Australia*] [*Airport symbol*] (OAG)
mkr .... Microroentgen (RU)
Mkr .... Mikroskop [*Microscope*] [*German*] (GCA)
mkr .... Mikroskopisch [*Microscopic*] [*German*]
MKR .... Militair Keuringsreglement [*Benelux*] (BAS)
MKR .... Minus Control Relay [*Railroads*] (RU)
mkrad .... Microrad (RU)
MKRD .... Blower Motor Jet Engines (BU)
MKRM ...... Interkolkhoz Repair Shop (RU)
MKRYe ...... International Commission on Radiological Units and Measurements [*ICRU*] (RU)
MKRZ .... International Commission on Radiological Protection [*ICRP*] (RU)
MKS .... Crossbar Switch [*Telephony*] (RU)
MKS .... International Conference on Commodities (BU)
MKS .... Junior Command Personnel (RU)
MKS .... Makedonski Kooperativen Sojuz [*Macedonian Cooperative Union*] (RU)
MKS .... Management-Kommunikationssystem [*German*] (ADPT)
MKS .... Maul- und Klauenseuche [*Hoof-and-Mouth Disease*] [*German*]
mks .... Maxwell (RU)
MKS .... Medunarodni Kongres Slavista [*International Congress of Specialists in Slavic Languages and Literature*] (YU)
MKS .... Mekane [*Ethiopia*] [*Airport symbol*] (OAG)
MKS .... Meter-Kilogram-Second [*System of units*] (RU)
MKS .... Metr-Kilogram-Sekunda [*Meter-Kilogram-Second*] [*Poland*]
MKS .... Miedzyszkolny Klub Sportowy [*Inter-School Sports Club*] (POL)
MKS .... Miedzyuczelniany Klub Studencki [*Intercollegiate Students' Club*] [*Poland*]
MKS .... Milicyjny Klub Sportowy [*Militia Sports Club*] (POL)
MKS .... Mugla Kirec Sanayii AS [*Mugla Lime Industry Corporation*] (TU)
mks .... Potion [*Pharmacy*] (RU)
MKSA .... Meter-Kilogram-Second-Ampere [*System of units*] (RU)
MKSAGS .. Meter-Kilogram-Second-Ampere-Degree Kelvin-Candle [*System of units*] (RU)
MKSB .... Ministry of Communal Economy and Public Works [*Obsolete*] (BU)
MKSBl .... Ministry of Communal Economy and Public Works [*Obsolete*] (BU)

MKSBP ..... Ministry of Communal Economy, Public Works, and Roads (BU)
MKSC........ Motorna Konjska Snaga-Cas [*Motor Horsepower-Hour*] (YU)
mksek........ Microsecond (RU)
MKSG .... Meter-Kilogram-Second-Degree Kelvin [*System of units*] (RU)
MKSK........ Meter-Kilogram-Second-Coulomb [*System of units*] (RU)
MKSO .... Interkolkhoz Construction Organization (RU)
MKSP .... International Confederation of Free Trade Unions [*ICFTU*] (RU)
MKSP........ International Conference of Free Trade Union (BU)
MKSP........ Magnetkartenspeicher [*German*] (ADPT)
MKSS........ Medunarodna Konferencija Slobodnih Sindikata [*International Conference of Free Trade Unions*] (YU)
MKSS........ Meter-Kilogram-Second-Candle [*System of units*] (RU)
MKSZ........ Magyar Kepzo - Es Iparmuveszek Szovetsege [*An association*] [*Hungary*] (EAIO)
MKSZ........ Magyar Kerekparos Szovetseg [*Hungarian Cyclists' Association*] (HU)
MKSZ........ Magyar Korhazszovetseg [*An association*] [*Hungary*] (EAIO)
MKT .... Magyar Kardiologusok Tarsasaga [*An association*] [*Hungary*] (EAIO)
MKT .... Magyar Kozgazdasagi Tarsasag [*Hungarian Economic Society*] (HU)
MKT .... Manufacture Khmere de Tabacs [*Cambodian Tobacco Manufacturing Company*] (CL)
MKT .... Milletlerarasi Kalkinma Teskilati [*Agency for International Development - AID*] (TU)
MKT .... Moscow Chamber Theater (RU)
MKT .... Tractor-Mounted Erection Crane (RU)
Mk Tf........ Makinali Tufek [*Machine Gun*] (TU)
MKTiR ...... Miedzyzakladowy Klub Techniki i Racjonalizacji [*Inter-Plant Technique and Rationalization Club*] (POL)
MKTIS ...... Magusa Genel Turk Isciler Sendikasi [*Famagusta Turkish Cypriot Workers Union*] (GC)
MKTs .... Interchamber Pillar [*Mining*] (RU)
MKTS........ Moscow Hard Alloys Kombinat (RU)
MKTU .... Small Public Address System of a Ship (RU)
MKU......... Cinephotomicrography Unit (RU)
MKU......... Long-Distance Cable Center, Toll Cable Center (RU)
MKU......... Makokou [*Gabon*] [*Airport symbol*] (OAG)
MKU......... Mary Kathleen Uranium Ltd. [*Australia*] (NRCH)
mkub .... Cubic Meter (BU)
MKV......... Microswitch (RU)
mkv .... Microvolt (BU)
MKV......... Mittelschueler-Kartellverband Katholischer Farbentraegender Korporationen Oesterreichs [*Union of the Austrian Catholic Student Associations*] (EG)
MKVE .... Magnetkontenverarbeitungseinheit [*German*] (ADPT)
MKVLKSM ... Moscow Committee of the VLKSM (RU)
MKVOKU ... Moscow "Red Banner" Higher Joint Command School Imeni Supreme Soviet of the RSFSR (RU)
mkvt .... Microwatt (BU)
MKW........ Manokwari [*Indonesia*] [*Airport symbol*] (OAG)
MKW........ Marles-Kuhlmann-Wyandotte [*Commercial firm*] [*France*]
m kw .... Metr Kwadratowy [*Square Meter*] [*Poland*]
MKW........ Munitionskraftwagen [*Ammunition Truck*] [*German military - World War II*]
MKWZZ ... Miedzynarodowa Konferencja Wolnych Zwiazkow Zawodowych [*International Conference of Free Trade Unions*] (POL)
MKY .... Mackay [*Australia*] [*Airport symbol*] (OAG)
MKY .... Manchufikuo Koku Yuso Kabushiki Kaisha [*Manchuria Aviation Corp.*]
MKY .... Monky Aerotaxis SA [*Mexico*] [*ICAO designator*] (FAAC)
Mkyuri....... Megacurie (RU)
mkyuri....... Millicurie (RU)
MKZ......... Malacca [*Malaysia*] [*Airport symbol*] (OAG)
MKZ......... Manganorudni a Kyzove Zavody [*Manganese Ore and Pyrite Plants*] [*Chvaletice*] (CZ)
MKZ......... Mbrojtja Kunder Zjarrit [*Albanian*]
MKZ......... Mesarija Kmetijske Zadruge [*Agricultural Cooperative of Butchers*] (YU)
MKZ......... Moscow Carburetor Plant (RU)
MKZhG..... International Cooperative Women's Guild (RU)
MKZhM..... International Harvester Company (RU)
MKZhT ..... International Rail Transport Committee (RU)
ml .... Junior (RU)
ML............. Luminescence Microscope (RU)
ML............. Maalaisliitto [*Agrarian League*] [*Finland*] (WEN)
ML............. Maaseutukeskusten Liitto [*An association*] [*Finland*] (EAIO)
ML............. Magnetic Tape (RU)
ML............. Mali [*ANSI two-letter standard code*] (CNC)
ml .... Manlik [*Masculine*] [*Afrikaans*]
ML............. Markierungsleser [*German*] (ADPT)
Ml .... Matmazel [*Miss*] [*Turkey*] (GPO)
ML............. Maule Aircraft Corp. [*ICAO aircraft manufacturer identifier*] (ICAO)
ML............. Maurer Lehrling [*Entered Apprentice*] [*Freemasonry*] [*German*]
ML............. Mechanikai Laboratorium [*Mechanical Laboratory*] (HU)
ML............. Mein Lieber [*My Dear*] [*German*]
ML............. Mere Loge [*Mother Lodge*] [*Freemasonry*] [*French*]
ml .... Meter Linear [*Albanian*]
ML............. Middle Latin [*Language, etc.*]
Ml .... Mikkelin Laani(a) [*Finland*]
m/L .... Mi Letra [*Spanish*]
ml .... Milha Maritima Internacional [*International Nautical Mile*] [*Portuguese*]
ml .... Mililitr [*Milliliter*] [*Poland*]
ml .... Mililitro [*Milliliter*] [*Portuguese*]
ml .... Millilitra(a) [*Milliliter*] [*Finland*]
ml .... Millilitre [*Milliliter*] [*French*] (GPO)
m/l .... Minha Letra [*My Letter*] [*Portuguese*]
ML............. Ministerstwo Lacznosci [*Ministry of Communications*] [*Poland*]
ML............. Ministerstwo Lesnictwa [*Ministry of Forestry*] (POL)
ML............. Mitchell Library [*Australia*] (ADA)
ML............. Mitgliedsland [*Member Country*] (EG)
ML............. Mlada Literatura [*New Literature*] [*A periodical Skopje*] (YU)
ML............. Mlade Leta (Vydavatelstvo Knih pro Mladez) [*Early Years (Publishing House for the Young)*] (CZ)
Ml .... Mladsi [*Junior*] [*Attached to a name*] (CZ)
ML............. Mladsi Lekar [*Junior Physician*] [*Military*] (CZ)
ml .... Mlodszy [*Junior*] [*Poland*]
Ml .... Molality of Solution (RU)
ML............. Moneda Legal [*Legal Tender*] [*Spanish*] [*Business term*]
ml .... Moottorilaiva [*Finland*]
M-L............ Moscow-Leningrad [*Bibliography*] (RU)
ml .... Mukaan Luettuna [*Finland*]
ML............. Muslim League [*Bangladesh*] [*Political party*] (FEA)
ml .... Youth (BU)
ML-12E....... Movimiento de Liberacion Doce de Enero [*12 January Liberation Movement*] [*Dominican Republic*] (LA)
MLA .... Interplanetary Vehicle (RU)
MLA .... Macedonian Literary Association [*Australia*]
MLA .... Malta [*Airport symbol*] (OAG)
MLA .... Malta Library Association (EAIO)
MLA .... Maramanga - Lac Alaotra
MLA .... Martial Law Administration [*Pakistan*]
MLA .... Member of the Legislative Assembly [*Namibia*] (AF)
MLA .... Mexican Librarians Association (EAIO)
MLA .... Mining Lease Application
MLA .... Motor Launch, Auxiliary [*NATO*]
MLA .... Movimento de Libertacao de Angola
MLA .... Movimiento Liberal Autonomo [*Autonomous Liberal Movement*] [*Colorado*] (LA)
MLAA .... Master Locksmiths Association of Australasia Ltd.
MLAANZ ... Maritime Law Association of Australia and New Zealand (ADA)
mladsh .... Junior (RU)
MLAL........ Movimento Laici America Latina
MLAP........ Muslim League Assembly Party [*Pakistan*] [*Political party*] (FEA)
MLAPU..... Marxist-Leninist Armed Propaganda Unit [*Turkey*]
mlat .... Mittellatein [*Medieval Latin*] [*German*]
MLB .... Melbourne [*Totalisator Agency Board code*] [*Australia*]
mlb .... Millilambert (RU)
MLBP........ Ministry of the Lumber and Paper Industries (RU)
MLC .... Mauritius Labour Congress (AF)
MLC .... Member, Legislative Council
MLC .... Methodist Ladies College [*Australia*] (ADA)
MLC .... Movimiento Liberal Constitucionalista [*Liberal Constitutionalist Movement*] [*Nicaragua*] (LA)
MLC .... Mutual Life and Citizens Assurance Co. Ltd. [*Australia*] (ADA)
MLCN .... Marxistisch-Leninistisch Centrum Nederland [*Marxist-Leninist Center, The Netherlands*] (WEN)
MLCV........ Mouvement de Liberation des Iles du Cap Vert [*Movement for the Liberation of the Cape Verde Islands*] (AF)
MLD .... Air Moldova [*ICAO designator*] (FAAC)
MLD .... Marineluchtvaartdienst [*Naval Air Force*] [*Netherlands*] (PDAA)
Mld .... Meldung [*Message*] [*German*] (GCA)
mld .... Miliard [*Billion*] [*Poland*]
MLD .... Minimalni Licni Dohodak [*Minimum Individual Income*] (YU)
MLD .... Moldavian Railroad (RU)
MLD .... Monarquicos Liberal Democratas [*Liberal Democratic Monarchists*] [*Spanish*] (WER)
MLD .... Mouvement pour la Liberation de Djibouti [*Movement for the Liberation of Djibouti*] (PD)
MLD .... Movimento di Liberazione della Donna [*Women's Liberation Movement*] [*Italian*] (WER)
MLD .... Movimiento de Liberacion Dominicana [*Dominican Liberation Movement*] [*Dominican Republic*] (LA)
MLDP .... Ministerstvo Lesu a Drevarskeho Prumyslu [*Ministry of Forests and the Lumber Industry*] (CZ)
MLE .... Magnetic Logical Element (RU)

MLE .... Male [*Maldives*] [*Airport symbol*]   (OAG)

Mle............. Modele [*Model*] [*French*]   (MTD)

MLEC........ Mouvement pour la Liberation de l'Enclave de Cabinda [*Movement for the Liberation of the Cabinda Enclave*] [*Angola*]   (AF)

MLegS .... Master of Legal Studies

MLEU .... Mouvement Liberal pour l'Europe Unie [*France*]   (FLAF)

MLF .... Malermestrenes Landsforbund [*An association*] [*Norway*]   (EAIO)

MLF .... Marxist-Leninistiske Front [*Marxist-Leninist Front*] [*Norway*]   (WEN)

MLF .... Marxist-Leninistisk Fraktion [*Marxist-Leninist Fraction*] [*Sweden*]   (WEN)

MLF .... Mauritius Labor Federation   (AF)

MLF .... Mauritius Labour Federation   (EAIO)

MLF .... Mauritius Liberation Front   (AF)

MLF .... Motor Launch, Fast [*NATO*]

MLF .... Mouvement de Liberation de la Femme [*Women's Liberation Movement*]

MLF .... Multilateral Force [*NATO*]

MLFF .... Manufacture de Laine et de Fibranne Filees [*Algeria*]

MLG .... Local Lecturer Groups   (BU)

MLG .... Malang [*Indonesia*] [*Airport symbol*]   (OAG)

MLG .... Marxist-Leninistiske Gruppene [*Marxist-Leninist Groups*] [*Norway*]   (WEN)

MLG .... Medical Librarians Group [*Australian Library and Information Association*]

MLG .... Middle Low German [*Language, etc.*]

MLG .... Movimento de Libertacao da Guine

MLG .... Youth Lecturer Groups   (BU)

MLGC ...... Mouvement de Liberation de la Guinee du Cap Vert [*Movement for the Liberation of Portuguese Guinea and the Cape Verde Islands*]

MLGC ...... Movimento de Libertacao da Guine e Cabo Verde [*Movement for the Liberation of Portuguese Guinea and the Cape Verde Islands*]

MLGCV ..... Mouvement de Liberation de la Guinee du Cap Vert [*Movement for the Liberation of Portuguese Guinea and the Cape Verde Islands*]

MLGCV ..... Movement for the Liberation of Portuguese Guinea and the Cape Verde Islands

MLGCV ..... Movimento de Libertacao da Guine e Cabo Verde [*Movement for the Liberation of Portuguese Guinea and the Cape Verde Islands*]

MLGP .... Movimento de Libertacao da Guine Portuguesa [*Movement for the Liberation of Portuguese Guinea*]

MLH.......... Mulhouse/Basel [*France*] [*Airport symbol*]   (OAG)

MLI .... Mali [*ANSI three-letter standard code*]   (CNC)

MLI .... Moscow Forest Institute   (RU)

ML i BP ..... Ministry of the Lumber and Paper Industries   (RU)

MLICV ..... Mouvement de Liberation des Iles du Cap Vert [*Movement for the Liberation of the Cape Verde Islands*] [*French*]

MLICV ..... Movimento de Libertacao das Ilhas de Cabo Verde [*Movement for the Liberation of the Cape Verde Islands*] [*Portuguese*]   (WER)

Mli MhTsk ... Milli Muhafiz Teskilati [*National Guard Organization*]   (TU)

MLiPD ...... Ministerstwo Lesnictwa i Przemyslu Drzewnego [*Ministry of Forestry and Timber Industry*] [*Poland*]

m lis............ Maille Lisiere [*Border Stitch*] [*Knitting*] [*French*]

mlk.............. Maalaiskunta [*Finland*]

MLK .... Mistni Lidova Knihovna [*Local People's Library*]   (CZ)

MLKE........ Marxistiki Leninistiki Kinisi Ellados [*Marxist-Leninist Movement of Greece*]   (GC)

ml k-r .... Junior Commander   (RU)

MLL .... Line Selector Electromagnet   (RU)

MLL .... Masarykova Letecka Liga [*Masaryk Aviation League*]   (CZ)

mll .... Mouillure [*Stain caused by moisture*] [*Publishing*] [*French*]

Mlle .... Mademoiselle [*Miss*] [*French*]   (GPO)

Mlle .... Muelle [*Mole*] [*Me*] [*See also*] [*Spanish*]   (NAU)

ml leyt .... Second Lieutenant   (RU)

MLLH .... Mezinarodni Liga Ledniho Hokeje [*International Ice Hockey League*]   (CZ)

MLM .... Military Liaison Mission [*Germany*]

MLM .... Morelia [*Mexico*] [*Airport symbol*]   (OAG)

MLM .... Movimento de Libertacao das Mulheres [*Women's Liberation Movement*] [*Portuguese*]   (WER)

MLMTT .... Marxism-Leninism-Mao Tse-Tung Thought [*Ideologies guiding the New People's Army, a guerrilla movement in the Philippines*]

MLN .... Melilla [*Spain*] [*Airport symbol*]   (OAG)

MLN .... Melilla Airport

mln .... Milion [*Million*] [*Poland*]

MLN .... Minerva Library Network [*Australia*]

MLN .... Mouvement de Liberation Nationale [*National Liberation Movement*] [*Burkina Faso Banned, 1974*] [*Political party*]

MLN .... Movimiento de Liberacion Nacional [*National Liberation Movement*] [*Uruguay*] [*Political party*]

MLN .... Movimiento de Liberacion Nacional [*National Liberation Movement*] [*Guatemala*] [*Political party*]   (PPW)

MLN .... Movimiento de Liberacion Nacional [*National Liberation Movement*] [*Argentina*]   (LA)

MLN .... Movimiento de Liberacion Nacional [*National Liberation Movement*] [*Mexico*]   (LA)

MLN .... Movimiento de Liberacion Nacional - Tupamaros [*National Liberation Movement - Tupamaros*] [*Uruguay*]   (LA)

MLN-29..... Movimiento de Liberacion Nacional 29 de Noviembre [*29 November National Liberation Movement*] [*Panama*]   (LA)

MLNA .... Movimento de Libertacao Nacional de Angola [*National Liberation Movement of Angola*]

ml nauchnsotr ... Junior Scientific Worker   (RU)

MLNC .... Mouvement de Liberation National des Comores [*National Liberation Movement of the Comoro Islands*]   (AF)

ml n s......... Junior Scientific Associate   (BU)

MLO .... Marxisten-Leninisten Oesterreichs [*Marxists-Leninists of Austria*] [*Political party*]   (PPE)

MLO .... Medical Liaison Officer [*Australia*]

MLO .... Mestni Ljudski Odbor [*Local People's Committee*]   (YU)

MLO .... Migrant Liaison Officer [*Australia*]

MLO .... Milos [*Greece*] [*Airport symbol*]   (OAG)

MLP .... Malabang [*Philippines*] [*Airport symbol*]   (OAG)

MLP .... Malta Labor Party [*Political party*]   (PPW)

MLP .... Mauritius Labor Party [*Political party*]   (PPW)

MLP .... Ministerstvo Lehkeho Prumyslu [*Ministry of Light Industry*]   (CZ)

MLP .... Ministry of Light Industry   (RU)

MLP .... Ministry of the Lumber Industry   (RU)

MLP .... Mouvement de Liberation du Peuple [*People's Liberation Movement*] [*Malagasy*]   (AF)

MLP .... Movimento Libertario Portugues [*Portuguese Anarchist Movement*]   (WER)

MLP .... Movimiento de Liberacion del Pueblo [*People's Liberation Movement*] [*El Salvador*] [*Political party*]   (PD)

MLP .... Movimiento de Liberacion Proletaria [*Proletarian Liberation Movement*] [*Mexico*] [*Political party*]   (PD)

MLPB .... Ministry of Light Industry, Belorussian SSR   (RU)

MLPC....... Mouvement de Liberation du Peuple Centrafricain [*Movement for the Liberation of the Central African People*]   (PD)

MLPD ...... Marxistische-Leninistische Partei Deutschlands [*Marxist-Leninist Party of Germany*]   (EG)

MLPN ...... Marxist-Leninist Party of the Netherlands   (WEN)

MLPOe...... Marxistische-Leninistische Partei Oesterreichs [*Marxist-Leninist Party of Austria*]   (WEN)

MLPS .... Ministrstvo za Lokalni Promet Slovenije [*Ministry of Local Transportation of Slovenia*]   (YU)

MLPU ...... Ministry of Light Industry, Ukrainian SSR   (RU)

MLQ .... Malalaua [*Papua New Guinea*] [*Airport symbol*]   (OAG)

MLR .... Madarska Ludova Republika [*Hungarian People's Republic*]   (CZ)

MLR .... Minimum Lending Rate

MlR........... Mladinska Revija [*Youth Review*]   (YU)

MLR .... Movimiento de Lucha Revolucionaria [*Revolutionary Struggle Movement*] [*Mexico*]   (LA)

MLR .... Movimiento Laboral Revolucionario [*Revolutionary Labor Movement*] [*Peru*]   (LA)

MLRC....... Multi-Language Resource Collection [*Western Australia*]

mlrd........... Billion   (RU)

mlrd/ME ... Billion International Units   (BU)

MLS.......... Lumber Machinery Station   (RU)

MLS.......... Malay Language Society   (ML)

MLS.......... Medical Libraries Section [*Library Association of Australia*]

MLS.......... Medilab Select [*Nuclear energy*] [*Belgium*]   (NRCH)

MLS.......... Mouvement de Liberation du Sanwi [*Movement for the Liberation of the Sanwi*] [*Ghana*]   (AF)

MLS.......... Movimento per le Liberta Statuarie [*Movement for Statutory Liberty*] [*Sanmarinese*]   (PPE)

MLS.......... Movimiento de Liberacion Sebta [*Ceuta Liberation Movement*] [*Spain*]   (PD)

MLSA....... Mines Local Staff Association

MLSA....... Mortlock Library of South Australiana

MLSOP .... Movement for the Liberation of Soa Tome and Principe [*Political party*]

MLSS .... Mechanized Letter Sorting System [*Hong Kong Post Office*]

MLSSA ..... Marine Life Society of South Australia

MLST .... Medico-Legal Society of Tasmania [*Australia*]

MLSTP ..... Mouvement pour la Liberation de Sao Tome et Principe [*Movement for the Liberation of Sao Tome and Principe*]   (AF)

MLSTP ..... Movimento de Libertacao de Sao Tome e Principe [*Movement for the Liberation of Sao Tome and Principe*] [*Portugal*]   (PPW)

Mlstrzm ..... Mladsi Strazmistr [*Warrant Officer, Junior Grade*]   (CZ)

MLSZ........ Magyar Labdarugo Szovetseg [*Hungarian Soccer League*]   (HU)

MLT .... Malta [*ANSI three-letter standard code*]   (CNC)

MLT .... Masarykova Liga Proti Tuberkulose [*Masaryk League for the Prevention of Tuberculosis*] (CZ)
MLT .... Multiplikation [*German*] (ADPT)
MLT .... Varnished Metal-Film Heat-Resistant (Resistor) (RU)
MLTAA..... Modern Language Teachers' Association of Australia
MLTI........ Moscow Forestry Engineering Institute (RU)
MLTM ...... Maktab Latehan Tentera Malaysia [*Malaysian Military Training College*] (ML)
MLU .... Masarykuv Lidovychovny Ustav [*Masaryk Institute of Public Education*] (CZ)
MLU .... Montlucon Air Service [*France*] [*ICAO designator*] (FAAC)
MLU .... Moroccan Labor Union
MLUH....... Martin-Luther-Universitaet Halle [*Martin Luther University, Halle*] (EG)
MLV .... Ministerstvo Lesniho a Vodniho Hospodarstvi [*Ministry of Forestry and Water Management*] (CZ)
MLW .... Monrovia [*Liberia*] [*Airport symbol*] (OAG)
MLX .... Malatya [*Turkey*] [*Airport symbol*] (OAG)
Mly .... National Library of Malaysia, Kuala Lumpur, Malaysia [*Library symbol*] [*Library of Congress*] (LCLS)
MlyKgM.... Sarawak Museum, Kuching, Malaysia [*Library symbol*] [*Library of Congress*] (LCLS)
MLZ .... Magnetostrictive Delay Line (RU)
Mlz............. Malzeme [*Materials, Equipment, Stock*] (TU)
MLZ .... Marxistische-Leninistische Zellen [*Marxist-Leninist Cells*] (WEN)
MLZ .... Melo [*Uruguay*] [*Airport symbol*] (OAG)
MLZhMS ... Women's International League for Peace and Freedom (RU)
MM............ Compagnie des Messageries Maritimes
MM............ International Society for the Interaction of Mechanics and Mathematics [*ICSU*]
mm .... Last Month (BU)
MM............ Local Air Mass (RU)
MM............ Maailmanmestaruus [*Finland*]
Mm .... Madam [*Madam*] [*Turkey*] (GPO)
MM............ Magic Millions [*Australia*]
MM............ Marina Militare [*Italian Navy*]
MM............ Marine Marchande [*France*] (FLAF)
MM............ Marker Beacon (RU)
MM............ Mars Matbaasi [*Mars Press*] [*Ankara*] (TU)
m/m........... Mas o Menos [*More or Less*] [*Spanish*]
MM............ Mathematical Model (RU)
mm .... Med Mera [*And So Forth*] [*Sweden*] (GPO)
mm .... Med Mere [*And So Forth*] [*Norway*] (GPO)
mm .... Med Mere [*And So Forth*] [*Denmark*] (GPO)
Mm .... Megameter (RU)
Mm .... Megametre [*Metric System*] [*French*] (GPO)
MM............ Melbourne Marathon [*Australia*]
MM............ Memoire Morte [*French*] (ADPT)
MM............ Mens en Maatschappij [*Benelux*] (BAS)
M/M........... Meritissimo [*Most Worthy*] [*Portuguese*]
MM............ Messageries Maritimes [*Forwarding agents*] [*French*]
MM............ Messieurs [*Plural of Mister*] [*French*]
MM............ Metal Manufacturers Ltd. [*Australia*]
MM............ "Metalna", Tovarna Konstrukcij in Strojnih Naprav, Maribor ["*Metalna" Machinery Factory in Maribor*] (YU)
mm .... Meta Mesimvrian [*Post Meridian*] (GC)
mm .... Metermazsa [*Quintal*] (HU)
MM............ Methodist Mission
mm .... Milimeter [*Albanian*]
mm .... Milimetr [*Millimeter*] (POL)
mm .... Milimetro [*Millimeter*] [*Portuguese*]
mm .... Milimetro [*Millimeter*] [*Spanish*]
MM............ Millet Meclisi [*Grand National Assembly*] [*BMM*] [*See also*] (TU)
Mm .... Millimeter [*German*] (GCA)
mm .... Millimetre [*Millimeter*] [*French*]
mm .... Millimetri [*Millimeters*] [*Italian*]
mm .... Millimetri(a) [*Millimeter*] [*Finland*]
mM .... Millimolarity (RU)
MM............ Mimar ve Muhendisler Ltd. [*Architects and Engineers Ltd.*] [*Manufacturers of aluminum kitchen ware*] (TU)
MM............ Ministerio da Marinha [*Admiralty*] [*Portuguese*]
MM............ Minister of Munitions [*British*] [*World War II*]
MM............ Ministerul Muncii [*Ministry of Labor*] (RO)
MM............ Ministry of Machinery Manufacture, USSR (RU)
Mm .... Miriametro [*Spanish*]
m/m........... Moi-Meme [*Myself*] [*French*]
MM............ Mois Maconnique [*Masonic Month*] [*Freemasonry*] [*French*]
MM............ Moravske Museum [*Moravian Museum*] [*Brno*] (CZ)
MM............ Moscow Subway (RU)
mm .... Motorized and Mechanized (RU)
MM............ Motor Method (RU)
MM............ Mozambique Metical [*Monetary unit*] (IMH)
mm .... Muiden Muassa [*Finland*]
MM............ Muistomitali [*Finland*]

mm .... Muun Muassa [*or Muuassa*] [*Among Other Things*] [*Finland*]
MM............ Muvelodesugyi Miniszterium/Miniszter [*Ministry/Minister of Cultural Affairs*] (HU)
mm² .... Milimetr Kwadratowy [*Square Millimeter*] [*Poland*]
Mm² .... Millimetre Carre [*Square Millimeter*] [*French*] (MTD)
mm³ .... Milimetr Szescienny [*Cubic Millimeter*] [*Poland*]
Mm³ .... Millimetre Cube [*Cubic Millimeter*] [*French*] (MTD)
MMA........ MacRobertson Miller Airline Services [*Australia*]
MMA........ Malaysian Medical Association (EAIO)
MMA........ Maldives Monetary Authority (GEA)
MMA........ Malmo [*Sweden*] [*Airport symbol*] (OAG)
MMA........ Mauritius Marine Authority (GEA)
MMA........ Methyl Methacrylate (RU)
MMA........ Metro Manila Airways International, Inc. [*Philippines*] [*ICAO designator*] (FAAC)
MMA........ Metropolitan Municipal Association [*Victoria, Australia*]
MMA........ Mine Management Associates
MMA........ Mines and Metals Association [*Australia*]
MMA........ Mothers and Midwives Action [*Australia*] [*An association*]
MMA........ Revised Product Form Algorithm (RU)
MMA........ Small Medical Apparatus (RU)
MMAA...... Acapulco/General Juan N. Alvarez Internacional [*Mexico*] [*ICAO location identifier*] (ICLI)
MMAA...... Methylol Methacrylamide (RU)
MMA/ADA ... Mahaica-Mahaicony-Abary/Agricultural Development Authority [*Guyana*] (LA)
MMAD...... Mikhanokinitos Monas Amesou Draseos [*Motorized Unit of Instant Action*] [*KAD*] [*See also*] (GC)
MMAJ....... Metal Mining Agency of Japan (PDAA)
MMAL ...... Mitsubishi Motors Australia Ltd.
MMAM..... Manufacture Marocaine d'Articles Metalliques
MMAN..... Aeropuerto del Norte [*Mexico*] [*ICAO location identifier*] (ICLI)
MMAS ..... Aguascalientes [*Mexico*] [*ICAO location identifier*] (ICLI)
MMB........ Meat Marketing Board
MMB........ Medicus Mundi Belgium (EAIO)
MMB........ Memanbetsu [*Japan*] [*Airport symbol*] (OAG)
MMB........ Metropolitan Milk Board [*South Australia*]
MMB........ Minimum Monthly Balance [*Finance*]
MMB........ Motorized and Mechanized Brigade (RU)
MMB........ Muzeum Mesta Bratislavy [*Bratislava Municipal Museum*] (CZ)
MMC........ Malaysia Mining Company
MMC........ Melbourne Magistrates Court [*Australia*]
MmC........ Millimetres Court [*French*] (MTD)
MMC........ Ministerial Meeting on Construction [*Australia*]
MMC........ Muhimbili Medical Centre
MMCA ..... Cananea [*Mexico*] [*ICAO location identifier*] (ICLI)
MMCA ..... Materials Management Council of Australia
MMCB ..... Cuernavaca [*Mexico*] [*ICAO location identifier*] (ICLI)
MMCB ..... Malaysia Mining Corp. Berhad (FEA)
MMCC ..... Ciudad Acuna [*Mexico*] [*ICAO location identifier*] (ICLI)
MMCC ..... Methodist Mission of Central Congo
MMCE ..... Ciudad Del Carmen [*Mexico*] [*ICAO location identifier*] (ICLI)
MMCG ..... Mid-Murray Citrus Growers [*Australia*]
MMCG ..... Nuevo Casas Grandes [*Mexico*] [*ICAO location identifier*] (ICLI)
MMCH..... Chilpancingo [*Mexico*] [*ICAO location identifier*] (ICLI)
MMCL ..... Culiacan [*Mexico*] [*ICAO location identifier*] (ICLI)
MMCM..... Chetumal [*Mexico*] [*ICAO location identifier*] (ICLI)
MMCN..... Ciudad Obregon [*Mexico*] [*ICAO location identifier*] (ICLI)
MMCP...... Campeche [*Mexico*] [*ICAO location identifier*] (ICLI)
MMCS ..... Ciudad Juarez/Abraham Gonzalez Internacional [*Mexico*] [*ICAO location identifier*] (ICLI)
MMCSEER ... Marjorie Mayrock Center for CIS [*Commonwealth of Independent States*] and East European Research [*Israel*] (EAIO)
MMCU...... Chihuahua/Internacional [*Mexico*] [*ICAO location identifier*] (ICLI)
MMCV ..... Ciudad Victoria [*Mexico*] [*ICAO location identifier*] (ICLI)
MMCY ..... Celaya [*Mexico*] [*ICAO location identifier*] (ICLI)
MMCZ ..... Cozumel/Internacional [*Mexico*] [*ICAO location identifier*] (ICLI)
MMCZ ..... Minerals Marketing Corp. of Zimbabwe
MMD........ Instantaneous Mine [*Navy*] (RU)
MMD........ Minami Daito Jima [*Volcano Islands*] [*Airport symbol*] (OAG)
MMD........ Movement for Multi-Party Democracy [*Zambia*] [*Political party*]
MMDI....... Middle Management Development Initiative
MMDM..... Ciudad Mante [*Mexico*] [*ICAO location identifier*] (ICLI)
MMDO ..... Durango [*Mexico*] [*ICAO location identifier*] (ICLI)
MME........ Madame [*Mrs.*] [*French*] (EY)
MME........ Mediterranean Medical Entente (EAIO)
MME........ Mercantile Marine Engineering and Graving Docks Co., NV [*Nuclear energy*] [*Belgium*] (NRCH)
MME........ Mikromesaies Epikheiriseis [*Small and Medium-Sized Enterprises*] (GC)

MME......... Ministerio de Minas e Energia [*Ministry of Mining and Energy*] [*Portuguese*]
MME......... Ministry of Mining and Energy [*Indonesia*]
MME......... Modern Mechanical Establishment [*Commercial firm*] [*Lebanon*]
MME......... Small Medical Encyclopedia (RU)
MMEA...... Metallic Mineral Exploration Agency [*Japan*] (PDAA)
MMEC...... Ministry to Middle East Christians [*Cyprus*]
MMEI...... Ministry of Machine Building and Electronics Industry [*China*]
MMEP...... Tepic [*Mexico*] [*ICAO location identifier*] (ICLI)
MMES...... Ensenada [*Mexico*] [*ICAO location identifier*] (ICLI)
MMES...... Mesdames [*Plural of Mrs.*] [*French*]
MMEX...... Mexico [*Mexico*] [*ICAO location identifier*] (ICLI)
MMF......... Makine ve Muhendislik Fakultesi [*Faculty of Mechanics and Engineering*] [*Istanbul Technical University*] (TU)
MMF........ Mamfe [*Cameroon*] [*Airport symbol*] (OAG)
MMF........ Meat and Dairy Farm (RU)
MMF........ Medunarodni Monetarni Fond [*International Monetary Fund*] [*Yugoslavian*] (YU)
MMF........ Ministry of the Maritime Fleet, USSR (RU)
MMF........ Mission Militaire Francaise [*French Military Mission*] (CL)
MMFB...... Melbourne and Metropolitan Fire Brigade [*Australia*]
MMFM..... Front des Journalistes [*Journalists Front*] [*Malagasy*] (AF)
MMFT...... Front des Enseignants [*Teachers Front*] [*Malagasy*] (AF)
MMG........ Mechanikai Meromuszerek Gyara [*Measuring Instruments Factory*] (HU)
MMG........ Milli Meclis Grupu [*National Assembly Group*] (TU)
MMG........ Mount Magnet [*Australia*] [*Airport symbol*] (OAG)
MMG........ Mouvement Mixte Gabonais
MMGA...... Mannequin and Models' Guild of Australia
MMGA...... Mannequins and Models Guild of Australia
MMGL...... Guadalajara/Miguel Hidalgo Y Costilla Internacional [*Mexico*] [*ICAO location identifier*] (ICLI)
MMGM..... Guaymas/General Jose Maria Yanez Internacional [*Mexico*] [*ICAO location identifier*] (ICLI)
MMGS...... Local Interdepartmental Geodetic Council (RU)
MMGT...... Guanajuato [*Mexico*] [*ICAO location identifier*] (ICLI)
MMgt........ Master of Management
MMGY...... Mechanikai Meromuszerek Gyara [*Measuring Instruments Factory*] (HU)
MMH........ Mercantile Mutual Holdings Ltd. [*Australia*]
MMH........ Mikromatika Air Cargo Ltd. [*Hungary*] [*ICAO designator*] (FAAC)
MMH........ Ministerio de Minas e Hidrocarburos [*Caracas, Venezuela*] (LAA)
MMHC...... Tehuacan [*Mexico*] [*ICAO location identifier*] (ICLI)
MMHO..... Hermosillo/Internacional [*Mexico*] [*ICAO location identifier*] (ICLI)
MMI......... Danish Association of Furniture Designers and Interior Architects (EAIO)
MMI......... Magyar Munkasmozgalmi Intezet [*Institute of the Hungarian Working Class Movement*] (HU)
MMI......... Malaysia Metal Industries [*Berhad*]
MMI......... Manufacturers Mutual Insurance Ltd. [*Australia*] (ADA)
MMI......... Materiel Mecanique et Industriel [*Morocco*]
MMI......... Medicus Mundi Internationalis [*International Organization for Cooperation in Health Care - IOCHC*] [*Nijmegen, Netherlands*] (EAIO)
MMI......... Moscow Mechanical Engineering Institute (RU)
MMI......... Moscow Medical Institute (RU)
MMIA....... Colima [*Mexico*] [*ICAO location identifier*] (ICLI)
MM IArch ... Munkasmozgalmi Intezet Archivuma [*Archives of the Institute of the Hungarian Working Class Movement*] (HU)
MMID....... Merida [*Mexico*] [*ICAO location identifier*] (ICLI)
MMidwif ... Master of Midwifery
MMIJ........ Mining and Materials Processing Institute of Japan
MMIJ........ [*The*] Mining and Metallurgical Institute of Japan (SLS)
MMIM...... Isla Mujeres [*Mexico*] [*ICAO location identifier*] (ICLI)
MMiMP.... Ministry of the Meat and Dairy Industry (RU)
m/min ...... Metro por Minuto [*Meters per Minute*] [*Portuguese*]
MMinMgt ... Master of Mining Management
MMIO....... Saltillo [*Mexico*] [*ICAO location identifier*] (ICLI)
MMiP........ Ministry of Machinery Manufacture and Instrument Making, USSR (RU)
MMiSKhP ... Ministry of Local and Shale-Chemical Industries [*ESSR*] (RU)
MMIT .... Iztepec [*Mexico*] [*ICAO location identifier*] (ICLI)
MMiTP..... Ministry of Local and Fuel Industries (RU)
MMJ .... Matsumoto [*Japan*] [*Airport symbol*] (OAG)
MMJA...... Jalapa [*Mexico*] [*ICAO location identifier*] (ICLI)
MMK........ International Maritime Committee [*IMC*] (RU)
MMK........ International Meteorological Committee (RU)
MMK........ Magnetomotorische Kraft [*Magnetomotive Force*] [*German*] (GCA)
MMK........ Magnitogorsk Metallurgical Kombinat (RU)
MMK........ Metallurgical and Metalworking Corp. [*Montenegro*] (EE)
mmk .... Miljoona(a) Markkaa [*Finland*]

mmk .... Millimicron (RU)
MMK........ Motorized and Mechanized Corps (RU)
MMK........ Murmansk [*Former USSR*] [*Airport symbol*] (OAG)
mmkf......... Millimicrofarad (RU)
MMKO..... Intergovernmental Maritime Consultative Organization [*IMCO*] (RU)
MMKR...... Interrayon Shop for Major Repair (RU)
MmL......... Millimetres Long [*French*] (MTD)
MMLA...... Malaysian Muslim Lawyers' Association
MMLA...... Military Mission of Liaison Administration [*World War II*]
MMLC...... Lazaro Cardenas [*Mexico*] [*ICAO location identifier*] (ICLI)
m ml l .... Assistant Surgeon, Battalion Surgeon (BU)
MMLM...... Los Mochis [*Mexico*] [*ICAO location identifier*] (ICLI)
MMLM...... Moroccan Marxist-Leninist Movement (AF)
MMLME .. Mediterranean, Mediterranean Littoral, and/or Middle East
Mml Me..... Muamelat Memuru [*Administrative Clerk*] (TU)
MMLO...... Leon [*Mexico*] [*ICAO location identifier*] (ICLI)
MMLP....... La Paz/General Manuel Marquez de Leon Internacional [*Mexico*] [*ICAO location identifier*] (ICLI)
MMLS...... Muhendislik-Mimarlik ve Lisans Sonrasi [*Engineering and Architectural Postgraduate Degree*] (TU)
MMLT ...... Loreto [*Mexico*] [*ICAO location identifier*] (ICLI)
MMLV...... Movimiento Marxista-Leninista de Venezuela [*Marxist-Leninist Movement of Venezuela*] (LA)
MMM........ Messe der Meister von Morgen [*Fair of the Masters of Tomorrow*] (EG)
MMM........ Middle Management Module
MMM........ Middlemount [*Australia*] [*Airport symbol*] (OAG)
MMM........ Minerals, Mining & Metallurgy Ltd. [*Australia*] (ADA)
MMM........ Ministerio de Minas y Metalurgia [*Ministry of Mines and Metallurgy*] [*Cuba*] (LA)
MMM........ Mouvement Militant Mauricien [*Mauritian Militant Movement*] [*Political party*] (PPW)
MMM........ Mouvement Mondial des Meres [*World Movement of Mothers - WMM*] [*Paris, France*] (EAIO)
MMM........ Muebles Metalicos Manizales (COL)
MMMA..... Matamoros Internacional [*Mexico*] [*ICAO location identifier*] (ICLI)
MMMD..... Merida/Lic. Manuel Crecencio Rejon Internacional [*Mexico*] [*ICAO location identifier*] (ICLI)
MMMG..... Mosonmagyarovari Mezogazdasagi Gepgyar [*Agricultural Machine Factory of Mosonmagyarovar*] (HU)
MMML..... Mexicali/General Rodolfo Sanchez Taboada Internacional [*Mexico*] [*ICAO location identifier*] (ICLI)
MMMM.... Morelia [*Mexico*] [*ICAO location identifier*] (ICLI)
MMMP..... Ministerio de la Marina Mercante y Puertos [*Ministry of Merchant Marine and Ports*] [*Cuba*] (LA)
MMMP..... Ministry of the Meat and Dairy Industry (RU)
MMMSP... Mouvement Militant Mauricien Socialiste Progressiste [*Mauritius Militant Socialist Progressive Movement*] (PPW)
MMMT ..... Magyar Mezogazdasagi Muvelodesi Tarsasag [*Hungarian Society for Agricultural Education*] (HU)
MMMT ..... Minatitlan [*Mexico*] [*ICAO location identifier*] (ICLI)
MMMV.... Monclova [*Mexico*] [*ICAO location identifier*] (ICLI)
MMMX..... Mexico/Lic. Benito Juarez Internacional [*Mexico*] [*ICAO location identifier*] (ICLI)
MMMY..... Monterrey/General Mariano Escobedo Internacional [*Mexico*] [*ICAO location identifier*] (ICLI)
MMMZ..... Magnitogorsk Metalware and Metallurgical Plant (RU)
MMMZ..... Mazatlan/General Rafael Buelna [*Mexico*] [*ICAO location identifier*] (ICLI)
MMN ...... Metallurgic et Mechanique Nucleaires [*Belgium*]
MMND ..... Analog Simulator (RU)
MMNG ..... Nogales/Internacional [*Mexico*] [*ICAO location identifier*] (ICLI)
MMNL...... Nuevo Laredo [*Mexico*] [*ICAO location identifier*] (ICLI)
MM(NSW) ... Milk Marketing (New South Wales) [*Australia*]
MMNU ..... Nautla [*Mexico*] [*ICAO location identifier*] (ICLI)
MMO .... International Meteorological Organization [*IMO*] (RU)
MMO .... Magasins du Monde-Oxfam [*Belgium*] (EAIO)
MMO .... Magnetic Meteorological Observatory (RU)
MMO .... Maio [*Cape Verde Islands*] [*Airport symbol*] (OAG)
MMO .... Makina Muhendisleri Odasi [*Chamber of Mechanical Engineers*] (TU)
MMO .... Meteoroloji Muhendisleri Odasi [*Chamber of Meteorological Engineers*] (TU)
mmo .... Middelbaar Middenstandsonderwijs [*Benelux*] (BAS)
MMO .... Moscow Mathematical Society (RU)
MMO .... Reclamation Machine Detachment (RU)
MMO .... Small Magellanic Cloud (RU)
MMOB...... Mimar, Muhendis Odalari Birligi [*The Chambers of Architecture and Engineering Association*] (TU)
MMOJMA ... Maizuru Marine Observatory/Japan Meteorological Agency (MSC)
mmol' .... Millimole (RU)
MMOX...... Oaxaca [*Mexico*] [*ICAO location identifier*] (ICLI)

MMP........ Magyar Megujulas Partja [*Party of Hungarian Renewal*] [*Political party*] (PPE)

MMP......... Makedonski Medicinski Pregled [*Macedonian Medical Survey*] [*A periodical Skopje*] (YU)

MMP........ Ministry of Local Industry (RU)

MMP........ Ministry of the Metallurgical Industry, USSR (RU)

MMP........ Molecular Beam Method (RU)

MMP........ Mompos [*Colombia*] [*Airport symbol*] (OAG)

MMPA...... Poza Rica [*Mexico*] [*ICAO location identifier*] (ICLI)

MMPB ...... Ministry of Local Industry, Belorussian SSR (RU)

MMPB ..... Puebla [*Mexico*] [*ICAO location identifier*] (ICLI)

MMPC ...... Market Milk Producers' Council [*Australia*]

MMPC ...... Pachuca [*Mexico*] [*ICAO location identifier*] (ICLI)

MMPE ...... Punta Penasco [*Mexico*] [*ICAO location identifier*] (ICLI)

MMPG ...... Ministerul Minelor, Petrolului, si Geologiei [*Ministry of Mines, Petroleum, and Geology*] (RO)

MMPG ...... Piedras Negras [*Mexico*] [*ICAO location identifier*] (ICLI)

MMPN...... Uruapan [*Mexico*] [*ICAO location identifier*] (ICLI)

MMPR ...... Puerto Vallarta/Lic. Gustavo Dias Ordaz Internacional [*Mexico*] [*ICAO location identifier*] (ICLI)

MMPS...... Manufacturing Message Format System

MMPS...... Puerto Escondido [*Mexico*] [*ICAO location identifier*] (ICLI)

MMPU...... Ministry of Local Industry, Ukrainian SSR (RU)

Mmq......... Millimetre Carre [*Square Millimeter*] [*French*] (MTD)

MMQT...... Queretaro [*Mexico*] [*ICAO location identifier*] (ICLI)

MMR........ Ministry of Material Reserves, USSR (RU)

MMRF...... Ministry of the Maritime and River Fleets, USSR (RU)

MMRWA .. Ministry of Mineral Resources and Water Affairs [*Botswana*]

MMRX ...... Reynosa/General Lucio Blanco Internacional [*Mexico*] [*ICAO location identifier*] (ICLI)

MMS........ International Mathematical Union (RU)

MMS........ International Music Council [*IMC*] (RU)

MMS........ Malayan Medical Service (ML)

MMS........ Manpower Management Staff [*NATO*] (NATG)

MMS........ Mazdoor Mahajan Sangh [*Textile Labor Association*] [*India*]

MMS........ Methodist Missionary Society

MMS........ Mexican Meteorological Service

MMS........ Militaermedizinische Sektion [*Military Medical Section*] [*German*] (EG)

MMS........ Motorized and Mechanized Unit (RU)

MMS........ Musical Masterpiece Society [*Record label*] [*USA, Europe*]

MMS........ Muslim Missionary Society [*Singapore*] (EAIO)

MMS........ Reclamation Machine Station (RU)

MMSAA ... Metals and Minerals Shippers Association of Australia

MMSC ...... Methodist Mission of South Congo

MMSC ...... Movimiento Magisterial Social-Cristiano [*Venezuela*] (EY)

MMSD ...... San Jose Del Cabo [*Mexico*] [*ICAO location identifier*] (ICLI)

MMSI....... Moscow Medical Stomatological Institute (RU)

MMSK ...... Mednogorsk Copper and Sulfur Kombinat (RU)

MMSM ..... Santa Lucia [*Mexico*] [*ICAO location identifier*] (ICLI)

MMSP....... Multinational Marine Science Project (MSC)

MMSP....... San Luis Potosi [*Mexico*] [*ICAO location identifier*] (ICLI)

MMSS....... Marine Meteorological Services System [*WMO*] (MSC)

MMSV ...... Magyar Mezogazdak Szovetkezete [*Hungarian Farmers' Cooperative*] (HU)

MMSW ..... International Union of Mine, Mill, and Smelter Workers [*Later, USWA*]

MMT......... Copper-Manganese Thermistor (RU)

MMT......... Magyar Meteorologiai Tarsasag [*Hungarian Meteorological Society*] (HU)

MMT......... Magyar Mikrobiologiai Tarsasag [*Hungarian Microbiological Society*] (SLS)

MMT......... Magyar Muveszeti Tanacs [*Hungarian Council of Arts*] (HU)

MMT......... Muenchner Mode-Tage [*Germany*]

MMTA ...... Tlaxcala [*Mexico*] [*ICAO location identifier*] (ICLI)

MMTB ...... Melbourne and Metropolitan Tramways Board [*Australia*]

MMTB ...... Tuxtla Gutierrez [*Mexico*] [*ICAO location identifier*] (ICLI)

MMTC ...... Metro Manila Transit Corp. [*Philippines*] (DS)

MMTC ...... Milton Margai Teachers College

MMTC ...... Minerals and Metals Trading Corporation [*India*]

MMTC ...... Mouvement Mondial des Travailleurs Chretiens [*World Movement of Christian Workers - WMCW*] [*Brussels, Belgium*] (EAIO)

MMTC ...... Torreon [*Mexico*] [*ICAO location identifier*] (ICLI)

MMTF....... Meat and Dairy Farm (RU)

MMTG...... Tuxtla Gutierrez [*Mexico*] [*ICAO location identifier*] (ICLI)

MMTJ....... Tijuana/General Abelardo L. Rodriguez Internacional [*Mexico*] [*ICAO location identifier*] (ICLI)

MMTL ...... Tulancingo [*Mexico*] [*ICAO location identifier*] (ICLI)

MMTM..... Tampico/General Francisco Javier Mina Internacional [*Mexico*] [*ICAO location identifier*] (ICLI)

MMTN...... Tamuin [*Mexico*] [*ICAO location identifier*] (ICLI)

MMTO...... Toluca [*Mexico*] [*ICAO location identifier*] (ICLI)

MMTP ...... Tapachula [*Mexico*] [*ICAO location identifier*] (ICLI)

MMTQ...... Tequesquitengo [*Mexico*] [*ICAO location identifier*] (ICLI)

MMTS....... Malaysian Military Training School (ML)

MMTSzSz ... Magyar Mernokok es Technikusok Szabad Szakszervezete [*Free Trade Union of Hungarian Engineers and Technicians*] (HU)

MMTX ...... Tuxpan [*Mexico*] [*ICAO location identifier*] (ICLI)

MMTY ...... Monterrey [*Mexico*] [*ICAO location identifier*] (ICLI)

MMU .... Municipal Mazdoor Union [*India*]

MMUA...... Major Mail Users of Australia

MMUN ..... Cancun [*Mexico*] [*ICAO location identifier*] (ICLI)

mmv........... Maximum Molecular Moisture-Absorption Capacity (RU)

MMV........ Millimetric Waves (RU)

MMV...,.... Milli Mudafaa Vekaleti [*National Defense Ministry*] [*MSB*] [*See also*] (TU)

MMVA ...... Villahermosa [*Mexico*] [*ICAO location identifier*] (ICLI)

MMVR ...... Veracruz/General Heriberto Jara [*Mexico*] [*ICAO location identifier*] (ICLI)

MMVZ ...... Minsk Motorcycle and Bicycle Plant (RU)

MMY........ Miyakojima [*Japan*] [*Airport symbol*] (OAG)

MMZ........ Magadan Machine Plant (RU)

MMZ........ Maimana [*Afghanistan*] [*Airport symbol*] [*Obsolete*] (OAG)

MMZ........ Moscow Machine Plant (RU)

MMZ........ Moscow Motorcycle Plant (RU)

MMZ........ Mytishchi Machinery Plant (RU)

MMZC ..... Zacatecas [*Mexico*] [*ICAO location identifier*] (ICLI)

MMZH...... Zihuatanejo [*Mexico*] [*ICAO location identifier*] (ICLI)

MMZM..... Zamora [*Mexico*] [*ICAO location identifier*] (ICLI)

MMZO...... Manzanillo [*Mexico*] [*ICAO location identifier*] (ICLI)

MMZP ..... Zapopan [*Mexico*] [*ICAO location identifier*] (ICLI)

MMZT...... Mazatlan [*Mexico*] [*ICAO location identifier*] (ICLI)

MN .... Bench Mark (RU)

MN .... Interdepartmental Standard (RU)

MN .... Macherey, Nagel [*& Co.*] [*Germany*]

MN .... Macherey, Nagel & Co. [*Germany*]

MN .... Machinery-Manufacturing Standard (RU)

MN .... Mae Nam [*River*] [*Thai*] (NAU)

MN .... Magnetic Saturation (RU)

MN .... Magyar Nephadsereg [*Hungarian People's Army*] (HU)

Mn .... Maison [*House*] [*French*]

Mn .... Mangan [*Manganese*] [*Chemical element*] [*German*]

Mn .... Manganes [*Manganese*] [*Chemical element*] [*Portuguese*]

MN .... Mantova [*Car registration plates*] [*Italian*]

mn .... Many (RU)

Mn .... Meganewton (RU)

MN .... Meteorologie Nationale [*French*] (MSC)

mn .... Met Name [*Namely*] [*Afrikaans*]

mn .... Million (OMWE)

mn .... Minute [*Minute*] [*French*]

mn .... Mnoga [*Plural*] (POL)

mn .... Mnozina [*Plural*] (YU)

M/N .... Moneda Nacional [*National Money*] [*Spanish*]

MN .... Mongolia [*ANSI two-letter standard code*] (CNC)

Mn .... Motonave [*Motor Vessel*] [*Italian*]

Mn .... Moulin [*Mill*] [*French*] (NAU)

MN .... Mouvement National [*Morocco*] [*Political party*] (EY)

MN .... Movimento Nonviolento [*Non-Violence Movement*] [*Italy*]

MN .... Movimiento Nacional [*Costa Rica*] [*Political party*] (EY)

MN .... Muzeum Narodowe [*National Museum*] (POL)

MN .... Nonlinear Model (RU)

mn .... Plural (RU)

m-n .... Shop, Store (RU)

MN .... Stationary Coupling (RU)

MNA......... Malawi News Agency (AF)

MNA......... Melanguane [*Indonesia*] [*Airport symbol*] (OAG)

MNA......... Merpati Nusantara Airlines PT [*Indonesia*] [*ICAO designator*] (FAAC)

Mna........... Mladina [*Youth*] [*A periodical*] (YU)

MNA......... Mouvement d'Action Politique et Sociale [*Political and Social Action Movement*] [*Switzerland*] [*Political party*] (PPW)

MNA......... Mouvement National Algerien [*National Algerian Movement*]

MNA......... Mouvement National Angolais [*Angolan National Movement*]

MNA......... Movimento Nacional de Angola [*Angolan National Movement*] (AF)

MNA......... Movimiento Nacional Arosemenista [*National Arosemena Movement*] [*Ecuador*] (LA)

MNA......... Movimiento Nueva Alternativa [*New Alternative Movement*] [*Venezuela*] (LA)

MNA......... Myanmar News Agency (EY)

MNADREG ... Movement of National Alliance for Democratic Restoration of Equatorial Guinea (AF)

Mnaznachenie ... Mobilization Assignment (BU)

MNB......... Magyar Nemzeti Bank [*Hungarian National Bank*] (HU)

MNB......... Magyar Nemzeti Bizottmany, New York [*Hungarian National Council, New York*] (HU)

MNB......... Maldives News Bureau (EY)

MNB......... Metal Tanker-Barge (RU)

MNB......... Ministerstvo Narodni Bezpecnosti [*Ministry of National Security*] (CZ)

MNB......... Moanda [*Zaire*] [*Airport symbol*]   (OAG)
MNB......... Moroccan News Bulletin
MNB......... Moscow Narodny Bank Ltd. [*Former USSR*]
MNB......... Movimento Nacionalista Brasileiro [*Brazilian Nationalist Movement*]   (LA)
MNBL....... Bluefields [*Nicaragua*] [*ICAO location identifier*]   (ICLI)
MNBR....... Los Brasiles/Carlos Ulloa [*Nicaragua*] [*ICAO location identifier*]   (ICLI)
MNBZ....... Bonanza [*Nicaragua*] [*ICAO location identifier*]   (ICLI)
MNC......... Ministerial Nomination Committee [*Australia*]
MNC......... Mouvement National Congolais [*Congolese National Movement*]
MNC......... Mouvement National du Congo-Lumumba [*Congo National Movement-Lumumba*] [*Zaire*]   (PD)
MNC......... Mouvement Nationaliste du Congo [*Congolese National Movement*]
MNC......... Movimiento Nacional Conservador [*National Conservative Movement*] [*Colorado*] [*Political party*]   (EY)
MNC......... Movimiento Nacionalista Cubano [*Cuban Nationalist Movement*] [*In exile*]   (LA)
MNCC....... Multinational Coordination Center [*NATO*]
MNCH...... Chinandega/German Pomares [*Nicaragua*] [*ICAO location identifier*]   (ICLI)
mn ch......... Plural   (RU)
MNCI....... Corn Island [*Nicaragua*] [*ICAO location identifier*]   (ICLI)
MNCIAWPRC ... Malaysian National Committee of the International Association on Water Pollution Research and Control   (EAIO)
MNC-K...... Mouvement National Congolais - Kalonji [*Congolese National Movement*] [*Kalonji Wing*]
MNC-L...... Mouvement National Congolais - Lumumba [*Congolese National Movement*] [*Lumumba Wing*]
MNCP....... Mbandzeni National Convention Party
MNCR....... Mouvement National Congolais de la Resistance
MND .... Ministry of National Development [*Guyana*]   (LA)
MND .... Ministry of National Development [*Singapore*]   (DS)
MND .... Movimento Nacional Democratico [*National Democratic Movement*] [*Portugal*] [*Political party*]   (PPE)
MNDAWA ... Motor Neurone Disease Association of Western Australia
MNDD ...... Mouvement National pour la Democratie et le Developpement [*Benin*] [*Political party*]   (EY)
MNDP....... Malawi National Democratic Party
mn dr........ Many Others   (RU)
MNDSZ .... Magyar Nok Demokratikus Szovetsege [*Hungarian Democratic Women's Union*]   (HU)
MNDSZ .... Magyarorszagi Nemetek Demokratikus Szovetsege [*Democratic Federation of Germans in Hungary*]   (HU)
MNE......... Mehr Nicht Erschienen [*No More Published*] [*German*]
MNE......... Ministerio de Negocios Estrangeiros [*Ministry of Foreign Affairs*] [*Portuguese*]   (WER)
MNE......... Ministry of National Education [*Burkina Faso*]
MNE......... Modern English [*Language, etc.*]
MNE......... Mouvement National d'Epargne [*France*]   (FLAF)
MNE......... Multinational Enterprise
MNE......... Superposed Epoch Method   (RU)
MNEAP .... Movimiento Nacional Estudiantil de Accion Popular [*National Student Movement of Popular Action*] [*Argentina*]   (LA)
MNEF ...... Mutuelle Nationale des Etudiants de France
MNERAM ... Members of New England Regional Art Museum
MNET ...... Magyar Nepkoztarsasag Elnoki Tanacsa [*Presidential Council of the Hungarian People's Republic*]   (HU)
MNF .... Mana [*Fiji*] [*Airport symbol*]   (OAG)
MNF .... Mizo National Front [*India*]   (PD)
MNF .... Multinational Force [*Eleven-nation peace-keeping force for the Sinai*]
MNFA ...... Mountaineers' and Nature Friends' Association [*Cyprus*]   (EAIO)
MNFF........ Magyar Nemzeti Fueggetlensegi Front [*Hungarian National Independence Front*] [*Political party*]
MNFO....... Mizo National Front Organisation [*Political party*] [*India*]
MNFP....... Magyar Nemzeti Fueggetlensegi Part [*Hungarian National Independence Party*] [*Political party*]   (PPE)
MNG .... Maningrida [*Australia*] [*Airport symbol*] [*Obsolete*]   (OAG)
MNG .... Mongolia [*ANSI three-letter standard code*]   (CNC)
MNG .... Movimiento Nueva Generacion [*New Generation Movement*] [*Panama*]   (LA)
MNG .... Movimiento Nueva Generacion [*New Generation Movement*] [*Venezuela*]   (LA)
MNHN...... Museum National d'Histoire Naturelle [*National Museum of Natural History*] [*French*]   (MSC)
MNHN(IGA) ... Museum National d'Histoire Naturelle, Laboratoire d'Ichtyologie Generale et Appliquee [*French*]   (ASF)
MNI.......... Malaysia National Insurance [*Subsidiary of PERNAS*]   (ML)
MNI.......... Montserrat [*West Indies*] [*Airport symbol*]   (OAG)
MNI.......... Moskovskii Neftyanoi Institut [*Moscow Petroleum Institute*]   (RU)
MNI.......... Movimento Nacional Independente
MNI.......... Movimiento Nacionalista de Izquierda [*Bolivia*]   (PPW)

MNIA .... Member of the National Institute of Accountants [*Australia*]
MNIB .... Marketing and National Importing Board [*Grenada*]   (GEA)
MNII .... Mari Scientific Research Institute   (RU)
MNIIEM... Moscow Scientific Research Institute of Epidemiology and Microbiology   (RU)
MNIIEMG ... Moscow Scientific Research Institute of Epidemiology, Microbiology, and Hygiene   (RU)
MNIILKh ... Moscow Scientific Research Institute of Forestry [*1932-1938*]   (RU)
MNIIP....... Moscow Scientific Research Institute of Prosthetics   (RU)
MNIIPTMash ... Interbranch Scientific Research, Planning, and Technological Institute for Mechanization and Automation in Machinery Manufacture   (RU)
MNIIVP.... Moscow Scientific Research Institute of Virus Preparations   (RU)
MNIIVS .... Moscow Scientific Research Institute of Vaccines and Serums Imeni I. I. Mechnikov   (RU)
MNIIYaLI ... Mordvinian Scientific Research Institute of Language, Literature, and History   (RU)
MNIL .... Malayan National Independence League   (ML)
MNiR........ Local Norms and Wages, Local Standards and Costs   (RU)
m-niye....... Deposit, Layer   (RU)
MNJ .... Mananjary [*Madagascar*] [*Airport symbol*]   (OAG)
MNJ .... Movimiento Nacional de la Juventud [*National Youth Movement*] [*Dominican Republic*]   (LA)
MNJ .... Movimiento Nacionalista Justicialista [*Justicialist Nationalist Movement - JNM*] [*Argentina*]   (PPW)
MNJ .... Movimiento Nacional Justicialista [*National Justicialista Movement*] [*Argentina*]   (LA)
MNJA ...... Movimiento Nacional de Juventudes Anticomunistas [*National Movement of Anticommunist Youth*] [*Argentina*]   (LA)
MNJD ...... Mouvement National de la Jeunesse Democratique [*National Movement of Democratic Youth*] [*Benin*]   (AF)
MNJR ...... Movimiento Nacional de la Juventud Revolucionaria [*National Movement of Revolutionary Youth*] [*Mexico*]   (LA)
MNJTS .... Mouvement National des Jeunes Travailleurs du Senegal [*National Movement of Young Workers of Senegal*]
MNK........ Magyar Nemzetgyules Konyvtara [*Library of the Hungarian National Assembly*]   (HU)
MNK........ Magyar Nepkoztarsasag [*Hungarian People's Republic*]   (HU)
MNK........ Maiana [*Kiribati*] [*Airport symbol*]   (OAG)
MNK......... Marine Nationale Khmere [*Cambodian National Navy*] [*Replaced MRK*]   (CL)
MNK........ Mesni Nacionalni Komitet [*Local National Committee*]   (YU)
MNK........ Multinationale Konzerne [*Multinational Concern*] [*German*]
mn-k.......... Polygon   (RU)
mnkem....... Magyar Nepkoztarsasag Erdemes Muvesze [*Meritorious Artist of the Hungarian People's Republic*]   (HU)
MNKK....... Magyar Nephadsereg Kozponti Klubja [*The Central Club of the Hungarian People's Republic*]   (HU)
mnkkm....... Magyar Nepkoztarsasag Kivalo Muvesze [*Eminent Artist of the Hungarian People's Republic*]   (HU)
MNL......... Manila [*Philippines*] [*Airport symbol*]   (OAG)
Mnl .... Middelnederlands [*Middle Dutch*] [*Language, etc.*] [*Afrikaans*]
MNL .... Miniliner SRL [*Italy*] [*ICAO designator*]   (FAAC)
MNL .... Movement for National Liberation [*Barbados*] [*Political party*]   (PPW)
MNL .... Movimiento Nacional y Latinoamericano [*National and Latin American Movement*] [*Argentina*]   (LA)
MNL .... National Liberation Movement [*Guatemala*] [*Political party*]   (PD)
MNL .... Small Pneumatic Boat   (RU)
MNLA ...... Malayan National Liberation Army [*Malayan Communist Party*]   (IN)
MNLA ...... Mon National Liberation Army [*Myanmar*] [*Political party*]   (EY)
MNLA ...... Movimento Nacional de Libertacao de Angola
MNLF ...... Malayan National Liberation Front [*Singapore*] [*Political party*]   (PD)
MNLF ...... Moro National Liberation Front [*Philippines*] [*Political party*]   (PD)
MNLGE .... Movimento Nacional da Libertacao de Guine Equatorial
MNLL ...... Malayan National Liberation League   (ML)
MNLN....... Leon/Fanor Urroz [*Nicaragua*] [*ICAO location identifier*]   (ICLI)
MNLT ...... Mouvement National de Liberation du Tchad
MN-M...... Small Nonlinear Electronic Simulator   (RU)
MNME...... Miskolci Nehezipari Muszaki Egyetem [*Heavy Industry Technical University of Miskolc*]   (HU)
MNMG .... Managua/Augusto Cesar Sandino [*Nicaragua*] [*ICAO location identifier*]   (ICLI)
MNMT .... Magyar Nepkoztarsasag Minisztertanacsa [*Council of Ministers of the Hungarian People's Republic*]   (HU)
MNO .... Manono [*Zaire*] [*Airport symbol*]   (OAG)
MNO .... Mesni Narodni Odbor [*Local People's Committee*]   (YU)
MNO .... Middelbaar Nijverheidsonderwijs [*Benelux*]   (BAS)

MNO .... Ministarstvo Narodne Odbrane [*Ministry of National Defense*] (YU)

MNO .... Ministerstvo Narodni Obrany [*Ministry of National Defense*] (CZ)

MNO .... Ministry of National Defense (BU)

MNO .... Moscow Numismatic Society (RU)

MNOFNRJ ... Ministarstvo Narodne Odbrane Federativne Narodne Republike Yugoslavije [*Ministry of National Defense of the Federal People's Republic of Yugoslavia*] (YU)

mnogokr ..... Iterative Aspect (RU)

mnogokr ..... Multicolor (RU)

mnogopromsoyuz ... Union of Multitrade Producers' Cooperatives (RU)

MNO/KS .. Ministerstvo Narodni Obrany/Kadrova Sprava [*Ministry of National Defense/Personnel Directorate*] (CZ)

MNOLO.... Moscow Scientific Society of Otolaryngologists (RU)

MNOO ...... Mesni Narodnooslobodilacki Odbor [*Local National Liberation Committee*] (YU)

MNO/SVU ... Ministerstvo Narodni Obrany/Stavebni Vyrobni Usek [*Ministry of National Defense/Building Production Sector*] (CZ)

MNOSZ .... Magyar Nepkoztarsasagi Orszagos Szabvany [*Hungarian National Standards*] (HU)

MNOT .... Magyar Nepkoztarsasagi Orszagos Tipusterv [*National Standards Plan of the Hungarian People's Republic*] (HU)

MNOT .... Magyar Nok Orszagos [*National Council of Hungarian Women*]

MNOT .... Magyar Nok Orszagos Tanacsa [*National Council of Hungarian Women*] (HU)

MNO/TAS ... Ministerstvo Narodni Obrany Tankova a Automobilova Sprava [*Ministry of National Defense/Tank and Automobile Directorate*] (CZ)

MNOTI ..... Magyar Nepkoztarsasag Orszagos Tervezesi Iranyelv [*Hungarian People's Republic, National Planning Directive*] (HU)

MNO/VL .. Ministerstvo Narodni Obrany/Velitelstvi Letectva [*Ministry of National Defense/Air Force Headquarters*] (CZ)

mnozh........ Plural (RU)

MNP .... Malay Nationalist Party (ML)

MNP .... Marine National Park [*Australia*]

MNP .... Milli Nizam Partisi [*National Order Party*] [*Ordered closed in May 1971*] (TU)

MNP .... Ministry of National Education (BU)

MNP .... Ministry of the Petroleum Industry (RU)

MNP .... Mouvement National des Pionniers [*National Pioneers Movement*] [*Congo*] (AF)

MNP .... Mouvement Nationale Patriotique [*Haiti*] [*Political party*] (EY)

MNP .... Movimiento Nacionalista Popular [*Popular Nationalist Movement*] [*Chile*] [*Political party*] (PD)

MNP .... Movimiento Nacional Petrolero [*National Petroleum Movement*] [*PEMEX Union*] [*Mexico*] (LA)

MNP .... Movimiento Nacional Poncista [*National Poncista Movement*] [*Ecuador*] (LA)

MNP .... Movimiento Nacional y Popular [*Paraguay*] [*Political party*] (EY)

MNP .... Movimiento No Partidarizado [*Peru*] [*Political party*] (EY)

MNP .... Northern Mariana Islands [*ANSI three-letter standard code*] (CNC)

MNP .... Ungrounded Loop Method (RU)

MNPA .... Malaysian Newspaper Publishers Association (EAIO)

MNPA .... Melbourne Newspaper Publishers Association [*Australia*]

MNPC .... Puerto Cabezas [*Nicaragua*] [*ICAO location identifier*] (ICLI)

MNPGD .... Mouvement National des Prisonniers de Guerre et des Deportes [*French*]

m npm .... Metrow Nad Poziomem Morza [*Meters above Sea Level*] [*Poland*]

MNPM ...... Ministarstvo na Narodnata Prosveta na Makedonija [*Ministry of Education of Macedonia*] (YU)

MNPS........ Movimiento Nazionale Pan-Somalo [*Pan-Somali National Movement*] [*Political party*]

MNPZ .... Moscow Petroleum-Processing Plant (RU)

MNQ .... Monto [*Australia*] [*Airport symbol*] (OAG)

MNR........ Mediese Navorsingsraad [*Medical Research Council*] [*South Africa*] (AF)

mnr............. Meneer [*Mister*] [*Afrikaans*]

MNR......... Milicias Nacionales Revolucionarias [*National Revolutionary Militias*] [*Cuba*] (LA)

MNR......... Ministry of National Resources [*Philippines*] (DS)

MNR......... Monair SA [*Switzerland*] [*ICAO designator*] (FAAC)

MNR......... Mongolian People's Republic (BU)

MNR......... Mongu [*Zambia*] [*Airport symbol*] (OAG)

MNR......... Mouvement National de la Revolution [*National Revolutionary Movement*] [*Congo*] (AF)

MNR......... Mouvement Nationaliste Revolutionnaire [*Revolutionary Nationalist Movement*] [*France*] [*Political party*] (PD)

MNR......... Mouvement National pour le Renouveau [*National Movement for Renewal*] [*Burkina Faso*] (AF)

MNR......... Movimiento Nacionalista Revolucionario [*National Revolutionary Movement*] [*Bolivia*] [*Political party*] (PPW)

MNR......... Movimiento Nacional Reformista [*National Reformist Movement*] [*Honduras*] [*Political party*]

MNR......... Movimiento Nacional Reformista [*National Reform Movement*] [*Argentina*] (LA)

MNR......... Movimiento Nacional Reformista [*National Reform Movement*] [*Guatemala*] (LA)

MNR......... Movimiento Nacional Revolucionario [*National Revolutionary Movement*] [*Mexico*] [*Political party*] (EAIO)

MNR......... Movimiento Nacional Revolucionario [*National Revolutionary Movement*] [*Spanish*] (WER)

MNR......... Movimiento Nacional Revolucionario [*National Revolutionary Movement*] [*El Salvador*] [*Political party*] (PPW)

MNR......... Mozambique National Resistance (AF)

MNR......... Mozambique National Resistance Movement

MNR......... Track-Setting Relay (RU)

MNRA ...... Mongolian People's Revolutionary Army (RU)

MNR-A...... Movimiento Nacionalista Revolucionario-Alianza [*Nationalist Revolutionary Movement-Alliance Faction*] [*Bolivia*] (LA)

MNRA .... Movimiento Nacionalista Revolucionario Autentico [*Authentic Nationalist Revolutionary Movement*] [*Bolivia*] (LA)

MNRCS..... Mouvement National pour la Revolution Culturelle et Sociale [*National Movement for the Cultural and Social Revolution*] [*Chad*] (AF)

MNRD...... Mouvement National de la Revolution Dahomeenne

MNRG....... Mouvement National de la Revolution Gabonaise [*Gabonese National Revolutionary Movement*] (AF)

MNRH....... Movimiento Nacionalista Revolucionario Historico [*Historic Revolutionary Nationalist Movement*] [*Bolivia*] [*Political party*] (PPW)

MNRI .... Movimiento Nacionalista Revolucionario de Izquierda [*National Revolutionary Movement of the Left*] [*Bolivia*] (LA)

MNRP .... Mongolian People's Revolutionary Party (BU)

MNRP .... Movimiento Nacionalista Revolucionario del Pueblo [*Nationalist Revolutionary People's Movement*] [*Bolivia*] [*Political party*] (PPW)

MNRPM ... Malay Nationalist Revolutionary Party of Malaya [*Partai Kebangsaan Melayu Revolusioner Malaya*] [*Political party*] (PPW)

MNRS ...... Machine for Continuous Pouring of Steel (RU)

MNR-U ..... Movimiento Nacional Revolucionario-Unido [*National Revolutionary Movement-United Faction*] [*Bolivia*] (LA)

MNRV .... Movimiento Nacionalista Revolucionario - Vanguardia Revolucionaria 9 de Abril [*Bolivia*] [*Political party*] (EY)

MNS .... Junior Command Personnel (RU)

MNS .... Local People's Council (BU)

MNS .... Mansa [*Zambia*] [*Airport symbol*] (OAG)

MNS .... Method of Steepest Descent (RU)

MNS .... Mladez Narodnich Socialistu [*National Socialist Party Youth*] (CZ)

MNS .... Monitor News Service [*Australia*]

MNS .... Mouvement National Somalien

MNS .... Movimiento Nacional de Salvacion [*National Movement of Salvation*] [*Dominican Republic*] [*Political party*] (PPW)

MNS .... Movimiento Nacionalista Salvadoreno [*Salvadoran Nationalist Movement*] (LA)

MNS .... Movimiento Nacional Suprapartidista [*National Supraparty Movement*] [*El Salvador*] (LA)

MNSC .... San Carlos/San Juan [*Nicaragua*] [*ICAO location identifier*] (ICLI)

MNSD ...... Mouvement National pour une Societe de Developpement [*Niger*] [*Political party*] (EY)

MNSDT .... Local People's Council of Deputies of the Working People (BU)

MNSI .... Siuna [*Nicaragua*] [*ICAO location identifier*] (ICLI)

MNSQ .... Motor Neurone Society of Queensland [*Australia*]

MNSSA ...... Motor Neurone Society of South Australia

MNST .... Motor Neurone Society of Tasmania [*Australia*]

MNSV .... Motor Neurone Society of Victoria [*Australia*]

MNSZ .... Zveno National Youth Union (BU)

MNT.......... Makedonski Naroden Teatar [*Macedonian National Theater*] (YU)

MNT.......... Montserrat Airways Ltd. [*Antigua and Barbuda*] [*ICAO designator*] (FAAC)

MNTK .... Mezhotraslevoi Naucho-Tekhni-Cheskii Kompleks [*Interdisciplinary Scientific-Technological Complex*] [*Russian*]

MNTK .... Movimiento Nacional Tupaj Katari [*Bolivia*] [*Political party*] (PPW)

MNTV .... Mistni Narodni Telovychovny Vybor [*Local Physical Education Board*] (CZ)

MNU .... Forced-Oil System (RU)

MNU .... Malayan Nurses Union (ML)

MNU .... Moulmein [*Myanmar*] [*Airport symbol*] (OAG)

MNU .... Movement for National Unity [*St. Vincentian*] (LA)

MNUC....... Mouvement National pour l'Unification du Congo

MNUR....... Mouvement National pour l'Union et la Reconciliation au Zaire [*National Movement for Union and Reconciliation in Zaire*] [*Political party*] (PD)

MNursing .. Master of Nursing
MNUT ...... Muslim National Union of Tanganyika
MNV .... Madarsky Narodny Vybor [*Hungarian National Committee*] (CZ)
mnv .... Met Noot Van [*Benelux*] (BAS)
MNV .... Mistni Narodni Vybor [*Local National Committee*] (CZ)
MNVN ...... Mien Nam Viet Nam [*South Vietnam*]
MNW .... Mittleres Niedrigwasser [*Mean Low Water Mark*] [*German*] (EG)
MNWSL .... Merchant Navy War Service League [*Australia*]
MNY .... Mono Island [*Solomon Islands*] [*Airport symbol*] (OAG)
MNYC ...... Maldives National Youth Council (EAIO)
MNYC ...... Mauritius National Youth Council (AF)
MNyT .... Magyar Nyelvtudomanyi Tarsasag [*Hungary*] (SLS)
MNZ .... Ministry of Public Health (BU)
MNZNRM ... Ministarstvo za Narodno Zdravje na Narodnata Republika Makedonija [*Ministry of Public Health of Macedonia*] (YU)
MNZS .... Ministrstvo za Notranje Zadeve Slovenije [*Ministry of the Interior of Slovenia*] (YU)
MNZSG .... Ministry of Public Health and Social Welfare (BU)
MO .... Deliberate Fire (RU)
MO .... Local Defense (RU)
MO .... Macau [*ANSI two-letter standard code*] (CNC)
Mo............. Maestro [*Master*] [*Italian*]
MO .... Magnetiese Observatorium [*Magnetic Observatory*] [*South Africa*] (RU)
mo............... Maio [*May*] [*Portuguese*]
MO .... Massed Fire [*Artillery*] (RU)
MO .... Megohm [*German*] (GCA)
mo............... Mesmo [*Same*] [*Portuguese*]
MO .... Meteorological Observatory (RU)
MO .... Methyl Orange (Indicator) (RU)
mo............... Met Onderschrift [*Benelux*] (BAS)
MO .... Middelbaar-Onderwijswet [*Benelux*] (BAS)
MO .... Middelbare Onderwys [*Secondary School*] [*Afrikaans*]
MO .... Milattan Once [*Before Christ*] (TU)
MO .... Milicja Obywatelska [*Citizens' Militia*] (POL)
MO .... Miner's Pick, Pick Hammer (RU)
m/o .... Minha Ordem [*My Orders*] [*Portuguese*]
MO .... Ministerstvo Obchodu [*Ministry of Trade*] (CZ)
MO .... Ministerstvo Oborony [*Ministry of Defense*] [*Former USSR*]
MO .... Ministerstwo Odbudowy [*Ministry of Reconstruction*] (POL)
MO .... Ministerstwo Oswiaty [*Ministry of Education*] (POL)
MO .... Minister van Onderwijs, Kunsten en Wetenschapen [*Benelux*] (BAS)
MO .... Minori Osservanti [*Italian*]
m/o .... Mi Orden [*Spanish*]
MO .... Mistni Organisace [*Local Organization*] (CZ)
MO .... Mobilization Section (RU)
MO .... Modena [*Car registration plates*] [*Italian*]
MO .... Moderato [*Moderate Speed*] [*Music*] (ADA)
MO .... Molecular Orbital (RU)
Mo............. Molibdenio [*Molybdenum*] [*Chemical element*] [*Portuguese*]
Mo............. Molybdaen [*Molybdenum*] [*Chemical element*] [*German*]
M/o .... Mon Ordre [*French*]
MO .... Mooney Aircraft, Inc. [*ICAO aircraft manufacturer identifier*] (ICAO)
MO .... Moravska Ostrava [*Moravian Ostrava*] (CZ)
Mo............. Morro [*Headland, Hill*] [*Spanish*] (NAU)
Mo............. Morro [*Headland, Hill*] [*Portuguese*] (NAU)
MO .... Morse Code Light [*or Fog Signal*] [*Navigation signal*]
MO .... Moscow Branch (RU)
MO .... Moscow Oblast (RU)
MO .... Motorized Detachment (RU)
mo............. Oil Separator, Lubricant Separator (RU)
MO .... Queueing Operation (RU)
MO .... Release Magnet (RU)
MO .... Submarine Chaser (RU)
MOA .... Mikti Orkhistra Athinon [*Athens Mixed Orchestra*] (GC)
MOA .... Milicias Obreras de la Alfabetizacion [*Literacy Workers Militias*] [*Nicaragua*] (LA)
MOA .... Ministry of Agriculture [*Philippines*] (DS)
MOA .... Misr Overseas Airways [*Egypt*]
MOA .... Moa [*Cuba*] [*Airport symbol*] (OAG)
MOA .... Mokichi Okada Association [*Japan*]
MOA .... Movimiento Obrero Autogestionario [*Self-Management Workers' Movement*] [*Spanish*] (WER)
MOA .... Municipal Officers' Association of Australia (ADA)
MOAA .... Municipal Officers' Association of Australia
MOAC ...... Movimiento Obrero de Accion Catolica [*Catholic Action Workers Movement*] [*Uruguay*] (LA)
MOAC .... Movimiento Obrero de Accion Catolica [*Catholic Action Workers Movement*] [*Argentina*] (LA)
MOAF .... Ministry of Agriculture and Forests [*Korea*] (PDAA)

MOARSAP ... Mains d'Or, Association pour le Rayonnement de la Sculpture et des Arts-Plastiques [*France*] (EAIO)
MOAU ...... Moscow Oblast Archives Administration (RU)
MOB......... International Refugee Organization (BU)
MOB......... Magyar Olympiai Bizottsag [*Hungarian Olympic Committee*] (HU)
MOB......... Major Organisations Board [*Australia Council*]
MOB......... Ministry of Budget [*Philippines*] (DS)
MOB......... Mistni Osvetova Beseda [*Local Cultural Group*] (CZ)
MOB........ Mobilisation Generale [*General Mobilization*] [*Cambodia*] (CL)
mob .... Mobilization (RU)
MOB......... Muemlekek Orszagos Bizottsaga [*National Committee on Historical Monuments*] (HU)
MOBBRIG ... Mobil Brigade [*Mobile Brigade*] (IN)
MOBEIRA ... Moagem de Beira Lda.
MOBIGALE ... Mobilisation Generale [*General Mobilization*] [*Cambodia*] (CL)
MOBLRKI ... Moscow Oblast Workers' and Peasants' Inspection [*1920-1934*] (RU)
MOBO....... Mobilization Section (RU)
mobovsu ..... Mobilization Section of the District Military Medical Directorate (RU)
MOBRAL ... Movimento Brasileiro de Alfabetizacao [*Adult education program*] [*Brazil*]
MOBSA..... Moscow Society for Combating Alcoholism (RU)
MOBSTYA ... Malayan Outward-Bound School Trained Youth Association (ML)
MOBUP .... Moskva-Oka Basin Administration of Waterways (RU)
MOC......... Malta Olympic Committee (EAIO)
MOC......... Management Opleidings Centrum
MOC......... Marcos Owners Club [*Formerly, Marcos Club*] (EA)
MOC......... Marine Operations Centre [*Commonwealth Department of Transport*] [*Australia*] (PDAA)
MOC......... Ministry of Constructions [*Korea*] (PDAA)
MOC......... Missionaries of Charity [*Australia*]
MOC......... Montes Claros [*Brazil*] [*Airport symbol*] (OAG)
MOC......... Mouvement des Ouvriers Chretiens [*Christian Workers Movement*] [*Belgium*] (WER)
MOC......... Movimiento de Objecion de Conciencia
MOC......... Movimiento Obrero Campesino [*Peasant Workers Union*] [*Argentina*] (LA)
MOC......... Movimiento Obrero Cristiano de Nicaragua [*Christian Labor Movement of Nicaragua*] (LA)
MOC......... Myanma Oil Corp. [*Myanmar*] (DS)
MOCAF .... Societe Motte Cordonnier Afrique
MOCAMA ... Molinos Caracas Maracaibo, SA [*Venezuela*]
MOCC....... MG Octagon Car Club [*Formerly, Octagon Car Club*] (EA)
MOCCA .... Minas de Oro de El Callao, CA [*Venezuela*] (LAA)
MOCI .... Ministry of Commerce and Industry [*Korea*] (PDAA)
MOCI .... Moniteur Officiel du Commerce et de l'Industrie [*France*] (FLAF)
MOCIL...... Mocambique Importadora (Beira) Lda.
MOCK....... Medunarodni Odbor Crvenog Krsta [*International Committee of the Red Cross*] (YU)
MOCN...... Machine-Outil a Commande Numerique [*French*] (ADPT)
MOCNA ... Maserati Owners Club of North America (EAIO)
MOD .... Mestske Oblastni Divadlo [*Municipal Regional Theater*] (CZ)
MOD .... Miedzynarodowa Organizacja Dziennikarska [*International Journalists' Organization*] (POL)
MOD .... Ministry of Defense [*Singapore*] (ML)
mod .... Model (RU)
Mod........... Modele [*Model*] [*French*] (MTD)
Mod........... Modell [*Pattern*] [*German*] (GCA)
Mod........... Moderato [*Moderately Fast*] [*Music*]
mod .... Modern (RU)
mod .... Modern [*Netherlands*]
mod .... Moderne [*Modern*] [*French*]
mod .... Moderno [*Modern*] [*Portuguese*]
mod .... Modifie [*Modify*] [*French*] (FLAF)
Mod........... Modifikation [*Modification*] [*German*] (GCA)
mod .... Modulator (RU)
MOD .... Mothers of the Disabled [*Australia*]
MOD .... Respiratory Minute Volume (RU)
MODA....... Ministry of Defence and Aviation [*Saudi Arabia*]
MODACAPI ... Movimiento de Accion Capitalina Independiente [*Movement for Capital Independent Action*] [*Dominican Republic*] (LA)
MODAS .... Modell-Datenbanksystem [*German*] (ADPT)
MODECAR ... Montajes Industriales del Caribe Ltda. [*Barranquilla*] (COL)
MODEF .... Mouvement de Defense des Exploitations Familiales [*Movement for the Defense of Family Farms*] [*French*] (WER)
MODELH/PRDH ... Mouvement pour la Liberation d'Haiti/Parti Revolutionnaire d'Haiti [*Political party*] (EY)
MODENI .. Movimiento Democratizador Nacionalista Independiente [*Nationalist Independent Democratizing Movement*] [*Honduras*] (LA)

MODEPANA ... Movimiento en Defensa del Patrimonio Nacional [*Movement for the Protection of National Resources*] [*Argentina*]   (LA)
MODEPAZ ... Movimiento Peruano de Soberania Nacional, Solidaridad Internacional, y Paz Mundial [*Peruvian Movement of National Sovereignty, International Solidarity, and World Peace*]   (LA)
MODEX .... Magyar Divataru Kulkereskedelmi Vallalat [*Hungarian Foreign Trade Enterprise for Fashionwear*]   (HU)
MODGER ... Moderne Geriewe [*Modern Convenience*] [*Afrikaans*]
Modifikat... Modifikation [*Modification*] [*German*]   (GCA)
MODN ...... Moorabbin, Oakleigh, Dandenong Valley Regional Library Service and Nunawading [*Library cooperative*] [*Australia*]
MODNE.... Mathitiki Organosi Dimokratikis Neolaias Ellados [*Student Organization of Democratic Youth of Greece*]   (GC)
MODNT.... Moscow Oblast House of Folk Art   (RU)
MODO ...... Mo Och Domsjo AB
MODPIK... Moscow Society of Playwrights and Composers   (RU)
mod praes... Modo Praescripto [*In the manner prescribed*] [*Latin*] [*Pharmacy*]   (BARN)
MODUR.... Movimiento de la Unidad Ruralista [*Uruguay*]   (LAA)
MODVF .... Moscow Society of Friends of the Air Force   (RU)
MOE......... Main-d'Oeuvre Etrangere   (BJA)
MOE......... Minister of Education [*Australia*]
MOE......... Ministry of Energy [*New Zealand*]
MOE......... Ministry of Energy [*Philippines*]   (DS)
MOE......... Momeik [*Myanmar*] [*Airport symbol*]   (OAG)
MoEA....... Ministry of Economic Affairs [*Taiwan*]
MOEAK .... Mystiki Organosis Ethnikis Apelevtheroseos Kyprou [*Secret Organization for the National Liberation of Cyprus*]   (GC)
moebl....... Moebliert [*Furnished*] [*German*]   (EG)
MOEC .... Movimiento de Obreros Estudiante y Campesinos [*Colombia*]
MOEC .... Movimiento Obrero, Estudiantil, y Campesino [*Worker-Student-Peasant Movement*] [*Colorado*]   (LA)
Moeglichk ... Moeglichkeit [*Possibility*] [*German*]   (GCA)
MOEK .... Moscow Oblast Power Engineering Committee   (RU)
MOEL .... Moscow Electric Bulb Plant   (RU)
MOF .... Maumere [*Indonesia*] [*Airport symbol*]   (OAG)
MOF .... Ministry of Finance [*Japan*]   (ECON)
MOF .... Ministry of Finance [*Philippines*]   (DS)
MOF .... Small Concentration Plant   (RU)
MOF .... Youth Fatherland Front   (BU)
MOFAC .... Marcus Oldham Farm Agricultural College [*Australia*]   (ADA)
MOFERT ... Ministry of Foreign Economic Relations and Trade [*China*]
MOFF....... Multiple Options Funding Facility [*Euronotes*]
MOFLOR ... Mocambique Florestal
MOFMC ... Marcus Oldham Farm Management College [*Australia*]   (ADA)
MOFTU .... MIG Operational Fighter Training Unit [*India*] [*Air Force*]
MOG .... Milicias Obreras Guatemaltecas [*Guatemalan Workers' Militia*]   (PD)
MOG .... Monghsat [*Myanmar*] [*Airport symbol*]   (OAG)
mog............ Tomb, Grave [*Topography*]   (RU)
MOGA....... International Civil Aviation Organization [*ICAO*]   (RU)
MOGAOR ... Moscow Oblast State Archives of the October Revolution   (RU)
MOGAS .... Sociedade Mocambicana de Gases Comprimidos
MOGES .... Moscow Association of State Electric Power Plants   (RU)
MOGIA ..... Moscow Oblast State Historical Archives   (RU)
MOGIZ ..... Moscow Branch of the Association of State Publishing Houses   (RU)
Mogl.......... Moeglich [*Possible*] [*German*]
MOGPIIYa ... Moscow Oblast State Pedagogical Institute of Foreign Languages   (RU)
MOGUR.... Movimiento Guerrillero Urbano [*Urban Guerrilla Movement*] [*Colorado*]   (LA)
MOGURT ... MOGURT Gepjarmu Kulkereskedelmi Vallalat [*MOGURT Foreign Trade Enterprise for Motor Vehicles*]   (HU)
Moguyde.... Mouvement Guyanais de Decolonisation [*Guiana Decolonization Movement*] [*France*] [*Political party*]   (PPW)
MOH .... Ministry of Health [*Egypt*]   (IMH)
MOHC .... Ministry of Housing and Construction [*Victoria, Australia*]
MOHOSZ ... Magyar Honvedelmi Sportszovetseg [*Hungarian Sports Federation for National Defense*]   (HU)
MOHOSZ ... Magyar Onkentes Honvedelmi Szovetseg [*Hungarian Voluntary Home Defense Association*]   (HU)
MOHOSZ ... Magyar Orszagos Horgasz Szovetseg [*Hungarian National Anglers' Association*]   (HU)
MOI.......... Main-d'Oeuvre Immigre   (BJA)
MOI.......... Main-d'Oeuvre Indigene [*Indigenous Manpower*] [*Congo - Leopoldville*]
MOI.......... Ministry of Irrigation [*Sudan*]
MOI.......... Mitiaro [*Cook Islands*] [*Airport symbol*]   (OAG)
MOI.......... Mouvement Ouvrier International   (BJA)
MOIC .... Malaysia Overseas Investment Corp.
MOID....... Moroccan Office of Information and Documentation
MOIDR ..... Moscow Society of Russian History and Antiquities   (RU)

MOIDS ..... Moscow Experimental Research Station for Sprinkler Watering   (RU)
MOIF .... Merkezi Odenekli Izin Fonu [*Central Compensation Fund*] [*Turkish Federated State of Cyprus*]   (GC)
MOIK....... Moscow Oblast Executive Committee   (RU)
MOIP .... Moscow Society of Naturalists   (RU)
MOIP .... Moskovskoye Obshchestvo Ispytateley Prirody [*Moscow Society of Testers of Nature*] [*Commonwealth of Independent States*]   (EAIO)
MOIR .... Movimiento Obrero Independiente Revolucionario [*Independent Revolutionary Workers' Movement*] [*Colorado*] [*Political party*]   (PPW)
MOIR .... Movimiento Obrero Izquierdista Revolucionario [*Colorado*] [*Political party*]   (PPW)
MOiSW ..... Ministerstwo Oswiaty i Szkolnictwa Wyzszego [*Ministry of Education and Higher Schools*]   (POL)
MOIUU..... Moscow Oblast Institute for the Advanced Training of Teachers   (RU)
MOIZMIRAN ... Murmansk Branch of the Institute of Terrestrial Magnetism, the Ionosphere, and Radio Wave Propagation (of the Academy of Sciences, USSR)   (RU)
MOJ .... Mojzeszowy [*Mosaic persuasion*] [*Polish*]
MOJA .... Movement for Justice in Africa [*Liberia*] [*Political party*]   (PPW)
MOJA-G ... Movement for Justice in Africa-Gambia [*Political party*]
MOK .... Copper Concentration Combine   (BU)
MOK .... International Coffee Organization   (RU)
MOK .... International Olympic Committee   (BU)
MOK .... Local Organizational Committee   (BU)
MOK .... Mora Ferenc Kiado [*Ferenc Mora Publishing House*]   (HU)
MOK .... Moscow Oblast Committee   (RU)
MOK .... Moscow Oblast Office   (RU)
MOK .... Mutuelle des Originaires de Krinjabo
MOK .... Muzeumok Orszagos Kozpontja [*National Museum Center*]   (HU)
MOKA .... Mystiki Organosi Kyprion Agoniston [*Underground Organization of Cypriot Fighters*]   (GC)
mokham ..... Mohammedan   (BU)
MOKI .... Magyar Orszagos Kozegeszsegugyi Intezet [*Hungarian National Institute of Public Health*]   (HU)
MOKI .... Moscow Oblast Clinical Scientific Research Institute   (RU)
MOKJ .... Mistni Odbor Kostnicke Jednoty [*Local Branch of the Union of Constance*]   (CZ)
MOKO ...... Moscow Oblast Department of Municipal Services   (RU)
mokt........... Millioctave   (RU)
mol .... Dairy [*Topography*]   (RU)
mol' .... Gram Molecule, Mole   (RU)
MOL......... Molde [*Norway*] [*Airport symbol*]   (OAG)
mol .... Molecular   (RU)
mol .... Molecule [*Molecule*] [*French*]
Mol .... Molekel [*or Molekuel*] [*Molecule*] [*German*]   (GCA)
Mol .... Molekuel [*or Molekul or Molekular*] [*Molecule or Molecular*] [*German*]
Mol .... Molekulargewicht [*Molecular Weight*] [*German*]   (GCA)
Mol-%........ Molprozent [*Molar Percent*] [*German*]   (GCA)
MOLA .... Moscow Society of Amateurs of Astronomy   (RU)
MOLAJ ..... Magyar-Szovjet Olaj Tarsasag [*Hungarian-Soviet Oil Enterprise*]   (HU)
mol art....... Dairy Artel   (RU)
MolASSR .. Moldavian Autonomous Soviet Socialist Republic [*1924-1940*]   (RU)
MOLB .... Moscow Oblast Lecture Bureau   (RU)
mold .... Moldavian   (RU)
Moldavgiz.. Moldavian State Publishing House   (RU)
MOLDEAGUA ... Molino Dagua Ltda. [*Colombia*]   (COL)
Mol-Dispers ... Molekulardispersion [*Molecular Dispersion*] [*German*]   (GCA)
MOLE .... Ministry of Labor and Employment [*Philippines*]   (IMH)
moleks........ Molecular Sieve   (RU)
molektronika ... Molecular Electronics   (RU)
Mol Gew .... Molekulargewicht [*Molecular Weight*] [*German*]
MOLGK .... Moscow "Order of Lenin" Conservatory Imeni P. I. Chaykovskiy   (RU)
MOLICA... Movimento de Libertacao da Cabinda [*Movement for the Liberation of Cabinda*] [*Angola*]   (AF)
MOLIDER ... Movimiento Liberal Democratico Revolucionario [*Revolutionary Democratic Liberal Movement*] [*Honduras*] [*Political party*]
MOLIFUGE ... Movimiento de Liberacion y Futuro de Guinea Ecuatorial
MOLIMO ... Movimento de Libertacao de Mocambique [*Mozambique Liberation Movement*]   (AF)
MOLINA .. Mouvement pour la Liberation Nationale [*Movement for National Liberation*]
MOLINACO ... Mouvement de Liberation Nationale des Comores [*National Liberation Movement of the Comoro Islands*]   (AF)
MOLIPO... Movimento de Libertacao Popular [*People's Liberation Movement*] [*Brazil*]   (LA)

Molirena .... Movimiento Liberal Republicano Nacionalista [*Nationalist Liberal Republican Movement*] [*Panama*] [*Political party*] (PPW)
MOLISV ... Movement for Liberation and Development [*Italy Political party*] (EAIO)
MOLKh ..... Moscow Society of Lovers of the Arts (RU)
molmash ..... Dairy Machinery Plant (RU)
MOLMI .... First Moscow "Order of Lenin" Medical Institute Imeni I. M. Sechenov (RU)
mol-myasn ... Dairy and Meat Sovkhoz [*Topography*] (RU)
MOLOM ... Mokhatlo Oa Lesotho Oa Matsema (EAIO)
Molotovneft' ... Molotov Petroleum Association (RU)
molprom ..... Dairy Industry (RU)
Molpromstroy ... All-Union Construction and Installation Trust of the Ministry of the Meat and Dairy Industry, USSR (RU)
Mol-Ref ..... Molekularrefraktion [*Molecular Refraction*] [*German*] (GCA)
Mol-Refr .... Molekularrefraktion [*Molecular Refraction*] [*German*]
MolSSR ..... Moldavian Soviet Socialist Republic (RU)
moltiss .... Moltissimo [*A Great Number*] [*Italian*]
mol v .... Molecular Weight (RU)
Mol-V .... Molvolum [*Molar Volume*] [*German*] (GCA)
Mol W .... Molekularwaerme [*Molecular Heat*] [*German*]
MOM .... Magyar Optikai Muvek [*Hungarian Optical Factory*] (HU)
m/o m .... Mas o Menos [*More or Less*] [*Spanish*]
Mom .... Megohm (RU)
MOM .... Men's Own Movement [*Australia*]
mom .... Milliohm (RU)
MOM .... Ministry of General Machinery Manufacture, USSR (RU)
MOM .... Musee Oceanographique de Monaco (ASF)
MOMA ...... Madagasikara Otronin'ny Malagasy [*Formerly, MONIMA*] [*Madagascar Led by Malagasy*]
MOMA ...... Miktai Omadai Mikhanimaton Anasyngrotiseos [*Joint Reconstruction Equipment Units*] [*SYKEA*] [*See also*] [*Greek*] (GC)
MOMB ...... Mombasa [*Island near Kenya*] (ROG)
MOM-OB-DER ... Meslek Okullari Mezun ve Ogrencileri Birlesme ve Dayanisma Dernegi [*Professional School Graduates and Students' Unity and Mutual Solidarity Association*] (TU)
MOMR ...... Ministry of Oil and Mineral Resources [*Yemen Arab Republic*]
MOMS ...... Mervardesskatt [*Value-Added Tax*] [*Sweden*] (WEN)
MOMS ...... Miestny Odbor Matice Slovenskej [*Local Branch of the Matica Slovenska (A Slovak cultural organization)*] (CZ)
MOMU ..... Missao Organizadora do Museu do Ultramar
MOMZ ...... Moscow Optical Instrument Plant (RU)
Mon .... Maison [*House, Firm, Family*] [*French*]
MON .... Makhitikai Omadai Neolaias [*Fighting Groups of Youth*] [*Greek*] (GC)
MON .... Member of the Order of the Niger
MON .... Metal-Oxide Low-Resistance (Resistor) (RU)
MON .... Mezinarodni Organisace Novinaru [*International Organization of Journalists*] (CZ)
MON .. Ministerstwo Obrony Narodowej [*Ministry of National Defense*] (POL)
Mon .... Monash University [*Australia*]
Mon .... Monastery, Cloister [*Topography*] (RU)
Mon .... Monday (EECI)
mon .... Monikko [*Finland*]
mon .... Monikollisesti [*Finland*]
mon .... Monikon [*Finland*]
mon .... Monocytes (RU)
Mon .... Monographie [*Monograph*] [*German*] (GCA)
Mon .... Monsieur [*Mister*] [*French*]
MON .... Mount Cook [*New Zealand*] [*Airport symbol*] (OAG)
MON .... Movimiento de Opinion Nacional [*National Opinion Movement*] [*Argentina*] (LA)
MONA ...... Marche des Options Negociables sur Actions [*Options exchange*] [*France*] (EY)
MONACA ... Molinos Nacionales CA [*Venezuela*] (DSCA)
MONALI .. Movement for National Liberation [*Barbados*] (LA)
MONALIGE ... Movimiento Nacional de Liberacion de la Guinea Ecuatorial
MONAP .... Movimiento Nacional de Pobladores [*National Settlers Movement*] [*Guatemala*] (LA)
MONARECO ... Movimiento Nacional Revolucionario de la Comunidad [*National Revolutionary Movement of the Community*] [*Argentina*] (LA)
MONAS .... Monumen Nasional [*National Monument*] (IN)
monasto ...... Monasterio [*Monastery*] [*Spanish*]
Monatsh ..... Monatshefte [*Monthly (As in a publication)*] [*German*]
Monatsschr ... Monatsschrift [*Monthly Publication*] [*German*]
Mon desInv ... Moniteur des Inventeurs [*France*] (FLAF)
Mond Jur ... Monde Juridique [*France*] (FLAF)
MONES .... Moniteur d'Entrees/Sorties [*French*] (ADPT)
MONEX .... Asian Monsoon Experiment [*WMO*] (PDAA)
mong .... Mongolian, Mongol (RU)
MONIAG ... Moscow Oblast Scientific Research Institute of Obstetrics and Gynecology (RU)

MONICT .. Monash Information and Communication Technology Centre [*Australia*]
MONIIAG ... Moscow Oblast Scientific Research Institute of Obstetrics and Gynecology (RU)
MONIIGS ... Moscow Branch of the State Scientific Research Institute of the Hydrolysis and Sulfite Liquor Industry (RU)
MONIKI ... Moscow Oblast Clinical Scientific Research Institute Imeni M. F. Vladimirskiy (RU)
MONIMA ... Mouvement National pour l'Independance de Madagascar [*National Movement for the Independence of Madagascar*] [*Political party*] (PPW)
MONIMI .. Moscow Oblast Scientific Research Methods Institute (RU)
MONIMPEX ... MONIMPEX Kulkereskedelmi Vallalat [*MONIMPEX Foreign Trade Enterprise*] (HU)
MONINFO ... Monash Information Service [*Monash University*] [*Australia*]
MONITI .... Moscow Oblast Scientific Research Institute of Tuberculosis (RU)
MONITO ... Moscow Branch of the All-Union Scientific, Engineering, and Technical Society (RU)
MONITOE ... Moscow Branch of the All-Union Scientific, Engineering, and Technical Society of Power Engineers (RU)
MONITOL ... Moscow Branch of the All-Union Scientific, Engineering, and Technical Society of Foundry Workers (RU)
MONITOMASh ... Moscow Branch of the All-Union Scientific, Engineering, and Technical Society of Machine Builders (RU)
MONITOVT ... Moscow Branch of the All-Union Scientific, Engineering, and Technical Society of Water Transportation (RU)
MONIZMIR ... Murmansk Branch of the Scientific Research Institute of Terrestrial Magnetism, the Ionosphere, and Radio Wave Propagation (RU)
Mon JudLyon ... Moniteur Judiciaire de Lyon [*France*] (FLAF)
Mon JugPaix ... Moniteur des Juges de Paix [*France*] (FLAF)
MONK ...... Commission on Mongolia (of the Academy of Sciences, USSR) (RU)
MONO ...... Moscow Department of Public Education (RU)
MONOCLE ... Mise en Ordinateur d'une Notice Catalographique de Livre [*MARC-format, Bibliotheque Universitaire de Grenoble*]
monogr .... Monografia [*Monograph*] [*Hungary*]
Monogr ...... Monogramm [*Monogram*] [*German*]
monogr .... Monogramma [*Monogram*] [*Italian*]
monogr .... Monogramme [*Monogram*] [*French*]
Monogr ...... Monographie [*Monograph*] [*German*]
monokl ...... Monoclinic (RU)
monokl s ...... Monoclinic Syngony (RU)
MoNRDEP ... Ministry of Natural Resources Development and Environmental Protection [*Ethiopia*] (ECON)
Mons .... Monsenhor [*Monsignor*] [*Portuguese*]
Mons .... Monsenor [*Monsignor*] [*Spanish*]
MONS .... Monsieur [*In France this form is considered contemptuous*] [*Preferred form is M*]
Mons .... Monsignore [*Monsignor*] [*Italian*]
MONSIG .. Monsignor [*Lord, Sir*] [*French*]
mont .... Electrician, Assembler, Fitter (RU)
mont .... Montiert [*Mounted*] [*Publishing*] [*German*]
Mont .... Montilla [*Record label*] [*USA, Spain, etc.*]
Montazhkhimzashchita ... Trust of the Glavteplomontazh of the Gosmontazhspetsstroy SSSR (RU)
Montazhlegmash ... Trust for the Installation of Technological Equipment of Establishments of Textile and Light Industries (RU)
Montazhsantekhsnab .. Supply Office for Sanitary Engineering Operations (RU)
Montazhstroymash ... Specialized Trust of the Glavstroy of the Ministry of the Machine Tool and Tool Industry, USSR (RU)
Monten ...... Montenegro
MONTO ... Moscow Oblast Administration of the Scientific and Technical Society (RU)
MONTRAC ... Movimiento Nacional de Trabajadores de Comunicaciones [*Venezuela*] (EY)
MONTRAL ... Montagargas y Tractores Ltda. [*Colombia*] (COL)
MONTRAL ... Movimiento Nacional de Trabajadores para la Liberacion [*National Movement of Workers for Liberation*] [*Venezuela*] (LA)
MONTREV ... Movimiento Nacional de Trabajadores Estatales de Venezuela (EY)
MONTRI . Movimiento Nacional de Trabajadores Independientes [*National Independent Workers Movement*] [*Venezuela*] (LA)
MONTSAME ... Mongolyn Tsahilgaan Medeeniy Agentlag [*Press agency*] [*Mongolia*]
MOO .... Macedonian-Odrin Volunteer Forces (BU)
MOO .... Moomba [*Australia*] [*Airport symbol*] [*Obsolete*] (OAG)
MOO .... Moscow Oblast Branch, Moscow Oblast Department (RU)
MOO .... Moscow Society of Hunters (RU)
MOOM ..... Monades Organoseos kai Methodon [*Organization and Methods Units*] [*Greek*] (GC)
MOOMP ... Moscow Oblast Department of Local Industry (RU)
MOONO ... Moscow Oblast Department of Public Education (RU)

MOOP....... Ministerstvo Okhrany Obshchestvennogo Poryadka [*Ministry for Maintenance of Public Order*] [*Former USSR*]   (LAIN)
MOOP....... Ministry for the Preservation of Public Order   (RU)
moor .... Moorig [*Peaty*] [*German*]   (GCA)
MooreTheol Coll ... Moore Theological College [*Australia*]
MOOSO.... Moscow Oblast Department of Social Security   (RU)
MOOT...... Moscow Oblast Labor Department   (RU)
MOOZ....... Moscow Oblast Department of Public Health   (RU)
MOP.......... Interbranch Association of Trade Unions   (RU)
MOP.......... International Organization of Employers [*IOE*]   (RU)
MOP.......... International Society of Soil Scientists   (RU)
MOP.......... Junior Maintenance Personnel   (BU)
MOP.......... Junior Service Personnel   (RU)
MOP.......... Metal Processing Industry   (BU)
MOP.......... Mezinarodni Organizace Prace [*International Labor Organization*]   (CZ)
MOP.......... Miedzynarodowa Organizacja Pracy [*International Labor Organization*]   (POL)
MOP.......... Ministerio das Obras Publicas [*Ministry of Public Works*] [*Portuguese*]   (WER)
MOP.......... Ministerio de Obras Publicas [*Ministry of Public Works*] [*Nicaragua*]   (MSC)
MOP.......... Ministerio de Obras Publicas [*Ministry of Public Works*] [*El Salvador*]
MOP.......... Ministerio de Obras Publicas [*Ministry of Public Works*] [*Venezuela*]   (LA)
MOP.......... Ministry of the Defense Industry, USSR   (RU)
MOP.......... Moscow Department of the Press   (RU)
MOP.......... Moscow Oblast Administration   (RU)
MOP.......... Mouvement d'Organisation du Pays [*Haiti*] [*Political party*]   (EY)
MOP.......... Mouvement Ouvriers-Paysans [*Workers' and Peasants' Movement*] [*Haiti*]   (PD)
MOP.......... Mouvement pour l'Ordre et la Paix [*Movement for Order and Peace*] [*New Caledonia*] [*Political party*]   (PD)
MOP.......... Small Experimental Underground Vault [*Permafrost investigation*]   (RU)
MOP.......... Trade Unions International   (RU)
MOPA....... Moderno Pazarlama ve Dagitim AS [*Modern Marketing and Distributing Corporation*]   (TU)
MOPAD.... Movement for Peace and Democracy
MOPALI... Movimiento Paraguayo de Liberacion [*Political party*]   (EY)
MOPARE ... Movimiento Patriotico de Renovacion [*Patriotic Renewal Movement*] [*Chile*]   (LA)
MOPBF..... International Organization of Aid to Fighters Against Fascism   (BU)
MOPED .... Ministry of Planning and Economic Development [*Ethiopia*]   (ECON)
moped........ Motor-Pedal [*Motorized Bicycle*]   (RU)
MOPEO.... Moscow Planning and Experimental Department   (RU)
MOPEX .... Mozgokep Kiviteli Vallalat [*Motion Picture Export Enterprise*]   (HU)
MOPG...... Materials for General and Applied Geology   (RU)
MOPG...... Miners' Trade Unions International   (RU)
MOPGC.... Malaysian Oil Palm Growers Council
MOPH....... Ministerio das Obras Publicas e Habitacao [*Ministry of Public Works and Housing*] [*Mozambique*]   (AF)
MOPI....... Moscow Oblast Pedagogical Institute Imeni N. K. Krupskaya   (RU)
MOPI .... Moscow Oblast Polytechnic Institute   (RU)
MOPI .... Movimiento Obrero Popular de Izquierda [*People's Labor Movement of the Left*] [*Colorado*]   (LA)
MOPKhN ... Trade Unions International of Chemical, Oil, and Allied Workers   (RU)
MOPLA .... Movimiento Popular por la Libertacao de Angola
MOPM...... Trade Unions International of Metal and Engineering Industries   (RU)
MOPOCO ... Movimiento Popular Colorado [*Colorado Popular Movement*] [*Paraguay*] [*Political party*]   (PD)
MOPP .... Miedzyszkolny Osrodek Prac Pozalekcyjnych [*Interschool Center for Extracurricular Work*]   (POL)
MOPP .... Miejski Osrodek Propagandy Partyjnej [*City Party Propaganda Center*]   (POL)
MOPR .... International Organization for Aid to Revolutionary Fighters [*1922-1947*]   (RU)
MOPR .... International Organization for Aid to Victims of the Revolution   (BU)
MOPR .... International Organization for Aid to Working People   (BU)
MOPR .... Miedzynarodowa Organizacja Pomocy Rewolucjonistom [*International Red Aid*]   (POL)
MOPS .... Multispectral Opium Poppy Sensor System   (TU)
MOPSD .... Trade Unions International of Workers of the Building, Wood, and Building Materials Industries   (RU)
MOPSh ..... Moscow Party School   (RU)
MOPShK... Moscow Experimental Model Commune School   (RU)
MOPSLKh ... Trade Unions International of Agricultural and Forestry Workers [*TUIAFW*]   (RU)

MOP(SP) .. Ministerstvo Ochrany Prace a Socialni Pece [*Ministry of Protection of Labor and of Social Welfare*]   (CZ)
MOPT .... Ministerio de Obras Publicas y Transportes [*Ministry of Public Works and Transportation*] [*Chile*]   (LAA)
MOPT .... Ministerio de Obras Publicas y Transportes [*Ministry of Public Works and Transportation*] [*Costa Rica*]   (LA)
MOPTT..... Postal, Telegraph, and Telephone International [*PTTI*]   (RU)
MOPU....... Moscow Oblast Assay Administration   (RU)
MOPUA.... Mouvement Populaire de l'Unite Angolaise [*Popular Movement of Angolan Unity*]   (AF)
MOPW ...... Ministry of Population Welfare [*Pakistan*]   (ECON)
MOQ .... Morondava [*Madagascar*] [*Airport symbol*]   (OAG)
MOR......... AS Morefly [*Norway*] [*ICAO designator*]   (FAAC)
MOR......... Medunarodna Organizacija Rada [*International Labor Organization - ILO*]   (YU)
MOR......... Mistni Odborova Rada [*Local Trade Union Council*]   (CZ)
mor .... Morador [*Dwelling, Resident*] [*Portuguese*]
MOR......... Morendo [*Gradually Softer*] [*Music*]
MOR......... Movimiento de Orientacion Reformista [*Reformist Orientation Movement*] [*Argentina*]   (LA)
MOR......... Movimiento Obrero Revolucionario Salvado Cayetano Carpio [*El Salvador*] [*Political party*]   (EY)
MOR......... Movimientos Oculares Rapidos [*Rapid Eye Movement*] [*Spanish*]
MOR......... Mundo Obrero Revolucionario [*Revolutionary Labor World*] [*Spanish*]   (WER)
mor .... Nautical Term   (BU)
mor .... Sea, Maritime, Naval   ·(RU)
Morak........ Naval Academy   (RU)
Morarkh .... Main Naval Archives   (RU)
MorASSR ... Mordovian Autonomous Soviet Socialist Republic   (RU)
MORD....... Ministry of Revolutionary Development [*Vietnam*]
MordASSR ... Mordvinian Autonomous Soviet Socialist Republic   (RU)
Mordgiz ..... Mordvinian State Publishing House   (RU)
MORE .... Movimiento Obrero Revolucionario [*Workers Revolutionary Movement*] [*Nicaragua*]   (LA)
MORECO ... Mozambique Revolutionary Council   (AF)
MOREHOB ... Mouvement de la Resistance des Hommes Bleus [*Blue Men Resistance Movement*] [*Morocco*]   (AF)
MORENA ... Mouvement de Redressement National [*Gabon*] [*Political party*]   (EY)
MORENA ... Mouvement de Renovation Nationale [*National Renewal Movement*] [*Malagasy*]   (AF)
MORENA ... Movimiento Revolucionario Nacional [*National Revolutionary Movement*] [*Brazil*]   (LA)
MORENA ... Movimiento de Renovacion Nacional [*National Renewal Movement*] [*Venezuela*] [*Political party*]   (PPW)
MORENA ... Movimiento de Restauracion Nacional [*National Restoration Movement*] [*Colorado*] [*Political party*]   (EY)
MORENA ... Movimiento Revolucionario Nacional [*National Revolutionary Movement*] [*Chile*]   (LA)
MORENURE ... Movimiento Revolucionario Nueva Republica [*New Republic Revolutionary Movement*] [*Dominican Republic*]   (LA)
morf............ Morphological, Morphology   (RU)
MORI .... Megyei Orvosi Rendelo Intezet [*County Medical Center*]   (HU)
MORIF...... Maros Research Institute for Food Crops [*Indonesia*] [*Research center*]   (IRC)
Moriskom .. Military History Commission for the Study and Utilization of the Experience of the 1914-1918 War at Sea   (RU)
MORKI ..... Moscow Branch of the Workers' and Peasants' Inspection   (RU)
morlet......... Naval Aviator   (RU)
Mormuz ..... Naval Museum   (RU)
Morozovsksel'mash ... Morozovsk Agricultural Machinery Plant   (RU)
MORP........ International Association of Revolutionary Writers   (RU)
MORP .... Metodyczny Osrodek Racjonalizacji Produkcji [*Production Rationalization Methods Center*]   (POL)
Morput'..... Administration of Sea Routes   (RU)
MORT .... International Association of Revolutionary Theaters   (RU)
Mortekhsnab ... State Procurement and Supply Office of the Ministry of the Maritime Fleet, USSR   (RU)
MORU....... Moscow Association of Accounting and Statistical Personnel   (RU)
MOS.......... International Organization for Standardization [*ISO*]   (BU)
MOS.......... Marine Observation Satellite [*Japan*]
MOS.......... Ministry of Supply [*Egypt*]   (IMH)
MOS.......... MISR Overseas Airways [*Egypt*] [*ICAO designator*]   (FAAC)
MOS.......... Mission Itinerante Ophtalmologique Saharienne
MOS.......... Mistni Osvetovy Sbor [*Local Cultural Council*]   (CZ)
MOS.......... Mobilni Operacni Sal [*Mobile Operations Van*]   (CZ)
MOS.......... Movimiento de Organizacion Socialista [*Socialist Organization Movement*] [*Mexico*]   (LA)
MoS.......... Museum of Sydney [*Australia*]
MOSA .... Ministry of Science and Arts [*US and Israel*]
MOSA .... Monash Orientation Scheme for Aborigines [*Australia*]
MOSA .... Moscow Branch of the Union of Architects, USSR   (RU)
MOSA .... Movimento de Solidariedade Africana

MOSAL..... Mocambique Sobresselentes e Accesorios Limitada
MOSAN.... Montaj ve Celik Imalat Ltd. Sti. [*Steel Manufacturing and Installation Corp.*] (TU)
MOSAN.... Movimiento Sindical Autonomo de Nicaragua [*Nicaragua*] (DSCA)
MOSANII ... Moscow Branch of the Arctic Scientific Research Institute (RU)
MOSAP..... Marine Oils Spill Action Plan [*New South Wales, Australia*]
Mosavtoremont ... Moscow City Trust of Automobile Repair Establishments (RU)
Mosavtotekhsnab ... Moscow City Trust of the Administration of Automobile Repair Plants and of Technical Supply of Automobile Transportation (RU)
Mosavtotrest ... Moscow Automobile Transportation Trust (RU)
Mosbass..... Moscow Coal Basin (RU)
MOSCH.... Moschus [*Musk*] [*Pharmacology*] (ROG)
Mosdachtrest ... Moscow City Dacha Trust (RU)
Mosdolproyekt ... Moscow Oblast Planning Institute for Housing, Civil Engineering, and Municipal Construction (RU)
Moselektrik ... Moscow Electrotechnical Plant (RU)
Moselektromontazh ... Moscow State Electrical Installation Trust (RU)
Moselektrotrans ... Moscow Power Supply Trust of the City Electric Transportation System (RU)
Moselektrotransproyekt ... Moscow Planning Office of the Administration of Passenger Transportation (RU)
Mosenergo ... Moscow Regional Administration of Power System Management (RU)
Mosenergoproyekt ... Planning Office of the Mosenergo (RU)
Mosenergosnab ... Materials and Equipment Supply Office of the Mosenergo (RU)
Mosenergostroy ... Moscow Trust for the Construction and Installation of Thermal Electric Power Plants (RU)
Mosfil .... Moscow State Philharmonic (RU)
Mosfilial .... Moscow Branch (RU)
MOSFIL'M ... Moscow Motion-Picture Studio (RU)
Mosfinotdel ... Moscow Finance Department (RU)
Mosfundamentstroy ... Moscow State Trust for Foundation Construction (RU)
Mosgaz ...... Trust of the Administration of the Gas Supply System of the Mosgorispolkom (RU)
Mosgazprovodstroy ... Moscow Trust for Gas Pipeline Construction (RU)
Mosgaztekhsnab ... Moscow City Trust of the Fuel and Power Supply System of the Mosgorispolkom (RU)
Mosgeo ...... Moscow Geological Administration (RU)
Mosgeolnerud ... Moscow Geological Exploration Trust for Nonmetallic Minerals (RU)
Mosgiprobum ... Moscow Branch of the State Institute for the Planning of Establishments of the Pulp, Paper, and Hydrolysis Industry (RU)
Mosgipromash ... Moscow Branch of the State Institute for the Planning of Machinery Plants (RU)
Mosgiprotrans ... Moscow State Planning and Surveying Institute of the State Industrial Committee for Transportation Construction, USSR (RU)
Mosgoraptekoupravleniye ... Pharmaceutical Administration of the Mosgorispolkom (RU)
Mosgorarbitrazh ... Moscow City Arbitration Commission (RU)
Mosgorbank ... Moscow City Bank (RU)
Mosgorbytkommunsnab ... Moscow City Trust of the Administration of Personal and Municipal Services (RU)
Mosgorbytkommunstroy ... Construction and Installation Trust of the Administration of Personal and Municipal Services of the Mosgorispolkom (RU)
Mosgordets ... Moscow City Children's Excursion and Tourist Station (RU)
Mosgorekskursbyuro ... Moscow City Excursion Office (RU)
Mosgorelektroprom ... Moscow City Electrotechnical Industry Trust (RU)
Mosgorfinupravleniye ... Moscow City Finance Administration (RU)
Mosgorgeotrest ... Moscow City Trust for Geological, Geodetic, and Cartographic Work (RU)
Mosgorispolkom ... Executive Committee of the Moscow City Soviet of Workers' Deputies (RU)
Mosgorkinoprokat ... Moscow City Office for Motion-Picture Distribution (RU)
Mosgorkom ... Moscow City Committee (RU)
Mosgorkoopinsoyuz ... Moscow City Union of Disabled Persons' Cooperatives (RU)
Mosgorkozhobuv'prom ... Moscow City Trust of the Leather and Footwear Industry (RU)
Mosgorles .. Moscow City Logging Trust (RU)
Mosgorleszag ... Moscow City Logging Trust (RU)
Mosgorlombard ... Administration of the Moscow City Pawnshop (RU)
Mosgormebel'prom ... Moscow City Trust of the Furniture Industry (RU)
Mosgormekhpogruz ... Mosgorispolkom Administration for the Mechanization of Loading and Unloading (RU)
Mosgormestprom ... Moscow City Local Industry Trust (RU)
Mosgormetalloprom ... Moscow City Trust of the Metals Industry (RU)
Mosgormetalloshirpotreb ... Moscow City Trust of the Consumers' Metalware Industry (RU)

Mosgormetrem ... Moscow City Trust for the Repair of Metalware, Watches, and Musical Instruments (RU)
Mosgorono ... Moscow City Department of Public Education (RU)
Mosgorotdelzags ... Department of the Civil Registry of the Mosgorispolkom (RU)
Mosgorplan ... Moscow City Planning Commission (RU)
Mosgorplastmass ... Moscow City Trust for the Manufacture of Plastic Consumers' Goods (RU)
Mosgorpogruz ... Moscow City Trust for Loading and Unloading (RU)
Mosgorpoligrafprom ... Moscow City Printing Trust (RU)
Mosgorpotrebsoyuz ... Moscow City Union of Consumers' Societies (RU)
Mosgorpromsnab ... Moscow City Trust for Industrial Supply (RU)
Mosgorpromsovet ... Council of Producers' Cooperatives of the City of Moscow (RU)
Mosgorshveyprom ... Moscow City Garment Industry Trust (RU)
Mosgorsobes ... Moscow City Department of Social Security (RU)
Mosgorsovet ... Moscow City Soviet of Workers' Deputies (RU)
Mosgorsovnarkhoz ... Council of the National Economy of the Moscow City Economic Region (RU)
Mosgorsovnarkhozstroy ... Construction and Installation Trust of the Mosgorsovnarkhoz (RU)
Mosgorspravka ... Moscow City Reference and Information Office (RU)
Mosgorstrakh ... Moscow City Administration of the Gosstrakh (RU)
Mosgorstromtrest ... Moscow City Building Materials Trust (RU)
Mosgorstroymontazh ... Moscow City Construction and Installation Trust (RU)
Mosgorsud ... Moscow City Court (RU)
Mosgorsvet ... Electric Power Supply Establishment for the Street Lighting of the City of Moscow (RU)
Mosgortekstil'prom ... Moscow City Textile Industry Trust (RU)
Mosgorteplo ... Moscow City Heat Engineering Office (RU)
Mosgortopsnab ... Moscow City Trust for Fuel Supply (RU)
Mosgortorgotdel ... Trade Department of the Ispolkom of the Mosgorsovet (RU)
Mosgortransproyekt ... Moscow Planning Office for Engineering, Industrial, and Electrotechnical Structures for City Transportation (RU)
Mosgortransstroy ... Construction Trust of the Administration of Passenger Transportation of the Mosgorispolkom (RU)
Mosgorvneshtek ... Moscow City Transportation and Forwarding Office for Out-of-Town Shipments (RU)
Mosgorvtek ... Moscow City Medical Commission for Determination of Disability (RU)
Mosgorzags ... Moscow City Department of the Civil Registry (RU)
Mosgorzdravotdel ... Moscow City Department of Public Health (RU)
Mosgosstrakh ... State Insurance Administration in the City of Moscow (RU)
MOSI .... Economic Data Machine Processing (BU)
MOSICP ... Movimiento Sindical Cristiano del Peru [*Christian Labor Movement of Peru*] (LA)
Mosinodezhda ... Trust for Custom-Tailoring (RU)
Mosinzhproyekt ... Moscow Institute for the Planning of Engineering Installations (RU)
MOs iSW ... Ministerstwo Oswiaty i Szkolnictwa Wyzszego [*Ministry of Education and Schools of Academic Rank*] [*Poland*]
Mosk......... Moscow (RU)
MOSK .... Moscow Railroad (RU)
Moskabel' ... Moscow Cable Plant (RU)
MOSKh..... Moscow Agricultural Society (RU)
MOSKh..... Moscow Branch of the Union of Artists of the RSFSR (RU)
Moskhimtrest ... Moscow State Chemical Trust (RU)
Moskhlebtorg ... Moscow State Organization for the Baked Goods and Confectionary Retail Trade (RU)
MOSKhOS ... Moscow Oblast Agricultural Experimental Station (RU)
Moskhoztorg ... Moscow City Trade Organization for Household Goods and Building Materials (RU)
Moskinap. Moscow Motion-Picture Equipment Plant (RU)
Moskip....... Moscow Control and Measuring Instruments Plant (RU)
MOSKIYeV ... Moscow-Kiev Railroad (RU)
Moskniga ... Moscow City Book Trade Office (RU)
Mosknigotorg ... Moscow Oblast Book Trade Office (RU)
MOSKOMONES ... Moscow Commission for Cases Concerning Minors (RU)
Moskovstroy ... Moscow Trust for the Capital Construction of Water Supply and Sewer System Installations (RU)
Moskozh .... Moscow Association of Leather Industry Establishments (RU)
Moskprofobr ... Moscow Subdivision of Vocational and Technical Education (RU)
Moskul'ttorg ... Moscow Organization for Trade in Goods for Cultural Purposes (RU)
Moskvugol' ... State Association of the Coal Industry of the Moscow Region Basin (RU)
Mosmashpriborstroy ... Moscow Construction Trust of the Glavstroy of the Ministry of Machinery Manufacture and Instrument Making, USSR (RU)
Mosmetroves ... Moscow Precision Scales and Measuring Instruments Plant (RU)
MosMGS... Moscow Interdepartmental Geodetic Council (RU)

Mosmoloko ... Moscow Milk and Dairy Products Trade Organization   (RU)
Mosmolzhivtrest ... Moscow Trust of Dairy and Livestock Breeding Sovkhozes   (RU)
Mosmoststroy ... Moscow Trust for Railroad Bridge Construction   (RU)
Mosmuzradio ... Moscow Plant for Guaranteed Repairing of Radio Equipment and Renting and Repairing of Musical Keyboard Instruments   (RU)
MOSNAV ... Moscow Lifesaving Society   (RU)
Mosneftekip ... Moscow Control and Measuring Instruments Plant for the Petroleum Industry   (RU)
Mosnezhilotdel ... Department of Nonresidential Buildings of the Mosgorsovet   (RU)
MOSNKh ... Moscow Oblast Council of the National Economy   (RU)
MOSO .... Moscow Department of Social Security   (RU)
Mosoblarbitrazh ... State Arbitration Commission at the Moscow Oblast Executive Committee   (RU)
Mosoblarkhivbyuro ... Moscow Oblast Archives Office   (RU)
Mosoblavtotek ... Moscow Oblast Automobile Transportation and Forwarding Office   (RU)
Mosobldorotdel ... Moscow Oblast Road Department   (RU)
Mosobldorstroy ... Moscow Oblast Road and Bridge Construction Trust   (RU)
Mosoblelektro ... Moscow Oblast Administration of Electric Power Plants and Networks   (RU)
Mosoblfinotdel ... Moscow Oblast Finance Department   (RU)
Mosoblgorlit ... Administration of Literature and Publishing Houses of the City of Moscow and Moscow Oblast   (RU)
Mosoblgosstrakh ... Administration of State Insurance in Moscow Oblast   (RU)
Mosoblispolkom ... Executive Committee of the Moscow Oblast Soviet of Workers' Deputies   (RU)
Mosoblkniga ... Moscow Oblast Book Trade Office   (RU)
Mosoblmestpromsnab ... Moscow Oblast Trust for Materials and Equipment Supply of the Moscow Oblast Administration of Local Industry   (RU)
Mosoblono ... Moscow Oblast Department of Public Education   (RU)
Mosoblpishcheprom ... Administration of the Food Industry of the Mosoblispolkom   (RU)
Mosoblplan ... Moscow Oblast Planning Commission   (RU)
Mosoblpromsovet ... Council of Producers' Cooperatives of Moscow Oblast   (RU)
Mosoblsovet ... Moscow Oblast Soviet of Workers' Deputies   (RU)
Mosoblsovnarkhoz ... Council of the National Economy of the Moscow Oblast Economic Administrative Region   (RU)
Mosoblsovprof ... Moscow Oblast Council of Trade Unions   (RU)
Mosoblspetsstroy ... Specialized Trust of the Construction Administration of the Mosoblispolkom   (RU)
Mosoblspravka ... Moscow Oblast Reference and Information Office   (RU)
Mosoblspravkontora ... Moscow Oblast Reference and Information Office   (RU)
Mosoblstatupravleniye ... Moscow Oblast Statistical Administration   (RU)
Mosoblstroy ... Moscow Oblast Construction Trust   (RU)
Mosoblstroymontazh ... Moscow Oblast Construction and Installation Trust   (RU)
MosoblstroyTsNIL ... Central Scientific Research Laboratory for Construction of the Glavmosoblstroy   (RU)
Mosobltekstil'prom ... Moscow Oblast Textile Trust   (RU)
Mosobltop ... Administration of the Fuel Industry and Local Building Materials of the Mosoblispolkom   (RU)
Mosoblvodokanal ... Moscow Oblast Water Supply and Sewer System Trust   (RU)
Mosoblzags ... Moscow Oblast Department of the Civil Registry   (RU)
Mosoblzdravotdel ... Moscow Oblast Department of Public Health   (RU)
Mosoblzhilprom ... Moscow Oblast Trust for Materials and Equipment Supply of the Housing Administration of the Mosoblispolkom   (RU)
Mosoblzhilupravleniye ... Moscow Oblast Housing Administration   (RU)
Mosobshchepitstroy ... Trust of the Main Administration of Public Eating Facilities of the Mosgorispolkom   (RU)
Mosochistvod ... Moscow Trust for Sewage Purification   (RU)
MOSOKR ... Moscow Belt Railroad   (RU)
Mosotdelstroy ... Moscow City Trust of the Administration of Finishing Work of the Glavmosstroy   (RU)
MOSP .... Moscow Branch of the Union of Writers   (RU)
MOSPB ..... Ministry of Public Construction, Roads, and Public Works   (BU)
Mosplastkozh ... Moscow Imitation Leather Plant   (RU)
Mosplastmass ... Moscow Scientific Research Institute of Plastics   (RU)
MOSPNI ... Moscow State Institute of Neuropsychology   (RU)
MOSPO ... Moscow Oblast Union of Consumers' Societies   (RU)
Mospochtamt ... Moscow Post Office   (RU)
Mospodzemproyekt ... Moscow Planning Institute of the Administration of the Mospodzemstroy   (RU)
Mospodzemstroy ... Moscow State Trust for the Construction of Underground Structures   (RU)
Mospodzemstroysnab ... Moscow City Trust for Materials and Equipment Supply of the Administration for the Construction of Underground Structures   (RU)

Mospoligraf ... Moscow State Association of Printing Industry Establishments   (RU)
MOSPOR ... Movement for the Struggle for Political Rights [*Uganda*]   (PD)
Mosprodsnab ... Moscow Office of Food Supply   (RU)
Mosprodstroy ... Construction and Installation Trust of the Second Main Construction Administration of the Ministry of the Foodstuffs Industry, USSR   (RU)
Mospromproyekt ... Moscow Institute of Industrial Planning   (RU)
Mospromtrans ... Administration for the Servicing of Industrial Establishments of the Glavmosavtotrans   (RU)
Mosproyekt ... Administration for the Planning of Housing, Civil Engineering, and Municipal Construction of the Mosgorispolkom   (RU)
Mosproyekt ... Institute for the Planning of Housing and Civil Engineering Construction in the City of Moscow   (RU)
MOSPS ..... Moscow Oblast Council of Trade Unions   (RU)
MOSPTTaR ... Mezinarodni Odborove Sdruzeni Zamestnancu Post, Telefonu, Telegrafu, a Rozhlasu [*International Federation of Trade Unions of Postal, Telephone, Telegraph, and Radio Employees*]   (CZ)
Mosrechtek ... Moscow River Transportation and Forwarding Office   (RU)
Mosremchas ... Moscow Watch Repair Plant   (RU)
Mosremelektrobytpribor ... Moscow Plant for the Repair of Electrical Household Appliances   (RU)
Mosremstanok ... Industrial and Technical Establishment for the Repair of Metal-Cutting Equipment of the Administration of Machinery Manufacture of the Mosgorsovnarkhoz   (RU)
Mosrestorantrest ... Moscow Trust of Model Restaurants   (RU)
MOSRYaZ ... Moscow-Ryazan' Railroad   (RU)
Mosrybtrest ... Moscow Oblast Fish Industry Trust   (RU)
MOSRYBVTUZ ... Moscow Technical Institute of the Fish Industry and Fisheries   (RU)
MOSS .... Market-Oriented, Sector-Selective [*or Specific*] [*Trade negotiations between United States and Japan*]
Mossangaltrikotazh ... Moscow Factory for the Manufacture of Sanitary Notions and the Repair of Knit Goods   (RU)
Mossannelektroprom ... Trust of the Administration of Installation, Electrical Installation, and Sanitary Engineering of the Glavmosstroy   (RU)
Mossantekhstroy ... Moscow State Sanitary Engineering Trust of the Glavmosstroy   (RU)
Mossel'elektro ... Moscow Oblast Trust of the Glavsel'elektro   (RU)
Mossel'energo ... Moscow Oblast Office for the Operation of Rural Electric Power Installations   (RU)
Mossel'khozaeros yemka ... Moscow Office of Aerogeodetic Establishments of the Ministry of Agriculture, USSR   (RU)
Mossel'khozpromstroy ... Moscow Construction and Installation Trust of the Moscow Oblast Administration of Agriculture   (RU)
Mossel'mash ... Moscow Agricultural Machinery Plant   (RU)
Mossel'prom ... Moscow Association of Establishments for Processing Products of the Agricultural Industry   (RU)
Mossel'proyekt ... Design and Planning Office of the Administration of Planning Organizations of the Ministry of Urban and Rural Construction, RSFSR   (RU)
Mossel'vodstroy ... Moscow Construction and Installation Office of Rural Water Management Projects   (RU)
Mosshakhtostroy ... Trust for the Construction of Mine Installations in the Moscow Region Coal Basin   (RU)
Mosshampanzavod ... Moscow Champagne Plant   (RU)
MOSSKh ... Moscow Branch of the Union of Soviet Artists   (RU)
Mosskuppromtorg ... Moscow City State Organization for Buying and Selling on Commission   (RU)
Mossnabsbytkino ... Moscow Oblast Office for the Supply and Marketing of Motion-Picture Goods   (RU)
Mossovet .... Moscow City Soviet of Workers' Deputies   (RU)
MOSSP ..... Moscow Branch of the Union of Soviet Writers   (RU)
Mosspirtotrest ... Moscow Alcohol Trust   (RU)
Mossredprom ... Moscow State Trust of Medium and Small Industries   (RU)
Mosstankin ... Moscow Institute of Machine Tools and Tools   (RU)
Mosstroy .... Moscow State Construction and Installation Trust   (RU)
Mosstroykanalizatsiya ... Moscow Construction Trust for Sewer System Facilities   (RU)
Mosstroymekhanizatsiya ... Moscow Trust for Mechanized Construction   (RU)
Mosstroytop ... Construction Office of the Administration of the Fuel Industry of the Mosoblispolkom   (RU)
Mosstroytrans ... Administration for Centralized Transportation of Construction Freight of the Glavmosavtotrans   (RU)
Mossvetstroy ... Specialized Construction and Installation Administration for the Installation of Moscow City Street Lighting   (RU)
most .... Bridge Crossing [*Topography*]   (RU)
MOST .... Militaeroberstaatsanwalt [*Military Senior Prosecutor*]   (EG)
MOST .... Ministry of Science and Technology of Korea   (ASF)
MOST .... Molonglo Observatory Synthesis Telescope [*University of Sydney*] [*Australia*]   (PDAA)

MOST .... Moskovskaya Assotsiatsiya Delovogo Sotrudnichestva c Organizatsiyami i Firmami Zarybezhom [*Moscow Association for Business Cooperation with Organizations and Firms of Foreign Countries*]   (EAIO)
Mostara ..... Moscow Trust for the Manufacture and Marketing of Packing Materials   (RU)
mostb.......... Bridge Battalion   (RU)
mostbr .... Bridge Brigade   (BU)
Mostekhfil'm ... Moscow Studio of Technical Films   (RU)
Mostekhtorgsnab ... Materials and Equipment Supply Office of the Main Administration of Trade of the Ispolkom of the Moscow City Soviet of Workers' Deputies   (RU)
Mostekstil' ... Moscow Oblast Textile Trust   (RU)
Mostekstil'torg ... Moscow Specialized Trade Office for Textile Goods   (RU)
Mostelefonstroy ... Moscow State Trust for the Construction of Telephone Structures   (RU)
Mosteploset'stroy ... Construction and Installation Administration of the Mosenergostroy Trust   (RU)
MOSTEU ... Moscow Tourist and Excursion Administration   (RU)
MOSTiW .. Miejski Osrodek Sportu, Turystyki, i Wypoczynku [*City Sports, Touring, and Rest Center*]   (POL)
Mostoremtonnel' ... All-Union Trust for the Reconstruction and Capital Repair of Bridges and Tunnels   (RU)
Mostorg ..... Moscow Oblast Trust for Wholesale and Retail Trade   (RU)
Mostorgin .. Moscow Disabled Persons' Trade and Producers' Cooperative Association   (RU)
Mostorgsnab ... Materials and Equipment Supply Office of the Department of Trade of the Ispolkom of the Moscow City Soviet of Workers' Deputies   (RU)
Mostorgstroy ... Construction and Installation Trust of the Main Administration of Trade of the Ispolkom of the Moscow City Soviet of Workers' Deputies   (RU)
Mostorgtrans ... Administration of Commercial Transportation of the Main Administration of Trade of the Ispolkom of the Moscow City Soviet of Workers' Deputies   (RU)
Mostostal... Panstwowe Przedsiebiorstwo Budowy Mostow i Konstrukcji Stalowych [*State Enterprise for Bridge Building and Steel Constructions*]   (POL)
Mostostroy ... Rayon Administration for Bridge Construction   (RU)
Mostostroyprom ... All-Union Trust of Industrial and Construction Establishments of the Glavmostostroy   (RU)
Mostotrest ... All-Union Trust for the Construction of Large and Supersize Bridges   (RU)
Mostransstroy ... Moscow Construction and Installation Trust of Transportation Construction   (RU)
mostsb........ Bridge-Building Battalion   (BU)
mostsr .... Bridge-Building Company   (BU)
Mostsvettorg ... Moscow Flower and Seedling Wholesale and Retail Trade Organization   (RU)
Mosugol'.... Oblast Administration of the Moscow Region Coal Basin   (RU)
MOSUKTEK ... Moscow Administration of Container Shipments and Transportation and Forwarding Operations   (RU)
MOSV .... Mednarodna Organizacija za Socialno Varstvo [*International Social Security Association*]   (YU)
MOSVIPE ... Mikti Omas Stratiotikis Voitheias Inomenon Politeion en Elladi [*Joint US Military Assistance Unit in Greece*]   (GC)
Mosvodokanalproyekt ... Institute for the Planning of Water Supply and Sewer System Installations of the Mosgorispolkom   (RU)
Mosvodokanalsnab ... Moscow Water Supply Trust of the Water Supply and Sewer System Administration of the Mosgorispolkom   (RU)
Mosvodoprovod ... Moscow Water Supply Trust of the Administration of Water Supply and Sewer Systems of the Mosgorispolkom   (RU)
Mosvodstroy ... Moscow Water Management Construction Trust   (RU)
Mosvuzstroy ... Moscow State All-Union Construction Trust of the Glavstroy of the Ministry of Higher Education, USSR   (RU)
MOSYuN .. Moscow Oblast Station for Young Naturalists   (RU)
MOSYuT... Moscow Oblast Station for Young Technicians   (RU)
MOSZ .... Magyar Orszagos Szabvany [*Hungarian National Standards*]   (HU)
MOSZ .... Magyar Orvos Szovetseg [*Hungarian Medical Association*]   (HU)
MOSZ .... Magyar Ottusa Szovetseg [*An association*] [*Hungary*]   (EAIO)
Moszagotstroy ... Moscow Specialized Construction and Installation Trust of the Glavzagotstroy   (RU)
Moszdravotdel ... Moscow Department of Public Health   (RU)
Moszelenstroy ... Moscow State Landscaping Trust   (RU)
Moszhilgoststroy ... Moscow Housing and Hotel Construction Trust   (RU)
Moszhilotdel ... Moscow Housing Department   (RU)
Moszhilproyekt ... Institute for the Planning of Major Housing Repair in the City of Moscow   (RU)
Moszhilremsnab ... Office of the Administration of Major Housing Repair of the Mosgorispolkom   (RU)
Moszhilspetsstroy ... Moscow Trust for Plastering and Other Special Finishing Operations   (RU)
Moszhilstroy ... Moscow Housing Construction Trust   (RU)

Moszhilupravleniye ... Moscow City Housing Administration   (RU)
Moszhivotnovodles ... Republic Office of the Administration for the Procurement of Building Materials and Structural Parts of the Ministry of Sovkhozes, RSFSR   (RU)
MOSZK..... Magyar Orszagos Szovetkezeti Kozpont [*National Center of Hungarian Cooperatives*]   (HU)
MOSZSZ .. Magyar Orvosok Szabad Szakszervezete [*Free Trade Union of Hungarian Physicians*]   (HU)
MOT......... Aeromonterrey SA [*Mexico*] [*ICAO designator*]   (FAAC)
MOT......... International Labor Organization [*ILO*]   (BU)
MOT......... Magyar Orszagos Tudosito Reszvenytarsasag [*Hungarian National News Agency Limited (Prewar)*]   (HU)
MOT......... Men of the Trees [*Australia*] [*An association*]
MOT......... Ministry of Tourism [*Philippines*]   (DS)
mot .... Motoring   (TPFD)
Mot .... Motorisiert [*Motorized*] [*German*]
mot .... Motorized   (RU)
Mot .... Motorlu [*Motorized*]   (TU)
MOT......... Movimiento Obrero Tradicionalista [*Traditionalist Labor Movement*] [*Spanish*]   (WER)
MOTAS..... Motorlu Araclar ve Aksamlari Subesi [*Motorized Vehicles and Parts Branch*] [*A subsidiary of ETI in the TFSC Turkish Cypriot*]   (TU)
MOTAT .... Museum of Transport and Technology [*New Zealand*]   (PDAA)
MOTC....... Ministry of Transport and Communications [*Philippines*]   (DS)
motd .... Mortar Section   (RU)
MOTESZ .. Magyar Orvostudomanyi Tarsasagok es Egyesuletek Szovetsege [*Federation of Hungarian Medical Science Societies and Associations*]   (HU)
MOTESZ .. Magyar Orvostudomanyi Tarsasagok Szovetsege [*Federation of Hungarian Medical Societies*]   (EAIO)
MOTEZ .... Moscow Transformer and Electric Motor Plant   (RU)
MOTF .... Milletlerarasi Ogrenci Teskilatlari Federasyonu [*Federation of International Student Organizations*]   (TU)
MOTH ...... Memorable Order of Tin Hats [*South Africa*]   (AF)
MOTI .... Magyar Orszagos Tervezesi Iranyelvek [*Hungarian National Planning Guidelines*]   (HU)
MOTI .... Moscow Oblast Institute of Tuberculosis   (RU)
MOTIM .... Magyarovar Timfold es Mukorundgyar [*Magyarovar Alumina and Alundum Factory*]   (HU)
MOTNE .... Meteorological Operational Telecommunications Network Europe
MOTNEG ... Meteorological Operational Telecommunication Network in Europe, Regional Planning Group [*ICAO*]   (PDAA)
MOTO...... Monatstonnen(metric) [*Metric Tons per Month*] [*German*]
MOTOCARSA ... Motores y Carrocerias de Colombia, Sociedad Anonima [*Colombia*]   (COL)
MOTOCOLDA ... Motos de Colombia Ltda. [*Colombia*]   (COL)
MOTOKOV ... Podnik Zahranicniho Obchodu pro Dovoz a Vyvoz Vozidel a Vyrobku Lehkeho Prumyslu [*Foreign Trade Enterprise for the Import and Export of Vehicles and Products of the Light Industry*]   (CZ)
MOTOPAR ... Motor Parcalari Imalati, Ticaret, ve Sanayi AS [*Motor Parts Manufacture, Trade, and Industry Corp.*]   (TU)
MOTORAGRI ... Societe pour le Developpement de la Motorisation de l'Agriculture [*Company for the Development and Mechanization of Agriculture*] [*Ivory Coast*]   (AF)
MOTORCOL ... Distribuidora de Automotores Colombianos Ltda. [*Colombia*]   (COL)
MOTOREP ... Motores y Repuestos Ltda. [*Colombia*]   (COL)
motorkm..... Motorovy Kilometr [*Motor-Kilometer*] [*Kilometer run by a motor-driven rail vehicle*]   (CZ)
MOTORLET ... Tovarna na Motory a Letadla [*Automobile and Aircraft Factory*] [*Janonice*]   (CZ)
MOTOTECHNA ... Narodni Podnik pro Prodej Jizdnich Kol a Motocyklu [*National Enterprise for the Retail Sale of Bicycles and Motorcycles*]   (CZ)
MOTOVALLE ... Motores del Valle [*Colombia*]   (COL)
MOTsKTI ... Moscow Branch of the Central Scientific Research, Planning, and Design Boiler and Turbine Institute Imeni I. I. Polzunov   (RU)
MOTsNIIRF ... Moscow Branch of the Central Scientific Research Institute of the River Fleet   (RU)
MOTZK .... Moscow Association of Theater and Show Ticket Offices   (RU)
MOU .... Metal-Oxide Ultrahigh-Frequency (Resistor)   (RU)
MOU .... Movimiento Obrero Unido [*United Worker Movement*] [*Puerto Rican*]   (LA)
mouch......... Mouchete [*Spotted*] [*French*]
mouil .... Mouillure [*Stain caused by moisture*] [*French*]
mouill .... Mouillure [*Stain caused by moisture*] [*French*]
MOULIAF ... Mouvement de Liberation Africaine [*African Liberation Movement*]   (AF)
MOULP ..... Moscow Oblast Administration of Light Industry   (RU)
MOUMS..... Moscow Oblast Administration of the Ministry of Communications, USSR   (RU)
MOUR....... Moscow Department of Criminal Investigation   (RU)

MOURAD ... Mouvement pour la Renovation et l'Action Democratique [*The Comoros*] [*Political party*]   (EY)
MOURP .... Moskva-Oka River Steamship Line Administration   (RU)
MOUS ...... Moscow Oblast Administration of Sovkhozes   (RU)
MOUSKh ... Moscow Oblast Administration of Agriculture   (RU)
Mouvcom ... Le Mouvement Communal [*Benelux*]   (BAS)
MOUVKh ... Moscow Oblast Administration of Water Management   (RU)
mov .... Met Onderschrift Van [*Benelux*]   (BAS)
MOV .... Mezinarodni Olympijsky Vybor [*International Olympics Committee*]   (CZ)
MOV .... Moranbah [*Australia*] [*Airport symbol*]   (OAG)
MOV .... Museum of Victoria [*Australia*]
MOV .... Reflected Wave Method   (RU)
MOVAGO ... Moscow Branch of the All-Union Astronomical and Geodetic Society   (RU)
MOVANO ... Moscow Branch of the All-Union Scientific Architectural Society   (RU)
MOVCORD ... Movement Coordinator
MOVE .... Motosyklistikos Omilos Voreiou Ellados [*Motorcyclists Club of Northern Greece*]   (GC)
MOVICAR ... Movilizadora de Cargamentos Ltda. [*Colombia*]   (COL)
MOVIU ..... Moscow District Military Engineering Directorate   (RU)
MOVLEK ... Moscow Oblast Visiting Medical and Epidemiological Consultation   (RU)
MOVNIIGS ... Moscow Branch of the All-Union Scientific Research Institute of the Hydrolysis and Sulfite Liquor Industry   (RU)
MOVOPC ... Mouvement de la Voix du Peuple Congolais
MOVS .... Manual Overseas Visa System
MOVSU .... Moscow District Military Medical Directorate   (RU)
Movzadt ..... Moscow Branch of the All-Union Correspondence Highway Technicum   (RU)
mow .... Mehr oder Weniger [*More or Less*] [*Commodities*] [*German*]
MOW .... Ministry of Works
MOW .... Moscow [*Former USSR*] [*Airport symbol*]   (OAG)
MOWD .... Ministry of Works and Development [*New Zealand*]   (PDAA)
MOZ .... Aerocharter GmbH [*Austria*] [*ICAO designator*]   (FAAC)
MOZ .... Mezhdunarodnaja Organizacija Zhurnalistov [*International Organization of Journalists*]
MOZ .... Miedzyzakladowa Organizacja Zwiazkowa [*Inter-Factory Labor Union Organization*]   (POL)
MOZ .... Miejscowa Organizacja Zwiazkowa [*Local Labor Union Organization*]   (POL)
MOZ .... Moorea Island [*French Polynesia*] [*Airport symbol*]   (OAG)
MOZ .... Mozambique [*ANSI three-letter standard code*]   (CNC)
MOZGOC ... Mozambique Gulf Oil Company
MOZh .... International Organization of Journalists [*IOJ*]   (RU)
Mozherez ... Moscow Railroad Repair Plant   (RU)
MOZM ...... International Organization for Legal Metrology   (RU)
MOZO ...... Moscow Land Department   (RU)
MOZU .... Magnetic Internal Storage   (RU)
MOZU .... Moscow Oblast Land Administration   (RU)
MP .... Bridge Train   (RU)
MP .... Council of Ministers Decree   (BU)
MP .... Crossing Point [*Topography*]   (RU)
MP .... Dead Space, Dead Ground [*Artillery*]   (RU)
MP .... Engine Drive   (RU)
MP .... Feed Mechanism [*Automation*]   (RU)
mp .... Local Production   (BU)
MP .... Machine Translation, Mechanical Translation   (RU)
MP .... Maciej Poleski [*Pen name of Polish author, Czeslaw Bielecki*]
MP .... Magnetic Bearing   (RU)
MP .... Magnetic Belt [*Weld inspection device*]   (RU)
MP .... Magnetic Field   (RU)
MP .... Magnetic Starter   (RU)
MP .... Magnetplatte [*German*]   (ADPT)
MP .... Magyar Posztogyar [*Hungarian Textile Factory*]   (HU)
mp .... Mainittu Paikka [*Finland*]
MP .... Mains Propres [*Personal Delivery*] [*French*]
MP .... Malayan Party   (ML)
mp .... Male Sex [*Statistics*]   (RU)
M-P .... Mandat-Poste [*Money Order*] [*French*]
MP .... Manu Propria [*In documents, after king's signature*] [*Italian*]
mp .... Mapa [*Chart, Map*] [*Publishing Former Czechoslovakia*]
MP .... Martens-Pensky Instrument [*For flash-point testing*]   (RU)
mp .... Masodperc [*Second*]   (HU)
MP .... Maximum Absorption   (RU)
mp .... Mechanized Regiment   (BU)
MP .... Medical Station   (RU)
Mp .... Megapond [*1,000 kilograms of thrust*]   (EG)
MP .... Meldungspuffer [*German*]   (ADPT)
MP .... Member of Parliament   (PWGL)
m/p .... Meses de Prazo [*Portuguese*]
MP .... Mesi Piesis [*Intermediate Pressure, Mean Pressure*]   (GC)
MP .... Mesto Pecata [*Place for Seal (Documents)*]   (YU)
mp .... Metru Patrat [*Square Meter*]   (RO)
MP .... Mexican Peso [*Monetary unit*]

MP .... Mezzo Piano [*Moderately Soft*] [*Music*]
MP .... Microswitch   (RU)
mp .... Miespuolinen [*Finland*]
MP .... Militaerpolizei [*Military Police*]   (EG)
MP .... Militere Polisie [*Military Police*] [*Afrikaans*]
MP .... Millet Partisi [*Nation Party*]   (TU)
MP .... Millia Passuum [*1,000 Paces; the Roman mile*]
MP .... Milli Partisi [*National Party*] [*Cyprus*]   (TU)
MP .... Minefield   (RU)
MP .... Ministarstvo Prosvete [*Ministry of Education*]   (YU)
MP .... Ministere Public [*France*]   (BAS)
MP .... Ministerio de Pesqueria [*Peru*]   (MSC)
MP .... Ministerstvo Paliv [*Ministry of Fuels*]   (CZ)
MP .... Ministerstvo Prumyslu [*Ministry of Industry*]   (CZ)
MP .... Ministry of Education   (RU)
MP .... Ministry of Industry [*Obsolete*]   (BU)
MP .... Ministry of Justice   (BU)
m/p .... Mi Pagare [*My Promissory Note*] [*Business term*] [*Spanish*]
MP .... Mitsubishi Plastics [*Japan*]   (PDAA)
MP .... Mizarsko Podjetje [*Cabinetmakers' Establishment*]   (YU)
MP .... Mlinsko Preduzece [*Military*]   (YU)
MP .... Mobilization Plan   (RU)
MP .... Mortar Regiment   (RU)
mp .... Mortar Unit   (RU)
M-P .... Moscow-Petrograd [*Bibliography*]   (RU)
MP .... Motherland Party [*Anatavan Partisi*] [*Turkey*] [*Political party*]   (PPW)
MP .... Motorized Infantry   (RU)
MP .... Motorized Regiment   (RU)
m/p .... Motor Sailer   (RU)
MP .... Mouvement Populaire [*Popular Movement*] [*Morocco*] [*Political party*]   (PPW)
MP .... Mouvement Progressif [*Cameroon*] [*Political party*]   (EY)
MP .... Movable Coupling   (RU)
MP .... Northern Mariana Islands [*ANSI two-letter standard code*]   (CNC)
MP .... Place for Seal   (RU)
MP .... Plastic Fuze for a Mine   (RU)
MP .... Polarizing Microscope   (RU)
MP .... Run Magnet   (RU)
MP .... Small-Caliber Pistol, Small-Bore Pistol   (RU)
MP .... Vertical Magnet   (RU)
MP .... Weather Post, Meteorological Post   (RU)
MPA .... Beef-Extract Agar   (RU)
MPA .... Magasins Populaires d'Arrondissement [*District People's Warehouses*] [*Guinea*]   (AF)
MPA .... Magazine Publishers Association [*Australia*]
MPA .... Main Political Administration [*Russian*]
MPA .... Malaysian Pediatric Association   (EAIO)
MPA .... Management Professionals Association [*Madras, India*]   (EA)
MPA .... Manevarska Protivavionska Artiljerija [*Maneuver Antiaircraft Artillery*]   (YU)
MPA .... Master Pastrycooks' Association [*Australia*]
MPA .... Master Printers' Association [*Singapore*]   (EAIO)
MPA .... Mercaptopropylamine   (RU)
MPA .... Miejskie Przedsiebiorstwo Autobusowe [*Municipal Bus Service Enterprise*]   (POL)
MPA .... Ministry of Peasant Affairs [*Burkina Faso*]
MPA .... Mission Presbyterienne Americaine
MPA .... Mission Publications of Australia   (ADA)
MPA .... Mouvement Panafricain Anticommuniste [*Pan-African Anti-Communist Movement*]   (AF)
MPA .... Mouvement Populaire Africain [*African People's Movement*] [*Burkina Faso*]   (AF)
MPA .... Movimiento Popular Argentino [*Argentine People's Movement*]   (LA)
MPA .... Multiple-Use Planning Area
MPAA .... Marasleios Paidagogiki Akadimia Athinon [*Marasleios Pedagogical Academy of Athens*]   (GC)
MPAA .... Mornaricka Protivavionska Artiljerija [*Navy Antiaircraft Artillery*]   (YU)
MPAA .... Movimento Popular Africano de Angola
MPAC .... Movimento do Povo Anticolonista [*People's Anticolonial Movement*] [*Portuguese*]   (WER)
MPAF .... Malaysian People's Action Front   (ML)
MPAIAC ... Movimiento para la Autodeterminacion y Independencia del Archipielago Canario [*Movement for the Self-Determination and Independence of the Canary Archipelago*] [*Canary Islands*] [*Spanish*]   (PD)
MPAJ .... Mouvement Panafricaine de la Jeunesse
MPAJA ..... Malayan People's Anti-Japanese Army   (ML)
MPAJU ..... Malayan People's Anti-Japanese Union   (ML)
MPAM ...... Missao de Pedologia de Angola e Mocambique, Junta de Investigacoes do Ultramar
MPANSW ... Master Patternmakers' Association of New South Wales [*Australia*]

MPANSW ... Master Poulterers' Association of New South Wales [*Australia*]

MPAS........ Ministerio da Previdencia e Assistencia Social [*Ministry of Welfare and Social Security*] [*Brazil*] (LA)

MPAT....... Ministere de la Planification et de l'Amenagement du Territoire [*Algeria*]

MPB .... Beef-Extract Broth (RU)

MPB .... Machine Rental Base (RU)

MPB .... Majlis Penimbangan Bersama [*Joint Consultative Council*] (ML)

MPB .... Mornington Peninsula Broadcasters Ltd. [*Australia*]

mpb .... Motorized Infantry Battalion (BU)

MPB .... Mouvement Progressiste de Burundi [*Progressive Movement of Burundi*]

MPB .... Musica Popular Brasileira [*Pop music*]

MPB .... Turret Traversing Mechanism (RU)

MPBO .... Bocas Del Toro [*Panama*] [*ICAO location identifier*] (ICLI)

mpbr.......... Motorized Infantry Brigade (RU)

MPBUJ ..... Modern Pentathlon and Biathlon Union of Japan (EAIO)

MPC .... Certificat de Mathematiques, Physique, et Chimie [*French*]

MPC .... Maharashtra Prajatantra Congress [*India*] [*Political party*] (PPW)

MPC .... Maharashtra Progressive Congress [*India*] [*Political party*] (PPW)

MPC .... Maison du Pneu et du Caoutchouc

MPC .... Makedonska Pravoslavna Crkva [*Macedonian Orthodox Church*] (YU)

MPC .... Metales Preciosos Colombianos [*Colombia*] (COL)

MPC .... Ministerstwo Przemyslu Chemicznego [*Ministry of the Chemical Industry*] (POL)

MPC .... Ministerstwo Przemyslu Ciezkiego [*Ministry of Heavy Industry*] (POL)

MPC .... Mitsubishi Petrochemical Co. [*Tokyo, Japan*]

MPC .... Monetary Policy Committee [*France*] (ECON)

MPC .... Mosul Petroleum Company (ME)

MPC .... Mouvement Patriotique Congolais [*Congo Patriotic Movement*] [*Political party*]

MPC .... Mouvement Progressive Congolais

MPC .... Movimiento Popular Colorado [*Paraguay*] (LAA)

MPC .... Movimiento Popular Cristiano [*Popular Christian Movement*] [*Bolivia*] (LA)

MPC .... Multicultural Psychiatric Center [*Australia*]

MPC .... Multi-Party Conference [*Namibia*] [*Political party*] (PPW)

MPC .... Mysore Power Corp. [*India*] (PDAA)

MPCA .... Manpower Citizens Association [*Guyana*] (LA)

MPCC....... Malta Pollution Control Center (ASF)

MPCD .... Mouvement Populaire Constitutionnel Democratique [*Popular Democratic Constitutional Movement*] [*Morocco*] [*Political party*] (PPW)

MPCF....... Campo De Francia/Enrique A. Jimenez [*Panama*] [*ICAO location identifier*] (ICLI)

MPCH .... Changuinola/Cap. Manuel Nino [*Panama*] [*ICAO location identifier*] (ICLI)

MPCh .... Maximum Usable Frequency (RU)

MPCh .... Ministerstwo Przemyslu Chemicznego [*Ministry of the Chemical Industry*] (POL)

MPCO .... Colon [*Panama*] [*ICAO location identifier*] (ICLI)

MPD......... Drill Feed Mechanism (RU)

MPD......... Magneto-Plasmadynamic (RU)

MPD......... Ministry of Popular Defence [*Burkina Faso*]

mpd .... Motorized Infantry Division (RU)

MPD......... Movement for Democratic Process [*Zambia*] [*Political party*] (EY)

MPD......... Movimento para Democracia [*Cape Verde*] [*Political party*] (EY)

MPD......... Movimiento Popular Democratico [*Popular Democratic Movement*] [*Ecuador*] [*Political party*] (PPW)

MPD......... Movimiento Popular Democratico [*Popular Democratic Movement*] [*El Salvador*] (LA)

MPD......... Movimiento Popular Dominicano [*Dominican Popular Movement*] [*Dominican Republic*] [*Political party*] (PPW)

MPD......... Portable Polarizing Microscope (RU)

MPDA .... David/Enrique Malek [*Panama*] [*ICAO location identifier*] (ICLI)

MPDA .... Motion Picture Distributors Association of Australia (ADA)

MPDAA .... Motion Picture Distributors' Association of Australia

MPDC .... Mouvement Populaire Democratique et Constitutionnel

MPDiP ...... Ministerstwo Przemyslu Drzewnego i Papierniczego [*Ministry of the Lumber and Paper Industry*] (POL)

MPDiRz .... Ministerstwo Przemyslu Drobnego i Rzemiosla [*Ministry of Small Scale and Handicraft Industry*] (POL)

MPDL .... Malayan People's Democratic League (ML)

MPDL .... Movimiento Pro-Democracia y Libertad [*Panama*] [*Political party*] (EY)

MPDSANSW ... Master Painters, Decorators and Signwriters' Association of New South Wales [*Australia*]

MPDU .... Malian People's Democratic Union

MPE .... Max-Planck-Institut fuer Extraterrestrische Physik [*Max Planck Institute for Extraterrestrial Physics*] [*Research center*] (IRC)

MPE .... Ministerstvo Paliv a Energetiky [*Ministry of Fuel and Power*] (CZ)

MPE .... Ministry for Planning and Environment [*Victoria, Australia*]

MPEA....... Mouvement Populaire d'Evolution Africaine [*African People's Evolution Movement*]

MPEC....... Miejskie Przedsiebiorstwo Energetyki Cieplnej [*Municipal Thermoelectric Power Enterprise*] (POL)

m pech'..... Open-Hearth Furnace (RU)

MPEDA..... Marine Products Export Development Authority [*India*] (ASF)

MPEG .... Museu Paraense Emilio Goeldi [*Emilio Goeldi Museum*] [*Research center*] [*Brazil*] (EAS)

MPE-HSE ... Ministerstvo Paliv a Energetiky - Hlavni Sprava Elektraren [*Chief Administration of Electric Power Stations of the Ministry of Fuel and Power*] (CZ)

MPEI........ Moscow Institute of Industry and Economics (RU)

MPENC..... Melbourne Poets, Playwrights, Essayists, Editors and Novelists Centre [*Australia*] (EAIO)

MPENC..... Montenegrin Poets, Playwrights, Essayists, Editors, and Novelists Centre [*Former Yugoslavia*] (EAIO)

MPF......... International Industrial Federation (RU)

MPF......... Malayan Patriotic Front (ML)

MPF......... Ministerio Publico Federal [*Federal Public Ministry*] [*Mexico*] (LA)

MPF......... Ministerium fuer Post und Fernmeldewesen [*Ministry for Postal Affairs and Telecommunications*] (EG)

MPF......... Moscow Printing Plant (of the Goznak) (RU)

MPFA....... Master Picture Framers Association [*Australia*]

MPFF .... Malay Police Field Force (ML)

MPFS .... Fuerte Sherman [*Panama*] [*ICAO location identifier*] (ICLI)

MPFS .... Magnetic Periodic Focusing System (RU)

MPG .... International Polar Year (RU)

MPG .... Maritime Patrol Group

MPG .... Maximum Backwater Level (RU)

MPG .... Max-Planck-Gesellschaft [*West German research organization*]

MPG .... Max Planck Gesellschaft zur Foerderung der Wissenschaft Eingetragener Verein [*Max Planck Society for the Promotion of Science*] [*Research center*] (WEN)

mpg .... Miles per Gallon (OMWE)

MPG .... Milice Populaire Guineenne [*Guinean People's Militia*] (AF)

mpg .... Myl per Gelling [*Miles per Gallon*] [*Afrikaans*]

MPG......... Piston Depth Gauge (RU)

MPGA ...... Beef-Extract Glucose Agar (RU)

MPGI .... Mouvement Populaire pour la Guadeloupe Independante [*Popular Movement for Independent Guadeloupe*] (PD)

MPGK .... Miejskie Przedsiebiorstwa Gospodarki Komunalnej [*Municipal Enterprises of Communal Economy*] (POL)

MPGP....... Mutuelle du Personnel de la Garde Provinciale [*Mutual Association of Provincial Guard Personnel*] [*Cambodia*] (CL)

MPGR .... Ministerstwo Panstwowych Gospodarstw Rolnych [*Ministry of State Farms*] (POL)

MPH .... Martinair Holland NV [*Netherlands*] [*ICAO designator*] (FAAC)

MPH .... Ministerstwo Przemyslu i Handlu [*Ministry of Industry and Trade*] (POL)

MPH .... Multi-Purpose Holdings [*Singapore*] [*Commercial firm*]

MPHO....... Howard Air Force Base [*Panama*] [*ICAO location identifier*] (ICLI)

MPHV .... Manufacture des Plastiques de Haute-Volta

M PhysSJ ... Member of the Physical Society of Japan

MPI .... International Patent Institute (RU)

MPI .... Magyar Pamutipar [*Hungarian Cotton Enterprise*] (HU)

MPI .... Mamitupo [*Panama*] [*Airport symbol*] (OAG)

MPI .... Management Partnerships International, Inc. (IID)

MPI .... Masyarakat Perhutanan Indonesia [*Indonesian Forestry Society*] (FEA)

MPI .... Matieres Premieres d'Importation [*Imported Raw Materials*] (CL)

MPI .... Max-Planck-Institut fuer Astronomie [*Max Planck Institute for Astronomy*] [*Germany*]

MPI .... Miejskie Przedsiebiorstwo Instalacji [*Municipal Installations Enterprise*] (POL)

MPI .... Miltarpsykologiska Institutet [*Military Psychology Institute*] [*Sweden*] (PDAA)

MPI .... Morrison Printing Ink & Machinery Ltd. [*New Zealand*]

MPI .... Moscow Pedagogical Institute (RU)

MPI .... Moscow Printing Institute (RU)

MPI .... Movimiento Patriotico Institucional [*Panama*] [*Political party*] (EY)

MPI .... Movimiento Pro-Independencia de Puerto Rico [*Pro-Independence Movement of Puerto Rico*] (LA)

MPI .... Moyennes et Petites Industries [*French*] (ADPT)

MPIA........ Max-Planck-Institut fuer Astronomie [*Max Planck Institute for Astronomy*] [*Germany*]

MPIA......... Miejskie Przedsiebiorstwo Imprez Artystycznych [*Municipal Show Business*] [*Poland*]
MPIA......... Movimento para a Independencia de Angola
MPIB......... Malaysian Pineapple Industry Board   (DS)
MPIEA...... Malayan Planting Industry Employers Association   (ML)
MPIGE...... Movimiento Pro-Independencia de Guinea Ecuatorial
MPIGM..... Milli Piyango Idaresi Genel Mudurlugu [*National Lottery Administration Directorate General*]   (TU)
MPiH........ Ministerstwo Przemyslu i Handlu [*Ministry of Industry and Trade*]   (POL)
MPII......... Magyar Parttorteneti Intezet Irattara [*Archives of the Hungarian Institute for Party History*]   (HU)
MPIIYa..... Moscow Pedagogical Institute of Foreign Languages   (RU)
MPiK........ Miedzynarodowa Prasa i Ksiazka [*International Press and Book Club*]   (POL)
MPIKRIMA ... Mpianatra Kristiana Malagasy [*Malagasy Christian Students*]   (AF)
MPiOS...... Ministerstwo Pracy i Opieki Spolecznej [*Ministry of Labor and Social Welfare*]   (POL)
MP i PL..... Machine Translation and Applied Linguistics [*Bibliography*]   (RU)
MPiSA....... Ministry of Instrument Making and Means of Automation, USSR   (RU)
MPiT .... Ministerstwo Poczt i Telegrafow [*Ministry of Posts and Telegraphs*]   (POL)
MPJ.......... Mouvement Panafricain de la Jeunesse [*Pan-African Youth Movement - PYAM*] [*Algeria*]
MPJ.......... Movimiento Popular Justicialista [*Popular Justicialist Movement*] [*Venezuela*]   (LA)
MPJE .... Jaque [*Panama*] [*ICAO location identifier*]   (ICLI)
MPK .... International Classification of Patents   (RU)
MPK .... International Convention Concerning the Carriage of Passengers and Luggage by Rail   (RU)
MPK .... International Preparatory Committee   (RU)
MPK .... Mechanized Movable Support [*Mining*]   (RU)
mpk .... Meripeninkulma(a) [*Finland*]
MPK .... Miejskie Przedsiebiorstwo Komunikacyjne [*Municipal Transportation Enterprise*]   (POL)
MPK .... Mining and Processing Combine   (BU)
MPK .... Ministry of Education and Culture [*Obsolete*]   (BU)
MPK .... Modernized Flotation Suit [*Military*]   (RU)
MPK .... Small Antisubmarine Ship   (RU)
MPKiO...... Moscow Park of Culture and Rest   (RU)
MPL .... Blade-Operating Mechanism [*Nautical term*]   (RU)
MPL .... Magnetplatte [*German*]   (ADPT)
MPL .... Mashonaland Progressive League
MPl........... Ministerstvo Planovani [*Ministry of Planning*]   (CZ)
MPL .... Ministerstwo Przemyslu Lekkiego [*Ministry of Light Industry*]   (POL)
M pl .... Ministre Plenipotentiaire [*French*]   (MTD)
MPL .... Montoneros Patria Libre [*Guerrila group*] [*Ecuador*]   (EY)
MPL .... Montpellier [*France*] [*Airport symbol*]   (OAG)
MPL .... Mouvement Politique Lulua [*Lulua Political Movement*] [*Political party*]
MPL .... Mouvement Populaire de Liberation [*People's Liberation Movement*] [*Djibouti*]   (AF)
MPL .... Movimento Politica dei Lavoratori [*Workers' Political Movement*] [*Italy*] [*Political party*]   (PPE)
MPL .... Movimiento Popular de Liberacion "Cinchoneros" [*"Cinchoneros" Popular Liberation Movement*] [*Honduras*] [*Political party*]
MPL .... Shunting Pneumatic Winch   (RU)
MPLA........ Malayan People's Liberation Army
MPLA........ Malaysian People's Liberation Army   (ML)
MPLA........ Metropolitan Public Libraries Association [*New South Wales, Australia*]
MPLA........ Mouvement Populaire de Liberation de l'Angola [*Popular Movement for the Liberation of Angola*]
MPLA...... Movimento Popular de Libertacao de Angola [*Popular Movement for the Liberation of Angola*] [*Political party*]
MPLA-AN ... Movimento Popular de Libertacao de Angola-Agostinho Neto
MPLAC..... Movimiento Popular Liberal del Archipielago Canario [*People's Liberal Movement of the Canary Islands*] [*Spanish*]   (WER)
MPlan........ Master of Planning
MPlanStudies ... Master of Planning Studies
MPLA-PT ... Movimiento Popular de Libertacao de Angola - Partido do Trabalho [*Popular Movement for the Liberation of Angola - Party of Labor*] [*Political party*]   (PPW)
MPLB........ Balboa/Albrook [*Panama*] [*ICAO location identifier*]   (ICLI)
MPLC........ Mouvement Populaire pour la Liberation du Congo
MPLC........ Movimento Popular de Libertacao de Cabinda [*Popular Movement for the Liberation of Cabinda*] [*Angola*] [*Political party*]   (PD)
MPLC........ Movimiento Popular de Liberacion Cinchonero [*Guerrilla forces*] [*Honduras*]   (EY)
MPLD .... Malorazni Protiletadlove Delostrelectvo [*Small Caliber Antiaircraft Artillery*]   (CZ)

MPLD .... Mouvement Populaire pour la Liberation de Djibouti [*Political party*]   (EY)
MPLF........ Malaysian People's Liberation Front   (ML)
MPLL........ Malayan People's Liberation League
MPLN ...... Movimento para a Libertacao Nacional [*National Liberation Movement*] [*Portuguese*]   (WER)
MPLN ...... Movimiento Popular de Liberacion Nacional [*People's National Liberation Movement*] [*Bolivia*]   (LA)
MPLO .... Malay Police Liaison Officer   (ML)
MPLP........ La Palma [*Panama*] [*ICAO location identifier*]   (ICLI)
MPLR........ Mongolska Partia Ludowo-Rewolucyjna [*Mongolian People's Revolutionary Party*] [*Poland*]
MPLR........ Mouvement pour la Liberation de la Reunion [*Movement for the Liberation of Reunion*]   (AF)
MPLT........ Mouvement Populaire pour la Liberation du Tchad [*Popular Movement for the Liberation of Chad*]   (AF)
MPLTT ..... Mouvement Populaire pour la Liberation Totale du Tchad [*Popular Movement for the Total Liberation of Chad*]   (AF)
MPM........ Junior Chamber International [*JCI*]   (RU)
MPM........ Majlis Pelajaran Melayu [*Malayan Education Council*]   (ML)
MPM........ Maputo [*Mozambique*] [*Airport symbol*]   (OAG)
MPM........ Materiel de Protection Moderne
MPM........ Mayotte People's Movement [*Comoros*]
MPM........ Milli Produktivite Merkezi [*National Productivity Center*]   (TU)
MPM........ Ministerstwo Przemyslu Maszynowego [*Ministry of the Machine Building Industry*]   (POL)
MPM........ Ministerstwo Przemyslu Metalowego [*Ministry of the Metal Industry*]   (POL)
MPM........ Mothers of the Plaza de Mayo [*Argentina*]   (EAIO)
MPM........ Mouvement Populaire Mahorais [*Mayotte People's Movement*] [*Comoros*] [*Political party*]   (PPW)
MPM........ Mouvement Populaire Marocain
MPM........ Movimiento Peronista Montonero [*Peronist Montonero Movement*] [*Dissolved, 1983*] [*Argentina*]   (LA)
MPMB ...... Ministerstwo Przemyslu Materialow Budowlanych [*Ministry of the Building Materials Industry*]   (POL)
MPMCANSW ... Master Plumbers and Mechanical Contractors Association of New South Wales [*Australia*]
MPMCAV ... Master Plumbers and Mechanical Contractors' Association of Victoria [*Australia*]
MPMCAWA ... Master Plumbers and Mechanical Contractors' Association of Western Australia
MPMG ...... Panama/Paitilla, Marco A. Gelabert [*Panama*] [*ICAO location identifier*]   (ICLI)
MPMI .... Moscow Fur and Peltry Institute   (RU)
MPMiM .... Ministerstwo Przemyslu Miesnego i Mleczarskiego [*Ministry of Meat and Dairy Industry*]   (POL)
MPMiMP ... Ministry of the Meat and Dairy Products Industry   (RU)
MPML....... Mid-Pacific Marine Laboratory   (MSC)
MPMM ..... Movimiento por un Mundo Mejor [*Movement for a Better World*] [*Venezuela*]   (LA)
MPMMG .. Marine Pollution Monitoring Management Group   (ASF)
MPMR ...... Movimiento Patriotica Manuel Rodriguez [*Manuel Rodriguez Patriotic Movement*] [*Chile*] [*Political party*]   (EY)
MPNC .... Mouvement pour le Progres National Congolais [*Movement for National Congolese Progress*]
MPO.......... Coast Guard, Coast Guard Service   (RU)
MPO.......... Intergovernmental Organization   (RU)
MPO.......... Magnetic Bearing of the Checkpoint   (RU)
MPO.......... Makedoniki Politiki Organosis [*Macedonian Political Organization*] [*Bulgarian anti-Greek organization*] [*Greek*]   (GC)
MPO......... Makedonska Politicka Organizacija [*Macedonian Political Organization*]   (YU)
MPO......... Miejskie Przedsiebiorstwa Ogrodnicze [*Municipal Garden Enterprises*]   (POL)
MPO......... Miejskie Przedsiebiorstwo Oczyszczania [*Municipal Sanitation Enterprise*]   (POL)
MPO......... Ministerstvo Post [*Ministry of Postal Service*]   (CZ)
MPO......... Moscow Consumers' Society   (RU)
MPO......... Motorisovany Prezvedny Oddil [*Motorized Reconnaissance Battalion*]   (CZ)
MPO......... Withholding Tax [*Indonesia*]   (IMH)
MPOA....... Puerto Obaldia [*Panama*] [*ICAO location identifier*]   (ICLI)
MPol......... Master of Policy
MPOM...... Miejskie Przedsiebiorstwo Oczyszczania Miasta [*Municipal Sanitation Enterprise*]   (POL)
MPOS .... Military Plans and Operations Staff
MPOZKZ ... Mesarsko Podjetje, Okrajna Zveza Kmetijskih Zadrug [*Butcher Establishment, District Union of Agricultural Cooperatives*]   (YU)
MPP .... Madjelis Perusahaan dan Perniagaan [*Chamber of Commerce and Industry*]   (IN)
MPP .... Manipur People's Party [*India*] [*Political party*]   (PPW)
MPP .... Mathematics Preparation Program [*University of New South Wales*] [*Australia*]
MPP .... Mechanized Field Laundry   (RU)

MPP .... Medical Aid Crossing Point   (BU)
MPP .... Medical Station at a Water Crossing   (RU)
MPP .... Melanesian Progressive Parti [*Vanuatu*] [*Political party*]   (EY)
MPP .... Mesarsko Preradivacko Preduzece [*Meat-Processing Establishment*]   (YU)
MPP .... Mestske Plynarenske Podniky [*Municipal Gas Works*]   (CZ)
MPP .... Mestske Prepravni Podniky [*Municipal Transportation Enterprises*]   (CZ)
MPP .... Ministerstvo Potravinarskeho Prumyslu [*Ministry of the Food Industry*]   (CZ)
MPP .... Ministry of the Food Industry   (RU)
MPP .... Mongol People's Party [*Mongolia*] [*Political party*]   (FEA)
MPP .... Mouvement pour le Progres du Peuple
MPP .... Movimento do Partido do Proletariado [*Proletariat Party Movement*] [*Portuguese*]   (WER)
MPP .... Movimento Popular Portugues [*Popular Portuguese Movement*]   (WER)
MPP .... Mulatupo [*Panama*] [*Airport symbol*]   (OAG)
MPP .... Programme of Mass Privatisation [*Poland*]   (ECON)
MPPA .... Beef-Extract Liver Agar   (RU)
MPPAV .... Master Poultry Processors' Association of Victoria [*Australia*]
MPPB .... Beef-Extract Liver Broth   (RU)
mppb .... Bridge Train of a Pontoon Battalion   (RU)
MPPC .... Panama [*Panama*] [*ICAO location identifier*]   (ICLI)
MPPD .... Ministry of Planning and Popular Development [*Burkina Faso*]
MPPP .... Mauritius People's Progressive Party
MPPP .... Meteorological Receiving-Sending Station   (RU)
MPPS .... Moroccan Party of Progress and Socialism [*Political party*]
MPPT .... Ministry of the Foodstuffs Industry   (RU)
m/pr .... Barely Noticeable Obstacles [*Topography*]   (RU)
m pr .... By the Way   (RU)
MPR .... Magnetic Bearing of a Radio Direction Finder   (RU)
MPR .... Magnetic Bearing of a Radio Navigation Point   (RU)
MPR .... Magnetic Bearing of a Radio Station   (RU)
MPR .... Magnetic Bearing of a Rocket   (RU)
MPR .... Majelis Permusyawaratan Rakyat [*People's Consultative Assembly*] [*Indonesia*]   (FEA)
MPR .... Mauritanian Party for Renewal [*Political party*]   (EY)
mpr .... Mine Disposal Company   (RU)
MPR .... Ministry of Food Reserves, USSR   (RU)
MPR .... Mongolian Peoples Republic
MPR .... Mouvement Populaire de la Revolution [*Popular Revolutionary Movement*] [*Zaire*] [*Political party*]   (PD)
MPR .... Mouvement Populaire Revolutionnaire [*Popular Revolutionary Movement*] [*Tunisia*] [*Political party*]   (PD)
MPR .... Movimento Popolare Rivoluzionario [*Popular Revolutionary Movement*] [*Italy*] [*Political party*]   (PD)
MPR .... Movimiento Popular Revolucionario [*Popular Revolutionary Movement*] [*Nicaragua*]   (LA)
MPR .... Movimiento Popular Revolucionario [*Popular Revolutionary Movement*] [*Ecuador*]   (LA)
MPRA .... Merit Protection and Review Agency [*Australia*]
MPRB .... Miejskie Przedsiebiorstwo Remontowo-Budowlane [*Municipal Repair and Construction Enterprise*]   (POL)
MPRB .... Miejskie Przedsiebiorstwo Robot Budowlanych [*Municipal Construction Enterprise*]   (POL)
MPRD .... Miejskie Przedsiebiorstwo Robot Drogowych [*Municipal Road Construction Enterprise*]   (POL)
MPRDiM .. Miejskie Przedsiebiorstwo Robot Drogowych i Mostowych [*Municipal Road and Bridge Construction Enterprise*]   (POL)
MPRH .... Rio Hato [*Panama*] [*ICAO location identifier*]   (ICLI)
MPRI .... Miejskie Przedsiebiorstwo Robot Inzynieryjnych (Dawna "Metrobudowa") [*Municipal Engineering Enterprise ("Metrobudowa")*] [*Formerly,*]   (POL)
MPRIA ...... Member of the Public Relations Institute of Australia
MPRI(Aust) ... Member of the Public Relations Institute of Australia   (ADA)
MPRiS .... Ministerstwo Przemyslu Rolnego i Spozywczego [*Ministry of the Agricultural and Food Industry*]   (POL)
MPRISA ... Member of the Public Relations Institute of Southern Africa   (AA)
MPros .... Ministry of Education   (RU)
MPR-P ...... Miejskie Przedsiebiorstwo Rozbiorkowo-Porzadkowe [*Municipal Demolition and Disposal Enterprise*]   (POL)
MPRP .... Mongolian People's Revolutionary Party [*Mongol Ardyn Khuv'sgalt Nam*] [*Political party*]   (PPW)
MPRP .... Moslem People's Republican Party [*Iran*] [*Political party*]   (PPW)
MPRS .... Madjelis Permusjawaratan Rakjat Sementara [*Provisional People's Consultative Congress*] [*Indonesia*]   (IN)
Mprv .... Mitprovisor [*German*]
MPRWiK .. Miejskie Przedsiebiorstwo Robot Wodociagowych i Kanalizacyjnych [*Municipal Water Supply and Sewer Construction Enterprise*]   (POL)
MPS .... International Chamber of Shipping [*ICS*]   (RU)
MPS .... International Industrial Secretariat   (RU)
MPS .... Machine Rental Station   (RU)

MPS .... Madagascar Pediatrics Society   (EAIO)
MPS .... Magasins-Pilotes Socialistes [*North African*]
MPS .... Magnetplatten-System [*German*]   (ADPT)
MPS .... Maschinenprogrammsystem [*Machine Program System*] [*German*]   (ADPT)
MPS .... Mashinoprokratnaia Stantsiia
MPS .... Mathematical Programming Society [*Voorburg, Netherlands*]   (EAIO)
MPS .... Medical Station of a Unit [*Military*]   (RU)
MPS .... Medunarodni Poljoprivredni Sajam [*International Agricultural Fair*] [*Novi Sad*]   (YU)
MPS .... Mestska Postovni Sprava [*City Postal Administration*]   (CZ)
MPS .... Methodist Philatelic Society   (EA)
MPS .... Mezhdunarodnoye Passazhirskoye Soglasheniye [*Agreement Concerning International Railroad Passenger Traffic (Between USSR and satellites)*]   (EG)
MPS .... Milicias Populares Sandinistas [*Sandinist People's Militias*] [*Nicaragua*]   (LA)
MPS .... Ministerstvo Pracovnich Sil [*Ministry of Manpower*]   (CZ)
MPS .... Ministry of Public Security [*Mongolia*]
MPS .... Ministry of Railroads, USSR   (RU)
MPS .... Mobile Police Station   (ML)
MPS .... Monte dei Paschi di Siena [*Bank*] [*Italian*]
MPS .... Mont Pelerin Society [*Sweden*]   (EAIO)
MPS .... Moroccan Paediatric Society   (EAIO)
MPS .... Moscow State Trust for the Construction of Underground Structures   (RU)
MPS .... Mouvement Patriotique du Salut [*Chad*] [*Political party*]   (EY)
MPS .... Mouvement Populaire Senegalais [*Senegalese Popular Movement*] [*Political party*]
MPS .... Movimiento de Patria Socialista [*Venezuela*] [*Political party*]   (EY)
MPS .... Movimiento Popular Socialista [*Socialist Popular Movement*] [*Colorado*]   (LA)
MPS .... Muy Poderoso Senor [*Spanish*]
MPS .... Scaling Circuit [*Computers*]   (RU)
MPS .... Society for Mucopolysaccharide Diseases   (EA)
MPS .... Track Machine Station [*Railroads*]   (RU)
MPSA .... Ministry of Instrument Making and Means of Automation, USSR   (RU)
MPSA .... Santiago [*Panama*] [*ICAO location identifier*]   (ICLI)
MPSC .... Movimiento Popular Socialcristiano [*Christian Social Popular Movement*] [*El Salvador*] [*Political party*]   (PD)
MPSD .... Moscow Proletarian Rifle Division   (RU)
MPSF .... Malayan People's Socialist Front   (ML)
MPSF .... Multi-Purpose Special Fund [*Asian Development Bank*] [*United Nations*]   (EY)
MPSIC ...... Madhya Pradesh State Industries Corp. [*India*]   (PDAA)
MPSM .... Maharashtra Prabodhan Seva Mandal [*India*]
MPSM .... Ministry of the Building Materials Industry   (RU)
MPSP .... Magnetplattenspeicher [*German*]   (ADPT)
MPSP .... Ministerstvo Prace a Socialni Pece [*Ministry of Labor and Social Welfare*]   (CZ)
MPSP .... Montazni Podnik Spoju [*Assembly Enterprise for Communications*]   (CZ)
MPSP .... Movimiento por la Paz y la Soberania de los Pueblos [*Movement for Peace and Sovereignty of Peoples*] [*Cuba*]   (LA)
MPSS .... Ministry of the Communications Equipment Industry, USSR   (RU)
MPSUD ..... Mouvement pour un Syndicalisme Uni et Democratique [*France*]   (FLAF)
MPSV .... Ministerstvo Prace a Socialnich Veci [*Ministry of Labor and Social Affairs*]   (CZ)
MPSZ .... Magyar Paraszt Szovetseg [*Hungarian Peasant Association*]   (HU)
MPSZ .... Magyar Penzugyi Szindikatus [*Hungarian Financial Syndicate*]   (HU)
MPT .... Direct-Current Machine   (RU)
MPT .... Madarska Partija Trudbenika [*Hungarian Workers' Party*]   (YU)
MPT .... Miejskie Przedsiebiorstwo Taksowkowe [*or Taksowek*] [*Municipal Taxicab Enterprise*]   (POL)
MPT .... Milk Pasteurization Tribunal [*Australia*]
MPT .... Ministerstvo Post a Telekomunikaci [*Ministry for Postal Affairs and Telecommunications*]   (CZ)
MPT .... Ministry of Posts and Telecommunications [*Japan*]   (PDAA)
MPT .... Ministry of Posts and Telecommunications [*People's Republic of China*]   (ECON)
MPT .... Ministry of Posts and Telecommunictions [*China*]   (ECON)
MPT .... Mouvement Populaire Tchadien [*Chadian Popular Movement*] [*Political party*]
MPT .... Mouvement Populaire Togolais [*Togolese Popular Movement*] [*Political party*]
MPT .... Mouvement pour le Progres et la Tolerance [*Burkina Faso*] [*Political party*]   (EY)
MPTO .... Tocumen/General Omar Torrijos H. [*Panama*] [*ICAO location identifier*]   (ICLI)

MPTShP ... Ministry of the Consumers' Goods Industry (RU)
MPTT....... Ministry of Post, Telegraph, and Telephone [*Obsolete*] (BU)
MPTTR..... Ministry of Post, Telegraph, Telephone, and Radio [*Obsolete*] (BU)
MPTU .... Technical Specifications of the Machinery Industry (RU)
MPTU .... Technical Specifications of the Metallurgical Industry (RU)
MPU......... Local Control Post (RU)
MPU......... Magnetic Track Angle (RU)
MPU......... Major Projects Unit [*Victoria, Australia*]
MPU......... Mapua [*Papua New Guinea*] [*Airport symbol*] [*Obsolete*] (OAG)
MPU......... Moscow Political Administration (RU)
MPU......... Movimiento del Pueblo Unido [*United People's Movement*] [*Nicaragua*] (LA)
mpuaz........ Millipoise (RU)
MPUAZO ... Naval Antiaircraft Artillery Fire Control Device (RU)
MPubAdmin ... Master of Public Administration
MPUK .... Local Industrial Training Center (RU)
mPV .... Maritime Polar Air (RU)
mpv............. Mine Disposal Platoon (RU)
MPV .... Moralno-Politicko Vaspitanje [*Moral and Political Education*] [*Military*] (YU)
MPV .... Refracted-Wave Method (RU)
MPV .... Small Time Constant (RU)
MPVKhO .. Local Antiaircraft and Chemical Defense (BU)
MPVO .... Mestnaia Protivovozdushnaia Oborona [*Local Anti-Air Defense*] [*Former USSR*]
MPVP....... International Traveling Exhibition of Instruments and Measuring Devices (RU)
MPVR ...... El Porvenir [*Panama*] [*ICAO location identifier*] (ICLI)
MPW .... Ministry of Public Works [*Vietnam*]
MPW .... Mouvement Populaire Wallon [*Walloon Popular Movement*] [*Belgium*] (WER)
MPWH..... Ministry of Public Works and Highways [*Philippines*] (DS)
MPWH..... Ministry of Public Works and Housing [*Saudi Arabia*] (IMH)
MPWU ...... Movement for Political World Union [*Blommenslyst, Fyn, Denmark*] (EA)
MPY .... Maatskappy [*Company, Society*] [*Afrikaans*]
MPYI........ Moble-Prefabrik Yapi Isletmesi [*Furniture-Prefabricated Structures Enterprise*] [*Turkish Cypriot*] (GC)
MPZ .... Mezinarodni Plachtarske Zavody [*International Glider Contests*] (CZ)
mpz............. Millipieze (RU)
mpz............. Millipoise (RU)
MPZ .... Mjesna Poljoprivredna Zadruga [*Local Agricultural Cooperative*] (YU)
MPZ .... Moravskoslezske Pletarske Zavody [*Moravian-Silesian Knitting Mills*] (CZ)
MPZh .... Beef-Extract Gelatin (RU)
MPZL........ Panama [*Panama*] [*ICAO location identifier*] (ICLI)
MPZU .... Permanent Storage Matrix (RU)
mq .... Manque [*Is Missing*] [*French*]
MQ .... Martinique [*ANSI two-letter standard code*] (CNC)
Mq.............. Metre Carre [*Square Meter*] [*French*] (MTD)
MQ .... Metro Quadrato [*Square Meter*] [*Italian*]
MQE........... Martinique [*West Indies*] (WDAA)
MQL........... Mildura [*Australia*] [*Airport symbol*] (OAG)
MQM .... Muhajir Qaumi Movement [*Pakistan*] [*Political party*] (ECON)
m-q-perf ..... Mais-Que-Perfeito [*Portuguese*]
Mqs............ Marquis [*Marquess*] [*French*] (MTD)
MQS .... Mustique [*Windward Islands*] [*Airport symbol*] (OAG)
Mqse........... Marquise [*Marchioness*] [*French*] (MTD)
MQSS........ Mary Queen of Scots Society (EAIO)
MQU .... Mariquita [*Colombia*] [*Airport symbol*] (OAG)
mquant .... Manquant [*Lacking*] [*French*]
mque........... Manque [*Is Missing*] [*French*]
MQV.......... Ministere de la Qualite de la Vie [*Ministry of the Quality of Life*] [*France*] (PDAA)
MQX.......... Makale [*Ethiopia*] [*Airport symbol*] (OAG)
MR............. Air Mauritanie [*Mauritania*] [*ICAO designator*] (ICDA)
MR............. Distance Scale (RU)
mr............... Gunner [*Artillery*] (BU)
MR............. High-Power Radio Station (RU)
MR............. Lever Micrometer (RU)
MR............. Magnetic Reverberator (RU)
m-r............. Major (RU)
MR............. Maldivian Rupee
m r............... Male Gender (BU)
MR............. Marca Registrada [*Registered Trademark*] [*Spanish*]
mr............... Martir [*Martyr*] [*Spanish*]
mr............... Masculine Gender (RU)
MR............. Mauritania [*ANSI two-letter standard code*] (CNC)
MR............. Mauritius Rupee
MR............. Maximum Relay, Over-Current Relay, Overload Relay (RU)
MR............. Mechanized Patrol (RU)
mr............... Meester [*Master*] [*Afrikaans*]
Mr............. Meester in de Rechten [*Academic qualification*] [*Netherlands*]

M/R............ Meine Rechnung [*My Calculations*] [*German*]
MR............. Metallurgy and Ore Mining (BU)
MR............. Meteorological Rocket (RU)
MR............. Microroentgenometer (RU)
mr............... Milliroentgen (RU)
M-r............. Minister [*Government*] (BU)
MR............. Ministerstwo Rolnictwa [*Ministry of Agriculture*] (POL)
MR............. Ministre Resident [*French*] (MTD)
MR............. Miniszteri Rendelet [*Ministerial Decree (Legal)*] (HU)
MR............. Mi Remesa [*My Remittance*] [*Spanish*] [*Business term*]
MR............. Mistni Rozhlas [*Local Radio Broadcasting*] (CZ)
MR............. Molto Reverendo [*Reverend*] [*Italian*]
MR............. Mondcivitan Republic [*Defunct*] (EAIO)
Mr............. Monsieur [*Mister*] [*French*] (MTD)
mr............... Mortar Company (RU)
mr............... Motorized Company (RU)
MR............. Movilizacion Republicana [*Republican Mobilization*] [*Nicaragua*]
MR............. Movimiento Renovacion [*Paraguay*] (LAA)
MR............. Museum of Revolution (RU)
MR............. Naval Reconnaissance (BU)
MR............. Naval Reconnaissance Aircraft (RU)
MR............. Radioisotope Manometer (RU)
MR............. Repair Shop (RU)
MR............. Route Relay (RU)
m r............. Sea Level (BU)
mr............... Slightly Soluble (RU)
MR-8 .... Movimiento Revolucionario 8 de Outubro [*8 October Revolutionary Movement*] [*Brazil*] (LA)
MR-13 .... Movimiento Revolucionario 13 de Noviembre [*13 November Revolutionary Movement*] [*Guatemala*] (LA)
MR-14J ..... Movimiento Revolucionario Catorce de Junio [*14 June Revolutionary Movement*] [*Dominican Republic*] (LA)
MR-24A..... Movimiento Revolucionario Veinticuatro de Abril [*24 April Revolutionary Movement*] [*Dominican Republic*] (LA)
MRA......... Manufacturing Resources of Australia (ADA)
MRA......... Market Research Africa
MRA......... Messtechnik, Regelungstechnik, Automatik [*Hoppenstedt Wirtschaftsdatenbank GmbH*] [*Germany*] [*Information service or system*] (CRD)
MRA......... Metropolitan Regional Abattoir [*Australia*]
MRA......... Ministerio da Republica para os Acores [*Ministry of the Republic for Azores*] [*Portuguese*] (WER)
MRA......... Mission pour la Reforme Administrative [*Administrative Reform Mission*] [*Chad*] (AF)
MRA......... Misurata [*Libya*] [*Airport symbol*] (OAG)
MRA......... Moral Re-Armament
MRA......... Motorcycle Riders' Association [*Australia*]
MRA......... Movimiento Revolucionario Autentico [*Authentic Revolutionary Movement*] [*Costa Rica*] (LA)
MRA......... Munich Reinsurance Co. of Australia
MRAA ...... Medical Record Association of Australia
MRAC...... Measurement Research Advisory Committee [*Australia*]
MRAC ...... Musee Royal de l'Afrique Centrale
MRACGP ... Member of the Royal Australasian College of General Practice (BABM)
MRACGP ... Member of the Royal Australian College of General Practitioners (ADA)
MRACO .... Member of the Royal Australasian College of Ophthalmologists [*British*] (BABM)
MRACP..... Member of the Royal Australasian College of Physicians (ADA)
MRACR ... Member of the Royal Australasian College of Radiologists [*British*] (BABM)
MRACS..... Member of the Royal Australasian College of Surgeons
mrad........... Millirad (RU)
mrae........... Naval Rocket-Launcher Air Squadron (RU)
MRAES ..... Member of the Royal Aeronautical Society [*South Africa*] (AA)
MRAJ....... Aranjuez [*Costa Rica*] [*ICAO location identifier*] (ICLI)
MRAL ...... Alajuela [*Costa Rica*] [*ICAO location identifier*] (ICLI)
MRAM...... Amubri [*Costa Rica*] [*ICAO location identifier*] (ICLI)
mram.......... Marble [*Quarry*] [*Topography*] (RU)
MRANZCP ... Member of the Royal Australian and New Zealand College of Psychiatrists [*British*] (BABM)
MRAP .... Mortgage and Rental Assistance Program [*Australia*]
MRAP .... Mouvement Contre le Racisme et pour l'Amitie Entre les Peuples [*Movement Against Racism and for Friendship between People*] (EAIO)
MRAP .... Movimiento de Resistencia Armada Puertorriquena [*Puerto Rican Armed Resistance Movement*] [*Political party*] (PD)
MRAP .... Naval Reconnaissance Air Regiment (RU)
MRAPI..... Member of the Royal Australian Planning Institute
MRAR ...... Atirro [*Costa Rica*] [*ICAO location identifier*] (ICLI)
MRAT .... Altamira De San Carlos [*Costa Rica*] [*ICAO location identifier*] (ICLI)
MRB .... Motorized Rifle Battalion [*Former USSR*]
MRB .... Mouvement de Resistance Bakongo

MRB .... Mouvement Rural du Burundi
MRBA .... Buenos Aires [*Costa Rica*] [*ICAO location identifier*]   (ICLI)
MRBB........ Babilonia [*Costa Rica*] [*ICAO location identifier*]   (ICLI)
MRBC .... Barra Del Colorado [*Costa Rica*] [*ICAO location identifier*]
               (ICLI)
MRBM ...... Bremen [*Costa Rica*] [*ICAO location identifier*]   (ICLI)
MRBN .... Bataan [*Costa Rica*] [*ICAO location identifier*]   (ICLI)
MRBO .... Boca Naranjo [*Costa Rica*] [*ICAO location identifier*]   (ICLI)
MRBP........ Barra De Parismina [*Costa Rica*] [*ICAO location identifier*]
               (ICLI)
MRBT........ Barra De Tortuguero [*Costa Rica*] [*ICAO location identifier*]
               (ICLI)
MRC .... Maintenance and Repair Craft [*Military*]
MRC .... Media Resource Center [*Adelaide, Australia*]
MRC .... Medical Relief Committee [*Israel*]
MRC .... Medical Research Council [*New Zealand*] [*Research center*]
               (IRC)
MRC .... Medical Research Council [*South Africa*] [*Research center*]
MRC .... Military Representatives Committee [*NATO*]   (NATG)
MRC .... Mission Resources Center [*Sydney, Australia*]
MRC .... Mobile Radio Communications
MRC .... Mouvement des Renovateurs Communistes [*France*] [*Political
               party*]   (EY)
MRC .... Movimiento de Restauracion Conservadora [*Colombia*]   (COL)
MRC .... Movimiento de Revolucion Cristiana [*Colorado*]   (LAA)
MRC .... Movimiento Rebelde Colombiano [*Colombian Rebel Movement*]
               (LA)
MRC .... Movimiento Revolucionario Campesino [*Peasant's
               Revolutionary Movement*] [*El Salvador*]   (LA)
MRCA ...... Canas [*Costa Rica*] [*ICAO location identifier*]   (ICLI)
MRCA ...... Multirole Combat Aircraft [*A joint English, German, and Italian
               project to develop a standard NATO fighter*]   (WEN)
MRCB .... Musee Royal du Congo Belge
MRCC .... Coto 47 [*Costa Rica*] [*ICAO location identifier*]   (ICLI)
MRCC .... Maritime Rescue Coordination Center [*Australia*]
MRCD .... Caledonia [*Costa Rica*] [*ICAO location identifier*]   (ICLI)
MRCE .... Carate [*Costa Rica*] [*ICAO location identifier*]   (ICLI)
MRCH ...... Chacarita [*Costa Rica*] [*ICAO location identifier*]   (ICLI)
MRCH ...... Murchison [*Botanical region*] [*Australia*]
MRCI........ Ciruelas [*Costa Rica*] [*ICAO location identifier*]   (ICLI)
MRCLABS ... Medical Research Council Laboratories [*Jamaica*]   (SLS)
MRCNZ .... Medical Research Council of New Zealand [*Research center*]
               (SLS)
MRCP........ Maoist Revolutionary Communist Party
MRCPA..... Member of the Royal College of Pathologists of Australia
MRCR .... Carrillo [*Costa Rica*] [*ICAO location identifier*]   (ICLI)
MRCSA..... Migrant Resource Center of South Australia
MRCV .... Cabo Velas [*Costa Rica*] [*ICAO location identifier*]   (ICLI)
MRCZ .... Carrizal [*Costa Rica*] [*ICAO location identifier*]   (ICLI)
MRD.......... Malaysian Rubber Development Corporation   (ML)
mrd .... Merced [*Grace, Mercy*] [*Spanish*]
MRD .... Merida [*Venezuela*] [*Airport symbol*]   (OAG)
mrd .... Miljardi(a) [*Finland*]
Mrd .... Milliarde [*Billion*] [*German*]   (WEN)
mrd .... Millirutherford   (RU)
MRD.......... Motorized Rifle Division [*Former USSR*]   (NATG)
MRD.......... Movement for the Restoration of Democracy [*Pakistan*]
               [*Political party*]   (PD)
MRD.......... Movement for the Restoration of Democracy [*Nepal*] [*Political
               party*]
MRD.......... Movimento Revolucionario Democratico [*Democratic
               Revolutionary Movement*] [*Brazil*]   (LA)
MRD.......... Movimiento de Reafirmacion Doctrinaria [*Movement of
               Doctrinaire Reaffirmation*] [*Argentina*]   (LA)
MRDB .... Museum of the Revolutionary Movement in Bulgaria   (BU)
MRDC .... Military Research and Development Center [*US-Thailand*]
MRDCC .... Metropolitan Refuse Disposal Consultative Committee
               [*Melbourne, Australia*]
MRDD...... Don Diego [*Costa Rica*] [*ICAO location identifier*]   (ICLI)
MRDL .... Mineral Respurces Development Laboratory [*Australia*]
MRDN...... Mouvement Revolutionnaire pour la Democratie Nouvelle
               [*Revolutionary Movement for New Democracy*] [*Senegal*]
               (PD)
MRDO....... Dieciocho [*Costa Rica*] [*ICAO location identifier*]   (ICLI)
MRDP....... Mezinarodni Ruda Delnicka Pomoc [*International Workers' Red
               Aid*]   (CZ)
MRE .... Mara Lodges [*Kenya*] [*Airport symbol*]   (OAG)
MRE .... Ministerio das Relacoes Exteriores [*Ministry of Foreign
               Relations*] [*Portuguese*]
MRE .... Movimiento Revolucionario Ecuatoriano [*Ecuadorean
               Revolutionary Movement*]   (LA)
MRE .... Movimiento Revolucionario Espartaco [*Bolivia*] [*Political party*]
               (PPW)
MRE .... Movimiento Revolucionario Estudantil [*Colorado*] [*Political
               party*]   (EY)
MREA .... Estero Azul [*Costa Rica*] [*ICAO location identifier*]   (ICLI)

MREAC..... Mon Repos Est au Ciel [*My Rest Is in Heaven*] [*Motto of Ludwig
               Philipp, Count of the Palatinate of Simmern (1602-1654)*]
               [*French*]
MREC .... El Carmen [*Costa Rica*] [*ICAO location identifier*]   (ICLI)
MRELB .... Malaysian Rubber Exchange and Licensing Board   (PDAA)
MRER .... El Ron Ron [*Costa Rica*] [*ICAO location identifier*]   (ICLI)
MResEnvS ... Master of Resource and Environmental Studies
MResEnvSt ... Master of Resource and Environmental Studies
MResSc ..... Master of Resource Science
MRET........ Esterillos [*Costa Rica*] [*ICAO location identifier*]   (ICLI)
mrezerford ... Millirutherford   (RU)
MRF .... Matabelaland Relief Force
MRF .... Medical Research Foundation [*France*]   (EAIO)
MRF .... Ministry of the River Fleet   (RU)
MRF .... Movement for Rights and Freedoms [*Bulgaria*] [*Political party*]
MRFB....... Malayan Rubber Fund Board   (PDAA)
MRFC....... Malawi Rural Finance Co. Ltd.
MRFD .... Finca Delicias [*Costa Rica*] [*ICAO location identifier*]   (ICLI)
MRFI........ Finca 10 (Nuevo Palmar Sur) [*Costa Rica*] [*ICAO location
               identifier*]   (ICLI)
MRFL....... Flamengo [*Costa Rica*] [*ICAO location identifier*]   (ICLI)
MRFP....... Finca La Promesa [*Costa Rica*] [*ICAO location identifier*]
               (ICLI)
MRFS .... Finca 63 [*Costa Rica*] [*ICAO location identifier*]   (ICLI)
MRG .... Miedzynarodowy Rok Geofizyczny [*International Geophysical
               Year*] [*Poland*]
MRG .... Mouvement de la Revolution Gabonaise
MRG .... Mouvement des Radicaux de Gauche [*Left Radical Movement*]
               [*Wallis and Futuna Islands*] [*Political party*]   (EY)
MRG .... Mouvement des Radicaux de Gauche [*Left Radical Movement*]
               [*Reunion*] [*Political party*]   (PPW)
MRG .... Mouvement des Radicaux de Gauche [*Left Radical Movement*]
               [*France*] [*Political party*]   (PPE)
MRG .... Municipal Reform Group [*Tasmania, Australia*]
mrg .... Myriagram   (RU)
MRGA ...... Garza [*Costa Rica*] [*ICAO location identifier*]   (ICLI)
MRGF .... Golfito [*Costa Rica*] [*ICAO location identifier*]   (ICLI)
MRGI .... Minority Rights Group International [*British*]   (EAIO)
MRGP .... Guapiles [*Costa Rica*] [*ICAO location identifier*]   (ICLI)
MRGT ...... Caterpillar Tractor Repair Shop   (RU)
MRGT ...... Guatuso [*Costa Rica*] [*ICAO location identifier*]   (ICLI)
MRGU ...... Guanacaste [*Costa Rica*] [*ICAO location identifier*]   (ICLI)
MRGV ...... Marine Research Group of Victoria [*Australia*]
MRH .... Mouvement Revolutionnaire Haitien [*Haiti*]   (LAA)
MRHG...... Hacienda Rancho Grande [*Costa Rica*] [*ICAO location
               identifier*]   (ICLI)
MRHJ ...... Hacienda Jaco (Harbor Land) [*Costa Rica*] [*ICAO location
               identifier*]   (ICLI)
MRHO ...... Hacienda Rio Cuarto [*Costa Rica*] [*ICAO location identifier*]
               (ICLI)
MRHP....... Hacienda Platanar [*Costa Rica*] [*ICAO location identifier*]
               (ICLI)
MRHS .... Hacienda La Suerte [*Costa Rica*] [*ICAO location identifier*]
               (ICLI)
MRHS ...... Macleay River Historical Society [*Australia*]
MRI .... Church of England in Australia Primate's Committee on Mutual
               Responsibility and Independence   (ADA)
MRI .... Mammal Research Institute [*University of Pretoria*] [*South
               Africa*]   (AA)
MRI .... Marine Research Institute [*Indonesian*]   (ASF)
MRI .... Megyei Rendelo Intezet [*County Ambulance Station*]   (HU)
MRI .... Meteorological Research Institute [*Ministry of Transport*]
               [*Research center*] [*Japan*]   (ERC)
MRI .... Microelectronics Research Institute [*South Africa*]
MRI .... Mitsubishi Research Institute, Inc. [*Research center*] [*Japan*]
               (ERC)
MRI .... Movimiento Republicano Independiente [*Independent
               Republican Movement*] [*Ecuador*]   (LA)
MRI .... Myer Retail Investments Proprietary Ltd. [*Australia*]
MRI .... Radioactive Isotope Method   (RU)
MRIC........ Revolutionary Movement of the Christian Left [*Ecuador*]
               [*Political party*]   (PPW)
MRIP........ Australian Marine Research in Progress [*Database*]
MRIP........ Imperio [*Costa Rica*] [*ICAO location identifier*]   (ICLI)
MRiRR ...... Ministerstwo Rolnictwa i Reform Rolnych [*Ministry of
               Agriculture and Agricultural Reforms*] [*Pre-World War II*]
               (POL)
MRIT........ Moscow Editing and Publishing Technicum   (RU)
MRK .... Interrayon Office (of the Soyuzpechat')   (RU)
MRK .... Local Wage Commission   (RU)
MRK .... Marine Royale Khmere [*Royal Cambodian Navy*] [*Replaced by
               MNK*]   (CL)
Mrk........... Merkez [*Central*]   (TU)
MRKCh ..... International Frequency Registration Board [*IFRB*]   (RU)
MRKF....... Miedzyzwiazkowa Rada Kultury Fizycznej [*Inter-Union Council
               of Physical Culture*]   (POL)

MRKI .... Moscow Workers' and Peasants' Inspection (RU)
MRL .... Aeromorelos SA de CV [*Mexico*] [*ICAO designator*] (FAAC)
MRL .... Madras Refineries Ltd. [*India*]
MRL .... Materials Research Laboratories [*Taiwan*] (IRC)
MRL .... Materials Research Laboratory [*Australia*] (IRC)
MRL .... Meat Research Laboratory [*Australia*]
MRL .... Minen-Raeum- und Legeboot [*Mine Sweeper and Layer*] (EG)
MRL .... Ministere de la Reconstruction et du Logement [*France*] (FLAF)
MRL .... Mongolska Republika Ludowa [*Mongolian People's Republic*] [*Poland*]
MRL .... Movimiento de Reintegracion Liberal [*Liberal Reintegration Movement*] [*Colombia*] (LA)
MRL .... Movimiento Revolucionario Liberal [*Liberal Revolutionary Movement*] [*Colorado*] (LA)
MRLA ...... La Paquita [*Costa Rica*] [*ICAO location identifier*] (ICLI)
MRLA ...... Malayan Races Liberation Army
MRLB........ Liberia/Tomas Guardia Internacional [*Costa Rica*] [*ICAO location identifier*] (ICLI)
MRLC........ Los Chiles [*Costa Rica*] [*ICAO location identifier*] (ICLI)
MRLE .... Laurel [*Costa Rica*] [*ICAO location identifier*] (ICLI)
MRLF .... La Flor [*Costa Rica*] [*ICAO location identifier*] (ICLI)
MRLG .... La Garroba [*Costa Rica*] [*ICAO location identifier*] (ICLI)
MRLI........ La Ligia [*Costa Rica*] [*ICAO location identifier*] (ICLI)
MRLIS ...... Mineral Resources Land Information System [*Australia*]
MRLL........ Las Lomas [*Costa Rica*] [*ICAO location identifier*] (ICLI)
MRLL........ Malay Races Liberation League (Communist) (ML)
MRLM ...... Limon/Limon Internacional [*Costa Rica*] [*ICAO location identifier*] (ICLI)
MRLPC ..... Mouvement de Regroupement et de Liberation du Peuple Congolais [*Movement for the Regroupment and Liberation of the Congolese People*]
MRLR .... La Roca [*Costa Rica*] [*ICAO location identifier*] (ICLI)
MRLT .... Las Trancas [*Costa Rica*] [*ICAO location identifier*] (ICLI)
MRLU ...... La Maruca [*Costa Rica*] [*ICAO location identifier*] (ICLI)
MRLV ...... La Cueva [*Costa Rica*] [*ICAO location identifier*] (ICLI)
MRLY ...... La Yolanda [*Costa Rica*] [*ICAO location identifier*] (ICLI)
MRM .... Engine Repair Shop (RU)
MRM .... Machine Repair Shop (RU)
MRM .... Manari [*Papua New Guinea*] [*Airport symbol*] (OAG)
MRM .... Marker Beacon (RU)
MRM .... Medical Microroentgenometer (RU)
MRM .... Metalurgija Raznobojnih Metala [*Nonferrous Metallurgy*] (YU)
MRM .... Ministerio da Republica para a Madeira [*Ministry of the Republic for Madeira*] [*Portuguese*] (WER)
MRM .... Movement for the Redemption of Liberian Muslims [*Political party*] (EY)
MRM .... Movimento da Resistencia de Mozambique [*Mozambique Resistance Movement*]
mrm .... Myriameter (RU)
MRMA ...... Montealto [*Costa Rica*] [*ICAO location identifier*] (ICLI)
MRMC ...... Murcielago [*Costa Rica*] [*ICAO location identifier*] (ICLI)
MRMJ .... Mojica [*Costa Rica*] [*ICAO location identifier*] (ICLI)
MRML ...... Montelimar O Los Sitios [*Costa Rica*] [*ICAO location identifier*] (ICLI)
MR/ML..... Movimiento Revolucionario/Marxista-Leninista [*Revolutionary Movement/Marxist-Leninist*] [*Portuguese*] (WER)
MRN .... Mental Retardation Nursing Certificate [*Australia*]
MRN .... Miejska Rada Narodowa [*Municipal People's Council*] (POL)
MRN .... Missions Gouvernementales Francaises [*France*] [*ICAO designator*] (FAAC)
MRN .... Mouvement de Renovation Nationale [*National Renovation Movement*] [*Haiti*] (LA)
MRN .... Mouvement pour la Reconstruction Nationale [*Haiti*] [*Political party*] (EY)
MRN .... Movimiento de la Reforma Nacional [*National Reform Movement*] [*Argentina*] (LA)
MRN .... Movimiento de Renovacion Nacional [*Movement for National Renovation*] [*Colorado*] [*Political party*] (PPW)
MRN .... Movimiento de Reorganizacion Nacional [*National Reorganization Movement*] [*Argentina*] (LA)
MRN .... Movimiento Reformista Nacional [*Honduras*] (LAA)
MRNC ...... Nicoya [*Costa Rica*] [*ICAO location identifier*] (ICLI)
MRND....... Mouvement Revolutionnaire National pour le Developpement [*National Revolutionary Movement for Development*] [*Rwanda*] [*Political party*] (PPW)
MRNJ .... Naranjo (Seveers) [*Costa Rica*] [*ICAO location identifier*] (ICLI)
MRNP .... Controlled Directional Reception Method (RU)
MRNS .... Nosara [*Costa Rica*] [*ICAO location identifier*] (ICLI)
MRO......... Interrayon Branch, Interrayon Department (RU)
Mro .... Maestro [*Master*] [*Spanish*]
MRO......... Masterton [*New Zealand*] [*Airport symbol*] (OAG)
MRO......... Medical Records Officer [*Australia*]
MRO......... Merit Review Office [*New South Wales, Australia*]
MRO......... Mistni Rada Osvetova [*Local Cultural Board*] (CZ)
MRO......... Movimiento Revolucionario Oriental [*Uruguayan Revolutionary Movement*] (LA)

MROC....... San Jose/Juan Santamaria Internacional [*Costa Rica*] [*ICAO location identifier*] (ICLI)
MROMIR ... Mroue Miroiterie
MROT .... Inter-American Regional Organization of Workers (RU)
MRP .... International Revolutionary Aid (RU)
MRP .... International Workers' Aid (RU)
MRP .... Magnetic Radio Bearing (RU)
MRP .... Magyar Radikalis Part [*Hungarian Radical Party*] (HU)
MRP .... Manufacture de Reconditionnement de Pneumatiques
MRP .... Marker Beacon Receiver (RU)
MRP .... Marla [*Australia*] [*Airport symbol*] (OAG)
MRP .... Medical Evacuation Distribution Station (RU)
MRP .... Mediterranean Regional Program
MRP .... Ministry of the Fish Industry (RU)
MRP .... Ministry of the Radiotechnical Industry, USSR (RU)
MRP .... Mobile RADAR Post
MRP .... Moscow River Steamship Line (RU)
MRP .... Mouvement Republicain Populaire [*Popular Republican Movement*] [*France*] [*Political party*] (PPE)
MRP .... Mouvement Revolutionnaire du Peuple [*Chad*] [*Political party*] (EY)
MRP .... Movimiento de la Revolucion Peruana [*Movement of the Peruvian Revolution*] (LA)
MRP .... Movimiento de Resistencia Popular [*Popular Resistance Movement*] [*Chile*] (LA)
MRP .... Movimiento Republicano Progresista [*Progressive Republican Movement*] [*Venezuela*] [*Political party*]
MRP .... Movimiento Revolucionario del Pueblo [*People's Revolutionary Movement*] [*Costa Rica*] (LA)
MRP .... Movimiento Revolucionario del Pueblo - Ixim [*People's Revolutionary Movement - Ixim*] [*Guatemala*] [*Political party*] (PD)
MRP .... Movimiento Revolucionario Pazestenssorista [*Paz Estenssoro Revolutionary Movement*] [*Bolivia*] (LA)
MRP .... Movimiento Revolucionario Popular [*Popular Revolutionary Movement*] [*Mexico*] (LA)
MRP .... Movimiento Revolucionario Popular [*Venezuela*] [*Political party*] (EY)
MRP .... Multi-Racial Party [*Zambia*] [*Political party*] (EY)
MRPA .... Punta Burica [*Costa Rica*] [*ICAO location identifier*] (ICLI)
MRPB........ Playa Blanca [*Costa Rica*] [*ICAO location identifier*] (ICLI)
MRPC....... Mouvement de Regroupement des Populations Congolaises [*Movement for the Regroupment of the Congolese People*] [*Political party*]
MRPC....... Paso Canoas [*Costa Rica*] [*ICAO location identifier*] (ICLI)
MRPD ...... Pandora [*Costa Rica*] [*ICAO location identifier*] (ICLI)
MRPE .... Palo Verde [*Costa Rica*] [*ICAO location identifier*] (ICLI)
MRPG .... Potrero Grande [*Costa Rica*] [*ICAO location identifier*] (ICLI)
Mr Ph ...... Magister der Pharmazie [*Master of Pharmacy*] [*German*]
MRPI........ Paissa [*Costa Rica*] [*ICAO location identifier*] (ICLI)
MRPJ .... Puerto Jimenez [*Costa Rica*] [*ICAO location identifier*] (ICLI)
MRPL........ Portalon [*Costa Rica*] [*ICAO location identifier*] (ICLI)
MRPM ...... Muito Reverendo Padre-Mestre [*Portuguese*]
MRPM ...... Palmar Sur [*Costa Rica*] [*ICAO location identifier*] (ICLI)
MRPN ...... Pelon Nuevo [*Costa Rica*] [*ICAO location identifier*] (ICLI)
MRPP........ Movimento Reorganizativo do Partido do Proletariado [*Movement for the Reorganization of the Proletariat Party*] [*Portuguese*] (WER)
MRPR....... Parrita [*Costa Rica*] [*ICAO location identifier*] (ICLI)
mrprof ...... Mimoradny Professor [*Associate Professor*] (CZ)
MRPS........ Paissa [*Costa Rica*] [*ICAO location identifier*] (ICLI)
MRPV ...... San Jose/Tobias Bolanos Internacional [*Costa Rica*] [*ICAO location identifier*] (ICLI)
MRQ......... Marinduque [*Philippines*] [*Airport symbol*] (OAG)
MRQP .... Quepos (La Managua) [*Costa Rica*] [*ICAO location identifier*] (ICLI)
MRR .... Macara [*Ecuador*] [*Airport symbol*] (OAG)
MRR .... Matthey Rustenburg Refiners [*South Africa*]
MRR .... Motorized Rifle Regiment [*Former USSR*]
MRR .... Movimento de Resistencia Republicana
MRR .... Movimento de Resistencia Revolucionaria [*Revolutionary Resistance Movement*] [*Brazil*] (LA)
MRRDB .... Malaysian Rubber Research and Development Board [*Research center*] (IRC)
MRRF........ Rio Frio O Progreso [*Costa Rica*] [*ICAO location identifier*] (ICLI)
MRRM ...... Rancho Del Mar [*Costa Rica*] [*ICAO location identifier*] (ICLI)
MRRN ...... Rancho Nuevo [*Costa Rica*] [*ICAO location identifier*] (ICLI)
MRRS .... Mortgage and Rent Relief Scheme [*Australia*]
MRRTA..... Long-Distance Radio-Relay Television Control Room (RU)
MRRTC..... Maligaya Rice Research and Training Center of the Philippines (IRC)
MRRX .... Roxana Farms [*Costa Rica*] [*ICAO location identifier*] (ICLI)
MRS .... Airline of the Marshall Islands [*ICAO designator*] (FAAC)
MRS .... Hungarian Badminton Association (EAIO)
MRS .... Machine Repair Station (RU)

mrs	Maravedises [*Old Spanish Coins*] [*Spanish*]
MRS	Marseille [*France*] [*Airport symbol*] (OAG)
mrs	Martires [*Martyrs*] [*Spanish*]
MRS	Mastectomy Rehabilitation Service [*Australia*]
MRS	Mechanized Fishing Station (RU)
MRS	Medical Reception Station [*Military*]
MRS	Mehrrechnersystem [*German*] (ADPT)
MRS	Mine-Detecting Service (RU)
Mrs	Moerser [*Mortar*] [*German*] (EG)
MRS	Motorized Fishing Station (RU)
MRS	Mouvement Republicain Senegalais [*Senegalese Republican Movement*] [*Political party*] (PPW)
MRS	Movimento Renovador Sindical [*Union Renewal Movement*] [*Brazil*] (LA)
MRS	Movimiento Reformista Salvadoreno [*Salvadoran Reformist Movement*] (LA)
MRS	Small Fishing Seiner (RU)
MRS	Speed Control Mechanism (RU)
MRSA	Market Research Society of Australia (ADA)
MRSA	San Alberto [*Costa Rica*] [*ICAO location identifier*] (ICLI)
MRSB	San Cristobal [*Costa Rica*] [*ICAO location identifier*] (ICLI)
MRSC	Santa Cruz [*Costa Rica*] [*ICAO location identifier*] (ICLI)
MRSG	Santa Clara De Guapiles [*Costa Rica*] [*ICAO location identifier*] (ICLI)
MRSh	Meridional Difference of Latitute (RU)
MRSH	Shiroles [*Costa Rica*] [*ICAO location identifier*] (ICLI)
MRSI	San Isidro De El General [*Costa Rica*] [*ICAO location identifier*] (ICLI)
MRSJ	San Jose [*Costa Rica*] [*ICAO location identifier*] (ICLI)
Mrsl	Maresal [*Marshal*] (TU)
MRSL	Member of the Republic of Sierra Leone
MRSM	Mongolian Revolutionary Youth League (RU)
MRSM	Mouvement du Renouveau Social Malgache
MRSM	Santa Marta [*Costa Rica*] [*ICAO location identifier*] (ICLI)
MRSN	Sirena [*Costa Rica*] [*ICAO location identifier*] (ICLI)
MRSO	Mining Research and Service Organization [*Taiwanese*] [*Research center*] (IRC)
MRSO	Santa Maria De Guacimo [*Costa Rica*] [*ICAO location identifier*] (ICLI)
MRSP	San Pedro [*Costa Rica*] [*ICAO location identifier*] (ICLI)
MRSR	Samara [*Costa Rica*] [*ICAO location identifier*] (ICLI)
MRSS	San Joaquin de Abangares [*Costa Rica*] [*ICAO location identifier*] (ICLI)
MR SSSR	Maritime Register of the USSR (RU)
MRST	San Agustin [*Costa Rica*] [*ICAO location identifier*] (ICLI)
MRSV	San Vito De Jaba [*Costa Rica*] [*ICAO location identifier*] (ICLI)
MRSX	Sixaola [*Costa Rica*] [*ICAO location identifier*] (ICLI)
MRSZ	Magyar Repulo Szovetseg [*Hungarian Aviation Association*] (HU)
MRT	Air Mauritanie [*Mauritania*] [*ICAO designator*] (FAAC)
mrt	Maart [*March*] [*Netherlands*] (GPO)
MRT	Magyar Radio es Televizio Vallalat [*Hungarian Radio and Television Enterprise*] (HU)
MRT	Makedonski Revolucionarni Teroristi [*Macedonian Revolutionary Terrorists*] (YU)
MRT	Mass Rapid Transit [*Singapore*] (FEA)
MRT	Mauritania [*ANSI three-letter standard code*] (CNC)
MRT	Miedzynarodowy Rajd Tatrzanski [*International Tatra Mountains Rally*] [*Poland*]
MRT	Ministere de la Recherche et de la Technologie [*French*]
MRT	Mirage Resorts Trust [*Australia*]
MRT	Moscow Revolutionary Tribunal (RU)
MRT	Mouvement Revolutionnaire Tchadien
MRT	Movimento Revolucionario Tiradentes [*Revolutionary Tiradentes Movement*] [*Brazil*] [*Political party*] (PD)
MRT	Small Fishing Trawler (RU)
MRTA	Movimiento Revolucionario Tupac Amaru [*Peru*] [*Political party*] (EY)
MRTA	Tamarindo de Bagaces [*Costa Rica*] [*ICAO location identifier*] (ICLI)
MRTB	Medical Radiological Technicians Belgium (EAIO)
MRTB	Movimiento Revolucionario de los Trabajadores Bolivianos [*Revolutionary Movement of Bolivian Workers*] (LA)
MRTB	Ticaban [*Costa Rica*] [*ICAO location identifier*] (ICLI)
MRTG	Taboga [*Costa Rica*] [*ICAO location identifier*] (ICLI)
MRTK	Movimiento Revolucionario Tupaj Katari [*Tupaj Katari Revolutionary Movement*] [*Bolivia*] [*Political party*] (PPW)
MRTM	Tamarindo de Santa Cruz [*Costa Rica*] [*ICAO location identifier*] (ICLI)
MRTO	International Workers' Theatrical Association (RU)
MRTO	Small Fishing Trawler with Refrigerated Holds (RU)
MRTP	Master of Regional and Town Planning
MRTP	Ministry of the Radiotechnical Industry, USSR (RU)
MRTP	Monopolies and Restrictive Trade Practices [*Act*] [*India*]
MRTP	Monopolies and Restrictive Trade Practices Act [*1969*] [*India*]

MRTPC	Monopolies and Restrictive Trade Practices Commission [*India*] (PDAA)
MRTR	Tambor [*Costa Rica*] [*ICAO location identifier*] (ICLI)
MRTs	Route Control Interlocking System [*Railroads*] (RU)
MRTU	Interrepublic Technical Specifications (RU)
MRTU	Moscow Radiotechnical Administration (RU)
MRTU	Moscow Radio Wire Broadcasting Center (RU)
MRU	Interrayon Center [*Telephony*] (RU)
MRU	Mano River Union [*See also UFM*] (EAIO)
MRU	Mauritius [*Airport symbol*] (OAG)
MRU	Ministere de la Reconstruction et de l'Urbanisme [*France*] (FLAF)
MRUP	Upala [*Costa Rica*] [*ICAO location identifier*] (ICLI)
MRV	Diaphragm Control Valve (RU)
MRV	Mercury-Water Gauge (RU)
MRV	Mineral Nyye Vody [*Former USSR*] [*Airport symbol*] (OAG)
MRV	Mouvement de Regroupement Voltaique [*Upper Volta Regroupment Movement*] [*Political party*]
MRW	Morioka [*Japan*] [*Airport symbol*] (OAG)
MRW	Motor- en Rijwielwet [*Benelux*] (BAS)
MRwCz	Muzeum Regionalne w Czestochowie [*Czestochowa Regional Museum*] (POL)
MRZ	Frost Resistance (RU)
MRZ	Metal Lattice Lagging [*Mining*] (RU)
MRZ	Moree [*Australia*] [*Airport symbol*] (OAG)
MRZ	Motor Repair Plant (RU)
MRZhK	Interrayon Livestock-Breeding Office (RU)
MRZP	Zapotal De Guanacaste [*Costa Rica*] [*ICAO location identifier*] (ICLI)
MS	Aircraft Position [*In flight*] (RU)
MS	Booby Trap (RU)
MS	Comparison Microscope (RU)
MS	Council of Ministers (BU)
MS	International Court of the United Nations (RU)
MS	Interplanetary Station (RU)
MS	Lubricating Oil (RU)
MS	Maandblad N. Samson NV Gewijd aan de Belangen der Gemeenteadministratie [*Benelux*] (BAS)
m/s	Maande na Sig [*Afrikaans*]
MS	Maatregel Schepen [*Benelux*] (BAS)
MS	Magnetstreifen [*German*] (ADPT)
MS	Magyar Szallodaszovetseg [*Hungary*] (EAIO)
ms	Mais [*More*] [*Portuguese*]
MS	Makrosprache [*German*] (ADPT)
MS	Manoscritto [*Manuscript*] [*Italian*]
MS	Mano Sinistra [*With the Left Hand*] [*Music*]
MS	Manuscrit [*Manuscript*] [*French*]
ms	Manuscrito [*Manuscript*] [*Portuguese*]
MS	Manuscrito [*Manuscript*] [*Spanish*]
Ms	Manuskrip [*Manuscript*] [*Afrikaans*]
Ms	Manuskript [*Manuscript*] [*German*] (EG)
ms	Manuskript [*Manuscript*] [*Danish/Norwegian*]
Ms	Marais [*Swamp*] [*Military map abbreviation World War I*] [*French*] (MTD)
Ms	Marcos [*Marks*] [*Spanish*]
MS	Marxistischer Studentenbund [*Marxist Student Federation*] (WEN)
MS	Masinska Radionica [*Machine Shop*] (YU)
MS	Massa [*Car registration plates*] [*Italian*]
MS	Mass Spectrometer (RU)
MS	Mastere Specialise [*French*]
MS	Matica Slovenska [*Slovenian Literary Society*] [*Ljubljana*] (YU)
MS	Matica Srpska [*Serbian Literary and Publishing Society*] [*Novi Sad*] (YU)
MS	Mechanization of Construction (RU)
MS	Mechanized Unit [*Military*] (RU)
MS	Medical Department [*of naval ship*], Medical Service (RU)
m/s	Medical Service (BU)
MS	Mellemfolkeligt Samvivke [*Danish Association for International Cooperation*] (EAIO)
MS	Mesi Sykhnotis [*Medium Frequency*] (GC)
MS	Metal Sarajevo [*Wholesale Metallurgical Trade Establishment, Sarajevo*] (YU)
MS	Metals Society [*Later, IOM*] (EAIO)
m/s	Meter je Sekunde [*Meters per Second*] (EG)
MS	Methylene Blue (RU)
m/s	Metro por Segundo [*Meters per Second*] [*Portuguese*]
MS	Mezzo Soprano [*Music*] (ROG)
MS	Milattan Sonra [*In the Year of Our Lord*] (TU)
MS	Millisekunde [*German*] (ADPT)
MS	Ministarstvo Saobracaja [*Ministry of Transportation*] (YU)
MS	Ministerio da Saude [*Ministry of Health*] [*Portuguese*]
MS	Ministerstvo Skolstvi [*Ministry of Education*] (CZ)
MS	Ministerstvo Spoju [*Ministry of Communications*] (CZ)
MS	Ministerstvo Spravedlnosti [*Ministry of Justice*] (CZ)
MS	Ministerstvo Stavebnictvi [*Ministry of Building*] (CZ)

MS .... Ministerstvo Strojirenstvi [*Ministry of the Machine Building Industry*] (CZ)
MS .... Ministerstwo Skupu [*Ministry of Procurement*] (POL)
MS .... Ministerstwo Sprawiedliwosci [*Ministry of Justice*] (POL)
MS .... Ministerul Sanatatii [*Ministry of Health*] (RO)
MS .... Ministry of Communications (RU)
MS .... Ministry of Construction (RU)
MS .... Ministry of Sovkhozes (RU)
MS .... Missionary Society
MS .... Missions to Seamen (EA)
MS .... Mistni Skupina [*Local Group*] (CZ)
MS .... Mittelsatz [*Middle Movement*] [*Music*]
MS .... Mittelschule [*Middle School*] [*German*]
ms .... Moins [*Less*] [*French*]
MS .... Molecular Sieve (RU)
MS .... Montserrat [*ANSI two-letter standard code*] (CNC)
MS .... Moscow Soviet of Workers', Peasants', and Red Army Deputies (RU)
ms .... Motorized Unit [*Military*] (RU)
ms .... Motorskip [*Motorboat*] [*Afrikaans*]
MS .... Moulins Sentenac [*Senegal*]
MS .... Musikschule [*Music School*] [*German*]
MS .... Mutation Spectrum (RU)
MS .... Mutuo Soccorso [*Mutual Aid*] [*Italian*]
MS .... Navy, Naval Forces (RU)
m/s .... Nurse (RU)
MS .... Parking Place [*Of aircraft*] (RU)
MS .... Screw Cap (RU)
MS .... Weather Service, Meteorological Service (RU)
MS .... Youth Union (BU)
MS .... Zeme Moravskoslezska [*Province (Land) of Moravia and Silesia*] (CZ)
MSA .... International Council on Archives [*ICA*] (RU)
MSA .... International Sociological Association [*ISA*] (RU)
MSA .... International Standard Atmosphere (RU)
MSA .... International Union of Architects (RU)
MSA .... Malacological Society of Australia (ADA)
MSA .... Malaysia-Singapore Airlines
MSA .... Management Selection Australia Proprietary Ltd. (ADA)
MSA .... Marine Stewards' Association [*Australia*]
MSA .... Maritime Safety Agent [*Japan*]
MSA .... Mauritius Sports Association
MSA .... Medical Scientists' Association [*Australia*]
MSA .... Medical Services Adviser [*Australia*]
MSA .... Medical Systems Association [*South Africa*] (AA)
MSA .... Mercury Singapore Airlines
MSA .... Ministry of Construction and Architecture [*Obsolete*] (BU)
MSA .... Mistral Air SRL [*Italy*] [*ICAO designator*] (FAAC)
MSA .... Monstakas Shipping Agencies Ltd. [*Cyprus*]
MSA .... Mouvement Socialiste Africain [*African Socialist Movement*] [*Political party*]
MSA .... Movimento dei Socialisti Autonomi [*Movement of Autonomous Socialists*] [*Italian*] (WER)
MSA .... Movimento Separatista Angolano
MSA .... Movimiento Socialista Andaluz [*Andalusian Socialist Movement*] [*Spanish*] (WER)
MSA .... Municipal Saleyards Association [*Victoria, Australia*]
MSA .... Musicological Society of Australia
MSA .... Mutual Security Agency [*Functions transferred to Foreign Operations Administration, 1953*]
MSAA ...... Membrane Structures Association of Australasia
MSAA .... Mower Specialists Association of Australia (ADA)
MSAAC..... Mower Specialists' Association of Australia Cooperative
MSAAIE ... Member of the South African Association of Industrial Editors (AA)
MSAARET ... Member of the South African Association of Registrable Engineering Technologists (AA)
MSAC........ Sonsonate/Acajutla [*El Salvador*] [*ICAO location identifier*] (ICLI)
MsaChemI ... Member of the South African Chemical Institute (AA)
MSACONSE ... Member of the South African Association of Consulting Engineers (AA)
MSACORRI ... Member of the South African Corrosion Institute (AA)
MSACPS... Member of the South African Coal Processing Society (AA)
MSAE........ Member of the Society of Automotive Engineers, Australasia (ADA)
MSAE-A.... Member of the Society of Automotive Engineers - Australasia
MSAFHE ... Member of the South African Federation of Hospital Engineering (AA)
MSAIA...... Member of the South African Institute of Auctioneers (AA)
MSAIAA ... Member of the South African Institute of Assayers and Analysts (AA)
MSAIB ...... Member of the South African Institute of Building (AA)
MSAICHE ... Member of the South African Institution of Chemical Engineers (AA)
MSAID...... Member of the South African Institute of Draughtsmen (AA)

MSAIE ...... Member of the South African Institute of Ecologists (AA)
MSAIEE ... Member of the South African Institute of Electrical Engineers (AA)
MSAIETE ... Member of the South African Institute of Electrical Technician Engineers (AA)
MSAIM..... Member of the South African Institute of Management (AA)
MSAIMARENA ... Member of the South African Institute of Marine Engineers and Naval Architects (AA)
MSAIMECHE ... Member of the South African Institute of Mechanical Engineers (AA)
MSAITINT ... Member of the South African Institute of Translators and Interpreters (AA)
MSAITRp ... Member of the South African Institute of Town and Regional Planners (AA)
MSAIW..... Member of the South African Institute of Welding (AA)
MSAN .... Morfotikoi Syllogoi Agrotikis Neolaias [*Agricultural Youth Educational Associations*] [*Greek*] (GC)
MS & LR ... Manchester, Sheffield & Lincolnshire Railway [*Later, Great Central*] [*British*] (ROG)
MSANO.... Ministerstvo Skolstvi a Narodni Osvety [*Ministry of Education and Culture*] (CZ)
MSAR........ Mouvement Solidarite Anti-Repression [*Solidarity and Anti-Repression Movement*] [*Mauritius*] (AF)
MSAS....... Malaysia Singapore Australia Society
ms as .... Muchos Anos [*Spanish*]
MSAS....... Musicians and Singers Association of Singapore (EAIO)
MSAS........ Slow Anticoincidence and Coincidence Circuit (RU)
MSAT....... International Road Transport Union [*IRU*] (RU)
MSAT....... Mutuelles Senegalaises d'Assurances des Transporteurs
MSAUD .... Muslim Students Association of the University of Dar Es Salaam
MSAV....... Medical Scientists' Association of Victoria [*Australia*]
MSAVP.... Moravsko-Slezska Akademie Ved Prirodnich [*Moravian and Silesian Academy of Natural Sciences*] (CZ)
MSB.......... Battalion Medical Service (BU)
msb............ Bridge Construction Battalion (RU)
MSB.......... International Socialist Bureau [*1900-1914*] (RU)
MSB.......... Machine Computation Office, Machine Calculating Office (RU)
MSB.......... Malaysian Special Branch (ML)
MSB.......... Maritime Safety Board [*Japan*]
MSB.......... Marxistischer Studentenbund [*Marxist Student Federation*] [*Austrian, West German*] (WEN)
MSB.......... Mededelingen van de Schoolraad voor de Scholen met de Bijbel [*Benelux*] (BAS)
MSB.......... Medical Battalion (RU)
MSB.......... Medicisko-Sanitetski Bataljoni [*Medical Hygiene Battalions*] (YU)
MSB.......... Medium Naval Bomber (RU)
MSB.......... Metal Dry-Cargo Barge (RU)
MSB.......... Milli Savunma Bakanligi [*National Defense Ministry*] [*MMV*] [*See also*] (TU)
msb............ Millistilb (RU)
MSB.......... Mine Subsidence Board [*New South Wales, Australia*]
msb............ Motorized Rifle Battalion (BU)
MSB.......... Motorized Rifle Brigade (RU)
MSB.......... Movimiento Sindical de Base [*Rank and File Labor Union Movement*] [*Argentina*] (LA)
MSB.......... Movimiento Socialista de Baleares [*Socialist Movement of the Balearic Islands*] [*Spanish*] (WER)
MSBIA ...... Member of Spa Bath Industry of Australia
MSBM....... Baltic Sea Naval Forces (RU)
MSBNSW ... Maritime Services Board of New South Wales [*Australia*]
MSBS........ Mer-Sol Balistique Strategique [*French submarine nuclear delivery system*]
MSC .... Maharashtra Socialist Congress [*India*] [*Political party*] (PPW)
MSC .... Malayan Service Corps (ML)
MSC .... Malaysian Solidarity Convention (ML)
MSC .... Maori Spiritualist Church [*New Zealand*]
MSC .... Marine Steering Committee [*IUCN*] (ASF)
MSC .... Maritime Safety Committee [*Advisory Committee on Pollution of the Sea*]
MSC .... Marquise [*Marchioness*] [*French*] (ROG)
MSc .... Master of Science (PWGL)
MSC .... Mediterranean Shipping Company
MSC .... Mediterranean Society of Chemotherapy (EAIO)
MSC .... Mediterranean Sub-Commission [*FAO*]
MSC .... Melbourne State College [*Australia*]
MSC .... Methylamines Sector Group [*Belgium*] (EAIO)
MSC .... Microcomputer Sound Club [*France*] (EAIO)
MSC .... Military Staff Committee [*United Nations*] (DLA)
MSC .... Minsk Strike Committee [*Byelorussia*] (EE)
MSC .... Moscow Airways [*Russian Federation*] [*ICAO designator*] (FAAC)
MSC .... Movimiento Socialista Catalan [*Catalan Socialist Movement*] [*Spanish*] (WER)
MSC .... Movimiento Socialista Colombiano [*Colombian Socialist Movement*] (LA)

MSC .... Muslim Supreme Council [*Uganda*]   (AF)
MSCAT ..... Minesweeper Catamaran [*Military*]
ms ch .... Bridge Unit   (BU)
MSCh .... Medical Unit   (RU)
MSCh .... Modified Gray Iron   (RU)
M Sch G ..... Markscheidegeraet [*Inclinometer*] [*German*]   (GCA)
MSChM .... Black Sea Naval Forces   (RU)
MSChPF ... International Union of Pure and Applied Physics [*IUPAP*]   (RU)
Mschr .... Monatsschrift [*Monthly Magazine*] [*German*]
MSChV ..... International Union of Private Railway Truck Owners'
             Associations   (RU)
MSCI .... Madrid Stock-Exchange Index [*Spain*]   (ECON)
MSCI .... Medical Services Committee of Inquiry [*Australia*]
MSCP .... Mesic Sovetsko-Ceskoslovenskeho Pratelstvi [*Soviet-
             Czechoslovak Friendship Month*]   (CZ)
MSCTDC .. Maharashtra State Cooperative Tribal Development Corp.
             [*India*]   (PDAA)
MSCX .... Maharashtra Sub-Contract Exchange [*Ministry of Industrial
             Development*] [*India*]
MSD .... Doctor Medicinae Scientariae [*Doctor of Scientific Medicine*]
             (CZ)
MSD .... Masarykuv Studentsky Domov [*Masaryk Students' Home*]   (CZ)
MSD .... Medical Battalion   (RU)
MSD .... Merck, Sharp & Dohme [*Australia*] Proprietary Ltd.   (ADA)
MSD .... Mines Safety Department [*Zambia*] [*Research center*]   (IRC)
MSD .... Minimal Lethal Dose   (RU)
MSD .... Motorized Rifle Division   (RU)
MSD .... Motostrelecka Divize [*Motorized Rifle Division*]   (CZ)
MSD .... Movimento Social Democrata [*Social Democrat Movement*]
             [*Portugal*] [*Political party*]   (PPE)
MSD .... Movimiento Social Democratico [*Social Democratic Movement*]
             [*Peru*]   (LA)
MSDC .... Movimiento Social Democrata Cristiano [*Christian Social
             Democrat Movement*] [*Paraguay*]   (LA)
MSDF .... Maritime Self-Defense Force [*Japan*]
MSDM ...... Ministry of Construction and Road Machinery Manufacture,
             USSR   (RU)
MSDP .... Mauritian Social Democratic Party
MSDP .... Mezinarodni Sdruzeni Demokratickych Pravniku [*International
             Association of Democratic Lawyers*]   (CZ)
ms dr .... Bridge Battalion   (BU)
MSDR .... Ministry of Supply and State Reserves   (BU)
MSDV .... Far Eastern Naval Forces   (RU)
MSE .... International Telecommunications Union [*ITU*]   (RU)
MSE .... Maandblad voor Sociaal Econ.- Wetenschappen [*Benelux*]
             (BAS)
MSE .... Mexican Stock Exchange   (MHDW)
MSE .... Monimoi Synodikai Epitropai [*Permanent Synodical
             Committees*] [*Greek*]   (GC)
MSE .... Movimiento Socialista Espanol [*Spanish Socialist Movement*]
             (WER)
MSE .... Mtibwa Sugar Estate Ltd.
MSEB .... Maharashtra State Electricity Board [*India*]   (PDAA)
m/sek .... Meter pro Sekunde [*Meters per Second*]   (EG)
msec .... Millisecond   (RU)
MSES .... Ministry of Construction of Electric Power Plants, USSR   (RU)
ms es .... Naval Squadron   (BU)
MSEUE ..... Mouvement Socialiste pour les Etats-Unies d'Europe [*Political
             party*]   (FLAF)
MSF .... Market Support Fund [*Australia*]
MSF .... Max Sea Food SA de CV [*El Salvador*] [*ICAO designator*]
             (FAAC)
MSF .... Medecins sans Frontieres [*Doctors without Borders - DWB*]
             [*France*]   (EAIO)
Msf. .... Mesafe [*Distance, Distant*]   (TU)
MSF .... Mouvement Sioniste de France   (BJA)
MSF .... Multilateral Scientific Fund
MSFK .... Moscow Union of Physical Culture   (RU)
MSFN .... Multipel Sklerose Forbundet i Norge [*Norway*]   (EAIO)
MSFNRJ... Ministarstvo Saobracaja Federativne Narodne Republike
             Jugoslavije [*Ministry of Transportation of the Federal
             People's Republic of Yugoslavia*]   (YU)
MSFNRJ... Muzejski Savet Federativna Narodna Republika Jugoslavija
             [*Museum Council of Yugoslavia*]   (YU)
MSFTS ..... Moscow Social Fund - Transportation Safety [*An association*]
             [*Commonwealth of Independent States*]   (EAIO)
MSG .... Maitrise de Sciences de Gestion [*French*]
MSG .... Makerere Students' Guild [*Uganda*]   (AF)
MSG .... Melanocyte-Stimulating Hormone   (RU)
MSG .... Merchant Service Guild of Australia
MSG .... Movimiento Socialista de Galicia [*Socialist Movement of
             Galicia*] [*Spanish*]   (WER)
MSG .... Movimiento Socialista Guineano [*Guinean Socialist Movement*]
MSGA .... Merchant Service Guild of Australia
MSGB .... Manorial Society of Great Britain   (EAIO)
MSGG .... International Union of Geodesy and Geophysics [*IUGG*]   (RU)

MSGNRM ... Ministarstvo za Socijalni Grizi na Narodnata Republika
             Makedonija [*Ministry of Social Assistance of Macedonia*]
             (YU)
Msgr .... Monsignore
MSGV .... International (Railway) Wagon Union   (RU)
MSH .... Maandblad voor Studeerenden in de Handels-Wetenschappen
             [*Benelux*]   (BAS)
MSH .... Ministerstvo Stavebnich Hmot [*Ministry of Building Materials*]
             (CZ)
MSh .... Nautical School   (RU)
MSh .... Naval Staff   (RU)
MSh .... Small Demolition Charge   (RU)
MShchU .... Local Control Board   (RU)
MShI .... Magnet of Step-by-Step Switch   (RU)
MSHR .... Missionary Sisters of Our Lady of the Holy Rosary [*Blackrock,
             County Dublin, Republic of Ireland*]   (EAIO)
MShT .... International Temperature Scale   (RU)
MShU .... Low-Noise Amplifier   (RU)
MShZ .... Moscow Tire Plant   (RU)
MSI .... Maintenance Supply Item
MSI .... Marine Science Institute [*Philippines*]   (IRC)
MSI .... Medunarodni Statisticki Institut [*International Statistical
             Institute*]   (YU)
MSI .... Moscow Institute of Sanitation   (RU)
MSI .... Mouvement Sociologique International
MSI .... Movimento Sociale Italiano [*Italian Social Movement*] [*Political
             party*]   (PPE)
MSI .... Second Independence Movement [*Ecuador*] [*Political party*]
             (PPW)
MSIA .... Member of the Safety Institute of Australia   (ADA)
MSIA .... Member of the Securities Institute of Australia
MSiDM ..... Ministry of Construction and Road Machinery Manufacture,
             USSR   (RU)
MSI-DN .... Movimento Sociale Italiano-Destra Nazionale [*Italian Social
             Movement-National Right*] [*Political party*]   (EY)
MSiIP .... Ministry of the Machine Tool and Tool Industry, USSR   (RU)
MSIM .... International Council for the Exploration of the Sea [*ICES*]
             (RU)
msin .... Magasin [*Store*] [*French*]
MSIP .... Ministry of the Machine Tool and Tool Industry, USSR   (RU)
MSIRI .... Mauritius Sugar Industry Research Institute   (AF)
MSJ .... Membrane Society of Japan   (EAIO)
MSJ .... Misawa [*Japan*] [*Airport symbol*]   (OAG)
MSK .... Card-Sorting Magnet   (RU)
MSK .... Dobrovol'noye Obshchestvo Moskovskiy Studencheskiy Klub
             [*Voluntary Society Moscow Student Club*] [*Commonwealth
             of Independent States*]   (EAIO)
MSK .... International Skating Union [*ISU*]   (RU)
MSK .... International Students' Conference   (BU)
MSK .... International Union of Crystallography [*IUCr*]   (RU)
MSK .... Local Scholarship Commission   (RU)
MSK .... Maritime Signal Book, Maritime Signal Code   (RU)
MSK .... Marketing Society of Kenya
MSK .... Masarykova Studentska Kolej [*Masaryk Students' Home*]   (CZ)
MSK .... Medical Team   (RU)
MSK .... Mistni Spravni Komise [*Local Administrative Commission*]
             (CZ)
MSK .... Mitsubishi Shoje Kaisha [*Japan*]   (PDAA)
MSK .... Mobile Construction Crane   (RU)
MSK .... Mobile Folding Crane   (RU)
MSK .... Moscow Time   (RU)
MSKh .... Freewheeling Mechanism   (RU)
MSKh .... Ministerstvo Sel'Skogo Khozyaistva Ministry of Agriculture
             [*Former USSR*]   (DSCA)
MSKh .... Ministry of Agriculture   (RU)
MSKhA ..... Moscow Agricultural Academy Imeni K. A. Timiryazev   (RU)
MSKhI ...... Moscow Agricultural Institute   (RU)
MSKhM .... Ministry of Agricultural Machinery Manufacture, USSR   (RU)
M-ski suv... Council of Ministers   (BU)
MSKP .... Maritime Disease Control Point   (RU)
Mskr .... Manuskript [*Manuscript*] [*German*]   (EG)
mskript....... Manuskript [*Manuscript*] [*Danish/Norwegian*]
MSKRP .... International Special Committee on Radio Interference   (RU)
MSL .... Measurement Specialities Ltd. [*Hong Kong*]
msl .... Mesela [*For Example*] [*Turkey*]   (GPO)
MSL .... Meson Science Laboratory [*Japan*]   (WND)
msl .... Mimo Sluzbu [*Retired, Inactive*]   (CZ)
MSL .... Mouvement des Sociaux-Liberaux [*Movement of Social Liberals*]
             [*France*] [*Political party*]   (PPW)
MSL .... Movimento Separatista Lusitano
MSI .... Muzeum Slaskie [*Silesian Museum*]   (POL)
MSL .... Small Collapsible Boat   (RU)
MSLA .... Missionary Sisters of Our Lady of the Angels [*Lennoxville, PQ*]
             (EAIO)
MSLP .... Malawi Socialist Labour Party [*Political party*]   (EY)

MSLP .... San Salvador/El Salvador Internacional [*El Salvador*] [*ICAO location identifier*] (ICLI)
MSM .... Maastricht School of Management [*Netherlands*]
MSM .... Mauritian Socialist Movement [*Political party*]
MSM .... Men Who Have Sex with Men [*Australia*] [*An association*]
MSM .... Mezinarodni Svaz Mladeze [*International Union of Youth*] (CZ)
MSM .... Ministry of Medium Machinery Manufacture (RU)
MSM .... Mouvement Social du Maniema
MSM .... Mouvement Socialiste Malgache [*Malagasy Socialist Movement*] (AF)
MSM .... Mouvement Socialiste Mauricien [*Mauritius Socialist Movement*] (AF)
MSM .... Mouvement Social Mohutu [*Mohutu Social Movement*]
MSM .... Mouvement Social Muhutu [*Hutu Social Movement*] [*Rwanda*] (AF)
MSM .... Mouvement Solidaire Muluba [*Muluba Solidarity Movement*] [*Political party*]
MSMA ...... Meteorological Services to Marine Activities [*WMO*] (MSC)
MSMAV.... Master Stone Masons' Association of Victoria [*Australia*]
MSMB....... Mortgage Secondary Market Board [*Australia*]
MSMC ...... Migrant Studies and Media Center [*Australia*]
MSMO...... International Union of Railway Medical Services (RU)
MSMPVO ... Medical Service of the Local Antiaircraft Defense (RU)
MSMS....... International Union of Socialist Youth [*IUSY*] (RU)
MSN .... Movimiento de Salvacion Nacional [*National Salvation Movement*] [*Nicaragua*] (LA)
MSN .... Movimiento de Salvacion Nacional [*National Salvation Movement*] [*Colorado*] [*Political party*] (EY)
MSND....... Mouvement Social pour la Nouvelle Democratie [*Cameroon*] [*Political party*] (EY)
MS-NK...... Matica Slovenska, Narodna Kniznica [*Matica Slovenska, National Library*] (CZ)
MSNK .... Small Council of People's Commissars [*1921-1930*] [*RSFSR*] (RU)
MSNKh ..... Moscow Council of the National Economy (RU)
MSNRM ... Ministerstvo za Sumarstvo na Narodnata Republika Makedonija [*Ministry of Forestry of Macedonia*] (YU)
MSNS....... International Council of Scientific Unions [*ICSU*] (RU)
MSO .... Inter-American Defense Board [*IADB*] (RU)
MSO .... Interkolkhoz Construction Organization (RU)
MSO .... International Economic Organizations (BU)
MSO .... International Tin Council [*ITC*] (RU)
MSO .... Local Construction Trust (BU)
MSO .... Malaysian Students' Organization [*Australia*]
MSO .... Medical Detachment (RU)
MSO .... Medical Section [*Military*] (RU)
MSO .... Mezinarodni Svaz Odborovy [*International Trade Union Federation*] (CZ)
MSO .... Ministerstvo Skolstvi a Osvety [*Ministry of Education and Culture*] (CZ)
MSO .... Ministry of Social Security (RU)
MSO .... Misto Specielni Ocisty [*Special Decontamination Point*] (CZ)
MSO .... Moulin du Sud-Ouest
MSO .... Mouvement Socialiste Occitan [*Occitanian Socialist Movement*] [*France*] [*Political party*] (PPE)
MSO .... Mozambique Solidarity Office (EA)
MSOA ...... Mine Surface Officials' Association of South Africa (AA)
MSOC ...... Maritime Sector Operations Center [*NATO*] (NATG)
MSocPol... Master of Social Policy
MSocSt...... Master of Social Studies
MSOF........ Fleet Medical Department (RU)
MSOGVD ... Local Council for Social Welfare and Children's Education (BU)
MSOH....... Members, Senators, and Office Holders [*Commonwealth Parliament*] [*Australia*]
Mson.......... Maison [*House, Firm*] [*Business term*] [*French*]
MSOP ...... International Union for the Protection of Nature [*IUPN*] (RU)
MSOS....... Meziministersky Sbor Obrany Statu [*Interdepartmental Committee for National Defense*] (CZ)
MSOT ...... International Union of Public Transport (RU)
MSOT ...... Magyar Sportorvosi Tanacs [*Hungarian Council of Sports Physicians*] (HU)
MSOTO .... International Union of Official Travel Organizations [*IUOTO*] (RU)
MSP.......... International Trade-Union Secretariat (RU)
MSP.......... Malacological Society of the Philippines (EAIO)
MSP.......... Manufacture Senegalaise de Papiers Transformes
MSP.......... Maximum Silo Price [*Farming terminology*]
MSP.......... Melanesian Soap Products Ltd. [*Papua New Guinea*]
m sp.......... Methyl Alcohol (RU)
MSP.......... Milli Selamet Partisi [*National Salvation Party*] (TU)
MSP.......... Ministerio de Salud Publica [*Ministry of Public Health*] [*Uruguay*] (LA)
MSP.......... Ministerstvo Socialni Pece [*Ministry of Social Welfare*] (CZ)
MSP.......... Ministerstvo Spotrebniho Prumyslu [*Ministry of Consumer Industry*] (CZ)

MSP.......... Ministerstvo Stavebniho Prumyslu [*Ministry of the Building Industry*] (CZ)
MSP.......... Ministry of Construction and Roads [*Obsolete*] (BU)
MSP.......... Ministry of the Machine Tool Industry, USSR (RU)
MSP.......... Ministry of the Shipbuilding Industry, USSR (RU)
MSP.......... Moderata Samlingspartiet [*Moderate Unity Party*] [*Sweden*] [*Political party*] (PPE)
MSP.......... Motorized Rifle Regiment (RU)
MSP.......... Motostrelecky Pluk [*Motorized Rifle Regiment*] (CZ)
MSP.......... Movimento Socialista Popular [*Popular Socialist Movement*] [*Portugal*] [*Political party*] (PPE)
MSP.......... Movimiento Sindical Peronista [*Peronist Union Movement*] [*Argentina*] (LA)
MSP.......... Servicio de Vigilancia Aerea del Ministerio de Seguridad Publica [*Costa Rica*] [*ICAO designator*] (FAAC)
MSPA....... Mauritius Sugar Producers Association (AF)
MSPA....... Mineral Sands Producers' Association [*Australia*]
MSPADD ... Mauritius Society for the Prevention of Alcohol and Drug Dependency (AF)
MSPAW.... Miedzynarodowe Stowarzyszenie Przyjaciele Angkor Wat [*International Association of Friends of Angkor Wat*] [*Multinational association based in Poland*] (EAIO)
MSPCA..... Mauritius Society for the Prevention of Cruelty to Animals
MSPD....... International Union for Child Welfare [*IUCW*] (RU)
MSPD....... Machine for Hoisting Operations (RU)
MSPD....... Mulheres Portuguesas Social-Democratas [*An association*] (EAIO)
MSpecEd ... Master of Special Education
MSpEd ...... Master of Special Education
MSPM....... Ministry of Construction of Machinery-Manufacturing Establishments, USSR (RU)
MSPMKhP ... Ministry of Construction of Establishments of the Metallurgical and Chemical Industries, USSR (RU)
MSPNP..... Ministry of Construction of Petroleum Industry Establishments, USSR (RU)
MSPO .... Moscow Union of Consumers' Societies (RU)
MSPR....... Maschinensprache [*German*] (ADPT)
MSpr.......... Ministerstvo Spravedlnosti [*Ministry of Justice*] (CZ)
MSPr .... Motostrelecky Prapor [*Motorized Rifle Battalion*] (CZ)
MSPS .... International Student Aid Service (BU)
MSpS......... Misioneros del Espiritu Santo [*Missionaries of the Holy Spirit*] [*Mexico*] (EAIO)
MSPT .... Movimientos Sindicales del Pueblo Trabajador [*Trade Union Movements of the Working People*] [*Nicaragua*] (LA)
MSPTI ...... Ministry of Construction of Heavy Industry Establishments, USSR (RU)
MSPUP..... Ministry of Construction of Coal Industry Establishments (RU)
MSQ.......... Minsk [*Former USSR*] [*Airport symbol*] (OAG)
ms r .... Bridge Company (BU)
MSR .... Bridge Construction District (RU)
MSR .... Egypt Air [*ICAO designator*] (FAAC)
MSR .... Independent Tripping Mechanism (RU)
MSR .... Malaysian Society of Radiographers (EAIO)
MSR .... Medical Company (RU)
MSR .... Montserrat [*ANSI three-letter standard code*] (CNC)
MSR .... Motorized Rifle Company (RU)
MSR .... Movement for Socialist Renewal [*Political and economic reform group*] [*Russian*]
MSR .... Movimiento Social de Reconstruccion [*Guatemala*] (LAA)
MSR .... Movimiento Socialista Revolucionario [*Revolutionary Socialist Movement*] [*Ecuador*] (LA)
MSR .... Movimiento Socialista Revolucionario [*Revolutionary Socialist Movement*] [*Panama*] [*Political party*] (PPW)
MSR .... Munster [*Germany*] [*Airport symbol*] (OAG)
MSR .... Shunting Signal Relay (RU)
MSRI........ Materials Science Research Institute [*Philippines*] [*Research center*] (IRC)
msrk .... Maaseurakunta [*Finland*]
MSRK iKD ... Moscow Soviet of Workers', Peasants', and Red Army Deputies (RU)
MSRKKA .. Naval Forces of the Workers' and Peasants' Red Army (RU)
MSRS........ Metapsychic Investigations and Scientific Research Society [*Turkey*] (EAIO)
MSS........... Hay-Cutting Machine Station (RU)
MSS........... Installation and Construction Station (RU)
MSS........... International Code [*Nautical term*] (RU)
MSS........... International Seismological Summary [*ISS*] (RU)
MSS........... International Union of Students [*IUS*] (RU)
MSS........... Machine Computation Station, Machine Calculating Station (RU)
Mss .... Manoscritti [*Manuscripts*] [*Italian*]
MSS .... Manuscripts (SCAC)
mss .... Manuscritos [*Manuscripts*] [*Portuguese*]
MSS .... Manuscritos [*Manuscripts*] [*Spanish*]
Mss .... Manuskripte [*Manuscript*] [*Afrikaans*]
MSS........... Medical Department [*of naval ship*], Medical Service (RU)

MSS........... Medical Station (RU)
MSS........... Medunarodni Studentski Savez [*International Students' Union*] (YU)
MSS........... Meter-Second-Candle [*System of units*] (RU)
MSS........... Metropolitan Speleological Society [*Australia*]
MSS........... Mezinarodni Svaz Studentstva [*International Students' Union*] (CZ)
MSS........... Ministerium fuer Staatssicherheit [*Ministry for State Security*] [*MfS, MISTASI*] [*See also*] (EG)
MSS........... Ministerstvo Statnich Statku [*Ministry of State Farms*] (CZ)
MSS........... Ministry for State Security [*China*]
MSS........... Ministry of Machine Tool Manufacture, USSR (RU)
MSS........... Missive van den Secretaris van Staat [*Benelux*] (BAS)
MSS........... Muzealna Slovenska Spolocnost [*Slovak Museum Society*] (CZ)
MSS........... Ship's Engineering Department (RU)
MSSA........ Merinostoettelersgenootskap van Suid Afrika [*Merino Stud Breeders' Society of South Africa*] (EAIO)
MSSB........ Mistni Skupina Svazu Brannosti [*Local Group of the Union for Military Preparedness*] (CZ)
MSSC........ Missionary Society of St. Columban (EAIO)
MSSC........ Mobile Service Switching Center
MSSh........ International Latitude Service [*ILS*] (RU)
MSSKh....... Moscow Union of Soviet Artists (RU)
MSSM....... Ministry of Construction and Construction Materials (BU)
MSSM....... Missionary Sisters of the Society of Mary [*Italy*] (EAIO)
MSSNSW ... Multiple Sclerosis Society of New South Wales [*Australia*]
MSSO........ Mount Stromlo and Siding Springs Observatories [*Australia*]
MSSP........ Magnetstreifenspeicher [*German*] (ADPT)
MSSP........ Missionary Society of Saint Paul [*Australia*]
MSSQ........ Multiple Sclerosis Society of Queensland [*Australia*]
MSSR........ Moldavian Soviet Socialist Republic (RU)
MSSRC ..... Mediterranean Social Science Research Council
MSSRZ ..... Moscow Shipyard (RU)
MSSS .... International Satellite Communications System (BU)
MSSS .... San Salvador/Ilopango Internacional [*El Salvador*] [*ICAO location identifier*] (ICLI)
MSSSh .... International Rapid Latitude Service (RU)
MSSSO ...... Mount Stromlo and Siding Springs Observatories [*Australia*]
MSST .... Multiple Sclerosis Society of Tasmania [*Australia*]
MSSU........ Malaysia Special Services Unit (ML)
MSSV .... Multiple Sclerosis Society of Victoria [*Australia*]
MSSVD...... Medical Society for the Study of Venereal Diseases [*Leeds, England*] (EAIO)
MSSWA .... Multiple Sclerosis Society of Western Australia
MSSZ .... Magyar Si Szovetseg [*Hungarian Skiing Association*] (HU)
MSSZh ...... International Sports Union of Railwaymen (RU)
MST........... Aeroamistad SA de CV [*Mexico*] [*ICAO designator*] (FAAC)
MST........... Maastricht [*Netherlands*] [*Airport symbol*] (OAG)
MST........... Maitrise de Sciences et Techniques [*French*]
MST........... Maladies Sexuelles Transmissibles [*Transmittable Sexual Diseases*] [*French*] (LA)
MST........... Mali Sorumluluk Tazminat [*Financial Responsibility Indemnification*] (TU)
mst .... Manuscrit [*Manuscript*] [*French*]
MST........... Marokanskii Soiuz Truda
mst .... Meistens [*In General*] [*German*] (GCA)
mst .... Meteorological Station (BU)
m st .... Miasto Stoleczne [*Capital City*] (POL)
mst .... Millistoke (RU)
MST........... Ministarstvo Spoljne Trgovine [*Ministry of Foreign Trade*] [*Yugoslavian*] (YU)
MST........... Ministerstvo Strojirenstvi [*Ministry of the Machine Building Industry*] (CZ)
MST........... Mise Sous-Tension [*French*] (ADPT)
MST........... Moravskoslezske Tiskarny [*Moravian-Silesian Printing Plant*] (CZ)
MST........... Moroccan Labor Union (RU)
MST........... Moscow Statistical Technicum (RU)
MST........... Movimiento Socialista de los Trabajadores [*Socialist Workers Movement*] [*Dominican Republic*] (LA)
MST........... Weather Station, Meteorological Station (RU)
MstB......... Bridge Battalion (RU)
Mstb.......... Masstab [*Rule, Standard*] [*German*] (GCA)
MSTC........ Mauritius Sugar Terminal Corporation
MSTG....... Marine Sciences and Technologies Grants [*Scheme*] [*Australia*]
MSTG....... Melbourne Screen and Theatre Guild [*Australia*]
MSTM....... Mafatlal Scientific and Technological Museum [*India*] (PDAA)
MSTM....... Movimiento de Sacerdotes para el Tercer Mundo
Mstr.......... Meister [*Master*] [*German*]
MSTS .... Moscow State Sanitary Engineering Trust of the Glavmosstroy (RU)
MSTSPACOM ... Mediterranean Military Sea Transportation Service Space Assignment Committee
MSU .... Bridge Construction Installation (RU)
MSU .... Machine Computation Installation, Machine Calculating Installation (RU)

MSU .... Maseru [*Lesotho*] [*Airport symbol*] (OAG)
MSU .... Messstellenumschalter [*German*] (ADPT)
MSU .... Migrant Services Unit [*Department of Social Services*] [*Australia*]
MSU .... Mindanao State University [*Philippines*] (ARC)
MSU .... Movimento Socialista Unificado [*Unified Socialist Movement*] [*Portuguese*] (WER)
MSUADC ... Mouvement Syndical Unifie Anti-Dictatorial/Collaborants [*Greece*] (EAIO)
MSUP........ Mouvement pour la Solidarite, l'Union et le Progres [*Benin*] [*Political party*] (EY)
MSurvMap ... Master of Surveying and Mapping
MSUS........ Mouvement Socialiste d'Union Senegalaise [*Senegalese Socialist Movement*] [*Political party*]
MSV .... Medical Platoon (RU)
MSv .... Ministerstvo Stavebnictvi [*Ministry of Building*] (CZ)
MSV .... Missionary Sisters of Verona
MSV .... Mistni Skolni Vybor [*Local School Committee*] (CZ)
MSV .... Moscow Shipyard (RU)
msv............ Motorized Rifle Platoon (RU)
MSV .... Musica sul Velluto (EAIO)
MSVU .... Ministerstvo Skolstvi, Ved, a Umeni [*Ministry of Education, Sciences, and Arts*] (CZ)
MSVU .... Moravskoslezske Sdruzeni Vytvarnych Umelcu [*Moravian-Silesian Association of Creative Artists*] (CZ)
MSVVMP ... Ministry of Construction of Military and Naval Establishments (RU)
MSW .... Massawa [*Ethiopia*] [*Airport symbol*] (OAG)
MSW .... Miejski Sztab Wojskowy [*City Military Headquarters*] (POL)
MSW .... Ministerstwo Spraw Wewnetrznych [*Ministry of Internal Affairs*] (POL)
MSW .... Ministerstwo Szkolnictwa Wyzszego [*Ministry of Higher Education*] (POL)
MSWiN ..... Ministerstwo Szkol Wyzszych i Nauki [*Ministry of Higher Schools and Science*] (POL)
MSX .... Mossendjo [*Congo*] [*Airport symbol*] (OAG)
MSY .... Massey University School of Aviation [*New Zealand*] [*ICAO designator*] (FAAC)
m sz .... Maganszektor [*Private Sector*] (HU)
MSZ .... Magyar Szabvany [*Hungarian Standard*] (HU)
MSZ .... Mednarodna Studentska Zveza [*International Students' Union*] (YU)
MSZ .... Ministerstvo pro Sjednoceni Zakonu [*Ministry for the Unification of Law*] (CZ)
MSZ .... Ministerstwo Spraw Zagranicznych [*Ministry of Foreign Affairs*] (POL)
MSZ .... Minsk Machine Tool Plant (RU)
MSZ .... Moscow Grinding Machine Plant (RU)
MSZ .... Mossamedes [*Angola*] [*Airport symbol*] (OAG)
MSzabadsagh Szov ... Magyar Szabadsagharcos Szovetseg [*Association of Hungarian Freedom Fighters*] (HU)
MSZB .... Magyar Szavatossagi Bank [*Hungarian Insurance Bank*] (HU)
MSZBH..... Magyar-Szovjet Baratsag Honap [*Hungarian-Soviet Friendship Month*] (HU)
MSZBT ..... Magyar-Szovjet Barati Tarsasag [*Hungarian-Soviet Friendship Society*] (HU)
MSZDP..... Magyar Szocial Demokrata Part [*Hungarian Social Democratic Party*] [*Political party*] (PPE)
MSZDSZ .. Magyarorszagi Szlovakok Demokratikus Szovetsege [*Democratic Association of Slovaks in Hungary*] (HU)
MSZh .... International Council of Women [*ICW*] (RU)
MSzH .... Magyar Szabvanyugyi Hivatal [*Hungarian Bureau of Standards*] (HU)
MSZH .... Magyar Szovjet Hirado [*Hungarian-Soviet News Agency*] (HU)
MSZHB..... Mezogazdasagi Szovetkezeti Hitelbank [*Agricultural Cooperative Credit Bank*] (HU)
MSZhD ..... International Union of Railways (RU)
MSzhSD... International Council of Social Democratic Women (RU)
MSZHSZ .. Magyar Szabadsagharcos Szovetseg [*Association of Hungarian Freedom Fighters*] (HU)
MSZI......... Magyar Szabvanyugyi Intezet [*Hungarian Bureau of Standards*] (HU)
MSZK....... Mezogazdasagi Szovetkezeti Kozpont [*Agricultural Cooperative Center*] (HU)
MSZKI ...... Meres- es Szamitas-Technikai Kutato Intezet [*Research Institute for Measurement and Computing*] [*Hungary*] (IRC)
MSZMP.... Magyar Szocialista Munkaspart [*Hungarian Socialist Workers' Party*] [*Political party*] (PPE)
MSZMT.... Magyar Szovjet Muvelodesi Tarsasag [*Hungarian-Soviet Cultural Society*] (HU)
MSzOSz .... Magyar Szakszervezetek Orszagos Szoevetsege [*National Confederation of Hungarian Trade Unions*] (EY)
MSZOSZ .. Mezogazdasagi Szakemberek Orszagos Szovetsege [*National Association of Agricultural Specialists*] (HU)
MSzP........ Magyar Szocialista Part [*Hungarian Socialist Party*] [*Political party*] (EY)
MSZSZ ..... Magyar Szabadsagharcos Szovetseg [*Association of Hungarian Freedom Fighters*] (HU)

MSzSz .... Mozgo Szakorvosi Szolgalat [*Special Mobile Medical Service*] (HU)

MSZSZ ..... Muveszeti Szakszervezetek Szovetsege [*Federation of Artists' Trade Unions*] (HU)

MSZSZOSZ ... Magyar Szabad Szakszervezetek Orszagos Szovetsege [*National Federation of Hungarian Free Trade Unions*] (HU)

MSZT........ Magyar Szenbanyaszati Troszt [*Hungarian Coal Mining Trust*]

MSZT .... Magyar-Szovjet Tarsasag [*Hungarian-Soviet Society*] (HU)

MT .... A Munka Torvenykonyve [*Labor Code*] (HU)

MT .... Dead Center (RU)

MT .... Estado de Mato Grosso [*State of Mato Grosso*] [*Brazil*]

MT .... Hoofdgroep Maatschappelijke Technologie [*Division for Technology in Society*] [*Netherlands Central Organization for Applied Natural Scientific Research*] (WED)

MT .... Internacia Asocio Monda Turismo [*International Association for World Tourism*] (EAIO)

MT .... Magnettrommel [*German*] (ADPT)

MT .... Maille Tombee [*Knitting*] [*French*]

mt .... Mainittu Teos [*Finland*]

MT .... Makinali Tufek [*Machine Gun*] (TU)

MT .... Malta [*IYRU nationality code*] [*ANSI two-letter standard code*] (CNC)

MT .... Mani Tese [*An association*] [*Italy*] (EAIO)

MT .... Manometric Thermometer (RU)

MT .... Marginal Toetsing [*Benelux*] (BAS)

MT .... Mariborska Tiskarna [*Maribor Printing House*] (YU)

MT .... Matera [*Car registration plates*] [*Italian*]

MT .... Matice Technicka [*Society for the Promotion of Technology*] (CZ)

Mt .... Megaton (RU)

MT .... Megyei Tanacs [*County Council*] (HU)

MT .... Meteor Construzioni Aeronautiche & Elettroniche SpA [*Italy*] [*ICAO aircraft manufacturer identifier*] (ICAO)

Mt .... Metre [*or Metreler*] [*Meter or Meters*] (TU)

MT .... Mikrotelegramm [*German*] (ADPT)

MT .... Milliers de Tonnes

MT .... Ministerio do Trabalho [*Ministry of Labor*] [*Portuguese*] (WER)

MT .... Ministerio do Trabalho [*Ministry of Labor*] [*Brazil*] (LA)

MT .... Ministerstvo Techniky [*Ministry of Technology*] (CZ)

MT .... Ministerul Turismului [*Ministry of Tourism*] (RO)

MT .... Ministry of Trade (RU)

MT .... Ministry of Transportation (BU)

MT .... Minisztertanacs [*Council of Ministers*] (HU)

MT .... Modosito Tervezet [*Modified Draft*] (HU)

mt .... Molecular Weight (BU)

Mt .... Mont [*Mount, Mountain*] [*French*] (NAU)

Mt .... Montant [*Amount*] [*Business term*] [*French*]

MT .... Mosaisk Troessamfund [*An association*] [*Denmark*] (EAIO)

M/t............. Motorni Tanker [*Motor Tanker*] (YU)

Mt .... Mount (IDIG)

MT .... Museo de Transporte [*Transport Museum*] [*Venezuela*]

MT .... Navigation Tables (RU)

MT .... Telephone Handset, Hand Microtelephone (RU)

MTA .... Macedonian Telegraph Agency (BU)

MTA .... Mack Trucks Australia

MTA .... Maden Tetkik ve Arama Genel Mudurlugu [*General Directorate of Mineral Research and Exploration*] [*Research center*] [*Turkey*] (IRC)

MTA .... Magyar Tudomanyos Akademia [*Hungarian Academy of Sciences*] (HU)

MTA .... Malaysian Territorial Army (ML)

MTA .... Marionette Theate of Australia

MTA .... Materiel Thermique Africain

MTA .... Mineral Research and Exploration Institute of Turkey (MENA)

MTA .... Ministry of Tourism and Aviation [*Seychelles*] (AF)

MTA .... Movimiento Teresiano de Apostolado [*Teresian Apostolic Movement - TAM*] [*Italy*] (EAIO)

mta .... Muita [*Portuguese*]

MTAA .... Motor Trades Association of Australia

MTAACT ... Motor Trades Association of the Australian Capital Territory

MTAC ...... Materials Technology and Application Centre [*Singapore*]

mtad .... Mine and Torpedo Aviation Division (BU)

MTAE .... Maden Tetkik ve Arastirma Enstitusu [*The Mining Research Institute*] [*MTA*] [*See also*] (TU)

mtae .... Mine and Torpedo Aviation Squadron (BU)

MTAIEA ... Motor Trade and Allied Industries Employers' Association [*Kenya*] (EAIO)

MTAIF ...... Member of the Australian Institute of Fund Raising

MTAK .... Magyar Tudomanyos Akademia Konyvtara [*Hungarian Academy of Sciences Library*] (IID)

MTAMEN-SEN ... Maden Tetkik ve Arastirma Enstitusu Genel Mudurlugu Isyeri Mensuplari Sendikasi [*Mining Technique and Research Institute Directorate General Site Employees Union*] [*Ankara*] (TU)

MTAMTO ... Magyar Tudomanyos Akademia Muszaki Tudomanyok Osztalya [*Hungarian Academy of Sciences, Division of Technical Sciences*] (HU)

MTANSW ... Motor Trades Association of New South Wales [*Australia*]

MTANSW ... Music Teachers Association of New South Wales [*Australia*]

MTANSW ... Music Teachers' Association of South Australia

MTAP........ Mine and Torpedo Air Regiment (RU)

mtap .... Mine and Torpedo Aviation Regiment (BU)

MTAS........ Ministry of Territorial Administration and Security [*Burkina Faso*]

MTASA..... Motor Trade Association of South Australia

MTAVA .... Mwananchi Tractor and Vehicles Assemblers Ltd.

MTAWA ... Motor Trade Association of Western Australia

MTB .... Monte Libano [*Colombia*] [*Airport symbol*] (OAG)

MTB .... Moscow Trolleybus (RU)

MTBA ...... Melbourne Tenpin Bowling Association [*Australia*]

MTC .... Manufacture de Tabac de la Cote-D'Ivoire

MTC .... Maritime Transport Committee [*OECD*] (DS)

MTC .... Mauritius Turf Club

MTC .... Medumurska Trikotaza (Cakovec) [*Medjumurje Knitted Goods Factory (Cakovec)*] [*YU*]

MTC .... Melbourne Technical College [*Australia*] (ADA)

MTC .... Microelectronics Technology Centre [*Royal Melbourne Institute of Technology*] [*Australia*]

MTC .... Military Transportation Committee [*NATO*] (NATG)

MTC .... Ministerio dos Transportes e Communicacoes [*Ministry of Transportation and Communication*] [*Portuguese*] (WER)

MTC .... Ministry pf Transport and Communications [*Burkina Faso*]

MTC .... Motor Trade Co. [*Jordan*]

MTC .... Mouvement des Travailleurs Chretiens (Charleroi) [*Benelux*] (BAS)

MTC .... Mouvement Traditionaliste Congolais [*Congolese Traditionalist Movement*]

MTC .... Murgian Trading Co. [*Yemen*]

MTC .... Murrumbidgee Turf Club [*Australia*]

MTCA ...... Cayes [*Haiti*] [*ICAO location identifier*] (ICLI)

MTCF....... Mes Tres Chers Freres [*Dearly Beloved Brethren*] [*French*]

MTCF....... Multilateral Technical Co-Operation Fund

MTCH....... Cap Haitien Internacional [*Haiti*] [*ICAO location identifier*] (ICLI)

MTCI........ Manufacture des Tabacs de la Cote-D'Ivoire

MTCOECD ... Maritime Transport Committee of the Organization for Economic Cooperation and Development [*France*] (EAIO)

MTCR .... Missile Technology Control Regime [*US, Canada, Britain, France, West Germany, Japan*]

MTCS....... Melbourne Theatre Cooperative Society [*Australia*]

MTD......... Macknight Airlines [*Australia*] [*ICAO designator*] (FAAC)

MTD......... Motor Transport Driver [*Royal Australian Navy*]

MTDC ...... Mineral Technology Development Centre [*Ministry of Mines and Energy, Directorate General of Mines*] [*Indonesia*]

MTDiL ...... Ministerstwo Transportu Drogowego i Lotniczego [*Ministry of Road and Air Transportation*] (POL)

MTD V-1 ... Mirovoy Tsentr Dannykh V-1 [*World Data Center B*] [*Russian*] (MSC)

MTE .... Magnetic Triode Element (RU)

MTE .... Maison Tunisienne de l'Edition

MTE .... Makina - Takim Endustrisi AS [*Machinery and Equipment Industry Corporation*] (TU)

MTE .... Materiel de Traction Eletrique [*France*] (PDAA)

MTE .... Mezogazdasagi es Elelmiszeripari Tudomanyos Egyesulet [*Scientific Institute for Agriculture and the Food Industry*] (HU)

MTE .... Minisztertanacs Elnoke [*Prime Minister, Chairman of the Council of Ministers*] (HU)

Mte............ Monte [*Mount, Mountain*] [*Italian*] (NAU)

Mte............ Monte [*Mount, Mountain*] [*Portuguese*] (NAU)

Mte............ Monte [*Mount, Mountain*] [*Spanish*] (NAU)

MTE .... Munkas Torna Egylet [*Workers' Athletic Association*] (HU)

MTEC....... Monash Timber Engineering Center [*Australia*]

MTEG .... Port-Au-Prince [*Haiti*] [*ICAO location identifier*] (ICLI)

MTEI........ Manufacture Tunisienne d'Exploitation Industrielle

MTEI........ Moscow Institute of Transportation Economics (RU)

MTEKSZ ... Magyar Tekezo Szovetseg [*Hungarian Bowling Association*] (HU)

M Termtud Tars ... Magyar Termeszettudomanyi Tarsasag [*Hungarian Natural Science Association*] (HU)

MTESZ ..... Muszaki es Termeszettudomanyi Egyesuletek Szovetsege [*Federation of Technical and Scientific Associations*] (HU)

MTEU .... Moscow Tourist and Excursion Administration (RU)

MTEWS/AD ... Mobile Tactical Early Warning System for Air Defense [*NATO*]

MTF .... Dairy Farm (RU)

MTF .... Materialteknisk Forening [*Association for Testing of Materials*] [*Norway*] (PDAA)

MTF .... Meat Production Farm (RU)

mtf............. Metaforikos [*Figuratively*] (GC)

MTF .... Mizan Teferi [*Ethiopia*] [*Airport symbol*] [*Obsolete*]   (OAG)
MTF .... Trimethyltrithiophosphite   (RU)
MTFL........ Man-Tended Free-Flying Laboratory [*European Space Agency*]
MTFL........ Moscow Television Branch Laboratory   (RU)
MTFP........ Marema Tlou Freedom Party [*Lesotho*]
MTFSC ..... Ministerial Task Force on Soil Conservation [*Australia*]
MTG .... Magusa Turk Gucu [*Famagusta Turkish Strength*] [*Soccer team*]   (TU)
MTG .... Marine Technik Planungsgesellschaft [*Institute for Naval Architecture*] [*Germany*]   (PDAA)
MTG .... Meldetextgeber [*German*]   (ADPT)
MTG .... Moscow Trust Group [*Former USSR*]
MtG .... Mount Gravatt College of Advanced Education [*Australia*]
MTG .... Muenchener Tieraerztliche Gesellschaft   (SLS)
Mtgl .... Mitglied [*Member*] [*German*]
MTGWU ... Mauritian Textile and Garment Workers' Union   (EY)
MT H........ A Munkaerotartalekok Hivatala Elnokenek Vegrehajtasi Utasitasa [*Decree of the President of the Office of Labor Reserves*]   (HU)
MTH......... Marine Technical Hull [*Royal Australian Navy*]
MTH......... Massachusetts Institute of Technology [*ICAO designator*]   (FAAC)
Mth .... Minisztertanacs Hatarozata [*Resolution of the Council of Ministers*]   (HU)
MT H........ Munkaerotartalekok Hivatala [*Office of Labor Reserves*]   (HU)
MThPast ... Maitre en Theologie Pastorale [*Master in Pastoral Theology*] [*French*]
MTI .... Magyar Tavirati Iroda [*Hungarian Telegraph Agency*]   (HU)
MTI .... Magyar Tavviati Iroda [*Hungarian News Agency*]   (BARN)
MTI .... Ministry of Trade and Industry [*Philippines*]   (IMH)
MTI .... Missionary Training Institute [*Philippines*]
MTI .... Moscow Peat Institute   (RU)
MTI .... Moscow Textile Institute   (RU)
MTI .... Mosteiros [*Cape Verde Islands*] [*Airport symbol*]   (OAG)
MTI .... Mouvement de la Tendance Islamique [*Islamic Trend Movement*] [*Tunisia*]   (PD)
MTIA .... Metal Trades Industry Association of Australia   (ADA)
MTIAA..... Metal Trades Industry Association of Australia
MTIB........ Malaysian Timber Industry Board
MTILP ..... Moscow Technological Institute of Light Industry   (RU)
MTIMMP ... Moscow Technological Institute of the Meat and Dairy Industry   (RU)
MTIMP..... Moscow Technological Institute of Local Industry   (RU)
MTiP .... Ministry of Trade and Industry   (RU)
MTIPP ...... Moscow Technological Institute of the Food Industry   (RU)
MTiSKhM ... Ministry of Tractor and Agricultural Machinery Manufacture, USSR   (RU)
MTiTM ..... Ministry of Transportation and Heavy Machinery Manufacture, USSR   (RU)
MTJA....... Jacmel [*Haiti*] [*ICAO location identifier*]   (ICLI)
MTJE....... Jeremie [*Haiti*] [*ICAO location identifier*]   (ICLI)
MTK......... Dairy Kolkhoz   (RU)
MTK......... International Commission on Terminology   (RU)
MTK......... International Telegraph Code   (RU)
MTK......... Maataloustuottajain Keskusliitto [*Agricultural Producers' Association*] [*Finland*]   (WEN)
MTK......... Magyar Tanacskoztarsasag [*Hungarian Soviet Republic*]   (HU)
MTK......... Makin [*Kiribati*] [*Airport symbol*]   (OAG)
MTK......... Medunarodna Trgovinska Komora [*International Chamber of Commerce*]   (YU)
MTK......... Metallurgie de Kolwezi
MTK......... Miedzynarodowe Targi Ksiazki [*International Book Fair*] [*Poland*]
MTK......... Shallow Tubular Well   (RU)
MTKhTU .. Moscow Theatrical Applied Art School   (RU)
MTKI........ Magyar Tejgazdasagi Kiserleti Intezet [*Hungarian Dairy Research Institute*]   (ARC)
MTkI .... Mernoki Tovabbkepzo Intezet [*Institute for Extension Courses in Engineering*]   (HU)
MTKI........ Munkavedelmi Tudomanyos Kutato Intezet [*Scientific Research Institute for Labor Safety*]   (HU)
MTKJ .... Mezogazdasagi Termekek Kereskedelmi Jegyzeke [*Commercial Register of Agricultural Products*]   (HU)
Mtkm .... Megatonnenkilometer [*Million Ton-Kilometers*]   (EG)
MTL .... Maaseudun Tyonantajaliitto [*Agricultural Employers' Association*] [*Finland*]   (WEN)
MTL .... Mainostoimistojen Liitto RY [*Finnish Association of Advertising Agencies*]   (EAIO)
MTL .... Maitland [*Australia*] [*Airport symbol*]   (OAG)
MTL .... Matjas Thomas Ltd. [*New Zealand*] [*Research center*]   (ERC)
mtl .... Monatlich [*Monthly*]   (EG)
MTL .... Mouvement pour le Triomphe des Libertes Democratiques [*Movement for the Triumph of Democratic Liberties*] [*Algeria*]
MTL .... Raf-Avia [*Latvia*] [*ICAO designator*]   (FAAC)

MTLD .... Mouvement pour le Triomphe des Libertes Democratiques [*Movement for the Triumph of Democratic Liberties*] [*Algeria*]
Mtlg .... Mitteilung [*Report*] [*German*]   (BJA)
MTM .... Machine and Tractor Shop   (RU)
MTM .... Maksutov Meniscus-Lens Telescope   (RU)
MTM .... Marches Tropicaux et Mediterraneens
MTM .... Metodtidmatning [*Methods Time Measurement*] [*Sweden*]   (WEN)
MTM .... Ministry of Heavy Machinery Manufacture, USSR   (RU)
MTM .... Ministry of Transportation Machinery Manufacture, USSR   (RU)
MTM .... Mouvement des Travailleurs Mauriciens [*Mauritian Workers Movement*]   (AF)
MTMA ..... Malaysian Textile Manufacturers' Association   (EAIO)
MTMA ..... Member of the Australian Institute of Taxation and Management Accountants
MTN .... Main Telecommunication Network [*United Nations*]   (EY)
MTN .... Multilateral Trade Negotiations
MTNG....... Mandated Territory of New Guinea [*Australia*]
MTO .... High-Powered Telephoto Lens   (RU)
MTO .... International Trade Organization   (RU)
MTO .... Maantutkimusosasto [*Department of Soil Science*] [*Research center*] [*Finland*]   (IRC)
MTO .... Maintenance Vehicle   (RU)
MTO .... Masuri Tehnice-Organizative [*Technical-Organizational Measures*]   (RO)
MTO .... Materials and Equipment Supply Department   (RU)
MTO .... Materiel Support [*Military*]   (RU)
MTO .... Mediterranean Theater of Operations
MTO .... Medunarodna Trgovinska Organizacija [*International Trade Organization*]   (YU)
MTO .... Milletlerarasi Ticaret Odasi [*International Chamber of Commerce*]   (TU)
MTO .... Milli Talebe Orgutu [*National Student Organization*]   (TU)
MTO .... Mouvement Togolais pour la Democratie [*Togolese Movement for Democracy*] [*Political party*]   (PD)
mto .... Muito [*Much*] [*Portuguese*]
MTO .... Thermomechanical Treatment   (RU)
MTO .... Weather Situation   (BU)
MTOA ...... Manufacture des Tabacs de l'Ouest Africain
MTOC ...... Movimiento de Trabajadores y Obreros de Clase [*Peru*]   (EY)
MTOP ...... Ministerio de Transporte y Obras Publicas [*Ministry of Transportation and Public Works*] [*Uruguay*]   (LA)
MTP .... International Chamber of Commerce [*ICC*]   (RU)
MTP .... Junior Technical Personnel   (RU)
MTP .... Magnetotelluric Profiling   (RU)
MTP .... Maktab Tentera Persekutuan [*Federation Military College*]   (ML)
MTP .... Manufacture Togolaise des Plastiques
MTP .... Marema Tlou Party [*Basotho*]   (AF)
MTP .... Marine Technical Propulsion [*Royal Australian Navy*]
MTP .... Miedzynarodowe Targi Poznanskie [*Poznan International Fair*]   (POL)
MTP .... Ministerstvo Tezkeho Prumyslu [*Ministry of Heavy Industry*]   (CZ)
MTP .... Ministry of Heavy Industry [*Obsolete*]   (BU)
MTP .... Ministry of the Fuel Industry   (RU)
MTP .... Ministry of the Textile Industry   (RU)
MTP .... Movimiento Todos par la Patria [*Argentina*] [*Political party*]   (EY)
MTPC....... Ministre des Travaux Publics [*Algeria*]
MTPEM... Ministere des Travaux Publics, Energie, et Mines [*Ministry of Public Works, Energy, and Mines*] [*Burundi*]   (EAS)
MTPP....... Moskoyskii Tekhnologicheskii Institut Pishchevoi Promyshlennosti [*Technological Institute of Food Industry*] [*Former USSR*]   (DSCA)
MTPP....... Port-Au-Prince/Internacional [*Haiti*] [*ICAO location identifier*]   (ICLI)
MTPP....... Tactical Infantry Training Methods   (RU)
MTPT........ Ministry of Commerce, Industry, and Labor [*Obsolete*]   (BU)
MTPX........ Port-De-Paix [*Haiti*] [*ICAO location identifier*]   (ICLI)
MTPY........ Metokhikon Tameion Politikon Ypallilon [*Civil Servants Pension Fund*] [*Greek*]   (GC)
MTQ......... CAAA Air Martinique [*France*] [*ICAO designator*]   (FAAC)
MTQ......... Martinique [*ANSI three-letter standard code*]   (CNC)
MTQ......... Mitchell [*Australia*] [*Airport symbol*]   (OAG)
MTR .... Magnetic Thermonuclear Reactor   (RU)
MTR .... Magyar Telefonhirmondo es Radio Reszvenytarsasag [*Hungarian Closed-Circuit Transmission and Radio Company Limited*]   (HU)
MTR .... Marginal Rate of Tax
MTR .... Mass Transit Railway [*Hong Kong*]
Mtr .... Metronome [*Record label*] [*Scandinavia, Germany, etc.*]
MTR .... Ministry of Labor Reserves   (RU)
MTR .... Monteria [*Colombia*] [*Airport symbol*]   (OAG)

MTR......... Naval Transport Aircraft (RU)
mt r............. Turbid Solution (RU)
MTransEc ... Master of Transport Economics
MTrans-TekhnB ... Ministry of Transportation, Technical Library (BU)
MTRC .... Mass Transit Railway Corporation [*Hong Kong*]
MTRCB..... Movie and Television Review and Classification Board
        [*Philippines*]
MTRK .... Makedonskiot Taen Revolucioneren Komitet [*Macedonian
        Secret Revolutionary Committee*] (YU)
Mtro........... Maestro [*Master*] [*Spanish*]
MTRZ .... Moscow Trolleybus Repair Plant (RU)
MTS.......... Long-Distance Telephone Communications (RU)
MTS.......... Long-Distance Telephone Exchange (RU)
MTS.......... Long-Distance Telephone Network, Trunk Network (RU)
MTS.......... Machine and Tractor Station (RU)
MTS.......... Machine-Tractor Stations (BU)
MTS.......... Magyar Testnevelesi es Sportmozgalom [*Hungarian Physical
        Education and Sports Movement*] (HU)
mts .... Mainittu Teos, Sivu [*Finland*]
MTS.......... Mantrust Asahi Airways PT [*Indonesia*] [*ICAO designator*]
        (FAAC)
MTS.......... Manzini [*Swaziland*] [*Airport symbol*] (OAG)
MTS.......... Maschinen-Traktoren-Station [*Machine-Tractor-Station*]
        [*German*]
MTS.......... Mashinno-Traktornye-Stantsii [*Machine-Tractor-Stations*]
        [*Russian*]
MTS.......... Masinsko-Traktorske Stanice [*Machine-Tractor-Stations*] (YU)
MTS.......... Materials and Equipment Supply (RU)
MTs .... Mechanical Interlocking [*Railroads*] (RU)
MTS.......... Message Transfer Service
MTS.......... Mestska Telekomunikacni Sprava [*City Administration for
        Telecommunications*] (CZ)
MTS.......... Meter-Ton-Second (RU)
MTS.......... Metokhikon Tameion Stratou [*Army Pension Fund*] [*Greek*]
        (GC)
MTS.......... Metre-Tonne-Seconde [*Meter-Ton-Second*] [*French*]
MTS.......... Miedzynarodowy Trybunal Sprawiedliwosci [*International Court
        of Justice*] [*Poland*]
MTS.......... Miedzynarodowy Tydzien Studenta [*International Students'
        Week*] (POL)
MTS.......... Ministerstvo Tezkeho Strojirenstvi [*Ministry of Heavy Machine
        Building Industry*] (CZ)
MTS.......... Ministry of Transportation Construction (RU)
MTs .... Mitotic Cycle (RU)
m-ts .... Month (RU)
MTS.......... Moscow Theater of Satire (RU)
MTsAOR .. Moscow Central Archives of the October Revolution (RU)
MTSB........ Megyei Testnevelesi es Sportbizottsag [*County Physical
        Education and Sports Committee*] (HU)
MTsB......... Motorcycle Battalion (RU)
MTSC........ Maritime Transit Services Corp. [*Ethiopia*]
MTsD .... World Data Centers (RU)
MTSE........ Munkas Testedzo es Sport Egylet [*Workers' Physical Education
        and Sports Association*] (HU)
MTsEM..... Mathematical Digital Electronic Computer (RU)
MTSG........ Ministry of Labor and Social Welfare [*Obsolete*] (BU)
MTSH .... Magyar Testnevelesi es Sporthivatal [*Hungarian Office of
        Physical Education and Sports*] (HU)
MTsK .... Centralized-Check Machine (RU)
MTsM .... Ministry of Nonferrous Metallurgy (RU)
MTSNRM ... Ministerstvo na Trgovijata i Snabduenjeto na Narodnata
        Republika Makedonija [*Ministry of Commerce and Supply
        of Macedonia*] (YU)
MTSP........ Magtnettrommelspeicher [*German*] (ADPT)
mtsp.......... Motorcycle Regiment (BU)
MTsR .... Interchain Reaction (RU)
mtsr........... Motorcycle Company (BU)
MTsRK..... Moscow Central Workers' Cooperative (RU)
MTSRTS... Maschinen-Traktoren-Station Reparatur-Technische Station
        [*Machine Tractor Station Repair and Technical Station*]
        (EG)
MTsSB ...... Central Bureau of the Association of Seismology and Physics of
        the Earth's Interior (RU)
MTST .... Magyar Testnevelesi es Sport Tanacs [*Hungarian Council for
        Physical Education and Sports*] (HU)
MTSU .... Malayan Technical Services' Union
mtsv.......... Motorcycle Platoon (RU)
MTsVIA .... Moscow Central Military History Archives (RU)
MTSZT ..... Magyar Termeszetbarat Szovetseg Tanacsa [*Council of the
        Hungarian Nature Study Association*] (HU)
MTT .... Magyar Taplalkozastudomanyi Tarsasag [*An association*]
        [*Hungary*] (EAIO)
MTT .... Magyar Tarsadalomtudomanyi Tarsulat [*Hungarian Social
        Science Association*] (HU)
MTT .... Magyar Tudomanyos Tanacs [*Hungarian Scientific Council*]
        (HU)
MTT .... Mediterranean Tours and Travel [*Egypt*]

MTT .... Milicias de Tropas Territoriales [*Territorial Troops Militia*]
        [*Cuba*] (LA)
MTT .... Minatitlan [*Mexico*] [*Airport symbol*] (OAG)
MTT .... Moscow Peat Technicum (RU)
mtt............. Multifrequency Voice-Frequency Telegraphy (RU)
MTT .... Orion SpA [*Italy*] [*ICAO designator*] (FAAC)
MTT .... Technical Installation Trust (RU)
MTT .... Telluric Current Method (RU)
MTTB........ Mauritius Tourist and Travel Bureau
MTTB........ Milli Turkiye Talebe Birligi [*Turkish National Student Union*]
        (TU)
MTTc......... Ministerul Transportului si Telecomunicatiilor [*Ministry of
        Transportation and Telecommunications*] (RO)
MTTE......... Malawi Traders Trust Extension
MTTH .... Minisztertanacs Tanacsi Hivatala [*Bureau for Local Councils of
        the Council of Ministers*] (HU)
MTTI......... Moscow Institute of Trade and the Science of Commodities
        (RU)
MTTI........ Muszaki Tudomanyos Tajekoztato Intezetben [*Hungarian
        Institute of Scientific and Technical Information*] (PDAA)
MTTK .... Maatalouden Tutkimuskeskus [*Agricultural Research Center*]
        [*Finland*] (IRC)
MTTP........ Ministere des Transports et des Travaux Publics [*Mali*]
MTTS........ Magyar Tancmuveszeti Tarsulasok Szovetsege [*An association*]
        [*Hungary*] (EAIO)
MTTs........ Moscow Television Center (RU)
MTTT........ Magyar Termeszettudomanyi Tarsasag [*Hungarian Natural
        Science Association*] (HU)
mtty........... Maaratty [*Finland*]
MTU......... Circuit Telecontrol [*Electricity*] (BU)
MTU......... Machine Technical School (BU)
MTU......... Mezimestska Telefonni Ustredna [*Long Distance Telephone
        Central*] (CZ)
MTU......... Mezinarodni Telekomunikacni Unie [*International
        Telecommunications Union*] (CZ)
MTU......... Motoren- und Turbinen Union [*Aerospace equipment
        manufacturer*]
MTU......... Motorinen Turbo-Union [*Germany*]
MTU......... Technical Installation Administration (RU)
MTU......... Weather Conditions (BU)
MTUC .... Macao Trade Union Council
MTUC .... Malayan Trades Union Congress
MTUC .... Malaysian Trades Union Congress (ML)
MTUC .... Mauritius Trades' Union Congress
M TudAkad ... Magyar Tudomanyos Akademia [*Hungarian Academy of
        Sciences*] (HU)
MTUF .... Mauritius Trades' Union Federation
MTUI .... Miners' Trade Unions Institute [*Poland*]
MTV......... Conference des Ministres Europeens du Travail [*Conference of
        European Ministers of Labour*] (EAIO)
mTV......... Maritime Tropical Air (RU)
MTV......... Materialtechnische Versorgung [*Procurement of Required
        Materials*] (EG)
mtv............. Megyei Tanacs ala Rendelt Varos [*Town Administered by a
        County Council*] (HU)
Mtv .... Mitverseher [*German*]
MTV......... Mota Lava [*Vanuatu*] [*Airport symbol*] (OAG)
MTV......... Motored Test Vehicle [*Weapons Research Establishment*]
        [*Australia*]
MTVA....... Metokhikon Tameion Vasilikis Aeroporias [*Royal Air Force
        Pension Fund*] [*Greek*] (GC)
MTVN....... Metokhikon Tameion Vasilikou Navtikou [*Royal Navy Pension
        Fund*] [*Greek*] (GC)
MTVO .... Regimental Shop for the Repair of Tank Armament and Optical
        Equipment (RU)
MTVRD..... Myanma Television and Radio Department (EY)
MTW......... Matthias-Thesen-Werft Wismar (VEB) [*Wismar Matthias-
        Thesen Shipyard (VEB)*] (EG)
MTWS....... Miedzynarodowe Towarzystwo Wagonow Sypialnych
        [*International Sleeping Car Association*] (POL)
MTY .... Monterrey [*Mexico*] [*Airport symbol*] (OAG)
MTYuZ ..... Moscow Young Spectator's Theater (RU)
MTZ .... Magnetotelluric Sounding (RU)
MTZ .... Materialne Technicke Zasobovani [*Technical and Material
        Procurement*] (CZ)
MTZ .... Moscow Brake Plant (RU)
MTZ .... Moscow Pipe Plant (RU)
MTZ .... Moscow Transformer Plant (RU)
MTZ .... "Tito" Metalski Zavod [*"Tito" Metal Institute*] [*Skopje*] (YU)
MTZ .... Tractor Made by the Minsk Tractor Plant (RU)
MU .... Akaflieg Muenchen Mitsubishi Heavy Industries [*Germany*]
        [*Japan*] [*ICAO aircraft manufacturer identifier*] (ICAO)
MU .... Installation Administration (RU)
MU .... Local Control [*Computers*] (RU)
MU .... Macquarie University [*Australia*]
MU .... Magnetic Amplifier (RU)
MU .... Masarykova Universita [*Masaryk University*] [*Brno*] (CZ)

MU .... Matematicky Ustav [*Mathematical Institute (of the Czechoslovak Academy of Sciences)*] (CZ)

MU .... Mauritius [*ANSI two-letter standard code*] (CNC)

MU .... Melbourne University [*Australia*]

MU .... Metrologicky Ustav [*Metrological Institute*] (CZ)

MU .... Mezinarodni Telefonni Ustredna [*International Telephone Exchange*] [*Prague*] (CZ)

MU .... Microphone Amplifier (RU)

MU .... Mie University [*Japan*] (MSC)

MU .... Monash University [*Australia*]

MU .... Montanni Unie [*European Coal and Steel Community*] (CZ)

MU .... Moviment Universitari [*University Movement*] [*Spanish*] (WER)

MU .... Multiplier [*Computers*] (RU)

mu .... Munkas [*Worker*] (HU)

MU .... Murdoch University [*Australia*]

MU .... Musicians' Union of Australia

mu .... Muszaki [*Technical, Engineering (Adjective)*] (HU)

MU .... Muzicka Akademija [*Music Academy*] (YU)

MU .... Mykologicky Ustav [*Institute of Mycology*] (CZ)

MU .... Naval Trainer, Naval Trainer Aircraft (RU)

MU .... Power Unit (RU)

MUA .... Maritime Union of Australia

MUA .... Mathematical Union of Argentina (EAIO)

MUA .... Mothers' Union in Australia

MUA .... Mouvement Universitaire Algerien [*Algerian University Movement*] (AF)

Mua .... Muavini [*Assistant, Deputy*] (TU)

MUA .... Mujeres Unidas en Accion [*Puerto Rico*] (EAIO)

MUA .... Munda [*Solomon Islands*] [*Airport symbol*] (OAG)

MUA .... Musicians' Union of Argentina (EAIO)

MUA .... Musicians' Union of Australia (ADA)

MU-AD ..... Magnetic Amplifier-Induction Motor (RU)

MUAG .... Central Agramonte [*Cuba*] [*ICAO location identifier*] (ICLI)

MUAKI ..... Muanyagipari Kutato Intezet [*Industrial Research Institute on Plastics*] (HU)

MUAN ...... Musterek Guvenlik ve Anlasmalar Dairesi Genel Mudurlugu [*Joint Security and Agreements Office Directorate General*] [*of Foreign Affairs Ministry*] (TU)

MUARC .... Monash University Accident Research Center [*Australia*]

MUART .... Muszaki Arut Ertekesito Vallalat [*Commercial Enterprise for Machines, Machine Tools, and Machine Products*] (HU)

MUAT .... Antilla [*Cuba*] [*ICAO location identifier*] (ICLI)

MUB .... Maun [*Botswana*] [*Airport symbol*] (OAG)

MUB .... Miejski Urzad Bezpieczenstwa [*Municipal Security Office*] (POL)

MUB .... Mouvement de l'Unite Basonge

MUBA ...... Baracoa/Oriente [*Cuba*] [*ICAO location identifier*] (ICLI)

MUBE ...... El Caribe [*Cuba*] [*ICAO location identifier*] (ICLI)

MUBEF ..... Mouvement Unifie Belge des Etudiants Francophones [*Belgian United Movement of French-Speaking Students*] (WER)

MUBI .... Cayo Mambi [*Cuba*] [*ICAO location identifier*] (ICLI)

MUBO .... Batabano [*Cuba*] [*ICAO location identifier*] (ICLI)

MUBY .... Bayamo [*Cuba*] [*ICAO location identifier*] (ICLI)

MUC .... Kandidat Mediciny [*Candidate for the Degree of Doctor of Medicine*] (CZ)

MUC .... Mezinarodni Umluva o Preprave Cestujicich po Zeleznici [*International Agreement on Railroad Passenger Transportation*] (CZ)

MUC .... Millions d'Unites de Compte [*Millions of Counting Units*] [*French Guiana*] (LA)

MUC .... Mission Universitaire et Culturelle Francaise en Tunisie

MUC .... Mouvement d'Union Camerounaise

MUC .... Movimiento Universitario Catolico [*Catholic University Movement*] [*Venezuela*] (LA)

MUC .... Movimiento Universitario del Centro [*Central University Movement*] [*Argentina*] (LA)

MUC .... Munich [*Germany*] [*Airport symbol*] (OAG)

MUCA .... Ciego De Avila [*Cuba*] [*ICAO location identifier*] (ICLI)

MUCB .... Caibarien [*Cuba*] [*ICAO location identifier*] (ICLI)

MUCC .... Cunagua [*Cuba*] [*ICAO location identifier*] (ICLI)

MUCECH ... Mivimiento Unitario Campesino y Etnias de Chile [*Trade union*] (EY)

MUCEU .... Makarere University College Employees Union [*Uganda*] (AF)

MUCF .... Cienfuegos [*Cuba*] [*ICAO location identifier*] (ICLI)

MUCF .... Mission Universitaire et Culturelle Francaise au Maroc

MUCG .... Macquarie University Caving Group [*Australia*]

MUCG .... Management/Union Consultative Group [*Australia*]

MUCL .... Cayo Largo Del Sur [*Cuba*] [*ICAO location identifier*] (ICLI)

MUCM ...... Camaguey/Ignacio Agramonte [*Cuba*] [*ICAO location identifier*] (ICLI)

MUCN .... Ciego De Avila Norte [*Cuba*] [*ICAO location identifier*] (ICLI)

MUCO .... Colon [*Cuba*] [*ICAO location identifier*] (ICLI)

MUCS .... Central Noel Fernandez [*Cuba*] [*ICAO location identifier*] (ICLI)

MUCS .... Movimiento de Unificacion y Coordinacion Sindical [*Union Unification and Coordination Movement*] [*Argentina*] (LA)

MUCU .... Santiago De Cuba/Antonio Maceo [*Cuba*] [*ICAO location identifier*] (ICLI)

MUCV .... Las Clavellinas [*Cuba*] [*ICAO location identifier*] (ICLI)

MUCY .... Cayajabo [*Cuba*] [*ICAO location identifier*] (ICLI)

MUD .... Ministarstvo Unutrasnjih Djela [*Ministry of Internal Affairs*] (YU)

MUD .... Mouvement pour l'Unite et la Democratie [*Djibouti*] [*Political party*] (EY)

MUD .... Mouvement Union Democratique [*Democratic Union Movement*] [*Monaco*] [*Political party*] (PPE)

MUD .... Movimento da Uniao Democratica [*Democratic Union Movement*] [*Portuguese*] (WER)

MUD .... Movimento Universitario de Desfavelamento [*University Antislum Movement*] [*Brazil*] (LA)

Mud .... Muddet [*Period*] [*of time*] (TU)

MUDA ...... Movimiento Universitario Democrata Argentino [*Argentine Democratic University Movement*] (LA)

MUDAR .... Mulheres por um Desenvolvimento Alternativo [*Development Alternatives with women for a New Era - DAWN*] [*Brazil*] (EAIO)

MUDel ...... Local Division Control [*Computers*] (RU)

MUDES .... Movimiento Universitario de Desenvolvimento Economico e Social [*University Movement for Economic and Social Development*] [*Brazil*] (LA)

MUDJ .... Movimiento de Unidade Democratica - Juvenil [*Democratic Union Movement - Youth*]

MUD-Juvenil ... Movimiento Uniao Democratica - Juvenil [*Democratic Union Movement - Youth*] [*Portuguese*] (WER)

MUDOK .... Muszaki Dokumentacios Kozpont [*Technical Documentation Center*] (HU)

MUDPAC ... Melbourne University Dual-Package Analog Computer [*Australia*] (ADA)

MUDr .... Doctor Medicinae Universae [*Doctor of Medicine*] (CZ)

MUE .... Maschinelle Uebersetzung [*German*] (ADPT)

MUE .... Movimiento de Unidad Estudiantil [*Movement of Student Unity*] [*Panama*] (LA)

Mue .... Muehle, Hammerwerk [*Mill, Foundry*] [*German*]

muegy .... Muegyetem [*Technical University*] (HU)

MUEL .... Mouvement pour l'Unite et l'Entente Lulua

MUERI ..... Murdoch University Energy Research Institute [*Australia*]

MUF .... Muting [*Indonesia*] [*Airport symbol*] (OAG)

MUF .... Ultraviolet Microscope (RU)

MUFC .... Central Amancio Rodriguez [*Cuba*] [*ICAO location identifier*] (ICLI)

MUFI .... Muszaki Fizikai Kutato Intezet [*Technical Physics Research Institute*] (HU)

MUFIS ...... Manisa Unlu Maddeler ve Firin Iscileri Sendikasi [*Manisa Farinaceous Products and Bakery Workers' Union*] (TU)

MUFL .... Florida [*Cuba*] [*ICAO location identifier*] (ICLI)

MUFLNG ... Mouvement pour l'Unification des Forces de Liberation de la Guadeloupe [*Movement for the Unification of National Liberation Forces of Guadeloupe*] [*Political party*] (PD)

MUFM ...... Mouvement Universal pour une Federation Mondiale [*World Association of World Federalists - WAWF*] [*Netherlands*]

MUFONOA ... Mutuelle des Fonctionnaires de l'Ordre Administratif [*Administrative Government Employees Mutual Association*] [*Cambodia*] (CL)

MUG .... Mulege [*Mexico*] [*Airport symbol*] [*Obsolete*] (OAG)

MUG .... Muszaki Gumigyar [*Industrial Rubber Factory*] (HU)

MUGI .... Melyepitoipari Uzemgazdasagi Iroda [*Industrial Management Bureau in Civil Engineering*] (HU)

MUGI .... Musterek Guvenlik Isleri Dairesi Genel Mudurlugu [*Joint Security Affairs Office Directorate General*] [*of Foreign Affairs Ministry*] (TU)

MUGM ...... Guantanamo, US Naval Air Base [*Cuba*] [*ICAO location identifier*] (ICLI)

MUGN ...... Giron [*Cuba*] [*ICAO location identifier*] (ICLI)

MUGT .... Guantanamo [*Cuba*] [*ICAO location identifier*] (ICLI)

Muh .... Muhabere [*Communications*] (TU)

Muh .... Muhasebe [*Accounting, Accountancy*] [*Turkish*] (TU)

muh .... Muhely [*Workshop*] (HU)

Muh .... Muhendis [*Engineer*] (TU)

Muh .... Muhtar [*Village Headman*] (TU)

MUHA .... Habana/Jose Marti [*Cuba*] [*ICAO location identifier*] (ICLI)

MUHE .... Ministere de l'Urbanisme, de l'Habitat, et de l'Environnement

MUHG ...... Holguin [*Cuba*] [*ICAO location identifier*] (ICLI)

Muh MimAka ... Muhendislik ve Mimarlik Akademisi [*Engineering and Architecture Academy*] (TU)

MUI .... Malaysian United Industries

MUI .... Maritime Union of India

MUI .... Movement for the Unity of the Left [*Ecuador*] [*Political party*] (PPW)

MUIN .... Movimiento Universitario Integralista Nacional [*National University Integral Movement*] [*Argentina*] (LA)

MUIS........ Isabella [Cuba] [ICAO location identifier]   (ICLI)
Muist .... Muistutus [Note] [Finland]   (GPO)
MUJ .... Mauritius Union of Journalists   (EAIO)
MUJ .... Movimiento Universitario Juvenil [University Youth Movement]
       [Costa Rica]   (LA)
MUJ .... Mui [Ethiopia] [Airport symbol]   (OAG)
MUJA .... Majana [Cuba] [ICAO location identifier]   (ICLI)
MUJCSA .. Mining Unions' Joint Committee of South Africa
MUJE....... Mechanics' Unions' Joint Executives [South Africa]
muk .... Flour Mill [Topography]   (RU)
MUK......... Local Control of Commands [Computers]   (RU)
MUK......... Magnetic Chart Angle   (RU)
MUK......... Marine Scientific Committee   (RU)
MUK......... Mauke [Cook Islands] [Airport symbol]   (OAG)
MUK......... Muk Air Taxi [Denmark] [ICAO designator]   (FAAC)
Mu K......... Muszaki Kiado [Publishing House of Technical Literature]
       (HU)
Muka .... Mukavele [Contract, Agreement]   (TU)
MUKhIN... Moscow Institute of Coal Chemistry   (RU)
MUL .... Maruti Udyog Ltd. [India]
mul .... Mit dem Urzeiger Laufend [Clockwise] [German]
MULA .... Monash University Law Alumni [Australia]
MULB .... Habana [Cuba] [ICAO location identifier]   (ICLI)
MULH .... Habana [Cuba] [ICAO location identifier]   (ICLI)
MULM...... La Coloma [Cuba] [ICAO location identifier]   (ICLI)
MULPOC ... Centre Multinational de Programme et d'Execution de Projets de
       l'Afrique de l'Ouest [Multinational Center for the
       Programming and Execution of West African Projects]
       (AF)
Mulr........... Muletier (Sentier) [Mule Path] [Military map abbreviation World
       War I] [French]   (MTD)
MULSF ..... Macquarie University Law School Foundation [Australia]
mult............ Mehrfach [Multiple] [German]
MULTICAP ... Australian Society for Multiply Handicapped Children
MULTICOR ... Multinational Finance Corp. [Indonesia]   (EY)
MULTIFERSELA ... Empresa Multinacional para la Comercializacion de
       Fertilizantes del Sistema Economico Latinoamericano
       [Multinational Enterprise for the Marketing of Fertilizers of
       the Latin American Economic System]   (LA)
MULTIFERT ... Multinacional de Fertilizantes
multigr .... Multigraferet [Multigraphed] [Publishing Danish/Norwegian]
multigr .... Multigrafie [Multilithed] [Publishing] [French]
mu m .... A Munkaugyi Miniszter Rendelete, Utasitasa [Decree of the
       Minister of Labor]   (HU)
MUM .... Methodology for Unmanned Manufacture [Robotics project]
       [Japan]
MuM......... Muhasebe Mudurlugu [Accounting Directorate] [of Foreign
       Affairs Ministry]   (TU)
MUM .... Mumias [Kenya] [Airport symbol] [Obsolete]   (OAG)
Mu M .... Munkaugyi Miniszter [Minister of Labor]   (HU)
MUMA....... Punta De Maisi [Cuba] [ICAO location identifier]   (ICLI)
MUMC...... Melbourne University Mountaineering Club [Australia]
MUMG..... Managua [Cuba] [ICAO location identifier]   (ICLI)
MUMH ..... Matahambre [Cuba] [ICAO location identifier]   (ICLI)
MUMI ...... Manzanillo [Cuba] [ICAO location identifier]   (ICLI)
MUMJ ...... Mayajigua [Cuba] [ICAO location identifier]   (ICLI)
MUMO ..... Moa [Cuba] [ICAO location identifier]   (ICLI)
MUMSU... Monash University Malaysian Students' Union [Australia]
MUMT...... Matanzas [Cuba] [ICAO location identifier]   (ICLI)
MUMZ...... Manzanillo [Cuba] [ICAO location identifier]   (ICLI)
MUN .... Maturin [Venezuela] [Airport symbol]   (OAG)
MUN .... Memorial Univeristy of Newfoundland   (PDAA)
MUN .... Metal-Film Ultrahigh-Frequency Unprotected (Resistor)   (RU)
MUN .... Mineworkers' Union of Namibia   (EY)
MUN .... Movimiento de Unidad Nacional [National Unity Movement]
       [Chile]   (LA)
MUN .... Movimiento de Unidad Nacional [National Unity Movement]
       [El Salvador]   (LA)
MUN .... Movimiento Universitario Nacional [National University
       Movement] [Argentina]   (LA)
mun .... Municipio [Municipality] [Portuguese]
Mun .... Munition [Ammunition]   (EG)
MUNA ...... La Cubana [Cuba] [ICAO location identifier]   (ICLI)
MUNA ...... United Nations Association of Mauritius   (EAIO)
MUNAF .... Movimento de Unidade Nacional Antifacista [National United
       Antifascist Movement] [Portugal] [Political party]   (PPE)
Munas........ Munasebetler [Relations]   (TU)
MUNAS..... Musjawarah Nasional [National Conference]   (IN)
MUNB....... San Nicolas De Bari [Cuba] [ICAO location identifier]   (ICLI)
MUNC....... Mouvement d'Union Nationale Congolaise
MUNC....... Nicaro [Cuba] [ICAO location identifier]   (ICLI)
MUNG...... Nueva Gerona [Cuba] [ICAO location identifier]   (ICLI)
MUNGE..... Movimiento de Union Nacional de Guinea Ecuatorial
MUNGE.... Movimiento para la Unificacion Nacional de Guinea Ecuatorial
       [Movement for National Unification of Equatorial Guinea]
       [Political party]   (EY)

MUNI........ Moscow Real Estate Administration   (RU)
MUNICROF ... Movimiento Universitario y Profesional para la Organizacion
       de la Comunidad [Colombia]   (COL)
MUNICS... Municipal Information Control System [Australia]
MUNOSZER ... Mutragya- es Novenyvedoszer Ertekesito Szovetkezeti
       Vallalat [Cooperative Enterprise for Selling Fertilizers and
       Products for Plant Protection]   (HU)
MUNSAL ... Municipalidad de San Salvador [El Salvador]   (LAA)
MUNU ...... Central Brasil [Cuba] [ICAO location identifier]   (ICLI)
MUOp .... Local Control of Operations [Computers]   (RU)
MUOpSdv ... Local Shift Control   (RU)
MUOSZ..... Magyar Ujsagirok Orszagos Szovetsege [National Federation of
       Hungarian Journalists]   (HU)
MUP......... Melbourne University Press [Australia]   (ADA)
MUP......... Mesno Usluzno Preduzece [Local Services Establishment]   (YU)
MUP......... Mezinarodni Urad Prace [International Labor Office]   (CZ)
MUP......... Ministarstvo Unutrasnjih Poslova [Ministry of Internal Affairs]
       (YU)
MUP......... Ministry of the Coal Industry   (RU)
MUP......... Mouvement de l'Unite Populaire [Popular Unity Movement]
       [Tunisia] [Political party]   (PD)
MUP......... Movimiento de Unidade Popular [Popular Unity Movement]
       [Portuguese]   (WER)
MUP......... Movimiento da Unidade Progressiva [Brazil] [Political party]
       (EY)
MUPA .... Punta Alegre [Cuba] [ICAO location identifier]   (ICLI)
MUPAS..... Melbourne University Programme in Antarctic Studies
       [Australia]
MUPB .... Baracoa Playa/Habana [Cuba] [ICAO location identifier]   (ICLI)
MUPGE .... Movimiento de Union Popular de Liberacion de la Guinea
       Ecuatorial
MUPL ...... Pilon [Cuba] [ICAO location identifier]   (ICLI)
MUPR ...... Pinar Del Rio [Cuba] [ICAO location identifier]   (ICLI)
MUPRA .... Macquarie University Postgraduate Representative Association
       [Australia]
MUPS....... Central Guatemala [Cuba] [ICAO location identifier]   (ICLI)
MUPT ...... Patria [Cuba] [ICAO location identifier]   (ICLI)
MUPV ...... Ministry of the Coal Industry of the Eastern Regions, USSR
       (RU)
MUPY ...... Micro et Processeur [French name, based on the Greek letters mu
       and pi, for a computer instruction program marketed by
       Info-Realite]
MUPZ ...... Ministry of the Coal Industry of the Western Regions, USSR
       (RU)
MUR......... Aerolinea Muri [Mexico] [ICAO designator]   (FAAC)
MUR......... Marudi [Malaysia] [Airport symbol]   (OAG)
MUR......... Melbourne University Rifles [Australia]
MUR......... Morski Urzad Rybacki [Deep Sea Fishing Administration]
       (POL)
MUR......... Moscow Office of Criminal Investigation   (RU)
MUR......... Mouvement Unifie de la Resistance
MUR......... Movimiento de Unidad Reformista [Reformist Unity Movement]
       [Dominican Republic]   (LA)
MUR......... Movimiento de Unidad Revolucionaria [Guerrilla forces]
       [Honduras]   (EY)
MUR......... Movimiento de Unidad Revolucionaria [Nicaragua] [Political
       party]   (EY)
MUR......... Movimiento Universitario Reformista [University Reform
       Movement] [Argentina]   (LA)
MUR......... Movimiento Universitario Revolucionario [Revolutionary
       University Movement] [Colorado]   (LA)
MUR......... Movimiento Universitario Revolucionario [Revolutionary
       University Movement] [Ecuador]   (LA)
MURBO.... Murray Basin Borehole Database [Australia]
MUrbRegPlg ... Master of Urban and Regional Planning
MURCEP ... Ministry of Urban and Rural Construction and Environmental
       Protection [China]   (PDAA)
Murd .... Murdoch University [Australia]   (ADA)
MUREBES ... Mutuelle des Ressortissants de Bengassou-Esseyakro
MURFAAMCE ... Mutual Reduction of Forces and Armaments and
       Associated Measures in Central Europe   (WER)
MURS .... Mouvement Universel de la Responsabilite Scientifique
       [Universal Movement for Scientific Responsibility - UMSR]
       (EAIO)
murt........... Murteellinen [Dialect] [Finland]
MUS.......... Magnetic Amplifier with Self-Magnetization   (RU)
MUS.......... Mauritius [ANSI three-letter standard code]   (CNC)
MUS.......... Multiprogramming Utility System [Regnecentralen] [Denmark]
Mus........... Musavir [Adviser]   (TU)
Mus........... Museum [Museum] [German]
MUS.......... Mushito [Race of maize] [Mexico]
mus............ Music   (TPFD)
Mus........... Musica [Music] [Portuguese]
mus............ Musiek [Music] [Afrikaans]
mus............ Musiikki [Music] [Finland]
Mus........... Musik [Music] [German]
mus............ Musique [French]   (TPFD)

Mus............ Muslim

mus............. Musor [*Schedule, Program*]   (HU)

MUSA .... San Antonio De Los Banos [*Cuba*] [*ICAO location identifier*] (ICLI)

MUSC .... Movimiento Universitario Social Cristiano [*Social Christian University Movement*] [*Dominican Republic*]   (LA)

MUSC .... Santa Clara [*Cuba*] [*ICAO location identifier*]   (ICLI)

MUSERMA ... Association Mutuelle de Secours des Ressortissants Manianga du Territoire de Songololo

MUSF........ Habana/Santa Fe [*Cuba*] [*ICAO location identifier*]   (ICLI)

MUSG .... Sagua La Grande [*Cuba*] [*ICAO location identifier*]   (ICLI)

MusH......... Music Hall [*Record label*] [*Argentina*]

M u-shte..... School of Music   (BU)

MUSICAM ... Masking Pattern Universal Sub-Band Integrated Coding and Multiplexing [*Broadcasting*]

MUSIL...... Multiprogramming Utility System Interpretive Language [*Regnecentralen*] [*Denmark*]

MUSJ........ San Julian (Escuela de Aviacion) [*Cuba*] [*ICAO location identifier*]   (ICLI)

MUSl........ Local Addition Control [*Computers*]   (RU)

MUSL........ Santa Lucia [*Cuba*] [*ICAO location identifier*]   (ICLI)

MUSN ...... Musician [*Royal Australian Navy*]

MUSN ...... Siguanea, Isla De La Juventud [*Cuba*] [*ICAO location identifier*]   (ICLI)

Muspaed .... Musisch-Paedagogisch [*Artistic-Educational*] [*German*]

MUSPIDA ... Musjawarah Pimpinan Daerah [*Regional Executive Council*]   (IN)

MUSR .... Simon Reyes [*Cuba*] [*ICAO location identifier*]   (ICLI)

MUSS........ Medunarodno Udruzenje za Socijalnu Sigurnost [*International Social Security Association (ISSA)*] [*YU*]

MUSS........ Sancti Spiritus [*Cuba*] [*ICAO location identifier*]   (ICLI)

MUST .... Meeting Updates in Skill Training [*International Labor Organization*] [*Information service or system United Nations*]   (DUND)

Must.......... Musterek [*Joint*]   (TU)

MUSZ .... Magyar Uszo Szovetseg [*Hungarian Swimming Association*]   (HU)

MUSZ .... Magyar Uttorok Szovetsege [*Hungarian Pioneers' Association*]   (HU)

musz .... Muszak [*Work Shift*]   (HU)

musz .... Muszaki [*Technical, Technological*]   (HU)

musz .... Muszeresz [*Mechanic*]   (HU)

MUSZ .... Muszertermelo Vallalat [*Synthetic Coal Production Enterprise*]   (HU)

MUSZI...... Mezogazdasagi Ugyvitelszervezesi Iroda [*Office for the Organization of Agricultural Business Management*]   (HU)

musz tuddoktora ... Muszaki Tudomanyok Doktora [*Doctor of Technical Sciences*]   (HU)

MUT.......... Magyar Urbanisztikai Tarsasag [*Hungary*]   (SLS)

MUT.......... Malta Union of Teachers   (SLS)

MUT.......... Multiservicios Aeronauticos SA de CV [*Mexico*] [*ICAO designator*]   (FAAC)

Mut .... Mutercim [*Translator*]   (TU)

Mutat........ Mutation [*German*]   (GCA)

MUTD........ Trinidad [*Cuba*] [*ICAO location identifier*]   (ICLI)

Mute.......... Mutehassis [*Specialist*]   (TU)

MUTI .... Manati [*Cuba*] [*ICAO location identifier*]   (ICLI)

MUTI .... Movimento Unitario dos Trabalhadores Intelectuais para a Defesa da Revolucao [*United Movement of Intellectuals for the Defense of the Revolution*] [*Portuguese*]   (WER)

mutilaz .... Mutilazione [*Mutilation*] [*Italian*]

MUTRACI ... Mutuelle des Transporteurs de Cote-D'Ivoire

MUUmn .... Local Multiplication Control [*Computers*]   (RU)

mUV.......... Maritime Moderate Air   (RU)

MUV.......... Mlynarsky Ustav Vyzkumny [*Flour Milling Research Institute*]   (CZ)

MUV.......... Modernized Simplified Fuze   (RU)

MUV.......... Universal Mine Fuze   (RU)

MUVA....... Central Primero De Enero [*Cuba*] [*ICAO location identifier*]   (ICLI)

MUVA....... Milchwirtschaftliche Untersuchungs- und Versuchsanstalt Kempten (Allgaeu) [*Allgaeu Institute for Dairying*]   (ARC)

muvez .... Muvezeto [*Foreman, Chief of Factory Unit*]   (HU)

MUVR....... Varadero [*Cuba*] [*ICAO location identifier*]   (ICLI)

MUVT....... Las Tunas [*Cuba*] [*ICAO location identifier*]   (ICLI)

MUW........ Mascara [*Algeria*] [*Airport symbol*]   (OAG)

MUW........ Moroccan Union of Work   (EAIO)

MUX........ Multan [*Pakistan*] [*Airport symbol*]   (OAG)

MUZ.......... Mezinarodni Umluva o Prepravre Zbozi po Zeleznicich [*International Agreement on Railroad Freight Transportation*]   (CZ)

MUZ.......... Mineworkers Union of Zambia   (AF)

muz........... Museum   (RU)

MUZ.......... Musoma [*Tanzania*] [*Airport symbol*]   (OAG)

Muz.......... Muzik [*Music*]   (TU)

Muz........... Muzyka [*or Muzyczny*] [*Music or Musical*]   (POL)

Muza .... Muza and Other Labels [*Record label*] [*Poland*]

Muzfond..... Music Fund of the USSR   (RU)

MUZG....... Zaragoza [*Cuba*] [*ICAO location identifier*]   (ICLI)

Muzgiz ...... State Music Publishing House   (RU)

muzhsk....... Masculine, Male   (RU)

muz-nauch .. Musicological   (BU)

MUZO....... Musical Education   (RU)

MUZO....... Music Department   (RU)

Muzpred .... State Music Trust (State Association of Music Establishments)   (RU)

MV............ Airlines of Western Australia [*Australia*] [*ICAO designator*]   (ICDA)

MV............ Cutter   (RU)

MV............ Driver-Mechanic   (RU)

MV............ Height Scale   (RU)

MV............ Low Water   (RU)

mv............. Maanviljelija [*Finland*]

MV............ Maldives [*ANSI two-letter standard code*]   (CNC)

mV............ Maritime Air   (RU)

MV............ Masking Agent [*Chemistry*]   (RU)

Mv............ Materialversorgung [*Material Supply, Procurement*]   (EG)

mv............. Measures of Weight   (RU)

MV............ Mechanical Rectifier   (RU)

MV............ Mechanized Troops   (RU)

mv............. Meervoud [*Plural*] [*Afrikaans*]

MV............ Megali Vretannia [*Great Britain*]   (GC)

MV............ Megawolt [*Megavolt*] [*Poland*]

MV............ Memoire Vive [*French*]   (ADPT)

Mv............ Mendelevio [*Mendelevium*] [*Chemical element*] [*Portuguese*]

MV............ Meter Waves, Metric Waves   (RU)

MV............ Methylviologen   (RU)

MV............ Mezzo Voce [*With Medium Fullness of Tone*] [*Music*]

MV............ Microswitch   (RU)

mV............ Milivolt [*Millivolt*] [*Portuguese*]

mV............ Miliwolt [*Millivolt*] [*Poland*]

MV............ Milletvekili [*Deputy*]   (TU)

mV............ Millivolt [*German*]   (GCA)

MV............ Mine Fuze   (RU)

MV............ Ministerstvo Vnitra [*Ministry of Interior*]   (CZ)

MV............ Ministry of Armaments, USSR   (RU)

mv............. Mint Vendeg [*Visiting Artist*]   (HU)

MV............ Mistni Velitelstvi [*Local Command Post*]   (CZ)

Mv............ Mitvergangenheit [*With Past Tense*] [*German*]

m/v............ Mois de Vue [*French*]

MV............ Molecular Weight   (RU)

MV............ Moonee Valley [*Australia*]   (ADA)

mv............. Moottorivene [*Finland*]

mv............. Mortar Platoon   (RU)

Mv............ Motovellero [*Sailing or fishing-boat with auxiliary motor*] [*Italian*]

mv............. Mrtva Vaha [*Dead Weight*]   (CZ)

MV............ Mudafaa Vekaleti [*Defense Ministry*]   (TU)

MV............ Multivibrator   (RU)

MV............ Music of the Vatican [*Record label*] [*France*]

Mv............ Naval Forces   (BU)

MV............ Oil Circuit Breaker, Oil Switch   (RU)

MV............ Rotary Magnet   (RU)

MV............ Small-Bore Rifle   (RU)

m-v............ Study of Materials   (RU)

MV............ Vacuum Gauge, Vacuum Manometer   (RU)

MVA.......... Magyar Vasuti Arudijszabas [*Hungarian Railroad Freight Rates*]   (HU)

MVA.......... Megavoltamper [*Megavolt-Ampere*]   (YU)

mva.......... Megavolt Ampere   (BU)

MvA.......... Memorie van Antwoord [*Benelux*]   (BAS)

MVA.......... Moscow Veterinary Academy   (RU)

MVA.......... Murray Valley Airlines [*Australia*]

MVA.......... Musica Viva Australia   (ADA)

MVA.......... Myvatn [*Iceland*] [*Airport symbol*] [*Obsolete*]   (OAG)

MvA I ...... Memorie van Antwoord aan de Eerste Kamer [*Benelux*]   (BAS)

MvA II...... Memorie van Antwoord aan de Tweede Kamer [*Benelux*]   (BAS)

mval.......... Milliaequivalent [*Milliequivalent*] [*German*]   (GCA)

MVAS....... Murray Valley Air Service [*Australia*]

MvB .... Maandblad voor Belastingrecht [*Benelux*]   (BAS)

MVB .... Marianas Visitors Bureau   (EAIO)

MVB .... Muziekverbond van Belgie [*Belgium*]   (EAIO)

MVB .... Mvengue [*Gabon*] [*Airport symbol*]   (OAG)

MvB en R.. Maandblad voor Berechtiging en Reclassering [*Benelux*]   (BAS)

MVBN ...... Mededelingen van het Verbond der Belgisch Nijverheid [*Belgium*]   (BAS)

MVCDGS ... Motor Vehicles and Components Development Grants Scheme [*Australia*]

MVCMB ... Murray Valley Citrus Marketing Board [*Australia*]

MVCS....... Motor Vehicle Certification System

MVD......... Air-Manganese Depolarization   (RU)

MvD.......... Minister van Defensie [*Minister of Defense*] [*Benelux*]   (BAS)

MVD......... Montevideo [*Uruguay*] [*Airport symbol*]   (OAG)

MvDeurw... Maandblad voor de Vereniging van Deurwaarders [*Benelux*] (BAS)

MVDLB..... Motor Vehicle Dealers' Licensing Board [*Western Australia*]

MVD-MGB ... Ministerstvo Vnutrennikh Del-Ministerstvo Gosudarstvennoe Bezopasnosti [*Later, KGB*]

MVDr .... Doctor Medicinae Veterinariae [*Doctor of Veterinary Medicine*] (CZ)

MVDr .... Veterinary Doctor [*Former Czechoslovakia*]

MVE .... Matravideki Eromu [*Power Plant of the Matra Region*] (HU)

MVETs...... Microhydraulic Power Plant (BU)

MVetSt ...... Master of Veterinary Studies

MVEU .... Moscow Higher School of Power Engineering (RU)

MVF .... International Monetary Fund [*IMF*] (RU)

MVFC....... Municipal Valuation Fees Committee [*Victoria, Australia*]

MVG.......... Magyar Vagon- es Gepgyar, Gyor [*Railroad Car and Machine Factory, Gyor*] (HU)

MVG.......... Mengenverbrauchsguttern [*Mass Consumption Goods*] [*German*]

MVGT .... Moscow Evening Mining Technicum (RU)

MVI .... Maandblad der Vereniging van Inspecteurs van Financien [*Benelux*] (BAS)

MVI .... Metallverarbeitende Industrie [*Metalworking Industry*] (EG)

MVI .... Moscow Veterinary Institute (RU)

MVIA .... Motor Vehicles Importers Association [*Cyprus*] (EAIO)

MVIS........ Murrumbidgee Irrigation Area Vine Improvement Society [*Australia*]

MV iSSO ... Ministry of Higher and Secondary Special Education (RU)

MVJ.......... Mandeville [*Jamaica*] [*Airport symbol*] [*Obsolete*] (OAG)

MvJ........... Minister van Justitie [*Minister of Justice*] [*Benelux*] (BAS)

MVK .... Magyar Voroskereszt [*Hungarian Red Cross*] (HU)

MVK .... Mevalonic Acid (RU)

Mvk........... Mevki [*Site, Locality*] (TU)

MVK .... Ministerstvo Vykupu [*Ministry for Bulk Purchases (of agricultural products)*] (CZ)

MVK .... Moscow-Volga Canal [*1937-1947*] (RU)

MVK .... Mulka [*Australia*] [*Airport symbol*] [*Obsolete*] (OAG)

MVKh........ Ministry of Water Management (RU)

MVKhPU .. Moscow Higher School of Industrial Art (RU)

MVKP .... Munisipale Vereniging van die Kaapprovinsie [*South Africa*] (AA)

MVKRCh .. Interdepartmental Commission on Radio Frequencies (RU)

MVL .... Magadan Airlines [*Russian Federation*] [*ICAO designator*] (FAAC)

MVL .... Maximal Pulmonary Ventilation (RU)

MVL .... Murray Valley League [*Australia*]

MVLDC..... Murray Valley League for Development and Conservation [*Australia*]

MVM........ Magyar Vegyimuvek [*Hungarian Chemical Factory*] (HU)

MvM........ Minister van Marine [*Benelux*] (BAS)

MVMF ...... Ministerstvo Voenno-Morskogo Flota [*Ministry of the Navy*] [*1950-53; merged into the MO*] [*Former USSR*]

MVMI ...... Moscow Evening Institute of Mechanical Engineering (RU)

MVMI ...... Moscow Evening Institute of Metallurgy (RU)

MVMU...... Murmansk Higher Nautical School (RU)

MVN........ Armed-Safe Mechanism (RU)

MVN........ Materialverbrauchsnorm [*Material Consumption Norm*] (EG)

MVNB ...... Mistni Velitelstvi Narodni Bezpecnosti [*Local Headquarters of the National Security Corps*] (CZ)

MVO......... Member of the Royal Victorian Order [*Australia*] (ADA)

MVO......... Ministerstvo Vnitrniho Obchodu [*Ministry of Domestic Trade*] (CZ)

MvO.......... Minister van Onderwijs [*Benelux*] (BAS)

MvO.......... Minister van Oorlog [*Benelux*] (BAS)

M-vo.......... Ministry (BU)

MVO......... Ministry of Higher Education (RU)

MVO......... Moscow Military District (RU)

M-voelektr i melior ... Ministry of Electrification and Land Reclamation [*Obsolete*] (BU)

M-voelektr vod prir bog ... Ministry of Electrification and Natural Resources [*Obsolete*] (BU)

M-vo fin ..... Ministry of Finance (BU)

M-vo indzan ... Ministry of Industry and Trades [*Obsolete*] (BU)

M-vo infizk ... Ministry of Information and the Arts [*Obsolete*] (BU)

M-vo narotbr ... Ministry of National Defense (BU)

M-vo narprosv ... Ministry of National Education (BU)

M-vo narzdr ... Ministry of Public Health (BU)

M-vo natransp ... Ministry of Transportation (BU)

M-voobsht sgr put blag ... Ministry of Public Buildings, Roads, and Public Works [*Obsolete*] (BU)

MVOP .... Ministerio da Viacao e Obras Publicas [*Ministry of Transportation and Public Works*] [*Portuguese*]

M-vo prav .. Ministry of Justice (BU)

M-vo sotspolit ... Ministry of Social Policy [*Obsolete*] (BU)

M-vo turg... Ministry of Commerce [*Obsolete*] (BU)

M-vo v .... Ministry of War [*Obsolete*] (BU)

M-vovunsh rab ... Ministry of Foreign Affairs (BU)

M-vovunsh rab i izpv ... Ministry of Foreign Affairs and Religious Faiths [*Obsolete*] (BU)

M-vo vutrrab ... Ministry of Internal Affairs (BU)

M-vozemed i durzh im ... Ministry of Agriculture and State Property [*Obsolete*] (BU)

M-vo zhelavtom vodni i vuzd suobsht ... Ministry of Railroads and Automobile, Water, and Air Communications [*Obsolete*] (BU)

M-vo zhelposht i telegr ... Ministry of Railroads, Posts, and Telegraphs [*Obsolete*] (BU)

MVP .... Correcting Mechanism (RU)

MVP .... Method of Induced Polarization (RU)

MVP .... Methylvinylpyridine (RU)

MVP .... Ministerstvo Verejnych Praci [*Ministry of Public Works*] (CZ)

MVP .... Mitsubishi Value Plan [*Japan*]

MVP .... Mitu [*Colombia*] [*Airport symbol*] (OAG)

MVP .... Refracted Wave Method, Refraction Method (RU)

MVPI........ Moscow Higher Pedagogical Institute (RU)

MVPP....... Metal Runway (RU)

MVR .... Maroua [*Cameroon*] [*Airport symbol*] (OAG)

MVR .... Ministry of Foreign Affairs (BU)

MVR .... Ministry of Internal Affairs (BU)

MVR .... Molecular-Weight Distribution (RU)

MVR .... Mongolische Volksrepublik [*Mongolian People's Republic*] (EG)

MVRDC .... Motor Vehicle Repair Disputes Committee [*New South Wales, Australia*]

MVRIAG... Murray Valley Rural Industry Assistance Group [*Australia*]

MVRIC...... Motor Vehicle Repair Industry Council [*New South Wales, Australia*]

MVR-UPPZ ... Ministry of Internal Affairs, Fire Prevention Administration (BU)

mvs .... Maanviljelysseura [*Finland*]

MVS .... Magnetic-Variation Station (RU)

MVS .... Masinska Visa Skola [*Advanced Machinery School*] (YU)

MVS .... Mezinarodni Vseodborovy Svaz [*International Federation of Trade Unions*] (CZ)

MVS .... Mine Ventilation Society of South Africa (AA)

MVS .... Ministerstvo Vooruzhennykh Sil [*Ministry of the Armed Forces*] [*1946-50; superseded by VM, MVMF*] [*Former USSR*]

MVS .... Ministerstvo Vseobecneho Strojirenstvi [*Ministry of Machine Building*] (CZ)

MVS .... Ministerstvo Vysokych Skol [*Ministry of Institutions of Higher Education*] (CZ)

MVS .... Ministry of the Armed Forces (RU)

MVS .... Mistni Vojenska Sprava [*Local Military Administration*] (CZ)

MVS .... Valence Bond Theory (RU)

MVSA....... Mediese Vereniging van Suid-Afrika [*South Africa*] (AA)

MVSA....... Misstofvereniging van Suid-Afrika [*South Africa*] (AA)

MVSN ...... Milizia Volontaria per la Sicurezza Nazionale [*Italian*]

MVSofSA .. Mine Ventilation Society of South Africa

MVSSO..... Ministry of Higher and Secondary Special Education (RU)

MVSSz ...... Magyar Vandorsport Szovetseg [*Hungarian Tourists Association*] (HU)

MVST....... Magyar Vallalkozasstrategiai Tarsasag [*Hungary*] (EAIO)

MVSz....... Magyar Vivo Szovetseg [*Hungarian Fencing Association*] (HU)

MVSZGA ... Mein Vertrauen Steht zu Gott Allein [*My Trust Is in God Alone*] [*Motto of Johann Adolf II, Duke of Saxony-Weissenfels (1649-97)*] [*German*]

MVSzPE.... Magyar Vasuti Szemely-, Poggyasz-, es Expresszarudijszabas [*Hungarian Railroad Passenger, Luggage, and Freight Rates*] (HU)

MVSZSZ... Magyar Vasutasok Szabad Szakszervezete [*Free Trade Union of the Hungarian Railroad Workers*] (HU)

MVT .... International Military Tribunal (RU)

MVT .... Mataiva [*French Polynesia*] [*Airport symbol*] (OAG)

Mvt .... Megawatt (RU)

MvT .... Memorie van Toelichting [*Benelux*] (BAS)

mvt .... Milliwatt (RU)

MVT .... Ministerstvo Vystavby a Techniky [*Ministry of Development and Technology*] (CZ)

MVT .... Ministry of Foreign Trade (BU)

MVT .... Ministry of Foreign Trade, USSR (RU)

MVT .... Ministry of Internal Trade (BU)

MVT .... Scale Rotary Transformer (RU)

Mvt-ch ...... Megawatt-Hour (RU)

MVTU .... Moscow Higher Technical School Imeni N. E. Bauman (RU)

MVTVS..... Mistni Vybor pro Telesnou Vychovu a Sport [*Local Committee for Physical Education and Sports*] (CZ)

MVU......... General-Purpose Wheatstone Resistance Bridge (RU)

MVU......... Musgrave [*Australia*] [*Airport symbol*] [*Obsolete*] (OAG)

MVunshRab ... Ministry of Foreign Affairs (BU)

MVunshTurg ... Ministry of Foreign Trade (BU)

MVutrTurg ... Ministry of Internal Trade (BU)

MVV .... Mynventilasievereniging van Suid-Afrika [*Mine Ventilation Society of South Africa*] (AA)

MVV .... Propellant, Low-Order Explosive (RU)

MVVS........ Modelarske Vyzkumne a Vyvojove Stredisko [*Model Research and Development Center (of the Union for Cooperation with the Army)*] (CZ)

MvW......... Minister van Waterstaat [*Benelux*] (BAS)

MVX......... Minvoul [*Gabon*] [*Airport symbol*] (OAG)

MVY......... Magyar Vitorlas Yachtszovetseg [*Hungarian Sailboat and Yachting Association*] (HU)

MVZ......... Ministerstvo Vyzivy [*Ministry of Food Supply*] (CZ)

MVZ......... Minsk Bicycle Plant (RU)

MVZ......... Moravskoklezske Vlnarske Zavody [*Moravian-Silesian Woolen Mills*] (CZ)

MVZG .... Mein Verlangen zu Gott [*My Desires (I Give) to God*] [*Motto of Anna Marie, Margravine of Brandenburg (1609-80)*] [*German*]

MVZI........ Moscow Higher Zootechnical Institute (RU)

MVZShPD ... Moscow Higher Correspondence School of Trade Unionism of the VTsSPS (RU)

MW........... Malawi [*ANSI two-letter standard code*] (CNC)

MW........... Marynarka Wojenna [*Navy*] (POL)

MW........... Maschinenwort [*German*] (ADPT)

MW........... Material Wybuchowy [*Explosive*] [*Poland*]

MW........... Maxwell Co. Ltd. [*Taiwan*]

MW........... Medium Wave (IDIG)

MW........... Megavat [*Megawatt*] (YU)

MW........... Megawat [*Megawatt*] [*Poland*]

MW........... Megawatt [*German*] (GCA)

mW........... Meines Wissens [*As Far as I Know*] [*German*] (EG)

MW........... Messwert [*Constant Value*] (EG)

MW........... Middle Welsh [*Language, etc.*]

mW........... Miliwat [*Milliwatt*] [*Poland*]

MW........... Minenwerfer [*Trench Mortar*] [*Military*] [*German*] (MTD)

MW........... Mine Warfare [*Royal Australian Navy*]

MW........... Mittelwasser [*Medium Water Level*] [*German*] (EG)

MW........... Moewe Flugzeugbau, Heini Dittmar [*Germany*] [*ICAO aircraft manufacturer identifier*] (ICAO)

MWA......... Metropolitan Waterworks Authority [*Thailand*]

MWAFG ... Media Workers Association of Free Grenada (LA)

MWASA.... Media Workers' Association of South Africa

MWc......... Megavat Cas [*Megawatt-Hour*] (YU)

MWC......... Melbourne Walking Club [*Australia*]

MWC......... Migrant Workers' Committee [*Australia*]

MWCB ...... Cayman Brac/Gerrard Smith [*Cayman Islands*] [*ICAO location identifier*] (ICLI)

MWCG ...... Grand Cayman [*Cayman Islands*] [*ICAO location identifier*] (ICLI)

MWCL ...... Little Cayman/Boddenfield [*Cayman Islands*] [*ICAO location identifier*] (ICLI)

MWCR ...... Georgetown/Owen Roberts International [*Cayman Islands*] [*ICAO location identifier*] (ICLI)

MWD........ Ministry of Works and Development [*New Zealand*] (PDAA)

MWDDEA .. Mutual Weapons Development Data Exchange Agreement [*NATO*]

MWDDEP ... Mutual Weapons Development Data Exchange Procedures [*NATO*]

MWDP ...... Mutual Weapons Development Program [*NATO*]

Mw d V ...... Mittelwort der Vergangenheit [*Past Participle*] [*German*]

MWE........ Merowe [*Sudan*] [*Airport symbol*] (OAG)

MWEIA.... Montessori World Educational Institute Australia

MWEU...... Motor Workshop Employees' Union (ML)

MWF........ Methodist Women's Fellowship [*Ghana*] (EAIO)

MWG........ Magyar Waggon- es Gepgyar, Ltd. [*Hungarian Railroad Car and Machine Plant Limited*] (HU)

MWG........ Miedzynarodowa Wspolpraca Geofizyczna [*International Geophysical Cooperation*] [*Poland*]

MWh .... Megawatt hour (EECI)

MWI......... Malawi [*ANSI three-letter standard code*] (CNC)

MWIA ...... Medical Women's International Association [*See also AIFM*] [*Cologne, Federal Republic of Germany*] (EAIO)

MWISA..... Member of the Water Institute of Southern Africa (AA)

MWJ .... Matthews Ridge [*Guyana*] [*Airport symbol*] (OAG)

MWL........ Malawi Women's League

MWL........ Muslim World League (BJA)

MWMC.... Metropolitan Waste Management Council [*Melbourne, Australia*]

MWO .... Mozambique Workers Organisation (EAIO)

m woj......... Miasto Wojewodzkie [*Capital of Province*] [*Poland*]

MWP .... Malta Workers Party [*Political party*] (PPE)

MWP .... Muzeum Wojska Polskiego [*Polish Army Museum*] [*Poland*]

MWPLF .... Malayan Workers and Peasants Labor Front (ML)

MWQ .... Magwe [*Myanmar*] [*Airport symbol*] (OAG)

MWR........ Ministry of Water Resources [*Burkina Faso*]

MWRC ..... Melbourne Western Region Commission [*Australia*]

MWSS ...... Metropolitan Waterworks and Sewerage System [*Philippines*] (DS)

MWT........ Mazurska Wytwornia Tytoniu [*Mazury (Masuria) Tobacco Plant*] (POL)

MWT........ Moolawatana [*Australia*] [*Airport symbol*] [*Obsolete*] (OAG)

MWU........ Maccabi World Union [*Ramat Gan, Israel*] (EAIO)

MWU........ Mine Workers Union [*South Africa*] (IMH)

MWU........ Mussau [*Papua New Guinea*] [*Airport symbol*] (OAG)

MWV........ Mineralolwirtschaftsverband eV [*Oil Industry Association*] [*Germany*] (PDAA)

MWWA .... Metropolitan Water Works Authority [*Thailand*] (DS)

MWWL .... Maori Women's Welfare League [*New Zealand*]

MWWV .... Movement of Working Women and Volunteers [*Tel Aviv, Israel*] (EAIO)

MWY........ Miranda Downs [*Australia*] [*Airport symbol*] [*Obsolete*] (OAG)

MWZ........ Mwanza [*Tanzania*] [*Airport symbol*] (OAG)

mx .... Au Mieux [*At Best*] [*French*]

Mx .... Makswel [*Maxwel*] [*Poland*]

mx .... Maximum [*Maximum*] [*German*]

MX .... Mexico [*ANSI two-letter standard code*] (CNC)

MX .... Wytwornia Maszyn Numer X [*Number X Machine Building Plant*] [*POL*]

MXA .... Compania Mexicana de Aviacion SA [*Mexico*] [*ICAO designator*] (FAAC)

MXB .... Masamba [*Indonesia*] [*Airport symbol*] (OAG)

MXC .... Mexair SA [*Switzerland*] [*ICAO designator*] (FAAC)

MXL .... Mexicali [*Mexico*] [*Airport symbol*] (OAG)

MXM........ Morombe [*Madagascar*] [*Airport symbol*] (OAG)

MXN......... Morlaix [*France*] [*Airport symbol*] (OAG)

MXP .... Milan [*Italy*] Malpensa Airport [*Airport symbol*] (OAG)

MXT .... Maintirano [*Madagascar*] [*Airport symbol*] (OAG)

MXU .... Mullewa [*Australia*] [*Airport symbol*] [*Obsolete*] (OAG)

MXX .... Merchant Express Aviation [*Nigeria*] [*ICAO designator*] (FAAC)

MXX .... Mora [*Sweden*] [*Airport symbol*] (OAG)

MXY .... Instituto de Misiones Extranjeras de Yarumal [*Foreign Missions of Yarumal*] [*Colombia*] (EAIO)

My............. Maatskappy [*Company*] [*Afrikaans*]

MY .... Malaysia [*IYRU nationality code*] [*ANSI two-letter standard code*] (CNC)

MYA .... Monoiodoacetate (RU)

MYA .... Moruya [*Australia*] [*Airport symbol*] (OAG)

MYA .... Myasishchev [*Aircraft*] [*Commonwealth of Independent States*]

MYA .... Myflug HF [*Iceland*] [*ICAO designator*] (FAAC)

MYAB ...... Clarence Bain, Andros Island [*Bahamas*] [*ICAO location identifier*] (ICLI)

MYAF....... Andros Town, Andros Island [*Bahamas*] [*ICAO location identifier*] (ICLI)

MYAG ...... Gorda Cay, Abaco Island [*Bahamas*] [*ICAO location identifier*] (ICLI)

MYAK....... Congo Town, Andros Island [*Bahamas*] [*ICAO location identifier*] (ICLI)

MYAM ...... Marsh Harbour, Abaco Island [*Bahamas*] [*ICAO location identifier*] (ICLI)

MYAN ...... San Andros, Andros Island [*Bahamas*] [*ICAO location identifier*] (ICLI)

MYAO ...... Moores Island, Abaco Island [*Bahamas*] [*ICAO location identifier*] (ICLI)

MYAP ...... Spring Point [*Bahamas*] [*ICAO location identifier*] (ICLI)

MYAS........ Sandy Point, Abaco Island [*Bahamas*] [*ICAO location identifier*] (ICLI)

myasn........ Meat Industry Kombinat [*Topography*] (RU)

myasn........ Meat Industry Plant [*Topography*] (RU)

myasokomb ... Meat Kombinat [*Topography*] (RU)

myasomolprom ... Meat and Dairy Industry (RU)

Myasomoltara ... Administration of Packing Materials Manufacture for the Meat and Dairy Industry (RU)

MYAT ...... Treasure Cay, Abaco Island [*Bahamas*] [*ICAO location identifier*] (ICLI)

MYAW ...... Walker Cay, Abaco Island [*Bahamas*] [*ICAO location identifier*] (ICLI)

MYB .... Mayoumba [*Gabon*] [*Airport symbol*] (OAG)

MYBC ...... Chub Cay, Berry Island [*Bahamas*] [*ICAO location identifier*] (ICLI)

MYBG ...... Bullocks Harbour/Great Harbour Cay, Berry Island [*Bahamas*] [*ICAO location identifier*] (ICLI)

MYBO ...... Ocean Cay, Bimini Island [*Bahamas*] [*ICAO location identifier*] (ICLI)

MYBS........ Alice Town/South Bimini, Bimini Island [*Bahamas*] [*ICAO location identifier*] (ICLI)

MYBT ...... Cistern Cay, Berry Island [*Bahamas*] [*ICAO location identifier*] (ICLI)

MYBW ...... Big Whale Cay, Berry Island [*Bahamas*] [*ICAO location identifier*] (ICLI)

MYBX ...... Little Whale Cay, Berry Island [*Bahamas*] [*ICAO location identifier*] (ICLI)

MYC .... Maadi Yacht Club

MYC .... Malayan Youth Council (ML)

MYC .... Maldives Youth Centre (EAIO)

MYC .... Maracay [*Venezuela*] [*Airport symbol*] (OAG)

MYCA .... Arthur's Town, Eleuthera Island [*Bahamas*] [*ICAO location identifier*] (ICLI)
MYCB .... New Bight, Cat Island [*Bahamas*] [*ICAO location identifier*] (ICLI)
MYCH ...... Hawks Nest Creek/Hawks Nest, Cat Island [*Bahamas*] [*ICAO location identifier*] (ICLI)
MYCI .... Colonel Hill, Crooked Island [*Bahamas*] [*ICAO location identifier*] (ICLI)
MYCL .... Mauritius Young Communist League (AF)
MYCP .... Pittsdown, Crooked Island [*Bahamas*] [*ICAO location identifier*] (ICLI)
MYCS .... Cay Sal [*Bahamas*] [*ICAO location identifier*] (ICLI)
MYCX .... Cutlass Bay, Cat Island [*Bahamas*] [*ICAO location identifier*] (ICLI)
MYD .... Malindi [*Kenya*] [*Airport symbol*] (OAG)
MYe .... International Unit (RU)
MYe .... Mass Unit (RU)
MYE .... Miyake Jima [*Japan*] [*Airport symbol*] (OAG)
MYEC .... Cape Eleuthera, Eleuthera Island [*Bahamas*] [*ICAO location identifier*] (ICLI)
MyeD .... International Unit of Activity [*Medicine*] (RU)
MYEG .... George Town, Exuma Island [*Bahamas*] [*ICAO location identifier*] (ICLI)
MYEH ...... North Eleuthera, Eleuthera Island [*Bahamas*] [*ICAO location identifier*] (ICLI)
MYEL .... Staniel Cay, Exuma Island [*Bahamas*] [*ICAO location identifier*] (ICLI)
MYEM ...... Governor's Harbour, Eleuthera Island [*Bahamas*] [*ICAO location identifier*] (ICLI)
MYEN .... Norman's Cay, Exuma Island [*Bahamas*] [*ICAO location identifier*] (ICLI)
MYER .... Rock Sound/International, Eleuthera Island [*Bahamas*] [*ICAO location identifier*] (ICLI)
MYES .... Lee Stocking Island, Exuma Island [*Bahamas*] [*ICAO location identifier*] (ICLI)
MYEY .... Hog Cay, Exuma Island [*Bahamas*] [*ICAO location identifier*] (ICLI)
MYFGSA .. Matadern y Frinorifico Guayaquil SA [*Ecuador*] (DSCA)
MYG .... Mayaguana [*Bahamas*] [*Airport symbol*] (OAG)
myg .... Myriagramme [*Myriagram*] [*French*]
MYGD .... Deep Water Cay, Grand Bahama Island [*Bahamas*] [*ICAO location identifier*] (ICLI)
MYGF .... Freeport/International, Grand Bahama Island [*Bahamas*] [*ICAO location identifier*] (ICLI)
MYGM ...... Grand Bahama Auxiliary Air Force Base, Grand Bahama Island [*Bahamas*] [*ICAO location identifier*] (ICLI)
MYGW ...... West End, Grand Bahama Island [*Bahamas*] [*ICAO location identifier*] (ICLI)
MYHA ...... Malaysian Youth Hostels Association (EAIO)
MYHA ...... Malta Youth Hostels Association (EAIO)
MYIG .... Matthew Town, Great Inagua Island [*Bahamas*] [*ICAO location identifier*] (ICLI)
MYJ .... Matsuyama [*Japan*] [*Airport symbol*] (OAG)
MYK .... Merkez Yonetim Kurulu [*Central Executive Committee*] [*of a political party*] (TU)
MYL .... Aeromyl SA de CV [*Mexico*] [*ICAO designator*] (FAAC)
myl .... Soap Plant [*Topography*] (RU)
MYLD .... Deadman's Cay, Long Island [*Bahamas*] [*ICAO location identifier*] (ICLI)
MYLR .... Diamond Roads, Long Island [*Bahamas*] [*ICAO location identifier*] (ICLI)
MYLS .... Stella Maris, Long Island [*Bahamas*] [*ICAO location identifier*] (ICLI)
MYM .... Monkey Mountain [*Guyana*] [*Airport symbol*] (OAG)
MYMM ..... Mayaguana Auxiliary Air Force Base, Mayaguana Island [*Bahamas*] [*ICAO location identifier*] (ICLI)
MYMSA.... Muslim Youth Movement of South Africa (EAIO)
MYN .... Mareb [*Yemen*] [*Airport symbol*] [*Obsolete*] (OAG)
MYNA .... Nassau [*Bahamas*] [*ICAO location identifier*] (ICLI)
MYNN .... Nassau/International, New Providence Island [*Bahamas*] [*ICAO location identifier*] (ICLI)
MYNW ...... Mynwese [*Mining*] [*Afrikaans*]
MYOD .... Malatya Yuksek Ogrenim Dernegi [*Malatya Higher Education Association*] (TU)
MYP .... Malawi Youth Pioneers (AF)
MYR .... Miriadair [*France*] [*ICAO designator*] (FAAC)
MYRA .... Multiyear Rescheduling Agreement [*Banking*]
MYRD .... Duncan Town, Exuma Island [*Bahamas*] [*ICAO location identifier*] (ICLI)
myriam ...... Myriametre [*Myriameter*] [*French*]
MYRP .... Port Nelson, Exuma Island [*Bahamas*] [*ICAO location identifier*] (ICLI)
MYS .... Malaysia [*ANSI three-letter standard code*] (CNC)
MYSM ...... Cockburn Town, San Salvador Island [*Bahamas*] [*ICAO location identifier*] (ICLI)
MYT .... Myitkyina [*Myanmar*] [*Airport symbol*] (OAG)
myt .... Mytologia [*Mythology*] [*Finland*]

myth .... Mythologie [*French*] (TPFD)
myth .... Mythology (TPFD)
MYu .... Ministry of Justice (RU)
MYuD .... International Youth Day [*1915-1945*] (RU)
MYuF .... Moscow Jewelry Factory (RU)
MYuI .... Moscow Law Institute (RU)
MYuS .... International Jurists' Union (BU)
MYuTAKE ... Materials of the South Turkmen Complex Archaeological Expedition (RU)
MYW .... Maendeleo ya Wanawake [*Women's Development Organization*] [*Kenya*] (AF)
MYW .... Mtwara [*Tanzania*] [*Airport symbol*] (OAG)
MYWF ...... Masonic Youth Welfare Fund [*Australia*]
MYX .... Menyamya [*Papua New Guinea*] [*Airport symbol*] (OAG)
MYY .... Miri [*Malaysia*] [*Airport symbol*] (OAG)
Mz .... Farmstead [*Topography*] (RU)
MZ .... Front des Artistes [*Artists Front*] [*Malagasy*] (AF)
MZ .... Machine Building Plant (BU)
MZ .... Mangels Zahlung [*For Non-Payment*] [*Business term*] [*German*]
Mz .... Mehrzahl [*Majority*] [*German*]
Mz .... Mesozoyik [*Mesozoic*] [*Geology*] (TU)
MZ .... Metallurgical Plant (BU)
mz .... Mezza [*Half*] [*Italian*]
MZ .... Mezzo [*Moderate*] [*Music*] (ROG)
MZ .... Microsonde (RU)
MZ .... Minelayer (RU)
MZ .... Ministerstvo Zeleznic [*Ministry of Railroads*] (CZ)
MZ .... Ministerstvo Zemedelstvi [*Ministry of Agriculture*] (CZ)
MZ .... Ministerstwo Zdrowia [*Ministry of Health*] (POL)
MZ .... Ministerstwo Zeglugi [*Ministry of Shipping*] (POL)
MZ .... Ministry of Agriculture [*Obsolete*] (BU)
MZ .... Ministry of Public Health (RU)
MZ .... Mizarska Zadruga [*Cabinetmakers' Cooperative*] (YU)
MZ .... Mlekarska Zadruga [*Milk Cooperative*] (YU)
MZ .... Mozambique [*ANSI two-letter standard code*] (CNC)
MZ .... Muzeum Ziemi [*Geological Museum*] (POL)
MZ .... Oil Dispenser, Servicing Truck (BU)
MZ .... Oil-Servicing Truck (RU)
mz .... Ointment, Salve (RU)
MZ .... Winter Oil (RU)
MZA .... Light Antiaircraft Artillery (BU)
MZA .... Moravsky Zemsky Archiv [*Moravian Provincial Archives*] (CZ)
MZA .... Small-Caliber Antiaircraft Artillery (RU)
MZA .... Small Refueling Unit (RU)
MZAL .... Minsk Plant of Transfer Machines and Standard-Unit Machine Tools (RU)
MZ-B .... Cluster Minefield (RU)
MZB .... Light Antiaircraft Battery (BU)
MZ bat ...... Light Antiaircraft Battery (BU)
MZBM ...... Miejski Zarzad Budynkow Mieszkalnych [*Municipal Administration of Residential Buildings*] (POL)
MZBZ .... Belize/International [*Belize*] [*ICAO location identifier*] (ICLI)
MZC .... Mitzic [*Gabon*] [*Airport symbol*] (OAG)
MZD .... Delayed-Action Mine (RU)
MZd .... Ministerstvo Zdravotnictvi [*Ministry of Public Health*] (CZ)
MZDI .... Ministry of Agriculture and State Property [*Obsolete*] (BU)
MZDS .... Moscow Woodworking Machine Plant (RU)
MZ-E .... Electromagnetic Minefield (RU)
MZFR .... Mehrzweck Forschungs [*Reactor*] [*Germany*] (NRCH)
MZFR .... Mehrzweck Forschungs Reaktor [*Nuclear energy*] (NRCH)
MZ-G .... Deep Minefield (RU)
MZG .... Makung [*Taiwan*] [*Airport symbol*] (OAG)
MZG .... Mazowieckie Zaklady Gastronomiczne [*Mazovian Catering Establishments*] [*Poland*]
MZG .... Ministry of Agriculture and Forests [*Obsolete*] (BU)
MZG .... Multiple Hardening Burner (RU)
MZGT .... Moscow Correspondence Mining Technicum (RU)
MZh .... Local Population (BU)
MZh .... Manufactured from Marine Animals (RU)
MZh .... Methyl Yellow (Indicator) (RU)
MZH .... Miejski Zarzad Handlu [*Municipal Administration of Trade*] [*Poland*]
MZhAVS... Ministry of Railroads, Automobiles, and Water Communications [*Obsolete*] (BU)
MZhD .... Murmansk Railroad (RU)
mzhdb .... Railroad Bridge Battalion (RU)
MZhDK..... International Railway Congress (RU)
mzhdp .... Railroad Bridge Regiment (RU)
MZhGS .... Ministry of Housing and Civil Engineering Construction (RU)
MZhK .... International Railway Transport Committee (RU)
MZhK .... Oil and Fats Kombinat (RU)
MZhKG .... International Cooperative Women's Guild [*ICWG*] (RU)
MZhP .... Oil and Fats Industry (RU)
mzhpb .... Railroad Bridge Battalion (BU)
mzhpp .... Railroad Bridge Regiment (BU)
MZhS .... Livestock-Breeding Machine Station (RU)

MZhSO ..... Women's International Zionist Organization [*WIZO*] (RU)
MZ-I .... Engineer Minefield (RU)
MZI .... Mopti [*Mali*] [*Airport symbol*] (OAG)
MZI .... Moscow Zootechnical Institute (RU)
MZIEI .... Moscow Correspondence Institute of Engineering Economics (RU)
MZIMP ..... Moscow Correspondence Institute of the Metalworking Industry (RU)
MZiOS ...... Ministerstwo Zdrowia i Opieki Spolecznej [*Ministry of Health and Social Welfare*] [*Poland*]
MZIShP .... Moscow Correspondence Institute of the Garment Industry (RU)
MZISSP .... Moscow Correspondence Institute of the Silicate and Construction Industries (RU)
MZK .... Interplant Cooperation, Interfactory Cooperation (RU)
MZK .... Marakei [*Kiribati*] [*Airport symbol*] (OAG)
MZK .... Miejskie Zaklady Komunikacyjne [*Municipal Transportation Establishments*] (POL)
mz k .... Military Band (BU)
MZKGG .... Miedzykomunalne Zaklady Komunikacyjne Gdansk-Gdynia [*Gdansk (Danzig)-Gdynia Inter-City Transportation Establishment*] (POL)
MZKhP ..... Ministry of Agriculture and Food Industry (BU)
MZL .... Magnetischer Zeichenleser [*German*] (ADPT)
MZL .... Manizales [*Colombia*] [*Airport symbol*] (OAG)
Mzl .... Mezarlik [*Cemetery*] (TU)
MZL .... Middle Zone League
MZM .... Metz [*France*] [*Airport symbol*] (OAG)
MZM .... Miejski Zaklad Mleczarski [*Municipal Dairy*] (POL)
MZ-M .... Sea Minefield (RU)
MZMA ...... Moscow Small Automobile Plant (RU)
MZn .... Mischzink [*Mixed Zinc*] [*German*] (GCA)
MZNRM ... Ministerstvo za Zemjodelie na Narodnata Republika Makedonija [*Ministry of Agriculture of Macedonia*] (YU)
MZO .... Manzanillo [*Cuba*] [*Airport symbol*] (OAG)
MZO .... Miejskie Zaklady Oczyszczania [*Town Cleaning Department*] [*Poland*]
MZO .... Ministerstvo Zahranicniho Obchodu [*Ministry of Foreign Trade*] (CZ)
MZO .... Ministerstwo Ziem Odzyskanych [*Ministry of Recovered Territories*] (POL)
MZO .... Ministry of Public Health (RU)
MZO .... Moscow Correspondence Branch (RU)
MZO .... Moscow Defense Zone [*1941-1942*] (RU)
MZO/HTS ... Ministerstvo Zahranicniho Obchodu/Hlavni Technicka Sprava [*Ministry of Foreign Trade/Main Technical Directorate*] (CZ)
MZOTsM ... Moscow Plant for the Processing of Nonferrous Metals (RU)
MZP .... Barely Perceptible Obstacle [*Military term*] (RU)
MZP .... Magyarorfzagi Zold Part [*Hungary*] (EAIO)
MZP .... Rabbit Wire, Concealed Wire [*Military term*] (RU)
MZP .... Small-Caliber Antiaircraft Machine Gun (RU)
MZPA .... Moscow Correspondence Industrial Academy (RU)
MZPD .... Miedzynarodowe Zrzeszenie Prawnikow Demokratow [*International Association of Democratic Lawyers*] (POL)
MZPI .... Moscow Correspondence Pedagogical Institute (RU)
MZPI .... Moscow Correspondence Printing Institute (RU)
MZPT .... Moscow Correspondence Technicum for Instrument Making (RU)
MZPUK .... Miejski Zarzad Przedsiebiorstw i Urzadzen Komunalnych [*City Administration of Municipal Enterprises and Establishments*] (POL)
MZPW ...... Mazowieckie Zaklady Przemyslu Welnianego [*Mazowsze (Masovia) Wool Plant*] (POL)
MZR .... Mazar-I-Sharif [*Afghanistan*] [*Airport symbol*] (OAG)
MZ-R .... River Minefield (RU)
MZRIP ...... Mazowieckie Zaklady Rafineryjne i Petrochemiczne [*Poland*]
MZS .... Interlibrary Loan Service (BU)
MZS .... Miedzynarodowe Zawody Szybowcowe [*International Glider Contest*] (POL)
MZS .... Miedzynarodowy Zwiazek Spoldzielczy [*International Cooperative Union*] (POL)
MZS .... Miedzynarodowy Zwiazek Studentow [*International Union of Students*] (POL)
MZS .... Ministerstvo na Zemjodelie i Sumarstvo [*Ministry of Agriculture and Forestry*] (YU)
MZS .... Motorized Station for Hunting Sea Animals (RU)
MZS .... Pile-Screwing Mechanism (RU)
MZS .... Winter Lubricating Oil (RU)
MZSh .... Moscow Grinding Accessories Plant (RU)
MZShV ...... Moscow Champagne Plant (RU)
MZSM .... Miedzynarodowe Zawody Sportowe Mlodziezy [*International Youth Games*] (POL)
MZST .... Moscow Correspondence Statistical Technicum (RU)
MZSZ .... Magyar Zenemuveszek Szovetsege [*Association of Hungarian Musicians*] (HU)
MZT .... Mazatlan [*Mexico*] [*Airport symbol*] (OAG)

MZTA .... Moscow Thermal Automation Plant (RU)
MZTI .... Moscow Correspondence Textile Institute (RU)
MZU .... Assembly Preparation Sector (RU)
MZU .... Magnetic Storage, Magnetic Memory (RU)
MZU .... Moravske Zemske Ustredi Obci, Mest, a Okresu [*Center of Communities, Towns, and Districts of the Province of Moravia*] (CZ)
MZU .... Small Floating Bucket Dredge (RU)
MZUB .... Magnetic Drum Storage (RU)
MZUL .... Magnetic Tape Storage (RU)
MZUMD ... Magnetic Disk Mini-Memory System (BU)
MZV .... Magyar Zsidok Vilagszovetsege [*World Federation of Hungarian Jews*] (EAIO)
MZV .... Ministerstvo Zahranicnich Veci [*Ministry of Foreign Affairs*] (CZ)
MZVZ .... Ministerstvo Zemedelstvi a Vyzivy [*Ministry of Agriculture and Food*] (CZ)
MZZ .... Barely Perceptible Obstacle [*Military term*] (RU)
MZZ .... Masinsko Zemjedelska Zadruga [*Agricultural Machinery Cooperative*] (YU)
MZZ .... Mesna Zemljoradnicka Zadruga [*Local Agricultural Cooperative*] (YU)
MZZhKT ... Moscow Correspondence Communal Housing Technicum (RU)

N

n .... Chief, Superior Officer (BU)
n .... Drehzahl, Umlaufzahl [*Number of Revolutions*] [*German*]
            (GCA)
N .... Electric Locomotive Made by the Novocherkassk Electric
            Locomotive Plant (RU)
N .... Flying Boat [*Russian aircraft symbol*]
N .... Gunner (RU)
N .... Leistung [*Output*] [*German*]
N .... Lower [*Toponymy*] (RU)
N .... Low Pressure [*Meteorology*] (RU)
N .... Nacelnik [*Chief*] (CZ)
n .... Nach [*After*] [*German*]
N .... Nachmittags [*Afternoon*] [*German*]
N .... Nachricht [*Report*] [*German*] (GCA)
N .... Nachts [*At Night*] [*German*]
n .... Nacido [*or Nacida*] [*Born*] [*Spanish*]
n .... Nad [*On*] [*In geographical names*] [*Poland*]
N .... Nada
N .... Naechst [*Next*] [*German*]
n .... Nagy [*Great, Big*] (HU)
N .... Nahgueterzug [*Local Freight Train*] (EG)
N .... Name [*Name*] [*German*]
n .... Namens [*In the Name Of*] [*Afrikaans*]
N .... Nan [*Phonetic alphabet*] [*World War II*] (DSUE)
n .... Narodni [*National*] (CZ)
N .... Nassdampf [*Wet (Saturated) Steam*] (EG)
n .... Nastepny [*Next, Following*] (POL)
N .... National [*National*] [*German*]
N .... Nato [*Born*] [*Italian*]
N .... Navire [*Ship*] [*French*] (MTD)
N .... Nehir [*River*] (TU)
n .... Nemzeti [*National*] (HU)
N/ .... Nen [*Albanian*]
N .... Neper Einheit der Daempfung [*German*] (ADPT)
n .... Nero [*Black*] [*Italian*]
n .... Netto [*Net*] [*Business term*] [*German*]
n .... Neu [*New*] [*German*]
n .... Neutral [*Neutral*] [*German*]
n .... Neutre [*Neutral*] [*French*]
n .... Neutron [*German*] (GCA)
n .... Neutrophils (RU)
N .... Neutrum [*Neutral*] [*Afrikaans*]
N .... New [*Toponymy*] (RU)
N .... New Persian
N .... New South Wales [*National Union Catalogue of Australia
            symbol*]
N .... Newton [*Finland*]
N .... Newton [*German*] (GCA)
N .... Ngultrum [*Monetary unit*] [*Bhutan*] (BARN)
N .... Nigeria Naira
N .... Nisos [*Island*] [*Greek*] (NAU)
N .... Nitrogenio [*Nitrogen*] [*Chemical element*] [*Portuguese*]
N .... Nitroglycerin (RU)
N .... Niuton [*Newton*] [*Poland*]
n .... Noche [*Night*] [*Spanish*]
n .... Noerdlich [*Northern*] [*German*]
n .... Noin [*About, Approximately*] [*Finland*] (GPO)
N .... Nom [*Name*] [*French*]
N .... Nombre Ignorado [*Spanish*]
n .... Nome [*Name*] [*Portuguese*]
N .... Nominal [*Nominal*] [*French*]
N .... Noord [*North*] [*Afrikaans*]
N .... Noordelik [*Northern*] [*Afrikaans*]
N .... Nord [*North*] [*German*]
N .... Nord [*North*] [*Italian*]
N .... Nord [*North*] [*Denmark*] (NAU)
N .... Nord [*North*] [*Sweden*] (NAU)
N .... Nord [*North*] [*Norway*] (NAU)

N .... Nord [*North*] [*French*] (MTD)
N .... Norm (RU)
N .... Normaal [*Normal*] [*Afrikaans*]
n .... Normal [*German*]
n .... Normalitaet [*Normality*] [*German*] (GCA)
N .... Norse [*Language, etc.*]
N .... Norte [*North*] [*Spanish*]
N .... Norte [*North*] [*Portuguese*]
N .... North (EECI)
N .... Northern (EECI)
N .... Norwegia [*Norway*] [*Poland*]
n .... Nosso [*Our*] [*Portuguese*]
N .... Nota [*Note*] [*Italian*]
N .... Notablemente Aprobado [*On an Examination: Credit*] [*Spanish*]
N .... Notar [*Notary*] [*German*]
n .... Note [*French*] (FLAF)
N .... Notos [*South*] (GC)
n/ .... Notre [*Our*] [*Business term*] [*French*]
n .... Noun (TPFD)
N .... Novelles [*Benelux*] (BAS)
N .... November [*Phonetic alphabet*] [*International*] (DSUE)
N .... Nowy [*New*] [*Poland*]
n .... Nuestro [*or Nuestra*] [*Our*] [*Spanish*]
n .... Numerato [*Numbered*] [*Publishing*] [*Italian*]
N .... Numero [*Number*] [*Finland*] (GPO)
N .... Nuts [*Phonetic alphabet*] [*Royal Navy World War I Pre-World
            War II*] (DSUE)
n .... Nutzeffekt, Wirkungsgrad [*Efficiency*] [*German*]
N .... Observation (RU)
N .... Observation, Surveillance, Supervision (BU)
N .... Observer (RU)
N .... People (BU)
N .... Plant Standard (RU)
N .... Rockwell International Corp. [*ICAO aircraft manufacturer
            identifier*] (ICAO)
N .... Stationary, Fixed (RU)
N .... Tight Fit, Drive Fit (RU)
n .... Uninhabited, Uninhabitable [*Topography*] (RU)
NA .... Ground Artillery (RU)
NA .... Nacelnik Artiljerije [*Chief of Artillery*] (YU)
Na .... Naira [*Monetary unit*] [*Nigeria*]
NA .... Namibia [*ANSI two-letter standard code*] (CNC)
NA .... Naples [*Car registration plates*] [*Italian*]
NA .... Napoleonic Association [*Enfield, Middlesex, England*] (EAIO)
NA .... National Action [*Australia*]
NA .... Nationalaktion Gegen die Ueberfremdung von Volk und Heimat
            [*National Action Against Foreign Domination of People and
            Homeland*] [*Switzerland*] (WEN)
NA .... National Assembly [*United Arab Republic*]
NA .... Nationale Aktion fuer Volk und Heimat [*National Action for
            People and Homeland*] [*Switzerland*] [*Political party*]
            (PPE)
NA .... Native Authority
Na .... Natrium [*Sodium*] [*Chemical element*] [*German*]
NA .... Navion Aircraft Co. [*ICAO aircraft manufacturer identifier*]
            (ICAO)
NA .... Nebenanschluss [*Extension*] [*German*] (GCA)
NA .... Nederlands Archievenblad [*Netherlands*] (BAS)
NA .... Neo-Assyrian [*or New Assyrian*] [*Language, etc.*] (BJA)
NA .... Neue Ausgabe [*or Auflage*] [*New Edition*] [*German*]
n/A .... Neuer Art [*Of New Type*] [*German*] (GCA)
NA .... New Alphabet (RU)
NA .... New Alternative Party [*Venezuela*] [*Political party*]
NA .... New [*South Wales*] Assumption [*Seminary*] [*Capuchin
            Franciscan Friars*]
NA .... Nitramine (RU)
NA .... Non-Attached [*European political movement*] (ECON)
NA .... Noord-Afrika [*North Africa*] [*Afrikaans*]

NA............ Noord-Amerika [*North America*] [*Afrikaans*]
NA............ Normal Markov Algorithms (RU)
NA............ Norske Atlanterhavskomite [*Norway*] (EAIO)
NA............ Norwegian AeroClub (EAIO)
na .... Nota del Autor [*Author's Note*] [*Spanish*]
na .... Not Available (EECI)
NA............ Noticias Argentinas SA [*News agency*] [*Argentina*] (EY)
NA............ Notioanatolikos [*Southeast*] (GC)
NA............ Nueva Alternativa [*Venezuela*] [*Political party*] (EY)
N/A........... Numerique/Analogique [*French*] (ADPT)
NA............ Ordinance on the Traffic With, Purchasing, and Storage of Containers in Commercial Circulation and Material and Technical Supply (BU)
na .... People's Artist (RU)
NA............ Rifled Artillery (RU)
Na .... Sodio [*Sodium*] [*Chemical element*] [*Portuguese*]
NAA........... Army Artillery Commander (RU)
NAA........... Narody Azii i Afriki
NAA........... Narrabri [*Australia*] [*Airport symbol*] (OAG)
NAA........... National Academy of Arts [*South Korea*] (EAIO)
NAA........... National Archery Association (OLYM)
NAA........... National Australian Association (ADA)
NAA........... National Oceanic and Atmospheric Administration [*Department of Commerce*] [*ICAO designator*] (FAAC)
NAA........... Naval Association of Australia (ADA)
NAA........... Netherlands Society of Allergology (EAIO)
NAA........... Nigerian Airport Authority (IMH)
NAA........... Normenausschuss Armaturen im DIN [*Deutsches Institut fuer Normung*] eV (SLS)
NAA........... North Atlantic Alliance
NAA........... Norwegian Association of Archivists (EAIO)
NAA........... Numismatic Association of Australia
NAAA....... National Association for Alopecia Areata [*Norway*] (EAIO)
NAAC....... New [*South Wales*] C B Alexander Agricultural College [*National Union Catalogue of Australia symbol*]
NAACAM ... National Association of Automotive Component and Allied Manufacturers
NAACIE.... National Association of Agricultural, Commercial, and Industrial Employees [*Guyana*] (LA)
NAAE....... National Affiliation of Arts Educators [*Australia*]
NAAE....... Nordic Association for Adult Education (EAIO)
NAAF....... North-African Air Force
NAAG....... Nordic Association of Applied Geophysics (EA)
NAALAS... Northern Australian Aboriginal Legal Aid Service
NAAM....... National Association for the Advancement of Muslims [*Uganda*] (AF)
NaamlVenn ... Naamlooze Vennootschap [*Benelux*] (BAS)
NAAMSA ... National Association of Automobile Manufacturers of South Africa
NAAO....... New [*South Wales*] Anglo-Australian Observatory [*National Union Catalogue of Australia symbol*]
NAAO....... North Africa Area Office
NAAP....... Netherlands Association for Animal Production (EAIO)
NAAR....... New [*South Wales*] Australian Archives - Regional [*Office*] [*National Union Catalogue of Australia symbol*]
NAAS .... Nordic Association for American Studies (EAIO)
NAASO..... Nigerian Afro-Asian People's Solidarity (AF)
NAASRA... National Association of Australian State Road Authorities (ADA)
NAAT....... National Association of Agricultural Teachers [*Australia*]
NAAUC.... National Association of Australian University Colleges (ADA)
NAAWS .... North American Association of Wardens and Superintendents (EAIO)
NAAWT .... National Action Against War Toys [*Australia*]
NAAWU.... National Automobile and Allied Workers Union [*UAW's sister union in South Africa*]
NAAWUL ... National Agricultural and Allied Workers' Union of Liberia (IMH)
NAB.......... Arnotts Biscuits Ltd. [*National Union Catalogue of Australia symbol*]
nab .... Embankment, Quay (RU)
nab .... Naberezhnaya [*Embankment, Quai*] (IDIG)
nab .... Nabozenstvi [*Religion*] (CZ)
NAB.......... National Apex Body [*India*] (PDAA)
NAB.......... National Assembly Bill
NAB.......... National Australia Bank
NAB.......... Nationaler AIDS-Beirat [*National Aids Committee*] [*Germany*] (EAIO)
NAB.......... National Security Agency [*NSA*] (RU)
NAB.......... Native Affairs Branch [*Northern Territory*]
NAB.......... News Agency of Burma
NAB.......... Nigeria-Arab Bank Ltd.
NAB.......... Nigerian Agricultural Bank
nab .... Observer (RU)
NAB.......... Unexploded Aerial Bomb (RU)

NABC........ New [*South Wales*] Australian Broadcasting Corporation [*Reference Library New South Wales*]
nabco.......... Naber & Co. [*Jordan*]
NABD....... Normenausschuss Bibliotheks- und Dokumentationswesen im DIN [*Deutsches Institut fuer Normung*] eV (SLS)
NABF .... Norges Ake-og Bob Forbund [*Norway*] (EAIO)
NABH....... New [*South Wales*] Albury Base Hospital [*Library*] [*National Union Catalogue of Australia symbol*]
NABIC...... National Alcoholic Beverages Industries Council [*Australia*]
NABK....... New [*South Wales*] Australian Bank [*Ltd.*] [*National Union Catalogue of Australia symbol*]
NABL .... New [*South Wales*] Association of Blind [*Citizens*] [*National Union Catalogue of Australia symbol*]
nabl .... Observation Tower [*Topography*] (RU)
NABLOC... Brussels Tariff Nomenclature for the Latin American Free Trade Association (BARN)
NABM....... New [*South Wales*] Australian Board of Missions [*Needham Memorial Library*]
NABO....... Nordic Literature and Library Committee [*Denmark*] (EAIO)
NABOCE .. National Bookkeeping Certificate
NABSO ..... Namibian Black Students Organization (AF)
NABT .... Nigerian Association of Building Technicians
NABTS...... North American Braodcast Teletext Standard (OSI)
NABWU... Namibia Building Workers' Union (EAIO)
NAC......... Astronomical Society of the Netherlands (EAIO)
NAC......... Natal Associated Collieries [*South Africa*] (PDAA)
NAC......... National Aboriginal Conference [*or Congress*] [*Australia*] (ADA)
NAC......... National Accelerator Centre [*South Africa*] [*Research center*] (IRC)
NAC......... National Action Committee (ML)
NAC......... National Advisory Council [*Sierra Leone*] (AF)
NAC......... National Advisory Council [*Somali*] (AF)
NAC......... National African Company
NAC......... National AIDS Committee [*Trinidad and Tobago*] (EAIO)
NAC......... National Air Charters Zambia Ltd.
NAC......... National Asthma Campaign [*Australia*]
NAC......... Native Anglican Church
NAC......... Netherlands Atlantics Commission (EAIO)
NAC......... Neutral-Aufbereitungs-Code [*German*] (ADPT)
NAC......... New Apostolic Church
NAC......... Nordic Academic Council [*Defunct*] (EA)
NAC......... Nordic Actors' Council (EAIO)
NAC......... Nordic Association for Campanology (EA)
NAC......... North Atlantic Shipping Conference (DS)
NAC......... Nyasaland African Congress [*Malawi*]
NACA .... National Advisory Committee on AIDS [*Fiji*] (EAIO)
NACA .... National Advisory Committee for Clean Air [*South Africa*] (SLS)
NACA .... New Australian Cultural Association (ADA)
NACA .... North Australian Canine Association
NACAF..... Northwest African Coastal Air Force
NACAIDS ... National Advisory Committee on AIDS [*Acquired Immune Deficiency Syndrome*] [*Australia*]
NACAL ..... North American Conference on Afroasiatic Linguistics
NACAR ..... National Advisory Committee on Aeronautical Research
NACB .... Nigerian Agricultural and Co-Operative Bank
NACBCS ... National Association of Community Based Children's Services [*Australia*]
NACC .... National Aboriginal Consultative Committee [*Australia*] (ADA)
NACC .... National Anti-Counterfeiting Committee [*Taiwan*] (EAIO)
NACC .... North American-Chilean Chamber of Commerce (EA)
NACCA ..... National Association of Chairmen of City Assemblies [*Japan*]
NACCES ... National Advisory Committee on the Commonwealth Employment Service [*Australia*]
NACCHO ... National Aboriginal Community-Controlled Health Organization [*Australia*]
NACCIMA ... Nigerian Association of Chambers of Commerce, Industry, Mines, and Agriculture
NACCME ... National Advisory and Coordinating Committee on Multicultural Education [*Australia*]
NACD....... New [*South Wales*] Australasian College of Dermatologists [*Librar y*] [*National Union Catalogue of Australia symbol*]
NACDA ..... National Cooperative Development Agency [*Grenada*] (LA)
NACE .... National Advisory Committee on Electronics [*India*] (PDAA)
NACE .... National Association for Conductive Education [*Australia*]
NACEM .... National Association of Catering Equipment Manufacturers [*France*] (EAIO)
NACES...... National Advisory Committee on Extension Services [*Australia*]
NACEW .... National Advisory Council on the Employment of Women [*New Zealand*]
NACF .... National Agricultural Cooperative Federation [*South Korea*] (FEA)
NACGHP.. Norwegian Association for Cartography, Geodesy, Hydrography, and Photogrammetry (EAIO)
nach........... Beginning (BU)
nach........... Beginning, Start, Source (RU)

nach............ Chief, Head, Commander (RU)
nach............ Initial, First, Elementary (RU)
nachart....... Artillery Commander (RU)
nachartdiv .. Division Artillery Commander (RU)
nachartkor .. Corps Artillery Commander (RU)
nachdiv....... Division Commander (RU)
Nachdr....... Nachdruck [*Reprint*] [*German*]
Nachf .... Nachfolger [*Successor*] [*German*] (WEN)
nachfin .... Chief of Finance [*Military term*] (RU)
Nachgiebigk ... Nachgiebigkeit [*Pliability*] [*German*] (GCA)
nachinsnab ... Chief of Engineer Supply [*Military term*] (RU)
nachinzh...... Chief of Engineer Service [*Military term*] (RU)
nachinzharm ... Chief of Engineer Service of an Army (RU)
NACHIPA ... Naviera Chilena del Pacifico [*Chile*] (LAA)
nachkants... Office Chief (RU)
nachkar ...... Guard Commander (RU)
nachkhim ... Chief of Chemical Service (RU)
nachkhoz... Chief of Administrative and Supply Department (RU)
nachkhoz.... Chief of Administrative and Supply Management (RU)
nachkhozupr ... Chief of Administrative and Supply Management (RU)
NACHM.... Nachmittags [*Afternoon*] [*German*]
nachmil ...... Chief of Militia (RU)
Nachn......... Nachnahme [*Surname*] [*German*]
NAChNII ... Scientific Archives of the Chuvash Scientific Research Institute of Language, Literature, History, and Economics (RU)
nachpo........ Chief of Political Section [*Military term*], Chief of Political Department (RU)
nachpoarm ... Chief of Political Section of an Army (RU)
nachpodiv... Chief of Political Section of a Division (RU)
nachprod .... Chief of Food Supply [*Military term*] (RU)
nachpu........ Chief of Political Directorate [*Military term*], Chief of Political Administration (RU)
Nachr .... Nachricht [*Report*] [*German*] (GCA)
NAChSANARM ... Chief Medical Administration of a Separate Army (BU)
nachsanarm ... Chief of Medical Service of an Army (RU)
nachsanbrig ... Chief of Medical Service of a Brigade (RU)
nachsandiv ... Chief of Medical Service of a Division (RU)
nachsankor ... Chief of Medical Service of a Corps (RU)
nachsanupr ... Chief of the Military Medical Directorate (RU)
nach sk .... Initial Velocity, Initial Speed (RU)
nachsnab.... Chief of Supply (RU)
nachsoch .... Chief of Secret Operations Unit (RU)
Nachtr........ Nachtrag [*Appendix*] [*Publishing*] [*German*]
nachveshch ... Chief of Clothing and Equipment Supply [*Military term*] (RU)
nachvoyendor ... Chief of Military Roads (RU)
nachvto....... Chief of Military Topographic Section (RU)
Nachw .... Nachweis [*Proof*] [*German*] (GCA)
Nachw .... Nachwirkung [*Aftereffect*] [*German*] (GCA)
Nachw .... Nachwort [*Epilogue*] [*German*]
NACIAD ... National Council for Integrated Area Development [*Philippines*] (EAS)
NACISA .... North Atlantic Communications and Information Systems Agency [*NATO*]
NACISO.... NATO Communications and Information Systems Organization (EAIO)
NACL .... Nippon Aviatronics Corp. Ltd. [*Japan*]
NACL .... North Australian Cement Limited (ADA)
NACLA ..... North American Congress on Latin America (LA)
NACLC..... National Association of Community Legal Centers [*Australia*]
NACLIS ... National Advisory Council for Library and Information Services [*Australia*]
NACO........ National Agricultural Company
NACOA..... Nacional de Combustible de Aviacion, SA [*National Aviation Fuel Corporation, Inc.*] [*Mexico*] (LA)
NACOA..... National Advisory Committee on Oceans and Atmosphere (ASF)
NACOEJ... North American Conference on Ethiopian Jewry (EAIO)
NACOL..... Nairobi Conveyors Ltd. [*Kenya*]
NACOLADS ... National Council on Libraries, Archives and Documentation Services [*Jamaica*] (PDAA)
NACP .... National Accounts Capability Programme [*United Nations*] (EY)
NACP .... National Association for Coloured People
NACP .... New [*South Wales*] Australian College of Physical [*Education*] [*National Union Catalogue of Australia symbol*]
NACP .... North Atlantic Consultive Process (OSI)
NACPA ..... National Association of Chairmen of Prefectural Assemblies [*Japan*]
NACPHO ... Nigeria Association of Creative Photographers
NACREL... National Chemical Research Laboratory
NACRO..... National Association of Charitable Recycling Organisations [*Australia*]
NACS .... National Assembly of Civil Society [*Chile*]
NACS .... New [*South Wales*] Australia Council [*Library*] [*National Union Catalogue of Australia symbol*]
NACSEX... North American Cuban Scientific Exchange

Nacst.......... Nacelnik Stabu [*Chief of Staff*] (CZ)
NACTU ..... National Council of Trade Unions [*South Africa*] (EAIO)
NACU:C .... New [*South Wales*] Australian Catholic University [*Castle Hill Campus*]
NACU:N.... New [*South Wales*] Australian Catholic University [*National Union Catalogue of Australia symbol*]
NACUSIP ... National Congress of Unions in the Sugar Industry of the Philippines
NACWE .... National Advisory Committee on Women and Education [*New Zealand*]
nacz .... Naczelny [*Chief, Main*] (POL)
NACZ....... National Arts Council of Zimbabwe (EAIO)
NAD.......... Air Division Commander (RU)
NAD.......... Division Artillery Commander (RU)
NAD.......... National Accountancy Diploma
NAD.......... New African Development
NAD.......... New [*South Wales*] Agriculture Department [*Head Office Library*]
NAD.......... Nicotinamide-Adenine Dinucleotide (RU)
NAD.......... Nobelair [*Turkey*] [*ICAO designator*] (FAAC)
NAD.......... Noradrenaline (RU)
NAD.......... Nordiska Namden for Alkohol- och Drogforskning [*Nordic Council for Alcohol and Drug Research - NCADR*] (EAIO)
NAD.......... Norwegian Association of the Deaf (EAIO)
NADA....... National Democratic Alliance [*Zambia*] [*Political party*] (EY)
NADA....... Network of Alcohol and Other Drugs Agencies [*Australia*]
NADA....... Norwegian Association of Double Amputees (EAIO)
NADB........ New [*South Wales*] Anti-Discrimination Board [*National Union Catalogue of Australia symbol*]
NADC....... Northern Australia Development Conference
NADCO..... National Agricultural Development Company [*Saudi Arabia*] (MENA)
NADE........ National Association for Drama in Education [*Australia*]
NADEC ..... National Agricultural Development Co. [*Saudi Arabia*] (PDAA)
NADECO.. National Development Corporation
NADEFCOL ... NATO Defense College [*Also, NADC, NDC*] [*Rome, Italy*]
NADEL ..... National Association of Democratic Lawyers [*South Africa*]
NADELCO ... Nacional de Comercio [*Colombia*] (COL)
NADEPA... National Democratic Party [*Solomon Islands*] [*Political party*] (PPW)
NADE(V)... National Association for Drama in Education (Victoria) [*Australia*]
NADF .... Nicotinamide-Adenine Dinucleotide Phosphate (RU)
NADGEMO ... NADGE [*NATO Air Defense Ground Environment*] Management Office [*Belgium*]
NADI........ Nomenclatura Arancelaria y Derechos de Importacion [*Tariff List and Customs Duties*] [*Argentina*] (LA)
NADI........ Scientific Research Highway Institute (RU)
NADIE ...... National Association for Drama in Education [*Australia*]
NADOC..... National Aborigines Day Observance Committee [*Australia*] (ADA)
NADR........ New [*South Wales*] Anglican Church Diocese of Riverina - Riverina Dioc esan Library [*National Union Catalogue of Australia symbol*]
NADREG.. National Alliance for Democratic Restoration in Equatorial Guinea [*Switzerland*] (EAIO)
NADS........ National Armament Directors [*NATO*]
nadt zagl..... Text Heading (BU)
NAEB .... North African Economic Board
NAEBM .... Normenausschuss Eisen- Blech- und Metallwaren im DIN [*Deutsches Institut fuer Normung*] eV (SLS)
NAEC .... National Aboriginal Education Committee [*Australia*] (ADA)
NAEDC ..... National Aboriginal Employment Development Committee [*Australia*] (ADA)
NAEETC... National Aboriginal Employment Education and Training Committee
NAEO........ New [*South Wales*] Australian Electoral Commission Office [*National Union Catalogue of Australia symbol*]
NAES........ Pumped Storage Electric Power Plant (RU)
NAEWS..... NATO Airborne Early Warning System
NAEX .... New [*South Wales*] Ampol Exploration [*Ltd.*] [*National Union Catalogue of Australia symbol*]
NAF .... Guilder [*Florin*] [*Monetary unit Netherlands Antilles*]
NAF .... Nederlandse Arbeidsfront [*Netherlands*] (BAS)
NAF .... Nordisk Anaesthesiologisk Forening [*Scandinavian Society of Anaesthesiologists - SSA*] (EA)
NAF .... Norsk Arbeidsgiverforening [*Norwegian Employers' Association*] (WEN)
NAF .... Norsk Astronautisk Forening [*Norwegian Astronautical Society*] (EAIO)
NAF .... Norske Anmonsorers Forening [*Norwegian Advertisers Association*] (IMH)
NAF .... North Anatolian Fault [*Geology*] [*Turkey*]
NAF .... Nouvelle Action Francaise [*New French Action*] [*Political party*] (PPE)
NAF .... Royal Netherlands Air Force [*ICAO designator*] (FAAC)
NAFA .... National Association of Furniture Agents [*Australia*]

NAFA .... National Automotive Fleet Administration Ltd. [*Australia*]
NAFA .... Night Aerial Camera   (RU)
NAFA .... Night Aerial Photographic Equipment   (BU)
NAFA .... Normenausschuss Fahrraeder im DIN [*Deutsches Institut fuer Normung*] e V   (SLS)
NAFAC..... Societe Nord-Africaine d'Arbitrages et de Changes [*Morocco*]
NAFBI....... National African Federation for the Building Industry [*South Africa*]   (AA)
NAFC .... New [*South Wales*] Australian Finance Conference [*National Union Catalogue of Australia symbol*]
NAFC .... North African Forestry Commission
NAFCA...... Nigeria Azania Friendship and Cultural Association
NAFCO ..... National Agricultural and Food Corporation [*Tanzania*]
NAFCO ..... National Airways and Finance Corporation
NAFCO ..... National Feed Company [*Egypt*]
NAFCOC... National African Federated Chamber of Commerce
NAFCON .. National Fertilizer Co. of Nigeria
NAFED ...... National Agricultural Cooperative Marketing Federation [*India*]
NAFEN ..... Near and Far East News Ltd.
NAFI........ National Association of Forest Industries [*Australia*]
NAFICOT ... National Fishing Corp. of Tuvalu [*Turkey*]   (EY)
NAFIN ...... Nacional Financiera, SA [*National Finance Bank, Inc.*] [*Mexico*]   (LAA)
NAFINSA ... Nacional Financiera Sociedad Anonima [*National Finance Bank, Incorporated*] [*Mexico*]   (LA)
NAFK .... Naphthofurancarboxylic Acid   (RU)
NAFLSSL ... National Assessment Framework for Languages at Senior Secondary Level [*Australia*]
NAFLU..... National Association of Free Labor Unions [*Philippines*]
NAFM .... National Australia Fund Management Ltd.
NAFMA .... NATO European Fighter Management Agency
NAFO .... Northwest Atlantic Fisheries Organization   (EA)
NAFOZ ...... National Fishermen Organization of Zambia
N-AFP ...... Nepal-Australia Forestry Project
NAFPP ...... National Accelerated Food Production Program
N Afr .... North Africa
NAFSLAC ... National Association of Federations of Syrian and Lebanese American Clubs
NAFTA...... New Zealand-Australia Free Trade Agreement   (ADA)
NAFTA...... North American Free Trade Agreement   (SCAC)
NAFTA...... Polnocno-Atlantycki Obszar Wolnego Handlu [*North Atlantic Free Trade Area*]   (POL)
NAFTU ..... National Association of Free Trade Unions [*Philippines*]   (FEA)
NAFU .... National African Federation of Unions [*Rhodesian*]   (AF)
NAFuO ...... Normenausschuss Feinmechanik und Optik im DIN [*Deutsches Institut fuer Normung*] e V [*Standards of Fine Mechanics and Optics in the German Institute of Standardization*]   (SLS)
NAG.......... Nagpur [*India*] [*Airport symbol*]   (OAG)
NAG.......... National Academy of Geography [*Argentina*]   (EAIO)
NAG.......... Nederlands Akoestisch Genootschap [*Netherlands*]   (EAIO)
NAG.......... Nederlands Architecten Genootschap [*Dutch Architects Association*]   (SLS)
NAG.......... New South Wales AUSINET Group [*Australia*]   (ADA)
NAG.......... Newtown Actors' Group [*Australia*]
NAGD........ New [*South Wales*] Attorney General's Department [*National Union Catalogue of Australia symbol*]
nagel.......... Nagelaten [*Posthumous*] [*Publishing*] [*Netherlands*]
NAGEMA ... Nahrungsmittel-, Genussmittel-, und Verpackungsmaschinen (VVB) [*Foodstuffs, Fancy Foodstuffs, and Packing Machines (VVB)*]   (EG)
NAGES...... Pumped Storage Hydro-Electric Power Plant   (RU)
nagl .... Naglowek [*Heading*]   (POL)
NAGM....... New [*South Wales*] Australian Graduate School of Management [*National Union Catalogue of Australia symbol*]
NAGPA ..... National Association of General Practitioners of Australia
NAGR........ New [*South Wales*] Agricultural Research Institute [*New South Wales Agriculture and Fisheries*]
NAGU .... Niederlaendische Aktiengesellschaft fuer die Abwicklung von Unternehmungen   (BJA)
nagyker v.... Nagykereskedelmi Vallalat [*Wholesale Commercial Enterprise*]   (HU)
NAH .... Ministry of Animal Health, Northern Region
NAH .... Naha [*Ryukyu Islands*] [*Airport symbol*]   (OAG)
Nah .... Nahum [*Afrikaans*]
NAH .... National Academy of History [*Argentina*]   (EAIO)
NAH .... New [*South Wales*] [*Royal Prince*] Alfred Hospital [*Susman Library*]
NAH .... Nordic Association for Hydrology   (EA)
NAH .... Nordic Association for the Handicapped   (EA)
NAH .... Nordic Association of Hairdressers [*Sweden*]   (EAIO)
NAHAL..... Noar Halutzi Lohem [*Pioneering Fighting Youth*] [*Israel*]
NAHCO ..... Nigerian Aviation Handling Company
NAHD .... Norwegian Association for Huntington's Disease   (EAIO)
Nahgef .... Nahgefecht [*Close Combat*]   (EG)
NAHGT..... National Aboriginal Health Goals and Targets [*Australia*]

NAHH .... Norwegian Association of Hard of Hearing People   (EAIO)
Nahk .... Nahkampf [*Close Combat*]   (EG)
nahk .... Nahkateollisuus [*Leather Industry*] [*Finland*]
NAHL........ New [*South Wales*] Auburn Hospital Library [*Auburn Hospital and Community Health Services*] [*National Union Catalogue of Australia symbol*]
NAHO .... National Aboriginal Health Organisation [*Australia*]
Nahr.......... Nahrung [*Food*] [*German*]   (GCA)
Nahrungsmittelvergift ... Nahrungsmittelvergiftung [*Food Poisoning*] [*German*]   (GCA)
NAHS....... National Aboriginal Health Strategy [*Australia*]
NAHS....... New [*South Wales*] Australian Council on Healthcare Standards [*National Union Catalogue of Australia symbol*]
NAHSWP ... National Aboriginal Health Strategy Working Party [*Australia*]
Nahz.......... Vereinigte Nieder- und Hochdruck-Dampfheizung [*Combined Low and High Pressure Steam Heating System*]   (EG)
NAI .... Annai [*Guyana*] [*Airport symbol*]   (OAG)
NAI .... National Archives of India
NAI .... National Association of Informatists [*Morocco*]   (EAIO)
NAI .... Nordiska Afrika Institutet
NAIA .... National Agricultural and Industrial Association [*Australia*]
NAIA .... National Association of Intercollegiate Athletics   (OLYM)
naib .... Greatest, Largest, Maximum   (RU)
NAIB .... Societe Nantaise d'Importation de Bois et de Quincaillerie [*Morocco*]
NAIC .... National Art Industry Council [*Australia*]
NAICO ...... Nacional de Ingenieria y Construcciones Ltda. [*Colombia*]   (COL)
NAID .... New [*South Wales*] AIDS [*Council*] [*National Union Catalogue of Australia symbol*]
NAIDC ...... New [*South Wales*] Australian Industry Development Corporation [*National Union Catalogue of Australia symbol*]
NAIDOC ... National Aboriginal and Islander Day Observance Committee [*Australia*]
NAIET....... Nord Africa Industria e Transporti
NAIF........ Nordiska Akademiska Idrottsforbund [*Scandinavian Federation for University Sport*]   (EA)
NAIG .... Nippon Atomic Industry Group [*Japan*]
NAIG .... Nippon Atomic Industry Group Co. Ltd. [*Japan*]
NAIHO...... National Aboriginal and Islander Health Organisation [*Australia*]
NAILG ...... National Awards for Innovation in Local Government [*Australia*]
NAILM ..... National Aboriginal and Islander Liberation Movement [*Australia*]
NAILS .... National Aboriginal and Islander Legal Service [*Australia*]
NAILSS.... National Aboriginal and Islander Legal Service Secretariat [*Australia*]
NAIM .... New [*South Wales*] Australian Institute of Management [*New South Wales Training Centre Ltd.*]
naim .... Smallest, Least, Minimum   (RU)
NAIPRC.... Netherlands Automatic Information Processing Research Centre (PDAA)
NAIPS .... New [*South Wales*] Australian Institute of Political Science [*National Union Catalogue of Australia symbol*]
NAIRU ...... Non-Accelerating Inflation Rate of Unemployment
NAISDA.... National Aboriginal Islander Skills Development Association [*Australia*]
NAITB....... National Automotive Industry Training Board [*Australia*]
NAITC....... National Arts Industry Training Council [*Australia*]
NAIU .... National Agro-Industrial Union [*Bulgaria*]   (IMH)
NAIZ .... Scientific Association for the Study of the Peoples of the West (RU)
NAJMWC ... New [*South Wales*] Australian Joint Maritime Warfare Centre [*National Union Catalogue of Australia symbol*]
NAJU .... Nordic Association of Journalists' Unions   (EA)
NAJWE..... New [*South Wales*] Australian Joint Warfare Establishment [*National Union Catalogue of Australia symbol*]
NAK.......... Corps Artillery Commander   (RU)
NAK.......... Naderlandsche Algemeene Keuringsdienst voor Landbouwzaden en Aardappelpootooed [*General Netherlands Inspection Service for Seeds of Field Crops and for Seed Potatoes*] [*Netherlands*]   (DSCA)
Nak .... Nakliyat [*or Nakliye*] [*Transport*]   (TU)
NAK.......... Nea Agrotiki Kinisis [*New Agrarian Movement*] [*Greek*]   (GC)
NAK.......... Nederlandsch Archief voor Kerkgeschiedenis
NAK.......... Nederlandse Algemene Keuringsdienst [*Netherlands*]   (BAS)
NAK.......... Neolaiistiko Andidiktatoriko Kinima [*Antidictatorial Movement of Youth*] [*Greek*]   (GC)
NAK.......... Neos Astikos Kodix [*New Code of Civil Procedure*]   (GC)
NAKA........ Valakinek A Partfogoltja [*or X. Y. ElvtarsNAK A KAdere*] [*Someone's Protege (slang)*]   (HU)
NAKASA... National Amateur Karate Association of South Africa
NAKB .... Nederlandse Algemene Keuringsdienst voor Boomkwekerinjproducten [*Netherlands*]   (BAS)
NAKG....... Nederlandse Algemene Keuringsdienst voor Groentezaden [*Netherlands*]   (BAS)

NAKI .... Nagynyomasu Kiserleti Intezet [*High Pressure Testing Institute*] (HU)
nakl .... Bill of Lading, Waybill, Invoice (RU)
nakl .... Mood [*Grammar*] (RU)
nakl .... Naklad [*Issue*] (POL)
nakl .... Naklada [*Edition*] (YU)
nakl .... Nakladatelstvi [*Publisher*] (CZ)
nakl .... Nakladem [*Published By*] (POL)
nakm .... Nakladni Kilometr [*Freight-Kilometer*] (CZ)
NaKo .... Nahrungs- und Konsumgueter [*Foodstuffs and Consumer Goods*] (EG)
NAKS .... Nederlandse Algemene Keuringsdienst voor Siergewassen [*Netherlands*] (BAS)
NAL .... National Acoustics Laboratory [*Australia*] (ECON)
NAL .... National Aeronautical Laboratory [*Council of Scientific and Industrial Research*] [*India*] [*Research center*] (ERC)
NAL .... National Aerospace Laboratory [*Research center*] [*Japan*] (PDAA)
NAL .... National Agricultural Laboratories
NAL .... National Alliance of Liberals [*Ghana*] (AF)
NAL .... Natsional'naia Afrikanskaia Liga
NAL .... Negociacion Azucarera Laredo Ltd. [*Peru*] (DSCA)
NAL .... Niue Airways Ltd. (EY)
NAL .... Normenausschuss Lebensmittel und Landwirtschaftliche Produkte im DIN [*Deutsches Institut fuer Normung*] eV [*Food and Agricultural Production Standards in the German Institute of Standardization*] (SLS)
NAL .... Norske Arkitekters Landsforbund [*Norwegian Architects Association*] (SLS)
NAL .... Norwegian America Line
NAL .... Notaufnahmelager [*Emergency Reception Camp*] (WEN)
NAL .... Scientific Automobile Laboratory [*1918-1920*] (RU)
NALAG ..... National Association for Loss and Grief [*Australia*]
NALBAT ... National Association of Licensed Buying Agents [*Nigeria*]
NALCO ...... National Association of Local Councils [*Ghana*]
NALDDH ... Encuentro Nacional de los Argentinos por las Libertades Democraticas y los Derechos del Hombre [*National Assembly of Argentines for Democratic Liberties and Human Rights*] (LA)
NALF .... Norges Arbeidslederforbund [*Norway*] (EAIO)
NALG .... National Association for Loss and Grief [*Australia*]
NALHC ...... National Acoustic Laboratories Hearing Center [*Australia*]
NALJS ...... Nordic Atomic Libraries Joint Secretariat [*Information service or system*] (IID)
NALL .... New [*South Wales*] Australian Listening Library [*National Union Catalogue of Australia symbol*]
NALLA ...... Agencia Nacional de Linhas a Longa Distancia [*National Agency for Long Distance Lines*] [*Portuguese*] (WER)
NALLS ...... National Aboriginal Literacy and Language Strategy [*Australia*]
NALMACO ... Nacional de Maquinas de Contabilidad Ltda. [*Colombia*] (COL)
NALN .... North African Liaison Section [*World War II*]
NALO .... Nasional Lotere [*National Lottery*] (IN)
NALO .... Naval Aircraft Logistics Office [*Department of Defence*] [*Australia*]
NALR .... New [*South Wales*] Australia Law Reform Commission [*National Union Catalogue of Australia symbol*]
NALSS ...... National Asian Languages Scholarship Scheme [*Australia*]
nam .... Namestek [*Deputy*] (CZ)
nam .... Namesti [*Square, Boulevard*] (CZ)
NAM .... Namibia [*ANSI three-letter standard code*] (CNC)
NAM .... Namlea [*Indonesia*] [*Airport symbol*] (OAG)
NAM .... Nederlandsche Aluminium Maatschappij NV
NAM .... Nederlandse Aardolie Maatschappij [*Netherlands Natural Gas Company*] (WEN)
NAM .... Nonaligned Movement (AF)
NAM .... Normenausschuss Maschinenbau im DIN [*Deutsches Institut fuer Normung*] eV [*Machine Building Standards in the German Institute of Standardization*] (SLS)
NAM .... North Africa Mission
NA-MA ..... Narodni Magazin [*People's Department Store*] (YU)
NAMA .... National Agenda for a Multicultural Australia
NAMA .... New [*South Wales*] Australian Medical Association [*Library*] [*Westmead Hospital*]
NAMAAWO ... National Union of Automotive Machineries, Appliances, and Allied Services Workers Organization [*Philippines*] (FEA)
NAMARCO ... National Marketing Corporation [*Philippines*]
NAMB ...... National Agricultural Marketing Board
NAMBOARD ... National Agricultural Marketing Board [*Zambia*]
NAMC .... New [*South Wales*] Australian Music Centre [*National Union Catalogue of Australia symbol*]
NAMC .... Nihon Aeroplane Manufacturing Co. [*Japan*]
NAMCAR ... North America/Caribbean
NAMCO.... Air-Cushion Vehicle built by Nakamura Seisakusho [*Usually used in combination with numerals*] [*Japan*]
NAMCPCM ... National Association of Metal Cans, Packagings, and Closures Manufacturers [*France*] (EAIO)

NAME....... New [*South Wales*] Adult Migrant English [*Service Resource Centre*] [*National Union Catalogue of Australia symbol*]
NAMED.... North African Medical Section [*World War II*]
NAMFREL ... National Citizens' Movement for Free Elections [*Philippines*] [*Political party*]
NAMI .... Automobile Designed by the Scientific Research Institute of Automobiles and Automobile Engines (RU)
NAMI .... Central Scientific Research Institute of Automobiles and Automobile Engines (RU)
naml .... Naemlich [*Namely*] [*German*] (GPO)
naml .... Namligen [*Namely*] [*Sweden*] (GPO)
NAML....... New [*South Wales*] Ashfield Municipal Library [*National Union Catalogue of Australia symbol*]
NAMM....... North African Military Mission [*World War II*]
namnt......... Namnteckning [*Signature (Name)*] [*Sweden*]
NAMOTI .. National Movement for True Independence [*Trinidadian and Tobagan*] (LA)
NAMP....... National Antibiotic Minimization Program [*Australia*]
NAMP....... NATO Annual Manpower Plan (NATG)
NAMP....... New [*South Wales*] Australian Mutual Provident [*Society Library*] [*National Union Catalogue of Australia symbol*]
NAMPA ..... NATO Maritime Patrol Aircraft Agency (NATG)
NAMPI..... National Archeological Museum in Plovdiv (BU)
NAMPO..... National Maize Producers Organisation [*South Africa*] (AA)
NAMS .... National Archeological Museum in Sofia (BU)
NAMSA .... NATO Maintenance and Supply Agency
NAMSO.... [*The*] Namibian Students Organization (AF)
NAMSO.... NATO Maintenance and Supply Organization [*Formerly, NATO Maintenance Supply Service Agency*] [*Luxembourg*]
NAMU ...... New [*South Wales*] Australian Museum [*National Union Catalogue of Australia symbol*]
NAMU ...... Nigerian African Mine Workers' Union
NAMUCAR ... Naviera Multinacional del Caribe [*Caribbean Multinational Shipping Line*] (LA)
NAN .... Nadi [*Fiji*] [*Airport symbol*] (OAG)
NAN .... National Association of Nurses [*Israel*] (EAIO)
NAN .... News Agency of Nigeria (EY)
NAN .... Normenausschuss Antriebstechnik im DIN [*Deutsches Institut fuer Normung*] eV [*Propulsion Technology Standards in the German Institute of Standardization*] (SLS)
NAN .... Ordinance on Amortization Norms (BU)
NANA........ New Africa News Agency
NANA........ Newsagents' Association of New South Wales and the Australian Capital Territory, Inc.
NANAI..... Dutch Actiongroup for Indians of North America
NANAU .... National Allied Unions [*Namibia*] (EY)
NANAW.... Naval Forces Northwest African Waters
NANC...... Nyasaland African National Congress
NANHPH ... National Association of Nursing Homes and Private Hospitals [*Australia*]
NANICA ... Naviera Nicaraguense [*Nicaraguan Shipping Co.*] (LA)
NANNP..... Nordic Association of Non-Commercial Phonogram Producers (EA)
NANP........ No Aircraft Noise Party [*Political party*]
NANPA ..... North American Nature Photography Association
NANS........ Air Navigation Service Manual (RU)
NANS........ National Association of Nigerian Students
NANS........ North Atlantic and Neighboring Seas
NAOC....... Nigerian Agip Oil Co.
NAOIG...... North African Inspector General's Section [*World War II*]
NAOP........ Artillery-Gunnery Manual (RU)
NAORD..... North African Ordnance Section [*World War II*]
NAORPB .. North Atlantic Ocean Regional Planning Board [*NATO*]
NAORPG .. North Atlantic Ocean Regional Planning Group [*NATO*] (NATG)
NAOU .... Northern Australia Observer Unit
NAP.......... Armed Proletarian Nuclei [*Italy*]
NAP.......... Bangladesh National Awami Party [*Political party*] (PPW)
nap .... Napis [*or Napisal*] [*Inscription or Written By*] [*Poland*]
NAP.......... Naples [*Italy*] [*Airport symbol*] (OAG)
nap .... Naponkent [*Daily*] (HU)
NAP.......... National Action Party [*Sierra Leone*] [*Political party*] (EY)
NAP.......... National Action Party [*Turkey*] [*Political party*] (PD)
NAP.......... National AIDS Program [*Guinea-Bissau*] (EAIO)
NAP.......... National Alliance Party [*Sierra Leone*]
NAP.......... National Appeals Panel [*Australia*]
NAP.......... National Association of Manufacturers [*US*] (RU)
NAP.......... National Audit Plan
NAP.......... National Awami Party [*Pakistan*] [*Political party*] (PD)
NAP.......... National Awami Party-Bashani [*Bangladesh*] [*Political party*] (FEA)
NAP.......... Nationales Aufbauprogramm [*National Reconstruction Program*]
NAP.......... Nelson Australia Paperbacks (ADA)
NAP.......... New Australian Party (ADA)
NAP.......... Niger Agricultural Project

NAP........... Nigeria Advance Party
NAP........... North Australia Program
NAP........... Nosokomeion Anapiron Polemou [*Nursing Home for War Handicapped*] [*Greek*] (GC)
NAP.......... Nouvelle Agence de Presse [*New Press Agency*] [*French*] (AF)
NAP.......... Nuclei Armati Proletari [*Armed Proletarian Nuclei*] [*Italian*] (PD)
NAP.......... Nucleos de Acao Partidaria [*Party Action Nuclei*] [*Brazil*] (LA)
NAP.......... Nucleos de Accion Popular [*Nuclei of Popular Action*] [*Spanish*] (WER)
NAP.......... Regimental Artillery Commander (RU)
NAP.......... Regimental Artillery Officer (BU)
NAPA....... Nyasaland African Progressive Association [*Malawi*]
NAPAC ..... Natal Performing Arts Council
NAPAC ..... Nigerian Anti-Piracy Action Committee
NAPAP...... Noyaux Armes pour l'Autonomie Populaire [*Armed Cells for Popular Autonomy*] [*France*] (PD)
NAPC .... North Aegean Petroleum Co. [*Greece*]
NAPCAN .. National Association for the Prevention of Child Abuse and Neglect [*Australia*]
NAPCh...... Nonlinear Active Frequency Transformer (RU)
NAPCO ..... National Production Company
NAPDO..... Namibian African People's Democratic Organisation
napech....... Printed, Published (BU)
NAPEDNC ... National Association of Political Ex-Deportees of the Nazi Camps [*Italy*] [*Political party*] (EAIO)
NAPEPA... Naviera Peruana del Pacifico [*Peru*] (LAA)
NAPG........ Nasionale Algemene Praktisynsgroep [*South Africa*] (AA)
NAPH....... New [*South Wales*] Astra Pharmaceuticals [*Proprietary Ltd. Medica l Library*] [*National Union Catalogue of Australia symbol*]
NAPHER .. Nigeria Association for Physical Health, Education, and Recreation
NAPIC...... National AIDS [*Acquired Immune Deficiency Syndrome*] in Prisons Informatio n Clear [*National Union Catalogue of Australia symbol*]
napk .... Napkozi [*During the Day, Daytime, Day-Care Center*] (HU)
NAPK .... National Agroindustrial Complex (BU)
NAPK .... Nea Anexartitos Politiki Kinisis [*New Independent Political Movement*] [*Greek*] (GC)
NAP-M...... National Awami Party-Muzaffar [*Bangladesh*] [*Political party*] (FEA)
NAPMG .... North African Provost Marshal General [*World War II*]
NAPMH.... National Association for Persons with Mental Handicap [*Germany*] (EAIO)
NAPMO.... NATO Airborne Early Warning and Control Programme Management Organization [*Brunssum, Netherlands*]
NAPO........ Chief of Political Section [*Military term*], Chief of Political Department (RU)
NAPOCOR ... National Power Corp. [*Philippines*] (DS)
(Na) podst ... (Na) Podstawie [*Based (On)*] (POL)
NAPOTS... National Aboriginal Project Officer Training Scheme [*Australia*]
NAPP .... Nacelnik Artiljerije Pesadiskog Puka [*Artillery Chief of an Infantry Regiment*] (YU)
Nappie .... Neuilly, Auteil, and Passy [*Elegant Paris neighborhoods; the term, Nappie, is used as a nickname for French Yuppies*]
napr........... For Example (BU)
napr........... For Example, For Instance (RU)
napr........... Na Priklad [*For Example*] (CZ)
napr........... Naprimer [*For Example*] (YU)
NAPR .... NATO Armaments Planning Review (NATG)
NAPRA ..... National Padi and Rice Authority (ML)
NAPRG ..... Norwegian Association for People with Restricted Growth (EAIO)
NAPRI...... National Animal Production Research Institute [*Nigeria*] [*Research center*] (IRC)
NAPROZA ... Nabavna in Prodajna Zadruga [*Buying and Selling Cooperative*] (YU)
NAPRW .... Northwest African Photographic Reconnaissance Wing [*World War II*]
NAPS........ Northern Australian Photo Survey
NAPSA...... National Association of Pharmaceutical Students of Australia (ADA)
NAPSA...... National Association of Psychology Students of Australia (ADA)
NAPT .... National Action on Public Transport [*Australia*]
NAPT .... Nordic Association of Plumbers and Tinsmiths (EAIO)
NAPTA...... National Association for the Prevention of Tuberculosis in Australia (ADA)
NAPTO ..... National Association of Private Transport Operators [*South Africa*] (AA)
napulnoprerab ... Completely Revised (BU)
NAPV .... Asynchronous Automatic Reclosing (RU)
NAQDC..... National Air Quality Data Center [*Australia*]
NAQMC.... North African Quartermaster Section [*World War II*]
nar............. Adverb (BU)
NAR.......... Beginning of Automatic Operation (RU)
NAR.......... Nare [*Colombia*] [*Airport symbol*] (OAG)

nar............. Narodni [*National*] (CZ)
nar............. Narozen [*Born*] (CZ)
NAR.......... National Alliance for Reconstruction [*Political party*] [*Trinidadian*]
NAR.......... National Archives of Rhodesia
NAR.......... Neo Aristero Revma [*Greece*] [*Political party*] (ECED)
NAR.......... Net Advertising Revenue [*Television*] [*British*]
NAR.......... Nordic Association for Rehabilitation [*Denmark*] (EAIO)
NAR.......... Nordiska Akademiker Radet [*Nordic Academic Council - NAC*] [*Defunct*] (EA)
NAR.......... Nordisk Amatorteaterrad [*Nordic Amateur Theatre Council*] [*Norway*] (EAIO)
NAR.......... Normanschlussregister [*German*] (ADPT)
NAR.......... Normenausschuss Radiologie im DIN [*Deutsches Institut fuer Normung*] eV [*Radiology Standards in the German Institute of Standardization*] (SLS)
NAR.......... North Australia Railway
NAR.......... Nuclei Armati Rivoluzionari [*Armed Revolutionary Nuclei*] [*Italian*] (PD)
nar............. People's, National (BU)
nar............. People's, Popular, National (RU)
NARA .... Nepal Association of Rafting Agents (EAIO)
NARA .... Nippon Australian Relations Agreement (ADA)
NARAL ..... National Association for the Repeal of Abortion Laws
NARAL ..... Net Advertising Revenue after Levy [*Television*] [*British*]
NARAT ..... NATO Request for Air Transport Support [*Military*]
NARBL...... Net Advertising Revenue before Levy [*Television*] [*British*]
NARC .... National Agricultural Research Center
NARC .... National Army Revolutionary Committee [*or Council*] [*Laos*]
NARCO ..... Narcotics Commission [*United Nations*]
NARCO ..... National Ranching Company [*Tanzania*] (AF)
NARD....... National Alliance for the Restoration of Democracy
NARD....... National Association of Resident Doctors [*Nigeria*]
nar-demokr rep ... People's Democratic Republic (BU)
NARE .... Norwegian Antarctic Research Expedition
NARESA... Natural Resources, Energy, and Science Authority of Sri Lanka [*Research center*] (EAS)
NARG....... Northern Areas Regional Group [*Australia*]
NARGA ..... National Association of Retail Grocers of Australia (ADA)
NARI .... Nanjing Automation Research Institute [*China*] [*Research center*] (IRC)
NARI .... Natal Agricultural Research Institute
NARI .... National Agricultural Research Institute of Guyana (IRC)
NARI .... National AIDS Research Institute [*India*]
NARIC...... National Rice and Corn Board [*Philippines*]
naris......... Painted, Drawn By (BU)
NAR-ISKoop ... Kibris Turk Narenciye Pazarlama Kooperatif [*Turkish Cypriot Citrus Fruit Marketing Cooperative*] (TU)
Narizdat.... People's Publishing House (BU)
NARKO..... Narenciye ve Tarim Urunleri Uretim ve Pazarlama Kooperatifi [*Citrus Fruit and Agricultural Products Producing and Marketing Cooperative*] [*Mersin*] (TU)
narkom...... People's Commissar [*1917-1946*] (RU)
narkomat.... People's Commissariat [*1917-1946*] (RU)
Narkomchermet ... People's Commissariat of Ferrous Metallurgy, USSR [*1939-1946*] (RU)
NARKOMELEKTRO ... People's Commissariat of Electric Power Plants and the Electrical Equipment Industry, USSR (RU)
NARKOMFIN ... People's Commissariat of Finance [*1924-1946*] (RU)
NARKOMGOSKON ... People's Commissariat of State Control [*1940-1946*] (RU)
Narkomindel ... Narodny Kommissariat Inostranikh Del [*People's Commissariat of Foreign Affairs*] [*1917-1946*] (RU)
narkomkhim ... People's Commissariat of the Chemical Industry [*1939-1946*] (RU)
Narkomkhimprom ... People's Commissariat of the Chemical Industry [*1939-1946*] (RU)
NARKOMKhOZ ... People's Commissariat of the Municipal Economy (RU)
Narkomkomkhoz ... People's Commissariat of the Municipal Economy (RU)
NARKOMLEGPROM ... People's Commissariat of Light Industry (RU)
NARKOMLES ... People's Commissariat of the Lumber Industry [*1932-1946*] (RU)
NARKOMMASh ... People's Commissariat of Machinery Manufacture, USSR (RU)
NARKOMMESTPROM ... People's Commissariat of Local Industry (RU)
Narkommyasomolprom ... People's Commissariat of the Meat and Dairy Industry (RU)
NARKOMNATs ... Narodny Kommissariat po Delam [*People's Commissariat for Nationalities, RSFSR*] (RU)
NARKOMNEFT' ... People's Commissariat of the Petroleum Industry, USSR [*1939-1946*] (RU)
NARKOMPIShChEPROM ... People's Commissariat of the Food Industry (RU)
NARKOMPOChTEL' ... People's Commissariat of Postal and Telegraphic Service (RU)
NARKOMPROD ... People's Commissariat of Food [*1917-1924*] (RU)

NARKOMPROS ... Narodny Kommissariat Prosveshcheniya [*People's Commissariat of Education*] [*1917-1946*] (RU)

NARKOMPUT' ... People's Commissariat of Railroads, USSR [*1922-1946*] (RU)

NARKOMRABKRIN ... People's Commissariat of Workers' and Peasants' Inspection [*1920-1934*] (RU)

NARKOMREChFLOT ... People's Commissariat of the River Fleet, USSR (RU)

Narkomrezinprom ... People's Commissariat of the Rubber Industry, USSR (RU)

NarkomRKI ... People's Commissariat of Workers' and Peasants' Inspection [*1920-1934*] (RU)

NARKOMRYBPROM ... People's Commissariat of the Fish Industry [*1939-1946*] (RU)

NARKOMSNAB ... People's Commissariat of Supply [*1930-1934*] (RU)

NARKOMSOBES ... People's Commissariat of Social Security [*1918-1946*] (RU)

NARKOMSOVKhOZOV ... People's Commissariat of Grain and Livestock-Breeding Sovkhozes (RU)

NARKOMSVYaZ' ... People's Commissariat of Communications, USSR [*1932-1946*] (RU)

Narkomtekstil' ... People's Commissariat of the Textile Industry (RU)

Narkomtop ... People's Commissariat of the Fuel Industry (RU)

Narkomtorg ... People's Commissariat of Foreign and Domestic Trade, USSR [*1924-1938*] (RU)

NARKOMTORG ... People's Commissariat of Trade [*1938-1946*] (RU)

NARKOMTRUD ... People's Commissariat of Labor [*1917-1933*] (RU)

Narkomtsvetmet ... People's Commissariat of Nonferrous Metallurgy, USSR [*1939-1946*] (RU)

NARKOMTYaZh ... People's Commissariat of Heavy Industry [*1932-1939*] (RU)

Narkomtyazhprom ... People's Commissariat of Heavy Industry, USSR [*1932-1939*] (RU)

NARKOMUGOL' ... People's Commissariat of the Coal Industry, USSR [*1939-1946*] (RU)

Narkomvneshtorg ... People's Commissariat of Foreign Trade, USSR [*1923-1925, 1930-1946*] (RU)

NARKOMVNUDEL ... Narodnyi Komissariat Vnutrennikh Del [*People's Commissariat of Internal Affairs (1917-1946)*] [*Also known as NKVD Soviet secret police organization*]

Narkomvnutorg ... People's Commissariat of Domestic Trade [*1924-1938*] (RU)

NARKOMVOD ... People's Commissariat of Water Transportation, USSR (RU)

Narkomvoyen ... People's Commissariat for Military Affairs [*1918-1923*] (RU)

Narkomvoyenmor ... People's Commissariat for Military and Naval Affairs, USSR [*1923-1934*] (RU)

Narkomvoyenmor ... People's Commissariat of the Navy, USSR [*1937-1946*] (RU)

Narkomyust ... People's Commissariat of Justice, USSR [*1936-1946*] (RU)

NARKOMZAG ... People's Commissariat of Procurement, USSR [*1938-1946*] (RU)

NARKOMZDRAV ... People's Commissariat of Public Health [*1936-1946*] (RU)

NARKOMZEM ... People's Commissariat of Agriculture (RU)

Narkoop ..... People's Cooperative (BU)

Narkoopizdat ... People's Cooperative Publishing House (BU)

narkot .... Narkotisch [*Narcotic*] [*German*] (GCA)

Nar kult ..... Narodna Kultura [*People's Culture*] [*A periodical*] (BU)

NARM .... North Australian Rubber Mills Ltd. (ADA)

Narmag ...... People's Store (BU)

NARMP .... National Antibacterial Residue Minimization Program [*Australia*]

NARO .... National Agricultural Research Organization [*Netherlands*] (ECON)

NARO .... National Association of Recycling Operations [*Australia*]

nar obr .... Public Education (RU)

Narobraz .... Department of Public Education (RU)

NARP .... New Australian Republican Party [*Political party*]

NARP .... Swedish Association of Registered Physical Therapists (EAIO)

nar pech ..... National Press (BU)

narpit .... Public Eating Facilities (RU)

NARPIT .... Trade Union of Workers of Public Eating Facilities (RU)

Nar prosv .... Narodna Prosveta [*Public Education*] [*A periodical*] (BU)

NARS .... National Agricultural Research Station

NARS .... Nigeria Amateur Radio Society (PDAA)

NARS .... Nyandarua Agricultural Research Station [*Kenya*] (DSCA)

NARS .... Unguided Aircraft-Launched Missile (RU)

Narsoc .... Narodni Socialiste [*National Socialists*] (CZ)

Nar subr ..... National Assembly (BU)

narsuvet ...... People's Council (BU)

NarTeatur ... National Theater (BU)

NARU .... North Australia Research Unit [*Australian National University*] (ADA)

NARUBIN ... Nasr Company for Rubber Industries

NARUS ..... Narodohospodarsky Ustav Slovensky [*Slovak Institute of Economics*] (CZ)

NARWA .... Nordic Agricultural Research Workers Association (EA)

NAS .... Nacelnik Automobilni Sluzby [*Chief, Motor Transport Service*] (CZ)

nas .... Nasionaal [*National*] [*Afrikaans*]

NAS .... Nassau [*Bahamas*] [*Airport symbol*] (OAG)

NAS .... Nationaal Arbeidssecretariaat [*Benelux*] (BAS)

NAS .... National Air School [*Australia*]

NAS .... National Alliance for Salvation [*Sudan*] [*Political party*] (MENA)

NAS .... National Art School [*Australia*]

NAS .... Navtikos Athlitikos Syndesmos [*Naval Athletic League*] [*Greek*] (GC)

NAS .... Nordisk Akustik Selskab [*Denmark*] (SLS)

NAS .... Normenausschuss Schweisstechnik im DIN [*Deutsches Institut fuer Normung*] eV [*Welding Technology Standards in the German Institute of Standardization*] (SLS)

nas .... Norwegian Association of Stutterers (EAIO)

nas .... Population (BU)

NASA .... National Agricultural Settlement Authority [*Libya*]

NASA .... Navegacion Atlantica SA [*Uruguay*] (LAA)

NASA .... North Atlantic Shippers Association (DS)

NaSa .... Nossa Senhora [*Our Lady*] [*Portuguese*]

NaSa .... Nuestra Senora [*Our Lady*] [*Spanish*]

NASAA ..... National Association for Sustainable Agriculture in Australia

NASACO .. National Shipping Agencies Company Ltd. [*Tanzania*] (AF)

NASAF ...... North African Strategic Air Force

NASAKOM ... Nasional, Agama, Kommunist [*Indonesian President Sukarno's policy of unity among National, Religious, and Communist forces*]

NASAKOM ... Nasionalis-Agama-Kimunis [*Nationalists, Religious Groups, Communists (Term symbolizing the apparent unity of principal political groups during the Sukarno era)*] (IN)

NASB .... National Animal Serum Bank [*Australia*]

NASBO ..... North African Shipping Board [*World War II*]

NASC .... New [*South Wales*] Albion Street Centre [*National Union Catalogue of Australia symbol*]

NASCIS ..... National Australian Schools Catalogue Information Service

NASCO ..... El Nasr Automotive Manufacturing Corporation [*Egypt*]

NASCO ..... National Safety Co. [*Saudi Arabia*]

NASCO ..... North Atlantic Salmon Conservation Organization [*Edinburgh, Scotland*] (EAIO)

NASDA ..... National Space Development Agency [*Japan*]

NASF .... National Aboriginal Sports Foundation [*Australia*]

NASGS ..... North African Secretary General Staff [*World War II*]

NASI .... Nigerian Army School of Infantry

NASIA .... National Association of Swedish Interior Architects (EAIO)

NASIG ...... North African Signal Section [*World War II*]

NASK .... New [*South Wales*] Askews [*Library Supplies*] [*National Union Catalogue of Australia symbol*]

NASK .... Normenausschuss Siebboeden und Kornmessung im DIN [*Deutsches Institut fuer Normung*] eV (SLS)

NASL .... Norwegian Academy of Science and Letters (EAIO)

nasl .... Successors (RU)

NASMA .... Parti Nasionalis Malaysia [*Political party*] (FEA)

NASME ..... Nigerian Army School of Military Engineering

NAS(MISC) ... North American Supply Committee, Miscellaneous [*World War II*]

NASP .... National Academy of Sciences of Panama (EAIO)

NaSPA .... National Systems Programmers Association (EAIO)

NASPED ... National Solar Photovoltaic Energy Demonstration Project [*Central Electronics Limited*] [*India*]

NASPO ..... National Armed Service Projects Organization [*Egypt*]

Na Sra .... Nuestra Senora [*Our Lady*] [*Spanish*]

NASS .... Nacelnik Aviosignalne Stanice [*Air Signal Station Chief*] (YU)

NASS .... North African Special Service Section [*World War II*]

NASS .... Nursing Area Support Service [*Australia*]

NASSA ...... National Art School Students' Association [*Australia*]

NASSA ...... National Association for the Study of Snow and Avalanches [*France*] (EAIO)

NASSDC .... National Social Science Documentation Centre [*Information service or system*] (IID)

NASST ...... National Union of Teachers in Sweden (EAIO)

nast .... Nastepny [*Next*] (POL)

nast .... Present (Tense) (RU)

NASTAR ... National Standard Races [*Skiing*] [*Australia*]

NASUTRA ... National Sugar Trading Corp. [*Philippines*] (IMH)

NASV .... International Academy of Sports Vision [*Formerly, National Academy of Sports Vision*] (EAIO)

NASVG ..... Nordic Association for Study and Vocational Guidance [*See also NRSY*] (EAIO)

NASX .... New [*South Wales*] Australian Stock Exchange [*Corporate Library*]

nasyshch ..... Saturated, Impregnated (RU)

nasz .... Naszierend [*Nascent*] [*German*]

Nat .... In der Natur [*In Nature*] [*German*]   (GCA)

N a T .... Name auf Titelblatt [*Name on the Title Page*] [*German*]

NAT .... Natal [*Brazil*] [*Airport symbol*]   (OAG)

nat .... Nationaal [*Benelux*]   (BAS)

nat .... National [*German*]   (GCA)

Nat .... National Party [*Australia*] [*Political party*]

nat .... Natuerlich [*Natural*] [*German*]   (GCA)

nat .... Natuurkunde [*Nature Study*] [*Afrikaans*]

NAT .... Navtikon Apomakhikon Tameion [*Seamen's Retirement Fund*] [*Greek*]   (GC)

NAT .... Normal Atmospheric Pressure   (RU)

NAT .... North African Theater [*World War II*]

NATA .... National Association of Teachers of Agriculture [*Australia*]

NATA .... National Association of Testing Authorities [*Australia*]   (SLS)

NATA .... Navy Air Technical Arsenal [*Aircraft manufacturer*] [*Japan*]

NATA .... Neighbors Aid to Asia   (CL)

NATAF ...... Northwest African Tactical Air Force [*World War II*]

NATBF ...... Northwest African Tactical Bomber Force [*World War II*]

Nat-Bibl ..... Nationalbibliothek [*National Library*] [*German*]

NATC .... National Aboriginal Tribal Council

NATC .... National Appropriate Technology Committee [*Malawi*]

NATC .... New [*South Wales*] Australian Tourist Commission [*National Union Catalogue of Australia symbol*]

NATC .... Nordic Amateur Theatre Council   (EAIO)

NATC .... Nordic Automobile Technical Committee [*Defunct*] [*Denmark*]   (EAIO)

NATC .... Northwest African Training Command [*World War II*]

NATCA ..... National Traffic Control Administration [*China*]

NATCC ..... Northwest African Troop Carrier Command [*World War II*]

NATCO ...... National Confectionery Company

NATCOL... Natural Food Colours Association [*Basel, Switzerland*]   (EAIO)

NATEX...... National Exhibition Trust [*Australia*]

NATEX...... National Textile Industries Corp. Ltd.

NATI .... State All-Union Scientific Research Institute of Tractors   (RU)

NATIDC.... Netherlands-Australia Trade and Industrial Development Council   (ADA)

NATIS ...... National Information System [*UNESCO*]

NATIS ...... National Information Systems [*Later, GIP*] [*UNESCO*]

NATIS ...... North Atlantic Treaty Information Service   (NATG)

NATIST .... National Translation Institute of Science and Technology of Japan

Nat'l .... National   (PWGL)

Natle .... Nationale [*National*] [*Military map abbreviation World War I*] [*French*]   (MTD)

NatLib....... National Liberal Party [*Australia*] [*Political party*]

NATO........ New [*South Wales*] Australian Taxation Office [*Sydney Tax Office Library*]

NATO........ North African Theater of Operations [*World War II*]

NATO........ North Atlantic Treaty Organization [*Facetious translation: "No Action, Talk Only"*] [*Brussels, Belgium*]

NATOA..... New [*South Wales*] Australian Taxation Office - Albury/ Wodonga Branch [*National Union Catalogue of Australia symbol*]

NATO-AGARD ... North Atlantic Treaty Organization - Advisory Group for Aeronautical Research and Development

NATOELLA ... North Atlantic Treaty Organization - European Long Lines Agency

NATO-Is ... Federation of NATO Workers Union   (TU)

NATO-LRSS ... North Atlantic Treaty Organization - Long-Range Scientific Studies

NATOMILOCGRP ... North Atlantic Treaty Organization - Military Oceanography Group   (NATG)

NATOP..... New [*South Wales*] Australian Taxation Office - Parramatta Branch [*National Union Catalogue of Australia symbol*]

NATO-RDPP ... North Atlantic Treaty Organization - Multilateral Research and Development Production Program

NATOS ..... New [*South Wales*] Australian Taxation Office - Sydney South Branch [*National Union Catalogue of Australia symbol*]

NATOSAT ... North Atlantic Treaty Organization Satellite

NATO-SC ... North Atlantic Treaty Organization - Science Committee

NATOUSA ... North African Theater of Operations, United States Army [*World War II*]

NATPN ..... North African Transportation Section [*World War II*]

NATR .... National Association of Technical Research [*France*]   (EAIO)

NatR .... Nationalrat [*Representative Assembly*] [*Switzerland*]

NATR .... Nordischer Amator Theater Rat [*Nordic Amateur Theatre Council - NATC*]   (EAIO)

NATREF ... National Petroleum Refiners of South Africa

NATROMOLDES ... Compania Nacional de Troquelado y Moldeo SA [*Colombia*]   (COL)

NAT-RPG ... North Atlantic Treaty Regional Planning Group   (NATG)

nats............ National   (BU)

NATS........ National Association of Technological Students [*Nigeria*]

NATS........ Nordisk Avisteknisk Samarbetsnaemnd [*Scandinavian Newspaper Technical Cooperation Council*]

NATS......... Nordisk Avisteknisk Samarbetsnamnd [*Nordic Joint Technical Press Board*] [*Sweden*]   (EAIO)

NATSAA... NATO Air Traffic Service Advisory Agency   (NATG)

NATSIEP ... National Aboriginal and Torres Strait Islander Education Policy [*Australia*]

NATSISU ... National Aboriginal and Torres Strait Islander Student Union [*Australia*]   (ADA)

nats k-t....... National Committee   (BU)

NAT-STD ... NATO STANAG International Standards

NATU........ National Association of Trade Unions [*Philippines*]

NATUC..... [*The*] National Trade Union Centre [*Trinidad and Tobago*]   (EY)

natuerl........ Natuerlich [*Natural*] [*German*]   (GCA)

NatuerlGroesse ... Natuerliche Groesse [*Full-Size*] [*German*]   (GCA)

Naturv........ Naturvorkommen [*Natural Occurrence*] [*German*]

Naturw....... Naturwissenschaft [*Natural Science*] [*German*]   (GCA)

NATV........ National Association of Towns and Villages [*Japan*]

NatWest..... National Westminster [*Bank*]

NAU .... Confederation Nordique des Cadres, Techniciens, et Autres Responsables [*Nordic Confederation of Supervisors, Technicians, and Other Managers*]   (EAIO)

NAU .... Napuka [*Marquesas Islands*] [*Airport symbol*]   (OAG)

NAU .... Natal Agricultural Union [*South Africa*]   (AF)

NAU .... Nordic Confederation of Supervisors, Technicians, and Other Managers [*Formerly, Nordic Union of Foremen*]   (EA)

NAUB........ New [*South Wales*] Auburn [*Municipal Library*] [*National Union Catalogue of Australia symbol*]

NAUCA..... Nomenclatura Arancelaria Uniforme Centroamericana [*Uniform Customs List of Central America*]   (LA)

nauch.......... Scientific   (BU)

nauch-issled ... Scientific Research   (RU)

nauch-izsl... Scientific Research   (BU)

nauch-popul ... Popular Science   (RU)

nauch-tekhn ... Scientific and Technical   (RU)

NAUI........ National Association of Underwater Instructors [*Australia*]

NAUOIS ... Netherlands Association of Users of Online Information Systems   (EAIO)

NAURP ..... Lower Amur River Steamship Line Administration   (RU)

NAUS........ New [*South Wales*] Ausonics [*Proprietary Ltd.*] [*National Union Catalogue of Australia symbol*]

Naut .... Nautica [*Nautical Science*] [*Portuguese*]

naut .... Nautical   (TPFD)

naut .... Nautique [*French*]   (TPFD)

NAUTS ..... National Union of Tanganyika Students [*Tanzania*]   (AF)

NAUW....... Nigeria Association of University Women

nav.............. Na Aanleiding Van [*With Reference To*] [*Afrikaans*]

nav............. Naar Aanleiding Van [*Benelux*]   (BAS)

NAV.......... Nederlandse Anthropogenetische Vereniging [*Netherlands*]   (SLS)

NAV.......... Normenausschuss Vakuumtechnik im DIN [*Deutsches Institut fuer Normung*] eV   (SLS)

NAV.......... Nurserymen's Association of Victoria [*Australia*]

NAV.......... Scientific Association of Oriental Studies   (RU)

NAV.......... Verband der Niedergelassenen Aerzte Deutschlands eV   (SLS)

NAVA....... National Association of Visual Arts [*Australia*]

NAVBALTAP ... Allied Naval Forces, Baltic Approaches [*NATO*]   (NATG)

NAVC........ New [*South Wales*] Avondale College [*National Union Catalogue of Australia symbol*]

NAVCENT ... Allied Naval Forces, Central Europe [*NATO*]

NAVDEP... Naval Deputy [*NATO*]   (NATG)

NAVDEPCENT ... Naval Deputy to Commander-in-Chief, Allied Forces, Central Europe [*NATO*]   (NATG)

NAVEA ..... Nationale Vereniging voor Auteursrechten [*Benelux*]   (BAS)

NAVENAL ... Compania Nacional de Navegacion [*National Shipping Company*] [*Colorado*]   (LA)

NAVF .... Norge Almenvitenskapelige Forskningsrad [*Norwegian Research Council for Science and the Humanities*]   (WEN)

NAVF .... Norges Allmennvitenskapelige Forskningsrad [*Norwegian Research Council for Science and the Humanities*] [*Information service or system*]   (IID)

NAVICONGO ... Syndicat des Cies de Navigation et Consignataires de Navires du Congo

NAVIDA ... Compania de Seguros la Nacional SA [*Colombia*]   (COL)

Navig.......... Navigable [*Navigable*] [*Military map abbreviation World War I*] [*French*]   (MTD)

NAVIGA ... Welt Organisation fur Schiffsmodellbau und Schiffsmodellsport [*World Organization for Modelship Building and Modelship Sport*] [*Austria*]   (EAIO)

NAVIM ..... Navigational Information for Mariners   (RU)

NAVIMAG ... Naviera Magallanes SA [*Chile*]   (EY)

NAVIP....... Narodno Vinarstvo i Podrumarstvo [*National Wine-Selling and Wine Cellars*] [*YU*]

NAVISAFE ... Naviera Santa Fe, SA [*Chile*]   (LAA)

NAVITOGO ... Syndicat des Compagnies de Navigation et des Consignataires de Navires du Togo

NAVLOMAR ... Intreprinderea de Navlosire, Agenturare, si Aprovizonare Nave [*Ship Supply Enterprise and Chartering Agency*] (RO)

NAVMAIRCOMCON ... Naval and Maritime Air Communications-Electronics Conference [*NATO*]

NAVNON ... Allied Naval Forces, North Norway [*NATO*]   (NATG)

NAVNORTH ... Allied Naval Forces, Northern Europe [*NATO*]

NAVO........ Noord-Atlantiese Verdragsorganisasie [*North Atlantic Treaty Organization*] [*Afrikaans*]

NAVO........ Noord-Atlantische Verdrags-Organisatie [*Benelux*]   (BAS)

NAVOCFORMED ... Naval On-Call Force, Mediterranean [*NATO*]   (NATG)

NAVRA ..... National Association of Volunteer Referral Agencies [*Australia*]

NAVROM ... Directia Generala a Navigatiei Civile [*General Directorate for Civil Navigation*]   (RO)

NAVROM ... Navigatia Maritima si Fluviala Romana [*Romanian Maritime and River Navigation*]   (RO)

NAVSCAP ... Allied Naval Forces, Scandinavian Approaches [*NATO*]   (NATG)

NAVSOUTH ... Allied Naval Forces, Southern Europe [*NATO*]   (NATG)

NAVSTAG ... Naval Standardization Agreement [*NATO*]

NAW......... Narathiwat [*Thailand*] [*Airport symbol*]   (OAG)

NAW......... National Arts Week [*Australia*]

NAW......... Nationales Aufbauwerk [*National Reconstruction Program (Voluntary, unpaid work)*]   (EG)

NAW......... Newair [*Denmark*] [*ICAO designator*]   (FAAC)

NAW......... Normenausschuss Wasserwesen im DIN [*Deutsches Institut fuer Normung*] eV   (SLS)

NAWA....... New [*South Wales*] AWA [*Defence Industries*] [*AWA Technical Library*]

NAWAL.... North American West African Line

NAWF....... National Aborigine Welfare Fund [*Australia*]   (ADA)

NAWFA .... North Atlantic Westbound Freight Association   (DS)

NAWGP.... National Agenda for Women's Grants Program [*Australia*]

NAWOA.... National Automobile Workshop Owners' Association

NAWTWPC ... Netherlands Association on Wastewater Treatment and Water Quality Management   (EAIO)

NAY.......... Navegacion y Servicios Aereos Canarios SA [*Spain*] [*ICAO designator*]   (FAAC)

NAYFARM ... National Youth Farmers' Movement of Nigeria [*Trade union*]

NAYLAMP ... Cooperativa de Trabajadores del Puerto de Pimental Ltda. [*Pimentel Port Workers Cooperative*] [*Peru*]   (LA)

NAYO........ National Youth Organization

NAZ.......... Emergency Supplies, Emergency Reserve   (RU)

NAZ.......... Nadvoitsy Aluminum Plant   (RU)

NAZ.......... National Archives of Zambia

NAZ.......... Netball Association of Zambia

NAZ.......... Servicios Aereos del Nazas SA de CV [*Mexico*] [*ICAO designator*]   (FAAC)

Nazavs .... Science for All [*Monograph series*]   (BU)

NAZhT...... Academy of Railroad Transportation   (RU)

NAZI .... Nationalsozialistische Deutsche Arbeiterpartei [*National Socialist German Workers' Party, 1919-45*] [*Political party*]

nazv........... Name, Title   (RU)

NaZw .... Nahrungsmittelzuweisung [*Foodstuffs Allotment*] [*German*]   (EG)

nazw .... Nazwisko [*Surname*] [*Poland*]

NB............. Magyar Nemzeti Bizottmany, New York [*Hungarian National Council, New York*]   (HU)

NB............. Nachbrief [*Postscript*] [*German*]   (GCA)

n/B............. Nad Becvou [*On the Becva River*]   (CZ)

nb .... Nagybecsu [*Esteemed*]   (HU)

NB............. Nagy-Britannia [*Great Britain*]   (HU)

NB............. Naoruzan Brod [*Armed Vessel*]   (YU)

NB............. Narodna Banka [*National Bank*] [*Yugoslavian*]   (YU)

NB............. Narodna Biblioteka [*National Library*]   (YU)

NB............. Narodni Bezpecnost [*National Security (Corps)*]   (CZ)

NB............. Ndermarrje Bujqesore [*Albanian*]

NB............. Neath and Brecon Railway [*Wales*]

NB............. Nemzeti Bajnoksag [*National Championship, National League (Soccer)*]   (HU)

NB............. Nemzeti Bank [*National Bank*] [*Hungarian*]

NB............. Nepbirosag [*People's Court*]   (HU)

NB............. Nepbolt [*People's General Store*]   (HU)

NB............. Netherlands-British Chamber of Commerce

NB............. New Britain   (ADA)

NB............. New Brunswick [*Canadian province*] [*Postal code*]

NB............. Nieuwebijdragen voor Rechtsgeleerdheid en Wetgeving [*Benelux*]   (BAS)

Nb............. Niobio [*Niobium*] [*Chemical element*] [*Portuguese*]

NB............. Nobel-Bozel

nB............. Noerdliche Breite [*North Latitude*] [*German*]

NB............. Nomenclature Board [*Tasmania, Australia*]

NB............. Nonlinear Block   (RU)

NB............. Nordiska Batradet [*Nordic Boat Council*] [*Sweden*]   (EAIO)

NB............. Nordlands Bank [*Norway*]

NB............. Normal Boy [*Normal (Average) Length*]   (TU)

NB............. North Borneo   (ADA)

NB............. Notez Bien [*Note Well*] [*French*]   (WER)

n/b............. Not Found [*On lists*]   (RU)

NB............. Scientific Library   (RU)

NB............. Tail Water   (RU)

NB............. Wage Scale   (BU)

NBA.......... National Bank of Australasia   (ADA)

NBA.......... National Broadcasting Authority [*Bangladesh*]   (EY)

NBA.......... Nepal Badminton Association   (EAIO)

Nba .... Neubauamt [*Office for New Construction*]   (EG)

NBA.......... Niger Basin Authority

NBA.......... Nigerian Bar Association

NBA.......... Night Bombardment Aviation   (RU)

NBA.......... North East Bolivian Airways [*ICAO designator*]   (FAAC)

NBA.......... Nuovo Banco Ambrosiano [*Italian*]

NBAA .... New [*South Wales*] BA Australia [*Ltd.*] [*Information Centre*]

NBAC....... Nigerian Bank for Agriculture and Co-Operatives

NBAD....... National Bank of Abu Dhabi

NBAD....... Night Bomber Division   (RU)

NBAIN ...... New [*South Wales*] Bain [*Securities Ltd.*] [*National Union Catalogue of Australia symbol*]

NBAKT ..... New [*South Wales*] Baker and Taylor [*National Union Catalogue of Australia symbol*]

NBANK..... New [*South Wales*] Bankstown [*City Library and Information Servic e*] [*National Union Catalogue of Australia symbol*]

NBAP .... Night Bomber Regiment   (RU)

NBAR....... New [*South Wales*] Barker [*College*] [*Sydney*]

NBAS........ New [*South Wales*] Bathurst Agricultural Research Station [*National Union Catalogue of Australia symbol*]

NBAT .... New [*South Wales*] Bathurst [*District Historical Society*] [*National Union Catalogue of Australia symbol*]

NBATT...... Nigerian Battalion

NBAU....... New [*South Wales*] Baulkham [*Hills Shire Library Service*] [*National Union Catalogue of Australia symbol*]

NBAY .... New [*South Wales*] Bayer [*Australia Ltd.*] [*National Union Catalogue of Australia symbol*]

NBB .... National Bank of Bahrain   (EY)

NBB .... National Bank of Brunei

NBB .... Nederlandse Boekverkopers Bond

NBBI......... Nederlands Bureau voor Bibliotheekwezen en Informatieverzorging [*Netherlands Organization for Libraries and Information Services*] [*Information service or system*]   (IID)

NBBL........ New [*South Wales*] Ballarat Branch Library [*National Union Catalogue of Australia symbol*]

NBC.......... Danish Agricultural Council   (EAIO)

NBC.......... Narodni Banka Ceskoslovenska [*Czechoslovak National Bank*]   (CZ)

NBC.......... National Ballet of Cuba

NBC.......... National Bank of Commerce [*Tanzania*]

NBC.......... National Bibliographic Control

NBC.......... National Book Council [*Australia*]   (PDAA)

NBC.......... National Business College [*Australia*]

NBC.......... Nederlands Bibliografisch Centrum

NBC.......... Newcastle Business College [*Australia*]

NBC.......... Newfoundland Base Command [*Army*] [*World War II*]

NBC.......... Nigerian Bottling Co.

NBC.......... Nigerian Broadcasting Corp.

NBC.......... Nordic Boat Council   (EA)

NBCA .... National Band Council of Australia

NBCAE...... North Brisbane College of Advanced Education [*Australia*]   (ADA)

NBCC .... National Bioethics Consultative Committee [*Australia*]

NBCC .... National Bureau for Co-Operation in Child Care [*British*]

NBCC .... Netherlands British Chamber of Commerce   (DS)

NBCC .... Nigerian British Chamber of Commerce [*London*]   (DCTA)

NBCDX ..... Nuclear, Biological, and Chemical Defense Exercise [*NATO*]   (NATG)

NBCG .... National Bulk Commodities Group [*Australia*]

NBCI .... Nigerian Bank for Commerce and Industry

NBCL........ New [*South Wales*] Bathurst City Library [*National Union Catalogue of Australia symbol*]

NBCR .... New [*South Wales*] Biological and Chemical Research Institute [*National Union Catalogue of Australia symbol*]

NBCRC...... National Biological Control Research Center [*Thailand*] [*Research center*]   (IRC)

NBCS........ New [*South Wales*] Blue Circle Southern [*Cement Ltd.*] [*National Union Catalogue of Australia symbol*]

NBD.......... National Bank for Development [*Egypt*]   (GEA)

NBD.......... National Bank of Dubai

NBD.......... Nederlandse Bibliotheekdienst [*'s-Gravenhage*]

NBD.......... Nordisk Byggedag [*Denmark*]   (SLS)

NBDB .... National Bibliographic Database [*Australia*]

NBDCS...... National Book Development Council of Singapore   (EAIO)

NBDL .... New [*South Wales*] Bathurst Diocesan Library [*Anglican Church Diocese of Bathurst*] [*Australia*]

NBDPL...... New [*South Wales*] Burwood-Drummoyne Public Library [*National Union Catalogue of Australia symbol*]
NBE........... National Bank of Egypt
NBE........... National Bank of Ethiopia   (AF)
NBEET...... National Board of Employment, Education, and Training [*Australia*]
NBEN....... New [*South Wales*] Bennett-Ebsco [*Subscription Services*] [*National Union Catalogue of Australia symbol*]
NBEV .... Bega Valley Shire Library [*National Union Catalogue of Australia symbol*]
NBF .... Nationaal Bibliotheek Fonds [*Netherlands*]
NBF .... Ndermarrje Bujqesore Frutore [*Albanian*]
Nbf............ Nebenform [*Secondary Form*] [*German*]   (GCA)
NBF .... Nordisk Barnkirurgisk Forening [*Scandinavian Association of Paediatric Surgeons - SAPS*] [*Denmark*]   (EAIO)
NBF .... Norges Badminton Forbund [*Norway*]   (EAIO)
NBF .... Norsk Bedriftsoekonomisk Forening [*Norway*]   (SLS)
NBF .... Norsk Bibliotekforening [*Norway*]   (SLS)
NBF .... Norsk Botanisk Forening [*Norway*]   (SLS)
NBFA .... National Bricklayers' Foundation of Australia   (ADA)
NBFGR..... National Bureau of Fish Genetic Resources [*India*]   (IRC)
NBFNRJ ... Narodna Banka Federativna Narodna Republika Jugoslavija [*National Bank of Yugoslavia*]   (YU)
NBG.......... National Bank of Greece
NBG.......... National Botanic Gardens [*India*]   (PDAA)
NBG.......... Neue Bach-Gesellschaft [*Music*]
NBGSA..... National Botanic Gardens of South Africa   (DSCA)
NBH .... National Bank of Hungary
NBH .... National Brewing Holdings [*Australia*]
NBH .... North Broken Hill Holdings [*Broken Hill Propiatary Co.*] [*Australia*]
NBHC....... New Broken Hill Consolidated [*Australia*]   (ADA)
NBHM ...... New [*South Wales*] Broken Hill Memorial [*Library*] [*Charles Rasp Memorial Library*]
NBHP....... National Better Health Program [*Australia*]
NBHP....... New [*South Wales*] BHP [*Steel International Group*] [*Rod an Bar Division*]
NBHP....... North Broken Hill Peko [*Australia*]
NBHV....... Dutch Federation of Traders in Livestock [*Netherlands*]   (EAIO)
NBI .... Nederlands Beheersinstituut [*Netherlands*]   (BAS)
NBI .... Niels Bohr Institute [*Denmark*]
NBI .... Norges Byggforskningsinstitutt [*Norwegian Building Institute*]
NBIMOD .. Naukowo-Badawczy Instytut Mechanicznej Obrobki Drewna [*Research Institute of the Mechanical Finishing of Lumber*]   (POL)
NBIO .... New [*South Wales*] Biotech [*Australia*] [*National Union Catalogue of Australia symbol*]
NBISS .... National Building Industry Specification System [*Australia*]
NBIW .... Naukowo-Badawczy Instytut Wlokienniczy [*Textile Scientific Research Institute*]   (POL)
NBK.......... Initial Point of Bomb Run   (RU)
NBK.......... National Bank of Kuwait
NBK.......... Nebelkerze [*Smoke-Candle*] [*German military - World War II*]
NBK.......... Nordisk Bilteknisk Kommitte [*Nordic Automobile Technical Committee - NATC*] [*Defunct*] [*Denmark*]   (EAIO)
NBKH....... New [*South Wales*] Bankstown Hospital [*Medical Library*]
NBL.......... National Basketball League [*Australia*]
NBL.......... Ndermarrje Bujqesore Lokale [*Albanian*]
NBL.......... Nigerian Breweries Limited
NBLA .... New [*South Wales*] Bland [*Shire Council*] [*National Union Catalogue of Australia symbol*]
NBLAC...... New [*South Wales*] Blackwells [*Regional Office*] [*National Union Catalogue of Australia symbol*]
NBLC......... Nederlands Bibliotheek- en Lectuur Centrum ['s-Gravenhage]
NBLH........ New [*South Wales*] Blacktown Hospital [*Medical Library*] [*National Union Catalogue of Australia symbol*]
NBM.......... Nederlandse Bond van Makelaars in Onroerende Goederen [*Netherlands*]   (BAS)
NBM.......... Niet Boek Materialen [*Netherlands*]
NBM.......... Nouvelle Boulangerie de M'Balmayo
NBMC....... New [*South Wales*] Blue Mountains City [*Library*] [*National Union Catalogue of Australia symbol*]
NBN.......... National Bank of Nigeria Ltd.
NBN.......... Newcastle Broadcasting Network [*Australian company broadcasting in Papua New Guinea*]   (FEA)
NBN.......... Normes Belges [*Belgium*]   (BAS)
NBNI........ Nasionale Bounavorsningsinstituut [*South Africa*]
NBO.......... Nairobi [*Kenya*] [*Airport symbol*]   (OAG)
NBO.......... National Bank of Oman Ltd. SAO   (EY)
NBO.......... National Broadcasting Organisation [*Australia*]
NBO.......... National Buildings Organisation [*India*]
NBO.......... Nordiska Kooperativa och Allmannyttiga Bostadsforetags Organisation [*Organization of Cooperative and Non-Profit Making Housing Enterprises in the Nordic Countries*]   (EAIO)
Nborba .... Narodna Borba [*National Struggle*] [*A journal*]   (YU)

NBOT........ New [*South Wales*] [*Royal*] Botanic [*Gardens*] [*Sydney*] [*Australia*]
NBOU........ New [*South Wales*] Bourke [*and District Historical Society*] [*National Union Catalogue of Australia symbol*]
NBP .... Initial Point of Bomb Run   (RU)
NBP .... Lower Sideband   (RU)
NBP .... Narodowy Bank Polski [*Polish National Bank*]   (POL)
NBP .... National Bank of Pakistan   (GEA)
NBP .... New [*South Wales*] Berger Paints [*National Union Catalogue of Australia symbol*]
NBP .... New Birth Party [*Cyprus*] [*Political party*]
nbp .... Zeroth Born Approximation   (RU)
NBPC........ National Black Playwrights Conference [*Australia*]
NBPDCh ... Lower Sideband of Doppler Frequencies   (RU)
NBPGR...... National Bureau of Plant Genetic Resources [*India*]
NBPU .... New [*South Wales*] Bourke Public [*Library*] [*National Union Catalogue of Australia symbol*]
nbr............. Nombre [*Number*] [*French*]
NBr .... Noorderbreedte [*North Latitude*] [*Afrikaans*]
nBr .... Nordliche Breite [*North latitude*] [*German*]
NBR .... North British Railway
NBR .... Unguided Ballistic Missile   (RU)
NBRA .... New [*South Wales*] Bathurst Regional Art [*Gallery*] [*National Union Catalogue of Australia symbol*]
NBRC .... New [*South Wales*] Barclays [*Bank Australia Ltd.*] [*National Union Catalogue of Australia symbol*]
NBRI .... National Building Research Institute [*South Africa*]
NBRI .... New [*South Wales*] Bread Research Institute [*of Australia*] [*National Union Catalogue of Australia symbol*]
NBRRI....... Nigerian Building and Road Research Institute [*Research center*]   (ERC)
NBRS........ National Building Research Station
NBS .... Chief of Ammunition Supply   (RU)
NBS .... National Broadcasting Service [*New Zealand*]
NBS .... National Broadcasting Service [*Trinidad and Tobago*]   (EY)
NBS .... Nemzetkozi Barati Sportjatekok [*International Friendship Games*]   (HU)
NBS .... Nigeria Building Society
NBS .... Nigerian Broadcasting Service
NBS .... Nordiska Byggforskningsorgans Samarbetsgrupp [*Nordic Building Research Cooperation Group*] [*Iceland*]   (EAIO)
NBS .... Normandy Base Section [*World War II*]
NBS .... Norsk Biokjemisk Selskap [*Norwegian Biochemical Society*]   (EAIO)
NBSA........ Nurses' Board of South Australia
NBSAE...... Norwegian-British-Swedish Antarctic Expedition [*1949-52*]
NBSH .... Ndermarrje Bujqesore Shteterore [*Albanian*]
NBSHU.... Ndermarrje Bujqesore Shteterore Ushtarake [*Albanian*]
NBSL .... National Biological Standards Laboratory [*Australia*]   (PDAA)
NBSS........ National Bible Society of Scotland   (SLS)
NBT .... Nederlandse Bond van Middelbare en Hogare Technici [*Netherlands Union of Professional Engineers*]
NBTA ...... New [*South Wales*] Bankers Trust Australia [*Ltd.*] [*Research Library*] [*National Union Catalogue of Australia symbol*]
NBTAA ..... National Baton Twirling Association of Australia   (ADA)
NBTC .... National Building Technology Centre [*Research center*] [*Australia*]   (IRC)
NBTVS...... National Broadcasting and Television Service [*Australia*]
NBU.......... Combat Sector Commander   (RU)
NBU.......... Nordiska Bankmannaunionen [*Confederation of Nordic Bank Employees' Unions*]   (EA)
NBUR........ New [*South Wales*] Burnside [*Library*] [*National Union Catalogue of Australia symbol*]
NBvGA ..... Nederlandse Bond van Gemeente-Ambtenaren [*Netherlands*]   (BAS)
NBX .... Nabire [*Indonesia*] [*Airport symbol*]   (OAG)
nC............... Na Christus [*After Christ*] [*Afrikaans*]
NC.............. Nastavni Centar [*Training Center*] [*Military*]   (YU)
NC.............. National Colonialist Party [*Australia*] [*Political party*]
NC.............. National Convention
NC.............. Native Commissioner
NC.............. Neighbourhood Centre [*Australia*]
NC.............. New Caledonia [*ANSI two-letter standard code*]   (CNC)
nc............... Non Chiffre [*Unnumbered*] [*Publishing*] [*French*]
NC.............. Non Classe [*Of soldiers who have not qualified at target practice*] [*French*]   (MTD)
nc............... Non Cote [*French*]
NC.............. NORDLEK Council   (EAIO)
n/c.............. Nossa Carta [*Portuguese*]
n/c.............. Nossa Casa [*Our House*] [*Portuguese*]
n/c.............. Nossa Conta [*Portuguese*]
n/c.............. Notre Compte [*Our Account*] [*French*]
NC.............. Nouveau Cedi
NC.............. Nouvelle Coutume [*French*]   (FLAF)
NC.............. Novo Cruzado [*Brazilian currency*]
NC.............. Nuestra Cuenta [*Our Account*] [*Business term*] [*Spanish*]

NC............. Numerus Clausus [*Designation for students*]
NC............. Societe en Nom Collectif [*France*]   (FLAF)
NCA........... Association of Norwegian Clothing, Shoe, Textile, Leather, and
      Sporting Goods Industries   (EAIO)
NCA........... NAIG [*Nippon Atomic Industry Group*] Critical Assembly
      [*Nuclear reactor*] [*Japan*]
NCA........... National Cancer Association of South Africa   (AA)
NCA........... National Coal Authority [*Australia*]
NCA........... National Commission on Agriculture [*India*]   (PDAA)
NCA........... National Committee for AIDS [*Mauritania*]   (EAIO)
NCA........... National Conference on AIDS [*Australia*]
NCA........... National Crime Authority [*Australia*]
NCA........... Network for Community Activities
NCA........... New [*South Wales - Department of*] Consumer Affairs [*National
      Union Catalogue of Australia symbol*]
NCA........... Nigeria's Constituent Assembly
NCA........... Nippon Cargo Airlines [*Japan*]
NCA........... Nippon Cargo Airlines Co. Ltd. [*Japan*] [*ICAO designator*]
      (FAAC)
NCA........... North Caicos [*British West Indies*] [*Airport symbol*]   (OAG)
NCA........... North Coast Airlines [*Australia*]
NCA........... Norwegian Canoe Association   (EAIO)
NCA........... Norwegian Church Aid
NCA........... Norwegian Society of Composers   (EAIO)
NCA........... Nursing Curricula Association of South Africa   (AA)
NCAA........ National Capital Attractions Association [*Australia*]
NCAA........ New South Wales Community Arts Association [*Australia*]
NCAAC..... National Consumer Affairs Advisory Council [*Australia*]
NC-AAPSO ... Nigerian Committee of the Afro-Asian People's Solidarity
      Organization   (AF)
NCAC .... National Cancer Advisory Committee [*Australia*]
NCAC .... Nordic Customs Administrative Council   (EA)
NCAC .... Northern Combat Area Command [*Myanmar*]
NCAE .... Newcastle College of Advanced Education [*Australia*]   (ADA)
NCAER ..... National Council of Applied Economic Research [*India*]   (SLS)
NCAFG ..... National Committee for Adult Fellowship Groups [*Australia*]
      (EAIO)
NCAI .... Aitutaki [*Cook Islands*] [*ICAO location identifier*]   (ICLI)
NCAJL...... National Council of Art in Jewish Life
NCAL .... National Constituent Assembly of Libya
NCAL .... National Council for Arts and Letters [*Sudan*]
N Cal......... New Caledonia
NCALAC... National Customs Agents Licensing Advisory Committee
      [*Australia*]
NCAMR .... Nordic Council for Arctic Medical Research   (EA)
NCAN....... New [*South Wales*] Canowindra [*and District Historical Society*]
      [*National Union Catalogue of Australia symbol*]
NCAO....... National Coalition of Aboriginal Organisations [*Australia*]
NCAOS ..... National Coalition of Aboriginal Organisations Secretariat
      [*Australia*]
NCAP .... National Cost Adjustment Provision [*Australia*]
NCAP .... New Careers for Aboriginal People [*Australia*]
NCAP .... Nordic Council for Animal Protection   (EA)
NCASC...... Nordic Council for Adult Studies in Church [*See also NKS*]
      (EAIO)
NCAT .... Atiu [*Cook Islands*] [*ICAO location identifier*]   (ICLI)
NCAT .... National Centre for Alternative Technology [*British*]
NCATC ..... Nigerian Civil Aviation Traning Centre   (PDAA)
NCAU....... Northern Cape Agricultural Union [*South Africa*]   (AA)
NCAV .... Nationaal Centrum voor Algemene Vorming van Jonge
      Werkmemers [*Belgium*]   (EAIO)
NCAV .... National Coursing Association of Victoria [*Australia*]
NCAW....... Nordic Council for Animal Welfare [*Denmark*]   (EAIO)
NCB.......... Nanyang Commercial Bank [*China*]
NCB.......... National Coal Board [*British*]
NCB.......... National Codification Bureau [*NATO*]   (NATG)
NCB.......... National Commercial Bank [*Jamaica*]
NCB.......... National Commercial Bank [*Saudi Arabia*]
NCB.......... National Commercial Bank [*St. Lucia*]   (LA)
NCB.......... National Computer Board [*Singapore*]   (DS)
NCB.......... National Council for Cement and Building Materials [*India*]
      [*Research center*]   (IRC)
NCB.......... Nationale Crisisbelasting [*Benelux*]   (BAS)
NCB.......... Nederlandse Consumentenbond [*Netherlands*]   (BAS)
NCB.......... Nederlandse Creditbank NV [*Financial institution*]
      [*Netherlands*]   (EY)
NCB.......... Nigeria Cocoa Board
NCB.......... Nippon Credit Bank [*Japan*]
NCB.......... North China Block [*Geology*]
NCBA .... National Children's Bureau of Australia
NCBO....... Nederlandse Christelijke Bond van Overheids-Personeel
      [*Netherlands*]   (BAS)
NCBR .... New [*South Wales*] Commonwealth Bank Research [*Library*]
      [*National Union Catalogue of Australia symbol*]
NCBT .... New [*South Wales*] Commonwealth Banking Technical [*Library*]
      [*National Union Catalogue of Australia symbol*]

NCBTA...... Nordic Cooperative of Brick and Tilemakers' Associations
      [*Denmark*]   (EAIO)
NCBWA .... National Congress of British West Africa
NCBY .... New [*South Wales*] Canterbury [*Hospital*] [*National Union
      Catalogue of Australia symbol*]
NCC.......... Namibia Council of Churches   (AF)
NCC.......... National Cadet Corps [*India*]
NCC.......... National Canefarming Committee [*Guyana*]   (LA)
NCC.......... National Capital Commission [*Canada*]
NCC.......... National Chamber of Commerce [*Bolivia*]   (EAIO)
NCC.......... National Communications Commission [*Uganda*]   (ECON)
NCC.......... National Construction Corporation Ltd.
NCC.......... National Consultative Council [*Uganda*]   (AF)
NCC.......... National Core Curriculum [*Australia*]
NCC.......... Nature Conservancy Council [*Scottish*]
NCC.......... Nederlandse Classificatie-Commissie ['s-Gravenhage]
NCC.......... New Conservative Club [*South Korea*]   (FEA)
NCC.......... Nordic Choral Committee   (EAIO)
NCC.......... North Calotte Committee [*See also NKK*] [*Nordic Council of
      Ministers*] [*Finland*]   (EAIO)
NCC.......... Norwegian Chamber of Commerce   (DCTA)
NCC.......... Norwegian Cultural Council   (EAIO)
NCC.......... Notre Cause Commune [*Benin*] [*Political party*]   (EY)
NCC.......... Nouvelle Cie. Commerciale
NCCA .... National Council of Chartered Accountants [*South Africa*]
      (PDAA)
NCCA .... New [*South Wales*] Cement and Concrete Association of
      Australia [*Federal Office Library*]
NCCA .... Nordic Committee for Central Africa [*Defunct*]   (EA)
NCC/AV.... Nederlandse Classificatie-Commissie/Algemene Vergadering
NCC/BV.... Nederlandse Classificatie-Commissie/Beleidsvoorbereiding
NCC/CGr .. Nederlandse Classificatie-Commissie/Studiecommissie voor
      Classificatie Grondslagen [*Waarinopgenomen Classificatie
      Research*]
NCCDCI.... Nordic Contact Committee Concerning Day Care Institutions
      [*Norway*]   (EAIO)
NCCdL ...... Nuova Camero Confederale del Lavoro [*New Confederated
      Chamber of Labor*] [*Italy - Trieste*]
NCCE .... Nordic Committee for Commercial Education [*See also NKH*]
      [*Odense, Denmark*]   (EAIO)
NCCI .... National Co. for Cooperative Insurance [*Saudi Arabia*]
NCC/IBL... Nederlandse Centrale Catalogus/Interbibliothecair Leenverkeer
      System [*Netherlands Central Catalogue/Interlibrary Loan
      System*] [*Consortium of the Royal Library and University
      Libraries*] [*Information service or system*]   (IID)
NCCIP....... Nordic Cooperation Committee for International Politics,
      Including Conflict and Peace Research   (EA)
NCCIR....... National Catholic Commission for Industrial Relations
      [*Australia*]
NCCK .... National Christian Council of Kenya
NCCM .... Nchanga Consolidated Copper Mines [*Zambia*]   (AF)
NCCO .... National Cold Chain Operations Ltd.
NCCP .... National Chinese Curriculum Project [*Australia*]
NCC/Plen ... Nederlandse Classificatie-Commissie/Plenaire Vergadering
NCCS........ Nordic Church Council for Seamen [*Denmark*]   (EAIO)
NCCS........ Nordic Council for Church Studies   (EA)
NCCSA...... Nature Conservation Council of South Australia
NCCSL...... National Center for Cross-Cultural Studies in Law [*Monash
      University*] [*Australia*]
NCCSL...... National Chamber of Commerce of Sri Lanka   (EAIO)
NCC/Thes ... Nederlandse Classificatie-Commissie/Thesaurusproblemen
NCC/UDC/Red ... Nederlandse Classificatie-Commissie/Redactiecommissie
      voor Herziening van de Nederlandse Teksten en voor de
      Tekst op een Register op de Nederlandse Verkorte UDC-
      Uitgave
NCD.......... National Christian Democratic Party [*Namibia*]   (AF)
NCD.......... National Commission for Democracy [*Ghana*] [*Political party*]
NCD.......... National Council of the Disabled [*Saint Lucia*]   (EAIO)
NCD.......... Non-Communicable Disease
NCD.......... Nordic Committee on Disability   (EAIO)
NCD.......... Nordic Council for the Deaf [*See also DNR*]   (EAIO)
NCDB .... National Commercial and Development Bank [*Dominica*]
NCDB .... National Co-Operative and Development Bank
NCDC........ National Coal Developement Corp. [*India*]   (PDAA)
NCDC........ National Coalition for a Democratic Constitution [*Political
      group*] [*South Korea*]
NCDC........ National Cooperative Development Corp. [*India*]
NCDDR..... National Committee for the Defence of Democratic Rights
      [*Ghana*]
NCDH .... New [*South Wales*] Camden District Hospital [*Penfold-Collins
      Medical Library*]
NCDP .... Namibie Christelike Demokratiese Party [*Namibian Christian
      Democratic Party*] [*Political party*]   (PPW)
NCDPIP.... National Council of Disabled Peoples International in Pakistan
      (EAIO)
NCDS .... National Centre for Development Studies [*Australian National
      University*]

NCDT........ National Centre for the Development of Telematics [*India*] (PDAA)
NCDTC ..... National Cooperative Development and Training Centre [*Sudan*]
NCDW....... National Confederation of Dominican Workers [*Dominican Republic*] (EAIO)
NCE.......... National Certificate of Education
NCE.......... National Chamber of Exporters [*Bolivia*] (EAIO)
NCE.......... Nice [*France*] [*Airport symbol*] (OAG)
NCE.......... Nigerian Certificates in Education
NCE.......... Nouvelles du Conseil de l'Europe (FLAF)
NCEF........ Nomads' Charitable and Educational Foundation [*Australia*]
NCELTR ... National Centre for English Language Teaching and Research [*Macquarie University*] [*Australia*]
NCEO........ New [*South Wales*] Catholic Education Office [*National Union Catalogue of Australia symbol*]
NCEPC...... National Committee on Environmental Planning and Coordination [*India*] (PDAA)
NCEPC...... National Council for Environmental Pollution Control [*India*] (PDAA)
NCEPH ..... National Centre for Epidemiology and Population Health [*Australia*]
NCERD ..... National Centre for Energy Research and Development [*University of Nigeria*] (WED)
NCERT...... National Council of Educational Research and Training [*India*]
NCES........ New [*South Wales*] Cessnock [*City Library*] [*National Union Catalogue of Australia symbol*]
NCETA...... National Center for Education and Training in Addictions [*Australia*]
NCF .... National Clothing Federation of South Africa (AA)
NCF .... NATO Composite Force
NCF .... Nepal Christian Fellowship
NCF .... Nigerian Conservation Foundation
NCF .... Nordisk Cerealistfoerbund (SLS)
NCF .... Nugget Coombs Foundation for Indigenous Studies [*Australia*]
NCFA .... Norwegian Cystic Fibrosis Association (EAIO)
NCFA .... Nurses' Christian Fellowship of Australia
NCFC........ Nigeria Construction & Furniture Co. Ltd.
NCFCA...... Nigeria Cuba Friendship and Cultural Association
NCFEI ...... National Center for Financial and Economic Information Services [*Ministry of Finance and National Economy*] [*Saudi Arabia*] (ECON)
NCFSA...... National Clothing Federation of South Africa (EAIO)
NCG.......... New Container Group [*C. H. Tung Co.*] [*Hong Kong*]
NCGA........ New [*South Wales*] Ciba-Geigy Australia [*Ltd.*] [*Yarrandoo Research Centre*]
NCGEB ..... National Center for Genetic Engineering and Biotechnology [*Thailand*] [*Research center*] (IRC)
NCGF .... New [*South Wales Renison*]Consolidated Goldfields Ltd. [*Technical Library*]
NCGG....... National Committee for Geodesy and Geophysics [*Pakistan*] (PDAA)
NCh .... Low Frequency (RU)
N Ch.......... Nach Christo [*After Christ*] [*German*]
NCH .... Nachingwea [*Tanzania*] [*Airport symbol*] (OAG)
nch............. Non Chiffre [*Unnumbered*] [*Publishing*] [*French*]
n/ch........... Nosso Cheque [*Our Check*] [*Business term*] [*Portuguese*]
NCHAA..... National Cutting Horse Association of Australia
NCHC....... National Cultural Heritage Committee [*Australia*]
NCHC....... New [*South Wales*] Coffs Harbour City [*Library*] [*National Union Catalogue of Australia symbol*]
NCHE....... National Council for Higher Education [*Sudan*]
NChK .... Neutralized Black Contact Substance (RU)
NCHP....... Navale et Commerciale Havraise Peninsulaire [*Malagasy*]
n Chr .... Nach Christus [*After Christ*] [*German*] (GPO)
n Chr G ..... Nach Christi Geburt [*After the Birth of Christ*] [*German*]
NChS........ Low-Frequency Seismic Exploration (RU)
NCHS .... National Centre for Health Statistics [*Australia*]
NChS .... Normal Human Serum (RU)
NCHSR ..... National Centre for HIV [*Human Immunodeficiency Virus*] Social Research [*Australia*]
NChSS....... Low-Frequency Seismic Station (RU)
NCHVR.... National Center for HIV [*Human Immunodeficiency Virus*] Virology Research [*Australia*]
Nchw.......... Nachweis [*Proof*] [*German*] (GCA)
NChZ......... Novacke Chemicke Zavody [*Chemical Factories at Novaky*] (CZ)
NChZ......... Science Reading Room (RU)
NCI .... National Cancer Institute [*Egypt*] [*Research center*] (IRC)
NCI .... National Chemical Industries
NCI .... Necocli [*Colombia*] [*Airport symbol*] (OAG)
NCI .... [*The*] Netherlands Cancer Institute
NCI .... New Community Instrument [*European Community*] (MHDB)
NCI .... No Currency Involved
NCI .... Norwegian Center for Information (EAIO)
NCID .... National Council on Intellectual Disability [*Australia*] (EAIO)

NCID .... New [*South Wales*] Council for Intellectual Disability [*National Union Catalogue of Australia symbol*]
NCIDB ...... North Coast Industry Development Board [*Australia*]
NCIE .... Nigerian Commercial & Industrial Enterprises Ltd.
NCIG .... New [*South Wales*] CIG [*Gases Technical Library*] [*National Union Catalogue of Australia symbol*]
NCIN .... New South Wales Curriculum Information Network [*Australia*]
NCIR .... New [*South Wales*] [*Australian*] Coal Industry Research Laborato ries Ltd. [*National Union Catalogue of Australia symbol*]
NCISA....... National Council of Independent Schools Associations [*Australia*]
NCITC....... National Clothing Industry Training Committee [*Australia*]
NCJC......... New [*South Wales*] Community Justice Centre [*National Union Catalogue of Australia symbol*]
NCJCS ...... National Conference of Jewish Communal Service
NCJT......... Nordic Committee of Journalism Teachers (EA)
NCJW........ National Council of Jewish Women Research Institute for Innovation in Education [*Israel*] [*Research center*] (IRC)
NCJWA..... National Council of Jewish Women of Australia
NCL .... National Chemical Laboratory [*India*] [*Research center*] (IRC)
NCL .... National Chemical Laboratory [*MITI*] [*Japan*] (PDAA)
NCL .... National Confederation of Labour [*Mauritius*]
NCL .... National Consolidated Limited [*Australia*] (ADA)
NCL .... New Caledonia [*ANSI three-letter standard code*] (CNC)
NCL .... Norwegian Caribbean Lines
NCLA .... New [*South Wales*] Centre for Languages - Australia [*National Union Catalogue of Australia symbol*]
NCLC .... New [*South Wales*] Commonwealth Law Courts [*Library*] [*Family Court of Australia*]
NCLDO ..... National Congress of Local Democratic Organs [*Guyana*] (LA)
NCLE......... National Commission for Law Enforcement and Social Justice [*Church of Scientology*] [*Australia*]
N'cle.......... University of Newcastle [*Australia*] (ADA)
NCLI .... National Chemical Laboratory for Industry [*Japan*]
NCLL......... National Council for the Liberation of Libya
NCLL......... New [*South Wales*] Clarence [*Regional*] Library [*National Union Catalogue of Australia symbol*]
NCLP........ Nyasaland Congress Liberation Party
NCLRSMQ ... National Campaign for Land Rights and Self-Management in Queensland [*Australia*]
NCLS........ National Conference of State Legislatures [*Australia*]
NCLTW..... National Confederation of Land Transport Workers [*Brazil*] (EAIO)
NCLY .... New [*South Wales*] Coopers and Lybrand [*Sydney Office*]
NCM......... National Comite Motorproeven [*Netherlands*]
NCM......... National Commission of Mathematics [*Portugal*] (EAIO)
NCM......... National Committee on Mathematics [*Australian Academy of Science*]
NCM......... Nederlandsche Creditverzekring Maatschappij [*Export credit agency*] [*Netherlands*]
NCM......... Newcastle Conservatorium of Music [*Australia*]
NCM......... New [*South Wales*] New Conservatorium of Music [*National Union Catalogue of Australia symbol*]
NCM......... Nicaraguan Campaign Medal
NCM......... Nippon Calculating Machine Co. [*Japan*] (PDAA)
NCM......... Nordic Council of Ministers (EAIO)
NCM......... Nordic Council on Medicines [*See also NLN*] (EAIO)
NCMB ...... Nigerian Cocoa Marketing Board
NCMB ...... Nordic Council for Marine Biology [*Denmark*] (ASF)
NCMC....... Nordic Council for Music Conservatories (EA)
NCMF .... New [*South Wales*] Chamber of Manufacturers [*National Union Catalogue of Australia symbol*]
NCMG....... Mangaia [*Cook Islands*] [*ICAO location identifier*] (ICLI)
NCMH ...... National Council for Mental Health [*South Africa*] (AA)
NCMI .... Naval Chemical and Metallurgical Laboratory [*India*] (PDAA)
NCMK....... Mauke [*Cook Islands*] [*ICAO location identifier*] (ICLI)
NCML....... New [*South Wales*] Canterbury Municipal Library [*National Union Catalogue of Australia symbol*]
NCMN...... Manuae [*Cook Islands*] [*ICAO location identifier*] (ICLI)
NCMP...... New [*South Wales*] Crooks Michell Peacock [*Stewart Proprietary Lt d.*] [*National Union Catalogue of Australia symbol*]
NCMR...... Matiaro [*Cook Islands*] [*ICAO location identifier*] (ICLI)
NCMR...... National Center for Marine Research [*Greece*] (IRC)
NCMR...... New [*South Wales*] Central Murray Regional [*Public Library*] [*National Union Catalogue of Australia symbol*]
NCMS .... National Convention and Management Services [*Australia*]
NCMV ...... National Christelijk Middenstands Verbond [*National Christian Middle Class Federation*] [*Belgium*] (WEN)
NCN.......... New [*South Wales*] College of Nursing [*Katie Zepps Nursing Library*]
NCNA........ New China News Agency
NCNC........ National Convention of Nigerian Citizens (AF)
NCNC........ National Council of Nigeria and Cameroon (AF)
NCNC........ National Council of Nigeria and the Cameroons [*Political party*]
NCNC........ National Council of Nigerian Citizens

NCND........ Neither Confirm nor Deny
NCNGO .... National Committee of Non-Governmental Organisations [*Australia*]
NCNL........ Nasionale Chemiese Navorsingslaboratorium [*South Africa*]
NCNS........ Nassau [*Cook Islands*] [*ICAO location identifier*]   (ICLI)
NCNSS...... National Commission on Nuclear Safety and Safeguards [*Mexico*]   (EAIO)
NCNU .... National Commission of Nigeria for UNESCO
NCO.......... National Commission for Information and Conscientization on Development Cooperation [*Netherlands*]
NCO.......... Non-Commissioned Officer   (EECI)
NCOB........ Nederlandstalig Centrum voor Openbare Bibliotheken
NCOB........ New [*South Wales*] Cobar [*Shire Library*] [*National Union Catalogue of Australia symbol*]
NCOBPS... National Conference of Black Political Scientists
NCOL........ New [*South Wales*] Condobolin Lachlan [*Shire Library*] [*National Union Catalogue of Australia symbol*]
NCOM....... Nchanga Consolidated Copper Mines Ltd. [*Zambia*]
NCOM....... New [*South Wales*] Compensation [*Court*]
NCON .... New [*South Wales*] Concord [*Library Service*] [*National Union Catalogue of Australia symbol*]
NCOO .... New [*South Wales*] Coonamble [*Shire Library*]
NCOP........ New [*South Wales*] Coopers [*Animal Health Australia Ltd.*] [*National Union Catalogue of Australia symbol*]
NCOR....... New [*South Wales*] - Corrective [*Services Department*] [*Corrective Services Academy*]
NCOS........ Comite de Liaison des Organisations Non-Gouvernmentales de Developpement aupres des Communautes Europeennes [*Liaison Committee of Development Non-Governmental Organizations to the European Communities*]   (EAIO)
NCOS........ New [*South Wales*] Coolah Shire [*Library*] [*National Union Catalogue of Australia symbol*]
NCOT........ New [*South Wales*] Cotter [*Harvey Library*] [*Institute of Respiratory Medicine*]
NCOTL ..... National Committee of Teacher-Librarians [*Australia*]
NCP .... National Chemical Products [*South Africa*]   (AA)
NCP .... National Convention Party [*Gambia*] [*Political party*]   (PPW)
NCP .... National Council of Priests of Australia   (ADA)
NCP .... National Country Party [*Australia*]   (ADA)
NCP .... National Curriculum Project
NCP .... Nepali Congress Party [*Political party*]   (EY)
NCP .... New [*South Wales*] College of Physicians [*Royal Australasian College of Physicians*]
NCPA .... National Capital Planning Authority [*Australia*]
NCPA .... National Centre for the Performing Arts [*India*]   (EAIO)
NCPA .... National Centre Party Australia
NCPA .... New [*South Wales*] Centre for Photography - Australia [*National Union Catalogue of Australia symbol*]
NCPC .... National Capital Planning Committee [*Australia*]
NCPC .... National Committee for the Protection of the Consumer [*Iran*]   (ME)
NCPC .... National Cooperative Planning Committee [*Mauritius*]   (AF)
NCPGG ..... National Center for Petroleum Geology and Geophysics [*Australia*]
NCPO .... Nordic Council for Physical Oceanography   (EA)
NCPP........ National Colored Peoples Party [*South Africa*]   (AF)
NCPT........ Navy Central Planning Team [*NATO*]   (NATG)
NCPW .... National Country Party of Western Australia [*Political party*]
NCPY .... Penrhyn [*Cook Islands*] [*ICAO location identifier*]   (ICLI)
NCR.......... Air Sur [*Spain*] [*ICAO designator*]   (FAAC)
NCR.......... National Cash Register Co. Proprietary Ltd. [*Australia*]   (ADA)
NCR.......... National Council for Research [*Sudan*]
NCR.......... National Council of Resistance for Liberty and Independence [*Iran*]   (PD)
NCR.......... National Council of the Revolution [*Syria*]
NCR.......... Nuclei Comunisti Rivoluzionari [*Communist Revolutionary Nuclei*] [*Italian*]   (WER)
NCRACPA ... National Center for Research, Animation and Creation in Plastic Arts [*France*]   (EAIO)
NCRC .... National Council of the Revolutionary Command [*Syria*]
NCRC .... North Coast Research Centre [*Australia*]   (DSCA)
NCRCH..... Nordic Committee of the Research Councils for the Humanities   (EA)
NCRD........ National Council for Research and Development [*NRDA*] [*Israel*] [*Later,*]
NCRDA ..... National Center for Research into Drug Abuse [*Australia*]
NCREA ..... National Council of Religious Education in Australia
NCRG .... Avarua/Rarotonga International [*Cook Islands*] [*ICAO location identifier*]   (ICLI)
NCRH........ New [*South Wales*] Church Records and Historical [*Society*] [*Uniting church archives and research centre*]
NCRI .... National Cereals Research Institute [*Nigeria*]
NCRK .... Rakahanga [*Cook Islands*] [*ICAO location identifier*]   (ICLI)
NCRL .... National Chemical Research Laboratory [*South Africa*]
NCRM .... Nordic Council for Railway Music   (EA)
NCRPD ..... National Committee on Recreation for People with Disabilities [*Australia*]

NCRR .... Nordic Council of Reindeer Research   (EAIO)
NCRV .... Nederlandse Christelijke Radio Vereniging [*Netherlands Christian Broadcasting Association*]   (WEN)
NCS .... National Catholic Secretariat
NCS .... National Council of Sports [*Uganda*]   (EAIO)
NCS .... Naval Control of Shipping [*NATO*]   (NATG)
NCS .... Newcastle [*South Africa*] [*Airport symbol*]   (OAG)
NCS .... Nghien Cuu Sinh [*Research Student*]
NCS .... Nigerian Chemical Services Ltd.
NCS .... Norsk Cardiologisk Sekskap [*Norway*]   (EAIO)
NCSA .... National Conservation Strategy for Australia
NCSA .... Newsagency Council of South Australia
NCSAHITAB ... National Community Services and Health Industry Training Advisory Board [*Australia*]
NCSATR ... National Council for Scientific and Technological Research [*Costa Rica*]   (EAIO)
NCSAV...... Nakladatelstvi Ceskoslovenske Akademie Ved [*Publishing House of the Czechoslovak Academy of Sciences*]   (CZ)
NCSB........ New [*South Wales*] Christian Services for the Blind [*National Union Catalogue of Australia symbol*]
NCSC........ National Companies and Securities Commission [*Australia*]
NCSD .... New [*South Wales*] CSR [*Colonial Sugar Refining Company*] Sugar Division Library [*National Union Catalogue of Australia symbol*]
NCSEES.... Nordic Committee for Soviet and East European Studies   (EA)
NCSF........ National Confederation of Small Farmers [*Italy*]   (EAIO)
NCSITSG ... National Community Services Industry Training Steering Group [*Australia*]
NCSJ .... Naval Communication Station, Japan
NCSL........ National Council of Sierra Leone
NCSMHC ... National Council for the Single Mother and Her Child [*Australia*]
NCSN .... North Coast Steam Navigation Co. [*Australia*]   (ADA)
NCSNE...... Naval Control of Shipping in Northern European Command Area [*NATO*]   (NATG)
NCSO .... New [*South Wales*] Catholic Schools' Office [*National Union Catalogue of Australia symbol*]
NCSP........ Nordic Committee on Salaries and Personnel [*Nordic Council of Ministers*] [*Copenhagen, Denmark*]   (EAIO)
NCSPD..... National Civic Service for Participation in Development
NCSR........ National Council for Scientific Research [*Zambia*]
NCSR........ National Council for Social Research
NCSS........ National Council of Social Service [*Singapore*]   (EAIO)
NCSS........ Nordic Council of Ski Schools   (EAIO)
NCSSW..... Nordic Committee of Schools of Social Work   (EAIO)
NCST........ National Committee of Science and Technology [*Department of Science and Technology*] [*India*]
NCST........ National Council for Science and Technology [*Ministry of Finance and Planning*] [*Barbados*]   (WED)
NCST........ National Council for Science and Technology [*Nepal*]
NCST........ Nigerian Council for Science and Technology   (PDAA)
NCSU........ Nigerian Civil Service Union
NCSU:A .... New [*South Wales*] Charles Stuart University [*National Union Catalogue of Australia symbol*]
NCSV........ Nederlandse Christen-Studenten Vereniging [*Dutch Christian Students' Union*]   (WEN)
NCSVU ..... Nakladatelstvi Ceskoslovenskych Vytvarnych Umelcu [*Publishing House of Czechoslovak Creative Artists*]   (CZ)
NCSW ...... National Council for Social Welfare [*Sudan*]
NCSY........ National Conference of Synagogue Youth
NCT .... National Corruption Tribunal [*Australia*]
NCT .... Nordic Cooperation on Telecommunications   (EAIO)
NCT .... Northern Cultural Trust [*South Australia*]
NCT .... Nucleo Comunista de Trabajadores [*Communist Nucleus of Workers*] [*Dominican Republic*]   (LA)
ncta............ Nuestra Cuenta [*Our Account*] [*Business term*] [*Spanish*]
NCTCT..... National Committee for Town/City Twinning [*France*]   (EAIO)
NCTL........ National Congress of Thai Labour
NCTR........ Nordic Council for Tax Research   (EA)
NCTS........ Nacelnik Centralne Telefonske Stanice [*Central Telephone Station Chief*] [*Military*]   (YU)
NCTS........ NADOW [*National Association for Training the Disabled in Office Work*] Computer Training Scheme [*Australia*]
NCTS........ National Center for Tourism Studies [*Australia*]
NCTU .... New [*South Wales*] Catholic Theological Union [*Colin Library*]
NCTUN..... National Council of Trade Unions of Nigeria
NCTVA ..... Norwegian Cable-TV Association   (EAIO)
NCTX .... New [*South Wales*] Caltex [*Refining Company*] [*Engineering Technical Library*]
NCU.......... National Commercial Union Ltd. [*Australia*]
NCU.......... National Conference for Unification [*South Korea*] [*Political party*]   (PPW)
NCU.......... Northern Co-Operative Union
NCUH .... New [*South Wales*] Cumberland Hospital [*Western Sydney Area Health Service*]
NCV.......... Nacelnik Centra Veze [*Chief of Communications Center*] [*Military*]   (YU)

NCVAW .... National Committee on Violence against Women [*Australia*]
NCVD .... Nacelnik Centra Vatre Divisiona [*Chief of a Divisional Fire Center*]   (YU)
NCVEVS ... Dutch Committee for European Security and Cooperation [*Pro-Moscow*]   (WEN)
NCVHS ..... National Committee on Health and Vital Statistics [*Australia*]
NCVV .... Natalse Christelike Vrouevereniging [*Afrikaans*]
NCW .... National Congress of Workers [*Philippines*]
NCW .... National Council of Women
NCW .... Nederlands Christelijk Werkgeversbond [*Dutch Christian Employers' Union*]   (WEN)
NCW .... Netherlands Council of Women   (EAIO)
NCW .... Non-Communist World
NCWA .... National Council of Women of Australia   (ADA)
NCWA .... Newsagency Council of Western Australia
NCWA .... Nigerian Citizens Welfare Association
NCW/ACT ... National Council of Women of the Australian Capital Territory
NCWC .... New [*South Wales*] Central Western Co-operative [*Public Library*] [*National Union Catalogue of Australia symbol*]
NCWD ...... National Council of Women in Development
NCWK ...... National Council of Women of Kenya
NCWNSW ... National Council of Women of New South Wales [*Australia*]
NCWP .... National Communications Working Party [*Australia*] [*Political party*]
NCWQ ...... National Council of Women of Queensland [*Australia*]
NCWR .... Nordic Council for Wildlife Research   (EAIO)
NCWS .... Nigerian Council of Women's Societies
NCWSA ..... National Council of Women of South Africa
NCWSA ..... National Council of Women of South Australia
NCWSBA ... National Council of Wool Selling Brokers of Australia
NCWT .... National Council of Women of Tasmania [*Australia*]
NCWTD .... Nationaal Centrum voor Wetenschappelijke en Technische Documentatie [*Belgium*]
NCWV .... National Council of Women of Victoria [*Australia*]
NCWWA ... National Council of Women of Western Australia
NCY .... Annecy [*France*] [*Airport symbol*]   (OAG)
NCY .... Nancy Aviation [*France*] [*ICAO designator*]   (FAAC)
NCYA .... New [*South Wales*] Cynamid [*Proprietary Ltd.*] [*National Union Catalogue of Australia symbol*]
NCYSSPA ... New South Wales Community Youth Support Scheme Projects Association [*Australia*]
NCYWA .... Nordic Child and Youth Welfare Alliance   (EA)
NCz .... New Cruzado [*Monetary unit*] [*Brazil*]   (BARN)
NCZO .... Nederlands Commissie voor Zee-Onderzoek [*Netherlands*]   (MSC)
ND .... Aerospatiale [*Societe Nationale Industrielle Aerospatiale*] [*France*] [*ICAO aircraft manufacturer identifier*]   (ICAO)
ND .... Directive on Concluding Contracts between Socialist Organizations   (BU)
ND .... Directive on Contracts   (BU)
nd .... Division Commander   (BU)
ND .... Low Pressure   (RU)
ND .... Naczelna Dyrekcja [*Central Administration, Main Directorate*]   (POL)
n/d .... Na Datum [*After Date*] [*Afrikaans*]
ND .... Narodni Divadlo [*National Theater*]   (CZ)
ND .... Narodowa Demokracja [*National Democratic Party*]   (POL)
ND .... Natuurdokter [*Afrikaans*]
ND .... Nea Demokratia [*New Democracy*] [*Greece*] [*Political party*]   (PPE)
Nd .... Neodimio [*Neodymium*] [*Chemical element*] [*Portuguese*]
Nd .... Neodym [*Neodymium*] [*Chemical element*] [*German*]
ND .... New Democracy [*European political movement*]   (ECON)
nd .... Niederdeutsch [*Low German*] [*German*]
Nd .... Niederdruck [*Low Pressure*] [*German*]   (EG)
Nd .... Niederschlag [*Precipitate*] [*German*]
ND .... Nomothetikon Diatagma [*Legislative Decree*]   (GC)
ND .... Non Disponible [*Not Available*] [*French*]
N/D .... Non-Drinker [*Medicine*]
ND .... Nontoxic Screening Smoke   (RU)
ND .... Normal Pressure   (RU)
ND .... Nostra Donna [*Our Lady*] [*Italian*]
ND .... Notiodytikos (Anemos) [*Southwesterly (Wind)*]   (GC)
N-D .... Notre Dame [*Our Lady*] [*French*]   (GPO)
ND .... Nova Doba [*New Time*] [*A periodical*]   (CZ)
ND .... Nov Den [*New Day*] [*A publishing establishment Skopje*]   (YU)
ND .... Ny Demokrati [*New Democracy*] [*Sweden*] [*Political party*]   (EY)
nd .... Observer   (BU)
ND .... Oil Field Exploitation   (RU)
n/D .... On the Dnepr [*Toponymy*]   (RU)
n/D .... On the Don [*Toponymy*]   (RU)
ND .... People's Militia   (RU)
ND .... Slant Range   (RU)
NDA .... Bandanaira [*Indonesia*] [*Airport symbol*]   (OAG)
NDA .... Dicyclohexylamine Nitrite   (RU)

NDA .... Naczelna Dyrekcja Administracyjna [*Chief Executive Administration*]   (POL)
NDA .... National Democratic Alliance [*Sierra Leone*] [*Political party*]   (EY)
NDA .... National Drama Association
NDA .... New [*South Wales*] [*Australian*] Dental Association [*New South Wales Branch*] [*National Union Catalogue of Australia symbol*]
NDA .... Nielsen Design Associates Ltd. [*Australia*]
NDA .... Nigerian Defence Academy
NDA .... Ninos de las Americas [*Children of the Americas*]   (EAIO)
NDA .... Norwegian Dyslexia Association   (EAIO)
NdA .... Nota dell'Autore [*Author's Note*] [*Italian*]
NDAC .... Nuclear Defense Affairs Committee [*NATO*]
N da D .... Nota da Direcao [*Portuguese*]
N da E .... Nota da Editora [*Editor's Note (Feminine)*] [*Portuguese*]
NDANC...... Nairobi District African National Congress
NDAP .... Naczelna Dyrekcja Archiwow Panstwowych [*Central Administration of State Archives*]   (POL)
NDAP .... Nationalsozialistische Deutsche Arbeiterpartei [*National Socialist German Workers' Party, 1919-45*] [*Political party*]   (PPW)
NDAR .... Algerian People's Democratic Republic   (RU)
NDAR .... Narodnaia Demokraticheskaia Alzhirskaia Respublika
N da R .... Nota da Redacao [*Editorial Note*] [*Portuguese*]
NDARC ..... National Drug and Alcohol Research Center [*University of New South Wales*] [*Australia*]
ndaw .... Nur Direkt ab Werk [*Only Directly from the Plant*]   (EG)
NDAZ .... National Drivers Association of Zambia
NDB .... Naczelna Dyrekcja Bibliotek [*Central Administration of Libraries*]   (POL)
NDB .... National Development Bank [*Sierra Leone*]   (GEA)
NDB .... Nomenclature Douaniere de Bruxelles
NDB .... Nouadhibou [*Mauritania*] [*Airport symbol*]   (OAG)
NDBC .... New [*South Wales Institute for*] Deaf and Blind Children [*National Union Catalogue of Australia symbol*]
NDC .... National Debt Commission [*Australia*]
NDC .... National Defence Committee [*Ghana*] [*Political party*]   (PPW)
NDC .... National Defense College [*Australia*]
NDC .... National Defense Council   (ML)
NDC .... National Democratic Congress [*Grenada*] [*Political party*]   (EY)
NDC .... National Democratic Congress [*Ghana*] [*Political party*]   (ECON)
NDC .... National Development Company [*Philippines*]   (GEA)
NDC .... National Development Corp. [*Saint Lucia*]   (EY)
NDC .... National Development Corp. [*Dominica*]   (EY)
NDC .... National Development Corporation [*Tanzania*]
NDC .... National Development Corporation [*Philippines*]
NDC .... National Documentation Center [*Laotian*]   (CL)
NDC .... National Drilling Co. [*United Arab Emirates*]   (MENA)
NDC .... Niger Delta Congress
NDC .... Nippon Decimal Classification
NDCA .... National Development Credit Agency
NDCC .... Ngie Development Consultative Committee
NDCG .... Naucno Drustvo Crne Gore [*Learned Society of Montenegro*] [*Cetinje*]   (YU)
NDD .... National Democratic Movement [*Portuguese*]   (RU)
NDD .... Newsagents Direct Distribution [*Australia*]
Ndd .... Niederschlaege [*Precipitates*] [*German*]
NdD .... Nota della Direzione [*Editor's Note*] [*Italian*]
NDD .... Sumbe [*Angola*] [*Airport symbol*]   (OAG)
NDDB .... National Dairy Development Board [*India*]
NDE.......... Mandera [*Kenya*] [*Airport symbol*]   (OAG)
NDE.......... National Directorate of Employment [*Nigeria*]
NdE .... Nota dell'Editore [*Publisher's or Editor's Note*] [*Italian*]
NDEC .... National Distance Education Centre [*Australia*]
N del A .... Nota del Autor [*Author's Note*] [*Spanish*]   (GPO)
N de la R .... Nota de la Redaccion [*Editorial Note*] [*Spanish*]   (GPO)
N del T .... Nota del Traductor [*Translator's Note*] [*Spanish*]   (GPO)
NdeM........ Nacionales de Mexico [*Mexican national railway*]   (IMH)
NDEP .... Nasionale Demokratiese Eenheids Party [*Namibia*]
NDF .... National Democratic Front [*Pakistan*] [*Political party*]   (FEA)
NDF .... National Democratic Front [*Philippines*] [*Political party*]   (FEA)
NDF .... National Democratic Front [*Myanmar*] [*Political party*]   (FEA)
NDF .... National Democratic Front [*Iran*] [*Political party*]   (PD)
NDF .... National Democratic Front [*Guyana*] [*Political party*]   (EY)
NDF .... National Democratic Front [*Yemen*] [*Political party*]   (PD)
NDF .... National Development Foundation
NDF .... New [*South Wales*] Dairy Farmers [*Cooperative Ltd.*] [*National Union Catalogue of Australia symbol*]
NDF .... Norges Doveforbund [*Norway*]   (EAIO)
NDF .... Norsk Dysleksiforbund [*Norway*]   (EAIO)
NDF .... Norske Dramatikeres Forbund [*Norway*]   (EAIO)
NDF .... Norwegian Diabetes Association   (EAIO)
NDFC .... National Development Finance Corporation [*Pakistan*]   (GEA)

NDFK .... Neon Dimokratikon Foititikon Kinima [*New Democracy Student Movement*] [*Greek*]   (GC)

NDG .... New [*South Wales*] Davis Gelatine [*(Australia) Proprietary Ltd.*] [*National Union Catalogue of Australia symbol*]

NDH .... Nezavisna Drzava Hrvatska [*Independent State of Croatia*] [*World War II*]   (YU)

NDI .... KS Nordic Air, Denmark [*ICAO designator*]   (FAAC)

NDI .... Namudi [*Papua New Guinea*] [*Airport symbol*]   (OAG)

NDI .... New [*South Wales*] Drug Information [*Centre*] [*National Union Catalogue of Australia symbol*]

NDI .... Normenausschuss der Deutschen Industrie [*Committee of Standards of the German Industry*]   (GCA)

NDIC .... New [*South Wales*] District Court [*Library*] [*National Union Catalogue of Australia symbol*]

NDIS .... National Document and Information Service [*Australia*]

NDIS .... National Drug Information Service [*Australian Commonwealth Department of Health*] [*Information service or system*]   (CRD)

NDJ .... N'Djamena [*Chad*] [*Airport symbol*]   (OAG)

NDK.......... Namorik [*Marshall Islands*] [*Airport symbol*]   (OAG)

NDK.......... Nemet Demokratikus Koztarsasag [*German Democratic Republic*]   (HU)

NDKhSh.... Nontoxic Screening Smoke Pot   (RU)

Ndl .... Nadel [*Needle*] [*German*]   (GCA)

NDL.......... National Diet Library [*Japan*]

Ndl .... Nederland [*Netherlands*] [*Netherlands*]   (GPO)

Ndl .... Nederlands [*Netherlands*] [*Afrikaans*]

NDL.......... Norddeutscher Lloyd [*German steamship company*]

NDL.......... Pneumatic Landing Boat   (RU)

NDLR .... Note de la Redaction [*Editorial Note*] [*French*]   (WER)

NDM .... Nadym Airlines [*Russian Federation*] [*ICAO designator*]   (FAAC)

NDM .... National Dried (Milk) [*Brand name for the British government's dried milk for babies - manufacturer undisclosed*]

NDMC ...... National Diamond Mining Company [*Sierra Leone*]   (AF)

NDMC ...... New Delhi Municipal Committee [*India*]   (PDAA)

NDMF .... National Development and Management Foundation

NDMiOZ .. Naczelna Dyrekcja Muzeow i Ochrony Zabytkow [*Central Administration of Museums and the Protection of Historical Relics*]   (POL)

NDMWC... National Domestic Meatworks Wholesalers Council [*Australia*]

NDN .... Nemzetkozi Demokratikus Noszovetseg [*International Federation of Democratic Women*]   (HU)

NDNA .... Navtiki Dioikisis Notiou Aigaiou [*Southern Aegean Naval Command*] [*Greek*]   (GC)

NDNRBiH ... Naucno Drustvo Narodne Republike Bosne i Hercegovine [*Learned Society of Bosnia and Hercegovina*]   (YU)

NDNSZ ..... Nemzetkozi Demokratikus Noszovetseg [*International Federation of Democratic Women*]   (HU)

NDO .... Naczelna Dyrekcja Ogolna [*Chief General Administration*]   (POL)

NDOA .... Narodnoe Dvizhenie za Osvobozhdenie Angoly [*People's Movement for the Liberation of Angola*] [*Russian*]

N do A .... Nota do Autor [*Author's Note*] [*Portuguese*]

N do D .... Nota do Diretor [*Portuguese*]

N do E .... Nota do Editor [*Editor's Note (Masculine)*] [*Portuguese*]

NDOH....... New [*South Wales*] - Department of Housing [*National Union Catalogue of Australia symbol*]

N do T .... Nota do Tradutor [*Translator's Note*] [*Portuguese*]

NDOZ....... Continuous Dipole Axial Sounding   (RU)

NDP.......... Narodno-Demokraticheskaia Partiia

NDP.......... National Democracy Party [*Thailand*] [*Political party*]   (PPW)

NDP.......... National Democratic Party [*Sierra Leone*] [*Political party*]   (EY)

NDP.......... National Democratic Party [*Grenada*] [*Political party*]   (PPW)

NDP.......... National Democratic Party [*Rhodesia and Nyasaland*] [*Political party*]

NDP.......... National Democratic Party [*Morocco*] [*Political party*]   (PPW)

NDP.......... National Democratic Party [*Iraq*] [*Political party*]   (BJA)

NDP.......... National Democratic Party [*India*] [*Political party*]   (PPW)

NDP.......... National Democratic Party [*Namibia*] [*Political party*]   (PPW)

NDP.......... National Democratic Party [*Egypt*] [*Political party*]   (PPW)

NDP.......... National Democratic Party [*Pakistan*] [*Political party*]   (PD)

NDP.......... National Democratic Party [*Solomon Islands*] [*Political party*]   (PPW)

NDP.......... National Democratic Party   (RU)

NDP.......... Nationaldemokratische Partei [*National Democratic Party*] [*Austria*] [*Political party*]   (PPW)

NDP.......... National Development Party [*Montserrat*] [*Political party*]   (EY)

NDP.......... National Development Plan

NDP.......... Nationalist Democracy Party [*Turkey*] [*Political party*]   (PPW)

NDP.......... Natsional'no-Demokraticheskaia Partiia

NDP.......... Neo-Destour Party [*Tunisia*]

NDP.......... New Democratic Party [*St. Vincent*] [*Political party*]   (PPW)

NDP.......... New Democratic Party [*Seychelles*] [*Political party*]   (EY)

NDP.......... New Democratic Party [*South Korea*] [*Political party*]   (PPW)

NDP.......... Noseci Dekontaminacioni Pribor [*Portable Decontamination Equipment*] [*Military*]   (YU)

NDP.......... Nuclear Disarmament Party [*Australia*] [*Political party*]

NDP.......... Vereniging van de Nederlandsche Dagbladpers [*Association of the Netherlands Daily Press*]   (WEN)

NDPA .... National Democratic Party of Australia   (ADA)

NDPC .... National Development Plan Council   (ML)

NDPD .... National-Demokratische Partei Deutschlands [*National-Democratic Party of Germany*] [*Berlin, East Germany*]   (EG)

NDPD .... Nationaldemokratische Partei Deutschlands [*German National Democratic Party*] [*Political party*]

NDPG .... National Democratic Party of Germany [*German Democratic Republic*]   (RU)

NDPL .... National Democratic Party of Liberia [*Political party*]   (EY)

NDPO .... Novosibirsk Volunteer Fire Society   (RU)

NDPP .... New [*South Wales*] [*State Office of the*] Director of Public Prosecutions [*National Union Catalogue of Australia symbol*]

ND(Q)....... Nominal Defendant (Queensland) [*Australia*]

NDR.......... Andrea Airlines SA [*Peru*] [*ICAO designator*]   (FAAC)

NDR.......... Narodnaia Demokraticheskaia Respublika Iemen

NDR.......... National Democratic Revolution [*Ethiopia*]   (AF)

NDR.......... Natsional'noe Dvizhenie Revoliutsii

NDR.......... Nemacka Demokratska Republika [*German Democratic Republic (East Germany)*]   (YU)

NDR.......... Nemecka Demokraticka Republika [*German Democratic Republic (East Germany)*]   (CZ)

ndr .... Nieder [*Down*] [*German*]   (GCA)

ndr .... Niedrig [*Low*] [*German*]   (GCA)

NDR.......... Norddeutscher Rundfunk [*Radio network*] [*Germany*]

NDR.......... Normenausschuss Druck- und Reproduktionstechnik im DIN [*Deutsches Institut fuer Normung*] eV [*Printing and Reproduction Technology Standards in the German Institute of Standardization*]   (SLS)

NdR.......... Nota della Redazione [*Editorial Note*] [*Italian*]   (WER)

NDRA .... Natural Disaster Relief Arrangements [*Australia*]

Ndrd.......... Niederdeutsch [*Low German*] [*Language, etc.*]

NDRE .... Norwegian Defense Research Establishment

NDRI .... National Dairy Research Institute [*India*] [*Research center*]   (IRC)

Ndrl........... Niederlassung [*Branch Establishment*] [*German*]   (CED)

NDRP .... New Democratic Republican Party [*South Korea*] [*Political party*]   (EY)

NDS .... Nakladatelstvi Dopravy a Spoju [*Publishing House for Literature on Transportation and Communications*]   (CZ)

NDS .... Neo-Democrates Senegalais [*Senegalese Neo-Democrats*]   (AF)

Nds........... Niedersachsen [*Lower Saxony*] [*German*]

NDS .... Nordic Demographic Society   (EA)

NDS .... Norsk Dermatologisk Selskap [*Norwegian Dermatological Society*]   (EAIO)

NDS .... Novinarsko Drustvo Slovenije [*Society of Journalists of Slovenia*]   (YU)

NDSA .... National Down's Syndrome Association [*India*]   (EAIO)

Ndschlg...... Niederschlag [*Precipitate*] [*German*]   (GCA)

NDSE .... New [*South Wales*] - Department of School Education [*Management Information Service*]

NDSG .... Northside District Safety Group [*Australia*]

NDSMK .... New Democratic Youth League of China   (RU)

NDSO .... Novodemokratski Savez Omladine [*New Democratic Youth Federation*] [*Vietnam*]   (YU)

NDSS........ Highest Permissible Degree of Compression   (RU)

NDT.......... Naczelna Dyrekcja Techniczna [*Chief Technical Administration*]   (POL)

NDT.......... Netherlands Dance Theater

NDT.......... New [*South Wales*] Department of Tourism [*Commission of New South Wales*]

NDT.......... Norwegian Defence Technology

NdT........... Nota del Traduttore [*Translator's Note*] [*Italian*]

NdT........... Note du Traducteur [*France*]   (FLAF)

NDTA .... Non-Destructive Testing Association of Australia

NDTAA ..... Non-Destructive Testing Association of Australia   (ADA)

NDTC .... National Dance Theater Company [*Jamaica*]

NDTP .... Namibia Democratic Turnhalle Party

NDU .... National Democratic Union [*Zimbabwe*] [*Political party*]   (PPW)

NDU .... Rundu [*Namibia*] [*Airport symbol*]   (OAG)

NDUF .... National Democratic United Front [*Later, FNDF*] [*Myanmar*] [*Political party*]   (PD)

NDUO ...... National Democratic Unity Organisation

NDV.......... Nacelnik Delostreleckeho Vyzbrojovani [*Chief, Artillery Ordnance*]   (CZ)

NDV.......... Nederlandse Dierkundige Vereniging [*Dutch Veterinarian Association*]   (SLS)

NDVSh ...... Scientific Reports of Schools of Higher Education   (RU)

NDYeF ...... People's Democratic United Front of China   (RU)

NDYL .... New Democratic Youth League   (ML)

NDZ.......... Nacelnik Delostreleckeho Zasobovani [*Chief of Artillery Supply Service*]   (CZ)

NDZ.......... Nontoxic Smoke Screen   (RU)
NDZR........ Natsional'noe Dvizhenie v Zashchitu Revoliutsii
ne............. Anno Domini [*In the Year of Our Lord*]   (RU)
Ne.............. Effektive Leistung [*Effective Horsepower*] [*German*]
NE.............. Fixed Electrode   (RU)
NE.............. Left Nationalists [*Spain*] [*Political party*]   (PPW)
Ne.............. Naheilgueterzug [*Local Express Freight Train*]   (EG)
NE.............. Narodna Enciklopedija Srpsko-Hrvatsko-Slovenacka (Stanojevic
       Stanoje) [*Stanoje Stanojevic's Serbo-Croatian-Slovenian
       National Encyclopedia*]   (YU)
NE.............. Nasa Era [*Our Era (In the Year of Our Lord)*]   (YU)
ne.............. Naszej Ery [*Our Era (In the Year of Our Lord)*]   (POL)
NE.............. Neiva [*Sociedade Construtora Aeronautica Neiva Ltda.*] [*Brazil*]
       [*ICAO aircraft manufacturer identifier*]   (ICAO)
ne.............. Nemet [*German*]   (HU)
Ne.............. Neon [*Neon*] [*Chemical element*] [*Portuguese*]
NE.............. Nepi Egyuttes [*Folk Ensemble*]   (HU)
NE.............. Neunkircher Eisenwerk AG [*Neuenkirch Foundry*]
NE.............. Nichtbundeseigene Eisenbahnen [*Non-Federal Railroads*]
       (WEN)
NE.............. Nichteisen [*Nonferrous*] [*German*]   (WEN)
NE.............. Niger [*ANSI two-letter standard code*]   (CNC)
NE.............. Ninkyo Eiga [*Chivalry Films*] [*Japan*]
NE.............. Niugini Earthmoving Ltd. [*Papua New Guinea*]
NE.............. Nomarkhiaki Epitropi [*Nome Committee*] [*Greek*]   (GC)
NE.............. Nomismatiki Epitropi [*Currency Committee*]   (GC)
ne.............. Non Ebarbe [*Untrimmed*] [*Publishing*] [*French*]
NE.............. Nonlinear Element   (RU)
NE.............. Nord-Est [*Northeast*] [*Italian*]
NE.............. Nord-Est [*Northeast*] [*French*]   (MTD)
NE.............. Nordeste [*Northeast*] [*Spanish*]
NE.............. Nordeste [*North-East*] [*Portuguese*]
NE.............. Nova Era [*Our Era (In the Year of Our Lord)*]   (YU)
NE.............. Standard Cell   (RU)
NEA.......... National Electrification Administration [*Philippines*]   (IMH)
NEA.......... National Energy Authority of Iceland [*Research center*]   (IRC)
NEA.......... Native Education Association
NEA.......... Nea Elliniki Aristera [*New Greek Left*] [*Greek*]   (GC)
NEA.......... Nebeneichamt [*Suboffice of Weights and Measures*] [*German*]
NEA.......... Newsletter Editors' Association [*Australia*]
NEA.......... Norwegian Educational Association   (EAIO)
NEA.......... Norwegian Epilepsy Association   (EAIO)
NEA.......... Nouvelles Editions Africaines [*New African Publishing
       Company*]   (AF)
NEA.......... Nuclear Energy Agency [*See also AEN*] [*Organization for
       Economic Cooperation and Development*]   (EAIO)
NEA.......... Numerotation Europeenne des Articles [*French*]   (ADPT)
NEAC........ National Environmental Awareness Committee [*South Africa*]
       (AA)
NEAC........ New [*South Wales*] Ethnic Affairs Commission [*National Union
       Catalogue of Australia symbol*]
NEACRP... Nuclear Energy Agency Committee on Reactor Physics [*OECD*]
       (EY)
NEAFC...... North-East Atlantic Fisheries Commission [*British*]   (EAIO)
NEAL........ New [*South Wales*] Esso Australia Ltd. [*Exploration Information
       Centre*]
NEAM....... New England [*Regional*] Art Museum [*National Union
       Catalogue of Australia symbol*]
NEANDC.. Nuclear Energy Agency Nuclear Data Committee [*OECD*]   (EY)
NEAQ....... Northern Electricity Authority of Queensland [*Australia*]
NEAS........ National ELICOS [*English Language Intensive Courses for
       Overseas Students*] Accreditation Scheme [*Australia*]
NEATO..... North East Asian Treaty Organization   (NATG)
NEB.......... National Electricity Board [*Malaysia*]   (ML)
NEB.......... National Enterprise Board [*Scottish*]
NEB.......... National Environment Board [*Thailand*]   (DS)
NEB.......... Navorsingseenheid vir Boerderybestuur [*University of the Orange
       Free State*] [*South Africa*]   (AA)
Neb.......... Nebel [*Fog, Smoke*] [*German*]   (GCA)
NEB.......... Nebelwerfer [*German six-barrelled mortar*]   (DSUE)
Neb.......... Neben [*Near*] [*German*]
NEB.......... Nepi Ellenorzesi Bizottsag [*People's Control Committee*]   (HU)
NEB.......... Scientific Experimental Center   (RU)
NEBA....... North East Bolivian Airways [*ICAO designator*]   (FAAC)
NEBAC...... National Ethnic Broadcasting Advisory Council [*Australia*]
Nebent...... Nebentitel [*Subtitle*] [*German*]
NEBVVS.. Scientific Experimental Center of the Air Force   (RU)
NEC......... National Economic Council [*Iran*]   (ME)
NEC.......... National Electoral Commission [*Nigeria*]   (ECON)
NEC.......... National Energy Commission [*Thailand*]   (PDAA)
NEC.......... National Energy Corporation [*Trinidadian and Tobagan*]
       (GEA)
NEC.......... National Engineering Center [*Philippines*]   (IRC)
NEC.......... National Evaluation Conference [*Australasian National
       Evaluation Society*]
NEC.......... National Executive Committee [*Malaysia*]   (ML)

NEC.......... National Executive Committee [*of the Revolutionary Council of
       Zanzibar*] [*Tanzania*]
NEC.......... National Executive Committee [*Mauritius*]   (AF)
NEC.......... National Executive Council [*Malaysia*]   (ML)
NEC.......... National Exhibition Centre Ltd. [*South Africa*]   (AA)
NEC.......... Necochea [*Argentina*] [*Airport symbol*]   (OAG)
NEC.......... Nederlands Elektrotechnisch Comite [*Netherlands*]
NEC.......... Nippon Electric Co. [*Japan*]
NEC.......... Non-Essential Consumer [*Philippine Standard Commodity
       Classification Manual*]   (IMH)
NEC.......... Northern European Command [*NATO*]   (NATG)
NEC.......... Northern European Countries
NEC.......... Northern Europe Committee [*NATO*]   (NATG)
NEC.......... Norwegian Employers' Confederation   (EAIO)
NECA....... Nigerian Employers Consultative Association
NECAL...... National Environmental Chemistry and Acoustics Laboratory
       [*New Zealand*]   (IRC)
NECAR..... New Electric Car [*Daimler-Benz AG*]   (PS)
NECC........ National Education Crisis Committee [*South Africa*]
NECCCRW ... Near East Christian Council Committee for Refugee Work
       (MENA)
NECCO..... Nigerian Engineering and Construction Company
NECDLC... Near East Commission for Desert Locust Control   (EAIO)
nech........... Odd   (RU)
NECK....... Nuclear Energy Committee of Kuwait   (PDAA)
NECLSA... North East Coalition for the Liberation of Southern Africa
NECM....... New England Conference Management [*Australia*]
NECO....... National Election Commission [*Nigeria*]
NECO....... National Iranian Industries Organization Export Co.   (EY)
NECO....... Nippon Electric Co.   (IAA)
NECOS..... Northern European Chiefs of Staff [*NATO*]   (NATG)
NECPP...... North Eastern Convention People's Party
NECTAR... Network of European CNS [*Central Nervous System*]
       Transplantation and Restoration
NECZAM ... National Educational Company of Zambia
NED.......... Naval Engineering Division [*Australian Defence Industries*]
NED.......... Nederduits [*Low German*] [*Afrikaans*]
Ned........... Nederlands [*Netherlands*] [*Netherlands*]   (CED)
NED.......... Nederlandse Emigratiedienst [*Netherlands*]   (BAS)
NED.......... Neolaia Ethnikis Draseos [*Youth for National Action*]   (GC)
NEDA....... National Economic and Development Authority [*Philippines*]
       (GEA)
NEDA....... Neolaia Eniaias Dimokratikis Arsteras [*Youth of the United
       Democratic Left*] [*EDA*] [*See also*]   (GC)
NEDAC..... Nuclear Energy Data Center [*Genshiryuoku Data Centre*]
       [*Japan*]   (WND)
NEDB....... National Economic Development Board [*Thailand*]   (FEA)
NEDC....... National Economic Development Council [*Benin*]
NEDC....... Near East Development Corp.   (OMWE)
NEDCO..... National Estates and Designing Company Ltd.
NEDE....... Nomos peri Eispraxeos Dimosion Esodon [*Law on Collection of
       Public Revenues*] [*Greek*]   (GC)
NEDEPA.. Nea Demokratiki Parataxi [*Cyprus*] [*Political party*]   (PPE)
NedGem..... De Nederlandse Gemeente [*Netherlands*]   (BAS)
NedGer(ef) ... Nederduits Gereformeerd [*Dutch Reformed*] [*Afrikaans*]
Ned Herv ... Nederduits Hervormd [*Dutch Reformed*] [*Afrikaans*]
NE DI K.... Neolaia Dimokratikou Kommatos [*Democratic Party Youth*]
       (GC)
NedInd....... De Nederlandse Industrie - Orgaan van het Verbond der
       Nederlandse Werkgevers [*Netherlands*]   (BAS)
NEDIPA.. Nea Demokratiki Parataxi [*Cyprus*] [*Political party*]   (PPW)
NEDIPA.... Neolaia Dimokratikis Parataxis [*Youth of the Democratic Front*]
       (GC)
NedJbl....... Nederlands Juristenblad [*Netherlands*]   (BAS)
NedJpd....... Nederlandse Jurisprudentie [*Netherlands*]   (BAS)
NEDKE..... Neon Ethnikon Dimokratikon Komma Ellinon [*New National
       Democratic Party of Greeks*] [*Greek*]   (GC)
NEDO....... Nederlands Documentatiecentrum voor Ontwikkelingslanden
NEDO....... New Energy Development Organization [*Japan*]
NEDP....... Neighbourhood Employment Development Program [*Australia*]
NedStcrt.... Nederlandse Staatscourant [*Netherlands*]   (BAS)
NEDUET .. NED University of Engineering and Technology [*Pakistan*]
       [*Research center*]   (ERC)
NEDYSI.... Neolaia Dimokratikou Synagermou [*Youth Organization of
       Democratic Rally*] [*Cyprus*]   (EAIO)
NEE.......... Navtikon Epimelitirion Ellados [*Merchant Marine Chamber of
       Greece*]   (GC)
NEE.......... Nukleer Enerji Enstitusu [*Nuclear Energy Institute*] [*Istanbul
       Technological University*]   (TU)
NEED........ Near East Emergency Donations
NEEDS-IR ... NIKKEI Economic Electronic Databank Service - Information
       Retrieval [*Information service or system*] [*Japan*]   (IID)
NEEDS-TS ... NIKKEI Economic Electronic Databank Service - Time
       Sharing [*Information service or system*] [*Japan*]   (IID)
NEEITC .... National Electrical and Electronic Industry Training Committee
       [*Australia*]

NEERI...... National Electrical Engineering Research Institute [*South Africa*] [*Research center*]   (IRC)
NEF .... Near East Foundation
NEF .... Nordiska Ekonomiska Forskningsradet [*Nordic Economic Research Council - NERC*]   (EAIO)
NEF .... Norsk Elektroteknisk Forening [*Norway*]   (SLS)
NEF .... Norsk Epilepsiforbund [*Norway*]   (EAIO)
NEFA .... New European Fighter Aircraft   (PS)
NEFA .... North-East Frontier Agency [*India*]
NEFC .... Near East Forestry Commission [*Italy*]   (DSCA)
NEFO .... New Emerging Forces   (IN)
NEFO .... Nordjylland Elektricitetsforsyning [*Denmark*]   (PDAA)
neft .... Oil Well [*Topography*]   (RU)
neft .... Petroleum, Oil   (RU)
neft .... Petroleum Production [*Topography*]   (RU)
Neft .... Petroleum Refinery [*Topography*]   (RU)
neft .... Petroleum Reservoir [*Topography*]   (RU)
Nefteburmashremont ... State Trust for the Repair of Drilling Equipment   (RU)
Neftekhimavtomat ... Scientific Research and Planning Institute for Complex Automation of Production Processes in the Petroleum and Chemical Industries   (RU)
NEFTEKIP ... Control and Measuring Instruments Plant for the Petroleum Industry   (RU)
neftepereg .. Petroleum-Refining   (RU)
Nefteprovodproyekt ... State All-Union Trust for Surveying and Planning of Petroleum Pipelines and Petroleum Storage Depots   (RU)
Neftezavodproyekt ... All-Union Trust for the Planning of Petroleum Industry Plants   (RU)
neg .... Negatif [*French*]   (TPFD)
neg .... Negative   (TPFD)
neg .... Negativo [*Negative*] [*Portuguese*]
neg .... Negociable [*Negotiable*] [*French*]
NEG .... Negril [*Jamaica*] [*Airport symbol*]   (OAG)
NEGAS...... NetzplangesteuertesAuftragsabwicklungsSystem [*German*]   (ADPT)
negat.......... Negativ [*Negative*] [*German*]   (GCA)
negt .... Negociant [*Merchant, Trader*] [*Business term*] [*French*]
negte.......... Negociante [*Wholesaler*] [*French*]
NEH .... Nederlandse Economische Hogeschool [*Netherlands*]   (BAS)
neh .... Nehai [*Late*]   (HU)
Neh .... Nehemia [*Afrikaans*]
NEH .... New [*South Wales*] [*Sydney*] Eye Hospital [*Medical Library*]
NEH .... Societe Nigerienne des Etablissements Herlicq
NEHA........ Nederlands Economisch Historisch Archief
Nehezip K .. Neheripari Kiado [*Publishing House on Heavy Industry*]   (HU)
NEHRC ..... New England History Resources Center [*University of New England*] [*Australia*]
NEHU .... North Eastern Hill University [*India*]   (PDAA)
NEI .... National Economics Institute [*Iceland*]
NEI .... Nature Expeditions International   (GNE)
NEI .... Nederlandsch Economisch Instituut [*Netherlands*]   (BAS)
NEI .... Netherlands East Indies
NEI .... Nordic Energy Index [*Database*] [*Nordic Atomic Libraries Joint Secretariat*] [*Denmark*] [*Information service or system*]   (IID)
NEI .... Nouvelles Equipes Internationales [*Later, European Christian Democratic Union*]
NEIA .... Northern Engineering Industries Africa [*Commercial firm*] [*South Africa*]
NEIB......... National Export Import Bank [*Egypt*]   (IMH)
NEIBR....... Norsk Institutt for By-og Regionforskning [*Norwegian Institute for Urban and Regional Research*]   (PDAA)
NEIC .... National Employers Industrial Council [*Australia*]
NEIC .... National Equivalence Information Centre [*Netherlands*]
NEIC .... Nuclear Energy Information Center [*Poland*]
NEIDA ...... Network of Educational Innovation for Development in Africa   (EAIO)
NEIM .... New [*South Wales*] Enterprise Information Management [*Proprietary Ltd.*] [*National Union Catalogue of Australia symbol*]
NEIS.......... National Electronic Interchange Services Proprietary Ltd. [*Australia*]
NEIS.......... New Enterprise Incentive Scheme [*Australia*]
NEIS.......... Novosibirsk Electrotechnical Institute of Communications   (RU)
NEITA....... National Excellence in Teaching Award [*Australia*]
neizv .... Unknown   (BU)
NEJWMC ... North Eastern Jewish War Memorial Centre [*Australia*]
NEK.......... Neo Elliniko Komma [*New Greek Party*] [*Greek*]   (GC)
NEK.......... Norsk Elektrotecnisk Komite [*Oslo, Norway*]
NEKA .... Nea Ergatiki Kinisis Athinon [*New Labor Movement of Athens*]   (GC)
NEKA .... Nomarkhiaki Epitropi Katapolemiseos Analfavitismou [*Nome Anti-Illiteracy Committee*] [*Greek*]   (GC)

NEKG .... Nova Hut Klementa Gottwalda [*New Metallurgical Works of Klement Gottwald*] [*Ostrava-Kuncice*]   (CZ)
NEKIN ...... Scientific Experimental Institute   (RU)
NEKOLIM ... Neocolonialist-Colonialist-Imperialist [*Indonesia*]
NEKOLIM ... Neokolonialisme, Kolonialisme, dan Imperialisme [*Neocolonialism, Colonialism, and Imperialism*] [*Indonesia*]   (IN)
NEKOSZ... Nepi Kollegiumok Orszagos Szovetsege [*National Association of People's Colleges*]   (HU)
nekr........... Obituary   (BU)
NEL .... National Emancipation League [*Nigeria*]
NEL .... Scientific Experimental Laboratory   (RU)
NELA .... National Environmental Law Association [*Australia*]
NELCONNZ ... National Electronics Conference, New Zealand [*IEEE*]
N(E)LE...... Nomarkhiaki (Eparkhiaki) Epitropi Laikis Epimorfosis [*Nomarchial (Provincial) Committee for Popular Advancement (Cultural, Vocational, Political, Recreational, etc.)*]   (GC)
nelle........... Nouvelle [*New*] [*French*]
NELSAK ... Nuclear Power Plants Institution [*Turkey*]   (MENA)
nem........... German   (RU)
NEM......... Nahrung, Einheit, Milch [*Nourishment, Unity, Milk*] [*German*]
NEM......... National Employers' Mutual Ltd. [*Australia*]
nem........... Nemet [*German*]   (HU)
NEM......... New Economic Mechanism [*Hungary*]
NEM......... Nichteisenmetall [*Non-Ferrous Metal*] [*German*]   (GCA)
NEM......... Northeastern Mediterranean
NEMA .... Netzschkauer Maschinenfabrik (VEB) [*Netzschkau Machine Factory (VEB)*]   (EG)
NEMA .... Nigerian Evangelical Missions Association
NEMAI ..... New [*South Wales*] Elizabeth Macarthur Agricultural Institute [*National Union Catalogue of Australia symbol*]
NEMAS..... Nouvelle Emaillerie Senegalaise
NEMC .... National Exemplary Materials Collection [*Australia*]
NEMC .... National Export Meatworks Council [*Australia*]
NEMEDRI ... Northeast and Mediterranean Route Instruction
NE-Metall ... Nichteisenmetall [*Nonferrous Metal*]   (EG)
nem ez .... German Language   (BU)
NEMH .... Navorsingseenheid vir Materiaalhantering [*University of the Witwatersrand*] [*South Africa*]   (AA)
NEMIC...... National Employment Manpower and Incomes [*Botswana*]
NEMKO.... Norges Elektriske Materiellkontrol [*Norwegian Electrical Control Board*]   (IMH)
NEMP .... National Energy Management Program [*Australia*]
NEMPl...... National Ethnographic Museum in Plovdiv   (BU)
nemz.......... Nemzeti [*National*] [*Hungary*]
nemzetk...... Nemzetkozi [*International*] [*Hungary*]
nemzk........ Nemzetkozi [*International*]   (HU)
NEN.......... Nederlandse Norm
NEN.......... Stichting Nederlands Normalisatie-Instituut
NENARACA ... Near East and North Africa Regional Agricultural Credit Association
nenasyshch ... Unsaturated   (RU)
NEO.......... New European Order [*Switzerland*]
NEOCALI ... Compania Cali Neon Ltda.   (COL)
neochishch ... Unpurified, Crude   (RU)
neodobr ...... Disapproving   (BU)
NEOF .... Nordic Engineer Officers' Federation   (EA)
neol............ Neologismo [*Neologism*] [*Portuguese*]
neopr.......... Indefinite (Pronoun)   (RU)
neopr .... Infinitive (Form of Verb)   (RU)
NEOVA..... Air-Cushion Vehicle built by Neoteric Engineering Affiliates [*Usually used in combination with numerals*] [*Australia*]
NEP .... Nea Ergatoypalliliki Parataxis [*or Nea Ergatiki Parataxis*] [*New Labor Faction*] [*Greek*]   (GC)
NEP .... Nemzeti Egyseg Partja [*Party of National Unity*] [*Hungary*] [*Political party*]   (PPE)
nep............. Neper   (RU)
NEP .... New Economic Policy [*Malaysia*]   (ML)
NEP .... New Economic Policy [*Israel*]   (IMH)
NEP .... New Economic Policy [*Program of former USSR, 1921-28; also US wage/price freeze and controls of Nixon Administration, 1971*]
NEP .... Novosadsko Elektricno Preduzece [*Novi Sad Electric Establishment*]   (YU)
NEPA .... National Electric Power Authority [*Nigeria*]
NEPA .... National Environmental Protection Agency [*China*]
NEPA .... New England Protected Area [*Australia*]
NEPA .... New [*South Wales*] - Environment Protection Authority [*National Union Catalogue of Australia symbol*]
NEPA .... Nigerian Electric Power Authority
NEPB........ Nigerian Enterprises Promotion Board [*or Bureau*]
NEPC........ Nigerian Export Promotion Council   (GEA)
NEPCO ..... National Export Promotion Council
neperekh .... Intransitive (Verb)   (RU)
neperiodich ... Nonperiodic   (RU)

NEPI......... National Exchange of Police Information [*Australia*]
NEPMUV MIN ... Nepmuvelesi Miniszterium/Miniszter [*Ministry/Minister of Public Education*] (HU)
NEPN........ Nepean [*Botanical region*] [*Australia*]
neprekh...... Intransitive (BU)
NEPRILS.. New Professionals in Information and Library Studies [*Western Australian institute of Technology*]
neprom....... Unchanged (BU)
nepsz......... Nepszeru [*Popular*] (HU)
NEPU........ Northern Elements Progression Union [*Nigeria*] [*Political party*]
NEPU........ Northern Elements Progressive Union [*Nigeria*]
nepul......... Incomplete (BU)
NER.......... Netherlands Electronic Radiogenootschap [*Netherlands*]
NER.......... Niger [*ANSI three-letter standard code*] (CNC)
NER.......... North Eastern Region
Nera.......... Nera & Musica [*Record label*] [*Norway*]
NERA........ New [*South Wales*] Energy Resources of Australia [*Ltd.*] [*National Union Catalogue of Australia symbol*]
NERC........ Nigeria Educational Research Council [*Research center*] (IRC)
NERC........ Nordic Economic Research Council (EA)
NERC........ Nuclear Energy Research Center [*Also, CEEN, SCK*] [*Belgium*]
NERC........ Regional Conference for the Near East [*UN Food and Agriculture Organization*]
NERC(NZ) ... National Electronics Research Council (New Zealand) (PDAA)
NERD........ National Engineering Research and Development Centre of Sri Lanka
NERD &D ... National Energy Research, Development, and Demonstration Program [*Australia*]
NERDDC .. National Energy Research Development and Demonstration Council [*Australia*] (PDAA)
NERG........ Nederlands Elektronica- en Radiogenootschap [*Netherlands*]
NEROAC .. Northeast Regional Office of Agriculture and Cooperatives [*Thai*] (ARC)
NERP .... Nicaraguan Exile Relocation Program [*CIA*]
NERPG...... Northern European Regional Planning Group [*NATO*] (NATG)
NERSA...... Centrale Nucleaire Europeenne a Neutrons Rapides SA [*France*] (PDAA)
ner-vo .... Inequality [*Mathematics*] (RU)
NES .... Netherlands' Ecological Society [*Multinational association*] (EAIO)
Nes............ Nisidhes [*Islet(s)*] [*Greek*] (NAU)
NES .... Nordeste, Linhas Aereas Regionais SA [*Brazil*] [*ICAO designator*] (FAAC)
NES .... Nordic Ergonomic Society (EAIO)
NES .... Nordiska Ergonomisallskapet [*Nordic Ergonomic Society*] (EAIO)
NES .... Nucleos Educativos Seleccionados [*Select Educational Centers*] [*Peru*] (LA)
NESA........ National Employment Strategy for Aboriginals [*Australia*]
NE/SA....... Near East/South Asia Council of Overseas Schools (EA)
NESAM..... Nucleo dos Estudantes Africanos Secundarios de Mocambique
NESB........ New [*South Wales*] [*St*] Edmond's School for the Blind [*St. Edmond's School for the Visually Impaired*]
NESBA...... National Executive of Small Business Agencies [*Australia*]
NESBIC .... Netherlands Students Bureau for International Cooperation
NESC........ National Economic and Social Council [*Dublin, Ireland*] (GEA)
NESDA...... Netherlands Electrostatic Discharge Association (EAIO)
NESDB...... National Economic and Social Development Board [*Thailand*] (DS)
NESh .... Train Commander, Echelon Commander (RU)
NESHS...... Narodna Enciklopedija Srpsko-Hrvatsko-Slovenacka [*Serbian-Croatian-Slovenian National Encyclopedia*] [*Zagreb*] (YU)
nesk.......... Several (RU)
neskl.......... Indeclinable (Word) (RU)
NESLATT ... National English Second Language Association for Teacher Training [*South Africa*] (AA)
NESP........ National Economic Survival Programme
NESPAK ... National Engineering Services of Pakistan
NEST........ New and Emerging Sciences and Technologies
NEST........ New [*South Wales*] East Sydney Technical [*College*] [*National Union Catalogue of Australia symbol*]
NEST........ New El Salvador Today [*An association*]
NEST........ New Era Schools Trust [*South Africa*]
NESTEC ... Societe d'Assistance Technique pour Produits Nestle SA [*Switzerland*] (ARC)
NESWA..... Netherlands Ex-Servicemen and Women's Association in Australia
NESZ........ Nephadsereg Egeszsegugyi Szolgalata [*Health Service of the People's Army*] (HU)
NET .... National Estate Tasmania [*Australia*]
NET .... Near East Tourist Agency [*Israel*]
NET .... Nepkoztarsasag Elnoki Tanacsa [*Presidium of the People's Republic*] (HU)
net .... Netto [*Net*] [*Afrikaans*]

NET .... Next European Torus [*Formerly, Joint European Torus (JET)*]
NET .... Nigerian External Telecommunications Ltd.
NET .... Nippon Educational Television [*Japan*]
NET .... Norme Europeene de Telecommunications [*Telecommunications*] (OSI)
NET .... Nouvelle Entreprise Togolaise
NETAS...... Northern Electric Telekomunikasyon Anonim Sirketi [*Northern Electric Telecommunication Corporation*] (TU)
NETh........ Nepkoztarsasag Elnoki Tanacsanak Hatarozata [*Resolution of the Presidential Council of the People's Republic*] (HU)
Neth Ant .... Netherlands Antilles
NETI......... Nehezipari Epulettervezo Iroda [*Construction Designing Office for Heavy Industry*] (HU)
NET Ltd .... Nigerian External Telecommunications Ltd. [*Lagos*]
NETS........ National Exhibition Touring Scheme [*Australia*]
NETSO..... Northern European Transhipment Organization [*NATO*] (NATG)
NETSS ...... National Exhibitions Touring Support Scheme [*Australia*]
NETT .... Network Environmental Technology Transfer [*Europe*] [*An association*]
Nettokm..... Nettotonnenkilometer [*Net Ton Kilometers (Product of the weight of the freight carried by a train multiplied by the kilometers traveled by that train)*] (EG)
NEU.......... National Employees' Union [*Sri Lanka*]
NEU.......... Transportes Aereos Neuquinos Sociedad de Estado [*Argentina*] [*ICAO designator*] (FAAC)
Neuausg ..... Neuausgabe [*Reprint*] [*German*]
neubearb .... Neubearbeitet [*Revised*] [*German*]
NEUCC .... Northern European Universities Computer Centre [*Denmark*] (PDAA)
neud........... Unsatisfactory (RU)
NEUM...... Non-European Unity Movement [*South Africa*] (PD)
neut .... Neuter (TPFD)
neut .... Neutre [*French*] (TPFD)
neut .... Neutrum [*Afrikaans*]
neutr......... Neutral [*German*] (GCA)
neutr......... Neutralisiert [*Neutralize*] [*German*]
neuw......... Neuwertig [*As Good as New*] [*German*]
neuzeitl...... Neuzeitlich [*Modern*] [*German*] (GCA)
n ev .... Naptari Ev [*Calendar Year*] (HU)
NEV.......... Neckarwerke Elektrizitats Versorgungs [*Germany*] (PDAA)
NEV.......... Nederlandse Ecologen Vereniging [*Netherlands Ecological Society*] [*Multinational association*] (EAIO)
NEV.......... Nederlandse Entomologische Vereniging [*Netherlands*] (SLS)
NEV.......... Nevis [*Leeward Islands*] [*Airport symbol*] (OAG)
Nevabs .... Nederlandse Vereniging van Ambtenaren van de Burgerlijke Stand [*Netherlands*] (BAS)
NEVAC ..... Nederlandse Vacuumvereniging [*Netherlands Vacuum Engineering Society*] (PDAA)
NEVEC...... Nederlandse Vereniging van Pelterijenfabrikanten en Groothandelaren in Bontvellen [*Dutch Association of Fur Manufacturers and Peltry Wholesalers*]
NEVEM .... Nederlandse Vereniging voor Logistiek Management [*Netherlands*] (SLS)
NEVIE....... Nederlandse Vereniging voor Inkoop-Efficiency [*Netherlands*] (SLS)
NEVIKI ..... Nehezvegyipari Kutato Intezet, Veszprem [*Research Institute for the Heavy Chemicals Industry, Veszprem*] (HU)
Nevkhimzavod ... Neva Chemical Plant (RU)
nevl........... Nevleges [*Nominal*] (HU)
Nevr .... Neurologist, Neurology (BU)
nevt........... Nevtelen [*Anonymous*] [*Publishing*] [*Hungary*]
NEVZ .... Novocherkassk Electric Locomotive Plant (RU)
N E Wbk.... Nieu-Engels Woordeboek [*New England Dictionary*] [*Afrikaans*]
NEX.......... Nynaes Energy-Chemicals Complex [*Project*] [*Sweden*]
NEY.......... Northeastern Yiddish [*Language, etc.*] (BJA)
neytr.......... Neutral, Inert (RU)
neytr-tsiya ... Neutralization (RU)
NEZA .... Nouvelles Entreprises Zairoises
nezameshch ... Unsubstituted (RU)
NEZhK .... Nonesterified Fatty Acids (RU)
NEZS........ North of England Zoological Society (SLS)
NF .... Air Vanuatu [*Airline code*] [*Australia*]
NF .... Impartable Fund (BU)
NF .... Inorganic Phosphate (RU)
NF .... Naphtoquinone (RU)
NF .... Narodna Fronta [*People's Front*] (YU)
NF .... Narodni Fronta [*National Front*] [*Former Czechoslovakia*] [*Political party*] (PPE)
NF .... Nationale Front [*National Front*] (EG)
NF .... National Front (RU)
NF .... Ne Fallor [*Doubtful*] (ROG)
NF .... Nemzeti Front [*National Front*] (HU)
NF .... Neue Folge [*New Series*] [*Bibliography*] [*German*]
NF .... New Forum [*An association*] [*Germany*] (EAIO)
NF .... Newfoundland (IDIG)

NF .... New French [*Language, etc.*]   (ROG)
NF .... Niederfrequenz [*Audio Frequency*] [*German military - World War II*]
NF .... Nieu-Foundland [*Newfoundland*] [*Afrikaans*]
NF .... Nieuw Front [*New Front*] [*Suriname*] [*Political party*]   (EY)
NF .... Nisko Frekventni [*Low Frequency*]   (YU)
NF .... Nobel Foundation   (EA)
NF .... Nordiska Fabriksarbetarefederationen [*Nordic Federation of Factory Workers Unions - NFFWU*]   (EAIO)
NF .... Nordmanns-Forbunder [*Norsemen's Federation*]   (EA)
NF .... Norfolk Island [*ANSI two-letter standard code*]   (CNC)
NF .... Norges Fredslag [*Norway*]   (EAIO)
NF .... Norman French [*Language, etc.*]
NF .... Norme Francaise [*French*]
NF .... Norsemen's Federation [*Norway*]   (EAIO)
NF .... Norsk Faglaererlag [*Norway*]   (SLS)
NF .... Norsk Front [*Norwegian Front*]   (PD)
NF .... Northern French [*Language, etc.*]   (ROG)
NF .... Nouveau Franc [*New Franc*] [*Monetary unit Introduced in 1960*] [*France*]
NF .... Nova Filatelija [*New Philately*] [*Ljubljana A periodical*]   (YU)
NF .... Nueva Fuerza [*New Force*] [*Venezuela*]   (LA)
nf .... Ny Foeljd [*New Series*] [*Sweden*]
NF .... People's Front   (BU)
NFA .... Naga Federal Army [*India*]
NFA .... National Fishermen's Association [*Australia*]
NFA .... National Food Authority [*Philippines*]   (DS)
NFA .... National Food Authority [*Australia*]
NFA .... National Front of Ahvaz [*Iran*]
NFA .... Native Fish Australia
NFA .... New South Wales Farmers' Association [*Australia*]
NFA .... Nitrophenyl Acetate   (RU)
NFA .... North Flying AS [*Denmark*] [*ICAO designator*]   (FAAC)
NFA .... Nutritional Foods Association [*Australia*]
NFA .... Swedish National Food Administration [*Research center*]   (IRC)
NFAA .... Neuro-Fibromatosis Association of Australia
NFAA .... Nordic Forwarding Agents Association [*Defunct*]   (EA)
NFAA .... Northern Federation of Advertisers Associations [*Stockholm, Sweden*]   (EAIO)
NFAC .... National Food and Agricultural Council [*Philippines*]   (DS)
NFADPI .... National Federation and Assembly of Disabled People in India   (EAIO)
NFAIS .... National Federation of American Information Services [*International Council of Scientific Unions*]
NFAM .... National Foundation for the Australian Musical
NFAP .... Nuclear Free Australia Party [*Political party*]
NFAPC ...... National Fisheries Adjustment Program Committee [*Australia*]
NFBCA ..... National Federation of Blind Citizens of Australia
NFBJ .... National Federation of Brazilian Journalists   (EAIO)
NFBW .... National Federation of Building Workers [*Israel*]   (EAIO)
NFBWW ... Nordic Federation of Building and Wood Workers   (EA)
NFC .... National Fertiliser Corp. [*Thailand*]
NFC .... National Fertilizer Corp. of Pakistan Ltd.
NFC .... National Fisheries Company [*Grenada*]   (LA)
NFC .... Nauru Finance Corporation   (GEA)
NFC .... Nordisk Forening for Cellforskning [*Nordic Society for Cell Biology - NSCB*]   (EAIO)
NFC .... Nouvelle Feuille de Coupons [*New Sheet of Coupons*] [*French*]
NFCA .... National Federation of Credit Associations [*Japan*]
NFCA .... New [*South Wales*] Family Court of Australia [*Principal Registry*]
NFCA .... Northern Fishing Companies' Association [*Australia*]
NFCD .... Nicaraguan Foundation for Conservation and Development   (EAIO)
NFCF .... Norsk Forening for Cystisk Fibrose [*Norway*]   (EAIO)
NFCGC ..... National Federation of Coffee Growers of Colombia   (EAIO)
NFCIS .... Nuclear Fuel Cycle Information System [*Database*] [*International Atomic Energy Agency*] [*United Nations*]   (DUND)
NFCP .... National Forest Conservation Program
NFD .... Eurowings (NFD & RFG Luftverhehrs AG) [*Germany*] [*ICAO designator*]   (FAAC)
NFD .... Northeast Frontier District [*Kenya*]   (AF)
NFD .... Northern Frontier District [*Kenya*]
NFD .... Northern Frontier Division
NFD .... Nueva Fuerza Democratica [*New Democratic Force*] [*Colombia*] [*Political party*]   (EY)
NfD .... Nur fuer den Dienstgebrauch [*For Official Use Only*]   (EG)
NFDC .... National Film Development Corp. [*India*]
NFDH........ New [*South Wales*] Fairfield Hospital [*National Union Catalogue of Australia symbol*]
NFDPS ...... National Flight Data Processing System [*ICAO*]   (DA)
NFDR .... National Front for the Defense of the Revolution [*Malagasy*]   (AF)
NFEAS ...... National Federation of Engineers, Architects, and Surveyors [*Israel*]   (EAIO)

NFEF .... National Free Enterprise Foundation [*Australia*]
NFER........ National Foundation for Educational Research in England and Wales   (SLS)
NFERG...... New [*South Wales*] Ferguson [*Memorial Library*] [*Presbyterian Church of Australia in New South Wales*]
NFF............ National Farmers' Federation [*Australia*]
NFF............ National Fatherland Front [*Afghanistan*] [*Political party*]   (FEA)
NFF............ Nemzeti Fueggetlensegi Front [*National Independence Front*] [*Hungary*] [*Political party*]   (PPE)
Nff.............. Nordisk Forening for Folkendansforskning [*Nordic Association for Folk Dance Research*] [*Sweden*]   (EAIO)
NFF............ Norges Farmaceutiske Forening [*Norway*]   (SLS)
NFF............ Norske Forskningsbibliotekarers Forening [*Norway*]   (SLS)
NFF............ Norske Fotterapeuters Forbund [*Norway*]   (SLS)
NFF............ Norske Fysioterapeuters Forbund [*Norway*]   (SLS)
NFF............ Norwegian Fibrositis Patients' Association [*Norway*]   (EAIO)
NFFA .... Ba [*Fiji*] [*ICAO location identifier*]   (ICLI)
NFFA .... National Foodcrop Farmers Association [*Trinidad and Tobago*]   (EAIO)
NFFF .... Nandi [*Fiji*] [*ICAO location identifier*]   (ICLI)
NFFF .... National Federation of Fish Friers
NFFN .... Nandi/International [*Fiji*] [*ICAO location identifier*]   (ICLI)
NFFO .... Malolo Lailai [*Fiji*] [*ICAO location identifier*]   (ICLI)
NFFR........ Norges Fiskeriforskningsrad [*Norwegian Fisheries Research Council*] [*Research center*]   (IRC)
NFFR........ Rabi [*Fiji*] [*ICAO location identifier*]   (ICLI)
NFFWU..... Nordic Federation of Factory Workers Unions   (EA)
NFG .... Nagaland Federal Government [*India*]
NFG .... National Freight Group
NFGD .... National Front of Democratic Germany   (RU)
NFH.......... Nacelnik Financniho Hospodarstvi [*Chief of Finance*] [*Military*]   (CZ)
NFHO........ Caaf Ho Nandi [*Fiji*] [*ICAO location identifier*]   (ICLI)
NFHP .... New [*South Wales*] Freehill Hollingdale and Page [*Solicitors*] [*National Union Catalogue of Australia symbol*]
NFHRD ..... National Foundation for Human Resource Developments [*Bangladesh*]
NFHS .... Nepean Family History Society [*Australia*]
NFI .... Naturfreunde-Internationale [*International Friends of Nature - IFN*]   (EAIO)
NFI .... News Features of India [*Press agency*]
NFI .... Nuclear Fuel Industries Ltd. [*Nuclear energy*] [*Japan*]   (NRCH)
NFI .... Nutrition Foundation of Italy   (ASF)
NFIA.......... National Finance Industry Association [*Australia*]
NFIA.......... National Forest Industries Association [*Australia*]
NFICA....... National Forest Industries Campaign Association [*Australia*]
NFIJ.......... National Federation of Israel Journalists
NFIK.......... Norske Forening for Industriell Kvalitetskontroll [*Norwegian Institute for Quality Control*]   (PDAA)
NFin.......... Directive on Financing, Crediting, and Controlling Capital Investments   (BU)
NFIP.......... Nuclear Free and Independent Pacific Coordinating Committee [*Australia*]
NFIP.......... Nuclear Free and Independent Pacific Movement [*Australia*]
NFIR.......... National Federation of Indian Railwaymen [*Trade union*]   (FEA)
NFIR.......... Norsk Forening for Internasjonal Rett [*Norway*]   (SLS)
NFIRF .... Nature Farming International Research Foundation   (EAIO)
NFITC .... National Forest Industries Training Council [*Australia*]
NFITU....... National Front of Independent Trade Unions [*India*]
NFIW .... Nationale Federatie der Informatie Weekbladen [*Belgium*]   (EAIO)
NFJ .... Narodna Fronta Jugoslavije [*National Front of Yugoslavia*]   (YU)
NFJU........ Nordic Federation of Journalists' Unions [*Norway*]   (EAIO)
NFK .... Norfolk Island [*ANSI three-letter standard code*]   (CNC)
NFK .... Novosadska Fabrika Kablova [*Novi Sad Cable Factory*]   (YU)
NFKA .... Norwegian Association for Classical Acupuncture   (EAIO)
NFKK .... Nordisk Forening for Klinisk Kemi [*Scandinavian Society for Clinical Chemistry - SSCC*] [*Finland*]   (EAIO)
NFKKK...... Directive on the Financial Crediting and Control of Capital Investments   (BU)
NFL .... National Confederation of Labour   (EAIO)
NFL .... National Football League of Australia
NFL .... Northern Federation of Labour [*Nigeria*]
NFLA........ National Front for the Liberation of Angola   (EA)
NFLC........ National Federation of Land Councils [*Australia*]
NFLSV ...... National Front for the Liberation of South Vietnam
NFLSVN ... National Front for the Liberation of South Vietnam [*Use NFLSV*]   (CL)
NFLU .... National Federation of Labor Unions [*Philippines*]
NFLUC...... National Free Labour Union Congress [*Thailand*]   (EY)
NFM .... Naroden Front na Makedonija [*People's Front of Macedonia*]   (YU)
NFM .... Narodni Front Makedonije
NFM .... North Flinders Mines [*Australia*]

NFMA .... Norwegian Furnishings Manufacturers' Association (EAIO)
NFMC .... National Federation of Milk Cooperatives [*France*] (EAIO)
NFME .... Nordic Federation for Medical Education [*Denmark*] (EAIO)
NFMI .... National Federation of the Milk Industry [*France*] (EAIO)
NFML .... New [*South Wales*] Fairfield Memorial Library [*National Union Catalogue of Australia symbol*]
NFMR .... Nordisk Forening for Medisinsk Radiologi [*Scandinavian Radiological Society - SRS*] (EAIO)
NFN .... Nouvelle Front NAZI [*New NAZI Front*] [*French*] (PD)
NFNA .... Nausori/International [*Fiji*] [*ICAO location identifier*] (ICLI)
NFNB .... Bureta [*Fiji*] [*ICAO location identifier*] (ICLI)
NFNC .... National Food and Nutrition Commission [*Zambia*] (SLS)
NFNCE...... Nucleus of Nonconventional Energy Sources of the Federal University of Ceara [*Brazil*]
NFND........ Deumba [*Fiji*] [*ICAO location identifier*] (ICLI)
NFNG........ Ngau [*Fiji*] [*ICAO location identifier*] (ICLI)
NFNH .... Lauthala Islands [*Fiji*] [*ICAO location identifier*] (ICLI)
NFNK .... Lakemba [*Fiji*] [*ICAO location identifier*] (ICLI)
NFNL .... Lambasa [*Fiji*] [*ICAO location identifier*] (ICLI)
NFNL .... Nasionale Fisiese Navorsingslaboratorium [*Council for Scientific and Industrial Research*] [*South Africa*] (AA)
NFNM .... Matei [*Fiji*] [*ICAO location identifier*] (ICLI)
NFNN........ Vanuabalavu [*Fiji*] [*ICAO location identifier*] (ICLI)
NFNO........ Koro [*Fiji*] [*ICAO location identifier*] (ICLI)
NFNP .... National Food and Nutrition Policy [*Australia*]
NFNR .... Rotuma [*Fiji*] [*ICAO location identifier*] (ICLI)
NFNS .... Savusavu [*Fiji*] [*ICAO location identifier*] (ICLI)
NFNU .... Bua [*Fiji*] [*ICAO location identifier*] (ICLI)
NFNV .... Vatukoula [*Fiji*] [*ICAO location identifier*] (ICLI)
NFNW .... Wakaya [*Fiji*] [*ICAO location identifier*] (ICLI)
NFOF .... Fiji [*Fiji*] [*ICAO location identifier*] (ICLI)
NFOG........ Nordisk Forening for Obstetrik och Gynekologi [*Finland*] (EAIO)
NFP .... National Federation Party [*Fiji*] [*Political party*] (PPW)
NFP .... Nationalist Front for Progress [*Solomon Islands*] [*Political party*] (FEA)
NFP .... Network for Fitness Professionals [*Australia*]
NFP .... New Frontier Party [*Japan*] [*Political party*]
NFP .... Northern Frontier Province [*Kenya*]
NFP .... Nutrition Foundation of the Philippines (EAIO)
NFP .... Physical Training Manual (RU)
NFP .... Science Fiction and Adventures (RU)
NFPAI .... Natural Family Planning Association of India (EAIO)
NFPC........ Nuclear Free Philippines Coalition (EAIO)
NFPJO ...... Nederlandse Federatie Plattelands Jongeren Organisaties [*Netherlands*] (EAIO)
NFPNS ...... Natural Family Planning National Secretariat [*Australia*]
NFPP .... National Family Planning Program
NFPTE ...... National Federation of Posts' and Telegraphs' Employees [*India*]
NFPTTE.... National Federation of Post, Telephone, and Telegraph Employees [*Trade union*] [*India*] (FEA)
NFPW........ National Federation of Peasant Women (EAIO)
NFPW........ National Federation of Petroleum Workers [*India*]
NFR .... Naturvetenskapliga forskingsradet [*Swedish Natural Science Research Council*]
NFR .... Naturvetenskapliga Forskningsradet [*Swedish Natural Science Research Council*] [*Research center*] (IRC)
NFR .... Navigatia Fluviala Romana [*Romanian River Navigation Agency*] (RO)
NFR .... Nordisk Forening for Rehabilitering [*Nordic Association for Rehabilitation*] (EAIO)
N FR .... Northern French [*Language, etc.*] (ROG)
NFR-90...... NATO Frigate for the 1990s
NFRA .... National Furniture Removers' Association [*Australia*]
NFRA .... Netherlands Foundation for Radio Astronomy
NFRC........ National Fund Raising Counsel of Australia Proprietary Ltd. (ADA)
NFRCC..... Nordic Forest Research Cooperation Committee [*Finland*] (EAIO)
NFRI........ National Food Research Institute [*Council for Scientific and Industrial Research*] [*South Africa*] (AA)
NFRI......... New [*South Wales Fisheries*] - Fisheries Research Institute [*National Union Catalogue of Australia symbol*]
NFS........... National Forest System (GNE)
NFS........... National Physical Culture Union (BU)
NFS........... Naturfreunde Schweiz [*Switzerland*] (EAIO)
NFS........... Nordens Fackliga Samorganisation [*Nordic Trade Union Council*] [*Sweden*]
NFS........... Nordiska Forbundet for Statskunskap [*Nordic Political Science Association - NPSA*] [*Norway*] (EAIO)
NFS........... Norsk Fysisk Selskap [*Norway*] (SLS)
NFSA .... National Film and Sound Archive [*Australia*]
NFSA .... National Food Standards Agreement [*Australia*]
NFSE........ Nederlandse Federatie Scouting Europa [*Netherlands*] (EAIO)
NFSHSA ... National Federation of State High School Associations (OLYM)
NFSL........ National Front for the Salvation of Libya

NFSN .... NATO French-Speaking Nations
NFSR........ National Fund for Scientific Research [*Belgium*] (EAIO)
NFSRA ..... National Fitness Southern Recreation Association [*Australia*]
NFSS .... National Fund for Social Security [*Arabian*]
NFSU........ Suva/Nausori [*Fiji*] [*ICAO location identifier*] (ICLI)
NFT .... National Film Theatre of Australia (ADA)
NFT .... Nefteyugansk Aviation Division [*Russian Federation*] [*ICAO designator*] (FAAC)
NFT .... Nigeria Trust Fund (AF)
NFT .... Norsk Forsvarsteknologi [*Norway*]
NFTA .... National Film Theatre of Australia (ADA)
NFTA .... Netherlands Foreign Trade Agency
NFTE........ Eua [*Tonga*] [*ICAO location identifier*] (ICLI)
NFTF........ Tongatapu/Fua'Amotu International [*Tonga*] [*ICAO location identifier*] (ICLI)
NFTL........ Ha'Apai Lifuka [*Tonga*] [*ICAO location identifier*] (ICLI)
NFTN .... Nuku'Alofa [*Tonga*] [*ICAO location identifier*] (ICLI)
NFTO........ Niuafo'Ou [*Tonga*] [*ICAO location identifier*] (ICLI)
NFTP........ Niuatoputapu [*Tonga*] [*ICAO location identifier*] (ICLI)
NFTV........ Niederfrequenz Television [*German*] (ADPT)
NFTV........ Vava'u [*Tonga*] [*ICAO location identifier*] (ICLI)
NFU........... New Zealand National Film Unit
NFV .... Nordischer Friseurverband [*Nordic Association of Hairdressers*] [*Sweden*] (EAIO)
NFVE........ Nordvestjysk Folkcenter for Vedvarende Energi [*Denmark*] (EAIO)
NFVorstufe ... Niederfrequenz Vorstufe [*Low Frequency Input Stage*] (EG)
NFVP........ National Film and Video Productions [*Australia*]
NF:W .... Forestry Commission of New South Wales [*National Union Catalogue of Australia symbol*]
NFW .... Narodowy Front Wyzwolenia [*National Liberation Front*] [*South Vietnam*] (POL)
NFWA .... Neuromuscular Foundation of Western Australia
NFWIR...... National Federation of Women's Institutes of Rhodesia
NFWO .... Nationale Fonds voor Wetenschappelijke Onderzoeking [*Benelux*] (BAS)
NFWO/FNRS ... Nationaal Fonds voor Wetenschappelijk Onderzoek/Fonds National de la Recherche Scientifique [*National Fund for Scientific Research*] [*Research center*] [*Belgium*] (IRC)
NFWP........ Nutritional Field Working Party
NFWWP.... Narodowy Front Wyzwolenia Wietnamu Poludniowego [*South Vietnam National Liberation Front*] (POL)
NFZ .... Narodni Fronta Zen [*National Women's Front*] (CZ)
NFZ .... National Front of Zimbabwe (PPW)
NG .... De Nederlandse Gemeente [*Netherlands*] (BAS)
NG .... Dumpy Level (RU)
NG .... Inert Gas (RU)
NG .... Nachrichtengrosesse [*German*] (ADPT)
NG .... Naoruzanje s Nastavom Gadanja [*Armament with Target Practice (Subject in training)*] (YU)
NG .... Narodni Galerie [*National Gallery of Art*] (CZ)
NG .... Nase Gradevinarstvo [*Our Construction*] [*A periodical*] (YU)
NG .... Nastava Gadanja [*Target Practice*] (YU)
NG .... Natural Gutta-Percha (RU)
NG .... NAZI Government (BJA)
NG .... Neurological Hospital (RU)
NG .... New Generation [*An association*] [*Bangladesh*] (EAIO)
ng .... Nicht Gezaehlt [*Not Counted*] [*Publishing*] [*German*]
NG .... Nigeria [*ANSI two-letter standard code*] (CNC)
NG .... Normenausschuss Grundlagen der Normung im DIN [*Deutsches Institut fuer Normung*] eV (SLS)
ng .... Post Commander (BU)
NGA........... Nationale Gesellschaft fuer Foerderung der Industriellen Atomstechnik [*Switzerland*] [*Nuclear energy*] (NRCH)
NGA........... National Gallery of Australia
NGA........... National Governors' Association [*Japan*]
NGA........... New [*South Wales*] Gosford Art Collection [*National Union Catalogue of Australia symbol*]
NGA........... Nigeria [*ANSI three-letter standard code*] (CNC)
NGA........... WAAC (Nigeria) Ltd. Nigeria Airways [*ICAO designator*] (FAAC)
NGA........... Young [*Australia*] [*Airport symbol*] (OAG)
NGAB........ Abaiang [*Kiribati*] [*ICAO location identifier*] (ICLI)
NGAC........ National Greenhouse Advisory Committee [*Australia*]
NGAL........ New [*South Wales*] Gardiner Library Service [*John Hunter Hospital*] [*National Union Catalogue of Australia symbol*]
NGAR........ Garvan Institute of Medical Research [*National Union Catalogue of Australia symbol*]
NGAS .... Naval Gunfire Air Spotting
NGB........... German State Library (RU)
NGB........... National Governing Bodies (OLYM)
NGB........... Naturforschende Gesellschaft in Bern [*Switzerland*] (SLS)
NGB........... Nemzeti Gondozo Bizottsag [*National Welfare Committee*] (HU)
NGB........... Nigerian Grains Board

NGB.......... Nippon Gijutsu Boeki Co. Ltd. [*Japan*] [*Information service or system*] (IID)
NGBH .... Griffith Base Hospital [*National Union Catalogue of Australia symbol*]
NGBR .... Beru [*Kiribati*] [*ICAO location identifier*] (ICLI)
NGC.......... National Gas Company [*Trinidadian and Tobagan*] (GEA)
NGC.......... National Gas Corporation Ltd.
NGC.......... Natural Gas Co. [*Australia*]
NGC.......... Newcastle Gas Company Ltd. [*Australia*] (ADA)
NGC.......... Nordic Geodetic Commission (EA)
NGC.......... Stichting Nederlands Graan-Centrum Netherlands Grain Centre [*Netherlands*] (DSCA)
NGCC .... North German Coal Control [*Post-World War II*]
NGCDO..... North German Coal Distribution Organization [*Post-World War II*]
NGCI .... Navorsingsgroep vir Chemiese Ingenieurswese [*Council for Scientific and Industrial Research*] [*South Africa*] (AA)
NGCL .... Gosford City Library [*National Union Catalogue of Australia symbol*]
NGD &MTC ... National Guide Dog and Mobility Training Centre [*Australia*]
NGDH .... Central Coast Area Health Service [*National Union Catalogue of Australia symbol*]
NGDR....... Nederlands Genootschap voor Document Reproductie
NGE.......... National Grain Exchange [*Australia*]
NGE.......... N'Gaoundere [*Cameroon*] [*Airport symbol*] (OAG)
NGE.......... Nigerian Guild of Editors
NGEB .... Nemzetkozi Gazdasagi Egyuttmukodesi Bank [*International Bank for Economic Cooperation (CEMA)*] (HU)
NGEF .... New Government Electric Factory [*India*] (PDAA)
N-Germ...... Noord-Germaans [*North-Germanic*] [*Language, etc.*] [*Afrikaans*]
ngez .... Nicht Gezaehlt [*By the Lot*] [*German*]
NGF.......... National Guarantee Fund [*Australia*]
NGF.......... Norsk Geofysisk Forening [*Norway*] (SLS)
NGF.......... Norsk Geoteknisk Forening [*Norway*] (SLS)
NGF.......... Northern Group of Forces [*Commonwealth of Independent States*] (NATG)
NGFF........ Funafuti [*Tuvalu*] [*ICAO location identifier*] (ICLI)
NGFO .... Nanumea [*Tuvalu*] [*ICAO location identifier*] (ICLI)
NGFTB...... Nordic Group for Forest Tree Breeding [*Norway*] (EAIO)
NGFU .... Funafuti/International [*Tuvalu*] [*ICAO location identifier*] (ICLI)
NGG .... Naturforschende Gesellschaft des Kantons Glarus [*Switzerland*] (SLS)
NGH .... Nepgondozo Hivatal [*People's Welfare Office*] (HU)
NGHD .... Gutteridge Haskins and Davey Proprietary Limited (New South Wales) [*National Union Catalogue of Australia symbol*]
NGI........... Glen Innes Municipal Council Library [*National Union Catalogue of Australia symbol*]
NGI........... Natural Gas Industry [*Australia*]
NGI........... Nederlandse Genootschap voor Informatica [*Netherlands Society for Informatics*] [*Information service or system*] (IID)
NGI........... Ngau [*Fiji*] [*Airport symbol*] (OAG)
NGI........... Norges Geotekniske Institutt [*Norwegian Geotechnical Institute*] [*Research center*] (IRC)
NGI........... Normal Histone (RU)
NGI........... Norsk Gerontologisk Institutt [*Norwegian Institute of Gerontology*] [*Research center*] (IRC)
NGID........ Garden Island Dockyard (Sydney) [*National Union Catalogue of Australia symbol*]
NGID........ Norwegian Group of Industrial Designers (EAIO)
NGIMIP.... Novosibirsk State Institute of Measures and Measuring Instruments (RU)
NGK.......... Nederduits Gereformeerde Kerk [*Dutch Reformed Church*]
NGK.......... Neutron-Gamma-Ray Logging (RU)
NGK.......... New Greek [*Language, etc.*]
Ng-Kabel.... Netzgruppenkabel [*Regional Cable*] (EG)
NGKB .... Nemzetkozi Gazdasagi Kapcsolatok Bizottsaga [*Committee of International Economic Relations*] (HU)
NGKVTs.... Directive on Border Control of Foreign Currency Valuables (BU)
NGL.......... Australian Gas light Cmpany Technical Library [*National Union Catalogue of Australia symbol*]
NGL.......... Inhomogeneous Lorentz Group (RU)
NGL.......... Natural Gas Liquids (OMWE)
NGL.......... Naturforschende Gesellschaft Luzern [*Switzerland*] (SLS)
NGL.......... Nederlands Genootschap van Leraren [*Netherlands*] (SLS)
NGL.......... Nigerian Green Line
NGL.......... Nitroglycol (RU)
Ngl .... Nitroglyzerin [*Nitroglycerin*] [*German*] (GCA)
ngl .... Nogle [*Some*] [*Danish/Norwegian*]
NGL.......... Normal Gliadin (RU)
NGL.......... Normenausschuss Gleitlager im DIN [*Deutsches Institut fuer Normung*] eV (SLS)
NGLS........ Great Lakes Shire Library [*National Union Catalogue of Australia symbol*]
NGMA....... Maiana [*Kiribati*] [*ICAO location identifier*] (ICLI)

NGMA....... National Geoscience Mapping Accord [*Australia*]
NGMB....... Nigerian Groundnuts Marketing Board
NGMK....... Marakei [*Kiribati*] [*ICAO location identifier*] (ICLI)
NGMN....... Makin [*Kiribati*] [*ICAO location identifier*] (ICLI)
NGMR....... Nederlands Genootschap voor Microgafie en Reprografie [*Formerly, NGDR*]
ngn .... Nanohenry (RU)
NGN .... Nargana [*Panama*] [*Airport symbol*] (OAG)
NGNB....... Lower Downstream Water Level (RU)
NGNU....... Nikunau [*Kiribati*] [*ICAO location identifier*] (ICLI)
NGO .... Nagoya [*Japan*] [*Airport symbol*] (OAG)
NGO .... Norges Geografiske Oppmaling [*Geographical Survey of Norway*] (EAS)
NGO .... Nur Gewerkschaftliche Opposition [*Trade-Union-Only Opposition*] (EG)
NGO .... Origin of Grouped Operation [*Computers*] (RU)
NGOC....... Naval Gunfire Operations Center
NGOC....... North German Oil Control [*Post-World War II*]
NGOMAT ... Ngomi-Matengo Cooperative Marketing Union
NGON .... Onotoa [*Kiribati*] [*ICAO location identifier*] (ICLI)
NGOT .... Natural Gas Organisation of Thailand (PDAA)
NGOVSA .. Nasionale Genootskap van Onkologiese Verpleging van Suid-Afrika [*South Africa*] (AA)
NGP.......... Neue Grosse Partei [*New Great Party*] [*Germany*] [*Political party*] (PPW)
NGP.......... New Guinea Party (ADA)
NGPG .... National General Practitioners Group [*South Africa*] (AA)
NGPI .... Novosibirsk State Pedagogical Institute (RU)
NGPR .... Nederlands Genootschap voor Public Relations
NGR.......... Newbold General Refractories Ltd. [*Australia*] (ADA)
N GR........ New Greek [*Language, etc.*] (ROG)
NGR.......... Nigerum [*Papua New Guinea*] [*Airport symbol*] (OAG)
NGR.......... Nuevas Generaciones Revolucionarias [*New Revolutionary Generations*] [*Guatemala*] (LA)
NGRC....... National Government of the Republic of China
NGRE........ Grenfell and District Public Library [*National Union Catalogue of Australia symbol*]
NGRI .... National Geophysical Research Institute [*India*]
NGRI .... Petroleum Institute of Geological Exploration [*Moscow*] (RU)
NGRI .... State All-Union Scientific Research Institute of Geological Exploration [*Leningrad*] (RU)
NGS.......... Directive on Chief Bookkeepers (BU)
NGS.......... General Air Services Ltd. [*Nigeria*] [*ICAO designator*] (FAAC)
NGS.......... Great Synagogue - Rabbi L A Falk Memorial Library [*National Union Catalogue of Australia symbol*]
NGS.......... Nacelnik Generalniho Stabu [*Chief of the General Staff*] (CZ)
NGS.......... Nagasaki [*Japan*] [*Airport symbol*] (OAG)
NGS.......... Nihon Gakujutsu Shinko-kai [*Japan*] (EAIO)
NGS.......... Normenausschuss Graphische Symbole im DIN [*Deutsches Institut fuer Normung*] eV (SLS)
NGSEE...... Nea Geniki Synomospondia Ergatoypallilon Ellados [*New Greek General Confederation of Labor*] (GC)
NGSK .... Nederduitse Gereformeerde Sendingkerk
NGSLO ..... Naval Gunfire Support Liaison Officer
NGSPA...... Nastava Gadanja Srednjokalibarska Protivavionska [*Target Practice for Medium Caliber Antiaircraft Guns*] (YU)
NGSS........ Non-Government Schools' Secretariat [*South Australia*]
NGSSO...... Naval Gunfire Support Staff Officer
NGSZ .... Nemzetkozi Gazdalkodo Szervezet [*Internationally Operating Organization*] (HU)
ngt .... Nagot [*Somewhat*] [*Sweden*]
Ngt .... Negociant [*Merchant*] [*French*] (MTD)
NGTA........ Tarawa/Bonriki International [*Kiribati*] [*ICAO location identifier*] (ICLI)
NGTB .... Abemama [*Kiribati*] [*ICAO location identifier*] (ICLI)
NGTE .... Tabiteuea (North) [*Kiribati*] [*ICAO location identifier*] (ICLI)
NGTM....... Tamana [*Kiribati*] [*ICAO location identifier*] (ICLI)
NGTO....... Nonouti [*Kiribati*] [*ICAO location identifier*] (ICLI)
NGTR....... Arorae [*Kiribati*] [*ICAO location identifier*] (ICLI)
NGTs........ Nitroglycerine (RU)
NGTS .... Tabiteuea (South) [*Kiribati*] [*ICAO location identifier*] (ICLI)
NGTT .... Tarawa/Betio [*Kiribati*] [*ICAO location identifier*] (ICLI)
NGTU....... Butaritari [*Kiribati*] [*ICAO location identifier*] (ICLI)
NGU .... Nachalnik Glavnoyo Upravlenia [*Chief of Main Directorate*] [*Soviet military rank*]
NGU .... Nizhniy Novgorod State University (RU)
NGU .... Norges Geologiske Undersokelse [*Geological Survey of Norway*] [*Research center*] (IRC)
NGU .... Novosibirsk State University (RU)
N GUI .... New Guinea Territory (WDAA)
N Guin .... New Guinea
NGUK....... Aranuka [*Kiribati*] [*ICAO location identifier*] (ICLI)
NGUY........ Guyra Shire Council Library - L T Starr Memorial Library [*National Union Catalogue of Australia symbol*]
NGV.......... Nederlands Genootschap van Vertalers [*Netherlands Association of Translators*]

NGVF .... Granville College of TAFE (Technical and Further Education) - S E Barratt Librar [*National Union Catalogue of Australia symbol*]
NGvF .... Nederlands Genootschap voor Fysiotherapie [*Netherlands Association for Physical Therapy*] (SLS)
NGWIZAKO ... Ngwizani a Kongo
NGWO ...... Non-Government Welfare Organisation [*Australia*]
NGZ.......... Naturforschende Gesellschaft in Zuerich [*Switzerland*] (SLS)
NH .... Editions Nouveaux Horizons [*US government imprint*]
Nh .... Hydraulischer Wirkungsgrad [*Hydraulic Efficiency*] [*German*] (GCA)
NH .... Nobil Uomo Homo [*Member of a Noble Family*] [*Italian*]
NH .... Normalhoehenpunkt [*Normal High*] [*German*]
NH .... Normenausschuss Heiz-, Koch- und Waermegeraete im DIN [*Deutsches Institut fuer Normung*] eV (SLS)
NH .... Nowa Huta (Przedsiebiorstwo Panstwowe) [*Nowa Huta (State Enterprise)*] (POL)
NHA .... National Hearing Aids Proprietary Ltd. [*Australia*]
NHA .... National Housing Authority [*Kuwait*]
NHA .... National Housing Authority [*Jamaica*] (LA)
NHA .... Natural Health Australia [*Natural Health Society of Australia*]
NHA .... New Humanity Alliance (EA)
NHA .... University of Western Sydney - Hawkesbury [*National Union Catalogue of Australia symbol*]
NHAA .... National Herbalists Association of Australia (ADA)
NHAM ...... Hambro Australia Limited [*National Union Catalogue of Australia symbol*]
NHAN .... National Hospital Association of the Netherlands (EAIO)
NHAO .... Nicaraguan Humanitarian Assistance Office
NHAS........ Hastings Municipal Library [*National Union Catalogue of Australia symbol*]
NHB .... National Housing Bank [*Brazil*]
NHC .... National Hotels Corp. [*Ethiopia*]
NHC .... National Housing Corporation [*Tanzania*]
NHC .... Nederlands Helsinki Comite [*Netherlands Helsinki Committee*] (EAIO)
NHCC....... Nursing Home Consultative Committee
NHCN .... Southern Sydney Area Health Service - St George Health Management Library [*National Union Catalogue of Australia symbol*]
NHCN:A ... New South Wales - Department of Health - Division of Analytical Laboratories - S [*National Union Catalogue of Australia symbol*]
NHCP........ A C Hatrick Chemicals Proprietary Limited [*National Union Catalogue of Australia symbol*]
NHCW ...... New South Wales - Department of Health - Central Western Region - Regional Heal [*National Union Catalogue of Australia symbol*]
NHD .... Naval Hydrographic Depot [*Burmese*] (MSC)
Nhd .... Neuhochdeutsch [*Modern High German*] [*Language, etc.*]
NHD .... New Housing District [*Australia*]
NHD .... Nieu-Hoogduits [*New High German*] [*Language, etc.*] [*Afrikaans*]
NHDC .... National Hotels Development Corporation Ltd.
NHDW ...... Hunter Water Board [*National Union Catalogue of Australia symbol*]
NHF.......... Nemzeti Harci Front [*Militant National Front*] (HU)
NHF.......... New Halfa [*Sudan*] [*Airport symbol*] (OAG)
NHF........ Nordiska Handikappforbundet [*Nordic Association for the Handicapped - NAH*] (EAIO)
NHF.......... Nordisk Herpetologisk Forening [*Scandinavian Herpetological Society - SHS*] (EAIO)
NHF.......... Nordisk Hydrologisk Forening [*Nordic Association for Hydrology - NAH*] [*Denmark*] (EAIO)
NHF.......... Norges Handelstands Forbund [*Norway*] (EAIO)
NHF.......... Norske Havforskeres Forening [*Norway*] (SLS)
NHFA........ National Heart Foundation of Australia (ADA)
NHFP .... New Hebrides Federal Party [*Political party*] (PPW)
NHG .... Naturhistorische Gesellschaft Hannover (SLS)
NHG .... Naturhistorische Gesellschaft Nuernberg eV (SLS)
NHG .... Natuurhistorisch Genootschap in Limburg [*Netherlands*] (SLS)
NHG .... Nederlands Historisch Genootschap [*Netherlands*] (SLS)
NHG .... Nederlands Huisartsen Genootschap [*Netherlands*] (SLS)
NHH.......... Historic Houses Trust of New South Wales - Lyndhurst Resource Centre [*National Union Catalogue of Australia symbol*]
NHH.......... Nagy Honvedo Haboru [*Great Patriotic War (of the Union of Soviet Socialist Republics)*] (HU)
NHIA........ National Hardware Institute of Australia
NHILL ...... Hills Library and Information Service [*National Union Catalogue of Australia symbol*]
NHIS .... Health Information Services (New South Wales) [*National Union Catalogue of Australia symbol*]
NHK .... Narodohospodarska Komise [*Economic Commission*] (CZ)
NHK .... Nederduits Hervormde Kerk van Afrika [*Dutch Reformed Church of Africa*] [*Namibian, South African*] (AF)
NHK .... Nihon/Nippon Hoso Kyokai [*Japan Broadcasting Corporation*]
NHK .... Nippon Hoso Kyokai [*Japan Broadcasting Corp.*] (PDAA)

NHKA .... Hornsby Ku-ring-gai Area Health Service [*National Union Catalogue of Australia symbol*]
NHKS........ Hawkesbury City Council Library [*National Union Catalogue of Australia symbol*]
NHL.......... Nittetsu High Living [*Commercial firm*] [*Japan*]
NHL.......... Nordic Federation of Heart and Lung Associations (EA)
NHL.......... Norges Hydrodynamiske Laboratorier [*Norwegian Hydrodynamic Laboratories*] (EAS)
NHL.......... Norsk Hydroteknisk Laboratorium [*Norwegian Hydrotechnical Laboratory*] [*Foundation of Scientific and Industrial Research*] (ERC)
NHLF .... North Harbor Labor Federation [*Philippines*] (EY)
NHLFRP.... National Health Labour Force Research Program [*Australia*]
NHLMAC ... National High-Level Manpower Allocation Committee
NHLS .... Macquarie Bank Limited - Central Records and Information Department [*National Union Catalogue of Australia symbol*]
NHM .... Nationale Maatschappij voor de Huisvesting [*Benelux*] (BAS)
NHM .... Nederlandsche Handelmaatschappij [*Netherlands*] (BAS)
NHMH...... Harden Murrumburrah Historical Society [*National Union Catalogue of Australia symbol*]
NHMRC.... National Health and Medical Research Council [*Australia*] (EAIO)
NHNP .... New Hebrides National Party [*Political party*] (FEA)
NHO.......... Northern Hemisphere Observatory [*Canary Islands*] (PDAA)
NH of GK .. Nederduits Hervormde of Gereformeerde Kerk [*Member of Dutch Reformed Church*] [*Afrikaans*]
NHOL .... Holroyd City Council Library Service [*National Union Catalogue of Australia symbol*]
NHOM ...... Hornsby Shire Public Library [*National Union Catalogue of Australia symbol*]
NHOR ...... Horwath and Horwath [*National Union Catalogue of Australia symbol*]
NHP.......... National Hotels and Properties Ltd. [*Jamaica*] (LA)
NHP.......... National Humanitarian Party [*Political party*] [*Australia*]
NHPA........ Australian College of Health Service Executives - New South Wales Branch - Healt [*National Union Catalogue of Australia symbol*]
NHPC........ National Hydroelectric Power Corp. [*India*]
NHPHA .... Nursing Homes and Private Hospitals Association [*Australia*]
NHPLO..... NATO HAWK Production and Logistics Organization [*France*] (NATG)
NHPM....... Narodni Hnuti Pracujici Mladeze [*National Movement of the Working Youth*] (CZ)
NHQTC..... New [*South Wales*] Headquarters Training Command Library [*Department of Defence*] [*National Union Catalogue of Australia symbol*]
NHR .... Nederlandse Huishoudraad [*Netherlands*] (BAS)
NHR .... Normenausschuss Heiz- und Raumlufttechnik im DIN [*Deutsches Institut fuer Normung*] eV (SLS)
NHRA .... Norwegian Hotel and Restaurant Association (EAIO)
NHRC........ National Human Rights Congress [*Australia*]
NHRC........ National Hydraulic Research Center [*Philippines*] [*Research center*] (IRC)
NHRE........ Human Rights and Equal Opportunity Commission [*National Union Catalogue of Australia symbol*]
NHRF........ Norsk Hotell-og Restaurantforbund [*Norway*] (EAIO)
NHRFRL... Nihonkai Regional Fisheries Research Laboratory [*Japan*] (MSC)
NHRI........ Nanjing Hydraulic Research Institute [*China*] [*Research center*] (IRC)
NHRKH .... Nauchno-Issledovatel'skiy Institut Rybnogo Khozyaystva [*Scientific Research Institute of Fisheries*] (MSC)
NHRSS..... Newcastle & Hunter River Steam Ship Co. [*Australia*]
NHS.......... National Housing Strategy [*Australia*]
NHS.......... Natural Health Society of Australia
NHSA .... Natural Health Society of Australia
NHSA .... Naval Historical Society of Australia
NHSCP ..... National Household Survey Capability Program [*United Nations*]
NHSE........ Goulburn Health Service - Regional Resource Centre [*National Union Catalogue of Australia symbol*]
NHSH .... Hastings District Historical Society [*National Union Catalogue of Australia symbol*]
NHSM .... Natural History Society of Malta (SLS)
NHT .... National Housing Trust [*Jamaica*] (LA)
NHTAP...... National Health Technology Advisory Panel [*Australia*]
NHTP........ Nursing Home-Type Patient
NHUR .... Hurstville City Library and Information Service [*National Union Catalogue of Australia symbol*]
NHV .... Nuku Hiva [*French Polynesia*] [*Airport symbol*] (OAG)
NHVPA..... Newcastle and Hunter Valley Pharmacists' Association [*Australia*]
NHW .... Neighbourhood Watch [*Australia*]
NHW .... Normenausschuss Hauswirtschaft im DIN [*Deutsches Institut fuer Normung*] eV (SLS)

NHW .... Royal Hospital for Women - Gordon Bradley Lowe Library [*National Union Catalogue of Australia symbol*]
NHYDRO ... RAN (Royal Australian Navy) Hydrographic Office [*National Union Catalogue of Australia symbol*]
Nhz. .... Niederdruckdampfheizung [*Low Pressure Steam Heating System*] (EG)
NHZ .... Niwano Heiwa Zaidan [*Japan*] (EAIO)
Ni .... Indizierte Leistung [*Indicated Output*] [*German*] (GCA)
NI .... Initial Pulse (RU)
NI .... Nacelnik Inzinjerije [*Engineering Corps Chief*] (YU)
NI .... Native Infantry [*Indian Armed Forces regiment*]
NI .... Nautical Institute [*British*] (EAIO)
NI .... Ndermarrje Industriale [*Albanian*]
NI .... Nepmuvelesi Intezet [*Institute of Public Education*] (HU)
NI .... Netherlands Indies [*Later, Republic of Indonesia*]
NI .... New India [*An association*] (EAIO)
NI .... Nicaragua [*ANSI two-letter standard code*] (CNC)
Ni .... Niquel [*Nickel*] [*Chemical element*] [*Portuguese*]
NI .... Non-Aligned [*Political group*] [*EC*] (ECED)
NI .... Nonlinear Distortion (BU)
NI .... Nonmetallic Minerals (RU)
NI .... Nonmineral Deposits (BU)
NI .... Norfolk Island [*Australia*] (ADA)
NI .... Normenausschuss Informationsverarbeitungssysteme im DIN [*Deutsches Institut fuer Normung*] eV (SLS)
NI .... Norsk Immunsviktforening [*Norway*] (EAIO)
NI .... North Island [*New Zealand*] (BARN)
NI .... Notes d'Information [*French*]
Ni .... Numeri [*Numbers*] [*Italian*] (GPO)
ni .... Output Norm (BU)
NI .... Position and Homing Indicator (RU)
NI .... Science and Art Publishing House (BU)
NI .... Scientific Institute (RU)
NI .... Scientific Research (RU)
NIA .... Naczelna Izba Aptekarska [*Chief Pharmacy Chamber*] (POL)
NIA .... National Institute of Accountants [*Australia*]
NIA .... National Institute of Administration [*Indonesia*]
NIA .... National Irrigation Administration [*Philippines*] (IMH)
NIA .... Nigerian Institute of International Affairs
NIA .... Nordic Institute in Aland [*Finland*] (EAIO)
NIA .... Norfolk Island Airlines [*Australia*] [*ICAO designator*] (FAAC)
NIA .... Scientific Institute of Architecture (RU)
NIAA .... National Independent Agents' Association [*Australia*]
NIAA .... Nursery Industry Association of Australia
NIAA-DTF ... National Industry Associations Anti-Dumping Task Force [*Australia*]
NIAB .... Air Research Bureau [*ARB*] (RU)
NIAD .... National Institute of Alcohol and Drugs [*Netherlands*] (IRC)
NIAES .... National Institute of Agro-Environmental Sciences [*Research center*] [*Japan*] (IRC)
NIAFIZ ..... Physics Scientific Research Association (RU)
NIAGAS .... National Institute of Atmospheric, Geophysical, and Astronomical Sciences [*Philippines*] [*Research center*] (EAS)
NIAI .... Scientific Research Aviation Institute (RU)
NIAI .... Scientific Research Institute of Batteries (RU)
NIAKhIM ... Chemical Scientific Research Association (RU)
NIAKUP .... Scientific Research Association of the Coal and Shale Industry (RU)
NIAL .... Scientific Research Automobile Laboratory (RU)
NIAM .... Nederlandsch-Indische Aardolie Maatschappij (OMWE)
NIAM .... Netherlands Institute for Audiovisual Media (MCD)
NIAM .... Scientific Research Association of Marxists (RU)
NIAMASh ... Scientific Research Association of Machinery Manufacture and Metalworking (RU)
NIAMET ... Scientific Research Association of Ferrous Metallurgy (RU)
NI & C .... Nippon Information and Communication [*Joint venture of IBM Corp. Japan and Nippon Telegraph and Telephone*]
NIANKP .... Scientific Research Association for the Study of National and Colonial Problems (RU)
NIANSW ... Nursery Industry Association of New South Wales [*Australia*]
NIAP .... Artillery Scientific Test Range (RU)
NIAR .... National Institute of Amateur Radio [*India*] (PDAA)
NIAS .... Automatic Nonlinear Sampled-Data System (RU)
NIAS .... Engineer Aviation Service Manual (RU)
NIAS .... National Institute of Agricultural Sciences [*Research center*] [*Japan*] (IRC)
NIAS .... National Institute of Airworthiness Surveyors [*Australia*]
NIAS .... National Institute of Atmospheric Sciences [*Philippines*] [*Research center*] (IRC)
NIAS .... Netherlands Institute for Advanced Study in the Humanities and Social Sciences (IRC)
NIAS .... Nordisk Institut for Asienstudier [*Nordic Institute of Asian Studies*] [*Denmark*] (EAIO)
NIAST .... National Institute for Aeronautics and System Technology [*South Africa*] (PDAA)

NIAT .... Nursery Industry Association of Tasmania [*Australia*]
NIAT .... Scientific Institute of Automobile Transportation (RU)
NIAT .... Scientific Research Institute of Aviation Technology (RU)
NIATsVETMET ... Scientific Research Association of Nonferrous Metallurgy (RU)
NIAWA ..... Nursery Industry Association of Western Australia [*Australia*]
NIB .... National Insurance Board [*Jamaica*] (LA)
NIB .... National Investment Bank [*Egypt*] (IMH)
NIB .... National Investment Bank [*Ghana*] (EY)
NIB .... National Investment Board [*Gambia*] (GEA)
NIB .... National Irrigation Board [*Kenya*]
NIB .... Nigeria International Bank Ltd.
NIB .... Nordic Investment Bank (GNE)
NiB .... Nordiska Investeringsbanken [*Nordic Investment Bank*]
NIB .... Scientific Research Office (RU)
NIBA .... National Insurance Brokers Association [*Australia*]
NIBAA ..... National Insurance Brokers' Association of Australia
NIBC .... Northern Ireland Base Command [*World War II*]
NIBEM-TNO ... Nationaal Instituut voor Brouwgerst, Mout, en Bier - Nederlands Centrale Organisatie voor Toegepast-Natuurwetenschappelijk Onderzoek [*National Institute for Malting Barley, Malt, and Beer - Netherlands Central Organization for Applied Natural Scientific Research*] (ARC)
NIBGE .... National Institute of Biotechnology and Genetic Engineering [*Pakistan*]
NIBID .... National Investment Bank for Industrial Development [*Greece*]
NIBM .... IBM Australia [*National Union Catalogue of Australia symbol*]
NIBMAR ... No Independence before Majority African Rule [*British policy in regard to Rhodesia*]
NIBS .... Nippon Institute of Biological Sciences (DAVI)
NIBTN ...... Scientific Research Office of Technical Standards (RU)
NIBV .... Scientific Research Office of Interchangeability (RU)
NIC .... Nastavna Intendantska Ceta [*Quartermaster Training Company*] (YU)
NIC .... Natal Indian Congress
NIC .... National Industrialization Company [*Saudi Arabia*] (MENA)
NIC .... National Industries Company [*Kuwait*]
NIC .... National Informatics Center [*India*] [*Information service or system*]
NIC .... National Insurance Co. [*Bahrain*] (EY)
NIC .... National Insurance Corporation [*Uganda*] (AF)
NIC .... National Insurance Corporation of Tanzania Ltd.
NIC .... National Intelligence Committee [*Malaysia*] (ML)
NIC .... National Interim Council [*Sierra Leone*] (AF)
NIC .... National Investigations Committee [*Ghana*]
NIC .... National Investment Commission [*Libya*]
NIC .... National Investment Council [*Honiara, Solomon Islands*] (GEA)
NIC .... Nauru Island Council [*Australia*]
NIC .... Nederlandse Informatie Combinatie ['*s-Gravenhage*]
NIC .... Netherlands Information Combine [*Delft*] [*Information service or system*] (IID)
NIC .... New Initial Commissions [*Business term*]
NIC .... Newly Industrialized [*or Industrializing*] Country
NIC .... Newly Industrializing Country (ECON)
NIC .... Nicaragua [*ANSI three-letter standard code*] (CNC)
NIC .... Nordic Immigration Committee [*Sweden*] (EAIO)
NIC .... Nuclear Industry Consortium [*Also known as GPIN*] [*Belgium*]
NICA .... Nicaragua Interfaith Committee for Action (EA)
NICA .... Nicaraguense de Aviacion SA [*Nicaragua*] [*ICAO designator*] (FAAC)
NICAMAR ... Compania Nicaraguense Mercantil e Industrial de Ultramar SA [*Nicaragua*] (DSCA)
NICAN ...... National Information Communication Awareness Network [*Australia*]
NICATELSAT ... Nicaraguan Telecommunication by Satellite [*Commercial firm*]
NICC .... National Industrial Construction Company [*Qatar*]
NICD .... National Institute of Communicable Diseases [*India*]
NICD .... National Institute of Community Development [*India*] (DSCA)
NICDAP .... National Information Centre for Drugs and Pharmaceutics [*Central Drug Research Institute*] [*India*]
NICE .... Nomenclature des Industries Etablies dans les Communautes Europeennes (FLAF)
NICEC .... National Iranian Copper Industries Co. (EY)
NICHIRINKYO ... Nihon Ringyo Gijutsu Kyokai [*Japan*] (EAIO)
nichtwss ..... Nichtwaessrig [*Nonaqueous*] [*German*] (GCA)
NICI .... ICI Australia Limited (New South Wales) [*National Union Catalogue of Australia symbol*]
NICI .... National Investment Company of Iran (ME)
NICIC .... National Iranian Copper Industries Co. (PDAA)
NICLAI ..... National Information Centre for Leather and Allied Industries [*Central Leather Research Institute*] [*India*]
NICMAP ... National Information Centre for Machine Tools and Production Engineering [*Central Machine Tool Institute*] [*India*]

NICNAS.... National Industrial Chemicals Notification and Assessment Scheme [*Australia*]
NICNet...... National Information Centre Network [*India*]
NICOD...... Northern Ireland Council for Orthopaedic Development, Inc. (SLS)
NICOL ...... National Insurance Corp. of Liberia   (EY)
NICON..... National Insurance Corporation of Nigeria   (AF)
NICR .... National Institute for Coal Research [*Council for Scientific and Industrial Research*] [*South Africa*]   (AA)
NICRO ...... National Institute for Crime Prevention and Rehabilitation of Offenders [*South Africa*]
NICSO....... NATO Integrated Communications System Organization [*Brussels, Belgium*]   (NATG)
NICSS .... Northern Ireland Council of Social Service   (SLS)
NICTLAN ... Scientific Research Centre for Technological Lasers [*Former USSR*]   (IRC)
NID........... Institute of Dental Research (New South Wales) [*National Union Catalogue of Australia symbol*]
nid .... Nidottu(na) [*Finland*]
NiD .... Niepodleglosc i Demokracja [*Independence and Democracy*] [*Political movement*]   (POL)
NID........... Norske Indusridesignere [*Norway*]   (EAIO)
NID........... Northern Ireland District
NID........... Nouvelle Imprimerie Dionysienne
NIDA .... National Institute for Development Administration [*Bangkok, Thailand*]
NIDA .... National Investment and Development Authority [*Papua New Guinea*]   (GEA)
NIDB .... Nigerian Industrial Development Bank   (AF)
NIDC .... National Industrial Development Corp. [*India*]
NIDC .... National Investment and Development Corp. [*Philippines*] (DS)
NIDC .... Nepal Industrial Development Corporation   (GEA)
Nidco.......... National Industrial Development Corporation [*Jamaica*]   (GEA)
NIDCS....... National Industrial Development Corporation of Swaziland
NIDE .... Identic Books Proprietary Limited [*National Union Catalogue of Australia symbol*]
NIDER ...... Nederlands Instituut voor Documentatie en Registratuur [*The Netherlands Institute of Documentation and Filing*]
NIDER ...... Nederlands Instituut voor Informatie, Documentatie, en Registratuur [*The Netherlands Institute of Information, Documentation, and Filing*] [*NOBIN*] [*Later,*]
NIDF .... Norwegian Immune Deficiency Foundation   (EAIO)
NIDI .... Nederlands Interuniversitair Demografisch Instituut [*Netherlands Interuniversity Demographic Institute*]
NiDI.......... Nickel Development Institute   (EAIO)
NIDI .... Scientific Research Diesel Institute   (RU)
NIDLR...... Office of the Director of Law Reform, Northern Ireland   (DLA)
NIDO........ Nationaal Instituut voor Diergengeskundig Onderzoek [*National Institute of Veterinary Research*] [*Belgium*]   (ARC)
NIDOC...... National Information and Documentation Centre [*Egypt*]
NIDP .... National Industrial Development Plan [*1979*] [*Mexico*]   (IMH)
NIDR .... Netherlands Institute for Dairy Research   (DSCA)
NIE .... Natal Institute of Engineers [*South Africa*]   (AA)
NIE .... National Index of Ecosystems [*Australia*]
NIE .... Netherlands Institute of Ecology
NIE .... Nonlinear Integrating Element [*Computers*]   (RU)
NIEC .... National Import and Export Corporation Ltd. [*Zambia*]
NIEC .... Northern Ireland Economic Council   (GEA)
niedr........... Niedrig [*Low*] [*German*]   (GCA)
niedrigsd .... Niedrigsiedend [*Low-Boiling*] [*German*]   (GCA)
NIEE......... New Sources of Electric Power   (RU)
NIEEI .... Scientific Research Institute of Electric Carbon Components (RU)
NIEFT .... Scientific Research Institute of Experimental Physiology and Therapy   (RU)
NIEI.......... Scientific Research Institute of Economics   (RU)
NIEIR........ National Institute of Economic and Industry Research [*Australia*]
NIEIRP ..... Scientific Research and Experimental Institute of the Rubber Industry   (RU)
NIEL......... Scientific Research Laboratory of Electric Automation   (RU)
niem .... Niemiecki [*German*]   (POL)
NIEM .... Scientific Research Institute of Epidemiology and Microbiology (BU)
NIEMS...... National Industrial Energy Management Scheme [*Australia*]
NIEN .... Nosilevtikon Idryma Emborikou Navtikou [*Maritime Workers Nursing Home*]   (GC)
NIEO .... New International Economic Order
NIEOK ...... National Institute of Education for Overseas Koreans [*South Korea*]   (EAIO)
nieokr........ Nieokreslony [*Indefinite*] [*Poland*]
NIER .... National Institute for Educational Research [*Research center*] [*Japan*]   (IRC)
NIERA...... Scientific Research and Experimental Work on Containers   (BU)
NIES.......... National Institute for Environmental Studies [*Japan*]   (IRC)

NIETh .... Nosilevtikon Idryma Ergaton Thalassis [*Maritime Workers Nursing Home*] [*Greek*]   (GC)
NIEX .... Institut National des Industries Extractives [*National Institute of Mining Industries*] [*Research center*] [*Belgium*]   (IRC)
NIF .... National Investment Fund [*Poland*] [*Finance*]
NIF .... National Iranian Front [*Political party*]
NIF .... National Islamic Front [*Sudan*] [*Political party*]
NIF .... Nomura International Finance [*Japan*]
NIF .... Nordiska Institutet foer Fargforskning [*Scandinavian Paint and Printing Ink Research Institute*] [*Research center*]   (IRC)
NIF .... Nordiska Institutet for Folkdiktning [*Nordic Institute of Folklore*] [*Finland*]   (EAIO)
NIF .... Not in Ferguson [*Bibliography of Australia*]
NIF .... Scientific Research Branch   (RU)
NIFA........ Nuclear Institute for Food and Agriculture [*Pakistan*] [*Research center*]   (IRC)
NIFF .... Nordiska Ickekommersielles Fonogramproducenters Forening [*Nordic Association of Non-Commercial Phonogram Producers - NANPP*]   (EAIO)
NIFI.......... National Inland Fisheries Institute [*Thai*]   (ASF)
NIFI.......... Scientific Research Institute of Finance   (RU)
NIFI.......... Scientific Research Institute of Physics (at the Leningrad State University Imeni A. A. Zhdanov)   (RU)
NIFKhI...... Physicochemical Scientific Research Institute Imeni L. Ya. Karpov   (RU)
NIFOR...... Nigerian Institute for Oil Palm Research
NIFS.......... Norsk Interesse Forening for Stamme [*Norway*]   (EAIO)
NIFTA....... Nouvelle Industrie de Filature et Tissage Algerienne
NIFTH ...... National Institute of Folk and Traditional Heritage [*Pakistan*] (EAIO)
NIG........... Aero Contractors Company of Nigeria Ltd. [*ICAO designator*] (FAAC)
NIG........... National Institute of Genetics [*Japan*]   (ARC)
NIG........... Nikunau [*Kiribati*] [*Airport symbol*]   (OAG)
NIG........... Scientific Research Group   (RU)·
NIGALEX ... Nigerian Aluminium Extrusions and Anodising
NIGC .... National Institute for Grain Crops [*South Africa*] [*Research center*]   (IRC)
NIGC .... National Iranian Gas Company   (ME)
NIGELEC ... Societe Nigerienne d'Electricite [*Niger Electric Power Company*] (AF)
NIGERCEM ... Nigerian Cement Company
NIG-GECIBA ... Societe Nigerienne de Genie Civil et Batiment
NIGI .... Scientific Research Institute of Hydraulic Engineering   (RU)
NIGIM ...... Central Scientific Research Institute of Geology and Mineralogy (RU)
NIGMI ...... Scientific Research Hydrometeorological Institute   (RU)
NIGPIPES ... Nigeria Pipes Ltd.
NIGRI........ Scientific Research Institute of Geological Exploration   (RU)
NIGRI....... Scientific Research Institute of Ore Mining   (RU)
NIGRIS ..... Scientific Research Ore-Mining Institute of the Lead and Zinc Industry   (RU)
NIGRIZoloto ... Scientific Research Institute of Geological Exploration for Gold   (RU)
NIGROUP ... Nigeria Industrial Group Ltd.
niH .... Nicht im Handel [*Not for Sale*] [*German*]
NIHERST ... National Institute of Higher Education (Research, Science, and Technology) [*Spain*]
NIHJ .... National Institutes of Health, Japan
NIHORT ... National Horticultural Research Institute [*Nigeria*] [*Research center*]   (IRC)
NIHRD...... National Institute of Health Research and Development [*Indonesia*]
NIHURST ... National Institute of Higher Education [*Trinidadian and Tobagan*]   (LA)
NII .... Nasionale Instituut vir Informatika [*Council for Scientific and Industrial Research*] [*South Africa*]   (AA)
NII .... Natal Institute of Immunology [*South Africa*] [*Research center*] (IRC)
NII .... National Institute of Immunology [*India*]
NII .... Negara Islam Indonesia [*Islamic State of Indonesia*]   (IN)
NII .... Scientific Research Institute   (BU)
NII .... Scientific Research Institute of Toys   (RU)
NIIA .... Nigerian Institute of International Affairs   (AF)
NIIA .... Scientific Research Institute of Aerial Surveying   (RU)
NIIA .... Scientific Research Institute of Architecture   (RU)
NIIAG .... Scientific Research Institute of Obstetrics and Gynecology   (RU)
NIIAK....... Scientific Research Institute of Aeroclimatology   (RU)
NIIAlmaz... State Scientific Research Institute of Diamond Tools and Diamond Machining Operations   (RU)
NIIAntropologii ... Scientific Research Institute of Anthropology   (RU)
NIIAP .... Scientific Testing Institute of Aviation Instruments   (RU)
NIIAR....... Nauchno-Issledovatelskii Institut Atomynych Reaktorov [*Atomic Reactor Scientific Research Institute*] [*Commonwealth of Independent States*]   (PDAA)
NIIAsbest.. Scientific Research Institute of the Asbestos-Processing Industry (RU)

NIIasbestotsement ... State Scientific Research Institute for Asbestos, Mica, Asbestos Cement Products, and for the Planning of Construction of Mica Industry Establishments (RU)

NIIASBESTTsEMENT ... Scientific Research Institute for Asbestos, Mica, Asbestos Cement Products, and for the Planning of Construction of Mica Industry Establishments (RU)

NIIasbotsement ... Scientific Research Institute for Asbestos, Mica, Asbestos Cement Products, and for the Planning of Construction of Mica Industry Establishments (RU)

NIIAT........ State Scientific Research Institute of Automobile Transportation (RU)

NIIAvtomatika ... Scientific Research Institute for the Automation of Production Processes in the Chemical Industry and Nonferrous Metallurgy (RU)

NIIAvtomatprom ... Scientific Research Institute for the Automation of Production Processes in Industry (RU)

NIIAvtopribor ... Scientific Research and Experimental Institute of Automobile and Tractor Electrical Equipment, Carburetors, and Instruments (RU)

NIIAvtopriborov ... Scientific Research and Experimental Institute of Automobile Electrical Equipment, Carburetors, and Instruments (RU)

NIIavtoprom ... Scientific Research Institute of the Automobile Industry (RU)

NIIB.......... Scientific Research Botanical Institute (RU)

NIIBP .... Scientific Research Institute of the Ferment Industry (RU)

NIIBUMDREVMASh ... Scientific Research Institute for Paper and Woodworking Machinery (RU)

NIIBUMMASh ... Scientific Research Institute of Paper Machinery (RU)

NIIChASPROM ... Scientific Research Institute of the Watchmaking Industry (RU)

NIIChERMET ... Scientific Research Institute of Ferrous Metallurgy (RU)

NIID .... Scientific Research Institute of Defectology (of the Academy of Pedagogical Sciences, RSFSR) (RU)

NIIDI......... Scientific Research Institute of Children's Infections (RU)

NIIDREVMash ... Scientific Research Institute of Woodworking Machinery (RU)

NIIE........... Scientific Research Institute of Electrification (BU)

NIIEE .... Scientific Research Institute for Electrification and Electrical Industry (BU)

NIIEE .... Scientific Research Institute of Power Engineering and Electrification (RU)

NIIEG........ Scientific Research Institute of Epidemiology and Hygiene (RU)

NIIEG........ Scientific Research Institute of Experimental Hygiene (RU)

NIIEKhAiI ... Scientific Research Institute of Experimental Surgical Equipment and Instruments (RU)

NIIEM....... Scientific Research Institute of Epidemiology and Microbiology (BU)

NIIEMG.... Scientific Research Institute of Epidemiology, Microbiology, and Hygiene (RU)

NIIES .... Scientific Research Institute of Economics of Construction (RU)

NIIF.......... Scientific Research Institute of Pharmacology (BU)

NIIF.......... Scientific Research Institute of Pharmacy (BU)

NIIF.......... Scientific Research Institute of Physics (at the Moscow State University) (RU)

NIIF.......... Scientific Research Institute of Physiology (RU)

NIIFK .... Scientific Research Institute of Finance and Credit (BU)

NIIFVUKh ... Scientific Research Institute for Physical Education and School Hygiene (BU)

NIIG .... Scientific Research Institute of Engineering Geology (RU)

NIIG .... Scientific Research Institute of Geography (RU)

NIIG .... Scientific Research Institute of Hydraulic Engineering (RU)

NIIGA .... Scientific Research Institute of Arctic Geology (RU)

NIIGAIK ... Novosibirsk Institute of Engineers of Geodesy, Aerial Surveying, and Cartography (RU)

NIIGGS ..... Scientific Research Institute of Forests and Forestry Resources (BU)

NIIGiM ..... Scientific Research Institute of Hydraulic Engineering and Reclamation (RU)

NIIGKRE ... Scientific Research Institute of the State Committee of the Council of Ministers, USSR, for Radio Electronics (RU)

NIIGMP.... Scientific Research Institute of Hydrometeorological Instruments (RU)

NIIGorsel'stroy ... Scientific Research Institute of Urban and Rural Construction (RU)

NIIGP........ Scientific Research Institute of Forestry Industry (BU)

NIIGP........ Scientific Research Institute of Urban Construction and District Planning (RU)

NIIGR........ Scientific Research Institute of Geophysical Exploration Methods (RU)

NIIGrad..... Scientific Research Institute of Urban Construction (RU)

NIIGradostroitel'stva ... Scientific Research Institute of Urban Construction and District Planning (RU)

NIIGrazhdanstroy ... Scientific Research Institute of Civil Engineering Construction (RU)

NIIGS........ State Scientific Research Institute of the Hydrolysis and Sulfite Liquor Industry (RU)

NIIGVF ..... Scientific Research Institute of the Civil Air Fleet of the USSR (RU)

NIIIAM..... Scientific Research and Testing Institute of Aviation Medicine (RU)

NIIInformstroydorkommunmash ... Scientific Research Institute of Information on Construction, Road, and Municipal Machinery Manufacture (RU)

NIIInfortyazhmash ... Scientific Research Institute of Information on Heavy, Power Engineering, and Transportation Machinery Manufacture (RU)

NIIIOM..... Scientific Research Institute of Industrial Economics and Organization in Machine Building (BU)

NIIK .... Scientific Research Institute of Culture (RU)

NIIKE........ Scientific Research Institute of Culture and Economics (RU)

NIIKF .... Scientific Research Institute for Health Resorts and Physiotherapy (BU)

NIIKh .... Scientific Research Institute of Chemistry (at the Khar'kov State University Imeni A. M. Gor'kiy) (RU)

NIIKhIM... Scientific Research Institute of Hydraulic Engineering and Land Reclamation (BU)

NIIKhIMMASh ... All-Union Scientific Research and Design Institute of Chemical Machinery (RU)

NIIKhIMPolimer ... Scientific Research Institute of Chemicals for Polymer Materials (RU)

NIIKhK..... Scientific Research Institute of Haematology and Blood Transfusion (BU)

NIIKhM .... Scientific Research Institute of Hydrology and Meteorology (BU)

NIIKhP...... Scientific Research Institute for Chemical Production (BU)

NIIKhP...... Scientific Research Institute of the Art Industry (RU)

NIIKhV...... Scientific Research Institute of Art Education (RU)

NIIKKh..... Scientific Research Institute of Potato Growing (RU)

NIIKKOP .. Scientific Research Institute for the Leather, Rubber, and Shoe Industries (BU)

NIIKMA.... Scientific Research Institute for Problems of the Kursk Magnetic Anomaly (RU)

NIIKP........ Scientific Research Institute of the Cable Industry (RU)

NIIKP........ Scientific Research Institute of the Coal Industry (BU)

NIIKP........ Scientific Research Institute of the Starch and Syrup Industry (RU)

NIIKRP ..... Scientific Research Institute of the Coal and Ore Mining Industries (BU)

NIIKS .... Novocherkassk Institute of Municipal Construction Engineers (RU)

NIIKS .... Scientific Research Institute of Motion-Picture Theater Construction (RU)

NIIKZ........ Scientific Research Institute of Rabbit Breeding and Fur Farming (RU)

NIIL........... Scientific Research Laboratory (RU)

NIILaborpribor ... Scientific Research Institute of Laboratory Instruments and Automation (RU)

NIILITMASH ... State Scientific Research Institute of Foundry Machinery and Technology (RU)

NIILK .... Scientific Research Institute of the Varnish and Paint Industry (RU)

NIILKh...... Scientific Research Institute of Forestry (RU)

NIILP .... Scientific Research Institute of Laboratory Instruments (RU)

NIILP .... Scientific Research Institute of the Lumber Industry (RU)

NIILTEKMASh ... Scientific Research Institute of Light and Textile Machinery (RU)

NIILV .... Scientific Research Institute of Bast Fibers (RU)

NIIM .... Scientific Research Institute of Mathematics (RU)

NIIM .... Scientific Research Institute of Metallurgy (RU)

NIIMASh ... Scientific Research Institute of Machinery Manufacture and Metalworking (RU)

NIIMash.... Scientific Research Institute of Technical Information on Machinery Manufacture (RU)

NIIMekhaniki ... Scientific Research Institute of Mechanics (RU)

NIIMESS ... Scientific Research Institute for the Mechanization and Electrification of Agriculture (BU)

NIIMESTTOPPROM ... Scientific Research Institute of Local and Fuel Industries (of the Gosplan UkrSSR) (RU)

NIIMetallurgkhimstroy ... Scientific Research Institute for Construction in the Metallurgical and Chemical Industries (RU)

NIIMETIZ ... Scientific Research Institute of Metalware Industry (RU)

NIIMF .... Scientific Research Institute of Mechanics and Physics (RU)

NIIMKSBP ... Scientific Research Institute of the Ministry of Communal Economy, Public Works, and Roads (BU)

NIIMM ..... Scientific Research Institute of Mathematics and Mechanics (RU)

NIIMontazhspetsstroy ... Scientific Research Institute for Installation and Specialized Construction Work (RU)

NIIMosstroy ... Scientific Research Institute of the Glavmosstroy (RU)

NIIMostov ... Scientific Research Institute of Bridge Construction (RU)

NIIMP....... Scientific Research Institute of the Fur Industry (RU)

NIIMP...... Scientific Research Institute of the Meat Industry   (RU)
NIIMRP.... Scientific Research Institute of Mechanization in the Fish Industry   (RU)
NIIMRTP ... Scientific Research Institute of the Ministry of the Radiotechnical Industry   (RU)
NIIMSK.... Scientific Research Institute of Monomers for Synthetic Rubber   (RU)
NIINAvtsel'khozmash ... Scientific Research Institute of Information on Automobile, Tractor, and Agricultural Machinery Manufacture   (RU)
NIINEFTEKhIM ... Scientific Research Institute of Petrochemical Industries   (RU)
NIINP........ Scientific Research Institute of the Petroleum Industry   (RU)
NIINSM.... Scientific Research Institute of New Building Materials, Structure Finishing, and Fitting   (RU)
NIINStroymaterialov ... Scientific Research Institute of New Building Materials, Structure Finishing, and Fitting   (RU)
NIIO .... National Iranian Industries Organization   (EY)
NIIO .... Scientific Research Institute for Education   (BU)
NIIO .... Scientific Research Institute of Reindeer Breeding   (RU)
NIIOGAZ ... State Scientific Research Institute for Gas Purification in Industry and Sanitation   (RU)
NIIOKh ..... Scientific Research Institute of Vegetable Growing   (RU)
NIIOMD ... Scientific Research Institute for the Protection of Motherhood and Childhood   (BU)
NIIOMES ... Scientific Research Institute for the Organization, Mechanization, and Economics of Construction   (RU)
NIIOMS.... Scientific Research Institute for the Economics, Organization, and Mechanization of Construction   (BU)
NIIOMS.... Scientific Research Institute for the Organization and Mechanization of Construction   (RU)
NIIOMSP ... Scientific Research Institute for the Organization and Mechanization of Construction Industry   (RU)
NIIOMTP ... Scientific Research Institute for the Organization, Mechanization, and Technical Aids in Construction   (RU)
NIIOPiK.... Scientific Research Institute of Organic Intermediates and Dyestuffs   (RU)
NIIORKh .. Scientific Research Institute of Lake and River Fisheries   (RU)
NIIOsnovaniy ... Scientific Research Institute of Foundations and Underground Structures   (RU)
NIIOSP ..... Scientific Research Institute of Foundations and Underground Structures   (RU)
NIIOT .... Scientific Research Institute of Labor Safety   (BU)
NIIOT .... Scientific Research Institute of Technology and Organization of Production   (RU)
NIIOZ .... Scientific Research Institute of Public Buildings and Structures   (RU)
NIIP.......... Scientific Research Institute of Apiculture   (RU)
NIIP.......... Scientific Research Institute of Fruit Growing Imeni I. V. Michurin   (RU)
NIIP.......... Scientific Research Institute of Poultry Raising   (RU)
NIIP.......... Scientific Research Institute of Soil Science   (RU)
NIIPG........ Scientific Research Institute of Applied Graphics   (RU)
NIIPI .... Scientific Research Institute of Zoonotic Infections in Specific Geographic Areas   (RU)
NIIPiN....... Scientific Research Institute of Planning and Standards   (RU)
NIIPIT....... Scientific Research Institute of Printing and Publishing Technology   (RU)
NIIPK........ Scientific Research Institute of Consumers' Cooperatives   (RU)
NIIPKh...... Scientific Research Institute of Applied Chemistry   (RU)
NIIPM....... Scientific Research Institute of Plastics   (RU)
NIIPM....... Scientific Research Institute of Printing Machinery   (RU)
NIIPOLIGRAFMASH ... Scientific Research Institute of Printing Machinery   (RU)
NIIPP .... Scientific Research Institute for the Prevention of Pneumoconiosis   (RU)
NIIPP .... Scientific Research Institute of Polymerization Plastics   (RU)
NIIPPIES ... Scientific Research, Planning, and Design Institute for Power Projects Construction   (BU)
NIIPRODMASh ... Scientific Research Institute of Food Machinery   (RU)
NIIPS .... Scientific Research Institute of Industrial Buildings and Structures   (RU)
NIIPT .... Scientific Research Institute of Direct Current   (RU)
NIIPT .... Scientific Research Institute of Hoisting and Conveying Installations   (RU)
NIIPT .... Scientific Research Institute of Industrial Transportation   (RU)
NIIPTMASh ... Scientific Research, Planning, and Technological Institute of Machinery Manufacture   (RU)
NIIPZiK .... Scientific Research Institute of Fur Farming and Rabbit Breeding   (RU)
NIIPZK ..... Scientific Research Institute of Fur Farming and Rabbit Breeding   (RU)
NIIR.......... Into Information Resources Proprietary Limited [*National Union Catalogue of Australia symbol*]
NIIR.......... National Institute of Industrial Research
NIIR.......... Scientific Research Institute of Rubber and Latex Products   (RU)

NIIRKh...... Scientific Research Institute of Fisheries   (RU)
NIIRP........ Scientific Research Institute of the Rubber Industry   (RU)
NIIRT........ Scientific Research Institute of Radio Broadcasting and Television   (RU)
NIIS.......... Scientific Research Institute for Construction   (BU)
NIIS.......... Scientific Research Institute of Communications   (RU)
NIIS.......... Scientific Research Institute of Shipbuilding   (RU)
NIIS.......... Scientific Research Institute of Suggestology   (BU)
NIISantekhniki ... Scientific Research Institute of Sanitary Engineering   (RU)
NIISChETMASH ... Scientific Research Institute of Calculating Machines   (RU)
NIISChETMAShMMiP ... Scientific Research Institute of Calculating Machines of the Ministry of Machinery and Instruments   (RU)
NIISel'stroy ... Scientific Research Institute of Rural Construction   (RU)
NIISEM .... Scientific Testing Institute of Communications and Electromechanics of the RKKA   (RU)
NIISF .... Scientific Research Institute for Constructional Physics   (RU)
NIISh......... Scientific Research Institute of the Wool Industry   (RU)
NIIShP ...... Scientific Research Institute of the Garment Industry   (RU)
NIIShP ...... Scientific Research Institute of the Tire Industry   (RU)
NIIShP ...... Scientific Research Institute of the Wool Industry   (RU)
NIISI .... Scientific Research and Testing Sanitation Institute of the RKKA   (RU)
NIISK .... Scientific Research Institute of Structural Parts   (RU)
NIISKhOM ... Scientific Research Institute of Agricultural Machinery   (RU)
NIISM....... Scientific Research Institute of Building Materials   (RU)
NIISM....... Scientific Research Institute of Forensic Medicine   (RU)
NIISMI...... Scientific Research Institute of Building Materials and Products   (RU)
NIISO....... Scientific Research Institute of Aircraft Equipment   (RU)
NIISP .... Scientific Research Institute of the Construction Industry   (RU)
NIISS........ Scientific Research Institute of Rural Buildings and Structures   (RU)
NIISS........ Scientific Research Institute of Shipbuilding and Ship Standards   (RU)
NIISS........ Scientific Research Institute of Synthetic Alcohols and Organic Products   (RU)
NIIST .... Scientific Research Institute of Sanitary Engineering   (RU)
NIIST .... Scientific Research Institute of Sorption Technology   (RU)
NIIStrommash ... State Scientific Research Institute of Machinery for the Building Materials Industry   (RU)
NIISTROY ... Scientific Research Institute for Construction   (RU)
NIIStroykeramika ... State Scientific Research Institute of Building Ceramics   (RU)
NIISV .... Scientific Research Institute of Glass Fibers   (RU)
NIISZhIMS ... Scientific Research Institute of Synthetic Fat Substitutes and Detergents   (RU)
NIIT.......... Scientific Research Institute of Labor   (RU)
NIIT.......... Scientific Research Institute of Remote Control   (RU)
NIIT.......... Scientific Research Institute of Transportation   (RU)
NIIT.......... Scientific Research Tobacco Institute   (BU)
NIITA........ Scientific Research Institute of the History and Theory of Architecture   (RU)
NIITAVTOPROM ... Scientific Research Institute of the Technology of the Automobile Industry   (RU)
NIITEIR.... All-Union Scientific Research Institute of Technical and Economic Research and Information on Radio Electronics   (RU)
NIITEKhIM ... Scientific Research Institute of Technical and Economic Research of the State Committee of the Council of Ministers, USSR, for Chemistry   (RU)
NIITekhmash ... Scientific Research Institute of Machinery-Manufacturing Technology   (RU)
NIItelevideniya ... Scientific Research Institute of Television   (RU)
NIITEPLOPRIBOR ... Scientific Research Institute of Heat Power Engineering Equipment   (RU)
NIITI .... Scientific Research Institute of the Theory and History of Architecture and Construction Engineering   (RU)
NIITIC ...... Ningxia Islamic International Trust & Investment Corporation [*Middle East*]
NIITIG ...... Scientific Research Institute for Technological Research on Fuels   (BU)
NIITII........ Scientific Research Institute of the Theory and History of the Fine Arts   (RU)
NIITIM ..... Kuban' Scientific Research Institute for Testing Tractors and Agricultural Machinery   (RU)
NIITIP ...... Scientific Research Institute of the Theory and History of Pedagogy   (RU)
NIITKh...... Scientific Research Institute of Labor Hygiene   (BU)
NIITM....... Scientific Research Institute of Automobile, Tractor, and Agricultural Machinery-Manufacturing Technology   (RU)
NIITM....... Scientific Research Institute of Machinery-Manufacturing Technology   (RU)
NIITMASh ... Scientific Research, Planning, and Design Institute of Machinery-Manufacturing Technology   (RU)
NIITN........ Scientific Research Institute of Technical Standardization   (RU)

NIITO .... Scientific Research Institute of Traumatology and Orthopedics (RU)

NIITOP ..... Scientific Research Institute of Trade and Public Eating Facilities (RU)

NIITP .... Scientific Research Institute for the Knitwear Industry (BU)

NIITP .... Scientific Research Institute of Knit Goods Industry (RU)

NIITraktorosel'khozmash ... Scientific Research Institute of Tractor and Agricultural Machinery-Manufacturing Technology (RU)

NIITraktorsel'khozmash ... Scientific Research Institute of Tractor and Agricultural Machinery-Manufacturing Technology (RU)

NIItransneft' ... Scientific Research Institute for Transportation and Storage of Petroleum and Petroleum Products (RU)

NIITruda ... Scientific Research Institute of Labor (RU)

NIITs .... Scientific Research Institute of the Cement Industry (RU)

NIITS .... Scientific Research Institute of Urban and Rural Telephone Communications (RU)

NIITsEMENT ... State All-Union Scientific Research Institute of the Cement Industry (RU)

NIITsemmash ... Scientific Research Institute of Cement Machinery (RU)

NIItsvetmet ... Scientific Research Institute of Nonferrous Metals (RU)

NIITU .... Scientific Research Institute of Packing Materials and Packaging (RU)

NIITVCh ... Scientific Research Institute of High-Frequency Currents (RU)

NIITyaZhMASh ... Scientific Research, Design, and Technological Institute of Heavy Machinery Manufacture (RU)

NIIUgleobogashcheniye ... State Planning, Design, and Scientific Research Institute of Coal Enrichment and Briquetting (RU)

NIIUIF ...... Scientific Research Institute of Fertilizers, Insecticides, and Fungicides (RU)

NIIV .... Scientific Research Institute of Synthetic Fibers (RU)

NIIV .... Scientific Research Institute of Viscose (RU)

NIIVESPROM ... Scientific Research Institute of Scales and Instruments (RU)

NIIVKh...... Scientific Research Institute of Water Management (RU)

NIIVS .... Scientific Research Institute of Vaccines and Serums (RU)

NIIVT .... Novosibirsk Institute of Water Transportation Engineers (RU)

NIIVT .... Scientific Research Institute of Foreign Trade (BU)

NIIVT .... Scientific Research Institute of High Temperatures (RU)

NIIVVS ..... Scientific Research Institute of the Air Force (RU)

NIIYaF ...... Scientific Research Institute of Nuclear Physics (of the Moscow State University) (RU)

NIIYaLI..... Scientific Research Institute of Language, Literature, and History (RU)

NIIZ........... Scientific Research Institute of Grain and Grain Products (RU)

NIIZ........... Scientific Research Institute of Zoology (RU)

NIIZarubezhgeologiya ... Scientific Research Laboratory of Geology of Foreign Countries (RU)

NIIZh .... Scientific Research Institute of Animal Husbandry (BU)

NIIZh .... Scientific Research Institute of Housing (RU)

NIIZh .... Scientific Research Institute of Livestock Breeding (RU)

NIIZhB...... Scientific Research Institute of Concrete and Reinforced Concrete (RU)

NIIZhELEZOBETON ... Scientific Research Institute of Reinforced Concrete Products and Building and Nonmetallic Materials (RU)

NIIZhS...... Scientific Research Institute for the Industrialization of Housing Construction (RU)

NIIZhT...... Novosibirsk Institute of Railroad Transportation Engineers (RU)

NIIZhT...... Scientific Research Institute of Railroad Transportation (RU)

NIIZhV...... Scientific Research Institute of Livestock Breeding and Veterinary Science (RU)

NIIZK........ Scientific Research Institute of Fur Farming and Rabbit Breeding (RU)

NIIZK........ Scientific Research Institute of Truck Gardening (BU)

NIIZKh...... Scientific Research Institute of Grain Farming (RU)

NIIZM....... Scientific Research Institute of Terrestrial Magnetism (RU)

NIJ............ Nigerian Institute of Journalism

NIJS .... Nuklearni Institut [*Jozef Stafan Nuclear Institute*] [*Yugoslavian*]

NIJS .... Nuklearni Institut Jozef Stefan [*Jozef Stefan Nuclear Institute*] [*Former Yugoslavia*]

NIK........... Naczelna Izba Kontroli [*Chief Board of Supervision*] [*Poland*]

NIK........... Najwyzsza Izba Kontroli [*Supreme Chamber of Control*] (POL)

NIK........... National Executive Committee (BU)

NIK........... Nehezipari Kozpont [*Heavy Industry Center*] (HU)

nik .... Nickel [*Mining location*] [*Topography*] (RU)

NIK........... Norsk Interesseforening for Kortvokste [*Norway*] (EAIO)

NIK........... Science, Art, and Culture (BU)

NIKE .... Nitrokemia Ipartelepek [*Nitrochemical Industrial Plants*] (HU)

NIKE .... Nosilevtikon Idryma Klirikon Ellados [*Nursing Home for Greek Clergy*] (GC)

NIKEX....... NIKEX Nehezipari Kulkereskedelmi Vallalat [*NIKEX Foreign Trade Enterprise for Heavy Industry Products*] (HU)

NIKFI .... All-Union Scientific Research Institute of Motion Pictures and Photography (RU)

NIKhB .... Khristo Botev Scientific Institute (BU)

NIKHEF.... Nationaal Instituut voor Kernfysica en Hoge Energie Fysica [*National Institute for Nuclear Physics and High Energy Physics*] [*Netherlands*] (IRC)

NIKhFI...... Scientific Research Chemical and Pharmaceutical Institute (RU)

NIKhI .... National General Art Exhibit (BU)

NIKhI .... Scientific Research Chemical Institute (RU)

NIKhI .... Scientific Research Cotton Institute (RU)

NIKhIMP ... All-Russian Scientific Research Chemical Institute of Local Industry (RU)

NIKhPZ..... Scientific Research Institute for Hygiene and Occupational Diseases (BU)

NIKI .... Scientific Research Institute of Business Cycles (RU)

NIKIIMP .. Scientific Research and Design Institute for Testing Equipment, Instruments, and for Mass Measurement Devices (RU)

NIKIIMRP .. Nauchno-Issledovatel'skij Institut Mekhanizatsii Rybnoi Promyshlennosti [*Research Institute of Mechanization of the Fishing Industry*] (ASF)

NIKIMP.... Scientific Research and Design Institute for Testing Equipment, Instruments, and for Mass Measurement Devices (RU)

NIKKATSU ... Nippon Katsudo Shashin [*Japan Cinematograph Company*]

NIKKEI..... Nihon Keizai Shimbun, Inc. [*Tokyo, Japan*] (IID)

NIKKEIREN ... Nihon Kejeisha Dantai Renme [*Japan Federation of Employers' Associations*] (EY)

Nikkokyo... Nihon Kotogakko Kyoshokuin Kumiai [*Japan Senior High School Teachers' Union*]

NIKP......... Scientific Research Institute of the Leather Industry (RU)

NIKTI........ Scientific Research, Design, and Technological Institute (RU)

NIKVI....... Scientific Research Institute of Dermatology and Venereal Diseases (RU)

NIL .... National Instituut voor Landbouwkrediet [*Benelux*] (BAS)

NIL .... Ndermarrje Industriale Lokale [*Albanian*]

NIL .... Nederlands Instituut voor Lastechniek [*Netherlands Welding Institute*] (PDAA)

NIL .... Niederlassung Import und Lagerung [*Import and Storage Branch*] (EG)

NIL .... Scientific Research Laboratory (RU)

NILAT....... Scientific Research Laboratory of Automobile Transportation (RU)

NILCO ...... Nationaal Instituut voor de Landbouwstudie in Congo

NILD .... Scientific Research Laboratory of Engines (RU)

NILET....... Scientific Research Laboratory of Experimental Therapy (RU)

NILK........ Scientific Research Institute of Varnishes and Paints (RU)

NILN .... Navorsingsinstituut vir die Leerynwerheid

NILNEFTEGAZ ... Scientific Research Laboratory of Geological Criteria for the Evaluation of Prospects of Oil and Gas Occurence (RU)

NILOME ... Research Institute on the Organization and Economics of Machinebuilding and Electronics [*Bulgarian*] (SLS)

NILOS....... Scientific Research Forest Experimental Station (RU)

NILP......... Ndermarrje Industriale Lokale e Prodhimeve [*Albanian*]

NILS .... National Institute of Labour Studies [*Australia*]

NILS .... Newsletter of International Labour Studies [*Netherlands*]

NILSI .... Scientific Research Laboratory of Machine Tools and Tools (RU)

NILST .... Nasionale Instituut vir Lugvaartkunde en Stelseltegnologie [*Council for Scientific and Industrial Research*] [*South Africa*] (AA)

NILT......... Labor Standards Research Laboratory (RU)

NILTara .... Scientific Research Laboratory of Packing Materials (RU)

NILtekmash ... Scientific Research Institute of Light and Textile Machinery (RU)

NILU .... Norsk Institutt for Luftforskning [*Norwegian Institute for Atmospheric Research*] (PDAA)

NILUSDP ... Scientific Research Laboratory of Structural Parts (RU)

NILW .... Naukowy Instytut Lekarsko-Weterynaryjny [*Scientific Institute of Veterinary Medicine*] (POL)

NILZC....... National Iranian Lead and Zinc Co. (EY)

NIM.......... Nationale Investeringsmaatschappij [*National Investment Society*] [*Belgium*] (GEA)

NIM.......... National Institute of Metallurgy [*South Africa*]

NIM.......... Nehezipari Miniszterium/Miniszter [*Ministry/Minister of Heavy Industry*] (HU)

NIM.......... New Ivanovo Textile Mill (RU)

NIM.......... Niamey [*Niger*] [*Airport symbol*] (OAG)

NIM.......... Nigerian Institute of Management

nim .... Nimitetty [*Finland*]

nim .... Nimittain [*Namely*] [*Finland*] (GPO)

NIMAA ..... National Indigenous Media Association of Australia

NIMBAS ... The Netherlands Insitute for MBA Studies

NIMD........ National Institute of Management Development [*Egypt*]

NIMDOK... Nehezipari Ministerium Muszaki Dokumentacios es Fordito Iroda [*Ministry of Heavy Industry Bureau of Technical Documentation and Translation*] (HU)

NIME .... Nehezipari Muszaki Egyetem [*Technical University for Heavy Industry*] (HU)

NIMEC...... National Iranian Mining Explorations Co. (EY)

NIMESS ... Nauchno-Izsledovatelski Institut po Mehanizatsia i Elektrificatsia na Selskoto Stopanstvo [*Institute of Mechanization and Electrification of Agriculture*] [*Bulgaria*] (IRC)

NIMEX ..... Nomenclature for Imports and Exports [*European Community*] (PDAA)

NIMGE ..... Marine Geophysical Scientific Research Expedition (RU)

NIMI .... Novocherkassk Institute of Reclamation Engineering (RU)

NIMI .... Scientific Research Institute of the Dairy Trade and Industry (RU)

NIMIGUSZI ... Nehezipari Miniszterium Ipargazdsagi es Uzemszervezesi Intezet [*Ministry of Heavy Industry Institute of Industrial Economics and Systems Analysis*] (HU)

nimim .... Nimimerkki [*Finland*]

NIMIS ...... Scientific Research Machine-Testing Station (RU)

NIM Kvt .... Nehezipari Miniszterium Muszaki Konyvtara [*Technical Library of the Ministry of Heavy Industry*] (HU)

NIML .... National Independence Movement of Latvia [*Political party*]

NIMMI ..... Naval Medical Scientific Research Institute (RU)

NIMMSC ... National Iranian Mines and Metal Smelting Co. (EY)

NIMN .... Nasionale Instituut vir Materiaalnavorsing [*Council for Scientific and Industrial Research*] [*South Africa*] (AA)

NIMPGJ ... Ndermarrje Industriale e Mallrave te Perdorimit te Gjere [*Albanian*]

NIMR .... National Institute for Materials Research [*South Africa*] [*Research center*] (IRC)

NIMR .... National Institute for Medical Research

Nimro .... Suid-Afrikaanse Nasionale Instituut Insake Misdaadvoorkoming En Rehabilitasie van Oortreders [*South Africa*] (AA)

NIMS .... Permafrost Scientific Research Station (RU)

NIMSA ...... Nigerian Medical Students Association

NIMTS ...... Nosilevtikon Idryma Metokhikou Tameiou Stratou [*Army Pension Fund Nursing Home*] [*Greek*] (GC)

NIMTSM ... Nauxhonolzsledovatelsci Institut po Mechanizatziva, Tractorno i Selskostopansko [*Research Institute of Mechanization, Tractor and Agricultural Machinery Construction*] [*Bulgaria*] (PDAA)

NIMVR ..... Nicholas Institute of Medical and Veterinary Research [*Australia*] (DSCA)

NIN .... National Institute of Nutrition [*India*] (PDAA)

NIN .... Nedeljne Informativne Novine [*Publisher*] [*Serbia*] (EY)

NIN .... Nederlands Instituut voor Navigatie [*Netherlands Institute of Navigation*] (EAIO)

NIN .... Normenausschuss Instandhaltung im DIN [*Deutsches Institut fuer Normung*] eV [*Repair Standards in the German Institute for Standardization*] (SLS)

NIN .... Nueva Izquierda Nacional [*New National Left*] [*Spanish*] (WER)

NIND .... Industrial Court of New South Wales [*National Union Catalogue of Australia symbol*]

NINE .... Information Edge Proprietary Limited [*National Union Catalogue of Australia symbol*]

NINFC ...... Heritage Library Infantry Centre [*National Union Catalogue of Australia symbol*]

NINGBN ... Army Malaria Research Unit - Ingleburn medical Library [*National Union Catalogue of Australia symbol*]

NINGRI .... Petroleum Scientific Research Institute of Geological Exploration (RU)

NINKhI ..... Scientific Research Institute of Neurosurgery (RU)

NINT .... Australian International Development Assistance Bureau - Centre for Pacific Deve [*National Union Catalogue of Australia symbol*]

NINV .... Inverell Public Library [*National Union Catalogue of Australia symbol*]

NIO .... National Institute of Oceanography [*India*] [*Research center*] (IRC)

NIO .... National Institute of Oceanography [*British*] (IID)

NIO .... National Institute of Oceanology [*Indonesian*] [*Research center*] (IRC)

NIO .... Naucno Istrazivacke Organizacije [*Scientific Research Organizations*] (YU)

NIO .... Nieuwe Internationale Orde [*Netherlands*]

NIO .... Nioki [*Zaire*] [*Airport symbol*] (OAG)

NIO .... Northern Ireland Office

NIOB .... Navorsingsinstituut vir Onderwysbeplanning [*University of the Orange Free State*] [*South Africa*] (AA)

NIOC .... National Iranian Oil Company

NIOC .... National Iron Ore Company [*Liberia*] (AF)

NIOHS ...... National Institute of Occupational Health and Safety [*Australia*]

NIOK .... Nederlands Instituut voor Onderzoek in de Katalyse [*Netherlands Institute for Catalysis Research*]

NIOKh ...... Scientific Research Institute of Vegetable Growing (RU)

NIOKhIM ... Scientific Research Institute of Basic Chemistry (RU)

NIOKR ...... Scientific Research and Experimental Design Work (RU)

NIOM .... Nordisk Institutt foer Odontologisk Materialprovning [*Scandinavian Institute of Dental Materials*] [*Research center*] (IRC)

NIOMC ..... Nigerian Iron Ore Mining Co.

NIOMR ..... Nigerian Institute for Oceanography and Marine Research (ASF)

NIOMTPS ... Scientific Research Institute for the Organization, Mechanization, and Technical Aids in Construction (RU)

NIOPIK ..... Scientific Research Institute of Organic Intermediates and Dyestuffs (RU)

NIOPR ...... Nigerian Institute for Oil Palm Research (DSCA)

NIORKh .... State Scientific Research Institute of Lake and River Fisheries (RU)

NIOSH ...... National Institute of Occupational Safety and Health [*Egypt*] [*Research center*] (IRC)

NIOT .... Scientific Research Institute of Work Safety (RU)

NIOZ .... Nederlands Instituut voor Onderzoek der Zee [*Netherlands Institute for Maritime Research*] (WEN)

NIP .... Namibia Independence Party [*Political party*] (PPW)

NIP .... National Independence Party [*Namibia*] [*Political party*] (PPW)

NIP .... National Information Policy [*Australia*]

NIP .... National Institute for Productivity

NIP .... National Integration Party [*Liberia*] [*Political party*] (EY)

NIP .... Ndermarrje Industriale e Prodhimeve [*Albanian*]

NIP .... New Industrial Policy [*Bangladesh*] (FEA)

NIP .... Novinarsko Izdavacko Poduzece [*Journalistic Publishing Establishment*] [*Zagreb*] (YU)

NIPA .... National Institute of Public Administration [*Pakistan*] [*Research center*] (IRC)

NIPA .... Nordens Institut pa Aland [*Nordic Institute in Aland - NIA*] [*Finland*] (EAIO)

NIP & TB .. Northern Ireland Postal and Telecommunications Board (DCTA)

NIPC .... Nagasaki Institute for Peace Culture [*Nagasaki Institute of Applied Sciences*] [*Japan*]

NIPC .... Nigerian Investment Property Company

NIPCO ...... Nile Petroleum Company [*Egypt*] (ME)

NI-pd .... Nacelnik Inzinjerije Pesadiske Divizije [*Chief Engineer of an Infantry Division*] (YU)

NIPF .... Northern Ireland Polio Fellowship (SLS)

NIPG .... Nederlands Instituut voor Praeventieve Gneeskunde [*Netherlands Institute for Preventive Medicine*] (PDAA)

NIPH .... National Institute of Public Health [*Norway*] (IRC)

NIPI .... Scientific Research Institute of Food Flavoring Industry (RU)

NIPIA .... Scientific Research Institute for Automation (BU)

NIPIGORMASh ... Scientific Research, Planning, and Design Institute of Mining and Concentrating Machinery (RU)

NIPINeftekhimavtomat ... Scientific Research and Planning Institute for Complex Automation of Production Processes in the Petroleum and Chemical Industries (RU)

NIPKEK .... Scientific Research Institute for Planning and Designing Electronic Calculators (BU)

NIPKIK ..... Scientific Research Planning and Design Institute for Shipbuilding (BU)

NIPKIMMI ... Scientific Research Planning and Design Institute for Metal Cutting Machines and Instruments (BU)

NIPKIRE... Scientific Research Planning and Design Institute for Radio Electronics (BU)

NIPM .... Ndermarrje Industriale e Prodhimeve Metalike [*Albanian*]

Nip M .... Nehezipari Miniszter [*Minister of Heavy Industry*] (HU)

NIPMPGJ ... Ndermarrje Industriale e Prodhimit te Mallrave te Perdorimit te Gjere [*Albanian*]

NIPN .... Nasionale Instituut vir Personeelnavorsing [*National Institute for Personnel Research*] [*Human Sciences Research Council*] [*South Africa*] (AA)

NIPO .... Netherlands Institute for Public Opinion (WEN)

NIPORT.... National Institute of Population Research and Training [*Bangladesh*] (IRC)

NIPOST .... Nigerian Postal Services

NI-pp .... Nacelnik Inzinjerije Pesadiskog Puka [*Chief Engineer of an Infantry Regiment*] (YU)

NIPP .... Scientific Institute of Neuropsychiatry and Mental Hygiene (RU)

NIPPA ...... Neonatal Intensive Care and Preterm Parents' Association

NIPPAN.... Nippon Shuppan Hanbai Inc. [*Japan*]

NIPPIES ... Scientific Research Planning and Design Institute for Power Systems (BU)

NIPPM ...... Nauchno Issledovatel'skiy Institut Polimerizationnykh Plasticheskikh Mass [*Polymerization Plastics Scientific Research Institute*] [*Former USSR*] (PDAA)

Nipporo...... Nihonhoso Rodokumiai [*Japan Broadcasting Workers' Union*]

NIPR........ National Institute for Personnel Research

NIPR........ National Institute of Polar Research [*Japan*] (MSC)

NIPROC.... Nigeria Industrial and Produce Company

NIPRORUDA ... Scientific Research Planning and Design Institute for Ore Mining and Concentration (BU)

NIPSSET .. Nigerian Institute of Plant Science and Solar Energy/Technology (IRC)

NIPT.......... New Information Processing Technology Project [*Japan*] (ECON)

NIQ........... Ndermarrje Industriale e Qumeshtit [*Albanian*]
NIR............ National Institute for Development Research and Documentation [*Botswana*] [*Research center*]   (IRC)
NiR............. Norms and Wages, Standards and Costs   (RU)
NIR............ Norskair [*Norway*] [*ICAO designator*]   (FAAC)
NIR............ Scientific Research and Development   (BU)
NIR............ Scientific Research Work   (RU)
NIRA........ National Institute for Research Advancement [*Research center*] [*Japan*]   (IRC)
NIRA........ Nucleare Italiana Reattori Avanzati [*Italian Nuclear Company for Advanced Reactors*]   (WER)
NIRC........ National Information Resources Centre [*Telecom Australia*]
NIRCSA .... National Institute for Research in Computer Science and Automation [*France*]   (EAIO)
NIRD........ National Institute of Rural Development [*India*] [*Research center*]   (IRC)
NIRD........ Scientific and Development Work   (BU)
NIRFI........ Scientific Research Institute of Radiophysics (at the Gor'kiy State University Imeni N. I. Lobachevskiy)   (RU)
NIRIA....... Nederlandse Ingenieursvereniging "NIRIA"
NIRIM....... National Institute for Research in Inorganic Materials [*Japan*]
NIRMMI... All-Union Scientific Research Institute of Vegetable Oils and Margarine   (RU)
NIRO........ Scientific Research Institute of Sea Fisheries and Oceanography   (RU)
NIROWI ... Nigerian-Rumanian Wood Industries
NIRP......... Scientific Research Institute of the Rubber Industry   (RU)
NIRR .... National Institute for Road Research
NIRS......... National Institute for Radiological Science [*Japan*]
NIRS......... National Irrigation Research Station [*Zambia*]   (ARC)
NIRSO....... Research Institute of Fisheries and Oceanography [*Bulgarian*]   (ASF)
NIRT .... National Iranian Radio and Television   (ME)
NIRTV...... National Iranian Radio and Television
NIS .... Chief of Engineer Service   (RU)
NiS............. Lookout and Communications [*Navy*]   (RU)
NIS .... Nacelnik Intendancni Sluzby [*Chief of Quartermaster Service*]   (CZ)
NIS .... Nagoya International School [*Japan*]
NIS .... National Institute for Standards [*Academy of Scientific Research and Technology*] [*Egypt*]
NIS .... National Insurance Scheme [*Jamaica*]   (LA)
NIS .... National Insurance Scheme [*Guyana*]   (LA)
NIS .... National Intelligence Service [*Bureau for State Security and Department of National Security*] [*South Africa*]
NIS .... Nepal Institute of Standards
NIS .... Newly-Independent States [*Of former Soviet Union*]
NIS .... Nicaraguense de Aviacion SA [*Nicaragua*] [*ICAO designator*]   (FAAC)
Nis.............. Nisis [*Islet(s)*] [*Greek*]   (NAU)
NIS .... Nordiska Ingenjoerssamfundet [*Scandinavian Society of Engineers*]
NIS .... Scientific Research Council   (BU)
NIS .... Scientific Research Department   (RU)
NIS .... Scientific Research Sector   (BU)
NIS .... Scientific Research Ship   (RU)
NIS .... Scientific Research Station   (RU)
NIS .... Standards Research Station   (RU)
NISC.......... Australian Institute of Steel Construction [*National Union Catalogue of Australia symbol*]
NISC......... National Iranian Steel Co.   (EY)
NISCO....... National Iranian Steel Company   (ME)
NISER .... Nigerian Institute for Social and Economic Research
NISH .... Ndermarrje Industriale Shtetore [*Albanian*]
NISHMN .. Ndermarrje Industriale Shtetore e Materialeve te Ndertimit [*Albanian*]
NISHMPGJ ... Ndermarrje Industriale Shtetore e Mallrave te Perdorimit te Gjere [*Albanian*]
NISHR(R)G ... Ndermarrje Industriale Shtetore Rroba te Gatshme [*Albanian*]
NISI........... National Institute of Sciences of India   (DSCA)
NISI........... Scientific Research Institute for Construction   (BU)
NISIC .... National Iranian Steel Industries Company   (ME)
NISIR .... National Institute for Scientific and Industrial Research [*Malaysia*]   (ML)
NISJOUR ... Nigerian School of Journalism
NISK......... Norsk Institutt foer Skogforskning [*Norwegian Forest Research Institute*] [*Research center*]   (IRC)
NISKhI...... Scientific Research Institute for Sanitation and Public Hygiene   (BU)
NISKhOZ ... Scientific Research Institute for Sanitation, Hygiene, and Organization of Public Health   (BU)
NISL......... National Indoor Soccer League [*Australia*]
NISM .... Lewisham Sports Medicine Clinic [*National Union Catalogue of Australia symbol*]
NISN .... Nasionale Instituut vir Steenkoolnavorsing [*Council for Scientific and Industrial Research*] [*South Africa*]   (AA)

NISO .... Lookout and Communications Service Section [*Navy*]   (RU)
NISO .... Scientific Institute of Aircraft Equipment   (RU)
NISP......... Lookout and Communications Service Station [*Navy*]   (RU)
NISPP .... Lookout and Communications Service Mobile Station [*Navy*]   (RU)
NISR......... Lookout and Communications Service Area [*Navy*]   (RU)
NISS .... Scientific Research Institute of Shipbuilding   (RU)
NISSAT..... National Information System for Science and Technology [*India*]   (PDAA)
NISSP....... National Integral Sample Survey Programme
NISSS........ National Information System for Social Sciences [*India*]   (PDAA)
NIST......... National Institute of Science and Technology [*Philippines*] [*Research center*]
NIST......... National Institute of Silicon Technology [*Pakistan*] [*Research center*]   (WED)
NISTADS ... National Institute of Science, Technology, and Development Studies [*India*] [*Research center*]   (IRC)
NISTEP..... National Institute of Science and Technology Policy [*Japan*]
NISTI .... North Institute for Scientific and Technical Information [*China*]   (IRC)
NISU .... National Injury Surveillance Unit [*Australia*]
NIT .... Notice d'Information Technique [*French*]   (ADPT)
NIT .... Numero de Identificacion Tributaria [*Tax Identification Number*] [*Colorado*]   (LA)
NITB......... Northern Ireland Tourist Board   (DCTA)
NITC......... National Information Technology Council [*Australia*]
NITC .... National Iranian Tanker Co.
NITECO.... Nigerian Technical Company Ltd.
NITEKhIM ... Scientific Research Institute of Technical and Economic Research of the State Committee of the Council of Ministers, USSR, for Chemistry   (RU)
NITEL....... Nigeria Telecommunications Ltd.
NITEX....... Societe Nigerienne des Textiles
NITGEO ... Scientific Research Institute of Heat and Water Power Engineering Equipment   (RU)
NITI.......... Scientific Research Institute for Textiles   (BU)
NITI.......... Scientific Research Technological Institute   (BU)
NITIE........ National Institute for Training in Industrial Engineering [*India*]   (PDAA)
NITIVPP... Scientific Research Technological Institute for the Wine Making and Brewing Industry   (BU)
NITKhI...... Scientific Research Institute of Chemical Technology   (RU)
NITKhIB ... Scientific Research Institute of Chemical Technology for Personal Services   (RU)
NITN .... Nasionale Instituut vir Telekommunikasienavorsing [*Council for Scientific and Industrial Research*] [*South Africa*]   (AA)
NITO .... Scientific, Engineering, and Technical Society   (RU)
NITOBUM ... Scientific, Engineering, and Technical Society of Paper Industry Workers   (RU)
NITOLES ... Scientific, Engineering, and Technical Society of the Lumber Industry   (RU)
NITOLesprom ... Scientific Technical Society of the Lumber Industry   (RU)
NITOLIT .. Scientific, Engineering, and Technical Society of Foundry Workers   (RU)
NITOM ..... Scientific, Engineering, and Technical Society of General Metallurgy   (RU)
NITON...... Scientific, Engineering, and Technical Society of Petroleum Workers   (RU)
NITP......... Nordic Institute for Theoretical Physics [*Denmark*]   (EAIO)
NITR .... National Institute for Telecommunications Research [*South Africa*]
NITR .... Nigerian Institute of Trypanosomiasis Research
NITRA...... Niger-Transit
NITROFERTIL ... Fertilizantes Nitrogenados do Nordeste SA [*Brazil*]
NITROVEN ... La Venezolana de Nitrogenos, SA [*Venezuelan Nitrogen Company, Inc.*]   (LA)
Nitroz......... Nitrozellulose [*Nitrocellulose*] [*German*]   (GCA)
NITRR...... National Institute for Transport and Road Research [*Council for Scientific and Industrial Research*] [*South Africa*]
NITsMP... Scientific Research Center for Machine Translation   (RU)
NiTU......... Norms and Technical Specifications   (RU)
NIU........... Niue [*ANSI three-letter standard code*]   (CNC)
NIU........... Scientific Institute for Fertilizers   (RU)
NIUE .... Alofi/Niue International [*Niue Island*] [*ICAO location identifier*]   (ICLI)
NIUGUGMS ... Nauchnyi Institut po Udobreniyam Glavnog Upravleniya Gidrometeorologicheskoi Sluzhby SSSR [*Scientific Institute for Fertilizers of the Main Administration of the Hydrometeorological Service ofthe Hydrometeorological Service of the USSR*] [*Former USSR*]   (DSCA)
NIUI .... Scientific Research Institute of Coal   (RU)
NIUIF....... Scientific Research Institute of Fertilizers, Insecticides, and Fungicides Imeni Ya. V. Samoylov   (RU)
NIURI .... National Interuniversity Research Institutes [*Japan*]
NIV........... Commander of Engineer Troops   (RU)

NIV .... Nederlands Indische Vakverbond [*Federation of Dutch Workers*] [*Indonesian*]
Niv .... Niveau [*Level*] [*German*]   (GCA)
Niv .... Nivose [*Fourth month of the "Calendrier Republicain", from December 21 to January 19*]   (FLAF)
NIvA .... Nederlands Instituut van Accountants [*Netherlands*]   (BAS)
NIVA .... Norsk Institutt foer Vannforskning [*Norwegian Institute for Water Research*] [*Research center*]   (IRC)
Nivages ...... Niva Hydroelectric Power Plant   (RU)
NIVB .... Navorsingsinstituut vir die Visserybedryf
NIVE .... Nederlands Instituut voor Efficiency [*Nederlandse Vereniging voor Management*] [*'s-Gravenhage*] [*Later,*]
NIVFO ...... Institut Norvegien de Recherche et d'Information Scientifiques [*Norwegian Institute of Scientific Research and Enlightenment*]   (EAIO)
NIVI .... Scientific Research Vacuum Institute   (RU)
NIVI .... Veterinary Scientific Research Institute   (RU)
NIVK .... Scientific Research Institute of Naval Shipbuilding   (RU)
NIVKhKI... Scientific Research Institute of Veterinary Hygiene and Control   (BU)
NIVMI...... Army Medical Scientific Institute   (BU)
NIVN .... Nasionale Voedselnavorsingsinstituut [*Council for Scientific and Industrial Research*] [*South Africa*]   (AA)
NIVNO ...... Nasionale Instituut vir Vuurpylnavorsingen-ontwikkeling [*South Africa*]
NIVOS...... Veterinary Scientific Research Experimental Station   (RU)
NIVOT ...... National Research Institute of Vegetables, Ornamental Plants, and Tea [*Research center*] [*Japan*]   (IRC)
NIVPN ...... Nasionale Instituut vir Vervoer- en Padnavorsing [*Council for Scientific and Industrial Research*] [*South Africa*]   (AA)
NIVR .... Nederlands Instituut voor Vliegtuigontwikkeling en Ruimtevaart [*Netherlands Institute for Aviation Research and Space Travel*]   (WEN)
NIVRA ...... Nederlands Instituut van Registeraccountants [*Dutch Institute of Accountants*]
NIVS......... Veterinary Scientific Research Station   (RU)
NIVTE....... Scientific Research Institute for Medical Determination of Disability   (RU)
NIVTEK .... Scientific Research Institute for Medical Determination of Disability   (RU)
NIVV .... Institute for Studies on Peace and Security [*Netherlands*]   (WEN)
NIWARS... Netherlands Interdepartmental Working Group on the Application of Remote Sensing
NIWIL....... Nigerian Wire Industries Limited
NIWN........ Nasionale Instituut vir Waternavorsing [*National Institute for Water Research*] [*Council for Scientific and Industrial Research*] [*South Africa*]   (AA)
NIWO........ (Stichting) Nederlandsche Internationale Wegvervoer Organisatie [*Netherlands*]   (BAS)
NIWR .... National Institute for Water Research [*Council for Scientific and Industrial Research*] [*South Africa*]
NIWTA ..... Northern Ireland Women Teacher's Association   (SLS)
NIX .... Nioro [*Mali*] [*Airport symbol*]   (OAG)
NIYaZ .... Scientific Research Institute of Linguistics   (RU)
NIZ .... Nacelnik Intendancniho Zasobovani [*Chief of Quartermaster Service*]   (CZ)
Niz.............. Nizina [*Plain*] [*Poland*]
NIZENP.... Antiaircraft Artillery Scientific Test Range   (RU)
Nizh .... Lower [*Toponymy*]   (RU)
NiZh .... Science and Life   (RU)
Nizhnevolgonneftegeofizika ... Administration of Geo-Physical Exploration of the Lower Volga Region   (RU)
NIZI.......... Scientific Research Institute of Zoology   (BU)
NIZISNP... Zonal Scientific Research Institute of Horticulture of the Non-Black Earth Belt   (RU)
nizm............ Lowland [*Topography*]   (RU)
NIZMIR.... Scientific Research Institute of Terrestrial Magnetism, the Ionosphere, and Radio Wave Propagation   (RU)
NIZO .... Nederlands Instituut voor Zuivelonderzoek [*Netherlands Institute for Dairy Research*]   (IRC)
nJ .... Naechsten Jahres [*or Naechstes Jahr*] [*Of Next Year or Next Year*] [*German*]   (EG)
NJ .... Namakwaland Lugdiens Bpk [*South Africa*] [*ICAO designator*]   (ICDA)
NJ .... Nas Jezik [*Our Language*] [*Belgrade A periodical*]   (YU)
NJ .... Neues Jahrbuch [*New Yearbook*] [*German*]   (GCA)
NJ .... New Japan Aircraft Maintenance Co. Ltd. [*Japan*] [*ICAO aircraft manufacturer identifier*]   (ICAO)
NJA .... Nepal Journalists Association   (EAIO)
NJA .... Norrbottens Jarnverk AB [*Norrbottens Ironworks*] [*Sweden*]   (WEN)
NJAC........ Jacksons Limited [*National Union Catalogue of Australia symbol*]
NJAC........ National Joint Action Committee [*Trinidadian and Tobagan*]   (LA)
NJB............ James Bennett Library Services Proprietary Limited [*National Union Catalogue of Australia symbol*]

NJB............ Nederlands Juristenblad [*Netherlands*]   (FLAF)
NJC .... Janssen-Cilag Proprietary Limited [*National Union Catalogue of Australia symbol*]
NJC .... National Jewish Center [*Australia*]
NJC .... Newcastle Jockey Club [*Australia*]
NJCCOE ... Nordic Joint Committee of Commercial and Office Executives   (EA)
NJCDE...... Nordic Joint Committee for Domestic Education   (EA)
NJCM........ Nederlands Juristen Comite voor de Mensenrechten [*Netherlands Jurists Committee for Human Rights*]   (EAIO)
NJCS .... National Jewish Committee on Scouting
NJF............ Nordiska Journalistforbundet [*Nordic Association of Journalists Unions - NAJU*]   (EAIO)
NJF............ Nordiske Jordbrugsforskeres Forening [*Nordic Agricultural Research Workers Association - NARWA*]   (EAIO)
NJFL .... New [*South Wales*] James Fletcher Library [*Hunter Area Health Service*] [*Division of Mental Health*] [*National Union Catalogue of Australia symbol*]
NJFX .... John Fairfax Group - Fairfax Editorial Library [*National Union Catalogue of Australia symbol*]
NJG .... Nachtjagugeschwader [*Night Fighter*] [*German*]
NJGFE ...... Nordic Joint Group for Forest Entomology   (EA)
NJH........... James Hardie and Company Proprietary Limited [*National Union Catalogue of Australia symbol*]
NJHS........ Australian Jewish Historical Society [*National Union Catalogue of Australia symbol*]
NJJ .... Johnson and Johnson Australia Proprietary Limited [*National Union Catalogue of Australia symbol*]
NJLP .... BHP Steel Coated Products Division - Central Library [*National Union Catalogue of Australia symbol*]
NJM .... New JEWEL [*Joint Endeavor for Welfare, Education, and Liberation*] Movement [*Grenada*]
NJMR .... Nordisk Verbane Musik Rad [*Nordic Council for Railway Music - NCRM*]   (EAIO)
NJP............ Narodni Jednota Posumavska [*National Society for the Sumava Area*]   (CZ)
NJR .... New JEWEL Regime [*Grenada*]
NJS............ Narodni Jednota Severoceska [*National Society for Northern Bohemia*]   (CZ)
NJSZT....... Neumann Janos Szamitastechnikai [*or Szamitogeptudomanyi*] Tarsasag [*Janos Neumann Society of Computer Technology*]   (HU)
NJT............ Societe Novajet [*France*] [*ICAO designator*]   (FAAC)
NJU .... Nordic Judo Union   (EAIO)
NJU .... Northern Jiaotong Univeristy [*China*]
NJUASCO ... New Juabeng Secondary-Commercial School
NJur........... Nederlandsche Jurisprudentie [*Netherlands*]   (BAS)
NJV .... Nederlandse Juristenvereniging [*Netherlands Lawyers Association*]   (ILCA)
NJW .... Neue Juristische Wochenschrift [*Germany*]   (FLAF)
NJYC......... National Jewish Youth Council
NK............. Air-Position Indicator   (RU)
NK............. Al Naqeeb & Khattar Co. [*Kuwait*]
NK............. Beginning of Curve [*Railroads*]   (RU)
Nk.............. Chief   (BU)
n-k............. Chief, Head, Commander   (RU)
NK............. Constant Storage   (RU)
NK............. Criminal Code   (BU)
NK............. Design Norms, Design Standards   (RU)
NK............. Naczelny Komitet [*Chief Committee*] [*Poland*]
NK............. Narodna Knjiznjica [*National Library*] [*Ljubljana*]   (YU)
NK............. Narodni Knihovna [*The National Library (Also, a publication series)*]   (CZ)
NK............. Narodopisny Kabinet [*Ethnological Section (of the Slovak Academy of Sciences)*]   (CZ)
NK............. "Nasza Ksiegarnia" (Instytut Wydawniczy) [*"Our Book-Shop" (Publishing Institute)*]   (POL)
NK............. National Committee   (RU)
NK............. Natural Rubber   (RU)
NK............. Naturkanten [*Edges as Fabricated*] [*German*]   (GCA)
NK............. Negative Culture   (RU)
nk............. Nemzetkozi [*International*]   (HU)
NK............. Neon Komma [*New Party*] [*Greek*] [*Political party*]   (PPE)
NK............. Netzknoten [*German*]   (ADPT)
NK............. Neutral Red (Indicator)   (RU)
NK............. Neutron Logging   (RU)
NK............. New Books   (RU)
NK............. Nickel-Cobalt   (RU)
nk............. Niin Kuin [*Finland*]
NK............. Niin Kutsuttu [*Finland*]
NK............. Nippon Kaiji Kyokai [*Japanese ship classification society*]   (DS)
NK............. Nogometni Klub [*Soccer Club*]   (YU)
NK............. No Ketones [*Organic chemistry*]   (DAVI)
NK............. Nomemklatur Kommission [*Commission on Nomenclature*] [*Germany*]   (DAVI)

NK............. Nomenklature Kommission [*Commission on Nomenclature*] [*Anatomy*] [*German*]

NK............. Nordiska Kemistradet [*Chemical Societies of the Nordic Countries*]   (EAIO)

NK............. Nordiska Kompaniet [*Merged with Ahlen & Holm AB to form NK-Ahlens AB*] [*Sweden*]   (IMH)

NK............. Normalkerze [*Candle Power*] [*German*]

NK............. Norsk Komponistforening [*Norway*]   (EAIO)

NK............. North Korean

NK............. Notarska Komora [*Notaries' Association*]   (CZ)

NK............. Nucleic Acids   (RU)

NK............. People's Commissariat [*1917-1946*]   (RU)

NK............. Scientific Committee   (RU)

NKA.......... Nordisk Kontaktorgan for Atomenergisporgsmal [*Nordic Liaison Committee for Atomic Energy*]   (EAIO)

NKA.......... North Korean Army

NKAF....... North Korean Air Force

NKAI........ Scientific Committee for Antarctic Research   (RU)

NKAO....... Nagorno-Karabakh Autonomous Oblast

NKAP....... People's Commissariat of the Aircraft Industry, USSR [*1939-1946*]   (RU)

NKAT....... People's Commissariat of Automobile Transportation   (RU)

NKAU....... National Committee of Automatic Control, USSR   (RU)

NKB.......... Nationale Kas voor Beroepskrediet [*Benelux*]   (BAS)

NKB.......... Nordiska Kommitten for Byggbestammelser [*Nordic Committee on Building Regulations - NCBR*] [*Finland*]   (EAIO)

NKB.......... Nordiske Kristne Buddhistmission [*Christian Mission to Buddhists - CMB*]   (EAIO)

NKB.......... Norges Kommunalbank [*Bank*] [*Norway*]

NKB.......... People's Commissariat of Ammunition, USSR   (RU)

NKBA....... National Kitchen and Bathroom Association [*Australia*]

NKBK....... National Committee of Bulgarian Members of Cooperatives   (BU)

NKC.......... Nouakchott [*Mauritania*] [*Airport symbol*]   (OAG)

NKChM..... People's Commissariat of Ferrous Metallurgy, USSR [*1939-1946*]   (RU)

NKCP....... North Kalimantan Communist Party [*Malaysia*] [*Political party*]   (PD)

NKD.......... Fixed Range Circle   (RU)

NKD.......... Najvyssi Kontrolny Dvor [*Supreme Accounting Office*]   (CZ)

NKD.......... Nukleardienst [*Germany*]   (PDAA)

NKDA....... Nea Kinisi Dikigoron Athinon [*New Movement of Athens Attorneys*]   (GC)

NKDP....... New Korea Democratic Party [*South Korean*]

NKDP....... North Korea Democratic Party

nke .... Normal Calomel Electrode   (RU)

NKe........... Normenausschuss Kerntechnik im DIN [*Deutsches Institut fuer Normung*] eV [*Nuclear Technology Standards in the German Institute of Standardization*]   (SLS)

NKEM....... Kempsey Shire Library [*National Union Catalogue of Australia symbol*]

NKEP....... People's Commissariat of the Electrical Equipment Industry, USSR   (RU)

NKES........ People's Commissariat of Electric Power Plants, USSR   (RU)

NKES iEP ... People's Commissariat of Electric Power Plants and the Electrical Equipment Industry, USSR   (RU)

NKF.......... Nene Kampffugzeng

NKF.......... Nordiske Kvinners Fredsnettverk [*Nordic Women's Peace Network*] [*Denmark, Finland, Norway, and Sweden*]   (EAIO)

NKF.......... Nordisk Konstforbund [*Nordic Art Association*] [*Norway*]   (EAIO)

NKF.......... Norges Kjott og Fleskesentral

NKF.......... People's Commissariat of Finance [*1924-1946*]   (RU)

NKFD....... Nationalkomitee Freies Deutschland [*National Free-Germany Committee*]   (WEN)

NKFin....... People's Commissariat of Finance [*1924-1946*]   (RU)

NKFO....... Nordisk Kollegium for Fysisk Oceanografi [*Nordic Council for Physical Oceanography - NCPO*]   (EAIO)

NKFV .... Nagyalfold Koolaj es Foldgastermelo Vallalat [*Great Plains Petroleum and Natural Gas Producing Enterprise*]   (HU)

NKG.......... Nanjing [*China*] [*Airport symbol*]   (OAG)

NKG.......... Neutralized Acid Sludge   (RU)

NKG.......... Neutron-Gamma-Ray Logging Method   (RU)

NKG.......... New Kenya Group

NKG.......... Nordic Geodetic Commission   (ASF)

NKGB....... People's Commissariat of State Security   (RU)

NKGB-NKVD ... Narodnyi Komissariat Gosudarstvennoe Bezopasnosti-Narodnyi Komissariat Vnutrennikh Del [*Later, KGB*]

NKGG....... Nationalkomitee fuer Geodaesie und Geophysik [*National Committee for Geodesy and Geophysics*]   (EG)

NKGK....... People's Commissariat of State Control [*1940-1946*]   (RU)

NKgP........ National Smallholders' Party [*Hungary*]   (EAIO)

NKGP....... People's Commissariat of the Mining Industry, USSR   (RU)

NKH .... Kinhill Engineers Proprietary Limited (New South Wales) [*National Union Catalogue of Australia symbol*]

NKH .... Nordisk Komite for Handelsundervisning [*Nordic Committee for Commercial Education - NCCE*] [*Odense, Denmark*]   (EAIO)

NKh .... Petroleum Industry   (RU)

NKhFI .... Scientific Chemical and Pharmaceutical Institute   (RU)

NKhGS...... National Art Gallery in Sofia   (BU)

NKhK....... Petrochemical Combine   (BU)

NKhS........ Chief of Chemical Service   (BU)

NKhV....... Commander of Chemical Troops   (RU)

n-ki............ Successors   (RU)

NKID........ Narodnyy Komissariat Inostrannykh Del [*People's Commissariat of Foreign Affairs*] [*Former USSR*]   (LAIN)

NKID........ People's Commissariat of Foreign Affairs [*1917-1946*]   (RU)

NKII .... Kwame N'Krumah Ideological Institute

NKJG .... Nederlandse Kring voor Joodse Genealogie [*Netherlands*]   (EAIO)

NKK......... Beginning of Belt Line [*Railroads*]   (RU)

NKK......... Narodni Kulturni Komise [*National Cultural Commission*]   (CZ)

NKK.......... Nepkonyvtari Kozpont [*Administrative Center for People's Libraries*]   (HU)

NKK.......... Nihon Kikaku Kyokai [*Japan*]   (EAIO)

NKK.......... Nippon Koka Kaisha [*Japanese shipbuilding company*]

NKK.......... Nippon Kokan [*Steel company*] [*Japan*]

NKK.......... Nordiska Kor Kommitten [*Denmark*]   (EAIO)

NKK.......... Nordkalottkommitten [*North Calotte Committee - NCC*] [*Finland*]   (EAIO)

NKKF .... Kurri Kurri College of TAFE (Technical and Further Education) [*National Union Catalogue of Australia symbol*]

NKKhP...... People's Commissariat of the Chemical Industry, USSR [*1939-1946*]   (RU)

NKKKh...... People's Commissariat of the Municipal Economy   (RU)

NKKU....... Negara Kesatuan Kalimantan Utara [*Unified State of North Kalimantan*]   (ML)

nkl .... Naklad [*Edition*] [*Publishing*] [*Poland*]

NKL.......... Namik Kemal Lise [*Namik Kemal Lycee*] [*High school Cyprus*]   (TU)

NKL.......... Norges Kooperative Landsforening [*Norway*]   (IMH)

NKL.......... People's Commissariat of the Lumber Industry [*1932-1946*]   (RU)

NKLEGprom ... People's Commissariat of Light Industry   (RU)

NKLes........ People's Commissariat of the Lumber Industry [*1932-1946*]   (RU)

NKLP........ People's Commissariat of Light Industry   (RU)

NKLU....... Noord-Kaaplandse Landbou-Unie [*South Africa*]   (AA)

nkm .... Najciezszy Karabin Maszynowy [*Heaviest Machine Gun*] [*Poland*]

NKM......... Nari Kendra Mumbai [*India*]   (EAIO)

NKM......... Non-Relativistic Quantum Mechanics   (RU)

NKM......... North Kalgurli Mines [*Australia*]

NKM......... People's Commissariat of Machinery Manufacture, USSR   (RU)

NKMash.... People's Commissariat of Machinery Manufacture, USSR   (RU)

NKMB....... Nederlandse Katholieke Middenstandsbond [*Netherlands Catholic Middle Class Association*]   (WEN)

NKMB....... Nordisk Kollegium for Marinbiologi [*Nordic Council for Marine Biology - NCMB*]   (EAIO)

NKMestprom ... People's Commissariat of Local Industry   (RU)

NKMF .... People's Commissariat of the Maritime Fleet, USSR   (RU)

NKMGG.... Nacionalne Komisije za Medunarodnu Geofizicku Godinu [*National Commissions for the International Geophysical Year*] [*1957-1958*]   (YU)

NKML....... Ku-ring-gai Library [*National Union Catalogue of Australia symbol*]

NKMMP ... People's Commissariat of the Meat and Dairy Industry   (RU)

NKMP....... People's Commissariat of Local Industry   (RU)

NKMTP ... People's Commissariat of the Local Fuel Industry   (RU)

NKMU....... National Kangaroo Monitoring Unit [*Australia*]

NKMV....... People's Commissariat of Mortar Weapons, USSR   (RU)

NKMZ....... New Kramatorsk Machinery Plant   (RU)

NKN .... Naczelny Komitet Narodowy [*Poland*]

NKN .... North Korean Navy

NKN .... People's Commissariat for Nationalities, RSFSR   (RU)

NK na OF .. National Committee of the Fatherland Front   (BU)

NKNLL ..... North Kalimantan National Liberation League   (ML)

NKNP....... People's Commissariat of the Petroleum Industry, USSR [*1939-1946*]   (RU)

NKO .... Narodnyi Komissariat Oborony [*People's Commissariat of Defense*] [*Existed until 1946*] [*Former USSR*]

NKO .... People's Commissariat of Defense [*1934-1946*]   (RU)

NKOF....... National Committee of the Fatherland Front   (BU)

NKOG .... Kogarah Municipal Library [*National Union Catalogue of Australia symbol*]

NKOJ .... Nacionalni Komitet Oslobodenja Yugoslavije [*National Committee for the Liberation of Yugoslavia*]   (YU)

NKOL........ Nacelnik Kadroveho Oddilu Letectva [*Air Force Personnel Chief*]   (CZ)

NKOM ...... People's Commissariat of General Machinery Manufacture, USSR   (RU)

NKOP .... People's Commissariat of the Defense Industry, USSR   (RU)

N-k otd ...... Section Chief   (BU)

NKOYu ...... National Committee for the Liberation of Yugoslavia   (RU)

NKP .... Commander's Observation Post   (RU)

NKP .... Nadi Ke Par   (EAIO)

NKP .... Nakorn Phanom [*Air base northeast of Bangkok*]

NKP .... Nasionale Konserwatiewe Party [*National Conservative Party*] [*South Africa*] [*Political party*]   (PPW)

NKP .... Nemet Kommunista Part [*German Communist Party*]   (HU)

NKP .... New Kenya Party

NKP .... Norges Kommunistiske Parti [*Norwegian Communist Party*] [*Political party*]   (PPE)

NKP .... Observation and Spotting Post [*Artillery*]   (RU)

NKP .... People's Commissariat of Education [*1917-1946*]   (RU)

NKPA .... North Korean People's Army

NKPishcheprom ... People's Commissariat of the Food Industry   (RU)

NKPiT .... People's Commissariat of Postal and Telegraphic Service   (RU)

NKPochtel' ... People's Commissariat of Postal and Telegraphic Service   (RU)

NKPP .... People's Commissariat of the Food Industry   (RU)

NKPROD .. People's Commissariat of Food [*1917-1924*]   (RU)

NKPros ...... People's Commissariat of Education [*1917-1946*]   (RU)

NKPRTAB ... Nakhon Phanom Royal Thai Air Base [*Leased by USAF during the Vietnam War*]   (VNW)

NKPS .... People's Commissariat of Railroads, USSR [*1922-1946*]   (RU)

NKPSM .... People's Commissariat of the Building Materials Industry   (RU)

NKPT .... People's Commissariat of Postal and Telegraphic Service   (RU)

NKPZA ...... Antiaircraft Artillery Observation and Spotting Post   (RU)

NKR .... Nordisk Konservatorierad [*Nordic Council for Music Conservatories - NCMC*]   (EAIO)

Nkr .... Norjan Kruunu(a) [*Finland*]

N KR .... Norwegian Krone [*Monetary unit*]

NKRC .... North Korean Red Cross

NKRF .... People's Commissariat of the River Fleet, USSR   (RU)

NKRKI ...... People's Commissariat of Workers' and Peasants' Inspection [*1920-1934*]   (RU)

NKRP .... People's Commissariat of the Fish Industry [*1939-1946*]   (RU)

NKRP .... People's Commissariat of the Rubber Industry, USSR   (RU)

NKrS .... Nacelnik Kurirske Stanice [*Courier Station Chief*] [*Military*]   (YU)

NKS .... National Koala Survey [*Australia*]

NKS .... Nordisk Kernesikkerhedsforskning [*Denmark*]   (EAIO)

NKS .... Nordisk Kirkelig Studierad [*Nordic Council for Adult Studies in Chruch - NCASC*]   (EAIO)

NKS .... Norsk Kjemisk Selskap [*Norwegian Chemical Society*]

NKS .... People's Commissariat of Communications, USSR [*1932-1946*]   (RU)

NKSC .... National Korean Studies Center [*Australia*]

NKSF .... Norske Kommuners Sentral Forbund [*Norwegian Local Authorities Association*]

NKSG .... National Committee of Soviet Geographers   (RU)

NKSKh ...... People's Commissariat of Grain and Livestock-Breeding Sovkhozes   (RU)

NKSM ...... People's Commissariat of Medium Machinery Manufacture, USSR   (RU)

NKSNAB ... People's Commissariat of Supply [*1930-1934*]   (RU)

NKSO .... People's Commissariat of Social Security [*1918-1946*]   (RU)

NKSP .... People's Commissariat of the Shipbuilding Industry, USSR   (RU)

NKSS .... People's Commissariat of Machine Tool Manufacture, USSR   (RU)

NKSvyazi ... People's Commissariat of Communications, USSR [*1932-1946*]   (RU)

nkt .... Lower Critical Temperature   (RU)

NKT .... Nordic Kabel Traadfabrikker [*Nordic Cable Manufacturer*] [*Denmark*]

NKT .... Normenausschuss Kommunale Technik im DIN [*Deutsches Institut fuer Normung*] eV [*Municipal Technology Standards in the German Institute of Standardization*]   (SLS)

NKT .... People's Commissariat of Labor [*1917-1933*]   (RU)

NKTF .... Norges Karttekniske Forbund [*Norway*]   (EAIO)

NKTF .... Norsk Kabel-TV Forbund [*Norway*]   (EAIO)

NKTG .... National Confederation of Workers of Guinea   (RU)

NKTiP ...... People's Commissariat of Trade and Industry   (RU)

NKTL .... Ground Ejection-Seat Trainer   (RU)

NKTM ...... People's Commissariat of Heavy Machinery Manufacture, USSR [*1939-1946*]   (RU)

NKTM ...... People's Commissariat of Transportation Machinery Manufacture, USSR [*1945-1946*]   (RU)

NKTOP ..... People's Commissariat of the Fuel Industry   (RU)

NKTorg ..... People's Commissariat of Foreign and Domestic Trade, USSR [*1924-1938*]   (RU)

NKTorg ..... People's Commissariat of Trade [*1938-1946*]   (RU)

NKTP .... People's Commissariat of Heavy Industry, USSR [*1932-1939*]   (RU)

NKTP .... People's Commissariat of the Fuel Industry   (RU)

NKTP .... People's Commissariat of the Tank Industry, USSR   (RU)

NKTP .... People's Commissariat of the Textile Industry   (RU)

NKTP .... People's Commissariat of Trade and Industry   (RU)

NKTrud ..... People's Commissariat of Labor [*1917-1933*]   (RU)

NKTsBP ..... People's Commissariat of the Pulp and Paper Industry, USSR   (RU)

NKTsM ..... People's Commissariat of Nonferrous Metallurgy, USSR [*1939-1946*]   (RU)

NKTyazhmash ... People's Commissariat of Heavy Machinery Manufacture [*1939-1946*]   (RU)

NKTYaZhprom ... People's Commissariat of Heavy Industry, USSR [*1932-1939*]   (RU)

NKU .... Nejvyssi Kontrolni Urad [*Supreme Accounting Office*]   (CZ)

NKU .... Nkaus [*Lesotho*] [*Airport symbol*]   (OAG)

N-k u-nie ... Department Chief   (BU)

NKUP .... People's Commissariat of the Coal Industry, USSR [*1939-1946*]   (RU)

NKV .... Nasionale Kankervereniging van Suid-Afrika [*South Africa*]   (AA)

NKV .... Nederlands Katholiek Vakverbond [*Netherlands Catholic Workers Federation*]   (WEN)

NKV .... People's Commissariat for Military Affairs [*1918-1923*]   (RU)

NKV .... People's Commissariat of Armaments, USSR   (RU)

NKVD .... Narodnyi Komissariat Vnutrennikh Del [*People's Commissariat of Internal Affairs (1917-1946)*] [*Also known as NARKOMVNUDEL Soviet secret police organization KGB*] [*Later,*]   (PD)

NKVD .... Neizvestino Kogda Vernesh'sia Domoi [*You Never Know When You Will Get Home*] [*Wordplay on NKVD, Soviet secret police organization*]

NKVM ...... People's Commissariat for Military and Naval Affairs, USSR [*1923-1934*]   (RU)

NKVMF .... Narodnyy Komissariat Voyenno-Morskogo Flota [*People's Commissariat of the Navy*] [*Former USSR*]   (LAIN)

NKVMF .... People's Commissariat of the Navy, USSR [*1937-1946*]   (RU)

NKVneshtorg ... People's Commissariat of Foreign Trade, USSR [*1923-1925, 1930-1946*]   (RU)

NKVnutorg ... People's Commissariat of Domestic Trade [*1924-1938*]   (RU)

NKVod .... People's Commissariat of Water Transportation, USSR   (RU)

NKVoyen ... People's Commissariat for Military Affairs [*1918-1923*]   (RU)

NKVoyenmor ... People's Commissariat for Military and Naval Affairs, USSR [*1923-1934*]   (RU)

NKVoyenmor ... People's Commissariat of the Navy, USSR [*1937-1946*]   (RU)

NKVP .... People's Commissariat of Munitions, USSR   (RU)

NKVR .... Narodni Komitet pro Vedeckou Radiotechniku [*National Committee for Scientific Radio Engineering*]   (CZ)

NKVT .... People's Commissariat of Domestic Trade [*1924-1938*]   (RU)

NKVT .... People's Commissariat of Foreign Trade, USSR [*1923-1925, 1930-1946*]   (RU)

NKVT .... People's Commissariat of Water Transportation, USSR   (RU)

NKW .... Naczelny Komitet Wykonawczy [*Chief Executive Committee*]   (POL)

NKW .... Narodowy Komitet Wyzwolenia [*National Liberation Committee*]   (POL)

NKWPSL ... Naczelny Komitet Wykonawczy Polskiego Stronnictwa Ludowego [*Chief Executive Committee of the Polish Peasant Party*]   (POL)

NKW SD ... Naczelny Komitet Wykonawczy Stronnictwa Demokratycznego [*Chief Executive Committee of the Democratic Party*]   (POL)

NKWV .... Nederlands Katholiek Werkgevers Verbond [*Netherlands Catholic Employers Association*]   (WEN)

NKWZSL ... Naczelny Komitet Wykonawczy Zjednoczonego Stronnictwa Ludowego [*Chief Executive Committee of the United Peasant Party*]   (POL)

NKY .... Nihon Kiseichu Yobokai [*Japan*]   (EAIO)

NKYu .... Narodnyy Komissariat Yustitsii [*People's Commissariat of Justice*] [*Former USSR*]   (LAIN)

NKYu .... People's Commissariat of Justice, USSR [*1936-1946*]   (RU)

NKYust ...... People's Commissariat of Justice, USSR [*1936-1946*]   (RU)

NKZ .... Narodno Kazaliste Zagreb [*Zagreb National Theater*]   (YU)

NKZ .... Netzkontrollzentrum [*German*]   (ADPT)

NKZ .... People's Commissariat of Agriculture   (RU)

NKZ .... People's Commissariat of Public Health [*1936-1946*]   (RU)

NKZag .... People's Commissariat of Procurement, USSR [*1938-1946*]   (RU)

NKzaUNICEF ... Nacionalna Komisija za UNICEF [*Yugoslav National Commission for UNICEF*]   (YU)

NKZdrav ..... People's Commissariat of Public Health [*1936-1946*]   (RU)

NKZem ...... People's Commissariat of Agriculture   (RU)

NKZM .... National Committee for the Defense of Peace   (BU)

NK ZSL ..... Naczelny Komitet Zjednoczonego Stronnictwa Ludowego [*Chief Committee of the United Peasants' Party*]   (POL)

NKZZhSKh ... People's Commissariat of Grain and Livestock-Breeding Sovkhozes   (RU)
NL .... Holandia [*Holland*] [*Poland*]
nl .... Naamlik [*Namely*] [*Afrikaans*]
nL .... Nad Labem [*On the Elbe River*]   (CZ)
nl .... Namelijk [*Namely*] [*Netherlands*]   (GPO)
NL .... Navigation Slide Rule   (RU)
NL .... Nebenlager [*Branch Camp*] [*German military - World War II*]
nl .... Nemlig [*Namely*] [*Norway*]   (GPO)
NL .... Neo Lao [*Hak Sat*] [*Lao Patriotic Front Use NLHS*]   (CL)
NL .... Netherlands [*International automobile identification tag*]
NL .... Netherlands [*ANSI two-letter standard code*]   (CNC)
nl .... Nicht Loeslich [*Not Soluble*] [*German*]
NL .... Niederlassung [*Branch Office, Field Office, Place of Business*] (EG)
NL .... Non-Lieu [*French*]   (FLAF)
NL .... Norsk Laererlag [*Norway*]   (EAIO)
NL .... Norsk Lektorlag [*Norway*]   (SLS)
NL .... Nouvelle Lune [*New Moon*] [*French*]
NL .... Nuevo Leon [*Mexican province*]
NL .... Pneumatic Boat   (RU)
NLA .... Naringslivets Arkivrad [*Sweden*]   (EAIO)
NLA .... National Liberation Army [*Bolivia*]
NLA .... National Library of Australia
NLA .... Navy League of Australia
NLA .... Ndola [*Zambia*] [*Airport symbol*]   (OAG)
NLA .... Nigerian Library Association
NLA .... Norske Landskapsarkitekters Forening [*Norwegian Association of Landscape Architects*]   (EAIO)
NLAB .... Labour Council of New South Wales [*National Union Catalogue of Australia symbol*]
NLAC .... National Library Advisory Council
NLAC .... National Literacy Advisory Committee
NLAF .... National Language Action Front   (ML)
NLAWS ..... Law Society of New South Wales [*National Union Catalogue of Australia symbol*]
NLB .... National Liquor Board
NLB .... Nepkoztarsasag Legfelso Birosaga [*Supreme Court of the People's Republic*]   (HU)
NLB .... New Lantau Bus Co. [*Hong Kong*]
nlb .... Nieliczbowane (Strony) [*Unpaged*]   (POL)
NLBF .... Norwegian Luge and Bob Federation   (EAIO)
NLBH .... Lismore Base Hospital Library [*National Union Catalogue of Australia symbol*]
NLBP .... Night Light Bomber Regiment   (RU)
NLC .... De Nederlandsche Landbouwcooperatie [*Netherlands*]   (BAS)
NLC .... Legal Aid Commission (New South Wales) [*National Union Catalogue of Australia symbol*]
NLC .... National Labour Congress [*Thailand*]   (EY)
NLC .... National Labour Congress [*Nigeria*]   (ECON)
NLC .... National Liberation Committee [*South Africa*]
NLC .... National Liberation Council [*Ghana*]   (AF)
NLC .... National Library of China
NLC .... National Liturgical Commission [*Catholic Church*] [*Australia*]
NLC .... New Liberal Club [*Shin Jiyu Club*] [*Japan*]   (PPW)
NLC .... Nigerian Labor Congress   (AF)
NLC .... Nordic Literature Committee [*Copenhagen, Denmark*]   (EAIO)
NLCC .... National Library Clearing Centre [*Australia*]
NLCD .... National Liberation Council Decree
NLCF .... National Livestock Cooperatives Federation [*South Korea*] (EAIO)
NLCOV ..... Lane Cove Public Library [*National Union Catalogue of Australia symbol*]
NLCS .... Nordic Leather Chemists Society [*Formerly, IVLIC Scandinavian Section*]   (EA)
NLD .... Namakwaland Lugdiens (EDMS) BPK [*South Africa*] [*ICAO designator*]   (FAAC)
NLD .... National League for Democracy [*Myanmar*] [*Political party*] (EY)
NLD .... Netherlands [*ANSI three-letter standard code*]   (CNC)
NLD .... New South Wales - Soil Conservation Service [*National Union Catalogue of Australia symbol*]
NLD .... Nuevo Laredo [*Mexico*] [*Airport symbol*]   (OAG)
NLDA .... National Livestock Development Authority [*Honiara, Solomon Islands*]   (GEA)
NLDH .... Lady Davidson Hospital - Medical Library [*National Union Catalogue of Australia symbol*]
NLDP .... National Liberal Democratic Party
NLDS .... National Library and Documentation Service [*Zinbabwe*] (PDAA)
NLE .... Northern Commuter Airlines [*New Zealand*] [*ICAO designator*] (FAAC)
NLEC .... Land and Environment Court (New South Wales) [*National Union Catalogue of Australia symbol*]
NLEE .... Leeton Shire Major Dooley Library [*National Union Catalogue of Australia symbol*]

NLEK .... L E K Parnership [*National Union Catalogue of Australia symbol*]
NLF .... National Front for the Liberation of South Vietnam [*Use NFLSV*]   (CL)
NLF .... National Labour Federation
NLF .... National Liberation Front [*Vietnam*] [*Political party*]
NLF .... National Liberation Front [*Aden*] [*Political party*]
NLF .... National Liberation Front [*South Africa*] [*Political party*]   (PD)
NLF .... National Liberation Front [*Myanmar*] [*Political party*]   (PD)
NLFPA ...... National Liberation Front Party Apparatus [*Algeria*]
NLFR .... National Liberation Front of Reunion
NLFR .... Nordisk Laederforskningsrad [*Denmark*]   (SLS)
NLFSV ...... National Liberation Front of South Vietnam [*Political party*]
NLG .... National Lecturers Group   (BU)
NLGC .... Nauru Local Government Council [*Australia*]
NLGTC ..... National Local Government Training Council [*Australia*]
NLH .... Liverpool Hospital [*National Union Catalogue of Australia symbol*]
NLH .... New Lao Hak [*Lao Patriotic Front*] [*Vietnam*] [*Political party*]
NLH .... New Life Hamlet [*See also NLHS, NLHZ*] [*Vietnam*] [*Military*]
NLH .... Norges Landbrukshoegskole [*Agricultural University of Norway*] (ARC)
NLHO ...... National Latina Health Organization   (EAIO)
NLHO .... Norwegian League of Handicap Organizations   (EAIO)
NLHR .... Australian Nuclear Science and Technology Organisation - Lucas Heights Research [*National Union Catalogue of Australia symbol*]
NLHS .... Neo Lao Hak Sat [*Lao Patriotic Front*]
NLHS .... New Lao Hak Sat [*New Life Hamlet*] [*See also NLH Vietnam*] [*Military*]
NLHX .... Neo Lao Hak Sat [*Lao Patriotic Front*] [*Use NLHS*]   (CL)
NLHZ .... New Lao Hak Zat [*New Life Hamlet*] [*See also NLH, NLHS Vietnam*] [*Military*]
NLI .... Norsk Lokalhistorisk Institutt [*Norwegian Local History Institute*]   (SLS)
NLIA .... National Languages Institute of Australia
NLID .... New South Wales - Department of Industrial Relations Employment Training and Fur [*National Union Catalogue of Australia symbol*]
NLIVL .... Liverpool City Library [*National Union Catalogue of Australia symbol*]
NLIVPL .... Department of Defence - Liverpool Area Library [*National Union Catalogue of Australia symbol*]
NLJ .... National Library of Jamaica   (PDAA)
NLJU .... New Liberal Jewish Union
NLK .... Norfolk Island [*Airport symbol*]   (OAG)
NLL .... National Luchtvaart Laboratorium [*Netherlands*]
NLL .... Norsk Logopedlag [*Norway*]   (SLS)
NLL .... Northern Limit Line [*Korea*]
NLL .... Nullagine [*Australia*] [*Airport symbol*]   (OAG)
NLLC .... National Languages and Literacy Council [*Australia*]
nlle .... Nouvelle [*New*] [*French*]
NLLO .... Lloyds Bank NZA [*National Union Catalogue of Australia symbol*]
NLM .... National Liberation Movement
NLM .... Nederlandse Luchtvaart Maatschappij [*Airline*] [*Netherlands*]
NLM .... Nile Liberation Movement [*Egypt*]
NLM .... Norwegian Lutheran Mission
NLMA ...... Nigerian Livestock and Meat Authority
NLMBBSA ... Norwegian LMBB's Syndrome Association   (EAIO)
NLMC .... Nordic Labour Market Committee   (EAIO)
NLMGB .... National Liberation Movement of Guinea-Bissau
NLMH .... Lidcombe Hospital - Medical Library [*National Union Catalogue of Australia symbol*]
NLML .... Leichhardt Municipal Library [*National Union Catalogue of Australia symbol*]
NLMPL ..... Lake Macquarie City Library [*National Union Catalogue of Australia symbol*]
NLMWT ... National Liberation Movement of Western Togoland
NLMZ .... New Lipetsk Metallurgical Plant   (RU)
NLN .... Nepean Libraries Network [*Australia*]
NLN .... Nordiska Lakemedelsnamnden [*Nordic Council on Medicines - NCM*]   (EAIO)
NLnet .... [*The*] Newfoundland and Labrador Network [*Canada*] [*Computer science*]   (TNIG)
NLO .... National Labour Organization [*India*]
NLO .... Workcover Authority of New South Wales - Londonderry Occupational Safety Centre [*National Union Catalogue of Australia symbol*]
NLOrLanyard ... Netherlands Orange Lanyard [*Military decoration*]
NLP .... Light Pneumatic Pontoon   (RU)
NLP .... Narodnoliberalna Partiia [*National Liberal Party*] [*Bulgaria*] [*Political party*]   (PPE)
NLP .... National Labour Party [*Sierra Leone*] [*Political party*]   (EY)
NLP .... National Language Policy [*Australia*]
NLP .... National Liberal Party [*Lebanon*]   (ME)

NLP .... National Liberal Party [Bermuda] [Political party]   (EY)
NLP .... National Liberation Party [Gambia] [Political party]   (PPW)
NLP .... Natural Law Party [Australia] [Political party]
NLP .... Nelspruit [South Africa] [Airport symbol]   (OAG)
NLP .... New Left Party [Political party] [Australia]
NLP .... Nigerian Labor Party   (AF)
NLPC .... National Libyan Petroleum Co.   (PDAA)
NLPC .... National Livestock Production Company
NLPC .... Nigerian Life and Pensions Consultants
NLPLG ...... National Language Policy Liaison Group [Australia]
NLR .... Nationaal Lucht- en Ruimtevaartlaboratorium [National Aeronautical and Astronautical Research Institute] [Research center] [Netherlands]   (WEN)
NLR .... Nemocnice Lehce Ranenych [Hospital for Slightly Wounded]   (CZ)
NLRC .... Law Reform Commission of New South Wales [National Union Catalogue of Australia symbol]
NLRC .... Narottam Lalbhai Research Centre [India] [Research center]   (IRC)
NLRC .... New Literatures Research Centre [University of Wollongong] [Australia]
NLRD .... National Hunting and Fishing Society   (BU)
NLRL .... Lithgow Regional Library [National Union Catalogue of Australia symbol]
NLRN .... National Library Record Number [Australia]
NLRS .... National Hunting and Fishing Union   (BU)
NLRU .... Nordens Liberale og Radikale Ungdom [Nordic Liberal and Radical Youth]   (EAIO)
NLS .... National Lending Service [Australia]
NLS .... Nordic Language Secretariat [See also SLN] [Norway]   (EAIO)
NLS .... Nordiske Laererorganisationers Samrad [Council of Nordic Teachers' Association] [Sweden]   (EAIO)
NLSB .... St Lucy's School for Blind and Visually Handicapped Children [National Union Catalogue of Australia symbol]
NLSC .... National Leather and Shoe Corporation
NLSH .... Ndermarrje Lokale Shteterore [Albanian]
NLU .... Natalse Landbou-Unie [Natal Agricultural University] [Afrikaans]
NLU .... National Labor Union [Philippines]
NlVenn....... Naamlooze Vennootschap [Benelux]   (BAS)
NLVF .... Norges Landbruksvitenskapelige Forskningsrad [Norwegian Agricultural Research Council] [Oslo, Norway]   (WEN)
NLWF .... Futuna/Pointe Vele [Wallis and Futuna Islands] [ICAO location identifier]   (ICLI)
NLWW ...... Wallis/Hififo [Wallis and Futuna Islands] [ICAO location identifier]   (ICLI)
NM .... Antidisturbance Mine, Antiremoval Mine   (RU)
NM .... De Nederlandsche Mercuur [Netherlands]   (BAS)
Nm .... Mechanischer Wirkungsgrad [Mechanical Efficiency] [German]
NM .... Nachmittag [Afternoon] [German]
NM .... Nacionalnite Malcinstva [National Minorities]   (YU)
nM .... Naechsten Monats [Of Next Month] [German]   (EG)
nm .... Namiddag [After Noon] [Netherlands]   (GPO)
NM .... Narodna Milicija [People's Militia] [Police]   (YU)
NM .... Narodna Mladina [People's Youth]   (YU)
NM .... Narodni Museum [National Museum]   (CZ)
NM .... Nasionale Merk [National Mark] [Afrikaans]
NM .... Nepjoleti Miniszterium/Miniszter [Ministry/Minister of Public Welfare]   (HU)
NM .... Newtonian Mechanics   (RU)
Nm .... Newtonmeter [Newton Meter (Unit of mechanical efficiency)]   (EG)
NM .... New World   (RU)
NM .... Nonmetallic Deposits   (RU)
NM .... Nordiska Metallarbetaresekretariatet [Nordic Metalworkers Secretariat - NMS]   (EAIO)
NM .... Nord Magnetique [French]   (MTD)
NM .... Norges Mallag [Norway]   (SLS)
Nm .... Normalmeter [Standard Meter]   (EG)
NM .... Normenstelle Marine im DIN [Deutsches Institut fuer Normung] eV [Marine Standards in the German Institute of Standardization]   (SLS)
NM .... Numerique Medical [French]   (ADPT)
NM .... Nuwe Maan [New Moon] [Afrikaans]
NM .... People's Militia   (BU)
NM .... People's Museum   (BU)
NM .... Pressure Gauge   (RU)
NM .... Vereniging tot Behoud van Natuurmonumenten in Nederland [Netherlands]   (SLS)
Nm³ .... Normkubikmeter [Normal Cubic Meter] [German]   (GCA)
NMA .... Chief of Medical Service of an Army   (RU)
NMA .... Natal Municipal Association [South Africa]   (AA)
NMA .... National Maritime Authority [Australia]
NMA .... National Marketing Authority [Fijian]   (GEA)
NMA .... National Monitoring Agency [India]
NMA .... National Museum of Australia

NMA .... National Music Academy [Australia]
NMA .... National Musicamp Association [Zimbabwe]   (EAIO)
NMA .... Nigerian Medical Association
NMA .... Nursing Mothers' Association of Australia   (ADA)
NMAA .... Nursing Mothers' Association of Australia
NMAC .... Macquarie Regional Library [National Union Catalogue of Australia symbol]
NMAK .... Makor Resource Centre of New South Wales [National Union Catalogue of Australia symbol]
NMAN ...... Manly Municipal Library [National Union Catalogue of Australia symbol]
NMARSC ... Army Maritime School [National Union Catalogue of Australia symbol]
NMB .... Bureau of Meteorology - Regional Office for New South Wales [National Union Catalogue of Australia symbol]
NMB .... Magnetic Drum Storage   (RU)
NMB .... Namib Air (Pty) Ltd. [Namibia] [ICAO designator]   (FAAC)
NMB .... National Meat Brokers [Australia]
NMB .... Nederlandsche Middenstandsbank NV [Bank] [Netherlands]
NMB .... Nigeria Marketing and Regional Production Development Board
NMB .... Scientific Medical Library   (RU)
NMBS .... Nationale Maatschappij der Belgische Spoorwegen [Railway] [Belgium]   (EY)
NMBT .... Burns Philp Research and Development Proprietary Limited [National Union Catalogue of Australia symbol]
NMC .... Nairobi Motor Club
NMC .... Nanjing Motor Corp. [China]
NMC .... National Memorials Committee [Australia]
NMC .... National Meteorological Center
NMC .... National Military Council [Surinam]   (PD)
NMC .... National Milling Corp. [Tanzania]   (EY)
NMC .... National Missionary Council [Australia]
NMC .... National Monuments Council [South Africa]   (AA)
NMC .... Nigerian Mining Corp.   (EAS)
nmc .... Norme de Munca Conventionale [Conventional Work Norms]   (RO)
NMC .... Northern Mining Corporation [Australia]
NMCA .... National Missionary Council of Australia
NMCC .... McCarthy Catholic Senior High School [National Union Catalogue of Australia symbol]
NMCC .... Nuclear Material Control Center [Nuclear energy] [Japan]   (NRCH)
NMCG .... NATO Maritime Coordination Group
NMCK .... McKinsey and Company Information Service [National Union Catalogue of Australia symbol]
NMCL .... Maitland City Library [National Union Catalogue of Australia symbol]
NMCM ...... Nigerian Motor Components Manufacturers
NMD .... Chief of Medical Service of a Division   (RU)
NMD .... New South Wales - Department of Mineral Resources [National Union Catalogue of Australia symbol]
NMDC .... National Mineral Development Corp. Ltd. [India]
NMDF .... National Movement for the Defense of the Fatherland [Replaced CDNI] [Lao]   (CL)
NMDR .... Murray-Darling Freshwater Research Centre [National Union Catalogue of Australia symbol]
NME .... Ndermarrje e Montimeve Elektrike [Albanian]
NME .... Newly Maturing Economy [Business term]
NMEP ...... Novyi Mezhduradnyi Ekonomicheskii Poriadok
NMERI ..... National Mechanical Engineering Research Institute [South Africa]
NMF .... Neuromuscular Foundation of Western Australia
NMF .... Nordiska Maskinbefalsfederationen [Nordic Engineer Officers' Federation - NEOF]   (EAIO)
NMF .... Norsk Meteorologforening [Norwegian Meteorological Association]   (SLS)
NmfL.......... National Microfilms Ltd., Dublin, Ireland [Library symbol] [Library of Congress]   (LCLS)
NMFM ...... National Mutual Funds Management Proprietary Ltd. [Australia]
NMFWA ... Neuromuscular Foundation of Western Australia
NMG .... MacPherson Greenleaf and Associates [National Union Catalogue of Australia symbol]
NMG .... San Miguel [Panama] [Airport symbol]   (OAG)
NMGC ...... Marriage Guidance Council of New South Wales [National Union Catalogue of Australia symbol]
NMHB ...... National Materials Handling Bureau [Australia]
NMI .... Ndermarrje e Montimeve Industriale [Albanian]
NMI .... Nederlands Mode Instituut [Netherlands]   (EAIO)
NMI .... Norsk Musikkinformasjon [Norway]   (EAIO)
NMIC .... Norwegian Music Information Centre   (EAIO)
NMIP .... New Major Investment Program [Australia]
NMIP .... Nordic Marine Insurance Pool [Norway]   (EAIO)
NMISF ...... Northern Mariana Islands Swimming Federation   (EAIO)
NMIU .... Nordic Meat Industry Union   (EA)

NMJ .... Narodna Mladina na Jugoslavija [*People's Youth of Yugoslavia*] (YU)
NMK.......... Chief of Medical Service of a Corps (RU)
NMK.......... Low-Molecular-Weight Component (RU)
NMK.......... Nasionale Mannekragkommissie [*National Manpower Commission*] [*South Africa*] (AA)
NMK.......... Nonequilibrium Molecular Constellation (RU)
NMK.......... Scientific Methodological Study Center (RU)
NMKh .... People's Museum in Khisar (BU)
NMKL .... Nordisk Metodikkommitte for Livsmedel [*Nordic Committee on Food Analysis*] (EAIO)
NMKN ...... Nationale Maatschappij voor Krediet aan de Nijverheid [*National Industrial Credit Society*] [*Belgium*] (GEA)
NML.......... Magnetic Tape Storage (RU)
nml .... Namelijk [*Benelux*] (BAS)
NMl .... Narodna Mladezh [*People's Youth*] [*A periodical*] (BU)
NMLA .... National Mutual Life Association of Australasia Ltd. (ADA)
NMLG .... Molong Historical Society [*National Union Catalogue of Australia symbol*]
NMLL .... Norske Musikklaereres Landsforbund [*Norwegian Music Teachers Association*] (SLS)
NMLN .... ILANET (Information and Libraries Access Network) [*National Union Catalogue of Australia symbol*]
NMLS........ Australian Meat and Livestock Corporation [*National Union Catalogue of Australia symbol*]
nmlvenn...... Naamloze Vennootschap [*Benelux*] (BAS)
NMLY .... Macleay College [*National Union Catalogue of Australia symbol*]
NMM .... Metal
nmm .... Naar Mijn Mening [*Benelux*] (BAS)
NMM .... Narodna Mladina na Makedonija [*People's Youth of Macedonia*] (YU)
NMM .... National Maritime Museum [*Australia*]
NMM .... Nepjoleti es Munkaugyi Miniszterium/Miniszter [*Ministry/Minister of Public Welfare and Labor*] (HU)
NMM .... Nepmuvelesi Miniszterium/Miniszter [*Ministry/Minister of Public Education*] (HU)
NMMA...... National Medium Miners Association [*Bolivia*] (EAIO)
NMN .... Ndermarrje e Materialeve te Ndertimit [*Albanian*]
NMN .... Nicotinamide Mononucleotide (RU)
NMNH ...... Nederlandsche Maatschappij voor Nijverheid en Handel [*Netherlands*] (EAIO)
NMO .... Forward Engine Room (RU)
NMO .... Norwegian Master-Painter Organization (EAIO)
NMO .... Scientific Methodological Department (RU)
NMOJMA ... Nagasaki Marine Observatory/Japan Meteorological Agency (MSC)
NMOS....... Mosman Library [*National Union Catalogue of Australia symbol*]
NMP.......... Chief of Medical Service of a Regiment (RU)
NMP.......... Movement Publications [*National Union Catalogue of Australia symbol*]
NMP........ National Maize Project
NMP........ National Mobilisation Programme [*Ghana*]
NMP.......... Nederlands Middenstands Partij [*Netherlands Middle Class Party*] [*Political party*] (PPE)
NMP........ Net Material Product (SCAC)
NMP........ New Management Policy [*IWC*] (ASF)
NMP.......... Normenausschuss Materialpruefung im DIN [*Deutsches Institut fuer Normung*] eV [*Material Testing Standards in the German Institute of Standardization*] (SLS)
NMPA ...... National Meat Processors Association [*Australia*]
NMPC .... Australasian Medical Publishing Company Limited [*National Union Catalogue of Australia symbol*]
NMPl........ People's Museum in Plovdiv (BU)
NMPO....... Nordic Master Painters' Organization (EA)
NMPP .... Nouvelles Messageries de la Presse Parisienne [*Paris press distribution agency*]
NMQH ...... Macquarie Hospital (North Ryde) - Medical Library [*National Union Catalogue of Australia symbol*]
NMQU ...... Macquarie University [*National Union Catalogue of Australia symbol*]
NMR.......... National Military Representatives with SHAPE [*NATO*]
NMR.......... National Movement for Renewal
NMRB .... National Mutual Royal Bank [*Australia*] (ADA)
NMRC....... National Meat Retail Council [*Australia*]
NMRE .... Moree Regional Library [*National Union Catalogue of Australia symbol*]
n mr s .... Commander of Naval Forces (BU)
NMS.......... Chief of Medical Service (RU)
NMS.......... Namsang [*Myanmar*] [*Airport symbol*] (OAG)
NMS.......... National Marine Services [*United Arab Emirates*] (MENA)
NMS.......... New Music Society [*Australia*]
NMS.......... Nigerian Meteorological Service (PDAA)
NMS.......... Nordic Metalworkers Secretariat (EA)
NMS.......... Scientific Medical Council (RU)
NMS.......... Scientific Methodological Council (RU)
NMS.......... Scientific Methodological Department (RU)

NMSA ...... Namibia Municipal Staff Association (EAIO)
NMSB .... Maritime Services Board of New South Wales - Reference Library [*National Union Catalogue of Australia symbol*]
NMSC .... Non-Melanoma Skin Cancer
NMSD .... Merck Sharp and Dohme (Australia) Proprietary Limited [*National Union Catalogue of Australia symbol*]
NMSH....... Ndermarrje Minerale Shteterore [*Albanian*]
NMSI .... Michell Sillar McPhee Meyer [*National Union Catalogue of Australia symbol*]
NMSJ........ McConnel Smith and Johnson Proprietary Limited [*National Union Catalogue of Australia symbol*]
NMSS....... New Mon State Party [*Myanmar*] [*Political party*]
NMSS........ Norway Multiple Sclerosis Society (EAIO)
NMSSA ..... National Multiple Sclerosis Society of Australia
NMST .... Mallesons Stephen Jaques - Sydney Office [*National Union Catalogue of Australia symbol*]
NMT.......... Bottom Dead Center (RU)
NMT.......... Nigerian Machine Tool Company
NMT.......... Nordic Mobile Telephone [*Radio-telephone system for car users*] [*Denmark, Finland, Norway, Sweden*]
NMTC .... Moore Theological College [*National Union Catalogue of Australia symbol*]
NMTC .... National Marine Tanker Company
NMTL .... Department of Defence - Materials Testing Laboratories [*National Union Catalogue of Australia symbol*]
NMTSC..... New Metals Technology Service Corp. [*China*]
NMU .... National Maritime Union [*Panama*] (LA)
NMU .... Nordic Musicians' Union (EA)
NMU .... Nuba Mountains Union
NMUD ...... Mudgee Shire Library [*National Union Catalogue of Australia symbol*]
NMUS....... Museum of Applied Arts and Sciences (Sydney) - Power House Museum [*National Union Catalogue of Australia symbol*]
NMV.......... Lower Low Water (RU)
NMV.......... Natalse Munisipale Vereniging [*South Africa*] (AA)
NMV.......... Nederlandse Malacologische Vereniging [*Netherlands*] (SLS)
NMV.......... Nederlandse Museumvereniging [*Dutch Museum Association*] (SLS)
NMV.......... Nederlandse Mycologische Vereniging [*Netherlands*] (SLS)
NMWA ...... National Mine Workers Association [*Liberia*] (AF)
NMWB...... Water Board (New South Wales) - Library and Information Service [*National Union Catalogue of Australia symbol*]
NMWM..... Moriah College - Fisher Library [*National Union Catalogue of Australia symbol*]
NMWU ..... National Mine Workers Union [*Liberia*] (AF)
NMWU ..... National Mining Workers' Union of Malaya
NMWU ..... Northern Mine Workers Union
NMX.......... University of Western Sydney - Macarthur - Milperra Campus - Information Resourc [*National Union Catalogue of Australia symbol*]
NMZhK..... Low-Molecular-Weight Fatty Acids (RU)
NN .... Anonimo [*Anonymous, Joint-Stock*] [*Portuguese*]
nN .... Gesamtwirkungsgrad [*Total Efficiency*] [*German*]
NN .... Ismeretlen Nevu [*Anonymous*] (HU)
NN .... Low Voltage (RU)
NN .... Nacht und Nebel [*Night and Fog*] [*Concentration camp inmates considered to be dangerous*] [*World War II*]
nN .... Nad Nisou [*On the Neisse River*] (CZ)
nn .... Nastepne (Strony) [*Next (Pages)*] (POL)
NN .... Ndermarrje e Ndertimeve [*Albanian*]
NN .... Nescio Nomen [*Name (of Father) Unknown (On birth certificates, etc.)*] [*Italian*]
NN .... New Nationals [*Political party*] [*Australia*]
NN .... Nigerian Navy
nn .... Nizke Napeti [*Low Voltage*] (CZ)
nn .... Non Numerato [*Unnumbered*] [*Publishing*] [*Italian*]
NN .... Normalnull [*Mean Sea Level*] [*German*]
NN .... Northern News
NN .... Notariele Nieuwsbode [*Benelux*] (BAS)
NN .... Nouvelle Normes [*New Standards*] [*French government hotel rating system*]
NNA .... Nationale-Nederlanden (Australia)
NNA .... National News Agency [*Lebanon*]
NNA .... National People's Army (RU)
NNA .... Nigerian National Alliance
NNA .... Nine Network Australia
NNA .... Notio-Notio-Anatolikos [*South-Southeast*] (GC)
NNAE....... University of Western Sydney - Nepean [*National Union Catalogue of Australia symbol*]
NNAK....... National Nurses Association of Kenya (EAIO)
NNBL....... George Weston Foods Laboratories Library [*National Union Catalogue of Australia s*]
NNC.......... Naga National Council [*India*] (PD)
NNC.......... Namibian National Council [*Africa*]
NNC.......... Native National Congress
NNC.......... Northern Nigerian Congress

NNCAE..... Nigerian National Council for Adult Education
NNCAMD ... RAAF (Royal Australian Air Force) 1 Central Ammunition Depot [*National Union Catalogue of Australia symbol*]
NNCC....... National Nursing Consultative Committee [*Australia*]
NNCIAWPRC ... Netherlands National Committee of the International Association on Water Pollution Research and Control (EAIO)
NNCIAWPRC ... Norwegian National Committee of the International Association on Water Pollution Research and Control (EAIO)
NNCT........ Newcastle Technical College [*National Union Catalogue of Australia symbol*]
NNCU:A.... University of Newcastle - Auchmuty Library [*National Union Catalogue of Australia symbol*]
NNCU:C.... University of Newcastle - Central Coast Campus Library [*National Union Catalogue of Australia symbol*]
NNCU:H ... University of Newcastle - Huxley Library [*National Union Catalogue of Australia symbol*]
NNCU:M... University of Newcastle - Newcastle Conservatorium of Music Library [*National Union Catalogue of Australia symbol*]
NND .... Nigerian National Diploma
NNDC....... New Nigeria Development Company Ltd.
NNDC....... Northern Nigeria Development Corporation
NNDH....... Nepean District Historical Society. (New South Wales) [*National Union Catalogue of Australia symbol*]
NNDL........ Noord-Nederland [*Northern Netherlands*] [*Afrikaans*]
NNDP........ Naga National Democratic Party [*India*] [*Political party*] (PPW)
NNDP........ Nigerian National Democratic Party (AF)
NNDTC..... National Nondestructive Testing Centre [*Atomic Energy Authority*] [*Information service or system*] (IID)
NNDW ...... Nandewar Historical Society [*National Union Catalogue of Australia symbol*]
NNE........... Nord-Nord-Est [*North Northeast*] [*French*] (MTD)
NNE........... Nord-Nord-Est [*North Northeast*] [*Italian*]
NNE........... Nornordeste [*North Northeast*] [*Spanish*]
NNEC....... National Nuclear Energy Commission [*Brazil*]
NNEI........ Nasionale Navorsingsinstituut vir Elektriese Ingenieurswese [*Council for Scientific and Industrial Research*] [*South Africa*] (AA)
NNF........... Namibia National Front [*Political party*] (PPW)
NNF........... National Science Foundation [*NSF*] (RU)
NNF........... Nordisk Neurokirurgisk Forening [*Scandinavian Neurosurgical Society - SNS*] (EAIO)
NNF........... Nordisk Neurologisk Forening [*Scandinavian Neurological Association - SNA*] (EAIO)
NNF........... Northern Nurses Federation [*Norway*]
NNFS .... Nordic Narrow/16mm Film Society (EA)
NNG .... Nanning [*China*] [*Airport symbol*] (OAG)
NNGC....... Het Nederlands Natuur - en Geneeskundig Congres
NNGG .... New Generations [*An association*] [*Spain*] (EAIO)
NNH .... Nordiska Namnden for Handikappfragor [*Nordic Committee on Disability - NCD*] [*Sweden*] (EAIO)
NNHM ...... National Natural History Museum [*Bulgarian Academy of Sciences*] [*Research center*] (EAS)
NNHO....... Nigerian Navy Hydrographic Office (MSC)
NNI........... Ndermarrje Ndertime Industriale [*Albanian*]
NNI........... Nederlands Normalisatie-Instituut [*Rijswijk*]
NNI........... Netherlands Standards Institute (EAIO)
NNI 82....... Normcommissie Informatieverzorging [*Netherlands*]
NNIL........ Northern Nigeria Investments Limited
NNIMI...... Nasionale Instituut vir Meganiese Ingenieurswese [*Council for Scientific and Industrial Research*] [*South Africa*] (AA)
NNIVS...... Nasionale Navorsingsinstituut vir Voedingsiektes [*South African Medical Research Council*] (AA)
NNK .... Neutron-Neutron Logging (RU)
NNK .... Nihon Noritsu Kyokai [*Japan*] (EAIO)
Nnl............. Nieu-Nederlands [*Modern Dutch*] [*Language, etc.*] [*Afrikaans*]
NNL........... Nigerian National Shipping Line
NNLC....... Ngwane National Liberation Congress [*Swaziland*] (AF)
NNLC....... Ngwane National Liberatory Congress [*Swaziland*]
NNM .... Ndermarrje e Ndertimit te Minierave [*Albanian*]
NNM .... Neutron-Neutron Method (RU)
NNMA ...... Nigerian National Merit Award
NNMC....... Nigerian Newsprint Manufacturing Company
NNML....... Norske Naturhistoriske Museers Landsforbund [*Norway*] (SLS)
NNN .... Nemzetkozi Nonap [*International Women's Day*] (HU)
NNNA ...... North Nyasa Native Association [*Malawi*]
NNO .... Naga Nationalist Organization [*India*]
NNO .... Nasionale Navorsingsinstituut vir Oseanologie [*Council for Scientific and Industrial Research*] [*South Africa*] (AA)
NNO .... Noord-Noordoos [*North Northeast*] [*Afrikaans*]
NNO .... Nord-Nord-Ouest [*North-Northwest*] [*French*]
NNO .... Nord-Nord-Ovest [*North-Northwest*] [*Italian*]
NNO .... Nornoroeste [*North-Northwest*] [*Spanish*]
NNOC....... Nigerian National Oil Company
NNOC....... Nigerian National Oil Corporation (AF)

NNP........... 'De Nederlandse Nieuwsbladpers' [*Netherlands Newspaper Press*] (EY)
NNP........... Nedre Norrlands Productfoerning [*Sweden*]
NNP........... New National Party [*Grenada*]
NNP........... Stationary Observation Post (RU)
NNP........... Vereniging van de Nederlandsche Nieuwsbladpers [*Association of the Netherlands Weekly Press*] (WEN)
NNPC....... Nigerian National Petroleum Company (AF)
NNPC....... Nigerian National Petroleum Corp. (ECON)
NNPC....... Northern Nigerian Publishing Company
NNPD........ Parke Davis Proprietary Limited - Medical Library [*National Union Catalogue of Australia symbol*]
NNPL .... Newcastle Region Public Library [*National Union Catalogue of Australia symbol*]
NNPW....... National Parks and Wildlife Service of New South Wales [*National Union Catalogue of Australia symbol*]
NNR........... Nordiska Nykterhetsradet [*Nordic Temperance Council - NTC*] (EAIO)
NNRA....... Newcastle Region Art Gallery [*National Union Catalogue of Australia symbol*]
NNRC....... National Nuclear Research Centre [*South Africa*]
NNRF .... Non-Negotiable Report of Findings [*Societe Generale de Surveillance SA*] (DS)
NNRI........ National Nutrition Research Institute
NNRL........ Namoi Regional Library [*National Union Catalogue of Australia symbol*]
NNRLNT .. Decree on Job Placement of Persons with Diminished Working Capacity (BU)
NNRO .... Den Norske Nasjonalkomite for Rasjonell Organisasjon [*Norway*] (SLS)
NNRTB ..... 1 Recruit Training Batallion [*National Union Catalogue of Australia symbol*]
NNS........... Netherlands Nuclear Society (EAIO)
NNS........... Nigeriiskii Natsional'nyi Soiuz
NNSAP..... Norwegian National Society for Autistic People (EAIO)
NNSC....... Nigerian National Supply Company
NNSD....... 2 Stores Depot (Royal Australian Air Force) [*National Union Catalogue of Australia symbol*]
NNSL .... Nigerian National Shipping Lines
NNSP........ Nachrichtennetz-Steuerungsprogramm [*German*] (ADPT)
NNST .... North Sydney College of TAFE (Technical and Further Education) [*National Union Catalogue of Australia symbol*]
NNSWD.... New South Wales - Defence Regional Library [*Department of Defence*] [*National Union Catalogue of Australia symbol*]
NNSYD ..... Municipality of North Sydney - Stanton Library [*National Union Catalogue of Australia symbol*]
NNT........... Nan [*Thailand*] [*Airport symbol*] (OAG)
NNTA....... National Trust of Australia (New South Wales) [*National Union Catalogue of Australia symbol*]
NNTs......... Low-Nitrated Cellulose (RU)
NN TTCC FF ... Nos Tres Chers Freres [*Dearly Beloved Brethren*] [*French*]
NNU .... Namibia National Union (AF)
NNU .... Nordic Numismatic Union (EAIO)
NNUM ...... Nordisk Numismatisk Union [*Denmark*] (EAIO)
NNUU ...... Naciones Unidas [*United Nations*] [*Use UN*] (LA)
NNV .... Nederlandse Natuurkundige Vereniging [*Dutch Natural History Association*] (SLS)
NNW .... Niedrigstes Niedrigwasser [*Minimum Low Water Level*] (EG)
NNW .... Noord-Noordwes [*North Northwest*] [*Afrikaans*]
NNW .... Nord Nord Ouest [*North Northwest*] [*French*] (MTD)
NNWL....... North Western Library Service [*National Union Catalogue of Australia symbol*]
NNWW ..... Nasionale Navorsingsinstituut vir Wiskundige Wetenskappe [*Council for Scientific and Industrial Research*] [*South Africa*] (AA)
NNY........... Nanyang [*China*] [*Airport symbol*] (OAG)
NNZ........... Auxiliary Charge Carriers (RU)
NO .... Chief of Operations Section (BU)
no............... Criminal Section (BU)
NO .... De Nederlandse Onderneming [*Netherlands*] (BAS)
NO .... Detachment Commander (RU)
NO .... Directive on Workers' and Employees' Leaves and Rest Periods (BU)
NO .... Nacelnik Oddeleni [*Chief of Department*] (CZ)
NO .... Nachalnik Otdelenia [*Chief of Department*] [*Soviet military rank*]
NO .... Nadbiskupski Ordinarijat [*Chancery of the Catholic Archbishopric*] (YU)
nO .... Nad Odrou [*On the Oder River*] (CZ)
no............... Nain T Niin Ollen [*Finland*]
NO .... Naroden Odbor [*People's Committee*] (YU)
NO .... Narodna Odbrana [*National Defense*] (YU)
NO .... Narodna Omladina [*People's Youth*] (YU)
NO .... Narodni Osvobozeni [*National Liberation*] [*A newspaper*] (CZ)
NO .... Narodnooslobodilacki [*National Liberation*] (YU)
NO .... National Okrug (RU)
NO .... National Opera (BU)

NO .... Navtikos Omilos [*Yacht Club*] (GC)
no............... Netto [*Net*] [*German*] (GPO)
NO .... Niederoesterreich [*or Niederoesterreichisch*] [*Lower Austria or Lower Austrian*] [*German*]
no............... Niet Ontvankelijk [*Benelux*] (BAS)
NO .... Nijverheidsonderwijs [*Benelux*] (BAS)
No .... Nobelio [*Nobelium*] [*Chemical element*] [*Portuguese*]
no............... Nommer [*Number*] [*Afrikaans*]
NO .... Noordoos [*Northeast*] [*Afrikaans*]
NO .... Nordosten [*Northeast*] [*German*] (EG)
NO .... Nord-Ouest [*Northwest*] [*French*]
NO .... Nord-Ovest [*Northwest*] [*Italian*]
NO .... Noroeste [*Northwest*] [*Spanish*]
NO .... Noroeste [*Northwest*] [*Portuguese*]
NO .... Norway [*ANSI two-letter standard code*] (CNC)
n/o .... Nossa Ordem [*Portuguese*]
n/o .... Notre Ordre [*Our Order*] [*Business term*] [*French*]
NO .... Nova Obzorja [*New Horizons*] [*Maribor A periodical*] (YU)
NO .... Novara [*Car registration plates*] [*Italy*]
no............... Novembro [*November*] [*Portuguese*]
No .... Novini [*News*] [*A newspaper*] (BU)
NO .... Nuestra Orden [*Our Order*] [*Spanish*] [*Business term*]
NO .... Null-Balance Device [*Computers*] (RU)
No .... Number (PWGL)
No .... Numer [*Number*] [*Poland*]
No .... Numero [*Number*] [*Italian*] (GPO)
no............... Numero [*Number*] [*Portuguese*]
no............... Numero [*Number*] [*Finland*]
No .... Numero [*Number*] [*German*] (GPO)
No .... Numero [*Number*] [*Spanish*]
no............... Numero [*Number*] [*Turkey*] (GPO)
No .... Numero [*Number*] [*French*]
No .... Nummer [*Number*] [*German*] (GCA)
n:o............. Numro [*Number*] [*Sweden*] (GPO)
n/o .... Over (RU)
NO .... Public Education (RU)
NOA .... Nueva Organizacion Anticomunista [*New Anticommunist Organization*] [*Guatemala*] (LA)
NOA .... Nueva Organizacion Antiterrorista [*New Anti-Terrorist Organization*] [*Guatemala*] (PD)
NOA .... People's Army of Liberation [*Chinese People's Republic*] (RU)
NOA .... Scientific Testing Airfield (RU)
NOAA....... National Oceanic and Atmospheric Administration (WER)
NOAC....... Nordic Committee for Accelerator Based Research [*Denmark*] (EAIO)
NOAH .... Narcotics, Opiates, Amphetamines, Heroin [*Police operation*] [*Australia*]
NOAK....... People's Army of Liberation of China (RU)
NOAKMO ... Narodni Odbor Autonomne Kosovo-Metohijske Oblasti [*People's Committee of the Autonomous Region of Kosovo-Metohija*] (YU)
No Amr ...... Nobetci Amiri [*Duty Officer*] (TU)
NOAP....... Ove Arup and Partners [*National Union Catalogue of Australia symbol*]
NoAptD ..... Novo Aptechno Delo [*New Pharmacy Affairs*] [*A periodical*] (BU)
NOAR....... Agricultural Research and Veterinary Centre [*New South Wales Department of Agriculture*] [*National Union Catalogue of Australia symbol*]
NOAR....... New South Wales - Department of Agriculture - Agricultural Research and Veterin [*National Union Catalogue of Australia symbol*]
NOAS....... National Organization for Agricultural Settling
NOASR ..... Netherlands Organization for Applied Scientific Research (EAIO)
NOB.......... Narodnooslobodilacka Borba [*National Liberation Struggle*] (YU)
NOB.......... Nationale Organisatie voor het Beroepsgoederenvervoer Wegtransport [*Benelux*] (BAS)
NOB.......... Nemzetkozi Olimpiai Bizottsag [*International Olympic Committee*] (HU)
Nob .... Nobile [*Nobleman*] [*Italian*]
NOB.......... Nobile [*Nobly*] [*Music*] (ROG)
NOB.......... Nuwe Onderwysbond [*Afrikaans*]
NOBIN...... Nederlands Orgaan voor de Bevordering van de Informatieverzorging [*'s-Gravenhage*]
NOBIN...... Stichting Nederlands Orgaan voor de Bevordering van de Informatieverzorging [*Netherlands Organization for Information Policy*] [*Information service or system*] [*Defunct*] (IID)
NObrigada ... People's Liberation Brigade (BU)
N Obs........ Nada Obsta [*Portuguese*]
NOBS .... Nasionale Ontwikkeling- en Bestuurstigting van Suid-Afrika [*South Africa*] (AA)
NOC.......... Ascor Flyservice AS [*Norway*] [*ICAO designator*] (FAAC)
NOC.......... National Oil Corporation [*Libyan, Nigerian*]

NOC.......... National Olympic Committee (OLYM)
NOC.......... National Operations Committee [*Malaysia*] (ML)
NOC.......... Naval Officer Commanding [*Australia*]
NOC.......... Netherlands Olympic Committee (EAIO)
NOC.......... No Objection Certificate [*Immigration*] [*Oman*] (IMH)
NOC.......... Norwegian Government Office of Culture [*Record label*]
NOC.......... Norwegian Olympic Committee (EAIO)
NOCG....... Narodna Omladina Crne Gore [*People's Youth of Montenegro*] (YU)
NOCG....... National Olympic Committee for Germany (EAIO)
NOCI........ Nederlandse Organisatie voor Chemische Informatie ['s-Gravenhage*]
NOCI........ Nomenclature Cambodgienne des Industries [*Cambodian Nomenclature of Industries*] (CL)
NOCIL ...... National Organic Chemicals Industries Limited [*India*]
NOCIRI..... National Olympic Committee Islamic Republic of Iran (EAIO)
NOCISEN ... Nouvelle Cimenterie du Senegal
NOCO ...... Norwegian Oil Company
NOCSA..... National Olympic Committee of South Africa (ECON)
NOD .... Chief of Railroad Section (RU)
NOD .... Greatest Common Divisor (RU)
NOD .... Natalse Onderwysdepartement [*Natal Education Department*] [*Afrikaans*]
NOD .... Norsk Oseanografisk Datasenter [*Norwegian Oceanographic Data Center*] (MSC)
NODB....... Nacelnik Odboru [*Branch Chief*] (CZ)
NODCO .... National Oil Distribution Company [*Umm Said, Qatar*] (MENA)
NODECA.. Norwegian Defense Communications Agency (NATG)
NODM ...... Ferrocarril Nor-Oeste de Mexico [*Mexico North Western Railroad*] [*AAR code*]
NODO ...... Narodnooslobodilacki Dobrovoljacki Odred [*National Liberation Volunteer Detachment*] [*World War II*] (YU)
NO-DO ...... Noticiarios y Documentales Cinematograficos [*Documentary Films and Newsreel Co.*] [*Spanish*] (WER)
NOE.......... Navtikos Omilos Ellados [*Yacht Club of Greece*] (GC)
NOE.......... Norden-Norddeich [*Germany*] [*Airport symbol*]
NOE.......... (Skholi) Nomikon kai Oikonomikon Epistimon [*(School of) Law and Economic Sciences*] [*SNOE*] [*See also*] (GC)
N-Oefen ..... Niederschachtoefen [*Low-Shaft Furnaces (Installed at the West Metallurgical Combine in Calbe/Saale)*] (EG)
NOEI........ Nouvel Ordre Economique International [*New International Economic Order*] [*Use NIEO*] [*French*] (AF)
NOEI........ Nuevo Orden Economico Internacional [*New International Economic Order*] [*Spanish*] (LA)
NOEL........ Naval Ordnance Electronics Laboratory
NOEM....... Netherlands Oil and Gas Equipment Manufacturers (EAIO)
noem.......... November (BU)
NOEP........ Neue Oekonomische Politik [*New Economic Policy*] [*Germany*]
noerdl........ Noerdlich [*Northern*] [*German*] (GCA)
NOeS .... Neues Oekonomisches System [*New Economic System*] (EG)
NOeSPL.... Neues Oekonomisches System der Planung und Leitung [*New Economic Planning and Managing System*] (EG)
NOF.......... Fonnafly AS [*Norway*] [*ICAO designator*] (FAAC)
NOF.......... Narodnooslobodilacka Fronta [*National Liberation Front*] (YU)
NOF.......... Narodnooslobodilacki Fond [*National Liberation Fund*] (YU)
NOF.......... People's Liberation Front (BU)
NOFPP...... National Family and Population Office [*Tunisia*] (EAIO)
NOFR .... New [*South Wales*] Orana and Far [*West*] Regional Health Se rvices Library [*National Union Catalogue of Australia symbol*]
NOFROA .. Compagnie Norvegienne et Francaise de l'Ouest Africain
NOFW....... New South Wales - Orana and Far Western Agricultural Research Centre [*Agriculture*] [*National Union Catalogue of Australia symbol*]
NOG .... Narodni Odbor Grada [*City People's Committee*] (YU)
NOG .... Nationaloekonomische Gesellschaft [*National Economic Association*] [*Austria*] (SLS)
NOG .... Nederlands Oogheelkundig Gezelschap [*Netherlands*] (SLS)
NOG .... Neue Organisationsmaschinengesellschaft [*German*] (ADPT)
NOG .... Normenausschuss Erdoel- und Erdgasgewinnung im DIN [*Deutsches Institut fuer Normung*] eV [*Oil and Natural Gas Production Standards in the German Institute of Standardization*] (SLS)
NOGEPA .. Netherlands Oil and Gas Exploration and Production Association
NOGI........ Ogilvy and Mather [*National Union Catalogue of Australia symbol*]
NOGO ...... Narodni Odbor Gradske Opstine [*Township People's Committee*] (YU)
NOGZ....... Narodni Odbor Grada Zagreba [*People's Committee of the City of Zagreb*] (YU)
NOHC....... National Occupational Health and Safety Commission [*Australia*]
NOHS....... Worksafe Australia [*National Union Catalogue of Australia symbol*]

NOHSC..... National Occupational Health and Safety Commission [*Australia*]
Noi............. Nisoi [*Islands*] [*N*] [*See also*] [*Greek*]   (NAU)
NOI............ Notice of Intention
NOIC......... National Organisation Investigation Committee, Printing and Allied Trades Employers' Federation of Australia   (ADA)
NOIK........ Nederlands-Oos-Indiese Kompanjie [*Dutch East Indies Company*] [*Afrikaans*]
NOIP........ National Office of Industrial Property
NOJ.......... Narodno Oslobodenje Jugoslavije [*National Liberation of Yugoslavia*]   (YU)
NOK.......... Narodni Odbor Kotara [*District People's Committee*]   (YU)
NOK.......... Nationales Olympisches Komitee [*National Olympic Committee*] (EG)
NOK.......... National Olympic Committee   (RU)
NOK.......... Nordostschweizerische Kraftwerke AG [*Switzerland*]
NOK.......... Norges Olympiske Komite [*Norwegian Olympic Committee*] (EAIO)
NOK.......... Norsk Oseanografisk Komite [*Norwegian Oceanographic Committee*]   (MSC)
NOK.......... Nywerheidsontwikkelingskorporasie [*Industrial Development Corporation*] [*Afrikaans*]
NOKW....... NAZI Oberkommando der Wehrmacht [*NAZI Armed Forces High Command*] [*World War II*] [*German*]   (BJA)
Nokyo........ Nogyo Kyodo Kumiai [*Japan*]
NOKZ........ Narodni Odbor Kotara Zagreba [*People's Committee of the District of Zagreb*]   (YU)
NOL........... National Overseas Airline Co. [*Egypt*] [*ICAO designator*] (FAAC)
NOL.......... Neptune Orient Lines [*Australia*]   (ADA)
NOLIT....... Nova Literatura, Izdavacko Preduzece [*New Literature, Publishing Establishment*] [*Belgrade*]   (YU)
NOLITAF ... Nouvelle Literie Africaine
NOM......... Nakuru Oils Mills Ltd. [*Kenya*]
NOM......... National Orientation Movement [*Nigeria*]
NOM......... Nisshin Oil Mills [*Japan*]
NOM........ Nomad River [*Papua New Guinea*] [*Airport symbol*]   (OAG)
nom........... Nominatief [*Nominative*] [*Afrikaans*]
nom........... Nominatif [*Nominative, Subject, Registered*] [*French*]
nom........... Nominatiivi [*Finland*]
Nom.......... Nominativ [*Nominative*] [*German*]
nom........... Nominative   (TPFD)
NOM........ Noordelijke Ontwikkelings Maatschappij [*Netherlands*]
NOM........ Norme Italiani per il Controllo degli Olii Minerali e Derivati [*Italian Standard for Mineral Oils and Derivatives*] (PDAA)
NOM........ Scientific Society of Marxists   (RU)
NOMACO ... Nouvelle Mauritanie Commerciale
nomb......... Nombreux [*Numerous*] [*French*]
NOMBA.... Nordic Molecular Biology Association [*Denmark*]   (EAIO)
nombr........ Nombreux [*Numerous*] [*French*]
NOMIS..... National Online Manpower Information System [*Manpower Services Commission*] [*Information service or system*] (IID)
nom kap ..... Nominale Kapitaal [*Afrikaans*]
nom nud ..... Nomen Nudum [*Invalid Name*] [*Biology, taxonomy*] [*Latin*]
NOMUS.... Nordic Music Committee [*Sweden*]   (EAIO)
NOMUS.... Nordisk Musikkomite [*Nordic Music Committee*]   (EAIO)
NON......... Nonouti [*Kiribati*] [*Airport symbol*]   (OAG)
NON......... North Norway   (NATG)
NON......... Nuevo Orden Nacional [*New National Order*] [*Ecuador*]   (LA)
NONAS..... Negroes Occidental National Agricultural School
NONE....... Network to Oust Nuclear Energy [*India*]   (EAIO)
NONSSA... National Oncology Nursing Society of South Africa   (EAIO)
NOO.......... Nacelnik Operacniho Oddeleni [*Chief of Operations Department*] (CZ)
NOO.......... Naoro [*Papua New Guinea*] [*Airport symbol*]   (OAG)
NOO.......... Narodni Odbor Opstine [*Municipal People's Committee*]   (YU)
NOO.......... Narodnooslobodilacki Odbor [*National Liberation Committee*] (YU)
NOOSR.... National Office of Overseas Skills Recognition [*Australia*]
NOP........... Narodnooslobodilacki Pokret [*National Liberation Movement*] [*World War II*]   (YU)
NOP........... Netherlands Association of Trade Unions   (RU)
NOP........... Novair-Aviacao Geral SA [*Portugal*] [*ICAO designator*]   (FAAC)
NOP........... Novy Operativni Plan [*New Operational Plan*]   (CZ)
NOPA........ Norske Populaerautorer [*Norway*]   (EAIO)
NOPAA..... National Office Products Association of Australia
NOPATO.. Nouvelle Papeterie Togolaise
NOPE........ New South Wales - Open Training [*Department of Technical and Further Education*] [*National Union Catalogue of Australia symbol*]
NOPEC..... Non-OPEC [*Oil producing countries which are not members of OPEC*]
NoPEF....... Nordiska Projektexportfonden [*Nordic Project Fund*] [*Finland*] (EAIO)

NOPiDO ... Narodnooslobodilacki Partizanski i Dobrovoljacki Odredi [*National Liberation Partisan and Volunteer Detachments*] [*World War II*]   (YU)
NOPiDV.... Narodnooslobodilacka Partizanska i Dobrovoljacka Vojska [*National Liberation Partisan and Volunteer Army*] [*World War II*]   (YU)
NOPiDVJ ... Narodnooslobodilacka Partizanska i Dobrovoljacka Vojska Jugoslavije [*National Liberation Partisan and Volunteer Army of Yugoslavia*] [*World War II*]   (YU)
NOPiD(vojska) ... Narodnooslobodilacka Partizanska i Dobrovoljacka (Vojska) [*National Liberation Partisan and Volunteer (Army)*] [*World War II*]   (YU)
NOP-N ...... Nordiska Publiceringsnamnden for Naturvetenskap [*Nordic Publishing Board in Science*]   (EAIO)
NOPO........ Narodnooslobodilacki Partizanski Odredi [*National Liberation Partisan Detachments*] [*World War II*]   (YU)
NOPOBiH ... Narodnooslobodilacki Partizanski Odredi Bosne i Hercegovine [*National Liberation Partisan Detachments of Bosnia and Hercegovina*] [*World War II*]   (YU)
NOPOJ ..... Narodnooslobodilacki Partizanski Odredi Jugoslavije [*National Liberation Partisan Detachments of Yugoslavia*] [*World War II*]   (YU)
NOPPMB ... Nigeria Oil Palm Produce Marketing Board
NOPTU ..... Scientific Organization of Production, Labor, and Management (BU)
NOPU........ Narodnooslobodilacki Partizanski Udarni [*National Liberation Partisan Shock Units*]   (YU)
NOPV........ Narodnooslobodilacka Partizanska Vojska [*National Liberation Partisan Army*] [*World War II*]   (YU)
NoPVDM .. N'Oubliez Pas Vos Decorations Maconniques [*Do Not Forget Your Masonic Regalia*] [*Freemasonry*] [*French*]
NOPWASD ... National Organization for Potable Water and Sanitary Drainage [*Egypt*]
NOR .... AS Norving [*Norway*] [*ICAO designator*]   (FAAC)
Nor............. Na-Oorlogse Rechtspraak [*Benelux*]   (BAS)
NOR .... Narodnooslobodilacki Rat [*National Liberation War*] [*World War II*]   (YU)
NOR .... Navtikos Omilos Rodou [*Rhodes Yacht Club*]   (GC)
NOR .... Nordfjordur [*Iceland*] [*Airport symbol*]   (OAG)
NOR .... Nordisk Organ for Reinforskning [*Nordic Council of Reindeer Research*] [*Norway*]   (EAIO)
NOR .... Norway [*ANSI three-letter standard code*]   (CNC)
NORA....... Orange Regional Gallery [*National Union Catalogue of Australia symbol*]
NORAD..... Norwegian Agency for Development
NorAE .... Norwegian Antarctic Expedition [*1956-*]
NORAID ... Norwegian Agency for International Development
NORAS ..... Norges Rad for Anvendt Samfunnsforskning [*NAVF Council for Applied Social Sciences*] [*Research center*] [*Norway*]   (IRC)
NORCEM ... Cement Company of Northern Nigeria
NORCEM ... Norwegian Cement Co.
NORCh...... Nonstandard Equipment and Spare Parts   (BU)
NORD .... Norsk Data [*Manufacturer and computer series*] [*Norway*]
NORDAF .. Northern Federation of Advertisers Associations [*Sweden*] (EAIO)
NORDCO ... Newfoundland Oceans Research and Development Corporation (MSC)
NORDEK .. Norway, Denmark, Finland, Sweden [*Nordic Economic Community*] [*Trade bloc*]
NORDEL .. Organization for Nordic Electrical Cooperation   (EA)
NORDFORSK ... Nordiska Samarbetsorganisationen foer Teknisk-Naturvetenskaplig Forskning [*Sweden*]   (SLS)
NORDIATRANS ... Association for Nordic Transplant and Dialysis Personnel   (EAIO)
NORDICOM ... Nordic Documentation Center for Mass Communication Research [*Database originator*] [*Finland*] [*Information service or system*]   (IID)
NORDINFO ... Nordiska Samarbetsorganet for Vetenskaplig Information [*Nordic Council for Scientific Information and Research Libraries*] [*Finland*]   (EAIO)
NORDISA ... Nordeste Industrial SA [*Brazil*]   (DSCA)
NORDITA ... Nordisk Institut for Teoretisk Atomfysik [*Nordic Institute for Theoretical Nuclear Physics*] [*Copenhagen, Denmark*] [*Research center*]   (WEN)
NORD/LB ... Norddeutsche Landsbank [*North Germany Federal Bank*]
NORDPLAN ... Nordic Institute for Studies in Urban and Regional Planning [*Sweden*]   (EAIO)
NordREFO ... Nordiska Institutet for Regionalpolitisk Forskning [*Nordic Institute of Regional Policy Research*] [*Finland*]   (EAIO)
NORDSAM ... Nordiska Samarbetskommitten for Internationell Politik [*Nordic Cooperation Committee for International Politics, Including Conflict and Peace Research*] [*Sweden*]   (EAIO)
NORDSAT ... Scandinavian Countries Broadcast Satellite   (MCD)
Nordser...... Nordisk Samkatalog foer Seriella Medicinska Publikationer [*Karolinska Institutets Bibliotek och Informationscentral*] [*Sweden*] [*Information service or system*]   (CRD)

NORDTEL ... Nordiskt Samarbete Inom Telekommunikation [*Nordic Cooperation on Telecommunications*] [*Finland*]   (EAIO)

NORESS ... Norwegian Regional Seismic Array

NOREX ..... Noranda Exploration Proprietary Ltd. [*Australia*]

NORG .... Nasserite Organisation Reform Group

NORGABON ... Societe Miniere du Nord-Gabon

NORIANE ... Normes et Reglements Informations Automatisees Accessibles en Ligne [*Automated Standards and Regulations Information Online*] [*Database French Association for Standardization*] [*Information service or system*]   (IID)

Noril'lag ..... Noril'sk Corrective Labor Camp   (RU)

NORINCO ... China North Industries Corp. [*China*]   (IMH)

NORINDOK ... Norwegian Committee for Information and Documentation

norj .... Norjaa [*or Norjaksi*] [*Finland*]

norj .... Norjalainen [*Finland*]

norl .... Norleucine   (RU)

NORL .... Northern Regional Library and Information Service [*National Union Catalogue of Australia symbol*]

NORLA ..... Northern Region Literature Agency

NorLantMedArea ... North Atlantic and Mediterranean Area

norm .... Normal [*German*]   (GCA)

norm .... Normen [*Standards*] [*German*]

NORMAC ... Northern Prawn Fishery Management Committee [*Australia*]

NORMANDOS ... Asociacion Colombiana de Criadores de Ganado Normando [*Colombia*]   (DSCA)

NORMATERM ... Normalisation, Automatisation de la Terminologie [*Standardization and Automation of Terminology*] [*Databank*] [*France*] [*Information service or system*]   (IID)

NORMED ... Chantiers du Nord et de la Mediterranee [*Shipbuilders*] [*French*]

NORMETAL ... Empresa Metalmecanica del Norte [*Northern Metalworking Enterprise*] [*Peru*]   (LA)

NOROIS ... Navires Oceanographiques de Recherches, d'Observation, d'Intervention, et de Soutien [*French*]   (MSC)

NORORIENTE ... Comision para el Desarrollo de la Region Nor-Oriental del Pais [*Venezuela*]   (DSCA)

NORPAC .. Cooperative Survey of the Northern Pacific   (MSC)

NORPRO .. Norwegian Committee on Trade Procedures   (PDAA)

NORQUISA ... Nordeste Quimica SA [*Brazil*]

NORS .... Norsk Operasjonsanalyse Foreningen [*Norwegian Operational Research Society*]   (PDAA)

NORS .... Office of New Vegetable Raw Materials   (RU)

NORSAM ... Nordiskt Samrad for en Aktiv Alderdom [*Nordic Association for Active Aging*] [*Finland*]   (EAIO)

NORSAR ... Norwegian Seismic Array [*Royal Norwegian Council for Scientific and Industrial Research*]

NORSS ...... Independent General Workers' Trade Union   (BU)

NORSWAM ... North Sea Wave Model   (MSC)

NORT .... Orange College of TAFE (Technical and Further Education) [*National Union Catalogue of Australia symbol*]

NORTEB ... Norwegian Telecommunications Users Group

NORTEC ... Northern Technical College [*Zambia*]

NORTHAG ... North [*European*] Army Group [*NATO*]

norv .... Norwegian   (RU)

NORVEN ... Comision Venezolana de Normas Industriales [*Standards Institute*] [*Venezuela*]   (PDAA)

NORWAID ... Norwegian Aid Society for Refugees and International Development

NORWESTLANT ... Northwestern Atlantic Environmental Study   (MSC)

NORWICH ... Knickers Off Ready When I Come Home [*Correspondence*]   (DSUE)

NorwP .... Norwegisches Patent [*Norwegian Patent*] [*German*]

NOS .... Chief of Axis of Communications   (RU)

NOS .... Irrigation and Drainage System   (BU)

NOS .... Nacelnik Operacni Skupiny [*Chief of Operational Detachment*]   (CZ)

NOS .... Narodna Omladina Srbije [*People's Youth of Serbia*]   (YU)

NOS .... Narodni Odbor Sela [*Village People's Committee*]   (YU)

NOS .... Narodni Odbor Sreza [*District People's Committee*]   (YU)

NOS .... Narodno Osvobojenje Slovenije [*National Liberation of Slovenia*] [*World War II*]   (YU)

NOS .... Nederlandse Omroep Stichting [*Netherlands Broadcasting Foundation*]   (WEN)

NOS .... Nederlandse Omroep Stichtung [*Radio and television network*] [*Netherlands*]

NOS .... Nordiska Odontologiska Studenter [*Council of Nordic Dental Students*] [*Sweden*]   (EAIO)

NOS .... Norges Offisielle Statistikk [*Norway*]

NOS .... Nossi-Be [*Madagascar*] [*Airport symbol*]   (OAG)

NOS .... Nouvel Ordre Social [*New Social Order*] [*Switzerland*]   (PD)

NOS .... Nulla Osta di Sicurezza [*Security Clearance*] [*Italian*]   (WER)

NOSA .... National Occupational Safety Association

NOSAB ..... Night Signal Bomb   (RU)

NOSALF ... Nordiska Samfundet for Latinamerika Forskning [*Nordic Association for Research on Latin America*] [*Sweden*]   (EAIO)

NoSAMF ... Nordiska Samarbetskommitten for Arktik Medicinsk Forskning [*Denmark*]   (SLS)

NOSAR ..... Norwegian Sesmic Array   (PDAA)

NOSCO ..... Ndola Oil Storage Company

NOSEBRIMA ... Nouvelle Societe d'Exploitation des Briqueteries du Mali [*Brick producer*] [*Mali*]

NOSEC ...... Nouvelle Societe Senegalaise de Commerce et d'Industrie

NOSFER ... Nouveau Systeme Fondamental pour la Determination de l'Equivalent de Reference [*OCITT*] [*New Masters System for Determining Reference Equivalents*]   (PDAA)

NOS-H ...... Nordiska Samarbetsnamnden for Humanistisk Forskning [*Nordic Committee of the Research Councils for the Humanities - NCRCH*]   (EA)

NOS-N ...... Samarbetsnamnden for de Nordiska Naturvetenskapliga Forskningraden [*Joint Committee of the Nordic Natural Science Research Councils - JCNNSRC*]   (EA)

NOSOCO ... Nouvelle Societe Commerciale Africaine

NOSONATRAM ... Nouvelle Societe Nationale des Transports Mauritaniens

NOSR .... New South Wales - Office of State Revenue [*Treasury*] [*National Union Catalogue of Australia symbol*]

NOS-S .... Nordiska Samarbetsnamnden for Samhallsforskning [*Joint Committee of Nordic Social Science Research Councils*] [*Denmark*]   (EAIO)

NOSWA .... National Organization of South-West Africa [*Namibia*]   (AF)

NOSZF ...... Nagy Oktoberi Szocialista Forradalom [*The Great October Socialist Revolution*]   (HU)

NOT .... Magyar Nok Orszagos Tanacsa [*National Council of Hungarian Women*]   (HU)

not .... Music [*Score of a composition*]   (RU)

NOT .... Nacionalna Organizacija Tehnicara [*National Organization of Technicians*]   (YU)

NOT .... Naczelna Organizacja Techniczna [*Chief Technical Organization*]   (POL)

NOT .... Nepbirosagok Orszagos Tanacsa [*National Council of People's Courts*]   (HU)

not .... Notaris [*Benelux*]   (BAS)

not .... Notice [*Annotation*] [*Publishing*] [*French*]

not .... Numerot [*Finland*]

NOT .... Orana Community College [*National Union Catalogue of Australia symbol*]

NOT .... Scientific Organization of Labor   (RU)

notaz .... Notazione [*Notation*] [*Publishing*] [*Italian*]

NOTC .... Overseas Telecommunications Corporation [*National Union Catalogue of Australia symbol*]

NOTCL ..... OTC (Overseas Telecommunications Corporation) Australia - Main Library [*National Union Catalogue of Australia symbol*]

NOTEKh ... Chief of Technical Department   (RU)

Notenanhg ... Notenanhang [*Music Appendix*] [*Publishing*] [*German*]

Notenbeil ... Notenbeilage [*Supplement(s) of Music*] [*Publishing*] [*German*]

Notenbeisp ... Notenbeispiel [*Musical Illustration*] [*Publishing*] [*German*]

notev .... Notevole [*Notable*] [*Italian*]

NOTh .... Navtikos Omilos Thessalonikis [*Salonica Yacht Club*]   (GC)

noti .... Text with Music   (BU)

Not il ed ..... Notlar Ilave Eden [*Notes Which Were Added*]   (TU)

notl .... Notlen [*Unmarried*]   (HU)

NoTNG ...... Norges Geologiske Undersoeklse Biblioteket [*Geological Survey of Norway*], Trondheim, Norway [*Library symbol*] [*Library of Congress*]   (LCLS)

NOTOX ..... No Toxic Incinerator Group [*Political party*]

NOTT .... National Office of Technology Transfer

NOTU .... National Organisation of Trade Unions [*Uganda*]

NOTU .... Nederlandsche Organisatie van Tijdschriften-Uitgevers [*Netherlands Organization of Periodical Publishers*]   (WEN)

NotW .... Notarieel Weekblad [*Benelux*]   (BAS)

Notw .... Wet op het Noterisambt [*Benelux*]   (BAS)

NOU .... Narodnooslobodilacki Udarni [*National Liberation Shock Troops*] [*World War II*]   (YU)

NOU .... Natalse Onderwysersunie [*Natal Teachers' Association*] [*Afrikaans*]

NOU .... Nederlandse Ornithologische Unie [*Dutch Ornithological Union*]   (SLS)

NOU .... Noumea [*New Caledonia*] [*Airport symbol*]   (OAG)

NOUB .... Narodnooslobodilacka Udarna Brigada [*National Liberation Shock Brigade*] [*World War II*]   (YU)

NOU(Korpus) ... Narodnooslobodilacki Udarni Korpus [*National Liberation Shock Corps*] [*World War II*]   (YU)

NOUP .... Narodnooslobodilacka Udarna Proleterska [*National Liberation Proletarian Shock (Unit)*]   (YU)

nouv .... Nouveau [*New*] [*French*]

Nouv DrYougosl ... Nouveau Droit Yougoslave   (FLAF)

NOUVELLE SIACA ... Societe Ivoirienne d'Ananas et de Conserves Alimentaires

Nouv Hol .... Nouvelles de Hollande [*Netherlands*]   (BAS)

Nouv Rep ... Nouveau Repertoire de Droit [*Dalloz*]   (FLAF)

Nouv RevDr Int Pr ... Nouvelle Revue de Droit International Prive [*Lapradelle*]   (FLAF)

NOUZ .... Narodni Odborove Ustredi Zamestnancu [*National Trade Union Employees' Center*] (CZ)
NOV .... Avianova SpA [*Italy*] [*ICAO designator*] (FAAC)
NOV .... Huambo [*Angola*] [*Airport symbol*] (OAG)
Nov............. Les Novelles [*Benelux*] (BAS)
NOV .... Narodna Omladina Vojvodine [*People's Youth of Vojvodina*] (YU)
NOV .... Narodnooslobodilacka Vojska [*National Liberation Army*] [*World War II*] (YU)
NOV .... Nederlandsche Orchideeen Vereniging [*Netherlands*] (EAIO)
NOV .... Nederlandse Orthopaedische Vereniging [*Netherlands*] (SLS)
Nov............. New [*Toponymy*] (RU)
NOV .... Nonpersistent Gas (RU)
NOV .... Noodwet Ouderdomsvoorziening [*Benelux*] (BAS)
Nov............. November [*German*] (GPO)
nov.............. November [*Hungary*] (GPO)
nov.............. November [*Denmark*] (GPO)
nov.............. November [*Netherlands*] (GPO)
nov.............. Novembre [*November*] [*Italian*]
nov.............. Novembre [*November*] [*French*]
nov.............. Novembro [*November*] [*Portuguese*] (GPO)
nov.............. Noviembre [*November*] [*Spanish*]
nov.............. Novum [*New*] [*Latin*] (MAE)
NOV .... People's Liberation Army (BU)
NOV .... Unstable Chemical Agents [*Military*] (BU)
NOVA........ Narodnooslobodilacka Vojska Albanije [*National Liberation Army of Albania*] [*World War II*] (YU)
NOVACAP ... Companhia Urbanizadora da Nova Capital do Brasil
NOVATOR ... Novye Torit [*Newly Flattened*] [*KGB term for newly recruited agent abroad*]
novbre .... Novembre [*November*] [*French*]
Novbre .... Noviembre [*November*] [*Spanish*]
Novciv .... Les Novelles (Droit Civil) [*Benelux*] (BAS)
Novcom ...... Les Novelles (Droit Commercial) [*Benelux*] (BAS)
NOVE........ NOMOS Verlagskatalog [*NOMOS Datapool*] [*Information service or system*] (IID)
nove .... Noviembre [*November*] [*Spanish*]
NOVELTA ... Nouvelle Societe Commerciale de Tamatave
NOVH .... Narodnooslobodilacka Vojska Hrvatske [*National Liberation Army of Croatia*] [*World War II*] (YU)
NOVI........ Nederlands Opleidingsinstituut voor Informatica [*Netherlands*]
NOVIB ...... Nederlandse Organisatie voor Internationale Ontwikkelingssamemwerking [*Netherlands Organization for International Development Cooperation*] (WEN)
NOVJ .... Narodnooslobodilacka Vojska Jugoslavije [*National Liberation Army of Yugoslavia*] [*World War II*] (YU)
NOVM ...... Narodnooslobodilacka Vojska Makedonije [*National Liberation Army of Macedonia*] [*World War II*] (YU)
NovNIKhI ... Scientific Research Institute of Cotton Growing in the New Regions (RU)
novo........... Novembro [*November*] [*Portuguese*]
NOVOK..... Nederlandse Organisatie van Olie- en Kolenhandelaren [*Netherlands*] (IMH)
novosib....... Novosibirsk (RU)
Novosibgiz ... Novosibirsk State Publishing House (RU)
Novosibirgiz ... Novosibirsk State Publishing House (RU)
Novosibproyekt ... Planning Institute of the Novosibirsk Gorispolkom (RU)
NOVOTEKS ... Tekstilna Tovarna, Novo Mesto [*Novo Mesto Textile Factory*] (YU)
NOVSlovenije ... Narodnoosvobodilna Vojska Slovenije [*National Liberation Army of Slovenia*] [*World War II*] (YU)
nov st .... New Style [*Gregorian calendar*] (RU)
NOW .... Narodowa Organizacja Wojskowa [*National Military Organization*] (POL)
NOW .... Royal Norwegian Air Force [*ICAO designator*] (FAAC)
NOX .... Air Nordic in Vasteras AB [*Sweden*] [*ICAO designator*] (FAAC)
NOZEMA ... Nederlandse Omroep Zender Maatschappij [*Netherlands Radio Broadcasting Company*] (WEN)
NOZh .... New Society of Painters [*1922-1924*] (RU)
NP .... Chief of Political Section [*Military term*], Chief of Political Department (RU)
NP .... Continuous Profiling (RU)
np .... Direction of Flight (RU)
NP .... Directive on Payments (BU)
NP .... Feed Pump (RU)
NP .... Forward Perpendicular [*Shipbuilding*] (RU)
NP .... Guide Plate (RU)
NP .... Irregular Semidiurnal Tides (RU)
NP .... Litter Post (RU)
NP .... Nacionalista Party [*Philippines*]
np .... Naispuolinen [*Finland*]
np .... Na Przyklad [*For Example*] (POL)
NP .... Narodnaia Partiia
np .... Narodni Podnik [*National Enterprise*] (CZ)
NP .... Narodni Pojisteni [*National Insurance*] (CZ)

NP .... Nasionale Party van Suid-Afrika [*National Party of South Africa*] [*Political party*] (PPW)
NP .... Nasionale Party van Suidwesafrika [*National Party of South West Africa*] [*Namibia*] [*Political party*] (PPW)
NP .... Nationalist Party [*Philippines*] [*Political party*] (PPW)
NP .... Nationalist Party [*Malta*] [*Political party*] (PPE)
NP .... National Party [*Papua New Guinea*] [*Political party*] (PPW)
NP .... National Party [*Nigeria*] (AF)
NP .... National Party [*Namibia*]
NP .... National Petroleum Co. [*Sierra Leone*]
NP .... National Press (BU)
NP .... Nation Party [*Turkey*] [*Political party*] (PPW)
NP .... Nauchen Pregled [*Scientific Review*] [*A periodical*] (BU)
NP .... Nebenprodukt [*Secondary Product, By-Product*] (EG)
np .... Nedsat Pris [*Reduced Price*] [*Danish, Norwegian*]
NP .... Nepal [*ANSI two-letter standard code*] (CNC)
np .... Neper [*Napier*] [*Poland*]
Np .... Neptunio [*Neptunium*] [*Chemical element*] [*Portuguese*]
np .... New Pence [*Monetary unit in Great Britain since 1971*]
NP .... News Publishers Ltd. [*Kenya*]
np .... Nome Proprio [*Proper Name*] [*Portuguese*]
NP .... Normalprofil [*Standard Cross Section*] [*German*] (GCA)
NP .... Normierte Programmierung [*German*] (ADPT)
NP .... Norsk Polarinstitutt [*Norwegian Polar Research Institute*] [*Ministry of the Environment*] (EAS)
NP .... Northern Province
NP .... North Pole [*Also, PN*]
NP .... Norwegisches Patent [*Norwegian Patent*] [*German*] (GCA)
NP .... Nova Proizvodnja [*New Production*] [*Ljubljana*] (YU)
NP .... Nowe Prawo [*New Law*] [*A periodical*] (POL)
NP .... Nucleoprotein (RU)
NP .... Nullpunkt [*Zero*] [*German*]
np .... Ny Pris [*List Price*] [*Danish, Norwegian*]
NP .... Observation Instrument (RU)
NP .... Observation Point, Observation Station (BU)
NP .... Observation Post (RU)
NP .... Petroleum Industry (RU)
NP .... Piston Jump (RU)
NP .... Populated Place (RU)
NP .... Settlements (BU)
NP .... Undetermined Frequency of Publication (BU)
NP .... Ungrounded Loop (RU)
NP .... Unpolished (RU)
NPA........... Artillery Observation Post (RU)
NPA .... Natalse Provinsiale Administrasie [*Natal Provincial Administration*] [*South Africa*] (AA)
NPA .... National Packaging Association [*Australia*] (PDAA)
NPA .... National Party of Australia (ADA)
NPA .... National Personnel Authority [*Japan*] (PDAA)
NPA .... National Pipeline Authority [*Australia*] (PDAA)
NPA .... National Police Agency [*Japan*]
NPA .... National Port Authority [*Cameroon*] (IMH)
NPA .... National Poultry Association [*Australia*]
NPA .... National Publishing Administration of China (FEA)
NPA .... New People's Army [*Philippines*] (PD)
NPA .... Nigerian Port Authority (MSC)
NPA .... Nigerian Port Authority Clerical Workers' Union
NPA .... Nigerian Publishers Association (EAIO)
NPA .... Nilsen Porcelains (Australia) Proprietary Ltd.
NPA .... Nine Pin Association [*Schauenburg, Federal Republic of Germany*] (EAIO)
NPA .... Norwegian Parkinson Association (EAIO)
NPA .... Norwegian Playwrights Association (EAIO)
NPAAC .... National Pathology Accreditation Advisory Council [*Australia*]
NPAACT... National Parks Association of the Australian Capital Territory
NPAC .... National Parks Advisory Council [*Australia*]
NPAC .... National Plantation Advisory Committee
NPAG .... New South Wales Police Academy - John K Avery Resource Centre [*National Union Catalogue of Australia symbol*]
NPAN .... National Plan for Australian Newspapers
NPAN .... Newspaper Proprietors Association of Nigeria
NPAP .... Niue People's Action Party [*Political party*] (EY)
NPAR .... New South Wales Parliamentary Library [*National Union Catalogue of Australia symbol*]
NPASOK ... Neolaia Panellinion Sosialistikon Kinima [*Panhellenic Socialist Movement Youth*] (GC)
NPAV .... National Parks Association of Victoria [*Australia*]
NPAV .... Nederlandse Patholoog Anatomen Vereniging [*Netherlands*] (SLS)
NPAWF.... National Parks and Wildlife Foundation [*Australia*]
NPAWT .... National Plan of Action for Women in TAFE [*Technical and Further Education*] [*Australia*]
NPB .... Coastal Lookout Station (RU)
NPB .... Nasionale Pers Beperk
NPB .... Nationale Plantentuin van Belgie [*National Botanic Garden of Belgium*] (ARC)

NPB .... National Productivity Board [*Australia*]
NPB .... National Productivity Board [*Singapore*]
NPB .... Scientific Educational Library   (RU)
NPC .... Nationaal Paritair Comite [*Benelux*]   (BAS)
NPC .... National People's Congress [*China*] [*Political party*]   (PPW)
NPC .... National People's Congress [*Nigeria*] [*Political party*]
NPC .... National Petrochemical Company [*Iran*]
NPC .... National Petroleum Corporation [*Barbados*]   (LA)
NPC .... National Philatelic Center [*Australia*]
NPC .... National Pipe Co. [*Saudi Arabia*]
NPC .... National Planning Commission [*Nepal*]   (GEA)
NPC .... National Power Corp. [*Philippines*]   (DS)
NPC .... National Preparatory Committee [*Guyana*]   (LA)
NPC .... National Printing Company Ltd.
NPC .... National Productivity Centre [*Turkey*]
NPC .... National Productivity Centre [*Ethopia*]
NPC .... National Productivity Centre [*Ministry of Trade and Industry*] [*Malaysia*]
NPC .... National Psychological Committee [*Malaysia*]   (ML)
NPC .... National Purchasing Corporation
NPC .... Nauru Phosphate Commission [*Australia*]
NPC .... Nauru Phosphate Corporation
NPC .... News and Periodicals Corporation [*Myanmar*]   (DS)
NPC .... Northern People's Congress [*Nigeria*]   (AF)
NPC .... Northern Petroleum Co. [*Iraq*]   (EY)
NPCA .... National Peanut Council of Australia   (ADA)
NPCC .... National Petroleum Construction Company Ltd. [*Abu Dhabi*]   (MENA)
NPCC .... National Pollution Control Commission [*Manila, Phillippines*]
NPCh .... Lowest Applicable Frequency   (RU)
NPCh .... Niezalezna Partia Chlopska [*Independent Peasant Party*]   (POL)
NPCIL ...... Nuclear Power Corp. of India Ltd.
NPCL .... Parramatta City Library [*National Union Catalogue of Australia symbol*]
NPCP .... Nairobi People's Convention Party
NPCS .... National Population Control Secretariat [*Australia*]
NPD .... Nationaldemokratische Partei Deutschlands [*National Democratic Party of Germany*] [*Germany*] [*Political party*]   (PPE)
NPD .... National Party for Democracy [*Zambia*] [*Political party*]   (EY)
NPD .... Nees Politikes Dynameis [*New Political Forces*] [*Greek*] [*Political party*]   (PPE)
NPD .... New South Wales - Police Headquarters [*National Union Catalogue of Australia symbol*]
NPD .... Norwegian Petroleum Directorate
NPDA .... National Pharmaceutical Distributors' Association [*Australia*]
NPDD .... Nomikon Prosopon Dimosiou Dikaiou [*Legal Entity of Public Law*] [*In reference to semi-government corporations*] [*Greek*]   (GC)
NPDMC .... National Property Development and Management Company
NPDN .... Nordic Public Data Network [*Denmark, Finland, Iceland, Norway and Sweden*]   (PDAA)
NPDP .... National Procurement Development Program [*Australia*]
NPE .... Napier [*New Zealand*] [*Airport symbol*]   (OAG)
NPE .... National Population Enquiry
NPE .... Nomarkhiaki Peitharkhiki Epitropi [*Nome Disciplinary Committee*] [*Greek*]   (GC)
NPEC....... National Pay Equity Coalition [*Australia*]
NPEC....... Native Plants Extracts Cooperative [*Australia*]
NPEN .... Penrith City Library [*National Union Catalogue of Australia symbol*]
NPF .... Narodni Pozemkovy Fond [*National Land Fund*]   (CZ)
NPF .... National Patriotic Front [*Guyana*]   (LA)
NPF .... National Police Force [*South Vietnam*]   (VNW)
NPF .... National Progressive Front [*Iraq*] [*Political party*]   (PPW)
NPF .... National Progressive Front [*Syria*] [*Political party*]   (PPW)
NPF .... National Provident Fund [*Zambia*]   (AF)
NPF .... Ndermarrje e Prodhimeve Farmaceutike [*Albanian*]
NPF .... Nicaragua Peace Fleet [*Denmark*]   (EAIO)
NPF .... Nigeria Police Force
NPF .... Niwano Peace Foundation [*Japan*]   (EAIO)
NPF .... Nordisk Plastikkirurgisk Forening [*Scandinavian Association of Plastic Surgeons - SAPS*]   (EAIO)
NPF .... Norges Parkinsonforbund [*Norway*]   (EAIO)
NPF .... Normenausschuss Pigmente und Fuellstoffe im DIN [*Deutsches Institut fuer Normung*] eV   (SLS)
NPF .... Norsk Psykologforening [*Norway*]   (SLS)
NPF .... Northern Progressive Front
NPFC....... Northwest Pacific Fisheries Commission   (ASF)
NPFI........ Institute of Theoretical and Applied Pharmacy   (RU)
NPFI........ Pfizer Proprietary Limited [*National Union Catalogue of Australia symbol*]
NPFL........ National Patriotic Front of Liberia [*Political party*]   (EY)
NPFMC.... Northern Prawn Fishery Management Committee [*Australia*]
NPG .... Narodowy Plan Gospodarczy [*National Economic Plan*]   (POL)
NPG .... Nederlands Psychoanalytisch Genootschap [*Netherlands*]   (SLS)

NPG .... Negative Population Growth
NPG .... Nile Provisional Government
NPG .... Normal Backwater Level   (RU)
NPG .... Normierte Programmierung [*German*]   (ADPT)
NPG .... Nuclear Planning Group [*NATO*]
NPH.......... Association of Nordic Paper Historians [*See also FNPH*] [*Sweden*]   (EAIO)
NPH.......... Napln Pohonych Hmot [*Gasoline Pump*]   (CZ)
NPH.......... Prince Henry Hospital - Medical Library [*National Union Catalogue of Australia symbol*]
NPHA....... Nanga Parbat/Haramosh Axis [*Himalayan geology*]
NPHI .... National Public Health Institute [*Research center*] [*Finland*]   (IRC)
NPHS........ Prince Henry Hospital - HRD (Human Resources Development) Resource Centre [*National Union Catalogue of Australia symbol*]
NPI .... Nasionale Produktiwiteitsinstituut [*National Productivity Institute*] [*South Africa*]
NPI .... National Pacific Insurance Ltd.
NPI .... National Pastoral Institute, Melbourne [*Australia*]
NPI .... National Pollutant Inventory
NPI .... Norwegian Pollution Inspectorate
NPI .... Novocherkassk Polytechnic Institute Imeni Sergo Ordzhonikidze   (RU)
NPIAW...... National Photographic Index of Australian Wildlife
NPID .... Nomikon Prosopon Idiotikou Dikaiou [*Legal Entity of Private Law*] [*Greek*]   (GC)
NPIT......... Pittwater Library Service [*National Union Catalogue of Australia symbol*]
NPITC....... National Plastics Industry Training Committee [*Australia*]
NPITC....... National Printing Industry Training Council [*Australia*]
NPK .... Beginning of Transition Curve [*Railroads*]   (RU)
NPK .... Criminal Procedure Code   (BU)
NPK .... Nationale Partij Kombinatie [*National Party Alliance*] [*Surinam*] [*Political party*]   (PPW)
NPK .... Nea Politiki Kinisis [*New Political Movement*] [*Greek*]   (GC)
NPK .... Punched-Card Storage   (RU)
NPK .... Scientific Production Combine   (BU)
NPKP........ Regimental Commander's Observation Post   (RU)
NPKS........ People's Political Advisory Council [*Chinese People's Republic*]   (RU)
NPKS........ People's Political Consultative Council   (BU)
NPKSK...... People's Political Advisory Council of China   (RU)
NPl............ Directive on Payments   (BU)
NPl............ Directive on Planning   (BU)
NPL .... National Physical Laboratory [*India*]   (PDAA)
NPL .... National Policy on Languages [*Australia*]
NPL .... National Properties Ltd. [*Australia*]
NPL .... Nauru Pacific Line
NPL .... Nederlandse Vereniging voor Produktieleiding [*Netherlands*]   (SLS)
NPL .... Nepal [*ANSI three-letter standard code*]   (CNC)
NPL .... New Plymouth [*New Zealand*] [*Airport symbol*]   (OAG)
NPL .... Nigeria Pipes Ltd.
npl .... Notre Place [*Our Town*] [*French*]
NPL .... Nueva Prensa Latinoamericana [*Nueva Prensa Latinoamericana*] [*Press agency*]   (LA)
NPL .... Punched-Tape Storage   (RU)
NPLAC...... National People Living with AIDS [*Acquired Immune Deficiency Syndrome*] Coalition [*Australia*]
NPLAN ... National Plan for Australian Newspapers
NPLATY ... RAN (Royal Australian Navy) Submarine School [*National Union Catalogue of Australia symbol*]
NPLF........ Namibia People's Liberation Front   (AF)
NPL-RPU ... National Physical Laboratory Radio Propagation Unit [*India*]   (PDAA)
npm .... Nad Poziomem Morza [*Above Sea Level*] [*Poland*]
NPM.......... Nazionalen Prirodonauchen Muzei [*National Natural History Museum*] [*Bulgaria*]   (IRC)
NpM .... Nepmuvelesi Miniszterium/Miniszter [*Ministry/Minister of Adult Education*]   (HU)
NPMA .... Australian Pharmaceutical Manufacturers' Association [*National Union Catalogue of Australia symbol*]
NpMAJ ..... Narodni Podnik Mistra Aloisa Jiraska [*Alois Jirasek National Enterprise*] [*Hronov*]
NPMC .... KPMG Peat Marwick (New South Wales) [*National Union Catalogue of Australia symbol*]
NPMC .... National Petroleum Marketing Company [*Trinidadian-Tobagan*]   (LA)
NPMC .... Nigerian Produce Marketing Company Ltd.
NPMCA .... National Paper Marketing Council of Australia
NPME .... Network for Peace in the Middle East [*Australia*]
NPMI .... Nordic Pool for Marine Insurance [*Helsinki, Finland*]   (EA)
NPML .... Pancontinental Mining Limited [*National Union Catalogue of Australia symbol*]
NPMO....... National Pasok Momogun Organization [*National Sons of the Soil Organization*] [*Sabah*]   (ML)

NPN.......... National Party of Nigeria [*Political party*] (PPW)
NPN.......... Ndermarrje e Prodhimeve te Ndryshme [*Albanian*]
NPNCA ..... National Parks and Nature Conservation Authority [*Australia*]
NPNRD..... Directive on the Non-Normed Work Day (BU)
NPO.......... Directive on Design Organizations (BU)
NPO.......... Nacelnik Planovaciho Oddeleni [*Chief of the Planning Section*] [*Military*] (CZ)
NPO.......... National Preservation Office [*National Library of Australia*]
NPO.......... Native Patrol Officer [*Australia*]
npo .... Navn paa Omslag [*Name on Wrapper*] [*Publishing Danish/ Norwegian*]
NPO.......... Nigerian Press Organisation
NPO.......... Nongovernmental Organizations (RU)
NPO.......... Northern Petroleum Organization [*Iraq*] (MENA)
NPO.......... Scientific Industrial Trust (BU)
npor .... Nadporucik [*Senior Lieutenant*] [*US equivalent: First Lieutenant*] (CZ)
NPOW....... Prince of Wales Hospital [*National Union Catalogue of Australia symbol*]
NPP .... Close Infantry Support (BU)
NPP .... Direct Support of Infantry (RU)
NPP .... Flight Manual (RU)
NPP .... Narodnaia Progressivnaia Partiia
NPP .... Nastavni Plan i Program [*Training Plan and Program*] [*Military*] (YU)
NPP .... National Patriotic Party [*Liberia*] [*Political party*] (EY)
NPP .... National People's Party [*Pakistan*] [*Political party*] (FEA)
NPP .... National Plastic Pipes Co. [*United Arab Emirates*] (MENA)
NPP .... National Progressive Party [*Iraq*] [*Political party*] (BJA)
NPP .... Nemzeti Paraszt Part [*National Peasant Party*] [*Hungary*] [*Political party*] (PPE)
NPP .... Nepohybliva Palebna Prehrada [*Fixed Fire Barrage*] (CZ)
NPP .... Neprosredna Podrska Pesadije [*Close Support of Infantry*] (YU)
NPP .... New Patriotic Party [*Ghana*] [*Political party*] (ECON)
NPP .... New People's Party [*North Korea*] [*Political party*] (FEA)
NPP .... New Progressive Party [*Puerto Rico*] [*Political party*]
NPP .... Nigerian People's Party [*Political party*] (PPW)
NPP .... Northern People's Party [*Ghana*]
NPP .... Nurse Practitioner Project
NPP .... People's Progressive Party [*British Guiana*] (RU)
NPPA .... National Parks and Primitive Areas
NPPA .... Norwegian Pulp and Paper Association
NPPB........ Mobile Field Hospital for Neurological Diseases (BU)
NPPB........ National Poisons and Pesticides Board [*Sweden*]
NPPF........ National Progressive Patriotic Front [*Iraq*] [*Political party*]
NPPG .... Neurological Mobile Field Hospital (RU)
NPPL........ National Parks and Public Lands [*Victoria, Australia*]
NPPL........ Placer Exploration Limited [*National Union Catalogue of Australia symbol*]
NPPM .... Northern Parks and Playgrounds Movement [*Australia*]
NPPN .... NUDO [*Namibia United Democratic Organization*] Progressive Party of Namibia [*Political party*] (PPW)
NPPPP ..... Northern Province Progressive People's Party
NPQTL...... National Project on the Quality of Teaching and Learning [*Australia*]
NPR .... Narodowa Partia Robotnicza [*National Workers' Party*] [*Poland*] [*Political party*] (PPE)
NPR .... Navy Public Relations [*Royal Australian Navy*]
NPRB .... Hand-to-Hand Combat Manual (RU)
NPRC .... Nederlandse Particuliere Rijnvaartcentrale [*Netherlands*] (BAS)
NPRC .... Nigerian Petroleum Refinery Company
NPRCG ..... Nuclear Public Reltions Contac Group [*Italy*] (PDAA)
NPRD .... New South Wales - Premier's Department - Library and Information Services [*National Union Catalogue of Australia symbol*]
NPRF........ National Priority Reserve Fund [*Australia*]
NPRK .... Parkes Shire Library [*National Union Catalogue of Australia symbol*]
NPRL........ National Physical Research Laboratory [*South Africa*]
NPRN .... Directive on Planning, Assigning, and Job Placement of Young Specialists with Higher Education (BU)
NPRO .... New South Wales - Property and Office Service [*Department of Courts Administration*] [*National Union Catalogue of Australia symbol*]
NPRSP ...... Narodowa Pozyczka Rozwoju Sil Polski [*National Loan for the Development of Poland's Resources*] (POL)
NPRT .... Nauru Phosphate Royalties Trust
NPRT .... New South Wales - Technical Service [*Department of Technical and Further Education*] [*National Union Catalogue of Australia symbol*]
NPRW ...... Price Waterhouse [*National Union Catalogue of Australia symbol*]
NPS .... Nationale Partij Suriname [*Surinam National Party*] [*Political party*] (PPW)
nps............. Navn paa en Side [*Name on a Page*] [*Publishing Danish/ Norwegian*]

nps............. Navn paa Smudsbladet [*Name on a Flyleaf*] [*Publishing Danish/ Norwegian*]
NPS .... New South Wales Police Academy - Headquarters Library [*National Union Catalogue of Australia symbol*]
NPS .... Normenausschuss Persoenliche Schutzausruestung und Sicherheitskennzeichnung im DIN [*Deutsches Institut fuer Normung*] eV (SLS)
NPS .... Norsk Parapsykologisk Selskap [*Norway*] (SLS)
NPS .... Norwegian Peace Society (EAIO)
NPS .... Nurses Personal Superannuation [*Australia*]
NPS .... Popular Science Series (RU)
NPS .... Scientific Pedagogical Section (RU)
NPSA........ Nordic Political Science Association [*Norway*] (EAIO)
NPSA........ Nouveau Programme Substantiel d'Action
NPSC........ Australian Police Staff College [*National Union Catalogue of Australia symbol*]
NPSC........ Nigeria Public Service Commission
NPSD .... Chief of Message Center (RU)
NPSFR ...... Net Public Sector Financing Requirement [*Business term*]
NPSK"NEI" ... Scientific Production Combine "New Energy Sources" [*Bulgarian*]
NPSL........ Narodnaia Partiia Seppa-Leone
NPSP........ National People's Salvation Party [*Zambia*] [*Political party*] (EY)
NPSRA..... Nuclear-Powered Ship Research Association [*Japan*]
NPSS .... Highest Useful Degree of Compression (RU)
NPSS .... Narodni Podnik Sberne Suroviny [*National Enterprise for the Collection of Raw Materials*] (CZ)
NPSS .... National Party of the Subjects of the Sultan of Zanzibar
NPSS .... National Police and Security Service [*Republic of Vietnam*]
NPSSh....... Staff Field Manual (RU)
NPST........ National Party of South Thailand (ML)
NPSU .... National Perinatal Statistics Unit [*Australia*]
NPSU .... Public Sector Union [*National Union Catalogue of Australia symbol*]
NPSZ........ Nemocenska Pojistovna Soukromych Zamestnancu [*Private Employees' Health Insurance Agency*] (CZ)
NPT .... Nationalpreistraeger [*National Prize Winner*] (EG)
NPT .... Nationwide Princesa Timber [*Philippines*]
npt .... Navn paa Titelblad [*Name on Title Page*] [*Publishing Danish/ Norwegian*]
NPT .... Netzplantechnik [*German*] (ADPT)
NPT .... State Rail Authority of New South Wales - Technical Library [*National Union Catalogue of Australia symbol*]
NPTC........ Presbyterian Theological Centre [*National Union Catalogue of Australia symbol*]
NPTZh ...... Directive on the Utilization of Women's Labor (BU)
NPU.......... Ground Transmitter (RU)
NPU.......... National People's Union [*Rhodesian*] (AF)
NPU.......... National Progressive Union [*Political party*] [*Egypt*]
npu .... Nehezpuska [*Heavy Rifle*] (HU)
NPU.......... Ne Plus Ultra [*No Further; i.e., the pinnacle of attainment*] [*French*]
NPU.......... Newspaper Press Union of South Africa
NPU.......... Nordic Postal Union (EA)
NPU.......... Normal Backwater Level (RU)
NPu.......... Normenausschuss Pulvermetallurgie im DIN [*Deutsches Institut fuer Normung*] eV (SLS)
NPU.......... Oil Field Administration (RU)
NPUA........ National Progressive Unionist Assembly [*Egypt*]
n pub .... Non Publie [*French*] (FLAF)
NPUD........ National Party for Unity and Democracy [*Mauritania*] [*Political party*] (EY)
NPUG........ National Progressive Unionist Grouping
NPUP .... National Progressive Unionist Party [*Egypt*] [*Political party*] (PPW)
NPV .... Lower High Water (RU)
NPV .... Naturpolitische Volkspartei [*People's Party for Nature Policy*] [*Germany*] [*Political party*] (PPW)
NPV .... Net Present Value
NPVCh ...... Lowest Applicable High Frequency (RU)
NPVO........ Air Defense Commander (RU)
NPW .... National Party of Western Australia [*Political party*]
NPW .... New South Wales - Public Works Department - Information Resources Unit [*National Union Catalogue of Australia symbol*]
NPWA ...... National Party of Western Australia
NPWAC .... National Parks and Wildlife Advisory Council [*Tasmania, Australia*]
NPWFNSW ... National Parks and Wildlife Foundation of New South Wales [*Australia*]
NPWP .... Nigerian People's Welfare Party
NPZ.......... Nabavljacke Prodajna Zadruga [*Buying and Selling Cooperative*] (YU)
NPZ.......... Nacelnik Proviantniho Zasobovani [*Chief of Food Supply*] [*Military*] (CZ)
NPz .... Nacelnik Pruzkumu [*Chief of Reconnaissance*] (CZ)

NPZ .... Petroleum-Processing Plant   (RU)
NPZ .... Petroleum Refinery   (BU)
NPZ .... Portable Contamination Apparatus [*Military term*]   (RU)
NPZDZh ... Directive on the Sale and Exchange of State Housing   (BU)
NPZFK ...... Directive on the Application of the Law on Financial Control
                  (BU)
NPZP........ Narodnaia Partiia Zanzibara i Pemby
NQ .... North Queensland [*Australia*]   (ADA)
NQB........... Queanbeyan-Yarrowlumla Library Service [*National Union
                  Catalogue of Australia symbol*]
NQC........... Northern Queensland Co. [*Australia*]
NQCC .... North Queensland Conservation Council [*Australia*]
NQIC .... National Quality Information Centre [*Institute of Quality
                  Assurance*] [*Information service or system*]   (IID)
NQL........... Nouveau Quartier Latin [*Paris bookstore*]
NQLA .... North Queensland Logging Association [*Australia*]
NQLP .... North Queensland Labour Party [*Australia*]   (ADA)
NQMFP .... North Queensland Multifunction Polis [*Australia*]
NQN .... Neuquen [*Argentina*] [*Airport symbol*]   (OAG)
NQN .... Transportes Aereos Neuquen [*Argentina*] [*ICAO designator*]
                  (FAAC)
NQNC .... North Queensland Naturalists Club [*Australia*]   (SLS)
NQP........... North Queensland Party [*Australia*]   (ADA)
NQPP .... National Quarantine Publicity Program [*Australia*]
NQR........... North Queensland Resources [*Australia*]
NQTGCA .. North Queensland Tobacco Growers Cooperative Association
                  [*Australia*]
NQTV .... North Queensland Television [*Australia*]
NQU .... Nuqui [*Colombia*] [*Airport symbol*]   (OAG)
NQUEENSD ... North Queensland [*Australia*]   (ROG)
NQUI........ Quirindi and District Historical Society and District Historical
                  Society [*National Union Catalogue of Australia symbol*]
NQX........... North Queensland Express [*Australia*]
NR.............. Chief of Intelligence   (BU)
nr................ Insoluble   (RU)
NR.............. Nachrichtenregiment [*Signal Regiment*] [*German military -
                  World War II*]
NR.............. Narodna Republika [*People's Republic*]   (YU)
NR.............. Narodni Rada [*National Council*]   (CZ)
NR.............. Nature Reserve
NR.............. Nauru [*ANSI two-letter standard code*]   (CNC)
nr................ Near   (EECI)
NR.............. Nederlandsche Rechtspraak [*Netherlands*]   (BAS)
NR.............. Nederlandse Regtspraak [*Netherlands*]   (BAS)
NR.............. Negro y Rojo [*Black and Red*] [*Spanish*]   (WER)
NR.............. Nieuwe Rechtspraak [*Benelux*]   (BAS)
NR.............. Nigerian Railway
NR.............. Nigerian Reinsurance Corp.
NR.............. Night Reconnaissance   (RU)
nr................ Nommer [*Number*] [*Afrikaans*]
nr................ Non Rogne [*Untrimmed*] [*Publishing*] [*French*]
NR.............. Noord-Rhodesie [*Northern Rhodesia*] [*Afrikaans*]
NR.............. Norges Rederiforbund [*Norway*]   (EAIO)
NR.............. Northern Rhodesia [*Later, Zambia*]
NR.............. Nuestra Remesa [*Our Remittance*] [*Spanish*] [*Business term*]
Nr.............. Numer [*Albanian*]
Nr.............. Nummer [*Number*] [*German*]   (GPO)
nr................ Nummer [*Number*] [*Denmark*]   (GPO)
nr................ Nummer [*Number*] [*Sweden*]   (GPO)
Nr.............. Nummer [*NumberDutch*]   (BAS)
NR.............. Nuwe Reel [*New Line*] [*Afrikaans*]
NR.............. People's Republic   (BU)
nr................ Service Company   (BU)
NR.............. Standard   (RU)
NRA .... Albanian People's Republic   (BU)
NRA .... Narodnaia Respublika Angola
NRA .... Narrandera [*Australia*] [*Airport symbol*]   (OAG)
NRA .... National Republican Alliance [*Australia*]
NRA .... National Resistance Army [*Uganda*]   (PD)
NRA .... National Retirement Association [*Australia*]
NRA .... National Rifle Association   (OLYM)
NRA .... Natural Resources Authority [*Jordan*]   (GEA)
NRA .... Nemzeti Repulo Alap [*National Aviation Fund*]   (HU)
NRA .... Normal Retirement Age
nra .... Nuestra [*Our*] [*Spanish*]
NRA .... People's Republic of Albania   (RU)
NRA .... People's Revolutionary Army of China [*1937-1945*]   (RU)
NRA .... Rheem Australia Limited - Research Centre Library [*National
                  Union Catalogue of Australia symbol*]
NRAA .... National Rifle Association of Australia
NRAC .... National Research Advisory Council [*New Zealand*]   (SLS)
NRAC .... Natural Resources Audit Council
NRAC .... Northern Rhodesia African Congress
NRAH .... Children's Hospital Camperdown - Medical Library [*National
                  Union Catalogue of Australia symbol*]
NRAJ........ National Recreation Association of Japan   (EAIO)

NRAMTU ... Northern Rhodesia African Mineworkers' Trade Union
NRAMU.... Northern Rhodesia African Mineworkers' Union
NRANC.... Northern Rhodesia African National Congress
NRAND..... Randwick City Library Service [*National Union Catalogue of
                  Australia symbol*]
NRANMM ... RAN [*Royal Australian Navy Missile Maintenance
                  Establishment*]
NRANSC... Royal Australian Navy Staff College [*National Union Catalogue
                  of Australia symbol*]
NRAS .... Northern Rhodesia Administrative Service
nras .... Nuestras [*Our*] [*Spanish*]
NRATUC .. Northern Rhodesian African Trades Union Congress
NRAWU.... Nyasaland Railways African Workers Union
NRB .... Bulgarian People's Republic   (BU)
NRB .... Narodnaia Respublika Benin
NRB .... Narodni Rada Badatelska [*National Research Council*]   (CZ)
NRB .... National Roads Board [*New Zealand*]   (PDAA)
NRB .... Natural Resources Board
NRB .... Nieuwe Rechterlijke Beslissingen [*Benelux*]   (BAS)
NRB .... People's Republic of Bulgaria   (RU)
NRB .... Radiation Safety Norms   (BU)
NRB .... State Bank of New South Wales - Research Library [*National
                  Union Catalogue of Australia symbol*]
NRBA .... Reserve Bank of Australia - Research Library [*National Union
                  Catalogue of Australia symbol*]
NRBC .... North Rocks [*Central School for*] Blind Children [*National
                  Union Catalogue of Australia symbol*]
NRBiH....... Narodna Republika Bosna i Hercegovina [*People's Republic of
                  Bosnia and Hercegovina*]   (YU)
NRBPNS ... Bulgarian People's Republic, National Assembly Presidium
                  (BU)
NRBQ .... Nurses' Registration Board of Queensland [*Australia*]
NRBS........ Royal Blind Society of New South Wales - Talking Book and
                  Braille Library [*National Union Catalogue of Australia
                  symbol*]
NRBS:R ..... Royal Blind Society of New South Wales - Reference Library
                  [*National Union Catalogue of Australia symbol*]
NRBulg...... Bulgarian People's Republic   (BU)
NRC.......... Ferrocarriles Nacionales de Colombia [*National Railroads of
                  Colombia*]   (LA)
NRC.......... Nacelnik Radio Centra [*Radio Center Chief*] [*Military*]   (YU)
NRC.......... Narodni Rada Ceskoslovenska [*Czechoslovak National Council*]
                  (CZ)
NRC.......... National Reconstruction Council
NRC.......... National Redemption Council [*Ghana*]   (AF)
NRC.......... National Referee Council [*Australia*]
NRC.......... National Reformation Council [*Sierra Leone*]   (AF)
NRC.......... National Republican Convention [*Nigeria*] [*Political party*]
NRC.......... National Research Centre [*Academy of Scientific Research and
                  Technology*] [*Egypt*] [*Research center*]
NRC.......... National Research Council [*Icelandic*] [*Research center*]   (IRC)
NRC.......... National Research Council of Ghana
NRC.......... Native Recruiting Corporation
NRC.......... Native Representative Council
NRC.......... Natural Resources College [*Malawi*]   (AF)
NRC.......... Nepal Resettlement Corporation   (GEA)
NRC.......... Nieuwe Rotterdamsche Courant [*Netherlands*]   (BAS)
NRC.......... Nigerian Railway Corporation
NRC.......... Niger River Commission
NRC.......... Nippon Research Center Ltd. [*Research center*] [*Japan*]   (IRC)
NRC.......... Norwegian Refugee Council
NRC.......... Nuclear Research Center [*Iran*] [*Research center*]   (IRC)
NRCB .... Readme Computer Books [*National Union Catalogue of
                  Australia symbol*]
NRCC .... Ndoleleji Rural Community Centre
NRCC .... Northern Riverina County Council [*Australia*]
NRCDP .... National Research Center for Disaster Prevention [*Research
                  center*] [*Japan*]   (IRC)
NRCE .... National Research Council of Egypt
NRCG .... Narodna Republika Crna Gora [*People's Republic of
                  Montenegro*]   (YU)
NRCL .... Natural Resources Conservation League of Victoria [*Australia*]
                  (SLS)
NRCO .... New Russian Chamber Orchestra   (BJA)
NRCP .... National Research Council of the Philippines [*Research center*]
                  (IRC)
NRCP .... Northern Rhodesia Commonwealth Party
NRCP .... Reckitt and Colman Pharmaceuticals [*National Union Catalogue
                  of Australia symbol*]
NRCRI...... National Root Crops Research Institute, Umudike [*Nigeria*]
                  [*Research center*]   (IRC)
NRCSA...... Neurological Resources Center of South Australia
NRCSH ..... Norwegian Research Council for Science and the Humanities
                  (EAIO)
NRCSTD... National Research Center for Science and Technology for
                  Development [*China*]   (IRC)

NRCT .... National Research Council, Thailand

NRD .... Aeronardi SpA [*Italy*] [*ICAO designator*]   (FAAC)

NRD .... Natsional'noe Revoliutsionnoe Dvizhenie

NRD .... Natural Resources Division [*An association*]   (EAIO)

NRD .... Niemiecka Republika Demokratyczna [*German Democratic Republic*]   (POL)

NRD .... Norderney [*Germany*] [*Airport symbol*]   (OAG)

NRD .... Normal Retirement Date

NRD .... People's Revolutionary Movement [*Ecuador*]   (RU)

NRDA .... National Research and Development Authority [*NCRD*] [*Israel*] [*Formerly,*]

NRDC .... National Research and Development Centre [*Philippines*] (ERC)

NRDC .... National Research Development Corporation of India

NRDC .... Natural Resources Defence Council

NRDC .... Northern Regional Development Corporation

NRDC-CPSC ... National Revolutionary Development Campaign and Central Planning Supreme Council [*Ethiopia*]   (GEA)

NRDP .... National Reconciliation and Development Program [*Philippines*]

NRDP .... National Rural Development Progress

NREA .... Natural Resources and Energy Agency [*Japan*]   (PDAA)

NREAN .... Northern Rivers Energy Action Network [*Australia*]

NREC .... Natural Resources and Environment Committee [*Victoria, Australia*]

N Recop ..... Nueva Recopilacion [*New Digest*] [*Spanish*]

NRED .... Sydney College of Advanced Education [*National Union Catalogue of Australia symbol*]

NREL .... CSIRO [*Commonwealth Scientific and Industrial Research Organisation*] News Releases [*Australia*] [*Information service or system*]   (CRD)

NREN .... Renwick College - Deaf and Blind Children's Centre [*National Union Catalogue of Australia symbol*]

NRES .... Residential Tenancies Tribunal (New South Wales) [*National Union Catalogue of Australia symbol*]

NRF .... National Research Fellowships [*Australia*]

NRF .... Neues Rotes Forum [*New Red Forum*] [*FRG student organization*]   (EG)

NRF .... New South Wales Retirement Fund [*Australia*]

NRF .... Niemiecka Republika Federalna [*German Federal Republic*] (POL)

NRF .... Nordisk Retsodontologisk Foerening [*Sweden*]   (SLS)

NRF .... Norges Rasjonaliseringsforbund [*Norway*]   (SLS)

NRF .... Nouvelle Revue Francaise [*Periodical title; initials also used on books published by Gallimard*]

NRF .... Nutrition Research Foundation [*Australia*]

NRF .... River Fleet Norms   (RU)

NRFI .... National Rail Freight Initiative [*Australia*]

NRFRL..... Nansei Regional Fisheries Research Laboratory [*Japan*]   (MSC)

NRG .... Northern Rhodesia Government

NRG .... Nuklearrohr-Gesellschaft [*Germany*]   (PDAA)

NRG .... Scientific and Editorial Group   (RU)

NRGG .... Nasionale Raad vir Geestesgesondheid [*South Africa*]   (AA)

NRGH .... Concord Repatriation General Hospital - Medical Library [*National Union Catalogue of Australia symbol*]

NRGSM .... National Research Group for the Structure of Matter [*Italy*] (EAIO)

NRH .... Narodna Republika Hrvatska [*People's Republic of Croatia*] (YU)

NRH .... Nouvelle Revue Historique de Droit Francais et Etranger (FLAF)

NRHA .... Northern Rivers Hydrophonic Association [*Australia*]

NRHH .... Ryde Hospital and Community Health Services - Hospital Library and Information S [*Hospital Library and Information Service*] [*National Union Catalogue of Australia symbol*]

NRHU .... National Rural Health Unit [*Australia*]

NRI .... Neuromuscular Research Institute [*Australia*]

NRI .... Nomura Research Institute [*Research center*] [*Japan*]   (IRC)

NRI .... Non-Resident Indian

NRIAE....... National Research Institute of Agricultural Engineering [*Research center*] [*Japan*]   (IRC)

NRIAG ...... National Research Institute of Astronomy and Geophysics [*Egypt*]   (IRC)

NRIAM ..... Nanjing Research Institute for Agricultural Mechanization [*Ministry of Agriculture, Animal Husbandry and Fishery*] [*China*]   (ERC)

NRIC .... National Resource Information Centre [*Department of Primary Industries and Energy*] [*Australia*]

NRIG .... Nurses Research Interest Group [*Australia*]

NRIH......... National Research Institute of Health [*Ethiopia*] [*Research center*]   (IRC)

NRIM .... National Research Institute for Metals [*Japan*]

NRIMS...... National Research Institute for Mathematical Sciences [*South Africa*]

NRIND...... National Research Institute for Nutritional Diseases [*South African Medical Research Council*]   (AA)

NRIO......... National Research Institute for Oceanography [*South Africa*] (MSC)

NRIPR....... National Research Institute for Pollution and Resources [*Agency for Industrial Science and Technology*] [*Japan*]   (EAS)

NRIT .... National Research Institute of Tea [*Research center*] [*Japan*] (IRC)

NRIV .... Riverina Community Library Service [*National Union Catalogue of Australia symbol*]

NRK.......... Narodnaia Respublika Kongo

NRK.......... Normenausschuss Rundstahlketten im DIN [*Deutsches Institut fuer Normung*] eV   (SLS)

NRK.......... Norrkoping [*Sweden*] [*Airport symbol*]   (OAG)

NRK.......... Norsk Rikskringkasting [*Norwegian Broadcasting Corporation*]

Nrk.......... Not Recommended (Term)   (RU)

NRKCh ..... Scientific Editing Map Compilation Department   (RU)

NRKE .... Latest Development in Quantum Electrodynamics   (RU)

NRKF .... Norsk Risiko Kapital Forening [*Norway*]   (EAIO)

NRKM...... Nederlandse Katholieke Middenstandsbond [*Netherlands*] (BAS)

NRL .... 3M Pharmaceuticals Proprietary Limited [*National Union Catalogue of Australia symbol*]

NRL .... National Radiation Laboratory [*Department of Health*] [*New Zealand*]   (WND)

NRL .... Nizhniy Novgorod Radio Laboratory   (RU)

NRL .... Norske Reindriftsamers Lansforbund [*Norway*]

NRLC .... National Research Laboratory for Conservation of Cultural Property [*India*] [*Research center*]   (IRC)

NRLM ...... National Research Laboratory of Metrology [*Research center*] [*Japan*]   (IRC)

NRLO .... Nationale Raad voor Landbouwkundig Onderzoek [*National Council for Agricultural Research*] [*Netherlands*]   (IRC)

NRLO-TNO ... Nationale Raad voor Landbouwkundig Onderzoek, Nederlands Centrale Organisatie voor Toegepast-Natuurwetenschappelijk Onderzoek [*National Council for Agricultural Research, Netherlands Central Organization for Applied Natural Scientific Research*]   (ARC)

NRLP........ Northern Rhodesia Liberal [*or Liberty*] Party

NRLTUC... Native Races Liquor Traffic United Committee

NRM.......... Nara [*Mali*] [*Airport symbol*]   (OAG)

NRM.......... Narodnaia Respublika Mozambik

NRM.......... National Resistance Movement [*Uganda*]   (PD)

NRM.......... National Revolutionary Movement [*France*]

NRM.......... Negara Republik Malaya [*State of the Republic of Malaya*]   (ML)

NRMA ...... National Roads and Motorists Association [*Australia*]   (PDAA)

NRMA ...... National Roads and Motorists' Association Public Policy Library [*National Union Catalogue of Australia symbol*]

NRMA ...... Northern Rivers Mathematical Association [*Australia*]

NRMC ...... Natural Resources Management Center [*Philippines*]   (ASF)

NRMG ...... Nederlands Rekenmachine Genootschap [*Netherlands*]

NRML ...... Rockdale City Library and Information Service [*National Union Catalogue of Australia symbol*]

NRMU...... Northern Rhodesia European Mineworkers' Union

NRMU...... Northern Rhodesia Mineworkers' Union

NRN .... Royal Netherlands Navy [*ICAO designator*]   (FAAC)

NRNS .... Royal North Shore Hospital and Area Health Service [*National Union Catalogue of Australia symbol*]

NRNTAU ... RAN (Royal Australian Navy) Trials and Assessing Unit [*National Union Catalogue of Australia symbol*]

NRO .... Directive on Registering Insurers   (BU)

NRO .... Narodni Rada Obchodnictva [*Merchants' National Council*] (CZ)

nro.............. Nuestro [*Our*] [*Spanish*]

Nro............. Numero [*Number*] [*Spanish*]

Nro............. Nummer [*Number*] [*German*]   (GCA)

NRO .... Riverview Observatory [*National Union Catalogue of Australia symbol*]

NROC....... National Revolutionary Operations Command [*Ethiopia*]   (AF)

NROS .... Nejvyssi Rada Obrany Statu [*Supreme Counil for National Defense*]   (CZ)

nros .... Nuestros [*Our*] [*Spanish*]

NROW...... Naczelna Rada Odbudowy Warszawy [*Chief Council for the Reconstruction of Warsaw*]   (POL)

NROW...... Naczelna Rada Organizowania Wystaw [*Chief Council for the Organization of Exhibitions*]   (POL)

NRP .... Narodni Ravnogorski Pokret [*Ravna Gora National Movement*] [*World War II*]   (YU)

NRP .... National Religious Party [*Hamiflaga Hadatit Leumit*] [*Israel*] [*Political party*]   (PPW)

NRP .... National Republican Party [*Guyana*] [*Political party*]   (EY)

NRP .... National Resistance Party [*Political party*]   (BJA)

NRP .... Nevis Reformation Party [*Political party*]

NRP .... New Republic Party [*South Africa*] [*Political party*]   (PPW)

NRP .... New Rhodesia Party [*Political party*]

NRP .... Nuwe Republiekparty [*New Republic Party*] [*Political party*] [*Afrikaans*]

NRP .... Observation and Reconnaissance Post   (RU)

NRP .... People's Republican Party [*Turkey*] [*Political party*]

NRP .... Roche Products Proprietary Limited [*National Union Catalogue of Australia symbol*]
NRPH .... Roussel Pharmaceuticals Proprietary Limited - Scientific Affiars Department [*National Union Catalogue of Australia symbol*]
NRPJ .... Nezavisna Radnicka Partija Jugoslavije [*Independent Labor Party of Yugoslavia*] [*Political party*]
NRPM .... People's Revolutionary Government of Mongolia (RU)
NRPS .... Independent Workers' Trade Union (BU)
NRR .... National Records Return [*Australia*]
NRR .... Net Reproduction Rate
NRR .... No Response Required
NRR .... Northern Rhodesia Regiment
NRR .... Romanian People's Republic (BU)
NRRA .... National Rail Regulatory Authority [*Australia*]
NRRC .... Natural Resources Research Council
NRRE .... Netherlands RADAR Research Establishment
Nr rej .... Numer Rejestracyjny [*Registration Number*] [*Poland*]
NRRPC ...... National Rural and Resources Press Club [*Australia*]
NRRR .... Royal Rehabilitation Centre Sydney [*National Union Catalogue of Australia symbol*]
NR(R)SH .... Ndermarrje Rritje Shpendesh [*Albanian*]
NRRTUC .. Northern Rhodesian Reformed Trades Union Congress
NRRU .... Northern Rivers Research Unit [*Australia*]
NRS .... Naczelna Rada Spoldzielcza [*Chief Council of Cooperatives*] (POL)
NRS .... Narodna Republika Slovenija [*People's Republic of Slovenia*] (YU)
NRS .... Narodna Republika Srbija [*People's Republic of Serbia*] (YU)
NRS .... National Refugee Service
NRS .... National Residue Survey [*Australia*]
NRS .... Nederlands Rundveestamboek [*Netherlands*] (BAS)
NRS .... Norsk Romsenter [*Norwegian Space Center*] (EAS)
NRS .... People's Radio Sofia (BU)
NRS .... Unguided Missile (RU)
NRSA .... National Remote Sensing Agency [*India*] (PDAA)
NRSA .... National Rose Society of Australia
NRSC .... Nansen Remote Sensing Centre [*Research center*] [*Norway*] (EAS)
NRSC .... National Remote Sensing Centre [*China*]
NRSC .... National Road Safety Council [*South Africa*]
NRSC .... Nordic Road Safety Council [*See also NTR*] [*Helsinki, Finland*] (EAIO)
NRSC .... Riverina Second Chance Project - Upper Murray Regional Library [*National Union Catalogue of Australia symbol*]
NRSE .... Narodna Radikalna Stranka u Egzilu [*National Radical Party in Exile*] (YU)
NRSl .... Narodna Republika Slovenija [*People's Republic of Slovenia*] (YU)
NRSY .... Nordiska Forbundet for Studie- och Yrkesvagledning [*Nordic Association for Study and Vocational Guidance - NASVG*] (EAIO)
nrt .... Net Registered Tons (EECI)
NRT .... Net Register Tonnage (RU)
NRT .... Net Register Tons (BU)
NRT .... Nettoregistertonne [*Net Register Tonnage*] [*German*]
NRT .... Neue Rumpftechnologie [*New Fuselage Technology*] [*Federal Ministry of Research and Technology*]
NRT .... Tokyo-Narita [*Japan*] [*Airport symbol*] (OAG)
NRTA .... New South Wales - Roads and Traffic Authority [*National Union Catalogue of Australia symbol*]
NRTAC ..... National Road Trauma Advisory Council [*Australia*]
NRTA:R .... New South Wales - Roads and Traffic Authority - Road Safety Library [*National Union Catalogue of Australia symbol*]
NRTH .... Rothschild Australia Limited [*National Union Catalogue of Australia symbol*]
NRTSS ...... Directive on Trying Labor Disputes by the Courts (BU)
NRTW .... Richmond-Tweed Regional Library [*National Union Catalogue of Australia symbol*]
NRU .... Hungarian People's Republic (BU)
NRU .... Nauru [*ANSI three-letter standard code*] (CNC)
NRUL .... Richmond-Upper Clarence Regional Library [*National Union Catalogue of Australia symbol*]
NRUTUC .. Northern Rhodesia United Trades Union Congress
NRV .... Growth Stimulant from Petroleum (RU)
NRV .... Nacelnik Radio Veze [*Radio Communications Chief*] [*Military*] (YU)
NRV .... National Reserve of Volunteers
NRV .... Net Register Tonnage (RU)
NRV .... Nigerian Revolutionary Vanguard (AF)
NRVS .... People's Revolutionary Military Council [*Chinese People's Republic*] (RU)
NRW .... Nordrhein-Westfalen [*North Rhine-Westphalia*] [*German*]
NRW .... Norwegian (ABBR)
NRWF .... Randwick College of TAFE (Technical and Further Education) [*National Union Catalogue of Australia symbol*]

n-ry .... Numery [*Numbers, Installments, Issues*] (POL)
NRY .... People's Republic of Yemen (BU)
NRYD .... Ryde City Library Service [*National Union Catalogue of Australia symbol*]
NRYF .... Ryde College of TAFE (Technical and Further Education) [*National Union Catalogue of Australia symbol*]
NRYH .... Ryde College of TAFE (Technical and Further Education) - Horticulture Library [*National Union Catalogue of Australia symbol*]
NRZ .... Ground Radar Interrogator (RU)
NRZ .... National Railways of Zimbabwe
NRZH .... Rozelle Hospital - Medical Library [*National Union Catalogue of Australia symbol*]
NRZK .... Naczelna Rada Zrzeszen Kupieckich [*Chief Council of Merchant Associations*] (POL)
NRZPHiU ... Naczelna Rada Zrzeszen Prywatnego Handlu i Uslug [*Chief Council of Private Trade and Service Associations*] (POL)
NS .... Chief Communications Officer, Chief Signal Officer (RU)
Ns .... Chief of Service (BU)
NS .... Chief of Signal Service (BU)
NS .... Chief of Supply (RU)
NS .... Command Personnel (RU)
NS .... Direct Stabilization (RU)
NS .... Initial Velocity, Initial Speed (RU)
NS .... Irregular Diurnal Tides (RU)
NS .... Irrigation System (BU)
ns .... Limited Service (BU)
NS .... Magnetizing Force (RU)
NS .... Nacelnik Saniteta [*Chief of Medical Corps*] (YU)
NS .... Nacelnik Staba [*Chief of Staff*] (YU)
NS .... Nacelnik Stabu [*Chief of Staff*] (CZ)
NS .... Nachalnik Sektora [*Chief of Sector*] [*Soviet military rank*]
NS .... Nachschrift [*Postscript*] [*German*] (EG)
NS .... Nach Sicht [*After Sight*] [*German*]
nS .... Nad Sazavou [*On the Sazava River*] (CZ)
nS .... Naechste Seite [*Next Page*] [*German*]
NS .... Nanosekunde [*German*] (ADPT)
NS .... Narodna Skupstina [*National Assembly*] (YU)
NS .... Narodna Stranka [*People's Party*] [*Montenegro*] [*Political party*] (EY)
NS .... Narodna Suma, Zagreb [*National Forests*] [*Zagreb A periodical*] (YU)
NS .... Narodne Starine [*National Antiquities*] [*Zagreb A periodical*] (YU)
NS .... Narodni Shromazdeni [*National Assembly*] (CZ)
NS .... Narodni Socialisticka Strana [*National Socialist Party*] (CZ)
NS .... Narodni Sourucenstvi [*National Unity Party (Fascist, 1939)*] (CZ)
ns .... Narodni Sprava [*or Spravce*] [*National Administration or Administrator*] (CZ)
NS .... Narodno Stopanstvo [*National Economy*] (YU)
NS .... Narodnye Sotsialisty [*Popular Socialists*] [*Former USSR*] [*Political party*] (PPE)
n/s .... Na Sig [*After Sight*] [*Afrikaans*]
NS .... Naskrif [*Post Script*] [*Afrikaans*]
NS .... National Assembly (BU)
NS .... National Council (BU)
NS .... National Union (BU)
NS .... Natjonal Samling [*National Union*] [*Norway*] (PD)
NS .... Navadeci Stanoviste [*Fire Direction Center or Forward Observer Post*] (CZ)
NS .... Nederlandsche Spoorwegen [*Netherlands Railways*] (WEN)
NS .... Nederlandse Spoorwegen [*Netherlands Railways*]
NS .... Nederlandse Staatscourant [*Netherlands*] (BAS)
NS .... Negri Sembilan (ML)
NS .... Nejvyssi Soud [*Supreme Court*] (CZ)
NS .... Nemzeti Segely [*National Relief*] (HU)
NS .... Neoi Sosialistai [*New Socialists*] [*Greek*] (GC)
NS .... Neue Sachlichkeit [*New Objectivity*] [*Pre-World War II group of German artists*]
NS .... New South Wales [*Australia*] (ADA)
ns .... New Style [*Gregorian calendar*] (RU)
NS .... Nieu-Seeland [*New Zealand*] [*Afrikaans*]
ns .... Niin Sanottu [*So Called*] [*Finland*] (GPO)
NS .... Nisandzija [*First Gunner*] (YU)
NS .... Nobelstiftelsen [*Nobel Foundation - NF*] (EAIO)
NS .... Noncombatant Duty (RU)
NS .... Nonlinear Resistance (RU)
NS .... Nordisk Speditorforbund [*Nordic Forwarding Agents Association - NFAA*] [*Defunct*] (EAIO)
NS .... Nordisk Svommeforbund [*Nordic Swimming Federations Association - NSFA*] (EAIO)
NS .... Nord Sud [*North-South*] [*On maps*] [*French*] (MTD)
NS .... Norges Sjokartneik [*Norway*] (MSC)
NS .... Norsk Skipsmeglerforbund [*Norway*] (EAIO)
n/s .... Nosso Saque [*Our Draft*] [*Business term*] [*Portuguese*]

NS	Nosso Senhor [*Our Lord*] [*Portuguese*]
Ns	Nostro [*Our*] [*Italian*]
NS	Nostro Signore [*Our Lord*] [*Italian*]
NS	Notre Seigneur [*Our Lord*] [*French*]
NS	Nouveau Style [*New Style*] [*French*]
ns	Nouvelle Serie [*New Series*] [*French*]
NS	Novi Sad [*Novi Sad*] (YU)
NS	Novi Svet [*New World*] [*Ljubljana A periodical*] (YU)
NS	Nudel'man-Suranov Aircraft Wing Gun (RU)
NS	Nuestra Senora [*Our Lady*] [*Spanish*] (GPO)
NS	Nuestro Senor [*Our Lord*] [*Spanish*]
ns	Nueva Serie [*New Series*] [*Spanish*]
NS	Numerische Steuerung [*German*] (ADPT)
NS	Nummernschalter [*German*] (ADPT)
ns	Nuorisoseura [*Finland*]
ns	Ny Serie [*New Series*] [*Sweden*]
NS	People's Council (BU)
N-S	Polnoc-Poludnie [*North-South*] [*Poland*]
NS	Scientific Council (BU)
NS	Staatsblad van het Koninkrijd der Nederlanden [*Netherlands*] (BAS)
ns	Train operates only on weekdays following Sundays and holidays [*See also S*] (EG)
n/s	Unclassified (RU)
NSA	Autoridade Nacional de Seguranca [*National Security Authority*] [*Portuguese*] (WER)
NSA	Chief of Medical Administration (BU)
NSA	Chief of Medical Service of an Army (RU)
NSA	Natal Society of Artists
NSA	National Security Agency [*Liberia*]
NSA	National Seniors' Association [*Australia*]
NSA	National Service Act [*Guyana*] (LA)
NSA	National Skill Share Association [*Australia*]
NSA	Navy Scientific Adviser [*Australia*]
NSA	Nederlandse Studenten Akkoord [*Netherlands Students' Accord*] (WEN)
NSA	Neurological Society of Australasia
NSA	Nile Safaris Aviation [*Sudan*] [*ICAO designator*] (FAAC)
NSA	Noosa [*Australia*] [*Airport symbol*] (OAG)
NSA	Norwegian Shipbrokers' Association (EAIO)
NSA	Norwegian Shipowners' Association (EAIO)
NSA	Norwegian Standards Association (EAIO)
NSa	Nossa Senhora [*Our Lady*] [*Portuguese*]
NSA	Nursery School Association [*Australia*]
NSA	Nutrition Society of Australia (ADA)
NSA	Standards Australia - Information Centre (Sydney) [*National Union Catalogue of Australia symbol*]
NSABA	National Spiritual Assembly of Baha'is of Australia
NSAC	Narodni Sdruzeni Americkych Cechu [*National Association of Czech Americans*] (CZ)
NSAC	National Space Activities Council
NSAC	St Andrew's College (University of Sydney) - Gillespie Divinity Library [*National Union Catalogue of Australia symbol*]
NSADP	Niger State Agricultural Development Project (ECON)
NSAG	Society of Australian Genealogy [*National Union Catalogue of Australia symbol*]
NSAGT	New South African Group Test [*Intelligence test*]
NSAH	Sydney Adventist Hospital Library [*National Union Catalogue of Australia symbol*]
NSAHS	Northern Sydney Area Health Service [*Australia*]
NSAHW	Nordic Secretariat for Agricultural and Horticultural Workers [*Denmark*]
NSAI	University of New South Wales - College of Fine Arts - Clement Semmler Library [*National Union Catalogue of Australia symbol*]
NSAJ	National Secretariat Australia Jaycees
NSAL	Nigerian South American Line
NSAP	Apia [*Western Samoa*] [*ICAO location identifier*] (ICLI)
NSAP	National Scouts Association of Panama (EAIO)
NSAPEA	Nordic Society Against Painful Experiments on Animals (EA)
NS:APR	CSIRO - Division of Animal Production - Ian Clunies Ross Animal Research Laborat [*National Union Catalogue of Australia symbol*]
NSAPV	Narodna Skupstina Autonomne Provincije Vojvodine [*People's Assembly of the Autonomous Province of Vojvodina*] (YU)
NS:APY	CSIRO - Division of Applied Physics [*National Union Catalogue of Australia symbol*]
NS:ARM	CSIRO - Division of Animal Production - Pastoral Research Laboratory [*National Union Catalogue of Australia symbol*]
NSARTY	North [*Head Barracks (Sydney)*] - School of Artillery [*National Union Catalogue of Australia symbol*]
NSAS	State Authorities Superannuation Board (New South Wales) [*National Union Catalogue of Australia symbol*]
NSASyd	National School of Art, Sydney [*Australia*]
NSAT	Institute of Technical and Adult Teacher Education (New South Wales) [*National Union Catalogue of Australia symbol*]
NSAU	Asau [*Western Samoa*] [*ICAO location identifier*] (ICLI)
NSAV	Nederlands-Suid-Afrikaanse Vereniging [*Dutch South African Association*] [*Afrikaans*]
NSB	Bimini-North [*Bahamas*] [*Airport symbol*] (OAG)
NSB	Narodni Svaz Brannosti [*National Association for Military Preparedness*] (CZ)
NSB	Nationaal-Socialistische Beweging [*National Socialist Movement*] [*Netherlands*] [*Political party*] (PPE)
NSB	National Shipping Board [*India*] (PDAA)
NSB	National Socialist Board [*Dutch National Socialist Party of 1931; later, Dutch NAZI Party*] [*Political party*]
NSB	National Standards Borad [*Ghana*] (PDAA)
NSB	Natsional'n Sel'skokhoziaistvenn Bank [*Arab*]
NSB	Nemzeti Sport Bizottsag [*National Sports Committee*] (HU)
NSB	Nordisk Sammanslutning for Barnavard [*Nordic Child and Youth Welfare Alliance - NCYWA*] (EA)
NSB	Nord-Sud [*Benin*] [*ICAO designator*] (FAAC)
NSB	Norges Statsbaner [*Norwegian State Railways*]
NSB	Nouvelle Societe du Bois
NSB	Nuclear Safety Bureau [*Australia*]
NSB	Nuclear Safety Bureau [*Japan*] (FEA)
NSBA	National Small Business Awards [*Australia*]
NSBE	St Benedict's Monastery (Arcadia) [*National Union Catalogue of Australia symbol*]
NS:BT	CSIRO - Division of Building Construction and Engineering [*National Union Catalogue of Australia symbol*]
NSC	Law Courts Library - Supreme Court of New South Wales [*National Union Catalogue of Australia symbol*]
NSC	National Safety Council of Australia (ADA)
NSC	National Science Council [*Taiwanese*] [*Research center*] (IRC)
NSC	National Science Council of Sri Lanka
NSC	National Security Council [*Malaysia*] (ML)
NSC	National Security Courts [*Somalia*]
NSC	National Settlement Convention
NSC	National Smallgoods Council [*Australia*]
NSC	National Sports Centre [*Australia*]
NSC	National Sports Club [*Australia*]
NSC	National Sports Commission
NSC	National Sports Council (ML)
NSC	National Standards Commission [*Australia*] (ADA)
NSC	National Standing Committee
NSC	National Steel Corp. [*Philippines*] (DS)
NSC	National Supply Corporation [*Libya*] (GEA)
NSC	NATO [*North Atlantic Treaty Organization*] Science Committee (EAIO)
NSC	Netherlands Shippers Council (DS)
NSC	Next Stop Commissioner [*Manila police slang*] [*Philippines*]
NSC	Nigerian Sugar Company Ltd.
NSC	Nippon Steel Corp. [*Japan*]
NSC	Noel-Schlosser & Compagnie
NSC	Norwegian Save the Children (EAIO)
NSC	Norwegian Shippers Council (DS)
NSC	Norwegian Society of Cardiology (EAIO)
NSCA	National Safety Council of Australia (ADA)
NSCA	National Society of Commercial Agents [*Australia*]
NSCAV	National Safety Council of Australia, Victoria Division
NSCB	National Savings and Credit Bank [*Ghana*]
NSCB	Nordic Society for Cell Biology (EA)
NSCC	Sydney Electricity [*National Union Catalogue of Australia symbol*]
NSCG	Neue Schweizerische Chemische Gesellschaft [*Switzerland*] (EAIO)
NSCH	Sisters of Charity Archives and Information Centre [*National Union Catalogue of Australia symbol*]
NSCHQ	Naval Support Command Headquarters [*Australia*]
NSCI	National Superannuation Committee of Inquiry [*Australia*]
NSCL	Sutherland Shire Libraries and Information Service [*National Union Catalogue of Australia symbol*]
NSCM	National Science Curriculum Materials Project [*Australia*] (PDAA)
NSCN	National Socialist Council of Nagaland [*India*] (PD)
NSCO	South Coast Cooperative Library Service [*National Union Catalogue of Australia symbol*]
NSCP	National Soil Conservation Program [*Australia*]
NSCP	Pasminco Limited - Research Library [*National Union Catalogue of Australia symbol*]
NSCS	Narodopisna Spolecnost Ceskoslovenska [*Czechoslovak Ethnographical Society*] (CZ)
NSCS	New South Wales - Soil Conservation Service [*Department of Conservation and Land Management*] [*National Union Catalogue of Australia symbol*]
NSCS	New Swiss Chemical Society [*Switzerland*] (EAIO)
NSCSA	National Shipping Company of Saudi Arabia [*Riyadh*] (MENA)
NSCSU	Nabozenska Spolecnost Ceskoslovenskych Unitaru [*Religious Society of Czechoslovak Unitarians*] (CZ)
NSCT	National Student Centre of Thailand (FEA)

NSCU .... National Software Coordination Unit [*Australia*]
NSCU:L...... Southern Cross University - Lismore Campus [*National Union Catalogue of Australia symbol*]
NSD .... Chief Signal Officer of a Division   (RU)
NSd .... Nasa Sodobnost [*Our Time*] [*Ljubljana A periodical*]   (YU)
NSD .... New South Wales - Department of Business and Regional Development [*National Union Catalogue of Australia symbol*]
NSD .... Norsk Samfunnsvitenskapelig Datatjeneste [*Norwegian Social Science Data Services*] [*Information service or system*]   (IID)
NSD .... Small Arms Field Manual   (RU)
NSDA .... National Space Development Agency [*Japan*]
NSDA .... Nigeria Steel Development Authority
NSDAJ ...... National Space Development Agency of Japan
NSDAP...... Nationalsozialistische Deutsche Arbeiterpartei [*National Socialist German Workers' Party, 1919-45*] [*Political party*]
NSDC .... National Scientific Documentation Center [*Indonesian Institute of Sciences*]
NSDC .... National Staff Development Committee [*Australia*]
NSDC .... Northern Shipowners' Defence Club [*See also NORDISK*]   (EAIO)
NSDFB ...... Nationalsozialistischer Deutscher Frontkaempferbund [*Germany*]
NSDP .... Independent Social Democratic Party of Germany   (RU)
NSDPG...... Independent Social Democratic Party of Germany   (RU)
NSDT .... Directive on Tax and Fee Collection   (BU)
NSDT .... People's Council of Working People's Deputies   (BU)
NSDV .... Directive on the Collection of Debts to the State   (BU)
NSE .... Nationalmuseets Skrifter, Etnografisk Raekke [*Copenhagen*]
NSE .... Nigerian Society of Engineers   (PDAA)
NSE .... Nigerian Stock Exchange
NSE .... Satena Servicios de Aeronavegacion A Territorios Nac [*Colombia*] [*ICAO designator*]   (FAAC)
NSEB .... Australian Bureau of Statistics New South Wales Office [*National Union Catalogue of Australia symbol*]
NSEC........ Australian Securities Commission - Chairman's Office Sydney Library [*National Union Catalogue of Australia symbol*]
NSEI .... Norsk Selskap for Elektronisk Informasjonsbehandling [*Norway*]   (SLS)
NSEI .... Norsk Selskap for Elektronisk Informasjonselskap [*Norwegian Computer Society*]
NSEM .... Nouvelle Societe Equatoriale de Mecanographie
NSEP .... Needle and Syringe Exchange Programme [*Australia*]
NS:ER........ CSIRO - Institute of Minerals Energy and Construction [*National Union Catalogue of Australia symbol*]
n ser........... New Series   (RU)
NSESA ...... Nomarkhiakon Symvoulion Exoskholikis Somatikis Agogis [*Nomarchy Council of Extracurricular Physical Education*] [*Greek*]   (GC)
NSF........... National Salvation Front [*Romania*] [*Political party*]
NSF........... Netherlands Sports Federation   (EAIO)
NSF........... Nordiska Skattevetenskapliga Forskningradet [*Nordic Council for Tax Research - NCTR*]   (EAIO)
NSF........... Norges Standardiseringsforbund [*Norwegian Standards Association*] [*Information service or system*]   (IID)
NSF........... Norske Siviloekonomers Forening [*Norway*]   (SLS)
NSF........... Norske Sosialoekonomers Forening [*Norway*]   (SLS)
NSF........... Norwegian Actors' Equity Association   (EAIO)
NSF........... Nurses Scholarship Foundation [*Lions Clubs*] [*Australia*]
NSFA........ Faleolo/International [*Western Samoa*] [*ICAO location identifier*]   (ICLI)
NSFA........ New Settlers Federation of Australia   (ADA)
NSFA........ Nordic Swimming Federations Association   (EA)
NSFC........ Natural Science Foudation of China
NSFC........ Nouvelle Societe France-Congo
NSFI .... Fagali'I [*Western Samoa*] [*ICAO location identifier*]   (ICLI)
NSFI .... Norges Skipsforskningsinstitutt [*Ship Research Institute of Norway*]   (ASF)
NSfK .... Nordiska Samarbetsradet for Kriminologi [*Scandinavian Research Council for Criminology - SRCC*] [*Finland*]   (EAIO)
NSFNRJ.... Narodna Skupstina Federativne Narodne Republike Jugoslavije [*People's Assembly of the Federal People's Republic of Yugoslavia*]   (YU)
NSFO .... National-Sozialistischer Fuersorge Offizier [*NAZI Guidance Officer*] [*German*]
NS:FR .... CSIRO - Division of Food Processing - Food Research Laboratory [*National Union Catalogue of Australia symbol*]
NSFS .... Nordiska Sallskapet for Stralskydd [*Nordic Society for Radiation Protection*] [*Norway*]   (EAIO)
NSFS .... People's Union for Physical Culture and Sports   (BU)
nsg............. Lower Horizontal Base Line   (RU)
NSG .... Narodni Strelecka Garda [*National Association of Riflemen*]   (CZ)
NSG .... Nippon Sheet Glass [*Commercial firm*] [*Japan*]
NSG .... North Shore Gas Co. [*Australia*]

NSG .... Nouvelle Societe du Gabon
NSG .... St George Hospital - J V Latham Medical Library [*National Union Catalogue of Australia symbol*]
NSGC .... National Safety Glazing Council [*South Africa*]   (AA)
NSGC .... Nostro Signore Gesu Cristo [*Our Lord Jesus Christ*] [*Italian*]
NSGF........ Norsk Samfunnsgeografisk Forening [*Norway*]   (SLS)
NSGLS ...... Nordisk Sekretariat for Gartneri- Land-, og Skovarbejderforbund [*Nordic Secretariat for Agricultural and Horticultural Workers - NSAHW*] [*Denmark*] [*Defunct*]   (EAIO)
NSGP........ Navtikon Stratologikon Grafeion Peiraios [*Piraeus Naval Recruiting Office*]   (GC)
NS:GR .... CSIRO - Division of Water Resources - Griffith Laboratory Library [*National Union Catalogue of Australia symbol*]
NSGS........ National Gymnastics and Sports Union   (BU)
NSGT .... Non-Self-Governing Territories [*United Nations*]
NSGT .... St George College of TAFE (Technical and Further Education) [*National Union Catalogue of Australia symbol*]
NSh............ Chief of Staff   (RU)
NSh............ Gear Pump   (RU)
NSH.......... Nadmorska Spoldzielnia Hydrotechnikow [*Coastal Region Hydraulic Engineers' Cooperative*]   (POL)
NSH.......... Ndermarrje Shteterore [*Albanian*]
NSH.......... Nordisk Samarbeidskomite for Husstellundervisning [*Nordic Joint Committee for Domestic Education - NJCDE*]   (EAIO)
NSH.......... Northern Star Holdings Ltd. [*Australia*]
NSh............ Public School   (RU)
NSh............ Pump Rod   (RU)
NSH.......... Sydney Hospital - Medical Library [*National Union Catalogue of Australia symbol*]
NSHC .... North Sea Hydrographic Commission [*of the International Hydrographic Organization*] [*Belgium*]
NSHC........ Shortland Electricity [*National Union Catalogue of Australia symbol*]
NSHE .... Shellharbour Municipal Library [*National Union Catalogue of Australia symbol*]
NSHF .... Ndermarrje Shteterore e Furnizimeve [*Albanian*]
NSHG........ Ndermarrje Shteterore e Grumbullimeve [*Albanian*]
NSHGJ...... Ndermarrje Shteterore Gjeologjike [*Albanian*]
NSHH .... Sacred Heart Hospice [*National Union Catalogue of Australia symbol*]
NSHIE....... Ndermarrje Shteterore Import Eksport [*Albanian*]
NSHK........ Newspaper Society of Hong Kong   (EAIO)
NSHL........ Northern Star Holdings Ltd. [*Australia*]
NSHMI ..... Ndermarrje Shteterore e Montimeve Industriale [*Albanian*]
NSHMI ..... Ndermarrje Shteterore Minerale Industriale [*Albanian*]
NSHN .... Ndermarrje Shteterore e Naftes [*Albanian*]
NSHN .... Ndermarrje Shteterore Ndertimi [*Albanian*]
NSHNG..... Ndermarrje e Shpimit dhe e Nxjerrjes se Gazit [*Albanian*]
NSHNI ...... Ndermarrje Shteterore Ndertime Industriale [*Albanian*]
NSHP .... Ndermarrje Shteterore Pyjore [*Albanian*]
NSHPMN ... Ndermarrje Shteterore e Prodhimeve Material Ndertimi [*Albanian*]
NSHR....... Sydney Church of England Grammar School (Shore) - Memorial Library [*National Union Catalogue of Australia symbol*]
NSHRAK .. Ndermarrje Shteterore per Riparimin e Automjeteve te (Ministrise se) Komunikacioneve [*Albanian*]
NShS .... Navigation Manual [*Aviation*]   (RU)
NSHSH ..... Ndermarrje Shteterore e Sharrave [*Albanian*]
NSHSH ..... Ndermarrje Shteterore e Sherbimeve [*Albanian*]
NSHSHK .. Ndermarrje Shteterore e Sherbimeve Komunale [*Albanian*]
NSHSHMI ... Ndermarrje Shteterore e Shperndarjes se Materialeve te Importit [*Albanian*]
NSht.......... Chief of Staff   (BU)
NSHT .... Sacred Heart Theological College [*National Union Catalogue of Australia symbol*]
NSHUM.... Ndermarrje Shteterore e Unifikuar Minerale [*Albanian*]
NShZO...... National Reserve Officers School   (BU)
NSI .... Dutch Society of Immunology [*Netherlands*]   (EAIO)
NSI .... National Sugar Institute [*India*]
NSI .... Nemzetkozi Statisztikai Intezet [*International Statistical Institute*]   (HU)
NSI .... Norsk Senter for Informatikk [*Norwegian Center for Informatics*] [*Information service or system*]   (IID)
NSIC......... National Small Industries Corporation
NSIC......... National Sport Information Centre [*Australia*]
NSIC......... St Ignatius' College (New South Wales) [*National Union Catalogue of Australia symbol*]
NSICC .... North Sea International Chart Commission   (MSC)
NSIDK...... Nederlandse Stichting Informatie- en Documentatiecentrum voor de Kartografie [*Utrecht*]
n sig............ Non Signe [*French*]   (FLAF)
NSIL......... Nouvelle Societe Immobiliere Librevilloise
NSIN .... Singleton Shire Library [*National Union Catalogue of Australia symbol*]
NSIS .... Systematics Information Systems [*National Union Catalogue of Australia symbol*]

NS:IT........ CSIRO - Division of Information Technology - Sydney Laboratory [*National Union Catalogue of Australia symbol*]

NSIT......... Netherlands Society for Industry and Trade   (EAIO)

NSIWP....... National Socialist Irish Workers' Party [*Political party*]

NSJ............ Narodna Skupstina na Jugoslavija [*National Assembly of Yugoslavia*]   (YU)

NSJ............ Nautical Society of Japan   (PDAA)

NSJC......... Nosso Senhor Jesus Cristo [*Our Lord Jesus Christ*] [*Portuguese*]

NSJC......... Notre Seigneur Jesus Christ [*Our Lord, Jesus Christ*] [*French*]

NSJC......... Nuestro Senor Jesucristo [*Our Lord Jesus Christ*] [*Spanish*]

NSJH........ St Joseph's College (New South Wales) [*National Union Catalogue of Australia symbol*]

NSK .... Chief Signal Officer of a Corps   (RU)

NSK .... National Council of Cartographers, USSR   (RU)

NSK .... Nihon Shinbun Kyokai [*Japan Newspaper Publishers and Editors Association*]   (EAIO)

NSK .... Nizi Sanitetski Kurs [*Elementary Medical Course*] [*Military*] (YU)

NSK .... Nomikon Symvoulion tou Kratous [*State Legal Council*] [*Greek*] (GC)

NSK .... Scientific Council for Coordination   (BU)

NSK .... Sinclair Knight [*National Union Catalogue of Australia symbol*]

NSKE........ Neolaia Sosialistikou Kommatos Ellados [*Youth of the Socialist Party of Greece*]   (GC)

NSKhI .... Novosibirsk Agricultural Institute   (RU)

NSKhI .... Scientific Research Institute of Sanitation and Public Hygiene (BU)

NSKIP....... Nordiska Samarbetskommitten for Internationell Politik [*Nordic Cooperation Committee for International Politics, Including Conflict and Peace Research*]   (EAIO)

NSKK .... Nationalsozialistischer Kraftfahr-Korps [*Germany*]

NSKK .... Nippon Sei Ko Kai [*Holy Catholic Church in Japan*] [*Church of England*]

NSKRS ..... Directive on Official Trips of Workers and Employees   (BU)

N skv......... Pressure Well   (RU)

NSL .... National Science Library [*India*]   (PDAA)

NSLB........ Nationalsozialistischer Lehrerbund [*NAZI Germany*]

NSL:D .... State Library of New South Wales - Dixson Library [*National Union Catalogue of Australia symbol*]

NSL:F .... State Library of New South Wales - Film and Video Service [*National Union Catalogue of Australia symbol*]

NSL:L .... State Library of New South Wales - Legal Information Access Centre [*National Union Catalogue of Australia symbol*]

NSL:M...... State Library of New South Wales - Mitchell Library [*National Union Catalogue of Australia symbol*]

NSL:P .... State Library of New South Wales - Public Libraries Branch [*National Union Catalogue of Australia symbol*]

NSL:PB ..... State Library of New South Wales - Preservation Branch [*National Union Catalogue of Australia symbol*]

NSL:R........ State Library of New South Wales - Document Delivery Service [*National Union Catalogue of Australia symbol*]

NSL:RB ..... State Library of New South Wales - Rare Books and Special Collections [*National Union Catalogue of Australia symbol*]

NSL:S .... State Library of New South Wales - Special Needs Service [*National Union Catalogue of Australia symbol*]

NSL:SY ..... State Library of New South Wales - Systems [*National Union Catalogue of Australia symbol*]

NSM .... German Peace Union [*Federal Republic of Germany*]   (RU)

NSM .... Nederlandse Stikstof Maatschappij NV [*Netherlands*]

NSM .... Norseman [*Australia*] [*Airport symbol*]   (OAG)

NSM .... Nutrition Society of Malaysia   (EAIO)

NSMA .... Maota [*Western Samoa*] [*ICAO location identifier*]   (ICLI)

NSMA .... Non-Smokers' Movement of Australia

NSMB .... Netherlands Ship Model Basin

NSMB .... Northern States Marketing Board

NSMB .... Sydney Missionary and Bible College - J T H Kerr Library [*National Union Catalogue of Australia symbol*]

NS:MCM .. CSIRO - Division of Animal Health - McMaster Laboratory [*National Union Catalogue of Australia symbol*]

NSME .... Snowy Mountains Engineering Corporation Limited [*National Union Catalogue of Australia symbol*]

NSMENG ... School of Military Engineering [*National Union Catalogue of Australia symbol*]

NSMH...... National Society for the Mentally Handicapped [*Denmark*] (EAIO)

NSMHE .... Snowy Mountains Hydro-Electric Authority - SMHEA Library [*National Union Catalogue of Australia symbol*]

NSML....... Strathfield Municipal Library [*National Union Catalogue of Australia symbol*]

NS:MOL ... CSIRO - Division of Biomolecular Engineering - Laboratory for Molecular Biology [*National Union Catalogue of Australia symbol*]

NSMPD..... Nordiska Samfundet Mot Plagsamma Dourforsok [*Sweden*] (EAIO)

NS:MS...... CSIRO - Division of Mathematics and Statistics Library [*National Union Catalogue of Australia symbol*]

NSMS........ Natsional'nyi Soiuz Marokkanskikh Studentov

NSN .... NATO Stock Number   (NATG)

NSN .... Nelson [*New Zealand*] [*Airport symbol*]   (OAG)

NSN .... Officer in Charge of Communications   (BU)

NSn .... Unguided Missile   (RU)

NSNA .... National Socialist Nederlandse Arbeiders Partij [*Netherlands group favoring integration of the Netherlands into the German reich*] [*World War II*]

NS:NAP.... CSIRO - Cotton Research Unit [*National Union Catalogue of Australia symbol*]

NSNG....... National Council of Nigerian Citizens   (RU)

NSNG....... Natsional'nyi Sovet Nigeriiskikh Grazhdan

NSNK .... Natsional'nyi Sovet Nigerii i Kameruna [*National Council of Nigeria and Cameroon*] [*Russian*]

NSNLC..... North Shore New Life Centre [*Australia*]

NSNRBiH ... Narodna Skupstina Narodne Republike Bosne i Hercegovine [*People's Assembly of the People's Republic of Bosnia and Hercegovina*]   (YU)

NSNRCG .. Narodna Skupstina Narodne Republike Crne Gore [*People's Assembly of the People's Republic of Montenegro*]   (YU)

NSNRM .... Narodno Sobranie na Narodnata Republika Makedonija [*People's Assembly of the People's Republic of Macedonia*] (YU)

NSNRS...... Narodna Skupstina Narodne Republike Slovenije [*People's Assembly of the People's Republic of Slovenia*]   (YU)

NSNRS..... Narodna Skupstina Narodne Republike Srbije [*People's Assembly of the People's Republic of Serbia*]   (YU)

NSNS........ National Union of People's Forces [*Morocco*]   (RU)

NSNS........ Natsional'nyi Soiuz Narodnykh Sil

NSNTI...... National Scientific and Technical Information System   (BU)

NSO.......... Chief of Communications of a Military District   (RU)

NSO.......... Directive on Bookkeeping Accountability   (BU)

NSO.......... National Security Organization [*Nigeria*]   (AF)

NSO.......... National Statistical Office

NSO.......... Nigerian Security Organisation

NSO.......... Nigerian Standards Organization [*Federal Ministry of Industries*]

NSO.......... Scone [*Australia*] [*Airport symbol*]   (OAG)

NSO.......... Standard Cost of Processing   (RU)

NSO.......... Student Scientific Society   (RU)

NSO.......... Sydney 2000 Olympic Committee [*National Union Catalogue of Australia symbol*]

NSOA .... Nouvelles Savonneries de l'Ouest Africain

NSODCC .. North Sumatra Oil Development Corp. Co. [*Japan*]   (PDAA)

NSOF .... National Council of the Fatherland Front   (BU)

NSOF .... Norwegian Shipping and Offshore Federation   (EAIO)

NSOH....... Sydney Opera House - Dennis Wolanski Library and Archives of the Performing Arts [*National Union Catalogue of Australia symbol*]

NSOL .... Norske Symfoni-Orkestres Lansforbund [*Norway*]   (EAIO)

nsolo.......... Sa Neogranicenom Solidarnom Odgovornoscu [*With Unlimited Joint Liability*] [*Former Yugoslavia*]   (CED)

NSOSA...... National Stationers and Office Suppliers Association [*Australia*]

NSOT .... Southern Tablelands Joint Library Service (New South Wales) [*National Union Catalogue of Australia symbol*]

NSP .... Nationalist Social Party [*Lebanon*]

NSP .... National Salvation Party [*Milli Selamet Partisi*] [*Turkey*] [*Political party*]   (PPW)

NSP .... National Security Planning [*Korean*]

NSP .... National Seoposengwe Party [*Bophuthatswana*] [*Political party*] (PPW)

NSP .... National Socialist Party [*New Zealand*] [*Political party*]   (PD)

NSP .... National Socialist Party of Australia   (ADA)

NSP .... Nederlandsch Scheepsbouwkundig Proefstation [*Netherlands Naval Testing Station*]   (WEN)

NSP .... Nordiska Sjoforsakringspoolen [*Nordic Pool for Marine Insurance - NPMI*]   (EA)

NSP .... Nosso Santo Padre [*Our Holy Father*] [*Portuguese*]

NS-P .... Notre Saint-Pere [*Our Holy Father*] [*French*]

NSP .... People's Socialist Party [*Republic of India*]   (RU)

NSP .... Routine Storage   (RU)

NSP .... Sandoz Australia Proprietary Limited [*National Union Catalogue of Australia symbol*]

NSP .... Sanitary Planning Norms   (RU)

NSPA........ National Socialist Party of Australia   (ADA)

NSPC........ St Paul's College (New South Wales) [*National Union Catalogue of Australia symbol*]

NSPCC ..... New South Wales - Environment Protection Authority [*National Union Catalogue of Australia symbol*]

NSPE .... Nouvelle Societe de Presse et d'Edition [*Publisher*] [*Madagascar*] (EY)

NSPK........ People's Socialist Party of Cuba   (RU)

NSPK........ Routine and Constant Storage   (RU)

NSPL........ Sydney City Library [*National Union Catalogue of Australia symbol*]

NSPM....... Catholic Institute of Sydney - Veech Library [*National Union Catalogue of Australia symbol*]

NSPN .... St Paul's National Seminary (New South Wales) [*National Union Catalogue of Australia symbol*]

NSP of A.... National Socialist Party of Australia (ADA)
NSPOGF ... Directive on Haymowing, Pastures, and Forest Resources (BU)
NSPP.......... New [*South Wales*] Slab and Plate Products Division [*Central Library*] [*BHP Steel International Group*] [*National Union Catalogue of Australia symbol*]
NSPRI .... Nigerian Stored Products Research Institute
NS priCSAV ... Narodopisna Spolecnost pri CSAV [*Former Czechoslovakia*] (EAIO)
NSqF.......... Norges Squashforbund [*Norway*] (EAIO)
NSR .... National Air Charter PT [*Indonesia*] [*ICAO designator*] (FAAC)
NSR .... National Shipping Report [*NATO*]
NSR .... Natsional'nyi Soiuz Ruandy
NSR .... Nederlands Studenten Raad [*National Student Council*] [*Netherlands*] (WEN)
NSR .... Nemecka Spolkova Republika [*German Federal Republic*] (CZ)
Nsr .... Nesriyat [*Publication*] (TU)
NSR .... Nordic Research Council on Forest Operations [*Finland*] (EAIO)
NSR .... Nordic Shooting Region (EAIO)
NSR .... Nordiska Skidskolans Rad [*Nordic Council of Ski Schools - NCSS*] [*Finland*] (EAIO)
NSR .... Nordiska Skogsarbetsstudiernas Rad [*Nordic Research Council on Forest Operations*] [*Sweden*] (EAIO)
NSR .... Nordisk Skuespillerrad [*Nordic Actors' Council - NAC*] [*Sweden*] (EAIO)
NSR .... Norske Samers Riksforbund [*Norway*]
n/sr............. Notre Sieur ... [*Our Sir ...*] [*French*]
NSR .... Nueva Sociedad Rural [*New Rural Society*] [*Spanish*] (WER)
NSR .... Soviet People's Republic [*1920-1924*] (RU)
NSRA .... National Shoe Retailers Association
NSRA .... Nigeria Squash Racket Association
NSRA .... Norwegian Squash Rackets Association (EAIO)
NSRA .... Nuclear Safety Research Association [*See also GAKK*] [*Japan*] (NRCH)
NSRA .... Shoalhaven Regional Art Collection [*National Union Catalogue of Australia symbol*]
NSRASA ... National Smallbore Rifle Association of South Africa
NSRC........ Narodni Shromazdeni Republiky Ceskoslovenske [*National Assembly of the Czechoslovak Republic*] (CZ)
NSRC........ National Science Research Council [*Guyana*]
NSRC........ NeoSynthesis Research Centre [*Sri Lanka*] (EAIO)
NSRF........ New South Wales - Department of Sport and Recreation - Sports House Library [*National Union Catalogue of Australia symbol*]
NSRF........ Norwegian Institute of State Authorized Public Accountants (EAIO)
NSRI.......... Nasionale Seereddingsinstituut [*Afrikaans*]
NSRI.......... National Sea Rescue Institute [*South Africa*] (PDAA)
NSRI.......... Nelspruit Subtropical Research Institute
NSRKP..... Nigeriiskaia Sotsialisticheskaia Raboche-Krest'ianskaia Partiia
NSRM........ National Strategy for Rangeland Management [*Australia*]
NS:RP........ CSIRO - Division of Radiophysics [*National Union Catalogue of Australia symbol*]
NSRP........ Nordic Society for Radiation Protection [*See also NSFS*] [*Helsinki, Finland*] (EAIO)
NSRR....... Nuclear Safety Research Reactor [*JAERI*] [*Japan*] (PDAA)
NSRS........ New South Wales Academy of Sport [*National Union Catalogue of Australia symbol*]
NSRT........ North South Roundtable (EAIO)
NSRZ........ Neva Ship Repair Yard (RU)
NSS............ National Science Statement [*Australia*]
NSS............ National Security Service [*Somali*]
NSS............ National Security Service [*Djibouti*] (AF)
NSS............ National Service Scheme [*India*]
NSS............ National Student Union (RU)
NSS............ Navtad Seva Sangh [*India*] (EAIO)
NSS............ Nederlandse Stichting voor Statistiek ['*s-Gravenhage*]
NSS............ Nejvyssi Spravni Soud [*Supreme Administrative Court*] (CZ)
NSS............ Nordiska Kommitten for Samordning av Elektriska Sakerhetsfragor [*Nordic Committee for Coordination of Electrical Safety Matters*] (EAIO)
NSS............ Nordiska Statistiska Sekretariatet [*Nordic Statistical Secretariat*] (EAIO)
NSS............ North Shore Synagogue [*Sydney - Rev Katz Library*]
NSSA........ Nematological Society of Southern Africa (EAIO)
NSSA........ Nichiren Shoshu Sokagakkai of Australia
NSSC........ Nuclear Safety Standards Commission [*Germany*] (EAIO)
NSSC........ Sancta Sophia College [*National Union Catalogue of Australia symbol*]
NSSD........ Department of Social Security - New South Wales Office [*National Union Catalogue of Australia symbol*]
NSSD........ National Strategy for Sustainable Development [*Australia*]
NSSF........ National Social Security Fund [*Kenya*]
NSSG........ National Statistical Service of Greece
NSSh .... Incomplete Secondary School, Seven-Year School (RU)

NSSL......... South Sydney City Library [*National Union Catalogue of Australia symbol*]
NSSM....... National Security Study Memorandum
NSSO .... National Sample Survey Organisation [*Economic research group*] [*India*]
NSSP .... National Syrian Socialist Party [*Lebanon*] [*Political party*]
NSSP .... Nava Sama Samaja Party [*New Equal Society Party*] [*Sri Lanka*] [*Political party*] (PPW)
NSSP .... Nosso Santissimo Padre [*Our Most Holy Father*] [*Portuguese*]
NSSR .... Royal Blind Society of New South Wales - Student and Special Transcriptions [*National Union Catalogue of Australia symbol*]
NSSS .... National Social Science Survey [*Australia*]
NSST......... National Sports and Technology Union (BU)
NST .... Aviacion Ejecutiva del Noroeste SA de CV [*Mexico*] [*ICAO designator*] (FAAC)
n st.............. Gregorian Calendar Dates (BU)
NST .... National Skills Training
N St .... Neuen Stils [*Of a New Style*] [*German*] (GCA)
NST .... New Straits Times [*Malaysia*]
n st.............. New Style [*Gregorian calendar*] (RU)
NST .... Nomenclature Statistique de Transport [*Benelux*] (BAS)
NST .... Nordens Samverkande Tegelforeningar [*Denmark*] (EAIO)
NST .... Sydney Institute of Technology (Ultimo) [*National Union Catalogue of Australia symbol*]
NSTA......... National Science and Technology Agency
NSTA......... National Science and Technology Authority [*Philippines*] [*Research center*]
NSTA........ State of the Art Communication Proprietary Limited [*National Union Catalogue of Australia symbol*]
NSTAG...... National Science and Technology Advisory Group [*Australia*]
NSTC........ National Science and Technology Centre [*Australia*]
NSTC........ North Sydney Technical College [*Australia*] (ADA)
NSTC........ Nyegezi Social Training Centre
NSTDA...... National Science and Technology Development Agency
NSTIC .... National Scientific and Technical Information Center [*Kuwait Institute for Scientific Research*]
NSTJ .... St John's College (New South Wales) [*National Union Catalogue of Australia symbol*]
NSTM .... Nordiska Skeppstekniska Mote [*Joint Committee of Nordic Marine Technology - JCNMT*] (EAIO)
NSTO .... Hunter Region Developmental Disability Service - Stockton Centre [*National Union Catalogue of Australia symbol*]
NSTR........ Sterling Pharmaceutical Proprietary Limited - Medical Library [*National Union Catalogue of Australia symbol*]
NSTU .... Pago Pago/International, Tutuila Island [*American Samoa*] [*ICAO location identifier*] (ICLI)
N-stvo .... Authorities, Chiefs, Superiors, Board of Trustees (BU)
NS:TXP ..... CSIRO - Division of Wool Technology - Sydney Laboratory [*National Union Catalogue of Australia symbol*]
NSU .... Neckarsulm [*Location in Wuerttemberg, Germany, of NSU Werke, automobile manufacturer; initialism used as name of its cars*]
NSU .... Novinarsky Studijni Ustav [*Research Institute of Journalism*] (CZ)
NSU .... Nuova Sinistra Unita [*New United Left*] [*Italy*] [*Political party*] (PPE)
NSU .... NV [*Naamloze Vennootschap*] Nederlandsche Scheepvaart Unie [*Netherlands*]
NSU .... Unidentified Vessel (RU)
NSUGAF... Nippon Suisan Gakkaishi [*Japanese Society of Scientific Fisheries*] (ASF)
NSUH........ Scone and Upper Hunter Historical Society [*National Union Catalogue of Australia symbol*]
NSUT .... Sutherland Hospital - Medical Library [*National Union Catalogue of Australia symbol*]
NSV .... Chief of Communications Center (BU)
NSV .... Nationalsozialistische Volkswohlfahrt [*Germany*]
NSV .... Nederlandsch Syndicalistisch Vakverbond [*Netherlands*] (BAS)
NSV .... Niersorgvereniging van Suid-Afrika [*Renal Care Society of South Africa*] (AA)
n/sv .... No Information (RU)
NSV .... St Vincent's Hospital (Sydney) - Walter McGrath Medical Library [*National Union Catalogue of Australia symbol*]
NSVA .... New South Wales Vigoro Association [*Australia*]
NSVN .... Nosokomeion Stelekhon Vasilikou Navtikou [*Royal Navy Cadre Hospital*] (GC)
NSVP........ St Vincent's Private Hospital (Sydney) [*National Union Catalogue of Australia symbol*]
NSVV .... Nederlandse Stichting voor Verlichtingskunde [*Netherlands Foundation for Illumination*] (PDAA)
NSW .... Ansett Airlines of New South Wales [*Australia*] [*ICAO designator*] (FAAC)
NSW .... New South Wales [*Australia*]
NSW .... Nichtsozialistisches Waehrungsgebiet [*Non-Socialist Monetary Area*] (EG)
NSW .... Nieu-Suid-Wallis [*New South Wales*] [*Afrikaans*]

NSW .... University of New South Wales [*Australia*]   (ADA)
NSWA .... Art Gallery of New South Wales [*National Union Catalogue of Australia symbol*]
NSWA .... New South Wales Archives [*Australia*]
NSWAAT ... New South Wales Association of Agricultural Teachers [*Australia*]
NSWABA ... New South Wales Amateur Boxing Association [*Australia*]
NSWAECG ... New South Wales Aboriginal Education Consultative Group [*Australia*]
NSWAEM ... New South Wales Assemblies' Evangelic Mission [*Australia*]
NSWAF..... New South Wales Agriculture and Fisheries [*Australia*]
NSWAFL.. New South Wales Australian Football League
NSWAGTC ... New South Wales Association of Gifted and Talented Children [*Australia*]
NSWAHP ... New South Wales Association of Health Professions [*Australia*]
NSWALC.. New South Wales Aboriginal Land Council [*Australia*]
NSWALC.. New South Wales Adult Literacy Council [*Australia*]
NSWAMES ... New South Wales Adult Migrant Education Service [*Australia*]
NSWAMH ... New South Wales Association for Mental Health [*Australia*]
NSWAPA ... New South Wales Amateur Pistol Association [*Australia*]
NSWAS..... New South Wales Association of Sephardim [*Australia*]
NSWASF .. New South Wales Amateur Soccer Federation [*Australia*]
NSWAWL ... New South Wales Animal Welfare League [*Australia*]
NSWAWPA ... New South Wales Amateur Water Polo Association [*Australia*]
NSWBA..... New South Wales Bar Association [*Australia*]
NSWBA..... New South Wales Basketball Association [*Australia*]
NSWBA..... New South Wales Bridge Association [*Australia*]
NSWBACE ... New South Wales Board of Adult and Community Education [*Australia*]
NSWBBA .. New South Wales Bloodhorse Breeders' Association [*Australia*]
NSWBCS .. New South Wales Bookmakers' Cooperative Society [*Australia*]
NSWBGA ... New South Wales Bowling Greenkeepers' Association [*Australia*]
NSWBIC ... New South Wales Banana Industry Committee [*Australia*]
NSWBJE... New South Wales Board of Jewish Education [*Australia*]
NSWBL..... New South Wales Basketball League [*Australia*]
NSWBS..... New South Wales Board of Surveyors [*Australia*]
NSWBSA .. New South Wales Board Sailing Association [*Australia*]
NSWC...... National South West Coalition [*Australia*]
NSWCA..... New South Wales Canoe Association [*Australia*]
NSWCA..... New South Wales Coal Association [*Australia*]
NSWCA..... New South Wales Council on the Aging [*Australia*]
NSWCAA ... New South Wales Community Arts Association [*Australia*]
NSWCC..... New South Wales Cancer Council [*Australia*]
NSWCC..... New South Wales Canine Council [*Australia*]
NSWCC..... New South Wales Council of Churches [*Australia*]
NSWCCFT ... New South Wales Council for Children's Films and Television [*Australia*]
NSWCCU ... New South Wales Churches Cricket Union [*Australia*]
NSWCF..... New South Wales Cycling Federation [*Australia*]
NSWCFA .. New South Wales Canning Fruitgrowers' Association [*Australia*]
NSWCFVI ... New South Wales Chamber of Fruit and Vegetable Industries [*Australia*]
NSWCGA ... New South Wales Cane Growers' Association [*Australia*]
NSWCGA ... New South Wales Cherry Growers' Association [*Australia*]
NSWCGA ... New South Wales Chicken Growers' Association [*Australia*]
NSWCGC ... New South Wales Citrus Growers' Council [*Australia*]
NSWCHS ... New South Wales Cooperative Housing Society [*Australia*]
NSWCID... New South Wales Council for Intellectual Disabilities [*Australia*]
NSWCMACA ... New South Wales Chinese Martial Arts and Cultural Association [*Australia*]
NSWCMC ... New South Wales Chicken Meat Council [*Australia*]
NSWCMOA ... New South Wales Coal Mine Owners' Association [*Australia*]
NSWCN .... New South Wales College of Nursing [*Australia*]
NSWCOA ... New South Wales Colliery Officials' Association [*Australia*]
NSWCOHO ... New South Wales Council of Heritage Organizations [*Australia*]
NSWCons Music ... New South Wales State Conservatorium of Music [*Australia*]
NSWCOTA ... New South Wales Council on the Aging [*Australia*]
NSWCPA.. New South Wales Coal Proprietors' Association [*Australia*]
NSWCPC.. New South Wales Child Protection Council [*Australia*]
NSWCSA .. New South Wales Churches Soccer Association [*Australia*]
NSWCSA .. New South Wales Cold Storage Association [*Australia*]
NSWCTA ... New South Wales Council of Tourist Associations [*Australia*]
NSW Ctof App ... New South Wales Court of Appeal [*Australia*]
NSWCUA ... New South Wales Credit Unit Association [*Australia*]
NSWCUA ... New South Wales Cricket Umpires' Association [*Australia*]
NSWCUEA ... New South Wales Credit Union Employers' Association [*Australia*]
NSWCYMCA ... New South Wales Council of the Young Men's Christian Associations [*Australia*]
NSWDAA ... New South Wales Domestic Abattoirs Association [*Australia*]
NSWDAA ... New South Wales Drug and Alcohol Authority [*Australia*]
NSWDBA ... New South Wales Deer Breeders' Association [*Australia*]
NSWDFA ... New South Wales Dairy Farmers' Association [*Australia*]
NSWDFA ... New South Wales Deer Farmers' Association [*Australia*]

NSWDFB.. New South Wales Dried Fruits Board [*Australia*]
NSWDIC... New South Wales Dairy Industry Conference [*Australia*]
NSWDPA ... New South Wales Dairy Products Association [*Australia*]
NSWDSC.. New South Wales Dam Safety Committee [*Australia*]
NSWDU.... New South Wales Debating Union [*Australia*]
NSWEEITC ... New South Wales Electrical and Electronic Industry Training Committee [*Australia*]
NSWEEU ... New South Wales Education Exports Unit [*Australia*]
NSWEPC.. New South Wales Egg Producers' Cooperative [*Australia*]
NSWEPOWA ... New South Wales Ex-Prisoners of War Association [*Australia*]
NSWETF .. New South Wales Education and Training Foundation [*Australia*]
NSWFA..... New South Wales Farmers' Association [*Australia*]
NSWFB..... New South Wales Fire Brigades [*Australia*]
NSWFBEU ... New South Wales Fire Brigade Employee's Union [*Australia*]
NSWFC..... New South Wales Film Corporation [*Australia*]   (ADA)
NSWFC..... New South Wales Fitness Council [*Australia*]
NSWFCA .. New South Wales Foster Care Association [*Australia*]
NSWFCHA ... New South Wales Farm and Country Holiday Association [*Australia*]
NSWFF..... New South Wales Folk Federation [*Australia*]
NSWFG..... New South Wales Furniture Guild [*Australia*]
NSWFGA ... New South Wales Flower Growers' Association [*Australia*]
NSWFGHC ... New South Wales Free Growers' Horticultural Council [*Australia*]
NSWFHU ... New South Wales Friends of the Hebrew University [*Australia*]
NSWFIA ... New South Wales Farmers' Industrial Association [*Australia*]
NSWFIC ... New South Wales Fishing Industry Council [*Australia*]
NSWFITC ... New South Wales Food Industry Training Council [*Australia*]
NSWFITC ... New South Wales Furniture Industry Training Council [*Australia*]
NSWFMC ... New South Wales Flour Millers' Council [*Australia*]
NSWFPA .. New South Wales Forest Products Association [*Australia*]
NSWFPCA ... New South Wales Federation of Parents and Citizens' Associations [*Australia*]
NSWFS..... New South Wales Fabian Society [*Australia*]
NSWFTO ... New South Wales Film and Television Office [*Australia*]
NSWG....... North Sea Working Group [*Advisory Committee on Pollution of the Sea*]
NSWGA .... New South Wales Golf Association [*Australia*]
NSWGA .... New South Wales Gymnastics Association [*Australia*]
NSWGB .... New South Wales Grains Board [*Australia*]
NSWGBOTA ... New South Wales Greyhound Breeders, Owners and Trainers Association [*Australia*]
NSWGC .... New South Wales Gun Club [*Australia*]
NSWGCB ... New South Wales Guild of Craft Bookbinders [*Australia*]
NSWGCHS ... New South Wales Group of Cooperative Housing Societies [*Australia*]
NSWGCSUA ... New South Wales Glass and Ceramic Silica Users' Association [*Australia*]
NSWGFL.. New South Wales Gridiron Football League [*Australia*]
NSWGFM ... New South Wales Guild of Furniture Manufacturers [*Australia*]
NSWGIS ... New South Wales Government Information Service [*Australia*]
NSWGMA ... New South Wales Girls' Marching Association [*Australia*]
NSWGMA ... New South Wales Glass Merchants' Association [*Australia*]
NSWGTC ... New South Wales Government Travel Center [*Australia*]
NSWHA .... New South Wales Hockey Association [*Australia*]
NSWHCA ... New South Wales Homeless Children's Association [*Australia*]
NSWHEA ... New South Wales Horticultural Exporters' Association [*Australia*]
NSWHGA ... New South Wales Hospital Group Apprentices Scheme [*Australia*]
NSWHPAC ... New South Wales Hospitals Planning Advisory Center [*Australia*]
NSWHRA ... New South Wales Hot Rod Association [*Australia*]
NSWHRC ... New South Wales Harness Racing Club [*Australia*]
NSWHS .... New South Wales Humanist Society [*Australia*]
NSWHTA ... New South Wales Hardcourt Tennis Association [*Australia*]
NSWIC...... New South Wales Industrial Commission [*Australia*]
NSWIC...... New South Wales Investment Corp. [*Australia*]
NSWICCA ... New South Wales Indo-China Chinese Association
NSWICCt S ... New South Wales Industrial Commission in Court Session [*Australia*]
NSWID...... New South Wales Institute of Dieticians [*Australia*]
NSWIER ... New South Wales Institute for Educational Research [*Australia*] (ADA)
NSWIP...... New South Wales Institute of Physiotherapy [*Australia*]
NSWIP...... New South Wales Institute of Psychotherapy [*Australia*]
NSWIT...... New South Wales Institute of Technology [*Australia*]   (ADA)
NSWJBD .. New South Wales Jewish Board of Deputies [*Australia*]
NSWJCU ... New South Wales Junior Cricket Union [*Australia*]
NSWJHS .. New South Wales Jersey Herd Society [*Australia*]
NSWJWM ... New South Wales Jewish War Memorial [*Australia*]
NSWL........ New South Wales Lotteries [*Australia*]
NSWLC..... New South Wales Leagues Club [*Australia*]

NSWLHPB ... New South Wales Ladies Highland Pipe Band [*Australia*]
NSWLRC .. New South Wales Law Reform Commission [*Australia*]   (ILCA)
NSWLSEA ... New South Wales Live Stock Exporters' Association [*Australia*]
NSWMA ... New South Wales Marching Association [*Australia*]
NSWMA ... New South Wales Midwives' Association [*Australia*]
NSWMB ... New South Wales Medical Board [*Australia*]
NSWMEA ... New South Wales Meat Exporters' Association [*Australia*]
NSWMEQB ... New South Wales Migrant Employment and Qualifications Board [*Australia*]
NSWMH... New South Wales Masonic Hospital [*Australia*]
NSWMIA ... New South Wales Meat Industry Authority [*Australia*]
NSWNA ..... New South Wales Netball Association [*Australia*]
NSWNCA ... New South Wales National Coursing Association [*Australia*]
NSWNGA ... New South Wales Nut Growers' Association [*Australia*]
NSWNPWS ... New South Wales National Parks and Wildlife Service [*Australia*]
NSWNRB ... New South Wales Nurses' Registration Board [*Australia*]
NSWODA ... New South Wales Oyster Distributors' Association [*Australia*]
NSWOTA ... New South Wales Occupational Therapy Association [*Australia*]
NSWOTA ... New South Wales Operating Theatre Association [*Australia*]
NSWOTA ... New South Wales Organic Traders' Association [*Australia*]
NSWP........ Non-Soviet Warsaw Pact   (NATG)
NSWPA..... New South Wales Poker Association [*Australia*]
NSWPA..... New South Wales Polo Association [*Australia*]
NSWPACC ... New South Wales Police Aero Club Company [*Australia*]
NSWPBA .. New South Wales Pipe Band Association [*Australia*]
NSWPC..... New South Wales Parachute Council [*Australia*]
NSWPC..... New South Wales Parents' Council [*Australia*]
NSWPC..... New South Wales Prices Commission [*Australia*]
NSWPEA .. New South Wales Physical Education Association [*Australia*]
NSWPGA ... New South Wales Professional Golfers' Association [*Australia*]
NSWPL..... New South Wales Police Legacy [*Australia*]
NSWPMOA ... New South Wales Public Medical Officers' Association [*Australia*]
NSWPOA ... New South Wales Property Owners' Association [*Australia*]
NSWPSPOA ... New South Wales Public Service Professional Officers' Association [*Australia*]
NSWPTC .. New South Wales Public Transport Commission [*Australia*]   (PDAA)
NSWPTCA ... New South Wales Professional Tennis Coaches Association [*Australia*]
NSWR .... South-West Regional Library (New South Wales) [*National Union Catalogue of Australia symbol*]
NSWRA .... New South Wales Rifle Association [*Australia*]
NSWRA .... New South Wales Rowing Association [*Australia*]
NSWRAA ... New South Wales Rural Assistance Authority [*Australia*]
NSWRCSA ... New South Wales Registered Cereal Seedgrowers' Association [*Australia*]
NSWRFAC ... New South Wales Recreational Fishing Advisory Council [*Australia*]
NSWRFL .. New South Wales Rugby Football League [*Australia*]
NSWRFS... New South Wales Rod Fishers' Society [*Australia*]
NSWRITC ... New South Wales Rural Industry Training Committee [*Australia*]
NSWRLIFA ... New South Wales Rugby League Insurance Finance Agency [*Australia*]
NSWRLMOA ... New South Wales Rugby League Medical Officers Association [*Australia*]
NSWRTA ... New South Wales Road Transport Association [*Australia*]
NSWRTEHF ... New South Wales Railway and Transport Employees' Hospital Fund [*Australia*]
NSWRTLA ... New South Wales Right to Life Association [*Australia*]
NSWRTM ... New South Wales Rail Transport Museum [*Australia*]
NSWRTTC ... New South Wales Road Transport Training Council [*Australia*]
NSWSA..... New South Wales Shooting Association [*Australia*]
NSWSA..... New South Wales Ski Association [*Australia*]
NSWSA..... New South Wales Softball Association [*Australia*]
NSWSA..... New South Wales Swimming Association [*Australia*]
NSWSACW ... New South Wales Standing Advisory Committee on Wheat [*Australia*]
NSWSBA .. New South Wales Sheepbreeders' Association [*Australia*]
NSWSCC .. New South Wales Society for Crippled Children [*Australia*]
NSWSCC .. New South Wales State Cancer Committee [*Australia*]
NSWSCL .. New South Wales Society for Computers and the Law [*Australia*]
NSWSDA ... New South Wales Soft Drink Association [*Australia*]
NSWSF ..... New South Wales Soccer Federation [*Australia*]
NSWSGA ... New South Wales Seed Growers' Association [*Australia*]
NSWSHS.. New South Wales School of Hypnotic Sciences [*Australia*]
NSWSJC... New South Wales Show Jumping Council [*Australia*]
NSWSK..... New South Wales Shorinjiryu Karate-do Association [*Australia*]
NSWSMBA ... New South Wales Stud Merino Breeders' Association [*Australia*]
NSWSO..... New South Wales Superannuation Office [*Australia*]
NSWSRCTG ... New South Wales Sales Representatives and Commercial Travellers' Guild [*Australia*]
NSWSS ..... New South Wales Supply Service [*Australia*]

NSWSSSA ... New South Wales Secondary Schools Soccer Association [*Australia*]
NSWSTC .. New South Wales Science and Technology Council [*Australia*]
NSWSTM ... New South Wales School of Therapeutic Massage [*Australia*]
NSWTA..... New South Wales Tennis Association [*Australia*]
NSWTA..... New South Wales Touch Football Association [*Australia*]
NSWTA..... New South Wales Typographical Association [*Australia*]
NSWTAFEC ... New South Wales Technical and Further Education Commission [*Australia*]
NSWTC..... New South Wales Taxi Council [*Australia*]
NSWTC..... New South Wales Tourism Commission [*Australia*]
NSWTC..... New South Wales Travel Center [*Australia*]
NSWTEC .. New South Wales Traffic Education Centre [*Australia*]
NSWTEU ... New South Wales Theatrical Employees' Union [*Australia*]
NSWTIA ... New South Wales Taxi Industry Association [*Australia*]
NSWTITC ... New South Wales Timber Industry Training Council [*Australia*]
NSWTLMB ... New South Wales Tobacco Leaf Marketing Board [*Australia*]
NSWTPA .. New South Wales Tennis Professionals Association [*Australia*]
NSWVCC ... New South Wales Vice Chancellors' Conference [*Australia*]
NSWVRA ... New South Wales Video Retailers' Association [*Australia*]
NSWWA ... New South Wales Wrestling Association [*Australia*]
NSWWAC ... New South Wales Women's Advisory Council [*Australia*]
NSWWASA ... New South Wales Women's Amateur Swimming Association [*Australia*]
NSWWJA ... New South Wales Women Justices' Association [*Australia*]
NSWWP.... New South Wales Water Polo [*Australia*] [*An association*]
NSWWSA ... New South Wales Water Ski Association [*Australia*]
NSWWSBA ... New South Wales Wool Selling Brokers' Association [*Australia*]
NSX .... Sydney College of the Arts [*National Union Catalogue of Australia symbol*]
NSYA .... Nomarkhiakon Symvoulion Ygeias kai Asfaliseos [*Nomarchy Health and Insurance Council*]   (GC)
NSYGA ..... Nigerian Seed-Yam Growers' Association
NSYN .... Syntex Australia Limited [*National Union Catalogue of Australia symbol*]
NSYO .... Nukleer Silahlarin Yayilmasinin Onlenmesi Antlasma [*Nuclear Arms Anti-Proliferation Agreement*]   (TU)
NSZ .... Narodowe Sily Zbrojne [*National Armed Forces*]   (POL)
NSZE......... Nemet Szocialista Egysegpart [*Socialist Unity Party of Germany*]   (HU)
NSZEP ...... Nemet Szocialista Egysegpart [*Socialist Unity Party of Germany*]   (HU)
nszhdv .... Chief Signal Officer of Railroad Troops   (RU)
NSZK........ Nemet Szovetseges Koztarsasag [*Federal Republic of Germany*]   (HU)
NSZK........ Nihon Seishonen Zendo Kyo-kai [*Japanese Youth Guidance Association*]
NSZP........ Nemzeti Szabadelvu Part [*National Liberal Party*] [*Hungary*] [*Political party*]   (PPE)
NT.............. Chief of Rear Services   (BU)
NT.............. Initial Point   (RU)
NT.............. Iraq-Saudi Arabia Neutral Zone [*ANSI two-letter standard code*]   (CNC)
NT.............. Low-Temperature   (RU)
NT.............. Nahradni Teleso [*Replacements Unit (Depot)*]   (CZ)
N-T .... Nal-Tel [*Race of maize*] [*Mexico*]
NT.............. Naphthotocopherol   (RU)
NT.............. Narodna Tehnika [*People's Technology*] [*A society*]   (YU)
NT.............. National Taranesc [*National Peasant Party*] [*Romania*] [*Political party*]   (PPE)
NT.............. National Trust of Australia   (ADA)
NT.............. Nea Taxis [*New Order*]   (GC)
NT.............. Nederlands Textielinstituut/Afdeling Textielveredeling [*Netherlands*]   (EAIO)
Nt .... Negociant [*Merchant*] [*French*]   (MTD)
nt .... Nel Testo [*In the Text*] [*Publishing*] [*Italian*]
nt .... Nem Tenyleges [*Nonprofessional, Irregular*] [*Military*]   (HU)
NT.............. Nepgazdasagi Tanacs [*People's Economic Council*]   (HU)
NT.............. Neues Testament [*New Testament*] [*German*]
NT.............. New Taiwan
NT.............. New Territories [*Hong Kong*]
NT.............. New Thailand Dollar [*Monetary unit*]
NT.............. Nikola Tesla [*Nikola Tesla*]   (YU)
NT.............. Nisanska Tacka [*Target Point*]   (YU)
nt .... Nit   (RU)
NT.............. Nomarkhiakon Tameion [*Nomarchy Fund*]   (GC)
NT.............. Nontransforme [*Military*] [*French*]   (MTD)
NT.............. Nordiska Transportarbetarefederationen [*Nordic Transportworkers' Federation - NTF*]   (EAIO)
NT.............. Nordisk Teater [*Denmark*]   (EAIO)
NT.............. Nordisk Traebeskyttelsesrad [*Nordic Wood Preservation Council - NWPC*]   (EAIO)
NT.............. Normaltemperatur [*Normal Temperature*] [*German*]   (GCA)
NT.............. Normal Temperature, Reference Temperature   (RU)
NT.............. Northern Territory [*Australia*]

NT .... Nota do Tradutor [*Translator's Note*] [*Portuguese*]
NT .... Nouveau Testament [*New Testament*] [*French*]
NT .... Novo Testamento [*New Testament*] [*Portuguese*]
NT .... Nuevo Testamento [*New Testament*] [*Spanish*]
NT .... Nula Tacka [*Zero Point*] (YU)
NT .... Nuovo Testamento [*New Testament*] [*Italian*]
NT .... Nuwe Testament [*New Testament*] [*Afrikaans*]
NT .... Oil Tanker (RU)
NT .... Superacoustic Telegraphy (RU)
Nt .... Thermischer Wirkungsgrad [*Thermal Efficiency*] [*German*]
nt .... Voetnoet [*Benelux*] (BAS)
NTA .... Australian and Overseas Telecommunications Corporation (New South Wales) [*National Union Catalogue of Australia symbol*]
NTA .... National Teachers Association
NTA .... National Tourism Administration [*China*] (EY)
NTA .... National Tourist Authority [*Papua New Guinea*] (GEA)
NTA .... National Trust of Australia (ADA)
NTA .... Nej til Atomvaben [*No to Nuclear Weapons*] [*An association*] [*Denmark*] (EAIO)
NTA .... New Turkish Alphabet (RU)
NTA .... Nigerian Television Authority
NTA .... Northern Territory, Australia
NTA .... Norwegian Telecommunications Administration [*or Agency*] [*Oslo*]
NTAA .... Tahiti/FAAA [*French Polynesia*] [*ICAO location identifier*] (ICLI)
NTAB .... Northern Territory Architects' Board [*Australia*]
NTAC .... Agricultural Research Centre (New South Wales Department of Agriculture) [*National Union Catalogue of Australia symbol*]
NTAC .... New South Wales - Agriculture - Agricultural Research Centre [*National Union Catalogue of Australia symbol*]
NTACF .... Northern Territory Anti-Cancer Foundation
NTAI .... Ndermarrje Tregtare e Artikujve Industriale [*Albanian*]
NTAIDSC ... Northern Territory AIDS [*Acquired Immune Deficiency Syndrome*] Council [*Australia*]
NTAN .... Ndermarrje Tregtare e Artikujve te Ndryshem [*Albanian*]
NTAR .... Greater Taree City Library [*National Union Catalogue of Australia symbol*]
NTAR .... Rurutu [*French Polynesia*] [*ICAO location identifier*] (ICLI)
NTAS .... Northern Territory Archives Service [*Australia*]
NTAS .... Norwegian Tracking Adjunct System
NTASH ..... Ndermarrje e Transportit Automobilistik Shteteror [*Albanian*]
NTAT .... Tubuai/Mataura [*French Polynesia*] [*ICAO location identifier*] (ICLI)
NTAW .... Northern Territory Aerial Work [*Australia*]
NTB .... Nachrichtentechnisches Buero [*Communications Office*] (EG)
NTB .... National Training Board Ltd. [*Australia*]
NTB .... Nederlandse Toonkunstenaarsbond [*Netherlands Musicians' Union*]
NTB .... Nederlandse Triathlon Bond (EAIO)
NTB .... Nigerian Tourist Board
NTB .... Norsk Telegrambyra [*Norwegian News Agency*]
NTB .... Norwegian News Bureau (RU)
NTB .... Nusatenggara Barat [*West Lesser Sundas*] (IN)
NTB .... Scientific and Technical Library (RU)
NTB .... Scientific and Technical Office (RU)
NTBA .... Northern Territory Bowls Association [*Australia*]
NTBH .... Tamworth Base Hospital Library [*National Union Catalogue of Australia symbol*]
NTBIC ...... Northern Territory Buffalo Industry Council [*Australia*]
NTBRB...... Northern Territory Building Referees' Board [*Australia*]
NTBS .... Northern Territory Board of Studies [*Australia*]
NTC .... National Telecommunications Commission [*Philippines*] (DS)
NTC .... National Telecommunications Company [*Senegal*]
NTC .... National Trading Company [*Sierra Leone*]
NTC .... National Trading Corporation [*Gambia*]
NTC .... National Transport Commission [*or Corporation*] [*South Africa*]
NTC .... National Tribal Council
NTC .... Newcastle Teachers' College [*Australia*] (ADA)
NTC .... Nigerian Tobacco Company
NTC .... Nordic Temperance Council (EA)
NTC .... Nordic Theater Committee [*Later, NTDC*] (EAIO)
NTC .... Northside Theatre Co. [*Australia*]
NTCA .... Northern Territory Cattlemen's Association [*Australia*]
NTCA .... Northern Territory Cricket Association [*Australia*]
NTCB .... Northern Territory Convention Bureau [*Australia*]
NTCC .... Northern Territory Conservation Commission [*Australia*]
NTCDC ..... Northern Territory Counter Disaster Council [*Australia*]
NTCF........ New South Wales Teachers' Federation [*National Union Catalogue of Australia symbol*]
NTCF........ Notre Tres Cher Frere [*Beloved Brother*] [*French*]
NTCFA...... Northern Territory Commercial Fishermen's Association [*Australia*]
NTCFA...... Northern Territory Crab Fishermen's Association [*Australia*]

NTCGA ..... Northern Territory Community Government Association [*Australia*]
NTCh........ Scientific and Technical Department (RU)
NTCIN ...... Northern Territory Curriculum Information Network [*Australia*]
NTCL........ Tamworth City Library [*National Union Catalogue of Australia symbol*]
NTCLP ...... Northern Territory Country Liberal Party [*Australia*] [*Political party*]
NTCMP..... Northern Territory Chamber of Mines and Petroleum [*Australia*]
NTCOGSO ... Northern Territory Council of Government School Organisations [*Australia*]
NTCOSS ... Northern Territory Council of Social Service [*Australia*]
NTCOTA .. Northern Territory Council on the Aging [*Australia*]
NTCPL...... TCPL Resources Limited [*National Union Catalogue of Australia symbol*]
NTCS........ National Teaching Co. Scheme [*Australia*]
NTCT .... National Tennis Center Trust [*Australia*]
NTCTA..... Northern Territory Clay Target Association [*Australia*]
NTD.......... Nordic Theatre and Dance [*Denmark*] (EAIO)
NTD.......... Scientific and Technical Society (BU)
NTDAB .... Northern Territory Drug and Alcohol Board [*Australia*]
NTDC .... Nordic Theatre and Dance Committee (EAIO)
NTDC .... Northern Territory Development Corporation [*Australia*]
NTDD....... New Territories Development Department [*Hong Kong*]
NTDG....... National Teaching Development Grant [*Australia*]
NTE .... Nantes [*France*] [*Airport symbol*] (OAG)
NTE .... Netztakteinheit [*German*] (ADPT)
NTE .... New Trade Engineering [*Qatar*]
NTED .... Northern Territory Education Department [*Australia*]
nteft........... Nel Testo e Fuori Testo [*In the Text and Outside the Text*] [*Publishing*] [*Italian*]
NTEL........ Telectronics Proprietary Limited [*National Union Catalogue of Australia symbol*]
NTEM ...... Temple Emanuel (Sydney) [*National Union Catalogue of Australia symbol*]
NTEN ...... Tenterfield and District Public Library [*National Union Catalogue of Australia symbol*]
NTEO .... Northern Territory Electoral Office [*Australia*]
NTES........ Northern Territory Emergency Service [*Australia*]
NTEU .... National Tertiary Education Union
NTF .... Australia Telescope National Facility - Paul Wild Observatory Library [*National Union Catalogue of Australia symbol*]
NTF .... Den Norske Tannlaegeforening [*Denmark*] (SLS)
NTF .... National Tidal Facility [*Flinders University*] [*Australia*]
NTF .... National Transport Federation [*Australia*]
Ntf............. Naturforscher [*Scientific Investigator*] [*German*]
NTF .... Nigerian Trust Fund [*African Development Bank*]
NTF .... Nordic Transportworkers' Federation [*See also NT*] (EAIO)
NTF .... Nordisk Thoraxkirurgisk Forening [*Scandinavian Association for Thoracic and Cardiovascular Surgery - SATCS*] (EAIO)
NTF .... Norges Tekstilforbund [*Norway*] (EAIO)
NTF .... Nucleotide Triphosphate (RU)
NTFC........ NATO Tactical Fighter Center
NTFI.......... Norsk Tekstil Forsknings Institutt [*Norwegian Textile Research Institute*] (PDAA)
NTFIC ...... Northern Territory Fishing Industry Council [*Australia*]
NTFITC .... Northern Territory Fishing Industry Training Committee [*Australia*]
NTFL........ Northern Territory Football League [*Australia*]
NTFNC..... Northern Territory Field Naturalists' Club [*Australia*]
NTFS........ Northern Territory Fire Service [*Australia*]
NTG.......... Nachrichtentechnische Gesellschaft im VDE (SLS)
NTG.......... Nederlands Tandheelkundig Genootschap [*Netherlands*] (SLS)
NTG.......... Neue Technologien GmbH [*Commercial firm*] [*Germany*]
NTG.......... Northern Territory Government [*Australia*]
NTG.......... Nukleartechnik GmbH & Co. KG [*Germany*] (WND)
NTGA .... Anaa [*French Polynesia*] [*ICAO location identifier*] (ICLI)
NTGB .... Fangatau [*French Polynesia*] [*ICAO location identifier*] (ICLI)
NTGC .... Tikehau [*French Polynesia*] [*ICAO location identifier*] (ICLI)
NTGD....... Apataki [*French Polynesia*] [*ICAO location identifier*] (ICLI)
NTGE .... Reao [*French Polynesia*] [*ICAO location identifier*] (ICLI)
NTGF .... Fakarava [*French Polynesia*] [*ICAO location identifier*] (ICLI)
NTGH .... Hikueru [*French Polynesia*] [*ICAO location identifier*] (ICLI)
NTGI .... Manihi [*French Polynesia*] [*ICAO location identifier*] (ICLI)
NTGJ .... Totegegie [*French Polynesia*] [*ICAO location identifier*] (ICLI)
NTGK .... Kaukura [*French Polynesia*] [*ICAO location identifier*] (ICLI)
NTGL .... Fakahina [*French Polynesia*] [*ICAO location identifier*] (ICLI)
NTGM....... Makemo [*French Polynesia*] [*ICAO location identifier*] (ICLI)
NTGMA .... Northern Territory Girls' Marching Association [*Australia*]
NTGMB .... Northern Territory Grain Marketing Board [*Australia*]
NTGN....... Napuka [*French Polynesia*] [*ICAO location identifier*] (ICLI)
NTGO....... Scientific and Technical Mining Society (RU)
NTGO....... Tatakoto [*French Polynesia*] [*ICAO location identifier*] (ICLI)
NTGP .... Northern Territory Government Publications [*Australia*]
NTGP .... Puka Puka [*French Polynesia*] [*ICAO location identifier*] (ICLI)
NTGPE...... Northern Territory Government Pipeline Executive [*Australia*]

NTGPO..... Northern Territory Government Printing Office [*Australia*]
NTGQ........ Pukarua [*French Polynesia*] [*ICAO location identifier*] (ICLI)
NTGR........ Aratica [*French Polynesia*] [*ICAO location identifier*] (ICLI)
NTGT........ Takapoto [*French Polynesia*] [*ICAO location identifier*] (ICLI)
NTGTB....... Northern Territory Government Tourist Bureau [*Australia*]
NTGU....... Arutua [*French Polynesia*] [*ICAO location identifier*] (ICLI)
NTGU........ Novosibirsk Territorial Geological Administration (RU)
NTGV........ Mataiva [*French Polynesia*] [*ICAO location identifier*] (ICLI)
NTGW....... Nukutavake [*French Polynesia*] [*ICAO location identifier*]
　　　　　　 (ICLI)
NTGY........ Tureia [*French Polynesia*] [*ICAO location identifier*] (ICLI)
NTH .... Norges Tekniske Hogskole [*Norwegian Institute of Technology*]
　　　　　　 (ASF)
NTHA....... Northern Territory Hockey Association [*Australia*]
NTHC....... National Trust Holding Co. [*Ghana*]
NTHC....... Newcastle Trades Hall Council [*Australia*]
NTHC....... Northern Territory Housing Commission [*Australia*]
NTHH....... Tweed Heads Private Hospital [*National Union Catalogue of Australia symbol*]
NTHU .... National Tsing Hua University [*Taiwan*] (WND)
NTI .... Bintuni [*Indonesia*] [*Airport symbol*] (OAG)
NTI .... Naucno Tekhniceskaja Informacija [*Science and Technical Information*] [*Former USSR*]
Nti.............. Neiti [*Miss*] [*Finland*] (GPO)
NTI .... Norsk Treteknisk Institutt [*Norwegian Institute of Wood Technology*] [*Research center*] (IRC)
NTI .... Scientific and Technical Publication (RU)
NTIOC ...... National Trade and Investment Outlook Conference [*Australia*]
NTIS.......... NEC [*Nippon Electric Company*]-Toshiba Information Systems, Inc. [*Japan*]
NTISSA..... Northern Territory Independent Schools Staff Association [*Australia*]
NTITC....... National Tourism Industry Training Council [*Australia*]
NTITS....... Northern Territory Interpreter and Translator Service [*Australia*]
NTJ............ National Theatre of Japan (EAIO)
NTK......... Directive on Workers' Record Books (BU)
NTK .... Lower Large Intestine (RU)
NTK .... Nordisk Teaterkomite [*Nordic Theater Committee - NTC*] (EAIO)
NTK .... Normenausschuss Transportkette im DIN [*Deutsches Institut fuer Normung*] eV (SLS)
NTK.......... Scientific and Technical Club (RU)
NTK.......... Scientific and Technical Committee (RU)
NTKR........ Takaroa [*French Polynesia*] [*ICAO location identifier*] (ICLI)
NTL .... National Testing Laboratories [*Australia*]
NTL .... National Textiles Ltd. [*Australia*]
NTL .... Newcastle [*Australia*] [*Airport symbol*] (OAG)
NTL .... News of Technical Literature (RU)
NTL .... New Tokaido Line [*Japanese rail system*]
NTL .... Northern Territory Library [*Australia*]
NTL .... Note Technique de Lancement [*French*] (ADPT)
NTLAI....... Ndermarrje Tregtare Lokale Artikuj Industriale [*Albanian*]
NTLAP....... Ndermarrje Tregtare Lokale Artikuj te Punuar [*Albanian*]
NTLAT....... Northern Territory Land Acquisition Tribunal [*Australia*]
NTLAU ..... Ndermarrje Tregtare Lokale Artikuj Ushqimore [*Albanian*]
NTLB......... Northern Territory Land Board [*Australia*]
NTLFZ....... Ndermarrje Tregtare Lokale e Furnizimeve te Zejtarise [*Albanian*]
NTLG .... National Tax Liaison Group [*Australia*]
NTLGA ..... Northern Territory Local Government Association [*Australia*]
NTLGGC... Northern Territory Local Government Grants Commission [*Australia*]
NTLGITC ... Northern Territory Local Government Industry Training Committee [*Australia*]
NTLLDG... Lend Lease Design Group Limited [*National Union Catalogue of Australia symbol*]
NTLPC...... Northern Territory Library Promotion Council [*Australia*]
NTLS........ Northern Territory Library Service [*Australia*]
NTLS........ TAFE (Technical and Further Education) New South Wales Library Services [*National Union Catalogue of Australia symbol*]
NTLSEA ... Northern Territory Live Stock Exporters' Association [*Australia*]
NTLUS....... Ndermarrje Tregtare Lokale Ushqimore Sociale [*Albanian*]
NTM.......... Narodni Technicke Museum [*National Museum of Technology*] (CZ)
NTMD....... Nuku Hiva [*French Polynesia*] [*ICAO location identifier*] (ICLI)
NTMI .... New [*South Wales*] Therapeutic Medicines Information Centre [*National Union Catalogue of Australia symbol*]
NTMK....... Nizhniy Tagil Metallurgical Kombinat (RU)
NTMN....... Hiva-Oa/Atuana [*French Polynesia*] [*ICAO location identifier*] (ICLI)
NTMP .... Ua Pou [*French Polynesia*] [*ICAO location identifier*] (ICLI)
NTMPA .... Northern Territory Marine and Ports Authority [*Australia*]
NTMU....... Ua Huka [*French Polynesia*] [*ICAO location identifier*] (ICLI)
NTMZ .... Novotul'skiy Metallurgical Plant (RU)

NTN........... Najwyzszy Trybunal Narodowy [*Supreme National Tribunal*] (POL)
NTN........... National Airways Corp. (Pty) Ltd. [*South Africa*] [*ICAO designator*] (FAAC)
NTN........... Network Termination Number [*Computer science*] (TNIG)
NTN........... Normanton [*Australia*] [*Airport symbol*] (OAG)
NTN........... Northern Territory News [*A publication*]
NTNA........ Northern Territory Nurserymen's Association [*Australia*]
NTNF .... Norges Teknisk-Naturvitenskapelige Forskningsrad [*Royal Norwegian Council for Scientific and Industrial Research*]
NTO.......... Nasionale Toneelorganisasie [*Afrikaans*]
NTO.......... National Theatre Organisation
n-to............ Net (RU)
nto .... Neto [*Net*] [*Spanish*]
NTO.......... Netto [*Net*] [*Afrikaans*]
NTO.......... Network Terminal Operator
NTO.......... Nordic Tele Organization [*Denmark*] (EAIO)
NTO.......... Santo Antao [*Cape Verde Islands*] [*Airport symbol*] (OAG)
NTO.......... Scientific and Technical Department (RU)
NTO.......... Scientific and Technical Society (RU)
NTOA........ Nigerian Transport Owners' Association
NTOB........ National Tourism Organization of Bangladesh (EAIO)
NTOBelmashprom ... Belorussian Republic Branch of the All-Union Scientific and Technical Society of the Machinery Industry (RU)
NTOC....... Northern Territory Open College [*Australia*]
NTOChM ... Scientific and Technical Society of Ferrous Metallurgy (RU)
NTOEP ..... Scientific and Technical Society of the Power Industry (RU)
NTOG....... National Tourist Organization of Greece
NTOGKh i AT ... Scientific and Technical Society of Urban Economy and Automobile Transportation (RU)
NTOLes..... Scientific and Technical Society of the Lumber Industry (RU)
NTOLesprom ... Scientific and Technical Society of the Lumber Industry (RU)
NTOLP...... Scientific and Technical Society of the Lumber Industry (RU)
NTOM....... National Tourist Organization of Malta (GEA)
NTOMASh ... Scientific and Technical Society of Machine Builders (RU)
NTOMashprom ... Scientific and Technical Society of the Machinery Industry (RU)
NTOMashpromlit ... Scientific and Technical Society of the Machinery Industry, Foundry Section (RU)
NTONGP ... Scientific and Technical Society of the Petroleum and Gas Industry (RU)
NTONP..... Scientific and Technical Society of the Petroleum Industry (RU)
NTOO .... Tooheys Limited [*National Union Catalogue of Australia symbol*]
NTORiE .... Scientific and Technical Society of Radio Engineering and Telecommunications Imeni A. S. Popov (RU)
NTOS .... Chief of Topographic Service (RU)
NTO SKh .. Scientific and Technical Society of Agriculture (RU)
NTOSP...... Scientific and Technical Society of the Shipbuilding Industry (RU)
NTOSS...... All-Union Scientific and Technical Society of Shipbuilding and Navigation (RU)
NTOSTIGKh ... Scientific and Technical Society of Sanitary Engineering and Urban Economy (RU)
NTOVT ..... Scientific and Technical Society of Water Transportation (RU)
NTP .... National Telephone Program [*Philippines*]
NTP .... National Tree Program [*Australia*]
NTP .... Naukowe Towarzystwo Pedagogiczne [*Pedagogical Learned Society*] (POL)
NTP .... Netzteilpruefgeraet [*German*] (ADPT)
NTP .... Normatywy Techniczne Projektowania [*Norms for Technical Planning*] (POL)
NTP .... Scientific and Technical Propaganda (RU)
NTP .... Technological Planning Norms (RU)
NTPA .... Northern Territory Planning Authority [*Australia*]
NTPA .... Northern Territory Police Association [*Australia*]
NTPA .... Northern Territory Port Authority [*Australia*]
NTPAC....... Northern Territory Planning Appeals Committee [*Australia*]
NTPC........ National Thermal Power Corp. [*India*] (PDAA)
NTPDLB .. Northern Territory Plumbers and Drainers Licensing Board [*Australia*]
NTPNC...... Northern Territory Place Names Committee [*Australia*]
NTPS........ Local Telegraphic Communications Post (RU)
NTPS........ Northern Territory Public Service [*Australia*]
NTPSA...... Northern Territory Public Service Association [*Australia*]
NTPWA .... Northern Territory Power and Water Authority [*Australia*]
NTQ.......... National Trust of Queensland [*Australia*]
NTR .... Nordiska Trafiksakerhetsradet [*Nordic Road Safety Council - NRSC*] [*Finland*] (EAIO)
NTR .... Nordiska Traskyddsradet [*Sweden*] (EAIO)
NTR .... Nordisk Tolladministrativt Rad [*Nordic Customs Administrative Council - NCAC*] (EAIO)
NTR .... Northern Territory Railway [*Australia*]
NTRA .... Northern Territory Rifle Association [*Australia*]

NTRA .... Norwegian Textile Retailers Association   (EAIO)
ntra .... Nuestra [Our] [Spanish]
ntras .... Nuestras [Our] [Spanish]
NTRC .... National Transport Research Center [Pakistan]   (IRC)
NTRC .... Northern Territory Rural College [Australia]
NTRGLB... Northern Territory Racing, Gaming and Liquor Board [Australia]
NTRI .... National Timber Research Institute [South Africa]   (ARC)
NTRL .... National Telecommunications Research Laboratory
NTRM .... Temora Rural Museum [National Union Catalogue of Australia symbol]
ntro .... Nuestro [Our] [Spanish]
ntros .... Nuestros [Our] [Spanish]
NTRU .... Northern Territory Rugby Union [Australia]
NTRU .... Northern Transvaal Rugby Union
NTS .... Chief of Technical Service   (RU)
NTs .... Directive on Prices   (BU)
NTS .... Nacelnik Telegrafske Stanice [Telegraph Station Chief] [Military] (YU)
NTS .... Narodno Trudovoi Soyuz [People's Labor Union] [Frankfurt, Federal Republic of Germany]   (PD)
NTS .... Natal Teacher's Society [South Africa]   (AA)
NTs .... National Center   (RU)
NTS .... National Labor Union   (RU)
NTS .... National Tourist Union   (BU)
NTS .... Netsionelno-Trudovoy-Soyuz [Union of Russian Solidarists]
NTs .... Nitrocellulose   (RU)
NTS .... Nordiska Tidningsutgivarnas Samarbetsnaemnd [Joint Council of Nordic Newspaper Publishers]
NTS .... Nordiske Teleansattes Samarbeidsorgan [Nordic Telecommunications Association]   (EAIO)
NTS .... Scientific and Technical Council   (RU)
NTS .... Scientific and Technical Union   (BU)
NTSA........ Northern Territory Softball Association [Australia]
NTSA........ Northern Territory Supervising Authority [Australia]
NTsAP...... National Weather Analysis Center [NAWAC]   (RU)
NTSB........ Northern Territory Surveyor Board [Australia]
NTSG .... University of Technology Sydney - Gore Hill Library [St. Leonards Campus] [National Union Catalogue of Australia symbol]
NTSGUGP ... Scientific and Technical Council of the Main Administration of the Mining Industry   (RU)
NTSH........ Ndermarrje Tregtare te Shitblerjes [Albanian]
NTSHAP... Ndermarrje Tregtare Shteterore Artikuj te Punuar [Albanian]
NTSHAU .. Ndermarrje Tregtare Shteterore Artikuj Ushqimore [Albanian]
NTSHFZ... Ndermarrje Tregtare Shteterore e Frutave dhe e Zarzavateve [Albanian]
NTSHUS... Ndermarrje Tregtare Shteterore Ushqimore Sociale [Albanian]
NTSI........ National Tribunal of Second Instance [Catholic Church] [Australia]
NTSK........ Nordiska Tele-Satelit Kommitton [Norway]
NTSK........ University of Technology Sydney - Kuring-gai Campus - George Muir Library [National Union Catalogue of Australia symbol]
NTSL........ University of Technology Sydney - St Leonards Campus - College of Law [National Union Catalogue of Australia symbol]
NTSM .... University of Technology Sydney - Markets Library [National Union Catalogue of Australia symbol]
NTSM:A.... University of Technology Sydney - Markets Library - Administration [National Union Catalogue of Australia symbol]
NTSM:Q ... University of Technology Sydney - Markets Library - Acquisitions [National Union Catalogue of Australia symbol]
NTSMSP ... Scientific and Technical Council of the Ministry of the Shipbuilding Industry   (RU)
NTSM:U ... University of Technology Sydney - Markets Library - User Services [National Union Catalogue of Australia symbol]
NTSRU...... Northern Territory Special Reconnaissance Unit
NTSS........ Directive on Trying Labor Disputes by the Courts   (BU)
NTSSC ...... Northern Territory School Sports Council [Australia]
NTsUVS.... Chief of the Central Directorate of Military Communications (RU)
NTT .... Nawas Trading & Transport Corp. [Jordan]
NTT .... Newton's Theory of Gravitation   (RU)
NTT .... Nihon Tengu To [Japan Goblin Party]
NTT .... Nippon Telegraph & Telephone Corp. [Telecommunications and videotex company] [Japan]
NTT .... Nuiatoputapu [Tonga] [Airport symbol]   (OAG)
NTT .... Nusatenggara Timur [East Lesser Sundas]   (IN)
NTTA .... Nigeria Table Tennis Association
NTTAB..... Northern Territory Totalizator Agency Board [Australia]
NTTB .... Bora Bora/Motu-Mute [French Polynesia] [ICAO location identifier]   (ICLI)
NTTE .... Tetiaroa [French Polynesia] [ICAO location identifier]   (ICLI)
NTTF........ Norsk Tekstil Teknisk Forbund [Norway]   (SLS)
NTTG .... Rangiroa [French Polynesia] [ICAO location identifier]   (ICLI)

NTTH........ Huahine/Fare [French Polynesia] [ICAO location identifier] (ICLI)
NTTLC...... Northern Territory Trades and Labor Council [Australia]
NTTM........ Moorea/Temae [French Polynesia] [ICAO location identifier] (ICLI)
NTTM .... Scientific and Technical Creativity among the Youth   (BU)
NTTO........ Hao [French Polynesia] [ICAO location identifier]   (ICLI)
ntto .... Netto [Net] [German]   (GPO)
NTTP........ Maupiti [French Polynesia] [ICAO location identifier]   (ICLI)
NTTPC...... Nippon Telegraph & Telephone Public Corp. [Telecommunications]   (IAA)
NTTR .... Raiatea/Uturoa [French Polynesia] [ICAO location identifier] (ICLI)
NTTT .... Tahiti [French Polynesia] [ICAO location identifier]   (ICLI)
NTTX .... Mururoa [French Polynesia] [ICAO location identifier]   (ICLI)
NTU.......... Namibia Trade Union   (EY)
NTU.......... Namibia Transnational Unit
NTU.......... National Taiwan University   (MSC)
NTU.......... Ndermarrje Tregtare e Ushqimeve [Albanian]
NTU.......... Nordisk Trafikskoleunion [Nordic Union of Motor Schools Associations - NUMSA] [Finland]   (EAIO)
NTU.......... Northern Territory University [Australia]
NTU.......... Scientific and Technical Administration   (RU)
NTU.......... Standard Technical Specifications   (RU)
NTUB .... Norges Tekniske Universitetsbibliotek [The Technical University Library of Norway]
NTUC .... Namibia Trade Union Council   (EY)
NTUC........ National Trade Union Congress [Singapore]
NTUC........ National Trade Union Council [Hungary]
NTUC........ Newcastle Technical and University College [Australia]
NTUC........ Nigerian Trade Union Congress
NTUC........ Nordic Trade Union Council
NTUC........ Nyasaland Trade Union Congress
NTUCB...... National Trades Union Congress of Belize   (EY)
NTUF........ Nigerian Trade-Union Federation   (AF)
NTUV........ Vahitahi [French Polynesia] [ICAO location identifier]   (ICLI)
NTV.......... National Television Authority
NTV.......... Nippon Television Network Corp. [Japan]
NTWA .... National Trust of Western Australia
NTWL .... Nederlandse Technische en Natuur Wetenschappelijke Literatuur
NTY .... Sun City [South Africa] [Airport symbol]   (OAG)
NTYRBA.... Northern Territory Young Readers' Book Award [Australia]
NTZ........... Iraq-Saudi Arabia Neutral Zone [ANSI three-letter standard code] (CNC)
NTZ........... New Pipe Plant   (RU)
Ntzl .... Nutzlast [Loading Capacity] [German]
NU .... Chief of Administration   (RU)
NU .... Lipnur [Indonesia] [ICAO aircraft manufacturer identifier] (ICAO)
NU .... Lower Level   (RU)
NU .... Nachalnik Uprovlenia [Chief of Directorate] [Soviet military rank]
NU .... Naciones Unidas [United Nations] [Spanish]
NU .... Nagasaki University [Japan]   (MSC)
NU .... Nahdlatul Ulama [Moslem Scholars Party]   (IN)
NU .... Nakhimov School [Navy]   (RU)
NU .... Naphthylacetic Acid   (RU)
NU .... Narodopisny Ustav [Ethnological Institute (of the Slovak Academy of Sciences)]   (CZ)
NU .... Natalse Universiteit [Natal University] [Afrikaans]
NU .... National Union
NU .... Nations Unies
NU .... Nazioni Unite [United Nations] [Italian]
NU .... Nepugyeszseg [Office of the People's Attorney]   (HU)
NU .... Nettezza Urbana [Municipal service for collecting rubbish, cleaning streets, etc.] [Italian]
Nu .... Ngultrum [Monetary unit] [Bhutan]   (BARN)
NU .... Niue [ANSI two-letter standard code]   (CNC)
Nu .... Numara [Number]   (TU)
NU .... Nuoro [Car registration plates] [Italian]
NU .... Scientific Establishment   (RU)
NU .... University of Sydney - Fisher Library [National Union Catalogue of Australia symbol]
NUA .... Nations Unies des Animaux [United Animal Nations - UAN] (EA)
NUA .... Nuna Air AS [Denmark] [ICAO designator]   (FAAC)
NUAA........ New South Wales Users and AIDS Association [Australia]
NUAD .... National Union of Actors and Directors Histadrut [Israel] (EAIO)
NUAE .... National Union of Afghanistan Employees   (EY)
NUAK........ National Aeronautics and Space Administration [NASA]   (RU)
NU:AM .... Alexander Mackie Library - University of Sydney [National Union Catalogue of Australia symbol]
NUAP........ Unilever Australia Limited - Information Services Department [National Union Catalogue of Australia symbol]

NU:AR....... University of Sydney - Architecture Library [*National Union Catalogue of Australia symbol*]

NUASA ..... Nairobi University Agriculture Students Association

NUAT........ Nordisk Union for Alkoholfri Trafikk [*Scandinavian Union for Non-Alcoholic Traffic - SUNAT*] (EA)

NUATFAC ... Nordiska Unionen for Arbetsledare, Tekniska Funktionarer och andra Chefer [*Nordic Confederation of Supervisors, Technicians and Other Managers*] (EAIO)

NUAUS ..... National Union of Australian University Students (ADA)

NUB.......... Nacizmus Uldozotteinek Bizottsaga [*Committee of the Victims of Nazism*] (HU)

NUB.......... Novacke Uholni Bane [*Novaky Coal Mines*] (CZ)

NU:B.......... University of Sydney - BISA [*Bibliographic Information on South-east Asia*]

NU:BA....... University of Sydney - Badham Library [*National Union Catalogue of Australia symbol*]

NUBE........ National Union of Bank Employees [*Philippines*] (ML)

NUBE........ National Union of Book Publishers [*Brazil*] (EAIO)

NUBEGW ... National Union of Building, Engineering, and General Workers

NU:BI........ University of Sydney - Biochemistry Department Library [*National Union Catalogue of Australia symbol*]

NUBIFI ..... National Union of Banks, Insurance, and Financial Institutions [*Nigeria*]

NUBIFIE... National Union of Bank, Insurance, and Financial Institutions Employees [*Nigeria*]

NU:BU....... University of Sydney - Burkitt Library [*National Union Catalogue of Australia symbol*]

NUC.......... Natal University College

NUC.......... Nationale UNESCO Commissie

NUC.......... National Unification Council [*Philippines*] [*Political party*] (FEA)

NUC.......... National Unity Council (ML)

NUC.......... National Universities Commission [*Nigeria*]

NUC.......... Nejvyssi Urad Cenovy [*Supreme Price Office*] (CZ)

NUC.......... Njala University College [*Sierra Leone*]

NU:CA....... University of Sydney - Camden Branch Library [*National Union Catalogue of Australia symbol*]

NUCC........ Nairobi University Chemical Club

NUCC........ National University Caving Club [*Australia*]

NUCCEW ... Nigerian Union of Construction and Civil Engineering Workers (EAIO)

NUCD........ National Union Catalogue of Library Materials for People with Disabilities [*Australia*]

NU CDI ..... Nations Unies, Commission du Droit International (FLAF)

NUCGIW .. National Union of Ceramics and Glass Industry Workers [*Israel*] (EAIO)

NU:CH ...... University of Sydney - School of Chemistry - A Boden Chemistry Library [*National Union Catalogue of Australia symbol*]

NUCLAM ... NUCLEBRAS Auxiliar de Mineracao, SA [*NUCLEBRAS Mining Assistance, Inc.*] [*Brazil*] (LA)

NUCLEBRAS ... Empresas Nucleares Brasileiras, SA [*Brazilian Nuclear Corporations*] [*Rio De Janeiro*] (LA)

NUCLEI.... NUCLEBRAS Enriquecimento Isotopico, SA [*NUCLEBRAS Isotope Enrichment, Inc.*] [*Brazil*] (LA)

NUCLEMON ... NUCLEBRAS de Monazita e Associados Ltda. [*NUCLEBRAS Monazite and Associated Elements Ltd.*] [*Brazil*] (LA)

NUCLEN .. NUCLEBRAS Engenharia, SA [*NUCLEBRAS Engineering, Inc.*] [*Brazil*] (LA)

NUCLENOR ... Centrales Nucleares del Norte, SA [*Nuclear energy*] [*Spanish*] (NRCH)

NUCLENOR ... Controles Nucleares del Norte, SA [*Spain*]

NUCLEP... NUCLEBRAS de Equipamentos Pesados, SA [*NUCLEBRAS Heavy Equipment, Inc.*] [*Brazil*] (LA)

NUCLIT.... Nucleare Italiana [*Government corporation*] [*Italian*] (NRCH)

NUC-N ...... National Union Catalogue: Nonbook Materials [*Australia*]

NUCOF..... National Union Catalogue of Films [*Australia*]

NUCON .... NUCLEBRAS Construtora de Centrais Nucleares, SA [*NUCLEBRAS Nuclear Plant Construction, Inc.*] [*Brazil*] (LA)

NUCOR..... Nuclear Development Corporation of South Africa (Pty.) Ltd.

NUCOS..... National Union Catalogue of Serials [*Australia*]

NUCPE ..... National Union of Public Corporated Employees [*Nigeria*]

NUCS .... National Union of Cameroon Students

NU:CU....... University of Sydney - Curriculum Resources Library [*National Union Catalogue of Australia symbol*]

NUCW....... National Union of Cameroon Workers (AF)

NUCW....... National Union of Cinema Workers (ML)

NUCW....... National Union of Commercial Workers [*Malayan*]

NUCWDF ... National Union of Civilian Workers in the Defence Forces [*Israel*] (EAIO)

NUDA .... Nigerian Union of Dispensing Assistants (AF)

NUDAC..... Nuclear Data Centre [*India*] (PDAA)

NU:DE....... University of Sydney - Faculty of Dentistry Library [*National Union Catalogue of Australia symbol*]

NU:DN ...... University of Sydney - Nursing Library [*National Union Catalogue of Australia symbol*]

NUDO .... National United Democratic Organization [*Namibia*] [*Political party*] (PPW)

NUDT........ National Union of Democratic Teachers [*Jamaica*] (EY)

NUDW ...... National Union of Diamond Workers [*Israel*] (EAIO)

NUE.......... Nachrichtenuebertragung [*German*] (ADPT)

NUE.......... Nuremberg [*Germany*] [*Airport symbol*] (OAG)

NU:E.......... University of Sydney - Engineering Library [*National Union Catalogue of Australia symbol*]

NUECA ..... Nomenclatura Uniforme de Exportacion para Centroamerica (LAA)

NUEE........ Nachrichtenuebertragungs-Steuereinheit [*German*] (ADPT)

NUEPI....... National Union of Employees in the Printing Industry (ML)

NUES .... Nachrichtenuebertragungssystem [*German*] (ADPT)

NUES .... National Union of Ethiopian Students

nuetzl.......... Nuetzlich [*Useful*] [*German*] (GCA)

NUEUS ...... National Union of Ethiopian University Students (AF)

NUEWMN ... National Union of Eritrean Women [*Ethiopia*]

NUF.......... National Unifying Force [*Zimbabwe*] [*Political party*] (PPW)

NUF.......... National Union of Foodworkers [*Israel*] (EAIO)

NUF.......... National United Front

NUF.......... National Unity Front [*Poland*] [*Political party*] (PPW)

NUF.......... Nordisk Urologisk Forening [*Scandinavian Association of Urology - SAU*] (EAIO)

NUFC .... National United Front of Cambodia [*Use FUNK*] (CL)

NUFCOR .. Nuclear Fuels Corporation [*South Africa*] (AF)

NUFFIC .... Netherlands Organisation for International Cooperation in Higher Education (EAIO)

NUFFIC .... Netherlands Universities Foundation for International Cooperation

NUFK .... National United Front of Cambodia [*Use FUNK*] (CL)

NUFO........ Norsk Undervisningsforbund [*Norway*] (EAIO)

NUFS........ National United Front of Somalia [*Political party*] (EY)

NUGAS ..... National Union of Greek Australian Students

NUGE........ National Union of Government Employees [*Israel*] (EAIO)

NU:GG ...... University of Sydney - Geogrpahy Library [*National Union Catalogue of Australia symbol*]

NUGHSS .. National Union of Graduates in Humanities and Social Sciences [*Israel*] (EAIO)

NU:GL....... University of Sydney - Geology Library [*National Union Catalogue of Australia symbol*]

NUGS........ National Union of Ghanaian Students (AF)

NUHA .... National Union of Hospital Assistants (ML)

NUHAW ... Union of Agricultural Workers [*Israel*] (EAIO)

NUHRW ... National Union of Hotel and Restaurant Workers [*Israel*] (EAIO)

NUHU .... Upper Hunter Regional Library [*National Union Catalogue of Australia symbol*]

NUHW ...... Nordic Union for Health and Work [*Denmark*] (EAIO)

NUIR .... National Union for Independence and Revolution [*Chad*] [*Political party*]

NUJ .... National Union of Journalists [*Malaysia*] (ML)

NUJ .... National Union of Journalists [*India*] (EAIO)

NUJ .... Nigerian Union of Journalists (AF)

NUJPS ...... National Union of Journalists in the Public Sector [*Israel*] (EAIO)

NUJS......... Novosadsko Udruzenje Jugoslovenskih Studenata [*Yugoslav Students Association in Novi Sad*] (YU)

NUK.......... Naphthylacetic Acid (RU)

NUK.......... Narodna in Univerzitetna Knjiznica [*National and University Library*] [*Ljubljana*] (YU)

NUK.......... Narodni a Universitni Knihovna [*National and University Library*] (CZ)

NUK.......... Nukutavake [*French Polynesia*] [*Airport symbol*] (OAG)

NUKEM.... Nuklear-Chemie und Metallurgie [*Germany*] (PDAA)

NUKS .... National Union of Kenya Students (AF)

NUKU .... Nejvyssi Ucetni Kontrolni Urad [*Supreme Accounting Office*] (CZ)

NUL.......... National and University Library [*Israel*] (BJA)

NUL.......... National Union for Liberation [*Philippines*] [*Political party*] (PPW)

NUL.......... National University of Lesotho

NU:L.......... University of Sydney - Law School Library [*National Union Catalogue of Australia symbol*]

NULF .... National United Liberation Front [*Myanmar*] [*Political party*] (FEA)

NULGE ..... Nigerian Union of Local Government Employees (AF)

NULL .... Nullarbor [*Botanical region*] [*Australia*]

NULT .... National Union of Liberian Teachers

num .... Above Sea Level (RU)

NUM .... National Union of Mineworkers [*South Africa*]

NUM .... National Unity Movement [*Sierra Leone*] [*Political party*] (EY)

num .... Nombre [*Numeral*] [*French*] (TPFD)

num .... Numerado [*Numbered*] [*Publishing*] [*Spanish*]

num .... Numeral [*Number*] [*Portuguese*]

num .... Numerato [*Numbered*] [*Publishing*] [*Italian*]

Num .... Numeri [*Numbers*] [*Afrikaans*]

num .... Numeriert [*Numbered*] [*Publishing*] [*German*]
num .... Numero [*Number*] [*Portuguese*]
num .... Numero [*Number*] [*Spanish*]
num .... Numerote [*Numbered*] [*French*]
NU:M .... University of Sydney - Medical Library [*National Union Catalogue of Australia symbol*]
NU:MA ..... University of Sydney - Mathematics Library [*National Union Catalogue of Australia symbol*]
NUMC ...... Newcastle University Mountaineering Club [*Australia*]
NUMCO ... Nigerian Uranium Mining Company
NU:ME ...... University of Sydney - Medical Society [*National Union Catalogue of Australia symbol*]
numer .... Numbered   (RU)
numer .... Numerato [*Numbered*] [*Publishing*] [*Italian*]
numer .... Numeriert [*Numbered*] [*Publishing*] [*German*]
numer .... Numerote [*Numbered*] [*French*]
numeraz ..... Numerazione [*Numbering*] [*Publishing*] [*Italian*]
numerosiss ... Numerosissimo [*Extremely Numerous*] [*Italian*]
numes .... Numerados [*Numbered*] [*Publishing*] [*Portuguese*]
Numism ..... Numismatica [*Numismatics*] [*Portuguese*]
NUMM ..... Chief of the Directorate for Mechanization and Motorization   (RU)
numm .... Nummereret [*Numbered*] [*Publishing Danish/Norwegian*]
nummr .... Nummereret [*Numbered*] [*Publishing Danish/Norwegian*]
NUMMS ... National Union of Malaysian Muslim Students   (ML)
numo .... Numero [*Number*] [*Spanish*]
NUMORD ... Australian Capital Territory Ordinances: Numbered [*Database*]
NUMP .... National Union of Medical Practitioners [*Israel*]   (EAIO)
NU:MP ...... University of Sydney - Graduate School of Management and Public Policy Library [*National Union Catalogue of Australia symbol*]
NUMR .... Upper Murray Regional Library [*National Union Catalogue of Australia symbol*]
NUMREG ... Australian Capital Territory Regulations: Numbered [*Database*]
NUMRUL ... Commonwealth Statutory Rules: Numbered [*Database*] [*Australia*]
NUMS .... National Union of Malaysian Students   (ML)
nums .... Numerados [*Numbered*] [*Publishing*] [*Portuguese*]
nums .... Numeros [*Numbers*] [*Spanish*]
NUMSA .... National Union of Metalworkers of South Africa
NUMSA .... Nordic Union of Motor Schools Associations [*Finland*]   (EAIO)
NU:MU ..... University of Sydney - Music Library [*National Union Catalogue of Australia symbol*]
NUN .... Nie Uit Nie [*Afrikaans*]
NUN .... University of New South Wales Libraries [*National Union Catalogue of Australia symbol*]
NUNBE ..... National Union of Nigerian Bank Employees   (AF)
NUNE:A .... University of New England - Dixson Library [*National Union Catalogue of Australia symbol*]
NUN:G ...... University of New South Wales - St George Campus [*National Union Catalogue of Australia symbol*]
NUNS .... National Union of Nigerian Students   (AF)
NUNW ...... National Union of Namibian Workers
NUNW ...... National Union of Newspaper Workers [*Malaysia*]   (ML)
NUN:W ..... University of New South Wales - Water Research Laboratories [*National Union Catalogue of Australia symbol*]
NU:NW ..... University of Sydney - Plant Breeding Institute [*National Union Catalogue of Australia symbol*]
NU:OA ...... University of Sydney - Orange Agricultural College [*National Union Catalogue of Australia symbol*]
NUOD .... Nationale Unie der Openbare Diensten [*Trade union*] [*Belgium*]   (EY)
NUOP .... National Union of Occupational Therapists [*Israel*]   (EAIO)
nuor .... Nuorempi [*Finland*]
NUP .... Nacionalno Udruzenje za Planiranje [*National Planning Association*] [*USA*]   (YU)
NUP .... Nationalist Unionist Party [*Sudan*]
NUP .... National Umma Party [*Sudan*] [*Political party*]
NUP .... National Union [*or Unionist*] Party [*Sudan*]
NUP .... National United Party [*Vanuatu*] [*Political party*]   (EY)
NUP .... Uncontrolled Repeater Station   (RU)
NU:P .... University of Sydney - Physics Library [*National Union Catalogue of Australia symbol*]
NUPAAWP ... National Union of Plantation, Agricultural and Allied Workers of the Philippines
NUPAW .... National Union of Plantation and Agricultural Workers [*Uganda*]   (AF)
NUPF .... National Union of Popular Forces [*Morocco*]
NU:PH ...... University of Sydney - Pharmacy Department [*National Union Catalogue of Australia symbol*]
NUPI .... Norsk Utenrikspolitisk Institutt [*Norwegian Institute of International Affairs*] [*Research center*]   (IRC)
NUPJ .... National Union of Private Journalists [*Cameroon*]
NUPMH .... National Union of Physically and Mentally Handicapped [*Mauritania*]   (EAIO)
NUPOD ..... Nakupna Ustredny Potravnych Druzstev [*Central Purchase Office of Food Cooperatives*]   (CZ)

NUPOSA .. National Undergraduate Program for Overseas Study of Arabic
NUPP .... National Unionist Progressive Party [*Egypt*]
NUPPCW ... National Union of Printing, Paper, and Cartonage Workers [*Israel*]   (EAIO)
NUPPW .... National Union of Physiotherapists and Para-Medical Workers [*Israel*]   (EAIO)
NU:PR .... University of Sydney - Power Research Library of Contemporary Art [*National Union Catalogue of Australia symbol*]
NUPS .... Nordic Union of Private Schools   (EA)
NUPSA ..... National Union of Pharmaceutical Students of Australia   (ADA)
NUPSE ...... National Union of Public Service Employees [*Guyana*]   (LA)
NUPSW .... National Union of Petrol Stations Workers [*Israel*]   (EAIO)
NUPTE ...... National Union of Port Trust Employees [*India*]
NU:PU .... University of Sydney - Public Health Library [*National Union Catalogue of Australia symbol*]
NUPW .... National Union of Plantation Workers [*Uganda*]
NUPW .... National Union of Plantation Workers in Malaya
NUPW .... National Union of Public Workers [*Barbados*]
NUR .... Unguided Missile   (RU)
NUR .... Unguided Rocket   (BU)
NURA .... National Union of Railwaymen of Australia
NURD .... Nueva Union Republicana-Democratica [*New Democratic Republican Union*] [*Venezuela*]   (LA)
NURDSR .. Directive on Extending the Working Day for Seasonal Work   (BU)
NURS .... National Union of Rhodesia Students   (AF)
NURS .... Unguided Missile   (RU)
NURS .... Unguided Rocket Projectile   (BU)
NURTIW .. National Union of Rubber and Tyre Industries Workers [*Israel*]   (EAIO)
NURTW .... National Union of Road Transport Workers [*Nigeria*]   (AF)
NUrV .... Lower Water Level   (RU)
NUS .... Chief of Communications Center   (RU)
NUS .... Nasionale Uitstalsentrum Bpk [*South Africa*]   (AA)
NUS .... National Union of Students [*Australia*]
NUS .... National University of Singapore   (PDAA)
NUS .... National Utility Services [*Australia*]
NUS .... Nonpartisan Teachers' Union   (BU)
NUS .... Norsup [*Vanuatu*] [*Airport symbol*]   (OAG)
NUSAS ...... Nasionale Unie van Suid-Afrikaanse Studente [*National Union of South African Students*]   (AF)
NUSAS ...... National Union of South African Students
NUSDE ..... National Union of Shop and Distributive Employees [*Nigeria*]   (AF)
NUSFDB ... NUS [*National University of Singapore*] Financial Database [*Information service or system*]   (IID)
NUSG .... National Union of Students of Ghana
NUSI .... National Union of Seamen of India
NUSP .... National Union of Students of the Philippines   (EAIO)
NUSPRAW ... National Union of Storeworkers, Packers, Rubber and Allied Workers [*Australia*]
NUSS .... National Union of Students of Sierra Leone
NUSS .... National Union of Syrian Students   (ME)
NUSU .... Nanyang University Students Union [*Singapore*]   (ML)
NUSWAS ... National Union of South-West African Students [*Namibia*]   (AF)
NUT .... Camden Theological Library - Centre for Ministry [*National Union Catalogue of Australia symbol*]
NUT .... National Union of Teachers [*Kenya*]   (AF)
NUT .... Nigerian Union of Teachers
NUT .... Norwegian Union of Teachers   (EAIO)
NUTA .... National Union of Tanganyika Workers [*Tanzania*]   (AF)
NUTAE ..... Nuffield Unit of Tropical Animal Ecology
NUTEC ..... Norwegian Underwater Technology Centre   (PDAA)
NUTGLW ... National Union of Textile, Garment, and Leather Workers [*Israel*]   (EAIO)
NUTPE ...... National Union of Technicians and Practical Engineers [*Israel*]   (EAIO)
NUTS .... New South Wales University Theatre Society [*Australia*]
NUTV .... Narodni Ustredni Telovychovny Vybor [*National Committee for Physical Education*]   (CZ)
NUTW .... National Union of Tanganyika Workers
NUTW .... National Union of Textile Workers
NUTWTC ... National Union of Transport Workers and Transport Cooperatives [*Israel*]   (EAIO)
NUUDC ..... Ndola Urban District Council [*Zambia*] [*Research center*]   (EAS)
NUUS .... National Union of Uganda Students   (AF)
NUUSFE ... National Union of United States Forces Employees [*South Korea*]
NUV .... Norges Unge Venstre [*Norway*]
NUW .... National Union of Woodworkers [*Israel*]   (EAIO)
NUW .... National Union of Workers [*Australia*]
NUWA .... National Urban Water Supply Authority
NUWCDW ... National Union of Watchmen, Cleaning, and Domestic Workers [*Israel*]   (EAIO)

NUWM ..... National Union of Workers in Mali
NU:WO ..... University of Sydney - Wolstenholme Library [*National Union Catalogue of Australia symbol*]
NUYC .... Nordic Union of Young Conservatives (EA)
NUYO .... National Union of Youth Organizations [*Uganda*] (AF)
NUZS .... National Union of Zambia Students (AF)
n/v .... Low-Voltage (RU)
NV .... Magnetizing Fork [*Weld inspection device*] (RU)
NV .... Minimum Moisture Capacity (of Soil) (RU)
NV .... Naamloze Vennootschap [*Limited Company, Corporation*] [*Netherlands*] (GPO)
NV .... Naamval [*Ease*] [*Afrikaans*]
NV .... Nacelnik Veze [*Communications Chief*] [*Military*] (YU)
NV .... Nachrichtenverarbeitung [*German*] (ADPT)
nV .... Nad Vahom [*On the Vah River*] (CZ)
nV .... Nad Vltavou [*On the Vltava River*] (CZ)
NV .... Narodni Vybor [*National Committee*] (CZ)
NV .... Nase Vojsko [*Our Army*] [*A publishing house*] (CZ)
NV .... Nas Vrt [*Our Garden*] [*Zagreb A periodical*] (YU)
NV .... Nederlandse Staatsmiinen [*Dutch State Mines*] (WEN)
NV .... Nemzetkozi Vasar [*International Fair*] (HU)
NV .... Neposredna Vatra [*Direct Fire*] [*Military*] (YU)
NV .... Nichtverbreitung [*Nonproliferation*] [*German*] (WEN)
NV .... Niski Vodostaj [*Low Tide*] (YU)
NV .... Norske Veritas [*Norwegian ship classification society*] (DS)
NV .... North Vietnam [*or North Vietnamese*] (CL)
n/v .... Notre Ville [*Our City*] [*French*] [*Business term*]
n/V .... On the Volga [*Toponymy*] (RU)
NV .... People's Army (BU)
NV .... Rotor, Main Rotor (RU)
nv .... Time Norm (BU)
NVA .... Australian Veterinary Association - Max Henry Memorial Library [*National Union Catalogue of Australia symbol*]
NVA .... Nationale Volksarmee [*National Peoples' Army*] [*Germany*]
NVA .... Native Vegetation Authority [*South Australia*]
NVA .... Nederlandsche Vereeniging van Antiquaren
NVA .... Nederlandse Vereniging voor Allergologie [*Netherlands*] (EAIO)
NVA .... Nederlandse Vereniging voor Anesthesiologie [*Dutch Association of Anesthesiologists*] (SLS)
NVA .... Neiva [*Colombia*] [*Airport symbol*] (OAG)
NVA .... Nemzetkozi Vasuti Arudijszabas [*International Railroad Freight Tariff*] (HU)
NVA .... Nile Valley Aviation Co. [*Egypt*] [*ICAO designator*] (FAAC)
NVA .... North Vietnamese Army
NVA .... Vietnam People's Army [*Use VPA*] [*North Vietnamese*] (CL)
NVAC .... North Vietnamese Army Captured
NVAD .... Department of Veterans' Affairs - New South Wales Branch Office [*National Union Catalogue of Australia symbol*]
NVAES ..... Novo-Voronezhskaya Atomnaya Energeticheskaya Stantisiya [*Novo-Voronezhskaya Atomic Power Station*] [*Former USSR*] (PDAA)
NVAF .... North Vietnamese Air Force
NVAM .... National Veterinary Association of Morocco (EAIO)
NVAS .... Nachrichtenverarbeitendes Anwender-System [*German*] (ADPT)
NVas .... Nasa Vas [*Our Village*] [*Ljubljana A periodical*] (YU)
NVAS .... North Vietnamese Army Suspect
NVB .... Narodni Vybor Bezpecnosti [*National Security Board*] (CZ)
NVB .... Nationale Vrouwenraad van Belgie [*National Council of Belgian Women*] (WEN)
NVB .... National Party Netherlands (WEN)
NVB .... National Security Brigade [*Netherlands*] (WEN)
NVB .... National Volunteer Brigade [*South African equivalent of the British Home Guard*]
NVB .... Nederlandse Vereniging van Bibliothecarissen
NVB .... Nederlandse Volksbeweging [*Dutch People's Movement*] [*Political party*] (PPE)
NVB .... Nederlandse Vrouwenbeweging [*Netherlands Women's Movement*] (WEN)
NVBA .... Nederlandse Vereniging van Bedrijfsarchivarissen ['s-Gravenhage]
NVB/CLO ... Sectie Centrum Literatuuronderzoekers van de Nederlandse Vereniging van Bibliothecarissen
NVBF .... Nordisk Vetenskapliga Bibliotekarie-Forbundet [*Scandinavian Federation of Research Librarians*] (EA)
NVB/SSB ... Sectie Speciale Bibliotheken van de Nederlandse Vereniging van Bibliothecarissen
NVB/SWB ... Sectie Wetenschappelijke Bibliotheken van de Nederlandse Vereniging van Bibliothecarissen
NVC .... Nederlandse Vakcentrale [*Netherlands Trade Union Central*]
NVC .... Nederlandse Vereniging voor Cardiologie [*Netherlands*] (EAIO)
NVC .... New Venture Company [*Australia*] (ADA)
NVC .... Nuriootpa Viticulture Center [*Australia*]
NVC .... Vianney College - Roman Catholic Seminary [*National Union Catalogue of Australia symbol*]
NVCB .... Newcastle Visitor and Convention Bureau [*Australia*]

NVCC .... Nederlandse Vereniging voor Cosmetische Chemie
NVD .... Chief of Military Roads (RU)
NVD .... Commander of Airborne Force (RU)
NVD .... Netherlands Dietetic Association (EAIO)
NVD .... Normal-Hub, Vier-Takt Dieselmotor [*Standard Stroke, Four-Cycle Diesel Engine*] (EG)
nvd .... Service Platoon (BU)
NVDAG ..... Nonviolent Direct Action Group [*Sri Lanka*] (EAIO)
NVDV .... Nederlandse Vereniging voor Dermatologie en Venereologie [*Netherlands*] (EAIO)
NVE .... Nationaal Verbond van Eierhandelaars [*Belgium*] (EAIO)
NVE .... Nederlandse Vereniging voor Ergonomie [*Netherlands Egonomics Society*] (PDAA)
NVE .... Nonviolent Erotica [*Video classification*] [*Australia*]
NVE .... Norges Vassdrags- og Elektrisitetsvesen [*Norwegian Water Resources and Electricity Board*] [*Ministry of Petroleum and Energy*] (WED)
nve .... Normal Hydrogen Equivalent (RU)
NVE .... Standard Hydrogen Electrode (RU)
NVEM .... Nederlandse Vereniging voor Electronenmicroscopie [*Netherlands*] (EAIO)
NVER .... Nederlandse Vereniging voor Europees Recht [*Netherlands*] (BAS)
NVETS ..... National Vocational Education and Training System [*Australia*]
NVF .... Lower-Volga Branch (RU)
NVF .... Nederlandse Vereniging van Fotojournalisten [*Netherlands Association of Photo Journalists*] (WEN)
NVF .... Nordisk Vejteknisk Forbund [*Nordic Association of Road and Traffic Engineering*] (EAIO)
NVF .... Notarisambt, Venduwezen en Fiscaalrecht [*Netherlands*] (BAS)
NVFL .... Nederlandse Vereningin van Fabrikanten van Landbouwwerktuigen [*Netherlands Association of Manufacturers of Agricultural Machinery*] [*Netherlands*] (DSCA)
NVFS .... Navorsingseenheid vir Vervoerekonomie en Fisiese Distribusiestudies [*Research Unit for Transport Economic and Physical Distribution Studies*] [*Rand Afrikaans University*] [*South Africa*] (AA)
NVG .... Nederlandse Vereniging voor Geodesie [*Netherlands*] (SLS)
NVG .... Nederlands Verbond van de Groothandel [*Netherlands*] (EAIO)
NVI .... Nederlandse Vereniging voor Immunologie [*Netherlands*] (EAIO)
NVI .... Nordic Volcanological Institute [*Iceland*] [*Research center*] (EAS)
NVII .... Noril'sk Evening Industrial Institute (RU)
NVIR .... Nederlandse Vereniging voor Internationaal Recht [*Dutch Association for International Rights*] (SLS)
NVj .... Nastavni Vjesnik [*Teaching Review*] [*Zagreb*] (YU)
NVJ .... Nederlandse Vereniging van Journalisten [*Netherlands*] (EAIO)
NVK .... Low-Voltage Contact (RU)
NVK .... Nacelnik Vojenskeho Klubu [*Military Club Officer*] (CZ)
NVK .... Narvik [*Norway*] [*Airport symbol*] (OAG)
nvkf .... Nemzeti Vallalat Korlatolt Felelosseggel [*National Enterprise with Limited Liability*] (HU)
NVKI .... Nederlandse Vereniging voor Kunstmatige Intelligentie [*Netherlands Association for Artifical Intelligence*] (PDAA)
NVL .... National Volleyball League [*Australia*]
NVL .... Nederlandse Vereniging voor Lastechniek [*Netherlands Welding Society*] [*NIL*] [*Later,*] (PDAA)
NVL .... Person Called Is Not Here [*Telephone*] (BU)
NVM .... Nationaal Verbond van de Magistraten van Eerste Aanleg [*Benelux*] (BAS)
NVM .... Nederlands Verbond van Middenstandsverenigingen [*Netherlands*] (BAS)
NVMA .... Nigeria Veterinary Medical Association (EAIO)
NVMB .... Naval Base Commander (RU)
NVN .... North Vietnam [*or North Vietnamese*] (CL)
NVNAF ..... North Vietnamese Air Force
NVNDO .... Nederlandse Vereniging voor Niet Destructief Onderzoek [*Netherlands Association for Non-Destructive testing*] (PDAA)
NVNIIGG ... Lower Volga Scientific Research Institute of Geology and Geophysics (RU)
NVNN .... North Vietnamese Navy
NVN/VC ... North Vietnamese/Viet Cong [*or North Vietnam/Viet Cong*] (CL)
NVO .... Low-Voltage Equipment (RU)
NVO .... Neuererverordnung [*Innovator Decree*] (EG)
NVo .... People's Army (BU)
NVOCC ..... Non-Vessel Operating Container Carrier
NVOI .... National Voice of Iran [*Clandestine, Soviet-backed radio station*]
NVOPNZh ... Directive Temporarily Restricting the Admission of New Residents in Large Cities and Other Settlements (BU)
NVOS .... Nederlandse Vereniging voor Orthodontische Studie [*Dutch Association for Orthodontic Studies*] (SLS)
NVP .... Nahverkehrspreisverordnung [*Price Regulation Governing Local Transportation*] (EG)

NVP .... Nationaal Verbond der Pluimveeslachthuizen [*Belgium*]   (EAIO)

NVP .... Nederlandse Vereniging van Persbureaux [*Netherlands Association of Press Bureaus*]   (WEN)

NVP .... Nederlandse Vereniging voor Personeelbeleid [*Netherlands*]   (SLS)

NVPOSL ... Nacelnik Protivzdusne Obrany Statu a Letectva [*Chief of National Air Defense and Aviation*]   (CZ)

NVP-U .... Nationale Volkspartij - Unie [*National United People's Party*] [*Netherlands Antilles*] [*Political party*]   (PPW)

NVR .... Nederlandse Vereniging van Rubber- en Kunstoffabrikanten [*Netherlands*]   (EAIO)

NVR .... Nederlandse Vredesraad [*Netherlands Peace Council*]   (WEN)

NVR .... Nederlandse Vrouwen Raad [*Netherlands*]   (EAIO)

NVRI .... Vom National Veterinary Research Institute

NVRIA ...... National Vision Research Institute of Australia

NVRL .... Nederlandse Vereniging van Radiologische Laboranten [*Dutch Association of Radiology Laboratories*]   (SLS)

NVRP .... Lower Volga River Steamship Line   (RU)

NVRZ .... Novorossiysk Railroad Car Repair Plant   (RU)

NVS .... Chief of Military Communications   (RU)

NVS .... Nacelnik Vycvikove Skupiny [*Chief of Training Detachment*]   (CZ)

NVS .... Nacelnik Vysadkove Sluzby [*Chief of Airborne Service*]   (CZ)

NVS .... Narodna Vlada Slovenije [*National Government of Slovenia*]   (YU)

NVS .... Nasionale Versnellersentrum [*Council for Scientific and Industrial Research*] [*South Africa*]   (AA)

NVS .... Nationaal Verbond van Slachthuizen en Vleesuitsnijderijen [*Belgium*]   (EAIO)

NVS .... Nederlandse Vereniging van Soepenfabrikanten [*Netherlands*]   (EAIO)

NVS .... Nejvyssi Vojensky Soud [*Supreme Military Court*]   (CZ)

NVS .... Norwegian Volunteer Service   (EAIO)

NVSA .... Ablow [*Vanuatu*] [*ICAO location identifier*]   (ICLI)

NVSA .... Natuurbestuurvereniging van Suidelike Afrika [*Southern African Wildlife Management Association - SAWMA*] [*Pretoria, South Africa*]   (EAIO)

NVSA .... Nematologiese Vereniging van Suidelike Afrika [*Nematological Society of Southern Africa*]   (EAIO)

NVSC .... Sola [*Vanuatu*] [*ICAO location identifier*]   (ICLI)

NVSD .... Lo-Linua [*Vanuatu*] [*ICAO location identifier*]   (ICLI)

NVSE .... Emae [*Vanuatu*] [*ICAO location identifier*]   (ICLI)

NVSF .... Graig Cove [*Vanuatu*] [*ICAO location identifier*]   (ICLI)

NVSG .... Longana [*Vanuatu*] [*ICAO location identifier*]   (ICLI)

NVSH .... Sara [*Vanuatu*] [*ICAO location identifier*]   (ICLI)

NVSKPT ... Nationaal Verbond der Syndikale Kamers der Praktici in de Tandheelkunde [*Belgium*]   (SLS)

NVSL .... Lamap [*Vanuatu*] [*ICAO location identifier*]   (ICLI)

NVSL .... Nasionale Vereniging vir Skoon Lug [*South Africa*]   (EAIO)

NVSM .... Lamen-Bay [*Vanuatu*] [*ICAO location identifier*]   (ICLI)

NVSN .... Maewo-Naone [*Vanuatu*] [*ICAO location identifier*]   (ICLI)

NVSO .... Lonorore [*Vanuatu*] [*ICAO location identifier*]   (ICLI)

NVSP .... Norsup [*Vanuatu*] [*ICAO location identifier*]   (ICLI)

NVSPZ ...... Nederlandse Vereniging voor Sociaal-Pedagogische Zorg [*Netherlands*]   (EAIO)

NVSR .... Redcliff [*Vanuatu*] [*ICAO location identifier*]   (ICLI)

NVSS .... Santo/Pekoa [*Vanuatu*] [*ICAO location identifier*]   (ICLI)

NVST .... Tongoa [*Vanuatu*] [*ICAO location identifier*]   (ICLI)

NVSU .... Ulei [*Vanuatu*] [*ICAO location identifier*]   (ICLI)

NVSV .... Valesdir [*Vanuatu*] [*ICAO location identifier*]   (ICLI)

NVSW .... Walaha [*Vanuatu*] [*ICAO location identifier*]   (ICLI)

NVSX .... South West Bay [*Vanuatu*] [*ICAO location identifier*]   (ICLI)

NVSZ .... North West Santo [*Vanuatu*] [*ICAO location identifier*]   (ICLI)

NVT .... National Veld Trust [*South Africa*]   (AA)

NVT .... Navegantes [*Brazil*] [*Airport symbol*]   (OAG)

NVT .... Nepokretne Vatrene Tacke [*Fixed Targets*] [*Military*]   (YU)

NVT .... Nie van Toepassing [*Not Applicable*] [*Afrikaans*]

NVTG .... Nederlandse Vereniging voor Tropische Geneeskunde [*Netherlands*]   (SLS)

NVTI .... National Vocational Training Institute [*Ghana*]

NVTO .... Nederlandse Vereniging voor Tekenonderwijs [*Netherlands*]   (EAIO)

NVTU .... Norwegian Vocational Teachers Union   (EAIO)

NVU .... Nederlandse Volksunie [*Dutch People's Union*]   (WEN)

NVU .... People's Military Academy   (BU)

NVV .... Nederlandse Bond van Vervoerspersoneel [*Netherlands Association of Transportation Personnel*]   (WEN)

NVV .... Nederlands Verbond van Vakverenigingen [*Netherlands Federation of Trade Unions*]   (WEN)

nvv .... Niet Verder Verschenen [*No More Published*] [*Netherlands*]

NVVA .... Anatom [*Vanuatu*] [*ICAO location identifier*]   (ICLI)

NVVA .... Nederlandse Vereniging van Automobielssuradeuren [*Netherlands*]   (BAS)

NVVB .... Aniwa [*Vanuatu*] [*ICAO location identifier*]   (ICLI)

NVVD .... Dillon's Bay [*Vanuatu*] [*ICAO location identifier*]   (ICLI)

NVvE .... Nederlandse Vereniging voor Ergonomie [*Netherlands*]   (SLS)

NVVF .... Futuna [*Vanuatu*] [*ICAO location identifier*]   (ICLI)

NVvGT ...... Nederlandse Vereniging van Gieterijtechnici [*Netherlands*]   (SLS)

NVVI .... Ipota [*Vanuatu*] [*ICAO location identifier*]   (ICLI)

NVVJ......... Forari [*Vanuatu*] [*ICAO location identifier*]   (ICLI)

NVVK .... Lenakel [*Vanuatu*] [*ICAO location identifier*]   (ICLI)

NVvL .... Nederlandse Vereniging voor Luchtvaarttechniek [*Netherlands*]   (SLS)

NVvM .... Nederlandse Vereniging voor Microbiologie [*Dutch Association for Microbiology*]   (SLS)

NVvN .... Nederlandse Vereniging van Neurochirurgen [*Dutch Association of Neurosurgeons*]   (SLS)

NVVQ .... Quoin Hill [*Vanuatu*] [*ICAO location identifier*]   (ICLI)

NVVR .... Nasionale Verkeersveiligheidsraad [*National Traffic Safety Council*] [*South Africa*]   (AF)

NVVS .... Chief of the Air Force   (RU)

NVVS .... Nederlandse Vereniging voor Slechthorenden [*Netherlands*]   (EAIO)

NVVSA...... Nasionale Vroueraad van Suid-Afrika [*South Africa*]   (AA)

NVvT .... Nederlandse Vereniging van Tandartsen [*Netherlands*]   (SLS)

NVVT .... Nederlandse Vereniging van Veiligheidstechnici [*Netherlands*]   (SLS)

NVVV .... Port-Vila/Bauerfield [*Vanuatu*] [*ICAO location identifier*]   (ICLI)

NVvW .... Nederlandse Vereniging van Wiskundeleraren [*Netherlands*]   (SLS)

NVW .... National Volunteer Week [*Australia*]

NVW .... Nederland in de Vijf Werelddeelen, Leyden 1947

NVvW .... Nota van Wijzigingen [*Benelux*]   (BAS)

n vz .... Chief of Aerostation   (BU)

NVZ .... Noninterchangeability   (RU)

n vz f .... Commander, Army Air Force   (BU)

nvzu .... Chief of Military School   (BU)

NW .... Naamwoord [*Nomen*] [*Afrikaans*]

NW .... Nederlandsche Werkgever [*Netherlands*]   (BAS)

NW .... Neighbourhood Watch [*Australia*]

NW .... Niedrigster Wasserstand [*Lowest Water Level*] [*German*]   (GCA)

NW .... Niedrigwasser [*Low Water Level*] [*German*]   (GCA)

nw .... Nieuw [*New*] [*Netherlands*]

NW .... Noordwes [*Northwest*] [*Afrikaans*]

NW .... Nord Ouest [*Northwest*] [*French*]   (MTD)

NW .... Nordwesten [*Northwest*] [*German*]   (EG)

NW .... Notarieel Weekblad [*Benelux*]   (BAS)

Nw............. Wirtschaftlicher Nutzeffekt Wirkungsgrad [*Economical Efficiency*] [*German*]

NWA .... Moheli [*Comoro Islands*] [*Airport symbol*]   (OAG)

NWA .... North-West Australia   (ADA)

NWA .... Norwegian Water Association   (EAIO)

NWA .... Norwich Winterthur Australia

NWAR .... Warringah Shire Library Service [*National Union Catalogue of Australia symbol*]

NWASCA ... National Water and Soil Conservation Authority [*New Zealand*]

NWAT .... Riverina Institute of TAFE (Technical and Further Education) - Wagga Wagga Colle [*National Union Catalogue of Australia symbol*]

NWATSN ... RAN (Royal Australian Navy) Tactical School [*National Union Catalogue of Australia symbol*]

NWAV .... Waverley Municipal Library (New South Wales) [*National Union Catalogue of Australia symbol*]

NWB .... Nederlandse Waterschapsbank NV [*Waterschaps Bank of the Netherlands*]

NWB .... Niedergeschwindigkeitswindkanal Braunschweig

NWB .... Normenausschuss Waagenbau im DIN [*Deutsches Institut fuer Normung*] eV [*Scale Building Standards in the German Institute of Standardization*]   (SLS)

NWBB .... Noumea [*New Caledonia*] [*ICAO location identifier*]   (ICLI)

NWBT .... Westpac Banking Corporation - Training Library [*National Union Catalogue of Australia symbol*]

NWC .... National Wage Case [*Australia*]

NWC .... National Wage Council [*Singapore*]

NWC .... National Workers' Congress [*Sri Lanka*]

NWC .... National Working Committee

NWC .... Nigerian Workers Council   (AF)

NWC .... Nigeria Wire & Cable Co. Ltd.

NWC .... Workcover Authority of New South Wales [*National Union Catalogue of Australia symbol*]

NWCA .... North-West Co-operative Association Ltd. [*Cameroon*]   (EY)

NWCA .... Wollongong City Gallery Library [*National Union Catalogue of Australia symbol*]

NWCC ...... National Women's Consultative Council of Australia

NWCC ...... North West County Council [*Australia*]

NWCC ...... Noumea/La Tontouta [*New Caledonia*] [*ICAO location identifier*]   (ICLI)

NWCH ...... Australian Asosciation for the Welfare of Children in Hospital [*National Union Catalogue of Australia symbol*]

NWCS ...... NATO-Wide Communications System   (NATG)

NWCTU .... Australian National Woman's Christian Temperance Union (EAIO)

NWD .... Northwest Air Services Ltd. [*Nigeria*] [*ICAO designator*] (FAAC)

NWDP .... Westpac Banking Corporation - Technology Library [*National Union Catalogue of Australia symbol*]

NWDR .... Nordwestdeutscher Rundfunk [*Northwest German Radio Network*] (WEN)

NWEL .... Wellcome Australia Limited - Library [*National Union Catalogue of Australia symbol*]

NWEN ...... Wentworth Shire Library [*National Union Catalogue of Australia symbol*]

NWER .... Western Riverina Community Library [*National Union Catalogue of Australia symbol*]

NWFP .... North-West Frontier Province [*Pakistan*] (PD)

NWF Pak... North West Frontier, Pakistan (ILCA)

NWG .... Niedergeschwindigkeitswindkanal Goettingen

Nw-G .... Nieuw-Guinea [*Benelux*] (BAS)

NWGA ...... National Wool Growers' Association [*South Africa*]

NWGA ofSA ... National Wool Growers' Association of South Africa (AA)

NWGDE.... Nordic Working Group on Development Education [*Nordic Council of Ministers*] [*Denmark*] (EAIO)

NWGSFW ... National Working Group on Screw Fly Worm [*Australia*]

NWH .... Nawa Air Transport [*Hungary*] [*ICAO designator*] (FAAC)

NWH .... Wollongong Hospital - Medical Library [*National Union Catalogue of Australia symbol*]

NWHS ...... Wentworth Area Health Service - Nepean Hospital [*National Union Catalogue of Australia symbol*]

NWI .... Netherlands West Indies

NWIB .... Northwestern Institute of Botany [*China*] (IRC)

NWIC .... Wingecarribee Shire Library [*National Union Catalogue of Australia symbol*]

NWICO ..... New World Information and Communications Order [*UNESCO*]

NWIO........ New World Information Order [*Term coined by the Nonaligned Countries at their Fifth Summit Meeting in 1976*]

NWITF ...... Netherlands Wholesale and International Trade Federation (EAIO)

NWK.......... Nordwestdeutsche Kraftwerke Aktiengesellschaft [*Northwest German Power Station Joint Stock Company*]

NWKV .... Nasionale Wolkwekersvereniging van Suid-Afrika [*National Wool Growers' Association of South Africa*]

NWKVvan SA ... Nasionale Wolkwekersvereniging van Suid-Afrika [*National Wool Growers' Association of South Africa*] (AA)

NWLC .... Walcha and District Historical Society [*National Union Catalogue of Australia symbol*]

NWM .... National Workers Movement [*St. Vincentian*] (LA)

NWM .... Normenausschuss Werkzeugmaschinen im DIN [*Deutsches Institut fuer Normung*] eV [*Machine-Tools Standards in the German Institute of Standardization*] (SLS)

NWML ...... Willoughby City Library [*National Union Catalogue of Australia symbol*]

NWMRS ... National Waste Minimization and Recycling Strategy [*Australia*]

NWO .... National Women's Organization [*Grenada*] (LA)

NWO .... Nederlandse Organisatie voor Wetenschappelijk Onderzoek [*Netherlands Organization for Scientific Research*] [*Netherlands*] (EAIO)

NWO .... New Work Opportunities [*A publication*]

NWOA ...... Wollongbar Agricultural Institute [*National Union Catalogue of Australia symbol*]

NWOI........ Nationaal Werk voor Oorlogsinvaliden [*Benelux*] (BAS)

NWOL....... Wollondilly Shire Library Service [*National Union Catalogue of Australia symbol*]

NWOO ...... NATO Wartime Oil Organization (NATG)

NWOOL.... Woollahra Municipal Library [*National Union Catalogue of Australia symbol*]

NWOS .... Nationaal Werk voor Oudstrijders en Oorlogslachtoffers [*Benelux*] (BAS)

NWP.......... Najwiekszy Wspolny Podzielnik [*Highest Common Divisor*] [*Poland*]

NWP.......... NATO and Warsaw Pact [*Projects*] (NATG)

NWP.......... Nederlandse Werkgroep van Praktizijns in de Natuurlijke Geneeskunst [*Netherlands*] (SLS)

NWPAG .... NATO Wartime Preliminary Analysis Group (NATG)

NWPC .... Nordic Wood Preservation Council [*Sweden*] (EAIO)

NWPL .... Wollongong City Library [*National Union Catalogue of Australia symbol*]

NWPN .... Nordic Women's Peace Network [*Denmark*] (EAIO)

NWPPWM ... National Working Party on Portrayal of Women in the Media [*Australia*]

NWR.......... North Western Railway [*India*]

NWRC ...... National Water Resources Council [*Philippines*] (DS)

NWRC ...... New South Wales - Department of Water Resources [*National Union Catalogue of Australia symbol*]

NWRC ...... New World Resource Center

NWRD .... Hongkong Bank of Australia [*National Union Catalogue of Australia symbol*]

NWRHB.... North West Regional Health Board [*Tasmania, Australia*]

NWRWA... North West Regional Water Authority [*Tasmania, Australia*]

NWS .... Nederlandse Werkelijke Schuld [*Netherlands*] (BAS)

NWS .... Waste Recycling and Processing (New South Wales) [*National Union Catalogue of Australia symbol*]

NWSH ...... Newcastle Western Suburbs Hospital [*Australia*]

NWSL........ Wyong Shire Library [*National Union Catalogue of Australia symbol*]

NWT.......... Normenausschuss Waermebehandlungstechnik Metallischer Werkstoffe im DIN [*Deutsches Institut fuer Normung*] eV [*Heat Technology of Metal Raw Material Standards in the German Institute of Standardization*] (SLS)

NWT.......... Nowata [*Papua New Guinea*] [*Airport symbol*] (OAG)

NWT.......... Wollongong College of TAFE [*Technical and Further Education*]

NWU .... National Workers Union [*Jamaica*] (LA)

NWU .... National Workers Union [*Dominican Republic*] (LA)

NWU .... National Workers Union [*St. Lucia*] (LA)

NWU .... National Workers Union [*Seychelles*] (AF)

NWU .... University of Wollongong - Michael Birt Library [*National Union Catalogue of Australia symbol*]

NWUA....... University of Wollongong Archives - Michael Birt Library [*National Union Catalogue of Australia symbol*]

NWUS .... National Workers' Union, Seychelles

NWW .... Najmniejsza Wspolna Wielokrotnosc [*Smallest Common Multiple*] [*Poland*]

NWW .... North West Airline [*Australia*] [*ICAO designator*] (FAAC)

NWWA...... Tiga, Iles Loyaute [*New Caledonia*] [*ICAO location identifier*] (ICLI)

NWWAof A ... National Water Well Association of Australia (ADA)

NWWC...... Ile Art/Wala, Iles Belep [*New Caledonia*] [*ICAO location identifier*] (ICLI)

NWWD...... Kone [*New Caledonia*] [*ICAO location identifier*] (ICLI)

NWWE...... Ile Des Pins/Moue [*New Caledonia*] [*ICAO location identifier*] (ICLI)

NWWF...... Voh [*New Caledonia*] [*ICAO location identifier*] (ICLI)

NWWH ..... Houailou/Nesson [*New Caledonia*] [*ICAO location identifier*] (ICLI)

NWWH ..... Wagga Wagga Base Hospital and District Health Service - Library and Information [*National Union Catalogue of Australia symbol*]

NWWI....... Hienghene/Henri Martinet [*New Caledonia*] [*ICAO location identifier*] (ICLI)

NWWJ ...... Poum [*New Caledonia*] [*ICAO location identifier*] (ICLI)

NWWK...... Koumac [*New Caledonia*] [*ICAO location identifier*] (ICLI)

NWWL...... Lifou/Ouanaham, Iles Loyaute [*New Caledonia*] [*ICAO location identifier*] (ICLI)

NWWM..... Noumea/Magenta [*New Caledonia*] [*ICAO location identifier*] (ICLI)

NWWN ..... Noumea [*New Caledonia*] [*ICAO location identifier*] (ICLI)

NWWO ..... Ile Ouen/Edmond-Cane [*New Caledonia*] [*ICAO location identifier*] (ICLI)

NWWQ ..... Mueo/Nickel [*New Caledonia*] [*ICAO location identifier*] (ICLI)

NWWR...... Mare/La Roche, Iles Loyaute [*New Caledonia*] [*ICAO location identifier*] (ICLI)

NWWS...... Plaine Des Lacs [*New Caledonia*] [*ICAO location identifier*] (ICLI)

NWWU ..... Touho [*New Caledonia*] [*ICAO location identifier*] (ICLI)

NWWV...... Ouvea/Ouloup, Iles Loyaute [*New Caledonia*] [*ICAO location identifier*] (ICLI)

NWWW..... Noumea/La Tontouta [*New Caledonia*] [*ICAO location identifier*] (ICLI)

NWWY...... Ouaco/Paquiepe [*New Caledonia*] [*ICAO location identifier*] (ICLI)

NWYE .... Wyeth Pharmaceuticals Proprietary Limited - Wyeth-Ayerst Library [*National Union Catalogue of Australia symbol*]

NY............. New York (IDIG)

NY............. Noorduyn Aviation Ltd. [*Canada ICAO aircraft manufacturer identifier*] (ICAO)

NY............. Nyasaland (ROG)

ny .... Nyilvanos [*Public*] (HU)

ny .... Nyilvantartas [*Record, Register*] (HU)

ny .... Nyomda [*Printing Office*] [*Hungary*]

ny .... Nyugalmazott [*Retired*] (HU)

Ny .... Nyugat [*West*] [*Hungary*] (GPO)

NYAB .... National Youth Association of Bhutan (FEA)

NYAC .... Yanco Agricultural Institute [*National Union Catalogue of Australia symbol*]

NYAL .... National Yugoslav Army of Liberation [*World War II*]

NYC........... Nigerian Youth Congress

NYC........... Nigerian Youth Council (AF)

NYCA .... National Youth Council of Australia (ADA)

NYCH........ National Youth Coalition on Housing [*Australia*]

NYCN .... National Youth Council of Nigeria

NYCS........ New South Wales - Department of Community Services [*National Union Catalogue of Australia symbol*]

NYCSMA ... National Young Christian Students' Movement of Australia
nyd .... Nydelig [*Nice*] [*Danish/Norwegian*]
NYE .... Nomiki Ypiresia tis Ekklisias [*Church Legal Service*] [*Greek*] (GC)
NYeZh .... Rudder, Propeller Designed by N. Ye. Zhukovskiy (RU)
NYF .... National Youth Foundation [*Australia*]
NYG .... Nyge Aero AB [*Sweden*] [*ICAO designator*] (FAAC)
NYI .... Sunyani [*Ghana*] [*Airport symbol*] (OAG)
nyilv .... Nyilvanos [*Public*] (HU)
nyilv rend ... Nyilvanos Rendes [*Full (Professor)*] (HU)
NYK .... Nippon Yusen Kaisha [*Japanese steamship company*]
nyk .... Nykyinen [*or Nykyisin*] [*Modern, In Our Days*] [*Finland*] (GPO)
ny kotv .... Nyeremenykotveny [*Premium Bond*] (HU)
NYKV .... Nyersborgyujto es Keszletezo Vallalat [*Raw Hide Collection and Storage Enterprise*] (HU)
NYLEXUSA ... New York Leather Exposition [*American European Trade and Exhibition Center*]
NYM .... National Youth Movement [*Sierra Leone*] (AF)
NYM .... Nigerian Youth Movement
NYMG .... National Youth Movement of Ghana
NYN .... Nyngan [*Australia*] [*Airport symbol*] (OAG)
NYO .... National Youth Organization [*Grenada*] (LA)
nyomt .... Nyomtatta [*Printed By*] (HU)
nyomtatv .... Nyomtatvany [*Printed Matter*] (HU)
Nyomtell .... Nyomtatvanyellato Vallalat [*Office Stationery Supply Enterprise*] (HU)
nyomtv .... Nyomtatvany [*Printed Matter*] (HU)
NYPC .... National Youth Pioneer Corps (ML)
NYPDOSZ ... Nyomda- es Papiripari Dolgozok Szakszervezete [*Trade Union of Workers and Employees of the Printing and Paper Industries*] (HU)
ny r .... Nyilvanos Rendes [*Full (Professor)*] (HU)
NYRBA ..... New York, Rio & Buenos Aires Airlines, Inc.
ny rk .... Nyilvanos Rendkivuli [*Associate (Professor)*] (HU)
nyrkk .... Nyrkkeily [*Boxing*] [*Finland*]
NYS .... National Youth Service
NYSC .... National Youth Service Corps [*Nigeria*] (AF)
NYSC .... National Youth Service Council [*Sri Lanka*] (EAIO)
NYTC .... Nigerian Youth Thinkers Club (AF)
NYTIL .... Nyanza Textile Industries Limited
nytr .... Nytryck [*Reprint*] [*Sweden*]
NYU .... National Youth Union
NYU .... Nyaung-U [*Myanmar*] [*Airport symbol*] (OAG)
Nyug pu ...... Nyugati Palyaudvar [*West Railway Station*] [*Budapest*] (HU)
NZ .... Air New Zealand Ltd. (Domestic Division) [*ICAO designator*] (ICDA)
NZ .... Criminal Law (BU)
Nz .... Nachzug [*Second Section of a Train (Operated separately)*] (EG)
NZ .... Nadnormativni Zasoby [*Supplies Exceeding the Standards*] (CZ)
nz .... Nagradni Zaloha [*Replacement Reserves*] (CZ)
NZ .... Narodna Zascita [*National Defense*] [*Slovenia*] (YU)
NZ .... Narodne Zhromazdenie [*National Assembly*] (CZ)
NZ .... Narody Zjednoczone [*United Nations*] (POL)
NZ .... Nasa Zena [*Our Woman*] [*Ljubljana A periodical*] (YU)
Nz .... National Library of New Zealand, Wellington, New Zealand [*Library symbol*] [*Library of Congress*] (LCLS)
NZ .... Na Znanje [*Take Note*] (YU)
NZ .... Nedotknutelna Zasoba [*War Reserve Supplies*] (CZ)
NZ .... Neutral Zone, No-Man's-Land (RU)
NZ .... New Zealand [*ANSI two-letter standard code*] (CNC)
NZ .... Nieuwezijds [*New Side*] [*Netherlands*] (CED)
NZ .... Nitrozellulose [*Nitrocellulose*] [*German*] (GCA)
NZ .... Normalzeit [*Standard Time*] [*German*]
NZ .... Normenausschuss Zeichnungswesen im DIN [*Deutsches Institut fuer Normung*] eV [*Design Standards in the German Institute of Standardization*] (SLS)
NZ .... Nova Zalozba [*New Publishing House*] (YU)
NZ .... Nova Zeta [*New Zeta*] [*Cetinje A periodical*] (YU)
NZ .... Plant Standard (RU)
NZ .... Reserve Supplies, Individual Reserves (RU)
NZA .... New Zealand Artillery (DMA)
NZAA .... Auckland/International [*New Zealand*] [*ICAO location identifier*] (ICLI)
NZAA .... New Zealand Archaeological Association (SLS)
NZAAC ..... New Zealand Army Air Corps (DMA)
NZAEC ...... New Zealand Army Educational Corps (DMA)
NZAEC ...... New Zealand Atomic Energy Committee (SLS)
NZAEI .... New Zealand Agricultural Engineering Institute (ARC)
NZAIRRD ... New Zealand Association for International Relief, Rehabilitation, and Development (EAIO)
NZAK .... Auckland [*New Zealand*] [*ICAO location identifier*] (ICLI)
NZAMC .... New Zealand Army Medical Corps (DMA)
NZANS ..... New Zealand Army Nursing Service (DMA)
NZAOC ..... New Zealand Army Ordnance Corps (DMA)

NZAP .... New Zealand Associated Press (BARN)
NZAP .... Taupo [*New Zealand*] [*ICAO location identifier*] (ICLI)
NZAPC ...... New Zealand Army Pay Corps (DMA)
NZAPMB ... New Zealand Apple and Pear Marketing Board (EAIO)
NZAQ .... Auckland [*New Zealand*] [*ICAO location identifier*] (ICLI)
NZAR .... Ardmore [*New Zealand*] [*ICAO location identifier*] (ICLI)
NZART ...... New Zealand Association of Radio Transmitters (PDAA)
NZASC ...... New Zealand Army Service Corps (DMA)
NZASM ..... Nederlandsch Zuid-Afrikaansche Spoorwegmaatschappij [*Afrikaans*]
NZASSMD ... New Zealand Association for the Scientific Study of Mental Deficiency (EAIO)
NZAV .... Nederlandsch Zuid-Afrikaansche Vereniging [*Dutch South African Association*] [*Afrikaans*]
NZB .... Royal New Zealand Ballet
NZBC .... New Zealand Book Council (PDAA)
NZBC .... New Zealand Broadcasting Corp. (PDAA)
NZBE .... New Zealand Buick Enthusiasts (EAIO)
NZBF .... New Zealand Badminton Federation (EAIO)
NZBr. .... Law on Marriage (BU)
NZBS .... New Zealand Broadcasting Service
NZBTO ..... New Zealand Book Trade Organization (PDAA)
NZCA .... Campbell Island [*New Zealand*] [*ICAO location identifier*] (ICLI)
NZCC .... New Zealand Cyclist Corps (DMA)
NZCCL ...... New Zealand Council for Civil Liberties (EAIO)
NZCER ...... New Zealand Council for Educational Research [*Research center*] (IRC)
NZCH .... Christchurch/International [*New Zealand*] [*ICAO location identifier*] (ICLI)
nzch .... Low Audio Frequency (RU)
NZCI .... Chatham Island/Tuuta [*New Zealand*] [*ICAO location identifier*] (ICLI)
NZCM ...... McMurdo Sound, Antarctica [*New Zealand*] [*ICAO location identifier*] (ICLI)
NZCO .... Christchurch [*New Zealand*] [*ICAO location identifier*] (ICLI)
NZCS .... New Zealand Concrete Society (EAIO)
NZCS .... New Zealand Corps of Signals (DMA)
NzCSI-A .... New Zealand Department of Scientific and Industrial Research, Antarctic Division, Christchurch, New Zealand [*Library symbol*] [*Library of Congress*] (LCLS)
NZCSICP ... New Zealand Committee for the Scientific Investigation of Claims of the Paranormal (EAIO)
NZCWPRC ... New Zealand Committee for Water Pollution Research and Control (EAIO)
NZD .... Normal-Hub, Zwei-Takt Dieselmotor [*Standard-Stroke, Two-Cycle Diesel Engine*] (EG)
NZd .... Nova Zadruga [*New Cooperative*] [*A periodical*] (YU)
NZDA .... New Zealand Dental Association (EAIO)
NZDB .... New Zealand Dairy Board
NZDC .... New Zealand Dental Corps (DMA)
NZDF .... Christchurch/International [*New Zealand*] [*ICAO location identifier*] (ICLI)
NZDN .... Dunedin [*New Zealand*] [*ICAO location identifier*] (ICLI)
NZDSIR .... New Zealand Department of Scientific and Industrial Research (PDAA)
NZE .... Corps of New Zealand Engineers (DMA)
NZED .... New Zealand Electricity Department (PDAA)
NZEF .... New Zealand Expeditionary Force
NZERDC ... New Zealand Energy Research and Development Committee
NZES .... New Zealnd Ecological Society (DSCA)
NZEVA ...... New Zealand Empire Veterans Association (DMA)
NZFA .... New Zealand Field Artillery (DMA)
NZFF .... New Zealand Fruitgrowers' Federation (EAIO)
NZFL .... New Zealand Federation of Labor
NZFMCAE ... New Zealand Federated Mountain Clubs Antarctic Expedition [*1962-63*]
NZFMRA ... New Zealand Fertiliser Manufacturers Research Association (SLS)
NZFOL ...... New Zealand Federation of Labour
NZFP .... New Zealand Forest Products
NZFPS ...... New Zealand Foundation for Peace Studies
NZFS .... New Zealand Forest Service
NZGA .... New Zealand Garrison Artillery (DMA)
NZGS .... Gisborne [*New Zealand*] [*ICAO location identifier*] (ICLI)
NZGS .... New Zealand Geographical Society (EAIO)
NZGSAE ... New Zealand Geological Survey Antarctic Expedition [*1957-*]
NZH .... Nakladni Zavod Hrvatske [*Publishing Institute of Croatia*] (YU)
NZH .... Narodna Zastita Hrvatske [*National Defense of Croatia*] (YU)
NZhDO ...... Chief of Railroad Guard (RU)
NZHK .... Hokitika [*New Zealand*] [*ICAO location identifier*] (ICLI)
NZHN .... Hamilton [*New Zealand*] [*ICAO location identifier*] (ICLI)
NZHO .... Wellington [*New Zealand*] [*ICAO location identifier*] (ICLI)
NZHS .... New Zealand Hydrological Society (SLS)
NZI .... Nationaal Ziekenhuis-Instituut [*Utrecht*]

NZI .... New Zealand Insurance Corp.
NZI .... NZI Insurance - Resource Centre [*National Union Catalogue of Australia symbol*]
NZIAS .... New Zealand Institute of Agricultural Sciences   (SLS)
NZIC .... New Zealand Institute of Chemistry
NZIE .... New Zealand Institution of Engineers   (PDAA)
NZIER .... New Zealand Institute of Economic Research   (PDAA)
NZIFST ..... New Zealand Institute of Food Science and Technology   (SLS)
NZIG .... New Zealand Industrial Gases Ltd.
NZIIA .... New Zealand Institute of International Affairs   (SLS)
NZIM .... New Zealand Institute of Management   (SLS)
NZIP .... [*The*] New Zealand Institute of Physics   (SLS)
NZIW .... New Zealand Institute of Welding   (EAIO)
nzk .... Sustained Oscillations   (RU)
NZKB .... Wellington/Kilbirnie [*New Zealand*] [*ICAO location identifier*] (ICLI)
NZKC .... New Zealand Kennel Club   (EAIO)
NZKI .... Kaikoura [*New Zealand*] [*ICAO location identifier*]   (ICLI)
NZKL .... Wellington/Kelburn [*New Zealand*] [*ICAO location identifier*] (ICLI)
NZKT .... Kaitaia [*New Zealand*] [*ICAO location identifier*]   (ICLI)
NZKTD ..... Directive on Collective Labor Contracts   (BU)
NZKX .... Kaitaia [*New Zealand*] [*ICAO location identifier*]   (ICLI)
NZL .... Neva Machinery Plant Imeni V. I. Lenin   (RU)
NZL .... New Zealand [*ANSI three-letter standard code*]   (CNC)
NZLA .... New Zealand Library Association   (SLS)
NZLP .... New Zealand Labour Party [*Political party*]   (PPW)
NZLR .... New Zealand League of Rights   (EAIO)
NZLVRA ... New Zealand Land Value Rating Association   (EAIO)
NZM .... Mount Cook Airlines [*New Zealand*] [*ICAO designator*]   (FAAC)
NZMACI ... New Zealand Maori Arts and Crafts Institute   (EAIO)
NZMC .... New Zealand Medical Corps   (DMA)
NZMF .... Milford Sound [*New Zealand*] [*ICAO location identifier*]   (ICLI)
NZMGC .... New Zealand Machine Gun Corps   (DMA)
NZMGS .... New Zealand Machine Gun Section   (DMA)
NZMP .... New Zealand Military Police   (DMA)
NZMR .... New Zealand Mounted Rifles   (DMA)
NZMTRB ... New Zealand Masonry Trades Registration Board   (EAIO)
NZN .... Niedersachsischer Zeitschriftennachweis [*Deutsches Bibliotheksinstitut*] [*Germany*] [*Information service or system*] (CRD)
NZNAC ..... New Zealand National Airways Corp.   (PDAA)
NZNC .... New Zealand Native Contingent   (DMA)
NZNCIAWPRC ... New Zealand National Committee of the International Association on Water Pollution Research and Control (EAIO)
NZNCOR .. New Zealand National Committee on Oceanic Research (PDAA)
NZNP .... New Plymouth [*New Zealand*] [*ICAO location identifier*] (ICLI)
NZNR .... Napier [*New Zealand*] [*ICAO location identifier*]   (ICLI)
NZNS .... Nelson [*New Zealand*] [*ICAO location identifier*]   (ICLI)
NZNV .... Invercargill [*New Zealand*] [*ICAO location identifier*]   (ICLI)
NZO .... Standing Barrage   (RU)
NZOC .... New Zealand Ordnance Corps   (DMA)
NZOCGA .. New Zealand Olympic and Commonwealth Games Association (EAIO)
NZOH .... Ohakea [*New Zealand*] [*ICAO location identifier*]   (ICLI)
NZOI .... New Zealand Oceanographic Institute [*New Zealand Department of Scientific and Industrial Research, Water Sciences Division*] (EAS)
NZOU .... Oamaru [*New Zealand*] [*ICAO location identifier*]   (ICLI)
NZPA .... New Zealand Ports Authority   (GEA)
NZPA .... New Zealand Press Association
NZP &TC ... New Zealand Post and Telegraph Corps   (DMA)
NZPB .... Directive on Payment for Work Stoppage and Waste in Industry, Transportation, and Construction   (BU)
NZPCI .... New Zealand Prestressed Concrete Institute   (PDAA)
NZPENC ... New Zealand PEN Centre   (EAIO)
NZPL .... Nadodrzanskie Zaklady Przemyslu Lniarskiego [*Odra River Linen Mills*] (POL)
NZPM .... Palmerston North [*New Zealand*] [*ICAO location identifier*] (ICLI)
NZPO .... New Zealand Post Office [*Telecommunications*]
NZPOA ..... New Zealand Purchasing Officers Association   (PDAA)
NZPP .... Najnoviji Nacrt Zakona o Parnicnom Postupku [*Most Recent Draft Law on Civil Procedure*] (YU)
NZPP .... Paraparaumu [*New Zealand*] [*ICAO location identifier*]   (ICLI)
NZPS .... New Zealand Pain Society   (EAIO)
NZPS .... New Zealand Permanent Staff   (DMA)
NZPsS .... New Zealand Psychological Society   (SLS)
NZQN .... Queenstown [*New Zealand*] [*ICAO location identifier*]   (ICLI)
NZR .... Nationale Ziekenhuisraad [*Utrecht*]
NZR .... New Zealand Railways   (PDAA)
NZR .... New Zealand Rifles   (DMA)
NZRB .... New Zealand Rifle Brigade   (DMA)
NZRN .... Raoul Island [*New Zealand*] [*ICAO location identifier*]   (ICLI)

NZRO .... Rotorua [*New Zealand*] [*ICAO location identifier*]   (ICLI)
NZS .... Nacelnik Zdravotnicke Sluzby [*Chief of Medical Service*] (CZ)
NZS .... Neobsluhovana Zesilovaci Stanice [*Unattended Booster Stations (Amplifier stations on coaxial cable line) (Underground metal tanks)*] (CZ)
NZS .... Netitalni Zarizeni Staveniste [*Unspecified Building Equipment (for current use)*] (CZ)
NZSA .... New Zealand Society of Accountants   (PDAA)
NZSA .... New Zealand Statistical Association   (EAIO)
NZSAB ..... New Zealand Ski Council   (EAIO)
NZSAP ...... New Zealand Society of Animal Production   (DSCA)
NZSAS ..... New Zealand Special Air Service   (DMA)
NZSC .... Australian Bibliographic Network Office Training [*National Union Catalogue of Australia symbol*]
NZSC .... New Zealand Staff Corps   (DMA)
NZSDST ... New Zealand Society of Dairy Science and Technology   (SLS)
NZSG .... Public Health and Social Welfare   (BU)
NZSH .... Ndermarrje Zooteknike Shteterore [*Albanian*]
NZSI .... New Zealand Standards Institute   (PDAA)
NZSIC .... New Zealand Standard Industrial Classification
NZSM .... New Zealand Submarine Mining Volunteers   (DMA)
NZSMT ..... New Zealand Society for Music Therapy   (EAIO)
NZSNA ..... New Zealand System of National Accounts
NZSO .... New Zealand Symphony Orchestra
NZSR .... Directive on the Substitution of Employees and Holding Several Jobs   (BU)
NZSRA ...... New Zealand Squash   (EAIO)
NZSSS ...... New Zealand Society of Soil Science   (SLS)
NZST .... New Zealand Standard Time
NZSTs .... Law on Supply and Prices   (BU)
NZTC .... New Zealand Tonnage Committee   (DS)
NZTD .... Law on Labor Contracts   (BU)
NZTG .... Tauranga [*New Zealand*] [*ICAO location identifier*]   (ICLI)
NZTS .... New Zealand Temporary Staff   (DMA)
NZTU .... Timaru [*New Zealand*] [*ICAO location identifier*]   (ICLI)
NZ UKCC ... New Zealand United Kingdom Chamber of Commerce (DCTA)
NZUVT ..... Law on the Regulation of Internal Trade   (BU)
NZV .... Nederlandse Zootechnische Vereniging [*Netherlands*]   (EAIO)
NZV .... Nepokretna Zaprecna Vatra [*Fixed Barrage Fire*] [*Military*] (YU)
NZVA .... New Zealand Veterinary Association   (SLS)
NZVC .... New Zealand Veterinary Corps   (DMA)
NZVC .... New Zealand Volunteer Corps   (DMA)
NZWA .... Chatham Island/Waitangi [*New Zealand*] [*ICAO location identifier*] (ICLI)
NZWB .... Woodbourne [*New Zealand*] [*ICAO location identifier*]   (ICLI)
NZWG .... New Zealand Writers Guild   (EAIO)
NZWG .... Wigram [*New Zealand*] [*ICAO location identifier*]   (ICLI)
NZWHN ... New Zealand Women's Health Network   (EAIO)
NZWIRI ... New Zealand Wool Industries Research Institute   (DSCA)
NZWK .... Whakatane [*New Zealand*] [*ICAO location identifier*]   (ICLI)
NZWN .... Wellington/International [*New Zealand*] [*ICAO location identifier*] (ICLI)
NZWP .... Whenuapai [*New Zealand*] [*ICAO location identifier*]   (ICLI)
NZWQ .... Wellington [*New Zealand*] [*ICAO location identifier*]   (ICLI)
NZWR .... Whangarei [*New Zealand*] [*ICAO location identifier*]   (ICLI)
NZWRAC ... New Zealand Women's Royal Army Corps   (DMA)
NZWS .... Westport [*New Zealand*] [*ICAO location identifier*]   (ICLI)
NZWU .... Wanganui [*New Zealand*] [*ICAO location identifier*]   (ICLI)
NZZA .... Auckland [*New Zealand*] [*ICAO location identifier*]   (ICLI)
NZZC .... Christchurch [*New Zealand*] [*ICAO location identifier*]   (ICLI)
NZZn .... Narodno Zemedelsko Zname [*People's Agrarian Banner*] [*A newspaper*] (BU)
NZZO .... Auckland [*New Zealand*] [*ICAO location identifier*]   (ICLI)
NZZW .... Wellington [*New Zealand*] [*ICAO location identifier*]   (ICLI)

O

o/ .... A l'Ordre De [French]
o .... Father [Ecclesiastic]   (RU)
O .... Flash Ranging   (RU)
O .... Gun   (RU)
o .... Island   (RU)
O .... Lake [Vessel class according to the river register]   (RU)
o .... Oben [Above] [German]   (EG)
O .... Ober [Upper] [German]
O .... Oblast [Governmental subdivision in USSR corresponding to a province or state]
O .... Oboe [Phonetic alphabet] [World War II]   (DSUE)
O .... Ocean [Ocean] [Poland]
O .... Odde [or Odden] [Point] [Norway]   (NAU)
o .... Oder [Or] [German]   (EG)
O .... Oeste [West] [Portuguese]
O .... Oeste [West] [Spanish]
O .... Oesterreich [or Oesterreichisch] [Austria or Austrian] [German] (GPO)
O .... Officiel [Official] [French]
O .... Officier [of the Legion of Honor] [French]   (MTD)
O .... Ohm [German]   (GCA)
o .... Ohne [Without] [German]   (EG)
O .... Ohne Fraktionszughoerigkeit [Independents] [German]
o .... Ojciec [Poland]
O .... Oklevel [Hungary]
O .... Okres [District]   (CZ)
o .... Oldal [Page]   (HU)
O .... Omnipol Foreign Trade Corp. [Former Czechoslovakia] [ICAO aircraft manufacturer identifier]   (ICAO)
o .... Omslag [Wrapper] [Publishing Danish/Norwegian]
O .... Onsydig [Neutral] [Afrikaans]
O .... Oos [East] [Afrikaans]
o .... Ora [Hour, Time]   (HU)
O .... Orange [Phonetic alphabet] [Royal Navy World War I Pre-World War II]   (DSUE)
o/ .... Ordem [Order] [Portuguese]
o .... Orden [Order] [Spanish]
o .... Ordentlich [Orderly] [German]
O/ .... Order [German]
o .... Ordinaer [Ordinary Grade] [German]
O .... Ordinaere Sorte [Ordinary Grade] [German]   (GCA)
O .... Ordinary [Level of General Certificate of Education] [Ghana]
O .... Ordonnance [Benelux]   (BAS)
O .... Ordonnanzoffizier [Special-Missions Staff Officer] [German military - World War II]
o/ .... Ordre [Order] [Business term] [French]
o .... Ore [Half Farthing] [Norway]   (GPO)
o .... Original [French]
O .... Original [German]
o .... Originale [Original] [Italian]
o .... Origineel [Original] [Publishing] [Netherlands]
O .... Ormos [Bay] [Greek]   (NAU)
o .... Oro [Gold] [Italian]
O .... Orszagos [National (Adjective)]   (HU)
O .... Ort [Place] [German]
o .... Ortho [Ortho] [German]
o .... Orvos [Physician]   (HU)
O .... Oscar [Phonetic alphabet] [International]   (DSUE)
O .... Oscilloscope   (RU)
O .... Ost [or Osten] [East] [German]   (EG)
O .... Osten [East] [German]
O .... Ostrov [or Ostrova] [Island or Islands] [Russian]   (NAU)
O .... Ostrov [or Ostrovu or Ostrovu] [River Island Romanian]   (NAU)
o .... Osztaly [Class, Department, Division]   (HU)
O .... Otocic [or Otocici] [Islet or Islets Former Yugoslavia]   (NAU)
O .... Otok [or Otoci] [Island or Islands Former Yugoslavia]   (NAU)
O .... Ouest [West] [French]
o .... Over [Over] [Danish/Norwegian]

O .... Overwegende [Benelux]   (BAS)
O .... Ovest [West] [Italian]
O .... Oxigenio [Oxygen] [Chemical element] [Portuguese]
O .... Oxygonon [Oxygen]   (GC)
O .... Oy [or Oya or Toy] [Island] [Norway]   (NAU)
O .... Splinter, Fragmentation   (RU)
O .... Tin   (RU)
OA .... Amplitude Limiter   (RU)
OA .... Antenna Mounting   (RU)
OA .... Axial Reinforcement   (RU)
OA .... Contaminated Atmosphere   (RU)
OA .... Obalska Artilerija [Coastal Artillery]   (YU)
OA .... Obec Architektu [Former Czechoslovakia]   (EAIO)
oa .... Och Andra [And Others] [Sweden]
oa .... Oder Aehnlich [Or Something Similar] [German]
oa .... Og Andre [And Others] [Danish/Norwegian]
oa .... Og Annet [And Others] [Norway]   (GPO)
OA .... Oklopni Automobil [Armored Car]   (YU)
OA .... Olymbiaki Aeroporia [Olympic Airlines]
oa .... Onder Andere [Among Others] [Netherlands]   (GPO)
OA .... Operational Airfield   (RU)
OA .... Order of Australia
O/A .... Original-Abfuellung [On estate-bottled German wine labels]
OA .... Oro Americano [American Gold] [Spanish] [Business term]
oa .... Orszagos Allatvasar [National Livestock Fair]   (HU)
OA .... Ost-Ausschuss [East Trade Committee]
OAA .... Office Automation Association [Australia]
OAA .... Office of Aboriginal Affairs [New South Wales, Australia]
OAA .... Omilos Andisfairiseos Athinon [Athens Lawn Tennis Club]   (GC)
OAA .... Order of Australia Association
OAA .... Organisation des Nations Unies pour l'Alimentation et l'Agriculture [Food and Agriculture Organization of the United Nations]
OAA .... Organizacion de Agricultura y Alimentacion [Food and Agriculture Organization] [Spanish]
OAA .... Orient Airlines Association   (EA)
OAA .... Orthoptic Association of Australia   (ADA)
OAA .... Oxley Aviation [Australia] [ICAO designator]   (FAAC)
OAAA .... Oceania Amateur Athletic Association   (EAIO)
OAAA .... Office Automation Association of Australia
OAAA .... Organismos Apaskholiseos kai Asfaliseos Anergias [or Organismos Apaskholiseos kai Asfaliseos Kata tis Anergias] [Organization for Unemployment Insurance and Employment] [Greek]   (GC)
OAAA .... Outdoor Advertising Association of Australia
OAACE ..... Organisation Afro-Asiatique de Cooperation Economique [Afro-Asian Organization for Economic Cooperation] [Use AFRASEC]   (AF)
OAAD .... Amdar [Afghanistan] [ICAO location identifier]   (ICLI)
OAAEE ..... Organosis Aoraton Agoniston Ellinikou Ethnous [Organization of Invisible Fighters of the Greek Nation] [SNNYS] [Also,]   (GC)
OAAH .... Organisation Afro-Asiatique pour l'Habitation [Afro-Asian Housing Organization] [Use AAHO]   (AF)
OAAH .... Orszagos Anyag es Arhivatal [National Material and Price Office]   (HU)
OAAK .... Andkhoi [Afghanistan] [ICAO location identifier]   (ICLI)
OAAPS ..... Organisation for Afro-Asian Peoples Solidarity
OAARR ..... Organisation Afro-Asiatique pour la Reconstruction Rurale [Afro-Asian Rural Reconstruction Organization] [Use AARRO]   (AF)
OAAS .... Asmar [Afghanistan] [ICAO location identifier]   (ICLI)
OAB .... Aerial Fragmentation Bomb   (RU)
OAB .... Ordem dos Advogados do Brasil [Brazilian Bar Association]   (LA)
OAB .... Organisation Africaine du Bois [African Timber Organization]   (EAIO)

883

OAB........... Orszagos Atomenergia Bizottsag [*National Atomic Energy Committee*] (HU)
OAB........... Separate Air Brigade (RU)
OABD........ Behsood [*Afghanistan*] [*ICAO location identifier*] (ICLI)
OABG........ Baghlan [*Afghanistan*] [*ICAO location identifier*] (ICLI)
OABK........ Bandkamalkhan [*Afghanistan*] [*ICAO location identifier*] (ICLI)
OABN........ Bamyan [*Afghanistan*] [*ICAO location identifier*] (ICLI)
OABR........ Bamar [*Afghanistan*] [*ICAO location identifier*] (ICLI)
oabr............ Gun Artillery Brigade (BU)
OABS........ Sarday [*Afghanistan*] [*ICAO location identifier*] (ICLI)
OABT........ Bost [*Afghanistan*] [*ICAO location identifier*] (ICLI)
OAC........... Obus en Acier a Amorcage de Culot [*Military*] [*French*] (MTD)
OAC........... Oost Afrikaansche Compagnie
OAC........... Orange Agricultural College [*Australia*] (ADA)
OAC........... Oriental Airlines Ltd. [*Nigeria*] [*ICAO designator*] (FAAC)
OAC........... Osservatorio Astronomico di Capodimonte [*Capodimonte Astronomical Observatory*] [*Research center*] [*Italy*] (EAS)
OACB........ Charburjak [*Afghanistan*] [*ICAO location identifier*] (ICLI)
OACC........ Chakhcharan [*Afghanistan*] [*ICAO location identifier*] (ICLI)
OACCF...... Orange Agricultural College Christian Fellowship [*Australia*]
OACDT...... Outback Areas Community Development Trust [*Australia*]
OACI......... Organisation de l'Aviation Civile Internationale [*International Civil Aviation Organization*] [*French United Nations*]
OACI......... Organizacion de Aviacion Civil Internacional [*International Civil Aviation Organization*] [*Spanish United Nations*] (DUND)
OACIE....... Oost Afrikaansche Compagnie
OACT........ Organisation Africaine de Cartographie et de Teledetection [*Algeria*] (EAIO)
OACV........ Office Algerien des Colonies de Vacances
OACV........ Operation Arachides et Cultures Vivrieres
OAD......... Bidirectional Amplitude Limiter (RU)
oad............. Gun Artillery Division (BU)
OAD......... Oficiul de Aprovizionare si Desfacere [*Office of Supply and Sales*] (RO)
OAD......... Organization of American States (BU)
OAD......... Orszagos Autobuszmenetrend es Dijszabas [*National Bus Timetable and Rate List*] (HU)
OAD......... Separate Artillery Battalion (RU)
OADA....... Organisation Arabe pour le Developpement Agricole [*Arab Agricultural Development Organization*] (AF)
OADD....... Dawlatabad [*Afghanistan*] [*ICAO location identifier*] (ICLI)
OADF........ Darra-I-Soof [*Afghanistan*] [*ICAO location identifier*] (ICLI)
OADMA..... Organismos Anegerseos Dikastikou Megarou Athinon [*Organization for Constructing the Athens Court House*] (GC)
oadn............ Separate Artillery Battalion (RU)
OADS........ Organisation Arabe de Defense Sociale (Contre le Crime)
OADV........ Devar [*Afghanistan*] [*ICAO location identifier*] (ICLI)
OADW....... Wazakhwa [*Afghanistan*] [*ICAO location identifier*] (ICLI)
OADZ........ Darwaz [*Afghanistan*] [*ICAO location identifier*] (ICLI)
OAE.......... Office d'Approvisionnement de l'Etat [*State Supply Office*] [*Benin*] (AF)
OAE.......... Omospondia Andistasiakon Ellados [*Greek Federation of Resisters*] (GC)
OAE.......... Organisasie van Afrika-Eenheid [*Organization of African Unity*] [*Use OAU*] (AF)
OAE.......... Organisatie voor Afrikaanse Eenheid [*South Africa*] (BAS)
OAE.......... Organisation der Afrikatischen Einheit
OAE.......... Organismos tis Afrikanikis Enotitos [*Organization of African Unity*] (GC)
OAE.......... Organizatiia Afrikanskovo Edinstva
OAE.......... Ormancilik Arastirma Enstitusu [*Forest Research Institute*] [*Turkey*] (IRC)
OAED....... Organismos Apaskholiseos Ergatikou Dynamikou [*Labor Force Employment Organization*] [*Greek*] (GC)
OAEK....... Keshm [*Afghanistan*] [*ICAO location identifier*] (ICLI)
OAEM....... Eshkashem [*Afghanistan*] [*ICAO location identifier*] (ICLI)
OAEP....... Office of Atomic Energy for Peace [*Thai*] [*Research center*] (IRC)
OAEQ........ Islam Qala [*Afghanistan*] [*ICAO location identifier*] (ICLI)
OAER....... Base Airfield (RU)
OAES....... Organisation d'Aide Economique et Sociale [*France*] (FLAF)
OAES....... Separate Air Communications Squadron (RU)
OAF.......... Austrian Air Ambulance [*ICAO designator*] (FAAC)
OAF.......... Occidentale Afrique Francaise [*French West Africa*]
OAFG....... Khost-O-Fering [*Afghanistan*] [*ICAO location identifier*] (ICLI)
OAFP....... Organisation of African Film Producers
OAFR....... Farah [*Afghanistan*] [*ICAO location identifier*] (ICLI)
OAFT....... Orszagos Allattenyesztesi es Takarmanyozasi Felugyeloseg [*National Animal Breeding and Fodder Inspectorate*] (HU)
OAFZ....... Faizabad [*Afghanistan*] [*ICAO location identifier*] (ICLI)
OAG......... Office of the Attorney-General
OAG......... Orange [*Australia*] [*Airport symbol*] (OAG)
OAG......... Organization of American States [*OAS*] (RU)
OAGA....... Ghaziabad [*Afghanistan*] [*ICAO location identifier*] (ICLI)

OAGD....... Gader [*Afghanistan*] [*ICAO location identifier*] (ICLI)
OAGG....... Oesterreichischer Arbeitskreis fuer Gruppentherapie und Gruppendynamik [*Austrian Association for Group Therapy and Group Dynamics*] (SLS)
OAGL....... Gulistan [*Afghanistan*] [*ICAO location identifier*] (ICLI)
OAGM...... Ghelmeen [*Afghanistan*] [*ICAO location identifier*] (ICLI)
OAGN...... Ghazni [*Afghanistan*] [*ICAO location identifier*] (ICLI)
OAGS....... Gasar [*Afghanistan*] [*ICAO location identifier*] (ICLI)
OAGZ....... Gardez [*Afghanistan*] [*ICAO location identifier*] (ICLI)
OAH .... Office of Aboriginal Health [*Australia*]
OAHE....... Hazrat Eman [*Afghanistan*] [*ICAO location identifier*] (ICLI)
OAHJ........ Hajigak [*Afghanistan*] [*ICAO location identifier*] (ICLI)
OAHN...... Khwahan [*Afghanistan*] [*ICAO location identifier*] (ICLI)
OAHR....... Herat [*Afghanistan*] [*ICAO location identifier*] (ICLI)
OAI........... Orszagos Allategeszsegugyi Intezet [*Central Veterinary Institute*] [*Hungary*] (ARC)
OAI........... Public Automobile Inspector (RU)
OAIC......... Office Algerien Interprofessionnel des Cereales [*Interoccupational Algerian Grains Office*] [*Algiers*] (AF)
OAIM....... Organisme Arabe pour l'Industrialisation Militaire
OAJ .... Opettajien Ammattijarjestoe [*Finland*] (SLS)
OAJL........ Jalalabad [*Afghanistan*] [*ICAO location identifier*] (ICLI)
OAJS........ Jabul Saraj [*Afghanistan*] [*ICAO location identifier*] (ICLI)
OAJW....... Jawand [*Afghanistan*] [*ICAO location identifier*] (ICLI)
OAK.......... Oesterreichische Aerztekammer [*Austrian Physicians Board*] (SLS)
OAK.......... Organismos Amerikanikon Kraton [*Organization of American States*] (GC)
oak .... Orszagos Allat- es Kirako [*or Kirakodo*] Vasar [*National Livestock and Merchandise Fair*] (HU)
OAK.......... Ostravsky Aeroklub [*Ostrava Aero Club*] (CZ)
OAKA....... Koban [*Afghanistan*] [*ICAO location identifier*] (ICLI)
OAKB....... Kabul Ad [*Afghanistan*] [*ICAO location identifier*] (ICLI)
OAKD....... Kamdesh [*Afghanistan*] [*ICAO location identifier*] (ICLI)
OAKG....... Khojaghar [*Afghanistan*] [*ICAO location identifier*] (ICLI)
OAKh....... Society of Architect Artists [*1903-1932*] (RU)
OAKJ........ Kajaki [*Afghanistan*] [*ICAO location identifier*] (ICLI)
OAKL....... Konjak-I-Logar [*Afghanistan*] [*ICAO location identifier*] (ICLI)
OAKM...... Kamar [*Afghanistan*] [*ICAO location identifier*] (ICLI)
OAKN...... Kandahar [*Afghanistan*] [*ICAO location identifier*] (ICLI)
OAKR....... Kaldar [*Afghanistan*] [*ICAO location identifier*] (ICLI)
OAKS ...... Khost [*Afghanistan*] [*ICAO location identifier*] (ICLI)
OAKT....... Kalat [*Afghanistan*] [*ICAO location identifier*] (ICLI)
OAKT....... Oesterreichische Arbeitskreise fuer Tiefenpsychologie [*Austrian Association for Psychology*] (SLS)
OAKX....... Kabul [*Afghanistan*] [*ICAO location identifier*] (ICLI)
OAKZ....... Karez-I-Mir [*Afghanistan*] [*ICAO location identifier*] (ICLI)
OAL.......... Oesterreichischer Arbeitsring fuer Laermbekaempfung [*Austrian Association for Combating Noise*] (SLS)
OAL.......... Olympic Airways SA [*Greece*] [*ICAO designator*] (FAAC)
OAL.......... Organisation pour l'Afrique Libre [*Organization for Free Africa*] (AF)
OAL.......... Special Automobile Laboratory (RU)
OALF........ Oromo Abo Liberation Front [*Ethiopia*] [*Political party*] (EY)
OALG....... Logar [*Afghanistan*] [*ICAO location identifier*] (ICLI)
OAL iMP ... Department of Mathematical Linguistics and Machine Translation (RU)
OALL....... Lal [*Afghanistan*] [*ICAO location identifier*] (ICLI)
o all............ Osszeallitotta [*Compiled By*] (HU)
OALN....... Laghman [*Afghanistan*] [*ICAO location identifier*] (ICLI)
OALS........ Organizacion Avanzada para la Liberacion del Sahara [*Forward Organization for the Liberation of the Sahara*] (AF)
OAM.......... Automatic Optimizer (RU)
OAM.......... Medal of the Order of Australia (ADA)
OAM.......... Oamaru [*New Zealand*] [*Airport symbol*] (OAG)
OAM.......... One Australian Movement [*Political party*]
OAM.......... Organisation Africaine et Malgache
OAM.......... Organization of Australian Midwives (ADA)
OAM.......... Relative Amplitude Modulation (RU)
OAMCAF ... Organisation Africaine et Malgache du Cafe [*African and Malagasy Coffee Organization*] (AF)
OAMCE .... Organisation Africaine et Malgache de Cooperation Economique [*Afro-Malagasy Organization for Economic Cooperation*] [*Common Afro-Malagasy Organization*] [*Later,*]
OAMJTB .. Organisation pour l'Afrique des Mouvements de Jeunesse et du Travail Benevole
OAMK ...... Mukur [*Afghanistan*] [*ICAO location identifier*] (ICLI)
OAMK ...... Okresni Auto-Motoklub [*District Motoring Club*] (CZ)
OAMN ...... Maimama [*Afghanistan*] [*ICAO location identifier*] (ICLI)
OAMNII ... Joint Scientific Research Institutes for Aviation Medicine (BU)
OAMO ...... Obshchaia Afro-Malagasiiskaia Organizatsiia
OAMPI ..... Office Africain et Malgache de la Propriete Industrielle
OAMS .... Mazar-I-Sharif [*Afghanistan*] [*ICAO location identifier*] (ICLI)
OAMT....... Munta [*Afghanistan*] [*ICAO location identifier*] (ICLI)
OAMTC .... Osterreichischer Automobil-, Motorrad-, und Touring Club [*Austria*] (EAIO)

OAN	Organismos Anelkyseos Navagion [*Ship Salvage Organization*] [*Greek*] (GC)	
OANA	Organization of Asian News Agencies	
OANA	Organization of Asia-Pacific News Agencies [*Malaysia*] (EY)	
OANI	Office of the Administrator of Norfolk Island [*Australia*]	
OANR	Nawor [*Afghanistan*] [*ICAO location identifier*] (ICLI)	
OANS	Salang-I-Shamali [*Afghanistan*] [*ICAO location identifier*] (ICLI)	
OAO	General Administrative Department (RU)	
OAO	Separate Air Detachment (RU)	
OAOA	Overnight Air Freight Operators Association [*Australia*]	
OAOB	Obeh [*Afghanistan*] [*ICAO location identifier*] (ICLI)	
OAOG	Urgoon [*Afghanistan*] [*ICAO location identifier*] (ICLI)	
OAOLPP	Oficina de Atencion a los Organos Locales del Poder Popular del Consejo de Ministros [*Local People's Government Department of the Council of Ministers*] [*Cuba*] (LA)	
OAOO	Deshoo [*Afghanistan*] [*ICAO location identifier*] (ICLI)	
OAP	Austrian Trade-Union Association (RU)	
oap	Gun Artillery Regiment (BU)	
OAP	Office Algerien de Peches [*Algerian Fishing Office*] (AF)	
OAP	Organisation Asienne de Productivite [*Asian Productivity Organization - APO*] [*French*]	
OAP	Organismos Apokhetevseos Protevousis [*Capital Area Drainage Organization*] [*Greek*] (GC)	
OAP	Organizacion Asiatica de Productividad [*Asian Productivity Organization - APO*] [*Spanish*]	
OAP	Osterreichische Arztegesellschaft fur Psychotherapie (EAIO)	
OAP	Separate Air Regiment (RU)	
OAPCKKPM	Odelenie za Agitacija i Propaganda pri Centralni Komitet na Komunistickata Partija na Makedonija [*Department of Agitation and Propaganda in the Central Committee of the Communist Party of Macedonia*] (YU)	
OAPEC	Oficina Administrativa para Programas Educativos Conjuntos [*ICCE*] [*Colombia*] [*Later,*] (COL)	
OAPEC	Organization of Arab Petroleum Exporting Countries [*See also OPAEP*] [*OPEC Kuwait*] [*Absorbed by*]	
OAPEP	Organisation Arabe des Pays Exportateurs de Petrole [*Organization of Arab Petroleum Exporting Countries*]	
OAPF	Main Motor Highway to the Front (BU)	
OAPG	Paghman [*Afghanistan*] [*ICAO location identifier*] (ICLI)	
OAPI	Organisation Africaine pour la Propriete Intellectuelle [*African Organization for Intellectual Rights*] (AF)	
OAPJ	Pan Jao [*Afghanistan*] [*ICAO location identifier*] (ICLI)	
OAPV	Single-Phase Automatic Reclosing (RU)	
OAPVO	Separate Antiaircraft Defense Army (BU)	
OAQD	Qades [*Afghanistan*] [*ICAO location identifier*] (ICLI)	
OAQK	Qala-I-Nyazkhan [*Afghanistan*] [*ICAO location identifier*] (ICLI)	
OAQM	Kron Monjan [*Afghanistan*] [*ICAO location identifier*] (ICLI)	
OAQN	Qala-I-Naw [*Afghanistan*] [*ICAO location identifier*] (ICLI)	
OAQQ	Qarqin [*Afghanistan*] [*ICAO location identifier*] (ICLI)	
OAQR	Qaisar [*Afghanistan*] [*ICAO location identifier*] (ICLI)	
OAR	Basic Repair Service (BU)	
OAR	Detached Motor Transport Company (BU)	
OAR	Obedinennaia Arabskaia Respublika [*United Arab Republic - UAR*]	
OAR	United Arab Republic (BU)	
OARB	Orient Airlines Research Bureau (PDAA)	
OARB	Separate Motor Vehicle Repair Battalion (RU)	
oaremb	Separate Motor Vehicle Repair Battalion (RU)	
OARG	Uruzgan [*Afghanistan*] [*ICAO location identifier*] (ICLI)	
OARI	Organizacion de Accion Revolucionaria Independiente [*Independent Revolutionary Action Organization*] [*Venezuela*] (LA)	
OARM	Dilaram [*Afghanistan*] [*ICAO location identifier*] (ICLI)	
OARM	District Motor Vehicle Repair Shop (RU)	
OARM	Organisation Arabe des Ressources Minieres [*Arab Organization for Mineral Resources*] [*Rabat, Moroccan*]	
OARN	Officine Allestimento e Riparazioni Navi [*Italian*] (MSC)	
OARP	Rimpa [*Afghanistan*] [*ICAO location identifier*] (ICLI)	
oarp	Separate Motor Transport Company (RU)	
OARS	Offenders Aid and Rehabilitation Services of South Australia	
OARTU	District Artillery Directorate (RU)	
OAS	Airfield Construction Section (RU)	
OAS	Airfield Service Section (RU)	
OAS	Aviation Supply Section (RU)	
O-as	Nullas [*Finest Quality*] (HU)	
OAS	Occupational Assistance Service [*Australia*]	
OAS	Oman Aviation Services Co. [*ICAO designator*] (FAAC)	
OAS	Organisacni Akciova Spolecnost [*Organizational Joint-Stock Company*] (CZ)	
OAS	Organisatie der Amerikaanse Staten [*Organization of American States*] [*Africaans*] (BAS)	
OAS	Organisation de l'Armee Secrete [*Secret Army Organization*] [*France*] (PD)	

OAS	Organismos Astikon Syngoinonion [*Urban Communications Organization*] [*Greek*] (GC)	
OAS	Organization of American State (SCAC)	
OAS	Organization of American States (IDIG)	
OAS	Orthopedic Appliance Service	
OAS	Other Approved Studies [*Australia*]	
OAS	Syrian Arab Bar Association (EAIO)	
OASB	Sarobi [*Afghanistan*] [*ICAO location identifier*] (ICLI)	
OASD	Shindand [*Afghanistan*] [*ICAO location identifier*] (ICLI)	
oase	Oaseged [*Deep-Grained Morocco*] [*Publishing Danish/ Norwegian*]	
OASG	Sheberghan [*Afghanistan*] [*ICAO location identifier*] (ICLI)	
oashr	Separate Army Disciplinary Company (RU)	
OASIS	Office Automation and School Information System [*Australia*]	
Oasis	Overseas Access for Information Systems	
OASK	Serka [*Afghanistan*] [*ICAO location identifier*] (ICLI)	
OASL	Olympic Airways Soccer League [*Australia*]	
OASL	Salam [*Afghanistan*] [*ICAO location identifier*] (ICLI)	
OASM	Samangan [*Afghanistan*] [*ICAO location identifier*] (ICLI)	
OASN	Sheghnan [*Afghanistan*] [*ICAO location identifier*] (ICLI)	
OASP	Sare Pul [*Afghanistan*] [*ICAO location identifier*] (ICLI)	
OASR	Sabar [*Afghanistan*] [*ICAO location identifier*] (ICLI)	
OASR	Separate Motorized Medical Company (RU)	
OASS	Salang-I-Junubi [*Afghanistan*] [*ICAO location identifier*] (ICLI)	
OAST	Shur Tepa [*Afghanistan*] [*ICAO location identifier*] (ICLI)	
OASTh	Organismos Astikon Syngoinonion Thessalonikis [*Organization of Salonica City Communications*] (GC)	
OAT	Obus en Acier a Amorcage de Tete [*Military*] [*French*] (MTD)	
OAT	Omades Andimetopiseos Tarachon [*Riot Control Groups*] [*MAT*] [*See also*] (GC)	
OAT	Organisation Arabe du Travail [*Arab Labor Organization*] [*North African*]	
OAT	Organizacion Arabe del Trabajo [*Arab Labor Organization - ALO*] [*Spanish*]	
OAT	Osservatorio Astronomico di Trieste [*Trieste Astronomical Observatory*] [*Ministero della Pubblica Istruzione*] [*Research center*] [*Italy*] (EAS)	
OAT	Ouvrages d'Art et Travaux	
OAT	Sogervair/Transoceanic Aviation [*France*] [*ICAO designator*] (FAAC)	
OATB	Separate Motor Transport Battalion (RU)	
oatbo	Separate Technical Support Battalion for an Airfield (BU)	
OATD	Toorghondi [*Afghanistan*] [*ICAO location identifier*] (ICLI)	
OATG	Tashkurghan [*Afghanistan*] [*ICAO location identifier*] (ICLI)	
OATh	Organismos Apokhetevseos Thessalonikis [*Salonica Drainage Organization*] (GC)	
OATK	Kotal [*Afghanistan*] [*ICAO location identifier*] (ICLI)	
OATN	Tereen [*Afghanistan*] [*ICAO location identifier*] (ICLI)	
OATQ	Taluqan [*Afghanistan*] [*ICAO location identifier*] (ICLI)	
oatro	Separate Technical Support Company for an Airfield (BU)	
OATS	Terminal Automatic Telephone Exchange (RU)	
OATUU	Organisation of African Trade Union Unity [*Formerly, AATUF, ATUC*] [*See also OUSA Accra, Ghana*] (EAIO)	
OATUU	Organization of African Trade Union Unity [*Accra, Ghana*] (AF)	
OATW	Tewara [*Afghanistan*] [*ICAO location identifier*] (ICLI)	
OATZ	Tesak [*Afghanistan*] [*ICAO location identifier*] (ICLI)	
OAU	Okrug Pharmaceutical Administration (BU)	
OAU	Organization of African Unity	
OAU	Organization of Artisans Unity [*Mauritius*]	
OAU	Oriol Avia [*Russian Federation*] [*ICAO designator*] (FAAC)	
OAULC	OAU [*Organization of African Unity*] Liberation Committee [*Addis Ababa, Ethiopia*] (EAIO)	
OAUZ	Kunduz [*Afghanistan*] [*ICAO location identifier*] (ICLI)	
OAV	Oesterreichische Arbeitsgemeinschaft fuer Volksgesundheit [*Austrian Association for Public Health*] (SLS)	
OAV	Oesterreichischer Alpen Verein [*Austrian Alpine Club*]	
OAV	Okresni Akcni Vybor [*District Action Committee*] (CZ)	
OAV	Omni-Aviacao e Tecnologia Lda. [*Portugal*] [*ICAO designator*] (FAAC)	
OAV	Organization Autonome de la Vallee [*Autonomous Organization of the Valley*] [*Senegal*] (AF)	
oavtb	Separate Motor Transport Battalion (RU)	
OAW	Oesterreichische Akademie der Wissenschaften [*Austrian Academy of Science*] (SLS)	
OAWU	Wurtach [*Afghanistan*] [*ICAO location identifier*] (ICLI)	
OAWZ	Wazirabad [*Afghanistan*] [*ICAO location identifier*] (ICLI)	
OAX	Oaxaca [*Mexico*] [*Airport symbol*] (OAG)	
OAX	Operational Aviation Services - Australia [*ICAO designator*] (FAAC)	
OAYQ	Yangi Qala [*Afghanistan*] [*ICAO location identifier*] (ICLI)	
oaz	Oasis (RU)	
OAZ	Odessa Automobile Assembly Plant (RU)	
OAZB	Zebak [*Afghanistan*] [*ICAO location identifier*] (ICLI)	
OAZG	Zaranj [*Afghanistan*] [*ICAO location identifier*] (ICLI)	
OB	Besluit op de Omzetbelasting [*Benelux*] (BAS)	

OB.............. Common Base (RU)
ob.............. Concentration (RU)
ob.............. Obacz [*See*] (POL)
ob.............. Oben [*Above*] [*German*] (GCA)
Ob.............. Ober [*Waiter*] [*Colloquial*] [*German*]
OB.............. Oberbuergermeister [*Lord Mayor*] [*German*]
OB.............. Oberlerchner [*Joseph Oberlerchner Holzindustrie*] [*Austria*] [*ICAO aircraft manufacturer identifier*] (ICAO)
ob.............. Obispo [*Bishop*] [*Spanish*]
OB.............. Oblast Library (RU)
ob.............. Obligation [*French*] [*Business term*]
ob.............. Obra [*Work*] [*Portuguese*]
ob.............. Obra [*Work*] [*Spanish*]
ob.............. Obywatel [*Citizen*] (POL)
O-B............. Oerlikon-Buehrle [*Switzerland*]
OB............. Officiele Bekendmakingen, Uitgave van de Vereniging van Nederlandse Gemeenten [*Netherlands*] (BAS)
OB.............. Offshore Banking [*Australia*]
oB.............. Ohne Befund [*Without Findings*] [*Medicine*] [*German*] (EG)
OB.............. Oktanski Broj [*Octane Number*] [*Navy*] (YU)
OB.............. Olympiai Bajnoksag [*Olympic Championship*] (HU)
OB.............. Omzetbelastingen [*Benelux*] (BAS)
O/B............. Oorgebring [*Bring Forward*] [*Afrikaans*]
OB.............. Openbare Bibliotheek [*Netherlands*]
OB.............. Operational Base [*Navy*] (RU)
OB.............. Optometrists' Board [*Australian Capital Territory*]
OB.............. Organizacao de Base [*Primary Organization*] [*Brazil*] (LA)
OB.............. Organosi Bolsevikon [*Organization of Bolsheviks*] [*Greek*] (GC)
OB.............. Orgelbuechlein [*Little Organ Book*] [*Bach Music*]
OB.............. Orszagos Bekebizottsag [*National Peace Committee*] (HU)
OB.............. Ortsbatterie [*Local Battery*] [*German military - World War II*]
OB.............. Ossewabrandwag
OB.............. Osterreichischer Betriebssportverband [*Austria*] (EAIO)
OB.............. Osvetova Beseda [*Cultural Center*] (CZ)
OB.............. Owena Bank [*Nigeria*]
OB.............. OXFAM - Belgique [*Belgium*] (EAIO)
ob.............. Revolution (RU)
OB.............. Uniovular Twins (RU)
ob.............. United, Joint (BU)
OBA........... Office of Business Affairs [*Northern Territory, Australia*]
OBA........... Old Boys' Association (ML)
OBA........... Outward Bound Australia
OBAD........ Obadja [*Obadiah*] [*Afrikaans*]
OBAD........ Report of the Bulgarian Archeological Society (BU)
OBAE........ Office des Bois d'Afrique Equatoriale [*Equatorial Africa Forestry Office*] (AF)
OBAE........ Separate Bomber Squadron (RU)
OBAI......... Report of the Bulgarian Archeological Institute (BU)
OBAP........ Office Belge pour l'Accroissement de la Productivitie [*Belgian Productivity Improvement Office*] (PDAA)
OBAR........ Office Beninois de l'Amenagement Rural [*Development organization*] [*Porto Novo, Benin*]
OBAS........ Obchodni Akciova Spolecnost [*Joint-Stock Trading Company*] (CZ)
OBATO..... Separate Airfield Technical Support Battalion (RU)
obats.......... Separate Tank Truck Battalion (RU)
OBB.......... Burgas Okrug Library (BU)
Obb........... Oberbayern [*Upper Bavaria*] (WEN)
OBB.......... Oesterreichische Bundesbahnen [*Austrian Federal Railways*]
OBB.......... Orszagos Bali Bizottsag [*National Social Dancing Committee*] (HU)
OBBB........ Bahrain [*Bahrain*] [*ICAO location identifier*] (ICLI)
OBBF........ Front Hospital Base Section (BU)
OBBI......... Bahrain/International [*Bahrain*] [*ICAO location identifier*] (ICLI)
Obbl.......... Obbligato [*Essential*] [*Music*]
Obbmo....... Obbligatissimo [*Your Obedient Servant*] [*Italian*]
OBC.......... Obock [*Djibouti*] [*Airport symbol*] (OAG)
OBC.......... Oceania Basketball Confederation [*Australia*] (EA)
OBC.......... Oeuvre Belge du Cancer [*Belgium*] (SLS)
OBCE........ Office Belge du Commerce Exterieur [*Belgian Overseas Trade Office*] (GEA)
OB-Centar ... Obavestajni Centar [*Information Center*] [*Military*] (YU)
ob ch.......... Part by Volume (RU)
ob cit......... Obra Citada [*Portuguese*]
Obczak....... Obcansky Zakon [*Civil Law Code*] (CZ)
OBD.......... Obecne Prospesne Bytove Druzstvo [*General Apartment Cooperative*] (CZ)
obdm .... Separate Area Decontamination Battalion (BU)
obdm .... Separate Ground Decontamination Battalion (RU)
OBE.......... Oberste Bauleitung fuer Elektrifizierung [*Construction Headquarters for Electrification*] (EG)
OBE.......... Relative Biological Effectiveness
OBEA........ Office Belge de l'Economie et de l'Agriculture [*Belgium*] (BAS)
OBEA........ Office of Economic Analysis Based on Public Participation (RU)

OBECI....... Office Beninois de Cinema [*Benin Cinema Office*] (AF)
obed........... Obediente [*Obedient*] [*Portuguese*]
Obekoso..... Oblast Economic Conference (RU)
OBEMAP ... Office Beninois des Manutentions Portuaires [*Beninese Office of Port Management*] (AF)
Oberfl........ Oberflaeche [*Surface*] [*German*] (GCA)
Oberflaechenspann ... Oberflaechenspannung [*Surface Tension*] [*German*] (GCA)
oberflaechl ... Oberflaechlich [*Superficial*] [*German*] (GCA)
OBERST ... Oberstimme [*Upper Part*] [*Music*]
OBERW .... Oberwerk [*Upper Work*] [*Music*]
Obes.......... Oblast Economic Conference (RU)
OBESSU ... Organising Bureau of European School Student Unions (EAIO)
obevak....... Oblast Evacuation Station (RU)
obg........... Detour [*Railroads*] (RU)
Ob G .... Obergericht [*Court of Appeal*] [*German*] (DLA)
OBG.......... Oesterreichische Bodenkundliche Gesellschaft [*Austrian Soil Science Association*] (SLS)
Obh .... Oberhalb [*Above*] [*German*]
OBH.......... Oerlikon-Buehrle Holding AG [*Switzerland*] (ERC)
OBI........... Office du Baccalaureat International [*International Baccalaureate Office - IBO*] (EAIO)
OBI........... Organisation du Baccalaureat International [*International Baccalaureate Organisation - IBO*] (EAIO)
OBI........... Outillage pour la Batiment et l'Industrie [*Morocco*]
OBiDN ...... Osrodek Bibliografii i Dokumentacji Naukowej [*Center for Bibliography and Scientific Documentation*] (POL)
OBIG .... Oesterreichisches Bundesinstitut fuer Gesundheitswesen [*Austrian National Institute for Public Health*] [*Information service or system*] (IID)
obikn .... Ordinary, Ordinarily (BU)
obit .... Separate Antitank Battalion (RU)
OBIV .... Separate Engineer Troops Battalion (RU)
obj .... Objek [*Object*] [*Afrikaans*]
obj .... Objekti [*Object*] [*Finland*]
obj .... Objektief [*Objective*] [*Afrikaans*]
obj .... Objeto [*Portuguese*]
obj .... Objetosc [*Size, Volume*] (POL)
obk .... Combat Ship Squadron (RU)
OBK.......... Office des Bauxites de Kindia
OBK.......... Organisation pour l'Amenagement et la Mise en Valeur du Bassin de la Kagera
OBK.......... Organisation pour l'Amenagement et le Developpement du Bassin de la Riviere Kagera [*Organization for the Management and Development of the Kagera River Basin - KBO*] (EAIO)
OBKE........ Orszagos Banyaszati es Kohaszati Egyesulet [*National Association for Mining and Metallurgy*] (HU)
ob/khs........ Approach Trench Adapted for Defense [*Topography*] (RU)
OBKhS ...... Department for Combating the Embezzlement of Socialist Property and Speculation (RU)
OBKhSS.... Department for Combating the Embezzlement of Socialist Property and Speculation (RU)
obkhz......... Separate Chemical Attack Protection Battalion (BU)
obkhz......... Separate Chemical Defense Battalion (RU)
OBKI .... Orszagos Balneologiai Kutato Intezet [*National Research Institute of Balneology*] (HU)
obl .... Cover (RU)
Obl .... Oblast [*Region*] [*Commonwealth of Independent States*] (EECI)
OBL .... Oblast [*Governmental subdivision in USSR corresponding to a province or state*]
obl .... Oblong [*Netherlands*]
obl .... Oblong [*French*]
obl .... Oblungo [*Oblong*] [*Publishing*] [*Italian*]
Oblarkhiv .. Oblast Archives Administration (RU)
Oblastop .... Oblast Fuel Administration (RU)
Oblbytpromsoyuz ... Oblast Producers' Union for Personal Services to the Population (RU)
obldortrans ... Oblast Administration of Highways, Dirt Roads, Trucking, and Carting (RU)
obldrevmebel'prom ... Oblast Administration of the Furniture and Woodworking Industry (RU)
oblekoso ..... Oblast Economic Conference (RU)
Oblfizkul't ... Oblast Committee for Physical Culture and Sport (RU)
Oblfo .... Oblast Finance Department (RU)
oblFU .... Oblast Finance Administration (RU)
oblgalkhimpromsoyuz ... Oblast Producers' Union of the Notions and Chemical Industries (RU)
Oblgalpromsoyuz ... Oblast Notions Producers' Union (RU)
Oblgiz .... Oblast State Publishing House (RU)
Oblgosstrakh ... Oblast Administration of State Insurance (RU)
oblig .... Obligation [*French*]
oblIUU....... Oblast Institute for the Advanced Training of Teachers (RU)
oblkhimpromsoyuz ... Oblast Producers' Union of the Chemical Industry (RU)
oblknigotorg ... Oblast Book Trade Office (RU)

Oblkomkhoz ... Oblast Department of Municipal Services   (RU)

oblkonupr... Oblast Administration of Horse Breeding   (RU)

Oblkoopinsoyuz ... Oblast Disabled Persons' Cooperative Union   (RU)

Oblkozhpromsoyuz ... Oblast Leather Producers' Union   (RU)

Obl k-t....... Oblast Committee   (BU)

Obllegprom ... Oblast Administration of Light Industry   (RU)

obllit........... Oblast Administration for the Protection of Military and State Secrets in the Press   (RU)

Oblmel'trest ... Oblast Rural Flour-Milling Trust   (RU)

oblmestprom ... Oblast Administration of Local Industry   (RU)

oblmesttopprom ... Oblast Administration of Local and Fuel Industries   (RU)

Oblmostorg ... Moscow Oblast Wholesale and Retail Trade Establishment   (RU)

Oblnitoles .. Oblast Scientific, Engineering, and Technical Society of the Sawmilling Industry   (RU)

ObLO........ Obcinski Ljudski Odbor [*Municipal People's Committee*]   (YU)

OBLO........ Oblastni Ljudski Odbor [*Regional People's Committee*]   (YU)

oblo............. Separate Light Flame-Thrower Battalion   (RU)

oblONO..... Oblast Department of Public Education   (RU)

oblorgnabor ... Oblast Department for Resettlement and Organized Recruitment of Workers   (RU)

oblosvod ..... Oblast Branch of the Society for Furthering the Development of Water Transportation and for the Safeguarding of Human Lives on Waterways   (RU)

oblpishcheprom ... Oblast Department of the Food Industry   (RU)

Oblplan...... Oblast Planning Commission   (RU)

oblpoligrafizdat ... Department of Publishing Houses and the Printing Industry of the Administration of Culture of an Oblispolkom   (RU)

oblpotrebsoyuz ... Oblast Union of Consumers' Societies   (RU)

oblprofsovet ... Oblast Council of Trade Unions   (RU)

oblpromstrom ... Oblast Administration of the Building Materials Industry   (RU)

oblpromtekhsnab ... Oblast Office of Materials and Equipment Supply of an Oblpromsovet   (RU)

oblproyekt ... Oblast Planning Office   (RU)

oblproyekt ... Planning Institute of an Oblispolkom   (RU)

oblRATAU ... Oblast Branch of the Ukrainian News Agency   (RU)

Oblrechtrans ... Oblast Administration for Transportation Development of Small Rivers   (RU)

Oblrybolovpotrebsoyuz ... Oblast Union of Fishermen's Cooperatives   (RU)

Oblsel'stroy ... Oblast Administration for Rural and Kolkhoz Construction   (RU)

oblSES....... Oblast Sanitary and Epidemiological Station   (RU)

Oblshveypromsoyuz ... Oblast Garment Producers' Union   (RU)

OblSNKh... Oblast Council of the National Economy   (RU)

Oblsobes .... Oblast Department of Social Security   (RU)

oblsortsemovoshch ... Oblast Office for the Procurement and Marketing of High-Quality Vegetable Seeds   (RU)

oblsovprof .. Oblast Council of Trade Unions   (RU)

oblsportsoyuz ... Oblast Council of the Union of Sports Societies and Organizations   (RU)

Oblstrompromsoyuz ... Oblast Producers' Cooperative Union for the Manufacture of Building Materials   (RU)

Oblstromtrest ... Oblast Trust of the Building Materials Industry   (RU)

Oblt........... Oberleutnant [*Lieutenant*] [*German*]

oblTEK ...... Oblast Transportation and Forwarding Office   (RU)

Obltekstil'promsoyuz ... Oblast Textile Producers' Cooperative Union   (RU)

obltekstil'shveypromsoyuz ... Oblast Producers' Union of the Textile and Garment Industries   (RU)

oblTEU ...... Oblast Tourist and Excursions Administration   (RU)

obltop.......... Oblast Administration of the Fuel Industry   (RU)

Obltrikotazhpromsoyuz ... Oblast Knit Goods Producers' Union   (RU)

obl ts.......... Oblast Center   (RU)

oblun .... Oblungo [*Oblong*] [*Publishing*] [*Italian*]

OBLUNKhU ... Oblast Administration of the Statistical Survey of the National Economy   (RU)

oblurs .... Oblast Administration of Workers' Supply   (RU)

oblUSKh.... Oblast Administration of Agriculture   (RU)

OblV .... Oblastni Velitelstvi [*Regional Headquarters (of the National Security Corps)*]   (CZ)

oblvodkhoz ... Oblast Administration of Water Management   (RU)

oblvoyenkomat ... Oblast Military Commissariat   (RU)

OblVTEK .. Oblast Medical Commission for Determination of Disability   (RU)

oblzags .... Oblast Department of the Civil Registry   (RU)

Oblzdrav .... Oblast Department of Public Health   (RU)

oblzo.......... Oblast Land Department   (RU)

Oblzoovetsnab ... Oblast Veterinary Technical Supply Office   (RU)

oblzu........... Oblast Land Administration   (RU)

OBM.......... Morobe [*Papua New Guinea*] [*Airport symbol*]   (OAG)

Obm .... Obmann [*German*]

OBM.......... Office Bugesera-Mayaga

OBM.......... Oxygen-Bottom Maxhutte   (PDAA)

ob/min........ Revolutions per Minute   (BU)

OBMP .... Separate Marine Battalion   (RU)

OBN.......... Department of Biological Sciences (of the Academy of Sciences, USSR)   (RU)

OBN.......... Osrodek Badan Naukowych [*Scientific Research Center*]   (POL)

obn .... Published, Made Public   (BU)

OBNI........ Orszagos Bor- es Nemikortani Intezet [*National Institute for Dermatology and Venereal Diseases*]   (HU)

OBNYH..... Orszagos Bunugyi Nyilvantarto Hivatal [*National Office of Criminal Records*]   (HU)

OB-O .... Obavestajno Odeljenje [*Information Department*] [*Military*]   (YU)

OBO.......... Obihiro [*Japan*] [*Airport symbol*]   (OAG)

OBO.......... Oddzial Budowy Osiedli [*Branch of Settlement Construction*]   (POL)

OBO.......... Oklopni Borbeni Odredi [*Armored Combat Detachments*]   (YU)

obo............. Separate Maintenance Battalion   (BU)

obo............. Separate Service Battalion   (RU)

Oborongiz .. State Scientific and Technical Publishing House of Literature on Defense   (RU)

obp .... Ammunition Supply Section   (RU)

OBP .... Combat Training Section   (RU)

OBP .... Ochrana Bezpecnosti Praca [*Labor Safety*]   (CZ)

OBP .... Reciprocal Bearing   (RU)

OBP .... Single Sideband   (RU)

OBP .... Total Lateral Displacement [*Navy*]   (RU)

OBPI .... Organisasi Buruh Perkebunan Indonesia [*Estate Workers' Union of Indonesia*]

obpo........... Obispo [*Bishop*] [*Spanish*]

OBQ .... Optometrists' Board of Queensland

obr............. Image, Face, Portrait   (BU)

obr .... Model [*Accompanied by year*]   (RU)

Obr............. Obavestenje Broj [*Information Number*]   (YU)

obr .... Obrot [*Revolution*] [*Poland*]

OBr .... Oklopna Brigada [*Armored Brigade*]   (YU)

Obr............. Originalbroschur [*Original Brochure Binding*] [*Publishing*] [*German*]

OBR.......... Overseas Business Reports

OBR .... Ruse Okrug Library   (BU)

obrab .... Revised   (BU)

obrabot .... Processed, Worked, Machined   (RU)

OBRET...... Old Breton [*Language, etc.*]

OBRIT....... Old British [*Language, etc.*]

obr/min ...... Obrotow na Minute [*Revolutions per Minute*] [*Poland*]

obrmo......... Obrigadissimo [*Most Obliged*] [*Portuguese*]

obro .... Obrigado [*Obliged*] [*Portuguese*]

Obro........... Originalbroschur [*Original Brochure Binding*] [*Publishing*] [*German*]

obro........... Outubro [*October*] [*Portuguese*]   (GPO)

obrs .... Separate Signal Brigade   (RU)

OBS .... Aubenas [*France*] [*Airport symbol*]   (OAG)

Obs............ Note d'Observations [*Benelux*]   (BAS)

obs............. Observacao [*Observation*] [*Portuguese*]

obs............. Observatie [*Benelux*]   (BAS)

Obs............ Observations [*French*]   (FLAF)

obs............. Observer [*Observe*] [*Denmark*]   (GPO)

obs............. Observera [*Observe*] [*Sweden*]   (GPO)

OBS .... Osterreichische Bundes Sportorganisation [*Austria*]   (EAIO)

OBS .... Outward-Bound Schools   (ML)

OBS .... Separate Signal Battalion   (RU)

OBSA .... Joint Standardization Office of the Aircraft Industry (TsAGI)   (RU)

OBSA .... Organizacion Boliviana de Sanidad Agropecuaria [*Bolivia*]   (LAA)

observ......... Observatory   (RU)

ObservContr ... Observations Contraires [*French*]   (FLAF)

obshch........ General, Common, Aggregate   (RU)

obshchedostup ... Moderately Priced, Open to All, Generally Accessible   (RU)

obshchepit ... Public Eating Establishment   (RU)

obshch titl ... General Title Page, Main Title Page   (RU)

obshtestv.... Social   (BU)

Obshtpodem ... Obshtestven Podem [*Social Uplift*] [*A periodical*]   (BU)

OBSI......... Organisasi Buruh Seluruh Indonesia [*Plantation Workers' Union of Indonesia*]

Obsre .... Observatoire [*Observatory*] [*Military map abbreviation World War I*] [*French*]   (MTD)

OBSS........ Office Beninois de Securite Sociale [*Benin Office of Social Security*]   (AF)

Obst .... Oberst [*German*]

Obstal' .... Obukhov Steel Foundry   (RU)

Obstlt .... Oberstleutnant [*Lieutenant Colonel*] [*German*]

OBSV........ Austrian Archery Association   (EAIO)

OBT .... One Billion Trees Program [*Australia*]

OBTI......... Association of Technical Publishing Houses   (RU)

OBTI......... Oblast Office of Technical Information   (RU)

OBTI......... Office of Technical Information Based on Public Participation   (RU)

OBTI......... Specialized Office of Technical Information   (RU)

OBTO .... Separate Armored Detachment   (RU)

obtrr .... Separate Loading-Unloading Operations Battalion   (BU)

OBU .... Oblastni Telefonni Ustredna [*Regional Telephone Exchange*] (CZ)

OBU .... Obvodny Bansky Urad [*District Mining Office*]   (CZ)

obuch .... Teaching, Instruction, Training   (RU)

OBulg .... Old Bulgarian [*Language*]   (BARN)

OBUV .... Operative Bakers' Union of Victoria [*Australia*]

obv .... De Ouderlijke Boedelverdeling [*Benelux*]   (BAS)

OBV .... Department for Agricultural Pest Control   (RU)

Obv .... Oberbauvorschriften [*Track Superstructure Regulations*]   (EG)

OBV .... Okresni Branny Vybor [*District Defense Committee*]   (CZ)

OBV .... Osterreichischer Badminton Verband [*Austria*]   (EAIO)

obv .... Separate Convalescent Battalion   (RU)

OBV .... Varna Okrug Library   (BU)

ob v .... Volumetric Weight   (RU)

OBVNO ..... Separate Battalion of People's Militia   (RU)

ob-vo .... Society, Company   (RU)

ObVS .... Obvodni Vybor Svazu [*Area Trade Union Committee*]   (CZ)

OBW .... Oberwerk [*Upper Work*] [*Music*]

obw .... Obwieszczenie [*Proclamation*]   (POL)

obw .... Obwoluta [*Book Jacket*]   (POL)

obwol .... Obwoluta [*Book Jacket*] [*Poland*]

obyasn .... Explained, Explanatory   (BU)

ob yasn .... Explanation   (RU)

ob yavl .... Announcement, Declaration   (RU)

ob yemn ...... Volume, Volumetric   (RU)

ob yemnch ... Part by Volume   (RU)

obyemnotsentrir ... Body-Centered   (RU)

ObZ .... Obranne Zpravodajstvi [*Counterintelligence*]   (CZ)

obz .... Separate Smokescreen Battalion   (BU)

OBZAMINI ... Ministerstvo Zahranicniho Obchodu [*Ministry of Foreign Trade (Cable address)*]   (CZ)

Oc .... Ocean [*Ocean*] [*Poland*]

OC .... Office Central pour la Cooperation Industrielle Internationale

oc .... Oktanove Cislo [*Octane Number*]   (CZ)

OC .... Ondes Courtes [*French*]

OC .... Ordnance Corps   (ML)

OC .... Outsiders Club   (EAIO)

OCA .... Aeroservicios Carabobo CA (ASERCA) [*Venzuela*] [*ICAO designator*]   (FAAC)

OCA .... Austrian Olympic Committee   (EAIO)

OCA .... Office de Commercialisation Agricole [*Senegal*]

OCA .... Office de Commercialisation Agricole [*Agricultural Marketing Bureau*] [*Guinea*]   (AF)

OCA .... Office of the Community Advocate [*Australian Capital Territory*]

OCA .... Oil Company of Australia No Liability   (ADA)

OCA .... Olympic Council of Asia [*Hawalli, Kuwait*]   (EAIO)

OCA .... Operational Control Authority [*NATO*]

OCA .... Operation Crossroads Africa

OCA .... Organisation Combat Anarchiste [*Anarchist Combat Organization*] [*France*] [*Political party*]   (PPW)

OCA .... Organizacao Cultural dos Angolanos

OCA .... Organizacao dos Comunistas de Angola

OCA .... Organizacion de Cooperativas Americanas [*Organization of American Cooperatives*]   (LA)

OCA .... Organizacion de las Cooperativas de America [*Organization of the Cooperatives of America - OCA*]   (EAIO)

OCAB .... Overseas Correspondents' Association Bangladesh   (FEA)

OCABE ...... Office de Coordination Atomique de Belgique [*Belgian Office of Atomic Coordination*]   (WER)

OCAD .... Office de Commercialisation Agricole du Dahomey

OCAD .... Oficiul Central de Aprovizionare si Desfacere [*Central Office for Supply and Sales*]   (RO)

OCAL .... Organization of Communist Action in Lebanon   (PD)

OCAL .... Overseas Containers Australia Ltd.   (DS)

OCAM .... Organisation Commune Africaine et Mauricienne [*African and Mauritian Common Organization*] [*Formerly, Organisation Commune Africaine et Malgache*]

OCAM .... Organisation de Cooperation Africaine et Malgache   (FLAF)

OCAM .... Organizacion Comun Africana y Mauriciana [*African-Mauritian Common Organization*] [*Spanish*]

OCAMM ... Organisation Commune Africaine, Malgache, et Mauricienne [*African, Malagasy, and Mauritian Common Organization*] [*Formerly, Organisation Commune Africaine et Malgache Later, OCAM*]

OCAPAM ... Office Central Africain de Productions Agronomiques et Medicinales

OCARM .... Order of Brothers of the Blessed Virgin Mary of Mount Carmel [*Rome, Italy*]   (EAIO)

OCAS .... Office de Commercialisation Agricole du Senegal [*Agricultural Marketing Office of Senegal*]   (AF)

OCAS .... Organization of Central American States [*See also ODECA*] [*San Salvador, El Salvador*]   (EAIO)

OCASA ...... Overseas Chinese Association of South Australia

OCATOUR ... Office National Centrafricain du Tourisme   (EY)

OCAU .... Office de Cooperation et d'Accueil Universitaire [*France*]

OCB .... Office Congolais des Bois [*Congolese Timber Office*]   (GEA)

OCB .... Olympic Committee of Bolivia   (EAIO)

OCB .... Organisation Camerounaise de la Banane [*Cameroon Banana Organization*]

OCBC .... Overseas Chinese Banking Corporation [*Singapore*]

OCBN .... Organisation Commune Benin-Niger des Chemins de Fer et des Transports [*Joint Benin-Niger Railroad and Transport Organization*]   (AF)

OCBV .... Office Communautaire du Betail et de la Viande [*Community Livestock and Meat Office*]   (AF)

OCC .... Coca [*Ecuador*] [*Airport symbol*]   (OAG)

occ .... Occasion [*Bargain*] [*French*]

OCC .... Occasional Care Campaign [*Australia*]

OCC .... Octagon Car Club [*Later, MOCC*]   (EAIO)

OCC .... Office Commercial Camerounais

OCC .... Office du Cafe et du Cacao [*Congolese coffee and cocoa marketing board*]

OCC .... Oficina de Circulacion Certificada [*Colombia*]   (COL)

OCC .... Olympic Committee of Czechoslovakia   (EAIO)

OCC .... Omuna Construction Co. Ltd. [*Nigeria*]

OCC .... Open Channel Cooperative

OCC .... Organic Consultative Committee [*Victoria, Australia*]

OCC .... Organisation Clandestine du Continent [*Algeria*]

OCC .... Organisation Combat Communiste [*Communist Combat Organization*] [*France*] [*Political party*]   (PPW)

OCC .... Organisation de Cooperation Commerciale [*France*]   (FLAF)

OCCA .... Fundacion Organizacion Civica Colombiana para la Alfabetizacion [*Colombia*]   (DSCA)

OCCA .... Oil and Colour Chemists' Association, Australia

OCCAA ..... Oil and Colour Chemists' Association, Australia   (ADA)

OCCASP ... Oficina de Cooperacion Costarricense Americana de Salud Publica [*Costa Rica*]   (LAA)

OCCE .... Office Congolais du Commerce Exterieur

OCCEDCA ... Organization for Co-Ordination in Control of Endemic Diseases in Central Africa   (EA)

OCCGE ..... Organisation de Coordination et de Cooperation pour la Lutte Contre les Grandes Endemies [*Organization for Co-Ordination and Co-Operation in the Control of Major Endemic Diseases*]   (EAIO)

OCCGE ..... Organisation de Coordination et de Cooperation pour la Lutte Contre les Grandes Endemies en Afrique de l'Ouest [*Organization for Coordination and Cooperation in the Control of Major Endemic Diseases in West Africa*] [*Burkina Faso*] [*Research center*]   (AF)

OCCGEAC ... Organisation de Coordination et de Cooperation Contre les Grandes Endemies en Afrique Centrale

occh .... Occhiello [*Half-Title Page*] [*Publishing*] [*Italian*]

OCCH .... Office Central de Credit Hypothecaire [*Benelux*]   (BAS)

OCCI .... Officer in Charge - Criminal Investigation   (ML)

OCCL .... Office Central des Contigents et Licences [*Benelux*]   (BAS)

OCCP .... Office of the Chief Commissioner of Police [*Victoria, Australia*]

OCCR .... Office Central de Chauffe Rationelle

OCD .... Office de Cooperation au Developpement [*Office of Cooperation in Developmental Activity*] [*Belgium*]   (AF)

OCD .... Olympic Committee of Denmark   (EAIO)

OCDE .... Organisation de Cooperation et de Developpement Economiques [*Organization for Economic Cooperation and Development - OECD*] [*France*]   (EAIO)

OCDE .... Organizacao de Cooperacao e Desenvolvimento Economico [*Organization for Economic Cooperation and Development - OECD*] [*Portuguese*]   (WER)

OCDE .... Organizacion de Cooperacion y Desarrollo Economicos [*Organization for Economic Cooperation and Development - OECD*] [*Spain*]   (MSC)

OCDN .... Organisation Commune Dahomey-Niger des Chemins de Fer et des Transports

OCDS .... Secular Order of Discalced Carmelites [*Rome, Italy*]   (EAIO)

OCE .... Helicocean [*France*] [*ICAO designator*]   (FAAC)

OCE .... Odessa Commodity Exchange [*Ukraine*]   (EY)

OCE .... Office de Commercialisation et d'Exportation [*Morocco*]

OCE .... Office de Controle et d'Exportation [*Control and Export Office*] [*Morocco*]   (AF)

OCE .... Officer Commanding Exercises [*Military*]

OCEAC ..... Organisation de Coordination pour la Lutte Contre les Endemies en Afrique Centrale [*Organization for Co-Ordination in Control of Endemic Diseases in Central Africa - OCCEDCA*]   (EAIO)

OCEAN ..... Organisation de la Communaute Europeenne des Avitailleurs des Navires [*Ship Suppliers' Organization of the European Community - SSOEC*] [*Hague, Netherlands*]   (EAIO)

OCEANLANT ... Ocean Subarea (Atlantic) [*NATO*]   (NATG)

OCE-BR .... Organizacion Comunista de Espana - Bandera Roja [*Communist Organization of Spain - Red Flag*]   (WER)

OCEC .... Office Central des Etudes Commerciales [*France*]   (FLAF)

OCEC .... Office of the Commissioner for Employees Compensation [*Australia*]
OCEL .... Overseas Container Europe Ltd. (DS)
OCEN .... Oce-Van der Grinten NV [*Netherlands*] [*NASDAQ symbol*]
OCEO .... Office of the Commissioner for Equal Opportunity [*Australia*]
OCEP .... Oficina Central de Estudios y Programas (del Ministerio de Hacienda) [*Peru*] (LAA)
OCEPA ...... Oficina Central de Estadisticas y Pronosticos Agricolas [*Santiago, Chile*] (LAA)
OCEPA ...... Organizacion Comercial Ecuatoriana de Productos Artesanales [*Ecuador*] (LAA)
OCEPLAN ... Oficina Central de Planificacion [*Central Planning Office*] [*Chile*]
O CF .... Office Central des Fournitures [*Benelux*] (BAS)
OCF .... Oficiul Central Farmaceutic [*Central Pharmaceutical Office*] (RO)
OCF .... Ozenji Critical Facility [*Nuclear reactor*] [*Japan*]
OCFA .... Overseas Christian Fellowship Australia
OCFL .... Office Congolaise des Chemins de Fer des Grands Lacs
OCFLN ...... Organisation Civile du Front de Liberation Nationale [*Algeria*]
OCF-ML ... Organisation Communiste de France - Marxiste-Leniniste [*Communist Organization of France - Marxist-Leninist*] (PPW)
OCFT .... Office du Chemin de Fer Transcamerounais
OCG .... Oesterreichische Computer Gesellschaft [*Austrian Computer Association*] (SLS)
OCG .... Ostry Casovy Granat [*Time Fuse Grenade*] (CZ)
OCGE .... Oficina para la Cooperacion con Guinea Ecuatorial (EY)
OCGM .... Office of Cabinet and Government Management [*Australia*]
OCh .... Ink Oscillograph (RU)
OCh .... Octane Number (RU)
OCH .... Office Congolais de l'Habitat [*Congolese Housing Office*] (AF)
och .... Very, Very Much, Greatly (RU)
ochishch .... Purified, Cleaned, Refined (RU)
OChK .... Detachable Wing Sections (RU)
OChM .... Relative Frequency Modulation (RU)
OChS .... General Libraries Association (BU)
OChS .... Okoliya Library Council (BU)
OChS .... Okrug Library Council (BU)
OChT .... Octane Number of Fuel (RU)
OChT .... Relative Frequency Telegraphy (RU)
OChZ .... Orel Watchmaking Plant (RU)
OChZ .... Ostravske Chemicke Zavody [*Ostrava Chemical Plants*] (CZ)
OChZ .... Public Reading Room (RU)
OCI .... Integrated Revolutionary Organizations [*Cuba*] (PPW)
OCI .... Office of Criminal Investigation (ML)
OCI .... Oficina Central de Informacion [*Central Information Office*] [*Venezuela*] (LA)
OCI .... Oficina Central de Informacion [*Central Information Office*] [*Peru*] (LA)
OCI .... Olympic Committee of Indonesia (EAIO)
OCI .... Organisation Communiste Internationaliste [*Internationalist Communist Organization*] [*France*] [*Political party*] (PPW)
OCI .... Organisation de la Conference Islamique [*Organization of the Islamic Conference - OIC*] [*Jeddah, Saudi Arabia*] (EAIO)
OCI .... Organisation pour la Cooperation Industrielle [*Industrial Cooperation Organization*] [*Algeria*] (AF)
OCI .... Organisme de Cooperation Industrielle
OCIBEC .... Office de Commerce et de l'Industrie de la Belgique et du Congo
OCIBU ...... Office des Cultures Industrielles du Burundi [*Burundi Industrial Crops Office*] [*Bujumbura*] (AF)
OCIC .... Office Cherifien Interprofessionnel des Cereales [*Morocco*]
OCIC .... Organisation Catholique Internationale du Cinema et de l'Audiovisuel [*International Catholic Organization for Cinema and Audiovisual*] (EAIO)
OCIEP ...... Office of the Commissioners of Inquiry for Environment and Planning [*Australia*]
OCIMF ...... Oil Companies International Marine Forum [*British*] (EAIO)
OCINAM .. Office Cinematographique National du Mali
OCIP .... Oficina Central de Informacion de Personas [*Missing Persons Information Center*] [*Uruguay*] (LA)
OCIP .... Organisme Commun des Institutions de Prevoyance [*Algeria*]
OCIPE .... Office Catholique d'Information sur les Problemes Europeens [*Catholic European Study and Information Center*] [*Belgium*] (IRC)
OCIR .... Office des Cultures Industrielles du Rwanda [*Rwandan Industrial Crops Office*] (AF)
OCIRU ...... Office des Cafes Indigenes du Ruanda et Burundi
OCIRU ...... Office des Cultures Industrielles du Ruanda-Urundi
OCI-TNO ... Organisch Chemisch Instituut, Nederlands Centrale Organisatie voor Toegepast-Natuurwetenschappelijk Onderzoek [*Institute for Organic Chemistry, Netherlands Central Organization for Applied Natural Scientific Research*] (ARC)
OCJ .... Ocho Rios [*Jamaica*] [*Airport symbol*] (OAG)

OCL .... Organizatia Comerciala Locala [*Local Trade Organization*] (RO)
OCL .... Over-Night Cargo Ltd. [*Nigeria*] [*ICAO designator*] (FAAC)
OCL .... Overseas Containers Limited [*Australia*] (ADA)
OCLAE ...... Organizacion Continental Latinoamericana de Estudiantes [*Latin American Continental Students' Organization*] (EAIO)
OCLALAV ... Organisation Commune de Lutte Antiacridienne et de Lutte Antiaviaire [*Joint Organization for the Control of Locusts and the Fowl Plague*] [*OCLAV*] [*Senegal*] [*Formerly,*] (AF)
OCLAV ..... Organisation Commune de Lutte Antiaviaire [*Joint Antiaviarian Organization*] [*OCLALAV*] [*Later,*]
OCLC .... Organizacion Comunista "Lucha de Clases" [*"Class Struggle" Communist Organization*] [*Spanish*] (WER)
OCLEAC ... Organisation de Coordination pour la Lutte Contre les Endemies en Afrique Centrale [*Organization for Coordination in Control of Endemic Diseases in Central Africa*] [*Use OCEAC*] (AF)
OCLPP ...... Oficiul pentru Construirea de Locuinte Proprietate Personala [*Office for the Construction of Privately Owned Housing*] (RO)
OCM .... Office des Changes Marocaines
OCM .... Office of Country Marketing [*Department of Commerce*] (IMH)
OCM .... Oficiul de Control al Marfurilor [*Office for the Control of Goods*] (RO)
OCM .... Organisation Civile et Militaire
OCMA .... Oil Companies' Materials Association [*London*]
OCMAD ..... Organizatia Cooperativei Mestesugaresti de Aprovizionare si Desfacere [*Artisan Cooperative Organization for Supply and Sales*] (RO)
OCMB .... Officer in Charge - Marine Branch (ML)
OCMC .... Office Congolais des Materiaux de Construction [*Construction agency*] [*Congo*]
OCMI .... Organisation Consultative Maritime Intergouvernementale [*France*] (FLAF)
OCMI .... Organizacion Consultiva Maritima Intergubernamental [*Intergovernmental Maritime Consultative Organization*] [*Use IMCO*] [*Spanish*] (LA)
OCM-LP ... Organizacao Comunista Marxista-Leninista Portuguesa [*Portuguese Communist Organization, Marxist-Leninist*] [*Political party*] (PPE)
OCMLR .... Organisation Communiste Marxiste-Leniniste de la Reunion [*Reunionese Communist Organization, Marxist-Leninist*] [*Political party*] (PPW)
OCN .... Oceanair-Transportes Aereos Regional SA [*Portugal*] [*ICAO designator*] (FAAC)
OCN .... Organizacion Contrasubversiva Nacional [*National Counter-Subversive Organization*] [*Spanish*] (WER)
OCNL .... Okonosco Co. (Nigeria) Ltd.
OCNSW .... Outdoor Club of New South Wales [*Australia*]
OCNZ .... Orchid Council of New Zealand (EAIO)
OCO .... Office Congolais de l'Okoume
OCO .... Office of Civil Operations [*Vietnam*]
OCO .... Old Cornish [*Language, etc.*]
OCOA .... Organismo Coordinador de Operaciones Antisubversivas [*Counter-Subversive Operations Coordinating Agency*] [*Uruguay*] (LA)
OCOD .... Officer Commanding Ordnance Directorate (ML)
OCOG .... Organizing Committees of the Olympic Games (OLYM)
OCOM ...... Oficina Central de Organizacion y Metodos [*Santiago, Chile*] (LAA)
OCORA ..... Office de Cooperation Radiophonique [*Office of Radio Cooperation*] [*French*] (AF)
OCOT .... Oficiul de Cadastru si Organizarea Teritoriului [*Office for Cadaster and Territorial Organization*] (RO)
OCP .... Office Cherifien des Phosphates [*Moroccan Phosphates Office*] [*Casablanca*] (AF)
OCP .... Oncocarciasis Control Programme
OCP .... Organisation Commerciale de la Production Bananiere de la Cote-D'Ivoire
OCP .... Organisation de Controle des Pollutions
OCP .... Organizacion Comunista Proletaria [*Proletarian Communist Organization*] [*Mexico*] (LA)
OCPC .... Officer in Charge of Police Circle (ML)
OCPE .... Office Communautaire de Promotion des Echanges [*Community Trade Promotion Office*] (AF)
OCPED ..... Office de Commercialisation du Poisson d'Eau Douce [*Freshwater Fish Marketing Corp. - FFMC*]
OCPHV ..... Office de Commercialisation des Produits de Haute Volta [*Marketing Office for Products of Upper Volta*] (AF)
OCPI .... Office Central de la Presse Illustree [*Illustrated Press Central Office*] [*French*] (AF)
OCPL .... Overseas Containers Pacific Ltd. (DS)
OCPT .... Office Congolais des Postes et Telecommunications
OCR .... Organisation des Chantiers de la Revolution [*Organization of Work Camps of the Revolution*] [*Guinea*] (AF)

OCR.......... Organisation for the Collaboration of Railways [*See also OSShD*] [*Warsaw, Poland*] (EAIO)
OCRA........ Organisation Clandestine de la Revolution Algerienne [*Clandestine Organization of the Algerian Revolution*] (AF)
OCRAP...... Oficina Central de Racionalizacion de la Administracion Publica [*Chile*] (LAA)
OCRBI....... Organization for Cooperation in the Roller Bearings Industry [*Warsaw, Poland*] (EAIO)
OCRCWA ... Outcare Civil Rehabilitation Council of Western Australia
OCRS........ Organisation Commune des Regions Sahariennes [*Common Organization of the Saharan Regions*]
OCS .... O'Connor Christian School [*Australia*]
OCS .... Office de la Canne et du Sucre [*Cane and Sugar Office*] [*Malagasy*] (AF)
OCS .... Office of the Chief Scientist
OCS .... Officer in Charge - Station (ML)
OCS .... Offshore Constitutional Settlement [*Australia*]
OCS .... Old Church Slavonic [*Language, etc.*]
OCS .... Ordine Civile di Savoia [*Decoration*] [*Italian*]
OCS .... Organe de Controle des Stupefiants [*Narcotic Drug Control Supervision*] [*French*]
OCS .... Organisme de Cooperation Scientifique [*Organization for Scientific Cooperation*] [*Algerian, French*] (AF)
OCS .... Oriental Ceramic Society (EA)
OCS .... Overseas Communication Service [*India*] (PDAA)
OCSA .... Orchid Society of South Australia
OCSB........ Officer in Charge - Special Branch (ML)
OCSE........ Organizzazione di Cooperazione e di Sviluppo Economico [*Organization for Economic Cooperation and Development*] [*Use OECD*] [*Italian*] (WER)
OCSMA .... Organisme Central du Service Militaire Adapte
OCSS .... Officer in Charge - Secret Societies (ML)
oct.............. October [*October*] [*Netherlands*] (GPO)
oct.............. Octobre [*October*] [*French*]
oct.............. Octubre [*October*] [*Spanish*]
OCT.......... Office de Cooperation du Travail [*Office of Labor Cooperation*] [*Zaire*] (AF)
OCT.......... Office du Commerce de Tunisie [*Tunisian Trade Office*] (AF)
OCT.......... Okresni Cirkevni Tajemnik [*District Church Secretary*] (CZ)
OCT.......... Organisation Communiste des Travailleurs [*Communist Organization of Workers*] [*France*] [*Political party*] (PPW)
octbre .... Octobre [*October*] [*French*]
Octbre .... Octubre [*October*] [*Spanish*]
octe............. Octubre [*October*] [*Spanish*]
OCTI .... Office Central des Transports Internationaux par Chemins de Fer [*Central Office for International Railway Transport*] (EAIO)
OCTK .... Office Central du Travail au Katanga
OCTNU..... Oficina de Cooperacion Tecnica de las Naciones Unidas [*United Nations Technical Cooperation Office*] (LA)
OCTRA ..... Office du Chemin de Fer Transgabonais [*Trans-Gabonese Railroad Office*] (AF)
OCTS........ Comite de Coordination des Telecommunications par Satellites [*Switzerland*] (WGAO)
OCTU .... Comite de Coordination des Telecommunications [*UNET*] (WGAO)
octup.......... Octuplus [*Eightfold*] [*Latin*] (MAE)
OCU.......... Odour Control Unit [*Sydney Water Board*] [*Australia*]
OCU.......... Organizacion de Consumidores y Usuarios [*Organization of Consumers and Users*] [*Spanish*] (WER)
OCV.......... Ocana [*Colombia*] [*Airport symbol*] (OAG)
OCV.......... Office des Cultures Vivrieres
OCV.......... Ordre des Chevaliers du Verseau [*Knights of Aquarius Order*] (EAIO)
OCV.......... Orszagos Cirkusz Vallalat [*National Circus Enterprise*] (HU)
OCWCIB... Organizing Committee of the World Congress on Implantology and Bio-Materials [*See also COCMIB*] [*Rouen, France*] (EAIO)
OD .... Aerovias Condor de Colombia Ltda. (AEROCONDOR) [*Colorado*] [*ICAO designator*] (ICDA)
OD .... Cutoff Throttle Valve (RU)
od................. Detachment (BU)
od................. Och Dylikt [*And the Like*] [*Sweden*] (GPO)
Od .... Odeon [*Record label*] [*Europe, etc.*]
od................. Oder [*Or*] [*German*] (EG)
OD .... Odessa Railroad (RU)
OD .... Oditur [*Judge Advocate*] (IN)
OD .... Ohne Dividende [*Without Dividend*] [*German*]
OD .... Oklopna Divizija [*Armored Division*] (YU)
OD .... Okonomisk Demokrati [*Economic Democracy*] [*Denmark*] (WEN)
OD .... Old Dutch [*Language, etc.*]
OD .... Onderwysdiploma [*Education Diploma*] [*Afrikaans*]
OD .... Onrechtmatige Daad [*Tort or Tortious Act*] [*Netherlands*] (ILCA)
OD .... Operacni Dustojnik [*Operations Officer*] (CZ)

OD .... Operations Duty Officer (BU)
OD .... Operations Duty Officer, Duty Officer (RU)
OD .... Optimal Distribution [*Linguistics*] (RU)
OD .... Optisches Drehungsvermoegen [*Optical Rotation*] [*German*]
OD .... Opus Dei [*Catholic Lay Organization*] [*Spanish*] (WER)
OD .... Order Dienst [*Netherlands first organized resistance group, 1940*] [*World War II*]
OD .... Ordnance Directorate (ML)
OD .... Ordnungsdienst [*Military Police Service*] [*German military - World War II*]
OD .... Orta Dalga [*Medium Wave*] (TU)
OD .... Osmotic Pressure (RU)
ODA .... Oblastni Dum Armady [*Regional Armed Forces Building*] (CZ)
ODA .... Oficina de Divulgacion Agricola [*Caracas, Venezuela*] (LAA)
ODA .... Okrug State Archive (BU)
ODA .... Overseas Development Administration [*British*] (EAIO)
ODA .... Overseas Development Aid
ODAA........ Aden/International [*People's Democratic Republic of Yemen*] [*ICAO location identifier*] (ICLI)
ODAB....... Beihan [*People's Democratic Republic of Yemen*] [*ICAO location identifier*] (ICLI)
ODAF .... Aden [*People's Democratic Republic of Yemen*] [*ICAO location identifier*] (ICLI)
ODAG....... Al-Gheida [*People's Democratic Republic of Yemen*] [*ICAO location identifier*] (ICLI)
ODA-IPER ... Ankara Ticaret Odalari Personnel Sendikasi [*Ankara Chamber of Commerce Personnel Union*] (TU)
ODAM...... Mukeiras [*People's Democratic Republic of Yemen*] [*ICAO location identifier*] (ICLI)
ODAMAP ... Office Dahomeen des Manutentions Portuaires
ODAN .... Kamaran [*People's Democratic Republic of Yemen*] [*ICAO location identifier*] (ICLI)
ODAN .... Old Danish [*Language, etc.*]
ODAP........ Perim [*People's Democratic Republic of Yemen*] [*ICAO location identifier*] (ICLI)
ODAQ .... Qishn [*People's Democratic Republic of Yemen*] [*ICAO location identifier*] (ICLI)
ODAR .... Riyan [*People's Democratic Republic of Yemen*] [*ICAO location identifier*] (ICLI)
ODAS........ Osrednji Drzavni Arhiv Slovenije [*Central State Archives of Slovenia*] (YU)
ODAS........ Socotra [*People's Democratic Republic of Yemen*] [*ICAO location identifier*] (ICLI)
ODASIR.... Oficina de Desarrollo Agricola de los Sistemas de Riego [*Venezuela*] (DSCA)
ODAT........ Ataq [*People's Democratic Republic of Yemen*] [*ICAO location identifier*] (ICLI)
OdAZ......... Odessa Automobile Assembly Plant (RU)
ODB.......... Air Service [*Mali*] [*ICAO designator*] (FAAC)
ODB.......... Cordoba [*Spain*] [*Airport symbol*] (OAG)
odb........... Odbitka [*Copy*] [*Poland*]
ODB.......... Ordinateur de Bureau [*French*] (ADPT)
ODB.......... Separate Decontamination Battalion (RU)
ODB.......... Separate Landing Battalion (RU)
odb........... Separate Smoke Battalion (BU)
odc............. Odcinek [*Section, Sector*] [*Poland*]
ODC.......... Office Douanier Congolais
ODC.......... Oficiul de Desfacere a Carnii [*Office for Meat Sales*] (RO)
ODCA........ Organizacion Democrata Cristiana de America [*Christian Democratic Organization of America - CDOA*] [*Caracas, Venezuela*]
ODCD........ Oficiul pentru Deservirea Corpului Diplomatic [*Office for Service to the Diplomatic Corps*] (RO)
ODD .... "Friends of Children" Society [*1924-1935*] (RU)
odd.............. Oddeleni [*Department*] (CZ)
odd.............. Oddil [*Battalion*] [*Military*] (CZ)
ODD .... Oodnadatta [*Australia*] [*Airport symbol*] (OAG)
ODD .... Organisation "Dienst fuer Deutschland" [*"Service for Germany" Organization*] (EG)
ODDEP ..... Organismos Dioikiseos kai Diakheiriseos Ekklisiastikis Periousias [*Organization for the Administration and Management of Church Property*] [*Greek*] (GC)
od dgl......... Oder Dergleichen [*Or the Like*] (EG)
ODDJEN .. Oditur Djenderal [*Judge Advocate General*] (IN)
ODDM ...... Organizacion pro Desarrollo de los Derechos de la Mujer [*Puerto Rico*] (EAIO)
ODDS........ Organizzazione delle Donne Democratiche Somale
oddz............ Oddzial [*Branch, Department, Section*] (POL)
ODE........... Odense [*Denmark*] [*Airport symbol*] (OAG)
ODE........... Oficiul de Documentare Energetica [*Office for Power Documentation*] (RO)
ODE........... Oil Drilling & Exploration Ltd. [*Australia*] (ADA)
ODE........... Ordem Dos Engenheiros [*Portugal*]
ODEAC...... Organisation des Etats d'Amerique Centrale [*Organization of Central American States - OCAS*] [*French*]

ODEACEC ... Organizacion de Asociaciones Contra el Comunismo [*Organization of Associations Against Communism*] [*Guatemala*]   (LA)

ODEB .... Separate Road Maintenance Battalion   (RU)

ODECA ..... Organizacion de los Estados Centroamericanos [*Organization of Central American States - OCAS*] [*San Salvador, El Salvador*]   (EAIO)

ODECABE ... Organizacion Deportiva Centroamericana y del Caribe [*Central American and Caribbean Sports Organization*] [*Guatemala*]   (LA)

ODECABE ... Organization Deportiva Centroamericana y del Caribe   (OLYM)

ODECOB .. Organismo de Desarrollo del Complejo Bayovar [*Agency for Development of the Bayovar Complex*] [*Peru*]   (LA)

ODEF .... Office National de Developpement et d'Exploitation des Ressources Forestieres [*National Agency for the Development and Exploitation of Forest Resources*] [*Togo*]   (AF)

ODEKA ..... Organisation pour l'Amenagement et le Developpement du Bassin de la Riviere Kagera

ODEM .... Office des Engins Mecaniques [*Office of Mechanical Equipment*] [*Cambodia*]   (CL)

ODEM .... Orta Dogu Etitim Merkezi [*Middle East Training Center*] [*Preparatory school*]   (TU)

ODEMO .... Organisation de Developpement du Moyen Ouest [*Middlewest Development Organization*] [*Malagasy*]   (AF)

ODEP .... Organismos Dioikiseos Ekklisiastikis Periousias [*Organization for the Administration of Church Property*] [*Greek*]   (GC)

ODEPA ..... Oficina de Planificacion Agricola [*Agriculture Planning Office*] [*Chile*]   (LA)

ODEPA ..... Organizacion Deportiva Panamericana [*Pan American Sports Organization - PASO*] [*Mexico City, Mexico*]   (EAIO)

ODEPA ..... Organization Deportiva Panamericana   (OLYM)

ODEPES ... Organismos Diakheiriseos Eidikon Poron Ergasiakon Somateion [*Organization for the Management of Labor Union Special Funds*]   (GC)

ODEPLAN ... Oficina de Planificacion Nacional [*National Planning Office*] [*Chile*]   (LA)

o dergl .... Oder Dergleichen [*Or the Like, Similarly*] [*German*]   (GCA)

ODESSA ... Organisation der Ehemaligen Schutzstaffel Angehoeriggen [*Organization of Former Members of the Elite Guard*] [*Founded after World War II to smuggle war criminals out of Germany and provide them with false identities*]

ODESUR ... Organizacion Deportiva Sudamericana [*An association*]   (EAIO)

ODETA ..... Organisation pour le Developpement du Tourisme Africain [*Organization for the Development of African Tourism*]   (AF)

ODF .... Department of Prerevolutionary Holdings [*In archives*]   (RU)

ODF .... Finishing Decorative Plywood   (RU)

OdF .... Opfer des Faschismus [*Victim of Fascism*]   (EG)

ODF .... South African Organ Donor Foundation   (AA)

ODG .... Oesterreichische Dermatologische Gesellschaft [*Austrian Dermatology Association*]   (SLS)

ODG .... Optical Index Head   (RU)

ODG .... Ordine del Giorno [*Order of the Day, Agenda*] [*Italian*]   (WER)

ODG .... Organosis Dimokratikon Gynaikon [*Organization of Democratic Women*] [*Cyprus*]   (GC)

ODG .... Reversible Generator   (BU)

o dgl .... Oder Dergleichen [*Or the Like*] [*German*]

ODH .... Onwettige Diamanthandel [*Illicit Diamond Buying*] [*Afrikaans*]

ODI .... Office pour le Developpement Industriel du Royaume du Maroc [*Rabat, Morocco*]

ODI .... Okresni Dopravni Inspektorat [*District Traffic Inspection Bureau*]   (CZ)

ODI .... Open Door International for the Economic Emancipation of the Woman Worker [*Brussels, Belgium*]   (EAIO)

ODI .... Orszagos Dietetikai Intezet [*National Dietetic Institute*]   (HU)

ODI .... Overseas Development Institute   (EA)

ODIN .... Online Dokumentations- und Informationsverbund [*Online Documentation and Information Affiliation*]

ODIPAC .... Office de Developpement Integre des Productions Arachidieres et Cerealieres [*Mali*]   (EY)

ODIS .... Olympic Day in the Schools   (OLYM)

ODISA .... Organization Development Institute of South Africa   (AA)

ODISY .... Organismos Diakheiriseos (Pleonazondos) Symmakhikou Ylikou [*Allied (Surplus) Materiel Management Organization*] [*Greek*]   (GC)

odj .... Odjezd [*Departure*]   (CZ)

ODJ .... Opinion des Jeunes

ODJR .... Organisation Democratique de la Jeunesse Reunionnaise [*Reunionese Democratic Youth Organization*]   (AF)

ODK .... Long-Term Credit Department   (RU)

ODK .... Obshchestvo Druzey Kino   (EAIO)

ODK .... Oesterreichische Dentistenkammer [*Austrian Dental Board*]   (SLS)

ODK .... Okregowa Dyrekcja Kolejowa [*District Railroad Administration*]   (POL)

ODK .... Orszagos Dokumentacios Kozpont [*National Documentation Center*]   (HU)

ODKD .... Organismos Dimosion Ktimaton Dodekanisou [*Organization of Public Properties of the Dodecanese*] [*Greek*]   (GC)

ODKO .... Osrodek Doskonalenia Kadr Oswiatowych [*Center for the Improvement of Teaching Personnel*]   (POL)

Odl .... Oberdispatcherleitung [*Head Dispatching Office*]   (EG)

ODLB .... Optical Dispensers' Licensing Board [*New South Wales, Australia*]

ODLT .... Oblastni Dum Lidove Tvorivosti [*Regional Folk Arts Center*]   (CZ)

ODM .... Organizacion pro Derechos de la Mujer [*Puerto Rico*]   (EAIO)

ODM .... Overseas Development Ministry

ODMA .... Optical Distributors and Manufacturers Association of Australia

ODMO ...... All-Union House of Clothing Models   (RU)

ODMP .... Organismos Diakheiriseos Monastiriakis Periousias [*Organization for Administration of Monastery Property*] [*Greek*]   (GC)

ODMTS .... Okoliya Depot of the Machine-Tractor Station   (BU)

ODN .... "Down with Illiteracy" Society   (RU)

ODN .... Long Seridan [*Malaysia*] [*Airport symbol*]   (OAG)

odnokr .... Momentary (Aspect of Verb)   (RU)

ODNT .... Oblast House of Folk Art   (RU)

ODO .... Bath and Disinfection Unit   (RU)

ODO .... Decontamination Unit   (RU)

ODO .... District House of Officers   (RU)

odobr .... Approved   (RU)

ODOKSAN ... Osmaneli Dokum Sanayi ve Ticaret AS [*Osmaneli Foundry Industry and Trade Corp.*]   (TU)

ODOL .... (Ontwerp) Onrechtmatige Daden Openbare Lichamen [*Benelux*]   (BAS)

ODOOS ..... Osrodek Dokumentacji Obrabiarek i Obrobki Skrawaniem [*Machine Tool and Machining Documentation Center*]   (POL)

odoram .... Odoramentum [*Perfume*] [*Latin*]   (MAE)

odorat .... Odoratus [*Odorous*] [*Latin*]   (MAE)

ODOT .... Orszagjaro Diakok Orszagos Talalkozoja [*National Meeting of Touring Students*]   (HU)

ODP .... Bath and Decontamination Station   (RU)

ODP .... Bird Pox-Diphtheria   (RU)

odp .... Foundations of the State and Law   (BU)

odp .... Odpoledne [*Afternoon*]   (CZ)

ODP .... Oekologisch-Demokratische Partei [*Ecological Democratic Party*] [*Germany*] [*Political party*]   (PPW)

ODP .... Office of Defence Production [*Australia*]

ODP .... Okrug State Enterprise   (BU)

odp .... Op Dit Punt [*Benelux*]   (BAS)

ODP .... Orderly Departure Program [*for Vietnamese refugees*] [*United Nations*]

OdP .... Ordnung der Planung [*Order on Planning*]   (EG)

ODP .... Organisation de Defense Populaire

ODP .... Organizacao da Defensa Popular [*People's Defense Organization*] [*Angola*]   (AF)

ODP .... Overall Documentation Plan [*NATO*]   (NATG)

ODP .... Supply and Maintenance Section   (BU)

ODPG .... Organisation du Developpement de la Plaine de Gonaives [*Organization for the Development of the Gonaives Plain*] [*Haiti*]   (LA)

ODPK .... Department of Long-Term Industrial Credit   (RU)

ODP/MT ... Organisation pour la Democratie Populaire/Mouvement du Travail [*Burkina Faso*] [*Political party*]   (EY)

ODPP .... Department of Long-Range Weather Forecasts   (RU)

ODPP .... Office of the Director of Public Prosecutions [*Australia*]

ODPT .... Oficiul de Documentare si Publicatii Tehnice [*Office for Documentation and Technical Publications*]   (RO)

odpto .... Separate Antitank Battalion   (RU)

odpvo .... Separate Air Defense Battalion   (RU)

ODR .... Bath and Disinfection Company   (RU)

ODR .... Organismo de Desarrollo Regional [*Regional Development Body*] [*Peru*]   (LA)

ODR .... Society of Friends of Radio   (RU)

ODRA .... Department of Ancient Manuscripts and Documents of the Institute of History of the Academy of Sciences, USSR   (RU)

ODRC .... Office of Disaster Relief Coordinator [*United Nations*]   (WDAA)

o drgl .... Oder Dergleichen [*Or the Like*] [*German*]

ODRL .... Department of Old Russian Literature   (RU)

ODRP .... Oblast House of Education Workers   (RU)

ODS .... Odessa [*Ukraine*] [*Airport symbol*]   (OAG)

ODS .... Optischer Dokumentensortierer [*German*]   (ADPT)

ODSB .... Separate Road-Building Battalion   (RU)

ODSK .... Society of Friends of Soviet Cinematography   (RU)

ODSNF ..... Joint Far Eastern Fleet Observation Service   (RU)

ODSP .... Consolidated State Economic Enterprises   (BU)

ODSS .... Society of Friends of the Soviet Union   (RU)

odst .... Odstavec [*Paragraph*]   (CZ)

ODSY .... Sayun [*People's Democratic Republic of Yemen*] [*ICAO location identifier*]   (ICLI)

ODSZ .... Obchod Drobnym Spotrebnim Zbozim [*Retail Store of Small Consumer Goods*]   (CZ)

ODT .... Organisation des Democrates Tunisiens [*Organization of Tunisian Democrats*]   (AF)

ODTA .... Organisation pour le Developpement du Tourisme Africain [*Organization for the Development of African Tourism*]   (AF)

ODTKA ..... Separate Motor Torpedo Boat Division   (RU)

ODTM .... Saponified Distilled Tall Oil   (RU)

ODTO .... Special Road Transportation Department   (RU)

ODTP .... Okrug State Commercial Enterprise   (BU)

ODTS .... Department of Scenery and Technical Equipment [*Motion-picture studio*]   (RU)

ODTU .... Orta Dogu Teknik Universitesi [*Middle East Technical University*] [*Ankara, Turkey*] [*Research center*]   (TU)

ODTU-DER ... Orta Dogu Teknik Universitesi Talebe Dernegi [*Middle East Technical University Student Association*]   (TU)

ODTUKMB ... Orta Dogu Teknik Universitesi Kibrisli Mezunlar Birligi [*Middle East Technical University Cypriot Graduates Union*]   (TU)

ODU .... Bath and Disinfection Installation   (RU)

ODU .... Integrated Dispatching Control   (RU)

ODU .... Old Dutch [*Language, etc.*]

ODUCAL .. Organizacion de las Universidades Catolicas de America Latina [*Organization of Catholic Universities of Latin America*] [*Santiago, Chile*]   (LAA)

ODV .... Okresni Doplnovaci Velitelstvi [*District Headquarters of Military Records and Reserves*]   (CZ)

ODVA .... Organisation du Developpement de la Vallee d'Artibonite [*Organization for the Development of the Artibonite Valley*] [*Haiti*]   (LA)

ODVA .... Special Far Eastern Army   (RU)

ODVF .... Society of Friends of the Air Fleet [*1923-1925*]   (RU)

ODVO .... Odessa Military District   (RU)

ODYE .... Omospondia Dikastikon Ypallilon Ellados [*Federation of Judiciary Employees of Greece*]   (GC)

ODZ .... Blinding Smoke Screen   (RU)

ODZS .... State Farms Trust   (BU)

OE .... Common Emitter   (RU)

Oe .... Ersted [*Oersted*] [*Unit of magnetizing intensity*] [*Poland*]

OE .... Oikonomiki Epitropi [*Finance Committee*] [*Greek*]   (GC)

OE .... Old English [*Language, etc.*] [*i.e., before 1150 or 1200*]

OE .... Omada "Epanastasi" [*"Revolution" Group*] [*Greek*]   (GC)

oe .... Omorrythmos Etaireia [*Unlimited General Partnership*]   (GC)

OE .... Oram Electric Industries Ltd. [*Israel*]

OE .... Order of Engineers [*Portugal*]   (EAIO)

OE .... Organo Espressivo [*Swell Organ*] [*Music*]

OE .... Otu Edo

Oe .... Oud-Engels [*Old English*] [*Language, etc.*] [*Afrikaans*]

OEA .... Automobile Operation Department   (RU)

OEA .... Office of Ethnic Affairs [*Victoria, Australia*]

OEA .... Office of Evaluation and Audit [*Aboriginal and Torres Strait Islander Commission*] [*Australia*]

OEA .... Organisasie vir Eenheid in Africa [*Organization of African Unity - OAU*] [*Afrikaans*]

OEA .... Organisation des Etats Africains   (FLAF)

OEA .... Organisation des Etats Americains [*Organization of American States - OAS*] [*French*]   (MSC)

OEA .... Organismos Epikourikis Asfaliseos [*Auxiliary Insurance Organization*] [*Greek*]   (GC)

OEA .... Organizacao dos Estados Americanos [*Organization of American States - OAS*] [*Portuguese*]

OEA .... Organizacion de los Estados Americanos [*Organization of American States - OAS*] [*Spanish*]

OEA .... Orszagos Energiagazdalkodasi Alap [*National Fund for Power Economy*]   (HU)

OEA .... Orszagos Epuletjavitasi Alap [*National Fund for Building Repairs*]   (HU)

OeAAB ...... Oesterreichischer Arbeiter- und Angestelltenbund [*Austrian Workers' and Employees' League*] [*OeVP affiliate*]   (WEN)

OEAB .... Abha [*Saudi Arabia*] [*ICAO location identifier*]   (ICLI)

OEAH .... Al-Ahsa [*Saudi Arabia*] [*ICAO location identifier*]   (ICLI)

OEALC ...... Oficina Regional de Educacion para America Latina y el Caribe [*Regional Office for Education in Latin America and the Caribbean-Chile*]   (IID)

OeAMC ..... Oesterreichische Alpine Montangesellschaft [*Austrian Alpine Mining Company*]   (WEN)

OEAQ .... Outdoor Educators' Association of Queensland [*Australia*]

OEAS .... Organisation Europaischer Aluminium Schmelzhutten [*Organization of European Aluminium Foundries*]   (PDAA)

OEAS .... Organismos Elengkhou ton di Aftokiniton Syngoinonion [*Organization for the Control of Automotive Communications*] [*Greek*]   (GC)

OEASA ...... Outdoor Educators' Association of South Australia

OEB .... Omospondia Ergodoton ke Viomichanon Kyprou [*Cyprus Employers and Industrialists Federation*]   (EAIO)

OEB .... Separate Evacuation Battalion   (RU)

OEBA .... El-Baha [*Saudi Arabia*] [*ICAO location identifier*]   (ICLI)

OeBB .... Oesterreichische Bauernbund [*Austrian Farmers' League*] [*OeVP affiliate*]   (WEN)

OeBB .... Oesterreichische Bundesbahnen [*Austrian State Railways*]   (WEN)

OEBH .... Bisha [*Saudi Arabia*] [*ICAO location identifier*]   (ICLI)

OEBI .... Oficina de Estadisticas Balleneras Internacionales [*Bureau of International Whaling Statistics - BIWS*] [*Spanish*]   (MSC)

OEBK .... Organisation pour l'Equipement Banana-Kinshasa

OEBM .... Organisation Europeenne de Biologie Moleculaire [*European Molecular Biology Organization - EMBO*] [*French*]   (ASF)

OEBM .... Organizacion Europea de Biologia Molecular [*European Molecular Biology Organization - EMBO*] [*Spanish*]   (ASF)

OEBU .... Organizacion de Exiliados Brasilenos en Uruguay [*Organization of Brazilian Exiles in Uruguay*]   (LA)

OEC .... Office des Etudiants Cambodgiens [*Office of Cambodian Students*]   (CL)

OEC .... Office d'Etudes sur le Caoutchouc [*Rubber Studies Office*]   (CL)

OEC .... Oil Exploration Company [*Iraq*]   (OMWE)

OEC .... Organisation Europeenne du Charbon [*European Coal Organization*] [*French*]   (WER)

OEC .... Overall Energy Council [*Japan*]   (PDAA)

OEC .... Overseas Employment Corporation [*Pakistan*]   (GEA)

OEC .... Oxford Editions of Cuneiform Texts

OECA .... Organisation des Etats Centro-Americains   (FLAF)

OECD .... Organization for Economic Cooperation and Development [*Formerly, OEEC*]

OECDC ..... Organization for Economic Cooperation among Developing Countries   (AF)

OECD-NEA ... Organization for Economic Cooperation and Development, Nuclear Energy Agency

OECE .... Organisation des Etats Caraibes de l'Est [*Organization of Eastern Caribbean States - OECS*] [*French*]

OECE .... Organisation Europeenne de Cooperation Economique [*Organization for European Economic Cooperation - OEEC*] [*Later, OECD See also OCDE France*]   (MSC)

OECE .... Organizacion de Estados Caribenos del Este [*Organization of Eastern Caribbean States - OECS*] [*Spanish*]

OECE .... Organizacion Europea de Cooperacion Economica [*Organization for European Economic Cooperation - OEEC*] [*Later, OECD Spain*]

OECEI ...... Oficina de Estudios para la Colaboracion Economica Internacional [*Research Office for International Economic Cooperation*] [*Buenos Aires*]   (LAA)

OECF .... Overseas Economic Cooperation Fund [*Japan*]

OECGD ..... Overseas Export Credit Guarantee Department

OECL .... Ordre des Experts Comptables Luxembourgeois [*Luxembourg*]   (EAIO)

OECQ .... Organisation Europeenne pour la Qualite [*European Organization for Quality -EOQC*] [*Switzerland*]

OECS .... Organisation of Eastern Caribbean States   (EAIO)

OECS .... Organization of Eastern Caribbean States   (LA)

OECSEAS ... Organisation of Eastern Caribbean States, Economic Affairs Secretariat [*St. Johns, Antigua*]   (EAIO)

OECT .... European Association of the Textile Wholesale Trade [*EC*]   (ECED)

oed .... Oper Edei Deixei [*Which Was To Be Demonstrated*]   (GC)

OEDE .... Omospondia Ergaton Dermatos Ellados [*Federation of Greek Leather Workers*]   (GC)

OEDOSZ ... Orvos-Egeszsegugyi Dolgozok Szakszervezete [*Trade Union of Workers and Employees in the Medical Services*]   (HU)

OEDR .... Dhahran/International [*Saudi Arabia*] [*ICAO location identifier*]   (ICLI)

OEDV .... Organismos Ekdoseos Didaktikon Vivlion [*Organization for the Publication of Textbooks*] [*OESV*] [*Formerly,*] [*Greek*]   (GC)

OEE .... Omospondia Efimeridopolon Ellados [*Federation of Greek Newspaper Vendors*]   (GC)

OEE .... Ordre de l'Etoile de l'Europe [*Huy, Belgium*]   (EAIO)

OEE .... Orszagos Erdeszeti Egyesulet [*National Forestry Association*]   (HU)

OEEC .... Organization for European Economic Cooperation [*Later, OECD*]

OEEPE ...... Organisation Europeenne d'Etudes Photogrammetriques Experimentales [*European Organisation for Experimental Photogrammetric Research*] [*Research Center Netherlands*]   (PDAA)

OEES .... Organisatie voor Europese Economische Samenwerking [*Benelux*]   (BAS)

OEESIO .... Omospondia Elevtheron Ergatikon Somateion Imikratikon Organismon [*Federation of Free Labor Unions of Semi-Governmental Organizations*]   (GC)

OEEYDKE ... Omospondia Ergatotekhniton kai Ektakton Ypallilon Dimon kai Koinotiton Ellados [*Federation of Workers, Technicians, and Temporary Employees of the Municipalities and Communes of Greece*] (GC)

oef............... Oefening [*Exercise*] [*Afrikaans*]

OEF .... Orszagos Erdeszeti Foigazgatosag [*National Directorate of Forestry*] (HU)

OEF .... Osterreichisches Energieforum [*Austria*] (EAIO)

OEFEK...... Omospondia Ethnikon Foititikon Enoseon Kyprou [*Federation of National Student Unions of Cyprus*] (GC)

OEFJ .... Orszagosan Egyseges Foglalkozasi Jegyzek [*Nationally Uniform Employment Register*] (HU)

OEFK........ Oikonomiki Eforia Forologias Klironomion [*Directorate of Inheritance Taxation*] [*Greek*] (GC)

OEFPN...... Department of Economic, Philosophical, and Legal Sciences (of the Academy of Sciences, USSR) (RU)

OEG........... Oesterreichische Ethnologische Gesellschaft [*Austrian Ethnological Association*] (SLS)

OEG.......... Osterreichische Exlibris-Gesellschaft [*Austria*] (EAIO)

OEGH .... Orszagos Energiagazdalkodasi Hatosag [*National Energy Management Authority*] (HU)

OEGI .... Oesterreichische Gesellschaft fuer Informatik [*German*] (ADPT)

OEGN........ Gizan [*Saudi Arabia*] [*ICAO location identifier*] (ICLI)

OEGS .... Gassim [*Saudi Arabia*] [*ICAO location identifier*] (ICLI)

OEGT........ Guriat [*Saudi Arabia*] [*ICAO location identifier*] (ICLI)

OEH .... Orszagos Energiagazdalkodasi Hatosag [*National Energy Management Authority*] (HU)

OEH .... Orszagos Epitesugyi Hivatal [*National Construction Office*] (HU)

OEHL........ Hail [*Saudi Arabia*] [*ICAO location identifier*] (ICLI)

OEHV........ Osterreichische Eis-hockey-Verband [*Austria*] (EAIO)

OEI .... Oficina de Educacion Iberoamericana [*Ibero-American Bureau of Education - IABE*] [*Madrid, Spain*] (EAIO)

OEI .... Organizacion de Estados Iberoamericanos para la Educacion, la Ciencia, y la Cultura [*Organization of Ibero-American States for Education, Science, and Culture*] (EAIO)

OEI .... Orszagos Epitoipari Igazgatosag [*National Directorate of the Building Industry*] (HU)

OEIA .... Office Equipment Industry Association of Australia

OEIAA ...... Office Equipment Industry Association of Australia

OEIC .... Overseas Economic Intelligence Committee [*Military*]

OEIFAE .... Omospondia Epangelmation Idioktiton Fortigon Avtokiniton Ellados [*Federation of Professional Truck Owners of Greece*] (GC)

OeIG .... Oesterreichische Industrieverwaltungs-Gesellschaft [*Austrian Industries Management Company*] (WEN)

OEIS........ Odessa Electrotechnical Institute of Communications (RU)

OEITFL..... Organisation Europeenne des Industries Transformatrices de Fruits et Legumes [*European Organization of Fruit and Vegetable Processing Industries*] [*Common Market*] [*Belgium*]

OEJB........ Jubail [*Saudi Arabia*] [*ICAO location identifier*] (ICLI)

OEJD........ Jeddah [*Saudi Arabia*] [*ICAO location identifier*] (ICLI)

OEJN .... Jeddah/King Abdul Aziz International [*Saudi Arabia*] [*ICAO location identifier*] (ICLI)

Oek .... Oekonomie [*Economy*] [*German*]

OEK.......... Oesterreichisches Elektrotechnisches Komitee [*Austria*]

OEK.......... Omospondia Ergodoton Kyprou [*Federation of Cypriot Employers*] (GC)

OEK.......... Organisation d'Etudiants Khmers [*Organization of Cambodian Students*] (CL)

OEK.......... Organismos Ellinikis Katoikias [*Greek Housing Organization*] (GC)

OEK.......... Organismos Ergatikis Katoikias [*Workers' Housing Organization*] [*Greek*] (GC)

OEK.......... Orszagos Epitesugyi Kormanybiztos [*National Commissioner of Construction*] (HU)

OEK.......... Orszagos Epuletjavitasi Kozpont [*National Center of Building Repairs*] (HU)

OEKAE ..... Omospondia Ergaton, Keramopoion, kai Angeioplaston Ellados [*Federation of Tile, Brick, and Ceramic Workers of Greece*] (GC)

OEKhVE ... Omospondia Ergatoypallilon Khimikis Viomikhanias Ellados [*Federation of Chemical Industry Workers of Greece*] (GC)

OEKJ........ Al-Kharj [*Saudi Arabia*] [*ICAO location identifier*] (ICLI)

OEKM .... Khamis Mushait [*Saudi Arabia*] [*ICAO location identifier*] (ICLI)

OEKULEI ... Oekonomisch-Kultureller Leistungsvergleich [*Economic-Cultural Comparison, Economic-Cultural Competition*] (EG)

OEKVE...... Omospondia Ergatoypallilon Kapnoviomikhanias Ellados [*Federation of Greek Tobacco Industry Workers and Employees*] (GC)

Oel .... Erdoelchemie [*Petrochemistry*] [*German*] (GCA)

OEL.......... Oil Exploration License

OeLB .... Oertlicher Landwirtschaftlicher Betrieb [*Local Agricultural Enterprise*] [*German*] (EG)

Oelleit........ Oelleitung [*Oil Pipeline or Line*] [*German*] (GCA)

oelloesl ...... Oelloeslich [*Oil-Soluble*] [*German*] (GCA)

OELMEK ... Omospondia Ellinon Leitourgon Mesis Ekpaidevseos Kyprou [*Federation of Greek Secondary School Teachers of Cyprus*] (GC)

OELRR...... Office of Economic Liaison and Regulatory Review [*Western Australia*]

OELTEK ... Omospondia Ellinon Leitourgon Tekhnikis Ekpaidevseos Kyprou [*Federation of Greek Technical School Teachers of Cyprus*] (GC)

OEM......... Omospondia Ergaton Metallou [*Metal Workers' Federation*] [*Greek*] (GC)

OEM......... Organizacion Editorial Mexicana [*Mexican Publishing Organization*] (LA)

OEMA....... Madinah [*Saudi Arabia*] [*ICAO location identifier*] (ICLI)

OEME....... Organotiki Epitropi Mathitikon Ekdiloseon [*Organizational Committee for Student Demonstrations*] [*Cyprus*] (GC)

OEMEE .... Omospondia Ergatotekhniton Metallevtikon Epikheiriseon Ellados [*Federation of Workers and Technicians of Mining Enterprises of Greece*] (GC)

OEMG....... Omospondia Ergaton Metaforon kai Georgias [*Federation of Transport and Farm Workers*] [*Cyprus*] (GC)

OEMI .... Oficina de Emergencia del Ministerio del Interior [*Interior Ministry Emergency Office*] [*Chile*] (LA)

OEML .... Organosi Ellinon Marxiston-Leniniston [*Organization of Greek Marxist-Leninists*] (GC)

OEMV....... Oesterreichische Mineralol-Verwaltung [*Austria*] (PDAA)

OEN.......... Organosis Ethnikis Neolaias [*Organization of Nationalist Youth*] [*Cyprus*] (GC)

OENA....... Oesterreichischer Normenausschuss [*Austrian Standards Committee*] [*Germany*] (GCA)

OENE....... Oesterreichische Gesellschaft zur Nutzing Nichtkonventioneller Energiequellen [*Austrian Society for the Use of Non-Conventional Energy Sources*]

OENG....... Nejran [*Saudi Arabia*] [*ICAO location identifier*] (ICLI)

OENO .... Omospondia Ellinikon Navtergatikon Organoseon [*Federation of Greek Maritime Worker Organizations*] (GC)

OENR....... Organization for European Nuclear Research

OEOA....... Office for Emergency Operations in Africa [*United Nations*] (EY)

OEOS .... Organismos Evropaikis Oikonomikis Synergasias [*Organization for European Economic Cooperation*] (GC)

OEP .... Consolidated Electric Power Enterprises (BU)

OeP .... Oekonomische Planinformation [*Economic Plan Information*] (EG)

Oe P .... Oesterreichisches Patent [*Austrian Patent*] (GCA)

OEP.......... Omospondia Epangelmation Peiraios [*Piraeus Tradesmen's Federation*] (GC)

OEP .... Organosi "Ergatiki Pali" [*"Worker Struggle" Organization*] [*Greek*] (GC)

OEPA .... Hafr Al-Batin Airport [*Saudi Arabia*] [*ICAO location identifier*] (ICLI)

OEPAC...... Office of the Economic Planning Advisory Council [*Australia*]

OEPD .... Organismos Ellinikou Papoutsiou kai Dermatos [*Greek Shoe and Leather Organization*] (GC)

OEPFC ...... Official Elvis Presley Fan Club (EAIO)

OEPL........ Organisation de l'Enseignement Prive Laic [*Private Lay Education Organization*] [*Cameroon*] (AF)

OEPP........ Organisation Europeenne et Mediterraneenne pour la Protection des Plantes [*European and Mediterranean Plant Protection Organization - EPPO*] (EAIO)

OEPT........ Office Equatorial des Postes et Telecommunications

OEQ.......... Organisation Europeenne pour la Qualite [*Switzerland*] (EAIO)

OER.......... Organizatsiia Ekonomicheskovo Razvitiia

OER.......... Ornskoldsvik [*Sweden*] [*Airport symbol*] (OAG)

OER.......... Separate Evacuation Company (RU)

OERAHA ... Organisation Europeenne pour des Recherches Astronomiques dans l'Hemisphere Austral [*European Southern Observatory - ESO*] (EAIO)

OeRF .... Oesterreichischer Rundfunk-Fernsehen [*Austrian Radio and Television System*] (WEN)

Oerf........ Rafha [*Saudi Arabia*] [*ICAO location identifier*] (ICLI)

Oerg.......... Oergermaans [*Primitive Germanic*] [*Language, etc.*] [*Afrikaans*]

OeRG........ Oesterreichischer Rundfunk GmbH [*Austrian Broadcasting Co.*] (WEN)

OERK .... Riyadh/King Khalid International [*Saudi Arabia*] [*ICAO location identifier*] (ICLI)

OERM .... Organisation Economique Regionale du Maghreb

OERN....... Organisation Europeenne de Recherche Nucleaire (FLAF)

OERR .... Arar [*Saudi Arabia*] [*ICAO location identifier*] (ICLI)

OERRPA... Outer Eastern Region Residential Planning Association for Intellectually Handicapped Children [*Melbourne, Australia*]

OERS........ Ordaisation des Etats Riverains du Fleuve Senegal [*Organization of Senegal River States*] (AF)

OERS........ Organisation des Etats Riverains du Senegal (EY)

OERS........ Organisation Europeenne de Recherches Spatiales

OERY .... Riyadh [*Saudi Arabia*] [*ICAO location identifier*]   (ICLI)
OES .... All-Union Institute for the Planning of Electric Power Projects
                     (RU)
OES .... Base-Load Electric Power Plant   (RU)
OES .... Integrated Power System, Grid System   (RU)
OES .... Oblast Economic Conference   (RU)
OES .... Organisation des Etats Sahariens
OES .... Organisation Europeenne des Scieries [*European Sawmills
                     Organization*] [*EC*]   (ECED)
OES .... Organotiki Epitropi Syndiaskepsis [*Conference Organization
                     Committee*]   (GC)
oes .... Osztrak Schilling [*Austrian Schilling*]   (HU)
OES .... San Antonio Oeste [*Argentina*] [*Airport symbol*]   (OAG)
OESCAND ... Old East Scandinavian [*Language, etc.*]
OESE......... Oficina de Estudios Socioeconomicos [*Venezuela*]   (LAA)
OESE......... Omospondia Ekdromikon Somateion Ellados [*Federation of
                     Hiking Clubs of Greece*]   (GC)
OESH .... Sharurah [*Saudi Arabia*] [*ICAO location identifier*]   (ICLI)
OESK....... Al-Jouf [*Saudi Arabia*] [*ICAO location identifier*]   (ICLI)
OESK....... Osteuropeiska Solidaritetskommitten [*East European Solidarity
                     Committee*]   (EAIO)
OESL......... Sulayel [*Saudi Arabia*] [*ICAO location identifier*]   (ICLI)
OESO .... Organisatie voor Economische Samenwerking en Ontwikkeling
                     [*Organization for Economic Cooperation and Development*]
                     [*Use OECD*] [*Netherlands*]   (WEN)
OESO .... Organisation Internationale d'Etudes Statistiques pour les
                     Maladies de l'Oesophage [*International Organization for
                     Statistical Studies on Diseases of the Esophagus*]   (EAIO)
OESR........ Organization for Economic Cooperation and Development
                     [*OECD*]   (RU)
OeSS........ Oekonomisches System des Sozialismus [*Economic System of
                     Socialism*]   (EG)
OESU .... Integrated Power System of the Ukrainian SSR   (RU)
OeSU .... Oesterreichische Studenten Union [*Austrian Students' Union*]
                     [*OeVP affiliate*]   (WEN)
OESV........ Organismos Ekdoseos Skholikon Vivlion [*Later, OEDV*] [*Greek*]
                     (GC)
OESVE...... Omospondia Ergoliptikon Syndesmon Voreiou Ellados
                     [*Federation of Contractors Associations of Northern Greece*]
                     (GC)
OeSWG ..... Oesterreichische Studiengesellschaft fur Wirtschaftliche
                     Guterbewegung [*Austrian Research Association for
                     Materials Handling*]   (PDAA)
OESz.......... Orvos-Egeszsegugyi Szakszervezet [*Medical Sanitation Trade
                     Union*]   (HU)
OET .... Occupational English Test [*Australia*]
OET .... Official Establishments Trust [*Australia*]
OET .... Organisation Europeenne des Transports   (FLAF)
OET .... Organizacion para Estudios Tropicales [*Organization for
                     Tropical Studies*]   (EAIO)
OET .... Orszagos Epitesugyi Tanacs [*National Council on Construction*]
                     (HU)
OETB .... Ocean Economics and Technology Branch [*United Nations*]
                     (MSC)
OETB .... Tabuk [*Saudi Arabia*] [*ICAO location identifier*]   (ICLI)
OETE .... Omospondia Ergaton Typou Ellados [*Federation of Greek Press
                     Workers*]   (GC)
OETF......... Taif [*Saudi Arabia*] [*ICAO location identifier*]   (ICLI)
OETI.......... Orszagos Elelmezes- es Taplalkozastudomanyi Intezet [*National
                     Institute of Food and Nutrition*] [*Budapest, Hungary*]
                     [*Research center*]   (HU)
OETO .... Ocean Economics and Technology Office [*United Nations
                     (already exists in GUS II database)*]   (ASF)
OETR .... Turaif [*Saudi Arabia*] [*ICAO location identifier*]   (ICLI)
OETs .... United Evangelical Churches   (BU)
OETTI....... Orszagos Elelmezes- es Taplalkozastudomanyi Intezet [*National
                     Institute of Food and Nutrition*]   (HU)
OeTV .... Oeffentlicher Dienst, Transport, und Verkehr [*Public Service,
                     Transportation, and Traffic (Trade Union)*]   (EG)
OETY .... Omospondiaki Epitropi Trapezikon Ypallilon [*Federative
                     Committee of Bank Employees*]   (GC)
OeUP .... Oesterreich-Ungarisches Patent [*Austro-Hungarian Patent*]
                     (GCA)
OEVA .... Office de l'Experimentation et de la Vulgarisation Agricoles
                     [*Tunisia*]
OEVA .... Omospondia Epangelmation kai Viotekhnon Athinon
                     [*Federation of Tradesmen and Craftsmen of Athens*] [*The
                     last initial varies according to location*]   (GC)
OeVB .... Oertlicher Volkseigener Betrieb [*Locally Administered State
                     Enterprise*]   (EG)
OeVP .... Oesterreichische Volkspartei [*Austrian People's Party*]   (WEN)
OeVW .... Oertliche Versorgungswirtschaft [*Local Public Utilities*]   (EG)
OeWB .... Oesterreichischer Wirtschaftsbund [*Austrian Business League*]
                     [*OeVP affiliate*]   (WEN)
Oe Wbk...... Oud-Engels Woordeboek [*Old English Dictionary*] [*Afrikaans*]
OEWJ........ Wejh [*Saudi Arabia*] [*ICAO location identifier*]   (ICLI)

OEY .... Omospondia Eforiakon Ypallilon [*Federation of Tax Assessors*]
                     (GC)
OEY .... Omospondia Emborikon Ypallilon [*Federation of Commercial
                     Employees*] [*Cyprus*]   (GC)
OEYN .... Yenbo [*Saudi Arabia*] [*ICAO location identifier*]   (ICLI)
OEYSK...... Omospondia Ergatotekhniton kai Ypallilon Stratiotikon
                     Katastimaton [*Federation of Military Establishment
                     Personnel*] [*Cyprus*]   (GC)
OEYTE...... Omospondia Ergatotekhniton-Ypallilon Tsimenton Ellados
                     [*Federation of Greek Cement Industry Workers and
                     Employees*]   (GC)
OEZ.......... Osteuropaeische Zeit [*East European Time*] [*German*]   (WEN)
of .... Commissioned Officer   (BU)
OF .... Concentration Plant   (RU)
OF .... Fast Airways BV [*Netherlands*] [*ICAO designator*]   (ICDA)
OF .... Fatherland Front [*People's Republic of Bulgaria*]   (RU)
OF .... High-Explosive Fragmentation [*Shell, Bomb*]   (RU)
Of .... Oferece [*Portuguese*]
OF .... Offensif Fusant [*Military*] [*French*]   (MTD)
of .... Oficina [*Office*] [*Spanish*]
of .... Oficina [*Office*] [*Portuguese*]
oF .... Ohne Fortsetzung [*No More*] [*German*]
OF .... Oil Facility [*International Monetary Fund*]
OF .... Old French [*Language, etc.*]
OF .... Openbare Financien [*Benelux*]   (BAS)
OF .... Organisation Fraternelle [*Fraternal Organization*] [*Mauritius*]
                     (AF)
OF .... Orta Frekans [*Medium Frequency*]   (TU)
OF .... Oslobodilacka Fronta [*Liberation Front*] [*World War II*]   (YU)
OF .... Otechestven Front [*Fatherland Front*] [*A periodical*]   (BU)
Of .... Oud-Frans [*Old French*] [*Language, etc.*] [*Afrikaans*]
OFA .... Omnium Forestier Africain
OFA .... Organizacion Farmaceutica Americana [*Colombia*]   (COL)
OFA .... Orienteering Federation of Australia
OFA .... Over Fifties Association [*Australia*]
OFAA .... Omilos Filon Astynomikon Athinon [*Association of Friends of
                     Athens Police Officers*]
OFAA .... Oyster Farmers' Association of Australia
OFAB .... Aerial High-Explosive Fragmentation Bomb   (RU)
OFAB .... Office d'Amenagement de Boke [*Boke Development Office*]
                     [*Guinea*]   (AF)
OFAEE...... Office Federal des Affaires Economiques Exterieures [*Federal
                     Office for Foreign Economic Affairs*] [*Switzerland*]
OFAI......... Oesterreichisches Forschungsinstitut fuer Artificial Intelligence
                     [*Austrian Research Institute for Artificial Intelligence*]
                     [*Research center*]   (IRC)
OFALAC ... Office Algerien d'Action Commerciale [*Algerian Office of
                     Business Activity*]   (AF)
OFALAC ... Office Algerien d'Action Economique et Touristique   (FLAF)
OFANSW ... Oyster Farmers' Association of New South Wales [*Australia*]
OFARES ... Office de l'Amenagement et de Reconstruction de la Zone
                     Hamma [*Construction, Housing, and Regional
                     Development Ministry*] [*Algeria*]
OFASA...... Obra Filantropica y Asistencia Social Adventista [*Santiago,
                     Chile*]   (LAA)
OFASA...... Organizacion Farmaceutica Americana Sociedad Anonima
                     [*OFA*] [*Colombia*] [*See also*]   (COL)
OFB .... Orszagos Foldbirtokrendezo Birosag [*Central Court for Land
                     Redistribution*]   (HU)
OFBO .... Hydroxyphenylbenzoxazole   (RU)
OFBT........ Orszagos Foldbirtokrendezo Tanacs [*National Council for Land
                     Redistribution*]   (HU)
OFBW .... Ozeanographische Forchungsanstalt der Bundeswehr [*Armed
                     Forces Oceanographic Research Establishment*]   (PDAA)
OFC .... Oceania Football Confederation
OFC .... Oceanography and Fisheries Committee   (ASF)
OFC .... Olayan Financing Co. [*Saudi Arabia*]   (PDAA)
OFCA .... Office d'Exploitation des Carrieres [*Office for the Exploitation of
                     Quarries*] [*Chad*]   (AF)
OFCA .... Organisation des Fabricants de Produits Cellulosiques
                     Alimentaires de la CEE [*Organization of Manufacturers of
                     Cellulose Products for Foodstuffs in the European Economic
                     Community*]
OFCSAV ... Orchardists and Fruit Cool Stores Association of Victoria
                     [*Australia*]
OFDE .... Organisation de Fraternite et de Developpement Economique
                     [*Organization for the Promotion of Fraternity and
                     Economic Development*] [*Mauritius*]   (AF)
OFDI .... Office of Foreign Direct Investment
OFE .... Omospondia Fortoekfortoton Ellados [*Federation of Greek
                     Longshoremen*]   (GC)
OFEDES ... Office des Eaux du Sous-Sol [*Office of Subsoil Water*] [*Niger*]
                     (AF)
OFEMA .... Office Francais d'Exportation de Materiel Aeronautique [*France*]
                     (PDAA)
OFENET ... Office des Entreprises de l'Etat [*Office of State Enterprises*]
                     [*Cambodia*]   (CL)

OFERMAT ... Office Francais de Cooperation pour les Chemins de Fer et les Materiels d'Equipement

OFEROM ... Office Central des Chemins de Fer d'Outre-Mer [*French Overseas Railroad Office*]

OFESA ...... Oficina de Estadisticas Agropecuarias [*Chile*]   (LAA)

OFET .... Organisation Francaise d'Enseignement de la Teledetection [*French Remote Sensing Training Organization*]   (PDAA)

OFF .... Freon Drier and Filter   (RU)

off .... Oeffentlich [*Public*] [*German*]

off .... Offentlig [*Public*] [*Danish/Norwegian*]

off .... Offert [*Offertory*] [*French*]

Off. .... Officier [*or Officiel*] [*Officer or Official*] [*French*]   (MTD)

Off. .... Offisier [*Officer*] [*Afrikaans*]

off .... Offizinell [*Official*] [*German*]   (GCA)

offentl .... Offentlig [*Public*] [*Sweden*]

OFFI .... Orszagos Fordito es Forditashitelesito Iroda [*National Office for Official Translations and Affidavits*]   (HU)

OFFINACO ... Office National de Cooperation [*National Cooperatives Office*] [*Replaced OROC Cambodia*]   (CL)

Off Nr .... Offerte Nummer [*Quotation Number*] [*German*]   (GCA)

off red .... Offres Reduites [*French*]

OFFWF ..... Osterreichischer Fonds zur Forderung der Wissenschaftlichen Forschung [*Austria*]   (EAIO)

Offz .... Offizier [*Officer*] [*German*]

Offzl .... Offizial [*Official*] [*German*]

OFGSA ...... Organic Farming and Gardening Society of Australia

OFGST ...... Organic Farming and Gardening Society of Tasmania [*Australia*]

OFH .... Orszagos Foldhivatal [*National Land Office*]   (HU)

OFI .... Office Francais d'Information [*Later, Agence France-Presse*]   (FLAF)

OFI .... Orientation a la Fonction Internationale

OFI .... Ornamental Fish International   (EAIO)

OFI .... Orszagos Foldhitelintezet [*National Agricultural Credit Bank*]   (HU)

OFIAGRO ... Oficina de Ingenieria Agronomica [*Venezuela*]   (DSCA)

ofic .... Oficina [*Print Shop*] [*Publishing*] [*Portuguese*]

OFICODA ... Oficinas de Control de Distribucion de Abastecimientos [*Supply Distribution Control Offices*] [*Cuba*]   (LA)

OFID .... OPEC [*Organization of Petroleum Exporting Countries*] Fund for International Development   (EAIO)

OFIDA .... Office des Douanes et Accises [*Customs and Excise Office*] [*French*]   (AF)

OFIGAN ... Oficina Nacional de Ganaderia [*Costa Rica*]   (DSCA)

OFIL .... Oficiul Filatelic [*Philatelic Office*]   (RO)

OFIMAD... Omnium Financier de Madagascar

OFIPA .... Societe Omnium Financier de Produits Alimentaires

OFIPLAN ... Oficina de Planificacion Nacional [*National Planning Office*] [*Costa Rica*]   (LA)

OFIS .... Operational Flight Information Service [*ICAO*]   (DA)

OFITEC .... Office Tunisien de l'Expansion Commerciale et du Tourisme

ofits .... Official   (RU)

ofits .... Official, Formal   (BU)

OFJ .... Olafsfjordur [*Iceland*] [*Airport symbol*]   (OAG)

OFK .... Oberfeldkommandantur [*Military government area headquarters*] [*German military - World War II*]

OFK .... Orthophosphoric Acid   (RU)

OFKO .... Omospondia Filathlon Kynigetikou Oplou [*Hunting Weapon Sportsmen's Federation*] [*Greek*]   (GC)

o fl .... Og Flere [*And So On*] [*Norway*]   (GPO)

OFL .... (Ortskomitee der) Organisation Freiwilliger Luftschutzhelfer [(*Local Committee of the*) *Organization of Volunteer Civil Defense Assistants*]   (EG)

OFLA........ Office des Fruits et Legumes d'Algerie [*Fruit and Vegetable Office of Algeria*]   (AF)

OFLAG...... Offizierslager [*Permanent Prison Camp for Captured Officers*] [*German military - World War II*]

OFLC........ Office of Film and Literature Classification [*Australia*]

OFlem .... Old Flemish [*Language, etc.*]   (BARN)

Ofm .... Oberforstmeister [*Chief Forest Supervisor*]   (EG)

OFM .... Oceanic Funds Management Proprietary Ltd. [*Australia*]

OFM .... Office of Financial Management [*New South Wales Treasury*] [*Australia*]

OFM .... Order of Friars Minor [*Italy*]   (EAIO)

OFM .... Ordine dei Frati Minori [*Order of Friars Minor*] [*Rome, Italy*]

OFM .... Relative Phase Modulation   (RU)

OFMAVINS ... Office Malgache des Vins

OFMI .... Orszagos Foldmerestani Intezet [*National Institute of Land Surveying*]   (HU)

OFMN....... Department of Physical and Mathematical Sciences (of the Academy of Sciences, USSR)   (RU)

OFN .... Operation Feed the Nation

OFNACER ... Office National des Cereales [*National Grain Office*] [*Burkina Faso*]

OFNACOM ... Office National de Commerce [*National Marketing Office*] [*Congo*]   (AF)

OFNCS...... Orange Field Naturalist and Conservation Society [*Australia*]

OFO.......... Oficir z Oruda [*Officer in Charge of Arms*]   (YU)

OFOD........ On-Flight Origin and Destination [*International Civil Aviation Organization*] [*Information service or system*]   (DUND)

OFOL .... Orivatikos Fysiolatrikos Omilos Lemesou [*Cyprus*]   (EAIO)

OFOM....... Office de la France d'Outre-Mer

OFOMENTO ... Oficina de Fomento [*Development Office*] [*Colorado*]   (LA)

OFON........ Officer of the Order of the Niger

OFOR........ October Revolution Holdings Department [*Archives*]   (RU)

oforandr ..... Ofoeraendrad [*Unchanged*] [*Sweden*]

OFOTERT ... Optikai, Finommechanikai, es Fotocikkeket Ertekesito Vallalat [*Marketing Enterprise for Optical, Fine Mechanical, and Photograhic Items*]   (HU)

OFP .... Obchodni-Financni Plan [*Business and Financial Plan*]   (CZ)

OFPE........ Office de la Formation Professionnelle et de l'Emploi [*Vocational Training and Employment Bureau*] [*Tunisia*]   (AF)

OFPRA...... Office Francais de Protection des Refugies et Apatrides [*France*]

OFR .... Officer of the Federal Republic [*Nigeria*]

OFR .... Oficiul Farmaceutic Regional [*Regional Pharmaceutic Office*]   (RO)

OFR .... Old French [*Language, etc.*]

OFR .... Opsonocytophagic Test   (RU)

OFR .... Order of the Federal Republic

OFRA .... O'Dochartaigh Family Research Association   (EA)

OFRAC...... On Farm Research Advisory Committee [*Australia*]

OFRATEME ... Office Francais des Techniques Modernes d'Education [*French Office of Modern Educational Techniques*]

OFRIS .... Old Frisian [*Language, etc.*]

OFRT......... Office Francaise de Radio-Television [*France*]   (PDAA)

ofs............... Offset   (RU)

OFS........... Oil from Sludge

OFS........... Orange Free State [*South Africa*]

OFS........... Ordre Franciscain Seculier

OFS........... Osvobodilna Fronta Slovenije [*Liberation Front of Slovenia*] [*YU*]

OFSA........ Ordo Fratrum Sancti Augustini [*Order of St. Augustine - OSA*] [*Rome, Italy*]   (EAIO)

OFSIT .... Orange Free State Investment Trust Ltd.

OFSSA ...... Orange Free State, South Africa   (ILCA)

OFSZSZK ... Orosz Federativ Sozcialista Szovjet Koztarsasag [*Russian Socialist Federative Soviet Republic*]   (HU)

OFT .... Obus en Fonte a Amorcage de Tete [*Military*] [*French*]   (MTD)

OFT .... Optical Fibre Technology

OFT .... Orszagos Foldbirtokrendezo Tanacs [*National Council for Land Redistribution*]   (HU)

OFT .... Orszagos Foldmuvelesugyi Tanacs [*National Agricultural Council*]   (HU)

OFT .... Relative Phase Telegraphy   (RU)

OFTA .... Office for the Aged [*Australia*]

oftalm......... Ophthalmology, Ophthalmologist   (BU)

OFTC......... Optical Fibre Technology Centre [*Australia*]

OFTC........ Overseas Finance and Trade Corp. [*Vietnam*]

OFTH....... Orszagos Foldugyi es Terkepeszeti Hivatal [*National Bureau of Geodesy and Cartography*]   (HU)

OFU.......... Ofu Island [*American Samoa*] [*Airport symbol*]   (OAG)

OFU.......... Organization for Free Ugandans   (AF)

OFUNC..... Organisation des Femmes de l'Union Nationale Camerounaise [*Women's Organization of the Cameroonian National Union*]   (AF)

OFV .... Obuka Oficira za Vatru [*Training of Fire Control Officer*] [*Military*]   (YU)

OFVK .... Oesterreichischer Fachverband fuer Volkskunde [*Austrian Folklore Society*]   (SLS)

Ofw .... Oberfeldwebel [*Sergeant-Major*] [*Air Corps rank*]

OFY .... Operation Feed Yourself [*Ghana*]

OFZS........ Oesterreichisches Forschungszentrum Seibersdorf GmbH [*Austrian Research Center Seibersdorf*] [*Research center*]   (IRC)

og............... Oben Genannt [*Above Named*] [*German*]

OG .... Obergericht [*Court of Appeal*] [*German*]   (DLA)

OG .... Oberstes Gericht [*Supreme Court*] [*German*]

OG .... Obudai Gazgyar [*Gas Works of Obuda*]   (HU)

OG .... Oddzial Glowny [*Main Branch*]   (POL)

OG .... Oesterreichischer Gemeindebund [*Union of Austrian Rural Municipalities*]

OG .... Official Gazette

OG .... Ogasawara Trench

Og .... Ogretmen [*Teacher*]   (TU)

OG .... Old German [*Language, etc.*]

OG .... Operation Chart   (RU)

OG .... Operativna Grupa [*Operational Group*] [*Military*]   (YU)

OG .... Organisation Gestosis [*Basel, Switzerland*]   (EAIO)

OG .... Organotikos Grammatevs [*Organizational Secretary*]   (GC)

OG .... Orientalische Gesellschaft [*Oriental Association*] [*Austria*]   (SLS)

OG .... Osaka Gas Kabushiki Kaisha [*Osaka Gas Co., Inc.*] [*Japan*]

og............... Osztag [*Detachment, Squad*]   (HU)

og............... Ova Godina [*This Year*]   (YU)

OG .... Reference Generator (RU)
OG .... Task Force, Task Group (RU)
OGA........... Oesterreichische Gesellschaft fuer Archaeologie [*Austria*] (SLS)
OGA........... Oesterreichische Gesellschaft fur Akupunktur [*Austrian Society of Acupuncture and Auricular Therapy*] (EAIO)
OGA........... Office General de l'Air
OGA........... Oficiul de Gospodarire a Apelor [*Water Management Office*] (RO)
OGA........... Organic Growers Association [*Australia*]
OGA........... Organizzazione Giovanile Africana
OGA........... Organosis Georgikon Asfaliseon [*Farm Insurance Organization*] [*Greek*] (GC)
OGA........... Orszagos Geodeziai Adattar [*National Documentation Center for Geodesy*] (HU)
OGABI ...... Omnium Gabonais Immobilier
OGAM....... Oesterreichische Gesellschaft fuer Allgemeinmedizin [*Austria*] (SLS)
OGANSW ... Organic Growers' Association of New South Wales [*Australia*]
OGAPROV ... Office Gabonais d'Amelioration et de Production de Viande
OGAR........ Omnium Gabonais d'Assurances et de Reassurances (EY)
OGAWA.... Organic Growers' Association of Western Australia [*Australia*]
OGB........... Oesterreichischer Gewerkschaftsbund [*Austrian Trade Union Federation*] [*Vienna*]
OGB........... Urban Improvement Department (RU)
OGBJO ...... Independent Trade Union Youth [*Luxembourg*] (EAIO)
OGB-L....... Onofhaengege Gewerkschaftsbond-Letzeburg [*Confederation of Independent Trade Unions*] [*Luxembourg*] (EY)
OGBTP...... Office General du Batiment et des Travaux Publics [*French*] (SLS)
OGC........... Office de Gestion, Compatibilite
OGC........... Oyeleke Group of Companies [*Nigeria*]
OGCF .... Oesterreichische Gesellschaft fuer China-Forschung [*Austria*] (SLS)
OGChPP ... Joint Numerical Weather Prediction Unit [*US*] (RU)
OGD .... Operativna Grupa Divizija [*Operational Group of the Divisions*] [*Military*] [*YU*]
OGDB........ Oesterreichische Gesellschaft fur Dokumentation und Bibliographie [*Austrian Association for Documentation and Bibliography*] (PDAA)
OGDC........ Oil and Gas Development Corporation [*Pakistan*] (GEA)
OGDI......... Oesterreichische Gesellschaft fuer Dokumentation und Information [*Austria*] (SLS)
OGE........... Chief Power Engineer Department (BU)
OGE........... Chief Power Engineer's Department (RU)
OGE........... Observer Group Egypt [*UN Truce Supervisor Organization*]
OGE........... Oesterreichische Gesellschaft fuer Ernaehrungsforschung [*Austria*] (SLS)
OGE........... Omospondia Gynaikon Ellados [*Federation of Greek Women*] (GC)
OGE........... Relative Genetic Effectiveness (RU)
OGEDEP... Office de Gestion de la Dette Publique [*Office for the Management of the Public Debt*] [*Zaire*] (AF)
OGEFA ..... Oesterreichische Gesellschaft fuer Arbeitstechnik und Betriebsrationalisierung [*Austria*] (SLS)
Ogefr.......... Obergefreiter [*Corporal*] [*Air Corps rank*]
OGEFUE... Oesterreichische Gesellschaft zur Foederung von Umweltschutz und Energieforschung [*Austria*] (SLS)
O Germ...... Oos-Germaans [*East Teutonic*] [*Language, etc.*] [*Afrikaans*]
Ogerm........ Oud-Germaans [*Old Teutonic*] [*Language, etc.*] [*Afrikaans*]
og esh .... Assault Echelon (BU)
OGEW....... Oesterreichische Gesellschaft fuer Erdoelwissenschaften [*Austria*] (SLS)
OGFKM .... Oesterreichische Gesellschaft fuer Filmwissenschaft, Kommunikations-, und Medienforschung [*Austria*] (SLS)
OGfM .... Oesterreichische Gesellschaft fuer Musik [*Austria*] (SLS)
OGFT .... Osterreichische Gesellschaft fur Weltraumforschung und Flugkorpertechnik [*Austrian Society for Space Exploration and Rocket and Technology*] (PDAA)
OGfU .... Oesterreichische Gesellschaft fuer Unfallchirurgie [*Austria*] (SLS)
OGFW .... Oesterreichische Gesellschaft fuer Angewandte Fremdenverkehrswissenschaft [*Austria*] (SLS)
OGG .... Oesterreichische Geographische Gesellschaft [*Austria*] (SLS)
OGG .... Oesterreichische Geologische Gesellschaft [*Austria*] (SLS)
OGG .... Oxyhemogram (RU)
OGGN .... Department of Geological and Geographical Sciences (of the Academy of Sciences, USSR) (RU)
OGH .... Oberster Gerichtshof [*Supreme Court*] [*German*]
OGH .... Oesterreichische Gesellschaft fuer Holzforschung [*Austria*] (SLS)
OGHMP.... Oesterreichische Gesellschaft fuer Hygiene, Mikrobiologie, und Praeventivmedizin [*Austria*] (SLS)
OGI .... Chief Engineer's Department (RU)
OGI .... Geodetic Surveying Organization (BU)
OGI........... Oesterreichisches Giesserei-Institut [*Austrian Foundry Institute*] [*Research center*] (IRC)
OGIA .... Office of Government Information and Advertising [*Australia*]

OGIL .... Koolaj es Foldgazbanyaszati Ipari Kutato Laboratorium [*Oil and Natural Gas Exploring Industrial Research Laboratory*] (HU)
OGIL .... Office General d'Information sur le Logement (FLAF)
ogiptd .... Separate Guards Antitank Battalion (RU)
OGIS .... Department of Geophysics and Seismology (of the Academy of Sciences, Turkmen SSR) (RU)
OGITH...... Organisation Generale Independante des Travailleurs et Travailleuses d'Haiti (EY)
OGIZ......... Association of State Publishing Houses [*1930-1949*] (RU)
OGK.......... Chief Designer's Department (RU)
OGK.......... Odessa State Conservatory Imeni A. V. Nezhdanova (RU)
OGK.......... Terminal Gas Logging (RU)
OGK-STO ... Chief Designers' Department for the Planning of Machine Tools and Technological Equipment (RU)
Ogl.............. Ogloszony [*Published*] (POL)
OGL........... Open General Licence [*Import classification*] [*India*]
ogl.............. Table of Contents (RU)
OGM .... Chief Mechanic Department (BU)
OGM .... Chief Mechanic's Department (RU)
OGM .... Osterreichische Gesellschaft fur Musik [*Austria*] (EAIO)
OGMA....... Oficinas Gerais de Material Aeronautico [*General Office of Air Material Workshops*] [*Portugal*]
OGMAC.... Oesterreichische Gesellschaft fuer Mikrochemie und Analytische Chemie [*Austria*] (SLS)
OGMD ...... Separate Guards Mortar Battalion (RU)
OGMET ..... Chief Metallurgist Department (BU)
OGMet ...... Chief Metallurgist's Department (RU)
OGMI....... Odessa Hydrometeorological Institute (RU)
OGMI........ Odesskii Gidrometeorologicheskii Institut [*Odessa Hydrometeorological Institute*] [*Ukraine*] (DSCA)
OGMkh ..... Chief Mechanic's Department (RU)
OGMW ...... Osterreichische Gesellschaft fur Musikwissenschaft [*Austria*] (EAIO)
OGN .... Department of Humanities (of the Academy of Sciences, USSR) (RU)
ogn.............. Firearm (BU)
OGN .... Yonagunijima [*Japan*] [*Airport symbol*] (OAG)
OGNB........ Odessa State Scientific Library Imeni A. M. Gor'kiy (RU)
ogneup........ Refractory Products Plant [*Topography*] (RU)
OGO .... Abengourou [*Ivory Coast*] [*Airport symbol*] (OAG)
OGO .... End of Grouped Operation [*Computers*] (RU)
OgOGM .... Ogretmen Okullari Genel Mudurlugu [*Teachers Schools Directorate General*] (TU)
ogp.............. Flame Thrower (BU)
OGP .... Oesterreichische Gesellschaft fuer Parapsychologie [*Austria*] (SLS)
OGPEC...... Officially Guaranteed Private Export Credits
OGPI .... Odessa State Pedagogical Institute Imeni K. D. Ushinskiy (RU)
OGPI .... Orel State Pedagogical Institute (RU)
OGPU........ O Gospodi, Pomogi Ubezhat [*O Lord, Help Me Escape*] [*Wordplay on OGPU, Soviet secret service organization*]
OGPU........ Otdelenie Gosudarstvenni Politcheskoi Upravi [*Special Government Political Administration*] [*Former Soviet secret service organization, also known as GPU Later, KGB*]
Ogr............. Ogrenci [*Student*] (TU)
OGRAPS... Opste Gradevinsko Preduzece Srbije [*General Construction Establishment of Serbia*] (YU)
Ogret-Bir ... Ogretmenler Yardim ve Dayanisma Birligi [*Teachers' Aid and Solidarity Union*] [*Cyprus*] (TU)
OGREVOPROMET ... Preduzece za Promet Ogrevnim Materijalom [*Fuel Trading Establishment*] [*YU*]
OGRR........ Oesterreichische Gesellschaft fuer Raumforschung und Raumplanung [*Austria*] (SLS)
Ogrt........... Ogretmen [*Teacher*] (TU)
OGS .... Oesterreichische Gesellschaft fuer Soziologie [*Austria*] (SLS)
OGS........... Oesterreichische Gesellschaft fuer Statistik [*Austria*] (SLS)
OGS........... Oesterreichische Gesellschaft fuer Strassenwesen [*Austria*] (SLS)
OGS........... Omospondia Georgikon Synetairismon [*Federation of Agricultural Cooperatives*] [*Greek*] (GC)
OGS........... Osservatoria Geofisico Sperimentale [*Geophysical Experimental Observatory*] [*Trieste, Italy*] (MSC)
OGSA .... Organisation de Gestion et de Securite Aeronautique [*Aeronautical Management and Safety Organization*] [*Algeria*] (AF)
ogsb........... Separate Guards Rifle Battalion (RU)
ogsbr .... Separate Guards Rifle Brigade (RU)
OGSD........ German-Soviet Friendship Organization (RU)
OGSE .... Omospondia Georgikon Synetairismon Ellados [*Federation of Greek Agricultural Cooperatives*] (GC)
OGSM .... Fuel and Lubricants Section (RU)
OGSS......... Organizzazione Generale degli Studenti Somali [*Organization of Somali Students*] [*Italian*]
OGSt.......... Oberstes Gericht Strafsachen [*Supreme Court for Criminal Cases*] (WEN)
OGT.......... Chief Technologist's Department (RU)
OGT.......... Orszagos Gazdasagi Tanacs [*National Economic Council*] (HU)

OGT.......... Ortak Gumruk Tarife No. [*Joint Customs Tariff Number*] [*As in EEC transactions*] (TU)

OGTsA ...... Organization of Central American States (RU)

Ogt Svy ...... Ogretim Seviyesi [*Level of Education*] (TU)

OGU .... Odessa State University Imeni I. I. Mechnikov (RU)

OGU .... Old Girls' Union [*Australia*]

OGV.......... Osterreichischer Golf-Verband [*Austria*] (EAIO)

OGVD....... Social Welfare and Education of Children (BU)

OGVF .... Civil Air Fleet Association (RU)

ogvl .... Rolling Barrage, Creeping Barrage (BU)

ogvsbr......... Separate Guards Rifle Brigade (RU)

OGVT .... Oesterreichische Gesellschaft zur Foerderung der Verhaltensforschung, -Modifikation, und Verhaltenstherapie [*Austria*] (SLS)

OGvTPP .... Separate Guards Break-Through Tank Regiment (RU)

OGW .... Oesterreichische Gesellschaft fuer Wirtschaftsraumforschung [*Austria*] (SLS)

OGX.......... Ouargla [*Algeria*] [*Airport symbol*] (OAG)

Ogy .... Orszaggyules [*National Assembly*] (HU)

OGYE .... Orszagos Gyogyszeresz Egyesulet [*National Association of Pharmacists*] (HU)

OGYIT ...... Orszagos Gyermek- es Ifjusagvedelmi Tanacs [*National Council for the Protection of Children and Youth*] (HU)

OGySSzK .. Orszagos Gyogynoveny- es Selyemguboforgalmi Szovetkezeti Kozpont [*National Cooperative for Medicinal Plants and Silk Cocoons*] (HU)

OGZ.......... Obst- und Gemuese-Zentrale [*Fruit and Vegetable Center*] (EG)

OGZ.......... Opci Gradanski Zakonik [*General Civil Code*] (YU)

OH .... Austrian National Union of Students (EAIO)

OH .... Olympijske Hry [*Olympic Games*] (CZ)

OH .... Outstretched Hands [*An association*] [*Italy*] (EAIO)

O/H .... Overzuche Handels Maatschappij [*Foreign Trade Company*] [*Dutch*] (ILCA)

OHA .... OH Aviationa [*France*] [*ICAO designator*] (FAAC)

OHAA .... Oral History Association of Australia (ADA)

OHAD .... Oral History and Antiquities Department

OHASA ..... Occupational Hygiene Association of South Africa (AA)

OHASA ..... Oral Hygienists' Association of South Africa (AA)

OHB .... Orszagos Honvedelmi Bizottmany [*National Defense Council*] (HU)

OHC .... Oral History Collection [*Monash University*] [*Australia*]

OHC .... Order of the Holy Cross, Liberian Mission

OHCF....... Office of Health Care Finance [*Australia*]

OHCSF...... Office of the Head of the Civil Service of the Federation [*Nigeria*]

OHD .... Ohrid [*Former Yugoslavia*] [*Airport symbol*] (OAG)

Ohd .... Oud-Hoogduits [*Old High German*] [*Language, etc.*] [*Afrikaans*]

OHE .... Office of Higher Education [*New South Wales, Australia*]

OHE .... Orszagos Hitelvedo Egylet [*National Credit Protection Association*] (HU)

ohellaerr..... Originalhellaerret [*Original Full Cloth*] [*Publishing Danish/Norwegian*]

OHES........ Okresni Hygienicko-Epidemiologicka Stanice [*District Public Health and Epidemiology Station*] (CZ)

OHF.......... Orszagos Halaszati Felugyeloseg [*National Fishing Inspectorate*] (HU)

Ohfranz...... Originalhalbfranz [*Original Half Calf*] [*Publishing*] [*German*]

Ohfrz......... Originalhalbfranz [*Original Half Calf*] [*Publishing*] [*German*]

OHG .... Oesterreichische Himalaya-Gesellschaft [*Austria*] (SLS)

OHG .... Oesterreichische Humanistische Gesellschaft fuer Steiermark [*Austria*] (SLS)

OHG .... Offene Handelsgesellschaft [*General Partnership*] [*German*]

OHG .... Old High German [*Language, etc.*]

OHH.......... Orszagos Hadigondozo Hivatal [*National War Relief Office*] (HU)

OHI .... Organisation Hydrographique Internationale [*International Hydrographic Organization - IHO*] [*Monte Carlo, Monaco*]

OHI .... Organizacion Hidrografica Internacional [*International Hydrographic Organization - IHO*] [*Spanish*] (ASF)

OHIS .... Organsko Hemijska Industrija [*Macedonia*] (EE)

OHJ.......... Oborova Hospodarska Jednorka [*Sectoral Economic Unit*] (CZ)

OHKI......... Orszagos Husipari Kutatointezet [*National Meat Industry Research Institute*] (HU)

OHL.......... Oberste Heeresleitung [*Supreme Command*] [*Military*] [*German*]

Ohldr .... Originalhalbleder [*Original Half Leather*] [*Publishing*] [*German*]

ohldr.......... Originalhellaeder [*Original Full Leather*] [*Publishing Danish/Norwegian*]

OHLM....... Office des Habitations a Loyer Moderes [*Office of Moderate Rent Housing*] [*Senegal*] (AF)

Ohlwd .... Originalhalbleinwand [*Original Half Cloth*] [*Publishing*] [*German*]

OHMcGF .. Odyssey House McGrath Foundation [*Australia*]

OHP.......... Observatoire de Haute Provence [*Haute Provence Observatory*] [*National Center for Scientific Research*] [*France*] (EAS)

OHP.......... Ochotnicze Hufce Pracy [*Volunteer Labor Brigades*] (POL)

OHP.......... Oral History Project [*Macquarie University*] [*Australia*]

OH PED .... Ohne Pedal [*Without Pedal*] [*Music*]

Ohprgt .... Originalhalbpergament [*Original Half Vellum*] [*Publishing*] [*German*]

OHSA....... Occupational Health and Safety Authority [*Victoria, Australia*]

OHSCSA... Occupational Health and Safety Commission of South Australia

OHSRC ..... Occupational Health Safety and Rehabilitation Council [*New South Wales, Australia*]

OHT .... Orszagos Halgazdasagi Tanacs [*National Council of Fisheries*] (HU)

OHT .... Orszagos Hitelugyi Tanacs [*National Council on Credit*] (HU)

OHT .... Otaibi & Harkan Transport [*Saudi Arabia*]

OHTA....... Organ Historical Trust of Australia

OHU .... Odborne Hornicke Uciliste [*Training Center for Mining Specialists*] (CZ)

OHV .... Osszetett Honvedelmi Verseny [*Combined National Defense Competition*] (HU)

OHY .... Onur Hava Tasimacilik AWMS [*Turkey*] [*ICAO designator*] (FAAC)

OHZ .... Hydroxylzahl [*Hydroxyl Number*] [*German*]

Ohz .... Ofenheizung [*Stove Heating*] (EG)

OI .... Actuating Element (RU)

OI .... Final Sum (RU)

OI .... Information Department (RU)

OI .... Information Processing (RU)

OI .... Oberingenieur [*Chief Engineer*] (EG)

Oi .... Oberirdisch [*Above Ground*] (EG)

OI .... Old Icelandic [*Language*] (BARN)

oi .... Onses Insiens [*In Our Opinion*] [*Afrikaans*]

OI .... Oos-Indiee [*East Indies*] [*Afrikaans*]

OI .... Orijentalni Institut [*Oriental Institute*] (YU)

OI .... Orvostovabbkepzo Intezet [*Institute for Postgraduate Medical Training*] (HU)

OI .... Oscillometric Index (RU)

OI .... Ote Iwapo [*All That Is Must Be Considered*] [*of OI Committee International, a third-world lobby opposing systematic birth control Swahili*]

OI .... Single Flash (RU)

OIA .... Omnium Industriel Africain

OIA .... Organizacion Internacional del Azucar [*International Sugar Organization - ISO*] (EAIO)

OIAA .... Abadan/International [*Iran*] [*ICAO location identifier*] (ICLI)

OIAB .... Boostan [*Iran*] [*ICAO location identifier*] (ICLI)

OIAB .... Ohara Institute for Agricultural Biology [*Japan*] (DSCA)

oiab........... Separate Engineer Airdrome Battalion (BU)

oiab........... Separate Engineer Aviation Battalion (RU)

OIAC .... Oboade Institute of African Culture

OIAC .... Organisation Interafricaine du Cafe [*Inter-African Coffee Organization*] [*Use IACO*] (AF)

OIAD .... Dezful [*Iran*] [*ICAO location identifier*] (ICLI)

OIAG .... Aghajari [*Iran*] [*ICAO location identifier*] (ICLI)

OIAG .... Oesterreichische Industrieholding AG [*Federal Austrian Holding Company*]

OIAG .... Oesterreichische Industrieverwaltungs-Aktiengesellschaft [*Austrian Industrial Management Joint Stock Company*] [*Vienna*]

OIAH........ Gachsaran [*Iran*] [*ICAO location identifier*] (ICLI)

OIAI .... Masjed Soleiman [*Iran*] [*ICAO location identifier*] (ICLI)

OIAJ .... Omidyeh [*Iran*] [*ICAO location identifier*] (ICLI)

OIAK .... Haft-Gel [*Iran*] [*ICAO location identifier*] (ICLI)

OIAL .... Lali [*Iran*] [*ICAO location identifier*] (ICLI)

OIAM .... Bandar Mahshahr [*Iran*] [*ICAO location identifier*] (ICLI)

OIAM .... Department for Testing Aviation Materials (RU)

OIAM .... Organisation Interafricaine et Malgache

OIAN........ Andimeshk [*Iran*] [*ICAO location identifier*] (ICLI)

OIAONI .... Department for the Study, Analysis, and Generalization of Scientific Information (of the All-Union Electrotechnical Institute Imeni V. I. Lenin) (RU)

OIAT .... Abadan [*Iran*] [*ICAO location identifier*] (ICLI)

OIAV .... Oesterreichischer Ingenieur- und Architekten-Verein [*Austria*] (SLS)

OIAW .... Ahwaz [*Iran*] [*ICAO location identifier*] (ICLI)

OIB .... Overseas Information Branch [*Department of Foreign Affairs*] [*Australia*]

OIBA .... Abumusa Island [*Iran*] [*ICAO location identifier*] (ICLI)

OIBB......... Bushehr/Bushehr [*Iran*] [*ICAO location identifier*] (ICLI)

OIBD .... Bandar Deylam [*Iran*] [*ICAO location identifier*] (ICLI)

OIBDI....... Osterreichisches Institut fur Bibliotheksforschung, Dokumentations und Inform ationswesen [*Austria*] (EAIO)

OIBF......... Forouz [*Iran*] [*ICAO location identifier*] (ICLI)

OIBF......... Oesterreichisches Institut fuer Bibliotheksforschung, Dokumentations-, und Informationswesen [*Austria*] (SLS)

OIBG........ Ganaveh [*Iran*] [*ICAO location identifier*] (ICLI)

OIBH........ Bastak [*Iran*] [*ICAO location identifier*] (ICLI)

OIBI......... Golbandi [*Iran*] [*ICAO location identifier*] (ICLI)

OIBK........ Kish Island [*Iran*] [*ICAO location identifier*] (ICLI)

OIBL......... Bandar Lengeh [*Iran*] [*ICAO location identifier*] (ICLI)

OIBN .... Borazjan [*Iran*] [*ICAO location identifier*] (ICLI)
OIBQ .... Khark Island [*Iran*] [*ICAO location identifier*] (ICLI)
OIBS .... Siri Island [*Iran*] [*ICAO location identifier*] (ICLI)
OIBT .... Bushehr [*Iran*] [*ICAO location identifier*] (ICLI)
OIBV .... Lavan Island [*Iran*] [*ICAO location identifier*] (ICLI)
OIBX .... Tonb Island [*Iran*] [*ICAO location identifier*] (ICLI)
OIC .... Oceanic International Corporation [*Uganda*]
OIC .... Office Central des Transports Internationaux par Chemin de Fer (FLAF)
OIC .... Office Ivoirien des Chargeurs
OIC .... Oficina de Investigacion Criminal [*Office of Criminal Investigation*] [*Ecuador*] (LA)
OIC .... Oost-Indische Compagnie [*Benelux*] (BAS)
OIC .... Organisation Internationale Catholique
OIC .... Organisation Internationale du Cafe [*International Coffee Organization*] [*French*] (AF)
OIC .... Organisation Internationale du Commerce [*International Organization for Commerce*] [*France*]
OIC .... Organizacion Internacional de Cafe [*International Coffee Organization*] [*Spanish*] (LA)
OIC .... Organizacion Izquierda Cristiana [*Christian Left Organization*] [*Chile*] (LA)
OIC .... Organization of the Islamic Conference [*See also OCI*] [*Jeddah, Saudi Arabia*] (EAIO)
OICA .... Azna [*Iran*] [*ICAO location identifier*] (ICLI)
OICA .... Organisation Internationale des Constructeurs d'Automobiles (EAIO)
OICB .... Baneh [*Iran*] [*ICAO location identifier*] (ICLI)
OICC .... Bakhtaran [*Iran*] [*ICAO location identifier*] (ICLI)
OICC .... Office International du Cacoa et du Chocolat [*International Office of Cocoa and Chocolate*] [*Established in 1930*]
OICC .... Organization of Islamic Capitals and Cities (EA)
OICD .... Abdanan [*Iran*] [*ICAO location identifier*] (ICLI)
OICE .... Bijar [*Iran*] [*ICAO location identifier*] (ICLI)
O ICE .... Old Icelandic [*Language, etc.*] (ROG)
OICE .... Organizacion de Izquierda Comunista de Espana [*Organization of the Communist Left of Spain*] (WER)
OICE .... Organizacion Interamericana de Cooperacion Economica [*Interamerican Economic Cooperation Organization*] (LAA)
OIcel .... Old Icelandic [*Language*] (BARN)
OICF .... Naft-E-Shah [*Iran*] [*ICAO location identifier*] (ICLI)
OICG .... Ghasre-Shirin [*Iran*] [*ICAO location identifier*] (ICLI)
OICH .... Islam Abad [*Iran*] [*ICAO location identifier*] (ICLI)
OICI .... Ilam [*Iran*] [*ICAO location identifier*] (ICLI)
OICI .... Oficina Internacional Catolica de la Infancia [*International Catholic Child Bureau*]
OICI .... Omnium Immobilier de Cote-D'Ivoire
OICI .... Organizacion Ibero-Americana de Cooperacion Intermunicipal [*Ibero-American Municipal Organization*] (EAIO)
OICI .... Organizacion Interamericana de Cooperacion Intermunicipal [*Interamerican Municipal Organization*]
OICJ .... Boroujerd [*Iran*] [*ICAO location identifier*] (ICLI)
OICK .... Khorram Abad [*Iran*] [*ICAO location identifier*] (ICLI)
OICL .... Sare Pole Zahab [*Iran*] [*ICAO location identifier*] (ICLI)
OICM .... Mehran [*Iran*] [*ICAO location identifier*] (ICLI)
OICM .... Organisation Internationale pour la Cooperation Medicale [*International Organization for Medical Cooperation*]
OICMA ..... Organisation Internationale Contre le Criquet Migrateur Africain [*International African Migratory Locust Organization*] (EAIO)
OICMA ..... Organisation Internationale pour le Controle du Criquet Migrateur Africain [*International African Migratory Locust Organization*] (AF)
OICNM ..... Organisation Intergouvernementale Consultative de la Navigation Maritime [*France*] (FLAF)
OICO .... Songhor [*Iran*] [*ICAO location identifier*] (ICLI)
OICP .... Paveh [*Iran*] [*ICAO location identifier*] (ICLI)
OICQ .... Takab [*Iran*] [*ICAO location identifier*] (ICLI)
OICR .... Dehloran [*Iran*] [*ICAO location identifier*] (ICLI)
OICRF ...... Office International du Cadastre et Regime Foncier
OICS .... Organe International de Controle des Stupefiants [*International Narcotics Control Board*] (EAIO)
OICS .... Sanandaj [*Iran*] [*ICAO location identifier*] (ICLI)
OICT .... Bakhtaran [*Iran*] [*ICAO location identifier*] (ICLI)
OICY .... Malavi [*Iran*] [*ICAO location identifier*] (ICLI)
OICZ .... Aligoodarz [*Iran*] [*ICAO location identifier*] (ICLI)
OID .... Ofensiva de Izquierda Democratica [*Offensive of the Democratic Left*] [*Bolivia*] (PPW)
OID .... Office of Industry and Development [*Australian Capital Territory*]
OIDB .... Oil Industry Development Board [*India*] (PDAA)
OIDE .... Oficiul de Informare Documentara Pentru Energetica [*Energy Documentary Information Office*] [*Romania*] (WED)
OIDMM .... Office Internationale de Documentation de Medecine Militaire [*International Office of Documentation on Military Medicine - IODMM*] (EAIO)

OIDR .... Society of History and Russian Antiquities (at the Moscow University) (RU)
OIDS .... Office of Intellectual Disability Services [*Australia*]
OIE .... Office International des Epizooties [*International Office of Epizootics*] [*Research center*] [*France*] (IRC)
OIE .... Omospondia Ilektrotekhniton Ellados [*Federation of Greek Electricians*] (GC)
OIE .... Organisation Internationale des Employeurs [*International Organization of Employers*]
OIE .... Organosis Inomenon Ethnon [*United Nations Organization*] (GC)
OIE .... Separate Fighter Squadron (RU)
OIEA .... Organismo Internacional de Energia Atomica [*International Atomic Energy Agency*] [*Spanish United Nations*] (DUND)
OIEA .... Organizacion Internacional de Energia Atomica [*International Atomic Energy Agency*] [*Use IAEA*] [*Spanish*] (LA)
OIEC .... Office International de l'Enseignement Catholique [*Catholic International Education Office - CIEO*] (EAIO)
OIEE .... Omospondia Idiotikon Ekpaidevtikon Ellados [*Federation of Private Teachers of Greece*] (GC)
OIEKO ...... Omospondia Ilektrismou kai Epikheiriseon Koinis Ofeleias [*Electric Power and Public Utilities Federation*] [*Greek*] (GC)
OIELE .... Omospondia Idiotikon Ekpaidevtikon Leitourgon Ellados [*Federation of Greek Private School Teachers*] (GC)
OIEN .... Organosis Ithikou Exoplismou Neotitos [*Youth Moral Rearmament Organization*] [*Greek*] (GC)
OIETA .... Office Inter-Etats du Tourisme Africain [*Inter-State Office for African Tourism*] (AF)
OIF .... Department of Historical Sciences and Philology (of the Academy of Sciences, USSR) (RU)
OIF .... Oesterreichisches Institut fuer Formgebung [*Austria*] (SLS)
OIF .... Oficiul de Imbunatatiri Funciare [*Land Improvement Office*] (RO)
OIF .... Opsti Investicioni Fond [*General Investment Fund*] (YU)
OIF .... Osrodek Informacji Firmowej [*Center of Information on Firms*] [*Poland*] (IMH)
OIFB .... Boroujen [*Iran*] [*ICAO location identifier*] (ICLI)
OIFC .... Ghamsar [*Iran*] [*ICAO location identifier*] (ICLI)
OIFD .... Ardestan [*Iran*] [*ICAO location identifier*] (ICLI)
OIFF .... Soffeh [*Iran*] [*ICAO location identifier*] (ICLI)
OIFG .... Golpaygan [*Iran*] [*ICAO location identifier*] (ICLI)
OIFH .... Esfahan [*Iran*] [*ICAO location identifier*] (ICLI)
OIFI .... Semirom [*Iran*] [*ICAO location identifier*] (ICLI)
OIFJ .... Najaf Abad [*Iran*] [*ICAO location identifier*] (ICLI)
OIFK .... Kashan [*Iran*] [*ICAO location identifier*] (ICLI)
OIFL .... Felavarjan [*Iran*] [*ICAO location identifier*] (ICLI)
OIFM .... Esfahan [*Iran*] [*ICAO location identifier*] (ICLI)
OIFN .... Naein [*Iran*] [*ICAO location identifier*] (ICLI)
OIFO .... Khomeini Shahr [*Iran*] [*ICAO location identifier*] (ICLI)
OIFPCA .... Oficiul de Imbunatatiri Funciare si Proiectare Constructii in Agricultura [*Office for Land Improvements and Construction Design in Agriculture*] (RO)
OIFR .... Ghomsheh [*Iran*] [*ICAO location identifier*] (ICLI)
OIFS .... Shahrekord [*Iran*] [*ICAO location identifier*] (ICLI)
OIFT .... Esfahan [*Iran*] [*ICAO location identifier*] (ICLI)
OIFU .... Fereidan [*Iran*] [*ICAO location identifier*] (ICLI)
OIFW .... Khomein [*Iran*] [*ICAO location identifier*] (ICLI)
OIFY .... Meymeh [*Iran*] [*ICAO location identifier*] (ICLI)
OIFZ .... Natanz [*Iran*] [*ICAO location identifier*] (ICLI)
OIG .... Oklopna Izvidacka Grupa [*Armored Reconnaissance Group*] (YU)
OIG .... Organisation Intergouvernementale
OIG .... Organizzazione Internazionale dei Giornalisti [*International Organization of Journalists*] [*Use IOJ*] [*Italian*] (WER)
OIGA .... Astara [*Iran*] [*ICAO location identifier*] (ICLI)
OIGF .... Fouman [*Iran*] [*ICAO location identifier*] (ICLI)
OIGG .... Rasht [*Iran*] [*ICAO location identifier*] (ICLI)
OIGH .... Hashtpar [*Iran*] [*ICAO location identifier*] (ICLI)
OIGIS .... Office of the Inspector-General of Intelligence and Security [*Australia*]
OIGK .... Khailkhal [*Iran*] [*ICAO location identifier*] (ICLI)
OIGL .... Langerood [*Iran*] [*ICAO location identifier*] (ICLI)
OIGM .... Manjil [*Iran*] [*ICAO location identifier*] (ICLI)
OIGN .... Lahijan [*Iran*] [*ICAO location identifier*] (ICLI)
OIGP .... Bandar Anzali [*Iran*] [*ICAO location identifier*] (ICLI)
OIGPE ...... Okregowy Inspektorat Gospodarki Paliwowo-Energetycznej [*District Fuel and Power Management Inspectorate*] (POL)
OIGR .... Office of Industrial Growth and Research [*of BDSA*]
OIGR .... Roodsar [*Iran*] [*ICAO location identifier*] (ICLI)
OIGT .... Rasht [*Iran*] [*ICAO location identifier*] (ICLI)
OIGU .... Roodbar [*Iran*] [*ICAO location identifier*] (ICLI)
OIH .... Orszagos Idegenforgalmi Hivatal [*National Tourist Office*] (HU)
OIHA .... Takestan [*Iran*] [*ICAO location identifier*] (ICLI)
OIHB .... Asad Abad [*Iran*] [*ICAO location identifier*] (ICLI)
OIHD .... Shahzand [*Iran*] [*ICAO location identifier*] (ICLI)

OIHF .... Tafresh [*Iran*] [*ICAO location identifier*] (ICLI)
OIHG........ Kharaghan [*Iran*] [*ICAO location identifier*] (ICLI)
OIHH .... Hamadan [*Iran*] [*ICAO location identifier*] (ICLI)
OIHJ .... Avaj [*Iran*] [*ICAO location identifier*] (ICLI)
OIHM....... Malayer [*Iran*] [*ICAO location identifier*] (ICLI)
OIHN .... Nahavand [*Iran*] [*ICAO location identifier*] (ICLI)
OIHP .... Office International d'Hygiene Publique [*United Nations*]
OIHQ .... Kangavar [*Iran*] [*ICAO location identifier*] (ICLI)
OIHR .... Arak [*Iran*] [*ICAO location identifier*] (ICLI)
OIHS .... Hamadan [*Iran*] [*ICAO location identifier*] (ICLI)
OIHT........ Hamadan [*Iran*] [*ICAO location identifier*] (ICLI)
OIHU .... Tooyserkan [*Iran*] [*ICAO location identifier*] (ICLI)
OII .... Department of Fine Arts (RU)
OIIA .... Abe-Ali [*Iran*] [*ICAO location identifier*] (ICLI)
OIIC.......... Kushke Nosrat [*Iran*] [*ICAO location identifier*] (ICLI)
OIIC.......... Oil Industry Industrial Committee [*Australia*]
OIID .... Tehran/Doshan Tappeh [*Iran*] [*ICAO location identifier*] (ICLI)
OIIE.......... Abyek [*Iran*] [*ICAO location identifier*] (ICLI)
OIIF.......... Firouzkouh [*Iran*] [*ICAO location identifier*] (ICLI)
OIIFDRES ... Oficina Internacional de Informacion del Frente Democratico Revolucionario de El Salvador [*International Information Office of the Democratic Revolutionary Front of El Salvador - IIODRFES*] [*San Jose, Costa Rica*] (EAIO)
OIIG .... Tehran/Ghaleh Morghi [*Iran*] [*ICAO location identifier*] (ICLI)
OIIH .... Mahallat [*Iran*] [*ICAO location identifier*] (ICLI)
OIII........... Tehran/Mehrabad International [*Iran*] [*ICAO location identifier*] (ICLI)
OIIJ .... Karaj [*Iran*] [*ICAO location identifier*] (ICLI)
OIIK .... Ghazvin [*Iran*] [*ICAO location identifier*] (ICLI)
OIIM .... Khoram Dareh [*Iran*] [*ICAO location identifier*] (ICLI)
OIIMF....... Odessa Institute of Engineers of the Maritime Fleet (RU)
OIIN .... Delijan [*Iran*] [*ICAO location identifier*] (ICLI)
OIIQ .... Ghom [*Iran*] [*ICAO location identifier*] (ICLI)
OIIR .... Garmsar [*Iran*] [*ICAO location identifier*] (ICLI)
OIIS .... Semnan [*Iran*] [*ICAO location identifier*] (ICLI)
OIIT.......... Tehran [*Iran*] [*ICAO location identifier*] (ICLI)
OIIU .... Damghan [*Iran*] [*ICAO location identifier*] (ICLI)
OIIV .... Seveh [*Iran*] [*ICAO location identifier*] (ICLI)
OIIVKh ..... Experimental Research Institute of Water Management (RU)
OIIW .... Varamin [*Iran*] [*ICAO location identifier*] (ICLI)
OIIX .... Tehran [*Iran*] [*ICAO location identifier*] (ICLI)
OIJ............ Organisation Internationale des Journalistes [*International Organization of Journalists - IOJ*] (EAIO)
OIJ............ Organismo de Investigacion Judicial [*Judicial Investigation Agency*] [*Costa Rica*] (LA)
OIK .... Accountability and Election Conferences (BU)
OIK .... Negative Impedance Converter (RU)
oik .... Oikealla [*Finland*]
oik .... Oikeastaan [*Really, Properly*] [*Finland*] (GPO)
OIKA .... Shahre Babak [*Iran*] [*ICAO location identifier*] (ICLI)
OIKB .... Bandar Abbas [*Iran*] [*ICAO location identifier*] (ICLI)
OIKD .... Darband/Ravar [*Iran*] [*ICAO location identifier*] (ICLI)
OIKE .... Anar [*Iran*] [*ICAO location identifier*] (ICLI)
oikeustkand ... Oikeustieteen Kandidaatti [*Finland*]
oikeustlis.... Oikeustieteen Lisensiaatti [*Finland*]
oikeusttri.... Oikeustieteen Tohtori [*Finland*]
OIKF......... Baft [*Iran*] [*ICAO location identifier*] (ICLI)
OIKh .... Tool Supply Department (RU)
OIKI .... Bandar Khamir [*Iran*] [*ICAO location identifier*] (ICLI)
OIKJ .... Jiroft [*Iran*] [*ICAO location identifier*] (ICLI)
OIKK .... Kerman [*Iran*] [*ICAO location identifier*] (ICLI)
OIKM........ Bam [*Iran*] [*ICAO location identifier*] (ICLI)
OIKN........ Narmashir [*Iran*] [*ICAO location identifier*] (ICLI)
OIKO........ Minab [*Iran*] [*ICAO location identifier*] (ICLI)
OIKQ........ Gheshm Island [*Iran*] [*ICAO location identifier*] (ICLI)
OIKR......... Rafsanjan [*Iran*] [*ICAO location identifier*] (ICLI)
OIKS......... Shahdad [*Iran*] [*ICAO location identifier*] (ICLI)
OIKT .... Kerman [*Iran*] [*ICAO location identifier*] (ICLI)
OIKU .... Hengam Island [*Iran*] [*ICAO location identifier*] (ICLI)
OIKW .... Kahnooj [*Iran*] [*ICAO location identifier*] (ICLI)
OIKX .... Hormoz Island [*Iran*] [*ICAO location identifier*] (ICLI)
OIKY .... Sirjan [*Iran*] [*ICAO location identifier*] (ICLI)
OIKZ .... Zarand [*Iran*] [*ICAO location identifier*] (ICLI)
OIL .... Oil India Ltd. (PDAA)
OIL .... Oil Insurance Ltd. [*Bermuda*]
OIL .... Organizzazione Internazionale del Lavoro [*International Labor Organization*] [*Use ILO*] [*Italian*] (WER)
OILB......... Organisation Internationale de Lutte Biologique Contre les Animaux et les Plantes Nuisibles [*International Organization for Biological Control of Noxious Animals and Plants - IOBC*] (EAIO)
OILE......... Office of Industry-Linked Education [*University of New South Wales*] [*Australia*]
OILP......... Odigoi Idiotikon Leoforeion Peiraios [*Drivers of Piraeus Privately Owned Buses*] (GC)

OIM.......... Organizatia Internationala a Muncii [*International Labor Organization*] (RO)
OIM.......... Oshima Island [*Japan*] [*Airport symbol*] (OAG)
OIM.......... Society of Marxist Historians (RU)
OIMA .... Torbat-E-Jam [*Iran*] [*ICAO location identifier*] (ICLI)
OIMB .... Birjand [*Iran*] [*ICAO location identifier*] (ICLI)
OIMC .... Sarakhs [*Iran*] [*ICAO location identifier*] (ICLI)
OIMD....... Goonabad [*Iran*] [*ICAO location identifier*] (ICLI)
OIME .... Esfarayen [*Iran*] [*ICAO location identifier*] (ICLI)
OIMF .... Ferdous [*Iran*] [*ICAO location identifier*] (ICLI)
OIMG .... Ghaen [*Iran*] [*ICAO location identifier*] (ICLI)
OIMH....... Torbat-E-Heidarieh [*Iran*] [*ICAO location identifier*] (ICLI)
OIMJ........ Emam Shahr [*Iran*] [*ICAO location identifier*] (ICLI)
OIMK .... Nehbandan [*Iran*] [*ICAO location identifier*] (ICLI)
OIML .... Janat Abad [*Iran*] [*ICAO location identifier*] (ICLI)
OIML .... Organisation Internationale de Metrologie Legale [*International Organization of Legal Metrology*] (EAIO)
OIMM ...... Mashhad [*Iran*] [*ICAO location identifier*] (ICLI)
OIMN....... Bojnord [*Iran*] [*ICAO location identifier*] (ICLI)
OIMO....... Ghoochan [*Iran*] [*ICAO location identifier*] (ICLI)
OIMP....... Taybad [*Iran*] [*ICAO location identifier*] (ICLI)
OIMQ....... Kashmar [*Iran*] [*ICAO location identifier*] (ICLI)
OIMR .... Fariman [*Iran*] [*ICAO location identifier*] (ICLI)
OIMS .... Sabzevar [*Iran*] [*ICAO location identifier*] (ICLI)
OIMS .... Society for the Study of Interplanetary Communications (RU)
OIMT .... Tabas [*Iran*] [*ICAO location identifier*] (ICLI)
OIMV .... Mashhad [*Iran*] [*ICAO location identifier*] (ICLI)
OIMW ...... Shirvan [*Iran*] [*ICAO location identifier*] (ICLI)
OIMX .... Shahr Abad [*Iran*] [*ICAO location identifier*] (ICLI)
OIMY .... Neishaboor [*Iran*] [*ICAO location identifier*] (ICLI)
OIN .... Department of Historical Sciences (of the Academy of Sciences, USSR) (RU)
OIN .... Oficinas de Impuestos Nacionales [*National Tax Offices*] [*Colorado*] (LA)
OIN .... Organisation Internationale de Normalisation [*International Organization for Standardization*]
OIN .... Organizacion Internacional de Normalizacion [*International Organization for Standardization - ISO*] [*Spanish*]
OIN .... Osrodek Informacji Naukowej [*Scientific Information Center*] [*Polish Academy of Sciences Warsaw*] [*Information service or system*] (IID)
OINA .... Amol [*Iran*] [*ICAO location identifier*] (ICLI)
OInAB ...... Separate Engineer Aviation Brigade (RU)
OINB .... Babolsar [*Iran*] [*ICAO location identifier*] (ICLI)
OINC........ Chalous [*Iran*] [*ICAO location identifier*] (ICLI)
OIND....... Minoo Dasht [*Iran*] [*ICAO location identifier*] (ICLI)
OINE .... Kalaleh [*Iran*] [*ICAO location identifier*] (ICLI)
OING .... Gorgan [*Iran*] [*ICAO location identifier*] (ICLI)
OINH .... Behshahr [*Iran*] [*ICAO location identifier*] (ICLI)
OINI .... Ghaem Shahr [*Iran*] [*ICAO location identifier*] (ICLI)
OINK .... Gonbad Ghabous [*Iran*] [*ICAO location identifier*] (ICLI)
OINL .... Alamdeh [*Iran*] [*ICAO location identifier*] (ICLI)
OINM........ Mahmood Abad [*Iran*] [*ICAO location identifier*] (ICLI)
OINN........ Noshahr [*Iran*] [*ICAO location identifier*] (ICLI)
OINO........ Noor [*Iran*] [*ICAO location identifier*] (ICLI)
OINP........ Azad Shahr [*Iran*] [*ICAO location identifier*] (ICLI)
OINQ........ Kelardasht [*Iran*] [*ICAO location identifier*] (ICLI)
OINR........ Ramsar [*Iran*] [*ICAO location identifier*] (ICLI)
OINS .... Sari [*Iran*] [*ICAO location identifier*] (ICLI)
OINV .... Tonkabon [*Iran*] [*ICAO location identifier*] (ICLI)
OINY .... Bandar Torkaman [*Iran*] [*ICAO location identifier*] (ICLI)
OINZ .... Dasht-E-Naz [*Iran*] [*ICAO location identifier*] (ICLI)
OIO........... Omospondia Imikratikon Organoseon [*Federation of Semi-Governmental Organizations*] [*Cyprus*] (GC)
OIOT .... Orszagos Ifjusagpolitikai es Oktatasi Tanacs [*National Youth Policy and Education Council*] (HU)
O i OV........ Errors and Misspellings Are Possible (RU)
OIP .... General True Bearing (RU)
OIP .... Oficina de Ingenieria del Proyecto [*Project Engineering Office*] [*Spanish*] (WER)
OIP .... Oklopna Izvidacka Patrola [*Armored Reconnaissance Patrol*] (YU)
OIP .... Organisation Internationale de la Paleobotanique [*International Organization of Paleobotany*]
OIP .... Organisation Internationale de Psychophysiologie [*International Organization of Psychophysiology - IOP*] (EAIO)
OIP .... Organisation Internationale pour le Progres [*Austria*] (EAIO)
OIP .... Organizacion Iberoamericana de Pilotos [*Ibero-American Organization of Pilots - IOP*] [*Mexico City, Mexico*] (EAIO)
OIP .... Organizacion Internacional de Periodistas [*International Organization of Journalists*] [*Use IOJ*] (LA)
OIP .... Reciprocal True Bearing (RU)
OIP .... True Bearing Reading (RU)

OIPC......... Organisation Internationale de la Police Criminelle [*International Criminal Police Organization*] [*Use INTERPOL*] [*French*]   (CL)

OIPC......... Organisation Internationale de Protection Civile [*International Civil Defense Organization - ICDO*]   (EAIO)

OIPC......... Organizacion Internacional de Policia Criminal [*International Criminal Police Organization*] [*Use INTERPOL*] [*Spanish*]   (LA)

OIPC......... Organizatia Internationala de Politie Criminala [*International Criminal Police Organization - INTERPOL*]   (RO)

OIPCh .... Single-Phase Gas Tube Frequency Converter   (RU)

OIPEEC .... Organisation Internationale pour l'Etude de l'Endurance des Cables [*International Organization for the Study of the Endurance of Wire Ropes - IOSEWR*]   (EAIO)

OIPI.......... Omsk Institute of Zoonotic Infections in Specific Geographic Areas   (RU)

OIPQA ...... Officina Internacional Permanente de Quimica Analitica para los Alimentos Humanos y Animales [*Permanent International Bureau of Analytical Chemistry of Human and Animal Food - PIBAC*] [*Spanish*]   (ASF)

oiptap .... Separate Antitank Artillery Regiment   (RU)

OIPTD....... Separate Antitank Battalion   (RU)

oiptd .... Separate Tank Destroyer Battalion   (BU)

OIR .... Institute of Workers Engaged in Joint Research   (RU)

OIR .... Oesterreichisches Institut fuer Raumplanung [*Austrian Institute for Regional Planning*] [*Research center*]   (IRC)

OIR .... Oficina de Informaciones y Radiodifusion de la Presidencia de la Republica [*Presidential Press and Radio Office*] [*Chile*]   (LA)

OIR .... Oficina Interamericana de Radio [*Inter-American Radio Office*]

OIR .... Okushiri [*Japan*] [*Airport symbol*]   (OAG)

OIR .... Old Irish [*Language, etc.*]

OIR .... Ontwerp Internationale Regeling van de Koopovereenkomst [*Benelux*]   (BAS)

OIR .... Organisation Internationale de Radiodiffusion [*International Radio Organization*] [*Later, OIRT*]

OIR .... Organisation Internationale pour les Refugies

OIR .... Slov-Air [*Slovakia*] [*ICAO designator*]   (FAAC)

OIRD......... Separate Engineer Reconnaissance Patrol   (RU)

OIRP......... Reciprocal True Radio Bearing   (RU)

OIRSA....... Organismo Internacional Regional de Sanidad Agropecuaria [*Regional International Organization of Plant Protection and Animal Health*] [*El Salvador*]

OIRT .... Organisation Internationale de Radiodiffusion et Television [*International Radio and Television Organization*] [*Formerly, OIR*]   (EAIO)

OIS .... Okoliya Statistics Inspector   (BU)

OIS .... Oncology Information Service [*University of Leeds*] [*England*] [*Information service or system*]   (IID)

OISA......... Abadeh [*Iran*] [*ICAO location identifier*]   (ICLI)

OISA......... Organization of Information Agencies of the Countries of Asia   (RU)

OISB......... Bavanat [*Iran*] [*ICAO location identifier*]   (ICLI)

OISB......... Orszagos Ifjusagi Sport Bizottsag [*National Committee for Physical Education of the Youth*]   (HU)

OISC......... Ardakan-E-Fars [*Iran*] [*ICAO location identifier*]   (ICLI)

OISC......... Office of the Insurance and Superannuation Commissioner [*Australia*]

OISCA....... Organization for Industrial, Spiritual, and Cultural Advancement International [*Tokyo, Japan*]   (EAIO)

OISD .... Darab [*Iran*] [*ICAO location identifier*]   (ICLI)

OISE......... Estahbanat [*Iran*] [*ICAO location identifier*]   (ICLI)

OISF......... Fasa [*Iran*] [*ICAO location identifier*]   (ICLI)

OISH .... Farashband [*Iran*] [*ICAO location identifier*]   (ICLI)

OISI .... Dehbid [*Iran*] [*ICAO location identifier*]   (ICLI)

OISJ .... Jahrom [*Iran*] [*ICAO location identifier*]   (ICLI)

OISK......... Kazeroun [*Iran*] [*ICAO location identifier*]   (ICLI)

OISL......... Lar [*Iran*] [*ICAO location identifier*]·   (ICLI)

OISM .... Mamassani [*Iran*] [*ICAO location identifier*]   (ICLI)

OISN .... Neiriz [*Iran*] [*ICAO location identifier*]   (ICLI)

OISP .... Persepolis/Marvdasht [*Iran*] [*ICAO location identifier*]   (ICLI)

OISQ .... Ghir/Karzin [*Iran*] [*ICAO location identifier*]   (ICLI)

OISR......... Lamerd [*Iran*] [*ICAO location identifier*]   (ICLI)

OISS......... Organisation Ibero-Americaine de Securite Sociale   (FLAF)

OISS......... Organizacion Iberoamericana de Seguridad Social [*Ibero-American Social Security Organization*]

OISS......... Shiraz/International [*Iran*] [*ICAO location identifier*]   (ICLI)

OIST......... Shiraz [*Iran*] [*ICAO location identifier*]   (ICLI)

OISTV....... Organisation Internationale pour la Science et la Technique du Vide

OISU .... Abarghou [*Iran*] [*ICAO location identifier*]   (ICLI)

OISW .... Kohkiloyeh [*Iran*] [*ICAO location identifier*]   (ICLI)

OISX .... Khonj [*Iran*] [*ICAO location identifier*]   (ICLI)

OISY......... Yasouj [*Iran*] [*ICAO location identifier*]   (ICLI)

OISZ .... Firouzabad [*Iran*] [*ICAO location identifier*]   (ICLI)

OIT .... Oficina Internacional del Trabajo [*International Labor Office*] [*Spanish*]

OIT .... Oita [*Japan*] [*Airport symbol*]   (OAG)

O IT .... Old Italian [*Language, etc.*]   (ROG)

OIT .... Organisation Internationale du Travail [*International Labor Organization*] [*French United Nations*]   (EAIO)

OIT .... Organizacion Internacional del Trabajo [*International Labor Organization*] [*Spanish United Nations*]   (DUND)

OIT .... Organization Iberoamericaine de Television   (NTCM)

OIT .... Orszagos Idegenforgalmi Tanacs [*National Council on Tourism*]   (HU)

OIT .... Orszagos Iparoktatasi Tanacs [*National Council on Industrial Training*]   (HU)

OIT .... Osrodek Informacji Turystycznej [*Tourist Information Center*] [*Poland*]

OITA .... Sarab [*Iran*] [*ICAO location identifier*]   (ICLI)

OITAF....... Organizzazione Internazionale dei Trasporti a Fune [*Italian*]   (SLS)

OITB......... Mahabad [*Iran*] [*ICAO location identifier*]   (ICLI)

OITC......... Sardasht [*Iran*] [*ICAO location identifier*]   (ICLI)

OITD........ Marand [*Iran*] [*ICAO location identifier*]   (ICLI)

OITDA ...... Optoelectronic Industry and Technology Development Association [*Japan*]

OITF......... Organisation Intergouvernementale pour les Transports Internationaux Ferroviaires [*Intergovernmental Organization for International Carriage by Rail*]   (EAIO)

OITG......... Naghadeh [*Iran*] [*ICAO location identifier*]   (ICLI)

OITH......... Khaneh/Piranshahr [*Iran*] [*ICAO location identifier*]   (ICLI)

OITI.......... Mianeh [*Iran*] [*ICAO location identifier*]   (ICLI)

OITI.......... Orszagos Idegsebeszeti Tudomanyos Intezet [*National Scientific Institute on Neurosurgery*]   (HU)

OITIS .... Overseas Industrial and Trade Investment Services

OITJ .... Julfa [*Iran*] [*ICAO location identifier*]   (ICLI)

OITK .... Khoy [*Iran*] [*ICAO location identifier*]   (ICLI)

OITK .... Special Corrective Labor Colony   (RU)

OITM .... Maragheh [*Iran*] [*ICAO location identifier*]   (ICLI)

OITN .... Meshgin Shahr [*Iran*] [*ICAO location identifier*]   (ICLI)

OITO .... Mian Do Ab [*Iran*] [*ICAO location identifier*]   (ICLI)

OITP......... Parsabad/Moghan [*Iran*] [*ICAO location identifier*]   (ICLI)

OITQ .... Ahar [*Iran*] [*ICAO location identifier*]   (ICLI)

OITR .... Corrective Labor Department   (RU)

OITR .... Uromiyeh [*Iran*] [*ICAO location identifier*]   (ICLI)

OITS......... Organizacion Internacional de Telecomunicaciones [*International Organization of Telecommunications*] [*Use IOTS*]   (LA)

OITS......... Saghez [*Iran*] [*ICAO location identifier*]   (ICLI)

OITT........ Tabriz [*Iran*] [*ICAO location identifier*]   (ICLI)

OITU .... Makou [*Iran*] [*ICAO location identifier*]   (ICLI)

OITV .... Tabriz [*Iran*] [*ICAO location identifier*]   (ICLI)

OITW .... Azar Shahr [*Iran*] [*ICAO location identifier*]   (ICLI)

OITX .... Sareskand [*Iran*] [*ICAO location identifier*]   (ICLI)

OITY .... Marivan [*Iran*] [*ICAO location identifier*]   (ICLI)

OITZ .... Oddeleni Inzenyrsko-Technickeho Zasobovani [*Engineer-Technical Supply Department*]   (CZ)

OITZ .... Zanjan [*Iran*] [*ICAO location identifier*]   (ICLI)

OIU............ Omdurman Islamic University [*Sudan*]

OIUK......... Hydroxyindoleacetic Acid   (RU)

OIV .... Oesterreichisches Institut fuer Verpackungswesen an der Wirtschaftsuniversitaet Wien [*Austria*]   (SLS)

OIV .... Office International de la Vigne et du Vin [*International Vine and Wine Office*]   (EAIO)

OIW .... Office of Indigenous Women [*Australia*]

OIYA .... Ardakan-E-Yazd [*Iran*] [*ICAO location identifier*]   (ICLI)

OIYaI........ Joint Institute of Nuclear Research   (RU)

OIYB .... Bafgh [*Iran*] [*ICAO location identifier*]   (ICLI)

OIYD .... Dehshir [*Iran*] [*ICAO location identifier*]   (ICLI)

OIYE .... Omospondia Idiotikon Ypallilon Ellados [*Greek Federation of Private Employees*]   (GC)

OIYF......... Taft [*Iran*] [*ICAO location identifier*]·   (ICLI)

OIYK .... Khor/Jandagh [*Iran*] [*ICAO location identifier*]   (ICLI)

OIYM .... Mehriz [*Iran*] [*ICAO location identifier*]   (ICLI)

OIYN......... Khore Beyabanak [*Iran*] [*ICAO location identifier*]   (ICLI)

OIYQ .... Khezr Abad [*Iran*] [*ICAO location identifier*]   (ICLI)

OIYT .... Yazd [*Iran*] [*ICAO location identifier*]   (ICLI)

OIYY .... Yazd [*Iran*] [*ICAO location identifier*]   (ICLI)

OIYZ .... Ashkezar [*Iran*] [*ICAO location identifier*]   (ICLI)

OIZ............ Joint Publishing House   (RU)

OIZ............ Opsti Imovinski Zakonik [*General Civil Code*]   (YU)

OIZ............ Organizatia Internationala a Ziaristilor [*International Organization of Journalists*]   (RO)

OIZ............ Publications Department (of the People's Commissariat of Defense)   (RU)

OIZ............ Society of Inventors   (RU)

OIZA .... Jalagh [*Iran*] [*ICAO location identifier*]   (ICLI)

OIZB .... Zabol [*Iran*] [*ICAO location identifier*]   (ICLI)

OIZC .... Chah Bahar/Konarak [*Iran*] [*ICAO location identifier*]   (ICLI)

OIZD .... Dashtyari [*Iran*] [*ICAO location identifier*]   (ICLI)

OIZG .... Ghasre Ghand [*Iran*] [*ICAO location identifier*]   (ICLI)

OIZH........ Zahedan [*Iran*] [*ICAO location identifier*]   (ICLI)
OIZI......... Iran Shahr [*Iran*] [*ICAO location identifier*]   (ICLI)
OIZJ........ Jask [*Iran*] [*ICAO location identifier*]   (ICLI)
OIZK .... Khash [*Iran*] [*ICAO location identifier*]   (ICLI)
OIZL........ Zabolee [*Iran*] [*ICAO location identifier*]   (ICLI)
OIZM ...... Mirjaveh [*Iran*] [*ICAO location identifier*]   (ICLI)
OIZN ...... Bazman [*Iran*] [*ICAO location identifier*]   (ICLI)
OIZO .... Sarbaz [*Iran*] [*ICAO location identifier*]   (ICLI)
OIZP........ Bampoor [*Iran*] [*ICAO location identifier*]   (ICLI)
OIZR .... Bask [*Iran*] [*ICAO location identifier*]   (ICLI)
OIZS........ Saravan [*Iran*] [*ICAO location identifier*]   (ICLI)
OIZT .... Zahedan [*Iran*] [*ICAO location identifier*]   (ICLI)
OIZY .... Nik-Shahr [*Iran*] [*ICAO location identifier*]   (ICLI)
OJ .... Ohne Jahr [*Without Date of Publication*] [*Bibliography*]
                 [*German*]
OJ .... Oklopna Jedinica [*Armored Unit*]   (YU)
OJ .... Osvetova Jizba [*Cultural Room*]   (CZ)
OJA .... Organizacja Jednosci Afrykanskiej [*Organization of African
                 Unity*] [*Poland*]
OJAC........ Amman [*Jordan*] [*ICAO location identifier*]   (ICLI)
OJAF........ Amman [*Jordan*] [*ICAO location identifier*]   (ICLI)
OJAI........ Amman/Queen Alia [*Jordan*] [*ICAO location identifier*]   (ICLI)
OJAM ...... Amman/Marka [*Jordan*] [*ICAO location identifier*]   (ICLI)
OJAQ .... Aqaba [*Jordan*] [*ICAO location identifier*]   (ICLI)
OJBD....... Irbid [*Jordan*] [*ICAO location identifier*]   (ICLI)
OJCE........ Orchestre des Jeunes de la Communaute Europeenne [*European
                 Community Youth Orchestra - ECYO*]   (EAIO)
OJE........... Okumenischer Jugendrat in Europa [*Ecumenical Youth Council
                 in Europe - EYCE*]   (EAIO)
OJE........... Organizacion Juvenil Espanola [*Spanish Youth Organization*]
                 (WER)
OJEC........ Official Journal of the European Communities
OJG .... Austrian Trade Union of Journalists   (EAIO)
OJHF .... Hotel Five [*Jordan*] [*ICAO location identifier*]   (ICLI)
OJHR ...... Hotel Four [*Jordan*] [*ICAO location identifier*]   (ICLI)
OJJO .... Jericho [*Jordan*] [*ICAO location identifier*]   (ICLI)
OJJR .... Jerusalem [*Jordan*] [*ICAO location identifier*]   (ICLI)
OJK .... Organisation de la Jeunesse Khmere [*Cambodian Youth
                 Organization*]   (CL)
OJM .... Olympiade Junger Mathematiker [*Olympiad of Young
                 Mathematicians*] [*Germany*]
OJM .... Organizacao da Juventude Mocambicana [*Mozambique Youth
                 Organization*]   (AF)
OJMF....... Mafraq [*Jordan*] [*ICAO location identifier*]   (ICLI)
OJN .... Organizacao Nacional dos Jornalistas [*Trade Union*]
                 [*Mozambique*]   (EY)
OJO .... Organizacion Juvenil de Octubre [*October Youth Organization*]
                 [*Spanish*]   (WER)
OJRL........ Optoelectronics Joint Research Laboratory [*Japan*]
OJT........... Orang Jahat Tempatan [*Local Bad Character*]   (ML)
OJZZ........ Amman [*Jordan*] [*ICAO location identifier*]   (ICLI)
OK............. Association for Educational Activities [*Finland*]   (EAIO)
OK............. Check Valve   (RU)
ok .... Circa   (BU)
OK............. Common Collector   (RU)
OK............. Compensating Winding   (RU)
OK............. Deflecting Coil   (RU)
OK............. Joint Command   (RU)
ok .... Near, About, Approximately   (RU)
OK............. Obchodni Komora [*Chamber of Commerce*]   (CZ)
OK............. Oblasni Komitet [*Regional Committee*]   (YU)
OK............. Oblast Committee   (RU)
ok .... Ocean   (RU)
OK............. Oceanographic Commission   (RU)
OK............. Odvodni Komise [*Draft Board*]   (CZ)
OK............. Ohne Kosten [*Without Cost*] [*German*]
ok .... Oka [*or Okades*] [*Unit of weight equal to 2.8 pounds*]   (GC)
ok .... Okoliya   (BU)
OK............. Okoliya Committee   (BU)
ok .... Okolnik [*Administrative Instruction*]   (POL)
ok .... Okolo [*Approximately*]   (POL)
OK............. Okresna Komisia [*District Commission*]   (CZ)
Ok .... Okrug [*District*] [*Commonwealth of Independent States*]   (EECI)
OK............. Okrug Committee   (BU)
OK............. Okruzni Komitet [*County Committee*]   (YU)
Ok .... Okulu [*School*]   (TU)
Ok .... Okunur [*Readable, Worthy of Being Read*]   (TU)
OK............. Ola Kala [*All Is Well*] [*Greek*]
OK............. Oliekonsumenternas Foerbund [*Oil company*] [*Merged with SP
                 to form OK Petroleum*] [*Sweden*]
OK............. Olympic Committee   (RU)
OK............. Onderkas [*Lowercase*] [*Afrikaans*]
OK............. Optical Quadrant   (RU)
OK............. Organizational Committee of the RSDRP   (RU)
OK............. Orszaggyules Konyvtara [*Library of the National Assembly*]
                 (HU)

ok .... Orszagos Kirako Vasar [*National Merchandise Fair*]   (HU)
OK............ Orszagos Kozpont [*National Center*]   (HU)
OK............. Oskar Kokoschka [*Austrian painter*] [*1886-1980*]
ok .... Osszekoto [*Liaison, Contact*]   (HU)
OK............. Personnel Department   (RU)
ok .... Reflux Condensate   (RU)
OK............. Release Key   (RU)
OK............. Reverse Course   (RU)
OKA.......... Okinawa [*Japan*] [*Airport symbol*]   (OAG)
OKA.......... Organismoi Koinonikis Asfaliseos [*Social Insurance
                 Organizations*] [*Greek*]   (GC)
OKA.......... Pulmotor, Resuscitating Oxygen Apparatus   (RU)
OKA.......... Separate Caucasian Army   (RU)
OKA.......... Separate "Red Banner" Army   (RU)
OKAA....... Kuwait Directorate General of Civil Aviation [*Kuwait*] [*ICAO
                 location identifier*]   (ICLI)
OKAB .... Oskarshamnsverkets Kraftgrupp [*Sweden*]   (PDAA)
OKAC....... Kuwait [*Kuwait*] [*ICAO location identifier*]   (ICLI)
OKAD....... Single-Phase Capacitive Induction Motor   (RU)
OKAE....... Separate Spotting Air Squadron   (RU)
OKAF....... Kuwait Air Force [*Kuwait*] [*ICAO location identifier*]   (ICLI)
OKAL-KOOP ... Omorfo Kalkinma Kooperatif Sirketi [*Omorfo Development
                 Cooperative*]   (TU)
OKAP........ Okrajna Avtoprevozniska Podjetja [*District Motor Transport
                 Establishments*]   (YU)
okap .... Surface Gunnery Support Force   (RU)
okarab .... Separate Machine Gun Artillery Battalion   (BU)
okart........... Originalkartonnage [*Original Paperboard Binding*] [*Publishing
                 Danish/Norwegian*]
OKB.......... Design Office Based on Public Participation   (RU)
OKB.......... Experimental Design Office   (RU)
OKB.......... Odeljak Korpusne Baze [*Detachment of Corps Depot*]   (YU)
OKB.......... Oesterreichische Kontrollbank [*Export credit agency*] [*Austria*]
OKB.......... Oesterreichischer Komponistenbund [*Austria*]   (SLS)
OKB.......... Orchid Beach [*Australia*] [*Airport symbol*]
OKB.......... Organizata e Kombeve te Bashkuara [*Albanian*]
OKB.......... Special Design Office   (RU)
OKBA....... Experimental Design Office for Automation   (RU)
OKBK....... Kuwait/International [*Kuwait*] [*ICAO location identifier*]   (ICLI)
OKBK....... Orszagos Konyvforgalmi es Bibliografiai Kozpont [*National
                 Book Circulation and Bibliography Center*]   (HU)
OK(b)P ...... Oroszorszagi Kommunista (Bolsevik) Part [*Russian Communist
                 Party (Bolsheviks)*]   (HU)
OKBT .... Orszagos Kozlekedesbiztonsagi Tanacs [*National Traffic Safety
                 Council*]   (HU)
OKChPH... Okresni Klub Chovatelu Postovnich Holubu [*District Club of
                 Carrier Pigeon Breeders*]   (CZ)
ok csop .... Osszekoto Csoport [*Liaison Group*]   (HU)
OKCT .... Odbor Klubu Ceskych Turistu [*Branch of the Czech Tourist
                 Club*]   (CZ)
OKD.......... Ostravsko-Karvinske Doly [*Ostrava-Karvina Mines*]   (CZ)
OKD.......... Ostravsko-Karvinske Kamenouhelne Doly [*Ostrava-Karvina
                 Coal Mines*]   (CZ)
OKD.......... Sapporo/Okadama [*Japan*] [*Airport symbol*]   (OAG)
OKDE....... Organosi Kommouniston Diethniston Elladas [*Organization of
                 Communist Internationalists of Greece*]   (GC)
OKDVA ..... Special "Red Banner" Far Eastern Army   (RU)
OKE........... Okino Erabu [*Japan*] [*Airport symbol*]   (OAG)
OKE........... Omas Koinovoulevtikou Ergou [*Group of Parliamentary Work*]
                 (GC)
OKE........... Omospondia Kafepolon Ellados [*Greek Coffee Merchants
                 Federation*]   (GC)
OKE........... Omospondia Klostoyfandourgon Ellados [*Federation of Greek
                 Textile Workers*]   (GC)
OKET .... Orszagos Kozegeszsegugyi Tanacs [*National Council of Public
                 Health*]   (HU)
OKF........... Photometric Ocular   (RU)
OK FJN ..... Ogolnopolski Komitet Frontu Jednosci Narodu [*All-Poland
                 National Unity Front Committee*]   (POL)
OKFN....... Obwodowy Komitet Frontu Narodowego [*District Committee of
                 the People's Front*]   (POL)
OKFN....... Ogolnopolski Komitet Frontu Narodowego [*All-Poland
                 Committee of the People's Front*]   (POL)
OKFP........ Oddzialowa Komisja Funduszu Posmiertnego [*Departmental
                 Commission of the Death Benefit Fund*]   (POL)
OKFS........ Okoliya Committee for Physical Culture and Sports   (BU)
OKFS........ Okrug Committee for Physical Culture and Sports   (BU)
OKG.......... Laser   (RU)
OKG.......... Obuv - Kuze - Guma [*Shoes - Leather - Rubber (A national
                 enterprise)*]   (CZ)
OKG.......... Oesterreichische Gesellschaft fuer Kommunikationsfragen
                 [*Austria*]   (SLS)
OKG.......... Okoyo [*Congo*] [*Airport symbol*]   (OAG)
OKG.......... Oskarshamnsverkets Kraft Grupp Aktiebolag [*Sweden*]
OKGT........ Orszagos Koolaj es Gazipari Troszt [*National Oil and Gas
                 Industry Trust*]   (HU)

OKGV........ Organismos Kypriakis Galakto-Viomikhanias [*Cypriot Dairy Industry Organization*] (GC)
OKh........... Fragmentation Chemical [*Shell*] (RU)
OKH.......... Oberkommando des Heeres [*Army High Command*] [*German military - World War II*]
OKH.......... Orszagos Kozellatasi Hivatal [*National Office of Public Supply*] (HU)
OKH.......... Orszagos Kozponti Hitelszovetkezet [*National Central Credit Society*] (HU)
OKhAB..... Fragmentation Chemical Aerial Bomb (RU)
okhb........... Separate Chemical Battalion (RU)
OKhEN...... Orthodoxos Khristianiki Enosis Neon [*Union of Orthodox Christian Youth*] [*Cyprus*] (GC)
OKhI.......... General Art Exhibit (BU)
OKhK......... Okhta Chemical Kombinat (RU)
OKhK......... Society of Book Artists (RU)
okhlazhd.... Cooled, Chilled, Refrigerated (RU)
okhmatdet... Institute of Mother and Child Care (RU)
OKhMK..... Orsko-Khalilovskiy Metallurgical Kombinat (RU)
OKhN........ Department of Chemical Sciences (of the Academy of Sciences, USSR) (RU)
OKhOA..... Organismos Khrimatodotiseos Oikonomikis Anaptyxeos [*Economic Development Funding Organization*] [*Greek*] (GC)
OKhOBR... Department of Art Education (RU)
okhot.......... Hunting (RU)
okhotn........ Hunter's Cabin [*Topography*] (RU)
OKhR........ Association of Realist Artists (RU)
OKhR........ Roadstead Defense (RU)
okhr............ Separate Chemical Company (RU)
okhr sl....... Security Service (BU)
okh rz......... Security Patrol [*Cavalry*] (BU)
OKhTs....... Department of Art Treasures (RU)
OKhVY...... Omospondia (Ergaton, Tekhniton, kai Ypallilon) Khimikis Viomikhanias kai Ygieinis [*Federation (of Workers, Technicians, and Employees) of the Chemical Industry and Sanitation*] [*Greek*] (GC)
OKhZ........ Administration of United State Chemical Plants (RU)
OKI........... Oki Island [*Japan*] [*Airport symbol*] (OAG)
OKI........... Okresni Kulturni Inspektorat [*Office of the District Inspector of Cultural Activities*] (CZ)
OKI........... Ontozesi Kutato Intezet [*Irrigation Research Institute*] [*Hungary*] (ARC)
OKI........... Organo Kemijska Industrija [*Former Yugoslavia*] (PDAA)
OKI........... Orszagos Kardiologiai Intezet [*National Institute of Cardiology*] (HU)
OKI........... Orszagos Kozegeszsegugyi Intezet [*National Institute of Public Health*] (HU)
OKIP......... Department of Control and Measuring Instruments (RU)
OKiP......... Oswiata, Ksiazka, i Prasa [*Education, Book, and Press (Club)*] (POL)
OKIS......... Organsko Kemijska Industrija Skopje [*Former Yugoslavia*]
OKISAR.... Special Committee for the Study of Union and Autonomous Republics (of the Academy of Sciences, USSR) (RU)
okisl pl....... Oxidizing Flame (RU)
OKISZ....... Kisipari Szovetkezetek Orszagos Szovetsege [*National Federation of Artisan Cooperatives*] (HU)
OKJ.......... Okada Airlines Ltd. [*Nigeria*] [*ICAO designator*] (FAAC)
OKJ.......... Okayama [*Japan*] [*Airport symbol*] (OAG)
OKJP........ Osterreichische Kommission Justitia et Pax [*Austria*] (EAIO)
okk............ Joint Force Command Code (RU)
OKK.......... Oblast Control Commission (RU)
OKK.......... Okregowa Komisja Ksiezy [*District Commission of Clergy*] (POL)
OKK.......... Omilos Kynofilon Kyprou [*Cyprus*] (EAIO)
OKK.......... Orszagos Kereskedelmi Kamara [*National Chamber of Commerce*] (HU)
OKK.......... Orszagos Konyvtari Kozpont [*National Library Center*] (HU)
OKK.......... Red Cross Society (RU)
OKKGM.... Orman Koylerini Kalkindirma Genel Mudurlugu [*Forest Villages Development Directorate General*] (TU)
OKKMA.... Special Commission for the Kursk Magnetic Anomaly (RU)
OKKPJ...... Okruzni Komitet Komunisticke Partije Jugoslavije [*County Committee of the Communist Party of Yugoslavia*] (YU)
OKKSC...... Okresni Komise Komunisticke Strany Ceskoslovenska [*District Commission of the Czechoslovak Communist Party*] (CZ)
OKL.......... Oesterreichisches Kuratorium fuer Landtechnik [*Austrian Governing Body for Agricultural Engineering*] (ARC)
okl............. Okladka [*Book Cover*] (POL)
okl............. Okleveles [*Certified, Possessing a Diploma (for example, Okl. Gepesz Mernok, Certified Mechanical Engineer)*] (HU)
OKL.......... Optikai es Finommechanikai Kozponti Kutato Laboratorium [*Central Research Laboratory for Optics and Precision Mechanics*] (HU)
OKLA........ Organismos Kendrikis Lakhanagoras Athinon [*Athens Central Vegetable-Market Organization*] (GC)

OKLE........ "Organosi Kommouniston Laiki Exousia" [*"Popular Power Organization of Communists"*] [*Greek*] (GC)
OKLK........ Okresni Komise Lidove Kontroly [*District Commission of People's Control*] (CZ)
oklot.......... Originalklotband [*Original Cloth Binding*] [*Publishing*] [*Sweden*]
oklotbd...... Originalklotband [*Original Cloth Binding*] [*Publishing*] [*Sweden*]
OKM......... Department of Clinical Medicine (RU)
OKM......... Oberkommando der Kriegsmarine [*Navy High Command*] [*German military - World War II*]
OKML...... District Courses for Junior Lieutenants (RU)
OKMP....... Oddeleni Kulturni-Masove Prace [*Cultural and Propaganda Department*] (CZ)
OKMZ....... Osvetova Komise Ministerstva Zemedelstvi [*Cultural Commission of the Ministry of Agriculture*] (CZ)
OKN.......... Okondja [*Gabon*] [*Airport symbol*] (OAG)
OKN.......... Okregowa Komisja Narciarska [*District Ski Commission*] (POL)
okn............ Reflux Condensate Pump (RU)
OK naSNM... Okoliya Committee of the People's Youth Union (BU)
OKNE....... Omospondia Kommounistikis Neolaias Ellados [*Federation of Greek Communist Youth*] (GC)
OKNO....... Kuwait International NOTAM Office [*Kuwait*] [*ICAO location identifier*] (ICLI)
OKNO....... Okruzni Komitet Narodne Omladine [*County Committee of the People's Youth*] (YU)
OKO.......... All-Russian Association of Cinematographic Societies (RU)
OKO.......... Oficer Kulturalno-Oswiatowy [*Culture and Education Officer*] (POL)
OKO.......... Plan Position Indicator (RU)
OKOK-DER... Ogretmen, Kolejliler, Ogretim, ve Kultur Dernegi [*Teachers', College Students', Teaching and Cultural Organization*] [*Cyprus*] (TU)
okol........... Okoliya (BU)
Okol k-t..... Okoliya Committee (BU)
Okol narsuvet... Okoliya People's Council (BU)
Okorg........ Okoliya Organizer (BU)
OKOS........ Officer Personnel Section (RU)
OKP.......... Citizens' Parliamentary Club [*Poland*] [*Political party*]
OKP.......... Compass Bearing Reading (RU)
OKP.......... LASER (RU)
OKP.......... Ogolnopolski Komitet Pokoju [*All-Poland Peace Committee*] [*Poland*]
OKP.......... Okresni Komunalni Podnik [*District Communal Enterprise*] (CZ)
OKP.......... Okrug Committee on Transportation (RU)
OKP.......... Oksapmin [*Papua New Guinea*] [*Airport symbol*] (OAG)
OKP.......... Olasz Kommunista Part [*Italian Communist Party*] (HU)
OKP.......... One Kameroon Party
OKP.......... Organismoi Koinonikis Politikis [*Social Policy Organizations*] [*Greek*] (GC)
OKP.......... Reciprocal Compass Bearing (RU)
OKP.......... Surface Support Force (RU)
OKP.......... United Peasants' Party [*Polish People's Republic*] (RU)
OKPG........ United Communist Party of Germany (RU)
okpp.......... Separate Border Control Post (RU)
OKPS........ General Leather Workers Trade Union (BU)
OKPS........ Okoliya Trade Unions Committee (BU)
OKPUV..... Oddil Kanonu Proti Utocne Vozbe [*Antitank Battalion*] (CZ)
OKQ.......... Okaba [*Indonesia*] [*Airport symbol*] (OAG)
OKR.......... Counterintelligence Section (RU)
OKR.......... Experimental Design Work (RU)
OKR.......... Major Repair Department, General Overhaul Department (RU)
okr............ Okreg [*District, Region*] (POL)
OKR.......... Okregowy Klub Racjonalizacji [*Regional Rationalization Club*] (POL)
okr............ Okres [*District*] (CZ)
okr............ Okrug (BU)
okr............ Okrug, District (RU)
OKR.......... Ostravsko-Karvinsky Revir [*Ostrava-Karvina Coal Basin*] (CZ)
OKR.......... Ostravsky Kamenouhelny Revir [*Ostrava Coal Basin*] (CZ)
okr............ Outskirts [*Topography*] (RU)
okrae......... Separate Spotting and Air Reconnaissance Squadron (RU)
okrae......... Separate Spotting and Reconnaissance Aviation Squadron (BU)
OKRAM..... Society of Marxist Students of Local Lore (RU)
OKRAP..... Separate Spotting and Air Reconnaissance Regiment (RU)
okrap......... Separate Spotting and Reconnaissance Aviation Regiment (BU)
Okres......... Okrug Economic Conference (RU)
okrfo.......... Okrug Finance Department (RU)
Okr KFS.... Okrug Committee for Physical Culture and Sports (BU)
okrkom....... Okrug Committee (RU)
Okr ns........ Okrug People's Council (BU)
okrono........ Okrug Department of Public Education (RU)
okrprofsovet... Okrug Council of Trade Unions (RU)
okrsobes..... Okrug Department of Social Security (RU)
OKRSPS.... Okrug Council of Trade Unions (RU)
okr ts......... Okrug Center (RU)
okrvetupr.... District Military Veterinary Directorate (RU)

okrzagot ..... Okrug Procurement Point (RU)
okrzdrav ...... Okrug Department of Public Health (RU)
okrZU .... Okrug Land Administration (RU)
oks .... Armed, Fuzed [*Ammunition*] (RU)
OKS .... Capital Construction Department (RU)
OKS .... Hydroxycorticosteroid (RU)
OKS .... Ohio Kache Systems Corp.
OKS .... Okresna Konzumna Sluzba [*District Consumers' Service*] (CZ)
OKS .... Okrug Cooperative Union (BU)
OKS .... Omospondia Katanalotikon Synetairismon [*Federation of Consumer Cooperatives*] [*Greek*] (GC)
OKS .... Orbital Space Station (RU)
OKS .... Organismos tou Kendrikou Symfonou [*Central Treaty Organization*] (GC)
OKS .... Single-Cable Logging Station (RU)
OKSD .... Sino-Soviet Friendship Society (RU)
OKSE .... Omospondia Kyvernitikon kai Stratiotikon Ergaton [*Federation of Government and Military Workers*] [*Cyprus*] (GC)
OKShR ...... Separate Telephone Construction Company (RU)
OKSKhOS ... Oblast Complex Agricultural Experimental Station (RU)
OKSKOJ ... Okruzni Komitet Saveza Komunisticke Omladine Jugoslavije [*County Committee of the League of Communist Youth of Yugoslavia*] (YU)
OKSMW ... Okregowy Komitet Stowarzyszenia Mlodziezy Wiejskiej [*District Committee of the Association of Peasant Youth*] (POL)
oksr .... Separate Telephone Construction Company (BU)
OKSS .... Okresni Sprava Spoju [*District Administration Office for Communications*] (CZ)
okt .... Octave (RU)
OKT .... October Railroad (RU)
okt .... Oktavo [*Octavo*] [*Afrikaans*]
Okt .... Oktober [*Afrikaans*]
okt .... Oktober [*Denmark*] (GPO)
Okt .... Oktober [*German*] (GPO)
Okt .... Oktyabr'skiy [*Toponymy*] (RU)
OKT .... Orszagos Konyvtarugyi Tanacs [*National Council on Libraries*] (HU)
OKT .... Orszagos Kozmuvelodesi Tanacs [*National Public Culture Council*] (HU)
OKT .... Orszagos Koznevelesi Tanacs [*National Council on Public Education*] (HU)
oktaedr .... Octahedral (RU)
OKTB .... Design and Technological Office Based on Public Participation (RU)
oktc .... Oktanove Cislo [*Octane Number*] (CZ)
OKThE ...... Organismos Kratikon Theatron Ellados [*Greek State Theater Organization*] (GC)
OKTI .... Orszagos Koranyi Tbc Intezet [*National Koranyi Tuberculosis Institute*] (HU)
oktr .... Separate Telephone Exchange Company (RU)
OKU .... Laser Amplifier (RU)
OKU .... Oblastni Kriminalni Ustredna [*Regional Criminal Investigation Bureau*] (CZ)
OKU .... Okrug Cooperative Administration (BU)
OKU .... Ozdi Kohaszati Uzemek [*Ozd Metallurgical Works*] (HU)
OKUD .... Omladinsko Kulturno Umjetnicko Drustvo [*Youth Cultural and Artistic Society*] (YU)
OKUOMS ... District Courses for Advanced Training of Medical Service Officers (RU)
OKV .... Odvolaci Karny Vybor [*Disciplinary Board of Appeal*] (CZ)
OKV .... Peasants' Mutual Aid Association [*German Democratic Republic*] (RU)
OKVB .... Osszoroszorszagi Kozponti Vegrehajto Bizottsag [*All-Union Central Executive Committee (USSR)*] (HU)
OKVDP ..... Acute Catarrhal Inflammation of Upper Respiratory System (RU)
OKVK .... Special Supreme Control Collegium for Land Disputes [*1922-1930*] (RU)
OKVT .... Orszagos Kornyezetvedelmi Tanacs [*National Council of Environmental Protection*] (HU)
OKW .... Oberkommando der Wehrmacht [*Armed Forces High Command*] [*German military - World War II*]
OKW .... Oesterreichische Kuratorium fur Wirtschaftlichkeit [*Austrian Management Board*] (PDAA)
OKWFN .... Okregowy Komitet Wyborczy Frontu Narodowego [*District Electoral Committee of the People's Front*] (POL)
OKWOM ... Ogolnopolski Komitet Wspolpracy Organizacji Mlodziezowych [*All-Poland Committee for the Cooperation of Youth Organizations*] (POL)
OKZ .... Opsti Krivicni Zakonik [*General Criminal Code*] (YU)
OKZ .... Short-Circuit Ratio (RU)
OKZVV ..... Okresni Komise Zemedelskych Vykrmen Vepru [*District Agricultural Commission for Hog Fattening Stations*] (CZ)
OKZZ .... Okregowa Komisja Zwiazkow Zawodowych [*District Commission of Trade Unions*] (POL)
OKZZ .... Okregowy Komitet Zwiazkow Zawodowych [*District Committee of Trade Unions*] (POL)

OL .... Base Line [*Of a ship*] (RU)
OL .... Clearing Lamp (RU)
OL .... Oberbaustofflager [*Superstructure Material Depot*] (EG)
OL .... Obrana Lidu [*People's Defense*] [*A newspaper*] (CZ)
OL .... O'Connors Air Services [*Airline code*] [*Australia*]
OL .... October League
oL .... Oestliche Laenge [*East Longitude*] [*German*]
OL .... Office Lady [*Japan*] (ECON)
oL .... Ohne Lieferplan [*Without Delivery Schedule*] (EG)
OL .... Oiseau-Lyre [*Record label*] [*France*]
ol .... Olasz [*Italian*] (HU)
OL .... Old Latin [*Language, etc.*]
OL .... Ons Leger [*Benelux*] (BAS)
OL .... Oos-Londen [*East London*] [*Afrikaans*]
OL .... Oosterlengte [*Eastern Longitude*] [*Afrikaans*]
OL .... Order of Lenin (RU)
OL .... Ordonnance-Loi [*Benelux*] (BAS)
OL .... Orszagos Leveltar [*National Archives*] (HU)
OL .... Ostfriesische Lufttransport GmbH [*Germany*] [*ICAO designator*] (ICDA)
OL .... Otravne Latky [*Chemical Agents, Toxicants*] (CZ)
Ol .... Oulun Laani [*Finland*]
OLA .... All-Slavic Linguistic Atlas (RU)
OLA .... Ogaden Liberation Army [*Ethiopia*] (AF)
OLA .... Orbital Space Vehicle, Orbital Spacecraft (RU)
OLA .... Organosis Laikis Amynis [*People's Defense Organization*] [*Greek*] (GC)
OLA .... Orland [*Norway*] [*Airport symbol*] (OAG)
OLADE ..... Organizacion Latinoamericana de Energia [*Latin American Energy Organization*] [*Quito, Ecuador*] (LA)
OLAFRIC ... Compagnie Huilerie Africaine
OLAG .... Oesterreichische Luftverkehrs Aktiengesellschaft [*Austrian Airlines*]
OlajertKirend ... Olajertekesito Vallalat Kirendeltsege [*Branch Office of the Oil Distribution Enterprise*] (HU)
OLAJTERV ... Koolaj es Gazipari Tervezo Vallalat [*Petroleum and Gas Industry Planning Enterprise*] (HU)
OLANI ...... Office du Lait du Niger
OLAS .... Organisatie voor Latijnsamerikaanse Solidariteit [*Benelux*] (BAS)
OLAS .... Organisation Locale des Affaires Sociales
OLAS .... Organizacion Latinoamericana de Solidaridad [*Latin American Solidarity Organization*] [*Use LASO*] (LA)
OLAS .... Organization of Latin American Solidarity [*Cuba*]
OLAVU ..... Organizacion Latinoamericana del Vino y de la Uva [*Montevideo, Uruguay*] (LAA)
OLB .... Olbia [*Italy*] [*Airport symbol*] (OAG)
OLB .... Orszagos Letszambizottsag [*National Census Committee*] (HU)
OLBA .... Beirut/International [*Lebanon*] [*ICAO location identifier*] (ICLI)
OLBS .... Separate Line Signal Battalion (RU)
OLBV .... Beirut [*Lebanon*] [*ICAO location identifier*] (ICLI)
OLC .... Organizacion para Liberacion del Comunismo [*Organization for Liberation from Communism*] [*El Salvador*] (LA)
OLC .... Orient Leasing Co. Ltd. [*Japan*]
OLC .... Overseas Liaison Committee
OLCP-EA ... Organisation de Lutte Contre le Criquet Pelerin dans l'Est Africain [*Desert Locust Control Organization for Eastern Africa*] [*Use DCLO-EA*] (AF)
old .... Oldal [*Page*] (HU)
Old .... Originalleinwand [*Original Cloth Binding*] [*Publishing*] [*German*]
OLDD .... Beirut [*Lebanon*] [*ICAO location identifier*] (ICLI)
OLDEPESCA ... Organismo Latinoamericano para el Desarrollo de la Pesca [*Latin American Organization for Developing Fishing*] (LA)
OLDP .... Society of Amateurs of Ancient Literature (RU)
OLDPI ...... Society of Amateurs of Literature and Art (RU)
Oldr .... Originalleder [*Original Leather*] [*Publishing*] [*German*]
OLDS .... Oddeleni Letecke Dopravni Spravy [*Department of Air Transport Directorate*] (CZ)
OLE .... Organosi Laikis Exousias [*Organization of Popular Sovereignty*] (GC)
OLEAHV .. Organisation Libre des Enseignants Africains de Haute Volta [*Free Organization of African Teachers of Upper Volta*] (AF)
O Leg .... Ordonnance Legislative [*Benelux*] (BAS)
OLEOCOL ... Oleaginosas Colombiana Ltda. [*Barranquilla*] (COL)
OLEOPAC ... Oleoducto del Pacifico, SA [*Colombia*] (COL)
OLESS ...... Open Learning Electronic Support Services [*Australia*]
OLEYIS .... Otel, Lokanta, ve Eglence Yerleri Iscileri Sendikasi [*Istanbul Hotel, Restaurant, and Amusement Places Workers' Union*] [*Turkey*]
OLEYIS .... Turkiye Otel, Lokanta, ve Eglence Yerleri Iscileri Sendikasi [*Hotel, Restaurant, and Amusement Places Employees Union of Turkey*] [*TOLEYIS*] [*See also*] (TU)
OLF .... Old Low Franconian [*Language, etc.*]

OLF .... Oromo Liberation Front [*Ethiopia*] [*Political party*]   (PD)
Olfm........... Oberlandforstmeister [*Chief Regional Forester*]   (EG)
OLG.......... Oberlandesgericht [*District Court of Appeal*] [*German*]   (DLA)
OLG.......... Oberlandsgericht [*Provincial Court*] [*German*]
OLG.......... Office of Local Government [*Northern Territory, Australia*]
OLG.......... Okoliya Lecture Group   (BU)
OLG.......... Okrug Lecture Group   (BU)
OLG.......... Old Low German [*Language, etc.*]
OLGC....... Office of the Local Government Commissioner (Queensland)
OLGR .... Oberlandesgerichtsrat [*Chief Regional Justice*] [*German*]
OLH.......... Oblastni Lidova Hvezdarna [*Regional Public Observatory*]   (CZ)
OLHSZ ..... Orszagos Lakasepitesi Hitelszovetkezet [*National Credit Cooperative for Housing Construction*]   (HU)
OLI .... Olafsvik [*Iceland*] [*Airport symbol*]   (OAG)
OLIC.......... Office de Liquidation des Interventions de Crise [*Benelux*]   (BAS)
OLICAR.... Oliveira et Cardoso
OLIE.......... Omospondia Leitourgon Idiotikis Ekpaidevseos [*Federation of Private School Teachers*] [*Greek*]   (GC)
Oliebond .... Nederlandse Bond van Belanghebbenden bij de Handel in Olien, Vetten en Oliezaden [*Netherlands*]   (BAS)
OLIMCH .. Open Learning Information and Materials Clearing House [*Australia*]
OLISS....... Online Information Services for Schools [*Australia*]
OLIZ.......... Specialized Laboratory of Electric Measurements   (RU)
OLK .... Okresni Lidova Knihovna [*District People's Library*]   (CZ)
OLK .... Organismos Limenon Kyprou [*Cyprus Port Authority*]   (GC)
OLK .... Osterreichische Lufstreitkrafte [*Austrian Military Airforce*]   (PDAA)
OLKK .... Tripoli [*Lebanon*] [*ICAO location identifier*]   (ICLI)
OLKO .... Omorfo, Lefke, ve Bolgesi Kooperatifleri Birligi [*Morfou, Lefka, and Regional Cooperatives Union*]   (TU)
OlKP .... Olasz Kommunista Part [*Italian Communist Party*]   (HU)
OLKV .... Tripoli [*Lebanon*] [*ICAO location identifier*]   (ICLI)
OLLA .... Organizacion de Lluita Armada [*Armed Struggle Organization*] [*Spanish*]   (WER)
OLLC........ Office of the Liquor Licensing Commissioner [*South Australia*]
OLLL......... Beirut [*Lebanon*] [*ICAO location identifier*]   (ICLI)
OLM .... Office des Logements Militaires [*North African*]
Olm .... Olumu [*Death*]   (TU)
Olm .... Olum Yili [*Year of Death*]   (TU)
OLM .... Organisation Locale Membre [*Local Member Organization*]   (AF)
OLMA ...... Ostschweizerische land - und milohwirtschafliche Ausstelung [*Switzerland*]   (DSCA)
OLME .... Omospondia Leitourgon Mesis Ekpaidevseos [*Federation of Secondary School Teachers*] [*Greek*]   (GC)
OLMUK .... Mukavva Sanayii ve Ticaret AS [*Cardboard Industry and Trade Corp.*]   (TU)
OLN.......... Oloton [*Race of maize*] [*Mexico*]
OLND....... Office de la Loterie Nationale pour le Developpement [*National Lottery Development Office*] [*Lao*]   (CL)
OLNE........ Organosis Leninistikis Neolaias Ellados [*Organization of Leninist Youth of Greece*]   (GC)
OLO.......... All-Army Hunting Organization   (BU)
OLO.......... Okrajni Ljudski Odbor [*District People's Committee*]   (YU)
OLO.......... Olotillo [*Race of maize*] [*Mexico*]
OLP .... Olympic Dam [*Australia*] [*Airport symbol*]   (OAG)
OLP .... Organisation de Liberation de Palestine [*Palestine Liberation Organization*] [*Use PLO*] [*French*]   (AF)
OLP .... Organismos Limenos Peiraios [*Piraeus Port Authority*]   (GC)
OLP .... Organizacao de Libertacao da Palestina [*Palestine Liberation Organization*] [*Use PLO*] [*Portuguese*]   (WER)
OLP .... Organizacion para la Liberacion de Palestina [*Palestine Liberation Organization - PLO*] [*Spanish*]
OLP .... Orszagos Legvedelmi Parancsnoksag [*National Air Defense Command*]   (HU)
OLP .... Separate Camp Station   (RU)
OLP .... Single-Wire Transmission Line   (RU)
OLPN .... Association of Persons Persecuted During the Nazism [*Federal Republic of Germany*]   (RU)
OLQ.......... Olsobip [*Papua New Guinea*] [*Airport symbol*]   (OAG)
OLR .... Organisation pour la Liberation du Rwanda [*Organization for the Liberation of Rwanda*]
OLRS........ General Hunting and Fishing Union   (BU)
olrs .... Separate Line Signal Company   (RU)
OLS .... Light Forces Detachment [*Navy*]   (RU)
OLS .... Odred Lekara Specijalista [*Medical Specialists Detachment*]   (YU)
OLS .... Okresny Ludovy Sud [*District People's Court*]   (CZ)
OLSA........ Otolaryngological Society of Australia
olsb............ Separate Telephone Construction Battalion   (BU)
OLSHOD.. Organization for the Liberation of Saguia El-Hamra and Oued El-Dheb [*Saharan*]
olszv .... Orszagos Lo- es Szamarvasar [*National Horse and Donkey Fair*]   (HU)

OLT .... Osjecka Ljevaonica i Tvornica Strojeva [*Osijek Foundry and Machinery Factory*]   (YU)
OLT .... Ostfriesische Lufttransport GmbH [*Germany*] [*ICAO designator*]   (FAAC)
OLTBr....... Separate Light Tank Brigade   (RU)
OLTEK...... Organosis Leitourgon Tekhnikis Ekpaidevsis Kyprou [*Organization of Technical Education Teachers of Cyprus*]   (GC)
OLTG .... Ordnung ueber den Lufttransport Gefaehrlicher Gueter [*Regulation on Air Transport of Hazardous Goods*]   (EG)
OLTh........ Organismos Limenos Thessalonikis [*Salonica Port Authority*]   (GC)
OLTL ImAM ... Oddzial Lodzki Towarzystwa Literackiego Imienia Adama Mickiewicza [*Lodz Branch of Adam Mickiewicz Literary Society*]   (POL)
OLTP........ Separate Light Tank Regiment   (RU)
OLV .... Oesterreichischer Lehrerverband [*Austria*]   (SLS)
olv.............. Olvasd [*Read*]   (HU)
OLV .... Onder Leiding Van [*Under the Leadership Of*] [*Afrikaans*]
olv.............. Orszagos Lovasar [*National Horse Fair*]   (HU)
Olw........... Originalleinwand [*Original Cloth Binding*] [*Publishing*] [*German*]
Olwd.......... Originalleinwand [*Original Cloth Binding*] [*Publishing*] [*German*]
OLY .... Olympic Aviation SA [*Greece*] [*ICAO designator*]   (FAAC)
OLYa........ Department of Literature and Language (of the Academy of Sciences, USSR)   (RU)
OLYeAiE... Society of Amateurs of the Natural Sciences, Anthropology, and Ethnography   (RU)
OLZ .... Besluit van den Opperbevelhebber van Landen Zeemacht [*Benelux*]   (BAS)
OM .... Het Openbaar Ministerie [*Benelux*]   (BAS)
OM .... Metal Settling Tank   (RU)
OM .... Militia Station   (RU)
OM .... Oberes Management [*German*]   (ADPT)
OM .... Obermanual [*Upper Manual*] [*Music*]
OM .... Obranci Miru [*Peace Defenders*]   (CZ)
OM .... Occupational Medal [*as used with special reference to Germany or Japan*] [*Military decoration*]
OM .... Octrooi en Merk [*Benelux*]   (BAS)
OM .... Odmorovaci Misto [*Decontamination Point*]   (CZ)
OM .... Officier Mecanicien
OM .... Officine Meccaniche [*Italian auto manufacturer*]
OM .... Officine Meccaniche [*Algeria*]
om.............. Ogsaa Med [*Bound Together With*] [*Publishing Danish/ Norwegian*]
OM .... Okresni Milice [*District Militia*]   (CZ)
OM .... Okrug Museum   (BU)
OM .... Oktatasugyi Miniszterium/Miniszter [*Ministry/Minister of Education*]   (HU)
OM .... Oman [*IYRU nationality code*] [*ANSI two-letter standard code*]   (CNC)
om.............. Omistaja [*Finland*]
OM .... Omospondia Metallorykhon [*Federation of Miners*] [*Cyprus*]   (GC)
om.............. Onder Meer [*Among Others*] [*Netherlands*]
OM .... Ontwerp-Meijers [*Benelux*]   (BAS)
OM .... Opera di Maria [*Work of Mary*] [*An association*]   (EAIO)
OM .... Opera Mundi [*Book-packaging firm based in Paris*]
OM .... Optionsmaeklarna [*Options market*] [*Sweden*]
OM .... Ordre de Modification [*French*]   (ADPT)
OM .... Organosi "Makhitis" ["*Fighter" Organization*] [*Greek*]   (GC)
OM .... Osadni Milice [*Hamlet Militia*]   (CZ)
OM .... Osrodek Maszynowy [*Machine Station*]   (POL)
OM .... Ostmark [*Monetary unit*] [*Germany*]
OM .... Ovce Mleko [*Sheep Milk*]   (YU)
om.............. Ovog Meseca [*Of This Month*]   (YU)
OM .... Power Governor   (RU)
OM .... Single-Band Modulation   (RU)
OM .... Small Offset   (RU)
OM .... Teaching Machine   (RU)
OMA.......... Department of Mechanization and Automation   (RU)
OMA.......... Inverse Matrix Algorithm   (RU)
OMA.......... Ocean Mining Associates
OMA.......... Office of Multicultural Affairs [*Australia*]
oma............. Og Mange Andre [*And Many Others*] [*Danish/Norwegian*]
oma............. Om Akustyczny [*Acoustical Ohm*] [*Poland*]
OMA.......... Organizacao das Mulheres Angolanas [*Organization of Angolan Women*]   (AF)
OMAA....... Abu Dhabi/International [*United Arab Emirates*] [*ICAO location identifier*]   (ICLI)
OMAAEEC ... Organisation Mondiale des Anciens et Anciennes Eleves de l'Enseignement Catholique [*World Organization of Former Pupils of Catholic Schools*]   (EAIO)
OMAB....... Buhasa [*United Arab Emirates*] [*ICAO location identifier*]   (ICLI)

OMAC....... Asab [*United Arab Emirates*] [*ICAO location identifier*]   (ICLI)
OMAD....... Abu Dhabi/Bateen [*United Arab Emirates*] [*ICAO location identifier*]   (ICLI)
OMADEX ... Office Malgache d'Exportation
OMAE....... Emirates Flight Information Region [*United Arab Emirates*] [*ICAO location identifier*]   (ICLI)
OMAG....... Armed Forces Supply and Repair Depot [*Portuguese*]   (WER)
OMAG....... Separate Naval Air Group   (RU)
OMAH....... Al Hamra [*United Arab Emirates*] [*ICAO location identifier*]   (ICLI)
OMAI........ Organisation Mondiale Agudath Israel [*Agudas Israel World Organization - AIWO*]   (EAIO)
OMAIR ..... Department of Mechanization and Automation of Information Work   (RU)
OMAJ .... Jebel Dhana [*United Arab Emirates*] [*ICAO location identifier*]   (ICLI)
OMAKhR ... Youth Society of the Association of Revolutionary Artists   (RU)
OMAL....... Al Ain [*United Arab Emirates*] [*ICAO location identifier*]   (ICLI)
OMAM...... Abu Dhabi/Al Dhafra [*United Arab Emirates*] [*ICAO location identifier*]   (ICLI)
OMANEXPO ... Oman Exhibition Center
OMAPAG ... Omnium Maghrebien de Participations et de Gestion
OMAQ ...... Quarmain [*United Arab Emirates*] [*ICAO location identifier*]   (ICLI)
OMAR....... Arzana [*United Arab Emirates*] [*ICAO location identifier*]   (ICLI)
omarb......... Omarbeidet [*Revised*] [*Publishing Danish/Norwegian*]
omarb......... Omarbetad [*Revised*] [*Sweden*]
OMAS....... Das Island [*United Arab Emirates*] [*ICAO location identifier*]   (ICLI)
OMAZ....... Zirku [*United Arab Emirates*] [*ICAO location identifier*]   (ICLI)
OMB......... Oblast Medical Library   (RU)
OMB......... Obshtina Mineral Baths   (BU)
OMB......... Omboue [*Gabon*] [*Airport symbol*]   (OAG)
OMB......... Openbare Muziek Bibliotheek [*Netherlands*]
OMB......... Organisation Moderne du Bureau
OMB......... Orszagos Munkabermegallapito Bizottsag [*or Orszagos Munkaber Bizottsag*] [*National Wage Board*]   (HU)
OMBEVI... Office Malien du Betail et de la Viande
OMBIT...... Okrug Interunion Office of Engineers and Technicians   (RU)
OMBKE .... Orszagos Magyar Banyaszati es Kohaszati Egyesulet [*National Hungarian Association of Mining and Metallurgy*]   (HU)
OMBN....... Department of Medical and Biological Sciences (of the Academy of Medical Sciences, USSR)   (RU)
OMBSN .... Separate Special-Purpose Medical Battalion   (RU)
OMBVI ..... Office Malien du Betail et de la Viande
OMC......... Ocean Minerals Company
OMC......... Office Mauritanien de Cereales [*Mauritanian Grain Office*]   (AF)
OMC......... Office Mechanization Centre [*Israel*]   (PDAA)
OMC......... Officina Macchine per Calzetteria [*Italy*]   (PDAA)
OMC......... Offshore Mining Company Ltd.
OMC......... Organizacion Medica Colegial [*Spanish*]
OMC......... Outboard Marine Corp. (Australia) Proprietary Ltd.
OMCE....... Orszagos Magyar Cecilia Egyesulet [*National Hungarian Cecilia Association (Music)*]   (HU)
OMCh .... Materiel Inspection   (RU)
OMCI .... Omnium Marocain Commercial et Industriel [*Moroccan Commercial and Industrial Trading Company*]   (AF)
OMCI .... Organisation Maritime Consultatif Intergouvernementale [*Intergovernmental Maritime Consultative Organization*]
OMCI .... Organisation Maritime Consultative Intergouvernementale [*Intergovernmental Maritime Consultative Organization*] [*Use IMCO*] [*French*]   (AF)
OMCO....... Ocean Minerals Company
OMCOM... Oficina de Mejoramiento Comunal [*Community Improvement Office*] [*El Salvador*]   (LA)
OMCT....... Organisation Mondiale Contre la Torture [*World Organization Against Torture*] [*Switzerland*]   (EAIO)
OMCT/SOST ... Organisation Mondiale Contre la Torture/SOS-Torture [*World Organization Against Torture/SOS-Torture*] [*Geneva, Switzerland*]   (EAIO)
OMD .... Institute of Mother and Child Care   (RU)
OMD .... Mother and Child Care   (RU)
OMD .... Oblastni Madarske Divadlo [*Hungarian Regional Theater*] (CZ)
OMD .... Ochrana Matek a Deti [*Mother and Child Care*]   (CZ)
OMDB....... Dubai [*United Arab Emirates*] [*ICAO location identifier*]   (ICLI)
OMDKRB ... Organization for the Management and Development of the Kagera River Basin
Ome........... Omega [*Record label*] [*Belgium, etc.*]
OME.......... Omospondia Metallevton Ellados [*Federation of Greek Miners*]   (GC)
OME.......... Organisation Mondiale de l'Emballage [*World Packaging Organization - WPO*]   (EAIO)
OMEA....... Office of Multicultural and Ethnic Affairs [*Australia*]
OMECA .... Office de Mecanographie

OMECH.... Oficina Meteorologica de Chile [*Chile*]   (LAA)
OMECOMS ... Organisation pour la Mecanographie, la Comptabilite, et le Secretariat
OMECSA ... Organization Mexicana de Construcciones SA
OMEH ...... Orszagos Munkaerogazdalkodasi Hivatal [*National Labor Institute*]   (HU)
OMEK....... Orszagos Mezogazdasagi es Elelmezesipari Kiallitas es Vasar [*National Agricultural and Food Industry Exhibition and Fair*]   (HU)
OMELF..... Office Marocain de l'Exportation de Legumes et Fruits
OMEP .... Organisation Mondiale pour l'Education Prescolaire [*World Organization for Early Childhood Education*]   (EAIO)
OMERA .... Societe d'Optique, de Mecanique, d'Electricite, et de Radio
OMERA .... Societe d'Optique, de Mecanique, d'Electricite et de Radio, Argenteuil [*France*]   (PDAA)
OMETI...... Orszagos Munkaegeszsegugyi Intezet [*National Institute for Workers' Health Protection*]   (HU)
OMF .... Omniflys SA de CV [*Mexico*] [*ICAO designator*]   (FAAC)
OMF .... Overseas Missionary Fellowship [*Singapore*]
OMFB .... Orszagos Muszaki Fejlesztesi Bizottsag [*National Technical Development Committee*]   (HU)
OMFI .... Orszagos Mezogazdasagi Fajtakiserleti Intezet [*National Agricultural Type-Experimentation Institute*]   (HU)
OMFJ........ Fujeirah/International [*United Arab Emirates*] [*ICAO location identifier*]   (ICLI)
OMFKI...... Orszagos Mezogazdasagi Fajtakiserleti Intezet [*National Agricultural Type-Experimentation Institute*]   (HU)
OMFMT ... Orszagos Mezogazdasagi Fajtaminosito Tanacs [*National Agricultural Type-Classifying Council*]   (HU)
OMFT .... Orszagos Mezogazdasagi Fajtaminosito Tanacs [*National Agricultural Type-Classifying Council*]   (HU)
OMG .... Oesterreichische Mathematische Gesellschaft [*Austria*]   (SLS)
OMG .... Oesterreichische Mineralogische Gesellschaft [*Austria*]   (SLS)
OMG .... Omega [*Namibia*] [*Airport symbol*]   (OAG)
OMGE....... Organisation Mondiale de Gastroenterologie [*World Organization of Gastroenterology - WOG*] [*Edinburgh, Scotland*]   (EAIO)
OMGE....... Organizacion de la Mujer de Guinea Ecuatorial
omgew .... Omgewerkt [*Revised*] [*Publishing*] [*Netherlands*]
OMGH ...... Orszagos Munkaero Gazdalkodasi Hivatal [*National Manpower Office*]   (HU)
Omgiz......... Omsk State Publishing House   (RU)
OMgK....... Orszagos Mezogazdasagi Konyvtar [*National Agricultural Library*]   (HU)
OMGR....... Department of Marine Geophysical Work [*of the VNIIGeofizika*]   (RU)
OMH .... Odbor Mistniho Hospodarstvi [*Local Economy Department*]   (CZ)
OMH .... Orszagos Meresugyi Hivatal [*National Scaling Office*]   (HU)
OMH .... Orumieh [*Iran*] [*Airport symbol*] [*Obsolete*]   (OAG)
omhdl .... Omhandler [*Deals With*] [*Danish/Norwegian*]
OMI .... Oblats de Marie Immaculee [*Oblates of Mary Immaculate*] [*Rome, Italy*]   (EAIO)
OMI .... Ocean Management, Incorporated
OMI .... Odessa State Medical Institute Imeni N. I. Pirogov   (RU)
OMI .... Office of Multicultural Interests [*Western Australia*]
OMI .... Omnium Marocain d'Investissement [*Moroccan Investment Trading Company*]   (AF)
OMI .... Organisation Maritime Internationale [*International Maritime Organization - IMO*]   (EAIO)
OMI .... Organisation Meteorologique Internationale
OMI .... Organizacion Maritima Internacional [*International Maritime Organization*] [*Spanish United Nations*]   (DUND)
OMI .... Orszagos Munkaegeszsegugyi Intezet [*National Institute for Workers' Health Protection*]   (HU)
OMI .... Ottica Meccanica Italiana [*Commercial firm*]
OMIAA ..... Orientation and Mobility Instructors' Association of Australasia
OMIC .... Omnium Marocain Industriel et Chimique [*Moroccan Industrial and Chemical Trading Company*]   (AF)
OMIH....... Orszagos Magyar Idegenforgalmi Hivatal [*Hungarian National Office of Tourism*]   (HU)
OmIIT....... Omsk Institute of Railroad Transportation Engineers   (RU)
OMIKE ..... Orszagos Magyar Izraelita Kozmuvelodesi Egyesulet [*Hungarian National Jewish Educational Association*]   (HU)
OMIKI ...... Orszagos Mezogazdasagi Ipari Kiserleti Intezet [*National Agricultural Experimental Station*]   (HU)
OMIKK ..... Orszagos Muszaki Informacios Kozpont es Konyvtar [*National Technical Information Center and Library*] [*Information service or system*]   (IID)
OMINC..... Ocean Management, Incorporated
OMIPE...... Office Mondial d'Information sur les Problemes d'Environnement [*French*]   (SLS)
OMIR .... Department of Mechanization of Engineering and Technical Calculations   (RU)
OMIT .... Organisation Mondiale Interarmees du Haut Commandement Francais [*French High Command telecommunications system*]

OMK......... General Mine Committee   (BU)
OMK......... Orszagos Muszaki Konyvtar [*National Technical Library*]   (HU)
OMKDK.... Orszagos Muszaki Konyvtar es Dokumentacios Kozpont [*National Technical Library and Documentation Center*]   (HU)
OMKER .... Orvosi Muszer es Fogaszati Cikk Kereskedelmi Vallalat [*Commercial Enterprise for Medical and Dental Instruments and Appliances*]   (HU)
OMKh ...... Society of Moscow Artists   (RU)
OMKMR... Department of Mechanization of Copying and Duplicating   (RU)
OML......... Fundamentals of Marxism-Leninism   (RU)
OML......... Oil Mining License
OML......... Oxley Memorial Library [*Australia*]   (ADA)
OMLE ...... Organization of Spanish Marxist-Leninists   (PD)
OMLE ...... Organosis Marxiston-Leniniston Elladas [*Organization of Marxist-Leninists of Greece*]   (GC)
o/m/m ...... A l'Ordre de Moi-Meme [*To Our Own Order*] [*French*] [*Business term*]
OMM .... Mother and Child Care   (RU)
OMM .... Operation Mils in Mali
OMM .... Organisation Meteorologique Mondiale [*World Meteorological Organization - WMO*]   (EAIO)
OMM .... Organizacao das Mulheres Mocambicanas [*Organization of Mozambique Women*]   (AF)
OMM .... Organizacion Meteorologica Mundial [*World Meteorological Organization - WMO*] [*United Nations (already exists in GUS II database)*] [*Spanish*]   (MSC)
OMM .... Orszagos Magyar Munkasbizottsag [*National Committee of Hungarian Workers*]   (HU)
OMM .... Scientific Research Institute of Mother and Child Care   (RU)
OMMI....... Orszagos Mezogazdasagi Minosegvizsgalo Intezet [*National Research Institute on Quality Standards in Agriculture*]   (HU)
OMMSA ... Organisation of Monuments, Museums, and Sites of Africa
OMMSS.... Oeuvres Mama Mobutu Sese Seko [*Mama Mobutu Sese Seko Projects*] [*Zaire*]   (AF)
OMN .... Department of Medical Sciences   (RU)
OMN .... Oman [*ANSI three-letter standard code*]   (CNC)
OMNIREX ... Omnium de Recherches et Exploitations Petrolieres [*Petroleum Exploration and Exploitation Company*] [*Algeria*]   (AF)
OMNIS ..... Office Militaire National pour les Industries Strategiques [*National Military Office for Strategic Industries*] [*Malagasy*]   (AF)
OMNIVI ... Omsk Veterinary Scientific Research Institute   (RU)
Omnl......... Omnilegie [*Benelux*]   (BAS)
omo............ Medical Support Detachment   (BU)
OMO .... Music Education Department   (RU)
OMO .... Offshore Mining Organisation [*Thailand*]   (FEA)
OMO .... Orman Muhendisleri Odasi [*Chamber of Forestry Engineers*] [*Turkish Cypriot*]   (GC)
OMO .... Separate Medical Detachment   (RU)
OMOCI.... Office de la Main-d'Oeuvre de Cote-D'Ivoire
OMOS....... Experimental Naval Aircraft Construction Section   (RU)
OMP......... Department of Local Industry   (RU)
OMP......... Magnetic Bearing Reading   (RU)
OMP......... Mass-Destruction Weapon   (RU)
OMP......... Officier du Ministere Public [*Benelux*]   (BAS)
omp .... Ominaispaino [*Finland*]
OMP......... Ordnance Maintenance Park   (ML)
OMP......... Reciprocal Magnetic Bearing   (RU)
omp .... Separate Mortar Regiment   (RU)
OMPA ...... Office of Marine Pollution Assessment [*National Oceanic and Atmospheric Administration*]   (ASF)
ompb .... Separate Motorized Pontoon Battalion   (RU)
OMPES..... Office of the Minister for Police and Emergency Services [*New South Wales, Australia*] [*Australia*]
OMPI .... Office Marocain de la Propriete Industrielle [*Morocco*]
OMPI .... Organisation Mondiale de la Propriete Intellectuelle [*World Intellectual Property Organization - WIPO*] [*Information service or system*]   (IID)
OMPI .... Organizacion Mundial de la Propiedad Intelectual [*World Intellectual Property Organization*] [*Spanish United Nations*]   (DUND)
OMPKA .... Organismos Mathitikis Pronoias kai Andillipseos [*Students' Training and Welfare Organization*] [*Greek*]   (GC)
OMPP .... Ochrana Majetku Proti Pozaru [*Protection of Property Against Fire*]   (CZ)
OMPSA..... Organisation Mondiale pour le Promotion Sociale des Aveugles [*World Council for the Welfare of the Blind - WCWB*]   (EAIO)
OMPTOB ... Separate Motorized Antitank Flamethrower Battalion   (RU)
OMPU...... Great Circle Magnetic Track Angle   (RU)
OMPU....... Oficina Municipal de Planeamiento Urbano [*Municipal Office of Urban Planning*] [*Venezuela*]   (LA)
OMR......... Obermedizinalrat [*Chief Public Health Officer (In the GDR, title awarded for special merit)*]   (EG)

OMR......... Objections en Monde Rural [*France*]   (EAIO)
OMR......... Office Mauritanien de la Radiodiffusion [*Mauritanian Broadcasting Office*]   (AF)
OMR......... Orad [*Romania*] [*Airport symbol*]   (OAG)
OMR......... Organizacion Magisterial Revolucionaria [*Revolutionary Teachers Organization*] [*El Salvador*]   (LA)
omr .... Separate Camouflage Company   (RU)
OMRE .... Orszagos Magyar Repulo Egyesulet [*Hungarian National Aviation Association*]   (HU)
OMRG...... Office Mauritanien de Recherches Geologiques [*Mauritania*]
OMRI .... Open Media Research Institute [*Non-profit news and analysis organization covering Eastern Europe and the former Soviet Union*]   (ECON)
OMRK...... Ras Al Khaimah/International [*United Arab Emirates*] [*ICAO location identifier*]   (ICLI)
OMRP...... Reciprocal Magnetic Radio Bearing   (RU)
OMRS ...... Orders and Medals Research Society   (EA)
OMS .... Experimental Reclamation Station   (RU)
OMS .... Oesterreichische Mineraloel und Stickstoffwerke AG [*Formed by merger of OMV and OSW*]
OMS .... Okresni Mericske Stredisko [*District Geodetic Center*]   (CZ)
OMS .... Okresni Myslivecky Svaz [*District Foresters' Union*]   (CZ)
oms .... Omsett [*Translated*] [*Publishing Danish/Norwegian*]
OMS .... Omsk [*Former USSR*] [*Airport symbol*]   (OAG)
OMS .... Omsk Railroad   (RU)
OMS .... Ordine Militare di Savoia [*Decoration*] [*Italian*]
OMS .... Organisation Mondiale de la Sante [*World Health Organization - WHO*] [*Switzerland*]
OMS .... Organizacao Mundial de Saude [*World Health Organization - WHO*] [*Portuguese*]
OMS .... Organizacion Mundial de la Salud [*World Health Organization*] [*Spanish United Nations*]   (DUND)
OMS .... Organizacni a Mobilizacni Sprava [*Organization and Mobilization Directorate*]   (CZ)
OMS .... Organization and Mechanization of Construction   (BU)
OMS .... Organizzazione Mondiale della Sanita [*World Health Organization*] [*Italian*]
OMS .... Organosi Mathitikou Syndikalismou [*Organization of Student Unionism*] [*Greek*]   (GC)
OMS .... Otdel Mezhdunarodnykh Svyazey [*International Relations Section*] [*Russian*]
OMS .... Telephone Call Canceled at Moment of Connection   (BU)
OMSB ...... Separate Bridge Construction Battalion   (RU)
omsb.......... Separate Medical Battalion   (RU)
omsb.......... Separate Motorized Rifle Battalion   (RU)
OMSC ...... Organisation Mondiale pour la Systemique et la Cybernetique [*World Organization of Systems and Cybernetics*]   (EAIO)
omsdON..... Separate Special-Purpose Motorized Rifle Division   (RU)
OMsektsiya ... General Mobilization Section   (BU)
OMSEN .... Omnium Senegal
OMSJ .... Sharjah/International [*United Arab Emirates*] [*ICAO location identifier*]   (ICLI)
OMSKhI ... Omsk Agricultural Institute Imeni S. M. Kirov   (RU)
omsl............ Omslag [*Wrapper*] [*Publishing*] [*Netherlands*]
omsl............ Omslag [*Wrapper*] [*Publishing*] [*Sweden*]
omsl............ Omslag [*Wrapper*] [*Publishing Danish/Norwegian*]
OMSR ...... Separate Medical Company   (RU)
omsr .... Separate Motorized Rifle Company   (RU)
OMSZ ...... Orszagos Mento Szolgalat [*National Ambulance Service*]   (HU)
OMSZ ...... Orszagos Meteorologiai Szolgalat [*National Meteorological Service*]   (HU)
OMSzK...... Orszagos Meheszeti Szovetkezeti Kozpont [*National Center of Beekeepers' Cooperatives*]   (HU)
OMT......... Organisation Mondiale du Tourisme [*World Tourism Organization*]   (CL)
OMTAG .... Oman Technical Agencies [*Commercial firm*]
OMTAS..... Otomotiv Transmisyon Aksami Sanayi ve Ticaret Anonim Sirketi [*Automotive Transmission Parts Industry and Commerce Corporation*]   (TU)
OMTI .... Omnium de Traitement de l'Information [*French*]   (ADPT)
OMTK....... Orszagos Magyar Tejertekesito Kozpont [*National Hungarian Center for Milk Distribution*]   (HU)
OMTKI ..... Orszagos Munkavedelmi Tudomanyos Kutato Intezet [*National Research Institute of Occupational Safety*] [*Hungary*]   (IRC)
OMTO....... Materiel Support Section [*Military term*], Materials and Equipment Supply Department   (RU)
omtr.......... Omtrykt [*Reprinted*] [*Publishing Danish/Norwegian*]
OMTS .... Materials and Equipment Supply Department   (RU)
OMTUR.... Organizacja Mlodziezy Towarzystwa Uniwersytetow Robotniczych [*Youth Organization of the Society of Workers' Universities (Extension courses)*]   (POL)
OMTVGE ... Omospondia Mikhanikon kai Thermaston Viomikhanias kai Georgias Ellados [*Federation of Greek Industrial and Agricultural Mechanics and Stokers*]   (GC)

OMTVK .... Omospondia Misthoton Typou kai Viomikhanias Khartou [*Federation of Salaried Press and Paper Industry Employees*] [*Greek*] (GC)

OMU .... Department for Stocktaking of Materials (RU)

OMU .... Operational Magnetic Amplifier (RU)

OMU .... Simultaneous Multiplier (RU)

OMUzmani ... Organizasyon ve Method Uzmani [*Organization and Methods Specialist*] (TU)

OMV.......... Oesterreichische Mineraloelverwaltung AG [*Austrian Oil Administration*] [*OMS*] [*Later,*]

OMV.......... Office de Mise en Valeur [*Development Office*] [*Cambodia*] (CL)

OMV.......... Optimaler Medienverbund [*German*] (ADPT)

OMV.......... Ordre des Medecins Veterinaires [*Belgium*] (SLS)

OMVA....... Office de Mise en Valeur Agricole [*Morocco*]

OMVG....... Organisation pour la Mise en Valeur du Fleuve Gambie [*Gambia River Basin Organisation*] (EAIO)

OMVK....... Okresni Mimoradna Vyzivovaci Komise [*District Special Food Commission*] (CZ)

OMVR....... Department of Mechanization of Computation (RU)

OMVS .... Organisation pour la Mise en Valeur du Fleuve Senegal [*Senegal River Development Organization*] [*Dakar*] (AF)

OMVSD .... Office de Mise en Valeur de Sategui-Deressia

OMVVM... Office de Mise en Valeur de la Vallee de la Medjerda [*Office for Developing the Medjerda Valley*] [*Tunisia*] (AF)

OMW .... Office of the Mining Warden [*Victoria, Australia*]

OMYeN..... Department of Mathematical and Natural Sciences (of the Academy of Sciences, USSR) (RU)

OMZ.......... Experimental Magnesium Plant (RU)

omz............. Omzendbrief [*Benelux*] (BAS)

OMZ.......... Optical Instrument Plant (RU)

OMZB .... Separate Small-Caliber Antiaircraft Battery (RU)

OMZD....... Delayed-Action Fragmentation Mine (RU)

OMZEST .. Omar Zawawi Establishment [*Commercial firm*] [*Oman*] (IMH)

omzhdb....... Separate Motorized Railroad Battalion (RU)

On .... Canon [*Cannon*] [*Short form used in commands only*] [*French*] (MTD)

on................ Concentrated Artillery Fire (RU)

ON .... League of Nations (BU)

ON .... Main Direction, Base Line (RU)

ON .... New Order [*Revolutionary group*] [*Italy*]

ON .... Observatoire de Neuchatel [*Switzerland*]

ON .... Observatorio Nacional do Brasil [*Brazil National Observatory*] [*Research center*] (EAS)

ON .... Oesterreichisches Normungsinstitut [*Austrian Standards Institute*] [*Research center*] (IRC)

ON .... Old Norse [*Language, etc.*]

On .... Onorevole [*Honorable*] [*Italian*] (GPO)

ON .... Ontario (IDIG)

ON .... Operativni Normy [*Operational Standards*] (CZ)

ON .... Orden Nuevo [*New Order*] [*Spanish*] (WER)

ON .... Ordine Nuovo [*New Order*] [*Italian*] (WER)

ON .... Ortsnetz [*Local Telephone Network*] (EG)

ON .... Osterreichisches Normungsinstitut [*Austrian Standards Institute*] (IRC)

On .... Oud-Noors [*Old Norse*] [*Language, etc.*] [*Afrikaans*]

on................ Overgeplaatst Naar [*Benelux*] (BAS)

ON .... Primary Direction [*Military*] (BU)

ON .... Reference Voltage (RU)

ON .... Specialized Standards (RU)

on................ Special-Purpose (RU)

ON .... Stress-Control Winding (RU)

ON .... Supercharger (RU)

ON .... United Nations (BU)

ONA .... Oesterreichisher Normenausschuss [*Austrian Standards Organization*] (PDAA)

ONA .... Office des Nouvelles Algeriennes [*Algerian News Office*] (AF)

ONA .... Office National d'Assurance Vieillesse [*Haiti*] (EY)

ONA .... Office of National Assessments [*Australia*]

ONA .... Of Naaste Aanbod [*Afrikaans*]

ONA .... Omnium Nord-Africain [*North African Trading Company*] [*Casablanca, Morocco*] (AF)

ONA .... Organisation des Nations Americaines (FLAF)

ONA .... Organizacion Nacional Agraria [*Peru*] (EY)

ONA .... Overseas National Airways [*Belgium*] [*ICAO designator*] (FAAC)

ONA .... Overseas National Airways, Inc.

ONA .... Overseas News Agency

ONAA........ Office National de l'Artisanat d'Art

ONAA........ Oficina Nacional de Apoyo Alimentario [*National Office for Food Support*] [*Peru*] (LA)

ONAAC..... Office National d'Alphabetisation et d'Action Communautaire [*National Office for Literacy and Community Action*] [*Haiti*] (LA)

ONAB........ Office National des Aliments du Betail [*Algeria*]

ONAB........ Office National du Bois [*Wood development and marketing board*] [*Cotonou, Benin*]

ONAC........ Oeuvre Nationale des Anciens Combattants et Victimes de la Guerre [*Benelux*] (BAS)

ONAC........ Office National d'Approvisionnement et de Commercialisation [*National Office of Supply and Marketing*] [*Djibouti*] (GEA)

ONAC........ Office National du Commerce Exterieur [*National Office of External Trade*] [*Burkina Faso*] (EY)

ONACER .. Office National des Cereales [*National Grain Office*] [*Zaire*] (AF)

ONACIBE ... Office National du Cinema du Benin

ONACO..... Office National Algerien de Commercialisation [*Algerian National Marketing Office*] (AF)

ONACT..... Organizacion Nicaraguense Americana de Cooperacion Tecnica [*Nicaraguan American Organization of Technical Cooperation*] (LA)

ONADEC.. Organisation Nationale des Entreprises Congolaises [*National Organization of Congolese Enterprises*] (AF)

ONAF........ Office National d'Affretements

ONAF........ Office National de Coordination des Allocations Familiales [*Benelux*] (BAS)

ONAF........ Office National des Forets [*National Forests Office*] [*Congo*] (AF)

ONAFEX... Office National Algerien des Foires et des Expositions Commerciales [*Algiers, Algeria*] (AF)

onafgesn..... Onafgesneden [*Uncut*] [*Publishing*] [*Netherlands*]

ONAFITEX ... Office National des Fibres Textiles [*National Textile Fiber Office*] [*Zaire*] (AF)

ONAFTI.... Office National d'Allocations Familiales pour Travailleurs Independants [*France*] (BAS)

ONAFTS... Office National d'Allocations Familiales pour Travailleurs Salaries [*France*] (BAS)

ONAGI...... Office National de Gestion des Biens Immobiliers de l'Etat [*National Office for Management of State Real Estate*] [*Zaire*] (AF)

ONAH .... Office National d'Hydrocarbures [*National Hydrocarbons Office*] [*Guinea*] (AF)

ONAHA .... Office National des Amenagements Hydro-Agricoles

ONAI........ Organisation of Nigerian Agricultural Industries

ONAJ .... Oficina Nacional de Asuntos Juridicos [*National Legal Affairs Office*] [*Peru*] (LA)

ONAKO..... Office National du Kouilou

ONAL........ Organisation Nouvelle pour l'Afrique Libre [*New Organization for Free Africa*] (AF)

ONALAI ... Office National du Lait et des Produits Laitiers [*Algeria*]

ONALAIT ... Office National du Lait et des Produits Laitiers [*Algeria*] (IMH)

ONALFA... Office National de l'Alfa [*North African*]

ONAMA.... Office National du Materiel Agricole [*National Agricultural Equipment Office*] [*Algeria*] (AF)

ONAMHYD ... Office National du Materiel Hydraulique [*Algiers, Algeria*]

ONAMO ... Office National Algerien de la Main-d'Oeuvre [*National Algerian Manpower Bureau*] (AF)

ONAMS.... Oficina Nacional de Apoyo a la Mobilizacion Social [*National Office for Support of Social Mobilization*] [*Peru*] (LA)

ONAP........ Oficina Nacional de Administracion Publica y Personal [*National Bureau for Personnel and Public Administration*] [*Dominican Republic*] (LA)

ONAP........ Oficina Nacional de Administracion y Personal [*Dominican Republic*]

ONAPARCS ... Office National des Parcs [*National Parks Office*] [*Algeria*] (IMH)

ONAPE ..... Oficina Nacional de Pesca [*Venezuela*] (DSCA)

ONAPED .. Organizacion Nacional de Periodistas Democraticos [*National Organization of Democratic Journalists*] [*Venezuela*] (LA)

ONAPLAN ... Oficina Nacional de Planificacion [*National Planning Office*] [*Dominican Republic*] (LAA)

ONAPO..... Office National des Produits Oleicoles [*National Olive Products Office*] [*Algeria*] (AF)

ONAREM ... Office National des Ressources Minieres [*National Office of Mineral Resources*] [*Niger*] (AF)

ONAREP .. Office National de Recherches et d'Exploitation Petroliers [*National Office for Petroleum Exploration and Mining*] [*Morocco*] (PDAA)

ONAREST ... Office National de la Recherche Scientifique et Technique [*National Office of Scientific and Technical Research*] [*Cameroon*] (AF)

ONAREXH ... Office National de Recherches et d'Exploitation des Hydrocarbures [*Morocco*]

ONAT........ Office National Algerien de l'Animation, de la Promotion et de l'Information Touristique [*Algeria*] (EAIO)

ONAT........ Office National Algerien du Tourisme [*Algerian National Tourist Office*] [*Algiers*] (AF)

ONATA..... Office National de l'Artisanat Traditionnel Algerien [*National Office of Algerian Traditional Handicrafts*] (AF)

ONATHO ... Office National du Tourisme et de l'Hotellerie [*National Tourism and Hotel Office*] [*Benin*] (AF)

ONATHOL ... Office National du Tourisme et de l'Hotellerie [*National Tourism and Hotel Office*] [*Guinea*]

ONATOUR ... Office de la Tourbe du Burundi [*Development organization*] [*Burundi*] (EY)

ONATRA .. Office National des Transports [*National Transportation Office*] [*Zaire*] (AF)

ONATRATE ... Oficina Nacional de Transporte Terrestre [*National Office for Land Transportation*] [*Dominican Republic*] (LA)

ONB......... Oesterreichischer Naturschutzbund [*Austria*] (SLS)

ONB......... Office National du Bois [*National Lumber Office*] [*Zaire*] (AF)

Onb .... Onbasi [*Corporal*] (TU)

onbed......... Onbeduidend [*Insignificant*] [*Netherlands*]

onbep......... Onbepaald [*Indefinite*] [*Afrikaans*]

onbeschr..... Onbeschreven [*Unused*] [*Netherlands*]

ONBG........ Office National des Bois du Gabon

ONBI .... Office National des Barrages et de l'Irrigation

ONC........... Office National de Commerce [*National Trade Office*] [*Burundi*] (AF)

ONC........... Office National des Cereales [*Chad*] (EY)

ONC........... Office National des Changes [*National Exchange Office*] [*Cambodia*] (CL)

ONC........... Office National du Cafe [*National Coffee Office*] [*Zaire*] (AF)

ONCA........ Office National de Commercialisation Agricole [*National Office for Agricultural Marketing*] [*Gabon*] (AF)

ONCAD..... Office National de Cooperation et d'Assistance pour le Developpement [*National Office of Cooperation and Assistance for Development*] [*Senegal*] (AF)

ONCC........ Organisme National des Congres et Conferences [*Algeria*] (IMH)

ONCE........ Oficina Nacional del Censo [*National Census Office*] [*Cuba*] (LA)

ONCF .... Office National des Chemins de Fer [*Moroccan Railways*]

ONCFG ..... Office National des Chemins de Fer de Guinee (EY)

ONCFM .... Office National des Chemins de Fer du Maroc [*Moroccan Railways*] (DCTA)

ONCIC ...... Office National pour la Commercialisation des Industries Cinematographiques [*National Marketing Bureau for the Cinematographic Industries*] [*Algeria*] (AF)

ONCL .... Office National Cinematographique du Laos [*National Motion Picture Office of Laos*] (CL)

ONCL .... Office National des Cereales et Legumineuses [*Morocco*] (IMH)

ONCN .... Office National de Construction Navale [*Algeria*] (IMH)

ONCPA ..... Office National de Commercialisation des Produits Agricoles [*National Office for the Marketing of Agricultural Products*] [*Congo*] (AF)

ONCPB ..... Office National de Commercialisation des Produits de Base [*National Basic Necessities Marketing Office*] [*Cameroon*] (AF)

ONCS .... Office National Catholique des Moyens de Communications Sociales

ONCSA ..... Orszagos Nep- es Csaladvedelmi Alap [*National Welfare Fund*] (HU)

ONCT........ Office National Congolais du Tourisme

ONCTA ..... Oficina Nacional des Catastro de Tierras y Aguas [*Venezuela*] (DSCA)

ONCV........ Office National de Commercialisation des Produits Viti-Vinicoles [*National Office for Marketing Wine and Wine Products*] [*Algiers, Algeria*] (AF)

OND .... Greatest Common Divisor (RU)

OND .... Office National du Diamant [*Central African Republic*] (EY)

OND .... Office National du Ducroire [*Export Credits Guarantee Office*] [*Belgium*] (GEA)

OND .... Office of the Nominal Defendant [*Australia*]

OND .... Ondangua [*Namibia*] [*Airport symbol*] (OAG)

OND .... Ordinary National Diploma [*Nigeria*]

OND .... Pressure Increase Limiter (RU)

ONDA ...... Office National du Droit d'Auteur [*Algeria*] (IMH)

ONDA ...... On-Line Dauerprogramm fuer den Sparkassenbetrieb [*German*] (ADPT)

ONDAH .... Office National des Debouches Agricoles et Horticoles [*French*] (BAS)

OndB........ Besluit op de Ondernemersbelasting [*Benelux*] (BAS)

ONDC........ Office National de Developpement de Cacao

ONDE........ Office National de Developpement de l'Elevage [*National Livestock Development Office*] [*Zaire*] (AF)

ONDEC..... Oficina Nacional de Educacion Catolica [*National Catholic Education Office*] [*Peru*] (LA)

ONDECOOP ... Oficina Nacional de Desarrollo Cooperativo [*Peru*]

ONDECOOP ... Oficina Nacional de Fomento Cooperativo [*National Cooperative Development Office*] [*Peru*] (LA)

ONDEPA .. Organizacion Nacional de Profesionales Agropecuarios [*National Agricultural and Livestock Professionals Association*] [*Colombia*] (LA)

ONDEPJOV ... Oficina Nacional de Desarrollo de Pueblos Jovenes [*National Office for the Development of New Settlements*] [*Peru*] (LA)

ondert......... Ondertitel [*Subtitle*] [*Publishing*] [*Netherlands*]

onderv .... Ondervoorsitter [*Vice-Chairman*] [*Afrikaans*]

onderw........ Onderwerp [*Subject*] [*Afrikaans*]

ONDR .... Office National Tchadien de Developpement Rural [*Chadian National Office for Rural Development*] (AF)

ONDRAF/NIRAS ... Organisme National de Dechets Radioactifs et des Matieres Fissiles [*Belgium*] (EY)

ONDS........ Office National du Sucre [*National Sugar Office*] [*Zaire*] (AF)

ONE........... Oeuvre Nationale d'Entraide [*National Welfare Fund*] [*Cambodia*] (CL)

ONE........... Office National de l'Electricite [*National Electricity Office*] [*Morocco*] (AF)

ONE........... Office National des Eaux [*National Water Office*] [*Ouagadougou, Burkina Faso*] (EY)

ONE........... Onepusu [*Solomon Islands*] [*Airport symbol*] [*Obsolete*] (OAG)

One........... Oyane [*or Oyene*] [*Islands*] [*Denmark*] (NAU)

One........... Oyane [*or Oyene*] [*Islands*] [*Norway*] (NAU)

ONEA .... Office National de l'Eau et de l'Assainissement [*Government body*] [*Burkina Faso*] (EY)

ONEC........ Oficina Nacional de Educacion Comunitaria [*National Community Education Bureau*] [*Haiti*] (LAA)

ONEC........ Oficina Nacional de Estadisticas y Censo [*National Office for Statistics and Census*] [*Peru*] (LA)

ONED....... Organismos Neolaias Enoseos Kendrou [*Center Union (Party) Youth Organization*] (GC)

Oneglag..... Onega Corrective Labor Camp (RU)

ONEI .... Organizacion Nacional de Estudiantes Independientes [*Spanish*]

ONEM....... Office National de l'Emploi [*France*] (BAS)

ONEO .... Office National d'Editions Officielles [*France*] (FLAF)

ONEP....... Office National d'Eau Potable [*National Drinking Water Office*] [*Rabat, Morocco*] (AF)

ONEP .... Office National d'Edition et de Presse [*News agency*] [*Niger*] (EY)

ONEPI...... Office National d'Edition, de Presse, et d'Imprimerie [*Publisher*] [*Benin*] (EY)

ONERA ..... Office National d'Etudes et de Recherches Aerospatiales [*National Office for Aerospace Studies and Research*] [*French*] (WER)

ONEREP... Omnium Cherifien de Negoce et de Representations Internationales

ONERN ..... Oficina Nacional de Evaluacion de Recursos Nacionales [*National Bureau for Evaluating National Resources*] [*Peru*] (LA)

ONERSOL ... Office Nigerien de l'Energie Solaire [*Nigerien Solar Energy Office*] [*Niger*] (AF)

ONEX........ Office National des Substances Explosives [*Algeria*] (IMH)

ONF........... Fatherland People's Front [*Hungarian People's Republic*] (RU)

ONF........... Ob'edinennyi Natsional'nyi Front

ONF........... Office National des Forets [*Central African Republic*] (EY)

ONF........... Okresny Narodny Front [*District National Front Organization*] (CZ)

ONF........... Old Norman French [*Language, etc.*]

ONF........... Old Northern French [*Language, etc.*]

ONFC .... Oman National Fisheries Company [*Muscat*] (MENA)

ONFP .... Office National de Formation Professionnelle

ONFP .... Office National Famille et Population [*Tunisia*] (EAIO)

ONFR .... Old Northern French [*Language, etc.*]

onfr........... Onfris [*Worn*] [*Netherlands*]

ONFR .... Oud-Nederfrankies [*Older Low Franconian*] [*Afrikaans*]

ONG .... Mornington Island [*Australia*] [*Airport symbol*] (OAG)

ONG .... Oesterreichische Numismatische Gesellschaft [*Austria*] (SLS)

ong............. Ongeveer [*About, Approximately*] [*Netherlands*] (GPO)

ONG .... Ongewoon [*Rare*] [*Afrikaans*]

ONG .... Organisation Non Gouvernementale

ONG .... Organisations Non-Gouvernementales [*Nongovernmental Organizations*] (AF)

ONGC........ Oil and Natural Gas Commission [*India*] (MCD)

ongedr .... Ongedrukt [*Unpublished*] [*Netherlands*]

ONGT........ Office National Gabonais du Tourisme [*Gabonese National Tourist Office*] (AF)

ONH.......... Office National de l'Huile [*National Olive Oil Office*] [*Tunisia*] (AF)

ONHA .... Office National de l'Huilerie d'Abeche

ONI........... Moanamani [*Indonesia*] [*Airport symbol*] (OAG)

ONI........... Office des Nouvelles Internationales [*International News Office*] [*French*] (AF)

ONI........... Office National de l'Ivoire

ONI........... Office National d'Immigration [*France*] (FLAF)

ONI........... Office National d'Irrigation [*National Irrigation Office*] [*Morocco*] (AF)

ONI........... Oficina Nacional de Informacion [*National Information Office*] [*Press agency Peru*]

ONI........... Oficina Nacional de Integracion [*National Integration Office*] [*Peru*] (LA)

ONI........... Organizacion Nacional Independiente [*National Independent Organization*] [*Venezuela*] (LA)

ONI........... Orszagos Nevelestudomanyi Intezet [*National Pedagogical Institute*] [*Kecskemet*] (HU)

ONI........... Oseanografiese Navorsingsinstituut [*Oceanographic Research Institute*] [*University of Natal*] [*South Africa*]   (AA)
ONIA........ Office National Industriel de l'Azote
ONIC........ Office National Interprofessionnel des Cereales [*France*]   (FLAF)
ONIDOL... Organisation Nationale Interprofessionnelle des Oleagineux [*France*]
ONIG......... Oeuvre Nationale des Invalides de la Guerre [*French*]   (BAS)
ONIG......... Opera Nazionale Invalidi di Guerra [*Italy*]
ONII.......... Institute of Scientific Research Based on Public Participation   (RU)
ONIITEM ... Oficina Nacional de Invenciones, Informacion Tecnica, y Marcas [*National Office for Inventions, Technical Information, and Trademarks*]   (LA)
ONIL........ Office National d'Industrialisation Libyen
ONIMET .. Organisme National Inter-Entreprises de Medecine du Travail [*Algeria*]   (IMH)
ONIS .... Oficina Nacional de Informacion Social [*National Social Information Office*] [*Peru*]   (LA)
ONISEP.... Office National d'Information sur les Enseignements et les Professions [*French*]
ONIT .... Oficina Nacional de Integracion [*National Integration Office*] [*Peru*]   (LA)
ONIT .... Organisation Nationale Independante des Travailleurs [*National Independent Organization for Workers*] [*Belgium*]
ONIVEG ... Office National d'Importation et de Vente de Viande en Gros [*Congo*]   (EY)
ONJ .... Organizacao Nacional de Jornalistas [*National Organization of Journalists*] [*Mozambique*]   (AF)
ONK .... Optimum Irregular Code   (RU)
ONK .... Oristikos Navtikos Katalogos [*Definitive Naval List*] [*Greek*]   (GC)
ONL........... Office National de Logement [*National Housing Office*] [*Zaire*]   (AF)
ONL........... Office National du Lait et de ses Derives [*French*]   (BAS)
ONL........... Oficina Nacional de Alojamiento [*National Housing Bureau*] [*Haiti*]   (LAA)
ONM .... Least Common Multiplier   (RU)
ONM .... Office du Niger au Mali
ONM .... Office National de la Meteorologie [*Algeria*]   (IMH)
ONM .... Office National de Modernisation [*National Modernization Office*] [*Central African Republic*]   (AF)
ONM .... Office National des Mines [*National Mines Office*] [*Tunisia*]   (AF)
ONM .... Office National Meteorologique [*French*]
ONM .... Organisation National des Moudjahidine [*National Veterans' Organization*] [*Algeria*]   (AF)
ONMB...... Oblast Scientific Medical Library   (RU)
ONMI........ Opera Nazionale Maternita e Infanzia [*National Institute for Mother and Child Welfare*] [*Italian*]   (WER)
ONMI........ Opera Nazionale per il Mezzogiorno d'Italia [*National Institute for the Improvement of Southern Italy*]   (WER)
ONMR...... Office National de la Modernisation Rurale [*National Office for Rural Modernization*] [*Morocco*]   (AF)
ONMT...... Office National Marocain de Tourisme [*Moroccan National Tourist Office*]   (AF)
ONMT...... Office National Mauritanien du Tourisme [*Mauritanian National Tourism Office*]   (AF)
ONNED .... Organosis Neon tis Neas Dimokratias [*Youth Organization of the New Democracy (Party)*] [*Greek*]   (GC)
ONO.......... Department of Public Education   (RU)
ONO.......... Oblasten Naroden Odbor [*Regional People's Committee*]   (YU)
ONO.......... Oesnoroeste [*West-Northwest*] [*Spanish*]
ONO.......... Office National de l'Okoume
ONO.......... Okruzni Narodni Odbor [*County People's Committee*]   (YU)
ONO.......... Oosnoordoos [*East-Northeast*] [*Afrikaans*]
ONO.......... Opstinski Narodni Odbor [*Municipal People's Committee*]   (YU)
ONO.......... Ovest-Nord-Ovest [*West-North-West*] [*Italian*]
ONOAKMO ... Okruzni Narodni Odbor Autonomne Kosovo-Metohiske Oblasti [*County People's Committee of the Autonomous Kosovo-Metohija Region*]   (YU)
ONOC ...... Oceania National Olympic Committee [*Australia*]
ONOC ...... Oceania National Olympic Committees [*New Zealand*]   (EAIO)
ONOO....... Okruzni Narodnooslobodilacki Odbor [*County National Liberation Committee*]   (YU)
ONOORG ... Onoorganklik [*Intransitive*] [*Afrikaans*]
ONOVAG ... Oeuvre Nationale des Orphelins, Veuves et Ascendants des Victimes de la Guerre [*Benelux*]   (BAS)
ONP.......... Association of German Trade Unions   (RU)
ONP.......... Office National de Peche [*National Fishing Office*] [*Zaire*]   (AF)
ONP.......... Office National de Peche [*National Fishing Office*] [*Algeria*]   (AF)
ONP.......... Office National de Peche [*National Fishing Office*] [*Tunis, Tunisia*]   (AF)
ONP.......... Office National des Peches [*National Fishing Office*] [*Morocco*]   (ASF)

ONP.......... Office National des Ports [*National Ports Office*] [*Cameroon*]   (MSC)
ONP.......... Office National des Ports [*National Ports Office*] [*Algiers-Port, Algeria*]   (AF)
ONP.......... Office National Pharmaceutique
ONP.......... Oficina Nacional de Pescas [*National Fishing Office*] [*Uruguay*]   (MSC)
ONP.......... Okresni Narodni Pojistovna [*District National Insurance Agency*]   (CZ)
ONP.......... Okresni Nemocenska Pojistovna [*District Health Insurance Agency*]   (CZ)
ONP.......... Scientific Propaganda Department   (RU)
ONP.......... Separate Observation Post   (RU)
ONPB .... Office National de Pharmacie du Benin [*National Pharmacy Office of Benin*] [*State enterprise Cotonou*]   (EY)
ONPC .... Office National des Ports du Cameroun [*Douala, Cameroon*]
ONPC .... Office National du Placement et du Chomage [*Benelux*]   (BAS)
ONPDD..... Omospondia Nomikon Prosopon Dimosiou Dikaiou [*Federation of Legal Entities of Public Law*] [*Greek*]   (GC)
ONPERS... Onpersoonlik [*Impersonal*] [*Afrikaans*]
ONPFEP... Office National du Planning Familial et de la Population
ONPFP..... Office National du Planning Familial et de la Population
ONPI .... Office National de la Propriete Industrielle [*National Office for Industrial Properties*] [*Algeria*]   (AF)
ONPM...... Office National des Peches Maritimes [*Morocco*]
ONPO....... Office National des Pensions pour Ouvriers [*France*]   (BAS)
ONPPC ..... Office National des Produits Pharmaceutiques et Chimiques [*National Office of Pharmaceutical and Chemical Products*] [*Niger*]   (AF)
ONPT .... Office National des Postes et Telecommunications [*National Postal and Telecommunications Office*] [*Congo*]   (AF)
ONPTI...... Office National des Pensions pour Travailleurs Independants [*France*]   (BAS)
ONPTS...... Office National des Pensions pour Travailleurs Salaries [*France*]   (BAS)
ONPTZ ..... Office National des Postes et Telecommunications du Zaire [*Zairian National Posts and Telecommunications Office*]   (AF)
ONPTZa .. Office National des Postes et Telecommunications du Zaire [*Zairian National Posts and Telecommunications Office*]   (AF)
ONPU........ Oficina Nacional de Planeamiento y Urbanismo [*National Planning and Urban Renewal Bureau*] [*Peru*]   (LA)
ONPUR..... Oficina Nacional de Planificacion Urbana y Regional [*National Office of Urban and Regional Planning*] [*Peru*]   (LAA)
ONPZ........ Obrtno Nabavna Prodajna Zadruga [*Handicraft Buying and Selling Cooperative*]   (YU)
ONR .... Oboz Narodowo-Radykalny [*Radical Nationalist Camp*] [*Poland*] [*Political party*]   (PPE)
ONR .... Oesterreichische Medizinische Gesellschaft fuer Neuraltherapie nach Huneke-Regulationsforschung [*Austria*]   (SLS)
ONR .... Organization for National Reconstruction [*Trinidadian and Tobagan*]   (LA)
ONRA....... Office National de la Reforme Agraire [*National Office for Agrarian Reform*] [*Algeria*]   (AF)
ONRA....... Oficina Nacional de la Reforma Agraria [*National Office for Agrarian Reform*] [*Peru*]   (LA)
ONRAP ..... Oficina Nacional de Racionalizacion y Capacitacion de la Administracion Publica [*National Office for Rationalization and Training in Public Administration*] [*Peru*]   (LAA)
ONRD .... Office National de Recherches et de Developpement [*National Research and Development Office*] [*Zaire*]   (AF)
ONRI........ Orde van Nederlandse Raadgevende Ingenieurs ['s-Gravenhage]
ONRR........ Office National Rail-Route [*Guinea*]
ONRS .... Office National de la Recherche Scientifique [*National Office for Scientific Research*] [*Algeria*]   (AF)
ONRSD ..... Office National de la Recherche Scientifique et du Developpement [*National Office for Scientific Research and Development*] [*Zaire*]   (AF)
ONS........... Oberste Nationale Sportkommission fur den Automobilsport in Deutschland [*Germany*]   (EAIO)
ONS........... Office National des Sports
ONS........... Okoliya People's Council   (BU)
ONS........... Okrug People's Council   (BU)
ONS........... Onslow [*Australia*] [*Airport symbol*] [*Obsolete*]   (OAG)
ons.............. Onsydig [*Neutral*] [*Afrikaans*]
ONS........... Ordinary National Assembly   (BU)
ONS........... Oriental Numismatic Society [*Reading, Berkshire, England*]   (EAIO)
ONSA .... Operasionele Navorsingvereniging van Suid-Afrika [*South Africa*]   (EAIO)
ONSC .... Oficina Nacional del Servicio Civil [*National Civil Service Office*] [*Uruguay*]   (LA)
ONSDT ..... Okoliya People's Council of Deputies of the Working People   (BU)
ONSDT ..... Okrug People's Council of Deputies of the Working People   (BU)

ONSER ..... Organisme National de Securite Routiere [*National Road Safety Organization*] [*Research Center France*]   (PDAA)
ONSiW ...... Osrodek Nauk Spolecznych i Wojskowych [*Social and Military Science Center*]   (POL)
ONSL .... Organisation Nationale des Syndicats Libres [*National Organization of Free Trade Unions*] [*Burkina Faso*]
ONSS .... Office National de la Securite Sociale [*National Office of Social Security*] [*Belgium*]   (WER)
ONSSU ..... Office National des Sports Scolaires et Universitaires [*National Office of Scholastic and University Sports*] [*Congo*]   (AF)
ONST .... Outline NATO Staff Target
ONT .... Department of Labor Standardization   (RU)
ONT .... Office National des Transports [*National Transportation Office*] [*Morocco*]   (AF)
ONT .... Office National de Textiles [*National Textiles Office*] [*Tunisia*]   (AF)
ONT .... Office National du Tourisme [*Macau*]
ONT .... Office Nationale du Tourisme [*Algeria*]   (EY)
ONT .... Oficiul National de Turism [*National Office for Tourism*]   (RO)
ONT .... Ombudsman of the Northern Territory [*Australia*]
ONT .... Ongaku No Tomo Sha Corp. [*Japan*]   (FEA)
ont .... Onteigening [*Benelux*]   (BAS)
ONT .... Orszagos Nepmuvelesi Tanacs [*National Council of Adult Education*]   (HU)
ONTA .... Office of National Tax Administration [*South Korea*]
ONTA .... Osei Nkanash Trade Agency [*Nigeria*]
ONTB .... Basic Scientific and Technical Library   (RU)
ONTB .... Specialized Scientific and Technical Library   (RU)
ontbr .... Ontbreekt [*Missing*] [*Netherlands*]
ONTEJ ...... Organizacion Nacional de Turismo Estudiantil y Juvenil [*National Organization of Student and Youth Tourism*] [*Peru*]   (LA)
ontelb .... Ontelbaar [*Numerous*] [*Netherlands*]
ONTF .... Office National des Travaux Forestiers [*National Office of Forest Workers*] [*Algeria*]
ONTI .... Association of Scientific and Technical Publishing Houses   (RU)
ONTI .... Department of Scientific and Technical Information   (RU)
ONTI .... Joint Scientific and Technical Publishing House   (RU)
ONTIZ ...... Association of Scientific and Technical Publishing Houses   (RU)
ontl .... Ontleding [*or Ontlening*] [*Derivation*] [*Afrikaans*]
ONTM .... Office National de Tourisme Marocaine
ONTP .... Office National des Transports Publics
ONTPiO .... Department of Scientific and Technical Information and Propaganda   (RU)
ONTS .... Oblast Scientific and Technical Council   (RU)
ONTS .... Office National du The et du Sucre [*National Tea and Sugar Office*] [*Morocco*]   (AF)
ontst .... Ontstaan [*Originate*] [*Netherlands*]
ONTT .... Office National du Tourisme et du Thermalisme [*National Office of Tourism and Thermal Springs*] [*Tunisia*]   (AF)
ONTT .... Office National Togolais du Tourisme
ONTV .... Okresni Narodni Telovychovny Vybor [*District Physical Education Committee*]   (CZ)
ontv .... Ontvang [*Received*] [*Afrikaans*]
Ontvbk ...... Ontvangen Boeken [*Benelux*]   (BAS)
ontw .... Ontworpen [*Designed*] [*Netherlands*]
OntwBW .... Ontwerp voor een Nieuw Burgerlijk Wetboek [*Benelux*]   (BAS)
OntwerpBW ... Ontwerp voor een Nieuw Burgerlijk Wetboek [*Benelux*]   (BAS)
OntwerpSE ... Ontwerp voor een Statuut van een Europese Naamloze Vennootschap [*Benelux*]   (BAS)
ONU .... Ono-I-Lau [*Fiji*] [*Airport symbol*] [*Obsolete*]   (OAG)
ONU .... Organisation des Nations Unies [*United Nations French*]
ONU .... Organizacao das Nacoes Unidas [*United Nations*] [*Use UN*] [*Portuguese*]   (WER)
ONU .... Organizacion de las Naciones Unidas [*United Nations*] [*Spanish*]   (DUND)
ONU .... Organizatia Natiunilor Unite [*United Nations*] [*Use UN*]   (RO)
ONU .... Organizzazione Nazioni Unite [*United Nations*] [*Italian*]
ONUC .... Organisation des Nations Unies au Congo [*United Nations Organization in the Congo*]
ONUDI ...... Organisation des Nations Unies pour le Developpement Industriel [*United Nations Industrial Development Organization*]
ONUDI ...... Organizacion de las Naciones Unidas para el Desarrollo Industrial [*United Nations Industrial Development Organization*] [*Spanish*]   (DUND)
ONUDI ...... Organizatia Natiunilor Unite pentru Dezvoltare Industriala [*United Nations Industrial Development Organization*] [*Use UNIDO*]   (RO)
ONUESC .. Organisation des Nations Unies pour l'Education, la Science et la Culture   (FLAF)
onuitg .... Onuitgegeven [*Unpublished*] [*Dutch*]   (BAS)
onuitgeg ...... Onuitgegeven [*Unpublished*] [*Netherlands*]
onumr .... Onumrerad [*Unnumbered*] [*Publishing*] [*Sweden*]
ONUST ..... Organisme des Nations Unies Charge de la Surveillance de la Treve [*En Palestine*]   (FLAF)

ONV .... Obvodni Narodni Vybor [*District National Committee*]   (CZ)
ONV .... Office National de la Vigne [*National Wine Office*] [*Tunisia*]
ONV .... Okresni Narodni Vybor [*District National Committee*]   (CZ)
onv .... Onveranderd [*Unrevised*] [*Publishing*] [*Netherlands*]
onverk .... Onverkort [*Unabridged*] [*Publishing*] [*Netherlands*]
onvolm .... Onvolmaak [*Imperfect*] [*Afrikaans*]
onvolt .... Onvoltooi(d) [*Imperfect*] [*Afrikaans*]
ONW .... Okreg Naukowy Warszawski [*Warsaw Academic District*]   (POL)
ONX .... Colon [*Panama*] [*Airport symbol*]   (OAG)
ONZ .... Least Common Denominator   (RU)
ONZ .... Main Charge Carriers   (RU)
ONZ .... Odbor za Narodno Zdravlje (SIV) [*Public Health Committee*]   (YU)
onz .... Onza [*Ounce*] [*Spanish*]
ONZ .... Organizacja Narodow Zjednoczonych [*United Nations*] [*Use UN*]   (POL)
OO .... Deviation Detection   (RU)
OO .... Oberoesterreich [*or Oberoesterreichisch*] [*Upper Austria or Upper Austrian*] [*German*]
OO .... Ohne Ort [*Without Place of Publication*] [*Bibliography*] [*German*]
oo .... Ojocowie [*Poland*]
OO .... Okresni Odbor [*District Branch*]   (CZ)
OO .... Okresni Organisace [*District Organization*]   (CZ)
OO .... Okruzni Odbor [*County Committee*]   (YU)
OO .... Oorsprokelijk Ontwerp [*Benelux*]   (BAS)
OO .... Operations Section   (RU)
OO .... Opstinski Odbor [*Municipal Committee*]   (YU)
OO .... Ordonnance Officier [*Ordnance Officer*] [*French*]
OO .... Organizational Department   (RU)
oo .... Originalt Omslag [*Original Wrapper*] [*Publishing Danish/Norwegian*]
OO .... Osnovna Organizacija [*Basic Organization*]   (YU)
OO .... Osobyi Otdel [*Counterintelligence surveillance unit in military formation until 1943*] [*Former USSR*]
OO .... Social Insurance   (BU)
OO .... Special Section, Special Department   (RU)
OOA .... Ochranna Organizace Autorska [*Authors' Protective Organization (Copyright)*]   (CZ)
OOB .... Okresni Osvetova Beseda [*District Cultural Group*]   (CZ)
OOB .... Separate Flamethrower Battalion   (RU)
OOBR .... Buraimi [*Oman*] [*ICAO location identifier*]   (ICLI)
OOC .... Office of Corrections [*Victoria, Australia*]
OOC .... Office of Olympic Coordination [*New South Wales, Australia*]
OOC .... Organisation des Operations Commerciales [*France*]   (FLAF)
OOC .... Osterreichisches Olympisches Comite [*Austrian Olympic Committee*]   (EAIO)
OOCL .... Orient Overseas Container Line   (ADA)
OOCL .... Overseas Ocean Carrier Limited [*Hong Kong*]
OOCNET .. Office of Corrections Network
OOD .... Company with Limited Liability   (BU)
OOD .... Movement Support Detachment   (RU)
OOD .... Office of Disability [*Australia*]
OOD .... Traffic Control Detachment   (BU)
oO Dr u J ... Ohne Ort, Druckernamen, und Jahr [*Without Place, Publisher, and Year*] [*German*]
OODS .... Okresna Organizacia Demokratickej Strany [*District Organization of the Democratic Party*]   (CZ)
OOD-vo ... Company with Limited Liability   (BU)
OOE .... Odiki Omospondia Ellados [*Greek Roads Federation*]   (GC)
OOE .... Office of Employment [*Victoria, Australia*]
OOE .... Office of Energy [*New South Wales, Australia*]
O Oe Prof ... Ordentlicher Oeffentlicher Professor [*Full Professor*] [*German*]   (GCA)
OOF .... Office of the Family [*Western Australia*]
OOFD .... Fahud [*Oman*] [*ICAO location identifier*]   (ICLI)
OOFQ .... Firq [*Oman*] [*ICAO location identifier*]   (ICLI)
OOG .... Oesterreichische Ophthalmologische Gesellschaft [*Austria*]   (SLS)
OOG .... Office of Gambling [*Victoria, Australia*]
OOGB .... Ghaba Central [*Oman*] [*ICAO location identifier*]   (ICLI)
OOGE .... Omospondia Oikodomon kai Genikon Ergaton [*Federation of Construction and General Workers*] [*Cyprus*]   (GC)
OOGM ...... Orta Ogretim Genel Mudurlugu [*Secondary Education Directorate General*]   (TU)
OOGSA ...... Omgewingsopvoedingsgenootskap van Suider-Afrika [*South Africa*]   (AA)
OOHA .... Haima [*Oman*] [*ICAO location identifier*]   (ICLI)
OOI .... Okresni Osvetovy Inspektorat [*Office of the District Inspector of Cultural Activities*]   (CZ)
OOI .... Orszagos Onkologiai Intezet [*National Oncological Institute*]   (HU)
OOIA .... Ibra [*Oman*] [*ICAO location identifier*]   (ICLI)
OOII .... Ibri [*Oman*] [*ICAO location identifier*]   (ICLI)
OOIZ .... Izki [*Oman*] [*ICAO location identifier*]   (ICLI)

OOJN .... Jarf North [*Oman*] [*ICAO location identifier*] (ICLI)
OOK .... Odred Obezbedenja Kretanja [*Movement Protecting Detachment*] [*Military*] (YU)
OOK .... Odred za Opravku Komunikacija [*Detachment for Communications Repair*] [*Military*] (YU)
OOK .... Okresni Odbor Kultury [*District Cultural Department*] (CZ)
OOK .... Orszagos Orvostorteneti Konyvtar [*National Library of Medical History*] (HU)
OOK .... Ovambo Ontwikkelingskorporasie [*Ovambo Development Corporation*] [*Namibia*] (AF)
OOKB .... Khasab [*Oman*] [*ICAO location identifier*] (ICLI)
OOKDK ..... Orszagos Orvostudomanyi Konyvtar es Dokumentacios [*National Medical Library and Center for Documentation*] [*Hungary*] (PDAA)
OOKiDKN ... Okregowe Osrodki Ksztalcenia i Doksztalcania Kadr Nauczycielskich [*District Centers for the Education and Improvement of Teaching Personnel*] (POL)
OOL .... Gold Coast [*Australia*] [*Airport symbol*] (OAG)
OOL .... Orient Overseas Line (DS)
OOLK .... Lekhwair [*Oman*] [*ICAO location identifier*] (ICLI)
OOM .... Cooma [*Australia*] [*Airport symbol*] (OAG)
OOMA ...... Masirah [*Oman*] [*ICAO location identifier*] (ICLI)
OOMM ..... Muscat [*Oman*] [*ICAO location identifier*] (ICLI)
OOMP........ Oblast Department of Local Industry (RU)
OOMS .... Muscat/Seeb International [*Oman*] [*ICAO location identifier*] (ICLI)
OON .... Department of Social Sciences (of the Academy of Sciences, USSR) (RU)
OON .... Obrerismo Organizado de Nicaragua [*Trade union*] [*Nicaragua*]
OON .... Order of the Niger
OON .... Organizacija na Obedinenite Narodi [*United Nations Organization*] (YU)
OON .... Organizatsiia Ob'edinennykh Natsii
OON .... Special-Purpose Detachment (RU)
OON .... United Nations Organization (BU)
OONAZ..... Special-Purpose Detachment (RU)
OONR .... Marmul/Nasir [*Oman*] [*ICAO location identifier*] (ICLI)
OONZ .... Nizwa [*Oman*] [*ICAO location identifier*] (ICLI)
OOO .... Office of the Ombudsman
OOOF........ Okrozni Odbor Osvobodilne Fronte [*County Committee of the Liberation Front*] (YU)
OOOID ..... Report of the Odessa Society of History and Antiquities (RU)
OOP.......... Oddzialowa Organizacja Partyjna [*Branch Party Organization*] (POL)
OOP.......... Okregowa Organizacja Partyjna [*District Party Organization*] (POL)
OOP.......... Primary Defense Zone (RU)
OOPEC ..... Office for Official Publications of the European Communities (ECED)
OOPP .... Opere Pubbliche [*Public Works*] [*Italian*]
OOR .... Obvodna Osvetova Rada [*District Cultural Council*] (CZ)
OOR .... Okresni Odborova Rada [*District Trade-Union Council*] (CZ)
OOR .... Separate Flamethrower Company (RU)
oordr.......... Oordrag [*Transfer*] [*Afrikaans*]
oordr.......... Oordragtelik [*Metaphorically*] [*Afrikaans*]
oorg .... Oorganklik [*Transitive*] [*Afrikaans*]
oorl .... Oorlede [*Late*] [*Afrikaans*]
OORM .... Rima [*Oman*] [*ICAO location identifier*] (ICLI)
OORQ .... Rostaq [*Oman*] [*ICAO location identifier*] (ICLI)
OORSFC... Only Official Rolling Stones Fan Club (EAIO)
oorspr........ Oorspronkelijk [*Original*] [*Publishing*] [*Netherlands*]
oorspr........ Oorspronklik [*Original*] [*Afrikaans*]
OORTR ...... Oortreffend [*Superlative*] [*Afrikaans*]
OOS .... Negative Feedback (RU)
OOS .... Okresni Osvetovy Sbor [*District Cultural Board*] (CZ)
OOSA .... Organismos Oikonomikis Synergasias kai Anaptyxeos [*Organization for Economic Cooperation and Development*] (GC)
OOSA .... Salalah [*Oman*] [*ICAO location identifier*] (ICLI)
OOSA .... Separate Detachment of Ambulance Motor Sleds (RU)
OOSB .... Okresni Odbor Svazu Brannosti [*District Branch of the Union for Military Preparedness*] (CZ)
OOSH....... Sohar [*Oman*] [*ICAO location identifier*] (ICLI)
OOSK .... Osnovna Organizacija Saveza Komunista [*Basic Organization of the League of Communists*] (YU)
OOSM ...... Sahma [*Oman*] [*ICAO location identifier*] (ICLI)
OOSMP .... Separate Specialized Medical Aid Detachment (RU)
OOSQ....... Saiq [*Oman*] [*ICAO location identifier*] (ICLI)
OOSR .... Sur [*Oman*] [*ICAO location identifier*] (ICLI)
OOSSNU .. Separate Dog-Team Sled-Litter Detachment (RU)
OOSSRN... Osnovna Organizacija Socijalisticki Savez Radnog Naroda [*Basic Organization of the Socialist Alliance of Working People*] (YU)
OOT.......... Onotoa [*Kiribati*] [*Airport symbol*] (OAG)
OOT.......... Work Safety Department (RU)
OOTC........ Oceania Olympic Training Center [*Australia*]

OOTH .... Thumrait [*Oman*] [*ICAO location identifier*] (ICLI)
OOUP........ Odbor za Organiziciono-Upravna Pitanja (SIV) [*Committee on Organizational and Administrative Problems*] (YU)
OOUR .... Osnovna Organizacija Udruzenog Rada [*Basic Organization of Workers*] [*Former Yugoslavia*] (CED)
oov .... Ontslagen op Verzoek [*Benelux*] (BAS)
OOVB........ Okresni Oddeleni Verejne Bezpecnosti [*District Department for Public Security*] (CZ)
OOYB........ Yibal [*Oman*] [*ICAO location identifier*] (ICLI)
OOZB........ Okrozni Odbor Zveze Borcev [*County Committee of the Union of Veterans*] (YU)
OP............. Bath Station (RU)
op.............. Experimental (RU)
OP............. Experimental Field [*Agriculture*] (RU)
OP............. Firing Position [*Artillery*] (BU)
OP............. Flight Control Section (RU)
OP............. Foam Fire Extinguisher (RU)
op.............. Inventory, List (RU)
op.............. List, Inventory of Goods, Schedule (BU)
OP............. N-Type Conductivity, Negative Conductivity (RU)
OP............. Obalna Plovidba [*Coastal Navigation*] (YU)
OP............. Obcansky Prukaz [*Citizen's Identification Card*] (CZ)
OP............. Objektprogramm [*German*] (ADPT)
OP............. Oborovy Podnik [*Sectoral Enterprise*] (CZ)
OP............. Obras Publicas [*Public Works*] [*Spanish*]
OP............. Obrtno Poduzece [*Handicraft Establishment*] (YU)
OP............. Observation Post (RU)
OP............. Observatoire de Paris [*France*]
op.............. Obvodni Podnik [*District Enterprise*] [*Former Czechoslovakia*] (CED)
OP............. Odbor za Privredu (SIV) [*Committee on Economics*] (YU)
OP............. Oddzial Powiatowy [*County Branch*] (POL)
OP............. Odevni Prodejny [*Clothing Stores*] (CZ)
OP............. Odevni Prumysl [*Garment Industry*] (CZ)
OP............. Officier de Police [*French*] (FLAF)
OP............. Okoliya Management (BU)
OP............. Okresni Pojistovna [*District Insurance Agency*] (CZ)
OP............. Okresni Poradna [*District Advisory Office*] (CZ)
OP............. Okrug Enterprise (BU)
OP............. Okrug Management (BU)
OP............. Old Persian [*Language, etc.*]
op.............. Olvadaspont [*Melting Point*] (HU)
OP............. Omospondia Pratirioukhon [*Federation of Gas Station Owners*] [*SP*] [*See also*] (GC)
OP............. Oostelike Provinsie [*Eastern Province*] [*Afrikaans*]
OP............. Operand [*Operator*] [*German*] (ADPT)
Op............. Operation [*German*] (GCA)
OP............. Operationnel [*Operational*] [*French*] (CL)
OP............. Operation Order (RU)
OP............. Operationssaal [*Operating Theater*] [*German*]
OP............. Operativni Planovani [*Operational Planning*] (CZ)
op.............. Opettaja [*Finland*]
op.............. Opusculo [*Small Work*] [*Portuguese*]
OP............. Opus Pacis [*Opus Pacis (Hungarian Catholic peace movement)*] (HU)
OP............. Orange People [*Australia*]
OP............. Orden de Predicadores [*Dominican Order*] [*Spanish*]
oP............. Ordentlicher Professor [*Full Professor*] [*German*]
OP............. Ordine dei Predicatori [*Dominican Order*] [*Italian*]
OP............. Ordre des Precheurs [*Dominicans*] [*French*]
OP............. Orient Press [*Press agency*] [*South Korea*]
OP............. Osnovni Pravac [*Main Direction*] [*Military*] (YU)
OP............. Osobni Prukaz [*Personal Identity Card*] (CZ)
OP............. Osvecova Prace [*Cultural Work*] [*A periodical*] (CZ)
OP............. Otets Paisiy [*Father Paisiy*] [*A periodical*] (BU)
OP............. Otkupno Preduzece [*Purchasing Establishment*] (YU)
OP............. Ouvriers Professionnels [*France*] (FLAF)
OP............. Overgangsperiode (EEG) [*Benelux*] (BAS)
OP............. Pneumatic Irrigator (RU)
OP............. Process Time (RU)
OP............. Propaganda Department (RU)
OP............. Reciprocal Bearing (RU)
OP............. Reflected and Refracted [*Wave*] (RU)
OP............. Rotary Converter (RU)
OP............. Stopping Point (RU)
OP............. Strongpoint (RU)
OP............. Supply Relay Point [*Military term*] (RU)
op-............. Telescopic Sight (RU)
OP............. Terminal Point (RU)
OPA .... Austrian Liberation Party (RU)
OPA .... Kopasker [*Iceland*] [*Airport symbol*] (OAG)
OPA .... Oesterreichisches Patentamt [*Austrian Patent Office*]
OPA .... Offre Publique d'Achat [*Public Offer to Purchase*] [*French*] (WER)
OPA .... Omada gia mia Proletariaki Aristera [*Group for a Proletarian Left*] [*Greek*] (GC)

OPA .... Onafhankelijke Partij [*Independent Party*] [*Netherlands*] [*Political party*] (PPW)

OPA .... Opal Air Pty Ltd. [*Australia*] [*ICAO designator*] (FAAC)

OPA .... Organisation des Pionniers Angolais [*Organization of Angolan Pioneers*] [*French*]

OPA .... Organismos Prolipseos Atykhimaton [*Accident Prevention Organization*] [*Greek*] (GC)

OPA .... Organizacao de Pioneiros Angolanos [*Organization of Angolan Pioneers*] [*Portuguese*] (AF)

OPA .... Organizacja Panstw Amerykanskich [*Organization of American States*] [*Poland*]

OPA .... Propaganda and Agitation Section (BU)

OPAB .... Abbottabad [*Pakistan*] [*ICAO location identifier*] (ICLI)

opab .... Separate Machine-Gun and Artillery Battalion (RU)

OPAC .... Office des Produits Agricoles de Costermansville

OPAC .... Online Public Access Catalogue [*Australia*]

OPAC .... Orana Policy Advisory Committee [*Australia*]

OPACA ..... Oil Palm Central Africa (EAIO)

OPACI .... Organisation Provisoire de l'Aviation Civile Internationale (FLAF)

OPACI .... Organizacion Paraguaya de Cooperacion Intermunicipal [*Paraguay*] (LAA)

OPAD .... Separate Gun Artillery Battalion (RU)

OPAEP ...... Organisation des Pays Arabes Exportateurs de Petrole [*Organization of Arab Petroleum Exporting Countries*] (EAIO)

OPAEP ...... Organisations des Pays Arabes Exportateurs de Petrole [*Organization of Arab Petroleum Exporting Countries - OAPEC*] [*French*]

OPAEP ...... Organizacion de Paises Arabes Exportadores de Petroleo [*Organization of Arab Petroleum Exporting Countries - OAPEC*] [*Spanish*]

opag .... Opaginerad [*Unnumbered*] [*Publishing*] [*Sweden*]

OPAIE .... Organismos Perithalpseos kai Apokatastaseos Israiliton Ellados [*Organization for Aid and Resettlement of Jews of Greece*] (GC)

OPAK .... Office des Produits Agricoles de Kivu [*Zaire*]

OPAKF ...... Optikai, Akusztikai es Filmtechnikai Egyesulet [*Optics, Acoustics, and Film Technology Association*] [*Hungary*] (SLS)

OPAKFI .... Optikai, Akusztikai, es Filmtechnikai Egyesulet [*Optics, Acoustics, and Film Technology Association*] (HU)

OPAL .... One People for Australia League (ADA)

OPALMA ... Oleos de Palma SA Agro-Industrial [*Brazil*] (DSCA)

OPAM .... Office des Produits Agricoles du Mali [*Malian Agricultural Products Office*] (AF)

OPANAL .. Organismo para la Proscripcion de las Armas Nucleares en la America Latina [*Agency for the Prohibition of Nuclear Weapons in Latin America*] (EAIO)

OPANAL .. Organizacion para la Proscripcion de Armas Nucleares en la America Latina [*Organization for the Prohibition of Nuclear Arms in Latin America*] [*Polanco, Mexico*] (LA)

OPANDAD ... Ortak Pazar Nezdinde Daimi Delegelik [*Turkish Permanent Delegation to the Common Market*] (TU)

OPAP .... Organismos Prognostikon Agonon Podosfairou [*Organization of Soccer Game Forecasters*] [*Greek*] (GC)

OPAPE ...... Organisation Pan-Africaine de la Profession Enseignante [*All Africa Teachers' Organization*] (EAIO)

Opappbd .... Originalpappband [*Original Boards*] [*Publishing*] [*German*]

OPAS .... Office des Produits Agricoles de Stanleyville

OPaS .... Okresni Poradna a Studovna [*District Advisory Bureau and Study Center*] (CZ)

OPAS .... Organisation de Propagande et d'Action Speciale [*Algeria*]

OPAT .... Office des Ports Aeriens de Tunisie [*Tunisian Airport Office*] (AF)

OPAT .... Office des Produits Agricoles du Togo [*Togo Agricultural Products Office*] (AF)

OPATTI .... Office de Promotion et d'Animation Touristique de Tahiti et ses Iles (EY)

Opb .... De Opbouw [*Benelux*] (BAS)

OPB .... Occupational Pensions Board [*British*] (DCTA)

OPB .... Old Picked Bumpers [*Choice cigarette butts*] [*Australian slang*]

OPB .... Open Bay [*Papua New Guinea*] [*Airport symbol*] (OAG)

OPB .... Optical Bombsight (RU)

OPB .... Security Service [*Civil defense*] (RU)

OPB .... Separate Machine-Gun Battalion (RU)

Opbd .... Originalpappband [*Original Boards*] [*Publishing*] [*German*]

OPBG .... Bhagtanwala [*Pakistan*] [*ICAO location identifier*] (ICLI)

OPBL .... Bela [*Pakistan*] [*ICAO location identifier*] (ICLI)

OPBM .... Okregowe Przedsiebiorstwa Barow Mlecznych [*District Milk Bar Enterprises*] (POL)

OPBN .... Bannu [*Pakistan*] [*ICAO location identifier*] (ICLI)

OPBR .... Bahawalnagar [*Pakistan*] [*ICAO location identifier*] (ICLI)

OPBW .... Bahawalpur [*Pakistan*] [*ICAO location identifier*] (ICLI)

OPC .... Oblast Union of Consumers' Societies (RU)

OPC .... Obras Publicas y Comunicaciones [*Dominican Republic*] (LAA)

OPC .... Oddil Polniho Cetnictva [*Military Police Battalion*] (CZ)

OPC .... Office of the Protective Commissioner [*Australia*]

OPC .... Oil Palm Company

OPC .... Oil Prices Committee [*India*] (PDAA)

OPC .... Ovamboland People's Congress

OPC .... Own Produce Consumed

OPCA .... Oficiul de Proiectari pentru Constructii in Agricultura [*Office for Design for Agricultural Constructions*] (RO)

OPCA .... Overseas Press Club of America (WDAA)

OPCC .... Office of Preschool and Child Care [*Victoria, Australia*]

OPCC .... Organisation of Petroleum Consuming Countries

OPCC .... Organisme Provincial de Cooperation et de Coordination [*Provincial Cooperation and Coordination Organization*] [*Cambodia*] (CL)

OPCH .... Chitral [*Pakistan*] [*ICAO location identifier*] (ICLI)

OPCh .... Optimum Working Frequency (RU)

op cit .... Opere Citato [*In the work quoted*] (SCAC)

op cit .... Ouvrage Cite [*French*] (FLAF)

OPCL .... Chilas [*Pakistan*] [*ICAO location identifier*] (ICLI)

OP-COM .. Opera-Comique [*Comic Opera*] [*Music*]

OPCR .... Chachro [*Pakistan*] [*ICAO location identifier*] (ICLI)

OPCT .... Chirat [*Pakistan*] [*ICAO location identifier*] (ICLI)

OPD .... Oberpostdirektion [*Main Postal Directorate*] (EG)

OpD .... Operativer Diensthabender [*Officer of the Day*] (EG)

OPDB .... Dalbandin [*Pakistan*] [*ICAO location identifier*] (ICLI)

OPDD .... Dadu [*Pakistan*] [*ICAO location identifier*] (ICLI)

opdesb .... Separate River Crossing Assault Battalion (RU)

OPDF .... One Percent for Development Fund [*Switzerland*] (EAIO)

OPDG .... Dera Ghazi Khan [*Pakistan*] [*ICAO location identifier*] (ICLI)

OPDI .... Dera Ismail Khan [*Pakistan*] [*ICAO location identifier*] (ICLI)

OPDK .... Daharki [*Pakistan*] [*ICAO location identifier*] (ICLI)

OPDO .... Oromo People's Democratic Organization [*Ethiopia*] [*Political party*] (EY)

OPDP .... Odbor za Perspektivni Drustveni Plan (SIV) [*Committee for the Prospective Economic Plan*] (YU)

opdr .... Opdracht [*Dedication*] [*Publishing*] [*Netherlands*]

OPDSNP ... General Regulations on the Procurement of Consumer Goods (BU)

OPDU .... Operative Painters and Decorators Union of Australia

OPDUA ..... Operative Painters amd Decorators' Union of Australia

OPE .... Office de la Protection de l'Enfance [*Benelux*] (BAS)

OPE .... Office de Promotion de l'Entreprise [*Enterprise Promotion Office*] [*Burkina Faso*] (GEA)

OPE .... Office of Projects Execution [*West Africa*] [*United Nations (already exists in GUS II database)*]

OPE .... Organismos Prolipseos Englimatos [*Organization for Crime Prevention*] [*Greek*] (GC)

OPE .... Organismos Proothiseos Exagogon [*Organization for Exports Promotion*] (GC)

OPE .... Organosis Pankypriakis Enotitas [*Organization for Pan-Cyprian Unity*] (GC)

OPE .... Oulamos Prolipseos Englimatos [*Crime Prevention Squad*] [*Cyprus*] (GC)

OPE .... Societe 3S Aviation (Aerope) [*France*] [*ICAO designator*] (FAAC)

OPEAGRO ... Organizacion de Paises Exportadores de Productos Agropecuarios [*Organization of Exporting Countries of Agricultural and Livestock Products*] (LA)

OPEB .... Experimental Model Excursion Center (RU)

OPEB .... Organizacao de Pesquisas Espaciais do Brasil [*Brazilian Space Research Organization*] (LA)

OPEC .... Organization of Petroleum Exporting Countries [*Also, OAPEC*] [*Vienna, Austria*]

OPECD ..... Organismos Populares de la Educacion, Cultura, y Deportes [*People's Educational, Cultural, and Sports Organizations*] [*Cuba*] (LA)

OPECNA .. OPEC [*Organization of Petroleum Exporting Countries*] News Agency [*See also APOPEC*] [*Vienna, Austria*] (EAIO)

OPEDC ..... Overseas Private Enterprise Development Corp. [*Proposed successor to Agency for International Development*]

OPEH .... Organizacion de Productores y Exportadores de Hierro (LAA)

OPEI .... Office National de Promotion d'Entreprise Ivoirienne [*National Office for the Promotion of Ivorian Enterprises*] (AF)

OPEK .... Organosis Prostasias Ellinon Kyprion [*Organization for the Protection of Greek Cypriots*] (GC)

OPEMA .... Office des Peches Maritimes [*Maritime Fishing Office*] [*Guinea*] (AF)

OPEMA .... Operacao Maua [*Ministerio dos Transportes*] [*Brazil*]

OPEN .... Office de Promotion de l'Entreprise Nigerienne [*Office for the Promotion of Nigerien Enterprises*] [*Niger*] (AF)

OPEN .... Organisation des Producteurs d'Energie Nucleaire [*Paris, France*] (EAIO)

openb .... Openbaar [*Public*] [*Afrikaans*]

Openb .... Openbaring [*Apocalypse*] [*Afrikaans*]

opengesn .... Opengesneden [*Cut Open*] [*Publishing*] [*Netherlands*]

OPEOE ...... Omospondia Pandopolon, Edodimopolon, kai Oinopandopolon Ellados [*Federation of Grocers, Food Dealers, and Wine Merchants of Greece*] (GC)

OPEP........ Omospondia Prosopikou Etaireion Petrelaioeidon [*Federation of Personnel of Petroleum Products Companies*] [*Greek*] (GC)

OPEP........ Organisation des Pays Exportateurs de Petrole [*Organization of Petroleum Exporting Countries*] [*Use OPEC*] [*French*] (AF)

OPEP........ Organismos Protypon kai Elenkhou Poiotitos [*Standards and Quality Control Organization*] (GC)

OPEP........ Organizacao dos Paises Exportadores de Petroleo [*Organization of Petroleum Exporting Countries*] [*Use OPEC*] [*Portuguese*] (WER)

OPEP........ Organizacion de Paises Exportadores de Petroleo [*Organization of Petroleum Exporting Countries*] [*Use OPEC*] [*Spanish*] (LA)

OPEP........ Unit of a Field Evacuation Station (RU)

OPer......... Old Persian [*Language*] (BARN)

OPERCOL ... Operaciones Comerciales Industriales Ltda. [*Barranquilla*] (COL)

OPers......... Old Persian [*Language*] (BARN)

OPERU ..... Transactions Office [*Gosbank*] (RU)

OPEV .... Office de Promotion de l'Entreprise Voltaique

OPEX .... Operational, Executive, and Administrative Personnel Program [*United Nations*]

OPEX .... Organization and Operations Executive

OPEZ........ Office pour la Promotion des Entreprises Zairoises [*Office for the Promotion of Zairian Enterprises*] (AF)

OPF .... Organisation Panafricaine des Femmes [*Pan-African Women's Organization*] (AF)

OPF .... Orszagos Penzugyi Felugyeloseg [*National Inspectorate of Revenue*] (HU)

OPFA........ Faisalabad [*Pakistan*] [*ICAO location identifier*] (ICLI)

OPFB........ Forward Front Logistical Installation Subsection (BU)

OPFB........ Unit of Advanced Front-Line Base (RU)

OPFPS....... Supply Relay Point Railhead for Courier Postal Communications (BU)

OPG.......... Ground Surface Mark (RU)

OPG.......... Oesterreichische Palaeontologische Gesellschaft [*Austria*] (SLS)

OPG.......... Oesterreichische Physikalische Gesellschaft [*Austria*] (SLS)

opg........... Opgave [*Table of Contents*] [*Publishing*] [*Netherlands*]

OPG.......... Ostry Prubojny Granat [*Armor-Piercing Grenade*] (CZ)

OPG.......... Overseas Property Group [*Commonwealth Department of Administrative Services*] [*Australia*]

OPGD........ Gwadar [*Pakistan*] [*ICAO location identifier*] (ICLI)

OPGT........ Gilgit [*Pakistan*] [*ICAO location identifier*] (ICLI)

OPHAM.... Office Pharmaceutique Malgache

OPhG........ Oesterreichische Pharmazeutische Gesellschaft [*Austria*] (SLS)

Ophn.......... Orpheon [*Record label*] [*Poland*]

OPHO .... Okregowe Przedsiebiorstwo Handlu Opalem [*District Fuel Trade Enterprise*] (POL)

OPHQ........ Karachi [*Pakistan*] [*ICAO location identifier*] (ICLI)

OPHS........ Office Public d'Hygiene Sociale [*France*] (FLAF)

OPI .... Odessa Pedagogical Institute Imeni K. D. Ushinskiy (RU)

OPI .... Odessa Polytechnic Institute (RU)

OPI .... Office de Promotion de l'Entreprise Ivoirienne

OPI .... Office of Public Information [*UNESCO*]

OPI .... Oposicion de Izquierda [*Leftist Opposition*] [*Spanish*] (WER)

OPIC........ Oficina Permanente Internacional de la Carne [*Permanent International Meat Office*] (EAIO)

OPIC........ Overseas Private Investment Corp. [*US International Development Cooperatio n Agency*] [*Washington, DC*]

OPIE........ Oficina de Planeamiento Integral de la Educacion [*Guatemala*]

OPIF......... Orient Press International Federation

OPIGIM.... Manuscript Department of the State Historical Museum (RU)

OPII.......... Institute of Planning and Research Based on Public Participation (RU)

OPINA ...... Opinion Nacional (Partido) [*National Opinion (Party)*] [*Venezuela*] (LA)

OPIR......... Organizacion Popular Independiente Revolucionaria [*Popular Independent Revolutionary Organization*] [*Venezuela*] (LA)

OPJ........... Office [*or Officier*] de la Police Judiciaire

OPJA........ Jacobabad [*Pakistan*] [*ICAO location identifier*] (ICLI)

OPJA........ Opasni Prostori u Jadranskom i Jonskom Moru [*Dangerous Areas in the Adriatic and Ionian Seas*] (YU)

OPJC........ Jacobabad [*Pakistan*] [*ICAO location identifier*] (ICLI)

OPJI......... Jiwani [*Pakistan*] [*ICAO location identifier*] (ICLI)

OPJM........ Organizacion de Pioneros Jose Marti [*Organization of Jose Marti Pioneers*] [*Cuba*] (LA)

OPK.......... Department of Blood Transfusion (RU)

OPK.......... Obrona Powietrzna Kraju [*Home Air Defense*] (POL)

OPK.......... Odbor za Prosvetu i Kulturu (SIV) [*Committee on Education and Culture*] (YU)

OPK.......... Oddeleni Pohranicni Kontroly [*Frontier Control Department*] (CZ)

OPK.......... Okoliya Industrial Combine (BU)

OPK.......... Orszagos Pedagogiai Konyvtar [*National Education Library*] (HU)

OPK .... Personnel-Training Department (RU)

OPK .... Separate Outguard (RU)

OPKA .... Cape Monze [*Pakistan*] [*ICAO location identifier*] (ICLI)

OPKC .... Karachi/International [*Pakistan*] [*ICAO location identifier*] (ICLI)

OPKD....... Hyderabad [*Pakistan*] [*ICAO location identifier*] (ICLI)

OPKE....... Chore [*Pakistan*] [*ICAO location identifier*] (ICLI)

OPKF....... Gharo [*Pakistan*] [*ICAO location identifier*] (ICLI)

OPKh....... Experimental Model Farm (RU)

OPKH....... Khuzdhar [*Pakistan*] [*ICAO location identifier*] (ICLI)

OPKhV ..... Omospondia Prosopikou Khimikis Viomikhanias [*Federation of Chemical Industry Personnel*] [*Greek*] (GC)

OPKI .... Onkopatologiai Kutato Intezet [*Research Institute in Tumor Pathology*] (HU)

OPKK .... Karachi/Korangi Creek [*Pakistan*] [*ICAO location identifier*] (ICLI)

OPKL........ Kalat [*Pakistan*] [*ICAO location identifier*] (ICLI)

opkl .... Opklaebet [*Mounted*] [*Publishing Danish/Norwegian*]

OPKN....... Kharan [*Pakistan*] [*ICAO location identifier*] (ICLI)

OPKO....... Kohat [*Pakistan*] [*ICAO location identifier*] (ICLI)

OPKR....... Karachi [*Pakistan*] [*ICAO location identifier*] (ICLI)

OPKT....... Kohat [*Pakistan*] [*ICAO location identifier*] (ICLI)

OPL .... Adjustable-Blade Reversible Runner (of a Hydraulic Turbine) (RU)

OPL .... Air Cote d'Opale [*France*] [*ICAO designator*] (FAAC)

OPL .... Obrana Proti Letadlum [*Antiaircraft Defense*] (CZ)

OPL .... Obrona Przeciw Lotnicza [*Antiaircraft Defense*] (POL)

OPL .... Occupational Priority List [*Immigration*] [*New Zealand*]

OPL .... Oil Prospecting License

opl .... Oplaag [*Edition*] [*Publishing*] [*Netherlands*]

opl .... Oplag [*Edition*] [*Publishing Danish/Norwegian*]

OPLA .... Lahore [*Pakistan*] [*ICAO location identifier*] (ICLI)

OPLA .... Oficina de Planificacion Agricola [*Agricultural Planning Office*] [*Chile*] (LA)

OPLA .... Omades Prostasias Laikou Agonos [*Units for the Protection of the People's Struggle*] [*Greek*] (GC)

OPLC .... Organizacion para la Liberacion de Cuba [*Organization for the Liberation of Cuba*] (PD)

OPLH....... Lahore/Walton [*Pakistan*] [*ICAO location identifier*] (ICLI)

OPLL....... Loralai [*Pakistan*] [*ICAO location identifier*] (ICLI)

OPLO....... Oromo People's Liberation Organization [*Ethiopia*] (AF)

OPLOH..... Organisation de Production et de Logistique OTAN [*Organisation du Traite de l'Atlantique Nord*] du HAWK

OPLot....... Obrona Przeciw Lotnicza [*Antiaircraft Defense*] [*Poland*]

OPLR....... Lahore [*Pakistan*] [*ICAO location identifier*] (ICLI)

opluv.......... Originalpluviusin [*Original Leatherette*] [*Publishing Danish/Norwegian*]

oplysn........ Oplysning [*Explanatory Note*] [*Publishing Danish/Norwegian*]

OPM......... First Aid Detachment (RU)

OPM......... Oberster Patent- und Markensenat [*German*]

OPM......... Oddeleni Prace a Mezd [*Labor and Wage Department*] (CZ)

OPM......... Oddzial Przedsiebiorstwa Mierniczego [*Branch of the Surveying Enterprise*] (POL)

OPM......... Office of Public Management [*New South Wales, Australia*]

OPM......... Okregowe Przedsiebiorstwo Miernicze [*District Surveying Enterprise*] (POL)

OPM......... Okresni Pece o Mladez [*District Youth Welfare Organization*] (CZ)

OPM......... Omwentelinge per Minuut [*Revolutions per Minute*] [*Afrikaans*]

Opm.......... Opmerking [*Remark*] [*Netherlands*] (GPO)

OPM......... Organisasi Papua Merdeka [*Papua Independent Organization*] [*Indonesia*] (PD)

OPM......... Organizacion Politico-Militar [*Politico-Military Organization*] [*Paraguay*] (PD)

OPM......... Single-Sideband Modulation (RU)

OPM......... Society of Marxist Teachers (RU)

OPMA....... Mangla [*Pakistan*] [*ICAO location identifier*] (ICLI)

OPMA....... Overseas Press and Media Association [*British*] (EAIO)

OPMF....... Muzaffarabad [*Pakistan*] [*ICAO location identifier*] (ICLI)

OPMI....... Mianwali [*Pakistan*] [*ICAO location identifier*] (ICLI)

OPMJ....... Moenjodaro [*Pakistan*] [*ICAO location identifier*] (ICLI)

OPMK....... Mir Pur Khas [*Pakistan*] [*ICAO location identifier*] (ICLI)

OPMN....... Miranshah [*Pakistan*] [*ICAO location identifier*] (ICLI)

OPMR....... Karachi/Masroor [*Pakistan*] [*ICAO location identifier*] (ICLI)

OPMS....... Miranshah [*Pakistan*] [*ICAO location identifier*] (ICLI)

OPMT....... Multan [*Pakistan*] [*ICAO location identifier*] (ICLI)

OPMT....... Organizacion Puertorriquena de la Mujer Trabajadora [*Puerto Rico*] (EAIO)

OPMW....... Mianwali [*Pakistan*] [*ICAO location identifier*] (ICLI)

OPN.......... Association of Trade Unions of Norway (RU)

opn .... Opnieuw [*Again, Anew*] [*Netherlands*]

OPNH....... Nawabshah [*Pakistan*] [*ICAO location identifier*] (ICLI)

OPNK....... Naushki [*Pakistan*] [*ICAO location identifier*] (ICLI)

OPNT....... Office des Ports Nationaux Tunisiens

OPO.......... Basic Plan of Operations [*Military term*] (RU)

OPO.......... Department for the Exchange of Production Experience (RU)

OPO........... Fire Prevention Department   (RU)
OPO........... Operations and Production Department   (RU)
OP-O........ Operativni Otsek [*Operation Section*] [*Military*]   (YU)
OPO........... Oporto [*Portugal*] [*Airport symbol*]   (OAG)
OPO........... Organization and Planning Department   (RU)
OPO........... Ortsparteiorganisation [*Local Party Organization*]   (EG)
OPO........... Oslobodilacki Partizanski Odred [*Partisan Liberation Detachment*]   (YU)
OPO........... Osnovnata Partiska Organizacija [*Basic Party Organization*]   (YU)
OPO........... Ovamboland People's Organisation
OPO........... Separate Border Guard Detachment   (RU)
OPOC....... Omnium Photo Optique Cinema
OPODD..... Omospondia Prosopikou Organismon Dimosiou Dikaiou [*Federation of Personnel of Public Law Organizations*] [*Greek*]   (GC)
OPOEKh ... Organosis Politikis kai Oikonomikis Epistratevseos tis Khoras [*Organization for the Political and Economic Mobilization of the Nation*] [*Greek*]   (GC)
OPOK....... Okara [*Pakistan*] [*ICAO location identifier*]   (ICLI)
OPOL....... Offshore Pollution Liability Association Ltd.   (EA)
OPOR....... Ormara [*Pakistan*] [*ICAO location identifier*]   (ICLI)
opow........... Opowiadanie [*Short Novel, Story*] [*Poland*]
OPOY....... Omospondia Perifereiakon Oikonomikon Ypallilon [*Federation of Regional Finance Employees*] [*Greek*]   (GC)
OPOYaZ ... Society for the Study of the Theory of Poetic Language [*1914-1923*]   (RU)
OPOZRz.... Okregowe Przedsiebiorstwa Obrotu Zwierzetami Rzeznymi [*District Slaughter Animal Trade Enterprise*]   (POL)
OPP .... Department of Industrial Establishments   (RU)
OPP .... Experimental Industrial Establishment   (RU)
OPP .... Mail Transportation Department   (RU)
OPP .... Main Direction-Finding Station   (RU)
OPP .... Office of Public Prosecutions [*Northern Territory, Australia*]
OPP .... Okrug Industrial Enterprise   (BU)
OPP .... Okrug Printing Enterprise   (BU)
OPP-O...... Omades Politikis Protovoulias [*Political Initiative Groups*] [*Greek*]   (GC)
opp .... Oppilas [*Finland*]
opp .... Opposant [*Benelux*]   (BAS)
opp .... Oppose [*French*]   (TPFD)
opp .... Opposite   (EECI)
OPP .... Organos de Poder Popular [*Organs of People's Government*] [*Cuba*]   (LA)
OPP .... Organoseis Prostasias Perivallondos [*Environmental Protection Organizations*]   (GC)
Opp .... Originalpappband [*Original Boards*] [*Publishing*] [*German*]
OPP .... Outline Perspective Plan [*Malaysia*]   (FEA)
OPP .... Political Propaganda Department   (RU)
OPP .... Propaganda and Press Department   (RU)
OPPA .... Party Propaganda and Agitation Department   (RU)
oppbd .... Originalpappbind [*Original Boards*] [*Publishing Danish/Norwegian*]
Oppbd .... Originalpappband [*Original Boards*] [*Publishing*] [*German*]
OPPC....... Parachinar [*Pakistan*] [*ICAO location identifier*]   (ICLI)
OPPE........ Omospondia Palaion Polemiston Ellados [*Federation of Greek Veterans*]   (GC)
OPPE........ Organismos Palaion Polemiston Ellados [*Organization of Greek Veterans*]   (GC)
OPPEM..... Organizacion para le Proteccion de las Plantas en Europa y en el Mediterraneo [*France*]   (DSCA)
OPPG .... Panjgur [*Pakistan*] [*ICAO location identifier*]   (ICLI)
opph .... Opphoeyde [*Raised*] [*Danish/Norwegian*]
OPPI......... Organisation of Pharmaceutical Producers of India
OPPI......... Pasni [*Pakistan*] [*ICAO location identifier*]   (ICLI)
OPPIR...... Portable Optical Pyrometer   (RU)
oppl .... Opplag [*Edition*] [*Publishing Danish/Norwegian*]
OPPME..... Office de Promotion des Petites et Moyennes Entreprises
OPPN .... Pishin [*Pakistan*] [*ICAO location identifier*]   (ICLI)
OPPP........ Organisation des Pays Producteurs de Petrole [*North African*]
OPPS........ Okoliya Fire-Fighting Service   (BU)
OPPS........ Optique Photo et Precision du Senegal
OPPS........ Peshawar [*Pakistan*] [*ICAO location identifier*]   (ICLI)
OPPU .... Association of Proletarian Writers of the Ukraine   (RU)
OPPV........ Experimental Model Ground of the Vsevobuch   (RU)
OPPWFA .. Operative Plasteres amd Plaster Workers' Federation of Australia
OPPZ........ Department for Resettlement and Preparation of an Area for Flooding [*Hydroelectric developments*]   (RU)
OPQCB ..... Office Professionel de Qualification et de Classification des Entreprises du Batiment
OPQS .... Qasim [*Pakistan*] [*ICAO location identifier*]   (ICLI)
OPQT .... Quetta/Samungli [*Pakistan*] [*ICAO location identifier*]   (ICLI)
OPR .... Basic Planned Repair   (BU)
OPR .... Covering Detachment, Covering Force   (RU)
OPR .... Field Repair Section   (RU)
OPR........... Odred za Pranje Rublja [*Laundry Detachment*] [*Military*]   (YU)

OPR........... Old Prussian [*Language, etc.*]
Opr............. Operator [*Surgeon*]   (TU)
opr .... Oprawa [*or Oprawiony*] [*Binding or Bound*]   (POL)
opr .... Oprindelig [*Original*] [*Publishing Danish/Norwegian*]
OPR .... Organisasi Perlawanan Rakjat [*People's Resistance Organization*]   (IN)
OPR .... Organisation du Peuple Rodriguais [*Organization of the Rodrigues People*] [*Mauritius*]   (AF)
Opr............. Supreme Court Decision   (BU)
OPR-33...... Organizacion Popular Revolucionaria-33 [*Popular Revolutionary Organization-33*] [*Uruguay*]   (LA)
oprac .... Opracowal [*or Opracowane*] [*Prepared By or Prepared*]   (POL)
OPRAG ..... Office des Ports et Rades du Gabon [*Gabon Ports and Roadsteads Office*]   (AF)
OPrem .... Ordre de Premontre [*Order of the Canons Regular of Premontre*] [*Rome, Italy*]   (EAIO)
OPREX...... Operational Exercise [*NATO*]   (NATG)
OPRI......... Office de la Propriete Industrielle [*Department of Industrial Property*] [*Ministry of Economic Affairs*]   (IID)
OPRK .... Rahimyarkhan [*Pakistan*] [*ICAO location identifier*]   (ICLI)
OPRN .... Islamabad/Chaklala [*Pakistan*] [*ICAO location identifier*]   (ICLI)
oProf .... Ordentlicher Professor [*Full Professor*] [*German*]   (WEN)
OPROL ..... Oddeleni Protiradiolokace [*Radar Countermeasures Department*]   (CZ)
oprol .... Oxyproline   (RU)
OPRON..... Organization of Progressive Nationals   (LA)
OProv........ Old Provencal [*Language*]   (BARN)
OPROVI.... Obra de Proteccion de Menores y Villas Infantiles [*Work of Protection of Minors' and Children's Villages*] [*Argentina*]   (LAA)
OPRP........ Organizacion Politica de la Revolucion Peruana [*Political Organization of the Peruvian Revolution*]   (LA)
OPRQ....... Shorekote/Rafiqui [*Pakistan*] [*ICAO location identifier*]   (ICLI)
OPRS........ Oddeleni Protiradiotechnicke Sluzby [*Counter Radiotechnical Service Department*]   (CZ)
OPRS........ Oil Palm Research Station
OPRS........ Overseas Public Relations Sub-Division [*Hong Kong*]
OPRS........ Risalpur [*Pakistan*] [*ICAO location identifier*]   (ICLI)
OPRT .... Rawalakot [*Pakistan*] [*ICAO location identifier*]   (ICLI)
OPruss....... Old Prussian [*Language*]   (BARN)
OPS .... Field Communications Section   (RU)
OPS .... General Rules of Signalization   (RU)
OPS .... Hydroxypropyl Alcohol   (RU)
OPS .... Oblasni Privredni Sud [*Regional Economic Court*]   (YU)
OPS .... OCBC [*Overseas Chinese Banking Corp.*] Property Services [*Singapore*]
OPS .... Ogledna Poljoprivredna Stanica [*Agricultural Experiment Station*]   (YU)
OPS .... Okresni Pedagogicky Sbor [*District Board of Education*]   (CZ)
OPS .... Okresni Pracovni Stredisko [*District Labor Center*]   (CZ)
OPS .... Okruhova Politicka Sprava [*Zonal Political Directorate*]   (CZ)
OPS .... Okruzni Privredni Sud [*County Economic Court*]   (YU)
OPS .... Operations [*Operations*] [*French*]   (CL)
OPS .... Operations Division [*NATO*]   (NATG)
ops............. Opusculos [*Small Works*] [*Portuguese*]
OPS .... Oral Protez Sanayii AS [*Oral Prosthetics Industry Corp.*]   (TU)
OPS .... Organisasi Perusahaan-Perusahaan Sedjenis [*Organization of Similar Enterprises*]   (IN)
OPS .... Organisation Panamericaine de la Sante [*Pan American Health Organization*]   (MSC)
OPS .... Organizacion Panamericana de la Salud [*Pan American Health Organization*] [*Use PAHO*]   (LA)
OPS .... Own Produce Sold
OPS .... Separate Signal Regiment   (RU)
OPS .... Single Flip-Flop   (RU)
OPS .... Underground Structures Department   (RU)
OPSA........ Oficina de Planeamiento del Sector Agropecuario [*Agricultural-Livestock Sector Planning Office*] [*Colorado*]   (LA)
OPSA........ Operavereniging van Suid-Afrika
OPSB........ Sibi [*Pakistan*] [*ICAO location identifier*]   (ICLI)
OPSC........ Office of the Public Service Commissioner [*Australia*]
OPSC........ Oil and Protein Seed Centre [*South Africa*]   (IRC)
OPSCO...... Operations Sub-Committee   (ML)
OPSD .... Skardu [*Pakistan*] [*ICAO location identifier*]   (ICLI)
OPSD .... Society of Polish-Soviet Friendship   (RU)
OPSF........ Karachi/Shara-E-Faisal [*Pakistan*] [*ICAO location identifier*]   (ICLI)
OPSh .... Shpagin Flare Pistol   (RU)
OPSJ .... Organisatie van Progressieve Studerende Jeugd [*Organization of Progressive Student Youth*] [*Netherlands*]   (WEN)
OPSK........ Sukkur [*Pakistan*] [*ICAO location identifier*]   (ICLI)
OPSM .... Office of Public Sector Management [*Australian Capital Territory*]
OPSM .... Optical Prescriptions Spectacle Makers Industries Ltd. [*Australia*]   (ADA)

OPSMB..... Organization of Progressive Socialists of the Mediterranean Basin
OPSP......... Operations Panel [*ICAO*]   (DA)
OPSP......... Shekhupura [*Pakistan*] [*ICAO location identifier*]   (ICLI)
OPSR......... Sargodha [*Pakistan*] [*ICAO location identifier*]   (ICLI)
OPSREP.... Operations Report [*NATO*]   (NATG)
OPSS........ Saidu Sharif [*Pakistan*] [*ICAO location identifier*]   (ICLI)
OPSSZZ.... Otkupno Preduzece Sreskog Saveza Zemljoradnickih Zadruga [*Purchasing Establishment of the District Agricultural Cooperatives Union*]   (YU)
OPSU ...... Sui [*Pakistan*] [*ICAO location identifier*]   (ICLI)
OPSUS...... Operasi Chusus [*Special Operations*]   (IN)
OPSW....... Sahiwal [*Pakistan*] [*ICAO location identifier*]   (ICLI)
OPSZS ...... Otkupno Preduzece Sreskog Zadruznog Saveza [*Purchasing Establishment of the District Cooperative Union*]   (YU)
OPT .... Joint Force Message Code Table   (RU)
OPT .... Office des Postes et des Telecommunications [*Postal and Telecommunications Office*] [*Gabon*]   (AF)
OPT .... Office of the Public Trustee [*Australian Capital Territory*]
OPT .... Optatief [*Optative*] [*Afrikaans*]
opt .... Optical, Optics   (RU)
opt .... Optics, Optical   (BU)
opt .... Optiikka [*Optics*] [*Finland*]
opt .... Optique [*French*]   (TPFD)
opt .... Optisch [*Optical*] [*German*]
OPT .... Osrodek Postepu Technicznego [*Technical Progress Center*] (POL)
OPT .... Society of Proletarian Tourism   (RU)
OPTA .... Terbela [*Pakistan*] [*ICAO location identifier*]   (ICLI)
optabr......... Separate Antitank Artillery Brigade   (RU)
OPTAD ..... Organisation for Pacific Trade and Development   (ADA)
opt akt ...... Optisch Aktiv [*Optically Active*] [*German*]   (GCA)
OPTD .... Separate Antitank Battalion   (RU)
OPTE........ All-Union Voluntary Society of Proletarian Tourism and Excursions [*1928-1936*]   (RU)
OPTH....... Talhar [*Pakistan*] [*ICAO location identifier*]   (ICLI)
OPTI......... Department of Industrial and Technical Information   (RU)
OPTI......... Orszagos Palyavalasztasi Tanacsado Intezet [*National Career Selection Advisory Institute*]   (HU)
optich .... Optical   (RU)
OPTICOM ... Optimum Community
OPTiE .... All-Union Voluntary Society of Proletarian Tourism and Excursions [*1928-1936*]   (RU)
OPTIMA... Organization for the Phyto-Taxonomic Investigation of the Mediterranean Area [*Berlin, Federal Republic of Germany*] (EAIO)
OPTINUTZ ... Optimale Nutzung von Laderaeumen [*German*]   (ADPT)
optorg......... Wholesale   (RU)
optr............. Optryk [*Reprint*] [*Publishing Danish/Norwegian*]
OPTRA...... Office Professionnel des Transports [*Professional Transportation Bureau*] [*French*]   (WER)
OPTS........ Office des Postes et des Telecommunications du Senegal [*Senegal Postal and Telecommunications Office*]   (AF)
OPTT........ Ob'edinenie Profsoiuzov Trudiashchikhsia Tunisa
OPTT........ Taftan [*Pakistan*] [*ICAO location identifier*]   (ICLI)
OPTU .... Turbat [*Pakistan*] [*ICAO location identifier*]   (ICLI)
OPU.......... Balimo [*Papua New Guinea*] [*Airport symbol*]   (OAG)
OPU.......... Experimental Model Institution   (RU)
OPU.......... Great Circle Track Angle   (RU)
opubl .... Published   (RU)
OPUDEMA ... Oficina de Planeamiento de la Universidad Tecnologica del Magdalena [*Colombia*]   (DSCA)
OPUL .... Organisasie van Petroleum-Uitvoerland [*Organization of Petroleum Exporting Countries - OPEC*] [*Afrikaans*]
opulab .... Separate Machine-Gun and Artillery Battalion   (RU)
opulap .... Separate Machine-Gun and Artillery Regiment   (RU)
opusc .... Opuscolo [*Pamphlet*] [*Publishing*] [*Italian*]
OPV .... Bedarfsflugunternehmen Dr. L. Polsterer [*Austria*] [*ICAO designator*]   (FAAC)
OPV .... Office Pharmaceutique Veterinaire
OPV .... Offshore Patrol Vessel [*India*] [*Military*]
OPVDC ..... Organizacao Provincial de Voluntarios e Defesa Civil
OPVDCA .. Organizacao Provincial de Voluntarios e Defesa Civil de Angola
OPVK .... Department of Industrial Veterinary Control   (RU)
OPVN........ Office des Produits Vivriers du Niger [*Nigerien Foodstuffs Office*] [*Niger*]   (AF)
OPVTR...... General Rules for Internal Work Order   (BU)
OPW......... Joint Freight Car Pool (Bloc) [*Russian*]   (EG)
OPW......... Ogolny Park Wagonow [*General Freight Car Pool*] [*Poland*] (CZ)
OPW......... Opuwa [*Namibia*] [*Airport symbol*]   (OAG)
OPWN....... Wana [*Pakistan*] [*ICAO location identifier*]   (ICLI)
OPWZ....... Oesterreichisches Produktivitaets- und Wirtschaftlichkeitszentrum [*Austria*]   (SLS)

OPXAE...... Omospondia Prosopikou Xenon Aeroporikon Etaireion [*Federation of Foreign Airline Company Personnel*] [*Greek*] (GC)
OPYK .... Omospondia Politon Ygron Kavsimon [*Federation of Liquid Fuel Dealers*] [*Greek*]   (GC)
OPYPA...... Oficina de Programacion y Politica Agropecuaria [*Uruguay*] (DSCA)
OPYRWA ... Office du Pyrethre au Rwanda [*Development organization*] [*Rwanda*]
opyt .... Experimental   (RU)
OPZ........... Obstacle-Forcing Detachment   (RU)
OPZ........... Obucarsko Preradivacka Zadruga [*Shoe Finishing Cooperative*] (YU)
OPZ........... Oesterreichisches Produktivitats Zentrum [*Austrian Productivity Centre*]   (PDAA)
OPZ........... Opca Poljoprivredna Zadruga [*General Agricultural Cooperative*] (YU)
OPZ........... Opca Privredna Zadruga [*General Economic Cooperative*]   (YU)
OPZB........ Olsztynskie Powiatowe Zjednoczenie Budowlane [*Olsztyn (Allenstein) County Construction Association*]   (POL)
OPZB........ Olsztynskie Przemyslowe Zjednoczenie Budowlane [*Olsztyn (Allenstein) Industrial Construction Association*]   (POL)
OPZB........ Zhob [*Pakistan*] [*ICAO location identifier*]   (ICLI)
OPZG........ Trade-Union Association of West Germany   (RU)
OPZHN..... Operacni Plan Zbrane Hromadneho Niceni [*Operations Plan for Weapons of Mass Destruction*]   (CZ)
OPZPHiU ... Ogolnopolskie Zrzeszenie Prywatnego Handlu i Uslug [*All-Poland Private Trade and Services Association*]   (POL)
OPZZ .... Department for Preparation of an Area for Flooding [*Hydroelectric developments*]   (RU)
OPZZ .... Ogolnopolskie Porozumienie Zwiazkow Zawodowych [*National Alliance of Trade Unions*] [*Poland*]
OQ .... Ouvrier Qualitie [*French*]
OR............. Controlled Member   (RU)
OR............. Danger Area   (RU)
OR............. Experimental Rocket [*Engine*]   (RU)
or .... Flamethrower Company   (RU)
or .... Greenhouse [*Topography*]   (RU)
or .... Gun   (RU)
or .... Gun, Piece   (BU)
or .... Landmark, Reference Point, Checkpoint   (BU)
OR............. Main Register   (RU)
OR............. Obligationsrecht [*Indispensable Right*] [*German*]
OR............. Oborove Reditelstvi [*Sectoral Directorate*]   (CZ)
OR............. Obvodni Rada [*District Council*]   (CZ)
OR............. Octrooiraad [*Rijswijk*]
Or.............. Octrooireglement [*Benelux*]   (BAS)
OR............. Odborova [*or Odborovy*] Rada [*Trade-Union Council or Trade-Union Counselor (Title of government official)*]   (CZ)
OR............. Odborove Riaditelstvo [*Sectoral Directorate*]   (CZ)
OR............. Odluka o Renti [*Land Rent Decision*] [*Law*]   (YU)
O-R .... Oesterreich-Reihe (Taschenbuecher) [*German*]
OR............. Officier de Reserve [*Reserve Officer*] [*French*]
OR............. Oklopne Rezerve [*Armored Reserves*]   (YU)
OR............. Okresni Referent [*District Official*]   (CZ)
OR............. Olah Raga [*Sports, Athletics*]   (IN)
OR............. Ondernemingsraad [*Benelux*]   (BAS)
OR............. Onderwijsraad
OR............. Open Registry [*Flag of convenience*] [*Shipping*]   (DS)
OR............. Operationsregister [*German*]   (ADPT)
or .... Op Rekening [*On Account*] [*Afrikaans*]
or .... Orderly, Messenger   (BU)
OR............. Order of the Rokel [*Sierra Leone*]
OR............. Ordonnance Royale [*Royal Ordinance*] [*Cambodia*]   (CL)
OR............. Organizacija Rada [*Organization of Work*]   (YU)
OR............. Organizacion de Revolucionarios [*Organization of Revolutionaries*] [*Venezuela*]   (LA)
or .... Original [*French*]
Or.............. Original [*German*]
or .... Original [*Danish/Norwegian*]
or .... Originale [*Original*] [*Italian*]
or .... Origineel [*Original*] [*Publishing*] [*Netherlands*]
OR............. Oristano [*Car registration plates*] [*Italy*]
or .... Orosz [*Russian*]   (HU)
Or.............. Orta [*Secondary*]   (TU)
or .... Orvosi Rendelo [*Medical Consultation Room*]   (HU)
Or.............. Reference Point, Marker   (RU)
OR............. Regulating Winding   (RU)
OR............. Roadstead Defense   (RU)
OR............. Separate Mounted Patrol   (RU)
OR............. Single Operating Mode [*Computers*]   (RU)
OR............. Telephone Call Canceled   (BU)
OR............. Working Winding   (RU)
ORA.......... All-Russian Association of Workers' Artels   (RU)
ORA.......... Office of Rural Affairs [*Victoria, Australia*]
ORA.......... Oramiral [*Vice Admiral*]   (TU)

ORA.......... Organisation de Resistance de l'Armee [*France*]
ORA.......... Organisation Revolutionnaire Anarchiste [*Revolutionary Anarchist Organization*] [*France*] [*Political party*] (PPE)
ORA.......... Organizacao Revolucionaria Armada [*Terrorist group*] [*Portugal*] (EY)
ORA.......... Organizacion de Reparaciones Automotoras [*Colombia*] (COL)
ORA.......... Organizacion de Resistencia Armada [*Organization of Armed Resistance*] [*Chile*] (LA)
ORAC....... Omnium de Refrigeration et Amenagements Coloniaux
ORACLE... Online Retrieval of Acquisitions, Cataloguing and Circulation Details for Library Enquiries [*State Library of Queensland*] [*Australia*] (PDAA)
ORAD....... Oficiul Regional de Aprovizionare si Desfacere [*Regional Office for Supply and Sales*] (RO)
ORAD....... Separate Artillery Reconnaissance Battalion (RU)
orad........... Separate Reconnaissance Artillery Battalion (BU)
ORAE....... Separate Air Reconnaissance Squadron (RU)
ORAF........ Organisation de la Resistance de l'Algerie Francaise
ORAF........ Organisation Regionale Africaine de la CISL
ORAF........ Ortadogu ve Afrika Dairesi Genel Mudurlugu [*Middle East and Africa Office Directorate General*] [*of Foreign Affairs Ministry*] (TU)
ORAMEI... Oeuvre Reine Astrid de la Mere et de l'Enfant Indigenes
ORAMS.... Oficina Regional de Apoyo a la Mobilizacion Social [*Regional Office of Support to Social Mobilization*] [*Peru*] (LA)
ORAN........ Organisation Regionale Africaine de Normalisation [*African Regional Organization for Standardization - AROS*] (EAIO)
OR-AN...... Orta Anadolu Insaat AS [*Central Anatolian Construction Corp.*] (TU)
ORANA..... Organisme de Recherches sur l'Alimentation et la Nutrition Africaines [*African Food and Nutrition Research Organization*] [*Senegal*]
ORAP........ Separate Air Reconnaissance Regiment (RU)
ORAQLE... Online Retrieval of Acquisitions, Cataloguing, and Circulation Details for Queensland Library Enquiries [*Australia*]
ORAREM... National Minerals Office [*Niger*] (IMH)
Orat........... Oratoire [*Oratory*] [*Military map abbreviation World War I*] [*French*] (MTD)
orato.......... Separate Airfield Technical Support Company (RU)
orats.......... Separate Tank Truck Company (RU)
ORAYCON... Organizacion Administrativa y Contable Draycon Ltda. [*Colombia*] (COL)
ORB.......... Offenders' Review Board [*New South Wales, Australia*]
ORB.......... Offsets Review Board [*New South Wales, Australia*]
ORB.......... Operaciske Recne Baze [*Operational River Bases*] [*Navy*] (YU)
ORB.......... Optometrists' Registration Board [*Victoria, Australia*]
Orb............ Orbis [*Record label*] [*Germany, etc.*]
ORB.......... Orebro [*Sweden*] [*Airport symbol*] (OAG)
ORB.... Orman Bakanligi [*Ministry of Forestry*] (TU)
orb.............. Separate Ammunition Supply Company (RU)
ORB.......... Separate Radio Battalion (RU)
ORB.......... Separate Reconnaissance Battalion (RU)
ORBA........ Erbil [*Iraq*] [*ICAO location identifier*] (ICLI)
ORBA........ Orde Baru [*New Order*] [*Indonesia*]
ORBACT... Optometrists' Registration Board of the Australian Capital Territory
ORBB........ Sirsenk/Bamarni [*Iraq*] [*ICAO location identifier*] (ICLI)
ORBC........ Baghdad/Soica Headquarters [*Iraq*] [*ICAO location identifier*] (ICLI)
ORBIS....... Polish Travel Office (IMH)
ORBM........ Mosul [*Iraq*] [*ICAO location identifier*] (ICLI)
ORBR........ Baghdad/Rasheed [*Iraq*] [*ICAO location identifier*] (ICLI)
ORBS......... Baghdad/Saddam International [*Iraq*] [*ICAO location identifier*] (ICLI)
ORBV........ Optometrists' Registration Board of Victoria [*Australia*]
ORBW....... Baghdad/Muthenna [*Iraq*] [*ICAO location identifier*] (ICLI)
ORBWA.... Optometrists' Registration Board of Western Australia
ORBZ........ Ain Zalah [*Iraq*] [*ICAO location identifier*] (ICLI)
ORC.......... Ocean Racing Club [*Australia*]
ORC.......... Office of Revenue Commissioners [*Ghana*]
ORC.......... Oficina de Registro de Consumidores [*Consumers Registration Office*] [*Cuba*] (LA)
ORC.......... Oilseeds Research Council [*Australia*]
ORC.......... Operations Review Committee [*New South Wales, Australia*]
ORCA........ Ocean Racing Club of Australia
ORCA........ Organisme Europeen de Recherche sur la Carie [*European Organization for Caries Research*] (EAIO)
ORCD........ Organisation for Regional Cooperation and Development [*Iran*]
ORCG........ Organe de Recherche des Criminels de Guerre
ORCh........ Optimum Working Frequency (RU)
ORCOREL... Organizacao Comercial de Representacoes Limitada
ORCSA....... Orange River Colony, South Africa (ILCA)
ORCV........ Outdoor Recreation Center Victoria [*Australia*]
ORD.......... CAP PA Gutierrez [*Hernando R.*] Ordonez [*Mexico*] [*ICAO designator*] (FAAC)

ORD.......... Oddil Rizeni Dopravy Verejne Bezpecnosti [*Highway Traffic Control Battalion of Public Security*] (CZ)
ORD.......... Office du Ranch de la Dihesse
ORD.......... Office of Rural Development [*South Korean*] [*Research center*] (IRC)
ORD.......... Offices Regionaux de Developpement [*Regional Development Offices*] [*Central African Republic*] (AF)
ORD.......... Okresni Rada Druzstev [*District Council of Cooperatives*] (CZ)
ord.............. Ordinaire [*Ordinary*] [*Type of rice Cambodia*] (CL)
ord.............. Ordinaire [*Ordinary*] [*French*]
Ord............ Ordnung [*Order*] [*German*]
Ord............ Ordonnance [*French*] (FLAF)
Ord............ Ordonnansie [*Ordinance*] [*Afrikaans*]
Ord............ Ordonnantie [*Benelux*] (BAS)
ORD.......... Organisation Rurale de Developpement [*Rural Development Organization*] [*Burkina Faso*] (AF)
ORD.......... Organisme Regional de Developpement
ORD.......... Organizacion de Revolucionarios Deshabilitados [*Nicaragua*] (EAIO)
ORD.......... Separate Reconnaissance Battalion (RU)
ORD.......... Separate Reconnaissance Patrol (RU)
ORDA........ Ober Ramstadt Depot Activity [*Germany*] [*Army*]
ORDEC..... Organismos Regionales de Desarrollo Comunal [*Venezuela*] (LAA)
ORDEN..... Organizacion Democratica Nacionalista [*Nationalist Democratic Organization*] [*El Salvador*] (LA)
ordentl........ Ordentlich [*Orderly*] [*German*]
ORDERSUR ... Oficina Regional de Desarrollo del Sur [*Peru*] (LAA)
ORDEZA .. Organismo Regional para Desarrollo de la Zona Afectada [*Regional Organization for the Development of the Earthquake Disaster Area*] [*Peru*] (LA)
ordin........... Ordinaire [*Ordinary*] [*Publishing*] [*French*]
ORDINEX ... Organisation Internationale des Experts [*International Organization of Experts*] [*France*] (EAIO)
ORDNA..... Organismes de Radiodiffusion des Pays NonAlignes [*Broadcasting Organizations of Non-Aligned Countries - BONAC*] (EAIO)
ORDO .... Ordinario [*Ordinarily*] [*Music*] (ROG)
ORDOK..... Orvostudomanyi Dokumentacios Kozpont [*Medical Documentation Center*] (HU)
Ord Pol ..... Ordonnance du Prefet de Police [*France*] (FLAF)
Ord Prof.... Ordinaryus Profesor [*Full Professor*] (TU)
ORDZh...... Ordzhonikidze Railroad (RU)
ORE........... Office de Recherches et d'Essais [*Office for Research and Experiments*]
ORE.......... Organisation Regionale Europeenne de la CISL
ORE.......... Organizacion Revolucionario de Estudiantes [*Revolutionary Organization of Students*] [*Spanish*] (WER)
ORE.......... Ornitologia Rondo Esperantlingva [*Esperantist Ornithologists' Association*] (EAIO)
OREALC... Regional Office for Education in Latin America and the Caribbean [*UNESCO*] [*Acronym is based on foreign phrase*]
OREAP...... Organisation Regionale de l'Est pour l'Administration Publique
ORE/ERO ... Organisation Regionale de la Federation Internationale Dentaire pour l'Europe [*European Regional Organization of the International Dental Federation*] (EAIO)
ORegl......... Octrooireglement [*Benelux*] (BAS)
OREL .... Organizacion de Relaciones Estudiantiles Latinoamericanas [*Organization for Latin American Student Relations*] (LA)
OREP .... Department for the Distribution and Dispatch of Publications (RU)
OREP .... Organization for Research and Educational Planning (EAIO)
ORF .... General Recursive Function (RU)
ORF .... Oceanic Research Foundation [*Australia*]
ORF .... Oesterreichischer Rundfunk [*Radio and television network*] [*Austria*]
ORF .... Oman Royal Flight [*ICAO designator*] (FAAC)
Orf.............. Orfeo [*Record label*]
ORF .... Orszagos Rendorfokapitanysag [*National Police Headquarters*] (HU)
ORFA/CSV ... Organizacao das Forcas Armadas Comites de Soldados Vermelhos [*Armed Forces Organization/Committee of Red Soldiers*] [*Portuguese*] (WER)
ORFI.......... Orszagos Reuma- es Furdougyi Intezet [*National Institute on Rheumatism and Curative Spas*] (HU)
ORFIDEM ... Organizacion y Financiacion de Empresas [*Colombia*] (COL)
ORFM .... Oficiul de Rezerve Forte de Munca [*Office for Labor Reserves*] (RO)
ORFS........ Organizacion de Rehabilitacion Fisico-Social [*Colombia*] (COL)
ORG.......... Office of Racing and Gaming [*Western Australia*]
ORG.......... Officer of the National Order of the Republic of the Gambia
ORG.......... Order of the Republic of Gambia
org.............. Organic (RU)
Org............ Organisation [*Organization*] [*German*] (GCA)
org............. Organisch [*Organic*] [*German*]
org............. Organizado [*Organized*] [*Portuguese*]
Org............ Organization (SCAC)

org .... Organizational (RU)
org .... Organization, Organizational (BU)
Org .... Orgeneral [*Full General*] (TU)
ORG .... Oriental Airlines (Gambia) Ltd. [*ICAO designator*] (FAAC)
ORG .... Paramaribo [*Surinam*] Zorg En Hoop Airport [*Airport symbol*] (OAG)
ORG .... Separate Reconnaissance Group (RU)
ORGA .... Organizacion Regional Gallega Autonoma [*Regional Galician Autonomy Organization*] [*Spain*] [*Political party*] (PPE)
ORGABON ... Compagnie des Mines d'Or du Gabon
ORGALIME ... Organisme de Liaison des Industries Metalliques Europeennes [*Liaison Group for the European Engineering Industries*] [*Brussels, Belgium*] (EAIO)
Orgametall ... Trust for the Rationalization of Production in the Machinery and Metalworking Industry (RU)
ORGAN ..... Organisation Regionale Africaine de Normalisation [*African Regional Organization for Standardization - AROS*] (EA)
organ .... Organisch [*Organic*] [*German*] (GCA)
Organa .... Organisch-Chemische Industrie (VVB) [*Organic Chemical Industry (VVB)*] (EG)
ORGANDA ... Organisasi Gabungan Angkutan Darat [*Federation of Transport Firms*] (IN)
ORGANIC ... Caisse de Compensation de l'Organisation Autonome Nationale de l'Industrie et du Commerce [*France*] (FLAF)
organich ..... Organic (RU)
Organism ... Organismus [*Organism*] [*German*] (GCA)
ORGATEC ... Societe Africaine d'Etudes Techniques
ORGAV ..... Organic Growers and Retailers Association of Victoria [*Australia*]
Orgavtoprom ... State All-Union Institute of Automobile Technology (RU)
Orgbyuro.... Organizational Bureau (BU)
Orgchermet ... Scientific Research Institute for the Organization of Ferrous Metallurgy (RU)
ORGECO .. Organisation Generale des Consommateurs [*French*]
ORGEL ..... Organique et Eau Lourde [*Organic liquid and heavy water nuclear reactor*]
Orgelektrotrans ... Republic Trust of the City Electric Transportation System Administration [*RSFSR*] (RU)
Orgenergostroy ... All-Union Institute for the Planning of Electric Power Projects (RU)
Org Exp ..... Organo Espressivo [*Swell Organ*] [*Music*]
Orggaz .... Republic Trust for the Adjustment and Control of Gas Equipment of the Urban Gas Supply System [*RSFSR*] (RU)
orgger .... Organizovani Gerilci [*Organized Guerrillas*] [*World War II*] (YU)
Orgkhim .... State All-Union Trust of the State Committee of the Chemical Industry, USSR (RU)
Orgmappe.. Originalmappe [*Original Portfolio*] [*Publishing*] [*German*]
Orgmashpribor ... All-Union Planning and Technological Experimental Institute of the Ministry of the Machinery and Tool Industry (RU)
Orgmashuchet ... Special Office for the Organization of Machine Accounting and Computing in Heavy Industry (RU)
orgnabor..... Department of Resettlement and Organized Recruitment of Workers (RU)
orgnabor..... Organized Recruitment (RU)
Or Gn Kh ... Ordu Genel Karargah [*Army General Staff*] (TU)
Orgotdel..... Organizational Department (BU)
Orgproyekttsement ... All-Union State Special Office for Starting, Adjustment, Planning, and Design Work in the Cement Industry (RU)
or gr .... Origem Grega [*Greek Origin*] [*Portuguese*]
orgraspred ... Organization and Distribution Department of the TsK VKP(b) (RU)
ORGREB... Organisation fuer Abnahme, Betriebsfuehrung, und Rationalisierung von Energieanlagen [*Organization for Acceptance, Operation, and Rationalization of Energy Facilities*] (EG)
ORGRES... State Trust for the Organization and Rationalization of Regional Electric Power Plants and Networks (RU)
ORGREZ... Organizace pro Racionalizaci Energetickych Zavodu [*Organization for Rationalization of Electric Power Plants*] (CZ)
Orgsekretar ... Organizational Secretary (BU)
Orgstankinprom ... State Planning, Technological, and Experimental Institute (for the Organization of the Machine-Tool and Tool Industry) (RU)
Orgstroy..... State Institute for the Introduction of Advanced Operational and Labor Methods in Construction (RU)
OrgVCMD ... Organizacijski Vestnik Cirilmetodijskega Drustva Katoliskih Duhovnikov LRS [*Organizational Review of the Cyril-Methodius Society of Catholic Priests of Slovenia*] [*Ljubljana*] (YU)
Orgvodokanal ... State Republic Adjustment and Repair Trust of the Water Supply and Sewer System Administration [*RSFSR*] (RU)

OrgVOFS .. Organizacijski Vestnik Osvobodilne Fronte Slovenije [*Organizational Review of the Liberation Front of Slovenia*] [*Ljubljana*] (YU)
Orgvosstroy ... Office for Organization and Standardization of Construction and Restoration Work (RU)
OrgVSZDL ... Organizacijski Vestnik Socijalisticne Zveze Delovnega Ljudstva Slovenije [*Organizational Review of the Socialist Union of Working People of Slovenia*] [*Ljubljana*] (YU)
orgy .... Ornagy [*Major*] [*Military*] (HU)
Orhfranz .... Originalhalbfranz [*Original Half Calf*] [*Publishing*] [*German*]
ORI .... Association of Workers in the Fine Arts (RU)
ORI .... Oceanographic Research Institute [*University of Natal*] [*South Africa*] (AA)
ORI .... Ocean Research Institute [*Japan*]
ORI .... Organizaciones Revolucionarias Integradas
ORI .... Organizacion Revolucionaria Integrada [*Cuba*] (LAA)
Ori .... Oriole [*Record label*] [*Great Britain*]
ORIA .... Ophthalmic Research Institute of Australia (ADA)
ORIA .... Outdoor Recreation in Australia
ORIC .... Oceanographic Research International Committee (ASF)
Orient........ Orientierung [*Orientation*] [*German*] (GCA)
Orientier ... Orientierung [*Orientation*] [*German*] (GCA)
ORIF.......... Oficiul Regional de Imbunatatire Funciara [*Regional Office for Land Improvement*] (RO)
orig .... Original [*Sweden*]
orig .... Original [*Former Czechoslovakia*]
Orig............ Original [*German*]
orig .... Original [*French*]
orig .... Originale [*Original*] [*Italian*]
orig .... Originalement [*French*] (TPFD)
orig .... Originally (TPFD)
orig .... Origineel [*Original*] [*Netherlands*]
origb........... Originalbind [*Original Binding*] [*Publishing Danish/Norwegian*]
origband ..... Originalband [*Original Binding*] [*Publishing*] [*Sweden*]
Origbd........ Originalband [*Original Binding*] [*Publishing*] [*German*]
orig bpodp ... Unsigned Original (BU)
orighafte..... Originalhaefte [*Original Issue*] [*Publishing*] [*Sweden*]
orighelkbd ... Originalhelklotband [*Original Full-Cloth Binding*] [*Publishing*] [*Sweden*]
Orighleinen ... Originalhalbleinen [*Original Half Cloth*] [*Publishing*] [*German*]
origin .... Original [*Original*] [*French*]
origin .... Originale [*Original*] [*Italian*]
origin .... Origineel [*Original*] [*Netherlands*]
origkart ...... Originalkartonnage [*Original Boards*] [*Publishing*] [*Sweden*]
origkbd .... Originalklotband [*Original Cloth Binding*] [*Publishing*] [*Sweden*]
Origleinen ... Originalleinen [*Original Cloth Binding*] [*Publishing*] [*German*]
origlinneband ... Originallinneband [*Original Linen Binding*] [*Publishing*] [*Sweden*]
Origlwd ...... Originalleinwand [*Original Cloth Binding*] [*Publishing*] [*German*]
orig savtogr ... Autographed Original (BU)
orig savtogr i pech ... Autographed and Sealed Original (BU)
orig spech ... Sealed Original (BU)
Origumschlag ... Originalumschlag [*Original Wrapper*] [*Publishing*] [*German*]
ORIK .... Organisation de la Region Industrielle du Koullou
ORIL.......... Oficina de Reglamentacion de la Industria Lechera [*Puerto Rico*] (DSCA)
ORINFOR ... Office Rwandaise d'Information [*Rwandan Information Office*] (AF)
ORINTAS ... Organize Insaat Sanayi ve Ticaret Ltd. Sti. [*Organized Construction Industry and Trade Corp.*] (TU)
Or-Is .... Turkiye Orman Iscileri Sendikasi [*Turkish Forestry Workers' Union*] [*Izmir*] (TU)
ORIT .... Organizacion Regional Interamericana de Trabajadores [*Inter-American Regional Organization of Workers*] [*Antigua*] (LA)
ORIT .... Organization Regional Interamericana de Trabdjadores [*Inter-American Labor Organization*] [*Spanish*] (BARN)
ORITU ...... Ocean Research Institute [*Japan*] (MSC)
ORJ .... Orinduik [*Guyana*] [*Airport symbol*] (OAG)
ORJUNA .. Organizacija Jugoslovenskih Nacionalista [*Organization of Yugoslav Nationalists*] (YU)
ORK .... Ob'edinennaia Respublika Kamerun
ORK .... Oekumenische Rate der Kirchen
ORK.......... Oesterreichische Rektorenkonferenz [*Austria*] (SLS)
ORK.......... Okresni Rolnicka Komise [*District Agricultural Commission*] (CZ)
ORK.......... Okresni Rozhodci Komise [*District Arbitration Commission*] (CZ)
ork.............. Orkiestra [*Orchestra*] [*Poland*]
ORK.......... Orszagos Rendorkapitanysag [*National Police Headquarters*] (HU)
ORK.......... Radio Compass Reading (RU)
ORKFiSp... Okregowa Rada Kultury Fizycznej i Sportu [*District Council of Physical Culture and Sport*] (POL)

orkhrr......... Separate Chemical and Radiation Reconnaissance Company (RU)
ORKhZ...... Separate Chemical Defense Company (RU)
orkhz.......... Separate Company for Protection Against Chemical Attacks (BU)
ORKI .... Ontozesi es Rizstermelesi Kutato Intezet [*Irrigation and Rice Cultivation Research Institute*] (HU)
ORKIMD .. Association of Revolutionary Composers and Personages Active in Music [*1924-1929*] (RU)
ORKLB..... Rare Book Division of the Lenin Library (RU)
ORKOY ..... Orman Koy Iliskileri Genel Mudurlugu [*Forest Village Affairs Directorate General*] (TU)
ORKOY ..... Orman Koyleri Projesi [*Forest Villages Project*] (TU)
ORL........... Institut fuer Orts-, Regional- und Landesplanung [*Institute for National, Regional, and Local Planning*] [*Switzerland*] [*Research center*] (IRC)
ORL........... Office de Radiodiffusion Lao [*Lao Radiobroadcasting Office*] (CL)
ORL........... Surveillance Radar (RU)
ORLA .... Orde Lama [*Old Order*] [*Indonesia*]
ORLAK ..... Orszagos Lakasepitesi Vallalat [*National Enterprise for Apartment Construction*] (HU)
or lat.......... Origem Latina [*Latin Origin*] [*Portuguese*]
ORLB .... Manuscript Division of the Lenin Library (RU)
orlpo.......... Separate Light Infantry Flame-Thrower Company (BU)
OR-LS .... Organizacion de Revolucionarios-Liga Socialista [*Organization of Revolutionarios-Socialist League*] [*Venezuela*] (LA)
orlsb .... Separate Radio-Relay Communications Battalion (BU)
Orlwd .... Originalleinwand [*Original Cloth Binding*] [*Publishing*] [*German*]
ORM.......... Experimental Jet Engine (RU)
ORM.......... Experimental Rocket Engine (RU)
ORM.......... Operation Riz Mopti [*Mali*]
ORM.......... Opytnyi Reaktivnyi Motor [*Experimental Reaction Motor*] [*Former USSR*]
Orm........... Orman [*or Ormancilik*] [*Forest or Forestry*] (TU)
orm .... Ormester [*Sergeant*] (HU)
Ormappe .... Originalmappe [*Original Portfolio*] [*Publishing*] [*German*]
ORMAS .... Organisasi Massa [*Mass Organization*] (IN)
ORMM...... Basrah/Magal [*Iraq*] [*ICAO location identifier*] (ICLI)
ORMN....... Oficina e Riparimit te Mjeteve te Ndertimit [*Albanian*]
ORMO ...... Ochotnicza Rezerwa Milicji Obywatelskiej [*Volunteer Reserve of Citizens' Militia*] (POL)
ORMS .... Basrah/Shaibah [*Iraq*] [*ICAO location identifier*] (ICLI)
ORMU....... Detached Company for Medical Reinforcement of the Army (BU)
ORMU....... Separate Medical Reinforcement Company (RU)
ORMVA .... Offices Regionaux de Mise en Valeur Agricole
ORMVAD ... Office Regional de Mise en Valeur Agricole des Doukkala [*Tunisia*]
ORMVAG ... Office Regional de Mise en Valeur Agricole du Gharb [*Morocco*]
ORMVAL ... Office Regional de Mise en Valeur Agricole de Loukkos
ORN .... Oran [*Algeria*] [*Airport symbol*] (OAG)
orn .... Orden [*Order*] [*Spanish*]
ORN .... Order of the River Niger
ORN .... Organization of Revolutionaries of the North [*Lebanon*] (PD)
ORN .... Orient Airways [*Pakistan*] [*ICAO designator*] (FAAC)
orn .... Ornamentale [*Ornamental*] [*Italian*]
orn .... Ornamentirt [*German*]
orn .... Ornato [*Decorated*] [*Italian*]
orn .... Orne [*Decorated*] [*Publishing*] [*French*]
ORN .... Osiedlowa Rada Narodowa [*People's Settlement Council*] [*Poland*]
ornam .... Ornamento [*Decoration*] [*Publishing*] [*Spanish*]
ORNAMO ... Finnish Association of Designers (EAIO)
ORNB....... Orenburg Railroad (RU)
ornem .... Ornemente [*Decorated*] [*Publishing*] [*French*]
ORNI........ L'Office Regulateur de la Navigation Interieure [*Benelux*] (BAS)
orni............ Ornithologie [*French*] (TPFD)
orni............ Ornithology (TPFD)
ORNIIMSK ... Orenburg Scientific Research Institute for the Breeding of Beef and Dairy Cattle (RU)
Ornit .... Ornitologia [*Ornithology*] [*Portuguese*]
ORNITS.... Society of Workers of Science and Technology for Assistance to the Building of Socialism in the USSR (RU)
ORNOGE ... Organizacion Nacional de la Oposicion de Guinea Ecuatorial en el Exilio [*National Organization of Opposition of Equatorial Guinea in Exile*] (AF)
ORO .... Official Receiver's Office [*Australia*]
ORO .... Okresni Rada Odboru [*District Trade-Union Council*] (CZ)
ORO .... Okresni Rada Osvetova [*District Cultural Council*] (CZ)
ORO .... Oorspronkelijk Regeringsontwerp [*Benelux*] (BAS)
ORO .... Organisation-Renseignement-Operation [*Algeria*]
ORO .... Organizacion Republicana Obrera [*Trade union*] [*Paraguay*]
oro .... Separate Maintenance Company (BU)
oro .... Separate Service Company (RU)

ORO .... Special Reconnaissance Detachment (RU)
ORO .... United Revolutionary Organizations of Cuba (RU)
OROAP..... Organizacion Regional del Oriente para la Administracion Publica [*Eastern Regional Organization for Public Administration*] (EAIO)
OROC....... Office Royal de Cooperation [*Royal Cooperatives Office*] [*Replaced by OFFINACO Cambodia*] (CL)
OROTEKS ... Oroslavska Tekstilna Industrija [*Oroslavlje Textile Industry*] (YU)
OROUBANGUI ... Societe d'Exploitation Auriferes de l'Oubangui
ORP........... Oddeleni Radu a Predpisu [*Department for Military Manuals and Regulations*] (CZ)
ORP........... Oficina de Regulacion de Precios [*Price Control Office*] [*Panama*] (LA)
ORP........... Okret Rzeczypospolitej Polskiej [*Polish Navy Ship*]
ORP........... Orange River Project
ORP........... Orapa [*Botswana*] [*Airport symbol*] [*Obsolete*] (OAG)
ORP........... Ordinary, Reasonable, and Prudent [*Legal term*] (BARN)
ORP........... Organisation de la Resistance Populaire [*Popular Resistance Organization*] [*Algeria*] (AF)
ORP........... Organization of the Rural Poor [*India*]
ORP........... Publications Distribution Department (RU)
ORP........... Reciprocal Radio Bearing (RU)
ORP........... Society of Revolutionary Poster Designers (RU)
ORPA .... Organizacion Revolucionaria del Pueblo en Armas [*Revolutionary Organization of the People in Arms*] [*Guatemala*] [*Political party*] (PD)
ORPADE... Organisation Panafricaine des Juristes et Economistes pour l'Assistance et le Developpement [*Pan-African Organization of Jurists and Economists for Assistance and Development*] (AF)
ORPAL...... Organizacion de Relaciones Publicas para America Latina (LAA)
ORPC .... Organizacion Revolucionaria Punto Critico [*Critical Point Revolutionary Organization*] [*Mexico*] (LA)
ORPC-ML ... Organizacao para a Reconstrucao do Partido Comunista-Marxista-Leninista [*Organization for the Reconstruction of the Communist Party/Marxist-Leninist*] [*Portuguese*] (WER)
ORPLAN... Oficina Regional de Planificacion [*Chile*] (DSCA)
ORPLANES ... Oficinas Regionales de Planificacion [*Chile*] (LAA)
ORPO....... Department of Leading Party Bodies (RU)
ORPO....... Office Regional des Produits Oleicoles du Centre [*Nationalized industry*] [*Algeria*] (EY)
ORPO....... Organization and Planning Department (RU)
ORPOL ..... Organisasi Politik [*Political Organization*] (IN)
ORPS........ General Workers' Trade Union [*People's Republic of Bulgaria*] (RU)
ORPV .... Office Regional de Produits Vivriers [*Regional Foodstuffs Office*] [*Togo*] (AF)
orpv .... Separate Field Water Supply Company (RU)
ORR.......... Separate Reconnaissance Company (RU)
orrb............ Separate Radio Relay Battalion (RU)
ORRCA ..... Organisation for the Rescue and Research of Cetaceans in Australia
ORRD........ River Traffic Control Department (RU)
orrd............ Separate Radio Relay Battalion (RU)
orreg.......... Separate Traffic Control Company (RU)
ORRO........ Separate Portable Flamethrower Company (RU)
ORRS .... Manpower Distribution Department (RU)
ORS .... Department of Workers' Supply (RU)
ORS .... General Workers Supply (BU)
ORS .... Irrigation System (RU)
ORS .... Obsluga Ratalnej Sprzedazy [*Installment Sales Service*] (POL)
ORS .... Oficiul de Rezerve de Stat [*Office for State Reserves*] (RO)
ORS .... Opci Radnicki Savez [*General Workers Union*] (YU)
ORS .... Operation Riz Segou [*Mali*]
ORS .... Operation Riz Sikasso [*Mali*]
ORS .... Operativna Ratna Sluzba [*Operational Military Service*] (YU)
ORS .... Orange River Sovereignty
ORS .... Orpheus Island [*Australia*] [*Airport symbol*]
ORS .... Separate Signal Company (RU)
ORS .... Separate Supply Company (RU)
ORS .... Society of Russian Sculptors [*1925-1932*] (RU)
ORSA .... Officiers de Reserve en Situation d'Activite sous Contrat [*Reserve Officers on Active Duty under Contract*] [*French*] (WER)
ORSC........ Office de la Recherche Scientifique Coloniale
ORSEC...... Organisation des Secours [*Disaster Relief Organization*] [*French*] (WER)
ORSI......... Operational Research Society of India (SLS)
ORSI......... Operations Research Society of Ireland (SLS)
ORSI-CONGO ... Societe Commerciale et Industrielle Orsi
ORSIS .... Operations Research Society of Israel (PDAA)
ORSJ......... Operations Research Society of Japan (PDAA)
ORSL........ Order of the Republic of Sierra Leone
ORSS......... General Workers Trade Union (BU)

ORSSA ...... Operations Research Society of South Africa   (AA)
ORSTOM ... Office de la Recherche Scientifique et Technique d'Outre-Mer [*Office of Overseas Scientific and Technical Research*] [*France*]
ORSV .... Austrian Federation of Roller Skating   (EAIO)
orsz .... Orszagos [*National*] [*Hungary*]
orszgy hat... Orszaggyulesi Hatarozat [*Resolution of the National Assembly*] (HU)
orsz ut........ Orszagut [*State Highway*]   (HU)
ORT .... Obsluga Ruchu Turystycznego [*Tourist Traffic Service*] [*Poland*]
ORT .... Organisation, Reconstruction, Travail
ORT .... Organizacion Revolucionaria de los Trabajadores [*Workers Revolutionary Organization*] [*El Salvador*]   (LA)
ORT .... Organizacion Revolucionaria de Trabajadores [*Workers Revolutionary Organization*] [*Spanish*]   (WER)
Ort............. Ortakligi [*Partnership*] [*Turkey*]   (CED)
Ort............. Ortaklik [*Partnership*]   (TU)
ort............. Orthodox   (HU)
ort............. Orthodromic   (RU)
ort............. Orthopedics, Orthopedist   (BU)
ort............. Ortograficzny [*Orthographic*]   (POL)
ORTB .... Office de Radiodiffusion et Television du Benin [*Radio and Television Broadcasting Office of Benin*]   (AF)
ORTB .... Separate Radio Battalion   (RU)
ortcheka ..... Special Extraordinary River Transportation Commission for Combating Counterrevolution and Sabotage   (RU)
ORTChK ... Rayon Branch of the Extraordinary Transportation Commission (RU)
ORTF........ Office de la Radio et de la Television Francaise [*State-owned radio and television network*] [*France*]
ORTF........ Office de Radiodiffusion et de Television Francaise [*Office of French Broadcasting and Television*]   (WER)
ORTF........ Office de Radiodiffusion-Television Francaise [*National Broadcasting Organization*] [*France*]   (NTCM)
ORTF........ Organization Radio Television France   (IAA)
ORTI .... Organization of Religious Teachers in Israel   (EAIO)
ORTM .... Office de Radiodiffusion et Television de Mauritanie [*Mauritanian radio and television station*]
ORTN .... Obrigacoes Reajustaveis do Tesouro Nacional [*National Treasury Readjustable Bonds*] [*Brazil*]   (LA)
ORTN .... Office de Radiodiffusion-Television du Niger [*Niger Radio and Television Broadcasting Office*]   (AF)
ORTN .... Officie Radiodiffusion Television du Niger [*Radio and television network*] [*Niger*]
ORTP .... Orthodromic Bearing   (RU)
ORTPN ..... Office Rwandais du Tourisme et des Parcs Nationaux [*Rwanda Tourism and National Parks Office*]
ortr .... Electronic Reconnaissance Detachment   (BU)
ortr .... Separate Radio Company   (RU)
ORTRAG .. Orbital Transport und Raketen Gesellschaft
ortrr............ Separate Loading-Unloading Works Company   (BU)
ORTS........ Office de Radiodiffusion-Television du Senegal [*Senegalese radio and television station*]
ORTZ .... Society for the Dissemination of Technical Knowledge   (RU)
ORU.......... Association of Accounting and Statistical Personnel   (RU)
ORU.......... Odborova Rada Ucitelska [*Teachers' Trade-Union Council*] (CZ)
ORU.......... Organizacion Revolucionaria Universitaria [*Revolutionary University Organization*] [*Dominican Republic*]   (LA)
ORU.......... Outdoor Distribution System [*Electricity*]   (RU)
ORUD....... Department of Rayon Administration of Roads   (RU)
ORUD....... Traffic Control Department   (RU)
ORUM...... Open-Pit Mining of Coal Deposits   (RU)
ORUS........ Orman Urunleri Sanayii Genel Mudurlugu [*Forest Products' Industry Directorate General*]   (TU)
ORuss .... Old Russian [*Language*]   (BARN)
ORV.......... Oceanographic Research Vessel
orv .... Orvos [*Physician*]   (HU)
orvb .... Separate Maintenance and Recovery Battalion   (RU)
orvb .... Separate Repair and Reconstruction (Engineer) Battalion   (BU)
ORVP .... Casualty Search and Evacuation Detachment   (RU)
orvr........... Separate Maintenance and Recovery Company   (RU)
ORW.......... Organizacja Rodzin Wojskowych [*Military Dependents Organization*]   (POL)
ORW.......... Orwex [*Poland*] [*ICAO designator*]   (FAAC)
ORWN....... Osrodek Rozpowszechniania Wydawnictw Naukowych [*Center for the Dissemination of Scientific Publications*]   (POL)
ORWNPAN ... Osrodek Rozpowszechniania Wydawnictw Naukowych Polskiej Akademii Nauk [*Polish Academy of Scientific Publications Dissemination Center*]   (POL)
ORX.......... Oryx Aviation [*South Africa*] [*ICAO designator*]   (FAAC)
ORY.......... Paris [*France*] Orly Airport [*Airport symbol*]   (OAG)
ORYa........ Gun Junction Box   (RU)
ORYaS...... Department of Russian Language and Literature (of the Academy of Sciences, USSR)   (RU)
oryg .... Oryginal [*or Oryginalny*] [*Original or Genuine*]   (POL)
ORZ.......... Orange Walk [*Belize*] [*Airport symbol*] [*Obsolete*]   (OAG)

ORZ.......... Organisations- und Rechenzentrum [*Organization and Computer Center*]   (EG)
ORZATU .. Department of Relay Protection, Automation, Remote Control, and Stability   (RU)
ORZZ .... Okregowa Rada Zwiazkow Zawodowych [*District Council of Trade Unions*]   (POL)
ORZZN ..... Zemedelske Zasobovani a Nakup, Oborove Reditelstvi [*Agricultural Supply and Purchasing, Sectoral Directorate*] (CZ)
o/s .... Argentine Gold Currency
OS.............. Axis of Communications   (RU)
OS.............. Experimental Station [*Agriculture*]   (RU)
OS.............. Experimental Vessel   (RU)
os.............. Expert Rifleman   (RU)
OS.............. Feedback   (RU)
OS.............. General Assembly, General Meeting   (BU)
OS.............. General Session (of the Academy of Sciences, USSR)   (RU)
OS.............. General Supply Depot   (RU)
OS.............. Insurance Department   (RU)
OS.............. Lean Caking [*Coal*]   (RU)
OS.............. Negative Resistance   (RU)
OS.............. Obchodni Skola [*Commercial School*]   (CZ)
OS.............. Oblasni Stab [*Regional Headquarters*] [*World War II*]   (YU)
OS.............. Oblastni Sberna [*Regional Depot*]   (CZ)
OS.............. Oblast Soviet   (RU)
OS.............. Odborna Skola [*Vocational School*]   (CZ)
OS.............. Odborna Skupina [*Group of Specialists*]   (CZ)
OS.............. Odborovy Svaz [*Trade Union*]   (CZ)
OS.............. Odvodni Soupis [*Conscription Inventory*]   (CZ)
OS.............. Oesterreichischer Staedebund [*Union of Austrian Towns*]
os.............. Ogleden Sonra [*Afternoon*]   (TU)
OS.............. Ogledna Stanica [*Experiment Station*]   (YU)
OS.............. Okoliya Council   (BU)
OS.............. Okresni Sekretariat [*District Secretariat*]   (CZ)
OS.............. Okresni Soud [*District Court*]   (CZ)
OS.............. Okrug Council   (BU)
OS.............. Old Saxon [*Language, etc.*]
os.............. Omaa Sukua [*Finland*]
OS.............. Omada "Gia ton Sosialismo" [*Group "For Socialism"*] [*Greek*] (GC)
OS.............. Omega Society [*Defunct*]   (EA)
o/s .... Onder Sorg [*In Charge Of*] [*Afrikaans*]
os.............. Onderstaande [*Following*] [*Afrikaans*]
OS.............. Operacni Sprava [*Operations Directorate*]   (CZ)
OS.............. Operativna Sala [*Operations Room*] [*Military*]   (YU)
OS.............. Optical Sensitizer   (RU)
OS.............. Optimal System   (RU)
OS.............. Orange Glass   (RU)
OS.............. Orange Light Filter   (RU)
OS.............. Orasul Stalin [*Stalin City*]   (RO)
OS.............. Order of Suvorov   (RU)
OS.............. Organisation Secrete [*Secret Organization*] [*Algeria*]
OS.............. Organisme Saharienne
OS.............. Organisme Stockeurs
OS.............. Organizacni Sluzba [*Organization Service*]   (CZ)
OS.............. Orkustofnun [*National Energy Authority*] [*Ministry of Industry Iceland*] [*Research center*]   (EAS)
OS.............. Oro Sellado [*Standard Gold*] [*Business term*] [*Spanish*]
OS.............. Orr Shalom [*Israel*]   (EAIO)
os.............. Osasto [*Finland*]
Os.............. Osiedle [*Settlement*] [*Poland*]
OS.............. Osjecki Sajam [*Osijek Fair*]   (YU)
OS.............. Osmatracka Stanica [*Observation Station*] [*Military*]   (YU)
Os.............. Osmio [*Osmium*] [*Chemical element*] [*Portuguese*]
OS.............. Osnovna Sredstva [*Fixed Assets*]   (YU)
os.............. Osoba [*Person*] [*Poland*]
OS.............. Osobni Spis [*Personal Record*]   (CZ)
os.............. Osoite [*Finland*]
OS.............. Otkupna Stanica [*Purchasing Station*]   (YU)
Os.............. Ou(d)-Saksies [*Old Saxon*] [*Language, etc.*] [*Afrikaans*]
OS.............. Ou Styl [*Old Style*] [*Afrikaans*]
OS.............. Ouvrier Specialise [*Specialized or Skilled Worker*] [*French*] (WER)
OS.............. Self-Excitation Winding   (RU)
OS.............. Single-Digit Adder   (RU)
OS.............. Special Conference   (RU)
OS.............. Special Worker   (RU)
OS.............. Supply Section, Supply Department   (RU)
OS.............. Support Force, Convoy Detachment [*Navy*]   (RU)
OS.............. Very Old   (RU)
OSA............ Aero Astra [*Mexico*] [*ICAO designator*]   (FAAC)
OSA............ Ochranny Svaz Autorsky [*Copyright Association*]   (CZ)
OSA............ Office of Special Affairs [*Australia*]
OSA............ Office of State Administration [*Australia*]
OSA............ Office Senegalais de l'Artisanat
OSA............ Oficerska Szkola Artylerii [*Artillery Officers' School*]   (POL)

OSA .... Oficina de Seguros Agricolas [*Puerto Rico*] (DSCA)
OSA .... Omnibus Services Authority
osa .... Om Svar Anhalles [*An Answer Is Requested*] [*Sweden*] (GPO)
OSA .... Ontwikkelingsvereniging van Suider-Afrika [*Development Society of Southern Africa*] (EAIO)
OSA .... Operation Sciences Appliquees [*Quebec*]
OSA .... Operativna Sala Aerodroma [*Operations Room of an Airport*] [*Military*] (YU)
OSA .... Order of St. Augustine [*See also OFSA*] [*Rome, Italy*] (EAIO)
OSA .... Organic Soil Association of Southern Africa
OSA .... Osaka [*Japan*] [*Airport symbol*] (OAG)
OSA .... Overseas Student Application [*Australia*]
OSA .... Society of Modern Architects (RU)
OSACI ...... Ecumenical Study and Action Centre on Investment [*Netherlands*]
osad .... Separate Self-Propelled Artillery Battalion (RU)
OSADC ..... Ogun State Agricultural Development Corporation
OSAE .... Separate Medical Air Squadron (RU)
OSAKVU .. Joint Central Asian "Red Banner" Military School (RU)
OSAL .... Oficina de Servicios para America Latina [*Colombia*] (DSCA)
OSAM ...... Separate Fixed Air Maintenance Depot (RU)
OSAN .... General Session of the Academy of Sciences, USSR (RU)
OSAP........ Aleppo/Neirab [*Syria*] [*ICAO location identifier*] (ICLI)
OSAP........ Oficerska Szkola Artylerii Przeciwlotniczej [*Antiaircraft Artillery Officer's School*] [*Poland*]
OSAP........ Oficerska Szkola Artylerii Przeciwpancernej [*Anti-Tank Artillery Officers' School*] (POL)
OSAP........ Separate Medical Air Regiment (RU)
OSAPlot .... Oficerska Szkola Artylerii Przeciwlotniczej [*Antiaircraft Artillery Officers' School*] (POL)
OSART...... Operational Safety Review Team [*International Atomic Energy Agency*]
OSAS........ Overseas Service Aid Scheme
OSAVE...... Oficina de Sanidad Vegetal [*Venezuela*] (DSCA)
OSAZ .... Okresni Sporitelna a Zalozna [*District Savings and Deposit Bank*] (CZ)
OSB .... Oesterreichischer Saengerbund [*Austria*] (EAIO)
OSB .... Office of Small Business [*New South Wales, Australia*]
OSB .... Orden de San Benito [*Order of St. Benedict*] [*Spanish*]
OSB .... Separate Combat Engineer Battalion (RU)
OSB .... Separate Rifle Battalion (RU)
osb .... Separate Signal Battalion (BU)
OSBC........ Ondo State Broadcasting Corporation [*Nigeria*]
OSBF......... Damascus [*Syria*] [*ICAO location identifier*] (ICLI)
OSBI......... General Union of Bulgarian Industrialists (BU)
osbr .... Separate Rifle Brigade (BU)
OSBT........ General Union of Bulgarian Merchants (BU)
OSBZK...... General Union of Bulgarian Agricultural Cooperatives (BU)
OSC .... Occupational Superannuation Commissioner [*Australia*]
OSC .... Office of Space Communications [*NASA*] (BARN)
OSC .... Ontwerp Staatscommissie [*Benelux*] (BAS)
OSC .... Organizacija Srpskih Cetnika [*Organization of Serbian Chetniks*] [*Chicago*] (YU)
OSC .... Overseas School Certificate (ML)
OSC .... Overseas Student Charge [*Australia*]
OSCA .... Office of State Corporate Affairs [*Western Australia*]
OSCAND .. Old Scandinavian [*Language, etc.*]
OSCAR...... Office of Special Clearances and Research [*Australia*]
OSCAS...... Office of Statistical Coordinating and Standards [*Philippines*] (PDAA)
OSCE........ Office Statistique des Communautes Europeennes [*Statistical Office of the European Communities - EUROSTAT*] [*Commission of the European Communities*]
OSCE........ Organisation for Security and Co-Operation in Europe (ECON)
OSCE........ Organization of the Petroleum Exporting Countries (EECI)
os ch .... Of Extreme Purity (RU)
o/sch .... Open Account (RU)
OSCI.......... Organizacion Simpatizante de la IV Internacional [*Organization Sympathizing with the Fourth International*] [*Spanish*] (WER)
OSCO .... Oil Service Company of Iran
OSCOM .... Oslo Commission (EAIO)
OSCOPROGASDE ... Oficina de Supervigilancia y Control de las Propiedades del General Anastasio Somoza y Debayle [*Office for the Supervision and Control of the Properties of General Anastasio Somoza Debayle*] [*Nicaragua*] (LA)
OSCP......... Ocean Sedimentary Coring Programme
OSD .... Okresni Spotrebni Druzstvo [*District Consumer Cooperative*] (CZ)
OSD .... Osrodek Szkolenia Dziennikarskiego [*Journalism Educational Center*] (POL)
OSD .... Ostersund [*Sweden*] [*Airport symbol*] (OAG)
OSDEC...... Orientacion Social de Dirigentes de Empresa Colombiana [*Colombia*] (COL)
OSDEM .... Society for Furthering Demilitarization and Disarmament (RU)

OSDI .... Damascus/International [*Syria*] [*ICAO location identifier*] (ICLI)
OSDT .... Damascus [*Syria*] [*ICAO location identifier*] (ICLI)
OSDZ .... Deir Ez Zor [*Syria*] [*ICAO location identifier*] (ICLI)
OSE .... Administracion de Obras Sanitarias del Estado [*State Board of Sanitation*] [*Uruguay*] (LA)
OSE .... Obras Sanitarias del Estado [*Uruguay*] (EY)
OSE .... Oeuvre Sociale pour Enfants [*Morocco*]
OSE .... Office of Special Employment [*Australia*]
OSE .... Oficina de Obras Sanitarias del Estado [*Uruguay*] (DSCA)
OSE .... Omospondia Syndaxioukhon Ellados [*Federation of Greek Pensioners*] (GC)
OSE .... Organismos Sidirodromon Ellados [*Railways Organization of Greece*] [*Sidirodromoi Ellinikou Kratous - SEK Athens*] [*Formerly,*] (GC)
OSE .... Organosi Sosialistikis Epanastaseos [*Socialist Revolutionary Organization*] [*Greek*] (GC)
OSE .... Osaka Stock Exchange [*Japan*]
Ose .... Oseraie [*Osier-Bed*] [*Military map abbreviation World War I*] [*French*] (MTD)
OSEA .... Ophthalmological Society of East Africa [*Kenya*] (SLS)
OSEB .... Orissa State Electricity Board [*India*] (PDAA)
OSEC........ Office Suisse d'Expansion Commerciale [*Swiss Office for the Development of Trade*]
OSECY...... Office of the Secretary to the Staff [*NATO*] (NATG)
OSEDT...... Oficiul Special pentru Editarea si Distribuirea Timbrelor [*Special Office for the Publication and Distribution of Stamps*] (RO)
Oseidenband ... Originalseidenband [*Original Silk Binding*] [*Publishing*] [*German*]
OSELMA .. Organismos Synetairistikis Ekmetallevseos Limnothalassis Mesolongiou kai Aitolikou [*Organization for the Cooperative Exploitation of the Mesolongion and Aitolikon Marshlands*] (GC)
OSEN .... Organization of Petroleum Exporting Countries [*OPEC*] (RU)
OSEO .... Sanitary and Epidemiological Detachment of a District (RU)
OSER........ Office de Securite Routiere
oset .... Ossetian, Ossetic (RU)
OSF............ Franciscan Sisters of Penance and Christian Charity [*Italy*] (EAIO)
OSF............ Odznaka Sprawnosci Fizycznej [*Physical Fitness Badge*] (POL)
OSF............ OPEC Special Fund
OSF............ Osaka Stock Futures [*Japan*] (ECON)
OSF............ Osrodek Sprawnosci Fizycznej [*Physical Fitness Center*] (POL)
OSFC........ Orissa State Financial Corporation [*India*]
OSFPS...... Railhead Section for Courier Postal Communications (BU)
OSFS .... Oblates of Saint Francis De Sales [*Roman Catholic religious order*]
OSG .... Fuel Supply Section, Fuel Supply Department (RU)
OSG .... Occupational Superannuation Group [*Australia*]
OSG .... Office of the Secretary General [*United Nations*]
OSG .... Organisationssysteme [*German*] (ADPT)
OSGA .... Department for Construction of Hydrogliders and Motor Sleds (RU)
OSGK .... General Assembly of the Civil Collegium (BU)
OSGK .... Oesterreichische Studiengesellschaft fuer Kybernetik [*Austrian Study Group for Cybernetics*] (SLS)
OSh........... Consumer Goods Department (RU)
OSh........... Feathering Hinge (RU)
OSh........... Fuze (RU)
OSH.......... Orden de San Jeronimo [*Order of St. Jerome*] [*Spain*] (EAIO)
OSH.......... Orszagos Sporthivatal [*National Sports Office*] (HU)
OShA .... Asphalt-Coated Fuze (RU)
oshb........... Separate Disciplinary Battalion (RU)
OSHCO..... Olayan Saudi Holding Co. [*Saudi Arabia*] (PDAA)
OShDA...... Double Asphalt-Coated Fuze (RU)
OSHE .... Office de Soutien de l'Habitat Economique [*Low-Cost Housing Support Office*] [*Ivory Coast*] (AF)
oshirt.......... Originalshirting [*Original Cloth Binding*] [*Publishing Danish/Norwegian*]
OShOSDOR ... Department of Highways (RU)
OShP .... Association of Swiss Trade Unions (RU)
oshr .... Separate Disciplinary Company (RU)
osht ar .... GHQ Reserve (BU)
osht ar rz.... GHQ Artillery (BU)
OShYu....... Oblast School of Young Correspondents (RU)
OShZ........ Omsk Tire Plant (RU)
OSI .... Aerosi SA de CV [*Mexico*] [*ICAO designator*] (FAAC)
OSI .... Deflecting System of Indicator (RU)
OSI .... Office of Samoa Information [*Press agency*]
OSI .... Office of Seniors' Interests [*Australia*]
OSI .... Office of Special Investigations
OSI .... Office Special d'Imposition
OSI .... Opitna Stanica za Impregnaciju [*Animal Impregnation Experiment Station*] [*Slavonski Brod*] (YU)

OSI .... Organizacion Sionistas Independientes [*Zionist organization in Chile*]

OSI .... Orszagos Sportorvosi Intezet [*National Institute of Sports Medicine*] (HU)

OSI .... Osijek [*Former Yugoslavia*] [*Airport symbol*] (OAG)

OSIM .... Oficiul de Stat pentru Inventii si Marci [*State Office for Inventions and Trademarks*] (RO)

OSISA ...... Openbare Skakelinstituut van Suidelike Afrika [*South Africa*] (EAIO)

OSJD........ Ordinis Sancti Joannis de Deo [*Order of St. John of God*]

OSK .... Offentlighets- och Sekretesslagsstiftningskommitten [*Sweden*]

OSK .... Okresna Spravna Komisia [*District Administrative Commission*] (CZ)

OSK .... Omospondia Syndaxioukhon Kapnergaton [*Federation of Pensioned Tobacco Workers*] [*Greek*] (GC)

OSK .... Organismos Skholikon Ktirion [*School Buildings Organization*] [*Greek*] (GC)

osk .... Orszagos Sertes es Kirako Vasar [*National Hog and Merchandise Fair*] (HU)

OSK .... Osaka Sanso [*Commercial firm*] [*Japan*]

OSK .... Osaka Syosen Karsha [*Japanese steamship company*]

OSK .... Oskarshamn [*Sweden*] [*Airport symbol*] (OAG)

osk .... Oskarzony [*The Accused*] [*Poland*]

osk .... Oskuren [*Uncut*] [*Publishing*] [*Sweden*]

OSK .... Osrodek Szkolenia Kadr [*Training Center of Personnel In*] (POL)

OSKhI .... Odessa Agricultural Institute (RU)

OSKL........ Kamishly [*Syria*] [*ICAO location identifier*] (ICLI)

oskm........ Osobovy Kilometr [*Passenger-Kilometer*] (CZ)

OSKOM .... Special Committee of the Council of Defense (RU)

Oskow....... Ogolnopolski Szkolny Komitet Odbudowy Warszawy [*All-Poland School Committee for the Reconstruction of Warsaw*] (POL)

OSKS........ General Students' Cooperative Association (BU)

OSL .... Oficerska Szkola Lacznosci [*Signal Officers' School*] (POL)

OSL .... Oficerska Szkola Lotnicza [*Air Force Officers' School*] (POL)

OSL .... Old [*Church*] Slavonic [*Language, etc.*]

OSL .... Oslo [*Norway*] [*Airport symbol*] (OAG)

OSL .... Single Pilot Lamp (RU)

OSLAM.... Organizacion de Seminarios Latinoamericanos [*Organization of Latin American Seminaries*] [*Colombia*] (LAA)

O Slav ...... Old [*Church*] Slavic [*Language*] (BARN)

OSLK........ Latakia/Latakia [*Syria*] [*ICAO location identifier*] (ICLI)

OSM .... Oberschaltmechaniker [*Chief Control Mechanic (At missile installation)*] (EG)

OSM .... Oficiul de Stat pentru Metrologie [*State Office for Metrology*] (RO)

OSM .... Okregowa Spoldzielnia Mleczarska [*District Dairy Cooperative*] (POL)

OSM .... Okresni Starostlivost o Mladez [*District Youth Welfare Organization*] (CZ)

OSM .... Orchid Society of Mauritius (EAIO)

OSM.......... Organizacion Submarina Mexicana, SA

Osm.......... Osmanlica [*Ottoman*] [*Historical*] (TU)

OSMA .... Opera Svizzera dei Monumenti d'Arte [*Switzerland*] (SLS)

OSME .... Ornithological Society of the Middle East (EAIO)

OSMP .... Specialized Medical Aid Detachment (RU)

OSMR .... Basic Single-Stage Decision Model (RU)

OSMU....... Separate Construction and Installation Administration (RU)

OSMU....... Special Construction and Installation Site (RU)

OSMW ...... Oficerska Szkola Marynarki Wojennej [*School for Naval Officers*] (POL)

OSN.......... Experimental Statistical Norms (RU)

osn............. Founded, Created (RU)

osn............. Fundamental, Basic, Principal (RU)

OSN.......... Obras Sanitarias de la Nacion [*National Sanitation Works*] [*Argentina*] (LAA)

OSN.......... Oficina de Seguridad Nacional [*Office of National Security*] [*Nicaragua*] (LA)

OSN.......... Organisace Spojenych Narodu [*United Nations*] (CZ)

OSN.......... Orzecznictwo Sadu Najwyzszego [*Decisions of the Supreme Court*] (POL)

OSN.......... Ottuv Slovnik Naucny [*Otto's Encyclopedia*] (CZ)

OSN.......... Standardization Department (RU)

OSNA .... Osmatranje Dejstva Neprijateljski Artiljerije [*Observation of Enemy Artillery Action*] (YU)

OSNAA ..... Organization for Afro-Asian Peoples Solidarity (RU)

OS naTPZK ... General Union of Labor Productive Cooperatives (BU)

Osnav....... Society for Lifesaving on Waterways of the USSR [*1928-1931*] (RU)

OSNAZ ..... Special-Purpose Detachment (RU)

OSNIE...... Omospondia Syllogon Nosilevtikon Idrymaton Ellados [*Federation of Greek Nursing Home Societies*] (GC)

OSNK .... General Assembly of the Criminal Law Collegium (BU)

osnov .... Founded, Created (RU)

OSNP .... All-China National People's Congress (BU)

OSNP .... Association of Free German Trade Unions (RU)

osn prerab .. Completely Revised (BU)

OSNS .... General Students' National Union (BU)

OSNSW.... Office of the Sheriff of New South Wales [*Australia*]

OSNU....... Dog-Team Sled - Litter Unit (RU)

OSO.......... Decontamination Section (RU)

OSO.......... Department of Social Security (RU)

OSO.......... Oessudoeste [*West-Southwest*] [*Spanish*]

OSO.......... Oossuidoos [*East-Southeast*] [*Afrikaans*]

OSO.......... Oposicion Sindical Obrera [*Workers Trade Union Opposition*] [*Spanish*] (WER)

OSO.......... Orange Symphony Orchestra [*Australia*]

OSO.......... Overseas Students Office [*Australia*]

OSO.......... Ovest-Sud-Ovest [*West-South-West*] [*Italian*]

OSO.......... Public Sanitation Officers (BU)

OSO.......... Ship Equipment Department (RU)

OSO.......... Society for Assistance to the Defense of the USSR [*1926-1927*] (RU)

Osoaviakhim ... Society for Assistance to the Defense, Aviation, and Chemical Construction of the USSR [*1927-1948*] (RU)

osobkm....... Osobni Kilometr [*Passenger-Kilometer (A unit of measure on railroads)*] (CZ)

Osobproyektmontazh ... State All-Union Special Planning and Installation Trust (RU)

Osodmil ..... Society for Assistance to the Militia (RU)

OSOMPP ... Okresni Sekce Organisacne-Masove Prace a Propagandy [*District Section for Mass Organizational Work and Propaganda*] (CZ)

OSOS .... Organizacion Secreta de Oficiales [*Secret Organization of Officers*] [*Guatemala*] (LA)

Osotop....... Special Conference on Fuel (RU)

OSOV .... Obalska Sluzba Obavestavanja i Veze [*Coastal Information and Communications Service*] [*Military*] (YU)

OsP .... Basic Regulations (BU)

OSP .... Consolidated Economic Enterprise (BU)

OSP .... Instrument-Landing Equipment (RU)

OSP .... Liaison Section with Infantry [*Artillery*] (RU)

OSP .... Limited Scope of Application [*Computer programing*] (RU)

osp............. Obciansky Sudny Poriadok [*Code of Civil Procedure*] (CZ)

OSP .... Obshtina Economic Enterprise (BU)

OSP .... Ochotnicza Straz Pozarna [*Volunteer Fire Brigade*] (POL)

OSP .... Office of the Special Prosecutor [*Queensland, Australia*]

OSP .... Oficerska Szkola Piechoty [*School for Infantry Officers*] (POL)

OSP .... Oficina de Seguridad Politica [*Office for Political Security*] [*Ecuador*] (LA)

OSP .... Oficina Sanitaria Panamericana [*Pan-American Sanitary Bureau - PASB*] [*Washington, DC*]

OSP .... Okresna Socialna Poistovna [*District Social Insurance Agency*] (CZ)

OSP .... Okresny Stavebny Podnik [*District Construction Enterprise*] (CZ)

OSP .... Okrug Economic Enterprise (BU)

OSP .... Orientarea Scolara/Profesionala [*Educational/Vocational Orientation*] (RO)

OSP .... Osrodek Szkolenia Partyjnego [*Party Training Center*] (POL)

osp............. Separate Signal Regiment (BU)

OSP .... Slupsk [*Poland*] [*Airport symbol*] (OAG)

OSP .... United Socialist Party [*French*] (RU)

OSPA......... Oficina Sectorial de Planificacion Agropecuaria [*Area Office for Agricultural-Livestock Planning*] [*El Salvador*] (LA)

OSPA........ Organisation Sanitaire Panamericaine [*Pan-American Sanitary Organization*] [*French*]

OSPAA...... Organisation de la Solidarite des Peuples Afro-Asiatiques [*Afro-Asian Peoples' Solidarity Organization*] [*Use AAPSO*] [*French*] (AF)

OSPAA...... Organizzazione di Solidarieta dei Popoli Afroasiatici [*Afro-Asian Peoples' Solidarity Organization*] [*Use AAPSO*] [*Italian*] (WER)

OSPAAAL ... Organisation de Solidarite des Peuples Afro-Asiatiques et d'Amerique Latine [*Afro-Asian Latin-American Peoples' Solidarity Organization*] [*Use AALAPSO*] [*French*] (AF)

OSPAAAL ... Organizacion de Solidaridad de los Pueblos de Africa, Asia, y America Latina [*Afro-Asian-Latin American Peoples' Solidarity Organization*] [*Use AALAPSO Havana, Cuba*] (LA)

OSPAAAL ... Organization of Solidarity of the Peoples of Africa, Asia, and Latin America

OSPAP ...... Odbytove Sdruzeni Papirenskeho Prumyslu [*Market Associations of the Paper Industry*] (CZ)

OSPB........ General Popular Banks' Union (BU)

OSPC........ Officer Superintending Police Circle (ML)

OSPF........ Oblasni Sekretarijat za Poslove Finansija [*Regional Secretariat of Finance*] [*Pristina*] (YU)

OSPK........ United Socialist Party of Catalonia (RU)

OSPN .... Oborove Stredisko pro Projektove Normy Spoju [*Sectoral Center for Planning Standards of Communications*] (CZ)

OSPO .... Oblast Union of Consumers' Societies (RU)

OSPO .... Okoliya Council of Trade Organizations (BU)
OSPR......... Palmyra [*Syria*] [*ICAO location identifier*] (ICLI)
OSPS .... General Council of Trade Unions (BU)
OSPS .... Oblast Council of Trade Unions (RU)
OSPS .... Okrug Council of Trade Unions (RU)
OSPT......... Osrodek Szkolnictwa Pocztowo-Telekomunikacyjnego [*Postal and Telecommunications Training Center*] (POL)
OSPVL ...... Organizace pro Spolupraci v Prumyslu Valivych Lozisek [*Organization for Cooperation in Ball Bearing Industry*] (CZ)
OSPZK ...... Okoliya Council of Consumers' Agricultural Cooperatives (BU)
OSR .... Comparison Element, Comparator (RU)
OSR .... Office of Sport and Recreation [*Australian Capital Territory*]
OSR .... Office of State Revenue [*New South Wales, Australia*]
OSR .... Oficerska Szkola Radiotechniczna (Jelenia Gora) [*Radio Engineering Officers' School (Jelenia Gora)*] (POL)
OSR .... Oktobarska Socijalisticka Revolucija [*October Socialist Revolution*] [*Russian Revolution, 1917*] (YU)
OSR .... Ortsschulrat [*German*]
Osr .... Osrodek [*Center*] [*Poland*]
OSR .... Ostrava [*Former Czechoslovakia*] [*Airport symbol*] (OAG)
OSR .... Separate Combat Engineer Company (RU)
OSR .... Special Construction Area (RU)
OSRB......... Overseas Services Resettlement Bureau
osrb .... Separate Signal Brigade (BU)
OSRG .... Okregowe Stacje Ratownictwa Gorniczego [*District Mine Rescue Stations*] (POL)
OSRO .... Office for the Sahelian Relief Operation [*UN Food and Agriculture Organization*]
OSROK ..... Office of Supply, Republic of Korea (IMH)
OSRV .... Rayon Terminal Broadcasting Station (RU)
OSS .... Experimental Selection Station (RU)
OSS .... General Union of Syndicates (BU)
OSS .... Land-Based Aircraft Section (of the TsKB of the Aviatrest) (RU)
OSS .... Obilna Spolocnost na Slovensku [*Grain Company in Slovakia*] (CZ)
OSS .... Oddzial Sprzetu Sanitarnego [*Sanitary Equipment Branch*] (POL)
OSS .... Office of the Supervising Scientist [*Australia*]
OSS .... Oficerska Szkola Samochodowa [*Motor Transport Officers' School*] (POL)
OSS .... Oficiul de Stat pentru Standarde [*State Office for Standards*] (RO)
OSS .... Okoliya Syndicate Council (BU)
OSS .... Organizace Spoluprace Socialistickych Zemi v Oboru Elektrickych a Postovnich Spoju [*Organization of Cooperation of Socialist Countries in the Field of Electrical and Postal Communications*] (CZ)
OSS .... Organization for Cooperation of Socialist Countries in the Domain of Posts and Telecommunications [*Defunct*] (EAIO)
OSS .... Overseas Shipping Services Proprietary Ltd. [*Australia*] (ADA)
Oss .... Wydawnictwo Zakladu Narodowego Imienia Ossolinskich [*Publishing House of the Ossolinski National Institution*] (POL)
OSSA .... Occupation Superannuation Standards Act [*Australia*]
OSSA .... Ophthalmological Society of South Africa (EAIO)
OSSA .... Order Secular of St. Augustine [*See also ASAS*] [*Rome, Italy*] (EAIO)
OSSC .... Oyo State Sports Council
OSSD......... Okresni Svaz Spotrebnich Druzstev [*District Union of Consumer Cooperatives*] (CZ)
OSSG......... Olympic Security Support Group (OLYM)
OSSh .... Single-Phase Dry-Type Mine Transformer (RU)
OSShD ...... Organisation fur die Zusammenarbeit der Eisenbahnen [*Organisation for the Collaboration of Railways - OCR*] (EAIO)
OSSM........ Oil Spill Simulation Model
OSSMM..... Office de Securite Sociale des Marins de la Marine Marchande [*Benelux*] (BAS)
OSSMRPF ... Organization for Swedish-Speaking Mentally Retarded Persons in Finland (EAIO)
OSSO .... Experimental Horticultural and Vegetable-Growing Station (RU)
OSSO .... Special Conference (RU)
OSSOM ..... Office de Securite Sociale d'Outre-Mer [*Benelux*] (BAS)
OSSS .... Damascus [*Syria*] [*ICAO location identifier*] (ICLI)
OSSSA ...... Ordine Supremo della Santissima Annunziata [*Decoration*] [*Italian*]
OSSU......... Office du Sport Scolaire et Universitaire [*France*] (FLAF)
OSSU......... Organisation du Sport Scolaire et Universitaire Togolais
OSSUC...... Organisation des Sports Scolaires et Universitaires du Cameroun
ossz.......... Osszes [*All*] [*Hungary*]
OST .... All-Union Standard [*1925-1940*] (RU)
ost............. Obsolete (BU)

OST .... Oddzial Sprzetowo-Transportowy [*Equipment and Transportation Department*] (POL)
OST .... Office for Science and Technology [*United Nations (already exists in GUS II database)*]
OST .... Onderstaande [*Following*] [*Afrikaans*]
OST .... Operationssteuerung [*German*] (ADPT)
OST .... Order of the Sons of Temperance [*Australia*]
OST .... Organisation Socialiste des Travailleurs [*Socialist Workers' Organization*] [*Senegal*] [*Political party*] (PPW)
OST .... Organizacion Socialista de los Trabajadores [*Socialist Workers' Organization*] [*Bolivia*] [*Political party*] (PPW)
OST .... Organizacion Socialista de los Trabajadores [*Socialist Workers' Organization*] [*Costa Rica*] [*Political party*] (PPW)
OST .... Osrodek Szkolenia Teatralnego [*Center for Dramatic Training*] (POL)
OST .... Ostend [*Belgium*] [*Airport symbol*] (OAG)
OST .... Society of Easel Painters [*1925-1932*] (RU)
ostar .... Obsolete Term (RU)
OSTB .... Office of the State Training Board [*Australia*]
OSTC......... Organisation Syndicale des Travailleurs du Cameroun [*Organization of Cameroon Workers' Unions*] (EAIO)
ostekhbyuro ... Special Technical Office (RU)
Osterr. .... Oesterreichisch [*Austria*] [*German*] (GPO)
OSTIV .... Organisation Scientifique et Technique Internationale du Vol a Voile [*International Technical and Scientific Organization for Soaring Flight*]
OSTiW ...... Osrodek Sportu, Turystyki, i Wypoczynku [*Sports, Tourism, and Recreation Center*] [*Poland*]
O St J......... Officer of the Order of St. John (ML)
ostl............. Oestlich [*Eastern*] [*German*]
ost p........... Railroad Stop [*Topography*] (RU)
OSTP......... Separate Sentry Post (RU)
Ostpr.......... Ostpreussen [*East Prussia*] [*German*]
OSTPZK ... General Union of Labor Productive Artisans' Cooperatives (BU)
OSTRAMEC ... Organizacion Sindical de Trabajadores de Medios de Comunicacion [*Trade Union Organization of Communication Media Workers*] [*Nicaragua*] (LA)
OSTT........ Damascus [*Syria*] [*ICAO location identifier*] (ICLI)
OSTT........ General Agreement on Tariffs and Trade [*GATT*] (RU)
OSTT........ Orszagos Sport- es Testnevelesi Tanacs [*National Council on Sports and Physical Education*] (HU)
OStZ .... Oesterreichisches Statistisches Zentralamt [*Austrian Central Statistical Office*]
OSTZ........ Separate Outpost Support (RU)
OSU .... Oficerska Szkola Uzbrojenia [*Ordnance Officers' School*] (POL)
OSU .... Okregowy Sad Ubezpieczen Spolecznych [*District Court of Social Security*] (POL)
OSU .... Okrug Statistical Administration (BU)
OSU .... Separate Construction Site (RU)
OSU .... Special Construction Administration (RU)
OSUS........ Okregowy Sad Ubezpieczen Spolecznych [*District Court of Social Security*] [*Poland*]
OSUZ .... Organization of Students of Secondary Educational Institutions (RU)
osv .... Och Sa Vidare [*And So Forth*] [*Sweden*]
OSV .... Oddeleni Sluzby Vojsk [*Troop Services Department*] (CZ)
osv .... Og Sal Videre [*And So Forth*] [*Norway*] (GPO)
osv .... Og Sa Videre [*And So Forth*] [*Denmark*] (GPO)
OSV .... Okresni Skolni Vybor [*District Board of Education*] (CZ)
OSV .... Opcinsko Sindikalno Vijece [*Municipal Trade-Union Council*] (YU)
OSV .... Organisatiewet Sociale Verzekering [*Benelux*] (BAS)
OSV .... Organisation Sociale des Volontaires [*Social Organization of Volunteers*] [*Burkina Faso*] (AF)
OSV .... Organismos tis Symfonou tis Varsovias [*Warsaw Pact*] (GC)
OSVA .... Organismos tis Synthikis tou Voreiou Atlandikou [*North Atlantic Treaty Organization*] (GC)
Osvag......... Information Agency (RU)
OSVIM...... Experimental Station of the All-Union Scientific Research Institute of Agricultural Mechanization (RU)
OSVO .... Oblastni Sprava Vychovy a Osvety [*Regional Educational and Cultural Administration*] (CZ)
OSVOD...... Obshchestvo Spaseniya na Vodakh RSFSR (EAIO)
OSVOD ..... Society for Furthering the Development of Water Transportation and for the Safeguarding of Human Lives on Waterways of the USSR [*1931-1956*] (RU)
OSVOK ..... Special Conference on the Restoration of Basic Industrial Capital (RU)
OSVS......... General Union of Water-Power Syndicates (BU)
OSVV .... Organization of the Soviet War Veterans (RU)
OSW .... Oesterreichische Stickstoffwerke AG [*Later, OMS*]
OSW .... Old Swedish [*Language, etc.*]
OSWA .... Orchid Society of Western Australia
OSWA .... Organ Society of Western Australia
OSWChem ... Oficerska Szkola Wojsk Chemicznych [*Chemical Warfare Officers' School*] (POL)

OSWP........ Oficerska Szkola Wojsk Pancernych [*Armored Troop Officers' School*] (POL)

OSWZ .... Oficerska Szkola Wojsk Zmechanizowanych [*Mechanized Troop Officers' School*] (POL)

OSY .... Namsos [*Norway*] [*Airport symbol*] (OAG)

OSYGO ..... Omospondia Synetairistikon Ypallilon Georgikon Organoseon [*Federation of Employees of Agricultural Cooperative Organizations*] [*Greek*] (GC)

OSZ .... Experimental Welding Plant (RU)

OSZ .... Koszalin [*Poland*] [*Airport symbol*] (OAG)

OSZ .... Okregowa Skladnica Zaopatrzenia [*District Supply Depot*] (POL)

OSZ .... Okresni Sporitelna a Zalozna [*District Savings and Deposit Bank*] (CZ)

OSZB........ Orszagos Szakmai Bertablazat [*National Occupational Wage Table*] (HU)

OSZB........ Orszagos Szamviteli Bizottsag [*National Committee on Accounting*] (HU)

OSZD(b)P ... Oroszorszagi Szocialdemokrata (Bolsevik) Part [*Russian Social Democratic Party (Bolsheviks)*] (HU)

OSZDMP ... Oroszorszagi Szocialdemokrata Munkaspart [*Russian Social Democratic Workers' Party*] (HU)

OSZFSZK ... Oroszorszagi Szovjet Foderativ Szocialista Koztarsasag [*Russian Socialist Federative Soviet Republic*] (HU)

OSZH .... Orszagos Szovetkezeti Hitelintezet [*National Cooperatives Credit Institute*] (HU)

OSZhD ...... Organization for Railroad Cooperation among Socialist Countries (BU)

OSZhD ...... Railroad Cooperation Organization (RU)

OSZI......... Orszagos Szamitastechnika Alkalmazasi Iroda [*National Computer Technology Application Office (A component of Kozponti Statisztikai Hivatal)*] (HU)

OSZJ .... Orszagos Szakmunkas Jegyzek [*National Skilled Worker Register*] (HU)

OSZK........ Oroszorszagi Szovjet Koztarsasag [*Russian Soviet Republic*] (HU)

OSzK........ Orszagos Szechenyi Konyvtar [*National Szechenyi Library*] [*Information service or system*] (IID)

OSZK(b)P ... Osszszovetsegi Kommunista (Bolsevik) Part [*All-Union Communist Party (Bolsheviks)*] (HU)

Osz KP ..... Osztrak Kommunista Part [*Austrian Communist Party*] (HU)

oszl .... Oszlop [*Column*] [*Military*] (HU)

OSZM .... Basic Single-Stage Maximum Problem (RU)

OSZP .... Olasz Szocialista Part [*Italian Socialist Party*] (HU)

OSZSZ ...... Orszagos Szabadsagharcos Szovetseg [*National Association of Freedom Fighters*] (HU)

OSZSZT.... Orszagos Szenbanyaszati Szaktanacs [*National Coal Mining Council*] (HU)

OSZT........ Orszagos Szakszervezeti Tanacs [*National Trade Union Council*] [*Budapest, Hungary*] (HU)

O SZ T ..... Orszagos Szovetkezeti Tanacs [*National Council of Cooperatives*] (HU)

oszt .... Osztaly [*Class, Department, Battalion*] (HU)

OSZT........ Ozdi Szenbanyaszati Troszt [*Coal Mining Trust of Ozd*] (HU)

osztr .... Osztrak [*Austria*] (HU)

Osztr KP .... Osztrak Kommunista Part [*Austrian Communist Party*] (HU)

OSZV........ Orszagos Szamitogeptechnikai Vallalat [*National Computer Technology Enterprise*] (HU)

OSZVB ...... Orszagos Szamviteli Bizottsag [*National Committee on Accounting*] (HU)

OSZZ........ Osnovni Savez Zemljoradnickih Zadruga [*Basic Union of Agricultural Cooperatives*] (YU)

OSZZSD ... Organizatsiya Sotrudnichestva Zheleznykh Dorog [*Organization for Cooperation among Railroads (of CEMA)*] (HU)

OT.............. All Clear Signal (RU)

OT.............. Current Limiter (RU)

OT.............. Current Winding (RU)

OT.............. Departure [*Railroads*] (RU)

OT.............. Emplacement (RU)

OT.............. Flamethrower Tank (RU)

ot .... Heating Load (RU)

OT.............. Labor Department (RU)

OT.............. Landmark, Reference Point (BU)

OT.............. Obojzivelne Tanky [*Amphibious Tanks*] (CZ)

OT.............. Obrneny Transporter [*Armored Personnel Carrier*] (CZ)

OT.............. Oddzial Terenowy [*Local Department*] (POL)

oT.............. Offener Tiegel [*Open Crucible*] [*German*] (GCA)

OT.............. Oikeustieteen Kandidaatti [*Finland*]

Ot.............. Olympus Tours Ltd. [*Cyprus*]

OT.............. Optical Theodolite (RU)

OT.............. Organisation Trotskiste [*Trotskyite Organization*] [*French*] (WER)

OT.............. Organizacion Trotskista [*Trotskyite Organization*] [*Spanish*] (WER)

OT.............. Orienteering Tasmania [*Australia*] [*An association*]

ot.............. Orszagos Tanacs [*National Council*] (HU)

OT.............. Orszagos Tervhivatal [*National Planning Office*] (HU)

Ot.............. Ortsteil [*Section (of town)*] (EG)

OT.............. Osnovna Tarifa [*Basic Tariff*] [*Railroads*] (YU)

OT.............. Osterreichischer Turnerbund [*Austria*] (EAIO)

OT.............. Ou Testament [*Old Testament*] [*Afrikaans*]

OT.............. Overland Telegraph [*Australia*] (DSUE)

ot .... Section, Division, Department (BU)

OT.............. Sectorial Standard (BU)

OT.............. Unidirectional Texture (RU)

OTA.......... Occupied Territory Administration [*World War II*]

OTA.......... Office Technique d'Assurances

OTA.......... Omnium Tchadien d'Alimentation

OTA.......... Organisation Mondiale du Tourisme et de l'Automobile [*World Touring and Automobile Organization*]

OTA.......... Organismoi Topikis Avtodioikiseos [*Organizations of Local Self-Government*] [*Greek*] (GC)

OTA.......... Orszagos Testnevelesi Alap [*National Fund for Physical Education*] (HU)

OTAAI ..... Oficina Tecnica de Asuntos Agricolas Internacionales [*Venezuela*] (DSCA)

OTAH....... Orszagos Tervhivatal, Arhivatal [*National Planning Office, Office of Price Control*] (HU)

OTAL........ OT Africa Line

OTAN....... Organisation du Traite de l'Atlantique Nord [*North Atlantic Treaty Organization - NATO*] [*Brussels, Belgium*]

OTAN....... Organizacao do Tratado do Atlantico Norte [*North Atlantic Treaty Organization*] [*Portuguese*]

OTAN....... Organizacion del Tratado del Atlantico Norte [*North Atlantic Treaty Organization*] [*Use NATO*] (LA)

OTAS .... Organizacion del Tratado del Atlantico Sur [*South Atlantic Treaty Organization*] [*Use SATO*] (LA)

OTASE...... Organisation du Traite de Defense Collective pour l'Asie du Sud-Est [*Southeast Asia Treaty Organization*] [*Use SEATO*] [*French*] (WER)

OTASE...... Organisation du Traite de l'Asie du Sud-Est (FLAF)

OTASE...... Organizacion del Tratado de Asia del Sudeste [*South-East Asia Treaty Organization - SEATO*] [*Spanish*]

OTASO ..... Organizacao do Tratado da Asia Sul-Oriental [*South-East Asia Treaty Organization*] [*Portuguese*]

OTAWA.... Occupational Therapy Association of Western Australia

O-TAWCS ... Okinawa Tactical Air Weapons Control System [*Japan*] (PDAA)

OTB.......... Office du The du Burundi [*Burundi Tea Office*] (AF)

OTB.......... Organisation du Traite de Bruxelles [*Belgium*] (FLAF)

OTB.......... Overseas Trust Bank [*Hong Kong*]

OTB.......... Separate Tank Battalion (RU)

OTB.......... Separate Transport Battalion (RU)

OTB.......... Special Technical Office (RU)

OTB.......... Technological Office Based on Public Participation (RU)

OTBD .... Doha/International [*Qatar*] [*ICAO location identifier*] (ICLI)

OTBP........ Department of Trade and Personal Service Facilities (RU)

OTBQ .... Occupational Therapists' Board of Queensland [*Australia*]

otbr............ Separate Tank Brigade (RU)

OTC.......... Office of Technical Cooperation [*United Nations*]

OTC.......... Operado de Terminal de Contenedores [*Container Terminal Operator*] [*Shipping*] [*Spanish*]

OTC.......... Operador de Transporte Combinado [*Combined Transport Operator*] [*Spanish*] [*Business term*]

OTC.......... Operatore di Trasporto Combinato [*Combined Transport Operator*] [*Italian*] [*Business term*]

OTC.......... Overseas Telecommunications Commission [*Australia*]

OTC.......... Overseas Telecommunications Commission of Australia (BARN)

OTCA .... Overseas Technical Cooperation Agency [*Japan*]

OTCI .... Overseas Telecommunications Commission International [*Australia*]

OTCZ .... Office des Transports en Commun du Zaire (AF)

OTD.......... Contadora [*Panama*] [*Airport symbol*] (OAG)

otd .... Department, Branch, Section (RU)

otd .... Department, Section, Separate, From Below (BU)

OTD.......... Office des Terres Domaniales [*National Land Office*] [*Tunis, Tunisia*] (AF)

otd .... Separate, Independent, Detached (RU)

otdavt .... Submachine-Gun Unit (RU)

Otdelstroy ... Trust for Special Finishing Work (RU)

OTDJEN... Oditurat Djenderal [*Office of the Judge Advocate General*] (IN)

otd l .... Separate Sheet (RU)

Otd mattekh snab .. Material and Technical Supply Department [*or Section*] (BU)

otd-niye ...... Department, Branch, Section (RU)

otd otpech... Separate Imprint (BU)

otd ott .... Offprint, Reprint, Separate Copy (RU)

otd prop iagit ... Propaganda and Agitation Section (BU)

otd svkh...... Sovkhoz Branch [*Topography*] (RU)

OTE .... Omospondia Thiroron Ellados [*Federation of Concierges of Greece*] (GC)

OTE.......... Operativne-Technicka Evidence [*Operational and Technical Reporting*] (CZ)

OTE.......... Organismos Tilepikoinonion Ellados [*Hellenic Telecommunications Organization*] [*Greek*]

OTE.......... Wage Rate and Economics Department (RU)

OTEC........ Ocean Thermal Exchange Conversion (LA)

OTECI....... Office Technique d'Etudes et de Cooperation Internationales [*France*]

OTEESC ... Oficina Tecnica de Estudios Economicos [*Venezuela*] (DSCA)

OTEF........ Office Tchadien d'Etudes Ferroviaires

OTEF........ Organisation Tunisienne de l'Education et de la Famille [*Tunisian Education and Family Organization*] (AF)

OTEINA.... Omnium Technique Electro-Industriel NA [*North African*]

OTEK........ Association of Transportation and Forwarding Offices (RU)

OTEK........ Consolidated Transportation and Shipping Offices (BU)

OTEM....... Otelcilik ve Turizm Egitim Merkezleri [*Hotel Operation and Tourism Training Centers*] [*Kyrenia*] (TU)

OTEMAS ... Osaka International Textile Machinery Show

OTEN........ Department of Technical Sciences (of the Academy of Sciences, USSR) (RU)

OTER........ Optical Target Engagement Recorder [*Australia*]

oter........... Separate Telegraph Operating Company (BU)

OTER........ Separate Telephone-Operating Company (RU)

OTERI....... Office Technique de Realisation Industrielle [*Lebanon*]

O TEUT..... Old Teutonic [*Language, etc.*] (ROG)

OTF.......... Organisasie van Teoretiese Fisici [*South Africa*] (AA)

OTF.......... Sheep-Breeding Farm (RU)

OTFB........ Service Section of Front Logistical Installation (BU)

OTFB........ Unit of a Rear Base of a Front (RU)

OTFZ........ Oddeleni Tylove Frontove Zakladny [*Rear Service Department of the Frontline Base*] (CZ)

otg............ From Above (BU)

OTG.......... Ogolnopolski Tygodnik Gospodarczy [*All-Poland Economic Weekly*] (POL)

OTG.......... Oklopna Takticka Grupa [*Armored Tactical Group*] (YU)

OTG.......... Olayan Transportation Group [*Saudi Arabia*]

OTG.......... Organismos Trofimon kai Georgias [*Food and Agriculture Organization (of the United Nations)*] (GC)

otg............ Responsible, In Charge (BU)

otglag........ Verbal (RU)

OTGS........ Department of City Telephone Networks (RU)

OTH.......... Orszagos Talalmanyi Hivatal [*National Patent Office*] (HU)

OTH.......... Orszagos Tervhivatal [*National Planning Office*] (HU)

OThAK...... Organismos Theatrikis Anaptyxeos Kyprou [*Organization for the Theatrical Development of Cyprus*] (GC)

OTI............ Department of Technical Information (RU)

OTI............ Department of Technical Information and Inventions (RU)

OTI............ Morotai Island [*Indonesia*] [*Airport symbol*] (OAG)

OTI............ Oesterreichisches Textil-Forschungsinstitut [*Austrian Textile Research Institute*] (SLS)

OTI............ Office of Trade and Investment [*Victoria, Australia*]

OTI............ Organizacion de Television Iberoamericana

OTI............ Orszagos Tarsadalombiztosito Intezet [*National Institute for Social Security*] (HU)

OTI............ Otonom Turk Idaresi [*Autonomous Turkish Administration*] [*Cyprus*] (TU)

OTIA........ Oficina Tecnica de Informacion Agricola [*Peru*] (DSCA)

OTIE........ Office des Transports Interieurs Europeens (FLAF)

OTIF......... Organisation Intergouvernementale pour les Transports Internationaux Ferrovaires [*Intergovernmental Organization for International Carriage by Rail*] (EAIO)

OTII.......... Department of Technical Information and Inventions (RU)

OTIPKhP .. Odessa Technological Institute of the Food and Refrigeration Industry (RU)

OTIR........ Department of Technical Information and Rationalization (RU)

OTiR......... Osrodek Techniki i Racjonalizacji [*Technology and Rationalization Center*] (POL)

OTIZ........ Department of Technical Information and Inventions (RU)

OTiZ......... Labor and Wages Department (RU)

OTIZ........ Specialized State Publishing House (RU)

OTK.......... Department of Technical Control (RU)

OTK.......... Main Transportation Commission (RU)

OTK.......... Obrona Terytorialna Kraju [*National Territorial Defense*] (POL)

OTK.......... Oddeleni Technicke Kontroly [*Technical Control Department*] (CZ)

OTK.......... Okresni Technicka Kontrola [*District Technical Control*] (CZ)

OTK.......... Omospondia Tourko-Kypriakou Kratous [*Turkish-Cypriot Federated State*] (GC)

otk............ Onallo Tanacsu Kozseg [*Village with Independent Council*] (HU)

OTK.......... Opatreni k Upevneni Technologicke Kazne [*Measures for the Strengthening of Technological Discipline*] (CZ)

OTK.......... Organisace Technicke Kontroly [*Technical Control Organization*] (CZ)

OTK.......... Organization of Technical Control (BU)

OTK.......... Osterreichischer Touristenklub [*Austria*] (EAIO)

OTK.......... Otdel Tekhnicheskogo Kontrolya [*Department of Technical Control*] [*Russian*]

OTK.......... Public Control by Members of the Communist Party (RU)

OTK.......... Separate Tank Corps (RU)

OTK.......... Special Transportation Commission (RU)

OTK.......... Technical Control Section (BU)

Otkomkhoz ... Department of Municipal Services (RU)

otl.............. Excellent [*Mark in school*] (RU)

OTL.......... Oberstleutnant [*Lieutenant Colonel*] (EG)

OTL.......... Oikeustieteen Lisensiaatti [*Finland*]

otm........... Mark, Notation, Reading [*Instrument*], Blip [*RADAR*] (BU)

otm........... Mark, Sign, Index (RU)

OTM.......... Ok Tedi Mining [*Papua New Guinea*]

OTM.......... Organizacao dos Trabalhadores de Mocambique [*Mozambique Workers' Organization*]

otm............ Revoked [*or Anulled or Abolished*] (BU)

OTM.......... Small Optical Theodolite (RU)

OTML........ Ok Tedi Mining Ltd. [*Papua New Guinea*]

OTMS........ Organization and Tactics of Medical Service (RU)

OTN.......... Department of Technical Sciences (of the Academy of Sciences, USSR) (RU)

OTN.......... Lastp-Linhas Aereas de Sao Tome e Principe [*ICAO designator*] (FAAC)

otn............ Relative (RU)

otnos......... Relative [*Pronoun*] (BU)

otnosit....... Relative (RU)

otnt........... Specific Gravity/Weight (BU)

otn vlazhn... Relative Humidity (RU)

otn yed....... Relative Unit (RU)

OTO.......... General Theory of Relativity (RU)

oto............. Oman Toimensa Ohella [*Finland*]

Oto............ Otomobil [*Automobile*] (TU)

OTO.......... Technical Training Department (RU)

OTOE........ Omospondia Trapezo-Ypallilikon Organoseon Ellados [*Federation of Greek Bank Employee Organizations*] (GC)

otol........... Otology, Otologist (BU)

otor........... Separate Flamethrower Tank Company (RU)

otorg......... Chief Organizer (RU)

OTP.......... Consolidated Commercial Enterprise (BU)

OTP.......... Department of Commercial Ports (RU)

OTP.......... Obalsko Transportno Preduzece [*Shore Transport Establishment*] [*Novi Sad*] (YU)

OTP.......... Oddeleni Technicke Pomoci [*Technical Assistance Department*] (CZ)

OTP.......... Office Togolais des Phosphates [*Togolese Phosphates Office*] (AF)

OTP.......... Okrug Commercial Enterprise (BU)

OTP.......... Omnium des Transports par Pipelines

OTP.......... Omnium Technique de Pipelines [*Sudan*]

OTP.......... Opce Trgovinsko Poduzece [*General Commercial Establishment*] [*YU*]

OTP.......... Optimum Temperature Sequence (RU)

OTP.......... Organismos Touristikis Pisteos [*Tourist Credit Organization*] [*Greek*] (GC)

OTP.......... Organization of Theoretical Physicists [*South Africa*] (AA)

OTP.......... Orszagos Takarekpenztar [*National Savings Bank*] (HU)

otp............ Separate Tank Regiment (RU)

otpech........ Printed, Print [*Offprint*] (BU)

OTPN........ Opolskie Towarzystwo Przyjaciol Nauk [*Poland*] (SLS)

OTPP........ Department of Technical Preparation of Production (RU)

OTPP........ Office of Transport, Policy and Planning [*South Australia*]

otpp........... Separate Breakthrough Tank Regiment (RU)

Otpr.......... Departure [*Railroads*] (RU)

OTPS........ General Labor Trade Union (BU)

OTR.......... Close Support Missile (RU)

OTR.......... Coto 47 [*Costa Rica*] [*Airport symbol*] (OAG)

otr............ Detachment (RU)

OTR.......... Group of Supply Ships, Convoy [*Navy*] (RU)

otr............. Negative [*Grammar*] (BU)

OTR.......... Oddeleni Technickych Rozboru [*Technical Analysis Department*] [*CZ*]

otr............ Separate Transport Company (RU)

otrab.......... Separate Transport Aviation Base (BU)

OTRACO .. Office des Transports du Congo [*Office of Transportation in the Congo*]

OTRACO .. Office de Transit de la Cote d'Afrique

OTRACO .. Office d'Exploitation des Transports Coloniaux

OTRADI.... Office de Transit de la Cote-D'Ivoire

OTRAG..... Orbital Transport- und Raketen-Aktiengesellschaft [*Rocket company*] [*Germany*]

OTRAZ..... Office d'Exploitation des Transports au Zaire

otrazhspos ... Reflectivity, Reflectance, Reflection Factor (RU)

otrazh sv.... Reflected Light (RU)

OTRBSA ... Occupational Therapists' Registration Board of South Australia

otremb........ Separate Tank Repair Battalion (RU)

OTrI............ Orszagos Traumatologiai Intezet [*National Institute of Traumatology*] (HU)
otritsat........ Negative (RU)
OTRYC..... Over the Reef Yacht Club [*Northern Mariana Islands*] (EAIO)
OTs........... Heating Plant (BU)
OTS .... Medium Optical Theodolite (RU)
OTS .... Negative Glow (RU)
OTs........... Officers' Training School [*Royal*] [*Australia*]
OTs........... Operational Center (BU)
OTS .... Orbital Test Satellite [*Communications satellite*] [*European Space Agency*]
OTS .... Organization for Tropical Studies [*Costa Rica*] (LAA)
OTS .... Tank Task Force (RU)
OTS .... Technical Supply Section, Technical Supply Department (RU)
OTS .... Terminal Telephone Exchange (RU)
OTsAG ..... Organization of Central American States [*OCAS*] (RU)
OTSB........ Orszagos Testnevelesi es Sportbizottsag [*National Committee for Sports and Physical Culture*] (HU)
OTsDP...... Operator of the Central Dispatcher's Station, Operator of the Central Control Post (RU)
otsekr .... Executive Secretary (RU)
Otsenkom .. Valuation Commission (RU)
OTSh .... Departure [*Nautical term*] (RU)
OTSH .... Orszagos Testnevelesi es Sport Hivatal [*National Office for Sports and Physical Education*] (HU)
OTShL....... Experimental Technical Sewing Laboratory (RU)
OTSI.......... Orszagos Testneveles- es Sportegeszsegugyi Intezet [*National Institute of Physical Education and Sports Hygiene*] (HU)
OTSI.......... Orszagos Testnevelesi es Sportorvosi Intezet [*National Physical Education and Sports Physician Institute*] (HU)
OTsK .... Body-Centered Cubic (RU)
OTsK .... United Central Committee (RU)
OTsR .... Basic Cysteine Reaction (RU)
otsr .... Separate Telegraph Construction Company (BU)
OTSSE ...... Omospondia Topikon Spoudastikon Syllogon Ellados [*Federation of Local Student Clubs of Greece*] (GC)
OT st.......... Emplacement for Heavy Machine Gun (RU)
otsv .... Signal Section, Communications Section (RU)
OTsZ .... Lead and Zinc Plant (BU)
OTT .... Basic Technical Requirements (RU)
ott.............. Copy, Print, Impression (RU)
OTT .... Ocean Transport and Trading
OTT .... Oikeustieteen Tohtori [*Finland*]
ott.............. Ottica [*Optics*] [*Italian*]
ott.............. Ottimo [*Excellent*] [*Italian*]
ott.............. Ottobre [*October*] [*Italian*]
OTT .... Single-Channel Carrier Telegraphy (RU)
OTT .... Society for Technical Creativity (BU)
OTTI......... Ostbayrisches Technologie-Transfer-Institut [*Information retrieval*]
OTTKT...... Orszagos Tavlati Tudomanyos Kutatasi Terv [*National Long-Range Scientific Research Plan*] (HU)
OTTP........ Omnium Technique des Transports par Pipelines
ottp............ Separate Heavy Tank Regiment (RU)
OTTU .... Odessa Streetcar and Trolleybus Administration (RU)
OTU.......... Office du Tourisme Universitaire [*France*]
OTU.......... Opetus-ja Tutkimusalan Unioni [*Teaching and Research Employees Union*] [*Finland*] (EY)
OTU.......... Otu [*Colombia*] [*Airport symbol*] (OAG)
OTU.......... Terminal Repeater (RU)
OTUA....... Office Technique pour d'Utilisation de l'Acier [*Technical Office for Steel Utilization*] [*France*] (PDAA)
OTUS .... Office Tunisien de Standardisation
OTUWA.... Organisation of Trade Unions of West Africa
otv.............. Hardening, Solidification (RU)
OTV .... Oeffentlicher Dienst, Transport, und Verkehr [*Public Service, Transportation, and Traffic (Trade union)*] (WEN)
otv.............. Responsible (RU)
OTVA .... Allied Tactical Air Force [*NATO*] (RU)
otvet.......... Responsible (RU)
OTVH .... Orszagos Termeszetvedelmi Hivatal [*National Bureau of Conservation*] (HU)
otv red .... Editor in Chief (RU)
otvruk........ Official in Charge (RU)
OTVT .... Orszagos Termeszetvedelmi Tanacs [*National Council for Plant and Wildlife Protection*] (HU)
OTWY ...... Otway [*Botanical region*] [*Australia*]
OTY .... Omospondia Takhydromikon Ypallilon [*Federation of Post Office Employees*] [*Greek*] (GC)
OTY .... Oria [*Papua New Guinea*] [*Airport symbol*] [*Obsolete*] (OAG)
OTYE .... Omospondia Trapezikon Ypallilon Ellados [*Federation of Bank Employees of Greece*] (GC)
OTZ .... Labor and Wages Department (RU)
OTZ .... Onega Tractor Plant (RU)
otzdrav ...... Department of Public Health (RU)
OU .... Administrative Department (RU)

OU .... Carbon Dioxide Fire Extinguisher (RU)
OU .... Control Device (RU)
OU .... Control Winding (RU)
OU .... Feedback Control (RU)
OU .... Lighting Device (RU)
OU .... Obalovy Ustav [*Packaging Institute*] (CZ)
OU .... Obecni Urad [*Community Office*] (CZ)
OU .... Oblast Center [*Communications*] (RU)
OU .... Obvodny Urad [*District Office*] (CZ)
OU .... Odborne Uciliste [*Vocational School*] (CZ)
OU .... Oductovaci Ustredna [*Accounting Center*] (CZ)
oU............. Ohne Umschlag [*Without Covers*] [*Publishing*] [*German*]
OU .... Okresni Telefonni Ustredna [*District Telephone Exchange*] (CZ)
OU .... Opisy Udoskonalen [*Descriptions of Improvements*] (POL)
OU .... Oposicion Unida [*United Opposition*] [*Dominican Republic*] (LA)
OU .... Opposition Unie [*United Opposition*] [*The Comoros*] [*Political party*] (EY)
OU .... Optical Goniometer (RU)
OU .... Optimal Control (RU)
OU .... Orientalni Ustav [*Institute of Oriental Studies (of the Czechoslovak Academy of Sciences)*] (CZ)
Ou .... Originalumschlag [*Original Wrapper*] [*Publishing*] [*German*]
OU .... Osidlovaci Urad [*Resettlement Office*] (CZ)
OU .... Osvetove Ustredie [*Cultural Center*] (CZ)
OU .... Replacement Section [*Military term*] (RU)
OU .... Terminal [*Computers*] (RU)
OUA .... Orchestre de l'Universite d'Abidjan
OUA .... Organisation de l'Unite Africaine [*Organization of African Unity - OAU*] (EAIO)
OUA .... Organizacao da Unidade Africana [*Organization of African Unity*] [*Use OAU*] [*Portuguese*] (WER)
OUA .... Organizacion de la Unidad Africana [*Organization of African Unity - OAU*] [*Spanish*] (MSC)
OUA .... Ouagadougou [*Burkina Faso*] [*Airport symbol*] (OAG)
OUA .... Relative Specific Activity (RU)
OUAT........ Orissa University of Agriculture and Technology [*India*] (DSCA)
OUB........... Overseas Union Bank [*Singapore*]
OUCFA ..... Office Universitaire et Culturelle Francaise en Algerie [*French Cultural and University Office in Algeria*] (AF)
OUD .... General Delivery Conditions [*Council for Economic Mutual Assistance*] (BU)
OUD .... Oujda [*Morocco*] [*Airport symbol*] (OAG)
OUD .... Separate Training Battalion [*Artillery*] (RU)
oudhk .... Oudheidkunde [*Archeology*] [*Afrikaans*]
oudl .... Ouderling [*Elder*] [*Afrikaans*]
OUDSI ...... General Conditions for the Procurement of Goods for Export (BU)
OUE........... Ouesso [*Congo*] [*Airport symbol*] (OAG)
OUED........ Organizacion Unitaria de Estudiantes de Deusto [*Unitary Organization of Deusto Students*] [*Spanish*] (WER)
OUF .... Orszagos Ugyvitelgepesitesi Felugyelet [*National Business Operations Mechanizing Supervision*] (HU)
OUF .... Overseas Union Finance [*Singapore*]
OUG .... Okrajna Uprava za Gozdarstvo [*District Forestry Administration*] (YU)
OUG .... Okregowe Urzedy Gornicze [*District Mining Administration*] (POL)
OUG .... Organisation de l'Unite Guineenne [*Organization of Guinean Unity*] (PD)
OUGK........ Oblastni Ustav Geodesie a Kartografie [*Regional Geodetic and Cartographic Institute*] (CZ)
OUGS........ Okrug Forestry Resources Administration (BU)
OUH .... Oudtshoorn [*South Africa*] [*Airport symbol*] (OAG)
OUI........... Organisation Universitaire Interamericaine [*Inter-American Organization for Higher Education*] (EAIO)
OUK .... Oblastna Uradovna Presidlovacej Komisie [*Regional Office of the Resettlement Commission*] (CZ)
OUK .... Okresni Ucitelska Knihovna [*District Teachers' Library*] (CZ)
OUK .... Okresni Uverova Komise [*District Loan Commission*] (CZ)
OUK .... Training Ship Detachment (RU)
OUL.......... Oulu [*Finland*] [*Airport symbol*] (OAG)
OULG........ Organisation Unifiee pour la Liberation de la Guinee [*Unified Organization for the Liberation of Guinea*] (AF)
OuLiPo ..... Ouvroir de Litterature Potentielle [*Workshop of Potential Literature*] [*French literary society*]
OUM .... Okregowy Urzad Miar [*District Office of Measures*] [*Poland*]
OUMEREP ... Outre-Mer Representation
OUMP........ Oblast Administration of Local Industry (RU)
OUMVR..... Okrug Administration of the Ministry of Internal Affairs (BU)
OUN .... Association of Ukrainian Nationalists (RU)
OUN .... Organisace Ukrajinskych Nacionalistu [*Organization of Ukrainian Nationalists*] (CZ)

OUN .... Organizacija Ujedinjenih Nacija [*United Nations Organization*] (YU)

OUN .... Organizacja Ukrainskich Nacjonalistow [*Organization of Ukrainian Nationalists*] (POL)

OUN .... Organizatsiia Ukrains'kykh Natsionalistiv [*Organization of Ukrainian Nationalists*] (CZ)

O und K ...... Orenstein und Koppel [*Commercial firm*] [*Germany*]

OUNZ .... Obvodni Ustav Narodniho Zdravi [*District Public Health Institute*] (CZ)

OUO .... Obalsko Utvrdenje Otseka [*Coastal Fortification Section*] (YU)

OUOP .... Okresny Urad Ochrany Prace [*District Labor Protection Office*] (CZ)

OUP .... Attended Repeater Station (RU)

OUP .... Odbor za Unutrasnju Politiku (SIV) [*Committee on Internal Policy*] (YU)

OUP .... Official Unionist Party [*Northern Ireland*] (PPW)

OUPP .... Separate Training Glider Regiment (RU)

OUPT .... Okregowy Urzad Pocztowy i Telekomunikacyjny [*District Post and Telecommunications Office*] (POL)

OUPZ .... Odborne Uciliste Pracovnich Zaloh [*Training School for Labor Reserves*] (CZ)

OUR .... Batouri [*Cameroon*] [*Airport symbol*] (OAG)

OUR .... Department of Criminal Investigation (RU)

OUR .... Organizacion de Unidad Revolucionaria [*Organization of Revolutionary Unity*] [*Bolivia*] [*Political party*] (PPW)

our .... Relative Specific Radioactivity (RU)

OURD .... Overseas Uranium Resources Development Company Ltd.

OUS .... Odborne Uciliste Spoju [*Center for Professional Instruction in Communications*] (CZ)

OUS .... Okregowe Urzedy Samochodowe [*District Automotive Vehicle Administration*] (POL)

OUS .... Ourinhos [*Brazil*] [*Airport symbol*] (OAG)

OUS .... Reference Repeater Station (RU)

OUSA .... Organisation de l'Unite Syndicale Africaine [*Organisation of African Trade Union Unity - OATUU*] [*Accra, Ghana*] (EAIO)

OUSA .... Organizacion de Unidad Sindical Africana [*Organization of African Trade Union Unity*] (LA)

OUSIV .... CEMA [*Council for Economic Mutual Assistance*] General Conditions (BU)

OUSKh ...... Oblast Administration of Agriculture (RU)

OUSPZ ...... Odborne Uciliste Statnich Pracovnich Zaloh [*Training School for State Labor Reserves*] (CZ)

OUT .... Organizacao Unida de Trabalhadores [*United Organization of Workers*] [*Portugal*] [*Political party*] (PPE)

OUT .... Orszagos Ugyvedi Tanacs [*National Council of Lawyers*] (HU)

out .... Outubro [*October*] [*Portuguese*]

OUTB .... Separate Training Tank Battalion (RU)

outo .... Outubro [*October*] [*Portuguese*]

ouv .... Ouverture [*French*]

ouv .... Ouvrage [*Work*] [*French*]

ouvr .... Ouvrage [*Work*] [*French*]

Ouvr .... Ouvrages Exterieurs [*Outworks*] [*Military map abbreviation World War I*] [*French*] (MTD)

OUVS .... District Directorate of Military Supply (RU)

OUZ .... Department of Educational Institutions (RU)

OUZ .... Zouerate [*Mauritania*] [*Airport symbol*] (OAG)

OUZD .... Okrozni Urad za Zavarovanje Delavcev [*District Office of Workers' Insurance*] (YU)

OV .... Chemical Warfare Agent (BU)

OV .... Dangerous Goods [*Railroads*] (RU)

OV .... Errors Are Possible (RU)

OV .... Field Winding (RU)

OV .... Firing Platoon (RU)

OV .... Flammable Substance (RU)

o-v .... Island (BU)

OV .... Obrnena Vozba [*Armored Corps*] (CZ)

OV .... Obvodni Vybor [*District Committee, Borough Committee*] (CZ)

ov .... Oeversatt [*Translated*] [*Sweden*]

OV .... Official Visitor [*Australia*]

OV .... Ohne Verpflegung [*Without Rations*] [*Military*] [*German*]

OV .... Ohne Verzoegerung [*Without Delay*] [*German*]

OV .... Okresni Velitelstvi [*District Headquarters*] (CZ)

OV .... Okresni Vybor [*District Committee*] (CZ)

OV .... Organic Matter (RU)

OV .... Orszagos Vezetoseg [*National Directorate*] (HU)

OV .... Ortsvereinigungen [*Local Associations*] (EG)

ov .... Osztalyvezeto [*Department Head/Chief*] (HU)

OV .... Ou Verbond [*Old Testament*] [*Afrikaans*]

Ov .... Ova [*Plain, Field*] (TU)

ov .... Over [*Over*] [*Danish/Norwegian*]

OV .... Process Time (RU)

ov .... Purified Water (RU)

OV .... Single-Shot Multivibrator (RU)

OV .... Toxic Agent (RU)

OVA .... Bekily [*Madagascar*] [*Airport symbol*] (OAG)

o-va .... Islands (RU)

OVA .... Obstbauversuchsanstalt [*Fruit Growing Experimental Station*] [*German*] (ARC)

OVA .... Organismos Viomikhanikis Anaptyxeos [*Organization for Industrial Development*] [*Greek*] (GC)

OVA .... Orissa Veterinary Association [*India*] (DSCA)

OV-ACAT ... Oecumenische Vereniging ACAT - Aktie van Christenen voor Afschaffing van Martelen [*Netherlands*] (EAIO)

OVAG .... Oesterreichische Volksbanken-Aktiengesellschaft [*Austrian bank*] (ARC)

OV Amst .... Beslissing van den Raad van Beroep voor de Ongevallen-Verzekering te Amsterdam [*Netherlands*] (BAS)

ovanst .... Ovanstaende [*Above-Described*] [*Publishing*] [*Sweden*]

OVAPAM ... Office de Valorisation Pastorale et Agricole du Mutara

OVATE ..... Okumenische Vereinigung der Akademien und Tagungzentren in Europa [*Ecumenical Association of Laity Centres and Academies in Europe - EALCAE*] [*Bad Boll, Federal Republic of Germany*] (EAIO)

OVB .... Novosibirsk [*Former USSR*] [*Airport symbol*] (OAG)

OVB .... Oddeleni Verejne Bezpecnosti [*Public Security Department*] (CZ)

OVB .... Onafhankelijk Verbond van Bedrijfsorganisaties [*Independent Federation of Industrial Organizations*] [*Netherlands*] (WEN)

OVB .... Organisatie ter Verbetering van de Binnenvisserij [*Organization for Improvement of Inland Fisheries*] [*Netherlands*] (ASF)

ovb .... Separate Reconstruction Battalion (RU)

OVBD .... Okresni Vystavbove Bytove Druzstvo [*District Association for Apartment Construction*] (CZ)

OVCI .... Organismo di Volontariato per la Cooperazione Internazionale la Nostra Famiglia [*Italy*] (EAIO)

OVD .... Motor Field Winding (RU)

OVD .... Office of Village Development [*SPATF*] [*Papua New Guinea*]

OVD .... Offizier vom Dienst [*Duty Officer*] (EG)

OVD .... Oviedo [*Spain*] [*Airport symbol*] (OAG)

OVDF .... Official Visitors to Departmental Facilities [*New South Wales, Australia*]

OVDNKh .. Oblast Exhibition of Achievements of the National Economy (RU)

OVE .... Oesterreichischer Verband fuer Elektrotechnik [*Austrian Association for Electrotechnology*] (SLS)

OVEF .... Orszagos Vetomagfelugyeloseg [*National Seed Inspectorate*] (HU)

O ve M .... Organizasyon ve Metot Grubu [*Organization and Methods Group*] [*In various ministries*] (TU)

overdr .... Overdruk [*Reprint*] [*Publishing*] [*Netherlands*]

overgeb .... Overgebonden [*Rebound*] [*Publishing*] [*Netherlands*]

overs .... Oeversaettning [*Translation*] [*Publishing*] [*Sweden*]

overs .... Oversat [*Translated*] [*Publishing Danish/Norwegian*]

overs .... Oversigt [*Summary*] [*Publishing Danish/Norwegian*]

OVET .... Orszagos Villamosenergiagazdalkodasi Tanacs [*National Council on the Utilization of Electric Power*] (HU)

OVF .... Orszagos Villamosenergia Felugyelet [*National Electric Power Authority*] (HU)

OVF .... Orszagos Vizugyi Foigazgato [*National Director General for Water Power and Hydraulic Engineering*] (HU)

OVG .... District Military Hospital (RU)

OVG .... Generator Field Winding (RU)

OVG .... Oberverwaltungsgericht [*Provincial Administrative Court of Appeal*] [*German*] (DLA)

OVG .... Oesterreichische Verkehrswissenschaftliche Gesellschaft [*Austrian Traffic Engineers Association*] (SLS)

OVG .... Office of the Valuer-General [*Northern Territory, Australia*]

OVGE .... Omospondia Viomikhanikon kai Genikon Ergaton [*Federation of Industrial and General Workers*] [*Cyprus*] (GC)

OVH .... Orszagos Vizgazdalkodasi Hivatal [*National Water Bureau*] (HU)

OVH .... Orszagos Vizugyi Hivatal [*National Bureau of Water Conservation*] (HU)

OVH .... Osztalyvezetohelyettes [*Deputy Department Head*] (HU)

OVI .... Clothing and Equipment Supplies (RU)

OVI .... Interior Installations Trust (BU)

OVI .... Okrug Water Installation (BU)

OVIBAR .... Office de la Valorisation de la Bananeraie Rwandaise [*Manufacturers of banana wine and juice*] [*Rwanda*]

OVIE .... Or Vert Ivoirien Societe d'Expansion

OVIKSh ..... Joint "Red Banner" Military Engineering School (RU)

OVILLEF ... Orszagos Villamosenergia Felugyelet [*National Electric Power Authority*] (HU)

OVIMU ..... Odessa Higher Engineering Nautical School (RU)

OVIR .... Office of Visas and Registrations [*Former USSR*]

OVIR .... Visa and Registration Department (RU)

OVIS .... Military Engineering Supply Section (RU)

OVIT .... Orszagos Villamostavvezetek Vallalat [*National Enterprise for Power Line*] (HU)

OVIU .... District Military Engineering Directorate (RU)

OvJ .... Officier van Justitie [*Benelux*] (BAS)

OVK .... Oblast Military Commissariat (RU)

OVK........... Orgaan van de Vereniging ter Beoefening van de Krijgswetenschap [*Benelux*] (BAS)

OVK........... Orszagos Vezetokepzo Kozpont [*National Management Training Center*] (HU)

OVKT........ Orszagos Vizgazdalkodasi Keretterv [*National General Plan on Water Economy*] (HU)

OVM.......... Congregation of the Oblates of the Virgin Mary [*Rome, Italy*] (EAIO)

OVM.......... Motor Field Winding (RU)

OVM.......... Society of Militant Materialists (RU)

OVMD...... Society of Militant Dialectical Materialists (RU)

Ov motart polk ... Combined Arms Motorized Artillery Regiment (BU)

ovnasl........ Ovojni Naslov [*Jacket Title*] (YU)

OVNI......... Objectos Volantes No Identicados [*Unidentified Flying Objects*] [*Spanish*]

OVNI......... Objeto Volador No Identificado [*Unidentified Flying Object*] [*Use UFO*] (LA)

OVNI......... Objet Volant Non-Identifie [*Unidentified Flying Object*] [*Use UFO*] (AF)

OVNS........ Oz Veshalom-Netivot Shalom [*Israel*] (EAIO)

OVO .... Oddeleni Vychovy a Osvety [*Department of (Political) Education and Culture*] [*Armed forces*] (CZ)

OVO .... Outside Service Department [*of a library*] (RU)

o-vo........... Society, Company (RU)

OVO .... Special Military District (RU)

OVOMA.... Omby Voafantina Malagasy

OVOS........ Okresny Vybor Odbojovych Sloziek [*District Committee of Resistance Units*] (CZ)

ovoshch...... Vegetable Storage [*Topography*] (RU)

ovoshchn .... Vegetable Sovkhoz [*Topography*] (RU)

OVP.......... Joint Force Training (RU)

OVP.......... Joint Rolling Stock [*Railroads*] (BU)

OVP.......... Oesterreichische Volkspartei [*Austrian People's Party*] [*Political party*] (PPW)

OVP.......... Okresni Vykupni Podnik [*District Bulk Purchasing Enterprise (for agricultural products)*] (CZ)

OVP.......... Oxidation-Reduction Potential (RU)

OVPP........ Military Field Post Section (RU)

OVPS........ Ob'edinennyi Velikii Progressivnyi Soiuz

OVR.......... Calling-Answering Relay (RU)

OVR.......... Harbor Defense (RU)

ovr .... Ravine [*Topography*] (RU)

OVR.......... Vereeniging tot Uitg. van Oud Vaderl. Rechtsbronnen [*Benelux*] (BAS)

OVRA....... Opera Volontaria per la Repressione dell'Antifascismo [*Fascist Secret Police*] [*Italian*]

OVRA....... Operazione di Vigilanza per la Repressione dell'Antifascismo [*Italian secret service agency*]

OVRI .... Oenological and Viticultural Research Institute [*South Africa*] [*Research center*] (IRC)

OVRK....... Okrug Military Revolutionary Committee (BU)

OVRP....... Organizacion de Voluntarios para la Revolucion Puertorriquena [*Organization of Volunteers for the Puerto Rican Revolution*] (PD)

OvRspr....... Overzicht Rechtspraak [*Benelux*] (BAS)

OVS........... Clothing and Equipment Depot (RU)

OVS........... Clothing and Equipment Supply (RU)

OVS........... Clothing and Equipment Supply Section (RU)

OVS........... Foreign Relations Section [*Military term*] (RU)

OVS........... Joint Armed Forces (RU)

OVS........... Joint Force Communications (RU)

OVS........... Oesterreichischer Verband fuer Strahlenschutz [*Austrian Association for Ray Protection*] (SLS)

OVS........... Official Visitors' Scheme

OVS........... Okresni Vojenska Sprava [*District Military Directorate*] (CZ)

OVS........... Oranje-Vrystaat [*Orange Free State*] [*Afrikaans*]

OVS........... Oxidation-Reduction Medium (RU)

OVS........... Separate Signal Platoon (RU)

OVSA .... Oftalmologiese Vereniging van Suid-Afrika [*Ophthalmological Society of South Africa*] (AA)

OVSA .... Omospondia Viotekhnikon Somateion Athinon [*Federation of Athens Handicrafts Associations*] (GC)

OVSB........ Oranje-Vrouesendingbond [*Afrikaans*]

OVSKK.... Osterreichischer Verein fur Suizidpravention, Krisenintervention, und Konfliktbewaltigung [*Austria*] (EAIO)

OVSL........ Organisation Voltaique des Syndicats Libres [*Voltan Organization of Free Trade Unions*] (AF)

OVSLU..... Oranje-Vrystaatse Landbou-Unie [*Orange Free State Agricultural Union*] [*Afrikaans*]

OVSOV .... Oranje-Vrystaatse Onderwysersvereniging [*Orange Free State Teachers Association*] [*Afrikaans*]

OVSR .... Separate Medical Company (RU)

OVSS........ Military Medical Service Section (RU)

OVSTM..... Operation Vallee du Senegal Tesekele-Magui

OVSU .... District Military Medical Directorate (RU)

OVSZ......... Orszagos Vertranszfuzios Szolgalat [*National Blood Transfusion Service*] (HU)

OVSZKTI ... Orszagos Vertranszfuzios Szolgalat Kozponti Tudomanyos Kutato Intezete [*Central Scientific Research Institute of the National Blood Transfusion Service*] (HU)

OVT.......... All Clear [*Air-raid warning*] (RU)

OVT.......... All-Clear Antiaircraft Defense Signal (BU)

OVT.......... Orszagos Villamos Tavvezetek Vallalat [*National Enterprise for Power Lines*] (HU)

OVTs .... Computation Service Center (RU)

ovts............ Sheep-Breeding Sovkhoz [*Topography*] (RU)

ovtsy......... Military Censorship Section (RU)

OVTT .... Orszagos Vezetotovabbkepzesi Tudomanyos Tanacs [*National Science Council for Advanced Management Training*] (HU)

OVTVS...... Okresni Vybor pro Telesnou Vychovu a Sport [*District Committee for Physical Education and Sports*] (CZ)

OVU .... Ocelarsky Vyzkumny Ustav [*Steel Research Institute*] (CZ)

OVU .... Optical Calculator (RU)

OVUZ....... Department of Higher Educational Institutions (RU)

OVV.......... Exciter Field Winding (RU)

OVV.......... Okresni Vojenske Velitelstvi [*District Military Headquarters*] (CZ)

OVV.......... Okresni Volebni Vybor [*District Election Committee*] (CZ)

Ovv............ Onverbindendverklaring [*Benelux*] (BAS)

OVV.......... Oranje-Vroue-Vereniging [*Afrikaans*]

OVV.......... Osterreichischer Volleyballverband [*Austria*] (EAIO)

OVVK....... District Military Medical Commission (RU)

OVZ.......... Expectation of External Start [*Computers*] (RU)

OVZ.......... Oesterreichisches Verpackungszentrum [*Austrian Wrapping Center*] (SLS)

OVZ.......... Orekhovo-Zuyevo Scales Plant (RU)

OW .... Obere Winkelgruppe [*Angles above 45*] [*German military - World War II*]

OW .... Octrooiwet [*Benelux*] (BAS)

OW .... Oel-Wasser [*Oil-in-Water*] [*German*] (GCA)

oW............ Oesterreichische Waehrung [*Austrian Currency*] [*German*]

OW .... Ohne Wert [*Without Value*] [*German*]

OW .... Okreg Wojskowy [*Military District*] (POL)

OW .... Old Welsh [*Language, etc.*]

OW .... Onder Wie [*Among Other Things*] [*Afrikaans*]

OW .... Ongevallenwet [*Benelux*] (BAS)

Ow............ Onteigeningswet [*Benelux*] (BAS)

O/W.......... Ontvangbare Wissels [*Bills Receivable*] [*Business term*] [*Afrikaans*]

OW .... Oorlogswet [*Benelux*] (BAS)

OW .... Openbare Werke [*Public Works*] [*Afrikaans*]

OW .... Osterreichischer Wasserskiverband [*Austria*] (EAIO)

OW .... Otto Wolff Aktiengesellschaft [*Otto Wolff Joint Stock Company*]

Owa........... Ostrov [*Islands*] [*O*] [*See also*] [*Russian*] (NAU)

OWAEC .... Organization for West African Economic Co-Operation

OWAL....... Oficina de Washington para America Latina [*Washington Office on Latin America*] [*Use WOLA*] (LA)

OWAS ...... Ovako Oy Working Posture Analysis System [*Finland*] (PDAA)

OWB......... Opleiding tot Wetenschappelijk Bibliothecaris

OWC......... One World Campaign [*Australia*]

OWD .... Ogolne Warunki Dostaw [*General Conditions of Delivery*] (POL)

OWF .... Oceania Weightlifting Federation [*Australia*] (EA)

OWG .... Ordnungswidrigkeiten-Gesetz [*Misdemeanors Law*] (EG)

OWI .... Oddzial Wykonawstwa Inwestycyjnego [*Investment Operations Branch*] (POL)

OWKS ...... Okregowy Wojskowy Klub Sportowy [*District Military Sport Club*] (POL)

OWL......... Online Western Libraries [*Perth, Australia*]

OWN .... Older Women's Network [*Australia*]

OWN .... Owens Group Ltd. [*New Zealand*] [*ICAO designator*] (FAAC)

OWP......... Oboz Wielkiej Polski [*Camp of Great Poland*] (PPE)

OWP......... Odrodzone Wojsko Polskie [*Restored Polish Army*] [*Poland*]

OWP......... Ogolnopolska Wystawa Plastyki [*All-Poland Exhibition of Plastic Arts*] (POL)

OWP......... Organization of Working People [*Guyana*] (LA)

OWPA....... Orchids - World Picture Agency [*France*] (EAIO)

OWRM...... Okregowe Warsztaty Remontowo-Montazowe [*District Repair and Assembly Shops*] (POL)

OWS......... Cargosur [*Spain*] [*ICAO designator*] (FAAC)

OWS......... Old West Saxon [*Language, etc.*] (ROG)

OWS......... Oxfam World Shops [*Belgium*] (EAIO)

OWSC ...... Old West Scandinavian [*Language, etc.*]

OWSI .... Open Water Scuba Instructor [*Australia*]

OWTU ...... Oil Workers Trade Union (LA)

OWU .... Out-of-Workers' Union [*Australia*]

Ox .... Oxydation [*Oxidation*] [*German*] (GCA)

Oxd .... Oxydation [*or Oxydieren*] [*Oxidation*] [*German*]

oxdd .... Oxydierend [*Oxidizing*] [*German*]

OXFAM .... Oxford Committee for Famine Relief [*Acronym is now organization's official name*] [*British*] (EA)

OXICOL.... Fabrica Colombiana de Oxigeno [*Colombia*] (COL)

OXIDOR ... Oxidaciones Organicas CA [*Venezuela*]

OXIQUIM ... Establecimientos Industriales Quimicos Ltda. [*Chemical Industrial Establishments Ltd.*] [*Chile*] (LA)

OXNE........ Organosis Xenonon Neotitos Ellados [*Youth Hostel Organization of Greece*] (GC)

Oxydat ...... Oxydation [*Oxidation*] [*German*] (GCA)

Oxydierbark ... Oxydierbarkheit [*Oxidizability*] [*German*] (GCA)

Oxyka .... Sauerstoffindustrie (VVB) [*Oxygen Industry (VVB)*] (EG)

Oy .... Osakeyhtioe [*Limited Company*] [*Finland*]

OYA.......... Goya [*Argentina*] [*Airport symbol*] (OAG)

OYAK .... Ordu Yardimlasma Kurumu [*Army Mutual Aid Association*] [*OYKGM*] [*See also*] (TU)

OYaP .... Generalized Programing Language (RU)

OYAS .... Abbs [*Yemen*] [*ICAO location identifier*] (ICLI)

OYBI .... Al-Beida [*Yemen*] [*ICAO location identifier*] (ICLI)

OYBO........ Al-Bough [*Yemen*] [*ICAO location identifier*] (ICLI)

OYBT .... Barat [*Yemen*] [*ICAO location identifier*] (ICLI)

OYC.......... Conair AS [*Denmark*] [*ICAO designator*] (FAAC)

OYCA .... Ocean Youth Club of Australia

OYE.......... Oyem [*Gabon*] [*Airport symbol*] (OAG)

OYeES...... Organization for European Economic Cooperation [*OEEC*] (RU)

OYEKO ..... Omospondia Ypallilon Epikheiriseon Koinis Ofeleias [*Federation of Public Utility Employees*] [*Greek*] (GC)

OYHD .... Hodeidah [*Yemen*] [*ICAO location identifier*] (ICLI)

OYI .... Organismos Ydrevseos kai Ilektrofotismou [*Water Supply and Electric Lighting Organization*] [*Followed by initial letter of location*] [*Greek*] (GC)

OYJ .... Opettajien Yhteisjaerjesto [*Finland*] (SLS)

OYK........... Omas Ypovrikhion Katastrofon [*Underwater Demolition Squad*] (GC)

OYKGM.... Ordu Yardimlasma Kurumu Genel Mudurlugu [*Army Mutual Aid Association Directorate General*] [*OYAK*] [*See also*] (TU)

OYKM....... Kamaran [*Yemen*] [*ICAO location identifier*] (ICLI)

OYMB....... Marib [*Yemen*] [*ICAO location identifier*] (ICLI)

OYMC....... Mokha [*Yemen*] [*ICAO location identifier*] (ICLI)

OYO .... Tres Arroyos [*Argentina*] [*Airport symbol*] (OAG)

OYPAE...... Omospondia Ypallilikou Prosopikou Avtokiniton Ellados [*Federation of Transport Personnel of Greece*] (GC)

OYSH........ Saada [*Yemen*] [*ICAO location identifier*] (ICLI)

OYSN .... Sanaa/International [*Yemen*] [*ICAO location identifier*] (ICLI)

OYSREA ... Office of Youth, Sport, Recreation and Ethnic Affairs [*Northern Territory, Australia*]

OYTh......... Organismos Ydrevseos Thessalonikis [*Salonica Water Supply Organization*] (GC)

OYTZ .... Taiz/Ganad [*Yemen*] [*ICAO location identifier*] (ICLI)

OYZM....... Al-Hazm [*Yemen*] [*ICAO location identifier*] (ICLI)

Oz.............. Australia [*Slang*] (ADA)

OZ.............. Barrage [*Artillery*] (RU)

OZ.............. Center of Contamination (RU)

OZ.............. Consolidated Plants (BU)

OZ.............. Department of Public Health (RU)

oz.............. Lake (RU)

OZ.............. Obrtna Zbornica [*Chamber of Craftsmen*] (YU)

OZ.............. Obstacle Detachment (RU)

OZ.............. Obucarska Zadruga [*Shoemakers Cooperative*] (YU)

OZ.............. Oddeleni Zbrani [*Weapons Department (Part of general staff)*] (CZ)

OZ.............. Odevne Zavody [*Clothing Enterprises*] (CZ)

OZ.............. Okregowy Zwiazek [*District Union*] [*Poland*]

OZ.............. Oktanzahl [*Octane Number*] [*German*] (GCA)

OZ.............. Operativna Zona [*Zone of Operation*] [*Military*] (YU)

OZ.............. Opravarenske Zavody [*Repair Shops*] (CZ)

OZ.............. Osvetove Zarizeni [*Equipment of Cultural Establishments*] (CZ)

Oz.............. Oudezijds [*Old Side*] [*Netherlands*] (CED)

Oz.............. Ozero [*Lake*] [*Russian*] (NAU)

oz.............. Reserve [*Military*] (BU)

oz.............. Troy Ounces (SCAC)

ozab .... Separate Antiaircraft Artillery Battery (RU)

OZAC....... Office Zairois de Controle [*Zairian Control Office*] (AF)

OZACAF... Office Zairois du Cafe [*Zairian Coffee Office*] (AF)

OZAD........ Separate Antiaircraft Artillery Battalion (RU)

OZAKOM ... Special Transcaucasian Committee [*1917-1920*] (RU)

OZAMS .... Oficina Zonal de Apoyo a la Mobilizacion Social [*Zonal Office of Support to Social Mobilization*] [*Peru*] (LA)

OZAP .... Obchodni Zarizeni [*Business Equipment*] (CZ)

OZAP .... Separate Antiaircraft Artillery Regiment (RU)

OZATE...... Ordzhonikidze Automobile and Tractor Electrical Equipment Plant (RU)

OZB .... Osnovni Zakon o Braku [*Basic Law on Marriage*] (YU)

OZBCO ..... Osobni Zdravotnicky Balicek Civilni Obrany [*Civil Defense First-Aid Kit*] (CZ)

OZBS......... Osnovni Zakon o Zastiti Bilja od Bolesti i Stetocina [*Basic Law on the Protection of Plants Against Diseases and Injurious Insects*] (YU)

OZBW .... Okregowy Zarzad Budownictwa Weglowego [*District Administration of Coal Industry Construction*] (POL)

OZC.......... Okregowy Zwiazek Cechow [*District Union of Guilds*] (POL)

OZC.......... Ozamis City [*Philippines*] [*Airport symbol*] (OAG)

OZCh........ Green Tea Infusion (RU)

OZCO....... Australia Council (EAIO)

OZD.......... Object Zvlastni Dulezitosti [*Specially Important Target*] (CZ)

OZDiP....... Child and Youth Health Care (RU)

OZE .... Osnovni Zakon o Ekspropriaciji [*Basic Law on Expropriation*] (YU)

OZEBiH .... Zavod za Ekonomsku Propagandu i Publicitet Bosne i Hercegovine [*Institute of Economic Propaganda and Publicity of Bosnia and Hercegovina*] [*Sarajevo*] (YU)

OZenAD .... Separate Antiaircraft Artillery Battalion (RU)

OZenAP ... Separate Antiaircraft Artillery Regiment (RU)

OZEPA...... Oesterreichische Vereinigung der Zellstoff- und Papierchemiker und -Techniker [*Austrian Association of Wood Pulp and Paper Chemists and Technicians*] (SLS)

O Zers........ Ohne Zersetzung [*Without Decomposition*] [*German*] (GCA)

OZET........ All-Union Society for Land Settlement of Jewish Workers in the USSR (RU)

ozetl........... Ozetleyen [*Summarized, Abridged*] (TU)

OZG.......... Okregowe Zaklady Gastronomiczne [*District Catering Establishments*] [*Poland*]

OzgurHaber-Is ... Turkish Postal, Telegraph, Telephone, Radio, and Television Workers Union (TU)

ozh........... Liquid Trap (RU)

OZH .... Oglasni Zavod Hrvatske [*Advertising Institute of Croatia*] [*Zagreb*] (YU)

OZH .... Ogrodnicze Zaklady Handlowe [*Garden Produce Sales Establishments*] (POL)

OZH .... Ogrodnicze Zaklady Hodowlane [*Horticultural Establishments*] (POL)

OZH .... Zaporozh'ye [*Former USSR*] [*Airport symbol*] [*Obsolete*] (OAG)

ozhad......... Separate Railroad Artillery Battalion (RU)

ozhdrb .... Separate Railroad Repair Battalion (RU)

OZHS....... Odbytova Zakladna Hlavni Spravy [*Main Administration, Distribution Unit*] (CZ)

oz i............ Ozel Isim [*Proper Noun*] (TU)

OZIPS .... General Artisan and Trade Union (BU)

Oz-Is .... Ozgur Is Sendikalar Konfederasyonu [*Confederation of Free Trade Unions*] (TU)

Oz Is.......... Turkiye Ozgur Isci Sendikalari Konfederasyonu [*Confederation of Free Trade Unions*] (TU)

OZK.......... Obchodni a Zivnostenska Komora [*Chamber of Commerce*] (CZ)

OZK.......... Odborna Zavodna Kniznica [*Factory Technical Library*] (CZ)

OZK.......... Odborna Zavodni Knihovna [*Factory Technical Library*] (CZ)

OZK.......... Odborova Zavodni Knihovna [*Trade Union Factory Library*] (CZ)

OZK.......... Oddzialy Zaopatrzenia Kolejowego [*Railroad Supply Branches*] (POL)

OZK.......... Okregowy Zarzad Kin [*District Movie Theatre Administration*] (POL)

OZK.......... Okresni Zivnostenska Komise [*District Trade Commission*] (CZ)

OZKZ........ Okrajna Zveza Kmetijskih Zadrug [*District Union of Agricultural Cooperatives*] (YU)

OZL .... Plant Laboratory (RU)

Oz lit .... Australian Literature (ADA)

OZLP........ Okregowy Zarzad Lasow Panstwowych [*District Administration of State Forests*] (POL)

OZM.......... Fragmentation Barrier Mine (RU)

OZMIN...... Australian Mineral Deposits [*Database*]

OZMO....... Opoczynskie Zaklady Materialow Ogniotrwalych [*Opoczno Fireproof Material Plant*] (POL)

OZMR ...... Opci Zakon o Morskom Ribolovu [*General Law on Sea Fishing*] (YU)

OZN.......... Oboz Zjednoczenia Narodowego [*National Unity Camp*] [*Pre-World War II*] (POL)

OZN.......... Organizacija Zdruzenih Narodov [*United Nations Organization*] (YU)

OZNNS .... Organization for the Protection of the Population and the National Economy (BU)

OZNO .... Opsti Zakon o Narodnim Odborima [*General Law on People's Committees*] (YU)

OZO.......... Correspondence Training Department (RU)

OZO.......... Odbor Zasobovaci a Odbytovy [*Supply and Marketing Department*] (CZ)

OZOE........ Osnovni Zakon o Ekspropriaciji [*Basic Law on Expropriation*] (YU)

ozog........... Harassing Fire (BU)

OZON .... Oboz Zjednoczenia Ogolno-Narodowego [*National Unity Camp*] [*Pre-World War II*] (POL)

OZORD..... Opsti Zakon o Odnosima Roditelja i Dece [*General Law on Parent and Child Relations*]   (YU)
OZOS........ Olsztynskie Zaklady Opon Samochodowych [*Olsztyn Tire Plant*]   (POL)
OZP........... Oddeleni Zahranicni Pomoci [*Foreign Aid Department*]   (CZ)
OZP........... Odraz Zabezpeceni Pohybu [*March Security Detachment*]   (CZ)
OZP........... Oglas za Pomorce [*Notice to Mariners*] [*A periodical*]   (YU)
OZP........... Osnovni Zakon o Prekrsajima [*Basic Law on Misdemeanors*]   (YU)
OZPGR ..... Okregowy Zarzad Panstwowych Gospodarstw Rolnych [*District Administration of State Farms*]   (POL)
OZPO........ Ostrowieckie Zaklady Przemyslu Odziezowego [*Ostrowiec Clothing Factory*]   (POL)
OZPP......... Ogolnopolskie Zrzeszenie Prywatnego Przemyslu [*All-Polish Association of Private Industry*]   (POL)
OZPP......... Osnovni Zakon o Drzavnim Privrednim Preduzecima [*Basic Law on State Economic Establishments*]   (YU)
OZPPChSiR ... Ogolnopolskie Zrzeszenie Prywatnego Przemyslu Chemicznego, Spozywczego, i Roznych [*All-Polish Association of Private Chemical, Food, and Miscellaneous Industries*]   (POL)
OZPS........ General Agrarian Trade Union   (BU)
OZR........... Oddzial Zaopatrzenia Robotniczego [*Workers' Supply Branch*]   (POL)
OZR........... Osrodek Zaopatrzenia Robotniczego [*Workers' Supply Center*]   (POL)
OZRA........ Plant Protection Department   (RU)
OZS........... Flame and Incendiary Agent   (RU)
OZS........... Oddeleni Zahranicnich Styku [*Foreign Affairs Department*]   (CZ)
OZS........... Okresni Zdravotni Sprava [*District Health Administration*]   (CZ)
OZS........... Osnovni Zakon o Starateljstvu [*Basic Law on Guardianship*]   (YU)
OZT........... Fragmentation Incendiary Tracer   (RU)
OZT........... Office Zairois du Tourisme
OZTs......... Waiting on Cement   (RU)
OZU........... Internal Storage, Internal Memory   (RU)
OZU........... Internal Storage System [*Computer science*]   (BU)
OZU........... Land Improvement Department   (RU)
OZU........... Opci Zakon o Univerzitetima [*General Law on Universities*]   (YU)
OZV........... Determination of Air Contamination   (RU)
OZV........... Flame and Incendiary Agent   (RU)
OZVD........ Otrokovicko-Zlinsko-Vizovicka Draha [*Otrokovice-Zlin-Vizovice Railroad*]   (CZ)
OZZ........... Okregowe Zaklady Zbozowe [*District Grain Elevators*]   (POL)
OZZ........... Opsta Zemjodelska Zadruga [*General Agricultural Cooperative*]   (YU)
OZZ........... Ouarzazate [*Morocco*] [*Airport symbol*]   (OAG)
OZZZ........ Osnovni Zakon o Zemljoradnickim Zadrugama [*Basic Law on Agricultural Cooperatives*]   (YU)

P

P	Advanced, Forward, Leading	(RU)
P	Apiary [*Topography*]	(RU)
P	Bound [*Bibliography*]	(RU)
p	Bystreet, Lane, Alley	(RU)
p	Case [*Grammar*]	(RU)
P	Democratic People's Republic of Korea [*Aircraft nationality and registration mark*]	(FAAC)
P	De Pacht [*Benelux*]	(BAS)
P	De Position [*Said of a battery*] [*Military*] [*French*]	(MTD)
P	Diamond Pyramid [*Vickers hardness test*]	(RU)
p	First Lieutenant	(BU)
P	Fixed Light [*Nautical term*]	(RU)
p	Folder, File, Dossier	(BU)
p	Food	(RU)
P	For Desert Backgrounds [*Designation of camouflage materials*]	(RU)
P	Fruit	(RU)
P	Infantry	(RU)
P	Instrument, Device, Apparatus	(RU)
p	Interference, Noise	(RU)
p	Kraft [*Force*] [*German*]	(GCA)
P	Padre [*Father*] [*Portuguese*]	
P	Padre [*Father*] [*Spanish*]	
P	Padre [*Father*] [*Italian*]	
p	Page [*Page*] [*French*]	
p	Page	(EECI)
p	Pagina [*Page*] [*Portuguese*]	(GPO)
p	Pagina [*Page*] [*Spanish*]	
p	Pagina [*Page*] [*Italian*]	
p	Pagina [*Page*] [*Hungary*]	
p	Pagina [*Page*] [*Netherlands*]	
p	Pagina [*Page*] [*Afrikaans*]	
p	Pagina [*Page*] [*Danish/Norwegian*]	
p	Painos [*Finland*]	
p	Pair [*French*]	
p	Pair, Couple	(RU)
P	Paise [*Monetary unit*] [*India*]	
p	Paiva(a) [*Day, Date*] [*Finland*]	(GPO)
P	Palmo [*Span*] [*Portuguese*]	
P	Palsta [*Finland*]	
P	Pan [*or Pani*] [*Sir, Madam, Miss*] [*Poland*]	
P	Papa [*Pope*] [*Spanish*]	
P	Papa [*Phonetic alphabet*] [*International*]	(DSUE)
P	Papier [*Paper*] [*German*]	
P	Papier [*Paper*] [*French*]	
p	Par [*By, Per, Through, From*] [*French*]	
P	Para [*Monetary unit*] [*Former Yugoslavia*]	
p	Paragraph, Clause	(RU)
P	Parameter	(RU)
P	Parc (a Bestiaux) [*Peak, Cattle Pen*] [*Military map abbreviation World War I*] [*French*]	(MTD)
P	Parkirozo (Hely) [*Parking Place*]	(HU)
P	Parkplatz [*Parking Place*] [*German*]	
P	Parlophone [*Record label*] [*Great Britain, Italy, Australia, etc.*]	
P	Parthian [*Language, etc.*]	
p	Partij [*Benelux*]	(BAS)
P	Pasir [*Part of place name, i.e. Pasir Puteh*]	(ML)
P	Pastor [*Pastor*] [*German*]	
P	Patent [*Russian*]	(RU)
P	Patent [*German*]	(GCA)
p	Patrz [*See*]	(POL)
P	Pawn [*Chess*]	(RU)
P	Paye [*Paid*] [*French*]	
P	Pe [*Foot*] [*Portuguese*]	
P	Pelle [*Leather*] [*Publishing*] [*Italian*]	
P	Pence [*Portuguese*]	
P	Pengo [*Monetary unit in Hungary until 1946*]	
p	Penni(a) [*Penny or Pence*] [*Monetary unit*] [*Finland*]	(GPO)

p	Per [*For*] [*Italian*]	
p	Perc [*Minute*]	(HU)
P	Pere [*Father*] [*French*]	
p	Pergamena [*Vellum*] [*Publishing*] [*Italian*]	
P	Permanent Stay [*in hospital*] [*British*]	
P	Persian	(DLA)
P	Personenzuglokomotive [*Passenger Train Locomotive, Local Passenger Train Locomotive*]	(EG)
p	Persoona [*Person*] [*Finland*]	
P	Perth [*Mint mark*] [*Australia*]	
P	Peseta [*Monetary unit*] [*Spain and Latin America*]	
P	Pesewa [*Monetary unit*] [*Ghana*]	
P	Peso [*Monetary unit*] [*Spain and Latin America*]	
P	Peta	(ADPT)
P	Peter [*Phonetic alphabet*] [*World War II*]	(DSUE)
P	Petrograd	(RU)
P	Pharmacien [*Apothecary*] [*French*]	
P...	Philips Electrologica	(ADPT)
P	Phosphor [*Phosphorus*] [*Chemical element*] [*German*]	
P	Piaggio Rinaldo [*Industria Aeronautiche & Meccaniche SpA*] [*Italy*] [*ICAO aircraft manufacturer identifier*]	(ICAO)
P	Pianissimo [*Very Softly*] [*Music*]	
P	Piano [*Softly*] [*Music*]	
P	Piaster [*Monetary unit*] [*Spain, Republic of Vietnam, and some Middle Eastern countries*]	
p	Piazza [*Place*] [*Italian*]	(CED)
P	Pic [*Peak*] [*Military map abbreviation World War I*] [*French*]	(MTD)
p	Piece [*Piece*] [*French*]	
P	Pied [*Foot*] [*French*]	
P	Pieno [*Full*] [*Italian*]	
p	Pietro [*Floor, Story*]	(POL)
p	Pieze	(RU)
P	Pip [*Phonetic alphabet*] [*Pre-World War II*]	(DSUE)
P	Piyade [*Infantry*]	(TU)
p	Plotno [*Cloth Binding*] [*Publishing*] [*Poland*]	
P	Plowland, Plowed Field [*Topography*]	(RU)
p	Poids [*Weight*] [*French*]	
p	Point, Post	(RU)
P	Poise [*German*]	(GCA)
p	Poise [*Russian*]	(RU)
p	Pole	(RU)
P	Polka [*Music*]	
P	Pond [*Gram of Thrust*] [*Kp (Kilopond) and Mp (Megapond)*] [*See also*]	(HU)
p	Pondus [*Weight*] [*Latin*]	(MAE)
P	Pont [*Bridge*] [*Military map abbreviation World War I*] [*French*]	(MTD)
P	Por [*Portuguese*]	
P%	Por Ciento [*Per Cent*] [*Spanish*]	
p	Porownaj [*Compare*] [*Poland*]	
P	Port [*Malaysia*]	(ML)
P	Port [*French*]	(NAU)
P	Portugalia [*Portugal*] [*Poland*]	
P	Pouce [*Inch*] [*French*]	
p	Pouls [*Pulse*] [*French*]	
P	Pour [*For*] [*French*]	
P	Powder [*Pharmacy*]	(RU)
P	Pozorovatelna [*Observation Post*]	(CZ)
P	Praca [*Square*] [*Portuguese*]	
P	Pregunta [*Question*] [*Spanish*]	
p	Prenez [*Take*] [*Pharmacy*]	
P	Prepositional [*Case*]	(RU)
P	Presshart [*Hard as Extruded*] [*German*]	(GCA)
p	Pression [*Pressure*] [*French*]	
p	Prime [*First, Prime*] [*French*]	
P	Princeps [*First Edition*] [*French*]	
p	Pro [*Per*] [*German*]	(GCA)

P .... Produktion [*Production*]   (EG)
P .... Professional Qualification [*Finland*]
P .... Professional Qualification [*Indonesian*]
P .... Program Module [*Computers*]   (RU)
P .... Proportionnel   (ADPT)
P .... Proteste [*I Protest*] [*French*]
P .... Protet [*Protest*] [*French*]
p .... Proximum [*Near*] [*Latin*]   (MAE)
P .... Ptychion [*Greek*]
P .... Puaz [*Poise*] [*Poland*]
P .... Pudding [*Phonetic alphabet*] [*Royal Navy World War I*]   (DSUE)
p .... Puhelin [*Telephone*] [*Finland*]
p .... Puissance [*Power*] [*French*]
P .... Pulau [*Part of place name, i.e. Pulau Penang/Pinang Malaysia*]   (ML)
p .... Punkt [*Point*] [*Poland*]
p .... Punto [*Stitch*] [*Spanish*]
p .... Pya [*Monetary unit*] [*Myanmar*]
P .... Pyha [*Finland*]
P .... Receiver   (RU)
P .... Regiment   (RU)
p .... Right, Right-Hand   (RU)
P .... Route, Track [*Topography*]   (RU)
P .... Sand [*Topography*]   (RU)
p .... Schlackenziffer [*Slag Ratio*] [*German*]   (GCA)
P .... Settlement [*Topography*]   (RU)
P .... Splinterproof Structures [*Topography*]   (RU)
P .... Square [*Topography*]   (RU)
p .... Stabnuclear   (RU)
P .... Starter Button   (RU)
P .... Steam Locomotive   (RU)
P .... Subcaliber   (RU)
P .... Suburb [*Topography*]   (RU)
P .... Switch   (RU)
P .... Trailer   (RU)
p .... Train   (RU)
P1 .... Teknikum Ingenior [*Professional qualification*] [*Denmark*]
P2 .... Akademingenior [*Professional qualification*] [*Denmark*]
P2 .... Papua New Guinea [*Aircraft nationality and registration mark*]   (FAAC)
P-2 .... Propaganda Due [*Secret Italian Masonic organization, allegedly tied to the Roman Catholic church*]
P3 .... Civilingenior [*Professional qualification*] [*Denmark*]
P3TP .... Pusat Penelitian dan Pengembangan Tanaman Pangan [*Central Research Institute for Food Crops*] [*Indonesian*]   (ARC)
P4 .... Aruba [*Aircraft nationality and registration mark*]   (FAAC)
P4 .... Nurse, Midwife [*Professional qualification*] [*Denmark*]
P4 .... Pegawai Pengangkutan Pasokan Polis [*Police Force Transport Officer*]   (ML)
P4TM .... Pusat Penelitian and Pengembangan Perkebunan Tanjung Morawa [*Rubber Research Center Tanjung Morawa*] [*Indonesian*]   (ARC)
PA .... Address Delivery Pulse [*Computers*]   (RU)
PA .... Anatomical Forceps   (RU)
PA .... Antenna Strip   (RU)
PA .... Black Prismatic Powder [*Symbol*] [*French*]   (MTD)
PA .... Estado do Para [*State of Para*] [*Brazil*]
PA .... Field Airdrome   (RU)
PA .... Field Army   (BU)
PA .... Field Artillery   (RU)
PA .... Field Balloon   (RU)
PA .... Intermediate Equipment [*Computers*]   (RU)
PA .... Jurisprudence du Port d'Anvers [*Belgium*]   (FLAF)
pA .... Micromicro Ampere [*Micromicro Ampere (1/10¹² Amperes)*]   (EG)
PA .... Mobile Directional Antenna   (RU)
PA .... Pacte de Solidarite Sociale [*Pact of Social Solidarity*] [*Belgium*]   (WER)
PA .... Pacto Andino [*Andean Pact*] [*Use Andean Group*]   (LA)
pa .... Paino Arkki [*Printed Sheet*] [*Finland*]   (GPO)
PA .... Palermo [*Car registration plates*] [*Italian*]
PA .... Palestinian Authority [*Political movement*]   (ECON)
PA .... Panama [*ANSI two-letter standard code*]   (CNC)
PA .... Panama [*Poland*]
PA .... Pan American World Airways, Inc. [*See also PAA, PAN-AM, PN*] [*ICAO designator*]   (MCD)
pa .... Para [*For, Toward*] [*Spanish*]
pa .... Para [*For, To, Just*] [*Portuguese*]
PA .... Par Amitie [*By Favor*] [*French*]
PA .... Par Autorite [*By Authority*] [*French*]
PA .... Parc d'Artillerie [*Military*] [*French*]   (MTD)
PA .... Parizsky Archiv [*Paris Archives (of the Ministry of Foreign Affairs)*]   (CZ)
PA .... Parti de l'Action [*Party of Action*] [*Morocco*] [*Political party*]   (PPW)
PA .... Partido Andalucista [*Spain*] [*Political party*]   (ECED)

PA .... Partido Arnulfista [*Panama*] [*Political party*]   (EY)
PA .... Partido Autentico [*Authentic Party*] [*Argentina*]   (LA)
PA .... Patentanmeldung [*Patent Application*]   (EG)
PA .... People's Alliance [*Althydubandalag*] [*Iceland*] [*Political party*]   (PPW)
PA .... People's Assembly [*Egypt*]
PA .... Peoples Association [*Singapore*]   (DS)
pa .... Per Adres [*Care Of*] [*Netherlands*]   (GPO)
PA .... Per Adresse [*Care Of*] [*German*]
pa .... Per Annum   (EECI)
PA .... Per Auguri [*Used on visiting cards to express congratulations, birthday wishes, etc.*] [*Italian*]
PA .... Personal Assistant [*British*]
PA .... Perwira [*Officer*]   (IN)
PA .... Petroleumaether [*Petroleum Ether*] [*German*]
PA .... Philippine Army
PA .... Piaster [*Monetary unit*] [*Spain, Republic of Vietnam, and some Middle Eastern countries*]
PA .... Pipeline Authority [*Australia*]
PA .... Piper Aircraft Corp. [*ICAO aircraft manufacturer identifier*]   (ICAO)
PA .... Pistolet Automatique [*Automatic Pistol*]   (CL)
PA .... Plataformas Anti-Capitalistas [*Anti-Capitalist Platforms*] [*Spanish*]   (WER)
Pa .... Playa [*Beach*] [*Spanish*]   (NAU)
PA .... Politische Abteilung [*Political Department*]   (EG)
PA .... Polyaethylen [*Polyethylene*] [*German*]   (GCA)
PA .... Polyamide   (RU)
PA .... Por Ausencia [*Because of Absence*] [*Spanish*]
PA .... Por Autoridad [*By Authority*] [*Spanish*]
PA .... Por Autorizacion [*For Authorization*] [*Spanish*]
PA .... Port Authority [*Western Australia*]
pa .... Postal Address   (RU)
PA .... Postamt [*Post Office*]   (EG)
PA .... Poste Administratif
PA .... Pour Ampliation [*Certified Copy*] [*French*]
Pa .... Praia [*Beach*] [*Portuguese*]   (NAU)
PA .... Presence Africaine
Pa .... Prima [*First Class*] [*Business term*] [*German*]
PA .... Prirocnik za Agitacija [*Handbook for Agitators*] [*A periodical*]   (YU)
PA .... Programmgesteuerte Anforderung [*German*]   (ADPT)
PA .... Proletariaki Aristera [*See also Omada gia mia Proletariaki Aristera (OPA)*]   (GC)
PA .... Propaganda and Agitation   (BU)
PA .... Propriete Assuree [*Insured Property*] [*French*]
PA .... Propyl Acetate   (RU)
PA .... Prospecting Authority [*Australia*]
PA .... Protestant Alliance [*Australia*] [*Political party*]
PA .... Protivavionski [*Antiaircraft*]   (YU)
Pa .... Protoactinio [*Chemical element*] [*Portuguese*]
Pa .... Pruefungsamt [*Inspection Office*]   (EG)
PA .... Psoriasis Association [*Australia*]
PA .... Regimental Artillery   (BU)
PA .... Sand-Oil Blender Unit [*Pet.*]   (RU)
PA .... Straightforward Algorithm   (RU)
PA .... Transverse Reinforcement   (RU)
PAA .... Pa-An [*Myanmar*] [*Airport symbol*]   (OAG)
PAA .... Pan African Airlines
PAA .... Pan American World Airways, Inc. [*See also PA, PAN-AM, PN*]
PAA .... Pharmaceutical Association of Australia   (ADA)
PAA .... Philippine Automotive Association   (DS)
PAA .... Plywood Association of Australia   (ADA)
PAA .... Polocrosse Association of Australia
PAA .... Port Autonome d'Abidjan [*The Ivory Coast*]   (EY)
PAA .... Proprietary Association of Australia   (ADA)
PAA .... Protezione Antiaereo [*Italian*]
PAA .... Protivavionska Artiljerija [*Antiaircraft Artillery*]   (YU)
PAA .... Prueba de Aptitud Academica [*Spanish*]
PAAB .... Field Army Air Base   (RU)
PAABS ..... Pan American Association of Biochemical Societies [*Venezuela*] [*ICSU*]
PAAECI .... Pan American Association of Educational Credit Institutions [*See also APICE*]   (EAIO)
PAAFL ..... Pan-African Air Freight Lines
PAAG .... Protivavionska Artiljeriska Grupa [*Antiaircraft Artillery Group*]   (YU)
PAANS...... Pan African Association of Neurological Sciences   (EAIO)
PAANSW ... Prisoners' Aid Association of New South Wales [*Australia*]
PAAORLBE ... Pan-American Association of Oto-Rhino-Laryngology and Broncho-Esophagology [*Mexico City, Mexico*]   (EAIO)
PAAP .... Public Accountants and Auditors Board [*South Africa*]   (PDAA)
paar .... Antiaircraft Artillery   (BU)
paarr.......... Army Mobile Ordnance Repair Depot   (BU)
PAAS...... Army Field Ammunition Depot   (RU)
PAAS........ Field Army Artillery Depot   (BU)

PAAS........ Polish Amateur Astronomical Society (EAIO)
PAASCU ... Philippine Accrediting Association of Schools, Colleges, and Universities
PAASOK... Pankyprion Agrotikon Koinoniko-Dimokratikon Komma [*Pan-Cyprian Agrarian Social-Democratic Party*] (GC)
paav............ Paaverbi [*Principial Verb*] [*Finland*]
PAAWA .... Pakistan Australia Association of Western Australia
PAAWA .... Progressive Axemen's Association of Western Australia
PAB .... Advanced Army Base (RU)
PAB .... Aerial Practice Bomb (RU)
PAB .... Gun Artillery Battery (RU)
PAB .... Mobile Army Base (RU)
PAB .... Parti des Paysans, Artisans, et Bourgeois [*Farmers', Artisans', and Burghers' Party*] [*Switzerland*] [*Political party*] (PPE)
PAB .... Performing Arts Board [*Australia Council*]
PAB .... Periscopic Aiming Circle [*Artillery*] (RU)
PAB .... Periskopska Artiljeriska Busola [*Periscopic Artillery Compass*] (YU)
PAB .... Planning Appeals Board [*Australia*]
PAB .... Plumbing Advisory Board [*South Australia*]
PAB .... Police Appeal Board [*South Australia*]
PAB .... Posto Agrario de Braga [*Portugal*] (DSCA)
PAB .... Poultry Advisory Board [*Queensland, Australia*]
PAB .... Promotions Appeal Board [*Victoria, Australia*]
PAB .... Semiautomatic Block System [*Railroads*] (RU)
PABAN...... Perwira Bantuan [*Officer Support Group*] (ML)
PABC........ Pan American Basketball Confederation [*See also CPB*] (EAIO)
PABEE ...... Proyecto Americano-Brasileno Ensino Elementar [*American-Brazilian Project for Training of Elementary Teachers*] (LAA)
PABEKO... Parti de l'Alliance des Bena-Koshi
PABFSA.... Pediatric Association of Black French-Speaking Africa (EAIO)
PABISA..... Party Bisamah' Sarawak (ML)
PABK........ Pan-American Coffee Bureau [*PACB*] (RU)
PABK........ Para-Aminobenzoic Acid (RU)
Pable .... Payable [*French*]
PABLI .... Pages Bleues Informatisees [*Commission of the European Communities*] [*Information service or system*] (CRD)
PABM........ Persatuan Asrama Belia Malaysia (EAIO)
PABMA..... Philippine Association of Battery Manufacturers, Inc. (DS)
PAB-PTC .. Promotion Appeal Board, Postal and Telecommunications Commission [*Australia*]
PAB(Q)...... Poultry Advisory Board (Queensland) [*Australia*]
PABR......... Gun Artillery Brigade (RU)
PAB(Tas)... Planning Appeals Board (Tasmania) [*Australia*]
PABX........ Private Automatic Branch Exchange
Pac .... Pacific [*Record label*] [*France*]
PAC .... Pacific Ocean
PAC .... Pacto de Alianza de Centro [*Chile*] [*Political party*] (EY)
PAC .... Pan-Africanist Congress [*South Africa*]
PAC .... Panama City [*Panama*] Paitilla Airport [*Airport symbol*] (OAG)
PAC .... Partido Accion Constitucional [*Constitutional Action Party*] [*Dominican Republic*] (LA)
PAC .... Partido Accion Cristiana [*Christian Action Party*]
PAC .... Partido Autentico Constitucional [*Authentic Constitutional Party*] [*El Salvador*] [*Political party*]
PAC .... Partido de Accion y Cambio [*Action and Change Party*] [*Costa Rica*] (LA)
PAC .... Patrulla Aerea Civil [*Colombia*] (COL)
PAC .... People's Army Congress
PAC .... Pesticides Advisory Committee [*Tasmania, Australia*]
PAC .... Piccole Apostole della Carita [*Italy*] (EAIO)
PAC .... Planning Advisory Council
PAC .... Poisons Advisory Committee [*Australia*]
PAC .... Politique Agricole Commune
PAC .... Pomocna Armadni Cesta [*Secondary Army Route*] (CZ)
PAC .... Port Autonome de Conakry [*Independent Port of Conakry*] [*Guinea*]
PAC .... Positive Action Campaign
PAC .... Preservation and Conservation Regional Office [*Australia*]
PAC .... Productivity Advisory Council
PAC .... Professional Advisory Committee [*South African Council for Professional Engineers*] (AA)
PAC .... Programa de Acao Concentrada [*Concentrated Action Program*] [*Brazil*] (LA)
PAC .... Programme Activity Center [*Advisory Committee on Pollution of the Sea*]
PAC .... Programme d'Action Commerciale
PAC .... Programme d'Application Courante [*French*] (ADPT)
PAC .... Prudential Assurance Co. Ltd. [*Australia*]
PAC .... Public Access Catalogue [*Australia*]
PAC .... Public Accounts Committee [*Mauritius*] (AF)
PAC .... Public Authority Contribution [*Australia*]
PAC .... Pulk Artylerii Ciezkiej
PACA........ Packard Automobile Club of Australia
PACA........ Pan-Africanist Congress of Azania [*South Africa*]

PACA......... Pastificio Ambato CA [*Ecuador*] (DSCA)
PACA........ Proyecto Ambiental para Centro America [*Environmental Project for Central America*] [*Spanish*] (ECON)
PACAust.... Packard Automobile Club of Australia
PACB........ Pan American Coffee Bureau [*New York*] (LAA)
PACB........ Poppy Advisory and Control Board [*Tasmania, Australia*]
PACB........ Portuguese Administrative Council of the Cahora Basa
PACCAL ... Petroleum and Chemicals Corporation (Australia) Limited (ADA)
PACCIOS ... Pan American Council of International Committee of Scientific Management
PACCOM ... Pacific Communications Network [*Computer science*] (TNIG)
PACE......... Committee for Promotion and Action in Community Education [*Australia*]
PACE......... Pan Arab Consulting Engineers [*Kuwait*]
PACE......... People against Child Exploitation [*Australia*]
PACE......... Planetary Association for Clean Energy (EA)
PACE......... Programme of Advanced Continuing Education [*Europe*]
PACE......... Promoting Aphasics Communicative Effectiveness [*Australia*]
PACE......... Publishers' Association for Cultural Exchange [*Japan*] (EAIO)
PACEC....... Pan-African Catholic Education Conference
PACGSR ... Pan American Center for Geographical Studies and Research [*See also CEPEIGE*] (EAIO)
PACIWU... Philippine Agricultural, Commercial, and Industrial Workers' Union (EY)
PACKFORSK ... Svenska Forpackningsforskningsinstitutet [*Swedish Packaging Research Institute*] [*Research center*] (IRC)
PACL........ Profound Assurance Co. Ltd. [*Nigeria*]
PACLA ..... Pan African Christian Leadership Assembly
PacO .... Pacific Ocean
PACO .... Pakistan Automobile Corp. (FEA)
PACO .... Peak Aboriginal Community Organisation [*Australia*]
PACOFS ... Performing Arts Council of the Orange Free State
PACOM .... Pacific Communications Group
PACOREDO ... Partido Comunista de la Republica Dominicana [*PCRD*] [*Communist Party of the Dominican Republic*] [*Also,*] (LA)
PACRA...... New Zealand Pottery and Ceramics Research Association (SLS)
PACREP... Pan African Centre for Research on Peace, Development, and Human Rights [*Nigeria*]
PACRIM ... Pacific Rim
PACSA...... Packaging Council of South Africa (AA)
PAC-SA .... Pan-Africanist Congress of South Africa (AF)
PACT........ Pacific Area Co-Operative Telecommunications [*Australia*]
PACT........ Parents Assist Children and Teachers [*Australia*]
PACT........ Performing Arts Council for the Transvaal
PACT........ Permaculture Australian Capital Territory
PACT........ Philippine Association of Chemistry Teachers (EAIO)
PACT........ Private Agencies Collaborating Together, Inc.
PACT........ Producers', Authors', Composers', and Talents' Cooperative Ltd. [*Australia*] (ADA)
PACT........ Professional Association of Classroom Teachers of the Australian Capital Territory
PACT........ Protect All Children Today [*Australia*]
PACT........ Publicly Accountable Classroom Teaching [*Australia*]
PACTEE.... Pakistan Christian Theological Education by Extension
PACTIV .... Principos Activos [*Ministerio de Sanidad y Consumo*] [*Spain*] [*Information service or system*] (CRD)
PACTS ...... Public Access Cordless Telephone Service [*Australia*]
PACTT ...... Planning the Australian Capital Territory Together
PACWID... Presidential Action Committee on Wood Industry Development [*Philippines*] (DS)
pad .... Case [*Grammar*] (RU)
PAD .... Gun Artillery Division (RU)
PAD .... Pacific Australia Direct
PAD .... Paderborn [*Germany*] [*Airport symbol*] (OAG)
PAD .... Partido Accion Democratica [*Democratic Action Party*] [*El Salvador*] [*Political party*] (PPW)
PAD .... Partido Autentico Democratico [*Authentic Democratic Party*] [*Guatemala*] (LA)
PAD .... Partido de Accion Democrata [*Democratic Action Party*] [*Spain*] [*Political party*] (PPW)
PAD .... Pedagogischer Austauschdienst [*Pedagogical Exchange Service*] [*German*]
PAD .... Port Autonome de Dakar [*Senegal*] (EY)
PAD .... Prime d'Adaptation Industrielle [*France*] (FLAF)
PAD .... Programmierbares Analog-und Digitalpruefsystem [*German*] (ADPT)
pad .... Ravine [*Topography*] (RU)
PAD .... Solid-Propellant Generator, Solid-Reactant Gas Generator (RU)
PADA .... Partico de Accion Democratica Anticomunista [*Anticommunist Democratic Action Party*] (LA)
PADAK ..... Papeterie Dakaroise SA
PADAP..... Philippine-Australian Development Assistance Program (ADA)

PADASA ... Pazarlama Dagitim ve Satis Ltd. Sti. [*Marketing, Distribution, and Sales Ltd. Corp.*] (TU)
PADC .... Philippine Aerospace Development Corp. (DS)
PADC .... Piccole Apostole della Carita [*Ponte Lambro, Italy*] (EAIO)
PADELPA ... Papeles del Pacifico Ltda. [*Colombia*] (COL)
PADENA ... Parti Democrate National [*National Democratic Party*]
PADENA ... Partido Democratico Nacional [*National Democratic Party*] [*Chile*] (LA)
PADEPA ... Papelera del Pacifico, SA [*Pacific Paper, Inc.*] [*Chile*] (LA)
PADES ...... Programa de Accion del Desarrollo Economico y Social [*Socioeconomic Development Action Program*] [*Bolivia*] (LA)
PADESM .. Parti des Desherites de Madagascar [*Party of the Deprived of Madagascar*] (AF)
PADI .... Parti pour l'Avancement de la Democratie en Ituri [*Party for Democratic Advancement in Ituri*] [*Political party*]
PADIK ...... Pankyprion Dimokratikon Kinima [*Pan-Cyprian Democratic Movement*] (GC)
Padin .... Partido de Integracion Nacional [*National Integration Party*] [*Peru*] [*Political party*] (PPW)
PADIS .... Pan-African Documentation and Information System [*Economic Commission for Africa*] [*United Nations*] (IID)
PADMU .... Pakistan Desertification Monitoring Unit [*Research center*] (IRC)
padn .... Gun Artillery Battalion (RU)
PADO .... Antiairborne Defense (RU)
PADOG ..... Plan d'Amenagement et d'Organisation
PADOG ..... Plan d'Amenagement et d'Organisation Generale de la Region Parisienne [*France*] (FLAF)
PADP .... Partido Accion Democratico Popular [*Popular Democratic Action Party*] [*Costa Rica*] (LA)
PADP .... Program of Aids for Disabled People [*Australia*]
PADPM ...... Pan-African Democratic Party of Malawi (AF)
PAdr .... Per Adresse [*Care Of*] (EG)
PADRES ... Padres Asociados para Derechos, Religiosos, Educativos, y Sociales [*Organization of Mexican-American priests*]
PADS .... People Against Dioxins in Sanitary Products [*An association*] [*Australia*]
PAE .... Paisajes Espanoles SA [*Spain*] [*ICAO designator*] (FAAC)
PAE .... Panellinios Aktoploiki Enosis [*Panhellenic Coastal Shipping Union*] (GC)
PAE .... Parataxis Agroton kai Ergazomenon [*Agrarian and Labor Faction*] [*Greek*] (GC)
PAE .... Preduzece za Automatizaciju i Elektroniku [*Establishment for Automation and Electronics*] (YU)
PAE .... Pret A Emettre [*Ready to Emit*] [*French*] (ADPT)
PAE .... Projets pour une Agriculture Ecologique [*Ecological Agriculture Projects - EAP*] [*Sainte Anne De Bellevue, PQ*] (EAIO)
PAEAC ...... Parliamentary Association for Euro-Arab Cooperation (EA)
PAEB .... Professional Accreditation and Education Board [*Australia*]
PAEC .... Pakistan Atomic Energy Commission (NRCH)
PAEC .... Philippines Atomic Energy Commission
PAECI .... Pan American Association of Educational Credit Institutions [*Bogota, Colombia*] (EAIO)
PAEEK ...... Podosfairiki Athlitiki Enosi Eparkhias Kyrineias [*Kyrenia District Athletic Soccer Union*] (GC)
PAEGAE ... Pronomioukhos Anonymos Etaireia Genikon Apothikon Ellados [*Chartered General Warehouses Joint Stock Company of Greece*] (GC)
PAEN .... Programa de Alimentacion y Educacion Nutricional [*Paraguay*] (DSCA)
paepstl ...... Paepstlich [*Papal*] [*German*]
PAF .... Mobile Photographic Laboratory (RU)
PAF .... Pakistan Air Force (PDAA)
PAF .... Panaf Airways Ltd. [*Gambia*] [*ICAO designator*] (FAAC)
PAF .... Pan-African Federation
PAF .... Pan-African Festival
PAF .... Permanent Air Force [*Australia*]
PAF .... Philippine Air Force
PAF .... Police de l'Air et des Frontieres [*Air and Frontier Police*] [*French*] (WER)
PAF .... Polyazophenylene (RU)
PAF .... Premature Anti-Fascist [*World War II designation used by Army Counterintelligence Department*]
PAF .... Prosjekt Alternativ Framtid [*Norway*] (EAIO)
PAF .... Puissance au Frein [*Brake Horse Power*] [*French*]
PAF .... Semiautomatic Apparatus for Packaging Lozenges (RU)
PAFA .... Pakistan Australia Friendship Association [*Australia*]
PAFA .... Philippine Australian Friendship Association
PAFAMS ... Pan American Federation of Associations of Medical Schools [*See also FEPAFEM*] [*Caracas, Venezuela*] (EAIO)
PAFATU ... Pan-African Federation of Agricultural Trade Unions (EA)
Pafawag ..... Panstwowa Fabryka Wagonow [*State Railroad Car Factory*] (POL)
PAFES .... Pan American Federation of Engineering Societies
PAFFWA ... Parents and Friends Federation of Western Australia

PAFIE .... Pacific Asian Federation of Industrial Engineering [*India*] (PDAA)
PAFLU ...... Philippine Association of Free Labor Unions
PAFMECA ... Pan-African Freedom Movement for East and Central Africa
PAFMECSA ... Pan African Freedom Movement for East, Central, and Southern Africa [*Superseded in 1963 by the liberation committee of the Organization of African Unity*] (PD)
PAFMI ...... Philippine Association of Feed [*or Flour*] Millers, Inc. (DS)
PAFNA ...... Pan-African News Agency (AF)
PAFT .... Pan-American Federation of Labor (RU)
pag .... Diving Gyro Horizon (RU)
PAG .... Gyro Horizon Converter (RU)
PAG .... I Pagliacci [*Opera*] (DSUE)
PAG .... Pagadian [*Philippines*] [*Airport symbol*] (OAG)
pag .... Pagina [*Page*] [*Italian*]
pag .... Pagina [*Page*] [*Spanish*]
pag .... Pagina [*Page*] [*Portuguese*]
pag .... Paginering [*Pagination*] [*Publishing Danish/Norwegian*]
Pag .... Paginierung [*Pagination*] [*Publishing*] [*German*]
pag .... Paginiran [*Paginated*] (YU)
PAG .... Panstwowy Arbitraz Gospodarczy [*State Office for Economic Arbitration*] (POL)
PAG .... Para-Aminohippuric Acid (RU)
PAG .... Party for the Autonomy of Gibraltar [*Political party*] (PPW)
PAG .... Prince Alfred's Guard
PAG .... Property Advisory Group [*British*] (DCTA)
PAG .... Protein Advisory Group [*United Nations*]
PAG .... Protivavionska Grupa [*Antiaircraft Group*] (YU)
PAG .... Pukovska Artiljeriska Grupa [*Regimental Artillery Group*] (YU)
PAG .... Regimental Artillery Group (RU)
PAGA .... Pan American Grace Airways, Inc. [*Also, PANAGRA*]
PAGART ... Polska Agencja Artystyczna [*Polish Art Agency*] (POL)
PAGASA ... Philippine Atmospheric, Geophysical and Astronomical Services Administration (PDAA)
pagdo .... Pagadero [*Payable*] [*Business term*] [*Spanish*]
PAGE .... Publish Australia Group Enterprise
Paged .... Polska Agencja Drzewna [*Polish Lumber Agency*] (POL)
PAGED ...... Polska Agencja Eksportu Drewna [*Polish Agency for the Export of Timber*] [*Poland*]
PAGENA ... Papeterie Generale de l'Afrique Occidentale
PAGENA ... Participation Generale Africaine
PAGENACI ... Participation Generale Africaine de la Cote-D'Ivoire
pagg .... Pagine [*Pages*] [*Italian*]
PAGI .... Photographic and Gelatin Industries [*Japan*]
PAGOR ...... Pailhoux et G. Goret [*R.*]
PAGRAL ... Proveedora Agroindustrial [*Colombia*] (COL)
pags .... Paginas [*Pages*] [*Spanish*]
pags .... Paginas [*Pages*] [*Portuguese*]
PAGS .... Parti de l'Avant-Garde Socialiste [*Socialist Vanguard Party*] [*Algeria*] [*Political party*] (PD)
PAGV .... Proefstation voor de Akkerbouw en de Groenteelt in de Vollegrond [*Arable Farming and Field Production of Vegetables Research Station*] [*Netherlands*] (ARC)
PAH .... Prince Alfred Hospital [*Australia*]
PAH .... Princess Alexandra Hospital [*Australia*]
PAHF .... Pan American Hockey Federation [*Winnipeg, MB*] (EAIO)
PAHR .... Permanent Assembly for Human Rights [*Argentina*] (EAIO)
PAHUB ..... Perwira Perhubungan [*Communications Officer*] (IN)
PAI .... Paideuma
PAI .... Panama Airways, Inc.
PAI .... Parti Africain de l'Independance [*African Independence Party*] [*Burkina Faso*] (AF)
PAI .... Parti Africain de l'Independance [*African Independence Party*] [*Senegal*] [*Political party*] (PPW)
PAI .... Partido Africano da Independencia da Guine Dita Portuguesa
PAI .... Partido Aragones Independiente [*Spain*] [*Political party*] (EY)
PAI .... People for Australian Independence (ADA)
PAI .... Plan de Accion Inmediata [*Plan for Immediate Action*] [*Peru*] (LA)
PAI .... Poale Agudat Israel (EAIO)
PAI .... Portable Aerosol Inhalator (RU)
PAI .... Port Adelaide Institute [*Australia*] (ADA)
PAI .... Property Agents International
PAIC .... Persia and Iraq Command [*World War II*]
PAIC .... Primary and Allied Industries Council [*Australia*]
PAICV ...... Parti Africain de l'Independance du Cap-Vert [*African Party for the Independence of Cape Verde*]
PAICV ...... Partido Africano da Independencia de Cabo Verde [*African Party for the Independence of Cape Verde*]
PAID .... Pan-African Institute for Development [*Geneva, Switzerland*]
PAIF .... Persia and Iraq Force [*World War II*]
PAIF .... Peter-Argo International Forwarders [*Greece*] [*Commercial firm*]
PAIGC .... Partido Africano da Independencia da Guine e do Cabo Verde [*African Party for the Independence of Guinea and Cape Verde*] [*Political party*] (PPW)

PAIGH ...... Pan American Institute of Geography and History [*Research center*] [*Mexico*]   (IRC)
PA IILTsK KPU ... Party Archives of the Institute of the History of the Party of the Central Committee of the Communist Party of the Ukraine   (RU)
paik .... Paikasta [*About a Place*] [*Finland*]
PAIM........ Parti Africain pour l'Independance des Masses [*African Party for the Independence of the Masses*] [*Senegal*] [*Political party*] (PPW)
PAIMEG ... Pan American Institute of Mining, Engineering, and Geology [*Defunct*]
Pain............ Prochain [*Next, Nearest*] [*French*]
paini .... Painissa [*Wrestling*] [*Finland*]
painoll .... Painollisena [*Stressed, Accented*] [*Finland*]
painott....... Painottomana [*Unaccented*] [*Finland*]
PAINT....... Primera Asociacion Internacional de Noticieros y Television [*First International Newsreel and TV Association*]
PAIP .... Parti Africain pour l'Independance du Peuple [*Senegal*]
PAIS .... Partido Amplio de Izquierda Socialista [*Chile*] [*Political party*] (EY)
PAIS .... Partido Autentico Institucional Salvadoreno [*Salvadoran Authentic Institutional Party*] [*Political party*]   (PPW)
PAIS .... Public Affairs Information Service
PAISA ...... Partido Autentico Institucional Salvadoreno [*Salvadoran Authentic Institutional Party*] [*Political party*]   (EY)
PAJ .... Press Association of Jamaica   (EY)
PAJ .... Protivavionska Odbrana Jedinice [*Antiaircraft Defense Units*] (YU)
PAJAR ...... Parti Rakyat Jati Sarawak [*Sarawak Native People's Party*] [*Malaysia*] [*Political party*]   (PPW)
PAJES...... Parents of Adult Jewish Singles
PAJG .... Procurement Agency of the Japanese Government
PAJU........ Pan-African Journalists Union   (AF)
PAK .... Industrial-Agrarian Complex   (BU)
PAK .... Paidagogiki Akadimia Kyprou [*Pedagogic Academy of Cyprus*] (GC)
pak .... Paketti [*Finland*]
PAK .... Pakistan [*Poland*]
PAK .... Pakistan [*ANSI three-letter standard code*]   (CNC)
PAK .... Panafrikanskii Kongress
PAK .... Panellinion Apelevtherotikon Kinima [*Panhellenic Liberation Movement*]   (GC)
PAK .... Pankyprio Andistasiako Kinima [*Pan-Cyprian Resistance Movement*]   (GC)
PAK .... Panzerabwehrkanone [*Antitank Gun*]   (EG)
PAK .... Panzer Abwehr Kanone [*Cannon Against Armor*] [*German antitank gun*]
PAK .... Pomiary - Automatyka - Kontrola [*Measurements - Automation - Control*] [*A monthlyperiodical*]   (POL)
PAK .... Projet Agricole de Kibuye
PAK .... Transfer of Instruction Address [*Computers*]   (RU)
PAKh .... Motorized Field Bakery   (BU)
PAKh .... Passenger Automobile Transportation Establishment   (RU)
PAKOE...... Panellinion Kendron Oikologikon Erevnon [*Panhellenic Center of Ecological Research*]   (GC)
PAKOMATIC ... Empacomatic de Colombia Ltda. [*Barranquilla*]   (COL)
PA KPE ..... Party Archives of the Central Committee of the Communist Party of Estonia   (RU)
PAKTAS ... Pamuk Ticaret ve Sanayi Anonim Sirketi [*Cotton Trade and Industry Corporation*]   (TU)
PAKuybobl ... Party Archives of the Kuybyshev Oblast   (RU)
Pal............. Chamber   (RU)
PAL........... Laboratory of Pathological Anatomy   (RU)
pal .... Palavra [*Word, Speech*] [*Portuguese*]
pal .... Palazzo [*Palace*] [*Italian*]   (CED)
PAL........... Parc d'Artillerie Lourde [*Military*] [*French*]   (MTD)
PAL........... Partido Agrario Laborista [*Chile*]   (LAA)
PAL........... Phase Alternation Line [*West German color television system*]
PAL........... Philippine Air Lines
PAL........... Philippine Air Lines, Inc. [*ICAO designator*]   (FAAC)
PAL........... Placi Aglomerate din Lemn [*Chipboard*]   (RO)
PAL........... Polska Akademia Literatury [*Polish Academy of Literature*] [*Pre-World War II*]   (POL)
PAL........... Polska Armia Ludowa [*Polish People's Army (1943-1944)*] [*Poland*]
PAL........... Polynesian Airlines Limited
PAL........... Pomocny Prumysl Automobilni a Letecky [*Instrument and Accessory Industry for Aircraft and Automobiles*]   (CZ)
PAL........... Portable Ambush Light [*Military*] [*Australia*]
PAL........... Povrchove Aktivni Latky [*Surface Active Agents (Oils)*]   (CZ)
PAL........... Progressive Alliance of Liberia [*Political party*]   (PPW)
PAL........... Transfer Machine Line   (RU)
Pala .... Partido Laborista [*Labor Party*] [*Panama*] [*Political party*] (PPW)
PALAD...... Peralatan Angkatan Darat [*Army Ordnance*]   (IN)
PALAPA ... Indonesian satellite
PALEA ...... Philippine Air Lines Employees' Association

Paleogr....... Paleografia [*Paleography*] [*Portuguese*]
paleol.......... Paleolithic   (RU)
paleon........ Paleontology   (RU)
Paleont....... Paleontologia [*Paleontology*] [*Portuguese*]
paleont .... Paleontology, Paleontological   (BU)
PALF .... Pyridoxal Phosphate   (RU)
PALGA...... Pathologisch-Anatomisch Landelijk Geautomatiseerd Archief [*Netherlands*]
Pali............ Partido Liberal [*Nicaragua*] [*Political party*]   (EY)
PALIKA .... Parti de Liberation Kanak [*New Caledonia*] [*Political party*] (EY)
PALM....... People's Action Labor Movement [*Grenada*]   (LA)
PALMC..... Philippine Airlines Mountaineering Club   (EAIO)
PALMEVEAS ... Palmiers et Heveas du Gabon
PALMITEX ... Industrias Textiles de Palmira   (COL)
PALMO .... Panellinios Organosis Laikis Symbarastaseos [*Panhellenic Organization of Popular Support*]   (GC)
Palms .... Paulian Association Lay Missionary Secretariat [*Australia*]
PALP .... Palebne Postaveni [*Firing Position*]   (CZ)
PALR .... Panzerabwehrlenkrakete [*Antitank Guided Rocket*]   (EG)
Pals .... Palais [*Palace*] [*Military map abbreviation World War I*] [*French*]   (MTD)
Pals .... Palheiros [*Fishing Village*] [*Portuguese*]   (NAU)
PALS .... People Against Lenient Sentences [*An association*] [*Australia*]
PALS .... Perth Automated Library Services [*Computer software*] [*Australia*]
PALSA ...... Philippine Air Lines Supervisors' Association
PALSS....... Physical and Life Sciences Society
PALU........ Parti Lumumbiste de l'Unite
PALU........ Progressive Arbeiders- en Landbouwersunie [*Progressive Workers' and Farm Laborers' Union*] [*Surinam*] [*Political party*]   (PPW)
PalvJust..... Het Paleis van Justitie [*Benelux*]   (BAS)
Pam .... Field Air Maintenance Shop   (RU)
PAM .... Mobile Air Maintenance Shop   (RU)
PAM .... Mobile Artillery Shop   (RU)
Pam .... Monument [*Topography*]   (RU)
PAM .... Pacto de Ayuda Mutua [*Mutual Aid Agreement*]   (LAA)
PAM .... Palestine Archaeological Museum [*Jerusalem*]   (BJA)
Pam .... Pampa [*Record label*] [*Brazil*]
PAM .... Panafricaine des Metaux
PAM .... Patriotikon Antidiktatorikon Metopon [*Patriotic Antidictatorial Front*] [*Greek*]   (GC)
PAM .... Patriotikon Apelevtherotikon Metopon [*Patriotic Liberation Front*] [*Greek*]   (GC)
PAM .... People's Action Movement [*Nevis*] [*Political party*]   (PPW)
PAM .... Periodistas Asociados de Manizales   (COL)
PAM .... Phoenicia Arab Hotel Management [*Saudi Arabia*]
PAM .... Phoenix Air Service GmbH [*Germany*] [*ICAO designator*] (FAAC)
PAM .... Pokrajinski Arhiv v Mariboru [*Provincial Archives in Maribor*] (YU)
PAM .... Pomorska Akademia Medyczna [*Pomeranian Medical Academy*] (POL)
PaM .... Prace a Mzdy [*Work and Wages*]   (CZ)
PAM .... Premier Acte Medical en Assurance Sociale-Maladie [*France*] (FLAF)
PAM .... Primary Association for Mathematics [*Australia*]
PAM .... Prioritaetsausgabemeldung [*German*]   (ADPT)
PAM .... Programme Alimentaire Mondial [*World Food Program*] [*Use WFP*]   (AF)
PAM .... Protivatomska Maska [*Antiatomic Mask*]   (YU)
PAM .... Protivavionski Mitraljez [*Antiaircraft Machine Gun*]   (YU)
PAM .... Puls-Amplituden Modulationsverfahren [*German*]   (ADPT)
PAM .... Regimental Artillery Shop   (RU)
PAMA ...... Perwira Pertama [*Junior Officer (Lieutenant to captain)*]   (IN)
PAME....... Pandemokratiki Agrotikon Metapon Ellados [*Pan-Democratic Agrarian Front of Greece*] [*Political party*]   (PPE)
PAME....... Pankyprion Ananeotikon Metopon [*Pan-Cyprian Renewal Front*]   (GC)
PAME....... Portuguese Association of Music Education   (EAIO)
PAMEN ... Perwira Menengah [*Field Grade Officer (Major to colonel)*]   (IN)
PAMF........ Pyridoxamine Phosphate   (RU)
PAMI........ Plan de Asistencia Medica Integral [*Comprehensive Medical Assistance Plan*] [*Argentina*]   (LA)
PAMI........ Pontificia Accademia Mariana Internazionalis [*Italian*]   (SLS)
PAMID...... Centrul de Calcul si Lucrari Auxiliare si Rare [*Center for Computation and Auxiliary and Rare Projects*]   (RO)
PAMIL...... Imo State Palm Industrial
PAMK .... Panellinia Agonistiki Mathitiki Kinisi [*Panhellenic Militant Student Movement*]   (GC)
PAMMD ... Public Administration, Manpower, and Management Division
PAMOL .... Plantations Pamol du Cameroun Ltd.
PAMP....... Pampero [*River Plate gale*] [*Nautical term*]   (DSUE)

PAMP........ Programa de Aperfeicoamento do Magisterio Primario [*Training Program for Primary School Teachers*] [*Rio De Janeiro, Brazil*] (LAA)
PAMS........ Army Field Medical Depot (RU)
PAMS........ Mobile Artillery Weather Station (RU)
PAMS........ Pacific Advanced Media Studies [*Australia*]
PAMSCAD ... Programme of Action for the Mitigation of the Social Consequences of the Adjustment for Development [*Ghana*]
PAMSS ..... Army Field Medical Depot (RU)
PAMTEKS ... Pamukkale Tekstil Sanayi ve Ticaret AS [*Pamukkale Textile Industry and Trade Corp.*] (TU)
PAMTS ..... Semiautomatic Long-Distance Telephone Communication (RU)
PAN........... Automatic Aiming Device [*Artillery*] (RU)
PAN........... Industrial-Agrarian Trust (BU)
PAN........... National Action Party [*Mexico*] [*Political party*] (PD)
PAN........... Panama [*ANSI three-letter standard code*] (CNC)
PAN........... Panitia [*Committee*] (IN)
Pan........... Pantheon [*Record label*] [*France, etc.*]
PAN........... Partido Agrario Nacional [*National Agrarian Party*] [*Bolivia*] (LA)
PAN........... Partido de Accion Nacional [*National Action Party*] [*Spanish*] (WER)
PAN........... Partido de Accion Nacional [*Nicaragua*] [*Political party*] (EY)
PAN........... Partiia Alzhirskovo Naroda
PAN........... Pattani [*Thailand*] [*Airport symbol*] (OAG)
PAN........... Pediatric Association of Nigeria (EAIO)
PAN........... Pesticides Action Network (EA)
PAN........... Peugeot Automobile of Nigeria
PAN........... Polska Akademia Nauk [*Polish Academy of Sciences*] [*Also, an information service or system*] (IID)
PAN........... Porte-Avion Nucleaire [*French*]
PAN........... Programa Alimentario Nacional [*National Food Program*] [*Nicaragua*] (LA)
PAN........... Project voor Automatische Namenverwerking [*Netherlands*]
PAN........... Pyridylazonaphthol (RU)
PAN........... Semiautomatic Aiming [*Artillery*] (RU)
PANA........ Pan-African News Agency [*Use PAFNA*] [*Dakar, Senegal*] (AF)
PANA........ Pan-Asia News Agency Ltd. [*Also, PANASIA*] [*Hong Kong*]
PANA........ Pan Asia News Alliance (CL)
PANA........ Parti Nationaliste
PANABANK ... Banco Panamericano [*Panama*] (EY)
PANAC ..... Parti National Chretien
PANAC ..... Plantations Association of Nigeria and the Cameroons
PANACH .. Pan-African Chemical Industries
PANACO .. Parti Nationaliste Congolais
PANACOL ... Panamericana de Comercio Ltda. [*Colombia*] (COL)
PANAF .... Pan-Africaine d'Affichage
PAN-AF .... Pan-African News Agency
PANAF..... Parti National Africain
PANAFTEL ... Pan-African Telecommunications (BARN)
PANAFTEL ... Pan-African Telecommunications Network (AF)
PANAGRA ... Pan American Grace Airways, Inc. [*Also, PAGA*]
PANAI...... Patronato Nacional de Ancianos e Invalidos [*Venezuela*]
PANAIR..... Panama Air Lines
PANAJECO ... Parti National de la Jeunesse Congolaise
PANAL..... Papuan National Alliance [*Political party*] (PPW)
PANALI.... Parti National de la Liberte
PANALO .. Philippine Alliance of Nationalist Labor Organizations (FEA)
PANALU... Parti National Lumumba [*Lumumba National Party*] [*Political party*]
PAN-AM... Pan American World Airways, Inc. [*See also PA, PAA, PN*]
PANAMAC ... Pan American World Airways Communications System
PANAMIN ... Private Association for National Minorities [*Philippines*]
PANANKO ... Parti Nationaliste Nkonga
PANARE... Parti National de Reconstruction
PANAS..... Parti Negara Sarawak [*Sarawak State Party*] (ML)
PANASA .. Productos Alimenticios Nacionales SA [*Costa Rica*] (DSCA)
PANASIA ... Pan-Asia News Agency Ltd. [*Also, PANA*] [*Hong Kong*]
PANATRA ... Parti National du Travail
PANBE...... Pansements du Benin
PANCAN .. [*The*] Panama Canal
PANCANCO ... Panama Canal Co. [*Superseded by Panama Canal Commission*]
Pancar-Is ... Turkiye Seker ve Seker Pancari Sanayii Iscileri [*Turkish Sugar and Sugar Beet Industry Workers' Union*] [*Ankara*] (TU)
Pand........... Pandectes Francaises (FLAF)
PANDA ..... Professional Association of Numismatic Dealers of Australasia (ADA)
PandB .... Pandectes Belges [*Belgium*] (BAS)
P & Cie....... Pictet & Compagnie [*Bank*] [*Switzerland*]
P & CYC .... Police and Citizens' Youth Club [*Australia*]
PANDDA .. Professional Association of Nurses in Developmental Disability Areas [*Australia*]
P & E.......... Pike and Eel [*A pub at Cambridge University*] [*British*] (DSUE)
P & E.......... Proof and Experimental [*Australian Army*]

PANDECA ... Partido Nacional para Democracia, Desarrollo, y Educacion Civica
P & F......... Parents and Friends [*An association*]
Pand FrPer ... Pandectes Francaises Periodiques (FLAF)
P & J......... Plaza y Janes [*Publisher*] [*Spain*]
P & P......... Papers and Proceedings [*Australia*]
P and P....... Payments and Progress Committee [*NATO*] (NATG)
PandPer...... Pandectes Periodiques [*Benelux*] (BAS)
P & RT....... Physical and Recreational Training [*Navy*] [*British*]
P & T.......... Direccion General de Correos y Telecommunicacion [*General Directorate of Posts and Telecommunications*] [*Spanish*] (WER)
P & T.......... Post and Telegraph Department [*India*] (IMH)
P & Z.......... Polensky & Zoeliner [*Contracting company*]
PANG........ Panglima [*Commander*] (IN)
PANGIS .... Pan-African Network for a Geological Information System [*UNESCO*] (DUND)
PANHONLIB ... Panama, Honduras, and Liberia [*Acronym used to refer to merchant ships operating under "flags of convenience"*]
PANI......... Patronato Nationale de la Infancia [*Costa Rica*]
PANIDA.... Societe de Panification de Doala
PANJU...... Pan-African Union of Journalists
Pankobirlik ... Pancar Kooperatifler Birligi [*Turkish Beet Producers' Union*] (TU)
PANLAR... PanAmerican League Against Rheumatism [*Canada*] (EAIO)
PANLIBHON ... Panama, Liberia, and Honduras [*Acronym used to refer to merchant ships operating under "flags of convenience"*]
PANLIBHONCO ... Panama-Liberia-Honduras-Costa Rica
PANP .... Prazska Akumulatorka [*Prague Battery Plant*] (CZ)
PANPA...... Pacific Area Newspaper Production Association [*Australia*] (PDAA)
PANPA...... Pacific Area Newspaper Publishers Association (EAIO)
PANPRA... Parti Nationaliste Progressiste Revolutionnaire [*Haiti*] [*Political party*] (EY)
Pans........... Pansiyon [*Pension, Boarding House*] (TU)
PANS......... Protivavionska Nisanske Sprave [*Antiaircraft Aiming Mechanism*] (YU)
PANSAR... Pan Sarawak Co. [*Malaysia*]
PANSDOC ... Pakistan National Scientific and Documentation Center [*Later, PASTIC*]
PANSEAFRON ... Panama Sea Frontier
panstw........ Panstwowy [*National, State*] (POL)
PANSW..... Playgroup Association of New South Wales [*Australia*]
PANSW..... Police Association of New South Wales [*Australia*]
PANT .... Police Association of the Northern Territory [*Australia*]
PANTEKS ... Pancevacka Tekstilna Industrija [*Pancevo Textile Industry*] (YU)
PANTEX... Textiles Panamericanos SA [*Colombia*] (COL)
PANTUR... Panamericana de Viajes y Turismo [*Colombia*] (COL)
PANZ .... Playwrights Association of New Zealand (EAIO)
PAO .... Panathinaikos Athlitikos Omilos [*Pan-Athenian Athletic Club*] (GC)
PAO .... Panellinios Apelevtherotiki Organosis [*Panhellenic Liberation Organization*] (GC)
PAO .... Panellinios Athlitiki Organosis [*Panhellenic Athletic Organization*] (GC)
PAO .... Polynesian Airline Operations Ltd. [*Western Samoa*] [*ICAO designator*] (FAAC)
PAO .... Preisanordnung [*Price Order*] [*German*] (EG)
PAO .... Protiatomova Ochrana [*Antinuclear Defense*] (CZ)
PAO .... Protivavionska Odbrana [*Antiaircraft Defense*] (YU)
PAO .... Provinsiale Administrasie van die Oranje-Vrystaat [*Orange Free State Provincial Administration*] [*South Africa*] (AA)
PAO .... Societe de Plantations de l'Afrique Occidentale
PAODYE... Pankyprios Anexartitos Omospondia Dimotikon Ypallilon kai Ergaton [*Pan-Cyprian Independent Federation of Civil Service Employees and Workers*] (GC)
PAOK .... Panthessalonikeios Athlitikos Omilos Konstandinoupoleos [*Pan-Salonica Athletic Club of Istanbul*] (GC)
PAOO........ Philippine Academy of Ophthalmology and Otolaryngology (PDAA)
PAOR .... Permanente Accion Organizada Revolucionaria [*Permanent Organized Revolutionary Action*] [*Peru*] (LA)
pa otb .... Antiaircraft Defense (BU)
PAOWU .... Port Authority and Other Workers Union [*Mauritius*] (AF)
PAP........... Agentia Polona de Presa [*Polish Press Agency*] (RO)
PAP........... Atypical Primary Pneumonia (RU)
PAP........... Gun Artillery Regiment (RU)
pap........... Paperiteollisuus [*Paper Industry*] [*Finland*]
Pap........... Papier [*Paper*] [*German*]
pap........... Papier [*Paper*] [*French*]
Pap........... Papierherstellung [*Papermaking*] [*German*] (GCA)
Pap........... Papua [*New Guinea*] (BARN)
PAP........... Paris-Afrique Presse [*Paris-Africa Press Agency*] [*French*] (AF)
PAP........... Parole au Peuple [*Voice to the People*] [*Belgium*] (WER)

PAP............ Parti d'Action Paysanne [*Farmers Actions Party*] [*Burkina Faso*]
     [*Political party*]
PAP............ Partido Accion Popular [*Popular Action Party*] [*Peru*] [*Political party*]
PAP............ Partido Accion Popular [*Popular Action Party*] [*Ecuador*]
     [*Political party*]
PAP............ Partido Aprista Peruano [*Aprista Party of Peru*] (LA)
PAP............ People's Action Party [*Ghana*] (AF)
PAP............ People's Action Party [*Papua New Guinea*] [*Political party*]
     (EY)
PAP............ People's Action Party [*Singapore*] [*Political party*] (PPW)
PAP............ People's Action Party [*Malaya*] [*Political party*]
PAP............ People's Alliance Party [*Solomon Islands*] [*Political party*]
     (PPW)
PAP............ Philippine Aid Plan
PAP............ Plano de Accao Politico [*Political Action Plan*] [*Portuguese*]
     (WER)
P a P............ Poco a Poco [*Little by Little*] [*Music*]
PAP............ Politiki Aneksartitos Parataksis [*Independent Political Front*]
     [*Greek*] [*Political party*] (PPE)
PAP............ Polska Agencja Prasowa [*Polish Press Agency*]
PAP............ Port-Au-Prince [*Haiti*] [*Airport symbol*] (OAG)
PAP............ Poultry and Animal Products Ltd.
PAP............ Powiatowe Archiwum Panstwowe [*County State Archives*]
     (POL)
PAP............ Progressive Australia Party (ADA)
PAP............ Pulk Artylerii Polowej [*Poland*]
PAPA........ Package de Paie [*French*] (ADPT)
PAPA........ Philippine Alien Property Administration [*Post-World War II*]
PAPA........ Philippines Alien Property Administration
PAPAS...... Partai Pesaka Anak Sarawak [*Sarawak Sons Pesaka Party*] (ML)
papbd........ Papbind [*Boards*] [*Publishing Danish/Norwegian*]
PAPC........ Processed Apple and Pear Committee [*Victoria, Austrial*]
PAPC........ Public Agricultural Production Corporation [*Sudan*]
PAPEC...... Societe Africaine de Production d'Articles en Papier et
     d'Emballages en Carton
PAPERI.... Parti Persaudaraan Islam [*Islamic Brotherhood Party*] (ML)
PAPF........ Philippine Association for Permanent Forests, Inc. (DSCA)
PAPHR...... Pancyprian Association for the Protection of Human Rights
     [*Cyprus*] (EAIO)
Papie.......... Papeterie [*Paper Manufactory*] [*Military map abbreviation World
     War I*] [*French*] (MTD)
PAPIR....... Programme d'Action Prioritaire d'Initiative Regionale
PAPIRPROMET ... Preduzece za Promet Papirom [*Paper Trade
     Establishment*] (YU)
papkart...... Papkartonnage [*Slipcase*] [*Publishing Danish/Norwegian*]
PaPL.......... W. and F. Pascoe Proprietory Ltd., Milsons Point, NSW,
     Australia [*Library symbol*] [*Library of Congress*] (LCLS)
PAPM........ Philippine Association of Paint Manufacturers, Inc. (DS)
PAPMAD ... Papeteries de Madagascar
Papo.......... Partido de Accion Popular [*Popular Action Party*] [*Panama*]
     [*Political party*] (PPW)
PAPOMO ... Partido Popular de Mocambique [*Mozambique Popular Party*]
     (AF)
PAPP........ Partido de Accion Patriotica Progresista [*Progressive Patriotic
     Action Party*] [*Ecuador*] (LA)
pappb........ Pappbind [*Boards*] [*Publishing Danish/Norwegian*]
PAPPE...... Unidade de Planejamento, Avaliacao, e Pesquisas de Programas
     Especiais [*Unit for Planning, Research, and Evaluation of
     Special Programs*] [*Rio De Janeiro, Brazil*] (LAA)
PAPS........ Army Field Food Depot (RU)
PAPS........ Partido Alianza Popular Socialista [*Socialist Popular Alliance
     Party*] [*Costa Rica*] (LA)
PAPSB....... Patent Attorneys' Professional Standards Body [*Australia*]
PAPU........ Pan-African Postal Union
paq............ Paquete [*Package*] [*Spanish*]
PAQ........... Port Authorities Queensland [*Australia*]
PAQS........ Pacific Association of Quantity Surveyors [*Australia*]
PAR .... Airfield Homing Radio Station (RU)
Par............. Ferry [*Topography*] (RU)
par............. Field Artillery (BU)
PAR .... Panstwowa Administracja Rolna [*State Administration of
     Agriculture*] (POL)
PAR .... Panzerabwehrreserve [*Antitank Reserve*] (EG)
PAR .... Paracel Islands [*ANSI three-letter standard code*] (CNC)
par............. Paragraaf [*Paragraph*] [*Afrikaans*]
par............. Paragraf [*Paragraph*] [*Poland*]
Par............. Paragrafo [*Paragraph*] [*Italian*]
par............. Paragrafos [*Paragraph*] (GC)
Par............. Paragraph [*German*] (GCA)
Par............. Paragraphe [*French*] (FLAF)
Par............. Paraguay
PAR .... Paris [*France*] [*Airport symbol*] (OAG)
par............. Paronimo [*Paronymous*] [*Portuguese*]
par............. Parrafo [*Paragraph*] [*Spanish*]

PAR .... Partido Accion Renovadora [*Renovation Action Party*] [*El
     Salvador*] (LA)
PAR .... Partido Accion Renovadora [*Renovation Action Party*] [*El
     Salvador*] (LA)
PAR .... Partido Accion Revolucionaria [*Revolutionary Action Party*]
     [*Nicaragua*] (LA)
PAR .... Partido Accion Revolucionaria [*Revolutionary Action Party*]
     [*Dominican Republic*] (LA)
PAR .... Partido Aragones Regionalista [*Aragonese Regional Party*]
     [*Spain*] [*Political party*] (PPE)
PAR .... Partito Anti-Reformista [*Anti-Reform Party*] [*Malta*] [*Political
     party*] (PPE)
par.............. Perfume Factory [*Topography*] (RU)
PAR .... Polska Agencja Reklamy [*Polish Advertising Agency*] (POL)
PAR .... Pool Atomico Portuguees [*Portuguese*] [*Nuclear energy*]
     (NRCH)
PAR .... Powszechna Agencja Reklamy [*General Advertising Agency*]
     [*Poland*]
PAR .... Predvaritelnaya Agenturnaya Razrabotka [*Preliminary
     Operational Elaboration*] [*Soviet State Security procedure*]
PAR .... Protivavionski Reflektori [*Antiaircraft Searchlights*] (YU)
PAR .... Pyridylazoresorcinol (RU)
PAR .... Regimental Artillery Repair Shop (BU)
PAR .... Spair [*Russian Federation*] [*ICAO designator*] (FAAC)
Par.............. Steamship Line (RU)
PAR .... Track Emergency Relay (RU)
para............ Paragrafos [*Paragraph*] (GC)
PARA......... Parti d'Action Revolutionnaire Angolaise
PARAC...... Parlementair Automatiserings Centrum
PARAG..... Paraguay [*or Paraguayan*] (WDAA)
PARAKOAD ... Para Komando Angkatan Darat [*Army Paracommando
     Troops*] (IN)
PARAKU... Pasokan Rakyat Kalimantan Utara [*North Kalimantan People's
     Forces*] [*Malaya*]
PARAKU... Pasukan Rakjat Kalimantan Utara [*North Kalimantan People's
     Forces*] (ML)
paral.......... Parallel (RU)
parall......... Parallel (RU)
Paralost...... Parametrisch Gesteuertes Programm zur Generierung von
     Speziellen Lochstreifen-Programmen [*German*] (ADPT)
PARAM..... Mobile Army Artillery Repair Shop (RU)
PARAMOSA ... Pastas Ramos y Semolas SA [*Colombia*] (COL)
PARAQUAD ... Paraplegic and Quadriplegic Association of New South Wales
     [*Australia*]
parash v...... Parachute Tower [*Topography*] (RU)
parashyut... Paratroop Field [*Topography*] (RU)
PARB........ Mobile Aircraft Repair Base (RU)
parb........... Mobile Automotive Repairs Battalion (BU)
PARB........ Mobile Motor Vehicle Repair Base (RU)
PARB........ Public Accountants Registration Board [*Australia*]
PARBICA ... Pacific Regional Branch of the International Council on Archives
     (EAIO)
PARC......... Pacific-Asia Resources Center [*Japan*] (EAIO)
PARC......... Pan-African Rinderpest Campaign [*Organization of African
     Unity*]
PARC......... Pan American Railway Congress Association [*Buenos Aires*]
     (LAA)
PARC......... Post Adoption Resource Centre [*Australia*]
parch .... Parchemin [*Parchment*] [*Publishing*] [*French*]
parchem .... Parchemin [*Parchment*] [*Publishing*] [*French*]
PARCOM ... Paris Commission [*See also CP*] (EAIO)
PARD .... Pakistan Academy for Rural Development (DSCA)
PARD .... People Against Racial Discrimination
PARDA...... Parca Dagitim Ticaret ve Sanayi AS [*Parts Distribution, Trade,
     and Industry Corp.*] (TU)
PARDIC .... Public Administration, Reconstructing, and Decentralisation
     Implement Committee [*Government body*] [*Ghana*]
PARE........ Price Adjusted Rates of Exchange [*Monetary conversion rate*]
     (ECON)
PARECO... Parti de Regroupement Congolais
parf............ Parfait [*Perfect*] [*French*]
PARGA...... Paris-Gabon
PARIBAS ... Compagnie Financiere de Paris et des Pays-Bas [*Paris and the
     Lower Regions Financial Company*] [*France*]
PARIS .... Pour l'Amenagement et le Renouveau Institutionel et Social
     [*France*] [*Political party*]
PARK........ Portable Radioactive Logging Equipment (RU)
PARKE...... Parataxis Kendrou [*Array of the Center*] (GC)
PARKINDO ... Partai Keristen Indonesia [*Indonesian Christian Party*] (IN)
parkrakhm ... Steam-Driven Starch Factory [*Topography*] (RU)
parl............ Parlamentti [*Parliamentary*] [*Finland*]
PARL........ Parlement [*Parliament*] [*Afrikaans*]
Parl .... Parliament (SCAC)
Parl .... Parliamentary (IDIG)
Parl .... Parliamentary (IDIG)
parl............ Parliamentary Expression (BU)

PARLB ...... Parliamentary Borough
ParlDoc ...... Parlementaire Documenten [*Benelux*]   (BAS)
ParlemBesch ... Parlementaire Bescheiden [*Benelux*]   (BAS)
ParlemHand ... Parlementaire Handelingen [*Benelux*]   (BAS)
par lesp ...... Steam-Driven Sawmill [*Topography*]   (RU)
PARLIKDER ... Partiya Litsom k Derevne [*The Party Face to Face with the Countryside*] [*Given name popular in Russia after the Bolshevik Revolution*]
ParlK .... Parlement en Kiezer [*Benelux*]   (BAS)
PARM .... Field Aircraft Repair Shop   (RU)
PARM .... Mobile Motor Vehicle Repair Shop   (RU)
PARM .... Partido Autentico de la Revolucion Mexicana [*Authentic Party of the Mexican Revolution*] [*Political party*]   (PPW)
PARM .... Regimental Aircraft Repair Shop   (RU)
PARM .... Regimental Artillery Repair Shop   (RU)
PARM .... Regimental Motor Vehicle Repair Shop   (RU)
PARMD .... Division Mobile Motor Vehicle Repair Shop   (RU)
PARMEHUTU ... Parti du Mouvement de l'Emancipation Hutu [*Hutu Emancipation Movement Party*] [*Rwanda*]   (AF)
Par mel'n .... Steam-Driven Mill [*Topography*]   (RU)
PARMP ..... Regimental Mobile Motor Vehicle Repair Shop   (RU)
Par muk ..... Steam-Driven Flour Mill [*Topography*]   (RU)
PARMUSI ... Partai Muslimin Indonesia [*Indonesian Moslem Party*]   (IN)
PARN .... Partido de Accion y Reconstruccion Nacional [*National Action and Reconstruction Party*] [*Guatemala*]   (LA)
Paro .... Paroco [*Parish Priest*] [*Portuguese*]
Parovozo-remont ... Locomotive Repair Shop [*Topography*]   (RU)
Parq .... Parquet [*French*]   (FLAF)
PARR .... Regimental Artillery Repair Shop   (BU)
PARRA ...... Parramatta [*Prison in New South Wales*] [*Australia*]   (DSUE)
PARS .... Produktions-Automations-Rationalisierungs-System [*German*]   (ADPT)
PARSA ..... Parasitological Society of Southern Africa   (EAIO)
PARSA ..... Postgraduate and Research Students' Association [*Australian National University*]
parsag .... Parancsnoksag [*Headquarters*] [*Military*]   (HU)
PARSAN ... Makina Parcalari Sanayii AS [*Machinery Spare Parts Industry Corp.*] [*Ankara*]   (TU)
parsek .... Parallax-Second, Parsec   (RU)
PARSOCILIBRE ... Parti Socialiste Libre du Burundi
P art .... Parc d'Artillerie [*Artillery Park*] [*French*]   (MTD)
Part .... Partei [*Party*] [*German*]   (GCA)
Part .... Parterre [*Ground Floor, Pit (Theater)*] [*German*]
part .... Participio [*Participle*] [*Portuguese*]
part .... Particula [*Particle*] [*Portuguese*]
Part .... Partida [*Certificate*] [*Spanish*]
part .... Partizan [*Partisan*]   (HU)
part .... Party   (BU)
part .... Party, Party Member   (RU)
partalk .... Partalkalmazott [*Party Employee*]   (HU)
PartArb ...... Particulier Arbitrage [*Benelux*]   (BAS)
partep .... Partepites [*Party Development*]   (HU)
Partex .... Participations and Explorations Corp.   (OMWE)
Partgruporg ... Party Group Organizer   (RU)
PARTICO ... Parti d'Interets Congolais [*Party for Congolese Interests*] [*Political party*]
PARTINDO ... Partai Indonesia [*Indonesian Party*]   (IN)
partis .... Partisiippi [*Participle*] [*Finland*]
partit .... Partitiivi [*Finland*]
Partizdat .... Communist Party Publishing House   (BU)
Partizdat .... Party Publishing House   (RU)
Partkom ..... Party Committee   (BU)
part k-t .... Party Committee   (RU)
Partorg .... Party Organizer   (BU)
Partorga ..... Party Organization   (BU)
parts .... Partial   (RU)
partsz .... Partszervezet [*Party Organization*]   (HU)
partszerv .... Partszervezet [*Party Organization*]   (HU)
partszolg .... Partszolgalat [*or Partszolgalatos*] [*Communist Party Activity or Participant in the Party Activity*]   (HU)
PartT .... Partizanska Tiskarna [*Partisan Printers*]   (YU)
PARU .... Semiautomatic Gain Control   (RU)
Paryadro .... Party Nucleus   (BU)
PARZ .... Mobile Motor Vehicle Repair Plant   (RU)
PAS .... Acid Para-Aminosalicilic [*Para-Aminosalicylic Acid*]   (RO)
PAS .... Advanced Ammunition Depot   (RU)
PAS .... Advanced Army Depot   (RU)
Pas .... Apiary [*Topography*]   (RU)
PAS .... Army Field Depot   (RU)
PAS .... Artillery Firing Regulations   (RU)
PAS .... Field Ammunition Depot   (RU)
PAS .... Panellinios Andialkooliki Stavroforia [*Panhellenic Anti-Alcohol Crusade*]   (GC)
PAS .... Paros [*Greece*] [*Airport symbol*]   (OAG)
PAS .... Partido de Accion Socialista [*Socialist Action Party*] [*Costa Rica*] [*Political party*]   (PPW)

PAS .... Parti Islam se Malaysia [*Islamic Party of Malaysia*] [*Political party*]   (PPW)
PAS .... Partito de Azione de Sardegna [*Sardinian Action Party*] [*Italy*] [*Political party*]   (PPW)
Pas .... Pasicrisie Belge [*Belgium*]   (BAS)
pas .... Pasture [*Topography*]   (RU)
PAS .... Pater Ahlbrinck Stichting [*Father Ahlbrinck Foundation*] [*Suriname*]   (EAIO)
PAS .... Pelita Air Service PT [*Indonesia*] [*ICAO designator*]   (FAAC)
PAS .... People's Association [*Singapore*]   (EAIO)
PAS .... Persatuan Agama Se-Melayu [*Pan-Malayan Religious Union*]   (ML)
PAS .... Personalabrechnungssystem [*German*]   (ADPT)
PAS .... Personalabrechnungs und Auskunftssystem [*German*]   (ADPT)
PAS .... Peruvian Astronomical Society
PAS .... Plano de Amparo Social [*Social Assistance Program*] [*Brazil*]   (LA)
PAS .... Polish Anatomical Society   (EAIO)
PAS .... Polish Anthropological Society   (EAIO)
PAS .... Polish Astronautical Society   (EAIO)
PAS .... Prisoners' Aid Society [*Australia*]
PAS .... Programmablauf-Steuerung [*German*]   (ADPT)
PAS .... Prozess-Automatisierungssprache [*German*]   (ADPT)
PAS .... Regimental Ammunition Depot   (RU)
PAS .... Regimental Artillery Depot   (BU)
PAS .... Soil and Agricultural Station   (RU)
PASA .... Petroquimica Argentina, Sociedad Anonima [*Argentina*]   (LAA)
PASA .... Pioneers' Association of South Australia
PASA .... Pipelines Authority of South Australia
PASA .... Playgroup Association of South Australia
PASA .... Police Association of South Australia
PASA .... Poligono do Acustica Submarina dos Acores [*Azores Submarine Acoustic Range*] [*Portuguese*]   (WER)
PASA .... Posto Agrario de Sotavento do Algarve [*Portugal*]   (DSCA)
PASB .... Pan American Sanitary Bureau [*Executive organ of PAHO*]
PASB .... Public Authorities Superannuation Board [*New South Wales, Australia*]
PASC .... Palestine Armed Struggle Command   (PD)
PASC .... Pan-African Student Conference   (AF)
PASC .... Pan American Sanitary Conference
PASC .... Pan American Standards Commission [*See also COPANT*]   (EAIO)
PASC .... Partido Socialista Autonomista de Canarias [*Autonomous Socialist Party of the Canary Islands*] [*Spanish*]   (WER)
PASCAL .... Programme Applique a la Selection et a la Compilation Automatique de la Litterature [*French*]
PascB .... Pasicrisie Belge [*Belgium*]   (BAS)
PASCH ...... Pascha [*Easter*] [*Church calendars*]   (ROG)
PascLxb ..... Pasicrisie Luxembourgeoise [*Luxembourg*]   (BAS)
PASCT ...... Pan American Society for Chemotherapy of Tuberculosis [*See also SAQT*] [*Buenos Aires, Argentina*]   (EAIO)
PASD .... Public Administration Studies Division
PASE .... Post-Apollo Space Electrophoresis [*European Space Agency*]
PASEGES ... Panellinios Anotati Synomospondia Enoseon Georgikon Synetairismon [*Panhellenic Supreme Confederation of Unions of Agricultural Cooperatives*]   (GC)
PASEP ...... Plano de Assistencia ao Servidor Publico [*Civil Servants Welfare Fund*] [*Brazil*]   (LA)
PASEV ...... Panellinios Syndesmos Ekdoton Vivliou [*Panhellenic Association of Book Publishers*]   (GC)
PASIC .... Percussive Arts Society International Convention [*Percussive Arts Society*]
Pasin .... Pasinomie [*Benelux*]   (BAS)
PASINKO ... Pasukan Induk Komando [*Main Marine Force*]   (IN)
PASISTE ... Pangyprios Syndesmos Idiotikon Scholon Tritovathmias Ekpedefsis [*Cyprus*]   (EAIO)
PASK .... Para-Aminosalicylic Acid   (RU)
PASKE ...... Panellinia Agonistiki Syndikalistiki Kinisi Ergazomenon [*Panhellenic Militant Workers Trade Union Movement*]   (GC)
PASKOARMA ... Pasukan Komando Armada [*Fleet Marine Force*]   (IN)
PasL .... Pasicrisie Luxembourgeoise [*Luxembourg*]   (BAS)
PASLIB ..... Pakistan Association of Specials Libraries   (PDAA)
Paslux .... Pasicrisie Luxembourgeoise [*Luxembourg*]   (BAS)
PASM .... Pan-African Student Movement   (AF)
Pasn .... Pasinomie [*Benelux*]   (BAS)
PASO .... Pan American Sanitary Organization
PASO .... Pan American Sport Organization   (OLYM)
PASO .... Pan American Sports Organization [*See also ODEPA*] [*Mexico City, Mexico*]   (EAIO)
PASO .... Partido Accion Socialista [*Socialist Action Party*] [*Costa Rica*]   (LA)
PASO .... Partido Socialista [*Socialist Party*] [*Honduras*]   (LA)
PASOA ...... Pan-African Students Organization in the Americas   (AF)
PASOC ...... Partido de Accion Socialista [*Party of Socialist Action*] [*Spain*] [*Political party*]   (PPW)

PASOCO... Parti Socialiste des Comores [*Socialist Party of Comoros*]
    [*Political party*] (EY)
PASOH ..... Partido de Accion Socialista de Honduras [*Political party*] (EY)
PASOH ..... Partido Socialista de Honduras [*Honduran Socialist Party*]
    [*Political party*]
PASOK...... Panellinion Sosialistikon Kinema [*Pan-Hellenic Socialist Movement*] [*Greek*] [*Political party*] (PPE)
PASP .... Panellinia Agonistiki Spoudastiki Parataxi [*Panhellenic Militant Student Faction*] (GC)
PASP .... Port Autonome de San Pedro [*The Ivory Coast*] (EY)
PASPE....... Pandeios Anotati Skholi Politikon Epistimon [*Pandeios Supreme School of Political Sciences*] [*Greek*] (GC)
PASPE....... Ptykhioukhoi tis Anotatis Skholis Politikon Epistimon [*Graduates of the Supreme School of Political Sciences*] [*Greek*] (GC)
PASS .... Army Field Medical Depot (RU)
pass .... Passade [*Portuguese*]
pass .... Passage [*Lane*] [*French*] (CED)
pass .... Passato [*Past*] [*Italian*]
pass .... Passenger (Train) (RU)
PASS .... Passief [*Passive*] [*Afrikaans*]
pass .... Passiivi(n) [*Passive Voice*] [*Finland*]
Pass........... Passim [*France*] (FLAF)
PASSAT.... Programm zur Automatischen Selektion von Stichwoertern aus Teksten [*German*]
PASS-B ..... Army Ammunition Dump (BU)
pass -tov ..... Passenger and Freight (Train) (RU)
PAST .... Ambulance Station (RU)
past........... Pastori [*Finland*]
PASTAGALLO ... Fabrica de Pastas el Gallo Ltda. [*Colombia*] (COL)
PASTCA.... Pasteurizadora Tachira, SA [*Venezuela*] (DSCA)
PASTIC..... Pakistan Scientific and Technical Information Center [*Formerly, PANSDOC*]
PASTIC..... Pakistan Scientific and Technological Information Center [*Formerly, PANSDOC*] [*Quaid-I-Azan University Campus Islamabad, Pakistan*]
PASU........ Pan-African Socialist Union [*Southern Rhodesia*]
PASUS ..... Pasukan Chusus [*Special Forces*] (IN)
PASV .... Partiia Arabskovo Sotsialisticheskovo Vozrozhdeniia
PASYDY ... Pankyprios Syndekhnia Dimosion Ypallilon [*Pan-Cyprian Union of Civil Servants*] (GC)
PAT .... Automation and Telemechanics Enterprise (BU)
PAT .... Papuan Air Transport
Pat............. Patent [*German*] (GCA)
Pat............. Pathe [*Record label*] [*France*]
pat .... Pathologic, Pathological, Pathology (RU)
PAT .... Patna [*India*] [*Airport symbol*] (OAG)
pat .... Patologia [*Pathology*] [*Italian*]
pat .... Patriarca [*Patriarch*] [*Spanish*]
PAT .... People's Action Team [*South Vietnam*]
PAT .... Petroleum Authority of Thailand (GEA)
PAT .... Pets as Therapy [*Australia*]
PAT .... Police Association of Tasmania [*Australia*]
PAT .... Polska Agencja Telegraficzna [*Polish Telegraph Agency*] (POL)
PAT .... Port Authority of Thailand (GEA)
PAT .... Prazska Akciova Tiskarna [*Prague Printing Joint-Stock Company*] (CZ)
PAT .... Priority Air Transport [*Army*] (FAAC)
PAT .... Produktions-datenerfassung, Auftragsueberwachung und Terminplanung [*German*] (ADPT)
PAT .... Programm-Ablauf Taeglich [*German*] (ADPT)
PATA........ Pacific Area Travel Association [*San Francisco, CA*]
PATA........ Pacific Association of Tax Administrators [*Australia*]
PATA........ Patagonia [*Region of South America*] (ROG)
PatA......... Patentamt [*Patent Office*] [*German*]
PATA........ P A Tiele Akademie [*'s-Gravenhage*]
PATADMIN ... Patent Administration System [*Australia*]
PATAIR .... Papuan Air Transport
pat -anat.... Pathologicoanatomical (RU)
PATC........ Philippine Aerial Taxi Company
PATC........ Programa de Asistencia Comunal (del MINVU) [*Ministerio de la Vivienda y Urbanismo*] [*Santiago, Chile*] (LAA)
PATCH ..... People Against Toxic Chemical Hazards [*An association*] [*Australia*]
PATDPA ... Deutsche Patent Datenbank [*German Patent Database*] [*German Patent Office*] [*Information service or system*] (IID)
PATEFA.... Printing and Allied Trades Employers' Federation of Australia (ADA)
PAT-ELS... Steam-Turbine Electric Power Plant (RU)
Patentabt ... Patentabteilung [*Patent Department*] [*German*] (GCA)
path........... Pathologie [*French*] (TPFD)
path........... Pathologisch [*Pathological*] [*German*]
path........... Pathology (TPFD)
PATI .... Perwira Tinggi [*General Officer*] (IN)
patin .... Patinato [*Coated Paper*] [*Publishing*] [*Italian*]
PATKh....... Passenger Automobile Transportation Establishment (RU)

patl .... Pataljoona [*Finland*]
PATNT...... Playgroup Association of the Northern Territory [*Australia*]
pato .... Patologia [*Pathology*] [*Finland*]
PATO .... Pattetico [*Pathetically*] [*Music*] (ROG)
patol .... Pathology, Pathologist (BU)
Patol.......... Patologia [*Pathology*] [*Portuguese*]
PATOLIS ... Patent Online Information System [*Database*] [*Japan*]
patologich .. Pathologic, Pathological (RU)
PATP .... Poets and the Pub [*Programme*] [*Australia*]
PATPOL ... Patent Attorney Office, Poland (IMH)
Patr .... Patriarca [*Patriarch*] [*Spanish*]
patr............ Patrio [*National, Paternal*] [*Portuguese*]
patr............ Patronimico [*Patronymic*] [*Portuguese*]
PATS .... Philippine Aeronautics Training School (PDAA)
PATU .... PanAfrican Telecommunications Union (EAIO)
PATU .... Police Anti-Terrorist Unit [*South Africa*]
PATWA ..... Playgroup Association of Western Australia
PATWA..... Professional and Technical Workers' Aliyah Association [*Promotes Jewish emigration to Israel*]
PATYOLAT ... Vegytisztito Vallalat [*Dry Cleaning Enterprise*] (HU)
PAtZ .... Protivatomska Zastita [*Antiatomic Defense*] (YU)
PAU .... Complete Author Index (RU)
PAU .... Field Automatic Welding Unit (RU)
PAU .... Mobile Nitrogen Unit (RU)
PAU .... Pan American Union [*Central organ and permanent secretariat of the OAS*]
PAU .... Pangkalan Angkatan Udara [*Air Force Base*] (IN)
PAU .... Pauk [*Myanmar*] [*Airport symbol*] (OAG)
PAU .... Personnel Autonome de l'Universite [*Autonomous University Staff Personnel*] [*Malagasy*] (AF)
PAU .... Polska Akademia Umiejetnosci [*Polish Academy of Sciences and Letters*] (POL)
Pau .... Poteau [*Fingerpost, Guidepost*] [*Military map abbreviation World War I*] [*French*] (MTD)
PAU .... Punjab Agricultural University [*India*] (ARC)
PAUJ........ Pan-African Union of Journalists
PAUP........ Automatic Program Setup Device (RU)
PAUSS ..... Pacto de Unidad Sindical Solidaridad [*Mexico*] (EY)
PAV .... Army Field Veterinary Depot (RU)
PAV .... Paksi Atomeroemue Vallalat [*Paks Nuclear Power Station*] [*Hungary*] (WND)
PaV .... Pathe-Vox [*Record label*] [*France*]
PAV .... Paulo Afonso [*Brazil*] [*Airport symbol*] (OAG)
pav............ Pavilion (RU)
PA(V)........ Police Association (Victoria) [*Australia*]
PAV .... Pomoc Americke Vlade [*US Government Economic Aid*] [*Tripartite Aid Program*] (YU)
PAV .... Poste-Avion [*Airmail*] [*French*]
PAV .... Programme d'Assistance Volontaire [*Voluntary Assistance Program*] [*Telecommunications Laotian*] (CL)
PAV .... Public Against Violence [*Former Czechoslovakia*] [*Political party*]
PAV .... Surface-Active Agents (BU)
PAV .... Surface-Active Substance (RU)
PAV .... Variable Attenuation Equalizer (RU)
PAVCO ..... Pisos de Asfalto y Vinilo SA [*Colombia*] (COL)
PAVCSS.... Principals' Association of Victorian Catholic Secondary Schools [*Australia*]
PAVES ...... Philippine Association of Vocational Education Superintendents
PAVETs .... Pumping-Storage Hydroelectric Plant (BU)
PAVINAL ... Pavimentadora Nacional [*Colombia*] (COL)
PAVI .... Pomoc Americke Vlade u Hrani [*US Government Aid in Food*] (YU)
PAVMP..... Fully Automatic High-Quality Machine Translation (RU)
PAVN .... People's Army of Vietnam
PAVN .... Vietnam People's Army [*Use VPA*] [*North Vietnamese*] (CL)
PAVS........ Army Field Veterinary Depot (RU)
PAVSA ...... Parasitologiese Vereniging van Suidelike Afrika [*Parasitological Society of Southern Africa*] (AA)
PAW .... Pambwa [*Papua New Guinea*] [*Airport symbol*] (OAG)
PAW .... Polska Agencja Wydawnicza [*Polish Publishing Agency*] (POL)
PAWA ...... Power and Water Authority [*Northern Territory, Australia*]
PAWC ...... Pan-African Women's Conference (AF)
PAWC ...... Pan-African Workers Congress (AF)
PAWWSWR ... Portuguese Association on Water, Wastewater and Solid Wastes Research (EAIO)
PAX .... Instytut Wydawniczy "Pax" [*"Pax" Publishing Institute*] (POL)
Pax........... Paxton [*Record label*] [*Great Britain*]
PAY .... Pamol [*Malaysia*] [*Airport symbol*] (OAG)
PAYCUEROS ... Paysandu Industria del Cuero [*Uruguay*] (DSCA)
PAYDS...... Panellinios Agon Yperaspiseos tis Dimokratias kai tou Syndagmatos [*Panhellenic Struggle for the Defense of Democracy and the Constitution*] (GC)
PAYLANA ... Paysandu Industria Lanera [*Uruguay*] (DSCA)
PAYM .... Pan-African Youth Movement (AF)
PAYO .... Pan-African Youth Organization (AF)

PAYP........ Prokekhorimeni Apothiki Ylikou Polemou [*Advanced Ordnance Depot*] [*Greek*] (GC)
PAZ .... Atomic Defense, Antiatomic Defense (RU)
PAZ .... Automobile Made by the Pavlovo Bus Plant Imeni A. A. Zhdanov (RU)
paz.............. Barrage Balloons Regiment (BU)
PAZ .... Nuclear Defense (BU)
PAZ .... Pavlovo Bus Plant Imeni A. A. Zhdanov (RU)
PAZ .... Plan d'Amenagement des Zones [*French*]
PAZ .... Podol'sk Battery Plant (RU)
PAZ .... Pohybliva Armadni Zakladna [*Mobile Army Base*] (CZ)
PAZ .... Poza Rica [*Mexico*] [*Airport symbol*] (OAG)
PAZ .... Protivavionska Zastita [*Antiaircraft Defense*] (YU)
PAZA........ Press Association of Zambia (EY)
PAZhK ..... Pan-American Railway Congress Association [*PARCA*] (RU)
PB .... Benzoyl Peroxide (RU)
PB .... Dive Bomber (RU)
PB .... Estado da Paraiba [*State of Paraiba*] [*Brazil*]
PB .... Etablissements Pierre Balet
PB .... Floating Base, Depot Ship, Tender (RU)
pb .... Infantry Battalion (RU)
PB .... Leading Battalion (BU)
pb .... Machine-Gun Battalion (RU)
PB .... Pachtbesluit [*Benelux*] (BAS)
PB .... Pandectes Belges [*Belgium*] (BAS)
PB .... Panzerbataillon [*Tank Battalion*] (EG)
Pb .... Pappband [*Bound in Pasteboard Covers*] [*Publishing*] [*German*]
PB .... Papua Besena [*Papua New Guinea*] [*Political party*] (FEA)
P/b .... Parabrod [*Steamer*] (YU)
PB .... Paris Bourse [*The French stock exchange*]
PB .... Parlementaire Bescheiden [*Benelux*] (BAS)
PB .... Parliamentary Broadcast Network [*Australia*]
PB .... Parole Board [*Australian Capital Territory*]
pb .... Partbizottsag [*Party Committee*] (HU)
pb .... Party Membership Card (RU)
P-B .... Pays-Bas [*Netherlands*] [*French*]
PB .... Pejabat Besar [*Head Office*] (ML)
PB .... Penzugyi Bizottsag [*Finance Committee*] (HU)
PB .... Perforateur de Bande [*French*] (ADPT)
PB .... Personele Belasting [*Benelux*] (BAS)
PB .... Pesadiski Bataljon [*Infantry Battalion*] (YU)
PB .... Peso Bruto [*Dead Weight*] [*Portuguese*]
PB .... Pharmaceutical Benefits Scheme [*Australia*]
PB .... Pharmacopoeia Britannica [*British Pharmacopoeia*]
PB .... Philosophiae Baccalaureus [*Bachelor of Philosophy*]
PB .... Physiotherapists Board [*Australian Capital Territory*]
PB .... Piso Bajo [*Ground Floor*] [*Spanish*]
pb .... Plus Bas [*French*]
PB .... Polis Besar [*Police District*] (ML)
PB .... Politburo (RU)
PB .... Politikai Bizottsag [*Political Committee*] (HU)
PB .... Poljska Bolnica [*Field Hospital*]
pb .... Pontoon Battalion (RU)
PB .... Premier Beer [*Premier Breweries Ltd.*] [*Onitsha, Nigeria*]
PB .... Presentation Brothers [*See also FPM*] (EAIO)
PB .... Prijzenbeschikking [*Benelux*] (BAS)
PB .... Privatbetrieb [*Private Enterprise*] [*German*] (EG)
PB .... Programmbibliothek [*Program Library*] [*German*] (ADPT)
PB .... Propan-Butan [*Propane-Butane*] (HU)
PB .... Proportional Unit [*Computers*]
PB .... Proprietes Baties
PB .... Prukaz Brance [*Conscription Certificate*] (CZ)
PB .... Prvni Brnenska Strojirna [*First Machine Factories in Brno*] (CZ)
PB .... Public (DSUE)
PB .... Publicatieblad (EEG) (BAS)
Pb .... Publicatieblad van de Europese Gemeenschappen [*Benelux*] (BAS)
PB .... Publicatieblad (van de Nederlandse Antillen) [*Netherlands*] (BAS)
pb .... Regimental Battery (RU)
PB .... Safety Regulations (RU)
PB .... Standing Bureau (BU)
pb .... Starboard (RU)
Pb .... St. Petersburg (RU)
PB .... Wet op de Personele Belasting [*Benelux*] (BAS)
PBA .... Floating Battery [*Artillery*] (RU)
PBA .... Mobile Drill Unit (RU)
PBA .... Pacific Broadcasting Association (EAIO)
PBA .... Partido Barrientista Autentico [*Bolivia*] [*Political party*] (PPW)
PBA .... Philippine Badminton Association (EAIO)
PBA .... Polska Bibliografia Analityczna [*Polish Analytical Bibliography*] (POL)
PBAA........ Private Businesses Association of Australia
PBAA........ Public Broadcasting Association of Australia (ADA)
PBAC........ Pharmaceutical Benefits Advisory Committee [*Australia*]

PBAS .... Property and Building Advisory Service [*Australia*]
pbatr........... Maintenance Battery (BU)
PBAV........ Power Boat Association of Victoria [*Australia*]
PBB........... Forward Hospital Base (BU)
PBB........... Paranaiba [*Brazil*] [*Airport symbol*] (OAG)
PBB........... Parti Pesaka Bumiputra Bersatu Sarawak [*United Bumiputra Party*] [*Malaysia*] [*Political party*] (FEA)
PBB........... Perserikatan Bangsa-Bangsa [*United Nations*] (IN)
PBB........... Petroquimica Bahia Blanca [*Argentina*]
PBB........... Private Blood Bank of Australia Ltd.
PBBATU ... Pastrycooks, Bakers, Biscuitmakers, and Allied Trades Union [*Australia*]
PBBM &A ... Pastrycooks, Bakers, Biscuit Makers, and Allied Trades Union [*Australia*]
PBBS .... Pertubuhan Bumiputera Bersatu Sarawak [*United Sarawak National Association*] [*Malaysia*] [*Political party*] (FEA)
PbBz............ Bleibronze [*Lead Bronze*] [*German*] (GCA)
PBC............ Pakistan Banking Council
PBC............ Pakistan Broadcasting Corp. (IMH)
PBC............ Panamerican Badminton Confederation (EAIO)
PBC............ People's Bank of China (ECON)
PBC............ Poljski Bolnicki Centar [*Field Hospital Center*] (YU)
PBC............ Portuguese Baptist Convention (EAIO)
PBC............ Provinciale Bibliotheek Centrale
PBCA........ Professional Business Colleges of Australia
PBCB .... Professional Boxing Control Board [*Victoria, Australia*]
Pbck .... Paperback [*Paperback*] [*Publishing*] [*German*]
Pbd .... Pappband [*Bound in Pasteboard Covers*] [*Publishing*] [*German*]
PBD .... Pomorsko-Brodarsko Drustvo [*Maritime Shipping Society*] (YU)
PBD .... Porbandar [*India*] [*Airport symbol*] (OAG)
PBDCT ...... Plano Basico de Desenvolvimento Cientifico e Tecnologico [*Basic Plan for Scientific and Technological Development*] [*Brazil*] (LA)
PBDS .... Parti Bansa Dayak Sarawak [*Malaysia*] [*Political party*] (FEA)
PBE........... Panstwowe Budownictwo Elektryczne [*State Power Engineering*] (POL)
PBE........... Pasar Biasa Eropa [*European Common Market*] (IN)
PBE........... Puerto Berrio [*Colombia*] [*Airport symbol*] (OAG)
PBE........... Regulation for the Safety and Operation of Hoisting Machinery (BU)
PBEC .... Pacific Basin Economic Council (FEA)
PbEG .... Publicatieblad Europese Gemeenschappen [*Benelux*] (BAS)
PBEIST .... Planning Board for European Inland Surface Transport [*NATO*] (PDAA)
PBF .... Fast Patrol Boat [*Ship symbol*] [*NATO*] (NATG)
PBF .... Pakistan Badminton Federation (EAIO)
PBF .... Pravoslavni Bogoslovski Fakultet [*Orthodox Theological Faculty*] (YU)
PBFL .... Planning for Better Family Living [*FAO*]
PBG .... Porphobilinogen (RU)
PBG .... Powszechny Bank Gospodarczy [*Poland*]
PBH .... Palm Beach Hotel [*Cyprus*]
PBI............ Plant Breeding Institute [*British*]
PBI............ Programme Biologique Internationale [*International Biological Program - IBP*] (MSC)
PBI............ Public Benevolent Institution [*Australia*]
PBI............ Purna Bina Indonesia PT
PBICSGH ... Permanent Bureau of International Congresses for the Sciences of Genealogy and Heraldry (EA)
PBinstitut ... Eastern Orthodox Theological Institute (BU)
PBK........... Mobile Pressure Chamber (RU)
PBK........... Pneumatic-Tired Tower Crane (RU)
PBK........... Przedsiebiorstwo Budowy Kopaln [*Mine Construction Enterprise*] (POL)
PBKA........ Persatuan Buruh Kereta Api [*National Railway Workers' Union*] [*Indonesia*]
PBKB........ Persatuan Buruh Kendaraan Bermotor [*Motorized Vehicle Workers' Union*] [*Indonesia*]
p bl .... Field Hospital (BU)
PBL........... Problem-Based Learning [*Australia*]
Pbl............. Publicatieblad van de Europese Gemeenschappen [*Benelux*] (BAS)
PBL........... Puerto Cabello [*Venezuela*] [*Airport symbol*] (OAG)
pble .... Payable [*Payable*] [*Business term*] [*French*]
pble .... Posible [*Possible*] [*Business term*] [*Spanish*]
PBLK .... Przedsiebiorstwo Budowy Linii Kablowych [*Cable Line Construction Enterprise*] (POL)
PBM .... Antitransmit-Receive Tube (RU)
PBM .... Paramaribo [*Surinam*] [*Airport symbol*] (OAG)
PBM .... Prozess-Betriebssystem [*German*] (ADPT)
PBM .... Przedsiebiorstwo Budownictwa Miejskiego [*Town Building Enterprise*] [*Poland*]
PBM .... Ranging Combat Vehicle (RU)
PBMA....... Plumbers and Builders Merchants Association [*Australia*]
PBMASA .. Paper Bag Manufacturers' Association of South Australia

PBMF........ Bulgarian Maritime Navigation Administration   (BU)
PBMUM ... Persatuan Bahasa Melayu Universiti Malaysia [*Malayan Language Association of the University of Malaysia*]   (ML)
PBN .... Non-Self-Propelled Floating Base   (RU)
PBN .... Porto Amboin [*Angola*] [*Airport symbol*]   (OAG)
PBn .... Poudres Brunes [*Symbol*] [*Military*] [*French*]   (MTD)
PBN .... Przeglad Bibliograficzny "Nafty" [*Bibliographical Review of the Journal "Nafta" (Petroleum)*]   (POL)
PBNII .... Perm' Biological Scientific Research Institute   (RU)
PBNP........ Observation Post Tank   (RU)
PBn S .... Poudre Brune de Siege [*Military*] [*French*]   (MTD)
PBNSW.... Pharmacy Board of New South Wales [*Australia*]
PBNSW.... Police Board of New South Wales [*Australia*]
PBNT........ Parole Board of the Northern Territory [*Australia*]
PBO .... Field Bath Detachment   (RU)
PBO .... Paraburdoo [*Australia*] [*Airport symbol*]   (OAG)
PBO .... Plan and Budget Organization [*Iran*]   (ME)
PBO .... Poor Bloody Observer [*British World War I military slang*]   (DSUE)
PBO .... Protibiologicka Ochrana [*Antibiological Defense*]   (CZ)
PBO .... Publiekrechtelijke Bedrijfsorganisatie [*Benelux*]   (BAS)
PBO .... Right Flank Protection   (RU)
PBO .... Single-Cotton Covered Wire   (RU)
PBoC........ People's Bank of China
PBOS........ Planning Board for Ocean Shipping [*Army*] [*NATO*]
PBP........... Ammunition Supply Point   (RU)
PBP........... Panstwowe Budownictwo Przemyslowe [*State Industrial Construction Enterprise*]   (POL)
PBP........... Pesadiska Borbena Pravila [*Infantry Combat Rules*]   (YU)
PBP........... Polskie Biuro Podrozy "Orbis" [*"Orbis" Polish Travel Bureau*]
PBP........... Powiatowe Biblioteki Pedagogiczne [*County School Libraries*]   (POL)
PBP........... Przedsiebiorstwo Budownictwa Przemyslowego [*Industrial Construction Enterprise*]   (POL)
PBPA .... Pharmaceutical Benefits Pricing Authority [*Australia*]
PBPOrbis ... Polskie Biuro Podrozy "Orbis" [*"Orbis" Polish Travel Bureau*]   (POL)
PBQ .... Pharmacy Board of Queensland [*Australia*]
PBQ .... Physiotherapists' Board of Queensland [*Australia*]
PBQ .... Podiatrists' Board of Queensland [*Australia*]
PBR........... Combat Deployment Point [*Aviation*]   (RU)
pbr............. Infantry Brigade   (RU)
PBR........... Panstwowy Bank Rolny [*State Agricultural Bank*]   (POL)
PBR........... Professional Board for Radiography [*South Africa*]   (EAIO)
PBR........... Programm zur Bekaempfung des Rassismus
PBR........... Prostor Bojoveho Rozmisteni [*Combat Deployment Sector*]   (CZ)
PBRG........ Primate Behaviour Research Group [*University of the Witwatersrand*] [*South Africa*]   (AA)
pbrgr .... Infantry Brigade Group   (RU)
PBRIS........ Pampanga-Bongabon Rivers Irrigation System [*Philippines*]   (PDAA)
pbro........... Presbitero [*Presbyter, Priest*] [*Spanish*]
PBRP........ Bulgarian River Navigation Administration   (BU)
PBRT........ Pharmaceutical Benefits Remuneration Tribunal [*Australia*]
PBrV .... Pomoc Britanske Vlade [*Economic Aid of British Government*] [*Tripartite Aid Program*]   (YU)
PBS........... Field Ballistic Station [*Artillery*]   (RU)
PBS........... Palestine Broadcasting Service   (BJA)
PBS........... Parti Bersatu Sabah [*Malaysia*] [*Political party*]   (ECON)
PBS........... Partner Bank System [*Capital Investment Coordinating Board*] [*Indonesia*]   (IMH)
PBS........... Persatuan Bawean Singapura [*Bawean Association of Singapore*]   (ML)
PBS........... Philippines Broadcasting Service   (FEA)
PBS........... Plattenbetriebssystem [*German*]   (ADPT)
PBS........... Popularna Biblioteka Sportowa [*Popular Sports Series*]   (POL)
PBS........... Poradkova a Bezpecnostni Sluzba [*Discipline and Security Service*] [*Civil defense*]   (CZ)
PBS........... Self-Propelled Floating Base   (RU)
PBSA .... Parole Board of South Australia
PBSA .... Pastoral Board of South Australia
PBSA .... Pharmacy Board of South Australia
PBSA .... Phylloxera Board of South Australia
PBSA .... Physiotherapists' Board of South Australia
PBSAA ...... Partially Blinded Soldiers' Association of Australia
PBSE .... Przedsiebiorstwo Budowy Sieci Elektrycznych [*Electrical Network Construction Enterprise*]   (POL)
PBSI .... Persatuan Bulutangkis Seluruh Indonesia [*Badminton Association of Indonesia*]   (EAIO)
PbSnBz ...... Bleizinnbronze [*Lead Tin Bronze*] [*German*]   (GCA)
PbSoBz ...... Bleisonderbronze [*Special Leaded Bronze*] [*German*]   (GCA)
PBSR .... Permanent Building Societies Registrar [*New South Wales, Australia*]
PBT........... Philippine Ballet Theater   (ECON)
PBTC .... Phayao Bible Training Center [*Thailand*]

PBTO........ Polsko-Brytyjskie Towarzystwo Okretowe
PBU .... Air-Burundi [*ICAO designator*]   (FAAC)
PBU .... High-Powered Magnifying Instrument   (RU)
PBU .... Poultry Breeders' Union [*Israel*]   (EAIO)
PBU .... Putao [*Myanmar*] [*Airport symbol*]   (OAG)
PBU .... Teacher's Pedagogical Library   (RU)
PBV........... Pharmacy Board of Victoria [*Australia*]
PBV........... Pomoc Belgiske Vlade [*Economic Aid of Belgian Government*]   (YU)
PBVl .... Pomoc Belgijske Vlade u Hrani [*Aid of Belgian Government in Food*]   (YU)
PBW .... Pedagogiczna Biblioteka Wojewodzka [*Voivodship Pedagogical Library*]   (POL)
PBWG .... Pakistan Bibliographical Working Group   (PDAA)
PBY........... Pearl Air Services (U) Ltd. [*Uganda*] [*ICAO designator*]   (FAAC)
PBZ........... Antibacteriological Defense   (BU)
PBZ........... Antibacteriological Protection, Bacteriological Protection   (RU)
PBZ........... Field Concrete Plant   (RU)
PBZ........... People's Bank of Zanzibar [*State bank*] [*Tanzania*]
PBZ........... Plettenberg [*South Africa*] [*Airport symbol*]   (OAG)
PBZ........... Pojizerske Bavlnarske Zavody, Narodni Podnik [*Jizera River Area Cotton Mills, National Enterprise*]   (CZ)
PBZPC ...... Przedsiebiorstwo Budowy Zakladow Przemyslu Ciezkiego [*Enterprise for the Construction of Heavy Industry Establishments*]   (POL)
PC .... Communist Party [*Peru*] [*Political party*]   (PD)
pc............... Pacote [*Bale, Bundle, Packet*] [*Portuguese*]
PC .... [*The*] Panama Canal
pc............... Pancelos [*Armored*]   (HU)
PC .... Paramount Chief
PC .... Parti Communiste [*Communist Party*] [*French*]
PC .... Parti Communiste [*Communist Party*] [*Luxembourg*] [*Political party*]   (PPW)
PC .... Parti de Conservation
PC .... Partido Carlista [*Carlist Party*] [*Spanish*]   (WER)
PC .... Partido Colorado [*Colorado Party*] [*Uruguay*] [*Political party*]   (PPW)
PC .... Partido Comunista [*Communist Party*] [*Brazil*]   (LAA)
PC .... Partido Comunista [*Communist Party*] [*Chile*]   (LAA)
PC .... Partido Comunista [*Communist Party*] [*Dominican Republic*]   (LAA)
PC .... Partido Comunista [*Communist Party*] [*Costa Rica*]   (LAA)
PC .... Partido Comunista [*Communist Party*] [*Spanish*]   (LA)
PC .... Partido Conservador [*Conservative Party*] [*Colombo*]   (LA)
PC .... Partido Conservador [*Conservative Party*] [*Nicaragua*] [*Political party*]   (EY)
PC .... Partido Conservador [*Conservative Party*] [*Ecuador*] [*Political party*]   (PPW)
pc............... Pas Cote [*French*]
pc............... Pas dans le Commerce [*Benelux*]   (BAS)
PC .... Patrolni Camac [*Patrol Boat*]   (YU)
pc............... Paye au Comptant [*Paid in Cash*] [*Business term*] [*French*]
PC .... Peace Corps
pc............... Peca [*Piece*] [*Portuguese*]
PC .... People's Committee
PC .... People's Conference [*India*] [*Political party*]   (PPW)
PC .... Per Condoglianza [*Used on visiting cards to express condolence*] [*Italian*]
PC .... Perfectae Caritatis [*Decree on the Appropriate Renewal of the Religious Life*] [*Vatican II document*]
PC .... Pesadiska Ceta [*Infantry Company*]   (YU)
PC .... Peuple et Culture [*France*]   (EAIO)
PC .... Philippine Constabulary
PC .... Piacenza [*Car registration plates*] [*Italian*]
pc............... Pied Carre [*Square Foot*] [*French*]
pc............... Pied Cube [*Cubic Foot*] [*French*]
PC .... Plaatselijke Commissie [*Benelux*]   (BAS)
PC .... Plaid Cymru [*Welsh national liberation party*] [*Political party*]
PC .... Points de Contact [*Military*] [*French*]   (MTD)
PC .... Police-Constable [*Scotland Yard*]
PC .... Policia de Control [*Colombia*]   (COL)
P/C............ Polizza di Carico [*Bill of Lading*] [*Shipping*] [*Italian*]
PC .... Pomocna Ceta [*Auxiliary Company*]   (YU)
PC .... Poor Classes [*British*]   (DSUE)
p/c .... Por Conta [*Portuguese*]
PC .... Portion Centrale [*French*]   (MTD)
PC .... Poste de Commandement [*Command Post*] [*Use CP*] [*French*]   (WER)
PC .... Poudre Composition [*Military*] [*French*]   (MTD)
pc............... Pour Cent [*Per Cent*] [*French*]
p/c .... Pour Compte [*By Cash*] [*Business term*] [*French*]
PC .... Pour Condoler [*To Offer Sympathy*] [*French*]
pc............... Praca [*Square*] [*Portuguese*]   (CED)
PC .... Prazske Cihelny [*Prague Brick Works*]   (CZ)
PC .... Preparatory Committee
PC .... Privy Counsellor   (SCAC)

PC .... Procaer SpA [*Italy*] [*ICAO aircraft manufacturer identifier*] (ICAO)
pc................ Procento [*Percent*] (CZ)
PC .... Producciones Colombia - Inravision [*Colombia*] (COL)
PC .... Productora de Controles Ltda. [*Colombia*] (COL)
PC .... Provincial Commissioner [*Kenya*] (AF)
PCA .... Packaging Council of Australia
PCA .... Parc de Corps d'Armee [*Military*] [*French*] (MTD)
PCA .... Parents' Centres Australia (ADA)
PCA .... Parti Communiste Algerien [*Algerian Communist Party*] [*Political party*]
PCA .... Partido Comunista de Angola [*Communist Party of Angola*] (AF)
PCA .... Partido Comunista de Argentina [*Communist Party of Argentina*] [*Political party*] (PD)
PCA .... Party of the Civic Alliance [*Romania*] [*Political party*] (EY)
p-ca............. Pecatnica [*Printing House*] (YU)
PCA .... Permanent Court of Arbitration [*See also CPA*] [*Hague, Netherlands*] (EAIO)
PCA .... Pest Control Association [*Australia*]
PCA .... Peugeot Concessionaires Australia
PCA .... Pharmacie Centrale Algerienne [*Algeria*] (IMH)
PCA .... Philippine Contractors Association (DS)
PCA .... Polish Community in Australia
PCA .... Pontificia Commissione di Assistenza [*Italian*]
PCA .... Pony Club Association [*Australia*]
PCA .... Pork Council of Australia
PCA .... Poste de Controle Administratif [*Administrative Control Post*] [*Congo*] (AF)
PCA .... Presidency of Civil Aviation [*Jeddah, Saudi Arabia*] (MENA)
PCAA .... Print Council of Australia
PCAA........ Portuguese Central Agriculture Association (EAIO)
PCA-CNRR ... Partido Comunista de Argentina - Comite Nacional para la Reivindicacion Revolucionaria [*Communist Party of Argentina - National Committee for Revolutionary Demands*] (LA)
PCAD .... Post de Commandement d'Artillerie Divisionnaire [*Military*] [*French*] (MTD)
PCAI......... Parliamentary Commissioner for Administrative Investigations [*Western Australia*]
PCAI......... Personal Care Assessment Instrument [*Australia*]
PCANSW .. Pest Control Association of New South Wales [*Australia*]
PCAQ .... Pony Club Association of Queensland [*Australia*]
PCARD...... Philippine Council for Agriculture Resources, Research, and Development (DS)
PCARR...... Philippines Council of Agricultural and Resources Research (PDAA)
PCAS........ Period Contract Awareness Service [*Australia*]
PCAS........ Produits Chimiques Auxiliaires et de Synthese [*France*]
PCAS........ Programa Credito Agricultor Supervisado [*Peru*] (DSCA)
PCASA ...... Pony Club Association of South Australia
PCAT........ Pakistan Council of Appropriate Technology (EAIO)
PCATT ..... Philippine Center for Appropriate Training and Technology
PCAU .... Philippine Civil Affairs Unit [*Army unit which supplied emergency subsistence after end of Japanese dominance*] [*World War II*]
PCAV........ Pony Club Association of Victoria [*Australia*]
PCAWA..... Pony Club Association of Western Australia
PCB........... Certificat de Physique, Chimie, Biologie [*Physics, Chemistry, and Biology Certificate*] [*French*] (WER)
PCB........... Parti Communiste de Belgique [*Communist Party of Belgium*] [*See also KPB*] [*Political party*] (PPE)
PCB........... Partido Comunista de Bolivia [*Communist Party of Bolivia*] [*Political party*] (PPW)
PCB........... Partido Comunista do Brasil [*Communist Party of Brazil*] [*Pro-Albanian*] [*Political party*] (PPW)
PCB........... People's Cooperative Bank [*Jamaica*] (LA)
PCB........... Perth Convention Bureau [*Australia*]
PCB........... Premier Commercial Bank Ltd. [*Nigeria*]
PCB........... Prix de Cession de Base [*Basic Wholesale Price*] [*French*]
PCBB .... Programme de Calcul de Bilan Brut [*French*] (ADPT)
PCB-ML.... Partido Comunista Marxista-Leninista de Bolivia [*Marxist-Leninist Communist Party of Bolivia*] [*Political party*] (PPW)
PCBR........ Partido Comunista Brasileiro Revolucionario [*Brazilian Revolutionary Communist Party*] (LA)
PCBR-TNO ... Plancommissie Bouwresearch TNO [*Planning Committee for Building Research TNO*] [*Netherlands Organization for Applied Scientific Research (TNO)*] [*Netherlands*] [*Research center*] (ERC)
PCC .... Panama Canal Co. [*Superseded by Panama Canal Commission*]
PCC .... Panama Canal Commission [*Independent government agency*]
PCC .... Partido Carlista de Cataluna [*Carlist Party of Catalonia*] [*Spanish*] (WER)
PCC........... Partido Comunista Canario [*Communist Party of the Canary Islands*] [*Spanish*] (WER)

PCC........... Partido Comunista Chileno [*Communist Party of Chile*] [*Political party*] (PD)
PCC........... Partido Comunista Cubano [*Communist Party of Cuba*] [*Political party*] (PPW)
PCC........... Partido Comunista de Colombia [*Communist Party of Colombia*] (LA)
PCC........... Partido Conservador Colombiano [*Conservative Party of Colombia*] [*Political party*] (PPW)
PCC........... Partie Communiste Chinois
PCC........... Party of Catalan Communists [*Political party*] (PPW)
PCC........... Pasteur Collection of Cyanobacteria [*France*]
PCC........... Pearcey Centre for Computing [*Chisholm Institute of Technology*] [*Australia*]
PCC........... People's Caretaker Council [*Rhodesian*] (AF)
PCC........... People's Caretakers' Council [*Rhodesian*]
PCC........... Pepper Community [*Later, IPC*]
PCC........... Per Copia Conforme [*True Copy*] [*Italian*]
PCC........... Period Contract Circular [*Australia*]
PCC........... Perth Chamber of Commerce [*Western Australia*]
PCC........... Perth City Council [*Australia*]
PCC........... Philippine Cotton Corp. (PDAA)
PCC........... Planetary Citizens' Council for Peace, Development, and the Environment [*Singapore*]
PCC........... Planning Consultative Council [*Victoria, Australia*]
PCC........... Planning Coordination Conference [*NATO*] (NATG)
PCC........... Polish Chamber of Commerce (EAIO)
PCC........... Pontifical Council for Culture [*Vatican City*] (EAIO)
PCC........... Pour Copie Conforme [*Certified True Copy*] [*French*]
PCC........... Pregnancy Crisis Centre [*Australia*]
PCC........... Price Control Center [*Iran*] (ME)
PCC........... Prisoners of Conscience Committee [*Estonia*] (EAIO)
PCC........... Production & Construction Corp. [*China*]
PCC........... Public Complaints Commission
PCCA........ Poste de Commandement de Corps d'Armee [*Military*] [*French*] (MTD)
PCCA........ Promotion of Community and Cultural Awareness [*Australia*]
PCCh .... Partido Comunista de Chile [*Chilean Communist Party*] [*Political party*] (EY)
PCCI .... Philippine Chamber of Commerce and Industry (IMH)
PCCI .... Portuguese Chamber of Commerce and Industry (EAIO)
PCCII .... Public Corporation for Construction and Industrial Installation [*Yemen*]
PCCM....... Permanent Consultative Committee of the Maghreb [*Tunisia*]
PCCM....... Portuguese Cultural Centre of Melbourne [*Victoria, Australia*]
PCCMCA .. Programa Cooperativo Centroamericano para el Mejoramiento de Cultivos Alimenticios (LAA)
PCC-ML.... Partido Comunista Colombiano - Marxista-Leninista [*Colombian Communist Party - Marxist-Leninist*] (LA)
PCCN .... Parti Congolais de Conscience Nationale
PCCNRR... Partido Comunista - Comite Nacional de Recuperacion Revolucionaria [*Communist Party - National Committee for Revolutionary Recovery*] [*Argentina*] (LA)
PCCS .... Parti Conservateur Chretien-Social [*Conservative Christian-Social Party*] [*Switzerland*] [*Political party*] (PPE)
PCD .... Democratic Conservative Party [*Nicaragua*] [*Political party*] (PD)
PCD .... Panstwowa Centrala Drzewna [*State Lumber Center*] (POL)
PCD .... Parti Communiste du Dahomey [*Communist Party of Dahomey*] [*Benin*] [*Political party*]
PCD .... Partido Comunista Dominicano [*Dominican Communist Party*] [*Dominican Republic*] [*Political party*] (PPW)
PCD .... Partido Conservador Democrata [*Democratic Conservative Party*] [*Nicaragua*] (LA)
PCD .... Patriotic Coalition for Democracy [*Political group*] [*Guyana*]
PCD .... Plataforma de Convergencia Democratica [*Platform of Democratic Convergence*] [*Spanish*] (WER)
PCD .... Programme Communal de Developpement [*Communal Development Program*] [*Algeria*] (AF)
PCD .... Pueblo, Cambio, y Democracia [*People, Change, and Democracy*] [*Ecuador*] (LA)
PCDA .... Partido Cristao Democratico de Angola [*Christian Democratic Party of Angola*] (AF)
PCDE........ Parent Council for Deaf Education [*Australia*]
PC de N...... Partido Comunista de Nicaragua [*Communist Party of Nicaragua*] (LA)
PCDF........ Programa Cooperativo para el Desarrollo Forestal [*Peru*] (DSCA)
PCDI......... Poste de Commandement de Division d'Infanterie [*Military*] [*French*] (MTD)
PCd'I (M-L) ... Partito Comunista d'Italia (Marxista-Leninista) [*Communist Party of Italy (Marxist-Leninist)*] (WER)
PCDO .... Provincial Community Development Officer
PCdoB....... Partido Comunista do Brasil [*Communist Party of Brazil*] [*Political party*] (PPW)
PCDP........ Parti Comorien pour la Democratie et le Progres [*Political party*] (EY)

PCD-PRP .. Pueblo, Cambio, y Democracia - Partido Roldosista Popular [*People, Change, and Democracy - Popular Roldosista Party*] [*Ecuador*] [*Political party*] (PPW)

PCE............ Parti Communiste Egyptien [*Communist Party of Egypt*]

PCE............ Partido Comunista de Espana [*Communist Party of Spain*] [*Political party*] (PPE)

PCE............ Partido Comunista Ecuatoriano [*Communist Party of Ecuador*] [*Political party*] (PPW)

PCE............ Petrozavodsk Commodity Exchange [*Russian Federation*] (EY)

PCE............ Polyarthrite Chronique Evolutive [*Chronic Evolutive Polyarthritis*] [*Medicine*] [*French*]

PCEA......... Parti Congolais de l'Entente Africaine

PCEA........ Presbyterian Church of East Africa

PCEA........ Presbyterian Church of Eastern Australia

PCEA........ Programa Cooperativo de Experimentacion Agropecuaria [*Lima, Peru*] (LAA)

Pceau........ Ponceau [*Culvert*] [*Military map abbreviation World War I*] [*French*] (MTD)

PCEC........ Philippine Cocoa Estates Corp.

PCEC........ Philippine Council of Evangelical Churches

PCEHS...... Publications du Comite des Etudes Historiques et Scientifiques de l'Afrique Occidentale Francaise

PCEI .... Partido Comunista de Espana (Internacional) [*Spanish Communist Party (International)*] (WER)

PCEM....... Parliamentary Council of the European Movement

PCEM....... Polish Commission for Electron Microscopy of the Polish Academy of Sciences (EAIO)

PCEM....... Premier Cycle d'Etudes Medicales [*French*]

PCE/ML ... Partido Comunista de Espana Marxista-Leninista [*Marxist-Leninist Spanish Communist Party*] (WER)

PCE-ML.... Partido Comunista del Ecuador-Marxista Leninista [*Communist Party of Ecuador-Marxist Leninist Faction*] [*Ecuador*] (LA)

PCE-R....... Partido Comunista de Espana - Reconstituido [*Reconstituted Spanish Communist Party*] [*Political party*] (PD)

PCES .... Partido Comunista de El Salvador [*Communist Party of El Salvador*] (LA)

PCEU........ Partido Comunista de Espana Unificado [*Unified Communist Party of Spain*] [*Political party*] (PPW)

PCF........... Pacific Cultural Foundation [*Taiwan*] (EAIO)

PCF........... Pakistan Christian Fellowship

PCF........... Parti Communiste Francais [*French Communist Party*] [*Political party*] (PPW)

PCF........... Pointer Club de France (EAIO)

PCF........... Population Center Foundation [*Philippines*] [*Research center*] (IRC)

PCFS .... Pax Christi - French Section (EAIO)

PCG .... Parti Communiste de Guadeloupe [*Communist Party of Guadeloupe*] [*Political party*] (PPW)

PCG .... Partido Carlista de Galicia [*Carlist Party of Galicia*] [*Spanish*] (WER)

PCGG .... Presidential Commission on Good Government [*Philippines*] (ECON)

pch.............. Ammunition Bearer [*or Carrier*] (BU)

pch.............. Because (RU)

PCh .... Digital Plethysmograph with Ink Registration (RU)

p ch .... Furnace/Hour (BU)

PCh .... Intermediate Frequency (RU)

PCH .... Panstwowa Centrala Handlowa [*State Trade Center*] (POL)

PCH .... Partido Comunista de Honduras [*Communist Party of Honduras*] [*Political party*] (PD)

p/ch............ Political Unit [*Military term*] (RU)

PCH .... Prince Charles Hospital [*Australia*]

PCh .... Program Clock (RU)

PCh .... Pseudorandom Number (RU)

PChM .... Frequency Manipulation Attachment [*Computers*] (RU)

PChM .... Program Clock Mechanism (RU)

PChO........ Protichemicka Ochrana [*Antichemical Defense*] (CZ)

pchor......... Podchorazy [*Ensign*] [*Poland*]

PChP........ Absorption Limiting Frequency (RU)

PChP........ Progressistskaia Chadskaia Partiia

P Chr......... Palais Chronologique [*France*] (FLAF)

PCHR .... Permanent Commission of Human Rights [*Nicaragua*] (EAIO)

PchU......... Printer [*Computers*] (RU)

PChZ .... Povazske Chemicke Zavody [*Chemical Plants of the Vah River*] (CZ)

PChZ .... Prazske Chemicke Zavody [*Prague Chemical Works*] (CZ)

PCI............ Parti Communiste Internationaliste [*Internationalist Communist Party*] [*France*] [*Political party*] (PPE)

PCI............ Partidul Comunist Italian [*Italian Communist Party*] (RO)

PCI............ Partito Comunista Italiano [*Italian Communist Party*] [*Political party*]

PCI............ Pax Christi International (EAIO)

PCI............ Paza Contra Incendiilor [*Fire Prevention*] (RO)

PCI............ Pecheries de Cote-D'Ivoire

PCI............ Prudential Cornhill Insurance Company of Australia Ltd.

PCIAC....... Petro-Canada International Assistance Corp.

PCIAOH ... Permanent Commission and International Association on Occupational Health (EAIO)

PCICS........ Permanent Council of the International Convention of Stresa on Cheeses (EAIO)

PCIJ.......... Permanent Court of International Justice

PCIM........ Parti du Congres de l'Independance

PCIM........ Parti du Congres de l'Independance de Madagascar [*Party of the Congress for Malagasy Independence*]

PCIM........ Programa Cooperativo de Investigaciones de Maiz [*Peru*] (LAA)

PCI/ML..... Partito Comunista d'Italia/Marxista-Leninista [*Italian Communist Party/Marxist-Leninist*] (WER)

PC-INP...... Philippine Constabulary - Integrated National Police (DS)

PCJ .... Partido Catorce de Junio [*14 June Party*] [*Dominican Republic*] (LA)

PCJ .... PEN Centre, Jamaica (EAIO)

PCJ .... Petroleum Corporation of Jamaica (GEA)

PCJC .... Parliamentary Criminal Justice Committee [*Queensland, Australia*]

PCJILMCC ... Philip C. Jessup International Law Moot Court Competition (EAIO)

PCK .... Pengarah Chawangan Khas [*Director Special Branch (Police)*] (ML)

PCK .... Pilotni Cvicna Kabina [*Pilot Training Cabin*] (CZ)

PCK .... Polski Czerwony Krzyz [*Polish Red Cross*] (POL)

PCK .... Portatif Celik Konstruksiyon Sanayi ve Ticaret AS [*Portable Steel Construction Industry and Trade Corp.*] (TU)

PCK .... Presbyterian Church of Korea (EY)

PCK .... Puna Cena Kostanja [*Full Cost*] (YU)

PCKD .... Pegawai Chawangan Khas Daerah [*District Special Branch Officer*] (ML)

PCKD .... Polski Centralny Komitet Doradczy [*Central Polish Advisory Committee*] (POL)

PCL........... Parti Communiste de Luxembourg [*Communist Party of Luxembourg*] [*Political party*] (PPE)

PCL........... Parti Communiste Libanais [*Lebanese Communist Party*] [*Political party*] (PPW)

PCL........... Philippine Cultural League [*Australia*]

PCL........... Pucallpa [*Peru*] [*Airport symbol*] (OAG)

PCLC........ Pest Control Licensing Committee [*New South Wales, Australia*]

PCLI .... Parti de la Convergence pour les Libertes et l'Integration [*Burkina Faso*] [*Political party*] (EY)

PCLLRC.... Post-Colonial Literatures and Languages Centre [*Macquarie University*] [*Australia*]

PCLPNLas ... Panstwowa Centrala Lesnych Produktow Niedrzewnych "Las" [*"Las" (Forest) State Agency of Non-Timber Forest Products*] (POL)

PCM .... Papeterie Cartonniere Moderne [*Algeria*]

PCM .... Par ces Motifs [*Benelux*] (BAS)

PCM .... Parti Communiste Malgache [*Malagasy Communist Party*] (AF)

PCM .... Parti Communiste Marocain [*Moroccan Communist Party*] [*Political party*]

PCM .... Parti Communiste Martiniquais [*Communist Party of Martinique*] [*Political party*] (PPW)

PCM .... Parti des Classes Moyennes [*Middle Class Party*] [*Luxembourg*] [*Political party*] (PPE)

PCM .... Partido Comunista Mexicano [*Mexican Communist Party*] [*Political party*] (PPW)

PCM .... Philippine Campaign Medal

PCM .... Pineapple Canning of Malaysia (ML)

PCM .... Polskie Centrum Muzyczne [*Poland*] (EAIO)

PCM .... Postgraduate Committee in Medicine [*Australia*]

PCM .... Pravoslavna Crkva vo Makedonija [*Orthodox Church in Macedonia*] (YU)

PCM .... Produits en Ciment Moule

PCMA .... Professional Conference Management Association [*Australia*]

PCMANSW ... Precast Concrete Manufacturers' Association of New South Wales [*Australia*]

PCMAV..... Precast Concrete Manufacturers' Association of Victoria [*Australia*]

PCMB........ Parents and Children after Marriage Breakdown [*Study*] [*Australia*]

PCMC....... Philippines Cement Manufacturers Corp. (EAIO)

PCMF....... Personnels des Cadres Militaires Feminins [*France*] (PDAA)

PCMIP ...... Pontifical Commission for Migrants and Itinerant Peoples [*See also PCMT*] [*Vatican City, Vatican City State*] (EAIO)

PCMIP ...... Pontifical Council for the Pastoral Care of Migrants and Itinerant People [*Vatican City*] (EAIO)

PC-ML ...... Marxist-Leninist Communist Party [*Bolivia*] [*Political party*] (PPW)

PCML........ Parti Communiste Marxiste-Leniniste [*Marxist-Leninist Communist Party*] [*France*] [*Political party*] (PPW)

PCML........ Partido Comunista Marxista-Leninista [*Marxist-Leninist Communist Party*] [*Argentina*] (LA)

PCML........ Partito Comunista Marxista-Leninista [*Marxist-Leninist Communist Party*] [*San Marino*] [*Political party*] (PPE)

PCMLB ..... Parti Communiste Marxiste-Leniniste de Belgique [*Marxist-Leninist Communist Party of Belgium*] (WER)
PCMLF ..... Parti Communiste Marxiste-Leniniste Francais [*French Marxist-Leninist Communist Party*] [*Dissolved, 1978*] [*Political party*] (PPW)
PC(ML)I .... Partito Comunista (Marxista-Leninista) de Italia [*Communist Party of Italy (Marxist-Leninist)*] [*Political party*] (PPE)
PCMPA ..... Programa Centroamericano de Mejoramiento de Produccion Animal (DSCA)
PCMT .... Pontificia Commissione Migrazioni e Turismo [*Pontifical Commission for Migrants and Itinerant Peoples - PCMIP*] [*Vatican City, Vatican City State*] (EAIO)
PCMU .... Plan Communal de Modernisation Urbaine
PCN .... Certificat de Physique, Chimie, Sciences Naturelles [*French*]
PCN .... Partido Comunista de Nicaragua [*Communist Party of Nicaragua*] [*Political party*] (PD)
PCN .... Partido Conservador Nicaraguense [*Nicaraguan Conservative Party*] [*Political party*] (PPW)
PCN .... Partido de Conciliacion Nacional [*National Reconciliation Party*] [*El Salvador*] [*Political party*] (PPW)
PCN .... Pitcairn Islands [*ANSI three-letter standard code*] (CNC)
PCNGO ..... Palestine Committee for Non-Governmental Organisations [*Tunisia*] (EAIO)
PCNU .... Positief Christelijk Nationale Unie [*Benelux*] (BAS)
PCO .... Parliamentary Counsel's Office [*Australia*]
PCO .... Partido Comunista Ortodoxo [*Orthodox Communist Party*] [*Dominican Republic*] (LA)
PCO .... Permanent Conservation Order [*Australia*]
Pco .... Picco [*Peak*] [*Italian*] (NAU)
Pco .... Pico [*Peak*] [*Po*] [*See also*] [*Portuguese*] (NAU)
Pco .... Pico [*Peak*] [*Po*] [*See also*] [*Spanish*] (NAU)
PCO .... Poste de Commandement Operationnel [*Operational Command Post*] [*Cambodia*] (CL)
PCO .... Pripraven k Civilni Obrane [*Prepared for Civil Defense (Badge)*] (CZ)
PCO .... Programme Complementaire Optionnel
PCO .... Protestants-Christelijke Onderwijsvakorganisatie [*Netherlands*] (SLS)
PCO .... Protiletecka Civilni Obrana [*Civil Air Defense*] (CZ)
PCOC .... Partit Comunista Obrero de Catalunya [*Communist Workers' Party of Catalonia*] [*Political party*] (PPW)
PCOD .... Permanente Commissie voor Overheids-Documentatie ['s-Gravenhage]
PCOE .... Partido Comunista Obrero de Espana [*Communist Workers' Party of Spain*] [*Political party*] (PPW)
PCP .... Palestinian Communist Party [*Political party*] (PD)
PCP .... Panafrican Congress of Prehistory
PCP .... Partido Communista Portugues [*Portuguese Communist Party*] [*Lisbon*] (WER)
PCP .... Partido Comunista Paraguayano [*Paraguayan Communist Party*] [*Political party*] (PD)
PCP .... Partido Comunista Peruano [*Peruvian Communist Party*] [*Political party*] (PPW)
PCP .... Partido Comunista Portugues [*Portuguese Communist Party*] [*Political party*] (PPE)
PCP .... Partido Comunista Puertorriqueno [*Puerto Rican Communist Party*] [*Political party*] (PPW)
PCP .... Partido Conservador Popular [*Popular Conservative Party*] [*Argentina*] (LAA)
p cp .... Petites Coupures [*French*]
PCP .... Practising Computer Professional [*Australian Computer Society*]
PCP .... Progressive Conservative Party [*Australia*] [*Political party*]
PCP .... Progressive Constitutionalist Party [*Malta*] [*Political party*] (PPE)
PCPAV ...... Pensioners-Combined Pensioners Association of Victoria [*Australia*]
PCPAZ ...... Permanente Commissie voor Post- en Archiefzaken ['s-Gravenhage]
PCPE .... Partido Comunista de los Pueblos de Espana [*Communist Party of the Peoples of Spain*] [*Political party*] (EY)
PCPI .... Permanent Committee on Patent Information [*World Intellectual Property Organization*] [*Information service or system*] (IID)
PCP-M ...... Partido Comunista Peruano - Mayoria [*Peruvian Communist Party - Majority Faction*] (LA)
PCP M-L ... Partido Comunista de Portugal, Marxista-Leninista [*Marxist-Leninist Communist Party of Portugal*] [*Political party*] (PPE)
PCP(R) ...... Partido Comunista Portugues Reconstruido [*Portuguese Communist Party - Reformed*] (WER)
PCP-U .... Partido Comunista Peruano - Unidad [*Peruvian Communist Party - Unidad Faction*] (LA)
PCPV .... Partido Comunista del Pais Valenciano [*Spain*] [*Political party*] (EY)
PCPV .... Partit Carli del Pais Valencia [*Carlist Party of the Valencian Country*] [*Spanish*] (WER)

PCR .... Parti Communiste Reunionnais [*Communist Party of Reunion*] [*Political party*] (PPW)
PCR .... Partido Comunista Revolucionario [*Revolutionary Communist Party*] [*Peru*] [*Political party*] (PPW)
PCR .... Partido Comunista Revolucionario [*Revolutionary Communist Party*] [*Argentina*] (LA)
PCR .... Partido Comunista Revolucionario [*Revolutionary Communist Party*] [*Chile*] (LA)
PCR .... Partido Comunista Revolucionario [*Revolutionary Communist Party*] [*Spanish*] (WER)
PCR .... Parti du Centre [*Center Party*] [*Mauritius*] (AF)
PCR .... Partidul Comunist Roman [*Romanian Communist Party*] [*Political party*] (PPE)
PCR .... Partito Comunista Rivoluzionario [*Revolutionary Communist Party*] [*Italian*] (WER)
PCR .... Program to Combat Racism
PCR .... Puerto Carreno [*Colombia*] [*Airport symbol*] (OAG)
PCRC .... Pacific Concerns Resource Center (EA)
PCRD .... Partido Comunista de la Republica Dominicana [*PACOREDO*] [*Communist Party of the Dominican Republic*] [*Also,*] (LA)
PCRDF ...... Philippine Coconut Research and Development Foundation
PCRH .... Provincial Cities and Rural Highways Program [*Australia*]
PCRMGPS ... Poor Clerks Regular of the Mother of God of the Pious Schools [*Rome, Italy*] (EAIO)
PCRML ..... Parti Communiste Revolutionnaire - Marxiste-Leniniste [*Revolutionary Marxist-Leninist Communist Party*] [*France*] [*Political party*] (PPW)
PCRV .... Parti Communiste Revolutionnaire Voltaique [*Voltan Revolutionary Communist Party*] (AF)
pcs .... Parancs [*Order, Command*] (HU)
PCS .... Parti Chretien-Social [*Christian Social Party*] [*Luxembourg*] [*Political party*] (PPW)
PCS .... Parti Communiste Senegalais [*Senegalese Communist Party*] (AF)
PCS .... Parti Communiste Suisse [*Communist Party of Switzerland*] [*Political party*] (PPE)
PCS .... Partido Comunista Salvadoreno [*Salvadoran Communist Party*] [*Political party*] (PPW)
PCS .... Partito Comunista Sammarinese [*Communist Party of San Marino*] [*Political party*] (PPE)
PCS .... Personal Care Subsidy [*Australia*]
PCS .... Petrochemical Corporation of Singapore
PCS .... Postupak Crkvenih Sudova [*Ecclesiastic Courts Procedure*] (YU)
PCS .... Pregnancy Counselling Service [*Australia*]
PCS .... Sabah Chinese Party [*Malaysia*] [*Political party*] (FEA)
PCSA .... Palm and Cycad Societies of Australia
PCSD .... Partido Cristao Social Democratico [*Christian Social Democratic Party*] [*Portugal*] [*Political party*] (PPE)
PCSF .... Pax Christi - Section Francaise [*France*] (EAIO)
PCSIR .... Pakistan Council of Scientific and Industrial Research [*Research center*] (IRC)
PCS/ML .... Parti Communiste Suisse/Marxiste-Leniniste [*Swiss Communist Party/Marxist-Leninist*] (WER)
PCSMQC .. Polish Committee for Standardization, Measures, and Quality Control (EAIO)
PCSP .... Permanent Commission of the Conference on the Use and Conservation of the Marine Resources of the South Pacific [*Peru*] (ASF)
PCSPE ...... Panama Canal Society of Professional Engineers (EAIO)
PCST .... Pakistan Council for Science and Technology (IRC)
PCST .... Public Corporation for Sugar Trade [*Sudan*]
PCSU .... Plan Communal Semi-Urbain [*Algeria*]
pct .... Panceltoro [*Armor-Piercing, Antitank (Shell, Gun)*] (HU)
PCT .... Parti Communiste Tunisien [*Tunisian Communist Party*] [*Political party*] (PD)
PCT .... Parti Congolais du Travail [*Congolese Labor Party*] [*Political party*] (PPW)
PCT .... Partido Comunista de los Trabajadores [*Communist Party of the Workers*] [*OPI*] [*Formerly,*] [*Spanish*] (WER)
PCT .... Partido Conservador Tradicional [*Traditionalist Conservative Party*] [*Nicaragua*] [*Political party*]
PCT .... Peace Air Togo [*ICAO designator*] (FAAC)
PCT .... Police Complaints Tribunal [*Australia*]
PCT .... Poste de Commandement Tir
PCT .... Programa de Cooperacion Tecnica [*Program of Technical Cooperation - PTC*] [*Organization of American States*] [*Washington, DC*]
p ct .... Prosent [*Percent*] [*Norway*] (GPO)
PCT .... Puangchon Chao Thai [*Thai Mass Party*] [*Thailand*] [*Political party*]
p/cta .... Por Cuenta [*On Account*] [*Spanish*]
PC-TNO .... Primatencentrum, Nederlands Centrale Organisatie voor Toegepast-Natuurwetenschappelijk Onderzoek [*Primate Center, Netherlands Central Organization for Applied Natural Scientific Research*] (ARC)

PCTP .... Partido Comunista dos Trabalhadores Portugueses [*Portuguese Workers' Communist Party*] [*Political party*] (PPW)
PCTUULAW ... Permanent Congress of Trade Union Unity of Latin American Workers [*See also CPUSTAL*] [*Mexico City, Mexico*] (EAIO)
PCU .... Partido Comunista del Uruguay [*Communist Party of Uruguay*] (LA)
PCU .... Partido Conservador Unido [*Chilean Catholic political party*]
PCU .... Policy Co-Ordination Unit [*Australia*]
PCUAA ..... Panhellenic Confederation of the Unions of Agricultural Associations [*Greece*] (EAIO)
PCUd'I....... Partito Comunista Unificato d'Italia [*United Communist Party of Italy*] [*Pro-Chinese*] (WER)
PCUI......... Partito Comunista Unificado de Italia [*Unified Communist Party of Italy*] [*Political party*] (PPE)
PCUK .... Produits Chimiques Ugine Kuhlmann [*French chemical company*]
PCUS........ Parti Communiste de l'Union Sovietique [*Communist Party of the Soviet Union*]
PCUS........ Partidul Comunist al URSS [*Communist Party of the USSR*] (RO)
PCV .... Groupement Petits Commercants Voltaique
PCV .... Partido Comunista Venezolana [*Venezuelan Communist Party*] [*Political party*] . (PPW)
PCV .... Per-Ce-Voir [*French*]
PCV .... Projektierung Chemische Verfahrenstechnik GmbH
PCV .... Prostitutes' Collective of Victoria [*Australia*]
PCVC........ Philippine Convention and Visitors Corp. (EAIO)
PCW .... Parti Communiste Wallon [*Walloon Communist Party*] [*Belgium*] (WER)
PCW .... Polichlorek Winylu [*Polyvinyl Chloride*] [*Poland*]
PCWA .... Pharmaceutical Council of Western Australia
PCWF....... Panstwowa Centrala Wychowania Fizycznego [*State Center of Physical Education*] (POL)
PCWF....... Philippine Communications Workers' Federation
PCWM ...... Panstwowe Centrum Wyszkolenia Morskiego [*State Center for Nautical Education*] (POL)
PCWTU..... Philippine Woman's Christian Temperance Union (EAIO)
PCWU .... Port Commissioners Workers' Union [*India*]
PCWU .... Public Cleansing Workers' Union [*Singapore*] (ML)
PCYC........ Police Citizens' Youth Club [*Australia*]
PCZ........... Canal Zone [*ANSI three-letter standard code*] [*Obsolete*] (CNC)
p cz .... Posrednia Czestotliwosc [*Intermediate Frequency*] [*Poland*]
PCZ........... Priroda, Clovek, Zdravje [*Nature, Man, Health*] [*A periodical Ljubljana*] (YU)
PD .... Democratic Party [*Ecuador*] [*Political party*] (PD)
PD .... Dispatcher's Console (RU)
PD .... Increased Pressure (RU)
PD .... Infantry Division (RU)
PD .... Padova [*Car registration plates*] [*Italian*]
Pd .... Paladio [*Palladium*] [*Chemical element*] [*Portuguese*]
PD .... Palaia Diathiki [*Old Testament*] (GC)
pd .... Par Delegation [*France*] (FLAF)
pd .... Partial Pressure (RU)
PD .... Parti Democratique [*Democratic Party*] [*Luxembourg Political party*] (EAIO)
PD .... Partido Democrata [*Democratic Party*] [*Costa Rica*] [*Political party*] (PPW)
PD .... Partido Democrata [*Democratic Party*] [*Chile*] [*Political party*]
PD .... Partido Democratico [*Democratic Party*] [*Brazil*] (LA)
PD .... Partido Democratico [*Democratic Party*] [*Spanish*] (WER)
PD .... Peak Detector (RU)
PD .... Pede Deferimento [*Portuguese*]
pd .... Peldany [*Copy*] (HU)
PD .... Pemangku Djabatan [*Acting (Manager, Chairman)*] (IN)
PD .... Per Dag [*Per Day*] [*Afrikaans*]
pd .... Per Deel [*Each Part, Volume*] [*Publishing*] [*Netherlands*]
PD .... Per Diem [*By the Day*] [*Latin*]
PD .... Perifereia Dimou [*Municipal District*] (GC)
PD .... Pesadiska Divizija [*Infantry Division*] (YU)
PD .... Petrol Dairesi [*Petroleum Office*] (TU)
PD .... Piece Detachee [*French*] (ADPT)
PD .... Piece Droite [*In a turret*] [*Military*] [*French*] (MTD)
pd .... Pied [*Foot*] [*French*]
PD .... Piezobirefringence (RU)
PD .... Piston Engine (RU)
PD .... Planinsko Drustvo [*Alpine Society*] (YU)
PD .... Poljoprivredno Dobro [*State Farm*] (YU)
Pd .... Poludnie [*or Poludniowy*] [*South or Southern*] [*Poland*]
pd .... Pond [*Pound*] [*Monetary unit*] [*Afrikaans*]
P/D .... Port Dickson (ML)
PD .... Port Du [*Carriage Forward*] [*French*]
PD .... Posdata [*or Post Data*] [*Postscript*] [*Spanish*] (GPO)
PD .... Potentiometric Transducer (RU)
PD .... Poverenictvo Dopravy [*Office of the Commissioner of Transportation*] (CZ)

PD .... Poverenictvo Dopravy a Verejnych Prac [*Office of the Commissioner of Transportation and Public Works*] (CZ)
PD .... Presernova Druzba [*Preseren Society*] (YU)
PD .... Pressedienst [*Press Service*] (EG)
pd .... Pressurized, Under Pressure (RU)
PD .... Prime Mover (RU)
PD .... Privatdozent [*Tutor*] [*German*]
PD .... Proedrikon Diatagma [*Presidential Decree*] [*Greek*] (GC)
PD .... Programa Democratico [*Democratic Program*] [*Spain*] [*Political party*] (PPE)
PD .... Program Transmitter [*Computers*] (RU)
PD .... Progressive Democrats [*Ireland*] [*Political party*]
PD .... Proportional Differentiator (RU)
PD .... Proportionnel et Derive [*French*] (ADPT)
PD .... Prosvetni Delavec [*Educational Worker*] [*A periodical Ljubljana*] (YU)
PD .... Protivdesantni [*Antilanding*] [*Military*] (YU)
PD .... Provisional District [*Church of England in Australia*]
PD .... Prussian Dollar [*Monetary unit*] (ROG)
PD .... Public Defender [*Australia*]
PD .... Pulse Pressure (RU)
PD .... Pushkin House (RU)
PD .... Semiconductor Diode (RU)
PD .... Starting Motor (RU)
PD .... Suspended Decontaminator (RU)
PD .... Switching Diode (RU)
pd .... Useful Effect (RU)
PDA .... Emergency-Signal Transmitter (RU)
PDA .... Pancyprian Dental Association [*Cyprus*] (EAIO)
PDA .... Parkinsons Disease Association of Victoria [*Australia*]
PdA .... Partei der Arbeit [*Labor Party*] [*Switzerland*] [*Political party*] (PPE)
PDA .... Parti Democratico da Angola [*Democratic Party of Angola*] [*Political party*]
PDA .... Partido Democratico Arubano [*Democratic Party of Aruba*] [*Political party*] (EY)
PDA .... Partit Democrata d'Andorra [*Andorran Democratic Party*] [*Political party*] (PPW)
Pd'A .... Partito d'Azione [*Action Party*] [*Italy*] [*Political party*] (PPE)
PDA .... Party of Democratic Action [*Bosnia-Herzegovina*] [*Political party*] (EY)
Pda .... Pedra [*Rock*] [*Portuguese*] (NAU)
PDA .... Perifereia Dimou Athinon [*Athens Municipal Area*] (GC)
PDA .... Peshawar Development Authority [*Pakistan*] (EY)
PDA .... Philippine Dental Association (EAIO)
Pda .... Piedra [*Rock*] [*Spanish*] (NAU)
PDA .... Population and Community Development Association [*Thailand*] (EAIO)
PDA .... Population and Community Development Association [*China*]
PDA .... Posadkovy Dum Armady [*Army Post Recreation Building*] (CZ)
PDA .... Pour Dire Adieu [*To Say Farewell*] [*On visiting cards*] [*French*]
PDA .... Preventive Detention Act [*Philippines*]
PDA .... Produktions- und Dienstleistungsabgabe [*Production and Services Tax (A type of turnover tax)*] [*German*] (EG)
PDA .... Professional Divers Association of Australia
PDA .... Proleter Devrimci Aydinlik Grubu [*Proletarian Revolutionary Enlightenment Group*] [*PDAG*] [*See also*] (TU)
PDA .... Puerto Inirida [*Colombia*] [*Airport symbol*] (OAG)
PDA .... Regulation on the Application of the Law on State Arbitration (BU)
PDAG .... Proleter Devrimci Aydinlik Grubu [*Proletarian Revolutionary Enlightenment Group*] [*PDA*] [*See also*] (TU)
PDA-KM ... Party of Democratic Action of Kosovo-Metohija [*Serbia*] [*Political party*] (EY)
PDAP......... Programa Autonomo de Desenvolvimento Agro-Pecuario [*Autonomous Agricultural-Livestock Development Program*] [*Portuguese*] (WER)
PDA-S .... Party of Democratic Action of the Sandjak [*Serbia*] [*Political party*] (EY)
PDAV .... Parkinson's Disease Association of Victoria [*Australia*]
PDAVO ..... Verordnung ueber die Produktionsabgabe und Dienstleistungsabgabe der VEW [*Ordinance Concerning the Production Tax and Services Tax of the State Economy*] (EG)
pdb .... Airborne Battalion (BU)
PDB .... Paradichlorobenzene (RU)
PDB .... Paratroop Battalion (RU)
PDB .... Partei der Deutschsprachigen Belgier [*Party of German-Speaking Belgians*] [*Political party*] (PPW)
PDB .... Parti Democrate du Burundi
PDB .... Partido Democrata Boliviano [*Bolivian Democratic Party*] (LA)
PDB .... Partido Democratico Brasileiro [*Brazilian Democratic Party*] (LA)
PDB .... Petrol Dairesi Baskanligi [*Petroleum Office Chairmanship*] (TU)
PDB .... Police Discipline Board [*New South Wales, Australia*]

PDB .... Production Dispatch Office   (RU)
PDBB .... Airdrop Fuel and Lubricant Tank   (RU)
pdbr .... Paratroop Brigade   (RU)
PDBS .... Parliamentary Database System [*Australia*]
PDC .... Mueo [*New Caledonia*] [*Airport symbol*]   (OAG)
PDC .... Pacte Democratica per Catalunya [*Democratic Pact for Catalonia*] [*Spain*] [*Political party*]   (PPE)
PDC .... Parti Democrate Chretien [*Christian Democratic Party*] [*Burundi*] [*Political party*]
PDC .... Parti Democrate Chretien [*Christian Democratic Party*] [*Malagasy*]   (AF)
PDC .... Parti Democrate Chretien du Burundi [*Christian Democratic Party of Burundi*]   (AF)
PDC .... Parti Democrate-Chretien Suisse [*Christian Democratic Party of Switzerland*] [*Political party*]   (PPE)
PDC .... Parti Democratique Camerounaise [*Political party*] [*Cameroon*]
PDC .... Parti Democratique Congolais
PDC .... Parti Democratique Constitutionel [*Constitutional Democratic Party*] [*Morocco*]   (AF)
PDC .... Parti Democratique de la Cote-D'Ivoire [*Democratic Party of the Ivory Coast*]
PDC .... Parti des Democrates Camerounais [*Political party*]   (EY)
PDC .... Partido da Democracia Cristao [*Christian Democratic Party*] [*Portugal*] [*Political party*]   (PPW)
PDC .... Partido Democracia Cristiana [*Christian Democratic Party*] [*Guatemala*] [*Political party*]   (PPW)
PDC .... Partido Democrata Cristiano [*Christian Democratic Party*] [*Paraguay*] [*Political party*]   (PPW)
PDC .... Partido Democrata Cristiano [*Christian Democratic Party*] [*Peru*] [*Political party*]   (PPW)
PDC .... Partido Democrata Cristiano [*Christian Democratic Party*] [*Honduras*] [*Political party*]   (PPW)
PDC .... Partido Democrata Cristiano [*Christian Democratic Party*] [*Bolivia*] [*Political party*]   (PPW)
PDC .... Partido Democrata Cristiano [*Christian Democratic Party*] [*Costa Rica*] [*Political party*]   (PPW)
PDC .... Partido Democrata Cristiano [*Christian Democratic Party*] [*El Salvador*] [*Political party*]
PDC .... Partido Democrata Cristiano [*Christian Democratic Party*] [*Panama*] [*Political party*]   (PPW)
PDC .... Partido Democrata Cristiano [*Christian Democratic Party*] [*Spain*]   (WER)
PDC .... Partido Democrata Cristiano [*Christian Democratic Party*] [*Mexico*]   (LA)
PDC .... Partido Democrata Cristiano [*Christian Democratic Party*] [*Uruguay*]   (LA)
PDC .... Partido Democrata de Confianza Nacional [*Nicaragua*] [*Political party*]   (EY)
PDC .... Partido Democratico Cristao [*Christian Democratic Party*] [*Brazil*] [*Political party*]
PDC .... Partido Democratico Cristiano [*Christian Democratic Party*] [*Argentina*] [*Political party*]   (PPW)
PDC .... Partido Democratico Cristiano [*Christian Democratic Party*] [*Chile*] [*Political party*]   (PPW)
PDC .... Partito della Democrazia Cristiana [*Christian Democratic Party*] [*Italy*] [*Political party*]
PDC .... People's Defence Committee [*Ghana*]   (PD)
PDC .... Population Documentation Center [*Food and Agriculture Organization*] [*United Nations Information service or system*]   (IID)
PDC .... Productivity and Development Center [*Philippines*]   (PDAA)
PDC .... Purchasing Development Center [*Australia*]
PDC .... Societe du Palace de Cocody
PDCAU ..... Pete Duel - Clube da Amizade do Universo [*Pete Duel Universal Friendship Club - PDUFC*]   (EAIO)
PDCG .... Partido Democracia Cristiana Guatemalteca [*Guatemalan Christian Democratic Party*] [*Political party*]   (PPW)
PDCh .... Doppler Frequency Converter   (RU)
PDCH .... Parti Democratique Chretien d'Haiti [*Political party*]   (EY)
PDCH .... Partido Democrata Cristiano de Honduras [*Honduran Christian Democratic Party*]   (LA)
PDCI .... Parti Democratique de la Cote-D'Ivoire [*Democratic Party of the Ivory Coast*] [*Political party*]   (PPW)
PDCL .... Partido Democrata de Castilla y Leon [*Democratic Party of Castille and Leon*] [*Spanish*]   (WER)
PDCM .... Parti Democrate Chretien de Madagascar [*Christian Democratic Party of Madagascar*]   (AF)
PDCN .... Partido Democratico de Cooperacion Nacional [*Democratic Party of National Cooperation*] [*Guatemala*] [*Political party*]
PDCP .... Private Development Corp. of the Philippines
PDCR .... Partido Democrata Cristiano Revolucionario [*Revolutionary Christian Democratic Party*] [*Bolivia*]   (LA)
PDCS .... Partito Democratico Cristiano Sammarinese [*Christian Democratic Party of San Marino*] [*Political party*]   (PPE)
PDD .... Maximum Permissible Dose   (RU)
PDD .... Panstwowy Dom Dziecka [*State Children's Home*]   (POL)

PDD .... Participacion Democratica de Tzquierda [*Chile*] [*Political party*]   (EY)
PDD .... Parti Democratique Dahomeen [*Benin*]
PDD .... Pertubohan Pemuda Daerah [*Rural Youth Organization*]   (ML)
PDD .... Posadkovy Dozorci Dustojnik [*Garrison Officer of the Day*]   (CZ)
PDD .... Proportional Pressure Transducer   (RU)
PDD .... Tree-Type Decoder [*Computers*]   (RU)
PDDD .... Protovathmion Dioikitikon kai Diaititikon Dikastirion [*First Instance Administrative and Arbitration Court*] [*Greek*]
PDE .... Pandie Pandie [*Australia*] [*Airport symbol*] [*Obsolete*]   (OAG)
PDE .... Partei fuer Deutschland und Europa [*Party for Germany and Europe*] [*Germany*] [*Political party*]   (PPW)
PDE .... Programma Dimosion Ependyseon [*Public Investments Program*]   (GC)
PDEB .... Partiia Dvizheniia za Emansipatsiiu Bakhutu
PDEG .... Panelliniki Dimokratiki Enosis Gynaikon [*Panhellenic Women's Democratic Union*]   (GC)
PDELAR ... Presidencia de la Republica [*Presidency of the Republic*] [*Mexico*]   (LA)
PDELB ...... Plumbers and Drainers' Examination and Licensing Board [*Queensland, Australia*]
P del E .... Penitenciaria del Estado [*State Penitentiary*] [*Spanish*]
PDelo .... Prosvetno Delo [*Cultural Journal*] [*A periodical Skopje*]   (YU)
pdesb .... River Crossing Assault Battalion   (RU)
pdesr .... River Crossing Assault Company   (RU)
pdesv .... River Crossing Assault Platoon   (RU)
PDF .... LAR Transregional, Linhas Aereas Regionais SA [*Portugal*] [*ICAO designator*]   (FAAC)
PDF .... Pakistan Democratic Front
PDF .... Panama Defense Forces [*Later, Public Forces*]
PDF .... Parti Democrate Francais [*French Democratic Party*] [*Political party*]   (PPW)
PDF .... Pasture Development Fund [*Iran*]
PDF .... Peat-Derived Fuel [*Finland*]
PDF .... People's Defense Force [*Singapore*]   (ML)
PDF .... People's Democratic Force [*The Bahamas*] [*Political party*]   (EY)
PDF .... Periscopic Long-Focus Camera   (RU)
PDF .... Pionniers de France [*French Pioneers*]   (WER)
PDF .... Popular Democratic Front [*Jordan*] [*Political party*]
PDFC .... People's Defense Force Command [*Singapore*]
PDFCI .... Perseroan Terbatas Private Development Finance Company of Indonesia   (IMH)
PDFLP ...... Popular Democratic Front for the Liberation of Palestine
PDG .... Padang [*Indonesia*] [*Airport symbol*]   (OAG)
PDG .... Parti Democratique de Guinee [*Democratic Party of Guinea*] [*Political party*]   (PPW)
PDG .... Parti Democratique Gabonais [*Gabonese Democratic Party*] [*Political party*]   (PPW)
PDG .... Partido Democrata Galego [*Galician Democratic Party*] [*Spanish*]   (WER)
PDG .... President Directeur General [*President Director General*] [*French*]
PDGA .... Producers' and Directors' Guild of Australia   (ADA)
PDGE .... Partido Democratico de Guinea Ecuatorial [*Democratic Party of Equatorial Guinea*] [*Political party*]   (EY)
PDH .... Pedagosko Drustvo Hrvatske [*Pedagogic Society of Croatia*]   (YU)
PDH .... Povjesno Drustvo Hrvatske [*Croatian Historical Society*]   (YU)
PDH .... Prirodoslovno Drustvo Hrvatske [*Croatian Natural Sciences Society*]   (YU)
PDHA .... Produktions-, Dienstleistungs-, und Handelsabgabe [*Production, Services, and Trade Tax*]   (EG)
PDHV-RDA ... Parti Democratique de la Haute Volta--Rassemblement Democratique Africain [*Democratic Party of Upper Volta-- African Democratic Rally*]   (AF)
PDI .... Padaeng Industry [*Thailand*]
PDI .... Partai Demokrasi Indonesia [*Indonesian Democratic Party*] [*Political party*]   (PPW)
PDI .... Parti Dahomeen de l'Independance
PDI .... Parti Democratique de l'Independance [*Democratic Independence Party*] [*Morocco*] [*Political party*]
PDI .... Partito Democratica Italiana [*Italian Democratic Party*] [*Political party*]   (PPE)
PDI .... Prime de Developpement Industriel [*France*]   (FLAF)
PDI .... Prise Ombilicale Derniers Instants   (MCD)
PDI .... Regulation on State Property   (BU)
PDIA .... Proprietary Dairy Industry Association [*South Africa*]   (AA)
PDiBM ...... Przedsiebiorstwo Detalu i Barow Mlecznych [*Milk Retail and Milk Bar Enterprise*]   (POL)
PDIC .... Public Demands Implementation Convention [*India*]   (PPW)
PDID .... Parti pour la Defense des Institutions Democratiques
PDII .... Pusat Dokumentasi dan Informasi Ilmiah [*Indonesian Center for Scientific Documentation and Information*] [*Information service or system*]   (IID)

PDIL......... Prueba del Desarrollo Inicial del Lenguaje [*Standardized test of Spanish language-speaking ability in children from three to seven years old*]
PDIN .... Pusat Dokumentasi Ilmiah Nasional [*Scientific and Technical Documentation Center*] [*Indonesia*]   (PDAA)
PDiRz .... Ministerstwo Przemyslu Drobnego i Rzemiosla [*Ministry of Small Scale and Handicraft Industry*]   (POL)
PDIS......... Pusat Dokumentasi Ilmu-Ilmu Sosial [*Social Sciences Documentation Center*] [*Indonesia*]   (PDAA)
PDIUM ..... Partito Democratico Italiano di Unita Monarchica [*Italian Democratic Party of Monarchical Unity*] [*Political party*]   (PPE)
PDJ............ Plaine Des Jarres [*South Vietnam*]
PDJTB....... Parti Democratique des Jeunes Travailleurs du Burundi
PDK .... Maximum Permissible Concentration   (RU)
PDK .... Panstwowy Dom Kultury [*State House of Culture*]   (POL)
PDK .... Party Democratic Kampuchea
PDK .... Phileleftheron Demokratikon Kendron [*Liberal Democratic Union*] [*Greek*]   (PPE)
PDK .... Phileleftheron Demokratikon Komma [*Liberal Democratic Party*] [*Greek*] [*Political party*]   (PPE)
PDK .... Planove-Dispecerska Kancelar [*Management and Plan Control Bureau*]   (CZ)
PDK .... Potentiometric Remote-Indicating Compass   (RU)
PDK .... Powiatowe Domy Kultury [*County Houses of Culture*]   (POL)
PDK .... Pres, Dokum, ve Kromaj Fabrikalari [*Stamping, Foundry, and Chrome Plating Factories*]   (TU)
PDk........... Primorski Dnevnik [*Maritime Region Daily*] [*Trieste*]   (YU)
PDKI......... Persatuan Pegawai Departemen Kesehatan Indonesia [*Union of Health Department Employees*] [*Indonesian*]
PDKN .... Maximum Permissible Concentration of Unidentified Radioactive Isotopes   (RU)
PDL .... Partido Democrata Liberal [*Liberal Democratic Party*] [*Spain*] [*Political party*]   (EY)
PDL .... People's Democracy of Laos [*Political party*]   (VNW)
PDL .... Ponta Delgada [*Portugal*] [*Airport symbol*]   (OAG)
PDL .... Poverty Datum Level [*or Line*]
PDL .... Proposta di Legge [*Parliamentary Bill*] [*Italian*]   (WER)
PD(LAO)... Public Defender (Legal Aid Office) [*Australia*]
PDLC........ Partido Liberal de Cataluna [*Liberal Democratic Party of Catalonia*] [*Political party*]   (PPW)
PDLM .... Direction des Peches Legunaires et Maritimes [*Lagoon and Marine Fishery Administration*] [*Ivory Coast*]   (AF)
PDLS......... Party of the Democratic Left of Slovakia [*Former Czechoslovakia*] [*Political party*]   (EY)
PDM .... Ground Decontamination Device   (RU)
PDM .... Parti Democratique Malgache
PDM .... Partido de los Democratas Melillenses [*Spanish North Africa*] [*Political party*]   (MENA)
PDM .... Partido Democratico Mexicano [*Mexican Democratic Party*]   (LA)
PDM .... People's Democratic Movement [*St. Vincentian*]   (LA)
PDM .... People's Democratic Movement [*Papua New Guinea*] [*Political party*]   (FEA)
PDM .... People's Democratic Movement [*Guyana*] [*Political party*]   (EY)
PDM .... People's Democratic Movement [*Turks and Caicos Islands*] [*Political party*]   (PPW)
PDM .... Persatuan Dermatologi Malaysia   (EAIO)
PDM .... Progres et Democratie Moderne [*Progress and Modern Democracy*] [*France*] [*Political party*]   (PPE)
PDM .... Railroad Track Maintenance Shops   (RU)
PDMA .... Propyldimethacrylamide   (RU)
PDMD....... Panstwowy Dom Malego Dziecka [*State Infants' Home*] [*Poland*]
PDMM...... Airdrop Flexible Bag   (RU)
PDMP .... Field Divisional Aid Station   (BU)
PDMS....... Point Defense Missile System [*NATO*]   (NATG)
PDMS....... Railroad Track Machinery Station   (RU)
PDN.......... Negative-Deciphering Apparatus   (RU)
PDN.......... Partido Democratico Nacional [*National Democratic Party*] [*Venezuela*] [*Political party*]
PDN.......... Partido Democratico Nacional [*National Democratic Party*] [*Chile*] [*Political party*]
PDN.......... Partito Democratico Nazionalista [*Democratic Nationalist Party (1921-1926)*] [*Malta*] [*Political party*]   (PPE)
PDN.......... Perusahaan Dagang Negara [*State Trading Company*]   (IN)
PDN.......... Programmsystem fuer Datenuebertragung und Netzsteurung [*German*]   (ADPT)
PDO.......... Advance Landing Detachment   (RU)
PDO.......... Antiamphibious Defense, Antilanding Defense   (RU)
PDO.......... Laundry and Disinfection Detachment   (RU)
PDO.......... Pankyprios Didaskaliki Organosis [*Pan-Cyprian Teachers Organization*]   (GC)
pdo .... Pasado [*Past*] [*Spanish*]
PDO.......... Perifereiaka Dioikitika Organa [*Regional Administrative Organs*] [*Greek*]   (GC)
PDO.......... Petroleum Development Oman [*Muscat*]   (ME)
pdo .... Philips and DuPont Optical GmbH [*Germany*]

PDO........... Prete dell'Oratorio [*Italian*]
PDO........... Principal Dental Officer [*New Zealand*]
PDO........... Production Dispatch Department   (RU)
PDO........... Production Dispatching Department   (BU)
PDO........... Prostor za Degazaciju Oruzja [*Arms Decontamination Area*]   (YU)
PDO........... Protivdesantna Odbrana [*Antilanding Defense*]   (YU)
PDO........... Public Defender's Office [*Australia*]
PDO........... Weapon Decontamination Site   (RU)
pd ob......... Supply Train [*Regimental*]   (BU)
PDOC........ Partido Democrata Obrero Campesino [*Democratic Worker-Peasant Party*] [*Dominican Republic*]   (LA)
PDOG........ Pankypriaki Dimokratiki Organosis Gynaikon [*Pan-Cyprian Democratic Women's Organization*]   (GC)
PDOIS....... People's Democratic Organisation for Independence and Socialism [*Senegambia*] [*Political party*]
PDOSOM ... Enterprise for the Extraction and Processing of Quarry-Lining Materials   (BU)
PDOV .... Prostor za Degazaciju Oruzja i Vozila [*Arms and Vehicles Decontamination Area*]   (YU)
PDoz .... Privatdozent [*University Lecturer*] [*German*]
pdp .... Airborne Regiment   (BU)
PDP .... Laundry and Disinfection Station   (RU)
PDP .... Mobile Control Tower [*Aviation*]   (RU)
PDP .... Pakistan Democratic Party [*Political party*]   (PD)
PDP .... Paratroop Regiment   (RU)
PDP .... Parliamentary Democratic Party [*Myanmar*] [*Political party*]
PDP .... Parti Democrate Populaire [*Popular Democratic Party*] [*France*] [*Political party*]   (PPE)
PDP .... Partido da Direita Portuguesa [*Party of the Portuguese Right*] [*Political party*]   (PPE)
PDP .... Partido de los Pobres [*Poor People's Party*] [*Mexico*]   (LA)
PDP .... Partido del Pueblo [*People's Party*] [*Panama*]   (LA)
PDP .... Partido Democrata Popular [*People's Democratic Party*] [*Argentina*]   (LA)
PDP .... Partido Democrata Popular [*Popular Democratic Party*] [*Spain*] [*Political party*]   (PPW)
PDP .... Partido Democrata Popular [*Popular Democratic Party*] [*Dominican Republic*] [*Political party*]   (PPW)
PDP .... Partido Democrata Progresista [*Progressive Democratic Party*] [*Argentina*]   (LA)
PDP .... Partido Democratico para o Progresso [*Democratic Progressive Party*] [*Guinea-Bissau*] [*Political party*]   (EY)
PDP .... Partido Democratico Populare [*Popular Democratic Party*] [*San Marino*] [*Political party*]   (PPE)
PDP .... Party for Democratic Prosperity [*Macedonia*] [*Political party*]
PDP .... People's Democratic [*Saint Christopher and Nevis*] [*Political party*]   (EY)
PDP .... People's Democratic Party [*Sudan*] [*Political party*]
PDP .... People's Democratic Party [*South Korea*] [*Political party*]   (EY)
PDP .... People's Democratic Party [*Netherlands Antilles*] [*Political party*]   (EY)
PDP .... People's Democratic Party [*Sierra Leone*] [*Political party*]   (EY)
PDP .... People's Democratic Party [*Bahamas*]   (LA)
PDP .... Philippine Democratic Party [*Pilipino Lakas Ng Bayan*] [*Political party*]   (PPW)
PDP .... Popular Democratic Party [*Puerto Rico*] [*Political party*]
PDP .... Poste de Donnees Pret [*French*]   (ADPT)
PDP .... Progressive Democratic Party [*Montserrat*] [*Political party*]   (PPW)
PDP .... Progressive Democratic Party [*St. Vincent*] [*Political party*]   (PPW)
PDP .... Punta Del Este [*Uruguay*] [*Airport symbol*]   (OAG)
PDP .... Suspended Decontamination Apparatus   (RU)
PDPA........ People's Democratic Party of Afghanistan [*Political party*]   (PPW)
PDPC........ Parti Democratique du Peuple Cabindais [*Democratic Party of the Cabindan People*] [*Angola*]   (AF)
PDPC........ Plant Diversity Protection Committee [*Total Environmental Centre, Sydney*] [*Australia*]
PDPL........ Programme pour le Developpement de la Production Laitiere [*Dairy Herd Development Program*] [*Mauritius*]   (AF)
PDPS........ Standing Production Conference   (RU)
PDPT........ Parti Democratique des Populations Togolaises [*Togolese Democratic People's Party*] [*Political party*]
PDQ.......... Perez De Cuellar [*Javier*] [*Peruvian diplomat Initialism is derived from the pronunciation of his last name*]
pdr............. Airborne Company   (BU)
pdr............. Infantry Battalion   (BU)
PDR .... Paratroop Company   (RU)
PDR .... Parti Democrate Rural
PDR .... Parti Democratique de la Reconstruction
PDR .... Parti Democratique Progressif [*Algeria*] [*Political party*]   (EY)
PDR .... Partido de la Democracia Radical [*Radical Democratic Party*] [*Chile*]   (LA)
PDR .... Partido Democratico Republicano [*Republican Democratic Party*] [*Brazil*]   (LA)

PDR .... Party of Democratic Reform [*Slovenia*] [*Political party*]　(EY)
PDR .... Personnes Deplacees et Refugiees
PDR .... Pharma-Dokumentationsring [*Pharma Documentation Ring*] [*Information service or system*]　(IID)
PDR .... Philippine Defense Ribbon [*Military decoration*]
PdR .... Praesident der Republic [*President of the Republic*]　(EG)
PDR .... Programme de Developpement Rural [*Tunisia*]
PDRE........ People's Democratic Republic of Ethiopia
PDREUF ... Public Daily-Rated Employees' Union Federation　(ML)
PDRH........ Partido Democratico Revolucionario Hondureno [*Revolutionary Democratic Party of Honduras*] [*Political party*]
PDRP........ Partido Democrata Reformista Peruano [*Peruvian Reformist Democratic Party*]　(LA)
PDRTs....... Radio Transmission Center　(RU)
PDRY .... People's Democratic Republic of Yemen [*Political party*]
pds........... Paratroop Gunner　(RU)
PDS........... Paratroop Service　(RU)
PDS........... Partei des Demokratischen Sozialismus [*Party of Democratic Socialism*] [*Germany Political party*]　(EAIO)
PDS........... Parti Democratique Senegalais [*Senegalese Democratic Party*] [*Political party*]　(PPW)
PDS........... Partido Democrata Socialista [*Socialist Democratic Party*] [*Panama*] [*Political party*]　(PPW)
PDS........... Partido Democratico Social [*Social Democratic Party*] [*Brazil*]　(LA)
PDS........... Partito Democratico della Sinistra [*Democratic Party of the Left*] [*Formerly, Italian Communist Party*] [*Political party*]　(EY)
PDS........... Partito di Democrazia Socialista [*Socialist Democracy Party*] [*San Marino*] [*Political party*]　(PPW)
PDS........... Party of Democratic Socialism [*Germany*] [*Political party*]
PDS........... Pedagosko Drustvo Srbije [*Pedagogic Society of Serbia*]　(YU)
PDS........... Planification des Systemes [*German*]　(ADPT)
PDS........... Plantations de la Savane de Dabou
PDS........... Plukovni Delostrelecka Skupina [*Regiment Artillery Group*]　(CZ)
PDS........... Poddustojnicka Skola [*Noncommissioned Officers School*]　(CZ)
PDS........... Preliminary Draft Standards for Special Libraries in Australia
PDS........... Private Database Service [*Australia*]
PDS........... Senior Roadmaster [*Railroads*]　(RU)
PDS........... Synchronization Transmitter　(RU)
PDSA........ People's Dispensary for Sick Animals [*South Africa*]　(AA)
PDSA........ Private Doctors' Society of South Australia
PDSC........ Parti Democrate et Social Chretien [*Zaire*] [*Political party*]　(EY)
PDSC........ Performers and Teachers Diploma, Sydney Conservatorium [*Australia*]　(ADA)
PDSC........ Population and Development Studies Center [*Korea*] [*Research center*]　(IRC)
PDSI........ Co-Phasing Pulse Transmitter　(RU)
PDSN .... Pnevmatikos Desmos Spoudaston tis Neolaias [*Cultural Bond of Student Youth*]　(GC)
PDSO .... Regulation on State Economic Organizations　(BU)
PDSO .... Voluntary Trade Union Sports Organization　(BU)
PDS-R....... Parti Democratique Senegalais - Renovation [*Senegalese Democratic Party - Reform*] [*Political party*]
PDSU........ Mobile Crushing and Grading Unit　(RU)
PDT .... Panstwowa Dyrekcja Tramwajowa [*State Administration of Streetcars*]　(POL)
PDT .... Panstwowy Dom Towarowy [*State Department Store*]　(POL)
PDT .... Partido Democratico Trabalhista [*Democratic Worker's Party*] [*Rio De Janeiro, Brazil*]　(LA)
PdT .... Parti du Travail [*Labor Party*] [*Switzerland*] [*Political party*]　(PPE)
PDT .... Powszechny Dom Towarowy [*General Department Store*]　(POL)
PDT .... Pretprijatie za Dalekovodi i Trasfostanici [*Establishment for Long-Distance Transmission Lines and Transformer Stations*] [*Skopje*]　(YU)
PDT .... Transportation Decontamination Site　(RU)
PDTC........ Petroleum Development [*Trucial Coast*]　(OMWE)
PDTZh ...... Container for Air-Dropping of Liquids　(RU)
PDU .... Control Transmitter　(RU)
PDU .... Maximum Permissible Level　(RU)
PDU .... Mobile Stone Crusher　(RU)
PDU .... Pacific Democrat Union　(EAIO)
PDU .... Parti Dahomeen de l'Unite [*Dahomean Unity Party*] [*Benin*] [*Political party*]
PDU .... Parti Democrate Unifie [*Unified Democratic Party*] [*Name replaced by Section Voltaique de Rassemblement Burkina Faso*] [*Political party*]
PDU .... Paysandu [*Uruguay*] [*Airport symbol*]　(OAG)
PDU .... Remote-Control Panel　(RU)
PDU .... Transmitting Installation　(RU)
PDUFC.... Pete Duel Universal Friendship Club　(EAIO)
PDUP .... Partito dell'Unita Proletaria [*Proletarian Unity Party*] [*Italian*]　(WER)

PdUP .... Partito di Unita Proletaria per il Comunismo [*Democratic Party of Proletarian Unity for Communism*] [*Italy*] [*Political party*]　(PPE)
PDUR .... Airdrop Packing Straps　(RU)
PDV .... Call Sender　(RU)
pdv........... Paratroop Platoon　(RU)
PDV .... Parti Democratique Voltaique [*Voltan Democratic Party*]　(AF)
PDV .... Petroleos de Venezuela
PdVP........ Praesidium der Volkspolizei [*People's Police Presidium*]　(EG)
PDVSA...... Petroleos de Venezuela Sociedade Anonima [*Venezuela*]
PDW .... Progress Dritte Welt
pd-wsch .... Poludniowo-Wschodni [*South-East*] [*Poland*]
PDZ .... Pedernales [*Venezuela*] [*Airport symbol*]　(OAG)
PDZ .... Penza Diesel Plant　(RU)
PDZ .... Pervoural'sk Dinas Brick Plant　(RU)
pd-zach...... Poludniowo-Zachodni [*South-West*] [*Poland*]
pdz/khs...... Underground Connecting Trench [*Topography*]　(RU)
Pe .... Aircraft Designed by V. M. Petlyakov　(RU)
PE .... British Aircraft Corp. Ltd. [*ICAO aircraft manufacturer identifier*]　(ICAO)
PE .... Electronic Psychrometer　(RU)
PE .... Electropneumatic Transducer　(RU)
PE .... Enameled Wire (Resistor)　(RU)
PE .... Estado de Pernambuco [*State of Pernambuco*] [*Brazil*]
PE .... Field Clearing Station　(RU)
Pe .... Padre [*Father*] [*Spanish*]
Pe .... Padre [*Father*] [*Portuguese*]
pe............. Parelthondos Etous [*Of the Past Year, Last Year's*]　(GC)
pe............. Par Exemple [*For Example*] [*French*]
PE .... Parlement Europeen　(FLAF)
PE .... Parni Elektrarna [*Steam Power Plant*]　(CZ)
PE .... Partidul Evreesc [*Rumania*]　(BJA)
pe............. Parts Egales [*Equal Parts*] [*French*]
PE .... Passeinheit [*Unit of Fit*] [*German*]
pe............. Pasta Espanola [*Leather-Covered Board Binding*] [*Publishing*] [*Spanish*]
PE .... Pedagogical Encyclopedia　(RU)
PE .... Perifereiaki Epitropi [*Regional Committee*]　(GC)
PE .... Periphere Einheit [*French*]　(ADPT)
pe............. Perjantai(na) [*Finland*]
PE .... Perspective Europeen　(FLAF)
PE .... Peru [*Poland*]
PE .... Peru [*ANSI two-letter standard code*]　(CNC)
PE .... Pescara [*Car registration plates*] [*Italian*]
PE .... Piyade Er [*Private, Infantry*]　(TU)
PE .... Police d'Etat [*State Police*] [*Algeria*]　(AF)
PE .... Polietilen [*Polyethylene*]　(TU)
PE .... Politischer Erzieher, Politische Erziehung [*Political Educator, Political Education*]　(EG)
PE .... Poljoprivredna Ekonomija [*Agricultural Economy*]　(YU)
PE .... Polyethylene　(RU)
PE .... Polytechnische Bildung und Erziehung [*Polytechnical Training and Education*]　(EG)
PE .... Pomorska Enciklopedija [*Marine Encyclopedia*]　(YU)
pe............. Ponte [*Bridge*] [*Portuguese*]　(CED)
pe............. Por Ejemplo [*For Example*] [*Spanish*]
PE .... Port Elizabeth
PE .... Poste d'Ecoute [*Listening Station*] [*Military*] [*French*]　(MTD)
PE .... Potencijalna Evaporacija [*Potential Evaporation*] [*Geography*]　(YU)
PE .... Problemes Economiques [*France*]　(FLAF)
PE .... Programmsteuereinheit [*German*]　(ADPT)
PE .... Prometheus-Europe [*Paris, France*]　(EAIO)
PE .... Protection de l'Enfance [*Benelux*]　(BAS)
PE .... Prozesseinheit [*German*]　(ADPT)
PE .... Semiconductor Element　(RU)
PE .... Threshold Element [*Computers*]　(RU)
PE .... Utricular Elements　(RU)
PEA .... Pan Europeenne Air Service [*France*] [*ICAO designator*]　(FAAC)
PEA .... Pankypriaki Enosis Apomakhon [*Pan-Cyprian Veterans Union*]　(GC)
PEA .... Penneshaw [*Australia*] [*Airport symbol*]　(OAG)
PEA .... People's Education Association
PEA .... Polish Ex-Servicemen's Association [*Australia*]
PEA .... Polyethylene Azelate
PEA .... Portuguese East Africa [*Mozambique*]
PEA .... Press Employees Association [*Mauritius*]　(AF)
PEA .... Programma Evropaikis Anorthoseos [*European Recovery Program*]　(GC)
PEA .... Proodevtiki Enosis Agoniston [*Progressive Fighters Union*] [*Cyprus*]　(GC)
PEA .... Provincial Electricity Authority [*Thailand*]　(IMH)
PEAC....... Pharmaceutical Education Advisory Committee [*Australia*]
PEAC....... Police Education Advisory Council [*New South Wales, Australia*]
PEACE...... Peace, Environment, and Community Efforts [*Australia*]

PEACESAT ... Pan-Pacific Educational and Cultural Exchange by Satellite Program [*University of Hawaii, Manoa*] [*Research center*] (RCD)

PEACESAT ... Pan-Pacific Education and Communications Experiment by Satellite (ADA)

PEACS ...... Instituto de Pesquisas e Experimentacao Agropecuaria do Centro-Sul [*Brazil*] (SLS)

PEAEA ...... Panellinios Enosis Agoniston Ethnikis Andistaseos [*Panhellenic Union of National Resistance Fighters*] (GC)

PEAK........ Panavstraliaki Epitropi Avtodiatheseos Kyprou [*Pan-Australian Committee for the Self-Determination of Cyprus*] (GC)

PEAK........ Panellinios Epitropi Avtodiatheseos Kyprou [*Panhellenic Committee for the Self-Determination of Cyprus*] (GC)

PEAKEL.... Panellinia Enosis Allilengyis ston Kypriako Lao [*Panhellenic Union of Solidarity with the Cypriot People*] (GC)

PEAM........ Pankypriako Ethniko Apelevtherotiko Metopo [*Pan-Cyprian National Liberation Front*] (GC)

PEAN ...... Panellinios Enosis Agonizomenon Neon [*Panhellenic Union of Fighting Youth*] (GC)

PEAN .... Patriotiki Enosis Agonizomenis Neolaias [*Patriotic Union of Fighting Youth*] [*Greek*] (GC)

PEAP........ Panellinios Enosis Apomakhon Polemou [*Panhellenic Union of War Veterans*] (GC)

PEAP........ Pankyprios Enosis Anakoufiseos Pathondon [*or Pankyprios Epitropi Apokatastaseos Pathondon*] [*Pan-Cyprian Union for Relief of the Distressed*] (GC)

PEAP........ Parent Education and Assistance Project [*Australia*]

PEAS........ Production Engineering Advisory Service [*Council for Scientific and Industrial Research*] [*South Africa*] (AA)

PEAT........ Programme Elargi d'Assistance Technique [*Expanded Program of Technical Assistance*] [*United Nations*]

PEAT........ Protypa Ergastiria Andikeimenon Tekhnis [*Model Art Craft Workshops*] [*Greek*] (GC)

PEATEA ... Panellinios Enosis Anapiron kai Travmation Ethnikis Andistaseos Periodou 1941-1944 [*Penhellenic Union of Wounded and Disabled of the National Resistance Period, 1941-1944*] (GC)

PEAThP .... Panellinios Enosis Anapiron kai Thymaton Polemou [*Panhellenic Union of Disabled and Victims of War*] (GC)

PEAYEA ... Panellinios Enosis Axiomatikon-Ypaxiomatikon Ethnikis Andistaseos [*Panhellenic Union of Officers and Noncommissioned Officers of the National Resistance*] (GC)

PEB............ Economic Planning Office (RU)

PEB............ Preduzece za Eksploataciju Boksita [*Bauxite Exploitation Establishment*] [*Cetinje*] (YU)

PEB............ Putno-Eksploatacioni Bataljon [*Road Maintenance Battalion*] [*Military*] (YU)

PeB............ Statni Pedagogicka Knihovna v Brne [*State Pedagogical Library in Brno*] (CZ)

PEBCO...... Port Elizabeth Black Civic Organization [*South Africa*] (PD)

PEBE........ Programa Especial de Bolsas de Estudio [*Special Scholarship Program*] (LAA)

PEC............ Pacific East Asia Cargo Airline, Inc. [*Philippines*] [*ICAO designator*] (FAAC)

PEC............ Pacific Economic Community (FEA)

PEC............ Palestine Economic Commission

PEC............ Partido Estat Catala [*Catalan State Party*] [*Spanish*] (WER)

PEC............ Parti pour l'Evolution des Comores [*Party for the Evolution of the Comoros*] (AF)

PEC............ Patriotic Election Coalition [*Hungary*] (EAIO)

PEC............ Peace Education Commission [*La Trobe University*] [*Australia*]

PEC............ Perfil de Evaluacion del Comportamiento [*Standardized test of elementary through high school students' behavior at school, at home, and with peers*]

PEC............ Polish Educational Committee [*Canberra, Australia*]

PEC............ Programme Exchange Centre [*Union of National Radio and Television Organisations of Africa*] [*Kenya*]

PEC............ Protocolo de Expansion Comercial [*Protocol Office for Trade Expansion*] [*Uruguay*] (LA)

PEC............ Prova Elementi Combustibili [*An Italian fast reactor*]

PEC............ Proyecto Electrico Campeche [*Campeche Electrification Project*] [*Mexico*] (LA)

PECA........ Process Engineers and Constructors' Association [*Australia*]

PECAM..... Pecheries Camerounaises

PECC........ Pacific Economic Cooperation Conference [*Australia*]

PECDAR ... Palestine Economic Council for Development and Reconstruction (ECON)

Pech .... Pechota [*Infantry*] (CZ)

pech........... Press (BU)

pech........... Printed (RU)

pech........... Printing Plant, Printed (BU)

Pechie....... Pecherie [*Fishery*] [*Military map abbreviation World War I*] [*French*] (MTD)

pech l......... Printer's Sheet (RU)

PECHOR .. Pechora Railroad (RU)

Pechorlag... Pechora Railroad Corrective Labor Camp (RU)

PechorNIUI ... Pechora Scientific Research Institute of Coal (RU)

PECI .... Plastiques et Elastomeres de la Cote-D'Ivoire

PECI .... Projects and Equipment Corp. of India (PDAA)

PECIG .... Pecheries Industrielles Gabonaises [*Gabonese Fishing Industries*] (AF)

PECIG .... Societe de Pecheries Industrielles du Gabon

PECO .... Centrala de Desfacere a Produselor Petroliere [*Central for the Sale of Petroleum Products*] (RO)

PECO .... Pakistan Engineering Co. Ltd. (FEA)

PECO .... Pays d'Europe Centrale et Orientale (ECON)

PECO .... Posto Experimental de Caprinos e Ovinos [*Brazil*] (DSCA)

PECOS ...... Pays D'Europe Centrale et Orientale

PEC(Qld).. Planning and Environment Court (Queensland) [*Australia*]

PECSAR..... Permanent Committee for Search and Rescue

PECTA ...... Programme des Emplois et des Competences Techniques pour l'Afrique [*Jobs and Skills Program for Africa - JASPA*] [*French*]

PED .... Pays en Developpement

ped............. Pedagogical (RU)

Ped .... Pedagoji [*Pedagogy*] (TU)

ped............. Pediatrics (BU)

PEDAEP ... Projet d'Experimentation et de Demonstration en Arboriculture, Elevage, et Paturage [*Tunisia*]

pedag.......... Pedagogical, Pedagogy (RU)

Pedag .... Professional Education Specialization (BU)

pedag u-shta ... Normal Schools (BU)

PEDCO ..... Petroleum Development Corporation [*South Korea*]

PEDE......... Programa Estrategico de Desenvolvimento [*Strategic Development Program*] [*Brazil*] (LA)

PEDEVESA ... Petroleos de Venezuela, Sociedad Anonima [*Venezuelan Petroleum, Incorporated*] (LA)

PEDIN....... National Petroleum Exploration Database [*Australia*]

pedin .... Pedagogical Institute (RU)

PEDMEDE ... Panellinios Enosis Diplomatoukhon Mikhanikon Ergolipton Dimosion Ergon [*Panhellenic Union of Licensed Engineer Public Works Contractors*] (GC)

PEDMIEDE ... Panellinios Enosis Diplomatoukhon Mikhanikon kai Ilektrologon Ergolipton Dimosion Ergon [*Panhellenic Union of Licensed Mechanical and Electrical Engineer Public Works Contractors*] (GC)

PEDP........ Pacific Energy Development Program [*Fiji*] [*United Nations*]

PEDPA...... Perifereiaki Dievthynsis Politikis Amynis [*Regional Civil Defense Directorate*] [*Cyprus*] (GC)

PEDRA ...... Palestine Economic Development and Reconstruction Agency (ECON)

PEDUC...... Professeurs d'Economie Domestique des Universites Canadiennes [*Canadian University Teachers of Home Economics - CUTHE*]

PEE........... Panellinia Enosis Ethnikofronon [*Panhellenic Union of Nationalists*] (GC)

PEE........... Pankypriaki Epitropi Eirinis [*Pan-Cyprian Peace Committee*] (GC)

PEE........... Pankypriaki Epitropi Englovismenon [*Pan-Cyprian Committee of Enclaved Persons*] (GC)

PEE........... Postes d'Expansion Economique [*French*]

PEEA .... Panellinios Enosis Efedron Axiomatikon [*Panhellenic Union of Reserve Officers*] (GC)

PEEA .... Pankyprios Enosis Epangelmation Avtokinitiston [*Pan-Cyprian Union of Professional Drivers*] (GC)

PEEA .... Pequenas Empresas de Extraccion de Anchoveta [*Small Enterprises for Anchovy Fishing*] [*Peru*] (LA)

PEEA .... Politiki Epitropi Ethnikis Apelevtheroseos [*Political Committee for National Liberation*] [*Greek*] (GC)

PEEEPP .... Panellinia Enosis Epanapatristhendon Ellinon Politikon Prosfygon [*Panhellenic Union of Repatriated Greek Political Refugees*] (GC)

PEEG .... Panellinios Enosis Ergazomenon Gynaikon [*Panhellenic Union of Working Women*] (GC)

PEEK .... Panellinios Epitropi Enoseos Kyprou [*Panhellenic Committee for the Union of Cyprus*] (GC)

PEEL .... Panellinios Enosis Epangelmation Logiston [*Panhellenic Union of Professional Accountants*] (GC)

Peer .... Peerless [*Record label*] [*USA, Mexico*]

PEETh....... Panellinios Enosis Elevtherou Theatrou [*Panhellenic Union of the Free Theater*] (GC)

PEF........... Palestine Endowment Funds [*Later, PEF Israel Endowment Funds*] (EA)

PEF........... Palestine Exploration Fund

PEF........... Panhellenic Association of Pharmacists [*Greece*] (EAIO)

PEF........... Por Especial Favor [*Portuguese*]

PEF........... Recurrent Figure Elements [*Cybernetics*] (RU)

PEFA .... Packaging Environment Foundation of Australia

PEFC........ Private Export Funding Corp. (IMH)

PEFCO...... Private Export Funding Corp.

PEFND...... Panellinios Enosis Filon Neas Dimokratias [*Panhellenic Union of Friends of New Democracy*] (GC)

PEFP .... Panellinios Enosis Filon ton Polyteknon [*Panhellenic Union of Friends of Parents of Large Families*] (GC)

Pefrogab..... Societe Nationale Petroliere Gabonaise (OMWE)

PEFTOK ... Philippine Expeditionary Force to Korea [*United Nations*]

PEFU .... Panel of Experts on Fish Utilization [*FAO*] (ASF)

PEG .... Panelladiki Enosis Gynaikon [*Panhellenic Women's Union*] (GC)

PEG .... Pegawai [*Officer, Official*] [*Malaysia*] (ML)

Peg .... Pegunungan [*Mountain Range*] [*Indonesian*] (NAU)

PEG .... Polyethylene Glycol (RU)

PEG .... Production Entitlement Guarantee [*International Agricultural Trade Research Consortium*] (ECON)

PEG .... Publicatieblad van de Europese Gemeenschappen [*Benelux*] (BAS)

pega........... Pegamoid [*Imitation Parchment*] [*Publishing*] [*French*]

PEGA........ Petrol ve Gas Endustrisi AS [*Petroleum and Gas Industry Corporation*] (TU)

PEGA........ Proodevtiki Enosis Gynaikon Ammokhostou [*Progressive Union of Famagusta Women*] (GC)

PEGAB..... Pecheries Gabonaises [*Fisheries of Gabon*] (AF)

PEGO .... Pankypriaki Ethniki Gynaikeia Organosis [*Pan-Cyprian National Women's Organization*] (GC)

PEGSAAA ... Pankypria Epitropi Goneon kai Syngenon Adiloton Aikhmaloton kai Agnooumenon [*Pan-Cyprian Committee of Parents and Relatives of Undeclared Prisoners and Missing Persons*] (GC)

PEGSAAAKT ... Panellinios Epitropi Goneon kai Syngenon Adiloton Aikhmaloton kai Agnooumenon tis Kypriakis Tragodias [*Panhellenic Committee of Parents and Relatives of Undeclared Prisoners and Missing Persons of the Cyprus Tragedy*] (GC)

PEGSM ..... Mobile Electric and Gas Welding Shop (RU)

PEGUPCO ... Persian Gulf Petroleum Company [*Iran*] (ME)

PEH .... Pehuajo [*Argentina*] [*Airport symbol*] (OAG)

PEHLA...... Prufung Elektrischer Hochleistungsapparate [*Joint Testing Laboratory for Electrical High-Power Equipment*] [*Germany*] (PDAA)

PEI............. Paul Ehrlich Institute [*Germany*]

PEI............. Pereira [*Colombia*] [*Airport symbol*] (OAG)

PEI............. Polyethyleneimine (RU)

PEI............. Pravno-Ekonomski Institut [*Law and Economic Institute*] (YU)

PEIAIKh ... Panellinios Enosis Idioktiton Avtokiniton Idiotikis Khriseos [*Panhellenic Union of Owners of Private Use Vehicles*] (GC)

PEIRA .... Public Employment Industrial Relations Authority [*New South Wales, Australia*]

PEIRS........ Public Employment Industrial Relations Services [*New South Wales, Australia*]

PEiZh .... Power and Damage Control Station [*Navy*] (RU)

PEJ .... Pejabat [*Office*] (ML)

pej.............. Pejoratif [*French*] (TPFD)

pej.............. Pejorative (TPFD)

pej.............. Por Ejemplo [*For Example*] [*Spanish*]

PEK........... Beijing [*China*] [*Airport symbol*] (OAG)

PEK........... Cohesive Energy Density (RU)

PEK........... Mailing Office (RU)

PEK........... Panagrotiki Enosis Kyprou [*Pan Agrarian Union of Cyprus*] (GC)

PEK........... Panellinios Enosis Kinimatografiston [*Panhellenic Cinematographers Union*] (GC)

PEK........... Pecsi Tudomanyegyetem Konyvtara [*Library of the University of Pecs*] (HU)

PEK........... Perifereiaki Epitropai Katanomon [*Regional Apportionment Committee*] [*Greek*] (GC)

PEK........... Politicka Ekonomie Kapitalismu [*Political Economics of Capitalism*] (CZ)

PEK........... Proodevtiki Enotiki Kinisi [*Progressive Union Movement*] (GC)

PEKA........ Pankyprios Enosis Kyprion Agoniston [*Pan-Cyprian Union of Cypriot Fighters*] (GC)

PEKA........ Panspoudastiki Epitropi Kypriakou Agonos [*All-Students Committee of the Cyprus Struggle*] [*Cyprus*] (GC)

PEKA........ Politiki Epitropi Kypriakou Agonos [*Political Committee of the Cyprus Struggle*] [*Cyprus*] (GC)

Pekachem .. Przedsiebiorstwo Konstrukcji Aparatury Chemicznej [*Chemical Equipment Designing Enterprise*] (POL)

PEKAM..... Parti Keadilan Masharakat [*Social Justice Party*] (ML)

PEKEMAS ... Pertubohan Kebangsaan Melayu Singapore [*Malayan National Organization in Singapore*] (ML)

pekh .... Infantry (RU)

PEKh .... Pankyprios Enosis Khimikon [*Pan-Cyprian Chemists Union*] (GC)

PEL............ Aeropelican Air Services Pty Ltd. [*Australia*] [*ICAO designator*] (FAAC)

Pel .... Parcel [*Shoal*] [*Portuguese*] (NAU)

PEL............ Past Economic Loss

PEL............ Pelajaran [*Education*] (ML)

PEL............ Pelaneng [*Lesotho*] [*Airport symbol*] (OAG)

pel............... Pelote [*Pin Cushion*] [*Sewing*] [*French*]

Pel .... Peloton [*Half of a Company, Quarter of a Squadron*] [*Military*] [*French*] (MTD)

PEL............ Petroleum Exploration Licence [*Australia*]

PEL............ Philatelic Esperanto League [*See also ELF*] [*Solna, Sweden*] (EAIO)

PEL............ Physics and Engineering Laboratory [*Department of Scientific and Industrial Research*] [*New Zealand*] (ERC)

PEL............ Production Equipment Limited [*Australia*]

PEL............ Programmes d'Equipements Locaux [*Algeria*]

peld............ Peldany [*Copy*] (HU)

PELDA ..... Pembantu Letnan Dua [*Second Sublieutenant*] (IN)

pelit .... Pelitermi [*Games*] [*Finland*]

PELITA ..... Pembangunan Lima Tahun [*5-Year Development (Plan)*] (IN)

PELMASI ... Pelopor Mahasiswa Sosialis Indonesia [*Indonesian Socialist College Student Pioneers*] (IN)

PELNI .... Pelajaran Nasional Indonesia [*Indonesian National Maritime Company*] (IN)

PELTU ..... Pembantu Letnan Satu [*First Sublieutenant*] (IN)

PEM .... Pankypriaki Enosis Mikrokatastimatarkhon [*Pan-Cyprian Union of Small Shopkeepers*] (GC)

PEM .... Pankypriakon Enotikon Metopon [*Pan-Cyprian Unifying Front*] (GC)

PEM .... Pankyprion Ergatoagrotikon Metopon [*Pan-Cyprian Labor Agrarian Front*] (GC)

PEM .... Partido Ecologista Mexicano [*Political party*] (EY)

PEM .... Petroleos Mexicanos [*Mexico*] (PDAA)

PEM .... Plast- und Elastverarbeitungsmaschinen [*Machines for Processing Plastic and Elastic Materials*] (EG)

PEM .... Puerto Maldonado [*Peru*] [*Airport symbol*] (OAG)

PEMA....... Pankyprion Eniaion Metopon Agoniston [*Pan-Cyprian United Fighters' Front*] (GC)

PEMAECO ... Societe de Peche Maritime du Congo [*Congo Maritime Fishing Company*]

PEMARZA ... Societe des Peches Maritimes du Zaire [*Zaire Maritime Fishing Company*] (AF)

PEME........ Programa de Expansao e Melhoria do Ensino [*Program for Expansion and Improvement of Education*] [*Brazil*] (LA)

PEME........ Proodevtiki Enosi Miteron Ellados [*Progressive Union of Greek Mothers*] (GC)

PEMEK..... Panellinios Enosis Mikhanikon Esoterikis Kavseos [*Panhellenic Union of Internal Combustion Engineers*] (GC)

PEMEN..... Panellinios Enosis Mikhanikon Emborikou Navtikou [*Panhellenic Union of Merchant Marine Engineers*] (GC)

PEMEX ..... Petroleos Mexicanos [*Mexican government petroleum operating company*]

PEMILU ... Pemilihan Umum [*General Election*] (IN)

PEMKO .... Profilo Elektrik Motorlari ve Kompresor Sanayii AS [*Profilo Electric Motors and Compressor Industry Corp.*] (TU)

PEMOEA ... Panellinios Enosis Makhiton Omadon Ethnikis Andistaseos [*Panhellenic Union of Fighter Groups of the National Resistance*] (GC)

PEMRam... Precision Electromagnetic Ram [*Denne Developments*] (PS)

PEMS........ Paris Evangelical Missions Society

PEN .... International PEN [*Official name; PEN, never spelled out in use, is said to stand for poets, playwrights, editors, essayists, novelists*] (EAIO)

PEN .... Panellinios Enosis Navton [*Panhellenic Seamen's Union*] (GC)

PEN .... Pankypriaki Ethniki Neolaia [*Pan-Cyprian Nationalist Youth*] (GC)

PEN .... Parti de l'Entente Nationale

PEN .... Penang [*Malaysia*] [*Airport symbol*] (OAG)

PEN .... Penang City [*Malaysia*] (ML)

Pen .... Peninsula [*Peninsula*] [*Spanish*] (NAU)

PEN .... Penolong [*Assistant*] (ML)

PEN .... Pnevmatiki Estia Nikaias [*Nikaia Cultural Home*] [*Greek*] (GC)

PEN .... Poder Ejecutivo National [*National Executive Body*] [*Argentina*] (LA)

PEN .... Provinciaal Elektriciteitsbedrijf van Noord-Holland [*Netherlands*] (BAS)

PENAD ..... Penerangan Angkatan Darat [*Army Information Office*] (IN)

PENAIC .... PEN All-India Centre (EAIO)

PENB......... PEN Clube do Brazil (EAIO)

PENC......... PEN Centre Catala [*Spain*] (EAIO)

PENCEE ... PEN Centre des Ecrivains en Exil [*Writers in Exile*] (EAIO)

PENCF ...... PEN Club Francais [*France*] (EAIO)

PENCH ..... PEN Club Hellenique [*Greece*] (EAIO)

PENCIA .... PEN Club Internacional de Argentina (EAIO)

PENCL ...... PEN Club Liechtenstein (EAIO)

PENCLO... PEN Club de Langue d'Oc [*France*] (EAIO)

PENCP ...... PEN Club del Paraguay (EAIO)

PENCS ...... PEN Club du Senegal (EAIO)

PENCS ...... PEN Club Skobje (EAIO)

PENCSN ... PEN Club du Senegal (EAIO)

PEND .... Low-Pressure Polyethylene (RU)

PENE........ Panellinios Ethniki Navtergatiki Enosis [*Panhellenic National Maritime Workers Union*] (GC)

PENEN ..... Panellinios Enosis Navtomageiron Emborikis Navtilias "O Agios Spyridon" [*Panhellenic Union of Merchant Marine Cooks*] (GC)

PENEN ..... Panellinios Enosis Navton Emborikis Navtilias [*Panhellenic Union of Merchant Marine Seamen*] (GC)

PENESA ... Pescas do Nordeste, Sociedad Anonima [*Brazil*] (LAA)

penit .... Penitente [*Penitent*] [*Spanish*]

penit .... Penitentiaire [*Benelux*] (BAS)

pen'k trep... Hemp Mill [*Topography*] (RU)

PENM ...... PEN Club de Mexico (EAIO)

PENM .... Penningmeester [*Treasurer*] [*Afrikaans*]

penn.......... Penningmeester [*Treasurer*] [*Afrikaans*]

PENP........ Partiia Edinstva i Natsional'novo Progressa

PENPRES ... Penetapan Presiden [*Presidential Decision*] (IN)

PENS........ Partido Espanol Nacional Socialista [*Spanish National Socialist Party*] (WER)

pent .... Pentek [*Friday*] (HU)

pentekspl.... Penteksemplar [*Fine Copy*] [*Publishing Danish/Norwegian*]

pentk .... Pentekening [*Pen and Ink Drawing*] [*Publishing*] [*Netherlands*]

Penz.......... Penza Railroad (RU)

PENZBD .. PEN Zentrum Bundesrepublik Deutschland [*Germany*] (EAIO)

Penzig .... Penzforgalmi Igazgatosag [*Directorate of Money Circulation*] (HU)

Penzkhimmash ... Penza Chemical Machinery Plant (RU)

Penzmash... Penza Machinery Plant (RU)

PEO .... Economic Planning Department (RU)

PEO .... Pankypria Ergatiki Omospondia [*Pancyprian Federation of Labour*] [*The "Old Trade Unions" Cyprus*]

PEO .... Pankyprios Ergatiki Omospondia [*or Pankypriaki Ergatiki Omospondia*] [*Pan-Cyprian Labor Federation*] (GC)

PEO .... Por Especial Obsequio [*Portuguese*]

PEO .... Principal Education Officer [*Australia*]

PEOIATA ... Panellinios Ethniki Omospondia Idioktiton Avtokiniton Taxi kai Agoraion [*Panhellenic National Federation of Owners of Taxis and Vehicles for Hire*] (GC)

PEOM .... Pankypria Ethniki Organosis Mathiton [*Pan-Cyprian National Students Organization*] (GC)

PEON .... Commission pour la Production d'Electricite d'Origin Nucleaire [*Commission for the Production of Electricity from Atomic Energy Sources*] [*France*] (PDAA)

PEON .... Pankyprios Ethniki Organosis Neolaias [*or Pankyprios Ethniki Organosis Neon*] [*Pan-Cyprian National Youth Organization*] (GC)

PEOPEF.... Panellinios Enosis Oikogeneion Politikon Exoriston kai Fylakismenon [*Panhellenic Union of Families of Political Exiles and Prisoners*] (GC)

PEP........... Converter of Electrical Quantities [*Computers*] (RU)

PEP........... Field Evacuation Station (RU)

PEP........... Pankyprios Epitropi Prosfygon [*Pan-Cyprian Refugee Committee*] (GC)

PEP........... Parti d'Emancipation Populaire

PEP........... Parti Ecologiste pour le Progres [*Burkina Faso*] [*Political party*] (EY)

PEP........... Parti Evangelique Populaire [*Popular Protestant Party*] [*Switzerland*] [*Political party*] (PPE)

PEP........... Pepitilla [*Race of maize*] [*Mexico*]

PEP........... Portfolio Evaluation Plan [*Australia*]

PEP........... Preduzece za Eksploataciju Pristanista [*Harbor Exploitation Establishment*] (YU)

PEP........... Private Enterprise Promotion (LAA)

PEP........... Professional Experience Program [*Australia*]

PEP........... Public Equity Partnership Program [*Housing scheme*] [*Australia*]

PEP........... Puslitbang Ekonomi dan Pembangunan [*Center for Economic and Development Studies*] [*Indonesia*] (IRC)

PEP........... Recurrent Representation Elements [*Cybernetics*] (RU)

PEP........... State All-Union Planning Institute for the Planning of Construction of Industrial Heat and Electric Power Plants for Supplying Power to Industrial Establishments in All Branches of the National Economy (RU)

PeP........... Statni Pedagogicka Knihovna v Praze [*State Pedagogical Library in Prague*] (CZ)

PEPA .... Philippine Educational Publishers' Association (EAIO)

PEPAS....... WHO [*World Health Organization*] Western Pacific Regional Centre for the Promotion of Environmental Planning and Applied Studies (EAIO)

PEPBNC ... Peninsula Enrichment Program for Bright Needy Children [*Queensland, Australia*]

PEPE .... People Persecuted by Pablo Escobar [*Colombia*] (ECON)

PEPEN ...... Panellinios Enosis Ploiarkhon Emborikis Navtilias [*Panhellenic Union of Merchant Marine Masters*] (GC)

PEPEN(PT) ... Panellinios Enosis Ploiarkhon Emborikis Navtilias (Pasis Taxeos) [*Panhellenic Union of Merchant Marine Masters (of All Classes)*] (GC)

PEPESCA ... Empresa Pesquera Mixta del Peru [*Peruvian Mixed Fisheries Enterprise*] (LA)

PEPG......... Pankyprios Enosis Proodevtikon Gynaikon [*Pan-Cyprian Union of Progressive Women*] (GC)

PEPG......... Port Emergency Planning Group [*NATO*] (NATG)

PEPOA...... Philippine Electric Plant Owners Association (DS)

Pepre......... Pepiniere [*Nursery Garden*] [*Military map abbreviation World War I*] [*French*] (MTD)

PEPSU ...... Patiala and East Punjab States Union

PEPSY....... Programmentwicklungs-und-Pflegesystem [*German*] (ADPT)

PEPU .... Protectorate Education Progress Union

peq............. Pequeno [*Small*] [*Spanish*]

peq............. Pequeno [*Small*] [*Portuguese*]

PEQUIVEN ... Petroquimica de Venezuela, CA [*Petrochemical Company of Venezuela*] (LA)

Per............. Alternating Light [*Nautical term*] (RU)

per............. Binding (RU)

per............. Bystreet, Lane, Alley [*Topography*] (RU)

Per............. Ferry, Water-Crossing Point [*Topography*] (RU)

Per............. Mountain Pass [*Topography*] (RU)

PER........... Partido Estadista Republicano [*Puerto Rico*] [*Political party*]

Per............. Perdendo [*Softer and Slower*] [*Music*]

PER........... Perikatan [*Alliance*] (ML)

per............. Period (RU)

PER........... Perth [*Australia*] [*Airport symbol*] (OAG)

PER........... Peru [*ANSI three-letter standard code*] (CNC)

PER........... Pharmaceutical Evaluation Report [*Australia*]

PER........... Plan d'Epargne Retraite [*Proposed tax-free retirement account plan*] [*French*]

per............. Premier [*First*] [*French*]

PER........... Programmereignisregistrierung [*German*] (ADPT)

PER........... Przedsiebiorstwa Elektryfikacji Rolnictwa [*Agriculture Electrification Enterprises*] (POL)

per............. Transitive [*Grammar*] (RU)

per............. Translation, Translator (RU)

PER........... Transmitter (RU)

PERAKU... Pergerakan Rakyat Kalimantan Utara [*North Kalimantan People's Movement*] (ML)

PER AN..... Per Annum [*By the Year*] [*Latin*]

Perap......... Perapohjola [*Finland*]

PERBARA ... Perhimpunan Bangsa-Bangsa Asia Tenggara [*Association of South East Asian Nations (ASEAN)*] (IN)

PERBUM ... Persatuan Buruh Minjak [*Federation of Oil Workers*] [*Indonesian*]

PERBUPRI ... Persatuan Buruh Perkebunan Republik Indonesia [*Plantation Workers' Union of Indonesia*]

PERBUTI ... Persatuan Buruh Textiel Indonesia [*Textile Workers' Union of Indonesia*]

perc .... Percalina [*Percaline*] [*Publishing*] [*Portuguese*]

perc .... Percaline [*Buckram*] [*Publishing*] [*French*]

PERCOMPASIA ... South East Asian Personal Computer Hardware and Software Show

Per con .... Per Contra [*On the Other Side*] [*Latin*]

PERD........ Perdendo [*or Perdendosi*] [*Softer and Slower Music*]

PERDEN... Perdendo [*or Perdendosi*] [*Softer and Slower Music*]

pereizd....... Reprint, Reprinted (RU)

perek .... Shoal [*Topography*] (RU)

perekh....... Transitive (Verb) (RU)

perem .... Alternating (Current) (RU)

peren .... Figurative (Sense) (RU)

perepech.... Reprinted (RU)

perepl .... Binding (RU)

perer .... Revised [*Bibliography*] (RU)

peresm....... Reviewed, Revised (RU)

perev......... Translation, Translator (RU)

perf........... Perfectum [*Perfect Tense*] [*Afrikaans*]

perf........... Perfeito [*Perfect*] [*Portuguese*]

perf........... Perfekti [*Perfect Tense*] [*Finland*]

perfett........ Perfettamente [*Perfectly*] [*Italian*]

perg .... Pergamena [*Vellum*] [*Publishing*] [*Italian*]

Perg........... Pergament [*Vellum*] [*Publishing*] [*German*]

perg .... Pergamin [*Parchment*] [*Publishing*] [*Poland*]

perg .... Pergaminho [*Parchment*] [*Publishing*] [*Portuguese*]

perg .... Pergamino [*Parchment*] [*Publishing*] [*Spanish*]

pergam ...... Pergamena [*Vellum*] [*Publishing*] [*Italian*]

Per Gr Pr ... Alternating Group-Flashing Light [*Nautical term*] (RU)

pergrygg..... Pergamentrygg [*Vellum Back*] [*Publishing*] [*Sweden*]

pergryggar ... Pergamentryggar [*Vellum Backs*] [*Publishing*] [*Sweden*]

Per GrZatm ... Alternating Group-Occulting Light [*Nautical term*] (RU)

Pergt.......... Pergament [*Vellum*] [*Publishing*] [*German*]

pergt.......... Pergament [*Vellum*] [*Publishing Danish/Norwegian*]

PERHIMI ... Perhimpunan Mahasiswa Indonesia [*Indonesia College Students Association*] (IN)

PERI .... Pakistan Economic Research Institute [*Research center*] (FEA)

PERI .... Protein Engineering Research Institute [*Japanese governmental and industrial consortium*] [*Later, BERI*]

PERIN....... Penalty Enforcement Registration of Infringement Notice [*Australia*]

PERINASIA ... Perkumpulan Perinatologi Indonesia [*Indonesian Society for Perinatology*] (EAIO)

period .... Periodical (BU)
period .... Periodic, Periodical, Recurring (RU)
period .... Periodisch [*Periodical*] [*German*] (GCA)
period dr ..... Repeating Decimal, Recurring Decimal (RU)
periodich .... Periodic, Intermittent (RU)
PERJAN ...... Perusahaan Jawatan [*Departmental Agency*] [*Indonesia*] (IMH)
perk .... Perkament [*Vellum*] [*Publishing*] [*Netherlands*]
PERKAPPEN ... Persatuan Karyawan Perusahaan Perkebunan Negara [*Association of Employees of State Plantations*] [*Indonesia*] (IN)
PERKARA ... Parti Perdapuan Kebangsaan Ra'ayat Brunei [*Brunei People's National United Party*] [*Political party*] (EY)
PERKATEXI ... Persatuan Karyawan Textil Indonesia [*Indonesian Textile Workers Union*] (IN)
PERKESO ... Pertubuhan Keselamatan Sosial [*Malaysia*]
PERKIM ... Pertubohan Kebajikan Islam Malaysia [*Malaysian Muslim Welfare Organization*] (ML)
perkt .... Perkament [*Vellum*] [*Publishing*] [*Netherlands*]
PERLA ...... Plan de Electrificacion Rural de Lobos y Alrededores [*Argentina*] (LAA)
perm .... Permanent (IDIG)
PERM .... Programmgesteuerte, Elektronische Rechenanlage Muenchen [*German*] (ADPT)
PERMAS .. Persatuan Rakyat Malaysian Sarawak [*Political party*] (EY)
PERMINA ... Pertambangan Minjak Nasional [*National Oil Company*] (IN)
PermNIUI ... Perm' Scientific Research Institute of Coal (RU)
PERMREP ... Permanent Representation to North Atlantic Council [*NATO*] (NATG)
Perm Rep ... Permanent Representative (EECI)
PERNAS ... Perbadanan Nasional [*National Corporation*] [*Malaysia*] (ML)
PERNIDA ... Perniagaan dan Perdagangan (Sharikat) [*Trade and Commerce Company*] (ML)
PERP .... Load Transfer Point (RU)
PERP .... Pan-Ethnic Republican Party of Australia [*Political party*]
perp .... Perpetuel [*Irredeemable*] [*Business term*] [*French*]
PERP .... Programma Elenkhou Rypanseos Perivallondos [*Pollution and Environment Control Program*] (GC)
Per P GrPr ... Alternating Fixed Light with a Group of Flashes [*Nautical term*] (RU)
Per P Pr ... Alternating Fixed Light with Flashes [*Nautical term*] (RU)
Per Pr .... Alternating Flashing Light [*Nautical term*] (RU)
PERPRES ... Peraturan Presiden [*Presidential Ordinance*] (IN)
Pers .... Persembe [*Thursday*] (TU)
pers .... Persiaa [*or Persiaksi*] [*Finland*]
pers .... Persialainen [*Finland*]
pers .... Persian (RU)
PERS .... Persies [*Persian*] [*Afrikaans*]
pers .... Persoenlich [*Personal*] [*German*] (GCA)
pers .... Person (TPFD)
pers .... Personale [*Personal*] [*Italian*]
PERS .... Personalinformations-System [*German*] (ADPT)
pers .... Personne [*French*] (TPFD)
PERS .... Personnel Dairesi Genel Mudurlugu [*Personnel Office Directorate General*] [*of Foreign Affairs Ministry*] (TU)
pers .... Persoona [*Person*] [*Finland*]
pers .... Persoonlik [*Personal*] [*Afrikaans*]
PERSAGI ... Persatuan Ahli Gizi Indonesia
Persa-Is ...... Perde ve Sahne Sanatcilari Sendikasi [*Screen and Stage Artists Union*] (TU)
PERSAL .... Physical Education Serials in Australian Libraries
PERSERO ... Perusahaan Perseroan [*Public Corporation*] [*Indonesia*] (IMH)
PERSERO ... Petrokimia Gresik PT [*Indonesia*]
PERSGA ... Red Sea and Gulf of Aden Environment Programme [*Saudi Arabia*]
PERSIT ..... Persatuan Isteri Tentara [*Army Wives Association*] (IN)
persoenl ...... Persoenlich [*Personal*] [*German*] (GCA)
Personenverz ... Personenverzeichnis [*Index of Persons*] [*German*]
pers pron ... Persoonapronomini [*Personal Pronoun*] [*Finland*]
PersStat ..... Personeel Statuut [*Benelux*] (BAS)
pers vnw ..... Persoonlike Voornaamwoord [*Personal Pronoun*] [*Afrikaans*]
PERTAMA ... Perkumpulan Tenaga Utama [*Association of Eminent Persons*] [*Malaysia*] (ML)
PERTAMIN ... Pertambangan Minjak Indonesia [*Indonesian Oil Company*] (IN)
PERTAMINA ... Pertambangan Minjak dan Gas Bumi Nasional [*National Oil and Natural Gas Company*] (IN)
Pertamina .. Perusahaan Tambangan Minyak dan Gas Bumi Negara a (OMWE)
PERTAS .... Perakende Giyim ve Tuketim Maddeleri Ticaret ve Sanayii [*Retail Wearing Apparel and Consumer Articles Industry and Trade Corp.*] (TU)
PERTI .... Persatuan Tarbijah Islamijah [*Islamic Education Union (Political party)*] (IN)
PERUM ..... Perusahaan Umum [*Public Company*] [*Indonesia*] (IMH)
PERUMTEL ... PERUM Telekomunikasi [*Provider of telephone and telegraph services*] [*Indonesia*] (IMH)

PERUMTEL ... Perushaan Umum Telekomunikasi [*Indonesia*] (PDAA)
perv .... Originally (RU)
perv .... Primary, Initial (RU)
pervonach... Originally (RU)
PERZA ...... Sistema de Control Periodo de Zafra [*Sugar Harvest Period Control System*] [*Cuba*] (LA)
Per Ztm ...... Alternating Occulting Light [*Nautical term*] (RU)
per zv .... Variable Star (RU)
PES .... Economic Planning Sector (RU)
PES .... Mobile Electric Power Plant (RU)
PES .... Partido Ecuatoriano Socialista [*Ecuadorean Socialist Party*] [*Political party*]
PES .... Peak-Load Electric Power Plant (RU)
pes .... Per Esempio [*For Example*] [*Italian*]
PES .... Plastiques et Elastomeres du Senegal
PES .... Politicka Ekonomie Socialismu [*Political Economics of Socialism*] (CZ)
PES .... Professional Employment Service [*Australia*]
Pes .... Sand [*Topography*] (RU)
PES .... Tidal Electric Power Plant (RU)
PESA .... Petroleum Exploration Society of Australia (ADA)
PESA .... Philippine Electrical Suppliers Association (DS)
PESABC .... Permanent Executive Secretariat of the Andres Bello Convention [*See also SECAB*] (EAIO)
PESCANGOLA ... Empresa de Pesca de Angola [*State fishing enterprise*] [*Luanda, Angola*]
PESCAPERU ... Empresa Publica de Produccion de Harina y Aceite de Pescado [*State Fishmeal and Fish Oil Production Agency*] [*Peru*] (LA)
PESCOCEAN ... Pesca Oceanica Ecuatoriana [*Ecuadorean Fishing Enterprise*] (LA)
PESCOM .. Empresa Mocambicana de Importacao e Exportacao de Produtos Pesqueiros [*Importer and exporter of fish products*] [*Mozambique*]
PESCONSA ... Pesquerias Espanoles Sovieticos Conjuntos [*Soviet-Spanish Joint Fisheries, Inc.*] [*Spanish*] (WER)
PESD .... Moderate-Pressure Polyethylene (RU)
PESEA ...... Panellinios Enosis Syndesmon Ethnikis Andistaseos [*Panhellenic Union of National Resistance Associations*] (GC)
PESEDE .... Panellinios Enosis Syndesmon Ergolipton Dimosion Ergon [*Panhellenic Union of Public Works Contractors Associations*] (GC)
PESEN ...... Panellinios Enosis Syndaxioukhon Emborikou Navtikou [*Panhellenic Union of Merchant Marine Pensioners*] (GC)
PESESY .... Syndekhnia Ypallilon Symvoulion Ydatopromitheias [*Union of Water Supply Boards Employees*] [*Cyprus*] (GC)
Peshch .... Cave, Cavern [*Topography*] (RU)
PESI .... Panellinia Enosi Sofronistikon Idrymaton [*Panhellenic Union of Correctional Institutions*] (GC)
PESIC .... Parti du Progres Economique et Social des Independants Congolais Luluabourg [*Party for Economic and Social Progress of the Congolese Independents in Luluabourg*] [*Political party*]
PESINE ..... Aluminum of Greece Corporation (GC)
PESK .... Panellinios Epitropi Symbarastaseos Kyprou [*Panhellenic Committee for Aid to Cyprus*] (GC)
PESL .... Petroleum Exploration Society of Libya (PDAA)
PESLA ...... Pekarsko Slasticarska Nabavna Zadruga [*Bakery and Cake Supply Cooperative*] (YU)
PESN .... Panellinios Ergazomeni kai Spoudazousa Neolaia [*Panhellenic Working and Studying Youth*] (GC)
PESP .... Pankypriaki Elliniki Sosialistiki Profylaki [*Pan-Cyprian Greek Socialist Vanguard*] (GC)
PESP .... Proodevtiki Ergatiki Syndikalistiki Parataxi [*Workers Progressive Trade Union Faction*] [*Greek*] (GC)
PESPEF .... Panellinios Enosis Syngenon Politikon Exoriston kai Fylakismenon [*Panhellenic Union of Relatives of Political Exiles and Prisoners*] (GC)
pess .... Pessoa [*or Pessoal*] [*Person or Personal*] [*Portuguese*]
PESU .... Electropneumatic Signal Device (RU)
PET .... Aeropetrel [*Chile*] [*ICAO designator*] (FAAC)
PET .... Panellinios Enosis Technikon [*Greek*] (SLS)
PET .... Pelotas [*Brazil*] [*Airport symbol*] (OAG)
PET .... People's Experimental Theatre
pet .... Petiitti(a) [*Finland*]
pet .... Petit [*Small*] [*French*]
pet .... Petrus [*Peter*] [*Afrikaans*]
PET .... Philippine Earth Terminal
PET .... Point Equitemps [*Point of Equal Time*] [*French*]
PET .... Politiets Efterretningstjeneste [*Police Intelligence Service*] [*Denmark*] (WEN)
PET .... Postes et Telecommunications [*French*] (ADPT)
PET .... Przepisy Eksploatacji Technicznej [*Rules for Technical Operation*] (POL)
PETA .... Pemuda Tanah Ayer [*National Youth Association*] [*Malayan*] (ML)
PETA .... People for the Ethical Treatment of Animals [*Australia*]

PETA......... Philippine Educational Theater Association
PETANI .... Persatuan Tani Nasional Indonesia [*Indonesian National Farmers Union*] (IN)
PETAR...... Pan European Television Audience Research
PETAS ...... Plastik Endustri ve Ticaret Anonim Sirketi [*Plastic Industry and Trade Corporation*] (TU)
PETC......... Parent Effectiveness Training Course [*Australia*]
p et ch......... Ponts et Chaussees [*Highways*] [*French*]
P et CV....... Parcs et Convois [*Military*] [*French*] (MTD)
PETE......... Parliamentary Education for Teacher Education [*Australia*]
PETF......... Polyethylene Terephthalate (RU)
PETGAZ ... Turkiye Petrol ve Urunleri Sanayii Nakil ve Satis Iscileri Sendikasi [*Turkish Petroleum and Products Industry Transport and Sales Workers Union*] (TU)
PETh.......... Panellinios Enosis Thalamipolon [*Panhellenic Union of Stewards*] (GC)
PETh.......... Pronoia Ergaton Thalassis [*Maritime Workers Welfare*] [*Greek*] (GC)
PEThGK.... Panellinios Enosis Thimaton Germanikis Katokhis "O Foinix" [*"Phoenix" Panhellenic Union of Victims of the German Occupation*] (GC)
PEThTh..... O Stefenson Panellinios Enosis Thermaston Thalassis [*Panhellenic Union of Sea Stokers*] (GC)
PETKIM ... Petrokimya Anonim Sirketi [*Petrochemical Corporation*] (TU)
PETKIM-IS ... Petroleum and Chemical Workers Union (TU)
p et m.......... Poids et Mesures [*Weights and Measures*] [*French*]
PETMARK ... PETROMIN Marketing [*Dhahran Airport, Saudi Arabia*] (MENA)
PETO......... Petrol Ofisi [*Petroleum Office*] (TU)
p et p......... Profits et Pertes [*Profits and Losses*] [*Business term*] [*French*]
petr............ Petrographic (RU)
PETRA ...... Program for the Vocational Training of Young People and their Preparation for Adult and Working Life [*EC*] (ECED)
PETRAMS ... Pernambuco Tramways and Power [*Brazil*] (LAA)
PETRANGOL ... Companhia de Petroleos de Angola [*Angola Petroleum Company*] [*Luanda*] (AF)
petr ef......... Petroleum Ether (RU)
PETRESA ... Petroquimica Espanola SA
PETRIN .... Petrographic Institute (of the Academy of Sciences, USSR) (RU)
PETROBEL ... Belayim Petroleum Co. [*Egypt*] (MENA)
PETROBRAS ... Petroleo Brasileiro, SA [*Brazilian Petroleum Corporation*] [*Rio De Janeiro*] (LA)
PETROCHIM ... Intreprinderea Petrochimica [*Petrochemical Enterprise*] (RO)
PETROCI ... Societe Nationale d'Operations Petrolieres de la Cote-D'Ivoire [*Ivorian Petroleum Company*] (AF)
PETROCID ... PETROMIN Sulphuric Acid Plant
PETROCORP ... Petroleum Corp. of New Zealand
PETROFERTIL ... PETROBRAS Fertilizantes SA [*State enterprise*] [*Brazil*] (EY)
PETROGAB ... Societe Nationale des Petroles Gabonais
PETROGAL ... Petroleos de Portugal, EP [*Portuguese Petroleum Co.*]
PETROKEMYA ... Arabian Petrochemical Co.
PETROLBER ... Petrolkemiai Beruhazasi Vallalat [*Petrochemical Investment Enterprise*] (HU)
petrolchem ... Petrolchemisch [*Petrochemical*] [*German*] (GCA)
PETROLGAS ... Petroleum and Gas Equipment Establishment [*Belgrade*] (YU)
PETROLIBER ... Compania Iberica Refinadora de Petroleos SA
Petrol-Is..... Turkiye Petrol, Kimya, Azot, ve Atom Iscileri Sendikasi [*Turkish Petroleum, Chemical, Nitrogen, and Atomic Workers Union*] (TU)
PETROLUBE ... PETROMIN Lubricating Oil Co. [*Saudi Arabia*] (MENA)
PETROMED ... Petroleos del Mediterraneo SA
PETROMIN ... General Petroleum and Mineral Organization [*Riyadh, Saudi Arabia*] (MENA)
Petromin .... General Petroleum and Mineral Organization of Saudi Arabia (OMWE)
PETROMINAS ... Empresa Nacional de Pesquisas e Exploracao Petroliferas e Mineiras [*National mineral regulatory agency*] [*Guinea-Bissau*]
PETROMISA ... PETROBRAS Mineracao Sociedade Anonima [*State enterprise*] [*Brazil*] (EY)
PETROMOC ... Empresa Nacional de Petroleos de Mocambique [*Oil refinery and distribution company*] [*Mozambique*]
PETRONAS ... Petroleum Nasional Bhd [*Malaysia*] (EY)
PETRONOR ... Refineria de Petroleos del Norte [*Spain*] (PDAA)
Petropar..... Petroleos Paraguayos [*Paraguayan Petroleum*] (GEA)
PETROPAR ... Societe de Participations Petrolieres [*North African*]
PETRO-PERU ... Petroleras de Peru [*Peruvian State Petroleum Agency*] (LA)
PETROPHIL ... Petroleum Philatelic Society International (EAIO)
PETROPLAS ... Plasticos Petroquimica [*Venezuela*]
PETROQUISA ... PETROBRAS Quimica, Sociedade Anonima [*PETROBRAS Chemical Corporation*] [*Rio De Janeiro, Brazil*] (LA)

PETROSERV ... PETROMIN Services Department [*Jeddah, Saudi Arabia*] (MENA)
PETROSHIP ... PETROMIN Tankers & Mineral Shipping Co. [*Saudi Arabia*] (MENA)
PETROSUL ... Sociedade Portuguesa De Refinacao de Petroleos SARL [*Portugal*] (PDAA)
PETROVEN ... Petroleos de Venezuela, SA [*Venezuelan Petroleum, Inc.*] (LA)
P et T......... Postes et Telecommunications [*Postal and Telecommunications Administration*] [*French*] (WER)
PETT......... Professeurs d'Enseignement Technique Theorique [*Theoretical Technical Education Teachers*] [*Senegal*] (AF)
pet vit .... Petit Vitesse [*Slow Speed*] [*Correspondence*] [*French*]
PEU .... Economic Planning Administration (RU)
PEU .... Epidemic Control Administration (RU)
PEU .... Paneuropa-Union [*Paneuropean Union*] (EAIO)
PEU .... Public Employees' Union [*Fijian*]
PEU .... Steam Power Plant [*Nautical term*] (RU)
PEV........... Enameled, Moisture-Resistant, Wire-Wound (Resistor) (RU)
PEV........... Panellinios Enosis Vasilofronon [*Panhellenic Union of Royalists*] (GC)
PEV........... Programme Elargi de Vaccination [*Expanded Vaccination Program*] [*Zaire*] (AF)
PEVA........ Piyasa Etud ve Arastirma Burosu [*Market Study and Research Bureau*] (TU)
PEVD......... High-Pressure Polyethylene (RU)
PEVE........ Prensa Venezolana [*Press agency*] [*Venezuela*]
PEVEV ...... Panellinios Ethniki Vasiliki Enosi Voreioelladiton [*Panhellenic National Royalist Union of Northern Greeks*] (GC)
PEVM........ Personal'naia Elektronnaia Vychislitel'naia Mashina [*Personal Computer*] [*Russian*]
PEVM........ Professional'naia Elektronnaia Vychislitel'naia Mashina [*Professional Computer*] [*Russian*]
PEVR........ Enameled, Moisture-Resistant, Adjustable Wire-Wound (Resistor) (RU)
PEVT......... Direct, Enameled, Heat-Resistant Wire-Wound (Resistor) (RU)
PEW .... Peshawar [*Pakistan*] [*Airport symbol*] (OAG)
PEW .... Popular Engineering Works Ltd. [*Fiji*]
PEWC........ Public Electricity and Water Corporation [*Sudan*]
pex............. Par Exemple [*For Example*] [*French*] (GPO)
p ex............ Por Exemplo [*For Example*] [*Portuguese*]
p ext.......... Por Extenso [*By Extension*] [*Portuguese*]
PEYAK...... Personel Yardimlasma Kooperatifi Ltd. [*Personnel Mutual Aid Cooperatives Corp.*] [*Cyprus*] (TU)
PEYKE ...... Panellinios Enosis Ypallilon Kinimatografikon Epikheiriseon [*Panhellenic Union of Employees of Motion Picture Enterprises*] (GC)
Pez............. Pezikon [*Infantry*] (GC)
PEZ........... Recurrent Sign Elements [*Cybernetics*] (RU)
Pezetcha..... Przemyslowo-Handlowa Zaklady Chemiczne [*Industrial and Commercial Chemical Establishments*] (POL)
Pezetgees ... Powiatowy Zwiazek Gminnych Spoldzielni [*County Union of Rural Communal Cooperatives*] (POL)
PEZh .... Power and Damage Control Station [*Navy*] (RU)
PEZZ......... Poljoprivredna Ekonomija Zemljoradnicke Zadruge [*Farm Economy of Agricultural Cooperatives*] (YU)
PF.............. Band Filter, Band-Pass Filter (RU)
PF.............. Field Fortifications (Manual) (RU)
PF.............. French Polynesia [*ANSI two-letter standard code*] (CNC)
PF.............. High-Explosive Cartridge (RU)
PF.............. Pacific Foam Ltd. [*Papua New Guinea*]
pf.............. Pacific Forum Line [*South Pacific island countries*]
pf.............. Pafta [*Section (of a map)*] (TU)
pf.............. Pancelos Fegyvernem [*Armored Forces*] (HU)
PF.............. Pandectes Francaises (FLAF)
PF.............. Patrimonio Forestal del Estado [*Spain*] (DSCA)
PF.............. Patriotic Front [*Zimbabwe*] [*Political party*] (PPW)
pf.............. Penzugyi Felugyelo [*Financial Inspector, Treasury Inspector*] (HU)
pf.............. Perfelvetel [*Appearance (In the court)*] (HU)
Pf.............. Peso Fuerte [*Heavy Weight*] [*Spanish*]
pf.............. Petits Fers [*Small Patterned Designs*] [*Publishing*] [*French*]
Pf.............. Pfarre [*German*]
Pf.............. Pfarrexpositur [*German*]
Pf.............. Pfennig [*Penny*] [*Monetary unit in Germany*] (GPO)
pf.............. Pfennigi(a) [*Finland*]
Pf.............. Pferd [*Horsepower*] [*German*]
PF.............. Pfund [*Pound*] [*Money, weight*] [*German*]
PF.............. Phase-Reversing Switch (RU)
PF.............. Pianoforte [*Soft, then Loud*] [*Music*]
pF.............. Pikofarad [*Picofarad*] [*Poland*]
PF.............. Piu Forte [*A Little Louder*] [*Music*]
PF.............. Plasticizer, Softener (RU)
PF.............. Polar Front (RU)

PF.............. POLISARIO [*Frente Popular para la Liberacion de Saguia El Hamra y Rio De Oro*] [*Popular Front for the Liberation of Saguia El Hamra and Rio De Oro Morocco*]   (PD)

PF.............. Poljoprivredni Fakultet [*Faculty of Agriculture*]   (YU)

PF.............. Polyphenylene   (RU)

pf .... Ponto de Fusao [*Melting Point*] [*Portuguese*]

PF.............. Por Favor [*Please*] [*Portuguese*]

Pf............... Postfach [*Post Office Box*] [*German*]   (CED)

pf .... Pour Feliciter [*To Congratulate*] [*French*]

PF.............. Poverenictvo pre Financie [*Office of the Commissioner of Finance*]   (CZ)

PF.............. Pravni Fakultet [*Faculty of Law*]   (YU)

PF.............. Prefecture [*Prefecture*] [*Military map abbreviation World War I*] [*French*]   (MTD)

PF.............. Prefilter   (RU)

PF.............. Presbyterian Foundation [*Australia*]

PF.............. Preterm Foundation [*Australia*]

pf .... Proximo Futuro [*Near Future*] [*Portuguese*]

PF.............. Puncher   (RU)

PF.............. Pyrophosphate   (RU)

PF.............. Underwater Lamp   (RU)

pf .... Vertical Photography [*Aviation*]   (RU)

PFA............ Parti de la Federation Africaine [*African Federation Party*] [*Political party*]

PFA............ Penang Football Association   (ML)

PFA............ Pension Fund Association [*Japan*]   (ECON)

PFA............ Perak Football Association   (ML)

PFA............ Philippine Foundry Association   (DS)

PFA............ Policia Federal Argentina [*Argentine Federal Police*]

PFA............ Portuguese Fiscal Association   (EAIO)

PFA............ Portuguese Foundry Association   (EAIO)

PFA............ Presbyterian Fellowship of Australia   (ADA)

PFA............ Preservatrice Fonciere d'Assurances [*Insurance*] [*France*]   (EY)

PFA............ Prisoner's Friends Association [*Israel*]   (EAIO)

PFA............ Prison Fellowship of Australia

PFA............ Produktionsfondsabgabe [*Production Fund Tax*]   (EG)

PFA............ Professional Fishermen's Association [*Tasmania, Australia*]

PFAC........ Parti Federal de l'Afrique Centrale

Pfadm........ Pfarradministrator [*German*]

PFAE........ Panstwowa Fabryka Aparatow Elektrycznych [*State Electrical Equipment Factory*]   (POL)

PFAG........ Pool Fencing Action Group [*Australia*]

PFANZ...... Police Federation of Australia and New Zealand

PFAT........ Private Forestry Association of Tasmania [*Australia*]

PFAWA..... Parents and Friends Association of Western Australia

PFAWA..... Poultry Farmers' Association of Western Australia

PFB........... Advanced Frontline Base   (RU)

PFB........... Advance Front Logistical Installation   (BU)

PFB........... Panstwowa Filharmonia Baltycka [*State Baltic Philharmonic Orchestras*]   (POL)

PFB........... Partei Freier Buerger [*Free Citizens' Party*] [*Germany*] [*Political party*]   (PPW)

PFB........... Passo Fundo [*Brazil*] [*Airport symbol*]   (OAG)

PFC........... Private Forestry Council [*Australia*]

PFC........... Progreso y Futuro de Ceuta [*Political party*]   (EY)

PFC........... Propellant Fuel Complex [*ISRO*] [*India*]   (PDAA)

PFCA........ Professional Freestyle Competitors of Australia   (ADA)

PFCI......... Peche et Froid de Cote-D'Ivoire

PFCRN...... Partido del Frente Cardenista de Reconstruccion Nacional [*Mexico*] [*Political party*]   (EY)

PFCV........ Patriotic Funds Council of Victoria [*Australia*]

PFD........... Demodulator Band Filter   (RU)

Pfd............ Pfund [*Pound*] [*Money, weight*] [*German*]

PFD........... Protovathmion Forologikon Dikastirion [*First Instance Tax Court*] [*Greek*]   (GC)

PFDA........ Philippine Fisheries Development Authority   (DS)

PFDF........ Plutonium Fuel Development Facility [*Power Reactor and Nuclear Fuel Development Corp.*] [*Japan*]   (PDAA)

PFDJ .... People's Front for Democracy and Justice [*Formerly, EPLF*] [*Eritrea*] [*Political party*]   (ECON)

PFE........... Partido Feminista de Espana [*Feminist Party of Spain*] [*Political party*]   (PPW)

PFE........... Popular Front of Estonia [*Political party*]

PFE........... Progetto Finalizzato Energetica [*Finalized Energy Program*] [*Research center*] [*Italian*]   (IRC)

p fel .... Penzugyi Felugyelo [*Financial Inspector, Treasury Inspector*]   (HU)

PFES......... Pakistan Fellowship of Evangelical Students

PFES......... Pan American Federation of Engineering Societies

PfExPrv ..... Pfarrexcurrendoprovisor [*German*]

PFF........... Police Field Force   (ML)

PFFF......... Plutonium Fuel Fabrication Facility [*Power Reactor and Nuclear Fuel Development Corp.*] [*Japan*]   (PDAA)

PFG........... Pfennig [*Penny*] [*Monetary unit*] [*German*]

PFHG .... Parkes Family History Group [*Australia*]

PFI............ Pakistan Forest Institute   (DSCA)

PFI .... Papirindustriens Forskningsinstitutt [*Pulp and Paper Research Institute*] [*Norway*]   (IRC)

PFI .... Presse Francaise et Internationale [*French and International Press*]   (AF)

PFI .... Pyatigorsk Pharmaceutical Institute   (RU)

PFIC .... Processed Food Industry Council [*Australia*]

PFIN .... Partido Frente de Liberacion Nacional [*Peru*]   (LAA)

PFITU .... Pancyprian Federation of Independent Trade Unions [*Cyprus*]   (EAIO)

PFJ .... Patreksfjordur [*Iceland*] [*Airport symbol*]   (OAG)

PFJM .... Policia Federal Judicial Mexicana [*Mexican Federal Judicial Police*]

PFK........... Field Physical Therapy Office   (RU)

PFK........... Pan-Foititikon Kinima [*Pan-Student Movement*]   (GC)

PFK........... Permanent Finance Commission   (BU)

PFKC .... Polish Federation of Korfball Clubs   (EAIO)

PFKK .... Polska Federacja Klubow Korfballu [*Poland*]   (EAIO)

PFKSZ....... Preliminary General Catalog of Fundamental Faint Stars   (RU)

PFL........... Laotian Patriotic Front   (RU)

PFL........... Pacific Forum Line [*South Pacific island countries*]

PFL........... Partido Frente Liberal [*Political party*] [*Brazil*]

Pfl............ Pflanze [*Plant*] [*German*]

Pfl............ Pflege [*Nursing*] [*German*]   (GCA)

PFL........... Philippine Federation of Labor   (EY)

PFL........... Placi Fibrolemnoase [*Fiberboard*]   (RO)

PFL........... Pol-Fly [*Poland*] [*ICAO designator*]   (FAAC)

pflanzl .... Pflanzlich [*Of the Plant*] [*German*]   (GCA)

PFLE .... Popular Front for the Liberation of Eritrea [*Ethiopia*]   (AF)

PFLKh ...... Polyphenol from Wood Chemicals   (RU)

PFLM .... People's Forces for the Liberation of Mozambique

PFLO .... Popular Front for the Liberation of Oman [*Political party*]   (PD)

PFLOAG ... Popular Front for the Liberation of Oman and the Arabian Gulf [*Political party*]   (PD)

PFLP......... Popular Front for the Liberation of Palestine [*Political party*]   (PD)

PFLP-GC... Popular Front for the Liberation of Palestine - General Command [*Political party*]   (PD)

PFLT .... People's Front of the Liberation Tigers [*Sri Lanka*] [*Political party*]   (EY)

PFM.......... Modulator Band Filter   (RU)

PFMAA .... Pet Food Manufacturers' Association of Australia

PFN .... Parti des Forces Nouvelles [*New Forces Party*] [*France*] [*Political party*]   (PPW)

PFNDAI .... Protein Foods and Nutrition Development Association of India   (EAIO)

PFNFP...... Philippines Federation of Natural Family Planning

PFNP......... Partido Federalista Nacionalista Popular [*Panama*] [*Political party*]   (EY)

PFNT........ Police Force of the Northern Territory [*Australia*]

PFO .... Financial Planning Department   (RU)

PFO .... Paphos [*Cyprus*] [*Airport symbol*]   (OAG)

PFO .... Ration and Forage Section [*Military term*]   (RU)

PFP .... Pakistan Trade-Union Federation   (RU)

PFP .... Partnership for Peace [*An organization of non-member countries which have established military cooperation with NATO*]   (ECON)

PFP .... Popular Front Party [*Ghana*] [*Political party*]   (PPW)

PFP .... Porcelain and Faience Industry   (BU)

PFP .... Progressiewe Federale Party [*Progressive Federal Party*] [*South Africa*] [*Political party*]   (PPW)

Pfprv .... Pfarrprovisor [*German*]

PFR........... Pfarrer [*Pastor*] [*German*]   (EY)

PFRB .... Publications and Films Review Board [*Western Australia*]

Pfrexprv ..... Pfarrexcurrendoprovisor [*German*]

Pfrmprv..... Pfarrmitprovisor [*German*]

Pfrmvk ...... Pfarrmitvikar [*German*]

PFS .... Farm Crop Rotation   (RU)

PFS .... Pakistan Foreign Service   (CL)

PFS .... Panellinios Farmakevtikos Syllogos [*Panhellenic Pharmaceutical Society*]   (GC)

PFS .... Pankyprios Farmakevtikos Syndesmos [*Pan-Cyprian Pharmaceutical Society*]   (GC)

PFS .... Projector for Facade Illumination, Floodlight   (RU)

PFS .... Ration and Forage Supply Depot   (RU)

pfsa............ Pour Faire Ses Adieux [*To Say Goodbye*] [*French*]   (GPO)

PFSh .... Partia Fashismit e Shqiperise [*Fascist Party of Albania*] [*Political party*]   (PPE)

PFSJ .... Panstwowa Fabryka Sztucznego Jedwabiu [*State Artificial Silk Factory*]   (POL)

Pf St .... Pfund Sterling [*Pound Sterling*] [*German*]   (GCA)

PFTE .... Pianoforte [*Soft, then Loud*] [*Music*]

PFTO......... Philippine Federation of Teachers' Organizations   (EY)

PFU .... Functional Block Using Film Circuits   (RU)

PFU .... Parti Feministe Unifie [*Unified Women's Party*] [*Belgium*]   (WER)

PFU .... Presbyterian Fellowship Union [*Australia*]

PFUJ .... Pakistan Federal Union of Journalists
PFUM .... Pabianicka Fabryka Urzadzen Mechanicznych [*Pabianice Machine Tool Factory*] (POL)
PFV .... Philippine Forces, Vietnam
PFV .... Pomoc Francuske Vlade [*French Government Economic Aid*] [*Tripartite Aid Program*] (YU)
pfv .... Pour Faire Visite [*To Make a Call*] [*French*]
PfVk .... Pfarrvikar [*German*]
PFVl .... Pomoc Francuske Vlade u Hrani [*Aid of French Government in Food*] (YU)
Pfvw .... Pfarrverweser [*German*]
PfVwes .... Pfarrverweser [*German*]
pfvzo .... Palyafelvigyazo [*Track Watchman*] (HU)
PFW .... Proefstation voor de Fruitteelt [*Fruit Growing Research Station*] [*Netherlands*] (ARC)
PFZ .... Panstwowy Fundusz Ziemi [*State Land Fund*] (POL)
PFZ .... Polni Frontove Zabezpeceni [*Frontline Field Support*] (CZ)
PFZ .... Post- und Fernmeldetechniches Zentralamt [*Central Office for Postal and Telecommunications Operations*] (EG)
PFZA .... Panstwowa Fabryka Zwiazkow Azotowych (w Chorzowie) [*State Nitrogen Compound Factory (in Chorzow)*] (POL)
PF-ZAPU .. Patriotic Front - Zimbabwe African People's Union [*Political party*] (PD)
PG .... Antitank Grenade (RU)
PG .... Carrier Pigeon, Homing Pigeon (RU)
PG .... Clamshell Loader, Grab Loader [*Mining*] (RU)
PG .... Field Hospital (RU)
PG .... Flash Absorber, Flash Eliminator, Flash Suppressor [*Artillery*] (RU)
PG .... Foam Generator (RU)
PG .... Hydraulic Press (RU)
pg .... Last Year (RU)
PG .... Machine-Gun Nest (RU)
pg .... Pago [*Paid*] [*Portuguese*]
PG .... Papua New Guinea [*ANSI two-letter standard code*] (CNC)
PG .... Paralysie Generale [*General Paralysis*] [*Medicine*] [*French*]
PG .... Paris Group [*See also GP*] [*France*] (EAIO)
PG .... Partido Galleguista [*Galician Party*] [*Spanish*] (WER)
PG .... Partido Garriques [*Garriques Party*] [*Spanish*] (WER)
PG .... Penang (ML)
Pg .... Pergament [*Vellum*] [*Publishing*] [*German*]
PG .... Perugia [*Car registration plates*] [*Italian*]
Pg .... Peso Guineen
Pg .... Petrograd (RU)
PG .... Pharmacopoeia Germanica [*German Pharmacopoeia*]
PG .... Piece Gauche [*In a turret*] [*Military*] [*French*] (MTD)
PG .... Pigment Granule (RU)
PG .... Pneumogram (RU)
PG .... Pokretna Grupa [*Mobile Group*] [*Military*] (YU)
PG .... Politechnika Gdanska [*Gdansk Polytechnical School*] (POL)
PG .... Politie-Gids [*Benelux*] (BAS)
PG .... Politikon Grafeion [*Politburo*] (GC)
PG .... Post-Grado [*Spanish*]
pg .... Pour Garder [*To Be Called For*] [*French*]
PG .... Prisonnier de Guerre [*Prisoner of War - POW*] [*French*]
PG .... Procuratore Generale [*Attorney General*] [*Italian*] (WER)
PG .... Procureur Generaal [*Public Attorney*] [*Dutch*] (ILCA)
PG .... Produktionsgenossenschaft [*Producer Cooperative*] (EG)
PG .... Pro-German [*Prisoner of war term*] [*World War I*] (DSUE)
PG .... Prokureur-Generaal [*Attorney-General*] [*Afrikaans*]
PG .... Propyl Gallate (RU)
pg .... Przez Grzecznosc [*Poland*]
PG .... Pyrolytic Graphite (RU)
PG .... Steam Generator [*Nuclear physics and engineering*] (RU)
PG .... Trigger Generator (RU)
PGA .... Mobile Army Group (RU)
PGA .... Pastoralists and Graziers Association [*Western Australia*]
PGA .... Pharmacy Guild of Australia (ADA)
PGA .... Pistachio Growers' Association [*Australia*]
PGA .... Port of Geelong Authority [*Victoria, Australia*]
PGA .... Portugalia, Companhia Portuguesa de Transportes Aeros SA [*Portugal*] [*ICAO designator*] (FAAC)
PGA .... Potato Growers of Australia
PGA .... Press Gallery Association
PGA .... Puppetry Guild of Australia
PGAI .... Poultry Growers' Association in Israel (EAIO)
PGANSW ... Potato Growers' Association of New South Wales [*Australia*]
PGAP .... Pneudraulic Autopilot (RU)
PGAP .... Poleodomikon Grafeion Athinon kai Perikhoron [*City Planning Office of Athens and Suburbs*] (GC)
PGASA ...... Playgroup Association of South Australia
PGAWA .... Pastoralists and Graziers' Association of Western Australia
PGAWA .... Potato Growers' Association of Western Australia
PGB .... Panglima Gagah Berani [*Federation Gallantry Decoration*] [*Malaysia*] (ML)
PGB .... Pusat Gerakan Bersama [*Joint Operations Center*] (ML)

PGC .... Persian Gulf Command [*World War II*]
pgcd .... Plus Grand Commun Diviseur [*Greatest Common Divider*] [*French*]
PGCVS ...... Postgraduate Committee in Veterinary Science [*Australia*]
PGDB .... Plumbers, Gasfitters, and Drainers' Board [*New South Wales, Australia*]
PGDip .... Postgraduate Diploma [*Australia*]
PGDipA ..... Postgraduate Diploma in Arts [*Australia*]
PGDipAgrSc ... Postgraduate Diploma in Agricultural Science [*Australia*]
PGDipDevTech ... Postgraduate Diploma in Development Technology [*Australia*]
PGDipEdSt ... Postgraduate Diploma in Educational Studies [*Australia*]
PGDipForSc ... Postgraduate Diploma in Forest Science [*Australia*]
PGDipIEM ... Postgraduate Diploma in Irrigation Engineering Management [*Australia*]
PGDipMath & MathEd ... Postgraduate Diploma in Mathematics and Mathematics Education [*Australia*]
PGDipMgtSt ... Postgraduate Diploma in Management Studies [*Australia*]
PGDipPhysio ... Postgraduate Diploma in Physiotherapy [*Australia*]
PGDipSc .... Postgraduate Diploma in Science [*Australia*]
pgd og .... Normal Barrage (BU)
PGDRB .... Plumbers, Gasfitters, and Drainers Registration Board [*Victoria, Australia*]
Pge .... Passage [*Passage*] [*Military map abbreviation World War I*] [*French*] (MTD)
PGEA .... Philippine Government Employees Association (FEA)
P Gen .... Parc du Genie [*Military*] [*French*] (MTD)
P Gen A .... Parc du Genie d'Armee [*Military*] [*French*] (MTD)
PGEUA .... Plumbers and Gasfitters Employees' Union of Australia
PGF .... Perpignan [*France*] [*Airport symbol*] (OAG)
PGF .... Praesentations-Graphische Funktionen [*German*] (ADPT)
PGF .... Precision Golf Forging Proprietary Ltd. [*Australia*] (ADA)
PGFVS .... Postgraduate Federation in Veterinary Science [*Australia*]
PGG .... Piston Gas Generator (RU)
PGG .... Przemysl Guzikarsko-Galanteryjny [*Haberdashery Goods Industry*] (POL)
PGG .... Steam and Gas Generator (RU)
PGH .... Pengarah [*Director*] (ML)
PGH .... Produktionsgenossenschaft des Handwerks [*Artisan Producer Cooperative*] (EG)
PGHMPR ... People's Great Hural of the Mongolian People's Republic
PGI .... Chitato [*Angola*] [*Airport symbol*] [*Obsolete*] (OAG)
PGI .... General Information Programme [*UNESCO*] [*Acronym is based on foreign phrase*]
PGI .... Paris District Gestion Informatique [*French*]
PGI .... Paris Gestion Informatique [*Paris Informatics Administration*] [*France*] [*Information service or system*] (IID)
PGI .... Partido Gallego Independiente [*Independent Galician Party*] [*Spanish*] (WER)
PGI .... Partido Galleguista de Izquierdas [*Galician Leftist Party*] [*Spanish*] (WER)
PGI .... Perfo Guide International [*French*] (ADPT)
PGI .... Philippine Geothermal, Incorporated
PGI .... Plast- och Gummitekniska Institutet [*Plastics and Rubber Institute*] [*Research center*] [*Sweden*] (IRC)
PGI .... Polar Geophysical Institute (of the Kola Branch of the Academy of Sciences, USSR) (RU)
PGI .... Programme de Gestion des Interruptions [*French*] (ADPT)
PGII .... Pergabungan Guru Islam Indonesia [*Islamic Teachers' Union*] [*Indonesia*]
Pgio .... Poggio [*Mound, Small Hill*] [*Italian*] (NAU)
PGJDF ...... Procuraduria General de Justicia del Distrito Federal [*Federal District Attorney General's Office*] [*Mexico*] (LA)
PGK .... Pangkalpinang [*Indonesia*] [*Airport symbol*] (OAG)
PGK .... Pflanzungsgesellschaft Kpeme
PGK .... Projectgroep Kernenergie [*Project Group for Nuclear Energy*] [*Netherlands Central Organization for Applied Natural Scientific Research*] (WND)
PGK .... Proodevtiki Gynaikeia Kinisi [*Progressive Women's Movement*] [*Cyprus*] (GC)
PGKI .... Persatuan Guru Katholik Indonesia [*Indonesian Catholic Teachers' Union*]
PGKU .... Pasukan Gerilja Kalimantan Utara [*North Kalimantan Guerrilla Force*] (IN)
PGL .... Panstwowe Gospodarstwa Lesne [*State Forest Properties*] (POL)
PGl .... Politechnika Gliwicka [*Engineering College of Gliwice*] [*Poland*]
PGL .... Proodevtikai Gynaikai Larnakos [*Progressive Women of Larnaca*] (GC)
PGM .... Persatuan Geologi Malaysia [*Geological Society of Malaysia*] (EAIO)
PGM .... Petroquimica General Mosconi [*Argentina*]
PGM .... Plovdiv City Museum (BU)
Pg(M) .... Posgraduacao (Mestrado) [*Academic degree*] [*Portuguese*]
PGMO .... Poltava Gravimetric Observatory (RU)
PGN .... Procurador General de la Nacion [*National Attorney General*] [*Colorado*] (LA)

PGN .... Procuraduria General de la Nacion [*Office of the National Attorney General*] [*Colorado*] (LA)
PGNP .... Pedal-Operated Parametric Generator (RU)
PGNU .... Provisional Government of National Union [*Laos*]
PGO .... Polar Geophysical Observatory (RU)
PGO .... Poltava Gravimetric Observatory (RU)
PGOA .... Pharmacy Guild of Australia
PGP .... Maximal Annual Penetration [*Radioactivity*] (BU)
PGP .... Parti Gabonais du Progres [*Political party*] (EY)
PGP .... Pomorsko Gradevno Preduzece [*Maritime Construction Establishment*] (YU)
PGPN .... Przedsiebiorstwo Geofizyki Przemyslu Naftowego [*Geophysical Enterprise of the Petroleum Industry*] (POL)
PGPP .... State Contract and Delivery Regulations (RU)
PGR .... Field Radiometer for Gamma-Beta Radiation (RU)
PGR .... Panstwowe Gospodarstwa Rolne [*State Farms*] (POL)
PGR .... Parental Guidance Recommended [*Movie rating*] [*Australia*]
pgr .... Pour Garder Recommandee [*French*]
PGR .... Procurador General Regional [*Regional Attorney General*] [*Colorado*] (LA)
PGR .... Procuradoria General Regional [*Office of the Regional Attorney General*] [*Colorado*] (LA)
PGRA .... Postgraduate Representative Association [*Australia*]
PGREIP ...... Prudential Global Real Estate Investment Program [*Australia*]
PGRI .... Persatuan Guru Republik Indonesia [*Union of Teachers of the Republic of Indonesia*]
PGRK .... Field Logging Radiometer for Gamma-Beta Radiation (RU)
PGRKU ..... Pasokan Gerilya Kalimantan Utara [*North Kalimantan Guerrilla Forces*] [*PGRS, changed June 1970 to conform with new CPNK, Communist Party of North Kalimantan*] [*Formerly*] (ML)
PGRM .... Parti Gerakan Rakyat Malaysia [*People's Action Party of Malaysia*] [*Political party*] (PPW)
P Gr Pr .... Fixed Light with a Group of Flashes [*Nautical term*] (RU)
PGRS .... Oil-Field Gas-Control Station (RU)
PGRS .... Pasokan Gerilya Rakyat Sarawak [*Sarawak People's Guerrilla Forces*] [*Replaced by PGRKU*] (ML)
PGRS .... Pergerakan Guerilja Rakyat Sarawak [*Sarawak People's Guerrilla Forces*] [*Malaya*]
PG Ryb ...... Panstwowe Gospodarstwa Rybackie [*State Fishing Farms*] [*Poland*]
PGS .... Battle Position, Battle Zone (RU)
pg s .... Frontier Sector (BU)
PGS .... Industrial Loudspeaker Communications (RU)
PGS .... Panellinios Gymnastikos Syllogos [*Panhellenic Gymnastic Club*] (GC)
PGS .... Panionios Gymnastikos Syllogos [*Pan-Ionian Gymnastic Club*] [*Greek*] (GC)
PGS .... Polish Geographical Society (EAIO)
PGS .... Pravila Garnizonske Sluzbe [*Garrison Service Rules*] (YU)
PGS .... Tauranga Aero Club, Inc. [*New Zealand*] [*ICAO designator*] (FAAC)
PGSD .... Partido Galego Social-Democrata [*Galician Social Democratic Party*] [*Spanish*] (WER)
PGSDN ...... Partido Galego Social-Democrata Nacionalista [*Nationalist Social Democratic Galician Party*] [*Spanish*] (WER)
PGT .... Micarta-Textolite Plastic (RU)
PGT .... Pacific Globe Trading Co. Ltd. [*Thailand*]
PGT .... Partido Guatemalteco del Trabajo [*Guatemalan Labor Party*] [*Political party*] (PD)
PGT .... Pasukan Gerak Tjepat [*Strike Troops (Air Force paratroops)*] (IN)
PGT .... Pegasus Hava Tasimaciligi AS [*Turkey*] [*ICAO designator*] (FAAC)
Pgt .... Pergament [*Vellum*] [*Publishing*] [*German*]
PGT .... Urban-Type Settlement (RU)
Pgtbd .... Pergamentband [*Vellum Binding*] [*Publishing*] [*German*]
PGTI .... Persatuan Guru Teknik Indonesia [*Technical Teachers' Union of Indonesia*]
PGTV .... Pecsi Geodeziai es Terkepeszeti Vallalat [*Geodesic and Cartographic Enterprise of Pecs*] (HU)
PGU .... Intercommunication Loudspeaker System (RU)
PGU .... Mobile Hydraulic Excavator [*Min.*] (RU)
PGU .... Peninsula Gas Utilization [*Malaysia*]
PGU .... Perm' State University Imeni A. M. Gor'kiy (RU)
PGU .... Underground Gasification of Coal (RU)
PGU .... Universal Hydraulic Blowout Preventer [*Pet.*] (RU)
PGV .... Checking Vertical-Flight Gyroscope (RU)
PGV .... Privatgueterwagen-Vorschriften [*Regulations for Private Freight Cars*] (EG)
PGWU .... Petroleum and General Workers' Union [*Aden*]
PGZ .... Physikalische Gesellschaft Zurich [*Physical Association of Zurich*] [*Switzerland*] (SLS)
PGZ .... Ponta Grossa [*Brazil*] [*Airport symbol*] (OAG)
PGZA .... Pravila Gadanja Zemaljske Artiljerije [*Ground Artillery Fire Rules*] (YU)

PH .... Paedagogische Hochschule [*Advanced School for Teacher Training*] (EG)
PH .... Parlementaire Handelingen [*Benelux*] (BAS)
ph .... Pecset Helye [*Seal*] (HU)
Ph .... Phare [*Lighthouse*] [*Military map abbreviation World War I*] [*French*] (MTD)
PH .... Philippines [*ANSI two-letter standard code*] (CNC)
ph .... Photographie [*Photography*] [*German*]
PH .... Photography [*Royal Australian Navy*]
PH .... Plantations Holdings Ltd. [*Barbados*]
ph .... Plus Haut [*French*]
PH .... Polynesian Airlines [*Airline code*] [*Australia*]
ph .... Postahivatal [*Post Office*] (HU)
pH .... Pouvoir Hydrogene [*Hydrogen Power*] [*Negative logarithm of effective H ion concentration Chemistry*]
PH .... Pre Hrista [*Before Christ*] (YU)
PH .... Presidential Medal of Honour [*Botswana*]
PH .... Produktionsmittelhandel [*Trade in Production Equipment*] (EG)
PH .... Provinciaal Hof [*Benelux*] (BAS)
PH .... Pruzkumna Hlidka [*Reconnaissance Patrol*] (CZ)
pH .... Wasserstoffexponent [*Hydrogen Exponent*] [*German*]
PH '96 .... Private House 1996 (OLYM)
PHA .... Permanente Hof van Arbitrage [*Benelux*] (BAS)
PHA .... Peruvian Hospital Association (EAIO)
PHA .... Pritikin Health Association of Australia
PHA .... Private Hospitals Association [*Australia*]
PHA .... Professional Hairdressers' Association [*Australia*]
PHA .... Professional Historians Association [*Australia*]
PHA .... Public Health Association [*Australia*]
PHA .... Pulshoehenanalyse [*German*] (ADPT)
PHAQ .... Private Hospitals' Association of Queensland [*Australia*]
PHARE ..... Poland and Hungary Assistance for Economic Restructuring [*EC*] [*ECED*]
Pharm .... Pharmazie [*Pharmacy*] [*German*]
Pharma ...... Pharmazeutische Industrie (VVB) [*Pharmaceutical Industry (VVB)*] (EG)
pharmak ..... Pharmakologisch [*Pharmacological*] [*German*] (GCA)
pharmakol ... Pharmakologisch [*Pharmacological*] [*German*] (GCA)
PHARMARIN ... Office National de Pharmacie [*Mauritania*]
pharmaz ..... Pharmazeutisch [*Pharmaceutical*] [*German*] (GCA)
pharmazeut ... Pharmazeutisch [*Pharmaceutical*] [*German*] (GCA)
PHARMEX ... Pharmaceutical Import Company [*Syria*] (ME)
PHASA ...... Professional Hunters Association of South Africa (EAIO)
PHAT .... Professional Historians' Association of Tasmania [*Australia*]
PHAV .... Private Hospitals' Association of Victoria [*Australia*]
PHAWA ..... Private Hospitals' Association of Western Australia
Ph B .... Bachelor of Pharmacy
Ph B .... Bachelor of Physical Culture
PHB .... Parnaiba [*Brazil*] [*Airport symbol*] (OAG)
PHB .... Perhubungan [*Communications*] (IN)
Ph B .... Philosophiae Baccalaureus [*Bachelor of Philosophy*]
Ph BD .... Doctor of Bible Philosophy
Ph Belg ...... Pharmakopoea Belgica [*Belgian Pharmacopoeia*] [*German*] (GCA)
Ph B inArch ... Bachelor of Philosophy in Architecture
Ph B inCom ... Bachelor of Philosophy in Commerce
Ph B inEd ... Bachelor of Philosophy in Education
PHC .... Pakistan High Command [*Military*]
PHC .... Petroleum Helicopters de Colombia SA [*ICAO designator*] (FAAC)
Ph C .... Philosopher of Chiropractic
PHC .... Port Harcourt [*Nigeria*] [*Airport symbol*] (OAG)
PHCA .... Parliament House Construction Authority [*Australia*]
PHCA .... Philippine Heart Center for Asia (PDAA)
PHCA .... Proyecto Hidrometeorologico Centroamericano [*Costa Rica*] (DSCA)
PHCI .... Plantations et Huileries de Cote-D'Ivoire [*Ivory Coast Plantations and Oil Works*] (AF)
PHCP .... Primary Health Care Programme
PHCS .... Pacific Hills Christian School [*Australia*]
PhD .... Doctor of Philosophy (PWGL)
Ph D .... Philosophiae Doctor [*Doctor of Philosophy*] [*Facetious translation: Piled Higher and Deeper*]
PhDr .... Doctor Philosofiae [*Doctor of Philosophy (PhD)*] (CZ)
PhDr .... Doktor der Philosophie [*Doctor of Philosophy (PhD)*] [*German*]
PHE .... Pawan Hans Ltd. [*India*] [*ICAO designator*] (FAAC)
PHE .... Port Hedland [*Australia*] [*Airport symbol*] (OAG)
PHEA .... Pan Hellenic Evangelical Alliance [*Greece*]
PHERP ..... Public Health Education and Research Program [*Australia*]
PHESF ..... Private Hospital Employees' Superannuation Fund [*Australia*]
PHF .... Pakistan Hockey Federation
PHF .... Pergamon Holding Foundation [*Liechtenstein*]
PHG .... Pahang (ML)
Ph G .... Pharmakopoea Germanica [*German Pharmacopoeia*] (GCA)

PHG .... Phenate-Hexamine Goggle [*British World War I anti-poison-gas helmet*]

Ph Helv ...... Pharmakopoea Helvetica [*Swiss Pharmacopoeia*] [*German*] (GCA)

Phi .... Philips [*Holland & International*] [*Record label*]

PHI .... Philips Aviation Services [*Netherlands*] [*ICAO designator*] (FAAC)

PHI .... Philosophie Informationsdienst [*Philosophy Information Service*] [*University of Dusseldorf*] [*Information service or system*] (IID)

PHI .... Programme Hydrologique International [*International Hydrological Program - IHP*] [*UNESCO*] (MSC)

PHIBEX .... Amphibious Exercise [*NATO*]

PHIC .... Pharmaceutical Industries Corporation [*Myanmar*] (DS)

PHIJ .... Permanente Hof van Internationale Justitie [*Benelux*] (BAS)

phil .... Philologie [*French*] (TPFD)

phil .... Philology (TPFD)

phil .... Philosophisch [*German*]

PHILCAG ... First Philippine Civic Action Group [*Deployed in 1964 to assist South Vietnam*] (VNW)

PHILCAG ... Philippine Civil Assistance Group

PHILCEMCOR ... Philippine Cement Corp. (FEA)

PHILCITE ... Philippine Center for International Trade and Exhibitions (DS)

PHILCOM ... Philippine Global Communications, Inc. [*Manila*] [*Telecommunications*]

PHILCOMSAT ... Philippiune Global Communications Satellite Corp. (PDAA)

PHILCON ... Philippine Contingent [*Military*]

PHILCONSA ... Philippine Constitution Association

PHILCONTU ... Philippine Congress of Trade Unions (FEA)

PHILCORIN ... Philippine Coconut Research Institute

PHIL I .... Philippine Islands (WDAA)

Philip .... Philippines

Philipp .... Philippines (BARN)

Phillip IT ... Phillip Institute of Technology [*Australia*]

PHILNABANK ... Philippine National Bank (FEA)

Philodril ..... Philippine Overseas Drilling & Oil Development Corp.

philol .... Philologisch [*German*]

philos .... Philosophie [*French*] (TPFD)

philos .... Philosophisch [*German*]

philos .... Philosophy (TPFD)

PHILPRO ... Philippine Committee on Trade Facilitation (PDAA)

PHILPUC ... Philippine Presidential Unit Citation Badge [*Military decoration*]

PHILSA .... Philippine Standards Association (PDAA)

PHILSEAFRON ... Philippine Sea Frontier

PHILSUCOM ... Philippines Sugar Commission (DS)

PHILSUCOM ... Philippine Sugar Commission (ARC)

PHILSUGIN ... Philippine Sugar Institute

PHIND ...... Pharmaceutical and Healthcare Industries News Database [*PJB Group Publications Ltd.*] [*Information service or system*] (IID)

PHIVOLC ... Philippine Institute of Volcanology [*National Science and Technology Authority*] [*Research center*] (EAS)

PHIVOLCS ... Philippine Institute of Volcanology and Seismology [*Department of Science and Technology*] [*Research center*] (EAS)

PHL .... Philippines [*ANSI three-letter standard code*] (CNC)

PHL .... Physisch Laboratorium [*Physics Laboratory*] [*Netherlands Central Organization for Applied Natural Scientific Research*] (WND)

PHL-TNO ... Physisch Laboratorium TNO [*Physics Laboratory TNO*] [*Netherlands Organization for Applied Scientific Research (TNO)*] [*Research center*] (ERC)

PhM .... Philips Minigroove [*Record label*]

PHM .... Pohonne Hmoty a Mazadla [*Petroleum Products and Lubricants*] (CZ)

PhMr .... Magister Farmaciae [*Pharmacist (Academic degree)*] (CZ)

PHO .... Principal House Officer [*Australia*]

phon .... Phonetics (TPFD)

PHOSBOUCRAA ... Phosphates de Boucraa SA [*Morocco*] (MENA)

Phot .... Photographie [*Photograph*] [*German*]

phot .... Photographie [*Photograph*] [*French*]

phot .... Photography (TPFD)

photogr .... Photographie [*Photograph*] [*Netherlands*]

Photogr ...... Photographie [*Photograph*] [*German*]

photot .... Phototypie [*Phototype*] [*Publishing*] [*French*]

PHP .... Peace and Happiness through Prosperity [*Spiritual and educational movement*] [*Japan*]

PHP .... Plantations du Haut-Penja

PHR .... Pacific Harbour [*Fiji*] [*Airport symbol*] (OAG)

PHR .... Peloton hors Range [*Military*] [*French*] (MTD)

phr .... Phrase [*French*] (TPFD)

PHRACT ... Print-Handicapped Radio, Australian Capital Territory

PHRI .... Peace and Human Rights Initiative [*Germany*] [*German Democratic Republic*] (EAIO)

PHRI .... Port and Harbor Research Institute [*Research center*] [*Japan*] (IRC)

PHS .... Peace and Humanity Society [*Australia*]

PHS .... Phitsanuloke [*Thailand*] [*Airport symbol*] (OAG)

PHS .... Progressive Hongkong Society [*Political party*]

PHSch .... Parteihochschule "Karl Marx" der SED [*"Karl Marx" Party Advanced School of the SED*] (EG)

PHSNZ .... Postal History Society of New Zealand [*Auckland*] (EA)

PHSR .... Przedsiebiorstwo Handlu Sprzetem Rolniczym [*Farm Equipment Trade Enterprise*] (POL)

PHU .... Postovni Hospodarska Ustredna [*Central Postal Management Office*] (CZ)

Phw .... Pandhuiswet [*Benelux*] (BAS)

PHW .... Phalaborwa [*South Africa*] [*Airport symbol*] (OAG)

PHWC .... Polish Helsinki Watch Committee (EAIO)

PHX .... Phoenix 2000 Airtaxi Ltd. [*Hungary*] [*ICAO designator*] (FAAC)

phys .... Physics (TPFD)

phys .... Physikal [*or Physikalisch*] [*Physical*] [*German*]

Phys .... Physikat [*or Physikus*] [*German*]

phys .... Physique [*French*] (TPFD)

physik .... Physikal [*or Physikalisch*] [*Physical*] [*German*]

physikal .... Physikalisch [*Physical*] [*German*] (GCA)

physiol .... Physiologie [*French*] (TPFD)

physiol .... Physiologisch [*Physiological*] [*German*] (GCA)

physiol ...... Physiology (TPFD)

PHZ .... Plan Hmotneho Zasobovani [*Materiel Procurement Plan*] (CZ)

Phz .... Presskohlenheizung [*Briquette Heating*] (EG)

PHZ .... Protivhemiska Zastita [*Antichemical Defense*] [*Military*] (YU)

PHZ .... Przedsiebiorstwo Handlu Zagranicznego [*Foreign Trade Enterprise*] (POL)

PI .... Design Institute (BU)

PI .... Estado do Piaui [*State of Piaui*] [*Brazil*]

PI .... Filipiny [*Philippines*] [*Poland*]

PI .... Information Transmission Device (RU)

PI .... Institute of Paleontology (RU)

PI .... Intermediate Total (RU)

PI .... La Propriete Industrielle [*Switzerland*] (FLAF)

PI .... Paedagogisches Institut [*Pedagogical Institute*] (EG)

pi .... Palaion Imerologion [*Old Calendar*] (GC)

PI .... Paracel Islands [*ANSI two-letter standard code*] (CNC)

PI .... Partido Independente [*Independent Party*] [*Costa Rica*] [*Political party*]

PI .... Partido Intransigente [*Intransigent Party*] [*Argentina*] [*Political party*] (PD)

PI .... Partido Intransigente [*Intransigent Party*] [*Uruguay*] (LA)

PI .... Parti Islam [*Islamic Party*] (ML)

PI .... Passeport International [*International Passport*] [*An association*] [*France*] (EAIO)

PI .... Paysans Independants

PI .... Pazarisen Inspektorat [*Market Inspectorate*] (YU)

PI .... Pedagogiai Intezet [*Pedagogical Institute*] (HU)

PI .... Pedagogical Institute (RU)

PI .... Permaculture International [*Australia*]

PI .... Personal Injury Accident [*British police term*]

PI .... Pharmacopoeia Internationalis [*International Pharmacopoeia*]

PI .... Photo International [*Defunct*] (EAIO)

PI .... Piaster [*Monetary unit*] [*Spain, Republic of Vietnam, and some Middle Eastern countries*]

PI .... Pisa [*Car registration plates*] [*Italian*]

PI .... Planning Institute (RU)

PI .... Point Initial [*Military*] [*French*] (MTD)

PI .... Polytechnic Institute (RU)

pi .... Posebno Izdanje [*Special or Separate Edition*] (YU)

PI .... Poverenictvo pre Informacie [*Office of the Commissioner of Information*] (CZ)

PI .... Precompte Immobilier [*Benelux*] (BAS)

PI .... Prehranbena Industrija [*Food Industry*] (YU)

PI .... Preselection, Preselector [*Telephony*] (RU)

PI .... Primary Meter (RU)

PI .... Proportional-Integral (Law) (RU)

PI .... Propriete Industrielle [*Benelux*] (BAS)

PI .... Pubblica Istruzione [*(Ministry of) Public Education*] [*Italian*]

PI .... Regimental Engineer (RU)

PI .... Sunshine Airlines [*Airline code*] [*Australia*]

PIA .... Pakistan International Airlines Corp. [*ICAO designator*] (FAAC)

PIA .... Piano [*Softly*] [*Music*]

PIA .... Plastics Industry Association [*Australia*]

PIA .... Plastics Institute of Australia (ADA)

PIA .... Polski Instytut Archeologiczny [*Polish Archeological Institute*] (POL)

PIA .... Primary Industry Association of Western Australia

PIA .... Public Information Adviser [*NATO*] (NATG)

PIA............ Public Intoxication Act [Australia]
PIAC.......... Partido de Integracion de America Central [Nicaragua] [Political party] (EY)
PIAC.......... Petroleum Industry Advisory Committee [British]
PIAC.......... Public Interest Advocacy Centre [Australia]
PIACC....... Pacific Islands Association of Chambers of Commerce [Fiji] (EAIO)
PIACT .... Programme International pour l'Amelioration des Conditions et du Milieu de Travail [International Program for the Improvement of Working Conditions and Environment] [French]
PIADP .... Palawan Integrated Area Development Project [Philippines]
PIAL.......... Patrick Intermarine Acceptances Limited [Australia] (ADA)
PIALLO .... Programa Alto Llano Occidental [Upper Western Plains Program] [Venezuela] (LA)
PIAN .... Institute of Paleontology (of the Academy of Sciences, USSR) (RU)
PIANC....... Permanent International Association of Navigation Congresses [Brussels, Belgium] (EAIO)
PIANG ...... Piangendo [Plaintive] [Music]
PIANISS ... Pianissimo [Very Softly] [Music]
PIAP.......... Printing Industries Association of the Philippines (DS)
PIAPUR .... Programa Interamericano de Planificacion Urbana y Regional [Inter-American Program for Urban and Regional Planning] [Lima, Peru] (LAA)
PIAR......... Piyasa Arastirma Merkezi [Market Research Center] (TU)
PIAR......... Proyectos Integrales de Asentamiento Rural [Integral Projects for Rural Settlement] [Peru] (LA)
PIARC ...... Permanent International Association of Road Congresses [See also AIPCR] [Paris, France] (EAIO)
PIAS .... Piaster [Monetary unit] [Spain, Republic of Vietnam, and some Middle Eastern countries]
PIAT......... Parizer Idisher Arbeiter Teater [Acronym is based on former name,] (BJA)
PIAWU..... Printing Industry and Allied Workers Union [Guyana] (LA)
PIB............ Papuan Infantry Battalion
PIB............ Partido Indio de Bolivia [Political party]
PIB............ Planning and Research Office (RU)
PIB............ Prices and Incomes Board
PIB............ Producto Interno Bruto [Gross Domestic Product] (LA)
PIB............ Produit Interieur Brut [Gross National Product] [Use GNP] (CL)
PIB............ Professional Integrity Branch [New South Wales Police Service] [Australia]
PIB............ Pukovska Intendantska Baza [Regimental Quartermaster Base] [YU]
PIBA......... Plan de Integracion de la Poblacion Aborigen [Peru] (DSCA)
PIBA......... Primary Industry Bank of Australia Ltd. (ADA)
PIBAC ...... Permanent International Bureau of Analytical Chemistry of Human and Animal Food [French] (ASF)
PIBAS........ Plastik Ip ve Bant Sanayi ve Tic Anonim Sirketi [Plastic Cord and Tape Industry and Trade Corporation] (TU)
PIBD......... Panstwowy Instytut Biologii Doswiadczalnej [State Institute of Experimental Biology] (POL)
PIBR......... Pig Industry Board of Rhodesia
PIBSL........ Panstwowy Instytut Badania Sztuki Ludowej [State Institute of Folk Art Research] (POL)
PIBTI........ Persatuan Industri Barang Jadi Tekstil Indonesia [Indonesian Association of Garment Industries]
PIBU......... Parti pour l'Independance du Burundi
PIC........... Pacific Airlines Holding Co. [Vietnam] [ICAO designator] (FAAC)
PIC............ Pacific Island Country [Australia]
PIC............ Pecheries Industrielles du Congo [Congo Industrial Fisheries] (AF)
PIC............ Petrochemical Industries Company [Kuwait] (ME)
PIC............ Petrochemical Industries Corp. [Myanmar] (DS)
PIC............ Piccadilly Saloon [London] (DSUE)
PIC............ Pig Improvement Co. [Australia]
PIC............ Pine Cay [British West Indies] [Airport symbol] [Obsolete] (OAG)
PIC............ Piping Industrial Contractors Ltda. [Colombia] (COL)
PIC............ Planification Industrielle Christian R. Champroux & Cie.
PIC............ Plantations Industrielles de Cocotiers
PIC............ Police Information Center [Jamaica] (LA)
PIC............ Policia de Investigacao Criminal [Criminal Investigation Police] [Mozambique] (AF)
PIC............ Puntos de Informacion Cultural [Spanish]
PICA......... Perth Institute of Contemporary Art [Australia]
PICA......... Printing Industry Craftsmen of Australia (ADA)
PICA......... Private Investment Co. for Asia SA
PICA......... Project for Integrated Catalogue Automation [Royal Netherlands Library] [Cataloging cooperative] (IID)
PICAO...... Provisional International Civil Aviation Organization [Later, ICAO]
PICC......... [The] People's Insurance Co. of China (EY)
PICC......... Philippines International Convention Center

picc............ Piccolo [Small] [Italian]
PICCAR .... Premier's Independent Commission for Change and Reform [Queensland, Australia]
PICG......... Pig Industry Consultative Group [Queensland, Australia]
PICG......... Programme International de Correlation Geologique [International Geological Correlation Programme - IGCP] (EAIO)
PICGC....... Permanent International Committee on Genetic Congresses [Japan] (DSCA)
PICIC .... Pakistan Industrial Credit Investment Corporation
PICM........ Party of the Independence Congress of Madagascar
PICM........ Permanent International Committee of Mothers
PICMME .. Provisional Intergovernmental Committee for Movement of Migrants in Europe (NATG)
PICO........ Pacific International Company Ltd.
PICO......... Partido Independiente de la Clase Obrera [Panama] [Political party] (EY)
PICOP....... Philippine Industries Corporation of the Philippines
PICOS .... Produktions-und Informations-Kontrollsystem [German] (ADPT)
PICPA ...... Philippine Institute of Certified Public Accountants (PDAA)
PICPSA ..... Permanent International Commission for the Proof of Small-Arms (EAIO)
PICS .... Passport Information and Control System [Australia]
PICSA .... Programa Interamericano para el Adiestramiento de Post-Graduados en Ciencias Sociales Aplicadas [Interamerican Program for the Training of Post-Graduate Students in Applied Social Sciences] [Mexico] (LAA)
PICSP .... Pro-Indian Commission of Sao Paulo [Brazil] (EAIO)
PIC(WA) ... Potato Industry Council (Western Australia)
PID .... Partido de Integracion Democrata [Democratic Integration Party] [Argentina] [Political party] (PPW)
PID .... Partido Institucional Democratico [Democratic Institutional Party] [Guatemala] (LA)
PID .... Partido Izquierda Democratica [Democratic Left Party] [Political party] (EAIO)
PID .... Planlama ve Insaat Dairesi [Planning and Construction Office] [Turkish Cypriot] (GC)
PID .... Planlama ve Insaat Dairesi Karayollari [Planning and Construction Office of Highways Directorate] [Turkish Cypriot] (GC)
PID .... Proletari in Divisa [Proletarians in Uniform] [Italian] (WER)
PID .... Proportionnel Integral et Derive [French] (ADPT)
PID .... Provision pour Investissements Diversifies
PID .... Publications and Information Directorate [CSIR] [India]
PIDBA ...... Programa Interamericano de Desarrollo de Bibliotecas Agricolas [Costa Rica] (DSCA)
PIDC........ Pakistan Industrial Development Corporation (GEA)
PIDC........ Precision Instrument Development Center [Taiwan] [Research center] (IRC)
PIDC........ Programme International de Developpement de la Communication
PIDE......... Pakistan Institute of Development Economics [Islamabad]
PIDE......... Policia Internacional e de Defesa do Estado [International and State Defense Police] [No longer in existence] [Portuguese] (WER)
PIDER ...... Programa de Inversiones para el Desarrollo Rural [Rural Development Investment Program] [Mexico] (LA)
pidgineng ... Pidginenglantia [Pidgin English] [Finland]
PIDI.......... Philippine Invention Development Institute [Research center] (IRC)
PID-regulyator ... Proportional-Integral-Differential Controller (RU)
PIDS......... Pacific Islands Industrial Development Scheme
PIDSA .... Population Information and Documentation System for Africa [Accra, Ghana]
PIE............ Pan Island Expressway [Singapore] (DS)
PIE............ Proto-Indo-European [Language] (BARN)
PIE............ Przedsiebiorstwo Instalacji Elektrycznych [Electrical Installations Enterprise] (POL)
PIEB .... Programa Interamericano de Estadisticas Basicas (LAA)
PIECE ...... Petroleum Institute Environmental Conservation Executive [Australia]
pieg............ Piegato [Folded] [Publishing] [Italian]
PIERT ...... Budapesti Papir es Irodaszer Ertekesito Vallalat [Budapest Trade Enterprise for Stationery and Office Supplies] (HU)
PIEU......... Pioneer Industries Employees Union (ML)
PIEUA...... Printing Industry Employees Union of Australia (ADA)
PIF .... Engineer Field Photographic Laboratory (RU)
PIF .... Pakistan Islamic Front [Pakistan] [Political party] (ECON)
PIF .... Public Investment Fund [Saudi Arabia]
PIFUSA.... Pilotos Fumigadores SA [Venezuela] (DSCA)
PIG .... Floating Integrating Gyroscope (RU)
PIG .... Panstwowy Instytut Geologiczny [State Geological Institute] (POL)
PIGM .... Panstwowa Inspekcja Gospodarki Materialowej [State Inspectorate for the Management of Materials] (POL)
PIGR......... Prefets Inspecteurs Generaux Regionaux [Algeria]

PIH .... Panstwowa Inspekcja Handlowa [*State Trade Inspectorate*] (POL)

PIH .... Panstwowy Instytut Higieny [*State Institute of Hygiene*] (POL)

PIHiSlJA .. Prirodoslovna Istrazivanja Hrvatske i Slavonije, Jugoslavenske Akademije [*National Science Studies of Croatia and Slavonia, Issued by the Yugoslav Academy of Sciences and Arts*] [*Zagreb*] (YU)

PIHM .... Panstwowy Instytut Hydrologiczno-Meteorologiczny [*State Institute of Hydrology and Meteorology*] (POL)

PIHPs........ Panstwowy Instytut Higieny Psychicznej [*State Institute of Mental Hygiene*] (POL)

PIHS.......... Panstwowy Instytut Historii Sztuki [*State Institute of the History of Art*] (POL)

PIHZ .... Polska Izba Handlu Zagranicznego [*Polish Chamber of Foreign Trade*] (POL)

PII .... Pelajar Islam Indonesia

PII .... Pemuda Islam Indonesia [*Indonesian Moslem Youth Organization*] (IN)

PIIA .... Pakistan Institute of Industrial Accountants (PDAA)

PIIMM iSKhP ... Planning and Research Institute of the Ministry of Local and Shale-Chemical Industries, ESSR (RU)

PIIO........... Poultry Industry Investigation Officer [*Australia*]

PIJR .... Programa Interamericano para la Juventud Rural [*Costa Rica*] (DSCA)

PIK............ Panstwowy Instytut Ksiazki [*State Book Institute*] (POL)

PIK............ Planning and Surveying Office (RU)

PIK............ Runway [*Airfield*] (BU)

PIKON ...... Film Corrosion Inhibitor for Petroleum-Extracting Equipment (RU)

pikor.......... Pioneer Correspondent (RU)

PIKPA .... Patriotikon Idryma Koinonikis Prononias kai Andilipseos [*Patriotic Institute of Social Aid and Welfare*] (GC)

PIL............ Pair Inter Langues [*Bourg La Reine, France*] (EAIO)

PIL............ Parti de l'Independance et de la Liberte [*Party for Independence and Liberty*] [*Congo*] [*Political party*]

PIL............ Petrochemical Industries Ltd. [*Australia*]

pil .... Pilot [*Pilot*] [*Poland*]

pil .... Pilula [*Pill*] [*Pharmacy*] (GPO)

PIL............ Polyolefins Industries Ltd. [*India*]

PIL............ Soil Adhesiveness Meter (RU)

PILB .... Pilbara [*Botanical region*] [*Australia*]

PILCAM ... Societe Camerounaise de Fabrication de Piles Electriques

PILEI........ Programa Interamericano de Linguistica y Ensenanza de Idiomas

PILL.......... Perth Inter-Library Loan Project [*Australia*]

PILOTUR ... Agencia de Viajes y Turismo [*Colombia*] (COL)

Pilr .... Pilier [*Pillar*] [*Military map abbreviation World War I*] [*French*] (MTD)

PILS.......... Pacific Information and Library Service [*Australia*]

PILSA........ Plastik Sanayi AS [*Plastic Industry Corporation*] (TU)

PIM .... Pacem in Maribus [*Secondary name for the International Ocean Institute*] (MSC)

PIM .... Packaging Industries (Malawi) Ltd.

PIM .... Pahalilik ve Issizlikle Mucadele Dernegi [*Association for the Struggle Against High Prices and Unemployment*] (TU)

PIM .... Panstwowa Inspekcja Materialowa [*State Inspectorate of Materials*] (POL)

PIM .... Panstwowy Instytut Meteorologiczny [*Poland*]

PIM .... Pasokan Infanteri Malaysia [*Malaysian Infantry Regiment*] (ML)

PIM .... Plan Indicativo Mundial [*Italy*] (DSCA)

PIM .... Pneumatic Actuator (RU)

PIM .... Presbyterian Inland Mission

PIM .... Principal Infirmier-Major

PIM .... Pro Independence Movement [*Puerto Rico*]

PIM .... Projekt Ivan Milutinovic [*Contractor*] [*Former Yugoslavia*]

PIM .... Safety Actuator (RU)

PIMA........ Petroleum Industries Marine Association [*Japan*] (MSC)

PIMA........ Photographic Industry Marketing Association [*Australia*]

PIMAG...... Pharmaceutical Industry Medical Advisers' Group [*South Africa*] (AA)

PIMAS ...... Plastik Insaat Malzemeleri Anonim Sirketi [*Plastic Construction Materials Corporation*] (TU)

PIMat .... Panstwowy Instytut Matematyczny [*State Mathematical Institute*] (POL)

PIMB......... Przemyslowy Instytut Maszyn Budowlanych [*Industrial Institute of Construction Machinery*] [*Research center*] [*Poland*] (IRC)

PIME......... Pontificum Institutum Mediolanese pro Missionibus Exteris [*Pontifical Institute for Foreign Missions*]

PIMEC ...... Programa Interamericano para Mejorar la Ensenanza de las Ciencias (de la OEA) [*Organizacion de Estados Americanos*] (LAA)

PIMM .... Pacific International Media Market [*Australia*]

PIMOT...... Przemyslowy Instytut Motoryzacji [*Automotive Industry Institute*] [*Ministry of Metallurgy and Machine Industry*] [*Research center*] [*Poland*] (ERC)

PIMR........ Przemyslowy Instytut Maszn Rolniczych [*Institute of Agricultural Machinery*] [*Poland*]

PIMS .... Personnel Information Management System [*Western Australia*]

PIMSA ...... Prensa Independiente Mexicana Sociedad Anonima [*Press agency*] [*Mexico*]

PIMUZ...... Paleontological Institute and Museum of the University of Zurich [*Switzerland*]

PIN .... Institute of Paleontology (of the Academy of Sciences, USSR) (RU)

PIN .... Philippine Investment Note

PIN .... Regulations and Standards for the Construction of Cities (RU)

PINA .... Pacific Islands News Association [*Australia*]

PINA .... Programa Integrado de Nutricion Aplicada [*Neiva*] (COL)

PINDAD ... Perindustrian Angkatan Darat [*Army Industrial Plant*] (IN)

PING .... Panstwowy Instytut Naukowo-Gospodarczy [*State Economic Research Institute*] (POL)

PINGW ..... Panstwowy Instytut Naukowy Gospodarstwa Wiejskiego [*State Research Institute of Rural Economy*] (POL)

PINM .... Planned Building of Settlements (BU)

PINRO ...... Polyarnyy Nauchno-Issledovatel'skiy Institut Morskogo Rybnogo Khozyaystva i Okeanografii [*Polar Scientific Research Institute of Sea Fisheries and Oceanography*] [*Russian*] (MSC)

PINSAL..... Pinturas Salvadorenas, SA [*Salvadoran Paints Corp.*]

PINSER..... Petites Industries Senegalaises Reunies

PINSTECH ... Pakistan Institute of Nuclear Science and Technology [*Nuclear energy*] (NRCH)

PINTUCO ... Pinturas Colombianas [*Colombia*] (COL)

PINU .... Partido de Innovacion y Unidad [*Innovation and Unity Party*] [*Honduras*] (LA)

PINZ......... Plastics Institute of New Zealand (PDAA)

PIO .... Information Reception from Operator [*Computers*] (RU)

PIO .... Poets International Organisation [*Bangalore, India*] (EAIO)

PIO .... Poverenictvo Informacii a Osvety [*Office of the Commissioner of Information and Culture*] (CZ)

PIOCC....... Province Intelligence and Operations Coordination Center [*Vietnam*] (VNW)

pion .... Pioneer (RU)

PIOSA .... Pan Indian Ocean Science Association

PIP............ Pan-Iranist Party [*Political party*] (PPW)

PiP............ Panstwo i Prawo [*State and Law*] [*A periodical*] (POL)

PIP............ Partido Independentista Puertorriqueno [*Puerto Rican Independence Party*] [*Political party*] (PPW)

PiP............ P. Ioannides Plastics Ltd. [*Cyprus*]

PIP............ Plantations Industrielles de Palmiers

PIP............ Policia de Investigaciones de Peru [*Peruvian Investigative Police*] (LA)

PIP............ Polski Instytut Prasoznawczy [*Polish Press Institute*] (POL)

PIP............ Primary Measuring Instrument (RU)

PIP............ Programa de Inversiones Publicas [*Public Investments Program*] [*Nicaragua*] (LA)

PIP............ Progressive Independent Party [*South Africa*] [*Political party*] (EY)

PIP............ Public Investment Programming [*Ministry of Finance and Economic Planning*] [*Ghana*]

PIP............ Puerto Rican Independence Party [*Political party*] (PD)

PIP............ Semiconductor Measuring Instrument (RU)

PIPA .... Pacific Islands Producers' Association [*South Pacific Bureau for Economic Co-Operation*] (EY)

PIPACE..... Peacetime Intelligence Plan, Allied Central Europe [*NATO*]

PIPES........ Program on International Politics, Economics, and Security [*University of Chicago*]

PIPICO ..... Panel on International Programs and International Cooperation in Ocean Affairs (MSC)

PIPMES.... Design Institute for Industrial, Mining, and Power Industry Construction (BU)

PIPR .... Polytechnic Institute of Puerto Rico

PIPS.......... Science and Technology Policies Information Exchange Programme [*SPINES*] [*UNESCO*] [*Superseded by*] [*Information service or system*] (IID)

PIPSA....... Productora e Importadora de Papel, Sociedad Anonima [*Paper Importer and Producer, Incorporated*] [*Mexico*] (LA)

piq .... Piqure [*Hole*] [*Publishing*] [*French*]

PIQ .... Plant Inspection and Quarantine [*Australia*]

piqq .... Piqures [*Holes*] [*Publishing*] [*French*]

PIR............ Engineer Reconnaissance Periscope, Trench Periscope (RU)

PIR............ Pacific Islands Regiments [*Australia*]

PIR............ Partido de Izquierda Radical [*Leftist Radical Party*] [*Chile*] (LA)

PIR............ Partido de la Izquierda Revolucionaria [*Party of the Revolutionary Left*] [*Bolivia*] [*Political party*] (PPW)

PIR............ People-Initiated Referendum [*Australia*]

PIR............ Philippine Independence Ribbon [*Military decoration*]

PIR............ Prakticna Izobrazba Rukovodioca [*Manager Training in Industry*] (YU)

PIR............ Prewarning Relay [*Railroads*] (RU)

PIR............ Prim-Air Aps [*Denmark*] [*ICAO designator*] (FAAC)

PIR............ Pukovska Intendantska Radionica [*Regimental Quartermaster Workshop*] (YU)
PIR............ Sound-Flash Survey Post [*Artillery*] (RU)
PIRA......... Postgraduate Industry Research Award [*Australia*]
PIRAI .... PIRA International [*British*] (EAIO)
Piram .... Pyramidal (RU)
PIRD......... People's Institute of Rural Development [*India*] (EAIO)
PIRDES..... Programme of Research for the Development of Solar Energy [*France*] (PDAA)
PIREN .... Programme Interdisciplinaire de Recherche en Environnement [*Interdisciplinary Program of Environmental Research*] [*National Scientific Research Center*] [*France*] (EAS)
PIREP....... Pilot Intensive Rural Employment Programme [*India*] (PDAA)
PIRIMLI ... Paper Industrial Research Institute [*China*] (IRC)
PIRM........ Pacific Institute of Resource Management [*New Zealand*]
PIROCEAN ... Programme Interdisciplinaire de Recherches Oceanographiques [*Interdisciplinary Program of Oceanographic Research*] [*National Scientific Research Center*] [*France*] (EAS)
PIRPSEV .. Programme Interdisciplinaire de Recherche sur la Prevision et la Surveillance des Eruptions Volcaniques [*Interdisciplinary Program of Research on the Predictionand Surveillance of Volcanic Eruptions*] [*National Scientific Research Center*] [*France*] (EAS)
PIRSA .... Psychological Institute of the Republic of South Africa (SLS)
PIRSEM.... Programme Interdisciplinaire de Recherche sur les Sciences pour l'Energie et les Matieres Premieres [*Interdisciplinary Program of Scientific Research in Energy and Raw Materials*] [*National Scientific Research Center*] [*France*] (EAS)
PIS............ Panellinios Iatrikos Syllogos [*Panhellenic Medical Association*] (GC)
PIS............ Pankyprios Iatrikos Syllogos [*Pan-Cyprian Medical Association*] (GC)
PIS............ Panstwowa Inspekcja Sanitarna [*State Sanitary Inspectorate*] (POL)
PIS............ Panstwowy Instytut Sztuki [*State Institute of Art*] (POL)
PIS............ Poitiers [*France*] [*Airport symbol*] (OAG)
PIS............ Prazska Informacni Sluzba [*Prague Information Service*] (CZ)
PIS............ Programa de Integracao Social [*Social Integration Program*] [*Brazil*] (LA)
PIS............ Przedsiebiorstwo Imprez Sportowych [*Sport Event Enterprise*] (POL)
PIS............ Pukovsko Intendantsko Slagaliste [*Regimental Quartermaster Depot*] (YU)
pisat .... Writer (RU)
PISC .... Philippine International Shipping Corp. (DS)
Pisch bum .. Paper Factory [*Topography*] (RU)
PISE .... Partido por la Independencia Socialista de Euzkadi [*Party for the Socialist Independence of the Basque Country*] [*Spanish*] (WER)
PISF.......... Printing Industry Superannuation Fund [*Australia*]
PISGA .... Palestinian Interim Self-Government Authority [*Proposed*] (ECON)
PISh.......... History Teaching in the School (RU)
pishch........ Food, Alimentary (RU)
pishch........ Food Industry Plant [*Topography*] (RU)
pishchemash ... Food Machinery Plant (RU)
pishcheprom ... Food Industry (RU)
Pishchepromizdat ... State Scientific and Technical Publishing House of the Food Industry (RU)
Pishchevkus ... Trade Union of Workers of the Food and Flavoring Industry of the USSR (RU)
pishchkonts ... Food Concentrates (RU)
pish mash... Typewriter (RU)
PISM .... Panstwowy Instytut Spraw Miedzynarodowych [*State Institute of International Affairs*] (POL)
PISM .... Polski Instytut Spraw Miedzynarodowych [*Polish Institute of International Affairs*] (POL)
PISO .... Philippine Investments Systems Organization (DS)
PISPESCA ... Asociacion Colombiana de Piscicultura y Pesca [*Colombia*] (COL)
PISS.......... Polskie Instalacje Sily i Swiatla [*Polish Power and Light Installations*] (POL)
PISS.......... Rules of the Economic and Social Council (BU)
PISSC....... Programme International sur la Securite des Substances Chimiques [*International Programme on Chemical Safety*] (EAIO)
PISUKI...... Pacific Islands Society of the United Kingdom and Ireland [*England*] (EAIO)
PISwL....... Polski Instytut Socjologiczny w Lodzi [*Polish Sociological Institute in Lodz*] (POL)
pit............. Drinking Water (RU)
pit............. Feeding, Nutrition (RU)
pit............. Nursery [*for plants or animals*] [*Topography*] (RU)
PIT............ Pacific Investment Trust
PIT............ Panair International SRL [*Italy*] [*ICAO designator*] (FAAC)

PIT............ Panstwowy Instytut Telekomunikacyjny [*State Institute of Communication*] (POL)
PIT............ Parti de l'Independance et du Travail [*Party of Independence and Labor*] [*Senegal*] [*Political party*] (PPW)
PIT............ Parti Ivoirien des Travailleurs [*Ivorian Workers' Party*] [*The Ivory Coast*] [*Political party*] (EY)
PIT............ Partners in Transition [*Poland, Czechoslovakia, and Hungary*] (ECON)
PIT............ Phillip Institute of Technology [*Australia*]
pit............. Pitaja [*Finland*]
PIT............ Preston Institute of Technology [*Australia*] (ADA)
PIT............ Przemyslowy Instytut Telekomunikacji [*Industrial Institute of Communication*] (POL)
PIT............ Public Information Terminal [*Australia*]
PIT............ Punkt Informacji Turystycznej [*Tourist Information Center*] [*Poland*]
PITAC ...... Pakistan Industrial Technical Assistance Centre
PITC .... Philippine International Trading Corporation (GEA)
PIT-CNT ... Plenario Intersindical de Trabajadores - Convencion Nacional de Trabajadores [*Inter-Trade Union Assembly - Workers' National Convention*] [*Uruguay*]
PITF .... Poultry Industry Trust Fund [*Australia*]
PITFC....... Potato Industry Trust Fund Committee [*Western Australia*]
pit frukt..... Fruit-Tree Nursery [*Topography*] (RU)
PITS .... Partners In Transition [*Poland, Czech, Hungary - called the Visegrad Trio*]
pitt............. Pittura [*Paint, painting*] [*Italian*]
PITTC .... Philips International Telecommunications Training Center (IAA)
PIU .... Breakdown Tester (RU)
PIU .... Pioneer Industries Union [*Singapore*] (ML)
PIU .... Piura [*Peru*] [*Airport symbol*] (OAG)
PIU .... Pneumatic Level Indicator (RU)
PIUC .... Parti pour l'Independance et l'Unite des Comores
PIUG .... Parti Independantiste de l'Unite Guyanaise [*Pro-Independence Party of Guyanese Unity*] [*Political party*] (PPW)
Piv .... Brewery [*Topography*] (RU)
PIV .... Pamutszovo Ipari Vallalat [*Cotton Mill*] (HU)
PIVE .... Regulations for the Manufacture of Explosion-Proof Electrical Equipment (RU)
Piv zav........ Brewery [*Topography*] (RU)
PIW .... Panstwowy Instytut Wydawniczy [*State Publishing Institute*] (POL)
PIWR........ Panstwowy Instytut Wydawnictw Rolniczych [*State Institute of Agricultural Publications*] (POL)
PIWU .... Pineapple Industry Workers Union (ML)
PIWWC.... Planetary Initiative for the World We Choose (EA)
PIX............ Pico Island [*Azores*] [*Airport symbol*] (OAG)
PIZO......... Societe Nationale de Distribution de Produits Petroliers [*Gabon*]
PIZOLUB ... Societe Pizo de Formulation de Lubrifiants
PIZZ.......... Pizzicato [*Plucked*] [*Music*]
PJ.............. Parteijargon [*Party Language*] [*German*]
Pj.............. Parteijargon [*Party Jargon*] (EG)
PJ.............. Partido Justicialista [*Justicialista Party*] [*Argentina*] (LA)
PJ.............. Pede Justica [*Portuguese*]
PJ.............. Pergamon Joinery Ltd. [*Ghana*]
pj.............. Per Jaar [*Yearly*] [*Afrikaans*]
PJ.............. Petaling Jaya [*Near Kuala Lumpur*] (ML)
PJ.............. Piece Jointe [*Enclosure*] [*French*] (NATG)
PJ.............. Police Judiciaire [*Criminal Investigation Police*] [*French*] (WER)
PJ.............. Poste de Jonction [*Military*] [*French*] (MTD)
PJ.............. Pouvoir Judiciaire [*Organe de l'union federale des magistrats, Paris*] (FLAF)
pj.............. Puheenjohtaja [*Finland*]
PJ.............. Puisne Judge [*Australia*]
PJA............ Pretprijatie za Javen Avtotransport [*Public Motor Transport Establishment*] (YU)
PJBD......... Permanent Joint Board on Defense [*US, Canada*]
PJC............ Parliamentary Joint Committee [*Australia*]
PJF............ Policia Judicial Federal [*Federal Judicial Police*] [*Mexico*] (LA)
PJG............ Panjur [*Pakistan*] [*Airport symbol*] (OAG)
PJG............ Pingat Jasa Gemilang [*Meritorious Medal*] [*Singapore*] (ML)
PJK............ Pingat Jasa Kebaktian [*Loyal Service Medal*] (ML)
PJKA......... Indonesian State Railways (IMH)
PJP............ Police Judiciaire des Parquets [*Investigatory Police of the Public Prosecutor*] [*Belgium*]
PJP............ Pusat Jabatan Polis [*Police Department Headquarters*] (ML)
PJPM......... Persatuan Jurutera Perunding Malaysia [*Association of Malaysian Consulting Engineers*] (EAIO)
PJS .... Jet Aviation, Business Jets AG [*Switzerland*] [*ICAO designator*] (FAAC)
PJXM......... Persatuan Juru X-Ray Malaysia [*Association of Malaysian Radiographers*] (EAIO)
PK .... Border Guard Commandant's Office (RU)
PK .... Border Guard Cutter (RU)

PK	Bypass Valve, Bypass (RU)
PK	Cavalry Support (RU)
PK	Check Button [*Telephony*] (RU)
p-k.............	Colonel (RU)
PK	Conciliation Commission (BU)
PK	Continuously Operating Coil Boiler, Single-Pass Boiler (RU)
PK	Cooking Kettle (RU)
PK	Coordinate Converter (RU)
pk	Correspondence Censorship (RU)
PK	Course Correction (RU)
PK	Entry-Driving Machine, Sinking Machine [*Mining*] (RU)
PK	Field Switchboard (RU)
PK	Fire Brigade (RU)
PK	Fire Hydrant (RU)
PK	Flotation Suit, Non-Sinkable Suit (RU)
PK	Forward Edge, Main Line of Resistance [*Military term*] (RU)
PK	Industrial Combine (BU)
PK	Intermediate Cascade (RU)
PK	Intermediate Switching (RU)
PK	Outguard (RU)
Pk	Pachtkamer [*Benelux*] (BAS)
PK	Paddle Steamer (RU)
PK	Pakistan [*ANSI two-letter standard code*] (CNC)
pk	Pakka(a) [*Finland*]
PK	Panzerkompanie [*Tank Company*] (EG)
pk	Parancsnok [*Commander*] (HU)
PK	Park Kultury [*Park of Culture*] (CZ)
pk	Partonkivuli [*Non-Party*] (HU)
PK	Party Commission [*or Committee*] (RU)
PK	Patriotiko Kinima [*Patriotic Movement*] [*Greek*] (GC)
PK	Pensions Commission (BU)
PK	Penyata Keadaan [*Situation Report*] (ML)
PK	Perak (ML)
pk	Perdekrag [*Horsepower*] [*Afrikaans*]
PK	Permanent Commission (BU)
Pk	Petrolatum, Acid (RU)
PK	Pferdekraft [*Horsepower*] [*German*]
PK	Phileleftheron Komma [*Liberal Party*] [*Greek*] [*Political party*] (PPE)
pk	Pikakivaari [*Finland*]
PK	Piston Compressor (RU)
PK	Pneumatic Contactor (RU)
PK	Poinikos Kodix [*Penal Code*] (GC)
PK	Pokrajinski Komitet [*Provincial Committee*] (YU)
PK	Polar Commission (of the Academy of Sciences, USSR) (RU)
PK	Politechnika Krakowska [*Technical University of Cracow*] [*Poland*]
PK	Politicka Knihovna [*Political Library*] (CZ)
PK	Politicki Komitet [*Political Committee*] (YU)
PK	Poljoprivredna Komora [*Chamber of Agriculture*] (YU)
PK	Polycarbonates (RU)
PK	Pomocne Kursy [*Auxiliary Courses*] (CZ)
Pk	Poskantoor [*Post Office*] [*Afrikaans*]
PK	Posta Kutusu [*Postbox*] [*Turkish*] (EY)
PK	Potassium Persulfate (RU)
PK	Poteau Kilometre [*Kilometer Post*] (CL)
PK	Powiatowy Komitet [*County Committee*] (POL)
PK	Prausnitz-Kuestner [*Reaction*] [*Immunology*]
PK	Prehranbeni Kombinat [*Food Combine*] (YU)
PK	Presernova Knjiznica [*Preseren Library*] [*Ljubljana*] (YU)
PK	Preventive Debugging [*Computers*] (RU)
PK	Primary Loop, Primary Circuit [*Nuclear physics and engineering*] (RU)
PK	Primrose Knitwear Ltd. [*Malawi*]
PK	Problems of Cybernetics [*Bibliography*] (RU)
PK	Proedros Kyverniseos [*President*] [*Automobile license plate designation*] (GC)
PK	Programmkapazitaet [*Program Capacity*] [*German*] (ADPT)
PK	Projektierung Kernkraftwerke [*Project Planning of Nuclear Power Plants*] (EG)
PK	Proodevtikon Komma [*Progressive Party*] (GC)
PK	Prothypourgos Kyverniseos [*Premier*] [*Automobile license plate designation*] (GC)
PK	Provinsiale Kennisgewing [*Provincial Note*] [*Afrikaans*]
PK	Provozni Komise [*Production Commission*] (CZ)
PK	Punched Card (RU)
pk	Putnicka Kola [*Passenger Car*] [*Railroads*] (YU)
PK	Pyrocatechol (RU)
pk	Regiment (BU)
PK	Relief Valve, Emergency Valve, Safety Valve (RU)
PK	Semiconductor Key (RU)
PK	Start Button (RU)
PK	Steam Boiler (RU)
PK	Steam Crane (RU)
p/k.............	Steamship (BU)
PK	Straight-Through Combine (RU)

p/k.............	Subcutaneously, Hypodermically [*Pharmacy*] (RU)
PK	Television Camera (RU)
PK	Transit Cascade (RU)
PK	Transit Curve, Transition Curve [*Railroads*] (RU)
PK	Transmitting Complex (RU)
PK	West Irian [*Aircraft nationality and registration mark*] (FAAC)
PKA	Equator Airlines Ltd. [*Kenya*] [*ICAO designator*] (FAAC)
PKA	Paket-Kontrollpostamt [*Parcel Post Inspection Office*] (EG)
PKA	Panstwowa Komisja Arbitrazowa [*State Arbitration Commission*] (POL)
P-ka............	Polyclinic (BU)
PKA	Pyrocatechol Monoacetate (RU)
PKAE	Politikon Komma Agroton Ellados [*Farmers' Political Party of Greece*] (GC)
PkAF..........	Pakistani Air Force
PKAS	Parti Kadazan Asli Sabah [*Malaysia*] [*Political party*] (FEA)
pkb	Area Road Traffic Control Battalion (BU)
PKB...........	Parti Kemajuan Brunei [*Brunei Progressive Party*] (ML)
PKB...........	Planning and Design Office (RU)
PKB...........	Projektierungs- und Konstruktionsbuero [*Project-Planning and Designing Office*] (EG)
PKbanken ..	Post- och Kreditbanken [*Bank*] [*Sweden*]
PKBAsboshifer ...	Planning and Design Office of the Asbestos Shingle, Mica, and Asphalt Roofing Industry (RU)
pkbr...........	Area Traffic Control Brigade (BU)
PKC	Panama Kennel Club (EAIO)
PKC	Panstwowa Komisja Cen [*State Price Commission*] (POL)
PKCh	Pilot-Frequency Receiver (RU)
PkCV	Pokretni Centar Veze [*Mobile Communications Center*] [*Military*] (YU)
PKD	Planlama ve Koordinasyon Dairesi [*Plans and Coordination Office*] [*of Turkish Electric Power Directorate General*] (TU)
PKD	Press for Annular Parts (RU)
PKD	Simple Cableway, Simple Ropeway (RU)
PKDB........	Partai Kebang-Saan Demokratik Brunei [*Brunei National Democratic Party*] [*Political party*] (EY)
PKDZ........	Posudkova Komise Duchodoveho Zabezpeceni [*Pension Review Commission*] (CZ)
PKE...........	Panstwowa Komisja Etatow [*State Personnel Commission*] (POL)
PKE...........	Parkes [*Australia*] [*Airport symbol*] (OAG)
PKEN	Pnevmatiki Kinisis Ellinikis Neolaias [*Intellectual Union of Young Greek Professionals*] (GC)
PKENNE...	Pnevmatiki Kinisis Ellinikis Neolaias Neon Epistimonon [*Intellectual Movement of Greek Youth and Young Professionals*] (GC)
pkesk.........	Puhelinkeskustelu [*Finland*]
PKF...........	Persatuan Karyawan Fadjarbhakti [*Fadjar Bhakti State Trading Enterprise Workers' Union*] [*Indonesian*]
PKF...........	Polska Kronika Filmowa [*Polish Film Chronicle*] (POL)
PK FJN......	Powiatowy Komitet Frontu Jednosci Narodu [*National Unity Front County Committee*] (POL)
PKG	Cardiopneumography (RU)
PKh...........	Ahead Running, Forward Running (RU)
pkh	Infantry (BU)
PKh...........	Interstage Cooler [*Refrigeration*] (RU)
p kh	Paradeigmatos Kharin [*For Example*] (GC)
PKh...........	Planned Economy (RU)
PKh...........	Pro Khristou [*Before Christ*] (GC)
p/kh..........	Steamship (RU)
PKh...........	Transfer Characteristic (RU)
PKhB........	Polychlorobenzene (RU)
PKhD........	Food, Clothing, and Equipment Supply Point (RU)
PKhL........	Chemical Field Laboratory (RU)
PKhL........	Field Chemical Laboratory (BU)
PKhM.......	Perchloromethyl Mercaptan (RU)
PKhN........	Chemical Observation Post (RU)
PKHO.......	Protivo-Khimicheskaia Oborona [*A Chemical Defense*] [*Former USSR*]
PKhOR	Chemical Defense Company (RU)
PKhP........	Chemical Defense Kit (RU)
PKhP........	Chemical Defense Training (RU)
PKhP........	Field Bakery (RU)
PKhR........	Chemical Agent Detection Kit (BU)
PKhR	Gas Detection Device, Chemical Monitoring Device, Chemical Reconnaissance Instrument (RU)
PKhS........	Chemical Defense Service (RU)
PKhV	Perchlorovinyl (RU)
PKhV	Polyvinyl Chloride (RU)
PKhZ........	Antichemical Defense (BU)
PKhZ........	Chemical Defense (RU)
PKhZ........	Field Bakery (RU)
PKhZR......	Chemical Defense Company (RU)
PKI...........	Information Command Converter [*Computers*] (RU)

PKI............ Partai Katolik Indonesia [*Catholic Party of Indonesia*] [*Political party*]

PKI............ Partai Komunis Indonesia [*Communist Party of Indonesia*] [*Political party*]

PKI............ Partai Kristen Indonesia [*Christian Party of Indonesia*] [*Political party*]

PKI............ Piackutato Iroda [*Marketing Research Office*] (HU)

PKI............ Posta Kiserleti Intezet [*Postal Service Experimental Institute*] (HU)

PKI............ Primary Cosmic Radiation (RU)

PKiEUWM ... Przedsiebiorstwo Konserwacji i Eksploatacji Urzadzen Wodno-Melioracyjnych [*Enterprise for the Conservation and Operation of Land Reclamation and Improvement Installations*] (POL)

PKiN.......... Palac Kultury i Nauki [*Palace of Culture and Science*] (POL)

PKiO.......... Park of Culture and Rest (RU)

PKIPishcheprom ... Planning and Design Institute for Complex Automation of Production Processes in the Food Industry (RU)

PKIU........ Printing and Kindred Industries Union [*Australia*] (ADA)

PKJ............ Pitanje Knjizevnosti i Jezika [*Literary and Linguistic Problems*] [*A periodical Sarajevo*] (YU)

PKJIF........ Prilozi za Knjizevnost, Jezik, Istoriju, i Folklor [*Contributions to Literature, Language, History, and Folklore*] [*A periodical*] (YU)

PKJU........ Posta Kozponti Javito Uzem [*Central Post Office Repair Shops*] (HU)

PKK........... Federatsiya Kinoklubov [*Federation of Film Societies*] [*Former USSR*] (EAIO)

PKK .... Kurdish Workers' Party [*Turkey*] [*Political party*] (PD)

PKK .... Pakokku [*Myanmar*] [*Airport symbol*] (OAG)

PKK .... Panstwowa Komisja Klasyfikacyjna [*State Qualification Commission*] (POL)

PKK .... Parteikontrollkommission [*Party Control Commission*] (EG)

PKK .... Pasokan Keselamatan Kawasan [*Area Security Unit*] (ML)

PKK .... Pilot Channel Receiver (RU)

PKK .... Planning and Design Office (RU)

PKK .... Political Consultative Committee [*of member countries of the Warsaw Treaty*] (RU)

PKKB........ Panstwowy Korespondencyjny Kurs Bibliotekarski [*State Correspondence Course for Librarians*] (POL)

PKKF........ Powiatowy Komitet Kultury Fizycznej [*County Committee on Physical Culture*] (POL)

PKKFiT ..... Powiatowy Komitet Kultury Fizycznej i Turystyki [*County Committee for Physical Culture and Tourism*] (POL)

PKKh .... Fireproof Chemical Composition (RU)

PKKP........ Powiatowa Komisja Kontroli Partyjnej [*County Party Control Commission*] (POL)

PKKPJ...... Pokrajinski Komitet Komunisticke Partije Jugoslavije [*Provincial Committee of the Communist Party of Yugoslavia*] (YU)

PKKPJ...... Politicki Komitet Komunisticke Partije Jugoslavije [*Political Committee of the Communist Party of Yugoslavia*] (YU)

PKKPJM... Pokrainski Komitet na Komunistickata Partija na Jugoslavija za Makedonija [*Regional Committee of the Communist Party of Yugoslavia for Macedonia*] (YU)

PKKR........ School for Improving Qualifications of Kolkhoz Managers [*1936-1941*] (RU)

PKL........... Panstwowa Komisja Lokalowa [*State Housing Commission*] (POL)

PKL........... Polskie Koleje Linowe [*Polish Funicular (or Cable) Railways*] (POL)

PKL........... Switch (RU)

pk lch .... Regimental Dispensary (BU)

PKM .... Parti des Kadihines de Mauritanie [*Party of Mauritanian Toilers*] (AF)

PKM .... Parti Komunis Malaya [*Malayan Communist Party*] (ML)

PKM .... Pasokan Kelengkapan Malaysia [*Malaysian Ordnance Corps*] (ML)

PKM .... Perkhidmatan Kajicuaca Malaysia [*Malaysian Meteorological Service*] [*Research center*] (EAS)

PKM .... Pneumatic Forging Hammer (RU)

PKM .... Pokrajinski Komitet Makedonije [*Provincial Committee of Macedonia*] [*Communist Party*] (YU)

PKM .... Pomocna Komanda Mesta [*City Auxiliary Military Command*] (YU)

PKM .... Projektierungs-, Konstruktions-, und Montagebuero [*Planning, Design, and Assembly Office*] (EG)

pkm .... Putnicki Kilometar [*Passenger-Kilometer*] (YU)

PKMB........ Pertubohan Kebangsaan Melayu Bersatu [*United Malayan National Organization*] (ML)

PKMS........ Pertubohan Kebangsaan Melayu Singapura [*Singapore Malays' National Organization*] [*Political party*] (FEA)

PKN.......... Number-to-Voltage Converter (RU)

PKN.......... Pangkalanbuun [*Indonesia*] [*Airport symbol*] (OAG)

PKN.......... Pekan [*Malaysia*] (ML)

PKN.......... Polski Komitet Normalizacyjny [*Polish Committee on Standardization*] (POL)

PKNIM...... Polish Committee for Standardization, Measure, and Quality Control

PKNM .... Partiia Kongressa Nezavisimosti Madagaskara

PKNMJ ..... Polski Komitet Normalizacji Miar i Jakosci [*Polish Committee for Standardization, Measures, and Quality Control*] (EAIO)

PKNPN ..... Regulation on Crediting Population Consumer Needs (BU)

PKNS........ Perbadanan Kemajuan Negeri Selangor [*Selangor State Development Organization*] (ML)

PKO........... Antisatellite Defense, Spacecraft Defense (RU)

PKO........... Defense Against Motor Torpedo Boats (RU)

PKO........... Differential Compound Winding (RU)

PKO........... Panellinios Kapnergatiki Omospondia [*or Pandelladiki Kapnergatiki Omospondia*] [*Panhellenic Tobacco Workers Federation*] (GC)

PKO........... Parakou [*Benin*] [*Airport symbol*] (OAG)

PKO........... Park Kultury a Oddechu [*Park of Culture and Recreation*] (CZ)

PKO........... Perdant par Knockout [*Losing by a Knockout*] [*French*]

PKO........... Polska Kasa Opieki [*Polish Security Bank*] (POL)

PKO........... Powszechna Kasa Oszczednosci [*General Savings Bank*] (POL)

PKO........... Regulation on Cooperative Organizations (BU)

pk ob .... Regimental Train (BU)

PKOE .... Panellinion Kendron Oikologikon Erevnon [*Panhellenic Center of Ecological Research*] [*PAKOE*] [*See also*] (GC)

PKOJF ...... Park Kultury a Oddechu Julia Fucika [*Julius Fucik Park of Culture and Recreation*] (CZ)

PKOl.......... Polski Komitet Olimpijski [*Polish Olympic Games Committee*] (POL)

pkom .... Politicki Komesar [*Political Commissar*] [*Communist Party*] (YU)

PKONS...... Pensions Commission of the Okrug People's Council (BU)

PKOP........ Polski Komitet Obroncow Pokoju [*Polish Committee of Partisans of Peace*] (POL)

PKO SA .... Polska Kasa Opieki Spolka Akcyjna [*Polish Guardian Bank Ltd.*] [*Poland*]

PKP........... Advanced Command Post (RU)

PKP........... Edge-Punched Card (RU)

PKP........... Infantry Heavy-Caliber Machine Gun (RU)

PKP........... Palestiner Komunistische Partei [*Palestine Communist Party*] [*Political party*] (BJA)

PKP........... Partido Komunista ng Pilipinas [*Communist Party of the Philippines*] [*Political party*] (PPW)

PKP........... Pegawai Kechil Polis [*Subordinate Police Officer*] (ML)

PKP........... Persatuan Karyawan Permorin [*Permorin Company Workers' Union*] [*Indonesia*]

PKP........... Perustuslaillinen Kansanpuolue [*Constitutional People's Party*] [*Finland*] [*Political party*] (PPE)

PKP........... Polityczny Komitet Porozumiewawczy [*Poland*]

PKP........... Poljoprivredno Komunalno Preduzece [*Communal Agricultural Establishment*] (YU)

PKP........... Polskie Koleje Panstwowe [*Polish State Railways*]

PKP........... Portuguese Communist Party (RU)

PKP........... Pukapuka [*French Polynesia*] [*Airport symbol*] (OAG)

PKP........... Simple Cableway, Simple Rope Crossing (RU)

PKPG........ Panstwowa Komisja Planowania Gospodarczego [*State Economic Planning Commission*] (POL)

PKPG........ Powiatowa Komisja Planowania Gospodarczego [*County Economic Planning Commission*] (POL)

PKPiW....... Przedsiebiorstwo Kolportazu Prasy i Wydawnictw [*Press and Publication Circulation Enterprise*] (POL)

PKPl.......... Panstwowa Komisja Plac [*State Wages Commission*] (POL)

PKPM........ Perserikatan Kebangsaan Pelajar Malaysia [*Malaysian Students National Association*] (ML)

PKPO........ Proletarian Cultural and Educational Organization (RU)

PKPP........ Epicyclic Gearbox [*Tanks*] (RU)

PKPP........ Pejabat Ketua Pegawai Polis [*Office of the Chief Police Officer*] (ML)

PKPR........ Panstwowa Komisja Planowania Rolniczego [*State Commission on Agricultural Planning*] (POL)

PKPR........ Polski Komitet Pomocy Repatriantom [*Polish Committee for Assisting Repatriates*] (POL)

PKPR........ Polski Korpus Przysposobienia i Rozmieszczenia [*Polish Training and Resettlement Corps (in exile)*] (POL)

PKPS........ Polski Komitet Pomocy Spolecznej [*Polish Social Assistance Committee*] (POL)

pkr............. Area Road Traffic Control Company (BU)

PKR .... Pokhara [*Nepal*] [*Airport symbol*] (OAG)

PKr............ Politechnika Krakowska [*Technical University of Cracow*] [*Poland*]

PKR .... Powiatowa Komenda Rejonowa [*District Army Command*] [*Poland*]

PKR .... Privremeni Komandni Racunar [*Temporary Staff Computer*] [*Military*] (YU)

PKR .... Switch Relay (RU)

pkr............. Winged Missiles Regiment (BU)

PKRDD ..... Pravitel'stvennaya Komissiya po Raketam Dalnego Deistviya [*State Commission for the Study of the Problems of Long-Range Rockets*] [*Former USSR*]
PKS .... Panstwowa Komisja Samochodowa [*Poland*]
PKS .... Panstwowa Komunikacja Samochodowa [*State Motor Transport*] (POL)
PKS .... Panstwowa Komunikacja Samolotowa [*State Airlines*] (POL)
PKS .... Parti Komunis Sarawak [*Sarawak Communist Party*] (ML)
PKS .... Parti Kongres Sarawak [*Malaysia*] [*Political party*] (EY)
PKS .... Periphery Communications Channel (RU)
PKS .... Political Consultative Council [*Chinese People's Republic*] (RU)
PKS .... Projekt-Kontrollsystem [*Project Control System*] [*German*] (ADPT)
PKS .... Regulation on Capital Construction (BU)
PKS .... Semiautomatic Logging Station (RU)
PKSCAT.... Parkes Catalogue of Radio Sources [*Australian National Radio Astronomy Observatory*] [*Information service or system*] (IID)
PKSh.......... Partia Komuniste e Shqiperise [*Communist Party of Albania*] [*Later, PPSh*] [*Political party*] (PPE)
PKSKOJ.... Politicki Komitet Saveza Komunisticke Omladine Jugoslavije [*Political Committee of the League of Communist Youth of Yugoslavia*] (YU)
PKSvJ .... Pucka Knjiznica Izdavana Drustvom Svetog Jeronima [*Popular Library Published by the Saint Jerome Society*] (YU)
PKT........... Partai Komunis Tjina [*Chinese Communist Party*] (IN)
PKT........... Passagers-Kilometres Transportes
PKT........... Penangkis Kapal Terbang [*Fighter Plane*] (ML)
pkt .... Punkt [*Center, Point*] [*German*] (POL)
PKTCh....... Assistant Commander for Technical Matters (RU)
PKTI .... Planning and Design Technological Institute (RU)
PKTP .... Regulation on Categorization of Labor for Pensioning (BU)
PKU .... Pekanbaru [*Indonesia*] [*Airport symbol*] (OAG)
PKU .... Powiatowa Komenda Uzupelnien [*County Military Reserve Headquarters*] (POL)
PKV .... Postupna Koncentracija Vatre [*Progressive Concentration of Fire*] [*Military*] (YU)
PKV .... Short-Wave Direction Finder (RU)
PKVD .... Panellinios Kinisis Vasilevomenis Dimokratias [*Panhellenic Movement for a Crowned Republic*] (GC)
PKVP........ Projekcne Konstrukcni Vyvojove Pracoviste [*Project Design and Development Center*] (CZ)
PKW .... Personenkraftwagen [*Automobile*] [*German*]
PKW .... Powiatowy Komitet Wykonawczy [*County Executive Committee*] (POL)
PKW .... Selebi-Phikwe [*Botswana*] [*Airport symbol*] (OAG)
PKWN .... Polski Komitet Wyzwolenia Narodowego [*Polish Committee of National Liberation*] (POL)
PKWZ........ Przedsiebiorstwo Kolportazu Wydawnictw Zagranicznych [*Enterprise for the Circulation of Foreign Publications*] (POL)
PKWZSL... Powiatowy Komitet Wykonawczy Zjednoczonego Stronnictwa Ludowego [*County Executive Committee of the United Peasant Party*] (POL)
PKY .... Palangkaraya [*Indonesia*] [*Airport symbol*] (OAG)
PKZ........... Pavlodar Combine Plant (RU)
PKZ........... Pedagosko-Knjizevni Zbor [*Pedagogic-Literary Society*] [*Zagreb*] (YU)
PKZ........... Penza Compressor Plant (RU)
PKZ........... Personenkennzeichen [*German*] (ADPT)
PkZC .... Pokretni Zicni Centar [*Mobile Wire Center*] [*Military*] (YU)
PKZD........ Antiaircraft Battalion Commander's Post (RU)
PKZh .... Iron Pentacarbonyl (RU)
PKZh .... Large Reinforced Concrete Slab (RU)
PKZhS....... Regulations on Housing Construction Crediting (BU)
PKZP .... Pracownicza Kasa Zapomogowo-Pozyczkowa [*Workers' Slate Club*] [*Poland*]
PKZSL....... Powiatowy Komitet Zjednoczonego Stronnictwa Ludowego [*District Committee of the United Peasants' Party*] [*Poland*]
PL .... Adjustable-Blade [*Nautical term*] (RU)
pl .... Colonel (BU)
Pl............... Flake (Powder), Plate (Powder) (RU)
PL .... Front Line [*Revolutionary group*] [*Italy*]
Pl............... Light-Press Fit (RU)
pl .... Melting (RU)
PL .... Mobile Laboratory (RU)
pl .... Mountain (BU)
pl .... Paaluokka [*Finland*]
PL .... Partido Laborista [*Labor Party*] [*Argentina*] (LA)
PL .... Partido Liberal [*Liberal Party*] [*Ecuador*] (LA)
PL .... Partido Liberal [*Liberal Party*] [*Bolivia*] (LA)
PL .... Partido Liberal [*Liberal Party*] [*Chile*] (LA)
PL .... Partido Liberal [*Liberal Party*] [*Paraguay*] [*Political party*] (PPW)
PL .... Partido Liberal [*Liberal Party*] [*Honduras*] [*Political party*]
PL .... Partido Liberal [*Liberal Party*] [*Colorado*] [*Political party*] (EY)
PL .... Partido Liberal [*Liberal Party*] [*Portugal*] [*Political party*] (PPE)

PL .... Partido Liberal [*Liberal Party*] [*Peru*] [*Political party*] (EY)
PL .... Partido Liberal [*Liberal Party*] [*Panama*] [*Political party*] (PPW)
PL .... Partido Liberal [*Liberal Party*] [*Spain*] [*Political party*] (PPE)
PL .... Partido Libertador [*Liberating Party*] [*Brazil*] [*Political party*]
PL .... Parti Liberal [*Liberal Party (1974-1979)*] [*Belgium*] [*Political party*] (PPE)
PL .... Pasicrisie Luxembourgeoise [*Luxembourg*] (BAS)
PL .... Pathet Lao (CL)
PL .... Pelatun [*Platoon*] (ML)
pl .... Peldaul [*For Example*] (HU)
PL .... Peso Liquido [*Liquid Weight*] [*Portuguese*]
Pl............... Piaza [*Place*] [*Italian*] (PWGL)
Pl............... Piazzale [*Place, Square*] [*Italian*] (CED)
PL .... Pilatus Flugzeugwerke AG [*Switzerland*] [*ICAO aircraft manufacturer identifier*] (ICAO)
pl .... Pills [*Pharmacy*] (RU)
PL .... Pilot's Parachute (RU)
pl .... Plaat [*Plate*] [*Publishing*] [*Netherlands*]
Pl............... Plac [*Square*] [*Poland*]
pl .... Place [*French*] (CED)
Pl............... Plan [*Plan, Design*] [*German*]
pl .... Plan [*or Planek or Planovani*] [*Plan or Planning*] (CZ)
pl .... Planche [*Plate*] [*Publishing*] [*French*]
pl .... Plane (RU)
PL .... Planimeter (RU)
pl .... Plano [*Design, Plan*] [*Spanish*]
pl .... Plansch [*Plate*] [*Publishing*] [*Sweden*]
pl .... Plass [*Place*] [*Norway*] (CED)
pl .... Plat [*Side of a Book*] [*Publishing*] [*French*]
pl .... Platinum (RU)
pl .... Plats [*Square*] [*Sweden*] (CED)
PL .... Platz [*Square*] [*German*] (EY)
Pl............... Plaza [*Square*] [*Spanish*]
pl .... Plein [*Full*] [*Publishing*] [*French*]
PL .... Pleine Lune [*Full Moon*] [*French*]
pl .... Plettet [*Spotted*] [*Publishing Danish/Norwegian*]
Pl............... Plicina [*Shoal*] [*Former Yugoslavia*] (NAU)
PL .... Ploshchad [*Square*] [*Russian*] (EY)
Pl............... Ploshtad [*Square*] [*Bulgarian*]
pl .... Plotno [*Cloth Binding*] [*Publishing*] [*Poland*]
pl .... Plural [*Plural*] [*Portuguese*]
pl .... Plural [*Plural*] [*German*]
pl .... Plurale [*Plural*] [*Italian*]
PL .... Pluralis [*Plural*] [*Afrikaans*]
pl .... Pluriel [*French*] (TPFD)
PL .... Poland [*ANSI two-letter standard code*] (CNC)
PL .... Politechnika Lodzka [*Engineering College of Lodz*] [*Poland*]
PL .... Polska [*Poland*] [*Poland*]
PL .... Postilokero [*Post Office Box*] [*Finland*]
PL .... Pravo Lidu [*The People's Right*] [*A newspaper*] (CZ)
pl .... Printer's Sheet (RU)
Pl............... Produktionsleitung [*Production Management*] (EG)
Pl............... Projection Lamp (RU)
PL .... Protiletecky [*Antiaircraft*] (CZ)
PL .... Punched Tape (RU)
pl .... Puolilihava [*Finland*]
Pl............... Raft [*Topography*] (RU)
pl .... Railroad Platform [*Topography*] (RU)
pl .... Square (BU)
Pl............... Square [*Topography*], Area (RU)
PL .... Submarine (RU)
PlA .... Amphibian (RU)
PLA........... Pakistan Liberation Army (PD)
PLA........... Pakistan Library Association (EAIO)
PLA........... Palestine Liberation Army
PLA........... Parlamento Latinoamericano [*Latin American Parliament - LAP*] [*Bogota, Colombia*] (EAIO)
PLA........... Partido Laborista Agrario [*Panama*] [*Political party*] (EY)
PLA........... Partido Liberal Autentico [*Panama*] [*Political party*] (EY)
PLA........... Party of Labor of Albania [*Political party*] (PPW)
PLA........... Patriotic Liberation Army [*Myanmar*] (PD)
PLA........... Pedro Leon Abroleda Brigade [*Colorado*] (PD)
PLA........... People's Liberation Army [*National Liberation Front*] [*North Vietnam*] (VNW)
PLA........... People's Liberation Army [*China*]
PLA........... People's Liberation Army [*India*] (PD)
Pla............. Plateau [*Tableland, Sunken Flat*] [*French*] (NAU)
PLA........... Polish Librarians Association (EAIO)
PLAA........ Partido de Luta dos Africanos de Angola [*Angola*]
PLAAF ..... People's Liberation Army Air Force
PLAB........ Aerial Depth Charge, Airborne Depth Charge (RU)
PLAC........ Philippine Labor Alliance Council [*Trade union*] (FEA)
PLAC........ Public Libraries Advisory Committee [*South Australia*]
PLACE ...... Programa Latinoamericano de Cooperacion Energetica [*Latin American Energy Cooperation Program*] (EAIO)

PLACO...... Technical Planning Committee [*ISO*] [*Switzerland*]   (PDAA)
plae............. Antisubmarine Air Squadron   (RU)
plae............. Antisubmarine Aviation Squadron   (BU)
PLAF........ People's Liberation Armed Forces [*South Vietnamese*]   (CL)
PLAF........ People's Liberation Armed Forces [*National Liberation Front*]
    [*North Vietnam*]   (VNW)
PLAIN....... Public Libraries Automated Information Network [*Australia*]
PLAKON... Platten-Konzentrator [*German*]   (ADPT)
PlAl........... Plattieraluminium [*Aluminum for Cladding*] [*German*]   (GCA)
PLAMAN ... Plano de Melhoramento da Alimentacao e do Manejo do Gado
    Leiteiro [*Brazil*]   (DSCA)
PLAMED.. Plantas Medicinales [*Ministerio de Sanidad y Consumo*] [*Spain*]
    [*Information service or system*]   (CRD)
PLAN .... People's Liberation Army Navy
PLAN .... People's Liberation Army of Namibia [*Political party*]   (PPW)
plan .... Planned, Planning, Plan   (RU)
PLAN .... Polska Ludowa Akcja Niepodleglosciowa [*Polish People's
    Independence Movement*]   (POL)
PLANAME ... Plano Nacional de Mecanizacao [*National Mechanization
    Program*] [*Brazil*]   (LA)
PLANAPAM ... Plano de Assistencia a Pecuaria Bovina do Amazonas [*Brazil*]
    (DSCA)
PLANARCO ... Planeacion Arquitectura Construccion [*Colombia*]   (COL)
PLANASEM ... Plano Nacional de Sementes do Ministerio da Agricultura
    [*Brazil*]   (DSCA)
PLANATES ... Plana Nacional de Assistencia Tecnica a Suinocultura [*Brazil*]
    (DSCA)
PLANAVE ... Plano Nacional de Avicultura. Ministerio de Agricultura
    [*Brazil*]   (DSCA)
PLANDES ... Sociedad Chilena de Planificacion y Desarrollo [*Chilean
    Association for Planning and Development*]   (LA)
PLANER ... Plano Nacional de Extensao Rural. Ministerio da Agricultura
    [*Brazil*]   (DSCA)
PLANHAP ... Plano Nacional de Habitacao Popular [*National Low-Cost
    Housing Plan*] [*Brazil*]   (LA)
PLANICOL ... Planificadora Industrial de Colombia [*Colombia*]   (COL)
PLANITEC ... Planeacion Tecnica [*Colombia*]   (COL)
Plankhozgiz ... State Publishing House of Literature on Planned Economy
    (RU)
Plankomtel' ... Telegraph Communications Planning Commission   (RU)
Plansk........ Planskizze [*Sketch Plan*] [*German*]
PLANTFACTS ... Steel Plants Information System [*German Iron and Steel
    Engineers Association*] [*Dusseldorf*] [*Information service or
    system*]   (IID)
plantk......... Plantkunde [*Botany*] [*Afrikaans*]
PLANVIRAL ... Planeamiento y Vivienda Rural [*Santiago, Chile*]   (LAA)
PLANYSA ... Planificacion y Servicios de Asesoramiento Agroeconomico
    SRL [*Venezuela*]   (DSCA)
PLANZO... All-Union Correspondence Institute of Planning   (RU)
PLAPIQUI ... Planta Pilanto de Ingeniera Quimica [*Universidad Nacional del
    Sur*] [*Argentina*]
plaq .... Plaquette [*Pamphlet*] [*Publishing*] [*French*]
pl ar........... Pack Artillery   (BU)
PLASAN ... Planlama Sanayi ve Ticaret Yatirim AS [*Planned Industrial and
    Commercial Investment Corp.*]   (TU)
PLASCO ... Plasticos Colombianos Ltda. [*Manizales*]   (COL)
PLASMEX ... International Plastics Exhibition
plast .... Plastic [*Danish/Norwegian*]
plast .... Plastico [*Plastic*] [*Spanish*]
plast .... Plastisch [*Plastic*] [*German*]   (GCA)
Plasta........ Betriebe zur Herstellung von Kunststoffen und Plastischen
    Massen (VVB) [*Plants for Production of Synthetic and
    Plastic Materials (VVB)*]   (EG)
PLASTEUROTEC ... Groupement Europeen des Fabricants de Pieces
    Techniques Plastiques [*European Group of Fabricators of
    Technical Plastics Parts*]   (EAIO)
PLASTICAM ... Plastique Camerounaise
PLASTICOL ... Plasticos Colombia Ltda. [*Palmira*]   (COL)
plastm .... Plastics Plant [*Topography*]   (RU)
Plastmasstroy ... State Trust for the Organization and Development of the
    Production of Plastics and Plastic Articles   (RU)
plastryggb .. Plastryggbind [*Plastic Back Binding*] [*Publishing Danish/
    Norwegian*]
PLAT........ Plan Lerma, Asistencia Tecnica [*Mexico*]   (DSCA)
plat .... Platinum [*Place of mining*] [*Topography*]   (RU)
Platf........... Platform [*Railroads, topography*]   (RU)
PLATIN .... Institute for the Study of Platinum and Other Precious Metals
    [*1918-1934*]   (RU)
Platrre........ Platriere [*Plaster Quarry*] [*Military map abbreviation World War
    I*] [*French*]   (MTD)
plattegr....... Plattegrond [*Map, Plan*] [*Publishing*] [*Netherlands*]
Plau........... Plateau [*Tableland*] [*Military map abbreviation World War I*]
    [*French*]   (MTD)
plav............ Smelting Works, Foundry [*Topography*]   (RU)
plavk .... Fusibility   (RU)
plavl .... Melting   (RU)
Plavmornin ... Floating Marine Scientific Research Institute   (RU)

PLAYDECA ... Plasticos y Derivados, Compania Anonima [*Venezuela*]
PLB............ Public Libraries Board [*Uganda*]   (EAIO)
PLB............ Public Libraries Branch [*Australia*]
PLB............ Short-Range Submarine   (RU)
PLC............ Parti de la Liberte du Citoyen [*Belgium*] [*Political party*]   (EY)
PLC............ Partido Liberal Constitucionalista [*Constitutionalist Liberal
    Party*] [*Nicaragua*] [*Political party*]   (PPW)
PLC............ Political-Legal Commission [*China*]
PLC............ Public Limited Company   (IDIG)
PLC............ Pymble Ladies College [*Australia*]   (ADA)
plchr.......... Planscher [*Plates*] [*Publishing*] [*Sweden*]
plchs.......... Planches [*Plates*] [*Publishing*] [*French*]
plCO .... Pluk Civilni Obrany [*Civil Defense Regiment*]   (CZ)
PLD .... Long-Range Submarine   (RU)
pld .... Mountain Infantry Division   (BU)
PLD .... Partido de la Liberacion Dominicana [*Dominican Liberation
    Party*] [*Dominican Republic*] [*Political party*]   (PPW)
PLD .... Partido Liberal Democratico [*Democratic Liberal Party*]
    [*Nicaragua*]   (LA)
PLD .... Parti Liberal-Democrate [*Cameroon*] [*Political party*]   (EY)
pld .... Peldany [*Copy, Sample*] [*HU*]
pld .... Poludnie [*or Poludniowy*] [*South or Southern*]   (POL)
PLD .... Protiletadlova Divize [*Antiaircraft Division*]   (CZ)
PLD .... Protiletadlove Delostrelectvo [*Antiaircraft Artillery*]   (CZ)
PLDO .... Antisubmarine Defense   (RU)
PLDO .... Protiletadlovy Delostrelecky Oddil [*Antiaircraft Artillery
    Battalion*]   (CZ)
PLDP........ Parti Liberal Democrate et Pluraliste [*Belgium*] [*Political party*]
    (PPW)
PLDP........ Political Leadership Development Program, AIPAC
PLDP........ Poverenictvo Lesneho a Drevarskeho Priemyslu [*Office of the
    Commissioner of the Forest and Lumber Industry*]   (CZ)
PLDS .... Polnohospodarske a Lesnicke Dokumentacne Stredisko
    [*Documentation Center for Agriculture and Forestry*]
    [*Kosice*]   (CZ)
PLDT........ Philippine Long Distance Telephone Co.
PLE........... Pipeline Engineering GmbH
Ple .... Pleiade [*Record label*] [*France*]
PLE........... Plesetsk [*Satellite launch complex*] [*Former USSR*]
pleb .... Plebeismo [*Plebianism*] [*Portuguese*]
pleg............ Plegado [*Folded*] [*Publishing*] [*Spanish*]
plem.......... Pedigreed   (RU)
Plemzagotkontora ... Office for Pedigreed Cattle Procurement   (RU)
Plenbezh .... Committee for Prisoner and Refugee Affairs   (RU)
PLEURO.... Pleuropneumonia [*Veterinary medicine*]   (DSUE)
PLEVANS ... Plascon-Evans [*Paint manufacturer*] [*South Africa*]
PLF .... Palestine Liberation Front [*Political party*]   (PD)
PLF .... People's Liberation Forces [*Ethiopia*] [*Political party*]   (AF)
PLF .... Philippine Labor Federation
PLF .... Pohjanmaan Lento OY [*Finland*] [*ICAO designator*]   (FAAC)
PLF .... Popular Liberation Front [*Ethiopia*]
PLF/GC..... People's Liberation Forces/General Command [*Ethiopia*]   (AF)
PLF-RC..... People's Liberation Forces - Revolutionary Committee
    [*Ethiopia*]
PLF-UO..... People's Liberation Forces - Unified Organization [*Ethiopia*]
PLG .... Center Lecturers Groups   (BU)
PLG .... Partido Liberal Galego [*Galician Liberal Party*] [*Spanish*]
    (WER)
PLG .... Provisional Libyan Government
PLGS .... Partita Liberale Giovani Somali [*Somali Liberal Youth Party*]
    [*Political party*]
PLGWU .... Progressive Labour and General Workers' Union [*Grenada*]
PLH .... Partido Liberal de Honduras [*Liberal Party of Honduras*]
    [*Political party*]   (PPW)
PLHDWU ... Port Louis Harbor and Dock Workers Union [*Mauritius*]   (AF)
PLI............ Empresa de Transporte Aereo del Peru [*ICAO designator*]
    (FAAC)
PLI............ Line-Pulse Receiver   (RU)
PLI............ Partido Liberal Independiente [*Independent Liberal Party*]
    [*Nicaragua*] [*Political party*]   (PPW)
PLI............ Partito Liberale Italiano [*Italian Liberal Party*] [*Political party*]
    (PPW)
PLI............ Payp-Layn Endustrisi [*Pipeline Industry*]   (TU)
PLI............ Public Law Institute [*Kenya*]   (EAIO)
PLIC .... Public Libraries and Information Council [*Proposed*] [*Australia*]
PLIDOS .... Persoenliches Literatur-Informations-und Dokumentations-
    System [*German*]   (ADPT)
PLI F........ Polo Laico Liberali-Repubblicani Federalisti [*Italy*] [*Political
    party*]   (ECED)
Plipdeco ..... Point Lisas Industrial Port Development Corporation
    [*Trinidadian and Tobagan*]   (GEA)
PLIS.......... Planungs Informations Systeme [*Netherlands*]
PLISA........ Plasticos Internacionales Ltda. [*Colombia*]   (COL)
PLIUN....... Partido Liberal Independiente de Unidad Nacional [*Nicaragua*]
    [*Political party*]   (EY)
plk .... Palkkausluokka [*Finland*]

plk	Plukovnik [Colonel] [US equivalent: Colonel] (CZ)	PLP	Parliamentary Labour Party [British]
PLK	Prazsky Linguisticky Krouzek [Prague Linguistic Circle] (CZ)	PLP	Parti de la Liberte et du Progres [Party of Liberty and Progress] [See also PVV] [Belgium] (PPE)
PLK	Protiletadlovy Kanon [Antiaircraft Cannon] (CZ)	PLP	Partido de Liberacion del Pueblo [People's Liberation Party] [Mexico] (LA)
PLK	Protiletecky Kryt [Antiaircraft Shelter] (CZ)	PLP	Partido de Liberacion Popular [Popular Liberation Party] [Ecuador] (LA)
plk	Pulkownik [Colonel] (POL)		
pl/khos	Ploiarkhos [Captain (Navy), Master (Merchant Marine)] (GC)	PLP	Partido de los Pobres [Poor People's Party] [Mexico] [Political party] (PD)
PLKI	Enterprise for Cast Stoneware (BU)	PLP	Partido Liberal Progresista [Progressive Liberal Party] [Guatemala] (LA)
pll	Planches [Plates] [Publishing] [French]		
PLL	Polskie Linie Lotnicze [Polish Air Lines] (POL)	PLP	Parti Liberal Progressiste [Liberal Progressive Party] [Morocco] [Political party] (PPW)
Plle	Passerelle [Footbridge] [Military map abbreviation World War I] [French] (MTD)	PLP	Parti pour la Liberation du Peuple [People's Liberation Party] [Senegal] [Political party] (PPW)
PLLG	Political-Legal Leading Group [China]	PLP	People's Liberation Party [Pakistan]
PLM	Aktiebolaget Platmanufaktur [Sweden]	PLP	People's Liberation Party [Liberia] (AF)
PLM	Pakistan Liberation Movement [Political party] (PD)	PLP	Podniky Lesneho Priemyslu [Enterprise of the Forest Industry] (CZ)
PLM	Palembang [Indonesia] [Airport symbol] (OAG)		
PLM	Paris-Lyon-Mediterranee [Railway] [Sometimes facetiously translated as "Pour les Morts"] [French] (MTD)	PLP	Poverenictvo Lahkeho Priemyslu [Office of the Commissioner of Light Industry] (CZ)
PLM	Partido de Libertacao de Mocambique	PLP	Progressive Labor Party [Bermuda] (LA)
PLM	Partido Leninista-Marxista [Leninist-Marxist Party] [Colorado] (LA)	PLP	Progressive Labor Party [St. Lucia] (LA)
PLM	Partij voor Landbouw en Middenstand [Benelux] (BAS)	PLP	Progressive Labour Party [Saint Lucia] [Political party] (EAIO)
PLM	People's Liberation Movement [Montserrat] [Political party] (PPW)	PLP	Progressive Liberal Party [Bahamas] [Political party] (PPW)
plm	Plnometr [Cubic Meter] (CZ)	PLP	Protiletadlovy Pluk [Antiaircraft Regiment] (CZ)
PLM	Progressive Labor Movement [Antigua] (LA)	PLP	Pusat Latehan Polis [Police Training Center] (ML)
plm	Prostorovy Metr [Cubic Meter] (CZ)	PLP	Soil Vacuum-Tube Potentiometer (RU)
plm	Small Submarine (RU)	PLPAR	Regulations on Internal Passports and Address Registration (BU)
PLMA	Pomoc Lekarska Mlodziezy Akademickiej [Medical Aid for University Youth] (POL)		
PLMA	Professional Librarians of Malta Association (SLS)	PL/PI	Proletarische Linke/Partei Initiative [Proletarian Left/Party Initiative] (WEN)
pl m-k	Lightship (RU)	plplt	Polplotno [Half-Cloth Binding] [Publishing] [Poland]
PLMN	Partido Marxista Leninista de Nicaragua [Political party] (EY)	PLPP	Pegawai Laut Pasokan Polis [Police Force Marine Officer] (ML)
PLMP	Progressive Labor Movement Party (LA)	PLPPH	Pusat Latehan Polis Pasokan Hutan [Police Field Force Training Center] (ML)
PLMR	Paris, Lyons, and Mediterranean Railway (ROG)		
PLN	Partido de Liberacion Nacional [National Liberation Party] [El Salvador] [Political party] (EY)	PLR	Constructions Metalliques Panz et Laon Reunis
		PLR	Partido Liberal Radical [Radical Liberal Party] [Paraguay] [Political party] (PPW)
PLN	Partido Liberacion Nacional [National Liberation Party] [Costa Rica] [Political party] (PPW)	PLR	Partido Liberal Radical [Radical Liberal Party] [Ecuador] [Political party] (PPW)
PLN	Partido Liberal Nacionalista [Nationalist Liberal Party] [Nicaragua]	PLR	Philippine Liberation Ribbon [Military decoration]
Pln	Pelabohan [Roadstead, Anchorage] [Indonesian] (NAU)	plr	Planscher [Plates] [Publishing] [Sweden]
Pln	Pelabohan [Roadstead, Anchorage] [Malaysia] (NAU)	PLR	Pusat Latehan Rikerut [Recruit Training Center] (ML)
PLN	Perusahaan Umum Listrik Negara [State Electricity Corp.] [Indonesia]	PLRA	Partido Liberal Radical Autentico [Authentic Liberal Radical Party][1] [Paraguay] [Political party] (PD)
PLN	Polnippon [Poland] [ICAO designator] (FAAC)	PLRO	Protiletecky Raketovy Oddil [Antiaircraft Rocket Battalion] (CZ)
pln	Polnoc [or Polnocny] [North or Northern] (POL)		
PLNC	Polish National Committee [International Association on Water Pollution Researchand Control] (EAIO)	PLRS	Protiletecke Ridici Strely [Air Defense Guided Missiles] (CZ)
		PLRT	Protiletadlova Raketova Technika [Air Defense Rocket Technology] (CZ)
PLNSW	Public Library of New South Wales [Australia] (ADA)	PLRV	Protiletadlove Raketove Vojsko [Antiaircraft Rocket Troops] (CZ)
PLO	Antisubmarine Defense (RU)		
PLO	Palestine Liberation Organization [Political party] (PD)	PLRZ	Protiletadlove Raketove Zbrane [Antiaircraft Rocket Weapons] (CZ)
PLO	Palestinian Lawyers' Organization		
PLO	Panstwowe Liceum Okretowe [State Merchant Marine School] (POL)	pls	Medium Submarine (RU)
		PLS	Palio Air Service [Italy] [ICAO designator] (FAAC)
PLO	Philippine Labor Organization	PLS	Parti de la Liberation et du Socialisme [Party of Liberation and Socialism] [Morocco] (AF)
PLO	Polskie Linie Oceaniczne [Polish Ocean Lines] (POL)		
PLO	Polskie Linie Okretowe [Polish Shipping Lines] (POL)	PLS	Parti Liberal Suisse [Liberal Party of Switzerland] [Political party] (PPE)
PLO	Port Lincoln [Australia] [Airport symbol] (OAG)		
PLO	Pravila Letacke Obuke [Flight Training Rules] [Air Force] (YU)	PLS	Plynarenska Sluzba [Gas Supply Service] [Civil defense] (CZ)
PLO	Principal Legal Officer [Australia]	PLS	Polish Language School [Canberra, Australia]
PLO	Protiletadlovy Oddil [Antiaircraft Battalion] (CZ)	PLS	Position Laterale de Securite
PLOB	Patrol Log Observations [Aviation] (DSUE)	PLS	Providenciales [British West Indies] [Airport symbol] (OAG)
Plodkoop	Fruit Cooperative (BU)	PLS	Public Libraries Section [Australia]
plodoovoshch	Fruit and Vegetable Sovkhoz [Topography] (RU)	PLS	Public Library Service [Australia]
Plon	Plantation [Plantation] [Military map abbreviation World War I] [French] (MTD)	plsbr	Mountain Rifle Brigade (BU)
		plschr	Planscher [Plates] [Publishing] [Sweden]
pl opt os	Optic Axial Plane (RU)	plsd	Mountain Rifle Division (BU)
pl or	Mountain Gun (BU)	plskg	Plateau (RU)
Pl OS	Pleven Oblast Court (BU)	plsp	Mountain Rifle Regiment (BU)
ploshch	Square [Topography], Area (RU)	PLST	Small Railroad Station [Topography] (RU)
PLOSU	Protiletadlova Obrana Statniho Uzemi [Air Defense of National Territory] (CZ)	PLT	Partido Liberal Teete [Teete Liberal Party] [Paraguay] [Political party] (PPW)
plot	Dam, Dike, Weir (RU)		
PLOT	People's Liberation Organization of Tamil Eelam [Sri Lanka] [Political party]	PLT	Pembantu Letnan [Sublieutenant] (IN)
		PLT	Permanent Labour Tribunal
plot	Plotno [Cloth Binding] [Publishing] [Poland]	plt	Plotno [Cloth Binding] [Publishing] [Poland]
PLOTE	People's Liberation Organization of Tamil Eelam [Sri Lanka] [Political party]	PLT	Portable Tank Lamp [Military term]
		PLT	Trenching Plow, Plow-Type Trench Excavator (RU)
plotn	Carpentry (RU)	PLTI	Volga Region Forestry Engineering Institute Imeni M. Gor'kiy (RU)
plotn	Density (RU)		
pl ou m	Plus ou Moins [More or Less] [French]	pltn	Platen [Plates] [Publishing] [Netherlands]
Plovmornin	Floating Marine Scientific Research Institute (RU)	PLTR	Polskie Lekarskie Towarzystwo Radiologiczne [Poland] (SLS)
PLOW	Petunia Lovers of the World	PLU	Lecturer's Projector Unit (RU)
PLP	La Palma [Panama] [Airport symbol] (OAG)	PLU	Partido Liberal Unificado [Unified Liberal Party] [Paraguay] [Political party] (PPW)
PLP	Panstwowe Liceum Pedagogiczne [State Pedagogical School] (POL)		

PLUA........	Partido da Luta dos Africanos de Angola [*Party for the Struggle of the Africans of Angola*] (AF)
PLUM	Philippine Labor Unity Movement [*of Federation of Industrial and Agrarian Workers*]
PLUNA	Primeras Lineas Uruguayas de Navegacion Aerea [*Uruguayan National Airlines*]
PLURO	Antisubmarine Guided Weapon (RU)
PLURS	Antisubmarine Guided Missile (RU)
plus............	Plusieurs [*Several*] [*French*]
PLUS	Prima Leben und Sparen [*Quality Living and Saving*] [*Brand name and discount store chain in West Germany and US*]
pluskv........	Pluskvamperfekti [*Pluperfect*] [*Finland*]
plut............	Plutonowy [*Sergeant*] [*Poland*]
PLUTO......	Pipeline under the Ocean [*British project*] [*World War II*]
Pluv	Pluviose [*Fifth month of the "Calendrier Republicain," from January 20 to February 19*] (FLAF)
pluv	Pluviusin [*Leatherette*] [*Publishing Danish/Norwegian*]
PLUZ........	Policy Land Use Zone [*Australian Capital Territory*]
PLV...........	Polaravia OY [*Finland*] [*ICAO designator*] (FAAC)
plv	Postilahetysvekseli [*Finland*]
PLV...........	Publicite sur le Lieu de Vente [*French*] (ADPT)
PL-VM	Pathet Lao - Viet Minh
PLW..........	Palau [*ANSI three-letter standard code*] (CNC)
PLW..........	Palu [*Indonesia*] [*Airport symbol*] (OAG)
PLW..........	Panstwowe Lecznice Weterynaryjne [*State Veterinary Hospitals*] (POL)
Plw	Polwysep [*Peninsula*] [*Poland*]
PLWA........	People Living with AIDS [*Acquired Immune Deficiency Syndrome*] [*Australia*]
PLWHA	People Living With HIV/AIDS [*Human Immunodeficiency Virus / Acquired Immune Deficiency Syndrome*] [*Australia*]
PLYF	Port Louis Youth Federation [*Reunionese*] (AF)
PLYMCHAN ...	Plymouth Subarea Channel [*NATO*] (NATG)
PLZ...........	Minelaying Submarine (RU)
PLZ...........	Plantations Lever au Zaire
PLZ...........	Polni Letistni Zabezpeceni [*Field Airfield Support*] (CZ)
PLZ...........	Port Elizabeth [*South Africa*] [*Airport symbol*] (OAG)
PLZ...........	Postleitzahl [*German*]
PLZ...........	Protiletalska Zascita [*Antiaircraft Protection*] [*Civil defense*] (YU)
PLZpriMINOT ...	Protiletalska Zascita pri MINOT [*Antiaircraft Defense in the Ministry of the Interior*] (YU)
PM	Antipersonnel Mine (RU)
PM	Blasting Unit, Blasting Machine (RU)
PM	Feeder, Feed Mechanism (RU)
PM	Field Shop [*Military term*] (RU)
PM	Field Weather Post (RU)
PM	Film (RU)
PM	Groupe Pierre Mariotte [*French*]
pm	Last Month (RU)
PM	Magnetic Starter (RU)
PM	Makarov Pistol (RU)
PM	Mechanical Packer [*Pet.*] (RU)
PM	Medical Aid Station (RU)
PM	Mobile Shop (RU)
PM	Padre Maestro [*Spanish*]
PM	Pak [*or Phak*] Mai [*New Party*] [*Political party*]
PM	Partito Monarchico [*Monarchist Party*] [*Italy*] [*Political party*] (PPE)
pm	Pasado Meridiano [*Spanish*] (GPO)
PM	Patriotikon Metopon [*Patriotic Front*] [*Greek Cyprus*] [*Political party*] (PPE)
PM	Penzugyminiszterium [*Ministry of Finance*] (HU)
pm	Per Maand [*Per Month*] [*Afrikaans*]
PM	Per Minuut [*Per Minute*] [*Afrikaans*]
pM	Per Monat [*Per Month*] [*German*]
pm	Pistolet Maszynowy [*Machine-Gun*] [*Poland*]
PM	Pistolet Mitrailleur [*Machine Pistol*] (CL)
PM	Plan-Methodik (Unterabteilung der Abteilung Plankoordinierung) [*Planning Methodology (A Subdivision of the Department of Plan Coordination)*] (EG)
PM	Plus-Minus [*Approximately*] [*Afrikaans*]
PM	Pneumatic Hammer (RU)
pm	Poids Mort [*Dead Weight*] [*French*]
PM	Policia Militar [*Military Police*] [*Portuguese*] (WER)
pm	Pomeridiane [*Afternoon*] [*Italian*] (GPO)
PM	Pontifex Maximus [*Italian*]
PM	Popular Movement Against the European Community (ECON)
PM	Posmeester [*Postmaster*] [*Afrikaans*]
PM	Post Mortem [*After Death*] [*Latin*]
PM	Powlesland & Mason [*Railway*] [*Wales*]
PM	Precizna Mehanika [*Precision Instruments*] (YU)
PM	Precompte Mobilier [*Benelux*] (BAS)
PM	Prefeitura Municipal [*Municipal Prefecture*] [*Portuguese*]
PM	Prehrada Mladeze ["*Youth*" *Dam*] (CZ)
PM	Preparation Militaire [*French*]
PM	Preteky Mieru [*Peace Race*] (CZ)
PM	Prevote Militaire [*Military Police*] [*Cambodia*] (CL)
PM	Programing Mechanism (RU)
PM	Proletarian Thought [*Publishing house*] (RU)
Pm	Promecio [*Chemical element*] [*Portuguese*]
PM	Promemoria [*Finland*]
pm	Pro Minute [*Per Minute*] [*German*]
PM	Przemysl Meblarski [*Furniture Industry*] (POL)
PM	Pseudomonoclinic (RU)
PM	Pubblico Ministero [*Public Prosecutor*] [*Italian*]
PM	Punjabi Muslim [*Pakistan*]
pm	Puscani Metak [*Rifle Bullet*] (YU)
PM	Ranging Mortar (RU)
PM	Repair Ship, Floating Shop (RU)
PM	Semisoft (RU)
PM	Societe pour le Developpement du Petrole Vert (Groupe Pierre Mariotte) [*France*]
PM	Steam Engine (RU)
PM	St. Pierre and Miquelon [*ANSI two-letter standard code*] (CNC)
PM	Vertical Magnet, Lifting Magnet (RU)
PM	Watering Truck, Sprinkler Truck (RU)
PMA	Pakistan Medical Association (SLS)
PMA	Pan Malaysian Air Transport [*ICAO designator*] (FAAC)
PMA	Panstwowe Muzeum Archeologiczne [*State Archaeological Museum*] (POL)
PMA	Pays les Moins Avances
PMA	Peace Movement Aotearoa [*New Zealand*] (EAIO)
PMA	Pemba Island [*Tanzania*] [*Airport symbol*] (OAG)
PMA	Performance Management Association (EAIO)
PMA	Perth Market Authority [*Australia*]
PMA	Perth Muslim Association [*Australia*]
PMA	Philippine Medical Association (SLS)
PMA	Photo Marketing Association [*Australia*]
PMA	Pigment Manufacturers of Australia Ltd.
PMA	Policia Militar Ambulante [*Mobile Military Police*] [*Guatemala*]
PMA	Polymethyl Acrylate (RU)
PMA	Port of Melbourne Authority [*Australia*]
PMA	Potato Marketing Authority [*Australia*]
PMA	Potato Merchants' Association [*Australia*]
PMA	Powder Metallurgy Association of South Africa (AA)
PMA	Precious Metals Australia
PMA	Programa Mundial de Alimentos [*UN World Food Program*] [*Use WFP*] (LA)
PMA	Propylmethacrylamide (RU)
PMAA	Proprietary Medicines Association of Australia
PMAC	Proprietary Medicines Advisory Committee [*Australia*]
PMAC	Provisional Military Administrative Council [*Ethiopia*] [*Political party*] (PD)
PMADK	Permanent International Association of Road Congresses [*PIARC*] (RU)
PMAEA	Port Management Association of Eastern Africa
PMAESA ..	Port Management Association of Eastern and Southern Africa (EA)
PMAKS.....	Permanent International Association of Navigation Congresses [*PIANC*] (RU)
PMAN	Prezidiul Marii Adunari Nationale [*Presidium of the Grand National Assembly*] (RO)
PMAV	Prazsky Mestsky Akcni Vybor [*Prague City Action Committee (of the National Front)*] (CZ)
PMAWCA ...	Port Management Association of West and Central Africa
PMB	Plan de Mestizacion Bovina [*Venezuela*] (DSCA)
pmb	Pontoon-Bridge Battalion (RU)
PMB	Private Mail Bag
PMB	Protivminobacacka Borba [*Antimortar Defense*] (YU)
PMB	Punkt des Maneuverbeginns [*Start of Maneuver (In intercepting enemy planes)*] (EG)
pmb	Road and Bridge Battalion (BU)
PMB	Turret Traversing Mechanism (RU)
PMBA.......	Progressive Music Broadcasting Association [*Australia*]
PMBC.......	Phuket Marine Biological Center [*Thailand*] [*Research center*] (IRC)
PMBr........	Pontoon-Bridge Brigade (RU)
PMBU	Personal Member of the Baptist Union [*British*]
PMC	Palabora Mining Company
PMC	Parents of Missing Children [*Australia*]
PMC	Parquets et Moulures du Cameroun
PMC	Pekarsko-Mesarska Ceta [*Bakers and Butchers Company*] (YU)
PMC	Planning and Management Consultancy [*Sudan*]
PMC	Planning Ministers' Conference [*Australia*]
PMC	Polish Music Centre (EAIO)
PMC	Polish Music Council (EAIO)
PMC	Pomorski Meteoroloski Centar [*Maritime Meteorological Center*] [*Former Yugoslavia*] (EAS)
PMC	Professional Musicians' Club [*Australia*]
PMC	Puerto Montt [*Chile*] [*Airport symbol*] (OAG)

PMCA .... Programa Multinacional de Ciencias Agropecuarias [*Costa Rica*] (DSCA)
PMCh .... Paramagnetic Particle   (RU)
PMCH .... Protection of Movable Cultural Heritage [*Australia*]
PMCI .... Phosphate Mining Corp. of Christmas Island   (EY)
PMCQ .... Paper Marketing Council of Queensland [*Australia*]
PMC (S) .... Pan Malaysia Cement Works (Singapore)   (ML)
PMCTF ..... Prime Minister's Country Task Force [*Australia*]
PMCU .... Personal Member of the Congregational Union [*British*]
PmCV .... Pomocni Centar Veze [*Auxiliary Communications Center*] [*Military*]   (YU)
PMCW ...... Pan Malaysia Cement Works   (ML)
PMD .... Padmotordiens [*Road Motor Service*] [*Afrikaans*]
PMD .... Pembangunan Masjarakat Desa [*Village Community Development*]   (IN)
PMD .... Protivpesadiska Mina-Drvena [*Wooden Anti-Infantry Mine*] (YU)
PMD .... Wooden Antipersonnel Mine   (RU)
PMDA .... Plastics Machinery Distributors Association [*British*]   (EAIO)
PMDB .... Partido do Movimento Democratico Brasileiro [*Brazilian Democratic Movement Party*]   (LA)
PMDC .... Pakistan Mineral Development Corporation   (GEA)
PMDK .... Machine-Gun and Mortar Decontamination Kit   (RU)
PME .... Petites et Moyennes Entreprises [*Small and Medium-Size Businesses*] [*French*]   (WER)
PME .... Plan de Modernisation et d'Equipement
PME .... Por Merce Especial [*By Special Favor*] [*Portuguese*]
PME .... Preparation Militaire Elementaire [*Combined Cadet Force - CCF*] [*French*]
PME .... Programa Mundial del Empleo [*World Employment Program - WEP*] [*Spanish*]
PME .... Programme Mondial de l'Emploi [*World Employment Program - WEP*] [*French*]
PME .... Pteryx Miktis Ekpaidevseos [*Mixed Training Wing*] [*Air Force*] [*Greek*]   (GC)
PMEC .... Postgraduate Medical Education Committee [*University of Queensland, Australia*]
pmet .... Puscani Metak [*Rifle Bullet*]   (YU)
PMEZ .... Pyshma Copper Electrolytic Plant   (RU)
PMF .... Full-Length Film, Feature Film   (RU)
PMF .... Pakistan Mazdoor Federation
PMF .... Philippine Missionary Fellowship
PMFAT ..... Personnel Militaire Feminin de l'Armee de Terre [*Army Female Military Personnel*] [*French*]   (WER)
PMG .... Pemangku [*Acting*]   (ML)
PMG .... Ponta Pora [*Brazil*] [*Airport symbol*]   (OAG)
PMG .... Population Monitoring Group [*New Zealand*]
PMG .... Posmeester-Generaal [*Postmaster General*] [*Afrikaans*]
PMG .... Provisional Military Government [*Ethiopia*]
PMG .... Przeladunki Morskie Gdansk [*Gdansk Cargo Handling Enterprise*]   (POL)
PMH .... Pari Mutuel sur les Hippodromes [*France*]   (FLAF)
PMH .... Polska Marynarka Handlowa [*Polish Merchant Marine*]   (POL)
Pm-Handel ... Produktionsmittelhandel [*Trade in Production Equipment*] (EG)
PMI .... Palma [*Mallorca Island*] [*Airport symbol*]   (OAG)
PMI .... Partai Muslimin Indonesia [*Indonesian Moslem Party (Same as PARMUSI)*]   (IN)
PMI .... Pensions Management Institute [*British*]   (EAIO)
PMI .... Petites et Moyennes Industries [*Small and Medium-Size Industries*]   (AF)
PMI .... Production Management Institute of South Africa   (AA)
PMI .... Protection Maternelle Infantile [*Service Nationale de*] [*(National) Infant and Maternal Protection (Department) Laotian*] (CL)
PMIA........ Powder Metal Industries Association [*Australia*]
PMIC........ Poultry Meat Industry Committee [*New South Wales, Australia*]
PMiM .... Applied Mathematics and Mechanics   (RU)
Pmin.......... Angle of Safety [*Artillery*]   (RU)
PMIP........ Pan-Malayan Islamic Party   (ML)
PMIS .... Projects Management Information System [*UNESCO*]   (DUND)
PMK .... Mobile Mechanized Column   (RU)
PMK .... Palair Macedonian [*Yugoslavia*] [*ICAO designator*]   (FAAC)
PMK .... Pecsi Moso- es Kokszmu [*Coal Processing and Coke Plant of Pecs*]   (HU)
PMK .... Polymethacrylic Acid   (RU)
PMK .... Popularni Motoristicka Knihovna [*Popular Publications Series on Motors*]   (CZ)
PMKh .... Mechanized Field Bakery   (RU)
PML .... Pakistan Muslim League [*Political party*]
PML .... Precision Mecanique Labinal SA [*French*]
PMLF........ Project Marketing Loan Facility [*Australia*]
PMLI........ Partito Marxista-Leninista Italiano [*Italian Marxist-Leninist Party*]   (WER)
PMLM....... Parti Marxiste-Leniniste Malgache

PMLM....... Parti Marxiste Leniniste Mauricien [*Mauritian Marxist-Leninist Party*]   (AF)
PML-TNO ... Prins Maurits Laboratorium TNO - Instituut voor Chemische en Technologische Research [*Prins Maurits Laboratory TNO - Institute for Chemical and Technological Research*] [*Netherlands*]   (ARC)
PMM .... Applied Mathematics and Mechanics   (RU)
PMM .... Mobile Machine Shop   (RU)
PMMA ...... Poly Methyl Methacrylate Association [*European Council of Chemical Manufacturers Federations*] [*Brussels, Belgium*] (EAIO)
PMMAPA ... Poly Methyl Methacrylate Producers Association [*Belgium*] (EAIO)
PMMC ...... Precious Minerals Marketing Company [*Exporter of diamonds and gold*] [*Sierra Leone*]
PMMT ...... Processeur Multiprotocole Multiligne des Transmissions [*French*]   (ADPT)
PMN .... Mine Observation [*Navy*]   (RU)
PMN .... Panglima Mangku Negara [*Knight of the Most Distinguished Order of the Defender of the Realm*]   (ML)
PMN .... Partido de Movilizacion Nacional [*National Mobilization Party*] [*Nicaragua*]   (LA)
PMN .... Progettazioni Meccanico Nucleare [*Nuclear Machinery Planning*] [*Italian*]   (WER)
PMN .... Pumani [*Papua New Guinea*] [*Airport symbol*]   (OAG)
PMO......... Mine Defense, Antimine Defense   (RU)
PMO......... Palermo [*Italy*] [*Airport symbol*]   (OAG)
PMO......... Pangosmios Meteorologikos Organismos [*World Meteorological Organization (of the United Nations)*]   (GC)
PMO......... Pianissimo [*Very Softly*] [*Music*]   (ROG)
PMO......... Portable Target Equipment   (RU)
pmo .... Proximo [*Next, Nearest*] [*Spanish*]
PMO......... Public Medical Officer [*Australia*]
PMOA .... Public Medical Officers Association [*Australia*]
PMOG....... Philippine Marine Officers' Guild
p mol .... Poids Moleculaire [*Molecular Weight*] [*French*]
PMP .... Bridge Train   (RU)
PMP .... Field Weather Post   (RU)
pmp .... Marine Regiment   (BU)
PMP .... Mechanized Field Laundry   (RU)
PMP .... Medical Aid Station   (RU)
PMP .... Pacific Magazines and Printing Ltd. [*Commercial firm*] [*Australia*]
PMP .... Partido ng Masang Pilipino [*Political party*]   (EY)
PMP .... Parti du Mouvement Populaire de la Cote Francaise des Somalis [*Popular Movement Party of French Somaliland*] [*Political party*]
PMP .... Partito Monarchico Popolare [*Popular Monarchist Party*] [*Italy*] [*Political party*]   (PPE)
PMP .... Pimaga [*Papua New Guinea*] [*Airport symbol*]   (OAG)
PMP .... Planetary Traversing Mechanism [*of a tank turret*]   (RU)
PMP .... Por Mao Propria [*Portuguese*]
PMP .... Preliminary Master Plan
PMP .... Property Management Plan [*Australia*]
PMP .... Regimental Aid Station   (BU)
PMP .... Regimental Medical Station   (RU)
PMP .... Semiconductor-Metal-Semiconductor [*Thin-film circuits*]   (RU)
PMPO .... Mechanized Field Laundry Detachment   (RU)
PMQ......... Perito Moreno [*Argentina*] [*Airport symbol*]   (OAG)
PMQ......... Permanent Married Quarters [*Canadian Forces*]
PMR .... Palmerston North [*New Zealand*] [*Airport symbol*]   (OAG)
PMR .... Partido Mariateguista Revolucionario [*Peru*] [*Political party*] (EY)
PMR .... Partidul Muncitoresc Roman [*Romanian Workers' Party*] [*Political party*]
PMR .... Partidul Muncitoresc Romin
PMR .... Polise-Air [*Russian Federation*] [*ICAO designator*]   (FAAC)
PMR .... Portable Microroentgenometer   (RU)
pmr............ Road and Bridge Company   (BU)
PMR .... Trailer Minelayer   (RU)
PMR-1 .... Protivpesadiska Mina-Rasprskava Juca [*Anti-Infantry Fragmentation Mine*]   (YU)
PMRC........ Pakistan Medical Research Council
PMRC........ Programa de Modernizacao e Reorganizacao da Comercializacao [*Marketing Reorganization and Modernization Program*] [*Brazil*]   (LA)
PMRGT..... Mobile Repair Shop for Artillery Caterpillar Tractors   (RU)
PMRN .... Prezydium Miejskiej Rady Narodowej [*Presidium of the People's Town Council*] [*Poland*]
PMRO .... Protivpesadiska Mina-Rasprskavajuca Otskocna [*Anti-Infantry Fragmentation Rebounding Mine*]   (YU)
PMRS........ Protivpesadiska Mina-Rasprskavajuca, Svetleca [*Anti-Infantry Fragmentation Flare Mine*]   (YU)
PMRV .... Plan Mobilizacniho Rozvinuti Vojsk [*Mobilization Plan for Troop Deployment*]   (CZ)
PMRW ...... Panstwowa Muzyczna Rada Wydawnicza [*State Musical Publication Council*]   (POL)

PMS........... Council of Ministers Decree (BU)
PMS........... Council of Ministers Letter (BU)
PMS........... Device for Determination of Mechanical Properties of Plants (RU)
PMS........... Field Weather Station (RU)
PMS........... Mine Service Regulations [Military term] (RU)
PMS........... Panstwowy Monopol Spirytusowy [State Alcohol Monopoly] (POL)
PMS........... Paranormal Music Society [Australia]
PMS........... Paris Missionary Society
PMS........... Partido Mexicano Socialista [Political party] (EY)
PMS........... Pavement Management System [Australia]
PMS........... Permanent-Magnet System Instrument [Metrology] (RU)
PMS........... Piccola Missione per il Sordomuti [Little Mission for the Deaf-Mute - LMDM] [Rome, Italy] (EAIO)
PMS........... Poljoprivredno-Masinska Stanica [Agricultural Machinery Station] (YU)
PMS........... Polski Monopol Solny [Polish Salt Monopoly] (POL)
PMS........... Polymethyl Siloxane (RU)
PMS........... Pontonova Mostova Souprava [Pontoon Bridging Section] (CZ)
PMS........... Preparation Militaire Superieure [Advanced Military Preparatory Training] [French] (WER)
PMS........... Presidential Management Staff [Philippines]
PMS........... Programmed Management Services [Australia]
PMS........... Track Machinery Station [Railroads] (RU)
PMSA....... Paddy's Market Stallholders' Association [Australia]
PMSC....... Prime Minister's Science Council [Australia]
PMSD....... Parti Mauricien Social-Democrate [Mauritian Social Democratic Party] [Political party] (PPW)
PMSMZ.... Ministry of Agriculture Pasture Reclamation Service (BU)
PMSP....... Proodevtiki Mathitiki Spoudastiki Parataxi [Progressive Student Faction] [Greek] (GC)
PMSP....... Proodevtiki Mathitiki Syndikalistiki Parataxi [Progressive Student Trade Union Faction] [Greek] (GC)
PMSU....... Partidul Muncitoresc Socialist Ungur [Hungarian Socialist Workers' Party] (RO)
PMT .... Instrument for Determination of Microhardness (RU)
PMT .... Panstwowy Monopol Tytoniowy [State Tobacco Monopoly] (POL)
PMT .... Partido Mexicano de los Trabajadores [Mexican Workers' Party] [Political party] (PPW)
PMT .... Partija Madarskih Trudbenika [Hungarian Workers' Party] (YU)
PMT .... Polski Monopol Tytoniowy [Polish Tobacco Monopoly] (POL)
PMT .... Post-Maastricht Tension [European community] (ECON)
PMT .... Productora Mexicana de Tuberia SA [Mexican Turbine Manufacturing Corp.]
PMT .... Prumyslova Tiskarna [Industrial Printing Plant] (CZ)
PMTF....... Applied Mechanics and Technical Physics (RU)
PMTs........ Copper-Zinc Solder (RU)
PMTZ....... Plan Materielne-Technickeho Zasobovani [Plan for the Procurement of Materiel and Equipment] (CZ)
PMU......... Fertilizer Containing Several Trace Elements (RU)
PMU......... Pari Mutuel Urbain [Legal Parimutuel System] [French] (WER)
PMU......... Peninsula Malay Union (ML)
PMU......... Police Mobile Unit [Zambia] (AF)
PMU......... Production-Installation Administration (BU)
PMU......... Programme de Modernisation Urbaine [Urban Modernization Program] [Algeria] (AF)
PMU......... Simple Meteorological Condition (BU)
PMUM...... Persatuan Mahasiswa Universiti Malaya [Students' Union, University of Malaya] (ML)
PMUM...... Societe d'Exploitation pour le Pari Mutuel Urbain au Maroc
PMUP....... Partidul Muncitoresc Unit Polonez [Polish United Workers' Party] (RO)
PMV......... Porlamar [Venezuela] [Airport symbol] (OAG)
PMV......... Pro Mundi Vita [Brussels, Belgium] [Defunct] (EAIO)
pm vl.......... Prearranged Barrage (BU)
PMV-LATA ... Passenger Motor Vehicle Labour Adjustment Training Arrangements [Australia]
PMVMP.... Passenger Motor Vehicle Manufacturing Plan [Australia]
PMW......... Polska Marynarka Wojenna [Polish Navy] [Poland]
PMWA...... Philippine Medical Women's Association (EAIO)
PMX .... Petroleos Mexicanos [Mexico] [ICAO designator] (FAAC)
PMZ .... Discontinuous Magnetic Recording, Intermediate Magnetic Recording (RU)
PMZ .... Industrial Installations Plant (BU)
PMZ .... Panstwowe Muzeum Zoologiczne [State Zoological Museum] (POL)
PMZ .... Panstwowy Monopol Zapalczany [State Match Monopoly] (POL)
PMZ .... Penza Machinery Plant (RU)
PMZ .... Pneumatic Stoker (RU)
PMZ .... Podol'sk Machine Plant (RU)
PMZD .... Delayed Action Railroad Mine (RU)
pmzhpb ...... Pontoon-Bridge Railroad Battalion (BU)

PN............. Actuating Pump, Starting Pump (RU)
PN............. Booster Pump [Aviation] (RU)
pn .... Cartridge (BU)
PN............. Direction Post (RU)
PN............. Guidance Point, Aiming Point (BU)
pn .... Monday (RU)
PN............. North Pole [Also, NP]
PN............. Observer's Parachute (RU)
pn .... Ordinal Number, Number in a Series, Atomic Number (RU)
PN............. Padre-Nosso [Our Father] [Portuguese]
PN............. Pakistan Navy
PN............. Pania Nord [A soil type] [Italy]
PN............. Partenavia Construzioni Aeronautiche SpA [Italy] [ICAO aircraft manufacturer identifier] (ICAO)
PN............. Partido Nacional [National Party] [Honduras] [Political party] (PPW)
PN............. Partido Nacional [National Party] [Dominican Republic] [Political party]
PN............. Partido Nacional [National Party] [Uruguay] [Political party] (PPW)
PN............. Partido Nacional [National Party] [Chile] (LA)
PN............. Partit Nazzjonalista [Nationalist Party] [Malta] [Political party] (EAIO)
PN............. Party Negara [National Party] (ML)
PN............. Passage a Niveau [Level Crossing] [French]
pn .... Patrz Nizej [See Below] [Poland]
PN............. Peace Now [Israel] [An association] (EAIO)
PN............. Personnel Navigant de l'Aviation Civile [France] (FLAF)
PN............. Perusahaan Negara [State Company] (IN)
PN............. Peti Nitrogenmuvek [Nitrogen Factory of Pet] (HU)
PN............. Philippine Navy
Pn............. Pinar [Spring, Fountain] (TU)
PN............. Pitcairn Islands [ANSI two-letter standard code] (CNC)
Pn............. Piton [Peak] [French] (NAU)
pn .... Pod Nazwa [Called] [Poland]
PN............. Pohlavni Nemoci [Venereal Diseases] (CZ)
PN............. Polemikon Navtikon [Navy] (GC)
PN............. Police Nationale [National Police] (CL)
PN............. Policia Nacional [National Police] [El Salvador] (LA)
PN............. Politicka Nastava [Political Training] [Military] (YU)
pn .... Polnoc [North] [Poland]
PN............. Polskie Normy [or Polska Norma] [Polish Standards] (POL)
PN............. Polynucleotide (RU)
PN............. Pordenone [Car registration plates] [Italy]
PN............. Preventive Adjustment, Preventive Maintenance (RU)
PN............. Projet de Norme (MCD)
PN............. Proviantni Nacelnik [Food Service Chief] (CZ)
PN............. Puolustusneuvosto [Defense Council] [Finland] (WEN)
PN............. Pyridine Nucleotide (RU)
PN............. Saturated Steam (RU)
PN............. Voltage Switch (RU)
pna .... Paivana [Finland]
PNA........... Pakistan National Alliance (PD)
PNA........... Palestinian National Authority [Political party] (ECON)
PNA........... Pamplona [Spain] [Airport symbol] (OAG)
PNA........... Pa-O National Army [Myanmar] [Political party] (EY)
PNA........... Parque Nacional de Araguaia [Brazil] (DSCA)
PNA........... Parti National Africain [African National Party] [Angola] (AF)
PNA........... Parti Nationale Africain [African National Party] [Chad] [Political party]
PNA........... Programa Nacional do Alcool [National Alcohol Program] [Brazil] (LA)
PNA........... Programmes Nationaux d'Applications [National Application Programs] [French] (ADPT)
PNA........... Temporary Directional Antenna (RU)
PNAM....... Padre-Nosso e Ave-Maria [Our Father and Hail Mary] [Portuguese]
PNAS........ Parque Nacional de Aparados da Serra [Brazil] (DSCA)
PNB .... Parque Nacional de Brasilia [Brazil] (DSCA)
PNB .... Partido ng Bayan [Party of the Nation] [Philippines] [Political party]
PNB .... Permodalan Nasional Bank [Malaysia]
PNB .... Philippine National Bank
PNB .... Product National Brut [Gross National Product - GNP] [Romanian] (RO)
PNB .... Produit National Brut [Gross National Product - GNP] [French]
PNB .... Proprietes Non Baties
PNBFT ...... Programa Nacional de Banano y Frutas Tropicales [National Banana and Tropical Fruit Program] [Ecuador] (LA)
PNC .... Pakistan National Congress [Political party]
PNC .... Palestine National Council (PD)
PNC .... Parque Nacional de Caparao [Brazil] (DSCA)
PNC .... Partido Nacional Ceuti [Ceuta National Party] [Political party] (PPW)
PNC .... Partido Nacional Conservador [Nicaragua] [Political party] (EY)

PNC .... Partido Nacional Cristiano [*National Christian Party*] [*Colorado*] [*Political party*] (EY)
PNC .... Partido Nacionalista Ceuti [*Political party*] (EY)
PNC .... Partidual Nationale Crestine [*National Christian Party*] [*Romania*] [*Political party*] (PPE)
PNC .... Parti National Caledonien [*Caledonian National Party*] [*Political party*] (PPW)
PNC .... People's National Congress [*Guyana*] (PD)
PNC .... Personnel Navigant Commercial
PNC .... Peruvian National Commission [*UNESCO*] (EAIO)
PNC .... Place Names Committee [*Victoria, Australia*]
PNC .... Power Reactor and Nuclear Fuel Development Corp. [*Japan*] (PDAA)
PNCA .... Programa Nacional de Capacitacion Agropecuaria [*Colombia*] (DSCA)
PNCB......... Pakistan Narcotics Control Board
PNCC .... Philippine National Construction Corp. (FEA)
PNCFN...... Permanent Nordic Committee on Food and Nutrition [*Copenhagen, Denmark*] (EAIO)
PNCH........ Partido Nacional Conservador de Honduras [*National Conservative Party of Honduras*] [*Political party*]
PNCIAWPRC ... Philippines National Committee of the International Association on Water Pollution Research and Control (EAIO)
PNCIAWPRC ... Portuguese National Committee of the International Association on Water Pollution Research and Control (EAIO)
PNCP......... Parti National de la Convention du Peuple
PNCS......... Programa Nacional de luta Contra a SIDA [*National AIDS Program*] [*Guinea-Bissau*] (EAIO)
pn d .... Engineer Combat Battalion (BU)
PND........... Low-Pressure Heater (RU)
PND........... Low-Pressure Polyethylene (RU)
PND........... Parti des Nationalistes du Dahomey [*Dahomean Nationalists Party*] [*Political party*]
PND........... Partido Nacional Democratico [*National Democratic Party*] [*Dominican Republic*] [*Political party*]
PND........... Partido Nacional Democratico [*National Democratic Party*] [*Costa Rica*] [*Political party*] (PPW)
PND........... Partidul National-Democrat [*National Democratic Party*] [*Romania*] [*Political party*] (PPE)
PND........... Parti National Democrate [*Morocco*] [*Political party*] (EY)
PND........... People for Nuclear Disarmament
PND........... Plano Nacional de Desenvolvimento [*National Development Plan*] [*Brazil*] (LA)
PND........... Punta Gorda [*Belize*] [*Airport symbol*] (OAG)
PND........... Slant-Range Correction (RU)
PNDA .... People for Nuclear Disarmament Australia [*An association*]
PNDB .... Pelerinage a Notre Dame de Beauraing [*An association*] (EAIO)
PNDC .... Partido Nacional de Democracia Centrista [*Chile*] [*Political party*] (EY)
PNDC .... Provisional National Defence Council [*Ghana*] (PD)
PNDD........ Parti National pour la Democratie et le Developpement [*Benin*] [*Political party*] (EY)
PNDT .... Parti Nationale pour la Developpement du Tchad [*National Party for the Development of Chad*]
PNDU........ Programa Nacional do Desenvolvimento Urbano [*National Urban Development Program*] [*Brazil*] (LA)
PNE .... Parque Nacional das Emas [*Brazil*] (DSCA)
PNE .... PASOK Nomarkhiaki Epitropi [*PASOK Nome Committee*] (GC)
PNE .... Polskie Normy Elektryczne [*Polish Electrical Standards*] (POL)
pne.............. Przed Nasza Era [*Before Our Era (Before Christ)*] (POL)
PNEB.......... Publishers National Environment Bureau [*Australia*]
PNed .... Pharmacopeia Nederlandsche [*Netherlands Pharmacopoeia*]
PNEM-APROME ... Partido Nacionalista Espanol de Melilla - Asociacion pro Melilla [*Spanish North Africa*] [*Political party*] (MENA)
PNEMEM ... Programa Nacional de Exportacao de Material de Emprego Militar [*National Policy for Export of Material for Military Use*] [*Brazil*] (LA)
PNEUROP ... European Committee of Manufacturers of Compressors, Vacuum Pumps, and Pneumatic Tools (EA)
pnev............ Pneumatic, Compressed-Air (RU)
PNF .... Palestine National Front [*Political party*] (PD)
PNF .... Palestine National Fund [*Palestine Liberation Organization*]
PNF .... Partito Nazionale Fascista [*National Fascist Party*] [*Italy*] [*Political party*] (PPE)
PNF .... Polynucleotide Phosphorylase (RU)
PNF .... Progressive National Front [*Syria*]
PNFTU...... Pakistan National Federation of Trade Unions
PNG.......... Papua New Guinea [*ANSI three-letter standard code*] (CNC)
PNG.......... Papua New Guinea Banking Corp.
PNG.......... Paranagua [*Brazil*] [*Airport symbol*] (OAG)
PNG.......... Partido Nacional Guevarista [*Ecuador*] [*Political party*] (PPW)
PNG.......... Philippine Newspaperworkers' Guild
PNGCC ..... Papua New Guinea Council of Churches (EAIO)
PNGDF ..... Papua New Guinea Defence Force [*Military*]

PNGI .... Papua New Guinea Institute of Chemistry
PNGPS...... Papua New Guinea Paediatric Society (EAIO)
PNGTUC .. Papua New Guinea Trade Union Congress
PNGWA .... Papua and New Guinea Workers' Association [*Australian New Guinea*]
PNH........... Partido Nacional Hondureno [*Honduran National Party*] [*Political party*]
PNH........... Parti National d'Haiti [*National Party of Haiti*] [*Political party*]
PNH........... Phnom Penh [*Cambodia*] [*Airport symbol*] (OAG)
PNI .... Aerovias de Poniente SA de CV [*Mexico*] [*ICAO designator*] (FAAC)
PNI .... Parque Nacional do Itatiaia [*Brazil*] (DSCA)
PNI .... Partai Nasional Indonesia [*Indonesian National Party*] (IN)
PNI .... Partai Nasionalis Indonesia [*Nationalist Party of Indonesia*] [*Political party*]
PNI .... Partido Nacional Independiente [*National Independent Party*] [*Costa Rica*] [*Political party*] (PPW)
PNI .... Partido Nacional Integracionista [*National Integration Party*] [*Venezuela*] (LA)
PNI .... Ponape [*Caroline Islands*] [*Airport symbol*] (OAG)
PNI .... Punjab Native Infantry [*India*]
PNIA .... Programa Nacional de Investigacion [*Honduras National Agricultural Research Program*] (EAS)
PNIC......... Pleasure Navigation International Joint Committee [*See also CINP*] [*The Hague, Netherlands*] (EAIO)
PNIG .... Parque Nacional de Iguacu [*Brazil*] (DSCA)
PNII.......... Pediatric Scientific Research Institute (RU)
PNIIIS....... Industrial and Scientific Research Institute for Engineering Surveys in Construction (RU)
PNIP......... Device for Beam Observation and Measurement [*Nuclear physics and engineering*] (RU)
PNIPA....... Plan Nacional de Integracion de la Poblacion [*National Plan for Integration of the Indian Population*] [*Lima, Peru*] (LAA)
PNIRO ...... Polar Scientific Research Institute of Sea Fisheries and Oceanography (RU)
PNIUI........ Moscow Region Scientific Research, Planning, and Design Institute of Coal (RU)
PNIUI........ Perm' Scientific Research Institute of Coal (RU)
p niz.......... Patrz Nizej [*See Below*] [*Poland*]
PNJALBB ... Peter Noone Just A Little Bit Better Promotion Club (EAIO)
pnk .... Peninkulma [*Finland*]
PNK .... Personalnummernkarte [*German*] (ADPT)
PNK .... Pontianak [*Indonesia*] [*Airport symbol*] (OAG)
PNKA .... Perusahaan Negara Kereta Api [*State Railway Company*] (IN)
PNKD .... Polski Narodowy Komitet Demokratyczny [*Polish National Democratic Committee*] [*In exile*] (POL)
PNL .... Aero Personal SA de CV [*Mexico*] [*ICAO designator*] (FAAC)
PNL .... Pakistan National League [*Political party*]
PNL .... Pantelleria [*Italy*] [*Airport symbol*] (OAG)
PNL .... Partidul National Liberal [*National Liberal Party*] [*Romania*] [*Political party*] (PPE)
PNL .... Parti National Liberal [*National Liberal Party*] [*Lebanon*] [*Political party*] (PPW)
PNL .... Philippine National Library (IMH)
PNL .... Prodotto Nazionale Lordo [*Gross National Product*] [*Use GNP*] [*Italian*] (WER)
PNLM .... Palestine National Liberation Movement [*Political party*] (BJA)
PNLRM..... Preferred National Land Rights Model [*Australia*]
PNM .... Pan-Somali Nationalist Movement [*Political party*]
PNM .... Partido Nacionalista de Mexicano [*Nationalist Party of Mexico*] [*Political party*]
PNM .... Partito Nazionale Monarchico [*National Monarchist Party*] [*Italy*] [*Political party*] (PPE)
PNM .... People's National Movement [*Trinidad and Tobago*] [*Political party*] (PD)
PNM-Aprome ... Partido Nacionalista de Melilla - Asociacion Pro Melilla [*Political party*] (EY)
PNN.......... Ground Observation Post (RU)
PNN.......... Low-Pressure Superheater (BU)
PNN.......... Prefectura Nacional Naval [*National Navy Prefecture*] [*Uruguay*] (LA)
PNN.......... Profesores Non Numerarios [*Extraordinary Professors*] [*Spanish*] (WER)
PNNV .... Net Positive Suction Head (RU)
PNO........... Assistant Chief of the Operations Section (RU)
PNO........... Deputy Chief of Staff for Operations (BU)
PNO........... Panellinios Navtiki Omospondia [*Panhellenic Seamen's Federation*] (GC)
PNO........... Pa-O National Organization [*Myanmar*] [*Political party*] (EY)
PNO........... Parti Nationaliste Occitan [*Occitanian Nationalist Party*] [*France*] [*Political party*] (PPE)
PNO........... Party for National Order [*Turkey*] [*Political party*] [*Defunct*] (MENA)
PNOC .... Philippine National Oil Company
PNOH .... Pozorista Narodnog Oslobodenja Hercegovine [*National Liberation Theaters of Hercegovina*] (YU)

PNOU........ Proleterska Narodnooslobodilacka Udarna [*Proletarian National Liberation Shock Troops*]   (YU)

PNOUB..... Proleterska Narodnooslobodilacka Udarna Brigada [*Proletarian National Liberation Shock Brigade*] [*World War II*]   (YU)

PNP .... Converter of Nonelectrical Parameters [*Computers*]   (RU)

PNP .... Forward Observation Post   (RU)

PNP .... Mobile Observation Post   (RU)

PNP .... Pakistan National Party [*Political party*]   (PD)

PNP .... Partido Nacionalista del Pueblo [*Bolivia*] [*Political party*]   (PPW)

PNP .... Partido Nacionalista ng Pilipinas [*Philippine Nationalist Party*] [*Political party*]   (EY)

PNP .... Partido Nacionalista Popular [*Popular Nationalist Party*] [*Panama*] [*Political party*]   (PPW)

PNP .... Partido Nacional Portugues [*Portuguese Nationalist Party*]   (WER)

PNP .... Partido Nashonal di Pueblo [*National People's Party*] [*Netherlands Antilles*] [*Political party*]   (EY)

PNP .... Partido Nuevo Progresista [*New Progressive Party*] [*Puerto Rico*] [*Political party*]   (PPW)

PNP .... Partidul National Poporului [*National People's Party*] [*Romania*] [*Political party*]   (PPE)

PNP .... Parti National du Progres [*National Progress Party*] [*Congo*] [*Political party*]

PNP .... Parti National Progressiste [*Haiti*] [*Political party*]   (EY)

PNP .... People's National Party [*Jamaica*] [*Political party*]   (PPW)

PNP .... People's National Party [*Ghana*] [*Political party*]   (PPW)

PNP .... Polish People's Republic   (BU)

PNP .... Popondetta [*Papua New Guinea*] [*Airport symbol*]   (OAG)

PNP .... Popular Nationalist Party [*Panama*] [*Political party*]   (PD)

PNP .... Progressive Nationalist Party [*Australia*]

PNP .... Progressive National Party [*Turks and Caicos Islands*] [*Political party*]   (PPW)

PNP .... Progressivnaia Nigerskaia Partiia

PNP .... Steam Reciprocating Pump, Steam Piston Pump   (RU)

PNPDD ..... Praxeis Nomikon Prosopon Dimosiou Dikaiou [*Acts of Legal Entities of Public Law*] [*Greek*]   (GC)

PNPG .... Parti National Populaire Guyanais [*French Guiana*] [*Political party*]   (EY)

PNPH .... Parti National Progressiste d'Haiti [*National Progressive Party of Haiti*] [*Political party*]

pn pk .... Engineer Combat Regiment   (BU)

PNPNOKDK ... Regulations on Imposing Fines by Organs of the State Control Commission   (BU)

PNPYO ...... People's National Party Youth Organization [*Jamaica*]   (LA)

PNQ.......... Poona [*India*] [*Airport symbol*]   (OAG)

PNQ.......... Provincial Newspapers (Queensland) Ltd. [*Australia*]

PNR .... Panair [*Spain*] [*ICAO designator*]   (FAAC)

PNR .... Partido Nacionalista Renovador [*Nationalist Renewal Party*] [*Guatemala*] [*Political party*]   (PPW)

PNR .... Partido Nacionalista Revolucionario [*Revolutionary Nationalist Party*] [*Ecuador*] [*Political party*]   (PPW)

PNR .... Partido Nacional Reformista [*Reformist National Party*] [*Guatemala*]   (LA)

PNR .... Partido Nacional Republicano [*National Republican Party*] [*Paraguay*] [*Political party*]

PNR .... Partido Nacional Republicano [*National Republican Party*] [*Portugal*] [*Political party*]   (PPE)

PNR .... Partido Nacional Revolucionario [*National Revolutionary Party*] [*Venezuela*] [*Political party*]

PNR .... Partij Nationalistische Republiek [*Nationalist Republic Party*] [*Surinam*] [*Political party*]   (PPW)

PNR .... Philippine National Railways   (DS)

PNR .... Pointe Noire [*Congo*] [*Airport symbol*]   (OAG)

PNR .... Policia Nacional Revolucionaria [*National Revolutionary Police*] [*Cuba*]   (LA)

PNR .... Polish People's Republic   (RU)

PNR .... Starting and Adjusting Operations   (BU)

PNR-44...... Partido Nacional Revolucionario de 44 [*National Revolutionary Party of 44*] [*Colorado*]   (LA)

PNRD .... Partido Nacionalista Revolucionario Democratico [*Democratic Revolutionary National Party*] [*Dominican Republic*]   (LA)

PNRS........ Programme National de Recherche sur le SIDA [*Syndrome Immuno-Deficitaire Acquis*] [*France*]

PNRSM..... Production Standards of Building Material Expenditure   (RU)

pn rt........... Engineer Combat Company   (BU)

PNS .... National Assembly Presidium   (BU)

PNS .... Observation and Signal Post   (RU)

PNS .... Pakistan National Shipping

PNS .... Philippines News Service

PNS .... Plovdiv People's Council   (BU)

PNS .... Pomocnik Nacelnika Stabu [*Assistant Chief-of-Staff*]   (CZ)

PNS .... Postovni Novinova Sluzba [*Postal Newspaper Subscription Service*]   (CZ)

PNS .... Prozatimni Narodni Shromazdeni [*Provisional National Assembly*]   (CZ)

PNS .... Survey Udara (Penas) PT [*Indonesia*] [*ICAO designator*]   (FAAC)

PNSC........ Pakistan National Shipping Corp.   (DS)

PNSC........ Parque Nacional de Sete Cidades [*Brazil*]   (DSCA)

PNSD .... Parti National pour la Solidarite et le Developpement [*Algeria*] [*Political party*]   (EY)

PNSFO ...... Pomocnik Nacelnika Staba za Fizicku Obuku [*Assistant to Chief of Staff for Physical Training*] [*Military*]   (YU)

PNSh .... Assistant Chief of Staff   (RU)

PNShR....... Assistant Chief of Staff for Intelligence   (RU)

PNSht .... Deputy Chief of Staff   (BU)

PNSJ .... Parque Nacional de Sao Joaquim [*Brazil*]   (DSCA)

PNSL .... Perbadanan Nasional Shipping Line Bhd [*Malaysia*]   (EY)

PNSO .... Parque Nacional de Serra dos Orgaos   (DSCA)

PNSO .... Plovdiv People's Sports Organization   (BU)

PNSS .... Philippine National Science Society   (IRC)

PNT .... Device for the Adjustment of Television Sets   (RU)

PNT .... It Is Clear [*Telegraphy*]   (RU)

Pnt............. Panart [*Record label*] [*Cuba, USA*]

PNT .... Parque Nacional de Tijuca [*Brazil*]   (DSCA)

PNT .... Partido Nacionalista de los Trabajadores [*Argentina*] [*Political party*]   (EY)

PNT .... Partidul National Taranesc [*National Peasant Party*]   (RO)

PNT .... Parti National du Travail [*Haiti*] [*Political party*]   (EY)

PNT .... Parti National du Travail [*Benin*] [*Political party*]   (EY)

PNT .... Party of New Turkey   (RU)

PNT .... Personnel Navigant Technique

Pnt............. Point [*Point*] [*Military map abbreviation World War I*] [*French*]   (MTD)

PNT .... Ponitrianske Tehelne [*Nitra Brick Works*]   (CZ)

PNTC........ Parti National Travailliste Camerounais [*Cameroonian National Labor Party*]   (AF)

PNTL........ Polskie Naukowe Towarzystwo Lesne [*Polish Scientific Society for Forestry*]   (POL)

PNTs........ Guidance and Target Identification Point   (RU)

PNU .... Mobile Magnetizer [*Weld inspection device*]   (RU)

PNU .... Palestine National Union   (BJA)

PNU .... Peasants' National Unity [*Afghanistan*] [*Political party*]   (EY)

PNU .... Postovni Novinovy Urad [*Postal Newspaper Subscription Office*] [*CZ*]

PNU.......... Regulations on Teachers' Appointments   (BU)

PNUA .... Partito Nazionale Unito Africa [*National Party of United Africans*] [*Somalia*] [*Political party*]

PNUC........ Provisional National Unity Council [*Romania*]   (EE)

PNUD........ Programa de las Naciones Unidas para el Desarrollo [*United Nations Development Program - UNDP*] [*Spanish*]   (MSC)

PNUD........ Programme des Nations Unies pour le Developpement [*United Nations Development Program*] [*Use UNDP*] [*French*]   (CL)

PNUD........ Programul Natiunilor Unite pentru Dezvoltare [*United Nations Development Program*]   (RO)

PNUDE ..... Programa das Nacoes Unidas para o Desenvolvimento [*United Nations Development Program*] [*Portuguese*]   (WER)

PNUE .... Programme des Nations Unies pour l'Environnement [*United Nations Environment Program*] [*Use UNEP*] [*French*]   (AF)

P/NUEE.... Programmierbare Nachrichtenuebertragungseinheit [*German*]   (ADPT)

PNUI .... Parti National Uni de l'Independance

PNULAD .. United Nations Program for Drug Abuse Control [*Use UNPDAC*]   (AF)

PNUMA .... Programa de las Naciones Unidas para el Medio Ambiente [*United Nations Environmental Programme Regional Office for Latin America*]   (EAIO)

PNUO....... Progressive National Unionist Organization [*Egypt*]   (ME)

PNV .... High Pressure Superheater   (BU)

PNV .... National Velasquista Party [*Ecuador*] [*Political party*]   (PPW)

PNV .... Night Vision Device   (RU)

PNV .... Panavia SA [*ICAO designator*]   (FAAC)

PNV .... Partido Nacionalista Vasco [*Basque Nationalist Party*] [*Spain*] [*Political party*]   (PPE)

PNV .... Partido Nacional Velasquista [*National Velasquista Party*] [*Ecuador*] [*Political party*]   (PPW)

PNV .... Parti National Voltaique [*Voltaic National Party*] [*Political party*]

PNV .... "Voltage-Time" Converter   (RU)

PNVC .... Partido Nacional de Veteranos Civiles [*Civilian Veterans National Party*] [*Dominican Republic*]   (LA)

pn-wsch...... Polnocno-Wschodni [*North-East*] [*Poland*]

PNYME..... Papir- es Nyomdaipari Muszaki Egyesulet [*Technical Association of the Paper and Printing Industry*]   (HU)

PNZ .... Panstwowe Nieruchomosci Ziemskie [*Poland*]

PNZ .... Petrolina [*Brazil*] [*Airport symbol*]   (OAG)

PNZ .... Poljoprivredni Nakladni Zavod [*Agricultural Publishing Institute*] [*Zagreb*]   (YU)

pn-zach....... Polnocno-Zachodni [*North-West*] [*Poland*]

PNZP........	Polnohospodarsky Nakupny a Zasobovaci Podnik [*Agricultural Supply and Purchase Enterprise*] (CZ)
PO..............	Advance Detachment (BU)
PO..............	Aircraft Designed by N. N. Polikarpov (RU)
PO..............	Auxiliary Organization (BU)
PO..............	Border Guard [*Detachment*] (RU)
PO..............	Bypass Switch (RU)
PO..............	Check Point Bearing (RU)
PO..............	Consumers' Society (RU)
PO..............	Cross Pollination (RU)
PO..............	Departure Yard, Advance Yard [*Railroads*] (RU)
PO..............	Exhaust Steam (RU)
PO..............	Foaming Agent, Frothing Agent (RU)
PO..............	Mobile Defense (RU)
po..............	Pachtovereenkomst [*Benelux*] (BAS)
PO..............	Pamiatnik Oslobodenia [*Liberation Memorial*] (CZ)
P-O..............	Paris-Orleans [*French*]
PO..............	Parliamentary Officer [*Australia*]
PO..............	Par Ordre De [*By Order Of*] [*In the context of signatures at the end of memos or documents*] [*French*] (CL)
po..............	Partisan Detachment (RU)
PO..............	Partizanski Odredi [*Partisan Detachments*] [*World War II*] (YU)
Po..............	Paseo [*Avenue*] [*Spanish*]
po..............	Pelniacy Obowiazki [*Acting Chief*] (POL)
PO..............	Permit Office [*British*] (ROG)
po..............	Pero [*But*] [*Spanish*]
PO..............	Petrol Ofisi [*Petroleum Office*] [*TPO*] [*See also*] (TU)
Po..............	Pico [*Peak*] [*Pco*] [*See also*] [*Spanish*] (NAU)
Po..............	Pico [*Peak*] [*Pco*] [*See also*] [*Portuguese*] (NAU)
PO..............	Pionyrska Organisace [*Pioneer Organization*] (CZ)
po..............	Pitaa Olla [*Finland*]
PO..............	Planning Department, Planning Section (RU)
PO..............	Poder Obrero [*Worker Power*] [*Argentina*] (LA)
PO..............	Podnikova Organisace [*Enterprise Organization*] [*A periodical*] (CZ)
PO..............	Podvodno Oruzje [*Underwater Weapons*] [*Military*] (YU)
PO..............	Political Department, Political Section (RU)
PO..............	Political Officer [*NATO*]
PO..............	Politicke Oddeleni [*Political Department*] (CZ)
PO..............	Politicky Oddil [*Political Department*] (CZ)
Po..............	Polonio [*Chemical element*] [*Portuguese*]
PO..............	Polskie Zaklady Lotnicze [*Poland*] [*ICAO aircraft manufacturer identifier*] (ICAO)
PO..............	Pom Operupolnomochennyy [*Junior Case Officer*] [*Soviet military rank*]
PO..............	Por Orden [*By Order*] [*Spanish*]
PO..............	Portugal [*NATO*]
po..............	Posebni Odtis [*Special Reprint*] (YU)
PO..............	Posorder [*Postal Order*] [*Afrikaans*]
PO..............	Poste d'Observation [*Military*] [*French*] (MTD)
PO..............	Post Office (RU)
Po..............	Postzug [*Mail Train*] (EG)
PO..............	Potere Operaio [*Workers' Power*] [*Italian*] (WER)
Po..............	Pouce [*Inch*] [*French*] (MTD)
Po..............	Pour Ordre [*French*] (MTD)
PO..............	Prednji Odred [*Advanced Detachment*] [*Military*] (YU)
PO..............	Presbyterorum Ordinis [*Decree on the Ministry and Life of Priests*] [*Vatican II document*]
PO..............	Privremeno Otsutan [*Temporarily Absent*] [*Census*] (YU)
PO..............	Processing Station (RU)
PO..............	Projektne Organizacije [*Industrial Designing Organizations*] (YU)
PO..............	Protiletecka Obrana [*Antiaircraft Defense*] (CZ)
PO..............	Provincie Ordonnantie [*Benelux*] (BAS)
PO..............	Pruzkumny Oddil [*Reconnaissance Battalion*] (CZ)
po..............	Puheena Oleva [*Finland*]
Po..............	Pulo [*Island*] [*Malay*] (NAU)
P-O..............	Pyrenees-Orientales [*French*]
PO..............	Receiving-Departure Yard [*Railroads*] (RU)
PO..............	Refracted and Reflected (Wave) (RU)
PO..............	Security on the March, March Security (RU)
PO..............	Starting Unit (RU)
p/o..............	Subdivision (RU)
PO..............	Turnover Period (RU)
PO..............	Verification Paid [*Telegraphy*] (RU)
POA...........	Le Point Air [*France*] [*ICAO designator*] (FAAC)
POA...........	Panellinios Omospondia Aliergaton [*Panhellenic Federation of Fishing Industry Workers*]
POA...........	Panellinios Omospondia Artergaton [*Panhellenic Federation of Bakery Workers*] (GC)
POA...........	Pankyprios Organosis Anapiron [*Pan-Cyprian Organization of the Disabled*] (GC)
POA...........	Pezoporikos Omilos Athinon [*Athens Walking Club*] (GC)
POA...........	Pontificia Opera di Assistenza [*Pontifical Relief Organization*]
POA...........	Porto Alegre [*Brazil*] [*Airport symbol*] (OAG)
POA...........	Portugees-Oos-Afrika [*Portuguese East Africa*] [*Afrikaans*]
POA...........	Prison Officers' Association [*A union*] [*British*] (DCTA)
POA...........	Public Order Act [*Mauritius*] (AF)
POAA........	Pankyprios Organosis Apokatastaseos Anapiron [*Pan-Cyprian Rehabilitation Organization for the Handicapped*] (GC)
POAA........	Post Office Agents' Association [*Australia*]
POAAP......	Panellinios Omospondia Astegon Aston Prosfygon [*Panhellenic Federation of Homeless Urban Refugees*] (GC)
POAAPS ...	Permanent Organization for Afro-Asian Peoples Solidarity
POAB........	Persatuan Olahraga Amatur Brunei [*Brunei Amateur Athletic Association*] (EAIO)
POAC	Port and Ocean Engineering Under Arctic Conditions International Committee (EAIO)
POAEA	Panellinios Organosis Agoniston Ethnikis Andistaseos [*Panhellenic Organization of National Resistance Fighters*] (GC)
POAM.......	Petty Officer Air Mechanician [*Australia*]
POANSW ...	Property Owners' Association of New South Wales [*Australia*]
POAP	Pangosmios Omospondia Adelfopoiimenon Poleon [*World Federation of Sister Cities*] (GC)
POAQ	Property Owners' Association of Queensland [*Australia*]
poarm........	Army Political Section (RU)
POAS........	Pankypria Omospondia Anexartiton Syntechnion [*Pancyprian Federation of Independent Trade Unions*] [*Cyprus*]
POAS........	Pankyprios Omospondia Anexartiton Syntekhnion [*Pan-Cyprian Federation of Independent Trade Unions*] (GC)
POAYA	Panellinios Omospondia Artergaton kai Ypallilon Artou [*Panhellenic Federation of Bakery Workers*] (GC)
POAYL......	Panellinios Omospondia Avtokinitiston Yperastikon Leoforeion [*Panhellenic Federation of Interurban Bus Drivers*] (GC)
POAYS......	Panellinios Omospondia Avtokinitiston Yperastikon Syngoinonion [*Panhellenic Federation of Drivers in Interurban Transportation*] (GC)
POB	Paris Opera Ballet
POB	Parti Ouvrier Belge [*Belgian Workers' Party*] [*Later, Belgian Socialist Party*] [*Political party*] (PPE)
POB	Partizansko Obavestajni Biro [*Partisan Information Bureau*] [*World War II*] (YU)
POB	Post Office Box (PWGL)
pober	Shore, Coast (RU)
POBNS......	Regulation on Relations with Banks in the National Economy (BU)
POC	Parti des Ouvriers Chretiens [*Christian Workers Party*] [*Belgium*] (WER)
POC	Parti d'Opposition Congolais [*Congolese Opposition Party*] [*Political party*]
POC	Pevecka Obec Ceskoslovenska [*Czechoslovak Choral Society*] (CZ)
POc	Porte-Oceane [*Record label*] [*France*]
POC	Proche-Orient Chretien (FLAF)
POC	Public Oil Co. [*Sudan*] (PDAA)
POC	Public Order Company (ML)
POCB	Philippine Overseas Construction Board (DS)
POCCC	Parents on Campus Childcare Centre [*Canberra, Australia*]
POCD	Petty Officer Clearance Diver [*Australia*]
POCH........	Progressiven Organisationen der Schweiz [*Progressive Organizations of Switzerland*] [*Political party*] (PPE)
poch..........	Spadix [*Botany*], Cop [*Textiles*] (RU)
po Chr	Po Chrystusie [*Poland*]
pocht	Post Office (RU)
pocht	Post, Postal, Mail (RU)
pocht -tel	Postal and Telegraphic, Post and Telegraph (RU)
pochv.........	Soil, Ground (RU)
pochv gidr ..	Soil Hydrology (RU)
pochvkompl ...	Soil Complex (RU)
pochvMin ...	Soil Mineralogy (RU)
pochvoobr...	Soil-Cultivating (RU)
POCM.......	Partido Obrero y Campesino de Mexico [*Mexico*] [*Political party*]
POCO.......	European Political Cooperation [*EC*] (ECED)
POCOX	Petty Officer Coxswain [*Australia*]
POCSM.....	Pionierska Organizacia Ceskoslovenskeho Svazu Mladeze [*Pioneer Organization of the Czechoslovak Union of Youth*] (CZ)
POCTA......	Prevention of Cruelty to Animals Society Member (DSUE)
pod	Approach Road, Porch, Entrance (RU)
POD..........	Division Dressing Detachment (RU)
POD..........	Podor [*Senegal*] [*Airport symbol*] (OAG)
POD..........	Pracownicze Ogrody Dzialkowe [*Employees' Garden Plots*] (POL)
POD..........	Preduzece za Obradu Duvana [*Tobacco Processing Establishment*] (YU)
pod	Signature (BU)
pod	Similar (BU)
pod	Similar, Like, Such (RU)
PODC	Philippine Oceanographic Data Center (MSC)

PODERI.... Programa de Desarrollo Rural Integral [*Integral Rural Development Program*] [*Nicaragua*]   (LA)

PODG........ Pangosmios Organismos Dimokratikon Gynaikon [*World Federation of Democratic Women*]   (GC)

podgot........ Preparation, Prepared   (RU)

podgr.......... Subgroup [*Artillery*]   (BU)

podigr......... Ironical   (BU)

podiv........... Political Section of a Division   (RU)

PODKO..... Powiatowy Osrodek Doskonalenia Kadr Oswiatowych [*County Center for Improvement of Educational Personnel*]   (POL)

Podlodkomin ... Minelaying Submarine   (RU)

PODN........ Pangosmios Organosis Dimokratikis Neolaias [*World Federation of Democratic Youth*]   (GC)

podn .... Podnaslov [*Subtitle*]   (YU)

podobr .... Improved   (BU)

Podolskhar ... Podol'sk Branch of the Sugar Trust   (RU)

podp .... Signature, Signed   (RU)

podp kpech ... Approved for Printing   (RU)

podplav...... Underwater Navigation   (RU)

podpolk...... Lieutenant Colonel   (RU)

podr .... Podrecznik [*Textbook*]   (POL)

pod red .... Edited By   (BU)

PODREM ... Rolling Stock Repair Train   (RU)

podrukovod ... Under the Leadership Of   (RU)

podsem .... Subfamily   (RU)

podst el....... Electric Substation   (RU)

podstroch ... Interlinear   (RU)

podstrochprimech ... Footnote   (RU)

podtyt......... Podtytul [*Subtitle*] [*Publishing*] [*Poland*]

podv........... Bound [*Book*]   (BU)

podv........... Underwater [*Topography*]   (RU)

podvizh....... Mobile, Movable   (RU)

PODY .... Pankyprios Organosis Dimokratikon Gynaikon [*Pan-Cyprian Organization of Democratic Women*]   (GC)

Podyemtranskomplekt ... Trust for Making Up Complete Sets of Hoisting and Conveying Equipment   (RU)

podzagl....... Subtitle   (BU)

podzagol..... Subtitle, Subhead   (RU)

Podzemgaz ... All-Union Experimental Office for the Surveying, Planning, and Construction of Experimental Mines for Underground Coal Gasification   (RU)

POE .... Pacific Orient Express   (WDAA)

POE .... Patriarkhiki Oikonomiki Epitropi [*Patriarchal Finance Committee*]   (GC)

POE .... Peace on Earth [*Australia*] [*Political party*]

POE .... Plan of Organization of Operations   (RU)

POE .... Polyoxyethylene Glycol   (RU)

POEA .... Pankypria Omospondia Efedron Axiomatikon [*Pan-Cyprian Federation of Reserve Officers*]   (GC)

POEA .... Philippines Overseas Employment Administration   (PDAA)

POE(AW) ... Petty Officer Electrician (Air Weapon) [*Australia*]

POED .... Pankyprios Organosis Ellinon Didaskalon [*Pan-Cyprian Greek Teachers Organization*]   (GC)

POEEYTE ... Panellinios Omospondia Ergaton Episistimou kai Ypallilon Touristikon Epangelmaton [*Panhellenic Federation of Food Supply and Tourist Trades Workers*]   (GC)

POEI......... Panellinios Omospondia Ergatoypallilon Imatismou [*Panhellenic Federation of Garment Workers and Employees*]   (GC)

POEK .... Panellinios Omospondia Ergatoypallilon Kreatos [*Panhellenic Federation of Meat Industry Workers and Employees*]   (GC)

POEKO ..... Panellinia Omospondia Emborikon Kladikon Organoseon [*Panhellenic Federation of Commercial Branch Organizations*]   (GC)

POELIME ... Pankyprios Organosis Ellinon Leitourgon Idiotikis Mesis Ekpaidevseos [*Pan-Cyprian Organization of Greek Private Secondary School Teachers*]   (GC)

POEM .... Panellinios Omospondia Ergaton Metallou [*Panhellenic Federation of Metal Workers*]   (GC)

POEM .... Petty Officer Electrical Mechanician [*Australia*]

POEO .... Panellinios Omospondia Ergatotekhniton Oikodomon [*Panhellenic Federation of Building Trades Workers*]   (GC)

POEOX ..... Panellinios Omospondia Ergatoypallilon Oikodomon kai Xylou [*Panhellenic Federation of Construction and Lumber Workers*]   (GC)

POES........ Pangosmios Omospondia ton Ergatikon Syndikaton [*World Federation of Trade Unions*]   (GC)

poet............ Poetic   (RU)

Poet .... Poetica [*Poetics*] [*Portuguese*]

poet............ Poetic Word   (BU)

poet............ Poetique [*French*]   (TPFD)

POETRI .... Programme on Exchange and Transfer of Information on Community Water Supply and Sanitation [*International Reference Center for Community Water Supply and Sanitation*] [*Information service or system*]   (IID)

POEYGTP ... Panellinios Omospondia Ergatotekhniton-Ypallilon Galaktos, Trofimon, kai Poton [*Panhellenic Federation of Milk, Food, and Beverage Personnel*]   (GC)

POEYPEPG ... Panellinios Omospondia Ergatotekhniton kai Ypallilon Paragogis, Epexergasias, kai Poliseos Galaktos [*Panhellenic Federation of Milk Production, Processing, and Sales Personnel*]   (GC)

POF .... Complete Evaluative Functions   (RU)

POF .... Fixed Capital Increment   (RU)

POF .... Pretres de l'Oratoire de France   (EAIO)

POFE......... Panellinios Organosis Filelevtheron Ellinidon [*Panhellenic Organization of Liberal Women*]   (GC)

POFI......... Pacific Oceanic Fishery Investigations   (ASF)

POFI......... Panellinios Omospondia Fotos kai Ikhou [*Panhellenic Federation of Light and Sound*]   (GC)

POFIS .... Postovni Filatelisticka Sluzba [*Postal Stamp Collector Service*]   (CZ)

POFNE...... Pankypria Omospondia Foititon kai Neon Epistimonon [*Pan-Cyprian Federation of Students and Young Professionals*]   (GC)

POG.......... Panelladiki Omospondia Gynaikon [*Panhelladic Federation of Women*]   (GC)

POG .... Port Gentil [*Gabon*] [*Airport symbol*]   (OAG)

POGaz .... Post Office Gazette [*British*] [*A publication*]   (DCTA)

POGEI...... Philippine Oil and Geothermal Energy Inc.

pogl .... Absorption   (RU)

pog m......... Linear Meter, Running Meter   (RU)

POGO....... Pankyprios Omospondia Gynaikeion Organoseon [*Pan-Cyprian Federation of Women's Organizations*]   (GC)

pogov......... Proverb   (RU)

pogresk ...... Border Guard Troop [*Cav.*]   (RU)

pogr kom .... Border Guard Commandant's Office [*Topography*]   (RU)

pogr st .... Frontier Post [*Marker*] [*Topography*]   (RU)

pogruz .... Loading and Unloading Platform [*Topography*]   (RU)

pogr zast..... Frontier Post   (RU)

POGSJAM ... Propagandno Odelenje pri Glavniot Stab na Jugoslovenskata Armija za Makedonija [*Propaganda Department in the General Headquarters of the Yugoslav Army of Macedonia*] [*World War II*]   (YU)

POH.......... Partizanski Odredi Hrvatske [*Croatian Partisan Detachments*] [*World War II*]   (YU)

pohj .... Pohjois [*Northern*] [*Finland*]

POHM....... Prisoner of His Majesty [*Australia*]

poHr........... Po Hrista [*In the Year of Our Lord*]   (YU)

POI .... Parti Oubanguien de l'Independance [*Ubangi Independence Party*] [*Political party*]

POIA .... Panstwowa Organizacja Imprez Artystycznych [*Poland*]

POIAArtos ... Panstwowa Organizacja Imprez Artystycznych "Artos" ["*Artos*" *State Organization for Artistic Performances*]   (POL)

POIAL....... Panellinios Omospondia Idioktiton Astikon Leoforeion [*Panhellenic Federation of Urban Bus Owners*]   (GC)

POIDON ... Regulation on Expropriation of Property for State and Public Needs   (RU)

POiE......... Pomorska Odlewnia i Emaliernia [*Pomerania Metal-Working and Enameling Plant*]   (POL)

POIEKO.... Panellinios Omospondia Ilektrismou kai Epikheiriseon Koinis Ofeleias [*Panhellenic Federation of Electric Power and Public Utility Enterprises*]   (GC)

POIT......... Powiatowy Osrodek Informacji Turystycznej [*District Tourist Information Center*] [*Poland*]

POJ........... Partizanski Odredi Jugoslavije [*Partisan Detachments of Yugoslavia*] [*World War II*]   (YU)

POJ........... Pionyrske Oddily Junaka [*Pioneer Units of the Junak Organization*]   (CZ)

poj .... Pojedynczy [*Single*]   (POL)

POK.......... Panellinion Oikologikon Kinima [*Panhellenic Ecological Movement*]   (GC)

pok .... Pokoj [*Room*]   (POL)

POK .... Postai Oktatasi Kozpont [*Postal Training Center*]   (HU)

POKB .... Panstwowy Osrodek Ksztalcenia Bibliotekarzy [*State Center for the Education of Librarians*]   (POL)

POKE .... Panellinios Organosis Kinimatografikon Epikheiriseon [*Panhellenic Organization of Motion Picture Enterprises*]   (GC)

POKh........ [*The*] Organic Chemistry Industry   (RU)

POKhI....... Plovdiv Okrug Art Exhibit   (BU)

POKLJDZ ... Preduzece za Opravku Kola i Lokomotiva Jugoslovanske Drzavne Zeleznice [*Car and Locomotive Repair Establishment of the Yugoslav Railroads*]   (YU)

Pokobank... Bank of Consumers' Cooperatives   (RU)

pok prel..... Index of Refraction, Refractive Index   (RU)

POKY .... Panellinios Omospondia Koinotikon Ypallilon [*Panhellenic Federation of Communal Employees*]   (GC)

pol .... Glade, Clearing [*Topography*]   (RU)

pol .... Half   (RU)

POL .... Pacific Ocean Lines   (DS)

POL .... Panellinios Omospondia Logiston [*Panhellenic Accountants Federation*] (GC)
POL .... Pemba [*Mozambique*] [*Airport symbol*] (OAG)
POL .... Petroleum, Oil, and Lubricants (CL)
POL .... Poland [*ANSI three-letter standard code*] (CNC)
POL .... Polar International Airlines, Inc. [*ICAO designator*] (FAAC)
pol .... Polarization (RU)
pol .... Polegada [*Inch*] [*Portuguese*]
pol .... Polert [*Polished*] [*Danish/Norwegian*]
pol .... Polish (BU)
Pol .... Political (PWGL)
pol .... Politics (TPFD)
pol .... Politie [*Benelux*] (BAS)
pol .... Politiikka [*Politics*] [*Finland*]
pol .... Politika [*or Politikai*] [*Politics or Political*] (HU)
pol .... Politique [*French*] (TPFD)
pol .... Politisch [*German*]
Pol .... Polizei [*German*]
pol .... Polones [*Portuguese*]
pol .... Polowa [*Half*] (POL)
pol .... Polski [*Polish*] (POL)
Pol .... Poluostrov [*Peninsula*] [*Pov*] [*See also*] [*Russian*] (NAU)
Pol .... Polydor & Deutsche Grammophon [*Record label*] [*Germany, Europe, etc.*]
Pol .... Polyphon [*Record label*] [*Denmark, etc.*]
pol .... Polytechnisch [*Polytechnical*] [*German*] (GCA)
Pol .... Tribunal de Police [*Benelux*] (BAS)
POLAG ..... Panellinios Omospondia Leoforeioukhon Agonon Grammon [*Panhellenic Federation of Unprofitable Bus Line Operators*] (GC)
polarograph ... Polarographisch [*Polarographic*] [*German*] (GCA)
POLAS ...... Polizei-Auskunftssystem [*Police Information System*] [*German*] (ADPT)
PolBer .... Politica Berichten [*Benelux*] (BAS)
PolBrux...... Jugement du Tribunal de Simple Police de Bruxelles [*Belgium*] (BAS)
POL-DER ... Polis Dernegi [*Police Association*] [*of a particular city*] (TU)
POLDOK .. Politische Dokumentation
polem......... Polemika [*Polemic*] (POL)
Pol Etr....... Politique Etrangere (FLAF)
POLEX-NORTH ... Polar Experiment in the Northern Hemisphere (MSC)
POLEX-SOUTH ... Polar Experiment in the Southern Hemisphere (MSC)
polg .... Polgari [*Civilian*] (HU)
polg m........ Polgarmester [*Mayor*] (HU)
Polgos .... Polskie Wydawnictwa Gospodarcze [*Polish Publishing House for Economics*] (POL)
Pol grad...... Polymerizationsgrad [*Degree of Polymerization*] [*German*]
POLICOLDA ... Poliolefinas Colombiana Ltda. [*Girardota-Antioquia*] (COL)
poligr......... Polygraphic (BU)
poligr......... Printing (RU)
poligr......... Printing Industry Factory [*Topography*] (RU)
Poligrafizdat ... Department of Publishing Houses and the Printing Industry (RU)
Poligrafkniga ... Book and Magazine Printing Trust (RU)
poligrafprom ... Printing Industry (RU)
Poligrafsoyuz ... Union of Printing Trade Workers (RU)
polikonom ... Political Economy (BU)
POLILAGO ... Polimeros del Lago CA [*Venezuela*]
POLINAL ... Policia Nacional [*National Police*] [*Colombia*] (COL)
Polinale...... Police Nationale [*National Police*] [*Cambodia*] (CL)
polir......... Polished (RU)
polir shl...... Polished Section (RU)
POLIS .... Politische Informations Systeme
POLISARIO ... Frente Popular para la Liberacion de Saguia El Hamra y Rio De Oro [*Popular Front for the Liberation of Saguia El Hamra and Rio De Oro*] [*Saharan*] (AF)
polit........... Political (BU)
polit........... Politisch [*German*]
POLITBUREAU ... Political Bureau [*of USSR*]
POLITBURO ... Politicheskoe Byuro [*Political Bureau of USSR*]
Politbyuro .. Political Bureau (BU)
Politbyurona TsK na BKP ... Politburo of the BCP [*Bulgarian Communist Party*] Central Committee (BU)
politekhn.... Polytechnic, Polytechnical (RU)
Politemigrant ... Political Exile (BU)
Politizdat.... Publishing House of Political Literature (RU)
politkom..... Political Commissar (RU)
politkom..... Politicki Komesar [*Political Commissar*] [*Communist Party*] (YU)
Politotdel ... Political Department (BU)
politprosvet ... Political Education Administration, Political Education Directorate, Political Education Committee (RU)
Politsekretar ... Political Secretary (BU)
politupr...... Political Administration, Political Directorate (RU)
Politupravlenie ... Political Administration (BU)
Politvod...... Political Administration of Water Transportation (RU)

Politzatvornik ... Political Prisoner (BU)
POLJCOPSKBA ... Poduzece za Opskrbu Poljoprivrede [*Agricultural Supply Establishment*] (YU)
POLJOOTKUP ... Poljoprivredno Otkupno Preduzece [*Agricultural Purchasing Establishment*] (YU)
POLJOPRODUKT ... Preduzece za Promet Poljoprivrednih Proizvoda [*Agricultural Products Trade Establishment*] (YU)
POLJOPROIZVOD ... Preduzece za Promet Poljoprivrednih Proizvoda [*Agricultural Products Trade Establishment*] (YU)
POLJOPROMET ... Preduzece za Promet Poljoprivrednih Proizvoda [*Agricultural Products Trade Establishment*] (YU)
POLJOTRGOVINA ... Preduzece za Promet Poljoprivrednih Proizvoda [*Agricultural Products Trade Establishment*] (YU)
polk .... Colonel (BU)
polkinzh ..... Regimental Engineer (RU)
polkom .... Political Commissar [*Communist Party*] (RU)
polkom .... Politicki Komesar [*Political Commissar*] [*Communist Party*] (YU)
polm .... Polymorph [*Polymorphous*] [*German*] (GCA)
POLMAR ... Plan de la Lutte Contre les Pollutions Marines Accidentelles [*French*] (MSC)
POLMO .... Zjednoczenie Przemyslu Motoryzacyjnego [*Automobile Industry Association*] [*Poland*]
Polnar .... Polska Wytwornia Narzedzi [*Polish Tool Plant*] (POL)
Poln P .... Polnisches Patent [*Polish Patent*] [*German*] (GCA)
Poln sobrsoch ... Complete Collection of Works, Complete Works (RU)
Polocean..... Polskie Linie Oceaniczne [*Polish Ocean Lines*] (POL)
POLOCENTRO ... Programa de Desenvolvimento dos Cerrados [*Scrublands Development Program*] [*Brazil*] (LA)
Polokr .... Politicky Okres [*Political District*] (CZ)
POLONORDESTE ... Programa de Desenvolvimento de Areas Integradas do Nordeste [*Program for the Development of Integrated Areas of the Northeast*] [*Brazil*] (LA)
Polotn......... Linen Factory [*Topography*] (RU)
polozh........ Positive (BU)
polozhit....... Positive (RU)
pol postsvkh ... Sovkhoz Field Structures [*Topography*] (RU)
Polpred....... Political Representative (BU)
polr............ Polrocznie [*Semiannual*] (POL)
POLRI .... Kepolisian Negara Republik Indonesia [*Republic of Indonesia State Police*] (IN)
Pol Sci........ Political Science (PWGL)
pol'sk......... Polish (RU)
polsk.......... Polskorek [*Half-Binding*] [*Poland*]
pol st .... Field Camp [*Topography*] (RU)
pol st .... Polar Station (RU)
polud .... Poludnie [*South*] [*Poland*]
polupl......... Poluplatno [*Half-Linen*] [*Binding*] (YU)
poluprovodn ... Semiconductor (RU)
Polw .... Polwysep [*Peninsula*] [*Poland*]
POLYAG... Panellinios Omospondia Leoforeioukhon Yperastikon Agonon Grammon [*Panhellenic Federation of Unprofitable Interurban Bus Line Operators*] (GC)
polyarograf ... Polarographic (RU)
polych........ Polychrome [*Multicolored*] [*French*]
polychr....... Polychrome [*Multicolored*] [*French*]
Polyg.......... Polygone [*Proving Ground, Artillery Range*] [*Military map abbreviation World War I*] [*French*] (MTD)
POLYMAT ... Polymer Materials [*Deutsches Kunststoff-Institut*] [*Germany*] [*Information service or system*] (CRD)
POLYMODE ... Polygon-MODE [*Mid-Ocean Dynamics Experiment*] [*Soviet-US cooperative undersea weather exploration*]
POLZAR ... Polis Pazari [*Police Market*] (TU)
pom .... Assistant (RU)
pom .... Assistant, Deputy (RU)
pom .... Building [*In addresses*] (RU)
POM.......... Panstwowe Osrodki Maszynowe [*State (Agricultural) Machine Stations*] (POL)
POM.......... Pays d'Outre-Mer (FLAF)
POM.......... Polisi Militer [*Military Police*] (IN)
pom .... Pomeridiane [*Afternoon*] [*Italian*] (GPO)
POM.......... Port Moresby [*Papua New Guinea*] [*Airport symbol*] (OAG)
POM.......... Postaugyi Miniszterium/Miniszter [*Ministry/Minister of the Post*] (HU)
POM.......... Prise des Origines Machine [*French*] (ADPT)
POMAG.... Societe de Grands Magasins de Pointe-Noire
pomb .... Pontoon-Bridge Battalion (RU)
pombr......... Pontoon-Bridge Brigade (RU)
pombrig...... Assistant Brigade Leader (RU)
POME .... Panellinios Omospondia Mousikon Ellados [*Panhellenic Federation of Greek Musicians*] (GC)
POME .... Prisoner of Mother England [*Nineteenth-century convict in penal colony of Australia, now a nickname for any Australian*]
pomgol .... Committee for Famine Relief [*1921-1922*] (RU)
pomkombat ... Assistant Battalion Commander (RU)
pomkombrig ... Assistant Brigade Commander (RU)

pomkomdiv ... Assistant Division Commander (RU)
pomkomroty ... Assistant Company Commander (RU)
pomkomvzod ... Assistant Platoon Commander (RU)
pomkomvzoda ... Assistant Platoon Commander (RU)
POMM ...... Panellinios Omospondia Milergato-Ypallilon kai Makaronotekhniton [*Panhellenic Federation of Mill and Macaroni Workers and Employees*] (GC)
pomnach ..... Assistant Chief (RU)
POMOA .... Provisional Office for Mass Organizational Affairs [*Ethiopia*] (AF)
pomocn .... Pomocniczy [*Auxiliary*] (POL)
pomp .... Pontoon-Bridge Regiment (BU)
POMR .... Partido Obrero Marxista Revolucionario [*Marxist Revolutionary Workers Party*] [*Peru*] (LA)
pomrezh ..... Assistant Producer (RU)
POMR/PST ... Partido Obrero Marxista Revolucionario/Partido Socialista de los Trabajadores [*Marxist Revolutionary Workers' Party/ Socialist Workers' Party*] [*Peru*] [*Political party*] (PPW)
POMSA ...... Post Office Management Staffs Association [*A union*] [*British*] (DCTA)
Pomvetsl .... Pomocna Veterinarska Sluzba [*Auxiliary Veterinary Service*] (CZ)
pomzav .... Assistant Manager, Assistant Chief (RU)
Pomzdrasl .. Pomocna Zdravotnicka Sluzba [*Auxiliary Medical Service*] (CZ)
PON .... Panellinios Omospondia Navtikon [*Panhellenic Seamen's Federation*] (GC)
PON .... Panellinios Organosis Neolaias [*Panhellenic Youth Organization*] (GC)
Pon .... Pavillon [*Pavilion*] [*Military map abbreviation World War I*] [*French*] (MTD)
PON .... Popularna Odznaka Narciarska [*Popular Ski Badge*] [*Poland*]
PON .... Portuguese Navy [*ICAO designator*] (FAAC)
ponb .... Pontoon-Bridge Battalion (BU)
ponbr .... Pontoon-Bridge Brigade (BU)
PONICS .... Police Operational Nominal Computer System [*Hong Kong*]
ponmostb .... Pontoon-Bridge Battalion (RU)
ponmostbr .. Pontoon-Bridge Brigade (RU)
ponmostp ... Pontoon-Bridge Regiment (RU)
pono .... Peso Neto [*Net Weight*] [*Spanish*]
ponp .... Pontoon-Bridge Regiment (RU)
PONTECO ... Societe Commerciale Pontenegrine-Oubangui
Po Nto .... Peso Neto [*Net Weight*] [*Spanish*]
ponv .... Pontoon Platoon (RU)
POO .... Pocos De Caldas [*Brazil*] [*Airport symbol*] (OAG)
POO .... Protivoklopna Odbrana [*Antiarmor Defense*] (YU)
POOC .... Pan Ocean Oil Corp. [*Nigeria*]
POOL .... Pollution of the Ocean Originating on Land [*Ad Hoc Group of Experts*] [*IOC*] (ASF)
POONSDT ... Design Organizations of Okrug People's Councils of Deputies of the Working People (BU)
POOP .... People Opposed to Ocean Pollution [*University of New South Wales*] [*Australia*]
POP .... Panstwowy Osrodek Pedagogiczny [*State Pedagogical Center*] (POL)
POP .... Partido de Orientacion Popular [*Popular Orientation Party*] [*Ecuador*] (LA)
POP .... Partido de Orientacion Popular [*Popular Orientation Party*] [*El Salvador*] [*Political party*] (PPW)
POP .... Parti Ouvrier et Paysan du Congo [*Congolese Workers' and Peasants' Party*] [*Zaire*] [*Political party*]
POP .... Parti Ouvrier et Populaire (Parti Suisse du Travail) [*Labor Party*] [*Switzerland*] (WER)
POP .... Patrullas de Orden Publico [*Public Order Patrols*] [*Cuba*] (LA)
POP .... Podstawowa Organizacja Partyjna [*Primary Party Organization (of the Polish United People's Party)*] (POL)
POP .... Poduzece za Odrzavanje Pruge JZ [*Yugoslav Railroads Track Maintenance Establishment*] (YU)
pop .... Populacao [*Population*] [*Portuguese*]
pop .... Popular [*Popular*] [*Portuguese*]
Pop .... Populare [*Record label*] [*Romania*]
POP .... Preduzece za Odrzavanje Puteva [*Road Maintenance Establishment*] (YU)
POP .... Predvaritelnaya Operativnaya Proverka [*Preliminary Operational Check*] [*Soviet State Security procedure*]
POP .... Prumysl-Obchod-Politika [*Industry-Commerce-Politics (The secretariats of the Communist Party)*] (CZ)
POP .... Puerto Plata [*Dominican Republic*] [*Airport symbol*] (OAG)
POP .... Regimental Supply Relay Point (RU)
POP .... Regulations on Social Assistance (BU)
POPCOM ... Population Commission [*Philippines*] (EAIO)
POPCRU ... Police and Prison Civil Rights Union [*Founded in 1989*] [*South Africa*] (ECON)
POPD .... Panellinia Omospondia Prosopikou Diylistirion [*Panhellenic Confederation of Refinery Employees*] (GC)
POP-DEI ... Panellinios Omospondia Prosopikou Dimosia Epikheirisis Ilektrismou [*Panhellenic Federation of Public Power Corporation Personnel*] (GC)

POPEO ...... Panellinios Omospondia Paragogis kai Emborias Oporokipevtikon [*Panhellenic Federation of Fruit and Vegetable Producers and Marketers*] (GC)
POPN .... Przedsiebiorstwo Obrotu Produktami Naftowymi [*Petroleum Products Marketing Enterprise*] (POL)
POPODD .. Panellinios Omospondia Prosopikou Organismon Dimosiou Dikaiou [*Panhellenic Federation of Personnel of Public Law Organizations*] (GC)
POPP .... Pangosmios Omospondia Palaion Polemiston [*World Veterans Federation*] (GC)
POPP .... Preduzece za Odrzavanje Plovnog Puta [*River Navigation Maintenance Establishment*] (YU)
POPPG ...... Party of the People's Progress Groups [*Trinidadian and Tobagan*] (LA)
popr .... Corrected (BU)
popr .... Poprawione [*Corrected*] (POL)
POPS .... Panellinios Omospondia Politikon Syndaxioukhon [*Panhellenic Federation of Civil Pensioners*] (GC)
POPsY .... Pangosmios Organismos Psykhikis Ygeias [*World Federation for Mental Health*] (GC)
popul .... Popular (RU)
populn .... Enlarged (BU)
p or .... Field Gun (BU)
Por .... Gunpowder Plant [*Topography*] (RU)
POR .... Partido Obrero Revolucionario [*Revolutionary Workers Party*] [*Peru*] [*Political party*]
POR .... Partido Obrero Revolucionario [*Revolutionary Workers Party*] [*Argentina*] [*Political party*]
POR .... Partido Obrero Revolucionario [*Revolutionary Workers Party*] [*Bolivia*] [*Political party*] (PPW)
POR .... Partido Operario Revolucionario [*Revolutionary Workers Party*] [*Brazil*] (LA)
POR .... Parti Ouvrier Revolutionnaire [*Revolutionary Workers Party*] [*Belgium*] (WER)
POR .... Pori [*Finland*] [*Airport symbol*] (OAG)
por .... Porig [*Porous*] [*German*] (GCA)
por .... Poroes [*Porous*] [*German*] (GCA)
por .... Porownaj [*Compare*] (POL)
por .... Porucik [*Lieutenant*] [*US equivalent: Second Lieutenant*] (CZ)
por .... Porucznik [*Lieutenant*] (POL)
POR .... Ranging Gun (RU)
Por .... Rapids [*Topography*] (RU)
POR .... Work Organization Plan (RU)
PORA .... Parti Ouvrier Revolutionnaire Arabe
PORAG ..... Presiding Officers' Review and Advisory Group [*Commonwealth Parliament*] [*Australia*]
PORAM .... Palm Oil Refiners Association of Malaysia (DS)
PORBISI ... Persatuan Organisasi Buruh Islam Seluruh Indonesia [*All-Indonesian Federation of Moslem Workers Organizations*] (IN)
PORC .... Partido Obrero Revolucionario-Combate [*Revolutionary Struggle Workers' Party*] [*Bolivia*] [*Political party*] (PPW)
porc .... Poradove Cislo [*Consecutive Number*] (CZ)
PORE .... Partido Obrero Revolucionario de Espana [*Revolutionary Labor Party of Spain*] (WER)
POREM .... Railroad Rolling-Stock Repair Train (RU)
PORF .... Public Opinion Research Foundation [*Taiwan*]
PORI .... Public Opinion Research of Israel Ltd. [*Research center*] (IRC)
PORIM ...... Palm Oil Research Institute of Malaysia
PORLA ...... Palm Oil Registration and Licensing Authority [*Malaysia*] (GEA)
PORM-PST ... Partido Obrero Revolucionario Marxista-Partido Socialista de los Trabajadores [*Peru*] [*Political party*] (EY)
por no .... Ordinal Number (BU)
por nom ...... Ordinal Number (BU)
Poroshkogr ... Powder Pattern (RU)
PORP .... Polish United Workers' Party (RU)
porph .... Porphyre [*Porphyry*] [*French*]
PORPISI ... Persatuan Organisasi Pemuda Islam Seluruh Indonesia [*All-Indonesia Federation of Moslem Youth Organizations*] (IN)
porpor .... Second Lieutenant (RU)
PORS .... Post-Acute Orthopaedic Rehabilitation Service [*Australia*]
Por skl .... Powder Magazine [*Topography*] (RU)
porssi .... Porssitermi [*Stock Exchange*] [*Finland*]
PORT .... Partido Obrero Revolucionario Trotskista [*Trotskyite Revolutionary Labor Party*] [*Peru*] (LA)
POR-T .... Partido Operario Revolucionario-Trotskista [*Trotskyite Revolutionary Labor Party*] [*Brazil*] (LA)
port .... Portada [*Title Page*] [*Publishing*] [*Spanish*]
port .... Portaikko [*Finland*]
port .... Portraet [*Portrait*] [*Danish/Norwegian*]
port .... Portrait [*French*]
Port .... Portugal [*Portugal*] [*Portuguese*]
port .... Portugalia [*or Portugaliksi*] [*Finland*]
port .... Portugalilainen [*Finland*]
Port .... Portugees [*Portugal*] [*Afrikaans*]

port.............	Portugues [*Portuguese*] [*Portuguese*]
port.............	Portuguese (RU)
portaf.........	Portafolio [*Portfolio*] [*Spanish*]
portef.........	Portefeuille [*Portfolio*] [*French*]
portf..........	Portfoelj [*Portfolio*] [*Sweden*]
Portf.......	Portfolio [*German*]
Portio........	Porticciolo [*Small Port*] [*Italian*] (NAU)
PORTOBRAS ...	Empresa de Portos do Brasil [*Brazilian Ports Enterprise*] (LA)
PORTP......	Partido Obrero Revolucionaria Trotskista Posadista [*Bolivia*] [*Political party*] (PPW)
Portr..........	Portraet [*Portrait*] [*German*]
portr..........	Portraet [*Portrait*] [*Danish/Norwegian*]
portr..........	Portrait [*French*]
portr..........	Portret [*Portrait*] [*Poland*]
portr..........	Portret [*Portrait*] [*Netherlands*]
portrn.........	Portretten [*Portraits*] [*Netherlands*]
portug.........	Portuguese (RU)
poryadk......	Ordinal (Number) (RU)
PORZOrbis ...	Przedsiebiorstwo Obslugi Ruchu Zagranicznego Orbis [*Orbis Foreign Travel Agency*] (POL)
pos..............	Adequate [*Mark in school*] (RU)
POS	Aeroposta SA [*Argentina*] [*ICAO designator*] (FAAC)
POS	Feedback Potentiometer (RU)
POS	Hunters' Trading Station (RU)
POS	Mirror-Image Firing Device (RU)
p-os.............	Paikallisosasto [*Finland*]
POS	Panellinios Odondiatrikos Syllogos [*Panhellenic Dental Society*] (GC)
POS	Panellinios Omospondia Sidirodromikon [*Panhellenic Railwaymen's Federation*] (GC)
POS	Parti de l'Objectif Socialiste
POS	Partido Obrero Socialista [*Socialist Labor Party*] [*Mexico*] (LA)
POS	Partiia Osvobozhdeniia i Sotsializma
POS	Plovdiv Oblast Court (BU)
POS	Polskie Organizacje Studenckie [*Polish Student Organizations*] (POL)
POS	Polytechnische Oberschule [*German*]
POS	Pomorski Obalski Sektor [*Naval Coastal Sector*] (YU)
POS	Port Of Spain [*Trinidad and Tobago*] [*Airport symbol*] (OAG)
POS	Posaune [*Trombone*] [*German*]
pos.............	Posel [*Deputy*] [*Poland*]
Pos	Position [*Position*] (EG)
POS	Professional Orchestra Society [*Chile*] (EAIO)
POS	Programmier-Optimierungssystem [*German*] (ADPT)
POS	Pskov Provincial Dictionary (RU)
POS	Publications de l'Office de Statistique [*Luxembourg*]
pos.............	Settlement (RU)
POS	Successive Concentration of Fire [*Artillery*] (BU)
POS	Tin-Lead Solder (RU)
POSB........	Post Office Savings Bank
POSCO......	Pohang Iron & Steel Co. (ECON)
POSCO.....	Pohang Iron & Steel Company [*South Korean*]
POSD	Panellinios Omospondia Syndesmon Dasoponon [*Panhellenic Federation of Forestry Workers' Associations*] (GC)
POSEIDON ...	Pacific Orient Seismic Digital Observation Network [*Japan*]
Posekr........	Political Secretariat (RU)
POSF........	Panstwowa Odznaka Sprawnosci Fizycznej [*State Badge for Physical Fitness*] [*Poland*]
POSG........	Panellinios Omospondia Syndesmon Geoponon [*Panhellenic Federation of Agriculturists' Associations*] (GC)
POSK........	Panellinios Omospondia Syndaxioukhon Kapnergaton [*Panhellenic Federation of Pensioned Tobacco Workers*] (GC)
POSK........	Polski Osrodek Spoleczno-Kulturalny [*Polish Social and Cultural Association - PSCA*] (EAIO)
POSKP......	Polski Osrodek Spoleczno-Kulturalny Posk [*Polish Social and Cultural Association - PSCA*] (EAIO)
POSL........	Parti Ouvrier Socialiste Luxembourgeois [*Luxembourg Socialist Workers' Party*] (EAIO)
Posl	Poslanec [*Member of the National Assembly*] (CZ)
posl.............	Proverb (RU)
poslbydl......	Posledni Bydliste [*Last Address*] (CZ)
posled.........	[*The*] Last One (BU)
Posledgol....	Central Commission for Combating the After-Effects of Famine (RU)
poslesl........	Epilogue (RU)
poslesl	Postword (BU)
posm............	Posthumous (BU)
POSM	Quarry Materials Processing Enterprise (BU)
posmert	Posthumous (RU)
POSNAA...	Permanent Organization for Afro-Asian Peoples Solidarity (RU)
Pos pl	Landing Site [*Helicopters*], Landing Area (RU)
pospo..........	Settlement Consumers' Society (RU)
PO(SPS& I)A ...	Professional Officers (State Public Service and Instrumentalities) Association [*Australia*]

posr	Adequate [*Mark in school*] (RU)
POSS........	Panellinios Omospondia Syndaxioukhon Sidirodromikon [*Panhellenic Federation of Railroad Pensioners*] (GC)
poss	Possessivo [*Possessive*] [*Portuguese*]
poss pron....	Possessivipronomini [*Possessive Pronoun*] [*Finland*]
posssuff......	Possessiivisuffiksi [*Finland*]
pos such	Opere Citato [*In the Work Cited*] (BU)
post.............	Decision, Resolution, Decree (RU)
post.............	Decree (BU)
post.............	Direct [*Current*], Permanent, Constant (RU)
post.............	Posterieur [*Of a Later Date*] [*French*]
post.............	Posterior [*Back*] [*Spanish*]
post.............	Posteriore [*Back*] [*Italian*]
POSTEC ...	Powder Science and Technology Research Association [*Norway*] (EAIO)
poster	Posterieur [*Of a Later Date*] [*French*]
poster	Posteriore [*Back*] [*Italian*]
posth	Posthume [*Posthumous*] [*French*]
POSTI	Przedsiebiorstwo Obrotu Spozywczymi Towarami Importowanymi [*Sales Enterprise for Imported Food Goods*] (POL)
posticc	Posticcio [*Imitation*] [*Italian*]
postitoim	Postitoimisto [*Finland*]
POSTiW....	Powiatowy Osrodek Sportu, Turystyki, i Wypoczynku [*County Sports, Touring, and Rest Center*] (POL)
Postkutiya ...	Post Office Box (BU)
Post naMin suvet ...	Council of Ministers Decree (BU)
postroykom ...	Construction Committee (RU)
Posyltorg....	Republic Mail Order Trade Office (RU)
poszczeg......	Poszczegolny [*Individual*] [*Poland*]
POT	Motor Vehicle Decontamination Site (RU)
POT	Pacific Overseas Trading Co. Ltd. [*Thailand*]
POT	Parish Organizing Teams [*Grenada*] (LA)
POT	Permis d'Occupation Temporaire [*Temporary Occupation Permit*] (CL)
POT	Port Antonio [*Jamaica*] [*Airport symbol*] (OAG)
Pot.............	Potamos [*River*] [*Greek*] (NAU)
pot.............	Potentiaali(n) [*Finland*]
POT	Pretprijatie za Obrabotka na Tutun [*Tobacco Processing Establishment*] (YU)
POT	Princess of Tasmania [*Ferry between mainland Australia and Tasmania*] (DSUE)
POT	Punkt Obslugi Turystycznej [*Tourist Service*] [*Poland*]
POTA	Prosopikon Organismon Topikis Avtodioikiseos [*Personnel of Local Self-Government Organizations*] [*Greek*] (GC)
POTAB......	Postal es Tavkozlesi Allando Bizottsag [*Standing Committee for Posts and Communications (CEMA)*] (HU)
potash	Potash Plant [*Topography*] (RU)
Potch..........	Potchefstroom [*Potchefstroom*] [*Afrikaans*]
potd	Machine-Gun Section (RU)
p/otd...........	Subdivision (RU)
POTE.........	Pecsi Orvostudomanyi Egyetem [*Medical University of Pecs*] (HU)
POTel	Petty Officer Telegraphist [*Australia*]
Potelin.......	Poskantoor Telektroniese Instituut [*Post Office Telectronic Institute*] [*South Africa*] (SLS)
potentiometr ...	Potentiometisch [*Potentiometrical*] [*German*] (GCA)
potents........	Potential (RU)
POTI..........	Postai Tervezo Iroda [*Postal Planning Office*] (HU)
POTKSPZ ...	Poduzece za Otkup i Trgovinu KSPZ [*Purchase and Trade Establishment, District Union of Agricultural Cooperatives*] (YU)
potloodaant ...	Potloodaantekening [*Pencil Note*] [*Netherlands*]
POTOR	Panstwowy Osrodek Technicznej Obslugi Rolnictwa [*State Center for Technical Services to Agriculture*] (POL)
potreb.........	Consumers' (RU)
potrebsoyuz ...	Union of Consumers' Societies (RU)
POTS.........	Petty Officer Telegraphist Special (DSUE)
POU..........	Mobile Desalting Unit (RU)
POU/AKO ...	Progressiewe Onderwysersunie / Aksiekomitee van Onderwysers [*South Africa*] (AA)
Poudie	Poudrerie [*Powder Works*] [*Military map abbreviation World War I*] [*French*] (MTD)
Poudre........	Poudriere [*Powdermill, Powder Magazine*] [*Military map abbreviation World War I*] [*French*] (MTD)
POUM.......	Partido Obrero de Unificacion Marxista [*Marxist Unification Labor Party*] [*Spanish*] (WER)
POUM.......	Partido Obrero de Unificacion Marxista [*Workers' Party of Marxist Unification, Former USSR*] (LAIN)
POUS	Partido Operario de Unidade Socialista [*Workers' Party for Socialist Unity*] [*Portugal*] [*Political party*] (PPW)
pov.............	Attorney (RU)
pov.............	Confidential (BU)
POV	Fuel and Lubricant Research Laboratory [*Finland*]
pov.............	Imperative Mood (RU)
POV	Pocatecni Obdobi Valky [*Initial Period of War*] (CZ)

POV .... Podminky Omezene Valky [*Limited Warfare Conditions*]   (CZ)
Pov .... Poluostrov [*Peninsula*] [*Pol*] [*See also*] [*Russian*]   (NAU)
pov .... Povolani [*Occupation*]   (CZ)
POV .... Principal Official Visitor [*Australia*]
POV .... Projekty Organisase Vystavby [*Organizational Plans for Construction*]   (CZ)
pov .... Raised, Increased, Stepped-Up   (RU)
POV .... Semipersistent Toxic Agent, Semipersistent War Gas   (RU)
POVA .... Promithevtikos Organismos Vasilikis Aeroporias [*Royal Air Force Procurement Organization*] [*Greek*]   (GC)
POVB .... Pohranicni Oddeleni Verejne Bezpecnosti [*Frontier Department of Public Security*]   (CZ)
POVC .... Probation Officers and Volunteers in Corrections [*Victoria, Australia*]
POVDOP .. Poverenictvo Dopravy [*Office of the Commissioner of Transportation*]   (CZ)
POVEK ...... Pankyprios Organosis Viotekhnon, Epangelmation, kai Katastimatarkhon [*Pan-Cyprian Organization of Artisans, Tradesmen, and Shopkeepers*]   (GC)
povel .... Imperative Mood   (RU)
poverkhn ... Surface, Superficial   (RU)
POVIR ...... Polar Branch of the All-Union Scientific Research Institute of Plant Growing   (RU)
povor .... Turning, Rotary   (RU)
POVP .... Statute of Military Crimes   (RU)
povr .... Damaged   (BU)
povstankom ... Insurrectionary Committee   (RU)
POW .... Polska Organizacja Wojskowa [*Polish Military Organization*]   (POL)
POW .... Pomorski Okreg Wojskowy [*Pomeranian Military District*]   (POL)
pow .... Powiat [*County*]   (POL)
pow .... Powierzchnia [*Surface*] [*Poland*]
POWCH .... Prince of Wales Children's Hospital [*Australia*]
powiel .... Powielany [*Mimeographed*]   (POL)
POWO .... Przedsiebiorstwo Obrotu Warzywami i Owocami [*Enterprise for Fruit and Vegetable Marketing*]   (POL)
POWTECH ... International Powder and Bulk Solids Technology Exhibition and Conference
POY .... Pangosmios Organosis Ygeias [*World Health Organization*]   (GC)
POYA .... Panellinios Omospondia Yperastikon Avtokinitiston [*Panhellenic Federation of Interurban Drivers*]   (GC)
poyasn .... Explanation   (RU)
poyasnit ..... Explanatory   (RU)
POYPA ...... Panellinios Omospondia Ypallilikou Prosopikou Avtokiniton [*Panhellenic Federation of Automotive Personnel*]   (GC)
POZ .... Mobile Obstacle Detachment   (RU)
POZ .... Mobile Obstacle Unit   (BU)
POZ .... Pohyblivy Odrad Zatarasovaci [*Mobile Detachment for Roadblocks*]   (CZ)
POZ .... Pokretni Odrdi za Zaprecavanje [*Mobile Barrage Detachments*]   (YU)
poz .... Positive   (RU)
POZ .... Poznan [*Poland*] [*Airport symbol*]   (OAG)
poz .... Pozycja [*Item*]   (POL)
pozh .... Fire Station [*Topography*]   (RU)
pozhch .... Fire Station, Firehouse   (RU)
pozh kal ...... Fire Tower [*Topography*]   (RU)
PozHL .... Pozorovaci Hlidka [*Observation Patrol*]   (CZ)
POZP .... Pretprijatie za Odrzavnje na Zeleznicki Prugi [*Railroad Track Maintenance Establishment*] [*Skopje*]   (YU)
pozv .... Fortification Platoon   (RU)
PP .... Antipersonnel   (BU)
PP .... Approach Area, Approach Zone [*Aviation*]   (RU)
PP .... Border Post   (RU)
PP .... Bridge Train   (RU)
PP .... Cartridge Carrier   (RU)
PP .... Compiler [*Computers*]   (RU)
PP .... Converting Substation   (RU)
PP .... Covered Space, Covered Surface   (RU)
PP .... Direct-Current Potentiometer   (RU)
PP .... Direct Wire   (RU)
PP .... Dressing Station   (RU)
PP .... Field Gun   (RU)
PP .... Field Mess [*Military*]   (RU)
PP .... Field Plotter [*Artillery*]   (RU)
PP .... Field Postal Service   (RU)
pp .... Field Post, Field Station   (RU)
PP .... Fire Fighting   (BU)
PP .... Floating (Observation and Communications) Post   (RU)
PP .... Food Industry   (RU)
PP .... Fuse   (RU)
PP .... Hydrant Base   (RU)
PP .... Industrial Enterprise   (BU)
PP .... Industrial Vacuum Cleaner   (RU)

PP .... Infantry Regiment   (BU)
PP .... Infantry Support   (RU)
pp .... In Order, In Sequence, In Succession   (RU)
PP .... Intermediate Product   (RU)
pp .... Intermediate Superheat, Intermediate Superheater   (RU)
PP .... Landing Site [*Helicopters*], Landing Area   (RU)
pp .... Lieutenant Colonel   (BU)
pp .... Loss on Calcination   (RU)
p/p .... Money Order, Postal Order   (RU)
p/p .... On the Instructions Of, On a Commission From, On Behalf Of   (RU)
p/p .... Original Signed   (RU)
PP .... Padres [*Fathers*] [*Spanish*]
pp .... Pages [*Pages*] [*French*]
pp .... Paginas [*Pages*] [*Portuguese*]   (GPO)
pp .... Paginas [*Pages*] [*Afrikaans*]
pp .... Paginas [*Pages*] [*Spanish*]
pp .... Pagine [*Pages*] [*Italian*]
Pp .... Pagine [*Pages*] [*Italian*]
Pp .... Pakketpos [*Parcel Post*] [*Afrikaans*]
PP .... Palebny Prumer [*Fire Diameter, Basic Load of Ammunition*]   (CZ)
PP .... Pandectes Periodiques [*Recueil Belge de Jurisprudence et de Legislation*] [*Belgium*]   (FLAF)
PP .... Panels Manufacturing Enterprise   (BU)
PP .... Pangu Pati [*Papua New Guinea*] [*Political party*]   (PPW)
PP .... Panowie [*or Panie or Panstwo*] [*Sirs, Madames*] [*Poland*]
Pp .... Pappe [*Pasteboard*] [*German*]
pp .... Paragraphs   (RU)
PP .... Parna Pekara [*Steam Bakery*]   (YU)
PP .... Parna Pivara [*Steam Brewery*]   (YU)
PP .... Parnicni Postupak [*Civil Procedure*]   (YU)
pp .... Par Procuration [*By Procuration*] [*French*]
PP .... Partia Popullore [*Popular Party*] [*Albania*] [*Political party*]   (PPE)
pp .... Participio Passato [*Past Participle*] [*Italian*]
PP .... Partido do Progresso [*Progress Party*] [*Portuguese*]   (WER)
PP .... Partido Panamenista [*Panamanian Party*] [*Political party*]   (PPW)
PP .... Partido Popular [*Popular Party*] [*Spain*] [*Political party*]   (PPE)
PP .... Partido Popular [*Popular Party*] [*Brazil*]   (LA)
PP .... Partido Populista [*Populist Party*] [*Argentina*] [*Political party*]
PP .... Parti du Peuple [*People's Party*] [*Burundi*] [*Political party*]
pp .... Partijen [*Benelux*]   (BAS)
pp .... Partisiipin Perfekti [*Past Participle*] [*Finland*]
PP .... Pasokan Peninjau [*Reconnaissance Corps*]   (ML)
PP .... Patrol Pengintip [*Reconnaissance Patrol*]   (ML)
pp .... Pawns [*Chess*]   (RU)
PP .... Pedal Switch   (RU)
PP .... Pegawai Penyiasat [*Investigation Officer*]   (ML)
PP .... Pekarsko Poduzece [*Baking Establishment*]   (YU)
PP .... Pengurus Pusat [*Central Executive Council*]   (IN)
PP .... People's Party [*Spain*] [*Political party*]   (ECON)
PP .... People's Party [*Halkci Partisi*] [*Turkey*] [*Political party*]   (PPW)
PP .... Peraturan Pemerintah [*Government Ordinance*]   (IN)
PP .... Perforating Gun, Gun Perforator   (RU)
PP .... Per Persoon [*Each*] [*Afrikaans*]
PP .... Perpustakaan Pusat [*Institut Teknologi Bandung*] [*Indonesia*]
PP .... Pesadiski Puk [*Infantry Regiment*]   (YU)
PP .... Pesurohjaya Polis [*Commissioner of Police*]   (ML)
PP .... Petgodisni Plan [*Five-Year Plan*]   (YU)
PP .... PETROPERU
PP .... Pianissimo [*Very Softly*] [*Music*]
pp .... Piena Pelle [*Full Leather*] [*Italian*]
PP .... Pjesacka Pukovnija [*Infantry Regiment*]   (YU)
PP .... Plachtarske Preteky [*Glider Contests*]   (CZ)
PP .... Plan Prace Podniku [*Factory Work Plan*]   (CZ)
PP .... Podnikovy Plan [*Factory Work Plan*]   (CZ)
pp .... Points, Paragraphs, Clauses   (RU)
pp .... Polgari Perrendtartas [*Civil Procedure, Code of Civil Procedure*]   (HU)
PP .... Police Parisienne [*France*]   (FLAF)
PP .... Policia de Proteccao [*Protective Police*] [*Mozambique*]   (AF)
PP .... Politechnika Poznanska [*Engineering College of Poznan*] [*Poland*]
PP .... Political Education Staff   (RU)
PP .... Poljoprivredno Preduzece [*Agricultural Establishment*]   (YU)
PP .... Popular Party [*European political movement*]   (ECON)
PP .... Por Poder [*Power of Attorney*] [*Legal term*] [*Spanish*]
pp .... Por Procuracao [*By Proxy, By the Action Of*] [*Legal term*] [*Portuguese*]
PP .... Portable Potentiometer   (RU)
PP .... Porte Pagado [*Carriage Paid*] [*Spanish*]
PP .... Portion Principale [*French*]   (MTD)
pp .... Port Paye [*Postage Paid*] [*Shipping*] [*French*]
PP .... Port Phillip [*Australia*]
PP .... Posa Piano [*Handle with Care*] [*Shipping*] [*Italian*]

pp	Posle Podne [*Afternoon*] (YU)
PP	Post Pagado [*Postage Paid*] [*Shipping*] [*Spanish*]
p-p	Post Scriptum (BU)
PP	Pour Presenter [*To Present*] [*French*]
PP	Powder Cartridge (RU)
P-P	Powietrze-Powietrze [*Air-to-Air (Missile)*] [*Poland*]
PP	Predionica Pamuka [*Cotton Mill*] (YU)
PP	Prehranbeno Preduzece [*Food Supply Establishment*] (YU)
PP	Prilepska Pivara [*Prilep Brewery*] (YU)
PP	Printer Switch [*Computers*] (RU)
PP	Private Jet Services AG [*Sweden*] [*ICAO designator*] (ICDA)
PP	Privredna Preduzeca [*Economic Establishments*] (YU)
PP	Privremena Pravila [*Provisional Rules*] [*Military*] (YU)
PP	Privremeno Prisutni [*Temporarily Present*] [*Census*] (YU)
PP	Productora de Papeles [*Yumbo-Valle*] (COL)
PP	Productos Philips [*Colombia*] (COL)
PP	Product Profile [*Department of Trade*] [*Australia*]
PP	Program Switch (RU)
PP	Progress [*or Progressive*] Party
PP	Projektno Preduzece [*Industrial Design Establishment*] (YU)
PP	Proodeftiki Parataxis [*Progressive Front*] [*Greek Cyprus*] [*Political party*] (PPE)
Pp	Protipechotni [*Anti-Infantry*] (CZ)
PP	Protivpesadiski [*Anti-Infantry*] (YU)
PP	Provisional Parish [*Church of England in Australia*]
pp	Proximo Passado [*Portuguese*]
PP	Prumysl Pradla [*The Undergarment Industry*] (CZ)
PP	Przedsiebiorstwo Panstwowe [*State Enterprise*] (POL)
pp	Publie Par [*Published By*] [*French*]
PP	Pulau-Pulau [*Group of Islands*] [*Malay*] (NAU)
PP	Receiving Device, Receiver (RU)
PP	Reception Sidings [*Railroads*] (RU)
PP	Recharging Station (RU)
pp	Second Lieutenant (BU)
PP	Semiconductor (RU)
p/p	Semifinished Material, Intermediate (RU)
PP	Semitrailer (RU)
PP	Small-Arms Ammunition Supply Point (RU)
PP	Standing Committee (BU)
pp	Steam Transformer (RU)
PP	Submachine Gun (RU)
PP	Superheated Steam (RU)
PP	Switching Station (RU)
pp	Teacher, Instructor (RU)
PP	Track Arrival [*Railroads*] (RU)
PP	Transfer Index (RU)
PP	Underwater Sound Detector (RU)
PP	Warning Post (RU)
pp a	Adjektiivina Kaytetty Partisiipin Perfekti [*Past Participle Used as an Adjective*] [*Finland*]
PPA	Longitudinal Transverse Reinforcement (RU)
PPA	Partido Panamenista Autentico [*Panama*] [*Political party*] (EY)
PPA	Partido Patriotico Arubano [*Aruban Patriotic Party*] [*Netherlands Antilles*] [*Political party*] (PPW)
PPA	Partido Peronista Autentico [*Authentic Peronist Party*] [*Argentina*] [*Political party*] (EY)
PPA	Parti du Peuple Algerien (FLAF)
PPA	Parti Populaire Africain
PPA	Parti Progressiste Africain [*African Progressive Party*] [*Senegal*] (AF)
PPA	Parti Progressiste Angolais [*Angolan Progressive Party*] (AF)
PPA	Pensioner Party of Australia [*Political party*]
PPA	Pensioner Power Association of Australia (ADA)
PPA	People's Progressive Alliance [*Gambia*] (AF)
PPA	Philippine Ports Authority (IMH)
PPA	Portland Port Authority [*Australia*]
PPA	Ports Public Authority [*Kuwait*]
PPA	Potato Processors' Association [*Australia*]
PPA	Press and Publications Administration [*China*]
PPA	Programa de Protecao Ambiental [*Environmental Protection Program*] [*Brazil*] (LA)
PPA	Programa para el Pequeno Agricultor [*Small Farmer Program*] [*Dominican Republic*] (LA)
PPA	Progressive Parties' Alliance [*Nigeria*]
PPA	Progressive Party of Australia (ADA)
PPA	Progress Presse Agentur GmbH [*Press agency*] [*Germany*]
PPAA	Professional Photographers Association of Australia
PPAB	Mobile Army Field Hospital (BU)
PPAC	Plant Protection and Agrochemistry Center [*Research center*] [*Hungary*] (IRC)
PPAC	Public Parks Advisory Committee [*South Australia*]
PP ACT	Pedal Power Australian Capital Territory
PPAG	Planned Parenthood Association of Ghana
PPAG	Program and Policy Advisory Group [*IUCN*] (ASF)
PPAM	Pasokan Perkhidmatan Am Malaysia [*Malaysian General Service Corps*] (ML)

PPAP	People's Party of Arunachal Pradesh [*India*] [*Political party*] (PPW)
p part	Participe Passe [*French*] (TPFD)
p part	Past Participle (TPFD)
PPASA	Planned Parenthood Association of South Africa (EAIO)
PPASM	Persatuan Perlindungan Alam Sekitar Malaysia [*Environmental Protection Society Malaysia*] (EAIO)
PPAWA	Poultry Producers' Association of Western Australia
PPB	Battalion Dressing Station (RU)
PPB	Field Ammunition Supply Point (RU)
PPB	Panstwowe Przedsiebiorstwo Budowlane [*State Construction Enterprise*] (POL)
PPB	Partido Popular Barrientista [*Barrientist People's Party*] [*Bolivia*] (LA)
PPB	Pertubohan Pembangunan Bandar [*City Development Organization*] (ML)
PPB	Police Paramilitary Battalion [*Zambia*] (AF)
PPB	Pres Prudente [*Brazil*] [*Airport symbol*] (OAG)
PPB	Regimental Ammunition Dump (BU)
PPB	Regimental Ammunition Supply Point (RU)
PPBANSW ...	Pasture Protection Boards' Association of New South Wales [*Australia*]
PPBB	Partai Pesaka Bumiputra Bersatu [*United Traditional Bumiputra Party*] [*Malaysia*] [*Political party*] (PPW)
PPBC	Plant Pathogenic Bacteria Committee (EA)
ppbd	Pappband [*Bound in Boards*] [*Sweden*]
Ppbd	Pappband [*Bound in Boards*] [*German*]
PPBDT	Persatuan Buruh Pengendara Betja Dokar dan Tjikar [*Dogcart and Bullock-Cart Drivers' Union*] [*Indonesia*]
PPB HiL....	Przedsiebiorstwo Przemyslowe Budowy Huty Imienia Lenina [*Industrial Enterprise for the Construction of Lenin Metallurgical Plant*] (POL)
PPBM	Panstwowe Przedsiebiorstwa Budowlano-Montazowe [*State Construction and Installation Enterprises*] (POL)
PPBM	Persatuan Penerbit Buku Malaysia [*Malaysian Book Publishers' Association*] (EAIO)
PP-BM	Persatuan Penjual-Penjual Buku Malaysia [*Malaysian Booksellers Association*] (EAIO)
PPBP	Pegawai Penjaga Balai Polis [*Officer in Charge - Police Station*] (ML)
PPBP	Privremena Pesadiska Borbena Pravila [*Temporary Infantry Combat Rules*] (YU)
PPBT	Panstwowe Przedsiebiorstwo Budownictwa Terenowego [*State Local Construction Enterprise*] (POL)
PPC	Partido Popular Catala [*Catalan People's Party*] [*Spanish*] (WER)
PPC	Partido Popular Cristiano [*Christian Popular Party*] [*Argentina*] (LA)
PPC	Partido Popular Cristiano [*Christian Popular Party*] [*Peru*] [*Political party*] (PPW)
PPC	Partido Progresista Cristiano [*Progressive Christian Party*] [*Dominican Republic*] (LA)
PPC	Parti Populaire Congolais
PPC	Parti Progressiste Congolais
PPC	Partitu Populare Corsu [*Corsica*] [*Political party*] (PD)
PPC	Petroleum Planning Committee [*Obsolete*] [*NATO*] (NATG)
PPC	Plateau Publishing Co. [*Nigeria*]
PPC	Pour Prendre Conge [*To Take Leave*] [*French*]
PPC	Pretoria Portland Cement [*Commercial firm*] [*South Africa*]
PPC	Program Planning Coordination Office [*United Nations*]
PPC	Public Petroleum Corp. [*Greece*] (PDAA)
PPC	Public Power Corp. [*Greece*] (IMH)
PPCA	Phonographic Performance Company of Australia
PPCA	Productivity Promotion Council of Australia (ADA)
PPCC	Port Phillip Conservation Council [*Australia*]
PPCDRP ...	Partido Pueblo, Cambio, y Democracia Roldosista del Pueblo [*People, Change, and Democracy Roldosist People's Party*] [*Ecuador*] (LA)
PPCEA	Parti Populaire Congolais de l'Entente Africaine
PPCK	Pegawai Penjaga Chawangan Khas [*Officer in Charge - Special Branch*] (ML)
ppcm	Plus Petit Commun Multiple [*Least Common Multiple*] [*French*]
PPCO	Parti Progressiste Congolais
PPCPL	Pegawai Penjaga Chawangan Polis Laut [*Officer in Charge - Marine Police Branch*] (ML)
PPCS	Primary Producers' Cooperative Society [*New Zealand*]
PPD	Degtyarev Submachine Gun (RU)
PPD	Humacao-Palmas [*Puerto Rico*] [*Airport symbol*] (OAG)
PPD	Maintenance of Reservoir Pressure, Repressuring (RU)
PPD	Message Center (RU)
PPD	Partido Popular Democratico [*Popular Democratic Party*] [*Portuguese*] (WER)
PPD	Partido Popular Democratico [*Popular Democratic Party*] [*Puerto Rico*] [*Political party*] (PPW)
PPD	Partido Popular Democratico [*Popular Democratic Party of Puerto Rico*] [*Spanish*] (BARN)

PPD .... Partido por la Democracia [*Democratic Party*] [*Chile*] [*Political party*]   (EY)

PPD .... Parti Populaire Djiboutien [*Djibouti People's Party*] [*Political party*]   (PPW)

PPD .... Parti Populaire du Dahomey

PPD .... Parti Progressiste Dahomeen [*Dahomey Progressive Party*] [*Political party*]

PPD .... Party for Peace and Democracy [*South Korea*] [*Political party*]

PPD .... Politieke Partij Democraten 66 [*Political Party Democrats 66*] [*Netherlands*]   (EAIO)

PPD .... Portuguese Popular Democrats

PPD .... Primary Production Department [*Singapore*]   (DS)

PPD .... Variable-Length Field   (RU)

PPDA........ Partido Popular Democratico Acoriano [*Azorean Popular Democratic Party*] [*Portuguese*]   (WER)

PPDC........ Paraguayan People's Documentation Center [*Mestre, Italy*]   (EAIO)

PPDC........ Partido Popular Democratica Cristiana [*Popular Christian Democratic Party*] [*Spain*] [*Political party*]   (PPE)

PPDC........ Partido Progresista Democrata Cristiano [*Christian Democratic Progressive Party*] [*Dominican Republic*]   (LA)

PPDDalmor ... Panstwowe Przedsiebiorstwo Dalekomorskie [*"Dalmor" State Maritime Enterprise*]   (POL)

PPDG .... Parti Progressiste Democratique Guadeloupeen [*Political party*]   (EY)

Ppd IIIKD ... Regulations on the Application of Title III of the Labor Code   (BU)

ppdo .... Proximo Pasado [*Last Month*] [*Spanish*]

PPDP........ Pegawai Penjaga Daerah Polis [*Officer in Charge - Police District*]   (ML)

PPE............ Electropneumatic Transducer   (RU)

PPE............ Partido Popular Extremeno [*Extremaduran People's Party*] [*Spanish*]   (WER)

PPE............ Parti Populaire Europeen [*European Peoples' Party - EPP*]   (EAIO)

PPE............ Protection des Plantes et Environnement - Centre d'Etudes et d'Informations [*Plant Protection and Environment Information Center*] [*French*]   (ARC)

PPE............ Supply and Evacuation Route   (RU)

PPEA........ Programa de Pesquisas e Educacao Agricola [*Brazil*]   (DSCA)

PPEA........ Proyecto Pro-Economia Agraria [*Argentina*]   (DSCA)

PPEC........ Panchayat Policy and Evaluation Committee [*Nepal*]

PPECB ..... Perishable Products Export Control Board [*South Africa*]   (PDAA)

PPEG .... Mobile Epidemic Control Group   (RU)

PPENC........ Portuguese PEN Centre   (EAIO)

PPEO........ Mobile Epidemic Control Detachment   (RU)

PPER........ Electrical Installation Plan   (RU)

PPF............ Ferrite-Testing Device   (RU)

PPF............ Parti Populaire Francais [*French Popular Party*] [*Political party*]   (PPE)

PPF............ Patriotic People's Front [*Hungary*] [*Political party*]

PPF............ People's Police Force

PPF............ Police Provident Fund [*Tasmania, Australia*]

PPF............ Privatefoeretagarnas Partioganisation i Finland [*Finnish Private Entrepreneurs' Party*] [*Political party*]   (PPE)

PPF............ Projet Pilote Forestier

PPF............ Protocole Relatif a Certaines Dispositions Interessant la France [*Annexe au traite Communaute Economique Europeenne*]   (FLAF)

PPFC .... People's Pearl and Fishery Cor. [*Government corporation*] [*Myanmar*]   (EY)

PPFG .... People's Progressive Front of Ghana

PPFK .... Planned Parenthood Federation of Korea   (EAIO)

PPFprepyatstviya ... Antipersonnel Fortification Obstacles   (BU)

PPG .... Mobile Field Hospital   (RU)

PPG .... Pago Pago [*Samoa*] [*Airport symbol*]   (OAG)

PPG .... Perde Praktisyn Groep [*South Africa*]   (AA)

PPG .... Pioneer Property Group [*Australia*]

PPG .... Psychophysikalische Gesellschaft eV   (SLS)

PPG .... Rectangular Hysteresis Loop   (RU)

PPGE........ Partido del Progreso de Guinea Ecuatorial [*Progressive Party of Equatorial Guinea*] [*Political party*]   (EY)

PPGK........ Panstwowe Przedsiebiorstwa Geodezji i Kartografii [*State Geodetic and Cartographic Enterprises*]   (POL)

PPH .... Pasokan Polis Hutan [*Police Field Force*]   (ML)

PPI............ Pakistan Press International

PPI............ Panitia Pemilihan Indonesia [*Indonesian Election Committee*]   (IN)

PPI............ Pan Pacific Institute [*Flinders University, Australia*]

PPI............ Partito Popolare Italiano [*Italian Popular Party*]   (WER)

PPI............ Pensioners for Peace International   (EAIO)

PPI............ Persatuan Peladjar Indonesia [*Indonesian Students Association*]   (IN)

PPI............ Persatuan Pelaut Indonesia [*Indonesian Seamen's Association*]   (IN)

PPI............ Port Pirie [*Australia*] [*Airport symbol*]   (OAG)

PPI............ Ports [*Harbors*] Performance Indicator [*Australia*]

PPI............ Professional Photographers of Israel   (PDAA)

PPI............ Program Philippines, Incorporated [*Television*]

PPIA .... Philippine Poultry Industry Association   (DS)

PPIB .... Prices, Productivity, and Incomes Board [*Nigeria*]

PPIC .... Personal Products Information Centre [*Australia*]

PPIC .... Pulp and Paper Industries Club [*Association of Thai Industries*]

PPICECA .. Protocole sur les Privileges et Immunites [*Annexe au traite Communaute Europeenne du Charbon et de l'Acier*]   (FLAF)

PPICEE..... Protocole sur les Privileges et Immunites [*Annexe au traite Communaute Economique Europeenne*]   (FLAF)

PPICEEA .. Protocole sur les Privileges et Immunites [*Annexes au traite Communaute Europeenne de l'Energie Atomique*]   (FLAF)

PPIE .... Panstwowe Przedsiebiorstwo Imprez Estradowych [*State Show Business*] [*Poland*]

PPINM...... Regulations on the Planned Construction of Settlements   (BU)

PPiPT(mine) ... Protivpesadiske i Protivtenkovske (Mine) [*Anti-Infantry and Antitank Mines*]   (YU)

PPIS.......... Panstwowe Przedsiebiorstwo Imprez Sportowych [*State Enterprise for Sporting Events*] [*Poland*]

PPiUR....... Przedsiebiorstwo Polowow i Urzadzen Rybackich [*Fisheries and Fishing Facilities Enterprise*]   (POL)

PPK............ G-Suit   (RU)

PPK............ Industrial and Political Courses   (RU)

PPK............ Panstwowe Przedsiebiorstwo Kolportazu [*State Enterprise for Circulation of Publications*]   (POL)

PPK............ Parti Progressiste Katangais [*Political party*]

PPK............ Pasokan Propaganda Khas [*Special Propaganda Force*]   (ML)

PPK............ Pegawai Pentadbir Kontijen [*Contingent Administrative Officer*]   (ML)

PPK............ Protiv Petokolonaski [*Anti-Fifth Column*]   (YU)

PPK............ Pusat Penyelidikan Kehutanan [*Forest Research Center*] [*Malaysia*]   (ARC)

PPK............ Regulations on Arbitration Commissions   (BU)

PPK............ Soil Absorbing Complex   (RU)

PPK............ Steam Superheater Channel   (RU)

PPKAM..... Panstwowe Przedsiebiorstwo Konserwacji Architektury Monumentalnej [*State Enterprise for the Conservation of Monumental Architecture*]   (POL)

PPKB......... Partai Perpaduan Kebang-Saan Brunei [*Brunei National United Party*] [*Political party*]   (EY)

PPKB......... Pertubohan Pasokmomogan Kadazan Bersatu [*United Kadazan Sons of the Soil Organization*] [*Sabah*]   (ML)

PPKEN...... Poinikos kai Peitharkhikos Kodix Emborikou Navtikou [*Merchant Marine Penal and Disciplinary Code*] [*Greek*]   (GC)

PPKh .... Mobile Field Bakery   (RU)

PPKIM ...... Persatuan Pelajar Kolej Islam Malaya [*Students Union of the Malayan Muslim College*]   (ML)

PPKK......... Panstwowe Przedsiebiorstwa Krawiecko-Kusnierskie [*State Enterprises for Tailoring and Furriery*]   (POL)

PPKLJDZ ... Pretprijatije za Popravka na Koli i Lokomotivi Jugoslovanske Drzavne Zeleznice [*Car and Locomotive Repair Establishment, Yugoslav State Railroads*]   (YU)

PPKO........ Pusat Pendidikan Komando [*Marine Training Center*]   (IN)

PPKRM..... Pusat Perjuangan Kebangsaan Rakyat Malaya [*Malayan People's National Struggle Center*]   (ML)

PPK Ruch .. Panstwowe Przedsiebiorstwo Kolportazu "Ruch" [*"Ruch" State Enterprise for the Circulation of Periodicals and Newspapers*]   (POL)

PPL............ Aid Station for the Slightly Wounded   (RU)

PPL............ Landing Area, Landing Field   (RU)

PPL............ Palach Press Ltd. [*British*]   (EAIO)

PPL............ Partido Popular de Liberacion [*Popular Liberation Party*] [*Argentina*]   (LA)

PPL............ Parti Populaire Liberal

PPL............ Partnership Pacific Limited [*Australia*]

Ppl............. Pesi Pluk [*Infantry Regiment*]   (CZ)

PPL............ Phak Pasason Lao [*Lao Communist Party*]   (CL)

PPL............ Poder Popular Local [*Local People's Government*] [*Cuba*]   (LA)

ppl .... Polplotno [*Half-Cloth Binding*] [*Publishing*]   (POL)

PPL............ Priez pour Lui [*Pray for Him*] [*French*]

PPL............ Private Property Listings of Australia

PPL............ Pruefanstalt der Elektrizitaetswerke Oesterreichs [*Electricity Supply Works of Austria Testing Laboratory*] [*Research center*] [*Austria*]   (ERC)

PPL............ Submarine Position   (RU)

pplk .... Podplukovnik [*Lieutenant Colonel*] [*US equivalent: Lieutenant Colonel*]   (CZ)

pplk .... Podpulkownik [*Lieutenant Colonel*]   (POL)

PPLP .... Pegawai Penjaga Latehan Polis [*Officer in Charge of Police Training*]   (ML)

PPM .... Antipersonnel Mine   (RU)

PPM .... First Aid Stations   (BU)

PPM .... Medical First Aid Station   (RU)

PPM .... Moving Permanent Magnet   (RU)

PPM .... Panstwowe Przedsiebiorstwo Melioracyjne [*State Land Reclamation Enterprise*] (POL)

PPM .... Panstwowe Przedsiebiorstwo Miernicze [*State Surveying Enterprise*] (POL)

PPM .... Particuliere Participatiemaatschappy [*Private Joint Stock Company*] [*Dutch*]

PPM .... Partido del Pueblo Mexicano [*Mexican People's Party*] [*Political party*] (PPW)

PPM .... Partido Popular Monarquico [*Popular Monarchist Party*] [*Portuguese*] (WER)

PPM .... Partido Proletario de Mexico [*Proletarian Party of Mexico*]

PPM .... Parti du Peuple Mauritanien [*Mauritanian People's Party*] (AF)

PPM .... Parti Pekerja-Pekerja Malaysia [*Workers' Party of Malaysia*] [*Political party*] (PPW)

PPM .... Parti Progressiste Martiniquais [*Progressive Party of Martinique*] [*Political party*] (PPW)

PPM .... Pasokan Perkhidmatan Malaysia [*Malaysian Service Corps*] (ML)

PPM .... Pattani People's Movement [*Thailand*] [*Political party*]

PPM .... Pemerentah Pasokan Meriam [*Battery Commander*] (ML)

PPM .... People's Popular Movement [*Trinidadian and Tobagan*] (LA)

PPM .... People's Pressure Movement [*Barbados*] (LA)

PPM .... Periode Principale de Maintenance [*French*] (ADPT)

PPM .... Persatuan Pediatric Malaysia [*Malaysian Pediatric Association*] (EAIO)

PPM .... Persatuan Pemakanan Malaysia [*Nutrition Society of Malaysia*] (EAIO)

PPM .... Persatuan Perpustakaan Malaysia [*Library Association of Malaysia*] (EAIO)

PPM .... Pingat Peringatan Malaysia [*Commemoration Medal - Malaysia*] (ML)

PPM .... Pneumatic Polishing Machine (RU)

PPM .... Poder Popular Municipal [*Municipal People's Government*] [*Cuba*] (LA)

PPM .... Policia Popular de Mocambique [*Mozambican People's Police*] (AF)

PPM .... Programme Prioritaire Minimal

PPM .... Protivpesadiske Mine [*Anti-Infantry Mines*] (YU)

PPM .... Pulkowe Pogotowie Medyczne [*Regimental Ambulance Services*] (POL)

PPM .... Pulspositions-Modulationsverfahren [*German*] (ADPT)

PPM .... Pusat Penelitian Marihat [*Marihat Research Center*] [*Indonesia*] [*Research center*] (IRC)

PPM .... Regimental Dressing Station (BU)

PPM .... Regimental Medical Aid Station (RU)

PPM .... Rock Loader, Dirt Loader [*Mining*] (RU)

PPM .... Turning Point [*Aviation*] (RU)

PPMFA ..... Pulp and Paper Manufacturers' Federation of Australia

PPMI........ Perserikatan Perhimpunan-Perhimpunan Mahasiswa Indonesia [*Federation of Indonesian College-Student Organizations*] (IN)

PP mini...... Antipersonnel Mines (BU)

PPMO .... Primary Party Mass Organization (BU)

PPMP....... Protipechotni Minove Pole [*Anti-Infantry Mine Field*] (CZ)

PPMS .... Programme and Project Management System [*United Nations Development Programme*] (DUND)

PPN .... Direct Legal Norms (BU)

PPN .... Flight Instruments, Flight Instrumentation (RU)

PPN .... Night Machine-Gun Sight (RU)

PPN .... Partido Patriotico Nobo [*New Patriotic Party*] [*Aruba*] [*Political party*] (EY)

PPN .... Partido Progreso Nacional [*National Progress Party*] [*Costa Rica*] [*Political party*] (PPW)

PPN .... Parti Progressiste Nigerien [*Nigerian Progressive Party*] [*Political party*]

PPN .... Perusahaan Perkebunan Negara [*State Plantation*] (IN)

PPN .... Pingat Pangkuan Negara [*Medal to the Orders of Chivalry - Malaysia*] (ML)

PPN .... Poder Popular Nacional [*National People's Government*] [*Cuba*] (LA)

PPN .... Popayan [*Colombia*] [*Airport symbol*] (OAG)

PPN .... Proizvodnja i Prerada Nafte [*Naphtha Production and Refining*] (YU)

PPNKM..... Pambansang Pederasyon ng Kababaihang Magbubukid [*National Federation of Peasant Women*] [*Malaysia*] (EAIO)

PPNUNPO ... Regulations on the Application of the Ukase on Naming and Renaming Sites of National and Local Significance (BU)

PPO .... Field Laundry Detachment (RU)

PPO .... Field Postal Section [*Military*] (RU)

PPO .... Fire-Fighting Equipment (RU)

PPO .... Periodicke Preventivni Opravy [*Periodical Preventive Repairs*] (CZ)

PPO .... Philippine Patent Office (IMH)

PPO .... Planovani a Provadeni Preventivnich Oprav [*Planning and Preventive Repair Work*] (CZ)

ppo .... Pouces [*Inches*] [*French*]

PPO .... Poverenictvo Priemyslu a Obchodu [*Office of the Commissioner of Industry and Commerce*] (CZ)

PPO .... Primary Party Organization (BU)

PPO .... Production Planning Department (RU)

PPO .... Promocion Professional Obrera [*Spain*] (PDAA)

PPO .... Protivpodmornicka Odbrana [*Antisubmarine Defense*] (YU)

PPO .... Scheduled Preventive Maintenance Inspection (RU)

PPOC....... Papeterie Principale de l'Oubangui-Chari

PPOK........ Premiowa Pozyczka Odbudowy Kraju [*Loan for the Reconstruction of the Country*] (POL)

p/polk .... Lieutenant Colonel (RU)

ppomslag.... Pappomslag [*Hard Paperboard Cover*] [*Sweden*]

p pon........... Par Procuration [*By Procuration*] [*French*]

PPOO .... Provisional People's Organizing Office [*Ethiopia*] (AF)

ppor........... Podporucik [*Junior Lieutenant*] [*US equivalent: Lieutenant, Junior Grade*] (CZ)

ppor .... Podporucznik [*Second Lieutenant*] [*Poland*]

PPOV........ Pripraven k Praci a Obrane Vlasti [*Prepared for Work and National Defense (Badge)*] (CZ)

PPOW .... Psychologists for the Prevention of War [*Australia*]

PPP............ Advanced Dressing Station (RU)

PPP............ Antipersonnel Obstacle (RU)

PPP............ Dressing Station and Field Mess (RU)

PPP............ First Aid Station (RU)

PPP............ Industrial Production Personnel (BU)

ppp .... Loss on Calcination (RU)

PPP............ Pakistan People's Party [*Political party*] (PD)

PPP............ Partai Persatuan Pembangunan [*United Development Party*] [*Indonesia*] [*Political party*] (PPW)

PPP............ Partido del Pueblo de Panama [*Panamanian People's Party*] [*Political party*] (PPW)

PPP............ Partido Patriotico Popular [*Popular Patriotic Party*] [*Ecuador*] (LA)

PPP............ Partido Popular Progresista [*Popular Progressive Party*] [*Honduras*] (LA)

PPP............ Parti du Progres du Peuple

PPP............ People's Patriotic Party [*Myanmar*] [*Political party*] (PD)

PPP............ People's Political Party [*St. Vincent*] [*Political party*] (PPW)

PPP............ People's Progressive Party [*Gambia*] [*Political party*] (PPW)

PPP............ People's Progressive Party [*Guyana*] [*Political party*] (PD)

PPP............ People's Progressive Party [*Mauritania*] [*Political party*] (EY)

PPP............ People's Progressive Party [*Solomon Islands*] [*Political party*] (PPW)

PPP............ People's Progressive Party [*Anguilla*] [*Political party*] (PPW)

PPP............ People's Progressive Party [*Malaysia*] (ML)

PPP............ People's Progressive Party [*Mauritius*] (AF)

PPP............ People's Progress Party [*Papua New Guinea*] [*Political party*] (PPW)

PPP............ Pianississimo [*As Softly As Possible*] [*Music*]

PPP............ Poder Popular Provincial [*Provincial People's Government*] [*Cuba*] (LA)

PPP............ Primary Products Promotion [*Australia*]

PPP............ Progressive People's Party [*Liberia*] [*Political party*] (PPW)

PPP............ Progressive People's Party [*Sierra Leone*] [*Political party*] (EY)

PPP............ Progressive People's Party [*Sudan*] [*Political party*] (EY)

PPP............ Proodevtiki Panspoudastiki Parataxi [*Progressive Pan-Student Faction*] [*Greek*] (GC)

PPP............ Proserpine [*Australia*] [*Airport symbol*] (OAG)

PPP............ Protestant People's Party [*Australia*] (ADA)

PPP............ Protivprojektilski Projektil [*Antimissile Missile*] (YU)

PPP............ Prumysl Polevkovych Pripravku [*Dehydrated Soup Industry*] (CZ)

PPP............ Public Policy Program [*Australian National University*]

PPP............ Ration Supply Point (RU)

PPP............ Receiving-Sending Post (RU)

PPP............ Regimental Small-Arms Ammunition Supply Point (RU)

PPP............ Send-Receive Switch (RU)

PPPAM ..... Persatuan Penerbit-Penerbit Akhbar Malaysia [*Malaysian Newspaper Publishers As sociation*] (EAIO)

PPPB .... Pegawai Penjaga Polis Bahagian [*Officer Superintending Police Sector*] (ML)

PP-PBM .... Persatuan Pengimpot-Pengimpot Buku Malaysia [*Malaysian Book Importers Association*] (EAIO)

PPPC .... Parti des Paysans et de Proletaires Congolais

PPPD......... Pegawai Penjaga Polis Daerah [*Officer in Charge - District Police*] (ML)

PPPD......... Per Persoon per Dag [*Per Person per Day*] [*Afrikaans*]

PPPFVM... Persatuan Pengeluar dan Pendegar Fonogram and Videogram Malaysia [*Malaysian Association of Phonogram and Videogram Producers and Distributors*] (EAIO)

PPPG .... People's Progressive Party of Guyana [*Political party*]

PPPG .... Pusat Penelitian dan Pengembangan Geologi [*Geological Research and Development Center*] [*Indonesia*] (EAS)

PPPM .... Persatuan Pandu Puteri Malaysia [*Girl Guides Association of Malaysia*] (EAIO)

PPPM .... Persatuan Ping Pong Malaysia [*Table Tennis Association of Malaysia*] (EAIO)
PPPP .... Pegawai Pengangkutan Pasokan Polis [*Police Force Transport Officer*] (ML)
PPPPC ...... Petroleum Products Pipeline Public Corporation [*Sudan*]
PPPPM ..... Persatuan Persuratan Pemuda Pemudi Melayu [*Malayan Youth Literary Association*] [*Singapore*] (ML)
PPPR .... Poverenictvo Podohospodarstva a Pozemkovej Reformy [*Office of the Commissioner for Agriculture and Land Reform*] (CZ)
PPPRF ...... Pan Pacific Public Relations Federation [*Thailand*] [*Defunct*]
PPQ .... Possible Parliamentary Question [*Australia*]
PPR........... Antirepeat Relay (RU)
PPR........... Clearing Station for the Wounded (BU)
P Pr .... Fixed Light with Flashes [*Nautical term*] (RU)
p/pr .... On Presentation, At Sight (RU)
ppr............ Papper [*Paper*] [*Sweden*]
ppr............ Participio Presente [*Present Participle*] [*Italian*]
PPR........... Partido Panamenista Republicano [*Panama*] [*Political party*] (EY)
PPR........... Partido Patriotico Revolucionario [*Mexico*] [*Political party*] (EY)
PPR........... Partido Proletariano Revolucionario [*Proletarian Revolutionary Party*] [*Portugal*] [*Political party*] (PPW)
PPR........... Parti Progresif Rakyat [*People's Progressive Party*] (ML)
PPR........... Pasokan Penchegah Rusohan [*Riot Prevention Unit*] (ML)
PPR........... Peste des Petits Ruminants [*Rinderpest-like disease*] [*Veterinary medicine*]
PPR........... Planned Preventive Repairs (BU)
PPR........... Planta Piloto de Ron [*Puerto Rico*] (DSCA)
PPR........... Poder Popular Regional [*Regional People's Government*] [*Cuba*] (LA)
ppr............ Podporucznik [*Second Lieutenant*] [*Poland*]
PPR........... Polish People's Republic
PPR........... Political Education Work (RU)
PPR........... Politieke Partij Radikalen [*Radical Political Party*] [*Netherlands*] [*Political party*] (PPE)
PPR........... Polska Partia Robotnicza [*Polish Workers' Party*] [*Political party*]
PPR........... Preliminary Work Preparation (RU)
PPR........... Price List by Rayon Rates (RU)
PPR........... River Crossing Point for the Wounded (RU)
PPR........... Scheduled Preventive Maintenance, Scheduled Overhaul, Regular Overhaul (RU)
p/pr .... Simple Portable Obstacles [*Military*] (RU)
PPR........... Work Plan (RU)
Pprap .... Pesi Prapor [*Infantry Battalion*] (CZ)
PPRC........ Panstwowe Przedsiebiorstwo Robot Czerpalnych [*State Enterprise for Dredging*] (POL)
PPRC........ Polish Peace Research Committee
PPRC........ Provincial People's Representative Conference [*China*]
PPRD........ Panstwowe Przedsiebiorstwo Robot Drogowych [*Poland*]
PPRETS .... Reformed Episcopal Seminary, Philadelphia, PA [*Library symbol*] [*Library of Congress*] [*Obsolete*]
PPRI .... Plant Protection Research Institute [*South Africa*] (ARC)
PPRI .... Plasma Physics Research Institute [*University of Natal*] [*South Africa*] (AA)
PPRK........ Panstwowe Przedsiebiorstwo Robot Komunikacyjnych [*State Enterprise for Transportation Projects*] (POL)
PPRN........ Prezydium Powiatowej Rady Narodowej [*Presidium of the People's District Council*] (POL)
PPRPiC ..... Panstwowe Przedsiebiorstwo Robot Podwodnych i Czerplanych [*State Enterprise for Underwater Work and Dredging*] (POL)
PPRV .... Peste des Petits Ruminants Virus [*Rinderpest-like disease*] [*Veterinary medicine*]
PPRV........ Recall Receiver (RU)
PPRV........ Regulations on Transporting Radioactive Substances (RU)
PPS .... Auroral Radio Wave Absorption (RU)
PPS .... Field Postal Station (RU)
PPS .... Fire Fighting Service (BU)
PPS .... Forward Message Center (RU)
PPS .... Mobile Post Offices (RU)
PPS .... Paper Publications Society [*Amsterdam, Netherlands*] (EA)
PPS .... Partia e Punes e Shqiperise [*Party of Labor of Albania - PLA*] [*Political party*] (PPW)
PPS .... Partido Popular Salvadoreno [*Salvadoran Popular Party*] [*Political party*] (PPW)
PPS .... Partido Popular Socialista [*Popular Socialist Party*] [*Mexico*] [*Political party*]
PPS .... Partido Popular Socialista [*Popular Socialist Party*] [*Argentina*] [*Political party*] (PPW)
PPS .... Parti du Progres et du Socialisme [*Party of Progress and Socialism*] [*Morocco*] [*Political party*] (PPW)
PPS .... Parti du Progres Social [*Burkina Faso*] [*Political party*] (EY)
PPS .... Partie Populaire Syrienne [*SNP, SSNP*] [*Lebanon*] [*See also*] (ME)

PPS .... Parti Populaire Senegalais [*Senegalese People's Party*] [*Political party*] (PPW)
PPS .... Parti Populaire Syrien [*Syrian People's Party*] [*Political party*] (BJA)
PPS .... Parti Progressiste Soudanais [*Sudanese Progressive Party*] [*Political party*]
PPS .... Pasokan Polis Sukarela [*Police Volunteer Reserve*] (ML)
PPS .... Performance Program Statement [*Australia*]
PPS .... Pingat Perkhidmatan Setia [*Federation Long Service and Good Conduct Medal - Malaysian*] (ML)
PPS .... Plovdiv Court of Reconciliation (BU)
PPS .... Polska Partia Socjalistyczna [*Polish Socialist Party*]
PPS .... Pozarna Preventivna Sluzba [*Fire Prevention Service*] (YU)
PPS .... Prazska Paroplavebni Spolecnost [*Prague Steamship Lines*] (CZ)
PPS .... Primary Collecting Point (RU)
PPS .... Primo-Predajna Sekcija [*Receiving and Transmitting Section*] [*Radio*] (YU)
PPS .... Produktionsplanungs-und Produktions-Steuerungssystem [*German*] (ADPT)
PPS .... Progressivnaia Partiia Svazilenda
PPS .... Projet "Production Primaire au Sahel"
PPS .... Proyecto Partido Socialista [*Socialist Party Project*] [*Dominican Republic*] (LA)
PPS .... Puerto Princesa [*Philippines*] [*Airport symbol*] (OAG)
PPS .... Regimental Food Supply Depot (RU)
PPS .... Rules for Sailing Competitions (RU)
PPS .... Sudayev Submachine Gun (RU)
PPSA .... Pan-Pacific Surgical Association (ADA)
PPSC .... Partido Popular Social Cristiano [*Popular Social Christian Party*] [*Nicaragua*] (LA)
PPSC .... Petroleum Products Supply Corporation [*Myanmar*] (DS)
PPSCA....... Partido Popular Social Cristiano Autentico [*Political party*] (EY)
PPSD .... Grupo Parlamentar do Partido Social-Democrata [*Parliamentary Group of the Social-Democratic Party*] [*Portugal*] (EAIO)
PPSD .... Polska Partia Socialno-Demokratyczna [*Polish Social-Democrat Party*] [*Political party*]
PPSEAWA ... Pan-Pacific and South-East Asia Women's Association [*Tokyo, Japan*] (EAIO)
PPSEI........ Progres Politique, Social, et Economique de l'Itasy [*Political, Social, and Economic Progress of the Itasy*]
PPSF .... Palestinian Popular Struggle Front [*Political party*] (BJA)
PPS-FR...... Polska Partia Socjalistyczna - Frakcja Rewolucyjna [*Polish Socialist Party - Revolutionary Faction*] [*Political party*] (PPE)
PPSh .... Partia e Punes e Shqiperise [*Labor Party of Albania*] [*Formerly, PKSh*] [*Political party*] (PPE)
PPSh .... Polar Cap Absorption (RU)
PPSh .... Shpagin Submachine Gun (RU)
PPSJ .... Pegawai Penjaga Siasatan Jenayat [*Criminal Investigation Officer*] (ML)
PPsluzhba ... Fire Fighting Service (BU)
PPSML...... Pusat Penelitian Sumberdaya Manusia dan Lingkungan [*Center for Research of Human Resources and the Environment*] [*Indonesia*] (IRC)
PPSP........ Proodevtiki Panspoudastiki Syndikalistiki Parataxi [*Progressive Pan-Student Trade Union Faction*] [*Greek*] (GC)
PPSS........ Regulations for Preventing Collisions at Sea (RU)
PPstantsiya ... Mobile Post Office (BU)
PPSV .... Printing and Publishing Services, Victoria [*Australia*]
PPSWA ...... Plant Protection Society of Western Australia [*Australia*]
PPS-WRN ... Polska Partia Socjalistyczna - Wolnosc, Rownosc, Niepodleglosc [*Polish Socialist Party - Freedom, Equality, Independence*] [*Political party*] (PPE)
PPT........... Papeete [*French Polynesia*] [*Airport symbol*] (OAG)
PPT........... Parti Progressiste du Tchad [*Progressive Party of Chad*] (AF)
PPT........... Parti Progressiste Tchadien [*Progressive Party of Chad*] [*Political party*]
PPT........... Pegawai Perisekan Tentera [*Military Intelligence Officer*] (ML)
PPT........... Poverenictvo pre Posty a Telegraf [*Office of the Commissioner of Postal and Telegraph Service*] (CZ)
PPT........... Przedsiebiorstwo Przemyslu Terenowego [*Local Industry Enterprise*] (POL)
PPT........... Pusat Penelitian Kependudukan dan Ketenagakerjaan [*Center for Population and Manpower Studies*] [*Indonesia*] (IRC)
PPT........... Semiconductor Triode (RU)
PPTA .... Pulp and Paper Technical Association [*Chile*] (EAIO)
Ppte.......... Propriete [*Property*] [*French*]
PPT-ISA.... Picture Personality Test for Indian South Africans
PPTiT .... Poczta Polska, Telegraf, i Telefon [*Polish Administration of Posts, Telegraphs, and Telephones*] (POL)
PPTM .... Partido Popular Trabajador Mexicano [*Mexican Working People's Party*] (LA)
PPTM .... Persatuan Perkhidmatan Tadbir Malaya [*Malayan Civil Service Association*] (ML)

PPTM........ Pusat Pengembangan Teknologi Mineral [*Mineral Technology Development Centre*] [*Indonesia*]

PPTN......... Pusat Penelitian Teknik Nuklir [*Nuclear Techniques Research Center*] [*Indonesia*]   (WND)

PPTOrbis ... Przedsiebiorstwo Podrozy i Turystyki Orbis [*Orbis Travel and Tourist Enterprise*]   (POL)

PPTR........ Pukovske Protivtenkovske Rezerve [*Regimental Antitank Reserves*]   (YU)

PPTS .... Panstwowe Przedsiebiorstwo "Totalizator Sportowy" [*State Enterprise "Sporting Pool"*] [*Poland*]

PP/TSD..... Post Placement and Training Support Program for People with Disabilities [*Australia*]

PPTT .... Persatuan Pegawai Tambang Timah [*Tin Mine Employees' Union*] [*Indonesia*]

PPTT .... Poczta Polska, Telegraf, i Telefon [*Polish Administration of Posts, Telegraphs, and Telephones*]

PPTV......... High-Resistance Direct-Current Potentiometer   (RU)

PPU .... Anti-G Device   (RU)

PPU .... Foam Polyurethane   (RU)

PPU .... Noise-Suppressing Device   (RU)

PPU .... Papun [*Myanmar*] [*Airport symbol*]   (OAG)

PPU .... Parti Populaire des Ueles [*Ueles People's Party*] [*Political party*]

PPU .... Planning and Production Administration   (RU)

PPU .... Planovita Preventivni Udrzba [*Planned Preventive Maintenance*]   (CZ)

PPU .... Starting and Switching Device   (RU)

PPU .... Steam Generating Unit, Steam Generating System   (RU)

Ppuk .... Potpukovnik [*Lieutenant Colonel*]   (YU)

PPUZhS .... Regulations on the Application of the Ukase on Encouraging and Assisting Cooperative and Individual Housing Construction   (BU)

PPV........... Advanced Veterinary Station   (RU)

PPV........... Maximal Field Moisture [*Agriculture*]   (BU)

PPV........... Maximum Field Moisture Capacity of Soil   (RU)

PPV........... Mobile Shot Point   (RU)

PPV........... Rules for the Use of Railroad Cars in International Passenger and Railroad Freight Traffic   (RU)

PPW.......... Panstwowe Przedsiebiorstwo Wydzielone [*State Exempted Enterprise Of*]   (POL)

PPWB........ Prairie Provinces Water Board   (PDAA)

PPWF........ Pakistan Petroleum Workers' Federation

PPWF........ Pulp and Paper Workers Federation of Australia

PPWFA ..... Pulp and Paper Workers Federation of Australia

PPWK........ Panstwowe Przedsiebiorstwo Wydawnictw Kartograficznych [*State Map Publication Enterprise*]   (POL)

PPWNH .... Przedsiebiorstwo Panstwowe Wyodrebnione "Nowa Huta" [*"Nowa Huta" State Exempted Enterprise*]   (POL)

PPWP .... Panstwowe Przedsiebiorstwo "Wiercenia Poszukiwawcze" [*State "Exploratory Drilling" Enterprise*]   (POL)

PPYa......... Armature-Testing Device   (RU)

PPYa......... Bee Venom Preparation   (RU)

PPYU........ Party of Popular Yemenite Unity [*Political party*]   (PD)

PPZ........... Fire Fighting   (BU)

PPZ........... Ignition Tester   (RU)

PPZ........... Papudziska Preradivacka Zadruga [*Slipper Production Cooperative*]   (YU)

PPZ........... Pneumatic Grain Elevator   (RU)

PPZB .... Poznanskie Przemyslowe Zjednoczenie Budowlane [*Poznan Industrial Construction Association*]   (POL)

PPZDA ...... Regulations on the Application of the Law on State Arbitration   (BU)

PPZDvP .... Regulations on the Application of the Law on Road Traffic   (BU)

PPZG........ Regulations on the Application of the Law on Forests   (BU)

PPZIR .... Regulations on the Application of the Law on Inventions and Rationalizations   (BU)

PPZM........ Polskie Przedsiebiorstwo Zeglugi Morskiej [*Polish Maritime Shipping Enterprise*]   (POL)

PPZNO...... Regulations on the Application of the Law on Rentals   (BU)

PPZNSNZ ... Regulations on the Application of the Law on Scientific Degrees and Titles   (BU)

PPZNZ...... Regulations on the Application of the Law on Public Health   (BU)

PPZP .... Regulations on the Application of the Law on Pensions   (BU)

PPZPZSK ... Regulations on the Application of the Law on the Pensioning of Cooperative Farmers   (BU)

PPZSG ...... Regulations on the Application of the Law on Citizens' Property   (BU)

PPZSt .... Regulations on the Application of the Law on Standardization   (BU)

PPZTSU.... Regulations on the Application of the Law on Territorial and Settlement Organization   (BU)

PPZVO...... Regulations on the Application of the Law on Higher Education   (BU)

PPZVT ...... Regulations on the Application of the Law on Foreign Trade   (BU)

PPZZ......... Poljoprivredno Preduzece Zemljoradnicke Zadruge [*Farm Establishment of an Agricultural Cooperative*]   (YU)

PQ............. Parti Quebecois [*Quebec separatist political party*]

PQ............. Premier Quartier [*First Quarter*] [*French*]

PQ............. Quebec   (IDIG)

PQANSW ... Paraplegic and Quadriplegic Association of New South Wales [*Australia*]

PQAQ........ Paraplegic and Quadriplegic Association of Queensland [*Australia*]

PQASA...... Paraplegic and Quadriplegic Association of South Australia

PQAV .... Paraplegic and Quadriplegic Association of Victoria [*Australia*]

PQAWA .... Paraplegic and Quadriplegic Association of Western Australia

PQD.......... Partido Quisqueyano Democrata [*Quisqueyan Democratic Party*] [*Dominican Republic*] [*Political party*]   (PPW)

PQPF........ Plusquamperfectum [*Pluperfect*] [*Afrikaans*]

PQQ.......... Port Macquarie [*Australia*] [*Airport symbol*]   (OAG)

PQRS........ Plant Quarantine Research Station [*Australia*]   (ARC)

PQU.......... Petroquimica Uniao [*Brazil*]

PQVS........ Platten-Quellenprogramm-Verwaltungssystem   (ADPT)

PR .... Aircraft Deployment Point   (RU)

pr............... Avenue   (RU)

pr............... Before   (BU)

pr............... Canal, Channel [*Topography*]   (RU)

PR .... Estado do Parana [*State of Parana*] [*Brazil*]

PR .... Flashing Light [*Nautical term*]   (RU)

PR .... Foaming Agent   (RU)

PR .... Homing Radio Station   (RU)

PR .... Infantry Company   (RU)

PR .... Infantry Reconnaissance   (RU)

pr............... Intermediate [*Nuclear physics and engineering*]   (RU)

PR .... Intermediate Relay   (RU)

PR .... Log Trailer   (RU)

PR .... Machine-Gun Company   (RU)

PR .... Maximum Load, Peak Level   (RU)

PR .... Mobile Radio Station   (RU)

pr............... Other   (RU)

PR .... Output Punch [*Computers*]   (RU)

pr............... Overloaded Operating Condition   (RU)

PR .... Paedagogischer Rat [*Pedagogical Council*] [*German*]   (EG)

PR .... Pakistan Railways   (DCTA)

PR .... Panthere Rose [*France*] [*An association*] [*Defunct*]   (EAIO)

PR .... Parma [*Car registration plates*] [*Italian*]

P/r............. Parni Remorker [*Steam Tugboat*]   (YU)

PR .... Parti de la Reconciliation

PR .... Partido Radical [*Radical Party*] [*Spain*] [*Political party*]   (PPE)

PR .... Partido Radical [*Radical Party*] [*Chile*] [*Political party*]

PR .... Partido Reformista [*Reformist Party*] [*Dominican Republic*] [*Political party*]   (PPW)

PR .... Partido Reformista [*Reformist Party*] [*Costa Rica*]   (LA)

PR .... Partido Republicano [*Republican Party*] [*Brazil*]   (LA)

PR .... Partido Republicano [*Republican Party*] [*Costa Rica*]   (LA)

PR .... Partido Republicano [*Republican Party*] [*Ecuador*] [*Political party*]   (EY)

PR .... Partido Republicano [*Republican Party*] [*Panama*] [*Political party*]   (EY)

PR .... Partido Revolucionario [*Revolutionary Party*] [*Guatemala*] [*Political party*]   (PPW)

PR .... Partido Riojano [*Spain*] [*Political party*]   (EY)

PR .... Parti Rakyat (Malaysia) [*People's Party of Malaysia*]   (ML)

PR .... Parti Republicain [*Republican Party*] [*France*] [*Political party*]   (PPW)

PR .... Parti Republicain [*Republican Party*] [*Reunion*] [*Political party*]   (EY)

PR .... Parti Republicain [*Republican Party*] [*Martinique*] [*Political party*]   (PPW)

PR .... Parti Republicain [*Republican Party*] [*New Caledonia*] [*Political party*]   (FEA)

PR .... Partito Radicale [*Radical Party*] [*Founded, 1955*] [*Italy*] [*Political party*]   (PPE)

PR .... Party Raayat [*Leftist organization in Singapore*]

pr............... Passage, Thoroughfare   (RU)

pr............... Past, Last   (RU)

PR .... Patria Roja [*Red Fatherland*] [*Peru*]   (PD)

PR .... Pekarska Radnja [*Bakery*]   (YU)

PR .... Perang Rakjat [*People's War*]   (IN)

PR .... Periodic Recording   (RU)

PR .... Periscope, Trench Periscope   (RU)

PR .... Per Ringraziamento [*With Thanks*] [*Italian*]

PR .... Philippine Reactor   (NRCH)

PR .... Piano Regolatore [*Zoning Regulations*] [*Italian*]   (WER)

PR .... Planned Repairs   (BU)

PR .... Pneumatic Relay   (RU)

PR .... Podkarpatska Rus [*Subcarpathian Ukraine*]   (CZ)

PR .... Podnikova Rada [*Factory Committee*]   (CZ)

PR .... Podnikove Reditelstvi [*Enterprise Management*]   (CZ)

PR .... Pojistovaci Rada [*Insurance Council*]   (CZ)

PR .... Polarized Relay   (RU)
PR .... Policejni Reditelstvi [*Police Headquarters*]   (CZ)
PR .... Polish Register [*Polish ship classification society*]   (DS)
PR .... Politierechter [*Benelux*]   (BAS)
PR .... Polskie Radio [*Polish Radio*]   (POL)
Pr .... Pond [*Topography*]   (RU)
pr .... Por [*By, Through*] [*Spanish*]
PR .... Position Area [*Artillery*]   (RU)
PR .... Positioning Relay   (RU)
PR .... Poste Recommandee [*Registered Post*]
PR .... Poste Restante [*French*]
pr .... Pour [*For*] [*French*]
PR .... Pour Remercier [*To Express Thanks*] [*French*]
PR .... Povolavaci Rozkaz [*Draft Order*]   (CZ)
pr .... Powder [*Pharmacy*]   (RU)
Pr .... Praesident [*President*] [*German*]
Pr .... Prairie [*Meadow*] [*Military map abbreviation World War I*] [*French*]   (MTD)
pr .... Praktisch [*Practical, Applied*] [*German*]
pr .... Praktoreion [*Agency, Agent's Office*]   (GC)
Pr .... Praseodimio [*Praseodymium*] [*Chemical element*] [*Portuguese*]
Pr .... Praseodym [*Praseodymium*] [*Chemical element*] [*German*]
PR .... Pravila (Nastava) [*Training Rules*] [*Military*]   (YU)
pr .... Prawy [*Right*] [*Poland*]
Pr .... Preis [*Price*] [*German*]
PR .... President de la Republique [*President of the Republic*]   (CL)
PR .... Presidente da Republica [*President of the Republic*] [*Portuguese*]   (WER)
Pr .... Presse [*Press*] [*German*]
pr .... Pressen [*Press*] [*German*]   (GCA)
Pr .... Press Fit   (RU)
PR .... Pretsednik Republike [*President of the Republic*]   (YU)
Pr .... Preussisch [*Prussian*] [*German*]
PR .... Prezydium Rzadu [*Presidium of the Government*]   (POL)
pr .... Prime [*First, Prime*] [*French*]
Pr .... Prince [*Prince*] [*French*]   (MTD)
PR .... Principe Real [*Royal Prince*] [*Portuguese*]
pr .... Pro [*Each, Per*] [*Sweden*]
pr .... Pro [*Each, Per*] [*Danish/Norwegian*]
Pr .... Probe [*Test, Trial*] [*German*]   (GCA)
pr .... Prochain [*Next, Nearest*] [*French*]
PR .... Procureur de la Republique [*France*]   (FLAF)
PR .... Proefstation voor de Rundveehouderij [*Research and Advisory Institute for Cattle Husbandry*] [*Research center*] [*Netherlands*]   (IRC)
Pr .... Professeur [*Professor or Teacher*]   (CL)
PR .... Profile, Section, Cross Section   (RU)
PR .... Programmierer [*Programer*] [*German*]   (ADPT)
PR .... Programmierung [*Programing*] [*German*]   (ADPT)
Pr .... Prolaz [*Passage*] [*Former Yugoslavia*]   (NAU)
PR .... Proportional Controller, Proportional Governor   (RU)
PR .... Propylene   (RU)
pr .... Prospekt [*or Praspekt*] [*Avenue*] [*Commonwealth of Independent States*]   (EECI)
PR .... Protestants [*Protestant*] [*Afrikaans*]
PR .... Provencal [*Language, etc.*]
PR .... Provinsiale Raad [*Provincial Council*] [*Afrikaans*]
PR .... Prozessrechner [*German*]   (ADPT)
Pr .... Pruefung [*Inspection*] [*German*]   (GCA)
PR .... Puerto Rico [*Spanish*]
PR .... Puerto Rico [*ANSI two-letter standard code*]   (CNC)
PR .... Puerto Rico [*Postal code*]
PR .... Radioactive Densimeter   (RU)
PR .... Receiver   (RU)
PR .... Repertoire General du Journal du Palais [*France*]   (FLAF)
PR .... Reproducing Puncher [*Computers*]   (RU)
pr .... Right, Right-Hand   (RU)
pr .... Right Tributary [*Topography*]   (RU)
PR .... Rubber-Covered Wire   (RU)
PR .... Solubility Product   (RU)
pr .... Spatial   (BU)
PR .... Starting Relay, Initiating Relay   (RU)
PR .... Starting Rheostat   (RU)
PR .... Station Bearing   (RU)
pr .... Strait, Sound   (RU)
PR .... Taxi Strip, Taxiway [*Aviation*]   (RU)
PR .... Test Relay   (RU)
pr .... Therefore, Hence, Then, And So Forth   (BU)
Pr .... Titulo de Profesor [*Spanish*]
PR .... Track Relay [*Railroads*]   (RU)
PR .... Trigger Register   (RU)
p/r .... Under the Leadership Of   (RU)
PR .... Zone of Destruction   (RU)
PRA .... Emergency-Pulse Receiver   (RU)
PRA .... Paint Research Association [*Israel*]   (SLS)
PRA .... Parana [*Argentina*] [*Airport symbol*]   (OAG)

PRA .... Parti de Regroupement Africain [*African Regroupment Party*] [*Zaire*]   (AF)
PRA .... Partido Revolucionario Autentico [*Authentic Revolutionary Party*] [*Bolivia*] [*Political party*]   (PPW)
PRA .... Parti du Regroupement Africain [*African Regroupment Party*] [*Banned, 1974 Burkina Faso*] [*Political party*]
PRA .... Parti du Regroupement Africain [*African Regroupment Party*] [*Niger*] [*Political party*]   (PD)
PRA .... People's Regional Assembly [*Sudan*]
PRA .... People's Republic of Angola
PRA .... People's Revolutionary Army [*Grenada*]
PRA .... Permanent Restricted Area [*Former USSR*]   (NATG)
PRA .... Petroleum Refineries (Australia) Proprietary Ltd.   (ADA)
PRA .... Pharmacy Restructuring Authority [*Australia*]
PRA .... Postrechnungsamt [*Postal Accounting Office*]   (EG)
Pr-A .... Prachtausgabe [*Deluxe Edition*] [*Publishing*] [*German*]
PRA .... Pubblico Registro Automobilistico [*Office where cars and other motor vehicles are registered*] [*Italian*]
PRA .... Start-Regulating Equipment   (RU)
PRAC .... Pacific Rim Advisory Council [*Australia*]
prac .... Pracownik [*Worker, Employee*] [*Poland*]
PRAC........ Production Research Advisory Committee [*Australia*]
PRAC........ Pyrethrum Research Advisory Committee [*Kenya*]
PRACA...... Programa de Adiestramiento y Estudios sobre Reforma Agraria del Itsmo Centroamericano   (DSCA)
P Racc .... Points de Raccordement [*Military*] [*French*]   (MTD)
Prachtausg ... Prachtausgabe [*Deluxe Edition*] [*Publishing*] [*German*]
Prachtex..... Prachtexemplar [*Splendid Copy*] [*German*]
prachtv .... Prachtvoll [*Wonderful*] [*German*]
PRACSAA ... Public Remote Access Computer Standards Association of Australia
Practijkg .... Maandblad De Praktijkgids [*Benelux*]   (BAS)
PRADA...... Partido Revolucionario Dominicano Autentico [*Dominican Republic*] [*Political party*]
PRADA...... Societe de Produits Agricoles du Dahomey
PRADHOTEL ... Compania Hotel del Prado SA [*Barranquilla*]   (COL)
pr Adr........ Per Adresse [*Care Of*] [*German*]
Praep......... Praeparat [*Substance*] [*German*]   (GCA)
PRAF........ People's Revolutionary Armed Forces [*Grenada*]   (LA)
PRAG .... Public Relations Association of Ghana
PRAGA...... Prevoyance et de Retraites des Agents Generaux d'Assurances [*France*]   (FLAF)
PRAI........ Proyecto de Reconstruccion y Accion Inmediata [*Reconstruction and Immediate Action Program*] [*Nicaragua*]   (LA)
PRAIEN .... Centre de Preparation Practique aux Applications Industrielles de l'Energie Nucleaire [*Center for Practical Preparations for Industrial Applications of Nuclear Energy*] [*France*]   (PDAA)
Prair.......... Prairial [*Ninth month of the "Calendrier Republicain", from May 20 to June 19*]   (FLAF)
PRAKLE .... Gesellschaft fuer Praktische Lagerstaettenforschung GmbH
prakt.......... Praktisch [*Practical, Applied*] [*German*]
pral........... Principal [*Spanish*]
pralte......... Principalmente [*Principally, Chiefly*] [*Spanish*]
PRAM ...... Partido Revolucionario Abril y Mayo [*April-May Revolutionary Party*] [*El Salvador*]   (LA)
PRAM ...... Partido Revolucionario Abril y Mayo [*April-May Revolutionary Party*] [*Guatemala*]   (LA)
PRAMEN ... Narodni Podnik pro Prodej Lahudkarskeho Zbozi [*National Enterprise for the Retail Sale of Delicatessen Merchandise*]   (CZ)
PRAMOB ... Pravila Mobilizacije [*Mobilization Regulations*]   (YU)
PRAMUKA ... Pradja Muda Karana [*The Youth Are the Hope of the State (State scouting organization)*]   (IN)
prap........... Prapor [*Battalion*]   (CZ)
PRAQ .... Playground and Recreation Association of Queensland [*Australia*]
PRAR........ Partido Republicano Argentino [*Argentine Republican Party*]   (LA)
PRAR........ Partido Revolucionario Autentico Rios [*Bolivia*] [*Political party*]   (PPW)
PRAS........ Pacific Regional Advisory Service [*South Pacific Bureau for Economic Co-Operation*]   (EY)
PRAS........ Parti du Regroupement Africain-Senegalais
Pras........... Praeses [*German*]
Pras........... Praesident [*President*] [*German*]
PRAT........ Parliamentary Retiring Allowances Trust [*Australia*]
PRATA...... Plano Regional de Assistencia Tecnica a Agricultura [*Brazil*]   (DSCA)
p rat aetat ... Pro Ratione Aetatis [*In Proportion to Age*] [*Latin*]   (MAE)
PRAUS...... Programme de Recherche sur l'Amiante de l'Universite de Sherbrooke [*Asbestos Research Program*] [*University of Sherbrooke Quebec*] [*Information service or system*]   (IID)
prav .... Correct, Accurate, True   (RU)
PRAV........ Playground and Recreation Association of Victoria [*Australia*]
prav........... Right, Right-Hand   (RU)
Prav........... Russian Orthodox Cemetery [*Topography*]   (RU)

pravl .... Administration, Management   (RU)

pravosl .... Russian Orthodox   (RU)

PravZZZI ... Regulations on the Application of the Law on Mandatory Property Insurance   (BU)

PRB............ Ammunition-Unloading Point   (RU)

PRB............ Distribution Planning Office   (RU)

PRB............ Mobile Repair Base   (RU)

PRB............ Painters' Registration Board [*Western Australia*]

PRB............ Partai Rakyat Brunei [*Brunei People's Party*]   (ML)

PRB............ Partido Republicano Brasileiro [*Brazil*] [*Political party*]   (EY)

PRB............ Partido Revolucionario Barrientista [*Barrientist Revolutionary Party*] [*Bolivia*]   (LA)

PRB............ Parti Rakyat Bersatu [*United People's Party*] [*Singapore*]   (ML)

PRB............ Physiotherapists' Registration Board [*New South Wales, Australia*]

PRB............ Podiatrists' Registration Board [*New South Wales, Australia*]

PRB............ Poudreries Reunies de Belgique [*Belgian United Powder Factories*]   (WER)

PRB............ Priorities Review Board [*Australian Capital Territory*]

PRB............ Professional Registration Boards of the Northern Territory [*Australia*]

PRB............ Proteus Air Systeme [*France*] [*ICAO designator*]   (FAAC)

PRB............ Psychosurgery Review Board [*Victoria, Australia*]

PRB............ Radio Direction-Finding Unit (Radiosonde)   (RU)

PRB............ Societe des Plantations Rhoniers-Bora

PRBC........ People's Revolutionary Broadcasting Corporation [*Libya*]

PRBiRS ..... Przedsiebiorstwo Remontowo-Budowlane i Robot Specjalnych [*Enterprise for Repair and Construction and for Special Projects*]   (POL)

PRBMECAB ... Permanent Regional Bureau of the Middle East Committee for the Affairs of the Blind [*Riyadh, Saudi Arabia*]   (EAIO)

pr br .... Antiarmored   (BU)

prbw .... Probeweise [*On Trial*] [*German*]   (GCA)

PRC............ Parti des Ressortissants Congolais

PRC............ Partido Regionalista de Cantabria [*Spain*] [*Political party*]   (EY)

PRC............ Partido Republicano Calderonista [*Calderonista Republican Party*] [*Costa Rica*] [*Political party*]   (PPW)

PRC............ Partido Revolucionario Comunista [*Brazil*] [*Political party*]   (EY)

PRC............ Partido Revolucionario Cristiano [*Christian Revolutionary Party*] [*Dominican Republic*]   (LA)

PRC............ Partido Revolucionario Cristiano [*Christian Revolutionary Party*] [*Argentina*]   (LA)

PRC............ Parti Republicain Caledonien [*New Caledonia*] [*Political party*]   (FEA)

PRC............ Parti Republicain Congolais

PRC............ Parti Revolutionnaire Centrafricain [*Central African Republic*]

PRC............ Peace Research Centre [*Australian National University*]

PRC............ People's Redemption Council [*Liberia*]   (PD)

PRC............ People's Republic of China [*Mainland China*]

PRC............ People's Republic of the Congo

PRC............ Polymer Research Centre [*Chisholm Institute of Technology*] [*Australia*]

PRC............ Revolutionary Socialist Party [*Peru*] [*Political party*]   (PD)

PRCA......... Pakistan Restaurant and Caterers Association   (EAIO)

PRCA........ People's Republic of China Army   (MCD)

PRCA........ Presbyterian Reformed Church of Australia

PRCAF ..... People's Republic of China Air Force

PrCHO ...... Prapor Chemicke Ochrany [*Chemical Defense Battalion*]   (CZ)

PRCI........ Parti Republicain de Cote-D'Ivoire

PRCI........ Parti Republicain de la Cote d'Ivoire [*Republicaqn Party of the Ivory Coast*] [*Political party*]   (EY)

PRCiP........ Przedsiebiorstwo Robot Czerpalnych i Podwodnych [*Enterprise for Dredging and Underwater Work*]   (POL)

pr compt ..... Pour Compte [*By Cash*] [*Business term*] [*French*]

PRCP........ Puerto Rican Communist Party [*Political party*]

PRCRTC ... Philippine Root Crop Research and Training Center [*Visayas State College of Agriculture*]

PRCS .... Palestinian Red Crescent Society

PRC(SVV) ... Peace Research Centre (Studiecentrum voor Vredesvraagstukken) [*Netherlands*]

PRD .... Parti Democratique Dahomeen [*Dahomey Democratic Party*] [*Political party*]

PRD .... Partido de la Revolucion Democratica [*Mexico*] [*Political party*]   (EY)

PRD .... Partido de Renovacion Democratica [*Democratic Renewal Party*] [*Costa Rica*] [*Political party*]   (PPW)

PRD .... Partido Radical Democrata [*Radical Democratic Party*] [*Ecuador*]   (LA)

PRD .... Partido Reformista Democratico [*Democratic Reformist Party*] [*Spain*] [*Political party*]   (PPW)

PRD .... Partido Renovador Democratico [*Democratic Renewal Party*] [*Portugal*] [*Political party*]   (EY)

PRD .... Partido Revolucionario Democratico [*Democratic Revolutionary Party*] [*Panama*] [*Political party*]   (PPW)

PRD .... Partido Revolucionario Dominicano [*Dominican Revolutionary Party*] [*Dominican Republic*] [*Political party*]   (PPW)

PRD .... Parti du Renouveau Democratique [*Benin*] [*Political party*]   (EY)

PRD .... Parti Radical-Democratique Suisse [*Radical Democratic Party of Switzerland*] [*Political party*]   (PPE)

PRD .... Parti Republicain du Dahomey

PRD .... Party of the Democratic Revolution [*Mexico*] [*Political party*]

PRD .... Powder Rocket Engine   (RU)

PRD .... Pribramske Rudne Doly, Narodni Podnik [*Pribram Ore Mines, National Enterprise*]   (CZ)

PRD .... Property Registration Department [*Iran*]   (ME)

PRD .... Proportional Pressure Regulator   (RU)

PRD .... Przedsiebiorstwo Robot Drogowych [*Road Construction Enterprise*]   (POL)

PRD .... Ramjet Engine   (RU)

PRD .... Transmitter   (RU)

PRDA .... Pony Riding for the Disabled Association [*Australia*]

PRDC........ Partido Revolucionario Democrata Cristiano [*Revolutionary Christian Democratic Party*] [*Venezuela*]   (LA)

PRDC........ Pig Research and Development Corp. [*Australia*]

PRDCYT ... Programa Regional de Desarrollo Cientifico y Tecnologico [*Regional Program of Scientific and Technological Development*] [*Spanish*]

PRDD .... Partiia Respublikanskovo Demokraticheskovo Dvizheniia

PrDI .... Regulation on State Property   (BU)

PRDM .... Parti pour le Rassemblement Democratique des Mahorais [*Mayotte*] [*Political party*]   (EY)

PRDN .... Partido de Reconciliacion Democratica Nacional [*Party of National Democratic Reconciliation*] [*Guatemala*] [*Political party*]

PRD-NR .... Partido Radical Democrata por una Nueva Republica [*Radical Democratic Party for a New Republic*] [*Ecuador*]   (LA)

PRDSP ...... Plan Regional para el Desarrollo del Sur del Peru [*Peru*]   (DSCA)

prd tr .... Supply Train [*Division and corps*]   (BU)

PRE............ Electromechanical Converter   (RU)

PRE............ Federation Europeenne des Fabricants de Produits Refractaires [*Zurich, Switzerland*]   (EAIO)

PRE............ Partido Republicano Evolucionista [*Republican Evolutionist Party*] [*Portugal*] [*Political party*]   (PPE)

PRE............ Partido Roldosista Ecuatoriano [*Ecuador*] [*Political party*]   (EY)

PRE............ Programme de Relevement Europeen [*European Recovery Program*]   (FLAF)

PRE............ Spanish Catalonian Battalion   (PD)

Preadv .... Preadvies [*Benelux*]   (BAS)

PREAG ...... Parks Residents Environmental Action Group [*Australia*]

PREAG ...... Preussische Elektrizitats AG [*Germany*]   (PDAA)

PREALC.... Programa Regional de Empleo para America Latina y el Caribe [*Regional Employment Program for Latin America and the Caribbean*] [*Spanish*]

PREALC.... Programme Regional d'Emploi pour l'Amerique Latine et les Caraibes [*Regional Employment Program for Latin America and the Caribbean*] [*French*]

prec .... Precedent [*Preceding*] [*French*]

prec .... Preciso [*Exact*] [*Portuguese*]

Prec........... Precite [*French*]

preced........ Precedent [*Previous*] [*Knitting*] [*French*]

pred .... Chairman   (RU)

pred .... Preceding, Previous, Foregoing   (RU)

pred .... Predicado [*Predicate*] [*Portuguese*]

pred .... Predicativo [*Predicative*] [*Portuguese*]

PRED.......... Predikaat [*Predicate*] [*Afrikaans*]

pred .... Predikant [*Reverend*] [*Afrikaans*]

pred .... Predikatiivinen [*Predicative*] [*Finland*]

Pred........... Prediker [*Ecclesiastes*] [*Afrikaans*]

pred .... Predseda [*Chairman*]   (CZ)

pred .... Preface, Foreword   (RU)

PREDESAL ... Programa de Estudios sobre Estilos de Desarrollo y Sistemas Alimentarios en America Latina

PREDESUR ... Programa Regional de Desarrollo del Sur del Ecuador   (EY)

predg .... Introduction [*or Preface*]   (BU)

predik .... Predicative   (BU)

predisl .... Preface   (BU)

predisl .... Preface, Foreword   (RU)

predl.......... Prepositional (Case)   (RU)

predlg .... Preposition   (BU)

predm........ Subject   (RU)

predsedrep ... Presidency of the Republic   (BU)

Predsprosbyuro ... Goods Supply and Demand Office   (RU)

predst .... Prefix   (BU)

PreduzecePTTSaobracaja ... Preduzece Postanskog, Telegrafskog, i Telefonskog Saobracaja [*Postal, Telegraph, and Telephone Establishment*]   (YU)

PreduzeceZOP ... Preduzece za Odrzavanje Pruge [*Railroad Track Maintenance Establishment*]   (YU)

predzavkom ... Chairman of a Plant Committee   (RU)

PREE......... Partido Revolucionario de Educadores Ecuatorianos [*Revolutionary Party of Ecuadorean Educators*]   (LA)

prees........... Preesens [*Present Tense*] [*Finland*]
pref........... Prefacao [*Preface*] [*Portuguese*]
pref........... Preface [*Preface*] [*French*]
pref........... Prefecture   (RU)
pref........... Prefeito [*Prefect*] [*Portuguese*]
pref........... Preference [*Preference*] [*French*]
pref........... Prefiksi, Etuliite [*Prefix*] [*Finland*]
pref........... Prefisso [*Prefix*] [*Italian*]
pref........... Prefix   (TPFD)
pref........... Prefixe [*French*]   (TPFD)
pref........... Prefixo [*Prefix*] [*Portuguese*]
PREFAB-CAMEROUN ... Societe de Prefabrication Camerounaise de
         Maisons Populaires
PREFANTIOQUIA ... Prefabricaciones Antioquia Ltda. [*Colombia*]   (COL)
prefaz......... Prefazione [*Preface*] [*Italian*]
preg........... Pregiato [*Esteemed*] [*Italian*]
pregev......... Pregevole [*Esteemed*] [*Italian*]
pregl........... Reviewed   (BU)
PREI.......... Professional Radio and Electronics Institute of Australia   (ADA)
PREIA....... Professional Radio and Electronics Institute of Australia
preim......... Mainly, Chiefly, Principally   (RU)
prejm......... Prejmenovan [*Renamed*]   (CZ)
prekh......... Transitive [*Verb*]   (BU)
prel........... Preliminaire [*Preliminary*] [*French*]
prel........... Preliminar [*Preliminary*] [*Portuguese*]
prel........... Preliminar [*Preliminary*] [*Spanish*]
prel........... Preliminare [*Preliminary*] [*Italian*]
PRELA ..... Prensa Latina, Angencia Informativa Latinoamericana [*Press
         agency*] [*Cuba*]
prelim........ Preliminaire [*Preliminary*] [*French*]
prelim........ Preliminare [*Preliminary*] [*Italian*]
PRELOG ... People's Revolutionary League of Ghana [*Political party*]
         (PPW)
prels .... Preliminares [*Preliminary Pages*] [*Publishing*] [*Portuguese*]
PREM....... Pakistan Railway Employees' Union   (FEA)
prem.......... Premier [*First*] [*French*]
PREMA..... Preservacao de Madeiras SA [*Brazil*]   (DSCA)
PREMAR.. Prefet Maritime [*Maritime Prefect*] [*French*]   (WER)
PREMOTO ... Promotion de Representation Automobile [*Ivory Coast*]
pren .... Figuratively   (BU)
prenebr....... Slighting   (BU)
prenebr....... Slighting, Scornful   (RU)
prep .... Copy, Transcript   (BU)
PREP .... Police Recruit Education Program [*Australia*]
prep .... Preparation [*French*]
prep .... Preposicao [*Preposition*] [*Portuguese*]
PREP .... Preposisie [*Preposition*] [*Afrikaans*]
prep .... Prepositio [*Preposition*] [*Finland*]
prep .... Preposition [*French*]   (TPFD)
prep .... Preposizione [*Preposition*] [*Italian*]
prep .... Teacher [*or Instructor*]   (BU)
PREPA ...... Societe de Prospection and d'Exploitation Petrolieres en Alsace
Prepak....... People's Revolutionary Party of Kungleipak [*India*] [*Political
         party*]   (PD)
PREPAL.... Societe Africaine de Preparations Alimentaires
PREPE ...... Plano de Reequipamento Especial para o Exercito [*Special
         Reequipment Plan for the Army*] [*Brazil*]   (LA)
prepech ...... Reprinted   (BU)
prep ichern ... Copy and Carbon Copy   (BU)
prepmashina ... Typewritten Copy   (BU)
prepod .... Teacher   (RU)
prerab......... Revised, Revised By   (BU)
prerab izd ... Revised Edition   (BU)
prerazk....... Retold By   (BU)
PREREPUBLIQUE ... President de la Republique [*President of the Republic*]
         [*Cambodia*]   (CL)
Pres .... Beslissing van den President eener Arrondissementsrechtbank in
         Kort Geding [*Benelux*]   (BAS)
PRES .... Plan de Reordenamiento Economico y Social [*Plan for Economic
         and Social Reordering*] [*Guatemala*]
PRES .... Presens [*Present (Tense)*] [*Afrikaans*]
pres .... Present [*French*]   (TPFD)
pres .... Presentation [*Presentation*] [*French*]
pres .... Presente [*Present*] [*Portuguese*]
Pres .... President [*Afrikaans*]
presb .... Presidente [*President*] [*Portuguese*]
presb .... Presbitero [*Presbyter, Priest*] [*Spanish*]
presbo........ Presbitero [*Presbyter, Priest*] [*Portuguese*]
PRESERVAM ... Preservacao de Madeiras Ltd. [*Brazil*]   (DSCA)
Pres Mem .. Presidential Member [*Australia*]
pres part..... Participe Present [*French*]   (TPFD)
pres part.... Present Pariciple   (TPFD)
PRESS....... Parti Republicain Social du Senegal [*Social Republican Party of
         Senegal*] [*Political party*]
pressl........... Presencni Sluzba [*Actual Military Service*]   (CZ)

PREST....... Comite pour la Politique de la Recherche Scientifique et
         Technique [*Luxembourg*]
PREST....... Party on Scientific and Technical Research Policy [*European
         community*]   (MHDB)
PRESTMO ... Prestissimo [*Very Fast*] [*Music*]   (ROG)
PRESTO ... Prestissimo [*Very Fast*] [*Music*]   (ROG)
pret........... Preterito [*Preterite*] [*Portuguese*]
PRET........ Preteritum [*Preterite*] [*Afrikaans*]
PRET........ Pretoria [*South Africa*]   (ROG)
PREUSSAG ... Preussische Bergwerks- und Huetten-AG [*PREUSSAG Mining
         and Metallurgical Corp.*]   (EG)
prev .... Prevedel [*Translated By*]   (YU)
prev .... Translator, Translated By, Translation   (BU)
PREVAC ... Promotora Nacional de Prevencion de Accidentes [*Colombia*]
         (COL)
prevoskhst ... Superlative Degree   (RU)
prev ot .... Translated From   (BU)
prev st......... Superlative   (BU)
PREXMIN ... Prospections et Exploitations Minieres [*Malagasy*]
prez .... President   (RU)
prez .... Prezes [*Chairman*] [*Poland*]
prez .... Prezydent [*President*] [*Poland*]
Prez........... Prezydium [*Presidium*] [*Poland*]
prezr........... Contemptuously   (BU)
prezr........... Contemptuous, Scornful, Disdainful   (RU)
Prf............. Academisch Proefschrift [*Benelux*]   (BAS)
PRF........... Palestine Rejection Front   (BJA)
PRF........... Partido Revolucionario Febrerista [*Febrerista Revolutionary
         Party*] [*Paraguay*] [*Political party*]   (PPW)
PRF........... Podjetje za Razdeljevanje Filmov [*Motion Picture Distributing
         Establishment*] [*YU*]
PRF........... Primitive Recursive Function   (RU)
PRFLP...... Popular Revolutionary Front for the Liberation of Palestine
         (ME)
prft .... Academisch Proefschrift [*Benelux*]   (BAS)
PRG .... Empresa Aero-Servicios Parrague Ltd. [*Chile*] [*ICAO designator*]
         (FAAC)
pr/g .... Last Year   (RU)
PRG .... Parachute Reconnaissance Group   (BU)
Prg............. Paragraf [*Paragraph*]   (TU)
PRG .... People's Revolutionary Government [*Grenada*]   (PD)
PRG .... Police des Renseignements Generaux [*General Investigation
         Police*]   (AF)
PRG .... Policy Research Group [*Australian Labor Party*]
PRG .... Prague [*Former Czechoslovakia*] [*Airport symbol*]   (OAG)
PRG .... Provisional Revolutionary Government [*Political arm of the
         Vietcong*]   (VNW)
PRG .... Provisional Revolutionary Government [*of the Republic of South
         Vietnam*] [*Use PRGRSV*]   (CL)
PRG/I .... Pick Resources Guide/International [*ALLM Books*] [*Information
         service or system*]   (IID)
PRGMTs ... Subregional Hydrometeorological Center   (RU)
PRGRSV ... Provisional Revolutionary Government of the Republic of South
         Vietnam   (CL)
Prgt .... Pergament [*Vellum*] [*Publishing*] [*German*]
PRGVN ..... Provisional Revolutionary Government of South Vietnam
         (VNW)
PRH........... Partido Revolucionario Hondureno [*Honduras Revolutionary
         Party*] [*Political party*]   (PPW)
PRH........... Patentti- ja Rekisterihallitus [*National Board of Patents and
         Registration*] [*Finland*]
PRH........... Phrae [*Thailand*] [*Airport symbol*]   (OAG)
PRI............ Parti de la Republique Islamique [*Iran*]
PRI............ Partido Revolucionario Independiente [*Independent
         Revolutionary Party*] [*Guatemala*]   (LA)
PRI............ Partido Revolucionario Institucional [*Party of the
         Institutionalized Revolution*] [*Mexico*] [*Political party*]
PRI............ Partito Repubblicano Italiano [*Italian Republican Party*]
         [*Political party*]   (PPW)
PRI............ Plastics and Rubber Institute [*Institution of the Rubber Industry
         and Plastics Institute*] [*Formed by a merger of*]   (EAIO)
PRI............ Praslin Island [*Seychelles Islands*] [*Airport symbol*]   (OAG)
PrI............ Precompte Immobilier [*Benelux*]   (BAS)
PRI............ Prevention Routiere Internationale [*International Road Safety
         Organization*] [*Luxembourg*]   (EAIO)
PRI............ Public Radio International
PRI............ Puerto Rico [*ANSI three-letter standard code*]   (CNC)
PRIA......... Public Relations Institute of Australia   (ADA)
PRIA......... Society for Participatory Research in Asia [*India*]   (EAIO)
prib............ Additional, Surplus   (RU)
prib............ Arrival   (RU)
pribalt .... Baltic Region   (RU)
pribav .... Added, Addition   (BU)
pribavl........ Addition, Supplement   (RU)
pribl........... Approximately   (RU)
PribVO ...... Baltic Military District   (RU)

prich .... Participle (BU)

PRICS .... Performers Releasing Information about Clean Syringes

PRIDA .... Programa Integral de Desarrollo Agricola [*Integral Agricultural Development Program*] [*Venezuela*] (LA)

PRIDECO ... Programa Integral de Desarrollo Comunal [*Integral Program of Community Development*] [*El Salvador*] (LA)

PRIF .... Peace Research Institute, Frankfurt [*Germany*] (IRC)

PrIF .... Precompte Immobilier Fictif [*Benelux*] (BAS)

Prig .... Suburb [*Topography*] (RU)

prij .... Prijezd [*Arrival*] (CZ)

prikl .... Applied (RU)

PrikVO ...... Carpathian Military District (RU)

pril .... Adjective (RU)

pril .... Priloha [*Appendix*] [*Former Czechoslovakia*]

pril .... Supplement (BU)

prim .... Annotation, Footnote, Remark (RU)

prim .... Primaer [*Primary*] [*German*]

PRIM .... Primarius [*Chief Delegate*] [*Afrikaans*]

Prim .... Primarius [*Chief Surgeon*] [*German*]

PRIMARCO ... Confecciones Primavera SA [*Colombia*] (COL)

PRIMAS ... Program fuer Rectorchieren und Indexieren mit Maschinenhilfe

PRIMCOM ... Pacific Rim Interactive Multimedia Computing [*Australia*]

primech ...... Annotation, Footnote, Remark (RU)

PRIMEX ... Promociones Industriales Mexicanas SA

Primizdat ... Primorskiy Kray Publishing House (RU)

primperev ... Translator's Note (RU)

primred ...... Primedba Redakcije [*Editorial Comment*] (YU)

prim ref ..... Abstractor's Note (RU)

PrimTASS ... Primorskiy Kray Branch of the News Agency of the Soviet Union (RU)

PRIMTEC ... Pacific Rim Interactive Multi-Media Technology

PRIN .... Partido Revolucionario de Integracion Nacional [*Revolutionary Party of National Integration*] [*Venezuela*] (LA)

PRIN .... Partido Revolucionario de la Izquierda Nacionalista [*National Leftist Revolutionary Party*] [*Bolivia*] [*Political party*] (PPW)

Prin .... Principal (SCAC)

prin .... Prinsipaal [*Principal*] [*Afrikaans*]

PRING .... Partido Revolucionario de Izquierda Nacional Gueiler [*Revolutionary Party of the National Left - Gueiler Wing*] [*Bolivia*] [*Political party*] (PPW)

PRIN-L ...... Partido Revolucionario de la Izquierda Nacional Laboral [*Political party*] (PPW)

PRINM ...... Partido Revolucionario de la Izquierda Nacional Moller [*Bolivia*] [*Political party*] (PPW)

print .... Printing (TPFD)

PRIO .... International Peace Research Institution, Oslo [*Norway*]

Prior .... Prioritaet [*Priority*] [*German*] (GCA)

Priorodo-mat fak ... Department of Natural History and Mathematics (BU)

pr i ot .... Arrival and Departure (RU)

prir .... Priredil [*Prepared By*] (YU)

PRiS .... Przemysl Rolny i Spozywczy [*Agricultural and Food Industry*] (POL)

PRISA .... Public Relations Institute of South Africa

PRISMA ... Prognose-und Informations-System fuer das Materialwesen [*German*] (ADPT)

Prist .... Landing Stage, Wharf, Pier [*Topography*] (RU)

prit .... Addition, Supplement (BU)

prit mest ... Possessive Pronoun (BU)

PRiTV .... Polskie Radio i Telewizja [*Polish Radio and Television*]

priv .... Privat [*Private*] [*Danish/Norwegian*]

Priv .... Privatdruck [*Privately Printed*] [*Publishing*] [*German*]

priv .... Privilegie [*Privileged, Licensed*] [*French*]

priv .... Privilegio [*Permit to Publish, Privilege*] [*Spanish*]

priv-dots ..... Privatdocent (RU)

Priv-Mitt.... Privat-Mitteilung [*Private Communication*] [*German*] (GCA)

PriVO .... Volga Military District (RU)

prizm .... Prismatic (RU)

PRJ .... Pede Recebimento e Justica [*Portuguese*]

PRK .... Democratic People's Republic of Korea [*ANSI three-letter standard code*] (CNC)

prk............ Enemy (RU)

PRK .... Mobile X-Ray Unit (RU)

PRK .... People's Republic of Kampuchea [*From 1979 to 1989*] [*Formerly, Cambodia*] [*Later, SOC*] (PD)

PRK .... Pneumatic Control Valve, Pneumatic Governor (RU)

PRK .... Przedsiebiorstwo Robot Kolejowych [*Railroad Construction Enterprise*] (POL)

PRK .... Radiation Monitoring Post (RU)

PRK .... Radio Control Point (BU)

PRK .... Semiautomatic Distributing Conveyor (RU)

PRK .... Straight Mercury-Quartz Discharge Lamp (RU)

PRKhM ..... Mobile Repair Shop for Chemical Equipment (RU)

pr Khr........ Before Christ (BU)

PRKhU ...... Field Collapsible Refrigeration Unit (RU)

PrKoop....... Regulation on Cooperative Organizations (BU)

PRKP .... Parachute Oxygen Apparatus (RU)

pr kub........ Simple Cubic Lattice (RU)

PRL............ Aviaprima [*Russian Federation*] [*ICAO designator*] (FAAC)

PRL............ Homing Radar (RU)

PRL............ Landing Radar (RU)

PRL............ Mobile Radiological Laboratory (RU)

PRL............ Partido Radical Liberal [*Radical Liberal Party*] [*Ecuador*] [*Political party*]

PRL............ Parti Reformateur Liberal [*Liberal Reform Party*] [*Belgium*] [*Political party*] (PPW)

PRL............ Parti Republicain de la Liberte [*Republican Party for Liberty*] [*Burkina Faso*] [*Political party*]

PRL............ Parti Republicain de la Liberte [*Republican Party for Liberty*] [*France*] [*Political party*] (PPE)

PRL............ Passive Radar (RU)

PRL............ Polska Rzeczpospolita Ludowa [*Polish People's Republic*] (POL)

PRL............ Pouvoir Revolutionnaire Local [*Local Revolutionary Authorities*] [*Guinea*] (AF)

PRLB .... Philips Research Laboratory Brussels [*NV Philips Gloeilampenfabrikken, Netherlands*] [*Research center*] [*Belgium*] (ERC)

PRLCA ...... Power Research Library of Contemporary Art [*University of Sydney, Australia*]

PRLU......... Portable Radiological Field Laboratory (RU)

PRLW........ Parti des Reformes et de la Liberte de Wallonie [*Belgium*] [*Political party*] (PPW)

PRM .... Field Oil-Reclaiming Plant (RU)

PRM .... Homing Beacon (RU)

pr m .... Last Month (RU)

PRM .... Mobile Repair Shop (RU)

PRM .... Partai Rakyat Malaya [*Malayan People's Party*] (ML)

PRM .... Parti de Regroupement Mauritanien [*Mauritanian Regroupment Party*] (AF)

PRM .... Polska Rada Muzyczna [*Polish Music Council*] (EAIO)

PRM .... Portable Microroentgenometer (RU)

PrM .... Precompte Mobilier [*Benelux*] (BAS)

PRM .... Prezes Rady Ministrow [*President of the Council of Ministers*] (POL)

PRM .... Prezydium Rady Ministrow [*Presidium of the Cabinet*] [*Poland*]

PRM .... Radio Beacon Signal Receiver (RU)

Prm .... Receiver (RU)

PRMC....... Programme de Restructuration des Marches Cerealieres [*Mali*]

PRMF........ Petroleum Retail Marketing Franchise Act [*Australia*]

PrMF .... Precompte Mobilier Fictif [*Benelux*] (BAS)

PRMH .... Parti Republicain Modere Haitien [*Political party*] (EY)

pr/min........ Idle Strokes per Minute (RU)

Prmj .... Proslog Mjeseca [*Preceding Month*] (YU)

PRN .... Parti de Regroupement National [*National Regroupment Party*] [*Burkina Faso*] (AF)

PRN .... Partido de la Resistencia Nicaraguense [*Political party*] (EY)

PRN .... Partido de la Revolucion Nacional [*Party of the National Revolution*] [*Bolivia*] [*Political party*] (PPW)

PRN .... Partido de Reconstrucao Nacional [*Brazil*] [*Political party*] (EY)

PRN .... Partido Republicano Nacional [*National Republican Party*] [*Costa Rica*] [*Political party*]

PRN .... Partido Revolucionario Nacionalista [*Nationalist Revolutionary Party*] [*Venezuela*] (LA)

PRN .... Powiatowa Rada Narodowa [*County People's Council*] (POL)

PRN .... Pristina [*Former Yugoslavia*] [*Airport symbol*] (OAG)

PRN .... Pro Re Nata [*When Required*] [*Pharmacy*]

PRNC .... Parti de Reconstruction Nationale du Congo

pr ne .... Before Christ (BU)

prne........... Pre Nase Ere [*Before Our Era (Before Christ)*] (YU)

PRNM ...... Parti de la Renaissance Nationale Mauritanienne

PRNM .... Pergerakan Revolusioner Nasional Malaya [*Malayan National Revolutionary Movement*] (ML)

PRNR .... Public Resort Nature Reserve

PRO .... Antimissile Defense (BU)

PRO .... Antimissile Defense, Missile Defense, Antirocket Defense (RU)

PRO .... Partido Revolucionario Ortodoxo [*Orthodox Revolutionary Party*] [*Honduras*] (LA)

PRO .... Partido Revolucionario Ortodoxo [*Orthodox Revolutionary Party*] [*Guatemala*] (LA)

PRO .... Passport Registration Department (RU)

PRO .... Polskie Ratownictwo Okretowe [*Polish Ship Salvage Enterprise*] (POL)

PRO .... Prostitutes' Rights Organisation [*Australia*]

PRO .... Protiraketova Obrana [*Antimissile Defense*] (CZ)

PROA .... Plantations Reunies de l'Ouest Africain

PROAGRO ... Comision Nacional de Promocion Agropecuaria [*Argentina*] (LAA)

PROAGRO ... Programa de Apoio a Atividade Agropecuaria [*Agriculture and Livestock Activity Support Program*] [*Brazil*] (LA)

PROAIBN ... Programa de Apoio as Industrias Basicas do Nordeste [*Northeast Basic Industry Support Program*] [*Brazil*] (LA)

PROAIUN ... Programa de Apoio a Infraestrutura Urbana do Nordeste [*Northeast Urban Infrastructure Support Program*] [*Brazil*] (LA)

PROALCOOL ... Programa Nacional do Alcool [*National Alcohol Program*] [*Brazil*] (LA)

PROAP...... Principal Regional Office for Asia and the Pacific [*UNESCO*]

PROAVES ... Procesadora del Valle SA [*Colombia*]   (COL)

PROAZU .. Asociacion de Productores de Azufre [*Sulfur Producers Association*] [*Chile*] (LA)

prob............ Proboszcz [*Parish-Priest*] [*Poland*]

PROBAB... Programa de Bibliotecas Agricolas do Brasil [*Brazil*] (DSCA)

Prob Eco .... Problemes Economiques [*La Documentation Francaise*]   (FLAF)

Probl .... Problem [*German*] (GCA)

probl............ Problema [*Problem*] [*Portuguese*]

probl............ Problems   (RU)

Probl Sov ... Problemes Sovietiques   (FLAF)

proc .... Procent [*Per Cent*] [*Poland*]

Proc............ Procent [*Percentage*] [*German*]   (GCA)

proc............ Procesion [*Procession*] [*Spanish*]

proc .... Processo [*Process*] [*Portuguese*]

proc .... Procuracao [*Procuration*] [*Portuguese*]

proc .... Procurador [*Proctor, Proxy*] [*Portuguese*]

PROCA...... Programa de Cooperacion con las Islas del Caribe [*Program of Cooperation with the Caribbean Islands*] [*Venezuela*]   (LA)

PROCACI ... Societe des Produits de Cacao de la Cote-D'Ivoire

PROCAER ... Progetti Costruzioni Aeronautiche [*Italian*]

PROCAMA ... Union des Producteurs de Cacao et de Cafe d'Akposo, Canton Ouma

PROCAMPO ... Asesoramiento Tecnico al Campo [*Technical Counseling for Rural Areas*] [*Nicaragua*]   (LA)

PROCANA ... Asociacion de Productores de Cana de Azucar [*Association of Sugarcane Producers*] [*El Salvador*]   (LA)

PROCAR... Productora de Carton Ltda. [*Colombia*]   (COL)

PROCARFAL ... Productora de Cartones Asfalticos Ltda. [*Colombia*]   (COL)

PROCAUCHO ... Productos de Caucho SA [*Colombia*]   (COL)

Proc civ ...... Code de Procedure Civile [*Code of Civil Proceedings*] [*French*]

PROCEBADA ... Asociacion para el Fomento del Cultivo de la Cebada [*Colombia*]   (COL)

PROCEMASA ... Procesadora del Mar, Sociedad Anonima [*Seafoods Processing Enterprise, Incorporated*] [*Ecuador*]   (LA)

Proc-Gen.... Procureur-Generaal bij de Hoge Raad der Nederlanden [*Netherlands*]   (BAS)

Proc Gen .... Procureur General [*France*]   (FLAF)

PROCHILE ... Instituto de Promocion de Exportaciones [*Institute for Export Promotion*] [*Chile*]   (LA)

PROCHIMAD ... Societe des Produits Chimiques de Madagascar

PROCHIMAT ... Compagnie de Produits Chimiques et Materiaux

prochit........ Read [*Bibliography*]   (RU)

PROCI...... Societe de Conditionnement de Produits Cote-D'Ivoire

PROCIDA ... Societe des Produits Chimiques, Industriels, et Agricoles

PROCO ..... Projects for Continental Operations [*World War II*]

PROCOHARINAS ... Productora Colombiana de Harinas [*Colombia*]   (COL)

PROCOLDER ... Proveedora Colombiana de Repuestos [*Colombia*]   (COL)

PROCOLMA ... Productos Colombianos de Madera [*Colombia*]   (COL)

PROCOLSA ... Productos Colombianos para Automotores [*Colombia*]   (COL)

PROCOLSA ... Promotora Colombiana Sociedad Anonima [*Colombia*]   (COL)

PROCON.. Proyectos y Construcciones [*Colombia*]   (COL)

PROCONSA ... Promotores de Containers SA [*Spain*]   (PDAA)

PROCONTROLES ... Productora de Controles Ltda. [*Colombia*]   (COL)

PROCOS... Produits Congeles au Senegal

PROCOTIP ... Promotion Cooperative du Transport Individuel Publique [*Public cars for private use to reduce traffic congestion*] [*Also known as TIP*] [*France*]

PROCOVEX ... Promotora de Ventas y Comercio Exterior Ltda. [*Colombia*]   (COL)

Proc Rep .... Procureur de la Republique [*France*]   (FLAF)

PROCUP... Partido Revolucionario Obrerista y Clandestino de Union Popular [*Mexico*] [*Political party*]   (EY)

prod............ Food   (RU)

Prod............ Produkt [*Product*] [*German*]

PRODA ... Project Development Institute [*Nigeria*]

PRODALUM ... Productos de Aluminio Arquitectonico Ltda. [*Colombia*]   (COL)

PRODAPAM ... Programa Setorial de Desenvolvimento Agropecuario do Amazonas [*Amazonas Agricultural and Stockraising Development Program*] [*Brazil*]   (LA)

PRODASEN ... Centro de Processamento de Dados do Senado Federal [*Federal Senate Data Processing Center*] [*Brazil*]   (LA)

PRODASTE ... Programm fuer die Datenanalyse Statistischer Erhebungen [*German*]   (ADPT)

PRODB ..... Supply Base   (BU)

PRODECO ... Programa de Promocion Educativa Comunal [*Program for the Promotion of Community Education*] [*Nicaragua*]   (LA)

PRODEFC ... Proyecto de Desarrollo Forestal Zonas Selectas [*Costa Rica*]   (DSCA)

PRODEL... Societe Frigorifique des Produits des Eleveurs Tchadiens

PRODELCO ... Promociones del Comercio [*Colombia*]   (COL)

PRODEMA ... Productores de Madera de El Salvador [*Wood Producers of El Salvador*]   (LA)

PRODEMA ... Productos de Madera Ltda. [*Colombia*]   (COL)

Proden........ Proyecto de Desarrollo Nacional [*Project for National Development*] [*Chile*]   (PPW)

PRODEPAL ... Productos de Papel Ltda. [*Colombia*]   (COL)

PRODESA ... Promotora Desarrollo Agricola [*Bolivia*]   (DSCA)

PRODESARROLLO ... Centro para la Promocion de la Ciencia y el Desarrollo Socioeconomico [*Center for Promotion of Socioeconomic Development and Science*] [*Costa Rica*]   (LA)

PRODESTE ... Programa de Desenvolvimento de Centro-Oeste [*Central-West Development Program*] [*Brazil*]   (LA)

PRODIAL ... Promotion des Usages Industriels de l'Alcool

Prodintorg ... All-Union Export-Import Association of the Ministry of Foreign Trade, USSR   (RU)

prodkom..... Food Committee   (RU)

prodmash..... Food Machinery Plant   (RU)

Prodmontazh ... State Planning and Installation Trust of the Glavtekhmontazh of the Ministry of Construction, RSFSR   (RU)

PRODOK .. Programmpaket fuer Projektbegleitende Dokumentation [*German*]   (ADPT)

prodolzh ..... Continuation, Sequel   (RU)

Prodrasmet ... Central Committee of the VSNKh for the Stocktaking, Distribution, and Sale of Heavy Ores and Metals   (RU)

Prodsnab.... Office of Food Supply for Workers and Employees   (RU)

produlzh ..... Continuation   (BU)

PRODUNAL ... Productos Nacionales [*Colombia*]   (COL)

PROE .... Programme Regional Oceanien de l'Environnement [*South Pacific Regional Environmental Programme - SPREP*]   (EAIO)

Proektneftespetsmontazh ... Planning Office of the Glavneftemontazh of the Ministry of Construction, RSFSR   (RU)

PROEMPAQUES ... Productora Nacional de Empaques Ltda. [*Colombia*]   (COL)

PROEXPA ... Promotora Espanola de Exportadores Alimentarios [*Trade association*] [*Spain*]   (EY)

PROEXPO ... Fondo de Promocion de Exportaciones [*Export Promotion Fund*] [*Colorado*]   (LA)

prof............ Profesor [*Professor*] [*Spanish*]

Prof .... Profesor [*Professor*] [*Albanian*]

Prof .... Profesor [*Professor*]   (TU)

prof............ Professional   (BU)

prof............ Professor [*Afrikaans*]

Prof .... Professor [*German*]

prof............ Professor [*Portuguese*]

Prof .... Professore [*Professor*] [*Italian*]

prof............ Professori [*Professor*] [*Finland*]

prof............ Profeta [*Prophet*] [*Spanish*]

prof............ Profusion [*Profusion*] [*Spanish*]

prof............ Trade-Union   (RU)

profa........... Professora [*Professor (Feminine)*] [*Portuguese*]

PROFAMILIA ... Centro de Planificacion Familiar [*Colombia*]   (COL)

PROFEM .. Federation Francaise du Pret a Porter Feminin [*France*]   (EAIO)

PROFERTIL ... Empresa de Produtos Quimicos e Fertilizantes Ltd. [*Brazil*]   (DSCA)

Profgrupa.... Trade Union Group   (BU)

Profgruporg ... Trade Union Group Organizer   (BU)

PROFI .... Programmiersystem fuer Profiltraeger-Bohrmaschinen [*German*]   (ADPT)

PROFICOL ... Productos Fitosanitarios de Colombia [*Colombia*]   (COL)

profilpunkt ... Prophylactic Station [*Topography*]   (RU)

Profintern... Profsoyuzny Internatsional [*Red International of Trade Unions*]   (RU)

Profizdat .... Trade-Union Publishing House   (RU)

Profkomitet ... Trade Union Committee   (BU)

profkor .... Trade-Union Correspondent   (RU)

PROFO...... Produksjonsteknisk Forskningsinstitutt [*Production Engineering Research Institute*] [*Norway*]   (ERC)

profobr .... Administration for Vocational Education of the Population   (RU)

PROFOG... Promotion du Foyer Guadeloupeen [*Promotion of the Guadeloupean Home*]   (LA)

Proforganizatsiya ... Trade Union Organization   (BU)

Profpredsedatel ... Trade Union Chairman   (BU)

Profsekretariat ... Trade Union Secretariat   (BU)

Profsoc.... Progres Social [*Benelux*]   (BAS)

Profsovet.... Council of Trade Unions   (RU)

Profsoyuz... Professionalnyl Soyuzi [*Association of Trade Unions*] [*Former USSR*]   (BU)

Profsozh.... Railroad Workers' Trade Union   (RU)

Prof-t......... Trade Union Committee   (BU)

Proftekhizdat ... All-Union Publishing House of Textbooks and Pedagogical Literature of the State Committee of the Council of Ministers, USSR, for Vocational and Technical Education (RU)
profus .... Profusamente [*Profusely*] [*Spanish*]
PROG .... Progressief [*Progressive*] [*Afrikaans*]
PROGAN .. Productos Ganaderos Chile Ltda. [*Chilean Livestock Products Ltd.*] (LA)
PROGAS ... Proveedora de Gas Ltda. [*Colombia*] (COL)
Progimn ...... Junior High School (BU)
PROGNO ... Prognosen-Trends-Entwicklungen [*Forecasts-Trends-Developments*] [*Society for Business Information*] [*Information service or system*] (IID)
Progr .... Programm [*Program*] [*German*]
Progr .... Programmschrift [*School Publication*] [*German*]
PROGRE... City Planning and Zoning Organization (BU)
PROHEVEA ... Projeto da Heveicultura da Amazonia [*Brazil*] (DSCA)
PROHUZA ... Centre d'Etudes et Informations des Problemes Humains dans les Zones Arides
PROI......... President of the Royal Institute of Oil Painters [*British*]
PROINCO ... Proyectos Ingenieria Construccion [*Colombia*] (COL)
PROINPA ... Promotora Industrial Panamericana [*Colombia*] (COL)
PROINSA ... Promociones de Credito e Inversiones Sociedad Anonima [*Colombia*] (COL)
proizn .... Pronounced (RU)
proizv .... Production (BU)
Proizv .... Scientific-Production Specialization (BU)
proizv-vo .... Production, Manufacture (RU)
proj............. Projekt [*Project*] [*Poland*]
proj............. Projektowal [*Designed By*] (POL)
proj............. Projet [*French*] (FLAF)
PROK .... Presbyterian Church in the Republic of Korea (EY)
Prok .... Prokuratur [*or Prokurist*] [*German*]
Prok .... Prokureur [*Attorney*] [*Afrikaans*]
PROKESA ... Fabrica de Sacos Productos de Kenaf SA [*Guatemala*] (DSCA)
Prok-Gen ... Prokureur-Generaal [*Attorney General*] [*Afrikaans*]
PROKOS... Universelles Programmsystem Kostenrechnung [*German*] (ADPT)
prol............. Prologo [*Preface*] [*Spanish*]
prol............. Strait, Sound (RU)
PROLACA ... Productos Lacteos de Lara, CA [*Venezuela*] (DSCA)
PROLECHE ... Procesadora de Leches SA [*Colombia*] (COL)
prolet......... Proletarian (RU)
Proletkul't ... "Proletarian Culture" [*1917-1932*] (RU)
proletstud... Proletarian Students (RU)
PROLOG .. Standardprogrammsystem Lohn und Gehalt [*German*] (ADPT)
prom........... Industrial (BU)
prom........... Industrial, Industry (RU)
PROM .... Promesse [*Promissory Note*] [*Afrikaans*]
Prom .... Promontorio [*Promontory*] [*Spanish*] (NAU)
prom .... Promotor [*Professor conferring a degree*] [*Poland*]
Prom .... Promulgue [*French*] (FLAF)
PROMECAR ... Productos Metalicos de Cartagena Ltda. [*Colombia*] (COL)
Promenergo ... Industrial and Technical Establishment for the Adjustment, Planning, and Repair of Power-Engineering Equipment (RU)
Promenergomontazh ... Industrial Power Installation (BU)
Promenergoproyekt ... State All-Union Planning Institute for the Planning of Construction of Industrial Heat and Electric Power Plants for Supplying Power to Industrial Establishments of All Branches of the National Economy (RU)
PROMETAL ... Entreprise Nationale de Produits Metalliques Utilitaires [*Commercial firm*] [*Algeria*]
PROMETAL ... Productos de Metal [*Colombia*] (COL)
PROMETALICOS ... Productos Metalicos de Colombia Ltda. [*Manizales*] (COL)
PROMETHEUS ... Program for European Traffic with Highest Efficiency and Unprecedented Safety (ECON)
PROMEXCOL ... Promotora de Explotaciones y Cultivos Ltda. [*Colombia*] (COL)
promezh ..... Intermediate, Interstitial (RU)
Promfinplan ... Industrial Finance Plan (BU)
Promgrazhdanstroy ... State Trust for Industrial and Civil Engineering Construction (RU)
PROMICA ... Productos Minerales CA [*Venezuela*] (DSCA)
PROMIDA ... Programmiersprache fuer die Mittlere Datentechnik [*German*] (ADPT)
PROMINEX ... Centre de Promotion des Investissements et des Exportations Haitiennes (EY)
PROMIV... Promotion Ivoirienne
Promizdat .. Industrial Publishing House (RU)
Promkombinat ... Industrial Combine (BU)
promkoop... Producers' Cooperatives (RU)
prommetsoyuz ... Union of Metal Producers' Cooperatives (RU)
Prommontazh ... Industrial Assemblies (BU)
PROMOCAM ... Societe Camerounaise de Promotion

PROMOCI ... Promotion des Cultures Industrielles
PROMOF ... Programmierte Modulare Finanzbuchhaltung [*German*] (ADPT)
PROMOGABON ... Agence Gabonaise de Promotion Industrielle et Artisanale [*Gabonese Agency for Industrial and Handicrafts Promotion*] (AF)
PROMOPLAST ... Societe de Promotion des Matieres Plastiques
PROMOSA ... Productos de Maiz SA [*Venezuela*] (DSCA)
PROMOTEC ... Producciones y Montajes Tecnicos Ltda. [*Colombia*] (COL)
promov .... Promoviert [*Graduated*] [*German*] (GCA)
PROMOVIL ... Propaganda Movil Ltda. (COL)
Promplan ... Industrial Planning Commission (RU)
prom prod... Intermediate Product (RU)
Promproekt ... Industrial Designs (BU)
prom sch..... Industrial Accounting (BU)
promsovet... Council of Producers' Cooperatives (RU)
promsoyuz ... Union of Producers' Cooperatives (RU)
prom-st'...... Industry (RU)
Promstal'konstruktsiya ... Planning Office of the Glavstal'konstruktsiya of the Ministry of Construction of Establishments of the Metallurgical and Chemical Industries, USSR (RU)
PROMSTRA ... Production Methods and Stress Research Association [*Netherlands*] (PDAA)
promstrakhkassa ... Mutual Insurance and Mutual Aid Fund of Producers' Cooperatives (RU)
promstrakhsovet ... Insurance Council of Artels of Producers' Cooperatives (RU)
Promstromenergomontazh ... All-Union Trust for the Installation of Power Engineering Equipment of the Glavstroymash of the Ministry of the Building Materials Industry, USSR (RU)
Promstroyizdat ... State Publishing House of Literature on Building Materials (RU)
Promstroyproyekt ... All-Union Trust of Construction Planning of Industrial Establishments and Structures of Ferrous and Nonferrous Metallurgy and Machinery Manufacture (RU)
Promstroyproyekt ... State Institute for Sanitary-Engineering and General-Construction Planning of Industrial Establishments [*Leningrad*] (RU)
Promstroyproyekt ... State Planning Institute for General-Construction and Sanitary-Engineering Planning of Industrial Establishments [*Moscow*] (RU)
Promsvyaz'montazh ... Trust for the Installation of Communications for Industrial Establishments (RU)
Promsyr'yeimport ... All-Union Import-Export Association for Industrial Raw Materials (RU)
Promtara.... Industrial Packing Materials Trust (RU)
promtekhsnab ... Department of Technical Supply at the Council of Producers' Cooperatives (RU)
promtorg .... Manufactured Goods Trade Organization (RU)
Promtransproyekt ... State Planning Institute for the Development of Plans of Structures and for the Organization of Industrial Transportation (RU)
Promvoyensovet ... Council of War Industry (RU)
Promzernoproyekt ... State Institute for the Planning of Flour-Milling and Groats Industry Establishments, Elevators, and Storage Facilities (RU)
promzhilstroy ... Industrial Housing Construction (RU)
PRON .... Patriotyczny Ruch Odrodzenia Narodowego [*Patriotic Movement for National Rebirth*] [*Poland*] (EY)
pron............ Pronom [*French*] (TPFD)
pron............ Pronome [*Pronoun*] [*Portuguese*]
PRON .... Pronomen [*Pronoun*] [*Afrikaans*]
pron............ Pronominal [*Pronominal*] [*Portuguese*]
pron............ Pronomini [*Pronoun*] [*Finland*]
pron............ Pronoun (TPFD)
PRONAN .. Programa Nacional de Alimentacao e Nutricao [*National Food and Nutrition Program*] [*Brazil*] (LA)
PRONASE ... Productura Nacional de Semillas [*National Seed Producers Organization*] [*Mexico*] (LA)
PRONENCA ... Programa Nacional de Educacao Nutricional y Complementacion Alimentaria [*Colorado*] (LAA)
PRONICA ... Productos Nicaraguenses, SA [*Nicaragua*] (DSCA)
PRONTEL ... Programa Nacional de Teleducacao [*National Television Education Program*] [*Brazil*] (LA)
PROP......... Panstwowa Rada Ochrony Przyrody [*State Council for the Protection of Nature*] (POL)
prop........... Propagandistic, Propaganda (RU)
PROP......... Propedeuties [*Preliminary*] [*Afrikaans*]
Prop .... Propeller [*German*] (GCA)
Prop .... Proponent [*Proponent*] [*Afrikaans*]
PrOP......... Regulation on Social Assistance (BU)
PROPAKASIA ... International Food Processing and Packaging Technology Exhibition and Conference for South East Asia
PROPAL... Productora de Papeles [*Yumbo-Valle*] (COL)
PROPAN... Productora de Pan [*Colombia*] (COL)
PROPASI ... Productores de Patata de Siembra, SL [*Spain*] (DSCA)
Prop Ind..... Propriete Industrielle [*Switzerland*] (FLAF)

PRO-PO .... Prognostika Podosfairou [*Soccer Forecasts*]   (GC)
propos .... Proposition [*French*]   (FLAF)
propr .... Proprieta [*Ownership, Property*] [*Italian*]
Propr .... Proprietor   (SCAC)
propriet ...... Proprietario [*Owner*] [*Italian*]
PROQUICOL ... Productos Quimicos Colombianos SA [*Colombia*]   (COL)
PROQUINAL ... Fabrica de Productos Quimicos Nacionales Ltda. [*Colombia*]   (COL)
pror .... Procurador [*Attorney, Procurator*] [*Spanish*]
PROROCHE ... Productos Roche SA [*Colombia*]   (COL)
PROS........ Proscenium [*Theater term*]   (DSUE)
pros .... Prosodia [*Prosody*] [*Portuguese*]
pros .... Prosodie [*French*]   (TPFD)
pros .... Prosody   (RU)
pros .... Prosonimo [*Portuguese*]
PROS........ Prostitutes Rights Organisation for Sex Workers [*Australia*]
PROSA...... Programmierungssystem mit Symbolischen Adressen [*German*]   (ADPT)
PROSAB ... Antiaircraft Bomb   (RU)
prosc.......... Proscenio [*Proscenium*] [*Portuguese*]
PROSE...... Prostitutes Rights Organisation for Sex Workers [*Australia*]
prosh .... Past (Tense)   (RU)
PROSI .... Public Relations Office of the Sugar Industry [*Mauritius*]
PROSID .... Transformation de Produits Siderurgiques
PROSIS..... Programmpaket Statistisches Informationssystem [*German*]   (ADPT)
prosm .... Reviewed, Revised   (RU)
prosmotr..... Reviewed   (RU)
prosp .... Avenue   (RU)
prosp .... Prospekt [*Leaflet*] [*Poland*]
PROSPEC ... Levantamentos, Prospecoes e Aerofotogrametria SA [*Brazil*]   (DSCA)
PROSSA ... Prosthodontic Society of South Africa   (AA)
prost .... Colloquial Expression   (RU)
prosv.......... Education   (BU)
prosvet........ Enlightening, Educational   (RU)
PROSY...... People's Republic of South Yemen   (BJA)
prot............ Canal, Channel [*Topography*]   (RU)
prot............ Minutes, Proceedings   (RU)
Prot .... Protectorat [*French*]   (FLAF)
prot............ Protestans [*Protestant*]   (HU)
Prot .... Protestant [*Afrikaans*]
prot............ Protestantisch [*Protestant*] [*German*]
PROT .... Protocol Dairesi Genel Mudurlugu [*Protocol Office Directorate General*] [*of Foreign Affairs Ministry*]   (TU)
PROT .... Protokol [*Protocol*] [*Afrikaans*]
PROTABACO ... Productora Tabacalera de Colombia SA [*Colombia*]   (COL)
Pro Tan...... Proje Tanzimi [*Organizing of Project*]   (TU)
PROTECO ... Productos Tecnicos Colombianos [*Buenaventura*]   (COL)
Prot ekz s ... Minutes of the Exarchy Council   (BU)
PROTELA ... Fabrica de Productos Textiles Protela Boger & Compania [*Colombia*]   (COL)
PROTENAL ... Productos Tecnicos Nacionales [*Colombia*]   (COL)
PROTERRA ... Programa de Redistribuicao de Terras e de Estimulo as Atividades Agro-Pecuarias do Nordeste e do Norte [*Land Redistribution and Agricultural and Livestock Incentive Program for the Northeast and North*] [*Brazil*]   (LA)
PROTEXSY ... Office de Promotion du Textile Synthetique en Cote-D'Ivoire
protez .... Protezione [*Protection*] [*Italian*]
PROTON .. Perusahaan Otomobile National [*Malaysian automobile manufacturer*]
PROTOS... Project Group voor Technische Ontwikkelingssamenwerking [*Project Group for Tec hnical development Cooperation*] [*Belgium*]   (EAIO)
prots .... Percent   (RU)
PROTZ...... Regulation on Recording and Reporting Labor Accidents   (BU)
prov .... Provedor [*Purveyor*] [*Portuguese*]
PROV .... Provencal [*Language, etc.*]
Prov.......... Province [*French*]   (MTD)
Prov.......... Provincia [*Province*] [*Spanish*]   (GPO)
PROV .... Provinciale [*Provincial*] [*Netherlands*]   (EY)
Prov.......... Provinsie [*Province*] [*Afrikaans*]
Prov.......... Provinz [*Province*] [*German*]   (EG)
prov .... Provisao [*Provision*] [*Portuguese*]
Prov.......... Provision [*Commission*] [*German*] [*Business term*]
prov .... Provisorio [*Provisional*] [*Portuguese*]
prov .... Provulok [*Lane*] [*Commonwealth of Independent States*]   (EECI)
prova .... Provincia [*Province*] [*Spanish*]
PROVALLE ... Promotora del Valle Ltda. [*Colombia*]   (COL)
Provbl........ Provinciaal Blad [*Benelux*]   (BAS)
provbr......... Provozni Brigada [*Traffic Brigade*] [*Motor pool for ministries*]   (CZ)
provd .... Provdana [*Married (Female)*]   (CZ)
PROVESA ... Produtos Veterinarios SA [*Brazil*]   (DSCA)
ProvHof..... Provinciaal Hof [*Benelux*]   (BAS)
PROVICALI ... Promotora de Vivienda de Cali   (COL)

PROVICO ... Promotora de Vivienda Popular [*Colombia*]   (COL)
PROVIEN ... Sociedad Protectora de Viviendas Economicas [*Programa "Alimentos para la Paz"*] [*Chile*]   (LAA)
PROVIMI ... Proteins, Vitamins, and Minerals [*Dutch manufacturing company*]
PROVINC ... PROVINC Kereskedelmi Egyesules [*PROVINC Trade Association*]   (HU)
PROVO ..... Provocateur   (DSUE)
PROVO ..... Provost Marshal [*Australia*] [*World War II*]   (DSUE)
PROVO ..... Stichting Proefbedrijf Voedselbestraling [*Experimental Station for Food Irradiation*] [*Netherlands*]   (PDAA)
Provol........ Wire Plant [*Topography*]   (RU)
provor........ Provisor [*Purveyor*] [*Spanish*]
ProvSt........ Provinciale Staten [*Benelux*]   (BAS)
Provw .... Provinciale Wet [*Benelux*]   (BAS)
provzheldor ... Cable Railway   (RU)
prox luc ...... Proxima Luce [*Day Before*] [*Latin*]   (MAE)
proxo .... Proximo [*Next, Nearest*] [*Spanish*]
Proyektgidromekhanizatsiya ... State Planning Institute for the Complex Planning of Hydraulic Mining Establishments of Nonmetallic Building Materials and for the Rendering of Technical Assistance in Putting Such Establishments in Operation and Servicing Them   (RU)
Proyektstal'konstruktsiya ... State Institute for the Planning, Research, and Testing of Steel Structures and Bridges   (RU)
Proz............ Prozent [*or Prozentig*] [*Percent or Percentage*] [*German*]
proz .... Versification   (BU)
Prozamet.... Biuro Projektowania Zakladow Przemyslu Metalowego i Elektrotechnicznego [*Bureau of Plans for Metal and Electrical Industry Plants*]   (POL)
prozodezhda ... Work Clothes   (RU)
PRP........... Manual Pneumatic Riveting Press   (RU)
PRP........... Parti de la Revolution Populaire [*People's Revolutionary Party*] [*Zaire*] [*Political party*]   (PD)
PRP........... Partido de Renovacion Puertorriqueno [*Puerto Rican Renewal Party*] [*Political party*]   (EY)
PRP........... Partido de Representacao Popular [*Brazil*] [*Political party*]
PRP........... Partido Renovacion Patriotica [*Honduras*] [*Political party*]   (EY)
PRP........... Partido Republicano Portugues [*Portuguese Republican Party*] [*Political party*]   (PPE)
PRP........... Partido Revolucionario do Proletariado [*Revolutionary Party of the Proletariat*] [*Brazil*]   (LA)
PRP........... Partido Revolucionario do Proletariado [*Revolutionary Party of the Proletariat*] [*Portuguese*]   (WER)
PRP........... Partido Revolucionario Popular [*Popular Revolutionary Party*] [*Portugal*] [*Political party*]   (PPE)
PRP........... Partido Revolucionario Proletario [*Proletarian Revolutionary Party*] [*Chile*]   (LA)
PRP........... Parti Republicain du Progres [*Republican Progress Party*] [*Central Africa*] [*Political party*]   (PD)
PRP........... Parti Republicain Progressif [*Algeria*] [*Political party*]   (EY)
PRP........... People's Redemption Party [*Nigeria*] [*Political party*]   (PPW)
PRP........... People's Reform Party [*Philippines*] [*Political party*]   (EY)
PRP........... People's Revolutionary Party [*Benin*] [*Political party*]
PRP........... People's Revolutionary Party [*North Vietnam*] [*Political party*]
PRP........... People's Revolution Party [*Singapore*]   (ML)
PrP............ Precompte Professionnel [*Benelux*]   (BAS)
PRP........... Prevencao Rodoviaria Portuguesa [*Portuguese*]   (SLS)
PRP........... Progressive Reform Party
PRP........... Track Relay Repeater   (RU)
PRPA........ Partido de Reunificacao do Povo Angolano [*Party for the Reunification of the Angolan People*]   (AF)
PRPB........ Parti de la Revolution Populaire du Benin [*Benin People's Revolutionary Party*] [*Political party*]   (PD)
PRP-BR ..... Partido Revolucionario do Proletariado-Brigadas Revolucionarias [*Revolutionary Party of the Proletariat-Revolutionary Brigades*] [*Portuguese*]   (WER)
PRPC........ Parti Republicain du Peuple Camerounais [*Political party*]   (EY)
PRPC........ Public Relations Policy Committee [*NATO*]   (NATG)
PrPCU-L ... Catholic University of Puerto Rico, Law Library, Ponce, Puerto Rico [*Library symbol*] [*Library of Congress*]   (LCLS)
PrPK .... Regulation on Conciliation Commissions   (BU)
pr pl .... Before Noon   (BU)
PRPL......... Light Sectional Floating Pier   (RU)
PRPL......... People's Democratic Republic of Laos
PrPS.......... Prapor Pohranicni Straze [*Border Guard Battalion*]   (CZ)
PRPS .... Relay and Broadcasting Equipment Enterprise   (BU)
PRPT .... Parti Revolutionnaire du Peuple Tunisien [*Revolutionary Party of the Tunisian People*] [*Political party*]   (PD)
PRPUC...... Philippine Republic Presidential Unit Citation [*Military decoration*]
PRPUCE..... Philippine Republic Presidential Unit Citation Emblem [*Military decoration*]
PRPUP...... Przedsiebiorstwo Robot Przemyslowych Urzadzen Podziemnych [*Industrial Underground Construction Enterprise*]   (POL)
PRR .... Mode Selector Switch   (RU)

PRR .... Philippine Research Reactor
PRR .... Poljoprivredna Remontna Radionica [*Agricultural Repair Shop*]
    (YU)
Prr.............. Privaatrecht [*Benelux*] (BAS)
PRRI .... Puerto Rico Rum Institute [*Later, PRRPA*]
PRRI-PERMESTA ... Pemerintah Revolusioner Republik Indonesia -
    Perdjuangan Semesta [*Revolutionary Government of the
    Republic of Indonesia - Total Struggle Movement*] (IN)
PRRM........ Philippine Rural Reconstruction Movement
PRRPA ...... Puerto Rico Rum Producers Association [*Defunct*] (EA)
PRRWM.... Przedsiebiorstwo Rejonowych Robot Wodno-Melioracyjnych
    [*Regional Irrigation and Land Reclamation Enterprise*]
    (POL)
PRS........... Antimissile Missile (RU)
PRS........... Homing Radio Station (RU)
PRS........... Mobile Regulating Station (RU)
PRS........... Parasi [*Solomon Islands*] [*Airport symbol*] (OAG)
PRS........... Parliamentary Research Service [*Tasmania, Australia*]
PRS........... Partai Rakyat Singapura [*Singapore People's Party*] (ML)
PRS........... Partei fuer Renten-, Steuer-, und Soziale Gerechtigkeit [*Party for
    Equitable Pensions, Taxation, and Social Services*]
    [*Germany*] [*Political party*] (PPW)
PRS........... Parti de la Revolution Socialiste [*Party of Socialist Revolution*]
    [*Senegal*] [*Political party*]
PRS........... Parti de la Revolution Socialiste [*Party of Socialist Revolution*]
    [*Benin*] [*Political party*]
PRS........... Parti de la Revolution Socialiste [*Party of Socialist Revolution*]
    [*Algeria*] (AF)
PRS........... Partido de la Revolucion Salvadorena [*Salvadoran Revolutionary
    Party*] (LA)
PRS........... Partido de la Revolucion Socialista [*Party of the Socialist
    Revolution*] [*Cuba*] [*Political party*]
PRS........... Partido para a Renovacao Social [*Party for Social Renovation*]
    [*Guinea-Bissau*] [*Political party*] (EY)
PRS........... Partido Revolucionario Socialista [*Mexico*] [*Political party*]
    (EY)
PRS........... Partido Revolucionario Socialista [*Socialist Revolutionary Party*]
    [*Colorado*] (LA)
PRS........... Parti du Regroupement Soudanais
PRS........... Parti Republicain Senegalais [*Senegalese Republican Party*]
    (AF)
PRS........... Partito Republicano Sammarinese [*Republican Party*] [*San
    Marino*] [*Political party*] (EY)
Prs.............. Personel [*Personnel*] (TU)
PRS........... Political Reference Service Group [*Australia*]
PRS........... Polski Rejestr Statkow [*Polish Register of Ships*] (POL)
PRS........... President of the Royal Society [*British*]
PRS........... Projet Rural de Sedhiou
PRS........... Radio Range Station (BU)
PRS........... Sailing Vessel (RU)
PRS........... Train Radio Station (RU)
PRSA........ Proportional Representation Society of Australia
PRSB........ Parti de la Revolution Socialiste du Benin
PRSC .... Partido Revolucionario Social Cristiano [*Christian Social
    Revolutionary Party*] [*Dominican Republic*] (LA)
pr sch.......... Proportional Counter (RU)
Prsdt........... Praesident [*President*] [*German*]
PRSF .... People's Revolutionary Struggle Force
PRSI .... Co-Phasing Pulse Receiver (RU)
PRSL .... Pedestrian's Road Safety League [*Australia*]
pr/smos...... Proypologismos [*Budget*] (GC)
PRSNT ...... Parti Republicain pour le Salut National Tchadien [*Republican
    Party for Chadian National Salvation*] (AF)
prspr........... Press-Spritzen [*Transfer Molding*] [*German*] (GCA)
PRSS .... Parti Republicain Social du Senegal
PRSS .... Powszechna Robotnicza Spoldzielnia Spozywcza [*General
    Worker's Consumer Cooperative*] (POL)
PrSt........... Predigtstation [*German*]
PRSTS....... Power Relay Satellite Transmission System [*Iceland*]
PRT.......... Device for Programed Temperature Control (RU)
Prt .... Parit [*Stream, Canal, Ditch*] [*Malay*] (NAU)
PRT.......... Parliamentary Remuneration Tribunal [*New South Wales,
    Australia*]
PRT.......... Partido Republicano Trabalhista [*Republican Workers Party*]
    [*Brazil*] (LA)
PRT.......... Partido Revolucionario de los Trabajadores [*Workers'
    Revolutionary Party*] [*Mexico*] (LA)
PRT.......... Partido Revolucionario de los Trabajadores [*Workers'
    Revolutionary Party*] [*Argentina*] [*Political party*] (PD)
PRT.......... Partido Revolucionario de los Trabajadores [*Revolutionary
    Workers Party*] [*Panama Political party*] (EY)
PRT.......... Partido Revolucionario de los Trabajadores [*Workers'
    Revolutionary Party*] [*Peru*] [*Political party*] (PPW)
PRT.......... Partido Revolucionario de los Trabajadores [*Workers'
    Revolutionary Party*] [*Uruguay*] [*Political party*] (PD)
PRT.......... Partido Revolucionario de los Trabajadores [*Revolutionary
    Workers' Party*] [*Costa Rica*] [*Political party*] (EY)

PRT........... Partido Revolucionario de Trabajadores [*Revolutionary Worker's
    Party*] [*Colorado*] [*Political party*] (EY)
PRT........... Partido Revolucionario dos Trabalhadores [*Workers'
    Revolutionary Party*] [*Portuguese*] (WER)
PRT........... Partido Rural Trabalhista [*Rural Labor Patry*] [*Brazil*] (LA)
PRT........... Patient Review Tribunal [*Queensland, Australia*]
PRT........... Plovni Recni Trenovi [*River Convoys*] [*Navy*] (YU)
PRT........... Portugal [*ANSI three-letter standard code*] (CNC)
PRT........... Proportional Temperature Control (RU)
PRT........... Prozessrechentechnik [*German*] (ADPT)
PRT........... Przedsiebiorstwo Robot Telekomunikacyjnych [*Communication
    Construction Enterprise*] (POL)
prtb............ Mobile Missile Maintenance Depot (BU)
PRTB .... Mobile Repair and Technical Base (RU)
PRTB .... Partido Revolucionario de Trabajadores Bolivianos [*Bolivian
    Workers' Revolutionary Party*] [*Political party*] (PD)
PRTBR ...... Partido Revolucionario de los Trabajadores de Bolivia Romero
    [*Bolivia*] [*Political party*] (PPW)
PRTC......... Partido Revolucionario de los Trabajadores Centroamericanos
    [*Revolutionary Party of Central American Workers*] [*El
    Salvador*] [*Political party*] (PD)
PRTC-H .... Partido Revolucionario de los Trabajadores Centroamericanos --
    Seccion de Honduras [*Revolutionary Party of Central
    American Workers -- Honduras*] [*Political party*]
PRTI .... Telemetering Receiver (RU)
PRTS .... Portable Radiotelegraph Station (RU)
PrTS .... Regulation on Hearing Labor Disputes (BU)
PRTZ......... Partisans, Guerrillas (BU)
PRU .... Control Pulse Receiver (RU)
PRU .... Manual Control Panel (RU)
PRU .... Mobile X-Ray Unit (RU)
PrU .... Model Statutes (BU)
PRU .... Palais Royal d'Ugarit [*Paris, France*] (BJA)
PRU .... Precambrian Research Unit [*University of Cape Town*] [*South
    Africa*] (AA)
PRU .... Prome [*Myanmar*] [*Airport symbol*] (OAG)
PRUC .... Partido Revolucionario de Union Civico [*Revolutionary Party
    for Civic Union*] [*Costa Rica*] [*Political party*]
Prud .... Conseil de Prud'Hommes [*French*] (BAS)
PRUD .... Partido Revolucionario de Unificacion Democratica
    [*Revolutionary Party of Democratic Unification*] [*El
    Salvador*] (LA)
PRUD .... Partido Revolucionario de Unification Democratica
    [*Revolutionary Party of Democratic Unification*] [*El
    Salvador*]
Prud App.... Conseil de Prud'Hommes d'Appel [*French*] (BAS)
Prud Brux .. Jugement Conseil de Prud'Hommes de Bruxelles [*Belgium*]
    (BAS)
PrUDP....... Regulation on the Application of the Ukase on State Pensions
    (BU)
Pruef .... Pruefung [*Test*] [*German*] (GCA)
Pruflsgg...... Pruefloesungen [*Testing Solutions*] [*German*]
PRUM .... Underground Working of Coal Deposits (RU)
PRUMO.... Progresso Unido de Mocambique [*United Progress of
    Mozambique*] (AF)
PRUN .... Partido Republicano de Unidad Nacional [*National Unity
    Republican Party*] [*Guyana*] (LA)
PrUNRM... Regulation on the Application of the Ukase on Encouraging a
    Higher Birth Rate and Large Families (BU)
PRUPC...... Parti Revolutionnaire de l'Union des Populations du Cameroun
PrUTKZS ... TKZS [*Labor Cooperative Farm*] Model Statutes (BU)
PrUZUP.... Regulation on the Structure and Tasks of the Pensions
    Administration and Its Local Organs (BU)
PRV .... Call Receiver (RU)
PRV .... Float-Type Regulating Valve (RU)
PRV .... Partido de la Revolucion Venezolana [*Party of the Venezuelan
    Revolution*] (LA)
PRV .... Pour Rendre Visite [*To Make a Call*] [*French*]
Prv.............. Proliv [*Channel, Strait*] [*Russian*] (NAU)
Prv.............. Provisor [*or Provisorisch*] [*German*]
pr-vo........... Government (RU)
pr-vo........... Representation, Delegation (RU)
PrVOBL.... Preisverordnungsblatt [*Price Regulations Gazette*] (EG)
PrVT......... Prosecutor of a Military Tribunal (RU)
PrVTAK .... Regulation on Proceedings before the Foreign Trade Arbitration
    Commission (BU)
PRW .... Przysposobienie Rolnicze i Wojskowe [*Agricultural and Military
    Training*] (POL)
PRWO .... Puerto Rican Revolutionary Workers Organization
PRWRA..... Puerto Rican Water Resources Authority
PRY .... Paraguay [*ANSI three-letter standard code*] (CNC)
pryam........ In the Direct Sense (RU)
prydl.......... Prydlig [*Neat*] [*Sweden*]
PRZ........... Locomotive Repair Plant (RU)
PRZ........... Przedsiebiorstwo Robot Zmechanizowanych [*Mechanized
    Construction Enterprise*] (POL)
Pr za opna kn ... Rules for Descriptive Cataloging in Public Libraries (BU)

PrZDA....... Regulation on the Implementation of the Law on State Arbitration (BU)

P Rz d/s ..... Pelnomocnik Rzadu do Spraw [*Government Plenipotentiary For*] [*Poland*]

przed Chr ... Przed Chrystusem [*Poland*]

przedr ... Przedruk [*Reprint*] (POL)

przedst....... Przedstawienie [*Performance*] [*Poland*]

przejrz .... Przejrzane [*Examined*] (POL)

przekl .... Przeklad [*Translation*] (POL)

przel .... Przelozyl [*Translated By*] [*Poland*]

przerob...... Przerobione [*Revised*] (POL)

przetl .... Przetlumaczyl [*Translated By*] [*Poland*]

przew......... Przewodniczacy [*President*] [*Poland*]

przew......... Przewodnik [*Guide*] [*Poland*]

PRZh .... Radioisotopic Liquid Density Meter (RU)

PrZhG....... Regulation for Accepting, Examining, and Settling Civil Grievances (BU)

PRZS .... Mobile Repair and Charging Station (RU)

przyg .... Przygotowal [*Prepared By*] [*Poland*]

przyp .... Przypisek [*Footnote, Postscript*] (POL)

PRZZ........ Powiatowa Rada Zwiazkow Zawodowych [*County Council of Trade Unions*] (POL)

PS............... Absorber (RU)

PS............... Adjustment Fire [*Artillery*] (RU)

PS............... Aiming Rest, Aiming Stand (RU)

PS............... Aircraft Bearing (RU)

PS............... Anti-Icing System (RU)

PS............... Bias Bleeder (RU)

PS............... Boom Position [*Nautical term*] (RU)

PS............... Card-Reader Punch [*Computers*] (RU)

PS............... Ceskoslovenska Lekarska Spolecnost J. E. Purkyne [*J. E. Purkyne Czechoslovak Medical Society*] (CZ)

ps............... Coast Guard Vessel (RU)

PS............... Communications Post (RU)

PS............... Corpo delle Guardie di Pubblica Sicurezza [*Corps of Public Security Guards*] [*Italian*] (WER)

PS............... Correction for Displacement [*Artillery*] (RU)

PS............... Direct Coupling (RU)

PS............... Dispatch Vessel (RU)

PS............... Field Crop Station (RU)

PS............... Field Service (RU)

PS............... Firing Regulations (RU)

ps............... Handwritten Pages (BU)

PS............... Intermediate Station (RU)

PS............... Interstage Cooler [*Refrigeration*] (RU)

PS............... Lines of Communication [*Military term*], Routes of Communication (RU)

PS............... Marshaling Yard, Classification Yard [*Railroads*] (RU)

PS............... Message Center (RU)

ps............... Opere Citato (BU)

PS............... Pakistan Standard (IAA)

PS............... Pandeios Skholi [*School*] [*PASPE*] [*See also*] (GC)

PS............... Pania Sud [*A soil type*] [*Italy*]

ps............... Parallax-Second, Parsec (RU)

PS............... Partecipazioni Statali [*State Participations*] [*Italian*] (WER)

PS............... Parteischule [*Party School*] (EG)

PS............... Partido Socialista [*Socialist Party*] [*Uruguay*] [*Political party*]

PS............... Partido Socialista [*Socialist Party*] [*Chile*] [*Political party*]

PS............... Partido Socialista Portuguesa [*Portuguese Socialist Party*] [*Political party*] (PPE)

PS............... Partido Socialista - Uno [*Socialist Party - One*] [*Also, PS-1 Bolivia*] [*Political party*] (PPW)

PS............... Parti Socialiste [*Socialist Party*] [*Belgium*] [*Political party*] (PPW)

PS............... Parti Socialiste - Federation de la Reunion [*Reunion Federation of the Socialist Party*] [*Political party*] (PPW)

PS............... Parti Socialiste Senegalais [*Senegal*]

Ps .... Pasa [*Pasha*] [*Turkey*] (GPO)

PS............ Pasca Sarjana [*Academic degree*] [*Indonesian*]

PS............ Pasne Skupnosti [*Pastures Held in Common*] (YU)

PS............ Passed School of Instruction [*of Officers*] [*British*]

PS............ Passenger Aircraft (RU)

PRS............ Patrol Vessel (RU)

PS............ Pavel Stepanek [*Czech ESP performer*]

PS............ Pedagogicky Sbor [*Board of Education*] (CZ)

PS............ Perifereiakon Symvoulion [*Regional Council*] (GC)

PS............ Persent [*Percent*] [*Afrikaans*]

PS............ Personeel Statuut [*Benelux*] (BAS)

PS............ Personenschutz [*Protection of Persons (MfS Department, supplies guards for officials, etc.)*] (EG)

PS............ Pesaro [*Car registration plates*] [*Italian*]

Ps .... Peseta [*Monetary unit*] [*Andorra and Spain*] (BARN)

PS............ Pferdestaerke [*Horsepower*] [*German*] (GPO)

PS............ Pharmaceutical Society [*Australia*]

PS............ Philippine Scouts

PS............ Picosekunde [*German*] (ADPT)

PS............... Pisnovy Soubor [*Choral Ensemble*] (CZ)

PS............... Plastic Scintillator (RU)

PS............... Plattenspeicher [*German*] (ADPT)

ps............... Ploshchad [*Square*] [*Commonwealth of Independent States*] (EECI)

PS............... Pocetnicka Sluzba [*Accounting Service*] (CZ)

PS............... Podaci Stanice [*Distribution Stations*] (CZ)

PS............... Poddustojnicka Skola [*Non-Commissioned Officers' School*] (CZ)

PS............... Podnikova Sprava [*Plant Management*] (CZ)

PS............... Pohranicni Straz [*Border Guard*] (CZ)

ps............... Poids Specifique [*Specific Gravity*] [*French*]

PS............... Pojistovaci Soud [*Insurance Court*] (CZ)

PS............... Police Sergeant [*Scotland Yard*]

PS............... Policia Sandinista [*Sandinist Police*] [*Nicaragua*] (LA)

PS............... Politechnika Szczecinska [*Engineering College of Szczecin*] [*Poland*]

PS............... Politicka Sprava [*Political Directorate*] (CZ)

PS............... Poljoprivredna Stanica [*Agricultural Station*] (YU)

PS............... Polni Soud [*Military Court*] (CZ)

PS............... Polni Straz [*Reconnaissance Unit*] (CZ)

PS............... Polyester Resin (RU)

PS............... Polystyrene (RU)

PS............... Polystyrene for Foaming (RU)

PS............... Popis Stanovnistva [*Population Census*] (YU)

PS............... Posadkova Sprava [*Garrison Directorate*] (CZ)

PS............... Pos-Escrito [*Postscript*] [*Portuguese*]

PS............... Position Speciale [*Special Appointment*] [*Cambodia*] (CL)

PS............... Positive Column [*Electricity*] (RU)

Ps............... Possak [*Mailbag*] [*Afrikaans*]

PS............... Poste de Secours [*Dressing Station*] [*Military*] [*French*] (MTD)

PS............... Postenska Stedilnica [*Postal Savings Bank*] (YU)

PS............... Post Office Station (RU)

PS............... Postovni Sporitelna [*Postal Savings Agency*] (CZ)

ps............... Postskriptum [*Postscript*] [*Denmark*] (GPO)

ps............... Postskriptum [*Postscript*] [*Sweden*] (GPO)

PS............... Postskriptum [*Postscript*] [*German*]

PS............... Povazske Strojarne [*Machine Building Factories of the Vah River Area*] (CZ)

PS............... Poverenictvo Spojov [*Office of the Commissioner of Communications*] (CZ)

PS............... Poverenictvo Spravodlivosti [*Office of the Commissioner of Justice*] (CZ)

PS............... Powszechna Samoobrona [*General Civil Defense*] (POL)

PS............... Pozemni Stavby [*Surface Construction*] [*A periodical*] (CZ)

PS............... Pravni Savet (SIV) [*Legal Council*] (YU)

PS............... Preduzece Soko [*Former Yugoslavia*] [*ICAO aircraft manufacturer identifier*] (ICAO)

P/S............. Pretovarne Stanice [*Transshipment Stations*] (YU)

P/S............. Pripusna Stanica [*Admission Station*] (YU)

PS............... Private Sak [*Private Bag*] [*Afrikaans*]

PS............... Privredni Savet [*Economic Council*] (YU)

PS............... Privredni Savetnik [*Economic Counselor*] [*A periodical*] (YU)

PS............... Privredni Sud [*Economic Court*] (YU)

PS............... Programmiersystem [*Programer System*] [*German*] (ADPT)

PS............... Progres Social [*Benelux*] (BAS)

PS............... Prumyslova Skola [*Industrial School*] (CZ)

PS............... Przedsiebiorstwo Samorzadowe [*Municipal Enterprise*] (POL)

Ps .... Psalm [*Psalm*] [*Afrikaans*]

ps............... Psaume [*Psalm*] [*French*]

ps- .... Pseudo- [*German*] (GCA)

PS............... Pseudoniem [*Pseudonym*] [*Afrikaans*]

ps............... Pseudonim [*Pseudonym*] [*Poland*]

PS............... Pubblica Sicurezza [*Police*] [*Italian*]

ps............... Puro-Sangue [*Pure-Blood*] [*Portuguese*]

PS............... Purple Glass (RU)

PS............... Pur Sang [*Thoroughbred*] [*Of a horse*] [*French*] (MTD)

PS............... Pyrosvestikon Soma [*Fire Corps*] (GC)

PS............... Recording Potentiometer (RU)

p/s............. Sailing Ship (RU)

PS............... Scaler (RU)

PS............... Settlement Soviet of Workers' Deputies (RU)

PS............... Signal Device (RU)

PS............... Signal Regiment (RU)

PS............... Solenoid Drive (RU)

PS............... Spontaneous Polarization (Method) (RU)

PS............... Starter Panel (RU)

PS............... Substation (RU)

ps............... Supply Wharf, Supply Pier (RU)

PS............... Total Correction [*Topography*] (RU)

PS............... Trade Union (RU)

PS............... Transport [*Russian aircraft symbol*]

PS............... Union of Consumers' Societies (RU)

PS............... Well Potential [*Pet.*] (RU)

PS₁ .... Indizierte Pferdestaerke [*Indicated Horsepower*] [*German*]

PS-1 .... Partido Socialista - Uno [Socialist Party - One] [Also, PS Bolivia] [Political party]   (PD)
PSA............ Pacific Island Aviation, Inc. [Mariana Islands] [ICAO designator]   (FAAC)
PSA............ Pacific Science Association [ICSU]
PSA............ Pangosmion Synedrion Apodimon [World Congress of Repatriates]   (GC)
PSA............ Pankyprios Syndesmos Agoniston [Pan-Cyprian League of Fighters]   (GC)
PSA............ Partido Socialista Aponte [Bolivia] [Political party]   (PPW)
PSA............ Partido Socialista Argentino [Socialist Party of Argentina] [Political party]
PSA............ Partido Socialista de Andalucia [Socialist Party of Andalusia] [Spanish]   (WER)
PSA............ Partido Socialista de Aragon [Socialist Party of Aragon] [Spanish]   (WER)
PSA............ Partido Solitario Africano
PSA............ Parti Socialiste Africain
PSA............ Parti Socialiste Autonome [Autonomous Socialist Party] [France] [Political party]   (PPE)
PSA............ Parti Solidaire Africain [African Solidarity Party] [Congo] [Political party]
PSA............ Parti Sportif Algerien
PSA............ Partito Socialista Autonomo [Autonomous Socialist Party] [Switzerland] [Political party]   (PPW)
PSA............ People's Supreme Assembly [Yemen] [Political party]   (PPW)
PSA............ Petites Soeurs de l'Assumption [Little Sisters of the Assumption - LSA] [Paris, France]   (EAIO)
PSA............ Peugeot Societe Anonyme [France]
PSA............ Peugot Societe Anonyme [Peugeot Co. Ltd.] [French]
PSA............ Pharmaceutical Society of Australia   (ADA)
PSA............ Philippine Shipbuilders Association   (DS)
PSA............ Philippine Standards Association   (IAA)
PSA............ Pisa [Italy] [Airport symbol]   (OAG)
PSA............ Port of Singapore Authority   (DS)
PSA............ Postsparkassenamt [Postal Savings Office]   (EG)
PSA............ Potters' Society of Australia
PSA............ Practical Socialism in Australia   (ADA)
PSA............ President of the Society of Antiquaries [British]
PSA............ Product Standards Agency [Ministry of Trade and Industry] [Philippines]   (IMH)
PSA............ Protective Security Attendant [Australia]
PSA............ Public Servants Association of South Africa   (AA)
PSA............ Public Service Association [Trade union] [New Zealand]
PSA............ Public Service Association [Western Samoa]
PSA............ Public Service Association [Guyana]
PSAA......... Panellinios Synomospondia Agoniston Andistaseos [Panhellenic Federation of Resistance Fighters]   (GC)
PSAA........ Polwarth Sheepbreeders' Association of Australia
PSAAThAX ... Panellinios Syndesmos Axiomatikon Asyrmatou Thalassis, Aeros kai Xiras [Panhellenic Association of Marine, Air, and Land Radio Officers]   (GC)
PSAAV ...... Provincial Sewerage Authorities Association of Victoria [Australia]
PSAB .... Pathology Services Accreditation Board [Victoria, Australia]
PSAC........ Pathology Services Advisory Committee [Australia]
PSAC........ Public Service Alliance of Canada [Labor union of federal government employees]
psag........... Parancsnoksag [Headquarters] [Military]   (HU)
PSAGE...... Partido Socialista de Guinea Ecuatorial [Equatorial Guinea]
PSAI .... Philippine Shipowners Association, Inc.   (DS)
PSAILIS.... Professional Member of the South African Institute for Librarianship and Information Science   (AA)
PSAIT....... Polish Society of Anaesthesiology and Intensive Therapy   (EAIO)
PSAJ......... Peace Studies Association of Japan
PSAN........ Partit Socialista d'Alliberament Nacional dels Paisos Catalans [National Liberation Socialist Party of the Catalan Regions] [Spanish]   (WER)
PSAPY ...... Panellinios Syndesmos Atmoploikon kai Praktoreiakon Ypallilon [Panhellenic Association of Shipping and Travel Agency Employees]   (GC)
P S ar .... Pur Sang Arabe [French]   (MTD)
PSAS .... Parti Senegalais d'Action Socialiste
PSASA...... Public Service Association of South Australia
PSAThP .... Panellinios Syndesmos Anapiron kai Thymaton Polemou 1912-1941 [Panhellenic Association of Disabled and Victims of Wars 1912 and 1941]   (GC)
PSB............ Partido Socialista Brasileiro [Brazilian Socialist Party]   (LA)
PSB............ Partido Socialista de Bolivia [Bolivian Socialist Party]   (LA)
PSB............ Parti Socialiste Belge [Belgian Socialist Party]   (WER)
PSB............ Police Superannuation Board [Australia]
PSB............ Public Service Board [Australia]   (PDAA)
psb............ Road Construction Battalion   (BU)
PSBA .... Pepsi Seven-Up Bottlers Australia Proprietary Ltd.
PSBK .... Poradni Sbor pro Bytovou Kulturu [Homemaking Advisory Council]   (CZ)

PSBU......... Public Sector and Broadcasting Union [Australia]
PSBV .... Public Service Board Victoria [Australia]
PSC............ Congolese Socialist Party [Zaire] [Political party]   (PD)
PSC............ Palaeontological Society of China   (SLS)
PSC............ Partido Social Conservador Colombiano [Colombian Social Conservative Party] [Political party]   (EY)
PSC............ Partido Social Cristiano [Social Christian Party] [Bolivia] [Political party]
PSC............ Partido Social Cristiano [Social Christian Party] [Guatemala] [Political party]   (PPW)
PSC............ Partido Social Cristiano [Social Christian Party] [Ecuador] [Political party]   (PPW)
PSC............ Partido Social Cristiano [Christian Social Party] [Spanish]   (WER)
PSC............ Partido Socialcristiano Nicaraguense [Nicaraguan Social Christian Party] [Political party]   (PPW)
PSC............ Partido Socialista de Catalunya [Catalan Socialist Party] [Spain] [Political party]   (PPE)
PSC............ Parti Social Chretien [Christian Social Party] [Belgium]   (WER)
PSC............ Parti Socialiste Caledonien [New Caledonia] [Political party]   (FEA)
PSC............ Parti Socialiste Camerounais [Cameroon Socialist Party] [Political party]
PSC............ Parti Socialiste Centrafricain [Central African Socialist Party] [Political party]   (PD)
PSC............ Parti Socialiste Congolais [Congolese Socialist Party]
PSC............ Parti Socialiste des Comores [Comoro Socialist Party]   (AF)
PSC............ Passed Staff College [Australia]
PSC............ Philippine Shippers Council   (DS)
PSC............ Philippine Sugar Commission   (EA)
PSC............ Photography Studies College [Australia]
PSC............ Police Service Commission [Jamaica]   (LA)
PSC............ Preparatory Studies Course [Australia]
PSC............ Price Stabilization Council [Philippines]   (DS)
PSC............ Production Sharing Contract [Petroleum Industry] [Indonesia]
PSC............ Product Safety Committee [New South Wales, Australia]
PSC............ Project Support Communication
PSC............ P. Soucail & Cie.
PSC............ Public Service Commission [Trinidadian and Tobagan]   (LA)
PSCA .... Pakistan Senior Citizens Association   (EAIO)
PSCA .... Polish Social and Cultural Association [British]   (EAIO)
PSCAV ...... Professional Squash Coaches' Association of Victoria [Australia]
PSCB .... Parliamentary Standing Committee on Broadcasting [Australia]
PSCLA...... Petroleum Supply Committee for Latin America
PSCN......... Partido Socialcristiano Nicaraguense [Nicaraguan Social Christian Party] [Political party]   (PPW)
PSC-PSOE ... Partit dels Socialistes de Catalunya [Party of Socialists of Catalonia] [Political party]   (PPW)
PSD............ Destour Socialist Party [Tunisia] [Political party]   (PD)
PSD............ Doctor of Political Science
Ps D .... Doctor of Psychology
Ps D .... Doctor of Psychology in Metaphysics
PSD............ Doctor of Public Service
PSD............ Medium-Pressure Heater   (RU)
PSD............ Message Center   (BU)
PSD............ Panglima Setia Di-Raja [First Grade of the Most Honorable Order of Setia Di-Raja]   (ML)
PSD............ Partido Socialdemocracia [Social Democratic Party] [Chile] [Political party]   (EY)
PSD............ Partido Social Democrata [Social Democratic Party] [Bolivia] [Political party]   (PPW)
PSD............ Partido Social Democrata [Social Democratic Party] [Spain] [Political party]   (PPE)
PSD............ Partido Social Democrata [Social Democratic Party] [Mexico] [Political party]   (PPW)
PSD............ Partido Social Democrata [Social Democratic Party] [Chile] (LA)
PSD............ Partido Social Democratico [Social Democratic Party] [Portuguese]   (WER)
PSD............ Partido Social Democratico [Social Democratic Party] [Brazil] [Political party]
PSD............ Partido Social Democratico [Social Democratic Party] [El Salvador] [Political party]
PSD............ Partido Social Democratico [Social Democratic Party] [Nicaragua] [Political party]   (PPW)
PSD............ Partido Socialista Democratico [Social Democratic Party] [Argentina] [Political party]   (PPW)
PSD............ Partido Socialista Democratico [Social Democratic Party] [Guatemala] [Political party]   (PD)
PSD............ Partido Socialista Democratico [Democratic Socialist Party] [Ecuador]   (LA)
PSD............ Partido Socialista Democratico [Democratic Socialist Party] [Venezuela]   (LA)
PSD............ Parti Social-Democrate [Social Democratic Party] [Luxembourg]   (WER)
PSD............ Parti Social-Democrate [Social Democratic Party] [Malagasy]   (AF)

PSD........... Parti Social-Democrate [Algeria] [Political party] (EY)
PSD........... Parti Social-Democrate [Social Democratic Party] [France] [Political party] (PPW)
PSD........... Parti Social Democrate de Madagascar et des Comores [Social Democratic Party of Madagascar and Comores]
PSD........... Parti Social-Democratie [Benin] [Political party] (EY)
PSD........... Parti Socialiste Democratique [Cameroon] [Political party] (EY)
PSD........... Parti Socialiste Democratique [Morocco]
PSD........... Parti Socialiste Destourien [Destourian Socialist Party] [Tunisia] (AF)
PSD........... Personal Services Department [Navy] [British]
PSD........... Polish Social Democracy (RU)
PSD........... Public Services Department [Malaysia] (ML)
PSD........... Punkt Sprzedazy Detalicznej [Retail Sales Center] (POL)
PSDB........ Partido da Social Democracia Brasiliera [Brazilian Social Democratic Party] [Political party] (EY)
PSDC........ Partido Social Democratico Cristiano [Christian Democratic Socialist Party] [Colorado] (LA)
PSDCL...... Partido Social Democrate de Castilla y Leon [Social Democratic Party of Castille and Leon] [Spanish] (WER)
PSDE........ Partido Social Democratico Espanol [Spanish Social Democratic Party] (WER)
PS de G...... Partido dos Socialistas de Galicia [Spain] [Political party] (EY)
PSDF........ People's Self-Defense Force [South Vietnamese militia force] (VNW)
PSDF........ People's Self-Defense Force [Vietnam]
PSDF........ Popular Self-Defense Force [Local armed units protecting Vietnamese hamlets]
PSDG........ Partido Social Democratico Gallego [Galician Social Democratic Party] [Spanish] (WER)
PSDI.......... Partido Social Democracia Independente [Independent Social Democratic Party] [Portugal] [Political party] (PPE)
PSDI.......... Partito Socialista Democratico Italiano [Italian Social Democratic Party] [Political party]
PSDIS....... Partito Socialista Democratico Indipendente Sammarinese [Independent Social Democratic Party of San Marino] [Political party] (PPE)
PSDMI...... Panellinios Syllogos Diplomatoukhon Mikhanologon-Ilektrologon [Panhellenic Association of Licensed Mechanics and Electricians] (GC)
PSDMR..... Partidul Social-Democrat al Muncitorilor din Romania [Social-Democratic Workers' Party of Romania] (RO)
PSDP........ Regimental Message Center (RU)
PSDP........ Regimental Sanitary and Decontamination Station (RU)
PSDS......... Packet Switch Data System [Information retrieval] (IID)
PSDS......... Partito Socialista Democratico Sammarinese [Social Democratic Party of San Marino] [Political party] (PPE)
PSDSP....... Pious Society of the Daughters of Saint Paul [See also FSP] [Rome, Italy] (EAIO)
PSDU........ Polish Social Democratic Union [Political party]
PSDV........ Portuguese Society for Dermatology and Venereology (EAIO)
PSE........... Aeroservicio Sipse SA de CV [Mexico] [ICAO designator] (FAAC)
PSe........... Effektive Pferdestaerke [Effective Horsepower] [German]
PSE........... Pacific School of English [Australia]
PSE........... Panellinios Syndesmos Exagogeon [Panhellenic Exporters Association] (GC)
PSE........... Pangosmion Symvoulion Ekklision [World Council of Churches] (GC)
PSE........... Pangosmios Synomospondia Ergaton [World Confederation of Labor] (GC)
PSE........... Pankyprion Symvoulion Eirinis [Pan-Cyprian Peace Council] (GC)
PSE........... Pankyprion Symvoulion Evimerias [Pan-Cyprian Welfare Council] (GC)
PSE........... Partido Socialista de Euskadi [Basque Socialist Party] [Spain] [Political party] (EY)
PSE........... Partido Socialista Ecuatoriano [Ecuadorean Socialist Party] [Political party] (PPW)
PSE........... Perth Stock Exchange [Australia]
PSE........... Phytochemical Society of Europe (EA)
PSE........... Ponce [Puerto Rico] [Airport symbol] (OAG)
PSE........... Producer Subsidy Equivalent [OECD model for the study of farm-support policies in the EC, Japan, America, Canada, Australia, and New Zealand]
PSEA........ Panellinios Synomospondia Efedron Axiomatikon [Panhellenic Confederation of Reserve Officers] (GC)
PSEA........ Politiki Skhediaseos Ektaktou Anangis [Emergency Planning Policy] (GC)
PSEAG...... Pancyprios Syndesmos +Epichirimation Anaptyxeos Gis [Cyprus Land and Building developers Association] (EAIO)
PSEB........ Punjab State Electricity Board [India] (PDAA)
PSEDN...... Pankyprion Soma Ethelondikis Douleias Neolaias [Pan-Cyprian Youth Corps for Volunteer Work] (GC)

PSEEPP.... Pankyprios Syndesmos Ellinon Ethelondon Palaion Polemiston [Pan-Cyprian League of Greek Volunteer Veterans] (GC)
PSEGS....... Panellinios Synomospondia Enoseon Georgikon Synetairismon [Panhellenic Confederation of Unions of Agricultural Cooperatives] (GC)
PSEGSE.... Panellinios Synomospondia Enoseon Georgikon Synetairismon Ellados [Panhellenic Confederation of Agricultural Cooperative Unions of Greece] (GC)
PSEM........ Polish Society for Electron Microscopy (EAIO)
PSEMA ..... Parti Social d'Education des Masses Africaines [African Party for Social Education of the Masses] [Burkina Faso]
PSEODM ... Panellinios Syndesmos Epikheiriseon Odikon Diethnon Metaforon [Panhellenic Association of International Road Transport Enterprises] (GC)
PSEPE....... Proodevtiki Syndikalistiki Ergatoypalliliki Parataxis Ellados [Progressive Labor Employee Faction of Greece] (GC)
PSEPP....... Proodevtiki Syndikalistiki Ergatoypalliliki Parataxis Peiraios [Progressive Labor Employee Faction of Piraeus] (GC)
PSESS ...... Public Senior Executive Service Scheme [Australia]
PSET .... Pre-Selection English Test [Australia]
pseud .... Pseudonim [Pseudonym] [Poland]
pseud .... Pseudonimo [Pseudonym] [Portuguese]
pseud .... Pseudonym [Danish/Norwegian]
Pseud......... Pseudonym [German]
Psevd......... Pseudonym (BU)
PSF .... Parti Social Francais [French Social Party] [Political party] (PPE)
PSF .... Philippine Sea Frontier
PSF .... Police Superannuation Fund [Australia]
PSF .... Popular Struggle Front [Palestine] [Political party] (PD)
PSF .... Problems of Modern Physics (RU)
PSF .... Progres Social Francais [French Social Progress] [Political party] (PPE)
PSF .... Prozesssignalformer [German] (ADPT)
PSFG .... Permanent Service on the Fluctuations of Glaciers [ICSU] [Research center] (IRC)
PSG........... Partido Social Guatemalteco [Guatemalan Social Party] (LA)
PSG........... Partido Socialista Galego [Galician Socialist Party] [Spanish] (WER)
PSG........... Parti Socialiste Guyanais [Guiana Socialist Party] [Political party] (PPW)
PSG........... Pechiney-Saint-Gobain [Commercial firm] [France]
PSG........... Peoples' Sacrifice Guerrillas [Iran] (ME)
PSG........... Phenol Sector Group [European Council of Chemical Manufacturers Federations] [Belgium] (EAIO)
PSG........... Planning and Estimate Group (RU)
PSG........... Program Services Group (OLYM)
PSG........... Property Services Group [New South Wales, Australia]
PSG........... Regimental Fuel Depot (RU)
PSG........... Search and Sorting Party [Military term] (RU)
PSGE .... Partido Socialdemocrata de Guinea Ecuatorial [Social Democratic Party of Equatorial Guinea] [Political party] (EY)
PSG-EG..... Partido Socialista Galego - Esquerda Galega [Spain] [Political party] (EY)
PSGII........ PSG Industrial Institute [India] [United Nations (already exists in GUS II database)]
PSGTCAEI ... Permanent Secretariat of the General Treaty on Central American Economic Integration (EAIO)
PSGTECH ... PSG College of Technology [India] [United Nations (already exists in GUS II database)]
PSh .... Hose Mask (RU)
PSH .... Partido Socialista de Honduras [Socialist Party of Honduras] (LA)
psh............. Per Shembull [Albanian]
Psh .... Pferdestaerkestunde [Horsepower-Hour] [German]
PSh .... Plug Switch (RU)
PSH .... Polish Society of History (EAIO)
PSh .... Regimental School (RU)
psh............. Rifle (BU)
PSh .... Wire-Stitching Machine (RU)
P S'ham ...... Port Swettenham (ML)
PShch......... Intermediate Distributing Frame [Telephony] (RU)
PShOK ...... Party Schools of Okrug Committees (BU)
PShP......... Ball-Bearing Suspension (RU)
PShS .... Navigation Service Regulations (RU)
PSI .... Collecting Point for Equipment (RU)
Psi .... Indizierte Pferdestaerke [Indicated Horsepower] [German] (GCA)
PSI .... Pakistan Standards Institute
PSI .... Pakistan Standards Institution (IAA)
PSI .... Partai Sosialis Indonesia [Indonesian Socialist Party] (IN)
PSI .... Partido Socialista de Izquierda [Workers Leftist Socialist Party] [Peru] (LA)
PSI .... Partido Socialista de Izquierda [Workers Leftist Socialist Party] [Mexico] (LA)

PSI .... Partido Socialista Interior [*Interior Socialist Party*] [*Spanish*] (WER)

PSI .... Parti Socialiste Ivoirien [*Ivorian Socialist Party*] [*The Ivory Coast*] [*Political party*] (EY)

PSI .... Partito Socialista Italiano [*Italian Socialist Party*] [*Political party*] (PPE)

PSI .... Pasni [*Pakistan*] [*Airport symbol*] (OAG)

PSI .... Paul Scherrer Institute [*Switzerland*] (IRC)

PSI .... Permanent Staff Instructor [*Military*] [*British*]

PSI .... Philippine Sugar Institute (DSCA)

PSI .... Photographic Society of Ireland (SLS)

PSI .... Polish Society for Immunology (EAIO)

PSI... .... Prozess-Steuerungs-und Informationssystem GmbH [*German*] (ADPT)

Psi .... Psikoloji [*Psychology*] (TU)

PSI .... Public Services International [*See also ISP*] [*Ferney Voltaire, France*] (EAIO)

PSI .... Purchasers' Strata Inspections Proprietary Ltd. [*Australia*]

PSI .... Static Test Device [*Artillery*] (RU)

PSIA .... Public Security Investigation Agency

Psic .... Psicanalise [*Psychoanalysis*] [*Portuguese*]

Psicol .... Psicologia [*Psychology*] [*Portuguese*]

PSIDC .... Punjab State Industrial Development Corporation [*India*] (PDAA)

PSIG .... Psigologie [*Psychology*] [*Afrikaans*]

PSII .... Partai Serikat Islam Indonesia [*Indonesian Islamic Union Party*] (IN)

psikh .... Psychiatry, Psychiatrist (BU)

PSIKH .... Psychology (BU)

psikhbol'n ... Psychiatric Hospital [*Topography*] (RU)

psikhol .... Psychological (RU)

PSIOE .... Pankyprios Syndesmos Idioktiton Okhimaton Enoikiaseos [*Pan-Cyprian Association of Car Rental Owners*] (GC)

PSIS .... Programme for Strategic and International Security Studies [*Switzerland*] (PDAA)

PSISC .... Port-Said International Sporting Club [*Egypt*]

PSIT .... Parti Socialiste Independant du Tchad

PSIUP .... Partito Socialista Italiano di Unita Proletaria [*Italian Socialist Party of Proletarian Unity (1945-1947)*] [*Political party*] (PPE)

PSIYM ...... Panellinios Syllogos Idiotikon Ypallilon Mikhanografiseos [*Panhellenic Association of Private Machine Accounting Employees*] [*Greek*] (GC)

PSJ .... Parti Socialista Jurassien [*Jura Socialist Party*] [*Switzerland*] (WER)

Psj .... Pasaj [*Passage, Arcade*] (TU)

PSJ .... Pegawai Siasatan Jenayat [*Criminal Investigation Officer*] (ML)

PSJ .... Petites Soeurs de Jesus [*Little Sisters of Jesus*] [*Italy*] (EAIO)

PSJ .... Poso [*Indonesia*] [*Airport symbol*] (OAG)

PSJM .... Popis Svjetionika Jadranskog i Jonskog Mora [*List of Lighthouses of the Adriatic and Ionian Seas*] (YU)

PSJU .... Privremeni Savet Juznoslovenskog Ujedinjenja [*Provisional Council of South Slavic Unification*] [*World War I*] (YU)

PSK .... Coast Guard Vessel (RU)

PSK .... Panellinion Sosialistikon Kinima [*Panhellenic Socialist Movement*] [*PASOK is preferred*] (GC)

PSK .... Panspoudastiki Syndikalistiki Kinisi [*Pan-Student Trade Union Movement*] [*Greek*] (GC)

PSK .... Parti Socialiste Koulamalliste

PSK .... Pasokan Simpanan Persekutuan [*Federal Reserve Unit (Police)*] (ML)

PSK .... Pharmaceutical Society of Kenya

PSK .... Postal Savings Office (BU)

PSK .... PostSparKasse [*Post Office Savings Bank*] [*Austria*]

PSK .... Proodevtiko Syndikalistiko Kinima [*Progressive Trade Union Movement*] [*Greek*] (GC)

PSK .... Przedsiebiorstwo Spedycji Krajowej [*Domestic Dispatching Enterprises*] (POL)

PSKh .... Precision Synchronoscope (RU)

PSKh .... Synchro Generator of a Transmitting Station (RU)

PSKhM ...... Panellinios Syllogos Khimikon Mikhanikon [*Panhellenic Association of Chemical Engineers*] (GC)

PSKhO ...... Food and Agriculture Organization of the United Nations [*FAO*] (RU)

PSKJ .... Pitanja Savremenog Knjizevnog Jezika [*Problems of the Modern Literary Language*] [*Sarajevo A periodical*] (YU)

PSKN .... Shipboard Regulations (RU)

PSL .... Collecting Point for Slightly Wounded (RU)

PSL .... Panellinios Synomospondia Logiston [*Panhellenic Confederation of Accountants*] (GC)

PSL .... Parti Social-Liberal [*Algeria*] [*Political party*] (EY)

PSl .... Politechnika Slaska [*Engineering College of Silesia*] [*Poland*]

PSL .... Polska Sztuka Ludowa [*Polish Folk Art*] (POL)

PSL .... Polskie Stronnictwo Ludowe [*Polish Peasant Party*] [*Political party*] (PPE)

PSL .... Professionnel Air Systems [*France*] [*ICAO designator*] (FAAC)

PSL .... Public Sector Liquidity

PSLA .... Pain and Suffering and Loss of Amenities [*Australia*]

PSLA .... Palaung State Liberation Army [*Myanmar*] [*Political party*] (EY)

PSLE .... Primary School Leaving Examination [*Singapore*] (FEA)

PSLI.......... Partito Socialista dei Lavoratori Italiani [*Socialist Party of Italian Workers*] [*Political party*] (PPE)

PSLINK.... Public Sector Labor Integrative Center [*Philippines*] (EY)

PSLIPI ...... Perpustakaan Sentral Lipi [*Indonesian Institute of Sciences*]

PSL-Lewica ... Polskie Stronnictwo-Lewica [*Polish Peasant Party-Left (1947-1949)*] [*Political party*] (PPE)

PSL-Lewica ... Polskie Stronnictwo Ludowe-Lewica [*Polish Peasant Party-Left (1913-1920)*] [*Political party*] (PPE)

PSL-NW.... Polskie Stronnictwo Ludowe-Nowe Wyzwolenie [*Polish Peasant Party-New Liberation*] [*Political party*] (PPE)

PSLO........ Palaung State Liberation Organization [*Myanmar*] [*Political party*] (EY)

PSL-Piast .. Polskie Stronnictwo Ludowe-Piast [*Polish Peasant Party-Piast*] [*Political party*] (PPE)

PSLV .... Polar Satellite Launch Vehicle [*India*]

PSL-Wyzwolenie ... Polskie Stronnictwo Ludowe-Wyzwolenie [*Polish Peasant Party-Liberation*] [*Political party*] (PPE)

PSM.......... Panglima Setia Mahkota [*Second Grade of Darjah Yang Mulia Setia Mahkota Malaysia*] (ML)

PSM.......... Panstwowa Szkola Morska [*State Maritime School*] (POL)

PSM.......... Parti Socialiste Malgache [*Malagasy Socialist Party*] (AF)

PSM.......... Parti Socialiste Mauricien [*Mauritian Socialist Party*] [*Political party*] (EY)

PSM.......... Parti Socialiste Monegasque [*Monaco Socialist Party*] [*Political party*] (PPW)

PSM.......... Pflanzenschutz- und Schaedlingsbekaempfungsmittel [*Plant Protection Products and Pesticides*] (EG)

PSM.......... Philatelic Society of Malaysia (EAIO)

PSM.......... Pious Society of Missions [*Australia*]

PSM.......... Politicke Skoleni Madaru [*Political Education of Hungarian Nationals*] (CZ)

PSM.......... Politicke Skoleni Muzstva [*Political Training of Enlisted Personnel*] (CZ)

PSM.......... Por Su Mandato [*By His Orders*] [*Spanish*]

PSM.......... Poznanska Spoldzielnia Mieszkaniowa [*Poznan Housing Cooperative*] (POL)

PSM.......... Public Sector Management Act [*Australia*]

PSM.......... Public Service Medal [*Australia*]

PSM.......... Pultschreibmaschine [*German*] (ADPT)

PSM.......... Simple Means of Mechanization (RU)

PSMA....... Proprietary Sugar Millers Association

PSMC....... Philippine Science and Mathematics Council (EAIO)

PSMC....... Public Sector Management Commission [*Australia*]

PSMC....... Public Sector Management Course [*Australia*]

PSME .... Partido Socialista de Melilla [*See also PSOE*] [*Spanish North Africa*] [*Political party*] (MENA)

PSME .... Philippine Society for Music Education (EAIO)

PSME-PSOE ... Partido Socialista de Melilla - Partido Socialista Obrero Espanol [*Political party*] (EY)

PSMP .... Pambansang Samahan ng Mag-aaral ng Pilipinas [*National Union of Students of th e Philippines*] (EAIO)

PSMS .... Construction Materials and Construction Industry (BU)

PSMS .... Poradni Sbor pro Mechanisaci Stavebnictvi [*Advisory Board for the Mechanization of the Construction Industry*] (CZ)

PSMSL...... Permanent Service for Mean Sea Level [*of the Federation of Astronomical and Geophysical Data Analysis Services*] [*Birkenhead, Merseyside, England*] (EAIO)

PSMU........ Pevecke Sdruzeni Moravskych Ucitelu [*Moravian Teachers' Choral Society*] (CZ)

PSMZH..... Progressivnyi Soiuz Marokkanskikh Zhenshchin

PSN .... Base-End Station (BU)

PSN .... Inflatable Life Raft (RU)

PSN .... Parent Support Network [*Australia*]

PSN .... Parti de la Solidarite Nationale [*Party of National Solidarity*] [*Luxembourg*] [*Political party*] (PPE)

PSN .... Partido Socialista Nicaraguense [*Nicaraguan Socialist Party*] [*Political party*] (PPW)

PSN .... Pharmaceutical Society of Nigeria

PSN .... Piano Spaziale Nazionale [*National Space Plan*] [*Italy*]

PSN .... Potosina del Aire SA de CV [*Mexico*] [*ICAO designator*] (FAAC)

PSN .... Premier Sports Network [*Australia*]

PSNC........ Pacific Steam Navigation Company (ADA)

PSNC........ Parti Socialiste de la Nouvelle Caledonie [*Socialist Party of New Caledonia*] [*Political party*] (PPW)

PSNI......... Pharmaceutical Society of Northern Ireland (SLS)

PSNL......... Poradny a Studovny Marxismu-Leninismu [*Advisory and Study Centers of Marxism and Leninism*] (CZ)

PSNS .... Poslovnik Savezne Narodne Skupstine [*Rules of Procedure of the Federal People's Assembly*] (YU)

PSNSW ..... Philatelic Society of New South Wales [*Australia*]

PSNV .... Partikulere Suiwelnywerheidsvereniging [*South Africa*] (AA)

PSNZ........ Perinatal Society of New Zealand (EAIO)

PSO .... Antisatellite Defense (RU)
PSO .... Decontamination Station (RU)
PSO .... Fire Watch Service (RU)
PSO .... Pankyprios Synergatiki Omospondia [*Pan-Cyprian Cooperative Federation*] (GC)
PSO .... Pasto [*Colombia*] [*Airport symbol*] (OAG)
PSO .... Personal Staff Officer [*Australia*]
PSO .... Personnel Services Organisation [*Australia*]
PSO .... Polymerizable Oligomer (RU)
PSO .... Portable Firing-Ground Equipment (RU)
PSO .... Port and Shipping Organization [*Iran*] (ME)
PSO .... Poverenictvo Skolstva a Osvety [*Office of the Commissioner of Education and Culture*] (CZ)
PSO .... Pratik Sanat Okulu [*Practical Trade School*] (TU)
PSO .... Presidential Security Office [*Republic of Vietnam*]
PSO .... Principal Staff Officer [*Pakistan*]
PSO .... Progressieve Studenten Organisatie [*Progressive Student Organization*] [*Netherlands*] (WEN)
PSO .... Proletarian Sports Society (RU)
PSO .... Psychiatric Services Officer [*Australia*]
PSO .... Public Service Obligation [*Australia*]
PSO .... Successive Concentration of Fire (BU)
PSO .... Successive Fire Concentration (RU)
PSOA .... Platre Sies de l'Ouest Africain
PSOA .... Postal Supervisory Officers' Association [*Australia*]
PSOC .... Pakistan State Oil Co. Ltd.
PSOE .... Partido Socialista Obrero Espanol [*Spanish Socialist Workers' Party*] [*See also PSME*] [*Political party*] (PPE)
PSOGWU ... Plate, Sheet, and Ornamental Glass Workers Union [*Australia*] (LA)
PSOJ .... Private Sector Organization of Jamaica (LA)
PSOKhS .... Panellinios Synomospondia Orthodoxon Khristianikon Syndikaton [*Panhellenic Confederation of Orthodox Christian Trade Unions*] (GC)
Pson .... Prison [*Prison*] [*Military map abbreviation World War I*] [*French*] (MTD)
PSOP .... Parti Socialiste des Ouvriers et Paysans [*Socialist Party of Workers and Peasants*] [*France*] [*Political party*]
PSOW .... Punkt Skupu Owocow i Warzyw [*Fruit and Vegetable Purchase Center*] (POL)
PSP .... Economic Marketing Enterprise (BU)
PSP .... Field Hospital Train (RU)
PSP .... Instrument Landing System Indicator (RU)
PSP .... Intermediate Patching Bay [*Telephony*] (RU)
PSP .... Intermediate Rendezvous Point [*Aviation*] (RU)
PSP .... Pacifistische Socialistische Partij [*Pacific Socialist Party*] [*Political party*] [*Netherlands*]
PSP .... Pacifistisch Socialistiche Partij
PSP .... Pacifistisch Socialistische Partij [*Pacifist Socialist Party*] [*Netherlands*] (WEN)
PSP .... Pacifist Socialist Party [*Netherlands*] (RU)
PSP .... Parti de la Solidarite du Peuple [*Cameroon*] [*Political party*] (EY)
PSP .... Partido Socialista del Peru [*Socialist Party of Peru*] [*Political party*] (PPW)
PSP .... Partido Socialista Popular [*Popular Socialist Party*] [*Dominican Republic*] (LA)
PSP .... Partido Socialista Popular [*Popular Socialist Party*] [*Argentina*] (LA)
PSP .... Partido Socialista Popular [*Popular Socialist Party*] [*Chile*] (LA)
PSP .... Partido Socialista Popular [*Popular Socialist Party*] [*Peru*] [*Political party*] (PPW)
PSP .... Partido Socialista Popular [*Popular Socialist Party*] [*Spain*] [*Political party*] (PPE)
PSP .... Partido Socialista Popular [*Popular Socialist Party*] [*Pre-1965*] [*Cuba*] [*Political party*] (PPW)
PSP .... Partido Socialista Portuguesa [*Portuguese Socialist Party*] [*Political party*] (PPW)
PSP .... Partido Socialista Puertorriqueno [*Puerto Rican Socialist Party*] (LA)
PSP .... Partido Social Progresista [*Social Progressive Party*] [*Brazil*] [*Political party*]
PSP .... Partido Social Progressista [*Social Progressive Party*] [*Brazil*] (LA)
PSP .... Parti Socialiste Polynesien [*Polynesian Socialist Party*] [*Political party*] (PPW)
PSP .... Parti Socialiste Progressiste [*Socialist Progressive Party*] [*Mauritius*] (AF)
PSP .... Parti Social pour le Progres [*Tunisia*] [*Political party*] (EY)
PSP .... Parti Soudanais Progressiste [*Sudanese Progressive Party*] [*Political party*]
PSP .... Pasokan Simpanan Persekutuan [*Federal Reserve Unit (Police)*] (ML)
PSP .... People's Socialist Party [*Political party*] [*Mauritius*]
PSp. .... Periodichesko Spisanie na Bulgarskoto Knizhovno Druzhestvo [*Periodical of the Bulgarian Learned Society*] (BU)
PSP .... Plattenspeicher [*German*] (ADPT)

PSP .... Ploigikos Stathmos Peiraios [*Piraeus Shipping Pilots Station*] (GC)
PSP .... Policia de Seguranca Publica [*Public Security Police*] [*Portuguese*] (WER)
PSP .... Postipankki [*National savings bank*] [*Finland*]
PSP .... Postupne Soustredeni Palby [*Rolling Fire Barrage*] (CZ)
PSP .... Pracownia Sztuk Plastycznych [*Plastic Arts Studio*] (POL)
PSP .... Praja Socialist Party [*India*] [*Political party*] (PPW)
PSP .... Pravnicka Skola Pracujicich [*Workers' Law School*] (CZ)
PSP .... Prazske Pevecke Sdruzeni [*Prague Choral Society*] (CZ)
PSP .... Predsednictvo Sboru Poverenikov [*Presidium of the Board of Commissioners*] (CZ)
PSP .... Programm-Struktur-Prozessor [*German*] (ADPT)
PSP .... Progressive Socialist Party [*Lebanon*] [*Political party*] (BJA)
PSP .... Proodevtiki Syndikalistiki Parataxis [*Progressive Labor Faction*] [*Greek*] (GC)
PSP .... Property Services Program [*Department of Administrative Services*] [*Australia*]
PSP .... Puerto Rican Socialist Party [*Political party*] (PD)
PSP .... Regular Hospital Train (RU)
PSP .... Rules of Formation Cruising (RU)
PSPA .... Professional School Photographers Association [*Australia*]
PSPC .... Partido Socialista del Pueblo de Ceuta [*Political party*] (EY)
ps pd og ...... Successive Concentration of Fire (BU)
PSPEYP ... Pancyprios Syndesmos Promitheuton Electronicon Ypolsgiston and Programmaton [*Cyprus Computer Hardware and Software Suppliers Association*] (EAIO)
PSPF .... Pokrajinski Sekretarijat za Poslove Finansija [*Provincial Secretariat of Finance*] [*Vojvodina*] (YU)
PSPG .... Partido Socialista do Povo Galego [*Socialist Party of the Galician People*] [*Spanish*] (WER)
PSPP .... Pambanssang Sanggunian sa Pananaliksik ng Pilipinas [*National Research Counci l of the Philippines*] (EAIO)
PSPP .... Pegawai Senjata Pasokan Polis [*Police Force Armament Officer*] (ML)
PSPPD ...... Partido Socialista Portugues de Ponta Delgada [*Portuguese Socialist Party of Ponta Delgada*] (WER)
PSPR .... Programmiersprache [*Programer Language*] [*German*] (ADPT)
PSPS .... Panellinios Syndesmos Politikon Syndaxioukhon [*Panhellenic League of Civil Pensioners*] (GC)
PSPS .... Pesticides Safety Precautions Scheme [*British*]
PSPS .... Private Sector Participation Scheme [*Housing*] [*Hong Kong*]
PSPU .... Pokrajinski Sekretarijat za Pravosudnu Upravu [*Provincial Secretariat of Justice*] [*Vojvodina*] (YU)
PSPV .... Partido Socialista del Pais Valenciano [*Spain*] [*Political party*] (EY)
PSPV .... Partit Socialista del Pais Valencia [*Socialist Party of the Valencian Country*] [*Spanish*] (WER)
PSPV .... Regimental Collecting Point for Prisoners of War (RU)
PSQC .... Philippine Society for Quality Control (PDAA)
PSR .... Partido Socialista Revolucionario [*Revolutionary Socialist Party*] [*Peru*] [*Political party*] (PPW)
PSR .... Partido Socialista Revolucionario [*Revolutionary Socialist Party*] [*Portugal*] [*Political party*] (PPE)
PSR .... Partido Socialista Revolucionario [*Revolutionary Socialist Party*] [*Mexico*] [*Political party*] (PPW)
PSR .... Parti Socialiste Republicain [*Socio-Republican Party*] [*Cambodia*] (CL)
PSR .... Parti Socialiste Reunionnais [*Reunionese Socialist Party*] (AF)
PSR .... Party Socialiste Revolutionnaire [*Socialist Revolutionary Party*] [*Lebanon*] [*Political party*] (PPW)
PSR .... Pescara [*Italy*] [*Airport symbol*] (OAG)
PSR .... Point Operating Relay [*Railroads*] (RU)
PSR .... Prioritaets-Statusregister [*German*] (ADPT)
PSR .... Programmes Sociaux de Relogement [*France*] (FLAF)
psr .... Road Construction Company (BU)
PSR .... Socialist Revolutionary Party (RU)
PSRD .... Woodworkers' Trade Union (RU)
PSRE .... Partido Socialista Revolucionario Ecuatoriano [*Socialist Revolutionary Party of Ecuador*] [*Political party*] (PPW)
PSRI .... Psycho-Social Rehabilitation International (EAIO)
PSRL .... Complete Collection of the Russian Chronicles (RU)
PSRM .... Panstwowa Szkola Rybolowstwa Morskiego [*State School of Deep-Sea Fishing*] [*Poland*]
PSRM .... Parti Sosialis Rakyat Malaya [*People's Socialist Party of Malaya*]
PSR-ML .... Partido Socialista Revolucionario - Marxista-Leninista [*Socialist Revolutionary Party - Marxist-Leninist*] [*Peru*] (LA)
PSR-ML/MIR ... Partido Socialista Revolucionario (Marxista-Leninista)/ Movimiento de Izquierda Revolucionaria [*Revolutionary Socialist Party (Marxist-Leninist)/Mi litant Movement of the Revolutionary Left*] [*Peru*] [*Political party*] (PPW)
PSRO .... Public Sector Recruitment Office [*Australia*]
PSRS .... Parti Socialiste Revolutionnaire Somalien [*Somali Revolutionary Socialist Party*] [*Use SRSP*] (AF)
PSRS .... Partito Socialista Rivoluzionario Somalo [*Somali Revolutionary Socialist Party*] [*Use SRSP*] (AF)
PSRSSKhP ... Agricultural and Food Industry Workers Trade Union (BU)

PSS	Mountain Rescue Service (BU)
PSS	Partia Socialiste e Shqiperise [*Socialist Party of Albania*] [*Political party*] (EAIO)
PSS	Parti de Solidarite Senegalaise [*Senegalese Solidarity Party*] [*Political party*]
PSS	Parti Socialiste Suisse [*Social Democratic Party of Switzerland*] [*Political party*] (PPE)
PSS	Partito Socialista Sammarinese [*Socialist Party of San Marino*] [*Political party*] (PPE)
PSS	Partito Socialista Somalo [*Somali Socialist Party*] [*Political party*]
PSS	Planungs-und Steuersystem [*Planning and Control System*] [*German*] (ADPT)
PSS	Poletno-Sletna Staza [*Take-Off and Landing Runway*] [*Military*] (YU)
PSS	Posadas [*Argentina*] [*Airport symbol*] (OAG)
PSS	Poverenictvo pre Socialnu Starostlivost [*Office of the Commissioner of Social Welfare*] (CZ)
PSS	Powszechna Spoldzielnia Spozywcow [*Universal Consumers' Cooperative*] [*Poland*]
PSS	Pregnancy Support Service [*Australia*]
PSS	Presbyteri Sancti Sulpicii [*Sulpicians*] [*Roman Catholic men's religious order*]
PSS	Prevention of Ship Collision at Sea (RU)
PSS	Privredni Savet Srbije [*Economic Council of Serbia*] (YU)
PSS	Public Sector Superannuation Scheme [*Australia*]
PSS	Station Operator's Link (RU)
PSSA	Packet Switching Services Australia
PSSA	Palaeontological Society of Southern Africa (AA)
PSSA	Pharmaceutical Society of South Africa (AA)
PSSA	Photogrammetric [*or Photographic*] Society of South Africa
PSSA	Private Secondary Schools Authority [*Mauritius*] (AF)
PSSA	Professional Ski Shops Association [*Australia*]
PSSA	Public State Services Association [*Australia*]
PSSAANDPS	Permanent Secretariat of the South American Agreement on Narcotic Drugs and Psychotropic Substances (EAIO)
PSSDM	Portuguese Society of Stomatology and Dental Medicine (EAIO)
Psse	Princesse [*Princess*] [*French*] (MTD)
PSSES	Public Service Senior Executive Service [*Australia*]
PSSF	Petites Soeurs de la Sainte-Famille [*Little Sisters of the Holy Family*] [*Sherbrooke, PQ*] (EAIO)
PSSh	Staff Field Service [*Regulations*] (RU)
PSSIIS	Partito Socialista: Sezione Italiana del Internazionale Socialista [*Socialist Party: Italian Section of International Socialism*] [*Political party*] (PPE)
PSS(Int)	Peace Science Society (International)
PSSLU	Philippine Social Security Labour Union (EY)
PSSM	Panstwowa Srednia Szkola Muzyczna [*State Secondary Music School*] (POL)
PSSNB	Pohranicni Straz Sboru Narodni Bezpecnosti [*National Security Corps Border Guard Troops*] (CZ)
PSST	Pakistan Society of Sugar Technologists
PSS(T)	Pregnancy Support Service (Tasmania) [*Australia*]
PST	Airwork (New Zealand) Ltd. [*ICAO designator*] (FAAC)
PST	Ambulance Loading Post, Ambulance Relay Post (RU)
P/St	Border Station (RU)
PST	Field Collecting Point (RU)
PST	Pancyprios Syndesmos Typographon [*Cyprus Master - Printers Association*] (EAIO)
PST	Pankyprios Syndesmos Tourkoplikton [*Pan-Cyprian Association of Victims of Turks*] (GC)
PST	Panstwowa Szkola Techniczna [*State Technical School*] [*Poland*]
PST	Partido Socialista de los Trabajadores [*Socialist Workers' Party*] [*Peru*] (LA)
PST	Partido Socialista de los Trabajadores [*Socialist Workers' Party*] [*Argentina*] (LA)
PST	Partido Socialista de los Trabajadores [*Socialist Workers' Party*] [*Venezuela*] (LA)
PST	Partido Socialista de los Trabajadores [*Socialist Workers' Party*] [*Mexico*] [*Political party*] (PPW)
PST	Partido Socialista de los Trabajadores [*Socialist Workers Party*] [*Panama*] [*Political party*] (EY)
PST	Partido Socialista de los Trabajadores [*Socialist Workers' Party*] [*Colorado*] [*Political party*] (PPW)
PST	Partido Social Trabalhista [*Social Workers Party*] [*Brazil*] (LA)
PST	Parti Suisse du Travail [*Swiss Labor Party*] [*Communist*] (WER)
PST	Patentstelle fuer die Deutsche Forschung [*Munich*] [*Information retrieval*]
PST	Pediatric Society of Thailand (EAIO)
PSt	Personeel Statuut [*Benelux*] (BAS)
PST	Peseta [*Monetary unit*] [*Spain and Latin America*]
Pst	Pferdestaerke [*Horsepower*] [*German*] (GCA)
pst	Pistil, Pistillate [*Botany*] (RU)
pst	Pond Sterling [*Pound Sterling*] [*Monetary unit*] [*Netherlands*] (GPO)
P st	Post Office Station [*Topography*] (RU)

P/St	Small Railroad Station, Flag Station, Whistle Stop [*Topography*] (RU)
P/St	Substation (RU)
PSTA	Packaging Science and Technology Abstracts [*International Food Information Service*] [*Germany*] [*Information service or system*]
PSTA	Partido Socialista Tito Atahuichi [*Bolivia*] [*Political party*] (PPW)
psta	Puolesta [*Finland*]
PSTE	Federation Protection Sociale-Travail-Emploi [*France*]
PSTR	Transportation Workers' Trade Union (RU)
PSTs	Steam Power Shop (RU)
PSTU	Private Secondary Teachers Union [*Mauritius*] (AF)
PSTUC	Pan-Sarawak Trade Union Congress (ML)
PSU	Control Signal Receiver (RU)
PSU	Parallel-Serien-Umsetzer [*German*] (ADPT)
PSU	Partido Socialista Unificado [*Socialist Unification Party*] [*Argentina*] [*Political party*] (PPW)
PSU	Partido Socialista Uruguayo [*Uruguayan Socialist Party*] [*Political party*] (PD)
PSU	Partidul Socialist Unitar [*Unitary Socialist Party*] [*Romania*] [*Political party*] (PPE)
PSU	Parti Socialiste Unifie [*Unified Socialist Party*] [*France*] [*Political party*] (PPW)
PSU	Partito Socialista Unificato [*Unified Socialist Party*] [*Italy*] [*Political party*] (PPE)
PSU	Partito Socialista Unitario [*Socialist Unity Party*] [*Italy*] [*Political party*] (PPE)
PSU	Philippine Seafarers' Union (EY)
PSU	Public Safety Unit [*Uganda*]
PSU	Public Sector and Broadcasting Union [*Australia*]
PSU	Public Sector Union [*Australia*]
PSU	Public Service Union [*Guyana*] (LA)
PSU	Public Service Union [*Australia*]
PSU	Steam Power Plant [*Nautical term*] (RU)
PSU	Universal Welding Transformer (RU)
PSUA	Partido Socialista Unificado da Alemanha [*Socialist Unity Party of East Germany*] [*Use SED*] (AF)
PSUC	Partit Socialista Unificat de Catalunya [*Unified Socialist Party of Catalonia*] [*Spain*] [*Political party*] (PPE)
PSULI	Partito Socialista Unitario de Lavoratori Italiani [*Unitary Socialist Party of Italian Workers*] [*Political party*] (PPE)
PSUM	Partido Socialista Unificado de Mexico [*Unified Socialist Party of Mexico*] (LA)
PSUP	Partido Socialista de Unidad Popular [*Socialist Party of Popular Unity*] [*Colorado*] (LA)
PSUP	Pokrajinski Sekretarijat za Unutrasnje Poslove (APV) [*Provincial Secretariat of Internal Affairs*] [*Vojvodina*] (YU)
PSUZ	Regulation on School Scholarships (BU)
PSV	Partido Socialista de Venezuela [*Socialist Party of Venezuela*] (LA)
PSV	Parti Socialiste Voltaique [*Voltan Socialist Party*] (AF)
PSV	Pilotage sans Visibilite [*French*]
PSV	Pilotage sans Visibilite Exterieure [*Blind Flying*] [*French*]
PSV	Polni Sled Veleni [*Field Command Echelon*] (CZ)
PSV	Poslovnik Saveznog Veca [*Rules of Procedure of the Federal Council*] (YU)
PSV	Pridruzena Stavebni Vyroba [*Subsidiary Construction Activity*] (CZ)
PSV	Progressieve Surinaamse Volkspartij [*Progressive Suriname People's Party*] [*Political party*] (PPW)
PSVB	Pomocna Straz Verejne Bezpecnosti [*Auxiliary Public Security Corps*] (CZ)
PSvHS	Poverenictvo Stavebnictva, Hlavna Sprava [*Office of the Commissioner of Construction, Main Administration*] (CZ)
PSVK	High-Frequency Intermediate Patching Bay [*Telephony*] (RU)
PSVPO	Preduzece za Spasavanje i Vadenje Potopljenih Objekata [*Establishment for Rescue and Salvage of Submerged Objects*] [*Shipping*] (YU)
PSVS	Polish Society of Veterinary Science (EAIO)
PSVS	Portuguese Society for Veterinary Sciences (EAIO)
PSVTI	Regimental Materiel Depot (RU)
PSVU	Poverenictvo Skolstva, Vied, a Umeni [*Office of the Commissioner of Education, Sciences, and Arts*] (CZ)
PSW	Programmierbares Schaltwerk [*German*] (ADPT)
PSWAD	Perspective Study of World Agricultural Development [*FAO*] [*United Nations*] (MSC)
PSWTUF	Public Service Workers' Trade Union Federation [*Sri Lanka*]
PSWU	Public Services Workers' Union [*Ghana*]
PSY	Port Stanley [*Falkland Islands*] [*Airport symbol*]
psych	Psychologie [*French*] (TPFD)
psych	Psychology (TPFD)
PsychJurGez	Psychiatrisch-Juridisch Gezelschap [*Benelux*] (BAS)
psyk	Psykologia [*Psychology*] [*Finland*]
PSZ	Pedagogiai Szeminarium [*Pedagogical Seminar*] (HU)
PSZ	Pedagogus Szakszervezet [*Teachers Trade Union*] (HU)

PSz............. Politechnika Szczecinska [*Engineering College of Szczecin*] [*Poland*]
PSZ............. Polskie Sily Zborjne [*Polish Armed Forces*]   (POL)
psz............. Probaszolgalatos [*On Probation*]   (HU)
PSz............. Przemysl Szklarski [*Glass Industry*]   (POL)
PSZ............. Puerto Suarez [*Bolivia*] [*Airport symbol*]   (OAG)
PSZdrRab ... Public Health Workers Trade Union   (BU)
PSzH......... Pancelozott Szalito Harcjarmu [*Armored Transport Vehicle*] [*Military*]   (HU)
PSZR........ Health Workers Trade Union   (BU)
PSZT........ Pecsi Szenbanyaszati Troszt [*Coal Mining Trust of Pecs*]   (HU)
PSzW........ Powiatowy Sztab Wojskowy [*County Military Headquarters*]   (POL)
PT .... Amphibious Personnel Carrier   (RU)
PT .... Amphibious Tank   (RU)
PT .... Antitank   (BU)
PT .... Brake Test [*Railroads*]   (RU)
PT .... Cable Trailer [*Oceanography*]   (RU)
PT .... Fire Alarm   (RU)
pt .... Friday   (RU)
PT .... Heavy-Duty Trailer, Giant Trailer   (RU)
PT .... Industrial Television   (RU)
PT .... Message Code Table   (RU)
P-T............. Palomero Toluqueno [*Race of maize*] [*Mexico*]
PT .... Partido de los Trabajadores [*Workers Party*] [*Dominican Republic*]   (LA)
PT .... Partido de los Trabajadores [*Paraguay*] [*Political party*]   (EY)
PT .... Partido del Trabajo [*Labor Party*] [*Spanish*]   (WER)
PT .... Partido dos Trabalhadores [*Workers Party*] [*Brazil*]   (LA)
PT .... Partido Trabajador [*Workers Party*] [*Argentina*]   (LA)
PT .... Partido Trabajador [*Mexico*] [*Political party*]   (EY)
PT .... Parti Travailliste [*Labor Party*] [*Mauritius*]   (AF)
PT .... Pataca [*Monetary unit*] [*Macau*]
PT .... Pegawai Turus [*Staff Officer*]   (ML)
PT .... Pelnym Tytulem [*Full-Titled*] [*Poland*]
PT .... Perseroan Terbatas [*Limited Company*] [*Indonesian*]   (IN)
Pt............. Personenzugtenderlokomotive [*Local Passenger Train Tender Locomotive*]   (EG)
PT .... Peseta [*Monetary unit*] [*Spain and Latin America*]
Pt............. Petit [*Small*] [*Military map abbreviation World War I*] [*French*]   (MTD)
PT .... Petrol Tractor [*British*]
PT .... Physical Training [*Royal Australian Navy*]
PT .... Piaster [*Monetary unit*] [*Spain, Republic of Vietnam, and some Middle Eastern countries*]   (IMH)
PT .... Pistoia [*Car registration plates*] [*Italian*]
Pt............. Platin [*Platinum*] [*Chemical element*] [*German*]
Pt............. Platina [*Platinum*] [*Chemical element*] [*Portuguese*]
PT .... Pleno Titulo [*Poland*]
pt .... Pod Tytulem [*Entitled, Under the Title*]   (POL)
PT .... Pogon na Plinsku Turbinu [*Gas Turbine Power*]   (YU)
pt .... Point [*Stitch*] [*Knitting*] [*French*]
PT .... Polartest Oy [*Commercial laboratory*] [*Finland*]   (WND)
PT .... Policia de Transito [*Traffic Police*] [*Mozambique*]   (AF)
PT .... Polis Tentera [*Military Police*]   (ML)
PT .... Polskie Towarzystwo [*Polish Society*]   (POL)
Pt............. Pont [*Bridge*] [*Military map abbreviation World War I*] [*French*]   (MTD)
Pt............. Port [*Harbor*] [*Military map abbreviation World War I*] [*French*]   (MTD)
PT .... Portugal [*ANSI two-letter standard code*]   (CNC)
PT .... Poste e Telecomunicazioni [*Post and Telecommunications*] [*Italian*]   (WER)
PT .... Poste e Telegrafi [*Post and Telegraph Service*] [*Italy*]
PT .... Potential Trigger   (RU)
PT .... Poverenictvo pre Techniku [*Office of the Commissioner of Technology*]   (CZ)
PT .... Prachakorn Thai [*Thai Citizens Party*] [*Political party*]
PT .... Precise Wire-Wound (Resistor)   (RU)
PT .... Predilnica i Tkalnica [*Spinning and Weaving Mills*] [*Maribor*]   (YU)
Pt............. President [*President*]   (AF)
PT .... Protitankovy [*Antitank*]   (CZ)
PT .... Protivtenkovski [*Antitank*]   (YU)
PT .... Publicidad Tecnica [*Colombia*]   (COL)
Pt............. Punt [*Point*] [*Netherlands*]   (NAU)
PT .... Putnicka Tarifa [*Passenger Rate*]   (YU)
Pt............. Pynt [*or Pynten*] [*Point*] [*Norway*]   (NAU)
Pt............. Pynt [*Point*] [*Denmark*]   (NAU)
PT .... Semiconductor Triode   (RU)
p/t .... Steamship   (RU)
PT .... Steam Turbine   (RU)
PT .... Textolite for Machine Parts   (RU)
PT .... Tokarev Pistol   (RU)
PT .... Training Parachute   (RU)
pT............. With Full Title [*Correspondence*] [*German*]

PTA .... Antitank Artillery   (RU)
PTA .... Asseccorz e Servicos a Projeto em Agriculture Alternativzs [*Consultants in Alt ernative Agriculture Projects*] [*Brazil*]   (EAIO)
PTA .... Parti du Travail Albanais [*Albanian Workers' Party (AWP)*] [*French*]   (WER)
PTA .... Passenger Transport Association [*South Africa*]   (AA)
PTA .... Passenger-Transport Authority [*Scottish*]
pta .... Pasta [*Cover*] [*Bookbinding*] [*Spanish*]
PTA .... Perifereiakon Tameion Agrofylakis [*Rural Police Regional Fund*] [*Greek*]   (GC)
PTA .... Peseta [*Monetary unit*] [*Spain and Latin America*]
PTA .... Petrograd News Agency [*1915-1918*]   (RU)
PTA .... Philippine Tourism Authority   (GEA)
PTA .... Plataformas de Trabajadores Anti-Capitalistas [*Platforms of Anti-Capitalist Workers*] [*Spanish*]   (WER)
PTA .... Platinum-Titanium Anode   (RU)
P-ta .... Poczta [*Post Office*] [*Poland*]
PTA .... Polish Telegraph Agency   (BU)
PTA .... Polish Tennis Association   (EAIO)
PTA .... Polskie Towarzystwo Akustyczne [*Polish Acoustical Society*] [*Poland*]
PTA .... Polskie Towarzystwo Anatomiczne [*Polish Anatomical Society*]   (EAIO)
PTA .... Polskie Towarzystwo Antropologiczne [*Polish Anthropology Society*]   (EAIO)
PTA .... Polskie Towarzystwo Archeologiczne [*Polish Archaeological Society*]   (POL)
PTA .... Polskie Towarzystwo Astronautyczne [*Poland*]   (SLS)
PTA .... Polskie Towarzystwo Astronomiczne [*Poland*]   (SLS)
Pta............. Ponta [*Point*] [*Portuguese*]   (NAU)
pta .... Porta [*Gate*] [*Italian*]   (CED)
PTA .... Poste Telephonique Artillerie [*Military*] [*French*]   (MTD)
PTA .... Pracovni Tabory [*Labor Camps*]   (CZ)
PTA .... Preferential Trade Agreement
PTA .... Preferential Trade Area
PTA .... Preferential Trade Arrangements [*ASEAN*]   (IMH)
PTA .... Property Trust of Australia
PTA .... Protivtenkovska Artiljerija [*Antitank Artillery*]   (YU)
Pta............. Punta [*Point*] [*Spanish*]   (NAU)
Pta............. Punta [*Point*] [*Italian*]   (NAU)
PTAA........ Professional Tattooists Association of Australia
PTAB........ Aerial Antitank Bomb   (RU)
PTAB........ Protivtenkovske Aviobombe [*Antitank Air Bombs*]   (YU)
PTAD .... Protivtenkovski Artiljeriski Divizion [*Antitank Artillery Division*] [*Military*]   (YU)
PTAiN .... Polskie Towarzystwo Archeologiczne i Numizmatyczne [*Poland*]   (SLS)
PTAITT..... Polskie Towarzystwo Anestezjologii i Intensywnej Terapii [*Polish Society of A naesthesiology and Intensive Therapy*]   (EAIO)
PTAL........ Professeur Technique d'Atelier de Lycee
PTAN .... Polskie Towarzystwo Numizmatyo [*Polish Numismatic Society*]   (EAIO)
PTAR........ Perpustakaan Tun Abdul Razak [*Mara Institute of Technology*] [*Malaysia*]
PTAr .... Polskie Towarzystwo Archeologiczne [*Polish Archaeological Society*]
PTARZ ...... Mobile Tank-Component Repair Plant   (RU)
ptas............ Pesetas [*Monetary units in Spain and Latin America*]
PTA-SA ..... Passenger Transport Association [*See also*]   (EAIO)
PTASKRINDO ... Perseroan Terbatas Asransi Kredit Indonesia [*Indonesia*]   (IMH)
PTB........... Antitank Battery   (RU)
PTB........... Industrial Safety Regulations   (BU)
PTB........... Parti des Travailleurs Burundi
PTB........... Partido Trabalhista Brasileiro [*Brazilian Labor Party*] [*Political party*]   (PPW)
PTB........... Parti du Travail de Belgique [*Belgian Labour Party*] [*Political party*]   (EY)
PTB........... Parti du Travail du Burkina [*Burkina Faso*] [*Political party*]   (EY)
PTB........... Physikalisch-Technische Bundesanstalt
PTB........... Physikalisch-Technische Bundesanstalt Braunschweig und Berlin [*Federal Physical-Technical Establishment in Braunschweig and Berlin*] [*Research center*]   (IRC)
PTB........... Polskie Towarzystwo Biochemiczne [*Polish Biochemical Society*]   (POL)
PTB........... Polskie Towarzystwo Botaniczne [*Polish Botanical Society*]   (POL)
PTB........... Pradelny a Tkalcovny Bavlny [*Cotton Spinning and Weaving Mills*]   (CZ)
PTB........... Producto Territorial Bruto [*Gross National Product*] [*Use GNP*]   (LA)
PTB........... Safety Engineering Regulations   (RU)
PTBA........ Proud to be Australian [*Political party*]
PTBat......... Protitankova Baterie [*Antitank Battery*]   (CZ)

PTBI .... PT Boats, Inc. (EAIO)

PTBT .... Partial Test-Ban Treaty

PTBW .... Przedsiebiorstwo Transportu Budownictwa Weglowego [*Mine Equipment Transportation Enterprise*] (POL)

PTC .... Panstwowe Teatry Czestochowskie [*Czestochowa State Theatres*] (POL)

PTC .... Partido de Trabajadores Colombianos [*Colombian Labor Party*] (LA)

PTC .... Parti Travailliste Congolais [*Congolese Labor Party*] [*Political party*]

PTC .... Peace Tax Campaign [*Australia*]

PTC .... Penang Turf Club (ML)

PTC .... Perak Turf Club (ML)

PTC .... Perth Technical College [*Australia*]

PTC .... Pioneer Tobacco Company

PTC .... Polskie Towarzystwo Cybernetyczne [*Polish Cybernetic Society*] [*Poland*]

PTC .... Polytechnology Transfer Centre [*CSIR*] [*India*]

PTC .... Posts and Telecommunications Corporation [*Myanmar*] (DS)

PTC .... Premium Tax Concession [*Australia*]

PTC .... Primary Teaching Certificate [*Australia*]

PTC .... Public Transport Corp. [*Victoria, Australia*]

PTCA .... Plains Tribal Council of Assam [*India*] [*Political party*] (PPW)

PTCA .... Professional Tennis Coaches' Association [*Australia*]

PTCCEA ... Philippine Technical, Clerical, Commercial Employees Association [*Trade union*] (FEA)

PTCh .... Polskie Towarzystwo Chemiczne [*Polish Chemical Society*] (POL)

PTD .... Antitank Battalion (RU)

PTD .... Panstwowe Teatry Dramatyczne [*State Drama Theatres*] (POL)

PTD .... Polskie Tonrarzystiro Dermotologiczna [*Polish Dermatological Association*] (EAIO)

PTD .... Polskie Towarzystwo Dermatologiczne [*Polish Dermatological Society*] (POL)

PTD .... Turboram Jet Engine (RU)

PTDC .... Pacific Trade and Development Conference [*OPTAD*] (FEA)

PTDC .... Pakistan Tourism Development Corporation Ltd. (GEA)

PTDD .... Support by Long-Range Tanks (RU)

PTDP .... Partido Trabalhista Democratico Portugues [*Portuguese Democratic Workers Party*] (WER)

PTDP .... Perifereia Teos Dioikiseos Protevousis [*Former Athens Administrative Area*] (GC)

PTDSC ...... Performers and Teachers Diploma, Sydney Conservatorium [*Australia*]

PTDWP ..... Panstwowy Teatr Domu Wojska Polskiego [*State Theatre of the House of the Polish Army*] (POL)

PTE .... Experimental Instruments and Techniques (RU)

PTE .... Pangosmios Takhydromiki Enosis [*Universal Postal Union*] (GC)

pte .... Parte [*Part*] [*Spanish*]

PTE .... Partido del Trabajo de Espana [*Spanish Labor Party*] (WER)

PTE .... Partido de Trabajadores Espanoles [*Spanish Workers' Party*] [*Political party*] (PPE)

PTE .... Partiia Togolezskovo Edinstva

PTE .... Passenger Transport Executive [*Scottish*]

PTE .... Permis Temporaires d'Exploitation

pte .... Perte [*Loss*] [*Bookkeeping*] [*French*]

Pte .... Petite [*Small*] [*Military map abbreviation World War I*] [*French*] (MTD)

Pte .... Pointe [*Point*] [*French*] (NAU)

PTE .... Politicno Teritorijalna Enota [*Political and Territorial Unit*] (YU)

PTE .... Polskie Towarzystwo Ekonomiczne [*Polish Economic Society*] (POL)

PTE .... Polskie Towarzystwo Elektryczne [*Polish Electrical Society*] (POL)

PTE .... Polskie Towarzystwo Entomologiczne [*Polish Entomological Society*] (SLS)

Pte .... Ponte [*Bridge*] [*Italian*] (NAU)

Pte .... Porte [*Gate*] [*Military map abbreviation World War I*] [*French*] (MTD)

PTE .... Port Stephens [*Australia*] [*Airport symbol*] (OAG)

Pte .... Poste [*Post*] [*Military map abbreviation World War I*] [*French*] (MTD)

Pte .... Private (EECI)

PTE .... Technical Operation Rules (RU)

PTE .... Technical Operations Regulations (BU)

Pte de D .... Poste de Douane [*Military map abbreviation*] [*World War I*] [*French*] (MTD)

PTEk .... Polskie Towarzystwo Ekonomiczne [*Polish Economic Society*] (POL)

PTEMPS ... Rules for Technical Operation of the Ministry of Railroads, USSR (RU)

Ptesi .... Pazartesi [*Sunday*] (TU)

PTETPC .... Party to Expose the Petrov Conspiracy [*Australia*] [*Political party*]

PTE-UC ..... Partido de los Trabajadores de Espana - Unidad Comunista [*Workers' Party of Spain - Communist Unity*] [*Political party*] (EY)

PTF .... Malololailai [*Fiji*] [*Airport symbol*] (OAG)

PTF .... Polskie Towarzystwo Farmaceutyczne [*Polish Pharmaceutical Society*] (POL)

PTF .... Polskie Towarzystwo Filologiczne [*Polish Philological Society*] (POL)

PTF .... Polskie Towarzystwo Filozoficzne [*Polish Philosophical Society*] (SLS)

PTF .... Polskie Towarzystwo Fizyczne [*Polish Physics Society*] (POL)

PTF .... Polskie Towarzystwo Fotograficzne [*Polish Photographic Society*] (POL)

PTF .... Poultry-Raising Farm (RU)

PTF .... Spinning and Weaving Factory (RU)

PTFE .... Polytetrafluoroethylene

PTFilozof ... Polskie Towarzystwo Filozoficzne [*Polish Philosophical Society*] (POL)

PTFiz .... Polskie Towarzystwo Fizyczne [*Polish Physics Society*] (POL)

PTFL .... Provincial Traders Foods Proprietary Ltd. [*Australia*]

PTG .... Amphibious Tracked Personnel Carrier (RU)

PTG .... Pietersburg [*South Africa*] [*Airport symbol*] (OAG)

PTG .... Pneumotachography (RU)

PTG .... Polskie Towarzystwo Geograficzne [*Polish Geographical Society*] (POL)

PTG .... Polskie Towarzystwo Geologiczne [*Polish Geological Society*] (POL)

PTG .... Polskie Towarzystwo Gleboznawcze [*Polish Soil Science Society*] (POL)

PTG .... Portuguese (ROG)

PTGU .... Steam-Turbine Generator Unit (RU)

PTGWO .... Philippine Transport and General Workers' Organization

PTH .... Philosophisch-Theologische Hochschule

PTH .... Polskie Towarzystwo Historyczne [*Polish Historical Society*] (POL)

pth .... Posta- es Tavirohivatal [*Post and Telegraph Office*] (HU)

PTHA .... Professional Trotting Horsemen's Association [*Australia*]

PTHZ .... Polskie Towarzystwo Handlu Zagranicznego [*Polish Society for Foreign Trade*] [*Poland*]

PTI .... Pedagogiai Tudomanyos Intezet [*Scientific Institute of Pedagogy*] (HU)

PTI .... Planning and Technological Institute (RU)

PTI .... Polskie Towarzystwo Immunologiczne [*Poland*] (SLS)

PTI .... Polytechnic Institute (RU)

PTI .... Poste Telephonique Infanterie [*Military*] [*French*] (MTD)

PTI .... Press Trust of India

PTI .... Publicacoes Tecnicas Internacionais Ltda. [*International Technical Publications Ltd.*] [*Information service or system*] (IID)

PTIC .... China National Postal and Telecommunications Industry Corp. (TCC)

PTIC .... Hangzhou Managing Division [*China*] (TCC)

PTIC .... Philippine Telecommunications Investment Corp.

PTIC .... Shanghai Managing Division [*China*] (TCC)

PTIMASh ... Khar'kov Planning and Design Technological Institute of Machinery Manufacture (RU)

Ptits .... Poultry-Raising Sovkhoz [*Topography*] (RU)

PTJ .... Policia Tecnica Judicial [*Judicial Technical Police*] [*Venezuela*] (LA)

PTJ .... Polskie Towarzystwo Jezykoznawcze [*Polish Philological Society*] [*Poland*]

PTJ .... Portland [*Australia*] [*Airport symbol*] (OAG)

PTK .... Channel Selector (RU)

PTK .... Field Telephone Cable (RU)

PTK .... Industrial and Technical Courses (RU)

PTK .... Panstwowe Technikum Korespondencyjne [*State Correspondence Technical School*] (POL)

PTK .... Polgari Torvenykonyv [*Civil Code*] (HU)

PTK .... Polskie Towarzystwo Kardiologiczne [*Poland*] (SLS)

PTK .... Polskie Towarzystwo Krajoznawcze [*Polish Local Studies Society*] (POL)

ptk .... Poytakirja [*Finland*]

PTK .... Protitankove Kanony [*Antitank Guns*] (CZ)

PTK .... Provozne-Technicke Knihovny [*Technical and Management Reference Libraries*] (CZ)

PTK .... Steam Turbocompressor (RU)

ptk .... Tank Commander's Panoramic Telescope (RU)

PTK .... Vocational and Technical Courses (RU)

PTKh .... Constant Table of Characteristics (RU)

PTKMPS... Regulations on Technical Control of Motor Vehicles (BU)

Ptkp .... Postatakarekpenztar [*Postal Savings Bank*] (HU)

PTKS .... Polskie Towarzystwo Kulturalno-Spoleczne [*Polish Cultural and Social Society*] (POL)

PTL .... Physikalisch-Technische Lehranstalt

PTL .... Polskie Towarzystwo Lekarskie [*Polish Medical Society*] [*Poland*]

PTL .... Polskie Towarzystwo Lesne [*Poland*] (SLS)

PTL............ Polskie Towarzystwo Ludoznawcze [*Polish Folklore Society*] (POL)
PTL............ Propeller-Turbinenluftstrahlmotor [*Turboprop Aircraft Engine*] (EG)
PTL............ Protivtenkovska Linija [*Antitank Line*] (YU)
PTM .... Antitank Mine (RU)
PTM .... Cloth Dust Mask (RU)
PTM .... Palmarito [*Venezuela*] [*Airport symbol*] (OAG)
PTM .... Panstwowe Technikum Mechaniczne [*State Mechanical Technical School*] (POL)
PTM .... Panstwowe Technikum Morskie [*State Maritime Technical School*] (POL)
PTM .... Parti Travailliste Mauricien
PTM .... Persekutuan Tanah Melayu [*Federation of Malaya*] (ML)
PTM .... Pocetna Tacka Marsrute [*Starting Point of a March*] [*Army*] (YU)
PTM .... Polis Tentera Malaysia [*Malaysian Military Police*] (ML)
PTM .... Polskie Towarzystwo Matematyczne [*Polish Mathematical Society*] (POL)
PTM .... Predilnica i Tkalnica [*Spinning and Weaving Mills*] [*Maribor*] (YU)
PTM .... Protivtenkovske Mine [*Antitank Mines*] (YU)
PTMA........ Polskie Towarzystwo Milosnikow Astronomii [*Polish Society of Friends of Astronomy*] (POL)
PTMA........ Poznanskie Towarzystwo Milosnikow Astronomii [*Poznan Society of Friends of Astronomy*] (POL)
PTMB........ Przemysl Terenowy Materialow Budowlanych [*Local Industry of Building Materials*] (POL)
PTMI........ Protitankova Mina [*Antitank Mine*] (CZ)
PT mini ...... Antitank Mines (BU)
PTMOW ... Polskie Towarzystwo Matematyczne, Oddzial Wroclawski [*Wroclaw (Breslau) Branch of the Polish Mathematical Society*] (POL)
PTMP........ Antitank Minefield (RU)
PTMP........ Protitankove Minove Pole [*Antitank Mine Field*] (CZ)
PTN .... Labor Party of the Netherlands (RU)
PTN .... Pantanal Linhas Aereas Sul-Matogrossenses SA [*Brazil*] [*ICAO designator*] (FAAC)
PTN .... Partido Trabalhista Nacional [*National Labor Party*] [*Brazil*] (LA)
PTN .... Polskie Towarzystwo Nautologiczne [*Poland*] (SLS)
PTN .... Polskie Towarzystwo Neofilologiczne [*Poland*] (SLS)
PTN .... Polskie Towarzystwo Neurologiczne [*Polish Neurological Society*] (POL)
PTN .... Regulations on Labor Norms (BU)
PTN .... Technical Observation Point (BU)
PTN .... Technical Observation Post (RU)
PTN .... Turbine-Driven Feed Pump (RU)
PTN .... Voice-Frequency Dialing Set [*Telephony*] (RU)
PTNII........ Planning, Technological, and Scientific Research Institute (RU)
PTNV .... Voice-Frequency Dialing and Ringing Set (RU)
PTNW .... Polskie Towarzystwo Nauk Weterynaryjnych [*Poland*] (SLS)
PTO .... Antitank Cannon, Antitank Gun (RU)
PTO .... Antitank Defense (BU)
PTO .... Antitorpedo Defense (RU)
PTO .... Hoisting and Conveying Equipment (RU)
PTO .... Industrial Transportation Department (RU)
PTO .... Part- es Tomegszervezeti Osztaly [*Party and Mass Organization Department*] (HU)
Pt O........... Partszervezesi Osztaly [*Department of Party Organization*] (HU)
pto .... Patio [*Court*] [*Portuguese*] (CED)
PTO .... Pato Branco [*Brazil*] [*Airport symbol*] (OAG)
PTO .... Polskie Towarzystwo Orientalistyczne [*Polish Society for Oriental Studies*] (POL)
Pto.............. Porto [*Port*] [*Portuguese*] (NAU)
Pto.............. Porto [*Port*] [*Italian*] (NAU)
PTO .... Post and Telegraph Office (RU)
PTO .... Principal Training Officer
PTO .... Production and Technical Department (RU)
PTO .... Protitankova Obrana [*Antitank Defense*] (CZ)
PTO .... Protitankovy Oddil [*Antitank Battalion*] (CZ)
PTO .... Protivo-Tankovaia Oborona [*Antitank Defense*] [*Former USSR*]
PTO .... Protivtenkovska Odbrana [*Antitank Defense*] (YU)
PTO .... Protivtorpedna Odbrana [*Antitorpedo Defense*] (YU)
PTO .... Public Trust Office [*Australia*]
Pto.............. Puerto [*Port*] [*Spanish*] (NAU)
PTO .... Technical Inspection Point (RU)
PTO .... Technical Production Department (BU)
PTO .... Technical Service Point (RU)
PTOiTr...... Polskie Towarzystwo Ortopedyczne i Traumatologiczne [*Poland*] (SLS)
PTOL........ Polskie Towarzystwo Otolaryngologiczne [*Poland*] (SLS)
PTOM .... Pays et Territoires d'Outre-Mer
Pton............ Ponton [*Pontoon*] [*Military map abbreviation World War I*] [*French*] (MTD)

PTOP......... Antitank Strongpoint (RU)
PTOR .... Antitank Cannon (BU)
PTOR .... Antitank Cannon, Antitank Gun (RU)
PTOR .... Antitank Defense Area (RU)
PTOZ........ Antitank Barrage Fire, Antitank Barrage (RU)
PTP........... Antitank Cannon, Antitank Gun (RU)
PTP........... Antitank Obstacle, Antitank Barrier (RU)
PTP........... Direct Heat Flow (RU)
PTP........... Pagdanan Timber Products [*Philippines*]
PTP........... Panstwowy Teatr Polski [*Polish State Theater*] (POL)
PTP........... Parent to Parent, Inc. [*Australia*]
PTP........... Parti Togolais du Progres [*Togolese Progress Party*] (AF)
PTP........... Plan de Trabajos Publicos [*Public Works Plan*] [*Argentina*] (LA)
PTP........... Pointe-A-Pitre [*Guadeloupe*] [*Airport symbol*] (OAG)
PTP........... Polskie Towarzystwo Pediatryczne [*Polish Pediatric Society*] [*Poland*]
PTP........... Polskie Towarzystwo Prehistoryczne [*Polish Prehistorical Society*] (POL)
PTP........... Polskie Towarzystwo Przyrodnikow [*Polish Naturalists' Society*] (POL)
PTP........... Polskie Towarzystwo Psychologiczne [*Polish Psychological Society*] (SLS)
PTP........... Pomocny Technicky Prapor [*Technical Support Battalion*] (CZ)
PTP........... Posto Telefonico Pubblico [*Public Telephone*] [*Italy*]
PTP........... Privremeni Tehnicki Propisi [*Provisional Technical Regulations*] (YU)
PTP........... Protitankova Puska [*Antitank Rifle*] (CZ)
PTP........... Protitankovy Pluk [*Antitank Regiment*] (CZ)
PTP........... Spot-Landing Parachute (RU)
PTP........... Step-Down Transformer Substation (RU)
PTP........... Technical Aid Point (RU)
PTP........... Television Program Selector (RU)
PtPb.......... Putnicki Parabrod [*Passenger Steamer*] (YU)
PTPI .... People to People International (EAIO)
PTPN........ Poznanskie Towarzystwo Przyjaciol Nauk [*Poznan Society of Friends of Science*] (POL)
PTP ONZ.. Polskie Towarzystwo Przyjaciol ONZ [*United Nations Association of Poland*] (EAIO)
PTPreh ...... Polskie Towarzystwo Prehistoryczne [*Polish Prehistorical Society*] (POL)
PTR........... Antitank Defense Area (RU)
PTR........... Antitank Ditch (RU)
PTR........... Antitank Fortified Area (BU)
PTR........... Antitank Rifle (RU)
PTR........... Partido Tercera Republica [*Chile*] [*Political party*] (EY)
PTR........... Parti Tindakan Ra'yat [*People's Action Party*] [*Singapore*] (ML)
PTR........... Parti Travailliste [*Labor Party*] [*Mauritius Use PT*] (AF)
ptr.............. Pietro [*Floor, Story*] (POL)
PTR........... Plan Technickeho Rozvoje [*Technical Development Plan*] (CZ)
PTR........... Pneumatic Friction Handsaw (RU)
PTR........... Polskie Towarzystwo Radiologiczne [*Polish Radiological Society*] [*Poland*]
PTR........... Polskie Towarzystwo Reumatologiczne [*Polish Rheumatological Society*] [*Poland*]
PTR........... Programa de Tecnologias Rurales [*Honduras*]
PTR........... Protivtenkovska Rezerva [*Antitank Reserve*] (YU)
PTR........... Pukovske Tenkovske Rezerve [*Regimental Tank Reserves*] (YU)
PTRB........ Field Tractor Repair Base (RU)
ptrb........... Mobile Tank Maintenance Battalion (BU)
PTRB........ Mobile Tank Maintenance Depot (BU)
PTRB........ Mobile Tank Repair Base (RU)
PTRD........ Degtyarev Antitank Rifle (RU)
PTrez........ Antitank Reserve (RU)
PTRI......... Philippine Textile Research Institute [*Research center*] (IRC)
PTRK........ Technical Radio Control Post (RU)
Ptrl............ Patrouillenfuehrer [*Patrol Leader*] [*German*]
PTRM....... Panstwowe Technikum Rybolowstwa Morskiego [*State Technical School for Deep-Water Fishing*] (POL)
PTRS .... Simonov Antitank Rifle (RU)
PTRU........ Antitank Line (RU)
PTRZ........ Mobile Tank Maintenance Plant (BU)
PTRZ........ Mobile Tank Repair Plant (RU)
PTRZ........ Planowo-Terminowe Remonty Zapobiegawcze [*Planned and Undeferrable Preventive Repairs*] (POL)
PTS........... Composite Video Signal (RU)
PTS........... Conveyor System (RU)
PTS........... Fish Receiving and Transport Vessel (RU)
PTS........... Heater Thermistor (RU)
PTS........... Mobile Television Unit (RU)
PTS........... Papiertechnische Stiftung fuer Forschung und Ausbildung in Papiererzeugung und Papierverarbeitung (SLS)
pts .... Parts [*Parts*] [*French*]
pts .... Pesetas [*Monetary units in Spain and Latin America*]
PTS........... Podohospodarska-Technicka Skola [*Agricultural School*] (CZ)

PTS .... Polskie Towarzystwo Semiotyczne [*Poland*] (SLS)
PTS .... Polskie Towarzystwo Socjologiczne [*Poland*] (SLS)
PTS .... Polskie Towarzystwo Statystyczne [*Polish Statistical Society*] (POL)
PTS .... Polskie Towarzystwo Stomatologiczne [*Poland*] (SLS)
PTS .... Polymerteknisk Selskab [*Denmark*] (SLS)
PTS .... Private Telecommunications Systems [*Radio-Suisse Ltd.*] [*Switzerland*] [*Telecommunications*]
PTS .... Puffertaktsteuerung [*German*] (ADPT)
Pts .... Puits [*Well*] [*Military map abbreviation World War I*] [*French*] (MTD)
PTS .... Pyrotechnic Agents (RU)
PTs .... Tank Trailer (RU)
PTS .... Telephone Relay Exchange (RU)
PTS .... Thermistor (RU)
PTS .... Tractor Trailer Snowplow (RU)
PTS .... Wire-Wound Resistance Tensometer (RU)
p-tsa .... Printing Press (BU)
PTSC .... Passed Technical Staff College [*Australia*]
PTSEEU .... Private Tea and Sugar Estates Employees Union [*Mauritius*] (AF)
pts et pts ..... Profits et Pertes [*Profits and Losses*] [*Business term*] [*French*]
Ptsi .... Pazartesi [*Sunday*] (TU)
PTS-K .... Thermistor with Indirect Heating (RU)
PTsKO .... Permanent Central Opium Board [*PCOB*] (RU)
pt sl .... Patrol Service (BU)
PTSL .... Przedsiebiorstwo Transportu Samochodowego Lacznosci [*Automotive Postal Service Enterprise*] (POL)
PTsN .... Gear-Driven Centrifugal Supercharger (RU)
PTsR .... Gear-Driven Centrifugal Governor, Gear-Driven Centrifugal Regulator (RU)
pts sl .... Military Police Service (BU)
PTsU .... Control Circuit Switch, Pilot Circuit Switch (RU)
PTsUK ...... Mobile Flight Control Center (RU)
PTsUK ...... Transfer to Central Command Control [*Computers*] (RU)
pts vd .... Military Police Platoon (BU)
PTT .... Intermediate Current Transformer (RU)
PTT .... Pasokan Pertahanan Tempatan [*Local Defense Corps*] (ML)
PTT .... Perth Theatre Trust [*Australia*]
PTT .... Politikai Tanacskozo Testulet [*Political Consultative Commission (of the Warsaw Pact)*] (HU)
PTT .... Polskie Towarzystwo Tatrzanskie [*Polish Tatra Mountains Society*] (POL)
PTT .... Postansko-Telegrafsko-Telefonski [*Postal, Telegraph, and Telephone*] (YU)
PTT .... Posta, Telefon, Telgraf [*Post, Telephone, and Telegraph Administration*] (TU)
PTT .... Posta, Telegraf, Telefon [*Post, Telegraph, Telephone*] (YU)
PTT .... Postes et Telecommunications [*Posts and Telecommunications*] (AF)
PTT .... Postes, Telegraphes, et Telediffusion [*Post, Telegraph, and Telephone*] [*General Post Office Facetious translation: Prostitution Telematique et Telephonique*] [*France*]
PTT .... Poste, Telegraf, e Telefon [*Post, Telegraph, and Telephone*] [*Albanian*]
PTT .... Posts, Telegraph, Telecommunications (PWGL)
PTT .... Post, Telegraph, and Telephone [*Saudi Arabia*] (ME)
PTT .... Post, Telephon und Telegraphenbetriebe [*Switzerland*] [*Telecommunications*]
PTT .... Post und Telegraphenverwaltung [*Postal and Telegraph Administration*] [*Austria*] [*Telecommunications*]
PtT .... Ptujski Tednik [*Ptuj Weekly*] [*A periodical*] (YU)
PTT .... Public Telephone and Telegraph
PTT .... Staatsbedrijf der Posterijen, Telegrafie en Telefonie [*Benelux*] (BAS)
PTT .... Television Picture Tube (RU)
PTT .... Tokarev Pistol (RU)
PTTI .... Postal, Telegraph, and Telephone International [*See also IPTT*] [*Geneva, Switzerland*] (EAIO)
PTTK .... Polskie Towarzystwo Turystyczno-Krajoznawcze [*Polish Tourist and Local Studies Society*] (POL)
PTTR .... Posta, Telegraf, Telefon, si Radio [*Posts, Telegraphs, Telephones, and Radio*] (RO)
PTTR .... Posts, Telegraphs, Telephones, and Radio (BU)
PTTS .... Postal, Telegraph, and Telephone Stations (BU)
PTU .... Fire-Fighting Technical School (RU)
PTU .... Industrial Television Unit (RU)
PTU .... Intermediate Repeater (RU)
PTU .... Polskie Towarzystwo Urologiczne [*Poland*] (SLS)
PTU .... Professional-Technical School [*Russian*]
PTU .... Remote-Control Board (RU)
PTU .... Steam Turbine Unit (RU)
PTU .... Technical Vocational School (BU)
PTU .... Television Receiver, Television Set (RU)
PTU .... Underwater Television Unit (RU)
PTU .... Vocational and Technical School (RU)

PTUA .... Public Transport Users' Association [*Australia*]
PTU/ACT ... Progressive Teachers Union / Action Committee of Teachers [*South Africa*] (AA)
PTUC .... Pacific Trade Union Community [*Australia*] (EAIO)
PTUC .... Philippine Trade Union Council
PTUF .... Pakistan Trade Union Federation
PTUMP ..... Antitank Controlled Mine Field (RU)
PTUR .... Antitank Guided Missile (RU)
PTURS ...... Antitank Guided Missile (RU)
PTUV .... Public Tenants' Union of Victoria [*Australia*]
PTV .... Parti Travailliste Voltaique [*Voltan Labor Party*] (AF)
PTV .... Programma Tekhnikis Voitheias [*Technical Assistance Program*] (GC)
PTV .... Programmierte Textverarbeitung [*German*] (ADPT)
PTV .... Voice-Frequency Ringing Receiver [*Telephony*] (RU)
PTV .... Workers' Party of Vietnam (RU)
PTVU .... Voice-Frequency Ringing and Control Receiver (RU)
PTWK .... Polskie Towarzystwo Wydawcow Ksiazek [*Polish Publishers' Association*] [*Poland*]
PTWMASA ... Private Treaty Wool Merchants' Association of South Australia
PTWMAV ... Private Treaty Wool Merchants' Association of Victoria [*Australia*]
PTWMAWA ... Private Treaty Wool Merchants' Association of Western Australia
PTWU .... Post and Telecommunications Workers Union [*Guyana*] (LA)
PTX .... Aereo Postal de Mexico SA de CV [*ICAO designator*] (FAAC)
PTY .... Panama City [*Panama*] [*Airport symbol*] (OAG)
Pty .... Proprietary (SCAC)
PTZ .... Polskie Towarzystwo Zootechniczne [*Polish Animal Husbandry Society*] (POL)
PTZ .... Protitankova Zaloha [*Antitank Reserve*] (CZ)
PTZO .... Antitank Barrage Fire (RU)
PU .... Adapter (RU)
PU .... Auxiliary Steering Equipment [*River vessels*] (RU)
PU .... Control Panel, Console (RU)
PU .... Control Post (RU)
PU .... Control Switch (RU)
PU .... Converter Unit [*Computers*] (RU)
PU .... Direct Control (RU)
PU .... Dust Extractor, Dust Allayer, Dust Trap [*Mining*] (RU)
PU .... Field Command (RU)
PU .... Field Service Regulations (RU)
PU .... Launcher [*Rocketry*] (RU)
PU .... Normal School (BU)
pu .... Paid Up (EECI)
PU .... Palackeho Universita [*Palacky University*] [*Olomouc*] (CZ)
pu .... Palyaudvar [*Railroad Station*] (HU)
PU .... Pangkalan Udara [*Air Base*] (IN)
PU .... Parametric Amplifier (RU)
PU .... Patentni Urad [*Patent Office*] (CZ)
PU .... Pechotni Uciliste [*Infantry School*] (CZ)
PU .... Pedagogicky Ustav [*Pedagogical Institute*] (CZ)
PU .... Per Uur [*Per Hour*] [*Afrikaans*]
PU .... Pijacna Uprava [*Market Administration*] (YU)
Pu .... Plutonio [*Plutonium*] [*Chemical element*] [*Portuguese*]
PU .... Plynarensky Ustav [*Gas Works*] [*Bechovice*] (CZ)
PU .... Polarograficky Ustav [*Polarographic Institute*] [*Czechoslovak Academy of Sciences*] (CZ)
PU .... Political Administration (BU)
PU .... Political Administration, Political Directorate (RU)
PU .... Polyurethane (RU)
PU .... Portable Photographic Enlarger (RU)
PU .... Potchefstroomse Universiteit [*Potchefstroom University*] [*Afrikaans*]
PU .... Pravnicky Ustav Ministerstva Spravedlnosti [*Law Institute of the Ministry of Justice*] (CZ)
PU .... Preamplifier (RU)
PU .... Precompte Unique [*Benelux*] (BAS)
PU .... Prehistoricky Ustav [*Prehistoric Institute*] [*Charles University Prague*] (CZ)
PU .... Printer [*Computers*] (RU)
PU .... Privredna Udruzenja [*Economic Associations*] (YU)
PU .... Privredne Ustanove [*Economic Institutions*] (YU)
PU .... Profesores Universitarios [*University Professors*] [*Spanish*] (WER)
PU .... Programer, Program Device (RU)
PU .... Programmierte Unterweisung [*German*] (ADPT)
PU .... Programmunterbrechung [*German*] (ADPT)
PU .... Proleterski Udarni [*Proletarian Shock Troops*] (YU)
PU .... Puetzer [*Germany*] [*ICAO aircraft manufacturer identifier*] (ICAO)
Pu .... Pulau [*or Pulu*] [*Island Malay*] (NAU)
Pu .... Punjab Regiment [*India*] [*Army*]
pu .... Puska [*Rifle*] (HU)
PU .... Receiver (RU)

PU .... Switching Device   (RU)
PU .... Testing Device   (RU)
PU .... Track Angle   (RU)
PU .... Universal Track-Shifting Machine [*Railroads*]   (RU)
PUA .... Accelerometer Tester   (RU)
PUA .... Parti de l'Unite Africaine
PUA .... Partido de Unificacion Anticomunista [*Anti-Communist Unification Party*] [*Guatemala*] [*Political party*]   (PPW)
PUA .... Primeras Lineas Uruguayas de Navegacion Aerea [*Uruguay*] [*ICAO designator*]   (FAAC)
PUAID ...... Parti d'Unite Arabe Islamique-Democratique [*Algeria*] [*Political party*]   (EY)
PUAO .... Fire Director [*Artillery*]   (RU)
Puarm .... Army Political Directorate   (RU)
PUAS .... Postal Union of the Americas and Spain [*See also UPAE*] [*Montevideo, Uruguay*]   (EAIO)
PUASP ...... Postal Union of the Americas, Spain, and Portugal [*Uruguay*]   (EAIO)
PUAZO ..... Antiaircraft Fire Control Instrument   (BU)
PUAZO ..... Antiaircraft Fire Director   (RU)
PUB .... Parti de l'Unite Basonge
PUB .... Partido Union Boliviana [*Bolivian Unity Party*] [*Political party*]   (PPW)
PuB .... Penzugyi Bizottsag [*Financial Committee*]   (HU)
PUB .... Prazska Uverni Banka [*Prague Credit Bank*]   (CZ)
PUB .... Public Utilities Board [*Singapore*] [*Barbados*]   (ML)
pub .... Publie [*Published*] [*French*]
pub .... Publiek [*Public*] [*Afrikaans*]
p/ub .... Shelter for Small-Arms Ammunition Supply Point [*Topography*]   (RU)
pubbl .... Pubblicazione [*Publication*] [*Italian*]
publ .... Public   (RU)
publ .... Publication, Published   (BU)
publ .... Publikacio [*Publication*] [*Hungary*]
publ .... Publikasjon [*Publication*] [*Danish/Norwegian*]
publ .... Publikation [*Publication*] [*Sweden*]
Publ .... Publikation [*Publication*] [*German*]
publ bibl ..... Public Library   (BU)
PublEurGem .. Publikatieblad der Europese Gemeenschappen [*Benelux*]   (BAS)
PublG .... PublizitatsGesetz [*Publicity Law*] [*Germany*]
PUBLICOM ... Agentia de Publicitate pentru Comertul Exterior [*Romanian Publicity Agency for Foreign Trade*]   (RO)
PUBLICONTA ... Contaduria Publica Ltda. [*Colombia*]   (COL)
PUBLIDELTA ... Delta Publicidad [*Colombia*]   (COL)
PUBLI-PERU ... Empresa de Publicidad del Peru [*Peruvian Advertising Enterprise*]   (LA)
publits .... Journalism   (RU)
Publr .... Publisher   (EECI)
PUBP .... Powiatowy Urzad Bezpieczenstwa Publicznego [*County Administration of Public Security*]   (POL)
PUBPS ...... Privredno Udruzenje Bioskopskih Preduzeca Srbije [*Economic Association of Motion Picture Theaters of Serbia*]   (YU)
PUC .... Pancyprian Union of Chemists [*Cyprus*]   (EAIO)
PUC .... Parti de l'Unite Congolaise [*Congolese Unity Party*] [*Political party*]
PUC .... Partido Union Civica [*Civic Union Party*] [*Dominican Republic*]   (LA)
PUC .... Pontificia Universidade Catolica [*Pontifical Catholic University*] [*Brazil*]   (LA)
PUC .... Popular Unity of Chile [*Political party*]
PUC .... Proteine Unicellulaire
PUC .... Public Utilities Commission [*Trinidadian and Tobagan*]   (LA)
PUCA .... Partido Unionista Centro Americana [*Nicaragua*] [*Political party*]   (EY)
PUCA .... Partido Unionista Centro Americano [*Central American Unionist Party*]   (LA)
PUCAM .... Por un Campo Argentino Mejor [*Argentina*]   (LAA)
PUCH .... Parti Uni des Communistes Haitiens [*United Party of Haitian Communists*]   (LA)
PUCHE ..... Potchefstroom University for Christian Higher Education
PUCO .... Partido Unificacion de Campesinos y Obreros [*Workers and Peasants Unification Party*] [*Guatemala*]   (LA)
PUD .... Partido Unificacion Democratica [*Democratic Unification Party*] [*Guatemala*]   (LA)
PUD .... Partido Union Democratica [*Guatemala*] [*Political party*]
PUD .... Plans d'Urbanisme Directeur [*Algeria*]
PUD .... Polish Union of the Disabled   (EAIO)
PUD .... Puerto Deseado [*Argentina*] [*Airport symbol*]   (OAG)
PUDH .... Parti d'Union des Democrates Haitiens [*Union Party of Haitian Democrats*]   (LA)
PUDN .... Partido Union Democratica Nacionalista [*National Democratic Union Party*] [*El Salvador*]   (LA)
PUDNOVJ ... Partizanska Udarna Divizija Narodnooslobodilacke Vojske Jugoslavije [*Partisan Shock Division of the National Liberation Army of Yugoslavia*]   (YU)

PUDOC ..... Centrum voor Landbouwpublikaties en Landbouwdocumentatie [*Center for Agricultural Publishing and Documentation*] [*Ministry of Agriculture and Fisheries*] [*Information service or system*]   (IID)
PUDR .... People's Union for Democratic Rights [*India*]   (EAIO)
PUE .... Physiotherapists' Union of Employees [*Australia*]
PUE .... Puerto Obaldia [*Panama*] [*Airport symbol*]   (OAG)
PUE .... Rules for Setting Up Electrical Installations   (RU)
PUF .... Partido Union Federal [*Federal Union Party*] [*Argentina*] [*Political party*]
PUF .... Pau [*France*] [*Airport symbol*]   (OAG)
PUF .... Peace Union of Finland   (EAIO)
PUF .... People's United Front [*Papua New Guinea*] [*Political party*]   (PPW)
PUF .... People's United Front [*Bangladesh*] [*Political party*]
PUF .... Presses Universitaires de France [*French University Press*]   (WER)
PUFO .... Pack Up and Fade Out [*End of military exercise*] [*British*]   (DSUE)
PUG .... Hunter-Killer Group [*Navy*]   (RU)
PUG .... Port Augusta [*Australia*] [*Airport symbol*]   (OAG)
PUG .... Przeglad Ustawodawstwa Gospodarczego [*Review of Economic Legislation*]   (POL)
PUGN .... Full Deflection [*Artillery*]   (RU)
puh .... Puhelin [*Telephone*] [*Finland*]
puhek .... Puhekieli [*Finland*]
puhkesk ..... Puhelinkeskustelu [*Finland*]
puhutt .... Puhutteluna [*Address*] [*Finland*]
PUI .... Engineer's Control Post   (RU)
PUI .... Model Statutes of the Labor Production Cooperatives of Disabled Persons   (BU)
PUI .... Partido Universitario Independiente [*Independent University Party*] [*Spanish*]   (WER)
PUJ .... Punta Cana [*Dominican Republic*] [*Airport symbol*]   (OAG)
PUK .... Parti d'Unite Katangaise [*Katanga Unity Party*] [*Political party*]   (PD)
PUK .... Patriotic Union of Kurdistan [*Iraq*] [*Political party*]   (PD)
PUK .... Pechiney-Ugine-Kuhlmann [*France*] [*Commercial firm*]
PUK .... Potchefstroomse Universiteitskollege [*Potchefstroom University College*] [*South Africa*]
PUK .... Pukarua [*French Polynesia*] [*Airport symbol*]   (OAG)
PUKO .... Propagacni Ustredi Kraje Olomouckeho [*Propaganda Headquarters for the Olomouc Region*]   (CZ)
PUL .... Linear Control Point [*Automation*]   (RU)
PUL .... Press Union of Liberia
PUL .... Pul. Przedsiebiorstwo Uslug Lotniczych [*Poland*] [*ICAO designator*]   (FAAC)
pulab .... Machine-Gun and Artillery Battalion   (RU)
PULADA .... Pusat Latehan Darat [*Army Training Center*]   (ML)
pulap .... Machine-Gun and Artillery Regiment   (RU)
pulm .... Pulmentum [*Gruel Pulmonary*] [*Latin*]   (MAE)
PULO .... Pattani United Liberation Organization [*Thailand*] [*Political party*]   (PD)
pul otd .... Machine-Gun Section   (RU)
PULPAPEL ... Celulosa y Papel de Colombia SA [*Colombia*]   (COL)
pulv .... Pulverisiert [*German*]   (GCA)
pulver .... Pulverig [*Powdery*] [*German*]   (GCA)
PUM .... Parti de l'Unite Marocaine
PUM .... Partido Unificado Mariateguista [*Peru*] [*Political party*]   (EY)
PUM .... Pomalaa [*Indonesia*] [*Airport symbol*]   (OAG)
PUMC .... Peking Union Medical College [*China*]
PUMC .... Public Utilities Management Company [*Kuwait*]   (GEA)
PUMGC .... Pious Union of Our Mother of Good Counsel [*See also SMBC*] [*Genazzano, Italy*]   (EAIO)
PUMO .... Mortar Fire Director   (RU)
PUMS .... Permanently Unfit for Military Service [*British*]
PUMS .... Pokrajinska Uprava Poljoprivrednih Masinskih Stanica [*Provincial Administration of Agricultural Machinery Stations*] [*Vojvodina*]   (YU)
PUMS .... Pravnicky Ustav Ministerstva Spravedlnosti [*Law Institute of the Ministry of Justice*]   (CZ)
PUMST ..... Polish Underground Movement (1939-1945) Study Trust   (EA)
PUMV ...... Publikacni Ustav Ministerstva Vnitra [*Publishing Institute of the Ministry of the Interior*]   (CZ)
PUMZ ...... Pervoural'sk Metalware Plant   (RU)
PUN .... Control and Guidance Post   (RU)
PUN .... Parti de l'Unite Nationale [*Party of National Unity*] [*Haiti*] [*Political party*]   (PPW)
PUN .... Partido de Unificacion Nacional [*National Unification Party*] [*Costa Rica*]   (LA)
PUN .... Partido Unico Nacional [*National Single Party*] [*Equatorial Guinea*]   (AF)
PUN .... Partido Union Nacional [*National Union Party*] [*Peru*]   (LA)
PUN .... Partido Union Nacional [*National Union Party*] [*Costa Rica*] [*Political party*]
PUNA .... Parti de l'Unite Nationale [*Party for National Unity*]
PUNC .... Partido de Unidad Nacional Conservadora [*Nicaragua*] [*Political party*]   (EY)

PUNG........ Parti de l'Unite Nationale de Guinee [*Party for Guinean National Unity*]
PUNGA..... Parti de l'Unite Nationale Gabonaise [*Party for Gabonese National Unity*] [*Political party*]
PUNGE..... Partido Unido Nacional de Guinea Ecuatorial
PUNIA...... Fighter Aviation Control and Guidance Post (RU)
PUNR........ Regulation on the Application of the Ukase on Encouraging the Birth Rate (BU)
PUNS .... Parti de l'Unite Nationale Sahraouie
PUNS .... Partido de Union Nacional del Sahara [*Western Sahara*] [*Political party*]
PUNS .... Permanently Unfit for Naval Service [*British*]
PUNSW .... Poets' Union of New South Wales [*Australia*]
PUNT .... Partido Unico Nacional de los Trabajadores [*Workers National Single Party*] [*Equatorial Guinea*] (AF)
PUNT .... Prisoners' United Front [*Australia*]
PUO........... Fire Direction Instrument (BU)
PUO........... Fire Director [*Artillery*] (RU)
PUOKR ..... Political Directorate of a Military District (RU)
puol .... Puolaa [*or Puolaksi*] [*Finland*]
puol .... Puolalainen [*Finland*]
PUOZA ..... Antiaircraft Fire Director (RU)
PUP .... Parti de l'Union Populaire [*People's Union Party*] [*Haiti*] (LA)
PUP .... Parti de l'Unite du Peuple
PUP .... Parti de l'Unite du Peuple Gabonais [*Political party*] (EY)
PUP .... Parti de l'Unite Populaire [*Tunisia*] [*Political party*] (EY)
PUP .... Partido da Unidade Popular [*Popular Unity Party*] [*Portuguese*] (WER)
PUP .... Partido Union Patriotica [*Patriotic Union Party*] [*Dominican Republic*] [*Political party*] (PPW)
PUP .... People's United Party [*Belize*] [*Political party*] (PPW)
PUP .... Popular Unity Party [*Bangladesh*] [*Political party*] (PPW)
PUP .... Pracovni Utvar Potrestanych [*Convict Labor Unit*] (CZ)
PUPch........ Intermediate-Frequency Preamplifier (RU)
PUPG .... Partido Union do Povo Galego [*United Party of the Galician People*] [*Spanish*] (WER)
PUPiK .... Przedsiebiorstwo Upowszechniania Prasy i Ksiazki [*Enterprise for Book and Press Distribution - "Ruch"*] [*Poland*]
PUPiKRuch ... Panstwowy Urzad Publikacji i Kolportazu "Ruch" [*"Ruch" State Bureau for Publishing and for Circulation of Publications*] (POL)
PUQ........... Punta Arenas [*Chile*] [*Airport symbol*] (OAG)
PUR .... Panstwowy Urzad Repatriacyjny [*State Repatriation Administration*] (POL)
PUR .... Partido de Unificacion Revolucionaria [*Party of Revolutionary Unification*] [*Guatemala*] [*Political party*]
PUR .... Political Directorate of the Revvoyensovet (RU)
PUR .... Polyurethan [*Polyurethane*] (EG)
PUR .... Przedsiebiorstwo Uplynnienia Remanentow [*Enterprise for Distribution of Surpluses*] (POL)
PUR .... Spurwing Airlines (Pty) Ltd. [*South Africa*] [*ICAO designator*] (FAAC)
PURA .... Partido de Union Republicana Autentica [*Authentic Republican Union Party*] [*Costa Rica*] (LA)
PuRD .... Pulse Jet Engines (BU)
purg........... Purgativus [*Cathartic, purgative*] [*Latin*] (MAE)
PURKKA... Political Directorate of the Workers' and Peasants' Red Army (RU)
PURNES... Regulation on the Management, Order, and Supervision of Floor Ownership (BU)
PURO .... Programa de Utilizacion de Recursos Oceanicos [*Ocean Resource Utilization Program - ORUP*] [*Spanish*] (ASF)
PURP......... Poljska Ujedinjena Radnicka Partija [*Polish United Workers Party*] (YU)
PURS........ Antitank Guided Missile (RU)
PURS........ Guided Missile Fire Director (RU)
PURS........ Partido de la Union Republicana Socialista [*Socialist Republican Union Party*] [*Bolivia*] (LA)
PURS........ Partido Unido de la Revolucion Sandinista [*United Party of the Sandinist Revolution*] [*Nicaragua*] (LA)
PURSC...... Partido Unido de la Revolucion Socialista Cubana [*Cuba*] [*Political party*] (EY)
Purvon....... First, Elementary (BU)
PUS........... Fire Director [*Artillery*] (RU)
PUS........... Panstwowy Urzad Samochodowy [*State Automobile Administration*] (POL)
PUS........... Permanent Under Secretary [*British*]
PUS........... Pile-Setting Device (RU)
PUS........... Plans d'Utilisation des Sols [*North African*]
PUS........... Postovni Urad Sekovy [*Postal Check Office*] (CZ)
PUS........... Przeglad Ubezpieczen Spolecznych [*Social Security Review*] [*A magazine*] (POL)
PUS........... Pusan [*South Korea*] [*Airport symbol*] (OAG)
PUSC......... Partido Unidad Social Cristiana [*Costa Rica*] [*Political party*] (EY)
PUSD......... Partido Unido Social Democratico [*United Social-Democratic Party*] [*Guinea-Bissau*] [*Political party*] (EY)

PUSD......... Polska Unia Socjaldemokratyczna [*Polish Social Democratic Union*] [*Political party*]
PUSF .... Rapid Film Drier (RU)
PUSKOPAD ... Pusat Koperasi Angkatan Darat [*Army Cooperative*] (IN)
PUSLITBANG AIR ... Pusat Penelitian dan Pengembangan Pengairan [*Hydraulic Engineering Research and Development Center*] [*Indonesia*] (ERC)
PUSLITBANGNAK... Pusat Penelitian dan Pengembangan Peternakan [*Central Research Institute for Animal Science - CRIAS*] [*Indonesian*] (ARC)
PUSM........ Pravnicky Ustav Ministerstva Spravedlnosti [*Law Institute of the Ministry of Justice*] (CZ)
PUSMM.... Parti d'Union Socialiste des Musulmans Mauritaniens [*Party for Socialist Unity of Moslems of Mauritania*] [*Political party*]
PUSO .... Decontamination Station (RU)
PUSO .... Sanitary Processing and Decontamination Centers (BU)
PUSPAMARA ... Pusat Perdagangan MARA [*MARA Sales Center*] (ML)
PUSPATI ... Pusat Penyelidikan Atom Tun Ismail [*Malaysia*] [*Nuclear energy*] (NRCH)
PUSPENAL ... Pusat Penerangan Angkatan Laut [*Navy Information Center*] (IN)
PUSRI .... Pupuk Sriwidjaja PT
Pust............ Desert [*Topography*] (RU)
PUST .... Panafrican Union of Science and Technology
PUSTEKGAN ... Pusat Teknologi Dirgantara [*Aerospace Technology Center*] [*Lembaga Penerbangan dan Antariksa Nasional Indonesia*] [*Research center*] (ERC)
PUT .... Aeroput [*Yugoslavia*] [*ICAO designator*] (FAAC)
PUT .... Parti de l'Unite Togolaise [*Togolese Unity Party*] (AF)
PUT .... Pekerdjaan Umum dan Tenaga [*Public Works and Power*] (IN)
PUTCO ...... Public Utility Transport Company
PUTERA ... Pusat Tenaga Ra'ayat [*Manpower Center*] [*Indonesia*] (ML)
PU-TKZS.. Model Statutes of the Labor Cooperative Farms (BU)
put p.......... Control Point [*Railroads*] (RU)
PUTPK ...... Model Statutes of Labor Productive Cooperatives (BU)
Put'rem ...... Administration of Railroad Track-Repair Plants (RU)
put'rem....... Track-Repair Train (RU)
PUTS......... Torpedo Director (RU)
PUTs.......... Vocational Training Center (BU)
PUU .... Puerto Asis [*Colombia*] [*Airport symbol*] (OAG)
puus........... Puusepantyot [*Carpentry*] [*Finland*]
puut .... Puutarhanhoito [*Horticulture*] [*Finland*]
PUV .... Pluk Utocne Vozby [*Combat Tank Regiment*] (CZ)
PUV .... Prazsky Ustredni Vybor [*Prague Central Committee*] (CZ)
PUV .... Predsednictvo Ustredniho Vyboru [*Presidium of the Central Committee*] (CZ)
PUVN .... Full Elevation [*Artillery*] (RU)
PuVRD ...... Pulsejet Engine (RU)
PUW .... Panstwowy Urzad Wydawniczy [*State Publishing Office*] (POL)
PUWF....... Panstwowy Urzad Wychowania Fizycznego [*State Office of Physical Education*] (POL)
PUWP .... Polish United Workers' Party [*See also PZPR*] [*Political party*] (PD)
PUY .... Pula [*Former Yugoslavia*] [*Airport symbol*] (OAG)
PUZ .... Portowy Urzad Zdrowia [*Port Health Administration*] (POL)
PUZ .... Presses Universitaires du Zaire et l'Office du Livre [*Publisher*] (EY)
PUZUP...... Regulation on the Organization and Tasks of the Pensions and Welfare Administration and Its Local Organs (BU)
PV .... Aircraft Sound Detector (RU)
PV .... Antiaircraft (BU)
pv................ Assistant Driver (RU)
PV .... Border Troops (RU)
PV .... Debarkation Point (RU)
PV .... Driving Engine (RU)
PV .... Drop Point [*Aviation*] (RU)
pv................ Feedwater (RU)
PV .... Field Railroad Car [*Military term*] (RU)
PV .... Final Bracket, Last Bracket [*Artillery*] (RU)
PV .... Full Moisture Capacity [*of soil*] (RU)
PV .... Fuse Link (RU)
PV .... General Delivery [*For telegrams*] (RU)
PV .... High Water, High Tide (RU)
PV .... Instituto de Promocion de la Vivienda Ltda. [*Colombia*] (COL)
PV .... Interference Field (RU)
PV .... Intermediate Waves (RU)
PV .... Machine-Gun Platoon (RU)
PV .... Military Port, Naval Port (RU)
PV .... Parachute Troops, Paratroops (RU)
PV .... Patraci Vozidlo [*Reconnaissance Vehicle*] (CZ)
PV .... Pavia [*Car registration plates*] [*Italian*]
PV .... Pendulo Vertical [*Vertical Pendulum*] [*Portuguese*]
p-v .... Peninsula (RU)
PV .... Periodieke Verzameling van Administratieve en Rechterlijke Beslissingen Betreffende het Openbaar Bestuur in Nederland [*Netherlands*] (BAS)

PV .... Petite Vitesse [*Goods train*] [*French*]
PV .... Phong Vien [*Signature on Newspaper Articles*]
pv............ Pienviljelija [*Finland*]
PV .... Planinski Vestnik [*Alpine Review*] [*Ljubljana A periodical*] (YU)
PV .... Planmaessig Vorbeugende Instandsetzung (System) [*Planned Preventive Maintenance*] (EG)
PV .... Plantations Villageoises
PV .... Planuebergang [*Grade Crossing*] [*German military - World War II*]
PV .... Polar Air (RU)
PV .... Polydor/Deutsche-Grammophon Variable Microgroove [*Record label*] [*Germany*]
PV .... Posadkove Velitelstvi [*Garrison Headquarters*] (CZ)
PV .... Posadkovy Velitel [*Garrison Commander*] (CZ)
PV .... Poverenictvo Vyzivy [*Office of the Food Commissioner*] (CZ)
PV .... Pradelny Vlny [*Woolen Mills*] (CZ)
PV .... Preignition (RU)
PV .... Proces-Verbal [*French*]
PV .... Proedros Voulis [*President of Chamber of Deputies*] [*Automobile license plate designation*] [*Greek*] (GC)
PV .... Protected Village
PV .... Prumyslove Vydavatelstvi [*Industrial Publishing House*] (CZ)
Pv............ Pulver [*Powder*] [*German*] (GCA)
P/V............ Pyrovolikon [*Artillery*] (GC)
PV .... Receiving Puncher [*Computers*] (RU)
PV .... Reclosure, Reclosing (RU)
PV .... Regulation on Entries (BU)
PV .... Relative Switching-In Duration (RU)
PV .... Rotary Switch (RU)
PV .... Semiconductor Rectifier (RU)
PV .... Shot Point [*Geophysics*] (RU)
PV .... Surface-Active Substance (RU)
PV .... Switching Time (RU)
PV .... Vertical Plotter (RU)
Pv3 .... Pretoriase Vereniging vir die Versorging van Vertraagdes [*South Africa*] (AA)
PVA .... Aerotransportes Privados SA de CV [*Mexico*] [*ICAO designator*] (FAAC)
PVA .... Longitudinal Helical Reinforcement (RU)
PVA .... Polyvinyl Acetate (RU)
PVA .... Providencia [*Colombia*] [*Airport symbol*] (OAG)
PVA .... Pukovska Veterinarska Ambulanta [*Regimental Veterinary Station*] (YU)
PVAE........ Polyvinyl Acetate Emulsion (RU)
PVAWG .... Pruefungsverband der Arbeiterwohnungsbaugenossenschaft [*Control Association of the Workers Housing Construction Cooperative*] (EG)
PVB........... Polyvinyl Bromide (RU)
PVBA......... Persoonlijke Vennootschap met Beperkte Aansprakelijkheid [*Limited Company*] [*Netherlands*] (CED)
PVC .... Partido de Veteranos Civiles [*Civilian Veterans' Party*] [*Dominican Republic*] [*Political party*] (PPW)
PVC .... Partido Vanguardia Comunista [*Communist Vanguard Party*] [*Argentina*] (LA)
PVC .... Pastoral Veterinary Centre [*Australia*] (ARC)
PVC .... Plantations Villageoises de Cocotiers
PVC .... Policlorura de Vinil [*Polyvinyl Chloride*] (RO)
PVC .... Polivinilklorur [*Polyvinylchloride*] [*By-product of Petro-Chemical Industry*] (TU)
PVD .... High-Pressure Heater (RU)
PVD .... Pays en Voie de Developpement [*Developing Countries*] [*French*] (WER)
PVD .... Pressure Head, Pitot-Static Head (RU)
PVD .... Ramjet, Ramjet Engine (RU)
PvdA .... Partij van de Arbeid [*Labor Party*] [*Netherlands*] [*Political party*] (PPE)
PvdA/PTA ... Partij van de Arbeid van Belgiee/Parti du Travail de Belgique [*Belgian Labor Party*] [*Political party*] (PPW)
pvdd........... Airborne Infantry Division (RU)
PVDE........ Policia de Vigilancia e Defesa do Estado [*Vigilance and State Defense Police*] [*Portuguese*] (WER)
PVDO....... Antiairborne Defense (RU)
PVDS........ Pravilnik o Vojno-Disciplinskim Sudovima [*Guide for Military Disciplinary Tribunals*] (YU)
PVDSK...... Regulation for Deposits at the State Savings Bank (BU)
PvdV .... Partij van de Vrijheid [*Party of Freedom*] [*Netherlands*] [*Political party*] (PPE)
PVE........... Porvenir [*Panama*] [*Airport symbol*] (OAG)
PVE........... Pteryga Vasikis Ekpaidevseos [*Basic Training Wing*] [*Greek*] (GC)
PVEE........ Pronoia Voreion Eparkhion Ellados [*Greek Northern Provinces Welfare*] (GC)
PVEN .... Primate Vaccine Evaluation Network
PVFSE....... Plano de Valorizacao Economica da Regiao da Fronteira Sudoeste do Pais [*Plan for Economic Promotion of the Southwest Border Region*] [*Brazil*] (LA)

PVFZ........ Planetary High-Altitude Frontal Zone (RU)
PVH........... Porto Velho [*Brazil*] [*Airport symbol*] (OAG)
PvJ .... Het Paleis van Justitie [*Benelux*] (BAS)
PVK........... Pedion Volis Kritis [*Crete Firing Range*] (GC)
PVK .... Preveza/Lefkas [*Greece*] [*Airport symbol*] (OAG)
PVK .... Pyruvic Acid (RU)
PVK .... Vibrating Roller Trailer (RU)
PVK .... Water-Resistant Pressboard (RU)
PVKh .... Polyvinyl Chloride (RU)
PVKhO ..... Air and Chemical Defense (RU)
PVKhO ..... Antiaircraft and Chemical Warfare Defense (BU)
PVKM ...... Steam-Air Forging Hammer (RU)
PVL........... Epidemic Pneumonia (RU)
PVL........... Papal Visit Ltd. [*Australia*]
PVL........... Regimental Veterinary Hospital (RU)
PVL........... Veterinary Field Hospital (RU)
pvm........... Paivamaara [*Finland*]
pvm........... Posta Vonalmester [*Postal Inspector*] (HU)
PVM .... Program-Timing Mechanism (RU)
PVM .... Punched-Card Computer, Punched-Tape Computer (RU)
PVM .... Suspension Footbridge (RU)
PVMA ...... Philippine Veterinary Medical Association (SLS)
PVMBA..... Personenvennootschap Met Beperkte Aansprakelijkheid [*Benelux*] (BAS)
PVN .... Air Observation Post (RU)
PVNOS..... Aircraft-Warning Service Post (RU)
PVO........... Air Defense (RU)
PVO........... Antiaircraft Defense (BU)
PVO........... Antiaircraft Gun (RU)
PVO........... People's Volunteer Organization [*Myanmar*] (FEA)
PVO........... Portoviejo [*Ecuador*] [*Airport symbol*] (OAG)
PVO........... Preisverordnung [*Price Regulation*] (EG)
PVO........... Principal Visiting Officer [*Australia*]
p-vo........... Production, Manufacture (RU)
PVO........... Protivo-Voxdushnaia Oborona [*Antiaircraft Defense*] [*Former USSR*]
PVO........... Protivvazdusna Odbrana [*Antiaircraft Defense*] (YU)
PVO........... Protivzdusna Obrana [*Air Defense*] (CZ)
PVOP........ Polgari Vedelem Orszagos Parancsnoksag [*National Civil Defense Command*] (HU)
PVOPP...... Air Defense of Loading Points (RU)
PVOS........ Protivzdusna Obrana Statu [*Territorial Air Defense Command*] (CZ)
PVOV .... Protivzdusna Obrana Vojsk [*Troop Air Defense*] (CZ)
PVOZN .... Air Defense of Population (RU)
PVP........... Approach Way, Approach Zone [*Aviation*] (RU)
PVP........... High-Density Polyethylene (RU)
PVP........... Padakovy Vysadkovy Pluk [*Airborne Parachute Regiment*] (CZ)
PVP........... Partido de la Victoria del Pueblo [*People's Victory Party*] [*Uruguay*] (LA)
PVP........... Partido Vanguardia Popular [*Popular Vanguard Party*] [*Costa Rican Communist Party*] (LA)
PVP........... Plantations Villageoises Palmiers
PVP........... Podjetje za Vzdrzavanje Prog [*Railroad Track Maintenance Establishment*] (YU)
PVP........... Polyvinylpyridine (RU)
PVP........... Polyvinylpyrrolidone (RU)
PVP........... Poslovnik Veca Proizvodaca [*Rules of Procedure of the Council of Producers*] (YU)
PVP........... Veterinary Aid Station (RU)
pvp............ Water-Soluble Powder [*Pharmacy*] (RU)
PVPJDZ.... Podjetje za Vzdrzevanje Proge Jugoslovanske Drzavne Zeleznice [*Rail Maintenance Establishment of the Yugoslav Railroads*] (YU)
pv pn........... Aid Station (BU)
PVPN........ Partido Vanguardia Popular Nacionalista [*Nationalist Popular Vanguard Party*] [*Venezuela*] (LA)
PVPr .... Padakovy Vysadkovy Prapor [*Airborne Parachute Battalion*] (CZ)
PVR........... Antiaircraft Reconnaissance [*Civil defense*] (RU)
PVR .... Posredna Vatra Rusenja [*Indirect Demolition Fire*] [*Military*] (YU)
PVR .... Puerto Vallarta [*Mexico*] [*Airport symbol*] (OAG)
PVRD .... Ramjet Engine (RU)
PVRD .... Ramjet, Ramjet Engine (RU)
PVRDT...... Solid-Fuel Ramjet Engine (RU)
PVRDZh.... Liquid-Fuel Ramjet Engine (RU)
PVRGS...... Regulation on Keeping State Civil Status Records (BU)
PVRZ........ Locomotive and Railroad Car Repair Plant (RU)
PVS........... Dust Vacuuming Service [*Industrial*] (BU)
PVS........... Ground-Air Liaison Post (RU)
pvs............ Ground-Air Panel (RU)
PVS........... Partido Vanguardia Socialista [*Socialist Vanguard Party*] [*Argentina*] (LA)
PVS........... Polyvinyl Alcohol (RU)

PVS............ Predsunute Velitelske Stanoviste [*Advance Command Post*] (CZ)
PVS............ Presidium of the Supreme Soviet (RU)
PVS............ Regimental Clothing and Equipment Depot (RU)
PVSA........ Paleontologiese Vereniging van Suider-Afrika [*Paleeontological Society of Southern Africa*] (AA)
PVSK........ Industrial Veterinary and Sanitary Control (BU)
PVSNRB ... Plenum of the Supreme Court of the Bulgarian People's Republic (BU)
PVSP........ Regular Military Hospital Train (RU)
PVSt.......... Paketvermittlungsstelle [*German*] (ADPT)
PVSV........ Permanent All-Union Construction Exhibition (RU)
PVT........... Par Voie Telegraphique [*By Telegraph*] [*French*]
PVT........... Planning and Reconstruction Trust (RU)
PVT........... Policia de Viacao e Transito [*Traffic and Highway Police*] [*Portuguese*] (WER)
Pvt............. Privat [*Private*] [*German*]
Pvt............. Private (IDIG)
PVTAEA ... Philippine Virginia Tobacco Administration Employees' Association
PVTAK...... Regulations of the Foreign Trade Arbitration Commission (BU)
Pvtdz.......... Privatdozent [*University Lecturer*] [*German*]
pv tpk .... Polgari Vedelmi Torzsparancsnok [*Civil Defense Staff Commander*] (HU)
PVTS......... Pravila Vazduhoplovne Tehnicke Sluzbe [*Air Technical Service Rules*] (YU)
PVU .... Calling and Ringing Device [*Telephony*] (RU)
PVU .... High-Resistance Indicating Converter (RU)
pvuch......... Air Defense Training Point (RU)
PVUZ .... Higher Pedagogical Educational Institution (BU)
PVV .... Fondation Europeenne "Pro Venetia Viva" [*European Foundation "Pro Venetia Viva"*] (EAIO)
PVV .... Partij voor Vrijheid en Vooruitgang [*Freedom and Progress Party*] [*See also PLP*] [*Belgium*] [*Political party*] (PPW)
PVV .... Passasiervervoervereniging [*Passenger Transport Association*] [*South Africa*] (EAIO)
PVV .... Prazsky Vzorkovy Veletrh [*Prague Sample Fair*] (CZ)
PVV .... Predsednictvo Vysokoskolskeho Vyboru [*Presidium of the University Committee*] (CZ)
PVV .... Prirodovedecke Vydavatelstvi [*Natural Sciences Publishing House*] (CZ)
PVVP........ Posadkove Velitelstvi Velke Prahy [*Garrison Headquarters for Greater Prague*] (CZ)
PVVPOVO ... Posadkove Velitelstvi Velke Prahy, Oddeleni Vychovy a Osvety [*Garrison Headquarters for Greater Prague, Department of Education and Culture*] (CZ)
PVZ........... High-Voltage Protection Station (RU)
PVZ........... Pancevacka Vodna Zajednica [*Pancevo Water Community*] (YU)
PVZ........... Perm' Bicycle Plant (RU)
PVZ........... Potiska Vodna Zajednica [*Potisje Water Community*] [*Zrenjanin*] (YU)
PVZ........... Poverenictvo pre Vyzivu a Zasobovanie [*Office of the Commissioner of Food Supply*] (CZ)
PVZ........... Protivvazdusna Zastita [*Antiaircraft Defense*] [*Army*] (YU)
Pvzl .... Provinzial [*Provincial*] [*German*]
PW............ Pachtwet [*Benelux*] (BAS)
PW............ Palau [*ANSI two-letter standard code*] (CNC)
PW............ Parti Wallon [*Walloon Party*] [*Belgium*] (WER)
PW............ Pensioenwet [*Benelux*] (BAS)
PW............ Periodiek Woordenboek der Registratie [*Benelux*] (BAS)
PW............ Periodiek Woordenboek van Administratieve en Gerechtelijke Beslissingen [*Benelux*] (BAS)
PW............ Politechnika Warszawska [*Warsaw Polytechnical School*] (POL)
PW............ Poolaritaetswechsel [*German*] (ADPT)
PW............ Positive Women [*An association*] [*Australia*]
PW............ Poswissel [*Money Order*] [*Afrikaans*]
PW............ Prasa Wojskowa [*Military Press*] [*Publishing house*] (POL)
pw............. Provinciale Wet [*Benelux*] (BAS)
PW............ Przemysl Weglowy [*Coal Industry*] (POL)
PW............ Przysposobienie Wojskowe [*Military Training*] (POL)
PWA .... Papierwerke Waldhof-Aschaffenburg AG [*Waldhof-Aschaffenburg Paper Works*] [*Business term*]
PWA .... Polish Women's Association [*Australia*]
PWA .... Power and Water Authority [*Northern Territory, Australia*]
PWASA ..... Poliomyelitis Welfare Association of South Australia
PWBBC..... Professional Wrestling and Boxing Board of Control
PWC .... Pacific War Council [*World War II*]
PWC .... Pentecostal World Conference [*Emmetten, Switzerland*] (EA)
PWC .... Provincial Warning Center [*NATO*] (NATG)
PWC .... Public Works Committee [*Australia*]
PWD .... Petroleum Warfare Department [*Ministry of Fuel and Power*] [*British*] [*World War II*]
PWDC........ Philippine War Damage Commission [*Post-World War II*]
PwF .... Produktionsgenossenschaften Werktaetiger Fischer [*Production Cooperatives of Working Fishermen*] (EG)

PWG .... Polskie Wydawnictwa Gospodarcze [*Polish Publishing House for Economics*] (POL)
PWH........ Department of Parks, Wildlife and Heritage [*Tasmania, Australia*]
PWI .... Alas Panamenas SA [*Panama*] [*ICAO designator*] (FAAC)
PWI .... Persatuan Wartawan Indonesia [*Indonesian Journalists Association*] (IN)
PWIF........ Plantation Workers' International Federation [*Later, IFPAAW*]
PWiT .... Przedsiebiorstwo Wystaw i Targow [*Exhibitions and Fairs Bureau*] [*Poland*]
PWKS....... Panstwowe Wydawnictwo Ksiazek Szkolnych [*State Publishing House for School Books*] (POL)
PWL........... Pensioenwet voor de Landmacht [*Benelux*] (BAS)
PWM .... Polskie Wydawnictwa Muzyczne [*Polish Music Publishing House*] (POL)
PWMM ..... Polly Woodside Maritime Museum [*Australia*]
PWN .... Panstwowe Wydawnictwo Naukowe [*State Publishing House for Scholarly Works*] (POL)
PWN .... Provinciaal Waterleidingsbedrijf van Noord-Holland [*Netherlands*] (BAS)
PWO......... Progressieve Werknemers Organizatie [*Progressive Workers' Organization*] [*Surinam*]
PWP.......... Peasants' and Workers' Party [*India*] [*Political party*] (PPW)
PWP.......... Polish Workers' Party
PWPMA.... Philippine Welding Products Manufacturers Association (PDAA)
PWPN ...... Panstwowe Wydawnictwo Popularno-Naukowe [*Popular Science State Publishing House*] (POL)
PWPW....... Panstwowa Wytwornia Papierow Wartosciowych [*State Office for the Printing of Bonds and Paper Money*] (POL)
PWr........... Politechnika Wroclawska [*Engineering College of Wroclaw*] [*Poland*]
PWR .... Powiatowa Wystawa Rolnicza [*County Agricultural Exhibition*] (POL)
PWRC....... Public Works Research Centre [*Greece*] (ERC)
PWRI....... Public Works Research Institute [*Ministry of Construction*] [*Research center*] [*Japan*] (EAS)
PWRiL...... Panstwowe Wydawnictwo Rolnicze i Lesne [*State Agriculture and Forestry Publishing House*] (POL)
PWRN ...... Prezydium Wojewodzkiej Rady Narodowej [*Presidium of the People's Province Council*] [*Poland*]
PWS .... Panstwowe Wydawnictwa Szkolne [*State School Publishing House*] (POL)
PWS.......... Psychological Warfare Society [*Birmingham, England*] (EA)
PWSA....... Panstwowa Wyzsza Szkola Aktorska [*State Higher School for Actors*] (POL)
PWSA....... Pheasant and Waterfowl Society of Australia
PWSAG..... Panstwowa Wyzsza Szkola Administracji Gospodarczej [*State Higher School for Economic Administration*] (POL)
PWSF .... Panstwowa Wytwornia Sprzetu Filmowego [*State Film Equipment Plant*] (POL)
PWSF .... Panstwowa Wyzsza Szkola Filmowa [*State Higher School of Motion Pictures*] (POL)
PWSM ...... Panstwowa Wyzsza Szkola Muzyczna [*State Higher School of Music*] (POL)
PWSP .... Panstwowa Wyzsza Szkola Pedagogiczna [*State Higher Pedagogical School*] (POL)
PWSSP...... Panstwowa Wyzsza Szkola Sztuk Plastycznych [*State Higher School of Plastic Arts*] (POL)
PWST .... Panstwowa Wyzsza Szkola Teatralna [*State Higher School of Dramatics*] (POL)
PWSTiF.... Panstwowa Wyzsza Szkola Teatru i Filmu [*State Higher School of Stage and Screen*] (POL)
PWSZ .... Panstwowe Wydawnictwa Szkolnictwa Zawodowego [*State Publishing House for Vocational Training*] (POL)
PWT .... Panstwowe Wydawnictwo Techniczne [*State Technical Publishing House*] (POL)
PWT .... Parti Wallon des Travailleurs [*Walloon Workers' Party*] [*Belgium*] (WER)
PWT .... Pasokan Wanita Tambahan [*Women's Auxiliary Corps*] (ML)
PWU......... Plantation Workers Union [*Mauritius*] (AF)
PWU......... Postal Workers Union [*Australia*]
PWU......... Public Workers Union [*Grenada*] (LA)
PWV .... Pretoria-Witwatersrand [*South Africa*]
PWV .... Pretoria, Witwatersrand, Vereeniging Industrial Area [*South Africa*] (AF)
PWWA ..... Provincial Water Works Authority [*Thailand*] (DS)
PWX .... Permanent Working Staff [*NATO*] (NATG)
p wyz .... Patrz Wyzej [*See Above*] [*Poland*]
PWZ .... Powiatowy Wydzial Zdrowia [*County Health Department*] (POL)
PX .... Pedro Ximenez [*A blending sherry*]
Px.............. Prix [*Prize*] [*French*]
PX .... Prumyslova Komise [*Industrial Commission*] (CZ)
PXD .... Post-Exercise Discussion [*NATO*] (NATG)
PXH........... Pacific Express Holdings Ltd. [*New Zealand*] [*ICAO designator*] (FAAC)

PXI............ Pax Christi International   (EA)
PXO........... Porto Santo [Portugal] [Airport symbol]   (OAG)
PXV .... Pedro Ximenez Viejo [A blending sherry]
PY .... Paraguay [ANSI two-letter standard code]   (CNC)
PY .... Paragwaj [Paraguay] [Poland]
PY .... Professional Year
PY .... Proto Yiddish   (BJA)
PYA .... Pioneer Youth Authority [Ghana]
pya............. Post-Office Box   (RU)
PYaZ.......... Antinuclear Defense, Nuclear Defense   (RU)
PYBURO... Pyrethrum Board of Kenya   (ARC)
PYC........... Aeropycsa SA de CV [Mexico] [ICAO designator]   (FAAC)
PYC............ Pale Yellow Candle [Baltic coffee-house] [London]   (DSUE)
PYC............ Pay Your Cash [Australian slang]
PYC............ Peace and Cooperation [Spain] [An association]   (EAIO)
PYC............ People's Youth Corps   (ML)
PYC............ Playon Chico [Panama] [Airport symbol]   (OAG)
PYC............ Presbyterian Youth Centre
PYE........... Protovathmios Ygeionomiki Epitropi [First Degree Medical Board] [Greek]   (GC)
PYF........... French Polynesia [ANSI three-letter standard code]   (CNC)
PYH........... Puerto Ayacucho [Venezuela] [Airport symbol]   (OAG)
PYM .... Pan-African Youth Movement   (EA)
PYMECO ... Asociacion de Pequenos y Medianos Comerciantes Autonomos [Association of Small and Medium Independent Businessmen] [Spanish]   (WER)
PYO .... Progressive Youth Organization [Guyana]   (LA)
PYP........... Professional Year Programme [Accounting] [Australia]
PYP........... Pyrosvestiki Ypiresia Poleos [Fire Department of the City Of] [Followed by initial letter of city name]   (GC)
PYR .... Pyramid Air Lines [Egypt] [ICAO designator]   (FAAC)
PYRESA.... Prensa y Radio Espanola Sociedad Anonima [Spanish Press and Radio, Incorporated]   (AF)
pyrolyt........ Pyrolytisch [Pyrolytical] [German]   (GCA)
PYS........... Praxis Ypourgikou Symvouliou [Act of the Ministerial Council]   (GC)
PYS........... Protovathmion Ypiresiakon Symvoulion [First Degree Service Council] [Greek]   (GC)
pys............. Pysakki [Finland]
PYSDE ...... Perifereiakon Ypiresiakon Symvoulion Dimotikis Ekpaidevseos [Regional Service Council for Elementary Education] [Greek]   (GC)
PYSME ..... Perifereiakon Ypiresiakon Symvoulion Mesis Ekpaidevseos [District Service Council for Secondary Education] [Greek]   (GC)
PYSSE....... Perifereiakon Ypiresiakon Symvoulion Stoikheiodous Ekpaidevseos [District Service Council for Elementary Education] [Greek]   (GC)
PYV .... Yaviza [Panama] [Airport symbol]   (OAG)
PZ .... Auxiliary Parachute   (RU)
PZ .... Canal Zone [ANSI two-letter standard code] [Obsolete]   (CNC)
pz............... Contamination Zone   (RU)
PZ .... Floating Point   (RU)
PZ .... Incendiary Bullet   (RU)
PZ .... Incendiary-Ranging   (RU)
PZ .... Loading Device   (RU)
Pz.............. Paleozoyik [Paleozoic] [Geology]   (TU)
PZ .... Panzerbrechend [Armor-Piercing] [German military - World War II]
PZ .... Passenger Building   (RU)
PZ .... Paterson, Zochonis & Co. [Liberia]
PZ .... Pekarska Zadruga [Baking Cooperative]   (YU)
pz............... Pieze   (RU)
PZ .... Pie Zeses [May You Live Piously] [Italian]
PZ .... Poale Zion [Labor federation] [Labor Zionist Alliance] [Later,]
pz............... Poise   (RU)
PZ .... Poljoprivredna Zadruga [Agricultural Cooperative]   (YU)
PZ .... Poljoprivredni Zavod [Agricultural Institute]   (YU)
PZ .... Postolarska Zadruga [Shoemakers' Cooperative]   (YU)
PZ .... Potenza [Car registration plates] [Italian]
PZ .... Potez [Establissements Henri Potez] [France] [ICAO aircraft manufacturer identifier]   (ICAO)
pz............... Praca Zbiorowa [Symposium]   (POL)
PZ .... Pracovni Zalohy [State Labor Reserves]   (CZ)
PZ .... Prazska Zelezarska Spolecnost, Narodni Podnik [Prague Iron Company, National Enterprise]   (CZ)
PZ .... Produktivitaetszentrale Saar eV [Saarbruecken] [Information retrieval]
PZ .... Proizvodacka Zadruga [Producers' Cooperative]   (YU)
PZ .... Projektantski Zavod [Industrial Design Institute]   (YU)
PZ .... Pulk Zmechanizowany [Mechanized Regiment]   (POL)
PZ .... Setup and Dismantling Time   (RU)
PZ .... Societe Paterson Zochonis and Co. Ltd.
PZ .... Statni Pracovni Zalohy [State Labor Reserves]   (CZ)
PZ .... Surinam [Aircraft nationality and registration mark]   (FAAC)
PZ .... Total Blackout Condition   (RU)

PZ .... Underwater Protection [of a ship]   (RU)
PZA .... Paz De Ariporo [Colombia] [Airport symbol]   (OAG)
pza............. Pieza [Piece] [Spanish]
PZA .... Polski Zwiazek Atletyczny [Polish Athletic Union]   (POL)
PZA .... Postzollamt [Postal Customs Office]   (EG)
PZANN ..... Pomorskie Zaklady Aparatury Niskiego Napiecia [Pomerania Enterprise for Low Tension Equipment]   (POL)
PZB........... Pietermaritzburg [South Africa] [Airport symbol]   (OAG)
PZB........... Poliski Zwiazek Badmintona [Poland]   (EAIO)
PZB........... Polski Zwiazek Bokserski [Polish Boxing Union]
PZB........... Przemyslowe Zjednoczenie Budowlane [Industrial Construction Association]   (POL)
PZBM........ Pomorskie Zaklady Budowy Maszyn [Pomerania Machine Construction Plant]   (POL)
PZBWP ..... Polski Zwiazek Bylych Wiezniow Politycznych [Polish Union of Former Political Prisoners]   (POL)
PzC............ Pruzkumna Ceta [Reconnaissance Platoon]   (CZ)
PZChK...... Panstwowe Zaklady Chowu Koni [State Horse-Breeding Stations]   (POL)
PZD........... Politische Zeitschriftendokumentation
PZD........... Poverenictvo Zdravotnictva [Office of the Commissioner of Health]   (CZ)
PZD........... Powiatowy Zarzad Drogowy [County Road Administration]   (POL)
PZDA .... Regulation on the Application of the Law on State Arbitration   (BU)
PzDB......... Pruzkumna Delostrelecka Baterie [Artillery Reconnaissance Battery]   (CZ)
pzdk........... Field Wood Structures Plant   (BU)
PzDO......... Pruzkumne Zpravodajske Delostrelecke Oddeleni [Artillery Intelligence Reconnaissance Detachment]   (CZ)
PZDV........ Panzer-Division [Armored Division] [German military]
PZE........... Panstwowy Zaklad Emerytalny [State Retirement Bureau]   (POL)
PZE........... Polski Zwiazek Esperantystow [Polish Association of Esperantists] [Poland]
PZEM........ Provinciale Zeeuwse Energie-Maatschappij [Netherlands]   (PDAA)
PZF........... Poljoprivredni Zemljisni Fond [Agricultural Land Fund]   (YU)
PZF........... Polski Zwiazek Filatelistow [Polish Association of Philatelists] [Poland]
PZFA .... Polski Zwiazek Fabryk Azotowych [Polish Union of Nitrogen Factories]   (POL)
PZG .... Panstwowe Zaklady Graficzne [State Printing Plants]   (POL)
PZG .... Polski Zwiazek Gimnastyczny [Polish Gymnastic Union] [Poland]
PZG .... Polski Zwiazek Gluchych [Polish Association of the Deaf] [Poland]
PZG .... Poznanskie Zaklady Gastronomiczne [Poznan Restaurant Enterprises]   (POL)
PZG .... Poznanskie Zaklady Graficzne [Poznan Printing Plant]   (POL)
PZGS .... Powiatowy Zarzad Gminnych Spoldzielni [County Administration of Rural Communal Cooperatives]   (POL)
PZGS........ Powiatowy Zwiazek Gminnych Spoldzielni [County Union of Rural Communal Cooperatives]   (POL)
PZGS .... Powiatowy Zwiazek Gminnych Spoldzielni "Samopomoc Chlopska" [District Association of the Village Cooperatives "Peasants' Self-Help"] [Poland]
PZGWiTS ... Polskie Zrzeszenie Gazownikow, Wodociagowcow, i Technikow Sanitarnych [Polish Association of Gas, Water Supply, and Sanitation Workers]   (POL)
PZH .... Panstwowy Zaklad Higieny [State Institute of Hygiene] [Warsaw, Poland] [Research center]   (POL)
PzH............ Pruzkumna Hlidka [Reconnaissance Patrol]   (CZ)
PZh............ Steam-Driven Locomotive Crane   (RU)
PZH .... Zhob [Pakistan] [Airport symbol]   (OAG)
PZhD......... Perm' Railroad   (RU)
pzhdb......... Railroad Track-Laying Battalion   (RU)
PZhG......... Horizontal Searchlight   (RU)
PZhI.......... Semi-Higher Railway Institute   (BU)
PZHK........ Polski Zwiazek Hodowcow Koni [Polish Union of Horse Breeders] [Poland]
PZHL .... Polski Zwiazek Hokeja na Lodzie [Polish Ice Hockey Union]   (POL)
pzhpb .... Railway Transportation Battalion   (BU)
PZHR .... Panstwowe Zaklady Hodowli Roslin [State Plant Breeding Station]   (POL)
PZhR......... Radioactive Liquid Density Meter   (RU)
PZhS......... Searchlight Station   (RU)
PZHT .... Polski Zwiazek Hokeja na Trawie [Polish Hockey Union]
PZhV......... Vertical Searchlight   (RU)
PZInz........ Panstwowe Zaklady Inzynierii [State Engineering Plant]   (POL)
PZITB ...... Polski Zwiazek Inzynierow i Technikow Budowlanych [Polish Union of Construction Engineers and Technicians]   (POL)
PZJ .... Polski Zwiazek Jezdziecki [Polish Riding Union]
PzJgdTrupp ... Panzerjagd Trupp [Tank Pursuit Squad]   (EG)
PZK........... Polski Zwiazek Kajakowy [Polish Kayak Union]   (POL)

PZK............ Polski Zwiazek Krotkofalowcow [*Polish Short-Wave Radio Operators Union*] (POL)
PZK............ Powder Chamber Measuring Device (RU)
PZK............ Underwater Protection of a Ship (RU)
PZKB........ Panstwowy Zaoczny Kurs Bibliotekarski [*State Correspondence Course for Librarians*] (POL)
PZKiOR..... Polish Union of Agricultural Circles and Organizations (PD)
PZKKR...... Panstwowy Zaklad Korespondencyjnego Ksztalcenia Rolniczego [*State Institute for Correspondence Courses on Agriculture*] (POL)
PZKKS ...... Polski Zwiazek Koszykowki, Siatkowki, i Szczypiorniaka [*Polish Basketball, Volleyball, and Handball Union*] (POL)
PZKO .... Polski Zwiazek Kulturalno-Oswiatowy [*Polish Culture and Education Union*] (POL)
PZKO .... Polski Zwiazek Kulturalno-Oswiatowy w Czechoslowacji [*Polish Union of Culture and Enlightenment in Czechoslovakia*] (CZ)
PZKol .... Polski Zwiazek Kolarski [*Polish Cycling Union*] (POL)
PZKosz ..... Polski Zwiazek Koszykowki [*Polish Basketball Union*]
PZKPFW... Panzerkampfwagen [*German tank*] [*World War II*]
PZKR........ Powiatowy Zwiazek Kolek Rolniczych [*District Union of Agricultural Co-Operatives*] [*Poland*]
PZKW....... Panzerkampfwagen [*German tank*] [*World War II*]
PZL............ Panstwowe Zaklady Lotnicze [*Poland*] [*ICAO designator*] (FAAC)
PZL............ Polskie Zaklady Lotnicze [*Polish Aviation Plant*] (POL)
PZL............ Polski Zwiazek Lowiecki [*Polish Hunting Union*] (POL)
PZL............ Polski Zwiazek Luczniczy [*Polish Archery Union*]
PZL............ Polski Zwiazek Lyzwiarski [*Polish Skaters' Union*] (POL)
PZL............ Powiatowy Zarzad Lacznosci [*County Communications Administration*] (POL)
PzL............. Pruzkumne Letectvo [*Reconnaissance Aviation (or Aircraft)*] (CZ)
PZLA........ Polski Zwiazek Lekkiej Atletyki [*Polish Light Athletic Union*] (POL)
PZLPO ...... Panstwowe Zenskie Liceum Przemyslu Odziezowego [*State Clothing Industry School for Women*] (POL)
PZLZ .... Panstwowy Zaklad Leczniczy dla Zwierzat [*State Animal Hospital*] (POL)
PZM .... Paleozoological Museum (of the Academy of Sciences, USSR) (RU)
PZM .... Panstwowy Zaklad Mleczarski [*Poland*]
PZM .... Polska Zegluga Morska [*Polish Steamship Company*] (POL)
PZM .... Polski Zwiazek Motocyklowy [*Polish Motorcyclists' Union*] (POL)
PZM .... Polski Zwiazek Motorowy [*Polish Motorists' Union*] (POL)
PZM .... Powiatowe Zaklady Mleczarskie [*County Dairies*] (POL)
PZMB....... Pruszkowskie Zaklady Materialow Biurowych [*Pruszkow Office Supplies Plant*] (POL)
PZMot .... Polski Zwiazek Motorowy [*Polish Motorists' Union*] (POL)
PZN .... Polski Zwiazek Narciarski [*Polish Ski Union*] (POL)
PZN .... Polski Zwiazek Niewidomych [*Polish Union of the Blind*] (POL)
PZNF........ Poznanskie Zaklady Nawozow Fosforowych [*Poznan Phosphorous Fertilizer Establishments*] (POL)
Pzo .... Pizzo [*Peak*] [*Italian*] (NAU)
PZO .... Podnik Zahranicniho Obchodu [*Foreign Trade Enterprise*] [*Czechoslovakian*] (CZ)
PZO .... Polskie Zaklady Optyczne [*Polish Optical Plants*] (POL)
PZO .... Pripraven k Zdravotni Obrane [*Prepared for Health Defense (Badge)*] (CZ)
PZO .... Protiletecka Zavodni Obrana [*Factory Antiaircraft Defense*] (CZ)
PzO .... Pruzkumny Odrad [*Reconnaissance Detachment*] (CZ)
PZO .... Puerto Ordaz [*Venezuela*] [*Airport symbol*] (OAG)
PZO .... Rolling Barrage, Creeping Barrage (BU)
PZOO .... Polski Zwiazek Obroncow Ojczyzny [*Polish Union for National Defense (Prewar)*] (POL)
PZP............ Poznanskie Zaklady Piekarnicze [*Poznan Bakeries*] (POL)
PZP............ Przedsiebiorstwa pod Zarzadem Panstwowym [*Enterprises under State Administration*] (POL)
PZPB .... Panstwowe Zaklady Przemyslu Bawelnianego [*State Cotton Plants*] (POL)
PZPB .... Panstwowe Zaklady Przemyslu Budowlanego [*State Construction Industry Plants*] (POL)
PZPB .... Prudnickie Zaklady Przemyslu Bawelnianego [*Prudnik (Neustadt) Cotton Plant*] (POL)
PZPI .... Pokrajinski Zavod za Poljoprivredna Istrazivanja [*Provincial Institute for Agricultural Research*] [*Novi Sad*] (YU)
PZPiT .... Panstwowy Zespol Piesni i Tanca [*State Song and Dance Ensemble*] [*Poland*]
PZPJG....... Panstwowe Zaklady Przemyslu Jedwabniczego i Galanterii [*State Silk and Haberdashery Plant*] (POL)
PZPN .... Polski Zwiazek Pilki Noznej [*Polish Soccer Union*] (POL)
PZPO......... Poznanskie Zaklady Przemyslu Odziezowego [*Poznan Clothing Plant*] (POL)
PZPR .... Polska Zjednoczona Partia Robotnicza [*Polish United Workers' Party - PUWP*] [*Political party*] (PPW)

PZPR......... Polski Zwiazek Pilki Recznej [*Polish Handball Union*] (POL)
PzPr.......... Pruzkumny Prapor [*Reconnaissance Battalion*] (CZ)
PZPS .... Panstwowe Zaklady Pomocy Szkolnej [*State School Supply Establishment*] (POL)
PZPS .... Poznanskie Zaklady Przemyslu Spirytusowego [*Poznan Alcohol Plant*] (POL)
PZPW....... Panstwowe Zaklady Przemyslu Welnianego [*State Wool Plants*] (POL)
PZR............ Powiatowy Zarzad Rolnictwa [*County Agricultural Administration*] (POL)
PzR........... Pruzkumna Rota [*Reconnaissance Company*] (CZ)
PZRK........ Perenosnyi Zenitnyi Raketnyi Kompleks [*Portable Air Defense Missile Complex*] [*Russian*]
PZS............ Field Battery Charging Station (RU)
PZS............ Mobile Battery Charging Station (RU)
PZS............ Panstwowa Zegluga Srodladows [*State Administration of Inland Navigation*] (POL)
PZS............ Panstwowe Zaklady Samochodowe [*State Automobile Plants*] (POL)
pzs .... Piezas [*Pieces*] [*Spanish*]
PZS............ Planinska Zveza Slovenije [*Alpine Union of Slovenia*] (YU)
PZS............ Poljodjelska Znanstvena Smotra [*Agricultural Scientific Survey*] [*Zagreb A periodical*] (YU)
PZS............ Polski Zwiazek Szermierczy [*Polish Fencing Union*] (POL)
PZS............ Prazska Zelezarska Spolecnost, Narodni Podnik [*Prague Iron Company, National Enterprise*] (CZ)
PzS............. Pruzkumna Skupina [*Reconnaissance Detachment*] (CZ)
PZSO........ Poznanskie Zaklady Srodkow Odzywczych [*Poznan Health Food Enterprise*] (POL)
PZSP......... Powiatowy Zwiazek Spoldzielni Produkcyjnych [*County Union of Producer Cooperatives (Collective farms)*] (POL)
PZSR .... Poznanskie Zaklady Surowcow Roslinnych [*Poznan Agricultural Raw Material Establishment*] (POL)
PZSz .... Polski Zwiazek Szermierczy [*Polish Fencing Union*]
P Z Sz I ..... Panstwowy Zaklad Szkolenia Inwalidow [*State Disabled Persons' Rehabilitation Institute*] (POL)
PZT............ Polski Zwiazek Tenisowy [*Polish Tennis Union*] (POL)
PZT............ Polski Zwiazek Turystyczny [*Polish Tourist Union*] (POL)
pzt .... Poza Tekstem [*Outside of the Text*] (POL)
PZTS .... Polski Zwiazek Tenisa Stolowego [*Polish Table Tennis Union*] (POL)
PZTW........ Polski Zwiazek Towarzystw Wioslarskich [*Polish Union of Rowing Associations*]
PZU .... Intermediate Storage (RU)
PZU .... Mobile Suction Dredge (RU)
PZU .... Panstwowy Zaklad Ubezpieczen [*Polish National Insurance*] (EY)
PZU .... Permanent Storage [*Computer science*] (RU)
PZU .... Permanent Storage System [*Computer science*] (BU)
PZU .... Port Sudan [*Sudan*] [*Airport symbol*] (OAG)
PZU .... Stability Margin Indicator (RU)
PZUW .... Powszechny Zadlad Ubezpieczen Wzajemnych [*General Mutual Insurance Company*] (POL)
PZV........... Ignition Delay Period (RU)
PZV........... Pokretna Zaprecna Vatra [*Mobile Barrage Fire*] [*Military*] (YU)
PZVA........ Postzeitungsvertriebsamt [*Postal Newspapers and Periodicals Distribution Office*] (EG)
PZVO .... Postzeitungsvertriebsordnung [*Postal Newspaper and Periodical Distribution Regulations*] (EG)
PZW .... Polski Zwiazek Wedkarski [*Polish Angling Union*] [*Poland*]
PZW .... Powiatowy Zarzad Weterynarii [*County Veterinary Administration*] (POL)
PZw........... Przeglad Zwiazkowy [*Union Review*] [*A periodical*] (POL)
PZWANN ... Pomorskie Zaklady Wytworcze Aparatury Niskiego Napiecia [*Pomerania Low Tension Apparatus Plant*] (POL)
PZWet .... Powiatowy Zarzad Weterynarii [*County Veterinary Administration*] (POL)
PZWL....... Panstwowy Zaklad Wydawnictw Lekarskich [*State Medical Publishing House*] (POL)
PZWM ...... Poznanskie Zaklady Wyrobow Metalowych [*Poznan Metal Products Plant*] (POL)
PZWME.... Pomorskie Zaklady Wytworcze Materialow Elektrotechnicznych [*Pomerania Electric Engineering Plant*] (POL)
PZWS .... Panstwowe Zaklady Wydawnictw Szkolnych [*State Textbook Publishing House*] (POL)
PZY............ Piestany [*Former Czechoslovakia*] [*Airport symbol*] (OAG)
PZZ............ Panstwowe Zaklady Zbozowe [*State Grain Elevators*] (POL)
PZZ............ Polski Zwiazek Zachodni [*Polish Union of the Western Territories*] (POL)
PZZ............ Polski Zwiazek Zapasniczy [*Polish Wrestling Union*] [*Poland*]
PZZ............ Polski Zwiazek Zeglarski [*Polish Sailing Union*] (POL)
PZZ............ Polski Zwiazek Zielarski [*Polish Union of Herbalists*] (POL)
PZZ............ Powiatowe Zaklady Zbozowe [*County Grain Elevators*] (POL)
PZZ............ Prodavnica Zemljoradnicke Zadruge [*Sales Department of Agricultural Cooperative*] (YU)

Q

Q .... Carre [*Square*] [*French*]   (MTD)
Q .... Elektrizitaetsmenge [*Electrical Quantity*] [*German*]
q .... Kwintal [*Quintal*] [*Poland*]
q .... Metermazsa [*Quintal*]   (HU)
q .... Metricky Cent [*Quintal*]   (CZ)
Q .... One Billion [*British thermal units*]   (GNE)
Q .... Qarar   (BARN)
Q .... Quadrat [*Square*] [*German*]
Q .... Quadrato [*Square*] [*Italian*]
q .... Quai [*Quay, Wharf*] [*French*]   (CED)
q .... Qualche [*A Few*] [*Italian*]
q .... Quantite [*Quantity*] [*French*]
q .... Que [*That, Which, Who, Whom, For, Because*] [*Spanish*]
Q .... Quebec [*Phonetic alphabet*] [*International*]   (DSUE)
Q .... Queen [*Phonetic alphabet*] [*Pre-World War II*] [*World War II*]
 .... (DSUE)
Q .... Queenie [*Phonetic alphabet*] [*Royal Navy World War I*]   (DSUE)
Q .... Queensland [*Australia*]
Q .... Queensland Fever [*Disease first noted in farmers of Queensland, Australia*]
q .... Quelques [*Some*] [*French*]
Q .... Quetzal [*Monetary unit*] [*Guatemala*]
q .... Quintal [*Quintal*] [*French*]   (GPO)
q .... Quintal (Kvintal) [*Quintal*]   (CZ)
Q .... Quintar [*Monetary unit*] [*Albania*]
Q .... Waermemenge [*Heat Quantity*] [*German*]
QA .... QANTAS Airways Ltd. [*Australia*]   (DS)
QA .... Qatar [*IYRU nationality code*] [*ANSI two-letter standard code*]
 .... (CNC)
QA .... Queensland State Archives [*Australia*]
QAA .... Queensland Athletic Association [*Australia*]
QAAA .... Queensland Amateur Athletic Association [*Australia*]
QAAR .... Queensland Australian Archives - Regional [*Office*] [*National Union Catalogue of Australia symbol*]
QAASCAE ... Queensland Association of Academic Staff in Colleges of Advanced Education [*Australia*]
QAAT .... Queensland Administrative Appeals Tribunal - [*Principal Registry Library*] [*National Union Catalogue of Australia symbol*]
QAAVNC .. Queensland Army Aviation National Centre [*Library (Department of Defence)*] [*National Union Catalogue of Australia symbol*]
QAB .... Queensland Agricultural Bank [*Australia*]
QAC .... Queensland Agricultural College [*J R Murray Library*] [*National Union Catalogue of Australia symbol*]
QAC .... Queensland AIDS Council [*Australia*]
QAC .... Queensland Arts Council [*Australia*]
QACU .... Queensland Australian Catholic University [*National Union Catalogue of Australia symbol*]
QADD .... Queensland Alcohol and Drug [*Services*] Department [*Department of Health*]
QADIE ...... Queensland Association of Drama in Education [*Australia*]
QAEO .... Queensland Australian Electoral [*Commission*] Office [*National Union Catalogue of Australia symbol*]
QAF .... Qatar Amiri Flight [*ICAO designator*]   (FAAC)
QAFCO ..... Qatar Fertilizer Company [*Umm Said*]   (ME)
QAFL .... Queensland Australian Football League
QAG .... Queensland Art Gallery [*Australia*]
QAG .... Queensland Attorney General [*Department*] [*National Union Catalogue of Australia symbol*]
QAGTC ..... Queensland Association for Gifted and Talented Children [*Australia*]
QAH .... Quick Airways Holland BV [*Netherlands*] [*ICAO designator*]   (FAAC)
QAHA .... Queensland Allergy and Hyperactivity Association [*Australia*]
QAI .... Quality Assurance International
QAIA .... Queen Alia International Airport [*Jordan*]
QAID .... Queensland Association of Industries for the Disabled [*Australia*]

QAILS .... Queensland Association of Independent Legal Services [*Australia*]
QAITAD .... Queensland Aboriginal and Islander Teacher Aide Development [*Australia*]
QAL .... Qintex Australia Ltd.
QAL .... Queensland Agen [*Ltd.*] Library [*National Union Catalogue of Australia symbol*]
QAL .... Queensland Airlines Proprietary Limited [*Australia*]   (ADA)
QAL .... Queensland Alumina Limited [*Australia*]   (ADA)
Qal .... Quintal [*Quintal*] [*French*]
QALB .... Queensland Albert [*Shire Library Service*] [*National Union Catalogue of Australia symbol*]
QAM .... Queensland Arts Movement [*Australia*]
QAMS ...... Queensland Air Museum Society [*Australia*]
QAMT ...... Queensland Association of Mathematics Teachers [*Australia*]
QAN .... Queensland Air Navigation Co. Ltd. [*Australia*]   (ADA)
QANTAS... Queensland & Northern Territory Aerial Service [*Later, QANTAS Airways Ltd.*] [*Australia*]
QAO .... Queensland Audit Office [*Australia*]
QAPBS ...... Queensland Association of Permanent Building Societies [*Australia*]
QAPCO ..... Qatar Petrochemical Company [*Doha, Qatar*]   (MENA)
QAR .... Queensland Animal Research [*Institute (Queensland Department of Primary Industries)*] [*National Union Catalogue of Australia symbol*]
QART .... Queensland Art [*Gallery*] [*National Union Catalogue of Australia symbol*]
QAS .... Queensland Academy of Sport [*Australia*]
QAS .... Queensland Ambulance Service [*Australia*]
QAS .... Quisqueya Airlines SA [*Haiti*] [*ICAO designator*]   (FAAC)
QASAR ..... Queensland Automated Serials Accession Register [*Australia*]
QASB .... Queensland Ambulance Service Board [*Australia*]
QASCO ..... Qatar Steel Company [*Umm Said, Qatar*]   (MENA)
QASS .... Queensland Academy of Space Sciences [*Australia*]
QAT .... Qatar [*ANSI three-letter standard code*]   (CNC)
QATA .... Queensland Art Teachers' Association [*Australia*]
QATARGAS ... Qatar Gas Co. [*QGPC*]   (MENA)
QATOB ..... Queensland Australian Taxation Office - Branch [*National Union Catalogue of Australia symbol*]
QAWU .... Queensland Australian Workers' Union [*National Union Catalogue of Australia symbol*]
qb .... Quantidade Bastante [*Sufficient Quantity*] [*Portuguese*]
QB .... Queensland Ballet [*Australia*]
QBA .... Queensland Band Association [*Australia*]
QBA .... Queensland Beekeepers' Association [*Australia*]
QBA .... Queensland Bridge Association [*Australia*]
QBB .... Queensland Barristers' Board [*Australia*]
QBBA .... Queensland Bloodhorse Breeders Association [*Australia*]
QBC .... Queensland Bible College [*W J Tunley Memorial Library*] [*National Union Catalogue of Australia symbol*]
QBCA .... Queensland Brisbane City [*Hall*] Art [*Gallery and Museum*] [*National Union Catalogue of Australia symbol*]
QBCC .... Queensland Bayside Community College [*National Union Catalogue of Australia symbol*]
QBCHS ..... Queensland Bush Children's Health Scheme [*Australia*]
QBCL......... Queensland Brisbane City [*Council*] Library [*Service*] [*National Union Catalogue of Australia symbol*]
QBD .... Queensland Book Depot [*Australia*]
QBES........ Queensland Bureau of Emergency Services [*Australia*]
QBFP .... Queensland Boating and Fisheries Patrol [*Australia*]
QBG .... Queensland Bookbinders' Guild [*Australia*]
QBHH .... Queesland Baillie Henderson Hospital [*Queensland Health Library*] [*National Union Catalogue of Australia symbol*]
QBL .... Queensland Baseball League [*Australia*]
QBNA .... Queensland Bush Nursing Association [*Australia*]
QBON........ Queensland Bond [*University*] [*National Union Catalogue of Australia symbol*]

QBON:L.... Queensland Bond [*University*] Law [*Library*] [*National Union Catalogue of Australia symbol*]

QBPH........ Queensland Belmont Private Hospital [*National Union Catalogue of Australia symbol*]

QBS .... Queensland Border Staff [*Australia*]

QBSA........ Queensland Blinded Soldiers' Association [*Australia*]

QBSM .... Que Besa Su Mano [*Who Kisses Your Hand*] [*Formal correspondence*] [*Spanish*]

QBSM .... Que Besa Sus Manos [*Kissing Your Hands*] [*Spanish*]

QBSM .... Queensland Boyne Smelters [*Ltd.*] [*National Union Catalogue of Australia symbol*]

QBSP........ Que Besa Sus Pies [*Who Kisses Your Feet*] [*Formal correspondence*] [*Spanish*]

QBTH........ Queensland Baptist Theological [*College - McConaghy Library*] [*National Union Catalogue of Australia symbol*]

qBtu......... Quadrillion British Thermal Units   (GNE)

QBWA ...... Queensland Braille Writing Association [*National Union Catalogue of Australia symbol*]

QBWUE.... Queensland Blind Workers Union of Employees [*Australia*]

QC............. Air Zaire SA [*Zaire*] [*ICAO designator*]   (ICDA)

QC............. Queen's Counsel

QCA.......... Queensland Coal Association [*Australia*]

QCA.......... Queensland College of Art [*Australia*]

QCA.......... Queensland Colonial Association [*Australia*]

QCA.......... Queensland Colostomy Association [*Australia*]

QCA.......... Queensland Cricket Association [*Australia*]

QCAL .... Queensland Comalco [*Minerals and Alumina - Mineral Products Division*] [*National Union Catalogue of Australia symbol*]

QCAN....... Queensland Community Arts Network [*Australia*]

QCAS .... Queensland Chamber of Agricultural Societies [*Australia*]

QCB.......... Queensland Coal Board [*Australia*]

QCBH....... Queensland Cairns Base Hospital [*National Union Catalogue of Australia symbol*]

QCC.......... Quality Control Circle [*Singapore*]

QCC.......... Queensland Cotton Corp. [*Australia*]

QCC.......... Queensland Council of Churches [*Australia*]

QCC.......... Queensland Cricketers' Club [*Australia*]

QCC.......... Queensland Cultural Centre [*Australia*]

QCCI .... Queensland Chamber of Commerce and Industry

QCCL .... Queensland Cairns City Library [*Service*] [*National Union Catalogue of Australia symbol*]

QCCT .... Queensland Cultural Centre Trust [*Australia*]

QCDRA ..... Queensland Caloundra [*City Library*] [*National Union Catalogue of Australia symbol*]

QCE .... Queensland Capricornia Electricity [*National Union Catalogue of Australia symbol*]

QCEA .... Quaker Council for European Affairs   (EA)

QCF .... Queensland Cancer Fund [*Australia*]

QCFCLB ... Queensland Council of Finance Counsellors and Lease Brokers [*Australia*]

QCGA....... Queensland Cane Growers' Association [*Australia*]

QCHL........ Queensland Cotton Holdings Ltd. [*Australia*]

QCHR....... Queensland Central Highlands Regional [*Library Service*] [*National Union Catalogue of Australia symbol*]

QCIN .... Queensland Curriculum Information Network [*Australia*]

QCJ........... Queensland Criminal Justice [*Commission*] [*National Union Catalogue of Australia symbol*]

QCJC........ Queensland Criminal Justice Commission [*Australia*]

QCL .... Queensland Cement Ltd. [*Australia*]

QCL .... Queensland Chemical Laboratory [*Australia*]

QCLE........ Queensland Continuing Legal Education [*Australia*]

qcm.......... Quadratcentimeter [*Square Centimeter*] [*German*]

QCM......... Queensland Chamber of Mines [*Australia*]

QCM......... Queensland Conservatorium of Music [*Griffith University*] [*National Union Catalogue of Australia symbol*]

QCMC....... Queensland Chicken Meat Council [*Australia*]

QCOI........ Queensland Chamber of Industry [*Australia*]

QCOO ...... Queensland Cooloola [*Shire Library Service*] [*National Union Catalogue of Australia symbol*]

QCOR....... Queensland Corrective [*Services Commission - Central Library*] [*National Union Catalogue of Australia symbol*]

QCOTA ..... Queensland Council on the Ageing [*Australia*]

QCP .... Queensland Country Party [*Australia*]   (ADA)

QCPA .... Queensland Country Press Association [*Australia*]

QCPCA...... Queensland Centre for Prevention of Child Abuse [*Australia*]

QCRF........ Queensland Children's Research Foundation [*Australia*]

QCSSO...... Queensland Council of State School Organisations [*Australia*]

QCT.......... Queensland Churches Together [*Australia*]

QCT.......... Queensland Coal Trust [*Australia*]

Q Ct of CrApp ... Queensland Court of Criminal Appeal [*Australia*]

QCX.......... Queensland-[*University of*] Central Queensland [*National Union Catalogue of Australia symbol*]

QCYC .... Queensland Cruising Yacht Club [*Australia*]

Qd .... Queensland [*Australia*]   (ADA)

QD .... Transbrasil SA Linhas Aereas [*Brazil*] [*ICAO designator*]   (ICDA)

QDA........... Qattara Depression Authority [*Egypt*]

QDAR........ Queensland Drug Awareness and Relief [*Movement*] [*National Union Catalogue of Australia symbol*]

QDDG .... Que de Dios Goce [*May He Rejoice in the Lord*] [*Spanish*]

QDEC .... Queensland Development Education Centre [*Australia*]

QDEC .... Queensland Distance Education College [*Basic Education Unit*] [*National Union Catalogue of Australia symbol*]

QDEH .... Queensland - Department of Environment and Heritage [*National Union Catalogue of Australia symbol*]

QDEHF ..... Queensland - Department of Environment and Heritage - Far [*Northern Regional Library*] [*National Union Catalogue of Australia symbol*]

QDF .... Queensland Department of Forestry [*Australia*]

QDG .... Que Dios Guarde [*Whom God Protects (used after mention of king)*] [*Spanish*]

QDH .... Queensland - Department of Health [*Central Library*] [*National Union Catalogue of Australia symbol*]

QDI .... Queensland Drug Information [*Centre*] [*National Union Catalogue of Australia symbol*]

QDID........ Queensland - Department of [*Business*] Industry and [*Regional*] De velopment [*National Union Catalogue of Australia symbol*]

qdm .... Quadratdecimeter [*Square Decimeter*] [*German*]

QDMS ...... Queensland - Department of Mapping and Surveying [*National Union Catalogue of Australia symbol*]

qdo............ Quando [*When*] [*Portuguese*]

QDO .... Queensland Dairyfarmers' Organisation [*Australia*]

QDOF .... Queensland Department of Forests [*Australia*]

QDOT....... Queensland - Department of Transport [*Central Library*] [*National Union Catalogue of Australia symbol*]

QDR.......... Dubai Riyal [*Monetary unit*]

QDS.......... Qantas Distribution Services [*Australia*]

QDSPA...... Queensland Dance Studio Proprietors' Association [*Australia*]

QDTAA ..... Queensland Dive Tourism Association of Australia

QDU .... Dusseldorf-Main RR [*Germany*] [*Airport symbol*]   (OAG)

QDVC....... Queensland Domestic Violence Resource Centre [*National Union Catalogue of Australia symbol*]

qe.............. Que [*That, Which, Who, Whom, For, Because*] [*Spanish*]

QE............. Question Ecrite [*French*]   (FLAF)

QE............. Question Ecrite avec Reponse [*French*]   (BAS)

QEA.......... Queensland Exporters' Association [*Australia*]

QEC .... Queensland Electricity Commission [*National Union Catalogue of Australia symbol*]

QEC .... Queensland Events Corp. [*Australia*]

QED .... Queensland Education Department [*Bibliographic Services*] [*National Union Catalogue of Australia symbol*]

QEDS .... Queensland Export Development Scheme

QEGE .... Que en Gloria Este [*Deceased, May He Be in Glory*] [*Spanish*]

QEIC .... Queensland Education Information Centre [*Australia*]

QEIC......... Queensland Egg Industry Council [*Australia*]

qepd.......... Que en Paz Descanse [*Rest in Peace*] [*Spanish*]

qer .... Quartier [*District*] [*French*]

QES .... Queensland Emergency Services [*National Union Catalogue of Australia symbol*]

QESC......... Queen Elizabeth Sports Center [*Bahamas*]   (LA)

QESISB..... Queensland Electricity Supply Industry Superannuation Board [*Australia*]

qesm .... Que Estrecha Su Mano [*Handshake*] [*Spanish*]

QEWDA..... Queensland Ethnic Welfare Development Association [*Australia*]

QF .... QANTAS Airways Ltd. [*Australia*] [*ICAO designator*]

QFA.......... Qantas Airways Ltd. [*Australia*] [*ICAO designator*]   (FAAC)

QFCA .... Queensland Family Court of Australia [*Brisbane Registry*] [*National Union Catalogue of Australia symbol*]

QFCC........ Qantas Flight Catering Centre [*Australia*]

QFD .... Queensland Forest Department [*Department of Primary Industries*]

QFDA .... Queensland Funeral Directors' Association [*Australia*]

QFDO........ Queensland Film Development Office [*Australia*]

QFEE......... Queensland Feez [*Ruthning*] [*National Union Catalogue of Australia symbol*]

QFF........... Queensland Farmers' Federation [*Australia*]

QFGA .... Queensland Farmers and Graziers' Association [*Australia*]

QFGA .... Queensland Flower Growers' Association [*Australia*]

QFHS .... Queensland Family History Society [*Australia*]

QFI .... Queensland Fisheries Industry [*Department of Primary Industries - Fisheries Library*]

QFIE......... Quotite Forfaitaire d'Impot Etranger [*French*]   (BAS)

QFITC .... Queensland Fishing Industry Training Committee [*Australia*]

QFITC .... Queensland Food Industry Training Council [*Australia*]

QFITC .... Queensland Furniture Industry Training Committee [*Australia*]

QFLGE...... Queensland Foundation for Local Government Engineering [*Australia*]

QFMA .... Queensland Fish Management Authority [*Australia*]

QFMA .... Queensland Flour Millers' Association [*Australia*]

QFNR .... Queensland Far Northern Regional [*Library*] [*Department of Primary Industries*]

QFPA......... Queensland Family Planning Association [*National Union Catalogue of Australia symbol*]

QFRI......... Queensland Fisheries Research Institute [*Australia*]   (PDAA)

QFS........... Queensland Fire Service [*Australia*]

QFS........... Queensland Forest Service [*Australia*]

QG .... Quartel-General [*Quarter General*] [*Portuguese*]

QG .... Quartier General [*Headquarters*] [*French*]   (WER)

QG .... Queensland Grains [*Australia*] [*Commercial firm*]

QGA........... Quartier General d'Armee [*Army Headquarters*] [*French*]   (MTD)

QGA........... Queensland Graingrowers' Association [*Australia*]

QGA........... Queensland Gymnastic Association [*Australia*]

QGAA....... Quartier General d'Administration et d'Accompagnement [*Administration and Support Headquarters*] [*Cambodia*]   (CL)

QG/AA ...... Quartier General de l'Armee Active [*Regular Army General Headquarters*] [*Cambodia*]   (CL)

QGAG....... Queensland Gladstone Art Gallery [*and Museum*] [*National Union Catalogue of Australia symbol*]

QGBES...... Queensland Government Bureau of Emergency Services [*Australia*]

QGBR....... Queensland Great Barrier Reef [*Marine Park Authority*] [*National Union Catalogue of Australia symbol*]

QGC........... Queensland Gold Coast [*University College of Griffith University*] [*Division of Information Science*]

QGCA....... Quartier General de Corps d'Armee [*Army Corps Headquarters*] [*French*]

QGCCL...... Queensland Gold Coast City Council Library [*Service*] [*National Union Catalogue of Australia symbol*]

QGCL........ Queensland Government Chemical Laboratory [*National Union Catalogue of Australia symbol*]

QG/DN...... Quartier General de la Defense Nationale [*National Defense General Headquarters*] [*Cambodia*]   (CL)

QG/EMG .. Quartier General de l'Etat Major General [*General Staff General Headquarters*] [*Cambodia*]   (CL)

QGFM .... Queensland Guild of Furniture Manufacturers [*Australia*]

qgg............. Que Gloria Goce [*Spanish*]

QGMS........ Qintex Group Management Services Proprietary Ltd. [*Australia*]

QGPC........ Qatar General Petroleum Company

QGPC........ Qatar General Petroleum Corporation [*Doha, Qatar*]   (MENA)

QGPO........ Qatari General Petroleum Organization   (ME)

QGU .... Queensland Golf Union [*Australia*]

QGU .... Queensland Griffith University [*Nathan Campus*] [*National Union Catalogue of Australia symbol*]

QGU:M ..... Queensland Griffith University Mount [*Gravatt Campus*] [*National Union Catalogue of Australia symbol*]

q/ha............ Quintal per Hectare [*100 Kilograms per Hectare*]   (HU)

QHC .... Queensland Housing Commission [*Australia*]

QHEA....... Queensland Horticultural Export Association [*Australia*]

QHO .... Queen's Hall Orchestra

QHOF........ Queensland [*Australian Stockman's*] Hall of Fame [*and Outback Heritage Centre*] [*National Union Catalogue of Australia symbol*]

QHP........... Queen's Honorary Physician [*Australia*]   (ADA)

QHS........... Queensland Historical Society [*Australia*]

QHSH .... Queensland Holy Spirit Hospital [*National Union Catalogue of Australia symbol*]

QHSIA ...... Queensland Hide and Skin Industries Association [*Australia*]

QHSS .... Queensland Healthy Soil Society [*Australia*]

QI.............. Queensland Insurance (Fiji) Ltd.

QI.............. Quotient Intellectuel [*Intelligence Quotient*] [*French*]

QIA .... Queensland Irish Association [*Australia*]

QIB .... Qatar Islamic Bank [*Doha*]   (MENA)

QIC .... Aero Quick [*Mexico*] [*ICAO designator*]   (FAAC)

QIC .... Queensland Industrial Commission [*Australia*]

QIC .... Queensland Investment Corp. [*Australia*]

QIC .... Queensland Isolated Children's [*Special Education Unit*]

QICA .... Queensland Immigration Control Association [*Australia*]

QICC .... Queensland Ipswich City Council [*Art Gallery*] [*National Union Catalogue of Australia symbol*]

QI Ct......... Queensland Industrial Court [*Australia*]

QIDC .... Queensland Industry Development Corp. [*Australia*]

QIEA .... Queensland Institute for Educational Administration [*Australia*]

QIER .... Queensland Institute for Educational Research [*Australia*]   (PDAA)

QIF .... Queensland Infantry Force [*Australia*]

QIMA .... Queensland Institute of Managerial Accountants [*Australia*]

QIMR .... Queensland Institute of Medical Research [*National Union Catalogue of Australia symbol*]

QIMS........ Queensland [*Australian*] Institute of Marine Science [*National Union Catalogue of Australia symbol*]

QINC .... Queensland Incitec [*Ltd.*] [*National Union Catalogue of Australia symbol*]

QINF .... Queensland Information [*Access Centre*] [*National Union Catalogue of Australia symbol*]

QIPS........ Queensland Ipswich [*Municipal Library*] [*National Union Catalogue of Australia symbol*]

QIRC .... Queensland Industrial Relations Commission [*Australia*]

QIS .... Queensland Industrial Steel Ltd. [*Australia*]

QIT .... Queensland Institute of Technolgy [*Australia*]   (EAS)

QIW .... Queensland Independent Wholesalers [*Australia*]

QJA .... Queensland Jockeys' Association [*Australia*]

QJA .... Queensland Justices' Association [*Australia*]

QJCCI .... Queensland Japan Chamber of Commerce and Industry [*Australia*]

QJCU .... Queensland James Cook University [*of North Queensland*] [*National Union Catalogue of Australia symbol*]

QJO .... Queensland John Oxley [*Library*] [*State Library of Queensland*]

QJST .... Queensland Johnstone [*Shire Library*] [*National Union Catalogue of Australia symbol*]

QJTTRE.... Queensland Joint Tropical Trials Research Establishment [*National Union Catalogue of Australia symbol*]

QKCC .... Queensland Kenmore Christian College [*Byard Library*] [*National Union Catalogue of Australia symbol*]

QKFA .... Queensland Keep Fit Association [*Australia*]

QKH .... Queensland Kinhill [*Cameron McNamara*] [*National Union Catalogue of Australia symbol*]

QKL .... Aeromaritime (CAAA) [*France*] [*ICAO designator*]   (FAAC)

QKL .... Cologne/Bonn-Main RR [*Germany*] [*Airport symbol*]   (OAG)

qkm .... Quadratkilometer [*Square Kilometer*] [*German*]   (EG)

ql .... Quantum Libet [*As Much as You Please*] [*Pharmacy*]   (GPO)

ql .... Quilate [*Carat*] [*Portuguese*]

QL............. Quoc-Lo [*Main national highway in South Vietnam*]   (VNW)

QLAO........ Queensland Legal Aid Office [*National Union Catalogue of Australia symbol*]

QLD.......... Queensland [*Australia*]

QLD.......... Queensland Lands Department [*National Union Catalogue of Australia symbol*]

Qld CollArt ... Queensland College of Art [*Australia*]

Qld ConsMusic ... Queensland Conservatorium of Music [*Australia*]

Qlder.......... Queenslander [*Australia*]

QLGD........ Queensland Local Government [*and Housing*] Department [*Information Resource Centre*]

QLGU....... Queensland Ladies Golf Union [*Australia*]

QLIRS ...... Queensland Legal Information Retrieval System [*Australia*]

QLP .... Queensland Labor Party [*Australia*]   (ADA)

QLRA .... Queensland Litter Research Association [*Australia*]

QLS........... Queensland Library Supplies [*Australia*]

QLSEA ...... Queensland Livestock Exporters' Association [*Australia*]

QLWC:...... Queensland Land Warfare Centre [*National Union Catalogue of Australia symbol*]

qm .... Quadratmeter [*Square Meter*] [*German*]   (EG)

QM .... Quartermaster [*Military*]   (VNW)

QM .... Queensland Museum [*Australia*]

QMA.......... Qatar Monetary Authority   (IMH)

QMA.......... Quarry Masters' Association [*Australia*]

QMAA....... Queensland Motel and Accommodation Association [*Australia*]

QMAC....... Queensland [*Kinhill Cameron*] McNamara [*National Union Catalogue of Australia symbol*]

QMANSW ... Quarry Masters' Association of New South Wales [*Australia*]

QMB.......... Queensland Meteorology Bureau [*Regional Office*] [*National Union Catalogue of Australia symbol*]

QMB.......... Queensland Milk Board [*Australia*]

QMBH....... Queensland Mackay Base Hospital [*National Union Catalogue of Australia symbol*]

QMC.......... Queensland Mackay City [*Library*] [*National Union Catalogue of Australia symbol*]

QMC.......... Queensland Metals Corp. [*Australia*]

QMC.......... Queensland Mining Council [*Australia*]

QMCB .... Queensland Mount Coot Brisbane [*City Council Library Service - the Botanic*] [*National Union Catalogue of Australia symbol*]

QMCC .... Queensland Multicultural Co-Ordinating Committee [*Australia*]

QMCHA.... Queensland Mechanical Cane Harvesters' Association [*Australia*]

QMCVDDH ... Que Me - Comite Vietnam pour la Defense des Droits de l'Homme [*Que Me - Vietnam Committee on Human Rights*]   (EAIO)

QMD .... Queensland - Minerals [*and Energy*] Department [*National Union Catalogue of Australia symbol*]

QMDA....... Centre for Quality Management and Decision Analysis [*Bond University*] [*Australia*]

QMEA .... Queensland Meat Exporters' Association [*Australia*]

QMG .... Quartermaster Gunner [*Royal Australian Navy*]

QMGC....... Queensland Marriage Guidance Council [*National Union Catalogue of Australia symbol*]

QMI........... Queensland Mount Isa [*City Library*] [*National Union Catalogue of Australia symbol*]

QMIA .... Queensland Meat Industry Award [*Australia*]

QMIBH..... Queensland Mount Isa Base Hospital [*National Union Catalogue of Australia symbol*]

QMIM .... Queensland MIM Holdings [*Ltd. - Information Research*] [*National Union Catalogue of Australia symbol*]

QMIS......... Queensland Medi-Data Information Service [*National Union Catalogue of Australia symbol*]
QML.......... Qayyum Moslem League [*Pakistan*]   (PD)
QML.......... Queensland Marble Ltd. [*Australia*]
QML.......... Queensland Medical Laboratory [*National Union Catalogue of Australia symbol*]
qmm .... Quadratmillimeter [*Square Millimeter*] [*German*]
QMM .... Queensland Maritime Museum [*Australia*]
QMM .... Queensland Mater Misericordiae [*Public Hospital*] [*School of Nursing*]
QMOC....... Queensland Mount Olivet Community [*Services Ltd.*] [*National Union Catalogue of Australia symbol*]
QMOR....... Queensland Moreton [*Shire Library*] [*National Union Catalogue of Australia symbol*]
QMR......... Qualitative Military Requirements [*NATO*]   (NATG)
QMSC .... Queensland Mathematical Sciences Council [*Australia*]
QMSL........ Queensland Maroochy Shire Library [*Service - Technical Services*] [*National Union Catalogue of Australia symbol*]
QMSSA ..... Queensland Merino Stud Sheepbreeders' Association [*Australia*]
QMU .... Queensland Museum [*Library*] [*National Union Catalogue of Australia symbol*]
qn .... Quien [*Who, Whom*] [*Spanish*]
QNA .... Qatar News Agency [*Doha*]   (ME)
QNA .... Queensland Netball Association [*Australia*]
QNC.......... [*The*] Queensland Naturalists' Club [*Australia*]   (SLS)
QNF.......... Queensland Newsagents' Federation [*Australia*]
QNFC .... Qatar National Fishing Co.   (IMH)
QNGH .... Queensland Nambour General Hospital [*Hospital Library*]
QNH .... Queensland Noosa [*District*] Hospital [*National Union Catalogue of Australia symbol*]
QNH .... Qui Nhon [*Vietnam*]   (VNW)
QNIA .... Queensland Nursery Industry Association [*Australia*]
QNIS .... Queensland Newspapers Information Services [*Australia*]
QNK.......... Kabo Air Travels [*Nigeria*] [*ICAO designator*]   (FAAC)
QNLS .... Queensland Noosa [*Council*] Library Service [*National Union Catalogue of Australia symbol*]
QNNTC ..... Qatar National Navigation & Transport Company Ltd. [*Doha*]   (MENA)
QNOO .... Queensland Noosa [*Gallery*] [*National Union Catalogue of Australia symbol*]
QNPL .... Queensland Nickel Proprietary Limited [*Australia*]   (ADA)
QNPWS .... Queensland National Parks and Wildlife Service [*Australia*]
QNQ .... Queensland-North Queensland [*Area Library*] [*Department of Defence*]
QNS........... Queensland Numismatic Society [*Australia*]
QNSC .... Queensland [*Division*] National Safety Council [*of Australia*] [*National Union Catalogue of Australia symbol*]
QNSC .... Qui Nhon Support Command [*Vietnam*]
Qnsld .... Queensland [*Australia*]   (BARN)
QNT.......... Qintex Ltd. [*Australia*]
QNU .... Queensland Nurses' Union [*National Union Catalogue of Australia symbol*]
QNUE....... Queensland Nurses' Union of Employees [*Australia*]
QO .... Question Orale [*French*]   (FLAF)
QOC.......... Queensland Opera Company [*Australia*]
QOCH .... Queen's Own Cameroon Highlanders
QOIB .... Queensland Office of International Business [*Australia*]
QOLP .... Queensland Open Learning Project [*Australia*]
QOLUG..... Queensland Online Users' Group [*Australia*]
QP............. Quantum Placet [*As Much as You Please*] [*Pharmacy*]
QP .... Queensland Pius [*XII Provincial Seminary*] [*National Union Catalogue of Australia symbol*]
QP............. Questions Prud'hommales [*France*]   (FLAF)
QPA .... Queensland Photolab Association [*Australia*]
QPA .... Queensland Potters Association [*Australia*]
QPAC .... Queensland Performing Arts Centre [*Australia*]
QPC .... Qatar Petroleum Company
QPC .... Queensland Philatelic Council [*Australia*]
QPC .... Queensland Police Club [*Australia*]
QPCH .... Queensland Prince Charles Hospital [*Medical Library*] [*National Union Catalogue of Australia symbol*]
QPD.......... Queensland - [*Department of the*] Premier [*Economic and Trade*] De velopment [*National Union Catalogue of Australia symbol*]
QPET........ Queensland Petroleum Exploration Trust [*Australia*]
QPF .... Queensland Producers' Federation [*Australia*]
QPH.......... Queensland Police [*Service*] - Headquarters [*Branch*] [*National Union Catalogue of Australia symbol*]
QPID .... Queensland - Primary Industries Department [*Agriculture Central Library*]
QPITC ...... Queensland Plastics Industry Training Committee [*Australia*]
qpl .... Quantum Placet [*As Much as You Please*] [*Pharmacy*]   (GPO)
QPL .... Queensland Press Ltd. [*Australia*]
QPMAA .... Quilted Products Manufacturers Association of Australia
QPO.......... Queensland Philharmonic Orchestra [*Australia*]
QPP .... Queensland People's Party [*Australia*] [*Political party*]

QPPA........ Qatar Petroleum Producing Authority [*QGPC*]   (MENA)
QPPD .... Queensland Parents of People with a Disability [*Australia*]
QPPL........ Queensland People's Progressive League [*Australia*]
QPPL........ Queensland Peter Pal Library [*Supplier*] [*National Union Catalogue of Australia symbol*]
QPPO .... Queensland Pork Producers' Organisation [*Australia*]
Q Prud ...... Questions Prud'hommales [*France*]   (FLAF)
QPS........... Queensland Purchasing and Sales [*Australia*]
QPSM....... Queensland Proprietary Sugar Millers' [*Association Proprietary Ltd.*] [*National Union Catalogue of Australia symbol*]
QPSNZ..... Quaker Peace and Service New Zealand
QPTR........ Queensland Perc Tucker Regional [*Gallery*] [*National Union Catalogue of Australia symbol*]
QPU .... Queensland Police Union [*Australia*]
qq .... Qualche [*A Few*] [*Italian*]
qq .... Quelques [*Some*] [*French*]
qq .... Quelqu'un [*Anyone, Someone*] [*Correspondence*] [*French*]
qq .... Quintales [*Hundredweights*] [*Spanish*]
QQC.......... Queensland Quality Centre [*Australia*]
QQC.......... Queensland - Queensland Cement [*Ltd.*] [*Medical Library*]
QQE.......... Queensland Queen Elizabeth [*II Jubilee Hospital*] [*National Union Catalogue of Australia symbol*]
Qqe........... Quelque [*Any, Some*] [*Correspondence*] [*French*]
qqf .... Quelquefois [*Sometimes*] [*French*]
QQHA .... Queensland Quarter Horse Association [*Australia*]
QQPA .... Queensland-Queensland Police Academy [*National Union Catalogue of Australia symbol*]
qques .... Quelques [*Some*] [*French*]
QR............. Qatar Riyal [*Monetary unit*]   (BJA)
QR............. Quantitative Restrictions [*International trade*]
Qr.............. Quartier [*Quarter*] [*Military map abbreviation World War I*] [*French*]   (MTD)
QRA.......... Queensland Rockhampton Art [*Gallery*] [*National Union Catalogue of Australia symbol*]
QRC .... Queensland Recreation Council [*Australia*]
QRGH ...... Queensland Repatriation General Hospital [*Greenslopes*]
QRHS........ Queensland Royal Historical Society [*Welsby Library*]
QRITC ...... Queensland Retail Industry Training Council [*Australia*]
QRMF ...... Quick Reacting, Mobile Force [*Military*] [*NATO*]   (NATG)
QRML ...... Queensland Rockhampton Municipal Library [*National Union Catalogue of Australia symbol*]
QRMN...... Qualified Registered Mental Nurses
QRS .... Queensland Rose Society [*Australia*]
QRS .... Queensland Royal Society [*National Union Catalogue of Australia symbol*]
QRSI......... Queensland Raw Sugar Industry [*Australia*]
QRSL........ Queensland Redland Shire [*Council*] Library [*National Union Catalogue of Australia symbol*]
QRTA ...... Queensland Road Transport Association [*Australia*]
QRTL........ Queensland Right to Life [*An association*] [*Australia*]
QRTSA ..... Queensland Retail Traders and Shopkeepers' Association [*Australia*]
QRV .... Qualified Valuer of the Real Estate Institute of New South Wales
QRZ........... Quaddel Reaktion Zeit [*Wheal Reaction Time*] [*German*]
QS .... Les Quatre Saisons [*Record label*] [*France*]
QS .... Qualitaetssicherung [*German*]   (ADPT)
QS .... Quecksilber-Saeule [*Mercury Column*] [*German*]
QS .... Quecksilber-Stand [*Mercury Level*] [*German*]
QSA .... Queensland State Archives [*National Union Catalogue of Australia symbol*]
QSA .... Queensland Swimming Association [*Australia*]
QSAL........ Quadripartite Standardisation Agreement List [*Australia*]
QSAT........ Queensland Scholastic Aptitude Test [*Australia*]
QSB .... Queensland Sugar Bureau [*Bureau of Sugar Experiment Stations*]
QSBC .... Queensland Small Business Council [*Australia*]
QSC .... African Safari Airways Ltd. [*Kenya*] [*ICAO designator*]   (FAAC)
QSC .... Al-Ahli Bank of Qatar   (MENA)
QSC .... Queensland Sugar Corp. [*Australia*]
QSC .... Queensland Supreme Court [*National Union Catalogue of Australia symbol*]
QSCA .... Queensland Specialist Contractors' Association [*Australia*]
QS:CAT ..... Queensland Centre for Advanced Technology [*National Union Catalogue of Australia symbol*]
QSCC........ Queensland Society for Crippled Children [*Australia*]
QSCR........ Queensland South Coast Regional [*Health Authority*] [*National Union Catalogue of Australia symbol*]
QSDMA .... Queensland Soft Drink Manufacturers' Association [*Australia*]
QSDR .... Queensland [*Corporation of the*] Synod of the Diocese of Rockhampton [*Rockhampton Diocesan Library*]
QSEC........ Queensland Security and Exchange Commission [*Australian Securities Commission*]
QSF........... Queensland Soccer Federation [*Australia*]
qsgh........... Que Santa Gloria Haya [*Rest in Peace*] [*Spanish*]
QSIC......... Queensland Sugar Industry Corp. [*Australia*]
QSIM........ Queensland Safety in Mines Testing [*and Research Station*] [*SIMTARS Information Centre*]

QSJC .... Queensland St Joseph's College [*National Union Catalogue of Australia symbol*]

QSJM .... Queen's Silver Jubilee Medal [*Australia*]

QSL .... Queensland State Library [*National Union Catalogue of Australia symbol*]

QSL .... Queensland Supercomputing Laboratories [*Australia*]

QS:LP .... Queensland CSIRO [*Commonwealth Scientific and Industrial Research Organization*] Long Po cket [*Laboratories*] [*National Union Catalogue of Australia symbol*]

QSMC .... Queensland Surveying and Mapping Advisory Council [*Australia*]

QSMVMAC ... Queen Street Mall and Valley Mall Advisory Committee [*Brisbane, Australia*]

QSN .... Queensland School of Nursing [*Library*] [*Royal Brisbane Hospital*]

QSNP .... Queensland Sullivan and Nicolaides and Partners [*National Union Catalogue of Australia symbol*]

QSPA .... Queensland Secondary Principals' Association [*Australia*]

QSPB .... Queensland [*Central*] Sugar [*Cane*] Prices Board [*National Union Catalogue of Australia symbol*]

QSPS .... Queensland Southport School [*National Union Catalogue of Australia symbol*]

QSR .... Queensland Sugar Research [*Institute*] [*E T S Pearce Library*]

QSRA .... Queensland Smallbore Rifle Association [*Australia*]

QSRFC ...... Queensland Sport and Recreational Fishing Council [*Australia*]

QSRTCG ... Queensland Sales Representatives and Commercial Travellers' Guild [*Australia*]

QSS .... Questions de Securite Sociale [*Revue mensuelle*] [*France*] (FLAF)

QSSS .... Quilon Social Service Society [*India*]

QSSU .... Queensland State Service Union [*Australia*]

QST .... Queensland Science and Technology Ltd. [*Australia*]

QS:TCP ..... Queensland CSIRO [*Commonwealth Scientific and Industrial Research Organization*] - [*Division of*] Tropical Crops and Pastures [*Cunningham Laboratory*]

QS:TFR ..... Queensland CSIRO [*Commonwealth Scientific and Industrial Research Organization*] Tropica l Forest Research Centre [*Division of Wildlife and Ecology*]

QSTV .... Queensland Satellite Television [*Australia*]

QSUG .... Queensland Sugar Corporation [*Australia*]

QSW .... Queensland Sly Weigall [*Cannan and Peterson*] [*National Union Catalogue of Australia symbol*]

QSWL .... Queensland Spastic Welfare League [*Australia*]

qt .... Quintal [*Quintal*] [*French*]

qta .... Quantia [*Quantity*] [*Portuguese*]

qta .... Quinta [*Farm, Estate*] [*Portuguese*] (CED)

QTAC .... Queensland Tertiary Admissions Centre [*Australia*]

qtaux .... Quintaux [*Quintals*] [*French*]

QTBH .... Queensland Toowoomba Base Hospital [*Dr Aeneas McDonnell Medical Library*]

QTBUE ..... Queensland Timber Board Union of Employees [*Australia*]

QTC .... Queensland Treasury Corp. [*Australia*]

QTCL .... Queensland Thuringowa City Libraries [*National Union Catalogue of Australia symbol*]

QTDC .... Queensland Training and Development Centre [*Corrective Services Commission*]

QTE .... Qualite [*Quality*] [*French*] (ROG)

QTEF .... Queensland Tertiary Education Foundation [*Australia*]

QTH .... Queensland Townsville [*General*] Hospital [*Medical Library*]

QTIA .... Queensland Tourism Industry Authority [*Australia*]

QTIEA ...... Queensland Timber Importers and Exporters' Association [*Australia*]

QTITC ...... Queensland Timber Industry Training Council [*Australia*]

QTLMB ..... Queensland Tobacco Leaf Marketing Board [*Australia*]

QTLN .... Queensland TAFE [*Technical and Further Education*] Library Network [*Devetir Library*]

QTM .... Queensland Titanium Mines Proprietary Ltd. [*Australia*] (ADA)

qto .... Quanto [*Whatever*] [*Portuguese*]

QTOL .... Queensland Toowoomba [*City*] Library [*National Union Catalogue of Australia symbol*]

qts .... Quilates [*Carats*] [*Spanish*]

QTSC .... Queensland Transmission and Supply Corp. [*Australia*]

QTSH .... Queensland Tape Service for the Handicapped [*National Union Catalogue of Australia symbol*]

QTSR .... Queensland - [*Department of*] Tourism Sport and Racing [*National Union Catalogue of Australia symbol*]

QTTA .... Queensland Table Tennis Association [*Australia*]

QTTC .... Queensland Tourist and Travel Corporation [*National Union Catalogue of Australia symbol*]

QTTE .... Quartette [*Music*]

QTTL .... Queensland Townsville Technical Library [*Townsville City Council - Town Planning Department*]

QTVL .... Queensland Townsville [*City*] Library [*National Union Catalogue of Australia symbol*]

QU .... Queensland University [*St Lucia Campus*]

qu .... Quer [*Oblong*] [*German*]

QUA .... Quassar de Mexico SA de CV [*ICAO designator*] (FAAC)

QuAC .... Queensland AIDS Council [*Australia*]

qual .... Qualitativ [*Qualitative*] [*German*]

Qual .... Qualiton & MHV [*Record label*] [*Hungary*]

QualCert .... Qualifying Certificate [*Australia*]

QUALCON ... National Australian Quality Conference

quant .... Quantitativ [*Quantitative*] [*German*]

QUARMUS ... Queensland University Architecture/Music Library [*St Lucia Campus*]

quart .... Quarteirao [*Quarter*] [*Portuguese*]

QUART ..... Quartetto [*Quartet*] [*Music*] (ROG)

QU BIOL... Queensland University Biological Sciences Library [*St. Lucia Campus*]

QUCA .... Queensland United Church in Australia [*Queensland Synod*]

Queb .... Quebrada [*Cut, Ravine*] [*Portuguese*] (NAU)

Queb .... Quebrada [*Cut, Ravine*] [*Spanish*] (NAU)

Queens ...... Queensland [*Australia*]

Queens ...... Queensway Studios [*Record label*] [*Great Britain*]

QUEENSL ... Queensland [*Australia*] (ROG)

Quell .... Quelle [*Source*] [*German*] (GCA)

Quell .... Quellung [*Swelling*] [*German*] (GCA)

quelq .... Quelques [*Some*] [*French*]

Quesco ...... Questions Commerciales et Administratives [*Benelux*] (BAS)

QUEST ...... Queensland Status of Exploration Titles [*Department of Mines*] [*Australia*]

QuestControv ... Question Controversee [*French*] (FLAF)

QuestPrud'h ... Questions Prud'hommales et Fiscales (FLAF)

Quest SS .... Questions de Securite Sociale [*Revue mensuelle*] [*France*] (FLAF)

QUGA .... Queensland United Graziers' Association [*Australia*]

QU HML... Queensland University Herston Medical Library [*National Union Catalogue of Australia symbol*]

QUI .... Aero Quimmco SA de CV [*Mexico*] [*ICAO designator*] (FAAC)

QUICK ...... Quotation Information Center KK [*Nihon Keizai Shimbun, Inc.*] [*Information service or system*] (IID)

quil .... Quilates [*Carats*] [*Spanish*]

Quim .... Quimica [*Chemistry*] [*Portuguese*]

QUIMAR .. Quimica del Mar SA [*Mexico*]

QUIMIDENT ... Industria Quimica Dental Ltda. [*Barranquilla*] (COL)

Quimigal .... Quimica de Portugal, EP (EY)

QUIMIMPORT ... Empresa Cubana Importadora de Productos Quimicos [*Cuban Enterprise for Import of Chemical Products*] (LA)

QUINACAM ... Quinquina du Cameroun

quinq .... Quinque [*Five*] [*Latin*] (MAE)

QUINT ...... Quintetto [*Quintet*] [*Music*] (ROG)

QUIP .... Quality in Policy Network [*Australia*]

QULOC ..... Queensland University Libraries Office of Cooperation [*Australia*]

QUNO .... Quaker United Nations Office (EAIO)

QUOLLS... Queensland Online Library System [*Australia*]

QUP .... Quellenprogramm [*German*] (ADPT)

QU PSE ..... Queensland University Physical Sciences and Engineering Library [*St Lucia Campus*]

QUR .... Queensland University Regiment [*Australia*]

QUSQ .... Queensland - University of Southern Queensland [*National Union Catalogue of Australia symbol*]

QUT .... Queensland University of Technology [*National Union Catalogue of Australia symbol*]

QUT CA .... Queensland University of Technology - Carseldine Campus [*National Union Catalogue of Australia symbol*]

QUT GP ... Queensland University of Technology - Gardens Point Campus [*National Union Catalogue of Australia symbol*]

QUT KG .... Queensland University of Technology - Kelvin Grove Campus [*National Union Catalogue of Australia symbol*]

QUT KP..... Queensland University of Technology - Kedron Park Campus [*National Union Catalogue of Australia symbol*]

QUT LS..... Queensland University of Technology - Library Science [*School of Information Systems*]

QU TRS..... Queensland University - Tape Reading Service [*National Union Catalogue of Australia symbol*]

QV .... Lao Aviation [*Laos*] [*ICAO designator*] (ICDA)

qv .... Quantum Vis [*As Much as You Wish*] [*Pharmacy*] (GPO)

QV.............. Quattrovalvole [*Four valves per cylinder*] [*Italian*]

qv .... Queira Ver [*Portuguese*]

qv .... Queira Voltar [*Portuguese*]

q.v.............. Quod Vide [*To Which Refer*] [*Latin*] (EECI)

QVFC......... Queensland Volunteer Flying Civilians [*Australia*]

QVH .... Queen Victoria Hospital [*Australia*]

QVM......... Queen Victoria Museum [*Tasmania, Australia*]

QVRF .... Queensland Victoria Research Foundation [*Australia*]

QWA .... Qwestair [*Australia*] [*ICAO designator*] (FAAC)

QWAAA.... Queensland Women's Amateur Athletic Association [*Australia*]

QWASC..... Queensland Women's Amateur Sports Council [*Australia*]

QWBBA .... Queensland Women's Basketball Association [*Australia*]

QWBBU .... Queensland Women's Basketball Union [*Australia*]

QWBM...... Queensland WBM [*Proprietary Ltd.*] [*National Union Catalogue of Australia symbol*]

QWC.......... Queensland Writers' Centre [*Australia*]
QWES .... Queensland Wesley [*Hospital Library*] [*National Union
             Catalogue of Australia symbol*]
QWHA ...... Queensland Women's Historical Association [*Australia*]
QWHC ...... Queensland Workers' Health Centre [*National Union Catalogue
             of Australia symbol*]
QWHS....... Queensland Women's Historical Society [*Australia*]
QWRC....... Queensland Water Resources Commission [*Australia*]
QWRC........ Queensland - Water Resources Commission [*National Union
             Catalogue of Australia symbol*]
QWRI .... Queensland Wheat Research Institute [*National Union
             Catalogue of Australia symbol*]
QX.............. Qatar Amiri Flight [*Qatar*] [*ICAO designator*]   (ICDA)
qx .... Quintaux [*Quintals*] [*French*]
QYA........... Queensland Yachting Association [*Australia*]

R

R .... Angle-Off (RU)
r .... Angulo Reto [*Right Angle*] [*Portuguese*]
R .... Basin, Bowl [*Topography*] (RU)
R .... Burst (RU)
r .... Company (BU)
R .... Control, Regulator, Governor (RU)
R .... De Rechtsstrijd [*Benelux*] (BAS)
R .... Distributor (RU)
R .... Elektrischer Widerstand [*Electrical Resistance*] [*German*]
r .... Gender [*Grammar*], Species, Kind (RU)
R .... Genitive (Case) (RU)
R .... Het Rechtsfront [*Benelux*] (BAS)
R .... Jet, Reactive (RU)
R .... Knife Switch (RU)
r .... Line, Order (BU)
R .... Parti Republicain Radical et Radical-Socialiste [*France*]
              [*Political party*] (ECED)
r .... Private (BU)
r .... Rada [*Series*] (CZ)
R .... Radfahrabteilung [*Bicycle Battalion*] [*German military - World
              War II*]
r .... Radikal [*Radical*] [*A newspaper*] (BU)
r .... Radius [*Radius*] [*German*]
R .... Rail (RU)
R .... Rand [*Monetary unit*] [*Botswana, Lesotho, South Africa, and
              Swaziland*]
R .... Rapido [*Express Train*] [*Italian*]
R .... Rat [*Counsel*] [*German*]
R .... Rayleigh [*German*] (GCA)
R .... Rayon, City District (RU)
r .... Real [*Monetary unit*] [*Spanish*]
R .... Reaumur [*Temperature scale*] [*German*]
R .... Reaumur Degree (RU)
R .... Reaumuria [*Finland*]
R .... Recessive (RU)
R .... Rechnung [*Calculation*] [*German*]
R .... Recht [*Law*] [*German*]
r .... Rechts [*Right-Hand Side*] [*German*] (GCA)
r .... Rechtsdrehend [*Clockwise*] [*German*]
r .... Recommande [*Recommend*] [*French*]
R .... Reconnaissance [*Aircraft*] (RU)
r .... Recu [*Received*] [*French*]
R .... Reducer (RU)
R .... Reel [*Line*] [*Afrikaans*]
r .... Referalo [*Reviewing*] (HU)
r .... Reggel [*Morning*] (HU)
r .... Registriert [*Registered*] [*German*]
R .... Reglement [*Benelux*] (BAS)
R .... Regs [*To the Right*] [*Afrikaans*]
R .... Regulating [*or Controlling*] (BU)
R .... Rei [*King*] [*Portuguese*]
R .... Reihe [*Series*] [*Publishing*] [*German*]
R .... Reisezugverkehr [*Passenger Train Transportation*] (EG)
R .... Reiz [*Stimulus*] [*German*] [*Psychology*]
R .... Reka [*River*] [*Russian*] (NAU)
r .... Rekke [*Series*] [*Publishing Danish/Norwegian*]
R .... Relay (RU)
r .... Relie [*Bound*] [*Publishing*] [*French*]
R .... Remotum [*Far Respiration*] [*Latin*] (MAE)
R .... Rendelet [*Decree (Legal)*] (HU)
R .... Rendor [*Policeman*] (HU)
r .... Rentgen [*Roentgen (Unit of radiation)*] [*Poland*]
R .... Repons [*Response*] [*French*]
R .... Report [*Carry Forward*] [*Bookkeeping*] [*French*]
R .... Reprobado [*On an Examination: Failed*] [*Spanish*]
R .... Reprovado [*Rejected*] [*Portuguese*]
R .... Reserve [*Officer's rating*] [*Danish Navy*]
r .... Resistance [*Resistance*] [*French*]

r .... Respiration [*Breathing*] [*French*]
R .... Responde [*Respond*] [*Spanish*]
R .... Respuesta [*Answer*] [*Spanish*]
r .... Resz [*Part*] [*Publishing*] [*Hungary*]
R .... Retarder [*Slow*] [*On clock-regulators*] [*French*]
R .... Reu [*Criminal, Defendant*] [*Portuguese*]
R .... Reverencia [*Reverence*] [*Spanish*]
R .... Reverendo [*Reverend*] [*Spanish*]
R .... Rey [*King*] [*Spanish*]
R$ .... Rhodesian Dollar [*Monetary unit*]
R .... Rial [*Monetary unit*] [*Iran, Saudi Arabia, etc.*]
R .... Richtkreis [*Aiming Circle*] [*Gunnery term*] [*German military -
              World War II*]
R .... Ridder [*Knight*] [*Denmark*] (GPO)
r .... Riisi(a) [*Finland*]
R .... Ring [*Cycle*] [*German*] (GCA)
R .... Rio [*River*] [*Portuguese*] (NAU)
R .... Rio [*River*] [*Spanish*] (NAU)
R .... River [*Type of boat*] (RU)
R .... Rivier [*River*] [*Netherlands*] (NAU)
R .... Riviere [*River*] [*French*] (NAU)
R .... Robert [*Phonetic alphabet*] [*Royal Navy World War I Pre-World
              War II*] (DSUE)
R .... Robin Avions [*Pierre Robin*] [*France*] [*ICAO aircraft
              manufacturer identifier*] (ICAO)
r .... Rodzaj [*Kind*] [*Poland*]
r .... Roentgen (RU)
R .... Roger [*Phonetic alphabet*] [*World War II*] (DSUE)
r .... Rok [*Year*] (CZ)
R .... Romac Pipe Fittings Ltd. [*Australia*]
R .... Roman
R .... Romania
R .... Romeo [*Phonetic alphabet*] [*International*] (DSUE)
R .... Rothschild & Associes Banque [*Bank*] [*France*]
R .... Rotte (Mehrere Haeuser in Lockerer Siedlung) [*German*]
r .... Route [*Road, Route*] [*French*]
r .... Rua [*Street*] [*Portuguese*] (CED)
R .... Rubin [*Name of inventor*] [*Found on fuses*] [*French*] (MTD)
R .... Ruble [*Monetary unit*] [*Former USSR*]
R .... Rud [*River*] [*Persian*] (NAU)
r .... Rudnichar [*Miner*] [*A periodical*] (BU)
R .... Rue [*Street*] [*French*]
R .... Ruhekontakt [*German*] (ADPT)
r .... Ruins [*Topography*] (RU)
R .... Ruled [*Followed by the dates of a monarch's reign*]
R .... Rumunia [*Romania*] [*Poland*]
R .... Rund [*Round*] [*German*]
R .... Rupee [*Monetary unit*] [*Ceylon, India, and Pakistan*]
R .... Russian (RU)
r .... Rustica [*Paperbound*] [*Publishing*] [*Spanish*]
R .... Rzeka [*River*] [*Poland*] (NAU)
R .... Siding Track [*Topography*] (RU)
R .... Stopien Reaumura [*Degree Reaumur*] [*Poland*]
r .... Was Born (RU)
R2E .... Realisations et Etudes Electronique [*Computer manufacturer*]
              [*France*]
RA .... Address Register [*Computers*] (RU)
RA .... Agglutination Reaction (RU)
RA .... De Rechtskundige Adviseur [*Benelux*] (BAS)
RA .... Emergency Relay (RU)
Ra .... Radical [*Chemistry*] (BU)
Ra .... Radio [*Radium*] [*Chemical element*] [*Portuguese*]
r/a .... Radioactivity (RU)
RA .... Radio Alger
RA .... Radio Australia (ADA)
RA .... Radionic Association (EA)
RA .... Radio Plate Battery (RU)
Ra .... Rainha [*Queen*] [*Portuguese*]

RA .... Rapport d'Activite [*French*]   (ADPT)
RA .... Ravenna [*Car registration plates*] [*Italian*]
RA .... Rdeca Armada [*Red Army*]   (YU)
RA .... Rechtsanwalt [*Attorney*] [*German*]
RA .... Rechtsgeleerde Adviezen [*Benelux*]   (BAS)
RA .... Reconnaissance Aviation   (BU)
RA .... Redacteur Adjoint
RA .... Refugee Agency [*NATO*]   (NATG)
RA .... Reims Aviation [*France*] [*ICAO aircraft manufacturer identifier*]
          (ICAO)
RA .... Rentgen Aparat [*X-Ray Apparatus*]   (YU)
RA .... Republica Argentina [*Argentine Republic*]
ra .... Repuloallomas [*Airport, Airbase*]   (HU)
RA .... Resguardo Aduanero [*Customs Police*] [*Peru*]   (LA)
RA .... Risque Aggrave [*Insurance*] [*France*]   (FLAF)
RA .... Robotnicka Akademia [*Workers' Academy*]   (CZ)
Ra .... Roca [*Rock*] [*Spanish*]   (NAU)
Ra .... Rocha [*Rock*] [*Portuguese*]   (NAU)
RA .... Rocket Artillery   (RU)
RA .... Royal Artillery   (ML)
RA .... Ruda Armada [*Red Army*]   (CZ)
RA .... Rudnik Antimona [*Antimony Mine*]   (YU)
RA .... Rueckwaertiges Armeegebiet [*Rear area of an army*] [*German military*]
RA .... Russian Archives   (RU)
RA .... Subscriber's Meter   (RU)
RAA .... Recueil des Actes Administratifs de l'Algerie
RAA .... Ricegrowers' Association of Australia
RAA .... Road Accidents Authority [*Australia*]
RAA .... Royal Australian Artillery   (ML)
RAA .... Royal Automobile Association [*Australia*]   (ADA)
RAA .... Royal Regiment of Australian Artillery   (DMA)
RAA .... Rural Assistance Authority [*New South Wales, Australia*]
RAAC .... Reference Areas Advisory Committee [*Victoria, Australia*]
RAAC .... Royal Australian Armoured Corps   (ADA)
RAACA .... Royal Australian Armoured Corps Association   (ADA)
RAACC ...... Royal Australian Armoured Corps Club   (ADA)
RAAChD ... Royal Australian Army Chaplains Department
RAADC ...... Royal Australian Army Dental Corps   (ADA)
RAAEC ...... Royal Australian Army Education Corps   (ADA)
RAAF .... Royal Australian Air Force [*ICAO designator*]   (FAAC)
RAAFA ...... Royal Australian Air Force Academy
RAAFA ...... Royal Australian Air Force Association
RAAFMS .. Royal Australian Air Force Medical Service   (ADA)
RAAFNS ... Royal Australian Air Force Nursing Service   (ADA)
RAALC ...... Royal Australian Army Legal Corps
raam .... Raamatussa [*or Raamatun Kielessa*] [*In the Bible or Biblical Phrase*] [*Finland*]
RAAM .... Refineria Argentina de Aceites Minerales SRL [*Argentina*]   (DSCA)
RAAMC .... Royal Australian Army Medical Corps   (ADA)
RAANC ..... Royal Australian Army Nursing Corps   (ADA)
RAANS ..... Royal Australian Army Nursing Service   (ADA)
RAAOC ..... Royal Australian Army Ordnance Corps   (ADA)
raap .... Reconnaissance Artillery Regiment   (BU)
RAAPC ..... Royal Australian Army Pay Corps
RAASC ..... Royal Australian Army Service Corps   (ADA)
raav .... Army Aviation Company   (BU)
RAB .... Raad van Advies voor Bedrijfsinformatie [*Rotterdam*]
rab .... Rabat [*Rebate*] [*Afrikaans*]
Rab .... Rabatt [*Discount*] [*German*]
rab .... Rabattre [*Pull Down*] [*Knitting*] [*French*]
RAB .... Rabaul [*New Britain Island*] [*Airport symbol*]   (OAG)
RAB .... Rasprskavajuce Aviobombe [*Fragmentation Air Bombs*]   (YU)
RAB .... Reichsautobahn [*Arterial Motor Road*] [*German*]
RAB .... Rentjana Anggaran Belandja [*Draft Budget*]   (IN)
RAB .... Republic Address Bureau   (RU)
RAB .... Republik Arab Bersatu [*United Arab Republic*]   (ML)
RAB .... Rijksarbeidsbureau [*Benelux*]   (BAS)
rab .... Worker   (RU)
RAbA .... Reichskanzlei-Akten Betreff Antisemitismus [*Acronym is based on former name,*]   (BJA)
rabatr .... Artillery Reconnaissance Battery   (RU)
RabbAss..... Rabbinatsassessor [*Acronym is based on former name,*]   (BJA)
rabbat........ Labor Battalion   (RU)
rabbrig ...... Work Brigade, Operating Crew   (RU)
Rabfak ...... Workers' School Department   (BU)
rab gor....... Workers' Settlement [*Topography*]   (RU)
RABIN...... Raad van Advies voor Bibliotheekwezen en Informatieverzorging [*Netherlands Council for Libraries and Information Services*]   (EAIO)
RABIS ...... Trade Union of Workers in the Arts   (RU)
Rabiz.......... Art Workers' Trade Union   (BU)
Rabkhim .... Trade Union of Chemical Industry Workers   (RU)
Rabkop....... Digger [*Mining*]   (BU)
Rabkor .... Workers' Newspaper Correspondent   (BU)

Rabkrin...... Narodny Kommissariat Rabochey i Krestyanskoy Inspeksii [*Workers' and Peasants' Inspection*] [*1920-1934*]   (RU)
rab pos....... Workers' Settlement [*Topography*]   (RU)
Rabpros...... Trade Union of Education Workers   (RU)
Rabsel .... Worker-Peasant Solidarity   (BU)
Rabselkor... Workers' and Peasants' Correspondent   (BU)
Rabshveyprom ... Trade Union of Garment Industry Workers   (RU)
Rabsnab ..... State Workers' Supply Enterprise   (BU)
rac .... Raccommodage [*Repair*] [*Publishing*] [*French*]
rac .... Racemisch [*Racemic*] [*German*]
rac .... Racine [*Root*] [*Pharmacy*]
RAC .... Recueil de Pieces sur l'Administration et le Commerce
RAC .... Regies d'Approvisionnement et de Commercialisation
RAC .... Registrar of Aboriginal Corporations [*Australia*]
RAC .... Representantes de Ambientes Cristianos [*Representatives of Christian Surroundings*] [*Spanish*]   (WER)
RAC .... Research Analysis Corporation
RAC .... Resource Assessment Commission [*Australia*]
RAC .... Rijks Advies Commissie voor de Openbare Bibliotheken
RAC .... Rotorua Aero Club [*New Zealand*] [*ICAO designator*]   (FAAC)
RAC .... Routiere Automobile Casablancaise
RAC .... Royal African Company
RAC .... Royal Air Cambodge [*Royal Air Cambodia*]   (CL)
RAC .... Rum Agriculture Co. [*Jordan*]
RACA .... Reckitt & Colman Australia Ltd.
RACA .... Royal Automobile Club of Australia   (ADA)
RACAB..... Real Academia de Ciencias y Artes de Barcelona [*Spanish*]   (SLS)
RACAM .... Rassemblement Camerounais
RACB........ Royal Automobile Club de Belgique [*Royal Automobile Club of Belgium*]   (EAIO)
racc........... Raccolta [*Collection*] [*Publishing*] [*Italian*]
RACC .... Rhodesian African Chamber of Commerce   (AF)
RACCAA... Refrigeration and Air Conditioning Contractors Association of Australia   (ADA)
RACDS..... Royal Australian College of Dental Surgeons   (ADA)
RACE........ Railways of Australia Container Express   (ADA)
RACE........ Real Automovil Club de Espana [*Royal Automobile Club of Spain*]
RACE........ Research and Development in Advanced Communications for Europe [*European Community*]   (MHDB)
RACE........ Research in Advanced Communications in Europe [*European Commission*]
racem......... Racemisch [*Racemic*] [*German*]   (GCA)
RACGP...... Royal Australian College of General Practitioners
RACGPFMP ... Royal Australian College of General Practitioners Family Medicine Program
RACI......... Royal Australian Chemical Institute
RACLA...... Resource and Action Committee for Latin America [*Australia*]
RACMA .... Royal Australian College of Medical Administrators
RACMP .... Royal Australian Corps of Military Police
RACMYP ... Real Academia de Ciencias Morales y Politicas [*Spanish*]   (SLS)
RACNSW ... Royal Aero Club of New South Wales [*Australia*]
RACO .... Royal Australian College of Ophthalmologists   (ADA)
RACOG .... Royal Australian College of Obstetricians and Gynaecologists
RACP........ Reunion des Amateurs de Chiens Pyreneens [*France*]   (EAIO)
RACP........ Royal Australasian College of Physicians   (ADA)
RACQ .... Radiological Advisory Council of Queensland [*Australia*]
RACR .... Royal Australasian College of Radiologists   (ADA)
RACS .... Royal Australasian College of Surgeons   (ADA)
RACS .... Royal Australian Corps of Signals   (DMA)
RACSA .... Royal Aero Club of South Australia
RACT........ Royal Australian Corps of Transport   (ADA)
RAC(WA) ... Royal Aero Club [*Western Australia*]
RAD........... Artillery Reconnaissance Battalion   (RU)
RAD........... Parti Radical [*Radical Party*] [*France*] [*Political party*]   (EAIO)
rad .... Radian   (RU)
rad .... Radical [*Radical*] [*Portuguese*]
rad .... Radiert [*Erased*] [*Publishing*] [*German*]
Rad .... Radierung [*Etching*] [*German*]
rad .... Radio [*Radio*] [*Finland*]
Rad .... Radioaktivitaet [*Radioactivity*] [*German*]   (GCA)
rad .... Radioallomas [*Radio Station*]   (HU)
rad .... Radioengineering   (BU)
rad .... Radiograma [*Radiotelegram*] [*Portuguese*]
Rad .... Radiola [*Record label*] [*Australia*]
rad .... Radio Plant [*Topography*]   (RU)
Rad .... Radyo [*Radio*]   (TU)
RAD........... Respect voor Arbeid en Democratie [*Belgium*] [*Political party*]   (EY)
RAD........... Royal Academy of Dancing [*British*]   (EAIO)
RADAM .... Radar da Amazonia [*Amazon Radar*] [*Aerial survey project*] [*Brazil*]   (LA)
RADAM .... RADAR of the Amazon [*Aerial survey project in Brazil*]

RADAR ..... Rassemblement des Democrates pour l'Avenir de la Reunion [*Rally of Democrats for the Future of Reunion*] [*Political party*] (PPW)

RADAUS... Radio-Austria AG

radb .... Radio Battalion (BU)

RADC .... Rome Air Development Center (ADPT)

radd .... Radio Battalion (RU)

RADDOL .. Raddolcendo [*Gradually Softer*] [*Music*]

RADECO .. Rassemblement des Democrats du Congo

RADELKISZ ... Radioaktiv es Elektronikus Merokeszulekeket Kivitelezo Kisipari Termeloszovetkezet [*Artisan Cooperative of Measuring Instruments for Radioactivity and Electronics*] (HU)

RADEM .... Regie Autonome de Distribution d'Eau et d'Electricite Meknes

RADEO ..... Rassemblement Democratique Congolais

RADER...... Rassemblement Democratique du Ruanda [*Democratic Rally of Rwanda*]

Radg .... Radierung [*Etching*] [*German*]

RADGAC .. Research and Development Grants Advisory Committee [*Australia*]

rad gen .... Radiation Genetics (RU)

Radi .... Radium [*Record label*] [*France*]

RADIAL.... Racoes, Distribuicao, e Assistencia Ltd. [*Brazil*] (DSCA)

Radierg ...... Radierung [*Etching*] [*German*]

RADIOBRAS ... Empresa Brasileira de Radiodifusao [*Brazilian Radiobroadcasting Company*] (LA)

Radiometeotsentr ... Radio-Meteorological Center (RU)

Radioprom ... Radio Industry (RU)

radiost .... Radio Station (RU)

Radiostroy ... Construction of Radio Stations (BU)

Radiostroy ... Trust of the Ministry of Communications, USSR (RU)

RADLL...... Royal Academy of Dutch Language and Literature [*Belgium*] (EAIO)

radn .... Reconnaissance Artillery Battalion (BU)

RADO........ Regional Agriculture Development Officer

radp .... Radio Regiment (BU)

RADP .... Republique Algerienne Democratique et Populaire [*Democratic and People's Republic of Algeria*] (AF)

RADPCO... Regional ADP [*Automatic Data Processing*] Contact Officer [*Australia*]

radr .... Radio Company (RU)

RADSA...... Recreation Association for the Disabled, South Australia

rad st .... Radio Station [*Topography*] (RU)

RadT .... Radiola-Telefunken [*Record label*] [*Australia*]

RAD-UDRT ... Respect voor Arbeid en Democratie/Union Democratique pour le Respect du Travail [*Respect for Labor and Democracy/Democratic Union for the Respect of Labor*] [*Belgium*] [*Political party*] (PPE)

RADWA .... Recreation Association for the Disabled of Western Australia

radz .... Radziecki [*Former USSR*] [*Poland*]

RAE .... Air Reconnaissance Squadron (RU)

RAE .... Arar [*Saudi Arabia*] [*Airport symbol*] (OAG)

RAE .... Radiodifusion Argentina al Exterior [*Broadcasting organization*] [*Argentina*]

RAe .... Rechtsanwalte [*Attorneys at Law*] [*German*]

RAE .... Republique Arabe d'Egypte

RAE .... Reunion Anual Especial (del CIES) [*Consejo Interamericano Economico y Social*] (LAA)

RAE .... Royal Australian Engineers (ADA)

RaEl .... Radium Element [*Radium Element*] [*German*]

RAEME..... Royal Australian Electrical and Mechanical Engineers (ADA)

RAeS........ Royal Aeronautical Society [*British*] (EAIO)

raeuml .... Raeumlich [*Spatial*] [*German*] (GCA)

RAF .... Radiofelderites [*Radio Reconnaissance*] (HU)

Raf .... Rafineri [*Refinery*] (TU)

RAF .... Real Academia de Farmacia [*Royal Academy of Pharmacy*] [*Spain*] (EAIO)

raf.............. Reconnaissance Aviation Squadron (BU)

RAF .... Reunion des Amateurs de Fox Terriers [*France*] (EAIO)

RAF .... Rhodesian Air Force (AF)

RAF .... Rote Armee Faktion [*Red Army Faction (Baader-Meinhof Group)*] [*Terrorist group*] [*Germany*]

RAF .... Royal Aircraft Factory [*World War I*] [*British*]

Rafa........... Refua at pi Halacha [*Medicine According to Jewish Law*] [*Israel*]

RAFA........ Royal Air Forces Association (EAIO)

RAFA........ Royal Australian Field Artillery (ADA)

RAFAMET ... Raciborska Fabryka Obrabiarek [*Raciborz Machine Tool Plant*] (POL)

RAFCOR... Rural Adjustment and Finance Corp. of Western Australia

RAFCWA.. Rural Adjustment and Finance Corp. of Western Australia [*Computer science*]

RAFE .... Regional Office for Asia and Far East [*FAO*] (ASF)

RAFECO... Rassemblement Federal Congolais

raff............. Raffigurante [*Showing*] [*Publishing*] [*Italian*]

Raff .... Raffination [*Refining*] [*German*] (GCA)

raff............. Raffiniert [*Refined*] [*German*]

Raffinat...... Raffination [*Refining*] [*German*] (GCA)

RAFI......... Political Party [*Israel*] (ME)

Rafie.......... Raffinerie [*Refinery*] [*Military map abbreviation World War I*] [*French*] (MTD)

RAFILM ... Radio- es Filmmechanikai Szolgalat [*Radio and Motion Picture Repair Service*] (HU)

RAFO .... Resident Air Force Officer [*Australia*]

RAFP......... Ryukyuan Armed Forces Police

RAFR........ Regional Office for Africa [*FAO*] (ASF)

RAFRC..... Revolutionary Armed Forces of the Republic of Cuba

RAFS........ Remote Area Families Service [*Uniting Church*] [*Australia*]

RAFT........ Campaign to Reunite in Australia the Families of Timor

RAFT........ Reunion des Amateurs de Fox Terriers [*An association*] (EAIO)

RAG........... Deep-Water Radiometer (RU)

RAG........... New South Wales Records Administration Group [*Australia*]

Rag .... Ragione [*Business Establishment*] [*Italian*] (CED)

Rag .... Ragioniere [*Accountant*] [*Italian*]

RAG.......... Rainforest Action Group [*Australia*]

RAG.......... Reconnaissance Air Group [*British*] (RU)

RAG.......... Referees Association of Ghana

RAG.......... Resident Action Group [*Australia*]

RAG.......... Rohoel-Aufsuchungs GmbH [*Austria*]

RAGA .... Royal Australian Garrison Artillery (ADA)

RAGAI...... Research Association of the German Apparel Industry (EAIO)

Ragaz .... Mixed Russian-American Compressed Gas Joint-Stock Company (RU)

RAGC .... Royal Adelaide Golf Club [*Australia*]

RAGE .... Read and Get Enjoyment Program [*Australia*]

RAGK .... High Command Artillery Reserve (RU)

RAH .... Rafha [*Saudi Arabia*] [*Airport symbol*] (OAG)

RAH........... Recuperation Assistee des Hydrocarbures [*Enhanced Oil Recovery*] [*French*]

RAHLO ..... Regional Aboriginal Health Liaison Officer [*Australia*]

RAHO ...... Royal Albert Hall Orchestra

RAHS .... Royal Australian Historical Society (ADA)

rahv .... Rahvaanomaista Kielta [*Vulgar*] [*Finland*]

RAI .... Baterai [*Battery (Artillery)*] (IN)

RAI .... Praia [*Cape Verde Islands*] [*Airport symbol*] (OAG)

RAI .... Radioactive Isotope (RU)

RAI .... Radiotelevisione Italiana [*Italian Radio and Television*] [*Rome*] [*Research center*] (ERC)

RAI .... Rassemblement Arabique-Islamique [*Algeria*] [*Political party*] (EY)

RAI .... Rede de Accao Interna [*Internal Action Net*] [*See MDLP*] [*Portuguese*] (WER)

RAI .... Registro Aeronautico Italiano [*Air Registration Board*] [*Italy*] (PDAA)

RAI .... Rijwiel- en Automobiel-Industrie [*Bicycle and Automobile Manufacturers' Organization*] [*Netherlands*] (WEN)

RAI .... Royal Air Inter [*Morocco*] (IMH)

RAI .... Royal Air Inter-Compagnie d'Exploitation de Lignes Aer Interieures [*Morocco*] [*ICAO designator*] (FAAC)

RAI .... Royal Australian Infantry (ADA)

RAIA .... Royal Australian Institute of Architects (ADA)

RAIC......... Red Andina de Informacion Comercial [*Andean Trade Information Network*] (EAIO)

RAIC......... Royal Australian Infantry Corps (DMA)

RAID .... Regie Autonome Intercommunale de Distribution d'Eau et d'Electricite [*Autonomous Intercommunal Administration for the Distribution of Water and Electricity*] [*Morocco*] (AF)

RAID .... Research, Assistance, Intervention, Dissuasion [*French antiterrorist police unit*]

RAID .... Residents against Industrial Development [*Australia*]

RAIDEX.... Antisurface Raiders Exercise [*NATO*] (NATG)

RAIMK...... Russian Academy of the History of Material Culture (RU)

RAIN .... Relatives Against the Intake of Narcotics [*Australia*]

RAIN .... Reversing Acidification in Norway

RAInf........ Royal Australian Infantry Corps

RAINS....... Regional Acidification Information and Simulation [*International Institute for Applied Systems Analysis*]

RAIP......... Rewe Abrechnungs-und Informationsprogramm [*German*] (ADPT)

RAIPA ...... Royal Australian Institute of Public Administration

RAIPLY..... Rai Plywood (Kenya) Ltd.

RAIPR....... Royal Australian Institute of Parks and Recreation (ADA)

RAIST .... Reseau Africain d'Institutions Scientifiques et Technologiques [*African Network of Scientific and Technological Institutions*] (EAIO)

RAI-TV...... Radio Audizioni Italiana-Televisione [*Italian Radio Broadcasting and Television Company*]

RAIZ.......... Russian-American Tool Plant (RU)

RAJ............ Raji Airlines [*Pakistan*] [*ICAO designator*] (FAAC)

RAJ............ Rajkot [*India*] [*Airport symbol*] (OAG)

rajz .... Rajzolta [*Drawn By*] (HU)

RAK .... Marrakech [*Morocco*] [*Airport symbol*] (OAG)

rak............. Observation Air Wing (BU)
rak............. Raken*taminen [*or Rakennustyot*] [*Building*] [*Finland*]
Rak............ Rakete [*Rocket*] [*German*] (GCA)
RAK.......... Rayon Administrative Commission (RU)
RAK.......... Regeln fuer die Alphabetische Katalogisierung [*Rules for Alphabetical Cataloging*] [*Information retrieval*]
RAK........ Rikets Allmanna Kartverk [*Geographical Survey Office*] [*Sweden*] (PDAA)
RAKAH..... New Communist List [*Israel*] (ME)
RAKhN..... Russian Academy of Art Sciences (RU)
rakp........... Rakpart [*Embankment*] (HU)
Ral............. Rallentando [*Gradually Slower*] [*Music*]
RAL.......... Republique Arabe Libyenne
RAL.......... Rotary Transfer Machine (RU)
RAL.......... Rutherford and Appleton Laboratory [*Observatory*] [*British*]
RALA........ Rannsoknastofnun Landbunadarins [*Agricultural Research Institute*] [*Icelandic*] [*Research center*] (IRC)
RALAC...... Refuse and Litter Advisory Committee [*Australia*]
RALAC...... Rehabilitation Artificial Limb, and Appliance Centre [*Australia*]
RALAC...... Repatriation Artificial Limb and Appliance Centre [*Australia*]
RALBEO... Regional Literacy and Basic Education Officer [*Australia*]
RALE........ Railway Association of Locomotive Enginemen
RALI......... Regimento de Artilharia Ligeira [*Light Artillery Regiment*] [*Portuguese*]
RALIE....... Rassemblement des Amateurs de Levriers d'Irlande et d'Ecosse [*France*] (EAIO)
RALIS....... Regimento de Artilharia de Lisboa [*Artillery Regiment of Lisbon*] [*Portuguese*] (WER)
RALMC..... Remote Aboriginal Language Management Committee [*Australia*]
RALSC ...... Rhodesian African Labor Supply Commission
RAM......... Ramenskoye [*US prefix for Soviet-Russian developmental aircraft flown at the Ramenskoye test facility*] (DOMA)
RAM......... Ramingining [*Australia*] [*Airport symbol*] (OAG)
RAM......... Reform the Armed Forces Movement [*Philippines*]
RAM......... Remote Area Media [*Australia*]
RAM......... Riverina and Murray Neighbourhood Centres Group [*Australia*]
RAM......... Royal Air Maroc [*Morocco*]
RAM......... Royal Air Maroc - Compagnie Nationale de Transports Aeriens [*Morocco*] [*ICAO designator*] (FAAC)
RAM......... Royal Australian Mint
RAM......... Rural and Agricultural Management Ltd. [*Australia*]
RAM......... "Russian Aircraft Engine" - Aircraft Engine Designed by A. D. Shvetsov [*1923*] (RU)
RAM......... Societe de Representation Automobile et Materiaux
RAMBO .... Remove Aquino from Malacanang before October [*Operation proposed by rebel military leader "Gringo" Honasan*] [*1987 Philippines*]
RAMO....... Rafinerie Mineralnich Oleju [*Mineral Oil Refinery*] (CZ)
RAMS........ Registered Australian Mortgage Securities Trust
RAMS........ Rights for All Male Sex Workers [*Australia*]
RAMS........ Rural Assessment/Manpower Study
RAMSA..... Radioaeronautica Mexicana, Sociedad Anonima [*Mexican Aeronautical Radio, Incorporated*] (LA)
RAN........... Power System Active Load Distributor (RU)
RAN........... Railway Abidjan-Niger
RAN........... Regie des Chemins de Fer Abidjan-Niger [*Abidjan-Niger Railway Administration*] (AF)
RAN........... Reseau Abidjan-Niger
RAN........... Resistencia Armada Nacionalista [*Nationalist Armed Resistance*] [*Brazil*] (LA)
RAN........... Royal Australian Navy (VNW)
RAN........... Russian Academy of Sciences [*1724-1925*] (RU)
RANA........ Rassemblement National Congolais
RANA........ Rhodesia & Nyasaland Airways
RANAS...... Royal Australian Naval Air Squadron (ADA)
RANATE... Royal Australian Naval Training Establishment (ADA)
RANBT..... Royal Australian Naval Bridging Train
RANC........ Royal Australian Naval College (ADA)
randbemerk ... Randbemerkning [*Margin Note*] [*Publishing Danish/Norwegian*]
R & I.......... Rural and Industries Bank of Western Australia (ADA)
R &IBWA .. Rural and Industries Bank of Western Australia
R & S......... Raben & Sjogren [*Publisher*] [*Sweden*]
RAN(E)...... Royal Australian Navy (Emergency)
RANEL..... Royal Australian Navy Experimental Laboratory (MCD)
RANF .... Royal Australian Nursing Federation (ADA)
RANFAN .. Rassemblement National des Francais Rapatries d'Afrique du Nord et d'Outre-Mer
RANFR...... Royal Australian Naval Fleet Reserve (DMA)
RangKoM .. [*The*] Rangkaian Komputer Malaysia [*Computer science*] (TNIG)
RANIION ... Russian Association of Scientific Research Institutes of Social Sciences [*1923-1930*] (RU)
RANION ... Russian Association of Scientific Research Institutes of Social Sciences [*1923-1930*] (RU)

ranis .... Science and Art Workers (RU)
RANMME ... Royal Australian Navy Missile Maintenance Establishment (ADA)
RANNS ..... Royal Australian Naval Nursing Service (DMA)
RANNS ..... Royal Australian Navy Nursing Service (ADA)
RANR .... Royal Australian Naval Reserve (ADA)
RANRL..... Royal Australian Navy Research Laboratory (ADA)
RANR(S)... Royal Australian Naval Reserve (Seagoing)
RANSA...... Royal Australian Navy Sailing Association
RANSA...... Rutas Aereas Nacionales Sociedad Anonima [*Cargo airline*] [*Venezuela*]
ransk .... Ranskaa [*or Ranskaksi*] [*Finland*]
ransk .... Ranskan Kielta [*or Ranskalainen*] [*French*] [*Finland*]
RANSW ... Ratepayers' Association of New South Wales [*Australia*]
RANSW ... Rationalist Association of New South Wales [*Australia*]
RANTAU .. Royal Australian Navy Trials and Assessing Unit
RANTE...... Royal Australian Navy Training Establishment
RANTME ... Royal Australian Navy Torpedo Maintenance Establishment
RAN(V)R... Royal Australian Naval (Volunteer) Reserve
RANVR(S) ... Royal Australian Naval Volunteer Reserve (Seagoing)
RANZCP... Royal Australian and New Zealand College of Psychiatrists (ADA)
rao .... Airfield Maintenance Company (RU)
RAO.......... Ribeirao Preto [*Brazil*] [*Airport symbol*] (OAG)
RAO.......... Russian Archaeological Society (RU)
RAOU........ Royal Australasian Ornithologists' Union (ADA)
RAP .... Air Reconnaissance Regiment (RU)
rap .... Artillery Reconnaissance Regiment (RU)
RAP .... Automatic Start Relay (RU)
RAP .... Radical Action for People
RAP .... Rapid Air [*France*] [*ICAO designator*] (FAAC)
rap .... Rapport [*French*] (FLAF)
RAP .... Rational Alternative to Pseudosciences [*Spain*] (EAIO)
RAP .... Rechner-Anpassungs-Prozessor [*German*] (ADPT)
RAP .... Recommended Area for Protection [*Australia*]
RAP .... Recycle Australia Project
RAP .... Regie Autonome des Petroles
RAP .... Regie des Agglomeres du Pays [*Saharan*]
RAP .... Regiment d'Artillerie Parachutiste [*Algeria*]
RAP .... Reglement Autovervoer Personen [*Benelux*] (BAS)
RAP .... Reglement d'Administration Publique [*North African*]
RAP .... Republik Arab Persatuan [*United Arab Republic*] (IN)
RAP .... Rezervni Delovi, Alata, i Pribora [*Spare Parts, Equipment, and Tools*] [*Military*] (YU)
RAP .... Rhodesian Action Party (AF)
RAP .... Robotnicza Agencja Prasowa [*Worker's Press Agency*] (POL)
RAP .... Royal Academy of Pharmacy [*Spain*] (EAIO)
RAP .... Rupees, Annas, Pies [*Monetary units*] [*India*]
RAP .... Rural Access Program [*Australia*]
RAPA........ Ramassage ou Paddy [*Paddy Harvesting*] [*Cambodia*] (CL)
RAPA........ Regional Office for Asia and the Pacific (ASF)
RAPAD..... Research Association for Petroleum Alternatives Development [*Japan*]
RAPAM..... Red de Accion sobre Plaguicidas y Alternativas en Mexico [*Member of the Pesticide Action Network*] (CROSS)
RAPC........ Regie d'Acconage du Port de Casablanca
Rap CS....... Rapport du Conseil de Securite [*L'Assemblee Generale des Nations Unies*] (FLAF)
RAPECA ... Rassemblement du Peuple Camerounais [*Camerounese People's Rally*]
RAPELU ... Rassemblement des Peuples Luba
RAPI......... Royal Australian Planning Institute (ADA)
RAPID....... Research and Professional Information Development [*University of New South Wales Libraries*] [*Australia*]
RAPIR ...... Radiation Pyrometer (RU)
RAPKh ..... Russian Association of Proletarian Artists [*1931-1932*] (RU)
RAPM .... Russian Association of Proletarian Musicians [*1923-1930*] (RU)
RAPO .... Russian Pharmaceutical Association (RU)
RAPP........ Rajasthan Atomic Power Project [*Atomic Energy Commission*] [*India*] (PDAA)
Rapp........... Rapporteur [*French*] (FLAF)
RAPP........ Russian Association of Proletarian Writers [*1923-1932*] (RU)
Rappr......... Rapprochez [*French*] (FLAF)
RAPRA...... RAPRA Technology [*Formerly, Rubber and Plastics Research Association*] (EA)
RAPS........ Rajasthan Atomic Power Station [*India*] (PDAA)
RAPS........ Recreation and Peer Support Group [*Australia*]
RAPSI ...... Remote Area Power Supply Investigation Branch [*Australia*]
RAQ........... Raha [*Indonesia*] [*Airport symbol*] (OAG)
RAQ........... Reglements sur l'Assurance de la Qualite [*Quality Assurance Regulation*] [*French*]
RAR........... Aviaross [*Russian Federation*] [*ICAO designator*] (FAAC)
RAR........... Rarotonga [*Cook Islands*] [*Airport symbol*] (OAG)
RAR........... Rhodesian African Rifles [*Military unit*]
RAR........... Royal Australian Regiment (VNW)

RARA .... Revolutionary Anti-Racism Action [*South Africa*] [*An association*]
R Arb .... Recht der Arbeit [*Right to Work*] [*German*] (DLA)
RARC .... Ruakura Agricultural Research Centre [*New Zealand*] (DSCA)
RARE........ Associated Networks for European Research [*EC*] (ECED)
RARE........ Reseaux Associes pour la Recherche Europeene [*Associated Networks for European Research*]
RARK .... Automatic Radiometer for Radioactive Logging (RU)
RARK .... Sectional Equipment for Radioactive Logging (RU)
RARU .... Rural Access Road Unit
RARZ .... Rayon Automobile Repair Plant (RU)
RARZ .... Riga Automobile Repair Plant (RU)
RAS........... Purified Alkyl Aryl Sulfonate (RU)
RAS........... Rasht [*Iran*] [*Airport symbol*] (OAG)
ras .... Rasurae [*Scrapings or Filings*] [*Latin*] (MAE)
RAS........... Reading Association Sydney [*Australia*]
RAS........... Relay-Controlled Automatic System (RU)
RAS........... Rien A Signaler [*Nothing to Singal*] [*French*] (ADPT)
RAS........... Rijks Archief School
RAS........... Riunione Adriatica di Sicurta SpA [*Insurance company*] [*Italian*]
RAS........... Rockhampton Aerial Services [*Australia*]
RAS........... Royal Academy of Science [*London*]
RAS........... Royal Adelaide Show [*Australia*]
RAS........... [*The*] Royal African Society (SLS)
RAS........... Royal Antiquarian Society [*Netherlands*] (EAIO)
RAS........... Rubber Association of Singapore
RAS........... Rural Adjustment Scheme [*Australia*]
RASA........ Refractarios Argentinos, SA [*Argentina*]
RASC........ Royal Agricultural Society of the Commonwealth
RASC........ Royal Australian Survey Corps (ADA)
RASCO...... Ras Lanuf Oil & Gas Processing Company [*Libya*]
RASCOM ... Regional African Satellite Communications System (ECON)
RASCOM ... Regional African Satellite Communication System for the Development of Africa [*ITU*] [*United Nations*] (DUND)
RASD........ Republique Arabe Sahraoui Democratique [*Saharan Democratic Arab Republic*] [*Use SDAR*] (AF)
RASD........ Royal Agricultural Society of Denmark (EAIO)
RASDS...... Regional Advisory Service in Demographic Statistics [*United Nations*] (EY)
RASE........ Royal Agricultural Society of England (SLS)
RASG........ Reunion des Amateurs de Setters Gordon [*France*] (EAIO)
RASigs....... Royal Australian Corps of Signals
RASILA..... Rannikko- ja Sisaevesiliikenteen Tvoenantajaliitto [*Employers' Federation of Coastal and Inland Waterways Transportation*] [*Finland*] (EY)
RASIOM... Raffinerie Siciliane Olii Minerali [*Italy*] (PDAA)
RASIT .... Radar de Surveillance au Sol
RASK........ Royal Agricultural Society of Kenya
RASNSW .. Royal Art Society of New South Wales [*Australia*]
RASNZ...... Royal Astronomical Society of New Zealand (SLS)
RASO .... Russian-British Raw Materials Company (RU)
rasp .... Disintegration, Decay [*Nuclear physics and engineering*] (RU)
rasp/min .... Disintegrations per Minute (RU)
raspredpunkt ... Distribution Center (RU)
rasp/sek ..... Disintegrations per Second (RU)
RASS .... Remote Area Services Subsidy Scheme [*Australia*]
rassh.......... Expanded (RU)
RASSL....... Royal Asiatic Society of Sri Lanka (EAIO)
RAST .... Analytical Computer Station (BU)
rast .... Plant [*Botany*] (BU)
rast .... Vegetation (RU)
rastsenkom ... Wage Commission (RU)
rastv .... Solubility (RU)
RASU .... Rangoon Arts and Science University [*Rangoon University*] [*Myanmar*] [*Later,*] (DS)
RASV........ Royal Agricultural Society of Victoria [*Australia*]
RASvy....... Royal Australian Survey Corps
RAT .... Institut de Recherches Agronomiques Tropicales et des Cultures Vivrieres [*Institute of Tropical Agronimic Research and Food Crops*] [*Togo*]
RAT .... Rad Anafalbetskih Tecajeva [*Program of Courses for Illiterates*] [*Military*] (YU)
RAT·.......... Radio Autotransformer (RU)
RAT .... Ratioflug Luftfahrtunternehmen GmbH [*Germany*] [*ICAO designator*] (FAAC)
RAT .... Raynaud's Association Trust (EA)
RAT .... Red Andina de Telecomunicaciones [*Andean Telecommunications Network*] (LA)
RAT .... Reichsangestellten-Tarifertrag [*Federal Employee's Tariff Revenue*] [*German*]
RAT .... Relay Autotransformer (RU)
RAT .... Reseau des Amis de la Terre [*Network of Friends of the Earth*] [*France*] [*Political party*] (PPE)
RAT .... Resistance Armee Tunisienne [*Tunisian Armed Resistance*] (PD)

RATAA...... Regione Autonoma Trentino Alto Adige [*Autonomous Region of Trentino South Tyrol*] [*Italian*] (WER)
RATAC...... Radar de Tir de l'Artillerie de Campagne
RATAO ..... Russian-Austrian Joint-Stock Trade Company (RU)
RATAU ..... Ukrainian News Agency (RU)
RATC........ Regie Autonome des Transports de la Ville de Casablanca [*North African*]
RATDA ..... Regional African Telecommunication Database [*International Telecommunication Union*] (DUND)
RATE........ Remote Area Teacher Education [*Australia*]
RATECO... Radio Tecnica Colombiana [*Colombia*] (COL)
RATEKSA ... Radiobranchens Tekniske og Kommercielle Sammenslutning [*Radio and Television Retailers Association*] [*Denmark*] (PDAA)
RATEP...... Remote Area Teacher Education Program [*Australia*]
rato .... Airfield Technical Support Company (RU)
RATO .... Russian-Austrian Joint-Stock Trade Company (RU)
RATP........ Regie Autonome des Transports Parisiens [*Paris Transport Authority*]
RATPP ...... Regie Autonome des Transports Publics Parisiens [*France*] (FLAF)
rats .... Rationalization, Efficiency-Expert (RU)
rats .... Rationalizer, Rationalization (BU)
Rats........... Ratsionalizatsiya [*Rationalization*] [*A periodical*] (BU)
RATS........ Rayon Automatic Telephone Exchange (RU)
RATS........ Remote Area Television Service [*Australia*]
Ratsbyuro... Rationalizations Bureau (BU)
ratsemich ... Racemic (RU)
ratsiya .... Radio Station [*Topography*] (RU)
Ratspredlozh ... Rationalization Suggestion (RU)
RATU .... Rated Atmospheric Temperature Conditions (RU)
RATV........ Remote Area Television Service [*Australia*]
RATZ........ Rustavi Nitrogen Fertilizer Plant (RU)
Rau............ Radeau [*Raft*] [*Military map abbreviation World War I*] [*French*] (MTD)
RAU.......... Railway African Union [*Uganda*] (AF)
RAU.......... Randse Afrikaanse Universiteit [*Rand Afrikaans University*] [*South Africa*]
RAU.......... Republica Arabe Unida [*United Arab Republic*] [*Spanish*]
RAU.......... Republique Arabe Unie [*United Arab Republic*] [*French*]
Rau............ Ruisseau [*Stream*] [*French*] (NAU)
rauch .... Rauchend [*Fuming*] [*German*] (GCA)
RAUK........ Reservialiupseerikoulu [*Finland*]
raut............ Rautatiet [*Railways*] [*Finland*]
RAV .... Cravo Norte [*Colombia*] [*Airport symbol*] (OAG)
RAV .... Rahmen-Absatzvertrag [*Basic Sales Contract*] (EG)
Rav .... Ravin [*Ravine*] [*Military map abbreviation World War I*] [*French*] (MTD)
RAVA .... Returned Australian Volunteers Abroad
RAVE .... Registro de Aspirantes a Viviendas de Emergencia [*Registry of Emergency Housing Candidates*] [*Uruguay*] (LA)
RAVEL...... Posta Radioveteltechnikai es Elektroakusztikai Uzeme [*Post Office Branch for Radio Reception and Acoustics*] (HU)
RAVISZ..... Radio es Villamossagi Szolgalat Kisipari Termeloszovetkezet [*Artisan Cooperative for Radio and Electric Service Enterprise*] (HU)
ravp .... Air Reconnaissance Regiment (RU)
Ravt........... Ravitaillement [*Revictualing*] [*Military*] [*French*] (MTD)
rav-vo .... Equality, Equation (RU)
RAW .... Arawa [*Papua New Guinea*] [*Airport symbol*] (OAG)
RAW .... Rationalisatie en Automatisering Wegenbouw [*Ede*]
RAW .... Regional Air (Pty) Ltd. [*South Africa*] [*ICAO designator*] (FAAC)
RAW .... Reichsbahnausbesserungswerk [*GDR Railroad Repair Yard*] (EG)
RAW .... Research and Analysis Wing [*Indian intelligence agency*] [*Sri Lanka*]
RAWA .... Revolutionary Association of the Women of Afghanistan
RAWB ...... Raad van Advies voor het Wetenschapsbeleid [*'s-Gravenhage*]
RAWU ...... Railway African Mineworkers Trade Union [*Southern Rhodesia*]
RAWU ...... Railway Associated Workers Union [*Rhodesian*] (AF)
RAWU ...... Railway Workers' Union of Malawi (EAIO)
Ray............ Rayon [*German*]
ray .... Rayon, City District (RU)
raydorkhoz ... Rayon Highway Department (RU)
rayfo.......... Rayon Finance Department (RU)
raygosstrakh ... Rayon State Insurance Inspection (RU)
rayGUMTO ... Rayon Office of the Main Administration of Materials and Equipment Supply (RU)
Raykom...... Rayon Committee (BU)
Raykoman ... Rayon Commandant's Office (BU)
Raykomisiya ... Rayon Commission (BU)
Raykomitet ... Rayon Committee (BU)
raykomkhoz ... City District Department of Municipal Services (RU)
raykommunkhoz ... City District Department of Municipal Services (RU)
raykomol.... Rayon Committee of the Young Communist League (RU)

raykompart ... Rayon Party Committee   (RU)
RAYKOMVOD ... Rayon Committee of the Water Transportation Workers' Trade Union   (RU)
Raykoop..... Rayon Cooperative Union   (BU)
raykprofsozh ... Rayon Committee of the Railroad Workers' Trade Union (RU)
raykul'tvod ... Rayon Committee for the Cultural Education of Water Transportation Workers   (RU)
raykurupr... Rayon Administration of Health Resorts   (RU)
rayles........ Rayon Forest Commission   (RU)
rayleskhoz ... Rayon Lumber Industry Establishment   (RU)
rayleskom .. Rayon Forest Commission   (RU)
raymag........ Rayon Store, City District Store   (RU)
raynarobraz ... Rayon Department of Public Education   (RU)
raynezhilotdel ... Rayon Department of Nonresidential Buildings   (RU)
rayONO..... Rayon Department of Public Education   (RU)
rayplan....... Rayon Planning Commission   (RU)
raypo.......... Rayon Consumers' Society   (RU)
raypotrebsoyuz ... Rayon Union of Consumers' Societies   (RU)
rayprofsovet ... Rayon Trade Union Council   (RU)
rayprofsozh ... Rayon Committee of the Railroad Transportation Workers' Trade Union   (RU)
raypromtrest ... Rayon Industry Trust   (RU)
raypur......... Rayon Administration   (RU)
raySES...... Rayon Sanitary and Epidemiological Station   (RU)
raysobes..... Rayon Department of Social Security   (RU)
raysovkhoz ... Rayon Sovkhoz Department   (RU)
Raysuvet .... Rayon Council   (RU)
raytekhsnab ... Rayon Office of Materials and Equipment Supply   (RU)
raytop......... Rayon Department of the Local Fuel Industry   (RU)
raytorgotdel ... Rayon Trade Department   (RU)
rayupolminzag ... Rayon Representative of the Ministry of Procurement   (RU)
Rayvetlechebnitsa ... Rayon Veterinary Hospital   (RU)
rayvodkhoz ... Rayon Water Management Department   (RU)
rayVTEK ... Rayon Medical Commission for Determination of Disability (RU)
rayzag........ Rayon Procurement Office   (RU)
rayzags....... Rayon Civil Registry Office   (RU)
Rayzankoop ... Rayon Artisans' Cooperative   (BU)
rayzdrav..... Rayon Department of Public Health   (RU)
rayzhilkommunotdel ... Rayon Communal Housing Department   (RU)
rayzhilupr .. Rayon Housing Administration   (RU)
Rayzo .... Rayon Land Department   (RU)
rayzu .... Rayon Land Administration   (RU)
raz .... Different [*or Various*]   (BU)
RAZ .... Referees Association of Zambia
RAZ .... Remise A Zero [*French*]   (ADPT)
RAZ .... Retour A Zero [*Return to Zero*] [*French*]   (ADPT)
RAZ .... Revolutionaere Aufbauorganisation Zurich [*Zurich Revolutionary Organizing Committee*] [*Switzerland*] (WEN)
RAZ .... Rijnmond Air Services BV [*Netherlands*] [*ICAO designator*] (FAAC)
raz .... Ruins [*Topography*]   (RU)
raz .... Siding Track [*Topography*]   (RU)
razb .... Diluted, Thinned   (RU)
RAZB........ Reconnaissance Battery   (RU)
razbat .... Reconnaissance Battalion   (BU)
Razch s/ka pri BNB ... Checking Account at the Bulgarian National Bank (BU)
razd .... Section, Chapter   (RU)
raz der .... Destroyed Village   (RU)
razd pag...... Broken Pagination   (BU)
razd pag...... Separate Pagination   (RU)
razg .... Colloquial   (BU)
razg .... Colloquial Word   (RU)
RAZh .... Radioactive Liquid Analyzer   (RU)
RAZhA ...... Regional'naia Assotsiatsiia Zhitelei Angoly
razm .... Dimensions, Proportions, Measures   (BU)
Raznoeksport ... All-Union Association for the Export of Miscellaneous Goods (RU)
Raznoimport ... All-Union Association for the Import of Miscellaneous Goods (RU)
Raznoiznos ... State Commercial Enterprise for Export and Import   (BU)
razr............ Class, Category   (RU)
razr............ Destroyed, Demolished [*Topography*]   (RU)
razrabot...... Development, Elaboration [*Bibliography*]   (RU)
razresh .... Authorized, Permitted   (RU)
razsh.......... Expanded [*Edition*]   (BU)
razv............ Ruins [*Topography*]   (RU)
razv d......... Village Ruins [*Topography*]   (RU)
razv kh ...... Farmstead Ruins [*Topography*]   (RU)
razv pos...... Settlement Ruins [*Topography*]   (RU)
razv ukr...... Fortification Ruins [*Topography*]   (RU)
raz zam....... Castle Ruins [*Topography*]   (RU)
Rb.............. Battalion Radio Station   (RU)

RB .... Biovular Twins   (RU)
Rb.............. Blocking Relay   (RU)
RB .... Bombing Manual   (RU)
rb.............. Diluted, Thinned   (RU)
Rb.............. Fishing Boat   (RU)
RB .... Hand Ram   (RU)
RB .... Labor Battalion   (RU)
rb.............. Missile Base   (BU)
RB .... Racunovodstveni Biro [*Accounting Bureau*]   (YU)
RB .... Rada Bezpecnosti [*Security Council*] [*United Nations*]   (CZ)
RB .... Radio Beograd [*Radio Belgrade*]   (YU)
RB .... Radio Brenner [*Radio network*] [*Germany*]
RB .... Radio Unit [*of a radiosonde*]   (RU)
Rb.............. Rannsoknastofnun Byggingaridnadarins [*Building Research Institute*] [*Iceland*]   (IRC)
RB .... Razvod Braka [*Divorce*]   (YU)
Rb.............. Rechtbank [*Benelux*]   (BAS)
RB .... Rechterlijke Beslissingen Arbeidsovereenkomst [*Benelux*] (BAS)
rb.............. Reconnaissance Battalion   (BU)
RB .... Red Brigades [*Revolutionary group*] [*Italy*]   (YU)
RB .... Redd Barna [*Norwegian Save the Children*]   (EAIO)
RB .... Regtsgeleerd Bijblad [*Benelux*]   (BAS)
RB .... Regular Budget [*United Nations*]
RB .... Regulating Unit   (RU)
Rb.............. Reichsbahn [*GDR Railroad*]   (EG)
Rb.............. Repair Base, Maintenance Base   (RU)
RB .... Republic Library   (RU)
R/b............ Ribarski Brod [*Fishing Boat*]   (YU)
RB .... Riksbibliotekjenesten [*National Agency for Research and Special Libraries and Documentation*] [*Norway*]   (PDAA)
Rb.............. Risicobank [*Benelux*]   (BAS)
RB .... Ritzaus Bureau [*Press agency*] [*Denmark*]
rb.............. Riz Blanc [*Polished Rice*]   (CL)
rb.............. Rok Biezacy [*or Roku Biezacego*] [*This Year*] [*Poland*]
rb.............. Rouble [*Ruble*] [*Monetary unit in the USSR*] [*French*]
RB .... Royal Burgh
rb.............. Rubel [*Ruble*]   (POL)
Rb.............. Rubidio [*Rubidium*] [*Chemical element*] [*Portuguese*]
RB .... Ruble [*Monetary unit*] [*Former USSR*]
RB .... Rucna Bomba [*Hand Grenade*]   (YU)
RB .... Rucni Bacac [*Hand Thrower*]   (YU)
RB .... Rudne Bane [*Mines for Non-Ferrous Metal Ores*]   (CZ)
RB .... Rudnik Bakra [*Copper Mine*] [*Majdanpek*]   (YU)
RB .... Rudnik Barita [*Barite Mine*]   (YU)
RB .... Rudnik Boksita [*Bauxite Mine*]   (YU)
RB .... Ruhazati Bolt [*Clothing Store*]   (HU)
RB .... Territorio do Rio Branco [*Territory of Rio Branco*] [*Portuguese*]
Rb.............. Vonnis van de Arrondissementsrechtbank [*Benelux*]   (BAS)
RBA .... Rabat [*Morocco*] [*Airport symbol*]   (OAG)
RBA .... Rabat Airport
RBA .... Rechterlijke Beslissingen Administratieve Rechtspraak [*Benelux*] (BAS)
RBA .... Rehoboth Baster Association [*Namibia*]   (PPW)
RBA .... Reichsbahnamt [*GDR Railroad Division*]   (EG)
RBA .... Reserve Bank Bulletin [*Database*] [*Australia*]
RBA .... Reserve Bank of Australia   (ADA)
RBA .... Royal Brunei Airlines [*ICAO designator*]   (FAAC)
RBAA .... Religious Booksellers Association of Australia
RBAF .... Royal Belgian Air Force
RBAF........ Royal Brunei Armed Forces
RBAU .... Robert Bosch (Australia) Proprietary Ltd. [*Melbourne, Australia*] [*Research center*]   (ERC)
RBB .... Bijdragen voor Rechtsgeleerdheid en Wetgeving en Bijblad [*Benelux*]   (BAS)
RBB .... Rabbit-Air AG, Zurich [*Switzerland*] [*ICAO designator*]   (FAAC)
RBb .... Rechtsgeleerd Bijblad [*Benelux*]   (BAS)
RBB .... Rental Bond Board [*New South Wales, Australia*]
RBB .... Sondervorschrift fuer die Regelung des Betriebes auf der Elektrischen Berliner S-Bahn [*Special Traffic Regulations for the Berlin Electric S-Bahn*]   (EG)
RbbD......... Reichsbahnbaudirektion [*GDR Railroad Construction Directorate*]   (EG)
Rbbu.......... Reichsbahnbauunion [*GDR Railroad Construction Enterprise*] (EG)
RBC .... Regional Border Committee [*Thai-Malay border*]   (ML)
RBC .... Rhodesia Broadcasting Company   (AF)
RBC .... Rhodesia Broadcasting Corp.
RBC .... Rotterdamsch Beleggingsconsortium, NV [*Rotterdam Investments Consortium*]
RBCO .... Regional Border Committee Office [*Thai-Malay border*]   (ML)
RBD .... Powder-Propelled Rocket Engine   (BU)
RBD .... Reichsbahndirektion [*GDR Railroad Directorate*]   (EG)
RBD .... Short-Range Missile   (RU)
RBDF......... Royal Bahamian Defense Force   (LA)
RBDM .... Registrar of Births Deaths and Marriages [*Australia*]

RBDP......... Rehoboth Bevryde Demokratiese Party [*Rehoboth Free Democratic Party or Liberation Front*] [*Namibia*] [*Political party*]   (EY)

RBDP......... Rehoboth Bevryder Demokratiese Party [*Rehoboth Free Democratic Party*] [*Namibia*]

RBE .... Arbet International Ltd. [*Hungary*] [*ICAO designator*]   (FAAC)

RBEI........... Revenu Brut des Entrepreneurs Individuels

RB en B...... Rechtsgeleerde Bijdragen en Bijblad [*Benelux*]   (BAS)

rbetr.......... Concrete Construction Company   (RU)

rbetr .... Concrete Works Company   (BU)

Rbf............. Rangierbahnhof [*Classification Yard*]   (EG)

RBF............ Recurrent Boolean Function   (RU)

RBF........... Retirement Benefits Fund [*Tasmania, Australia*]

RBFB........ Retirement Benefits Fund Board [*Australia*]

RBFIT....... Retirement Benefits Fund Investment Trust [*Australia*]

RBFM........ Reglement van het Beamtenfonds voor het Mijnbedrijf [*Benelux*]   (BAS)

RBFT .... Romanian Bank of Foreign Trade   (IMH)

RBG .... Reactor-Brennelemente GmbH [*Germany*]   (PDAA)

RBg .... Rechtsreglement Buitengewesten [*Benelux*]   (BAS)

RBG .... Reichsbuergergesetz [*German National Law*] [*1935*] [*Acronym is based on former name,*]   (BJA)

RBGDT..... Royal Botanic Gardens and Domain Trust [*Australia*]

RBGNH..... Royal Botanic Gardens and National Herbarium [*Australia*]

RBGS........ Royal Botanic Gardens Sydney [*Australia*]

RBH........... Regal Bahamas International Airways Ltd. [*ICAO designator*]   (FAAC)

RBH........... Royal Blind Homes [*Australia*]

RBI............. Rabi [*Fiji*] [*Airport symbol*]   (OAG)

RBI............. Radio Berlin International

RBI............. Radiobiologisch Instituut [*Radiobiological Institute*] [*Netherlands Central Organization for Applied Natural Scientific Research*]   (WND)

RBI............. Reserve Bank of India   (ECON)

RBI............. Ruder Boskovic Institut [*Former Yugoslavia*]   (MSC)

RBI............. Rudjer Boskovic Institute [*Croatia*]   (EAIO)

RB II .... Radio Beograd II [*Radio Belgrade, Station 2*]   (YU)

RBJ........... Rebun [*Japan*] [*Airport symbol*] [*Obsolete*]   (OAG)

RBL............ Research Bureau Limited

RBL............ Ruble [*Monetary unit*] [*Former USSR*]

rbl.............. Szovjet Rubel [*Soviet Ruble*]   (HU)

RBLAC...... Regional Bureau for Latin America and the Caribbean [*United Nations*]   (ECON)

RBM .... Richards Bay Minerals

RBMECAB ... Regional Bureau of the Middle East Committee for the Affairs of the Blind [*An association*]   (EAIO)

RBMR .... Royal Brunei Malay Regiment   (DS)

RBMU .... Regions Beyond Missionary Union

RBN .... Radioisotope Blocking Attachment   (RU)

RBNZ .... Reserve Bank of New Zealand

RBO .... Rainbow Cargo Express [*Ghana*] [*ICAO designator*]   (FAAC)

RBO .... Retirement Benefits Office [*Australia*]

RBO .... Russian Botanical Society   (RU)

RBOMU.... Russian Bibliographic Society at the Moscow State University   (RU)

RBP........... Raba Raba [*Papua New Guinea*] [*Airport symbol*]   (OAG)

RBP........... Radar Bombsight   (RU)

RBP........... Raffinerie Belge des Petroles [*Belgium*]   (BAS)

RBPB........ Raffles and Bingo Permits Board [*Victoria, Australia*]

RBPC........ Roads and Bridges Public Corporation [*Sudan*]

RBQ .... Rurrenabaque [*Bolivia*] [*Airport symbol*]   (OAG)

rbr .... Missile Brigade   (BU)

RBR .... Rio Branco [*Brazil*] [*Airport symbol*]   (OAG)

rbrtr........... Armored Carrier Company   (RU)

RBS........... Radiolosko Borbena Sredstva [*Radiological Combat Equipment*]   (YU)

RBSNSW .. Royal Blind Society of New South Wales [*Australia*]

RBT .... Roadstead Diesel Tugboat   (RU)

RBT .... Robinton Aereo CA [*Dominican Republic*] [*ICAO designator*]   (FAAC)

RBtg......... Rechtsreglement Buitengewesten [*Benelux*]   (BAS)

rbtr .... Armored Carrier Company   (RU)

RBU .... Concrete Mortar Unit   (RU)

RBU .... Depth-Charge Rocket Launcher   (RU)

RBU .... Radioisotope Blocking Device   (RU)

RBU .... Reaktor Brennelement Union [*Combustible Element Reactor Union*]

RBU .... Revirni Bansky Urad [*Coal Basin Mining Office*]   (CZ)

RBV .... Radiologiai, Biologiai, es Vegyi Vedelem [*Radiological, Biological, and Chemical Defense*]   (HU)

RBVA .... Rhodesian Bantu Voters' Association

RBvN .... Het Rechtskundig Blad voor het Notaris-Ambt [*Benelux*]   (BAS)

rbvO.......... Rechtbank van Ommegang [*Benelux*]   (BAS)

RBVZ........ Russian-Baltic Railroad-Car Plant   (RU)

RBW .... Rainbow Group [*European political movement*]   (ECON)

RC .... Catholique [*French*] [*FRC*]   (TPFD)

RC .... Centro Studi Russia Cristiana [*Italian*]   (SLS)

RC .... Chiny [*China*] [*Poland*]

RC .... Congregation de Notre Dame de la Retraite au Cenacle [*Congregation of Our Lady of the Retreat in the Cenacle*]   (EAIO)

RC .... Congregation of Our Lady of the Retreat in the Cenacle [*Roman Catholic women's religious order*] [*Italy*]

RC .... Radice Cubica [*Cube Root*] [*Italian*]

RC .... Radio Centar [*Radio Center*] [*Military*]   (YU)

RC .... Radio-Cevi [*Radio Tubes*]   (YU)

RC .... Rassemblement Congolais [*Congolese Rally*] [*Buakvu*]

RC .... Rechter-Commissaris [*Benelux*]   (BAS)

RC .... Red China

RC .... Reggio Calabria [*Car registration plates*] [*Italian*]

RC .... Registrar of Companies

RC .... Registre du Commerce [*French*]

RC .... Reparaturcode [*German*]   (ADPT)

RC .... Responsabilite Civile [*France*]   (FLAF)

RC .... Rest Camp

RC .... Retenues Collinaires

RC .... Revolutionary Council [*Ethiopia*]

RC .... Ribolovni Centar [*Fishing Center*]   (YU)

RC .... Ridici Cviceni [*Exercise Umpires*]   (CZ)

RC .... Riz Cargo [*Brown Rice*] [*Cambodia*]   (CL)

RC .... Roads Corp. [*Victoria, Australia*] [*Commercial firm*]

RC .... Roman Catholic   (TPFD)

RC .... Roman Catholic Church

RC .... Route Coloniale [*Colonial Highway*]   (CL)

RCA .... Reformed Church in Africa

RCA .... Regional Committee for Africa

RCA .... Republique Centrafricaine [*Central African Republic*] [*Use CAR*]   (AF)

RCA .... Residential Care Assistant [*Australia*]

RCA .... Restaurant and Catering Association of New South Wales [*Australia*]

RCA .... Retailers' Council of Australia

RCA .... Revival Centres of Australia

RCA .... Rostrum Clubs of Australia

rca .... Rustica [*Paperbound*] [*Publishing*] [*Spanish*]

RCAA .... Racing Commission Agents' Association [*Australia*]

RCAC .... Regional Civil Aviation Conference   (LAA)

RCADXC... Radio Club Amsterdam Dx Certificate   (IAA)

RCAE........ Riverina College of Advanced Education [*Australia*]   (ADA)

RCAGA ..... Royal Commission on Australian Government Administration   (ADA)

RCANSW .. Registered Clubs Association of New South Wales [*Australia*]

RCANSW ... Restaurant and Caterers' Association of New South Wales [*Australia*]

RCAQ .... Restaurant and Caterers' Association of Queensland [*Australia*]

RCASA...... Royal Commission on Australia's Security and Intelligence Agencies

RCASNSW ... Radio Controlled Aircraft Society of New South Wales [*Australia*]

RCAV .... Restaurant and Caterers' Association of Victoria [*Australia*]

RCAY .... Gangshan [*China*] [*ICAO location identifier*]   (ICLI)

RCB .... Rationalisation des Choix Budgetaires [*Rationalization of Budgetary Choices*] [*French*]   (WER)

RCB .... Richards Bay [*South Africa*] [*Airport symbol*]   (OAG)

RCBS........ Jinmen [*China*] [*ICAO location identifier*]   (ICLI)

RCC .... Reglement pour la Conservation du Cadastre [*Belgium*]   (BAS)

RCC .... Research Center of Crete

RCC .... Residual Oil Catalytic Conversion Process [*Libya*]

RCC .... Revolutionary Command Council [*Iraq*]   (PD)

RCC .... Revolution Command Council [*Libya*]   (ME)

RCC .... Revolution Command Council [*Liberia*]   (AF)

RCC .... Right to Choose Coalition [*Australia*]

RCC .... Rijks Computer Centrum

RCCC........ Regiment Colonial de Chasseurs de Chars

RCCI......... Romanian Chamber of Commerce and Industry   (EAIO)

RCCKP..... Rassemblement des Chefs Coutumiers du Kongo Portugais

RCD .... Rassemblement Constitutionnel Democratique [*Tunisia*] [*Political party*]   (ECON)

RCD .... Rassemblement pour la Culture et la Democratie [*Algeria*] [*Political party*]   (EY)

RCD .... Regional Cooperation for Development [*Iran, Pakistan, Turkey*]

RCDC .... Pingdong (South) [*China*] [*ICAO location identifier*]   (ICLI)

RCDI .... Longtan [*China*] [*ICAO location identifier*]   (ICLI)

RCDM .... Regional Centre for Drama and Music [*University of New England, Australia*]

RCDS........ Ring Christlich-Demokratischer Studenten [*Christian-Democratic Student Ring*]   (WEN)

RCDTC..... Regional Cooperative Development and Training Centre [*Sudan*]

RCE .... Aerocer SA [*Mexico*] [*ICAO designator*]   (FAAC)

RCE .... Radiocadena Espanola   (EY)

RCE .... Union Restaurants Collectifs Europeens [*European Catering Association*] (EAIO)
RCF............ Rassemblement Communautaire Francais (FLAF)
RCF............ Retriever Club de France (EAIO)
RCFM......... Regie du Chemin de Fer du Mali
RCFN........ Taidong/Fengnian [*China*] [*ICAO location identifier*] (ICLI)
RCFS .... Jiadong [*China*] [*ICAO location identifier*] (ICLI)
RCFS .... Regie des Chemins de Fer du Senegal
RCFZ .... Fengshan [*China*] [*ICAO location identifier*] (ICLI)
RCG .... Rhodesia Christian Group
RCGC .... Royal Canberra Golf Club [*Australia*]
RCGI......... Ludao [*China*] [*ICAO location identifier*] (ICLI)
RCGM .... Taoyuan [*China*] [*ICAO location identifier*] (ICLI)
RCH........... Chile [*Chile*] [*Poland*]
RCh........... Number Register (RU)
RCH........... Riohacha [*Colombia*] [*Airport symbol*] (OAG)
RCH........... Royal Canberra Hospital [*Australia*]
RCH........... Ruhrchemie AG [*Germany*] (WED)
RCh........... Working Drawing (RU)
RCh........... Worm Reducer (RU)
RChG .... Partial Group Relay (RU)
RChK .... Rayon Extraordinary Commission for Combating Counterrevolution and Sabotage (RU)
RCHK........ Reform Club of Hong Kong (EAIO)
Rchn.......... Rechnung [*Calculation*] [*German*]
RChO......... Rota Chemicke Ochrany [*Chemical Defense Company*] (CZ)
RChPz........ Rota Chemickeho Pruzkumu [*Chemical Reconnaissance Company*] (CZ)
RChPzH .... Radiacni a Chemicka Pruzkumna Hlidka [*Radiation and Chemical Reconnaissance Patrol*] (CZ)
RCHRA ..... Regional Council on Human Rights in Asia (EAIO)
RChRPz..... Rota Chemickeho a Radiacniho Pruzkumu [*Chemical and Radiation Reconnaissance Company*] (CZ)
RChS .... Solution for Cleaning Firearm Barrels (RU)
RCHSI....... Riverland Community Health Services, Inc. [*Australia*]
RChV .... Sensitivity Time Control (RU)
RCI .... Republique de la Cote d'Ivoire [*Republic of the Ivory Coast*] (BARN)
RCIA......... Rite for Christian Initiation of Adults [*Australia*]
RCIADIC .. Royal Commission into Aboriginal Deaths in Custody [*Australia*]
RCIC......... Red Cross International Committee
RCiK .... Rada Czytelnictwa i Ksiazki [*Council on Reading and Books*] [*Poland*]
RCIUA...... Regional Council of the Independent Unions of Algeria [*Union Regionale des Syndicats Independants d'Algerie*]
RCIVS .... Regional Conference on International Voluntary Service [*Commercial firm*] (EAIO)
RCJ........... Recontre Chretiens et Juifs [*Acronym is based on former name,*] (BJA)
RCK .... Rada Czytelnictwa i Ksiazki [*Council on Reading and Books*] (POL)
RCK .... Rasinski Cetnicki Korpus [*Rasina Chetnik Corps*] [*World War II*] (YU)
RCKH........ Gaoxiong [*China*] [*ICAO location identifier*] (ICLI)
rcks .... Rueckseitig [*On the Verso*] [*Publishing*] [*German*]
RCKU .... Jiayi [*China*] [*ICAO location identifier*] (ICLI)
RCKW .... Hengchun [*China*] [*ICAO location identifier*] (ICLI)
RCL............ Railway Construction Law [*Japan*]
RCL............ Redcliff [*Vanuatu*] [*Airport symbol*] (OAG)
RCL............ Regional Container Line (DS)
RCL............ Ricegrowers' Cooperative Ltd. [*Australia*]
RCL............ Royal Caribbean Line (DS)
RCLB........ Revolutionary Communist League of Britain [*Political party*] (PPW)
RCLC........ Xiao Liu Qiu [*China*] [*ICAO location identifier*] (ICLI)
RCLG........ Taizhong [*China*] [*ICAO location identifier*] (ICLI)
RCLS .... Lishan [*China*] [*ICAO location identifier*] (ICLI)
RCLU .... Jilong [*China*] [*ICAO location identifier*] (ICLI)
RCLWUNE ... Regional Commission on Land and Water Use in the Near East (EA)
RCLY........ Lanyu [*China*] [*ICAO location identifier*] (ICLI)
RCM .... La Republique des Citoyens du Monde [*Commonwealth of World Citizens*]
RCM .... Rassemblement Chretien de Madagascar [*Christian Rally of Madagascar*]
RCM .... Richmond [*Australia*] [*Airport symbol*] (OAG)
RCM .... Roan Consolidated Mines [*Zambia*]
RCM .... Roman Catholic Missions
RCMAC..... Raw Cotton Marketing Advisory Committee [*Australia*]
RCME .... Russian Commodity and Raw Materials Exchange [*Russian Federation*] (EY)
RCMF........ Royal Commonwealth Military Forces (ADA)
RCMJ........ Donggang [*China*] [*ICAO location identifier*] (ICLI)
RCMQ....... Qingquangang [*China*] [*ICAO location identifier*] (ICLI)
RCMS........ Ilan [*China*] [*ICAO location identifier*] (ICLI)

RCN .... Radio Cadena Nacional [*Colombia*] (COL)
RCN .... Reactor Centrum Nederland [*Netherlands Reactor Center*] [*ECN*] [*Later,*] (WEN)
RCN .... Residential Care Nurse [*Australia*]
RCNA .... Royal College of Nursing, Australia
RCNN........ Tainan [*China*] [*ICAO location identifier*] (ICLI)
RCNO........ Dongshi [*China*] [*ICAO location identifier*] (ICLI)
RCNP .... Research Center for Nuclear Physics [*Osaka University*] [*Japan*] (PDAA)
RCO .... Aero Renta de Coahuila SA de CV [*Mexico*] [*ICAO designator*] (FAAC)
RCO .... Regional Catering Officer [*British*] (DCTA)
RCO .... Rota Civilni Obrany [*Civil Defense Company*] (CZ)
RCOA .... Refugee Council of Australia
RCP............ Regiment de Chasseurs Parachutistes [*Algeria*]
RCP............ Regional Cooperation Program [*Australia*]
RCP............ Republican Colored Party [*South Africa*] (AF)
RCP............ Reseau Experimental a Commutation par Paquets [*French*] (ADPT)
RCP............ Revolutionary Communist Party of India [*Political party*] (PPW)
RCP............ Romanian Communist Party [*Political party*]
RCP............ Rural Counselling Program [*Australia*]
RCPA .... Regional Colleges Principals' Association of Victoria [*Australia*]
RCPA .... Royal College of Pathologists of Australia (ADA)
RCP(B)....... Romanian Communist Party (Bolshevik) [*Political party*]
RCP(b)....... Russian Communist Party (Bolsheviks) [*Political party*]
RCPI .... Revolutionary Communist Party of India [*Political party*] (PPW)
RCPO .... Xinzhu [*China*] [*ICAO location identifier*] (ICLI)
RCQ .... Reconquista [*Argentina*] [*Airport symbol*] (OAG)
RCQC .... Magong [*China*] [*ICAO location identifier*] (ICLI)
RCQS........ Taidong/Zhihang [*China*] [*ICAO location identifier*] (ICLI)
RCR .... Riaditelstvo pre Cestovny Ruch [*Central Bureau for the Promotion of Tourist Trade*] (CZ)
RCRA .... Zouying [*China*] [*ICAO location identifier*] (ICLI)
RCRF........ Rei Cretariae Romanae Fautores [*Society of Roman Ceramic Archeologists*]
RCRS........ Remote Control Radio Service [*Australia*]
RCS........... Regiment de Commandement et de Soutien [*Headquarters and Support Regiment*] [*Burkina Faso*] (AF)
RCS........... Registrar of Cooperative Societies [*New South Wales, Australia*]
RCS........... Renal Care Society of South Africa (AA)
RCS........... Republika Ceskoslovenska [*Czechoslovak Republic (until 1960)*] (CZ)
RCS........... Rizzoli Corriere della Sera [*Publisher*]
RCS........... Royal Choral Society
RCSC......... Huwei [*China*] [*ICAO location identifier*] (ICLI)
RCSE .... Royal College of Surgeons of England (SLS)
RCSI .... Rede CONSISDATA de Servicos Integrados [*CONSISDATA Integrated Services Network*] [*Consultoria, Sistemas, e Processamento de Dados Ltda.*] [*Brazil*] [*Information service or system*] (CRD)
RCSI .... Royal College of Surgeons in Ireland (SLS)
RCSM........ Ri Yue Tan [*China*] [*ICAO location identifier*] (ICLI)
RCSP .... Royal Commission on Social Policy [*Australia*]
RCSQ........ Pingdong (North) [*China*] [*ICAO location identifier*] (ICLI)
RCSQ........ Royal Commonwealth Society of Queensland [*Australia*]
RCSS........ Taibei/Songshan [*China*] [*ICAO location identifier*] (ICLI)
RCSSA .... Regional Centre for Seismology for South America (EAIO)
RCSSMRS ... Regional Centre for Services in Surveying, Mapping, and Remote Sensing [*West Africa*]
RCT .... Internationalt Rehabiliterings- og Forskningscenter foer Torturofre [*International Rehabilitation and Research Center for Torture Victims*] [*Research center*] (IRC)
RCT .... Rehabilitation and Research Center for Torture Victims (EAIO)
RCTA......... Resource Centre Teachers Association [*Australia*]
RCTI .... Rajawali Citra Televisi Indonesia (EY)
RCTL......... Regio Corpo Truppe Libiche
RCTP........ Taibei City/Taibei International Airport [*China*] [*ICAO location identifier*]
RCTV........ Radio Caracas Television [*Venezuela*] (EY)
RCU .... Regional Coordinating Unit [*Advisory Committee on Pollution of the Sea*]
RCU .... Rio Cuarto [*Argentina*] [*Airport symbol*] (OAG)
RCU .... Rungwe Central Union
RCU .... Rural Cooperative Union [*Iran*]
RCUK .... Bakuai [*China*] [*ICAO location identifier*] (ICLI)
RCV .... Regie Cassette Video [*Software distributor*] [*French*]
RCV .... Rezervni Centar Veze [*Reserve Communications Center*] [*Military*] (YU)
RCVV .... Rhodesiese Christelike Vrouevereniging
RCWAT..... Retarded Citizens' Welfare Association of Tasmania [*Australia*]
RCWK .... Xinshe [*China*] [*ICAO location identifier*] (ICLI)
RCWS........ Research Centre for Women's Studies [*University of Adelaide, Australia*]

RCWT .... Reseau des Chemins de Fer et du Wharf du Togo [*Togo Railroad and Wharf Network*]   (AF)
RCXY........ Guiren [*China*] [*ICAO location identifier*]   (ICLI)
RCY .... Red Cross and Red Crescent Youth [*Geneva, Switzerland*]
RCYU .... Hualian [*China*] [*ICAO location identifier*]   (ICLI)
RD............. Difference of Longitudes   (RU)
RD............. "Distance Record" [*Aircraft designed by A. N. Tupolev, also called ANT-25*]   (RU)
RD............. Distributing Board   (RU)
RD............. Jet Engine   (RU)
RD............. Long-Range Reconnaissance Aircraft   (RU)
RD............. Maternity Home   (RU)
rd.............. Missile Battalion   (BU)
RD............. Observation Battalion [*Artillery*]   (RU)
RD............. Pressure Regulator   (RU)
RD............. Pressure Relay   (RU)
RD............. Rabotnichesko Delo [*Workers' Affairs*] [*A periodical*]   (BU)
Rd............. Rad [*Wheel*] [*German*]   (GCA)
rd.............. Radian [*Radian (Unit of arc measure)*] [*Poland*]
rd.............. Radiano [*Radian*] [*Portuguese*]
RD............. Radio Battalion   (RU)
RD............. Radio-Frequency Two-Frequency [*Cable*]   (RU)
RD............. Radioisotopic Pickup   (RU)
RD............. Radiologische Dienst [*Radiological Service*] [*Netherlands Central Organization for Applied Natural Scientific Research*]   (WND)
Rd............. Rand
RD............. Real Decreto [*Royal Decree*] [*Spanish*]
RD............. Recemment Degorgee [*Recently Disgorged*] [*Refers to aging of wine*] [*French*]
RD............. Reception des Donnees [*Data Reception*] [*French*]   (ADPT)
RD............. Reconnaissance Patrol   (BU)
RD............. Reditelstvi Drah [*Railroad Directorate*]   (CZ)
Rd............. Reduktion [*Reduction*] [*German*]
RD............. Reforma Democratica [*Democratic Reform*] [*Spanish*]   (WER)
RD............. Regio Decreto [*Royal Decree*] [*Italian*]
RD............. Republica Democratica [*Democratic Republic*]   (RO)
RD............. Republike Demokratike [*Democratic Republic*] [*Albanian*]
Rd............. Reverend [*Reverend*] [*French*]
RD............. Reversible Diesel Engine, Reversible Engine   (RU)
RD............. Rive Droite [*Right Bank*] [*French*]
RD............. Rizeni Dopravy [*Transport Direction Center*]   (CZ)
Rd............. Road   (PWGL)
RD............. Rocket Engine   (BU)
RD............. Rocket Engine, Rocket Motor   (RU)
RD............. Rolnicke Druzstvo [*Agricultural Cooperative*]   (CZ)
RD............. Route Departementale [*Departmental Route*] [*French*]
rd.............. Rund [*About, Approximately*] [*German*]
rd.............. Rutherford   (RU)
RD............. Rychla Divise [*Assault Division*]   (CZ)
RD............. Ryksdaalder [*Rix-Dollar*] [*Afrikaans*]
RD............. Taxiway   (RU)
RD-1J .... Rucni Dvogled Prvi Jugoslovenski [*Hand Binocular, 1st Yugoslav Model*]   (YU)
RDA .... Automatic Pressure Regulator   (RU)
RDA .... Manual Respirator   (RU)
RDA .... Racial Discrimination Act [*Australia*]
RDA .... Rassemblement Democratique Afar
RDA .... Rassemblement Democratique Africain [*Niger*] [*Political party*]   (PD)
RDA .... Rassemblement Democratique Africain [*Ivory Coast*] [*Political party*]   (PPW)
RDA .... Rassemblement Democratique Algerien
RDA .... Regional Dailies of Australia   (ADA)
RDA .... Regional Development Agency [*de CARIFTA*] [*Caribbean Free Trade Association*]   (LAA)
RDA .... Regional Development Authority [*Victoria, Australia*]
RDA .... Republica Democratica Alema [*German Democratic Republic*] [*Use GDR*] [*Portuguese*]   (WER)
RDA .... Republique Democratique Allemande [*German Democratic Republic - GDR*]   (CL)
RDA .... Royal Danish Aeroclub   (EAIO)
RDA .... Rufdatenaufzeichnung [*German*]   (ADPT)
RDA .... Rural Development Academy [*Bogra, Bangladesh*]   (ECON)
RDA .... Rural Development Administration [*Korea*] [*Research center*]   (IRC)
RDA .... Rural Development Area [*Swaziland*]   (IMH)
RDA .... Rural Doctors' Association [*Australia*]
RDA .... Ruvuma Development Association
RDA .... TK Travel Ltd. [*Gambia*] [*ICAO designator*]   (FAAC)
RDAA .... Riding for the Disabled Association of Australia
RDAA .... Rural Doctors' Association of Australia
RDAAC ..... Research into Drug Abuse Advisory Committee [*Australia*]
RDAC .... Royal Dutch Agricultural Committee   (EAIO)
RDAF .... Regional Director of Agriculture and Fisheries [*Australia*]
RDAF .... Royal Danish Air Force

RDAG....... Rassemblement Democratique Africain de la Guinee
Rda M........ Reverenda Madre [*Reverend Mother*] [*Spanish*]
RD & D ..... Research, Development, and Demonstration Program [*Australia*]
RD & P....... Research, Development, and Production [*NATO*]   (NATG)
RDAQ....... Riding for Disabled Association of Queensland [*Australia*]
RDASL...... Royal Danish Academy of Sciences and Letters   (EAIO)
RDB .... Racecourses Development Board [*South Australia*]
RdB .... Rat des Bezirkes [*Bezirk Council*]   (EG)
RDB .... Reddingsdaadbond [*Aid Society*] [*South Africa*]   (AF)
RDB .... Reisebeschreibungen von Deutschen Beamten und Kriegsleuten im Dienst der Niederlaendischen West- und Ost-Indischen Kompagnien [*The Hague*]
RDC .... Racecourse Development Committee [*New South Wales*]
RDC .... Radiodiffusion du Cameroun
RDC .... Rassemblement Democratique Caledonien [*Caledonian Democratic Rally*] [*Political party*]   (PPW)
RDC .... Rassemblement Democratique Centrafricain [*Central African Republic*] [*Political party*]
RDC .... Refugee Documentation Centre [*Information service or system*]   (IID)
RDC .... Republique Democratique du Congo
RDC .... Revolutionary Development Cadre [*South Vietnam*]
RdC .... Rez-de-Chaussee [*First Floor*] [*French*]
RDC .... Rural Development Centre [*Sudan*]
RDC .... Rural Development Centre [*University of New England, Australia*]
RDC .... Rural Development Corporation of Zambia   (GEA)
RDC .... Saudi Company for Research and Development   (ME)
RDCAA ..... Registered Dairy Cattle Association of Australia
RDCAP...... Research and Development Center for Applied Physics [*Indonesia*] [*Research center*]   (IRC)
RDCG .... Research and Development Center for Geotechnology [*Indonesia*]   (IRC)
RDCJ .... Research Development Corporation of Japan
RDD.......... Long-Range Missile   (RU)
RDD.......... Rassemblement Democratique Dahomeen [*Dahomean Democratic Rally*]
RDD.......... Regional Development Director
RDD.......... Republik Demokratik Djerman [*German Democratic Republic*]   (IN)
RDD.......... Rolnicke Dobytkarske Druzstvo [*Farmers' Livestock Cooperative*]   (CZ)
RDEC .... Research, Development, and Evaluation Commission [*Taiwanese*]   (GEA)
RDETS ..... Republic Children's Excursion and Tourist Station   (RU)
RDF .... Reddingsdaafonds
Rdfk .... Rundfunk [*Radio*] [*German*]
RDFWA..... Regular Defence Force Welfare Association [*Australia*]
RDG.......... Reference Drawing Group [*NATO*]   (NATG)
RDG.......... Republica Democratica Germana [*German Democratic Republic*]   (RO)
RDG.......... Smoke Hand Grenade   (RU)
RDGS .... Royal Dutch Geographical Society   (EAIO)
RDHM ...... Royal Dental Hospital, Melbourne [*Australia*]
RDI .... Rassemblement des Democrates Liberaux pour la Reconstruction Nationale [*Benin*] [*Political party*]   (EY)
RDI .... Relief and Development Institute [*Formerly, International Disaster Institute*] [*Defunct*]   (EA)
RDJ........... Rudne Doly Jesenik [*Jesenik Mines for Non-Ferrous Metal Ores*]   (CZ)
RDJA........ Rassemblement Democratique de la Jeunesse Angolaise
RDK.......... Rayon House of Culture   (RU)
RDKA .... Royal Dutch Korfball Association   (EAIO)
RDL .... Raadslid [*Councillor*] [*Afrikaans*]
RDL .... Regio Decreto Legge [*Law Promulgated by Royal Decree*] [*Italian*]
RDLGE...... Reunion Democratica para la Liberacion de Guinea Ecuatorial [*Democratic Movement for the Liberation of Equatorial Guinea*] [*Political party*]   (PD)
RDLK .... Rassemblement Democratique du Lac du Kwango et Kwilu
rdm........... Company Decontamination Area   (BU)
rdm........... Ground Decontamination Company   (RU)
RDM......... Incremental-Code Modulation   (RU)
RDM......... Rand Daily Mail
RDM......... Republique Democratique de Madagascar [*Democratic Republic of Madagascar*]   (AF)
RDM......... Retail Distribution Management [*Australia*]
RDM......... Rotterdamsche Droogdok Maatschappij [*Shipyard*] [*Netherlands*]
RDMOA.... Repatriation Department Medical Officers' Award [*Australia*]
RDN.......... Dinar SA [*Argentina*] [*ICAO designator*]   (FAAC)
RDN.......... Low-Pressure Relay   (RU)
rdn............ Missile Battalion   (BU)
Rdnot .... Randnoten [*Marginal Notes*] [*German*]

RDNP .... Rassemblement Democratique Nationaliste et Progressiste [*Progressive Nationalist and Democratic Assembly*] [*Haiti*] (PD)
RDNS .... Royal District Nursing Service of Victoria [*Australia*]
RDNS .... Royal District Nursing Society of South Australia
RDNSSA ... Royal District Nursing Society of South Australia
RDNT .... Workers' House of Folk Art (RU)
RDNU .... Rally for Democracy and National Unity [*Mauritania*] [*Political party*] (EY)
RDO.......... Reaction to Moving Object (RU)
Rdo .... Reverendo [*Reverend*] [*Spanish*]
RDO .... Rostered Day Off [*Australia*]
RDOEI ...... Research and Development Organization for Electrical Industry [*India*] (PDAA)
Rdo P .... Reverendo Padre [*Reverend Father*] [*Spanish*]
RDP .... Area Traffic Control Point (RU)
RDP .... Direct Action Pressure Regulator (RU)
RDP .... Manual Decontamination Apparatus (RU)
RDP .... Pilot Pressure Regulator [*Oil equipment*] (RU)
RDP .... Portable Decontamination Apparatus (BU)
RDP .... Radiodifusao Portuguesa [*State Broadcasting Service*]
RDP .... Rassemblement Democratique Paysan
RDP .... Rassemblement pour la Democratie et le Progres [*Mali*] [*Political party*] (EY)
RDP .... Regiment de Dragons Parachutistes [*Algeria*]
RDP .... Regional Development Program [*Australia*]
RDP .... Rehoboth Democratic Party [*Namibia*] (AF)
RDP .... Reunification Democracy Party [*Political party*] [*South Korea*]
RDP .... Snorkel (RU)
RDPA .... Rayon House of Party Activists (RU)
RDPC........ Rassemblement Democratique des Peuples Comoriens [*Democratic Rally of Comoro Peoples*] (AF)
RDPC........ Rassemblement Democratique du Peuple Camerounais [*Cameroon*]
RDPTS ...... Rassemblement Democratique et Populaire Thomas Sankara [*The Thomas Sankara Popular and Democratic Rally*] [*Burkina Faso*]
RDPTT ...... Radionica Direkcije PTT [*Workshop of the Postal, Telegraph, and Telephone Administration*] (YU)
RDR .... Rada Delegatow Robotniczych [*Council of Workers' Delegates*] (POL)
RDR .... Radiation Reconnaissance (BU)
RDR .... Rassemblement Democratique et Revolutionnaire [*France*] (FLAF)
RDR .... Ruf-Daten-Rechner [*German*] (ADPT)
RDRK .... Republik Demokratik Rakjat Korea [*Korean People's Democratic Republic*] (IN)
RDRS........ Rangpur/Dinajpur Rural Service [*Bangladesh*] (EAIO)
RDS .... Area Traffic Control Service (RU)
RDS .... Has Worked with Radio Stations of the Democratic Countries [*Diploma for amateur radio operators*] (BU)
RDS .... Long-Range Radio Station (RU)
RDS .... Pressure Signal Relay (RU)
RDS .... RADAUS [*Radio-Austria AG*] Data-Service [*Telecommunications*]
RDS .... Records Data Services [*Australia*]
RDS .... Reperimento Documentazione Siderurgica [*Iron and Steel Documentation Service*] [*Information service or system*] (IID)
RDS .... Repubblica Democratica Somala
RDS .... Royal Dublin Society [*Irish*] (SLS)
RDS .... Traffic Control Area (RU)
RDS .... Two-Chamber Oxygen Pressure Reducer (RU)
RDS .... "Worked with All Countries of People's Democracy" [*Amateur radio operator's diploma*] (RU)
RDSAP ...... Royal Dutch Society for Advancement of Pharmacy (EAIO)
Rdsch .... Rundschau [*Survey*] [*German*] (GCA)
RDSD .... Revolutionary Development Support Division [*South Vietnam*]
RDSO .... Research, Design, and Standardization Organization [*Indian Railways*] [*India*] (PDAA)
RDSP........ Revolutionary Development Support Plan [*or Program*] [*South Vietnam*]
RDT .... Repubblica Democratica Tedesca [*German Democratic Republic*] [*Use GDR*] [*Italian*] (WER)
RDT .... Richard-Toll [*Senegal*] [*Airport symbol*] (OAG)
RDT .... Rolniczy Dom Towarowy [*Agricultural Department Store*] (POL)
RDT .... Solid-Propellant Rocket Engine (RU)
RDTF........ Revolutionary Development Task Force [*South Vietnam*]
RDTT .... Solid-Propellant Rocket Engine (RU)
RDV .... Air Reducer (RU)
RDV .... High-Pressure Relay (RU)
RDV .... Reglement Dienstvoorwaarden [*Benelux*] (BAS)
RDV .... Republica Democratica Vietnam [*Democratic Republic of Vietnam*] (RO)
RDV .... Republik Demokratik Vietnam [*Democratic Republic of Vietnam*] (IN)

RDV .... Republique Democratique du Viet-Nam [*Democratic Republic of Vietnam*] [*Use DRV or North Vietnam*] (CL)
RDVN........ Republique Democratique du Viet-Nam [*Democratic Republic of Vietnam*] [*Use DRV or North Vietnam*] (CL)
rd-vs .... Rendez-Vous [*Appointment, Meeting-Place*] [*French*]
Rdy Nsr...... Radyo Nesriyati [*Radio Broadcast*] (TU)
RDZ .... Ringier Dokumentationszentrum [*Ringier Documentation Center*] [*Switzerland*] [*Information service or system*] (IID)
RDZ .... Rodez [*France*] [*Airport symbol*] (OAG)
RE .... Capacitance Regulator (RU)
RE .... Electromagnetic Relay (RU)
RE .... Fuel-Flow Regulator (RU)
RE .... Rada Europejska [*Council of Europe*] [*Poland*]
RE .... Radio-Eireann [*Eire*] [*Record label*]
RE .... Radio Engineering and Electronics (RU)
RE .... Randeinheit [*German*] (ADPT)
Re .... Receita Medica [*Medical Prescription*] [*Portuguese*]
RE .... Rechner [*Computer*] [*German*] (ADPT)
re .... Rechts [*To the Right*] [*German*]
Re .... Recipe [*Portuguese*]
Re .... Recipe [*Spanish*]
RE .... Reconnaissance Squadron [*Aviation*] (RU)
Re .... Regelleistung [*Standard Capacity*] (EG)
RE .... Reggio Emilia [*Car registration plates*] [*Italian*]
RE .... Regimento de Engenharia [*Engineering Regiment*] [*Portuguese*] (WER)
RE .... Regulating Element, Control (RU)
RE .... Rekeneenheden [*Benelux*] (BAS)
Re .... Renio [*Rhenium*] [*Chemical element*] [*Portuguese*]
RE .... Renovacion Espanola [*Spanish Renovation*] (PPE)
RE .... Retirado [*Retired*] [*Argentina*] (LA)
RE .... Reunion [*ANSI two-letter standard code*] (CNC)
Re .... Reynolds Number (RU)
Re .... Reynold's Zahl [*Reynold's Number*] [*German*] (GCA)
RE .... Rijkseenheid [*Benelux*] (BAS)
Re .... Roche [*Rock*] [*French*] (NAU)
RE .... Roupie Mauricienne [*Mauritius*]
RE .... Royal Engineers (ML)
RE .... Rupee [*Monetary unit*] [*Ceylon, India, and Pakistan*]
REA .... Raad voor Economische Aangelegenheden [*Benelux*] (BAS)
REA .... Radio and Electronic Equipment (RU)
REA .... Radioelectronic Apparatus (BU)
REA .... Rauchgasentschwefelungs-Anlage [*Flue Gas Desulfurization Unit*] [*German*]
REA .... Reao [*French Polynesia*] [*Airport symbol*] (OAG)
REA .... Regie des Eaux Agricoles [*Agricultural Water Administration*] [*Tunisia*] (AF)
REA .... Rural Electrification Authority [*Egypt*] (IMH)
REAAA...... Road Engineering Association of Asia and Australasia
REAB........ Radiotechnikai es Elektronikai Ipari Allando Bizottsaga (Kolcsonos Gazdasagi Segitseg Tanacsa) [*Council for Mutual Economic Assistance Permanent Committee for the Radio Technology and Electronics Industry*] (HU)
reabr........... Rocket Artillery Brigade (RU)
reabr........... Rocket-Launching Artillery Brigade (BU)
ReAC .... Reinsurance Australia Corp. [*Commercial firm*]
REACH .... Review and Analysis of Companies in Holland [*Database*] (IID)
READ .... Rehabilitation, Education, Access for the Disabled [*Australia*]
read .... Rocket-Launching Artillery Battalion (BU)
REA et A... Rite Ecossais Ancien et Accepte [*Ancient and Accepted Scottish Rite*] [*Freemasonry*] [*French*]
REAF........ Royal Egyptian Air Force
Reakt......... Reaktion [*Reaction*] [*German*] (GCA)
REAL........ Recherches et Expansion d'Alimentation [*Nutrition Research and Expansion*] [*Ivory Coast*] (AF)
Realsch ...... Realschule [*Secondary School*] [*German*] (GCA)
REAMERICA ... Representaciones America Ltda. [*Colombia*] (COL)
REAN .... Royal Exchange Assurance (Nigeria) Ltd.
REANSW ... Real Estate Association of New South Wales [*Australia*]
reap .... Rocket Artillery Regiment (RU)
reap .... Rocket-Launching Artillery Regiment (BU)
REAP........ Rural Education Access Program [*Australia*]
REAP........ Rural Education Activities Programme [*New Zealand*]
REAV .... Renewable Energy Authority of Victoria [*Australia*]
REB .... Maintenance and Operation Base (RU)
reb .... Roentgen Equivalent Man (RU)
REB .... Royal Exhibition Buildings [*Melbourne, Australia*]
REB .... Rural Electricity Board
REBAR..... Regie des Batiments du Rwanda
REBASB.... Real Estate and Business Agents' Supervisory Board [*Western Australia*]
rebatr.......... Rocket Battery (RU)
rebatr .... Rocket-Launching Battery (BU)
REBIA .... Regional Building Institute for Africa
REBIA .... Regional Educational Building Institute for Africa

REBK......... Repertoire des Banques de Donnees en Conversationnel [*Association Nationale de la Recherche Technique*] [*Information service or system*]

REBUS...... Reseau des Bibliotheques Utilisant SIBIL [*Library Network of SIBIL Users*] [*University of Lausanne Switzerland*] [*Information service or system*] (IID)

rec............. Receita [*Receipt*] [*Portuguese*]

rec............. Recensie [*Benelux*] (BAS)

rec............. Recenzja [*or Recenzent*] [*Critic, Review or Reviewer*] [*Poland*]

REC .... Recife [*Brazil*] [*Airport symbol*] (OAG)

rec............. Reconventie [*Benelux*] (BAS)

Rec .... Recours [*Benelux*] (BAS)

Rec .... Recueil [*Benelux*] (BAS)

REC .... Regiment Etranger de Cavalerie [*Foreign Cavalry Regiment*] [*French*]

REC .... Regroupement des Etudiants Camerounais [*Regrouping of Cameroonese Students*]

REC .... Rural Electrification Corp. [*India*] (PDAA)

RECAST.... Research Centre for Applied Science and Technology [*Nepal*] (IRC)

RECAST.... Rural Energy Centre for Appropriate Science and Technology [*Nepal*]

RECC........ Rhine Evacuation and Control Command [*NATO*] (NATG)

Rec CourCE ... Recueil de la Jurisprudence de la Cour de Justice des Communautes Europeennes [*A publication*] (FLAF)

RECE........ Representacion Cubana del Exilio [*Cuban Representation of Exiles*]

rech .... Fluvial, River (RU)

Rech .... Recherche [*Research*] [*French*]

Rechizdat ... "River Transportation" Publishing House (RU)

rechn .... River, Fluvial (RU)

rechner....... Rechnerisch [*Mathematical*] [*German*] (GCA)

Rechsudotrest ... All-Union River Shipbuilding Trust (RU)

RechtbAntwerpen ... Vonnis van de Rechtbank van Antwerpen [*Belgium*] (BAS)

RechtbKooph ... Vonnis van de Rechtbank van Koophandel [*Benelux*] (BAS)

Rechtek...... River Transportation and Forwarding Office (RU)

rechtsdr...... Rechtschrehend [*Dextrorotatory*] [*German*] (GCA)

Rechtsw...... Rechtswesen [*or Rechtswissenschaft*] [*Jurisprudence*] [*German*] (GCA)

recipr.......... Reciproco [*Reciprocal*] [*Italian*]

Rec Jur CCom Eur ... Recueil de la Jurisprudence de la Cour de Justice des Communautes Europeennes [*A publication*] (FLAF)

Recl .... Reclasseering [*Benelux*] (BAS)

reco............ Recebido [*Portuguese*]

RECOCIDI ... Representation Commerciale de Cote-D'Ivoire

RECODEX ... Report Collection Index [*Studsvik Energiteknik AB*] [*Database Nykoping, Sweden*]

RECOFLOR ... Reforma Colombiana de la Flor [*Colombia*] (COL)

RECOL...... Representacoes Comerciais Lda.

Recomm...... Recommandation [*Benelux*] (BAS)

RECOPE ... Refinadora Costarricense de Petroleo [*Costa Rican Oil Refinery*] (LA)

RECP........ International College of Real Estate Consulting Professionals (EAIO)

RECRAS ... Retrieval System for Current Research in Agricultural Sciences [*Japan*]

RECSAM .. Regional Center for Education in Science and Mathematics [*Subsidiary of SEAMEC*] (CL)

Rect........... Rectificatif [*French*] (FLAF)

RECTAS.... Regional Centre for Training in Aerial Surveys (EAIO)

RECTAS.... Regional Centre for Training in Aerospace Surveys [*Nigeria*] (EAIO)

Rectif......... Rectificatif [*Benelux*] (BAS)

RecWet ...... Recente Wetenswaardigheden [*Benelux*] (BAS)

RED .... Comite International de La Croix-Rouge [*Switzerland*] [*ICAO designator*] (FAAC)

red .... Redactie [*Editorship*] [*Publishing*] [*Netherlands*]

Red............. Redaction [*French*] (FLAF)

red .... Redagowal [*Edited By*] [*POL*]

red .... Redakce [*Editorial Staff*] (CZ)

red .... Redakcja [*Editorial Board, Editorial Office*] (POL)

RED .... Redaksi/Redaktur [*Editorial Staff/Editor*] (IN)

RED .... Redakteur [*Editor*] [*Afrikaans*]

Red............. Redakteur [*or Redaktion*] [*Editorship*] [*German*]

red .... Redaktor [*Editor*] [*Sweden*] (GPO)

red .... Redaktor [*Editor*] [*Denmark*] (GPO)

Red............. Redan [*Military map abbreviation*] [*World War I*] [*French*] (MTD)

RED .... Redasksie [*Editorial Staff*] [*Afrikaans*]

red .... Redigiert [*Edited*] [*Publishing*] [*German*]

red .... Reditel [*Director, Manager*] (CZ)

red .... Reducao [*Reduction*] [*Portuguese*]

Red............. Reduktion [*Reduction*] [*German*]

red .... Reduziert [*Reduced*] [*German*] (GCA)

RED .... Regional Economic Development [*Center*] (CL)

red .... Regular (BU)

red .... Rocket Battalion (RU)

RED .... Thread Tolerance Unit (RU)

Redakt....... Redakteur [*Editor*] [*German*] (GCA)

Redakt....... Redaktion [*Editorial Office*] [*German*] (GCA)

REDAN ..... Redes e Artefactos Nacionais Lda.

redbr.......... Redni Broj [*Ordinal Number*] (YU)

redd .... Reduzierend [*Reducing*] [*German*]

Rede .... Redoute [*Redoubt*] [*Military map abbreviation World War I*] [*French*] (MTD)

REDEC...... Research & Development Corporation [*Saudi Arabia*]

red gimnu-tel ... Regular High School Teacher (BU)

redig .... Redigerad [*Edited*] [*Sweden*]

redig .... Redigiert [*Edited*] [*Publishing*] [*German*]

redizdat ...... Editorial and Publishing Section (RU)

redkol......... Editorial Board (RU)

Redkolegiya ... Editorial Board (BU)

red k-t........ Editorial Committee (BU)

redn .... Rocket-Launching Battalion (BU)

red nachu-ka ... Regular Woman Elementary School Teacher (BU)

red nachu-l ... Regular Male Elementary School Teacher (BU)

red nacz...... Redaktor Naczelny [*Chief Editor*] [*Poland*]

red nauk ..... Redaktor Naukowy [*Scientific Supervisor*] [*Poland*]

REDO .... Red Documental [*Ministerio de Educacion Publica*] [*Chile*] [*Information service or system*] (CRD)

REDP........ Rada Ekonomiczna Drog Publicznych [*Economic Council on Public Roads*] (POL)

REDP........ Rejony Eksploatacji Drog Publicznych [*Public Road Exploitation Districts*] (POL)

red prit .... Regular Supplement (BU)

redprof .... Redni Profesor [*Full Professor*] (YU)

redprogimn u-l ... Regular Junior High School Teacher (BU)

REDSO....... Regional Economic Development Services Office

REDSO/ESA ... Regional Economic Development Services Office for East and Southern Africa

red sost....... Editor-Compiler (RU)

red-stop...... Editor and Owner (BU)

REDUC ..... Red Latinoamericana de Documentacion en Educacion [*Latin American Education Documentation Network*] (PDAA)

redupl........ Reduplikasie [*Reduplication*] [*Afrikaans*]

redverbet .... Redactie Verbetering [*Benelux*] (BAS)

REE .... Radio Exterior Espana (EY)

REEC........ Radical Environmental Education Collective [*Australia*]

reed .... Reedition [*New Edition*] [*Publishing*] [*French*]

REEFNSW ... Real Estate Employers Federation of New South Wales [*Australia*]

ref.............. Abstract, Paper (RU)

ref.............. Referat [*or Referent*] [*Section or Section Head*] [*Poland*]

Ref............. Referate [*Reports, Abstracts*] [*German*]

Ref............. Refere [*French*] (FLAF)

ref.............. Reference [*Reference, Allusion*] [*French*]

ref.............. Referensie [*Reference*] [*Afrikaans*]

Ref............. Referent [*Expert Adviser*] [*German*]

ref.............. Referowal [*Report Made By*] (POL)

ref.............. Refondu [*French*] (FLAF)

ref.............. Reformado [*Protestant*] [*Portuguese*]

Ref............. Reformation [*German*] (GCA)

ref.............. Reformatus [*Reformed (Church)*] (HU)

ref.............. Reformiert [*Reformed*] [*German*] (GCA)

ref.............. Refundido [*Recast*] [*Publishing*] [*Portuguese*]

REF........... Repertoire Fiscal [*Benelux*] (BAS)

ref.............. Roentgen Equivalent Physical (RU)

REFAMOL ... Representacoes Farmaceuticas de Mocambique Lda.

refce.......... Reference [*Australia*]

refl............. Reflechi [*French*] (TPFD)

REFL........ Refleksief [*Reflexive*] [*Afrikaans*]

refl............. Refleksiivi(nen) [*Finland*]

refl............. Refleksiiviverbi [*Reflexive Verb*] [*Finland*]

refl............. Reflexive (TPFD)

reflex .... Reflexivo [*Reflexive*] [*Portuguese*]

refr .... Refractometry (RU)

REFTTA.... Return Endorsement for Travel to Australia

REG .... Electrohydraulic Regulator (RU)

REG .... Hydroelectric Steering Apparatus (RU)

REG .... Maintenance and Recovery Group (RU)

Reg .... Regal, Branch of EMI [*Record label*] [*Spain*]

reg .... Regenerator (RU)

Reg .... Regens [*Rain*] [*German*]

reg .... Regeny [*Novel*] (HU)

reg .... Regering [*Government*] [*Afrikaans*]

REG .... Reggio Calabria [*Italy*] [*Airport symbol*] (OAG)

Reg .... Regie [*French*] (FLAF)

reg .... Regierte [*Regulate*] [*German*]

Reg .... Regiment [*Regiment*] [*French*] (MTD)

reg .... Regimento [*Regiment*] [*Portuguese*]

reg .... Regione [*Italian*] (CED)

reg .... Register [*Index*] [*Publishing*] [*Netherlands*]
Reg .... Register [*Index*] [*Publishing*] [*German*]
reg .... Register [*Index*] [*Publishing*] [*Sweden*]
reg .... Register   (EECI)
reg .... Registratie [*Benelux*]   (BAS)
reg .... Registriert [*Registered*] [*German*]
reg .... Regiszter [*Index*] [*Hungary*]
REG .... Regourd Aviation [*France*] [*ICAO designator*]   (FAAC)
reg .... Regular [*Regular*] [*Portuguese*]
REG .... Remontno Evakuaciona Grupa [*Repair and Evacuation Group*] [*Military*]   (YU)
reg .... Repair and Evacuation Group   (BU)
REGALCO ... Etablissements Regal & Compagnie
regd .... Registered   (EECI)
Reg-Dir ...... RegierungsDirektor [*Senior Civil Servant*] [*German*]
reg dv .... Traffic Control   (RU)
Regel .... Regelung [*Control*] [*German*]   (GCA)
regelm .... Regelmaessig [*Regular*] [*German*]   (GCA)
Regenerier ... Regenerierung [*Regeneration*] [*German*]   (GCA)
REGIC .... Regie Generale d'Industries du Cameroun
REGIDESO ... Regie de Distribution d'Eau et d'Electricite [*Water and Power Distribution Administration*] [*French*]   (AF)
REGIFERCAM ... Regie des Chemins de Fer du Cameroun [*Cameroonian Railway Administration*]   (AF)
Registerbd ... Registerband [*Index Volume*] [*Publishing*] [*German*]
Registerbl ... Registerblatt [*Index Page*] [*Publishing*] [*German*]
Regl .... Reglement [*Administrative Ordinance or Rule of Procedure*] [*French*]   (ILCA)
Regl Add .... Reglement Additionnel [*French*]   (FLAF)
Regl de Pr .. Reglement de Procedure [*French*]   (FLAF)
REGLES ...... Repartition du Surproduit Petrolier Particuliere a la Saoura et aux Oasis
Reglg-Duc .. Reglement Grand-Ducal [*Benelux*]   (BAS)
ReglMin ..... Reglement Ministeriel [*Benelux*]   (BAS)
reglt .... Reglement [*Settlement, Adjustment, Regulation*] [*French*]
REGM .... Randfontein Estates Gold Mine [*South Africa*]
RegO .... Regentschapsordonnantie [*Benelux*]   (BAS)
rego .... Registrado [*Registered*] [*Portuguese*]
REGO .... Registration [*Of a motor vehicle*] [*Australia*]   (DSUE)
rego .... Registro [*Register*] [*Portuguese*]
rego .... Regulamento [*Regulation*] [*Portuguese*]
Regord .... Regentschapsordonnantie [*Benelux*]   (BAS)
Regotmas ... All-Union Office for Regeneration of Used Petroleum Lubricants   (RU)
Reg-R .... Regierungsrat [*Government Counsel*] [*German*]   (GCA)
Regr Afr ..... Regroupement Africain   (FLAF)
Reg-Rat ...... Regierungsrat [*Administrative Advisor*] [*German*]
regsg .... Regsgeleerde [*Jurist*] [*Afrikaans*]
regt .... Regiment [*Regiment*] [*Afrikaans*]
reg t .... Register Ton   (RU)
Reg-T .... Registertonne [*Register Ton*] [*German*]   (GCA)
Regwet .... Registratiewet [*Benelux*]   (BAS)
REH .... Radioelektronikai Hadviseles [*Radio Electronic Warfare*]   (HU)
reh .... Rehausse [*Decorated*] [*Publishing*] [*French*]
REHOTELES ... Reservacion de Hoteles [*Colombia*]   (COL)
REHVA ..... Representatives of European Heating and Ventilating Associations
REI .... Radio Espana Independiente [*Radio Independent Spain*]   (WER)
REI .... Rat der Europaeischen Industrieverbaende [*Council of European Industrial Federations*]
REI .... Regie Exploitations Industrielles [*Morocco*]
REI .... Regiment Etranger d'Infanterie [*Foreign Infantry Regiment*] [*French*]
REI .... Renewable Energy Index [*Energy Information Service*] [*Information service or system*] [*Australia*]
REIA .... Real Estate Institute of Australia   (ADA)
Reib .... Reibung [*Friction*] [*German*]   (GCA)
reichvergold ... Reichvergoldet [*Richly Gilt*] [*Publishing*] [*German*]
Reif .... Reifung [*Ripening*] [*German*]   (GCA)
REI(M) ...... Regiment Etranger d'Infanterie (de Marche) [*Foreign Marching Infantry Regiment*] [*French*]
reimp .... Reimpression [*Reprint*] [*Publishing*] [*French*]
reimpr .... Reimpression [*Reprint*] [*Publishing*] [*French*]
reimpres ..... Reimpression [*Reprint*] [*Publishing*] [*French*]
Reinheitspruef ... Reinheitspruefung [*Purity Test*] [*German*]   (GCA)
Reinig .... Reinigung [*Purification*] [*German*]   (GCA)
Reinschr ..... Reinschrift [*Clean Copy*] [*German*]   (GCA)
REIS .... Reseau Europeen Integre d'Image et de Services [*European Integrated Network of Image and Services*]   (EAIO)
REIV .... Real Estate Institute of Victoria [*Australia*]
REIV(Aust) ... Valuer, Real Estate and Stock Institute of Australia   (ADA)
rej .... Rejet [*French*]   (FLAF)
REJ .... Rejimen [*Regiment*]   (ML)
REJECO ...... Regroupement de la Jeunesse Congolaise
rek .... Being Recommended, Recommended   (RU)
REK .... Rekening [*Account*] [*Afrikaans*]

Rek .... Reklamcilik [*Advertising, Publicity*]   (TU)
REK .... Reykjavik [*Iceland*] [*Airport symbol*]   (OAG)
REKENK .. Rekenkunde [*Arithmetic*] [*Afrikaans*]
REKMEK ... Russian Electrotechnical Committee of the International Electrotechnical Commission   (RU)
Rekput' ..... All-Union Trust for the Reconstruction of Railroads   (RU)
rekt .... Rector   (RU)
rekt .... Rekisteritonni(a) [*Finland*]
rektn .... Rekisteritonni(a) [*Finland*]
REL .... Rassemblement Europeen de la Liberte [*European Liberty Rally*] [*France*] [*Political party*]   (PPE)
REL .... Raziel Enterprises Ltd. [*Ghana*]
REL .... Relais   (ADPT)
rel .... Relatief [*Relative*] [*Afrikaans*]
rel .... Relatif [*French*]   (TPFD)
Rel .... Relations   (PWGL)
rel .... Relative   (TPFD)
rel .... Relativo [*Relative*] [*Portuguese*]
Rel .... Relatore [*Reporter*] [*Italian*]   (ILCA)
REL .... Relie [*Bound*] [*Publishing*] [*French*]
rel .... Religion   (BU)
REL .... Resrutturazione Elettronica [*Electrical Reconstruction*] [*Italy*]
REL .... Trelew [*Argentina*] [*Airport symbol*]   (OAG)
RELAP ...... Replaciones Publicas y Tecnicas Publicitarias Ltda. [*Colombia*]   (COL)
relat .... Relativ [*Relative*] [*German*]   (GCA)
RELC .... Regional English Language Center [*Subsidiary of SEAMEC*]   (CL)
RELC .... Regional Language Centre [*SEAMEO*] [*Singapore*] [*Research center*]   (IRC)
RELIA ...... Regional European Long Lines Agency   (IAA)
relig .... Religious   (RU)
relyativ ...... Relativistic   (RU)
REM .... Raster Elektron Mikroskopie [*Scanning Electron Microscopy*] [*German*]
rem .... Remanie [*French*]   (BAS)
Rem .... Remington [*Record label*] [*USA, Europe, etc.*]
Rem .... Remise [*Remittance*] [*Business term*] [*French*]
rem .... Repair   (RU)
REM .... Resort Militer [*Military Area (KOREM)*]   (IN)
REMA ...... Societe de Reception et de Magasin
remabatr ..... Rocket-Launching Mortar Battalion [*Artillery*]   (BU)
REMAC ...... Reconhecimento da Margem Continental Brasileira [*Brazil*]   (MSC)
remadn .... Rocket-Launching Mortar Battalion [*Artillery*]   (BU)
remap .... Rocket-Launching Mortar Regiment   (BU)
REMAR ..... Representaciones Maritimas [*Colombia*]   (COL)
remarg .... Remarginado [*Margins Reworked*] [*Publishing*] [*Spanish*]
remb .... Maintenance Battalion   (RU)
remb .... Remboursable [*Repayable, Redeemable*] [*French*]
Rembt .... Remboursement [*Reimbursement*] [*Business term*] [*French*]
REME .... Royal Electrical and Mechanical Engineers [*Jordan*]   (ME)
remesl .... Trade, Artisan   (RU)
remletuchka ... Mobile Repair Shop   (RU)
Remmashtrest ... Trust for the Repair of Metal-Cutting Machine Tools and Forging and Pressing Equipment   (RU)
rem mast ..... Repair Shop [*Topography*]   (RU)
Remmekh .. Machine Repair Plant   (RU)
REMO .... Societe Ouest Africaine de Distribution Ets. Rene Montenay & Cie.
REMOL .... Representacoes de Mocambique Limitada
remont .... Repair Shop [*Topography*]   (RU)
REMP .... Research Group for European Migration Problems [*Netherlands*]   (SLS)
rempl .... Remplie [*Folded on Itself*] [*Publishing*] [*French*]
REMPOD ... Radio-Elektromehanisko Podjetje [*Radio and Electrical Engineering Establishment*]   (YU)
remzavod .... Repair Plant   (RU)
REN .... Aero-Rent SA de CV [*Mexico*] [*ICAO designator*]   (FAAC)
RENA ...... Rede Nacional de Abastecimento [*National Supply Network*] [*Brazil*]   (LA)
RENAB ..... Empresa Estatal de Reparacoes Navais de Beira
RENAC ..... Retele Nationale de Calculatoare [*National Computer Networks*]   (RO)
RENAIBAKO ... Renaissance du Bas-Kongo
RENAICAM ... Renaissance Camerounaise
Renaiss .... Renaissance [*German*]
RENAMO ... Resistencia Nacional Mocambicana [*Mozambique*]
RENAPE ... Rede Nacional de Pesca [*National Fishing Network*] [*Brazil*]   (LA)
RENAT ...... Revolutsiya, Nauka, Trud [*Revolution, Science, Labor*] [*Given name popular in Russia after the Bolshevik Revolution*]
RENAVE ... Empresa de Reparos Navais [*Ship Repair Company*] [*Brazil*]   (LA)
rend .... Rendelet [*Decree (Legal)*]   (HU)
rendk .... Rendkivuli [*Extraordinary*]   (HU)

rend pu.......	Rendezo Palyaudvar [*Marshalling Yards (Railway)*] (HU)
RENEC......	Rede Nacional das Emissoras Catolicas [*National Association of Catholic Radio Stations*] [*Brazil*] (LAA)
RENEC......	Registraduria Nacional del Estado Civil [*National Civil Registry Office*] [*Colorado*] (LA)
RENEC......	Regroupement National des Etudiants Camerounais [*National Regrouping of Cameroonese Students*]
renf............	Renforce [*Reinforced*] [*Publishing*] [*French*]
RENFE......	Red Nacional de los Ferrocariles Espanoles [*Spanish National Railways*] (EY)
RENFE......	Red Nacional de los Ferrocarriles Espanoles [*Spanish National Railroads*] (WER)
RENOR.....	Regiao de Producao do Norte [*Belem, Brazil*] (LAA)
rentg..........	X-Ray, Roentgen (RU)
REO..........	Regional Education Officer
REO..........	Rio Airways, Inc. [*ICAO designator*] (FAAC)
REO..........	Russian Economic Society (RU)
reorg.........	Reorganized (EECI)
REP...........	Die Republikaner [*Republican Party*] [*Germany*] [*Political party*] (PPW)
REP...........	Distribution and Shipping of Printed Matter (BU)
REP...........	Distribution Clearing Station [*Military*] (BU)
REP...........	Evacuation Distribution Station (RU)
REP...........	Exploration and Extraction Establishment (RU)
REP...........	Radioelektronnoye Podavleniye [*Radio Electronic Suppression*] [*Soviet counterintelligence*] (LAIN)
REP...........	Regiment Etranger de Parachutistes [*Foreign Paratroop Regiment*] (AF)
REP...........	Regional Environmental Plan [*Australia*]
rep............	Repare [*Repaired*] [*French*]
rep............	Repareret [*Repaired*] [*Danish/Norwegian*]
rep............	Repariert [*Repaired*] [*German*]
Rep...........	Reparticao [*Partition*] [*Portuguese*]
rep............	Repartition [*Allotment*] [*French*]
Rep...........	Repertoire [*Benelux*] (BAS)
rep............	Report [*French*]
Rep...........	Report [*German*]
rep............	Reportaz [*or Reporter*] [*Report or Reporter*] [*Poland*]
Rep...........	Representative (PWGL)
rep............	Reprovado [*Rejected*] [*Portuguese*]
Rep...........	Republic (EECI)
Rep...........	Republican (SCAC)
REP...........	Republiek [*Republic*] [*Afrikaans*]
rep............	Repulo [*Flying, Flyer, Aircraft*] (HU)
REP...........	Subscription System for the Distribution of the Daily Press (BU)
REPA........	Rural Environment Planning Association [*Australia*]
REPAHA...	Regional Educational Program for Animal Health Assistants [*Guyana*] (LA)
repar.........	Reparation [*Repair*] [*French*]
repar.........	Repariert [*Repaired*] [*German*]
reparat.......	Reparation [*Repair*] [*French*]
RepColin....	Repertoire de Jurisprudence Congolaise [*Congo*] (BAS)
Rep DrInt Prive ...	Repertoire de Droit International Prive [*Fonde par de La Pradelle et Niboyet*] [*A publication*] (FLAF)
REPELITA ...	Rentjana Pembangunan Lima Tahun [*5-Year Development Plan (1969-1973)*] (IN)
REPEM-CEAAL ...	Red de Educacion Popular Entre Mujeres Afiliada al Consejo de Educacion de A dultos de America Latino [*Women's Network of the Council for Adult Education in Latin American*] [*Ecuador*] (EAIO)
Repert	Repertorium [*Compendium*] [*German*] (GCA)
repertkom ..	Repertoire Committee (RU)
REPESA....	Refineria de Petroleos de Escombreras SA [*Spain*]
repet.........	Repetition [*Repetition*] [*Knitting*] [*French*]
RepF.........	Repertoire Fiscal [*Benelux*] (BAS)
RepFisc	Repertoire Fiscal [*Benelux*] (BAS)
REPIDISCA ...	Red Panamericana de Informacion y Documentacion en Ingenieria Sanitaria y Ciencias del Ambiente [*Pan American Network for Information and Documentation in Sanitary Engineering and Environmental Sciences*] [*WHO*] [*United Nations*] (DUND)
repl............	Replie [*Folded on Itself*] [*Publishing*] [*French*]
REPLEK....	Republicko Pretprijatie za Promet so Lekovi [*Republican (i.e., Macedonian) Pharmaceutical Trade Establishment*] [*Skopje*] (YU)
REPMC.....	Representative to the Military Committee [*NATO*]
REPOSA ...	Resinas Poliesteres SA [*Spain*]
RepPrat......	Repertoire Pratique du Droit Belge [*Belgium*] (BAS)
RepPratDrB ..	Repertoire Pratique du Droit Belge [*Belgium*] (BAS)
repr...........	Reproductie [*Reproduction*] [*Publishing*] [*Netherlands*]
repr...........	Reproduction [*Reproduction*] [*Publishing*] [*French*]
REPRECOL ...	Representacoes e Construcoes Lda.
reprod........	Reproductie [*Reproduction*] [*Publishing*] [*Netherlands*]
reprod........	Reproduction [*Publishing*] [*French*]
Reprod	Reproduktion [*Reproduction*] [*Publishing*] [*German*]

REPSA	Refineria Paraguaya, Sociedad Anonima [*Paraguay Refineries, Incorporated*] (LA)
repter..........	Repuloter [*Airfield*] (HU)
Rept MtgAAAS ...	Report. Meeting of the Australasian Association for the Advancement of Science [*A publication*]
Repub........	Republic (SCAC)
Req............	Chambre des Requetes [*French*]
RER	Radioelektronnaya Razvedka [*Reconnaissance and Intelligence*] [*Soviet counterintelligence*] (LAIN)
RER	Reseau Express Regional [*Paris subway*]
Rer	Rocher [*Rock*] [*French*] (NAU)
RER	Rural Economy Research
RERAN	Reunion Especial de Representantes Gubernamentales de Alto Nivel para Fortalecer al CIES [*Consejo Interamericano Economico y Social*] (LAA)
RERF........	Radiation Effects Research Foundation [*Research center*] [*Japan*] (IRC)
RERIC	Renewable Energy Resources Information Center [*Asian Institute of Technology*] [*Thailand*]
RERU	Rural Economy Research Unit
RES...........	Centre for Resource and Environmental Studies [*Australian National University*] (ARC)
RES...........	Electric Contact-Roller Welding (RU)
RES...........	Rayon Electric Power Plant (RU)
RES...........	Reformed Ecumenical Synod [*South Africa*] (AF)
RES...........	Regional Environmental Study [*Australia*]
res.............	Reserva Militar [*Military Reserve*] [*Portuguese*]
Res	Reserve [*German*]
Res	Residencia [*Residence*] [*Portuguese*]
res.............	Residentie [*Resident*] [*Benelux*] (BAS)
RES...........	Resistencia [*Argentina*] [*Airport symbol*] (OAG)
Res	Resmi [*Official*] (TU)
Res	Resolu [*Resolved, Decided*] [*French*] (ILCA)
Res	Resolution [*Benelux*] (BAS)
RES...........	Restauraciones Aeronauticas SA de CV [*Mexico*] [*ICAO designator*] (FAAC)
RES...........	Reticuloendothelial System (RU)
RES...........	Royal Easter Show [*Australia*]
RESACENT ...	Remote Sensing Applications Centre [*Pakistan*] [*Research center*] (IRC)
RESADOC ...	Reseau Sahelien d'Information et de Documentation Scientifiques et Techniques [*Sanelian Scientific and Technical Information and Documentation Network*] [*Bamako, Mali*]
RESAV	Real Estate Salespersons' Association of Victoria [*Australia*]
RESAWA ..	Real Estate Salespersons' Association of Western Australia
RESC	Real Estate Services Council [*Australia*]
RESELCO ...	Fabrica de Resistencias Electricas Colombianas [*Colombia*] (COL)
Res etIura ...	Res et Iura Immobilia [*Benelux*] (BAS)
REShD.......	Electric Reaction Step Motor (RU)
RESHUS...	Reseau Documentaire en Sciences Humaines de la Sante [*Network for Documentation in the Human Sciences of Health*] [*Institut de l'Information Scientifique et Technique*] [*Information service or system*] (IID)
RESIBA.....	Resinas Sinteticas da Bahia SA [*Brazil*]
Resid	Residence [*or Resident*] [*Residence or Resident*] [*French*] (MTD)
RESIDA	Reporteros Sindicalizados de Antioquia [*Colombia*] (COL)
Res Im........	Res et Jura Immobilia [*Benelux*] (BAS)
RESIV	Real Estate and Stock Institute of Victoria [*Australia*]
Res JuraImm ...	Res et Jura Immobilia [*Benelux*] (BAS)
RESKRIM ...	Reserse Kriminil [*Criminal Investigations*] (IN)
RESMAC ..	Red Sismica Mexicana de Apertura Continental [*Continental Mexican Seismic Network*] (LA)
resol...........	Resolution [*French*] (FLAF)
RESOLCOL ...	Resortes de Colombia Ltda. [*Palmira*] (COL)
RESOS	Radio-Electrical Equipment and Communications Station (RU)
resp	Republic (RU)
resp	Respectively (BU)
resp	Respektieflik [*Respectively*] [*Afrikaans*]
Resp	Respektive [*Respectively*] [*German*]
RESPOL....	Resguardo y Policia Aduanera [*Customs Security and Police*] [*Chile*] (LA)
Respta	Respuesta [*Answer*] [*Spanish*]
REST	Relief Society of Tigre [*Ethiopia*]
rest	Restaurato [*Repaired*] [*Italian*]
rest	Restaure [*Restored*] [*Publishing*] [*French*]
rest	Restauriert [*Repaired*] [*German*]
REST	Retail Employees Superannuation Trust [*Australia*]
restaur........	Restaurato [*Repaired*] [*Italian*]
RESTEC....	Remote Sensing Technology Centre [*Japan*]
Restitut	Restitution [*French*] (FLAF)
reszl...........	Reszleg [*Section, Detachment*] (HU)
RET	Radiation-Effective Temperatures (RU)
RET	Radioellentevekenyseg [*Radio Countermeasures*] (HU)

RET .... Renewable Energy Technology [*Project of the Botswana Technology Group*]
Ret .... Retorica [*Rhetoric*] [*Portuguese*]
ret .... Retoriikka [*Rhetoric*] [*Finland*]
ret .... Retrato [*Portrait*] [*Portuguese*]
RET .... Rost [*Norway*] [*Airport symbol*]   (OAG)
RETD .... Red Especial de Transmision de Datos [*Spanish telephone co.*]
retd .... Retired   (EECI)
RETE .... Radioellentevekenyseg Elharitasa [*Defense Against Radio Countermeasures*]   (HU)
RETE .... Real Estate Title Exchange [*Australia*]
RETECSA ... Representaciones Tecnicas, Sociedad Anonima [*Venezuela*]
RETI .... Communaute de Travail des Regions Europeennes de Tradition Industrielle [*Association of Traditional Industrial Regions of Europe*] [*Lille, France*]   (EAIO)
RETIS .... Regional Technological Information Service [*India*]
Retrnt .... Retranchement [*Intrenchment*] [*Military map abbreviation World War I*] [*French*]   (MTD)
rets .... Recessive   (RU)
rets .... Review, Reviewer   (RU)
Rett .... Rettung [*Rescue*] [*German*]   (GCA)
RETU .... River Technical Operations Administration   (RU)
REU .... Air Reunion [*France*] [*ICAO designator*]   (FAAC)
REU .... Reunion [*ANSI three-letter standard code*]   (CNC)
REU .... Reus [*Spain*] [*Airport symbol*]   (OAG)
REU .... Rhodesia Electoral Union
REUNIR.... Reseau des Universites et de la Recherche [*Network of Universities and Research*] [*French*] [*Computer science*]   (TNIG)
REUR .... Regional Office for Europe [*FAO*]   (ASF)
REUS........ Importadora de Repuestos Usados Ltda. [*Colombia*]   (COL)
REUV .... Universal Electronic Explosionproof Relay   (RU)
Rev .... Cour de Revision [*Monaco*]   (DLA)
REV .... Rechnungseinzugsverfahren [*Invoice Collection System (Cashless system of paying bills)*]   (EG)
REV .... Register of Encumbered Vehicle [*Australia*]
REV .... Reventador [*Race of maize*] [*Mexico*]
Rev .... Reverend   (SCAC)
Rev .... Reverendo [*Reverend*] [*Portuguese*]
Rev .... Revident [*or Revier*] [*German*]
rev .... Revideret [*Revised*] [*Publishing Danish/Norwegian*]
rev .... Revidiert [*Revised*] [*Publishing*] [*German*]
rev .... Revisao [*Revision*] [*Portuguese*]
Rev .... Revista [*Review*] [*Portuguese*]
Rev .... Revisyon [*Revision*]   (TU)
rev .... Revolver   (RU)
rev .... Revu [*Revised*] [*Publishing*] [*French*]
REV .... Rural Enterprise Victoria [*Australia*]
Reva .... Reverencia [*Reverence*] [*Portuguese*]
REVALCO ... Remaches y Valvulas Colombianas Ltda. [*Colombia*]   (COL)
REVCOM ... Revolutionary Committee [*China*]
Revd .... Reverend [*Reverend*] [*French*]
REV DEV .. Revolutionary Development [*South Vietnam*]
Revdo .... Reverendo [*Reverend*] [*Portuguese*]
revid .... Reviderad [*Revised*] [*Sweden*]
revid .... Revidiert [*Revised*] [*Publishing*] [*German*]
REVIMA ... Societe pour la Revision et l'Entretien du Materiel Aeronautique [*French*]
Revis .... Revisor [*German*]
reviz........... Inspector, Auditor   (RU)
rev kom ..... Revolutionary Committee   (RU)
Revmo .... Reverendissimo [*Most Reverend*] [*Portuguese*]
revol .... Revolutionary   (BU)
RevTar ...... Revenue Tariff [*Australia*] [*Political party*]
rev var .... Revenu Variable [*Variable Income*] [*French*]
Revvoyensovet ... Revolutionary Military Council [*1918-1934*]   (RU)
revvoyentribunal ... Revolutionary Military Tribunal   (RU)
REVY........ Royal Edward Victualling Yard [*Royal Australian Navy*]
REW .... Reichsbahnentwicklungswerk [*GDR Railroad Development Works*]   (EG)
REX .... Reynosa [*Mexico*] [*Airport symbol*]   (OAG)
REXS........ Radio Exploration Satellite [*Japan*]
REY .... Aero-Rey SA de CV [*Mexico*] [*ICAO designator*]   (FAAC)
REY .... Reyes [*Bolivia*] [*Airport symbol*]   (OAG)
REYA .... Revolutionary Ethiopian Youth Association
REYDIN.... Representaciones y Distribuciones Industriales Ltda. [*Colombia*]   (COL)
rez............. Electrified Wire Entanglement Company   (RU)
REZ .... Radioelektronnaya Zashchita [*Radioelectronic Defense*] [*Soviet counterintelligence*]   (LAIN)
rez............. Reserve   (RU)
rez............. Reservoir, Tank, Cistern   (RU)
rez............. Resume, Summary   (BU)
rez............. Reziprok [*Reciprocal*] [*German*]   (GCA)
rez............. Rezyser [*Director*] [*Poland*]
REZ .... Riga Electrical Machinery Plant   (RU)

rez.............. Rubber   (RU)
rez.............. Rubber Products Plant [*Topography*]   (RU)
rez.............. Rutherford   (RU)
Rezinoproyekt ... State Institute for the Planning of Establishments of the Rubber Industry   (RU)
Rezinotekhnika ... Industrial Rubber Products Plant   (RU)
Rezinotrest ... State Trust of the Rubber Industry   (RU)
Rezinproyekt ... State Institute for the Planning of Establishments of the Rubber Industry   (RU)
rez ras........ Resonance Scattering   (RU)
rf................ Abstract, Paper   (RU)
RF .... Distribution Feeder   (RU)
RF .... Forcing Relay   (RU)
RF .... Fournier [*France*] [*ICAO aircraft manufacturer identifier*]   (ICAO)
RF .... Franc [*Monetary unit*] [*Rwanda*]
RF .... Radio France   (IAA)
rf................ Radphot   (RU)
RF .... Rechnerfamilie [*German*]   (ADPT)
rf................ Refractometry   (RU)
RF .... Republique Francaise [*French Republic*]
RF .... Responsibilite Familiale [*Insurance*] [*French*]   (FLAF)
rf................ Revenu Fixe [*Fixed Income*] [*French*]
RF .... Rhodesian Front [*Later, Republican Front*]
Rf .... Rif [*Reef*] [*Netherlands*]   (NAU)
Rf .... Riff [*Reef*] [*German*]   (NAU)
RF .... Rinforzando [*With Special Emphasis*] [*Music*]
RF .... Routes Forestieres [*Forested Routes*] [*French*]   (BARN)
RF .... Rwanda Franc
RF .... Sveriges Riksidrottsforbund [*Swedish Sports Confederation*]   (EAIO)
RFA .... Rainforest Foundation Australia
RFA .... Reglement Forfaitaire Anticipe [*France*]   (FLAF)
RFA .... Republica Federal Alema [*Federal Republic of Germany*] [*Use FRG*] [*Portuguese*]   (WER)
RFA .... Republique Federale d'Allemagne [*Federal Republic of Germany*] [*Use FRG*]   (AF)
RFA .... Retard a la Fermeture de l'Admission [*French*]   (MTD)
RFA .... Royal Field Artillery [*Australia*]
RFACA ...... Royal Federation of Aero Clubs of Australia   (ADA)
RFB.......... Air-Cushion Vehicle built by Rhein Flugzeugbau [*Usually used in combination with numerals*] [*Germany*]
RFB.......... Reaktorbau Forschungs und Baugesellschaft mbH & Co. [*Nuclear energy*] [*Austria*]   (NRCH)
RFB.......... Registrar of Finance Brokers [*Victoria, Australia*]
RFB.......... Roter Frontkaempferbund [*League of Red Front Fighters*]   (WEN)
RFBR .... Russian Foundation for Basic Research
RFC.......... Rajasthan Financial Corp. [*India*]   (PDAA)
RFC.......... Raljska Fabrika Cementa [*Ralja Cement Factory*]   (YU)
RFC.......... Resource Finance Corp. [*Australia*]
RFC.......... Royal Flying Corps [*Australia*]
RFC.......... Rural Finance Corp. [*Australia*]
RFCA........ Rare Fruit Council of Australia
RFCA........ Retail Floor Coverings Association of New South Wales [*Australia*]
RFCV .... Rural Finance Council of Victoria [*Australia*]
RFCWA..... Regional Fisheries Commission for Western Africa   (MSC)
RFD .... Republik Federal Djerman [*Federal Republic of Germany*]   (IN)
RFD .... Reserve Forces Decoration [*Australia*]
RFDK........ Republic Long-Term Credit Fund   (RU)
RFDS........ Royal Flying Doctor Service [*Australia*]
RFE.......... Aero Fe SA [*Mexico*] [*ICAO designator*]   (FAAC)
RFE.......... Retard a la Fermeture de l'Echappement [*French*]   (MTD)
RFEI .... Rostov-Na-Donu Institute of Finance and Economics   (RU)
RFET......... Real Federacion Espanola de Tenis [*Royal Spanish Tennis Federation*]   (EAIO)
RFF........... Rede Ferroviaria Federal [*Federal Railway Network*] [*Brazil*]   (LA)
RFF........... Rocket Fabrication Facility [*ISRO*] [*India*]   (PDAA)
RFFG .... Reserve Fund for Future Generations [*Finance Ministry*] [*Kuwait*]
RFFSA...... Rede Ferroviaria Federal Sociedad Anonima [*Brazil*]
RFFSA...... Rede Ferroviaria Federal Sociedade Anonima [*Federal Railway Corporation*] [*Brazil*]   (EY)
RFG .... Follicle-Stimulating Hormone Reaction   (RU)
RFG .... Rayon Physical Culture Group   (BU)
RFG .... Referendum First Group [*Australia*]
RFG .... Reise und Industrieflug [*Airline*] [*Germany*]
RFG .... Republica Federala Germana [*Federal Republic of Germany*]   (RO)
RFGC........ Royal Fremantle Golf Club [*Australia*]
RFH .... Reichsfinanzhof [*Reich Finance Court*] [*German*]   (ILCA)
RfH .... Riksfoerbundet foer Hembygdsvard [*Sweden*]   (SLS)
RFI .... Radio France Internationale [*Proposed French equivalent to England's BBC*]

RFI............ Republicki Finansiski Inspektorat [*Republic Financial Inspectorate*]   (YU)
RFI............ Richmond Fellowship International [*British*]   (EAIO)
RFIC......... Republique Federale Islamique des Comores [*Islamic Federal Republic of the Comoros*]   (AF)
RFJ .... Ring Freiheitlicher Jugend [*Liberal Students Organization*] [*FPOe affiliate*] [*Austria*]   (WEN)
RFK........... Radio Free Kabul [*British*] [*Defunct*]   (EAIO)
RFK........... Ribosephosphoric Acid   (RU)
RFKhO ...... Russian Physicochemical Society [*1878-1930*]   (RU)
RFM .... Reserve Force Medal [*Military decoration*] [*Australia*]
RFMA....... Rassemblement Franco-Musulman Algerien
RFN .... Raufarhofn [*Iceland*] [*Airport symbol*]   (OAG)
RFN .... Rybnicka Fabryka Maszyn [*Rybnik Machine Factory*]   (POL)
RFNRE...... Revolving Fund for Natural Resources Exploration [*United Nations*]   (EY)
RFO .... Air Royal [*France*] [*ICAO designator*]   (FAAC)
RFO .... Radiodiffusion Francaise d'Outre-Mer [*Radio broadcasting company*] [*French*]   (FEA)
RFO .... Radio France d'Outre-Mer [*Mayotte, Comoros*]
RFO .... Rayon Finance Department   (RU)
RFO .... Russian Photographic Society   (RU)
RFO .... Russian Physical Society   (RU)
RFP........... Raiatea [*French Polynesia*] [*Airport symbol*]   (OAG)
RFP........... Rassemblement des Forces Patriotiques [*Chad*]
RF/PF....... Regional Forces - Popular Forces [*Republic of Vietnam*] [*Army*]
RFPOS ...... Rada Federalna Polskich Organizacji Studenckich [*Federal Council of Polish Student Organizations*]   (POL)
RFQ .... Request for Quotation
Rfr............. Ranskan Frangi(a) [*Finland*]
RFR........... Rio Frio [*Costa Rica*] [*Airport symbol*]   (OAG)
RFRN .... Redeemable Floating Rate Note
RFS........... Radio Broadcasting Station   (RU)
RFS........... Ring Freiheitlicher Studenten [*Liberal Party Students Circle*] [*Austria*]   (WEN)
RFS........... Rossair Pty Ltd. [*Australia*] [*ICAO designator*]   (FAAC)
RFS........... Rossendorfer Forschungs-Reaktor [*Rossendorf Research Reactor*] [*German*]
RFS........... Rural Fire Service [*Australia*]
RFSB .... Regional Forward Scatter Branch [*Supreme Allied Commander, Europe*]   (NATG)
RFSP .... Radet foer Forskning foer Samfunnsplanlegging [*NAVF Council for Research for Societal Planning*] [*Research center*] [*Norway*]   (IRC)
RFSRR ...... Rosyjska Federacyjna Socjalistyczna Republika Radziecka [*Russian Soviet Federated Socialist Republic*]   (POL)
RFSS......... Reichsfuehrerschutzstaffel [*German*]   (BJA)
RFT........... Reactor for Physics and Engineering Research   (RU)
RFT........... Repubblica Federale Tedesca [*Federal Republic of Germany*] [*Use FRG*] [*Italian*]   (WER)
RFT........... Rundfunk- und Fernmeldetechnik [*Radio and Telecommunications Technology*]   (EG)
RFTO........ Russian Physicotechnical Society   (RU)
RFV........... Excitation Fixation Relay   (RU)
RFWCHS.. Royal Far West Children's Homes Scheme [*Australia*]
RFZ........... Rinforzando [*With Special Emphasis*] [*Music*]
RFZ........... Rundfunk- und Fernsehtechnisches Zentralamt [*Radio and Television Central Office*]   (EG)
RG............. Hand Grenade   (RU)
RG............. Rada Glowna [*Central Council*]   (POL)
RG............. Rada Gospodarcza [*Economic Council*]   (POL)
RG............. Ragusa [*Car registration plates*] [*Italian*]
rg............... Rang [*Row*] [*Knitting*] [*French*]
RG............. Rdultovskiy Point Detonation Fuze   (RU)
RG............. Reaktionsgeschwindigkeit [*Reaction Velocity*] [*German*]   (GCA)
RG............. Realgymnasium [*German*]
RG............. Rechtsgeschichte [*German*]   (ILCA)
RG............. Reconnaissance Group   (RU)
Rg............. Regierung [*German*]
RG............. Reichsgericht [*Reich Supreme Court*] [*German*]   (ILCA)
RG............. Renseignements Generaux [*General Information (Intelligence)*] [*French Secret Police*]   (CL)
RG............. Revolutionary Government [*Vietnam*]
RG............. Rhombic Horizontal [*Antenna*]   (RU)
rg............... Rive Gauche [*Left Bank*] [*French*]
RG............. Rotglut [*Red Heat*] [*German*]   (GCA)
RG............. Rueckgang [*Return*] [*Music*]
RG............. Volume Control   (RU)
RGA .... Hemagglutination Reaction   (RU)
Rga............ Rangieraufseher [*Classification Yard Supervisor*]   (EG)
RGA .... Region Air [*Seychelles*] [*ICAO designator*]   (FAAC)
RGA .... Regional Galleries Association of New South Wales [*Australia*]
RGA .... Rio Grande [*Argentina*] [*Airport symbol*]   (OAG)
RGA .... Rubber Growers' Association [*Later, TGA*]   (EAIO)
RGAQ........ Regional Galleries Association of Queensland [*Australia*]
rgb............. Deep Drilling Company   (RU)

RGB .... Rechtsreglement Buitengewesten [*Benelux*]   (BAS)
RGB .... Republic of Guinea-Bissau
RGBL........ Reichsgesetzblatt [*Federal Legal Press*] [*German*]   (BJA)
RGB-MB ... Resistencia da Guine-Bissau Movimento Bafata [*Political party*]   (EY)
RGC .... Renison Goldfields Consolidated Ltd. [*Australia*]
RGCFTP.... Regie Generale de Chemins de Fer et de Travaux Publics [*General Railroad and Public Works Agency*] [*Cameroon*]   (AF)
RGCL........ Reunion General Confederation of Labor
RGD.......... Degtyarev Hand Grenade   (RU)
RGD.......... Depth Remote Flow Meter   (RU)
RGD.......... Double Rhombic Horizontal [*Antenna*]   (RU)
RGD.......... Rijks Geologische Dienst [*Netherlands*]   (MSC)
RGda......... Radio Grenada
RGDAA ..... Royal Guide Dogs Association of Australia
RGDAT .... Royal Guide Dogs Association of Tasmania [*Australia*]
RGDU........ Rassemblement General pour le Desarmement Universel
RGE .... Gamma-Electron Relay   (RU)
RGE .... Porgera [*Papua New Guinea*] [*Airport symbol*]   (OAG)
RGE .... Rat der Gemeinden Europas [*Council of European Municipalities*]
Rge .... Refuge [*Shelter*] [*Military map abbreviation World War I*] [*French*]   (MTD)
RGE .... Regroupement des Guineens a l'Exterieur [*Rally of Guineans Abroad*]   (PD)
Rgel MagTh ... Rechtsgeleerde Magazijn Themis [*Benelux*]   (BAS)
RGEM .... Representantes des Gouvernements des Etats Membres [*Au Sein du Conseil*] [*French*]
RGFS......... Religiose Gesellschaft der Freunde (Quaker) in der Schweiz [*Religious Society ofFriends (Quakers) in Switzerland*]   (EAIO)
Rgg............. Regentschapsgerecht [*Benelux*]   (BAS)
RGGA .... State Riga City Archives of the Latvian SSR   (RU)
RGI .... Rangiroa [*French Polynesia*] [*Airport symbol*]   (OAG)
RGI .... Regional Airlines [*France*] [*ICAO designator*]   (FAAC)
RGI .... Russian Hydrological Institute   (RU)
RGK.......... City District Committee   (RU)
RGK .... General Headquarters Reserve   (BU)
RGK .... Reserv Glavnogo Komandovaniia [*Reserve of the High Command*] [*Former USSR*]
RGKDAI.... RomischGermanische Kommission des Deutschen Archaologischen Instituts [*Roman-Germanic Commission of the German Archaeological Institute*] [*Germany*]   (EAIO)
RGL .... Rio Gallegos [*Argentina*] [*Airport symbol*]   (OAG)
RGLC........ Racing, Gaming, and Liquor Commission [*Northern Territory, Australia*]
rglm........... Regelmaessig [*Regular*] [*German*]   (GPO)
RGM......... Rdultovskiy Membrane-Type Point Detonating Fuze   (RU)
RGM......... Rijksmuseum van Geologie en Mineralogie [*National Museum of Geology and Mineralogy*] [*Rijksuniversiteit Leiden*] [*Netherlands*]   (EAS)
RGMI .... Rostov State Medical Institute   (RU)
RGMTs....... Regional Hydrometeorological Center   (RU)
RGN........... Raad vir Geesteswetenskaplike Navorsing [*Afrikaans*]
RGN........... Rada Gospodarki Narodowej [*Council on the National Economy*]   (POL)
RGN........... Rangoon [*Myanmar*] [*Airport symbol*]   (OAG)
RG NOT .... Rada Glowna Naczelnej Organizacji Technicznej [*High Council of the Chief Technical Organization*] [*Poland*]
RGNU........ Royal Government of National Union of Cambodia [*Use GRUNK*]   (CL)
RGNUC ..... Royal Government of National Union of Cambodia [*Use GRUNK*]   (CL)
RGO.......... Argo SA [*Dominican Republic*] [*ICAO designator*]   (FAAC)
RGO.......... Rada Glowna Opiekuncza [*Main Charity Council*] [*World War II*]   (POL)
RGO.......... Realisation de Grands Ouvrages [*Algeria*]
RGO.......... Regelungstechnik, Geraetebau und Optik [*Regulating Technology, Appliance and Optical Tools Industry*]   (EG)
RGO.......... Revolutionaere Gewerkschafts-Opposition [*Revolutionary Trade-Union Opposition*]   (EG)
RGO.......... Russian Geographic Society [*1845-1924*]   (RU)
RGP.......... Rhodesian Government Party
RGP.......... Rijksgeschied-Kundige Publicaties
RGPH .... Rada Glowna Przyjaciol Harcerstwa [*Chief Council of Friends of Scouting*]   (POL)
RGR.......... Rassemblement des Gauches Republicaines [*Assembly of the Republican Left*] [*France*] [*Political party*]
RGR.......... Rassemblement des Gaullistes Reunionnais
RGS .... Horizontal Welded Petroleum Tank   (RU)
RGS .... Reforma General de Salarios [*General Wage Reform*] [*Cuba*]   (LA)
RGSA........ Royal Geographical Society of Australasia   (ADA)
RGSKhOS ... Republic State Agricultural Experimental Station   (RU)

RGSSA ...... Royal Geographical Society of Australasia, South Australian Branch
Rgt............. Regiment [*Regiment*] [*Military*] [*French*]   (MTD)
RGT .... Rengat [*Indonesia*] [*Airport symbol*]   (OAG)
RGT .... Reuniao Geral de Trabalhadores [*General Meeting of Workers*] [*Portuguese*]   (WER)
RgtB .... Regentsbesluit [*Benelux*]   (BAS)
RGT-Regel ... Reaktionsgeschwindigkeit-Temperatur Regel [*Reaction-Rate-Temperature Rule*] [*German*]   (GCA)
RGU .... Rostov State University   (RU)
RGUB .... Revolutionary Government of the Union of Burma
RGV .... Estimated Water Level, Rated Water Level   (RU)
RGV .... Rauhfuttergrossvieheinheit [*500 Kilograms of Live Weight of Domestic Animals Feeding on Coarse Fodder*]   (EG)
RGVV .... Estimated High-Water Level, Rated High-Water Level   (RU)
RGW .... Rat fuer Gegenseitige Wirtschaftshilfe [*Council for Economic Mutual Assistance (CEMA)*] [*German*]   (WEN)
RGZKP...... Rada Glowna Zwiazku Kompozytorow Polskich [*Main Council of the Union of Polish Composers*]   (POL)
RG ZLZS... Rada Glowna Zrzeszenia Ludowych Zespolow Sportowych [*Chief Council of Peasant Sports and Athletics Clubs Association*] [*Poland*]
RH .... Air Zimbabwe [*Zimbabwe*] [*ICAO designator*]   (ICDA)
RH .... Haiti [*Haiti*] [*Poland*]
Rh............. Rechtsherstel [*Benelux*]   (BAS)
rh.............. Residence Habituelle [*Benelux*]   (BAS)
RH .... Revisionist History [*Taby, Sweden*]   (EAIO)
Rh............. Rhein [*Rhine River*] [*German*]
rh.............. Rhonchi [*Rales*] [*Latin*]   (MAE)
rh.............. Rovid Hullamu [*Shortwave*]   (HU)
RH .... Rueckwaertiges Heeresgebiet [*Rear area of a group of armies*] [*German military*]
RH .... Southern Rhodesia [*ANSI two-letter standard code*] [*Obsolete*]   (CNC)
RH .... Wet tot Bevordering van de Rigtige Heffing der Directe Belastingen [*Benelux*]   (BAS)
RHA.......... Racial Hygiene Association [*Australia*]
RHA.......... Rental Housing Association [*Australia*]
RHA.......... Resmi Hizmet Arac [*Official Service Vehicle*]   (TU)
RHA.......... Resort Hotels of Australia
RHA.......... Reykholar [*Iceland*] [*Airport symbol*] [*Obsolete*]   (OAG)
RHA.......... Rural Housing Authority [*Western Australia*]
RHAAP ..... Rural Housing Assistance for Aborigines Program [*Australia*]
RHAPP ..... Rental Housing Assistance for Pensioners Program [*Australia*]
RHE.......... Reims [*France*] [*Airport symbol*]   (OAG)
rhein .... Rheinisch [*Of the Rhine River*] [*German*]   (GCA)
Rheinbraun ... Rheinische Braunkohlenwerke AG [*Germany*]   (WED)
RHEINHYP ... Rheinische Hypothekenbank AG [*Germany*]   (EY)
RHENO..... Rhodamine Experiment in the North Sea [*ICES*]   (MSC)
Rhet.......... Rhetoric   (TPFD)
rhet........... Rhetorique [*French*]   (TPFD)
RHFF........ Richard Hatch Fan Fellowship [*Defunct*]   (EAIO)
RHI........... Royal Hall of Industries [*Sydney Showground*] [*Australia*]
RHIC .... Rouse Hill Infrastructure Consortium Proprietary Ltd. [*Australia*]
Rhiz.......... Rhizom [*Rhizome*] [*German*]   (GCA)
Rhj .... Rechnungshalbjahr [*Half of Fiscal Year*]   (EG)
RHKJC...... Royal Hong Kong Jockey Club
RHKP .... Royal Hong Kong Police
Rhld .... Rheinland [*Rhineland*] [*German*]
RHN .... Rhonavia [*France*] [*ICAO designator*]   (FAAC)
RHO .... Reichshaushaltsordnung [*Federal Budget Order*] [*German*]
RHO .... Rhodes Island [*Greece*] [*Airport symbol*]   (OAG)
RHO .... Southern Rhodesia [*ANSI three-letter standard code*] [*Obsolete*]   (CNC)
Rhod.......... Rhodesia
Rhod.......... Rhodesiee [*Zimbabwe*] [*Afrikaans*]
RHOKAT .. Rhodesia-Katanga Company Limited
RHONICK ... Rhodesian Nickel Corporation Ltd.
RHP .... Regiment de Hussards Parachutistes [*Algeria*]
RHSET...... Rural Health Support Education and Training Program [*Australia*]
RHSNSW ... Royal Humane Society of New South Wales
RHSQ .... Royal Historical Society of Queensland [*Australia*]   (SLS)
RHSQld..... Royal Historical Society of Queensland [*Australia*]
RHSSA ...... Royal Humane Society of South Australia [*Australia*]
RHSV .... Royal Historical Society of Victoria [*Australia*]   (SLS)
RHSV .... Royal Horticultural Society of Victoria [*Australia*]
RHSVic...... Royal Historical Society of Victoria [*Australia*]
Rhuzi......... Rhodesian Uzi
RHV.......... Rada Hospodarska Vsestatni [*National Economic Council*]   (CZ)
rhW .... Rheinische Waehrung [*Rhenish Currency*] [*German*]
rhythm ...... Rhythmisch [*Rhythmical*] [*German*]   (GCA)
RI .... Computing Engineer   (RU)
RI .... Indonezja [*Indonesia*] [*Poland*]

RI .... Insulation Rubber   (RU)
RI .... Pulse Distributor   (RU)
RI .... Pulse Relay   (RU)
RI .... Pulse Storing Device   (RU)
RI .... Radioactive Isotope   (RU)
RI .... Rapport d'Intervention [*French*]   (ADPT)
ri .... Rechterlijke Inrichting [*Benelux*]   (BAS)
RI .... Recommended Inventions   (RU)
Ri.............. Redpath Industries Ltd. [*New Zealand*]
RI .... Regiment d'Infanterie [*Infantry Regiment*] [*French*]   (WER)
RI .... Register Selector   (RU)
RI .... Registro Italiano [*Italian ship classification society*]   (DS)
RI .... Rendelo Intezet [*Clinic for Ambulatory Patients*]   (HU)
RI .... Repubblica Italiana [*Republic of Italy*] [*Italian*]
RI .... Republicains Independants [*Independent Republicans*] [*French*]   (WER)
RI .... Republik Indonesia [*Republic of Indonesia*]   (IN)
RI .... Resistance International   (EA)
RI .... Rieti [*Car registration plates*] [*Italian*]
ri .... Rigging International Saudi Arabia Ltd.
RI .... Rio-Sul, Servicos Aereos Regionais SA [*Brazil*] [*ICAO designator*]   (ICDA)
RI .... Rithofundasamband Islands [*Writers' Union of Iceland*]   (EAIO)
RI .... Rockwell International
RI .... Selector Relay   (RU)
RI .... Servo Relay   (RU)
RIA .... Regiment d'Infanterie Autonome [*Autonomous Infantry Regiment*] [*Cambodia*]   (CL)
RIA .... Regiment Interarmes d'Appui [*Inter-Service Support Regiment*] [*Burkina Faso*]   (AF)
RIA .... Royal Irish Academy   (SLS)
RIA .... Rupin Institute of Agriculture [*Israel*]   (DSCA)
RIA .... Santa Maria [*Brazil*] [*Airport symbol*]   (OAG)
RIAACM... Research Institute of the Association of the Austrian Cement Industry   (EAIO)
RIAD .... Rencontres Internationales des Assureurs Defense [*Genoa, Italy*]   (EA)
RIAF........ Royal Indian Air Force
RIAF........ Royal Iraqi Air Force
RIALIDE... Red de Informacion de Alide
RIAM .... Regiment Interarmes Malgache [*Malagasy Inter-Service Regiment*]   (AF)
RIAM .... Royal Irish Academy of Music   (SLS)
RIAN .... Radium Institute Imeni V. G. Khlopin of the Academy of Sciences, USSR   (RU)
RIAOM ..... Regiment Interarmes d'Outre-Mer [*Overseas Inter-Service Regiment*] [*French*]   (AF)
RIAP .... Research Institute for Asia and the Pacific [*Australia*]
RIAS .... Research Institute for Animal Science
RIAS .... Research Institute for Applied Sciences [*Japan*]   (IRC)
RIAS .... Rundfunk im Amerikanischen Sektor Berlins [*Radio in American Sector*] [*Germany*]
RIAT........ Ramogi Institute of Advanced Technology
RIB........... Riberalta [*Bolivia*] [*Airport symbol*]   (OAG)
RIB........... Rijksinkoopbureau [*Government Purchasing Office*] [*Netherlands*]   (PDAA)
RIB........... Rural and Industries Bank of Western Australia [*Commercial firm*]
RIB........... "Russian Historical Library" [*1872-1927*]   (RU)
RIC .... Rainforest Information Centre [*Australia*]   (EAIO)
RIC .... Regiment d'Infanterie Commando [*Infantry Commando Regiment*] [*Burkina Faso*]   (AF)
RIC .... Reglement International Concernant le Transport des Containers [*Benelux*]   (BAS)
RIC .... Regolamento Internazionale Carrozze [*International Carriage and Van Union*]
RIC .... Rehabilitation Industries Corporation [*India*]   (GEA)
RIC .... Repertoire Bibliographique des Institutions Chretiennes [*Bibliographical Repertory of Christian Institutions*] [*Centre de Recherche et de Documentation des Institutions Chretiennes*] [*French*] [*Information service or system*]   (CRD)
RIC .... Reuniao Inter-Camaras [*Inter-Chamber Meeting*] [*Portuguese*]   (WER)
Ric .... Ricevuta [*Received*] [*Italian*]
RIC .... Rural Innovation Centre [*Western Australia*]
RICA........ Rural Industry Council of Australia
RICAT ...... Recherches Internationales Concertees dans l'Atlantique Tropical [*International Cooperative Investigation of the Tropical Atlantic - ICITA*] [*French*]   (MSC)
RICC........ Regie Industrielle de la Cellulose Coloniale [*France*]   (FLAF)
ricc.......... Riccamente [*Richly*] [*Italian*]
RICC........ Rice Industry Coordination Committee [*New South Wales, Australia*]
riccam....... Riccamente [*Richly*] [*Italian*]
ricchiss....... Ricchissimo [*Very Rich*] [*Italian*]

RICE.......... Rice Information Cooperative Effort University of the Philippines (DSCA)
RICHE....... Reseau d'Information et de Communication Hospitalier (OSI)
richem .... Richement [*Richly*] [*French*]
RICM......... Regiment d'Infanterie Coloniale de Maroc
RICM......... Registre International des Citoyens du Monde [*International Registry of World Citizens*]
RICOCI..... Representations Industrielles et Commerciales de l'Ouest de la Cote-D'Ivoire
RICOM ..... Comptoir du Rip
ricop .... Ricoperto [*Recovered*] [*Italian*]
RICPLA..... Reunion de la Ingenieria de la Cuenca del Plata [*Uruguay*] (DSCA)
RICU .... Reformed Industrial and Commercial Workers' Union
RID .... Radioisotopic Engine (RU)
RID .... Reactor Instituut te Delft [*Delft Reactor Institute*] [*Netherlands*] (WEN)
RID .... Regiment d'Infanterie Derive [*Derived Infantry Regiment*] [*French*] (WER)
RID .... Reglement International Concernant le Transport des Marchandises Dangereuses [*International Regulation Governing the Carriage of Dangerous Goods*]
RID .... Repatriement Integral des Devises [*Full Repatriation of Foreign Exchange*] (CL)
RID .... Report-Identifikationsnummer [*German*] (ADPT)
RID .... Rijksinstituut voor Dirkwatervoorziening [*State Institute for Drinking Water Research*] [*Netherlands*] (PDAA)
RID .... Royal Irrigation Department [*Thailand*] (DS)
RIDA .... Rural and Industrial Development Authority [*Malaysia*] (ML)
RIDE.......... Research in Distance Education [*Seminar*] [*Australia*]
RIDEP ...... Regional Integrated Development Project
RIDGE....... Ridge Interaction and Downstream Gradient Experiment [*International Southern Ocean Studies*] (MSC)
RIE............. Recognised Investment Exchange [*British*]
RIE............. Reglement International Concernant le Transport des Colis Express [*Benelux*] (BAS)
RIE............. Reseau Informatique Europeen [*French*] (ADPT)
RIE............. Royal Institute of Engineers [*Netherlands*] (EAIO)
RIEC......... Research Institute for Estate Crops [*Indonesian*] [*Research center*] (IRC)
RIEDA....... Reseau d'Innovations Educatives pour le Developpement en Afrique [*Network of Educational Innovation for Development in Africa*] (EAIO)
RIEG......... Radioisotopic Electrogenerator (RU)
RIEM........ Republic Institute of Experimental Medicine (BU)
RIEM........ Rostov Institute of Epidemiology and Microbiology (RU)
RIENA....... Rassegna Internazionale Elettronica Nucleare ed Aerospaziale [*Nuclear energy*] [*Italian*] (NRCH)
RIEP .... Research Institute for Education Planning [*South Africa*] (SLS)
RIEU .... Research Institute for Energy Utilization [*Germany*] (EAIO)
RIEx .... Reglement International Concernant le Transport des Colis Express [*International Regulation for the Transportation of Express Freight*] (EG)
RIF............. Radgivende Ingeniorers Forening [*Association of Consulting Engineers*] [*Norway*] (EAIO)
RIF............. Resistance Interieure Francaise (FLAF)
rif.............. Rifatto [*Rewritten*] [*Italian*]
RIFFI........ Riksforbundet Internationella Foereningen foer Invandrarkvinnor [*Sweden*]
rifil .... Rifilato [*Trimmed*] [*Publishing*] [*Italian*]
rifior .... Rifioriture [*Foxing*] [*Publishing*] [*Italian*]
rifl .... Riflessivo [*Reflexive*]
RIFP .... Research Institute for Fundamental Physics [*Kyoto University*] [*Japan*] (WND)
RIFR .... Radio Pulse Phase Discriminator (RU)
RIFT .... Regiment d'Infanterie des Forces du Territoire [*Territorial Forces Infantry Regiment*] [*French*] (WER)
RIG .... Editing and Publishing Group (RU)
RIG .... Reaktorinstitut des Vereines zur Forderung der Anwendung der Kernenergie [*Reactor Institute of the Association for the Advancement of Nuclear Energy Application*] [*Research center*] [*Austria*] (WND)
RIG .... Reaktor-Interessen-Gemeinschaft [*Austria*] (PDAA)
RIG .... Reference Interest Group [*Australia*]
RIG .... Riga Airlines [*Latvia*] [*ICAO designator*] (FAAC)
Rig.............. Rigole [*Gully*] [*Military map abbreviation World War I*] [*French*] (MTD)
RIG .... Rio Grande [*Brazil*] [*Airport symbol*] (OAG)
RIG .... Route d'Interet General [*General Use Highway*] (CL)
Rigasel'mash ... Riga Agricultural Machinery Plant (RU)
RIGOPS .... Rayon Forest and Environmental Protection Inspectorate (BU)
RIGPN....... Rayon State Fire Inspection (RU)
Rigt .... Rigters [*Judge*] [*Afrikaans*]
RIH........... Roboty Inzynierskie i Hydrotechniczne [*Engineering and Hydraulic (Enterprise)*] (POL)
RIHED ...... Regional Institute for Higher Education and Development (CL)

RIHES....... Research Institute for Health Sciences [*Thailand*] [*Research center*] (IRC)
RIIA.......... Reuniones de Intercambio de Informacion Agropecuaria [*Argentina*] (LAA)
RIIA.......... Royal Institute of International Affairs, London
RIIAM....... Research Institute of Investment Analysts Malaysia
RIIC.......... Rural Industries Innovation Centre [*Botswana*]
RIICO....... Rajasthan State Industrial Development & Investment Corporation Ltd. [*India*]
RIIEC .... Research Institute for International Economic Cooperation [*China*] (IRC)
RIIGVF ..... Riga Institute of Civil Air Fleet Engineers (RU)
RIITKhPZ ... Republic Scientific Research Institute for Labor Hygiene and Occupational Diseases (BU)
RIIZh........ Rayon Animal Husbandry Research Institute (BU)
RIIZh........ Republic Animal Husbandry Research Institute (BU)
RIIZhT...... Rostov Institute of Railroad Transportation Engineers (RU)
RIJ .... Rioja [*Peru*] [*Airport symbol*] (OAG)
RIJ .... Romano Internacionalno Jekhethanibe [*International Romani Union*] (EA)
RIK .... Radiofonikon Idryma Kyprou [*Cyprus Broadcasting Corporation*] (GC)
RIK .... Rayon Executive Committee (RU)
RIL............ Regulating Artificial Line (RU)
RIL............ Reliance Industries Ltd. [*India*]
ril.............. Rilegato [*Bound*] [*Publishing*] [*Italian*]
RIL............ Royal Interocean Line [*Australia*]
rilegat........ Rilegatura [*Binding*] [*Publishing*] [*Italian*]
RILEM ...... Reunion Internationale des Laboratoires d'Essais et de Recherches sur les Materiaux et les Constructions [*International Union of Testing and Research Laboratories for Materials and Structures*] (EAIO)
RILKO....... Research into Lost Knowledge Organisation Trust (EAIO)
RIM .... Quantized Pulse Modulation (RU)
RIM .... Regimiento de Infanteria Motorizada [*Motorized Infantry Regiment*] [*Cuba*] (LA)
RIM .... Republique Islamique de Mauritanie [*Islamic Republic of Mauritania*] (AF)
RIM .... Rhodesian Institute of Management
Rim........... Rimesse [*Remittance*] [*Business term*] [*German*]
RIMA .... Regiment d'Infanterie de la Marine [*Marine Corps Regiment*] [*French*] (WER)
RIMCU ..... Research Institute for Mindanao Culture [*Philippines*]
RIMDC...... Rajasthan State Industrial and Mineral Development Corp. [*India*] (PDAA)
RIME........ Research in the Middle East [*Cyprus*] [*Research center*] (IRC)
rim-kat...... Roman Catholic (RU)
RIMPAC ... Rim of the Pacific [*Naval exercise; name refers to the four participating countries: Australia, Canada, New Zealand, and the United States*]
RIMS........ Research Institute for Mathematical Sciences [*Kyoto University*] (MCD)
RIN .... Non-Unified Characteristics Selector Relay (RU)
RIN .... Resimen Induk [*Training Regiment*] (IN)
Rin............. Rhinology, Rhinologist (BU)
RIN .... Rijksinstituut voor Natuurbeheer [*Research Institute for Nature Management*] [*Research center*] [*Netherlands*] (ARC)
RIN .... Ringi Cove [*Solomon Islands*] [*Airport symbol*] (OAG)
RIN .... Royal Institute of Navigation (DS)
RINA .... Registro Italiano Navale ed Aeronautica [*Italy*]
RIND .... Research Institute of National Defense [*Sweden*]
RINE .... Research Institute of the National Economy [*Japan*]
RINF......... Rinforzando [*With Special Emphasis*] [*Music*]
rinf........... Rinforzato [*Reinforced*] [*Italian*]
rinforz .... Rinforzato [*Reinforced*] [*Italian*]
RINFZ....... Rinforzando [*With Special Emphasis*] [*Music*]
ringfoerm ... Ringfoermig [*Cyclical*] [*German*] (GCA)
RINI.......... Riz du Niger (EY)
rinnov .... Rinnovato [*Renewed*] [*Italian*]
RINPO ...... Research Institute of Nuclear Power Operation [*China*] (IRC)
RInS.......... Ratna Intendantska Sluzba [*War Quartermaster Service*] (YU)
RINSE....... Records Information Service [*Australia*]
RINTI i P... Republic Institute of Scientific and Technical Information and Propaganda (RU)
RIO .... Editorial and Publishing Section (RU)
RIO .... Inspection Department (RU)
RIO .... Rijecka Industrija Odjece [*Rijeka Clothing Industry*] (YU)
RIO .... Rio De Janeiro [*Brazil*] [*Airport symbol*] (OAG)
RIO .... Routine Information Processing (RU)
RIO .... Russian Historical Society [*1866-1917*] (RU)
RIO .... Unified Characteristics Selector Relay (RU)
RIOE .... Research Institute for Ocean Economics [*Japan*] (IRC)
RionGES.... Rion Hydroelectric Power Plant (RU)
RIP........... Reglement International Concernant le Transport des Wagons de Particuliers [*Benelux*] (BAS)
rip.............. Ripiegato [*Folded*] [*Publishing*] [*Italian*]

RIP............ Ripieno [*Additional*] [*Music*]
RIP............ Route Intraprovinciale [*Intraprovincial Highway*] (CL)
RIP............ Rural Industries Promotions [*Botswana*]
RIPA......... HCM [*Harish Chandra Mathur*] Rajasthan State Institute of Public Administration [*India*] [*Research center*] (IRC)
RIPAA....... Royal Institute of Public Administration Australia [*Australia*]
ripar .... Riparato [*Repaired*] [*Italian*]
riparaz........ Riparazione [*Repair*] [*Italian*]
RIPC.......... Regiment d'Infanterie Parachutiste de Choc [*Algeria*]
RIPC.......... Regroupement des Independants et Paysans Camerounais [*Regrouping of Independents and Farmers of the Cameroons*]
ripet........... Ripetuto [*Repeated*] [*Italian*]
RIPI .... Research Institute of the Paper Industry [*Hungary*]
ripieg......... Ripiegato [*Folded*] [*Publishing*] [*Italian*]
RIPN......... Controlled Direct-Current Power Supply (RU)
RIPP .... Russian-American Institute for President Programs [*For technology transfer*]
ripr .... Riproduzione [*Reproduction*] [*Italian*]
riprod .... Riproduzione [*Reproduction*] [*Italian*]
riproduz...... Riproduzione [*Reproduction*] [*Italian*]
RIPS.......... Regional Institute for Population Studies [*Accra, Ghana*]
RIPSA .... Rutas Internacionales Peruanas, Sociedad Anonima [*Peruvian International Routes, Incorporated*] (LA)
RIPT .... Research Institute for Polymers and Textiles [*Japan*] (PDAA)
RIRDC....... Rural Industries Research and Development Corp. [*Australia*]
RIRF .... Rural Industry Research Funds [*Australia*]
RIS............ Air Services Ltd. [*Czechoslovakia*] [*ICAO designator*] (FAAC)
ris .... Drawing (BU)
ris .... Drawing, Illustration, Diagram (RU)
RIS............ Editing and Publishing Council (BU)
RIS............ Impulse Signal Relay (RU)
RIS............ Ratna Intendantska Sluzba [*War Quartermaster Service*] (YU)
ris .... Rice [*Topography*] (RU)
RIS............ Rishiri [*Japan*] [*Airport symbol*] [*Obsolete*] (OAG)
RIS............ Synchronization Pulse Separator (RU)
RISC .... Rotterdam International Safety Centre [*Netherlands*]
RISCO....... Rhodesian Iron and Steel Company
RISCOM ... Rhodesian Iron and Steel Commission
RISCPT ..... Registre International des Sustances Chimiques Potentiellement Toxiques [*International Register of Potentially Toxic Chemicals - IRPTC*] [*French*] (ASF)
RISD.......... Rural Institutions and Services Division [*FAO*]
RISDA .... Rubber Industry Smallholders Development Authority [*Malaysia*] (GEA)
Rise .... Remise [*Military map abbreviation*] [*World War I*] [*French*] (MTD)
RISEAP..... Regional Islamic Da'Wah Council of Southeast Asia and the Pacific (EAIO)
RISI .... Resource Information Systems, Inc. (IID)
RISI .... Rostov-Na-Donu Construction Engineering Institute (RU)
RISKh........ Rostov Institute of Agricultural Machinery (RU)
RISKhI ...... Republic Scientific Research Institute of Sanitation and Hygiene (BU)
RISO......... Editorial and Publishing Council (RU)
RISO......... Riso National Laboratory [*Denmark*]
RISOL....... Risoluto [*Resolutely*] [*Music*] (ROG)
RISONPALM ... Rivers State Nigerian Palm Ltd.
RISPA .... Research Institute of the Sumatra Planters Association [*Indonesia*] (DSCA)
rist............. Ristampa [*Reprint*] [*Italian*]
RISVD....... Risvegliato [*Reanimated*] [*Music*] (ROG)
RIT............ Radioactive Thickness Gauge (RU)
RIT............ Rassemblement Interprofessionnel du Togo
RIT............ Recherche et Industrie Therapeutiques [*Belgium*]
RIT............ Rede Interamericana de Telecomunicaciones (LAA)
RIT............ Red Interamericana de Telecomunicaciones [*Inter-American Telecommunication Network*] (NTCM)
RIT............ Regiment d'Infanterie Territoriale [*Territorial Infantry Regiment*] [*French*]
RIT............ Regiment Interarmes Togolais [*Togolese Inter-Service Regiment*] (AF)
RIT............ Rio Tigre [*Panama*] [*Airport symbol*] (OAG)
RIT............ Ritardando [*Gradually Slower*] [*Music*]
RIT............ Ritenuto [*Immediately Slower*] [*Music*]
RIT............ Royal Institute of Technology [*Sweden*] (MCD)
RITA......... Red Informatica de Tratamiento de la Administracion [*Spanish*]
RITA......... Registered Industry Training Agent [*Australia*]
RITA......... Reseau Integre de Transmission Automatique [*French*]
RITA......... Reseau Integre de Transmissions de l'Armee de Terre [*Integrated Communications Network of the Army*] [*French*] (WER)
RITA......... Russian Information Telegraph Agency [*Formerly, TASS*]
RITAL....... Red Internacional de American Latina [*International Telecommunication Network for Latin America*] (NTCM)
RITAR...... Ritardando [*Gradually Slower*] [*Music*]
RITARD.... Ritardando [*Gradually Slower*] [*Music*]

RITARO.... Ritardando [*Gradually Slower*] [*Music*] (ROG)
RITEN...... Ritenuto [*Immediately Slower*] [*Music*]
RITENA .... Reunion Internacional de Tecnicos de la Nutricion Animal [*International Meeting of Animal Nutrition Experts*] (EAIO)
RITENO.... Ritenuto [*Immediately Slower*] [*Music*] (ROG)
RITES....... Rail India Technical and Economic Services
RITLA ...... Red Tecnologica Latinoamericana [*Latin American Technological Network*] (LA)
RITM........ Research Institute for Tropical Medicine [*Philippines*] [*Research center*] (IRC)
ritor .... Rhetorical (RU)
ritr .... Ritratto [*Portrait*] [*Italian*]
RITU .... Red International of Trade Unions [*Russian*]
RITU .... Regional Information Technology Unit [*Australia*]
RIU .... Radioactive Level Indicator (RU)
riun............ Riunito [*Combined*] [*Publishing*] [*Italian*]
RIV .... Regolamento Internazionale Veicoli [*Italian generic term meaning "International Regulation of Vehicles"*] [*Initialism also refers to International Wagon Union*]
RIV .... Republicko Izvrsno Vece [*Republic Executive Council*] (YU)
riv .... Riveduto [*Revised*] [*Italian*]
Riv............ Riviera [*Record label*] [*France*]
Riv............ Riviere [*River*] [*French*] (NAU)
Riv............ Rivista [*Review*] [*Italian*] (BJA)
RIV .... Rus in Vrede [*Rest in Peace*] [*Afrikaans*]
RIV .... Time Pulse Relay (RU)
RIVAN ...... Radio Interference Van [*Weapons Research Establishment*] [*Australia*]
Rivatex....... Rift Valley Textiles Ltd. [*Kenya*]
rived .... Riveduto [*Revised*] [*Italian*]
RIVO .... Rijksinstituut voor Visserijonderzoek [*Government Institute for Fishery Research*] [*Netherlands*] (WEN)
RIVON ...... Rijiksinsteut voor Veldbiologish Onderzoek ten behoeve van het Natuurbehoud [*State Institute for Nature Conservation Research*] [*Netherlands*] (DSCA)
RIVR......... Riverina [*Botanical region*] [*Australia*]
RIVRO....... Rijksinstituut voor het Rassenonderzoek van Cultuurgewassen [*Government Institute for Research on Varieties of Cultivated Plants*] [*Netherlands*] (ARC)
RIW .... Radiowy Instytut Wydawniczy [*Radio Publishing Institute*] (POL)
RIX .... Riga [*Former USSR*] [*Airport symbol*] (OAG)
RIZ........... Radio Industry Zagreb [*Former Yugoslavia*]
RIZ........... Rio Alzucar [*Panama*] [*Airport symbol*] (OAG)
RIZIV .... Rijksinstituut voor Ziekte- en Invaliditeits-Verzekering [*Benelux*] (BAS)
RIzsllZhiv St Z ... Rayon Animal Husbandry Research Institute in Stara Zagora (BU)
RJ............. Estado do Rio De Janeiro [*State of Rio De Janeiro*] [*Brazil*]
RJ............. Rio de Janeiro (IDIG)
RJA........... Rhodesian Judo Association
RJA........... Royal Jordanian [*ICAO designator*] (FAAC)
RJAA......... Royal Jordanian Air Academy (PDAA)
RJAA .... Tokyo/New Tokyo International [*Japan*] [*ICAO location identifier*] (ICLI)
RJAF .... Matsumoto [*Japan*] [*ICAO location identifier*] (ICLI)
RJAF .... Royal Jordanian Air Force
RJAH .... Hyakuri [*Japan*] [*ICAO location identifier*] (ICLI)
RJAI .... Ichigaya [*Japan*] [*ICAO location identifier*] (ICLI)
RJAK .... Kasumigaura [*Japan*] [*ICAO location identifier*] (ICLI)
RJAM........ Minamitorishima [*Japan*] [*ICAO location identifier*] (ICLI)
RJAO......... Chichijima [*Japan*] [*ICAO location identifier*] (ICLI)
RJAT .... Takigahara [*Japan*] [*ICAO location identifier*] (ICLI)
RJAW....... Iwo Jima [*Japan*] [*ICAO location identifier*] (ICLI)
RJB .... Rajbiraj [*Nepal*] [*Airport symbol*] [*Obsolete*] (OAG)
RJBD........ Nanki-Shirahama [*Japan*] [*ICAO location identifier*] (ICLI)
RJCA .... Asahikawa [*Japan*] [*ICAO location identifier*] (ICLI)
RJCB .... Obihiro [*Japan*] [*ICAO location identifier*] (ICLI)
RJCC .... Sapporo/Chitose [*Japan*] [*ICAO location identifier*] (ICLI)
RJCG........ Sapporo [*Japan*] [*ICAO location identifier*] (ICLI)
RJCH .... Hakodate [*Japan*] [*ICAO location identifier*] (ICLI)
RJCK .... Kushiro [*Japan*] [*ICAO location identifier*] (ICLI)
RJCM........ New Memanbetsu [*Japan*] [*ICAO location identifier*] (ICLI)
RJCN .... Nakashibetsu [*Japan*] [*ICAO location identifier*] (ICLI)
RJCO........ Sapporo/Okadama [*Japan*] [*ICAO location identifier*] (ICLI)
RJCR .... Rebun [*Japan*] [*ICAO location identifier*] (ICLI)
RJCS .... Kushiro/Kenebetsu [*Japan*] [*ICAO location identifier*] (ICLI)
RJCT .... Radio Jugoslovanske Cone Trsta [*Radio of Yugoslav Zone of Trieste*] (YU)
RJCT .... Tokachi [*Japan*] [*ICAO location identifier*] (ICLI)
RJCW........ Wakkanai [*Japan*] [*ICAO location identifier*] (ICLI)
RJCY .... Muroran/Yakumo [*Japan*] [*ICAO location identifier*] (ICLI)
RJDA........ Rassemblement des Jeunesses Democratiques Africaines [*Rally of African Democratic Youth*]

RJDA......... Recueil de Jurisprudence du Droit Administratif et du Conseil
　　　　　　d'Etat [*Benelux*]　(BAS)
RJDB......... Iki [*Japan*] [*ICAO location identifier*]　(ICLI)
RJDC......... Yamaguchi-Ube, Honshu Island [*Japan*] [*ICAO location
　　　　　　identifier*]　(ICLI)
RJDG........ Fukuoka [*Japan*] [*ICAO location identifier*]　(ICLI)
RJDK........ Kamigoto [*Japan*] [*ICAO location identifier*]　(ICLI)
RJDM...... Metabaru [*Japan*] [*ICAO location identifier*]　(ICLI)
RJDO........ Ojika [*Japan*] [*ICAO location identifier*]　(ICLI)
RJDT........ Tsushima [*Japan*] [*ICAO location identifier*]　(ICLI)
RJEB .... Monbetsu [*Japan*] [*ICAO location identifier*]　(ICLI)
RJEC .... Asahikawa [*Japan*] [*ICAO location identifier*]　(ICLI)
RJEO........ Okushiri [*Japan*] [*ICAO location identifier*]　(ICLI)
RJER .... Rishiri Island [*Japan*] [*ICAO location identifier*]　(ICLI)
RJFA .... Ashiya [*Japan*] [*ICAO location identifier*]　(ICLI)
RJFB........ Gannosu/Brady [*Japan*] [*ICAO location identifier*]　(ICLI)
RJFC .... Yakushima [*Japan*] [*ICAO location identifier*]　(ICLI)
RJFE........ Fukue [*Japan*] [*ICAO location identifier*]　(ICLI)
RJFF......... Fukuoka [*Japan*] [*ICAO location identifier*]　(ICLI)
RJFG .... Tanegashima [*Japan*] [*ICAO location identifier*]　(ICLI)
RJFK........ Kagoshima [*Japan*] [*ICAO location identifier*]　(ICLI)
RJFM .... Miyazaki [*Japan*] [*ICAO location identifier*]　(ICLI)
RJFN........ Nyutabaru [*Japan*] [*ICAO location identifier*]　(ICLI)
RJFO........ Oita [*Japan*] [*ICAO location identifier*]　(ICLI)
RJFR .... Kitakyushu [*Japan*] [*ICAO location identifier*]　(ICLI)
RJFT......... Kumamoto [*Japan*] [*ICAO location identifier*]　(ICLI)
RJFU .... Nagasaki [*Japan*] [*ICAO location identifier*]　(ICLI)
RJFY .... Kanoya [*Japan*] [*ICAO location identifier*]　(ICLI)
RJFZ .... Tsuiki [*Japan*] [*ICAO location identifier*]　(ICLI)
RJI .... Res et Jura Immobilia [*Benelux*]　(BAS)
RJImm...... Res et Jura Immobilia [*Benelux*]　(BAS)
RJK........... Rijeka [*Former Yugoslavia*] [*Airport symbol*]　(OAG)
RJKA .... Amami [*Japan*] [*ICAO location identifier*]　(ICLI)
RJKB .... Okierabu [*Japan*] [*ICAO location identifier*]　(ICLI)
RJKI .... Kikai/Kikaigashima Island [*Japan*] [*ICAO location identifier*]
　　　　　　(ICLI)
RJKN........ Tokunoshima Island [*Japan*] [*ICAO location identifier*]　(ICLI)
RJMSS...... Rama Janambhoomi Mukti Sangharsh Samiti [*Society to
　　　　　　Liberate Rama's Birthplace*] [*India*]
RJN .... Rada Jednosci Narodowej [*Council of National Unity*]　(POL)
RJNF .... Fukui [*Japan*] [*ICAO location identifier*]　(ICLI)
RJNG .... Gifu [*Japan*] [*ICAO location identifier*]　(ICLI)
RJNH........ Hamamatsu [*Japan*] [*ICAO location identifier*]　(ICLI)
RJNK........ Kanazawa/Komatsu [*Japan*] [*ICAO location identifier*]　(ICLI)
RJNN........ Nagoya [*Japan*] [*ICAO location identifier*]　(ICLI)
RJNO .... Oki [*Japan*] [*ICAO location identifier*]　(ICLI)
RJNT........ Toyama [*Japan*] [*ICAO location identifier*]　(ICLI)
RJNY .... Yaizu/Shizuhama [*Japan*] [*ICAO location identifier*]　(ICLI)
RJO .... Revolutionary Justice Organization [*Lebanese terrorist group*]
RJOA........ Hiroshima [*Japan*] [*ICAO location identifier*]　(ICLI)
RJOB........ Okayama [*Japan*] [*ICAO location identifier*]　(ICLI)
RJOC........ Izumo [*Japan*] [*ICAO location identifier*]　(ICLI)
RJOE........ Akeno [*Japan*] [*ICAO location identifier*]　(ICLI)
RJOF .... Hofu [*Japan*] [*ICAO location identifier*]　(ICLI)
RJOH........ Miho [*Japan*] [*ICAO location identifier*]　(ICLI)
RJOI......... Iwakuni [*Japan*] [*ICAO location identifier*]　(ICLI)
RJOK........ Kochi [*Japan*] [*ICAO location identifier*]　(ICLI)
RJOM .... Matsuyama [*Japan*] [*ICAO location identifier*]　(ICLI)
RJOO .... Osaka/International [*Japan*] [*ICAO location identifier*]　(ICLI)
RJOP........ Komatsujima [*Japan*] [*ICAO location identifier*]　(ICLI)
RJOR........ Tottori [*Japan*] [*ICAO location identifier*]　(ICLI)
RJOS .... Tokushima [*Japan*] [*ICAO location identifier*]　(ICLI)
RJOT........ Takamatsu [*Japan*] [*ICAO location identifier*]　(ICLI)
RJOY .... Osaka/Yao [*Japan*] [*ICAO location identifier*]　(ICLI)
RJOZ........ Ozuki [*Japan*] [*ICAO location identifier*]　(ICLI)
RJR .... Radio Jamaica Rediffusion Ltd.
RJS .... Richard Jeffries Society　(EAIO)
RJSA .... Aomori [*Japan*] [*ICAO location identifier*]　(ICLI)
RJSC .... Yamagata [*Japan*] [*ICAO location identifier*]　(ICLI)
RJSD .... Sado [*Japan*] [*ICAO location identifier*]　(ICLI)
RJSH........ Hachinohe [*Japan*] [*ICAO location identifier*]　(ICLI)
RJSI .... Hanamaki [*Japan*] [*ICAO location identifier*]　(ICLI)
RJSK........ Akita [*Japan*] [*ICAO location identifier*]　(ICLI)
RJSM .... Misawa [*Japan*] [*ICAO location identifier*]　(ICLI)
RJSN .... Niigata [*Japan*] [*ICAO location identifier*]　(ICLI)
RJSO .... Ominato [*Japan*] [*ICAO location identifier*]　(ICLI)
RJSS .... Sendai [*Japan*] [*ICAO location identifier*]　(ICLI)
RJST......... Matsushima [*Japan*] [*ICAO location identifier*]　(ICLI)
RJSU .... Kasuminome [*Japan*] [*ICAO location identifier*]　(ICLI)
RJT .... Rassemblement des Jeunes Togolais [*Togolese Youth Rally*]
RJTA .... Atsugi [*Japan*] [*ICAO location identifier*]　(ICLI)
RJTC .... Tachikawa [*Japan*] [*ICAO location identifier*]　(ICLI)
RJTD .... Tokyo [*Japan*] [*ICAO location identifier*]　(ICLI)
RJTE .... Tateyama [*Japan*] [*ICAO location identifier*]　(ICLI)
RJTF......... Chofu [*Japan*] [*ICAO location identifier*]　(ICLI)
RJTG .... Tokyo [*Japan*] [*ICAO location identifier*]　(ICLI)

RJTH......... Hachijojima [*Japan*] [*ICAO location identifier*]　(ICLI)
RJTI .... Tokyo [*Japan*] [*ICAO location identifier*]　(ICLI)
RJTJ......... Iruma [*Japan*] [*ICAO location identifier*]　(ICLI)
RJTK .... Kisarazu [*Japan*] [*ICAO location identifier*]　(ICLI)
RJTL .... Shimofusa [*Japan*] [*ICAO location identifier*]　(ICLI)
RJTO .... Oshima [*Japan*] [*ICAO location identifier*]　(ICLI)
RJTQ .... Miyakejima [*Japan*] [*ICAO location identifier*]　(ICLI)
RJTR .... Zama/Rankin [*Japan*] [*ICAO location identifier*]　(ICLI)
RJTT .... Tokyo/International [*Japan*] [*ICAO location identifier*]　(ICLI)
RJTU .... Utsunomiya [*Japan*] [*ICAO location identifier*]　(ICLI)
RJTW .... Zama [*Japan*] [*ICAO location identifier*]　(ICLI)
RJTY .... Yokota [*Japan*] [*ICAO location identifier*]　(ICLI)
RJTZ .... Fuchu [*Japan*] [*ICAO location identifier*]　(ICLI)
RJZ .... Royal Jordanian Air Force [*ICAO designator*]　(FAAC)
RK............. Air Afrique [*Ivory Coast*] [*ICAO designator*]　(ICDA)
RK............. Capital Repair　(RU)
RK............. Channel Distributor　(RU)
RK............. Command Register　(RU)
RK............. Compounding Regulator　(RU)
RK............. Compressor Relay　(RU)
RK............. Discharge Cascade　(RU)
RK............. Distributing Head　(RU)
RK............. Final Relay, Operating Relay　(RU)
RK............. Logging Radiometer　(RU)
r-k .... Mine　(RU)
RK............. Natural Rubber　(RU)
RK............. Oxygen Reducer　(RU)
RK............. Pocket Radiometer　(RU)
RK............. Quota in Physical Quantity [*Former Yugoslavia*]　(IMH)
RK............. Rade Koncar, Tvornica Elektricnih Strojeva [*Rade Koncar
　　　　　　Electric Machinery Works*] [*Zagreb*]　(YU)
RK............. Radiation Circuit　(RU)
RK............. Radiation Monitor　(RU)
RK............. Radioactive Logging　(RU)
RK............. Radio Compass　(RU)
RK............. Radio Klub [*Radio Club*]　(YU)
rk............. Raekke [*Series*] [*Publishing Danish/Norwegian*]
RK............. Rassemblement Katangais [*Katanga Rally*]
RK............. Rayon Committee　(RU)
RK............. Rdeci Kriz [*Red Cross*]　(YU)
Rk............. Reaktion [*Reaction*] [*German*]
RK............. Rechnerkopplung [*German*]　(ADPT)
rk............. Rechterkolom [*Benelux*]　(BAS)
RK............. Reglement Betreffende de Krijgstucht [*Benelux*]　(BAS)
RK............. Regulator Box　(RU)
R/K........... Rekening-Koerant [*Current Account*] [*Business term*] [*Afrikaans*]
RK............. Remote-Konzentrator [*French*]　(ADPT)
rk............. Rendkivuli [*Extraordinary*]　(HU)
RK............. Repair Office　(RU)
RK............. Republic Committee　(RU)
RK............. Republic Office　(RU)
RK............. Rimsko-Katolicky [*Roman Catholic*]　(CZ)
RK............. Robna Kuca, Trgovinsko Poduzece [*Store*] [*Commercial*]　(YU)
rk............. Romai Katolikus [*Roman Catholic*]　(HU)
RK............. Roman Catholic
RK............. Rooms-Katoliek [*Roman Catholic*] [*Afrikaans*]
RK............. Runner　(RU)
RK............. Separation Capacitor　(RU)
RK............. Supervisory Relay, Control Relay　(RU)
RK............. Workers' and Peasants'　(RU)
RKA .... Air Afrique [*Ivory Coast*] [*ICAO designator*]　(FAAC)
RKA .... Fish Gelatin Agar　(RU)
RKAF........ Royal Khmer Air Force [*Cambodia*]
R Kb......... Vereniging De Rotterdamsche Korenbeurs [*Benelux*]　(BAS)
RKChF...... Workers' and Peasants' Black Sea Fleet　(RU)
RKD.......... Pressure Control Relay　(RU)
RKD.......... Rijksbureau voor Kunsthistorische Documentatie [*Netherlands*]
　　　　　　(SLS)
RkD........... Rocket Engine, Rocket Motor　(RU)
RKD........... X-Ray Diffraction Chamber　(RU)
RKE .... Roskilde [*Denmark*] [*Airport symbol*]　(OAG)
RKED......... Revoliutsionnyi Komitet Edinstva i Deistviia
RKF........... Focusing X-Ray Camera　(RU)
RKF........... Oxygen-Flux Cutter　(RU)
RKF........... Workers' Congress of Philippines　(RU)
RKFS .... Rayon Committee for Physical Culture and Sports　(BU)
RKG.......... Royal Khmer Government [*Cambodia*]
RKGTO ..... Republic Program "Ready for Work and Defense"　(BU)
RKh........... Birth of Christ [*BC in dates*]
RKh........... Forward Stroke, Driving Stroke　(RU)
R Kh .... Vonnis van de Rechtbank van Koophandel [*Benelux*]　(BAS)
RKhA .... Russian Art Archives　(RU)
rkhch......... Radiochemically Pure　(RU)
RKhK .... Rubezhnoye Chemical Kombinat　(RU)
RKhO .... Russian Chemical Society　(RU)
RKhP .... Receiver Performance　(RU)

RKhR .... Radiation and Chemical Reconnaissance (RU)
rkhrr .... Chemical and Radiation Reconnaissance Company (RU)
rkhrr.......... Chemical and Radio Reconnaissance Company (BU)
rkh s .... Supply Dump, Distributing Point (BU)
RKhT .... Republic Office for Wholesale Trade in Household Goods [*RSFSR*] (RU)
RKhZ......... Chemical Barrage Area (RU)
rkhz............ Chemical Defense Company (RU)
RKI .... Workers' and Peasants' Inspection [*1920-1934*] (RU)
RKIE.......... Reformatus Kereszteny Ifjusagi Egyesulet [*Reformed Church Christian Youth Association*] (HU)
RK i KD ..... Of Workers', Peasants', and Red Army Deputies (RU)
RKJJ.......... Kwangju [*South Korea*] [*ICAO location identifier*] (ICLI)
RKJK .... Kunsan [*South Korea*] [*ICAO location identifier*] (ICLI)
RKJM........ Mokpo [*South Korea*] [*ICAO location identifier*] (ICLI)
RKJO......... Hongjungri [*South Korea*] [*ICAO location identifier*] (ICLI)
RKJU......... Jhunju [*South Korea*] [*ICAO location identifier*] (ICLI)
RKJY .... Yeosu [*South Korea*] [*ICAO location identifier*] (ICLI)
RKK .... Air-Regenerating Gas Mask Designed by Kovshov and Kuz'menko (RU)
RKK .... Mediation Commission for Price Adjustment (BU)
RKKR .... Radiation-Induced Catalytic Cracking (RU)
Rkk .... Reaktionen [*Reactions*] [*German*]
RKK .... Requisitioning Commission (BU)
RKK .... Wage Rate and Dispute Commission (RU)
RKK .... Workers' and Peasants' Control (RU)
RKKA .... Raboche-Krest'ianskaia Krasnaia Armiia [*Workers' and Peasants' Red Army*] [*Redesignated Soviety Army*] [*Former USSR*]
RKKA .... Workers' and Peasants' Red Army [*1918-1946*] (RU)
RKKAF..... Workers' and Peasants' Red Army and Navy (RU)
RKKF........ Workers' and Peasants' Red Navy (RU)
RKKh .... Rayon Department of Municipal Services (RU)
RKKM ...... Workers' and Peasants' Red Militia (RU)
rk kov .... Rendkivuli Kovet [*Ambassador Extraordinary*] (HU)
RKKS........ Workers' and Peasants' Red Armed Forces (RU)
RKKVF...... Workers' and Peasants' Red Air Force (RU)
RKL .... Line Control Relay (RU)
rkl............. Ruokalusikallinen [*Finland*]
RK-LS- ...... Radioactive Logging with Luminescent Counters (RU)
RKM .... Cable Trunk Region (RU)
rkm........... Mounted Militia Reserve (RU)
RKM .... Radiographic Camera-Monochromator (RU)
rkm............ Rakennusmestari [*Finland*]
RKM .... Reczny Karabin Maszynowy [*Light Machine Gun*] (POL)
RKM .... Relativistic Quantum Mechanics (RU)
RKM .... Rendorsegi Korzeti Megbizott [*District Policeman*] (HU)
RKM .... Rezervno Komandno Mesto [*Reserve Command Post*] (YU)
RKM .... Workers' and Peasants' Militia (RU)
RKN .... Standard Round Relay (RU)
RKN .... Voltage Control Relay (RU)
RKNC .... Chunchon [*South Korea*] [*ICAO location identifier*] (ICLI)
RKND........ Sokcho [*South Korea*] [*ICAO location identifier*] (ICLI)
RKNH........ Heongsung [*South Korea*] [*ICAO location identifier*] (ICLI)
RKNI .... Injae [*South Korea*] [*ICAO location identifier*] (ICLI)
RKNK .... Kwandaeri [*South Korea*] [*ICAO location identifier*] (ICLI)
RKNN........ Kangnung [*South Korea*] [*ICAO location identifier*] (ICLI)
RKNP .... Republican Peasants' National Party [*Turkish*] (RU)
RKNW........ Wonju [*South Korea*] [*ICAO location identifier*] (ICLI)
RKNY .... Yangku [*South Korea*] [*ICAO location identifier*] (ICLI)
RKO........... Disconnection Circuit Control Relay (RU)
RKO........... Operation Code Register (RU)
RKO........... Rayon Municipal Department (RU)
RKO........... Reichskassenordnung [*Federal Finance Regulations*] [*German*]
rkp............. Manuscript (RU)
rkp............. Rakpart [*Embankment*] (HU)
RKP .... Rejonowe Komitety Porozumiewawcze [*Regional Consultative Committees*] (POL)
rkp............. Rekopis [*Manuscript*] (POL)
RKP .... Roman Kommunista Part [*Romanian Communist Party*] (HU)
RKP .... Ruotsalainen Kansanpuolue [*Finland*]
RKP .... Russian Communist Party (RU)
RKP(b)....... Ruska Komunisticka Partija (Boljsevici) [*Russian Communist Party (Bolsheviks)*] [*1918-1925*] (YU)
RKPB......... Workers' and Peasants' Party of Burma (RU)
RKPC........ Cheju/International [*South Korea*] [*ICAO location identifier*] (ICLI)
RKPD .... Chedong [*South Korea*] [*ICAO location identifier*] (ICLI)
RKPE........ Chinhae [*South Korea*] [*ICAO location identifier*] (ICLI)
RKPK .... Kimhae/International [*South Korea*] [*ICAO location identifier*] (ICLI)
RKPM .... Cheju/Mosulpo [*South Korea*] [*ICAO location identifier*] (ICLI)
RKPN .... Rooms Katholieke Partij Nederland [*Roman Catholic Party of the Netherlands*] [*Political party*] (PPE)
RKPP........ Busan [*South Korea*] [*ICAO location identifier*] (ICLI)
Rk-Prod ..... Reaktionsprodukt [*Reaction Product*] [*German*] (GCA)

RKPS .... Rayon Committees for Production Consultation (BU)
RKPS .... Sachon [*South Korea*] [*ICAO location identifier*] (ICLI)
RKPS .... Working Committees of the Trade Union (BU)
RKPS .... Ulsan [*South Korea*] [*ICAO location identifier*] (ICLI)
RKPU .... Ulsan [*South Korea*] [*ICAO location identifier*] (ICLI)
RKPZ......... Rabotnicki Kulturno-Prosvetni Zavod [*Workers Cultural and Educational Institute*] (YU)
RKR .... Reversible Annular Register (RU)
Rkr .... Ruotsin Kruunu(a) [*Finland*]
RKRT........ Rejonowe Kierownictwo Robot Telekomunikacyjnych [*District Management of Telecommunications Construction Work*] (POL)
RKRWM ... Rejonowe Kierownictwo Robot Wodno-Melioracyjnych [*District Administration for Irrigation and Land Reclamation Work*] (POL)
RKS........... Control Radio Station (RU)
RKS........... End-of-Count Relay (RU)
RKS........... Lubrication Control Relay (RU)
RKS........... Raadet foer Kaernkraftsaekerhet [*Nuclear energy*] [*Sweden*] (NRCH)
RKS........... Radiometric Control Station (RU)
RKS........... Raeum- und Kuestensicherungsdivision [*Mine-Sweeping and Coastal Security Division*] (EG)
RKS........... Rayon Communications Office (RU)
RKS........... Rayon Cooperative Union (BU)
RKS........... Record Keeping System (LA)
RKS........... Robotniczy Klub Sportowy [*Workers' Sports Club*] (POL)
RKS........... Synchronism Control Relay (RU)
RKS........... Velocity Control Relay, Speed Control Relay (RU)
RKSA......... Ascom City [*South Korea*] [*ICAO location identifier*] (ICLI)
RKSB......... Uijeongbu [*South Korea*] [*ICAO location identifier*] (ICLI)
RKSC......... Cheongokri [*South Korea*] [*ICAO location identifier*] (ICLI)
RKSD........ Kanamni [*South Korea*] [*ICAO location identifier*] (ICLI)
RKSE......... Paekryoungdo Beach [*South Korea*] [*ICAO location identifier*] (ICLI)
RKSF .... Republic of Korea Air Force Headquarters [*South Korea*] [*ICAO location identifier*] (ICLI)
RKSG......... Pyongtaek [*South Korea*] [*ICAO location identifier*] (ICLI)
RKSH .... Kwanak [*South Korea*] [*ICAO location identifier*] (ICLI)
RKSh .... Rayon Kolkhoz School (RU)
RKSI .... Chajangni [*South Korea*] [*ICAO location identifier*] (ICLI)
RKSK .... Susaek [*South Korea*] [*ICAO location identifier*] (ICLI)
RKSL........ Seoul City [*South Korea*] [*ICAO location identifier*] (ICLI)
RKSM........ Russian Young Communist League [*1918-1924*] (RU)
RKSM........ Seoul East [*Sinchonri*] [*South Korea*] [*ICAO location identifier*] (ICLI)
RKSO .... Osan [*South Korea*] [*ICAO location identifier*] (ICLI)
RKSP........ Paekryoungdo Site [*South Korea*] [*ICAO location identifier*] (ICLI)
RKSP .... Rooms Katholieke Staatspartij [*Roman Catholic State Party*] [*Netherlands*] [*Political party*] (PPE)
RKSR........ Yeongdongri [*South Korea*] [*ICAO location identifier*] (ICLI)
RKSS .... Seoul/Kimpo International [*South Korea*] [*ICAO location identifier*] (ICLI)
RKST........ Tongoucheon [*South Korea*] [*ICAO location identifier*] (ICLI)
RKSU........ Yeoju [*South Korea*] [*ICAO location identifier*] (ICLI)
RKSW....... Suwon [*South Korea*] [*ICAO location identifier*] (ICLI)
RKSX........ Song San-Ri [*South Korea*] [*ICAO location identifier*] (ICLI)
RKSY........ Seoul/Yungsan [*South Korea*] [*ICAO location identifier*] (ICLI)
rkt............. Jet Propulsion Technology (RU)
RKT .... Ras Al Khaymah [*United Arab Emirates*] [*Airport symbol*] (OAG)
RKT .... Workers' and Peasants' Theater (RU)
RKTA .... Andong [*South Korea*] [*ICAO location identifier*] (ICLI)
RKTC........ Chungju [*South Korea*] [*ICAO location identifier*] (ICLI)
RKTD........ Taejon [*South Korea*] [*ICAO location identifier*] (ICLI)
RKTH........ Pohang [*South Korea*] [*ICAO location identifier*] (ICLI)
RKTJ........ Kyungju [*South Korea*] [*ICAO location identifier*] (ICLI)
RKTM .... Seosan [*South Korea*] [*ICAO location identifier*] (ICLI)
RKTN .... Taegu [*South Korea*] [*ICAO location identifier*] (ICLI)
RKTO........ Nonsan [*South Korea*] [*ICAO location identifier*] (ICLI)
RKTOF..... Workers' and Peasants' Pacific Fleet (RU)
RKTs......... Relay-Code Central Control (RU)
RKTS .... Sangju [*South Korea*] [*ICAO location identifier*] (ICLI)
RKTT........ Taegu [*South Korea*] [*ICAO location identifier*] (ICLI)
RKTY........ Yechon [*South Korea*] [*ICAO location identifier*] (ICLI)
RKU.......... Radiokomunikacni Kontrolni Urad [*Radio Communications Control Office*] (CZ)
RKU.......... Rejonowa Komenda Uzupelnien [*District Headquarters of Military Reserves*] (POL)
RKU.......... Relative Bearing (RU)
RKU.......... Reonska Katastarska Uprava [*Regional Cadastre Administration*] (YU)
RKU.......... Rudnik Kamenog Uglja [*Coal Mine*] (YU)
RKU.......... Yule Island [*Papua New Guinea*] [*Airport symbol*] (OAG)
RKUD........ Radnicko Kulturno Umetnicko Drustvo [*Workers' Cultural and Artistic Society*] (YU)

RKV .... Oxygen-Air Mixture Regulator   (RU)
RKV .... Raad vir Kernveiligheid [*South Africa*]   (AA)
RKV .... Rahmenkollektivvertrag [*Skeleton Collective Labor Agreement*] (EG)
RKVMF ..... Workers' and Peasants' Navy   (RU)
RKVolksbond ... Rooms-Katholieke Volksbond [*Benelux*]   (BAS)
RKVP .... Rooms Katholieke Volkspartij [*Roman Catholic People's Party*] [*Netherlands*] [*Political party*]   (PPE)
RKVT .... Rada Klubu Vojenskeho Telesa [*Committee of the Military Post Club*]   (CZ)
RKW .... Rationalisierungs-Kuratorium der Deutschen Wirtschaft [*German Productivity and Management Association*] [*Research center*]   (IRC)
RKW .... Rooms-Katholieke Werkliedenverbond [*Benelux*]   (BAS)
Rk Wkbl .... Rechtskundig Weekblad [*Benelux*]   (BAS)
RKWV .... Roomsch-Katholiek Werkliedenverbond in Nederland [*Netherlands*]   (BAS)
RKY .... Rokeby [*Australia*] [*Airport symbol*] [*Obsolete*]   (OAG)
RKZ .... Charging Control Relay   (RU)
RKZM .... Rosyjski Komunistyczny Zwiazek Mlodziezy [*Russian Communist Youth Union*]   (POL)
rl .... Demarcation Line   (RU)
r-l .... Leader, Manager   (BU)
RL .... Liban [*Lebanon*] [*Poland*]
RL .... Line Relay   (RU)
RL .... Manual Laboratory   (RU)
RL .... Radar   (RU)
RL .... Radiaal [*Radial*] [*Afrikaans*]
RL .... Radioactivni Latky [*Radioactive Agents*]   (CZ)
RL .... Radio Link, Wire Broadcasting Line   (RU)
RL .... Radiolokator [*RADAR*]   (CZ)
rl .... Rajoitettu Lisamaksuvollisuus [*Finland*]
RL .... Reactance Tube   (RU)
Rl .... Real [*Real, Royal*] [*Spanish*]
RL .... Rechenlocher [*German*]   (ADPT)
RL .... Regtspleging bij de Landmagt [*Benelux*]   (BAS)
RL .... Relativen Luftfeuchtigkeit [*Relative Humidity*] [*German*]
RL .... Rial [*Monetary unit*] [*Iran, Saudi Arabia, etc.*]
RL .... Richtlinien [*Instructions, Directions*] [*German*]   (ILCA)
RL .... Rikoslaki [*Finland*]
RL .... Route Laterale [*Secondary Road*]   (CL)
RL .... Rudnik Lignita [*Lignite Mine*]   (YU)
rl .... Rulla(a) [*Finland*]
RL .... X-Rays, Roentgen Rays   (RU)
RLA .... Lar-Liniile Aeriene Romance [*Romania*] [*ICAO designator*] (FAAC)
RLA .... Radar Devices   (RU)
RLA .... Rocket Vehicle   (RU)
RLA .... Royal Lao [*or Laotian*] Army [*Laos*]
RLAF .... Royal Laotian Air Force
RLAT .... Regional Office for Latin America [*FAO*]   (ASF)
RLB .... Racecourses Licences Board [*Victoria, Australia*]
rlb .... Radar Battalion   (BU)
RLB .... Radar Battery   (BU)
RLB .... Radar Complex   (BU)
RLC .... Avial (Russian Co. Ltd.) [*Former USSR*] [*ICAO designator*] (FAAC)
RLC .... Radio Liberty Committee [*Later, RFE/RL*]   (EA)
RLC .... Revival Life Centre [*Australia*]
RLCP .... Redfern Legal Centre Publishing Ltd. [*Australia*]
RLD .... Republika Ludowo-Demokratyczna [*People's Democratic Republic*]   (POL)
RLD .... Rheinland Air Service [*Germany*] [*ICAO designator*]   (FAAC)
RLD .... Rijksluchtvaartdienst [*Civil Aviation Authority*] [*Netherlands*] (PDAA)
RLF .... Rabotnicheski Literaturen Front [*Workers' Literary Front*] [*A periodical*]   (BU)
RLF .... Riksforbundet Landsbygdens Folk [*National Farmers Union*] [*Sweden*]   (WEN)
RLF .... Royal Laotian Forces
RLG .... Luteinizing Hormone Reaction   (RU)
rlg .... Rilegato [*Bound*] [*Publishing*] [*Italian*]
RLG .... Royal Lao Government   (CL)
RLG .... Royal Laotian Government
RLI .... Rhodesia Light Infantry
RLj .... Radio Ljubljana   (YU)
RLJM .... Repertoire de Legislation et de Jurisprudence Marocaines (FLAF)
RLK .... Air Nelson Ltd. [*New Zealand*] [*ICAO designator*]   (FAAC)
RLK .... Rada Lidovych Komisaru [*Council of People's Commissars*] (CZ)
rlk .... Radar   (RU)
rlk .... Radlux   (RU)
RLKSM ..... Russian Lenin Young Communist League [*1924-1926*]   (RU)
RL Lu .... Rechtspleging bij de Land- en Luchtmacht [*Benelux*]   (BAS)

RLM .... Reichsleftfahrt Ministerium [*German Air Ministry*] [*World War II*]
RLN .... External Line Disconnecting Switch   (RU)
RLN .... Raete fuer Landwirtschaftliche Produktion und Nahrungsgueterwirtschaft [*Councils for Agricultural Production and the Foodstuffs Industry*]   (EG)
RLNR .... Research Laboratory for Nuclear Reactors [*Japan*]   (WND)
RLO .... Rajonski Ljudski Odbor [*Precinct People's Committee*]   (YU)
RLP .... Radar Post   (RU)
RLP .... Rally of the Lao People   (CL)
RLP .... Rassemblement Liegeois pour la Paix [*Liege Assemblage for Peace*] [*French*]   (WER)
RLP .... Rejon Lasow Panstwowych [*State Forest District*]   (POL)
RLP .... Rhodesian Labor Party
RLP .... Rosella Plains [*Australia*] [*Airport symbol*] [*Obsolete*]   (OAG)
RLPB .... Rural Land Protection Board [*Australia*]
RLPS .... Russian Lumber Industry Council   (RU)
RLR .... Radar Company   (BU)
RLR .... Radio Liberty Research [*Research center*]   (IRC)
RLR .... Rumunska Lidova Republika [*Romanian People's Republic*] (CZ)
RLS .... Estimated Resistance Line   (RU)
RLS .... Radar Station   (RU)
RLS .... Radar System   (BU)
RLS .... Radio Relay Communications Line   (RU)
RLS .... Raketenleitstation [*Missile Control Center*]   (EG)
RLS .... Regional Library Service [*Australia*]
RLS .... Rustenburg Layered Suite [*or Sequence*] [*Bushveld Complex, South Africa Geology*]
RLSS .... Red Lion and Sun Society [*Red Cross*] [*Iran*]   (ME)
RLSS .... Royal Life Saving Society [*Studley, Warwickshire, England*] (EAIO)
RLSS .... Royal Life Saving Society of Australia
RLSS-A ..... Royal Life Saving Society of Australia   (ADA)
RLSVD ...... Superhigh-Pressure Mercury-Vapor Lamp   (RU)
RLSWA ..... Royal Life Saving Society of Western Australia
RLT .... Arlit [*Niger*] [*Airport symbol*]   (OAG)
RLTA .... Rhodesian Lawn Tennis Association
Rltb .... Realitaetenbesitzer [*German*]
RLTDC ...... Rokel Leaf Tobacco Development Company [*Sierra Leone*]
rlto .... Airdrome Maintenance Support Company   (BU)
rlts .... Stigma   (RU)
RLU .... Rozhlasova Ludova Univerzita [*People's Radio University (Extension courses)*]   (CZ)
RLU .... Workers' Literature University   (RU)
RLV .... Real Aviation Ltd. [*Ghana*] [*ICAO designator*]   (FAAC)
RLZ .... Reditelstvi Lesnich Zavodu [*Directorate of Forest Enterprises*] (CZ)
RM .... Company Mortar   (RU)
RM .... Design Model   (RU)
RM .... Fix [*Aviation*]   (RU)
RM .... Magnetic Relay   (RU)
RM .... Main-Line Reserve   (RU)
RM .... Maximum Relay   (RU)
rm .... Militia Reserve   (RU)
RM .... Overload Relay, Over-Current Relay   (RU)
RM .... Power Disconnecting Switch   (RU)
RM .... RAAF [*Royal Australian Air Force*] Museum
RM .... Rada Miejska [*Town Council*] [*Poland*]
RM .... Rada Ministrow [*Council of Ministers*]   (POL)
RM .... Radio Beacon   (RU)
RM .... Radio Marti [*Cuba*]
RM .... Rand Mines Group [*South Africa*]
RM .... Rare Metals   (BU)
RM .... Ratna Mornarica [*Navy*]   (YU)
rm .... Raummeter [*Cubic Meter*] [*German*]
RM .... Rechenmaschine [*German*]   (ADPT)
RM .... Rede Mulher [*An association*] [*Brazil*]   (EAIO)
RM .... Region Militaire [*Military Region*]   (CL)
RM .... Registre des Metiers [*France*]   (FLAF)
RM .... Reichsmarine [*German Navy*]
RM .... Reichsmark [*Later, DM*] [*Monetary unit*] [*German*]
RM .... Repair Shop   (RU)
RM .... Reponse Ministerielle [*France*]   (FLAF)
RM .... Resident-Magistraat [*Resident Magistrate*] [*Afrikaans*]
RM .... Resident Minister [*Church of England in Australia*]
RM .... Retenue a la Source sur les Revenus des Capitaux Mobiliers [*France*]   (FLAF)
RM .... Reverenda Madre [*Reverend Mother*] [*Spanish*]
RM .... Ricchezza Mobile [*(Tax on) Income*] [*Italian*]
RM .... River Mine   (RU)
RM .... Robni Magazin [*Store*] [*Commercial*]   (YU)
RM .... Roentgenometer   (RU)
Rm .... Room   (EECI)
Rm .... Rotmetall [*Red Metal*] [*German*]   (GCA)
RM .... Roupie Mauricienne

RM............ Royal Marines (ML)
RM............ Rudarstvo i Metalurgija [*Mining and Metallurgy*] (YU)
RM............ Steering Engine (RU)
RMA.......... Regiment de Marche d'Afrique [*African Marching Regiment*] [*French*]
RMA.......... Roma [*Australia*] [*Airport symbol*] (OAG)
RMA.......... Royal Mail Aircraft [*Australia*]
RMA.......... Royal Monetary Authority [*Bhutan*] (GEA)
RMAA....... Records Management Association of Australia (ADA)
RMAA....... Rubber Manufacturers' Association of Australia
RMAF........ Royal Malayan Air Force (ML)
RMAF....... Royal Moroccan Air Force
RMALAN ... Royal Malaysian Navy
RMALC..... Red Mexicana de Accion Frente al Libre Comercio [*Mexican Action Network on Free Trade*] (CROSS)
RMB.......... Machine Repair Base (BU)
RMB.......... Rand Merchant Bank [*South Africa*]
RMB.......... Renminbi [*Monetary unit*] [*China*]
RMB.......... Roulement Miniatures, Bienne [*Switzerland*] (PDAA)
RMBC....... Regional Marine Biological Center [*Singapore*] (ASF)
RMBNSW ... Rice Marketing Board of New South Wales [*Australia*]
RMBQ....... Rice Marketing Board of Queensland [*Australia*]
RMC.......... Radiation Medicine Centre [*BARC*] [*India*] (PDAA)
RMC.......... Radio Monte Carlo [*Monaco*] (EY)
RMC.......... Regional Meteorological Center [*WMO*] (ASF)
RMC.......... Resource Materials Centre [*Australia*]
RMC.......... Revue du Marche Commun [*Review of the Common Market*] [*French*]
RMCC....... Regional Ministers Conference on Cooperatives [*Australia*]
RM-CEAAL ... Red de Mujeres del Consejo de Educacion de Adultos de Americana Latina [*Women's Network of the Council for Adult Education in Latin America - WN-CAELA*] [*Quito, Ecuador*] (EAIO)
RMcraftN .. Registered Mothercraft Nurse [*Australia*]
RMCRS..... Royal Motonautique Club de Rabat Sale [*Morocco*]
RMCS....... Russian Mendeleev Chemical Society
RMD......... Resident Medical Doctor [*Australia*]
RMD......... Rhine-Main-Danube Navigation System (DS)
RME......... Armenian International Airlines [*ICAO designator*] (FAAC)
RMEF....... Reponse du Ministre de l'Economie et des Finances [*France*] (FLAF)
RMF......... Reponse du Ministre des Finances [*France*] (FLAF)
RMF......... Rhodesian Mining Federation
RMF......... Royal Malaysian Air Force [*ICAO designator*] (FAAC)
RMFAE..... Reponse du Ministre des Finances et des Affaires Economiques [*France*] (FLAF)
RMHDDHG ... Regiere Mich Herr durch Deinen Heiligen Geist [*Rule Me, Lord, Through Thy Holy Spirit*] [*Motto of Ann, Margravine of Brandenburg (1575-1612)*] [*German*]
RMI .... Reich Ministry of Interior
RMI .... Rostov Institute of Mechanical Engineering (RU)
RMI .... Rudarsko-Metalurski Inspektorat [*Mining and Metallurgic Inspectorate*] (YU)
RMIA .... Retail Management Institute of Australia (ADA)
rmint .... Mine Sweeper Company (RU)
RMIP........ Region Militar de Isla de Pinos [*Isle of Pines Military Region*] [*Cuba*] (LA)
rmisk......... Mine Detector Company (RU)
RMIT........ Royal Melbourne Institute of Technology Ltd. [*Australia*]
RMITTV ... Royal Melbourne Institute of Technology Television [*Australia*]
RMJ.......... Reponse du Ministre de la Justice [*France*] (FLAF)
RMK......... Dismountable Metal Pile Driver (RU)
RMK......... Renmark [*Australia*] [*Airport symbol*] (OAG)
RMKI .... Reszecske es Magfizkai Kutato Intezet [*Research Institute for Particle and Nuclear Physics*] [*Hungary*] (WND)
RML......... Revolutionaere Marxistische Liga [*Marxist Revolutionary League*] [*Switzerland*] (WEN)
RMLE....... Regiment de Marche de la Legion Etrangere [*Foreign Legion Marching Regiment*] [*French*]
RMM........ Dismountable Metal Bridge (RU)
RMM........ Mechanical Repair Shop (RU)
RMM........ Rakosi Matyas Muvek, Csepel [*Matyas Rakosi Works, Csepel*] (HU)
RMM........ Rum Milli Muhafiz [*Greek National Guard (on Cyprus)*] (GC)
RMMO...... Rum Milli Muhafiz Ordusu [*Greek Cypriot National Guard Army*] (GC)
RMMZ...... Revda Metalware and Metallurgical Plant (RU)
r mn........... Genitive Plural (RU)
RMN........ Maximum Voltage Relay (RU)
RMN........ Regiao Militar do Norte [*Northern Military Region*] [*Portuguese*] (WER)
RMN........ Royal Malayan Navy (ML)
RMNO....... Rozkaz Ministra Narodni Obrany [*Order by the Minister of National Defense*] (CZ)
RMNSW ... Railway Museum of New South Wales [*Australia*]
RMNV....... Multianode Mercury-Arc Rectifier (RU)

RMO......... Rafinerie Mineralnich Oleju [*Mineral Oil Refinery*] (CZ)
Rmo......... Reverendissimo [*Most Reverend*] [*Italian*]
RMO......... Rezerwa Milicji Obywatelskiej [*Citizens' Militia Reserve*] (POL)
RMO......... Russian Musical Society (RU)
RMP......... Company Medical Station (RU)
rmp........... Marine Company (RU)
rmp........... Motorized Infantry Company (RU)
RMP......... Rand Mines Property Ltd. [*South Africa*]
RMP......... Resource Management Project [*Australia*]
RMP......... Roman Munkaspart [*Romanian Workers' Party*] (HU)
RMP......... Roodepoort Mission Press [*Baptist Union*] [*South Africa*]
RMP......... Royal Malaysian Police (ML)
RMPI....... Mining of Subsurface Mineral Deposits (RU)
RMPR....... Rassemblement Mahorais pour la Republique [*Mayotte Rally for the Republic*] [*Political party*] (PPW)
RM PRL .... Rada Ministrow Polskiej Rzeczpospolitej Ludowej [*Council of Ministers of the Polish People's Republic*] (POL)
RMPS....... Royal Melbourne Philharmonic Society [*Australia*]
RMR......... Malraux Society (EAIO)
RMr......... Radio Mreza [*Radio Network*] (YU)
RMR......... Royal Malay Regiment (ML)
RMS .... Council of Ministers Decision (BU)
RMS .... Mechanical Repair Station (RU)
RMS .... Motorized Fishing Station (RU)
RMS .... Radical Mass Spectrometer (RU)
RMS .... Radio-Frequency Mass Spectrometer (RU)
RMS .... Region Militaire Speciale [*Special Military Region*] [*Cambodia*] (CL)
RMS .... Republik Maluku Selatan [*Republic of South Moluccas*] (IN)
RMS .... Revised Management Scheme [*International Whaling Commission*]
RMS .... Risk Management Services [*Oman*]
RMS .... Workers' Youth League [*Bulgarian*] (RU)
RMS .... Workers' Youth Union (BU)
RMSA....... Rural Marketing and Supply Association [*Australia*]
RMSD .... Royal Mail Special Delivery [*British Post Office facility*] (DCTA)
RMT......... Maximum Current Tripping Device (RU)
RmT......... Minimum Current Tripping Device (RU)
RMT......... Regiment de Marche du Tchad
RMTC....... Royal Melbourne Technical College [*Australia*]
RM Th ...... Rechtsgeleerd Magazijn Themis [*Netherlands*] (FLAF)
RMTO....... Regional Motor Transport Officer [*British*] (DCTA)
RMTs .... Distance between Centers (RU)
RMTs .... Mechanical Repair Shop (RU)
RMTs .... Radio-Meteorological Center (RU)
RMTs .... Workers' Youth Center (BU)
rmu........... Bridge Launcher Company (RU)
RMU......... Rudnik Mrkog Uglja [*Brown Coal Mine*] (YU)
RMU......... Small-Angle X-Ray Scattering (RU)
RMV......... Romania [*Romania*] [*ICAO designator*] (FAAC)
RMVE .... Regiment de Marche de Volontiers Etrangers [*Foreign Volunteers Marching Regiment*] [*French*]
RM WP ..... Rada Mlodziezowa Wojska Polskiego [*Youth Council, Polish Army*] (POL)
RMZ......... Machine Repair Plant (BU)
RMZ......... Mechanical Repair Plant (RU)
RMZ......... Repair and Assembly Plant (RU)
RMZ......... Riga Machine Plant (RU)
RMZ......... Rijksdienst voor Maatschappelijke Zekerheid [*Benelux*] (BAS)
RMZ......... Rostov Machine Plant (RU)
RMZ......... Workers' Youth Detachment (BU)
RN............ Carrier Rocket (RU)
RN............ Estado do Rio Grande Do Norte [*State of North Rio Grande*] [*Brazil*]
RN............ Load Regulator (RU)
RN............ Load Resolution (RU)
RN............ Neutralization Reaction (RU)
RN............ Neutron Radiation Meter, Neutron Detector (RU)
RN............ Noncombatant Private (RU)
RN............ Rada Naczelna [*Chief Council*] (POL)
RN............ Rada Narodowa [*National Council (in London); People's Council (in Poland)*] (POL)
RN............ Radio Filament Battery (RU)
RN............ Radio National [*Australian Broadcasting Corp.*]
Rn............ Radom [*Portuguese*]
Rn............ Radon [*Radon*] [*Chemical element*] [*German*]
Rn............ Radonio [*Radon*] [*Chemical element*] [*Portuguese*]
RN............ Rafinerija Nafte [*Naphtha Refinery*] (YU)
r-n............ Rayon, City District, Area (RU)
RN............ Regia Nave [*Royal Ship*] [*Italian*]
RN............ Regular Miner's Lamp (RU)
RN............ Renovacion Nacional [*National Renovation*] [*Chile*] [*Political party*] (EY)
RN............ Resistencia Nacional [*National Resistance*] [*El Salvador*] (LA)
RN............ Revenu National [*North African*]
RN............ Revolucion Nacional [*Spain*] [*Political party*] (EY)

RN............ Riserva Navale [*Naval Reserve*] [*Italian*]
RN............ Rodoviaria Nacional, EP [*Portugal*]   (EY)
RN............ Route Nationale [*National Highway*] [*French*]   (WER)
RN............ Stress Relaxation   (RU)
RN............ Voltage Regulator   (RU)
RN............ Voltage Relay   (RU)
RN............ Work Norm   (RU)
RN............ Zero Relay   (RU)
RNA.......... Rassemblement National Arabe [*Arab National Rally*] [*Tunisia*]   (PD)
RNA.......... Repulogepes Novenyvedo Allomas [*Agricultural Air Station*]   (HU)
RNA.......... Rhodesian Native Association
RNA.......... Royal Naval Association [*Australia*]
RNA.......... Royal Nepal Academy   (EAIO)
RNA.......... Royal Nepal Airlines Corp. [*ICAO designator*]   (FAAC)
RNA.......... Royal Netherlands Army
RNA.......... Royal Norwegian Army   (MCD)
RNAA....... Royal Netherlands Aeronautical Association   (EAIO)
RNAAF..... Royal Norwegian Army and Air Force
RNAAS...... Royal Netherlands Academy of Arts and Sciences   (EAIO)
RNAC....... Royal Newcastle Aero Club [*Australia*]
RNAF .... Royal Netherlands Air Force
RNAF .... Royal Norwegian Air Force
RNAIA ...... Royal National Agricultural and Industrial Association [*Australia*]
RNAM....... Regional Network for Agricultural Machinery [*Institute of Agricultural Engineering and Technology*] [*Philippines*]
RNASS...... Royal North Australian Show Society
RNB.......... Reditelstvi Narodni Bezpecnosti [*National Security Directorate*]   (CZ)
RNB.......... River Tank Barge   (RU)
RNB.......... Ronneby [*Sweden*] [*Airport symbol*]   (OAG)
RNB.......... Worker of the New Bulgaria   (BU)
RNbA........ Reichsbahn-Neubauamt [*GDR Railroad Office for New Construction*]   (EG)
RNBN....... Non-Self-Propelled River Tank Barge   (RU)
RNBS........ Self-Propelled River Tank Barge   (RU)
RNC........ Royal Natal Carbineers
RNC........ Royal Niger Co. [*British*]
RNCC .... Royal Nepal Chamber of Commerce   (EAIO)
RNCF........ Royal Netherlands Chemical Foundation
RNCFC...... Regie Nationale des Chemins de Fer du Cameroun [*Railway system*] [*Cameroon*]   (EY)
RNCFM..... Reseau National de Chemins de Fer Malgache [*Malagasy National Railroad System*]   (AF)
RNCSIR .... Royal Norwegian Council for Scientific and Industrial Research   (EAIO)
RNCV .... Radio Nacional de Cabo Verde [*National Radio of Cape Verde*]   (EY)
RND.......... Arc Voltage Regulator   (RU)
RND.......... Low-Pressure Rotor   (RU)
RND.......... Rassemblement National Democratique [*National Democratic Rally*] [*Senegal*] [*Political party*]   (PPW)
RND.......... Rassemblement National pour la Democratie [*Benin*] [*Political party*]   (EY)
RND.......... Rijks Nijverheids Dienst [*Netherlands*]
RNDP .... Rassemblement National Democratique et Populaire [*Chad*]
RNDr......... Doktor Prirodnich Ved [*Doctor of Natural Sciences*]   (CZ)
RNE.......... Radio Nacional de Espana [*Spanish National Radio*]   (WER)
RNE.......... Register of the National Estate [*Australia*]
RNE.......... Roanne [*France*] [*Airport symbol*]   (OAG)
Rne........... Ruine [*Ruins*] [*Military map abbreviation World War I*] [*French*]   (MTD)
RNEA .... Regional Office for the Near East [*FAO*]   (ASF)
RNEIA...... Royal Netherlands East Indies Army
RNET .... Regie Nationale des Eaux du Togo
R NethAF ... Royal Netherlands Air Force
RNF .... Refounded National Party [*South Africa Political party*]   (EAIO)
RNFL........ Rhodesia National Football League
RNFU .... Rhodesian National Farmers Union   (AF)
RNG.......... Raad vir Nasionale Gedenkwaardighede [*National Memorial Council*] [*Afrikaans*]
rng .... Roentgen   (RU)
RNGC........ Royal Nairobi Golf Club
RNH.......... Royal Newcastle Hospital [*Australia*]
RNI .... Rassemblement National des Independants [*National Rally of Independents*] [*Morocco*]   (AF)
RNI .... Rural Nutrition Institute [*South Korean*] [*Research center*]   (IRC)
RNIFI .... Republic Pharmaceutical Scientific Research Institute   (BU)
RNII.......... Scientific Research Institute of Jet Propulsion   (RU)
RNIIAKKh ... Rostov Scientific Research Institute of the Academy of Municipal Services Imeni K. D. Pamfilov   (RU)
RNIIEM.... Republic Scientific Research Institute of Epidemiology and Microbiology   (BU)

RNIIKF ..... Republic Scientific Research Institute of Health Resorts and Physiotherapy   (BU)
RNIIKhK... Republic Scientific Research Institute of Bone Surgery   (BU)
RNIKF....... Republic Scientific Research Institute for Clinical Physiology   (BU)
RNIKVI..... Republic Scientific Research Institute of Skin and Venereal Diseases   (BU)
RNITI....... Republic Scientific Research Institute on Tuberculosis   (BU)
r-niye.......... Plant   (RU)
RNJ .... Rektorskommitten for de Nordiska Journalist Hogskolorna [*Committee for Nordic Universities of Journalism - CNUJ*] [*Defunct*]   (EAIO)
RNJ .... Yoron-Jima [*Japan*] [*Airport symbol*]   (OAG)
RNK.......... Radiodiffusion Nationale Khmere [*Cambodian National Radio*]   (CL)
RNK.......... Ribonucleic Acid   (RU)
RNK.......... Roman Nepkoztarsasag [*Romanian People's Republic*]   (HU)
RNK-aza .... Ribonuclease   (RU)
RNL.......... Radiodiffusion Nationale Lao [*Lao National Radio*]   (CL)
RNL.......... Rennell Island [*Solomon Islands*] [*Airport symbol*]   (OAG)
RNL.......... Riso National Laboratory [*Research center*] [*Denmark*]   (IRC)
RNLA .... Royal Netherlands Army
RNLAF..... Royal Netherlands Air Force
RNM........ Minimum Voltage Relay   (RU)
RNM........ Radiodiffusion Nationale Marocaine
RNM........ Rassemblement National Malgache [*Malagasy National Rally*]   (AF)
RNM........ Resistencia Nacional Mocambicana [*Mozambican National Resistance*]   (PD)
RNMB...... Republic Scientific Medical Library   (RU)
RNMC...... Royal Netherlands Marine Corps
RNN......... Ronne [*Denmark*] [*Airport symbol*]   (OAG)
RNN......... Royal Netherlands Navy
RNN......... Royal Norwegian Navy
RNN......... Zero Voltage Relay   (RU)
RNNAS .... Royal Netherlands Naval Air Service
RNO .... Air Normandie [*France*] [*ICAO designator*]   (FAAC)
RNO .... Reseau National d'Observation de la Qualite du Milieu Marin [*French*]   (MSC)
RNO .... Riddare af Nordstjerne Order [*Knight of the Polar Star*] [*Sweden*]
RNO .... Riddare of Nordstjerne [*Knight of the Order of the Polar Star*] [*Norway*]
RNO .... Single-Phase Voltage Regulator   (RU)
RNOA....... Royal Norwegian Army   (NATG)
RNOAF ..... Royal Norwegian Air Force
RNOC....... Resistencia Nicaraguense de Organizacion Civica [*Political party*]   (EY)
RNON ...... Royal Norwegian Navy   (NATG)
RNORA..... Royal Norwegian Army
RNORN..... Royal Norwegian Navy
RNP.......... Controlled Directional Reception   (RU)
RNP .... Radio Navigation Point   (RU)
RNP .... Rassemblement National Populaire [*National People's Rally*] [*France*]
RNP .... Regie Nationale des Palmeraies
RNP .... Revista Nacional da Pesca [*Brazil*]   (DSCA)
RNP .... Rhodesia National Party   (AF)
RNP .... Rongelap [*Marshall Islands*] [*Airport symbol*]   (OAG)
RNPC .... Regie Nationale des Palmeraies du Congo
RNPE .... Regie Nationale des Plantations de l'Equateur
RNPISMP ... Republic Scientific and Practical Institute for Emergency Medical Aid
RNPS........ Regie Nationale des Plantations de la Sangha
RNR.......... Registru Naval Roman   (DS)
RNR.......... Robinson River [*Papua New Guinea*] [*Airport symbol*]   (OAG)
RNR.......... Romanian People's Republic   (BU)
RNS .... Nonlogical Combinations Relay   (RU)
RNS .... Radio Navigation Station [*or System*]   (RU)
RNS .... Radio Navigation System   (BU)
RNS .... Rated-Speed Relay   (RU)
RNS .... Rayon People's Councils   (BU)
RNS .... Recherche du Numero de Sequence [*French*]   (ADPT)
RNS .... Rennes [*France*] [*Airport symbol*]   (OAG)
RNS .... Ribonukleiensuur [*Ribonucleic Acid*] [*Afrikaans*]
RNS .... Services Aeronautiques Roannais [*France*] [*ICAO designator*]   (FAAC)
RNS .... Starter Voltage Relay   (RU)
RNS .... Start-of-Count Relay   (RU)
RNSA .... Royal Netherland Shipowners Association   (EAIO)
RNSAS...... Royal Netherlands Society for Agricultural Science   (EAIO)
RNSS........ Royal Norwegian Society of Sciences
RNT .... Radiodiffusion Nationale Tchadienne [*Chadian National Broadcasting*]   (AF)
RNT .... Radio Navigation Point   (RU)
RNT .... Rentavion CA [*Venezuela*] [*ICAO designator*]   (FAAC)
RNT .... Three-Phase Voltage Regulator   (RU)

RNT .... Zero Current Relay (RU)
RNTA .... Rassemblement National des Travailleurs Algeriens [*National Rally of Algerian Workers*] (AF)
RNTA .... Regie Nationale des Tabacs et Allumettes
RNTB .... Regie Nationale des Transports Brazzavillois
RNTB .... Republic Scientific and Technical Library (RU)
RNTP .... Regie Nationale des Transports et des Travaux Publics [*Congo*]
RNU .... Lower Level Relay (RU)
RNU .... Ranau [*Malaysia*] [*Airport symbol*] (OAG)
RNUR .... Regie Nationale des Usines Renault
RNVA .... Royal Netherlands Veterinary Association (EAIO)
RNVR .... Royal Naval Volunteer Reserve (ML)
RNW .... Radio Nederland Wereldomroep [*Radio Netherlands World Broadcasting Foundation*] (WEN)
r-nyy .... Rayon, City District, Area (RU)
RNZ .... Radio New Zealand
RNZ .... Royal New Zealand
RNZA .... Royal New Zealand Army (VNW)
RNZA .... Royal Regiment of New Zealand Artillery (DMA)
RNZAC ...... Royal New Zealand Aero Club (EAIO)
RNZAC ...... Royal New Zealand Armoured Corps (DMA)
RNZAEC ... Royal New Zealand Army Educational Corps (DMA)
RNZAF ...... Royal New Zealand Air Force
RNZAMC .. Royal New Zealand Army Medical Corps (DMA)
RNZAOC .. Royal New Zealand Army Ordnance Corps (DMA)
RNZASC ... Royal New Zealand Army Service Corps (DMA)
RNZBOWiD ... Rada Naczelna Zwiazku Bojownikow o Wolnosc i Demokracje [*Chief Council of the Association of Combatants for Liberty and Democracy*] [*Poland*]
RNZChD ... Royal New Zealand Chaplains Department (DMA)
RNZCS ..... Royal New Zealand Corps of Signals (DMA)
RNZDC ..... Royal New Zealand Dental Corps (DMA)
RNZE .... Royal New Zealand Engineers
RNZEME ... Corps of Royal New Zealand Electrical and Mechanical Engineers (DMA)
RNZIH ...... Royal New Zealand Institute of Horticulture (DSCA)
RNZIR .... Royal New Zealand Infantry Regiment (VNW)
RNZN .... Royal New Zealand Navy
RNZNC ..... Royal New Zealand Nursing Corps (DMA)
RNZN(V)R .. Royal New Zealand Naval (Volunteer) Reserve
RNZPC ..... Royal New Zealand Pay Corps (DMA)
RNZSP ..... Rada Naczelna Zrzeszenia Studentow Polskich [*Chief Council of the Polish Student Association*] (POL)
RO .... Biro [*Bureau*] (IN)
RO .... Cutting-Off Relay, Disconnecting Relay (RU)
RO .... Electronic Equipment, Electronic and Radio Equipment [*Aircraft maintenance*] (RU)
RO .... Fallout Radiometer (RU)
RO .... Flamethrower Company (RU)
RO .... Intelligence Agency (RU)
RO .... Intelligence Service Department (BU)
RO .... Limiting Relay (RU)
RO .... Manual Sprinkler (RU)
RO .... Omani Rial [*Monetary unit*] (IMH)
RO .... Portable Flamethrower (RU)
RO .... Raastuvanoikeus [*Finland*]
RO .... Rada Okregowa [*District Council*] [*Poland*]
RO .... Radial-Axial (RU)
RO .... Radio Marker Beacon (RU)
RO .... Radio Officer [*Australia*]
RO .... Radio Operator [*Royal Australian Navy*]
RO .... Radio Orient (IAA)
RO .... Radna Organizacija [*Organization of Workers*] [*Former Yugoslavia*] (CED)
RO .... Raketometny Oddil [*Rocket Launcher Battalion*] (CZ)
RO .... Rayon Department, City District Department (RU)
RO .... Real Orden [*Royal Decree*] [*Spanish*]
RO .... Rechenoperation [*Computer Operation*] [*German*] (ADPT)
RO .... Recherche Operationnelle [*Operational Research*] [*French*] (ADPT)
RO .... Reconnaissance Detachment (BU)
RO .... Regeringsontwerp [*Benelux*] (BAS)
RO .... Regulator, Adjusting Device (RU)
RO .... Republiski Odbor [*Republic Committee*] (YU)
RO .... Rock [*Germany*] [*ICAO aircraft manufacturer identifier*] (ICAO)
RO .... Rocket Launcher (RU)
RO .... Rocket Weapon (RU)
RO .... Romania [*ANSI two-letter standard code*] (CNC)
RO .... Rovigo [*Car registration plates*] [*Italian*]
RO .... Stopping Relay (RU)
RO .... Territorio de Rondonia [*Territory of Rondonia*] [*Portuguese*]
RO .... Wet op de Regterlijke Organisatie en het Beleid der Justitie [*Benelux*] (BAS)
RoA .... Railways of Australia (ADA)

ROA .... Real Instituto y Observatorio de la Armada [*Royal Naval Institute and Observatory*] [*Ministry of Defense*] [*Spain*] (EAS)
ROA .... Rehabilitation of Offenders Act [*1974*] [*British*] (DCTA)
ROA .... Retard a l'Ouverture de l'Admission [*French*] (MTD)
ROA .... Ruska Oslobodilacka Armija [*Russian Liberation Army*] [*Organized by the Germans from Soviet prisoners*] [*World War II*] (YU)
ROAC .... Railways of Australia Committee
ROAD .... Ruch Obywatelski-Akcja Demokratyczna [*Civil Movement for Democratic Action*] [*P oland*] [*Political party*]
ROAH .... Naha [*Ryukyu Islands*] [*ICAO location identifier*] (ICLI)
ROAK .... Ruch Oporu Armii Krajowej [*Resistance Movement of the Home Army*] (POL)
ROAR .... Run for Aquino and Resignation [*Event organized by Philippine joggers to protest the assassination of Benigno Aquino*]
ROARS ...... Royal Oman Amateur Radio Society (PDAA)
ROB .... Monrovia [*Liberia*] Roberts International Airport [*Airport symbol*] (OAG)
ROB .... Reserveoffizier-Bewerber [*Reserve officer applicant*] [*German military - World War II*]
ROB .... Robertsfield [*Liberia*] [*Airport symbol*]
ROBAN ..... Manuscript Division of the Library of the Academy of Sciences, USSR (RU)
ROBECO .. Rotterdamsch Beleggingsconsortium, NV [*Business term*]
ROBIN ...... Register of Business Opportunities in New South Wales [*Australia*]
RO BIS ...... Manuscript Division of the State Public Library Imeni Saltykov-Shchedrin (RU)
ROC .... Reconnaissance Optique de Caracteres [*Optical Character Recognition*] [*French*]
ROC .... Regional Operating Center [*NATO Integrated Communications System*] (NATG)
ROC .... Regional Organisation of Councils [*Australia*]
ROC .... Regroupement des Officiers Communistes [*Burkina Faso*] [*Political party*] (EY)
ROC .... Republic of China
ROC .... Rhodesia Omnibus Company
roc .... Rocne [*Annually*] [*Publishing Former Czechoslovakia*]
ROCAF ...... Republic of China Air Force
ROCAP ..... Regional Office for Central American and Panamanian Affairs [*Guatemala*] (LAA)
ROCC .... [*The*] Regional Oil Combating Center for the Mediterranean (ASF)
ROCCON ... Road Construction Company of Nigeria Ltd.
ROCH .... Ruch Oporu Chlopskiego [*Movement of Peasant Resistance*] [*Poland*] [*Political party*] (PPE)
ROCI .... Rickman Owners Club International (EAIO)
ROCKSTORE ... International Symposium on Storage in Excavated Rock Caverns (PDAA)
ROCMAGV ... Republic of China, Military Assistance Group, Vietnam
ROCMC .... Republic of China Marine Corps
ROCN .... Republic of China Navy
ROCOCO ... Rocailles, Coquilles, et Cordeau [*Rocks, Shells, and String*] [*French*]
ROCPEX ... Republic of China Philatelic Exhibition
ROCSOC ... Republic of China Society of Cardiology (SLS)
roczn .... Rocznie [*Yearly*] (POL)
roczn .... Rocznik [*Yearbook*] (POL)
rod .... Born (RU)
rod .... Genitive [*Case*] (RU)
rod .... Spring, Source [*Topography*] (RU)
roddom ...... Maternity Home (RU)
RODE .... Iejima United States Air Force Base [*Ryukyu Islands*] [*ICAO location identifier*] (ICLI)
RODK .... Russian Book Friends' Society (RU)
RODN .... Kadena Air Base [*Ryukyu Islands*] [*ICAO location identifier*] (ICLI)
rodn .... Spring, Source [*Topography*] (RU)
rodz .... Rodzaj [*Type*] [*Publishing*] [*Poland*]
ROE .... Resistencia de Obreros y Estudiantes [*Worker and Student Resistance Group*] [*Uruguay*] (LA)
ROE .... Sedimentation Rate [*Medicine*] (RU)
ROEFEX ... Rotterdam Energy Futures Exchange [*Netherlands*] (EY)
Roentgenbeug ... Roentgenbeugung [*X-Ray Diffraction*] [*German*] (GCA)
roentgenograph ... Roentgenographisch [*Radiographic*] [*German*] (GCA)
ROEP .... Restore our Endangered Platteland [*South Africa*] (AA)
ROF .... Aerofrance [*France*] [*ICAO designator*] (FAAC)
ROF .... Rayon Physical Culture Organization (BU)
ROF .... Reformed Ogboni Fraternity [*Nigeria*]
ROFA .... Radio of Free Asia (NTCM)
ROG .... General-Group Relay (RU)
ROG .... Rijksopvoedingsgesticht [*Benelux*] (BAS)
ROG .... Rogel [*C.C. Sergio Gonzales*], Ing. [*Mexico*] [*ICAO designator*] (FAAC)
rog .... Rogne [*Trimmed*] [*Publishing*] [*French*]
ROGBL ..... Manuscript Division of the State Library Imeni Lenin (RU)

RO GIM .... State Historical Museum. Manuscript and Old Book Division (RU)
ROGN........ Flamethrower Company (RU)
rogn .... Rogne [*Trimmed*] [*Publishing*] [*French*]
RO GPB..... Manuscript Division of the State Public Library Imeni Saltykov-Shchedrin (RU)
ROH .... Revolucne Odborove Hnutie [*Revolutionary Trade-Union Movement*] (CZ)
ROH .... Robinhood [*Australia*] [*Airport symbol*] [*Obsolete*] (OAG)
ROHK....... Royal Observatory, Hong Kong [*Research center*] (EAS)
ROI .... Religious Observance Index (BJA)
ROIG .... Ishigaki Jima [*Ryukyu Islands*] [*ICAO location identifier*] (ICLI)
RO IRLI .... Manuscript Division of the Institute of Russian Literature (RU)
ROIT .... Regionalny Osrodek Informacji Turystycznej [*Regional Tourist Information Center*] [*Poland*]
ROJ .... Republic Observatory, Johannesburg [*South Africa*]
ROK .... Republic of Korea
ROK.......... Rockhampton [*Australia*] [*Airport symbol*] (OAG)
ROKA .... Republic of Korea Army
ROKAF..... Republic of Korea Air Force
ROKAMS ... Republic of Korea Army Map Service (PDAA)
ROKAP ..... Republic of Korea Civic Action Program
ROKDTF.. Republic of Korea Division Task Force
ROKF .... Republic of Korea Forces
ROKFV...... Republic of Korea Forces in Vietnam
ROKG .... Republic of Korea Government
ROKJ........ Kume Jima [*Ryukyu Islands*] [*ICAO location identifier*] (ICLI)
ROKK .... Red Cross Society of the RSFSR (RU)
ROKMC .... Republic of Korea Marine Corps
ROKN........ Republic of Korea Navy
ROKPUC... Republic of Korea Presidential Unit Citation Badge [*Military decoration*]
ROKPUCE ... Republic of Korea Presidential Unit Citation [*Military decoration*]
ROKW....... Yomitan [*Ryukyu Islands*] [*ICAO location identifier*] (ICLI)
ROL........... Royal Overseas League [*British*] (EAIO)
ROLAC...... Regional Office for Latin America and the Caribbean [*United Nations Environment Programme*] (EAIO)
ROLTEX ... Rovidaru es Lakastextil Kiskereskedelmi Vallalat [*State Dry Goods Stores*] (HU)
ROM.......... City District Militia Department (RU)
ROM.......... City District Militia Station (RU)
ROM.......... Empresa Aeromar [*Dominican Republic*] [*ICAO designator*] (FAAC)
ROM.......... Magnetic Revolution Regulator (RU)
ROM.......... Open-Sea Reconnaissance Aircraft (RU)
Rom........... Roemisch [*Roman*] [*German*]
Rom........... Romain [*French*] (TPFD)
rom .... Roman [*Romanian*] (HU)
ROM.......... Romania [*ANSI three-letter standard code*] (CNC)
rom .... Romaniaa [*or Romaniaksi*] [*Finland*]
rom .... Romanialainen [*Finland*]
rom .... Romantique [*Binding tooled in the romantic style*] [*Publishing*] [*French*]
ROM.......... Rome [*Italy*] [*Airport symbol*] (OAG)
Rom........... Romeine [*Roman*] [*Afrikaans*]
rom .... Romeinse Lettertipe [*Roman Type*] [*Afrikaans*]
Rom........... Romorker [*Trailer*] (TU)
ROMAMPAS ... Review of Migrant and Multicultural Programs and Services [*Australia*]
roman .... Romanisch [*Norman*] [*German*]
Rom &Jul ... Romeo and Juliet [*Shakespearean work*] (BARN)
romant........ Romantique [*Binding tooled in the romantic style*] [*Publishing*] [*French*]
romboedr.... Rhombohedral (RU)
romb s .... Rhombic Syngony (RU)
ROMCONSULT ... Institutul Roman de Consulting [*Romanian Consulting Institute*] (RO)
ROMD....... Minami Daito Jima [*Ryukyu Islands*] [*ICAO location identifier*] (ICLI)
ROMINVENT ... Bureau of Foreign Patents and Inventions of Romania (IMH)
rom kat....... Romai Katolikus [*Roman Catholic*] (HU)
rom-kath .... Roemisch-Katholisch [*Roman Catholic*] [*German*]
ROMO ...... Republic General Machinery Manufacture Association [*RSFSR*] (RU)
ROMPETROL ... Company for Oil and Gas Cooperation of Romania (IMH)
ROMTRANS ... Intreprinderea de Stat pentru Transporturi si Expeditii Internationale [*State Enterprise for International Transportation and Shipments*] (RO)
RO/MVD .. Investigating Section of the Ministry of Internal Affairs (RU)
ROMVD...... Rayon Branch of the Ministry of Internal Affairs (RU)
ROMW...... Recreation Opportunities for Migrant Women [*Australia*]
ROMY....... Miyako [*Ryukyu Islands*] [*ICAO location identifier*] (ICLI)
RON .... Air Nauru [*ICAO designator*] (FAAC)
RON .... Eskadron [*Squadron*] (IN)

RON .... Rondon [*Colombia*] [*Airport symbol*] [*Obsolete*] (OAG)
RONA........ Naha United States Naval Base [*Ryukyu Islands*] [*ICAO location identifier*] (ICLI)
RONCAST ... Royal Nepal Academy for Science and Technology
RONFIN ... Republic of Nauru Finance Corp.
RONO .... Rayon Department of Public Education (RU)
rontg........... Rontgen [*Roentgen (unit of radiation)*] (HU)
ROO .... Rondonopolis [*Brazil*] [*Airport symbol*] (OAG)
roodsn .... Roodsneden [*Red Edges*] [*Publishing*] [*Netherlands*]
roomal........ Roomalainen [*Finland*]
roomkat...... Roomalais-Katolinen [*Finland*]
ROOP....... Portable Pneumatic Fire Extinguisher-Sprinkler (RU)
rop .... Company Strong Point (RU)
ROP .... Field Failure Relay (RU)
ROP .... Referat Ochrony Przemyslowej [*Industrial Security Office*] (POL)
ROP........... Republic of Panama
ROP........... Republic of the Philippines
ROP .... Rota [*Mariana Islands*] [*Airport symbol*] (OAG)
ROP .... Royal Oman Police [*ICAO designator*] (FAAC)
ROP .... Russian Society of Pathologists (RU)
ROPIK...... Russian Society for the Study of the Crimea (RU)
ROPIT....... Russian Steamship Line and Trade Society (RU)
ROPME .... Regional Organization for the Protection of the Marine Environment [*Safat, Kuwait*] (EAIO)
ROPWiM .. Rada Ochrony Pomnikow Walki i Meczenstwa [*Council for Conservation of Monuments of Struggle and Martyrdom*] (POL)
ROR........... Koror [*Palau Islands*] [*Airport symbol*] (OAG)
RORA .... Aguni [*Ryukyu Islands*] [*ICAO location identifier*] (ICLI)
RORE .... Iejima [*Ryukyu Islands*] [*ICAO location identifier*] (ICLI)
RORG........ Naha [*Ryukyu Islands*] [*ICAO location identifier*] (ICLI)
RORH........ Hateruma [*Ryukyu Islands*] [*ICAO location identifier*] (ICLI)
RORI .... Russian Society of Radio Engineers [*1918-1929*] (RU)
RORK .... Kitadaito [*Ryukyu Islands*] [*ICAO location identifier*] (ICLI)
ro-ro .... Roll-On Roll-Off (IDIG)
RO-RO ...... Rolls Royce [*Automobile*] [*Slang*] (DSUE)
RORS .... Shimojishima [*Ryukyu Islands*] [*ICAO location identifier*] (ICLI)
RORT .... Residents Opposed to Runway Three [*at Sydney Airport*] [*Australia*]
RORT .... Tarama [*Ryukyu Islands*] [*ICAO location identifier*] (ICLI)
RORY .... Yoron [*Ryukyu Islands*] [*ICAO location identifier*] (ICLI)
ros .... Area Communications Section (RU)
ROS .... ATS-Servicii de Transport Aerian [*Italy*] [*ICAO designator*] (FAAC)
ROS .... General-Signal Relay (RU)
ROS .... Operating Exchange Capacity [*Nuclear energy*] (BU)
ROS .... Radarska Osmatracka Stanica [*RADAR Observation Station*] (YU)
ROS .... Radiova Odposlouchavaci Sluzba [*Radio Monitoring Service*] (CZ)
ROS .... Remontowa Obsluga Statkow [*Ship Repair Service*] (POL)
ROS .... Rosario [*Argentina*] [*Airport symbol*] (OAG)
ros .... Rosyjski [*Russian*] (POL)
ROS .... Speed-Limiting Relay (RU)
ROSA .... Federation of Rose Societies of South Africa (AA)
ROSA .... Review of Structural Arrangements [*Australian telecommunications*]
ROSAGROBIRZHA ... Russian Commodity Exchange of the Agro-Industrial Complex (EE)
Rosavtoobsluzhivaniye ... Republic Trust of Filling Stations and Automobile Service Stations (RU)
Rosavtoremont ... Republic Trust of Automobile Repair Plants and Shops (RU)
Rosbakaleya ... Republic Office of the Wholesale Trade in Sugar, Confectionery, Canned Goods, Tobacco, Salt, and Other Groceries [*RSFSR*] (RU)
Rosbriket ... Republic Briquette Trust [*RSFSR*] (RU)
Rosdrozhzhi ... Republic Trust of Yeast Industry [*RSFSR*] (RU)
ROSE......... Research Open Systems in Europe [*Computer science*] (BARN)
Rosformomaterialy ... State Republic Trust for the Extraction of Casting Sand and Clay (RU)
Rosgalantereya ... Republic Office of the Wholesale Trade in Notions, Perfume, Cosmetics, and Soap [*RSFSR*] (RU)
Rosgazstroy ... Republic Trust for the Construction of Gas Networks [*RSFSR*] (RU)
Rosgiprogorsel'stroy ... Republic State Planning Institute for the Planning of Urban and Rural Construction of the RSFSR (RU)
Rosgiprosel'khozstroy ... Republic State Planning Institute for the Planning of Agricultural Construction [*RSFSR*] (RU)
Rosgiprosovkhozstroy ... Republic State Institute for the Planning of Sovkhoz Construction [*RSFSR*] (RU)
Rosgiprovodkhoz ... Republic State Institute for the Planning of Water-Management and Reclamation Construction of the Gosvodkhoz RSFSR (RU)

Rosgiprozem ... Republic State Planning Institute for Land Use Measures [*RSFSR*]   (RU)

Rosgizmestprom ... State Publishing House of Local Industry of the RSFSR (RU)

Rosglavavtotraktorosnabsbyt ... Main Administration for the Supply and Marketing of Automobiles, Tractors, Motors, Agricultural Machinery, and Spare Parts [*RSFSR*]   (RU)

Rosglavbumprom ... Main Administration of the Paper Industry [*RSFSR*]   (RU)

Rosglavbumsnabsbyt ... Main Administration for the Supply and Marketing of Products of the Pulp and Paper, Wood Chemistry, and Furniture Industries   (RU)

Rosglavchermetsnabsbyt ... Main Administration of Supply and Marketing of Ferrous Metals, Metalware, Ores, Fluxes, By-Product Coke, and Refractory Products [*RSFSR*]   (RU)

Rosglavelektrosnabsbyt ... Main Administration of Supply and Marketing of Electrotechnical Equipment, Cable Products, and Electrotechnical Consumer Goods   (RU)

Rosglavfil'm ... Main Administration of Motion-Picture Production [*RSFSR*]   (RU)

Rosglavgosrybvod ... Main State Inspection for Fish Conservation and Reproduction and for Control of Fishing [*RSFSR*]   (RU)

Rosglavkhimkomplekt ... Main Administration for Supplying Complete Sets of Equipment, Devices, Cables, and Other Products and Basic Materials to Chemical Industry Establishments Being Constructed or Repaired [*RSFSR*]   (RU)

Rosglavkhimsnabsbyt ... Main Administration of Supply and Marketing of Chemical, Rubber, and Asbestos Products [*RSFSR*]   (RU)

Rosglavkniga ... Main Administration of the Book Trade [*RSFSR*]   (RU)

Rosglavkonserv ... Main Administration of the Canning and Vegetable Drying Industry [*RSFSR*]   (RU)

Rosglavkoopkhoztorg ... Main Administration for Trade in Building Materials, Hardware, and Goods Used in Industry   (RU)

Rosglavkoopkul'ttorg ... Main Administration for Trade in Goods for Cultural Purposes [*RSFSR*]   (RU)

Rosglavkoopmyasoptitsa ... Main Administration for the Procurement, Processing, and Marketing of Meat, Eggs, and Dairy Products [*of the Rospotrebsoyuz*]   (RU)

Rosglavkooppromtorg ... Main Administration for Trade in Industrial Goods [*of the Rospotrebsoyuz*]   (RU)

Rosglavkoopsnab ... Main Administration of Materials and Equipment Supply [*of the Rospotrebsoyuz*]   (RU)

Rosglavkoopzhivsyr'ye ... Main Administration for the Procurement, Processing, and Marketing of Livestock Raw Materials, Secondary Raw Materials, Livestock Products, and Fur (RU)

Rosglavkozh ... Main Administration of the Leather Industry [*RSFSR*]   (RU)

Rosglavkul'tsnabsbyt ... Main Supply and Marketing Administration of the Ministry of Culture, RSFSR   (RU)

Rosglavlegsnab ... Main Administration of Materials and Equipment Supply of the Ministry of Light Industry, RSFSR   (RU)

Rosglavlegsnabsbytsyr'ye ... Main Administration for Supplying and Marketing Raw Materials of Light Industry   (RU)

Rosglavlen ... Main Administration of the Flax and Hemp Industry [*RSFSR*]

Rosglavles ... Main Administration of the Lumber Industry [*RSFSR*]   (RU)

Rosglavlesosbyt ... Main Administration for the Marketing of Lumber [*RSFSR*]   (RU)

Rosglavlesosnab ... Main Administration of Materials and Equipment Supply of the Ministry of the Lumber Industry, RSFSR   (RU)

Rosglavlessnabsbyt ... Main Administration for Supply and Marketing of Products of the Logging and Woodworking Industry [*RSFSR*]   (RU)

Rosglavmashdetal' ... Main Administration of Machine Part Manufacture [*RSFSR*]   (RU)

Rosglavmashsnabsbyt ... Main Administration for the Supply and Marketing of Machinery [*RSFSR*]   (RU)

Rosglavmaslosyrprom ... Main Administration of the Butter and Cheese Industry [*RSFSR*]   (RU)

Rosglavmedsnab ... Main Medical Supply Administration [*RSFSR*]   (RU)

Rosglavmekh ... Main Administration of the Fur and Sheepskin-Coat Industry [*RSFSR*]   (RU)

Rosglavmyasomolsnab ... Main Administration of Materials and Equipment Supply of the Ministry of the Meat and Dairy Products Industry, RSFSR   (RU)

Rosglavmyasomolstroy ... Main Construction Administration of the Ministry of the Meat and Dairy Products Industry, RSFSR   (RU)

Rosglavmyasoptitseprom ... Main Administration of the Meat and Poultry Processing Industry [*RSFSR*]   (RU)

Rosglavneftesnabsbyt ... Main Administration of Supply and Marketing of Petroleum and Petroleum Products   (RU)

Rosglavoboronsnabsbyt ... Main Supply and Marketing Administration of the Defense Industry [*RSFSR*]   (RU)

Rosglavobuv' ... Main Administration of the Footwear Industry [*RSFSR*]   (RU)

Rosglavparfyumer ... Main Administration of the Perfume, Cosmetics, and Essential-Oil Industry   (RU)

Rosglavpishchesnabsbytsyr'ye ... Main Administration of Supply and Marketing of Food Raw Materials   (RU)

Rosglavpivo ... Main Administration of the Brewing and Soft Drink Industry [*RSFSR*]   (RU)

Rosglavpriborsnabsbyt ... Main Administration of Supply and Marketing of Instruments and Automation Equipment [*RSFSR*]   (RU)

Rosglavprodsnab ... Main Administration of Materials and Equipment Supply of the Ministry of the Foodstuffs Industry, RSFSR   (RU)

Rosglavradiosnabsbyt ... Main Administration of Supply and Marketing of Communications Equipment and Radiotechnical Products [*RSFSR*]   (RU)

Rosglavraszhirmaslo ... Main Administration of the Oil and Fats Industry [*RSFSR*]   (RU)

Rosglavrybsnab ... Main Administration of Materials and Equipment Supply of Fish Industry Establishments [*RSFSR*]   (RU)

Rosglavrybsnabsbyt ... Main Administration of Supply and Production Marketing of the Fish Industry [*RSFSR*]   (RU)

Rosglavrybstroy ... Main Construction Administration of the Ministry of the Fish Industry, RSFSR   (RU)

Rosglavrybtara ... Main Administration of Logging and Manufacture of Packing Materials of the Ministry of the Fish Industry, RSFSR   (RU)

Rosglavsadpitomnik ... Main Administration of Horticulture, Nurseries, Sericulture, and Apiculture [*RSFSR*]   (RU)

Rosglavsakhar ... Main Administration of the Sugar Industry [*RSFSR*]   (RU)

Rosglavsel'snab ... Main Administration of Materials and Equipment Supply of the Ministry of Agriculture, RSFSR   (RU)

Rosglavsetesnast' ... Main Administration of the Netting and Rigging Industry [*RSFSR*]   (RU)

Rosglavsherst' ... Main Administration of the Wool Industry [*RSFSR*]   (RU)

Rosglavshveyprom ... Main Administration of the Garment Industry [*RSFSR*]   (RU)

Rosglavsol' ... Main Administration of the Salt Industry [*RSFSR*]   (RU)

Rosglavspirt ... Main Administration of the Alcohol, Liqueur, and Vodka Industry   (RU)

Rosglavstankoinstrumentsnabsbyt ... Main Administration of Supply and Marketing of Machine Tools, Forging-and-Pressing Equipment, Tools, and Abrasives [*RSFSR*]   (RU)

Rosglavsteklo ... Main Administration of the Glass Industry [*RSFSR*]   (RU)

Rosglavstromsnab ... Main Supply Administration of the Building Materials Industry [*RSFSR*]   (RU)

Rosglavstroy ... Main Construction Administration [*RSFSR*]   (RU)

Rosglavstroysnabsbyt ... Main Administration of Supply and Marketing of Building Materials and Sanitary Engineering Equipment [*RSFSR*]   (RU)

Rosglavtabak ... Main Administration of the Tobacco and Tea Industries (RU)

Rosglavtekstil'galantereya ... Main Administration of the Textile and Notions Industries [*RSFSR*]   (RU)

Rosglavtekstil'snabsbytsyr'ye ... Main Administration of Supply and Marketing of Textile Industry Raw Materials [*RSFSR*]   (RU)

Rosglavtopmash ... Main Administration of Fuel Machinery [*RSFSR*]   (RU)

Rosglavtorfbriket ... Main Administration of the Peat and Peat-Briquette Industry [*RSFSR*]   (RU)

Rosglavtrikotazh ... Main Administration of the Knit Goods Industry [*RSFSR*]   (RU)

Rosglavtselinstroy ... Main Administration of Sovkhoz Construction on Virgin and Fallow Lands [*RSFSR*]   (RU)

Rosglavtsvetmetsnabsbyt ... Main Administration of Supply and Marketing of Nonferrous and Rare Metals, Nonferrous Rolled Products, and Metalware [*RSFSR*]   (RU)

Rosglavtyazhmashsnabsbyt ... Main Administration of Supply and Marketing of Products of Heavy Transportation, Construction, and Road Machinery [*RSFSR*]   (RU)

Rosglavugleneft' ... Main Administration of the Coal and Petroleum Industries [*RSFSR*]   (RU)

Rosglavuglesnabsbyt ... Main Administration of Supply and Marketing of Coal Fuel, Shale, and Peat [*RSFSR*]   (RU)

Rosglavvalprom ... Main Administration of the Felt Industry [*RSFSR*]   (RU)

Rosglavvino ... Main Administration of the Wine-Making Industry [*RSFSR*]   (RU)

Rosglavvitaminprom ... Main Administration of the Vitamin Industry [*RSFSR*]   (RU)

Rosglavvodsnab ... Main Administration of Materials and Equipment Supply of the Ministry of Water Management, RSFSR   (RU)

Rosgorstroy ... Republic Trust of Civil Engineering and Housing Construction [*RSFSR*]   (RU)

Rosgosstrakh ... Administration of State Insurance for the RSFSR   (RU)

Roskhlebtorg ... Main Administration of the Grain Trade [*RSFSR*]   (RU)

Roskhmel' ... Russian Republic Office for Hop Growing   (RU)

Roskhoztorg ... Republic Office for Wholesale Trade in Household Goods [*RSFSR*]   (RU)

Roskhoztrans ... Main Administration of Automobile Transportation of the Ministry of Sovkhozes, RSFSR   (RU)

Roskombank ... Russian Commercial Bank   (RU)

Roskonservlestara ... Trust for the Procurement and Processing of Lumber and for the Manufacture of Packing Materials of the Rosglavkonserv [*RSFSR*]   (RU)

Roskooplestara ... Republic Trust for the Procurement of Lumber and for the Manufacture of Packing Materials of the Rosglavkoopsnab   (RU)

Roskoopprodkontora ... Republic Office for Food Trade   (RU)

Roskooppromproyekt ... Republic Planning Office of the Rospromsovet   (RU)

Roskul'ttorg ... Republic Office for Wholesale Trade in Goods for Cultural Purposes and Sporting Goods [*RSFSR*]   (RU)

Roslegpromstroy ... State Republic Construction and Installation Trust of the Ministry of Light Industry, RSFSR   (RU)

Roslesotopsbyt ... Administration of Fuel Marketing and Lumber Supply [*RSFSR*]   (RU)

Roslesstroytorg ... Republic Office for the Trade in Lumber and Building Materials [*RSFSR*]   (RU)

Rosleszag ...   Republic Logging Trust [*RSFSR*]   (RU)

ROSM .... Revolutionary Organization of Socialist Muslims   (EAIO)

Rosmashdortrest ... Republic Trust for the Management of Road Machine Stations [*RSFSR*]   (RU)

Rosmaslosindikat ... All-Russian Syndicate of the Vegetable Oil Industry   (RU)

Rosmedsnabtorg ... Office for Purchasing, Procurement, and Supply of Chemicopharmaceutical Goods, Reagents, Sanitation and Hygiene Articles, and Other Pharmaceutical Products [*RSFSR*]   (RU)

Rosmetalloproyekt ... Office for the Planning of Machinery and Metalworking Plants [*RSFSR*]   (RU)

Rosmyasomolproyekt ... Republic Planning and Surveying Office of the Ministry of the Meat and Dairy Products Industry, RSFSR   (RU)

Rosmyasorybtorg ... Republic Office for the Wholesale Trade in Meat, Butter, and Fish   (RU)

ROSNIIMS ... Republic Scientific Research Institute of Local Building Materials [*RSFSR*]   (RU)

Rosobuv'torg ... Republic Office of the Wholesale Trade in Footwear [*RSFSR*]   (RU)

Rosokhotsoyuz ... Union of Hunters' Societies of the RSFSR   (RU)

Rosoptpromtorg ... Republic Office of the Wholesale Trade in Industrial Goods [*RSFSR*]   (RU)

Rospotrebsoyuz ... Union of the Consumers' Societies of the RSFSR   (RU)

Rosprodproyekt ... Republic Planning Office of the Ministry of the Foodstuffs Industry, RSFSR   (RU)

Rospromsovet ... Council of Producers' Cooperatives of the RSFSR   (RU)

Rospromtorg ... Main Administration for Trade in Industrial Goods [*RSFSR*]   (RU)

Rosproyekt ... Institute for Publication and Distribution of Standard Designs for Rural Construction [*RSFSR*]   (RU)

ROSS .... Roudnicke Strojirny a Slevarny [*Roudnice Engineering Works and Foundries*]   (CZ)

Rossel'khoztekhnika ... All-Russian Association of the Council of Ministers of the RSFSR for the Sale of Agricultural Machinery, Spare Parts, Mineral Fertilizers, and Other Materials and Equipment, Repair Organization, and Machine Utilization in Kolkhozes and Sovkhozes   (RU)

Rossel'stroy ... Republic Construction Trust of the Ministry of Agriculture, RSFSR   (RU)

Rosshelk .... Russian Republic Office for Sericulture   (RU)

Rosskotsyr'ye ... Republic Office for Supply of Animal Raw Materials and for Fattening of Cattle [*RSFSR*]   (RU)

Rossnabso ... Administration of Materials and Equipment Supply of the Ministry of Social Security, RSFSR   (RU)

Rossortsemovoshch ... Republic Office for the Procurement and Marketing of High-Quality Vegetable Seeds [*RSFSR*]   (RU)

Rossovkhozstroy ... Republic Construction Trust of the Ministry of Sovkhozes, RSFSR   (RU)

Rossovkhoztrans ... Main Administration of Automobile Transportation of the Ministry of Sovkhozes, RSFSR   (RU)

Rosspetsstroy ... Republic Specialized Trust of the Glavspetsstroy [*RSFSR*]   (RU)

Rosstromproyekt ... State Planning Institute for the Planning of Building Materials Plants [*RSFSR*]   (RU)

Rosstroymontazh ... Republic Construction and Installation Trust [*RSFSR*]   (RU)

ROSTA ...... Regional Office for Science and Technology in Africa [*UNESCO*] [*See also BRUSTA*] [*Nairobi, Kenya*]   (EAIO)

ROSTA ...... Rossiskoye Telegrafnaye Agenstvo [*Russian News Agency (1918-1935)*]   (RU)

ROSTAS ... Regional Office for Science and Technology in the Arab States [*UNESCO*]   (ASF)

ROSTE ...... Regional Office for Science and Technology for Europe [*UNESCO*] [*Italy*]   (EAIO)

Rostekhizdat ... Publishing House of Scientific and Technical Literature of the RSFSR   (RU)

Rostekstil'torg ... Republic Office for Wholesale Trade in Textiles [*RSFSR*]   (RU)

Rostizdat .... Rostov Publishing House   (RU)

ROSTLA ... Regional Office for Science and Technology in Latin America [*UNESCO*]   (ASF)

ROSTLAC ... Regional Office of Science and Technology for Latin America and the Caribbean   (MSC)

Rostorgmestprom ... Rostov City Administration of Local Industry   (RU)

Rostorgmontazh ... Republic Specialized Trust for the Installation of the Refrigeration and Trade Equipment [*RSFSR*]   (RU)

Rostorgodezhda ... Republic Office of Wholesale Clothing Trade [*RSFSR*]   (RU)

Rostorgreklama ... Republic Office of Trade Advertising [*RSFSR*]   (RU)

Rostorgsnab ... Main Administration of Materials and Equipment Supply of the Ministry of Trade, RSFSR   (RU)

Rostorgstroy ... Construction and Installation Trust of the Ministry of Trade, RSFSR   (RU)

Rostovenergo ... Rostov Power System   (RU)

ROSTSCA ... Regional Office of Science and Technology for South and Central Asia [*UNESCO*]   (IRC)

ROSTSEA ... Regional Office of Science and Technology for Southeast Asia [*UNESCO*]   (IRC)

Rostsel'mash ... Rostov Agricultural Machinery Plant   (RU)

Rosvalmashproyekt ... Design, Planning, and Installation Office of the State Committee on Light Industry of the Gosplan SSSR   (RU)

Rosvattrest ... Republic Cotton and Wadding Trust [*RSFSR*]   (RU)

Rosvodstroy ... Republic Reclamation Construction Trust [*RSFSR*]   (RU)

Rosvuzizdat ... Publishing House of the Ministry of Higher and Secondary Special Education, RSFSR   (RU)

Rosyuvelirtorg ... Republic Office for Jewelry Manufacture and Trade [*RSFSR*]   (RU)

Roszoovetsnab ... Republic Office for the Supply of Veterinary and Zootechnical Equipment, Instruments, and Drugs [*RSFSR*]   (RU)

ROT .... Reverse-Current Relay   (RU)

ROT .... Reverse-Current Tripping Device   (RU)

ROT .... Rotorua [*New Zealand*] [*Airport symbol*]   (OAG)

ROT .... Tarom, Romanian Air Transport [*ICAO designator*]   (FAAC)

ROT .... Temperature Regulator   (RU)

ROTA .... Rats of Tobruk Association [*Australia*]

ROTEL ...... Rolling Hotel [*European bus-tour system*]

ROTERO .. Roterodamum [*Rotterdam*]   (ROG)

rotgedr .... Rotgedruckt [*Printed in Red*] [*German*]

ROTM .... Futema [*Ryukyu Islands*] [*ICAO location identifier*]   (ICLI)

rotoc .... Rotocalco [*Rotogravure*] [*Publishing*] [*Italian*]

ROTs .... Cycle Termination Relay   (RU)

ROTS .... Royal Officers' Training School [*Australia*]

ROTTER ... Rotterdam   (ROG)

Rotverschieb ... Rotverschiebung [*Red Shift*] [*German*]   (GCA)

ROTZ .... Reactor with a Heat-Transfer Agent and Organic Moderator   (RU)

ROU .... Manual Carbon Dioxide Fire Extinguisher   (RU)

ROU .... Pressure-Reducing and Cooling Unit   (RU)

ROU .... Republica Oriental del Uruguay

ROU .... Russe [*Bulgaria*] [*Airport symbol*]   (OAG)

Roubne .... Roubine [*Military map abbreviation*] [*World War I*] [*French*]   (MTD)

ROUE .... Revolutionary Organization of Uganda   (AF)

roul .... Roulette [*Circular Design*] [*Publishing*] [*French*]

rouss .... Rousseurs [*Red Spots*] [*Publishing*] [*French*]

ROV .... Rostov [*Former USSR*] [*Airport symbol*]   (OAG)

rov .... Rovat [*Newspaper Column*]   (HU)

rov .... Rovidites [*Abbreviation*] [*Hungary*]

ROVA .... Returned Overseas Volunteers of Australia   (EAIO)

ROVS .... Russkiy Obshche-Voyenskiy Soyuz [*Russian Armed Forces Union*]   (LAIN)

ROW .... Residents of Woolloomooloo [*Australia*]

ROW .... Rest of World [*Newly industrialized countries of Asia*]

ROW .... Rheinische Olefinwerke

ROW .... Rybnicki Okreg Weglowy [*Rybnik Coal Basin*] [*Poland*]

ROY .... Rio Mayo [*Argentina*] [*Airport symbol*]   (OAG)

roy .... Royaume [*Kingdom*] [*French*]

RoyCom ..... Royal Commission [*Australia*]

ROYN .... Yonagunijima [*Ryukyu Islands*] [*ICAO location identifier*]   (ICLI)

ROZ .... Research-Oktanzahl [*Research Octane Number*] [*German*]   (GCA)

roz .... Rozebrano [*Out-of-Print*] [*Publishing Former Czechoslovakia*]

roz .... Rozena [*Nee (Maiden name)*]   (CZ)

rozdz .... Rozdzial [*Chapter*]   (POL)

rozp .... Rozporzadzenie [*Instruction*]   (POL)

rozsz .... Rozszerzone [*Enlarged*]   (POL)

Rp .... Bench Mark   (RU)

RP .... Casualty Sorting Station   (RU)

RP .... Company Machine Gun   (RU)

RP .... Distinctive Attributes   (RU)

RP .... Distribution Field   (RU)

RP .... Distribution Point [*Electricity*]   (RU)

RP .... Excavations and Studies   (BU)

RP	Field Radiometer (RU)
rp	Genitive Case (RU)
RP	Initiating Relay (RU)
RP	Intermediate Relay (RU)
RP	Light Machine Gun (RU)
RP	Loading Point, Entrucking Point (RU)
RP	Miner's Lamp with Increased Reliability (RU)
rp	Observation Post, Reconnaissance Post (RU)
RP	Operating Field [*Computers*] (RU)
RP	Polarized Relay (RU)
RP	Precipitation Test (RU)
RP	Precision Roentgen Meter (RU)
RP	Rada Panstwa [*State Council*] [*Poland*]
RP	RADAR Plotter [*Royal Australian Navy*]
RP	Radiation Pyrometer (RU)
RP	Radio Direction Finder (BU)
RP	Radio Director Finder, Radiogoniometer (RU)
RP	Radio Patrulha [*Radius Patrol*] [*Portuguese*]
RP	Radio Prijemnik [*Radio Receiver*] (YU)
rp	Rakpart [*Embankment*] (HU)
Rp	Rampe [*Ramp, Loading Platform*] (EG)
RP	Rappen [*Monetary unit*] [*Switzerland*]
Rp	Rapport [*French*] (FLAF)
RP	Rayon Substation (RU)
RP	Recette Principale [*Principal Returns*] [*French*]
RP	Reconnaissance by Radio Direction Finding (RU)
RP	Recorder (RU)
RP	Reditelstvi Post [*Postal Directorate*] (CZ)
RP	Region Parisienne (FLAF)
RP	Regulating Post, Commanding Post (RU)
RP	Reichs Patent [*State Patent*] [*German*]
rp	Rekopis [*Manuscript*] (POL)
RP	Reponse Payee [*Prepaid Reply*] [*French*] (CL)
RP	Representation Proportionnelle [*Proportional Representation*] [*French*]
RP	Republican Party [*Iraq*] [*Political party*] (BJA)
RP	Republic of Panama
RP	Republic of Portugal (BARN)
RP	Republic of the Philippines
RP	Republikeinse Party van Suidwesafrika [*Republican Party of South West Africa*] [*Namibia*] [*Political party*] (PPW)
RP	Republike Popullore [*Albanian*]
RP	Resolver (RU)
RP	Reverendo Padre [*Reverend Father*] [*Spanish*]
RP	Reverend Pere [*Reverend Father*] [*French*]
RP	Rhodesian Party
RP	Ribarsko Poduzece [*Fishing Establishment*] (YU)
RP	Rijksproefstation [*Benelux*] (BAS)
RP	Rocni Plan [*Year Plan*] (CZ)
RP	Route Provinciale [*Provincial Highway*] (CL)
RP	Rude Pravo [*The Red Right*] [*A newspaper*] (CZ)
RP	Rudny Projekt [*Mining Investments Planning Office*] (CZ)
RP	Rupiah [*Monetary unit*] [*Indonesia*]
RP	Rzeczpospolita Polska [*Polish Republic*] (POL)
RP	Searchlight Radar (RU)
RP	Unloading Platform, Detrucking Platform (RU)
RP	Workers' Party (BU)
rp	Workers' Settlement (RU)
RPA	Lure-Distributing Truck (RU)
RPA	Parabolic Horn Antenna (RU)
RPA	Provence Aero Service [*France*] [*ICAO designator*] (FAAC)
RPA	Radio Reception Equipment Room (RU)
RPA	Rassemblement Populaire Africain
RPA	Rationalist Press Association [*British*] (EAIO)
RPA	Rechapage Pneus Afrique
RPA	Register of Private Agents [*Victoria, Australia*]
RPA	Republican Party of Australia [*Political party*]
RPA	Republica Populara Albania [*Albanian People's Republic*] (RO)
RPA	Republica Popular de Angola
RPA	Republika Poludniowej Afryki [*Republic of South Africa*] [*Poland*]
RPA	Republik Persatuan Arab [*United Arab Republic*] (IN)
RPA	Republique Populaire d'Angola
RPA	Retired Police Association [*Australia*]
RPA	Rice Producers Association [*Guyana*] (LA)
RPA	Rolpa [*Nepal*] [*Airport symbol*] (OAG)
RPAA	Radiata Pine Association of Australia (ADA)
RPAC	Research Policy Advisory Committee [*Department of Agriculture*] [*South Australia*]
RPAC	Resistencia do Povo Anti-Colonista [*Peoples Anti-Colonialist Resistance*] [*Portuguese*] (WER)
RPAH	Royal Prince Alfred Hospital [*Australia*]
RPAJ	Radnicke Protivavionske Jedinice [*Workers' Antiaircraft Units*] [*Army*] (YU)
RPAL	Rubber Planters Association of Liberia
RPAYC	Royal Prince Alfred Yacht Club [*Australia*]
RPB	Company Ammunition Supply Point (RU)
RPB	Nonceramic Polarized Relay (RU)
RPB	Radar Bombsight (RU)
rpb	Radio Direction-Finding Battalion (BU)
RPB	Rassemblement Populaire du Burundi
RPB	Repair and Rental Base (RU)
RPB	Republica Populara Bulgara [*Bulgarian People's Republic*] (RO)
RPB	Republique Populaire du Benin
RPb	Rohrblei [*Tube Lead*] [*German*] (GCA)
RPB	Workers' Party of Burma (RU)
RPBA	Regiao de Producao da Bahia [*Brazil*] (LAA)
RPBS	Repatriation Pharmaceutical Benefits Scheme [*Australia*]
RPC	Radiation Protection Committee [*South Australia*]
RPC	Regiment de Parachutistes Coloniaux [*Algeria*]
RPC	Regiment Parachutiste Commando [*Paratrooper Commando Regiment*] [*Burkina Faso*] (AF)
RPC	Regional Police Commander
RPC	Remuneration Planning Corp. [*Australia*]
RPC	Republica Populara Chineza [*China*] (RO)
RPC	Republique Populaire de Chine
RPC	Request the Pleasure of Your Company [*On invitations*] (DSUE)
RPC	Research Priorities Committee for Human Sciences Research [*Human Sciences Research Council*] [*South Africa*] (AA)
RPC	Retrait du Permis de Conduire [*France*] (FLAF)
RPC	Reunionese Peace Committee
RPC	Rivers People's Congress
RPC	Rural Political Cadre [*Vietnam*]
RPC	Russian Privatization Center (ECON)
RPCh	Frequency Starting Relay (RU)
RPCh	Manual Heterodyne Frequency Trim (RU)
RPCh	Radio Pulse Frequency Converter (RU)
RPCI	Regroupement des Partis de la Cote-D'Ivoire [*Regroupment of the Parties of the Ivory Coast*]
RPCM	Rassemblement Populaire Caledonien et Metropolitain [*Caledonian and Metropolitan Popular Rally*] [*Political party*] (PPW)
RPCQ	Rural Press Club [*Queensland, Australia*]
RPCR	Rassemblement pour la Caledonie dans la Republique [*Popular Caledonian Rally for the Republic*] [*Political party*] (PPW)
RPCV	Rural Press Club of Victoria [*Australia*]
RPCWA	Rural Press Club of Western Australia
RPD	Degtyarev Light Machine Gun (RU)
RPD	Direct-Action Controller (RU)
RPD	Electronic Radio Countermeasures (BU)
RPD	Pressure Regulator (RU)
RPD	Radio Countermeasures (RU)
RPD	Ramjet Engine (RU)
RPD	Repertoire Pratique Dalloz [*France*] (FLAF)
RPD	Rijksplanologische Dienst [*National Physical Planning Agency*] [*Research center*] [*Netherlands*] (IRC)
RPD	Rotary Piston Engine (RU)
RPD	Ruchnoi Pulemet Degtyarev [*Light Machine Gun*] [*Former USSR*]
RPDB	Repertoire Pratique du Droit Belge [*Belgium*] (BAS)
RPDC	Republique Populaire Democratique de Coree [*Democratic People's Republic of Korea - DPRK*] [*North Korea*] (CL)
RPDK	Republica Populara Democrata Coreeana [*Korean Democratic People's Republic*] (RO)
RPDLMG	Ruchnoy Pulemyot Degtyaryov Light Machine Gun [*Soviet-made weaponry*] [*Also, RPDM, RPDM LMG*] (VNW)
RPDM	Ruchnoy Pulemyot Degtyaryov Light Machine Gun [*Soviet-made weaponry*] [*Also, RPD LMG, RPDM LMG*] [*Military*] (VNW)
RPDMLMG	Ruchnoy Pulemyot Degtyaryov Light Machine Gun [*Soviet-made weaponry*] [*Also, RPD LMG, RPDM*] [*Military*] (VNW)
rpdn	Missile Maintenance Battalion (BU)
RPENC	Romanian PEN Centre (EAIO)
RPEYC	Royal Prince Edward Yacht Club [*Australia*]
RPF	Front Distribution Port (RU)
RPF	Rally for the Republic [*French*] [*Political party*] (ECON)
RPF	Rassemblement du Peuple Francais [*Rally of the French People*] (WER)
RPF	Reformatorische Politieke Federatie [*Reformist Political Federation*] [*Netherlands*] [*Political party*] (PPE)
RPF	Rwandan Patriotic Front [*Political party*]
RPG	Antitank Hand Grenade (RU)
RPG	Antitank Rocket Launcher (RU)
RPG	Fire Chief (BU)
rpg	Radio Direction-Finding Group (BU)
RPGC	Royal Perth Golf Club [*Australia*]
RPH	Radio for the Print Handicapped [*Australia*]
RPHM	Referent Zasobovani Pohonne Hmoty a Mazadla [*Officer-in-Charge of Petroleum Products and Lubricants*] (CZ)
RPI	Radiation Protection Inspectorate [*Ministry of Health*] [*Singapore*] (WND)

RPI............ Rassemblement du Peuple Issa [*Somali*]
RPI............ Rassemblement Populaire pour l'Independance [*People's Rally for Independence*] [*Djibouti*] [*Political party*]   (PPW)
RPI............ Rayon Fire Inspector   (RU)
RPI............ Registro de la Propiedad Industrial [*Spanish Patent Office*] [*Information service or system*]   (IID)
RPI............ Relay Selector Panel   (RU)
RPI............ Republican Party of India [*Political party*]   (PPW)
RPI............ Republican Party of Italy   (RU)
RPI............ Riga Polytechnic Institute   (RU)
RPI............ Rostov Pedagogical Institute   (RU)
RPIMA...... Regiment Parachutiste d'Infanterie de Marine [*Naval Infantry Paratrooper Regiment*] [*French*]   (AF)
RPK .... Automatic Direction Finder   (RU)
RPK .... Command Radio Transmitter   (RU)
RPK .... Rayon Industrial Kombinat   (RU)
RPK .... Rayon Party Committee   (RU)
RPK .... Rayon Studbook   (RU)
rpk............ Rem-Perdekrag [*Brake Horsepower*] [*Afrikaans*]
RPK .... Rumunska Partia Komunistyczna [*Communist Party of Romania*] [*Poland*]
RPKAD...... Resimen Para Komando Angkatan Darat [*Army Para Commando Regiment*] [*India*]   (IN)
rpkhz......... Chemical Defense Company   (RU)
RPKO .... Automatic Direction Finder-Recorder   (RU)
RP-Kredite ... Richtsatz-Plankredite [*Standard Planned Credits*]   (EG)
RPL........... Radiophysics Laboratory [*CSIRO*] [*Australia*]   (PDAA)
RPL........... Rassemblement du Peuple Lao [*Rally of the Lao People*] [*Use RLP*]   (CL)
RPL........... Rejon Przemyslu Lesnego [*Forest Industry District*]   (POL)
RPL........... Reliance Petrochemicals Ltd. [*Reliance Industies*] [*India*]
RPl .... Richtlinie des Plenums des Obersten Gerichts [*Guidelines of the Plenum of the Supreme Court*]   (EG)
rpl............. Rupla(a) [*Finland*]
RPM .... Company Aid Station   (BU)
RPM .... Mantissa Transfer Register [*Computers*]   (RU)
RPM .... Neutral Flat Magnetic Relay   (RU)
RPM .... Ngukurr [*Airport symbol*]
RPM .... Oil-Pumping Relay   (RU)
RPM .... Radio Programas de Mexico [*Radio network*]
RPM .... Republica Populara Mongola [*Mongolian People's Republic*]   (RO)
RPM .... Republica Popular de Mocambique
RPM .... Reverendo Padre Maestro [*Spanish*]
rpm............ Revoluciones por Minuto [*Revolutions per Minute*] [*Spanish*]
RPM .... Rivers People's Movement
rpm............ Rotacao por Minuto [*Revolutions per Minute*] [*Portuguese*]
RPM .... Rotary Loader   (RU)
RPM .... Sorting and Selecting Machine   (RU)
RPMB........ Cubi Naval Air Station, Bataan [*Philippines*] [*ICAO location identifier*]   (ICLI)
RPMC........ Cebu/Lahug, Cebu [*Philippines*] [*ICAO location identifier*]   (ICLI)
RPMK .... Clark Air Base, Pampanga [*Philippines*] [*ICAO location identifier*]   (ICLI)
RPML........ Laoag/International, Ilocos Norte [*Philippines*] [*ICAO location identifier*]   (ICLI)
RPMM ...... Manila/International [*Philippines*] [*ICAO location identifier*]   (ICLI)
RPMP........ Legazpi, Albay [*Philippines*] [*ICAO location identifier*]   (ICLI)
RPMR........ Romblon, Tablas Island [*Philippines*] [*ICAO location identifier*]   (ICLI)
RPMS........ Sangley Point Naval Station, Cavite [*Philippines*] [*ICAO location identifier*]   (ICLI)
RPMT........ Lapu-Lapu/Mactan International [*Philippines*] [*ICAO location identifier*]   (ICLI)
RPMZ........ Zamboanga/International [*Philippines*] [*ICAO location identifier*]   (ICLI)
RPN .... Load-Supply Relay   (RU)
RPN .... Manual Fire Pump   (RU)
RPN .... Radio Philippines Network
RPN .... Regulation Under Load   (RU)
RPN .... Rosh-Pina [*Israel*] [*Airport symbol*]   (OAG)
RPN .... Standard Flat Relay   (RU)
RPNE .... Regiao de Producao do Nordeste [*Brazil*]   (LAA)
RPO .... Constant-Speed Governor   (RU)
RPO .... Intermediate Disconnection Relay   (RU)
rpo .... Radio Direction-Finding Detachment   (BU)
RPO .... Russian Palestine Society   (RU)
RPO .... Starting Revolution Relay   (RU)
RPP........... Company Small-Arms Ammunition Supply Point   (RU)
RPP........... Mercury-Arc Rectifier Substation   (RU)
RPP........... Mobile Radio Direction-Finding Station   (RU)
RPP........... Number Sequence Transfer Register [*Computers*]   (RU)
RPP........... Polarity Reversal Relay   (RU)

RPP........... Rassemblement Populaire pour le Progres [*Popular Rally for Progress*] [*Djibouti*] [*Political party*]   (PPW)
RPP........... Rayon Public Telephone   (RU)
RPP........... Republican People's Party [*Cumhuriyet Halk Partisi - CHP*] [*Turkey*] [*Political party*]
RPP........... Republica Populara Polona [*Polish People's Republic*]   (RO)
RPP........... Rocket Propellant Plant [*ISRO*] [*India*]   (PDAA)
RPP........... Workers Progressive Party [*Canada*]   (BU)
RPPI .... Resurgence Party of the People of Iran [*Rastakhiz Party*] [*Iran*]   (ME)
RPPS .... Robotnicza Partia Polskich Socjalistow [*Workers Party of Polish Socialists*] [*Political party*]   (PPE)
RPPS-Lewica ... Robotnicza Partia Polskich Socjalistow - Lewica [*Workers Party of Polish Socialists - Left*] [*Political party*]   (PPE)
RPPT .... Regroupement des Partis Politiques du Tchad
RPQPT...... Registro de Productos Quimicos Potencialmente Toxicos [*International Register of Potentially Toxic Chemicals - IRPTC*] [*Spanish*]   (ASF)
RPR .... Company Antitank Defense Area   (RU)
RPR .... Federation Guadeloupeenne du Rassemblement pour la Republique [*Guadeloupe Federation of the Rally of the Republic*] [*Political party*]   (PPW)
rpr .... Radio Direction-Finding Company   (BU)
RPR .... Raipur [*India*] [*Airport symbol*]   (OAG)
RPR .... Rassemblement pour la Republique [*Rally for the Republic*] [*Wallis and Futuna Islands*] [*Political party*]   (PD)
RPR .... Rassemblement pour la Republique [*Rally for the Republic*] [*France*] [*Political party*]   (ECON)
RPR .... Rassemblement pour la Republique [*Rally for the Republic*] [*French Guiana*] [*Political party*]   (PPW)
RPR .... Rassemblement pour la Republique [*Rally for the Republic*] [*Mayotte*] [*Political party*]   (EY)
RPR .... Rassemblement pour la Republique [*Rally for the Republic*] [*Martinique*] [*Political party*]   (PPW)
RPR .... Rassemblement pour la Republique [*Rally for the Republic*] [*Reunion*] [*Political party*]   (PPW)
RPR .... Rassemblement pour la Republique [*Rally for the Republic*] [*French Polynesia*] [*Political party*]   (PPW)
RPR .... Republique Populaire de Roumanie [*France*]   (FLAF)
RPr............ Rodopski Pregled [*Rhodope Mountains Review*] [*A periodical*]   (BU)
RPRD .... Australian Reinforced Plastics Research and Development, Inc.   (ADA)
RPRG........ Republique Populaire Revolutionnaire de Guinee
RPRI........ Radiata Pine Research Institute [*Australia*]
RPS........... Intermediate Lock-On Relay   (RU)
RPS........... Intermediate Signal Relay   (RU)
RPS........... Portable Reconnaissance Station   (RU)
RPS........... Radio Direction-Finding Station   (RU)
RPS........... Radio Program Standard [*Australian Broadcasting Tribunal*]
RPS........... Rayon Union of Consumers' Societies   (RU)
RPS........... Referat Pracovnich Sil [*Manpower Department (attached to the National Committees)*]   (CZ)
RPS........... Reunion Presse Service [*Reunion Press Service*]   (AF)
RPS........... Reversible Scaling Circuit   (RU)
RPS........... Rhone-Poulenc Sante [*Pharmaceutical company*] [*France*]
RPS........... Rijkspostspaarbank [*Benelux*]   (BAS)
rps .... Rotacao por Segundo [*Revolutions per Second*] [*Portuguese*]
RPS........... Steady-Speed Regulator [*Computers*]   (RU)
RPS........... Warning Signaling Relay   (RU)
RPSh......... Manually Controlled Saw Frame   (RU)
RPSH........ Republika Popullore e Shqiperise [*Albanian*]
rpsh .... Shpagin Light Machine Gun   (RU)
RPSN........ Radiometric Device for Automatic Determination of Sulfur in a Stream of Petroleum Products   (RU)
RPSNT ...... Republican Party for Chadian National Salvation [*Use PRSNT*]   (AF)
rpsv .... Psychological Warfare Company   (BU)
RPT........... Alternating-Current Intermediate Relay   (RU)
RPT........... Fuel-Pumping Relay   (RU)
RPT........... Limit Current Regulator   (RU)
RPT........... Radioisotopic Portable Thickness Gauge   (RU)
RPT........... Rassemblement du Peuple Togolais [*Rally of the Togolese People*] [*Political party*]   (PPW)
RPT........... Rayon Food Trade Organization   (RU)
RPT........... Reactor for Physical and Technical Investigations [*Former USSR*] [*Nuclear energy*]
RPT........... Rural Property Trust [*Australia*]
RPTI .... Ryazan' Planning and Technological Institute   (RU)
RPTOP...... Company Antitank Strong Point   (RU)
RPTT .... Post, Telegraph, and Telephone Workers   (BU)
RPU .... Radio Propagation Unit [*National Physical Laboratory*] [*India*]   (PDAA)
RPU .... Republica Populara Ungara [*Hungarian People's Republic*]   (RO)
RPU .... Wire Broadcasting Adapter   (RU)
RPUA .... Aparri, Cagayan [*Philippines*] [*ICAO location identifier*]   (ICLI)

RPUB......... Baguio, Benguet [*Philippines*] [*ICAO location identifier*]   (ICLI)

RPUC .... Cabanatuan, Nueva Ecija [*Philippines*] [*ICAO location identifier*] (ICLI)

RPUD .... Daet, Camarines Norte [*Philippines*] [*ICAO location identifier*] (ICLI)

RPUE......... Lucena, Quezon [*Philippines*] [*ICAO location identifier*]   (ICLI)

RPUF......... Floridablanca Air Base, Pampanga [*Philippines*] [*ICAO location identifier*] (ICLI)

RPUG .... Lingayen, Pangasinan [*Philippines*] [*ICAO location identifier*] (ICLI)

RPUH........ San Jose, Occidental Mindoro [*Philippines*] [*ICAO location identifier*] (ICLI)

RPUI.......... Iba, Zambales [*Philippines*] [*ICAO location identifier*] (ICLI)

RPUJ .... Castillejos, Zambales [*Philippines*] [*ICAO location identifier*] (ICLI)

RPUK .... Calapan, Oriental Mindoro [*Philippines*] [*ICAO location identifier*] (ICLI)

RPUL......... Lipa/Fernando Air Base, Batangas [*Philippines*] [*ICAO location identifier*] (ICLI)

RPUM .... Mamburao, Occidental Mindoro [*Philippines*] [*ICAO location identifier*] (ICLI)

RPUN .... Naga, Camarines Sur [*Philippines*] [*ICAO location identifier*] (ICLI)

RPUO .... Basco, Batanes Island [*Philippines*] [*ICAO location identifier*] (ICLI)

RPUP......... Jose Panganiban/PIM, Camarines Norte [*Philippines*] [*ICAO location identifier*] (ICLI)

RPUQ .... Vigan, Ilocos Sur [*Philippines*] [*ICAO location identifier*] (ICLI)

RPUR .... Baler, Aurora Sub-Province [*Philippines*] [*ICAO location identifier*] (ICLI)

RPUS......... San Fernando, La Union [*Philippines*] [*ICAO location identifier*] (ICLI)

RPUT........ Tuguegarao, Cagayan [*Philippines*] [*ICAO location identifier*] (ICLI)

RPUU .... Bulan, Sorsogon [*Philippines*] [*ICAO location identifier*] (ICLI)

RPUV .... Virac, Catanduanes [*Philippines*] [*ICAO location identifier*] (ICLI)

RPUW .... Marinduque/Gasan, Marinduque [*Philippines*] [*ICAO location identifier*] (ICLI)

RPUX .... Plaridel, Bulacan [*Philippines*] [*ICAO location identifier*] (ICLI)

RPUY .... Cauayan, Isabela [*Philippines*] [*ICAO location identifier*] (ICLI)

RPUZ .... Bagabag, Neuva Viscaya [*Philippines*] [*ICAO location identifier*] (ICLI)

rpv .... Field Water-Supply Company   (RU)

RPV .... Intermediate Switching on Relay   (RU)

RPV .... Reclosure Relay   (RU)

RPV .... Water-Pumping Relay   (RU)

RPVA......... Tacloban/Daniel Z. Romualdez, Leyte [*Philippines*] [*ICAO location identifier*] (ICLI)

RPVB........ Bacolod, Negros Occidental [*Philippines*] [*ICAO location identifier*] (ICLI)

RPVC........ Calbayog, Western Samar [*Philippines*] [*ICAO location identifier*] (ICLI)

RPVC........ Racionalni Provozne-Vycvikovy Cykl [*Rational Temporary Training Cycle*] (CZ)

RPVD .... Dumaguete/Sibulan Negros Oriental [*Philippines*] [*ICAO location identifier*] (ICLI)

RPVE......... Caticlan, Aklan [*Philippines*] [*ICAO location identifier*] (ICLI)

RPVE........ Reflets et Perspectives de la Vie Economique [*Benelux*]   (BAS)

RPVF .... Catarman, Northern Samar [*Philippines*] [*ICAO location identifier*] (ICLI)

RPVG .... Guiuan, Eastern Samar [*Philippines*] [*ICAO location identifier*] (ICLI)

RPVH .... Hilongos, Leyte Del Norte [*Philippines*] [*ICAO location identifier*] (ICLI)

RPVI.......... Iloilo, Iloilo [*Philippines*] [*ICAO location identifier*]   (ICLI)

RPVK........ Kalibo, Aklan [*Philippines*] [*ICAO location identifier*]   (ICLI)

RPVL......... Roxas/Del Pilar, Palawan [*Philippines*] [*ICAO location identifier*] (ICLI)

RPVM .... Masbate [*Philippines*] [*ICAO location identifier*]   (ICLI)

RPVN .... Medellin, Cebu [*Philippines*] [*ICAO location identifier*]   (ICLI)

RPVO .... Ormoc, Leyte [*Philippines*] [*ICAO location identifier*]   (ICLI)

RPVP......... Puerto Princesa, Palawan [*Philippines*] [*ICAO location identifier*] (ICLI)

RPVR......... Roxas, Capiz [*Philippines*] [*ICAO location identifier*]   (ICLI)

RPVS .... San Jose De Buenavista/Antique [*Philippines*] [*ICAO location identifier*] (ICLI)

RPVT......... Tagbilaran, Bohol [*Philippines*] [*ICAO location identifier*] (ICLI)

RPvZ.......... Rijksproefstation voor Zaadcontrole [*Government Seed Testing Station*] [*Netherlands*] (ARC)

RPWA .... Surallah/Allah Valley, Cotabato (South) [*Philippines*] [*ICAO location identifier*] (ICLI)

RPWB........ Buayan/General Santos, Cotabato (South) [*Philippines*] [*ICAO location identifier*] (ICLI)

RPWC........ Cotabato, North Cotabato [*Philippines*] [*ICAO location identifier*] (ICLI)

RPWD .... Davao/Francisco Bangoy International [*Philippines*] [*ICAO location identifier*] (ICLI)

RPWE........ Butuan, Agusan [*Philippines*] [*ICAO location identifier*]   (ICLI)

RPWG .... Dipolog, Zamboanga Del Norte [*Philippines*] [*ICAO location identifier*] (ICLI)

RPWI......... Ozamis, Misamis Oriental [*Philippines*] [*ICAO location identifier*] (ICLI)

RPWJ .... Jolo, Sulu [*Philippines*] [*ICAO location identifier*]   (ICLI)

RPWK........ Tacurong/Kenram, Cotabato [*Philippines*] [*ICAO location identifier*] (ICLI)

RPWL........ Cagayan De Oro, Misamis Oriental [*Philippines*] [*ICAO location identifier*] (ICLI)

RPWM ...... Malabang, Lanao Del Sur [*Philippines*] [*ICAO location identifier*] (ICLI)

RPWN .... Bongao/Sanga-Sanga, Sulu [*Philippines*] [*ICAO location identifier*] (ICLI)

RPWP........ Pagadian, Zamboanga Del Sur [*Philippines*] [*ICAO location identifier*] (ICLI)

RPWS........ Surigao, Surigao Del Norte [*Philippines*] [*ICAO location identifier*] (ICLI)

RPWT........ Del Monte, Bukidnon [*Philippines*] [*ICAO location identifier*] (ICLI)

RPWV........ Buenavista, Agusan [*Philippines*] [*ICAO location identifier*] (ICLI)

RPWW ...... Tandag, Surigao Del Sur [*Philippines*] [*ICAO location identifier*] (ICLI)

RPWX........ Iligan, Lanao Del Norte [*Philippines*] [*ICAO location identifier*] (ICLI)

RPWY........ Malaybalay, Bukidon [*Philippines*] [*ICAO location identifier*] (ICLI)

RPWZ........ Bislig, Surigao Del Sur [*Philippines*] [*ICAO location identifier*] (ICLI)

RPXC......... Tarlac (Crow Valley) [*Philippines*] [*ICAO location identifier*] (ICLI)

RPXG......... Lubang, Occidental Mindoro [*Philippines*] [*ICAO location identifier*] (ICLI)

RPXI.......... Itbayat, Batanes [*Philippines*] [*ICAO location identifier*]   (ICLI)

RPXJ .... Jomalig, Quezon [*Philippines*] [*ICAO location identifier*]   (ICLI)

RPXM........ Fort Magsaysay, Nueva Ecija [*Philippines*] [*ICAO location identifier*] (ICLI)

RPXP......... Poro Point, La Union [*Philippines*] [*ICAO location identifier*] (ICLI)

RPXR......... Corregidor, Cavite [*Philippines*] [*ICAO location identifier*] (ICLI)

RPXT......... Alabat, Quezon [*Philippines*] [*ICAO location identifier*]   (ICLI)

RPXU .... Sorsogon, Sorsogon [*Philippines*] [*ICAO location identifier*] (ICLI)

RPYa.......... Gas Mask Repair Box   (RU)

RPYS .... Republique Populaire du Yemen du Sud

RPZ............. Rada Pomocy Zydom

RPz............. Radiovy Pruzkum [*Radio Reconnaissance*]   (CZ)

RPZB......... Rzeszowskie Przemyslowe Zjednoczenie Budowlane [*Rzeszow Industrial Construction Association*] (POL)

RPzP .... Radiovy Pruzkumny Pluk [*Radio Reconnaissance Regiment*] (CZ)

RQ.............. Ravitaillement Quotidien [*Daily Revictualing*] [*Military*] [*French*] (MTD)

RQAC .... Royal Queensland Aero Club [*Australia*]

RQAS .... Royal Queensland Art Society [*Australia*]

RQBCHS... Royal Queensland Bush Children's Health Scheme [*Australia*]

RQGC .... Royal Queensland Golf Club [*Australia*]

RQLTA...... Royal Queensland Lawn Tennis Association [*Australia*]

RQTC .... Royal Queensland Theatre Co. [*Australia*]

RQX........... Air Engiadina [*Switzerland*] [*ICAO designator*]   (FAAC)

RR.............. Cutoff Relay   (RU)

RR.............. Deployment Area [*Military term*]   (RU)

r-r .... Dimensions, Size   (RU)

RR.............. Discharge Relay   (RU)

RR.............. Labor Company   (RU)

rr .... Manual Control   (RU)

RR.............. Manual Control Rheostat   (RU)

RR.............. Rada Robotnicza [*Workers' Council*] [*Poland*]

RR.............. Radial Rada Ltda.   (COL)

RR.............. Radio Renascenca [*Radio Station*] [*Portuguese*]   (WER)

RR.............. Radioteleviziunea Romana [*Romanian Radiotelevision*]   (RO)

RR.............. Rad Republiky [*Order of the Republic (a decoration)*]   (CZ)

RR.............. Rannsoknarad Rikisins [*National Research Council*] [*Iceland*] (EAIO)

RR.............. Rattanakosin Rice Co. Ltd. [*Thailand*]

RR.............. Reclasseringsregeling [*Benelux*]   (BAS)

RR.............. Reconcentracion Revolucionaria [*Revolutionary Reconcentration*] [*Peru*]   (LA)

rr .... Reconnaissance Company   (BU)

RR.............. Regulating Relay   (RU)

RR.............. Remontna Radionica [*Repair Shop*]   (YU)

RR.............. Repair Shop   (BU)

RR.............. Republic at Romania   (BARN)

RR	Reversing Relay (RU)
RR	Revirni Reditelstvi [*Coal Basin Directorate*] (CZ)
RR	Rhodesian Railways
RR	Rhodesia Regiment
r-r	Richtiger [*More Correctly*] [*German*] (GCA)
RR	Rijecka Revija [*Rijeka Review*] [*A periodical*] (YU)
rr	Rivers (RU)
RR	Rodna Rech [*Native Language*] [*A periodical*] (BU)
Rr	Rruga [*Albanian*]
RR	Rumanian Register of Shipping (DS)
r-r	Solution (RU)
rr	Species, Kinds (RU)
R/r	Traffic Control Company (RU)
RR	Turcja [*Turkey*] [*Poland*]
RRA	Automobile Regulating Relay (RU)
RRA	Rubber Research Association [*Israel*] (SLS)
RRAB	Rotary-Scattering Aerial Bomb (RU)
RRAF	Royal Rhodesian Air Force
RRAP	Residents for Responsible Airport Planning [*Australia*]
rrazm	Mine Clearance Company (RU)
RRB	RAAF [*Royal Australian Air Force*] Radio Butterworth
RRB	Radiographers Registration Board [*Tasmania, Australia*]
RRB	Radio Regulatory Bureau [*Japan*] (PDAA)
rrb	Radio-Relay Battalion (BU)
RRB	Radio Research Board [*CSIRO*] [*Australia*] (PDAA)
RRC	Ethiopian Relief and Rehabilitation Commission
RRC	Rapid Results College [*Nigeria, Ghana*]
RRC	Relief and Rehabilitation Committee [*Sudan*]
RRC	Research Registration Centre [*Australia*]
RRC	Rhodesian Reformed Church
RRC	Rubber Research Center [*Thai*] (ARC)
RRCBC	Regional Research Centre of the British Caribbean [*Trinidad*] (DSCA)
RRCh	Manual Frequency Control (RU)
RRCS	Royal Rehabilitation Centre Sydney [*Australia*]
RRD	Dilution, Scattering, and Decontamination (RU)
rrd	Radio Relay Battalion (RU)
RRD	Rocket Jet Engine (RU)
RRD	Rocket Jet Engines (BU)
rrd	Traffic Control Company (RU)
RRE	Marree [*Australia*] [*Airport symbol*] [*Obsolete*] (OAG)
RRESA	Registered Real Estate Salespersons' Association [*Australia*]
RRF	Recna Ratna Flotila [*Naval River Flotilla*] (YU)
RRF	Red Resistance Front [*Netherlands*] [*Political party*]
RRFO	Rhine River Field Organization [*Post-World War II*]
RRG	Manual Volume Control (RU)
RRG	Rodrigues Island [*Mauritius*] [*Airport symbol*] (OAG)
RRHS	Richmond River Historical Society [*Australia*]
RRI	Barora [*Solomon Islands*] [*Airport symbol*] (OAG)
RRI	Radio Republic Indonesia (IAA)
RRI	Radio Republik Indonesia [*Radio network*]
RRI	Rubber Research Institute [*Malaysia*] (ML)
RRI	Ryazan' Radiotechnical Institute (RU)
RRII	Rubber Research Institute of India (DSCA)
RRIM	Rubber Research Institute of Malaysia (FEA)
r-rimost'	Solubility (RU)
RRIMP	Roche Research Institute of Marine Pharmacology [*Australia*] (ADA)
RRIN	Rubber Research Institute of Nigeria
RRIP	Rural Research in Progress [*CSIRO*] [*Information service or system*] [*Australia*]
RRIPMU ...	Royal Ryde Inpatient Pain Management Unit [*Australia*]
RRISL	Rubber Research Institute of Sri Lanka [*Research center*] (IRC)
r-ritel'	Solvent (RU)
RRK	Radiodiffusion de la Republique Khmere [*Radio of the Cambodian Republic*] (CL)
RRK	Regulator-Distributor Box (RU)
RRL	Radio Relay Line (RU)
RRL	Radio Research Laboratory [*Japan*] (PDAA)
RRL	Rumunska Republika Ludowa [*Romanian People's Republic (1952-1965)*] [*Poland*]
RRLH	Regional Research Laboratory Hyderabad [*CSIR*] [*India*]
RRLJ	Regional Research Laboratory, Jorhat [*India*] [*Research center*] (IRC)
RRN	Serra Norte [*Brazil*] [*Airport symbol*] (OAG)
RRO	Rechnungslegungsordnung fuer das Reich [*Germany*]
RROCA	Rolls Royce Owners' Club of Australia
RRP	Republican Reliance Party [*Cumhuriyetci Guven Partisi - CGP*] [*Turkey*] [*Political party*] (PPW)
RRP	Rudnik Rjavega Premoga [*Brown Coal Mine*] (YU)
RRP	Rumunska Radnicka Partija [*Rumanian Labor Party*] (YU)
RRPP	Reverends Peres [*Reverend Fathers*] [*French*]
rrr	Radio-Relay Company (BU)
RRRC	Resettlement, Relief, and Rehabilitation Commission [*Sudan*]
RRRPD	Reseau de Radio Rurale des Pays en Developpement [*Developing Countries Farm Radio Network*] (EAIO)
RRS	Radio Relay Station (RU)
RRS	Roros [*Norway*] [*Airport symbol*] (OAG)
RRS	Rural Reconstruction Scheme [*Australia*]
RRSA	Radio Republic of South Africa
RRSA	Radio Republic South Africa (IAA)
RRSP	Regional Remote Sensing Programme [*Asia*]
RRSS	Ruska Ratna Sluzba Stabova [*Russian War Staff Service*] (YU)
RR SSSR ...	River Register of the USSR (RU)
RRT	Braking Reverse Relay (RU)
RRT	Repatriation Review Tribunal [*Australia*]
RRT	Republik Rakjat Tiongkok [*China*] (IN)
RRT	Tank Regulating Relay (RU)
RRT	Tractor Regulating Relay (RU)
RRTI	Ryazan' Radiotechnical Institute (RU)
RRU	Company Ultrashort-Wave Radio (RU)
RRU	Manual Amplification Control (RU)
RRU	Regulation Review Unit [*Victoria, Australia*]
RRWU	Rhodesia Railway Workers' Union
RRZ	Mining Equipment Repair Plant (RU)
RRZD	Rolniczy Rejonowy Zaklad Doswiadczalny [*Regional Agricultural Experimental Station*] (POL)
RS	Arrest van de Raad van State [*Benelux*] (BAS)
RS	Bent Rhombic [*Antenna*] (RU)
RS	Counting Relay (RU)
RS	De Rechtstrijd [*Benelux*] (BAS)
r/s	Design Computation (RU)
RS	Discharge Resistance (RU)
RS	Estado do Rio Grande Do Sul [*State of South Rio Grande*] [*Brazil*]
RS	Flow Relay (RU)
RS	Intelligent Service Section (BU)
RS	Medium Repair (RU)
RS	Mixture Controller (RU)
RS	Privates, Rank and File (RU)
RS	Radial Drill (RU)
RS	Radio Communications (RU)
R/s	Radio Net (RU)
RS	Radio Sarajevo (YU)
RS	Radio Slovenija [*Radio Slovenia*] (YU)
r/s	Radio Stanica [*Radio Station*] (YU)
RS	Radio Station (RU)
RS	Radna Snaga [*Manpower*] [*Army*] (YU)
RS	Radnicki Sindikat [*Trade-Union*] (YU)
RS	Radnicko-Sluzbenicki [*Workers and Employees*] (YU)
rs	Radnih Sati [*Working Hours*] (YU)
RS	Ratio Controller (RU)
RS	Ratio Relay (RU)
RS	Ratna Sluzba [*Military Service*] (YU)
RS	Rayon Council (BU)
RS	Rayon Soviet of Workers' Deputies (RU)
Rs	Reales [*Spanish*]
RS	Realschule [*German*]
RS	Real Servicio [*Royal Service*] [*Spanish*]
RS	Recette Subordonnee [*Subordinate Revenue (Office)*] [*Cambodia*] (CL)
RS	Reconstruccion Socialista [*Socialist Reconstruction*] [*Spanish*] (WER)
RS	Register of Shipping of the USSR [*Ship classification society*] (DS)
RS	Register of the USSR (RU)
RS	Regular Session (BU)
RS	Regulating Station (RU)
Rs	Reis [*Money*] [*Portuguese*]
RS	Reizstoff [*Tear Gas*] [*German military*]
RS	Relaxation Strength (RU)
RS	Repair Ship, Floating Repair Base (RU)
RS	Republicains Sociaux [*Social Republicans*] [*France*] [*Political party*] (PPE)
RS	Republic Council (RU)
RS	Republike Socialiste [*Socialist Republic*] [*Albanian*]
Rs	Resolutie [*Benelux*] [*French*] (BAS)
RS	Reversive Counter (RU)
RS	Revolutionary Council (RU)
RS	Rheinflugzeugbau [*Germany*] [*ICAO aircraft manufacturer identifier*] (ICAO)
RS	Rocket, Missile (RU)
RS	Rocket Shell (BU)
RS	Rumah Sakit [*Hospital*] (IN)
RS	Seiner [*Boat*] (RU)
RS	Signal Company (RU)
RS	Signal Relay (RU)
rs	Silver Ruble (RU)
RS	Sliding Relay (RU)
RS	Speed Regulator (RU)
RS	Speed Relay (RU)
Rs	Sri Lanka Rupee [*Monetary unit*] (IMH)

RS .... Starter Relay   (RU)
RS .... Turret Lathe   (RU)
RS .... Wire Broadcasting Network   (RU)
RS .... Workers' Supply   (RU)
RSA........... Air Service Affaires [*France*] [*ICAO designator*]   (FAAC)
RSA........... Army Regulating Station   (RU)
RSA........... Artillery Reconnaissance Service   (RU)
RSA........... Radio South Africa
RSA........... Railway Security Agency [*South Vietnam government security*] (VNW)
RSA........... Rationalist Society of Australia
RSA........... Regional Studies Association [*British*]   (EAIO)
RSA........... Renal Society for Australasia
RSA........... Republic of South Africa [*Use SA*]   (AF)
RSA........... Republiek van Suid-Afrika [*Republic of South Africa*] [*Afrikaans*]
RSA........... Retirement Savings Account [*Australia*]
RSA........... Returned Services Association [*Australia*]
RSA........... Royal Society of Australia   (BARN)
RSA........... Russian Space Agency
RSA........... Santa Rosa [*Argentina*] [*Airport symbol*]   (OAG)
RSAA........ Rail Sleeper Association (Australia)   (ADA)
RSAA........ Remote Sensing Association of Australia   (ADA)
RSAAF ...... Royal South African Air Force
RSABA ..... Royal South Australia Bowling Association
RSABA ..... Royal South Australian Bowling Association
RSAF .... Republic of Singapore Air Force   (PDAA)
RSAF .... Royal Saudi Air Force
RSAIC ...... Romanian Society for Anaesthesia Intensive Care   (EAIO)
RSAO .... Riksforbundet Sveriges Amatororkestrar [*Association of Swedish Amateur Orchestras*]   (EAIO)
RSAP .... Revolutionaire Socialistische Arbeiders Partij [*Revolutionary Socialist Workers' Party*] [*Netherlands*] [*Political party*] (PPE)
RSASA ...... Royal Society of Arts of South Australia
RSAT........ Real Sociedad Arqueologica Tarraconense [*Spanish*]   (SLS)
rsau .... Self-Propelled Gun Company   (RU)
rsb .... Battalion Radio   (RU)
RS-B .... Bomber Radio   (RU)
RSB........... Regionale Steun Bibliotheek [*Bibliotheek met een regionale steunfunctie*]
RSB........... Regional Shipping Boards [*NATO*]   (NATG)
RSB........... Registered Schools Board [*Victoria, Australia*]
RSB........... Roseberth [*Australia*] [*Airport symbol*] [*Obsolete*]   (OAG)
RSB........... Royal Swedish Ballet
RSB........... Royal Swedish Ballet
RSB........... Samaero SA [*Romania*] [*ICAO designator*]   (FAAC)
RSBCA ..... Regional School Building Centre for Africa
RSB(E)...... Regional Shipping Board (East) [*NATO*]
RSBKE ..... Dictionary of the Contemporary Bulgarian Literary Language (BU)
RSBS .... Research School of Biological Sciences [*Australian National University*]
RSB(W) ..... Regional Shipping Board (West) [*NATO*]
RSC........... Rada Svobodneho Ceskoslovenska [*Council of Free Czechoslovakia*]   (CZ)
RSC........... Reactor Safety Commission [*Germany*]
RSC........... Regional Safety Coordinator [*Australia*]
RSC........... Remote Sensing Center [*Egypt*] [*Research center*]   (IRC)
RSC........... Republica Socialista Cehoslovaca [*Czechoslovak Socialist Republic*]   (RO)
RSC........... Riga Skulte Airport [*Former USSR*] [*Airport symbol*] [*Obsolete*] (OAG)
RSC........... Road Safety Council [*Australia*]
RSC........... Royal Society of Chemistry [*Chemical Society and Royal Institute of Chemistry*] [*Formed by a merger of*]   (EAIO)
RSCACT ... Road Safety Council of the Australian Capital Territory
RSC & G .... Roux Seguela Cayzac & Goudard [*French advertising agency*]
RSCDS ...... Royal Scottish Country Dance Society [*Australia*]
Rsch .... Rueckenschild [*Back Label*] [*Publishing*] [*German*]
Rschild...... Rueckenschild [*Back Label*] [*Publishing*] [*German*]
RSCN........ Royal Society for the Conservation of Nature [*Jordan*]   (EAIO)
RSCNT...... Road Safety Council of the Northern Territory [*Australia*]
RSCsl........ Rodopisna Spolecnost Ceskoslovenska [*Czechoslovak Genealogy Society*]   (CZ)
RSD .... Medium-Range Missile   (RU)
RSD .... Radio Science Division [*National Physical Laboratory*] [*India*] (PDAA)
RSD .... Rassemblement des Socialistes et des Democrates [*Rally of Socialists and Democrats*] [*Reunion*] [*Political party*] (PPW)
RSD .... Reditelstvi Statnich Drah [*State Railroad Directorate*]   (CZ)
RSD .... Rock Sound [*Bahamas*] [*Airport symbol*]   (OAG)
RSD .... Rolnicke Skladistni Druzstvo [*Agricultural Warehouse Cooperative*]   (CZ)
RSD .... Romanian Society of Dermatology   (EAIO)

RSDB........ SCB [*Statistika Centralbyran*] Regional Statistical Data Base [*Sweden*] [*Information service or system*]   (CRD)
RSDLP ...... Russian Social-Democratic Labor Party [*Political party*]
RSDLP(B) ... Russian Social-Democratic Labor Party (Bolsheviks) [*Political party*]
RSDP .... Rural School Development Program [*Australia*]
RSDP .... Russian Social Democratic Party   (BU)
RSDP(o) .... Workers' Social Democratic Party (United)   (BU)
RSDRF ...... Russian Social Democratic Workers' Faction   (RU)
RSDRP ...... Rossiiskaia Sotsial-Demokraticheskaia Rabochaya Partiia [*Russian Social Democratic Workers' Party*] [*Political party*]   (PPE)
RSDRP(b) ... Russian Social Democratic Workers' Party (of Bolsheviks) [*1912-1918*]   (RU)
RSE........... Radio Slobodna Europa [*Radio Free Europe*]   (CZ)
RSE........... Raggruppamento Selenia Elsag [*Integrated air-defense systems company*] [*Italian*]
RSE........... Reforma Social Espanola [*Spanish Social Reform*]   (WER)
rse.............. Remise [*Remittance*] [*Business term*] [*French*]
RSE........... Romanian Society for Electroencephalography   (EAIO)
RSE........... Sydney-Rose Bay [*Australia*] [*Airport symbol*]   (OAG)
RSEA .... Ret-Ser Engineering Agency [*Taiwan*]
RSEB .... Response du Secretaire d'Etat au Budget   (FLAF)
RSER .... Optimalizing-Control Relay Systems, Extremum Relay Systems (RU)
RSF .... Front Regulating Station   (RU)
RSF .... Real Sociedad Fotografica [*Spanish*]   (SLS)
RSF .... Rhodesia Settlement Forum
RSF .... Rocket Sled Facility [*ISRO*] [*India*]   (PDAA)
RSFI .... Republica Socialista Federativa Iugoslavia [*Socialist Federal Republic of Yugoslavia*]   (RO)
RSFS .... Religious Society of Friends [*Quakers*] in Switzerland   (EAIO)
RSFSR...... Republique Socialiste Federative Sovietique de Russie
RSFSR...... Ruska Sovjetska Federativna Socijalisticka Republika [*Russian Soviet Federative Socialist Republic*]   (YU)
rsg .... Residentsgerecht of Residentiegerecht [*Benelux*]   (BAS)
RSGB........ Radio Society of Great Britain [*Potters Bar, Hertfordshire, England*]   (EAIO)
RSGC........ Royal Sydney Golf Club [*Australia*]
RSh .... Block Terminal, Control Box   (RU)
rsh .... Deciphering   (RU)
RSh .... Difference of Latitudes   (RU)
RSh .... Loudspeaker Cord   (RU)
RSh .... Miner's Measuring Tape   (RU)
RSHA .... Reichssicherheitshauptampt [*Central Security Office of the Reich*] [*NAZI Germany*]
RShch .... Control Board   (RU)
RShch .... Distributing Board   (RU)
RShN .... Manual Bull Pump   (RU)
rsh og .... Destruction Fire   (BU)
RS-I........... Fighter Radio   (RU)
RSI............ Mixing Relay Selector   (RU)
RSI............ Pulse-Counting Relay   (RU)
RSI............ Pulse Pickup Relay   (RU)
RSI............ Religious Science International   (EAIO)
RSI............ Repubblica Sociale Italiana [*Italian Socialist Republic*] [*Founded by Mussolini 1943-1945*]
RSI............ Rio Sidra [*Panama*] [*Airport symbol*]   (OAG)
RSI............ Royal Sanitary Institute   (ROG)
RSITA .... Reglement du Service International des Telecommunications de l'Aeronautique
RSJ .... Sisters of Saint Joseph of the Sacred Heart [*Australia*]   (EAIO)
RSK........... Complement-Fixation Reaction   (RU)
RSK........... Rayon Savings Bank   (RU)
RSK........... Reaktorsicherheitskommission [*Reactor Safety Commission*] [*Nuclear energy*]   (NRCH)
RSK........... Repair and Construction Office   (RU)
RSKh .... Rayon Seed Production Farm   (RU)
RSKU........ Reza Shah Kibur University [*Iran*]
RSL........... Reditelstvi Statnich Lesu [*Directorate of State Forests*]   (CZ)
RSL........... Reditelstvi Statnich Loterii [*State Lottery Directorate*]   (CZ)
RSL........... Returned Services League of Australia   (ADA)
RSL........... Rio-Sul, Servicos Aereos Regionais SA [*Brazil*] [*ICAO designator*]   (FAAC)
RSL........... Trunk Line Relay   (RU)
RSL........... Workers' Union of Lithuania   (RU)
RSLA .... Returned Services League of Australia   (ADA)
RSL-DS ..... Trunk Line and Four-Wire Termination Relay   (RU)
RSLK........ Rubber-Glass-Lacquer Tissue   (RU)
RSLMF .... Republic of Sierra Leone Military Forces
RSLO........ Terminal Trunk Line Relay   (RU)
RSLT .... Tandem Trunk Line Relay   (RU)
RSLU........ Multiplex Trunk Line Relay   (RU)
RSLUI ...... Outgoing Multiplex Trunk Line Relay   (RU)
RSLUIM ... Outgoing Long-Distance Multiplex Trunk Line Relay   (RU)
RSLUV ...... Incoming Multiplex Trunk Line Relay   (RU)

RSLUVM .. Incoming Long-Distance Multiplex Trunk Line Relay (RU)
RSM .... Clarity, Audibility, Quality of Modulation (RU)
RSM .... Mantissa Sum Register [*Computers*] (RU)
RSM .... Regliment-Sersant-Major [*Regiment Sergeant Major*] [*Afrikaans*]
RSM .... Repubblica di San Marino [*Car registration plates*] [*Italian*]
RSM .... Revolution Socialiste Malgache [*Malagasy Socialist Revolution*] (AF)
RSM .... Robotnicza Spoldzielnia Mieszkaniowa [*Workers' Housing Cooperative*] (POL)
RSM .... Rostov Agricultural Machinery Plant (RU)
RSM .... Rotterdam School of Management [*Netherlands*] (ECON)
RSM .... Ruf- und Signalmaschine [*Telephone and Signal Equipment*] (EG)
RSMA .... Reinforcing Steel Manufacturers' Association [*Australia*]
RSMAD ..... Remote Sensing and Meteorological Division [*ISRO*] [*India*] (PDAA)
RSMD .... Remote Sensing and Meteorological Applications Division [*Scientific Advisory Committee, IAEA*] (ASF)
RSME .... Real Sociedad Matematica Espanola [*Spanish*] (SLS)
RSMK .... Repair, Construction, and Installation Office (RU)
RSMLC ..... Red de Salud de las Mujeres Latinoamericanas y del Caribe [*Latin American and Caribbean Women's Health Network*] (EAIO)
RSMML .... Rajasthan State Mines and Mineral Ltd. [*India*] (PDAA)
RSMPS ...... Romanian Society for Mathematical and Physical Sciences
RSN .... Rassemblement pour le Salut National [*Rally for National Salvation*] [*Senegal*] (PD)
RSN .... Royal Swazi National Airways Corp. [*Swaziland*] [*ICAO designator*] (FAAC)
RSNA .... Royal Society of Northern Antiquaries (ROG)
RSNAE ...... Regional Superintendent Naval Armament Engineering [*Department of Defence*] [*Australia*]
RSNB .... Royal Spanish National Ballet
RSNDT ...... Rayon People's Councils of Deputies of the Working People (BU)
RSNKh ...... Rayon Council of National Economy (RU)
RSNT .... Revised Single Negotiating Text
RSNZ .... Royal Society of New Zealand (SLS)
RSO .... Aero Asia [*Pakistan*] [*ICAO designator*] (FAAC)
RSO .... Building and Repair Organization (BU)
RSO .... Radio Identification System (RU)
RSO .... Revolutionaere Sozialisten (Oesterreichs) [*Revolutionary Socialists (Austria)*] [*Political party*] (PPE)
RSON .... Detection and Guidance Radar Station (RU)
RSOP .... Rzeszowska Spoldzielnia Ogrodniczo-Pszczelarska [*Rzeszow Gardening and Beekeeping Cooperative*] (POL)
RSP .... Communications Company with Infantry (RU)
RSP .... Number Sequence Sum Register [*Computers*] (RU)
RSP .... Radioisotope Society of the Philippines (SLS)
RSP .... Radioisotopic Object Counter (RU)
RSP .... Rassemblement Socialiste Progressiste [*Tunisia*] [*Political party*] (EY)
RSP .... Rayon Construction Enterprise (BU)
RSP .... Recessive, Sex-Linked [*Biology*] (RU)
RSP .... Research Society of Pakistan (EAIO)
RSp .... Resolution of Coincidence (RU)
RSP .... Reversible Counter-Converter (RU)
RSP .... Revolutionaire Socialistische Partij [*Revolutionary Socialist Party*] [*Netherlands*] [*Political party*] (PPE)
RSP .... Revolutionary Socialist Party [*India*] [*Political party*] (PPW)
RSPA .... Reparticao Sanitaria Pan-Americana (LAA)
RSPAS ...... Research School of Pacific and Asian Studies [*Australian National University*]
RSpB .... Resolution of Coincidence on a Magnetic Drum (RU)
RSPI .... Rzemieslnicza Spoldzielnia Pracy Introligatorow [*Labor Cooperative of Book-Binders*] (POL)
RSpL .... Resolution of Coincidence on Magnetic Tapes (RU)
RSPN .... Royal Society for Protection of Nature [*Bhutan*] (EAIO)
Rspr .... Rechtspraak [*Case Law, Judicial Decisions*] [*Netherlands*] (ILCA)
Rspr .... Rechtsprechung [*Court Practice*] [*German*] (ILCA)
Rspr Arb .... Rechtsprechung in Arbeitssachen [*Labor Court Reports*] [*German*] (ILCA)
rsprov .... Rechtspraakoverzicht [*Benelux*] (BAS)
Rspr SV ..... Rechtspraak Sociale Verzekering [*Benelux*] (BAS)
RSPS .... Republic Trade-Union Council (RU)
RSPV .... Reconstruccio Socialista del Pais Valencia [*Socialist Reconstruction of the Valencian Country*] [*Spanish*] (WER)
RSQLd .... Royal Society of Queensland [*Australia*]
RSR .... Republica Socialista Romana [*Socialist Republic of Romania*] (RO)
RSR .... Republica Socialista Romania [*Socialist Republic of Romania*] (EY)
rsr .... Residentieraad [*Benelux*] (BAS)
rsrto .... Radio Technical Support Signal Company (BU)

RSS .... Rashtriya Swayamsevak Sangh [*National Union of Selfless Servers*] [*Militant Hindu organization India*]
RSS .... Rastriya Sambad Samiti [*Press agency*] [*Nepal*]
RSS .... Recreation and Sports Service [*Hong Kong*]
RSS .... Remote Sensing Society [*Nottingham, England*] (EAIO)
RSS .... Republike Socialiste Sovjetike [*Soviet Socialist Republic*] [*Albanian*]
RSS .... Resolving Coincidence Circuit (RU)
RSS .... Ribbed Smoked Sheets [*of Rubber*] (CL)
RSS .... Rok Stranickeho Skoleni [*Party Indoctrination Year*] (CZ)
RSS .... Roseires [*Sudan*] [*Airport symbol*] (OAG)
rss .... Rousseurs [*Red Spots*] [*Publishing*] [*French*]
RSS .... Royal Scientific Society [*Jordan*] [*Research center*] (IRC)
RSS .... Signal Pickup Relay (RU)
RSS .... Stop-Signal Relay (RU)
RSS .... Tracking Radio Station (RU)
RSSA .... Rockwell Ship Systems Australia Proprietary Ltd.
RSSA .... Royal Scottish Society of Arts (SLS)
RSSAF .... Royal Society of South Africa (AA)
RSSAILA .. Returned Sailors', Soldiers', and Airmen's Imperial League of Australia (ADA)
RSSILA ..... Returned Sailors' and Soldiers' Imperial League of Australia (ADA)
RSSM .... Republica Sovietica Socialista Moldova [*Soviet Socialist Republic of Moldavia*] (RO)
RSSS .... Rashtriya Swayamseyak Sangh [*National Union of Selfless Servers*] [*Militant Hindu organization India*] (PD)
r st .... Mercury Column (RU)
R St .... Raad van State [*Benelux*] (BAS)
RST .... Radio Sistema Tricolar (COL)
RSt .... Radio Station (RU)
RST .... Rassemblement Socialiste Tunisien [*Tunisia*] (MENA)
RST .... Rechenstanzer [*German*] (ADPT)
RST .... Repair and Construction Trust (RU)
RST .... Revolutia Stiintifico-Tehnica [*Scientific-Technical Revolution*] (RO)
RST .... Rhodesian Selection Trust
Rst .... Rostock (EG)
RST .... Royal Society of Tasmania [*Australia*]
RSTas .... Royal Society of Tasmania [*Australia*]
rstca .... Rustica [*Paperbound*] [*Publishing*] [*Spanish*]
RSTMH .... Royal School of Tropical Medicine and Hygiene
RSTMH .... Royal Society of Tropical Medicine and Hygiene [*British*] (EAIO)
RSTO .... Radiotechnical and Illuminating Engineering Support [*Aviation*] (RU)
RSTPK ...... Rayon Union of Labor Productive Cooperatives (BU)
rstv .... Solubility (RU)
RSU .... Amplified Power Ratio Regulator (RU)
RSU .... Radioisotopic Follow Level Gauge (RU)
RSU .... Repair and Construction Administration (RU)
RSU .... Royal Salvage Unit [*Australia*]
RSv .... Company Communications (RU)
RSV .... Rechtspraak Sociale Verzekering [*Benelux*] (BAS)
RSV .... Restaurants and Sleeping Cars [*Railroads*] (BU)
RSV .... Rijn-Schelde-Verolme [*Commercial firm*] [*Netherlands*]
RSV .... Rimamurany- Salgotarjani Vasmu Reszvenytarsasag [*Rimamurany- Salgotarjan Iron Works Limited*] (HU)
RSV .... Rude Skov [*Denmark*] [*Geomagnetic observatory code*]
RSV .... Troop Assembly Area (RU)
RSVic .... Royal Society of Victoria [*Australia*]
RSVP .... Repondez, s'Il Vous Plait [*The Favor of an Answer is Requested*] [*French*]
RSVP .... Royal St. Vincent Police (LA)
RSVPL .... Repondez, s'Il Vous Plait [*The Favor of an Answer is Requested*] [*French*] (FLAF)
RSW .... Rada Szkol Wyzszych [*Council on Higher Schools*] (POL)
RSW .... Robotnicza Spoldzielnia Wydawnicza [*Poland*]
RSW .... Rolnicza Spoldzielnia Wytworcza [*Agricultural Production Cooperative*] (POL)
RSWB .... Raumordnung, Stadtebau, Wohnungswesen, Bauwesen [*Fraunhofer Society*] [*Germany*] (IID)
RSWK .... Reglement voor Sumatra's Westkust [*Benelux*] (BAS)
RSWPrasa ... Robotnicza Spoldzielnia Wydawnicza "Prasa" [*"Prasa" (Press) Worker's Cooperative Publishing House*] (POL)
RSYe .... Radio Station "Free Europe" (RU)
RSZ .... Air Service State Co. [*Hungary*] [*ICAO designator*] (FAAC)
RSZ .... Equisignal Zone (RU)
RSZ .... Rada Slovenskych Zien v Exile [*Council of Slovak Women in Exile*] (CZ)
RSZ .... Ratarsko Sjemenska Zadruga [*Agricultural Seed Cooperative*] (YU)
RSZ .... Rektorat Sveucilista u Zagrebu [*Rectorate of the University of Zagreb*] (YU)
RSZ .... Repulogepes Szolgalat [*Aviation Service (of Ministry of Agriculture and Food Industry)*] (HU)

RSZ............ Repulo Szovetseg [*Aviation Association*]   (HU)
RSZ............ Revolutionaere Studentenschaft Zuerich [*Revolutionary Student Organization of Zurich*] [*Switzerland*]   (WEN)
RSZ............ Riaditelstvo Statnych Zeleznic [*State Railroads Directorate*] (CZ)
RSZ............ Ryazan' Machine Tool Plant   (RU)
RSZB......... Reonska Stanica za Zastitu Bilja [*Regional Plant Protection Station*]   (YU)
r szk............ Rok Szkolny [*School Year*] [*Poland*]
RT .... Air Tungaru (Gilbert Islands) [*British*] [*ICAO designator*] (ICDA)
RT .... Electric Current Recording   (RU)
RT .... Electric Current Relay
RT .... Exploration Theodolite   (RU)
RT .... Expulsion-Type Arrester   (RU)
RT .... Fishing Trawler   (RU)
RT .... Fuel Regulator   (RU)
RT .... Magyarorszagi Rendeletek Tara [*Collection of Decrees of Hungary*]   (HU)
RT .... Radio Engineering   (RU)
RT .... Radioisotopic Thermoregulator   (RU)
RT .... Radio Tank, Tank Radio   (RU)
RT .... Radiotelegrafia [*or Radiotelegrafo*] [*Wireless Telegraph*] [*Italian*]
RT .... Radiotelegrafista [*Wireless Operator*] [*Italian*]
R-T .... Radio-Telephonie [*Radio-Telephony*] [*French*]
RT .... Rangement du Tampon [*French*]   (ADPT)
RT .... Rangoon Institute of Technology [*Myanmar*]   (DS)
Rt .... Rashed Travel Agency [*Yemen*]
RT .... Raumteil [*Part by Volume*] [*German*]
RT .... Raumtemperatur [*Room Temperature*] [*German*]   (GCA)
RT .... Recueillis Temporaires [*Temporarily Taken In*] [*Of unadoptable children*] [*French*]
r/t .... Refereer na Trekker [*Refer to Drawer*] [*Afrikaans*]
RT .... Reference Point   (RU)
RT .... Registertonne [*Register Ton*] [*German*]
RT .... Reglement de Travail [*Benelux*]   (BAS)
RT .... Relay Transformer   (RU)
RT .... Reperforator Transmitter   (ADPT)
rt................ Reszvenytarsasag [*Corporation*]   (HU)
RT .... Rift Valley Textiles Ltd. [*Kenya*]
Rt .... Right   (IDIG)
RT .... Robna Tarifa [*Commodity Freight Rates*] [*Railroads*]   (YU)
RT .... Rocket Engineering   (RU)
RT .... Rukun Tetangga [*Neighborhood Association*]   (IN)
RT .... Sound Corrector   (RU)
RT .... Temperature Regulator   (RU)
RT .... Temperature Relay, Thermal Relay   (RU)
RT .... X-Ray Tube   (RU)
RTA .... Page-Printing Apparatus   (RU)
RTA .... Radiodiffusion-Television Algerienne   (FLAF)
RTA .... Radio-Television Algerienne [*Algerian Radio and Television*] (AF)
RTA .... Retail Television Association [*Australia*]
RTA .... Returned to Australia
RTA .... Rhodesian Tobacco Association   (AF)
RTA .... Roads and Traffic Authority [*New South Wales, Australia*]
RTA .... Road Trains of Australia
RTA .... Rotuma [*Fiji*] [*Airport symbol*]   (OAG)
RTAB....... Royal Thai Air Force Base [*Also, RTAFB*]   (VNW)
RTAC........ Regional Technical Assistance Center [*Mexico*]   (LAA)
RTAFB...... Royal Thai Air Force Base [*Also, RTAB*]   (VNW)
RTAQ .... Remedial Teachers' Association of Queensland [*Australia*]
RTAV .... Retail Traders Association of Victoria [*Australia*]
RTAV .... Royal Thai Army in Vietnam
RTAVF ..... Royal Thai Army Volunteer Force   (VNW)
RTAWA .... Retail Traders' Association of Western Australia
rtb.............. Radio Battalion   (RU)
RTB .... Radiodiffusion-Television Belge [*Belgian Radio Broadcasting and Television System*]
rtb.............. Radioengineering Battalion   (BU)
RTB .... Radio Television Brunei
RTB .... Rassemblement des Travailleurs Burundi
RTB .... Roatan [*Honduras*] [*Airport symbol*]   (OAG)
RTB .... Rudarsko-Topionicki Basen [*Mining and Foundry Basin*] [*Bor*] (YU)
RTBF .... Radio-Television Belge de la Communaute Culturelle Francaise [*Broadcasting organization*] [*Belgium*]   (EY)
RTBISC.... Radiodiffusion-Television Belge - Institut des Services Comuns [*Belgian Radio Broadcasting and Television - Common Services Institute*]
rtbr .... Radioengineering Brigade   (BU)
RTC .... La Radiotechnique-Compelec [*French*]
RTC .... Radiodiffusion-Television Congolaise [*Congolese Radio and Television*]   (AF)
RTC .... Radio Tecnica Colombiana

RTC .... Regional Training Center for Inland Fisheries Operatives [*India*] (ASF)
RTC .... River Transport Corporation [*North Khartoum, Sudan*]
RTC .... Road Transport Commission [*Australia*]
RTC .... Ronde Tafel-Conferentie [*Benelux*]   (BAS)
RTCA....... Rural Training Council of Australia
rtca........... Rustica [*Paperbound*] [*Publishing*] [*Spanish*]
RTCAC..... Regional Transport Coordination Advisory Committee [*New South Wales, Australia*]
RTChK ..... Rayon Transportation Extraordinary Commission for Combating Counterrevolution and Sabotage   (RU)
RTCV........ Rural Training Council of Victoria [*Australia*]
RTCWA..... Rural Training Council of Western Australia
RTD .... Radiodiffusion-Television de Djibouti
RTD .... Radio Tanzania Dar Es Salaam
RTD .... Roentgen Technische Dienst BV [*Nuclear energy*] [*Netherlands*] (NRCH)
RTD .... Turbojet Engine   (RU)
RTDE .... Revue Trimestrielle de Droit Europeen [*French*]
RTE .... Aeronorte - Transportes Aereos Lda. [*Portugal*] [*ICAO designator*]   (FAAC)
rte .... Remite [*or Remitente*] [*Sender, From*] [*Spanish*]
Rte............. Route [*Road, Route*] [*French*]
Rte............. Route Nationale [*National Road*] [*Military map abbreviation World War I*] [*French*]   (MTD)
RTF........... Radiodiffusion-Television Francaise [*French Radio Broadcasting and Television System*]
RTF........... Radiotelefonia [*Radio Communication*] [*Spanish*]
RTF........... Radiotelephone   (RU)
RTF........... Road Transport Forum [*Australia*]
RTG.......... Radiodiffusion-Television Gabonaise [*Gabonese radio and television network*]
RTG .... Radiodiffusion-Television Guineenne [*Guinean radio and television network*]
RTg........... Radiotelegrafija [*Radiotelegraphy*]   (YU)
RTG .... Reaktor Tevsii Proje Grubu [*Reactor Distribution Project Group*] (TU)
RTG .... Reglement Telegraphique [*Telegraph Regulations*] [*French*]
RTG .... Rentgen [*Roentgen (Unit of radiation)*]   (YU)
RTG .... River Transport Group [*South Vietnamese Navy*]   (VNW)
RTG .... Ruteng [*Indonesia*] [*Airport symbol*]   (OAG)
RTGA .... Hemagglutination-Inhibition Test   (RU)
RTgC .... Radiotelegrafska Centrala [*Radiotelegraphic Center*]   (YU)
RTGR .... Radiotelegraph   (RU)
RTGW ...... Rettungsgeraetewagen [*Rescue Equipment Truck (Used by fire department)*]   (EG)
RTH.......... Radio Thailand   (FEA)
RTHK .... Radio Television Hong Kong
Rthr........... Reichsthaler [*German*]
RTHS .... Raymond Terrace Historical Society [*Australia*]
RTI............ Industrial Rubber Products [*Plant*]   (RU)
RTI............ Radiodiffusion-Television Ivoirienne [*Ivory Coast Radio and Television*]   (AF)
RTI............ Radiotechnical Equipment   (RU)
RTI............ Roti [*Indonesia*] [*Airport symbol*]   (OAG)
RTI............ Rural Technology Institute [*India*]
RTI............ Ruska Tekstilna Industrija [*Ruse Textile Industry*]   (YU)
RTIC......... RadioTechnique Industrielle et Commerciale [*Industrial and Commercial Radio Technic*] [*France*]
RTIF......... Road Transport Industry Forum [*Australia*]
RTISC....... River Torrens Improvement Standing Committee [*Australia*]
RTJ .... Rad Tovarysstva Jezisova [*Society of Jesus*]   (CZ)
RTJ .... Robotnicka Telocvicna Jednota [*Workers' Gymnastic Association*]   (CZ)
RTK .... City District Theater Box Office   (RU)
RTK .... Radiation-Induced Thermal Cracking   (RU)
RTK .... Repulestudomanyi es Tajekoztato Kozpont [*Center for Aviation Science and Information*]   (HU)
RTK .... Wheel Trench Digger   (RU)
RTL........... Radio Television Luxembourgeoise [*Radio Television Luxembourg*] [*French*]
RTL........... Regeleing Toezicht Luchtvaart [*Benelux*]   (BAS)
RTL........... Regeling van het Rijkstoezicht op de Luchtvaart [*Benelux*] (BAS)
RTL........... Rheintalflug-Rolf Seewald [*Austria*] [*ICAO designator*]   (FAAC)
RTL........... Road Signs & Traffic Contol Equipment (Auckland) Ltd. [*New Zealand*]
RTM .... Guiding Technical Materials   (RU)
RTM .... Istituto per le Ricerche de Tecnologia Meccanica e per l'Automazione [*Italian*]   (SLS)
RTM .... Maximum Thermal Relay   (RU)
RTM .... Radio Television Malaysia
RTM .... Radio-Television Malgache [*Malagasy Radio and Television*] (AF)
RTM .... Radio-Television Marocaine [*Moroccan Radio and Television*] (AF)

RTM .... Rassemblement des Travaillistes Mauriciens [*Mauritius*] [*Political party*]   (EY)
RTM .... Regie Belge des Transports Maritimes [*Belgium*]   (DCTA)
RTM .... Regie des Transports du Mali [*Mali Transportation Administration*]   (AF)
RTM .... Regimen de Tiralleurs Marocains
RTM .... Rio Tinto Minera [*Spanish copper mines*]
Rtm .... Rittmeister [*Cavalry Captain*] [*German*]
rtm.............. Rotmistrz [*Captain (of Horse)*] [*Poland*]
RTM .... Rotterdam [*Netherlands*] [*Airport symbol*]   (OAG)
RTM .... Rotterdamse Tramweg Maatschappij [*Netherlands*]   (BAS)
RTM .... Trans Am Compania Ltda. [*Ecuador*] [*ICAO designator*]   (FAAC)
RTN .... Forcing Temperature Regulator   (RU)
RTNA .... Regional Television News Australia
RTNB .... Radio-Television Nationale du Burundi   (EY)
RTNC .... Radio-Television Nationale Congolaise
RTN/HD ... Royal Thai Navy/Hydrographic Department   (MSC)
RTO .... Radio Equipment   (RU)
RTO .... Radio Telegraph Installation   (BU)
RTO .... Radio Telegraph Section   (RU)
RTO .... Russian Technical Society [*1866-1929*]   (RU)
RTO .... Technical Service Company   (RU)
RTO .... Technical Support Company   (RU)
RTP......... Fire-Fighting Instructor   (RU)
RTP......... Radioengineering Post   (BU)
rtp.............. Radioengineering Regiment   (BU)
RTP.......... Radio Post   (RU)
rtp.............. Radio Regiment   (RU)
RTP.......... Radiotechnical Industry   (RU)
RTP.......... Radio Televisao Portuguesa [*Portuguese Radio-Television System*]
RTP.......... Recno Transportno Preduzece [*River Transport Establishment*]   (YU)
RTP.......... Reference Telephonique [*French*]   (ADPT)
RTP.......... Republican Turkish Party [*Cyprus*] [*Political party*]
RTP.......... Rutland Plains [*Australia*] [*Airport symbol*] [*Obsolete*]   (OAG)
RTPA........ Regie des Transports de la Province de l'Atlantique
RTPD........ Direct Action Temperature Regulator   (RU)
RTPD........ Radio Countermeasures   (RU)
RTPD........ Robotnicze Towarzystwo Przyjaciol Dzieci [*Workers Society of Friends of Children*]   (POL)
RTPR........ Radiotechnicky Prapor [*Radiotechnical Battalion*]   (CZ)
RTPS .... Research Unit for Transport Economic and Physical Distribution Studies [*Rand Afrikaans University*] [*South Africa*]   (AA)
RTPz.......... Radiotechnicky Pruzkum [*Radiotechnical Reconnaissance*]   (CZ)
RTPzP .... Radiotechnicky Pruzkumny Pluk [*Radiotechnical Reconnaissance Regiment*]   (CZ)
rtr .... Radio Company   (RU)
rtr .... Radioengineering Company   (BU)
RTR .... Royal Tank Regiment   (ML)
RTR .... Sociedade Brazileira de Turismo (ROTATUR) [*Brazil*] [*ICAO designator*]   (FAAC)
RTRI......... Railway Technical Research Institute [*Research center*] [*Japan*]   (IRC)
RTRL........ Richmond-Tweed Regional Library [*Australia*]
RTs .... Centrifugal Relay   (RU)
RTs .... Expanding Cement   (RU)
RTS........... Manual Exchange   (RU)
RTS........... Radiodiffusion-Television du Senegal [*Radio and television network*] [*Senegal*]
RTS........... Radioengineering Station   (BU)
RTS........... Radiotechnical Equipment   (RU)
RTS........... Radiotechnical Personnel   (RU)
RTS........... Radiotechnical Service   (RU)
RTS........... Radiotelegraph Station   (BU)
RTS........... Radiotelemetering Station   (RU)
RTS........... Radiotelemetering System   (RU)
RTS........... Radio-Television Scolaire [*French*]
RTS........... Radio Television Seychelles
RTS........... Radio-Television Singapore
RTS........... Radiotelevizija Srbije [*Serbia*]   (EY)
RTS........... Radio Wire Broadcasting Network
RTs .... Rayon Center   (RU)
RTS........... Rayon Telephone Network   (RU)
RTs .... Reactor Shop   (BU)
RTS........... Rechnergesteuertes Text-System [*German*]   (ADPT)
RTS........... Regie des Transports du Senegal [*Senegal Transportation Administration*]   (AF)
RTS........... Regiment des Transmissions et Services [*Signals and Services Regiment*] [*Malagasy*]   (AF)
RTS........... Remontno-Tehnicke Stanice [*Technical Repair Stations*]   (YU)
RTS........... Repair and Technical Station   (RU)
RTS........... Reparaturtechnische Station [*Equipment Repair Station*]   (EG)

RTS........... Reparatur-Technische Station [*Repair and Technical Station*] [*German*]
rts .... Review, Critique   (RU)
RTS........... Rottnest Island [*Australia*] [*Airport symbol*]   (OAG)
RTS........... Rueti-Te Strake BV [*Robot-Technological Systems*] [*Research center*] [*Netherlands*]   (ERC)
RTS........... Television Relay Station   (RU)
RTs .... Track Circuit   (RU)
RTSA .... Remote Telephone Subscribers' Association [*Australia*]
r-tsa........... Workshop   (BU)
RTSh......... Workers' Technical School   (RU)
RTShch..... Roadstead Mine Sweeper   (RU)
r-tsiya....... Reaction   (RU)
RTSK........ Rayon Transportation and Warehouse Kombinat   (RU)
RTSM....... Republic Trust for the Manufacture of Building Materials   (RU)
RTsO .... Centralized Disconnecting Relay   (RU)
rt st........... Mercury Column   (RU)
RTsT......... Radial-Flow Centripetal Turbine   (RU)
RTsU .... Recording Digital Unit   (RU)
RTT .... Radet for Teknisk Terminologi [*Norwegian Council for Technical Terminology*] [*Oslo*] [*Information service or system*]   (IID)
RTT .... Radio Television Tunisien [*Tunisian Radio and Television*]   (AF)
RTT .... Regie des Telegraphes et des Telephones [*Telegraph and Telephone Administration*] [*Belgium*]   (WER)
RTT .... Regiment de Tirailleurs Tunisiens
RTT .... Residential Tenancies Tribunal [*New South Wales, Australia*]
RTT .... Temperature Regulator of Heat-Transfer Agent   (RU)
Rttm .... Rittmeister [*Cavalry Captain*] [*German*]
RTTs......... Radio Relay Center   (BU)
RTTs......... Riga Television Center   (RU)
RTTsS .... Radio Relay Station   (BU)
RTU .... Development and Technical Improvements Fund   (BU)
RTU .... Radiotechnical Installations   (RU)
RTU .... Radio Wire Broadcasting Center   (RU)
RTU .... Rayon Radio Wire Broadcasting Installation   (RU)
RTU .... Relay Center   (RU)
RTU .... Remote-Control Relay   (RU)
RTU .... Repair and Technical Administration   (RU)
RTU .... Republic Technical Specifications   (RU)
RTUC .... Reformed Trade Union Congress
RTUF....... Revolutionary Trade Unions Federation [*Cyprus*]   (EAIO)
RTV .... Direccion General de Radiodifusion y Television [*Directorate General of Radio Broadcasting and Television*] [*Spanish*]   (WER)
RTV .... Radiodiffusion-Television (Upper Volta) [*Radio and television network*]
RTV .... Radio Relay Point   (BU)
RTV .... Radiotechnicke Vojsko [*Radiotechnical Troops*]   (CZ)
RTV .... Radio Television
RTV .... Radio Troops   (RU)
RTV .... Rhodesian Television   (AF)
RTV .... Rikstrygdeverket [*National Social Insurance System*] [*Norway*]
RTV .... Ruhaipari Tervezo Vallalat [*Designing Enterprise of the Clothing Industry*]   (HU)
RTV .... Thermal Time Relay   (RU)
RTV .... Valve-Type Lightning Arrester   (RU)
RTVA .... Radio Television de Andalucia [*Spain*]   (EY)
RTVD .... Radiotelevision Dominicana [*Dominican Radio and Television*] [*Dominican Republic*]
RTVE........ Radiotelevision Espanola [*Spanish*]
RTVM .... Radio Television Madrid [*Spain*]   (EY)
RTVMU ... Radiotelevision Murciana [*Spain*]   (EY)
RTVV........ Radiotelevision Valencia [*Spain*]   (EY)
RTY .... Merty [*Australia*] [*Airport symbol*] [*Obsolete*]   (OAG)
RTZ .... Radio Tanzania Zanzibar
RTZ .... Radiotechnicke Zabepeceni [*Radiotechnical Support (Security)*]   (CZ)
RTZ .... Rakovnicke Tukove Zavody, Narodni Podnik [*Rakovnik Fat Rendering Factories, National Enterprise*]   (CZ)
RTZ .... Rio Tinto Zinc Corp. [*Uranium mining company*] [*British, Namibian*]   (AF)
RTZ .... Rota Tezkych Zbrani [*Heavy Weapons Company*]   (CZ)
RTZ .... Ruzomberske Textilne Zavody [*Ruzomberok Textile Mills*]   (CZ)
RTZ .... Tank Repair Plant   (RU)
RU .... Accelerating Relay   (RU)
RU............. Control Relay   (RU)
RU............. Decision Amplifier   (RU)
RU............. Demagnetizing Device   (RU)
RU............. Directorate of Intelligence   (RU)
RU............. Distribution System [*Electricity*]   (RU)
RU............. Estimated Angle   (RU)
RU............. Gain Control   (RU)
RU............. Guiding Regulations   (RU)

RU............. Indicator Relay (RU)
Ru............. Knife Switch (RU)
RU............. Level Regulator (RU)
RU............. Manual Control (RU)
RU............. Ore Mining Administration (BU)
RU............. Radio Center (RU)
RU............. Radio Control (RU)
RU............. Rasinjski Ugljenokop [Rasinja Coal Pit] (YU)
RU............. Rayon Center [Communications] (RU)
RU............. Recno Uporiste [River Stronghold] [Navy] (YU)
RU............. Recognition Device (RU)
RU............. Reconnaissance Device (RU)
RU............. Recorder (RU)
RU............. Reduction-Cooling Unit (RU)
RU............. Regulator, Controller (RU)
RU............. Reserve Unit [Equal to one US dollar] [International finance] [Former USSR]
RU............. Revolutionary Union
RU............. Rhodes University
RU............. River Navigation School (RU)
Ru............. Rubha [Point] [Gaelic] (NAU)
RU............. Rudnik Uglja [Coal Mine] (YU)
RU............. Rugby-Unie [Rugby Union] [Afrikaans]
Ru............. Ruine [German]
RU............. Runic [Language, etc.] (ROG)
Ru............. Rutenio [Ruthenium] [Chemical element] [Portuguese]
RU............. Scanner (RU)
RU............. Separate Balancing (RU)
RU............. Separation Node (RU)
RU............. Steering Gear (RU)
RU............. Trade School (RU)
RU............. Unit Rheostat (RU)
RU............. X-Ray Unit (RU)
RUA.......... Arua [Uganda] [Airport symbol] (OAG)
RUA.......... Photo Reproducing and Enlargement Apparatus (RU)
RUA.......... Resistenca Unida Angolesa
RUAM...... Radio-Controlled Model Airplane (BU)
RuB........ Ring um Berlin [Ring around Berlin (Railroad)] (EG)
r ub........... Rok Ubiegly [or Roku Ubieglego] [Last Year] [Poland]
RUB........ Ruble [Monetary unit] [Former USSR]
rubr .... Heading, Column (RU)
Rubr .... Rubrik [Heading, Column] [German]
rubr .... Rubrik [Heading, Column] [Danish/Norwegian]
rubr .... Rubriziert [Rubricated] [Publishing] [German]
rubr .... Rubryka [Column] [Poland]
rubriz......... Rubriziert [Rubricated] [Publishing] [German]
RUBSSO ... Rossendale Union of Boot, Shoe, and Slipper Operatives [British] (DCTA)
RUC .... Republique Unie du Cameroun
RUCA .... Rijks Universitair Centrum Antwerpen
RUCATSE ... Runway Capacity to Serve the South East [Airport planning group] [British] (ECON)
ruch .... Brook, Stream [Topography] (RU)
Ruckenvergold ... Rueckenvergoldung [Back Gilding] [Publishing] [German]
Rucks....... Rueckseite [Verso] [German]
Ruckvergoldg ... Rueckenvergoldung [Back Gilding] [Publishing] [German]
ruckw......... Rueckwaertig [Back] [Publishing] [German]
RUCS........ Remote or Underserved Communities Scheme [Australia]
RUD.......... Diagnostic X-Ray Unit (RU)
RUD.......... Engine Control Lever (RU)
rud .... Mine [Topography] (RU)
RUD.......... Republicka Uprava za Dohotke [Republic Revenue Administration] (YU)
RUD.......... Rosicke Uhelne Doly [Rosice Coal Mines] (CZ)
RUD.......... Rosicko-Oslavanske Uhelne Doly [Rosice-Oslavany Coal Mines] (CZ)
RUD.......... Street Traffic Control (RU)
Rudmetal.... State Commercial Enterprise for Import and Export of Metal Ores (BU)
rudn........... Mine (RU)
RUDNAP .. Rudarsko Nabavno Prodajno Preduzece Eksport-Import [Export-Import Mining Establishment] [Belgrade] (YU)
RUDT....... Rassemblement pour l'Unite et la Democratie Tchadienne [Chad]
Rueckst ...... Rueckstoss [Recoil, Repulse] (EG)
Ruecktr ...... Ruecktritt [Back Pedal, Reversal] [German] (GCA)
Ruestg .... Ruestung [Armament] [German] (GCA)
RUF .... Revolutionary United Front [Sierra Leone] [Political party] (EY)
RUFE......... Zeitschrift fuer Rundfunk und Fernsehen [Journal for Radio and Television] [NOMOS Datapool] [Information service or system]
RUFMAN ... Research Unit for Farm Management [University of the Orange Free State] [South Africa] (AA)
RUG.......... Rijks Universiteit Gent
RUG.......... Rijks Universiteit Groningen

RUGSh ...... Intelligence Directorate of the General Staff (RU)
RUH .... Riyadh [Saudi Arabia] [Airport symbol] (OAG)
RUH .... Statni Vyzkumny Ustav Rybarsky a Hydrologicky [State Research Institute of Fishing and Hydrology] (CZ)
Ruhest........ Ruhestand [Retirement] [German] (GCA)
RUK........... Commander's Radio Center (RU)
ruk............. Leader, Manager, Instructor (RU)
ruk............. Manager (BU)
ruk............. Manuscript (RU)
RUK........... Reserviupseerikoulu [Finland]
RUK .... Rhodes-Universiteitskollege [Rhodes University College] [Afrikaans]
ruk............. River Branch [Topography] (RU)
RUKH........ Ukrainian Popular Movement for the Restructuring (EAIO)
rukop......... Manuscript (BU)
rukov .... Manual, Textbook (RU)
rukovod ..... Manager, Management (BU)
RUL .... Rejonowy Urzad Likwidzcyjny [District Liquidation Office] (POL)
RUL .... Research and University Librarians [Finland] (EAIO)
rum .... Controlled-Mine-Laying Company (RU)
RUM......... Medical X-Ray Unit (RU)
RUM......... Radio-Controlled Mechanism (RU)
RUM......... Radio-Controlled Model (RU)
RUM......... Railwayman's Union of Malaysia
RUM......... Ranger Uranium Mines [Commercial firm] [Australia]
RUM......... Rayon Militia Administration (RU)
RUM......... Recinto Universitario [Puerto Rico] (DSCA)
rum .... Romanian (BU)
RUM......... Rumjartar [Nepal] [Airport symbol] [Obsolete] (OAG)
RUMA...... Rayon Mechanization and Motor Vehicle Transport Administration (BU)
rum ez........ Romanian Language (BU)
RuMVKP... Vsesoiuznaia Knizhnaia Palata [All-Union Book Chamber], Ulitsa Oktiab r Skaia, Moscow, Soviet Union [Library symbol] [Library of Congress] (LCLS)
RUN........... Carbon Voltage Regulator (RU)
RUN........... Normal Level Relay (RU)
RUN........... Rassemblement pout l'Unite Nationale [Cameroon] [Political party] (EY)
RUN........... Reunion Island [Airport symbol] (OAG)
RUN........... Rol Unico Nacional [Centralized National Registry] [Chile] (LA)
RUNI........ Rayon Real Estate Administration (RU)
RUNV....... Rada Ustredniho Narodniho Vyboru [Council of the Central National Committee] (CZ)
RUO........... Manual Carbon-Dioxide Fire Extinguisher (RU)
ruots.......... Ruotsalainen [Finland]
ruots.......... Ruotsalaiset [Finland]
ruots.......... Ruotsia [or Ruotsiksi] [Finland]
RUP .... Field Acceleration Relay (RU)
RUP .... Industrial X-Ray Unit (RU)
RUP .... Position Indicator Rheostat (RU)
rup............. Rupia [Rupee] [Portuguese]
RUP .... Ukrainian Revolutionary Party (RU)
RUP .... Universal Field Radiometer (RU)
RUPD .... Republiska Uprava za Posredovanje Dela [Republic Employment Agency] (YU)
RUPR .... Republicka Uprava za Posredovanje Rada [Republic Employment Agency] (YU)
RUPSh....... Sleeve Float Level Regulator (RU)
RUR .... Reduction Cooling System [Nuclear energy] (BU)
RURALCO ... Rurutu Island [French Polynesia] [Airport symbol] (OAG)
RURALCO ... Construcciones Rurales [Argentina] (DSCA)
RURALMINAS ... Fundacao Rural Mineira [Minas Gerais Rural Foundation] [Brazil] (LA)
RURT .... Rayon Administration of River Transportation (RU)
RUS .... Air Russia Airlines [Russian Federation] [ICAO designator] (FAAC)
RUS .... Air-Search Radar (RU)
RUS .... Marau [Solomon Islands] [Airport symbol] (OAG)
RUS .... Regional Communications Center (RU)
Rus .... Rusca [Russian] (TU)
Rus .... Russies [Russian] [Afrikaans]
RUS .... Universal Scintillation Radiometer (RU)
Rusavstrotorg ... Mixed Russian-Austrian Trading and Industrial Company (RU)
Rusavsttorg ... Mixed Russian-Austrian Trading and Industrial Company (RU)
rus ez.......... Russian Language (BU)
Rusgertorg ... Russian-German Trading and Industrial Company (RU)
RuSHA ...... Rasse und Siedlungshauptamt [NAZI] (BJA)
ruskindbd... Ruskindbind [Suede Binding] [Publishing Danish/Norwegian]
Rusl............ Rusland [Russia] [Afrikaans]
RUSN .... Switching and Busing Arrangement Supplying the Station Auxiliaries (RU)

rus per .... Russian Translation (RU)
russ .... Russian (RU)
RUSSICA ... Russian Information and Communications Agency (IID)
russk .... Russian (RU)
Russl .... Russland [*Russia*] [*German*] (GCA)
Russ P .... Russisches Patent [*Russian Patent*] [*German*] (GCA)
rust .... Rustica [*Paperbound*] [*Publishing*] [*Spanish*]
rust .... Rustica [*Paperbound*] [*Publishing*] [*Italian*]
RUSTAN ... Russian Text Analyzer
RUT .... Carbon Current Regulator (RU)
RUT .... Rejonowy Urzad Telekomunikacyjny [*District Office of Telecommunication*] [*Poland*]
RUT .... Remote-Control Device Distributor (RU)
RUT .... Therapeutic X-Ray Unit (RU)
rutkod .... Russian Universal Telegraph Code (RU)
RUTT .... Rejonowy Urzad Telefoniczno-Telegraficzny [*District Telephone and Telegraph Office*] [*Poland*]
RUU .... Rentjana Undang-Undang [*Draft Law*] (IN)
RUU .... Rijksuniversiteit Utrecht [*Netherlands*]
RUV .... Manual Fuze Setter (RU)
RUV .... Rikisutvarpid-Sjonvarp [*Iceland*] (PDAA)
RUV .... Time-Dependent Gain Control (RU)
RUV .... Water Level Regulator (RU)
RUVAT ..... Ruhaipari Anyagellato Vallalat [*Clothing Industry Supply Enterprise*] (HU)
ruz .... Ruzny [*Various*] (CZ)
ruzh .... Rifle (RU)
Ruzh .... Rifle Plant [*Topography*] (RU)
RU ZSP ..... Rada Uczelniana Zrzeszenia Studentow Polskich [*College Council of the Polish Students' Association*] [*Poland*]
RV .... Air Controller (RU)
RV .... Call Distributor, Traffic Distributor [*Telephony*] (RU)
RV .... Control Screw (RU)
rv .... Convalescent Company (RU)
rv .... Corporal of the Guards (BU)
RV .... Excitation Regulator (RU)
RV .... Explosion-Proof Miner's Lamp (RU)
RV .... Humidity Regulator (RU)
RV .... Israel Aircraft Industries Ltd. [*ICAO aircraft manufacturer identifier*] (ICAO)
RV .... Mercury-Arc Rectifier (RU)
RV .... Radical Left [*Denmark*] (WEN)
RV .... Radikale Venstre [*Radical Liberals*] [*Denmark*] [*Political party*] (PPE)
RV .... Radioactive Contamination, Radioactive Substance (RU)
RV .... Radioactive Substance (BU)
RV .... Radio Altimeter (BU)
RV .... Radio Altitude (RU)
RV .... Radio Vatican [*Vatican State*] (PDAA)
RV .... Radio Veze [*Radio Communications*] (YU)
RV .... Radio Wave (RU)
RV .... Railroad Car Repair (RU)
RV .... Ratno Vazduhoplovstvo [*Air Force*] (YU)
RV .... Reactor Venezolano [*Venezuela*] (NRCH)
Rv. .... Rechtsvraag [*Benelux*] (BAS)
rv .... Reconnaissance Platoon (RU)
RV .... Reducing Substance (RU)
RV .... Reduktionsvermoegen [*Reduction Ability*] [*German*] (GCA)
R-V .... Rendez-Vous [*Appointment, Meeting-Place*] [*French*]
RV .... Richtverband [*Radio Relay*] (EG)
RV .... Rod Valgallianse [*Red Electoral Alliance*] [*Norway*] (PPE)
RV .... Rotary Viscosimeter (RU)
RV .... Rotary Voltmeter (RU)
Rv .... Rueckenvergoldung [*Back Gilding*] [*Publishing*] [*German*]
RV .... Timing Relay (RU)
RV .... Waiting Area [*Military term*] (RU)
RV .... Wassermann Reaction (RU)
Rv .... Wetboek van Burgerlijke Rechtsvordering [*Benelux*] (BAS)
RVA .... Farafangana [*Madagascar*] [*Airport symbol*] (OAG)
RVA .... Missile Troops and Artillery (BU)
RvA .... Raad van Arbeid [*Benelux*] (BAS)
RVA .... Regie des Voies Aeriennes [*Airlines Administration*] [*Zaire*] (AF)
RVA .... Regroupements des Villages Animes
RVA .... Retirement Village Association [*Australia*]
RVA .... Rijksdienst voor Arbeidsvoorziening [*Benelux*] (BAS)
Rva .... Rouva [*Madam*] [*Finland*] (GPO)
RVAC .... Royal Victorian Aero Club [*Australia*]
RVAHJ ...... Royal Victorian Association of Honorary Justices [*Australia*]
RVANSW ... Retirement Village Association of New South Wales [*Australia*]
RVA/RLW ... Regie des Voies Aeriennes/Regie der Luchtwegen [*Airports and Airways Agency of Belgium*] [*Ministry of Transport*] [*Research center*] [*Belgium*] (EAS)
RVB .... Maintenance and Recovery Battalion (RU)
RVB .... Maintenance and Recovery Brigade (RU)
RvB .... Raad van Beroep [*Benelux*] (BAS)

rvb .... Repair and Reconstruction Battalion (BU)
RVB .... Rijksverzekeringsbank [*Benelux*] (BAS)
RvB .... Wet, Houdende Instelling van Raden van Beroep voor de Directe Belastingen [*Benelux*] (BAS)
RvB (SV) .... Raad van Beroep (Sociale Verzekering) [*Benelux*] (BAS)
RvC .... Raad van Commissarissen [*Benelux*] (BAS)
RVC .... Rapport Valeur-Cout
RVC .... Reditelstvi Vodnich Cest [*Waterways Directorate*] (CZ)
RVC .... Republicki Vazduhoplovni Centar [*Republic Aviation Center*] (YU)
RVCM .... Republic of Vietnam Campaign Medal [*Military decoration*]
RVD .... Air Traffic Control (BU)
RVD .... Auxiliary Two-Coil Relay (RU)
RVD .... High-Pressure Relay (RU)
RVD .... High-Pressure Rotor (RU)
RVD .... Reglement Dienstvoorwaarden Spoorwegen [*Benelux*] (BAS)
RvdW .... Rechtspraak van de Week [*Benelux*] (BAS)
RVE .... Electronic Timing Relay (RU)
RVE .... Reichsvereinigung der Juden in Deutschland [*A publication*] (BJA)
RVE .... Saravena [*Colombia*] [*Airport symbol*] (OAG)
Rverg .... Rueckenvergoldung [*Back Gilding*] [*Publishing*] [*German*]
Rvergold .... Rueckenvergoldung [*Back Gilding*] [*Publishing*] [*German*]
RVF .... Regie des Voies Fluviales [*River Lines Administration*] [*Zaire*] (AF)
RVG .... Reichsversorgungsgesetz [*Federal Assistance Law*] [*German*]
RVG .... Richtverbindungsgeraete [*Microwave Relay Set*] (EG)
Rvg .... Rueckenvergoldung [*Back Gilding*] [*Publishing*] [*German*]
RVGK .... Reserve of the Supreme Command (RU)
rvh .... Raad van Hoofden [*Benelux*] (BAS)
RVHP .... Rada Vzajemne Hospodarske Pomoci [*Council of Economic Mutual Aid*] (CZ)
RVHS .... Royal Victorian Historical Society [*Australia*]
RVI .... Interval Switch-On Relay (RU)
RVI .... Raad van Indie [*Benelux*] (BAS)
RVI .... Ratni Vojni Invalidi [*Disabled Veterans*] (YU)
RVI .... Renault Vehicules Industriels [*Commercial firm*] [*France*]
RVI .... Renault Vehicules Industriels [*Renault Industrial Vehicles*] [*Finland*]
RVI .... RV-Aviation [*Finland*] [*ICAO designator*] (FAAC)
RvJ .... Raad van Justitie [*Benelux*] (BAS)
RVJD .... Reichsvereinigung der Juden in Deutschland [*A publication*] (BJA)
RVK .... Has Worked with All Continents [*Diploma for amateur radio operators*] (BU)
RVK .... Rayon Military Commissariat (RU)
RVK .... Rijksstation voor Kleinveetelt [*Government Research Station for Small Stock Husbandry*] [*Belgium*] (ARC)
RVK .... Rugby-Voetbalklub [*Rugby Football Club*] [*Afrikaans*]
RVK .... Vertical Riveted Petroleum Tank (RU)
RVKV .... Rada Vytvarne Kultury Vyroby [*Council for Creative Designing of Products*] [*CID*] [*See also*] (CZ)
RVL .... Airvallee SpA-Services Aeriens de Val d'Aoste [*Italy*] [*ICAO designator*] (FAAC)
RVL .... Reditelstvi Vojenskych Lesu [*Directorate of Military Forests*] (CZ)
RVL .... Rijksstation voor Landbouwtechniek [*Government Research Station for Agricultural Engineering*] [*Belgium*] (ARC)
RVL .... Royal Viking Line [*Kloster Cruises of Norway*]
RVM .... Excitation Regulator with a Motor Drive (RU)
RVM .... Pendular Timing Relay (RU)
RVM .... Regie des Voies Maritimes [*Shiplines Administration*] [*Zaire*] (AF)
RVM .... Rohrenvoltmeter [*Vacuum Tube Voltmeter*] (EG)
RVMYC ..... Royal Victorian Motor Yacht Club [*Australia*]
RVN .... Republic of Vietnam
RVN .... Rovaniemi [*Finland*] [*Airport symbol*] (OAG)
RVNAF ...... Republic of Vietnam Air Force
RVNAF ...... Republic of Vietnam Armed Forces
RVNAFHMFC ... Republic of Vietnam Armed Forces Honor Medal, First Class [*Military decoration*]
RVNAFHMSC ... Republic of Vietnam Armed Forces Honor Medal, Second Class [*Military decoration*]
RVNCAMFC ... Republic of Vietnam Civil Actions Medal, First Class [*Military decoration*]
RVNCAMSC ... Republic of Vietnam Civil Actions Medal, Second Class [*Military decoration*]
RVNCM .... Republic of Vietnam Campaign Medal [*Military decoration*]
RvNE .... Rijksstation voor Nematologie en Entomologie [*Government Research Station for Nematology and Entomology*] [*Belgium*] (ARC)
RVNF .... Republic of Vietnam Forces
RVNGCUCW/P ... Republic of Vietnam Gallantry Cross Unit Citation with Palm [*Military decoration*]
RVNMC .... Republic of Vietnam Marine Corps
RVNN .... Republic of Vietnam Navy

RVO........... Rabaul Volcano Observatory [*Papua New Guinea*]
RvO........... Reglement van Orde [*Benelux*]   (BAS)
RVO........... Reichsversicherungsordnung [*Federal Insurance Laws*]
    [*German*]
RVO........... Rijksverdedigingsorganisatie [*National Defense Research
    Organization*] [*Netherlands*]   (WEN)
RVOG....... Radio Voice of the Gospel
Rvoir........ Reservoir [*Tank*] [*Military map abbreviation World War I*]
    [*French*]   (MTD)
rvp.............. Military Police Company   (BU)
RVP........... Pneumatic Timing Relay   (RU)
rvp.............. Raad van Politie [*Benelux*]   (BAS)
RvP........... Rijksstation voor Plantenveredeling [*Government Research
    Station for Plant Breeding*] [*Belgium*]   (ARC)
RVP........... Rolnicka Vzajomna Pokladnica [*Agricultural Mutual Savings
    Bank*]   (CZ)
RVPAFS.... Register of Veterinary Preparations and Animal Feeding Stuffs
    [*Australia*]
RvPop........ Rijksstation voor Populierenteelt [*Government Research Station
    for Poplar Breeding*] [*Belgium*]   (ARC)
RvPZ........... Rijksstation voor Plantenziekten [*Government Research Station
    for Phytopathology*] [*Belgium*]   (ARC)
RVR........... Maintenance and Recovery Company   (RU)
rvr............... Rechtsvraag [*Benelux*]   (BAS)
RVRME..... Rift Valley Research Mission in Ethiopia [*Anthropology*]
RVS........... Audio Signal Cut-In Relay   (RU)
RVS........... Diving Station with Manual Equipment   (RU)
RvS........... Raad van State, Geschillen van Bestuur [*Benelux*]   (BAS)
RVS........... Radio Broadcasting Station   (RU)
RVS........... Radiove Vysilaci Stredisko [*Radio Broadcast Center*]   (CZ)
RVS........... Rechnerverbundsystem [*German*]   (ADPT)
RVS........... Reifengewerbe-Verband der Schweiz [*Swiss Association of the
    Tyre Industry*]   (PDAA)
RVS........... Revolutionary Military Council (of the Union of SSR) [*1922-
    1934*]   (RU)
RvS............. Rijksstation voor Sierplantenteelt [*Government Research Station
    for Ornamental Plant Growing*] [*Belgium*]   (ARC)
RVS........... Rollfuhrversicherungsschein [*Freight Insurance Policy*]   (EG)
RVS........... Rotterdamsche Verzekering-Societeiten [*Netherlands*]   (BAS)
RVS........... Vertical Welded Petroleum Tank   (RU)
RVSA........ Rekenaarvereniging van Suid-Afrika [*Computer Society of South
    Africa*]   (AA)
RVSN........ Raketny Voiska Strategicheskovo Naznacheniya [*Strategic
    Rocket Forces*] [*Russian*]   (PDAA)
RVSN........ Strategic Missile Troops   (BU)
RVSR........ Republic Revolutionary Military Council [*1918-1922*]   (RU)
RvSt........... Raad van State [*Benelux*]   (BAS)
RVSU........ Distributing Shaft of the Servomechanism   (RU)
RVSU........ Rakety Vojensko-Strategickeho Urceni [*Strategic Missiles*]   (CZ)
RVSVP...... Repondez Vite, s'Il Vous Plait [*Please Reply at Once*] [*French*]
RVT........... High-Voltage Traction Disconnector   (RU)
RVT........... Reditelstvi Vodnich Toku [*Watercourse Directorate*]   (CZ)
RVT........... Revolutionary Military Tribunal   (RU)
RVT........... Rozvoj Vedy a Techniky [*Development of Science and
    Technology*]   (CZ)
RVTD........ Decimeter-Range Radio Altimeter   (RU)
RVTU........ Republic Provisional Technical Specifications   (RU)
RVU........... Mercury-Arc Rectifier Unit   (RU)
RVU........... Radio Broadcasting Center   (RU)
RVU........... Upper-Level Relay   (RU)
RVV........... Excitation Switch-On Relay   (RU)
RVV........... Rectifier Switch-On Relay   (RU)
RVV........... Reeve Aleutian Airways, Inc. [*ICAO designator*]   (FAAC)
RVV........... Reglement Verkeersregels en Verkerstekens [*Benelux*]   (BAS)
RVV........... Respublika Verkhnaia Vol'ta
RvV............ Rijksstation voor Veevoeding [*Government Research Station for
    Animal Nutrition*] [*Belgium*]   (ARC)
RVV-TNO ... Researchgroep voor Vlees en Vleeswaren Nederlands Centrale
    Organisatie voor Toegepast-Natuurwetenschappelijk
    Onderzoek [*Research Group for Meat and Meat Products
    Netherlands Central Organization for Applied Natural
    Scientific Research*]   (ARC)
RVY........... Rivera [*Uruguay*] [*Airport symbol*]   (OAG)
RVYC........ Royal Victorian Yacht Club [*Australia*]
RVZ........... Radiosonde Observation   (RU)
RVZ........... Riga Railroad Car Plant   (RU)
RvZ............ Rijksstation voor Zeevisserij [*Government Research Station for
    Sea Fisheries*] [*Belgium*]   (ARC)
RVZI........ Rijksfonds voor Verzekering tegen Ziekte en Invaliditeit
    [*Benelux*]   (BAS)
RW............. Hughes Air Corp. [*ICAO designator*]   (ICDA)
RW............. Rassemblement Wallon [*Walloon Rally*] [*Belgium*]   (WER)
RW............. Rechenwerk [*German*]   (ADPT)
RW............. Rechtskundig Weekblad [*Belgium*]   (BAS)
RW............. Rechtswissenschaft [*Jurisprudence*] [*German*]   (ILCA)
RW............. Registratiewet [*Benelux*]   (BAS)

RW............. Reichswaehrung [*German Currency*] [*German*]
RW............. Rijkswaterstaat [*Netherlands*]   (MSC)
RW............. Ringsdorff-Werke, GmbH [*Nuclear energy*]   (NRCH)
RW............. Rukun Warga [*Precinct Association (Composed of Rukun
    Tetanggas - RT)*]   (IN)
RW............. Rwanda [*ANSI two-letter standard code*]   (CNC)
RWA......... Aligiulia SpA [*Italy*] [*ICAO designator*]   (FAAC)
RWA......... Raoul Wallenberg Association [*See also RWF*]   (EA)
RWA......... Rwanda [*ANSI three-letter standard code*]   (CNC)
RWAAC .... Rural Workers Accommodation Advisory Committee [*New
    South Wales, Australia*]
RWABA .... Royal Western Australian Bowling Association
RWAG ...... Rural Women's Access Grants [*Australia*]
RWAHS .... Royal Western Australian Historical Society
RWAIB...... Royal Western Australian Institute for the Blind [*Australia*]
RWC......... Rural Water Commission [*Australia*] [*Research center*]   (EAS)
RWD......... Air Rwanda [*ICAO designator*]   (FAAC)
RWD......... Reichswetterdienst [*State Weather Service*] [*German*]
RWE......... Rheinisch-Westfaelisches Electrizitaetswerk AG [*Rheine-
    Westphalian Electricity Co.*] [*Germany*]
RWeek...... Rechtskundig Weekblad [*Benelux*]   (BAS)
RWF......... Raoul Wallenberg Foreningen [*Raoul Wallenberg Association -
    RWA*]   (EAIO)
RwF.......... Rwandan Franc [*Monetary unit*]   (IMH)
RWG......... Regional Work Group
RWI.......... Rheinisch-Westfaelische Institut
RWI.......... Rijkswerkinrichting [*Benelux*]   (BAS)
RWMC...... Committee on Radioactive Waste Management [*Organization
    for Economic Cooperation and Development*]   (ERC)
RWMC...... Radioactive Waste Management Centre [*Japan*]   (WND)
RWP......... Rawalpindi/Islamabad [*Pakistan*] [*Airport symbol*] [*Obsolete*]
    (OAG)
RWP......... Romanian Workers' Party [*Political party*]
RWPG....... Rada Wzajemnej Pomocy Gospodarczej [*Council for Economic
    Mutual Assistance*]   (POL)
RWS......... Air Whitsunday [*Australia*] [*ICAO designator*]   (FAAC)
RWS......... Rhodesian Women's Service
RWTF........ RAAF [*Royal Australian Air Force*] Welfare Trust Fund
    [*Australia*]
RWTH...... Rheinisch-Westfaelische Technische Hochschule Aachen
    [*Rhineland-Westphalia Technical University, Aachen*]
    (ARC)
RWU......... Railway Workers Union [*Uganda*]   (AF)
RWU......... Rural Workers Union [*Australia*]
RWUZ....... Railway Workers Union of Zambia
RWW......... Rijksgroepsregeling Werkloze Werknemers [*Benelux*]   (BAS)
RXA........... Arax Airlines Ltd. [*Nigeria*] [*ICAO designator*]   (FAAC)
RXA........... Rank Xerox Australia   (ADA)
RXL........... Air Exel [*France*] [*ICAO designator*]   (FAAC)
RXS........... Roxas City [*Philippines*] [*Airport symbol*]   (OAG)
ry................ Rahayksikko [*Finland*]
RY.............. Rakas Ystava (Kirjeissa) [*Finland*]
RY.............. Redcoat Air Cargo Ltd. [*British*] [*ICAO designator*]   (ICDA)
ry................ Rehuyksikko(a) [*Finland*]
ry................ Rekisteroity Yhdistys [*Registered Association*] [*Finland*]
RY.............. Riley Aeronautics Corp. [*ICAO aircraft manufacturer identifier*]
    (ICAO)
r-y.............. Size, Dimensions   (RU)
r-y.............. Solutions   (RU)
ryad........... Rare   (BU)
RYaNSh ... Russian Language in the National School [*Bibliography*]   (RU)
RYaS......... Russian Language and Literature [*Bibliography*]   (RU)
RYaSh....... Russian Language in the School [*Bibliography*]   (RU)
Ryazmekhzavod ... Ryazan' Machine Plant   (RU)
Ryazsel'mash ... Ryazan' Agricultural Machinery Plant   (RU)
Ryaztsvetmet ... Ryazan' Plant for the Production and Processing of
    Nonferrous Metals   (RU)
ryb.............. Fish Culture   (RU)
ryb.............. Fish Industry Plant, Fishery [*Topography*]   (RU)
ryb dv........ Fisherman's Yard [*Topography*]   (RU)
rybkop........ Fish Smokehouse [*Topography*]   (RU)
rybol.......... Fishing [*Topography*]   (RU)
Rybosudoproyekt ... Central Design Office for Shipbuilding of the Ministry of
    the Fish Industry, USSR   (RU)
Rybosudostroy ... Administration of Fishing-Boat Building   (RU)
rybov.......... Fish Culture   (RU)
ryb pos........ Fishermen's Settlement [*Topography*]   (RU)
ryb pr......... Fisheries [*Topography*]   (RU)
rybtrest....... State Fish Trust   (RU)
rybzavod..... Fish Product Plant   (RU)
ryb zim....... Fishermen's Winter Camp [*Topography*]   (RU)
RYC........... Royal Yacht Club [*Australia*]
ryc.............. Rycina [*Illustration*]   (POL)
RYCCA...... Residential Youth and Child Care Association of Australia
    (ADA)
RYFO........ Ryan Foundation International [*India*]   (EAIO)

Rygawar..... Warszawsko-Ryska Fabryka Wyrobow Gumowych [*Warsaw-Riga Rubber Products Plant*]   (POL)

rygforg........ Rygforgyldning [*Gold Tooling on Back*] [*Publishing Danish/Norwegian*]

rygforgyldn ... Rygforgyldning [*Gold Tooling on Back*] [*Publishing Danish/Norwegian*]

ryggdekor... Ryggdekoration [*Ornamentation on Spine*] [*Publishing Danish/Norwegian*]

RYIS .... Rural Youth Information Service [*Australia*]

rykm........... Rykmentti [*Finland*]

RYMSA..... Rural Youth Movement of South Australia

RYO........... Rio Turbio [*Argentina*] [*Airport symbol*]   (OAG)

RYONSW ... Rural Youth Organisation of New South Wales [*Australia*]

RYOQ....... Rural Youth Organisation of Queensland [*Australia*]

RYOT .... Rural Youth Organisation of Tasmania [*Australia*]

RYS........... Religious Youth Service [*Australia*]

rys .... Rysowal [*Drawn By*]   (POL)

rys .... Rysunek [*Drawing*]   (POL)

Ryt.............. Rytmi [*Record label*] [*Finland*]

RZ .... Company Reserve   (RU)

RZ .... Contaminated Area   (RU)

RZ .... Delay Regulator   (RU)

RZ .... Grounding Relay, Protective Relay   (RU)

RZ .... Land Surveyor's Tape   (RU)

RZ .... Rada Zakladowa [*Works Committee*] [*Poland*]

RZ .... Radioactive Contamination   (RU)

RZ .... Radiosonde   (RU)

RZ .... Radio Zagreb   (YU)

RZ .... Raketna Zrna [*Rocket Shells*]   (YU)

RZ .... Rare Earths   (RU)

RZ .... Ratni Zlocini [*War Crimes*]   (YU)

RZ .... Rdeca Zastava [*Red Flag*]   (YU)

RZ .... Rdeca Zvezda [*Red Star*]   (YU)

RZ .... Rechenzentrum [*Computer Center*]   (EG)

RZ .... Referativity Zhurnal-Informaties

RZ .... Regal-Zonophone [*Record label*] [*Great Britain*]

RZ .... Regiment de Zouaves

RZ .... Regtspleging bij de Zeemagt [*Benelux*]   (BAS)

RZ .... Repair Plant   (RU)

rz .... Reserve   (BU)

RZ .... Retour Zero [*French*]   (ADPT)

RZ .... Revolutionary Legality   (RU)

RZ .... Ribarska Zadruga [*Fishing Cooperative*]   (YU)

RZ .... Rozvodovy Zavod Elektricke Energie [*Electric Power Distributing Plant*]   (CZ)

rz .... Rueckzieland [*Returning, Aiming Backward*] [*German*]   (GCA)

rz .... Rzeka [*River*] [*Poland*]

RZA .... Santa Cruz [*Argentina*] [*Airport symbol*]   (OAG)

RZAP........ Reserve Air Regiment   (RU)

rzd .... Siding Track [*Topography*]   (RU)

RZDR .... Rechenzentrum der Deutschen Reichsbahn [*GDR Railroad Computer Center*]   (EG)

RZE .... Rare-Earth Elements   (RU)

RZE .... Rzeszow [*Poland*] [*Airport symbol*]   (OAG)

r-zh........... Boundary, Line   (RU)

RZhO......... Rayon Housing Department   (RU)

RZhU........ Railroad Trade School   (RU)

RZhU........ Rayon Housing Administration   (RU)

RZIV.......... Rijksinstituut voor Ziekte- en Invaliditeits-Verzekering [*Benelux*]   (BAS)

RZJD........ Rejonowe Zjednoczenie Jajczarsko-Drobiarskie [*District Egg and Poultry Cooperative*]   (POL)

RZK .... Ruski Zastitni Korpus [*Russian Defense Corps*] [*World War II*]   (YU)

RZKT........ Republic Correspondence Cooperative Technicum of the Rospotrebsoyuz   (RU)

RZM .... Loader-Unloader   (RU)

RZM .... Radomskie Zaklady Miesne [*Radom Meat Establishment*]   (POL)

RZM .... Rare-Earth Metals   (RU)

RZM .... Reservation de Zones en Memoire [*French*]   (ADPT)

RZM .... Rewolucyjny Zwiazek Mlodziezy [*Revolutionary Union of Youth*]   (POL)

RZMO .... Rogoznickie Zaklady Materialow Ogniotrwalych [*Rogoznik (Rosenig) Fireproof Materials Plant*]   (POL)

RZMP........ Rozdelovna Zemedelskych Mechanisacnich Potreb [*Distribution Agency of Agricultural Mechanization Equipment*] [*Prague*]   (CZ)

RZNO........ Rada Zidovskych Nabozenskych Obci [*Council of Jewish Religious Congregations*]   (CZ)

RZO .... Radomskie Zaklady Obuwia [*Radom Shoe Plant*]   (POL)

RZO .... Rayon Land Department   (RU)

RZO .... Rechenzentrum der Ortskrankenkassen [*German*]   (ADPT)

Rz P........... Rzeczpospolita Polska [*Polish Republic*]   (POL)

RZPD........ Radomszczanskie Zaklady Przemyslu Drzewnego [*Radomsko Lumber Plant*]   (POL)

Rzpl........... Rzeczpospolita [*Republic*] [*Poland*]

Rzplita........ Rzeczpospolita [*Republic*] [*Poland*]

RZPT .... Radomskie Zaklady Przemyslu Terenowego [*Radom Local Industry Plant*]   (POL)

RZPW........ Rudzkie Zaklady Przemyslu Weglowego [*Ruda Coal Plant*]   (POL)

RZPW........ Rybnickie Zjednoczenie Przemyslu Weglowego [*Rybnik Coal Industry Association*]   (POL)

RZR .... Rhodesia Zimbabwe, Registrar of Pension and Provident Fund

RZR .... Rudnik Zeljezne Rude [*Iron Ore Mine*]   (YU)

RZS............ Audio Signal Relay   (RU)

RZS............ Mercury-Arc Rectifier Charging Station   (RU)

RZS............ Republicki Zavod za Statistiku [*Republic Statistical Institute*]   (YU)

RZS............ Rijkszuivelstation [*Government Station for Research in Dairying*] [*Belgium*]   (ARC)

RZS............ Robotnicze Zespoly Spoldzielcze [*Poland*]

RZS............ Rolnicze Zrzeszenie Spoldzielcze [*Agricultural Cooperative Association*]   (POL)

RZS............ Rolniczy Zespol Spoldzielczy [*Agricultural Cooperative Union*]   (POL)

RZSI........... Rudnik Zivega Srebra [*Mercury Mine*] [*Idrija*]   (YU)

RZSI........... Royal Zoological Society of Ireland   (SLS)

RZSSh........ Republic Correspondence Secondary School   (RU)

RZSZL....... Republiski Zavod za Socialno Zavarovanje v Ljubljani [*Republic Institute of Social Insurance in Ljubljana*]   (YU)

RZU .... Radio Zpravodajsky Utvar [*Radio Intelligence Regimental Unit*]   (CZ)

RZV .... Antiaircraft Reconnaissance Platoon   (RU)

RZV .... Rudnici Zlata i Volframa [*Gold and Tungsten Mines*] [*Kucevo*]   (YU)

RZZ .... Rejonowa Zbiornica Zlomu [*District Scrap Metal Collection Point*]   (POL)

Rz Z G........ Rzeszowskie Zaklady Gastronomiczne [*Rzeszow Restaurant Establishments*]   (POL)

S

S .... Adder [*Computers*]   (RU)
S .... Aerospatiale [*Societe Nationale Industrielle Aerospatiale*] (Sud Aviation) [*France*] [*ICAO aircraft manufacturer identifier*] (ICAO)
S .... Ambulance Aircraft   (RU)
S .... Balance   (RU)
S .... Bishop [*Chess*]   (RU)
S .... Coupling   (RU)
S .... Displacement [*Artillery*]   (RU)
S .... Esses [*Phonetic alphabet*] [*Pre-World War II*]   (DSUE)
S .... For Snow Background [*Camouflage*]   (RU)
s .... Kind, Quality, Grade   (RU)
S .... Medical (Department of a Ship)   (RU)
S .... Nakladatelstvi Svoboda [*Svoboda Publishing House*]   (CZ)
S .... Neuter [*Gender*]   (RU)
s .... North   (BU)
S .... North, Northern   (RU)
s/ .... Sa [*Their, Your*] [*French*]
S .... Saba Shipping & Stevedoring Corp. [*Yemen*]
S .... Sac [*Sack*] [*French*]
S .... Saeure [*Acid*] [*German*]
s .... Sahife [*Page*] [*Turkey*]   (GPO)
S .... Saint [*Saint*] [*French*]   (MTD)
s .... Saldo [*Balance*] [*Afrikaans*]
S .... San [*or Santo*] [*Saint*] [*Spanish*]
S .... San [*Saint*] [*Spanish*]   (EECI)
s .... Sana [*Word*] [*Finland*]
s .... Sans [*Without*] [*French*]
S .... Santa [*or Santo*] [*Saint*] [*Portuguese*]
S .... Sao [*Saint*] [*Portuguese*]   (GPO)
S .... Sarjana [*Academic degree*] [*Indonesian*]
S .... Satz [*German*]   (ADPT)
S .... Scandia
S .... Schilling [*Monetary unit*] [*Austria*]
S .... Schip en Schade [*Benelux*]   (BAS)
S .... Schloss [*Castle*] [*German*]
S .... Schnellzuglokomotive [*Fast Express Train Locomotive*]   (EG)
S .... Schule [*School*] [*German*]
S .... Schwefel [*Sulphur*] [*Chemical element*] [*German*]
s .... Schwer [*Heavy, Difficult*] [*German*]   (GCA)
s .... Second [*French*]
S .... Seconde [*French*]   (MTD)
s .... Seged [*Assistant*]   (HU)
S .... Seguente [*And Following*] [*Italian*]   (ILCA)
S .... Segundo [*Second*] [*Portuguese*]
S .... Sehen [*See*] [*German*]
S .... Sehid [*Martyr*]   (TU)
S .... Seite [*Page*] [*German*]   (GPO)
S .... Sekonde [*Second*] [*Afrikaans*]
s .... Sekunda [*or Sekundy*] [*Second or Seconds*] [*Poland*]
S .... Sekunde [*Second*] [*German*]
s .... Sekunti(a) [*Finland*]
S .... Self-Propelled   (RU)
s/ .... Sem [*Without*] [*Portuguese*]
s .... Senza [*Without*] [*Italian*]
s .... Seria [*Series*] [*Publishing*] [*Poland*]
s/ .... Ses [*Their, Your*] [*French*]
s/ .... Seus [*His*] [*Portuguese*]
s .... Sever [*North*]   (CZ)
S .... Shipboard [*Nuclear physics and engineering*]   (RU)
S .... Shushi [*Japan*]
S .... Siam Steel Group [*Thailand*]
s .... Sida [*Page*] [*Sweden*]   (GPO)
s .... Side [*Page*] [*Norway*]   (GPO)
s .... Side [*Page*] [*Denmark*]   (GPO)
s .... Sider [*Pages*] [*Denmark*]   (GPO)
S .... Siecle [*Century*] [*French*]
S .... Siege [*Siege*] [*French*]   (MTD)

s .... Siehe [*See*] [*German*]   (EG)
S .... Siemens [*Afrikaans*]
S .... Sierra [*Phonetic alphabet*] [*International*]   (DSUE)
s .... Siglo [*Century*] [*Spanish*]
s .... Signe [*Signed*] [*French*]
s .... Sillinki [*Finland*]
S .... Sily
s .... Sin [*Without*] [*Spanish*]
S .... Sinif [*Class*]   (TU)
s .... Sivu [*Page*] [*Finland*]   (GPO)
s .... Sivuilla [*Finland*]
s .... Sivu(lla) [*Finland*]
s .... Sivut [*Finland*]
s .... Sjieling [*Shilling*] [*Monetary unit*] [*Afrikaans*]
s/ .... Sobre [*On, Upon*] [*Portuguese*]
s/ .... Sobre [*On, Upon*] [*Spanish*]
S .... Sobresaliente [*On an Examination: Distinction*] [*Spanish*]
S .... Socialdemokratiet [*Social Democratic Party*] [*Denmark*]   (WEN)
S .... Socialist Group [*EC*]   (ECED)
S .... Sofia   (BU)
S .... Soir [*Evening*] [*French*]
s .... Sokak [*Street*] [*Turkey*]
s/ .... Son [*Their, Your*] [*French*]
s .... Sondre [*South*] [*Norway*]   (GPO)
S .... Soudruh [*or Soudruzka*] [*Comrade*]   (CZ)
S/ .... Sous [*Sub or Under*] [*Prefix*] [*French*]   (CL)
S .... South   (IDIG)
S .... South Australia [*National Union Catalogue of Australia symbol*]
S .... Southern   (EECI)
S .... Spartacus [*Sports society*]   (RU)
S .... Staatsblad van het Koninkrijk der Nederlanden [*Netherlands*]   (BAS)
S .... Staz Szpitalny [*Hospital Practice*] [*Poland*]
s .... Ster [*Stere*] [*Poland*]
s .... Stere [*Cubic Meter*] [*French*]
S .... Stokes [*German*]   (GCA)
s .... Stron [*Pages*]   (POL)
S .... Studien [*Benelux*]   (BAS)
s/ .... Su [*Your*] [*Spanish*]
S .... Su [*Water, Stream*]   (TU)
s/ .... Sua [*Portuguese*]
S .... Subtitled
S .... Sucre [*Monetary unit*] [*Ecuador*]
S .... Sud [*South*] [*French*]   (ROG)
S .... Sudska Uprava [*Judicial Administration*]   (YU)
S .... Sued [*or Sueden*] [*South*] [*German*]   (EG)
S .... Sugar [*Phonetic alphabet*] [*Royal Navy World War I Pre-World War II*] [*World War II*]   (DSUE)
S .... Suid [*South*] [*Afrikaans*]
s .... Suivants [*French*]   (FLAF)
S .... Sul [*South*] [*Portuguese*]
S .... Superhigh [*Bearing precision grade*]   (RU)
s/ .... Sur [*Geography*] [*French*]
S .... Sur [*South*] [*Spanish*]
S .... Surface [*Surface*] [*French*]
S .... Sveriges Socialdemokratiska Arbetareparti [*Social Democratic Party*] [*Sweden*]   (WEN)
s .... Swiety [*Saint*] [*Poland*]
s .... Symmetrisch [*Symmetric*] [*German*]
S .... Syn [*Son*] [*Poland*]
s .... Syntyaan [*Finland*]
s .... Syntynyt [*Finland*]
S .... Syria   (BARN)
S .... Szwecja [*Sweden*] [*Poland*]

S .... Trains Run Only on Sundays and the Following Holidays: New Year, Good Friday, Easter Monday, 1 May, 8 May (Day of Liberation), 7 October (Day of the Republic), 1st and 2nd day of Christmas, Ascension Day, Day of Penitence, Whit-Monday (EG)

s .... Village (BU)

s .... Village, Settlement (RU)

S .... Wetboek van Strafrecht [*Benelux*] (BAS)

S .... Whistle [*Railroads*] (RU)

S2 .... Bangladesh [*Aircraft nationality and registration mark*] (FAAC)

S2A3 .... Southern African Association for the Advancement of Science (EAIO)

S3R .... Societe de Reassurance des Risques Spatiales [*French*]

S7 .... Seychelles [*Aircraft nationality and registration mark*] (FAAC)

S9 .... Sao Tome and Principe [*Aircraft nationality and registration mark*] (FAAC)

SA .... Agricultural Academy (BU)

SA .... Ammunition Depot (RU)

SA .... Djaksa [*Government Prosecuting Attorney*] (IN)

SA .... Power Unit (RU)

Sa .... Saari [*or Saaret*] [*Island or Islands*] [*Finland*] (NAU)

Sa .... Saat [*Hour*] (TU)

Sa .... Sachsen [*Saxony*] [*German*]

Sa .... Saege [*German*]

sa .... Sajto Alatt [*In Press*] (HU)

sa .... Saka [*Jocular*] (TU)

SA .... Salerno [*Car registration plates*] [*Italian*]

SA .... Salgotarjani Acelarugyar [*Salgotarjan Steel Factory*] (HU)

sa .... Sama [*Finland*]

SA .... Samohodna Artiljerija [*Self-Propelled Artillery*] (YU)

sa .... Sans Annee [*Without Year*] [*French*]

SA .... Saterdag [*Saturday*] [*Afrikaans*]

SA .... Saudi Advertising [*Commercial firm*] [*Saudi Arabia*]

SA .... Saudi Arabia [*ANSI two-letter standard code*] (CNC)

SA .... Saunders Aircraft Corp. Ltd. [*Canada ICAO aircraft manufacturer identifier*] (ICAO)

SA .... Scottish Amicable [*Insurance company*]

SA .... Scouts' Association [*Lithuania*] (EAIO)

SA .... Self-Propelled Artillery (RU)

Sa .... Senora [*Mrs., Madam*] [*Spanish*]

sa .... Senz'anno [*Without Year of Publication*] [*Italian*]

SA .... Separatabdruck [*Reprint*] [*German*]

Sa .... Serra [*Mountain Range*] [*Portuguese*] (NAU)

SA .... Service Automobile [*Military*] [*French*] (MTD)

SA .... Service Auxiliaire [*Military*] [*French*] (MTD)

s/a .... Seu Aceite [*His, or Her, Esteemed*] [*Portuguese*]

Sa .... Shima [*Island*] [*Japan*] (NAU)

sa .... Siehe Auch [*See Also*] [*German*] (EG)

Sa .... Sierra [*Mountain Range*] [*Spanish*] (NAU)

SA .... Signaling Device (RU)

sa .... Sin Ano [*Without Year*] [*Publishing*] [*Spanish*]

SA .... Slovenian Association [*Australia*]

SA .... Slovenska Akademija Znanosti in Umetnosti [*Slovenian Academy of Sciences and Arts*] [*Ljubljana*] (YU)

SA .... Sociedad Anonima [*Stock Company*] [*Spanish*]

SA .... Sociedade Anonima [*Stock Company*] [*Portuguese*]

SA .... Societe Anonyme [*Stock Company*] [*French*]

SA .... Societe Asiatique de Paris [*France*] (SLS)

SA .... Society of Allergology [*Former Czechoslovakia*] (EAIO)

SA .... Soil Association [*Bristol, England*] (EAIO)

SA .... Soloists Association [*Denmark*] (EAIO)

SA .... Son Altesse [*His, or Her, Highness*] (CL)

SA .... Sonderabdruck [*Separate Printing*] [*German*]

SA .... Sortie Accumulateur [*French*] (ADPT)

SA .... Sosyete Anonim [*Stock Company*] (TU)

SA .... South Africa (AF)

SA .... South Australia [*State in Australia*] (BARN)

SA .... Southbank Aviation [*Australia*]

SA .... Soviet Archaeology (RU)

SA .... Soviet Arctic (RU)

SA .... Soviet Army (RU)

SA .... Soviet Automatic Coupling (RU)

SA .... Spiritual Assembly of the Baha'is of Argentina (EAIO)

SA .... Spolka Akcyjna [*Company Limited*] [*Poland*]

SA .... Squash Australia

SA .... Srpska Akademija [*Serbian Academy*] (YU)

SA .... Standard Atmosphere (RU)

SA .... Standards Australia

SA .... State Archives [*Australia*]

SA .... Statni Arbitraz [*State Arbitration Office*] (CZ)

SA .... Stichting Agromisa [*Agromisa Foundation*] [*Netherlands*] (EAIO)

SA .... Sturmabteilung [*German*] [*Political party*] (PPE)

SA .... Sua Alteza [*His, or Her, Highness*] [*Portuguese*]

SA .... Sua Altezza [*His, or Her, Highness*] [*Italian*]

SA .... Su Alteza [*His, or Her, Highness*] [*Spanish*]

SA .... Sudamerica [*South America*] [*Spanish*]

SA .... Sudan Airways [*Khartoum*] (MENA)

SA .... Sudanese Army

SA .... Suid-Afrika [*South Africa*] [*Afrikaans*]

SA .... Suid-Amerika [*South America*] [*Afrikaans*]

SA .... Suomen Akatemia [*Finland*] (SLS)

SA .... Suomen Ampumahitoliito [*Biathlon Association*] [*Finland*] (EAIO)

SA .... Svenska Arkivsamfundet [*Swedish Archival Association*] (EAIO)

SA .... Syntactic Analysis (RU)

Sa .... Train Operates Only on Saturday (EG)

SA3TM ...... South African Association for Accident and Traffic Medicine (AA)

SAA .... Saudia Arabia Airlines

SAA .... Saudi Arabian Army (ME)

SA-A .... Scientific Adviser - Army [*Australia*]

SAA .... Scout Association of Argentina (EAIO)

SAA .... Scout Association of Australia

SAA .... Secretaries' Association of Australia

SAA .... Service des Activites Aeriennes [*Aerial Activities Service*] [*French*] (WER)

SAA .... Singapore Aftercare Association

SAA .... Sociedad Argentina de Agronomia [*Argentine Society of Agronomy*] [*Buenos Aires*] (LAA)

SAA .... Sociedad Argentina de Antropologia [*Argentine Anthropological Society*] [*Buenos Aires*] (LAA)

SAA .... Sociedad de Amigos del Arbol [*Panama*] (DSCA)

SAA .... Societe Aefienne d'Assurances

SAA .... Societe Africaine d'Ambulances

SAA .... Societe Agricole de l'Agneby

SAA .... Societe Algerienne d'Assurance

SAA .... Societe Auxiliaire Africaine pour le Developpement du Commerce, de l'Industrie, et de l'Agriculture en Afrique Occidentale

SAA .... South African Airways [*ICAO designator*] (FAAC)

SAA .... South African Alliance (PPW)

SAA .... South African Army

SAA .... South African Artillery

SAA .... South African Aviation Corps

SAA .... South Australia Art [*Gallery*] [*National Union Catalogue of Australia symbol*]

SAA .... South Australian Archives

SAA .... Southern Africa Association [*British*] (EAIO)

SAA .... Spanish Atlantic Association (EAIO)

SAA .... Special Advisory Authority [*Australia*]

SAA .... Sportsmen's [*or Sportswomen's*] Association of Australia (ADA)

SAA .... Standards Association of Australia (BARN)

SAA .... State Aboriginal Affairs [*South Australia*]

SAA .... Swedish Archival Association (EAIO)

SAA .... Syndesmos Apostraton Axiomatikon [*Alliance of Retired Officers*] [*Followed by initial letter of service branch name*] [*Greek*] (GC)

SAA .... Syndicat Agricole Africain

SAA .... Syrian Arab Airlines

SAA .... San Antonio De Areco [*Argentina*] [*ICAO location identifier*] (ICLI)

SAAA........ Sarawak Amateur Athletes Association (ML)

SAAA........ South African Association of Arts

SAAA........ Southern Africa Accounting Association (EAIO)

SAAA........ Southern African Association of Archaeologists (AA)

SAAA........ Sport Aircraft Association of Australia

SAAA....... Sudanese Amateur Athletic Association

SAAAMI ... Southern African Association for the Advancement of Medical Instrumentation (AA)

SAAAPEA ... South African Association Against Painful Experiments on Animals (AA)

SAAAS ...... South African Association for the Advancement of Science

SAAAU ..... South African Amateur Athletic Union

SAAB........ Saudi Arabian Agricultural Bank [*Riyadh*] (MENA)

SAAB........ South African Association of Botanists (AA)

SAAB........ Svenska Aeroplan Aktiebolaget [*Swedish automobile manufacturer; acronym used as name of its cars*]

SAAB........ Syndicat des Agents de l'Administration du Burundi [*Burundi Union of Administrative Employees*] (AF)

SAABA...... South Australian Amateur Basketball Association

SAABED ... Societe Africaine d'Application des Bitumes et Derives

SAABL...... South Australian Amateur Basketball League

SAABMI ... Suider-Afrikaanse Assosiasie vir die Bevordering van Mediese Instrumentasie [*South Africa*] (AA)

SAABU..... South African Amateur Body-Building Union

SAAC........ Concordia/Commodoro Pierrest Egui [*Argentina*] [*ICAO location identifier*] (ICLI)

SAAC........ Societe Africaine d'Automobile et de Courtage

SAAC........ South African Army Corps

SAAC........ South American Athletic Confederation (EAIO)

SAAC......... South Australian Agricultural Consulting [*and Management Company Proprietar y Ltd.*] [*National Union Catalogue of Australia symbol*]
SAAC......... Swiss-American Aircraft Corp. (IAA)
SAACA...... Servicio Agropecuaria Aereo, CA [*Venezuela*] (DSCA)
SAACB...... South African Association of Clinical Biochemists (EAIO)
SAACCA ... South Australian Aboriginal Child Care Agency
Saace......... South African Association for Clinical Engineering (AA)
SAACE...... South African Association for Co-Operative Education (AA)
SAACE...... South African Association of Consulting Engineers
SAACI...... Southern African Association for the Conference Industry (AA)
SAACI...... Syndicat Agricole Africain de la Cote-D'Ivoire
SAAD........ Societe des Amis d'Alexandre Dumas (EA)
SAADCO... Saudi Arabian Agriculture & Dairy Co.
SAAE........ Societe Algerienne d'Accumulateurs Electriques
SAAEB...... South African Atomic Energy Board (AF)
SAAECE ... Southern African Association for Early Childhood Educare (EAIO)
SAAELC.... South Australian Agricultural Equipment Liaison Committee
SAAF........ Saudi Arabian Air Force
SAAF........ South African Air Force (AF)
SAAFA...... South African Air Force Association
SAAFA...... South African Amateur Fencing Association
SAAFA...... Special Arab Aid Fund for Africa
SAAFARI ... South African Airways Fully Automatic Reservations Installations (PDAA)
SAAFL...... South Australian Amateur Football League
SAAFoST .. South African Association for Food Science and Technology (SLS)
SAAG........ Gualeguaychu [*Argentina*] [*ICAO location identifier*] (ICLI)
SAAGA...... South African Avocado Growers' Association (EAIO)
SAAGTC.... South Australian Association for Gifted and Talented Children
SAAGU..... South African Amateur Gymnastics Union
SAAHP...... South African Association for Health Promotion (AA)
SAAI......... Punta Indio [*Argentina*] [*ICAO location identifier*] (ICLI)
SAAI......... Sociedad Argentina de Alergia e Inmunopatologia [*Argentina*] (SLS)
SAAI......... South African Acoustics Institute (EAIO)
SAAIE...... Southern African Association of Industrial Editors (EAIO)
SAAJ........ Junin [*Argentina*] [*ICAO location identifier*] (ICLI)
SAAJA...... South African Amateur Judo Association
SAAK........ Synetairismoi Apokatastaseos Aktimonon Kalliergiton [*Cooperatives for the Rehabilitation of Landless Farm Workers*] [*Greek*] (GC)
SAAKV...... Suid-Afrikaanse Avokadokwekersverening [*South African Avocado Growers Association*] (EAIO)
SAAL........ South Australian Athletic League
SAAL........ Syrian Arab Airlines Limited (ME)
SAALA...... Southern African Applied Linguistics Association (AA)
SAAlAS..... South African Association for Laboratory Animal Science (AA)
SAALED ... Southern African Association for Learning and Educational Disabilities (EAIO)
SAAM....... Mazaruca [*Argentina*] [*ICAO location identifier*] (ICLI)
SAAMA..... South African Agricultural Manufacturers' Association (AA)
SAAMBR .. South African Association for Marine Biological Research
SAAME..... Southern African Association for Medical Education (AA)
SAAMLS... Southern African Association for Movement and Leisure Sciences (EAIO)
SAAMS..... Suid-Afrikaanse Assosiasie vir Massaspektrometrie [*South African Association for Mass Spectrometry*] (AA)
SAAMSAT ... South African Amateur Radio Satellite Association (AA)
SAAN........ Pergamino [*Argentina*] [*ICAO location identifier*] (ICLI)
SAAN........ South African Associated Newspapers
SA & F...... Southern Airlines and Freighters [*Australia*]
SAANDT... South African Association for Non-Destructive Testing (AA)
saann.......... Saannollinen [*Regular*] [*Finland*]
SAANZ...... Sociological Association of Australia and New Zealand (ADA)
SAANZ...... Speleological Association of Australia and New Zealand (ADA)
SAAO .... Societe Auxiliaire d'Afrique Occidentale
SAAO .... South African Astronomical Observatory
SAAOC..... Saudi Arabia Army Ordnance Corps
SAAOT...... South African Association of Occupational Therapists (EAIO)
SAAP......... Parana/Gral Urquiza [*Argentina*] [*ICAO location identifier*] (ICLI)
SAAP........ Sociedad Argentina de Artes Plasticas [*Argentine Society of Plastic Arts*] (LA)
SAAP........ South Australian Adoption Panel
SAAP........ Suid-Afrikaanse Arbeiders-Party [*South African Labor Party*] [*Afrikaans*]
SAAP........ Supported Accommodation Assistance Program [*Australia*]
SAAPBS.... South Australian Association of Permanent Building Societies
SAAPC ...... Sudanese Animal & Agricultural Production Company
SAAPMB .. South African Association of Physicists in Medicine and Biology (EAIO)
SAAPPA.... South African Apple and Pear Producers' Association (AA)

SAAPPV.... Suid-Afrikaanse Appel en Peerprodusentevereniging [*South Africa*] (AA)
SAAPS....... South African Association of Paediatric Surgeons (EAIO)
SAAPSA.... South Australian Apple and Pear Shippers' Association
SAAR........ Rosario [*Argentina*] [*ICAO location identifier*] (ICLI)
SAAR........ Societe Africaine des Artisans Reunis
SAARA...... South African Angora Rabbits Breeders' Association (AA)
SAARBS.... South African Angora Ram Breeders' Society
SAARC...... South Asian Association for Regional Cooperation
SAARDT... South African Amateur Radio Development Trust (AA)
SAARDT ... Syndicat Autonome des Agents de la Radiodiffusion du Togo [*Autonomous Union of Radiobroadcasting Workers of Togo*]
SAARET ... South African Association for Registerable Engineering Technologists
SAARIT .... Suid-Afrikaanse Assosiasie van Registreerbare Ingenieurstegnoloe [*South African Association of Registrable Engineering Technologists*] (AA)
SAAROS ... Suid-Afrikaanse Amateur Radio Ontwikkelings Stigting [*South African Amateur Radio Development Trust*] (AA)
SAARP...... South African Association of Retired Persons and Pensioners (AA)
SAARU...... South African Amateur Rowing Union
SAAS........ South African Archaeological Society (SLS)
SAAS........ South African Association for Stuttering (AA)
SAASC...... Soviet Afro-Asian Solidarity Committee
SAASigs .... South African Army Signals
SAASPER ... South African Association for Sport Science, Physical Education, and Recreation (AA)
SAASRA ... South Australian Aboriginal Sports and Recreation Association
SAASS...... South African Aloe and Succulent Society (AA)
SAATC...... Southern African Air Transport Council
SAATE ..... South Australian Association for the Teaching of English
SAATU..... South African Amateur Trampoline Union
SAATVE ... South African Association for Technical and Vocational Education (SLS)
SAAU .... South African Agricultural Union
SAAU .... South African Artistes United
SAAU .... South African Athletic Union
SAAU .... Villaguay [*Argentina*] [*ICAO location identifier*] (ICLI)
SAAUW .... South African Association of University Women (EAIO)
SAAV........ Santa Fe/Sauce Viejo [*Argentina*] [*ICAO location identifier*] (ICLI)
SAAVV...... Suid-Afrikaanse Aalwyn- en Vetplantvereniging [*South African Aloe and Succulent Society*] (AA)
SAAWF ..... South African Amateur Wrestling Federation
SAAWPA .. South Australian Amateur Water Polo Association
SAAWU .... South African Allied Workers Union (AF)
SAAWU .... South African Amateur Weight-Lifting Union
SAB........... Air-Dropped Parachute Flare (BU)
SAB........... Illuminating Aerial Bomb (RU)
SAB........... Saba [*Netherlands Antilles*] [*Airport symbol*] (OAG)
sab............. Sabado [*Saturday*] [*Spanish*]
SAB........... SABENA [*Societe Anonyme Belge d'Exploitation de la Nav Aerienne*] [*Belgium*] [*ICAO designator*] (FAAC)
SAB........... Saiuz na Artistite v Balgaria [*Union of Bulgarian Actors*] (EAIO)
SAB........... Scout Association of Belize (EAIO)
SAB........... Self-Propelled Artillery Brigade (RU)
SAB........... Singapore Armoured Brigade (ML)
SAB........... Sociedad Argentina de Biologia [*Argentine Biological Society*] [*Buenos Aires*] (LAA)
SAB........... Sociedad Arqueologica de Bolivia [*Archaeological Society of Bolivia*] [*La Paz*] (LAA)
SAB........... Societe Africaine de Bonneterie
SAB........... Societe Africaine des Bois
SAB........... Societe Anonyme Belge pour le Commerce du Haut-Congo
SAB........... Societe des Allumettes du Benin
SAB........... Society of Applied Botany [*Germany*] (EAIO)
SAB........... South African Bond
SAB........... South African Breweries
SAB........... South Australian Brewing
SAB........... Staf Angkatan Bersendjata [*Armed Forces Staff*] (IN)
SAB........... Sveriges Allmaenn Biblioteksfoerening [*Sweden*] (SLS)
SAB........... Svetleca Aviobomba [*Flare Aerial Bomb*] (YU)
SABA........ Buenos Aires [*Argentina*] [*ICAO location identifier*] (ICLI)
SABA........ Societe Abidjanaise de Batiment
SABA........ Societe Agricole Bananiere de l'Agneby
SABA........ Societe Anonyme des Barytes Algeriennes
SABA........ South African Black Alliance [*Political party*] (PPW)
SABA........ South African Brick Association (PDAA)
SABA........ South Australian Badminton Association
SABA........ South Australian Bowling Association
SABAIC..... Societe Anonyme de Batiments Ivoiro-Celtique
SABAM..... Societe Belge des Auteurs, Compositeurs, et Editeurs [*Belgium*] (SLS)

SABAP ...... Southern African Bird Atlas Project [*South Africa*] [*Research center*] (IRC)
SABC......... Buenos Aires (Edificio Condor) [*Argentina*] [*ICAO location identifier*] (ICLI)
SABC......... Societe Anonyme des Brasseries du Cameroun [*Cameroon Brewery Company*] (AF)
SABC......... South Africa Broadcasting Corporation (AF)
SABC......... South African Broadcasting Corp.
SABC......... South Australia Brewing Co. [*Commercial firm*]
SABCA ...... Societe Anonyme Belge de Constructions Aeronautiques [*Belgium*] (PDAA)
SABCI .... Societe d'Application des Bois a la Construction et a l'Industrie en Cote-D'Ivoire
SABDN...... Societe Agricole et Bananiere de Divo Nord
SABDR...... South Australian Birth Defects Registry
SABE......... Buenos Aires/Aeroparque, Jorge Newbery [*Argentina*] [*ICAO location identifier*] (ICLI)
SABE......... Societe Africaine de Beton Equatoriaux
SABE......... Societe Africaine des Bois de l'Est
SABE......... Societe Africaine des Bois Equatoriaux
SABE......... Societe Africaine d'Exploitation des Brevets "Eries"
SABEA ...... Societa Alimentari Bevande e Affini [*Italy*] (PDAA)
SABEK ...... Suid-Afrikaanse Besigheidkamer [*South Africa*] (AA)
SABENA ... Societe Anonyme Belge d'Exploitation de la Navigation Aerienne [*Belgian World Airlines*] [*Facetious translation: Such a Bad Experience, Never Again*]
SABET ...... Scottish Association for Building Education and Training (SLS)
SABEX ...... Societe Abidjanaise d'Expertises
SABF .... South African Brandy Foundation (EAIO)
SABF .... Syrian Arab Badminton Federation (EAIO)
SABH .... South Australian Brewing Holdings [*Commercial firm*]
SABI .... Societe Africaine de Biscuiterie
SABI .... Societe Africaine de Bordelaise Industrielle [*Morocco*]
SABI .... Suid-Afrikaanse Brandweerinstituut [*South Africa*] (AA)
SABIC .... Saudi Basic Industries Corporation [*Riyadh*] (MENA)
SABIC .... Societe Africaine des Bois Industrielle et Commerciale
SABIMA ... Societe Abidjanaise d'Importation de Materiel Industriel
SABIMET ... Sociedad Abastecedora de la Industria Metalurgica [*Chile*] (LAA)
SABINE .... Systeme d'Acces a la Banque Informatique des Nomenclatures Europeennes [*Database*] [*EC*] (ECED)
SABISA..... South African Building Interior Systems Association (AA)
SABITA..... Southern African Bitumen and Tar Association (AA)
SABL......... Societe des Sciences, Arts, et Belles-Lettres de Bayeux [*France*] (SLS)
SABL......... South Australian Bookmakers' League
SABLI........ Societe Agro-Animale Benino-Arabe-Libyenne
Sablre......... Sabliere [*Sand Pit*] [*Military map abbreviation World War I*] [*French*] (MTD)
SABM........ Buenos Aires (Servicio Meteorologico Nacional) [*Argentina*] [*ICAO location identifier*] (ICLI)
SABM........ Societe Africaine de Beton Manufacture
SABM........ Societe Africaine des Bois du M'bam
SABO .... Societe Agricole d'Abobo
SABOA...... Southern African Bus Operators Association (AA)
SABOGAB ... Societe Anonyme des Bois du Gabon
sabr .... Self-Propelled Artillery Brigade (RU)
SABRA ...... Suid-Afrikaanse Bureau vir Rasse Aangeleenthede [*South African Bureau of Racial Affairs*]
SABRAO... Society for the Advancement of Breeding Researches in Asia and Oceania (ADA)
SABRE ...... Sweden and Britain RADAR Auroral Experiment [*Ionospheric physics*]
SABRE ...... System for Autonomous Bodies Reporting and Evaluation [*Joint project of the Government of Bangladesh and United Nations Department of Technical Co-operation for Development*] [*Information service or system*]
SABRI .... Serikat Buruh Rokok Indonesia [*Cigarette Workers' Union of Indonesia*]
SABS .... Congregation of the Sisters of the Adoration of the Blessed Sacrament [*Kerala, India*] (EAIO)
SABS .... Senior [*Secondary*] Assessment Board of South Australia [*National Union Catalogue of Australia symbol*]
SABS .... Suid-Afrikaanse Buro vir Standaarde [*South African Bureau of Standards*]
SABSA ...... South African Billiards and Snooker Association
SABSA ...... South Australian Brake Specialist Association
SABSWA .. South African Black Social Workers Association (AF)
SABTA ...... South African Bitumen and Tar Association (AA)
SABTA ...... South African Black Taxi Association (AA)
SABTA ...... South African Bus and Taxi Association
SABTP .... Societe Africaine de Batiments et de Travaux Publics
SABTS....... South African Blood Transfusion Service
SABU......... South Africa Badminton Union (EAIO)
SABV .... Suid-Afrikaanse Bybelvereniging
SABV-CP .. Societe Africaine de Betail et Viande, Cuirs, et Peaux

SAC........... Missionary Sisters of the Catholic Apostolate [*Italy*] (EAIO)
sac .... Sacerdote [*Priest*] [*Portuguese*]
SAC........... Saint Aloysius College [*Australia*] (ADA)
SAC........... Schweizer Alpen Club [*Swiss Alpine Club*]
SAC........... Scientific Advisory Council to the Prime Minister
SAC........... Service d'Action Civique [*Civic Action Service*] [*French*] (WER)
SAC........... Servicio de Asesoramiento Ciudadano [*Civic Advisory Service*] [*Spanish*] (WER)
SAC........... Singapore Arts Council (EAIO)
SAC........... Sociedad Argentina de Criminologia [*Argentine Criminological Society*] [*Buenos Aires*] (LAA)
SAC........... Sociedad de Agricultores de Colombia [*Farmers Association of Colombia*] (LA)
SAC........... Societe Africaine de Chaussures
SAC........... Societe Africaine de Confection
SAC........... Societe Africaine de Constructions
SAC........... Societe Africaine de Culture
SAC........... Societe Agricole Constant et Compagnie
SAC........... Societe d'Achat et de Commission
SAC........... Societe d'Action Coloniale
SAC........... Societe d'Action Cooperative avec les Territoires d'Outre-Mer
SAC........... Societe d'Assistance Comptable
SAC........... Society of African Culture [*France*] (EAIO)
SAC........... South African College
SAC........... South Australian Club
SAC........... Southern Africa Committee
SAC........... Space Activities Commission [*Japan*]
SAC........... Space Applications Centre [*Indian Space Research Organization*] [*Research center*] (ERC)
SAC........... Sport for All Clearinghouse [*Belgium*] (EAIO)
SAC........... Standing Armaments Committee [*NATO*] (NATG)
SAC........... Starptautiskas Apmainas Centrs [*International Exchange Center*] [*Latvia*] (EAIO)
SAC........... State Aboriginal Council [*Australia*]
SAC........... Structural Adjustment Committee [*Commonwealth Cabinet*] [*Australia*]
SAC........... Student Access Centre [*Australia*]
SAC........... Sudan Air Cargo
SAC........... Sudanese Aeronautical Services Co. Ltd. [*Sudan*] [*ICAO designator*] (FAAC)
SAC........... Sudanese African Congress [*Political party*] (MENA)
SAC........... Sudania Aviation Co. [*Sudan*] [*ICAO designator*] (FAAC)
SAC........... Sugar Association of the Caribbean [*Port Of Spain, Trinidad*] (EAIO)
SAC........... Suore Missionarie dell'Apostolato Cattolico [*Missionary Sisters of the Catholic Apostolate*] [*Rome, Italy*] (EAIO)
SAC........... Supreme Agricultural Council
SAC........... Sveriges Arbetares Central-Organisation [*Central Organization of Swedish Workers*] (WEN)
SAC........... Swiss Aero Club (EAIO)
SAC........... Sydney Airport Centre [*Australia*]
SACA........ Cordoba/Area de Material [*Argentina*] [*ICAO location identifier*] (ICLI)
SACA........ Societa per Azioni Costruzioni Aeronavali [*Italy*] (PDAA)
SACA........ Societe Agricole de Cote-d'Afrique
SACA........ Societe Anonyme Commerciale Agricole [*Paris Representantes Bogota*] (COL)
SACA........ Societe Auxiliaire de Commerce Africain
SACA........ Societe des Automobiles de la Cote-d'Afrique
SACA........ South African Council for Architects (AA)
SACA........ South African Cricket Association
SACA........ South Australian Canine Association
SACA........ South Australian Council on the Ageing
SACAA...... South African Coal Ash Association (AA)
SACAB ..... Scandinavian Aircraft Construction AB [*Sweden*]
SACAB ..... Societe Anonyme Camerounaise de Bonneterie
SACAC...... South African Council for Automation and Computation (SLS)
SACAE ..... South Australian College of Advanced Education (PDAA)
SACAF ...... Societe Anonyme de Constructions en Afrique
SACAF ...... Societe Centrafricaine du Sac
SACAM..... Societe Africaine de Carreaux Agglomeres de Marbre
SACAM..... Societe Agricole du Cameroun
SACAM..... South Australian Committee on Access and Mobility
SACANGO ... Southern Africa Committee on Air Navigation and Ground Operation
SACAPH... Societe Agricole des Caoutchoucs d'Anphu-Ha
SACAR...... Societe Abidjanaise de Carrelage
SACB........ South African Cricket Board
SACB........ South African Criminal Bureau
SACBA ..... South Australian Cat Breeders' Association
SACBC ...... South Australian Children's Ballet Company
SACBC ...... Southern Africa Catholic Bishops' Conference
SACBC ...... Southern African Catholic Bishops' Conference (EAIO)
SACBC-JPC ... Southern African Catholic Bishops' Conference - Justice and Peace Commission (EAIO)
SACBS....... South Australian Cell Biology Society

SACBTP.... Societe Africaine de Construction de Batiments et Travaux Publics
SACC......... La Cumbre [*Argentina*] [*ICAO location identifier*] (ICLI)
SACC......... Societe Anonyme Camerounaise de Chaussures et Valises
SACC......... Societe Artisanale Camerounaise de Chaussures
SACC......... South African Council of Churches (AF)
SACC......... South Australian Council of Churches
SACCA...... Servicio Agronomico de los Cultivadores de Cana de Azucar [*Venezuela*] (DSCA)
SACCAM.. Societe Artisanale des Coutures Camerounaises
SACCAP ... South African Council for Conservation and Anti-Pollution (AA)
SACCAR ... Southern African Centre for Co-Operation in Agricultural Research (EY)
SACCB ...... Societe Anonyme des Cultures au Congo Belge
SACCI .... South African Council of Civil Investigators (AA)
SACCI .... Swiss-Australian Chamber of Commerce and Industry [*Australia*]
SACCIE..... Societe Algerienne de Commission, Consignation, Courtage d'Import-Export
SACCS ...... Shipping and Air Cargo Commodity Statistics [*Australia*]
SACD........ Coronel Olmedo [*Argentina*] [*ICAO location identifier*] (ICLI)
SACD........ Societe des Auteurs et Compositeurs Dramatiques [*Society of Dramatic Authors and Composers*] [*Paris, France*] (EAIO)
SACD........ South African Container Depot (DS)
SACDA...... South African Copper Development Association
SACDC...... South African Coastal Defence Corps
SACE........ Cordoba [*Argentina*] [*ICAO location identifier*] (ICLI)
SACE........ Sezione Special per l'Assicurazione del Credito all'Exportazione [*Export credit agency*] [*Italian*]
SACE........ Social and Cultural Education [*Northern Territory, Australia*]
SACE........ Sociedad de Amistad Cubana-Espanola [*Spanish-Cuban Friendship Society*] (LA)
SACE........ South Australian Certificate of Education
SACE........ South Australian Christian Education [*Anglican Board of Christian Education*]
SACE........ South Australian College of English
SACEC...... Societe Africaine de Cooperation Economique [*Senegal*]
SACEG...... Societe Africaine de Constructions et d'Entreprises Generales
SACEL ...... Societe Anonyme Camerounaise d'Electronique
SACEM..... Societe Anonyme Cherifienne d'Etudes Minieres [*Moroccan Mining Studies Corporation*] (AF)
SACEM..... Societe des Auteurs, Compositeurs, et Editeurs de Musique [*Society of Authors, Composers, and Music Publishers*] [*French*] (WER)
SACER...... Servicio de Asesoramiento, Clinica, y Extension Rural [*Argentina*] (LAA)
SACER...... Societe Africaine de Commerce et de Representation
SACER...... Societe Africaine de Constructions Economiques et Rapides
SACES....... South Australian College of External Studies (ADA)
SACEUR ... Supreme Allied Commander, Europe [*NATO*]
SACEUREP ... Supreme Allied Commander, Europe Representative [*NATO*] (NATG)
SACF........ Cordoba [*Argentina*] [*ICAO location identifier*] (ICLI)
SACF........ Sociedad Argentina de Ciencias Fisiologicas [*Argentina*] (SLS)
SACF........ South African Canoe Federation
SACF........ South Australian Cycling Federation
SACFA...... South Australian Canning Fruitgrowers' Association
SACFER.... Societe Africaine de Construction et de Fabrication d'Engins Roulants
SACFM ..... South Australian Centre for Manufacturing
SACFS....... South Australian Country Fire Service
SACFVI..... South Australian Chamber of Fruit and Vegetable Industries
SACG........ Cordoba [*Argentina*] [*ICAO location identifier*] (ICLI)
SACG........ Societe d'Alimentation et de Commerce Generale
SACH .... Sociedad Agronomica de Chile [*Agronomical Society of Chile*] (LAA)
SACHD ..... South Australian Centre for Human Development
sachl.......... Saechlich [*German*]
Sachs.......... Saechsisch [*Saxon*] [*German*]
Sachv......... Sachverstaendiger [*German*]
Sachw........ Sachwalter [*German*]
SACI.......... Andre Pagliano et Cie., Societe Africaine de Commission et d'Importation
SACI.......... Pilar [*Argentina*] [*ICAO location identifier*] (ICLI)
SACI.......... Societe Africaine de Commerce et d'Industrie [*African Trade and Industry Company*] [*Ivory Coast*] (AF)
SACI.......... Societe Auxiliaire de Constructions Immobilieres
SACI.......... [*The*] South African Chemical Institute (SLS)
SACI.......... State Administration of Commodity Inspection [*China*]
SACI.......... Suid-Afrikaanse Chemiese Instituut [*South African Chemical Institute*] (AA)
SACIA .... Societe Africaine pour le Commerce, l'Industrie, et l'Agriculture
SACIA .... Societe Agricole, Commerciale, et Industrielle de l'Agneby
SACIA .... Societe Auxiliaire du Commerce et de l'Industrie en Afrique

SACIACI... Societe Africaine Commerciale, Industrielle, et Agricole de Cote-D'Ivoire
SACIET..... Societe Africaine de Commerce, Import, Export, Transport
SACIL .... Sociedade Agricola & Comercial (Imala) Limitada
SACIM...... Society in Aid of Children Inoperable in their Motherland [*Australia*]
SACIM...... Southern African Center for Ivory Marketing
SACIN....... South Australian Curriculum Network
SACJK...... Societe Africaine des Comptoirs J. A. Klein
SACK........ Scientific Advisory Committee on Kangaroos [*Australia*]
SACL........ Laguna Larga [*Argentina*] [*ICAO location identifier*] (ICLI)
SACL........ South African Confederation of Labor (AF)
SACL........ South Australian [*National*] Acoustic Laboratories [*National Union Catalogue of Australia symbol*]
SACLA ...... South African Computer Lecturers' Association (AA)
SACLA ...... South African Confederation of Labour
SACLANT ... Supreme Allied Atlantic Command (WER)
SACLANT ... Supreme Allied Commander, Atlantic [*NATO*]
SACLANTCEN ... Saclant Anti-Submarine Warfare Research Centre [*La Spezia*] [*Italian*] [*Research center*] (ERC)
SACLANTCEN ... Supreme Allied Atlantic Command Anti-Submarine Warfare Research Centre [*NATO*] [*Italy*]
SACLANTCEN ... Supreme Allied Commander, Atlantic, Antisubmarine Warfare Research Center [*NATO*]
SACLANTREPEUR ... Supreme Allied Commander, Atlantic, Representative in Europe [*NATO*]
SACLAU ... SACLANT [*Supreme Allied Commander, Atlantic*] Authentification System [*NATO*] (NATG)
SACLEX.... SACLANT [*Supreme Allied Commander, Atlantic*] Standing Exercise Orders [*NATO*] (NATG)
SACM........ Societe Abidjanaise de Constructions Mecaniques
SACM........ Societe Africaine de Constructions Metalliques
SACM........ Societe Alsacienne de Constructions Mecaniques
SACM........ Societe Anonyme de Confection Malgache
SACM........ South Arabian Common Market
SACM........ South Australian Centre for Manufacturing [*National Union Catalogue of Australia symbol*]
SACM........ Villa Gral, Mitre [*Argentina*] [*ICAO location identifier*] (ICLI)
SACMC..... South Australian Chicken Meat Council
SACME..... South Australian Chamber of Mines and Energy
SACN .... Ascochinga [*Argentina*] [*ICAO location identifier*] (ICLI)
SACNA...... South African Citrus Nurserymen's Association (AA)
SACNA...... South African Clinical Neuropsychological Association (AA)
SACNA...... South African Club of North America
SACNSW .. Society for Arts and Crafts New South Wales [*Australia*]
SACO .... Cordoba [*Argentina*] [*ICAO location identifier*] (ICLI)
SACO .... Service Administratif Canadien Outre-Mer
SACO .... Servicio Aereo Colombiano [*Colorado*]
SACO .... Societe Abidjanaise de Construction
SACO .... Societe Africaine de Cacao
SACO .... Societe Africaine de Commerce
SACO .... Societe Anonyme de la Carrosserie d'Oloumi
SACO .... Sveriges Akademikers Central-Organisation [*Swedish Confederation of Professional Associations*] (WEN)
SACO .... Swedish Confederation of Professional Associations (EAIO)
SACOB...... South African Chamber of Business (AA)
SACOCI .... Societe Africaine de Commerce et d'Industrie en Cote-D'Ivoire
SACOD ..... Societe Anonyme de Commercialisation d'Or et de Diamants
SACOD ..... South African Congress of Democrats
SACOL...... South African Confederation of Labour
SACOM .... Societe Agricole et Commerciale de la Mananjeba
SACOM .... Societe Anonyme Cherifienne d'Organisation Moderne [*Morocco*]
SACOMAIT ... Societe Algerienne de Construction, de Materiel Agricole Industriel, et de Travaux Publics [*Algerian Construction, Agricultural and Industrial Equipment, and Public Works Company*] (AF)
SACOMAT ... Societe Africaine de Construction et Materiaux
SACOME ... Societe Africaine de Constructions Metalliques et d'Entreprise
SACOMI... Societe Africaine de Commerce et d'Industrie
SACOMINE ... Societe Agricole, Commerciale, et Miniere
SACOMM ... Southern African Communication Association (AA)
SACON ..... SACON [*Technical Library*] [*National Union Catalogue of Australia symbol*]
SACOOP... Sociedad Auxiliadora de Cooperativas [*Cooperatives Assistance Agency*] [*Chile*] (LA)
SACOPECA ... Salazones y Conservas de Pescado CA [*Venezuela*] (DSCA)
SACOPS.... Societa Anonima Case Operaie Petrolibia Silca
SACOR...... Sociedad Agricola CORFO [*Corporacion de Fomento a la Produccion*] [*Chile*] (LAA)
SACOR...... Sociedad Concessionaria de Rafinacao de Petroleos em Portugal
SACORRI ... South African Corrosion Institute (AA)
SACOS...... South African Council for Sport (AF)
SACOS...... State Assurance Corp. of Seychelles (EY)
SACOTA ... South Australian Council on the Ageing
SACOTRA ... Societe Africaine de Consignation et de Transit

SACOTRAPDA ... Societe Arabe pour le Commerce, le Transport Public, et le Developpement Agricole
SACP .... Chepes [*Argentina*] [*ICAO location identifier*]   (ICLI)
SACP .... South Africa Communist Party   (AF)
SACP .... State Administration of Commodity Prices [*Chinese*]   (GEA)
SACP .... Systeme d'Armes Courte Portee [*Short-Range Weapons System*] [*French*]   (WER)
SACPA ...... South African Cement Producers Association   (AA)
SACPAC ... South African Co-Ordinating Performing Arts Council
SACPE ...... South African Council for Professional Engineers
SACPO ...... South African Coloured People's Organization
SACPS ...... South African Coal Processing Society   (AA)
SACQ .... Monte Quemado [*Argentina*] [*ICAO location identifier*]   (ICLI)
SACRA ...... Societe Africaine de Courtage et de Representation d'Assurances
SACRA ...... Societe Nord Africaine de Construction et de Representation Agricole et Mecanique
SACRS ...... South African Crystallographic Society   (AA)
SACS .... Sino-American Cultural Society   (SLS)
SACS .... Societe Agricole et Commerciale de la Sangha
SACS .... South African Ceramic Society   (EAIO)
SACS .... South African College School
SACS .... South African Corps of Signals
SACS .... Villa De Soto [*Argentina*] [*ICAO location identifier*]   (ICLI)
SACSA ...... South African Conservative Students Association   (AF)
SACSA ...... Standing Advisory Committee for Scientific Advice [*Oslo Commission*]   (DCTA)
SACSDAC ... South Australian Conference of the Seventh-Day Adventist Church
SACSEA .... Supreme Allied Command, South-East Asia [*Australia*]   (ADA)
SACSIR ..... South African Council for Scientific and Industrial Research
SACSJ .... Student and Academic Campaign for Soviet Jewry
SACSOS .... South Australian Coloured Sheep Owners Society
SACSS .... South Australian Council of Social Service
SACSS .... Staff Association of Catholic Secondary Schools [*Australia*]
SACSSR .... Svaz Architektu Ceskoslovenske Socialisticke Republiky [*Union of Architects of the Czechoslovak Socialist Republic*]   (CZ)
SACT .... Gobernador Gordillo [*Argentina*] [*ICAO location identifier*]   (ICLI)
SACT .... Societe Africaine de Commerce et de Transports
SACT .... Societe Algerienne de Construction Telephonique
SACTA ...... Societe Agricole de Collecte de Tabac
SACTU ...... South African Congress of Trade Unions   (AF)
SACTW ..... South African Council of Transport Workers   (AF)
SACU .... Cordoba [*Argentina*] [*ICAO location identifier*]   (ICLI)
SACU .... Sociedad de Avicultores y Cunicultores del Uruguay [*Uruguay*]   (DSCA)
SACU .... Society for Anglo-Chinese Understanding [*British*]   (EAIO)
SACU .... South African Cricket Union
SACU .... South African Customs Union
SACUA ...... Southern African Customs Union Agreement
SACUGS ... South African Committee for the International Union of Geological Sciences   (AA)
SACV .... Villa Maria Del Rio Seco [*Argentina*] [*ICAO location identifier*]   (ICLI)
SACW .... South Australian Creative Workshops
SACY .... Societe Anonyme des Anciens Ets. Cauvin-Yvose
SAD .... Composite Air Division   (RU)
sad .... Composite Aviation Division   (BU)
SAD .... Dubai Insurance Co. [*United Arab Emirates*]   (MENA)
SAD .... Schweizerischer Aufklaerungsdienst [*Swiss Intelligence Service*]   (WEN)
SAD .... Self-Propelled Artillery Battalion   (RU)
SAD .... Servicios Aereos de La Capital [*Colombia*] [*ICAO designator*]   (FAAC)
SAD .... Servicos de Accao Directa [*Services for Direct Action*] [*Portuguese*]   (WER)
SAD .... Single Administrative Document [*European trade contract*] [*1986*]   (DCTA)
SAD .... Sistema Automatizado de Direccion [*Automated Data Addressing System*] [*Cuba*]   (LA)
SAD .... Sjedinjene Americke Drzave [*United States of America*]   (YU)
SAD .... Societe Africaine de Detergents
SAD .... Societe Africaine de Domiciliation
SAD .... Societe Agricole de Diby
SAD .... Societe des Artistes Decorateurs [*French*]   (SLS)
SAD .... South Australia - Department [*of Primary Industries*] [*Agriculture Library*]
SAD .... Sowjetische Administration Deutschlands [*Soviet Administration of Germany*]   (EG)
SAD .... Spanish Academy of Dermatology   (EAIO)
SAD .... Spolecnost Antonina Dvoraka [*Antonin Dvorak Society*]   (CZ)
SAD .... Swedish Association of Dietitians   (EAIO)
SAD .... Swedish Association of Dyers   (EAIO)
SAD .... Systems Assessment Division [*Weapons Research Establishment*] [*Australia*]

SADA .... Sendikalararasi Dayanisma Konseyini [*Inter-Union Solidarity Council*]   (TU)
SADA .... Servico de Apoio e Desenvolvimento Agrario [*Service for Agrarian Support and Development*] [*Portuguese*]   (WER)
SADA .... Sinai Arastirma Danisma Ajansi [*Industrial Research Advisory Agency*] [*Ankara*]   (TU)
SADA .... Sociedad Argentina de Apicultores [*Argentina*]   (LAA)
SADA .... Societe Agricole d'Ampombilawa
SADA .... Sortie Acces Direct Aleatoire [*German*]   (ADPT)
SADA .... South African Diabetes Association   (EAIO)
SADA .... South Australian Darts Association
SADA .... South Australian Debating Association
SADAB ...... Societe Africaine des Automobiles M. Berliet
SADACEB ... Societe Anonyme des Anciens Chantiers d'Entreprise Borsetti
SADACEM ... Applications de la Chime de l'Electricite et des Metaux SA [*Belgium*]
SADAEA ... Societe Anonyme des Anciens Etablissements Amouroux
SADAF ...... Saudi Petrochemical Co.
SADAF ...... Sociedad Argentina de Analisis Filosofico [*Argentine Society of Philosophical Analysis*]   (EAIO)
SADAIC .... Sociedad Argentina de Autores, Interpretes, y Compositores de Musica [*Argentine Society of Songwriters, Singers, and Composers*]   (LA)
SADAMI ... Service Auxiliaire de l'Assistance Medicale aux Indigenes
SADAPE ... Sociedad Anonima de Aplicaciones Electronicas [*Colombia*]   (COL)
SADAR ...... Societe Anonyme d'Appareillage Radioelectrique [*France*]   (PDAA)
SADARET ... Societe Anglaise d'Etudes et de Realisations d'Energie et de Telecommunications
SADAS ...... Syllogos Architktonon Diplomatouchon Anotaton Scholon [*Greek*]   (SLS)
SADBA ...... South Australian Deer Breeders' Association
SADC .... Adelaide Medical Centre for Women and Children - Medical Library [*National Union Catalogue of Australia symbol*]
SADC .... Singapore Air Defence Command   (ML)
SADC .... Sociedad Agraria Departamental del Cuzco [*Peru*]   (DSCA)
SADC .... Southern African Development Community   (ECON)
SADCA ...... Societe Anonyme des Conserves Alimentaires [*Tunisia*]
SADCA ...... South African Defence Campaign of Australia
SADCC ...... South African Development Coordination Committee [*Australia*]
SADCC ...... Southern African Development Coordination Committee
SADCC ...... Southern African Development Co-Ordination Conference [*Gaborone, Botswana*] [*Formed in 1979*]
SADCOP ... Petroleum Products Distribution Organization [*Syria*]   (ME)
SADD .... Buenos Aires/Don Torcuato [*Argentina*] [*ICAO location identifier*]   (ICLI)
SADE .... Services, Agriculture, Developpement, Elevage
SADE .... Sociedad Argentina de Escritores [*Argentine Writers Association*]   (LA)
SADE .... Suramericana de Electrificacion [*Colombia*]   (COL)
SADEC ...... Societe Africaine d'Etudes et Constructions
SADEC ...... Societe Auxiliaire d'Entreprises de Constructions en Afrique
SADEC ...... South Australian Development Education Centre   (EAIO)
SADEC-CI ... Societe Auxiliaire d'Entreprises de Constructions en Cote-D'Ivoire
SADECHaute-Volta ... Societe Auxiliaire d'Entreprises de Constructions en Haute-Volta
SADECO ... Seychelles Agricultural Development Company   (GEA)
SADECO ... Societe Africaine pour le Developpement du Commerce
SADELCA ... Sociedad Aerea del Caqueta [*Airline*] [*Colombia*]
SADEM ..... Sindicato Argentino de Musicos [*Musicians' Union of Argentina*]   (EAIO)
SADEM ..... Societe Africaine des Eaux Minerales
SADEMI ... Sociedad Abastecedora de la Mineria [*Mining Supply Company*] [*Chile*]   (LA)
SADEO ..... Synergazomenoi Agonistikoi Dimokratikoi Organismoi Ergazomenon [*Cooperating Democratic Militant Workers and Employee Organizations*]   (GC)
SADER ...... Societe Africaine de Deroulage des Etablissements Fils
SADER ...... Societe d'Amenagement et du Developpement Regional du Gharb
SADEVO ... Societe Nationale d'Amenagement et de Developpement de la Vallee de l'Oueme
SADEYA ... Sociedad Astronomica de Espana y America [*Hispano-American Astronomical Society*]   (EAIO)
SADF .... San Fernando [*Argentina*] [*ICAO location identifier*]   (ICLI)
SADF .... South African Defense Forces   (AF)
SADFA ...... South African Dyers' and Finishers' Association   (AA)
SADG .... Monte Grande [*Argentina*] [*ICAO location identifier*]   (ICLI)
SADG .... Societe des Architectes Diplomes par le Gouvernement [*French*]   (SLS)
SADHEA .. South African Dietetics and Home Economics Association   (AA)
SADI .... Saratov Highway Institute   (RU)

SADI......... Service d'Approvisionnement et de Distribution des Produits Importes [*Imports Distribution and Supply Department*] [*Subsidiary of OROC--replaced by EPS Cambodia*]   (CL)
SADI......... Societe Africaine de Developpement Industriel
SADIA...... Societe Africaine de Diffusion Industrielle et Automobile
SADIA....... Societe Auxiliaire de l'Industrie de l'Azote [*France*]   (DSCA)
SADIAMIL ... Societe Africaine du Developpement de l'Industrie Alimentaire du Millet et du Sorgho [*African Society for the Development of the Millet- and Sorghum-Based Food Industry*]   (AF)
SADIC....... Societe Anonyme pour le Developpement Interieur Commercial et Industriel
SADICO.... Societe Africaine de Diffusion de Cosmetiques
SADICOM ... Distribuidora Comercial SA [*Colombia*]   (COL)
SADIF....... Societe Africaine de Diffusion
SADIH...... Societe Algerienne pour le Developpement de l'Industrie Hoteliere et Touristique
SADIKS..... Soviet Association of Friendship and Cultural Cooperation with the Countries of Latin America   (RU)
SADIL....... Sociedad Anonima e Industrias Laneras [*Uruguay*]   (DSCA)
SADIM...... Societe Anonyme pour le Developpment Immobilier de Monaco   (PDAA)
SADIN...... Societe Africaine de Distillation Industrielle [*Morocco*]
SADIO....... Sociedad Argentina de Investigacion Operativa [*Argentina*]   (SLS)
SADIS ...... Southern African Documentation and Information System   (PDAA)
SADITA .... Societe Africaine d'Importation et de Distribution de Tabacs et Articles Divers
SADITEX ... Societe d'Approvisionnement et de Distribution Textiles
SADITEX-Mauritanie ... Societe Mauritanienne d'Approvisionnement et de Distribution Textiles
SADIVOIRE ... Societe Africaine de Diffusion Ivoire
SADJ .... Jose C. Paz/Dr. Mariano More [*Argentina*] [*ICAO location identifier*]   (ICLI)
SADL........ La Plata [*Argentina*] [*ICAO location identifier*]   (ICLI)
SADL........ Sterilization Advance Development Laboratory [*Japan*]
SADM ...... Moron [*Argentina*] [*ICAO location identifier*]   (ICLI)
SADM ...... Sociedad Argentina de Derechos de las Mujeres [*Women's Rights Association*] [*Argentina*]   (LA)
SADME..... South Australia Department of Mines and Energy   (EAS)
SADMN .... Sociedad Argentina de Medicina Nuclear [*Argentina*]   (SLS)
SADO .... Sistemas de Adquisicion de Datos Oceanicos [*Ocean Data Acquisition Systems - ODAS*] [*Spanish*]   (ASF)
SADO .... Societe Agricole d'Offa
SADO .... Systeme d'Aquisition de Donnees Oceaniques [*Ocean Data Acquisition System - ODAS*] [*French*]   (MSC)
SADOI...... Sociedad Argentina de Organizacion Industrial [*Argentine Association of Industrial Organization*]   (LA)
SADP........ Double-Side Photostat Machine   (RU)
SADP........ El Palomar [*Argentina*] [*ICAO location identifier*]   (ICLI)
SADP........ Scandinavian Association of Directory Publishers   (EAIO)
SADPMA ... South Australian Dairy Products Manufacturers' Association
SADQ .... Quilmes [*Argentina*] [*ICAO location identifier*]   (ICLI)
SADR........ Merlo [*Argentina*] [*ICAO location identifier*]   (ICLI)
SADR........ Saharan Arab Democratic Republic [*Morocco*]   (PD)
SADRA...... South Australian Drag Racers' Association
SADRAC... South African Defence Research Advisory Committee
SADRCB ... South Australian Dog Racing Control Board
SADS........ San Justo/Aeroclub Argentino [*Argentina*] [*ICAO location identifier*]   (ICLI)
SADS........ South Australian Dental Service
SADSSC... South Australian Deaf Sports and Social Club
SADTA...... South African Dancing Teachers' Association
SADTC...... SHAPE [*Supreme Headquarters Allied Powers Europe*] Air Defense Technology Center [*Later, STC*] [*NATO*]
SADV .... Suid-Afrikaanse Diabetesvereniging [*South African Diabetes Association*]   (EAIO)
SADZ........ Matanza/Aeroclub Universita Rio [*Argentina*] [*ICAO location identifier*]   (ICLI)
sae .... Composite Air Squadron   (RU)
sae .... Composite Aviation Squadron   (BU)
SAE........... Medical Air Ambulance Squadron   (RU)
SAE........... School of Audio Engineering [*Australia*]
SAE........... Signal-Abfrag-Einrichtung [*German*]   (ADPT)
SAE........... Skyways Africa Ltd. [*Kenya*] [*ICAO designator*]   (FAAC)
SAE........... Societe Africaine d'Edition
SAE........... Societe Anonyme Egyptienne
SAE........... Societe Auxiliaire d'Entreprises
SAE........... Son Altesse Electorale [*His Highness the Elector*] [*French*]   (ROG)
SAE........... Son Altesse Eminentissime [*His Most Eminent Highness*] [*French*]
SAE........... Soviet Antarctic Expedition   (RU)
SAE........... Standard Australian English
SAEA........ Society of Automotive Engineers - Australasia   (ADA)
SAEA........ South Australian Exporters Association

SAEB........ Societe Africaine d'Entreprises et de Batiment [*Dakar*]
SAEB .... Societe Africaine d'Exploitation des Bois
SAEC........ Societe Abidjanaise d'Expansion Chimique
SAEC........ Societe Africaine d'Expansion Chimique
SAEC........ South African Engineers' Corps
SAEC........ South African Exchange Control   (IMH)
SAEC........ South Australian Energy Council
SAEC........ South Australian Equestrian Centre
SAEC........ State Administration of Exchange Control [*China*]
SAECC ...... South African Electrolytic Corrosion Committee   (AA)
SAEC-CAMEROUN ... Societe Africaine d'Expansion Chimique - Cameroun
SAECO...... Societe Abidjanaise d'Exploitations Commerciales
SAECP...... Societe Africaine d'Exportation de Cuirs et Peaux
SAECS....... Southern African Europe Container Service   (DS)
SAED........ Societe Africaine d'Etudes et de Developpement [*African Society for Study and Development*] [*Burkino Faso*]
SAED........ Societe d'Agriculture et d'Elevage du D'jiminy
SAED........ Societe d'Amenagement et d'Exploitation des Terres du Delta du Fleuve Senegal [*Senegal River Delta Lands Development and Exploitation Agency*]   (GEA)
SAED........ Societe des Amis d'Eugene Delacroix   (EAIO)
SAED........ South Australia Education Department
SAEE........ Syndesmos Anaptyxeos Ellinikon Exoplismon [*Association for the Development of Greek Armaments*]   (GC)
SAEEI ...... Societe Africaine d'Equipement Electrique et Industriel des Etablissements Verger et Delporte
SAEF........ Ezeiza [*Argentina*] [*ICAO location identifier*]   (ICLI)
SAEF........ Societe Anonyme des Entreprises J. Fornero
SAEG........ Societe Africaine des Entreprises Girardin [*Morocco*]
SAEGHT... Societe Africaine d'Exploitation et de Gestion Hoteliere et Touristique
SAEI......... Service des Affaires Economiques et Internationales [*Economic and International Affairs Service*] [*French*]   (WER)
SAEI......... Sumitomo Atomic Energy Industries Ltd.
SAEIS....... South African Energy Information System [*South African Council for Scientific and Industrial Research*]   (WED)
SAEKK...... Suid-Afrikaanse Elektrolitiese Korrosiekomitee [*South Africa*]   (AA)
SAEL........ Sociedad Argentina de Estudios Linguisticos [*Argentine Society of Linguistic Research*] [*Buenos Aires*]   (LAA)
SAELPA.... Sociedad Anonima de Eletrificacao da Paraiba [*Brazil*]   (LAA)
SAEm........ Son Altesse Eminentissime [*His Most Eminent Highness*] [*French*]
SAEM........ Synergazomenon Andidictatorikon Ergatiko Kinima [*Cooperating Antidictatorial Labor Movement*] [*AEM*] [*See also*]   (GC)
SAEMG..... Secretaria de Agricultura do Estado de Minas Gerais [*Brazil*]   (DSCA)
SAEN........ Societe des Anciens Etablissements Nicolas & Cie.
SAENET ... South Australian Advanced Educational Computer Network
SAEO .... South Australian Electoral [*Commission*] Office [*National Union Catalogue of Australia symbol*]
SAEP........ Societe Africaine d'Editions et de Publicite
SAEP........ Societe d'Agriculture et d'Elevage du Pool
SAEP........ Societe l'ACTION d'Edition et de Presse [*Tunisia*]
SAEPA..... Societe Arabe des Engrais Phosphates et Azotes [*Arab Phosphoric Fertilizer and Nitrogen Co.*] [*Tunisian Chemical Group*]
SAER........ Srpsko-Austriski i Evropski Rat [*Serbo-Austrian and European War*] [*World War I*]   (YU)
SAERO...... Societe des Anciens Etablissements A. Reymond de Ouagadougou
saertr.......... Saertryk [*Reprint*] [*Publishing Danish/Norwegian*]
saerudg....... Saerudgave [*Special Edition*] [*Publishing Danish/Norwegian*]
SAES .... Swiss Academy of Engineering Sciences   (EAIO)
SAESA ...... Compania de Servicios Aereos SA [*Spain*] [*ICAO designator*]   (FAAC)
SAESA ...... Servicios Aereos Especiales SA [*Mexico*]   (PDAA)
SAESP...... Secretaria de Agricultura do Estado de Sao Paulo [*Brazil*]   (DSCA)
SAEST....... Society for the Advancement of Electrochemical Science and Technology [*India*]   (PDAA)
SAET........ Societe Africaine d'Etudes Topographiques
SAET........ South Australian Electricity Trust
SAETA ...... SA Ecuatoriana de Transportes Aereos [*Airline*] [*Ecuador*]
SAETI .... Societe Algerienne d'Etudes d'Infrastructure [*Algeria*]
SAETO...... Sociedad Aereo del Tolina [*Colorado*]
Saett........... Saettigung [*Saturation*] [*German*]   (GCA)
Saettig........ Saettigung [*Saturation*] [*German*]   (GCA)
saeurebestaend ... Saeurebestaendig [*Acid-Resistant*] [*German*]   (GCA)
Saeurelsg ... Saeureloesung [*Acid Solution*] [*German*]   (GCA)
SAEV........ Ezeiza [*Argentina*] [*ICAO location identifier*]   (ICLI)
SAEWA..... South African Electrical Workers' Association
SAEZ........ Buenos Aires [*Argentina*]/Ezeiza [*Argentina*] [*ICAO location identifier*]   (ICLI)
SAF........... Republic of Singapore Air Force [*ICAO designator*]   (FAAC)

SAF............ Service Administratif et Financier [*Administrative and Financial Service*] [*French*] (WER)
SAF........... Singapore Armed Forces (ML)
SAF............ Sistema de Asesoramiento y Fiscalizacion [*Advisory and Inspection System*] [*Peru*] (LA)
SAF............ Small Arms Factory [*Australia*]
SAF........... Societe Africaine des Etablissements Fakhry
SAF........... Societe Africaine Forestiere [*Libreville*]
SAF........... Societe Agricole de Foumbo
SAF........... Societe Agricole et Forestiere
SAF........... Societe Alimentaire Fine
SAF........... Societe Astronomique de France [*French*] (SLS)
SAF........... Societe Automobile Fassie [*Morocco*]
SAF........... Societe des Agriculteurs de France [*French*] (SLS)
SAF........... Soudure Autogene Francaise [*France*] (PDAA)
SAF........... South African Foundation
SAF........... Speicher-Ausgabe-Anforderung [*German*] (ADPT)
SAF........... Sultan's Armed Forces [*Oman*] (ME)
SAF........... Superannuation Accumulation Fund [*Tasmania, Australia*]
SAF........... Svenska Arbetsgivareforeningen [*Swedish Employers' Confederation*] [*Stockholm*] (WEN)
SAF........... Svensk Anestesiologisk Foerening [*Sweden*] (SLS)
SAF........... Swedish Air Force
SAF........... Swiss Athletic Federation (EAIO)
SAF........... Syrian Air Force (BJA)
SAFA........ Societe Africaine Forestiere et Agricole
SAFA........ Societe d'Achats France-Afrique
SAFA........ South African Foundry Association (AA)
SAFA........ South African Freedom Association
SAFA........ South Australian Football Association
SAFA........ Southern Amateur Football Association
SAFA........ Suomen Arkkitehtiliitto - Finlands Afkitektforbund [*Finnish Association of Architects*] (EAIO)
SAFACAM ... Societe Africaine Forestiere et Agricole Cameroun
SAFAF...... South Arabian Federal Air Force
SAFAL....... Societe Africaine de Fonderie d'Aluminium
SAFAMI ... Societe Africaine de Fabrications Metalliques Industrielles
SAFAR ...... Societe Africaine de Fabrication des Automobiles Renault [*Ivory Coast*]
SAFARI..... South African Fundamental Atomic Reactor Installation (PDAA)
SAFARI..... Systeme Automatise pour les Fichiers Administratifs et de Repertoire des Individus [*French*] (ADPT)
SAFARRIV ... Societe Africaine d'Assurances et de Reassurances en Republique de Cote-D'Ivoire
SAFAS....... Saf Plastik Sanayi ve Ticaret Anonim Sirketi [*Clear Plastic Industry and Trade Corporation*] (TU)
SAfB .... Schweizerische Arbeitsgemeinschaft fuer Bevoelkerungsfragen [*Switzerland*] (SLS)
SAFB .... Suid-Afrikaanse Federasie van Byeboervereinigings [*South African Federation of Beekeepers' Associations*] (EAIO)
SAFBA ...... South African Federation of Beekeepers' Associations (EAIO)
SAFBAIL .. Societe Africaine de Credit Bail
SAFBITC .. South Australian Food and Beverage Industry Training Council
SAFBV ...... SuiderAfrikaanse Federasie vir Beweging en Vryetydwetenskoppe [*Southern African Association for Movement and Leisure Sciences*] (EAIO)
SAFC .... Societe Africaine Financiere de Commission et de Courtage
SAFC .... South Australian Film Corporation
SAFC .... Swiss Association for Friendship with China (EAIO)
SAFCA ...... Societe Africaine de Courtage d'Assurances
SAFCA ...... Societe Africaine de Credit Automobile
SAFCA ...... Societe Africaine de Fabrication de Cahiers
SAFCA ...... Societe Africaine de Fabrication de Cycles et Accessoires
SAFCA ...... South African Society of Composers, Authors, and Music Publishers
SAF-CAP .. Sistema de Asesoramiento y Fiscalizacion para las Cooperativas Agrarias de Produccion [*Advisory and Supervisory System for Agrarian Production Cooperatives*] [*Peru*] (LA)
SAFCI....... Societe Administrative et Financiere de Cote-D'Ivoire
SAFCI....... Societe Africaine Financiere, Commerciale, et Immobiliere
SAFCO...... Saudi Arabian Fertilizers Company (ME)
SAFCO...... Societe Africaine Colombani & Cie.
SAFCO...... Societe Africaine de Conserverie
SAFCO...... Societe Africaine de Construction
SAFCO...... Societe Afrique Commerce
SAFCO...... Standing Advisory Committee on Fisheries [*Puerto Rican*] (ASF)
SAFCOM .. Societe Africaine de Constructions Metalliques
SAFCOP ... Societe Africaine de Commercialisation des Produits de la Mer
SAFD........ Societe des Ateliers et Fonderies Denis-Huet
SAFE .... Safety Advice for the Elderly [*Australia*]
SAFE .... Santa Fe [*Argentina*] [*ICAO location identifier*] (ICLI)
SAFE .... Save Animals from Exploitation [*Australia*]
SAFE .... Secured Asset Funding Entity Ltd. [*Australia*]
SAFE .... Serrature Auto Ferroviarie Edili SpA [*Turin, Italy*]

SAFE .... Servicio Auxiliar Femenino del Ejercito [*Army Women's Auxiliary Service*] [*Chile*] (LA)
SAFE .... Societe Africaine d'Entreposage
SAFE .... Societe d'Analyse Financiere et Economique [*French*]
SAFE .... South African Friends of England
SAFE .... Stop Arms for Export [*Australia*]
SAFE .... Straits Air Freight Express [*Australia*]
SAFECOL ... Safe Colombiana, SA [*Colombia*] (COL)
SAFEFCON ... South Africa Far East Freight Conference
SAFEGE..... Societe Anonyme Francaise d'Etudes, de Gestion, et d'Entreprise
SAFEL...... Sociedad Anonima, Fabricante de Electrodomesticos [*Spanish*]
SAFEL...... Societe Africaine de Fruits et Legumes
SAFEL...... Societe Africaine d'Elevage
SAFELEC ... Societe Africaine d'Electricite
SAFEM ..... Societe Africaine de Froid Electro-Menager
SAFER ...... Societe d'Amenagement Foncier et d'Etablissement Rural [*Real Estate and Rural Development Company*] [*French*] (WER)
Saff............ Saffian [*Morocco*] [*Publishing*] [*German*]
SAFF .... South African Field Force
SAFFA ...... SpA Fabbriche Fiammiferi ed Affini-Saffa [*Italian*]
SAFFARRIV ... Societe Africaine d'Assurance et de Reassurances en Republique de Cote d'Ivoire (EY)
s-affl........... Sous-Affluent [*Sub-Tributary*] [*French*]
SAFFUC..... Sudan African Freedom Fighters Union of Conservatives
SAFG......... Suid-Afrikaanse Federasie van Groeptelers [*South African Federation of Group Breeders*] (EAIO)
SAFGA ...... South Australian Flower Growers' Association
SAFGB ...... South African Federation of Group Breeders (AA)
SAFGIV ..... Suid-Afrikaanse Fotogrammetrie en Geo-Inligting Vereniging [*South Africa*] (AA)
SAFGRAD ... Semi-Arid Food Grain Research and Development [*West Africa*]
SAFHE...... South African Federation of Hospital Engineering (AA)
SAFHI....... Suid-Afrikaanse Federasie van Hospitaal-Ingenieurswese [*South African Federation of Hospital Engineering*] (AA)
SAFI .... Saudi Arabian Financial Institution Company (ME)
SAFI .... Societe Africaine de Fabrication Industrielle
SAFI .... Societe Africaine d'Investissements
SAFIAC..... South Australian Film Investment Advisory Committee
SAFIC....... Societe Africaine Forestiere Industrielle et Commerciale
SAFIC....... South Australian Fishing Industry Council
SAFICA..... Societe Africaine de Fabrication et d'Impression de Cahiers
SAFICO ... Sistema Andino de Financiamiento de Comercio [*Andean Commercial Financing System*] (LA)
SAFICOCI ... Societe Abidjanaise de Fournitures pour l'Industrie et les Constructions en Cote-D'Ivoire
SAFICOM ... Societe Africaine pour l'Industrie et le Commerce
SAFIE....... Societe Africaine d'Installations Electriques
SAFIEX..... Societe Africaine d'Importation et d'Exportation
SAFIL....... Societa Agricola Fondiaria Italo-Libica
SAFIL....... Societe Africaine de Filterie
SAFIL....... South African Filtration Society (AA)
SAFIM ...... Societa per Azioni Finanziaria Industria Manufatturiera [*Italian*]
SAFINA .... Societe Africaine Industrielle et Agricole de Sebikotane
SAFINELEC ... Societe Africaine d'Injection et d'Electricite
SAFIR........ Societe Africaine de Fabrications Industrielles et de Representation
SAFISC ..... South Australian Film Industry Standing Committee
SAFITC ..... South Australian Fishing Industry Training Council
SAFM .... Societe Africaine de Fabrication Metallique
SAFMARINE ... South African Marine Corp. Ltd.
SAFMC ..... South Atlantic Fishery Management Council (ASF)
SAFMSA... Sudanese Armed Forces Military Sports Association
SAFO .... Societe Anonyme des Safaris Jean d'Orgeix
SAFO........ Swedish Atomic Forum [*Nuclear energy*] (NRCH)
SAFO........ Systeme Automatique du Fret Orly [*Automatic Freight System*] [*French*] (ADPT)
SAFONKS ... Societe Anonyme des Anciens Etablissements Maurice Fonks
SAFOP...... Societe Africaine de Formation Professionnelle
SAFOR...... Societe Sanaga Forestiere
SAFR .... Schweizerische Arbeitsgemeinschaft fuer Raumfahrt [*Swiss Association for Work on Space Travel*] [*Lucerne*] [*Research center*] (ERC)
SAFR .... Societe Anonyme Francaise de Reassurance [*Insurance*] (EY)
S Afr........... South Africa
SAFRA....... Societe Africaine d'Assurances
SAFRA ...... Storekeepers and Food Retailers of Australia (ADA)
SAFRAR.... Sociedad Anonima Franco-Argentina de Automotores [*Argentina*] (LAA)
SAfrD .... South African Dutch
SAFRED ... Societe Africaine d'Emballage et de Demenagement
SAFREP.... Societe Anonyme Francaise de Recherches et d'Exploitation de Petrole [*French Petroleum Exploration and Exploitation Corporation*] [*Algeria*] (AF)
SAFREX.... Societe Africaine d'Exploration Petroliere
SAFRI....... South African Forestry Research Institute (ARC)

SAFRIC..... Societe Africaine de Confection
SAFRIC..... Societe Africaine de Cooperation Commerciale [*Morocco*]
SAFRICA.. Societe Africaine de Representations Industrielles, Commerciales, et d'Assurances
SAFRICO ... Societe Africaine de Construction
SAFRIM.... Societe Africaine de Mecanographie
SAFRIMEX ... Sociedade Africana de Importacao e Exportacao Lda.
SAFRINEX ... Societe Africaine d'Exploitation Vinicole
SAFRING ... South African Bird Ringing Unit   (EAIO)
SAFRIPA .. Societe Africaine de Parfumerie
SAFRITEX ... Societe Africaine de Textile
SAFRITIS ... Societe Africaine "Les Tissandiers"
SAFSI....... South African Fire Services Institute   (AA)
SAFT .... Societe Africaine de Filature et de Tissage [*Morocco*]
SAFT .... Societe d'Affretement Maritime du Togo   (EY)
SAFT .... Societe des Accumulateurs Fixes et de Traction [*France*]   (PDAA)
SAFTAS.... Society of Australian Film and Television Arts and Sciences
SAFTEL.... Societe Africaine d'Electronique et de Telecommunications
SAFTI .... Singapore Armed Forces Training Institute   (ML)
SAFTO ...... South African Foreign Trade Organization   (AF)
SAFTU ...... South African Federation of Trade Unions
SAFUES.... South African Federation of University Engineering Students
SAFUIS..... Suid-Afrikaanse Federasie vir Universiteitsingenieurstudente [*South African Federation of University Engineering Students*]   (AA)
SAFV .... Sociedad Argentina de Fisiologia Vegetal [*Argentina*]   (DSCA)
SAFV .... Suid Afrikaanse Farmakologie Vereniging [*South African Pharmacological Society*]   (EAIO)
SAFV .... Suid-Afrikaanse Fisioterapie Vereniging [*South Africa*]   (AA)
SAFVC....... South Australian Film and Video Centre
SAFVCA.... South African Fruit and Vegetable Canners' Association   (EAIO)
SAFVSEMV ... Suid-Afrikaanse Federasie van Siersteen- en Mineralogiese Verenigings [*South African Federation of Gem and Mineralogical Societies*]   (EAIO)
SAFWA ..... South African Furniture Removers and Warehousemen's Association   (AA)
Sag .... Sagaria [*Zechariah*] [*Afrikaans*]
Sag .... Saglik [*Health*]   (TU)
SAG .... Sammlung von Algenkulturen [*Germany*]
SAG .... Scandinavian Association of Geneticists   (DSCA)
SAG .... Schweizerische Afrika-Gesellschaft [*Swiss Society of African Studies*]   (EAIO)
SAG .... Schweizerische Astronomische Gesellschaft [*Switzerland*]   (SLS)
SAG .... Scierie, Atelier, et Garage
SAG .... Secretaria de Agricultura y Ganaderia [*Secretariat of Agriculture and Livestock*] [*Mexico*]   (LA)
SAG .... Secretaria de Estado de Agricultura y Ganaderia de la Nacion [*Argentina*]   (LAA)
SAG .... Servicio Agricola y Ganadero [*Agriculture and Livestock Service*] [*Chile*]   (LA)
SAG .... Sociedad de Agricultores y Ganaderos [*Colombia*]   (COL)
SAG .... Societa Agricoltori Ginba [*Italy*]   (DSCA)
SAG .... Societe Africaine de Groupage
SAG .... Societe Agricole de Guinee [*Agricultural Company of Guinea*]   (AF)
SAG .... Societe Agricole du Gabon
SAG .... Societe Algerienne de Geophysique [*Algerian Geophysics Company*]   (AF)
SAG .... Society of Australian Genealogists   (ADA)
SAG .... South Australian Gas Co. [*Commercial firm*]
SAG .... Sowjetische Aktiengesellschaft [*Soviet Corporation*] [*SAGs were plants confiscated by the USSR after WWII and operated under Soviet auspices until the mid-50's*]   (EG)
SAG .... Sozialistische Arbeitsgemeinschaft [*Socialist Work Group*]   (EG)
SAG .... Statistical Advisory Group [*Cultural Advisory Council*] [*Australia*]
SAG .... Swedish Air Ambulance [*ICAO designator*]   (FAAC)
SAG .... Systemanschlussgruppe [*German*]   (ADPT)
SAGA .... Savonnerie du Gabon
SAGA .... Schweizerische Aertzgesellschaft for Akupunktur [*Swiss Medical Society of Acupunktur*]   (EAIO)
SAGA .... Screen Actors Guild of Australia
SAGA .... Societa Applicazioni Gomma Antivibranti [*Italy*]   (PDAA)
SAGA .... Societe Africaine de Groupement d'Achats
SAGA .... Societe Anonyme de Gerance et d'Armement
SAGA .... Societe Suisse d'Etudes Anglaises [*Switzerland*]   (SLS)
SAGA .... South African Guide Dogs Association for the Blind   (AA)
SAGA .... South African Gymkhana Association
SAGA .... South Australian Gymnastic Association
SAGA .... Students Against Greiner's Attacks [*Australia*]
SAGACE ... Systeme Automatique pour la Gestion et l'Echange des Comptes Economiques [*French*]   (ADPT)
SAGAL...... Sociedade Agricola Algodoeira
SAGAPE ... Societe d'Approvisionnement de Gaz Algerien pour l'Europe [*Company for Supplying Algerian Gas to Europe*]   (AF)

SAGBAE ... Swedish Association of Graduates in Business Administration and Economics   (EAIO)
SAGC........ Societe Africaine de Genie Civil
SAGCA...... Societe Auxiliaire de Garantie et de Courtage d'Assurances
SAGCE...... South African Gold Coin Exchange [*Johannesburg*]
SAGCI...... Societe d'Affretement et de Groupage de Cote-D'Ivoire
SAGD .... Suid-Afrikaanse Geneeskundige Dienst
SAGDIC .... Swedish Association of Graduates in Documentation, Information and Culture   (EAIO)
SAGE........ Senior Australians for Growth and Exploration
SAGE........ Simulateur d'Apprentissage de la Gestion des Entreprises [*French*]   (ADPT)
SAGE........ Societe Africaine de Gestions d'Entreprises
SAGE........ South Australian Group of Chief Executives of Tertiary Institutions
SAGE........ Soviet-American Gallium Experiment [*Particle physics*]
SAGE........ Swedish Association of Graduate Engineers   (EAIO)
SAGE........ Symvoulion Arkhigon Genikon Epiteleion [*General Staff Officers Council*] [*Greek*]   (GC)
SAGEC...... Societe Africaine de Genie Civil
SAGECCOM ... Societe Africaine de Genie Civil et de Constructions Metalliques
SAGECI .... Societe d'Agriculture et d'Elevage de la Cote-D'Ivoire
SAGECO ... Societe Abidjanaise de Gerance et d'Exploitation Commerciale
SAGEM.... Societe Africaine des Articles Galvanises et Emailles
SAGEM..... Societe d'Applications Generales d'Electricite et de Mecanique [*French*]
SAGEM..... Sumerbank Arastirma Gelistirme ve Egitim Muessesesi [*Sumerbank Research Development and Training Establishment*] [*Turkey*]   (IRC)
SAGEMAR ... Societe d'Agence de Marques
SAGES ...... South African Gastroenterology Society   (AA)
SAGGA ..... South Australian Grape Growers' Association
SAGGBS ... Salvation Army Guides and Guards, Brownies, and Sunbeams   (EAIO)
SAGHS...... South Australian Genealogy and Heraldry Society, Inc.
SAGI......... South African Garrisons Institutes
SAGICAM ... Societe Agro-Industrielle du Cameroun
SAGICOE ... Societe Agricole et Industrielle de la Cote Est
SAGIS ...... Societe Agricole et Industrielle de Sassandra
Saglik-Is.. Turkiye Saglik Iscileri Sendikasi [*Turkish Health Workers Union*]   (TU)
SAGM .... South African General Mission
SAGMACS ... Sociedade de Analises Graficas e Mecanograficas Aplicadas aos Complexos Sociais [*Brazil*]   (LAA)
SAGO .... Latin America Center [*Acronym is based on foreign phrase*] [*Belgium*]
SAGO .... Sociedad Agricola Ganadera de Osorno [*Chile*]   (DSCA)
SAGO .... Studie en Aktiegroep voor Ontwikkelingssamenwerking
SAGP......... Suid-Afrikaanse Genootskap van Plantkundiges [*South Africa*]   (AA)
SAGRCB ... South Australian Greyhound Racing Control Board
SAGRICOL ... Societe Agricole et d'Elevage Khmero-Chinoise [*Cambodian-Chinese Agricultural and Livestock Company*]   (CL)
SAGRINA ... Societe Agricole de la Nanoua
SAGROCOL ... Sociedad Agrologica Colombiana Ltda. [*Colombia*]   (COL)
SAGS........ South African Geographical Society   (SLS)
SAGS........ South African Geriatric Society   (AA)
SAGU .... Central Asian State University Imeni V. I. Lenin   (RU)
SAGU .... South African Golf Union
SAGUF...... Schweizerische Arbeitsgemeinschaft fuer Umweltforschung [*Swiss Association for Environmental Studies*]   (WEN)
SAGV........ Suid-Afrikaanse Geografiese Vereniging [*South African Geographical Society*]   (AA)
SAGV........ Suid-Afrikaanse Geriatriese Vereniging [*South African Geriatric Society*]   (AA)
Sah............ Sahachivin [*Mr. or Ms.*] [*Literally Comrade; formerly used as a term of address for a member of the Sangkum Reastr Niyum (Prince Sihanouk's party) Cambodia*]   (CL)
Sah............ Sahara
SAH.......... Sanaa [*Yemen Arab Republic*] [*Airport symbol*]   (OAG)
SAH.......... Sayakhat [*Kazakhstan*] [*ICAO designator*]   (FAAC)
SAH.......... Secteur d'Administration et d'Habitation
SAH.......... Servicio de Agrometeorologia e Hydrologia [*Peru*]   (ASF)
SAH.......... Sociedad Argentina de Hematologia [*Argentine Society of Hematology*]   (SLS)
SAH.......... Society of Aeronautical Historians [*Netherlands*]   (EAIO)
SAHA .... South African Heavy Artillery
SAHA .... South African Homoeopathic Association   (AA)
SAHA .... South Australia Hockey Association
SAHC .... Chosmadal [*Argentina*] [*ICAO location identifier*]   (ICLI)
SAHC .... Scottish Australian Heritage Council
SAHC .... Scottish Australian Horse Council
SAHCTL ... South Australian Hard Court Tennis League
SAHDA .... South Australian Huntingtons Disease Association
SAHDGA .. South African Hot Dip Galvanizers' Association   (AA)

SAHE .... Society of Anatomists, Histologists and Embryologists [*Bulgaria*] (EAIO)
SAHF .... South African Haemophilia Foundation (AA)
sahk. .... Sahkotekniikka [*Electricity*] [*Finland*]
SAHL .... Salvation Army Home League [*See also LF*] (EAIO)
SAHM .... Societe Africaine des Halles Modernes
SAHM .... Societe Algerienne des Huiles Minerales
SAHNOS .. South African Head and Neck Oncology Society (AA)
SAHOP ..... Secretaria de Asentamientos Humanos y Obras Publicas [*Secretariat for Human Settlements and Public Works*] [*Mexico*] (LA)
SAHP .... Societe Anonyme de l'Hotel du Plateau
SAHR .... Fuerte Gral Roca [*Argentina*] [*ICAO location identifier*] (ICLI)
SAHRA ..... South Australian Herd Recorders' Association
SAHRC ...... South Australian Harness Racing Club
SAHS .... Southern African Hypertension Society (PDAA)
SAHS .... Suid-Afrikaanse Hemofiliestigting [*South African Hemophilia Foundation*] (AA)
SAHSA ...... Servicio Aereo de Honduras SA (PDAA)
SAHSPA ... South Australian High School Principals' Association
SAHT .... South Australian Housing Trust [*National Union Catalogue of Australia symbol*]
SAHV .... Suid-Afrikaanse Homeopatiese Vereniging [*South African Homoeopathic Association*] (AA)
SAI .... Service des Affaires Indigenes [*Bureau of Native Affairs*]
SAI .... Servicio Agricola Interamericano [*Interamerican Agricultural Service*] [*Bolivia*] (LAA)
SAI .... Shaheen Air International [*Pakistan*] [*ICAO designator*] (FAAC)
SAI .... Sindicato de Auxiliares de Ingenieria [*Union of Engineering Assistants*] [*El Salvador*] (LA)
SAI .... Singapore Aircraft Industries (PDAA)
SAI .... Societa Assicuratrice Industriale SpA [*Insurance*] [*Italy*] (EY)
SAI .... Societe Africaine d'Importation
SAI .... Societe Arabe d'Investissements
SAI .... South African Infantry
SAI .... Sports Authority of India (EAIO)
SAI .... Students for Australian Independence (ADA)
SAI .... Su Alteza Imperial [*His, or Her, Imperial Highness*] [*Spanish*]
SAIA .... School of Aboriginal and Islander Administration [*Australia*]
SAIA .... Societe Agricole et Industrielle de l'Ankara [*Malagasy*]
SAIA .... Solidariedade Africana para a Independencia de Angola
SAIA .... South African Institute of Auctioneers (AA)
SAIAA ...... South African Institute of Assayers and Analysts (AA)
SAIAE ...... South African Institute of Aeronautical Engineers (EAIO)
SAIAE ...... South African Institute of Agricultural Engineers (AA)
SAIAeE ..... South African Institute of Aeronautical Engineers (SLS)
SAIAO ...... Societe Auxiliaire Immobiliere d'Afrique Occidentale
SAIAT ...... Societa Attivita Immobiliari Ausliarie Telefoniche [*Italy*] (PDAA)
SAIB .... Saudi Investment Bank (MENA)
SAIB .... Societa Agricola Industriale Bengasi
SAIB .... Societe Africaine des Industries du Batiment
SAIB .... Societe Algerienne pour l'Industrie du Batiment
SAIB .... Societe Arabe Internationale de Banque [*Bank*] [*Egypt*]
SAIB .... Suid-Afrikaanse Instituut vir Bestuurswese [*South Africa*] (AA)
SAIB .... Suider-Afrikaanse Instituut van Boswese [*South Africa*] (AA)
SAIBE ...... Societe Automobile et Industrielle du Benin
SAIBI .... Suid-Afrikaanse Instituut van Bedryfsingenieurs [*South Africa*] (AA)
SAIBI .... Suid-Afrikaanse Instituut vir Biblioteek en Inligtingwese [*South African Institute for Librarianship and Information Science*] (EAIO)
SAIC .... Secretaria de Agricultura, Industria, e Comercio [*Brazil*] (DSCA)
SAIC .... Shanghai Aviation Industrial Corporation
SAIC .... Signalement et Archivages des Information Courantometriques [*French*] (MSC)
SAIC .... South African Indian Congress (PD)
SAIC .... South African Indian Council (AF)
SAIC .... South African Institute of Computer Scientists (AA)
SAIC .... South Australian Industrial Commission
SAIC .... State Actuary and Insurance Commissioner [*Queensland, Australia*]
SAIC .... State Administration for Industry and Commerce [*China*] (IMH)
SAICA ...... Societa Algherese Industrie Chimiche Agricole
SAICA ...... Societa Anonima Industriale Commerciale Automobilistica
SAICA ...... Societe Africaine Industrielle, Commerciale, et Agricole
SAICA ...... Societe Agricole et Industrielle de la Cote d'Afrique
SAICA ...... South African Institute of Chartered Accountants (AA)
SAICCOR ... South African Industrial Cellulose Corporation (Pty) Ltd.
SAICE ...... South African Institute of Civil Engineers
SAICET .... South African Institute of Civil Engineering Technicians and Technologists (EAIO)

SAICETT .. South African Institute of Civil Engineering Technicians and Technologists (EAIO)
SAICHE .... South African Institution of Chemical Engineers (AA)
SAIChemE ... South African Institution of Chemical Engineers
SAICHI ..... Suid-Afrikaanse Instituut van Chemiese Ingenieurs [*South African Institute of Chemical Engineers*] (AA)
SAICI .... Societe Agricole et Industrielle de la Cote-D'Ivoire
SAICIC ...... South Australian Industrial Court and Industrial Commission
SAICO ...... South African Institute for Cooperatives (AA)
SAICOS ... Societe Agricole, Industrielle, et Commerciale du Senegal
SAICS .... South African Institute of Computer Scientists (AA)
SAICt .... South Australian Industrial Court
SAID .... South African Institute of Draughtsmen (AA)
SAID .... South [*Australian*] AIDS [*Council*] [*Darling House Library*]
SAID .... Swiss Agency for International Development
SAIDA ...... Societa Anonima Italiana Distilleria Agraria
SAIDA ...... Southern African Inherited Disorders Association (AA)
SAIDC ...... South African Inventions Development Corporation
SAIDCOR ... South African Inventions Development Corp. [*Research center*] (ERC)
SAIDE .... Services Aeriens Internationaux d'Egypte
SAIDI .... Southern African Institute of Driving Instructors (AA)
SAIDSA ...... South African Intruder Detection Systems Association (AA)
SAIE .... South Africa Institute of Engineers
SAIE .... Suid-Afrikaanse Instituut van Ekoloe [*South African Institute of Ecologists*] (AA)
SAIEA ...... Societe Auxiliaire Immobiliere des Etats d'Afrique
SAIEA ...... South Africa Institute Employers' Association
SAIEA ...... Suid-Afrikaanse Instituut van Essaieurs en Analitici [*South African Institute of Assayers and Analysts*] (AA)
SAIEE .... South Africa Institute of Electrical Engineers
SAIEG .... South African Institute of Engineering Geologists (AA)
SAIEI .... Suid-Afrikaanse Instituut van Elektriese Ingenieurs [*South African Institute of Electrical Engineers*] (AA)
SAIEP .... Sociedad Anonima Importadora y Exportadora de la Patagonia [*Argentina*] (LAA)
SAIER ...... South Australian Institute of Educational Research
SAIERE ..... South African Institute of Electronic and Radio Engineers (AA)
SAIET ...... Societa Anonima Impianti Elettrici Tripoli
SAIET ...... Societe Africaine d'Importation et d'Exportation Tchadienne
SAIETE ..... South African Institute of Electrical Technician Engineers (AA)
SAIETI ...... Suid-Afrikaanse Instituut van Elektrotegniese Tegnikusingenieurs [*South African Institute of Electrical Technician Engineers*] (AA)
SAIF .... South African Industrial Federation
SAIF .... South African Institute of Forestry (SLS)
SAIF .... South African Institute of Foundrymen
SAIF .... Suid-Afrikaanse Instituut vir Fisika [*South Africa*] (AA)
SAIF .... Suid-Afrikaanse Instituut vir Fotograwe [*South Africa*] (AA)
SAIFECS ... SpA Industria Fibre e Cartoni Speciali [*Italy*] (PDAA)
SAIG .... Suid-Afrikaanse Instituut vir Gieterywese [*South Africa*] (AA)
SAIGE .... Societa di Architettura Industriale per gli Impiantidi Generazione di Energia, SpA [*Nuclear energy*] [*Italian*] (NRCH)
SAIGER .... Suid-Afrikaanse Instituut van Geoktrooieerde Rekenmeesters [*South Africa*] (AA)
SAIGG .... Suid-Afrikaanse Intydsgebruikergroep [*South Africa*] (AA)
SAIGIMS ... Central Asian Scientific Research Institute of Geology and Mineral Raw Materials (RU)
SAIGR .... Suid-Afrikaanse Instituut van Geoktrooieerde Rekenmeesters [*South Africa*] (AA)
SAIH .... Societe Africaine Immobiliere et Hoteliere
SAIH .... Studentenes og Akademikernes Internasjonale Hjelpefond [*Norway*]
SAIHBTH ... South African Institute of Health and Beauty Therapists (AA)
SAII .... Central Asian Industrial Institute (RU)
SAII .... Societe Africaine d'Impressions Industrielles
SAIIA .... South African Institute of International Affairs (AA)
SAIIA .... Suid-Afrikaanse Instituut van Internasionale Aangeleenthede [*South African Institute of International Affairs*] (AF)
SAIIE .... South African Institute of Industrial Engineers (AA)
SAIIG .... Suid-Afrikaanse Instituut van Ingenieursgeoloe [*South Africa*] (AA)
SAIL .... Steel Authority of India Ltd. [*Commercial firm*]
SAIL .... Survey of Australian Interlibrary Lending
SAILI .... Suid-Afrikaanse Instituut van Landbou-Ingenieurs [*South Africa*] (AA)
SAILI .... Suid-Afrikaanse Instituut van Lugvaartkundige Ingenieurs [*South Africa*] (AA)
SAILIS ...... South African Institute for Librarianship and Information Science (EAIO)
SAILL .... Survey of Australian Interlibrary Lending
SAILLE ..... Systeme de Generation Automatique d'Instructions Logiques en Langages Evolues [*French*] (ADPT)
SAILugI ..... Suid-Afrikaanse Instituut vir Lugvaartkundige Ingenieurs [*South African Institute of Aeronautical Engineers*] (EAIO)

SAIM......... South African Institute of Management (PDAA)
SAIMAN... Societa Anonima Industrie-Meccaniche Aeronautiche Navali [*Italian*]
SAIMarENA ... South African Institute of Marine Engineers and Naval Architects (AA)
SAIMC...... South African Institute for Measurement and Control (PDAA)
SAIMCI .... Societe Anonyme Immobiliere des Magasins de Cote-D'Ivoire
SAIME...... Central Asian Scientific Research Institute for the Mechanization and Electrification of Irrigation Farming (RU)
SAIMechE ... South African Institute of Mechanical Engineers
SAIMENA ... South African Institute of Marine Engineers and Naval Architects (PDAA)
SAIMH ..... South African Institute of Materials Handling (AA)
SAIMI .... Societe des Amis de l'Institut Metapsychique International [*Society of Friends of the International Metaphysical Institute*] (EAIO)
SAIM-KEBE ... Societe Anonyme Immobiliere - Kebe
SAIMM..... South African Institute of Mining and Metallurgy
SAIMN...... Suid-Afrikaanse Instituut vir Mediese Navorsing [*South Africa*] (AA)
SAIMO...... South African Indian Missionary Outreach
SAIMR..... South African Institute for Medical Research
SAINA .... Societe Anonyme Industrielle Nord-Africaine [*North African Industrial Company*] [*Tunisia*] (AF)
SAInstE ..... Southern African Institute of Energy (AA)
SAIO......... Sociedad Argentina de Investigacion Operativa [*Society for Operational Research*] [*Argentina*] (PDAA)
SAIOM...... Southern African Institute of Organization and Methods (AA)
SAIOR...... South African Institute of Oceanographic Research (MSC)
SAIP .... South African Institute of Physics (SLS)
SAIP .... South African Institute of Printing (SLS)
SAIPA .... Sociedad Argentina para la Investigacion de Productos Aromaticos [*Argentina*] (DSCA)
SAIPA .... South African Institute of Patent Agents (AA)
SAIPA .... South African Institute of Public Administration (AA)
SAIPA .... Suid-Afrikaanse Instituut vir Patent Agente [*South African Institute of Patent Agents*] (AA)
SAIPA .... Suid-Afrikaanse Instituut vir Publieke Administrasie [*South African Institute for Public Administration*]
SAIPAS..... Sociedad Argentina para la Investigacion de Productos Aromaticos [*Argentina*] (LAA)
SAIPE....... South African Institute for Production Engineering (AA)
SAIR......... Societe Agricole et Industrielle de la Ruzizi
SAIR......... Societe Anonyme Industrielle de Resines [*France*]
SAIR......... Son Altesse Imperiale Royale [*French*] (MTD)
SAIRAC .... South African Institute of Refrigeration and Air-Conditioning
SAIRI .... Supreme Assembly for the Islamic Revolution in Iraq [*Political party*] (ECON)
SAIRR ...... South African Institute of Race Relations (AF)
SAIRW...... Suid-Afrikaanse Instituut van Rekenaarswetenskaplikes [*South Africa*] (AA)
SAIS .... Sociedad Agricola de Interes Social [*Social Interest Agricultural Organization*] [*Peru*] (LA)
SAIS .... Societa Agricola Italo-Somala
SAIS .... Societe Agricole et Industrielle du Soja [*Morocco*]
SAIS .... South African Immunology Society (AA)
SAIS .... South African Information Service (AF)
SAIS .... South African Institute of Security (AA)
SAIS .... South African Interplanetary Society
SAIS .... Suid-Afrikaanse Instituut vir Sweiswese [*South Africa*] (AA)
SAISA ...... South African Ice-Skating Association
SAISB....... South African Individual Scale for the Blind [*Intelligence test*]
SAISB....... South Australian Independent Schools' Board
SAISC....... South African Institute of Steel Construction
SAISI .... Suid-Afrikaanse Instituut van Siviele Ingenieurs [*South African Institute of Civil Engineers*] (AA)
SAISIT ...... Suid-Afrikaanse Instituut van Siviele Ingenieurs-Tegnici en - Tegnoloe [*South African Institute of Civil Engineering Technicians and Technologists*] (EAIO)
SAISS........ Suid-Afrikaanse Instituut van Stads- en Streekbeplanners [*South African Institute of Town and Regional Planners*] (AA)
SAISSB ..... Suid-Afrikaanse Instituut van Stads- en Streekbeplanners [*South African Institute of Town and Regional Planners*] (AA)
SAIT .... Societa per l'Africa Italiana Tripoli
SAIT .... Societe Africaine d'Importation de Textiles
SAIT .... South African Institute of Translators
SAIT .... South Australian Institute of Technology (ERC)
SAITE .... Saudi Arabian International & Trading Establishment [*Commercial firm*]
SAITINT... South African Institute of Translators and Interpreters (AA)
SAITIS...... South Australian Institute of Technology Information Service
SAITRP..... South African Institute of Town and Regional Planners (AA)
SAITT .... Suid-Afrikaanse Instituut vir Teatertegnologie [*South African Institute of Theatre Technology*] (AA)
SAIV .... South African Institute of Valuers
SAIV .... Suid-Afrikaanse Immunologie Vereniging [*South African Immunology Society*] (AA)

SAIVA .... Societe Anonyme d'Importation et de Vente d'Alimentation
SAIVERT ... Suid-Afrikaanse Instituut van Vertalers en Tolke [*South Africa*] (AA)
SAIW........ South African Institute of Welding
SAiW .... Stowarzyszenie Ateistow i Wolnomyslicieli [*Association of Atheists and Freethinkers*] (POL)
SAIW........ Suid-Afrikaanse Instituut van Waardeerders [*Die*] [*South Africa*] (AA)
SAIZR ...... Central Asian Institute for the Protection of Plants (RU)
saj.............. Sajat [*Personal, Private*] (HU)
SAJ .... Shipbuilders Association of Japan (PDAA)
SAJ .... Society for the Advancement of Judaism
SAJ .... Sozialistische Arbeiterjugend [*Socialist Workers Youth*] (WEN)
SAJA .... Sociedad de Agricultores Japoneses [*Palmira*] (COL)
SAJA .... South African Jewellers Association
SAJB .... South African Jukskei Board
SAJM .... Schweizerische Arbeitsgemeinschaft fuer Jugendmusik und Musikerziehung [*Swiss Association for Young Musicians and Music Education*] (SLS)
SAK .... Composite Air Corps (RU)
sak............. Composite Aviation Corps (BU)
SAK .... Coupled Subscriber's Line Equipment (RU)
SaK .... Medical Launch (RU)
SAK .... Saudarkrokur [*Iceland*] [*Airport symbol*] (OAG)
SAK .... Slovensky Autoklub [*Slovak Automobile Club*] (CZ)
SAK .... Socialisticka Akademie [*Socialist Academy*] (CZ)
SAK .... Societe Agricole de la Kaedi
SAK .... Spolecnost Aplikovane Kybernetiky [*Society for Applied Cybernetics*] (CZ)
SAK .... Spoudastiki Andi-Imperialistiki Kinisi [*Student Anti-Imperialist Movement*] [*Greek*] (GC)
SAK .... Strategic Air Command (BU)
SAK .... Suomen Ammattiilittojen Keskusforfesto [*Finnish National Trade Union Confederation*] (DCTA)
SAK .... Suomen Ammattiliittojen Keskusjarjesto [*Central Organization of Finnish Trade Unions*]
SAK .... Sveriges Allmaenna Konstfoerening [*Sweden*] (SLS)
SAK .... Sveriges Arbetarepartiet Kommunisterna [*Swedish Workers' Communist Party*] [*Political party*] (PPW)
SAKB........ Special Architectural Design Office (RU)
SAKB........ Suid-Afrikaanse Kriminele Buro [*South Africa*] (AA)
SAKB........ Suider Afrikaanse Katolieke Biskopsraad [*Southern African Catholic Bishops' Conference - SACBC*] (EAIO)
SAKELA ... Societe Agricole de l'Ekela
SAKF........ Svenska Akustikkonsulenters Foerening [*Sweden*] (SLS)
SAKGG..... Suid-Afrikaanse Koppelgebruikersgroep [*South Africa*] (AA)
SAKh .... Mean Aerodynamic Chord (RU)
sakh........... Sugar Plant [*Topography*] (RU)
Sakharles... All-Union Office for Wooden Packing Materials of the Glavsakhar (RU)
SAKhKNII ... Sakhalin Complex Scientific Research Institute (of the Siberian Department of the Academy of Sciences, USSR) (RU)
Sakhremsnab ... Trust for the Supply of Sugar Industry Establishments of the Rosglavsakhar with Materials and Equipment (RU)
sakh trost ... Sugarcane [*Topography*] (RU)
SAKI .... Saudi Arabia - Kuwait - Iraq
sakki .... Sakkipeli [*Chess*] [*Finland*]
SAKOMM ... Suider-Afrikaanse Kommunikasievereniging [*South African Communication Association*] (AA)
SAKorrI .... Suid-Afrikaanse Korrosie-Instituut [*South African Corrosion Institute*] (AA)
SAKOV...... Kerkorrelistevereniging van Suid-Afrika [*South Africa*] (AA)
SAKRV...... Suid-Afrikaanse Kristallografiese Vereniging [*South African Crystallographic Society*] (AA)
saks .... Saksaa [*or Saksaksi*] [*Finland*]
saks .... Saksalainen [*or Saksan Kielta*] [*German*] [*Finland*]
SAKU .... Central Asian Communist University Imeni V. I. Lenin (RU)
SAKV......... Suid-Afrikaanse Keramiekvereniging [*South African Ceramic Society*] (EAIO)
SAKV......... Suid-Afrikaanse Kwekersvereniging [*South Africa*] (AA)
SAKVA...... Suid-Afrikaanse Konfederasie van Arbeid [*South African Labor Confederation*] (AF)
SAL............ Aktiebolaget Svenska Amerika Linien [*Swedish American Line*] [*Sweden*]
SAl .... Aluminiumschweissdraht [*Aluminum Welding Wire*] [*German*] (GCA)
SAL............ Caspair Ltd. [*Kenya*] [*ICAO designator*] (FAAC)
SAL............ Laboratory Drier (RU)
Sal .... Saline [*Salt Pit*] [*Military map abbreviation World War I*] [*French*] (MTD)
SAL............ Salisbury [*Public Library Service*] [*National Union Catalogue of Australia symbol*]
SAL............ San Salvador [*El Salvador*] [*Airport symbol*] (OAG)
SAL............ School of Australian Linguistics [*Darwin Community College*] [*Australia*]
Sal .... Signal [*Signal*] [*Military map abbreviation World War I*] [*French*] (MTD)

SAL........... Societat Arqueologica Lulliana [*Spanish*] (SLS)
SAL........... Societe Africaine de Lubrifiants
SAL........... Societe Anonyme Libanaise
SAL........... Societe Astronomique de Liege [*Belgium*] (SLS)
SAL........... Societe d'Anthropologie de Lyon
SAL........... South African Pound
SAL........... South American Program Library (ADPT)
SAL........... South Arabian League
SAL........ Southern Airlines [*Australia*]
SAL........ Subsecretaria de Asuntos Legislativos [*Undersecretariat of Legislative Affairs*] [*Argentina*] (LA)
SAL........... Suid-Afrikaanse Lugdiens [*South African Airways*] (AF)
SAL........... Suid-Afrikaanse Lugmag [*South African Air Force*] [*See also SALM, SAAF*]
SAL........... Winch Power Unit (RU)
SALA........ Sammenslutningen af Landbrugets Arbejdsgiverforeninger [*Agricultural Employers' Federation*] [*Denmark*] (EY)
SALA........ Secret Army for the Liberation of Armenia
SALA........ South African Library Association
SALACO... Saudi Arabian Lube Additives Co.
SALAM...... Societe Africaine de Lampes et d'Appareils Menagers
SALB........ South African Library for the Blind (PDAA)
SALC........ Secret Army for the Liberation of Corsica
SALCI...... Societe Alsacienne de la Cote-D'Ivoire
SALCI...... Societe des Ananas de la Cote-D'Ivoire
SALDRU... Southern Africa Labour and Development Research Unit
SALE........ Syndesmos Anaptyxeos Larnakos kai Eparkhias [*Larnaca City and District Development Association*] (GC)
SALEA...... South Australian Livestock Exporters' Association
SALEC...... Salinera Ecuatoriana SA [*Ecuador*] (DSCA)
SALF........ Somali Abo Liberation Front [*Ethiopia*] [*Political party*] (PD)
SALF........ Sveriges Arbetsledareforbund [*Swedish Association of Supervisors*] (EAIO)
SALGA...... South Australian Local Government Association
SALGGC... South Australian Local Government Grants Commission
SALGITC ... South Australian Local Government Industry Training Committee
SALH........ Svetove Akademicke Letni Hry [*World Student Summer Sports Games*] (CZ)
SALIE........ Sydney Area Library Information Exchange [*Australia*] (ADA)
SALIGNA ... Comercio Reflorestamento e Servicos Tecnicos Ltd. [*Brazil*] (DSCA)
SALINTO ... Societe des Salines du Togo
SALLG...... South Australian Law Librarians Group
SALM........ Salvation Army League of Mercy [*British*] (EAIO)
SALM........ Suid-Afrikaanse Lugmag [*South African Air Force*] [*Use SAAF*] (AF)
SALMA..... South African Agricultural Machinery Association (AA)
SALMAR .. Societe Algerienne des Travaux Publics et Maritimes [*Algerian Public and Maritime Works Company*] (AF)
SALP........ Societe Africaine de Librairie et de Papeterie
SALP........ South African Labour Party
Salpie........ Salpetrerie [*Saltpeter Works*] [*Military map abbreviation World War I*] [*French*] (MTD)
SALS........ South African Logopedic Society
SALS........ Southern African Literature Society [*Botswana*] (EAIO)
SAlSi.......... Aluminium-Legierungs-Schweissdraht mit Silizium [*Aluminum Alloy Welding Wire with Silicon*] [*German*] (GCA)
SALT........ Sammenslutningen af Leverandoerer af Tilsaetningsstoffer i Danmark [*Denmark*] (EAIO)
SALT........ Societe Agricole Logone Tchad
SALT........ South Australian Library Technicians [*Committee*]
SALTA...... South Australian Lawn Tennis Association
SALTU...... South African Lawn Tennis Union
SALU......... Suid-Afrikaanse Landbou-Unie [*South African Agricultural Union*] [*Afrikaans*]
SAM .... Fixed Air Maintenance Depot (RU)
SAM .... Institut fuer Meeresgeologie und Meeresbiologie "Senckenberg" ["*Senckenberg" Institute for Oceanology and Ocean Biology*] (MSC)
SAM .... Punched-Card Machine (RU)
SAM .... Punched-Card Machine Plant (RU)
SAM .... Sahabat Alam Malaysia [*Friends of the Earth - Malaysia*] (EAIO)
SAM .... Salamo [*Papua New Guinea*] [*Airport symbol*] (OAG)
Sam........... Samoa (BARN)
Sam........... Samuel [*Samuel*] [*Afrikaans*]
SAM .... Seccao de Amparo a Mulher [*Brazil*]
SAM .... Senegal Agricole Materiel
SAM .... Servico Aereo de Mocambique
SAM .... Sindicato Argentino de Musicos [*Argentine Musicians Union*] (LA)
SAM .... Sistema Alimentario Mexicano [*Mexican Food Supply System*] [*Mexico*] (LA)
SAM .... Slaska Akademia Medyczna [*Silesian Academy of Medicine*] [*Poland*]

SAM .... Slavomakedonikon Apelevtherotikon Metopon [*Slav-Macedonian People's Liberation Front*] [*Greek*] (GC)
SAM .... Sociedad Aeronautica de Medellin [*Colombia*] [*ICAO designator*] (FAAC)
SAM .... Sociedad Aeronautica de Medellin Consolidada [*Colorado*]
SAM .... Sociedad Argentina de Metales [*Argentine Society of Metals*] (LAA)
SAM .... Sociedade Africana de Mocambique [*African Society of Mozambique*]
SAM .... Societa Anonima Meccanidraulica
SAM .... Societe Abidjanaise Metallurgique
SAM .... Societe Africaine de Menuiserie
SAM .... Societe Africaine de Mines [*African Mines Company*] [*French*] (AF)
SAM .... Societe Agricole de la Mambere
SAM .... Societe Agricole de M'banga
SAM .... Societe Automobile et Mecanique
SAM .... Societes Auxiliaires de Materiel [*France*] (FLAF)
SAM .... Society of Americanists [*Paris, France*] (EA)
SAM .... South American
SAM .... South Australian Micrographics Seminar and Exhibition
SAM .... Specialites Automobiles de Meknes
SAM .... Speicherausgabemeldung [*German*] (ADPT)
SAM .... Squadre di Azione Mussolini [*Mussolini Action Squads*] [*Italian*] (WER)
S AM .... Suid-Amerika [*South America*] [*SA*] [*See also*] [*Afrikaans*]
SAMA .... Gral Alvear [*Argentina*] [*ICAO location identifier*] (ICLI)
SAMA .... Saudi Arabian Monetary Agency [*Riyadh*]
SAMA .... Sociedad de Amistad Mexico Albania [*Mexico-Albania Friendship Society*] (EAIO)
SAMA .... Societe d'Approvisionnement Maritime (Adams & Cie.)
SAMA .... Societe d'Assurances Millot Andre pour les Pays d'Outre-Mer
SAMA .... Societe d'Avitaillement Maritime d'Abidjan
SAMA .... South Australian Medical Association [*National Union Catalogue of Australia symbol*]
SAMA .... South Australian Mining Association
SAMA .... Southern African Museums Association (SLS)
SAMA .... Stati Africani e Malgascio Associati
SAMAC..... Societe Africaine de Manufacture et de Commerce
SAMAC..... Societe Africaine de Materiaux Ceramiques
SAMAF..... Societe Auxiliaire du Manganese de Franceville
SAMAFORTAL ... Societe Auxiliaire de Materiel Africain Ortal
SAMAG .... Societe Algerienne des Magasins Generaux
SAMALIDA ... Societe Arabe Mauritano-Libyenne de Developpement Agricole (EY)
SAMAN .... Sociedad Anonima, Molineros Arroceros Nacionales [*Uruguay*] (DSCA)
SAMANGOKY ... Societe Malgache d'Amenagement et la Mise en Valeur de la Vallee du Bas Mangoky [*Malagasy Company for the Development and Utilization of the Lower Mangoky Valley*] (AF)
SAMAO .... Societe Auxiliaire de Materiel pour l'Afrique Occidentale
SAMAPA .. Servicio Municipal de Agua Potable y Alcantarillado [*Municipal Waterworks and Sewerage Service*] [*Bolivia*] (LA)
SAMAR..... Societe Agricole de Marambitsy
samarb .... Samarbeid [*Collaboration*] [*Publishing Danish/Norwegian*]
SAMARCO ... Saudi Arabian Maritime Company Ltd. [*Jeddah*] (ME)
SAMAREC ... Saudi Arabian Marketing & Refining Co. (EY)
SAMARTO ... Societe Anonyme Martini Pinto et Cie.
SAMAT..... Societe Africaine de Representation de Materiel Automobile et Technique
SAMATAGOR ... Societe Auxiliaire de Materiel Agricole Ortal [*Senegal*]
sambo......... Self-Defense without Weapons (RU)
SAMC....... Cristo Redentor [*Argentina*] [*ICAO location identifier*] (ICLI)
SAMC....... South African Medical Corps
SAMCO .... Saudi Methanol Co.
SAMCO .... Societe Anonyme de Manufacture de Confection
SAMCOA ... Syndicat des Agents Maritimes de la Cote Occidentale d'Afrique
SAMCOR ... South Australian Meat Corporation (ADA)
SAMDU .... Servico de Assistencia Medica Domiciliar e de Urgencia [*Home and Emergency Medical Assistance Service*] [*Brazil*] (LA)
SAME........ Mendoza/El Plumerillo [*Argentina*] [*ICAO location identifier*] (ICLI)
SAME........ South Australian Matriculation Examination
SAME........ Spanish Association for Medical Education [*British*] (EAIO)
SAMEA..... South Australian Meat Exporters' Association
SAMEAC.. South Australian Multicultural and Ethnic Affairs Commission
SAMEC..... Societe Africaine de Materiel d'Entreprise et de Construction
SAMED..... South African Medical Literature [*South African Research Council*] [*Information service or system*] (CRD)
SAMEGE.. Societe Anonyme Marocaine d'Etudes, de Gestion, et d'Entreprise
SAMEIA ... Sociedade Anonima de Maquinas e Equipamentos Industriais Agropecuarios [*Brazil*] (DSCA)
SAMELA .. Societe des Ateliers Metalliques et d'Entreprises de Laon-Afrique
samengest .. Samengesteld [*Compiled*] [*Publishing*] [*Netherlands*]

samenw ...... Samenwerking [*Collaboration*] [*Publishing*] [*Netherlands*]
SAMER..... Societe d'Armament et de Manutention de la Mer Rouge [*Red Sea Shipping Company*] [*Djibouti*] (AF)
S Amer....... South America
SAMES..... Societe Anonyme des Machines Electrostatiques [*Electrostatic Machines Corporation*] [*French*] (WER)
SAMET..... Societe Africaine de Menuiserie Ebenisterie et Tapisserie
SAMF....... Mendoza [*Argentina*] [*ICAO location identifier*] (ICLI)
SAMF....... Societe Africaine de Mobilier et Ferronnerie
SAMF....... Swedish Association of Masters in Forestry (EAIO)
SAMFS..... South Australian Metropolitan Fire Service
SAMG .... Sociedad Argentina de Mineria y Geologia [*Argentine Society of Minerals and Geology*] [*Buenos Aires*] (LAA)
SAMGGM ... Sehit Aileleri Malul Gaziler ve Gorev Malulleri Dernegi [*Society for the Families of Those Killed and Wounded in Action*] [*Turkish Cypriot*] (GC)
SamGU ...... Samarkand State University Imeni Alisher Navoi (RU)
SAMH....... Valle Hermoso [*Argentina*] [*ICAO location identifier*] (ICLI)
SAMI........ Central Asian Medical Institute (RU)
SAMI........ San Martin [*Argentina*] [*ICAO location identifier*] (ICLI)
SAMI........ Service de l'Assistance Medicale aux Indigenes
SAMI........ Sistema Aereo Militar Interamericano [*Inter-American Military Air System*] (LA)
SAMI........ Societe Africaine de Materiel Industriel
SAMI........ Svenska Artisters och Musikers Intresseorganisation [*Swedish Artists And Musicians Interest Organization*] (EAIO)
SAMIA...... Societe Arabe des Industries Metallurgiques Mauritano-Koweitienne [*Mauritanian-Kuwaiti Arab Metallurgical Industries Company*] (AF)
SAMIEA ... South African Motor Industry Employers' Association (AA)
SAMIN...... Societe d'Exploitation de Sables et Mineraux [*French*]
SAMINE... Societe Anonyme d'Entreprises Minieres [*Morocco*]
SAMIPAC ... Societe Auxiliaire et Miniere du Pacifique [*France*] (PDAA)
SAMI-PRADEC ... Societe Anonyme de Miroiterie, Peinture, Ravalement, Decoration
SAMIR...... Societe Anonyme Marocaine Italienne de Raffinage [*Moroccan-Italian Refining Corporation*] (AF)
SAMI-TCHAD ... Societe Africaine de Materiel Industriel du Tchad
SAMJ........ Jachal [*Argentina*] [*ICAO location identifier*] (ICLI)
SAML........ Nationella Samlingspartiet [*National Coalition Party*] [*Finland*] [*Political party*] (PPE)
saml........... Samling [*Collection*] [*Sweden*]
saml........... Samling [*Collection*] [*Danish/Norwegian*]
SAML........ Sociedad Anonima Mercantil de Lima [*Import-export company*] [*Peru*]
samlingsbd ... Samlingsband [*Collective Volume*] [*Sweden*]
sam lpb....... Independent Light Antiaircraft Battery (BU)
SAMM ...... Malargue [*Argentina*] [*ICAO location identifier*] (ICLI)
SAMM ...... Servicos de Assistencia Medica Militar [*Military Medical Assistance Services*] [*Angola*] (AF)
SAMM ...... Societe d'Applications des Machines Motrices [*French*]
SAMM ...... South Australian Maritime Museum
SAMMA ... Societe Anonyme d'Acconage et de Manutention en Mauritanie
sammenfold ... Sammenfoldet [*Folded*] [*Publishing Danish/Norwegian*]
sammetsbd ... Sammetsband [*Velvet Binding*] [*Publishing*] [*Sweden*]
Samml...... Sammlung [*Collection*] [*German*]
Sammlg...... Sammlung [*Collection*] [*German*]
SAMNAM ... Samradet for Nordisk Amatormusik [*Arhus, Denmark*] (EAIO)
SAMO .... Swedish Association of Military Officers (EAIO)
SAMOA .... Societe Agence Maritime de l'Ouest Africain [*Senegal*]
SAMOA .... Societe Agence Maritime de l'Ouest Africain Cameroun
SAMOA .... Societe Anonyme des Metaux Oeuvres en Afrique [*Morocco*]
SAMOA-CI ... Societe Agence Maritime de l'Ouest Africain - Cote d'Ivoire [*Shipping*] [*Ivory Coast*]
SAMOR .... Societe d'Approvisionnement du Monde Rural
SAMOREM ... Societe Africaine de Montage et de Reparation Mecanique
SAMP........ La Paz [*Argentina*] [*ICAO location identifier*] (ICLI)
SAMP........ Sociedad Suramericana de Metales Preciosos SA [*Colombia*] (COL)
SAMPA..... South African Modern Pentathlon Association
SAMPI ...... Suid-Afrikaanse Mielieprodusente-Instituut [*South African Corn Producing Institute*] (AF)
SAMQ .... Mendoza Aeroparque [*Argentina*] [*ICAO location identifier*] (ICLI)
SAMR........ San Rafael [*Argentina*] [*ICAO location identifier*] (ICLI)
SAMR........ South African Mounted Riflemen
SAMRA..... South African Market Research Association (SLS)
SAMRAF .. South African Military Refugee Aid Fund
SAMREF... South Australian Mines Reference [*Database*]
SAMRO ..... South African Music Rights Organisation
SAMS........ San Carlos [*Argentina*] [*ICAO location identifier*] (ICLI)
SAMS........ Saudi Arabian Mining Syndicate
SAMS........ Scottish Association for Marine Science
SAMS........ Society of Advanced Motorists Sydney [*Australia*]
SAMS........ [*The*] South African Mathematical Society (SLS)
SAMS........ South American Missionary Society

SAMS........ Swiss Academy of Medical Sciences (EAIO)
SAMSA ..... Serrature Auto Meridionali Stampi Attrezzature SpA [*Avellino, Italy*]
SAMSO ..... Suid-Afrikaanse Mieliespesialiteite Organisasie [*South African Corn Specialty Organization*] (AF)
SAM-SOFRATOP ... Societe Auxiliaire de Materiel de la Societe Francaise de Travaux Topographiques et Photogrammetriques
samt........... Saemtliche [*Complete*] [*German*]
samt........... Samtidig [*Contemporary*] [*Danish/Norwegian*]
SAMTA..... South Australian Music Teachers Association
SAMTAS .. Supervisory and Management Training Association of Singapore (PDAA)
samtid .... Samtidig [*Contemporary*] [*Danish/Norwegian*]
samtl .... Saemtliche [*All*] [*German*]
SAMU .... Uspallata [*Argentina*] [*ICAO location identifier*] (ICLI)
SAMUS..... South African Medical Ultrasound Society (AA)
SAMV....... Mendoza [*Argentina*] [*ICAO location identifier*] (ICLI)
SAMV....... Suider Afrikaanse Museumvereniging [*Southern African Museums Association*] (EAIO)
SAMVIC ... Surveying and Mapping Victorian Industrial Council [*Australia*]
SAMW ...... Schweizerische Akademie der Medizinischen Wissenschaften [*Swiss Academy of Medical Science*] (SLS)
SAMWU ... South African Mineworkers Union (AF)
SAN .... Pump Power Unit (RU)
San .... Sanaat [*Art, Craft*] (TU)
san .... Sanatorium [*Topography*] (RU)
San .... Sanayi [*Industry*] (TU)
San .... Sanitaets [*Medical*] (EG)
san .... Sanitation, Sanitary, Medical (RU)
san .... Sanomalehdet [*Journalism*] [*Finland*]
San .... Santiye [*Construction Site*] (TU)
SAN .... Science Association of Nigeria
SAN .... Senior Advocate of Nigeria
SAN .... Servicio Aerofotografico Nacional [*National Aerophotographical Service*] [*Peru*] (LAA)
SAN .... Servicios Aereos Nacionales [*Ecuador*] [*ICAO designator*] (FAAC)
SAN .... Slovak Academy of Sciences (RU)
SAN .... South [*Australian Government*] Analytical [*Laboratories*] [*National Union Catalogue of Australia symbol*]
SAN .... South Australian Navy
SAN .... Srpska Akademija Nauka [*Serbian Academy of Sciences*] (YU)
SANA .... Scientists Against Nuclear Arms [*Australia*]
SANA .... South African Nurserymen's Association (AA)
SANA .... South African Nursing Association (AA)
SANA .... Southern Afrikan News Agency
SANA .... Syrian Arab News Agency (ME)
SANAA ...... Servicio Autonomo Nacional de Agua y Alcantarillado [*National Water and Sewage Service*] [*Honduras*] (LAA)
SANAB...... South African Narcotics Bureau
SANAE...... South African National Antarctic Expedition
SANA(NZ) ... Scientists Against Nuclear Arms (New Zealand)
sanap......... Medical Aviation Regiment (RU)
SANAR...... Sanitaere Einrichtungen und Armaturen [*Sanitary Plumbing Equipment and Fittings*] (EG)
SANAS..... Service d'Alimentation et Nutrition Appliquee du Senegal
Sanat........ Sanatorium [*Sanatorium*] [*Military map abbreviation World War I*] [*French*] (MTD)
SANAUTOS ... Compania Santandereana de Automoviles Ltda. [*Bucaramanga*] (COL)
SANB......... Sanayi ve Teknoloji Bakanligi [*Ministry of Industry and Technology*] (TU)
SANB......... Societe Agricole du Nasso et de la Bia
SANB......... South African National Bibliography
SANBIM... Santral Bilgi Islem Merkezi, AS [*Central Data Processing Headquarters, Inc.*] (TU)
SANBRA ... Sociedade Algodoeira do Nordeste Brasileiro, SA [*Northeast Brazil Cotton Association, Inc.*] (LA)
SANC .... Catamarca [*Argentina*] [*ICAO location identifier*] (ICLI)
SANC .... Sanctuary [*Naval cadet's hiding place for smoking*] [*Slang*] [*British*] (DSUE)
SANCA...... South African National Council on Alcoholism and Drug Dependence
SANCAR... South African National Council for Antarctic Research
SANCAR... South African National Council for Antarctic Research
SANCB...... South African National Council for the Blind (AA)
SANCC..... South African Nature Conservation Centre (AA)
SANCD ..... South African National Council for the Deaf (AA)
sancha...... Medical Unit [*Military term*] (RU)
SANCHED ... South African Association for Health Education (AA)
SANCI....... South African National Committee on Illumination
SANCIAHS ... South African National Committee for the International Association of Hydrological Sciences
SANCIAWPRC ... South African National Committee of the International Association on Water Pollution Research and Control (EAIO)

SANCOLD ... South African National Committee on Large Dams (AA)
SANCOR... South African National Commission for Oceanographic Research (MSC)
SANCOT... South African National Committee on Tunnelling
SANCS ...... State Authorities Non-Contributory Superannuation Scheme [*Australia*]
SANCST ... Saudi Arabian National Center for Science and Technology [*Riyadh*] (IMH)
SANCU ..... South African National Consumer Union (AA)
SANCWEC ... South African National Committee of the World Energy Conference (PDAA)
S & CI .... Silicate and Chemical Industries Pty. Ltd. [*South Africa*] (AA)
Sand Isls .... Sandwich Islands
SANDRAMINE ... Compagnie Miniere Haut Sassandra [*Haut Sassandra Mining Company*] [*Ivory Coast*] (AF)
Sandruzhina ... Medical Battalion (BU)
SANE........ Santiago Del Estero [*Argentina*] [*ICAO location identifier*] (ICLI)
SANE........ Society Against Nuclear Energy [*South Africa*] (AA)
SANE........ Students Aware of the Natural Environment [*Australia*]
SANECOR ... South African National Committee for the Engineering Committee on Oceanic Research (AA)
SANEF ...... South African National Equestrian Federation (AA)
SANEGRAM ... Plano de Saneamento de Grande Sao Paulo [*Greater Sao Paulo Sanitation Plan*] [*Brazil*] (LA)
SANEL...... Suid-Afrikaanse Nasionale Epilepsieliga [*South African National Epilepsy League*] (AA)
SANEPID ... Centrul Sanitaro-Anti-Epidemic [*Health and Anti-Epidemic Center*] (RO)
Sanepidstantsiya ... Medical Epidemiological Station (BU)
SANF........ Salvation Army Nurses' Fellowship (EAIO)
SANF........ South African Naval Forces
SANF........ Sudan African National Front
SANG .... Saudi Arabian National Guard
SANG .... South Australian Network Group
SANGORM ... South African National Group of the International Society for Rock Mechanics (SLS)
SANH........ Rio Hondo/Las Termas [*Argentina*] [*ICAO location identifier*] (ICLI)
SANI........ Tinogasta [*Argentina*] [*ICAO location identifier*] (ICLI)
SANIGMI ... Central Asian Scientific Research Hydrometeorological Institute (RU)
SANIIRI.... Central Asian Scientific Research Institute of Irrigation (RU)
SANIISh.... Central Asian Scientific Research Institute of Sericulture (RU)
SANIKIS... Central Asian Scientific Research Complex Institute of Structures (RU)
SaNIS .... Observation and Communication Aircraft (RU)
SANKIGHW ... Suid-Afrikaanse Nasionale Komitee vir die Internasionale Genootskap van Hidrologiese Wetenskappe [*South African National Committee for the International Association of Hydrological Sciences*] (AA)
SANKO ..... Santral Konfeksiyon Sanayii ve Ticaret AS [*Central Ready-Made Clothing Industry and Trade Corp.*] (TU)
sankom....... Sanitary Commission (RU)
SANKON .. Suid-Afrikaanse Nasionale Komitee vir Oseanografiese Navorsing [*South Africa*] (AA)
SANKV...... Suid-Afrikaanse Nasionale Komitee vir Verligting [*South Africa*] (AA)
SANKWEK ... Wereldenergiekonferensie (Nasionale Komitee) [*South Africa*] (AA)
SANL......... La Rioja/Cap. V. Almandos Almonacid [*Argentina*] [*ICAO location identifier*] (ICLI)
SANLAM ... Suid-Afrikaanse Nasionale Lewensassuransie-Maatskappy [*South African National Life Assurance Co. Ltd.*]
SANLC...... South African Native Labor Corps
SANLF ...... Saudi Arabian National Liberation Front [*Political party*] (BJA)
SANMIG ... San Miguel Beer (DSUE)
SANNC ..... South African Native National Congress
SANO........ Chilecito [*Argentina*] [*ICAO location identifier*] (ICLI)
SANO .... Medical Section, Sanitary Department (RU)
SANOS...... Servicio Autarquico Nacional de Obras Sanitarias [*Paraguay*] (LAA)
SANOVNO ... Medical Section of a Military Scientific Society (RU)
SANP........ Sociedad de Anatomia Normal y Patologica [*Normal and Pathological Surgery Society*] [*Buenos Aires, Argentina*] (LAA)
SANPA...... Turk Sanayi Arastirma, Nesriyat, ve Pazarlama Merkezi [*Turkish Industrial Research, Publicity, and Marketing Center*] (TU)
SANPER ... Systeme d'Analyse de Performances [*French*] (ADPT)
Sanpost ...... Medical Center (BU)
sanprosvet ... Sanitary Education (RU)
SANRA...... South African National Rifle Association
SANRA...... Suid-Afrikaanse Nasionale Raad Insake Alkoholisme en Afhanklikheid van Verdowingsmiddels [*South African National Council on Alcoholism and Drug Dependence*] (AA)

San-Rat...... Sanitaetsrat [*Member of the Board of Health*] [*German*]
SANRB...... Suid-Afrikaanse Nasionale Raad vir Blindes [*South African National Council for the Blind*] (AA)
SANRD ..... Suid-Afrikaanse Nasionale Raad vir Dowes [*South Africa*] (AA)
SANROC... South African Non-Racial Open Committee for Olympic Sports (AF)
Sans .... Sanskrit [*Sanskrit*] [*Afrikaans*]
SANS........ Slovensko-Ameriski Narodni Svet [*Slovenian-American National Council*] (YU)
SANS........ South African Naval Service
SANS........ Sudano-Afrikanskii Natsional'nyi Soiuz
Sans Et....... Sansur Edilmistir [*Censored*] (TU)
SANSW..... Shires Association of New South Wales [*Australia*]
SANT........ Tucuman/Teniente Benjamim Matienzo [*Argentina*] [*ICAO location identifier*] (ICLI)
SANTA...... Sociedade Anonima Nacional de Transportes Aereos [*Brazil*]
SANTA...... South African National Tuberculosis Association
SANTAM ... Suid-Afrikaanse Trust- en Assuransie-Maatskappy
Santekhproyekt ... State Planning Institute for Industrial Sanitary Engineering Planning of the Gosstroy SSSR (RU)
Santekhstroy ... State Trust of Sanitary Engineering Construction (RU)
SANTUR... Compania Santandereana de Turismo [*Bucaramanga*] (COL)
SANTV...... Suid-Afrikaanse Nasionale Tuberkulosevereniging [*South Africa*] (AA)
SANU .... San Juan [*Argentina*] [*ICAO location identifier*] (ICLI)
SANU .... Slovenacka Akademija na Naukite i Umetnosta [*Slovenian Academy of Sciences and Arts*] [*Ljubljana*] (YU)
SANU .... Somali African National Union (AF)
SANU .... Special Anti-Narcotics Unit [*Colorado*]
SANU .... Sudan African National Union
SANUM .... South Africa National Union for Mineworkers
SANUM .... Suid-Afrikaanse Vereniging vir Numeriese Wiskunde [*South African Society for Numerical Mathematics*] (AA)
sanupr .... Sanitary Administration (RU)
SANVU ..... Suid-Afrikaanse Nasionale Verbruikersunie [*South Africa*] (AA)
SANW .... Ceres [*Argentina*] [*ICAO location identifier*] (ICLI)
SANY .... Societe Auxiliaire de N'Gor Yoff
SANZ .... Standards Association of New Zealand
SAO .... Automatic Optimization System (RU)
SAO .... Sahel Aviation Service [*Mali*] [*ICAO designator*] (FAAC)
SAO .... Sao Paulo [*Brazil*] [*Airport symbol*] (OAG)
SAO .... Societe Agricole de l'Ouest
SAO .... South Asian Outreach
SAO .... Strafor Afrique Occidentale [*Dakar*]
SAOA .... South African Orthopaedic Association (EAIO)
SAOA .... South Australian Ornithological Association (SLS)
SAOB .... Stuurgroep Automatisering Openbare Bibliotheken
SAOBTA ... Societe Anonyme Oddos Bois Tozan Agneby
SAOC .... Rio Cuarto/Area de Material [*Argentina*] [*ICAO location identifier*] (ICLI)
SAOC .... South African Olympic Committee
SAOC .... South African Orchid Council (AA)
SAOC .... South African Ordnance Corps
SAOC .... South Australian Olympic Council
SAOD .... Villa Dolores [*Argentina*] [*ICAO location identifier*] (ICLI)
SAOE .... Embalse Rio Tercero [*Argentina*] [*ICAO location identifier*] (ICLI)
SAOGIDEP ... Central Asian Branch of the Gidroenergoproyekt (RU)
SAOHSC... South Australian Occupational Health and Safety Commission
SAOI......... Sindicato Autonomo del Omnibus Interdepartmental [*Autonomous Union of Interdepartmental Bus Drivers*] [*Uruguay*] (LA)
SAOKU ..... Suid-Afrikaanse Ontwikkelingskorporasie vir Uitvindings [*South Africa*] (AA)
SAOL......... Laboulaye [*Argentina*] [*ICAO location identifier*] (ICLI)
SAOM .... Marcos Juarez [*Argentina*] [*ICAO location identifier*] (ICLI)
SAON .... Sindicato Argentino de Obreros Navales [*Argentine Union of Shipyard Workers*] (LA)
SAON .... Socialist Academy of Social Sciences (RU)
SAONGA .. South African Olympic and National Games Association
SAOR .... Suid-Afrikaanse Orgideeraad [*South African Orchid Council*] (AA)
SAOR .... Villa Reynolds [*Argentina*] [*ICAO location identifier*] (ICLI)
SAOS........ South African Optical Society (AA)
SAOS........ South Southern African Ornithological Society (SLS)
SAOT........ Swedish Association of Occupational Therapists (EAIO)
SAOU .... San Luis [*Argentina*] [*ICAO location identifier*] (ICLI)
SAOU .... Suid-Afrikaanse Onderwysersunie
SAOUG .... South African Online User Group (AA)
SAOV .... Suid-Afrikaanse Optiese Vereniging [*South African Optical Society*] (AA)
SAOV .... Suid-Afrikaanse Ortopediese Vereniging [*South African Orthopaedic Association*] (EAIO)
SAOV .... Symvoulion Amoivaias Oikonomikis Voitheias [*Council for Mutual Economic Assistance*] (GC)
SAP........... Automatic Search System (RU)

sap	Composite Air Regiment (BU)
SAP	Nouvelle Societe Africaine de Plastiques
SAP	Sabah Alliance Party (ML)
SAP	San Pedro Sula [Honduras] [Airport symbol] (OAG)
sap	Saper [Combat Engineer] [Poland]
SAP	Schweizer Automatik Pool [German] (ADPT)
SAP	Schweizerische Arztegesellschaft fur Psychotherapie (EAIO)
SAP	Seccao de Agitacao e Propaganda [Agitation and Propaganda Section] [Of PCB] [Brazil] (LA)
sap	Self-Propelled Artillery Regiment (RU)
SAP	Servicio de Aprovisionamientos [Supply Department] [Spanish] (WER)
SAP	Servicos Aereos Portugueses Ltda. [Portugal]
SAP	Seychelles Agence de Presse [News agency] (EY)
SAP	Sidirodromoi Athinon-Peiraios [Athens-Piraeus Railways] (GC)
SAP	Sintered Aluminum Powder (RU)
SAP	Slovenija Avtopromet [Slovenian Motor Transport] [Ljubljana] (YU)
SAP	Social Action Party [Thailand] [Political party] (FEA)
SAP	Socialistische Arbeiderspartij [Socialist Workers' Party] [Netherlands] [Political party] (PPW)
SAP	Sociedad Agronomica de Panama [Panama] (DSCA)
SAP	Sociedad Argentina de Pediatria [Argentine Pediatric Society] [Buenos Aires] (LAA)
SAP	Sociedade Anatomica Portuguesa [Portuguese Anatomical Society] (SLS)
SAP	Societe Africaine de Peinture
SAP	Societe Africaine de Pneumatique
SAP	Societe Africaine des Peaux
SAP	Societe Africaine des Petroles [African Petroleum Company] [Senegal] (AF)
SAP	Societe Africaine Pigeon et Compagnie
SAP	Societe Agricole de Prevoyance [Algeria]
SAP	Societe Algerienne des Polymeres
SAP	Societe d'Anthropologie de Paris [Anthropological Society of Paris] [French] (SLS)
SAP	[The] Society of Analytical Psychology (SLS)
SAP	Soma Amesou Paramvaseos [Instant Intervention Corps] (GC)
SAP	Soma Astynomias Poleon [Cities Police (Corps)] [Greek] (GC)
SAP	South African Party [Political party] (PPW)
SAP	South African Police (ECON)
SAP	South African Police Force
SAP	Soysal Adelet Partisi [Social Justice Party] [Turkish Cyprus] [Political party] (PPE)
SAP	Sozialistische Arbeiterpartei [Socialist Workers' Party] (WEN)
SAP	Special Action Programme
SAP	Stowarzyszenie Architektow Polskich [Association of Polish Architects] (POL)
SAP	Structural Adjustment Package [Australia]
SAP	Structural Adjustment Programme [Nigeria]
SAP	Suid-Afrikaanse Partij
SAP	Suid-Afrikaanse Polisie [South African Police] [Afrikaans]
SAP	Suid-Afrikaanse Produkte [South African Product] [Afrikaans]
SAP	Suramericana de Promociones Ltda. [Colombia] (COL)
SAP	Sveriges Socialdemokratiska Arbetareparti [Swedish Social Democratic Labor Party] [Political party] (PPW)
SAP	Symvoulion Ambelourgikon Proiondon [Vine Products Council] [Cyprus] (GC)
SAP	Syndesmos Anapiron Polemou [League of War Disabled] [Greek] (GC)
SAPA	Security and Property Assurance SpA [Italy] (EY)
SAPA	Sociedad Anonima Petrolera Argentina [Argentina] (LAA)
SapA	Societa in Accomandita per Azioni [Limited Partnership with Shares] [Italian] (IMH)
SAPA	Societe Africaine de Produits Alimentaires
SAPA	Societe Africaine des Peches de l'Atlantique
SAPA	South African Polo Association
SAPA	South African Poultry Association
SAPA	South African Powerboat Association
SAPA	[The] South African Psychological Association (SLS)
SAPA	South African Publishers' Association
SAPA	Suid-Afrikaanse Press Agentskaap [South African Press Agency] (AF)
SAPAC	Societe Anonyme de Peche, d'Armement et de Conservation
SAPAC	Societe Parisienne d'Achats en Commun [Purchasing agency] [France] (IMH)
SAPA-CAMEROUN	Societe d'Application de Peintures en Afrique - Cameroun
SAPACI	Societe des Papeteries de Cote-D'Ivoire
SAPAL	Societe Africaine de Produits Alimentaires [Senegal]
SAPAL	Societe Agro-Pastorale et de Legumes
SAPAM	Swedish Association for the Protection of Ancient Monuments (EAIO)
SAPARC	South Australian Performing Arts Resource Centre
SAPAT	South African Picture Analysis Test
sapb	Combat-Engineer Battalion (RU)
SAPB	Societe Anonyme Plantations Guy de Brecey & Cie.
SAPB	South Australian Psychological Board
SAPC	Societe Africaine de Plomberie et de Couverture
SAPC	South Australian Philatelic Council
SAPC	South Australian Planning Commission
SAPCA	Societe Anonyme de Pecheries et Conserves Alimentaires [Morocco]
SAPCAM	Societe Africaine de Produits Chimiques Agricoles et Menagers
SAPCE	Societe Algerienne de Produits Chimiques et d'Engrais [Algerian Chemical and Fertilizer Products Company] (AF)
SAPCO	Societe d'Amenagement de la Petite Cote
SAPCO	Sudanese African People's Congress [Political party] (EY)
SAPCS	Societe Africaine des Produits Chimiques Shell [Ivory Coast]
SAPD	Sammenslutningen af Praktiserande Dyrlaeger [Denmark] (SLS)
sape	Combat Engineer Troop (RU)
SAPE	Societe Anonyme Participations et d'Etudes [French]
SAPEA	Syndesmos Agoniston Poleos kai Eparkhias Ammokhostou [Famagusta Town and District Fighters League] (GC)
SAPEBA	Societe Agricole pour l'Exploitation de la Banane
SAPEC	Societe de Peche et Conserves [Fishing and Canning Company] [Tunisia] (AF)
SAPECO	Societe Africaine de Promotion Economique
SAPEF	Societe Africaine de Publicite et d'Editions Fusionnees
SAPEGA	Societe d'Approvisionnement et de Peche du Gabon
SAPEL	Syndesmos Agoniston Poleos kai Eparkhias Lemesou [Limassol Town and District Fighters League] (GC)
SAPELEC	Societe Africaine des Piles Electriques
SAPERI	Societe d'Application et de Perfectionnement Industriel
SAPEVA	Syndicat des Producteurs de Vanille [Vanilla Growers Trade Union] [Malagasy] (AF)
SAPF	Auxiliary Front Motor Road (BU)
SAPF	South African Permanent Force (AF)
SAPF	South African Pioneer Force
SAPF	Suider-Afrika Padfederasie [Southern Africa Road Federation - SARF] (EAIO)
SAPFOR	Southern Australia Perpetual Forests Ltd. (ADA)
SAPGIS	South African Photogrammetry and Geo-Information Society (AA)
SAPH	Societe Africaine de Plantations d'Heveas [African Rubber Plantation Company] [Ivory Coast] (AF)
SAPI	Societe Africaine de Peche Industrielle
SAPI	Societe Africaine des Produits pour l'Industrie
SAPIC	Societe Anonyme des Plantations d'Industries et de Commerce
SAPICS	South African Production and Inventory Control Society (AA)
SAPIG	Sociedad Anonima Pesquera Industrial Gallega [Galician Industrial Fishing Corporation] [Spanish] (WER)
SAPK	Societe Anonyme des Plantations de Komono
SAPLE	Societe Anonyme de Peintures, Liants, et Enduits
SAPLOCAM	Sanitaires et Plomberie au Cameroun
SAPM	Societe Africaine de Produits Manufactures [Senegal]
SAPMA	South African Paint Manufacturers' Association (AA)
SAPN	Societe Agricole et Pastorale du Niari
SAPO	Samocinny Pocitac [Computer] (CZ)
SAPO	Sarawak People's Organization [Malaysia] [Political party] (PPW)
SAPO	South African Post Office (PDAA)
SAPOA	South Africa Property Owners' Association
SAPOAD	Systemes Applications Projet Operation Action Detail [French] (ADPT)
SAPONET	South African Post Office Network
sap otd	Combat Engineer Squad (RU)
SAPP	Skholi Anapiron Paidon "Parnassou" [Parnassos Crippled Children's School] [Greek] (GC)
SAPPCO	Saudi Plastics Products Co. (PDAA)
SAPPI	South African Pulp and Paper Industries Ltd.
sapr	Combat-Engineer Company (RU)
SAPRAF	Societe d'Achats de Produits de l'Afrique Francaise
SAPRAK	Samakum Pravatitu Khmer [Cambodian Historians Association] (CL)
Sapre	Sapiniere [Firwood] [Military map abbreviation World War I] [French] (MTD)
SAPREF	South African Petroleum Refineries Ltd. [Shell and British Petroleum Oil Companies]
SAPRESSE	Societe Africaine de Presse, d'Edition, et de Publicite [Publisher] [Senegal]
SAPRHS	South African Plan for Research in the Human Sciences [Human Sciences Research Council] (AA)
SAPRIM	Societe Abidjanaise de Promotions Industrielles et Immobilieres
SAPRITC	South Australian Plastics and Rubber Industry Training Committee
SAPROC	Societe d'Achats de Produits du Cameroun
SAPROCHIM	Societe Africaine de Produits Chimiques
SAPROCSY	Societe Africaine de Produits Chimiques et de Synthese
SAPROLAIT	Societe Africaine de Produits Laitiers
SAPROMA	Societe Africaine de Produits Manufactures

SAPROV ... Societe pour l'Exploitation des Procedes Velut
SAPROZI ... Societe d'Amenagement et de Promotion de la Zone Franche Industrielle
SAPRUCA ... Servicios Aereos de los Productores Agricolas [*Venezuela*] (DSCA)
SAPS .... Scandinavian Association of Paediatric Surgeons (EAIO)
SAPS .... Scandinavian Association of Plastic Surgeons [*See also NPF*] (EAIO)
SAPS .... Servico de Alimentacao da Previdencia Social [*Social Welfare Food Service*] [*Brazil*] (LA)
SAPS .... South African Pharmacological Society (EAIO)
SAPS .... South African Price Schedule
SAPSA ..... Public Service Association of South Australia
SAPSFA .... South Australian Professional Shark Fishermen's Association
SAPSI .... Algorithm Designing for Textual Information Processing (RU)
SAPT .... Societe Africaine de Photogrammetrie et de Topographie
SAPT .... Societe Anonyme Pierre Treche & Cie.
SAPT .... Societe d'Astronomie Populaire de Toulouse [*French*] (SLS)
SAPT .... Swedish Association of Pre-School Teachers (EAIO)
SAPTCO ... Saudi Public Transport Company [*Riyadh*]
SAPTI .... South Australian Panel for Translators and Interpreters
SAPU .... South African Police Union (ECON)
sapv .... Combat Engineer Platoon (RU)
SAPV .... Suid-Afrikaanse Pluimvee Vereniging
SAPWW .... Spanish Association for Purification of Water and Wastewater (EAIO)
SAQ .... San Andros [*Bahamas*] [*Airport symbol*] (OAG)
SAQ .... Schweizerische Arbeitsgmeneinschaft fur Qualitatsbeforderung [*Swiss Association for the Promotion of Quality*] (PDAA)
SAQT .... Sociedad Panamericana de Quimioterapia de la Tuberculosis [*Pan American Society for Chemotherapy of Tuberculosis - PASCT*] (EA)
SAR .... Automated Control System (BU)
SAR .... Automatic Control Station (RU)
SAR .... Automatic Control System (RU)
Sar .... Sarnic [*Cistern, Reservoir, Tank*] (TU)
SAR .... Saudi Arabian Riyal [*Monetary unit*] (DS)
SAR .... Schemas d'Armature Rurale [*North African*]
SAR .... School Achievement Record [*Australia*]
SAR .... Secteur d'Amelioration Rurale [*Rural Development Sector*] [*Algeria*] (AF)
SAR .... Section Artisanale Rurale
SAR .... Serbian Autonomous Region [*Commonwealth of Independent States*] (EECI)
SAR .... Servicios Aereos de Pilotos Ejecutivos [*Colombia*] [*ICAO designator*] (FAAC)
sar .... Shed, Barn [*Topography*] (RU)
SAR .... Siriiskaia Arabskaia Respublika
SAR .... Sjednocena Arabska Republika [*United Arab Republic (UAR)*] (CZ)
SAR .... Societe Africaine de Raffinage [*African Refining Company*] [*Senegal*] (AF)
SAR .... Societe Africaine de Ravitaillement
SAR .... Societe Africaine de Representation
SAR .... Societe Africaine Radioelectrique
SAR .... Societe Algeroise du Radiateur
SAR .... Societes d'Amenagement Regional [*France*] (FLAF)
SAR .... Son Altesse Royale [*His or Her Royal Highness*] [*French*]
SAR .... SONAR Acoustique Remorque [*Acoustic imaging system*] [*French*]
SAR .... South African Railways
SAR .... South Africa Rand
SAR .... South Australian Government Railways
SAR .... South Australian Recordings
SAR .... Special Administrative Region [*Hong Kong*]
SAR .... Speicherauswahlregister [*German*] (ADPT)
SAR .... Srpska Autonomna Oblast [*Serb Autonomous Region*] (EE)
SAR .... Students at Risk [*Australia*]
SAR .... Sua Altezza Reale [*His, or Her, Royal Highness*] [*Italian*]
SAR .... Su Alteza Real [*His, or Her, Royal Highness*] [*Spanish*]
SAR .... Suedlicher Aussenring [*(Berlin) Southern Outer Freight Ring*] (EG)
SAR .... Suid-Afrikaanse Republiek [*South African Republic*] [*Afrikaans*]
SAR .... Svenska Arkitekters Riksfoerbund [*Swedish Architects Association*] (SLS)
SAR .... Synthese-Gas-Anlage Ruhr GmbH
SAR .... Syrian Arab Republic (ME)
SARA .... Saratoga Trunk (DSUE)
SARA .... Servico de Assistencia aos Refugiados de Angola
SARA .... Sleep Apnoeia Research Association [*Australia*]
SARA .... Sociedad Agricola de Reforma Agraria [*Chile*] (DSCA)
SARA .... Societe Abidjanaise de Ravitaillement et d'Alimentation
SARA .... South African-Rhodesian Association
SARA .... South Australian Restaurant Association
SARA .... South Australian Rowing Association
SARA .... Stichting Academisch Rekencentrum Amsterdam

SARA .... Suid-Afrikaanse Raad vir Argitekte [*South Africa*] (AA)
SARA .... Systeme Accelerateur Rhone-Alpes [*Rhone-Alpes Accelerator*] [*Research center*] [*French*] (WND)
SARAC ..... South Australian Rural Advisory Council
SARAH ..... Search and Rescue Aid to Homing [*Australia*]
SAR & H... South African Railways and Harbors
SARARA ... Southern African Rock Art Research Association (AA)
SARAS ...... SpA Raffinerie Sarde [*Sarde Refinery Corporation*] [*Italy*]
Saratovgaz ... Saratov Gas Industry Trust (RU)
SARB .... South African Reserve Bank
SARB .... South African Rugby Board
SARBICA ... Southeast Asian Regional Branch of the International Council on Archives (EAIO)
SARBIM ... Serikat Buruh Industri Bahan Makanan Rakjat [*People's Food Processors' Union*] [*Indonesian*]
SARBUBSI ... Serikat Buruh Betjak Seluruh Indonesia [*Pedicab Workers' Union of Indonesia*]
SARBUFIS ... Serikat Buruh Film Senidrama Indonesia [*Union of Film Artists of Indonesia*]
SARBUKRI ... Serikat Buruh Kristen Indonesia [*Union of Christian Workers of Indonesia*]
SARBUKSI ... Serikat Buruh Kehutanan Seluruh Indonesia [*Forestry Workers' Union of Indonesia*]
SARBUMRI ... Serikat Buruh Metaal Republik Indonesia [*Metal Workers' Union of Indonesia*]
SARBUMUSI ... Sarekat Buruh Muslimin Indonesia [*Indonesian Moslem Workers Union*] (IN)
SARBUPRI ... Sarekat Buruh Perkebunan Republik Indonesia [*Republic of Indonesia Plantation Workers Union*] (IN)
SARBUTRI ... Serikat Buruh Textil Republik Indonesia [*Textile Workers' Union of Indonesia*]
SARC .... Corrientes [*Argentina*] [*ICAO location identifier*] (ICLI)
SARC .... Sarcasm (DSUE)
SARC .... Sociedad de Aprovechamiento de los Recursos Naturales de Colombia [*Colombia*] (LAA)
SARCAS.... Societe Arachides Casamance
SARCCUS ... Southern African Regional Committee for the Conservation and Utilisation of the Soil
SARCI .... Societe Abidjanaise de Representation Commerciale Industrielle
SARCO ...... Saudi Arabian Refining Company (ME)
SARCO ...... Societe d'Exploitation des Etablissements Raoul de Comarmond
SARCU ...... Sociedad Argentina por las Relaciones Culturales con la Union Sovietica [*Argentine Society for Cultural Relations with the USSR*] (LA)
SARD .... Resistencia (Ciudad) [*Argentina*] [*ICAO location identifier*] (ICLI)
sard .... Sardoba [*Water reservoir in Central Asia*] [*Topography*] (RU)
SARDA ...... Sociedad de Amigos de la Republica Democratica Alemana [*Society of Friends of the German Democratic Republic*] [*Ecuador*] (LA)
SARDA ...... Sokoto Agricultural and Rural Development Authority [*Africa*]
SARDU ..... South Australian [*Aircraft*] Research and Development Unit [*National Union Catalogue of Australia symbol*]
SARE .... Resistencia [*Argentina*] [*ICAO location identifier*] (ICLI)
SAREC ...... Societe Africaine de Revetements, d'Etancheite, de Carrelages
SAREC ...... Styrelsen foer u-Landsforskning [*Swedish Agency for Research Cooperation with Developing Countries*] (WED)
SAREC ...... Swedish Agency for Research and Co-Operation with Developing Countries (ASF)
SARECCI ... Societe Africaine de Revetements, d'Etancheite, de Carrelages de Cote-D'Ivoire
SARECO ... Societe Africaine de Restauration Collective
SARED ...... Societe Anonyme de Representations et de Diffusions
SAREDIS ... Societe Anonyme de Representation et de Distribution
SAREM ..... Societe Africaine Radio Electro-Menager
SAREMCA ... Societe Anonyme de Recherches et d'Explorations Minieres en RCA
SAREMCI ... Societe Anonyme de Recherches et d'Exploitation Minieres en Cote-D'Ivoire [*Ivory Coast Mining Exploration and Exploitation Corporation*] (AF)
s a rend ...... Sajto ala Rendezte [*Prepared for Publication By*] (HU)
SAREP ...... Societe Africaine de Representation
SAREP ...... Southern African Refugee Education Project
SAREPA.... Societe Africaine de Recherches et d'Etudes pour Aluminium
SARET ...... Societe Africaine de Recuperation et de Transformation
SARF .... Formosa [*Argentina*] [*ICAO location identifier*] (ICLI)
SARF .... Southern Africa Road Federation [*See also SAPF*] (EAIO)
sarg .... Sargento [*Sergeant*] [*Portuguese*]
SARG .... Societe Africaine de Representations Generales
SARGRE ... Service des Assurances sur Risques de Guerre et Risques Exceptionnels [*War and Special Risks Insurance Department*] [*Cambodia*] (CL)
SarGRES... Saratov State Regional Electric Power Plant (RU)
SARGS ...... Sociedade Avicola do Rio Grande do Sul [*Brazil*] (DSCA)
SARH .... Secretaria de Agricultura y Recursos Hidraulicos [*Secretariat of Agriculture and Water Resources*] [*Mexico*] (LA)

SARI......... Iguazu/Cataratas Del Iguazu [*Argentina*] [*ICAO location identifier*]   (ICLI)
SARI......... Societe Africaine de Representations Industrielles
SARI......... Societe pour la Riz et l'Industrie
SARI......... South Australian Recreation Institute
SARIA...... Societe Anonyme de Realisations Industrielles en Afrique
SARIACI... Societe Anonyme de Realisations Industrielles en Afrique-Cote-D'Ivoire
SARIA-Haute-Volta ... Societe Anonyme de Realisations Industrielles en Afrique-Haute-Volta
SARIA-Niger ... Societe Anonyme de Realisations Industrielles en Afrique-Niger
SARICECO ... Sanaga Rice Corporation
SARIF....... Sukarami Research Institute for Food Crops [*Indonesia*] [*Research center*]   (IRC)
SARITC..... South Australian Retail Industry Training Council
SARK........ Suid-Afrikaanse Raad van Kerke [*South African Council of Churches*] [*Afrikaans*]
Sarkombayn ... Saratov Combine Plant   (RU)
SARL......... Paso De Los Libres [*Argentina*] [*ICAO location identifier*]   (ICLI)
SARL......... Sociedade Anonima de Responsabilidade Limitada [*Joint Stock Company*] [*Portuguese*]   (CED)
SARL......... Societa a Responsabilita Limitata [*Limited Liability Company*] [*Italian*]
SARL......... Societe Anonyme a Responsabilite Limitee [*Limited Liability Company*] [*French*]   (WER)
SARL......... South African Radio League
SARL......... South Australia Rugby League
SARLA...... South African Rock Lobster Association
SARM....... Fixed Aircraft Repair Shop   (RU)
SARM........ Monte Caseros [*Argentina*] [*ICAO location identifier*]   (ICLI)
SARM........ Societe Anonyme de Ravitaillement Maritime [*Morocco*]
SARMA..... Societe Anonyme de Recherches de Mecanique Appliquee [*French*]
SARMAG ... Societe Africaine de Ravitaillement Maritime et d'Approvisionnements Generaux
SARMC..... Search and Rescue Mission Coordinator [*Australia*]
SARMG..... Southeast Asian Research Materials Group   (ADA)
SARN ...... Automatic Voltage Regulator Frame   (RU)
SARO .... Ituzaingo [*Argentina*] [*ICAO location identifier*]   (ICLI)
SAROB...... Suid-Afrikaanse Raad vir Outomatisasie en Berekening [*South African Council for Automation and Computation*]   (AA)
SAROJ ...... Savez Astronautickih i Raketnih Organizacija [*Former Yugoslavia*]   (SLS)
SAROM ..... Societa Azionaria Raffinazione Olii Minerali [*Italian*]
SARP......... Posadas [*Argentina*] [*ICAO location identifier*]   (ICLI)
SARP......... Stowarzyszenie Architektow Rzeczypospolitej Polskiej [*Association of Architects of the Polish Republic*]   (POL)
SARPA...... South Australian Revolver and Pistol Association
SARPAP.... Societe d'Application et de Recherches de Produits Anti-Parasitaires [*France*]
SARPI ...... Societe Algerienne de Realisation et de Promotion Industrielle [*Algerian Industrial Development Company*]   (AF)
SARR........ Resistencia [*Argentina*] [*ICAO location identifier*]   (ICLI)
SARRAL ... South African Recording Rights Association Ltd.   (AA)
SARRC...... South Australian Road Runners Association
SARS........ Presidencia R. Saenz Pena [*Argentina*] [*ICAO location identifier*]   (ICLI)
Sars........... Sarsenetteinband [*Cloth Binding*] [*Publishing*] [*German*]
SARS........ Student Association for the Rights of Students [*Australia*]
SARSA...... Societa Anonima Raccolta Sparta Alfa
SARST....... Societe Auxiliaire de la Recherche Scientifique et Technique
SART....... Societe Africaine de Realisations Touristiques
SART........ Societe Algerienne de Radio-Television
SART....... South African Railway Troops
SARTA ...... Societe Anonyme Roumaine de Transport Aerien [*Romania*]
SARTITC.. South Australian Road Transport Industry Training Committee
SARTOC... South Africa Regional Tourism Council
SARTOC... Southern Africa Regional Tourism Council   (EAIO)
sartr........... Saertryck [*Offprint*] [*Publishing*] [*Sweden*]
SARU .... Resistencia [*Argentina*] [*ICAO location identifier*]   (ICLI)
SARU .... South African Rugby Union
SARU .... South Australian Rugby Union
SARV......... Suider-Afrikaanse Rekeningkundige Vereniging [*South Africa*]   (AA)
SARZ........ Spornoye Automobile Repair Plant   (RU)
SAS........... Ammonium Nitrate-Superphosphate   (RU)
SAS........... Composite Air Unit   (RU)
SAS........... Medical Aviation Station   (RU)
SAS........... Sahne Artistleri Sendikasi [*Theatre Artists Union*] [*Izmir*]   (TU)
SAS........... Sanidad y Asistencia Social [*Health and Social Welfare*] [*Venezuela*]   (LA)
SAS........... Saudi Automotive Services Co.
SAS........... Scandinavian Airlines System [*Sweden*] [*ICAO designator*]   (FAAC)

SAS........... Secondary Assistance Scheme [*Australia*]
SAS........... Section Administrative Specialisee
SAS........... Servicio Nacional de Asistencia Social [*SENDAS*] [*Colombia*] [*Formerly,*]   (COL)
SAS........... Servizio Attivita Spaziale [*Space Activity Service*] [*Italian*]   (WER)
saS............. Siehe Auch Seite [*See Also Page*] [*German*]
SAS........... Slovak Architects' Society [*Former Czechoslovakia*]   (EAIO)
SAS........... Slovensky Abstinentny Svaz [*Slovak Temperance Union*]   (CZ)
SAS........... Sociedad de Agricultores de Santander [*Colombia*]   (DSCA)
SAS........... Societa Adriatica di Scienze [*Italian*]   (SLS)
SAS........... Societa in Accomandita Semplice [*Limited Partnership*] [*Italian*]
SAS........... Societe Africaine des Silicates
SAS........... Societe Alimentaire Sucriere
SAS........... Societe Astronomique de Suisse [*Astronomical Society of Switzerland*]   (EAIO)
SAS........... Societe Automobile Senegalaise
SAS........... Solomons Ano Sagufenua [*Solomon Islands*] [*Political party*]   (FEA)
SAS........... Son Altesse Serenissime [*His or Her Serene Highness*] [*French*]
SAS........... South African Ship
SAS........... South Asian Seas
SAS........... Special Access Scheme [*Pharmaceuticals*] [*Australia*]
SAS........... Special Air Services [*Australia*]   (VNW)
SAS........... Spolok Architektov Slovenska [*Slovak Architects' Society*] [*Former Czechoslovakia*]   (EAIO)
SAS........... St. Andrew Society [*Edinburgh, Scotland*]   (EAIO)
SAS........... State Authorities Superannuation Board [*New South Wales, Australia*]
SAS........... State Auxiliary Services
SAS........... Su Alteza Serenisima [*His, or Her, Most Serene Highness*] [*Spanish*]
SAS........... Suid-Afrikaanse Skip [*South African Ship*] [*Afrikaans*]
SAS........... Suid-Afrikaanse Spoorwee
SAS........... Suomen Automaatioseura [*Society of Automation*] [*Finland*]   (EAIO)
SAS........... Suomi Albania Seura [*Finnish - Albanian Friendship Association*]   (EAIO)
SAS........... Superintendencia de Armazens e Silos   (LAA)
SAS........... Svenska Akustiska Saellskapet [*Sweden*]   (SLS)
SAS........... Svenska Arkeologiska Samfundet [*Swedish Archaeological Society*]   (EAIO)
SAS........... SverigeAmerika Stiftelsen [*Sweden-American Foundation*]   (EAIO)
SAS........... Sveti Arhijerejski Sinod [*Holy Synod of Bishops*] [*Serbian Orthodox Church*]   (YU)
SAS........... Swedish Archaeological Society   (EAIO)
SAS........... Swedish Association of Scientists   (EAIO)
SAS........... Swiss Astronomical Society   (EAIO)
SAS........... Syndicat pour l'Amelioration des Sols et des Cultures [*Soils and Crops-Improvement Syndicate*] [*French*]   (ARC)
SAS........... Ukrainian Soviet Socialist Republic Author's Certificate [*Patent*]   (RU)
SASA .... Salta [*Argentina*] [*ICAO location identifier*]   (ICLI)
SASA .... Security Association of South Africa   (AA)
SASA .... Semilleros Argentinos SA [*Argentina*]   (DSCA)
SASA .... Servicio Agricola SA [*Mexico*]   (DSCA)
SASA .... Slovenian Academy of Sciences and Arts   (EAIO)
SASA .... Soil Association of South Australia
SASA .... South African Skating Association
SASA .... South African Society of Anaesthetists   (AA)
SASA .... South African Softball Association
SASA .... South African Statistical Association   (AA)
SASA .... South African Sugar Association   (AF)
SASA .... South Asian Studies Association of Australia and New Zealand
SASA .... South Australian Sawmillers' Association
SASA .... Southern African Stomatherapy Association   (AA)
SASA .... Suni ve Sentetik Elyaf Sanayi Anonim Sirketi [*Artificial and Synthetic Fibers Industry Corporation*]   (TU)
SASAE ...... South African Society for Agricultural Extension   (AA)
SASAP...... South African Society of Animal Production
SASAQS.... Southern Africa Society of Aquatic Scientists   (EAIO)
SASAR ...... Singapore Association of Shipbuilders and Repairers [*Singapore Port Authority*]
SASAS...... South African Society for Atmospheric Sciences   (AA)
SASAS...... Southern Africa Society of Aquatic Scientists   (EAIO)
SASAV ...... Suid-Afrikaanse Steenkool-as Vereniging [*South Africa*]   (AA)
SASB .... South Australian Superannuation Board
SASB .... State Authorities Superannuation Board [*New South Wales, Australia*]
SASBANK ... Suid-Afrikaanse Spaar- en Voorskotbank
SASBFIT... South Australian Superannuation Board Fund Investment Trust
SASC .... Salta [*Argentina*] [*ICAO location identifier*]   (ICLI)
SASC .... South African Service Corps
SASC .... South Australian Securities Commission [*National Union Catalogue of Australia symbol*]

SASC .... Statutory Authorities Service Commission [*Trinidadian and Tobagan*] (LA)
SASC .... Sydney Amateur Sailing Club [*Australia*]
SASC .... Sydney Amateur Sport Club [*Australia*]
SASC .... Sydney Anglican Schools Corp. [*Commercial firm*]
SASCA ...... Sassandra-Cavally
SASCA ...... South African Support Campaign Australia
SASCAM .. South African Society for the Care of Mentally Handicapped
SASCAR.... South African Scientific Committee for Antarctic Research (MSC)
SASCE....... South African Society for Cooperative Education (AA)
SASCO ...... Saudi Arabian Shipping Co. Ltd.
SASCO ...... Sudanese Aeronautical Services Co. Ltd. [*Sudan*] [*ICAO designator*] (FAAC)
SASCON ... Southern African Solidarity Congress [*Zimbabwe*] [*Political party*] (PPW)
SASCP....... South African Society of Crop Production (AA)
SASDT ...... South African Society of Dairy Technology (AA)
SASEDIN ... South Asia Socio-Economic Development Information Network [*Proposed*]
SASEM ..... Societe Africaine de Stockage et d'Embarquement
SAS en H ... Suid Afrikaanse Spoorwee en Hawens [*South African Railways and Harbors*] [*Use SAR and H*] (AF)
SASEP....... Societe Africaine de Serigraphie et de Publicite [*Morocco*]
SASES .... South Australian State Emergency Services
SASET....... Societe Auxiliaire Senegalaise des Exploitations de Thies
SASEV ...... South African Society for Enology and Viticulture (EAIO)
SASF .... Scientific Agricultural Society of Finland (EAIO)
SASFA....... South Australian School Football Association
SASFA....... South Australian Shark Fishermen's Association
SASFED.... South African Security Federation (AA)
SASFIT ..... South Australian Superannuation Fund Investment Trust
SASG .... Sosialistiske Arbeids og Studie Grupper [*Socialist Labor and Study Groups*] [*Norway*] (WEN)
SASH......... South African Society for Haematology (AA)
SAShLP..... Stalingrad Aviation School for Pilots (RU)
SASHS ...... Southern African Society for Horticultural Science (AA)
SASht .... United States of America (BU)
SASI .... South African Standards Institution
SASI .... South Australian Sports Institute [*Coaching Resource Centre*]
SASIF .... Societe Africaine de Sondages, Injections, Forages
SASIF-CI .. Societe Africaine de Sondages, Injections, Forages de Cote-D'Ivoire
SASIO .... South African Society of Insurance Officials
SASJ.......... Jujuy [*Argentina*] [*ICAO location identifier*] (ICLI)
SASJ.......... South African Society of Journalists
SASK .... Suid-Afrikaanse Seinkorp
SASKV ...... Suid-Afrikaanse Sitruskwekeryvereniging [*South African Citrus Nurserymen's Association*] (AA)
SASL .... Swedish Association of School Leaders (EAIO)
SASLA....... South Australian Salaried Lawyers' Association
SASLA....... South Australian School Libraries Association
SASLHA ... South African Speech-Language-Hearing Association (AA)
SASLO ..... South African Scientific Liaison Office
SASM........ South African Society for Microbiology (AA)
SASM........ South African Student Movement
SASM........ Southern African Students Movement (AF)
SASM........ Suid-Afrikaanse Staande Mag [*South African Permanent Force*] [*Use SAPF*] (AF)
SASMA ..... Silk and Art Silk Mills Association [*India*]
SASMA ..... South African Sports Medicine Association (AA)
SASMAL... South African Sugar Millers Association Limited
SASMB ..... South Australian Stock Medicines Board
SASMC ..... South Australian Sports Medicine Centre
SASMFOS ... South African Society of Maxillo-Facial and Oral Surgeons (EAIO)
SASMI ...... Sindacato Autonomo Scuola Media Italiana [*Italian*] (SLS)
SASMIRA ... Silk and Art Silk Mills' Research Association [*India*] [*Research center*] (IRC)
SASMO..... Syrian Arab Organization for Standardization and Metrology
SASMSA... South Australian Stud Merino Sheepbreeders' Association
SASNA ...... Syllogikon Amyndikon Symfonon Notioanatolikis Asias [*Southeast Asia Treaty Organization*] (GC)
SASO......... Oran [*Algeria*] [*ICAO location identifier*] (ICLI)
SASO......... Saudi Arabian Standards Organization (IMH)
SASO........ South African Society of Orthodontists (AA)
SASO......... South African Students' Organization (PD)
SASOG...... South African Society of Obstetricians and Gynaecologists (AA)
SASOL ...... Suid-Afrikaanse Steenkool- Olie- en Gaskorporasie [*South African Coal, Oil, and Gas Corporation*] (AF)
SASOM..... South African Society of Marketers (AA)
SASORT ... South African Society of Radiotherapists (AA)
SASP .... South African Society of Physiotherapy
SASP .... Southern African Student Program
SASP .... Swedish Association for Share Promotion

SA-SPM .... Socialist Alliance - Socialist Party of Macedonia [*Political party*] (EY)
SASPP....... South African Society for Plant Pathology (AA)
SASPY....... Syndesmos Allilovoitheias Syndaxioukhon Politikon Ypallilon [*Mutual Aid Society for Pensioned Civil Employees*] [*Greek*] (GC)
SASQ......... La Quiaca [*Argentina*] [*ICAO location identifier*] (ICLI)
SASQ........ South African Society for Quality (AA)
SASQC...... South African Society for Quality Control (AA)
SASQUA ... Southern African Society for Quaternary Research (EAIO)
SASR .... Rivadavia [*Argentina*] [*ICAO location identifier*] (ICLI)
SASR .... Sri Aurobindo Society Research [*India*] (EAIO)
SASRA ...... South African Surf Riders' Association
SASS......... Sino-American-Shanghai Squibb Pharmaceuticals [*China*]
SASS......... Special Anti-Smuggling Squad [*Sierra Leone*]
SASS......... Su Atento y Seguro Servidor [*Yours Very Sincerely*] [*Spanish*]
SASS......... Surveillance and Army Support Ship [*Australia*]
SASSA....... Schweizerische Arbeitsgemeinschaft der Schulen fuer Sozialarbeit [*Swiss Association of Schools for Social Work*] (SLS)
SASSA....... South Australian Stock Salesmen's Association
SASSAR .... South African Spoorwee, South African Railways
SASSDA.... Southern Africa Stainless Steel Development Association (AA)
SASSE....... Servico de Assistencia e Seguro Social dos Economiarios [*Assistance and Social Security Service for Domestic Servants*] [*Brazil*] (LA)
SASSH ...... South African Society of Surgery of the Hand (AA)
SASSh .... United States of America [*USA*] (RU)
SASSO ...... Saudi Arabian Standards and Specifications Organisation
SAST .... Tartagal/Gral Mosconi [*Argentina*] [*ICAO location identifier*] (ICLI)
SASTA ...... South African Sugarcane Technologists Association
SASTA ...... South Australian Secondary Teachers Association
SASTROUF ... Senegalaise de Transports Routieres et Fluviaux
SASUKO... Saudi Sulfur Co.
SASUTA ... Southern African Society of University Teachers of Accounting (EAIO)
SASV .... Schweizerischer Akademischer Sportverband [*Switzerland*] (EAIO)
SASV .... Suid-Afrikaanse Statistiese Vereniging [*South Africa*] (AA)
SASV .... Suid-Afrikaanse Suikervereniging [*South Africa*] (AA)
SASVIA..... Suid-Afrikaanse Studente Vereeniging in Amsterdam
SASVS....... Swallows Association for Social Voluntary Service [*Denmark*] (EAIO)
SASVV ...... Suid-Afrikaanse Steenkoolverwerkingsvereniging [*South Africa*] (AA)
SAT........... Acoustic Homing Torpedo (RU)
SAT........... Kesatuan/Saruan [*Unit, Organization (Military)*] (IN)
SAT........... Salamaua Aerial Transport [*Australia*]
SAT........... Salaries and Allowances Tribunal [*Australia*]
Sat............. Saterdag [*Saturday*] [*Afrikaans*]
sat.............. Satira [*Satire*] [*Portuguese*]
sat.............. S A Tobbi [*Et Cetera*] (HU)
Sat............. Saturn [*Record label*] [*France*]
sat.............. Satynowy (Papier) [*Satin (Paper)*] (POL)
SAT........... Security Appeals Tribunal [*Australia*]
SAT........... Sennacieca Asocio Tutmonda [*Nationless Worldwide Association*] (EAIO)
SAT........... Servico Acoriana de Transportes Aereos [*Portugal*] [*ICAO designator*] (FAAC)
SAT........... Shakespearean Authorship Trust [*England*] (EAIO)
SAT........... Societe Abidjanaise des Tabacs
SAT........... Societe Abidjanaise de Torrefaction
SAT........... Societe Abidjanaise de Transports
SAT........... Societe Africaine de Transit
SAT........... Societe Africaine de Transports Routiers
SAT........... Societe Africaine de Travaux
SAT........... Societe Amar Taleb
SAT........... Societe Anonyme de Telecommunications [*French*]
SAT........... Societe Archeologique de Touraine [*Touraine Archeological Association*] [*French*] (SLS)
SAT........... South Atlantic
SAT........... Sports Authority of Thailand (EAIO)
SAT........... Syndicat Autonome du Tchad
SAT........... World Vision of Australia (ADA)
SATA........ Servicio Alcoreano de Transportes Aereos [*Korean Air Transport Service*]
SATA........ Servicios Auxiliares de Transportes [*ICAO designator*] (FAAC)
SATA........ Sociedade Acoriana de Transportes Aereos Ltda. [*Airline*] [*Portugal*]
SATA........ Societe Africaine de Transit et d'Affretement
SATA........ Societe Africaine de Transports Automobiles
SATA........ Societe Algero-Tunisienne Alfatiere
SATA........ South African Teachers' Association
SATA........ South Australian Tennis Association
SATA........ Swiss Association for Technical Assistance
SATAB...... South Australian Totalisator Board

SATAC...... Societe d'Applications Techniques Agricoles et Caoutchoutieres
SATAC...... South Australian Tertiary Admissions Centre
SATACI..... Societe Africaine de Transit et d'Affretement Cote-D'Ivoire
SATA-CONGO ... Societe Africaine de Transit et d'Affretement Congo
SATAER..... Societe Algerienne de Transports Aeriens
SATA-GABON ... Societe Africaine de Transit et d'Affretement au Gabon
SATAK...... Societe Anonyme de Transports et d'Acconage de Kribi
SATAM..... Societe Anonyme pour Tous Appareillages Mecaniques
SATAR...... Societe Africaine de Transport et d'Affretement Routier
SATAS ...... Societe Anonyme des Transports Automobiles du Souss
SATA-SENEGAL ... Societe Africaine de Transit et d'Affretement Senegal
SATB........ South African Tourism Board
SATBC...... South Australian Trailer Boat Club
SATC........ Clorinda [*Argentina*] [*ICAO location identifier*]   (ICLI)
SATC........ Societe Abidjanaise de Tissus et Confections
SATC........ Societe d'Applications Techniques au Cameroun
SATC........ South African Tank Corps
SATCC...... South African Trade Union Coordination Council
SATCC...... Southern African Transport and Communications Commission
SATCO...... Societe Africaine de Terrassements et Constructions [*Morocco*]
SATCO...... South African Air Traffic Controllers' Association   (AA)
SATCO...... South Australian Timber Corp.
SATCO...... Swiss African Trading Corp. [*Liberia*]
SATCP ...... Sol-Air Tres Courte Portee [*Very Short Range Ground to Air*] [*Missile*] [*French*]
SATCRIS .. Semi-Arid Tropical Crops Information Service   (IID)
SATCS....... Scandinavian Association for Thoracic and Cardiovascular Surgery   (EA)
SATD........ El Dorado [*Argentina*] [*ICAO location identifier*]   (ICLI)
SATD........ Society of Australian Teachers of Dancing   (ADA)
SATE........ Ekonomiese Vereniging van Suid-Afrika [*Economic Society of South Africa*]   (EAIO)
SATEBA.... Societe Anonyme de Traverse en Beton Arme [*Morocco*]
SATEBA.... Societe des Tuileries et Briqueteries Africaines
SATEC ...... Shamir Advanced Technologies Engineering Centre [*Israel*]
SATEC ...... Sociedade Angolana de Tecidos Estampados [*Printed Fabric Company of Angola*]   (AF)
SATEC ...... Societe Africaine de Traitements Electrochimiques
SATEC ...... Societe d'Aide Technique et de Cooperation [*Technical Aid and Cooperation Company*] [*French*]   (AF)
SATEC ...... Societe d'Assistance Technique et de Credit Social d'Outre-Mer
SATEG...... Societe Anonyme de Transports et d'Exploitations Generales
SATEL ...... Societe Africaine des Techniques Electroniques
SATELIT .. Societe des Telecommunications Internationales du Togo [*International Telecommunications Company of Togo*] (AF)
SATELM... Societe Africaine de Transport et de Location de Materiel
SATEM ..... Societe Anonyme de Terrassements Mecaniques
SATENA ... Servicio de Aeronavegacion en Territorios Nacionales [*National Territorial Aerial Service*] [*Colorado*]   (LA)
SATEP ...... Service d'Achat, de Traitement, et d'Ecoulement des Poissons de Mer [*Salt Water Fish Purchasing, Processing, and Distribution Department*] [*Cambodia*]   (CL)
SATEP ...... South Australian Touring Exhibitions Program
SATEP ...... Southern African Team for Employment Promotion
SATERCO ... Societe Anonyme de Terrassements et de Constructions [*Belgium*]   (PDAA)
SATET ...... Societe Africaine de Travaux et d'Etudes Topographiques [*African Topographic Projects and Studies Company*] [*Congo*]   (AF)
SATET-GABON ... Societe Gabonaise de Travaux et d'Etudes Topographiques [*Gabonese Topographic Projects and Studies Company*]
SATET-TCHAD ... Societe Tchadienne de Travaux et d'Etudes Topographiques [*Chadian Topographic Projects and Studies Company*]
SATEX ...... Societe Africaine de Textiles
SATEX-CI ... Societe Africaine de Textiles de Cote-D'Ivoire
SATEXCO ... Compania Textil Colombiana SA [*Colombia*]   (COL)
SATF .... Societe des Anciens Textes Francais [*Society of Ancient French Texts*]   (SLS)
SATFL....... Societe d'Affretements et des Transports Fluviaux Lao [*Lao River Transport and Charter Company*]   (CL)
SATG........ Goya [*Argentina*] [*ICAO location identifier*]   (ICLI)
SATGA...... South African Timber Growers Association   (AA)
SATI .... Bernardo De Irigoyen [*Argentina*] [*ICAO location identifier*] (ICLI)
SATI .... Servicio de Asistencia Tecnica a la Industria [*Service for Technical Assistance to Industry*] [*Argentina*]   (LA)
SATI .... Societe Africaine de Torrefaction Industrielle
SATI .... Sudan American Textile Industry
SATI .... Surinam Association of Trade and Industry
SATIM ...... Societe Africaine de Tissage et d'Impressions, Morocco
SATIS....... Scientific and Technical Information Service [*New Zealand*]
SATIS........ Socially Appropriate Technology Information System [*Tool Foundation*] [*Netherlands*]

SAT-IS ...... Turkiye Satis Isicleri Sendikasi [*Turkish Sales Workers Union*] [*Erzurum*]   (TU)
SATITC..... South Australian Timber Industry Training Council
SATK........ Las Lomitas [*Argentina*] [*ICAO location identifier*]   (ICLI)
SATK........ Suid-Afrikaanse Toeristekorporasie
SATL........ Suomen Autoteknillinen Litto [*Finland*]   (SLS)
SATM....... Mercedes [*Argentina*] [*ICAO location identifier*]   (ICLI)
SATM....... Societe Auxiliaire de Transport et de Materiel
SATMACI ... Societe d'Assistance Technique pour la Modernisation Agricole de la Cote-D'Ivoire [*Technical Assistance Company for the Agricultural Modernization of the Ivory Coast*]   (AF)
SATMAR.. South African Torbanite Mining and Refining Co.
SATNUC... Societe pour l'Applications Techniques dans le Domaine de l'Energie Nucleaire [*Nuclear energy*] [*French*]   (NRCH)
SATO .... Obera [*Argentina*] [*ICAO location identifier*]   (ICLI)
SATO .... Societe Anonyme de Torrefaction de l'Oubangui
SATOC...... Societe Anonyme Travaux Oubangui Chari
SATOER ... Suid-Afrikaanse Toeristekorporasie [*See also SATK*] [*Afrikaans*]
SATOM..... Societe Anonyme de Travaux d'Outre-Mer [*Overseas Construction Corporation*] [*Algeria*]   (AF)
SATOP ...... South Australian Taxation Office - Pulteney Branch [*National Union Catalogue of Australia symbol*]
SATOUR... South African Tourist Corporation
SATP .... Societe Africaine de Travaux Publics
SATP .... Southern African Training Program
SATPEC.... Societe Anonyme Tunisienne de Production et d'Expression Cinematographique [*North African*]
SATR .... Reconquista [*Argentina*] [*ICAO location identifier*]   (ICLI)
SATRA ...... Societe Africaine de Travaux
SATRACOM ... Societe Africaine pour le Transport et le Commerce
SATRAM .. Societe Africaine de Travaux Maritimes et Fluviaux
SATRAM .. Societe Auxiliaire de Transports et de Materiel
SATRAP.... Societe Africaine de Travaux Publics et Prives
SATRAR ... Service d'Achat, de Transformation, et de Reconditionnement du Riz [*Rice Purchasing and Processing Department*] [*Cambodia*]   (CL)
SATRECO ... Societe Africaine de Terrassements et Routes Economiques
SATS .... Societe Africaine de Tolerie et Soudure
SATS .... South African Training Ship
SATS .... South African Transport Services
SATS .... South Australian [*Adelaide*] Theosophical Library [*National Union Catalogue of Australia symbol*]
SATS .... Union of Actors and Theater Employees   (BU)
SATSA ...... South African Tour and Safari Association
SATSF....... Special Assistance to Students Fund [*Australia*]
SATSS....... South Australian Transport Subsidy Scheme
SATT .... Scout Association of Trinidad and Tobago   (EAIO)
SATT .... Societe Africaine des Transports Tropicaux [*Algeria*]
SATT .... Societe Africaine de Transports et de Terrassements
SATT .... Societe Africaine de Travaux et de Transports [*Ivory Coast*]
SATTA ...... Societe Africaine de Transactions, Transports, et Automobiles
SATTA ...... South Australian Table Tennis Association
SATTs .... Sofia Direct Dialing Telephone Exchange   (BU)
SATU........ Curuzu Cuatia [*Argentina*] [*ICAO location identifier*]   (ICLI)
SATU........ Singapore Association of Trade Unions   (ML)
SATU........ South African Tennis Union
SATU........ South African Theatre Union
SATU........ South African Typographical Union
SATU........ Specialist Anti-Terrorist Unit [*Liberia*]
SATUC...... South African Trade Union Council   (AF)
SATUCC ... Southern African Trade Union Coordination Council [*Gaborone, Botswana*]   (EAIO)
SATUDAS ... Sakarya Tarim Urunleri Uretme ve Degerlendirme Anonim Sirketi [*Sakarya Agricultural Products Cultivation and Enhancement (Improvement) Corporation*]   (TU)
SATURO... Societe Africaine de Tubes et Robinetterie [*Morocco*]
SATW........ Schweizerische Akademie der Technischen Wissenschaften [*Swiss Academy of Engineering Sciences*]   (EAIO)
SATY........ Suomen Analyyttinen Trilogia Yhdistys [*Finnish Society of Analytical Trilogy*]   (EAIO)
SAU .... Abbreviated Author Index   (RU)
SAU .... Aircraft Power Plant   (RU)
SAU .... Automatic Control System   (RU)
SAU .... Saudi Arabia [*ANSI three-letter standard code*]   (CNC)
SAU .... Sawu [*Indonesia*] [*Airport symbol*]   (OAG)
SAU .... Scandinavian Association of Urology   (EA)
SAU .... Sections Administratives Urbaines [*Algeria*]
SAU .... Self-Propelled Artillery   (BU)
SAU .... Self-Propelled Gun   (RU)
SAU .... Societe d'Architecture et d'Urbanisme
SAU .... Surface Agricole Utile [*Algeria*]
SAU .... United Aviation Services SA [*Spain*] [*ICAO designator*]   (FAAC)
SAUAC..... South Australian Uranium Advisory Committee
saub........... Sauber [*Clean*] [*German*]
SAUCAF ... Societe d'Achats et d'Usinage de Cafe
SAUCM..... Societe Anonyme des Usines a Cafe du Mungo

SAUCO ..... Servicios de Automacion Contable, SA [*Automatic Data Processing Services, Inc.*] [*Spanish*]   (WER)
SAUDENA ... Sociedad Anonima Uruguaya de Navegacion [*Uruguay*]   (LAA)
SAUDIA .... Saudi Arabian Airlines   (ME)
SAUDICORP ... Saudi Capital Corporation
SAUDUG .. South Australian Dynix Users' Group
SAUG .... Sydney Apple Users Group [*Australia*]
SAUJ .... South African Union of Journalists   (EAIO)
SAUJS .... South African Union of Jewish Students
SAUK .... Suid-Afrikaanse Uitsaaikorporasie [*South Africa Broadcasting Corporation*] [*Use SABC*]   (AF)
SAULT ...... South Australian Urban Land Trust
SAUM .... South African Unity Movement
SAUP .... Automated Management System   (RU)
SAUPCI .... Societe d'Achats et d'Usinage des Produits de la Cote-D'Ivoire
SAUR .... Societe d'Amenagement Urbain et Rural
SAUR-AFRIQUE ... Societe d'Amenagement Urbain et Rural pour l'Afrique
SAUS .... Sausage   (DSUE)
SAus .... South Australia   (ADA)
S AUS .... South Australia   (BARN)
S Aust .... South Australia
SAUT .... Swedish Association of University Teachers   (EAIO)
SAUTRAC ... Societe Auxiliaire pour la Fourniture d'Energie Electrique de Traction [*Benelux*]   (BAS)
SAUU .... South African Underwater Union
SAUV .... Suid-Afrikaanse Uitgewersvereniging [*South African Publisher Association*]   (EAIO)
SAUXAF ... Societe Auxiliaire de Afrique Francaise
SAV .... Savanna [*Zaria*]
sav .... Savart   (RU)
SAV .... Slovenska Akademia Vied [*Slovak Academy of Sciences*]   (CZ)
SA'V .... Stathmos Proton Voitheion [*First Aid Station*]   (GC)
SAV .... Strollad ar Vro [*Country Party*] [*France*] [*Political party*]   (PPW)
SAV .... Sudania Aviation Co. [*Sudan*] [*ICAO designator*]   (FAAC)
SAVA .... Piedra Del Aguila [*Argentina*] [*ICAO location identifier*]   (ICLI)
SAVA .... Savonneries Associees [*Kinkala*]
SAVA .... Servicios do Aerotaxisa e Abastecimento do Vale Amazonica [*Airline*] [*Brazil*]
SAVA .... Societe Africaine de Vehicules Automobiles
SAVA .... South African Veterinary Association   (AA)
SAVA .... Suid-Afrikaanse Vereniging vir Afgetredenes [*South Africa*]   (AA)
SAVA .... Suid-Afrikaanse Vereniging vir Hakkel [*South Africa*]   (AA)
SAVA .... Suider-Afrikaanse Vereniging van Argeoloe [*South Africa*]   (AA)
SAVAC ...... South Australian Visual Arts Committee
SAVAG ...... Sociedade Anonima Viacao Aerea Gavzha [*Brazil*]
SAVAK ...... Sazemane Attalat Va Anmiyate Keshvar [*Iranian security and intelligence organization*]
SAVAK ...... Sazman-e Ettela'at va Amniyat-e Keshvar [*National Intelligence and Security Organization*] [*Iran*]   (ME)
SAVAL ...... Suid-Afrikaanse Vereniging vir Algemene Literatuurwetenskap [*South Africa*]   (AA)
SAVAP ...... Societe Anonyme de Vente et d'Application de Peinture
SAVAS-IS ... Askeri Savas Tesisleri Iscileri Sendikasi [*Military Encounter Installations Workers' Union*] [*Sinop*]   (TU)
SAVAT ...... Suid Afrikaanse Vereniging van Arbeidsterapeute [*South African Association of Occupational Therapists*]   (EAIO)
SAVAW ..... Suid-Afrikaanse Vereniging vir Atmosferiese Wetenskappe [*South African Society for Atmospheric Sciences*]   (AA)
SAVB .... El Bolson [*Argentina*] [*ICAO location identifier*]   (ICLI)
SAVBMN ... Suid-Afrikaanse Vereniging vir Marine-Biologiese Navorsing [*South Africa*]   (AA)
SAVBR ...... SuiderAfrikaanse Vereniging vir Bedryfsredakteurs [*Southern African Association of Industrial Editors*]   (EAIO)
SAVC .... Comodoro Rivadavia/Gral Mosconi [*Argentina*] [*ICAO location identifier*]   (ICLI)
SAVC .... South African Veterinary Corps
SAVCA ...... Savonneries S. Calafatas & Cie. [*Cameroon*]
SAVCO ...... Servicios Aereos Virgen de Copacabana [*Bolivia*]   (PDAA)
SAVCONGO ... Savonnerie du Congo
SAVD .... El Maiten [*Argentina*] [*ICAO location identifier*]   (ICLI)
SAVD .... Suid-Afrikaanse Vervoerdienste [*South Africa*]   (AA)
SAVDH ..... Suid-Afrikaanse Vereniging vir Dieetkunde en Huishoudkunde [*South Africa*]   (AA)
SAVDP ...... Suid-Afrikaanse Vereniging vir Diereproduksie [*South Africa*]   (AA)
SAVE .... Esquel [*Argentina*] [*ICAO location identifier*]   (ICLI)
SAVEC ...... Societe Africaine de Vente et de Consignation
SAVECAO ... Societe d'Achats et de Ventes de Cacao et de Cafe
SAVES .... South Australian Voluntary Euthanasia Society
SAVF .... Comodoro Rivadavia [*Argentina*] [*ICAO location identifier*]   (ICLI)
SAVF .... Suid-Afrikaanse Vroue-Federasie [*Afrikaans*]

SAVFGB ... Suid-Afrikaanse Vereniging van Fisici in Geneeskunde en Biologie [*South African Association of Physicists in Medicine and Biology*]   (EAIO)
SAVG .... Suid-Afrikaanse Vereniging vir Gesondheidsbevordering [*South Africa*]   (AA)
SAVGB ...... Suid-Afrikaanse Vereniging vir Gehaltebeheer [*South Africa*]   (AA)
SAVGP ...... Suid-Afrikaanse Vereniging vir Gewasproduksie [*South Africa*]   (AA)
SAVH .... Las Heras [*Argentina*] [*ICAO location identifier*]   (ICLI)
SAVH .... Suid-Afrikaanse Vereniging vir Hematologie [*South African Society for Haematology*]   (AA)
SAVHC ..... Suid-Afrikaanse Vereniging van Handchirurgie [*South African Society for Surgery of the Hand*]   (AA)
SAVI .... Society for the Advancement of the Vegetable Industry [*Philippines*]   (SLS)
SAVI .... Suid-Afrikaanse Vertalers-Instituut
SAVIA .... Sociedad Agronomica Viveros Industriales Argentinos [*Argentina*]   (DSCA)
SAVIC .... Services Apres-vente Industriels et Commerciaux [*After Sale Industrial and Commercial Services*] [*French*]   (ADPT)
SAVIEM ... Societe de Vehicules Industriels et d'Equipements Mecaniques [*Industrial Vehicles and Mechanical Equipment Company*] [*French*]   (WER)
SAVIL .... Societe Abidjanaise de Vente pour les Importations de Luxe
SAVIMO ... Societe Agricole et Vinicole Maghrebine
SAVK .... Suid-Afrikaanse Vereniging van Kinderchirurge [*South African Association of Pediatric Surgeons*]   (EAIO)
SAVK .... Suid-Afrikaanse Vereniging vir Kwaliteit [*South Africa*]   (AA)
SAVKB ...... Suid-Afrikaanse Vereniging van Kliniese Biochemici [*South African Association of Clinical Biochemists*]   (AA)
SAVKGM ... Suid-Afrikaanse Vereniging van Kaak-Gesigs en Mondchirurgie [*South Africa*]   (AA)
SAVKI .... Suid-Afrikaanse Vereniging vir Kliniese Ingenieurswese [*South Africa*]   (AA)
SAVKN ...... Suid-Afrikaanse Vereniging vir Kop- en Nekonkologie [*Die*] [*South Africa*]   (AA)
SAVKO ...... Suid-Afrikaanse Vereniging vir Kooperatiewe Onderwys [*South Africa*]   (AA)
SAVKO ...... Suid-Afrikaanse Vereniging vir Kooperatiewe Opleiding [*South Africa*]   (AA)
SAVKWA ... Suider-Afrikaanse Vereniging vir Kwaternere Navorsing [*South African Society for Quaternary Research*]   (AA)
SAVL .... Suid-Afrikaanse Vereniging vir Landbouvoorligting [*South Africa*]   (AA)
SAVLOM ... Suider-Afrikaanse Vereniging vir Leer- en Opvoedingsmoeilikhede [*South Africa*]   (AA)
SAVM .... Lago Musters [*Argentina*] [*ICAO location identifier*]   (ICLI)
SAVM .... Suid-Afrikaanse Vereniging van Mondhigieniste [*South Africa*]   (AA)
SAVM .... Suid-Afrikaanse Vereniging vir Mikrobiologie [*South Africa*]   (AA)
SAVMBN ... Suid-Afrikaanse Vereniging vir Marine-Biologiese Navorsing [*South Africa*]   (AA)
SAVMO .... Suid-Afrikaanse Vereniging van Musiekonderwysers [*Die*] [*South Africa*]   (AA)
SAVMO .... Suidelike Afrikaanse Vereniging vir Mediese Onderwys [*South Africa*]   (AA)
SAVN .... Societe d'Amenagement de la Vallee du Niari
SAVN .... Suid-Afrikaanse Vereniging vir Narkotiseurs [*South Africa*]   (AA)
SAVO .... San Antonio Oeste [*Argentina*] [*ICAO location identifier*]   (ICLI)
SAVO .... Suider-Afrikaanse Vereniging vir Onkruidwetenskap [*South Africa*]   (AA)
SAVOGO .. Suid-Afrikaanse Vereniging vir Opleiding van Geskiedenisonderwysers [*South Africa*]   (AA)
SAVOS ...... Suidelike Afrikaanse Vereniging vir Oorgeerfde Siektes [*South Africa*]   (AA)
SAVOT ...... Suidelike Afrikaanse Vereniging vir Oorerflike Toestande [*South Africa*]   (AA)
SAVOW .... Suider-Afrikaanse Vereniging vir Onkruidwetenskap [*South Africa*]   (AA)
SAVP .... Paso De Indios [*Argentina*] [*ICAO location identifier*]   (ICLI)
SAVP .... Suid-Afrikaanse Vereniging vir Patoloe [*South Africa*]   (AA)
SAVP .... Suid-Afrikaanse Vereniging vir Plantpatologie [*South African Society for Plant Pathology*]   (AA)
SAVP .... Suid-Afrikaanse Vereniging vir Proefdierwetenskap [*South Africa*]   (AA)
SAVQ .... Maquinchao [*Argentina*] [*ICAO location identifier*]   (ICLI)
SAVR .... Alto Rio Senguerr [*Argentina*] [*ICAO location identifier*]   (ICLI)
SAVRA ...... South African Vehicle Renting Association
SAVRI .... Suid-Afrikaanse Vereniging van Raadgewende Ingenieurs [*South Africa*]   (AA)
SAVRT ...... Suid-Afrikaanse Vereniging van Radioterapeute [*South African Society of Radiotherapists*]   (AA)
SAVS .... Sierra Grande [*Argentina*] [*ICAO location identifier*]   (ICLI)

SAVSLOR ... Suid-Afrikaanse Vereniging vir Sportwetenskap, Liggaamlike Opvoedkunde, en Rekreasiekunde [*South African Association for Sport Science, Physical Education, and Recreation*] (AA)

SAVST ...... Suid-Afrikaanse Vereniging vir Suiweltegnologie [*South Africa*] (AA)

SAVSTG .... Suid-Afrikaanse Vereniging van Spraak-Taal-Gehoor [*South Africa*] (AA)

SAVT .... Trelew/Almirante Zar [*Argentina*] [*ICAO location identifier*] (ICLI)

SAVTBO ... Suid-Afrikaanse Vereniging vir Tegniese en Beroepsonderwys [*South Africa*] (AA)

SAVTW ..... Suider-Afrikaanse Vereniging vir Tuinbouwetenskappe [*South Africa*] (AA)

SAVU .... Comodoro Rivadavia [*Argentina*] [*ICAO location identifier*] (ICLI)

SAVU .... Servo-Assisted Vinten Unit Camera [*Australia*]

SAVU .... Slovenska Akademia Vied a Umeni [*Slovak Academy of Sciences and Arts*] (CZ)

SAVU .... System Automatizace ve Veleni [*Automated System of Troop Command*] (CZ)

SAVUV ...... Suid-Afrikaanse Vereniging van Universiteitsvroue [*South African Association of University Women*] (EAIO)

SAVV .... Suid-Afrikaanse Verpleegstersvereniging [*South Africa*] (AA)

SAVV .... Suid-Afrikaanse Veterinere Vereniging [*South Africa*] (AA)

SAVV .... Viedma/Gobernador Castello [*Argentina*] [*ICAO location identifier*] (ICLI)

SAVVG ...... Suid-Afrikaanse Vereniging van Verloskundiges en Ginekoloe [*South Africa*] (AA)

SAVVO ..... Suider-Afrikaanse Vereniging vir Voorskoolse Opvoeding [*South Africa*] (AA)

SAVVoT .... Suid-Afrikaanse Vereniging vir Voedselwetenskap en -Tegnologie [*South Africa*] (AA)

SAVY .... Puerto Madryn [*Argentina*] [*ICAO location identifier*] (ICLI)

SAW .... Saechsische Akademie der Wissenschaften zu Leipzig [*Saxon Academy of Science at Leipzig*] (SLS)

SAW .... [*The*] Second Automobile Works [*China*] (TCC)

SAW .... Sterling Airways Ltd. [*Denmark*] [*ICAO designator*] (FAAC)

SAW .... Suid-Afrikaanse Weermag [*South African Defense Force*] [*Use SADF*] (AF)

SAWA .... Lago Argentino [*Argentina*] [*ICAO location identifier*] (ICLI)

SAWA .... Society of Anaesthetists of West Africa [*Nigeria*] (EAIO)

SAWA .... South African Water-Ski Association

SAWAS .... South African Women's Auxiliary Services

SAWAU .... South African Women's Agricultural Union

SAWB .... Base Marambio [*Argentina*] [*ICAO location identifier*] (ICLI)

SAWBA ..... South African Womens' Bowling Association

SAWC .... South Australian Writers' Centre

SAWD .... Puerto Deseado [*Argentina*] [*ICAO location identifier*] (ICLI)

SAWE .... Rio Grande [*Argentina*] [*ICAO location identifier*] (ICLI)

SAWEDO ... Samenwerkende Werkplaats-Technische Documentatiediensten

SAWEUNSW ... Shop Assistants and Warehouse Employees Union of New South Wales [*Australia*]

SAWFA ..... South African Wine Farmers Association

SAWFD ..... South Australian Woods and Forests Department

SAWG .... Rio Gallegos [*Argentina*] [*ICAO location identifier*] (ICLI)

SAWGU .... South African Wattle Growers Union

SAWH .... Ushuaia [*Argentina*] [*ICAO location identifier*] (ICLI)

SAWHA .... South African Women's Hockey Association

SAWIC ...... South African Water Information Centre [*Information service or system*] (IID)

SAWJ .... San Julian/Cap. D. J. D. Vasquez [*Argentina*] [*ICAO location identifier*] (ICLI)

SAWKAN ... Suid-Afrikaanse Wetenskaplike Komitee vir Antarktiese Navorsing [*South Africa*] (AA)

SAWL .... Singapore Association of Women Lawyers (EAIO)

SAWLT ..... South African Written Language Test [*Educational test*]

SAWM .... Rio Mayo [*Argentina*] [*ICAO location identifier*] (ICLI)

SAWMA .... Southern African Wildlife Management Association [*See also NVSA*] (EAIO)

SAWMC .... South Australian Waste Management Commission

SAWNA .... South African Women's Netball Association

SAWP .... Perito Moreno [*Argentina*] [*ICAO location identifier*] (ICLI)

SAWP .... Socialist Alliance of the Working People [*Serbia*] [*Political party*]

SAWPA ..... South African Word Processing Association (AA)

SAWPY ..... Socialist Alliance of the Working People of Yugoslavia [*Political party*] (EY)

SAWR .... Gobernador Gregores [*Argentina*] [*ICAO location identifier*] (ICLI)

SAWR .... South Australian Wine Research [*Institute*] [*John Fornachon Memorial Library*]

SAWRC ..... South Australian Water Resources Council

SAWS .... Jose De San Martin [*Argentina*] [*ICAO location identifier*] (ICLI)

SAWS .... Seventh Day Adventist Welfare Service (CL)

SAWSO ..... Salvation Army World Service Office

SAWSS ...... Southern African Weed Science Society (AA)

SAWT .... Rio Turbio [*Argentina*] [*ICAO location identifier*] (ICLI)

SAWTNI ... Suid-Afrikaanse Wol- en Tekstielnavorsingsinstituut [*Council for Scientific and Industrial Research*] [*South Africa*] (AA)

SAWTRI ... South African Wool Textile Research Institute

SAWU .... Santa Cruz [*Argentina*] [*ICAO location identifier*] (ICLI)

SAWV .... Suid-Afrikaanse Wiskundevereniging [*South African Mathematical Society*] (EAIO)

SAWV .... Suid-Afrikaanse Woordverwerkingsvereniging [*South Africa*] (AA)

SAWWV .... Suid-Afrikaanse Wingerd en Wynkundevereniging [*South African Society for Enology and Viticulture*] (EAIO)

SAX .... Sabah Air [*Malaysia*] [*ICAO designator*] (FAAC)

SAX .... Sambu [*Panama*] [*Airport symbol*] (OAG)

Sax .... Saxony

SAY .... Salisbury [*Zimbabwe*] [*Airport symbol*] [*Obsolete*] (OAG)

SAY .... Suomen Anestesiologiyhdistys [*Finland*] (SLS)

SAY .... Suomi-Amerikka Yhdistys [*Finnish-American Society*] (WEN)

SAYA .... Sarawak Advanced Youth Association (Communist) (ML)

SAYA .... South African Yachting Association

SAYC .... Southern Association of Youth Clubs [*Mauritius*] (AF)

SAYCO ..... Sociedad de Autores y Compositores de Colombia [*Colombia*] (COL)

SAYeZhD ... Union of European Railways Road Services (RU)

SAYOS .... Salvation Army Youth Outreach Service [*Australia*]

SAYRH ..... Secretaria de Agricultura y Recursos Hidraulicos [*Secretariat of Agriculture and Water Resources*] [*Mexico*] (LA)

SAZ .... Sasstown [*Liberia*] [*Airport symbol*] (OAG)

SAZ .... Sporitelna a Zalozna [*Savings and Deposit Bank*] (CZ)

SAZ .... Sumgait Aluminum Plant (RU)

SAZ .... Swiss Air-Ambulance Ltd. [*ICAO designator*] (FAAC)

SAZA .... Azul [*Argentina*] [*ICAO location identifier*] (ICLI)

SAZB .... Bahia Blanca/Comdte. Espora [*Argentina*] [*ICAO location identifier*] (ICLI)

SAZC .... Cnel. Suarez [*Argentina*] [*ICAO location identifier*] (ICLI)

SAZD .... Dolores [*Argentina*] [*ICAO location identifier*] (ICLI)

SAZE .... Pigue [*Argentina*] [*ICAO location identifier*] (ICLI)

SAZF .... Olavarria [*Argentina*] [*ICAO location identifier*] (ICLI)

SAZG .... General Pico [*Argentina*] [*ICAO location identifier*] (ICLI)

SAZh .... Flyer's Life Jacket (RU)

sazh .... Sagene (RU)

SAZH .... Svetove Akademicke Zimni Hry [*World Student Winter Sports Games*] (CZ)

SAZH .... Tres Arroyos [*Argentina*] [*ICAO location identifier*] (ICLI)

SAZhU ...... Automatic Rigid Control System (RU)

SAZI .... Bolivar [*Argentina*] [*ICAO location identifier*] (ICLI)

SAZJ .... Benito Juarez [*Argentina*] [*ICAO location identifier*] (ICLI)

SAZK .... Cerro Catedral [*Argentina*] [*ICAO location identifier*] (ICLI)

SAzK .... Schweizerische Aerztekommission fuer Notfallhilfe und Rettungswesen [*Swiss Medical Commission for Emergency Help and Rescue*] (SLS)

SAZL .... Santa Teresita [*Argentina*] [*ICAO location identifier*] (ICLI)

SAZM .... Mar Del Plata [*Argentina*] [*ICAO location identifier*] (ICLI)

SAZN .... Neuquen [*Argentina*] [*ICAO location identifier*] (ICLI)

SAZO .... Necochea [*Argentina*] [*ICAO location identifier*] (ICLI)

SAZP .... Pehuajo/Comodoro P. Zanni [*Argentina*] [*ICAO location identifier*] (ICLI)

SAZPI .... Central Asian Polytechnic Institute (RU)

SAZQ .... Rio Colorado [*Argentina*] [*ICAO location identifier*] (ICLI)

SAZR .... Santa Rosa [*Argentina*] [*ICAO location identifier*] (ICLI)

SAZS .... San Carlos De Bariloche [*Argentina*] [*ICAO location identifier*] (ICLI)

SAZT .... Tandil [*Argentina*] [*ICAO location identifier*] (ICLI)

SAZU .... Puelches [*Argentina*] [*ICAO location identifier*] (ICLI)

SAZU .... Slovenska Akademija Znanosti in Umetnosti [*Slovenian Academy of Sciences and Arts*] [*Ljubljana*] (YU)

SAZV .... Villa Gesell [*Argentina*] [*ICAO location identifier*] (ICLI)

SAZW .... Cutral-Co [*Argentina*] [*ICAO location identifier*] (ICLI)

SAZX .... Nueve De Julio [*Argentina*] [*ICAO location identifier*] (ICLI)

SAZY .... San Martin De Los Andes/Chapelco [*Argentina*] [*ICAO location identifier*] (ICLI)

sb .... Collection [*Bibliography*] (RU)

sb .... Construction Battalion (RU)

SB .... Convergence of Meridians, Grid Declination (RU)

SB .... Distress Signal (RU)

SB .... Het Schoolbestuur [*Benelux*] (BAS)

SB .... High-Speed Bomber (RU)

SB .... Medium Bomber (RU)

SB .... Rendezvous Point [*Aviation*] (RU)

SB .... Rifle Battalion (BU)

SB .... SAAB-Scania AB [*Sweden*] [*ICAO aircraft manufacturer identifier*] (ICAO)

SB .... Samaritan Befrienders [*Australia*] (EAIO)

sb .... Saturday (RU)

SB .... Savannah Bank of Nigeria

sb .... Sbirka [*Collection*] (CZ)

Sb .... Sbirka Zakonu Ceskoslovenske Socialisticke Republiky [*Laws of the Czechoslovak Socialist Republic*]   (CZ)
sb .... Selbstaendig [*Independent*] [*German*]   (GCA)
SB .... Shanti Bahini [*Peace Force*] [*Bangladesh*] [*Political party*]
SB .... Siedebeginn [*Initial Boiling Point*] [*German*]   (GCA)
Sb .... Signalbuch [*Signal Book*]   (EG)
SB .... Sitzungsbericht [*Transaction*] [*German*]
SB .... Slovenska Bibliografija [*Slovenian Bibliography*]   (YU)
SB .... Sluzba Bezpieczenstwa [*Security Service*] [*Poland*]   (POL)
SB .... Solicitors' Board [*Queensland, Australia*]
SB .... Solomon Islands [*ANSI two-letter standard code*]   (CNC)
s/b .... Son Billet [*His Bill*] [*French*]
SB .... Sotsialisticheska Borba [*Socialist Struggle*] [*A periodical*]   (BU)
SB .... South [*Australia*] Burleigh [*College*] [*Branson Library*]
SB .... Soviet Botany   (RU)
SB .... Sowjetische Botschaft [*Soviet Embassy*]   (EG)
SB .... Spravce Budov [*Superintendent of Buildings*]   (CZ)
SB .... Statni Banka Ceskoslovenska [*Czechoslavak State Bank*]   (CZ)
SB .... Statni Studijni Knihovna Dra. Zdenka Nejedleho, Ceske Budejovice [*Dr. Zdenek Nejedly State Research Library in Ceske Budejovice*]   (CZ)
SB .... Stettarsamband Baenda [*Iceland*]   (EAIO)
sb .... Stilb   (RU)
Sb .... Subay [*Officer*]   (TU)
Sb .... Sube [*Branch*]   (TU)
Sb .... Subesi [*Branch*] [*Turkey*]   (CED)
sb .... Substantiivi [*Noun*] [*Finland*]
SB .... Suedliche Breite [*South Latitude*] [*German*]
SB .... Suiderbreedte [*South Latitude*] [*Afrikaans*]
SB .... Sumerbank [*Sumer Bank*]   (TU)
sb .... Sur Bois [*On Wood*] [*Publishing*] [*French*]
SB .... Svaz Banictva [*Slovak Mining Association*]   (CZ)
SB .... Svaz Brannosti [*Association for Military Preparedness*]   (CZ)
SB .... Sydney Bitter Beer [*Australia*]
SB .... Systembereich [*German*]   (ADPT)
SB1 .... Statens Byggeforskningsinstitut [*Danish Building Research Institute*] [*Ministry of Housing*] [*Research center*]   (ERC)
SBA .... Bulgarian Automobile Association   (BU)
SBA .... Sick Berth Attendant [*Australia*]
SBA .... Singapore Badminton Association   (EAIO)
SBA .... Singapore Base Area   (ML)
SBA .... Singapore Booksellers Association   (EAIO)
SBA .... Small Business Association [*St. Lucia*]   (LA)
SBA .... Small Business Association [*Barbados*]   (LA)
SBA .... Small Businesses' Association [*Jamaica*]   (EY)
SBA .... Social Bridge Australia
SBA .... Sociedade Brasileira de Automatica [*Brazilian Society of Automatics*]   (EAIO)
SBA .... Societe Belge de l'Azote and des Produits Chimiques du Marly [*Belgium*]
SBA .... Societe Bordelaise Africaine
SBA .... Societe des Bois d'Assinie
SBA .... STA-Mali [*ICAO designator*]   (FAAC)
SBA .... Sudan Basketball Association
SBA .... Sweet Bugger All [*An exclamation*] [*Slang*] [*British*]   (DSUE)
SBAA .... Conceicao Do Araguaia [*Brazil*] [*ICAO location identifier*]   (ICLI)
SBAA .... Small Business Association of Australia
SBAA .... Swedish Business Archives Association   (EAIO)
SBAC .... Small Business Advisory Center [*Ministry of Trade and Industry*] [*Philippines*]
SBAC .... Societe des Tabacs, Cigars, et Cigarettes J. Bastos de l'Afrique Centrale
SBAF .... Rio De Janeiro/Afonsos [*Brazil*] [*ICAO location identifier*]   (ICLI)
S-Bahn .... Schnellbahn [*High-Speed Railway*] [*German*]
SBAL .... [*South Australia*] Balaklava [*Community Library*] [*National Union Catalogue of Australia symbol*]
SBAL .... Sociedade Bandeirante de Avicultura Ltd. [*Brazil*]   (DSCA)
SBAM .... Amapa [*Brazil*] [*ICAO location identifier*]   (ICLI)
SBAN .... Anapolis (Base Aerea) [*Brazil*] [*ICAO location identifier*]   (ICLI)
SBANK ...... State Bank [*of South Australia*] [*National Union Catalogue of Australia symbol*]
sbap .... High-Speed Bomber Regiment   (RU)
SBAP .... Schweizerischer Berufsverband fuer Angewandte Psychologie [*Swiss Professional Association for Related Psychology*]   (SLS)
SBAR .... Aracaju/Santa Maria [*Brazil*] [*ICAO location identifier*]   (ICLI)
SBASA ...... Spina Bifida Association of South Australia
SBAT .... Service Botanique et Agronomique de Tunisie
SBAT .... Spina Bifida Association of Tasmania [*Australia*]
sbatr .... Launching Battery   (RU)
SBAU .... Aracatuba [*Brazil*] [*ICAO location identifier*]   (ICLI)
SBAV .... Small Business Association of Victoria [*Australia*]
SBAV .... Spina Bifida Association of Victoria [*Australia*]

SBAV .... Teodoro Sampaio/Usina Porto Primavera [*Brazil*] [*ICAO location identifier*]   (ICLI)
SBAWA ...... Spina Bifida Association of Western Australia
SBB .... Saudi-British Bank
SBB .... Schweizer Bundesbahnen [*Swiss Federal Railroad*]
SBB .... Societe Belge des Betons [*Belgium*]   (PDAA)
SBB .... Societe des Brasseries de Bouake [*Ivory Coast*]
SBBA .... Boca Do Acre [*Brazil*] [*ICAO location identifier*]   (ICLI)
SbBAN ...... Sbornik na Bulgarskata Akademiya na Naukite [*Collection of the Bulgarian Academy of Sciences*] [*A periodical*]   (BU)
SBBE .... Belem/Val-De-Caes [*Brazil*] [*ICAO location identifier*]   (ICLI)
SBBG .... Baje/Cmt. Gustavo Kraemer [*Brazil*] [*ICAO location identifier*]   (ICLI)
SBBH .... Belo Horizonte/Pampulha [*Brazil*] [*ICAO location identifier*]   (ICLI)
SBBI .... Curitiba/Bacacheri [*Brazil*] [*ICAO location identifier*]   (ICLI)
SBBL .... Belem [*Brazil*] [*ICAO location identifier*]   (ICLI)
SBBQ .... Barbacena [*Brazil*] [*ICAO location identifier*]   (ICLI)
SBBR .... Brasilia/Internacional [*Brazil*] [*ICAO location identifier*]   (ICLI)
SBBS .... Brasilia [*Brazil*] [*ICAO location identifier*]   (ICLI)
SBBSI .... Serikat Buruh Bank Seluruh Indonesia [*All-Indonesia Bank Employees Union*]   (IN)
SBBT .... Barretos [*Brazil*] [*ICAO location identifier*]   (ICLI)
SBBU .... Bauru [*Brazil*] [*ICAO location identifier*]   (ICLI)
SBBV .... Boa Vista/Internacional [*Brazil*] [*ICAO location identifier*]   (ICLI)
SBBW .... Barra Do Garcas [*Brazil*] [*ICAO location identifier*]   (ICLI)
SBC .... Sibasa [*South Africa*] [*Airport symbol*]   (OAG)
SBC .... Singapore Baptist Convention   (EAIO)
SBC .... Singapore Bible College
SBC .... Singapore Broadcasting Corp.
SBC .... Small Business Computer Co. Proprietary Ltd. [*Australia*]   (ADA)
SBC .... Sociedade Brasileira de Cartografia [*Brazil*]   (DSCA)
SBC .... Societe de Batiments et de Constructions
SBC .... Society of Business Communicators [*Australia*]
SBC .... State Bicycle Committee [*New South Wales, Australia*]
SBC .... Stichting Bouwcentrum Ratiobouw
SBC .... Swiss Bank Corporation
SBC .... Swiss Broadcasting Corp.
SBC .... Sydney Basketball Council [*Australia*]
SBCA .... Cascavel [*Brazil*] [*ICAO location identifier*]   (ICLI)
SBCA .... SBC [*Swiss Bank Corp.*] Australia
SBCA .... Small Business Combined Association [*Australia*]
SBCAO .... State Business and Corporate Affairs Office [*South Australia*]
SBCBC ...... Societe de Bitumes et Cut-Backs du Cameroun
SBCC .... Cachimbo [*Brazil*] [*ICAO location identifier*]   (ICLI)
SBCCPA .... Sociedade Brasileira de Ciradores de Caes Pastores Alemaes [*Brazil*]   (DSCA)
SBCD .... Campo Grande [*Brazil*] [*ICAO location identifier*]   (ICLI)
SBCE .... Concordia [*Brazil*] [*ICAO location identifier*]   (ICLI)
SBCF .... Belo Horizonte/Confins [*Brazil*] [*ICAO location identifier*]   (ICLI)
SBCG .... Campo Grande/Internacional [*Brazil*] [*ICAO location identifier*]   (ICLI)
SBCH .... Chapeco [*Brazil*] [*ICAO location identifier*]   (ICLI)
SBCI .... Carolina [*Brazil*] [*ICAO location identifier*]   (ICLI)
SBCI .... Societe Bamakoise du Commerce et de l'Industrie
SBCI .... Swiss Bank Corp. International
SBCIC .... Small Business Credit Insurance Corp. [*Japan*]
SBCJ .... Maraba/Carajas [*Brazil*] [*ICAO location identifier*]   (ICLI)
SBCL .... Cruz Alta/Carlos Ruhl [*Brazil*] [*ICAO location identifier*]   (ICLI)
SBCM .... Criciuma [*Brazil*] [*ICAO location identifier*]   (ICLI)
SBCO .... Porto Alegre/Canoas [*Brazil*] [*ICAO location identifier*]   (ICLI)
SBCP .... Campos/Bartolomeu Lisandro [*Brazil*] [*ICAO location identifier*]   (ICLI)
SBCR .... Corumba/Internacional [*Brazil*] [*ICAO location identifier*]   (ICLI)
SBCS .... Statna [*or Statni*] Banka Ceskoslovenska [*Czechoslovak State Bank*]   (CZ)
SBCSA ...... Small Business Corp. of South Australia [*Commercial firm*]
SBCT .... Curitiba/Afonso Pena [*Brazil*] [*ICAO location identifier*]   (ICLI)
SBCV .... Caravelas [*Brazil*] [*ICAO location identifier*]   (ICLI)
SBCW .... Curitiba [*Brazil*] [*ICAO location identifier*]   (ICLI)
SBCY .... Cuiaba/Marechal Rondon [*Brazil*] [*ICAO location identifier*]   (ICLI)
SBCZ .... Cruzeiro Do Sul/Internacional [*Brazil*] [*ICAO location identifier*]   (ICLI)
SBD .... Samenwerking Bedrijfseconomische Documentatie
SBD .... Societe de Bauxite de Dabola [*Dabola Bauxite Company*] [*Guinea*]   (AF)
SBD .... Srpsko Biolosko Drustvo [*Serbian Biological Society*]   (YU)
SBD .... Srpsko Brodarsko Drustvo [*Serbian Shipping Establishment*]   (YU)
SBD .... Stavebni Bytove Druzstvo [*Association for Apartment Construction*]   (CZ)

SBDA......... Stichting Bibliotheek- en Documentatie-Academies ['s-Gravenhage]
SBDC......... Small Business Development Corp. [Australia]
SBDH .... Sociedade Brasileira de Discos Historicos J. Leon [Record label] [Brazil]
SBDJ .... Savez Biokemijskih Drustava Jugoslavije [Samoa]   (EAIO)
SBDK....... Solombala Paper and Woodworking Kombinat   (RU)
SBDN ...... Presidente Prudente [Brazil] [ICAO location identifier]   (ICLI)
SBDP .... Soviet Battlefield Development Plans
SBDS .... Stichting Bibliotheek- en Documentatie-Scholen [Later, SBDA]
SBE .... Pimpinan Pusat Serikat Buruh Es [Ice Workers' Union] [Indonesia]
SBE .... Selebi-Pikwe [Botswana] [Later, PKW] [Airport symbol]   (OAG)
SBE .... Sociedade Brasileira de Entomologia [Brazilian Entomological Society]   (SLS)
SBE .... Societe Belge d'Ergologie [Belgium]   (SLS)
SBEE .... Societe Beninoise d'Electricite et d'Eau [Benin Water and Electricity Company]   (AF)
SBEG .... Manaus/Eduardo Gomes [Brazil] [ICAO location identifier]   (ICLI)
SBEK .... Jacare-Acanga [Brazil] [ICAO location identifier]   (ICLI)
SBEN .... Campos/Plataforma SS-17 [Brazil] [ICAO location identifier]   (ICLI)
SBER .... Eirunepe [Brazil] [ICAO location identifier]   (ICLI)
Sber........... Sitzungsbericht [Transaction] [German]   (BJA)
SBES .... Sao Pedro Da Aldeia [Brazil] [ICAO location identifier]   (ICLI)
SBET .... Pedregulho/Estreito [Brazil] [ICAO location identifier]   (ICLI)
SBF .... Brandfoersvarsfoereningen [Sweden]   (SLS)
SBF .... Salvo Buon Fine [Under Usual Reserve] [Formula used in acknowledging receipt of checks] [Business term] [Italian]
sbf.............. Sauf Bonne Fin [Under Usual Reserve] [Formula used in acknowledging receipt of checks] [Business term] [French]
SBF .... Siyasi Bilgileri Fakultesi [Political Science Faculty of Ankara University]   (TU)
SBF .... Sociedade Brasileira de Fisica [Brazilian Physics Association] (LA)
SBF .... Sociedade Brasileira de Floricultura [Brazil]   (DSCA)
SBF .... Societe Burundaise de Financement [Development bank]   (EY)
SBF .... Societe des Bourses Francaises [France]   (ECON)
SBF .... Spanish Badminton Federation   (EAIO)
SBF .... Svenska Bergmannafoereningen [Sweden]   (SLS)
SBF .... Sveriges Begravningsbyraers Forbund [Sweden]   (EAIO)
SBF .... Sveriges Bildelsgrossisters Forening [Sweden]   (EAIO)
SBF .... Swedish Badminton Association   (EAIO)
SBF .... Swiss Badminton Federation   (EAIO)
SBFB .... Suomen Betoniyhdistys Finska Betongforeningen [Finland] (EAIO)
SBFC .... Franca [Brazil] [ICAO location identifier]   (ICLI)
SBFI.......... Foz Do Iguacu/Cataratas [Brazil] [ICAO location identifier] (ICLI)
SBFKB...... Siyasal Bilgiler Fakultesi Kibrislilar Birligi [Cypriot Union of Ankara University School of Political Sciences] [Turkish Cypriot]   (GC)
SBFL......... Florianopolis/Hercilioluz [Brazil] [ICAO location identifier] (ICLI)
SBFN .... Fernando De Noronha [Brazil] [ICAO location identifier] (ICLI)
SBFT .... Fronteira [Brazil] [ICAO location identifier]   (ICLI)
SBFU .... Alpinopolis/Furnas [Brazil] [ICAO location identifier]   (ICLI)
SBFZ .... Fortaleza/Pinto Martins [Brazil] [ICAO location identifier] (ICLI)
Sbg .... Salzburg [or Salzburger or Salzburgisch] [German]
SBG........... Schweizerische Botanische Gesellschaft [Swiss Botanical Association]   (SLS)
SBG........... Sociale Beleggings Gemeenschap [Benelux]   (BAS)
SBG........... Societe Belge de Geologie [Belgian Society of Geology]   (SLS)
SBG........... Societe Boucherie Generale
SBG........... Societe des Bois du Gabon
SBG........... Svenska Bergmannafoereningen [Sweden]   (SLS)
SBGA....... Brasilia/Gama [Brazil] [ICAO location identifier]   (ICLI)
SBGE........ Societe Belge de Gastro-Enterologie [Belgian Society of Gastroenterology]   (SLS)
SBGG........ Societe de Boissons Gazeuses du Gabon
SBGL........ Rio De Janeiro/Internacional Galeao [Brazil] [ICAO location identifier]   (ICLI)
SBGM....... Guajara-Mirim [Brazil] [ICAO location identifier]   (ICLI)
SBGO .... Goiania/Santa Genoveva [Brazil] [ICAO location identifier] (ICLI)
SBGP .... Campos/Plataforma PNA-1 [Brazil] [ICAO location identifier] (ICLI)
SBGR........ Sao Paulo/Internacional Guarulhos [Brazil] [ICAO location identifier]   (ICLI)
SBGS .... Ponta Grossa [Brazil] [ICAO location identifier]   (ICLI)
SBGW....... Guaratingueta [Brazil] [ICAO location identifier]   (ICLI)
SBH .... St. Barthelemy [Leeward Islands] [Airport symbol]   (OAG)
SBHED...... Sociedade Brasileira de Herbicidas e Ervas Daninhas [Brazil] (DSCA)

SBHO........ Societe des Brasseries du Haut-Ogooue [Gabon]
SBHT........ Altamira [Brazil] [ICAO location identifier]   (ICLI)
SBI .... Science-Based Industries
SB-I........... Service de Bibliographie sur l'Informatique [Paris Gestion Informatique] [France] [Information service or system] (CRD)
SBI .... Sociedad Brasileira de Instrucao [Rio De Janeiro, Brazil]   (LAA)
SBI .... Societa Botanica Italiana [Italian Botanical Society]   (SLS)
SBI .... Societe Belge d'Investissement International
SBI .... Societe des Bois de Sassandra-Issia
SBI .... Societe des Bois Ivoiriens
SBI .... Society for Business Information [Germany]   (EAIO)
SBI .... Stalbyggnadsinstitutet [Swedish Institute of Steel Construction] [Research center]   (IRC)
SBI .... State Bank of India   (PDAA)
SBI .... Statens Byggeforskningsinstitut [Danish Building Research Institute]   (WED)
SBI .... Sugarcane Breeding Institute [India]   (DSCA)
SBIA .... Spa Bath Industry of Australia
SBII .... Serikat Buruh Islam Indonesia [Central Islamic Labor Union of Indonesia]
SBIL .... Ilheus [Brazil] [ICAO location identifier]   (ICLI)
SBIM........ Serikat Buruh Industri Metal [Metal Industries Workers' Union] [Indonesian]
SBIP .... Ipatinga/Usiminas [Brazil] [ICAO location identifier]   (ICLI)
SBIR .... Serikat Buruh Industri Ringan [Small Industry Workers' Union] [Indonesian]
SBIT .... Itumbiara/Hidroelectrica [Brazil] [ICAO location identifier] (ICLI)
SBIZ .... Imperatriz [Brazil] [ICAO location identifier]   (ICLI)
SBJ .... Serikat Buruh Jodium [Iodine Factory Workers' Union] [Indonesian]
SBJC......... Belem/Julio Cesar [Brazil] [ICAO location identifier]   (ICLI)
SBJF......... Juiz De Fora/Francisco De Assis [Brazil] [ICAO location identifier]   (ICLI)
SBJP......... Joao Pessoa/Presidente Castro Pinto [Brazil] [ICAO location identifier]   (ICLI)
SBJR......... Rio De Janeiro/Jacarepagua [Brazil] [ICAO location identifier] (ICLI)
SBJV......... Joinville [Brazil] [ICAO location identifier]   (ICLI)
SBK.......... Bibliographic Information File   (RU)
SBK.......... Construction Tower Crane   (RU)
SBK.......... Schnellbrueterkraftwerksgesellschaft [Nuclear energy]
SBK.......... Serikat Buruh Kehutanan [National Forestry Workers' Union] [Indonesia]
SBK.......... Serikat Buruh Kependjaaran [Prisons Workers' Unions] [Indonesia]
SBK.......... Societe des Brasseries de Kinshasa
SBK.......... Spezialbaukombinat [Special Constructions Combine]   (EG)
SBK.......... Stationary Pressure Chamber   (RU)
SBK.......... St. Brieuc [France] [Airport symbol]   (OAG)
SBK.......... Storm, Van Bentem & Kluywer [Netherlands]
SBK.......... Union of Bulgarian Composers   (BU)
SBKA........ Serikat Buruh Kereta Api [Railway Workers Union]   (IN)
SBKB .... Serikat Buruh Kendaraan Bermotor [Motor Vehicle Workers Union]   (IN)
SBKG........ Campina Grande/Joao Suassuna [Brazil] [ICAO location identifier]   (ICLI)
SBKhSS..... Office for Combating the Embezzlement of Socialist Property and Speculation   (RU)
SBKI .... Reinforced Concrete Structures and Goods   (BU)
SBKM....... Reinforced Concrete Structures and Installations   (BU)
SBKM....... Spezialbaukombinat Magdeburg [Magdeburg Special Construction Combine]   (EG)
SbKNV ...... Sbirka Obezniku pro Krajske Narodni Vybory [Collection of Directives for Regional National Committees]   (CZ)
SBKP .... Sao Paulo (Campinas)/Viracopos [Brazil] [ICAO location identifier]   (ICLI)
SBKP .... Serikat Buruh Kementerian Pertahanan [Defense Ministry Union] [Indonesia]
SBKR........ Safeman Banader va Keshti Rani [Iran]   (MSC)
SBKU .... Cucui [Brazil] [ICAO location identifier]   (ICLI)
SBL........... Santa Ana [Bolivia] [Airport symbol] [Obsolete]   (OAG)
SBL........... Serikat Buruh Logam [Metal Workers' Union] [Indonesia]
SBL........... Slovenski Biografski Leksikon [Slovenian Biographical Dictionary]   (YU)
SBLB .... Labrea [Brazil] [ICAO location identifier]   (ICLI)
SBLGI ...... Serikat Buruh Listrik dan Gas Indonesia [Indonesian Gas and Electrical Workers Union]   (IN)
SBLJ......... Lajes [Brazil] [ICAO location identifier]   (ICLI)
SBLN........ Lins [Brazil] [ICAO location identifier]   (ICLI)
SBLO .... Londrina [Brazil] [ICAO location identifier]   (ICLI)
SBLP .... Bom Jesus Da Lapa [Brazil] [ICAO location identifier]   (ICLI)
SBLS .... Lagoa Santa [Brazil] [ICAO location identifier]   (ICLI)
SBM.......... Societe Bananiere du Mambe
SBM.......... Societe Belge de Musicologie [Belgian Society of Musicology] (EAIO)

SBM.......... Societe Bois et Metal [*Tunisia*]
SBM.......... Societe des Bains de Mer [*Monaco*]
SBMA....... Maraba [*Brazil*] [*ICAO location identifier*]   (ICLI)
SBMC....... State Building Materials Company
SBMD....... Soviet-Bulgarian Mining Company   (BU)
SBME........ Macae [*Brazil*] [*ICAO location identifier*]   (ICLI)
SBME........ Societe Belge de Microscopie Electronique [*Belgium*]   (SLS)
SBMG....... Maringa [*Brazil*] [*ICAO location identifier*]   (ICLI)
SBMI........ Societe Belge de Medecine Interne [*Belgium*]   (SLS)
SBMK....... Montes Claros [*Brazil*] [*ICAO location identifier*]   (ICLI)
SBML........ Marilia [*Brazil*] [*ICAO location identifier*]   (ICLI)
SBMN ...... Manaus/Ponta Pelada [*Brazil*] [*ICAO location identifier*]   (ICLI)
SBMO ...... Maceio/Palmares [*Brazil*] [*ICAO location identifier*]   (ICLI)
SBMO ...... Sociedade Brasileira de Microondas [*Brazilian Microwave Society*]   (EAIO)
SBMQ ...... Macapa/Internacional [*Brazil*] [*ICAO location identifier*]   (ICLI)
SBMR....... Manoel Ribas [*Brazil*] [*ICAO location identifier*]   (ICLI)
SBMS....... Mocoro/Dix-Sept Rosado [*Brazil*] [*ICAO location identifier*]   (ICLI)
SBMT....... Sao Paulo/Marte [*Brazil*] [*ICAO location identifier*]   (ICLI)
SBMU ...... Manaus [*Brazil*] [*ICAO location identifier*]   (ICLI)
SBMV....... Sociedade Brasileira de Medicina Veterinaria [*Brazil*]   (DSCA)
SBMY....... Manicore [*Brazil*] [*ICAO location identifier*]   (ICLI)
SBMZ....... Porto De Moz [*Brazil*] [*ICAO location identifier*]   (ICLI)
SBNF........ Navegantes [*Brazil*] [*ICAO location identifier*]   (ICLI)
SBNL........ Bulgarian National Legions Union   (BU)
SBNM ...... Santo Angelo [*Brazil*] [*ICAO location identifier*]   (ICLI)
SBNOR ..... Savez Boraca Narodnooslobodilackog Rata [*Union of Combatants of the National Liberation War*]   (YU)
SBNOV ..... Sojuz na Borcite od Narodnoosloboditelnata Vojna [*Union of Combatants of the National Liberation War*]   (YU)
SBNSW ..... State Bank of New South Wales [*Australia*]
SBNT........ Natal/Augusto Severo [*Brazil*] [*ICAO location identifier*]   (ICLI)
SbNU........ Sbornik za Narodni Umotvoreniya, Nauka, i Knizhnina [*Collection of Folklore, Science, and Literature*] [*A periodical*]   (BU)
SBO .... Jet Flame Blasthole Drill   (RU)
SBO .... Societe Auxiliaire pour la Brasserie d'Outre-Mer
SBO .... Stichting Bloedgroepenonderzoek Foundation for Blood Group Studies in Animals [*Netherlands*]   (DSCA)
SBO .... Stoleczne Biuro Odbudowy [*Warsaw Reconstruction Office*]   (POL)
SBOA .... Stop Banking on Apartheid
Sbob .... Sbirka Obezniku [*Collection of Directives (for Regional People's Committees)*]   (CZ)
SBOI......... Oiapoque [*Brazil*] [*ICAO location identifier*]   (ICLI)
SBOL........ Stihaci Bombardovaci Letectvo [*Fighter-Bomber Airforce (or Aircraft)*]   (CZ)
SBOLD...... Stihaci Bombardovaci Letecka Divize [*Fighter-Bomber Airforce Division*]   (CZ)
SBOM ...... Societe des Brasseries de l'Ogooue Maritime [*Gabon*]
SBOT........ Stoleczne Biuro Obslugi Turysty [*Warsaw Tourist Service Office*]   (POL)
SBOU .... Ourinhos [*Brazil*] [*ICAO location identifier*]   (ICLI)
SBP........... Pile-Driver Ferry   (RU)
SBP........... Societe Belge de Photogrammetrie et de Teledetection [*Belgium*]   (SLS)
SBP........... Societe Belge de Psychologie [*Belgium*]   (SLS)
SBP........... Societe Beneluxienne de Phlebologie [*Benelux Phlebology Society - BPS*]   (EA)
SBP........... Solidarity Between Peoples [*France*]   (EAIO)
SBP........... Sosyalist Birlik Partisi [*Socialist Unity Party*] [*Turkey*] [*Political party*]   (EY)
SBP........... Soziale Buergerpartei [*Social Citizen's Party*] [*Germany*] [*Political party*]   (PPW)
SBP........... Sprava Bojove Pripravy [*Combat Training Directorate*]   (CZ)
SBP........... Srpska Bratska Pomoc [*Serbian Fraternal Aid*] [*USA*]   (YU)
SBP........... Stowarzyszenie Bibliotekarzy Polskich [*Polish Librarians' Association*]   (POL)
SBP........... Suore del Buon Pastore [*Italy*]   (EAIO)
SBP........... Union of Bulgarian Writers   (BU)
SBPA .... Porto Alegre/Salgado Filho [*Brazil*] [*ICAO location identifier*]   (ICLI)
SBPA .... Singapore Book Publishers' Association   (EAIO)
SBPB .... Federation des Scouts Catholiques [*Belgium*]   (EAIO)
SBPB .... Parnaiba [*Brazil*] [*ICAO location identifier*]   (ICLI)
SBPC .... Pocos De Caldas [*Brazil*] [*ICAO location identifier*]   (ICLI)
SBPC .... Small Business Promotion Corp. [*Japan*]   (PDAA)
SBPC .... Sociedade Brasileira para o Progresso da Ciencia [*Brazilian Society for the Advancement of Science*]   (LA)
SBPF......... Passo Fundo/Lauro Kurtz [*Brazil*] [*ICAO location identifier*]   (ICLI)
SBPF......... Union of Fighters Against Fascism   (BU)
SBPG .... Paranagua [*Brazil*] [*ICAO location identifier*]   (ICLI)
SBPH........ Porto Velho [*Brazil*] [*ICAO location identifier*]   (ICLI)

SBPI .... Petropolis/Pico do Couto [*Brazil*] [*ICAO location identifier*]   (ICLI)
SBPK .... Pelotas [*Brazil*] [*ICAO location identifier*]   (ICLI)
SBPK .... Staatsbibliothek Preussischer Kulturbesitz [*Library of the Prussian Cultural Foundation*] [*Berlin*] [*Information retrieval*]
SBPL .... Petrolina [*Brazil*] [*ICAO location identifier*]   (ICLI)
SBPN........ Porto Nacional [*Brazil*] [*ICAO location identifier*]   (ICLI)
SBPN........ Societe des Boulangeries et Patisseries Nouvelles
SBPO........ Sick Berth Petty Officer [*Australia*]
SBPP .... Ponta Pora/Internacional [*ICAO location identifier*]   (ICLI)
SBPP .... Societe Belgo-Francaise de Presse et de Promotion [*Publisher*] [*Belgium*]   (EY)
SBPPI........ Serikat Buruh Pelajaran dan Pelabuhan Indonesia [*Indonesian Harbor and Maritime Workers Union*]   (IN)
SBPR .... Piracaba [*Brazil*] [*ICAO location identifier*]   (ICLI)
SBPT .... Serikat Buruh Perhubungan dan Transpor [*Transport and Communications Workers Union*]   (IN)
SBPT .... Societe Beninoise pour la Promotion du Tourisme   (EY)
SBPUT ...... Serikat Buruh Pekerdjaan Umum dan Tenaga [*Public Works and Power Workers Union*]   (IN)
SBPV .... Porto Velho [*Brazil*] [*ICAO location identifier*]   (ICLI)
SBPW........ Pindamonhangaba/Visaba [*Brazil*] [*ICAO location identifier*]   (ICLI)
SBQ .... Surveyors' Board of Queensland [*Australia*]
SBQV....... Vitoria Da Conquista [*Brazil*] [*ICAO location identifier*]   (ICLI)
SBR........... Bomb Release   (RU)
SBR........... Deliver Only to the Addressee [*Telegraphy*]   (RU)
SBR........... Society of Bead Researchers   (EA)
s Br........... Suedliche Breite [*South Latitude*] [*German*]
SBRAC ...... Sociedade Brasileira de Realizacoes Artistico Culturais [*Brazil*]   (EAIO)
SBRB .... Rio Branco/Presidente Medici [*Brazil*] [*ICAO location identifier*]   (ICLI)
SBRE .... Recife [*Brazil*] [*ICAO location identifier*]   (ICLI)
SBRF .... Recife/Guararapes [*Brazil*] [*ICAO location identifier*]   (ICLI)
SBRJ.......... Rio De Janeiro/Santos Dumont [*Brazil*] [*ICAO location identifier*]   (ICLI)
SBRP .... Ribeirao Preto/Leite Lopes [*Brazil*] [*ICAO location identifier*]   (ICLI)
SBRQ........ Sao Roque [*Brazil*] [*ICAO location identifier*]   (ICLI)
SBRS .... Resende [*Brazil*] [*ICAO location identifier*]   (ICLI)
SBRU........ Sectional Switching Structure   (RU)
SBS .... Saoud Brothers & Sons Ltd. [*Ghana*]
SBS .... Secretaria de Bienestar Social [*Guatemala*]   (DSCA)
SBS .... Servicios Aereos Barsa SA de CV [*Mexico*] [*ICAO designator*]   (FAAC)
SBS .... Sevastopol' Biological Station Imeni A. O. Kovalevskiy   (RU)
SBS .... Singapore Bus Service   (DS)
SBS .... Sociedad Brasileira de Silvicultura [*Brazil*]   (DSCA)
SBS .... Societe de Banques Suisse
SBS .... Societe des Bois de la Sanaga
SBS .... Soeurs de Bon Sauveur [*France*]   (EAIO)
SBS .... Speicherbereichsschutz [*German*]   (ADPT)
SBS .... Spojene Strojirny a Slevarny Bohumira Smerala, Narodni Podnik [*Bohumir Smeral Consolidated Machine Building Plants and Foundries, National Enterprise*]   (CZ)
SBS .... Svaz Bojovniku za Svobodu [*Union of Fighters for Freedom*]   (CZ)
SBS .... Svenska Bibliotekariesamfundet [*Sweden*]   (SLS)
SBS .... Swiss Botanical Society   (EAIO)
SBSA .... Sao Carlos/Francisco Pereira Lopez [*Brazil*] [*ICAO location identifier*]   (ICLI)
SBSA .... Savings Bank of South Australia   (ADA)
SBSA .... Societe Bottin   (EAIO)
SBSA .... Standard Bank of South Africa
SBSA .... State Bank of South Australia
SBSA .... Swedish Board for Space Activities   (EAS)
SBSC .... Rio De Janeiro/Santa Cruz [*Brazil*] [*ICAO location identifier*]   (ICLI)
SBSD .... School Based School Development [*Australia*]
SBSD .... Union of Bulgarian-Soviet Societies
SBSF .... Statens Biologiske Stasjon Flodevigen [*State Biological Station Flodevigen*] [*Research center*] [*Norway*]   (IRC)
SBSI .... Sugar Beet Seed Institute [*Iran*]   (IRC)
SBSJ .... Sao Jose Dos Campos [*Brazil*] [*ICAO location identifier*]   (ICLI)
SBSK .... Samakhom Bokkholik Seksa Khmer [*Association of Cambodian Education Personnel*]   (CL)
SBSL........ Sao Luis/Marechal Cunha Machado [*Brazil*] [*ICAO location identifier*]   (ICLI)
SBSM .... Santa Maria [*Brazil*] [*ICAO location identifier*]   (ICLI)
SBSN .... Santarem/Internacional [*Brazil*] [*ICAO location identifier*]   (ICLI)
SBSP .... Sao Paulo/Congonhas [*Brazil*] [*ICAO location identifier*]   (ICLI)
SBSR .... Sao Jose Do Rio Preto [*Brazil*] [*ICAO location identifier*]   (ICLI)
SBSR .... Society of Biological Sciences of Romania   (EAIO)

SBST .... Santos [*Brazil*] [*ICAO location identifier*]   (ICLI)
sbst .... Selbststaendig [*Independent*] [*German*]   (GCA)
SBStJ........ Serving Brother of the Order of St. John   (ML)
SBSV .... Salvador/Dois de Julho [*Brazil*] [*ICAO location identifier*]   (ICLI)
SBSV .... Suomen Biologian Seura Vanamo [*Finland*]   (EAIO)
SBSY .... Cristalandia/Santa Isabel do Morro [*Brazil*] [*ICAO location identifier*]   (ICLI)
SBT .... Savings Bank of Tasmania [*Australia*]
SBT .... Schools Board of Tasmania [*Australia*]
SBT .... Shakespeare Birthplace Trust   (EA)
SBT .... Shanghai Book Traders
SBT .... Societe de Batelage de Tulear
SBT .... Societe de Bois Tropicaux
SBTA .... Sydney Business and Travel Academy [*Australia*]
SBTB .... Statens Bibiotek og Trykkeri Blinde [*State Library and Printing House for the Blind*] [*Denmark*]   (PDAA)
SBTC .... Sino-British Trade Council   (DS)
SBTC .... Tapuruquara [*Brazil*] [*ICAO location identifier*]   (ICLI)
SBTE .... Teresina [*Brazil*] [*ICAO location identifier*]   (ICLI)
SBTF .... Tefe [*Brazil*] [*ICAO location identifier*]   (ICLI)
SBTI .... Armored Equipment Depot   (RU)
SBTK .... Tarauaca [*Brazil*] [*ICAO location identifier*]   (ICLI)
SBTMA..... Swedish Brick and Tile Manufacturers   (EAIO)
sb tr .... Collection of Transactions   (RU)
SBTS .... Sistema Brasileiro de Comunicacao por Satelites [*Brazilian System for Satellite Communication*]   (LA)
SBTT .... Tabatinga/Internacional [*Brazil*] [*ICAO location identifier*]   (ICLI)
SBTU......... Tucurui [*Brazil*] [*ICAO location identifier*]   (ICLI)
SBU .... Sociedade Brasileira de Urbanismo, SA [*Brazilian Urban Development Company, Inc.*]   (LA)
SBU .... Sociedades Biblicas Unidas
SBU .... Springbok [*South Africa*] [*Airport symbol*]   (OAG)
SBU .... Starwelt Airways [*Burundi*] [*ICAO designator*]   (FAAC)
SBUA........ Sao Gabriel Da Cachoeira [*Brazil*] [*ICAO location identifier*]   (ICLI)
sbucciat ...... Sbucciatura [*Peeling*] [*Publishing*] [*Italian*]
SBUF......... Paulo Afonso [*Brazil*] [*ICAO location identifier*]   (ICLI)
SBUG .... Uruguaiana/Rubem Berta [*Brazil*] [*ICAO location identifier*]   (ICLI)
SBUI......... Carauari [*Brazil*] [*ICAO location identifier*]   (ICLI)
SBUL......... Uberlandia [*Brazil*] [*ICAO location identifier*]   (ICLI)
SBUP........ Castilho/Urubupunga [*Brazil*] [*ICAO location identifier*]   (ICLI)
SBUR........ Uberaba [*Brazil*] [*ICAO location identifier*]   (ICLI)
SBV........... Sabah [*Papua New Guinea*] [*Airport symbol*]   (OAG)
SbV .... Sammlung Betrieblicher Vorschriften [*Collection of Operational Regulations*]   (EG)
SBV........... Schweiz Basketball-Verband [*Swiss Basketball Society*]   (EAIO)
SBV........... Senaat-Beknoptverslag [*Benelux*]   (BAS)
SBV........... State Bank of Victoria [*Australia*]
SBV........... Stredisko Branne Vychovy [*Military Education Center*]   (CZ)
SBV........... Svaz Branne Vychovy [*Union for Military Education*]   (CZ)
SBVG........ Varginha/Jam Brigadeiro Trompowsky [*Brazil*] [*ICAO location identifier*]   (ICLI)
SBVH .... Vilhena [*Brazil*] [*ICAO location identifier*]   (ICLI)
SBVM........ Societe de la Bourse de Valeurs Mobilieres de Bruxelles [*Stock exchange*] [*Belgium*]   (EY)
Sb VS .... Collection of Supreme Court Practice   (BU)
SBVT......... Vitoria/Goiabeira [*Brazil*] [*ICAO location identifier*]   (ICLI)
SBW.......... Sibu [*Malaysia*] [*Airport symbol*]   (OAG)
SBWA........ Standard Bank of West Africa Ltd.
SBWP........ Stowarzyszenie Bylych Wiezniow Politycznych [*Association of Former Political Prisoners*]   (POL)
SBXG........ Barra Do Garcas/Xingu [*Brazil*] [*ICAO location identifier*]   (ICLI)
SBXV......... Xavantina [*Brazil*] [*ICAO location identifier*]   (ICLI)
SBY........... BFS [*Berliner Spezial Flug*], Luftahrtunternehmen GmbH [*Germany*] [*ICAO designator*]   (FAAC)
SBYA........ Iauarete [*Brazil*] [*ICAO location identifier*]   (ICLI)
SBYS .... Piracununga/Campo Fontenelle [*Brazil*] [*ICAO location identifier*]   (ICLI)
Sbytminvod ... All-Union Mineral Water Marketing Office   (RU)
SBZ............ Scibe Airlift [*Zaire*] [*ICAO designator*]   (FAAC)
SBZ............ Sdruzene Bavlnarske Zavody [*United Cotton Mills*]   (CZ)
SBZ............ Sibiu [*Romania*] [*Airport symbol*]   (OAG)
SBZ............ Slezske Bavlnarske Zavody [*Silesian Cotton Mills*]   (CZ)
SBZ............ Slovenske Bavlnarske Zavody [*Slovak Cotton Mills*]   (CZ)
SBZ............ Sowjetische Besatzungszone [*Soviet Zone of Occupation*]   (EG)
Sbzaknar.... Sbirka Zakonu a Narizeni Republiky Ceskoslovenske [*Collection of Laws and Degrees of the Czechoslovak Republic*]   (CZ)
SBZh.......... Union of Bulgarian Journalists   (BU)
SC .... Catalan Solidarity [*Political party*]   (PPW)
Sc .... Escandio [*Chemical element*] [*Portuguese*]
SC .... Estado de Santa Catarina [*State of Santa Catarina*] [*Brazil*]
Sc .... Nederlandse Staatscourant [*Netherlands*]   (BAS)

sc .... Sans Couverture [*Without Cover*] [*Publishing*] [*French*]
SC .... Sawasdichote Ltd. [*Thailand*]
sc .... Scene [*Scene*] [*French*]
Sc .... Scogliera [*Ridge of Rocks*] [*Italian*]   (NAU)
SC .... Scottish Aviation Ltd. [*ICAO aircraft manufacturer identifier*]   (ICAO)
SC .... Secretaria de Comercio [*Secretariat of Commerce*] [*Mexico*]   (LA)
SC .... Sekretarijat Centra za Unapredenje Gradevinarstva [*Secretariat of the Center for Advancement of Building*]   (YU)
SC .... Senatus-Consulte [*France*]   (FLAF)
SC .... Senior Certificate [*Queensland, Australia*]
SC .... Senior Consultus [*Afrikaans*]
SC .... Senior Counsel
SC .... Service en Campagne [*Military*] [*French*]   (MTD)
sc .... Seul Cours [*Sole Quotation*] [*Stock exchange*] [*French*]
SC .... Seychelles [*ANSI two-letter standard code*]   (CNC)
SC .... Shire Council [*Australia*]   (ADA)
SC .... Soccer Club [*Australia*]
SC .... Societatea de Cardiologie [*Romania*]   (EAIO)
SC .... Societe Cooperative [*French*]   (BAS)
S/C .... Son Compte [*His, or Her, Account*] [*French*]
SC .... Sons of Charity [*France*]   (EAIO)
s/c .... Sous le Couvert [*Under Cover*] [*French*]
SC .... State Constituency
SC .... State Counsel
SC .... Steering Committee [*NATO*]
SC .... Strazarski Camac [*Patrol Boat*]   (YU)
SC .... Stronnictwo Chlopskie [*Peasants' Party*] [*Poland*] [*Political party*]   (PPE)
s/c .... Sua Carta [*Your Letter*] [*Portuguese*]
s/c .... Sua Conta [*Your Account*] [*Business term*] [*Portuguese*]
SC .... Su Cargo [*Your Debit*] [*Business term*] [*Spanish*]
SC .... Su Casa [*His, or Her, House*] [*Spanish*]
SC .... Su Cuenta [*Your Account*] [*Business term*] [*Spanish*]
SC .... Suez Canal
SCA............ Sabah Chinese Association   (ML)
SCA............ Sarawak Chinese Association   (ML)
SCA............ Save the Children Alliance [*Gentofte, Denmark*]   (EAIO)
SCA............ Senegal Cultural Archives   (EAIO)
SCA............ Sheepmeat Council of Australia
SCA............ Sociedad Colombiana de Arquitectos [*Colombia*]   (COL)
SCA............ Sociedade Cultural de Angola
SCA............ Sociedad en Comandita por Acciones [*Limited Company*]
SCA............ Societa Anonima Strade Costruzioni Asfalti
SCA............ Societe Camerounaise pour l'Automobile
SCA............ Societe Centrale d'Achats [*Purchasing agency*] [*France*]   (IMH)
SCA............ Societe Commerciale Africaine
SCA............ Societe Commerciale d'Assurances
SCA............ Societe des Ciments d'Abidjan [*Ivory Coast*]
SCA............ Societe en Commandite par Actions [*Benelux*]   (BAS)
SCA............ Society for Coptic Archaeology [*Egypt*]   (EAIO)
SCA............ Society of Czech Architects   (EAIO)
SCA............ Soil Conservation Authority [*Australia*]
SCA............ Statiune de Cercetare Agricola [*Agricultural Research Station*]   (RO)
SCA............ Suez Canal Authority
SCA............ Svenska Cellulosa Aktiebolaget [*Sweden*]
SCA............ Swedish Concrete Association   (EAIO)
SCA............ Sydney College of the Arts [*Australia*]
SCA............ Sydney Cove Authority [*Australia*]
SCA............ Sydney Cricket Association [*Australia*]
SCAA.......... Service de Coordination des Affaires Algeriennes   (FLAF)
SCAAP ...... Special Commonwealth African Assistance Plan
SCAAS ...... Sindicato de Carpinteros, Armadores, Albaniles, y Similares [*Trade Union of Carpenters, Fitters, Masons, and Related Trades Workers*] [*Nicaragua*]   (LA)
SCAB........ Sociedad Cooperativa de Agronomos de Bolivia [*Bolivia*]   (DSCA)
SCAB........ Societe Centrale des Architectes Belges [*Belgium*]   (SLS)
SCAB........ Societe des Chantiers et Ateliers du Bassin de Diego-Suarez
SCAC........ Ancud/Pupelde [*Chile*] [*ICAO location identifier*]   (ICLI)
SCAC........ Societe Commerciale d'Affretements et de Combustibles
SCAC........ Societe Commerciale et Agricole du Cameroun
SCAC........ Societe de Carrieres Africaines et de Constructions
SCACN...... Sociedad Cooperativa Anonima de Cafeteros de Nicaragua [*Nicaragua*]   (DSCA)
SC (ACT)... Supreme Court (Australian Capital Territory)   (DLA)
SCACT ...... Supreme Court of the Australian Capital Territory
SCAD........ Societe Centrafricaine de Deroulage
SCAD......... Systeme Communautaire d'Acces a la Documentation [*Database*] [*EC*]   (ECED)
SCADA...... Salisbury Council of Alcoholism and Drug Addiction [*Zimbabwe*]
SCADOA... Service Commun d'Armements Desservant l'Ouest Africain
SCADTA ... Sociedad Colombo-Alemena de Transportes Aereos

SCAE .... Salisbury College of Advanced Education [*Australia*] (ADA)
SCAEPC .... Societe Centrafricaine d'Engrais et de Produits Chimiques
SCAER ...... Societe de Credit Agricole et d'Equipement Rurale du Mali [*Agricultural Credit and Rural Supply Organization of Mali*]
SCAF .... Compagnie des Scieries Africaines [*Ivory Coast*]
SCAF .... Societe des Conserves Africaines Alimentaires
SCAF .... Supreme Council of the Armed Forces [*Sudan*]
SCAFA ...... Societe Centrafricaine d'Affretements et d'Acconage
SCAFO ...... Spolek Commerciale d'Afrique Occidentale
SCAFR ...... Societe Centrale d'Amenagement Foncier Rural [*France*] (FLAF)
SCAG .... Saigon Civil Assistance Group [*Vietnam*]
SCAG .... Societe Commerciale et Agricole de Guinee
SCAG .... Societe Cooperative des Artisans de la Guyane [*Cooperative Association of Artisans of French Guiana*] (LA)
SCAG .... Standing Committee of Attorneys-General [*Australia*]
SCAH .... Secteur de Commerce, Artisanat, et Habitation
SCAHUR .. Societe Congolaise d'Amenagement de l'Habitat Urbain et Rural
SCAI .... Societe Commerciale Abidjanaise d'Importation
SCAL .... Societe Commerciale Andre Le Tellier
SCALA ...... Societa Coloniale Anonima Lavori Africa
SCALOM ... Societe Camerounaise de Location de Materiel et de Travaux Publics
SCALS ...... South Coast Aboriginal Legal Service Ltd. [*Australia*]
SCAM .... Societe Civile des Auteurs Multimedia [*France*] (EAIO)
SCAM .... Societe Commerciale Afrique-Maroc
SCAM .... Societe Commerciale d'Applications Mecanographiques [*France*] (PDAA)
SCAM .... Societe Cooperative Agricole Marocaine
SCAM .... Societe de Colonisation Agricole au Mayumbe
SCAM .... Standing Committee on Agricultural Machinery
SCAMAT .. Societa Commercio Attrezzi Macchinari Affini Tripoli
SCAMIC ... Societe Camerounaise pour l'Expansion Industrielle et Commerciale
SCAMP ..... Sperry Computer-Aided Message Processor [*British*]
SCAMTRA ... Societe Camerounaise de Manutention, de Transport, et de Transit
SCAN .... Scanfile [*Database*] [*Australia*]
SCAN .... Sufferers of Compulsive Anxiety Neurosis [*Australia*]
Scanaustral ... Scandinavian Australia Carriers Ltd. (ADA)
SCANDEFA ... Scandinavian Dental Fair [*Danish Dental Association*]
SCANDOC ... Scandinavian Documentation Centre
SCAN-Test ... Scandinavian Pulp, Paper and Board Testing Committee [*Sweden*] (EAIO)
SCAO .... Standing Conference of Atlantic Organisations [*British*] (EAIO)
SCAP .... Alto Palena/Alto Palena [*Chile*] [*ICAO location identifier*] (ICLI)
SCAP .... Societe Centrale d'Aquiculture et de Peche (ASF)
SCAPA ...... Sociedade de Comercializacao e Apoio a Pesca Artesanal [*Company for Marketing and Support for Industrial Fishing*] [*Cape Verde*] (AF)
SCAR .... Arica/Internacional Chacalluta [*Chile*] [*ICAO location identifier*] (ICLI)
SCAR .... Scandinavian Council for Applied Research [*Netherlands*] (DSCA)
SCAR .... Scientific Committee on Antarctic Research [*ICSU*] [*Cambridge, England*] (EAIO)
SCAR .... Society of Comparative Art Research [*Austria*] (EAIO)
SCAR .... Special Committee on Antarctic Research [*Australia*]
SCAROMINES ... Societe Centrafricano-Roumaine des Mines
SCARS ...... Social Conscience against Rape and Sexual Assault [*Australia*]
SCAS .... Statiunea Centrala de Apicultura si Sericicultura [*Central Station for Apiculture and Sericulture*] (RO)
SCASA ...... Servicio de Cooperacion Agricola Salvadoreno-Norteamericano [*El Salvador*] (LAA)
SCAT .... Societa Ceirano Automobili Torino [*Early Italian auto manufacturer*]
SCAT .... Societe Centrafricaine des Tabacs [*Tobacco association*] [*Central African Republic*]
SCAT .... Societe Commerciale Andre Testas
SCATRA ... Societe Centrafricaine de Travaux
SCAUL ...... Standing Conference of African University Libraries [*Lagos, Nigeria*]
SCAULEA ... Standing Conference of African University Libraries, Eastern Area
SCAULWA ... Standing Conference of African University Libraries (EAIO)
SCAULWA ... Standing Conference of African University Libraries, Western Area
SCAV .... Societe Cherifienne d'Articles de Voyages
SCAW .... Subcommittee on Animal Welfare [*Animal Health Committee*] [*Australia*]
SCB .... Savings and Credit Bank [*Cambodia*] (CL)
Sc B .... Scientiae Baccalaureus [*Bachelor of Science*] (GPO)
SCB .... Siam Commercial Bank [*Thailand*]
SCB .... Societe Camerounaise de Banque [*Cameroonian Banking Company*] (AF)

SCB .... Societe Camerounaise des Bois
SCB .... Societe Chimique de Belgique [*Belgium*] (SLS)
SCB .... Societe Commerciale de Bouake
SCB .... Societe de Constructions des Batignolles
SCB .... Societe des Ciments du Benin [*Benin Cement Company*] (AF)
SCB .... Societe d'Etude et de Developpement de la Culture Bananiere
SCB .... Soeurs de la Charite de Besancon [*Sisters of Charity*] [*France*] (EAIO)
SCB .... South China Block [*Geology*]
SCB .... Spolek Ceskych Bibliofilu [*Society of Czech Bibliophiles*] (CZ)
SCB .... Statistiska Centralbyran [*National Central Bureau of Statistics*] [*Research center*] [*Sweden*] (IRC)
SCB .... Statni Vedecka Knihovna, Ceske Budejovice [*State Research Library in Ceske Budejovice*] (CZ)
SCB .... Syndicat Chretien du Burundi [*Christian Labor Union of Burundi*] (AF)
SCBA .... Balmaceda/Balmaceda [*Chile*] [*ICAO location identifier*] (ICLI)
SCBA .... Societe du Chien de Berger Allemand [*France*] (EAIO)
SCBAL ...... Standard Chartered Bank Australia Ltd. (ADA)
SCBCL-C... Societe Commerciale de Banque Credit Lyonnais-Cameroun (EY)
SCBE .... Societe Camerounaise de Bois Equatoriaux
SCBI .... Societe Commerciale des Bois Ivoirienne
SCBI .... Societe de Banque en Cote-D'Ivoire
SCBK .... Societe Congolaise des Brasseries Kronenbourg
SCBL .... Quilpue/Mil el Belloto [*Chile*] [*ICAO location identifier*] (ICLI)
SCBM .... Societe Camerounaise de Beton Manufacture
SCBQ .... Santiago/Mil el Bosque [*Chile*] [*ICAO location identifier*] (ICLI)
SC/BSE ..... Scientific Co-Operation Bureau for the European and North American Region [*United Nations*] (EA)
SCBT .... Shirika la Chakula Bora Tanzania
SCC .... Saudi Cable Co. [*Saudi Arabia*] (PDAA)
SCC .... Schweizer Computer Club [*Swiss Computer Club*] [*German*] (ADPT)
SCC .... Seed Certification Committee [*Queensland, Australia*]
SCC .... Severoceske Cihelny [*North Bohemian Brick Works*] (CZ)
SCC .... Seychelles Construction Company
SCC .... Siam Cement Co. [*Thailand*]
SCC .... Sisters of the Cross of Chavanod [*France*] (EAIO)
SCC .... Small Cause Court [*India*] (DLA)
SCC .... Small Claims Court [*Northern Territory, Australia*]
SCC .... Societe Camerounaise de Construction
SCC .... Societe Commerciale Camerounaise
SCC .... Societe des Centres Commerciaux [*Commercial firm*] [*France*]
SCC .... Soeurs de la Croix de Chavanod [*Sisters of the Cross of Chavanod*] [*France*] (EAIO)
SCC .... Soil Conservation Council [*South Australia*]
SCC .... Soweto Community Council [*South Africa*] (AF)
SCC .... Spanish Chamber of Commerce (DS)
SCC .... Standstill Coordinating Committee [*for government-owed debts*] [*South Africa*]
SCC .... State Cinema Corporation [*Sudan*]
SCC .... State Crime Commission [*New South Wales, Australia*]
SCC .... State/Territories Consultative Committee [*Australia*]
SCC .... Sudan Chamber of Commerce (EAIO)
SCC .... Sudan Council of Churches
SCC .... Suore della Carita Cristiana [*Sisters of Christian Charity*] [*Italy*] (EAIO)
SCC .... Swedish Cooperative Centre
SCC .... Swiss Committee of Chemistry (EAIO)
SCC .... Sydney Coastal Council [*Australia*]
SCCA .... Saab Car Club of Australia
SCCA .... Society of Company and Commercial Accountants [*Edgbaston, Birmingham, England*] (EAIO)
SCCA .... Sprint Car Control Council of Australia [*Oversees Sprint car racing*]
SCCAM ..... Standing Committee of Consumer Affairs Ministers
SCCARCF ... Societe Centrale Canine pour l'Amelioration des Races de Chiens en France (EAIO)
SCCAS ...... Statiunea Centrala de Cercetari pentru Apicultura si Sericicultura [*Central Research Station for Apiculture and Sericulture*] (RO)
SCCB .... Sociedad Cubana de Ciencias Biologicas [*Cuban Biological Sciences Society*] (LA)
SCCB .... State Contracts Control Board [*New South Wales, Australia*]
SCCC .... Chile Chico/Chile Chico [*Chile*] [*ICAO location identifier*] (ICLI)
SCCC .... Sociedad Chilena de Ciencia de la Computacion [*Chile*] (EAIO)
SCCC .... Societe Cinematographique et Commerciale de Casamance
SCCC .... Societe de Coulee Continue de Cuivre
SCCC .... Syndicat Chretien des Communications et de la Culture [*Belgium*] (EAIO)
SCCCE ...... Statie Centrala de Cercetari pentru Combaterea Eroziunii [*Central Research Station for Combatting Soil Erosion*] (RO)
SCCD .... Iquique/Los Condores [*Chile*] [*ICAO location identifier*] (ICLI)

SCCE......... Societe Camerounaise de Conditionnement et d'Entreposage
SCCF......... Calama/El Loa [*Chile*] [*ICAO location identifier*]   (ICLI)
SCCG......... Societe Camerounaise pour le Commerce General
SCCGA...... Societe Camerounaise de Controle et de Gestion Administrative
SCCH........ Chillan/Gral, Bernardo O'Higgins [*Chile*] [*ICAO location identifier*]   (ICLI)
SCCH........ Sociedad Cientifica de Chile [*Chile*]   (DSCA)
SCCI.......... Punta Arenas/Internacional Carlos Ibanez Del Campo [*Chile*] [*ICAO location identifier*]   (ICLI)
SCCI.......... Societe de Construction de Cote-D'Ivoire
SCCI.......... Societe pour le Compoundage en Cote-D'Ivoire
SCCI.......... State Committee for Cooperation and Investment [*Vietnam*]
SCCI.......... Supreme Court of Christmas Island [*Australia*]
SCCI.......... Surinam Chamber of Commerce and Industry
SCC(K)I..... Supreme Court of Cocos (Keeling) Islands [*Australia*]
SCCM........ Societe de Courtage et de Consignation Maritime
SCC(NSW) ... State Chamber of Commerce [*New South Wales*] [*Australia*]
SCCOM..... Societe de Courtage et de Consignation Maritime
SCCOP...... State Consulting Company for Oil Projects [*Iraq*]   (PDAA)
SCCP......... Sabah Chinese Consolidated Party [*Malaysia*] [*Political party*]   (FEA)
SCCP......... Statiunea de Cercetari pentru Cresterea Porcinelor [*Research Station for Hog Breeding*]   (RO)
SCC(Q)...... State Chamber of Commerce [*Queensland*] [*Australia*]
SCCRM..... Sacra, Cesarea, Catolica, Real Majestad [*Spanish*]
SCCS......... Sociedad Colombiana de la Ciencia del Suelo [*Colorado*]   (SLS)
SCCSA...... Society of Cosmetic Chemists of South Africa   (EAIO)
SCCT......... Societe Cambodgienne de Cultures Tropicales [*Cambodian Tropical Crop Company*]   (CL)
SCCT........ Societe Camerounaise de Commerce et de Transports
SCCTP....... Societe Congolaise de Construction et de Travaux Publics
SCCTU...... Swiss Confederation of Christian Trade Unions   (EAIO)
SCCUK...... Swedish Chamber of Commerce for the United Kingdom   (DS)
SCCWASP ... State Contracting Company for Water & Sewerage Projects [*Iraq*]
SCCY......... Coyhaique/Teniente Vidal [*Chile*] [*ICAO location identifier*]   (ICLI)
SCCZ......... Punta Arenas [*Chile*] [*ICAO location identifier*]   (ICLI)
SCD.......... Scottish Country Dance Club [*Australia*]
SCD.......... Service de Cooperation au Developpement [*France*]   (EAIO)
SCD.......... Servicio Central de Documentacion [*Central Documentation Service*] [*Venezuela*]   (LA)
SCD.......... Slovenian Christian Democrats [*Political party*]
SCD.......... Sociedad Chilena del Derecho de Autor [*Chile*]   (EAIO)
SCD.......... Sociedad Colombiana de Dermatologia [*Colombia*]   (EAIO)
SCD.......... Societe Commerciale de Dolisie
SCD.......... Societe des Ciments du Dahomey
SCD.......... Sporting Club Dakarois
SCD.......... Studie Centrum voor Documentatie [*NIDER*]
SCDA........ Iquique/Gral Diego Aracena [*Chile*] [*ICAO location identifier*]   (ICLI)
SCDA........ Sullivans Cove Development Authority [*Tasmania, Australia*]
SCDC........ Societe Camerounaise de Diffusion Commerciale
SCDE........ Societe Camerounaise d'Expansion Economique
SCDF......... Sdruzeni Ceskych Demokratickych Federalistu [*Association of Czech Democratic Federalists*]   (CZ)
SCDP........ Societe Camerounaise des Depots Petroliers
SCDPIS..... Swiss Conference of Directors of Professional and Industrial Schools   (EAIO)
SCDSD...... Scientific Clearinghouse and Documentation Services Division [*National Science and Technology Authority*] [*Information service or system*]   (IID)
SCDU .... Svaz Ceskoslovenskych Divadelnich Umelcu [*Union of Czechoslovak Theater Artists*]   (CZ)
SCDV........ Sociedad Chilena de Dermatologia y Venereologia [*Chile*]   (EAIO)
SCE............ Severoceske Energeticke Zavody [*North Bohemian Electric Power Plants*]   (CZ)
SCE............ Siberia Commodity Exchange [*Russian Federation*]   (EY)
SCE............ Sky Care Ltd. [*New Zealand*] [*ICAO designator*]   (FAAC)
SCE............ Societe Camerounaise d'Equipement
SCE............ Societe Cherifienne d'Engrais et de Produits Chimiques [*Morocco*]
Sce............. Source [*Spring*] [*Military map abbreviation World War I*] [*French*]   (MTD)
SCE............ St. Petersburg Commodity Exchange [*Russian Federation*]   (EY)
SCE............ Stredoceske Elektrarny, Narodni Podnik [*Central Bohemian Electric Power Works, National Enterprise*]   (CZ)
SCEA......... Societe Cooperative d'Entreprise Africaine
SCEA......... Supreme Committee for Energy Affairs [*Iraq*]   (ME)
SCEA......... Swedish Christian Educational Association   (EAIO)
SCEB......... SHAPE [*Supreme Headquarters Allied Powers Europe*] Communications Electronics Board [*NATO*]   (NATG)
SCEC........ Secondary Computer Education Committee [*Victoria, Australia*]
SCEC........ Societe Commerciale d'Exploitation de Carrieres
SCEC......... Societe de Compatibilite et d'Expertises Comptables

SCEC........ Sydney Conference and Exhibition Centre [*Australia*]
SCECA...... Servicio Cooperativo de Educacion Colombo Americana [*Colombia*]   (COL)
SCECGI..... Standing Committee of the EC Glass Industries [*Belgium*]   (EAIO)
SCECO...... Saudi Consolidated Electric Co.
SCECSAL ... Standing Conference of Eastern, Central, and Southern African Librarians
SCED........ Sociedade Comercial de Exportacaos e Distribuicas, SARL
SCED........ Societe Centrafricaine d'Exploitation Diamantifere [*Central African Company for Diamond Mining*]   (AF)
SCED........ Svaz Ceskobratrskeho Evangelickeho Duchovenstva [*Association of the Clergy of the Church of the Bohemian Brethren*]   (CZ)
SCEDP...... South Coast Employment Development Project Ltd. [*Australia*]
SCEES....... Service Central des Enquetes et Etudes Statistiques [*Central Service for Statistical Inquiries and Studies*] [*Ministry of Agriculture Paris, France*]
SCEF .... Isla Rey Jorge/Centro Meteorologico Antartico Presidente Frei [*Chile*] [*ICAO location identifier*]   (ICLI)
SCEF .... Societe Camerounaise d'Exploitation Forestiere
SCEFL....... Societe Camerounaise Equatoriale de Fabrication de Lubrifiants
SCEI .... Society for Clinical and Experimental Immunology [*Germany*]   (EAIO)
SCEIBF ..... Standing Conference for Europe of the International Basketball Federation   (EAIO)
SCEL .... Santiago/Internacional Arturo Merino Benitez [*Chile*] [*ICAO location identifier*]   (ICLI)
scel .... Scellino [*Shilling*] [*Monetary unit*] [*Italian*]
SCELF .... Societe Civile de l'Edition Litteraire Francaise   (FLAF)
SCEM .... Santiago/Arturo Merino Benitez (Edificio Direccion Meteorologica) [*Chile*] [*ICAO location identifier*]   (ICLI)
SCEMA ..... Steering Committee on Environmental Monitoring and Assessment [*ASF*]
SCEMory & Cie ... Societe Camerounaise des Ets. Mory & Compagnie
SCEN........ Santiago/Edificio Navegacion Aerea Arturo Merino Benitez [*Chile*] [*ICAO location identifier*]   (ICLI)
SCEP .... Servicio Cooperativo del Empleo del Peru [*Lima, Peru*]   (LAA)
SCEP .... Societe Commerciale des Ets. J. V. Piraube
SCEPAG ... Societe pour le Conditionnement et l'Exportation des Produits Agricoles
SCEPC....... Senior Civil Emergency Planning Committee [*NATO*]   (NATG)
SCEPOM .. Societe de Construction et d'Exploitation du Pont de Moossou
SCER........ Quintero [*Chile*] [*ICAO location identifier*]   (ICLI)
SCESB....... State Casual Employees Superannuation Board [*Victoria, Australia*]
SCESO ...... Societe de Cabotage et d'Entreposage du Sud-Ouest
SCET .... Societa Cooperativa Eoilizia Tripoli
SCET .... Societe Centrafricaine d'Equipement Touristique
SCET .... Societe Centrale pour l'Equipement du Territoire [*Central Company for Territorial Equipment*] [*Algiers, Algeria*]   (AF)
SCETA ...... Societe de Controle et d'Exploitation de Transports Auxiliaires [*France*]   (PDAA)
SCET-INTERNATIONAL ... Societe Centrale pour l'Equipement du Territoire International
SCET-Ivoire ... Societe Centrale pour l'Equipement du Territoire en Cote-D'Ivoire
SCETO ...... Societe Centrale pour l'Equipement Touristique
SCEZ .... Santiago [*Chile*] [*ICAO location identifier*]   (ICLI)
SCF .... Save the Children Fund [*British*]   (EAIO)
SCF .... Schipperkes Club de France   (EAIO)
SCF .... Skywings AB [*Sweden*] [*ICAO designator*]   (FAAC)
SCF .... Sociedad Centroamericana de Farmacologia [*Central American Society of Pharmacology - CASP*]   (EAIO)
SCF .... Societe Chimique de France [*French*]   (SLS)
SCF .... Societe de Comptabilite de France [*French*]   (SLS)
SCF .... Societe des Ciments Francais [*Cement producer*] [*France*]
SCF .... Spaniel Club Francais [*France*]   (EAIO)
SCF .... Svenska Civilekonomfoereningen [*Sweden*]   (SLS)
SCF .... Swiss Canoe Federation   (EAIO)
SCFA .... Antofagasta/Internacional Cerro Moreno [*Chile*] [*ICAO location identifier*]   (ICLI)
SCFA .... Save the Children Fund Australia
SCFA .... Skin and Cancer Foundation of Australia
SCFCEF .... Syndicat des Constructeurs Francaise de Condensateurs Electrique Fixes [*France*]   (PDAA)
SCFCS...... Standing Committee on the Free Circulation of Scientists [*International Council of Scientific Unions*]
SCFF......... Syndicat General des Fondeurs de France   (EAIO)
SCFFC....... Societe Commerciale et Forestiere Fouet & Compagnie
SCFG .... Societe Commerciale et Forestiere Gabonaise
SCFM .... Porvenir/Capitan Fuentes Martinez [*Chile*] [*ICAO location identifier*]   (ICLI)
SCFM .... Societe de Conserves Franco-Mauritaniennes
SCFSEC .... Standing Committee of French-Speaking Ethnical Communities [*EA*]

SCFT .... Futaleufu/Futaleufu [*Chile*] [*ICAO location identifier*]   (ICLI)
SCFT .... Societe Commerciale France-Tropiques
SCFZ .... Antofagasta [*Chile*] [*ICAO location identifier*]   (ICLI)
SCG .... Siam Cement Group [*Thailand*]
SCG .... Sitra Cargo Systems [*Peru*] [*ICAO designator*]   (FAAC)
SCG .... Societe Canadienne de Geotechnique [*Canadian Geotechnical Society*]   (EAIO)
SCG .... Societe Colas de Guinee
SCG .... Southern Cross Group [*Australia*]
SCG .... Special Consultative Group [*NATO*]
Sc Gael...... Scotch Gaelic [*Language*]   (BARN)
SCGB......... Societe des Caoutchoucs de Grand Bereby [*Ivory Coast*]
SCGI .... Societe Congolaise de Gaz Industriels [*Congolese Industrial Gas Company*]   (AF)
SCGNC...... Societe de Commerce General N'Dingue & Compagnie
SCGWTUF ... Sudan Central Government Workers' Trade-Union Federation
SCGZ........ Puerto Williams/Guardia-Marina Zanartu [*Chile*] [*ICAO location identifier*]   (ICLI)
sch .... Bill, Account   (RU)
s/ch .... Combat Unit   (RU)
SCH .... Friend or Foe [*Identification*]   (RU)
SCh .... Gray Pig Iron   (RU)
SCh .... Medical Unit   (RU)
SCh .... Medium Frequency   (RU)
SCh .... Natural Frequency   (RU)
SCh .... Random Number   (RU)
Sch .... Reading, Readout [*Computers*]   (RU)
SCh .... Samopomoc Chlopska [*Peasants' Mutual Aid*]   (POL)
SCH .... Schalter [*Switch*] [*German*]   (ADPT)
Sch .... Scheidsgerecht [*Benelux*]   (BAS)
Sch .... Scheidsman of Bindend-Adviseur [*Benelux*]   (BAS)
sch .... Scherma [*Fencing*] [*Italian*]
SCH .... Schilling [*Monetary unit*] [*Austria*]
SCH .... Schreiner Airways BV [*Netherlands*] [*ICAO designator*]   (FAAC)
Sch .... Schwerin [*One of the GDR Railroad Directorate units*]   (EG)
s/ch .... Secret Unit   (RU)
SCH .... Societe Commerciale et Hoteliere
SCH .... Society of Classical Homeopathy [*Australia*]
sch .... Strain Purity, Varietal Purity   (RU)
SCH .... Svaz Ceskeho Herectva [*Union of Czech Actors*]   (CZ)
sch .... Today, This Day   (RU)
SCHA .... Copiapo/Chamonate [*Chile*] [*ICAO location identifier*]   (ICLI)
SChA .... "Man-Machine" System   (RU)
SCHA .... Scottish Catholic Historical Association   (SLS)
Schad .... Schadwagenzug [*Damaged-Car Train*]   (EG)
schadh........ Schadhaft [*Damaged*] [*German*]
schaedl....... Schaedlich [*Destructive*] [*German*]   (GCA)
Schallm...... Schallmessung [*Sound Ranging*] [*German*]   (GCA)
scharn .... Scharnier [*Hinge, Joint*] [*Netherlands*]
Schbw........ Schiessbaumwolle [*Guncotton*] [*German*]   (GCA)
SCHDR ..... Schnelldrucker [*Rapid Printer*] [*German*]   (ADPT)
SCHE .... Society for Christian Higher Education [*South Africa*]   (AA)
ScheidsrBessliss ... Scheidsrechterlijke Besslissing [*Benelux*]   (BAS)
SchenSch ... Schip en Schade [*Benelux*]   (BAS)
Schernachgiebgk ... Schernachgiebigkeit [*Shear Pliability*] [*German*]   (GCA)
SCHG .... Chilean Society of History and Geography   (EAIO)
SchG .... Schiedsgericht [*Arbitration Court*] [*German*]   (ILCA)
Schger .... Scheidsgerecht [*Benelux*]   (BAS)
SchgtVAB ... Scheidsgerecht voor de Vermogensaanwasbelasting [*Benelux*]   (BAS)
SCHGUSSR ... Comite de Soutien aux Groupes Helsinki en URSS [*Support Committee for the Helsinki Groups of the USSR*] [*France*]   (EAIO)
Schh .... Schutzhaus [*German*]
SchK .... Control Counter, Instruction Counter   (RU)
SChK .... Four-Wire Patching Rack   (RU)
SchK .... Schiedskommission [*Arbitration Commission*]   (EG)
SchKh .... Drafting Facilities   (RU)
SChK iChP ... Soviet Red Cross and Red Crescent   (BU)
SchKK .... Checking-Code Counter   (RU)
SchKO .... Schiedskommissionsordnung [*Arbitration Commission Regulations*]   (EG)
Schl .... Schliesse [*Clasp*] [*German*]
Schl .... Schloss [*Castle*] [*German*]   (NAU)
Schlackenfuehr ... Schlackenfuehrung [*Slag Duct*] [*German*]   (GCA)
Schliessf..... Schliessfach [*Post Office Box*] [*German*]   (CED)
SCHLS ...... Schluszsatz [*Finale*] [*Music*]
Schlussbl..... Schlussblatt [*Last Leaf*] [*German*]
Schlussschr ... Schlussschrift [*Colophon*] [*German*]
Schlusst...... Schlusstitel [*Colophon*] [*German*]
SChM .... "Man-Machine" System   (RU)
SChM .... Modified Gray Pig Iron   (RU)
schm .... Schmelzend [*Melting*] [*German*]
schm .... Schmilzt [*Melts*] [*German*]
Schmelzp.... Schmelzpunkt [*Melting Point*] [*German*]   (GCA)
Schmelzpt .. Schmelzpunkt [*Melting Point*] [*German*]   (GCA)

Schmerzstill ... Schmerzstillung [*Relieving Point*] [*German*]   (GCA)
Schmier...... Schmierung [*Lubrication*] [*German*]   (GCA)
Schmp....... Schmelzpunkt [*Melting Point*] [*German*]
Schmpt...... Schmelzpunkt [*Melting Point*] [*German*]
Schmutztit ... Schmutztitel [*Half Title*] [*Publishing*] [*German*]
SCHO .... Societe Commerciale et Hoteliere de l'Ouest
SChP......... Four-Wire Switching Bay   (RU)
SchP......... Schmelzpunkt [*Melting Point*] [*German*]
SCHR .... Cochrane/Cochrane [*Chile*] [*ICAO location identifier*]   (ICLI)
schr .... Schreiben [*or Schriftlich*] [*To Write or In Writing*] [*German*]
schr .... Schrijver [*Author*] [*Netherlands*]
Schrb......... Schraube [*Screw*] [*German*]   (GCA)
SCHREG... Schieberegister [*German*]   (ADPT)
Schr Gew.... Schraubengewinde [*Thread*] [*German*]   (GCA)
Schriftst .... Schriftsteller [*Author*] [*German*]   (GCA)
Schriftwiedergab ... Schriftwiedergabe [*Reproduction of Handwriting*] [*Publishing*] [*German*]
Schrp......... Schrankenposten [*Crossing Guard, Guarded Crossing*]   (EG)
Schr-Verz... Schriftenzerzeichnis [*Bibliography*] [*German*]   (GCA)
SChS........ Black Sea Medium Seiner   (RU)
SChS........ Medium-Frequency Seismic Exploration   (RU)
SChSD...... Union of Czechoslovak-Soviet Friendship   (RU)
sch sr .... Flank Guard   (BU)
SCHT .... Schalttafel [*German*]   (ADPT)
SCHT .... Sindrome de Choque Toxico [*Toxic Shock Syndrome*] [*Spanish*]
Schuerf....... Schuerfung [*Scrape*] [*German*]   (GCA)
Schupo....... Schutzpolizist [*Policeman*] [*German*]
schutbl........ Schutblad [*Flyleaf*] [*Publishing*] [*Netherlands*]
SchV .... Time Counter   (RU)
Schw......... Schwach [*Weak*] [*German*]
schw......... Schwarz [*Black*] [*German*]
Schw......... Schwedisch [*Swedish*] [*German*]
Schw......... Schweizerisch [*Switzerland*] [*German*]
Schw......... Schwer [*Heavy*] [*German*]
Schw......... Schwerin [*One of the GDR Railroad Directorate units*]   (EG)
Schw......... Schwester [*Sister, Nun*] [*German*]   (EG)
Schwank .... Schwankung [*Deviation*] [*German*]   (GCA)
schwed...... Schwedisch [*Swedish*] [*German*]   (GCA)
Schwed P.... Schwedisches Patent [*Swedish Patent*] [*German*]   (GCA)
schweiz....... Schweizersich [*Switzerland*] [*German*]   (GCA)
schweizer.... Schweizerisch [*Switzerland*] [*German*]   (GCA)
Schwel....... Schwelung [*Smoldering*] [*German*]   (GCA)
schwerl...... Schwerloeslich [*Only Slightly Soluble*] [*German*]
Schwfwst.... Schwefelwasserstoff [*Hydrogen Sulfide*] [*German*]   (GCA)
Schwg........ Schwingung [*Vibration, Oscillation*] [*German*]   (GCA)
Schwis....... Schwefelsaeure [*Sulfuric Acid*] [*German*]   (GCA)
Schwk .... Schwefelkohlenstoff [*Carbon Disulfide*] [*German*]   (GCA)
Schwldr..... Schweinsleder [*Pigskin*] [*German*]
Schwnsl...... Schweinsleder [*Pigskin*] [*German*]
Schwp........ Schwerpunkt [*Center of Gravity*] [*German*]   (GCA)
Schwsldr .... Schweinsleder [*Pigskin*] [*German*]
Schww .... Schwellenwerk [*Tie Factory (or Shop), Tie Concentration Yard, Tie Storage Depot*]   (EG)
Schwz P..... Schweizerisches Patent [*Swiss Patent*] [*German*]   (GCA)
SCI............ Sand Collectors International   (EAIO)
sci.............. Science   (TPFD)
sci.............. Scientifique [*French*]   (TPFD)
Sci............. Scogli [*Rock(s), Reef(s)*] [*Italian*]   (NAU)
SCI............ Service Civil International [*Australia*]
SCI............ Service Civil International [*International Voluntary Service*] [*India*]
SCI............ Servicio Central de Inteligencia [*Central Intelligence Service*] [*Spanish*]
SCI............ Shipping Corp. of India
SCI............ Siam Cast Iron Works Co. Ltd. [*Thailand*]
SCI............ Silicate de Cote-D'Ivoire
SCI............ Smorgon Consolidated Industries [*Australia*]
SCI............ Sociedad Colombiana de Ingenieros [*Colombian Engineers Association*]   (LA)
SCI............ Societe Camerounaise d'Impregnation
SCI............ Societe Camerounaise Industrielle
SCI............ Societe Commerciale Interoceanique
SCI............ Societe de Chimie Industrielle   (EA)
SCI............ Special Cargo Airlines [*Russian Federation*] [*ICAO designator*]   (FAAC)
SCIA .... Servicio Cooperativo de Instituciones Agropecuarias [*Quito, Ecuador*]   (LAA)
SCIA .... Societe Civile Immobiliere Africaine
SCIA .... Societe Commerciale et Immobiliere de l'Atlantique
SCIA .... Societe Commerciale, Industrielle, et Agricole
SCIAB ...... Service Civil International, Austrian Branch   (EAIO)
SCIAC .... Societe Commerciale, Industrielle, et Agricole Centrafricaine
SCIAGI .... Sociedad Cooperativa Indigenista de Agricultura, Ganaderia, e Industrias [*Bolivia*]   (DSCA)
SCIAOD.... Swedish Council for Information on Alcohol and Other Drugs   (EAIO)

SCIAS....... Societa Commerciale Italiana Africa Settentrionale
SCIBE....... Societe de Construction Ivoirienne de Batiment et Entretien
SCIBP....... Special Committee for the International Biological Program [*ICSU*]
SCIC .... Curico/General Freire [*Chile*] [*ICAO location identifier*] (ICLI)
SCIC .... Societe Centrale Immobiliere de la Caisse des Depots [*Et consignations*] (FLAF)
SCIC .... Sudanese Chemical Industries Company
SCICA ...... Societe Chimique et Industrielle Camerounaise
SCICAS..... Servicio Cooperativo Interamericano de Credito Agricola Supervisado [*Guatemala*] (DSCA)
SCICD ...... Societe Centrale Immobiliere de la Caisse des Depots
SCICFNDT ... Standing Committee for International Cooperation within the Field of Non-Destructive Testing (EA)
SCID......... Societe Commerciale et Industrielle Dahomeenne
SCIDA .... Servicio Cooperativo Interamericano de Agricultura [*Guatemala*] (DSCA)
SCIDE .... Servicio Cooperativo Interamericano de Educacion (LAA)
SCIE .... Concepcion/Carriel Sur [*Chile*] [*ICAO location identifier*] (ICLI)
Scie............ Scierie [*Sawmill*] [*Military map abbreviation World War I*] [*French*] (MTD)
SCIE .... Societe Camerounaise d'Importation et d'Exportation
SCIE .... Societe Camerounaise d'Installations Electriques
SCIE .... Societe Commerciale et Industrielle d'Expansion [*Hotel de France*]
SCIEC....... Societe Civile et Immobiliere des Entrepots de Coton
SCIEC....... Syndicat des Commercants Importateurs et Exportateurs du Cameroun
SCIENCE ... Societe des Consultants Independants et Neutres de la Communaute Europeenne [*Belgium*] (PDAA)
SCIENCE ... Stimulation des Cooperations Internationaux et des Echanges Necessaires aux Chercheurs Europeennes [*Stimulation of International Cooperation and the Necessary Exchanges of European Scientists*] [*EEC*]
SCIF .... Servicio Cooperativo Interamericano de Fomento y Vias de Comunicacion [*Peru*] (DSCA)
SCIF .... Societe Cherifienne de Materiel Industriel et Ferroviaire
Sci Fa adDis Deb ... Scire Facias ad Disprobandum Debitum [*Latin*] (DLA)
SCIFE....... Servicio Cooperativo Interamericano de Fomento Economico (LAA)
SCIG......... Societe Commerciale et Industrielle du Gabon
SCII .... Societe Commerciale Ivoirienne d'Importation
SCIK .... Savezni Centar za Izobrazbu Kadrova [*Federal Center for Instruction of Cadres*] (YU)
SCIL .... Societe Commerciale et Industrielle de Lambarene
SCIMO...... Societe Commerciale et Industrielle pour la Metropole et Outre-Mer
SCIMPEX ... Syndicat des Commercants Importateurs et Exportateurs [*Importers and Exporters Union*] [*Burkina Faso*]
SCIMPEX-COTE-D'IVOIRE ... Syndicat des Commercants Importateurs et Exportateurs de la Cote-D'Ivoire [*Importers and exporters union of the Ivory Coast*]
SCIMPEXDA ... Syndicat des Commercants Importateurs et Exportateurs du Dahomey [*Importers and exporters union of Dahomey*]
SCIMPEX-HAUTE VOLTA ... Syndicat des Commercants Importateurs et Exportateurs de Haute-Volta [*Importers and exporters union of Upper Volta*]
SCIMPEX-MALI ... Syndicat des Commercants Importateurs et Exportateurs du Mali [*Importers and exporters union of Mali*]
SCIMPEXNI ... Syndicat des Commercants Importateurs et Exportateurs du Niger [*Importers and exporters union of Niger*]
SCIMPEXRIM ... Syndicat des Commercants Importateurs et Exportateurs de la Republique Islamique de Mauritanie [*Importers and exporters union of Mauritania*]
SCIMPEXTO ... Syndicat des Commercants Importateurs et Exportateurs du Togo [*Importers and exporters union of Togo*] (AF)
SCIMPOS ... Societe Camerounaise d'Injection et de Modelage de Produits Organiques et Synthetiques
SCIN......... Springvale Community Information Network [*Australia*]
SCIO......... Sarawak Communist International Organization [*Also known as SCO*] (ML)
SCIOZ....... Service Civil International, Osterreichische Zweig [*Austrian Branch*] (EAIO)
SCIP .... Isla De Pascua/Mataveri [*Easter Island*] [*Chile*] [*ICAO location identifier*] (ICLI)
SCIP .... Societe Civile Immobiliere du Plateau
SCIP .... South Chad Irrigation Project
SCIP .... Student Community Involvement Program [*Australia*]
SCIPA .... Servicio Cooperativo Interamericano de Produccion de Alimentos [*Peru*] (LAA)
SCIPLAC .. Societe Sciages et Placages Centrafricains
SCIPP....... South Chad Irrigation Pilot Project
SCIPS....... Servicio Cooperativo Interamericano Plan del Sur [*Peru*] (DSCA)
SCIRAWN ... Scientific Research Applied to World Needs [*ICSU*]
SCIRIKA ... Societe Commerciale et Industrielle "Rika"

SCIS .... School Cataloguing Information Service [*Australia*]
SCISP........ Servicio Cooperativo Interamericano de Salud Publica [*Inter-American Cooperative Public Health Service*] [*Paraguay*] (LAA)
SCISP........ Servicio Cooperativo Interamericano de Salud Publica [*Colombia*] (COL)
SCI/SR ...... Shakaichosa-Kenkyusho Consumer Index Summary Report [*Marketing Intelligence Corp.*] [*Japan*] [*Information service or system*] (CRD)
SCITL........ Servicio Comercial de la Industria Textil Lanera [*Spain*] (EY)
sciup.......... Sciupato [*Worn*] [*Italian*]
SCIZ .... Isla De Pascua [*Easter Island*] [*Chile*] [*ICAO location identifier*] (ICLI)
SC J .... Court of Justiciary Cases [*Scotland*] (DLA)
SCJ .... Priests of the Sacred Heart of Jesus [*Italy*] (EAIO)
SCJ .... Scanjet AB [*Sweden*] [*ICAO designator*] (FAAC)
SCJ .... Science Council of Japan (MCD)
SCJ .... Service Civique de la Jeunesse
SCJ .... Standing Committee on Japan [*Australia*]
SCJM .... Sisters of Charity of Jesus and Mary [*See also ZLJM*] [*Belgium*] (EAIO)
SCJO .... Osborno/Canal Bajo [*Chile*] [*ICAO location identifier*] (ICLI)
SCK.......... Studiecentrum voor Kernenergie [*Also, CEEN, NERC*] [*Center for Nuclear Energy Studies*] [*Belgium*] (NRCH)
SCK.......... Svaz Ceskych Knihovniku [*Union of Czech Librarians*] (CZ)
SCKN....... Societe Commerciale du Kouilou Niari
SCKN........ Svaz Ceskych Knihkupcu a Nakladatelu [*Union of Czech Booksellers and Publishers*] (CZ)
SCKN-CENTRAFRIQUE ... Societe Commerciale du Kouilou Niari - Centrafrique
SCKN-CONGO ... Societe Commerciale du Kouilou Niari - Congo
SCL........... Santiago [*Chile*] [*Airport symbol*] (OAG)
SCL........... Society for Caribbean Linguistics [*St. Augustine, Trinidad*] (EAIO)
SCL........... Society for Computers and Law [*Abingdon, Oxfordshire, England*] (EAIO)
SCL........... Somali Confederation of Labour
SCL........... Southern Copper Ltd. [*Commercial firm*] [*Australia*]
SCL........... Spolek Ceskych Lekaru [*Society of Czech Physicians*] (CZ)
SCLAT ...... Service Central de la Lutte Anti-terroriste [*Central Anti-Terrorist Service*] [*France*] (ECON)
SCLC .... South Coast Labour Council [*Australia*]
SCLE .... Santiago/Los Leones [*Chile*] [*ICAO location identifier*] (ICLI)
SCLFC...... Sydney Children's Libraries' Film Circuit [*Australia*] (ADA)
SCLL .... Vallenar/Vallenar [*Chile*] [*ICAO location identifier*] (ICLI)
SCLP .... Santiago/Lo Prado [*Chile*] [*ICAO location identifier*] (ICLI)
SCM .... Aero Servicio de Carga Mexicana SA de CV [*Mexico*] [*ICAO designator*] (FAAC)
SCM .... Korea-US Security Consultative Meeting
SCM .... Sacra Catolica Majestad [*Spanish*]
SCM .... Social Change Media [*Australia*]
SCM .... Sociedad Colombiana de Matematicas [*Colorado*] (SLS)
SCM .... Societe Camerounaise de Machines
SCM .... Societe Camerounaise de Minoterie
SCM .... Societe Camerounaise Michelin
SCM .... Societe Canine de Madagascar (EAIO)
SCM .... Societe de Caution Mutuelle
SCM .... Societe de Construction de Madagascar
SCM .... Society of Clinical Masseurs [*Australia*]
SCM .... Society of Community Medicine [*Later, SPH*] (EAIO)
SCM .... Sous-Commission de Co-Ordination des Questions Forestieres Mediterraneennes [*FAO*]
SCM .... State Committee Member of Communist Terrorist Organization (CTO) [*Malaysia*] (ML)
SCM .... Svaz Ceskoslovenske [*or Ceske*] Mladeze [*Union of Czechoslovak (or Czech) Youth*] (CZ)
SCM .... Sydney Conservatorium of Music [*Australia*]
SCMA....... Servicio Colombiano de Meteorologia e Hidrologia [*Colombia*] (COL)
SCMB....... Societe de Construction Metallique de Bouake
SCMB....... Standard Chartered Merchant Bank [*Singapore*]
SCMBZ..... Spojene Ceske a Moravske Bavlnarske Zavody [*United Czech and Moravian Cotton Mills*] (CZ)
SCMC....... Sociedad Cubana de Matematica y Computacion [*Cuba*] (EAIO)
SCMCI ...... Societe Commerciale de la Moyenne Cote-D'Ivoire
SCMD .... Santiago/Ministerio de Defensa Nacional [*Chile*] [*ICAO location identifier*] (ICLI)
SCMDBMC ... Standing Committee of the Murray-Darling Basin Ministerial Council [*Australia*]
SCME........ Surgut Commodity and Raw Materials Exchange [*Russian Federation*] (EY)
SCMIC ...... State Constructional Materials Import Company [*Iraq*] (ME)
SCMO .... Societe pour une Confederation au Moyen-Orient [*Society for Middle East Confederation - SMEC*] [*Israel*] (EAIO)
SCMO .... Studie- en Informatiecentrum TNO voor Milieu-Onderzoek [*TNO Study and Information Center on Environmental Research*] [*Information service or system*] (IID)

SCMO-TNO ... Studie- en Informatiecentrum voor Milieu-Onderzoek - Nederlands Centrale Organisatie voor Toegepast-Natuurwetenschappelijk Onderzoek [*Study and Information Center on Environmental Research - Netherlands Central Organization for Applied Natural Scientific Research*]   (ARC)

SCMT .... Standing Committee of Ministers Responsible for Transportation of the Caribbean Community [*Guyana*]   (EAIO)

SCN .... Saarbrucken [*Germany*] [*Airport symbol*]   (OAG)

SCN .... Sindicato de Carreteras Nacionales [*National Highways Union*] [*Colorado*]   (LA)

SCN .... Slovenske Cirkevne Nakladatelstvo [*Slovak Church Publishing House*]   (CZ)

SCN .... Sociedad Chilena de Nutricion [*Chile*]   (EAIO)

SCN .... South American Airlines [*Peru*] [*ICAO designator*]   (FAAC)

SCN .... Svaz Ceskych Novinaru [*Union of Czech Journalists*]   (CZ)

SCNC .... Sociedad de Ciencias Naturales Caldas [*Colombia*]   (DSCA)

SCNCM .... Standing Committee of Nature Conservation Ministers [*Australia*]

SCNEA ...... Sealing Commission for the Northeast Atlantic   (ASF)

SCNI .... Supreme Court of Norfolk Island [*Australia*]

SCNO .... Srpski Centralni Narodni Odbor [*Serbian Central National Committee*] [*Chicago*]   (YU)

SCNOCB ... Societe Cooperative Nationale Ouvriere de Construction et de Batiment [*Tunisia*]

SCNPWC .. Standing Committee for Nobel Prize Winners' Congresses   (EA)

SCNR .... Scientific Committee of National Representatives [*NATO*]

SCNSM ..... Special Committee for National Security Measures [*Terminated*] [*South Korea*]   (FEA)

SCNSW ..... Spastic Centre of New South Wales [*Australia*]

SCNSW ..... Supreme Court of New South Wales [*Australia*]

SCNT .... Suez Canal Net Ton [*of oil tankers*]

SCNT .... Supreme Court of the Northern Territory [*Australia*]

SCNVYO ... Standing Conference of National Voluntary Youth Organizations [*Zimbabwe*]   (EAIO)

SCNWA ..... Sealing Commission for the Northwest Atlantic   (ASF)

SCNZ .... Shipping Corporation of New Zealand

SCO .... Euro Air Helicopter Service AB [*Sweden*] [*ICAO designator*]   (FAAC)

SCO .... Sarawak Communist Organization [*Also known as SCIO*]   (ML)

Sco .... Scoglio [*Rock(s), Reef(s)*] [*Italian*]   (NAU)

SCO .... Shell Company of Qatar   (OMWE)

SCO .... Societe Commerciale de l'Ogooue

SCO .... Societe des Ciments d'Onigbolo

SCO .... Societe des Ciments d'Owendo

SCO .... State Coroners' Office [*Australia*]

SCOA .... Societe Commerciale de l'Ouest Africain [*West African Trading Company*]   (AF)

SCOA .... Superannuated Commonwealth Officers' Association [*Australia*]

SCOA .... Sydney College of the Arts [*Australia*]

SCOC .... Societe Commerciale de l'Ouest Cameroun

SCOC .... Spanish Chamber of Commerce [*Taiwan*]   (EAIO)

SCOCAM ... Standing Committee of Consumer Affairs Ministers [*Australia*]

SCOD .... Societe Cooperative Oecumenique de Developpement [*Ecumenical Development Cooperative Society - EDCS*] [*Netherlands*]   (EAIO)

SCODAP ... Sous-Comite de Defense et d'Action Psychologique [*Defense Psychological Action Subcommittee*] [*In the Ministry of Agriculture Cambodia*]   (CL)

SCODI ...... Societe de Conserves de la Cote-D'Ivoire

SCOFA ...... Societe Commerciale France-Afrique

SCOFIDEX ... Societe Commerciale Federale Camerounaise d'Importation et d'Exportation

SCOG .... Service Central d'Organisation et de Gestions [*Central Organization and Management Department*] [*Burundi*]   (AF)

SCOG .... Sociedad Colombiana de Obstetricia y Ginecologia [*Colorado*]   (SLS)

SCOI .... Societe Charbonniere de l'Ocean Indien

SCOLMA ... Standing Conference on Library Materials on Africa

SCOM .... Scientific Committee [*NATO*]   (NATG)

SCOM .... Service Central d'Organisation et de Methodes du Ministere de la Fonction Publique

SCOM .... Societe Commerciale de l'Ouest Mauritanien

SCOM ...... State Co. for Oil Marketing [*Iraq*]   (EY)

SCOMA .... Sydney College of Makeup Art [*Australia*]

SCOMAD ... Service de Controle du Conditionnement de Madagascar

SCOMB ..... Societe Cooperative de Meubles et de Batiments

scomp .... Scomparti [*Sections*] [*Italian*]

scompl .... Scompleto [*Incomplete*] [*Italian*]

SCON .... Quellon/Ad Quellon [*Chile*] [*ICAO location identifier*]   (ICLI)

SCON .... Santiago/Quinta Normal [*Chile*] [*ICAO location identifier*]   (ICLI)

SCOP .... State Co. for Oil Projects [*Iraq*]   (EY)

SCOPAL ... Standing Committee on Pacific Libraries [*Australia*]

SCOPE ...... Scientific Committee on Problems of the Environment [*ICSU*]   (EA)

SCOPE ...... Small Cooperative Enterprises Scheme [*New Zealand*]

SCOPE ...... Standing Conference of Public Enterprises [*India*]   (FEA)

SCOPEC ... Societe Industrielle et Commerciale de la Petite Cote

SCOPED ... Societe Commerciale du Petit Diboum

SCOPSS .... Societe Cooperative-Ouvriere de Production de Sidi-Salem [*Algeria*]

SCOR .... Scientific Committee on Oceanic Research [*ICSU*] [*Halifax, NS*]   (EAIO)

SCOR .... Societe Commerciale de Reassurance [*Paris, France*]

SCORE ..... Service Corps of Retired Employees [*Australia*]

SCORE ...... Survey and Comparison of Research Expenditures [*Dept. of Science*] [*Australia*]   (PDAA)

SCORESA ... Societe Commerciale de la Region des Savanes

SCORRAD ... Standing Committee on Resources Research and Development [*IPFC*]   (ASF)

SCOSA ...... Spastic Centres of South Australia

SCOSTEP ... Scientific Committee on Solar Terrestrial Physics [*ICSU*]

SCOT .... Shipborne SATCOM Terminal [*British*]

SCOT .... Soweto Committee of Ten [*South Africa*]   (AF)

SCOT .... Standing Committee on Technology [*Australian Book Trade Committee*]

SCOT .... Swinburne College of Technology [*Australia*]   (ADA)

SCOT .... Syrian Company for Oil Transport [*Banias*]   (ME)

SCOTL ..... State Committee of Teacher-Librarians [*Australia*]

Scots .... Scots   (TPFD)

Scott .... Scottish   (TPFD)

SCOTT ...... Shipping Corporation of Trinidad and Tobago   (LA)

SCOV .... Svaz Ceskoslovenskych Oslepenych Vojinu [*Union of Czechoslovak Blind Veterans*]   (CZ)

SCP .... Samoa Coconut Products Ltd.

SCP .... Saudi Civil Police   (ME)

SCP .... Scottish Conservative Party [*Political party*]

SCP .... Sdruzeni Ceskych Partyzanu [*Association of Czech Partisans*]   (CZ)

SCP .... Sociedad Colombiana de Pediatria [*Colombia*]   (EAIO)

SCP .... Sociedad Colombiana de Planificacion [*Colombian Planning Society*]   (LA)

SCP .... Societe Camerounaise de Publications

SCP .... Societe Cherifienne de Petrole [*Moroccan Petroleum Company*]   (AF)

SCP .... Societe de Chimie Physique [*French*]   (SLS)

SCP .... Societe de Commercialisation des Peaux

SCP .... Standing Committee on Packaging [*Australia*]

SCP .... Sudanese Communist Party [*Political party*]   (PD)

SCP .... Syrian Communist Party [*Political party*]   (PPW)

SCPA .... Singapore Country People's Association [*Pro-Communist Barisan Sosialis Front organization*]   (ML)

SCPA .... Societe Commerciale des Potasses et de l'Azote

SCPC .... Societe Camerounaise de Collecte des Peaux et Cuirs

SCPDR ..... Scientific Council on Peace and Disarmament Research   (EAIO)

SCPE .... Swedish Confederation of Professional Employees   (EAIO)

SCPENC ... Shanghai Chinese PEN Centre [*China*]   (EAIO)

SCPF .... Societe Commerciale Panayotis Freres

SCPI .... Societe Civile de Participation Immobiliere [*North African*]

SCPL .... Societe Camerounaise Pierre Lemonnier

SCPM .... Societe Cherifienne des Produits Manufactures

SCPMA ..... Statiuhea de Cercetari pentru Plante Medicinale si Aromatice [*Medicinal and Aromatic Plants Research Station*] [*Romanian*]   (ARC)

SCPRI .... Service Central de Protection Contre les Radiations Ionisantes [*France*]

SCPS .... Supreme Council for Popular Sports [*Sudan*]

SCPT .... Sydney Cove Passenger Terminal [*Australia*]

SCPUvN .... Sdruzeni Ceskoslovenskych Politickych Uprchliku v Nemecku [*Association of Czechoslovak Political Refugees in Germany*]   (CZ)

SCQ .... Santiago De Compostela [*Spain*] [*Airport symbol*]   (OAG)

SCQ .... Sociedad Chilena de Quimca

scr .... Sanscrito [*Sanskrit*] [*Language, etc.*] [*Portuguese*]

SCR .... Service Central de Renseignements [*Secret police*] [*Rwanda*]

SCR .... Si-Chang Flying Service Co. Ltd. [*Thailand*] [*ICAO designator*]   (FAAC)

SCR .... Societe Centrale de Representation

Scra .... Scogliera [*Ridge of Rocks*] [*Italian*]   (NAU)

SCRATA ... Steel Castings Research and Trade Association [*Sheffield, England*]   (EAIO)

SCRC .... Spanish Colonial Research Center [*University of New Mexico*] [*Research center*]   (RCD)

SCRCC ...... Soil Conservation and Rivers Control Council [*New Zealand*]   (DSCA)

SCRCSA .... Statiunea Centrala de Reproductie si Combatere Sterilitatii la Animale [*Central Station for Reproduction and Combating Sterility in Animals*]   (RO)

SCRD .... Vina Del Mar/Rodelillo [*Chile*] [*ICAO location identifier*]   (ICLI)

SCRE......... Syndicat des Constructeurs de Relais Electriques [*France*] (PDAA)

SCREG...... Societe Chimique Routiere et d'Entreprise Generale [*French*]

SCREM..... Societe Campinoise de Recherches et Exploitations Minerales [*Benelux*] (BAS)

SCRES....... State Commission for Restructuring the Economic System [*China*] (IMH)

SCRG......... Rancagua/De La Independencia [*Chile*] [*ICAO location identifier*] (ICLI)

SCRG........ Societe Chimique et Routiere de la Gironde

SCRIPT..... Support for Creative Independent Production Talent [*EC*] (ECED)

SCRM........ Isla Rey Jorge/Base Aerea Teniente R. Marsh Martin [*Chile*] [*ICAO location identifier*] (ICLI)

SCRN........ Sociedad Colombiana de Repursos Naturales [*Colombia*] (DSCA)

SC/ROSTENA ... Bureau Regional de Science et de Technologie pour l'Europe et l'Amerique du Nord [*Regional Office for Science and Technology for Europe and North America*] (EAIO)

SCRP......... Severocesky Rudny Pruzkum [*North Bohemian Ore Prospecting*] (CZ)

SCS............ Science Council of Singapore (SLS)

SCS........... Scientific Control Systems Akademie (SLS)

SCS........... Scottish Combined Societies [*Australia*]

SCS........... Screening and Costing Staff [*NATO*] (NATG)

SCS........... Singapore Cosmos Shipping Co. Pty. Ltd. (DS)

SCS........... Slovensky Cyklisticky Svaz [*Slovak Cycling Association*] (CZ)

SCS........... Societe Camerounaise de Sacherie

SCS........... Societe Commerciale Senegalaise

SCS........... Societe de Construction du Senegal

SCS........... Societe en Commandite Simple [*Simple Partnership*] [*Belgium*]

SCS........... Society of Cypriot Studies [*Cyprus*] (EAIO)

SCS........... Soil Conservation Service [*Puerto Rico*] (DSCA)

SCS........... Solicitud de Certificado de Solvencia [*Settlement Application Certificate*] [*Venezuela*]

SCS........... Svaz Ceskoslovenskych Skladatelu [*Czechoslovak Composers' Union*] (CZ)

SCS........... Swedish Cartographic Society (EAIO)

SCS........... Swiss Cardiac Society (EAIO)

SCS........... Syndikat Ceskych Spisovatelu [*Czech Writers' Syndicate*] (CZ)

SCSA........ Secondary Colleges Staff Association [*Tasmania, Australia*]

SCSA......... Ski Club of South Africa

SCSA......... Spastic Centres of South Australia

SCSA......... Supreme Council for Sport in Africa [*See also CSSA*] [*Yaounde, Cameroon*] (EAIO)

SCSBCVG ... Suore di Carita delle Sante Bartolomea Capitanio e Vincenza Gerosa [*Sisters of Charity of Saints Bartholomew Capitanio And Vincent Gerosa*] [*Italy*] (EAIO)

SCSC......... Santiago/Ciudad [*Chile*] [*ICAO location identifier*] (ICLI)

SCSC......... Standing Committee on Soil Conservation [*Australia*]

SCSCB....... Sisters of Charity of St. Charles Borromeo [*See also LCB*] (EAIO)

SCSE......... La Serena/La Florida [*Chile*] [*ICAO location identifier*] (ICLI)

SCSE......... State Committee for the State of Emergency [*Commonwealth of Independent States*] (EE)

SCSF......... Svaz Ceskoslovenskych Filatelistu [*Union of Czechoslovak Philatelists*] (CZ)

SCSFA....... Sunset Coast Sub-tropical Fruits Association [*Queensland, Australia*]

SCSFUT.... Syndikat Ceskoslovenskych Filmovych Umelcu a Techniku [*Czechoslovak Film Artists and Technicians Trade Union*] (CZ)

SCSH......... Svaz Ceskoslovenskeho Hasicstva [*Union of Czechoslovak Firemen*] (CZ)

SCSH......... Svaz Ceskoslovenskych Horolezcu [*Czechoslovak Mountain Climbers' Association*] (CZ)

SCSHC...... South China Sea Hydrographic Commission (MSC)

SCSI.......... Svaz Ceskoslovenskych Invalidu [*Union of Czechoslovak Disabled Persons*] (CZ)

SCSIN....... Service Central de Surete des Installations Nucleaires [*Nuclear energy*] [*French*] (NRCH)

SCSJAT.... Sisters of Charity of St. Jeanne Antide Thouret [*Italy*] (EAIO)

SCSK........ Shellfish Commission for the Skagerrak-Kattegat (ASF)

SCSKU...... Svaz Ceskych Skladatelu a Koncertnich Umelcu [*Former Czechoslovakia*] (SLS)

SCSN......... Santo Domingo/Santo Domingo [*Chile*] [*ICAO location identifier*] (ICLI)

SCSN......... Svaz Ceskoslovenskych Novinaru [*Czechoslovak Journalists' Union*] (CZ)

SCSP......... Societe de Scientifique et Cultural de Pakistan (EAIO)

SCSP......... Svaz Ceskoslovensko-Sovietskeho Priatelstva [*Czechoslovak-Soviet Friendship League*] (CZ)

SCSPS....... Standing Committee on the Safeguard of the Pursuit of Science [*International Council of Scientific Unions*]

SCSR......... Segundo Corral/Segundo Corral Alto [*Chile*] [*ICAO location identifier*] (ICLI)

SCSS.......... Svaz Ceskoslovenskych Spisovatelu [*Czechoslovak Writers' Union*] (CZ)

SCST........ Castro/Gamboa [*Chile*] [*ICAO location identifier*] (ICLI)

SCST......... State Committee for Science and Technology [*Former USSR*] (IMH)

SCSV......... Svaz Ceskoslovenskych Vytvarniku [*Union of Czechoslovak Creative Artists*] (CZ)

SCSVU...... Svaz Ceskoslovenskych Vytvarnych Umelcu [*Union of Czechoslovak Creative Artists*] (CZ)

SCSWA...... Spanish Cotton Spinners and Weavers Association (EAIO)

SCT........... Saab Aircraft AB [*Sweden*] [*ICAO designator*] (FAAC)

SCT........... Secretaria de Comunicaciones y Transportes [*Secretariat of Communications and Transport*] [*Mexico*] (LA)

Sct............. Section [*Section, Division*] [*Military*] [*French*] (MTD)

SCT........... Service de Calcul par Telephone [*French*] (ADPT)

SCT........... Servicio de Cooperacion Tecnica [*Technical Cooperation Service*] [*Chile*] (LA)

SCT........... Severoceske Tiskarny [*North Bohemian Printing Plants*] (CZ)

SCT........... Societe Camerounaise du Tabac

SCT........... Societe Cotonniere Transoceanique

SCT........... Societe de Chimie Therapeutique [*French*] (SLS)

SCT........... Sous-Commission des Cartes Tectoniques [*Subcommittee for Tectonic Maps of the Commission for the Geological Map of the World - STMCGMW*] (EAIO)

SCT........... Swinburne College of Technology [*See also SCOT*] [*Australia*] (EAIO)

SCT........... Swiss Committee Against Torture (EAIO)

SCTA........ Societe Camerounaise de Transport et d'Affretement

SCTA........ Societe Commerciale de Transport des Amis

s/cta.......... Su Cuenta [*Your Account*] [*Business term*] [*Spanish*]

SCTAA...... Shopping Centre Tenants' Association of Australia

SCTB......... Santiago/Eulogio Sanchez [*Chile*] [*ICAO location identifier*] (ICLI)

SCTC......... Societe de Commerce et de Transports du Cameroun

SCTC......... Temuco/Maquehue [*Chile*] [*ICAO location identifier*] (ICLI)

SCTE......... Puerto Montt/Internacional El Tepual [*Chile*] [*ICAO location identifier*] (ICLI)

SCTF......... SHAPE [*Supreme Headquarters Allied Powers Europe*] Centralized Training Facility [*NATO*] (NATG)

SCTG........ Societe Cotiere de Transport de Grumes

SCTI.......... Santiago/Internacional Los Cerillos [*Chile*] [*ICAO location identifier*] (ICLI)

SCTI.......... Servicio de Cooperacion Tecnica Industrial [*Santiago, Chile*] (LAA)

SCTI.......... Soviet Chamber of Trade and Industry

SCTIP....... Service de Cooperation Technique Internationale de Police [*International Police Technical Cooperation Service*] (CL)

SCTM....... Societe Commerciale et de Travaux Mecaniques [*Cameroon*]

SCTN........ Chaiten/Chaiten [*Chile*] [*ICAO location identifier*] (ICLI)

SCTN........ Societe Cherifienne de Transports et de Navigation

SCTNB...... Societe Commerciale des Techniques Nouvelles du Batiment

SCTO........ Societe Cotonniere Transoceanique

SCTRH...... Societe Camerounaise de Transports Routiers d'Hydrocarbures

SCTS......... Societe Centrafricaine des Transports de la Haute-Sangha

SCTS......... Societe des Cooperatives de Transportateurs du Senegal

SCTT........ Societe Commerciale de Transports Transatlantiques

SCTTAO... Societe Commerciale de Transports Transatlantiques Afrique Occidentale

SCTT-CI.... Societe Commerciale de Transports Transatlantiques Cote-D'Ivoire

SCTTM..... Societe Commerciale de Transports Transatlantiques Madagascar

SCTT-MAURITANIENNE ... Societe Commerciale de Transports Transatlantiques Mauritanienne

SCTTOI.... Societe Commerciale de Transports Transatlantiques Ocean Indien

SCTT-TAMATAVE ... Societe Commerciale de Transports Transatlantiques de Tamatave

SCTW....... Study Center for the Third World [*Italy*] (EAIO)

SCTZ......... Puerto Montt [*Chile*] [*ICAO location identifier*] (ICLI)

SCU........... Salvadoran Communal Union (EAIO)

SCU........... Santiago [*Cuba*] [*Airport symbol*] (OAG)

SCU........... Supreme Council of Universities [*Saudi Arabia*] (ME)

SCU........... Syndicat Central Unique [*Trade union*] [*Cameroon*]

SCUA........ Suez Canal Users Association

SCUB........ Societe pour le Commerce et l'Usinage des Bois

SCUG........ Svaz Ceskych Umelcu a Grafiku [*Union of Czech Artists*] (CZ)

SCUGH..... Sdruzeni Ceskych Umelcu Grafiku "Hollar" [*Hollar Association of Czech Graphic Artists*] (CZ)

SCUMRA ... Societe Centrale de l'Uranium et des Mineraux et Metaux Radioactifs [*Nuclear energy*] [*French*] (NRCH)

SCV........... Savez Drustava za Cistocu Vazduha (EAIO)

SCV........... Schweiz Chorvereinigung [*Switzerland*] (EAIO)

SCV........... Service de la Carte de la Vegetation [*Vegetation Map Service*] [*French*] (WER)

SCV........... Sindicatos Cap Verde

SCV........... Societe Commerciale Voltaique "La Moderne"

SCV............ Societe Credit et Vente
SCV............ State College of Victoria [*Australia*]   (ADA)
SCV............ Stato della Citta del Vaticano [*Vatican City*]
SCV............ Suceava [*Romania*] [*Airport symbol*]   (OAG)
SCV-B........ State College of Victoria - Burwood [*Australia*]
SCVB........ Sydney Convention and Visitors' Bureau [*Australia*]
SCVC........ State College of Victoria at Coburg [*Australia*]   (ADA)
SCVD........ Valdivia/Pichoy [*Chile*] [*ICAO location identifier*]   (ICLI)
SCV-F........ State College of Victoria - Frankston [*Australia*]
SCV-H........ State College of Victoria - Hawthorn [*Australia*]
SCVHU ..... Svaz Ceskych Vykonnych Hudebnich Umelcu [*Czech Musicians' Union*]   (CZ)
SCV-ICE ... State College of Victoria - Institute of Catholic Education [*Australia*]   (ADA)
SCV-IECD ... State College of Victoria - Institute of Early Childhood Development [*Australia*]
SCVM........ Service Central des Ventes du Mobilier de l'Etat [*France*]   (FLAF)
SCVPB ..... Slovenska Centralna Vojno-Partizanska Bolnisnica [*Slovenian Central Partisan Military Hospital*]   (YU)
SCVPH ...... Sub-Committee on Veterinary Public Health [*Australia*]
SCV-R........ State College of Victoria - Rusden [*Australia*]
SCV-T........ State College of Victoria - Toorak [*Australia*]
SCVTMS... Suez Canal Vessel Traffic Management System   (MENA)
SCVZO ...... Svaz Ceskoslovenskych Vojaku Zahranicniho Odboje [*Union of Czechoslovak Veteran Partisans Abroad*]   (CZ)
SCW .... Malmo Aviation AB [*Sweden*] [*ICAO designator*]   (FAAC)
SCWA........ Supreme Court of Western Australia
SC (WA)..... Supreme Court (Western Australia)   (DLA)
SCWG....... Satellite Communications Working Group [*NATO*]   (NATG)
SCWO ...... Singapore Council of Women's Organizations
SCWR....... Scientific Committee on Water Research [*ICSU*]   (ASF)
SCWR....... Standing Committee on Water Resources [*Australia*]
SCZ.......... Santa Cruz [*Solomon Islands*] [*Airport symbol*]   (OAG)
SCZ............ Svaz Ceskoslovenskeho Zivnostnictva [*Czechoslovak Small Business Association*]   (CZ)
SCZ............ Svaz Ceskych Zen [*Union of Czech Women*]   (CZ)
SCZA........ Station Centrale de Zoologie Agricole [*France*]   (DSCA)
SCZV .... Svaz Ceskoslovenskych Zahranicnich Vojaku [*Union of Czechoslovak Veterans of Foreign Wars*]   (CZ)
SD .... Aircraft and Engine [*Aircraft maintenance*]   (RU)
s/d .... Children's Show   (RU)
s/d .... Daily Ration   (RU)
SD .... Degtyarev Heavy Machine Gun   (RU)
SD .... Flank Patrol   (BU)
SD .... Lethal Dose   (RU)
SD .... Mean Pressure, Medium Pressure   (RU)
SD .... Medical Unit   (RU)
SD .... Rifle Division   (RU)
SD .... Sadr Diwani Adalat Court [*Bengal, India*]   (DLA)
sd............... Samma Dag [*The Same Day*] [*Sweden*]   (GPO)
sd............... Samme Dato [*Same Date*] [*Denmark*]   (GPO)
sd............... Sans Date [*No Date (of publication)*] [*French*]
SD .... Schemas Directeurs [*Morocco*]
SD .... Schnelldrucker [*German*]   (ADPT)
SD .... Sciere de Duckoue
SD .... Se Despide [*Spanish*]
SD .... Sehr Dringend [*Very urgent, used preceding German coded messages*]
SD .... Sekolah Dasar [*Elementary School*]   (IN)
sd............... Sem Data [*Without Date (of Publication)*] [*Portuguese*]
sd............... Senza Data [*Without Date (of Publication)*] [*Italian*]
SD .... Service de Documentation [*Agence de Promotion des Investissements*] [*Tunisia*]
SD .... Service Detectif [*Haiti*]
SD .... Servomotor   (RU)
SD .... Sicherheitsdienst [*Police Duty*] [*NAZI Germany*]
sd............... Siedend [*Boiling*] [*German*]
Sd............... Siedepunkt [*Boiling Point*] [*German*]
sd............... Siedet [*Boils*] [*German*]   (GCA)
sd............... Siehe Dies [*See This, Which See*] [*German*]
sd............... Siehe Dort [*See There*] [*German*]
sd............... Sine Dato [*Benelux*]   (BAS)
sd............... Social Democrat   (BU)
SD .... Socialdemokratiet i Danmark [*Social Democratic Party of Denmark*] [*Political party*]   (PPE)
SD .... Socialisme en Democratie [*Benelux*]   (BAS)
SD .... Socialne Demokraticka Strana Delnicka [*Social Democratic Workers' Party*]   (CZ)
SD .... Societa de Dermatologie [*Romania*]   (EAIO)
SD .... Solar Engine   (RU)
SD .... Solar Pickup   (RU)
Sd............... Sonderdruck [*Separate Printing*] [*German*]
sd............... Sosiaalidemokraatti(nen) [*Finland*]
SD .... Sous-Directeur
SD .... Speciale Diensten [*Special Service*] [*Dutch Navy*]

SD .... Spontaneous Fission   (RU)
SD .... Sportsko Drustvo [*Sport Society*]   (YU)
SD .... Spotrebni Druzstvo [*Consumers Cooperative*]   (CZ)
SD .... Stathmos Dioikiseos [*Command Post*]   (GC)
SD .... Stokta Degil [*Not in Stock*]   (TU)
SD .... Streifendrucker [*Line Printer*] [*German*]   (ADPT)
SD .... Stronnictwo Demokratyczne [*Democratic Party*] [*Poland*] [*Political party*]   (PPE)
SD .... Stycny Dustojnik [*Courier Officer*]   (CZ)
SD .... Sudan [*ANSI two-letter standard code*]   (CNC)
Sd............... Sund [*Sundet*] [*Sound*] [*Denmark*]   (NAU)
Sd............... Sund [*Sundet*] [*Sound*] [*Norway*]   (NAU)
SD .... Superheterodyne Demodulator   (RU)
SD .... Svensk Dietistforening [*Sweden*]   (EAIO)
SD .... Sy Deurlugtigheid [*Afrikaans*]
SD .... Synchronous Motor   (RU)
SD .... Synchronous Transducer   (RU)
sd............... Today   (RU)
SD .... Transmitting Selsyn   (RU)
SDA .... Baghdad-Saddam [*Iraq*] [*Airport symbol*]   (OAG)
SDA .... Schweizerische Depeschenagentur AG [*Swiss News Agency*]   (EY)
SDA .... Self-Defence Agency [*Japan*]   (ECON)
SDA .... Self-Propelled Sprinkler   (RU)
SDA .... Sjedinjene Drzave Amerike [*United States of America*]   (YU)
SDA .... Social-Democratic Association [*Political party*]   (EAIO)
SDA .... Societe de l'Aerotrain [*France*]   (PDAA)
SDA .... Somali Democratic Alliance [*Political party*]   (EY)
SDA .... Sozialistische Demokratische Aktion [*Socialist Democratic Action*] [*Switzerland*]   (WEN)
SDA .... Staff Development Association [*Australia*]
SDA .... Stranka Demokratske Akcije [*Party of Democratic Action*] [*Bosnia-Herzegovina*] [*Political party*]   (EY)
SDA .... Stratiotiki Dievthynsis Athenon [*Athens Military Directorate*]   (GC)
SDA .... Swedish Dental Association   (EAIO)
SDA .... Swedish Diabetic Association   (EAIO)
SDA .... Syrian Dental Association   (EAIO)
SDAA .... Scottish Dancing Association of Australia
SDAC........ Societe d'Application Cinematographique
SDAEA ..... Shop, Distributive and Allied Employees' Association [*Australia*]
SDAG .... Sowjetisch-Deutsche Aktiengesellschaft [*Soviet-German Corporation (Wismut)*]   (EG)
SDAI......... Societe de Developpement Agricole et Industriel [*Agricultural and Industrial Development Company*] [*Senegal*]   (AF)
SDAJ .... Savez Drustava Anatoma Jugoslavije [*Former Yugoslavia*]   (EAIO)
SDAJ .... Savez Drustava Arhitekta Jugoslavije [*Federation of Architects' Societies of Yugoslavia*]   (YU)
SDAJ .... Sozialistische Deutsche Arbeiterjugend [*Socialist German Workers Youth*]   (WEN)
SDAM ...... Seventh Day Adventist Mission
SDAM ...... Social Democratic Alliance of Macedonia [*Political party*]   (EY)
SDAM ...... Stratiotiki Dioikisis Anatolikis Mesogeiou [*Military Directorate for the Eastern Mediterranean*] [*Greek*]   (GC)
SDAN .... Skholi Diakonisson Adelfon kai Nosokomon [*School for Deaconesses and Nurses*] [*Greek*]   (GC)
SDAP........ Sociaal-Democratische Arbeiders Partij [*Social Democratic Workers' Party*] [*Netherlands*] [*Political party*]   (PPE)
SDAR........ Saharan Democratic Arab Republic   (AF)
SDAR........ Savez Drustava Arhivskih Radnika Jugoslavije [*Former Yugoslavia*]   (SLS)
SDARFNRJ ... Savez Drustava Arhivskih Radnika Federativna Narodna Republika Jugoslavija [*Federation of Archivists' Societies of Yugoslavia*]   (YU)
SDAT........ Sociedad Dasonomica de America Tropical [*Costa Rica*]   (LAA)
SDAT........ Societe pour le Developpement Agricole du Togo
sdat op........ Inventory, Transfer List   (RU)
SDB .... Les Scieries du Baoule Anciens Ets. Jean Nivet
SDB .... Salesians of Don Bosco
SDB .... Selection de Debit Binaire [*French*]   (ADPT)
SDB .... Sex Discrimination Board [*South Australia*]
SDB .... Sociaal-Democratische Bond [*Social Democratic League*] [*Netherlands*] [*Political party*]   (PPE)
SDB .... Societe Dahomeenne de Banque
SDB .... Spesiale Diensbataljon [*Special Service Battalion*] [*Afrikaans*]
SDB .... State Development Bank [*Hungary*]
SDBM........ Sojuz na Drustvata na Bibliotekarite na Makedonija [*Macedonia*]   (EAIO)
SDBO .... Societe de Banque Occidentale [*France*]   (EY)
SDBRJ....... Savez Drustava Bibliotecnih Radnika Jugoslavije [*Former Yugoslavia*]   (EAIO)
SDC .... Secretarial Diploma College [*Australia*]
SDC .... Social Development Commission [*Jamaica*]   (LA)
SDC .... Societe de Developpement et de Confection [*Morocco*]
SDC .... State Disasters Committee [*Australia*]

SDC .... Sudan Development Corporation [*Khartoum*]
SDC .... Sugar Development Corporation
SDC .... Swedish Airforce [*ICAO designator*]   (FAAC)
SDC .... Sydney Dance Co. [*Australia*]
SDCA........ Societe de Conserves Africaines [*Senegal*]
SDCA........ Society of Dyers and Colourists of Australia   (ADA)
SDCA........ Square Dance Callers Association [*Australia*]
SDCANZ... Society of Dyers and Colourists of Australia and New Zealand
                   (ADA)
SDCI......... Servico Director e Coordinador de Informacoes [*Director and
                   Coordinator of Information Service*] [*Portuguese*]   (WER)
SDCM .... Societe Dahomeenne de Ciments et Materiaux
SDCP........ Service de Diffusion Cinematographique Populaire [*People's
                   Movie Dissemination Service*] [*Algeria*]   (AF)
SDD .... Collection of Effective Treaties, Agreements, and Conventions
                   Concluded with Foreign States   (RU)
SDD .... Lubango [*Angola*] [*Airport symbol*]   (OAG)
SDD .... Second Development Decade [*United Nations*]
SDD .... Skola Dustojnickeho Dorostu [*Officers' Candidate School*]   (CZ)
SDD .... Srpsko Dobrotvorno Drustvo [*Serbian Welfare Society*]
                   [*Chicago*]   (YU)
SDD .... Two-Cycle Light Range Finder   (RU)
SDDE .... Societe Dahomeenne pour le Developpement Economique
SDDF........ Sosyal Demokrasi Dernekleri Federasyonu [*Federation of Social
                   Democracy Organizations*]   (TU)
SDDOM .... Societe pour le Developpement des Departements d'Outre-Mer
SDE .... Santiago Del Estero [*Argentina*] [*Airport symbol*]   (OAG)
SDE .... Savez Drustva Ekologa   (EAIO)
SDE .... Service de Documentation Economique
SDE .... Societe Dakaroise d'Entreposage
SDE .... Sosialistiki Dimokratiki Enosis [*Socialist Democratic Union*]
                   [*Greek*]   (GC)
SDE .... Statiunea Didactica si Experimentala [*Teaching and
                   Experimental Station*]   (RO)
SDE .... Symvoulion Dimosion Ergon [*Public Works Council*] [*Greek*]
                   (GC)
SDEC........ Sudan Desert Encroachment Control and Rehabilitation
                   Programme
SDECE ...... Service de Documentation Exterieure et de Contre-Espionnage
                   [*Foreign Intelligence and Counterintelligence Service*]
                   [*French*]   (WER)
SDEE........ Sindicato Democratico de Estudiantes de Espana [*Democratic
                   Union of Students of Spain*]   (WER)
SDEJ .... Savez Drustava Ekonomista Jugoslavije [*Federation of Societies
                   of Economists of Yugoslavia*]   (YU)
SDEM........ Societe d'Entreprise de Montages
SDEPM ..... Syndicat des Directeurs des Etablissements d'Enseignement
                   Prive de Madagascar [*Malagasy Union of Principals of
                   Private Education Institutions*]   (AF)
SDEPP ...... Societe Dahomeenne d'Entreposage de Produits Petroliers
S de RL ...... Sociedad de Responsabilidad Limitada [*Private Limited
                   Company*] [*Business term*] [*Spanish*]
SDF........... Sammenslutningen af Danmarks Forskningsbiblioteker
                   [*Denmark*]   (SLS)
SDF........... Saudi Development Fund   (ME)
SDF........... Self-Defense Force [*Vietnam*]   (VNW)
SDF........... Social Democratic Federation [*Iceland*] [*Political party*]   (PPW)
SDF........... Social Democratic Federation [*Japan*] [*Political party*]   (PPW)
SDF........... Social Democratic Front [*Ghana*] [*Political party*]   (PPW)
SDF........... Social Democratic Front [*Cameroon*] [*Political party*]   (EY)
SDF........... Sofia State Philharmonic   (BU)
SDF........... Sudan Defence Forces
SDF........... Svenska Datafoereningen [*Sweden*]   (SLS)
SDF........... Svenska Diabetesforbundet [*Sweden*]   (EAIO)
SDFD........ Societe Africaine de Distribution de Fournitures Dentaires
SDFK........ Swiatowa Demokratyczna Federacja Kobiet [*Women's
                   International Democratic Federation*]   (POL)
SDFM........ World Federation of Democratic Youth   (BU)
SDG .... Aerosierra de Durango [*Mexico*] [*ICAO designator*]   (FAAC)
SDG .... Societe de Diamant de Guinee [*Diamond mining organization*]
                   [*Guinea*]
SDG .... Societe de Droguerie du Gabon
SDG .... Soli Deo Gloria Szovetseg [*Soli Deo Gloria Association*]   (HU)
SDG .... Syllogos Dimokratikon Gynaikon [*Association of Democratic
                   Women*] [*Greek*]   (GC)
SDGDR ..... Society for Dermatology in the German Democratic Republic
                   (EAIO)
SDGK .... Supreme Command Signal Battalion   (BU)
SDGS......... Srpska Drzavna Granicna Straza [*Serbian Frontier Guard*]
                   [*World War II*]   (YU)
SDH.......... Servicio de Helicopteros SL [*Spain*] [*ICAO designator*]   (FAAC)
SDH.......... Spoldzielczy Dom Handlowy [*Cooperative Department Store*]
                   [*Poland*]
SDH.......... Sy Deurlugtige Hoogheid [*Afrikaans*]
SDHP .... Sosyal Demokrasi Halkci Partisi [*Social Democratic Populist
                   Party*] [*Turkey*] [*Political party*]   (MENA)
SDI............ Saidor [*Papua New Guinea*] [*Airport symbol*]   (OAG)

SDI............ Service de Documentation Interministerielle [*Interministerial
                   Documentation Service*] [*National Telecommunications
                   Research Center*] [*Information service or system*]   (IID)
SDI............ Sivitanideion Dimosion Idryma [*Sivitanideios Public
                   Foundation*] [*Greek*]   (GC)
SDI............ Societa Dantesca Italiana [*Italian*]   (SLS)
SDI............ Societe d'Etudes pour le Developpement des Industries Agricoles
                   au Senegal
SDI............ Stars of David International   (EAIO)
SDI............ Statni Drevarska Inspekce [*State Inspection Office for Wood and
                   Wood Products*]   (CZ)
SDIAS .... Societe pour le Developpement des Industries Agricoles au
                   Senegal
SDIBC .... Syndicat de Defense des Interets Bananiers au Cameroun
SDIC.......... Societe de Developpement Industriel du Cameroun
SDICS .... Societe de Developpement des Industries Chimiques de Sud
                   [*Chemical Industries of the South Development Co.*]
                   [*Tunisia*]
SDIEGEE ... Somateion Daktylografon Idiotikon Epikheiriseon-Grafeion kai
                   Elevtheron Epangelmaton [*Union of Typists of Private
                   Enterprises, Offices, and Liberal Professions*] [*Greek*]   (GC)
SDIH .... Societe Dakaroise Immobiliere d'Habitations
SDIM........ Systeme de Documentation et d'Information Metallurgique [*EG*]
                   [*Luxembourg*]
S Dist .... Section de Distribution [*Military*] [*French*]   (MTD)
SDJ............ Sendai [*Japan*] [*Airport symbol*]   (OAG)
SDJAP....... Sportsko Drustvo Jugoslovenske Armije Partizan [*The Partisan
                   Sport Club of the Yugoslav Army*]   (YU)
SDJO .... Service de Distribution de Jus d'Orange [*Orange Juice
                   Distribution Department*] [*In SKD Cambodia*]   (CL)
SDK .... Sandakan [*Malaysia*] [*Airport symbol*]   (OAG)
SDK .... Schweizerische Direktoren-Konferenz Gewerblich Industrieller
                   Berufsund Fach schulen [*Switzerland*]   (EAIO)
SDK .... Seljacko-Demokratska Koalicija [*Peasant-Democratic Coalition*]
                   [*Former Yugoslavia*] [*Political party*]   (PPE)
SDK .... Social Accounting Service [*Former Yugoslavia*]   (IMH)
SDK .... Sociedad Aerea del Caqueta Ltd. [*Colombia*] [*ICAO designator*]
                   (FAAC)
SDK .... Sprava Dalkovych Kabelu [*Administration Office for Long-
                   Distance Cables*]   (CZ)
SDK .... Srpski Dobrovoljacki Korpus [*Serbian Volunteer Corps*] [*World
                   War II*]   (YU)
SDKhA ...... Sofia State Art Academy   (BU)
SDKP........ Socjaldemokracja Krolestwa Polskiego [*Social-Democratic Party
                   of the Kingdom of Poland (1893-1900)*]
SDKPiL..... Socjal-Demokracja Krolestwa Polskiego i Litwy [*Social-
                   Democratic Party of the Kingdom of Poland and of
                   Lithuania (Before World War I)*]   (POL)
SDKU .... Decoding Device   (RU)
SDL............ Collapsible Landing Boat   (RU)
SDL............ Senza Data o Luogo [*No Date or Place (of Publication)*] [*Italian*]
SDL............ Social Democratic Party of Latvia   (RU)
SDL............ Sprava Dopravnich Letist [*Administration Office for Transport
                   Plane Airports*]   (CZ)
SDL............ Sprava Dopravniho Letectva [*Transport Airforce Directorate*]
                   (CZ)
sdl.............. Suedlich [*Southern*] [*German*]   (GCA)
SDL............ Sundsvall [*Sweden*] [*Airport symbol*]   (OAG)
SDL............ Wooden Engineer Boat   (RU)
Sdlg .... Siedlung [*Settlement*] [*German*]
SDLP .... Social Democratic and Labour Party [*Northern Ireland*] [*Political
                   party*]   (PPW)
SDLP .... Social Democratic and Liberal Party [*British*] [*Political party*]
SDLZ......... Skola Dustojniku Letectva v Zaloze [*School for Reserve Air Force
                   Officers*]   (CZ)
SDLZ......... Slovenske Divadelne a Literarne Zastupitelstvo [*Slovak
                   Theatrical and Publishing Agency*]   (CZ)
SDM .... Diesel Pile Hammer   (RU)
SDM .... Sienkiewiczowska Dzielnica Mieszkaniowa [*Sienkiewicz
                   Residential District*]   (POL)
SDM .... Societe Diallo Moctar & Cie. [*Senegal*]
SDM .... Somali Democratic Movement [*Political party*]   (EY)
SDM .... Su Divina Majestad [*Spanish*]
SDM .... Synetairismoi Dytikis Makedonias [*Cooperatives of Western
                   Macedonia*]   (GC)
SDM .... Szczecinska Dzielnica Mieszkaniowa [*Szczecin (Stettin)
                   Residential District*]   (POL)
SDM .... Ten-Key Adder   (RU)
SDME........ Sous-Direction des Moyens d'Essais [*Sub-Directorate of Means of
                   Testing*] [*French*]   (WER)
SDMFAJ... Savez Drustava Matematicara, Fizicara, i Astronoma Jugoslavije
                   [*Former Yugoslavia*]   (SLS)
SDMH .... Shoalhaven District Memorial Hospital [*Australia*]
SDMJ........ Savez Drustava Mikrobiologa Jugoslavije [*Samoa*]   (EAIO)
SDMMA ... Sakarya Devlet Muhendislik ve Mimarlik Akademesi [*Sakarya
                   State Engineering and Architecture Academy*]   (TU)
SDN .... Sandane [*Norway*] [*Airport symbol*]   (OAG)

SDN .... Secretaria de la Defensa Nacional [*Secretariat of National Defense*] [*Mexico*]   (LA)

SDN .... Sendirian [*Private Business Company*] [*Malaysia*]   (ML)

SDN .... Societa delle Nazioni [*League of Nations*] [*Italian*]

SDN .... Societe Demographique Nordique [*Nordic Demographic Society - NDS*]   (EAIO)

SDN .... Societe des Nations [*League of Nations*] [*French*]

SDN .... Sudan [*ANSI three-letter standard code*]   (CNC)

Sdn Bhd ..... Sendirian Berhad [*Private Limited Company*] [*Malaysia*]

SDNL .... Suomen Demokraattinen Nuorisoliitto [*Finnish Democratic Youth League*]   (WEN)

SDO .... Clothing Decontamination Station   (RU)

SDO .... Early-Warning System   (RU)

SDO .... Streans Diamond Organisation [*Retail jewelry chain*] [*South Africa*]

SDO .... Subdivisional Officer [*India*]

Sdo .... Suido [*Channel*] [*Japan*]   (NAU)

sdo. .... Supply Section   (BU)

SDOE .... Syndesmos Diplomatoukhon Oikonomikon kai Emborikon Epistimon [*League of Economic and Commercial Sciences Graduates*]   (GC)

S-Don .... Northern Donets Railroad   (RU)

SDOP .... Spolecnost Dunajsko-Oderskeho Pruplavu [*Danube-Oder Canal Company*]   (CZ)

SDP .... Aero Sudpacifico SA [*Mexico*] [*ICAO designator*]   (FAAC)

SDP .... Dominican Society of Pediatrics   (EAIO)

SDP .... Double-Track Snowplow   (RU)

SDP .... Mean Square Dynamic Error   (RU)

SDP .... Remote Feeder Transmission Bay   (RU)

SDP .... Sanitary and Decontamination Station   (RU)

SDP .... Savannah Development Project [*Sudan*]

SDP .... Savezni Drustveni Plan [*Federal Economic Plan*]   (YU)

SDP .... Schwestern von der Gottlichen Vorsehung [*Sisters of Divine Providence*] [*Germany*]   (EAIO)

SDP .... Serb Democratic Party [*Croatia*] [*Political party*]   (EY)

SDP .... Serbian Democratic Party [*Bosnia-Herzegovina*] [*Political party*]   (EY)

SDP .... Seychelles Democratic Party   (AF)

Sdp .... Siedepunkt [*Boiling Point*] [*German*]

SDP .... Singapore Democratic Party [*Political party*]   (PPW)

SDP .... Sinnbilder fuer Datenflussplane [*German*]   (ADPT)

SDP .... Skill Development Program [*Australia*]

SDP .... Social Democratic Party [*Hungary*] [*Political party*]

SDP .... Social Democratic Party [*Albania*] [*Political party*]   (EY)

SDP .... Social Democratic Party [*Philippines*] [*Political party*]   (PPW)

SDP .... Social Democratic Party [*Nigeria*] [*Political party*]

SDP .... Social Democratic Party [*Germany*] [*Political party*]

SDP .... Social Democratic Party [*Trinidad and Tobago*] [*Political party*]   (PPW)

SDP .... Social Democratic Party [*Thailand*] [*Political party*]   (PPW)

SDP .... Social Democratic Party [*Australia*] [*Political party*]

SDP .... Social Democratic Party [*Iceland*] [*Political party*]   (PPW)

SDP .... Social-Democrat Party [*Zambia*] [*Political party*]   (EY)

SDP .... Socialdemokratska Partija [*Social Democratic Party*]   (YU)

SDP .... Socialist Democratic Party [*South Korea*] [*Political party*]   (EY)

SDP .... Sosyal Demokrat Partisi [*Social Democratic Party*] [*Turkish Cyprus*] [*Political party*]   (EY)

SDP .... Sosyalist Devrimci Partisi [*Revolutionary Socialist Party*]   (TU)

SDP .... Sozial Demokratesch Partei [*Social Democratic Party*] [*Luxembourg*] [*Political party*]   (PPE)

SDP .... Sports Development Program [*Australia*]

SDP .... Steyr-Daimler-Puch AG [*Research center*] [*Austria*]   (ERC)

SDP .... Stowarzyszenie Dziennikarzy Polskich [*Polish Journalist Association*]

SDP .... Stranka Demokratskih Reformi [*Party of Democratic Reform*] [*Slovenia*] [*Political party*]   (EY)

SdP .... Sudetendeutsche Partei [*Sudeten German Party*] [*Former Czechoslovakia*] [*Political party*]   (PPE)

SDP .... Suomen Sosialidemokraattinen Puolue [*Finnish Social Democratic Party*] [*Political party*]   (EAIO)

SDP .... Supervision Development Project [*Australia*]

SDP .... Swaziland Democratic Party   (AF)

SDPC .... Social Democratic Party of Croatia [*Political party*]

SDPE .... Sistema de Direccion y Planificacion de la Economia [*Economic Management and Planning System*] [*Cuba*]   (LA)

SDPF .... Social Democratic Party of Finland   (RU)

SDPG .... Social Democratic Party of Germany   (RU)

SDPH .... Social Democratic Party of Hungary [*Political party*]   (EAIO)

SDPITFNRJ ... Savez Drustava Poljoprivrednih Inzenjera i Tehnicara Federativna Narodna Republika Jugoslavija [*Federation of Societies of Agricultural Engineers and Technicians of Yugoslavia*]   (YU)

SDPJ .... Social Democratic Party of Japan [*Political party*]   (EAIO)

SDPL .... Social Democratic Party of Lithuania [*1896-1935*]   (RU)

SDPL .... Suomen Demokratian Pioneerien Liitto [*Finnish League of Democratic Pioneers*]   (WEN)

SDPLS .... Service de Distribution de Parfumerie, Liqueur, et Spiritueux [*Perfumes, Liqueurs, and Alcoholic Beverages Distribution Department*] [*Cambodia*]   (CL)

SDPM .... Societe Dakaroise des Petroles Mory

SDPNS ..... Stenographic Records of the First National Assembly   (BU)

SDPP .... Social Democracy Popularist Party [*Turkey*] [*Political party*]

SDP-PDR .. Social Democratic Party - Party of Democratic Reform [*Croatia*] [*Political party*]

SDPRR(b) ... Socjaldemokratyczna Partia Robotnicza Rosji (Bolszewikow) [*Social-Democratic Workers' Party of Russia (Bolsheviks)*] [*Poland*]

SDPS .... Social Democratic Party of Slovenia [*Political party*]   (EY)

SDPSh .... Social Democratic Party of Sweden   (RU)

SDPU .... Socialist and Democratic People's Union [*Mauritania*] [*Political party*]   (EY)

SDPV .... Social Democratic Party of Hungary   (RU)

SDPV .... Societe pour le Developpement du Petrole Vert [*Groupe Pierre Mariotte*] [*France*]

SDQ .... Santo Domingo [*Dominican Republic*] [*Airport symbol*]   (OAG)

SDR .... Santander [*Spain*] [*Airport symbol*]   (OAG)

SDR .... Societe de Developpement Regional [*Regional Development Company*] [*Belgium*]   (WER)

SDR .... Societe de Developpement Rural [*Rural Development Company*] [*Ivory Coast*]   (IMH)

SDR .... Somali Democratic Republic   (AF)

SDR .... Special Drawing Right   (EECI)

SDR .... Special Drawing Rights [*International Monetary Fund*]

SDR .... Strelecke Druzstvo [*Rifle Squad*]   (CZ)

SDR .... Syder [*Bulgaria*] [*ICAO designator*]   (FAAC)

SDR .... System Design Report [*NATO*]   (NATG)

SDR .... System for Data Retrieval [*Information retrieval*]

SDRA .... Service de Documentation, Renseignement, et Action [*Documentation, Intelligence, and Action Service (Security and Counterintelligence Branch)*] [*Belgium*]   (WER)

SDRA .... Societe pour le Developpement de la Riviera Africaine [*Company for the Development of the African Riviera*] [*Ivory Coast*]   (AF)

SDRB .... Societe de Developpement Regional de Bruxelles [*Brussels Regional Development Agency*] [*Belgium*]   (GEA)

SDRC .... Service de Documentation, Renseignement, et Chiffre [*Documentation, Intelligence, and Cipher Service (Ciphers Branch)*] [*Belgium*]   (WER)

SDRDP ...... South Darfur Rural Development Programme [*Sudan*]

SDRI .... Service de Documentation, Renseignement, et Information [*Documentation, Intelligence, and Information Service (Intelligence Branch)*] [*Belgium*]   (WER)

SDRL .... Semiconductor Device Research Laboratory [*Chulalongkorn University*] [*Thai*] [*Research center*]   (ERC)

SDRM ...... Societe de Developpement Rural de Medouneu

SDRM ...... Societe pour l'Administration du Droit de Reproduction Mecanique des Auteurs, Compositeurs et Editeurs [*France*]   (FLAF)

SDrog .... Staatliches Erfassungs- und Absatzkontor fuer Arznei- und Gewuerzpflanzen [*State Procurement and Sales Office for Medicinal Plants and Herbs*]   (EG)

SDRP .... Social Democratic Workers' Party   (RU)

SDRP .... Societe Dahomeenne de Rechapage de Pneumatiques

SDRP .... Socjaldemokracja Rzeczypospolitej Polskiej [*Social Democracy of the Republic of Poland*] [*Political party*]   (EY)

SDRPL ...... Social Democratic Workers' Party of Latvia [*1917-1934*]   (RU)

SDRPR ...... Socijal-Demokratska Radnicka Partija Rusije [*Social-Democratic Workers Party of Russia*]   (YU)

SDRS .... Societe de Developpement Rizicole du Senegal

SDRS .... Societe pour le Developpement des Regions Sahariennes [*Saharan Regional Development Company*] [*Algeria*]   (AF)

SDRT .... Sous-Direction des Recherches Techniques [*Sub-Directorate of Technological Research*] [*French*]   (WER)

SDRT .... Technical Research Sub-Department [*French*] [*Acronym is based on foreign phrase*]

sdruc. .... Sdrucito [*Worn-Out*] [*Italian*]

SDS .... Listened to Democratic Radio Stations [*Amateur radio operator's diploma*]   (BU)

SDS .... Long-Distance Service Office   (RU)

SDS .... Saltens Dampskipsselskap AS [*Commercial firm*] [*Norway*]

SDS .... Samostalna Demokratska Stranka [*Independent Democratic Party*] [*Former Yugoslavia*] [*Political party*]   (PPE)

Sds .... Sandsack [*Sand Bag*] [*German*]   (GCA)

SdS .... Servizio di Sicurezza [*Internal Security Service*] [*Anti-Terrorism*] [*Italian*]   (WER)

SDS .... Ship Remote-Indicating Station   (RU)

SDS .... Slovenska Demokraticka Strana [*Slovak Democratic Party*]   (CZ)

SDS .... Slovenska Demokratska Stranka [*Slovenian Democratic Party*]   (YU)

SDS .... Societas Divini Salvatoris [*Society of the Divine Saviour*]   (EAIO)

SDS .... Socijal Demokratska Stranka [*Social-Democratic Party*]   (YU)

SDS .... Sosyal Demokrat Sendikalari [*Social Democrat Unions*]   (TU)

SDS........... Sozialistischer Deutscher Studentenbund [*German Socialist Students Association*] (EG)

SDS........... Srpska Demokratska Stranka [*Serb Democratic Party*] [*Political party*]

SDS........... Srpska Drzavna Straza [*Serbian State Guard*] [*World War II*] (YU)

SDS........... Statni Divadelni Studio [*State Theater Studio*] (CZ)

SDS........... Stratiotiki Dioikisis Sidirodromon [*Military Administration of Railroads*] [*Greek*] (GC)

SDS........... Svenska Dermatologiska Saellskapet [*Sweden*] (SLS)

SDSA........ Selangor Democratic Students Association (Communist) (ML)

SDSA........ Societe pour la Diffusion des Sciences et des Arts [*Society for the Spread of the Sciences and Arts*] [*France*] (PDAA)

SDSC........ Strategic and Defence Studies Centre [*Research center*] [*Australia*] (IRC)

SDSI......... Scientific Data Systems Israel

SDSK........ Sosyal Demokrat Sendikacilar Konseyi [*Council of Social Democrat Unionists*] (TU)

SDSM........ Socijaldemokratski Savez Makedonije [*Social Democratic Alliance of Macedonia*] [*Political party*] (EY)

SDSO........ Students' Voluntary Sports Society (RU)

SDSPF....... Savezni Drzavni Sekretarijat za Poslove Finansija [*Federal State Secretariat for Financial Affairs*] (YU)

SDT .... (Program) Compiling Diagnostic Tables (RU)

SDT .... Saidu Sharif [*Pakistan*] [*Airport symbol*] (OAG)

SDT .... Service de la Documentation Technique [*Ministere du Plan, du Developpement Industriel, et de la Reforme Administrative*] [*Togo*]

SDT .... Simplification du Travail [*France*] (FLAF)

SDT .... Societe Dahomeenne de Transports

SDT .... Spoldzielczy Dom Towarowy [*Cooperative Store*] [*Poland*]

SDT .... Stations for Decontamination and Deactivation of Transport (BU)

SDT .... Terrain SDP SA [*Spain*] [*ICAO designator*] (FAAC)

SDT .... Transport Decontamination Station (RU)

SDTA........ Scottish Dance Teacher's Alliance [*Glasgow, Scotland*] (EAIO)

SDTAQ...... Speech and Drama Teachers Association of Queensland [*Australia*]

SDTC........ South Darfur Transport Company [*Sudan*]

SDTI......... Societe pour le Developpement Touristique Interafricain

SDTJ .... Svaz Delnickych Telocvicnych Jednot Ceskoslovenskych [*Federation of Czechoslovak Workers' Gymnastic Associations*] (CZ)

SDTJC....... Svaz Delnickych Telocvicnych Jednot Ceskoslovenskych [*Federation of Czechoslovak Workers' Gymnastic Associations*] (CZ)

SDTs......... Moving-Target Selector [*or Selection*] (RU)

SDU .... Rio De Janeiro-Dumont [*Brazil*] [*Airport symbol*] (OAG)

SDU .... Savezna Drzavna Uprava [*Federal State Administration*] (YU)

SDU .... Secondary Girls School (BU)

SDU .... Social Development Unit [*Singapore*] (PDAA)

SDU .... Sociedad de Dermatologia del Uruguay [*Society of Dermatology of Uruguay*] (EAIO)

SDU .... Sofia State University (BU)

SDU .... Soziale Demokratische Union [*Social Democratic Union*] [*Germany*] [*Political party*] (PPW)

SDU .... Standardized Pressure Indicator (RU)

SDUE .... Schnelle Datenuebertragung [*Rapid Data Transmission*] [*German*] (ADPT)

SDU-NDP ... Slovenian Democratic Union - National Democratic Party [*Political party*] (EY)

SDV .... Kombinat of Synthetic Fragrant Substances (RU)

SDV .... Scule, Dispozitive, si Verificatoare [*Tools, Devices, and Controls*] (RO)

SDV .... Servicios Aereos del Vaupes Ltd. [*Colombia*] [*ICAO designator*] (FAAC)

SDV .... Sprava Delostreleckeho Vyzbrojovani [*Artillery Ordnance Directorate*] (CZ)

SDV .... Sprava Doplnovani Vojsk [*Directorate for Troop Replacements*] (CZ)

SDV .... Synthetic Fragrant Substances (RU)

SDV .... Tel Aviv/Yafo [*Israel*] [*Airport symbol*] (OAG)

SDVNS...... Stenographic Records of the Grand National Assembly (BU)

SDVU .... Statny Drevarsky Vyskumny Ustav [*State Research Institute for Wood*] (CZ)

SDW .... Schutzmeinschaft Deutscher Wald [*German Association for the Protection of Forests and Woodlands*] (PDAA)

SDYA........ Selangor Democratic Youth Association (Communist) (ML)

SDYaV....... Extremely Toxic Poisons (RU)

SDZ .... Skola Dustojniku v Zaloze [*School for Reserve Officers*] (CZ)

SDZ .... Slovenska Demokratska Zveza [*Slovenian Democratic Union*] [*Trieste*] (YU)

SDZ .... Slovenska Dijaska Zveza [*Slovenian Student Union*] (YU)

SDZ .... Svaz Dopravnich Zamestnancu [*Transport Employees' Union*] (CZ)

SDZS......... Svaz Dopravnych Zamestnancov Slovenska [*Slovak Transport Employees' Union*] (CZ)

SE .... British Charter [*British*] [*ICAO designator*] (ICDA)

SE .... Electric Meter (RU)

SE .... Electromagnetic Separator (RU)

SE .... Estado de Sergipe [*State of Sergipe*] [*Brazil*]

SE .... Ferroelectric (RU)

SE .... Free-Electron [*Method*] (RU)

se .... Launcher [*Rocket-Firing*] Squadron (BU)

SE .... Opaque Screen (RU)

SE .... Saad Establishment for General Trading [*Oman*]

Se .... Sable [*Sand*] [*Military map abbreviation World War I*] [*French*] (MTD)

SE .... Salvo Erro [*Error Free*] [*Portuguese*]

SE .... Sanat Enstitusu [*Trade Institute*] (TU)

se .... Sans Nom d'Editeur [*French*] (FLAF)

SE .... Schaltelement [*German*] (ADPT)

SE .... Schleicher-Bruns [*Germany*] [*ICAO aircraft manufacturer identifier*] (ICAO)

SE .... Scieries de l'Equateur

Se .... Secca [*or Secche*] [*Shoal or Shoals*] [*Italian*] (NAU)

SE .... Secretaria de Estado [*Secretariat of State*] [*Portuguese*] (WER)

SE .... Secretariat [*or Secretaire*] d'Etat

Se .... Seine [*or Seiner*] [*His*] [*German*]

Se .... Selen [*Selenium*] [*Chemical element*] [*German*]

Se .... Selenio [*Selenium*] [*Chemical element*] [*Portuguese*]

Se .... Sema [*or Schema*] [*Sketch, Drawing*] (TU)

se .... Senza Editore [*Without Publisher*] [*Italian*]

SE .... Siberian Ethnography (RU)

SE .... Siedeende [*Final Boiling Point*] [*German*] (GCA)

SE .... Siemens-Einheit [*Siemens Unit*] [*German*] (GCA)

S-E .... Skandinaviska Enskilda Banken [*Scandinavian Private Bank*] [*Sweden*]

SE .... Skholi Evelpidon [*Army Cadets Academy*] (GC)

SE .... Slovenske Elektrarne [*Slovak Electric Power Plants*] (CZ)

SE .... Smallpox Eradication Programme

SE .... Societas Europea (Europese NV) [*Benelux*] (BAS)

SE .... Solar Cell (RU)

SE .... Solidaridad Espanola [*Spanish Solidarity*] [*Political party*] (PPW)

SE .... Soma Edonopoulon [*United Democratic Youth Organization Corps*] [*Cyprus*]

SE .... Son Eminence [*His, or Her, Eminence*] [*French*] (MTD)

SE .... Son Excellence [*His, or Her, Excellency*] [*French*] (CL)

SE .... Sovetskaia Etnografiia [*Soviet Ethnography*]

SE .... Speichereinheit [*German*] (ADPT)

SE .... Sport Egylet [*Athletic Club*] (HU)

SE .... Statisticko-Ekonomicke Oddeleni [*Statistical and Economic Department*] (CZ)

SE .... Sua Eccellenza [*His, or Her, Excellency*] [*Italian*]

SE .... Sud-Est [*Southeast*] [*French*] (MTD)

SE .... Sud-Est [*Southeast*] [*Italian*]

SE .... Sudeste [*Southeast*] [*Spanish*]

SE .... Sueste [*Southeast*] [*Portuguese*]

SE .... Su Excelencia [*His, or Her, Excellency*] [*Spanish*]

SE .... Suomen Elainlaakariliitto [*Finland*] (EAIO)

SE .... Suomen Ennatys [*Finland*]

SE .... Survival Equipment [*Royal Australian Navy*]

SE .... Sweden [*ANSI two-letter standard code*] (CNC)

SE .... Sy Eksellensie [*His, or Her, Excellency*] [*Afrikaans*]

SE .... Symvoulevtiki Epitropi [*Consultative Committee*] (GC)

SE .... Symvoulion Epikrateias [*Council of State*] [*Greek*] (GC)

SE .... Synchronous Electric Motor (RU)

SE .... Syndikalistiki Enotita [*Syndicalist Unity*] (GC)

SE .... Systemeinheit [*German*] (ADPT)

SEA .... Research and Analysis Laboratory [*Belgium*] (ARC)

SEA .... Scandinavian Endodontic Association [*Sweden*] (EAIO)

SEA .... Scottish Epilepsy Association (SLS)

SEA........... Secondary Education Authority of Western Australia

SEA........... Service Economique Africain [*African Economic Service*] [*Tunisia*] (AF)

SEA........... Servicio de Extension Agropecuaria (del INTA) [*Instituto Nacional de Tecnologia Agropecuaria*] [*Argentina*] (LAA)

SEA........... Servicios Especiales Aereos Ltda. [*Cucuta*] (COL)

SEA........... Sheltered Employment Allowance [*Australia*]

SEA........... Sindicato de Educadores Argentinos [*Argentine Teachers Union*] (LA)

SEA........... Single European Act [*EEC*]

SEA........... Skholai Efedron Axiomatikon [*Reserve Officers Schools*] [*Greek*] (GC)

SEA........... Skholi Ethnikis Amynis [*National Defense School*] [*Greek*] (GC)

SEA........... Sociedad de Economistas Agrarios [*Association of Agrarian Economists*] [*Chile*] (LA)

SEA........... Sociedad de Estudios y Accion Ciudadana [*Civic Action and Studies Group*] [*Argentina*] (LA)

SEA........... Sociedad Entomologica Argentina [*Argentina*] (DSCA)

SEA........... Sociedad Espanola de Acustica [*Spanish Society of Acoustics*] (PDAA)

SEA........... Societe d'Electronique et d'Automatisme [*Electronic and Automation Society*] [*French*]   (ADPT)
SEA........... Societe d'Entreprises Africaines [*Cameroon*]
SEA........... Societe d'Equipement pour l'Afrique
SEA........... Societe d'Etudes Ardennaises [*French*]   (SLS)
SEA........... Societe Equatoriale d'Assurances
SEA........... Societe Europeenne Automatique [*European Automation Society*] [*French*]   (ADPT)
SEA........... Society for Engineering in Agriculture [*Australia*]
SEA........... Society of Engineering Associates [*Australia*]
SEA........... Soma Ellinon Alkimon [*Corps of Valiant Greeks*]   (GC)
SEA........... Southeast Asia
SEA........... South East Asia Insurance, Berhad [*Malaysia*]
SEA........... Station d'Essais et d'Analyses [*CERIA Research and Analysis Station*] [*Research center*]   (IRC)
SEA........... Strumentazione Elettronica Avanzata [*Research center*] [*Italy*]   (WND)
SEA........... Syllogos Emboroypallilon Athinon [*Association of Athens Commercial Employees*]   (GC)
SEA........... Syndesmos Efedron Axiomatikon [*Reserve Officers Association*] [*Cyprus*]   (GC)
SEA........... Syndesmos Ellinikis Anexartisias [*Greek Independence League*]   (GC)
SEAA........ Social Education Association of Australia
SEAAKh.... Skholi Epimorfoseos Anoteron Axiomatikon Khorofylakis [*Gendarmerie Senior Officer Training School*] [*Greek*]   (GC)
SEAANZ... Small Enterprise Association of Australia and New Zealand
SEAAPP.... Syndesmos Eispraktoron Avtokiniton Athinon-Peiraios-Perikhoron [*Union of Bus Collectors for Athens, Piraeus, and Suburbs*]   (GC)
SEAAS ...... Syllogos Ellinon Apofoiton Anotaton Skholon [*Society of Greek Graduates of Advanced Schools*] [*Cyprus*]   (GC)
SEABC ...... Southeast Asia Business Council   (ML)
SEABM ..... Societe d'Exploitation Agricole du Bas-Mangoro
SEABOARD ... Seaboard World Airways   (MHDB)
SEAC........ Societe d'Equipement pour l'Afrique-Cameroun
SEAC........ Societe Economique Africaine du Congo
SEAC........ South and East African Conference
SEAC........ Southeast Asia Command   (ML)
SEACA ...... Sociedad Ecuatoriana de Alergia y Ciencias Afinas [*Ecuador*]   (SLS)
SEACE ...... Systeme Europeen d'Assurance-Credit a l'Exportation [*European System of Assurance Credit for Export*] [*Belgium*]
SEACI .... Societe d'Equipement pour l'Afrique, Cote-D'Ivoire
SEACI .... Societe Eurafricain pour le Commerce et l'Industrie
SEACO...... Societe d'Equipement pour l'Afrique-Congo
SEACOM ... South East Asia Commonwealth Telephone Cable   (ADA)
SE/ACT..... Southern Europe - ACTISUD [*Authority for the Coordination of Inland Transport in Southern Europe*] [*NATO*]   (NATG)
SEADAG... Southeast Asia Development Advisory Group   (CL)
SEADEX... Seaward Defense Exercise [*NATO*]   (NATG)
SEADZ..... Southeastern Agricultural Development Zone [*Ethiopia*]   (IRC)
SEAE........ Service des Etudes et de l'Analyse Economique
SEAF........ Servicio de Empleo y Accion Formativa [*Employment and Training Action Service*] [*Venezuela*]   (LA)
SEAF........ Sveriges El-och Elektronikagenters Forening [*Swedish Electrical and Electronics Agents Association*]   (PDAA)
SEAFDC.... South East Asian Fisheries Development Centre   (EAIO)
SEAFDEC ... Southeast Asian Fisheries Development Center [*Research center*]   (IRC)
SEAFDEC ... South East Asian Fisheries Development Centre
SEAG........ Societe d'Equipement pour l'Afrique-Gabon
SEAGS ...... Southeast Asian Geotechnical Society   (EAIO)
SEA-HV .... Societe d'Equipement pour l'Afrique-Haute-Volta
SEAIR .... Southeast Asia Airlift System [*Vietnam*] [*Also, SEAAS*] [*Air Force*]   (VNW)
SEAISI ...... South East Asia Iron and Steel Institute   (EA)
SEAK........ Spoudastiki Enotiki Andi-Imperialistiki Kinisi [*Student Unifying Anti-Imperialist Movement*] [*Greek*]   (GC)
SEAK........ Syndonistiki Epitropi Agoniston Kyprou [*Coordinating Committee of Cypriot Fighters*]   (GC)
SEAKEE.... Syndonistiki Epitropi Andidiktatorikis Kinisis Ekpatrismenon Ellinidon [*Coordinating Committee for the Antidictatorial Movement of Expatriated Greek Women*]   (GC)
SEAL......... Los Alamos [*Ecuador*] [*ICAO location identifier*]   (ICLI)
SEAL......... Scandinavian East Africa Line [*Reunionese*]   (AF)
SEAL......... Solicitors Estate Agencies Ltd. [*Australia*]
SEAL......... Southeast Asian Learners   (MEDA)
SEALS...... Stirling's Easy Automated Library System [*Australia*]
SEAM....... Ambato [*Ecuador*] [*ICAO location identifier*]   (ICLI)
SEAM....... Servicios Agricolas Mecanizados [*Mechanized Agricultural Services*] [*Chile*]   (LA)
SEAM....... Societe d'Equipement pour l'Afrique-Mauritanie
SEAMEC .. Southeast Asia Ministers of Education Council   (CL)
SEAMEC .. Southeast Asian Ministers of Education Council

SEAMEO ... Southeast Asia Ministers of Education Organization [*Bangkok, Thailand*]   (CL)
SEAMEO-BIOTROP ... Southeast Asia Ministers of Education Organization Regional Center for Tropical Biology [*Indonesian*]   (ARC)
SEAMES... Southeast Asia Ministers of Education Secretariat   (CL)
SEAMES... Southeast Asian Ministers of Education Secretariat [*Thailand*]
SEAMES... South East Asian Ministers of Education Secretariat [*Australia*]
SEAMO... Southeast Asian Ministers of Education Organization
SEAMP ..... Southeast Asia Microform Project   (ML)
SEAMS ..... Southeast Asian Mathematical Society [*Singapore, Singapore*]
SEAN........ Ana Maria [*Ecuador*] [*ICAO location identifier*]   (ICLI)
SEAN........ Skholi Episkeptrion Adelfon Nosokomon [*Visiting Nurses School*]   (GC)
SEAN........ Societe d'Equipement pour l'Afrique-Niger
SEANA...... Societe d'Etudes pour l'Amelioration de la Nutrition en Afrique
SEA/NWFZ ... Southeast Asian Nuclear-Weapons-Free Zone
SEANZ..... Small Enterprise Association of Australia and New Zealand
SEANZA ... South-East Asia, New Zealand, Australia   (ADA)
SEAP .... Arapicos [*Ecuador*] [*ICAO location identifier*]   (ICLI)
SEAP .... Secretaria Especial de Abastecimento e Precos [*Special Secretariat for Supply and Prices*] [*Brazil*]   (LA)
SEAP .... Securities and Exchange Authority of Pakistan   (IMH)
SEAP .... Social Environment Assessment Policy [*Australia*]
SEAP .... Sociedad Economica de Amigos del Pais [*Economic Society of Friends of the Country*] [*Colorado*]   (LA)
SEAP .... Southeast Asian Peninsula   (CL)
SEAP .... Syndikalistiki Ergatiki Agonistiki Parataxi [*Labor Union Struggle Faction*] [*Greek*]   (GC)
SEAPA ...... Seaports Authority [*Riyadh, Saudi Arabia*]   (MENA)
SEAPCTIT ... Southeast Asia Promotion Center for Trade, Investment, and Tourism   (CL)
SEAPK ...... Syllogos Exoriston kai Apofylakisthendon Politikon Kratoumenon [*Association of Exiled and Released Political Prisoners*] [*Greek*]   (GC)
SEAPTIT .. Southeast Asia Promotion Center for Trade, Investment, and Tourism [*Use SEAPCTIT*]   (CL)
SEAR........ Arajuno [*Ecuador*] [*ICAO location identifier*]   (ICLI)
SEAR........ Southeast Asian Refugees   (MEDA)
SEARCA ... SEAMEO [*Southeast Asia Ministers of Education Organization*] Regional Center for Graduate Study and Research in Agriculture [*Philippines*] [*Research center*]   (IRC)
SEARCA ... Southeast Asia Regional Center for Agriculture [*Subsidiary of SEAMEC*]   (ML)
SEARCC ... Southeast Asia Regional Computer Confederation   (EA)
SEARCH... System to Select Entries and Report to Customs Houses [*Australia*]
SEARCHEX ... Sea/Air Search Exercise [*NATO*]   (NATG)
SEARFS.... South East Asia Regional Feeder Service   (DS)
SEARNG... South East Asian Region Network for Geosciences [*International Council of Scientific Unions*]
SEAS .... Ascazubi [*Ecuador*] [*ICAO location identifier*]   (ICLI)
SEAS .... Committee for Scientific Exploration of the Atlantic Shelf   (ASF)
SEAS .... Secretaria de Estado dos Assuntos Sociais [*State Secretariat for Social Affairs*] [*Angola*]   (AF)
SEAS .... Societe d'Equipement pour l'Afrique-Senegal
SEAS .... South East Afforestation Services [*Australia*]
SEAS .... Speicher-Eingabe/Ausgabe-Steuerung [*Memory-Input/Output-Control*] [*German*]   (ADPT)
SEASA ...... Science and Engineering Academy of South Africa
SEASCO ... Science Co-Operation Office for Southeast Asia [*UNESCO*]   (ASF)
SEASOE ... Syndonistiki Epitropi Andidiktatorikon Organoseon Ellados [*Coordinating Committee of Antidictatorial Organizations of Greece*]   (GC)
SEASS...... Southeast Asia Airlift System [*Vietnam*] [*Also, SEAIR*] [*Air Force*]   (VNW)
SEAT .... Atacames [*Ecuador*] [*ICAO location identifier*]   (ICLI)
SEAT .... Sociedad Espanol de Automoviles de Turismo [*Spanish automobile manufacturer; acronym used as name of its cars*]
SEAT .... Societa Elenchi Ufficiali Abbonati al Telefono [*Official Telephone Directory Company*] [*Italian*]
SEAT .... Syndekhnia Ergatoypallilon tis Arkhis Tilepikoinonion [*Union of Telecommunications Authority Employees*] [*Cyprus*]   (GC)
SEATAC ... Southeast Asian Agency for Regional Transport and Communications Development   (EAIO)
SEATAC ... Southeast Asia Transportation and Communications   (CL)
SEATEC.... South East Asia Technology Co. Ltd. [*Thailand*]   (DS)
SEATLAS ... Compania de Seguros Atlas SA [*Manizales*]   (COL)
SEATO...... Southeast Asia Treaty Organization [*International organization formed to combat the spread of Communism*]   (VNW)
SEATRAD ... Southeast Asia Tin Research and Development Center [*Malaysia*]   (IRC)
SEATS...... Stock Exchange Automated Trading System [*Australia*]
SEA-URICA ... South East Asia Universal Realtime Information Cataloging and Administration System
SEAUSO... Southeast Asian University Students Organization   (ML)

SEAV......... Superintendencia de Ensino Agricola e Veterinario [*Rio De Janeiro, Brazil*] (LAA)
SEAVOM ... Societe d'Etudes et d'Applications Vide Optique Mecanique [*France*] (PDAA)
SEB............ Clearing and Evacuation Base (RU)
SEB............ Marshaling Evacuation Hospital (BU)
SEB............ Medical Evacuation Base (RU)
SEB............ Sebha [*Libya*] [*Airport symbol*] (OAG)
SEB............ Sociedad Espanola de Bioquimica [*Spanish*] (SLS)
SEB............ Societe des Etudes Bloyennes [*France*] (EAIO)
SEB............ Societe d'Exploitation du Parc a Bois de Belabo
SEBA......... Babahoyo [*Ecuador*] [*ICAO location identifier*] (ICLI)
SEBA......... Severoceske Bavlnarske Zavody [*North Bohemian Cotton Mills*] (CZ)
SEBA......... Stichting tot Exploitatie en Bescherming van Auteursrechten [*Benelux*] (BAS)
SEBAC...... State Ethnic Broadcasting Advisory Council [*Australia*]
SEBACAM ... Societe des Bauxites du Cameroun [*Cameroon Bauxite Company*] (AF)
SEBAM..... Societe Eburneenne d'Armement
SEBAT...... Societe Eburneenne de Batiment
SEBC......... Bahia De Caraquez [*Ecuador*] [*ICAO location identifier*] (ICLI)
SEBC......... Societe d'Exploitation des Bois du Cameroun
SEBC......... Societe d'Exploitation des Bois du Congo
SEBCA...... Societe d'Exploitation des Bois et Contreplaques en Algerie
SEBD........ Bola De Oro [*Ecuador*] [*ICAO location identifier*] (ICLI)
SEBE......... La Beata [*Ecuador*] [*ICAO location identifier*] (ICLI)
SEBF......... Slovenska Evanjelicka Bohoslovecka Fakulta [*Slovak Protestant Theological School*] [*Modra*] (CZ)
SEBH........ Balao Chico [*Ecuador*] [*ICAO location identifier*] (ICLI)
SEBI.......... Boliche [*Ecuador*] [*ICAO location identifier*] (ICLI)
SEBI.......... Securities and Exchange Board of India (ECON)
SEBICOB ... Societe Industrielle de Biscuiterie et Confiserie du Benin
SEBIMA ... Societe d'Exploitation des Bitumes du Maroc
SEBL.......... Single European Banking Licence
SEBLIMA ... Societe d'Exploitation des Bitumes et Lubrifiants Irano-Marocaine
SEBM........ Societe d'Exploitation des Briqueteries du Mali
SEBOGA... Societe pour l'Expansion des Boissons Hygieniques au Gabon
SEBRIMA ... Societe d'Exploitation des Briqueteries du Mali
SEBS-m..... Societe Europeenne de Biomedecine Sous-Marine [*French*] (ASF)
SEBSO...... Societe d'Exploitation des Bois du Sud-Ouest
SEBT......... El Batan [*Ecuador*] [*ICAO location identifier*] (ICLI)
SEBT......... Societe d'Exportation des Bois Tropicaux
SEBUMI ... Serikat Buruh Minjak Indonesia [*Indonesian Oil Workers Union*] (IN)
SEC............ Scandinavian Episcopal Conference [*Norway*] (EAIO)
sec............. Secante [*Secant*] [*French*]
Sec............. Secolo [*Century*] [*Italian*]
sec............. Seconde [*Second (of Time)*] [*French*]
sec............. Secondo [*Second*] [*Italian*]
Sec............. Secretary (EECI)
sec............. Section [*Section*] [*French*]
sec............. Seculo [*Century*] [*Portuguese*]
sec............. Sekundaer [*Secondary*] [*German*] (GCA)
sec............. Sekunde [*Second*] [*German*] (GCA)
SEC............ Service Entretien Clients [*French*] (ADPT)
SEC............ Sindicato de Educadores Costarricenses [*Costa Rican Educators Union*] (LA)
SEC............ Sociedad Espanola de Cardiologia [*Spanish*] (SLS)
SEC............ Societe d'Echanges Commerciaux
SEC............ Societe d'Expertise Comptable
SEC............ Societe Europeenne de Culture [*European Society of Culture - ESC*] (EAIO)
SEC............ Solar Energy Commission [*Saudi Arabia*] (PDAA)
SEC............ State Economic Commission [*China*] (IMH)
SEC............ State Economic Corp. [*Bulgaria*] (IMH)
SEC............ State Education Commission [*Chinese*]
SEC............ State Electoral Council [*Australia*]
SEC............ State Enterprise for Food Canning [*Iraq*]
SEC............ Supply Executive Committee [*NATO*] (NATG)
SEC............ Swedish Employers' Confederation (EAIO)
SEC............ Sydney Entertainment Centre [*Australia*]
SEC............ Syndicat des Employes du Commerce
SEC............ Systeme Europeen de Comptes Economiques Integres [*European Integrated Economic Accounting System*] (WER)
SECA......... Catarama [*Ecuador*] [*ICAO location identifier*] (ICLI)
SECA......... Secretariado de Enlace de Comunidades Autogestionarias [*Argentina*] (EAIO)
SECA......... Servicios de Conservacion de Estabilizacion Agricola [*Puerto Rico*] (DSCA)
SECA......... Societe d'Eco-Amenagement [*Commercial firm*] [*France*] (ECON)
SECA......... Societe d'Exploitation Commerciale et Agricole

SECA......... Societe d'Exploitation des Carrieres d'Azaguie
SECA......... Societe d'Exploitation et de Constructions Aeronautiques [*French*]
SECA......... Societe pour l'Expansion Commerciale Africaine
SECA......... Societe pour l'Exportation des Cafes du Sud
SECAB...... Secretaria Ejecutiva Permanente del Convenio Andres Bello [*Permanent Executive Secretariat of the Andres Bello Convention*] (EAIO)
SECAB...... Secretaria Permanente del Convenio Andres Bello [*Colombia*] (COL)
SECADRA ... Servicio de Coordenacao das Atividades das Delegacias Regionais Agricolas [*Brazil*] (DSCA)
SECAM..... Sequentiel Couleurs a Memoire [*Sequential Memory Color*] [*Television system*] [*French*] (WER)
SECAM..... Symposium of Episcopal Conferences of Africa and Madagascar
SECAN...... Societe d'Etudes et de Constructions Aero-Navales [*French*]
SECAN...... Societe d'Expertises Comptables en Afrique Noire
SECAP...... Servicio Ecuatoriano de Capacitacion Profesional [*Ecuadorean Professional Training Service*] (LA)
SECARTYS ... Asociacion Espanola de Exportadores de Electronica e Informatica (EY)
SECAS....... Sociedad de Estudiantes de Ciencias Agronomicas Salvadorenas [*El Salvador*] (DSCA)
SECAT...... Societe d'Exploitation Cinematographique du Tchad
SECBA...... Societe des Exportateurs et Commissionnaires en Bois Africains
SECC......... Condorcocha [*Ecuador*] [*ICAO location identifier*] (ICLI)
SECC......... Societe d'Etude de la Cellulose du Congo (IMH)
SECCA...... Sociedad Ecuatoriana del Carbon [*Ecuadorean Coal Company*] (LA)
SECCO...... Societe d'Etudes Contre la Corrosion
SECE......... Santa Cecilia [*Ecuador*] [*ICAO location identifier*] (ICLI)
SECED...... Servicio Central de Documentacion de la Presidencia del Gobierno [*Central Service Organization for the Prime Minister's Office (Intelligence Unit)*] [*Spanish*] (WER)
SECF......... Serviciul de Exploatare Cai Ferate [*Railway Utilization Service*] (RO)
SECF......... Somali Eastern and Central Front [*Political party*] (EY)
SECFFASEN ... Societe d'Expertises Comptables Fiduciaires France-Afrique-Senegal
SECGPS.... Syndicat des Employes de la CGPS
SECH........ Chone [*Ecuador*] [*ICAO location identifier*] (ICLI)
sech............ Section (RU)
SECh.......... Sociedad de Escritores de Chile [*Writers Association of Chile*] (LA)
SECI......... Societa Elettrica Coloniale Italiana
SECI......... Societe d'Equipement de la Cote-D'Ivoire
SECI......... Societe d'Exploitation des Carrieres Ivoiriennes
SECI......... Societe Equatoriale de Commerce et d'Industrie
SECIG....... Service d'Etudes et de Coordination de l'Information Gouvernementale [*Service for Research and Coordination of Government Information*] [*Congo*] (AF)
SECL......... Chiles [*Ecuador*] [*ICAO location identifier*] (ICLI)
SECLF...... Station d'Essais Combustibles et Lubrifiants de la Flotte [*French Navy*] (PDAA)
SECM....... Clementina [*Ecuador*] [*ICAO location identifier*] (ICLI)
SECMA..... Societe d'Exploitation Cinematographique Africaine
SECMI...... Societe d'Entreprise de Constructions et Montage Ivoirienne
SECN........ Societe d'Etudes des Caissons Nucleaires [*France*] (PDAA)
SECO......... Bureau de Controle pour la Securite de la Construction en Belgique [*Office for Research on Safety Precautions in Belgian Construction Work*] (PDAA)
SECO......... Coca [*Ecuador*] [*ICAO location identifier*] (ICLI)
SECO......... Societe d'Elevage et de Commerce
SECO......... Societe d'Entreprises Congolaises
SECOBI.... Servicio de Consulta a Bancos de Informacion [*Database Consultation Service*] [*Information service or system*] [*Mexico*] (IID)
SECOFI..... Secretaria de Comercio y Fomento Industrial [*Secretariat of Trade and Industrial Promotion*] [*Mexico*] (CROSS)
SECOFIN ... Secretaria de Comercio y Fomento Industrial [*Secretariat of Commerce and Industrial Development*] [*Mexico*] (LA)
SECOINSA ... Sociedad Espanola de Comunicaciones e Informatica, Sociedad Anonima [*Spanish Company of Communications and Data Processing, Incorporated*] (WER)
SECOLAS ... Societe d'Expansion Commerciale de l'Atlas
SECOLAS ... Southeastern Conference on Latin American Studies [*United States*]
SECOM..... Secretaria de Comercio [*Secretariat of Commerce*] [*Spanish*] (LA)
SECOM..... Secretaria de Comunicacao Social [*Mass Media Secretariat*] [*Brazil*] (LA)
SECONOM ... Service de Coordination de la Normalisation Maghrebine
SECONS ... Sector de Construccion [*Construction Sector*] [*Cuba*] (LA)
SECOR...... Societe Equatoriale de Commerce et de Representation [*Pointe Noire*]
SECOREB ... Secretariat de la Conference des Ordinaires du Rwanda et du Burundi

SECP .... Societe Eburneenne de Cuirs et Peaux
SecPac .... Security Pacific Bank [*Hong Kong*]
SECPANE ... Servicio Cooperativo Peruano-Norteamericano de Educacion [*Peru*]   (DSCA)
SECPR .... Sociedad Ecuatoriana de Cirugia Plastica y Reconstructiva [*Ecuador*]   (EAIO)
SECR .... Curaray [*Ecuador*] [*ICAO location identifier*]   (ICLI)
Secr .... Secretariat   (EECI)
secr .... Secretario [*Secretary*] [*Portuguese*]
SECRAC .... Societe d'Entreprises Chimiques et Routieres au Cameroun
SECRAE .... Societe d'Entreprises Chimiques et Routieres de l'Afrique Equatoriale
SECRE ...... Societe d'Etudes et de Construction Electroniques [*French*]   (ADPT)
SECREN ... Societe d'Exploitation pour la Construction et la Reparation Navale [*Naval Construction and Repair Company*] [*Malagasy*]   (AF)
secreta ...... Secretaria [*Secretariat*] [*Spanish*]
SECS .... Sociedad Espanola de Ciencia del Suelo [*Spain*]   (DSCA)
Sec soc .... Securite Sociale [*Social Security*] [*French*]
SECT .... Firing Field Equipment Service [*French*] [*Acronym is based on foreign phrase*]
Sect .... Secretariat   (IDIG)
sect .... Section [*Section*] [*French*]
Sect .... Section du Contentieux [*Du Conseil d'Etat*] [*France*]   (FLAF)
SECT .... Service des Equipements de Champs de Tir [*DRME*] [*France*]   (PDAA)
SECT .... Societe d'Exploitation des Cultures Tropicales
SECT .... South East Cultural Trust [*South Australia*]
SECT .... Syndicat des Enseignants Catholiques du Togo [*Catholic Teachers Union of Togo*]   (AF)
SECTA ...... Societe d'Entreprise de Construction et de Travaux en Afrique
SECTCI ..... Societe d'Exploitations de Carrieres et de Transports de la Cote-D'Ivoire
SECTO ...... Syndicat des Employes du Commerce du Togo [*Commercial Employees Union of Togo*]   (AF)
SECTUR ... Secretaria de Cultura y Turismo [*Secretariat of Culture and Tourism*] [*Honduras*]   (LA)
SECU .... Cuenca [*Ecuador*] [*ICAO location identifier*]   (ICLI)
SECU .... Screening Evaluation Coordination Unit [*Australian Institute of Health*]
SECV .... State Electricity Commission of Victoria [*Australia*]   (PDAA)
SECWA ..... State Energy Commission of Western Australia [*Energy Research Branch*]   (WED)
SECWG ..... South Eastern Conservation Working Group [*Australia*]
Sec'y .... Secretary   (PWGL)
SECYNEI ... Secretaria de Comercio y Negociaciones Economicas Internacionales [*Secretariat of Commerce and International Economic Negotiations*] [*Argentina*]   (LA)
sed .... Sans Editeur [*French*]   (BAS)
SED .... Secretaria de Educacao e Cultura [*Brazil*]
Sed .... Sedes [*A Stool*] [*Medicine*]
SED .... Service des Enquetes Douanieres [*France*]   (FLAF)
SED .... Societe d'Equipement du Dahomey
SED .... Sozialistische Einheitspartei Deutschlands [*Socialist Unity Party of Germany*] [*Political party*]   (PPW)
SED .... Soziolistische Linheitspartei Deutschlands [*Socialist Unity Party*] [*German*]   (BARN)
SED .... Stathmoi Elengkhou Diavatirion [*Passport Control Stations*]   (GC)
SEd .... Sy Edele [*His Honorable*] [*Afrikaans*]
SED .... Syndesmos Ellinon Diaititon [*League of Greek Arbitrators*]   (GC)
SED .... Syndikalistiki Ergatiki Dimokratia [*Labor Union Democracy*] [*Greek*]   (GC)
SED .... Systeme d'Enregistrement des Donnees [*French*]   (ADPT)
SEDA .... Societe des Etablissements Donzel Andre & Cie.
SEDA .... Societe d'Etudes pour le Developpement de l'Afrique
SEDAC ..... Societe des Etablissements Donzel Andre & Compagnie
SEDAGB ... Sy Edelagbare [*The Honorary*] [*Afrikaans*]
SEDAGRI ... Societe d'Etudes et de Developpement Agricole
SEDAL ...... Societe des Eaux de l'Agglomeration Algeroise [*Algeria*]   (IMH)
SEDAM ..... Societe d'Etudes et de Development des Aeroglisseurs Marins Terrestres et Amphibies [*French*]   (MCD)
SEDAM ..... Societe d'Etudes et de Developpement des Aeroglisseurs Marins, Terrestres, et Amphibies
SEDAR ...... Sociedad Espanola de Anestesiologia y Reanimacion [*Spanish*]   (SLS)
SEDAS ...... Sociedad Elaboradora de Articulos de Seda [*Colombia*]   (COL)
SEDB .... SEAMEO Education Development Bonds   (CL)
SEDB .... Singapore Economic Development Board   (DS)
SEDC .... Sarawak Economic Development Corp. [*Malaysia*]
SEDC .... Societe d'Exploitation Dorland et Cedolin
SEDC .... State Economic Development Corporations   (ML)
SEDCI ...... Societe d'Etudes pour le Developpement de la Cote-D'Ivoire
SEDCO ...... Small Enterprises Development Corporation [*Zimbabwe*]
sedd .... Sans Engagement de Dates [*French*]

SEDEC ...... Secretaria de Estado de Educacao e Cultura [*Brazil*]
SEDEC ...... Societe d'Edition de Documentation Economique et Commerciale [*France*]
SEDECA ... Societe Senegalaise d'Exploitation de Carrieres
SEDECO ... Sindicato de Empleados de Desarrollo Comunal [*Trade Union of Community Development Employees*] [*Costa Rica*]   (LA)
SEDEFITA ... Societe d'Etude et de Developpement des Perimetres du Fiherenana et de la Taheza [*Fiherenana and Taheza Area Planning and Development Company*] [*Malagasy*]   (AF)
SEDEIS ..... Societe d'Etudes et de Documentation Economiques, Industrielles, et Sociales [*Economic, Industrial, and Social Studies Company*] [*Paris, France*]
SEDEPAC ... Servicio, Desarrollo y Paz [*Service, Development, and Peace*] [*An association*] [*Mexico*]   (CROSS)
SEDES ...... Sociedade de Estudos para Desenvolvimento Economico e Social [*Economic and Social Development Studies Company*] [*Portuguese*]   (WER)
SEDES ...... Societe d'Etudes pour le Developpement Economique et Social [*Society for the Study of Economic and Social Development*] [*Information service or system*] [*France*]   (IID)
SEDES ...... Synomospondia Elevtheron Dimokratikon Ergatikon Syndikaton [*Confederation of Free Democratic Labor Unions*] [*Greek*]   (GC)
SEDESAF ... Societe Seydou Demba Samake Fils & Cie.
SEDEX ...... Servicio de Extension Agricola y Desarrollo de Comunidades [*Bolivia*]   (LAA)
SEDF .... SEAMEO Education Development Fund   (CL)
SEdGestr ... Sy Edelgestrenge [*The Right Honorable*] [*Afrikaans*]
SEDI .... Secretaria de Desarrollo Industrial [*Secretariat of Industrial Development*] [*Argentina*]   (LA)
SEDI .... Societe d'Etudes de Developpement Industriel [*Company for Studies of Industrial Development*] [*Ivory Coast*]   (AF)
SEDIA .... Sociedad Ecuatoriana de Ingenieros y Arquitectos [*Ecuadorean Society for Engineers and Architects*]   (LA)
SEDIA .... Societe d'Etude du Developpement Industriel et Agricole [*Algeria*]
SEDIA .... Societe d'Etudes et de Distribution Interafricaine
SEDIAC .... Societe pour l'Etude et le Developpement de l'Industrie, l'Agriculture, et le Commerce [*Company for the Study and the Development of Industry, Agriculture, and Commerce*] [*French*]   (AF)
SEDIC .... Sociedade de Distribuicao Industrial e Commercial Lda.
SEDIC .... Sociedad Espanola de Documentacion e Informacion Cientifica [*Spanish Society for Documentation and Information Sciences*] [*Information service or system*]   (IID)
SEDICAL ... Societe d'Exploitation et de Distribution de Carburants et Lubrifiants
SEDICO .... Societe d'Industrie et de Commerce
SEDICSS .. Societe Senegalaise pour le Developpement Industriel et Commercial du Sine Saloum
SEDIEK ..... Syndekhnia Ergatoypallilon Dimon kai Imidimosion Epikheiriseon Kyprou [*Union of Employees of Municipal and Semi-Public Enterprises of Cyprus*]   (GC)
SEDIEX ..... Societe Senegalaise de Distribution Import-Export
SEDIGEP ... Synergatiki Enosis Diatheseos Georgikon Proiondon [*Agricultural Products Cooperative Marketing Union*] [*Cyprus*]   (GC)
SEDIP .... Societe Senegalaise de Distribution de Primagaz
SEDIS .... Service Information-Diffusion [*Information Dissemination Office*] [*National Institute for Research in Informatics and Automation*] [*Information service or system*]   (IID)
SEDITEX ... Societe d'Etudes pour le Developpement de l'Industrie Textile
SEDITRO ... Societe Senegalaise d'Importation et de Distribution des Fruits Tropicaux
SEDJI .... Service d'Etudes et de Documentation Juridique Internationale [*Benelux*]   (BAS)
sedm .... Weekly   (BU)
SEDMEK .. Syndesmos Ellinon Dievthyndon Mesis Ekpaidevseos Kyprou [*League of Greek Secondary School Principals of Cyprus*]   (GC)
SEDN .... Syndesmos Ellinon Dimokratikon Nomikon [*League of Greek Democratic Lawyers*]   (GC)
SEDO .... Sociedad Espanola de Optica [*Spanish*]   (SLS)
SEDO .... Societe d'Entreprise et de Debardage de l'Ogooue
SEDO .... Syndonistiki Epitropi Dimosio-Ypallilikon Organoseon [*Coordinating Committee of Public Employee Organizations*] [*Greek*]   (GC)
SEDOC ...... European System for the International Clearing of Vacancies and Applications for Employment [*EC*]   (ECED)
SEDOC ...... Service de Documentation [*Documentation Service*] [*Cameroon*]   (AF)
SEDOC ...... Service d'Etudes et de Documentation [*Studies and Documentation Department*] [*Cambodia*]   (CL)
SEDOCAR ... Service de Documentation Scientifique et l'Armement [*French*]
SEDP .... Strategic Economic Development Package [*Australia*]
SEDRE ...... Societe d'Equipement du Departement de la Reunion
SEDTA ...... Sociedad Ecuatoriana de Transportes Aereos [*Ecuador*]

SEDUM .... Sindicato Democratico de Estudiantes de la Universidad de Madrid [*Democratic Student Union of the University of Madrid*] [*Spanish*] (WER)
SEDYK...... Syndekhnia Epistimonon Ypallilon Kyprou [*Union of Professional Civil Servants of Cyprus*] (GC)
SEE............ Service de l'Energie de l'Etat [*Luxembourg*]
SEE............ Societe des Electriciens et des Electroniciens [*French*]
SEE............ Societe d'Etudes et d'Expansion [*Studies and Expansion Society - SES*] [*Later, Et Ex*] (EAIO)
SEE............ Society of Electronic Engineers [*India*] (PDAA)
SEE............ Sosialistiki Epanastatiki Enosi [*Socialist Revolutionary Union*] [*Greek*] (GC)
SEE............ State Economic Enterprise [*Turkey*] (ECON)
SEE............ Statement of Environmental Effects [*Australia*]
SEE............ Surgical Eye Expeditions International (EAIO)
SEE............ Symvoulion Evropaikis Enoseos [*European Union Council*] [*Greek*] (GC)
SEE............ Symvoulion Exoterikou Emboriou [*Foreign Trade Council*] [*Greek*] (GC)
SEE............ Syndesmos Ellinidon Epistimonon [*League of Greek Professional Women*] (GC)
SEEA .... Southeast European Airlines [*Greece*] [*ICAO designator*] (FAAC)
SEEB .... Societe d'Exploitation et d'Exportation de Bois
SEE-BG ..... See-Berufsgenossenschaft [*Seamans' Industrial Welfare Association*] [*Germany*] (PDAA)
SEECCIASDI ... Standing EEC [*European Economic Community*] Committee of the International Association of the Soap and Detergent Industry [*See also CPCEAISD*] [*Brussels, Belgium*] (EAIO)
SEED........ Sustainable Energy and Environment Division [*United Nations*]
SEEDC ...... South East Economic Development Council [*Australian Capital Territory*]
SEEE .... Societe Equatoriale d'Energie Electrique
SEEEE....... Societe Europeenne d'Etudes et d'Essais d'Environnment [*France*] (PDAA)
SEEF .... Service des Etudes Economiques et Financieres [*France*] (FLAF)
SEEF .... Servico de Estatistica Economica e Financieira [*Rio De Janeiro, Brazil*] (LAA)
SEEF .... Societe Eburneenne d'Exploitation Forestiere
SEEFA....... Syndonistiki Epitropi Ellinon Foititon Anglias [*Coordinating Committee of Greek Students in England*] (GC)
SEEG .... Societe d'Energie et d'Eau du Gabon [*Gabon Power and Water Company*] (AF)
SEEG .... Syndonistiki Epitropi Ergazomenon Gynaikon [*Coordinating Committee of Working Women*] [*Greek*] (GC)
SEEGE ...... Syndonistiki Epitropi Ergazomenon Gynaikon Ellados [*Coordinating Committee of Working Women of Greece*] (GC)
SEEI .... Savet za Energetiku i Ekstraktivnu Industriju [*Council on Power and the Extractive Industry*] (YU)
SEEL .... Singapore Electronic and Engineering, Ltd. (IAA)
seem .... Seemaennisch [*Nautical*] [*German*]
SEEM........ Seemyl [*Nautical Mile*] [*Afrikaans*]
SEEM........ Sociedad Espanola de Estudios Medievales [*Spain*] (EAIO)
SEEM........ Societe d'Exploitation des Ets. Moubarack
SEEN........ Syndicat d'Etudes d'Energie Nucleaire [*Nuclear Energy Research Union*] [*Belgium*] (WER)
SEENE...... Syndonistiki Epitropi Ergazomenon Neon Ellados [*Coordinating Committee of Working Youth of Greece*] (GC)
SEENGP ... Syndesmos Ellinon Exagogeon Nopon Georgikon Proiondon [*League of Greek Exporters of Fresh Agricultural Products*] (GC)
SEEO........ Salvis Erroribus et Omissis [*Errors and Omissions Excepted*] [*Latin*]
SEEP .... Sociedad Espanola para el Estudio de los Pastos [*Spain*] (DSCA)
SEEPE....... Section des Rencontres des Etudiants Portugais a l'Etranger
SEEPZ....... Santa Cruz Electronics Export Processing Zone [*India*] (IMH)
SEER .... Servico de Eletrificacao Rural [*Brazil*] (DSCA)
SEerw......... Sy Eerwaarde [*Reverend*] [*Afrikaans*]
SEES .... Esmeraldas/General Rivadeneira [*Ecuador*] [*ICAO location identifier*] (ICLI)
SEES .... Societe d'Entreprises Electriques et Sanitaires
SEES .... Synomospondia Elevtheron Ergatikon Syndikaton [*Confederation of Free Labor Unions*] [*Cyprus*] (GC)
Seesa.......... Societe d'Expansion Economique du Satikana
SEET .... Showlag Establishment for Exchange & Trading [*Yemen Arab Republic*]
SEETS...... South Eastern Employment Training Service [*Australia*]
Seew.......... Seewesen [*Nautics*] [*German*] (GCA)
SEEY .... (Pankypria) Syndekhnia Ergaton Ependysis kai Ypodisis [*(Pan Cyprian) Union of Garment and Shoe Workers*] (GC)
SEF............ Sefanja [*Zephaniah*] [*Afrikaans*]
SEF............ Serviciul de Exploatare Feroviar [*Railway Utilization Service*] [*RO*] (RO)
SEF............ Societa Ecologica Friulana [*Italian*] (SLS)
SEF............ Societe d'Ethnologie Francaise [*French*] (SLS)

SEF............ Societe d'Exploitation Forestiere
SEF............ Syndesmos Ellinoaigyptiakis Filias [*Greek-Egyptian Friendship Association*] (GC)
SEFA .... Secretaria de Estado do Fomento Agrario [*Secretariat of State for Agricultural Development*] [*Portuguese*] (WER)
SEFA .... Societe d'Exploitations Forestieres Africaines
SEFA .... South East Forest Alliance [*Australia*]
SEFA .... Syllogos Ergaton Fotaeriou Athinon [*Athens Gas Workers Union*] (GC)
SEFAC...... Societe d'Etudes Franco-Africaine des Constructions
SEFAC...... Societe d'Exploitation Forestiere et Agricole du Cameroun
SEFAN ..... Societe des Entreprises Frigorifiques de l'Afrique du Nord [*Morocco*]
SEFBT....... Societe d'Exploitation Forestiere de Bois du Togo
SEFCA...... Societe des Entrepots Frigorifiques de la Casamance
SEFCAM.... Societe d'Exploitation Forestiere du Cameroun
SEFCO...... Societe d'Etudes Folkloriques du Centre-Ouest [*French*] (SLS)
SEFEL....... Secretariat Europeen des Fabricants d'Emballages Metalliques Legers [*European Secretariat of Manufacturers of Light Metal Packages*] (EA)
SEFERIF... Societe d'Exploitation du Fer du Rif [*Morocco*]
SEFG .... Syllogos Ellinon Foititon Gallias [*Club of Greek Students in France*] (GC)
SEFI .... Societe d'Exploitation Forestiere d'Issia
SEFI .... Societe d'Exploitations Forestieres et Industrielles
SEFI .... Societe Europeenne pour la Formation des Ingenieurs [*European Society for Engineering Education*] (EA)
SEFI.......... Syndicat des Entreprises Francaises de Travaux Publics a Vocation Internationale
SEFIC....... Societe d'Exploitations Forestieres et Industrielles du Cameroun
SEFIM...... Societe des Etudes Financieres et Meunieres [*French*] (SLS)
SEFITA ..... Societe d'Effilochage, Filature, Tissage, et Apprets [*Morocco*]
SEFLI .... Societe d'Equipement et de Fabrication pour la Luminescence et l'Incandescence [*Morocco*]
SEFOC ..... Societe d'Exploitations Forestieres du Comoe
SEFS .... Societe d'Exploitation des Frigorifiques Survif [*Mauritania*]
SEFS.......... Syllogos Ergazomenon Foititon Spoudaston [*Association of Working Students*] [*A fifth letter is added for name of city in which located*] (GC)
SEFT .... Section d'Etudes et de Fabrications des Telecommunications [*France*] (PDAA)
SEFTRA .... Societe d'Exploitations Forestieres et de Transports Routiers Africains
SEG............ Clearing and Evacuation Hospital (RU)
seg .... Present [*Tense*] (BU)
SEG............ Segno [*Sign*] [*Music*]
Seg .... Seguente [*Following*] [*Italian*]
seg .... Seguinte [*Following*] [*Portuguese*]
seg .... Segundo [*Second*] [*Portuguese*]
SEG............ Skyline [*Norway*] [*ICAO designator*] (FAAC)
SEG............ Societe d'Exploitations Gabonaises
SEG............ Swiss Ethnological Society (EAIO)
SEG............ Syllogos Ellinon Geologon [*Greek Geologists Association*] (GC)
SEG............ Syndesmos Ellinon Germanias [*Association of Greeks in Germany*] (GC)
SEG............ Systemerweiterungsbruppe [*German*] (ADPT)
SEGA........ Societe d'Entreprises Generales Africaines
SEGA........ Societe d'Etudes Gabonaises
SEGA........ Societe d'Exploitation des Gravieres en Afrique
Segal .... Secretaire General [*Secretary General*] (CL)
SEGAMO ... Societe d'Etudes du Gazoduc de la Mediterranee Occidentale
SEGANS ... Societe d'Etude du Transport et de la Valorisation des Gaz Naturels du Sahara
SEGAS ..... Syndesmos Ellinikon Gymnastikon kai Athlitikon Somateion [*Association of Greek Gymnastic and Athletic Clubs*] (GC)
SEGAZCAM ... Societe Camerounaise du Gaz
SEGAZCAM ... Societe d'Etudes pour la Mise en Valeur du Gaz Naturel Camerounais
SEGBA ...... Servicios Electricos del Gran Buenos Aires SA [*Argentina*] (EY)
SEGD......... (Pankypria) Syndekhnia Ergaton Georgias kai Dason [*(Pan-Cyprian) Union of Farm and Forest Workers*] (GC)
SEGE......... Guale [*Ecuador*] [*ICAO location identifier*] (ICLI)
SEGECI..... Societe d'Entreprises Generales et de Constructions Industrielles
SEGECO.... Societe d'Entreprise Generale Equatoriale de Constructions
SEGECOT ... Societe d'Etudes Generales et de Cooperation Technique
SEGEDAN ... Societe d'Etudes et de Gestion de l'Afrique Noire
SEGENI .... Societe Generale Senegalaise pour le Negoce et l'Industrie
SEGEPLAN ... Secretaria General del Consejo Nacional de Planificacion Economica [*State Planning Council*] [*Guatemala*]
SEGESA.... Societe d'Etudes Geographiques, Economiques, et Sociologiques Appliquees
segg .... Seguente [*Following*] [*Italian*]
SEGGTH... Service des Etudes Generales des Grands Travaux de l'Hydraulique [*Major Construction and Water Works General Studies Service*] [*Algeria*] (AF)
SEGI.......... Societe d'Exploitation du Granit Ivoirien

SEGIC .... Societe d'Etudes Generales de Constructions Industrielles et Civiles
SEGL .... Gul [*Ecuador*] [*ICAO location identifier*]   (ICLI)
SEGMA ..... Societe d'Etudes du Gaz Marin [*Tunisia*]
segn .... Segnatura [*Signature*] [*Publishing*] [*Italian*]
SEGO .... Societe d'Exploitation des Grumes de l'Ouest
SEGOA ...... Societe Senegalaise d'Oxygene et d'Acetylene
SEGOR ...... Societe d'Etudes de Gestion et d'Organisation
SEGP .... Socialist Unity Party of Germany   (BU)
SEGR .... Guarumal [*Ecuador*] [*ICAO location identifier*]   (ICLI)
SEGR .... Societe d'Exploitation de la Gare Routiere
SEGRA ...... System of Elements of the Hydraulic Control Automation   (RU)
SEGRAM ... Societe Equatoriale des Grands Magasins
SEGRE ...... Fuerzas Hidroelectricas del Segre SA [*Spain*]   (PDAA)
SEGS .... Galapagos (Baltra) [*Ecuador*] [*ICAO location identifier*]   (ICLI)
SEGU .... Guayaquil/Simon Bolivar [*Ecuador*] [*ICAO location identifier*]   (ICLI)
SEGZ .... Gualaquiza [*Ecuador*] [*ICAO location identifier*]   (ICLI)
SEH .... Secretariat d'Etat a l'Hydraulique [*Secretariat of State for Hydraulic Engineering*] [*Algeria*]   (AF)
Seh .... Sehir [*City, Town*]   (TU)
SEHA .... Societe d'Exploitation Hoteliere en Afrique [*Congo*]
SEHCI .... Societe pour l'Equipement Hydraulique en Cote-D'Ivoire
SEHI .... Cotacachi [*Ecuador*] [*ICAO location identifier*]   (ICLI)
Sehlite .... Sydney Eye Hospital Library Literature [*Australia*]   (ADA)
SEHOBAREST ... Sindicato de Empleados de Hoteles, Bares, y Restaurantes [*Trade Union of Hotel, Bar, and Restaurant Employees*] [*Dominican Republic*]   (LA)
SEHOMA ... Societe de Conseil et d'Expansion Commerciale Hollando-Malienne
SEHPG ...... Societe d'Exploitation Hoteliere de Port-Gentil
SEHR .... Societe d'Exploitation des Hydrocarbures de Hassi R'Mel [*Algeria*]
SEHT .... Hacienda Taura [*Ecuador*] [*ICAO location identifier*]   (ICLI)
SEI .... Electric-Pulse Counter   (RU)
SEI .... Secretaria Especial de Informatica [*Special Secretariat of Informatics*] [*Brazil*]   (LA)
SEI .... Senhor Do Bonfim [*Brazil*] [*Airport symbol*]   (OAG)
SEI .... Servico de Estatistica e Informacoes [*Brazil*]   (DSCA)
SEI .... Sibirskiy Energeticheskiy Institut [*Siberian Power Engineering Institute*] [*Former USSR*]   (IRC)
SEI .... Societas Ergophthalmologica Internationalis [*International Ergophthalmological Society*] [*Stockholm, Sweden*]   (EAIO)
SEI .... Societe de Constructions et d'Embranchements Industriels
SEI .... Societe d'Etudes Speciales et d'Installations Industrielles
SEI .... Societe Senegalaise d'Entreprises Industrielles
SEI .... Somateion Ellinon Ithopoion [*Greek Actors Association*]   (GC)
SEI .... Statni Energeticka Inspekce [*State Power Inspectorate*]   (CZ)
SEI .... [*The*] Stockholm Environment Institute [*Sweden*]
SEIB .... Ibarra [*Ecuador*] [*ICAO location identifier*]   (ICLI)
SEIB .... Societe d'Electricite Industrielle et Batiments
SEIB .... Societe Electrique et Industrielle de Baol [*Senegal*]
SEIC .... Societe d'Etudes et d'Informations Charbonnieres [*French*]   (SLS)
SEIC .... Societe d'Exploitation Industrielle et Commerciale
SEIC .... Societe Electrique et Industrielle de la Casamance
SEICI .... Societe d'Exportation et d'Importation de la Cote-D'Ivoire
SEIDE .... Sociedad de Estudios Internacionales de la Democracia Espanola [*Society of International Studies of Spanish Democracy*]   (WER)
Seidenp ...... Seidenpapier [*Tissue Paper*] [*German*]
SEIFSA ..... Steel and Engineering Industries Federation of South Africa   (AF)
SEIG .... Intag [*Ecuador*] [*ICAO location identifier*]   (ICLI)
Seihororen ... Zenkoku Seimei Hoken Rodokumiai Rengokai [*National Federation of Life Insurance Workers' Unions*] [*Japan*]
Seikyororen ... Zenkoku Seikyo Rodokumiai Rengokai [*National Federation of Consumers' Cooperative Society Workers' Unions*] [*Japan*]
SEIM .... Isla San Miguel [*Ecuador*] [*ICAO location identifier*]   (ICLI)
SEIM .... Secretaria de Intereses Maritimos [*Secretariat of Maritime Interests*] [*Argentina*]   (LA)
SEIM .... Syndicat des Entreprises et Industries du Mali
SEIMAD ... Societe d'Equipement Immobilier de Madagascar [*Realty Equipment Company of Madagascar*]   (AF)
SEIMAF .... Societe d'Exportation et d'Importation de Materiel en Afrique
SEIN .... Societe d'Electronique Industrielle et Nucleaire [*France*]   (PDAA)
SEIN .... Societe d'Encouragement pour l'Industrie Nationale [*Society for the Encouragement of National Industry*] [*French*]   (SLS)
SEINA ...... Societe Europeenne d'Instruments Numeriques et Analogiques [*French*]   (ADPT)
SEIO .... Sociedad Espanola de Investigacion Operativa, Estadistica, e Informatica [*Spanish*]   (SLS)
SEIR .... Societe Senegalaise d'Energie et d'Irrigation
Seirokyo ..... Seifu Kankei Tokushu Hojin Rodokumiai Kyogikai [*Council of Governmental Special Corporation Employees*] [*Japan*]

SEIS .... Sociedad de Estudiantes de Ingenieria y Arquitectura Salvadorenos [*Society of Salvadoran Engineering and Architecture Students*]   (LA)
Seishi .... Seinen Shiso Kenkyn-kai [*Youth Ideological Study Association*] [*Japan*]
SEIT .... Servicio Especializado de Informacion Tecnica [*Programa de Asistencia Tecnica a la Industria Metalica del Servicio Nacional de Aprendizaje*] [*Colorado*]
SEIT .... Societe Electrique et Industrielle de Tambacounda
SEITA .... Service d'Exploitation Industrielle des Tabacs et des Allumettes [*Commercial Tobacco and Match Manufacturing Agency*] [*Paris, France*]   (WER)
Seit Abw ..... Seitenabweichung [*Drift*] [*German*]   (GCA)
SEITC .... Section d'Etudes et d'Information des Troupes Coloniales
SEITRA ...... Societe d'Etudes Industrielles et de Travaux
SEIVA .... Sindicato de Empleados de la Industria del Vidrio y Afines [*Union of Employees of the Glass and Related Industries*] [*Argentina*]   (LA)
SE/IWT ..... Southern Europe - Inland Waterways Transport [*NATO*]   (NATG)
SEJ .... Slovenska Evanjelicka Jednota [*Slovak Evangelical Union*]   (CZ)
SEJA .... Jaramillo [*Ecuador*] [*ICAO location identifier*]   (ICLI)
SEJCR ...... Societe Europeenne des Jeunes de la Croix-Bleue [*European Society for Blue Cross Youth - ESBCY*]   (EAIO)
SEJEF ...... Societe d'Etudes Juridiques, Economiques, et Fiscales [*French*]   (SLS)
SEJI .... Jipijapa [*Ecuador*] [*ICAO location identifier*]   (ICLI)
SEJS .... Secretariat d'Etat a la Jeunesse et aux Sports
SEK .... Economic Power Combine   (BU)
SEK .... International Electric Power Conference   (BU)
sek .... Sekonde [*Second*] [*Afrikaans*]
SEK .... Sekretariat [*or Sekretaris*] [*Secretariat or Secretary*]   (IN)
sek .... Sekunda [*or Sekundy*] [*Second or Seconds*] [*Poland*]
Sek .... Sekundaer [*Secondary*] [*German*]
Sek .... Sekunde [*Second*] [*German*]
SEK .... Sekundus [*Alternate*] [*Afrikaans*]
sek .... Sekunnissa [*Finland*]
sek .... Sekunti(a) [*Finland*]
SEK .... Sidirodromoi Ellinikou Kratous [*Greek State Railways*] [*OSE*] [*See also*]   (GC)
SEK .... Sut Endustrisi Kurumu [*Dairy Industry Association*]   (TU)
SEK .... Svenska Elektriska Kommissionen [*Sweden*]
SEK .... Svensk Exportkredit AB [*Swedish Export Credit Corp.*]
SEK .... Symvoulion Ethnikon Klirodotimaton [*National Bequests Council*] [*Greek*]   (GC)
SEK .... Syndesmos Ergodoton Kyprou [*Cyprus Employers Association*]   (GC)
SEK .... Synomospondia Ergaton Kyprou [*Cyprus Workers' Confederation*]   (GC)
SEKA .... Syndonistiki Epitropi Kypriakou Agonos [*Coordinating Committee of the Cyprus Struggle*]   (GC)
SEKA .... Turkiye Seluloz ve Kagit Fabrikalari Isletmesi [*Turkish Cellulose and Paper Factories Administration*]   (TU)
SEKA-IS .... Turkiye Seluloz, Kagit, ve Mamulleri Iscileri Sendikasi [*Turkish Cellulose, Paper, and Paper Products Workers' Union*]   (TU)
SEKAM ..... Syndonistiki Epitropi Kanonismou Anatheseos Meleton [*Coordinating Committee for Regulation of Research Assignments*] [*Greek*]   (GC)
SEKBERGOLKAR ... Sekretariat Bersama Golongan Karya [*Joint Secretariat of Functional Groups*]   (IN)
SEKDJEN ... Sekretaris Djenderal [*Secretary General*]   (IN)
SEKE .... Sosialistikon Ergatikon Komma tis Elladas [*Socialist Labor Party of Greece*] [*Forerunner of Greek Communist Party (KKE)*]   (PPE)
SEKE .... Synetairistiki Enosis Kapnoparagogon Ellados [*Cooperative Union of Greek Tobacco Growers*]   (GC)
SEKEP ...... Symvoulio Emborias Kypriakon Elaiokomikon Proiondon [*Cypriot Olive Products Marketing Council*]   (GC)
Seker-Is ..... Turkiye Seker Sanayii Iscileri Sendikasi [*Sugar Industry Workers Union of Turkey*]   (TU)
SEKF .... Syndonistiki Epitropi Kyprion Foititon [*Cypriot Students Coordinating Committee*] [*Greek*]   (GC)
SEKI .... Somateion Ellinon Kyprion Ithopion [*Greek-Cypriot Actors Association*]   (GC)
SEKO .... Syndonistiki Epitropi Kommaton kai Organoseon [*Coordinating Committee of Parties and Organizations*] [*Cyprus*]   (GC)
SEKOVE ... Synetairistika Ergostasia Konservopoiias Voreiou Ellados [*Northern Greece Cooperative Canning Factories*]   (GC)
SEKP .... Symvoulion Emborias Kypriakon Pataton [*Cyprus Potato Marketing Council*] [*SEP*] [*See also*]   (GC)
sekr .... Confidential, Confidentially   (RU)
sekr .... Secretary   (RU)
Sekr. .... Sekretaer [*or Sekretariat*] [*Secretary or Secretariat*] [*German*]
sekr .... Sekretaris [*Secretary*] [*Afrikaans*]
sekr .... Sekretarz [*Secretary*] [*Poland*]
sekre .... Sekretaresse [*Secretary*] [*Afrikaans*]

Sekret........ Sekretion [Secretion] [German] (GCA)
SEKRIMA ... Sendika Kristianina Malagasy [Christian Confederation of
　　　　　Malagasy Trade Unions] [Madagascar]
SEks........... Sy Eksellensie [His, or Her, Excellency] [Afrikaans]
seksot........ Secret Agent (RU)
Sekt........... Sektion [Section, Dissection] [German]
Sekundaerstrahl ... Sekundaerstrahlung [Secondary Radiation] [German]
　　　　　(GCA)
SEKXA ...... Syndikaton Ergatotekhniton Katergasias Xylou Athinon [Athens
　　　　　Union of Technicians and Workers in Wood Processing]
　　　　　(GC)
Sel .... Ducret-Thomson [Formerly, Ducretet Selmer] [Record label]
　　　　　[France]
SEL........... Sanitary and Epidemiological Laboratory (RU)
SEL........... Scouts' Esperanto League (EA)
SEL........... Selangor (ML)
sel.............. Selective, Selection (RU)
sel.............. Selig [Deceased] [German] (GPO)
sel.............. Selis [or Selides] [Page or Pages] (GC)
SEL........... Seoul [South Korea] [Airport symbol] (OAG)
SEL........... Sindicato de Ensenanza Libre [Trade Union of Free Education]
　　　　　[Spanish] (WER)
SEL........... Skolta Esperanto-Ligo [Scouts' Esperanto League] (EAIO)
SEL........... Socialist Electoral League [Norway] (PPW)
SEL........... Societe d'Exploitation Limonadiere
SEL........... Special Environmental Levy [Sydney Water Board] [Australia]
SEL........... Standard Elektrik Lorenz
SEL........... Stichting Experimentale Landbouwnedryven Foundation for
　　　　　Experimental Farms [Surinam] (DSCA)
SEL........... Syndesmos Efedron Lemesou [League of Limassol Reserves]
　　　　　(GC)
SEL........... Syndesmos Ellinon Logotekhnon [League of Greek Writers]
　　　　　(GC)
sel.............. Village (RU)
SELA .... Lago Agrio [Ecuador] [ICAO location identifier] (ICLI)
SELA .... Systeme Economique Latino-Americain [Latin American
　　　　　Economic System - LAES] [French]
SELACJ .... Secretariado Latinoamericano de la Compania de Jesus [Latin
　　　　　American Bureau of Society of Jesus] (EAIO)
SELAF ...... Societe d'Etudes Linguistiques et Anthropologiques de France
　　　　　[French Society for the Study of Linguistics and
　　　　　Anthropology] (SLS)
SELAF ...... Societe pour l'Etudes des Langues Africaines [Paris]
SELAVIP .. Servicio Latinoamericano y Asiatico de Vivienda Popular [Latin
　　　　　American and Asian low Income Housing Service] [Chile]
　　　　　(EAIO)
selb .... Selbst [Self] [German] (GCA)
selbst .... Selbstaendig [Independent] [German] (GCA)
Selbstverl ... Selbstverlag [Published by the Author] [German]
Selbstvlg .... Selbstverlag [Published by the Author] [German]
SELC .... La Cecilia [Ecuador] [ICAO location identifier] (ICLI)
SELCA ...... Societe d'Exploitation la Cascade [Cameroon]
SELCON..... Seleccion Contable [Argentina] (LAA)
SELEC...... Societe d'Etude des Electrocompresseurs [France] (PDAA)
SELEK...... Synergatiki Enosi Lemonoparagogon Kyrineias [Kyrenia Lemon
　　　　　Growers Marketing Union] (GC)
Sel'elektro ... Main Administration of Rural Electrification (RU)
Sel'elektrostroy ... Moscow Construction and Installation Trust of the
　　　　　Glavsel'elektrostroy (RU)
SELETE .... Skholi Ekpaidevtikon Leitourgon Epangelmatikis kai Tekhnikis
　　　　　Ekpaidevseos [School for Teachers in Trades and Technical
　　　　　Education] [Greek] (GC)
SELF........ Societe d'Ergonomie de Langue Francaise [French] (SLS)
SELFCI ..... Societe des Etablissements Louis Feltrin de Cote-D'Ivoire
SEL-FZ...... Standard Elektrik Lorenz AG - Forschungszentrum [Standard
　　　　　Elektrik Lorenz - Research Center] [International
　　　　　Telephone and Telegraph Corporation, USA Stuttgart]
　　　　　[Research center] (ERC)
sel'ges........ Rural Hydroelectric Power Plant (RU)
SELI .... Limoncocha [Ecuador] [ICAO location identifier] (ICLI)
SELIS .... Societe d'Equipement pour l'Infrastructure Saharienne [Saharan
　　　　　Infrastructure Equipment Company] [Algeria] (AF)
Selitr .... Saltpeter Plant [Topography] (RU)
SELJ .... La Julia [Ecuador] [ICAO location identifier] (ICLI)
Sel'khozaerofotos'yemka ... Administration of Agricultural Aerial Surveying
　　　　　(RU)
Sel'khozgiz ... State Publishing House of Agricultural Literature, Journals, and
　　　　　Posters (RU)
Sel'khozizdat ... Publishing House of Agricultural Literature, Journals, and
　　　　　Posters [Moscow] (RU)
sel'khozuch ... Agricultural Training School (RU)
Sel'khozVNITO ... All-Union Scientific, Engineering, and Technical Society of
　　　　　Agriculture (RU)
SELKIM.... Seluloz Kimya Sanayi ve Ticaret AS [Cellulose Chemical
　　　　　Industry and Trade Corporation] (TU)
Sel'kolkhozgiz ... State Agricultural, Cooperative, and Kolkhoz Publishing
　　　　　House (RU)

Selkoop ...... Village Cooperative (BU)
Selkor......... Village Correspondent (BU)
SELL .... Llurimaguas [Ecuador] [ICAO location identifier] (ICLI)
s ell .... Segedellenor [Assistant Supervisor] (HU)
Sel'leszag... Logging Administration of the Ministry of Agriculture, USSR
　　　　　(RU)
SELM .... Loma Larga [Ecuador] [ICAO location identifier] (ICLI)
Sel'mash .... All-Russian Syndicate of Agricultural Machines and Implements
　　　　　(RU)
Sel'mashsnabsbyt ... All-Union Office for Supply of Agricultural Machinery
　　　　　Plants and for Marketing of Their Production (RU)
SELN........ Limon [Ecuador] [ICAO location identifier] (ICLI)
SELNI .... Societa Elettronucleare Italiana [Nuclear energy] [Italian]
　　　　　(NRCH)
SELO........ Loja (La Toma) [Ecuador] [ICAO location identifier] (ICLI)
SELO .... Societa Elettronica Lombarda [Nuclear energy] [Italian]
　　　　　(NRCH)
SELP .... Senior Executive Leadership Program [Australia]
SELPE...... Syndesmos Epikheiriseon Lianikis Poliseos Ellados [Association
　　　　　of Retail Enterprises of Greece] (GC)
SELSA...... Science and Environment Library System Australia
SELSA...... Servicio de Lucha Sanitaria [Health Promotion Service]
　　　　　[Argentina] (LA)
SELSA...... Sindicato de Empresa La Laguna, Sociedad Anonima [Union of
　　　　　the La Laguna Enterprise, Inc.] [El Salvador] (LA)
Sel'skosovet ... Council of Agricultural Cooperative Centers (RU)
Sel'skosoyuz ... All-Russian Union of Agricultural Cooperatives (RU)
sel st .... Plant Breeding Station [Topography] (RU)
sel stop ...... Agricultural (BU)
Selsuvet...... Village People's Council (BU)
SELT .... Latacunga [Ecuador] [ICAO location identifier] (ICLI)
SELT .... Syndicat d'Enseignants Laics du Togo [Lay Teachers Union of
　　　　　Togo] (AF)
SELTA ...... Societe Electro-Technique Africaine
SELTI....... Sudan English Language Teaching Institute
Seluloz-Is ... Turkiye Seluloz ve Mamulleri Iscileri Sendikasi [Turkish
　　　　　Cellulose and Cellulose Products Workers Union] (TU)
SEM........... Aircraft Electric Meteorograph (RU)
sem .... Family [Biology] (RU)
sem .... Seed (RU)
sem .... Semana [Week] [Portuguese]
Sem .... Semaphore [Semaphore] [Military map abbreviation World War
　　　　　I] [French] (MTD)
SEM........... Semboyan [Signals (Army)] (ML)
sem .... Semelhante [Similar] [Portuguese]
sem .... Semence [Seed] [Pharmacy]
sem .... Semestre [Half Year] [Portuguese]
Sem .... Semestriel [French] (FLAF)
SEM........... Servicio de Equipos Mecanicos [Mechanical Equipment Service]
　　　　　[Peru] (LA)
SEM........... Servicio Nacional de Erradicacion de la Malaria [National
　　　　　Service for Malaria Eradication] [Colorado] (LA)
SEM........... Servicios Electromecanicos Ltda. [Colombia] (COL)
SEM........... Sila Elektromotoryczna [Electromotive Force] [Poland]
SEM........... Single European Market
SEM........... Sociedade de Estudos de Mocambique
SEM........... Sociedad Espanola de Microbiologia [Spanish Society of
　　　　　Microbiology] (SLS)
SEM........... Societe d'Economie Mixte (FLAF)
SEM........... Societe d'Emaillage et de Galvanisation du Mali
SEM........... Societe d'Energie de Madagascar
SEM........... Societe d'Equipement de la Mauritanie
SEM........... Societe Senegalaise d'Etudes Maritimes
SEM........... Society for Ethnic Missions [Australia]
SEM........... Soma Efodiasmou kai Metaforon [Supply and Transportation
　　　　　Corps] [Army] [Greek] (GC)
S Em .... Son Eminence [His, or Her Eminence] [French]
SEM........... Son Excellence Monsieur ———— [His Excellency Mr.
　　　　　————] (AF)
SEM........... Statie de Evidenta Mecanizata [Station for Mechanized Records]
　　　　　(RO)
SEM........... Station Experimentale de Marienau [Marienau Experimental
　　　　　Center] [Institut de Recherche de la Siderurgie] [France]
　　　　　(EAS)
SEM........... Stochastisch-Ergodische Messelektronik [German] (ADPT)
SEm .... Sua Eminenza [His Eminence] [Italian]
SEm .... Sy Eminensie [His Eminence] [Afrikaans]
SEMA....... Macara [Ecuador] [ICAO location identifier] (ICLI)
SEMA....... Secretaria Especial do Meio-Ambiente [Special Secretariat for the
　　　　　Environment] [Brazil] (LA)
SEMA....... Secteurs Experimentaux de Modernisation Agricole
SEMA....... Societe d'Economie et de Mathematiques Appliquees
SEMA....... Societe de Materiaux de Construction
SEMA....... Societe d'Equipement de Materiel Aeronautique
SEMA....... Societe d'Equipement du Mali
SEMA....... Societe d'Etudes Minieres Africaines

SEMA........ Societe d'Exploitation Miniere de l'Androy
S Ema........ Sua Eminencia [*His Eminence*] [*Portuguese*]
SEMAB..... Secteur Experimental de Modernisation Agricole de Bongor
SEMABLE ... Secteur Experimental de Modernisation Agricole du Ble
SEMAC..... Societe d'Exploitation des Magasins et Ateliers Casino
SEMACO ... Societe d'Exploitation de Materiaux de Construction
SEMADCO ... Societe El-Nasr d'Engrais and d'Industries Chimiques [*Egypt*]
SEMAG..... Societe Senegalaise des Grands Magasins
SEMALK .. Secteur Experimental de Modernisation Agricole de Lai et Kelo
SEMARP .. Societe d'Etude du Marche du Plateau
SEMAS ..... Standart Elektrik Malzemesi Ticaret ve Sanayii Anonim Sirketi [*Standard Electrical Equipment Trade and Industry Corporation*] (TU)
SEMC........ Macas [*Ecuador*] [*ICAO location identifier*] (ICLI)
SEMC........ State Emergency Management Committee [*New South Wales, Australia*]
SEMCA..... Secteur Experimental de Modernisation des Cultures d'Altitude
SEMCAM ... Sydney Electrical Machines, Controls, and Applied Magnetics [*Research consortium*] [*Australia*]
SEMCENTRE ... Secteur Experimental de Modernisation Agricole du Centre
SEMCI ...... Societe Ebenisterie, Menuiserie de Cote-D'Ivoire
SEME........ Sociedad Espanola de Microscopia Electronica [*Spain*] (EAIO)
SEME........ Societe d'Entreprise et de Materiel Electrique
SEMECA .. Sociedad de Estudiantes de Medicina Emilio Alvarez [*Emilio Alvarez Association of Medical Students*] [*El Salvador*] (LA)
SEMEDE .. Servicio Medico para Empleados Departamentales [*Colombia*]
SEMEFO .. Servicio Medico Forense [*Forensic Medicine Service*] [*Mexico*] (LA)
Semenovodsoyuz ... All-Russian Seed-Growing Union of Agricultural Cooperatives (RU)
SEMEO..... Southeast Asia Ministers of Education Organization [*Bangkok, Thailand*] [*Use SEAMEO*] (CL)
semes.......... Semestral [*Semiannual*] [*Spanish*]
SEMEST... Secteur Experimental de Modernisation Agricole de l'Est
SEMEYK .. Syndekhnia Epistimonon Mikhanikon Ekpaidevtikis Ypiresias Kyprou [*Union of Professional Engineers of the Cyprus Educational Service*] (GC)
SEMF........ State Enterprise Mutual Fund [*Pakistan*] (PDAA)
SEMH .... Machala [*Ecuador*] [*ICAO location identifier*] (ICLI)
Sem Hop .... Semaine des Hopitaux (FLAF)
semi........... Semis [*One-Half*] [*Latin*] [*Pharmacy*] (MAE)
SEMI........ Societe des Eaux Minerales Ivoiriennes
SEMI........ Societe d'Etudes de Marche et d'Informatique [*Society for the Study of Marketing and Informatics*] [*Information service or system*] [*Defunct*] (IID)
SEMI........ Societe d'Expertises Maritimes et Industrielles
SEMI........ State Enterprise for Mechanical Industries in Iskandariyah [*Iraq*]
semid.......... Semidrachma [*Half a Drachm*] [*Latin*] [*Pharmacy*] (MAE)
SEMIKON ... Seminare/Konferenzen [*Seminars/Conferences*] [*Society for Business Information*] [*Information service or system*] [*Defunct*] (IID)
Semin........ Seminaire [*Seminary*] [*Military map abbreviation World War I*] [*French*] (MTD)
SEMIPI..... Preparatory School for Student Officers [*Malagasy*] (AF)
SEMIRA ... System of Electronic Marks' Interrogation, Registration, and Administration [*Database*] [*WIPO*] [*United Nations*] (DUND)
Sem Jur...... La Semaine Juridique (FLAF)
SEMK........ Syndesmos Epistimonon Michanikon Kyprou [*Cyprus*] (EAIO)
SEMKO..... Svenska Electriska Materielkontrollanstalten [*Swedish Institute for Testing and Approval of Electrical Equipment*] (PDAA)
SEMKUR ... Sebze ve Meyva Kurutma Sanayii AS [*Fruit and Vegetable Drying Industry Corp.*] (TU)
SEML........ Manglaralto [*Ecuador*] [*ICAO location identifier*] (ICLI)
seml........... Semleges [*Neutral*] (HU)
SEMM....... Societe Europeenne de Materials Mobiles [*France*] (PDAA)
SEMMARITIME ... Secteur Experimental de Modernisation Maritime
SEMME.... Syllogos Ergazomenon Mathiton Mesis Ekpaidevseos Athinon [*Association of Working Students in Secondary Education*] [*Greek*] (GC)
SEMNORD ... Secteur Experimental de Modernisation et d'Action Rurale du Nord [*North Modernization and Rural Action Experimental Sector*] [*Cameroon*] (AF)
SEMO .... Montalvo [*Ecuador*] [*ICAO location identifier*] (ICLI)
SEMO .... Societe Belgo-Francaise d'Energie Nucleaire Mosane [*Nuclear energy*] [*Belgium*] (NRCH)
SEMO .... State Emergency Management Organisation [*New South Wales, Australia*]
SEMO .... Syndesmos Eisagogeon Michanokiniton Ochimaton [*Cyprus*] (EAIO)
SEMO .... Syndonistiki Epitropi ton Metallourgikon Organoseon [*Coordinating Committee of Metallurgical Organizations*] [*Greek*] (GC)
SEMP........ Mopa [*Ecuador*] [*ICAO location identifier*] (ICLI)
SEMP........ Senior Executive Management Program [*Australia*]

SEMP........ Societe d'Editions Medico-Pharmaceutiques [*Medical-Pharmaceutical Publishing Co.*] [*France*] [*Information service or system*] (IID)
SEMP .... Statens Etnografiska Museum. Publications
SEMPA ..... Syndicat des Entrepreneurs de Manutention du Port d'Abidjan [*Ivory Coast*]
SEMPAO .. Syndicat des Entreprises de Manutention de Ports d'Afrique Occidentale [*West African Port Handling Enterprises Union*] [*Senegal*] (AF)
SEMPIMA ... Sendikan'ny Mpivarotra Malagasy [*Malagasy Businessmen's Association*] (AF)
SEMPOK.. Syndicat des Entreprises de Manutention du Port de Kaolack
SEMRY ..... Societe d'Expansion et de Modernisation de la Riziculture de Yagoua
SEMS .... Monjas Sur [*Ecuador*] [*ICAO location identifier*] (ICLI)
SEMT .... Manta [*Ecuador*] [*ICAO location identifier*] (ICLI)
SEMT .... Skholi Ekpaideveos Mikhanikon Tilepikoinonias [*Training School for Telecommunications Engineers*] [*Greek*] (GC)
SEMT .... Societe d'Etude des Machines Thermiques
SEMU .... Servicio Electrico Municipal
SEMULTRA ... Servicio Multimodal Transismico [*Transisthmian Multimodal Service*] [*Mexico*] (LA)
SEMUP..... Self-Excited Magnetized Dynamoelectric Amplifier (RU)
SEMVGC.. Societe d'Etudes pour la Mise en Valeur du Gaz Camerounaise
Sen .... Senaat [*Senate*] [*Afrikaans*]
sen .... Senare [*Later*] [*Sweden*]
Sen .... Senat [*Senate*] [*German*]
Sen .... Senator [*Senator*] [*Afrikaans*]
Sen .... Senatore [*Senator*] [*Italian*]
SEN .... Senegal [*ANSI three-letter standard code*] (CNC)
Sen .... Senior [*Netherlands*] (GPO)
sen .... Senior [*Poland*]
sen .... Seno [*Sine*] [*Portuguese*]
SEN .... Sistema Energetico Nacional [*National Power System*] [*Cuba*] (LA)
SEN .... Sistemul Energetic National [*National Power System*] (RO)
SEN .... Skholi Emborikou Navtikou [*Merchant Marine Academy*] (GC)
SEN .... Sociedad de Equipamiento Nacional [*National Equipment Company*] [*Haiti*] (LAA)
SEN .... Societe Equatoriale de Navigation
SEN .... Societe Europeenne de Neuro+radiologie [*European Neuroradiological Association*] [*France*] (EAIO)
SEN .... Societe Europeenne de Neuroscience [*European Neuroscience Association - ENA*] (EA)
SEN .... Soma Ellinon Navtoproskopon [*Greek Sea Scouts*] (GC)
SEN .... Soma Elpidoforon Neon [*Corps of Hopeful Youth*] [*Cyprus*] (GC)
SEN .... Somateion Ellinidon Nomikon [*Association of Greek Women Attorneys*] (GC)
SEN .... Symvoulion Emborikou Navtikou [*Merchant Marine Council*] [*Greek*] (GC)
SEN .... Syndicat des Enseignants du Niger [*Union of Nigerian Teachers*] (GC)
SENA........ Nor Antizana [*Ecuador*] [*ICAO location identifier*] (ICLI)
SENA........ Servicio Nacional de Aprendizaje [*National Apprenticeship Service*] [*Colorado*] (LA)
SENA....... Societe d'Energie Nucleaire Franco-Belge des Ardennes [*Nuclear energy*] [*French*] (NRCH)
SENA....... Societe d'Etudes Numismatiques et Archeologiques [*Society of Numismatic and Archeological Studies*] [*French*] (SLS)
SENA....... Symvoulion Elengkhou Navtikon Atykhimaton [*Council for the Control of Marine Accidents*] [*Greek*] (GC)
SENAA...... Syndonistiki Epitropi Neolaion Andimonarkhikou Agona [*Coordinating Committee of Youth of the Antimonarchical Struggle*] [*Greek*] (GC)
SENAC...... Servico Nacional de Aprendizagem Comercial [*National Service for Commercial Training*]
SENAC...... Servico Nacional do Comercio [*National Trade Service*] [*Brazil*]
SENAC...... Societe Senegalaise de l'Amiante Ciment
SENACA ... Servicio Nacional del Control Animal [*National Animal Control Service*] [*Uruguay*] (LA)
SENADEM ... Secretaria Nacional de Educacion Media [*National Secretariat of Intermediate Education*] [*Venezuela*] (LA)
SENAFER ... Servicio Nacional de Fertilizantes [*National Fertilizer Service*] [*Peru*] (LA)
SENAI .... Servico Nacional da Aprendizagem Industrial [*National Industrial Apprenticeship Service*] [*Brazil*] (LA)
SENALFA ... Servicio Nacional de Lucha Contra la Fiebre Aftosa [*Asuncion, Paraguay*] (LA)
SENAM..... Servico Nacional de Assistencia aos Municipios [*National Municipal Aid Service*] [*Brazil*] (LA)
SENAM..... Societe Senegalaise de Navigation Maritime
SENAMEHI ... Servicio Nacional de Meteorologia e Hidrologia [*National Meteorological and Hydrographic Service*] [*Peru*] (LA)
SENAPET ... Servicio Nacional de Programacion y Evaluacion Tecnica [*National Technical Programing and Evaluation Service*] [*Argentina*] (LA)

SENAPI .... Servicio Nacional de Artesanias y Pequenas Industrias [*Panama*] (LAA)
SENARA ... Servicio Nacional de Radiodifusion [*National Broadcasting Service*] [*Argentina*] (LA)
SENASA ... Servicio Nacional de Sanidad Animal [*National Animal Health Service*] [*Argentina*] (LA)
Senatarkh ... Senate Archives (RU)
SENATI .... Servicio Nacional de Adiestramiento en Trabajo Industrial [*National Service for Industrial Work Training*] [*Peru*] (LA)
SENC........ Nor Cayambe [*Ecuador*] [*ICAO location identifier*] (ICLI)
SENCIE .... Societe Senegalaise de Scierie
Sen-Cons ... Senatus-Consulte (FLAF)
S en CPA ... Societe en Commandite par Actions (FLAF)
SENDAS ... Servicio Nacional de Asistencia Social [*SAS*] [*Colombia*] [*Later,*] (COL)
SENDE...... Servicio Nacional del Empleo [*Chile*] (LAA)
SENDET ... Secretaria Ejecutiva Nacional de Detenidos [*National Executive Secretariat of Prisoners*] [*Chile*] (LA)
SENDIP .... Secretaria Nacional de Informacion Publica [*National Public Information Secretariat*] [*Ecuador*] (LA)
SENDOC... Small Enterprises National Documentation Centre [*India*]
SENDU ..... Servicio Nacional de Desarrollo Urbano [*National Urban Development Service*] [*Bolivia*] (LA)
SENE......... Syndonistiki Epitropi Neon Ergazomenon [*Coordinating Committee of Working Youth*] [*Greek*] (GC)
SENEAM ... Servicios a la Navegacion en el Espacio Aereo Mexicano [*Mexico*] [*ICAO designator*] (FAAC)
Seneg.......... Senegal
SENEGALAP ... Societe Senegalaise de Diffusion d'Appareils Electriques
SENELEC ... Societe Senegalaise de Distribution d'Energie Electrique
SENEPESCA ... Societe Senegalaise pour l'Expansion de la Peche Cotiere, Surgelation, et Conditionnement des Aliments
SENEPHARMA ... Societe Pharmaceutique Senegalaise
SENEPNEU ... Societe Senegalaise de Pneumatiques
SENETEX ... Societe Senegalaise des Textiles
SENETRANSCARS ... Senegalaise de Transports par Cars
SENETRANSFIL ... Societe Senegalaise de Transformation du Fil de Metal
SENFOR ... Servicio Nacional de Formacion Profesional [*Paraguay*] (LAA)
SENG .... Secretaria de Estado dos Negocios do Governo [*Brazil*]
SENGA...... Societe d'Entreposage du Gabon
SENGAZ... Societe Senegalaise des Gaz
SENI.......... Nor Iliniza [*Ecuador*] [*ICAO location identifier*] (ICLI)
SENICOM ... La Senegalaise Industrielle Commerciale
SENIMCO ... Senegalaise Immobiliere et Commerciale
SENIMEX ... Senegal Import-Export
SENINFOR ... Societe Senegalaise de Travaux Informatiques
Sen-i-Roren ... Nihon Sen-i-Sangyo Rodokumiai Rengokai [*Japan Federation of Textile and Clothing Workers' Union*]
SENKEN ... Senko Seiren Kenkyusho [*Research Institute of Mineral Dressing and Metallurgy*] [*Research center*] [*Japan*] (IRC)
SENN .... Societa Elettronucleare Nazionale [*Italian*]
SENO .... Syndonistiki Epitropi Neon Oikodomon [*Coordinating Committee of Young Construction Workers*] [*Greek*] (GC)
s en/of vt .... Schending en/of Verkeerde Toepassing [*Benelux*] (BAS)
SENOTEL ... Societe Anonyme de Construction et de Gestion Immobiliere et Hoteliere
SENPA ...... Servicio Nacional de Productos Agrarios [*National Service for Agricultural Products*] [*Spanish*] (WER)
SENPRUC ... Secretaria Nacional de Preuniversitarios Cristianos [*Colombia*] (COL)
SENRAC ... South Australian State Energy Research Advisory Committee
S en S .... Schip en Schade [*Benelux*] (BAS)
Sensibilizier ... Sensibilisierung [*Sensitizing*] [*German*] (GCA)
Sent .... Sentenza [*Decision, Judgment*] [*Italian*] (ILCA)
sent............ Sentido [*Sorry*] [*Portuguese*]
sent............ September (RU)
s-ent............ Sous-Entendu [*Understood*] [*French*]
SENTA...... Societe d'Etudes Nucleaires et de Techniques Advancees [*Nuclear energy*] [*French*] (NRCH)
Sent Arb..... Sentence Arbitrale [*Benelux*] (BAS)
SENTOKYO ... Senmon Toshokan Kyogikai [*Special Libraries Association*] [*Japan*] (PDAA)
SENU .... Neuvo Rocafuerte [*Ecuador*] [*ICAO location identifier*] (ICLI)
SENU .... Societe Luxembourgeoise d'Energie Nucleaire SA
SEO .... Department of Sanitation and Epidemiology (RU)
SEO .... Salvo Erro ou Omissao [*Errors and Omissions Excepted*] [*Portuguese*]
SEO .... Sanitary and Epidemiological Detachment (RU)
SEO .... Sauf Erreur ou Omission [*Errors or Omissions Excepted*] [*French*] (GPO)
SEO .... Seguela [*Ivory Coast*] [*Airport symbol*] (OAG)
SEO .... Senior Education Officer [*Australia*]
SEO .... Sin Errores y Omisiones [*Errors and Omissions Excepted*] [*Business term*] [*Spanish*]
SEO .... Societe des Etudes Oceaniennes [*French*] (SLS)

SEO .... Societe Electrique de l'Our [*Luxembourg*]
SEO .... Soma Ellinidon Odigon [*Greek Women Drivers Corps*] (GC)
SEO .... State Electoral Office [*Australia*]
SEO .... Symvoulion Epilogis Opliton [*Soldier Selection Council*] [*Greek*] (GC)
SEO .... Syndesmos Ellinon Oreivaton [*Greek Mountain Climbers League*] (GC)
SEOA .... Pasochoa [*Ecuador*] [*ICAO location identifier*] (ICLI)
SEOC......... State Emergency Operations Centre [*New South Wales, Australia*]
SEOED...... Skholi Eidikon Oplon Enoplon Dynameon [*Armed Forces Special Weapons School*] [*Greek*] (GC)
SEOI .... Secretaria de Estado da Ordem Interna [*State Secretariat for Internal Security*] [*Angola*] (AF)
SEOIL ...... Syndesmos Ergazomenon kai Odigon Idioktiton Leoforeion [*Association of Employees and Drivers of Privately Owned Buses*] [*Greek*] (GC)
SEOL........ Olmedo [*Ecuador*] [*ICAO location identifier*] (ICLI)
SEOO .... Sauf Erreur ou Omission [*Errors and Omissions Excepted*] [*French*]
SEOP......... SHAPE [*Supreme Headquarters Allied Powers Europe*] Emergency Operating Procedures [*NATO*] (NATG)
SEOPP ...... Syndonistiki Epitropi Organoseon Prostasias tou Perivalondos [*Coordinating Committee of Organizations for the Protection of the Environment*] [*Greek*] (GC)
SEOPT ...... Secretaria de Estado de Obras Publicas y Transporte [*Argentina*] (LAA)
SEOR......... Oro [*Ecuador*] [*ICAO location identifier*] (ICLI)
SEOr.......... Senola Europea d'Orgonoteragia [*Italian*] (SLS)
SE ou O...... Sauf Erreur ou Ommission (FLAF)
SEP............ Medical Evacuation Point (RU)
SEP............ Samenwerkende Elektriciteit Produktie Bedrijven [*Electric utility*] [*Netherlands*]
SEP............ Secretaria de Educacion Publica [*Secretariat of Public Education*] [*Mexico*] (LA)
SEP............ Secretaria de Estado das Pescas [*Cape Verde*] (EY)
SEP............ Secretariat d'Etat au Plan [*Algeria*]
SEP............ Semenwerkende Electriciteits-Produktiebedrijven [*Benelux*] (BAS)
sep............ Separado [*Separate*] [*Portuguese*]
sep............ Separat [*Separate*] [*Danish/Norwegian*]
sep............ Separata [*Reprint, Separate*] [*Portuguese*]
sep............ Septiembre [*September*] [*Spanish*]
SEP............ Servico de Estatistica de Producao [*Rio De Janeiro, Brazil*] (LAA)
SEP............ Skholi Epangelmatikou Prosanatolismou [*Trade Orientation School*] [*Greek*] (GC)
SEP............ Smallpox Eradication Programme
SEP............ Sociedad Entomologica del Peru [*Peru*] (DSCA)
SEP............ Societe d'Economie Politique de Belgique [*Belgium*] (BAS)
SEP............ Societe Equatoriale Pharmaceutique
Sep............ Societe Europeenne de Planification a Long Terme [*Belgium*] (SLS)
SEP............ Societe Europeenne de Propulsion [*European Propellant Society*] [*French*] (WER)
SeP............ Solidarite et Participation [*Political party*] [*Belgium*]
SEP............ Soma Ellinon Proskopon [*Greek Boy Scouts*] (GC)
SEP............ Sosialistiki Epanastatiki Pali [*Socialist Revolutionary Struggle*] [*Greek*] (GC)
SEP............ Special Electrotechnical Regulations (RU)
SEP............ Special Environmental Programme [*Australia*]
SEP............ Stichting Economische Publikaties
SEP............ Stowarzyszenie Elektrykow Polskich [*Association of Polish Electrical Engineers*] (POL)
SEP............ Structural Efficiency Principle [*Australia*]
SEP............ Studiegroup voor Europese Politiek (EA)
SEP............ Suboticko Elektricno Preduzece [*Subotica Electrical Establishment*] [*YU*]
SEP............ Sumadisko Elektricno Preduzece [*Sumadija Electrical Establishment*] [*Vreoci*] (YU)
SEP............ Surrendered Enemy Personnel (ML)
SEP............ Symfonia Emboriou kai Pliromon [*Commerce and Payments Agreement*] [*Greek*] (GC)
SEP............ Symvoulion Elaiokomikon Proiondon [*Olive Oil Products Council*] [*Greek*] (GC)
SEP............ Symvoulion Emborias Pataton [*Potato Marketing Council*] [*SEKP Cyprus*] [*See also*] (GC)
SEP............ Symvoulion Exagogikis Politikis [*Export Policy Council or Board*] (GC)
SEP............ Systima Enorganis Prosgeioseos [*Instrument Landing System*] (GC)
SEPA .... Pastaza [*Ecuador*] [*ICAO location identifier*] (ICLI)
SEPA .... Science Education Program for Africa (AF)
SEPA .... Servicios Periodisticos Asociados [*Associated Journalistic Services*] [*Chile*] (LA)
SEPA .... Societe d'Edition et de Presse Africaine

SEPA .... Societe des Engrais Phosphates Azotes [*Phosphate and Nitrate Fertilizer Company*] [*Tunisia*]   (AF)
SEPAA ...... Sheepskin Export Packers' Association of Australia
SEPAC ...... Secretaria de Promocion y Asistencia de la Comunidad [*Volunteer Service of the Secretariat of Community Assistance and Development*] [*Argentina*]   (LA)
SEPAC ...... Systeme d'Evolution Progressive et Automatisee des Connaissances [*French*]   (ADPT)
SEPACAM ... Societe d'Exploitation pour l'Assainissement du Cameroun
SEPAFIN .. Secretaria de Patrimonio y Fomento Industrial [*Mexico*]
SEPAM ...... Societe d'Exportation des Produits Animaux du Mali
SEPAMA .. Societe d'Exploitation des Produits d'Arachides du Mali
SEPAN ...... Servicio Publicitario de Alimentos y Nutricion [*Colombia*] (COL)
SEPANAL ... Secretaria del Patrimonio Nacional [*Secretariat of National Patrimony*] [*Mexico*]   (LA)
SEPANI .... Societe d'Exploitation des Produits d'Arachides du Niger
SEPAP ...... Severoceske Papirny [*North Bohemian Paper Works*]   (CZ)
separ .... Separatum [*Separately*] [*Latin*]   (MAE)
SEPARC .... Societe d'Etudes pour la Promotion de l'Architecture et des Oeuvres d'Oscar Niemeyer [*French*]   (SLS)
SE/PB .... Southern Europe - Ports and Beaches [*NATO*]   (NATG)
SEPB .... Swedish Environmental Protection Board   (MSC)
SEPBA ...... Societe d'Exploitation du Parc a Bois d'Abidjan [*Ivory Coast*]
SEPBC ...... Societe d'Exploitation des Parcs a Bois du Cameroun
sepbre .... Septiembre [*September*] [*Spanish*]
SEPC .... Societe d'Exploitation des Produits de Cote-D'Ivoire
SEPCAE .... Societe des Engrais et des Produits Chimiques d'Afrique Equatoriale
SEPCEM ... Societe d'Etude pour la Promotion de la Culture et l'Exploitation du Mais au Cameroun
SEPCM ..... Societe d'Engrais et de Produits Chimiques de Madagascar
SEPCOM ... Somali Export Promotion Co.
SEPCON ... Saudi Economic and Petroleum Consulting Group
SEPDTh .... Syndikalistiki Epitropi dia tin Prostasian ton Dimokratikon Thesmon [*Trade Union Committee for the Defense of Democratic Institutions*] [*Greek*]   (GC)
SEPE .... Pechichal [*Ecuador*] [*ICAO location identifier*]   (ICLI)
SEPE .... Secretariat pour l'Etude des Problems de l'Eau [*Secretariat for the Study of Water Problems*] [*France*]   (PDAA)
SEPEA ...... Societe Europeene de Psychiatrie de l'Enfant et de l'Adolescent [*European Society of Child and Adolescent Psychiatry - ESCAP*]   (EAIO)
SEPECAT ... Societe Europeenne de Production de l'Avion Ecol de Combat et d'Appaui Tactique [*France*]   (PDAA)
SEPEL .... Sementeira e Pecuaria Lider SA [*Brazil*]   (DSCA)
SEPEM ..... Societe d'Exploitation de Peche en Mer
SEPEN ..... Secretariat d'Etat au Plan et a l'Economie Nationale [*Tunisia*]
SEPEO ...... Syndonistiki Epitropi Provolis Ellinikis Oikonomias [*Coordinating Committee for the Promotion of the Greek Economy*]   (GC)
SEPFA .... South East Professional Fishermen's Association [*Australia*]
SEPFI .... Societe d'Etudes et de Participation Financieres et Immobilieres [*North African*]
SEPG .... Societe d'Energie de Port-Gentil
SEPH .... State Establishment for Prefabricated Housing [*Iraq*]
SEPHA ...... Special Emergency Programme for the Horn of Africa [*World Food Programme*] [*United Nations*]
SEPHOS ... Societe d'Etudes et de Participations Phosphatieres [*Phosphate Studies and Participations Company*] [*French*]   (WER)
SEPI .... Pichincha [*Ecuador*] [*ICAO location identifier*]   (ICLI)
SEPI .... State Establishment for Petrochemical Industries [*Iraq*]
SEPIA .... Societe d'Etudes de Production Industrielle en Afrique
SEPIC .... Societe d'Etude et de Promotion des Industries de la Cellulose
SEPICA ..... Societe d'Etudes et de Promotion Industrielle des Camerounais
SEPIPSA ... Servicio Peruano de Ingenieros de Petroleo del Oriente, Sociedad Anonima [*Peruvian Service of Petroleum Engineers for Eastern Peru, Incorporated*]   (LA)
SEPL .... Playas [*Ecuador*] [*ICAO location identifier*]   (ICLI)
SEPLACODI ... Secretaria de Planamiento, Coordinacion, y Difusion [*Information, Coordination, and Planning Secretariat*] [*Uruguay*]   (LA)
SEPLAN ... Secretaria de Planejamento [*Planning Secretariat*] [*Brazil*]   (LA)
SEPLIS ...... Secretariat Europeen des Professions Liberales, Independantes et Sociales [*European Secretariat of the Liberal, Independant and Social Professions*] [*EC*]   (ECED)
SEPM .... Statiunea Experimentala de Preparate Microbiologice [*Experimental Station for Microbiological Preparations*] (RO)
SEPMI ...... Sociedad para la Educacion Patriotico-Militar [*Society for Patriotic-Military Education*] [*Cuba*]   (LA)
SEPO .... Posorja [*Ecuador*] [*ICAO location identifier*]   (ICLI)
SEPO .... Societe d'Exploitation des Produits Oleagineaux [*Morocco*]
SEPOGA ... Societe d'Exploitation des Produits Oleagineux du Gabon [*Gabonese Oleaginous Products Exploitation Company*] (AF)

SEPOM ..... Societe d'Exploitation des Produits Oleagineux du Mali [*Malian Oleaginous Products Exploitation Company*]
SEPP .... Societe d'Entreposage des Produits Petroliers
SEPPIC .... Section de Peche et de Pisciculture du Cameroun
SEPR .... Sociedad Espanola de Proteccion Radiologica [*Spanish Society for Radiological Protection*]   (WND)
SEPR .... Societe d'Etudes de la Propulsion a Reaction [*French*]
SEPR .... Societe Europeenne des Produits Refractaires [*French*]
SEPRA ...... Sociedad Explotadora de Productos Agricolas Ltda. [*Agricultural Products Promotional Company Ltd.*] [*Chile*]   (LA)
SEPREP .... Secretaria de Prensa de la Presidencia de la Republica [*Press Secretariat of the Presidency*] [*Peru*]   (LA)
SEPRIC ..... Societe d'Etudes pour la Promotion de l'Industrie Cafeiere
SEPRONAL ... Sociedad Explotadora de Productos Nacionales Ltda. [*Colombia*]   (COL)
SEPS .... Pasaje [*Ecuador*] [*ICAO location identifier*]   (ICLI)
SEPSEIC ... Secretaria Ejecutiva de Planificacion del Sector Economia Industria y Comercio [*Costa Rica*]
SEPT .... Putumayo [*Ecuador*] [*ICAO location identifier*]   (ICLI)
sept .... Septem [*Seven*] [*Latin*]   (MAE)
sept .... September [*Denmark*]   (GPO)
Sept .... September [*Afrikaans*]
Sept .... September [*German*]   (GPO)
sept .... September [*Netherlands*]   (GPO)
sept .... Septembre [*September*] [*French*]
sept .... Septentrional [*Northern*] [*French*]
sept .... Septiembre [*September*] [*Spanish*]
SEPT .... Servico de Estatistica de Provedencia e do Trabalho [*Rio De Janeiro, Brazil*]   (LAA)
SEPT .... Societe d'Etude de Psychodrame Pratique et Theorique [*French*]   (SLS)
SEPT .... Syndicat des Enseignants Protestants Togolais [*Togolese Protestant Teachers Union*]   (AF)
septbre .... Septembre [*September*] [*French*]
septe .... Septiembre [*September*] [*Spanish*]
SEPU .... Puna [*Ecuador*] [*ICAO location identifier*]   (ICLI)
SEPUP ...... Science Education for Public Understanding Project [*Australia*]
SEPV .... Portoviejo [*Ecuador*] [*ICAO location identifier*]   (ICLI)
SEPVPS .... Somateion Ergatikou Prosopikou Viomikhanion Plastikon Ylon kai Synafon Athinon-Peiraios-Perikhoron [*Union of Working Personnel of the Plastics and Related Industries of Athens, Piraeus, and Suburbs*]   (GC)
SEPY .... Puyo [*Ecuador*] [*ICAO location identifier*]   (ICLI)
SEQC .... Sociedad Espanola de Quimicos Cosmeticos [*Spanish*]   (SLS)
SEQE .... Quevedo [*Ecuador*] [*ICAO location identifier*]   (ICLI)
SEQN .... Quininde [*Ecuador*] [*ICAO location identifier*]   (ICLI)
SEQU .... Quito/Mariscal Sucre [*Ecuaor*] [*ICAO location identifier*] (ICLI)
SER .... Aerocalifornia SA [*Mexico*] [*ICAO designator*]   (FAAC)
ser .... Middle   (RU)
ser .... Seria [*Series*]   (POL)
ser .... Serial   (RU)
ser .... Serie [*Series*] [*Sweden*]
ser .... Serie [*Series*] [*French*]
Ser .... Serie [*Series*] [*German*]
ser .... Serie [*Series*] [*Portuguese*]
ser .... Serine   (RU)
SER .... Servicio Estatal de Radiodifusion [*State Radiobroadcasting Service*] [*Panama*]   (LA)
SER .... Servico de Economia Rural [*Brazil*]   (LAA)
SER .... Servico de Radiodifusao Educativa [*Educational Radiobroadcasting Service*] [*Brazil*]   (LA)
ser .... Silver   (RU)
SER .... Sociaal Economische Raad [*Social Economic Council*] [*Netherlands*]   (WEN)
SER .... Sociedad Espanola de Radiodifusion [*Spanish North Africa*] (MENA)
SER .... Sociedad Espanola de Rehabilitacion [*Spanish*]   (SLS)
SER .... Societe Equatoriale de Raffinage [*Equatorial Refining Company*] [*Gabon*]   (AF)
SER .... Societe Europeenne de Radiologie [*European Society of Radiology*]   (SLS)
SER .... Svenska Elektro- och Data- Ingenjoerers Riksforening [*Sweden*]
SER .... System of Optimizing Control   (RU)
SERA .... Social and Economic Revolutionary Army
SERA .... Socialist Environment and Resources Association [*Russian*]
SERA .... Sociedad para el Estudio de la Reproduccion Animal [*Argentina*] (DSCA)
SERA .... Societe d'Etudes et de Realisations Agricoles
SERA .... Societe d'Etudes et de Representation en Afrique
SERAC ...... South East Racing Association [*Australia*]
SERAC ...... State Energy Research Advisory Committee [*Australia*]
SERADIS ... Societe Senegalaise de Representation, d'Approvisionnement et de Distribution
SERAF ...... Schaktentreprenoerernas Arbetsgivarefoerbund [*Employers' Association of Swedish Earth Moving Contractors*]   (EY)

SERAM..... Service d'Etudes et de Recherches Antimalariennes
SERAO...... Societe d'Engineering et de Realisations en Afrique de l'Ouest
SERAS...... Societe d'Exploitation des Ressources Animales du Senegal
SERB......... Riobamba [Ecuador] [ICAO location identifier]   (ICLI)
serb............ Serbiaa [or Serbiaksi] [Finland]
serb............ Serbialainen [Finland]
SERB......... Societe d'Etudes et de Recherches Biologiques [French]   (SLS)
SERB......... Societe Europeene de Radiobiologie [European Society for Radiation Biology - ESRB]   (EAIO)
SERBAUD ... Serikat Buruh Angkatan Udara [Air Transport Workers Union]   (IN)
SERBB...... State Employees' Retirement Benefits Board [Australia]
SERBIUM ... Serikat Buruh Industri dan Umum [General and Industrial Workers Union]   (IN)
serbskokhorv ... Serbo-Croatian   (RU)
SERC......... Saudi-Egyptian Reconstruction Company   (ME)
SERC......... Seccion Especial de Repression del Comunismo [Argentine police]
SERC......... Societe d'Equipement de la Republique du Congo
SERC......... Structural Engineering Research Centre Madras [Council of Scientific and Industrial Research] [India]   (ERC)
SERCA...... Secteur Experimental de Rationalisation du Circuit de l'Arachide [Senegal]
SERCA...... Servicios de Carga Aerea [National Airlines] [Costa Rica]   (EY)
SERCA...... Societe d'Exploitation de la Republique Centrafricain
SERCH...... Societe d'Etudes et de Recherches pour la Connaissance de l'Homme [French]   (SLS)
SERCO...... Service et Commerce
SERCOBE ... Servicio Tecnico Comercial de Constructores de Bienes de Equipo [Spain]   (PDAA)
SERCOGIM ... Societe de Services Communs et de Gestion Immobiliere
SERCOMETAL ... Servicio Tecnico Comercial de Construcciones Metalicasy de Caldereria [Spain]   (PDAA)
SERCOTEC ... Servicio de Cooperacion Tecnica [Technical Cooperation Service] [Chile]   (LA)
SERDF...... State Energy Research and Development Fund [New South Wales, Australia]
SERDI....... Societe d'Etude et de Realisation pour le Developpement Industriel [Organization for the Study and Implementation of Industrial Development] [Malagasy]   (GEA)
SEREB...... Societe pour l'Etude et la Realisation d'Engins Balistiques [French]
SEREC...... Societe d'Etudes de Representation et de Controle
SEREC-CI ... Societe d'Etudes, de Recherches, et d'Exploitations de Carrieres en Cote-D'Ivoire
SEREG...... Societe d'Etudes, de Realisations, et de Gestion
SEREL....... Societe d'Exploitation et de Recherches Electroniques [France]   (PDAA)
SEREM..... Societe d'Etudes, de Recherches, et l'Exploitation Minieres
SEREMA .. Sendika Revolisakionera Malagasy [Revolutionary Malagasy Trade Union] [Madagascar]
SEREPCA ... Societe de Recherches et d'Exploitation des Petroles du Cameroun [Petroleum Prospecting and Exploitation Company of Cameroon]   (AF)
SEREPT.... Societe Francaise d'Exploitation et de Recherches Petroliers en Tunisie [French Company for Petroleum Exploitation and Prospecting in Tunisia]   (AF)
SERES...... Societe d'Etudes et de Recherches en Sciences Sociales [French]   (SLS)
SERESA.... Societe d'Etudes de la Realisation Economique et Sociale en l'Agriculture
SEREX...... Secretaria Ejecutiva de Relaciones Economicas Externas [Executive Secretariat for Foreign Economic Relations] [Chile]   (LA)
SERF......... Study of Energy Release in Flares [International Council of Scientific Unions]
SERFHAU ... Servico Federal de Habitacao e Urbanismo [Federal Housing and Urban Planning Service] [Brazil]   (LA)
Serg........... Sergente [Sergeant] [Italian]
SERG........ Solar Energy Research Group [Lebanon]   (EAIO)
SERGAL ... Sociedade de Exportacoes, Representacoes Gerais, e Agencias Limitada
SERGS...... Sociedade de Engenharia do Rio Grande Do Sul [Brazil]   (SLS)
SERGTHI ... Societe d'Etudes et de Realisation des Grands Travaux Hydrauliques et Industriels [Algeria]
SERH .... Servicio de Empleo y Recursos Humanos [Employment and Human Resource Service] [Peru]   (LAA)
serh ed........ Serh Eden [Annotated]   (TU)
SERI......... Aguarico [Ecuador] [ICAO location identifier]   (ICLI)
SERI .... Societe d'Etudes et de Realisations Industrielles [Morocco]
SERIA ...... Societe d'Etudes et de Realisations Industrielles d'Abidjan
SERIAO ... Societe d'Equipement Rural et Industriel d'Afrique Occidentale
SERIC .... Societe d'Etudes et de Realisation pour l'Industrie Cafeiere et Cacaoyere
SERIC ...... Societe pour l'Exploitation de Representations Industrielles et Commerciales

SERICC..... Societe d'Etudes et de Recherches pour l'Industrie et le Commerce Camerounais
SERICODI ... Societe d'Etudes et de Realisations Industrielles de Cote-D'Ivoire
SERIM ...... Societe d'Etudes et de Realisations Industrielles Modernes
SERI-RENAULT ENGINEERING ... Societe d'Etudes et de Realisations Industrielles Renault-Engineering
SERIWA ... Solar Energy Research Institute, Western Australia
SERIX .... Swedish Environmental Research Index [Swedish National Environmental Protection Board] [Database]   (IID)
SERM........ Sociedad Espanola de Radiologia y Electrologia Medicas y de Medicina Nuclear [Spanish]   (SLS)
SERM........ Societe d'Etudes et de Recherches Minieres de Madagascar [Mining Studies and Prospecting Company of Madagascar]   (AF)
Serma........ Serenisima [Most Serene] [Spanish]
SERMAN ... Societe d'Exploitation et de Recherches Minieres dans l'Afrique du Nord
SERMENA ... Servicio Medico Nacional de Empleados [National Employees Medical Service] [Chile]   (LA)
SERMI ...... Societe d'Etudes et de Realisations Minieres et Industrielles
SERMIS ... Societe d'Etudes et de Recherches Minieres du Senegal
Sermo........ Serenisimo [Most Serene] [Spanish]
SERNAGEOMIN ... Servicio Nacional de Geologia y Mineria [National Geology and Mining Service] [Chile] [Research center]   (IRC)
SERNAM ... Service National des Messageries [France]   (PDAA)
SERNAP ... Servicio Nacional de Pesca [Chile]   (ASF)
Sernatur ..... Servicio Nacional de Turismo [National Tourism Service] [Chile]   (GEA)
SERO......... Santa Rosa [Ecuador] [ICAO location identifier]   (ICLI)
SEROA...... Societe Algerienne d'Etudes et de Realisation d'Ouvrages d'Art [Algeria]   (IMH)
SERO-EST ... Societe d'Etudes et de Realisation d'Ouvrages d'Art de l'Est [Algeria]   (IMH)
SEROR...... Societe d'Etudes et de Realisation d'Ouvrages d'Art de l'Ouest [Algeria]   (IMH)
SERP .... Sindicato de Educadores de la Revolucion Peruana [Union of Educators of the Peruvian Revolution]   (LA)
SERP .... Syndicat de l'Enseignement de la Region Parisienne   (FLAF)
SERPAJ ... Servicio Paz y Justicia [Chile]   (EAIO)
SERPAJ .... Servicio Paz y Justicia en America Latina [Justice and Peace Service in Latin America] [Brazil]
SERPAL.... Servicio Radiofonico para America Latina [Radio Service for Latin America] [Costa Rica]   (LA)
SERPAR.... Servicio de Parques [Park Service] [Peru]   (LA)
SERPED.... Service d'Etudes et de Recherches Pedagogiques pour les Pays en Voie de Developpement
serpr.......... Serprent [Offprint, Separate] [Publishing Danish/Norwegian]
SERPRO ... Servico Federal de Processamento de Dados [Federal Data Processing Service] [Brazil]   (LA)
SE/RRT..... Southern Europe - Railroad Transport [NATO]   (NATG)
SERS .... Rio Saloya [Ecuador] [ICAO location identifier]   (ICLI)
sers............ Sersant [Sergeant] [Afrikaans]
SERS-MAJ ... Sersant-Majoor [Sergeant Major] [Afrikaans]
SERST....... Secretariat d'Etat a la Recherche Scientifique
SERT .... Sertifikaat [Certificate] [Afrikaans]
SE/RT .... Southern Europe - Road Transport [NATO]   (NATG)
SERT .... State Enterprise for River Transport [Iraq]
SERT .... Systeme d/Enregistreurs sur Reseau Telephonique [French]   (ADPT)
SERTAF.... Services Techniques Africains Cote-D'Ivoire
SERTEC.... Societe d'Etudes et de Realisations Techniques
SERTECI .. Syndicat des Entreprises de Remorquage et de Transport par Eau de la Cote-D'Ivoire
SERTEL.... Servicios Telereservacios SA de CV [ICAO designator]   (FAAC)
SERTI........ Societe d'Etudes et de Realisations pour le Traitement de l'Information [German]   (ADPT)
SERTI........ Studio-Ecole de la Radiodiffusion Television Ivoirienne
SERTID..... Societe d'Etudes et de Realisation pour le Textile et les Industries Diverses
SERVIGAS ... Servicio de Gas a Domicilio [Colombia]   (COL)
SERVITEC ... Empresa de Servicios Tecnicos de Computacion [Enterprise for Technical Computation Services] [Cuba]   (LA)
SERVITECO ... Servicio Tecnico y Comercial Ltda. [Pereira]   (COL)
SERVIVENSA ... Empresa Servicicious Avensa SA [Venezuela] [ICAO designator]   (FAAC)
servo.......... Servicio [Service] [Spanish]
servor .... Servidor [Servant] [Spanish]
Serv Soc ..... Le Service Social [Benelux]   (BAS)
SERY .... Sarayacu [Ecuador] [ICAO location identifier]   (ICLI)
serzh.......... Sergeant   (RU)
SES .... Butt Resistance Electric Welding   (RU)
SES .... Medical Epidemiological Station   (BU)
SES .... Samarbetsorganisationen for Emballagefragor i Skandinavien [Scandinavian Packaging Association] [Sweden]   (EA)

SES .... Sanitarno Epidemioloske Stanice [*Sanitary Epidemic Stations*] (YU)
SES .... Sanitary and Epidemiological Station (RU)
SES .... Sekretaris [*Secretary*] (IN)
SES .... Senior Executive Service [*Australia*]
SES .... Senior Experten Service [*Germany*] (EAIO)
SES .... Servicio Especial de Seguridad [*Special Security Police*] [*Bolivia*]
SES .... Ship Earth Station [*INMARSAT*]
SES .... Societe Europeenne des Satellites [*Luxembourg*]
SES .... Solar Energy Society [*Australia*] (PDAA)
SES .... Special Exploitation Service [*South Vietnamese studies and observations group*] [*Military*] (VNW)
SES .... Standardliste Eisen und Stahl [*Standard List for Iron and Steel Products*] (EG)
SES .... Station Operating Department [*Railroads*] (RU)
SES .... Stock Exchange of Singapore
SES .... Studies and Expansion Society [*See also SEE*] (EAIO)
SES .... Sumska Eksperimentalna Stanica [*Forestry Experiment Station*] [*Erdelija*] (YU)
SES .... Suomen Egyptologinen Seura [*Finland*] (SLS)
SES .... Sydney Esperanto Society [*Australia*]
SES .... Syndesmos Ethnikofronon Somateion [*or Synomospondia Ethnikon Somaton*] [*League of Nationalist Associations or League of Nationalist Groups Cyprus*] (GC)
SES .... Syndicat des Enseignants du Senegal [*Teachers Union of Senegal*] (AF)
SESA .... Salinas [*Ecuador*] [*ICAO location identifier*] (ICLI)
SESA .... Societe d'Etudes des Systemes d'Automation [*French*]
SESA .... Software et Engineering des Systemes d'Informatique et d'Automatique [*French*] (ADPT)
SESA .... Standard Electrica, Sociedad Anonima [*Brazilian affiliate of ITT*]
SESAC ...... Society of European Stage Authors and Composers
SESAF ...... Societe Anonyme pour les Echanges entre la Suisse et l'Afrique
SESAM ..... Symbolische Eingabesprache fuer Automatische Mess-Systeme [*German*] (ADPT)
SESAM ..... Symbolisches Eingabesystem fuer Anweisungen bei Multiprogramming [*German*] (ADPT)
SESAM ..... Systeme Electronique de Selection Automatique de Microfilms
SESAME... Systeme d'Etudes pour un Schema d'Amenagement [*French*]
SESB .... Sibambe [*Ecuador*] [*ICAO location identifier*] (ICLI)
SESC .... Saudi Eastern Shipping Co.
SESC .... Servico Social do Comercio [*Commercial Social Service*] [*Brazil*] (LA)
SESC .... Sucua [*Ecuador*] [*ICAO location identifier*] (ICLI)
SESCO ..... Sarawak Electricity Supply Corporation (ML)
SESCO ..... Societe Europeenne des Semiconducteurs [*France*] (PDAA)
SESCYP.... Societe d'Exploitation des Salons de Coiffure Yetty et Patricia
SESD .... Santo Domingo De Los Colorados [*Ecuador*] [*ICAO location identifier*] (ICLI)
SESDA ...... Secretariat de Sante Dentaire de l'Afrique
SESE .... Secadal [*Educador*] [*ICAO location identifier*] (ICLI)
SESEP....... Societe d'Etudes et de Soins pour les Enfants Paralyses [*French*] (SLS)
SESG .... Sangay [*Ecuador*] [*ICAO location identifier*] (ICLI)
SESG .... Southern Europe Shipping Group [*NATO*] (NATG)
SESH........ San Honorato [*Ecuador*] [*ICAO location identifier*] (ICLI)
SESI.......... Servico Social da Industria [*Industrial Social Service*] [*Brazil*] (LA)
SESI .... Solar Energy Society of Ireland [*International Solar Energy Society*]
SESI.......... Sur Iliniza [*Ecuador*] [*ICAO location identifier*] (ICLI)
SESIM....... Secours Social aux Invalides Militaires [*Social Aid for Disabled Military Personnel*] [*Cambodia*] (CL)
SESIN .... Service Central de Surete des Installations Nucleaires [*Nuclear Installation Central Safety Service*] [*French*] (WER)
SESJ .... San Jose [*Ecuador*] [*ICAO location identifier*] (ICLI)
SESK .... Silok [*Ecuador*] [*ICAO location identifier*] (ICLI)
SESKO ...... Suomen Sahkoteknillinen Standardisoimisyhdistys [*Finnish Electro-technical Standards Association*] (EAIO)
SESKOABRI ... Sekolah Staf dan Komando Angkatan Bersendjata Republik Indonesia [*Republic of Indonesia Armed Forces Staff and Command School*] (IN)
SESL.......... San Lorenzo [*Ecuador*] [*ICAO location identifier*] (ICLI)
SESM .... Samborondon [*Ecuador*] [*ICAO location identifier*] (ICLI)
SESM .... Special-Purpose Electronic Computer (RU)
SESMD ..... Sudan Stock Exchange and Securities Market Developments
SESN .... San Carlos [*Ecuador*] [*ICAO location identifier*] (ICLI)
SESO .... La Estrella [*Ecuador*] [*ICAO location identifier*] (ICLI)
SESO .... Studiecentrum voor Economisch en Sociaal Onderzoek [*Center for Economic and Social Research*] [*University of Antwerp*] [*Research center*] [*Belgium*] (IRC)
SESP.......... Servicio Especial de Salud Publica [*Special Public Health Service*] [*Guatemala*] (LAA)
SESP.......... Servico Especial de Saude Publica [*Special Public Health Service*] [*Brazil*] (LA)
SESR .... Esperantists' Union of Soviet Republics (RU)

SESR .... San Rafael [*Ecuador*] [*ICAO location identifier*] (ICLI)
SESR .... Societe Europeenne de Sociologie Rurale [*Germany*] (DSCA)
SESRTCIC ... Statistical, Economic, and Social Research and Training Center for Islamic Countries [*Research center*] [*Turkey*] (IRC)
SESS......... Secretaria de Estado de Seguridad Social [*Argentina*] (LAA)
SESSA ...... Solar Energy Society of Southern Africa (AA)
Sessh........ Sesshaftigkeit [*Persistency*] [*German*] (GCA)
SESSIA ..... Societe d'Etudes, de Constructions de Souffleries, Simulateurs et Instrumentation Aerodynamique [*France*] (PDAA)
SEST .... San Cristobal (Galapagos) [*ICAO location identifier*] (ICLI)
SEST .... Swedish-ESO Submillimetre Telescope [*Observatory*]
SESTICOM ... South Easterners Scientific and Technical Information Consortium of Melbourne [*Australia*]
SESTICON ... South Eastern Scientific and Technical Information Consortium [*Australia*]
SESTM...... Societe Europeenne de la Science et de la Technologie des Membranes [*European Society of Membrane Science and Technology - ESMST*] (EA)
SESUAM .. Societe d'Etudes Sucrieres en Afrique et a Madagascar
SESUCHARI ... Societe d'Etudes Sucrieres du Chari
SESUHV... Societe d'Etudes Sucrieres de Haute-Volta
SESY .... Sur Cayambe [*Ecuador*] [*ICAO location identifier*] (ICLI)
SESZ .... Sur Antizana [*Ecuador*] [*ICAO location identifier*] (ICLI)
SET........... Aircraft Electric Tachometer (RU)
SET........... Securities Exchange of Thailand
SET........... Sekretariat [*Secretariat*] (IN)
set............. Setembro [*September*] [*Portuguese*] (GPO)
SET........... Skholai Ekpaidevseos Tekhniton [*Technicians Training Schools*] [*Greek*] (GC)
SET........... Sociedad Ecuatoriana de Transportes Aereos Ltda. [*Ecuador*] [*ICAO designator*] (FAAC)
SET........... Societa Esercizi Telefoni [*Telephone Company*] [*Italian*]
SET........... Societe d'Entreprises de Transport et de Transit [*Burkina Faso*]
SET........... Societe d'Etudes et de Travaux Topographiques
SET........... South East Trawl [*Australia*]
SET........... Standard d'Exchange et de Transfert [*Computer graphics*] [*French*]
SET........... Suboticki Elektricni Tramvaj [*Subotica Electric Streetcar*] (YU)
SET........... System Entwicklungs-Techniken [*German*] (ADPT)
SETA .... Sociedad Tecnica Agropecuaria Ltda. [*Bucaramanga*] (COL)
SETA .... Societa Esercizi Telefonici Ausiliari [*Italy*] (PDAA)
SETA .... Societe d'Equipements Techniques et Automobiles
SETA .... Societe des Ets. Tanoh
SETA .... Societe d'Etudes Topographiques Africaines
SETA .... Societe Electronique Africaine
SETA .... Taura [*Ecuador*] [*ICAO location identifier*] (ICLI)
SETAC ...... Syndicat des Entrepreneurs de Batiments, Travaux Publics, et Activites Connexes de la Republique du Congo
SETACI..... Societe Ivoirienne d'Equipements Techniques et Automobiles
SETAF....... Southern European Task Force [*NATO*]
SETAF....... Southern European Task Forces [*NATO powers headquarters in Italy*]
SETAM ..... Societe d'Etudes et de Travaux d'Art du Maroc
SETAO...... Societe d'Etudes et de Travaux pour l'Afrique de l'Ouest [*Ivoirian*]
SETAO...... Societe d'Etudes et de Travaux pour l'Afrique Occidentale
SETAP ...... Societe pour l'Etude Technique d'Amenagement Planifie
SETA-UITA ... Syndicat Europeen des Travailleurs de l'Alimentation, de l'Hotellerie, et des Branches Connexes dans l'UITA [*European Committee of Food, Catering, and Allied Workers' Unions within the IUF - ECF-IUF*] (EAIO)
SETB .... Timbre [*Ecuador*] [*ICAO location identifier*] (ICLI)
SETBOG ... Syndicat des Exploitants et Transformateurs du Bois de Guyane [*Trade Union of Growers and Processors of the French Guianese Forest*] (LA)
SETCA ...... Societe d'Etudes pour le Tourisme en Casamance
SETCA ...... Syndicat des Employes Techniciens et Cadres [*Technical Employees and Cadres Trade Union*] [*Belgium*] (WER)
SETCI....... Societe d'Extrusion et de Tissage de Cote-D'Ivoire
SETCO ...... Societe d'Editions Techniques Coloniales
sete .... Setiembre [*September*] [*Spanish*]
SETE .... Tena [*Ecuador*] [*ICAO location identifier*] (ICLI)
SETEC....... Societe d'Etudes Techniques et de Coordination du Batiment
SETEC....... Societe d'Etudes Techniques et Economiques [*Technical and Economic Studies Company*] [*French*] (AF)
SETEF....... Societe d'Etudes Economiques et Financieres
SETEGA ... Servicios Tecnicos y Ganaderos [*Colombia*] (COL)
SETEL....... Societe Europeenne de Teleguidage [*France*] (PDAA)
SETELEC ... Societe d'Etudes et Travaux d'Electricite
SETEM ...... Societe d'Etudes et de Travaux Electromecaniques
SETEM ..... Syndesmos Ergolipton Tekhnikon Ergon Makedonias [*Association of Macedonia Technical Projects Contractors*] (GC)
SETEN ...... Secretariat d'Etat Tunisien a l'Education Nationale
SETER ...... Societe d'Etudes et de Travaux pour l'Electronique et la Radio

SETETh .... Syndesmos Ergolipton Tekhnikon Ergon Thessalonikis [*Association of Salonica Technical Projects Contractors*] (GC)
SETFIA ..... South East Trawl Fishing Industry Association [*Australia*]
SETG .... Tenguel [*Ecuador*] [*ICAO location identifier*] (ICLI)
SETH. .... Societe d'Etudes et de Travaux Hydrauliques
SETH. .... Taisha [*Ecuadaor*] [*ICAO location identifier*] (ICLI)
SETHEM ... Societe d'Etudes Hydrauliques, Electriques, et Mecaniques
SETI .... Service d'Etudes et Travaux d'Infrastructure [*Infrastructure Studies and Construction Service*] [*Algeria*] (AF)
SETI .... Societe d'Exploitation des Techniques Industrielles [*Industrial Techniques Exploitation Company*] [*Tunisia*] (AF)
SETI .... Societe Europeenne pour le Traitement de l'Information [*European Society for the Processing of Information*]
SETI .... Tiputini [*Ecuador*] [*ICAO location identifier*] (ICLI)
SETIA .... Sindicato de Empleados Textiles de la Industria y Afines de la Republica Argentina [*Union of Employees of the Textile and Related Industries of the Argentine Republic*] (LA)
SETIC .... Societe d'Etudes des Industries du Ciment [*Senegal*]
SETIF .... Societe d'Etudes Techniques Industrielles et Frigorifiques
SETIM ...... Service des Equipements et des Techniques Instrumentales de la Meteorologie [*Meteorology Technology and Materials Center*] [*France*] (EAS)
SETIM ...... Societe d'Etudes et de Coordination Industrielle Marocaine [*Moroccan Industrial Studies and Coordination Company*] (AF)
SETIMEG ... Societe Anonyme d'Etudes, de Travail Immobilier, et de Gestion
SETIS .... Societe Europeenne pour l'Etude et l'Integration des Systemes Spatiaux [*France*] (PDAA)
SETM .... Societe d'Etudes et de Travaux Mecanographiques
SETMAC .. South East Trawl Fishery Management Advisory Committee [*Australia*]
Set'mash .... Khar'kov Electrical Network and Installation Machinery Plant (RU)
SETMC ..... Societe d'Etudes Topographiques Maffone & Cie.
SETO. .... Pacto [*Ecuador*] [*ICAO location identifier*] (ICLI)
S et O .... Seine-et-Oise (FLAF)
seto .... Setembro [*September*] [*Portuguese*]
SETOM. .... Societe d'Etudes de Travaux d'Outre-Mer [*Overseas Projects Studies Company*] [*French*] (AF)
SETOP ...... Secretaria de Transporte y Obras Publicas [*Secretariat of Transportation and Public Works*] [*Argentina*] (LA)
SETP .... Tandapi [*Ecuador*] [*ICAO location identifier*] (ICLI)
SETPI .... Society of Engineers and Technicians of the Paper Industry [*Samoa*] (EAIO)
SETR .... Societe d'Expansion et de Transformation des Resines
SETR .... Tarapoa [*Ecuador*] [*ICAO location identifier*] (ICLI)
SETRA ...... Service d'Etudes Techniques des Routes et Autoroutes [*Road and Motorway Study Department*] [*French*]
SETRA ...... Societe d'Etudes et de Travaux
SETRABES ... Secretaria do Trabalho e Bem Estar Social [*Brazil*]
SETRA-Congo ... Societe d'Etudes et de Travaux au Congo
SETRAPEM ... Societe Equatoriale de Travaux Petroliers Maritimes
sett. .... Settembre [*September*] [*Italian*]
SETT .... Societe d'Exploitation de Transports et de Taxis
SETT .... Teniente Ortiz [*Ecuador*] [*ICAO location identifier*] (ICLI)
SETTAO ... Syndicat des Entrepreneurs de Transports et Transitaires de l'Afrique Occidentale
SETTD ...... Syndicat des Entrepreneurs de Transport et Transitaires de Dakar
SETTE. ...... Societe d'Entreprise de Travaux Topographiques et d'Edition
SETU .... Societe d'Equipement des Terrains Urbains [*Ivory Coast*]
SETU .... Societe d'Etudes et de Travaux pour l'Uranium [*Nuclear energy*] [*French*] (NRCH)
SETU. .... Tulcan [*Ecuador*] [*ICAO location identifier*] (ICLI)
SETUBA ... Societe d'Etudes et de Travaux pour l'Utilisation du Beton Arme
SETUBA-Bangui ... Societe d'Etudes et de Travaux pour l'Utilisation du Beton Arme en Oubangui
SETUBA-Cameroun ... Societe d'Etudes et de Travaux pour l'Utilisation du Beton Arme en Cameroun
SETUBA-TCHAD ... Societe d'Etudes et de Travaux pour l'Utilisation du Beton Arme au Tchad
SETUFCO ... Sindicato de Empleados y Trabajadores de la United Fruit Co. [*Guatemala*] (DSCA)
SETUG ...... Societe d'Etudes et de Gestion [*North African*]
setzag .... Netlayer [*Navy*] (RU)
SEU .... Servicio de Extension Universitaria [*Paraguay*] (LAA)
SEU .... Sindicato Espanol Universitario [*Spanish University Union*] (WER)
SEU .... Sociedad Editorial Uruguaya [*Uruguayan Publishing Society*] (LA)
SEU .... Socio-Ecological Union (EAIO)
SEU .... Studia Ethnographica Upsaliensia
seud .... Seudonimo [*Pseudonym*] [*Spanish*]
SEUL .... Servicio Europeo de Universitarios Latinoamericanos [*Belgium*]
seul .... Seulement [*Only*] [*French*]
SE u O .... Salvo Error u Omision [*Errors or Omissions Excepted*] [*Spanish*]

seur .... Seuraava [*Following, Next*] [*Finland*] (GPO)
SEURECA ... Societe d'Etudes pour l'Urbanisme, l'Equipement, et les Canalisations
SEURMAD ... Societe d'Equipement Urbain et Rural de Madagascar
SEUSS. .... Sociedad de Estudiantes Universitarios San Salvador [*Association of San Salvador University Students*] [*El Salvador*] (LA)
SEUY .... Chanduy [*Ecuador*] [*ICAO location identifier*] (ICLI)
SEV .... Council for Mutual Economic Assistance [*CMEA*] (RU)
SEV .... Northern Railroad (RU)
Sev. .... North, Northern (RU)
SEV .... Schweizerischer Elektrotechnischer Verein [*Swiss Electrotechnical Association*]
SEV .... Sekundaer-Elektronvervielfacher [*Secondary Electron Emission Multiplier*] (EG)
sev .... Severen [*Northern*] (YU)
SEV .... Slovenske Energeticke Vyrobne [*Slovak Electric Power Producing Plants*] (CZ)
SEV .... Societe d'Ethologie Veterinaire [*Society for Veterinary Ethology - SVE*] [*Edinburgh, Scotland*] (EAIO)
SEV .... Societe d'Exploitation de Viandes
SEV .... Soviet Ekonomicheskoj Vzaimopomshchi [*Council for Mutual Economic Assistance - CMEA*] [*Former USSR*] (ASF)
SEV .... Srednje Evropsko Vreme [*Middle European Time*] (YU)
SEV .... Statens Energiverk [*National Energy Board*] [*Sweden*] (WED)
SEV .... Swiss Electrotechnical Association (EAIO)
SEV .... Syndesmos Ellinon Viomikhanon [*Association of Greek Industrialists*] (GC)
SEVA .... Valdez [*Ecuador*] [*ICAO location identifier*] (ICLI)
SEVAP ...... Syndesmos Ergaton Vyrsodepson Athinon-Peiraios [*Union of Athens-Piraeus Tannery Workers*] (GC)
Sev Dobr .... North Dobrudzha (BU)
Sevdvinlag ... Northern Dvina Corrective Labor Camp (RU)
SEVE .... (Pankypria) Syndekhnia Emborikon kai Viomikhanikon Ergatoypallilon [*(Pan-Cyprian) Union of Commercial and Industrial Workers*] [*Cyprus*] (GC)
SEVE .... Syndesmos Ergatotekhniton Viomikhanias Elastikou [*Union of Rubber Industry Workers and Technicians*] [*Greek*] (GC)
SEVEGEP ... Synergatiki Etaireia Viomikhanikis Epexergasias Agrotikis Paragogis [*Cooperative Company for Industrial Processing of Agricultural Produce*] [*Cyprus*] (GC)
Severenergo ... Northern Power Administration (BU)
SEVI .... Villano [*Ecuador*] [*ICAO location identifier*] (ICLI)
SEVIMA ... Societe d'Exploitation de la Viande a Madagascar
Sev-Kav ..... North Caucasian (RU)
Sevl O S ..... Sevlievo Oblast Court (BU)
Sevmorbaza ... Sevastopol' Naval Base (RU)
Sevmorput' ... Northern Sea Route (RU)
Sevmorzavod ... Sevastopol' Shipyard (RU)
SEVN .... Vinces [*Ecuador*] [*ICAO location identifier*] (ICLI)
SevNIIGiM ... Northern Scientific Research Institute of Hydraulic Engineering and Reclamation (RU)
SevNIIGM ... Northern Scientific Research Institute of Hydraulic Engineering and Reclamation (RU)
SevNIIP ..... Northern Scientific Research Industrial Institute (RU)
SEVOL ...... Societe d'Equipement de la Haute-Volta
SEVOP ...... Syndesmos Ellinon Viomikhanon Oinon kai Poton [*Association of Greek Industrialists of Wines and Beverages*] (GC)
SEVSA ...... Sonenergie Vereniging van Suidelike Afrika [*Solar Energy Society of Southern Africa*] (AA)
SEVT .... Statisticke a Evidencni Vydavatelstvi Tiskopisu [*Publishing House for Statistical and Record Forms*] (CZ)
SEVT .... Ventanas [*Ecuador*] [*ICAO location identifier*] (ICLI)
Sevurallag .. Northern Ural Corrective Labor Camps (RU)
sev-vost ...... Northeast, Northeastern (RU)
Sevvostlag. .. Northeastern Corrective Labor Camps (RU)
sev-zap .... Northwest, Northwestern (RU)
Sevzapgiprogorsel'stroy ... Northwestern State Planning Institute for the Planning of Urban and Rural Construction (RU)
SEVZAPPROYeKTPORTIZ ... Administration for the Study and Planning of the Northern and Western Ports (RU)
Sevzaptransles ... Northwestern Lumber Transportation Trust (RU)
Sevzheldorlag ... Northern Railroad Corrective Labor Camp (RU)
SEW .... Sociaal-Economische Wetgeving [*Netherlands*] [*Benelux*] (BAS)
SEW .... Societe des Etablissements Wanner
SEW .... Sozialistische Einheitspartei Westberlins [*Socialist Unity Party of West Berlin*] [*Germany*] [*Political party*] (PPW)
SEWA .... Self Employed Women's Association [*India*] (EAIO)
SEWMRPG ... Southern European Western Mediterranean Regional Planning Group [*NATO*] (NATG)
SEWURG ... State Enterprise Worker Unions Relations Group [*Thailand*]
S Exa .... Sua Excelencia [*Your Excellence*] [*Portuguese*]
S ExaRevma ... Sua Excelencia Reverendissima [*Your Most Reverend Excellence*] [*Portuguese*]
S Exc. .... Son Excellence [*His, or Her, Excellency*] [*French*] (CL)
S Excia .... Sua Excelencia [*His, or Her, Excellency*] [*Portuguese*]

SEXENA ... Sociedad de Exalumnos de la Escuela Nacional de Agricultura [*El Salvador*]   (DSCA)

s expr........ Sine Expressione [*Without Expressing*] [*Latin*]   (MAE)

SEXV .... Syndesmos Ergodoton Xylourgikis Viomichanias [*Cyprus*] (EAIO)

SEY .... Air Seychelles [*ICAO designator*]   (FAAC)

SEY .... Selibaby [*Mauritania*] [*Airport symbol*]   (OAG)

SEYA .... Yaupi [*Ecuador*] [*ICAO location identifier*]   (ICLI)

SEYCO .... Seleccion y Comercio de Patata SA [*Spain*]   (DSCA)

SEYCOM ... Seychelles National Commodity Company

SEYD .... Subay Esleri Yardimlasma Dernegi [*Officers Wives Mutual Aid Society*]   (TU)

SEYET .... Syndikalistiki Enotita Ypallilon Ethnikis Trapezis [*Syndicalist Unity of National Bank Employees*] [*Greek*]   (GC)

Seynic........ Seychelles National Investment Corporation   (GEA)

SEYTIM.... Seychelles Timber Co.

Seytour....... Seychelles Tourist Board   (GEA)

SEZ .... Mahe Island [*Seychelles Islands*] [*Airport symbol*]   (OAG)

Sez............. Sezione [*Division*] [*Italian*]   (ILCA)

SEZ .... Slovenske Elektrotechnicke Zavody [*Slovak Electrical Equipment Plants*]   (CZ)

SEZ .... Special Economic Zones [*China*]   (TCC)

SEZA .... Zamora [*Ecuador*] [*ICAO location identifier*]   (ICLI)

SEZb .... Srpski Etnografski Zbornik [*Serbian Ethnographic Papers*] [*Issued by the Serbian Academy*]   (YU)

SEZEB...... Societe d'Ethnozoologie et d'Ethnobotanique [*French*]   (SLS)

SEZID .... Societe d'Equipement des Zones d'Industrialisation Decentralisee [*Decentralized Industrialization Area Equipment Company*] [*French*]   (WER)

SEZP .... Zumba-Pucupamba [*Ecuador*] [*ICAO location identifier*]   (ICLI)

SF .... Northern Fleet   (RU)

SF .... Photon Counter   (RU)

SF .... Provisional Sinn Fein [*Northern Ireland*] [*Political party*] (PPW)

SF .... Sameignarfelag [*Partnership*] [*Icelandic*]   (CED)

SF .... Samfundet Folkhalsan [*Finland*]   (EAIO)

SF .... Sans Frais [*Without Cost*] [*French*]

sf............... Sauerstoffrei [*Oxygen-Free*] [*German*]   (GCA)

SF .... Scheibe-Flugzeugbau GmbH [*Germany*] [*ICAO aircraft manufacturer identifier*]   (ICAO)

SF .... Security Forces [*Malaysia*]   (ML)

s/f............. Seu Favor [*Your Favor*] [*Portuguese*]

Sf.............. Sforzando [*With Additional Accent*] [*Music*]

SF .... Shanghai Foodstuffs Branch [*of China National Cereals, Oils & Foodstuffs Import/Export Corp.*]

SF .... Sicherungs- und Fernmeldewesen [*Protective Devices and Telecommunications*] [*SFW, SuF*] [*See also*]   (EG)

sf............... Sin Fecha [*No Date*] [*Spanish*]

SF .... Slovenska Filharmonia [*Slovak Philharmonic Orchestra*]   (CZ)

SF .... Socialist Front [*Malaysia*]   (ML)

SF .... Socialistisk Folkeparti [*Socialist People's Party*] [*Denmark*] (WEN)

SF .... Soma Frondiston [*Quartermaster Corps*]   (GC)

SF .... Sosialistisk Folkepartiet [*Socialist People's Party*] [*Norway*] [*Political party*]   (PPE)

SF .... Sosialokonomenes Forening [*Norway*]   (EAIO)

SF .... Soviet Fleet   (RU)

SF .... Spectrophotometer   (RU)

SF .... Sport Fotanacs [*Main Sports Council*]   (HU)

SF .... State Forces [*India*] [*Army*]

SF .... Statni Filharmonie [*State Philharmonic*]   (CZ)

SF .... Statsantaelldas Foerbund [*Trade union*] [*Sweden*]

SF .... Sunbird [*Airline code*] [*Australia*]

SF .... Svenska Fornminnesforeningen [*Sweden*]   (EAIO)

SF .... Sveriges Fredsraad [*Sweden*]   (EAIO)

SF .... Sveriges Skolledarforbund [*Sweden*]   (EAIO)

SF .... Swiss Franc [*Monetary unit*]

SF .... Systeme Francais [*French System*]

SF2M........ Societe Francaise de Metallurgie et de Materiaux [*France*] (EAIO)

SFA .... Aerotransportes Entre Rios SRL [*Argentina*] [*ICAO designator*] (FAAC)

SFA .... Sarawak Farmers Association (Communist)   (ML)

SFA .... Sfax [*Tunisia*] [*Airport symbol*]   (OAG)

SFA .... Socialist Federation of Australasia [*or Australia*]   (ADA)

SFA .... Societe Forestiere d'Azingo

SFA .... Societe Francaise d'Acoustique [*French Society of Acoustics - FSA*]   (EAIO)

SFA .... Societe Francaise d'Angeiologie [*France*]   (EAIO)

SFA .... Societe Francaise d'Archeologie [*French Society of Archeology*] (SLS)

SFA .... Societe Francaise d'Astronautique [*France*]

SFA .... Soviet Philatelic Association   (RU)

SFA .... Sudan Football Association

SFA .... Swedish Foundries' Association   (EAIO)

SFA .... Swiss Football Association   (EAIO)

SFAB .... Societe Franco-Africaine des Bois

SFAB .... Svenska Flygmotor AB [*Swedish Airplane Motor Corp.*]   (WEN)

SFAC .... Societe des Forges et Ateliers du Creusot [*French*]

SFAD .... Societe Forestiere Andre Desbrosses

SFADECO ... Societe Franco-Africaine d'Expansion Commerciale

SFAE .... Societe Franco-Africaine d'Exploitation

SFAE .... Swiss Federation for Adult Education   (EAIO)

SFAF .... Societe Francaise des Analystes Financiers [*French*]   (SLS)

SFAG .... Societe Financiere et Auxiliaire de Gestion

SFAG .... Societe Forestiere et Agricole du Gabon

SFAHD..... Society of the Friends of Ancient and Historical Dubrovnik [*Croatia*]   (EAIO)

SFAI .... Steel Furnace Association of India   (PDAA)

SFAK .... Selskabet for Analytisk Kemi [*Denmark*]   (SLS)

SFAL .... Societe Forestiere Africaine de la Louali

SFAL .... Stanley Airport [*Falkland Islands*] [*ICAO location identifier*] (ICLI)

SFAM .... Syndicat Francais de l'Aquaculture Marine [*France*]   (EAIO)

SFA-PP..... Slovenian Farmers' Association - People's Party   (EY)

SFAR .... Societe Francaise d'Anesthesie et de Reanimation [*France*] (EAIO)

SFAS .... Schweizerischer Fachverband fuer Schweiss- und Schneidmaterial [*Swiss association*]   (SLS)

sfasc......... Sfasciato [*Loosened*] [*Italian*]

SFAT .... Societe Franco-Africaine de Transports

SFB .... Air Sofia [*Bulgaria*] [*ICAO designator*]   (FAAC)

SfB .... Samarbetskommitten for Byggnadsfragor [*Cooperative Committee for the Building Industry*] [*Sweden*]   (PDAA)

SFB .... Sea Fisheries Branch [*South Africa*]   (MSC)

SFB .... Sender Freies Berlin [*Radio Free Berlin*]   (WEN)

SFB .... Sonderforschungsbereiche [*German*]

SFBC .... Societe Francaise de Biologie Clinique

SFBL .... Societe Forestiere Bertrand-Lupo

SFBO .... Societe Forestiere du Bas-Ogooue

SFBP .... Society Francaise des Petroles BP

SFBS......... Spoleczny Fundusz Budowy Stolicy [*People's Fund for the Construction of Warsaw*]   (POL)

SFBS......... Spoleczny Fundusz Budowy Szkol [*Social School Construction Fund*]   (POL)

SFBSiI ...... Spoleczny Fundusz Budowy Szkol i Internatow [*Social Fund for the Construction of Schools and Boarding Schools*]   (POL)

SFBW .... Spoleczny Fundusz Budowy Warszawy [*People's Fund for the Construction of Warsaw*]   (POL)

SFC .... School Furniture Complex [*Department of Education, New South Wales*] [*Australia*]

SFC .... Securities and Futures Commission [*Hong Kong*]

SFC .... Societa Filosofica Calabrese [*Italian*]   (SLS)

SFC .... Societe Forestiere du Cameroun

SFC .... Societe Francaise de Ceramique [*French Society of Ceramics*] (SLS)

SFC .... Societe Francaise de Chimie [*French Chemical Society - FCS*] (EAIO)

SFC .... Societe Francaise de Cosmetologie [*French Society of Cosmetology*]   (SLS)

SFC .... Societe Frederic Chopin [*International Frederic Chopin Foundation*]   (EAIO)

SFC .... Society of Finnish Composers   (EAIO)

SFC .... State Farms Corporation [*India*]

SFC .... State Financial Corp. [*India*]   (PDAA)

SFC .... State Fishing Corp. [*Ghana*]

SFC .... Swiss Federation of Choirs   (EAIO)

SFC .... Towarzystwo imienia Fryderyka Chopina [*Poland*]   (EAIO)

SFCA .... Sudan Fertility Care Association   (EAIO)

SFCCI....... Singapore Federation of Chambers of Commerce and Industry

SFCE .... Societe Francaise du Commerce Europeen

SFCI .... State Farms Corp. of India   (PDAA)

SFCM .... Societe Francaise de Chronometrie et de Microtechnique [*French*]   (SLS)

SFCM .... Societe Francaise de Commerce a Madagascar

SFCN......... Societe Francaise de Construction Navales [*France*]   (PDAA)

SFCP .... Societe Francaise de Chirurgie Pediatrique [*French Society of Pediatric Surgery*]   (SLS)

SFCPR...... Societe Francaise de Chirurgie Plastique et Reconstructive [*French Society of Plastic and Reconstructive Surgery*] (SLS)

SFCT .... Societe Franco-Camerounaise des Tabacs

SFCT .... State Fire Commission of Tasmania [*Australia*]

SFCV .... State Film Centre of Victoria [*Australia*]

SFD .... Diffraction Spectrophotometer   (RU)

SFD .... San Fernando [*Venezuela*] [*Airport symbol*]   (OAG)

SFD .... Saudi Fund for Development   (IMH)

SFD .... Suore Francescane di Dillingen [*Sisters of St. Francis of Dillingen - SSFD*] [*Italy*]   (EAIO)

SFD .... Sydney Fire District [*Australia*]

SFDA .... Small Farmers' Development Agency [*India*]

SFDAS ...... Societe Francaise de Droit Aerien et Spatial [*French*]   (SLS)

SFDC........ Societe Financiere pour le Developpement du Cameroun

SF/DE/SKKE ... Sosialismos Filelevtheron/Dimokratiki Enosis/Sosialistiko Komma Kinima Ellados [*Liberals' Socialism/Democratic Union/Socialist Party Movement of Greece*] [*Greek*]   (GC)

SFDI......... Societe Francaise pour le Droit International [*French*]   (SLS)

SFDIC....... Societe Francaise des Distilleries d'Indochine [*French Distillery Company of Indochina*]   (CL)

SFDM........ Svetova Federace Demokraticke Mladeze [*World Federation of Democratic Youth*]   (CZ)

SFDO........ Svetska Federacija Demokratske Omladine [*World Federation of Democratic Youth*]   (YU)

SFDP......... Societe Francophone de Primatologie [*Francophone Primatological Society - FPS*] [*France*]   (EAIO)

SFDTUC ... Sarawak First Division Trade Union Congress   (ML)

SFDZ........ Svetova Federace Demokratickych Zen [*World Federation of Democratic Women*]   (CZ)

SFE........... Scottish Financial Enterprise

SFE........... Societe Financiere Europeenne

SFE........... Societe Francaise d'Egyptologie [*French Society of Egyptology*]   (SLS)

SFE........... Societe Francaise des Electriciens [*French*]

SFE........... Soviet Far East   (FEA)

SFE........... Sydney Futures Exchange [*Australia*]   (ADA)

SFEB........ Societe Francaise d'Etudes du Batiment

SFECCM... State Foreign Economic Commission of the Council of Ministers [*Former USSR*]

SFEDTP... Societe Francaise d'Entreprises de Dragages et de Travaux Publics

SFEE......... Societe Francaise d'Etudes pour l'Electricite [*French*]   (SLS)

SFEI.......... Servicio de Fomento de la Economia Indigena de la Direccion General de Investigacion y Extension Agricola [*Guatemala*]   (LAA)

SFEM........ Second-Tiered Foreign Exchange Market

SFEN........ Societe Francaise d'Energie Nucleaire [*Nuclear energy*] [*French*]   (NRCH)

SFENA...... Societe Francaise d'Equipement pour la Navigation Aerienne   (FLAF)

sfenoid....... Sphenoidal   (RU)

SFER........ Societe Francaise d'Economie Rurale [*French Society of Rural Economics*]   (SLS)

SFERMA... Societe Francaise d'Entretien et de Reparation de Materiel Aeronautique [*French*]

SFERT....... Systeme Fundamental Europeen de Reference pour la Transmission Telephonique [*European master telephone reference system*]

SFES......... Sindicato de Fotografos de El Salvador [*Union of Photographers of El Salvador*]   (LA)

SFF........... Santana Furniture Factory Ltd. [*Nigeria*]

SFF........... Science Fiction Foundation   (EA)

SFF........... Senior Firefighter [*Australia*]

SFF........... Skopski Filozofski Fakultet [*Faculty of Philosophy in Skopje*]   (YU)

SFF........... Sociedad de Fomento Fabril [*Chile*]   (LAA)

SFF........... Societa Filologica Friulana "G. I. Ascoli" [*Italian*]   (SLS)

SFF........... Society of Filipino Foresters   (DSCA)

SFF........... Staatlicher Futtermittelfonds [*State Fodder Fund*]   (EG)

SFF........... Svenska Folkbibliotekarie Foerbundet [*Swedish Public Library Association*]   (SLS)

SFF........... Svenska Forsakringsforeningen [*Sweden*]   (EAIO)

SFF........... Sveriges Farmacevtforbund [*Sweden*]   (EAIO)

SFF........... Swiss Footpaths Federation   (EAIO)

SFF........... Sydney Film Festival [*Australia*]

SFFA......... System der Fehlerfreien Arbeit [*System of Error-Free Work*]   (EG)

SFFAI....... Societe Francaise de Fournitures pour l'Automobile et l'Industrie

SFFF......... Scandinavian Association of Zone-Therapeutists [*Denmark*]   (EAIO)

SFFF......... Societas pro Fauna et Flora Fennica [*Finland*]   (SLS)

SFFL........ Svensk Foerening foer Foniatri och Logopedi [*Sweden*]   (SLS)

SFG.......... Societe Francaise de Gynecologie [*French Gynecological Association*]   (SLS)

SFG.......... Staatliches Forschungsinstitut fuer Geochemie [*State Research Institute of Geochemistry*] [*Germany*]   (WND)

SFG.......... St. Maarten [*Netherlands Antilles*] [*Airport symbol*]   (OAG)

SFG.......... Sudflug Suddeutsche Fluggesellschaft MbH [*Germany*] [*ICAO designator*]   (FAAC)

SFHM....... Societe Francaise d'Histoire de la Medecine [*French Society of Medical History*]   (SLS)

SFHOM.... Societe Francaise d'Histoire d'Outre-Mer [*French*]   (SLS)

SFI........... Savezni Finansiski Inspektorat (DSPF) [*Federal Financial Inspectorate*]   (YU)

SFI........... Silikose-Forschungsinstitut [*Silicosis Research Institute*] [*Germany*]   (EAS)

SFI........... Sindacato Ferrovieri Italiani [*Union of Italian Railroad Workers*]

SFI........... Skipsteknisk Forsknings Institutt [*Ship Research Institute*] [*Norway*]   (PDAA)

SFI........... Sky Freighters NV [*Belgium*] [*ICAO designator*]   (FAAC)

SFI........... Societa Filosofica Italiana [*Italian*]   (SLS)

SFI........... Societe de Froid et d'Importation

SFI........... Societe Financiere Internationale [*International Finance Corporation - IFC*] [*French*]   (CL)

SFI........... Societe Francaise d'Ichtyologie [*French*]   (SLS)

SFI........... Society of Friends of Icons [*Germany*]   (EAIO)

SFI........... Sports Federation of Israel   (EAIO)

SFI........... Stenindustrins Forskningsinstitut [*Swedish Stone Industry Research Institute*] [*Research center*]   (IRC)

SFIB.......... Syndicat National des Fabricants d'Ensembles de Information et des Machines de Bureau [*National Federation of Data Handling Equipment and Office Machines Manufacturers*] [*France*]   (PDAA)

SFIC........ Societe et Federation Internationale de Cardiologie [*International Society and Federation of Cardiology*] [*Switzerland*]   (EAIO)

SFIC........ Societe Francaise de l'Internationale Communiste [*Old French Communist Party*]   (FLAF)

SFID......... Section Francaise de l'Internationale Ouvriere [*French Section of the Workers International*]

SFID......... Societe Forestiere et Industrielle de la Doume [*Cameroon*]

SFIE......... Sociedad Feminina Israelita de Ecuador   (EAIO)

SFIM........ Societe de Fabrication d'Instruments de Mesure [*French*]

SFIO........ Section Francaise de l'Internationale Ouvriere [*French Section of the Workers International (French Socialist Party)*]   (WER)

SFIP......... Societe Francaise des Ingenieurs Plasticiens [*France*]

SFIT........ Societe Franco-Ivoirienne de Transports

SFIT........ Superannuation Fund Investment Trust [*Australia*]

SFIT........ Swiss Federal Institute of Technology   (IAA)

SFITV....... Societe Francaise des Ingenieurs et Techniciens Vide [*French Society of Vacuum Engineers and Technicians*]   (PDAA)

SFJ........... Savez Filatelista Jugoslavije [*Federation of Yugoslav Philatelists*]   (YU)

SFJ........... Sondre Stromfjord [*Greenland*] [*Airport symbol*]   (OAG)

SFJA......... Service de la Formation des Jeunes en Algerie

SFK........... Council of Physical Culture   (RU)

SFK........... Northern Fergana Canal   (RU)

SFK........... Rural Physical Culture Collective   (BU)

SFK........... Satelliten Fuellfaktor Klausel [*German*]   (ADPT)

SFK........... Savet za Fizicku Kulturu (SIV) [*Council on Physical Culture*]   (YU)

SFK........... Selbstfahrkanone [*Self-Propelled Gun*]   (EG)

SFK........... Sosyalist Fikir Klubu [*Socialist Idea Club*]   (TU)

SFKD........ Swiatowa Federacja Kobiet Demokratycznych [*Poland*]

SFKh.......... Collection of Regulations, Orders, and Instructions on Financial and Economic Problems   (RU)

SFKhV....... Collection of Regulations, Orders, and Instructions on Financial and Economic Problems   (RU)

SFKp......... Selbstfahrerlafettenkompanie [*Assault Gun Company*]   (EG)

SFL........... Sao Filipe [*Cape Verde Islands*] [*Airport symbol*]   (OAG)

SFL........... Selbstfahrlafette [*Self-Propelled Carriage (Self-propelled gun)*]   (EG)

SFL........... Southflight Aviation Ltd. [*New Zealand*] [*ICAO designator*]   (FAAC)

SFL........... Statens Forskingsstasjoner i Landbruk [*Norwegian State Agricultural Research Stations*] [*Research center*]   (IRC)

SFL........... Suomen Farmasialiitto [*Finland*]   (SLS)

SFL........... Svenska Facklaerarfoerbundet [*Swedish Teachers Association*]   (SLS)

SFL........... Svenska Finlands Laerarfoerbund [*Swedish Teachers Association of Finland*]   (SLS)

SFL........... Syndicat des Fonctionnaires du Laos [*Lao Government Employees Union*]   (CL)

SFLG........ Societe Forestiere du Lac Gome

SFLG........ Societe Forestiere du Littoral Gabonais

SFM.......... Signal- und Fernmeldemeisterei [*Signal and Telecommunications Group*]   (EG)

SFM.......... Societe Forestiere du Maine

SFM.......... Societe Francaise de Malacologie [*French*]   (SLS)

SFM.......... Societe Francaise de Mesotherapie [*French*]   (SLS)

SFM.......... Societe Francaise de Metallurgie [*French Society of Metallurgy*]   (PDAA)

SFM.......... Societe Francaise de Musicologie [*France*]   (EAIO)

SFM.......... Societe Francaise des Mecaniciens

SFM.......... Swedish Free Mission

SFM.......... Sydney Fund Managers Ltd. [*Australia*]

SFMANSW ... Stock Feed Manufacturers' Association of New South Wales [*Australia*]

SFMAQ..... Stock Feed Manufacturers' Association of Queensland [*Australia*]

SFMASA.... Stock Feed Manufacturers' Association of South Australia

SFMAV .... Stock Feed Manufacturers' Association of Victoria [*Australia*]

SFMAWA ... Stock Feed Manufacturers' Association of Western Australia

SFMB........ Swiatowa Federacja Miast Blizniaczych [*World Federation of Twin Cities*] [*Poland*]

SFMD........ Swiatowa Federacja Mlodziezy Demokratycznej [*World Federation of Democratic Youth*]   (POL)
SFMD........ Swiatowy Festiwal Mlodziezy Demokratycznej [*World Festival of Democratic Youth*]   (POL)
SFME........ Societe Francaise de Medecine Esthetique   (SLS)
SFME........ Societe Francaise de Microscopie Electronique [*French Society of Electron Microscopy*]   (SLS)
SFMex....... Sociedad Forestal de Mexico
SFMG........ Societe Francaise de Medecine Generale [*French Society of General Medicine*]   (SLS)
SFMI .... Societe Francaise de Moteurs a Induction [*France*]   (PDAA)
SFMK........ Societe Forestiere de Mouyondzi Kintouka
SFML .... Sydney Fish Markets Ltd. [*Australia*]
SFMO........ Societe Forestiere du Moyen Ogooue
SFMS .... Societe Forestiere du Maine-Senegal
SFMS .... Societe Francaise de Medecine du Sport [*French Society of Sports Medicine*]   (SLS)
SFMT .... Societe Francaise de Medecine du Trafic [*French*]   (SLS)
SFN........... Safiran Airlines [*Iran*] [*ICAO designator*]   (FAAC)
SFN........... Santa Fe [*Argentina*] [*Airport symbol*]   (OAG)
SFN........... Sistema Financiero Nacional [*National Financial System*] [*Nicaragua*]   (LA)
SFN........... Societe Forestiere du Niari
SFN........... Societe Francaise de Numismatique [*French*]   (SLS)
SFN........... Svenska FN-Forbundet [*Sweden*]   (EAIO)
SFNAe .... Societe Francaise de Navigation Aerienne [*France*]
SFNCTU ... Swiss Federation of National-Christian Trade Unions
SFND........ Societatea Franceza de Navigatie Danubiana [*French Society for Navigation of the Danube*]   (RO)
SFNG........ Societe Forestiere de la N'gounie
SFNI .... Suikerfabrieknavorsingsinstituut
SFNL .... Societe Forestiere du Nyong et Lobo
SFNO .... Sklad Fondu Narodni Obnovy [*Depot of the National Reconstruction Fund*]   (CZ)
SFO........... Seefrachtordnung [*Ocean Freight Regulation*]   (EG)
SFO........... Socialist Force Ouvriere [*French*]
SFO........... Societe Francaise d'Ophtalmologie [*French Society of Ophthalmology*]   (SLS)
SFO........... Societe Francaise d'Orchidophilie [*France*]   (EAIO)
SFO........... Spoleczny Fundusz Oszczedzania [*People's Savings Fund*]   (POL)
SFO........... Svenska Foreningen OIKOS [*Sweden*]   (EAIO)
SFO........... Svetova Federace Odboru [*World Federation of Trade-Unions*]   (CZ)
SFOA........ Societe Financiere de l'Ouest Africain [*Senegal*]
SFOA......... Spoudazousa Foititiki Organosis Athinon [*Athens Organization of Enrolled Students*]   (GC)
SF ofNSW ... Schizophrenia Fellowship of New South Wales [*Australia*]
sfogl........... Sfogliato [*Pages Torn Loose*] [*Publishing*] [*Italian*]
SFOI .... Saint-Freres Ocean Indien
SFOKiS ..... Spoleczny Fundusz Odbudowy Kraju i Stolicy [*Social Fund for Rebuilding the Counry and the Capital (1948-1956)*] [*Poland*]
SFOM........ Societe Financiere pour les Pays d'Outre-Mer [*Overseas Finance Company*] [*French*]   (AF)
SFOM........ Societe Francaise d'Optique et de Mecanique [*France*]   (PDAA)
SFOPP....... Spoleczny Fabryczny Osrodek Propagandy Partyjnej [*Plant Social Party Propaganda Center*]   (POL)
SFOR........ Spoleczny Fundusz Oszczednosciowy Rolnictwa [*Farmers' Community Savings Fund*]   (POL)
Sforz........... Sforzando [*With Additional Accent*] [*Music*]
SFOS .... Societe Francaise d'Organo-Synthese [*France*]   (PDAA)
SFOS .... Spoleczny Fundusz Odbudowy Stolicy [*People's Fund for the Reconstruction of Warsaw*]   (POL)
SFP .... Sforzato Piano [*Sudden change from forte to piano*] [*Music*]   (ROG)
SFP .... Siam Food Products [*Thailand*]
SFP .... Sociedade Financeira Portuguesa [*Portuguese Financial Society*]   (WER)
SFP .... Societe Francaise de Pedagogie [*French Society of Pedagogy*]   (SLS)
SFP .... Societe Francaise de Physique [*French Society of Physics*]   (SLS)
SFP .... Societe Francaise de Production [*French Society of Production*]
SFP .... Societe Francaise de Psychologie [*French Society of Psychology*]   (SLS)
SFP .... Svaz Filmovych Pracovniku [*Union of Film Workers*]   (CZ)
SFP .... Svenska Folkpartiet [*Swedish People's Party*] [*Finland*] [*Political party*]   (PPE)
SFP .... Syllogos Foititon Peiraios [*Piraeus Students Club*]   (GC)
SFP .... World Federation of Trade Unions   (BU)
SFPA .... Servico Federal de Promocao Agropecuaria [*Brazil*]   (DSCA)
SFPH .... Societe Francaise des Physiciens d'Hopital [*French Society of Hospital Physicians*]   (SLS)
SFPH .... Svenska Foereningen foer Psykisk Haelsovard [*Sweden*]   (SLS)
SFPI .... Societe de Fabrication des Portes Isolantes [*Benin*]   (EY)
SFPI .... Societe Francaise de Participations Industrielles [*France*]

SFPMAC... Societe Francaise de Physiologie et de Medecine Aeronautiques et Cosmonautiques [*French*]   (SLS)
SFPN .... Swiatowa Federacja Pracownikow Nauki [*World Federation of Scientific Workers*]   (POL)
SFPP.......... Sanidad de las Fuerzas Policiales del Peru [*Health Service of the Peruvian Police Forces*]   (LA)
SFPR .... Servico Federal de Prevencao e Repressao (aos Crimes Contra e Fazenda Nacional) [*Federal Service for Prevention and Suppression of Crimes Against the National Treasury*)] [*Brazil*]   (LA)
SFPS.......... Postal Courier Communications Station   (BU)
SFPS.......... World Federation of Trade-Unions   (BU)
SFPTU ...... Swiss Federation of Protestant Trade Unions
SFR........... Calculation of Financial Estimate   (RU)
SFR........... Safair Freighters (Pty) Ltd. [*South Africa*] [*ICAO designator*]   (FAAC)
sFr............. Schweizer Frank [*Swiss Franc*] [*Monetary unit*]
SFR........... Schweizerischer Friedensrat [*Switzerland*]   (EAIO)
SFR........... Societe Francaise de Radioprotection [*French Society of Radio Protection*] [*ICSU*] [*Nuclear energy*]
SFR........... Sotto Fascia Raccomandata [*Registered Printed Matter*] [*Italian*]
SFR........... Streak Camera   (RU)
SFR........... Svenska Faergeritekniska Riksfoerbundet [*Sweden*]   (SLS)
SFR........... Sveriges Forskollarares Riksforening [.*Sweden*]   (EAIO)
SFRA .... Societe Francaise de Representation pour l'Afrique
SFRI .... Swiss Forest Research Institute   (DSCA)
SFRJ......... Socjalistyczna Federacyjna Republika Jugoslawii [*Socialist Federative Republic of Yugoslavia*] [*Poland*]
SFRJ .... Sozialistische Foederative Republik Jugoslawien [*Socialist Federative Republic of Yugoslavia*]   (WEN)
SFRM .... Societe de Fabrications Radioelectriques Marocaines
SFRP .... Societe Francaise de Radioprotection [*French Society of Radio Protection*] [*ICSU*] [*Nuclear energy*]   (NRCH)
SFRS .... Sea Fisheries Research Station [*Israel*]   (MSC)
SFRV .... Schweizerische Fernseh- und Radio-Vereinigung [*Swiss Television and Radio Broadcasting Association*]   (WEN)
SFRYu .... Socialist Federated Republic of Yugoslavia   (BU)
SFS .... School for Field Studies [*Kenya*]
SFS .... Sektion fuer Systementwicklung [*GID*] [*Information retrieval*]
SFS .... Societe Forestiere de Sangha
SFS .... Societe Francaise de Sociologie [*French Society of Sociology*]   (SLS)
SFS .... Sotto Fascia Semplice [*Unregistered Printed Matter*] [*Italian*]
SFS .... Srpska Fabrika Stakla [*Serbian Glass Factory*] [*Paracin*]   (YU)
SFS .... State Fleet Services [*New South Wales, Australia*]
SFS .... Suomen Standardisomisliitto [*Finnish Standards Association*] [*Information service or system*]   (IID)
SFS .... Svenska Fornskriftsaellskapet [*Sweden*]   (SLS)
SFS .... Sveriges Forenade Studentkarer [*Swedish United Student Union*]   (WEN)
SFS .... Sydney Football Stadium [*Australia*]
SFSF .... Svenska Freds ochs Skiljedomsforeningen [*Swedish Society for Peace Arbitration*]   (WEN)
SFSM .... Societe Fonciere du Sud de Madagascar
SF-SN .... Smrt Fasizmu - Sloboda Narodu [*Death to Fascism - Freedom to the People*] [*Standard phrase in official documents*]   (YU)
SFSN .... Society of French-Speaking Neurosurgeons   (EA)
SFT .... Scierie, Foret, Transport
SFT .... Skelleftea [*Sweden*] [*Airport symbol*]   (OAG)
SFT .... Societe Forestiere Tropicale
SFT .... Societe Francaise des Thermiciens [*French*]   (SLS)
SFT .... Societe Francaise des Traducteurs [*French Society of Translators*]
SFT .... Sport Fotanacs [*Main Sports Council*]   (HU)
SFT .... Standard Fuel Tonnes [*Arab*]
SFT .... Sudanese Flight [*Sudan*] [*ICAO designator*]   (FAAC)
SFTB .... Societe Forestiere Tailleur & Baizet
SFTC .... Shanghai Foreign Trade Corporation
SFTI.......... Siberian Physicotechnical Institute   (RU)
SFTS.......... Swinburne Film and Television School [*Australia*]
SFTTU ...... Sudanese Federation of Teachers' Trade Union
SFTU .... Somali Federation of Trade Unions   (EAIO)
SFTU .... Swaziland Federation of Trade Unions
SFU........... Safia [*Papua New Guinea*] [*Airport symbol*]   (OAG)
SFU........... Societe de Fluoration de l'Uranium [*A joint company formed by governmental and industrial organisations in eight European countries*]   (PDAA)
SFU........... Societe Francaise des Urbanistes [*French*]   (SLS)
SFU........... Sport for Understanding [*Australia*]
SFU........... Statni Fotomericky Ustav [*State Institute of Photogrammetry*]   (CZ)
SFUFNRJ ... Savez Farmaceutskih Udruzenja FNRJ [*Federation of Pharmaceutical Associations of Yugoslavia*]   (YU)
SFUP .... Swidnicka Fabryka Urzadzen Przemyslowych [*Swidnica (Schweidnitz) Industrial Equipment Factory*]   (POL)
SFV........... Schizophrenia Fellowship of Victoria [*Australia*]

SFV .... Schweizerische Franchising-Vereinigung [*Swiss Franchising Union*] (SLS)
SFV .... Schweizerischer Forstverein [*Swiss Forest Society*] (SLS)
SFV .... Schweizerischer Fussballverband [*Switzerland*] (EAIO)
SFV .... Societe de la Flore Valdotaine [*Italian*] (SLS)
SFV .... Societe Francaise du Vide [*French*] (SLS)
SFV .... Sports Federation of Victoria [*Australia*]
SFV .... Sveriges Film- och Videoamatorer [*Swedish Federation of Film and Video Amateurs*] (EAIO)
SFV .... Swedish Federation of Film and Video Amateurs [*Sweden*] (EAIO)
SFVH........ Svenska Foereningen foer Vetenskaplig Homeopati [*Sweden*] (SLS)
SFVP .... Svetova Federacia Vedeckych Pracovnikov [*World Federation of Scientific Workers*] (CZ)
SFVU........ Slovensky Fond Vytvarnych Umeni [*Slovak Creative Arts Foundation*] (CZ)
SFW.......... Sante Fe [*Panama*] [*Airport symbol*] (OAG)
SFW.......... Sicherungs- und Fernmeldewesen [*Blocking and Telecommunications (Railroad) System*] (EG)
SFW.......... Signal- und Fernmeldewesen [*Signal and Telecommunications System*] (EG)
SFW.......... Stellenbosch Farmers' Winery
SFWA....... Soccer Federation of Western Australia
SFWISA .... Senior Fellow of the Water Institute of Southern Africa (AA)
SFWTU ..... Sudan Federation of Workers' Trades Unions
SFY........... Special Fund for Youth [*UNESCO*] (EAIO)
SFY........... Suomen Filosofinen Yhdistys [*Finland*] (SLS)
Sfz............. Sforzando [*With Additional Accent*] [*Music*]
SFZZ .... Swiatowa Federacja Zwiazkow Zawodowych [*World Federation of Trade Unions*] [*Poland*]
S-G .... Besluit van den Secretaris-Generaal [*Benelux*] (BAS)
sg............... Centigram (RU)
SG .... Cophasal Horizontal [*Antenna*] (RU)
SG .... Depth Recorder (RU)
SG .... Goryunov Heavy (Machine Gun) (RU)
SG .... Sa Grace [*His or Her Grace*] [*French*]
SG .... Sa Grandeur [*His Grace*] [*French*] (MTD)
sg............... Same Year (BU)
Sg.............. Schnellgueterzug [*Fast Freight Train*] (EG)
SG .... Secondo Grandezza [*According to Size of Portion*] [*On restaurant menus*] [*Italian*]
SG .... Secretaire General [*Secretary General*] (CL)
SG .... Secretaria de Gobernacion [*Secretariat of Government*] [*Mexico*] (LA)
SG .... Secretariat General [*Secretariat General*] (CL)
SG .... Secretary-General [*United Nations*]
SG .... Service Geographique
Sg.............. Sgeir [*Rock*] [*Gaelic*] (NAU)
SG .... Sicherheitsgruppe [*Security Group*] (EG)
SG .... Siebelwerke ATG GmbH [*Germany*] [*ICAO aircraft manufacturer identifier*] (ICAO)
SG .... Signal Generator (RU)
sg............... Signalman (BU)
SG .... Singapore [*ANSI two-letter standard code*] (CNC)
sg............... Singulaari, Yksikko [*Singular*] [*Finland*]
SG .... Skolsko Gadanje [*Target Practice*] (YU)
SG .... Social Hygiene (RU)
SG .... Socialistische Gids [*Benelux*] (BAS)
SG .... Societe Generale de Credit
SG .... Society for Geography [*South Africa*] (EAIO)
SG .... Society of Genealogists (EA)
SG .... Sogenaamd [*So-Called*] [*Afrikaans*]
sg............... Sogenannt [*So-Called*] [*German*]
SG .... Solidarite Guineenne [*France-based Guinean political organization*]
sg............... Soortlike Gewig [*Specific Gravity*] [*Afrikaans*]
SG .... Sozialgericht [*Social Security Court*] [*German*] (ILCA)
SG .... Special Group [*NATO*]
sG.............. Spezifisches Gewicht [*Specific Gravity*] [*German*]
SG .... Spoldzielnia Gminna [*Rural Commune Cooperative*] (POL)
S-G .... Staten-Generaal [*Benelux*] (BAS)
Sg.............. Streckung [*Stretching*] [*German*] (GCA)
SG .... Sua Graca [*Your Grace*] [*Portuguese*]
SG .... Sua Grandeza [*Your Eminence*] [*Portuguese*]
SG .... Substitut du Procureur General (FLAF)
SG .... Sudan Government
S/G .... Su Giro [*Your Draft*] [*Spanish*] [*Business term*]
SG .... Sumsko Gazdinstvo [*Forestry Management*] (YU)
SG .... Sveriges Grossistforbund [*Sweden*] (EAIO)
SG .... Sydney Greens [*Political party*] [*Australia*]
SG .... Synchronous Generator (RU)
sg............... This Year, Current Year (RU)
SG .... Welding Torch (RU)
SG43MMG ... Stankovyi Goryunova 1943 Medium Machine Gun [*Soviet made*] (VNW)

SGA .... Air Saigon [*Vietnam*] [*ICAO designator*] (FAAC)
SGA .... Main Air Depot (RU)
SGA .... Schweizerische Gesellschaft fuer Asienkunde [*Switzerland*] (SLS)
SGA .... Schweizerische Gesellschaft fuer Aussenpolitik [*Switzerland*] (SLS)
SGA .... Schweizerische Gesellschaft fuer Automatik [*Switzerland*] (SLS)
SGA .... Sekolah Guru Atas [*Senior Teachers School*] (IN)
SGA .... Showmen's Guild of Australia
SGA .... Slavic Gospel Associations
SGA .... Societe de Geologie Appliquee aux Gites Mineraux [*Society for Geology Applied to Mineral Deposits*] [*ICSU*] (EAIO)
SGA .... Societe Gabonaise d'Assainissement
SGA .... Societe Generale Australia
SGA .... Societe Generale d'Alimentation [*Importer and distributor of food*] [*Zaire*]
SGA .... Swiss Golf Association (EAIO)
SGAC........ Secretariat General d'Aviation Civile [*Secretariat General for Civil Aviation*] [*French*] (CL)
SGAC........ Secretariat General for Civil Aviation [*French*]
SGAC........ Societe Gabonaise d'Assurances et Courtage
SGACC..... Secretariat General a l'Aviation Civile et Commerciale (FLAF)
SGAE........ Sociedad General de Autores de Espana [*Spain*] (EAIO)
SGAE........ Studiengesellschaft fuer Atomenergie, GmbH [*Nuclear energy*] [*Austria*] (NRCH)
SGAEI ...... Societe Gabonaise d'Amenagement et d'Equipement Immobiliers
SGAG .... Schweizerische Gesellschaft fuer Angewandte Geographie [*Switzerland*] (SLS)
SGAHE ..... Schweizerische Gesellschaft fuer Anatomie, Histologie und Embryologie [*Switzerland*] (EAIO)
SGAI .... Schweizerische Gesellschaft fuer Allergologie und Immunologie [*Switzerland*] (EAIO)
SGAMS..... Services Generaux Autonome de la Maladie du Sommeil
SGAP........ Society for Growing Australian Plants (ADA)
SGAR....... Schweizerische Gesellschaft fuer Anaesthesiologie und Reanimation [*Switzerland*] (SLS)
SGAS........ Asuncion/Presidente General Stroessner [*Paraguay*] [*ICAO location identifier*] (ICLI)
SGAU .... Sofia City Pharmacy Administration (BU)
SGAV....... Statisztikai Gepi Adatfeldolgozo Vallalat [*Enterprise for Mechanical Processing of Statistical Data*] (HU)
SGAW ...... Subgroup on Assessment of Weapons [*NATO*] (NATG)
SGAY........ Ayolas [*Paraguay*] [*ICAO location identifier*] (ICLI)
SGB........... Schweizerischer Gewerkschaftsbund [*Swiss Federation of Trade Unions*]
SGB........... Schweizerisches Gewerkschaftsbund [*Swiss Trade Union Federation*] (WEN)
SGB........... Sociedade Geografica Brasileira [*Brazil*] (SLS)
SGB........... Societe Gabonaise des Bois
SGB........... Societe Generale de Banque [*Bank Society*] [*Information service or system*] (IID)
SGB........... Societe Generale de Banque au Cameroun
SGB........... Societe Generale de Belgique [*Belgium*]
SGB........... Societe Geologique de Belgique [*Belgium*] (SLS)
SGB........... Societe Nationale des Grands Barrages [*National Large Dam Company*] [*Use SNGB Cambodia*] (CL)
SGB........... Sozialistischer Grosshandelsbetrieb [*Socialist Wholesale Enterprise*] (EG)
SGB........... Sudan Gezira Board
SGBA........ Societe Generale de Banque aux Antilles [*Guadeloupe*] (EY)
SGBC........ Societe Generale de Banques au Cameroun [*General Banking Company of Cameroon*] (AF)
SGBC........ Societe Generale de Banques au Congo [*General Banking Company of the Congo*]
SGBCI ...... Societe Generale de Banques en Cote-D'Ivoire [*General Banking Company of the Ivory Coast*] (AF)
SGBD........ Systeme de Gestion de Base de Donnees [*French*] (ADPT)
SGBM....... Societe Guineenne de Beton Manufacture
SGBS .... Societe General de Banque du Senegal [*General Banking Company of Senegal*] (AF)
SGBS .... Strathelyde Graduate Business School [*Toulouse, France*] (ECON)
SGBV........ Bella Vista [*Paraguay*] [*ICAO location identifier*] (ICLI)
SGC .... Service de Geodesie et de Cartographie [*Haiti*] (DSCA)
SGC .... Sociedad Geografica de Colombia [*Colombia*] (DSCA)
SGC .... Societe Generale Cooperative [*Benelux*] (BAS)
SGC .... Societe Generale de Construction [*General Construction Company*] [*Zaire*] (AF)
SGC .... State Grants Commission [*Tasmania, Australia*]
SGCA........ Secretariat General a l'Aviation Civile [*French Civil Aviation Secretariat*]
SGCE........ Syndicat General de la Construction Electrique (FLAF)
SGCEC ..... Standing Group Communications-Electronics Committee [*Later, MCEWG*] [*NATO*] (NATG)
SGCFG ..... Societe de Gestion de la Compagnie Francaise du Gabon
SGCH .... Sociedad de Genetica de Chile [*Chile*] (DSCA)

SGCI .... Schweizerische Gesellschaft fuer Chemische Industrie [*Switzerland*] (EAIO)
SGCI .... Societe Generale de la Cote-D'Ivoire
SGCO .... Concepcion [*Paraguay*] [*ICAO location identifier*] (ICLI)
SGCTP ...... Societe Gabonaise de Constructions de TP
SGD .... Sonderborg [*Denmark*] [*Airport symbol*] (OAG)
SGD .... Srpsko Geografsko Drustvo [*Serbian Geographical Society*] (YU)
SGD .... Storehouse for Finished Parts (RU)
SGDG .... Sans Garantie du Gouvernement [*Without Government Guarantee*] [*French*] (WER)
SGDL........ Societe des Gens de Lettres [*Association of Men of Letters*] [*French*]
SGDN .... Secretariat General de la Defence Nationale [*France*] (PDAA)
SGDR .... Societe Gabonaise de Developpement Rural
SGDT........ Societe de Gestion du Depot de Tamatave
SGE .... All-Union Helminthological Expedition (RU)
SGE .... Schweizerische Gesellschaft fuer Ernaehrungsforschung [*Switzerland*] (SLS)
SGE .... Scientific Glass Engineering [*Melbourne, Australia*]
SGE .... Service de Lutte Contre les Grandes Endemies
SGE .... Societe Gabonaise d'Entreposage
SGE .... Societe Gabonaise d'Entreprises
SGE .... Societe Generale d'Electricite
SGE .... Societe Generale d'Entreprise [*French*]
SGE .... Societe Guineenne d'Equipement [*Guinean Equipment Company*] (AF)
SGEA .... Societe Generale d'Entreprise d'Algerie
SGEEM ...... Societe Generale d'Entreprises Electromecaniques
SGEFE ...... Syndonistikon Grafeion Ellinon Foititon Exoterikou [*Coordinating Bureau of Greek Students Abroad*] (GC)
SGEFI....... Syndonistikon Grafeion Ellinon Foititon Italias [*Coordinating Office for Greek Students in Italy*] (GC)
SGEG........ Syndicat General de l'Education en Guadeloupe (PD)
SGEH .... Societe Gabonaise d'Etude Hoteliere
SGEI .... Societe Gabonaise d'Etudes et Interventions
SGEK .... Stathmoi Georgikis Erevnis kai Ktinotrofias [*Agricultural Research and Animal Breeding Stations*] [*Greek*] (GC)
SGEN .... Encarnacion [*Paraguay*] [*ICAO location identifier*] (ICLI)
SGEN .... Syndicat General de l'Education Nationale [*French*]
SGEP .... Sindicatura General de Empresas Publicas [*General Trusteeship of Public Enterprises*] [*Argentina*] (LA)
SGEP .... Socialist Group in the European Parliament [*See also GSPE*] (EAIO)
SGEP .... Syndicat General de l'Enseignement Public [*French*] (SLS)
SGEPC ...... Societe Guineenne d'Engrais et de Produits Chimiques
SGEPP ...... Societe Gabonaise d'Entreposage de Produits Petroliers
SGES .... Centimeter/Gram/Erg/Second (RU)
SGES .... Societa Generale Esercize Siciliano Finanziaria [*Italian*]
SGET........ Sofia City Electric Transport (BU)
SGETP ...... Societe Gabonaise d'Entreprises de Travaux Publics
SGETPI..... Societe Generale d'Entreprises pour les Travaux Publics & Industriels
SGF .... Societe Ganamet Freres
SGF .... Societe Generale de Fonderie [*General Society of Foundries*] [*French*]
SGF .... Societe Generale Fonciere
SGF .... Societe Geologique de France (SLS)
SGF .... Svenska Geofysiska Foereningen [*Sweden*] (SLS)
SGF .... Svenska Geotekniska Foereningen [*Sweden*] (SLS)
SGF .... Svenska Gjuteriforeningen [*Sweden*] (EAIO)
SGF .... Sveriges Gjuteritekniska Foerening [*Sweden*] (SLS)
SGF .... Sveriges Gummitekniska Foerening [*Sweden*] (SLS)
SGF .... Sydney Garden Festival [*Australia*]
SGFA .... Asuncion [*Paraguay*] [*ICAO location identifier*] (ICLI)
SGFF .... Schweizerische Gesellschaft fuer Familienforschung [*Switzerland*] (SLS)
SGFI .... Filadelfia [*Paraguay*] [*ICAO location identifier*] (ICLI)
SGFT........ Schweizerische Gesellschaft fuer Feintechnik [*Switzerland*] (SLS)
SGG .... Schweizerische Geisteswissenschaftliche Gesellschaft [*Switzerland*] (SLS)
SGG .... Schweizerische Gesellschaft fuer Gerontologie [*Switzerland*] (SLS)
SGG .... Schweizerische Gesellschaft fuer Gynaekologie [*Switzerland*] (SLS)
SGGG .... Societe Generale du Golfe de Guinee
SGGiD .... Collection of State Deeds and Treaties (RU)
SGGP......... Schweizerische Gesellschaft fuer Gesundheitspolitik [*Switzerland*] (SLS)
SGGR .... Guaira [*Paraguay*] [*ICAO location identifier*] (ICLI)
SGGW .... Szkola Glowna Gospodarstwa Wiejskiego [*Central School of Agriculture*] (POL)
SGH .... Szkola Glowna Handlowa [*Main School of Commerce*] (POL)
SGHC .... Societe des Grands Hotels du Cameroun
SGHMP .... Service Generale d'Hygiene Mobile et de Prophylaxie

SGI .... Sabah Gas Industries [*Malaysia*] [*Commercial firm*]
SGI .... Servicio Geodesico Interamericano [*Inter-American Geodetic Survey - IAGS*] [*United States*]
SGI .... Sheriff Guards International [*Nigeria*] (EAIO)
SGI .... Societa Generale Immobiliare di Lavori di Utilita Pubblica ed Agricola SpA [*Italian*]
SGI .... Societa Geologica Italiana [*Italian*] (SLS)
SGI .... Societe de Gestion d'Interets
SGI .... Soka Gakkai International [*An association*]
SGI .... Statens Geotekniska Institut [*Swedish Geotechnical Institute*] [*Research center*] [*Sweden*] (IRC)
SGI .... Sverdlovsk Mining Institute Imeni V. V. Vakhrushev (RU)
SGIA .... Societe de Gerances Industrielles et Agricoles
SGIA .... Sporting Goods Importers' Association of Japan (EAIO)
SGIB .... Itaipu [*Paraguay*] [*ICAO location identifier*] (ICLI)
SGIC .... State Government Insurance Commission [*Australia*]
SGICF .... Syndicat General de l'Industrie Cotonniere Francaise (FLAF)
SGIEC .... State Government Information and Enquiry Centre [*Western Australia*]
SGIFK .... Smolensk State Institute of Physical Culture (RU)
SGiP......... Soviet State and Law (RU)
SGJ .... Sagarai [*Papua New Guinea*] [*Airport symbol*] (OAG)
SGJ .... Syndicat General des Journalistes [*France*] (EAIO)
SGJN .... San Juan Nepomuceno [*Paraguay*] [*ICAO location identifier*] (ICLI)
SGK .... Horizontal Seismograph Designed by Kirnos (RU)
SGK .... Savezna Gradevinska Komora [*Federal Chamber of Construction*] (YU)
SGK .... Schweizerische Gesellschaft der Kernfachleute [*Switzerland*] (SLS)
SGK .... Schweizerische Gesellschaft fuer Kartographie [*Switzerland*] (EAIO)
SGK .... Staatliche Geologische Kommission [*State Geological Commission*] (EG)
SGKB........ Societe Generale-Komercni Banka [*Former Czechoslovakia*] (EY)
SGKGS ...... Schweizerische Gesellschaft fuer Kulturguterschutz [*Switzerland*] (EAIO)
SGKV........ Studiengesellschaft fuer den Kombinierten Verkehr eV (SLS)
SGL .... Schulgemeinschaftsleitung [*School Community Leadership*] (EG)
S/Gl .... Secretaire General [*Secretary General*] [*Cambodia*] (CL)
SGL .... Senegalair [*Senegal*] [*ICAO designator*] (FAAC)
sgl .... Sklad Glowny [*Main Warehouse*] (POL)
SGL .... Sociedad Geografica de Lima [*Peru*] (EAIO)
SGLMGA ... Sydney Gay and Lesbian Mardi Gras Association [*Australia*]
SGLO .... Lobrego, Fortin [*Paraguay*] [*ICAO location identifier*] (ICLI)
SGLP .... Standing Group Representative Liaison Paper to the International Staff [*Obsolete*] [*NATO*] (NATG)
SGLV .... La Victoria (Ex Casado) [*Paraguay*] [*ICAO location identifier*] (ICLI)
SGM .... Goryunov Modernized Heavy (Machine Gun) (RU)
SGM .... Schweizerischen Verbandes der Grosshandler und Importeure der Motorfahrzeugbranche [*Switzerland*] (EAIO)
SGM .... Scripture Gift Mission [*Myanmar*]
SGM .... Service de Geologie et des Mines [*Haiti*] (DSCA)
SGM .... Servicio Geografico Militar [*Uruguay*] (DSCA)
SGM .... Societe Gabonaise de Mecanique
SGM .... Societe Generale de Minerais [*General Ores Company*] [*Zaire*] (AF)
SGM .... Standing Group Memorandum [*Obsolete*] [*NATO*] (NATG)
SGM .... Syndicat des Gens de Mer
SGMB .... Societe Generale Marocaine de Banques
SGMB .... Societe Geologique et Mineralogique de Bretagne [*French*] (SLS)
SGMC .... Standing Group Meteorological Committee [*Obsolete*] [*NATO*] (NATG)
SGMC .... State Gold Mining Corporation [*Ghana*]
SGME........ Mariscal Estigarribia [*Paraguay*] [*ICAO location identifier*] (ICLI)
SGMGA .... Sydney Gay Mardi Gras Association [*Australia*]
SGMI........ Saratov State Medical Institute (RU)
SGMI........ Sverdlovsk State Medical Institute (RU)
SGMK .... Schweizerische Gesellschaft fuer Muskelkrankheiten [*Switzerland*] (SLS)
SGML........ Standard Generalized Markup Language [*Also, GSML*] [*International Standards Organization*]
SGMM ...... Secretariat General de la Marine Marchande [*France*] (PDAA)
SGMMC .... Saudi-German Mechanical & Maintenance Company
SGMT .... Societe Generale des Moulins du Togo
SGMT........ Sverdlovsk Mining and Metallurgical Technicum Imeni I. I. Polzunov (RU)
SGMTP ..... Service de Gestion du Materiel des Travaux Publics [*Public Works Equipment Management Department*] [*Zaire*] (AF)
SGN .... Group Carrier Bay (RU)
SGN .... Ho Chi Minh [*Vietnam*] [*Airport symbol*] (OAG)

SGN .... Nephelometer (RU)
SGN .... Saint Gobain Techniques Nouvelles [*France*] (PDAA)
SGN .... Service Geologique National [*National Geological Survey*] [*Bureau of Geological and Mining Research*] [*Information service or system*] (IID)
SGN .... Servicio Geologico Nacional [*National Geological Survey*] [*Bogota, Colombia*] (LAA)
SGN .... Sheriff Guards International, Nigeria (EAIO)
SGN .... Societe de Genie Nucleaire [*Nuclear energy*] [*French*] (NRCH)
SGN .... Societe Gabonaise de Negoce
sgn .... Sogenaamd [*So-Called*] [*Afrikaans*]
SGNA .... Nueva Asuncion [*Paraguay*] [*ICAO location identifier*] (ICLI)
SGNB .... Schweizerische Gesellschaft fuer ein Neues Bodenrecht [*Switzerland*] (SLS)
SGNCh ...... Low-Frequency Seismic Generator (RU)
SGNS .... Sofia City People's Council (BU)
SGNSDT ... Sofia City People's Council of Working People's Deputies (BU)
SGO .... Group Equipment Bay (RU)
SGO .... Saint George [*Australia*] [*Airport symbol*] (OAG)
SGO .... Societe Gabonaise de l'Okoume
SGO .... Solicitor-General's Office [*Australia*]
SGO .... Suomalaisen Tiedeakatemian Geofysiikan Observatorio [*Sodankyla Geophysical Observatory of the Finnish Academy of Science and Letters*] [*Research center*] (EAS)
SGO .... Superintendent-Generaal van Onderwys [*Superintendent-General of Education*] [*Afrikaans*]
SGODA ..... Sofia City and Okrug State Archives (BU)
SGOL .... Olimpo [*Paraguay*] [*ICAO location identifier*] (ICLI)
SGOM .... Societe de Gestion pour l'Outre-Mer
SGOMSEC ... Scientific Group on Methodologies for the Safety Evaluation of Chemicals [*International Council of Scientific Unions*]
SGOPC ...... Sindicato Gremial de Obreros de Productos de Cemento [*Union of Cement Products Workers*] [*El Salvador*] (LA)
SGP .... Gas-Pressure Welding Machine (RU)
SGP .... Group Conversion Bay (RU)
SGP .... Schweizerische Gesellschaft fuer Personalfragen [*Switzerland*] (SLS)
SGP .... Servicos Geologicos de Portugal [*Portuguese*] (SLS)
SGP .... Sindicato Gremial de Peleteros [*Union of Leather Workers*] [*El Salvador*] (LA)
SGP .... Singapore [*ANSI three-letter standard code*] (CNC)
SGP .... Sistema General de Preferencias [*General Preference System*] (LA)
SGP .... Sociedad Geologica del Peru [*Peru*] (SLS)
SGP .... Staatkundig Gereformeerde Partij [*Netherlands*] [*Political party*] [*Benelux*]
SGP .... Storehouse for Finished Products (RU)
SGP .... Stowarzyszenie Geodetow Polskich [*Association of Polish Geodesists*] (POL)
SGP .... Sumsko Gradevinsko Preduzece [*Forestry Construction Establishment*] (YU)
SGP .... Systeme Generalise de Preferences [*French*]
SGPA .... Sovjetska Glavna Pomorska Agencija [*Soviet Central Maritime Agency*] [*Belgrade*] (YU)
SGPF .... Spencer Gulf Prawn Fishery [*Australia*]
SGPI .... Pilar [*Paraguay*] [*ICAO location identifier*] (ICLI)
SGPI .... Saratov State Pedagogical Institute (RU)
SGPI .... Smolensk State Pedagogical Institute Imeni Karl Marx (RU)
SGPI .... Stalinabad State Pedagogical Institute Imeni T. G. Shevchenko (RU)
SGPI .... Sverdlovsk State Pedagogical Institute (RU)
SGPIS .... Szkola Glowna Planowania i Statystyki [*Main School of Planning and Statistics*] (POL)
SGPK .... All-Union Geological Exploration Office (RU)
SGPO .... Puerto Pinasco [*Paraguay*] [*ICAO location identifier*] (ICLI)
SGPS .... Ciudad Presidente Stroessner [*Paraguay*] [*ICAO location identifier*] (ICLI)
SGPT .... Societe Generale de Photo-Topographie
SGPU .... Northern Mining Industry Administration (RU)
S Gr .... Sa Grandeur [*French*]
SGR .... Saudi Government Railroad
SGR .... Service General du Renseignement [*General Intelligence Service*] [*Belgium*] (WER)
Sgr .... Sgeir [*Rock*] [*Gaelic*] (NAU)
Sgr .... Silbergroschen [*Old Prussian coin worth about 2 1/2 cents*] [*German*]
SGR .... Societe Guineenne de Revetements
SGR .... Spanski Gradanski Rat [*Spanish Civil War*] (YU)
SGRA .... Special Horizontal Photographic Reproduction Apparatus (RU)
SGRNM .... Schweizerische Gesellschaft fuer Radiologie und Nuklearmedizin [*Swiss Society for Radiology and Nuclear Medicine*] (WND)
SGRO .... Rosario [*Paraguay*] [*ICAO location identifier*] (ICLI)
SGRRO ...... Saudi Government Railroad Organization
SGRT .... Societe Gabonaise de Radio et Television
SGS .... Centimeter-Gram-Second [*System of units*] (RU)

SGS .... Hydrographic Service Vessel (RU)
SGS .... School of General Studies [*Australian National University*]
SGS .... Sisters of the Good Shepherd [*Italy*] (EAIO)
SGS .... Societa Generale di Sorveglianza [*Italy*]
SGS .... Societa Generale Semiconduttori [*Italy*] (PDAA)
SGS .... Societe Gabonaise de Sciace
SGS .... Societe Generale de Surveillance [*General Surveillance Co.*] [*Switzerland*]
SGS .... Sudan Gezira Scheme
SGS .... Svenska Gymnastiklaeraresaellskapet [*Sweden*] (SLS)
SGSB .... Staatliches Guss- und Schmiedebuero, Berlin [*Berlin State Casting and Forging Office*] (EG)
SGSC .... Standing Group Security Committee [*Obsolete*] [*NATO*] (NATG)
SGSE .... Cgs Electrostatic System (RU)
SGSG .... Schweizerische Gesellschaft fuer ein Soziales Gesundheitswesen [*Switzerland*] (SLS)
SGSM .... Cgs Electromagnetic System (RU)
SGSM .... Fuel and Lubricants Depot (RU)
SGSNR .... Shadanhojin Gaaru Sukauto Nihon Renmei [*Japan*] (EAIO)
SGSR .... Generator and Compressor-Expander Frame (RU)
SGSR .... Scientific Group for Space Research [*Greece*] (EAIO)
SGSS .... Schweizerische Gesellschaft fuer Skandinavische Studien [*Switzerland*] (SLS)
SGSZ .... Szkola Glowna Sluzby Zagranicznej [*Main School for the Foreign Service*] (POL)
SGT .... Schweizerische Galvanotechnische Gesellschaft [*Switzerland*] (SLS)
sgt .... Segedtiszt [*Adjutant, Aide-de-Camp*] (HU)
Sgt .... Sergeant (SCAC)
Sgt .... Sergent [*Sergeant*] [*Military*] [*French*] (MTD)
SGT .... Societa' Aerotaxi SUD [*Italy*] [*ICAO designator*] (FAAC)
SGT .... Societe des Garde-Temps [*Switzerland*] (PDAA)
SGT .... Societe Generale de Transports [*Morocco*]
SGT .... Societe Guineenne de Transport
SGT .... Spencer Gulf Telecasters Ltd. [*Australia*]
SGTC .... Service General des Troupes Coloniales
SGTC .... Societe Gabonaise de Transports et de Carrieres
sgte .... Siguiente [*Following*] [*Spanish*]
SGTE .... Societe Generale de Techniques et d'Etudes
SGTE .... Societe Generale de Traction et d'Exploitations
SGTIA ...... Standing Group Technical Intelligence Agency [*NATO*] (NATG)
SGTICES .. Sindicato General de Trabajadores de la Industria de la Construccion de El Salvador [*General Union of Workers of the Construction Industry of El Salvador*] (LA)
SGTK .... Schweizerische Gesellschaft fuer Theaterkultur [*Switzerland*] (SLS)
SGTM .... Societe Generale des Transports Maritimes [*French*]
SGTM .... Titanium Dioxide Manufacturers Sector Group (EAIO)
SGTMA ..... Societe Gabonaise de Transports Maritimes et d'Affretement
SGTS .... Scottish Gaelic Texts Society (SLS)
SGTS .... Societe Generale Textiles et Soieries
SGU .... Northern Geodetic Administration (RU)
SGU .... Saratov State University Imeni N. G. Chernyshevskiy (RU)
SGU .... Savezna Geodetska Uprava [*Federal Geodetic Administration*] (YU)
SGU .... Schweizerische Gesellschaft fuer Umweltschutz [*Swiss Association for Environmental Protection*] (WEN)
SGU .... Slovensky Geologicky Urad [*Slovak Geological Office*] (CZ)
SGU .... Smolensk State University (RU)
SGU .... Statni Geologicky Ustav CSR [*State Geological Institute of the Czechoslovak Republic*] (CZ)
SGU .... Sveriges Geologiska Undersoekning [*Geological Survey of Sweden*] (ARC)
SGU .... Sveriges Geologiska Undersokning [*Geological Survey of Sweden*] [*Uppsala*] [*Information service or system*] (IID)
SGV .... Northern Group of Armed Forces (RU)
SGV .... Sierra Grande [*Argentina*] [*Airport symbol*] (OAG)
SGWM ...... Standing Group Working Memorandum [*NATO*] (NATG)
SGWTU ..... Sudan Government Workers' Trade Union
SGWTUF .. Sudan Government Workers' Trade-Union Federation
SGX .... Songea [*Tanzania*] [*Airport symbol*] (OAG)
SGYR .... Yasyreta [*Paraguay*] [*ICAO location identifier*] (ICLI)
SGZ .... Srpski Gradanski Zakonik [*Serbian Civil Code*] (YU)
SGZ .... Suedwestdeutsche Genossenschafts-Zentralbank AG [*Bank*] [*Frankfurt, West Germany*]
SGZP .... Schweizerische Gelleschaft fur Zerstorungsfrei Prufung [*Swiss Association for Non-Destructive Testing*] (PDAA)
Sh .... Aircraft Designed by V. B. Shavrov (RU)
Sh .... Glider Designed by Sheremet'yev (RU)
sh .... Highway (RU)
sh .... Latitude (RU)
Sh .... Loose Fit (RU)
Sh .... Powdered Coal (RU)
SH .... Sa Hautesse [*His, or Her, Highness*] [*French*]
Sh .... Sahife [*Page*] (TU)

Sh.............. Sahra [*Field*]   (TU)
SH.............. Sanayi Holding [*Industrial Holding Corporation*] [*Turkish Cypriot*]   (GC)
SH.............. Sardjana Hukum [*Bachelor of Laws*]   (IN)
Sh.............. Schutzhaltesignal [*Protective Stop Signal*]   (EG)
SH.............. Schweizer Heimatwerk [*Switzerland*]   (EAIO)
SH.............. Scripophila Helvetica   (EA)
SH.............. Service de l'Hydraulique [*Water Management Department*] [*French*]   (ARC)
sh.............. Shillinki(a) [*Finland*]
SH.............. Short Brothers & Harland Ltd. [*ICAO aircraft manufacturer identifier*]   (ICAO)
Sh.............. Shturmovik [*Attack aircraft*]   (RU)
SH.............. Siam Hardware Industry Co. Ltd. [*Thailand*]
SH.............. Son Honneur [*His Honor*] [*French*]
Sh.............. Staff, Headquarters
Sh.............. St. Helena [*ANSI two-letter standard code*]   (CNC)
SH.............. Svaz Zamestnancu v Hornictvi [*Mineworkers Union*]   (CZ)
SH.............. Sy Heiligheid [*His Highness*] [*Afrikaans*]
SH.............. Sy Hoogheid [*Her Highness*] [*Afrikaans*]
ShA.............. Attack Aviation   (RU)
SHA.............. Servicio Aereo de Honduras SA [*ICAO designator*]   (FAAC)
SHA.............. Shanghai [*China*] [*Airport symbol*]   (OAG)
SHA.............. Sociedad de Historia Argentina [*Argentine Historical Society*] [*Buenos Aires*]   (LAA)
SHA.............. Sosyal Hizmetler Akademisi [*Social Services Academy*]   (TU)
SHA.............. State Housing Authority [*Australia*]
SHA.............. Swiss Hospital Association   (EAIO)
ShAAZ...... Shadrinsk Automobile Subassembly Plant   (RU)
Shabak...... Sherut Bitahon Kelali [*General Security Service*] [*Israel*]
SHAC...... Societe Havraise Africaine de Commerce
SHAC...... Societe Hoteliere d'Afrique Centrale
SHAC...... Societe Hussein Ayad & Cie.
ShAD........ Attack Air Division   (RU)
SHADCOM ... Shipping Advisory Committee [*NATO*]
ShAE...... Attack Air Squadron   (RU)
SH-AF...... Shelter-Afrique   (EAIO)
SHAG....... Share Holder Action Group [*Australia*]
ShAGES.... Shatura State Electric Power Plant   (RU)
shakh........ Checkerboard Arrangement   (RU)
shakh........ Mine, Shaft [*Topography*]   (RU)
shakhm...... Chess   (RU)
ShakhtNIUI ... Shakhty Scientific Research, Planning and Design Institute of Coal   (RU)
Shakhtospetsstroy ... State Trust for Construction and Sinking of Shafts of the Glavspetspromstroy [*RSFSR*]   (RU)
Shaks........ Shakespearella [*Shakespeare*] [*Finland*]
ShAL.......... Extensive Air Shower, Auger Shower [*An*]   (RU)
SHAL....... Societe d'Histoire et d'Archeologie de la Lorraine [*French*]   (SLS)
SHALCO... Sharjah Liquefied Gas Company [*Saudi Arabia*]
SHAMIR... Association of Jewish Religious Professionals from the Commonwealth of Independent States and Eastern Europe [*Israel*]   (EAIO)
SHAMIR... Organization of Religious Russian Immigrants [*Israel*]   (EAIO)
SHANZ..... Soil and Health Association of New Zealand   (EAIO)
ShAP.......... Attack Air Regiment   (RU)
SHAPE..... Supreme Headquarters, Allied Powers Europe [*NATO*]
SHAPEX ... SHAPE [*Supreme Headquarters Allied Powers Europe*] Annual Command Exercise [*NATO*]   (NATG)
SHAR .... Sriharikota Island Launch Complex [*India*]
SHAR .... Sriharikota Rocket Range [*ISRO*] [*India*]   (PDAA)
SHARE...... School, Home, and Reading Enjoyment [*Australia*]
Sharyorokyo ... Sharyo-Sangyo Rodokumiai Kyogikai [*Federation of Rolling Stock Industry Workers' Unions*] [*Japan*]
SHAS........ Sephardi Torah Guardians [*Israeli political party*]
SHAT .... Sociedad Horticola para America Tropical [*Costa Rica*]   (LAA)
ShAU .... Wide-Band Antenna Amplifier   (RU)
ShB .... Disciplinary Battalion   (RU)
SHB .... Nakashibetsu [*Japan*] [*Airport symbol*]   (OAG)
SHB .... Samenwerkende Havenbedrijven [*Co-operating Harbor Concerns*] [*Netherlands*]   (WEN)
SHB .... Schindler Haerter AG [*Zuerich, Switzerland*] [*Research center*]   (ERC)
SHB .... Shabair [*Zaire*] [*ICAO designator*]   (FAAC)
shb........... Shirtingsbind [*Cloth Binding*] [*Publishing Danish/Norwegian*]
SHB .... Societe Hoteliere du Barachois
SHB .... Societe Hotelleries de Bamako
SHB .... Societe Hydroelectrique de Boali
SHB .... Sozialdemokratischer Hochschulbund [*Social Democratic University Student Association*]   (EG)
SHB .... Svenska Handelsbanken [*Bank*] [*Sweden*]
SHBA .... Shtetet e Bashkuara te Amerikes [*Albanian*]
ShBM .... Drum-Type Ball Mill   (RU)
SHC .... Service Hydrographique de la Cote [*Belgium*]   (MSC)
SHC .... Shire Indaselassie [*Ethiopia*] [*Airport symbol*]   (OAG)

SHC .... Societe Hoteliere du Cambodge [*Hotel Company of Cambodia*]   (CL)
SHC .... State Housing Corporation
SHC .... Swiss Craft Foundation   (EAIO)
Shch .... Crushed Stone [*Road-paving material*] [*Topography*]   (RU)
ShchDU ..... Remote-Control Panel   (RU)
ShchE .... Aircraft Designed by S. O. Shcherbakov   (RU)
shchel .... Alkaline   (RU)
shchel-zem .. Alkaline-Earth   (RU)
shchet .... Brush   (RU)
ShchKD ..... Jaw Crusher   (RU)
ShchMPB ... Alkaline Meat-Peptone Bouillon   (RU)
shch oks ..... Alkali Metal Oxalate   (RU)
ShchOM .... Crushed Stone Cleaning Machine   (RU)
ShchSP ...... Fuse Panel of the Switch Control Relay [*Railroads*]   (RU)
ShchU .... Control Panel   (RU)
shch/ub ...... Slit Shelter [*Topography*]   (RU)
ShchUK ..... Oxalacetic Acid   (RU)
ShchVP ...... Auxiliary Instrument Panel   (RU)
SHCJ .... Society of the Holy Child Jesus
SHCP .... Secretaria de Hacienda y Credito Publico [*Secretariat of Finance and Public Credit*] [*Mexico*]   (LA)
SHD .... Seehydrographischer Dienst [*Maritime Hydrographic Service*]   (EG)
SHD .... Severoceske Hnedouhelne Doly [*North Bohemian Lignite (Brown Coal) Mines*]   (CZ)
SHD .... Societe d'Histoire du Droit [*French*]   (SLS)
SHD .... Srpsko Hemisko Drustvo [*Serbian Chemical Society*]   (YU)
ShD .... Step Motor [*Automation*], Step-by-Step Motor [*Electric machines*]   (RU)
SHDC .... Student Homeland Defense Corps [*South Korea*]
ShDM .... School of Peasant Youth [*Uzbekistan and Tadzikistan*]   (RU)
SHDM .... Sportovni Hry Delnicke Mladeze [*Young Workers' Athletic Games*]   (CZ)
ShDMRTs ... Centralized Interlocking Relay Mine Traffic Control   (RU)
ShDRTs ..... Centralized Relay Mine Traffic Control   (RU)
ShE .... Bypass Element   (RU)
ShE .... Scotch Encephalitis   (RU)
SHE .... Scrutineers for Honest Elections [*Australia*]
SHE .... Shah Establishment [*Saudi Arabia*]
SHE .... Shenyang [*China*] [*Airport symbol*]   (OAG)
SHE .... Sy Hoogedele [*The Right Honourable*] [*Afrikaans*]
SHEDCO .. Sharjah Economic Development Corporation [*United Arab Emirates*]   (MENA)
SHEerw ..... Sy Hoogeerwaarde [*The Right Reverend*] [*Afrikaans*]
SHEF .... Societe Holding Economique et Financiere [*Economic and Financial Holding Company*] [*France*]
sheg .... Jocular   (BU)
SHEHFA... Societe Hoteliere et d'Exploitation Hoteliere Franco-Africaine
SHEHGYD ... Sakarya Halk Egitimi Hizmetlerini Gelistirme Yayma Dernegi [*Sakarya Organization for the Development and Spread of Popular Educational Services*] [*Turkish Cypriot*]   (GC)
shelk........... Sericultural Sovkhoz [*Silk-Reeling Factory*] [*Topography*]   (RU)
ShELKOPRAVLENIYe ... Administration of Associated Silk Factories   (RU)
SHELLBENINREX ... Societe Shell Beninoise de Recherches et d'Exploitation
SHELL-CAMREX ... Societe Shell Camerounaise de Recherches et d'Exploitation
SHELL-DAHOREX ... Societe Shell Dahomeenne de Recherches et d'Exploitation
SHELL-IVOREX ... Societe Shell Ivoirienne de Recherches et d'Exploitation
SHELL-MAUREX ... Societe Shell Mauritanienne de Recherches et d'Exploitation
SHELL-NIGEREX ... Societe Shell Nigerienne de Recherche et d'Exploitation
SHELL-SENREX ... Shell Senegalaise de Recherches et d'Exploitation
SHELL-TOGOREX ... Societe Shell Togolaise de Recherches et d'Exploitation
SHEMA .... Organization for the Education and Rehabilitation of Hearing-Impaired Children and Youth [*Israel*]   (EAIO)
SHEw........ Sy Hoogeerwaarde [*The Right Reverend*] [*SHEerw*] [*See also*] [*Afrikaans*]
Shf............. Sahife [*Page*]   (TU)
SHF .... Societe Hydrotechnique de France [*Hydraulic Engineering Society*] [*France*]   (PDAA)
ShFZO....... Industrial Training School   (BU)
ShG .... Noise Generator   (RU)
SHG .... Schweizerische Heilpadagogische Gesellschaft [*Switzerland*]   (EAIO)
SHG .... Schweizerische Heraldische Gesellschaft [*Switzerland*]   (EAIO)
SHG .... Swiss Society for the Mentally Disabled   (EAIO)
SHGNA ...... Sydney Hospital Graduate Nurses Association [*Australia*]
Shh............. Sihhiye [*Hygiene*]   (TU)
SHH .... Society of Homes for the Handicapped [*Hong Kong*]   (EAIO)
SHHA........ Self Help Housing Agency
ShI .... Boarding School   (RU)
SHI .... Shimojishima [*Japan*] [*Airport symbol*]   (OAG)

SHI .... Societe Hoteliere Ivoirienne
ShI .... Step-by-Step Switch   (RU)
SHI .... Sumitomo Heavy Industries Ltd. [*Nuclear energy*] [*Japan*] (NRCH)
SHIA .... Handikapporganisationernas Internationella Bistandsstiftelse [*Swedish Organization of the Handicapped-International Aid Foundation*] [*Sweden*]   (EAIO)
SHIAL....... Societe pour l'Histoire des Israelites d'Alsace-Lorraine
SHIC.......... Societe Hoteliere et Immobiliere du Congo
SHICA....... Societe Hoteliere et Immobiliere de la Chaine des Alizes
SHICO ...... Shire Co. [*Somalia*]
shif .... Slate Plant [*Topography*]   (RU)
Shigenroren ... Zen-Nihon Shigen-Sangyo Rodokumiai Rengokai [*Japan Federation of Minerals Resources Industry Workers' Unions*]
Shiginren ... Shichuginko Jugyoin-Kumiai Rengokai [*Federation of City Bank Employees' Unions*] [*Japan*]
SHIHATA ... Shirika la Habari la Tanzania [*Tanzania News Agency*]   (AF)
shil .... Shilling   (RU)
ShIM .... Impulse Duration Modulation   (RU)
SHINBET ... Israel General Security Service [*Acronym represents Hebrew phrase*]
Shinbunroren ... Nihon Shinbun Rodokumiai Rengo [*Japanese Federation of Press Workers' Unions*]
SHINSAMBETSU ... Zenkoku Sangyobetsu Rodo Kumiai Rengo [*Japan*] (FEA)
SHINUI..... Political Party [*Israel*]   (ME)
SHIO .... Sveriges Hantverks- och Industriorganisation-Familjefoeretagen [*Federation of Trades, Industries, and Family Enterprises*] [*Sweden*]   (EY)
SHIP.......... State Heritage Inventory Project [*New South Wales, Australia*]
SHIPCON ... Shipping Control [*NATO*]   (NATG)
SHIPS .... Satellite Housing Integrated Programmed Support [*Australia*]
ShIR.......... Cord Register Finder   (RU)
shir .... Width   (RU)
ShIRAS ..... Artillery Shell Burst Simulator   (RU)
shirt............ Shirting [*Cloth*] [*Publishing Danish/Norwegian*]
shirtingsbd ... Shirtingsbind [*Cloth Binding*] [*Publishing Danish/Norwegian*]
shirtomsl .... Shirtingsomslag [*Cloth Wrapper*] [*Publishing Danish/Norwegian*]
shiv............. Rapids [*Topography*]   (RU)
SHIZO .... Penal Isolation Cell   (RU)
SHJ............ Sharjah [*United Arab Emirates*] [*Airport symbol*]   (OAG)
SHJ............ Sharjah Ruler's Flight [*United Arab Emirates*] [*ICAO designator*] (FAAC)
SHJO .... Slechthorende Jongeren Organisatie [*Netherlands*]   (EAIO)
ShK .... Broad Gauge   (RU)
ShK .... Cord Set Assembly   (RU)
ShK .... Pilot Balloon Set   (RU)
shk .... School   (RU)
SHK .... Schweizerische Hochschulkonferenz [*Switzerland*]   (SLS)
SHK .... Sehonghong [*Lesotho*] [*Airport symbol*]   (OAG)
SHK .... Shorouk Air [*Egypt*] [*ICAO designator*]   (FAAC)
SHK .... Societe Hoteliere du Kouilou
SHK .... Societe Hydroelectrique du Kouilou
SHK .... Statni Vedecka Knihovna, Hradec-Kralove [*State Scientific Library in Hradec-Kralove*]   (CZ)
SHK .... Sun Hung Kai Securities [*Hong Kong*]
ShK .... Track Gauge   (RU)
ShKAS....... Shpital'nyy, Komarnitskiy Rapid-Fire Aircraft (Machine Gun) (RU)
shkh .... Mine, Shaft   (RU)
ShKM .... Kolkhoz Youth School   (RU)
ShKM .... Peasant Youth School   (RU)
ShKN......... Primary School   (RU)
Shkolfil'm .. Central Motion Picture Laboratory of the Ministry of Education, RSFSR
shkrab........ Teacher, School Worker   (RU)
ShKU .... Plug-In Switchboard   (RU)
ShKU .... School of Cook Apprenticeship and Course Organization   (RU)
ShL .... Headset   (RU)
shl .... Lock, Sluice [*Topography*]   (RU)
SHL .... Saarberg-Hoelter-Lurgi GmbH
SHL .... Seltrust Holdings Limited [*Australia*]
Shl.............. Slag [*Road-paving material*] [*Topography*]   (RU)
shl-bet .... Slag Concrete   (RU)
SHLF........ Societe d'Histoire Litteraire de la France [*French*]   (SLS)
SHLRC...... Speech and Hearing Language Research Centre [*Macquarie University, Australia*]
ShM .... Ball Mill   (RU)
ShM .... Helmet-Mask (Gas Mask)   (RU)
ShM .... Mine Mill   (RU)
SHM .... Nanki Shirahama [*Japan*] [*Airport symbol*]   (OAG)
ShM .... Plastering Machine   (RU)
SHM .... Societe de la Haute-Mondah [*Gabon*]
SHM .... Societe des Hotelleries du Mali

SHM.......... Societe Hoteliere de Mauritanie
SHM.......... Spoldzielcze Hurtownie Miedzypowiatowe [*Intercounty Cooperative Wholesale Warehouses*]   (POL)
SHM.......... Sportovne [*or Sportovni*] Hry Mladeze [*Young People's Athletic Games*]   (CZ)
ShMA .... Axial Shaft Mill   (RU)
ShMAS..... School for Junior Aviation Specialists   (RU)
ShMO....... Nautical Training School   (RU)
ShMO....... Odessa Nautical School   (RU)
SHMP....... Service d'Hygiene Mobile et de Prophylaxie du Cameroun
ShMT .... Shaft-Mill Furnace   (RU)
ShMT .... Tangential Shaft Mill   (RU)
ShMU....... Nautical Apprenticeship School   (RU)
SHMU...... Statny Hydrologicky a Meteorologicky Ustav [*State Hydrological and Meteorological Institute*] [*Bratislava*]   (CZ)
shmutstit .... Half Title   (RU)
ShMVU..... School of Masters of Abundant Harvests   (RU)
SHMZ .... Savezni Hidrometeoroloski Zavod [*Federal Hydrometeorological Institute*] [*Belgrade*]   (YU)
SHN.......... Service Hydrologique National [*Guinean National Hydrological Service*] [*Research center*]   (EAS)
SHN.......... Servicio de Hidrografia Naval [*Naval Hydrographic Service*] [*Argentina*]   (ASF)
SHN.......... Shaheen Airport Services [*Pakistan*] [*ICAO designator*]   (FAAC)
SHN.......... Societe des Huileries du Niger
SHN.......... St. Helena [*ANSI three-letter standard code*]   (CNC)
SHNC....... Societe Hoteliere Nord-Cameroun
SHNFZ...... Southern Hemisphere Nuclear Free Zone [*Australia*]
SHNP....... Sydney Harbour National Park [*Australia*]
SHNUM... Shoqeria per Ndihme Ushtrise dhe Mbrojtje [*Albanian*]
ShO............ Assault Force   (RU)
ShO............ Bifilar Oscillograph, Soft-Iron Oscillograph   (RU)
ShO............ Cryptographic Section   (RU)
SHO........... North Shore Aero Club, Inc. [*New Zealand*] [*ICAO designator*] (FAAC)
SHO........... Societe Commerciale Industrielle et Agricole du Haut-Ogooue
SHO........... Societe du Haut-Ogooue [*Chadian trading company*]
SHOA .... Societe Hoteliere de l'Ouest Africain
SHOC....... SHAPE [*Supreme Headquarters Allied Powers Europe*] Operations Center [*NATO*]   (NATG)
SHOC....... Societe Horlogerie du Congo
SHODB ..... Seyir Hidrografi ve Osinografi Dairesi Baskanligi [*Department of Navigation, Hydrography, and Oceanography*] [*Turkey*] (MSC)
ShOK........ Siauliai Footwear Kombinat   (RU)
SHOM....... Service Hydrographique et Oceanographique de la Marine [*Naval Hydrographic Service*] [*French*]   (ASF)
SHORTIE ... Short-Range Thermal Imaging Equipment
S Hos .... Section d'Hospitalisation [*Military*] [*French*]   (MTD)
shoss .... Highway   (RU)
shotl .... Scottish   (RU)
SHOUT ..... Self Help Organisations United Together [*Australia*]
ShOV .... Shunt Field Winding   (RU)
ShP .... Cord Switch   (RU)
ShP .... Hachure Device   (RU)
ShP .... Listening Sonar   (RU)
ShP .... Pilot Balloon   (RU)
SHP .... Satellite Housing Program [*Australia*]
SHP .... Service Aerien Francais [*France*] [*ICAO designator*]   (FAAC)
SHP .... Societe d'Histoire de la Pharmacie [*French*]   (SLS)
SHP .... Sosyal Demokrasi Halkci Partisi [*Social Democratic Populist Party*] [*Turkey*] [*Political party*]   (EAIO)
SHP .... Special Humanitarian Programme [*Australia*]
SHPA .... Society of Hospital Pharmacists of Australia   (ADA)
SHPB........ Specijalizovana Hirurska Poljska Bolnica [*Field Hospital for Specialized Surgery*]   (YU)
SHPF....... Societe de l'Histoire du Protestantisme Francais [*French*]   (SLS)
ShPI......... Siauliai Pedagogical Institute   (RU)
ShPM .... Tie Tamper [*Railroads*]   (RU)
SHPN .... Savez Hrvatskih Privatnih Namjestenika [*Federation of Croatian Private Employees*]   (YU)
ShPO .... Full Hole Joint   (RU)
ShPP......... Detection Band Width   (RU)
ShPP......... Mine Surface Substation   (RU)
ShPR......... Hand-Operated Ship Steam Windlass   (RU)
ShPS......... Listening Sonar Station   (RU)
ShPSS....... Wide-Band Seismic Station   (RU)
ShPT......... Swiss Labor Party   (RU)
SHPz.......... Skupina Hloubkoveho Pruzkumu [*Deep Reconnaissance Detachment*]   (CZ)
SHQ........... Supreme Headquarters
ShR........... Bypass Relay   (RU)
ShR........... Bypass Rheostat   (RU)
ShR........... Circuit Resonator   (RU)
ShR........... Connecting Cord Relay   (RU)
ShR........... Plug-and-Jack   (RU)

SHR .... Severcesky Hnedouhelny Revir [*North Bohemian Lignite (Brown Coal) Basin*] (CZ)
SHR .... Shire Highlands Railway Co.
shr .... Shirtingrygg [*Half-Cloth*] [*Publishing Danish/Norwegian*]
shr .... Shrapnel (BU)
ShR .... Shunt Regulator (RU)
SHR .... Statni Hospodarska Rada [*State Economic Council*] (CZ)
ShR .... Step-by-Step Distributor (RU)
ShR .... Step Monitor [*Computers*] (RU)
SHR .... Student Homelessness Rate [*Australia*]
shr .... Type [*Printing*] (BU)
ShR .... Wall Socket (RU)
SHRA .... Spanish Human Rights Association (EAIO)
ShRB .... Tire-Repair Base (RU)
SHRCS ...... Svaz Horolezcu Republiky Ceskoslovenske [*Mountain Climbing Association of the Czechoslovak Republic*] (CZ)
SHRD .... Svaz Zamestnancu Hutniho Prumyslu a Rudnych Dolu [*Union of Employees in the Metallurgical Industry and Ore Mines*] (CZ)
ShRD .... Total Band Width (RU)
SHRH .... Servicios Hidraulicos de la Republica de Haiti [*Water Service of the Republic of Haiti*] (LAA)
SHRM .... Sportovne Hry Robotnickej Mladeze [*Athletic Games for Young Workers*]
ShRM .... Workers' Youth School (RU)
ShRS .... School of Helmsmen and Signalmen (RU)
ShRV .... Bypass Rheostat of an Exciter (RU)
ShRV .... Radio Broadcasting Station (RU)
ShRYu .... Young Workers' School (RU)
SHS .... Kraljevina Srba, Hrvata, i Slovenaca [*Kingdom of Serbs, Croats, and Slovenes*] (YU)
ShS .... Mine Construction (RU)
SHS .... Scandinavian Herpetological Society [*Denmark*] (EAIO)
SHS .... Scieries du Haut-Sassandra
SHS .... Shashi [*China*] [*Airport symbol*] (OAG)
SHS .... Slovenska Historicka Spolocnost [*Slovak Historical Society*] (CZ)
SHS .... Slovensky Hokejovy Svaz [*Slovak Ice Hockey Association*] (CZ)
SHS .... Societas Heraldica Scandinavica [*Denmark*] (EAIO)
SHS .... Srbi, Hrvati, i Slovenci [*Serbs, Croats, and Slovenes*] (YU)
SHS .... Stowarzyszenie Historykow Sztuki [*Poland*] (SLS)
SHS .... Sudan Horticultural Society
SHS .... Sunshine Aviation SA [*Switzerland*] [*ICAO designator*] (FAAC)
SHS .... Suomen Hammaslaeaekaeriseura [*Finland*] (SLS)
SHS .... Svaz Hokejistov Slovenska [*Slovak Ice Hockey Association*] (CZ)
SHS .... Swiss Heraldry Society (EAIO)
SHSBF ...... Societe des Huiles et Savons du Burkina Faso [*Producer of oils and soaps*]
SHS/DC .... Social and Human Sciences Documentation Centre [*UNESCO*] (DUND)
ShShS .... Headquarters Cryptographic Service (RU)
SHSHV ..... Societe des Huiles et Savohs de Haute-Volta
SHSiKA ..... Sekcja Historii Sztuki i Krytyki Artystycznej [*Section on the History of Art and Art Criticism*] (POL)
ShSK .... Samajaya ha Samaika Kendraya [*Sri Lanka*] (EAIO)
SHSKM ..... Stowarzyszenie Historykow Sztuki i Kultury Materialnej [*Association of Historians of Art and Material Culture*] (POL)
ShSM .... Rural Youth School (RU)
SHSM ...... Sportovni Hry Skolni Mladeze [*Student Athletic Games*] (CZ)
sht .... Adit, Gallery [*Topography*] (RU)
sh t .... Hardness Scale (RU)
sht .... Piece (RU)
SHT .... Societe Hoteliere de Treichville
SHT .... Societe Hoteliere du Tchad
sht .... Staff, Headquarters (BU)
sht .... State, Staff (RU)
SHT .... Sydney Harbour Tunnel [*Australia*]
ShT .... Tanzanian Shilling
shta .... Army Headquarters (BU)
ShtA .... Ground Attack Aviation (BU)
shtabokr..... District Headquarters (RU)
shtabrig...... Brigade Headquarters (RU)
shtadiv....... Division Headquarters (RU)
shtaesk....... Squadron Headquarters (RU)
shtakor....... Corps Headquarters (RU)
Shtalvo....... Leningrad Military District Headquarters (RU)
Shtamorsichern ... Black Sea Naval Headquarters (RU)
SHTAMPOZHEST' ... Stamped Sheet Metalware Plant (RU)
Shtamvo ..... Moscow Military District Headquarters (RU)
ShtAO........ Instrument Section Control Panel [*Nuclear energy*] (BU)
shtarm .... Army Headquarters (RU)
Shtbobm..... Baltic Sea Coast Defense Headquarters (RU)
shtd .... Division Headquarters (BU)
shtda .... General Headquarters (BU)

Shtergres.... Shterovka State Regional Electric Power Plant (RU)
SHTFNRJ ... Savez Hemicara-Tehnologa Federativna Narodna Republika Jugoslavija [*Union of Chemical Technologists of Yugoslavia*] (YU)
shtks.......... Corps Headquarters (BU)
Shtl............ Sehitlik [*Cemetery*] [*Mzl*] [*Military*] [*See also*] (TU)
SHTM .... Societe des Hotelleries et du Tourisme du Mali
shtoa.......... Separate Army Headquarters (BU)
ShTP......... Braided Telephone Cord (RU)
shtpk......... Regimental Headquarters (RU)
SHTR .... Societe pour les Reacteurs Nucleaires HTR [*France*] (PDAA)
ShTS .... Connection Contact (RU)
ShTsV .... Water Chromaticity Scale (RU)
SHTT .... Societe Hoteliere et Touristique de Tunisie
ShTT .... Tank Technicians' School (RU)
ShTU .... Trade Apprenticeship School (RU)
ShTV .... Twisted Telephone Cord (RU)
SHU .... Saarberg-Hoelter-Umwelttechnik GmbH
SHU .... Scandinavian Hydrographic Union (MSC)
ShU .... Shilling Ugandan
SHU .... Statni Historicky Ustav [*State Historical Institute*] (CZ)
ShUMP ...... Apprenticeship School in Mass-Employment Skills (RU)
ShUNS .... School for Advanced Training of the Command Staff (RU)
Shuppanroren ... Nihon Shuppan Rodokumiai Rengokai [*Japan Federation of Publishing Workers' Unions*]
SHURE ..... Save the Hawkesbury's Unique River Environment [*Australia*]
s/hv .... Sort/Hvitt [*Black and White*] [*Publishing Danish/Norwegian*]
SHV .... Statni Hudebni Vydavatelstvi [*State Music Publishing House*] (CZ)
SHV .... Steenkolen-Handelsvereeniging NV [*Netherlands*]
shv............ Swedish (RU)
ShVAK...... Shpital'nyy-Volkov Aircraft Wing Cannon (RU)
SHVD .... Sportovni Hry Vojenskeho Dorostu [*Junior Military Athletic Games*] (CZ)
SHVEYPROM ... Garment Industry (RU)
SHVEYPROMSOYUZ ... Producers' Union of the Garment Industry (RU)
shveyts .... Swiss (RU)
ShVLP .... School of Advanced Flight Training (RU)
SHVM .... Sportovni Hry Vysokoskolske Mladeze [*University Youth Sports Games*] (CZ)
SHVP........ Societe Hoteliere Victory Palace
ShVZ .... Siauliai Bicycle Plant (RU)
SHW .... Sharurah [*Saudi Arabia*] [*Airport symbol*] (OAG)
SHY .... Shinyanga [*Tanzania*] [*Airport symbol*] (OAG)
SHZ .... Savezni Hidrometeoroloski Zavod [*Federal Hydrometeorological Institute*] (YU)
SHZ .... Seshute's [*Lesotho*] [*Airport symbol*] (OAG)
Shz .... Sounding Balloon (RU)
SHZ .... Sportovni Hry Zactva [*Student Athletic Games*] (CZ)
SHZ .... Sulfat-Huettenzement [*Sulfate Blast Furnace Cement*] (EG)
SHZ .... Svaz Zamestnancu v Hornictvi [*Union of Employees in the Mining Industry*] (CZ)
ShZh .... Silk Gland (RU)
ShZO .... Reserve Officers School (BU)
SI.............. Hunting Switch (RU)
si............... Inertia (RU)
SI.............. Infrared Spectroscopy (RU)
SI.............. International System of Units (RU)
SI.............. Northeast (BU)
SI.............. Pulse Counter (RU)
Si.............. Saki [*Cape, Point*] [*Japan*] (NAU)
SI.............. Sanitarni Inspektorat [*Sanitary Inspectorate*] (YU)
si............... Sans Interet [*Ex-Dividend*] [*Stock exchange*] [*French*]
SI.............. Sekretarijat za Industriju (SIV) [*Secretariat of Industry*] (YU)
SI.............. Sekretarijat za Informacije (SIV) [*Secretariat of Information*] (YU)
SI.............. Seksi [*Section*] (IN)
SI.............. Senter for Industriforskning [*Center for Industrial Research*] [*Norway*] (EAS)
SI.............. Sentralinstitutt foer Industriell Forskning [*Central Institute for Industrial Research*] [*Research center*] [*Norway*] (IRC)
SI.............. Servicio de Informaciones [*Information Service*] [*Peru*] (LA)
SI.............. Severo-Istok [*Northeast*] (YU)
SI.............. Sezione Italiana [*Italy*] (EAIO)
SI.............. Sicherung [*German*] [*Computer science*] (ADPT)
Si.............. Sidi [*Tomb*] [*Arabic*] (NAU)
SI.............. Siena [*Car registration plates*] [*Italian*]
Si.............. Sikh Regiment [*India*] [*Army*]
Si.............. Silicio [*Silicon*] [*Chemical element*] [*Portuguese*]
Si.............. Silizium [*Silicon*] [*Chemical element*] [*German*]
SI.............. Skholi Ippikou [*Cavalry School*] [*Greek*] (GC)
SI.............. Skovteknisk Institut [*Danish Institute of Forest Technology*] (ARC)
SI.............. Smith, Imossi & Co. Ltd. [*Gibraltar*]
SI.............. Social Independiente [*Netherlands Antilles*] [*Political party*] (EY)

SI.............. Socialist International [*Political party*]   (EAIO)
SI.............. Sociedad de Industrias [*Industrial Association*] [*Peru*]   (LA)
SI.............. Societe d'Intervention
SI.............. Society of Indexers   (EAIO)
SI.............. Solomon Islands   (BARN)
SI.............. Soroptimist International [*Cambridge, England*]   (EAIO)
SI.............. South Island [*New Zealand*]   (BARN)
SI.............. Spratly Islands [*ANSI two-letter standard code*]   (CNC)
SI.............. Staroslovenski Institut [*Institute for Church Slavonic Studies*] (YU)
SI.............. Statni Inspekce [*State Inspection*]   (CZ)
SI.............. Statutory Instrument
SI.............. Sub-Inginer [*Romanian*]
Si.............. Sungai [*or Sungei*] [*River Malay*]   (NAU)
Si.............. Sungai [*or Sungei*] [*River Indonesian*]   (NAU)
SI.............. Survival International [*British*]   (EAIO)
SI.............. Svenska Institutet [*Sweden*]   (SLS)
SI.............. Synchronizing Pulse, Timing Pulse   (RU)
SI.............. Syndicat d'Initiative [*French*]
si.............. Synns Insiens [*In His Opinion*] [*Afrikaans*]
SI.............. Systeme International d'Unites [*International System of Units*] [*Also, SIU*]
SI.............. Szkola Inzynierska [*Engineering School*]   (POL)
Si.............. True North   (RU)
SI.............. Union of Industrialists   (BU)
SI3T.......... Syndicat des Industries Francaises du Telephone, du Telegraphe et de Leurs Applications Telematiques [*Association of French Telephone, Telegraph, and Related Telematics Industries*] [*France*]   (EAIO)
SIA.............. Safety Institute of Australia   (ADA)
SIA.............. Secretatiat of Industrial Approvals [*India*]   (PDAA)
SIA.............. Securities Institute of Australia   (ADA)
SIA.............. Service Intercontinental d'Assurances [*Morocco*]
SIA.............. Servico de Informacao Agricola [*Agricultural Information Service*] [*Rio De Janeiro, Brazil*]   (LAA)
SIA.............. Servizio Informazioni Aeronautiche [*Air Intelligence*] [*Italian*]
SIA.............. Singapore Airlines Ltd. [*ICAO designator*]   (FAAC)
SIA.............. Singapore Institute of Architects   (SLS)
SIA.............. Singapore International Airlines   (PDAA)
SIA.............. Skholi Iptamenon Aeroporon [*Air Force Flying School*] [*Greek*] (GC)
SIA.............. Societa Italiana di Anatomia [*Italy*]   (EAIO)
SIA.............. Societa Italiana di Andrologia [*Italian*]   (SLS)
SIA.............. Societa Italiana di Audiologia e Foniatria [*Italian*]   (SLS)
SIA.............. Societe des Ingenieurs Civils de France
SIA.............. Societe des Ingenieurs de l'Automobile [*France*]   (EAIO)
SIA.............. Societe d'Investissements Africains
SIA.............. Societe Immobiliere Africaine
SIA.............. Societe Interafricaine d'Assurances
SIA.............. Societe Internationale d'Acupuncture [*French*]   (SLS)
SIA.............. Societe Ivoirienne d'Assurances
SIA.............. Solkanska Industrija Apna [*Solkan Lime Industry*] [*Nova Gorica*] (YU)
SIA.............. Spolek Ceskoslovenskych Inzenyru a Architektu [*Society of Czechoslovak Engineers and Architects*]   (CZ)
SIA.............. Statiunea de Intretinere Auto [*Automotive Maintenance Station*] (RO)
SIA.............. Steel Industry Authority [*Australia*]
SIA.............. Sugar Industry Authority [*Jamaica*]   (GEA)
SIA.............. Swiss Society of Engineers and Architects   (IAA)
SIA.............. Xian [*China*] [*Airport symbol*]   (OAG)
SIAA.......... Seed Industry Association of Australia
SIAA.......... Singapore Industrial Automation Association   (EAIO)
SIAA.......... Societe Ivoirienne d'Appareils Automatiques
SIAAC....... Syndicat des Intermediaires d'Assurances Agrees au Cameroun
SIAAP....... Sugar Industry Adjustment Assistance Program [*Australia*]
SIAB.......... Sociedad de Ingenieros Agronomos de Bolivia [*Bolivia*]   (DSCA)
SIAB.......... Societe Industrielle et Automobile Bennouna [*Morocco*]
SIABC....... Sociedad Iberoamericana de Biologia Celular [*Ibero-American Society for Cell Biology - IASCB*]   (EAIO)
SIAC.......... Secretariado Interamericano de Accion Catolica [*Inter-American Secretariat of Catholic Action*] [*Santiago, Chile*]   (LAA)
SIAC.......... Servicio de Informacion Agricola y Comercial [*Mexico*]   (DSCA)
SIAC.......... Societa Italiana Additivi per Carburanti [*Italy*]   (PDAA)
SIAC.......... Societe d'Applications de l'Informatique et du Calcul [*French*] (ADPT)
SIAC.......... Societe Immobiliere Africaine et de Commerce
SIAC.......... Societe Internationale des Artistes Chretiens [*International Society for Christian Artists*] [*Lydiate, Merseyside, England*]   (EAIO)
SIAC.......... Societe Nationale des Industries Algeriennes de la Chaussure
SIACA........ Societe Immobiliere Africaine de Courtage et d'Assurances
SIACA........ Societe Ivoiro-Allemande de Conserves d'Ananas
SIACAF..... Societe Industrielle et Agricole Centrafricaine
SIACI .... Societe des Industries Alimentaires en Cote-D'Ivoire

SIACI .... Societe Intercontinental d'Assurances pour le Commerce et l'Industrie [*Intercontinental Assurance Company of Commerce and Industry*] [*France*]
SIA-Congo ... Societe Industrielle et Agricole du Congo
SIACRE..... Societe Inter-Africaine de Courtage de Reassurances [*Senegal*] (EY)
SIAC='s.... Specialized Information Analysis Centres
SIAD.......... Societa Italiana Acetilene e Derivati
SIAD.......... Societa Italiana Autori Drammatici [*Italian*]   (SLS)
SIADA....... Societe Industrielle et Agricole pour le Developpement de l'Alaotra
SIADES..... Sociedad de Ingenieros Agronomos de El Salvador [*Association of Salvadoran Agricultural Engineers*]   (LA)
SIAE.......... Scottish Institute of Adult Education   (SLS)
SIAE.......... Societa Italiana degli Autori ed Editori [*Italian Authors' and Publishers' Association*]
SIAE.......... Societa Italiana per l'Antropologia e la Etnologia [*Italian*]   (SLS)
SIAE.......... Societe Abidjanaise Import-Export
SIAE.......... Societe Italienne des Auteurs et Editeurs   (FLAF)
SIAEK ...... Syndesmos Ilektonikon Asfaleias Enaerias Kykloforias [*Association of Air Traffic Controllers*]   (GC)
SIAEX ...... Societe Ivoirienne d'Achat et d'Exportation
SIAF.......... Societe Internationale Africaine [*Morocco*]
SIAG.......... Societe Industrielle et Automobile de Guinee
SIAGRUZ ... Inversiones Agropecuarias SA [*Colombia*]   (COL)
SIAIEX...... Societe Inter-Africaine d'Import-Export
SIAL .... Sociedade Imobiliaria e de Administracoes Limitada
SIAL .... Societe Industrielle et Agricole de la Lobaye
SIAM......... Sociedad Industrial de Articulos Metalicos Ltda. [*Colombia*] (COL)
SIAM......... Societe d'Investissements Agricoles a Madagascar
SIAM......... Societe Industrielle Alimentaire de Magaria
SIAM......... Societe Ivoirienne d'Acconage et de Manutention
SIAMA...... Society for Interests of Active Missionaries in Asia, Africa, and America   (EAIO)
SIAMAR ... Societe d'Investissements Agricoles au Maroc
SIAMO...... Syndicat Interprofessionnel pour l'Acheminement de la Main-d'Oeuvre
SIAN......... Institute of Seismology of the Academy of Sciences, USSR   (RU)
SIAN......... Societe Industrielle d'Adjame Nord
SIAN......... Societe Industrielle et Agricole du Niari [*Niari Industrial and Agricultural Company*] [*Congo*]   (AF)
SIANI .... Societe Industrielle et Automobile du Haut-Niger
SIANS ...... Societa Italiana Attivita Nervosa Superiore [*Italian*]   (SLS)
SIAO.......... Societe d'Investissement d'Affaires Occidentales [*Paris, France*]
SIAO.......... Societe Immobiliere de l'Afrique Occidentale
SIAOC....... Societe d'Investissement d'Affaires Occidentales [*Paris, France*]
SIAP .... Sociedad Interamericana de Planificacion [*Inter-American Planning Society - IAPS*] [*San Juan, Puerto Rico*]   (LAA)
SIAP .... Societe Industrielle Africaine de Plastiques
SIAP .... Statistical Institute for Asia and the Pacific [*Research center*] [*Japan*]   (IRC)
SIAP .... Statistical Institute for Asia and the Pacific [*United Nations*] (ECON)
SIAP-CONGO ... Societe Industrielle d'Articles en Papier du Congo
SIAPE....... Societa Industriale Automatismo Prodotti Electronici [*Industrial Firm for Automatic Electronic Equipment*] [*Italian*] (WER)
SIAPE....... Societe Industrielle d'Acide Phosphorique et d'Engrais [*Phosphoric Acid and Fertilizer Manufacturing Company*] [*Tunisia*]   (AF)
SIAR......... Siviele Ingenieurswese-Adviesraad [*South Africa*]   (AA)
SIAR......... Societa Italiana di Anestesiologia Rianimazione e Terapia del Dolore [*Italian*]   (SLS)
SIAR......... Societe de la Surveillance Industrielle [*France*]   (PDAA)
SIARA ...... Societe Interafricaine de Representations Automobile
SIARM ..... Societe Ivoirienne d'Approvisionnement et de Restauration Maritime
SIAS .... Scandinavian Institute of African Studies   (AF)
SIAS .... Scandinavian Institute of Asian Studies [*See also CINA*] [*Later, NIAS*]   (EAIO)
SIAS .... Siemens Ablaufsimulator [*Siemens Course Simulator*] [*German*] (ADPT)
SIAS .... Small Industries Advisory Service
SIAS .... Societe Ivoirienne Azar et Salame
SIASA ...... Societa Italiana per l'Archeologia e la Storia delle Arti [*Italian*] (SLS)
SIASO .... Societa Italiana per gli Archivi Sanitari Ospedalieri [*Italian*] (SLS)
SIASP....... Societa Istriana di Archeologia e Storia Patria [*Italian*]   (SLS)
SIAT .... Seccion Investigacion de Accidentes del Transito [*Traffic Accidents Investigation Section*] [*Chile*]   (LA)
SIAT .... Societa Italiana Assicurazioni Trasporti [*Italy*]   (EY)
SIAT .... Societa Italiana di Ingegneria Aerofotogrammetria e Topografia [*Italian*]   (SLS)
SIAT .... Societe d'Investissement Arabe de Tunisie [*Arab Investment Company of Tunisia*]   (AF)

SIAT .... Societe Immobiliere d'Afrique Tropicale
SIAT .... Societe Industrielle et Agricole du Tabac Tropical
SIAT .... Societe Ivoirienne Agricole de Tiassale
SIATE .... Servicios de Informacion y Asistencia Tecnica a las Empresas [*Instituto Centroamericano de Investigacion y Tecnologia Industrial*] [*Guatemala*]
SIATSA ..... Servicios para la Investigacion Agricola Tropical Sociedad Anonima [*Tropical Agriculture Research Services*] [*Honduras*]   (ARC)
SIB .... Saudi International Bank
SIB .... Servico de Informacoes Bibliograficas [*Brazil*]
sib .... Siberia, Siberian   (RU)
SIB .... Sibiti [*Congo*] [*Airport symbol*]   (OAG)
SIB .... Sidang Injil Borneo
SIB .... Sistema de Informacion Bursatil [*Stock Exchange Information System*] [*Madrid Stock Exchange*] [*Information service or system*]   (IID)
SIB .... Sociedade Interplanetaria Brasileira [*Brazil*]
SIB .... Societa Italiana di Biogeografia [*Italian*]   (SLS)
SIB .... Societa Italiana di Biometria [*Italian*]   (SLS)
SIB .... Societa' Siba Aviation [*Italy*] [*ICAO designator*]   (FAAC)
SIB .... Societe Industrielle Bobolaise
SIB .... Societe Industrielle des Bois
SIB .... Societe Industrielle du Boina
SIB .... Societe Internationale de Biometeorologie [*International Society of Biometeorology*]   (EAIO)
SIB .... Societe Ivoirienne de Banque [*Ivorian Banking Company*]   (AF)
SIB .... Sovjetski Informativni Biro [*Soviet Information Bureau*]   (YU)
SIB .... Special Investigations Bureau   (ML)
SIB .... Statens Institut foer Byggnadsforskning [*National Swedish Institute for Building Research*] [*Research center*]   (IRC)
SIBA .... Societe d'Importation de Beaux Ameublements
SIBA .... Societe Industrielle de Bois Africains
SIBA .... Societe Industrielle de Briqueteries Africaines
SIBA .... Societe Industrielle des Blanchisseries Africaines
SIBA .... Societe Intercontinentale de Banque Societe Anonyme
SIBACI ..... Societe Industrielle des Beaux-Arts de l'Ameublement de Cote-D'Ivoire
SIBACO .... Societe Immobiliere de la Baie de Cocody
SibADI ...... Siberian Highway Institute Imeni V. V. Kuybyshev   (RU)
SIBAF .... Societe Industrielle de Bois Africains
SIBAG ...... Societe d'Industries de Bois au Gabon
SIBAGEC ... Societe Ivoirienne de Batiment et de Genie Civil
SIBAT .... Societe Industrielle du Batiment
SIBAT .... Societe Ivoirienne Burguiere & Ambrosino des Transports
SIBC .... Societe Immobiliere du Boulevard Carde [*Ivory Coast*]
SIBC .... Societe Internationale de Bibliographie Classique [*French*]   (SLS)
Sibe .... Sicherheitsbeauftragter [*Security Officer*]   (EG)
SIBE .... Societe d'Importation des Bois Exotiques
SIBEK .... Second International Biomass Experiment   (MSC)
SIBEKA ..... Societe d'Entreprise et d'Investissement du Beceka [*Belgium*]
SIBEX .... Singapore International Building Exhibition
SIBEX .... Submillimetre-Infrared Balloon Experiment [*Joint Enterprise Between NPL (DoI) and University of Florence*] [*Italy*]   (PDAA)
SIBF .... Stiftelsen Stockholms Studentkarers Internationella Bistandsfond [*Swedish Students' International Assistance Fund*] [*Sweden*]
Sibgiprobum ... State Institute for the Planning of Pulp and Paper Industry Establishments in Siberia and the Far East   (RU)
Sibgiprogormash ... Siberian State Planning, Design, and Experimental Institute of Mining Machinery   (RU)
Sibgiprotorg ... Siberian State Planning Institute of Trade   (RU)
Sibgiprotrans ... Siberian State Planning and Surveying Institute of the State Industrial Committee for Transportation Construction of the USSR   (RU)
SIBIA .... Societe Ivoirienne des Boulangeries et des Industries Alimentaires
SIBICOB... Societe Industrielle de Biscuiterie et Confiserie du Benin
SIBIL .... Systeme Integre pour les Bibliotheques Universitaires de Lausanne [*Integrated System for the University of Lausanne Libraries*] [*Switzerland*]   (IID)
SIBIL .... System Informatise pour Biblitheques [*Information System for Libraries*]   (EAIO)
SibIZMIR ... Siberian Institute of Terrestrial Magnetism, Ionosphere and Radio Wave Propagation (of the Siberian Department of the Academy of Sciences, USSR)   (RU)
SibIZRA .... Siberian Institute for the Protection of Plants   (RU)
SIBKIS ...... Siberian Complex Institute of Structures and Building Materials   (RU)
SIBM .... Societa Italiana di Biologia Marina [*Italian*]   (SLS)
SIBM .... Societe Internationale de Biologie Mathematique [*International Society of Mathematical Biology*]   (EAIO)
SIBMAS.... Societe Internationale des Bibliotheques et Musees des Arts du Spectacle [*International Association of Libraries and Museums of the Performing Arts*]   (EAIO)

SibNIA ...... Siberian Scientific Research Aviation Institute   (RU)
SibNIILKhE ... Siberian Scientific Research Institute of Forestry and Forest Utilization   (RU)
SIBNIISKhOZ ... Siberian Scientific Research Institute of Agriculture   (RU)
SibNIIZh... Siberian Scientific Research Institute of Livestock Breeding   (RU)
SIBNIIZKhOZ ... Siberian Scientific Research Grain Institute   (RU)
SibNIVI..... Siberian Scientific Research Veterinary Institute   (RU)
SIBO.......... Societa Italiana di Bioterapia e di Omeopatia [*Italian*]   (SLS)
SIBO.......... Societe Industrielle de Bonneterie
SIBO.......... Societe Ivoirienne des Bois de l'Est
SIBOIS..... Societe Industrielle Ivoirienne des Bois
SIBOL .... Sweden Integrated Banking On-Line [*Computer science*]   (ADPT)
SIBOR ...... Singapore Interbank Offer Rates
SIBP .... Societe Industrielle Belge des Petroles [*Belgium*]   (BAS)
SIBP .... Societe Ivoirienne des Petroles BP
SIBRAS..... Societe Industrielle de Brasseries du Senegal
Sibrybvod... Administration of Fish Conservation and Fisheries in Siberia   (RU)
SIBS.......... Societa Italiana di Biologia Sperimentale [*Italian*]   (SLS)
SIB-SA ...... Societe Immobiliere du Benin
Sibsantekhmontazh ... Siberian Sanitary Engineering Installation Trust   (RU)
Sibsel'mash ... Novosibirsk Agricultural Machinery Plant   (RU)
SIBT .... Societe Ivoirienne des Bois de Tiassale
Sibtyazhmash ... Siberian Heavy Machinery Plant   (RU)
SIBVO ...... Siberian Military District   (RU)
SIC............ La Specialisation Industrielle et Chimique
SIC............ Sabah Indian Congress   (ML)
SIC............ Science de l'Intelligence Creatrice
SIC............ Scientific Information Centre of the Bulgarian Academy of Sciences   (EAIO)
SIC............ Secretaria de Industria y Comercio [*Secretariat of Industry and Commerce*]   (LA)
SIC............ Servei d'Informacio Catala [*Catalan Information Service*] [*Spanish*]   (WER)
SIC............ Servicio de Inteligencia Colombiano [*Colombian Intelligence Service*]   (LA)
SIC............ Servicio de Inteligencia Criminal [*Criminal Intelligence Service*] [*Ecuador*]   (LA)
SIC............ Servicio de Intercambio Cientifico [*Panamerican*]   (LAA)
SIC............ Servicio Informativo Continental [*Press agency*] [*Argentina*]
SIC............ Sinhala Institute of Culture [*Sri Lanka*]   (EAIO)
SIC............ Small Industries Corporation [*Guyana*]   (LA)
SIC............ Sociedade Intercontinental de Comercio Lda.
SIC............ Societa Italiana Cauzioni [*Italy*]   (EY)
SIC............ Societa Italiana di Chemioterapia [*Italian*]   (SLS)
SIC............ Societe d'Import et de Commission
SIC............ Societe Immobiliere du Cameroon [*Cameroon Real Estate Company*]   (AF)
SIC............ Societe Immobiliere du Cameroun [*Cameroon*]   (IMH)
SIC............ Societe Industrielle des Cacaos [*Cameroon*]
SIC............ Societe Industrielle et Commerciale [*Industrial and Commercial Company*] [*Senegal*]   (AF)
SIC............ Societe Industrielle pour le Traitement des Caroubes [*North African*]
SIC............ Societe Intercontinentale des Containers [*France*]   (PDAA)
SIC............ Societe Internationale de Cardiologie [*Switzerland*]   (SLS)
SIC............ Societe Internationale de Chirurgie [*International Society of Surgery - ISS*] [*Basel, Switzerland*]   (EA)
SIC............ Societe Internationale de Criminologie [*International Society of Criminology*]   (EA)
SIC............ Societe Ivoirienne de Cinema
SIC............ Society of Icelandic Composers   (EAIO)
SIC............ Sports Industries Commission [*New South Wales, Australia*]
SIC............ Srp i Cekic [*Hammer and Sickle*]   (YU)
SIC............ State Insurance Corporation [*Nigeria*]
SIC............ State Investment Corp. Ltd. [*Mauritius*]   (EY)
SIC............ Systeme Informatique pour la Conjoncture [*Information System for the Economy*] [*INSEE*] [*France*] [*Information service or system*]   (IID)
SICA .... Sociedade Industrial e Comercial Africana Lda. [*Nampula*]
SICA .... Societe d'Interet Collectif Agricole   (FLAF)
SICA .... Societe Immobiliere Centrafricaine
SICA .... Societe Immobiliere de la Cote-d'Afrique
SICA .... Societe Industrielle de l'Est Camerounais
SICA .... Societe Industrielle et Commerciale Africaine
SICA .... Societe Industrielle et Commerciale d'Approvisionnements
SICAB ...... Societe Immobiliere Cocody Abidjan
SICAB ...... Societe Industrielle Camerounaise des Bois
SICABAG ... Societe d'Interet Collectif Agricole de Guadeloupe [*Guadeloupe*]   (DSCA)
SICABAM ... Societe d'Interet Collectif Agricole Bananiere de la Martinique   (EY)
SICABLE .. Societe Ivoirienne de Cables
SICABO .... Societe Cooperative Agricole de Bonoua

SICABO .... Societe Ivoirienne de Carrosserie Bois
SICAC .... Societe Industrielle Commerciale Agricole de la Casamance
SICAF........ Societe Industrielle Chimique Africaine
SICAF........ Societe Industrielle de Couvertures Africaines
SICAF........ Societe Ivoirienne de Culture d'Ananas Frais
SICAFE ..... Sindicato de la Industria del Cafe [*Union of the Coffee Industry*] [*El Salvador*]   (LA)
SICAG .... Societe Industrielle Commerciale et Agricole de Guinee
SICAG .... Societe Industrielle de Cautionnement de Garantie
SICAH .... Societe Internationale pour le Credit Agricole Hypothecaire (FLAF)
SICA-HR... Societe d'Interet Collectif Agricole-Habitat Rural [*Rural Agriculture-Habitat Collective Interest Society*] [*Guadeloupe*]   (LA)
SICAI .... Societa d'Ingegneria e Consulenza Attivita Industriali
SICAI .... Societa Italo-Congolese Attivita Industriali
SICAI .... Societe Italo-Congolaise d'Aide a l'Industrie
SICAL .... Societe Industrielle, Commerciale, et Agricole de la Likouala
SICAN........ Societe Industrielle et Commerciale de l'Afrique du Nord d'Engrais et Produits Agricoles [*Algeria*]
SICAO........ Societe Industrielle et Commerciale de l'Afrique de l'Ouest
SICAP .... Servicio Interamericano de Cooperacion Agricola Panamena [*Panama*]   (LAA)
SICAP .... Societe Immobiliere du Cap-Vert
SICAPE...... Societe Italo-Congolaise d'Armement et de Peche
SICAPEB .. Societe d'Interet Collectif Agricole des Planteurs et Producteurs-Exportateurs de Bananes [*Guadeloupe*]   (DSCA)
SICAR .... Societe Ivoirienne de Courtage, d'Assurances, et de Reassurances
SICAT .... Societe Immobiliere et Commerciale de l'Afrique Tropicale
SICAV .... Societe d'Investissement a Capital Variable [*Variable-Capital Investment Co.*] [*French*]   (WER)
SICC .... Secours International de Caritas Catholica [*Belgium*]   (EAIO)
SICC .... Singapore International Chamber of Commerce
SICC .... Standards Information Center of China [*Library*]
SICCA .... Societe Industrielle des Cuirs et Caoutchouc
SICCACAOS ... Societe Industrielle Camerounaise des Cacaos [*Producer of cocoa and cocoa butter*] [*Cameroon*]
SICCI........ Societe Industrielle et Commerciale de Cote-D'Ivoire
SICCRA..... Singapore International Chamber of Commerce Rubber Association
SICCT........ Secretaria da Industria, Comercio, Ciencia, e Tecnologia do Estado de Sao Paulo [*Brazil*]
SICE .... Sistema Informativo Commercio Estero [*Italy*]
SICE .... Societe Industrielle et Commerciale de l'Emyrne
SICEJ .... Society of Instrument and Control Engineers of Japan   (IAA)
SICELP ..... Societa Italiana Costruzioni e Lavori Pubblici
SICES........ Sindicato de la Industria del Cemento de El Salvador [*Union of the Cement Industry of El Salvador*]   (LA)
SICF .... Societe Ivoirienne des Chemins de Fer [*Railway system*] [*The Ivory Coast*]   (EY)
SICFA........ Societa Italiana Commercio Ferramenta e Affini nelle Colonie
SICFA........ Societe Industrielle et Commerciale Franco-Africaine
SICFOM ... Societe Immobiliere et Commerciale pour la France et l'Outre-Mer
SICH.......... Sociedad Internacional de la Ciencia Horticola [*Netherlands*]   (DSCA)
SICHILMA ... Sindicato de Chicleros y Laborantes en Madera [*Guatemala*]   (DSCA)
sichtb.......... Sichtbar [*Visible*] [*German*]   (GCA)
Sichtbarmach ... Sichtbarmachung [*Rendering Visible*] [*German*]   (GCA)
SICI .... Societe Immobiliere et Commerciale Ivoirienne
SICK .... Societe Immobiliere et Commerciale du Kouilou
SICLIES.... Secretaria Interuniversitaria de Coordinacion Latinoamericana para la Investigacion Economico-Social   (LAA)
SICM .... Societe Internationale de Construction et de Menuiserie
SICM .... Societe Ivoirienne de Ciments et Materiaux
SICMA ...... Societe Industrielle et Commerciale de Materiel Aeronautique [*French*]
SICMEOS ... Societe Industrielle et Commerciale de Materiel d'Equipement d'Organisation et de Securite [*Senegal*]
SICMI .... Societe Internationale pour le Check-Up Medical Interdisciplinaire [*Belgium*]   (SLS)
SICN.......... Societe Industrielle de Combustibles Nucleaires [*French*]
SICN.......... Societe Industrielle et Commerciale Nigerienne
SICN.......... Syndicate for Fabrication of Fuel Elements [*French*] [*Acronym is based on foreign phrase*]
SICN.......... Systeme Ivoirien de Compatibilite Nationale
SICNA....... Societe Industrielle et Commerciale Nord-Africaine d'Engrais et Produits Agricoles [*Morocco*]
SICND....... Societe Immobiliere du Comptoir National du Diamant
SICO.......... Sociedad Importadora Comercial [*Colombia*]   (COL)
SICO.......... Societe Industrielle et Commerciale en Oubangui
SICO.......... Societe Ivoirienne pour le Commerce avec l'Om
SICOA....... Societe Immobiliere et Commerciale de l'Ouest Africain Cote-D'Ivoire

SICOB .... Salon des Industries du Commerce et de l'Organisation du Bureau [*Exposition of Office and Business Supply Industries and Office Organization*] [*French*]   (WER)
SICOBOIS ... Societe Industrielle et Commerciale des Bois Tropicaux
SICOC .... Societe Industrielle et Commerciale des Oleagineux Centrafricains
SICOCAM ... Societe Industrielle et Commerciale du Cameroun
SICOD....... Societe Industrielle de Cosmetiques et Derives
SICODEM-CI ... Societe Industrielle et Commerciale pour le Developpement du Mais en Cote-D'Ivoire
SICOE .... Societe Industrielle et Commerciale de la Cote Est
SICOF .... Societe de l'Industrie de la Confection de Fes [*Morocco*]
SICOF .... Societe Industrielle, Commerciale, et Financiere
SICOFAA ... Sistema de Cooperacion entre las Fuerzas Aereas Americanas [*System of Cooperation among American Air Forces*]   (LA)
SICOFEM ... Societe Ivoirienne de Confections Feminines et Masculines
SICOFREL ... Societe Ivoirienne pour la Commercialisation des Fruits et Legumes
SICOGERE ... Societe Ivoirienne de Copropriete et de Gerance
SICOGI ..... Societe Ivoirienne de Construction et de Gestion Immobiliere
SICOL .... Sociedade Importadora Commercial Limitada
SICOM..... Societe Industrielle de Constructions Metalliques
SICOM..... Societe Industrielle et Commerciale
SICOM..... Societe Industrielle et Commerciale de Marrakech
SICOM..... Societe Industrielle et Commerciale de M'Balmayo
SICOM..... State Industrial and Investment Corp. of Maharashtra [*India*]   (PDAA)
SICOMA... Societe Immobiliere et Commerciale Africaine
SICOMA... Societe Industrielle et Commerciale de Mauritanie
SICOMA... Societe Ivoirienne de Construction et de Materiaux
SICOMAD ... Societe Industrielle de la Cote Ouest de Madagascar
SICOMAR ... Societe Ivoirienne de Consignation, de Manutention, et d'Armement
SICOME... Societe Industrielle de Confection a Meknes [*Morocco*]
SICOMED ... Societe Ivoirienne de Construction Medicale
SICOMI .... Societe Immobilieres pour le Commerce et l'Industrie [*France*]   (PDAA)
SICOMO... Societe Industrielle de Confection Moderne
SICON....... Societe Industrielle et Commerciale du Niger
SICONEXIM ... Societe Intercontinentale de Constructions et d'Exploitations Immobiliers, Madagascar
SICONGO ... Societe Immobiliere du Congo
SICONIEX ... Societe Industrielle Commerciale Nigerienne d'Import-Export
SICONIGER ... Societe Industrielle et Commerciale du Niger
SICOP .... Sistemul Integrat de Conducere a Productiei de Constructii-Montaj [*Integrated Management System for the Production of Constructions and Assemblies*]   (RO)
SICOPECHE ... Societe Ivoirienne de Cooperation Internationale pour la Peche
SICOPEG ... Societe Internationale de Conditionnement, de Participation, et d'Entreprise Generale
SICOPHAR ... Societe Industrielle du Coton Pharmaceutique
SICOR....... Societe Ivoirienne de Coco Rape
SICOS .... State Insurance Co. of Somalia [*Djibouti*]   (EY)
SICOT .... Societe Internationale de Chirurgie Orthopedique et de Traumatologie [*International Society of Orthopaedic Surgery and Traumatology*] [*Brussels, Belgium*]   (EAIO)
SICOTOUR ... Societe Casamance Investissement Touristique
SICOTP..... Societe Ivoirienne Commerciale Ouvriere de Travaux Publics et de Batiments
SICOVAM ... Societe Interprofessionnelle de Compensation des Valeurs Mobiliers   (FLAF)
SICOVO.... Societe Industrielle et Commerciale Voltaique
SICPAD .... Societe Industrielle Centrafricaine des Produits Alimentaires et Derives
SICR .... Service d'Irrigation et de Controle des Rivieres [*Haiti*]   (DSCA)
SICREO .... Societa Italiana Calcolo Ricerca Economica Operativa SpA [*Italian*]   (SLS)
SICRO .... Societe d'Informatique de Conseil et de Recherche Operationnelle [*French*]   (ADPT)
SICRUS..... Societe Ivoirienne de Crustaces
SICRYS..... Sydney Indochinese Refugee Youth Support Group [*Australia*]
SICS .... Societe Immobiliere de la Cote Sauvage
SICSC........ State Intelligence Counter-Subversive Committee   (ML)
SICT .... Societe Industrielle Chimique de Tiko
SICT .... Societe Industrielle et Commerciale du Tchad
SICTA .... Societe Ivoirienne de Controle Technique Automobile et Industriel
SICTLM.... Solomon Islands Cultural Traditional Leaders Movement
SICTU .... Solomon Islands Council of Trade Unions   (EY)
SICY .... Societe Industrielle et Commerciale du Yatenga
SID............. Sal Island [*Cape Verde Islands*] [*Airport symbol*]   (OAG)
SID............. Secretaria de Imprensa e Divulgacao [*Secretariat of Press and Publishing*] [*Brazil*]   (LA)
SID............. Service d'Information et de Documentation [*Information and Documentation Service*] [*Haiti*]   (LA)

SID............. Servicio de Informacion de la Defensa [*Defense Intelligence Service*] [*Uruguay*]   (LA)

SID............. Servizio Informazioni della Difesa [*Defense Intelligence Service*] [*Italian*]   (WER)

sid.............. Sida [*or Sidor*] [*Page or Pages*] [*Sweden*]

SID............. Sidfin Air Ltd. [*Zambia*] [*ICAO designator*]   (FAAC)

sid.............. Sidottu(na) [*Finland*]

SID............. Sociedad Industrial Dominicana [*Dominican Industrial Association*] [*Dominican Republic*]   (LA)

SID............. Societe Industrielle Dakaroise

SID............. Societe Internationale pour le Developpement [*Society for International Development*]

SID............. Societe Ivoirienne de Distribution

SID............. Society for International Development   (EA)

SID............. Standard Industrial Development Co. Ltd.

SIDA.......... Service d'Information et de Documentation de l'Apprentissage et de la Formation Professionnelle   (FLAF)

SIDA.......... Societa Italiana di Assicurazioni SpA [*Italy*]   (EY)

SIDA.......... Societe d'Information et de Diffusion Abidjanaise

SIDA.......... Societe Industrielle des Derives d'Acetylene

SIDA.......... Societe Internationale Fernand de Vischer pour l'Histoire des Droits de l'Antiquite   (EA)

SIDA.......... Society of Interior Designers of Australia

SIDA.......... Sudden Infant Death Association [*Australia*]

SIDA.......... Swedish International Development Agency

SIDA.......... Swedish International Development Authority   (AF)

SIDA.......... Syndrome Immuno-Deficitaire Acquis [*Acquired Immune Deficiency Syndrome*] [*French*]

SIDADT .... Societe Industrielle pour le Developpement Automobile au Dahomey et au Togo

SIDAL....... Societe Ivoirienne d'Ascenseurs et d'Appareils de Levage

SIDAM...... Societe Ivoirienne d'Assurances Mutuelles

SIDAM...... Somali Institute of Development Administration and Management

SIDAM-MAT ... Societe Ivoirienne d'Assurances Mutuelles-Mutuelle d'Assurances Transports [*The Ivory Coast*]   (EY)

SIDAT .... Societe Industrielle pour le Developpement Automobile au Dahomey et au Togo

SIDB.......... Societe Industrielle Dakaroise du Bois

SIDB.......... Societe Industrielle des Bois [*Congo*]

SIDC.......... Societe Industrielle Dahomeenne de Confection

SIDC.......... Space Industry Development Centre [*Australia*]

SIDC.......... Swaziland Industrial Development Corp.   (EY)

SIDCA....... Societe Industrielle Dakaroise de Conserves Alimentaires

SIDC-PAV .. Special Interdepartmental Committee on Protection Against Violence [*Australia*]

SIDE.......... Secretaria de Informacion de Estado [*State Intelligence Secretariat*] [*Argentina*]   (LA)

SIDE.......... Servicio de Inteligencia del Ejercito [*Army Intelligence Service*] [*Uruguay*]   (LA)

SIDE.......... Servicio de Investigaciones de Crimenes Economicos [*Investigating Service for Economic Crimes*] [*Chile*]   (LA)

SIDE.......... Sistemul Informational Demografic [*Demographic Information System*]   (RO)

SIDE.......... Sociedad de Ingenieria del Ecuador [*Ecuadorean Engineering Society*]   (LA)

SIDE.......... Societe Ivoirienne d'Entreprises

SIDEA .... Societa Italiana di Economia Agraria [*Italian Society of Agrarian Economy*]   (SLS)

SIDEAC .... Societe Industrielle d'Engrais de l'Afrique Centrale

SIDEB .... Societe Ivoirienne de Distribution et d'Equipement de Bureaux

SIDEC .... Societe Senegalaise d'Importation, de Distribution, et d'Exploitation Cinematographique

SIDEC .... Stanford International Development Education Center

SIDECI...... Societe Ivoirienne pour le Developpement de la Construction Industrialisee

SIDECO .... Sindicato Profesional de Duenos de Establecimientos Comerciales de Chile [*Professional Union for Proprietors of Chilean Commercial Establishments*]   (LA)

SIDEFCOOP ... Sociedad Interamericana de Desarrollo de Financiamiento Cooperativo [*Inter-American Society for the Development of Cooperative Financing*] [*Buenos Aires, Argentina*]   (EAIO)

SIDEL .... Sociedad Industrial de Ladrillo Ltda. [*Colombia*]   (COL)

SIDELAF .. Societe Ivoirienne d'Electrification

SIDELPA.. Siderurgica del Pacifico SA [*Colombia*]   (COL)

SIDEM...... International Desalination Company [*French*]   (WER)

SIDEM...... Societe Ivoirienne d'Entreprises Maritimes

SIDEMA ... Societe Industrielle pour le Developpement du Machinisme Agricole [*Industrial Company for the Development of Agricultural Mechanization*] [*Malagasy*]   (AF)

SIDEMA ... Societe Ivoirienne d'Electro-Menager et d'Ameublement

SIDEMAS ... Sivas Demiryol Makina Sanayii ve Muessesi [*Sivas Railway Machinery Industry Establishment*] [*Under Turkish State Railways*]   (TU)

SIDEMPA ... Servicio Internacional de Marcas y Patentes [*Colombia*]   (COL)

SIDENA .... Siderurgia Nacional [*National Iron and Steel Company*] [*Mexico*]   (LA)

SIDEPAR ... Siderurgia Paraguaya   (EY)

SIDER .... Entreprise Nationale de Siderurgie [*Algeria*]

SIDERAFRIC ... Centre d'Information et de Promotion des Produits Siderurgiques et des Tubes d'Acier Francais en Afrique

SIDERAMA ... Companhia Siderurgica da Amazonia [*Amazon Iron and Steel Company*] [*Brazil*]   (LA)

SIDERBRAS ... Siderurgica Brasileira, SA [*Brazilian Iron and Steel Corp.*] [*Brasilia*]   (LA)

SIDERFIL ... Siderurgica de Filadelphia Ltda. [*Bucaramanga*]   (COL)

Sidermex.... Siderurgica Mexicana [*Mexican Steel Company*]   (GEA)

SIDERMEX ... Siderurgica Mexicana, SA de C   (EY)

SIDERNA ... La Siderurgie Nationale [*Zaire*]

SIDERPERU ... Empresa Siderurgica del Peru [*Peruvian State Iron and Steel Enterprise*]   (LA)

SIDERRIO ... Acerias Paz Del Rio SA Siderurgica Paz Del Rio [*Colombia*]   (COL)

SIDERSA ... Empresa Siderurgica Boliviana, SA [*Bolivian Iron and Steel Enterprise*] [*La Paz*]   (LA)

SIDES....... Societa Italiana di Dermatologia e Sifilografia [*Italian*]   (SLS)

SIDeS .... Societa Italiana pro Deontologia Sanitaria [*Italian*]   (SLS)

SIDES....... Societe Industrielle pour le Developpement de la Securite en Algerie [*Industrial Company for the Development of Security in Algeria*]   (AF)

SIDESA..... Siderurgica de la Sabana [*Colombia*]   (COL)

SIDEST..... Societe Independante de Documentation et d'Editions Scientifiques et Techniques [*French*]

SIDETRA ... Societe Industrielle de Deroulage et de Tranchage

SIDEV .... Societa Italiana di Dermatologia e Venereologia [*Italian Society of Dermatology and Venereology*]   (EAIO)

SIDEX .... Societe d'Importation de Distribution et d'Exportation

SIDEXCA ... Societe Ivoirienne d'Exportation et de Transformation de Cafe, de Cacao, et de Produits Agricoles et Industriels

SIDF .... Saudi Industrial Development Fund   (ME)

SIDF .... Societe Ivoirienne de Developpement et de Financement

SIDFA .... Senior Industrial Development Field Adviser [*United Nations*]

SIDI .... Service d'Information et de Documentation Industrielles [*Centre National de Promotion des Petites et Moyennes Entreprises*] [*Togo*]

SIDI .... Societe Ivoirienne de Developpement Industriel

SIDIA .... Sistema Integrado de Direccion de la Industria Azucarera [*Sugar Industry Integrated Management System*] [*Cuba*]   (LA)

SIDIAMIL ... International Company for the Development of Food Industries Using Sorghum and Millet [*African*]

SIDICAS ... Societe Immobiliere de Distribution de Carburants au Sahara

SIDICO .... Societe Ivoirienne d'Exportation et de Diffusion des Colas

SIDIMAG ... Societe Ivoirienne de Distribution de Marchandises Generales

SIDINSA... Siderurgica Integrada, Sociedad Anonima [*Integrated Iron and Steel Company, Incorporated*] [*Argentina*]   (LA)

SIDITEX ... Societe Internationale pour le Developpement de l'Industrie Textile

S i DM .... Construction and Road Machinery Manufacture   (RU)

SIDM......... Societa Italiana di Musicologia [*Italian Society of Musicology*]   (SLS)

SIDO .... Small Industries Development Organization [*Tanzania*]   (AF)

SIDO .... Small-Scale Industries Development Organization [*State agency to promote development of small industry*] [*Zambia*]

SIDO .... Societe Internationale pour le Developpement des Organisations [*International Society for the Development of Organizations*]   (EAIO)

SIDOR....... Siderurgica del Orinoco [*Orinoco Iron and Steelworks*] [*Venezuela*]   (EY)

SIDP .... Societe Ivoirienne de Distribution Petroliere

SIDRF .... Sudden Infant Death Research Foundation [*Australia*]

SIDRO....... Societe Internationale d'Energie Hydro-Electrique [*International Society of Hydroelectric Energy*] [*Belgium*]

SIDS .... Societe Internationale de Defense Sociale [*International Society for Social Defence - ISSD*] [*Paris, France*]   (EAIO)

SIDS .... Societe Internationale de Droit Social   (FLAF)

SIDT .... Servicio de Informacion y Documentacion Tecnica [*Instituto Tecnico de Capacitacion y Productividad*] [*Guatemala*]

SIDT......... Societe Industrielle de Transformation

S(id)TPR .. Transistorized Scintillation Counter (with an Integrating Discriminator)   (RU)

SIDUCAM ... Sindicato de Duenos de Camiones [*Truckowners Union*] [*Chile*]   (LA)

SIDUCO.... Societe Industrielle d'Usinage et de Conditionnement

SIDUO ...... International Society for Ophthalmic Ultrasound [*Germany*]   (EAIO)

SIDUO ...... International Society on Ultrasonic Diagnostics in Ophthalmology [*Belgium*]   (SLS)

SIE............. Seminarios de Investigacion Economica [*Spain*]   (DSCA)

Sie .... Serie [*French*]   (FLAF)

SIE............. Service Import Export [*Import-Export Department*] [*In SKD Cambodia*]   (CL)

SIE............. Servicio de Informaciones del Ejercito [*Army Intelligence Service*] [*Argentina*]   (LA)

SIE............ Servicio de Informaciones del Ejercito [*Army Intelligence Service*] [*Peru*]   (LA)

SIE............ Societa Italiana di Endocrinologia [*Italian Society of Endocrinology*]   (SLS)

SIE............ Societa Italiana di Ergonomia [*Italian*]   (SLS)

SIE............ Societe Immobiliere ELAEIS

SIE............ Societe Ivoirienne des Etiquettes

SIE............ Soroptimist International d'Europe [*Soroptimist International of Europe*]   (EAIO)

SIEB......... Societe Ivoirienne d'Exploitation Bananiere

SIEBA....... Societe Industrielle d'Exploitation des Bois Africains [*Douala*]

SIEBEG..... Societe Ivoirienne d'Exploitation des Bois en Grumes

SIEC......... Societe Internationale pour l'Enseignement Commercial [*International Society for Business Education*] [*Lausanne, Switzerland*]   (EAIO)

SIEC......... Societe d'Expansion Commerciale

SIECA....... Secretaria de Integracion Economica Centroamericana [*Secretariat of Central American Economic Integration*]   (LA)

SIECA....... Secretariat Permanent du Traite General d'Integration Economique de l'Amerique Centrale   (FLAF)

SIECA....... Societe Ivoirienne d'Exploitation de Carrieres

SIECAP..... Seminario sobre la Integracion Economica Centroamericana y la Alianza para el Progreso   (LAA)

SIEC-Benin ... Societe Immobiliere pour l'Equipement et la Construction au Benin

SIECD....... Societe Internationale d'Education Continue en Dentisterie [*International Society of Continuing Education in Dentistry - ISCED*] [*Brussels, Belgium*]   (EAIO)

SIEC-Dahomey ... Societe Immobiliere pour l'Equipement et la Construction au Dahomey

sied............ Siedend [*Boiling*] [*German*]

SIED......... Societe Ivoirienne d'Ebenisterie et Decoration

SIED......... Societe pour l'Importation et l'Exportation de Metaux Precieux au Dahomey

Siedep........ Siedepunkt [*Boiling Point*] [*German*]   (GCA)

Siedeverh ... Siedeverhalten [*Boiling Characteristics*] [*German*]   (GCA)

SIEDS....... Societa Italiana di Economia Demografia e Statistica [*Italian Society of Economic Demography and Statistics*]   (SLS)

SIEDS....... Societe Internationale d'Etude du Dix-Huitieme Siecle [*International Society for Eighteenth-Century Studies - ISECS*]   (EAIO)

SIEFA....... Syndesmos Idioktiton Elafron Fortigon Aftokiniton [*League of Light Weight Truck Owners*] [*Greek*]   (GC)

SIEF-CONGO ... Societe Immobiliere et Fonciere Congo

SIEFP....... Societe Industrielle d'Exploitation Forestiere du Plateau

SIEF-RCA ... Societe Immobiliere et Fonciere RCA

SIEF-Tchad ... Societe Immobiliere et Fonciere Tchad

SIEG......... Societe Industrielle d'Emaillage et de Galvanisation

SIEHT....... Societe Ivoirienne d'Equipement Hotelier et Touristique

SIEI.......... Specialized Institute for Engineering Industries [*Iraq*]

SIEID........ Syndicat Interprofessionnel des Entreprises Industrielles du Dahomey

SIEIT....... Syndicat Interprofessionnel des Entreprises Industrielles du Togo

SIEL......... Sociedad Industrial Electronica Ltda. [*Colombia*]   (COL)

SIEL......... Syllogos Idiotikon Ekpaidevtikon Leitourgon [*Association of Private School Teachers*]   (GC)

SIELOR..... Societe Ivoirienne d'Electronique, Optique, et Radio

SIELTE..... Societa Impianti Elettrici e Telefonici Sistema "Ericsson"

SIEM......... Sindicato da Industria de Extracao de Madeiras [*Brazil*]   (DSCA)

SIEM......... Societa Italiana per l'Educazione Musicale [*Italian Society of Musical Education*]   (SLS)

SIEM......... Societe Industrielle Electro-Mecanique

SIEM......... Societe Ivoirienne d'Emballages Metalliques

SIEMENS ... Siemens Aktien-Gesellschaft (Berlin-Muenchen) [*Siemens Corporation (Berlin-Munich)*]   (EG)

SIEMI....... Societe d'Importation et d'Exportation de Materiel Industriel

SIEMI-RCA ... Societe d'Importation et d'Exportation de Materiel Industriel en RCA

SIEN......... Sistema de Informacion Estadistica Nacional [*National Statistical Information System*] [*Cuba*]   (LA)

SIEN......... Societe Internationale d'Etudes Neroniennes [*French*]   (SLS)

SIEPM...... Societe Internationale pour l'Etude de la Philosophie Medievale [*International Society for the Study of Medieval Philosophy*]   (EAIO)

SIER......... Societa Italo-Espanola de Resinas SA

SIERA....... Scierie et Ebenisterie de l'Ira

SIERI........ Societe Internationale d'Etude et de Recherche Industrielle [*Morocco*]

SIERI........ Societe Ivoirienne d'Etudes et de Realisations Industrielles

SIEROMCO ... Sierra Leone Ore and Metal Company

SIEROMOCO ... Sierra Leone Ore and Metal Company

SIERS....... Societe Industrielle d'Etudes et Realisations Scientifiques [*France*]   (PDAA)

SIERTA..... Societe Ivoirienne d'Etudes et de Realisation de Travaux Agricoles

sierz........... Sierzant [*Sergeant*] [*Poland*]

SIES........... Secretariat for International Ecology, Sweden

SIES........... Sindicato de la Industria Electrica de El Salvador [*Union of the Electrical Industry Workers of El Salvador*]   (LA)

SIES........... Societa Italiana di Ergonomia Stomatologica [*Italian*]   (SLS)

SIES........... Societe Industrielle d'Engrais au Senegal

SIES........... Soils and Irrigation Extension Service [*Australia*]   (DSCA)

SIESC........ Secretariat International des Enseignants Secondaires Catholiques [*International Secretariat of Catholic Secondary School Teachers*] [*Acronym used in association name, SIESC Pax Romana Nijmegen, Netherlands*]   (EAIO)

SIESCA..... Societe Ivoirienne d'Elevage, de Salasion, et de Commerce Alimentaire

SIET .... Small Industry Extension Institute [*India*]

SIETA .... Societe Internationale d'Etudes et de Travaux en Afrique

SIETHO.... Societe Ivoirienne d'Expansion Touristique et Hoteliere

SIETI........ Small Industry Extension Training Institute [*India*]

SIETRANS ... Ivorian Maritime Transport and International Logistics Engineering

Siex .... Superintendencia de Inversiones Extranjeras [*Supervisory Authority for Foreign Investments*] [*Venezuela*]   (GEA)

SIEXI........ Societe Ivoirienne d'Exportation et d'Importation

SIF .... Simra [*Nepal*] [*Airport symbol*]   (OAG)

SIF .... Skycy Freighters International Ltd. [*Kenya*] [*ICAO designator*]   (FAAC)

SIF .... Sociedad Iberoamericana de Filosofia [*Spain*]   (EAIO)

SIF .... Societa Italiana di Fisica [*Italian*]   (SLS)

SIF .... Societe Ivoirienne de Financement

SIF .... Societe Sondages-Injections-Forages

SIF .... Society of Israeli Foresters   (DSCA)

SIF .... Suncorp Insurance and Finance [*Commercial firm*] [*Australia*]

SIF .... Survival International - France   (EAIO)

SIF .... Sveriges Industriforbund [*Federation of Swedish Industries*]   (WEN)

SIFA .... Seguridad e Inteligencia de las Fuerzas Armadas [*Security and Intelligence of the Armed Services*] [*Venezuela*]

SIFA .... Servicio de Inteligencia de la Fuerza Aerea [*Air Force Intelligence Service*] [*Argentina*]   (LA)

SIFA .... Servicio de Inteligencia de la Fuerza Aerea [*Air Force Intelligence Service*] [*Chile*]   (LA)

SIFA .... Servicio de Inteligencia de las Fuerzas Armadas [*Armed Forces Intelligence Service*] [*Dominican Republic*]   (LA)

SIFA .... Servicio de Inteligencia de las Fuerzas Armadas [*Armed Forces Intelligence Service*] [*Venezuela*]   (LA)

SIFA .... Societe Industrielle Forestiere et des Allumettes

SIFA .... Statens Institutt for Alkohol- og Narkotikaforskning [*National Institute for Alcohol and Drug Research*] [*Norway*]   (IRC)

SIFA .... Syndesmos Idioktiton Fortigon Avtokiniton [*League of Truck Owners*] [*Greek*]   (GC)

SIFAC....... Societe Industrielle Forestiere en Afrique Centrale

SIFAC....... Societe Industrielle Forestiere et Agricole de la Casamance

SIFACE..... Societe Ivoirienne de Fabrication et de Commercialisation d'Appareillages Electriques et Electroniques

SIFACOL ... Societe Ivoirienne de Fabrication de Colles et Liants

SIFADS..... Singapore Indian Film, Arts, and Dramatic Society   (EAIO)

SIFAL........ Societe Ivoirienne de Fabrication de Lubrifiants

SIFAR....... Servizio Informazioni delle Forze Armate [*Armed Forces Intelligence Service*] [*Italian*]   (WER)

SIFAS........ Sentetik Iplik Fabrikalari Anonim Sirketi [*Synthetic Silk Factories Corporation*] [*Bursa*]   (TU)

SIFAS........ Societe Industrielle de Fabrication d'Articles Scolaires [*School Supplies Manufacturing Company*] [*Cambodia*]   (CL)

SIFAV....... Societe Industrielle de Fabrication d'Articles de Voyage

SIFC .... Sparks International Official Fan Club   (EAIO)

SIFC .... Summa International Finance Corp. [*Hong Kong*]

SIFCAM..... Societe Industrielle et Forestiere du Cameroun

SIFCCA..... Societe Immobiliere Financiere et Commerciale de la Cote-d'Afrique

SIFCCA..... Societe Industrielle Forestiere et Commerciale Camerounaise

SIFCI........ Societe Industrielle et Forestiere de Cote-D'Ivoire [*Ivory Coast Industrial and Forestry Company*]   (AF)

SIFCODER ... Societe Ivoirienne d'Importation et d'Exportation, de Fabrication, Construction, Confection, Distribution, d'Echanges, et de Representations

SIFCODI... Societe Ivoirienne de Fabrication, Conditionnement, et Distribution

SIFCP........ Societe Industrielle de Fabrication de Chaussures Plastuques

SIFD......... Societa Italiana del Flauto Dolce [*Italian*]   (SLS)

SIFEC........ Societe d'Isolation Frigorifique et d'Entreprise de Construction

SIFEDIB ... Societe Ivoirienne Forestiere et de Developpement des Industries du Bois

SIFEL....... Societe Ivoirienne de Fabrication d'Elastiques

SIFELEC... Societe Ivoirienne de Fabrication de Materiel Electrique et de Compteurs a Eau

SIFEP........ Societe d'Importation Fruits et Primeurs

SIFERCOM ... Societe Ivoirienne d'Entreprise et de Construction

SIFET........ Societa Italiana di Fotogrammetria e Topografia [*Italian*]   (SLS)

SIFF.......... Societe Ivoirienne Farhat Freres
SIFF.......... Statens Institutt for Folkehelse [*National Institute of Public Health*] [*Norway*]   (ARC)
SIFF.......... Stock Index Futures Fund
SIFI........... Societe Immobiliere Financiere et Industrielle
SIFIDA...... Societe Internationale Financiere pour les Investissements et le Developpement en Afrique [*International Financial Company for Investments and Development in Africa*] [*Geneva, Switzerland*]
SIFLI........ Societe Ivoirienne de Fabrication de Lubrifiants et d'Insecticides
SIFMA ..... Societe Ivoirienne de Fabrication et de Montage Automobile
SIFMAP.... Somateion Idioktiton Fortigon kai Motosykletton Athinon-Peiraios [*Association of Athens-Piraeus Truck and Motorcycle Owners*]   (GC)
SIFMCOL ... Siemmens Colombiana Ltda. [*Colombia*]   (COL)
SIFO.......... Small Industries Finance Office [*Thai*]   (GEA)
SIFO.......... Sociedad Industrial de Fundicion de Occidente   (COL)
SIFO.......... Societa Italiana di Farmacia Ospedaliera [*Italian*]   (SLS)
SIFO.......... Statens Institutt for Forbruksforskning [*National Institute for Consumer Research*] [*Research center*] [*Norway*]   (IRC)
SIFO.......... Svenska Institutet for Opinions-Undersokningar [*Swedish Institute for Public Opinion Polls*]   (WEN)
SIFOMAT ... Societe Ivoirienne de Fournitures et de Materiaux
SIFOR ...... Societe Industrielle de Fort-Dauphin
SIFRA....... Societe Industrielle des Fruits Africains [*Guinea*]
SIFRIA...... Societe Immobiliere de Fria
SIFROID... Societe Industrielle du Froid du Benin
SIFT.......... Societe Industrielle et Forestiere de Tchanga
SIFT.......... Spanish Institute of Foreign Trade   (EAIO)
SIFTAM.... Societa Immobiliare Fondiaria Tripolina Ahmed Muntasser
SIG........... San Juan/Isla Grande [*Puerto Rico*] [*Airport symbol*]   (OAG)
SIG........... Sichtgeraet [*German*]   (ADPT)
Sig............. Signal [*German*]   (GCA)
SIG........... Signalman [*Royal Australian Navy*]
sig............. Signatura [*Signature*] [*Spanish*]
Sig .... Signore [*Sir or Mister*] [*Correspondence*] [*Italian*]
Sig .... Sigorta [*Insurance*]   (TU)
SIG........... Societa Italiana di Glottologia [*Italian*]   (SLS)
SIG........... Societe Industrielle Generale [*General Industrial Company*] [*Tunisia*]   (AF)
SIG........... Societe Ivoirienne de Gaufretterie
SIG........... Societe Ivoirienne de Gerances
SIG........... Societe Ivoirienne de Groupage
SIG........... State Intelligence Group [*New South Wales Police Service*] [*Australia*]
SIG........... Systeme Informatique de Gestion [*French*]   (ADPT)
Siga .... Signora [*Madam*] [*Italian*]
SIGA......... Societa Italiana di Genetica Agraria [*Italian*]   (SLS)
SIGA......... Societe Ivoirienne de Gestion Agricole
SIGAC ...... Sindicato de la Industria Gastronomica y Actividades Conexas [*Union of Workers in the Restaurant Industry and Related Activities*] [*El Salvador*]   (LA)
SIGAL...... Societe Ivoirienne de Galvanisation
SIGAMA... Societe Italo-Gabonaise des Marbres
SIGAP ...... Societe d'Information et de Gestion-d'Analyse et de Programmation [*French*]   (ADPT)
SIGAS ...... Societe d'Ingenierie, de Gestion, et de Service en Afrique
SIGC.......... Servicio de Investigacion de la Guardia Civil [*Investigation Service of the Civil Guard*] [*Spanish*]   (WER)
SIGE .... Societa Italiana di Gastroenterologia [*Italian Society of Gastroenterology*]   (SLS)
SIGEBAN ... Sindicato de la Industria General de Empresas Bancarias y Asociaciones de Ahorro y Prestamo [*Trade Union of the General Industry of Banking and Savings and Loan*] [*El Salvador*]   (LA)
SIGEFOR ... Societe Ivoirienne de Gestion et d'Exploitation Forestiere
SIGEM ...... Salon International du Genie et de l'Equipement Municipal
SIGEN....... Societa Impianti Generazione Energia Nucleare, SpA [*Nuclear energy*] [*Italian*]   (NRCH)
SIGES....... Societe Ivoirienne de Gestion, d'Etudes, et des Services
SIGEXA .... Societe Ivoirienne de Gestion et d'Exploitation Automobiles
Sigg .... Signori [*Sirs*] [*Italian*]
SIGI .... Societe Ivoirienne de Gestion Immobiliere
SIGIRD ..... Systeme Integre de Gestion Informatise des Ressources Documentaires [*Integrated System for the Management of Documentary Resources*] [*University of Quebec, Montreal*] [*Information service or system*]   (IID)
Sigl............ Signal [*Signal*] [*Military map abbreviation World War I*] [*French*]   (MTD)
SIGLE .... System for Information on Grey Literature in Europe [*European Association for Grey Literature Exploitation*] [*Commission of the European Communities*] [*Information service or system*]   (IID)
SIGLOI ..... Societe d'Importation et de Distribution de Gaz Liquefies pour l'Ocean Indien
SIGM......... Societa Italiana di Ginnastica Medica [*Italian*]   (SLS)

SIGMA...... Fabrika Signalnih Uredaja i Masina [*Signal Equipment and Machinery Factory*] [*Subotica*]   (YU)
SIGMA...... Saudi Investment Group & Marketing Co.
SIGMA...... Societe Industriale Generale de Mecanique Appliquee [*France*]   (PDAA)
SIGMATP ... Societe Industrielle Gabonaise de Materiaux de Travaux Publics
Sign .... Call Number [*Book*]   (BU)
sign............. Signeret [*Signed*] [*Publishing Danish/Norwegian*]
sign............. Signiert [*Signed*] [*German*]
SIGNA....... Signora [*Madam*] [*Italian*]   (ROG)
Signa .... Signorina [*Miss*] [*Italian*]
signat......... Signature [*Signature*] [*Publishing*] [*French*]
signat......... Signatuur [*Signature*] [*Publishing*] [*Netherlands*]
SIGNETEL ... Societe de Signalisation Electronique et de Telecommunications
SIGP .... Societe Industrielle de la Grande Peche
SIGRA ...... Sociedad Industrial de Grasas SA [*Colombia*]   (COL)
SIGRAG.... Societe Industrielle d'Exploitation des Granits Guineens
SIGS .... Signals Corps [*Australia*]
sigs .... Siguientes [*Following, Next*] [*Spanish*]
sigte........... Siguiente [*Following, Next*] [*Spanish*]
SIGTTO .... Society of International Gas Tanker and Terminal Operators   (EAIO)
SIGUE...... Society for Developments in Guinea
SIH .... Sakekamer Industrie und Handelskammer [*Namibia*]   (EAIO)
SIH .... Schweizerisches Institut fuer Hauswirtschaft [*Swiss Institute for Domestic Economy*]   (SLS)
SIH .... Silgarhi Doti [*Nepal*] [*Airport symbol*]   (OAG)
SIH .... Societe Internationale d'Hematologie [*International Society of Hematology - ISH*] [*Buenos Aires, Argentina*]   (EA)
SIH .... Societe Ivoirienne d'Habillement
SIH .... Societe Ivoirienne d'Hotellerie
SIH .... Society for Italic Handwriting   (EA)
SIHAM...... Sy Imperiale Hoogheid [*His Imperial Highness*] [*Afrikaans*]
SIHAM ...... Societe Industrielle des Huiles au Maroc
SIHTCO.... Societe Ivoirienne Hoteliere et Touristique de la Comoe
SII .... Siimes Aviation AB [*Finland*] [*ICAO designator*]   (FAAC)
SII .... Societe d'Imprimerie Ivoirienne
SII .... Standards Institution of Israel [*Research center*]   (IRC)
SII .... Structural Impediments Initiative [*US-Japan trade negotiations*]
SII .... Sveriges Industriforbund Industriforbundet [*Sweden*]   (EAIO)
SIIAEC...... Secretariat International des Ingenieurs, des Agronomes, et des Cadres Economiques Catholiques [*International Secretariat of Catholic Technologists, Agriculturists, and Economists*] [*Paris, France*]   (EAIO)
SIICR........ Sistema de Informacion Industrial de Costa Rica [*Consejo Nacional de Investigaciones Cientificas y Tecnologicas*] [*Costa Rica*]
SIIFT........ Sociedad Internacional de Ingenieros Forestales Tropicales [*International Society of Tropical Foresters*]   (EAIO)
SIII .... Societa Italiana di Immunologia e di Immunopatologia [*Italian Society of Immunology and Immunopathology*]   (SLS)
SIII .... Societe Industrielle et Immobiliere Ivoirienne
SIIS........... Shanghai Institute for International Studies [*China*]   (IRC)
SIITS .... Societa Italiana di Immunoematologia e Trasfusione del Sangue [*Italian*]   (SLS)
SIJ .... Siglufjordur [*Iceland*] [*Airport symbol*]   (OAG)
SIJADEP .. International Secretariat of Jurists for an Amnesty and Democracy in Paraguay [*Paris, France*]   (EAIO)
SIJAU ...... Secretariat International des Juristes pour l'Amnistie en Uruguay [*France*]
SIJVPP...... Statni Inspekce Jakosti Vyrobku Potravinarskeho Prumyslu [*State Inspection Office for Quality of Food Industry Products*]   (CZ)
SIJZV........ Statni Inspekce Jakosti Zemedelskych Vyrobku [*State Inspection Office for Quality of Agricultural Products*]   (CZ)
SIK............ Savezna Industriska Komora [*Federal Chamber of Industry*]   (YU)
SIK............ Schweizerisches Institut fuer Kunstwissenschaft [*Swiss Institute for Aesthetics*]   (SLS)
SIK............ Societe Immobiliere de Koutou
SIK............ Sostanjska Industrija Konfekcije [*Sostanj Ready-Made Clothing Industry*]   (YU)
SIK............ Svenska Institutet for Konserveringsforskning [*Swedish Institute for Food Preservation Research*]   (PDAA)
SIK............ Svenska Livsmedelsinstitutet [*The Swedish Food Institute*]   (ASF)
SIKD"Njegos" ... Srpsko Istorisko-Kulturno Drustvo "Njegos" [*"Njegos" Serbian Historical and Cultural Society*] [*Chicago*]   (YU)
SIKN......... Societe Immobiliere du Kouilou-Niari
SIKO......... Societe Industrielle du Kouilou
SIL .... Salon Internacional del Libro [*Spanish*]
SIL .... Schools/Industry Link [*Australia*]
SIL .... Singapore Islands Line   (DS)
SIL .... Societas Internationalis Limnologiae [*International Association for Limnology*] [*ICSU*]   (ASF)

SIL............ Societas Internationalis Limnologiae Theoreticae et Applicae [*International Association of Theoretical and Applied Limnology*]
SIL............ Societe Internationale de la Lepre
SIL............ Special Import License [*Sri Lanka*]   (IMH)
SIL............ Suomen Ilmailuliitto [*Finland*]   (SLS)
sil.............. Tower Silo [*Topography*]   (RU)
SILA.......... Sistema Informativo Latinoamericano [*Latin American Information System*]   (LA)
SILAAB..... Summer Institute of Linguistics, Australian Aborigines Branch (ADA)
SILAP....... Sindacato Nazionale Dipendenti Ministero del Lavori Pubblici [*National Union of Employees in the Ministry of Public Welfare*] [*Italy*]
SILAS....... Singapore-based Integrated Library Automation System   (PDAA)
SILATU .... Servicio de Informacion de Latu [*Laboratorio Tecnologico del Uruguay*] [*Uruguay*]
SILC.......... Sheep Industry Liaison Committee [*New South Wales, Australia*]
SILCA .... Sindacato Italiano Lavoratori Cappellai ed Affini [*Italian Federation of Hat and Allied Workers*]
SILCA .... Societa Italo-Libica Commercio Automobili
SILCO .... Societe Ivoiro-Libanaise de Commerce
SILDA ...... Sociedad Industrial Litografica Ltda. [*Colombia*]   (COL)
SILE .... Service d'Information de la Legion Etrangere
SILETI ...... Sierra Leone Timber Industry and Plantation Company
SILF.......... Societe Internationale de Linguistique Fonctionelle [*International Society of Functional Linguistics*]   (EAIO)
SILI .... Sindacato Nazionale Lavoratori Italcable [*National Union of Cable Workers*] [*Italy*]
silik .... Silicate Industry Plant [*Topography*]   (RU)
SILIKAT ... Svenska Silikatforskningsinstitutet [*Swedish Institute for Silicate Research*] [*Research center*]   (IRC)
SILIORIOS ... Silicatos y Viorios Ltda. [*Colombia*]   (COL)
SILK .... System fuer Integrierte Lokale Kommunikation [*German*]   (ADPT)
sill .... Sillabe [*Syllable*] [*Afrikaans*]
S Ilma........ Sua Ilustrissima [*Your Most Illustrious*] [*Portuguese*]
SILMT ...... Syndesmos Idioktiton Leoforeion Meizonos Typou [*League of Owners of Large Buses*] [*Greek*]   (GC)
silogr .... Silografia [*Wood-Block Print*] [*Italian*]
silograf....... Silografia [*Wood-Block Print*] [*Italian*]
SILOM...... Societe d'Investissements Laitiers Outre-Mer
SILP.......... Societe Ivoirienne de Librairie et de Papeterie
SILP.......... Solomon Islands Liberal Party [*Political party*]   (EY)
SILPA....... Societa Industria Lavorazione Pietra Azizia
SILS.......... Societe d'Investissements Libano-Senegalaise
SILTE........ Sindacato Italiano Lavoratori Telecomunicazioni [*Italian Union of Telecommunications Workers*]
SILTS .... Sindacato Italiano Lavoratori Telefoni di Stato [*Italian Union of Government Telephone Workers*]
SILU .... Sugar Industry Laborers Union [*Mauritius*]   (AF)
SILULAP .. Sindacato Italiano Lavoratori Uffici Locali ed Agenzie Postelegrafonici [*Italian Union of Local Post and Telegraph Office Workers*]
SILWF....... Sugar Industry Labor Welfare Fund [*Mauritius*]   (AF)
SILWFC.... Sugar Industry Labour Welfare Fund Committee [*Guyana*]
SiM .... "Hammer and Sickle" Plant   (RU)
SIM........... Servicio de Informacion Militar [*Military Intelligence*] [*Spanish*]
SIM........... Servicio de Inteligencia Militar [*Military Intelligence Service*] [*Dominican Republic*]   (LA)
SIM........... Servicio de Inteligencia Militar [*Military Intelligence Service*] [*Chile*]   (LA)
SIM........... Servicio Industrial de la Marina [*Peru*]   (PDAA)
SIM........... Servizio Informazioni Militare [*Military Intelligence Service*] [*Italian*]   (WER)
SIM........... Shanghai Institute of Metallurgy, Academia Sinica [*China*]   (IRC)
SIM........... Siberian Scientific Research Institute of Metals   (RU)
sim............. Siemens   (RU)
SIM........... Simbai [*Papua New Guinea*] [*Airport symbol*]   (OAG)
SIM........... Slovenska Izseljenska Matica [*Slovenian Emigration Society*]   (YU)
SIM........... Sociedad Industrial de Materiales [*Colombia*]   (COL)
SIM........... Sociedad Industrial Metalica Ltda. [*Manizales*]   (COL)
SIM........... Societa di Intermediazione Mobiliare [*Finance*] [*Italy*]   (ECON)
SIM........... Societa Italiana Manufatti [*Italian clothing manufacturer*]
SIM........... Societe d'Importation et d'Achat du Mali
SIM........... Societe Immobiliere de Madagascar
SIM........... Societe Industrielle de Menuiserie
SIM........... Societe Senegalaise d'Investissements Maritimes
SIM........... Somali Islamic Movement [*Political party*]
SIM........... Spolka Inzynierow Mechanikow [*Mechanical Engineers Company*]   (POL)
SIM........... Standards Institution of Malaysia   (ML)
SIM........... Studie en Informatiecentrum Mensenrechten [*Netherlands Institute of Human Rights*]   (EAIO)
SIM........... Sudan Interior Mission

sim............. Symmetrical   (RU)
SIM........... Synthetisches Informationsmodell [*German*]   (ADPT)
SIMA........ Servicio Industrial de Marina [*Maritime Industrial Service*] [*Peru*]   (LA)
SIMA........ Servico de Informacao do Mercado Agricola [*Agricultural Marketing Information Service*] [*Rio De Janeiro, Brazil*]   (LAA)
SIMA........ Sociedad de Intercambio Mercantil Ltda. [*Colombia*]   (COL)
SIMA........ Societa Italiana di Meteorologia Applicata [*Italian Society of Applied Meteorology*]   (SLS)
SIMA........ Societe d'Importation et d'Exportation Centrafricaine
SIMA........ Societe Industrielle de Metaux pour l'Afrique
SIMA........ Societe Ivoirienne de Menuiserie et d'Ameublement
SIMA........ Southern India Millowners Association   (PDAA)
SIMA........ Sydney Improvised Music Association [*Australia*]
SIMAA...... Societe d'Importation de Materiel Automobile et Agricole
SIMAC...... Societe Immobiliere d'Afrique Centrale
SIMACO... Societe Ivoirienne de Materiaux de Construction
SIMAF...... Societe Industrielle Moderne d'Ameublement et de Ferronnerie
SIMAFCI.. Societe Immobiliere Africaine de la Cote-D'Ivoire
SIMAFRUIT ... Societe Interprofessionnelle Maritime et Fruitiere
SIMAI ...... Servicio Industrial de la Marina de Iquitos [*Iquitos Industrial Marine Service*] [*Peru*]   (LA)
SIMAP ...... Servicio de Informacion de Mercadeo Agropecuario [*Peru*]
SIMAR...... Societe Ivoirienne de Maroquinerie
SIMAS ...... Sindicato de la Industria de Muebles, Accesorios, y Similares [*Union of the Furniture and Related Industries*] [*El Salvador*]   (LA)
SIMAVIN ... Societe d'Importation Africaine Vinicole
SIMC........ Societa Internazionale di Medicina Cibernetica [*International Society of Cybernetic Medicine*] [*Italian*]   (SLS)
SIMC........ Societe Immobiliere Congolaise
SIMC........ Societe Immobiliere du Moyen-Congo
SIMC........ Societe Internationale de Medecine de Catastrophe [*International Society for Disaster Medicine - ISDM*] [*Switzerland*]   (EA)
SIMC........ Societe Ivoirienne de Montages et de Constructions
SIMCA ...... Societe Industrielle de Mecanique et de Carrosserie Automobile [*French automobile manufacturer; acronym used as name of its cars*]
SIMCI ...... Societe Industrielle de Matelas de Cote-D'Ivoire
SIMCO...... Societe Immobiliere et de Constructions du Tchad
SIMCOA... Silicon Metal Co. of Australia Ltd. [*Australia*]
SIMDA...... Sociedad de Importaciones Ltda. [*Bucaramanga*]   (COL)
SIME......... Industria Sideromecanica [*Steelworking Industry*] [*Cuba*]   (LA)
SIME......... Servicio Integral de Medicina Escolar. Universidad del Valle [*Colombia*]   (COL)
SIME......... Societe d'Importation de Materiel Electrique
SIME......... Societe Industrielle de Materiaux et d'Etancheite
SIMEA...... Societa Italiana Meriodionale per l'Energia Atomica [*Italian*]
SIMEA...... Societe Ivoirienne de Montage et d'Exploitation Automobile
SIMECA ... Sociedade Importadora de Maquinas, Equipamentos, Carros, e Acessorios Lda.
SIMECO... Societe Ivoirienne de Menuiserie, d'Ebenisterie, et de Constructions Immobilieres
SIMEE ...... Shanghai Institute of Mechanical and Electrical Engineering [*China*]   (IRC)
SIMEF...... Societe des Industries Mecaniques et Electriques de Fes
SIMEI ...... Societe Ivoirienne de Materiaux Etanches et Isolants
SIMENT ... Societe Imerinienne d'Entreprises
SIMESA ... Siderurgica de Medellin Sociedad Anonima   (COL)
SIMEUBLES ... Societe Ivoirienne de Meubles
SIMEX ...... Singapore International Monetary Exchange
SIMEX ...... Singapore Monetary Exchange   (ECON)
SIMEX ...... Societe d'Importation et d'Exportation
SIMEX ...... Syrian Import and Export Company   (ME)
SIMEXCO ... Societe Ivoirienne d'Importation, d'Exportation et de Commission
SIMFER.... Societa Italiana di Medicina Fisica e Riabilitazione [*Italian*]   (SLS)
SIMG........ Societas Internationalis Medicinae Generalis [*International Society of General Practice*] [*Klagenfurt, Austria*]   (EAIO)
SIMGAL ... Societe d'Importation du Senegal
SIMHA ..... Societe Internationale de Mycologie Humaine et Animale [*International Society for Human and Animal Mycology - ISHAM*] [*British*]   (EA)
SIMI .... Societa Italiana di Medicina Interna [*Italian Society of Internal Medicine*]   (SLS)
SIMI .... Societa Italiana Macchine Idrauliche [*Italy*]   (PDAA)
SIMI .... Societa Italo-Svizzeva Metalli Iniettati [*Italy*]   (PDAA)
SIMI .... Societe Internationale de Materials Industriels [*France*]   (PDAA)
SIMI .... Societe Ivoirienne de Machettes Industrielles
simili .... Similigravure [*Halftone Engraving*] [*Publishing*] [*Netherlands*]
similigrav ... Similigravure [*Halftone Engraving*] [*Publishing*] [*French*]
SIMITAS .. Sosyal Isletmeler ve Mesken Insaati Turk Anonim Sirketi [*Social Administration and Housing Construction Corporation*]   (TU)

SIMKh....... Saratov Institute of Agricultural Mechanization Imeni M. I. Kalinin   (RU)
SIMLA ...... Societa Italiana di Medicina Legale e delle Assicurazioni [*Italian*] (SLS)
SIMO .... Societe Imprimerie de l'Ogooue [*Publisher*] [*Gabon*]
SIMO .... Societe Ivoirienne des Materiels d'Organisation
SIMO .... Somateion Ithopion Melodramatos kai Operas [*Association of Musical Stage and Opera Performers*] [*Greek*]   (GC)
SIMOCA... Societe Industrielle du Moyen-Orient au Cameroun [*Arab*]
SIMOPA ... Societe Industrielle Moderne de Parfumerie
SIMOTUR ... Sindicato de Motoristas del Transporte Urbano [*Trade Union of Urban Transportation Drivers*] [*Nicaragua*]   (LA)
SIMP........ Simpleton   (DSUE)
SIMP......... Simpson [*Botanical region*] [*Australia*]
SIMP......... Societa Italiana di Medicina Psicosomatica [*Italian Society of Psychosomatic Medicine*]   (SLS)
SIMP......... Societa Italiana di Mineralogia e Petrologia [*Italian*]   (SLS)
SIMP......... Stowarzyszenie Inzynierow i Technikow Mechanikow Polskich [*Association of Polish Mechanical Engineers and Technicians*]   (POL)
SIMPA ...... Societe Industrielle Moderne de Plastiques Africains
SIMPAFRIC ... Societe d'Impressions Africaines
SIMPEX.... Stowarzyszenie Inzynierow i Technikow Mechanikow Polskich [*Polish Mechanical Engineers Association*]   (EAIO)
SIMPEX.... Syndicat des Importateurs et Exportateurs du Gabon
SIMPOL .... Societe Ivoirienne de Mousse Polyester
SIMPROFRANCE ... Comite Francaise pour la Simplification de Procedures du Commerce Internationale [*French Committee for the Simplification of International Commerce Procedures*]   (PDAA)
SIMPS....... Societa Italiana di Medicina Preventiva e Sociale [*Italian Society of Preventative and Social Medicine*]   (SLS)
SIMR........ Societe Internationale de Mecanique des Roches [*International Society for Rock Mechanics - ISRM*]   (EAIO)
sim/ros..... Simaioforos [*Ensign*] [*Navy rank*]   (GC)
SIMS .... Skandinaviska Simuleringssaellskapet [*Scandinavian Simulation Society*] [*Also, SSS*]   (EA)
SIMS .... Societa Italiana di Medicina Sociale [*Italian*]
SIMSA ...... Servicios a la Industria Maderera SA [*Spain*]   (DSCA)
SIMSGA ... Sugar Industry Manufacturers and Service Group of Australia
SIMSI........ Societa Italiana di Medicina Subacquea ed Iperbarica [*Italian*] (SLS)
SIMSKh .... Saratov Institute of Agricultural Mechanization Imeni M. I. Kalinin   (RU)
SIMSOC ... Societe Immobiliere Socomotra & Cie.
SIMSTF .... Societe Internationale de Mecanique des Sols et de Travaux de Fondations [*International Society for Soil Mechanics and Foundation Engineering - ISSMFE*]
SIMT .... Societa Italiana di Medicina del Traffico [*Italian*]   (SLS)
SIMTA ...... Societa Italiana Medica del Training Autogeno [*Italian*]   (SLS)
SIMTARS ... Safety in Mines Testing and Research Station [*Australia*]
SIMU........ Local Control Synchronizing Pulse [*Computers*]   (RU)
SIMUN ...... Empresa Siderurgica del Muna SA [*Colombia*]   (COL)
SIN .... Schweizerisches Institut fuer Nuklearforschung [*Swiss Institute for Nuclear Research*] [*Nuclear energy*]   (NRCH)
SIN .... Servicio de Informaciones Navales [*Naval Intelligence Service*] [*Argentina*]   (LA)
SIN .... Servicio de Inteligencia Nacional [*National Intelligence Service*] [*Peru*]   (LA)
SIN .... Servizio Informazioni Navali [*Naval Intelligence*] [*Italian*]
SIN .... Sinair [*France*] [*ICAO designator*]   (FAAC)
sin.............. Sinaleiro [*Signal Corps Soldier*] [*Portuguese*]
SIN .... Singapore [*Airport symbol*]   (OAG)
sin.............. Sinonimo [*Synonym*] [*Portuguese*]
Sin............. Sinter [*Record label*] [*Brazil*]
SIN .... Sinus [*Sinus*] [*Afrikaans*]
SIN .... Sistemul Informatic National [*National Data Processing System*]   (RO)
SIN .... Societa Italiana di Neurochirurgia [*Italian Society of Neurosurgery*]   (SLS)
SIN .... Societe Industrielle de Nouveautes [*North African*]
sin.............. Synonym   (RU)
SINA......... Sindicato de la Industria Nacional del Azucar [*Union of the National Sugar Industry*] [*El Salvador*]   (LA)
SINA......... Societe Ivoirienne de Navigation
SINA......... Sports Injury Nurses Association [*Australia*]
SINABAN ... Sindicato Nacional de Empleados Bancarios de Panama [*National Union of Bank Employees of Panama*]   (LA)
SINACAM ... Sistema Nacional de Controle Ambiental [*National Environmental Control System*] [*Brazil*]   (LA)
SINACHOD ... Sindicato Nacional de Choferes Dominicanos [*National Trade Union of Dominican Drivers*] [*Dominican Republic*]   (LA)
SINACITI ... Sistema Nacional de Informacion Cientifica y Tecnologica [*Consejo Nacional de Investigaciones Cientificas y Tecnologicas*] [*Venezuela*]

SINACMA ... Sindacato Nazionale Dipendenti Corte dei Conti e Magistrature Amministrative [*National Union of General Accounting Office Employees*] [*Italy*]
SINADEPS ... Sistema Nacional de Desarrollo de Propiedad Social [*National System for Social Property Development*] [*Peru*]   (LA)
SINADI..... Sistema Nacional de Informacion [*National Information System*] [*Peru*]   (LA)
SINAES..... Societe Industrielle des Applications de l'Energie Solaire [*Industrial Society for Applications of Solar Energy*] [*Senegal*]
SINAF .... Sindacato Nazionale Dipendenti Ministero Agricoltura e Foreste [*National Union of Ministry of Agriculture and Forestry Employees*] [*Italy*]
SINAFCO ... Societe Inter-Africaine pour la Cooperation Commerciale [*Senegal*]
SINAFORP ... Sistema Nacional de Formacion Profesional [*National System for Professional Training*] [*Nicaragua*]   (LA)
SINAMIL ... Sindacato Nazionale Dipendenti Ministero del Lavoro e Previdenza Sociale [*National Union of Ministry of Labor and Social Security Employees*] [*Italy*]
SINAMN... Sindacato Nazionale Dipendenti Marina Mercantile [*National Union of Merchant Marine Workers*] [*Italy*]
SINAMOS ... Sistema Nacional de Apoyo a la Mobilizacion Social [*National System for Support to Social Mobilization*] [*Peru*]   (LA)
SINAP .... Sistema Nacional de Ahorros y Prestamos [*National Savings and Loan System*] [*Italy*]   (LA)
SINARA ... Sistema Nacional de Radiodifusion [*National Broadcasting System*] [*Argentina*]   (LA)
SINAREX ... Societe Nationale de Recherche et d'Exploitation Minieres
SINART .... Sistema Nacional de Radio y Television Cultural [*National System for Cultural Radio and Television*] [*Costa Rica*]   (LA)
SINASBI... Sistema Nacional de Servicios de Bibliotecas e Informacion [*Venezuela*]   (PDAA)
SINASCEL ... Sindacato Nazionale Scuola Elementare [*National Union of Elementary School Teachers*] [*Italy*]
SINATRA ... Sindicato Nacional de Trabajadores de la Radio [*National Radio Workers Union*] [*Colorado*]   (LA)
SINATRASTEDO ... Sindicato Autonomo de Trabajadores de Sacos y Tejidos Dominicanos [*Autonomous Trade Union of Dominican Sacking and Textile Workers*] [*Dominican Republic*]   (LA)
SINBI .... Societe Nouvelle de Broderies et d'Impressions [*North African*]
SINC.......... Nicaraguan International Rescue from Communism   (PD)
SINC.......... Servei d'Informacio Nacional Catala [*Catalan National Information Service*] [*Spanish*]   (WER)
SINCAP .... Societe Industrielle du Cap-Vert [*Senegal*]
SINCAT .... Societa Industria Catanese
SINCATEX ... Societe Industrielle Camerounaise des Textiles
SINCO...... Societa Incremento e Commerciale
SINCO...... Societe Internationale de Commerce
SINCOE..... Sindacato Nazionale Dipendenti Ministero Industria e Commercio Estero [*National Union of Ministry of Industry and Foreign Commerce Employees*] [*Italy*]
SINCOLIT ... Societe Industrielle et Commerciale de Literie
SINCONI ... Societe Industrielle Commerciale Nigerienne
SINCRO.... Societe Informatique, de Conseils, et de Recherches Operationnels
Sind............ Statens Industriverk [*National Industry Board*] [*Sweden*]   (GEA)
sind............ Syndicate   (RU)
SINDACO ... Sindicato Angolano dos Camponeses e Operarios
SINDAF .... Sindacato Nazionale Dipendenti Amministrazioni Finanziarie [*National Union of Financial Administration Employees*] [*Italy*]
SINDARMA ... Sindicato Nacional das Empresas de Navegacao Maritima [*Brazil*]   (LAA)
SINDEIT... Sindicato de Empleados del Instituto Tecnologico [*Trade Union of Technological Institute Employees*] [*Costa Rica*]   (LA)
SINDELEN ... Sociedad de Industrias Electricas Nacionales [*Society of National Electrical Industries*] [*Chile*]   (LA)
SINDEMU ... Sociedad Industrial de Muebles Ltda. [*Colombia*]   (COL)
SINDEP .... Sindicato Nacional de la Empresa Privada [*National Private Enterprise Union*] [*Costa Rica*]   (LA)
SINDEU.... Sindicato de Trabajadores de la Universidad de Costa Rica [*Trade Union of Costa Rica University Workers*]   (LA)
SINDICOL ... Sindicato Unico de Trabajadores de Coltejer [*Colombia*]   (COL)
SINDICONS ... Sindicato Obrero de la Construccion de Antioquia [*Colombia*]   (COL)
SINDU ...... Servicio Interamericano sobre el Desarrollo Urbano [*Inter-American Urban Development Information Service*]   (LA)
SINEC .... Siemens Netzwerk fuer Minicomputer [*Siemens Network to Minicomputers*] [*German*]   (ADPT)
SINECELH ... Sindicato Nacional de Empleados de Comunicaciones Electricas de Honduras [*National Union of Electrical Communication Employees of Honduras*]   (LA)
SINEG....... Societe Ivoirienne de Negoce

SINE-IS..... Turkiye Sinema Iscileri Sendikasi [*Turkish Cinema Workers Union*] [*Istanbul*]   (TU)

SINEPUDERH ... Sindicato de Empleados Publicos de Educacion Rural en Honduras [*Trade Union of Honduran Rural Education Public Employees*]   (LA)

SINETIC... Siemens Netzplantechnik [*Siemens Net Plan Technology*] [*German*]   (ADPT)

SINFDOK ... Statens Rad for Vetenskaplig Information och Dokumentation [*Swedish Council for Scientific Information and Documentation*]   (IID)

SINFELTA ... Sindicato Ferroviario del Pacifico [*Colombia*]   (COL)

sing............ Singular [*Singular*] [*Portuguese*]

SING .... Singularis [*Singular*] [*Afrikaans*]

sing............ Singulier [*French*]   (TPFD)

s-ing .... Sous-Ingenieur [*Sub-Engineer*] [*French*]

SINGLISH ... Singapore English

Sinh............ Sinhalese [*Language*]   (BARN)

SINIE .... Sistema Nacional de Informacion Documental en Educacion [*National System of Documentary Information on Education*] [*Information service or system*]   (IID)

SININCA .. Sub-Sistema Nacional de Informacion en Ciencias Agropecuarias [*Maracay, Venezuela*]

SINK.......... Individual Carrier-Channels and Pilot-Frequency Bay   (RU)

SINMUH .. Sindicato Musical de Honduras [*Honduran Musical Trade Union*] [*Honduras*]   (LA)

SINN .... Societe de l'Imprimerie Nationale du Niger

SINOCHART ... China National Chartering Corp. [*China*]   (FEA)

SINOCHEM ... China National Chemicals Import & Export Corp. [*China*]   (IMH)

Sinod k-vo ... Synodic Publishing House   (BU)

SINOMAPE ... Sindicato Nacional de Operadores de Maquinas Pesadas [*National Union of Heavy Machinery Operators*] [*Dominican Republic*]   (LA)

sinon........... Sinonimo [*Synonym*] [*Portuguese*]

SINOPEC ... China Petrochemical International Co.   (TCC)

SINOPTAL ... Societe Industrielle d'Optique Algerie

SINOTASHIP ... Sino-Tanzanian Joint Shipping Company

SINOTRANS ... China National Foreign Trade Transportation Corp. [*China*]   (FEA)

SINP.......... Saha Institute of Nuclear Physics [*India*] [*Research center*]   (WND)

SINPA .... Societe d'Interet National des Produits Agricoles [*National Agricultural Products Company*] [*Malagasy*]   (AF)

SINPAR .... Servicio Investigativo Particular [*Colombia*]   (COL)

SINPEP..... Sindicato Nacional de Profesores de Educacion Primaria [*National Union of Elementary Education Teachers*] [*Peru*]   (LA)

SINPES ..... Sindicato Nacional de Profesores de Educacion Secundaria [*National Union of Secondary School Teachers*] [*Peru*]   (LA)

SINPET..... Sindicato Nacional de Profesores de Educacion Tecnica [*National Union of Technical Education Teachers*] [*Peru*]   (LA)

SINPI .... Societa Italiana di Neuropsichiatria Infantile [*Italian*]   (SLS)

SINPOCAF ... Sindicato Nacional dos Trabalhadores dos Portos e Caminhos de Ferro [*Trade union*] [*Mozambique*]   (EY)

SINR.......... Swiss Institute for Nuclear Research

SINS .... Societa Italiana di Neurosonologia [*Italian*]   (SLS)

SINSW ...... Security Institute of New South Wales [*Australia*]

S INT........ Senza Interruzione [*Without Interruption or Pause*] [*Music*]

sint .... Synthetic   (RU)

SINTA .... Servicio de Informacion en Tecnologia de Alimentos [*Fundacion Centro de Investigaciones del Estado para la Produccion Experimental Agroindustrial*] [*Venezuela*]

SINTAC .... Sindicato Nacional dos Trabalhadores da Aviacao Civil, Correios, e Comunicacoes [*Trade union*] [*Mozambique*]   (EY)

SINTAE .... Sindicato Nacional de Trabajadores de Artes y Espectaculos [*National Union of Entertainment Workers*] [*Cuba*]   (LA)

SINTAF..... Sindicato Nacional dos Trabalhadores Agro - Pecuarios e Florestais [*Trade union*] [*Mozambique*]   (EY)

SINTAL .... Servicio de Informacion Tecnica para la Industria de Alimentos [*Instituto de Investigaciones Tecnologicas*] [*Colorado*]

SINTAS..... Sosyal Sehircilik Insaat ve Ticaret Anonim Sirketi [*Social City Planning Construction and Trade Corporation*]   (TU)

SINTCOBASE ... Sindicato Nacional dos Trabalhadores do Comercio, Banca, e Seguros [*Trade union*] [*Mozambique*]   (EY)

SINTEC .... Servicio de Informacion Tecnica [*Corporacion Financiera Popular SA*] [*Colorado*]

SINTECO ... Sociedad Industrial Tecnica Ltda. [*Colombia*]   (COL)

SINTEF..... Stiftelsen for Industriell og Teknisk Forskning [*Foundation of Scientific and Industrial Research*] [*Norway*]

SINTEL..... Sindicato de Telecomunicacoes [*Telecommunications Workers Union*] [*Portuguese*]   (WER)

Sinter .... Sinterung [*Sintering*] [*German*]   (GCA)

sintetich ..... Synthetic   (RU)

SINTEVEC ... Sindicato Nacional dos Trabalhadores da Industria Textil Vestuario, Couro, e Calcado [*Trade union*] [*Mozambique*]   (EY)

SINTHOTS ... Sindicato Nacional dos Trabalhadores da Industria Holeleira, Turismo e Similares [*Trade union*] [*Mozamique*]   (EY)

SINTIA ..... Sindicato Nacional dos Trabalhadores da Industria do Acucar [*Trade union*] [*Mozambique*]   (EY)

SINTIAB... Sindicato Nacional dos Trabalhadores da Industria Alimentar e Bebidas [*Trade union*] [*Mozambique*]   (EY)

SINTIC...... Sindicato Nacional dos Trabalhadores da Industria de Caju [*Trade union*] [*Mozamb ique*]   (EY)

SINTICIM ... Sindicato Nacional dos Trabalhadores da Industria de Construcao Civil, Madeira, e Minas [*Trade union*] [*Mozambique*]   (EY)

SINTIME ... Sindicato Nacional dos Trabalhadores da Industria Metalurgica, Metalomecanica, e Energia [*Trade union*] [*Mozambique*]   (EY)

SINTIQUIGRA ... Sindicato Nacional dos Trabalhadores da Industria Quimica, Borracha, Papel, e Grafica [*Trade union*] [*Mozambique*]   (EY)

SINTMAP ... Sindicato Nacional dos Trabalhadores da Marinha Mercante e Pesca [*Trade Union*] [*Mozambique*]   (EY)

SINTO....... System Informaccji Naukowej Technicznej i Organizacyjnej [*Poland*]   (PDAA)

SINTP .... Societe d'Interet National des Travaux Publics [*National Public Works Company*] [*Malagasy*]   (AF)

SINTRA .... Societe Industrielle des Nouvelles Techniques Radioelectriques et de l'Electronique Francaise [*France*]

SINTRABANCOL ... Sindicato Nacional de Trabajadores del Banco de Colombia [*Colombia*]   (COL)

SINTRABE ... Sindicato de Trabajadores de Editorial y Tipografia Bedout [*Colombia*]   (COL)

SINTRAFEC ... Sindicato de Trabajadores de la Federacion Nacional de Cafeteros de Colombia [*Chinchina-Caldas*]   (COL)

SINTRAFERRAT ... Sindicato de Trabajadores Ferrocarriles del Atlantico [*Atlantico Railroad Workers Union*] [*Colorado*]   (LA)

SINTRAIMEC ... Sindicato de Trabajadores de las Industrias Metalicas de Colombia [*Colombian Metal Workers Union*]   (LA)

SINTRAQUIN ... Sindicato Nacional de Trabajadores de la Industria Quimica [*Colombia*]   (COL)

SINTRASALUD ... Sindicato de Trabajadores de Salud [*Trade Union of Health Workers*] [*Dominican Republic*]   (LA)

SINTRAT ... Sindicato Nacional dos Trabalhadores dos Transportes Rodoviarios e Assistencia Tecnica [*Trade union*] [*Mozambique*]   (EY)

SINTRAVA ... Sindicato Nacional de Trabajadores de Avianca [*Colombia*]   (COL)

SINU .... Solomon Islands National Union of Workers   (FEA)

SINUW ..... Solomon Islands National Union of Workers

SIO .... Aircraft Icing Gauge   (RU)

SIO .... Individual Equipment Bay   (RU)

SIO .... Random Information Processing   (RU)

SIO .... Rural Election District   (RU)

SIO .... Sekretarijat za Industrijo in Obrt [*Secretariat of Industry and Trade*]   (YU)

SIO .... Smithton [*Australia*] [*Airport symbol*]   (OAG)

SIO .... Social Insurance Organization [*Saudi Arabia*]   (ME)

SIO .... Societa per l'Industria dell'Ossigeno e di Altri Gas SpA [*Nuclear energy*] [*Italian*]

SIO .... Societe Industrielle d'Owendo

SIO .... Studio za Industrijsko Oblikovanje [*Studio for Industrial Design*] [*Zagreb*]   (YU)

SIO .... Surinaamse Islamitische Organisatie   (EY)

SIOC.......... Shanghai Institute of Organic Chemistry [*Chinese*]

SIOCMF ... Societa Italiana di Odontostomatologia e Chirurgia Maxillo-Facciale [*Italian*]   (SLS)

SIODC....... Swaziland Iron Ore Development Company Ltd.

SIOeChCF ... Societa Italiana di Otorinolaringologia e Chirurgia Cervico-Facciale [*Italian*]   (SLS)

SIOG .... Societa Italiana di Ostetricia e Ginecologia [*Italian Society of Obstetrics and Gynecology*]   (SLS)

SIOG .... Societe Internationale d'Ophtalmologie Geographique [*International Society of Geographic Opthalmology*]   (EAIO)

SIOI........... Societa Italiana di Odontoiatria Infantile [*Italian*]   (SLS)

SIOI........... Societa Italiana per l'Organizzazione Internazionale [*Italian*]

SIOM .... Societe Industrielle Oleicole Marocaine

SIOMA...... Societe Impressions Ofset Maroc

SIOP.......... Societa Italiana di Otorinolaringologia Pediatrica [*Italian*]   (SLS)

SIOP.......... Societe Internationale d'Oncologie Pediatrique [*International Society of Pediatric Oncology*] [*Leeds, England*]   (EAIO)

SIORBA .... Societe Immobiliere Ornano-Jean-Bart [*Morocco*]

SIOS.......... Servizio Informazioni Operativa e Situazione [*Operational Intelligence and Situation Services*] [*Italian*]   (WER)

SIOS.......... Stichting Industrie Outwikkeling Suriname [*Surinam*]   (DSCA)

SIOSA .... Sicula Oceanicas SA [*Shipping line*] [*Italy*]   (EY)

SIOT......... All-Union Scientific Research Institute of Work Safety of the VTsSPS [*All-Union Central Trade-Union Council*] (Sverdlovsk)   (RU)

SIOT......... Societa Italiana di Ortopedia e Traumatologia [*Italian*]   (SLS)

SIP............ Individual Frequency-Converter Bay   (RU)

SIP............ Secretaria de Informacion Publica [*Secretariat of Public Information*] [*Argentina*]   (LA)

sip.............. Senza il Prezzo [*Without Price*] [*Publishing*] [*Italian*]

SIP............ Servicio de Investigacion Prehistorica y Museu de Prehistoria [*Spanish*]   (SLS)

SIP............. Simferopol [*Former USSR*] [*Airport symbol*]   (OAG)

SIP............. Sindacato Italiano Pescatori [*Italian Union of Fishermen*]

SIP............. Sindicato de Industriales Panamenos [*Panamanian Industrialists Union*]   (LA)

SIP............. Sindicato de la Industria del Pescado [*Fishing Industry Union*] [*Argentina*]   (LA)

SIP............. Sindicato de la Industria Pesquera [*Fishing Industry Union*] [*El Salvador*]   (LA)

SIP............. Sisterhood for International Peace [*Australia*]

SIP............. Sociedad Interamericana de Prensa [*Inter-American Press Association*] [*Use IAPA*]   (LA)

SIP............. Societa Italiana di Parapsicologia [*Italian*]   (SLS)

SIP............. Societa Italiana di Pediatria [*Italian Pediatric Society*]   (SLS)

SIP............. Societa Italiana di Psichiatria [*Italian Society of Psychiatry*]   (SLS)

SIP............. Societa Italiana per Esercizio delle Telecomunicazioni SpA [*Italy*]

SIP............. Societa Italiana per l'Esercizio Telefonico [*Italian Society for Telephone Use*] [*Information service or system*]   (IID)

SIP............. Societe Genevoise d'Instruments de Physique [*Switzerland*]

SIP............. Societe Indigene de Prevoyance

SIP............. Societe Industrielle Pharmaceutique

SIP............. Societe Internationale Pirelli SA [*Switzerland*]

SIP............. Societe Ivoirienne de Peche

SIP............. Societe Ivoirienne de Peinture

SIP............. Societes Indigenes de Prevoyance [*North African*]

SIP............. Solar and Interplanetary Programme [*International Council of Scientific Unions*]

SIP............. Spoleczne Inspekcje Pracy [*People's Labor Inspectorate*]   (POL)

SIP............. Spoleczny Inspektor Pracy [*People's Labor Inspector*]   (POL)

SIP............. Step Pulse Interrupter   (RU)

SIP............. Sumsko Industrisko Poduzece [*Forestry Industrial Establishment*]   (YU)

SIP............. Svensk-Internationella Pressbyran [*Swedish-International Press Bureau*]   (EY)

SIPA......... Science-Based Industrial Park Administration [*National Science Council*] [*Taiwan*] [*Research center*]   (ERC)

SIPA......... Secao de Informacoes e Publicadade Agricola [*Brazil*]   (DSCA)

SIPA......... Servicio de Investigacion y Promocion Agrarias [*Agrarian Research and Development Service*] [*Peru*]   (LA)

SIPA......... Servico de Informacao da Producao Agricola [*Agricultural Production Information Service*] [*Brazil*]   (LAA)

SIPA......... Societa Italiana di Patologia Aviare [*Italian*]   (SLS)

SIPA......... Societe d'Importation des Pieces Automobiles

SIPA......... Societe Industrielle de Produits Africains

SIPA......... Societe Industrielle des Plastiques Abidjanais

SIPA......... Solomon Islands Ports Authority   (GEA)

SIPA......... Somali Institute of Public Administration

SIPAC...... Societe Ivoirienne de Plomberie, Assainissement, et Canalisation

SIPAD...... Preduzece za Izvoz Drveta, Sarajevo (Sumsko Industrisko Preduzece Akcionarsko Drustvo) [*Wood Export Establishment*] [*Sarajevo*]   (YU)

SIPAG...... Societe Industrielle de Panification de Guinee

SIPAG...... Syndicat des Instituteurs, Professeurs, et Agents de la Guadeloupe   (PD)

SIPAI........ Societa Italiana di Psicoterapia Analitica Immaginativa [*Italian*]   (SLS)

SIPAL....... Societe Industrielle de Preparations Alimentaires [*Togo*]

SIPALAC.. Sindicato de la Industria de Productos Alimenticios, Lacteos, y Actividades Conexas [*Union of the Food, Dairy, and Related Industries*] [*El Salvador*]   (LA)

SIPAM...... Societe Industrielle de Peche a Madagascar

SIPAM...... Societe Industrielle des Produits Alimentaires du Nord-Marocain

SIPAMA ... Servico de Inspecao de Produtos Agropecuarios e Materiais Agricolas [*Brazil*]   (DSCA)

SIPAOC .... Societa Italiana di Patologia e di Allevamento degli Ovini e dei Caprini [*Italian*]   (SLS)

SIPAR .... Societe Ivoirienne de Peche et d'Armement [*Ivorian Fishing and Shipping Company*]   (AF)

SIPARCO ... Societe Industrielle de Parfumerie et de Cosmetique

SIPAROCI ... Societe Industrielle de Parfumerie et de Cosmetique

SIPC .... Societa Italiana di Psicopedagogia Clinica [*Italian*]   (SLS)

SIPCA .... Saudi International Petroleum Carriers Ltd.

SIPCA .... Societe Industrielle de Produits Chimiques et Aromatiques

SIPCI........ Societe Ivoirienne de Promotion Commerciale et Industrielle

SIPCO .... Societe Ivoirienne de Produits Congeles

SIPCP........ Sociedad de Ingenieros Profesionales del Canal de Panama   (EAIO)

SIPE .... Savezni Institut za Poljoprivrednu Ekonomiku [*Federal Institute of Agricultural Economics*]   (YU)

SIPE .... Sociedade Industrial de Produtos Electricos [*Industrial Company for Electrical Products*] [*Portuguese*]   (WER)

SIPE .... Societa Italiana di Psicoterapie Energetiche [*Italian*]   (SLS)

SIPEC........ Societe Industrielle des Peches au Cameroun

SIPEC........ Societe Ivoirienne de Peintures et Colorants

SIPECO...... Societe Industrielle des Peintures de Conakry

SIPEGA..... Societe Industrielle des Peches du Gabon

SIPER........ Societe Ivoirienne de Peinture et Revetement

SIPES........ Sindicato de la Industria Portuaria de El Salvador [*Union of Port Workers of El Salvador*]   (LA)

SIPEU .... Solomon Islands Public Employees' Union

SIPG .... Societe Internationale de Participation et de Gestion

SIPG .... Societe Internationale de Pathologie Geographique [*International Society of Geographical Pathology*] [*Australia*]   (EAIO)

SIPH......... Scandinavian International Property Holdings

SIPH.......... Societe Indochinoise de Plantations d'Heveas [*Indochinese Rubber Plantation Industry*]

SIPHAC .... Societe Industrielle Pharmaceutique du Cameroun

SIPHO....... Societe Immobiliere de Promotion d'Etudes et de Realisations Hotelieres

SIPI .... Shanghai Institute of the Pharmaceutical Industry [*China*]   (IRC)

SIPI .... Societa Italiana di Psicologia Individuale [*Italian*]   (SLS)

SIPI .... Societe Ivoirienne de Promotion Industrielle [*Ivorian Company for Industrial Promotion*]   (AF)

SIPIHO ..... Societe Ivoirienne pour l'Industrie Hoteliere

SIPJB .... Societe Industrielle de Parfumerie Jazzar Bitar

SIPL.......... Societe Industrielle de Produits Laitiers

SIPLA....... Societe Immobiliere et de Placement

SIPMAD .... Societe Industrielle de Peche de Madagascar

SIPMAG ... Societe Ivoirienne de Papiers et Materiels d'Arts Graphiques

SIPO......... Sicherheitspolizei [*Security Police*] [*NAZI*]   (BJA)

SIPO......... Sindicato Profesional Orquestal [*Chile*]   (EAIO)

SIPO......... Swiss Intellectual Property Office [*Bern*] [*Information service or system*]   (IID)

SIPOA ...... Servico de Inspecao de Produtos de Origem Animal [*Brazil*]

SIPOA ...... Societe Industrielle Pharmaceutique de l'Ouest Africain

SIPOL ...... Seccion de Investigacion Policiaca [*Police Investigation Section*] [*Mexico*]   (LA)

SIPPO ...... Societe Ivoirienne des Pieces et Pneumatiques d'Occasion

SIPPTAL... Sindicato de Productores Propietarios de Tierras Agropecuarias del Litoral [*Union of Coastal Agricultural and Livestock Landowners and Producers*] [*Ecuador*]   (LA)

SIPR .... Societe Ivoirienne de Plomberie et Revetements

SIPRA .... Societa Italiana Pubblicita Per Azioni [*Italian radio and television advertising company*]

SIPRA .... Societe Ivoirienne de Productions Animals

SIPRAG .... Societe Ivoirienne de Promotion Agricole

SIPREDI ... Societe Internationale de Presse, d'Edition, et de Diffusion

SIPRI .... Stockholm International Peace Research Institute [*Solna, Sweden*]   (EAIO)

SIPRIM..... Societe Ivoirienne de Promotion et de Realisations Immobilieres

SIPRO .... Servicios Informativos Procesados [*Processed Information Services*] [*Mexico*]   (CROSS)

SIPROA .... Societe Ivoirienne de Produits Agricoles

SIPROM .... Societe Industrielle des Produits Metallurgiques [*Morocco*]

SIPRON .... Sistema de Protecao ao Programa Nuclear Brasileiro [*Protective System for the Brazilian Nuclear Program*]   (LA)

SIPROSEM ... Societe Ivoirienne de Production de Sel Marin

SIPRO-TOURIST ... Societe Ivoirienne de Promotion Touristique

SIPRT........ Societe Internationale pour les Plantes-Racines Tropicales

SIPS.......... Science Innovation Program [*Australia*]

SIPS.......... Societa Internazionale di Psicologia della Scrittura [*International Society of Psychology of Handwriting - ISPII*]   (EAIO)

SIPS .... Societa Internazionale di Psicologia dello Sport [*Italian*]   (SLS)

SIPs .... Societa Italiana di Psicologia [*Italian*]   (SLS)

SIPS.......... Societa Italiana di Psicologia Scientifica [*Italian*]   (SLS)

SIPS.......... Societa Italiana per il Progresso delle Scienze [*Italian Society for the Advancement of Science*]   (ASF)

SIPS.......... Societe Industrielle de Papeterie au Senegal

SIPS.......... Societe Internationale de Psychologie des Sports [*International Society of Sports Psychology*]   (EAIO)

SIPS.......... Societe Ivoirienne de Plomberie Sanitaire

SIPSEC ..... Syndicat des Importateurs de Produits Petrolieres du Sud-Est and du Centre de France

SIPT .... Societa Italiana di Psicosintesi Terapeutica [*Italian*]   (SLS)

SIPTP........ Societe Industrielle de Plomberie, Travaux Publics, et Particuliers [*Senegal*]

SIPV .... Societa Italiana di Patologia Vascolare [*Italian*]   (SLS)

sir .... Namely   (BU)

SIR............ Selective Investerings Regeling [*Selective Investment Law*] [*Netherlands*]   (IMH)

SIR............ Singapore Infantry Regiment   (ML)
SIR............ Sion [*Switzerland*] [*Airport symbol*]
Sir .... Sirius [*Record label*] [*Sweden*]
sir .... Sirop [*Syrup*] [*Pharmacy*]
SIR............ Societa Italiana Resine SpA [*Italy*]
SIR............ Societe Ivoirienne de Raffinage [*Ivorian Refining Company*]
  (AF)
SIR............ Standarization, Interoperability, and Readiness [*NATO*]   (MCD)
SIR............ Stratified Indexing and Retrieval [*Japan*] [*Computer science*]
SIR............ Svenska Inredningsarkitekters Riksforbund [*Sweden*]   (EAIO)
SIRAMA ... Societe Siramamy Malagasy [*Malagasy Sugar Company*]   (AF)
SIRAPS ̇.... Sistema Intersectorial Regional de Apoyo a la Propiedad Social
  [*Intersectoral Regional System for Support of Social
  Property*] [*Peru*]   (LA)
SIRAT .... Societe Ivoirienne de Realisations Artisanales et Touristiques
SIRATAC ... Commonwealth Scientific and Industrial Research Organisation
  and Agriculture Department Tactics for Growing Cotton in
  Australia
SIRCA ...... Societe des Importateurs Reunis du Cameroun
SIRCA ...... Societe Industrielle de la Republique Centrafrique
SIRCE .... Societa per l'Incremento Rapporti Commerciali con l'Estero
  [*Italy*]   (PDAA)
SIRCOM ... Societe Ivoirienne de Representation et de Commission
SIRCOMA ... Societe Industrielle de Representations et Commerciale en
  Mauritanie
SIRDI .... Societe Immobiliere de Representation et de Distribution
SIREGCI ... Societe Immobiliere et de Representations Generales de Cote-
  D'Ivoire
SIREG-Dakar ... Societe Immobiliere et de Representations Generales de
  Dakar
SIREL........ Societe Industrielle et Routiere des Entreprises Lair
SIRELE..... Societe Ivoirienne de Realisation Electrique
SIREMAR ... Sicilia Regionale Marittima SpA [*Italy*]   (EY)
SIRENE .... Systeme Informatique du Repertoire des Entreprises et des
  Etablissements [*German*]   (ADPT)
SIREP........ Societe Internationale pour la Recherche et l'Exploitation du
  Petrole
SIRESP ..... Sindicato da Industria de Resinas Sinteticas do Estado de Sao
  Paulo [*Brazil*]
SIRG.......... Schleudergegossener Rotguss [*Centrifugally Cast Red Brass*]
  [*German*]   (GCA)
SIRI .... Societa Italiana per la Robotica Industriale [*Italian Society of the
  Robotics Industry*]   (SLS)
SIRI .... Societe Ivoirienne de Representation Industrielle
SIRI .... Soil and Irrigation Research Institute [*South Africa*]   (ARC)
SIRI .... Sugar Industry Research Institute [*Jamaica*]
SIRIEM..... Societa Italiana Ricerche Idriche e Minerarie
SIRIM .... Societe Internationale de Recherche Interdisciplinaire sur la
  Maladie
SIRIM .... Standards and Industrial Research Institute of Malaysia
  [*Research center*]   (IRC)
SIRIP........ Societe Irano-Italienne des Petroles [*Irano-Italian Petroleum
  Company*]   (ME)
SIRLEJ ..... Societe Internationale de Recherche en Litterature d'Enfance et
  de Jeunesse [*International Research Society for Children's
  Literature - IRSCL*]   (EA)
SIRMCE.... Societe Internationale pour la Recherche sur les Maladies de
  Civilisation et l'Environment [*International Society for
  Research on Civilization Diseases and Environment*]
  [*Brussels, Belgium*]   (EAIO)
SIRO.......... CSIRO [*Commonwealth Scientific and Industrial Research
  Organisation*] Research in Progress [*Australia*]
  [*Information service or system*]   (CRD)
SIROS .... Schnelles Informations-und Retrieval-System [*German*]
  (ADPT)
SIROWET ... CSIRO Wall Exposure Test [*Australia*]
SIRS .... Saztec Information Retrieval Services [*Australia*]
SIRT .... Servicio de Informacion y Recursos Tecnicos [*Honduras*]
SIRTDO .... Small Industries Research Training and Development
  Organisation [*India*]   (PDAA)
SIRTI........ Societa Italiana Reti Telefoniche Interurbane [*Italy*]   (PDAA)
SIRU.......... Singapore Industrial Research Unit   (PDAA)
SIRWA ...... Societe Industrielle du Rwanda
SIS .... Reference and Information Service   (RU)
SIS .... Scientific Instrument Society   (EA)
SIS .... Secteur Industriel Socialiste [*Socialist Industrial Sector*] [*Algeria*]
  (AF)
SIS .... Seddick Isehak Saleh [*Yemen*] [*Commercial firm*]
SIS .... Sentencing Information System [*Judicial Commission of New
  South Wales*] [*Australia*]
SIS .... Settlement Information Strategy [*Australia*]
SIS .... Seychelles International Safari Air Ltd. [*ICAO designator*]
  (FAAC)
SIS .... Share Information Service [*British*]   (DCTA)
SIS .... Sishen [*South Africa*] [*Airport symbol*]   (OAG)
SIS .... Societa Internazionale Scotista [*International Scotist Society -
  ISS*] (EAIO)

SIS .... Societa Italiana di Statistica [*Italian Statistical Society*]   (SLS)
SIS .... Societa Italo-Somala [*Italian-Somalian Society*] [*Commercial
  firm*]
SIS .... Societe d'Informatique et de Systemes Compagnie Bancaire
  [*France*]   (PDAA)
SIS .... Societe Immobiliere du Senegal
SIS .... Societe Industrielle de Sacherie
SIS .... Societe Ivoirienne de Spectacles
SIS .... Sovetska Informacni Sluzba [*Soviet Information Service*]   (CZ)
SIS .... Soviet Intelligence Services
SIS .... Special Industrial Services [*United Nations Industrial
  Development Organization*]
SIS .... Special Investigation Section   (ML)
SIS .... Standardiseringskommissionen i Sverige [*Swedish Standards
  Institution*]   (ARC)
SIS .... State Information Service [*Australia*]
SIS .... Statens Institutt for Stralehygiene [*Ministry of Health and Social
  Affairs*] [*Norway*]   (WND)
SIS .... Stratiotiki Iatriki Skholi [*Army Medical School*] [*Greek*]   (GC)
SIS .... Sveriges Standardiseringskommission [*Swedish Standards
  Institution*] [*Also, an information service or system*]   (IID)
SIS .... Swedish Inteplanetary Society   (IAA)
SIS .... Symvoulion Iatrikon Syllogon [*Medical Associations Council*]
  (GC)
SIS .... Well Induction Seismic Detector   (RU)
SISA......... Seguros e Inversiones, Sociedad Anonima [*Insurance and
  Investments Corporation*] [*El Salvador*]
SISA .... SITRAM [*Societe Ivoirienne de Transport Maritime*]
  International Shipping Agencies [*Ivory Coast*]   (AF)
SISA .... Societa Italiana per le Scienze Ambientali: Biometeorologia,
  Bioclimatologia, ed Ecologia [*Italian*]   (SLS)
SISA .... Societa Italiana per lo Studio dell'Arteriosclerosi [*Italian Society
  for the Study of Arteriosclerosis*]   (SLS)
SISA .... Societa Italiana Servizi Aerei [*Italy*]
SISA .... Societa Italiana Strade Africa
SISAL........ Sistema de Informacion Siderurgica para America Latina
  [*Instituto Latinoamericano del Fierro y el Acero*] [*Chile*]
SISAL....... Sport Italiana Societa a Responsabilita Limitata [*Original
  founder of football pools in Italy*]
SISALTEX ... Industrias Textiles de Sisal [*Venezuela*]   (DSCA)
SISAP........ Societe d'Installations Sanitaires, d'Assainissement, et de
  Plomberies
SISC .... Societe Industrielle Senegalaise de Confections
SISC .... South India Shipping Corp. Ltd.   (DS)
SISCA....... Societa Italiana per lo Studio della Cancerogenesi Ambientale ed
  Epidemiologia dei Tumori [*Italian*]   (SLS)
SISCOMA ... Societe Industrielle Senegalaise de Constructions Mecaniques et
  de Materiels Agricoles
SISEA........ Sugar Industry Staff Employees Association [*Mauritius*]   (AF)
SISEF .... Societe Industrielle de Sciage et d'Exploitation Forestiere
SISEP .... Societe Ivoirienne de Soufflage et d'Emballage Plastique
SISF .... Societa Italiana di Scienze Farmaceutiche [*Italian*]   (SLS)
SISFER ..... Societe Ivoirienne de Serrurerie et Ferronerie
SISH......... Societe Internationale de la Science Horticole [*International
  Society for Horticultural Science - ISHS*]   (EAIO)
SISI........... Small Industries Service Institute [*India*]   (PDAA)
SISIR........ Singapore Institute of Standards and Industrial Research   (ML)
SISK .... Sosyalist Isci Sendikalari Konfederasyonu [*Confederation of
  Socialist Worker Unions*]   (TU)
S Isl........... Sandwich Islands
SISMED.... Societa Italiana di Storia della Medicina [*Italian*]   (SLS)
SISMES .... Societa Italiana di Statistica Medico-Sanitaria [*Italian*]   (SLS)
SISO .... Schema voor de Indeling van de Systematische Catalogus in
  Openbare Bibliotheken [*Netherlands*]
SISP.......... Servicio Cooperativo Interamericano de Salud Publica [*Inter-
  American Cooperative Public Health Service*] [*Paraguay*]
  (LAA)
SISS.......... Societa Italiana della Scienza del Suolo [*Italian*]   (SLS)
SISS.......... Societe Industrielle des Silicones [*French*]
sist............. Make, System, Systematic   (RU)
SISUGA .... Societe d'Investissements Sucriers au Gabon
SISVet .... Societa Italiana delle Scienze Veterinarie [*Italian Society of
  Veterinary Science*]   (SLS)
SISWO ...... Stichting Interuniversitair Institut voor Sociaal-Weten-
  Schappelijk Onderzoek [*Netherlands Universities' Joint
  Social Research Center*] [*Research center*]   (IRC)
SISWP....... Soroptimist International of the South West Pacific [*Sydney,
  NSW, Australia*]   (EAIO)
SIT .... Coeducational Technical School of Economics   (BU)
sit .... Es Igy Tovabb [*Et Cetera*]   (HU)
SIT .... School of Industrial Technology [*University of Mauritius*]
SIT .... Service d'Information Technologique [*Institut Algerien de
  Normalisation et de Propriete Industrielle*] [*Algeria*]
SIT .... Servicio de Informacion Tecnica [*Centro de Desarrollo Industrial
  del Ecuador*] [*Ecuador*]
SIT .... Sindicato Industria Textil [*Union of the Textile Industry*] [*El
  Salvador*]   (LA)

SIT .... Singapore Improvement Trust   (ML)
sit .... Sin Indicaciones Tipograficas [*Without Name of Publisher*] [*Spanish*]
SIT .... Sistemul Informatic Teritorial [*Territorial Data Processing System*]   (RO)
SIT .... Societe Indochinoise de Transports [*Indochinese Transport Company*]   (CL)
SIT .... Societe Industrielle de Transports
SIT .... Societe Industrielle Thanry
SIT .... Societe Interafricaine de Transports
SIT .... Societe International de Telecommunications Aeronautiques [*Belgium*] [*ICAO designator*]   (FAAC)
SIT .... Societe Ivoirienne de Topographie
SIT .... Societe Ivoirienne de Transit
SIT .... Societe Ivoirienne de Transports
SIT .... Soma Ippikou kai Tethorakismenon [*Cavalry and Armored Corps*]   (GC)
SIT .... State Information Technology [*Western Australia*]
SIT .... Statiile de Intretinere Tehnica [*Technical Maintenance Stations*]   (RO)
SIT .... Stowarzyszenie Inzynierow i Technikow [*Association of Engineers and Technicians*]   (POL)
SIT .... Swinburne Institute of Technology [*Australia*]
SiT .... Wydawnictwo "Sport i Turystyka" [*"Sport and Turystyka" (Sport and Tourism) Publishing House*]   (POL)
SITA .... Sociedade Internacional de Trilogia Analitica [*International Society of Analytical Trilogy - ISAT*] [*Sao Paulo, Brazil*]   (EAIO)
SITA .... Societe de Transports Automobile de l'Imerina
SITA .... Societe Industrielle de Transports Automobiles
SITA .... Societe Internationale des Telecommunications Aeronautiques [*International Society of Aeronautical Telecommunications*] [*London, England*]
SITA .... Solomon Islands Tourist Authority   (EAIO)
SITAB .... Societe Ivoirienne des Tabacs
SITAC .... Societe Internationale des Tabacs au Cameroun
SITAF .... Societe Industrielle des Transports Automobiles Africains
SITAG .... Sindicato Industrial de Trabajadores de Artes Graficas [*Mexico*]   (LAA)
SITAM ...... Societe Industrielle des Tabacs Malgaches
SITAO ...... Societe Immobiliere et Touristique de l'Afrique de l'Ouest
SITAOF ..... Syndicat d'Initiative et de Tourisme de l'AOF
SITAP .... Syndesmos Idioktiton Taxi Athinon kai Proasteion [*Athens and Suburbs Taxi Owners Association*]   (GC)
SITB .... Societe Ivoirienne de Transformation du Bois
SITC .... Shenzhen Industry and Trade Centre [*China*]   (TCC)
SITC .... Standard Industrial Trade Classification [*United Nations*]
SITC .... Sultan Idris Training College   (ML)
SITCA .... Secretaria de Integracion Turistica Centroamericana [*Secretariat for Central American Tourism Integration*] [*Nicaragua*]   (LAA)
SITCE .... Servicio de Informacion sobre Traducciones Cientificas en Espanol [*Argentina*]   (DSCA)
SITCEN .... Situation Center [*NATO*]   (NATG)
SITCHAD ... Societe Immobiliere du Tchad
SITCIB ...... Societe Ivoirienne de Transport, de Commerce, et d'Industrie du Bois
SITCO .... Saudi International Transport Co.
SITCO .... Science, Industry, and Technology Council [*Western Australia*]
SITCOG .... Societe Ivoirienne de Transformation de Corps Gras
SITE .... Satellite Instructional Television Experiment [*NASA/Indian Space Research Organization, 1974*]
SITE .... Sindicato Independiente de Trabajadores de la Ensenanza [*Independent Trade Union of Educational Workers*] [*Spanish*]   (WER)
SITE .... Societa Italiana di Ecologia [*Italy*]   (EAIO)
SITEB .... Societe Industrielle de Travaux en Batiments [*Chad*]
SITECO .... Sociedad de Investigaciones Tecnicas Colombianas [*Society of Colombian Technical Research*]   (LA)
SITECOHDEFOR ... Sindicato de Trabajadores de la Corporacion de Desarrollo Forestal [*Trade Union of the Forestry Development Corporation Workers*] [*Honduras*]   (LA)
SITEF .... Societe Ivoirienne de Tacheronnage et d'Exploitation Forestiere
SITEK .... Sindikato di Trahado den Edukashon na Korsov [*Curacao Schoolteachers' Trade Uni on*] [*Netherlands Antilles*]   (EY)
SITEL .... Societe Belge des Ingenieurs de Telecommunication et d'Electronique [*Belgian Society of Telecommunication and Electronic Engineers*]   (PDAA)
SITEL .... Societe des Ingenieurs do Telecommunication [*Belgium*]
SITEL .... Societe Ivoirienne de Telecommunications
SITELESC ... Syndicat des Industries de Tubes Electroniques et Semiconducteurs [*France*]   (PDAA)
SITEP .... Societe Italo-Tunisienne d'Exploitation Petroliere [*Italian-Tunisian Petroleum Exploitation Company*]   (AF)
SITER .... Societe Ivoirienne de Technique Electronique et de Radio

SITET .... Sindicato Industrial de Trabajadores Electricos y de Telecomunicaciones [*Industrial Union of Electrical and Telecommunications Workers*] [*Costa Rica*]   (LA)
SITEX .... Societe Ivoirienne des Textiles
SITG .... Stowarzyszenie Inzynierow i Technikow Gornictwa [*Association of Mining Engineers and Technicians*]   (POL)
SITH .... Societe Internationale de Technique Hydrothermale
SITHA .... Salon International du Textile et de l'Habillement
SITI .... Swan International Tours, Inc. [*China*]   (TCC)
SITI .... Swiss Institute for Technical Information [*Information service or system*]   (IID)
SITIAMAH ... Sindicato de Trabajadores de la Industria Azucarera, Mieles, Alcoholes, y Similares de Honduras [*Trade Union of Honduran Sugar, Molasses, Alcohol, and Related Industries Workers*] [*Honduras*]   (LA)
SITIAMAH ... Sindicato de Trabajadores de la Industria del Acero, Metales, y Similares [*Trade Union of Steel, Metal, and Related Industries Workers*] [*Honduras*]   (LA)
SITIEF ...... Societe Ivoirienne de Travaux Topographiques et Fonciers
SITIM .... Societe Internationale des Techniques d'Imagerie Mentals [*International Society for Mental Imagery Techniques in Psychotherapy and Psychology*] [*Paris, France*]   (EAIO)
SITIYO ..... Sisli Iktisadi Ticari Ilimler Yuksek Okulu [*Sisli College of Economic and Commercial Science*] [*Istanbul*]   (TU)
SITJ .... Savez Inzenjera i Tehnicara Jugoslavije [*Union of Engineers and Technicians of Yugoslavia*]   (YU)
SITK .... Stowarzyszenie Inzynierow i Technikow Komunikacji [*Association of Transportation Engineers and Technicians*]   (POL)
SITLD .... Stowarzyszenie Inzynierow i Technikow Lesnictwa i Drzewnictwa [*Association of Forestry and Lumber Engineers and Technicians*]   (POL)
SITLiD ..... Stowarzyszenie Inzynierow i Technikow Lesnictwa i Drzewnictwa [*Association of Forestry and Lumber Engineers and Technicians*]   (POL)
SITMA ...... Societe Ivoirienne de Transports de Materiaux
SITO .... Societe Industrielle de Traitement des Oleagineux
SITO .... Societe Ivoirienne des Transports de l'Ouest
SITOM ...... Societe Industrielle de Traitement des Ordures Menageres
SITP .... Aircraft Temperature Pulsation Gauge   (RU)
SITP .... Societe Ivoirienne de Transports Publics
SITPCh ...... Stowarzyszenie Inzynierow i Technikow Przemyslu Chemicznego [*Association of Engineers and Technicians of the Chemical Industry*]   (POL)
SITPChem ... Stowarzyszenie Inzynierow i Technikow Przemyslu Chemicznego [*Association of Engineers and Technicians of the Chemical Industry*]   (POL)
SITPH .... Stowarzyszenie Inzynierow i Technikow Przemyslu Hutniczego [*Association of Engineers and Technicians of the Metallurgical Industry*]   (POL)
SITPN .... Stowarzyszenie Inzynierow i Technikow Przemyslu Naftowego [*Association of Engineers and Technicians of the Petroleum Industry*]   (POL)
SITPP .... Stowarzyszenie Inzynierow i Technikow Przemyslu Papierniczego [*Association of Engineers and Technicians of the Paper Industry*]   (POL)
SITPP .... Stowarzyszenie Naukowo-Techniczne Inzynierow i Technikow Przemyslu Papierniczego [*Scientific and Technical Association of Engineers and Technicians of the Paper Industry*]   (POL)
SITPPP ..... Stowarzyszenie Inzynierow i Technikow Przemyslu Papierniczego w Polsce [*Scientific and Technical Association of Engineers and Technicians of the Paper Industry of Poland*]   (EAIO)
SITPPW .... Stowarzyszenie Inzynierow i Technikow Polskiego Przemyslu Weglowego [*Association of Engineers and Technicians of the Polish Coal Industry*]   (POL)
SiTPSpoz ... Stowarzyszenie Inzynierow i Technikow Przemyslu Spozywczego [*Association of Food Industry Engineers and Technicians*]   (POL)
SITPW ...... Stowarzyszenie Inzynierow i Technikow Przemyslu Wlokienniczego [*Association of Engineers and Technicians of the Textile Industry*] [*Poland*]   (PDAA)
SITPWl ..... Stowarzyszenie Inzynierow i Technikow Przemyslu Wlokienniczego [*Association of Engineers and Technicians of the Textile Industry*]   (POL)
SITR .... Stowarzyszenie Inzynierow i Technikow Rolnictwa [*Association of Engineers and Technicians in Agriculture*]   (POL)
SITRA .... Seoul International Trade Fair [*South Korean*]
SITRA .... Societe Ivoirienne de Transit
SITRA .... Societe Ivoirienne de Travaux
SITRA .... South India Textile Research Association
SITRA .... Suomen Itsenaisyyden Juhlavouden Rahasto [*Finnish Independence Jubilee Fund*]   (PDAA)
SITRABA ... Societe Ivoirienne des Travaux Publics et Travaux Publics et Batiments

SITRAC..... Sindicato da Trabajadores Concord [*Concord Workers Union*] [*Argentina*] (LA)

SITRAC..... Sindicato de Trabajadores Cordoba [*Trade Union of Cordoba Workers*] [*Argentina*] (LA)

SITRAC..... Societe Industrielle de Transformation Centrafricaine

SITRACA ... Sindicato de Trabajadores del Calzado [*Trade Union of Footwear Workers*] [*Costa Rica*] (LA)

SITRACO ... Societe Interprofessionnelle de Transit et de Commissariat en Douane

SITRACOCS ... Sindicato de Trabajadores de la Construccion y Conexas Salvadorenas [*Trade Union of Salvadoran Workers in Construction and Related Activities*] (LA)

SITRACOCS ... Sindicato Gremial de Maestros de Cora de la Construccion y de Occupaciones Similares [*Trade union*] [*El Salvador*]

SITRADIQUE ... Sindicato de Trabajadores de la Division de Quepos [*Union of Workers of the Quepos Division*] [*Costa Rica*] (LA)

SITRAFENAT ... Sindicato de Trabajadores Ferrocarrileros y Portuarios [*Trade Union of Railroad and Port Workers*] [*Costa Rica*] (LA)

SITRAHCONAV ... Sindicato de Trabajadores Hondurenos de Companias Navieras [*Trade Union of Honduran Shipping Companies Workers*] (LA)

SITRAICE ... Sindicato de Trabajadores de la Industria Ceramica [*Trade Union of Ceramic Industry Workers*] [*Nicaragua*] (LA)

SITRAIM ... Sindicato de Trabajadores de la Industria de Muebles [*Trade Union of Furniture Industry Workers*] [*Nicaragua*] (LA)

SITRAINA ... Sindicato de Trabajadores del Instituto Nacional Agrario [*Workers Union of the National Agrarian Institute*] [*Honduras*] (LA)

SITRAM ... Sindicato de Trabajadores Materfer [*Materfer Workers Union*] [*Argentina*] (LA)

SITRAM ... Societe Industrielle de Transformation des Metaux

SITRAM ... Societe Ivoirienne de Transport Maritime [*Ivorian Marine Transport Company*] (AF)

SITRANE ... Societe Ivoirienne de Transport et de Nettoiement

SITRANS-BOIS ... Societe Ivoirienne de Transformation des Bois

SITRAPOSTH ... Sindicato de Trabajadores Postales de Honduras [*Trade Union of Honduran Postal Workers*] (LA)

SITRAPROVEC ... Sindicato Nacional de Trabajadores de Empresas de Produccion, Extraccion, Venta, y Mercadeo de Materiales de la Construccion [*National Union of Workers of Companies Producing, Selling, and Marketing Contruction Materials*] [*Panama*] (LA)

SITRASFCO ... Sindicato Industrial de la Standard Fruit Company [*Industrial Union of the Standard Fruit Company*] [*Costa Rica*] (LA)

SITRATERCO ... Sindicato de Trabajadores de la Tela Railroad Company [*Union of Tela Railroad Company Workers*] [*Honduras*] (LA)

SITRATEX ... Sindicato de Trabajadores de la Industria Textil [*Trade Union of Textile Industry Workers*] [*Nicaragua*] (LA)

SITRECO ... Sindicato de Trabajadores de Empresas Comerciales [*Trade Union of Commercial Enterprise Workers*] [*Nicaragua*] (LA)

SITS........... Engineering and Technical Personnel Section (RU)

SITS........... Societa Italiana Telecommunicazione Siemens [*Italy*] (PDAA)

SITS........... Societe Internationale de Transfusion Sanguine [*International Society of Blood Transfusion - ISBT*] [*Paris, France*] (EA)

SITS........... Syndicat des Ingenieurs et Techniciens du Senegal [*Engineers and Technicians Union of Senegal*] (AF)

SITSDIJ.... Savez Inzenjera i Tehnicara Sumarstva i Drvne Industrije Jugoslavije [*Union of Engineers and Technicians of the Forestry and Wood-Working Industries of Yugoslavia*] (YU)

SITsU .... Central Control Synchronizing Pulse [*Computers*] (RU)

SITT .... Servicio de Informacion y Transferencia de Tecnologia [*Centro Nacional de Productividad*] [*El Salvador*]

SITT .... Societe d'Industrie Textile Togolaise

SITTELCOM ... Sindicato Nacional de Trabajadores de la Empresa Nacional de Telecomunicaciones [*National Union of Workers of the National Telecomunications Enterprise*] [*Colorado*] (LA)

SITU .... Systeme d'Information des Trajets Urbains [*Computerized transit routing information service in Paris*]

SITUAM ... Sindicato Independiente de Trabajadores de la Universidad Autonoma Metropolitana [*Independent Trade Union of Workers of the Metropolitan Autonomous University*] [*Mexico*] (LA)

SITUN...... Sindicato de Trabajadores de la Universidad Nacional [*Trade Union of National University Workers*] [*Costa Rica*] (LA)

SITUS .... Sindicato de Trabajadores Universitarios Salvadorenos [*Trade Union of Salvadoran University Workers*] (LA)

Sitz............ Sitzung [*Conference*] [*German*] (GCA)

Sitzber........ Sitzungsberichte [*Proceedings*] [*German*] (GCA)

SIU .... Societa Italiana di Urologia (SLS)

SIU .... Societe Internationale d'Urologie [*International Society of Urology - ISU*] [*Paris, France*] (EAIO)

SIU .... Special Investigation Unit [*Australia*]

SIU .... Systeme International d'Unites [*International System of Units*] [*Also, SI*]

SIUB.......... Societe Ivoirienne d'Usinage des Bois

SIUCHODISNA ... Sindicato Unido de Choferes del Distrito Nacional [*United Trade Union of National District Drivers*] [*Dominican Republic*] (LA)

SIUP.......... Seychelles Islands United Party (AF)

SIUPA....... Solomon Islands United Party [*Political party*] (PPW)

SIV............ Council for Economic Mutual Assistance (BU)

SIV............ Savezno Izvrsno Vece [*Federal Executive Council*] (YU)

SIV............ Sistema de Inspeccion de Vuelo [*Flight Inspection System*] [*Venezuela*] (LA)

Siv .... Sivil [*Civil*] (TU)

siv .... Sivulla [*Pages*] [*Finland*] (GPO)

SIV............ Societa Italiana Vetro [*Glass manufacturer*] [*Italy*]

SIV............ Societe Immobiliere de la Volta

SIV............ Societe Immobiliere de Vridi

SIV............ Societe Senegalaise pour l'Industrie du Vetement

SIVA.......... Sociedad Importadora de Vehiculos (COL)

SIVA.......... Societe Industrielle de Vetements en Afrique

SIVA.......... Societe Ivoirienne d'Agriculture

SIVA.......... Societe Ivoirienne du Village d'Azuretti

SIVAE .... Societe Ivoirienne d'Amenagement et d'Entretien

SIVAK .... Societe Ivoirienne Agricole et Industrielle du Kenaf

SIVAM...... Statia de Incercari si Verificari de Aparatura Medicala [*Station for Testing and Checking Medical Apparatus*] (RO)

SIVE .... Societe Ivoirienne d'Importation de Vehicules et d'Equipement

SIVEL....... Societe Ivoirienne d'Electricite

SIVELEC .. Societe Ivoirienne d'Electricite

SIVEM....... Societe Ivoirienne d'Emballage

SIVENG.... Societe Ivoirienne d'Engrais

SIVENSA ... Siderurgica Venezolana Steel, Sociedad Anonima

SIVETI...... Societe Ivoirienne de Vetements sur Mesures Industrielles

SIVIE........ Societe Ivoirienne d'Installations Electriques

SIVIMEX ... Societe Ivoirienne d'Importation et d'Exportation

SIVIT........ Societe des Industries de la Viande du Tchad

SIVITOUR ... Societe Senegalo-Suedoise de Villages Touristiques

SIVOA....... Societe Ivoirienne d'Oxygene et d'Acetylene

SIVOITEX ... Societe Industrielle Ivoirienne de Textiles

SIVOMAR ... Societe Ivoirienne de Navigation Maritime [*Ivory Coast*] (EY)

SIW............ Spoldzielczy Instytut Wydawniczy [*Cooperative Publishing Institute*] (POL)

SIWA......... Scottish Inland Waterways Association (SLS)

SIWIS........ Siemens-Werkstaetten-Informations-System [*German*] (ADPT)

SIWU......... Shoe Industry Workers' Union (ML)

SIX............ Singleton [*Australia*] [*Airport symbol*] (OAG)

SIXATAF .. Sixth Allied Tactical Air Force, Southeastern Europe [*NATO*] (NATG)

SIXPOOL ... Sdruzeni Sesti Leteckych Spolecnosti Socialistickych Zemi [*Association of Six Airline Companies of Socialist Countries*] (CZ)

SIZ............. Community of Self-Interest [*Former Yugoslavia*] (IMH)

SIZ............. Sestroretsk Tool Plant Imeni Voskov (RU)

SIZ............. Sportske Igre Ucenika i Ucenica Srednjih i Strucnih Skola Zagreba [*School Games of Secondary and Technical Schools in Zagreb*] (YU)

SIZAI .... Societe Italo-Zairese Attivita Industriali

SIZB .... Savezni Institut za Zastitu Bilja [*Federal Institute for Plant Protection*] (YU)

SIZK .... Samara Institute of Grain Crops (RU)

SIZSK........ Savezni Institut za Zastitu Spomenika Kulture [*Federal Institute for the Preservation of Cultural Monuments*] (YU)

SJ............... La Semaine Judiciaire [*Switzerland*] (FLAF)

SJ............... La Semaine Juridique (FLAF)

SJ............... SJ Huvudkontor [*Swedish State Railways*] (DCTA)

sj................. Sjieling [*Shilling*] [*Monetary Unit*] [*Afrikaans*]

SJ............... Society of Jesus [*Italy*] (EAIO)

SJ............... Sonder Jaartal [*Without Year*] [*Afrikaans*]

SJ............... Sozialistische Jugend [*Socialist Youth*] [*Austria*] (WEN)

SJ............... Svalbard and Jan Mayen Islands [*ANSI two-letter standard code*] (CNC)

SJ............... Sveriges Statens Jarnvagar [*Swedish State Railways*] (WEN)

SJA .... Servicios Aereos Especiales de Jalisco SA de CV [*Mexico*] [*ICAO designator*] (FAAC)

SJA .... Society for Japanese Arts [*Netherlands*] (EAIO)

SJAA .... St. John's Ambulance Association (ML)

SJAB .... St. John's Ambulance Brigade (ML)

SJAC .... Society of Japanese Aerospace Companies Inc. (EY)

SJAC .... Society of Japanese Aircraft Constructors (PDAA)

sjaeld.......... Sjaelden [*Seldom Found*] [*Danish/Norwegian*]

sjagr .... Sjagreng [*Shagreen*] [*Publishing Danish/Norwegian*]

SJB .... Surinaams Juristenblad [*Benelux*] (BAS)

SJC .... Sisters of St. Joseph of Cluny [*France*] (EAIO)

SJC .... Socorro Juridico Cristiano [*El Salvador*] (EAIO)

SJC .... Sydney Journalists' Club [*Australia*]

SJCC.......... Social Justice Consultative Council [*Victoria, Australia*]

SJCC......... Suburban Jewish Community Center

SJCC......... Sydney Junior Chamber of Commerce [*Australia*]

SJD........... Los Cabos [*Mexico*] [*Airport symbol*]   (OAG)

SJE............ San Jose Del Guaviaro [*Colombia*] [*Airport symbol*]   (OAG)

SJE .... Savez Jugoslovenske Elektroprivrede [*Yugoslav Electric Industries Union*] [*Belgrade*]   (YU)

sjev .... Sjeverni [*Northern*]   (YU)

SJF............ Saint John [*Virgin Islands*] [*Airport symbol*]   (OAG)

SJF............ Statens Jordbrugstekniske Forsog [*National Agricultural Engineering Institute*] [*Denmark*]   (ARC)

SJF............ Suburban Jewish Folkshul

SJFR......... Statens Rad foer Skogs- och Jordbruksforskning [*Swedish Council for Forestry and Agricultural Research*] [*Research center*]   (IRC)

SJFR......... Sveriges Jagmastares och Forstmastares Riksforbund [*Sweden*]   (EAIO)

SJH........... San Juan Del Cesar [*Colombia*] [*Airport symbol*]   (OAG)

SJI .... San Jose [*Philippines*] [*Airport symbol*]   (OAG)

SJI .... Statni Jakostni Inspekce [*State Quality Inspection*]   (CZ)

SJIA........... Saint Joan's International Alliance [*See also AIJA*]   (EAIO)

SJJ............ Sarajevo [*Former Yugoslavia*] [*Airport symbol*]   (OAG)

SJJR......... Societe Jean-Jacques Rousseau [*Switzerland*]   (EAIO)

SJK............ Sao Jose Dos Campos [*Brazil*] [*Airport symbol*]   (OAG)

SJL............ Savez Jugoslovenskih Laboratorija [*Union of Yugoslav Laboratories*]   (YU)

SJM .... Svalbard and Jan Mayen Islands [*ANSI three-letter standard code*]   (CNC)

SJMJ......... Societe de Jesus, Marie et Joseph [*Society of Jesus, Mary and Joseph*] [*Netherlands*]   (EAIO)

SJO............ San Jose [*Costa Rica*] [*Airport symbol*]   (OAG)

SJP............ Sao Jose Do Rio Preto [*Brazil*] [*Airport symbol*]   (OAG)

SJP............ Savezno Javno Pravobraniostvo [*Federal Body of Government Attorneys*]   (YU)

SJP .... Singapore Justice Party [*Political party*]   (PPW)

SJP .... Socialist Janata Party [*India*] [*Political party*]   (ECON)

SJP .... Social Justice Party [*Malaysia*]   (ML)

SJSD......... Soviet Jewry Solidarity Day   (BJA)

SJT .... Savezno Javno Tuziostvo (SIV) [*Federal Public Prosecutors*]   (YU)

SjT .... Sokerijuurikkaan Tutkimuskeskus [*Sugar Beet Research Center*] [*Finland*]   (ARC)

SJTF......... Sveriges Jarnvagars Tjanstemannaforbund [*Sweden*]   (EAIO)

SJU............ San Juan [*Puerto Rico*] [*Airport symbol*]   (OAG)

SJU............ Schweizerische Journalistennen und Journalisten Union [*Switzerland*]   (EAIO)

SJV............ Societe Jules Verne [*France*]   (EAIO)

SJX............ Sartaneja [*Belize*] [*Airport symbol*]   (OAG)

SJZ............ Sao Jorge Island [*Azores*] [*Airport symbol*]   (OAG)

SJZ............ Sueddeutsche Juristenzeitung [*German*]   (ILCA)

SK .... Classified Catalog   (RU)

SK .... Column Counter   (RU)

Sk .... Compass North   (RU)

SK .... Composers' Union   (RU)

SK .... Compounding System   (RU)

SK .... Conic Separator   (RU)

sk.............. Declension   (RU)

sk.............. Economic Combine   (BU)

SK .... End of Communication   (RU)

SK .... Express Train   (RU)

SK .... Family Code   (BU)

SK .... Feeble-Prisoner Crew [*Corrective labor camps*]   (RU)

SK .... Jib Crane   (RU)

SK .... Patrol Cutter   (RU)

sk.............. Rifle Corps   (BU)

sk.............. Rock, Cliff [*Topography*]   (RU)

sk.............. Sajat Kezevel [*Signed*] [*Hungary*]   (GPO)

sk.............. Sajatkezuleg [*In One's Own Handwriting*]   (HU)

sk.............. Sa Kallad [*So Called*] [*Sweden*]   (GPO)

sk.............. Sakki(a) [*Finland*]

SK .... Salicylic Acid   (RU)

SK .... Saobracajna Kontrola [*Transportation Control*]   (YU)

SK .... Sarajevski Kiseljak, Preduzece za Eksploataciju Lekovitog Vrela "Kiseljak" [*"Kiseljak" Mineral Spring Enterprise*] [*Sarajevo*]   (YU)

SK .... Savet za Kulturu [*Cultural Council*]   (YU)

SK .... Savez Komunista [*League of Communists*]   (YU)

SK .... Scierie de Koumassi

sk.............. Sector   (BU)

Sk............. Sekil [*Figure, Sketch*]   (TU)

sk.............. Sekunde [*Second*] [*German*]

SK .... Sikorsky Aircraft Division [*United Aircraft Corp.*] [*ICAO aircraft manufacturer identifier*]   (ICAO)

Sk............. Skar [*or Skaret*] [*Rock above Water*] [*Sweden*]   (NAU)

sk.............. Sketch   (BU)

Sk............. Skizze [*Sketch*] [*German*]

SK .... Skladnica Ksiegarska [*Book Store*] [*Poland*]

sk............. Skola, Skolni, Skolsky, Skolstvi [*School (noun and adjective), Education*]   (CZ)

Sk.............. Skolj [*Skoljic*] [*Island, Reef Former Yugoslavia*]   (NAU)

Sk.............. Skolni Knihovna [*School Library*]   (CZ)

SK .... Skolska Knjiga [*A textbook publishing establishment*] [*Zagreb*]   (YU)

Sk.............. Skopelos [*Skopeloi*] [*Reef(s)*] [*Greek*]   (NAU)

sk.............. Skora (Oprawa) [*Leather (Binding)*] [*Poland*]

SK .... Slavic Committee   (BU)

SK .... Slovanska Knihovna [*Slavic Library*]   (CZ)

SK .... Slovenska Kniha [*The Slovak Book (part of the Czechoslovak National Bibliography)*]   (CZ)

SK .... Slovenska Koroska [*Slovenian Carinthia*] [*A periodical*]   (YU)

Sk.............. Sokak [*Street*] [*Sok*] [*See also*]   (TU)

SK .... Solana Kreka [*Kreka Salt Mine*] [*Tuzla*]   (YU)

SK .... Soldatenkommitte [*Soldiers' Committee*] [*Switzerland*]   (WEN)

SK .... Solenoid Valve   (RU)

SK .... South Korea

SK .... Sovetskyaya Kolonia [*Soviet Colony*]

SK .... Soviet Books   (RU)

SK .... Special Committee   (RU)

sk.............. Speed, Velocity   (RU)

SK .... Sport Kor [*Sport Club*]   (HU)

S K .... Sport Lap- es Konyvkiado [*Publishers of Sports Periodicals and Books*]   (HU)

SK .... Sportovni Klub [*Sports Club*]   (CZ)

SK .... Sports Club   (RU)

SK .... Staatlichen Kunstschule [*National College of Art*] [*German*]

SK .... Stabilizing Circuit   (RU)

SK .... Stadtsparkasse Koeln [*Bank*]

SK .... Stammauftragskarte [*German*]   (ADPT)

SK .... Statens Kulturrad [*Sweden*]   (EAIO)

SK .... Station Commandant   (RU)

SK .... Suomen Kaupunkilutto [*Association of Town Councils*] [*Finland*]

SK .... Suomen Kennelliitto [*Finland*]   (EAIO)

SK .... Suomen Kirjastoseura [*Finland*]   (EAIO)

SK .... Surat Kabar [*Newspaper*]   (IN)

SK .... Survey of Kenya

SK .... Sveriges Korforbund [*Sweden*]   (EAIO)

SK .... Synchronous Compensator   (RU)

SK .... Synthetic Rubber   (RU)

SKA .... "Academy" Sports Club   (RU)

s-ka .... Account   (BU)

SKA .... Army Sports Club   (RU)

SKA .... Patrol Cutter   (RU)

SKA .... Schweizerische Kreditanstalt [*Bank*] [*Switzerland*]

SKA .... Slovenska Kulturna Akcija [*Slovenian Cultural Action*] [*Buenos Aires*]   (YU)

SKA .... Somateion Ktiston Athinon [*Union of Athens Builders*]   (GC)

s-ka .... Spolka [*Partnership, Company*]   (POL)

SKA .... Srednjokalibarska Artiljerija [*Medium Caliber Artillery*]   (YU)

SKA .... Srpska Kraljevska Akademija [*Serbian Royal Academy*]   (YU)

SKA .... Studienkommission for Atomenergie [*Switzerland*]

SKA .... Symvoulion Koininikis Asfaliseos [*Social Insurance Council*] [*Greek*]   (GC)

SKA .... Syndesmos Koniaston Athinon [*Union of Athens Plasterers*]   (GC)

SKA .... Syndonistikon Klimakion Arogis [*Detachment for Coordination of Assistance*] [*Greek*]   (GC)

s-ka akc...... Spolka Akcyjna [*Joint Stock Company*] [*Polish*]   (POL)

SKAAL....... Solidaritaets-Komitee fuer Afrika Asien und Lateinamerika

skad........... Skadad [*Damaged*] [*Sweden*]

SKAF......... Schweizerische Katholische Arbeitsgemeinschaft fuer Auslaenderfragen [*Switzerland*]   (SLS)

SKAF......... Swedish Paperboard Research Group

SKAF......... Syndikalistiki Kinisis Aristeron Filelevtheron [*Labor Movement of Leftist Liberals*] [*Greek*]   (GC)

SKAI......... International Special Committee on Antarctic Research   (RU)

skalenoedr ... Scalenohedral   (RU)

SKAN .... Solidariteits Komitee Argentiniee [*Netherlands*]

SKAN .... Srpska Kraljevska Akademija Nauka [*Serbian Royal Academy of Sciences*]   (YU)

skand......... Scandinavian   (RU)

skand......... Skandinaavinen [*Finland*]

SKAND ..... Skandinawie [*Scandinavia*] [*Afrikaans*]

SKANDSF ... Skandinaviska Seglarforbundet [*Scandinavian Yachting Association - SYA*]   (EAIO)

SKAP........ Armedia/El Elden [*Colorado*] [*ICAO location identifier*]   (ICLI)

SKAPP ...... North Caucasian Union of Associations of Proletarian Writers   (RU)

SKAR........ Svenska Kommunalarbetare Foerbund [*Trade union*] [*Sweden*]

SKAS .... Puerto Asis [*Colorado*] [*ICAO location identifier*]   (ICLI)

SKAT .... Schweizerische Kontaktstelle fuer Angepasste Technik [*Swiss Center for Appropriate Technology*]

SKATV ...... St. Kilda Access Television [*Australia*]

skaz............ Predicate (RU)
SKAZ......... Samara Carburetor and Fittings Plant (RU)
SKB............ Independent Design Office (RU)
SKB............ Machine Tool Design Office (RU)
SKB............ Saint Kitts [Leeward Islands] [Airport symbol] (OAG)
skb............. Skindbind [Leather Binding] [Publishing Danish/Norwegian]
SKB............ Special Design Office (RU)
SKB............ Synthetic Butadiene Rubber (RU)
SKBADGL ... St. Karl Borromaus Association for the Dissemination of Good Literature (EAIO)
SKBANN... Special Design Office for the Automation of Petroleum Processing and Petrochemistry (RU)
SKBAP ...... Special Design Office of Analytical Instrument Making (RU)
SKBC......... El Banco/Los Flores [Colorado] [ICAO location identifier] (ICLI)
SKBF .... Schweizerische Koordinationsstelle fuer Bildungsforschung [Swiss Coordination Center for Research in Education] [Information service or system] (IID)
SKBG......... Bucaramanga/Palo Negro Sur [Colorado] [ICAO location identifier] (ICLI)
SKBIB........ Samengeschakelde Besluiten over de Inkomsten-Belastingen [Benelux] (BAS)
SKBiH .... Savez Komunista Bosne i Hercegovine [League of Communists of Bosnia and Hercegovina] (YU)
SKBKOM ... Special Design Office for the Planning of Leather and Footwear Machines (RU)
SKBM........ Serikat Kaum Buruh Minjak [Federation of Oil Unions] [Indonesian]
SKBM........ Synthetic Butadiene-Sodium Rubber with High Frost Resistance (RU)
SKBNM..... Special Design Office of Petroleum Machinery (RU)
SKBO......... Bogota/Eldorado [Colorado] [ICAO location identifier] (ICLI)
SKBProdmash ... Special Design Office of Food Machinery (RU)
SKBPSA.... Independent Design Office of Automation Instruments and Devices (RU)
SKBQ......... Barranquilla/Ernesto Cortissoz [Colorado] [ICAO location identifier] (ICLI)
SKBS .... Bahia Solano/Jose Celestino Mutis [Colorado] [ICAO location identifier] (ICLI)
SKBSiI....... Spoleczny Komitet Budowy Szkol i Internatow [Social Committee for the Building of Day and Boarding Schools] [Poland]
SKBSN ...... Special Design Office for the Standardization of Instrument Making (RU)
SKBTM ..... Special Design Office of Textile Machinery (RU)
SKBTO...... Special Design Office of Weaving Equipment (RU)
SKBU......... Buenaventura [Colorado] [ICAO location identifier] (ICLI)
SKC............ Schweizerisches Komitee fur Chemie [Swiss Committee on Chemistry] [Switzerland] (EAIO)
SKC............ Suki [Papua New Guinea] [Airport symbol] (OAG)
SKCC......... Cucuta/Camilo Daza [Colorado] [ICAO location identifier] (ICLI)
SKCD......... Condoto/Mandinga [Colorado] [ICAO location identifier] (ICLI)
SKCG......... Cartagena/Rafael Nunez [Colorado] [ICAO location identifier] (ICLI)
SKCG......... Savez Komunista Crne Gore [League of Communists of Montenegro] (YU)
SKChF....... Black Sea Fleet Sports Club (RU)
SKCL......... Cali/Alfonso Bonilla Aragon [Colorado] [ICAO location identifier] (ICLI)
SKCO .... Tumaco/La Florida [Colorado] [ICAO location identifier] (ICLI)
SKCZ......... Corozal/Las Brujas [Colorado] [ICAO location identifier] (ICLI)
SKD .... Reference Documentation Files (RU)
SKD .... Samarkand [Former USSR] [Airport symbol] (OAG)
SKD .... Self-Adjusting Two-Cantilever Crane (RU)
SKD .... Severoceske Konsumni Druzstvo [North Bohemian Consumer Cooperative] (CZ)
SKD .... Slovenske Komorne Divadlo [Slovak Chamber Theater] (CZ)
SKD .... Slovensko Kemijsko Drustvo [Slovenian Chemical Society] (YU)
SKD .... Societe Khmere des Distilleries [Cambodian Distilleries Company] (CL)
SKDA .... Sportkomitee der Befreundeten Armeen [Sports Committee of the Allied Armies] (EG)
SKDA .... Sports Committee of Friendly Armies (RU)
SKDL......... Suomen Kansan Demokraattinen Liitto [Finnish People's Democratic League] [Political party] (PPW)
sk dv .... Cattle Yard [Topography] (RU)
SKE............ Scandinavian Cooperative Exports (RU)
SKE............ Skien [Norway] [Airport symbol] (OAG)
SKE............ Sosialistikon Komma Ellados [Socialist Party of Greece] (GC)
SKE............ Steinkohleneinheit [Hard Coal Unit] (EG)
SKE............ Svetska Konferencija za Energiju [World Power Conference] (YU)
SKE .... World Energy Conference (BU)

SKEA......... Staatliches Komitee fuer Erfassung und Aufkauf [State Committee for Procurement and Purchase] (EG)
SKEC......... Barranquilla [Colorado] [ICAO location identifier] (ICLI)
SKED........ Bogota [Colorado] [ICAO location identifier] (ICLI)
SKEETK.... Syndesmos Kataskevaston Eliacon & Electricon Thermoloutiron Kyprou [Cyprus] (EAIO)
SKEF .... Societe Khmere d'Exploitation Forestiere [Cambodian Forest Exploitation Company] (CL)
skeik........... Skeikunde [Chemistry] [Afrikaans]
SKEJ......... Barrancabermeja/Yariguis [Colorado] [ICAO location identifier] (ICLI)
SK-ELD..... Sosialistikon Komma - Enosis Laikis Dimokratias [Socialist Party - Union of Popular Democracy] [Greek] (GC)
SKEPA ...... Syndonistiki Kinisis tou Ethnikou Pandimokratikou [Coordinating Movement for the National Democratic Struggle] [Greek] (GC)
SKF............ AB Svenska Kullagerfabrik [Swedish Ballbearing Works] (WEN)
SKF............ Navy Sports Club (RU)
SKF............ Sosialistiko Kinima Foititon [Student Socialist Movement] [Greek] (GC)
SKF............ Staatliches Komitee fuer Forstwirtschaft [State Forestry Committee] (EG)
SKF............ Svenska Kullager Frabikon [Swedish Ball Bearing Manufacturing]
SKF............ Svenska Kullargerfabriken [Sweden] (PDAA)
SKF............ Svensk Kirurgisk Foerening [Sweden] (SLS)
SKFCM ..... Statni Komise pro Finance, Ceny, a Mzdy [State Commission for Finance, Prices, and Wages] (CZ)
SKFL .... Florencia/Capitolio [Colorado] [ICAO location identifier] (ICLI)
SKFP .... Soviet Motion-Picture and Photo Industry (RU)
SKG .... Caterpillar Jib Crane (RU)
SKG .... Sekretarijat za Kmetijstvo in Gozdarstvo (ISLRS) [Secretariat of Agriculture and Forestry] (YU)
SKG .... Srpski Knjizevni Glasnik [Serbian Literary Bulletin] [A periodical] (YU)
SKG .... Thessaloniki [Greece] [Airport symbol] (OAG)
SKGI......... Girardot/Santiago Vila [Colorado] [ICAO location identifier] (ICLI)
SKGJ .... Stalna Konferencija Gradova Jugoslavije [Permanent Conference of Yugoslav Towns] (YU)
SKGP........ Guapi [Colorado] [ICAO location identifier] (ICLI)
SkGSM...... Fuels and Lubricants Depot (RU)
SKGU .... North Caucasian Geological Administration (RU)
SKGU .... North Caucasian State University (RU)
s/kh........... Agricultural (RU)
SKh .... Agricultural Aircraft (RU)
skh .... Agriculture (RU)
SKh .... Artists' Union (RU)
skh .... Diagram, Circuit (RU)
SKh .... Painters' Union (BU)
SKH .... Savez Komunista Hrvatske [League of Communists of Croatia] (YU)
skh .... Scheme, Plan, Project (BU)
SKH .... Seine Koenigliche Hoheit [His Royal Highness] [German]
SKh .... Socialist Economy (RU)
SKh .... Stathmos Khorofylakis [Gendarmerie Station] (GC)
SKh .... Steady-State Characteristic (RU)
SKH .... Surkhet [Nepal] [Airport symbol] (OAG)
SKH .... Sy Koninklike Hoogheid [His Royal Highness] [Afrikaans]
SKhA .... Agricultural Academy (RU)
SkhB .... Block Diagram (RU)
SKhB .... Union of Bulgarian Painters (BU)
SKhE......... Agricultural Encyclopedia (RU)
SkhE .... Elementary Diagram (RU)
SKhEM...... Syndikaton Khersaion Emborevmatikon Metaforon [Land Commercial Transports Trade Union] [Greek] (GC)
SkhF .... Functional Circuit (RU)
SKhG .... State Publishing House of Agricultural Literature, Journals, and Posters (RU)
SKhI.......... Agricultural Institute (RU)
s-kh inv ...... Agricultural Implements (RU)
SKhIU........ Sofia School of Industrial Art (BU)
SKhKB....... Special Artistic Design Office (RU)
SKhL......... Cast Chromium Steel (RU)
SKhL......... Medical Chemistry Laboratory (BU)
SKhL......... Medico-Chemical Laboratory (RU)
SKHL........ Siipikarjanhoitajain Liitto Ry [Poultry Breeders Association] [Finland] (ARC)
SKhLR....... Agricultural Workers' and Lumbermen's Trade Union (RU)
SKhM .... Syllogos Khimikon Mikhanikon [Association of Chemical Engineers] [Greek] (GC)
SKhM......... Wiring Diagram (RU)
s-kh mekh .. Agricultural Mechanics (RU)
s-kh mel ..... Agricultural Reclamation (RU)

s-kh met ..... Agricultural Meteorology (RU)
s-kh min ..... Agricultural Mineralogy (RU)
SKhOS ...... Agricultural Experimental Station (RU)
SKhPK ...... Agricultural Producers' Cooperative (RU)
SKhPPG .... Specialized Surgical Mobile Field Hospital (RU)
SKhR .... Chemical Scout Kit (RU)
SKhR .... Special Chemical Reconnaissance (RU)
SKhRU ...... Sofia School of Fine Arts (BU)
SKhS .... Agricultural Station (RU)
SKHS .... Sri Kapila Humanitarian Society (EAIO)
SKHS .... Suomen Kirkkohistoriallinen Seura [*Finland*] (SLS)
SKhSp .... Coincidence Circuit (RU)
SKhU .... Agricultural Apprenticeship School (RU)
s kh-vo .... Agriculture (RU)
SKhZ .... Medico-Chemical Defense (RU)
SKI .... Channel Test Bay (RU)
SKI .... Schweizerisches Krankenhausinstitut [*Switzerland*] (SLS)
SKI .... Selective System Equipment Endframe (RU)
Ski .... Seriki [*Partner*] [*Turkey*] (CED)
SKI .... Soma Ktiniatrikou kai Ipponeion [*Veterinary and Remount Corps*] (GC)
SKI .... Spolek Komercnich Inzenyru [*Society of Graduates of Schools of Business Administration*] (CZ)
SKI .... Staten Kaernkraftinspektion [*Swedish Nuclear Power Inspectorate*] (WND)
SKI .... Syndikalistiki Kinisi Iatrikis [*Medical Trade Union Movement*] [*Greek*] (GC)
SKI .... Synthesis of Isoprene Rubber (RU)
SKIA .... Staatliches Kontrollinstitut fur Immunbiologische Arzneimittel [*Institute for the State Control of Immunobiological Pharmacology*] [*Germany*] (IRC)
SKIB .... Ibague/Perales [*Colombia*] [*ICAO location identifier*] (ICLI)
SKIF .... Svenska Konsultfoereningen [*Sweden*] (SLS)
SKIKhA ..... Syllogos Katokhon Idiotikis Khriseos Avtokiniton [*Society of Private Automobile Owners*] [*Greek*] (GC)
skindtit .... Skindtitel [*Leather Title Piece*] [*Publishing Danish/Norwegian*]
skinnbd ...... Skinnband [*Leather Binding*] [*Publishing*] [*Sweden*]
skinnryggbd ... Skinnryggband [*Bound with Leather Back*] [*Publishing*] [*Sweden*]
SKIP .... Ipiales/San Luis [*Colombia*] [*ICAO location identifier*] (ICLI)
SKIP .... Skills for Progress [*India*] (EAIO)
SKIP .... Strojno-Kovinsko Industrijsko Podjetje [*Machinery and Metallurgical Works*] [*Ljubljana*] (YU)
Skip .... Turpentine Plant [*Topography*] (RU)
SKIS .... St. Kilda Income Stretchers [*Australia*]
SKJ .... Savez Kompozitora Jugoslavije [*Union of Composers of Yugoslavia*] (YU)
SKJ .... Savez Komunista Jugoslavije [*League of Communists of Yugoslavia*] (YU)
SKJ .... Skyjet, Inc. [*Antigua and Barbuda*] [*ICAO designator*] (FAAC)
SKJ .... Sojuzot na Komunistite na Jugoslavija [*League of Communists of Yugoslavia*] (YU)
SKJ .... Statystyczna Kontrola Jakosci [*Statistical Quality Control*] [*Poland*]
SKJP .... Vereinigung Schweizerischer Kinder- und Jugendpsychologen [*Switzerland*] (SLS)
SKK .... Allied Control Commission (BU)
SKK .... Showa Kenkyu Kai [*Showa Research Association*] [*Japan*]
SKK .... Sowjetische Kontrollkommission [*Soviet Control Commission*] (EG)
SKK .... Spoleczna Komisja Kontroli [*People's Control Commission*] (POL)
SKK .... Staatliche Kontrollkommission [*State Control Commission*] (EG)
SKK .... Staatliches Kohle-Kontor [*State Coal Office*] (EG)
SKK .... Stichting Kernvoortstuwing Koopvaardijschepen [*Foundation for Nuclear Propulsion of Merchant Ships*] [*Netherlands*] (PDAA)
SKK .... Swiatowy Kongres Kobiet [*World Congress of Women*] (POL)
SKK .... Szkola Kadr Kierowniczych [*School for (Party) Leaders in ————*] (POL)
SKKF .... Stoleczny Komitet Kultury Fizycznej [*Warsaw Committee on Physical Culture*] (POL)
SKKF .... Syndesmos Kypro-Koreatikis Filias [*League of Cypriot-Korean Friendship*] (GC)
SKKZ .... Spoleczna Komisja Kontroli Zaopatrzenia [*People's Control Commission on Supplies*] (POL)
skl .... Declension (RU)
SKL .... Schwermaschinenbau "Karl Liebknecht," Magdeburg (VEB) [*"Karl Liebknecht" Heavy Machine Construction Plant, Magdeburg (VEB)*] (EG)
SKL .... Seismic Logging Laboratory (RU)
skl .... Storehouse, Depot [*Topography*] (RU)
SKL .... Suomen Kristillinen Liitto [*Finnish Christian League*] [*Political party*] (PPE)
SKL .... Union of Finnish Writers (EAIO)
SKLC .... Los Cedros/Uraba [*Colombia*] [*ICAO location identifier*] (ICLI)

Skl gor .... Fuel Depot [*Topography*] (RU)
SKLM .... La Mina/Riohacha [*Colombia*] [*ICAO location identifier*] (ICLI)
SKLOEXPORT ... Podnik Zahraniciniho Obchodu pro Vyvoz Skla [*Foreign Trade Enterprise for the Export of Glass*] (CZ)
sklon .... Declension (RU)
SKLP .... St. Kitts Labor Party (LA)
SKLT .... Leticia/Alfredo Vasquez Cobo [*Colombia*] [*ICAO location identifier*] (ICLI)
SKM .... Savez Komunista Makedonije [*League of Communists of Macedonia*] (YU)
SKM .... Signalbuch der Kaiserlichen Marine [*Imperial Marine Code Book*] [*German military - World War I*]
SKM .... Sojuz na Komunistite na Makedonija [*League of Communists of Macedonia*] (YU)
SKM .... Statny Kulturny Majetok [*State Cultural Properties*] (CZ)
SKM .... Szybkobiezna Kolej Miejska [*Municipal Express Railroad*] (POL)
SKM .... Young Communist League (RU)
SKMA .... Societe Khmere de Montage Automobile [*Cambodian Automobile Assembly Company*] (CL)
SKMG .... Magangue/Baracoa [*Colombia*] [*ICAO location identifier*] (ICLI)
SKMGG ...... Special Committee for the International Geophysical Year (RU)
SKMJ .... Sojuz na Komunistickata Mladina na Jugoslavija [*Union of Communist Youth of Yugoslavia*] (YU)
SKMQ .... Mariquita/Mariquita [*Colombia*] [*ICAO location identifier*] (ICLI)
SKMR .... Monteria/Los Garzones [*Colombia*] [*ICAO location identifier*] (ICLI)
SKMR .... Szkolenie Kadr Mechanizacji Rolnictwa [*Training of Personnel for the Mechanization of Agriculture*] (POL)
SKMS .... Svaz Komunistickych Mladorobotnikov Slovenska [*Union of Young Communist Workers of Slovakia*] (CZ)
SKMU .... Mitu/Mitu [*Colombia*] [*ICAO location identifier*] (ICLI)
SKMZ .... Manizales/La Nubia [*Colombia*] [*ICAO location identifier*] (ICLI)
SKMZ .... Old Kramatorsk Machinery Plant Imeni S. Ordzhonikidze (RU)
SKN .... Sanockie Kopalnictwo Naftowe [*Sanok Oil Wells*] (POL)
SKN .... Sekuaderan [*Squadron*] (ML)
SKN .... Stokmarknes [*Norway*] [*Airport symbol*] (OAG)
SKN .... Studencka Konferencja Naukowa [*Students' Scientific Conference*] (POL)
SKN .... Symvoulion Kriseos Nomarkhon [*Council for Judging Nomarchs*] [*Greek*] (GC)
SKN .... Syndekhnia Kyvernitikon Nosokomon [*Union of Government Nurses*] [*Cyprus*] (GC)
SKN .... Synthetic Butadienenitrile Rubber (RU)
SKNDO ..... Stichting Kwalificatie van Niet-Destructief Onderzoekers [*Foundation for Qualification of Non-Destructive Testing Personnel*] [*Netherlands*] (PDAA)
SKNE .... Savezna Komisija za Nuklearnu Energiju [*Federal Commission for Nuclear Energy*] (YU)
Skne .... Skjerane [*or Skjaerane*] [*Rocks above Water*] [*Norway*] (NAU)
SKNII .... Sakhalin Complex Scientific Research Institute (of the Academy of Sciences, USSR) (RU)
SKNIVI ..... North Caucasian Scientific Research Veterinary Institute (RU)
SKNO .... Sreski Komitet Narodne Omladine [*District Committee of the People's Youth*] (YU)
SKNV .... Neiva/La Manguila [*Colombia*] [*ICAO location identifier*] (ICLI)
SKNY .... Suomen Kliinisen Neurofysiologian Yhdistys [*Finland*] (EAIO)
SKO .... Association of Sanatoriums and Health Resorts (RU)
SKO .... Compander-Equipment Bay (RU)
SKO .... Construction and Billeting Section (RU)
SKO .... Saobracajno-Komercijalno Odeljenje [*Transportation Commercial Department*] [*Railroads*] (YU)
SKO .... Serial Production Design Department (RU)
SKO .... Sieges-Kilometres Offerts
SKO .... Sokoto [*Nigeria*] [*Airport symbol*] (OAG)
SKO .... Surveillance Radar (RU)
SKO .... Szkolna Kasa Oszczednosci [*School Savings Bank*] [*Poland*]
SKO .... Szkolne Kola Oszczednosciowe [*School Savings Circles*] (POL)
SKO .... Szkolny Komitet Opiekunczy [*School Assistance Committee*] (POL)
SKOC .... Ocana/Aguas Claras [*Colombia*] [*ICAO location identifier*] (ICLI)
SKODAM ... Staf Komando Daerah Militer [*Staff of Military Region Command*] (IN)
SkOE .... Skopevtiki Omospondia Ellados [*Marksmen's Federation of Greece*] (GC)
SKOGA ..... Soviet-Chinese Civil Aviation Society (RU)
SKOI .... Suomen Konsulttitoimistojen Liitto [*Finnish Association of Consulting Firms*] (EY)
SKOJ .... Savez Komunisticke Omladine Jugoslavije [*Union of Communist Youth of Yugoslavia*] (YU)
SKOJ .... Soupravy pro Kontrolu Ozareni Jednotlivce [*Detectors of Radiation in Personnel*] (CZ)

SKOK	Commission for Admittance to Sanatoriums and Health Resorts (RU)
SKOL	Suomen Konsulttitoimistojen Liitto [*Finnish Association of Consulting Firms*] (EY)
SKOM	Stratiotiki Kommounistiki Organosis Makronisou [*Makronisos Communist Army Organization*] [*Greek*] (GC)
SKOO	Scandinavian Cooperative Wholesale Society (RU)
SKOP	Slasko-Krakowski Okreg Przemyslowy [*Industrial Region of Cracow and Silesia*] [*Poland*]
SKOP	Swiatowy Komitet Obroncow Pokoju [*World Committee of Partisans of Peace*] (POL)
SKOP	Symvoulion Koinonikis kai Oikonomikis Politikis [*Social and Economic Policy Council*] (GC)
skor	Express [*Railroads*] (RU)
skot	Cattle-Breeding [*Topography*] (RU)
SKOT	Otu/Otu [*Colorado*] [*ICAO location identifier*] (ICLI)
SKOT	Stredni Kolovy Obrneny Transporter [*Medium APC (Armored Personnel Carrier)*] (CZ)
skotl	Skotlantilainen [*Scotch*] [*Finland*]
Skotob	Slaughterhouse [*Topography*] (RU)
Skotoimport	Office for the Import of Cattle (RU)
skot ov	Cattle Barn, Stable [*Topography*] (RU)
SKOW	Szkolny Komitet Odbudowy Warszawy [*School Committee on the Reconstruction of Warsaw*] (POL)
SKP	Accounting and Clerical Personnel (RU)
SKP	Disease Control Station (RU)
SKP	Flank Control Post (BU)
SKP	Flight Command Post (RU)
SKP	Launcher [*Rocket-Firing*] Command Post (BU)
SKP	Medical Control Point (BU)
SKP	Savet za Komunalne Poslove [*Communal Affairs Council*] (YU)
SKP	Savezna Komisija za Plate [*Federal Wage Commission*] (YU)
SKP	Sine-Cosine Potentiometer (RU)
SKP	Skopje [*Former Yugoslavia*] [*Airport symbol*] (OAG)
SKP	Societe Khmere de Pneumatiques [*Cambodian Tire Company*] (CL)
SKP	Soma Kyprion Proskopon [*Boy Scouts of Cyprus*] (GC)
SKP	Spanyol Kommunista Part [*Spanish Communist Party*] (HU)
SKP	Startkontrollpunkt [*Take-Off Control Center*] (EG)
SKP	Statni Katalog Prace [*State Labor Catalog*] (CZ)
SKP	Stowarzyszenie Ksiegarzy Polskich [*Association of Polish Booksellers*] [*Poland*]
SKP	Stowarzyszenie Ksiegowych Polskich [*Association of Polish Accountants*] (POL)
SKP	Suomen Kommunistinen Puolue [*Communist Party of Finland*] [*Political party*] (PPW)
SKP	Sveriges Kommunistiska Partiet [*Communist Party of Sweden*] [*Political party*] (PPE)
SKP	Svesavezna Komunisticka Partija [*All-Union Communist Party*] (YU)
SKPB	Puerto Bolivar/Riohacha [*Colorado*] [*ICAO location identifier*] (ICLI)
SKP(b)	Sovjetska Komunisticka Partija (Boljsevika) [*Soviet Communist Party (Bolsheviks)*] (YU)
SKP(b)	Svesavezna Komunisticka Partija (Boljsevika) [*All-Union Communist Party (Bolsheviks)*] (YU)
SKPC	Puerto Carreno [*Colorado*] [*ICAO location identifier*] (ICLI)
SKPD	Savez Kulturno-Prosvetnih Drustava [*Federation of Cultural and Educational Societies*] (YU)
SKPDS	Savez Kulturno-Prosvetnih Drustava Srbije [*Federation of Cultural and Educational Societies of Serbia*] (YU)
SKPE	Pereira/Matecana [*Colorado*] [*ICAO location identifier*] (ICLI)
SKPF	Savezna Komisija za Pregled Filmova [*Federal Commission for Film Censorship*] (YU)
SKPF	Svenska Kyrkans Personalforbund [*Sweden*] (EAIO)
SKPH	Societe Khmere de Plantations d'Heveas [*Cambodian Rubber Plantation Company*] (CL)
SKPI	Pitalito [*Colorado*] [*ICAO location identifier*] (ICLI)
SK-PJ	Savez Komunista - Pokret za Jugoslaviju [*League of Communists - Movement for Yugoslavia*] [*Political party*]
SKPP	Popayan/Guillermo Leon Valencia [*Colorado*] [*ICAO location identifier*] (ICLI)
SKPP	Savezna Komisija za Plate u Privredi [*Federal Commission on Industrial Wages*] (YU)
SKPPE	Union for Coordinating Production and Distribution of Electricity (RU)
SKPS	Pasto/Antonio Narino [*Colorado*] [*ICAO location identifier*] (ICLI)
skpt	Stabni Kapitan [*Senior Captain*] [*Military rank*] (CZ)
SKPU	Savet za Komunalne Poslove i Urbanizam (SIV) [*Council on Communal Affairs and City Planning*] (YU)
SKPV	Providencia/Providencia [*Colorado*] [*ICAO location identifier*] (ICLI)
SKPZSSR	Szkolne Kolo Przyjaciol ZSSR [*School Circle of Friends of the USSR*] (POL)
SKQ	Sekakes [*Lesotho*] [*Airport symbol*] (OAG)
skr	Abbreviated, Abbreviation (BU)
SKR	Corona Stabilitron Tube (RU)
SKR	Cruise Missiles (BU)
SKR	Escort Ship (RU)
SKR	Raman Spectrum (RU)
Skr	Sekretariat [*Secretariate*] [*German*]
Skr	Skaer [*or Skjaer*] [*Rock above Water*] [*Denmark*] (NAU)
skr	Skinnrygg [*Half-Leather*] [*Publishing Danish/Norwegian*]
Skr	Skjaer [*or Skjer or Skjeret*] [*Rock above Water*] [*Norway*] (NAU)
skr	Skrywer [*Author*] [*Afrikaans*]
SKR	Slovenska Kniznicna Rada [*Slovak Library Council*] (CZ)
SKR	Societe Khmere de Raffinage de Petrole [*Cambodian Petroleum Refining Company*] [*Use SKRP*] (CL)
SKR	Staatliches Komitee fuer Nichtmetallische Rohstoffreserven [*State Committee for Non-Metallic Raw Material Reserves*] (EG)
skr	Sved Korona [*Swedish Krona*] (HU)
S KR	Swedish Krona [*Monetary unit*]
skrab	Skrabet [*Scraped*] [*Danish/Norwegian*]
SKRB	Stoleczny Klub Racjonalizatorow Budownictwa [*Warsaw Club of Construction Rationalizers*] (POL)
skrbd	Skinnryggband [*Bound with Leather Back*] [*Publishing*] [*Sweden*]
SKRG	Rio Negro/Jose Maria Cordova [*Colorado*] [*ICAO location identifier*] (ICLI)
SKRH	Rio Hacha, Guajira [*Colorado*] [*ICAO location identifier*] (ICLI)
SKRK	Spoleczny Komitet Radiofonizacji Kraju [*People's Committee on Country-Wide Radio Installation*] (POL)
SKRO	Statni Komise pro Rizeni a Organizaci [*State Commission for Management and Organization*] (CZ)
SKRP	Societe Khmere de Raffinage de Petrole [*Cambodian Petroleum Refining Company*] (CL)
Skrt	Sanskrit [*Language*] (BARN)
SKRU	Combined Motion-Picture and Radio Installation (RU)
SKS	Savez Komunista Slovenije [*League of Communists of Slovenia*] (YU)
SKS	Savez Komunista Srbije [*League of Communists of Serbia*] (YU)
SKS	Savezna Komisija za Standardizaciju [*Federal Commission on Standardization*] (YU)
SKS	Schweizerische Konferenz fuer Sicherheit im Strassenverkehr [*Switzerland*] (SLS)
SKS	Self-Propelled Compressor Station (RU)
SKS	Self-Propelled Logging Station (RU)
SKS	Services Kataeb de Securite
SKS	Simonov Self-Loading Carbine (RU)
SKS	Skrydstrup [*Denmark*] [*Airport symbol*] (OAG)
SKS	Sky Service [*Belgium*] [*ICAO designator*] (FAAC)
SKS	Slovenska Katoliska Skupnost [*Slovenian Catholic Unity*] [*USA*] (YU)
SKS	Soren Kierkegaard Society [*Copenhagen, Denmark*] (EA)
SKS	Soviet Committee of Slavicists (RU)
SKS	Sovieto-Kypriakos Syndesmos [*Soviet-Cypriot Association*] (GC)
SKS	Spoldzielczy Klub Sportowy [*Cooperative Sport Club*] (POL)
SKS	Staendige Kommission des RGW fuer Standardisierung [*CEMA Permanent Commission for Standardization*] (EG)
SKS	Suomalaisen Kirjallisuuden Seura [*Finnish Literary Society*] (WEN)
SKS	Suomalaisten Kemistien Seura [*Finland*] (SLS)
SKS	Suomen Kardiologinen Seura [*Finland*] (EAIO)
SKS	Suomi-Kiina Seura [*Finland-China Society*] (WEN)
SKS	Sveriges Kyrkliga Studieforbund [*Sweden*] (EAIO)
SKS	Svetoveho Kongresu Slovakov [*Canada*] (EAIO)
SKS	Synthetic Butadiene Styrene Rubber (RU)
SKS	Szkolne Kolo Sportowe [*School Sports and Athletics Circle*] [*Poland*]
SKS	Szkolny Klub Sportowy [*School Sports and Athletics Club*] [*Poland*]
SKSA	Saravena/Saravena El Eden [*Colorado*] [*ICAO location identifier*] (ICLI)
SKSE	(Pankypria) Syndeknhia Kyvernitikon kai Stratiotikon Ergaton [(*Pan-Cyprian*) *Union of Government and Military Workers*] [*Cyprus*] (GC)
SKSG	Santagueda/Santagueda [*Colorado*] [*ICAO location identifier*] (ICLI)
SKSJ	San Jose Del Guaviare/S. J. Del Guaviore [*Colorado*] [*ICAO location identifier*] (ICLI)
SKSM	Santa Marta/Simon Bolivar [*Colorado*] [*ICAO location identifier*] (ICLI)
SKSO	Union of Communes of the Northern Oblast [*1936-1937*] (RU)
SKSP	San Andres/Sesquicentenario, San Andres [*Colorado*] [*ICAO location identifier*] (ICLI)
SKSP	Skupina Svepomoci [*Self-Help Group*] (CZ)
SKSRRCM	Smeshannaya Komissiya po Primeneniyu Soglasheniya o Regulirovanii Rybolovstva na Chernom More [*Joint Commission for Regulation of Fishing in the Black Sea*] (ASF)

SKSRRD ... Smeshannaya Komissiya po Primeneniyu Soglasheniya o Regulirovanii Rybolovstva v Vodakh Dunaya [*Joint Commission for Regulation of Fishing on the Danube*] (ASF)
SKSV .... San Vicente Del Caguan [*Colorado*] [*ICAO location identifier*] (ICLI)
SKSV .... Statni Knihovna Spolecenskych Ved [*State Social Science Library*] [*Prague*] (CZ)
Skt............. Sankt [*Saint*] [*German*] (GPO)
SKT............ Sanskrit [*Afrikaans*]
Skt............. Skalenteil [*Scale Graduation*] [*German*] (GCA)
SKT............ Spoldzielnia Komunikacyjno-Transportowa [*Transportation Cooperative*] (POL)
SKT............ Statni Komise pro Techniku [*State Commission for Technology*] (CZ)
SKT............ Synergatiki Kendriki Trapeza [*Cooperative Central Bank*] [*Cyprus*] (GC)
SKTB .... Special Design and Technological Office (RU)
SKTBSP .... Independent Design and Technological Office for the Planning of Glass Devices and Apparatus (RU)
SKTC .... Sydney Kindergarten Teachers College [*Australia*] (ADA)
SKTD........ Trinidad [*Colorado*] [*ICAO location identifier*] (ICLI)
SKTF .... Sveriges Kommunaltjanstemannaforbund [*Sweden*] (EAIO)
SKTF .... Sveriges Kvalitetstekniska Forening [*Swedish Organisation for Quality Control*] (PDAA)
SKTM....... Tame [*Colorado*] [*ICAO location identifier*] (ICLI)
SKTP .... Preassembled Transformer Substation Set (RU)
SKTU........ Turbo, Gonzalo Mejia [*Colorado*] [*ICAO location identifier*] (ICLI)
SKU .... Coding Device (RU)
SKU .... Housing Construction Administration (RU)
SKU .... Medical Health Resort Administration (BU)
SKU .... Standardized Jib Crane (RU)
SKUC........ Arauca/Santiago Perez [*Colorado*] [*ICAO location identifier*] (ICLI)
SKUD .... Sindikalno Kulturno-Umetnisko Drustvo [*Trade-Union Cultural and Artistic Society*] (YU)
SKUGMS ... North Caucasian Administration of the Hydrometeorological Service (RU)
SKUI......... Quibdo/El Carano [*Colorado*] [*ICAO location identifier*] (ICLI)
SKUPDBiH ... Savez Kulturno-Umjetnickih i Prosvjetnih Drustava Bosni i Hercegovine [*Federation of Cultural, Artistic, and Educational Societies of Bosnia and Hercegovina*] (YU)
skv .... Drill Hole, Oil Well (RU)
SKV........... Salzburger Kulturvereinigung [*Austria*] (SLS)
SKV........... Santa Katarina [*Egypt*] [*Airport symbol*] (OAG)
SKV........... Savezna Komisija za Vodoprivredu [*Federal Commission for Water Power*] (YU)
SKV........... Schweizerischer Kanu-Verband [*Switzerland*] (EAIO)
SKV........... Union of Shortwave Amateur Radio Operators (RU)
SKVH .... Svatni Komise pro Vedecke Hodnosti [*State Commission for Scientific Awards*] (CZ)
SKVO .... Military District Sports Club (RU)
SKVO .... North Caucasian Military District (RU)
SKVP .... Short Takeoff and Landing Aircraft (RU)
SKVP .... Valledupar/Alfonso Lopez [*Colorado*] [*ICAO location identifier*] (ICLI)
SKVT........ Sine-Cosine Rotating Transformer (RU)
SKVT........ Statni Komise pro Rozvoj a Koordinaci Vedy a Techniky [*State Commission for Development and Coordination of Science and Technology*] (CZ)
SKVUZ...... Council of Commissars of Higher Educational Institutions (RU)
SKVV........ Soviet Committee of War Veterans (RU)
SKVV........ Villavicencio/Vanguardia [*Colorado*] [*ICAO location identifier*] (ICLI)
SKVVI ...... Stathmos Koinonikon Voitheion Vasilikou Idrymatos [*Social Assistance Station of the Royal Foundation*] [*Greek*] (GC)
SKW .... Schlauchkraftwagen [*Hose-Equipped Truck (Fire Department equipment)*] (EG)
SKW .... Syndicate of North Germany Electric Utilities [*Germany*] [*Acronym is based on foreign phrase*]
SKW .... Szkolne Komisje Wspolzawodnictwa [*School Competition Commissions*] (POL)
SKX .... Skyways AB [*Sweden*] [*ICAO designator*] (FAAC)
SKY........... Cooper Skybird Air Charters Ltd. [*Kenya*] [*ICAO designator*] (FAAC)
SKYaD...... Holding Release of Toxic Smoke (RU)
SKYP .... Skholi Klostikis Yfandikis kai Plektikis [*Spinning, Weaving, and Knitting School*] [*Greek*] (GC)
SKYP .... Suomen Kansan Yhtenaeisyyden Puolue [*People's Unity Party*] [*Finland*] [*Political party*] (PPW)
SKYP .... Yopal/Yopal [*Colorado*] [*ICAO location identifier*] (ICLI)
SKYu......... Union of Communists of Yugoslavia (RU)
SKZ........... Slovenski Knjizni Zavod [*Slovenian Book Institute*] [*Ljubljana*] (YU)
SKZ........... Srpska Knjizevna Zadruga [*Serbian Literary Society*] [*Society and publishing house*] (YU)

SKZ........... Sueddeutsches Kunststoff-Zentrum (SLS)
SKZ........... Sukkur [*Pakistan*] [*Airport symbol*] (OAG)
SKZ........... Sveucilisna Knjiznica, Zagreb [*University Library, Zagreb*] (YU)
SKZ........... Syzran' Combine Plant (RU)
SKZA........ Medium-Caliber Antiaircraft Artillery (BU)
SKZM....... Soviet Committee for the Protection of Peace (RU)
SKZP .... Staatliches Kontor fuer Zellstoff und Papier [*State Office for Pulp and Paper*] (EG)
sl............... Centiliter (RU)
SL.............. Collapsible Boat (RU)
SL.............. Decoy Ship, Q-Ship (RU)
sl............... Follow, Following (BU)
sl............... Following, Next (RU)
Sl............... Large Village, Settlement [*Toponymy*] (RU)
sl............... Sans Lieu [*Without Place (of publication)*] [*French*]
SL.............. Satzlaenge [*German*] (ADPT)
sl............... Sauf Livraison [*Safe Delivery*] [*French*]
SL.............. Schutte Lanz [*World War I German aircraft designation*]
sl............... Schwer Loeslich [*Only Slightly Soluble*] [*German*]
SL.............. Sea-Land Service Ltd. [*Taiwan*]
sl............... Sem Lugar [*Without Place (of publication)*] [*Portuguese*]
SL.............. Sendero Luminoso [*Shining Path*] [*Peru*] (PD)
sl............... Senza Luogo [*Without Place (of publication)*] [*Italian*]
sl............... Service [*Telephony*] (RU)
s/l............. Seu Lancamento [*Your Bidding*] [*Portuguese*]
SL.............. Sierra Leone [*ANSI two-letter standard code*] (CNC)
SL.............. Signal Lamp (RU)
SL.............. Silvaire [*ICAO aircraft manufacturer identifier*] (ICAO)
sl............... Sin Lugar [*Without Place (of publication)*] [*Spanish*]
SL.............. Skibsteknisk Laboratorium [*Danish Maritime Institute*] [*Akademiet for de Tekniske Videnskaber - ATV*] [*Research center*] (ERC)
sl............... Slang (TPFD)
sl............... Slangia [*Slang*] [*Finland*]
Sl............... Slecna [*Miss*] (CZ)
SL.............. Slesvigske Parti [*Schleswig Party*] [*Denmark*] [*Political party*] (PPE)
Sl............... Slovensko [*Slovakia*] (CZ)
sl............... Slovensky [*Slovak*] (CZ)
SL.............. Sluzbeni List [*Official Gazette*] (YU)
s/l............. Sobreloja [*Portuguese*]
SL.............. Sociedad de Responsabilidad Limitada [*Private Limited Company*] [*Spanish*]
SL.............. Societas Liturgica (EA)
SL.............. Sport Leicht [*Sports Lightweight (Car)*] [*German*]
SL.............. Starsi Lekar [*Senior Physician*] [*Army*] (CZ)
SL.............. Statni Studijni Knihovna [*State Research Library in Liberec*] (CZ)
SL.............. Statni Vedecka Knihovna, Liberec [*State Research Library in Liberec*] (CZ)
SL.............. Steeloscope (RU)
SL.............. Stihaci Letectvo [*Fighter Airforce (or Aircraft)*] (CZ)
SL.............. Stor-Stockholms Lokalttrafiken [*Sweden*] (PDAA)
SL.............. Streifenleser [*German*] (ADPT)
SL.............. Stronnictwo Ludowe [*Peasant Party*] [*Poland*] [*Political party*] (PPE)
s/l............. Sua Letra [*Your Letter*] [*Portuguese*]
SL.............. Suomen Laeaekintaevoimistelijaliitto [*Finland*] (SLS)
SL.............. Supplementary List [*Royal Australian Navy*]
SL.............. Svaz Lyzaru [*Skiing Association*] (CZ)
SL.............. Sveriges Laerarforbund [*Sweden*] (SLS)
SL.............. Sveriges Lantbruksforbund [*Federation of Swedish Farmers' Associations*] (WEN)
SL.............. Swaziland Lilangeni
SL.............. Syrian Lira
sl............... Syyslukukausi [*Finland*]
SL.............. Trunk [*Telephony*] (RU)
sl............... Weakly, Slightly, Lightly (RU)
sl............... Word (RU)
SLA............ Sabi-Limpopo Authority
SLA............ Salta [*Argentina*] [*Airport symbol*] (OAG)
SLA............ Scandinavian Lead Association [*Sweden*] (EAIO)
SLA............ Sekolah Landjutan Atas [*Senior Secondary School*] (IN)
SLA............ Sierra Leone Airlines
SLA............ Sierra National Airlines [*Sierra Leone*] [*ICAO designator*] (FAAC)
SLA............ South Lebanon Army
SLA............ Sudanese Liquid Air Co.
SLA............ Svenska Lantarbetsgivareforeningen [*Swedish Agricultural Employers' Association*] (WEN)
SLA............ Swiss Labour Assistance (EAIO)
SLA............ Swiss Lifesaving Association (EAIO)
SLAAA ...... St. Lucia Amateur Athletic Association (EAIO)
SLAALIS .. Sierra Leone Association of Archivists, Librarians, and Information Scientists (EAIO)

slaav .... Slaavilainen [*Finland*]
SLAB .... Abopo [*Bolivia*] [*ICAO location identifier*]   (ICLI)
SLAC .... Structures Lamellees d'Afrique Centrale
SLAC .... Suburban Law Association Convention [*Victoria, Australia*]
SLACS ...... School Libraries and Computer Systems Group [*New South Wales Department of Education*] [*Australia*]
Sladkoop .... Confectioners' Cooperative   (BU)
SLAEA ..... Society of Licensed Aircraft Engineers (Australia)   (ADA)
SLAEAA ... (Pankypria) Syndekhnia Limenergaton, Akhthoforon, kai Ergaton Apothikon kai Alieias [*(Pan-Cyprian) Union of Port Workers, Porters, and Warehouse and Fishing Workers*]   (GC)
SLAG .... Monteagudo [*Bolivia*] [*ICAO location identifier*]   (ICLI)
SLAIA ...... Sociedad Latinoamericana de Ingenieria Agricola   (DSCA)
SLAIC ...... Soweto Local Authority Interim Committee
SLAJ .... Sierra Leone Association of Journalists
SLAM .... Sierra Leone Alliance Movement   (PD)
SLAM .... St. Lucia Labor Action Movement   (LA)
SLAM .... Supersonic Low-Altitude Missile [*Later, LASV*] [*NATO*]   (NATG)
SLAMI ...... Societe Lyonnaise Agricole, Miniere, et Industrielle
SLAMS ..... Syndicat des Constructeurs d'Appareils de Levage, de Manutention et de Materials de Stockage [*France*]   (PDAA)
SLAN .... Angora [*Bolivia*] [*ICAO location identifier*]   (ICLI)
SLANT ...... School Library Association of the Northern Territory [*Australia*]   (SLS)
slants .... Shale Field [*Topography*]   (RU)
SLAP .... Apolo [*Bolivia*] [*ICAO location identifier*]   (ICLI)
SLAPCO ... Sierra Leone Production Company
SLAQ .... Aiquile [*Bolivia*] [*ICAO location identifier*]   (ICLI)
SLARG ...... Slargando [*Slackening*] [*Music*]
SLAS .... Ascencion De Guarayos [*Bolivia*] [*ICAO location identifier*]   (ICLI)
SLASA ...... School Library Association of South Australia
SLASP ...... Syndicat Liberal des Agents de Services Publics [*Benelux*]   (BAS)
SLAST ...... Sierra Leone Association of Science Teachers   (EAIO)
SLAU .... San Aurelio [*Bolivia*] [*ICAO location identifier*]   (ICLI)
SLAV .... Avicaya [*Bolivia*] [*ICAO location identifier*]   (ICLI)
slav .... Slavic   (RU)
SLAVCA ... Sindacato Nazionale Lavoratori Vetro e Ceramica [*National Union of Glass and Ceramics' Workers*] [*Italy*]
Slavizdat .... Slavic Publishing House   (BU)
SLAW .... School of Land Air Warfare [*Australia*]
SLAW .... Slawies [*Slavic*] [*Afrikaans*]
slaw .... Slawisch [*German*]
SLAX .... Ay-Luri [*Bolivia*] [*ICAO location identifier*]   (ICLI)
SLB .... Solomon Islands [*ANSI three-letter standard code*]   (CNC)
SLB .... Studia ad Tabulas Cuneiformes Collectas a FMTh de Liagre Boehl Pertinentia [*Leiden*]
SLBA .... Sri Lanka Badminton Association   (EAIO)
SLBC .... Boca Chapare [*Bolivia*] [*ICAO location identifier*]   (ICLI)
SLBC .... Societe Luxembourgeoise de Biologie Clinique   (EAIO)
SLBC .... Sri Lanka Broadcasting Corporation   (IMH)
SLBF .... Blanca Flor [*Bolivia*] [*ICAO location identifier*]   (ICLI)
SLBFE ...... Sri Lanka Bureau of Foreign Employment
SLBH .... Buena Hora [*Bolivia*] [*ICAO location identifier*]   (ICLI)
SLBJ .... Bermejo [*Bolivia*] [*ICAO location identifier*]   (ICLI)
SLBN .... Bella Union [*Bolivia*] [*ICAO location identifier*]   (ICLI)
Slbr .... Sluzbeno Broj [*Official Number*]   (YU)
SLBS .... Sierra Leone Broadcasting Service
SLBU .... Baures [*Bolivia*] [*ICAO location identifier*]   (ICLI)
SLBV .... Villa Vista [*Bolivia*] [*ICAO location identifier*]   (ICLI)
SLBW .... Buena Vista [*Bolivia*] [*ICAO location identifier*]   (ICLI)
SLBY .... Boyuibe [*Bolivia*] [*ICAO location identifier*]   (ICLI)
SLC .... Scandinavian Library Center [*Denmark*]   (SLS)
SLC .... Schoool Leaving Certificate [*British*]   (BARN)
SLC .... Sport Leicht Coupe [*Sports Lightweight Coupe*] [*German*]
SLC .... Surf Life Saving Club [*Australia*]
SLC .... Swiftlines Ltd. [*Kenya*] [*ICAO designator*]   (FAAC)
SLCA .... Camiri [*Bolivia*] [*ICAO location identifier*]   (ICLI)
SLCB .... Cochabamba/Jorge Wilsterman [*Bolivia*] [*ICAO location identifier*]   (ICLI)
SLCC .... Copacabana [*Bolivia*] [*ICAO location identifier*]   (ICLI)
SLCF .... Societe le Chauffrage Francais [*France*]   (PDAA)
SLCG .... Charagua [*Bolivia*] [*ICAO location identifier*]   (ICLI)
SLCH .... Chapacura [*Bolivia*] [*ICAO location identifier*]   (ICLI)
SLCI .... Clara Rios [*Bolivia*] [*ICAO location identifier*]   (ICLI)
SLCJ .... Cavinas [*Bolivia*] [*ICAO location identifier*]   (ICLI)
SLCL .... Collpani [*Bolivia*] [*ICAO location identifier*]   (ICLI)
SLCL .... Sierra Leone Council of Labour
SLCM .... Camiare [*Bolivia*] [*ICAO location identifier*]   (ICLI)
SLCN .... Charana [*Bolivia*] [*ICAO location identifier*]   (ICLI)
SLCO .... Cobija [*Bolivia*] [*ICAO location identifier*]   (ICLI)
SLCP .... Concepcion [*Bolivia*] [*ICAO location identifier*]   (ICLI)

SLCP .... Standing Liaison Committee of Physiotherapists within the EEC [*European Economic Community*)] [*See also CPLK*] [*Copenhagen, Denmark*]   (EAIO)
SLCQ .... Copaquilla [*Bolivia*] [*ICAO location identifier*]   (ICLI)
SLCR .... Comarapa [*Bolivia*] [*ICAO location identifier*]   (ICLI)
SLCS .... Cerdas [*Bolivia*] [*ICAO location identifier*]   (ICLI)
SLCT .... Choreti [*Bolivia*] [*ICAO location identifier*]   (ICLI)
SLCV .... Cavinas [*Bolivia*] [*ICAO location identifier*]   (ICLI)
SLCY .... Collpa [*Bolivia*] [*ICAO location identifier*]   (ICLI)
SLCZ .... Santa Cruz/El Trompillo [*Bolivia*] [*ICAO location identifier*]   (ICLI)
SLD .... Savez Lekarskih Drustava Jugoslavije [*Federation of Medical Societies of Yugoslavia*]   (SLS)
SLD .... Savezno Lovacko Drustvo [*Federal Hunting Society*]   (YU)
SLD .... Sea Landing Division [*NATO*]
SLD .... Skholi Limenikon Dokimon [*Port Cadets School*] [*Greek*]   (GC)
SLD .... Sliac [*Former Czechoslovakia*] [*Airport symbol*]   (OAG)
SLD .... Sofia Hunting Association   (BU)
SLD .... State Library Division [*South Australia*]
SLD .... Stihaci Letecka Divize [*Fighter Airforce Division*]   (CZ)
SLD .... Union of Hunting Societies   (YU)
SLDA .... Society for Librarianship and Documentation in Agriculture [*Germany*]   (EAIO)
SLDC .... Sierra Leone State Development Corporation
SLDD .... Scientific Library and Documentation Division [*National Science and Technology Authority*] [*Philippines*] [*Information service or system*]   (IID)
SLDJ .... Savez Lekarskih Drustava Jugoslavije [*Federation of Medical Societies of Yugoslavia*]   (YU)
SLDN .... El Desengano [*Bolivia*] [*ICAO location identifier*]   (ICLI)
SLDP .... Loma Del Porvenir [*Bolivia*] [*ICAO location identifier*]   (ICLI)
SLDP .... Sierra Leone Democratic Party [*Political party*]   (EY)
SLE .... Sierra Leone [*ANSI three-letter standard code*]   (CNC)
SlE .... Slovenski Etnograf [*The Slovenian Ethnographer*] [*Ljubljana A periodica*]   (YU)
SLE .... Societas Linguistica Europaea [*Linguistic Society of Europe*] [*Austria*]   (EAIO)
SLE .... Society of Land Economists [*Australia*]
sle .... Succursale [*Branch Agency, Sub-Office*] [*French*]
SLEB .... Societe Laiterie d'Elevage de Brazzaville
SLEC .... El Cairo [*Bolivia*] [*ICAO location identifier*]   (ICLI)
SLED .... El Dorado [*Bolivia*] [*ICAO location identifier*]   (ICLI)
sled .... Follows, Next, Consequently   (BU)
sled .... Therefore, Consequently, Following, Next   (RU)
sled obr ...... In the Following Way, As Follows   (RU)
SLEE .... Societe Lyonaise des Eaux et de l'Eclairage [*French*]
SLEF .... El Triunfo [*Bolivia*] [*ICAO location identifier*]   (ICLI)
sleg .... Slegato [*Binding Broken*] [*Publishing*] [*Italian*]
SLEJ .... El Jovi [*Bolivia*] [*ICAO location identifier*]   (ICLI)
SLEJS ...... Sri Lanka Eksath Jatheenge Sangamaya   (EAIO)
SLEL .... El Roseda [*Bolivia*] [*ICAO location identifier*]   (ICLI)
SLENA ...... Sierra Leone News Agency
SLENCA ... Sierra Leone Nature Conservation Association
SLEO .... El Paraiso [*Bolivia*] [*ICAO location identifier*]   (ICLI)
SLEP .... El Peru [*Bolivia*] [*ICAO location identifier*]   (ICLI)
SLES .... Espiritu [*Bolivia*] [*ICAO location identifier*]   (ICLI)
SLET .... Sierra Leone External Telecommunications Co.
SLEU .... Eucaliptos [*Bolivia*] [*ICAO location identifier*]   (ICLI)
SLEV .... El Salvador [*Bolivia*] [*ICAO location identifier*]   (ICLI)
SLEZ .... La Esperanza [*Bolivia*] [*ICAO location identifier*]   (ICLI)
SLF .... Fidgenoessisches Institut fuer Schnee- und Lawinenforschung [*Federal Institute for Snow and Avalanche Research*] [*Research center*] [*Switzerland*]   (IRC)
SLF .... Sammenslutningen af Lokalhistoriske Foreninger [*Denmark*]   (SLS)
SLF .... Selon la Formule [*According to Formula*] [*Pharmacy*]
SLF .... Simplicial Linear Function   (RU)
SLF .... Skandinaviska Lackteknikers Forbund [*Federation of Scandinavian Paint and Varnish Technologists*] [*Sweden*]   (EAIO)
SLF .... Skolledarfbundet [*Sweden*]   (SLS)
SlF .... Slovenska Filharmonie [*Slovak Philharmonic*]   (CZ)
SLF .... Slovensky Literarny Fond [*Slovak Literary Foundation*]   (CZ)
SLF .... Somali Liberation Front   (AF)
SLF .... Sveriges Lakarforbund [*Sweden*]   (EAIO)
SLF .... Svetova Luteranska Federacia [*Lutheran World Federation*]   (CZ)
SLFA .... Fatima [*Bolivia*] [*ICAO location identifier*]   (ICLI)
SLFA .... Sierra Leone Football Association
SLFC .... Supervisor of Loan Fund Companies [*New South Wales, Australia*]
SLFL .... Sierra Leone Federation of Labour
SLFP .... Sri Lanka Freedom Party [*Political party*]   (PPW)
Slg .... Sammlung [*Collection*] [*German*]
SLG .... School Libraries Group [*Australian Library and Information Association*]

SLG........... Schweizerische Lichttechnische Gesellschaft [*Switzerland*] (SLS)

SLgE......... Schweizerische Liga Gegen Epilepsie [*Switzerland*] (SLS)

SLGJ .... Guadalajara [*Bolivia*] [*ICAO location identifier*] (ICLI)

SLGMS..... Snow Avalanche Hydrometeorological Station (RU)

SLGR........ Sri Lanka Government Railway (PDAA)

SLGRU..... State Local Government Relations Unit [*South Australia*]

SLGY......... Guayaramerin [*Bolivia*] [*ICAO location identifier*] (ICLI)

SLH .... Secteur de Loisir et d'Habitation

SLH .... Sociedade Latinoamericana de Hepatologia [*Latin American Society of Hepatology - LASH*] (EAIO)

SLH .... Sola [*Vanuatu*] [*Airport symbol*] (OAG)

SLH .... Sprava Lesniho Hospodarstvi [*Forest Management Administration*] (CZ)

SLHJ .... Huacaraje [*Bolivia*] [*ICAO location identifier*] (ICLI)

SLHN .... Chane Bedoya [*Bolivia*] [*ICAO location identifier*] (ICLI)

SLHRC..... Sri Lankan Human Rights Campaign [*Australia*]

SLHT......... Colquechaca [*Bolivia*] [*ICAO location identifier*] (ICLI)

SLHU .... Huachi [*Bolivia*] [*ICAO location identifier*] (ICLI)

SLHY......... Caquiaviri [*Bolivia*] [*ICAO location identifier*] (ICLI)

SLI .... China National Light Industrial Products Import & Export Corp., Shanghai Branch [*China*]

SLI .... Servicios Aeroes Litoral SA de CV [*Mexico*] [*ICAO designator*] (FAAC)

SLI .... Societa di Linguistica Italiana [*Italian*] (SLS)

SLI .... Statni Letecka Inspekce [*State Air Inspection Office*] (CZ)

SLIA .... School Libraries in Australia

SLIC .... Coroico [*Bolivia*] [*ICAO location identifier*] (ICLI)

SLIC .... Saudi Light Industry Company

SLiC .... Save Libraries Coalition [*Victoria, Australia*]

SLIC .... Special Libraries in Civic [*Australia*]

SLIG .... Inglaterra [*Bolivia*] [*ICAO location identifier*] (ICLI)

SLIH......... Samaihuate [*Bolivia*] [*ICAO location identifier*] (ICLI)

SLIJ .... Iniguazu [*Bolivia*] [*ICAO location identifier*] (ICLI)

SLIK .... Slovansky Literarni Klub [*Slavic Literary Club*] (CZ)

SLIM .... Sierra Leone Independence Movement

SLIM .... Societe Librairie Imprimerie Messagerie [*Tunisia*]

SLIP .... Sociedad Latinoamericana de Investigadores de Papa (LAA)

SLIP.......... Special Libraries in Parramatta [*Australia*]

SLIR .... Ibori [*Bolivia*] [*ICAO location identifier*] (ICLI)

SLIRE........ Societa Libica Incremento Razze Equine

SLIRI .... Shanghai Light Industry Research Institute [*China*] (IRC)

SLIS.......... School of Library and Information Studies [*Kuring-Gai College of Advanced Education*] [*Australia*]

SLIS.......... State Land Information System [*New South Wales, Australia*]

SLIT .... Itaguazurenda [*Bolivia*] [*ICAO location identifier*] (ICLI)

SLITA....... Societe Lilloise d'Imprimerie de Tananarive

SLITUF.... Sri Lanka Independent Trade Union Federation

SLIV .... Isla Verde [*Bolivia*] [*ICAO location identifier*] (ICLI)

SLIX .... Ixiamas [*Bolivia*] [*ICAO location identifier*] (ICLI)

SLIZ .... Izozog [*Bolivia*] [*ICAO location identifier*] (ICLI)

SLJD .... El Jordan [*Bolivia*] [*ICAO location identifier*] (ICLI)

SLJE .... San Jose [*Bolivia*] [*ICAO location identifier*] (ICLI)

SLJM .... San Juan De Fribal [*Bolivia*] [*ICAO location identifier*] (ICLI)

SLJN .... San Juan (Estancias) [*Bolivia*] [*ICAO location identifier*] (ICLI)

SLJO .... San Joaquin [*Bolivia*] [*ICAO location identifier*] (ICLI)

SLJPSM.... Sri Lanka Jathika Pusthakala Seva Mandalaya (EAIO)

SLJT......... Santa Juanita [*Bolivia*] [*ICAO location identifier*] (ICLI)

SLJV.......... San Javier [*Bolivia*] [*ICAO location identifier*] (ICLI)

SLK........... Line Distribution Bay (RU)

SLK .... Red Signal Lamp (RU)

SLK .... Silkair (Singapore) Pte Ltd. [*ICAO designator*] (FAAC)

SLK .... Slovenska Lekarska Kniznica [*Slovak Medical Library*] (CZ)

SLK .... Statni Lekarska Knihovna [*State Medical Library*] [*Prague*] (CZ)

Sl-Kh.......... Chemical Service (RU)

sl Khr .... After Christ (BU)

SLKQ........ San Miguel [*Bolivia*] [*ICAO location identifier*] (ICLI)

Sl Kuv....... Silahli Kuvvetler [*Armed Forces*] (TU)

SLKV......... Sport Lap- es Konyvkiadovallalat [*Publishing House for Sport Periodicals and Books*] (HU)

SLKY .... Puerto Yuca [*Bolivia*] [*ICAO location identifier*] (ICLI)

SLL .... Saarland Airlines AG [*Germany*] [*ICAO designator*] (FAAC)

SLL .... Salalah [*Oman*] [*Airport symbol*] (OAG)

SLL .... Sarawak Liberation League [*Communist - Same leadership as NKCP*] (ML)

sll................ Sehr Leicht Loeslich [*Very Easily Soluble*] [*German*]

SLL........... Statens Lantbrukskemiska Laboratorium [*National Laboratory for Agricultural Chemistry*] [*Sweden*] (IRC)

SLL .... Suomen Laeaekaeriliitto [*Finland*] (SLS)

SLL .... Supplemented Living Level [*South Africa*]

SLLA .... La Asunta [*Bolivia*] [*ICAO location identifier*] (ICLI)

SLLA .... Sri Lanka Library Association (EAIO)

SLLC .... La China [*Bolivia*] [*ICAO location identifier*] (ICLI)

SLLC .... Sierra Leone Labour Congress (EAIO)

SLLE .... La Ele [*Bolivia*] [*ICAO location identifier*] (ICLI)

SLLI........... La India [*Bolivia*] [*ICAO location identifier*] (ICLI)

SLLJ .... Laja [*Bolivia*] [*ICAO location identifier*] (ICLI)

SLLL.......... Laguna Loa [*Bolivia*] [*ICAO location identifier*] (ICLI)

SLLP.......... La Paz/Kennedy Internacional [*Bolivia*] [*ICAO location identifier*] (ICLI)

SLLT .... Los Tajibos [*Bolivia*] [*ICAO location identifier*] (ICLI)

SLLU .... San Lorenzo [*Cordillera*] [*ICAO location identifier*] (ICLI)

SLLV .... La Selva [*Bolivia*] [*ICAO location identifier*] (ICLI)

SLLZ .... San Lorenzo [*Bolivia*] [*ICAO location identifier*] (ICLI)

SLM .... Dry Leucocytes (RU)

SLM........... Magnetic Recording Logometer (RU)

SLM........... Schweizerische Lokomotiv- und Maschinenfabrik [*Locomotive manufacturer*] [*Switzerland*]

SLM .... Simplicial Linear Methods (RU)

SLM .... Sociedad Latinoamericana de Maiz [*Latin American Corn Society*] [*Mexico*] (LAA)

SLM .... Sul Livello del Mare [*Above Sea Level*] [*Italian*]

SLM .... Surinaamse Luchtvaart Maatschappij NV [*Surinam*] [*ICAO designator*] (FAAC)

SLMC........ School Library Media Centre [*Australia*]

SLMD........ Madidi [*Bolivia*] [*ICAO location identifier*] (ICLI)

SLMG........ Magdalena [*Bolivia*] [*ICAO location identifier*] (ICLI)

SLML........ La Madre [*Bolivia*] [*ICAO location identifier*] (ICLI)

SLMP........ Mapiri [*Bolivia*] [*ICAO location identifier*] (ICLI)

SLMR........ Memore [*Bolivia*] [*ICAO location identifier*] (ICLI)

SLMV........ Monte Verde [*Bolivia*] [*ICAO location identifier*] (ICLI)

SLMW........ Mategua [*Bolivia*] [*ICAO location identifier*] (ICLI)

SLMWAK ... Sierra Leone Muslim Women's Association - Kankaylay (EAIO)

SLMX........ Monos Arana [*Bolivia*] [*ICAO location identifier*] (ICLI)

SLN .... Secretariat Lingiustiques Nordiques [*Norway*] (EAIO)

SLN .... Secretariat Linguistiques Nordiques [*Nordic Language Secretariat - NLS*] [*Oslo, Norway*] (EAIO)

SLN .... Societe le Nickel [*France*] (FEA)

SLN .... Sri Lanka Navy

slna............ Senza Luogo ne Autore [*Without Place or Author*] [*Publishing*] [*Italian*]

SLNA......... Sierra Leone News Agency

slna............ Sin Lugar ni Ano [*Without Place or Year (of publication)*] [*Spanish*]

slnd............ Sans Lieu ni Date [*Without Place or Date (of publication)*] [*French*]

slnd............ Sem Lugar nem Data [*Without Place or Date (of publication)*] [*Portuguese*]

slnd............ Senza Luogo ne Data [*Without Place or Date (of publication)*] [*Italian*]

SLNE......... Nueva Era [*Bolivia*] [*ICAO location identifier*] (ICLI)

sln ed.......... Sans Lieu ni Editeur [*Benelux*] (BAS)

slnif............ Sin Lugar ni Fecha [*Without Place or Date (of publication)*] [*Spanish*]

SLNLSB.... Sri Lanka National Library Services Board (EAIO)

SLNO .... Nuevo Mundo [*Bolivia*] [*ICAO location identifier*] (ICLI)

SLNP......... Nueva Esperanza [*Bolivia*] [*ICAO location identifier*] (ICLI)

SLNQ .... Nueva Esperanza (Marban) [*Bolivia*] [*ICAO location identifier*] (ICLI)

SLNSW ..... State Library of New South Wales [*Australia*] (ADA)

SLNV......... Nieve [*Bolivia*] [*ICAO location identifier*] (ICLI)

SLO .... Sarawak Labor Organization (ML)

SLO .... Socialist Liberals' Organization [*Egypt*]

sl ob............ Afternoon (BU)

sl obr .... In the Following Way, As Follows (RU)

SLOC......... School Libraries' Organising Council [*Australia*]

SLOC......... Sea Lines of Communication [*NATO*] (NATG)

SLOCA....... Service to Livestock Owners in Communal Areas

SLO-FITES ... Svaz Slovenskych Filmovych a Televiznych Umelcov [*Union of Slovak Film and Television Artists*] (CZ)

SLOI.......... Orialsa [*Bolivia*] [*ICAO location identifier*] (ICLI)

Slon............ Solovetskiy Special Camp (RU)

SLOOC....... Seoul Olympic Organizing Committee [*South Korea*] (EAIO)

SLOR......... Oruro [*Bolivia*] [*ICAO location identifier*] (ICLI)

SLORC....... State Law and Order Restoration Council [*Myanmar*]

SLOT......... Sinaota [*Bolivia*] [*ICAO location identifier*] (ICLI)

SLOTFOM ... Service de Liaison des Originaires des Territoires de la France d'Outre-Mer

slov............ Dictionary, Glossary (RU)

slov............ Slovene, Slovenian (BU)

Slov .... Slovenia

SLOVUC... Slovensky Urad pre Veci Cirkevne [*Slovak Office for Church Affairs*] (CZ)

SLOVZAKU ... Slovensky Zememericsky a Kartograficky Ustav [*Slovak Geodetic and Cartographic Institute*] (CZ)

slow .... Slowenisch [*German*]

slowen........ Slowenisch [*German*]

SlOZA .... Slaski Okregowy Zwiazek Atletyczny [*Silesian Regional Athletic Association*] [*Poland*]

SlOZB........ Slaski Okregowy Zwiazek Bokserski [*Silesian Regional Boxing Association*] [*Poland*]

SLP .... Salpa Aviation Co. Ltd. [*Sudan*] [*ICAO designator*]   (FAAC)

SLP .... San Luis Potosi [*Mexican state*]

SLP .... Scottish Liberal Party [*Political party*]

SLP .... Simanovskiy, Lebedev, and Prokof'yev Gun Camera   (RU)

SLP .... Socialist Labor Party [*Egypt*] [*Political party*]   (PPW)

SLP .... St. Lucia Labor Party   (LA)

SLPA .... Sierra Leone Ports Authority

SLPA .... Sri Lanka Ports Authority   (GEA)

SLPA .... State Lamb Producers' Association [*Queensland, Australia*]

SLPIM...... Sierra Leone Progressive Independence Movement

SLPK .... Slovenska Planovacia Komisia [*Slovak Planning Commission*]   (CZ)

sl pl............. Afternoon   (BU)

SLPM .... Palmira [*Bolivia*] [*ICAO location identifier*]   (ICLI)

SLPMB ..... Sierra Leone Produce Marketing Board

SLPO......... Potosi [*Bolivia*] [*ICAO location identifier*]   (ICLI)

SLPP.......... Paraparau [*Bolivia*] [*ICAO location identifier*]   (ICLI)

SLPP.......... Sierra Leone People's Party [*Political party*]   (PD)

SLPP.......... Sri Lanka People's Party [*Political party*]   (PPW)

SLPR .... Puerto Rico [*Bolivia*] [*ICAO location identifier*]   (ICLI)

SLPS .... Puerto Suarez [*Bolivia*] [*ICAO location identifier*]   (ICLI)

Sl PS.......... Sliven Court of Reconciliation   (BU)

SLPT .... Peta [*Bolivia*] [*ICAO location identifier*]   (ICLI)

SLPT .... Socialist Labor Party of Turkey [*Turkiye Sosyalist Isci Partisi*] [*Political party*]   (PPW)

SLPU......... Puchuni [*Bolivia*] [*ICAO location identifier*]   (ICLI)

SLPV .... Puerto Villa-Roel [*Bolivia*] [*ICAO location identifier*]   (ICLI)

SLPZ .... Village Medical Prophylactic Center   (BU)

SLQ........... State Library of Queensland [*Australia*]   (ADA)

SLQY......... Curichi [*Bolivia*] [*ICAO location identifier*]   (ICLI)

Sl-R........... Radiotechnical Service   (RU)

SLR .... Sierra Leone Railway   (MHDB)

SLR .... Sierra Leone Regiment

SLR............ SOBELAIR [*Societe Belge de Transport Aeriens*] [*Belgium*] [*ICAO designator*]   (FAAC)

SLR............ Sport Leicht Renn [*Sports Lightweight·Racing (Car)*] [*German*]

SLRA .... San Ramon [*Bolivia*] [*ICAO location identifier*]   (ICLI)

SLRB .... Robore [*Bolivia*] [*ICAO location identifier*]   (ICLI)

SLRC .... School Library Resource Centre [*Australia*]

SLRE .... El Remate [*Bolivia*] [*ICAO location identifier*]   (ICLI)

SLRG......... Schweizerische Lebensrettungs-Gesellschaft [*Switzerland*]   (EAIO)

SLRH......... Rancho Alegre [*Bolivia*] [*ICAO location identifier*]   (ICLI)

SLRI .... Riberalta [*Bolivia*] [*ICAO location identifier*]   (ICLI)

SLRP .... Rosapata [*Bolivia*] [*ICAO location identifier*]   (ICLI)

SLRP .... Society for Strategic and Long Range Planning [*Later, Strategic Planning Society - SP*]   (EAIO)

SLRQ......... Rurrenabaque [*Bolivia*] [*ICAO location identifier*]   (ICLI)

SLRR .... Retiro [*Bolivia*] [*ICAO location identifier*]   (ICLI)

SLRS .... Rio Seco [*Bolivia*] [*ICAO location identifier*]   (ICLI)

SLRT .... Santa Rita [*Bolivia*] [*ICAO location identifier*]   (ICLI)

SLRY .... Reyes [*Bolivia*] [*ICAO location identifier*]   (ICLI)

SLS .... Aeroservicios Ejecutivos Sinaloenses SA [*Mexico*] [*ICAO designator*]   (FAAC)

SLS .... Schweizerischer Landesverband fuer Sport [*Switzerland*]   (EAIO)

SLS .... Securities Lending Service [*Australian Stock Exchange*]

SLS .... Silistra [*Bulgaria*] [*Airport symbol*]   (OAG)

SLS .... Slovenska Lekarska Spolecnost [*Former Czechoslovakia*]   (SLS)

SLS .... Slovenska Ljudska Stranka [*Slovene People's Party*] [*Former Yugoslavia*] [*Political party*]   (PPE)

SL'S .... Slovenska L'Udova Strana [*Slovak People's Party*] [*Also, HSL'S*] [*Political party*]   (PPE)

SLS .... Statne [*or Statni*] Lesy a Statky [*State Forests and Farms*]   (CZ)

SLS .... Stowarzyszenie Lekarzy Sportowych [*Association of Sports Physicians*]   (POL)

SLS .... Svenska Laekaresaellskapet [*Sweden*]   (SLS)

SLS .... Svenska Litteratursaellskapet i Finland [*Finland*]   (SLS)

SLSA .... Santa Ana De Yacuma [*Bolivia*] [*ICAO location identifier*]   (ICLI)

SLSA .... State Library of South Australia   (ADA)

SLSAA...... Surf Life Saving Association of Australia

SLSB .... San Borja [*Bolivia*] [*ICAO location identifier*]   (ICLI)

SLSC......... Santa Clara (Moxos) [*Bolivia*] [*ICAO location identifier*]   (ICLI)

SLSC......... Surf Lifesaving Club [*Australia*]

SLSD .... San Carlos Gutierrez [*Bolivia*] [*ICAO location identifier*]   (ICLI)

SLSF .... San Francisco (Moxos) [*Bolivia*] [*ICAO location identifier*]   (ICLI)

SLSG .... Sipuati [*Bolivia*] [*ICAO location identifier*]   (ICLI)

SLSH......... Santa Ana De Huachi [*Bolivia*] [*ICAO location identifier*]   (ICLI)

SLSI.......... San Ignacio De Velasco [*Bolivia*] [*ICAO location identifier*]   (ICLI)

SLSJ .... Salinas [*Bolivia*] [*ICAO location identifier*]   (ICLI)

SLSK .... Sauces [*Bolivia*] [*ICAO location identifier*]   (ICLI)

SLSL......... Santa Lucia (Cliza) [*Bolivia*] [*ICAO location identifier*]   (ICLI)

SLSM .... San Ignacio De Moxos [*Bolivia*] [*ICAO location identifier*]   (ICLI)

SLSN .... Sanandita [*Bolivia*] [*ICAO location identifier*]   (ICLI)

SLSO .... Santa Barbara De Parra [*Bolivia*] [*ICAO location identifier*]   (ICLI)

SLSP .... Syndicat Liberal des Services Publics [*Benelux*]   (BAS)

SLSQ .... Saahaqui [*Bolivia*] [*ICAO location identifier*]   (ICLI)

SLSR .... Santa Rosa De Yacuma [*Bolivia*] [*ICAO location identifier*]   (ICLI)

SLSS......... Sasasama [*Bolivia*] [*ICAO location identifier*]   (ICLI)

SLST......... San Antonio [*Bolivia*] [*ICAO location identifier*]   (ICLI)

SLST......... Sierra Leone Selection Trust   (AF)

SLSTIC ..... Sri Lanka Scientific and Technical Information Centre [*National Science Council of Sri Lanka*]

SLSU .... Sucre [*Bolivia*] [*ICAO location identifier*]   (ICLI)

SLSW .... Santa Barbara (Versalles) [*Bolivia*] [*ICAO location identifier*]   (ICLI)

SLSW .... Verband Schweizerischer Langlauf- und Ski-Wanderschulen [*Switzerland*]   (SLS)

SLSX .... San Ramon De Senac [*Bolivia*] [*ICAO location identifier*]   (ICLI)

Slt .... Selat [*Strait*] [*Malay*]   (NAU)

slt .... Sous le Titre [*Benelux*]   (BAS)

S Lt .... Sous-Lieutenant [*Second Lieutenant*] [*French*]   (MTD)

SLT .... State Library of Tasmania [*Australia*]   (ADA)

SLTA .... Sudan Lawn Tennis Association

SLTB .... Sri Lanka Tourist Board   (EAIO)

SLTB .... St. Lucia Tourist Board   (EAIO)

SLTB .... Syndicat Libre des Travailleurs du Burundi [*Free Union of Workers of Burundi*]   (AF)

SLTC .... Society of Leather Technologists and Chemists [*South Africa*]   (AA)

SLTE .... Teoponte [*Bolivia*] [*ICAO location identifier*]   (ICLI)

SLTF.......... San Telmo (Cordillera) [*Bolivia*] [*ICAO location identifier*]   (ICLI)

SLTG .... Santiago [*Bolivia*] [*ICAO location identifier*]   (ICLI)

SLTH......... Tumichucua [*Bolivia*] [*ICAO location identifier*]   (ICLI)

SLTI .... San Matias [*Bolivia*] [*ICAO location identifier*]   (ICLI)

SLTJ .... Tarija [*Bolivia*] [*ICAO location identifier*]   (ICLI)

SLTP .... Tipuani [*Bolivia*] [*ICAO location identifier*]   (ICLI)

SLTR .... Trinidad [*Bolivia*] [*ICAO location identifier*]   (ICLI)

SLTs .... Aircraft Colored Lamp   (RU)

SLTS .... Todos Santos [*Bolivia*] [*ICAO location identifier*]   (ICLI)

SLTT .... Total Bolivia [*Bolivia*] [*ICAO location identifier*]   (ICLI)

SLTTCO ... Saudi Livestock Transportation and Trading Co.   (PDAA)

SLTU .... Tucavaca [*Bolivia*] [*ICAO location identifier*]   (ICLI)

SLTY .... Tiguipa [*Bolivia*] [*ICAO location identifier*]   (ICLI)

SLTZ .... Tupiza [*Bolivia*] [*ICAO location identifier*]   (ICLI)

SLU........... St. Lucia [*West Indies*] [*Airport symbol*]   (OAG)

SLU........... Svenska Landsbygdens Ungdomsforbund [*Swedish Rural Youth Association*]   (WEN)

SLU........... Sveriges Lantbruksuniversitet [*Swedish University of Agricultural Sciences*]   (ARC)

SLUB......... Svaz Ludovych Protifasistickych Bojovnikov [*People's Union of Fighters of Fascism*]   (CZ)

SLUC......... Uncia [*Bolivia*] [*ICAO location identifier*]   (ICLI)

sluch.......... Sluchacz [*Student*] [*Poland*]

sluch.......... Sluchowisko [*Radio Play*] [*Poland*]

SLUFAE.... Surface-Launched Fuel Air Explosive

SLUJ .... Savez Likovnih Umetnika Jugoslavije [*Yugoslav Association of Representational Artists*]   (YU)

SLUK .... Slovensky Ludovy Umelecky Kolektiv [*Slovak People's Artistic Ensemble*]   (CZ)

SLUKO...... Studijni a Lidovychovny Ustav Olomouckeho Kraje [*Research Institute for Adult Education in Olomouc Region*]   (CZ)

SLUSZ ...... Slovensky Urad Socialneho Zabezpecenia [*Slovak Social Security Office*]   (CZ)

SLUT........ Soutez Lidove Umelecke Tvorivosti [*Folk Arts Contest*]   (CZ)

SLUV........ Uvas Verdes [*Bolivia*] [*ICAO location identifier*]   (ICLI)

SLUY........ Uyuni [*Bolivia*] [*ICAO location identifier*]   (ICLI)

sluzh.......... Employee   (RU)

sluzh.......... Office, Business   (RU)

SLV............ El Salvador [*ANSI three-letter standard code*]   (CNC)

SLV............ Schweizerischer Lehrerverein [*Switzerland*]   (SLS)

SLV............ Schweizerischer Leichtathletikverband [*Switzerland*]   (EAIO)

SLV............ Southern Launch Vehicle [*Australia*]

SLV............ State Library of Victoria [*Australia*]   (ADA)

SLV............ Statens Livsmedelsverk [*National Food Administration*] [*Sweden*]   (ARC)

SLvA .... Slovenska Liga v Amerike [*Slovak League in America*]   (CZ)

SLVA .... Villa Aroma [*Bolivia*] [*ICAO location identifier*]   (ICLI)

SLVD......... Covendo [*Bolivia*] [*ICAO location identifier*]   (ICLI)

SLVE .... Venecia [*Bolivia*] [*ICAO location identifier*]   (ICLI)

SLVG......... Valle Grande [*Bolivia*] [*ICAO location identifier*]   (ICLI)

SLVI .... Caranavi [*Bolivia*] [*ICAO location identifier*]   (ICLI)

SLVM........ Villa Montes [*Bolivia*] [*ICAO location identifier*]   (ICLI)

SLVN........ Valencia [*Bolivia*] [*ICAO location identifier*]   (ICLI)
SLVOM..... Slovensky Vybor Obrancov Mieru [*Slovak Committee of the Defenders of Peace*]   (CZ)
SLVR........ Viru Viru [*Bolivia*] [*ICAO location identifier*]   (ICLI)
SlVTS....... Slovenska Viedeckotechnicka Spolocnost [*Slovak Scientific-Technical Society*]   (CZ)
SlVTVS ..... Slovensky Vybor pre Telesnu Vychovu a Sport [*Slovak Physical Education and Athletic Committee*]   (CZ)
SLW.......... Society for Walloon Language and Literature Study [*Belgium*]   (EAIO)
SLWA....... Santa Rosa De Abuna [*Bolivia*] [*ICAO location identifier*]   (ICLI)
SLWD........ Seis De Agosto [*Bolivia*] [*ICAO location identifier*]   (ICLI)
SL-WolaLudu ... Stronnictwo Ludowe-Wola Ludu [*Peasant Party-People's Will*] [*Poland*] [*Political party*]   (PPE)
SLX........... Salt Cay [*British West Indies*] [*Airport symbol*]   (OAG)
SLY........... Sky Line for Air Services Ltd. [*Sudan*] [*ICAO designator*]   (FAAC)
slya........... Sin Lugar y Ano [*Without Place or Year (of publication)*] [*Spanish*]
SLYA........ Yacuiba [*Bolivia*] [*ICAO location identifier*]   (ICLI)
SLYB........ El Bato [*Bolivia*] [*ICAO location identifier*]   (ICLI)
SLYI......... Yapacani [*Bolivia*] [*ICAO location identifier*]   (ICLI)
SLYP .... Muyupampa [*Bolivia*] [*ICAO location identifier*]   (ICLI)
SLYY .... San Yo Yo [*Bolivia*] [*ICAO location identifier*]   (ICLI)
SLZ........... Green Signal Lamp   (RU)
SLZ........... Sao Luiz [*Brazil*] [*Airport symbol*]   (OAG)
SLZA .... Scandinavian Lead Zinc Association [*Stockholm, Sweden*]   (EAIO)
SLZB .... San Pedro [*Bolivia*] [*ICAO location identifier*]   (ICLI)
SLZF........ San Francisco (Naciff) [*Bolivia*] [*ICAO location identifier*]   (ICLI)
SLZG .... San Agustin [*Bolivia*] [*ICAO location identifier*]   (ICLI)
SLZJ .... San Pedro (Richard) [*Bolivia*] [*ICAO location identifier*]   (ICLI)
SLZK .... San Lucas [*Bolivia*] [*ICAO location identifier*]   (ICLI)
SLZR .... San Rafael (Isidoro) [*Bolivia*] [*ICAO location identifier*]   (ICLI)
SLZX .... San Pedro (Salvatierra) [*Bolivia*] [*ICAO location identifier*]   (ICLI)
SM .... Aircraft Meteorograph   (RU)
SM .... Blue Camouflage Lamp   (RU)
SM .... Calculator, Calculating Machine   (RU)
sm.............. Centimeter   (BU)
SM .... Council of Ministers   (RU)
SM .... Drilling Machine   (RU)
SM .... Drone Aircraft   (RU)
SM .... Economic Militia   (BU)
SM .... Machine Builder's Handbook   (RU)
SM .... Machine for the Manufacture of Building Materials   (RU)
Sm .... Magnetic North   (RU)
SM .... Medal of Service of the Order of Canada
SM .... Membrane Signaler   (RU)
SM .... Middle Marker Beacon   (RU)
sm.............. Mixed   (BU)
sm.............. Mixed, Mixer   (RU)
SM .... Padri Maristi [*Italy*]   (EAIO)
SM .... (Pankypria) Syndekhnia Metallorykhon [*(Pan-Cyprian) Miners Union*]   (GC)
SM .... Sa Majeste [*His, or Her, Majesty*] [*French*]   (CL)
Sm .... Samario [*Samarium*] [*Chemical element*] [*Portuguese*]
SM .... Samarkand Museum
sm.............. Same Month   (BU)
SM .... San Marino [*ANSI two-letter standard code*]   (CNC)
SM .... Santimetre [*Centimeter*]   (TU)
SM .... Sarjana Muda [*Academic degree*] [*Indonesian*]
Sm .... Schmelzpunkt [*Melting Point*] [*German*]
Sm............. Schmilzt [*Melts*] [*German*]
sm.............. Seemeile [*Nautical Mile*] [*German*]   (EG)
SM .... Seine Majestaet [*His Majesty*] [*German*]
SM .... Sekundenmeter [*Meters per Second*] [*German*]
SM .... Servomotor   (RU)
SM .... SIAI-Marchetti SpA [*Italy*] [*ICAO aircraft manufacturer identifier*]   (ICAO)
SM .... Siege et Montague [*Military*] [*French*]   (MTD)
SM .... Signal Mine   (RU)
SM .... Skholi Mathiteias [*Apprenticeship School*] [*Greek*]   (GC)
SM .... Slovenske Muzeum [*Slovak Museum*] [*Bratislava*]   (CZ)
sm.............. Smukt [*Handsomely*] [*Danish/Norwegian*]
SM .... Snowplow   (RU)
SM .... Sociaal Maandblad [*Benelux*]   (BAS)
SM .... Socialist Youth   (BU)
SM .... Societa Altair [*Italy*] [*ICAO designator*]   (ICDA)
SM .... Society of Malawi   (EAIO)
SM .... Society of Mary [*Italy*]   (EAIO)
SM .... Soldiers' Memorial Hospital [*Australia*]
SM .... Sortiermaschine [*German*]   (ADPT)
SM .... Southern Cross Medal

SM .... Soviet Mission   (RU)
SM .... Soviet Music   (RU)
SM .... Splosno Mizarstvo [*General Cabinetmaking*]   (YU)
SM .... Stasiemeester [*Station Master*] [*Afrikaans*]
SM .... Station Magasin [*Military*] [*French*]   (MTD)
SM .... Statne Majetky [*State Farms*]   (CZ)
SM .... Stopwatch   (RU)
SM .... Student Youth   (BU)
SM .... Studio SM [*Record label*] [*France*]
SM .... Sua Maesta [*His, or Her, Majesty*] [*Italian*]
SM .... Submarine Services [*Royal Australian Navy*]
SM .... Su Majestad [*His, or Her, Majesty*] [*Spanish*]
SM .... Sumska Manipulacija [*Forestry Management*]   (YU)
sm.............. Suomalainen [*Finland*]
sm.............. Suomea [*or Suomeksi*] [*Finland*]
SM .... Suomen Mestaruus [*Finland*]
SM .... Surete Militaire [*Military Security*]   (AF)
SM .... Svenska Museiforeningen [*Sweden*]   (EAIO)
SM .... Sy Majesteit [*His Majesty*] [*Afrikaans*]
SM .... Synchronous Machine   (RU)
SM .... Systema Malykh [*Small System*] [*Russian*] [*Computer science*]
SM .... Sztandar Mlodych [*Banner of the Young*] [*Poland*]
sm.............. This Month   (RU)
SM .... Twelve-Sports Event   (BU)
SM .... Washing Machine   (RU)
SmA .... Address Adder [*Computers*]   (RU)
SMA .... Automatic Washing Machine   (RU)
SMA .... European Convention on International Highways   (BU)
SMA .... Sa Majeste Aulique [*His, or Her, Austrian Majesty*] [*French*]   (ROG)
SMA .... Santa Maria [*Azores*] [*Airport symbol*]   (OAG)
SMA .... Satzmarke [*German*]   (ADPT)
SMA .... Schweizerische Meteorologische Anstalt [*Swiss Meteorological Institute*]   (ARC)
SMA .... Scouts Musulmans Algeriens [*Algerian Moslem Scouts*]   (AF)
SMA .... Secteurs de Modernisation Agricole
SMA .... Section de Munitions d'Artillerie [*Military*] [*French*]   (MTD)
SMA .... Segnalamento Marittimo ed Aereo [*Maritime and Aviation Signaling*] [*Commercial firm*] [*Italy*]
SMA .... Sekolah Menengah Atas [*Senior Middle School*]   (IN)
SMA .... Servicio Meteorologico de la Armada [*Chile*]   (MSC)
SMA .... Servicio Militar Activo [*Active Military Service*] [*Cuba*]   (LA)
SMA .... Servico Meteorologico de Angola
SMA .... Singapore Manufacturers Association   (EAIO)
SMA .... Singapore Medical Association   (PDAA)
SMA .... Singapore Monetary Authority   (ML)
SMA .... Skholi Mikhanikon Aeroporias [*Air Force Engineer School*]   (GC)
SMA .... Sociaal Maandblad Arbeid [*Benelux*]   (BAS)
SMA .... Sociedad Mexicana de Antropologia [*Mexico*]   (SLS)
SMA .... Sociedad Mineira de Agricultura [*Brazil*]   (DSCA)
SMA .... Sowjetische Militaerische Administration [*Soviet Military Administration*]   (EG)
SMA .... Statiuni pentru Mecanizarea Agriculturii [*Stations for the Mechanization of Agriculture*]   (RO)
SMA .... Stichting Mondiaal Alternatief [*Foundation for Ecological Development Alternatives*] [*Netherlands*]   (EAIO)
SMA .... Stredisko Automatizace a Mechanizace [*Automation and Mechanization Center*]   (CZ)
SMA .... Su Majestad Apostolica [*Spanish*]
SMA .... Swedish Medical Association   (EAIO)
SMA .... Swedish Museums Association   (EAIO)
SMA .... Swiss Mini-Golf Association   (EAIO)
SMA .... Swiss Musicians' Association   (EAIO)
SMA .... Sydney Market Authority [*Australia*]
SMA .... Sydney Metropolitan Area [*Australia*]
SMA .... Union of International Associations [*UIA*]   (RU)
SMAA .... Secretaries and Managers' Association of Australia
SMAC....... Societe Maghrebine de Courtage et d'Assurances
SMAC....... Societe Miniere Ajax & Cie.
SMAC....... State Minerals Advisory Council [*Australia*]
SMACA ..... Societe Marocaine d'Approvisionnement Carrosserie Automobile
SMACI ...... Societe Miniere et Agricole de la Cote-D'Ivoire
SMACP ..... Sociedad Mexicana de Amistad con China Popular [*Mexican Society of Friendship with People's China*]   (LA)
SMACT ..... Societe Marocaine d'Affretement de Consignation et de Tourisme
SMAD .... Sowjetische Militaradministration in Deutschland [*Soviet Military Administration in Germany*]   (EG)
SMAE........ Collection of the Museum of Anthropology and Ethnography   (RU)
SMAE........ Servicos Municipalizados de Agua et Electricidade
SMAEI ...... Societe Malgache d'Entreprises Industrielles
SMAF........ Afobaka [*Surinam*] [*ICAO location identifier*]   (ICLI)

SMAG .... Salaire Minimum Agricole Garanti [*Agricultural Guaranteed Minimum Wage*] [*French*] (AF)
SMAG .... Societe Meuniere et Avicole du Gabon
SMAGF ..... Societe Medicale des Antilles-Guyane Francaises [*Medical Society of Antilles-French Guiana*] (LA)
SMAJ .... [*The*] Sugar Manufacturers' Association of Jamaica Ltd. (DSCA)
SMAM ...... Amotopo [*Surinam*] [*ICAO location identifier*] (ICLI)
SMAM ...... Servizio Meteorologico dell'Aeronautica Militare [*Italian*] (MSC)
SMAP .... Societe Malgache de Peinture
SMAP .... Swiss Medical Association for Psychotherapy (EAIO)
SMAQ .... Stipendiary Magistrates Association, Queensland [*Australia*]
SMAR....... Societe Malgache d'Assurances et de Representations
SMAR....... Societe Mauritanienne d'Assurances et de Reassurances
SMARA..... Servicio Meteorologico de la Armada Argentina [*Naval Meteorological Service*] [*Argentina*] (PDAA)
SMARC..... Southern Mindanao Agricultural Research Center [*Philippines*] (ARC)
smarg .... Smarginato [*Trimmed Margin*] [*Publishing*] [*Italian*]
smaskr .... Smaaskrifter [*Miscellanea*] [*Publishing Danish/Norwegian*]
SMAT....... Societe de Machines et Appareils Techniques [*French*] (ADPT)
SMAT....... Societe Maritime du Togo
SMATA ...... Sindicato de Mecanicos y Afines del Transporte Automotor [*Union of Mechanics and Related Automotive Transport Workers*] [*Argentina*] (LA)
SMATAGOR ... Societe Auxiliaire de Materiel Agricole Ortal
SMATEC .. Societe Marocaine d'Agglomeres et de Tuyaux en Ciment
SMb .... (Abteilung) Schwermaschinenbau (der Staatlichen Plankomission) [*Heavy Machine-Building Department (of the State Planning Commission)*] (EG)
SMB.......... Lightproof and Weatherproof Camouflage Paper (RU)
SMB.......... Sa Majeste Britannique [*His or Her Britannic Majesty*] [*French*]
SMB.......... Seychelles Marketing Board (EY)
SMB.......... Societas Missionaria Bethlehem [*Bethlehem Mission Society*] (EAIO)
SMB.......... Societe Mauritanienne de Banque
SMB.......... Societe Miniere des Bandamas [*Bandamas Mining Company*] [*Ivory Coast*] (AF)
SMB.......... Societe Multinationale de Bitumes [*Ivory Coast*]
SMB.......... Stock Medicines Board [*Australia*]
SMB.......... Su Majestad Britanica [*Spanish*]
SMB.......... Union of Bulgarian Musicians (BU)
SMBA........ Singapore Merchant Bankers' Association (EAIO)
SMBA....... Societe Anonyme des Mines de Bou Arfa
SMBC....... Saehan Merchant Bank Corp. [*South Korea*]
SMBC....... Santuario Madre del Buon Consiglio [*Pious Union of Our Mother of Good Counsel - PUMGC*] [*Genazzano, Italy*] (EAIO)
SMBG........ Bakhuys [*Surinam*] [*ICAO location identifier*] (ICLI)
SMBN .... Albina [*Surinam*] [*ICAO location identifier*] (ICLI)
SMBO .... Botopasie [*Surinam*] [*ICAO location identifier*] (ICLI)
SMBPA ..... Societe Malienne de Biscuiterie et Pates Alimentaires
SMBS .... Societe des Mines de Bou-Skour [*Morocco*]
SMBSA ...... Stock Medicines Board of South Australia
SMBW....... Bronsweg [*Surinam*] [*ICAO location identifier*] (ICLI)
SMC .... Sabang Merauke Raya Air Charter PT [*Indonesia*] [*ICAO designator*] (FAAC)
SMC .... Sa Majeste Catholique [*His or Her Catholic Majesty*] [*of Spain*] [*French*]
SMC .... Saudi Medical Co. [*Saudi Arabia*]
SMC .... Savings and Mortgage Corporation [*Ethiopia*] (AF)
SMC .... Severomoravske Cihelny [*North Moravian Brick Works*] (CZ)
SMC .... Shobokshi Maritime Co. [*Saudi Arabia*]
SMC .... Siam Maison Co. Ltd. [*Thailand*]
SMC .... Singapore Maritime Command (ML)
SMC .... Small and Medium Industry Promotion Corp. [*South Korea*]
SMC .... Sociedad Mexicana de Cactalogia [*Mexico*] (DSCA)
SMC .... Societe Malgache de Cultures
SMC .... Societe Mathematique du Congo (EAIO)
SMC .... Societe Mediterraneenne de Chimiotherapie [*Mediterranean Society of Chemotherapy - MSC*] [*Italy*] (EAIO)
SMC .... State Motor Corporation
SMC .... Statni Maloobchodni Ceny [*State Retail Prices*] (CZ)
SMC .... Sudan Military College
SMC .... Sugar Marketing Co. [*Sierra Leone*]
SMC .... Su Majestad Catolica [*Spanish*]
SMC .... Supreme Military Council [*Nigeria*] (AF)
SMC .... Surveyor Menninger Chenevet [*North African*]
SMC .... Swiss Council of Music (EAIO)
SMCA........ Cayana [*Surinam*] [*ICAO location identifier*] (ICLI)
SMCA........ Societe de Manutention de Carburants Aviation [*France*]
SMCA........ Societe Malgache de Conteneurs et d'Affretement
SMCADY ... Societe de Manutention de Carburants Aviation de Dakar-Yoff
SMCD .... Supreme Military Council Decree [*Ghana*] (DLA)
SMCh .... Modified Gray Pig Iron (RU)
SMCI........ Coeroeni [*Surinam*] [*ICAO location identifier*] (ICLI)
SMCM ...... Societe Marocaine Charbonniere et Maritime

SMCO .... Coronie [*Surinam*] [*ICAO location identifier*] (ICLI)
SMCP........ Societe Mauritanienne pour la Commercialisation du Poisson (EY)
SMCPP ..... Societe Mauritanienne de Commercialisation des Produits Petroliers (EY)
SMCS .... Sociedad Mexicana de la Ciencia del Suelo [*Mexico*] (DSCA)
SMCT....... Cottica [*Surinam*] [*ICAO location identifier*] (ICLI)
SMCV....... Scierie, Menuiserie Charpente de Haute-Volta Georges Jacob
SMD .... Societe des Mines du Djado
SMD .... Societe Marocaine de Distribution d'Eau, de Gaz, et d'Electricite
SMDA .... Drietabbetje [*Surinam*] [*ICAO location identifier*] (ICLI)
SMDA .... Skandinavisk Museumsforbund Danske Afdeling [*Denmark*] (EAIO)
SMDJ .... Djoemoe [*Surinam*] [*ICAO location identifier*] (ICLI)
SMDK ...... Donderskamp [*Surinam*] [*ICAO location identifier*] (ICLI)
SMDN ...... Societe Miniere du Dahomey Niger
SMDO .... Ladoeanie [*Surinam*] [*ICAO location identifier*] (ICLI)
SMDP........ Societe Maghrebine de Distribution de Papiers
SMDR .... Societe Mutuelle de Developpement Rural
SME.......... Severomoravske Energeticke Zavody [*North Moravian Electric Power Plants*] (CZ)
SME.......... Siemens Mikrocomputer Entwicklungssystem [*Siemens Microcomputer Development System*] [*German*] (ADPT)
SME.......... Sindicato Mexicano de Electricistas [*Mexican Electricians Union*] (LA)
SME.......... Skholi Metekpaidevseos Enilikon [*Advanced Training School for Adults*] [*Greek*] (GC)
SME.......... Societa Meridionale Finanziaria SpA [*Italian*]
SME.......... Societe des Mission Evangeliques de Paris
SME.......... Societe Malgache d'Edition
SME.......... Societe Malgache Electronique
SME.......... Stato Maggiore dell' Esercito [*Army General Staff*] [*Italian*] (WER)
SME.......... Systeme Monetaire Europeen [*European Monetary System*] [*Use EMS*] (AF)
SMEA....... Sociedade Mineira de Engenheiros Agronomos [*Brazil*] (DSCA)
SMEA........ Stratiotikai Monades Ethnofylakis Amynis [*National Guard Military Defense Units*] [*Greek*] (GC)
SMEC....... Snowy Mountains Engineering Corporation [*Australia*] (ADA)
SMEC....... Societe de Menuiserie, Ebenisterie, et Charpente
SMEC....... Society for Middle East Confederation [*Israel*] (EAIO)
SMECA ...... Societe Malgache d'Exploitation des Calcaires de l'Ankaratra
SMECMA ... Societe Malienne d'Etude et de Construction de Materiel Agricole
SMEF .... Societe Generale Malgache d'Exploitations Forestieres
SMEI .... Society of Municipal Engineers of Israel (EAIO)
SMEITJ .... Savez Masinskih i Elektrotehnickih Inzenjera i Tehnicara Jugoslavije [*Union of Mechanical and Electrical Engineers and Technicians of Yugoslavia*] (YU)
SMEK....... Economic Mining and Power Complex (BU)
SMEK....... Suomalaisen Mutoilun Edistamiskeskus [*Finland*] (EAIO)
SM elj .... Siemens Martin Eljaras [*Siemens-Martin Process*] (HU)
SMEM....... Societe Marocaine d'Engrainages et de Mecanique
SMEO ...... Societe Miniere de l'Est Oubangui [*Paris*]
SMEP .... Societe de Menuiserie et d'Ebenisterie du Port
SMEP........ Societe des Missions Evangeliques de Paris
SMEP........ Societe Marocaine des Engrais Pulverises
SMER........ Societe Maghrebine de Construction et d'Entretien des Routes [*Morocco*]
SMERSH .. Smert' Shpionam [*Death to the Spies*] [*Former Soviet Union state security organization, often referred to in the popular James Bond espionage stories*]
SMERT ..... Societe Malienne d'Exploitation des Ressources Touristiques [*Tourist Development Organization of Mali*]
SMETO..... Staff Meteorological Officer [*NATO*] (NATG)
SMEX....... Singapore International Monetary Exchange
SMEX........ Societe Malgache d'Expertises
SMF.......... Service Maritime et Fluvial [*Gabon*] (MSC)
SMF.......... Sociedad Mexicana de Fitopatologia [*Mexico*] (SLS)
SMF.......... Societe Mathematique de France
SMF.......... Societe Meteorologique de France [*French*] (SLS)
SMF.......... Special Mobile Force [*Mauritius*] (AF)
SMF.......... Su Majestad Fidelisima [*Spanish*]
SMF.......... Svenska Missionsforbundet [*Swedish Missionary Society*] (WEN)
SMF.......... Svenska Musikerforbundet [*Sweden*] (EAIO)
SMF.......... Syllogos Megareon Foititon [*Association of Megara Students*] [*Greek*] (GC)
SMFELE.... Service du Moral et Foyer d'Entraide de la Legion Etrangere
SMg .... Magnesium-Schweissdraht [*Magnesium Welding Wire*] [*German*] (GCA)
SMG .... Schweizerische Mathematische Gesellschaft [*Switzerland*] (SLS)
SMG .... Servicio Militar General [*General Military Service*] [*Cuba*] (LA)
SMG .... Sistemik Mayi Gubre [*Systemic Liquid Fertilizer*] (TU)
SMG .... Social Monitoring Group [*New Zealand*]
SMG .... Sociedad Minera del Guainia [*Colorado*] (EY)

SMG .... Societe de Mecanique de Gennevilliers [*Ball-bearing manufacturer*] [*French*]
SMG .... Societe Mecanique Gabonaise
SMG .... Societe Mesnil et Gajewski
SMG .... Sortier-Mischgenerator [*German*] (ADPT)
SMG .... Stato Maggiore Generale [*General Staff*] [*Italian*]
SMGC .... Societe Miniere Gabon-Congo
SMGE .... (Pankypria) Syndeknia Metaforon kai Genikon Ergaton [*(Pan-Cyprian) Union of Transport and General Workers*] (GC)
SMGE .... Sociedad Mexicana de Geografia y Estadistica [*Mexico*] (DSCA)
SMGI .... Societe des Minerais de la Grande-Ile
SMGI .... Societe Mauritanienne des Gaz Industriels
SMGL .... Scieries Modernes de Grand-Lahou [*Grand-Lahou Modern Sawmills*] [*Ivory Coast*] (AF)
SMGS .... Abkommen ueber den Internationalen Eisenbahngueterverkehr (Abk d Russ Bez) [*Agreement on International Railroad Freight Traffic (Russian abbreviation)*] (EG)
SMGS .... Agreement on International Railroad Freight Traffic (RU)
SMH .... Schroeder, Muenchmeyer, Hengst [*Bank*] [*Obsolete*]
SMH .... Service de Meteorologie et d'Hydrologie [*Haiti*] (DSCA)
SMH .... Societe Suisse de Microelectronique et d'Horlogerie [*Commercial firm*] (ECON)
SMHEA .... Snowy Mountains Hydro Electric Authority [*Australia*] (PDAA)
SMHI .... Sveriges Meteorologiska och Hydrologiska Institut [*Swedish Meteorological and Hydrological Institute*] [*Research center*] (IRC)
SMHN .... Sociedad Mexicana de Historia Natural [*Mexico*] (DSCA)
SMHR .... Societe Mecanique du Haut-Rhin [*Upper Rhine Mechanical Co.*]
SMI .... Aero Sami SA de CV [*Mexico*] [*ICAO designator*] (FAAC)
SMI .... (Pankypria) Syndekhnia Mikhanotekhniton kai Ilektrotekhniton [*(Pan-Cyprian) Union of Machinists and Electricians*] (GC)
SMI .... Sa Majeste Imperiale [*His, or Her, Imperial Majesty*] [*French*]
SMI .... Samos Island [*Greece*] [*Airport symbol*] (OAG)
SMI .... Sanidad del Ministerio del Interior [*Interior Ministry Health Service*] [*Peru*] (LA)
SMI .... Saratov State Medical Institute (RU)
SMI .... Section de Munitions d'Infanterie [*Military*] [*French*] (MTD)
SMI .... Siberian Institute of Metallurgy (RU)
SMI .... Smolensk State Medical Institute (RU)
SMI .... Societa Metallurgica Italiana [*Manufacturer of electronic components*] [*Italian*]
SMI .... Societe Miniere Intercoloniale
SMI .... Societe Miniere Intertropicale
SMI .... Su Majestad Imperial [*His, or Her, Imperial Majesty*] [*Spanish*]
SmI .... Summing Integrator (RU)
SMI .... Swiss Market Index (ECON)
SMI .... Swiss Meteorological Institute [*Research center*] [*Switzerland*] (IRC)
SMI .... Systeme des Methodes Integrees [*French*] (ADPT)
SMIA .... Social Marketing International Association [*Queretaro, Mexico*] [*Defunct*] (EAIO)
SMIA .... Societe Marocaine pour l'Industrie Agricole
SMIB .... Small and Medium Industry Bank [*South Korea*]
SMIC .... New South Wales Survey and Mapping Industry Council [*Australia*]
SMIC .... Salaire Minimum Interprofessionnel de Croissance [*Interoccupational Minimum Growth Wage*] [*French*] (WER)
SMIC .... Societe Malgache d'Investissement et de Credit
SMIC .... Sorghum and Millets Information Center [*ICRISAT*] [*India*]
SMID .... Council of Ministers of Foreign Affairs [*1945-1955*] (RU)
SMID .... Danish Association for Mass Communication Research (EAIO)
SMIE .... Societe Mauritanienne d'Importation et d'Exportation
SMIEC ...... China National Machinery Import/Export Corporation, Shanghai Branch [*China*]
SMIER ...... Societe Medicale Internationale d'Endoscopie et de Radiocinematographie [*French*] (SLS)
SMIG .... Salaire Minimum Interprofessionnel Garanti [*Interoccupational Guaranteed Minimum Wage*] [*French*] (CL)
SMII .... Societe Malgache d'Impressions Industrielles
SMIL .... Statistics and Market Intelligence Library [*Department of Trade*] [*British*] (DCTA)
SMIP .... Mass Information and Propaganda Media (BU)
SMIREE(Aust) ... Senior Member, Institution of Radio and Electronics Engineers, Australia (ADA)
SMIS .... Special Military Intelligence Staff (ML)
SMISB .... Societe Mauritanienne des Industries Secondaires du Batiment
SMISO ...... Systeme Mondial Integre de Station Oceaniques [*Integrated Global Ocean Station System*] (MSC)
SMITH ...... Societe Mauritanienne du Tourisme et d'Hotellerie
S Mitr .... Section de Mitrailleuses [*Military*] [*French*] (MTD)
SMIVE ...... Syllogos Mikhanologon-Ilektrologon Voreiou Ellados [*Association of Engineers-Electricians of Northern Greece*] (GC)
SMJ .... Salvo Melhor Juizo [*Portuguese*]
SMJ .... Sim [*Papua New Guinea*] [*Airport symbol*] (OAG)

SMJ .... Spoldzielnie Mleczarsko-Jajczarskie [*Milk and Egg Cooperatives*] (POL)
SMJCM .... Societe de Caution Mutuelle des Jeunes Commercants du Mungo [*Cameroon*]
SMJK .... Njoeng Jakob Kondre [*Surinam*] [*ICAO location identifier*] (ICLI)
SMK .... Construction and Installation Combine (BU)
SMK .... Construction and Installation Crane (RU)
SMK .... Construction and Installation Office (RU)
SMK .... Shokuryo-Mondai Kenkyukai [*Japan*] (EAIO)
SMK .... Societe Miniere de Kisenge
SMK .... Statni Mzdova Komise [*State Wage Board*] (CZ)
Smk .... Suomen Markka(a) [*Finland*]
SMKA........ Kabalebo [*Surinam*] [*ICAO location identifier*] (ICLI)
SMKE........ Kayser [*Surinam*] [*ICAO location identifier*] (ICLI)
SMKS .... Shina Mondai Kenkyo Sho [*China Problems Research Institute*] [*Pre-World War II*] [*Japan*]
SMKW ...... Paramaribo/Kwatta [*Surinam*] [*ICAO location identifier*] (ICLI)
SML........... Forensic Medicine Laboratory (RU)
sml............. Sammenlign [*Compare*] [*Denmark*] (GPO)
SML........... Station Motors Ltd. (Uganda)
SML........... Stella Maris [*Bahamas*] [*Airport symbol*] (OAG)
SML........... Stichting Mechanische Landbouw in Surinam Foundation for Mechanized Agriculture [*Surinam*] (DSCA)
SML........... Suomen Maalaiskuntien Litto [*Union of Rural Municipalities*] [*Finland*]
SML........... Suomen Museoliitto [*Finland*] (SLS)
SML........... Suomen Musiikkionpilaitosten Liitto [*Finland*] (EAIO)
SML........... Survey Motor Launch [*Royal Australian Navy*]
SMLA........ Kamala Soela [*Surinam*] [*ICAO location identifier*] (ICLI)
Smlg........... Sammlung [*German*]
SMLT .... Langatabbetje [*Surinam*] [*ICAO location identifier*] (ICLI)
SMLT .... Societe du Metro Leger de Tunis [*Railway system*] [*Tunisia*] (MENA)
SMLTSA ... Society of Medical Laboratory Technologists of South Africa (EAIO)
SmM .... Mantissa Adder [*Computers*] (RU)
SMM .... Missionaries of the Company of Mary [*Italy*] (EAIO)
SMM .... Semporna [*Malaysia*] [*Airport symbol*] (OAG)
SMM .... Servicio Meteorologico de Mocambique
SMM .... Ship, Machinery, Marine Technology International Exhibition
SMM .... Societe Miniere de M'Passa
SMM .... Sucreries Marseillaises de Madagascar
SMMCZ... Sociedad Mexicana de Medicina y Cirugia Zootecnicas [*Mexico*] (DSCA)
SMMI........ Salesian Missionaries of Mary Immaculate [*See also SSMMI*] [*Gentilly, France*] (EAIO)
SMMI........ Siberian Institute of Mechanics and Machinery Manufacture (RU)
SMMM ..... Sindicato de Mecanicos y Metalurgicos de Managua [*Trade Union of Managua Mechanics and Metalworkers*] [*Nicaragua*] (LA)
SMMO ...... Moengo [*Surinam*] [*ICAO location identifier*] (ICLI)
SMN .... Senior Naval Commander (RU)
SMN .... Seri Maharajah Mangku Negara [*Grand Knight of the Most Distinguished Order of the Defender of the Realm*] (ML)
SMN .... Servicio de Meteorologia Nacional [*National Meteorological Service*] [*Mexico*] (MSC)
SMN .... Servicio Meteorologico Nacional [*National Meteorological Service*] [*Argentina*] (LAA)
SMN .... Servicio Minero Nacional [*National Mining Survey*] [*Ministerio de Economia, Secretaria de Industria y Mineria*] [*Research center*] [*Argentina*] (EAS)
SMN .... Societe des Melasses du Niari
SMN .... Societe des Mines du Niger [*Niger Mining Company*] (AF)
SMNI .... New Nickerie/Nickerie [*Surinam*] [*ICAO location identifier*] (ICLI)
SMNL........ Sudan Movement for National Liberation
SMNO .... Singapore Malays National Organization [*Pertubohan Kebangsaan Melayu Singapore*] [*Political party*] (PPW)
SMNS........ Senior Medical Officer of a Sector (RU)
SMNZ ...... Societe des Mines du N'Zako
SMO .... Service Militaire Obligatoire [*Obligatory Military Service*] [*Cambodia*] (CL)
SMO .... Servicio Militar Obligatorio [*Obligatory Military Service*] [*Peru*] (LA)
SMO .... Sevastopol' Naval Observatory (RU)
SMO .... Sportnomedicinske Objave [*Sport Medicine News*] [*Ljubljana A periodical*] (YU)
SMO .... Svetova Meteorologicka Organizace [*World Meteorological Organization*] (CZ)
SMO .... Svetska Meteoroloska Organizacija [*World Meteorological Organization*] (YU)
SMOA .... Societe des Mines d'Or de l'Andavkoera [*Malagasy*]
SMOA .... Societe Marocaine d'Oxygene et d'Acetylene
SMOA .... Soviet Mineral Oil Administration [*Commonwealth of Independent States*]

SMOA .... Specialized Automation Installations Organization (BU)
SM-OCIC ... Service Missionaire de l'Organisation Catholique Internationale du Cinema [*Missionary Service of the International Catholic Organization for Cinema and Audiovisual*] [*Vatican City*] (EAIO)
SMOCM ... Sculpture, Monuments and Outdoor Cultural Material [*Australian Institute for the Conservation of Cultural Material*]
smoezel....... Smoezelig [*Dirty*] [*Netherlands*]
SMOF....... Slavomakedonski Osloboditelniot Front [*Slavo-Macedonian National Liberation War*] (YU)
SMOG .... Smelost', Mysl', Obraz, Glubina [*Boldness, Thought, Image, Depth*] or Samoye Molodoye Obyedinenie Geniev [*Youngest Federation of Geniuses*] [*Clandestine group of writers in Moscow, USSR*]
SMOL .... Oelemari [*Surinam*] [*ICAO location identifier*] (ICLI)
SMOL .... Societe Miniere de l'Ogooue-Lobaye
SMOL .... Suomen Musiikinopettajain Liitto [*Finland*] (SLS)
smol............ Tar Works [*Topography*] (RU)
Smolgiz ...... Smolensk State Publishing House (RU)
SMOM ...... Sovrano Militare Ordine di Malta [*Sovereign Military Order of Malta*] [*Italian*]
SMOMPK ... Collection of Materials Describing Localities and Tribes of the Caucasus (RU)
SMON .... Subacute Myelo-Optic Neuropathy [*Medicine*]
SMOS........ Samorzad Mieszkancow Osiedla Studenckiego [*Residents' Autonomous Administration of the Students' Settlement*] (POL)
SMOSJJ ... Sovereign Order of Saint John of Jerusalem (EAIO)
SMOT .... Free Interprofessional Association of Soviet Workers (PD)
SMOTIG... Service de la Main-D'Oeuvre des Travaux d'Interet General
SMP.......... Code of Marine Regulations (RU)
SMP.......... Construction and Installation Train (RU)
SMP.......... First Aid (RU)
SMP.......... Northern Sea Route (RU)
SmP.......... Number Sequence Adder [*Computers*] (RU)
SMP.......... Rivet Gun (RU)
SMP.......... Salinity Management Plan [*Australia*]
SMP.......... Samahang Malakolohiya ng Pilipinas [*Philippines*] (EAIO)
SMP.......... Samahang Manggagawang Pilipino [*National Alliance of Teachers and Office Workers*] [*Philippines*] (EY)
Smp.......... Schmelzpunkt [*Melting Point*] [*German*] (GCA)
SMP.......... Second Malaysia Plan (ML)
SMP.......... Secteur Experimental de Modernisation des Palmeraies
SMP.......... Secteurs de Modernisation du Paysannat [*North African*]
SMP.......... Sekolah Menengah Pertama [*Junior Middle School*] (IN)
SMP.......... Semiautomatic Washing Machine (RU)
SMP.......... Sempati Air Transport PT [*Indonesia*] [*ICAO designator*] (FAAC)
SMP.......... Sociedad Mejoramiento de Praderas [*Uruguay*] (DSCA)
SMP.......... Societe des Magasins Prisunic
SMP.......... Societe des Mines de Poura
SMP.......... Societe Malgache de Publicite
SMSI........ Societe Marocaine de Pediatrie [*Morocco*] (EAIO)
SMP.......... Societe Moderne de Peche
SMP.......... Somalia Marine Products [*Commercial firm*]
SMP.......... Sosialistiki Mathitiki Parataxi [*Socialist Student Faction*] [*Greek*] (GC)
SMP.......... Soviet Military Power [*A publication 1981-1991; changed in 1992 to Forces in Transition*] (DOMA)
SMP.......... Sprava Materialniho Planovani [*Materiel Planning Directorate*] (CZ)
SMP.......... Suomen Maaseudun Puolue [*Finnish Rural Party*] [*Political party*] (PPW)
Sm p.......... Tar Furnace [*Topography*] (RU)
SMPA........ Paloemeu/Vincent Fajks [*Surinam*] [*ICAO location identifier*] (ICLI)
SMPB........ Paramaribo [*Surinam*] [*ICAO location identifier*] (ICLI)
SMPC........ Societe des Mines et Produits Chimiques [*French*]
SMpec........ Siemens-Martinova Pec [*Open-Hearth Furnace*] (CZ)
SMPG........ Poesoegroenoe [*Surinam*] [*ICAO location identifier*] (ICLI)
SMPI........ Societe Mauritanienne de Presse et d'Impression [*Publisher*] (EY)
SMPL........ Smiseny Letecky Pluk [*Mixed Aircraft Regiment*] (CZ)
SMPL........ Societe Malgache de Produits Laitiers
SMPM....... Paramaribo [*Surinam*] [*ICAO location identifier*] (ICLI)
SMPMG.... Societe Mauritanienne de Papeterie et Mobilier General
SMPP .... Societe de Mecanique du Port de Peche
SMPP .... Societe Marocaine des Produits du Petrole
SMPR .... Secteur de Modernisation et de Production Rurale
SMPR .... Societes Mutuelles de Production Rurale
SMPS .... Abkommen ueber den Internationalen Eisenbahnpassagier-Verkehr [*Agreement on International Railroad Passenger Traffic (Russian abbreviation)*] (EG)
SMPS .... Convention for International Road Communications (BU)
SMPT........ Apentina [*Surinam*] [*ICAO location identifier*] (ICLI)

SMR .... Construction and Installation Work (BU)
SMR .... Mechanically Recording Seismograph (RU)
SMR .... Sa Majeste Royale [*His, or Her, Royal Majesty*] [*French*]
SMR .... San Marino [*ANSI three-letter standard code*] (CNC)
SMR .... Santa Marta [*Colombia*] [*Airport symbol*] (OAG)
SMR .... Schweizer Musikrat [*Switzerland*] (EAIO)
SMR .... Serviciul Maritim Roman [*Romanian Maritime Service*] (RO)
SMR .... Societe Malgache de Raffinerie [*Malagasy Refining Company*] (AF)
SMR .... South Molucca Republic
SMR .... Standardised Minimum Rules [*For the treatment of prisoners*] [*Australia*]
SMR .... Standard Malaysia Rubber (ML)
SMR .... Su Majestad Britanica [*Spanish*]
SMR .... Svenska Mejeriernas Riksfoerening Centrallaboratoriet [*Swedish Dairies' Association Central Laboratory*] (ARC)
SMR .... Washing Machine with Manual Wringer (RU)
SMRA........ Raleighvallen [*Surinam*] [*ICAO location identifier*] (ICLI)
SMRE........ Societe de Marie Reine d'Ecosse [*Mary Queen of Scots Society*] (EAIO)
SMRI........ Sugar Milling Research Institute [*South Africa*]
SMRL........ Sudan Medical Research Laboratories (PDAA)
SMRSSZZ ... Servisna Masinska Radionica (SSZZ) [*Machine Servicing Shop*] (YU)
SMRT........ Societes Mutuelles Rurales Togolaises
SMS.......... Saeed Mohammed Saeed Establishment [*Saudi Arabia*] [*Commercial firm*]
SMS.......... Saint Marie [*Madagascar*] [*Airport symbol*] (OAG)
SMS.......... Sa Majeste Suedoise [*His, or Her, Swedish Majesty*] [*French*] (ROG)
SMS.......... Saudi Medical Services [*Saudi Arabia*]
SMS.......... Scandinavian Migraine Society (EA)
SMS.......... Schloemann-Siemag [*Steel plant and processing supplier*]
SMS.......... Seiner Majestaet Schiff [*His Majesty's Ship*] [*German*]
SMS.......... Servicios Aerolineas Mexicanas SA de CV [*Mexico*] [*ICAO designator*] (FAAC)
SMS.......... Serviciul Medical si Sanatate [*Medical and Health Service*] (RO)
SMS.......... Sinatra Music Society (EAIO)
SMS.......... Sindicatul Muncitorilor din Sanatate [*Union of Health Workers*] (RO)
SMS.......... Skandinavisk Migraeneselskab [*Scandinavian Migraine Society*] (EAIO)
SMS.......... Slovak Medical Society [*Former Czechoslovakia*] (EAIO)
SMS.......... Snowy Mountains Scheme [*Australia*]
SMS.......... State Mail Service [*New South Wales, Australia*]
SMS.......... Stredni Mostova Souprava [*Medium Bridging Section*] (CZ)
SMS.......... Suomen Maataloustieteelinen Seura [*Finland*] (EAIO)
sms .... Synthesis of Systems That Are Optimal in the Minimax Sense (RU)
SMS.......... Syro-Mesopotamian Studies
SMSA........ Sudan Medical Students Association (EAIO)
SMSASQ .. Senior Member of the South African Society for Quality (AA)
SMSI........ Sipaliwini [*Surinam*] [*ICAO location identifier*] (ICLI)
sm sledkart ... See the Following Card (RU)
SMSM....... Kwamalasoemoetoe [*Surinam*] [*ICAO location identifier*] (ICLI)
SMSM....... Missionary Sisters of the Society of Mary
SMSM....... Societe Miniere du Sud de Madagascar
SMSM....... Soeurs Missionnaires de la Societe de Marie [*Missionary Sisters of the Society of Mary*] (EAIO)
SMSP .... Societe Miniere du Sud-Pacifique [*State-owned industries*] [*New Caledonia*] (EY)
SMSR .... Servicio Medico Social Rural [*Rural Medical-Social Service*] [*Cuba*] (LA)
SMST........ Stoelmanseiland [*Surinam*] [*ICAO location identifier*] (ICLI)
SMST........ System of Modular Jet-Type Elements (RU)
SMT.......... Intercity Television Service (RU)
SMT.......... Multiple Telephony System (RU)
SMT.......... Sistema Multimodal Transistmico [*Transisthmian Multimodal System*] [*Mexico*] (LA)
smt .... Smudstitel [*Half-Title*] [*Publishing Danish/Norwegian*]
SMT.......... Spoljna Mrtva Tacka [*Outer Dead Center*] (YU)
SMT.......... Sri Muang Thai Labels Weaving Factory Co. Ltd. [*Thailand*]
SMT.......... Stacion per Maqina e Traktore [*Albanian*]
SMT.......... Statiuni de Masini si Tractoare [*Machine and Tractor Stations*] (RO)
SMTA........ Tabiki [*Surinam*] [*ICAO location identifier*] (ICLI)
SMTB........ Tafelberg/Rudi Kappel [*Surinam*] [*ICAO location identifier*] (ICLI)
SMTC........ Sa Majeste Tres Chretienne [*His, or Her, Most Christian Majesty*] [*French*]
SMTF........ Sa Majeste Tres Fidele [*His, or Her, Most Faithful Majesty*] [*French*]
SMTF .... Societe Miniere de Tenke-Fungurume [*Tenke-Fungurume Mining Company*] [*Zaire*] (AF)
SMTH .... Societe Mauritanienne du Tourisme et d'Hotellerie

SMTI........ Tibiti [*Surinam*] [*ICAO location identifier*]   (ICLI)

SMTK....... Standardna Medunarodna Trgovinska Klasifikacija [*Standard International Trade Classification*]   (YU)

SMTM....... Societe Malgache de Transports Maritimes [*Malagasy Marine Transport Company*]   (AF)

SMTP........ Tepoe [*Surinam*] [*ICAO location identifier*]   (ICLI)

SMTs........ Sofia Interurban Telephone Exchange   (BU)

SMTT........ Societe Marocaine de Transports Touristiques

SMTT........ Societe Miniere de Tassa N'Taghalgue [*Uranium mining company*] [*Niger*]

SMTTs...... Capital Interurban Telephone Exchange   (BU)

SMTWL.... Stichting voor Moeilijk Toegankelijke Wetenschappelijke Literatuur [*Netherlands*]

SMU .... Adverse Meteorological Conditions   (RU)

SMU .... Blackout Device   (RU)

SMU .... Complex Meteorological Conditions   (BU)

SMU .... Construction and Installation Administration   (RU)

SMU .... Samraadet for Musikundervisning [*Denmark*]   (EAIO)

SMU .... Science Mapping Unit [*New Zealand*]

SMU .... Sindicato Medico del Uruguay [*Medical Labor Union of Uruguay*]   (LA)

SMU .... Statni Meteorologicky Ustav [*State Meteorological Institute*]   (CZ)

SMU .... Swedish Musicians' Union   (EAIO)

smugr .... Suomalais-Ugrilainen [*Finland*]

SMUH....... Savez Muzickih Udruzenja Hrvatske [*Federation of Musical Associations of Croatia*]   (YU)

SMUH....... Secretariat des Missions d'Urbanisme et d'Habitat

SMUR ...... Construction and Installation Administration for the Development of Radio Facilities   (RU)

SMUS....... Soviet Mission to the United States   (WDAA)

smusst .... Smusstitel [*Half-Title*] [*Publishing Danish/Norwegian*]

SMUW ...... Seminarium Matematyczne Uniwersytetu Warszawskiego [*Mathematics Seminar of Warsaw University*]   (POL)

SMV .... Centimeter Waves   (RU)

SMV .... Schweizerischer Musikerverband [*Switzerland*]   (SLS)

SMV .... Sociedad de Medicina Veterinaria [*Argentina*]   (DSCA)

S-MV .... Sprava Ministerstva Vnitra [*Directorate of the Ministry of Interior (Directorates are designated by numbers)*]   (CZ)

SMV .... Surveying and Mapping Victoria [*Australia*]

SMVCH .... Sociedad de Medicina Veterinaria de Chile [*Chile*]   (DSCA)

SMVK....... Syndesmos Metallourgicon Viomichanion Kyprou [*Cyprus*]   (EAIO)

SMVO ...... Avanavero [*Surinam*] [*ICAO location identifier*]   (ICLI)

SMVU ...... Sociedad de Medicina Veterinaria del Uruguay [*Uruguay*]   (DSCA)

SMW .... Smara [*Morocco*] [*Airport symbol*]   (OAG)

SMW .... Stowarzyszenie Mlodziezy Wiejskiej [*Association of Peasant Youth*]   (POL)

SMWA ...... Southern Mercantile Workers Association [*Trinidad and Tobago*]   (EAIO)

SMWA ...... Wageningen [*Surinam*] [*ICAO location identifier*]   (ICLI)

SMWS....... Washabo [*Surinam*] [*ICAO location identifier*]   (ICLI)

SMY .... Simenti [*Senegal*] [*Airport symbol*]   (OAG)

SMY .... Skholi Monimon Ypaxiomatikon [*Regular Noncommissioned Officers School*] [*Greek*]   (GC)

SMY .... Suomen Muinaismuistoyhdistys [*Finland*]   (SLS)

SMYa .... Union of International Fairs   (RU)

SMZ .... Schweizerische Musikzeitung [*Switzerland*]

SMZ .... Serikali ya Mapinduzi ya Zanzibar

SMZ .... Serpukhov Motorcycle Plant   (RU)

SMZ .... Slovenska Misionska Zveza [*Slovenian Missionary Union*] [*Buenos Aires*]   (YU)

SMZ .... Slovenske Magnezitove Zavody [*Slovak Magnesite Plants*]   (CZ)

SMZ .... Societe Miniere du Zamza

SMZ .... Solikamsk Magnesium Plant   (RU)

SMZ .... Sonmez Airlines [*Turkey*] [*ICAO designator*]   (FAAC)

SMZ .... Stocarska Mlekarska Zadruga [*Cattle and Dairy Cooperative*]   (YU)

SMZ .... Stoelmanseiland [*Surinam*] [*Airport symbol*]   (OAG)

SMZhS...... Convention on International Railroad Communications   (BU)

SMZO ...... Paramaribo/Zorg en Hoop [*Surinam*] [*ICAO location identifier*]   (ICLI)

SMZY....... Paramaribo/Zandery [*Surinam*] [*ICAO location identifier*]   (ICLI)

SN .... Bench Adjustment   (RU)

SN .... Combined Observation, Bilateral Observation   (RU)

SN .... Combined Observation, Bilateral Spotting   (BU)

SN .... Construction Norms   (RU)

Sn .... Estanho [*Tin*] [*Chemical element*] [*Portuguese*]

sn .... From the Bottom   (RU)

SN .... Homing   (RU)

SN .... House Supplies [*Electric power plant*]   (BU)

sn .... Medic, Stretcher Bearer   (BU)

SN .... Medium Voltage   (RU)

SN .... Observation Service   (RU)

SN .... Sad Najwyzszy [*Supreme Court*]   (POL)

sn............ Samoin [*Finland*]

Sn .... San [*Saint*] [*Spanish*]

Sn .... San [*Mountain*] [*Japan*]   (NAU)

SN .... SAN [*Societe Aeronautique Normande*] [*France*] [*ICAO aircraft manufacturer identifier*]   (ICAO)

Sn .... Saniye [*Second*] [*of time*]   (TU)

Sn .... Santo [*Saint*] [*Spanish*]

Sn .... Sayin [*Esteemed*]   (TU)

SN .... Securite Nucleaire [*Nuclear Security Service*] [*Belgium*]   (WER)

sn............ Sem Numeracao [*Without Number*] [*Publishing*] [*Portuguese*]

Sn .... Sene [*Year*]   (TU)

SN .... Senegal [*ANSI two-letter standard code*]   (CNC)

SN .... Sertoma Nacional [*Mexico*]   (EAIO)

SN .... Servicio Nacional [*Spanish*]

sn............ Seun [*Son*] [*Afrikaans*]

SN .... Severoceske Nakladatelstvi [*North Bohemian Publishing House*]   (CZ)

s/n .... Sin Numero [*Without Number*] [*Publishing*] [*Spanish*]   (CED)

SN .... Skarb Narodowy [*Poland*]

SN .... Slovanske Nakladatelstvi [*Slavic Publishing House*]   (CZ)

S/n .... Sobre Nosotros [*On Us*] [*Business term*] [*Spanish*]

SN .... Societe Nationale [*Nationalized industry*] [*French*]

SN .... Souvenir Napoleonien [*France*]   (EAIO)

SN .... Soviet of Nationalities   (RU)

SN .... Spojene Narody [*United Nations*]   (CZ)

SN .... Spojovaci Nacelnik [*Communications Chief*]   (CZ)

SN .... Spolecnost Narodu [*League of Nations*]   (CZ)

SN .... Statni Nakladatelstvi [*State Publishing House*]   (CZ)

sn............ Sthene   (RU)

SN .... Stores Naval [*Royal Australian Navy*]

SN .... Stratiotikos Nomos [*Military Law*] [*Greek*]   (GC)

SN .... Stronnictwo Narodowe [*Nationalist Party*] [*Poland*] [*Political party*]   (PPE)

SN .... Studium Nauczycielskie [*Teachers' College*] [*Poland*]

SN .... Sunbeam Flower Nurseries Ltd. [*New Zealand*]

SN .... Surete Nationale [*National Security*] [*French*]

SN .... Sveriges Naturvetareforbund [*Sweden*]   (EAIO)

SN .... Systemnormausschuss [*German*]   (ADPT)

SN .... Systemnummer [*System Number*] [*German*]   (GCA)

SN .... Voltage Stabilizer   (RU)

SNA ...... Saudi News Agency   (ME)

SNA ...... Scandinavian Neurological Association [*Denmark*]   (EAIO)

SNA ...... Secretary of Native Affairs

SNA ...... Service de Navigation Aerienne   (FLAF)

SNA .... Servico Nacional de Ambulancia [*National Ambulance Service*] [*Portuguese*]   (WER)

SNA .... Sindicato Nacional Agricola [*National Agricultural Union*] [*Cuba*]   (LA)

SNA .... Sociedade Nacional de Agricultura [*National Agricultural Society*] [*Rio De Janeiro, Brazil*]   (LAA)

SNA .... Sociedad Nacional Agraria [*National Agrarian Society*] [*Peru*]   (LA)

SNA .... Sociedad Nacional de Agricultura [*National Agricultural Society*] [*Chile*]   (LA)

SNA .... Societe Nationale d'Allumettes [*National Match Company*] [*Malagasy*]   (AF)

SNA .... Societe Nationale d'Assurances [*Algeria*]   (EY)

SNA .... Societe Nationale d'Assurances [*National Insurance Company*] [*Cambodia*]   (CL)

SNA .... Societe Nationale d'Assurances et de Reassurances de la Republique de Guinee

SNA ...... Somalia National Alliance

SNA ...... Somali National Army   (AF)

SNA ...... Sudan News Agency   (BJA)

SNA ...... Surinaams Nieuws Agentschap [*Surinam News Agency*]   (EY)

SNA ...... Syndesmos Neon Axiomatikon [*League of Young Officers*] [*Greek*]   (GC)

SNA .... Syrian News Agency   (BJA)

SNA ...... System of National Accounts [*United Nations*]

SNA ...... Union of the Peoples of Angola [*Party*]   (RU)

SNAA ...... Servicio Nacional de Acueductos y Alcantarillados [*National Water and Sewerage Service*] [*San Jose, Costa Rica*]   (LAA)

SNAB........ Syndicat National des Architectes de Belgique [*Belgium*]   (BAS)

snabd.......... Supplied   (BU)

Snabprommontazh ... Office of Materials and Equipment Supply of the Soyuzprommontazh Trust   (RU)

snabsbyt..... Supply and Marketing Administration   (RU)

Snabstroymost ... Supply Office of the Mostotrest   (RU)

Snabstroyvuz ... All-Union Office of the Main Administration of Capital Construction of the Ministry of Higher Education, USSR   (RU)

SNABT...... Societe Nationale d'Amenagement de la Baie de Tanger

Snabtoprom ... Office for the Supply of Fuel Industry Establishments   (RU)

SNAC .... Societe Nationale de Confection [*North African*]

SNAC .... Societe Nord-Africaine de Construction [*Morocco*]
SNAC .... Societe Nouvelle d'Assurance du Cameroun
SNAC .... Syndicat National des Auteurs et Compositeurs de Musique [*French*]   (SLS)
SNACH ..... Sociedad Nacional de Agricultura de Chile [*Chile*]   (DSCA)
SNACI .... Societe Nouvelle d'Assurances de Cote-D'Ivoire
SNAD .... Sindacato Nazionale Autori Drammatici [*Italian*]   (SLS)
SNAE........ Societe Nord Africaine des Eaux
SNAF........ Societe Nationale des Antiquaires de France   (EAIO)
SNAF........ Societe Nord Africaine de Constructions Mecaniques et Ferroviaires [*Algeria*]
SNAF........ Student National Action Front   (ML)
SNAFOR... Societe Nationale pour le Developpement Forestier [*National Company for Forestry Development*] [*Benin*]   (AF)
SNAGSGP ... Syndicat National des Armateurs de Grands Chalutiers Surgelateurs de Grande Peche [*France*]   (EAIO)
SNAHDA .. Societe Nationale des Huileries du Dahomey
SNAI........ Jawhar Sugar Factory [*Somalia*]
SNAI......... Societa Nazionale per l'Agricoltura e l'Industria
SNAICC .... Secretariat of National Aboriginal and Islander Child Care [*Australia*]
SNALS ...... Sindacato Nazionale Autonomo Lavoratori della Scuola [*Italy*]   (EY)
SNAM .... Societa Nazionale Metanodotti [*National Gas Pipeline Company*] [*Italian*]   (WER)
SNAM .... Societe Nigerienne d'Application Mecanique
SNAP........ Sarawak National Party [*Malaysia*] [*Political party*]   (PPW)
SNAP........ Servicio Nacional de Agua Potable y Saneamiento Rural [*National Service for Water Supply and Rural Sanitation*] [*Argentina*]   (LAA)
SNAP........ Societe Nigerienne d'Application de Peinture
SNAP........ Special Needs Access Project [*Australia*]
SNAP........ Students for Nuclear Awareness and Disarmament [*Australia*]
SNAP........ Support Network for Aboriginal Parents [*Australia*]
SNAPM..... Society of Norwegian Authors of Popular Music   (EAIO)
SNAPP ...... Servico de Navegacao da Amazonia e Administracao do Porto de Para [*Brazil*]   (LAA)
SNAR .... Artillery Ground Reconnaissance Station   (RU)
SNAR .... Servicio Nacional de Acueductos Rurales [*National Service for Rural Aqueducts*] [*Dominican Republic*]   (LA)
SNAR .... Societe Nationale d'Assurances et de Reassurances de la Republique de Guinee [*Insurance*] [*Guinea*]
SNARI .... Societe Nouvelle Algerienne de Representation Internationale [*New Algerian International Representation Company*]   (AF)
SNAS........ Singapore National Academy of Science   (SLS)
SNAS........ Societe Nord Africaine du Sac [*Algeria*]
SNASA ...... Sociedad Nacional de Agricultura, SA [*Mexico*]   (DSCA)
SNASE ...... Sindacato Nazionale Autonomo Scuola Elementare [*Primary teachers association*] [*Italy*]   (EY)
SNASP ...... Servico Nacional de Seguranca Popular [*National People's Security Service*] [*Mozambique*]   (AF)
SNAT........ Societe Nationale d'Acconage et de Transit
SNAT........ Societe Nationale de l'Artisanat Traditionnel [*Algiers, Algeria*]
SNATC...... Syndicat National des Armateurs de Thoniers-Congelateurs [*France*]   (EAIO)
SNATCH... Societe Nationale Algerienne de Transport et de Commercialisation des Hydrocarbures [*Algerian National Hydrocarbons Transportation and Marketing Company*]   (AF)
SNATRAC ... Syndicat National des Travailleurs du Commerce
SNAV .... Shell Nederlandse Antillen Verkoopmij NV
SNAV .... Union of Lifesaving Societies   (RU)
SNAVR...... Rescue and Emergency Damage Repair Work   (BU)
SNB .... Battery Combined Observation   (RU)
snb.............. Battery Observation Service   (RU)
SNB .... Lateral Observation Post   (BU)
SNB .... Savezna Narodna Banka [*Federal National Bank*]   (YU)
SNB .... Sbor Narodni Bezpecnosti [*National Security Corps*]   (CZ)
SNB .... Sekcja Naukowo-Badawcza [*Scientific Research Section*]   (POL)
SNB .... Sinif Numara Birinci [*Number One Quality*]   (TU)
SNB .... Slovenska Narodna Bibliografia [*Slovak National Bibliography*] [*Former Czechoslovakia*]   (PDAA)
SNB .... Snake Bay [*Australia*] [*Airport symbol*]   (OAG)
SNB .... Straz Narodni Bezpecnosti [*National Security Guard*]   (CZ)
SNB .... Superintendencia Nacional de Bancos [*National Superintendency of Banks*] [*Colorado*]   (LA)
SNBA......... Societe Nationale des Beaux-Arts [*French*]   (SLS)
SNBATI .... Syndicat National du Beton Arme et des Techniques Industrialisees
SNBC........ Sucreries de Nossi-Be et de la Cote Est SA
SNBG .... Societe Nationale des Bois du Gabon
SNBG .... Societe Nouvelle des Bois en Grumes
SNBM .... Societe Nicoise des Bains de Mer [*Nice Sea Baths Company*] [*France*]
SNBO .... Senior Commander of Coastal Defense   (RU)
SNBP......... Servico de Navegacao da Bacia do Prata [*Brazil*]   (LAA)

SNBr .... Brigade Combined Observation   (RU)
SNBTRAPAL ... Societe Nationale du Batiment et de Travaux Publics d'Alger [*Algeria*]   (IMH)
SnBz......... Zinnbronze [*Tin Bronze*] [*German*]   (GCA)
SNC .... Servicio Nacional de Caminos [*Bolivia*]
SNC .... Siam Navaco Ltd. [*Siam Cast Iron Works*] [*Thailand*]
SNC .... Societa in Nome Collettivo [*Partnership*] [*Italian*]
SNC .... Societe en Nom Collectif [*Partnership*] [*French*]   (BAS)
SNC .... Societe Nationale de Cimenterie [*Niger*]
SNC .... Societe Nationale de Cinema
SNC .... Societe Nationale de Comptabilite [*National Accounting Society*] [*Algeria*]
SNC .... Societe Nationale de Construction [*National Construction Company*] [*French*]   (AF)
SNC .... Societe Nationale du Cameroun
SNC .... Societe Navale Caennaise [*Caen Shipbuilding Company*] [*French*]   (WER)
SNC .... Societe Nigerienne des Ciments [*Nigerien Cement Company*]   (AF)
SNC .... Supreme National Council [*Cambodia*]
SNC .... Swazi National Council   (AF)
SNC .... Swiss Nonvaleurs Club [*Later, Scripophila Helvetica - SH*]   (EAIO)
SNCA .... Societe Navale de l'Ouest Africain
SNCA .... Syndicat National des Courtiers d'Assurances   (FLAF)
SNCASE ... Societe Nationale de Construction Aeronautique du Sud-Est [*French*]
SNCASO... Societe Nationale de Construction Aeronautique du Sud-Ouest [*French*]
SNCB........ Societe Nationale des Chemins de Fer Belges [*Belgian National Railroads*]   (WER)
SNCC........ Selected Non-Communist Countries
SNCC........ Societe Nantaise de Cultures Cafeieres
SNCCA...... Swedish National Council for Cultural Affairs   (EAIO)
S$NCD ...... Singapore Dollar Negotiable Certificate of Deposit
SNCDR...... Societe Nationale Congolaise de Developpement Rural [*Congolese National Enterprise for Rural Development*]   (AF)
SNCDV...... Societe Navale Chargeurs Delmas-Vieljeux
SNCE........ Societe Nationale du Commerce Exterieur
SNCE........ Societe Nouvelle des Conduites d'Eau [*Steel and iron pipe fabricator*] [*Rabat, Morocco*]   (MENA)
SNCF........ Societe Nationale des Chemins de Fer Francais [*French National Railroad Company*]   (AF)
SNCF........ Syndicat National des Chirugiens Francais [*French*]   (SLS)
SNCFA ...... Societe Nationale des Chemins de Fer Algeriens [*Algerian National Railroad Company*]   (AF)
SNCFB ...... Societe Nationale des Chemins de Fer Belges [*Belgium*]   (BAS)
SNCFF ...... Societe Nationale des Chemins de Fer Francais [*French National Railroad Co.*]
SNCFL ...... Societe Nationale des Chemins de Fer Luxembourgeois [*Luxembourg*]   (BAS)
SNCFT ...... Societe Nationale des Chemins de Fer Tunisiens [*Tunisian National Railroad Company*]   (AF)
SNCFV ...... Societe Nationale des Chemins de Fer Vicinaux [*Benelux*]   (BAS)
SNCG .... Societe Nationale de Corps Gras [*Algeria*]
SNCh......... Carrier-Frequency Mixing   (RU)
SNCh......... Union of People's Libraries   (BU)
SNCI......... Service National des Champs Intenses [*National Department of Intense Fields*] [*Research center*] [*France*]   (WED)
SNCI......... Societe Nationale de Credit a l'Industrie [*National Industrial Credit Society*] [*Belgium*]   (GEA)
SNCI......... Societe Nationale de Credit et d'Investissement [*Credit institution*] [*Luxembourg*]   (EY)
SNCIAWPRC ... Singapore National Committee of the International Association on Water Pollution Research and Control   (EAIO)
SNCIAWPRC ... Swedish National Committee of the International Association on Water Pollution Research and Control   (EAIO)
SNCIAWPRC ... Swiss National Committee of the International Association on Water Pollution Research and Control   (EAIO)
SNCIP .... Societe Nationale de Construction et de Travaux Publics [*National Construction and Public Works Company*] [*Algeria*]   (AF)
SNCLF ...... Societe de Neuro-Chirurgie de Langue Francaise [*Society of French-Speaking Neurosurgeons - SFSN*]   (EA)
SNCM .... Societe Nationale des Constructions Mecaniques [*Algeria*]
SNCMEC.. Societe Nationale des Constructions Mecaniques [*Algeria*]
SNCMETAL ... Societe Nationale de Construction Metalliques [*Algeria*]
SNCOTEC ... Societe Nationale de Commercialisation des Textiles et des Cuirs [*North African*]
SNCS......... Syndicat National des Chercheurs Scientifiques [*French researchers' trades union*]
SNCST ...... Saudi National Centre for Science and Technology   (PDAA)
SNCT......... Societe Nationale Centrafricaine de Travaux

SNCTP ...... Societe Nationale de Construction et de Travaux Publics [*National Construction and Public Work Company*] [*Benin*] (AF)

SNCUNESCO ... Swedish National Commission for UNESCO (EAIO)

SNCV .... Societe Nationale des Chemins de Fer Vicinaux [*National Local Railroads*] [*Belgium*] (WER)

SNCV .... Societe Nouvelle de Confiserie de Vridi

SNCVA ...... Syndicat National des Constructeurs de Vehicules Agricoles (FLAF)

SNCZ .... Societe Nationale des Chemins de Fer du Zaire [*Zairian National Railroad Company*] (AF)

SND .... Battalion Combined Observation [*Artillery*] (RU)

snd .... Battalion Observation Service [*Artillery*] (RU)

SND .... Dutch Deaf Association (EAIO)

SND .... Severoceske Narodni Divadlo [*North Bohemian National Theater*] (CZ)

SND .... Skholi Navtikon Dokimon [*Naval Academy*] [*Greek*] (GC)

SND .... Slezske Narodni Divadlo [*Silesian National Theater*] [*Opava*] (CZ)

SND .... Slovenske Narodne Divadlo [*Slovak National Theater*] (CZ)

SND .... Srpsko Naucno Drustvo [*Serbian Learned Society*] (YU)

SND .... Stronnictwo Narodowo-Demokratyczne [*Poland*]

SND .... Student Scientific Society (BU)

SNDA .... Scottish National Dancing Association [*Australia*]

SNDA .... Secretaria Nacional de Defesa Agropecuaria [*National Secretariat for Agricultural Protection*] [*Brazil*] (LA)

SNDE .... Societe Nationale de Distribution d'Eau

SNDF .... Second National Development Plan

SNDK .... Slovenske Nakladatelstvo Detskej Knihy [*Slovak Publishing House of Juvenile Literature*] (CZ)

SNDK .... Statni Nakladatelstvi Detske Knihy [*State Publishing House of Juvenile Literature*] (CZ)

SNdl .... Suid-Nederland [*South Netherlands*] [*Afrikaans*]

SNDL .... Suomen Naisten Demokraattinen Liitto [*Finnish Women's Democratic League*] (WEN)

SNDLF ...... Societe de Nutrition et de Dietetique de Langue Francaise [*French-Language Society of Nutrition and Dietetics - FLSND*] [*France*] (EAIO)

SNDN .... Sisters of Notre Dame de Namur [*Roman Catholic religious order*] [*Rome, Italy*] (EAIO)

SNDP .... Second National Development Plan [*Zambia*] (IMH)

sndp .... Sin Nota de Precio [*Without Indication of Price*] [*Publishing*] [*Spanish*]

SNDT .... Shreemati Nathibai Damodar Thackersey Women's University [*India*]

SNDV .... Societe Navale Delmas-Vieljeux

SNDY .... Sandy Deserts [*Botanical region*] [*Australia*]

SNE .... All-Union Association for the Export and Import of Petroleum and Petroleum Products (RU)

SNE .... Sao Nicolau [*Cape Verde Islands*] [*Airport symbol*] (OAG)

SNE .... Servicios Aereos Norte Sur SA de CV [*Mexico*] [*ICAO designator*] (FAAC)

SNE .... Servico Nacional de Emprego [*National Employment Service*] [*Portuguese*] (WER)

SNE .... Sistema Nacional de Estadisticas [*National Statistics Service*] [*Peru*] (LA)

SNE .... Sociedad Nuclear Espanola [*Nuclear energy*] [*Spanish*] (NRCH)

SNE .... Societe Nationale d'Electricite [*National Electric Company*] [*Guinea*] (AF)

SNE .... Societe Nationale d'Energie

SNE .... Societe Nationale d'Equipement [*National Supply Company*] [*Benin*] (GEA)

SNE .... Societe Nationale des Eaux

SNE .... Sojuznefteexport

SNEA .... Societe Nationale d'Exploitation Agricole

SNEA .... Societe Nationale ELF [*Essences et Lubrifiants de France*] Aquitaine [*National ELF (Essences et Lubrifiants de France) Aquitaine Company*] [*Paris, France*] [*Research center*] (AF)

SNEA .... Syndicat National des Enseignants Angolais

SNEAHV .. Syndicat National des Enseignants Africains de Haute Volta [*National Union of African Teachers of Upper Volta*] (AF)

SNEB .... Societe Nationale d'Exploitation des Bois [*National timber industry*] [*Congo*]

SNEC .... Nouvelle Societe Commerciale des Ets. Charbonneau

SNEC .... Societe Nationale des Eaux du Cameroun [*Cameroon*] (IMH)

SNEC .... Syndicat National de l'Education et de la Culture [*National Educational and Cultural Association*] [*Mali*] (AF)

SNEC .... Syndicat National des Enseignants du Cameroun [*Trade union*] [*Cameroon*]

SNECC ...... Syndicat National des Employes et Cadres du Commerce

SNECI .... Sindicato Nacional dos Empregados do Comercio e da Industria de Provincia de Mocambique

SNECIPA ... Sindicato Nacional dos Empregados do Comercio e da Industria da Provincia de Angola [*Trade union*] [*Angola*]

SNECMA ... Societe Nationale d'Etude et de Construction de Moteurs d'Avion [*France*] (EY)

SNED .... Societe Nationale d'Edition et de Diffusion [*Algeria*]

snee .... Snede [*Edge*] [*Publishing*] [*Netherlands*]

SNEELD ... Syndicat National des Enseignants des Ecoles Libres du Dahomey

SNEF .... Singapore National Employers' Federation

SNEF .... Societe Nouvelle des Ets. Farner & Cie.

SNEFAC ... Societe Nouvelle d'Entreprises Franco-Africaines de Constructions

SNEFCA ... Syndicat National des Entreprises du Froid et du Conditionnement de l'Air [*France*] (PDAA)

SNEG .... Servicio Nacional de Estadistica Ganadera [*Santiago, Chile*] (LAA)

SNEG .... Syndicat National des Enseignants de Guinee [*National Teachers Union of Guinea*] (AF)

SNEHM .... Societe Nationale d'Exploitation des Huileries du Mali

SNEI .... Societe Nouvelle d'Editions Industrielles

SNEI .... Societe Nouvelle d'Editions pour l'Industrie [*Industrial News Publishing Company*] (IID)

SNEL .... Sindicato Nacional de Editores de Livros [*National Publishers' Association*] [*Brazil*] (LAA)

SNEL .... Societe Nationale d'Electricite [*Zaire*]

SNEM .... Servicio Nacional de Erradicacion de la Malaria [*National Malaria Eradication Service*] [*Ecuador*] (LA)

SNEM .... Servicio Nacional de Erradicacion de la Malaria [*National Malaria Eradication Service*] [*Nicaragua*] (LA)

SNEMA ..... Societe Nationale des Eaux Minerales Algeriennes [*National industry*] [*Algiers, Algeria*]

SNEN .... Syndicat National des Enseignants du Niger [*National Teachers Union of Niger*] (AF)

SNEP .... Saudi Naval Expansion Program (IMH)

SNEP .... Servicio Nacional de Erradicacion del Paludismo [*National Service for Eradication of Malaria*] [*Cuba*] (LA)

SNEP .... Societe Nationale d'Edition et de Publicite [*Algeria*]

SNEP .... Societe Nationale d'Electrolyse et de Petrochimie [*Morocco*]

SNEP .... Societe Nationale des Entreprises de Presse

SNEP .... Stredisko pro Normovani a Ekonomiku Prace [*Center for Standardization and Economics of Labor*] (CZ)

SNEP .... Syndicat National de l'Edition Phonographique [*France*] (EAIO)

SNEPIA .... Syndicat National des Ecoles Privees d'Informatique et d'Automatique [*French*] (ADPT)

SNEPPCI .. Syndicat National de l'Enseignement Primaire Public de Cote-D'Ivoire [*Ivory Coast National Public Primary Education Union*] (AF)

SNERI .... Societe Nationale d'Etudes, de Gestion, de Realisations, et d'Exploitation Industrielles [*National Company for Industrial Studies, Management, Achievement, and Exploitation*] [*Algeria*] (AF)

SNES .... Symmetric Nonlinear Electrical Resistance (RU)

SNES .... Syndicat National de l'Enseignement Secondaire [*National Union of Secondary School Teachers*] [*French*]

SNES .... Syndicat National de l'Enseignement Superieur [*National Union of Advanced Education Teachers*] [*Morocco*] (AF)

SNESup ..... Syndicat National de l'Enseignement Superieur [*National Union of Advanced Education Teachers*] [*French*] (WER)

SNET .... Syndicat National de l'Enseignement Technique [*National Union of Technical School Teachers*] [*French*]

SNETA ...... Societe Nationale pour l'Etude des Transports Aeriens [*Belgium*]

SNETHA... Societe Nationale d'Etudes et de Travaux Hydrauliques et Agricoles du Niger

Snf .... Sinif [*Class*] (TU)

SNF .... Slovensky Narodny Front [*Slovak National Front*] (CZ)

SNF .... Somali National Front [*Political party*] (EY)

SNF .... Statens Naturvidenskabolige Forskningsrad [*Danish Natural Science Research Council*] [*Research center*] (ERC)

SNF .... Sudanese National Front [*Political party*] (PD)

SNF .... Svenska Naturskyddsfoereningen [*Sweden*] (SLS)

SNFBP ...... Syndicat National des Fabricants de Bouillons et Potages [*France*] (EAIO)

SNFGE ...... Societe Nationale Francaise de Gastro-Enterologie [*French*] (SLS)

SNFK .... Compensation-Type Ferromagnetic Voltage Stabilizer with Magnetized Actuating Mechanisms (RU)

SNFP .... Parametric-Type Ferromagnetic Voltage Stabilizer (RU)

SNFPH ...... Sindicato Nacional de Frutos y Productos Horticolas [*Spain*] (DSCA)

SNFQ .... Syndicat National des Fabricants de Quincaillerie [*France*]

SNFS .... Syndicat National des Fabricants de Sucre de France [*Institut de Recherches de l'Industrie Sucriere*] [*France*]

SNG .... San Ignacio De Velasco [*Bolivia*] [*Airport symbol*] (OAG)

SNG .... Sans Notre Garantie [*Without Our Guarantee*] [*French*] [*Business term*]

SNG .... Santierul Naval Galati [*Galati Naval Shipyard*] (RO)

SNG .... Schweizerische Naturforschende Gesellschaft [*Switzerland*] (SLS)

SNG .... Schweizerische Neurologische Gesellschaft [*Switzerland*] (SLS)

SNG .... Senckenbergische Naturforschende Gesellschaft (SLS)

SNG .... Singapore (WDAA)
SNG .... Slovenska Narodna Galeria [*Slovak National Art Gallery*] (CZ)
SNG .... Slovensko Narodno Gledalisce [*Slovenian National Theater*] (YU)
SNGB .... Societe Nationale des Grands Barrages [*National Large Dam Company*] [*Cambodia*] (CL)
SNGE .... Societe Nationale Gabonaise d'Etudes
SNGIAPL ... Swiss National Group of International Association of Penal Law (EAIO)
SNGM .... Servicio Nacional de Geologia y Mineria [*National Department of Geology and Mining*] [*Quito, Ecuador*] (LAA)
SNGOD ..... Special NGO [*Nongovernmental Organization*] Committee on Disarmament (EA)
SNGOSAR ... Swedish NGO Secretariat on Acid Rain (EAIO)
SNGSO ...... Societe Nationale du Gaz de Sud-Ouest
SNGTN ..... Societe Nationale de Grands Travaux du Niger
SNH .... Societe Nationale de l'Habitat [*National Housing Company*] [*Central African Republic*] (AF)
SNH .... Societe Nationale des Hydrocarbures [*National Hydrocarbons Corporation*] [*Cameroon*]
SNHBM .... Societe Nationale des Habitations a Bon Marche [*Benelux*] (BAS)
SNHF .... Societe Nationale d'Horticulture de France [*Paris, France*] (SLS)
SNHU .... Societe Nationale Algerienne de l'Hotellerie Urbaine [*Algeria*] (IMH)
SNI .... National Intelligence Service [*Zaire*] (PD)
SNi .... Nickelschweissdraht [*Nickel Welding Wire*] [*German*] (GCA)
SNI .... Secretariado Nacional da Informacao [*National Secretariat of Information*] [*Portuguese*] (WER)
SNI .... Secretaria Nacional Internacional [*National-International Secretariat*] [*Argentina*] (LA)
SNI .... Servico Nacional de Informacoes [*National Intelligence Service*] [*Brazil*] (LA)
SNI .... Sinoe [*Liberia*] [*Airport symbol*] (OAG)
SNI .... Sistema Nacional de Informacion [*National Information System*] [*Colorado*] (IID)
SNI .... Sistema Nacional de Informacion [*National Information System*] [*Peru*] (LA)
SNI .... Sociedad Nacional de Industrias [*National Association of Industries*] [*Peru*] (LA)
SNI .... Societa Nazionale Italiana [*Italian*]
SNJ .... Societa Nucleare Italiana [*Italian Nuclear Society*] (WND)
SNI .... Societe Nationale d'Investissement [*Banking*] [*Belgium*] (EY)
SNI .... Societe Nationale d'Investissement du Cameroun (EY)
SNI .... Societe Nationale d'Investissement et Fonds Annexes [*Development bank*] [*Togo*]
SNI .... Societe Nationale d'Investissements [*National Investment Company*] [*Cameroonian, Malagasy, Moroccan*] (AF)
SNI .... Societe Nigerienne de Transports Aeriens [*Niger*] [*ICAO designator*] (FAAC)
SNI .... Soogdiernavorsingsinstituut [*Mammal Research Institute*] [*University of Pretoria South Africa*] (AA)
SNI .... Staatsblad Nederlands-Indie [*Benelux*] (BAS)
SNI .... Studieselskapet for Norsk Industri [*Association for the Development of Norwegian Industry*] (PDAA)
SNI .... Syndicat National des Instituteurs [*National Union of Teachers*] [*French*]
SNIA .... Servicio Nacional de Investigaciones Agropecuarias [*Panama*] (DSCA)
SNIA .... Sindacato Nazionale Istruzione Artistica [*Italian*] (SLS)
SNIACE .... Sociedad Nacional Industrias Aplicaciones Celulosa Espanola SA [*Spanish*]
SNIAS .... Societe Nationale Industrielle Aerospatiale [*French*]
SNIAVISCOSA ... Societa Nazionale Industria Applicazioni Viscosa SpA [*Spanish*]
SNIB .... Societe Nationale des Industries du Bois [*North African*]
SNIC .... Sindicato Nacional de la Industria de la Carne [*National Union of the Meat Industry*] [*El Salvador*] (LA)
SNIC .... Singapore National Institute of Chemistry
SNIC .... Sistem National Informational pentru Conducere [*Natonal Data Processing System for Management*] (RO)
SNIC .... Societe Nationale des Industries Chimiques [*Production and distribution of chemical products*] [*Algeria*]
SNIC .... Societe Nationale des Industries de la Cellulose
SNIC .... Societe Nouvelle de l'Imprimerie Centrale
SNICA .... Sistema Nacional de Informacion en Ciencias Agropecuarias [*Buenos Aires, Argentina*]
SNICS ...... Societe Nationale pour l'Industrie et le Commerce au Senegal
SNIE .... Servicio Nacional de Identificacion y Extranjeria [*National Identification and Alien Service*] [*Venezuela*] (LA)
SNIE .... Societe Navale d'Importation et d'Exportation
SNIEM ...... Societe Nationale d'Importation et Exportation Mauritanienne
SNI-FA ...... Societe Nationale d'Investissement et Fonds Annexes [*National Investment Corporation and Associated Fund*] [*Togo*] (GEA)
SNII .... Council of Scientific Research Institutes (BU)

SNIIGGIMS ... Siberian Scientific Research Institute of Geology, Geophysics, and Mineral Raw Materials (RU)
SNIIGiM ... Northern Scientific Research Institute of Hydraulic Engineering and Reclamation (RU)
SNIIGM .... Northern Scientific Research Institute of Hydraulic Engineering and Reclamation (RU)
SNIILP ...... Sverdlovsk Scientific Research Institute of the Lumber Industry (RU)
SNIING ..... Stalingrad Scientific Research Institute of Petroleum and Gas (RU)
SNIIP .... All-Union Scientific Research Institute of Instrument Making (RU)
SNIISPP ... All-Union Scientific Research Institute of the Synthetics and Perfume Industry (RU)
SNIITMASh ... Stalingrad Scientific Research Institute of Machinery-Manufacturing Technology (RU)
SNIL .... Selangor National Independence League (ML)
SNILPI ...... Sindacato Nazionale Ingegneri Liberi Professionisti Italiana [*Liberal Professionals-Engineers*] (EY)
SNIM .... Societe Nationale Industrielle et Miniere [*National Industrial and Mining Company*] [*Mauritania*] (AF)
SNIMA ...... Service de Normalisation Industrielle Marocaine [*Morocco*]
SNIMAB ... Syndicat National des Importateurs de Materiels de Bureau et d'Informatique [*French*] (ADPT)
SNIMC ...... Stichting Nederlandse Informatie Managers Combinatie [*Netherlands*] (EAIO)
SNIO .... Servicio Nacional de Instrumentacion Oceanografica [*Mexico*] (MSC)
SNIP .... Construction Norms and Regulations (RU)
SNIP .... Societe Nationale de Financement des Recherches de Petrole [*National Petroleum Prospecting Financing Company*] [*Algeria*] (AF)
SNI-PEGC ... Syndicat National des Instituteurs et Professeurs d'Enseignement General de College [*France*] (EAIO)
SNIPS .... Skillshare National Information Processing System [*Australia*]
SNIS .... Guidance and Liaison Aircraft (RU)
SNIS .... Lookout and Communications Service [*Navy*] (RU)
SNIT .... Societe Nationale Immobiliere de Tunisie [*Tunisian National Real Estate Company*] (AF)
SNIV .... Societe Nationale des Industries Verrieres [*National Glass Industries Company*] [*Algeria*] (AF)
SNJ .... Savez Novinara Jugoslavije [*Federation of Journalists of Yugoslavia*] (YU)
SNJNV ...... Servico Nacional de Justica e Nao Violencia [*National Service for Justice and Non-Violence*] [*Brazil*]
SNJP .... Schweizerische Nationalkommission Justitia et Pax [*Switzerland*] (EAIO)
SNK .... Carrier and Control Frequencies Bay (RU)
SNK .... Cooperative Dutch Choral Society [*Netherlands*] (EAIO)
SNK .... Council of People's Commissars [*1917-1946*] (RU)
SNK .... Soiuz Narodov Kameruna
SNK .... Soviet Narodnykh Komissarov [*Council of People's Commissars*] [*Former USSR*] (LAIN)
SNKh .... Council of the National Economy (RU)
SNKhB ..... Bulgarian National Choral Union (BU)
SNKL .... Statni Nakladatelstvi Krasne Literatury [*State Publishing House of Belles-Lettres*] (CZ)
SNKLHU .. Statni Nakladatelstvi Krasne Literatury, Hudby, a Umeni [*State Publishing House of Belles-Lettres, Music, and Art*] (CZ)
SNKom ...... Council of People's Commissars [*1917-1946*] (RU)
SNL .... Societe des Naturalistes Luxembourgeois [*Luxembourg*] (SLS)
SNL .... Societe Nationale des Lieges [*North African*]
SNL .... Societe Nationale du Logement [*Benelux*] (BAS)
SNL .... Somali National League
SNL .... Syndicat National des Lyceens [*Morocco*]
SNLB .... Societe Nationale des Industries des Lieges et du Bois [*National Cork and Wood Industries Company*] [*Algiers, Algeria*] (AF)
SNLE .... Sous-Marin Nucleaire Lanceur d'Engins [*Missile-Launching Nuclear Submarine*] [*French*] (WER)
SNLP .... Societe Nationale Libyenne des Petroles
SNM .... German Free Youth League (RU)
SNM .... People's Youth Union (BU)
SNM .... Sindacato Nazionale Medici [*Doctors association*] [*Italy*] (EY)
SNM .... Slovenske Narodne Muzeum [*Slovak National Museum*] [*Turciansky Sv. Martin*] (CZ)
SNM .... Slovenske Narodopisne Muzeum [*Slovak Ethnographic Museum*] [*Turciansky Sv. Martin*] (CZ)
SNM .... SNAM SpA [*Italy*] [*ICAO designator*] (FAAC)
SNM .... Sociedad Nacional de Mineria [*National Mining Association*] [*Chile*] (LA)
SNM .... Societe Nantaise de Madagascar
SNM .... Somali National Movement [*Political party*] (PD)
SNM .... Spolecnost Narodniho Muzea [*National Museum Society*] (CZ)
snm .... Sthene-Meter (RU)
SNMA .... Servicios Nacionales de Meteorologia y Aerofotografia [*Peru*] (DSCA)

SNMAREP ... Societe Nationale de Materiel pour la Recherche et l'Exploitation du Petrole
SNMC .... Societe Nationale des Materiaux de Construction [*National Building Materials Company*] [*Algiers, Algeria*] (AF)
SNMD .... Union of Scientific Medical Societies (BU)
SNMES ...... Syndicat National Marocain de l'Enseignement Superieur
SNMETAL ... Societe Nationale des Constructions Metalliques [*National Metal Construction Company*] [*Algiers, Algeria*] (AF)
SNMFM .... Sindicato Nacional dos Motoristas, Ferroviarios, e Metallurgicos
SNMFSMSN ... Syndicat National des Medecins Francais Specialistes des Maladies du Systeme Nerveux [*Paris, France*] (SLS)
SNMH .... Servicio Nacional de Meteorologia e Hidrologia [*Ecuador*] (DSCA)
SNMOF .... Syndicat National des Medecins Osteotherapeutes Francais [*Paris, France*] (SLS)
SNMS .... Syndicat National des Medecins du Sport [*Paris, France*] (SLS)
SNMTs ..... List of Settlements in the Bulgarian Kingdom (BU)
SNMVT ..... Societe Nationale de Mise en Valeur du Sud Tunisien
SNNA .... Somali National News Agency
SNNGA ..... Societe Nationale des Materiaux de Construction [*National Construction Materials Company*] [*Algeria*] (AF)
SNNIS .... Observation, Guidance, and Liaison Aircraft (RU)
SNNMCC ... Sistema Nacional de Normalizacion, Metrologia, y Control de Calidad [*National System of Standardization, Weights and Measures, and Quality Control*] [*Cuba*] (LA)
SNO .... Ground Support Equipment (RU)
sn o .... Medical Section (BU)
SNO .... Societe Nantaise d'Outre-Mer
SNO .... Sreski Narodni Odbor [*District People's Committee*] (YU)
SNO .... Srpska Narodna Odbrana [*Serbian National Defense*] [*A society Chicago*] (YU)
SNO .... Students' Scientific Society (RU)
SNO .... Svaz Narodniho Osvobozeni [*National Liberation League*] (CZ)
SNOA .... Societe Nationale des Ouvrages d'Art [*Algeria*] (IMH)
SNOA .... Srpska Narodna Odbrana u Americi [*Serbian National Defense Council in America*] [*Chicago*] (YU)
SNOA .... Syndicat des Negociants de l'Ouest Africain
SNOAT ..... Societe Nouvelle d'Ouvrages d'Art et Travaux
SNOB .... Slovenska Narodnoosvobodilna Borba [*Slovenian National Liberation Struggle*] (YU)
SNOBrigada ... Sofia People's Liberation Brigade (BU)
SNOC .... Singapore National Oil Company
SNOE .... Skholi Nomikon kai Politikon Epistimon [*School of Law and Political Sciences*] [*MOE*] [*See also*] (GC)
SNOF .... Societe Nouvelle d'Organisation Forestiere
SNOI .... Sumarski Naucno Opiten Institut [*Forestry Scientific Research Institute*] (YU)
SNOO .... Slovenski Narodnoosvobodilni Odbor [*Slovenian National Liberation Committee*] (YU)
SNOO .... Sreski Narodnooslobodilacki Odbor [*District National Liberation Committee*] (YU)
SNOS .... Slovenski Narodnoosvobodilni Svet [*Slovenian National Liberation Council*] (YU)
s/note .... Sous-Note (FLAF)
SNOUB ..... Slovenska Narodnoosvobodilna Udarna Brigada [*Slovenian National Liberation Shock Brigade*] [*World War II*] (YU)
SNOW .... Operation Peace for the Galilee [*Acronym from the Hebrew title for the invasion of Lebanon, 1982*]
SNP .... Concealed Observation Post (RU)
SNP .... Free People's Party [*Federal Republic of Germany*] (RU)
SNP .... Internordic Plant Breeding [*Sweden*] (EAIO)
SNP .... Regimental Combined Observation (RU)
SNP .... Samnordisk Planteforedling [*Internordic plant breeding*] [*An association*] [*Sweden*] (EAIO)
SNP .... Servicio Nacional de Pesca [*Argentina*] (MSC)
SNP .... Sindicato Nacional de Paisanos [*Trade union*] [*Paraguay*] (EY)
SNP .... Sindicato Nacional de Periodistas [*Costa Rica*] (EAIO)
SNP .... Sistema Nacional de Pensiones [*National Pensions System*] [*Peru*] (LA)
SNP .... Slovak National Party [*Former Czechoslovakia*] [*Political party*] (EY)
SNP .... Slovenske Narodne Povstanie [*Slovak National Uprising*] (CZ)
SNP .... Socialist People's Party [*Denmark, Norway*] (RU)
SNP .... Social Nationalist Party [*Lebanon*] (ME)
SNP .... Sociedad Nacional de Pesca [*National Fishing Society*] [*Chile*] (LA)
SNP .... Sociedad Nacional de Pesqueria [*Peru*]
SNP .... Somali National Police (AF)
SNP .... Sudanese National Party [*Political party*] (EY)
SNPA .... Servico Nacional de Pesquisas Agronomicas [*Brazil*] (LAA)
SNPA .... Societe Nationale des Petroles d'Aquitaine [*Aquitaine National Petroleum Company*] [*French*] (AF)
SNPA &ER ... Service National de la Production Agricole et de l'Enseignement Rurale [*National Service for Agricultural Production and Education*] [*Haiti*] (LAA)

SNPAE ...... Syndesmos Neon dia ton Pyrinikon Afoplismon kai tin Eirinin "Bertrand Russell" [*Youth League for Nuclear Disarmament and Peace*] [*Frequently referred to as the "Bertrand Russell League"*] [*Greek*] (GC)
SNPDES ... Syndicat National des Personnels de Direction de l'Enseignement Secondaire [*Paris, France*] (SLS)
SNPE .... Societe Nationale de Presse et d'Edition [*National Press and Publishing Company*] [*Mauritania*] (AF)
SNPE .... Societe Nationale des Poudres et Explosifs [*National Powder and Explosives Company*] [*French*] (WER)
SNPEN ...... Syndicat National des Professeurs des Ecoles Normales d'Instituteurs [*Paris, France*] (SLS)
SNPEP ...... Secretaria Nacional de Propaganda y Educacion Politica [*National Secretariat for Political Propaganda and Education*] [*Nicaragua*] (LA)
SNPF .... Syndicat National des Pediatres Francais [*French*] (SLS)
SNPG .... Societe Nouvelle des Pecheries Gabonaises
SNPH .... Syndicat National des Psychiatres des Hopitaux [*Paris, France*] (SLS)
SNPI .... Servicio Nacional de Productividad Industrial [*Spain*] (DSCA)
SNPJ .... Slovenska Narodna Podporna Jednota [*Slovenian National Welfare Society*] (YU)
SNPK .... Syndesmos Navtikon Praktoron Kyprou [*Association of Cypriot Shipping Agents*] (GC)
SNPL .... Statni Nakladatelstvi Politicke Literatury [*State Publishing House of Political Literature*] (CZ)
SNPL .... Syndicat National des Pilotes de Lignes [*French*] (MCD)
SNPLM ..... Societe Nationale des Petroles de Languedoc Mediterraneen
SNPM .... Societe Nationale de Presse Marocaine [*Moroccan National Press Company*] (AF)
SNPMT ..... Syndicat National Professionnel des Medecins du Travail [*Paris, France*] (SLS)
SnPn .... Powder for Siege and Fortress Guns [*Symbol*] [*French*] (MTD)
SNPN .... Societe Nationale de Protection de la Nature et d'Acclimatation de France [*Paris, France*] (SLS)
SNPP .... Sindicato Nacional de Periodistas Profesionales [*National Union of Professional Journalists*] [*Dominican Republic*] (LA)
SNPP .... Societe Nationale des Produits Petroliers [*National Petroleum Products Company*] [*Morocco*] (AF)
SNPPT ...... Societe Nationale de la Petite Propriete Terrienne [*Benelux*] (BAS)
SNPQR ..... Syndicat National de la Presse Quotidienne Regionale (FLAF)
SNPS .... Societe Nouvelle de Promotion Cinematographique [*West Africa*]
SNPSB ...... Servico Nacional de Producao de Sementes Basicas [*National Service for Producing Basic Seeds*] [*Brazil*] (LA)
SNPT .... Societe Nationale de Promotion Touristique
SN PTT ..... Sekcja Narciarska Polskiego Towarzystwa Tatrzanskiego [*Ski Section of the Polish Tatra Mountains Society*] (POL)
SNR .... Aero Sonora SA de CV [*Mexico*] [*ICAO designator*] (FAAC)
SNR .... Missile Guidance Station (RU)
SNR .... Saint Nazaire [*France*] [*Airport symbol*] (OAG)
SNR .... Section of Scientific Workers (RU)
Snr .... Senhor [*Mister or Lord*] [*Portuguese*] (GPO)
SNR .... Slovenska Narodna Rada [*Slovak National Council*] (CZ)
SNR .... Societatea Numismatica Romana [*Romanian*] (SLS)
SNR .... Societe Nationale de Raffinage [*National Refining Company*] [*Algeria*] (AF)
SNR .... Societe Nouvelle de Roulements [*French*]
SNR .... Svaz Narodni Revoluce [*National Revolution League*] (CZ)
SNR .... Union of Scientific Workers (BU)
Snra .... Senhora [*Madam*] [*Portuguese*] (GPO)
SNRA .... Servicio Nacional de Reforma Agraria [*Bolivia*] (DSCA)
SNRB .... Union of Bulgarian Scientific Workers (BU)
SNRDO ..... Servicio Nazionale Raccolta Dati Oceanografici [*Italian*] (MSC)
SNREGMA ... Societe Nationale de Promotion, de Realisation, et de Gestion des Marches de Gros [*Algeria*] (IMH)
SNREPAL ... Societe Nationale de Recherches et d'Exploitation des Petroles en Algeria [*National Company for Petroleum Prospecting and Exploitation in Algeria*] (AF)
SN Repal.... Societe Nationale de Recherches et d'Exploitation des Petroles en Algerie (OMWE)
SNRH .... Sabor Narodne Republike Hrvatske [*Assembly of Croatia*] (YU)
SNRSS .... Societatea Nationala Romana pentru Stiinta Solului [*Romanian*] (SLS)
Snrta .... Senhorita [*Miss*] [*Portuguese*] (GPO)
SNRvZ .... Slovenska Narodna Rada v Zahranici [*Slovak National Council in Exile*] (CZ)
SNS .... Ground Stereophotogrammetry (RU)
SNS .... Samarbeidsnemden for Nordisk Skogforskning [*Nordic Forest Research Cooperation Committee - NFRCC*] [*Finland*] (EAIO)
SNS .... Savezna Narodna Skupstine [*Federal People's Assembly*] (YU)
SNS .... Scandinavian Neurosurgical Society (EA)
SNS .... Self-Adjusting System (RU)
SNS .... Servicio Nacional de Salud [*National Health Service*] [*Chile*] (LA)

SNS............ Sindacato Nazionale Scrittori [*Italian*] (SLS)
SNS............ Singapore Newspaper Services [*Singapore Press Holdings*]
SNS............ Slovak National Party [*Political party*] (ECON)
SNS............ Societe Centrafricaine de Transport Aerien [*Central African Republic*] [*ICAO designator*] (FAAC)
SNS............ Societe Nationale de Siderurgie [*National Steel Company*] [*Algiers, Algeria*] (AF)
SNS............ Societe Niger-Soudan
SNS............ Societe Nouvelle Safric
SNS............ Sofia People's Council (BU)
SNS............ Spanish Nuclear Society [*Also, SNE*] (EAIO)
SNS............ Special Night Squads [*Palestine*] (BJA)
SNS............ Srpski Narodni Savez [*Serbian National Federation*] [*Chicago*] (YU)
SNS............ Studieforbundet Naringsliv och Samhalle [*Research Association for Industry and Society*] (WEN)
SNS............ Suomi-Neuvostoliitto-Seura [*Finland-Soviet Union Society*] (WEN)
SNS............ Village People's Council (BU)
SNSEMPAC ... Societe Nationale de Semouleries, Meuneries, Fabrique de Pates Alimentaires Couscous [*Algeria*]
SNSF .... Swiss National Science Foundation [*Research center*] [*Switzerland*] (IRC)
SNSO .... Union of People's Sports Organizations (BU)
SNSOGATRA ... Societe Nouvelle Societe Gabonaise de Travaux
SNSRC ...... Swedish Natural Science Research Council (DSCA)
SNST .... Societe Nationale Sucriere du Tchad [*Chadian National Sugar Co.*]
SNT .... Navigation Light (RU)
SNT .... Secretaria Nacional de Transportes [*Brazil*] (EY)
SNT .... Societe Nationale de Transports [*National Transportation Company*] [*Tunisia*] (AF)
SNT .... Societe Nigerienne de Television
SNT .... Stowarzyszenie Naukowo-Techniczne [*Scientific and Technical Association*] [*Poland*]
SNTA........ Sindicato Nacional de Trabajadores Azucareros [*National Trade Union of Sugar Industry Workers*] [*Cuba*] (LA)
SNTA........ Sindicato Nacional de Trabajadores de Salud [*National Health Workers Union*] [*Cuba*] (LA)
SNTA........ Societe Nationale des Tabacs et Allumettes [*Algeria*]
SNTA........ Societe Nigerienne de Transports Automobiles
SNTA......... Syndicat National des Transporteurs Aeriens [*Airlines association*] [*France*] (EY)
SNTAF ...... Sindicato Nacional de Trabajadores Agricolas y Forestales [*National Union of Agricultural and Forestry Workers*] [*Cuba*] (LA)
SNTAG...... Sindicato Nacional de Trabajadores de Artes Graficas [*National Union of Workers in the Graphic Arts Industry*] [*Cuba*] (LA)
SNTAP ...... Sindicato Nacional de Trabajadores de Administracion Publica [*National Union of Public Administration Workers*] [*Cuba*] (LA)
SNTC........ Sindicato Nacional de Trabajadores de Comercio [*National Commercial Workers Union*] [*Cuba*] (LA)
SNTC........ Sindicato Nacional de Trabajadores de la Construccion [*National Union of Construction Workers*] [*Cuba*] (LA)
SNTC........ Sindicato Nacional de Trabajadores del Calzado [*National Footwear Workers Union*] [*Costa Rica*] (LA)
SNTC........ Societe Nationale Tunisienne de Cellulose
SNTCA...... Sindicato Nacional de Trabajadores del Comercio y la Administracion [*National Union of Workers in Commerce and Administration*] [*Cuba*] (LA)
SNTCFAR ... Sindicato Nacional de Trabajadores Civiles de las Fuerzas Armadas Revolucionarias [*National Union of FAR Civilian Workers*] [*Cuba*] (LA)
SNTCG...... Sindicato Nacional de Trabajadores del Comercio y Gastronomia [*National Commercial and Restaurant Workers Union*] [*Cuba*] (LA)
SNTD .... Union of Scientific and Technical Societies (BU)
SNTE........ Sindicato Nacional de Trabajadores de la Educacion [*National Trade Union of Education Workers*] [*Mexico*] (LA)
SNTEC...... Sindicato Nacional de Trabajadores de la Educacion y Cultura [*National Union of Education and Cultural Workers*] [*Cuba*] (LA)
SNTF........ Societe Nationale des Transports Ferroviaires [*Algeria*]
SNTF........ Societe Nigerienne de Transports Fluviaux et Maritimes [*Niger*]
SNTFM..... Societe Nationale des Transports Ferroviaires Mauritaniens [*Mauritanian National Railroad Transportation Company*] (AF)
SNTFM..... Societe Nigerienne des Transports Fluviaux et Maritimes (EY)
SNTGP...... Stowarzyszenie Naukowo-Techniczne Geodetow Polskich [*Scientific and Technical Association of Polish Geodesists*] (POL)
SNTH .... Societe Nationale des Travaux d'Hydraulique
SNTI......... Societe Nationale de Tomates Industrielles
SNTI......... Stowarzyszenie Naukowo-Techniczne Inzynierow [*Scientific and Technical Association of Engineers*] (POL)

SNTI......... Systeme Numerise de Transmissions Interieures [*French*]
SNTIA....... Sindicato Nacional de Trabajadores de la Industria Azucarera [*National Union of Sugar Industry Workers*] [*Cuba*] (LA)
SNTIAL .... Sindicato Nacional de Trabajadores de la Industria Alimenticia [*National Food Industry Workers Union*] [*Cuba*] (LA)
SNTIiTG ... Stowarzyszenie Naukowo-Techniczne Inzynierow i Technikow Gornictwa [*Scientific and Technical Association of Mining Engineers and Technicians*] (POL)
SNTIiTP.... Stowarzyszenie Naukowo-Techniczne Inzynierow i Technikow Przemyslu [*Scientific and Technical Association of Engineers and Technicians of the Industry*] (POL)
SNTIL .... Sindicato Nacional de Trabajadores de la Industria Ligera [*National Union of Light Industry Workers*] [*Cuba*] (LA)
SNTIQE .... Sindicato Nacional de Trabajadores de las Industrias Quimica y Energetica [*National Chemical and Energy Industry Workers Union*] [*Cuba*] (LA)
SNTIT .... Sindicato Nacional de Trabajadores de la Industria de Transporte [*National Transportation Industry Workers Union*] [*El Salvador*] (LA)
SNTIT .... Sindicato Nacional de Trabajadores de la Industria Tabacalera [*National Union of Tobacco Industry Workers*] [*Cuba*] (LA)
SNTITK .... Stowarzyszenie Naukowo-Techniczne Inzynierow i Technikow Komunikacji [*Scientific and Technical Association of Transportation Engineers and Technicians*] (POL)
SNTITP..... Stowarzyszenie Naukowo-Techniczne Inzynierow i Technikow Przemyslu [*Scientific and Technical Association of Engineers and Technicians of the Industry*] (POL)
SNTITPCh ... Stowarzyszenie Naukowo-Techniczne Inzynierow i Technikow Przemyslu Chemicznego [*Scientific and Technical Association of Engineers and Technicians of the Chemical Industry*] [*Poland*] (PDAA)
SNTITPP .. Stowarzyszenie Naukowo-Techniczne Inzynierow i Technikow Przemyslu Papierniczego [*Scientific and Technical Association of Paper Industry Engineers and Technicians*] (POL)
SNTITWM ... Stowarzyszenie Naukowo-Techniczne Inzynierow i Technikow Wodno-Melioracyjnych [*Scientific and Technical Association of Irrigation and Land Reclamation Engineers and Technicians*] (POL)
SNTL......... Statne Nakladatelstvo Technickej Literatury [*State Publishing House of Technical Literature*] (CZ)
SNTM .... Sindicato Nacional de Trabajadores de la Medicina [*National Medical Workers Union*] [*Cuba*] (LA)
SNTM-CNAN ... Societe Nationale de Transportes Maritimes et Campagnie Nationale Algerienne de Navigation (EY)
SNTM-HYPROC ... Societe Nationale de Transportes Maritimes des Hydrocarbures et des Produits Chimiques [*Algeria*] (EY)
SNTMM ... Sindicato Nacional de Trabajadores Mineros y Metalurgicos [*National Union of Miners and Metalworkers*] [*Cuba*] (LA)
SNTMMP ... Sindicato Nacional de Trabajadores de la Marina Mercante y Puertos [*National Union of Merchant Marine and Port Workers*] [*Cuba*] (LA)
SNTMVCI ... Syndicat National des Transports de Marchandises et Voyageurs de la Cote-D'Ivoire
SNTN .... Societe Nationale des Transports Nigeriens
SNTO .... Students' Scientific and Technical Society (RU)
SNTP......... Low-Frequency Transit and Channel Transfer Bay (RU)
SNTP......... Sindicato Nacional de Trabajadores de la Prensa [*National Press Workers Union*] [*Venezuela*] (LA)
SNTP......... Sindicato Nacional de Trabajadores de Petroleo [*National Union of Oil Workers*] [*Cuba*] (LA)
SNTP......... Sindicato Nacional Textil y de las Pieles [*National Union of Textile and Leather Workers*] [*Cuba*] (LA)
SNTP......... Societe Nationale de Travaux Publics [*Algeria*]
SNTPL ...... Sindicato Nacional de Trabajadores de la Prensa y el Libro [*National Press and Book Workers Union*] [*Cuba*] (LA)
SNTPVO ... Council for Science, Technical Progress, and Higher Education (BU)
SNTQE...... Sindicato Nacional de Trabajadores de la Quimica y la Energetica [*National Union of Chemical and Power Industries Workers*] [*Cuba*] (LA)
SNTR........ Societe Nationale des Transports Routiers [*Algeria*]
SN TRAV .. Societe Nationale de Travaux d'Amenagement et de Viabilisation [*Rouiba, Algeria*] (IMH)
SNTRI .... Societe Nationale de Transport Rural et Interurbain [*Tunisia*] (MENA)
SNTRM..... Sindicato Nacional de Trabajadores Petroleros de la Republica Mexicana [*Mexican National Oil Workers Union*] (LA)
SNTS .... Service Nationale de Transfusion Sanguine [*French blood transfusion service*]
SNTS .... Sindacato Nazionale Telefonici di Stato [*National Union of State Telephone Workers*] [*Italian*]
SNTS .... Sindicato Nacional de Trabajadores de la Salud [*National Trade Union of Health Workers*] [*Cuba*] (LA)

SNTS .... Sindicato Nacional de Trabajadores Sastres [*National Union of Tailors*] [*Ecuador*]   (LA)

SNTS .... Store Nordiske-Telegraf-Selskap Fabriken A/S [*Great Northern Telegraph Co. Factory Ltd.*] [*Denmark*]   (WEN)

SNTS .... Studiorum Novi Testamenti Societas [*Society for New Testament Study*]

SNTSS ...... Sindicato Nacional de Trabajadores del Seguro Social [*National Trade Union of Social Security Workers*] [*Mexico*]   (LA)

SNTTC ..... Sindicato Nacional de Trabajadores de Transportes y Comunicaciones [*National Union of Transportation and Communications Workers*] [*Cuba*]   (LA)

SNTU .... Societe Nigerienne de Transport Urbain

SNTUC ..... Singapore National Trades Union Congress   (FEA)

SNTUC ..... Singapore National Trade Unions Congress   (ML)

SNTV .... Societe Nationale des Transports de Voyageurs [*Algeria*]

SNTZ .... Syndicat National des Travailleurs Zairois

SNU .... Seoul National University [*South Korea*]

SNU .... Skopski Naroden Univerzitet [*Skopje People's University*]   (YU)

SNU .... Snunit Aviation [*Israel*] [*ICAO designator*]   (FAAC)

SNU .... Somali National Union

SNUD .... Syndicat National Unifie des Douanes [*French*]

SNUJ .... Singapore National Union of Journalists   (ML)

SNUM ...... Spilka Nezalezhnoy Ukrains'koy Molodi   (EAIO)

SNUP .... Sahara National Union Party

SNUS .... Sistema Nacional Unico de Salud [*Sole National Health Program*] [*Nicaragua*]   (LA)

SNV .... Aero Servicio del Norte SA de CV [*Mexico*] [*ICAO designator*]   (FAAC)

SNV .... Sabiraliste Neispravnih Vozila [*Assemblage of Defective Vehicles*] [*Military*]   (YU)

SNV .... Santa Elena [*Venezuela*] [*Airport symbol*]   (OAG)

SNV .... Sbor Napravne Vychovy [*Correctional Training Corps*]   (CZ)

SNV .... Schweizerische Normen-Vereinigung [*Swiss Standards Agreement*]   (SLS)

SNV .... Statens Naturvardsverk [*National Swedish Environment Protection Board*]   (ARC)

SNVI .... Societe Entreprise Nationale de Vehicules Industriels [*Nationalized industry*] [*Algeria*]   (EY)

SNVS .... Societe Nationale de Vente des Surplus   (FLAF)

SNVV .... Stichting voor de Nederlandse Vlasteelt en Vlasbewerking [*Foundation for Growing and Processing of Flax in the Netherlands*] [*Netherlands*]   (DSCA)

SNW .... Sandoway [*Myanmar*] [*Airport symbol*]   (OAG)

snw .... Selfstandige Naamwoord [*Noun*] [*Afrikaans*]

SNYS .... Seychelles National Youth Service

SNZ .... Savet za Narodno Zdravlje [*Public Health Council*]   (YU)

SNZ .... Sekretarijat za Narodno Zdravlje (SIV) [*Secretariat of Public Health*]   (YU)

SNZ .... Sprava Napravneho Zarizeni [*Correctional Facilities Directorate*]   (CZ)

SNZSP ...... Savet za Narodno Zdravlje i Socijalnu Politiku [*Council on Public Health and Social Policy*]   (YU)

SO .... Angle Horaire Sideral Origine [*Greenwich Hour Angle of Aries*] [*French*]

SO .... Austrian Air Services [*Austria*] [*ICAO designator*]   (ICDA)

SO .... Concentrated Fire   (RU)

SO .... Convergent Fire [*or Concentrated Fire*]   (BU)

SO .... Deviation Signaling   (RU)

SO .... Economic Trust   (BU)

SO .... Flank Guard, Flank Detachment   (BU)

so .... Launching [*Rocket-Firing*] Detachment   (BU)

SO .... Medical Aid Section   (RU)

SO .... SAI Ambrosini SpA [*Italy*] [*ICAO aircraft manufacturer identifier*]   (ICAO)

SO .... Saobracajno Odeljenje [*Transportation Department*]   (YU)

so .... Sauf Omission [*Omissions Excepted*] [*French*]

SO .... Savezni Odbor [*Federal Committee*]   (YU)

SO .... Savezni Organi [*Federal Organs*]   (YU)

SO .... Schienenoberkante [*Top of Rail*]   (EG)

SO .... Seasonal Servicing [*of automobiles*]   (RU)

SO .... Second Class Open [*Train ticket*]   (DCTA)

SO .... Secret Department, Secret Section   (RU)

SO .... Secteur Operationnel [*Operational Sector*]   (CL)

SO .... Security at the Halt or in Bivouac   (RU)

s/o .... Self-Propelled Cannon   (BU)

SO .... Self-Propelled Gun   (RU)

so .... Se On [*That Is*] [*Finland*]   (GPO)

SO .... Sergo Ordzhonikidze [*Locomotive series*]   (RU)

so .... Service Officiel [*On Official Service*] [*French*]

so .... Servo [*Serve*] [*Portuguese*]

So .... Seto [*Strait*] [*Japan*]   (NAU)

SO .... Siberian Department (of the Academy of Sciences, USSR)   (RU)

SO .... Siehe Oben [*See Above*] [*German*]   (GPO)

so .... Siemens Oesterreich [*Nuclear energy*] [*Austria*]   (NRCH)

SO .... Social Security   (RU)

so .... Soevereiniteitsoverdracht (Indonesie) [*Benelux*]   (BAS)

SO .... Somalia [*ANSI two-letter standard code*]   (CNC)

So .... Sondag [*Sunday*] [*Afrikaans*]

SO .... Sondrio [*Car registration plates*] [*Italian*]

s/o .... Son Ordre [*His Order*] [*French*] [*Business term*]

SO .... Sortierer [*Sorter*] [*German*]   (ADPT)

SO .... Speicherorganisation [*Memory Organization*] [*German*]   (ADPT)

SO .... Spojene Ocelarny [*United Steel Works*] [*Kladno*]   (CZ)

SO .... Sports Society   (RU)

SO .... Srpski Odbor [*Serbian Committee*]   (YU)

SO .... Standard Model, Standard Sample   (RU)

so .... Standard Purification [*of gases*]   (RU)

SO .... Statni Studijni Knihovna v Ostrave [*State Research Library in Ostrava*]   (CZ)

SO .... Statni Vedecka Knihovna v Ostrave [*State Research Library in Ostrava*]   (CZ)

SO .... Studijni Oddeleni [*Study Section*]   (CZ)

s/o .... Sua Ordem [*Your Order*] [*Portuguese*] [*Business term*]

SO .... Sudoeste [*Southwest*] [*Portuguese*]

SO .... Sudoeste [*Southwest*] [*Spanish*]

SO .... Suedosten [*Southeast*] [*German*]   (EG)

SO .... Suidoos [*Southeast*] [*Afrikaans*]

SOA .... Scandinavian Orthopaedic Association   (EA)

SOA .... Skoda Air [*Czechoslovakia*] [*ICAO designator*]   (FAAC)

SOA .... Societe Occidentale Africaine

SOA .... Societe Omnisports de l'Armee

SOA .... Soldats de l'Opposition Algerienne [*Soldiers of the Algerian Opposition*]   (AF)

SOA .... Special Olympics Australia

SOACAM ... Societe Avicole de l'Ouest Cameroun

SOACIA ... Societe Auxiliaire pour le Commerce et l'Industrie en Afrique

SOACO ..... Societe Anonyme de Constructions

SOACO ..... Societe Ouest-Africaine de Commission

SOADIP ... Societe Africaine de Diffusion et de Promotion

SOAE .... State Organization for Administration and Employment [*Iran*]   (ME)

SOAEM ..... Societe Ouest-Africaine d'Entreprises Maritimes

SOAEM-CI TRANSIT ... Societe Ouest-Africaine d'Entreprises Maritimes et de Transit en Cote d'Ivoire [*Shipping*] [*Ivory Coast*]

SOAF .... Sultan of Oman Air Force

SOAFCO ... Societe Africaine de Commerce et de Courtage

So Afr .... South Africa

SOAG .... Stichting Ontwikkeling van de Automatisering bij de Gemeenten ['s-Gravenhage]

SOAGA ..... Sindicato Obrero de Artes Graficas Autonomo [*Autonomous Trade Union of Graphic Arts Workers*] [*Dominican Republic*]   (LA)

SOAGCI .... Societe d'Affretement et de Groupage de Cote-D'Ivoire

SOAGE ...... Sindicatos de Obreros y Administrativos de General Electric [*Union of General Electric Workers*] [*Uruguay*]   (LA)

SOAGRIL ... Sociedade de Administracao Agricola Itubera Ltd. [*Brazil*]   (DSCA)

SOALCO ... Societe Nationale des Conserveries Algeriennes

SOAM .... Societe d'Oxygene et d'Acetylene de Madagascar

SOAM .... Stratiotikos Oikos tis Avtou Megaleiotitos [*His Majesty's Military Aides*] [*Greek*]   (GC)

SOAN .... Siberian Department of the Academy of Sciences, USSR   (RU)

SOAO .... North Ossetian Autonomous Oblast [*1924-1936*]   (RU)

SOAP .... Societe Ouest-Africaine de Presse

SOAS .... School of Oriental and African Studies [*University of London*]

SOASSR .... North Ossetian Autonomous Soviet Socialist Republic   (RU)

SOAT .... Public Automotive Transportation Association   (BU)

SOATO ..... Societe Africaine de Torrefaction

SOAVES ... Sociedade Avicola de Distribuicao e Abate Ltd. [*Brazil*]   (DSCA)

SOAVI ...... Sociedade Avicola Paraminense Ltd. [*Brazil*]   (DSCA)

soavt .... Coauthor   (RU)

SOB .... Lead-Covered Armored Signal Cable   (RU)

SOB .... Sanayi Odalari Birligi [*Union of Chambers of Commerce*]   (TU)

SOB .... Senior Battery Officer [*Artillery*]   (BU)

SOB .... Silly Old Bugger [*Officer over the age of 39*] [*British*]   (DSUE)

SOB .... Sluzbena Obvestila [*Official Announcements*]   (YU)

SOB .... Soviet Order of Battle   (DOMA)

SOB .... State Organization for Buildings [*Iraq*]

SOBAB ..... Societe de Bois d'Abengourou

SOBAKA ... Societe Bananiere de la Kavi

SOBAKI .... Societe Belgo-Africaine du Kivu

SOBAMAD ... Societe Bananiere de Madagascar

SOBANO ... Societe du Batelage de Nossi-Be

SOBANOA ... Societe Bananiere de la Nonoa

SOBCOT ... Societe Belge de Chirurgie Orthopedique et de Traumatologie [*Belgium*]   (SLS)

SOBECOV ... Societe de Stockage et de Commercialisation des Produits Vivriers [*Development organization*] [*Burundi*]   (EY)

SOBEFI ..... Societe Bertrand Fils

SOBEGI .... Societe Beninoise des Gaz Industries

SOBEK ...... Societe Beninoise du Kenaf

SOBELAIR ... Societe Belge de Transports Pan Air [*Airline*] [*Belgium*]
SOBEMAC ... Societe Beninoise des Materiaux de Construction [*Beninese Construction Material Company*] [*Cotonou*]   (AF)
SOBENA... Sociedade Brasileira de Engenharia Naval [*Brazilian Naval Engineering Society*]   (LA)
SOBEPALH ... Societe Beninoise de Palmier a Huile [*Beninese Oil Palm Company*] [*Porto-Novo*]   (AF)
sobes .... Social Security   (RU)
SOBETEX ... Societe Beninoise des Textiles [*Beninese Textile Company*]   (AF)
SOBIASCO ... Societe Bitume et de l'Asphalt du Congo
SOBIL .... Sociedade de Administracoes de Bens e Mobiliarios Lda.
sobir .... Collective Noun   (RU)
SOBOA ... Societe des Brasseries de l'Ouest Africain
SOBOCA... Societe des Bois du Sud Ouest Cameroun
SOBOCAM ... Societe de Conditionnement, de Fabrication, et de Transformation de Boissons du Cameroun
SOBOCI.... Societe des Boissons Hygieniques de la Cote-D'Ivoire
SOBOCO .. Societe de Bonnetterie et Confection Dakaroise
SOBOFRI ... Societe Bobolaise de Friperie
SOBOGAZ ... Societe des Boissons Gazeuses du Benin
SOBOHA .. Societe des Bois de la Hana
SOBOMA ... Societe Bonnetiere Malagasy
SOBOMA ... Societe des Bois de la Manzan
SOBOMA ... Societe des Boissons de Mauritanie
SOBP........ Sentral Organisasi Buruh Pantjasila [*Central Organization of Pantjasila Labor*] [*Indonesia*]
sobr .... Collection   (RU)
SOBRABAND ... Societe des Brasseries du Bandundu [*Zaire*]   (IMH)
SOBRACON ... Sociedade Brasileira de Comando Numerico e Automatizacao Industrial [*Brazil*]   (EAIO)
SOBRADO ... Societe des Brasseries du Dahomey
SOBRAGA ... Societe des Brasseries du Gabon
SOBRAGUI ... Societe des Brasseries de Guinee
SOBRAT ... Societe des Brasseries du Tchad
SOBRI .... Sentral Organisasi Buruh Republik Indonesia [*Republic of Indonesia Federation of Workers Organizations*]   (IN)
SOBRICI... Societe de Briqueteries de Cote-D'Ivoire
SOBRIMA ... Societe des Briqueteries du Mali
sobr soch ... Collected Works   (RU)
SobrUzak ... Collection of Laws and Decrees of the Workers' and Peasants' Government of the RSFSR   (RU)
SOBSI .... Sentral Organisasi Buruh Seluruh Indonesia [*Central All-Indonesia Workers' Organization*]
sobst izd ..... Private Publication   (BU)
sobstv .... Proper, Properly, Strictly   (RU)
SOBUMINES ... Societe Burundaise des Mines
SOBV........ Svaz Obcanu Bez Vyznani [*Union of Citizens without Religious Affiliation*]   (CZ)
Soc.............. Chambre Sociale [*French*]
SOC .... Secundaria Obrera-Campesina [*Workers and Peasants Secondary School*] [*Cuba*]   (LA)
Soc.............. Socialisme [*Socialism*] [*Benelux*]   (BAS)
SOC .... Socialist Objectives Committee [*Australian Labor Party*]
Soc............. Sociedad [*Society, Company*] [*Spanish*] [*Business term*]
Soc............. Sociedade [*Society, Company*] [*Portuguese*] [*Business term*]
SOC .... Sociedad Odontologica de Concepcion [*Chile*]   (SLS)
Soc.............. Societe [*French*]   (FLAF)
Soc.............. Society   (EECI)
SOC .... Solar Observers Society [*Poland*]   (EAIO)
SOC .... Solidaritat Obrera da Catalunya [*Workers Solidarity of Catalonia*] [*Spanish*]   (WER)
SOC .... Solo [*Indonesia*] [*Airport symbol*]   (OAG)
SOC .... Southern Oceans Survey [*ISOS*]   (MSC)
SOC .... Superacion Obrera-Campesina [*Workers and Peasants Educational Improvement*] [*Cuba*]   (LA)
SOC .... Surinaams Olympisch Comite [*Suriname Olympic Committee*] [*Suriname*]   (EAIO)
SOC .... Swiss Olympic Committee   (EAIO)
SOC .... Syrian Olympic Committee   (EAIO)
SOC .... Systeme d'Ordinateurs Connectes [*French*]   (ADPT)
SOCA .... Cayenne/Rochambeau [*French Guiana*] [*ICAO location identifier*]   (ICLI)
SOCA .... Societe Commerciale Africaine
SOCA .... Societe de Carrosserie Abidjanaise
SOCA .... Societe des Compteurs Africains
SOCA .... Societe Olympic Centrafricaine pour le Diamant et Metaux Precieux
SOCA .... State Organisation for Civil Aviation [*Iraq*]
SOCAB..... Societe Agricole du Bandama
SOCAB..... Societe Camerounaise de Bonneterie
SOCAB..... Societe de Construction Automobile du Benin
SOCABAIL ... Societe Camerounaise de Credit Bail
SOCABEX ... Societe d'Application des Bois Exotiques
SOCABO... Societe Camerounaise des Boulangers
SOCABU... Societe d'Assurances du Burundi [*Bujumbura, Burundi*]

SOCACAO ... Societe Camerounaise de Cacaos
SOCACENTRO ... Sociedad de Canicultores del Centro [*Venezuela*]   (DSCA)
SOCACI .... Societe Commerciale et Agricole de la Cote-D'Ivoire
SOCACIG ... Societe Centrafricaine de Cigarettes
SOCACOLIE ... Societe Camerounaise de Commerce Local d'Importation et d'Exportation
SOCACOTRA ... Societe Camerounaise de Commerce et de Transport
SOCAD ..... Societe Camerounaise de Dietetique et d'Alimentation
SOCAD ..... Societe de Commercialisation et de Credit Agricole du Dahomey
SOCADA... Societe Centrafricaine de Developpement Agricole [*Agricultural development organization*] [*Central African Republic*]
SOCADE... Societe Camerounaise de Developpement
SOCADEM ... Societe Camerounaise d'Emballages Metalliques
SOCADI.... Societe Centrafricaine de Diamant Industriel
SOCADIESEL ... Societe Camerounaise du Diesel
SOCADIMO ... Sociedad de Canicultores del Distrito Moran [*Venezuela*]   (DSCA)
SOCADIMP ... Societe Abidjanaise d'Importation
SOCADIS ... Societe Camerounaise de Distribution
SOCAF...... Societe Cinematographique de l'Ouest Africain
SOCAF...... Societe Commerciale Africaine [*Ivory Coast*]
SOCAFER ... Societe Camerounaise de Plomberie et de Ferronerie
SOCAFIC ... Societe Camerounaise de Fournitures pour l'Industrie et les Constructions
SOCAFIEX ... Societe Commerciale Africaine d'Importation et d'Exportation
SOCAFLI ... Societe Africaine de Librairie "Les Heures Claires"
SOCAFRIC ... Societe Camerounaise de Representation Industrielle et Commerciale
SOCAFRICA ... Societe Africaine d'Achats
SOCAFROID-Ivoire ... Societe Africaine du Froid Cote-D'Ivoire
SOCAGEL ... Societe Gabonaise de Cellulose
SOCAGI.... Societe Centrafricaine des Gaz Industriels
SOCAHIT ... Societe Camerounaise Hoteliere, Immobiliere, et Touristique
SOCAHO ... Societe Camerounaise Hoteliere
SOCAJU ... Sociedade Comercial e Industrial de Caju
SOCAL...... Sociedad de Cultivos Agricolas Limitada   (COL)
SOCAL...... Sociedade de Calcado [*Shoe factory*] [*Cape Verde*]
SOCAL...... Societe des Conserves Alimentaires
SOCALDET ... Societe Algerienne de Developpement Touristique
SOCALDEX ... Societe Algerienne de Developpement et d'Expansion
SOCALIMINES ... Societe Mixte Centrafricano-Arab-Libyenne des Mines [*Joint Central African-Arab-Libyan Mining Company*]   (AF)
SOCALTRA ... Societe Alsacienne d'Etudes et Travaux [*France*]   (PDAA)
SOCAM .... Societe Camerounaise de Menuiserie
SOCAM .... Societe Commerciale Africaine d'Importation
SOCAM .... Societe des Conserves Alimentaires du Mali
SOCAMA ... Societe Agricole de Mandigou [*Congo*]   (DSCA)
SOCAMAC ... Societe Camerounaise de Manutention et d'Acconage   (EY)
SOCAMBOIS ... Societe Camerounaise des Bois
SOCAMCAP ... Societe Camerounaise d'Elevage et de Capture d'Animaux Sauvages
SOCAMCO ... Societe Camerounaise de Conserveries
SOCAME ... Societe Camerounaise des Engrais
SOCAMEC ... Societe Camerounaise d'Expansion de la Culture
SOCAMETA ... Societe Camerounaise de Construction Metallique
SOCAMEX ... Societe Camerounaise d'Exportation
SOCANA .. Societe Camerounaise de Navigation
SOCANA .. Societe des Plantations de Cafe Nana de Carnot
Soc Ane ...... Societe Anonyme [*Stock Company*] [*French*] [*Business term*]   (GPO)
SOCANIGER ... Societe des Allumettes du Niger
SOCAPA ... Societe Camerounaise de Produits Africains
SOCAPA ... Societe Camerounaise des Anciens Ets. Joseph Paris
SOCAPA ... Societe Camerounaise pour le Developpement de l'Automobile
SOCAPALM ... Societe Camerounaise de Palmeraies
SOCAPAR ... Societe Camerounaise des Anciens Ets. Joseph Paris
SOCAPE ... Societe Camerounaise de Presse et d'Edition
SOCAPET ... Societe Camerounaise des Petroles
SOCAPROD ... Societe Camerounaise de Production et de Distribution de Boissons Hygieniques
SOCAPS.... Societe Camerounaise des Produits Shell
SOCAR...... Societe Camerounaise d'Assurances et de Reassurances
SOCAR...... Societe Camerounaise de Carrosserie
SOCARAGUA ... Sociedad Canicultores del Estado Aragua [*Venezuela*]   (DSCA)
SOCAREC ... Societe Africaine de Rectification
Soc aResp Lim ... La Societe a Responsabilite Limitee   (FLAF)
SOCARET ... Societe Camerounaise de Reparations et Transports
SOCARMAR ... Sociedade de Cargas e Descargas Maritimas, SARC [*Maritime Loading and Unloading Society*] [*Portuguese*]   (WER)
SOCARP ... Societe Commerciale Agricole du Rip [*Senegal*]
SOCARSEL ... Societe Camerounaise de Raffinage de Sel
SOCAS ...... Sociedades de Cooperacion Agricola [*Agricultural Cooperation Associations*] [*Chile*]   (LA)

SOCAS...... Societe de Conserves Alimentaires du Senegal
SOCASE ... Societe Commerciale Agricole Senegalaise
SOCASEP ... Societe Camerounaise de Sepultures et Transports Speciaux
SOCAT...... Societe Cherifienne d'Articles Transformes
SOCATCI ... Societe des Caoutchoucs de Cote-D'Ivoire
SOCATEM ... Societe Camerounaise de Tresses d'Eponges Menageres
SOCATEX ... Societe Camerounaise de Confection et de Bonneterie
SOCATI .... Societe Centrafricaine de Telecommunications Internationales
SOCATOUR ... Societe Camerounaise de Tourisme   (EY)
SOCATRAF ... Societe Centrafricaine de Transports Fluviaux [*Central African Republic*]   (EY)
SOCATRAL ... Societe Camerounaise de Transformation de l'Aluminium
SOCATUC ... Societe Camerounaise de Tuyauteries et de Cordes en Plastique
SOCATUR ... Sociedad de Canicultores del Turbio [*Venezuela*]   (DSCA)
SOCAVER ... Societe Camerounaise de Verrerie
Soc BelgeEtudes ... Societe Belge d'Etudes et d'Expansion [*Belgium*]   (BAS)
SOCC........ Solidaridad Obrera Cristiana de Cataluna [*Christian Workers Solidarity of Catalonia*] [*Spanish*]   (WER)
SOCCA...... Societe Camerounaise de Credit Automobile
SOCCDE... Societe Commerciale Camerounaise pour le Developpement et l'Economie
SOCCONAT ... Societe Cambodgienne de Consignation de Navires et de Transit [*Cambodian Ship Consignment and Transit Company*]   (CL)
SOCCP...... Societe de l'Ouest Cameroun pour le Commerce et la Photographie
Socd........... Sociedad [*Society, Company*] [*Spanish*] [*Business term*]
Socdem....... Socialni Demokrat [*Social Democrat*]   (CZ)
SOCDYL.... Sarawak Overseas Chinese Democratic Youth League   (ML)
SOCEA...... Societe Eau et Assainissement
SOCECO... Societe Camerounaise d'Etudes et de Constructions
SOCECO... Societe Senegalaise de Commerce
SOCECOD ... Societe Senegalaise pour le Commerce et le Developpement
SOCECOM ... Societe Commerciale de Keur Soce
Soc Ec RAdv ... Sociaal-Economische-Raad-Adviezen [*Benelux*]   (BAS)
Soc EcWetg ... Sociaal Economische Wetgeving [*Benelux*]   (BAS)
SOCEF ...... Societe de Construction et d'Exploitation des Installations Frigorifiques [*Refrigeration Plant Construction and Operation Company*]   (AF)
SOCEFI..... Societe Centrafricaine d'Exploitations Forestieres et Industrielles
SOCEI...... Societe Commerciale Camerounaise d'Exportation et d'Importation
SOCEL ...... Sociedade Industrial de Celuloses [*Industrial Society of Cellulose*] [*Portuguese*]   (WER)
Soc enComm par A ... Societe en Commandite par Actions   (FLAF)
SOCEPA ... Societe Anonyme d'Etudes et de Participations Immobilieres
SOCEPAR ... Sociedad de Celadores Particulares [*Colombia*]   (COL)
SOCEPAR ... Societe Anonyme d'Etudes et de Participations Immobilieres
SOCEPPAR ... Sociedade Cerealista Exportadora de Produtos Paranaenses [*Brazil*]   (DSCA)
SOCERAM ... Societe Malgache de Ceramique
SOCETEC ... Societe d'Etudes Techniques
SOCETODAK ... Societe d'Etudes du Thon Dakarois
SOCEXPLAN ... Societe d'Exploitation de Plantations Societe Socfinol
SOCFEIC ... Societe Khmero-Francaise d'Entreprises Industrielles et Commerciales [*Cambodian-French Industrial and Commercial Enterprises Company*]   (CL)
Soc Gen...... Societe Generale Australia
SOCh......... Secret Operations Unit   (RU)
soch........... Works [*Bibliography*]   (RU)
SOCHAMAD ... Societe Anonyme de Confection Malgache
SOCHEGIC ... Societe Cherifienne de Gestion Industrielle et Commerciale
SOCHETI ... Societe Cherifienne d'Etudes et d'Entreprises
SOCHOT .. Societe Hoteliere du Cambodge [*Hotel Company of Cambodia*]   (CL)
SOCI......... Societe de l'Ouest de la Cote-D'Ivoire
SOCI......... State Organisation for Construction Industries [*Iraq*]
SOCIA...... Societe Commerciale Industrielle et Agricole
SOCIA....... Societe pour l'Industrie Atomique [*Nuclear energy*] [*French*]   (NRCH)
SOCIABE ... Societe Agricole de M'Be
SOCIACI... Societe Commerciale et Industrielle Africaine de la Cote-D'Ivoire
SOCIAGRI ... Societe Ivoirienne d'Expansion Agricole
SOCIAL .... Sociedade Comercial, Industrial, e de Agencias Limitada
SOCIBEMA ... Societe des Ciments et Betons Manufactures
SOCICA .... Societe Cinematographique Africaine
SOCICO.... Societe Immobiliere de la Communaute
SOCICO.... Societe Immobiliere et Commerciale du Congo
SOCIDA.... Societe Commerciale et Industrielle Dakaroise
SOCIDIS... Societe Ivoirienne d'Importation et de Distribution
SOCIE....... Societe Commerciale d'Import Export [*Dakar*]
SOCIEM ... Societe de Commerce General d'Importation et d'Exportation de Mauritanie
SOCIEP..... Societe d'Importation et d'Exportation des Produits
SOCIFRANCE ... Societe Immobiliere Francaise
SOCIGA.... Societe de Cigarettes du Gabon

SOCIGA.... Societe des Ciments du Gabon [*Cement producer*] [*Gabon*]   (IMH)
SOCIGAB ... Societe Commerciale et Industrielle au Gabon
SOCIGLACE ... Societe des Glacieres d'Abidjan
SOCIM...... Societe Centrafricaine d'Investissements Immobiliers
SOCIM...... Societe Commerciale et Industrielle de Mauritanie [*Mauritanian Commercial and Industrial Company*]   (AF)
SOCIMA... Societe des Ciments du Mali
SOCIMAD ... Societe Cinema de Madagascar
SOCIMAF ... Societe Commerciale et Mobiliere de l'Afamba
SOCIMAT ... Societe des Ciments et Materiaux
SOCIMEX ... Societe d'Importation et d'Exportation de l'Ocean Indien
Sociol .... Sociologia [*Sociology*] [*Portuguese*]
SOCIP .... Societe Cristal Pailin SA [*Pailin Crystal Company, Inc.*] [*Cambodia*]   (CL)
SOCIPAR ... Societe Ivoirienne de Participation
SOCIPEC ... Societe Ivoirienne de Participations Economiques
SOCIPECHE ... Societe Cote Ivoirienne de Peche
SOCIPRA ... Societe Industrielle de Peinture et Ravalement
SOCIR...... Societe Congolaise Italienne de Raffinage
Soc Is .... Society Islands   (BARN)
Soc Isl .... Society Islands
SOCITAS ... Societe Ivoirienne de Textiles Artificiels et Synthetiques
SOCITEL ... Societe Ivoirienne des Telephones
SOCITO.... Societe Industrielle Togolaise
SOCITOUR ... Societe Casamancaise d'Investissement Touristique
SOCITRABAR ... Societe Commerciale et Industrielle des Transports de Banjoun Reunis
SOCITRACAM ... Societe Camerounaise Interprofessionnelle pour la Fourniture des Traverses et de Bois Debites au Transcamerounais
SOCIVEL ... Societe Ivoirienne de Vetements du Luxe
SOCIVER ... Societe Ivoirienne de Verrerie
SOCIVIM ... Societe Ivoirienne d'Importation
SocK.......... Socialisticno Kmetijstvo [*Socialist Agriculture*] [*Ljubljana A periodical*]   (YU)
SOCLEEN ... Society for Clean Environment [*India*]   (PDAA)
SocM.......... Socialisticna Misel [*Socialist Thought*] [*Ljubljana A periodical*]   (YU)
SOCMA .... Societe Commerciale de Materiel Automobile [*Automobile Equipment Company*] [*Cambodia*]   (CL)
Soc Mbl...... Sociaal Maandblad [*Benelux*]   (BAS)
SOCMEQ ... Societe Cambodgienne de Materiels Electriques et de Quincaillerie [*Cambodian Electrical Equipment and Hardware Company*]   (CL)
SOCO .... Societe Commerciale et Hoteliere du Gabon
SOCOAF... Societe Cinematographique de l'Ouest Africain
SOCOAF... Societe Commerciale Africaine du Sine Saloum
SOCOAGRO ... Sociedad de Construcciones y Operaciones Agropecuarias, SA [*Agriculture and Livestock Construction and Operations Association, Inc.*] [*Chile*]   (LA)
SOCOB ..... Societe Commerciale des Woulad Boussaba
SOCOB ..... Societe Cooperative Ouvriere de Batiments de Bamako
SOCOBA... Societe Commerciale du Baol
SOCOBA... Societe Commerciale Voltaique Raymond et Abid Bachour
SOCOBA... Societe Congolaise du Batiment
SOCOBA... Societe de Construction de Batiments [*Gabon*]
SOCOBACAM ... Societe Commerciale du Baleng du Cameroun
SOCOBAM ... Societe Commerciale du Mbam
SOCOBANQUE ... Societe Congolaise de Banque
SOCOBAO ... Societe Commerciale de Balumbi-Ouest
SOCOBE... Societe Commerciale du Benin
SOCOBIS ... Societe Confiserie et Biscuitiere
SOCOBLE ... Societe Cooperative de Ble de Tunisie
SOCOBO .. Societe Cooperative de Bonoua
SOCOBOD ... Societe Commerciale Bock-Dieuf
SOCOBOIS ... Societe Congolaise des Bois
SOCOBOM ... Societe Commerciale Mauritanienne Boussahab et Mouloud
SOCOC ..... Societe Commerciale de l'Ouest Cameroun
SOCOCANIC ... Sociedad Cooperativa Anonima de Cafeteros de Nicaragua [*Managua*]   (LAA)
SOCOCI.... Societe Commerciale de la Cote-D'Ivoire
SOCOCIM ... Societe Ouest-Africaine des Ciments [*West African Cement Company*] [*Senegal*]   (AF)
SOCOCO .. Sociedad Colombiana de Construcciones Ltda. [*Colombia*]   (COL)
SOCOCOM ... Compania Nacional de Combustibles SA [*Colombia*]   (COL)
SOCODA ... Sociedad Constructora Ltda. [*Colombia*]   (COL)
SOCODAK ... Societe Commerciale Dakaroise
SOCODESE ... Societe Commerciale et de Decorticage du Senegal
SOCODEXCO ... Sociedad Colombiana de Expansion Comercial [*Colombia*]   (COL)
SOCODI.... Societe Commerciale de Distribution
SOCODI.... Societe Congolaise de Disques
SOCODIA ... Societe Commerciale pour le Developpement Industriel en Afrique

SOCODIM ... Societe Commerciale d'Importation
SOCODIMA ... Societe de Construction et Distribution de Materiaux
SOCODROG ... Societe de Courtage pour la Droguerie
SOCOFADIS ... Societe Commerciale Famille Dimelente du Senegal
SOCOFAM ... Sociedad Colombiana de Fabricantes Mecanicos [*Duitama-Boyaca*] (COL)
SOCOFAOCAM ... Societe Commerciale Familiale de l'Ouest-Cameroun
SOCOFEL ... Sociedade Comercial de Ferragens Limitada
SOCOFER ... Societe Coloniale du Fer
SOCOFFA ... Societe Commerciale et Financiere Franco-Africaine [*Franco-African Trading and Finance Company*] (AF)
SOCOFI.... Societe Commerciale Financiere et Industrielle
SOCOFI.... Societe Commerciale Franco-Ivoirienne
SOCOFI.... Societe J. Corsetti et Fils
SOCOFIAM ... Societe Cooperative Forestiere Industrielle et Agricole de la Marahoue
SOCOFIDE ... Societe Congolaise de Financement du Developpement [*Congo*]
SOCOFOA ... Societe Commerciale Francaise de l'Ouest Africain
SOCOFOR ... Societe Commerciale et Forestiere du Saloum
SOCOFRA ... Societe Commerciale Francaise
SOCOFRACIM ... Societe Commerciale Franco-Africaine des Ciments
SOCOFRALE ... Societe de Courtage de la France Australe
SOCOFRAN ... Societe du Congo Francais
SOCOFROID ... Societe Congolaise de Conservation et de Congelation
SOCOGABON ... Societe Commerciale et Hoteliere du Gabon
SOCOGECI ... Societe de Constructions du Genie Civil
SOCOGEDA ... Societe de Construction Generale de Danane
SOCOGEL ... Societe de Commerce General
SOCOGIF ... Societe de Constructions Giraudel Freres
SOCOGIM ... Societe de Construction et de Gestion Immobiliere [*Benin*] (EY)
SOCOGIM ... Societe de Construction et de Gestion Immobiliere de Mauritanie
SOCOGRASAS ... Sociedad Colombiana de Grasas Vegetales Ltda. [*Barranquilla*] (COL)
SOCOGUI ... Sociedad Colonial de Guinea
SOCOIMA ... Societe Commerciale et Industrielle du Mali
SOCOIMPORT ... Societe Commerciale d'Importation du Sine Saloum
SOCOINAF ... Societe des Commercants Industriels et Agriculteurs Africains
SOCOINCO ... Ingenieros Constructores Contratistas [*Colombia*] (COL)
SOCOL...... Societe de Construction d'Entreprises Generales [*Belgium*] (PDAA)
SOCOLA... Societe Commerciale de Lamina
SOCOLAG ... Societe Commerciale du Laghem
SOCOLDA ... Sociedad Colombiana de Administradores de Empresas [*Colombian Managers Society*] (LA)
SOCOLETRA ... Societe Coloniale d'Etudes et de Travaux
SOCOLEX ... Societe Coloniale d'Expansion Economique
SOCOLOR ... Sociedad Colombiana de Orquideologia [*Colombia*] (DSCA)
SOCOM.... Societe Commerciale du Mungo
SOCOMA ... Societe Commerciale de Keur-Madiabel
SOCOMA ... Societe Commerciale de la Mauritanie
SOCOMA ... Societe Commerciale du Mayumba
SOCOMA ... Societe Commerciale Marocaine
SOCOMA ... Societe des Conserves du Mali
SOCOMAB ... Societe Congolaise de Manutention des Bois [*Congolese Company for the Administration of Forests*] (AF)
SOCOMAF ... Societe Commerciale Africaine
SOCOMAGAZ ... Societe Commerciale et Agricole d'Azaguie
SOCOMAL ... Societe Commerciale d'Alimentation
SOCOMAN ... Societe Commerciale et Miniere pour l'Afrique du Nord [*Morocco*]
SOCOMAR ... Societe Commerciale et Maritime
SOCOMASS ... Societe de Construction, Montage, et Appareillage de Station Services
SOCOMATHA ... Societe Commerciale Mauritanienne Thaofique
SOCOMAUM ... Societe Commerciale Mauritanienne Mohamed Moloud et Cie.
SOCOME ... Societe de Constructions Metalliques, Chad
SOCOMEC ... Societe Cooperative Mecanographique
SOCOMELA ... Societe de Constructions Metalliques
SOCOMELEC-Ivoire ... Societe Commerciale de Materiel Electrique [*Ivory Coast*]
SOCOMENA ... Societe du Complexe Industriel et Maritime de Menzel Bourguiba [*Morocco*]
SOCOMENA ... Societe Tunisienne Commerciale, Mecanique, et Maritime [*Tunisian Commercial, Mechanical, and Maritime Company*] (AF)
SOCOMETAL ... Sociedad de Construcciones Metalicas, SA [*Metal Construction Company, Inc.*] [*Chile*] (LA)
SOCOMETAL ... Societe de Constructions Metalliques
SOCOMETRA ... Societe Commerciale d'Etudes et de Travaux
SOCOMI... Societe Commerciale de Materiel Industriel
SOCOMIA ... Societe Commerciale pour l'Equipement Industriel et Agricole, Madagascar

SOCOMO ... Societe Commerciale de l'Oubangui
SOCOMO ... Societe Commerciale de Morondava
SOCOMO ... Societe Commerciale Moderne
SOCOMOL ... Sociedade Comercial de Mocambique Limitada
SOCOMOR ... Societe Commerciale Moramangaise [*Malagasy*]
SOCONA.. Societe de Constructions Navales
SOCONAF ... Societe Commerciale Nord-Africaine [*Morocco*]
SOCONDOF ... Societe Commerciale de N'Doffane [*Senegal*]
SOCONOCA ... Societe de Constructions du Nord Cameroun
SOCONOMAR ... Societe Commerciale d'Affretements Maritimes
SOCONORD ... Societe Commerciale du Nord
SOCONOVILLE ... Societe Commerciale Nouvelle de Treichville
SOCONTI ... Sociedad Colombiana de Contadores Publicos Titulados [*Colombia*] (COL)
SOCONY .. Societe Commerciale du Nyong
SOCOODER ... Societe Cooperative de Developpement Rural
SOCOODJALO ... Societe Commerciale Ondona du Dja et Lobo
SOCOOPED ... Societes Cooperatives d'Epargne et de Developpement
SOCOPAF ... Societe Commerciale de Produits Africains
SOCOPAL ... Societe des Conserves des Poissons a l'Huile [*Tunisia*]
SOCOPAN ... Sociedad Constructora de Pavimentos America [*Colombia*] (COL)
SOCOPAP ... Societe Commerciale de Papeterie [*Commercial Paper Company*] [*French*] (WER)
SOCOPASS ... Societe Commerciale de Passy [*Senegal*]
SOCOPECRO ... Societe Commerciale de Peche au Crocodile
SOCOPEIN ... Societe Commerciale de Peintures
SOCOPEINT ... Societe Congolaise de Peinture
SOCOPETROL ... Societe Congolaise d'Entreposage de Produits Petroliers
SOCOPIM ... Societe Commerciale pour l'Industrie au Maroc
SOCOPRE ... Societe Senegalaise de Commercialisation des Produits de l'Elevage
SOCOPRISE ... Societe Africaine d'Entreprises Industrielles et Immobilieres
SOCOPRO ... Societe de Commerce et de Produits
SOCOPSA ... Societe Cooperative des Planteurs de Saa
SOCORA... Sociedad de Comercializacion de la Reforma Agraria [*Agrarian Reform Marketing Association*] [*Chile*] (LA)
SOCORAM ... Societe de Constructions Radio-Electriques du Mali
SOCORAP ... Societe de Cocos Rapes
SOCOREP ... Societe Congolaise de Recherche de Petrole
SOCORINA ... Societe de Constructions et de Reparations Industrielles et Navales
SOCORP... Sociedad Colombiana de Ralaciones Publicas [*Barranquilla*] (COL)
SOCORWA ... Societe de Confection du Rwanda
SOCOSA... Societe du Commerce Sarakole
SOCOSAC ... Societe Commerciale et Industrielle du Sac [*Senegal*]
SOCOSAL ... Societe Commerciale du Saloum [*Senegal*]
SOCOSE... Societe de Constructions Senegalaises
SOCOTA... Societe Commerciale de Tananarive
SOCOTA... Societe Commerciale de Transactions
SOCOTCHAD ... Societe Commerciale du Tchad
SOCOTEC ... Societe de Controle Technique et d'Expertise de la Construction
SOCOTEIN ... Sociedad Colombiana de Tecnicos Industriales [*Colombia*] (COL)
SOCOTEL ... Societe Mixte pour le Developpement de la Technique de la Commutation dans le Domaine des Telecommunications [*France*] (PDAA)
SOCOTEX ... Societe de Commercialisation des Textiles [*Tunisia*]
SOCOTIC ... Societe Commerciale de Transports et d'Importation au Cameroun
SOCOTO .. Societe Commerciale du Togo
SOCOTOB ... Societe Commerciale Tournebize
SOCOTOU ... Societe Commerciale de Toumodi
SOCOTRAM ... Sociedade de Comercializacao e Transformacao de Madeira [*Lumber Processing and Marketing Company*] (AF)
SOCOTRAN ... Societe de Compatibilite Transit Gestion Divers [*Senegal*]
SOCOTRANS ... Societe Congolaise de Transports [*Riverway transport company*] [*Congo*]
SOCOTRAV ... Societe Cooperative des Transporteurs Voltaiques
SOCOVACK ... Societe Commerciale de Vack Ngouna [*Senegal*]
SOCOVI.... Societe Commerciale Vivriere du Mungo
SOCOVIA ... Societe Comorienne des Viandes [*The Comoros*] [*Commercial firm*] (EY)
SOCOVIAS ... Sociedad Constructora de Vias [*Colombia*] (COL)
SOCOWAG ... Societe Commerciale Wague Freres & Cie.
SOCPA...... Societe Congolaise de Produits Alimentaires
SOCRAA... Societe de Commerce et de Representation Automobile et Assurances
SOCRARROZ ... Sociedad de Cultivos y Recoleccion de Arroz Ltda. [*Neiva*] (COL)
SOCRAT ... Societe de Constructions Radiotelephoniques [*French*]
SOCRATAL ... Societe Camerounaise pour la Transformation de l'Aluminium

SOCREC ... Societe de Constructions, Representations, et Etudes du Cambodge [*Cambodian Construction, Sales, and Studies Company*] (CL)

SOCREDO ... Societe pour le Credit et le Developpement en Oceanie [*Commercial bank*] [*French Polynesia*] (EY)

SocStandp ... Socialistische Standpunten [*Benelux*] (BAS)

SOCTROPIC ... Societe Khmere des Cultures Tropicales [*Cambodian Tropical Crop Company*] (CL)

SOCUMA ... Societe des Mines de Cuivre de Mauritanie

SOCUTCHAD ... Societe Sucriere du Tchad

Soc Verz ..... Sociale Verzekering [*Benelux*] (BAS)

SOCZOO .. Sociedad Cubana de Zoologia [*Cuba*] (EAIO)

SOD .... Sekondere Onderwysdiploma [*Secondary Education Diploma*] [*Afrikaans*]

SOD .... Skholi Opliton Diavivaseon [*Enlisted Men's Signal Corps School*] [*Greek*] (GC)

SOD .... Societe d'Etudes pour l'Obtention du Deuterium [*Nuclear energy*] [*French*] (NRCH)

SOD .... State Organization for Dams [*Iraq*]

SOD .... Studencki Osrodek Dyskusyjny [*Students' Discussion Center*] (POL)

SOD .... Studiekring voor Documentatie en Administratieve Organisatie der Overheid ['s-Gravenhage]

SOD .... Synchronous Single-Phase Motor (RU)

SODACA ... Societe Dahomeenne de Credit Automobile

SODACA-LITIME ... Societe de Developpement et d'Approvisionnement du Canton d'Akposso-Litime

SODACAP ... Societe de Distribution d'Articles en Caoutchouc et Plastiques

SODACI .... Societe Dahomeenne Cinematographique

SODACO .. Societe Dahomeenne de Comptabilite

SODACOM ... Societe Dahomeenne de Commerce

SODACOM ... Societe Dakaroise de Constructions Metalliques

SODACOT ... Societe Dahomeenne de Consignation et de Transit

SODACRUS ... Societe Dahomeenne de Crustaces

SODAF ...... Societe Dahomeenne d'Ananas et Fruits

SODAF ...... Somali Democratic Action Front (AF)

SODAFE ... Societe pour le Developpement de l'Afrique Equatoriale

SODAGA .. Societe Dakaroise des Boissons Gazeuses

SODAGA .. Societe Generale d'Approvisionnement du Dahomey

SODAGRI ... Societe de Developpement Agricole et Industriel du Senegal [*Agricultural and Industrial Development Agency of Senegal*]

SODAI .... Societe Dahomeenne pour le Developpement Industriel et Commercial

SODAIC .... Societe Dahomeenne pour le Developpement de l'Industrie et du Commerce

SODAICA ... Societe de Developpement Agricole et Industriel de la Casamanca

SODAK ..... Societe Dahomeenne Agricole et Industrielle du Kenaf

SODAK ..... Societe Dakaroise de Negoce

SODAL ...... Societe de Diffusion d'Articles de Luxe

SODAMETRO ... Societe Dahomeenne de Messageries et de Transports Routiers

SODAMI ... Societe Dahomeenne de Minoterie

SODAP ...... Synergatikos Organismos Diatheseos Ambelourgikon Proiondon [*Vine Products Cooperative Marketing Union Ltd.*] (GC)

SODAPE ... Joao Dario Agropecuaria Ltd. [*Brazil*] (DSCA)

SODAPEC ... Societe Dahomeenne de Peintures et Colorants

SODA-PECHE ... Societe Dahomeenne de Peche

SODA-PECHE ... Societe Dakaroise de Peche

SODA-PLASTICA ... Societe Dahomeenne de Plastique

SODAS ...... Sodyum Sanayii Anonim Sirketi [*Sodium Industry Corporation*] [*Ankara*] (TU)

SODASEL ... Societe Dahomeenne de Sel

SODATEX ... Societe Dahomeenne de Textiles

SODATOURISME ... Societe d'Equipement et d'Exploitation Hoteliere et Touristique du Dahomey

SODATRA ... Societe Dakaroise de Transit

SODB .... Sdruzeni pro Odbyt Dehtovych Barviv [*Association for Marketing of Aniline Dyes*] (CZ)

SODEA ..... Societe de Developpement Agricole [*Agricultural Development Company*] [*Rabat, Morocco*] (EY)

SODE(A) ... Synergatikos Organismos Diatheseos Esperidoeidon (Ammokhostos) [*Famagusta Citrus Fruit Cooperative Marketing Union*] (GC)

SODEAM ... Societe pour le Developpement de l'Electricite en Afrique et a Madagascar

SODEBATEL ... Societe de Developpement pour le Batiment et l'Electricite

SODEBLE ... Societe de Developpement pour la Culture et la Transformations du Ble [*Cameroon*]

SODEC ...... Societe de Decorticage [*Senegal*]

SODECA ... Societe pour le Developpement de l'Elevage et des Cultures de l'Alaotra [*Malagasy*]

SODECAO ... Societe de Developpement du Cacao [*Cameroon*]

SODECCO ... Societe de Developpement Regional-Centre [*France*]

SODECI .... Societe de Distribution d'Eau de la Cote-D'Ivoire

SODECO .. Societe Dakaroise d'Entreprises et de Constructions

SODECO .. Societe pour le Developpement du Commerce

SODECOTON ... Societe de Developpement du Coton [*Cameroon*]

SODEFEL ... Societe pour le Developpement de la Production des Fruits et Legumes [*Company for the Development of Fruit and Vegetable Production*] [*Ivory Coast*] (AF)

SODEFITEX ... Societe de Developpement des Fibres Textiles

SODEFOR ... Societe pour le Developpement des Plantations Forestieres [*Forest Cultivation Development Company*] [*Ivory Coast*] (AF)

SODEFRAMA ... Societe des Echanges Franco-Marocaines

SODEGBESS ... Societe de Developpement et de Gestion des Sites de Sali

SODEGIC ... Societe d'Entreprises Generales Industrielles et Commerciales

SODEINCO ... Societe de Developpement Industriel et Commercial

SODELAC ... Societe de Developpement du Lac Chad

SODELAC ... Societe d'Exploitation du Lac Tchad

SODELEC ... Societe d'Electrification et de Canalisation

SODE(M) ... Synergatikos Organismos Diatheseos Esperidoeidon (Morfou) [*Morfou Citrus Fruit Cooperative Marketing Union*] (GC)

SODEMA ... Societe de Credit pour le Developpement de la Martinique (EY)

SODEMA ... Societe d'Etudes pour le Developpement de l'Industrie Mechanique en Algerie

SODEMHE ... Societe de Mise Hors d'Eau

SODEMI ... Societe pour le Developpement Minier de la Cote-D'Ivoire [*Ivory Coast Mining Development Company*] (AF)

SODEMO ... Societe pour le Developpement de la Region de Morondava [*Company for the Development of Morondava Region*] [*Malagasy*] (AF)

SODENI .... Societe d'Embouteillage du Niger

SODENIA ... Societe de Developpement des Niayes (Thies) [*Senegal*]

SODENICOB ... Societe de Developpement Regional de la Vallee du Niari et de Jacob

SODENKAM ... Societe de Developpement du Nkam [*Nkam Development Company*] [*Cameroon*] (AF)

Sodep .... Social Democratic Party [*Turkey*] [*Political party*] (PPW)

SODEP ...... Societe d'Extrusion des Plastiques

SODEP ...... Sosyal Demokrasi Partisi [*Social Democratic Party*] [*Ankara, Turkey*] (MENA)

SODEPA ... Committee on Society, Development, and Peace, Kenya

SODEPA ... Societe de Developpement et d'Exploitation des Produits Animaux [*Cameroon*]

SODEPAC ... Societe de Developpement de la Peche Artisanale des Comores [*Fisheries Development Corporation of the Comoros*]

SODEPALM ... Societe pour le Developpement et l'Exploitation du Palmier a Huile [*Company for the Development and Exploitation of Oil Palm*] [*Ivory Coast*] (AF)

SODEPAX ... Exploratory Committee on Society, Development, and Peace of the Roman Catholic Church and the World Council of Churches

SODEPRA ... Societe pour le Developpement des Productions Animales [*Company for the Development of Animal Production*] [*Ivory Coast*] (AF)

SODERA ... Societe de Developpement des Ressources Animales [*State enterprise*] [*Cotonou, Benin*] (AF)

SODERAG ... Societe de Developpement Regional Antilles-Guyane [*Martinique*] (EY)

SODERDA ... Societe de Developpement de la Republique du Dahomey

Sodere .... Societe de Developpement Economique de la Reunion [*Economic Development Organization of Reunion*] (GEA)

SODERIM ... Societe de Developpement de la Riziculture dans la Plaine des Mbo [*Cameroon*]

SODERIZ ... Societe pour le Developpement de la Riziculture

SODERMAN ... Sociedad de Desarrollo Regional de La Mancha [*Company for Regional Development of La Mancha*] [*Spanish*] (WER)

SODERN .. Societe Anonyme d'Etudes et Realisations Nucleaires [*Industrial company*] [*French*] [*Research center*] (ERC)

SODERO .. Societe de Developpement Regional des Pays de Loire [*France*]

soderzh .... Content, Contents (RU)

SODES ... Societe d'Ethanol de Synthese

SODESUCRE ... Societe pour le Developpement des Plantations de Canne a Sucre, l'Industrialisation et Commercialisation du Sucre [*Company for the Development of Sugar Cane Plantations, and the Industrialization and Marketing of Sugar*] [*Ivory Coast*] (AF)

SODETCHAD ... Societe de Developpement du Tchad

SODETEG ... Societe d'Etudes Techniques et d'Entreprises Generales [*Technical Studies and General Enterprises Company*] [*French*] (WER)

SODETEGAO ... Societe d'Etudes Techniques d'Entreprises Generales Afrique de l'Ouest

SODETEL ... Sociedad de Tejidos Limitada [*Colombia*] (COL)

SODETEX ... Societe de Developpement des Fibres Textiles [*Government cotton development organization*] [*Senegal*]

SODETI .... Sociedad de Desarrollo de Tecnico Industrial [*Spanish*]

SODETO ... Societe des Detergents du Togo

SODETODAK ... Societe d'Etudes du Thon Dakarois

SODETRAF ... Societe pour le Developpement des Transports Aeriens en Afrique

SODETRAM ... Societe d'Etudes pour Realisations en Outre-Mer

SODEVA... Societe de Developpement de l'Elevage [*Cameroon*] (EY)

SODEVA... Societe de Developpement et de Vulgarisation Agricole [*Agricultural Development and Diversification Agency*] [*Senegal*]

SODEVEA ... Societe pour le Developpement et l'Exploitation de l'Hevea

SODEXA... Societe d'Exploitation Agricole

SODEXAFRIC ... Societe d'Exploitation de Magasins en Centrafrique

SODEXHO ... Societe d'Exploitations Hotelieres, Maritimes, Aeriennes, et Terrestres

SODEZONN ... Societe de Developpement de la Zone Njock-Nkoue

SODF......... Synergatikos Organismos Diatheseos Ftharton [*Cooperative Organization for the Marketing of Perishables*] [*Cyprus*] (GC)

SODI .... Sport Organization for the Deaf in Israel (EAIO)

SODIACAM ... Societe de Distribution Alimentaire de Cameroun

SODIACE ... Societe pour le Developpement de l'Industrie et l'Agriculture de la Cote Est

SODIAL.... Societe de Diffusion d'Articles de Luxe

SODIAM... Societe Diamantifere Centrafricaine de Diamants

SODIAMA ... Societe de Diffusion Automobile de Madagascar

SODIAMCI ... Societe Diamantifere de la Cote-D'Ivoire

SODIAN ... Sociedad para el Desarrollo Industrial de Andalucia [*Company for the Industrial Development of Andalusia*] [*Seville, Spain*] (WER)

SODIAR.... Sociedad Industrial de Armenia (COL)

SODIC...... Societe de Developpement Industriel et Commercial (FLAF)

SODIC...... Societe de Developpement Ivoirien de la Construction

SODIC...... Societe de Distribution Industrielle et Commerciale [*Morocco*]

SODIC...... Societe pour la Conversion et le Developpement Industriels [*France*] (PDAA)

SODICAM ... Societe Generale de Distribution au Cameroun

SODICAN ... Sociedad para el Desarrollo Industrial Canario [*Company for Industrial Development of the Canary Islands*] [*Madrid, Spain*] (WER)

SODICONGO ... Societe Diamantaire du Congo

SODIEX .... Sociedad para el Desarrollo Industrial de Extremadura [*Company for Industrial Development of Extremadura*] [*Caceres, Spain*] (WER)

Sodiga .... Sociedad para el Desarrollo Industrial de Galicia [*Galicia Industrial Development Society*] [*Spanish*] (GEA)

SODIMA... Societe de Distribution de Materiel Automobile et Technique

SODIMAF ... Societe de Distribution des Grandes Marques pour l'Africa

SODIMICO ... Societe de Developpement Industriel et Miniere du Congo

SODIMIZA ... Societe de Developpement Industriel et Miniere du Zaire [*Industrial Development and Mining Company of Zaire*] (AF)

SODIMPEX ... Societe Commercial d'Import-Export

SODIM-TP ... Societe de Distribution de Materiel de Travaux Publics

SODIPA .... Societe de Diffusion et Importation de Produits Alimentaires [*Senegal*]

SODIPHAC ... Societe de Diffusion Pharmaceutique en Afrique Centrale

SODIREP ... Societe de Diffusion et de Representation

SODIS....... Societe de Diffusion Industrielle et Scientifique

SODISHUIL ... Societe de Distribution de l'Huile

SODISSER ... Societe de Distribution et de Services

SODISTAR ... Societe de Diffusion des Produits de la Star

SODITAL ... Societe de Developpement de l'Industrie Touristique en Algerie (EY)

SODITAS ... Solvent Distributorlugu Anonim Sirketi [*Solvent Distributorship Corporation*] (TU)

SODITEX ... Sociedad Distribuidora de Textiles [*Colombia*] (COL)

SODIZI ..... Societe du Domaine Industriel de Ziguinchor

SODMC .... Sdruzeni Organizaci Deti a Mladeze CSR [*Association of Organizations of Children and Youth of the Czech Socialist Republic*] (CZ)

SODOJEL ... Societe du Domaine des Ouled Jellal

SodP.......... Sodobna Pedagogika [*Contemporary Pedagogy*] [*Ljubljana A periodical*] (YU)

SODRANOR ... Societe de Dragage du Nord

SODRE...... Servicio Oficial de Difusion Radioelectrica [*Official Radio Broadcasting Service*] [*Uruguay*] (LA)

SODSC...... Secretariado de Orientacion de la Democracia Social Catalana [*Orientation Secretariat for the Social Democracy of Catalonia*] [*Spanish*] (WER)

SODUCAF ... Societe d'Usinage de Cafe du Cameroun

SODUCO.. Societe Durand et Compagnie

SODY .... Stegastikos Organismos Dimosion Ypallilon [*Civil Servants' Housing Organization*] [*Greek*] (GC)

SOE .... Erythrocyte Sedimentation Rate (RU)

soe .... Socially Dangerous Element (RU)

SOE .... Souanke [*Congo*] [*Airport symbol*] (OAG)

SOE .... State of Environment [*Australia*]

SOE .... State Organization for Electricity [*Iraq*]

SOE .... State-Owned Enterprise [*Ghana*]

SOEC......... Statistical Office of the European Communities (DCTA)

Soeh .... Soehne [*Sons*] [*German*] (GCA)

SOEI......... Syndicat des Ouvriers et Employes des Industries

SOEKOR... Southern Oil Exploration Company [*South Africa*] (MSC)

SOEKOR... Suidelike Olie-Eksplorasie-Korporasie [*Southern Oil Exploration Corporation*] [*South Africa*] (AF)

SOELACI ... Societe Agriculture de Cote-D'Ivoire

SOEME..... Sindicato de Obreros y Empleados del Ministerio de Educacion [*Union of Workers and Employees of the Ministry of Education*] [*Argentina*] (LA)

SOEMO .... Services d'Observation et d'Education en Milieu Ouvert [*Algeria*]

SOEMPEDRO ... Sociedad Empacadora de Drogas [*Colombia*] (COL)

SOERAC... Systemes et Peripheriques Associes aux Calculateurs [*French*] (ADPT)

SOERNI.... Societe d'Etudes et de Representations Navales Industrielles RCA

SOEXAL ... Societe d'Exploitation des Anciens Ets. Luiz

SOEXCO... Sociedad Exportadora de Confecciones Ltda. [*Colombia*] (COL)

SOF........... Societe Ornithologique de France [*Ornithology Society of France*] (SLS)

SOF........... Sofia [*Bulgaria*] [*Airport symbol*] (OAG)

sof.............. Sofort [*or Sofortigen*] [*Immediate*] [*German*]

SOF........... Soldier of Fortune

SOF........... Svenska Officersforbundet [*Sweden*] (EAIO)

SOF........... Svetova Odborova Federace [*World Federation of Trade Unions*] (CZ)

SOFAC...... Societe de Financement d'Achats a Credit

SOFACAM ... Societe Familiale Africaine du Cameroun

SOFACAMA ... Societe de Fabrication de Canalisations de Madagascar

SOFACO... Societe Africaine de Fabrication, de Formulation, et de Conditionnement

SOFALCA ... Societe de Fabrication d'Alcaloides

SOFAM..... Societe Franco-Africaine de Metallurgie

SOFAMAR ... Sociedade de Fainas de Mar e Rio, SARC [*Sea and River Labor Society, Inc.*] [*Portuguese*] (WER)

SOFAMI ... Societe de Fabrication Metallique Ivoirienne

SOFAN...... Societe et Fournisseurs d'Afrique Noire et de Madagascar

SOFAR...... Sociedade de Farinhos [*Flour Company*] [*Angola*] (AF)

SOFARIN ... Sociedad Farmaceutica Internacional [*Colombia*] (COL)

SOFAS ...... Sonnenenergie-Fachverband Schweiz [*Solar Energy Department of Switzerland*] (SLS)

SOFASA ... Sociedad de Fabricantes de Automotores [*Envigado-Antioquia*] (COL)

SOFBA ...... Societe Francaise des Bois Africains

Sofbas .... Sofia Basin (BU)

SOFCAR ... Societe de Fabrication de Carbones

SOFCOT ... Societe Francaise de Chirurgie Orthopedique et de Traumatologie [*French*] (SLS)

SOFE......... Swedish Options and Futures Exchange

SOFEM..... Societe Forestiere et d'Elevage de Mouyondzi Soffer & Cie.

SOFEMOL ... Sociedade de Ferragens e Motores Limitada

Sofenergo .. Sofia Electric Power Administration (BU)

SOFFEX.... Swiss Options and Financial Futures Exchange

SOFFIN .... Societe Financiere France-Ingelheim

SOFFO...... Societe Financier pour la France et les Pays d'Outre-Mer

SOFGM..... Societe Algerienne de Fabrication Electro-Mecanique

SOFI .... Soziologisches Forschungsinstitut Goettingen [*Sociological Research Institute of Goettingen*] (SLS)

SOFI .... Systeme d'Ordinateurs pour le Fret International

SOFIA .... Systeme d'Ordinateurs pour le Fret International Aerien [*French*] (ADPT)

SOFIBEL .. Societe Forestiere et Industrielle de Belabo

SOFIBOI.. Societe Forestiere et Industrielle des Bois Ivoiriens

SOFIBOIS ... Societe Financiere des Bois Tropicaux

SOFICA .... Societe de Fournitures pour l'Industrie et les Constructions Africaines [*Senegal*]

SOFICA .... Societe Forestiere Industrielle et Commerciale [*Cameroon*]

SOFICAL ... Societe de Financement Industriel Commercial et Agricole

SOFICAR ... Societe des Fibres de Carbone

SOFICO .... Societe des Fibres Coloniales (Matsende)

SOFICO .... Societe Industrielle de Fournitures et de Chaussures "L'Ours" [*Tunisia*]

SOFICOMAF ... Societe Financiere et Commerciale Africaine

SOFICRIN ... Societe Francaise des Crins Vegetaux [*Morocco*]

SOFIDAK ... Societe de la Foire Internationale de Dakar

SOFIDE .... Societe Financiere de Developpement [*Finance Company for Development*] [*Zaire*] (AF)

SOFIDEG ... Societe Financiere de Developpement Economique en Guyane [*Financial Society for the Economic Development of French Guiana*] (LA)

SOFIFA..... Societe Financiere et Immobiliere Franco-Africaine

SOFIGES.. Societe Financiere et de Gestion [*Tunisia*] (IMH)

SOFIHDES ... Societe Financiere Haitienne de Developpement (EY)

SOFIKE..... Societe Forestiere et Industrielle de la Nkebe

SOFIM ...... Service d'Ordinateurs pour le Fret International Maritime [*French*]   (ADPT)
SOFIMEC ... Societe de Fibres et Mecanique
SOFIMEC ... Societe Francaise pour l'Industrie Miniere au Cameroun [*French Mining Industry Company in Cameroon*]   (AF)
SOFIMO... Societe Financiere pour le Moyen-Orient
SOFINA .... Societe Financiere de Transports et d'Entreprises Industrielles [*French*]
SOFIOM... Societe Francaise des Ingenieurs d'Outre-Mer
SOFIPA..... Societe Financiere Internationale de Participation
SOFIRAD ... Societe Francaise de Radiodiffusion [*France*]
SOFIRAN ... Societe Francaise des Petroles d'Iran [*French Petroleum Company of Iran*]   (ME)
SOFIREP.. Societe Franco-Ivorienne de Representation
SOFISEDIT ... Societe Financiere Senegalaise pour le Developpement de l'Industrie et du Tourisme [*Senegalese Financial Company for the Development of Industry and Tourism*]   (AF)
SOFITEX.. Societe des Fibres Textiles [*Textile Fiber Company*] [*Benin*]   (AF)
SOFITEX.. Societe Voltaique des Fibres Textiles [*Fiber manufacturer*] [*Burkina Faso*]
SOFITIS ... Societe de Filature et Tissage
SOFITRANS ... Societe Financiere pour le Developpement des Transports et du Tourisme
SOFLUMAR ... Societe d'Armement Fluvial et Maritime [*Shipping line*] [*France*]   (EY)
SOFMA..... Societe Francais de Materiels d'Armement [*France*]   (PDAA)
SOFOCI.... Societe Forestiere de la Cote-D'Ivoire
SOFODECI ... Societe Forestiere de la Cote-D'Ivoire
SOFOFA ... Sociedad de Fomento Fabril [*Industrial Development Association*] [*Chile*]   (LA)
SOFOHI.... Societe pour le Forestiere du Hein
SOFOMECA ... Societe de Fonderies et Mecanique [*Tunisia*]   (IMH)
SOFONAL ... Societe de Fonderie des Alliages Legers
SOFOPLAST ... Societe de Fabrication d'Objets en Plastique
SOFOR...... Societe Forestiere
SOFOR-IS ... Turkiye Soforler ve Otomobilciler Federasyonu [*Turkish Chauffeurs and Automobile Drivers Federation*]   (TU)
SOFORMA ... Societe Forestiere du Mayumbe
SOFOTE ... Societe Forestiere de la Tene
SOFRACIMA ... Societe Franco-Africaine de Cinema
SOFRACO ... Societe Francaise de Constructions
SOFRACOL ... Sociedad Franco Colombiana de Especialidades Farmaceuticas Limitada [*Colombia*]   (COL)
SOFRADI ... Societe Francaise de Distribution [*Senegal*]
SOFRAFIMEX ... Societe Franco-Africaine d'Importation et d'Exportation
SOFRAMAC ... Societe Francaise pour le Developpement des Entreprises et leur Adaptation au Marche Commun   (FLAF)
SOFRAMER ... Societe Francaise d'Achats pour l'Outre-Mer
Sofrapel...... Societe Francaise des Petroles Elwerath   (OMWE)
SOFRATEP ... Societe Franco-Tunisienne d'Exploitation Petroliere
SOFRATI ... Societe Franco-Africaine de Tissus
SOFRATOME ... Societe Francaise d'Etudes et de Realisations Nucleaires [*Nuclear Studies and Realizations Society of France*]   (WND)
SOFRATOP ... Societe Francaise de Travaux Topographiques et Photogrammetriques [*French Topographic and Photogrammetric Projects Company*]   (AF)
SOFRA-TP ... Societe Francaise de Travaux Publics [*French Public Works Company*]   (AF)
SOFRAVIN ... Societe Francaise des Vins
SOFRECOM ... Societe Francaise d'Etudes des Telecommunications [*French Telecommunications Studies Company*]   (CL)
SOFRECOM ... Societe Francaise d'Etudes et de Realisations d'Equipements de Telecommunications [*French communications engineering company*] [*Telecommunications*]
SOFRED ... Societe Francaise d'Etudes et de Developpement [*French Research and Development Company*]   (AF)
SOFREDOC ... Societe Francaise d'Etudes et d'Editions Documentaires
SOFREGAZ ... Societe Francaise d'Etudes et de Realisations d'Equipements Gaziers
SOFREL.... Societe des Fruits et Legumes
SOFRELEC ... Societe Francaise d'Etudes et de Realisations d'Equipements Electriques
SOFREMINES ... Societe Francaise d'Etudes Minieres
SOFREPAL ... Societe Francaise de Recherches et d'Exploitation des Petroles en Algerie
Sofrepal...... Societe Francaise pour la Recherche et l'Exploitation des Petroles en Algerie   (OMWE)
SOFRERAIL ... Societe Francaise d'Etudes et de Realisations Ferroviaires [*French Railroad Design and Construction Company*]   (AF)
SOFRES.... Societe Francaise d'Enquetes par Sondage [*French Opinion Polling Company*]   (WER)
SOFRES.... Societe Francaise d'Etudes Statistiques
SOFRESID ... Societe Francaise d'Etude d'Installations Siderurgiques [*France*]

SOFRETES ... Societe Francaise d'Etudes Thermique et d'Energie Solaire
SOFRETRANSPORTS-URBAINS ... Societe Francaise d'Etudes et des Realisations de Transports Urbains [*French*]
SOFRETU ... Societe Francaise d'Etudes et des Realisations de Transports Urbains [*French*]
SOFRIGAL ... Societe des Frigorifiques du Senegal
SOFRIMA ... Societe des Frigorifiques de Mauritanie
SOFRINA ... Societe Francaise pour l'Industrie en Afrique [*French Company for Industry in Africa*]   (AF)
SOFRINOR ... Societe des Entrepots Frigorifiques du Nord
SOFRITAO ... Societa Franco-Italiana per l'Africa Occidentale [*Senegal*]
SOFRO........ Societe Francaise de Recherche Operationnelle
SOFRUIPRIM ... Societe Primeurs Frais Nouveaux Selectionnes
SOFRUMA ... Societe Marocaine de Navigation Fruitiere [*Morocco*]   (MENA)
Sofstroy...... Sofia Construction Administration   (BU)
SOFT......... Australian Software Locator [*John Fairfax & Sons Ltd.*] [*Information service or system*]   (CRD)
SOFT......... Software Locator [*Database*] [*Australia*]
SOFUMAD ... Societe des Futs Metalliques de Madagascar
Sof u-t........ Sofia University   (BU)
SOFV......... Societe Okoume du Fernan-Vaz
Sofzhilfond ... Sofia Housing Facilities   (BU)
SOG.......... Schweizerische Ophthalmologische Gesellschaft [*Swiss Ophthalmological Society*]   (SLS)
SOG.......... Schweizerische Orchideen-Gesellschaft [*Swiss Orchid Society*]   (EAIO)
SOG.......... Sindicato de Obreros del Gas [*Gas Workers Union*] [*Uruguay*]   (LA)
SOG.......... Sindicato de Obreros Gallegos [*Trade Union of Galician Workers*] [*Spanish*]   (WER)
SOG.......... Societe Ouvriere Gabonaise
sog............ Sogenannt [*So-Called*] [*German*]   (GPO)
SOG.......... Sogndal [*Norway*] [*Airport symbol*]   (OAG)
SOG.......... Suedosteuropa-Gesellschaft eV [*Southeastern European Association*]   (SLS)
SOGA........ Society of General Affairs, SA [*Cambodia*]   (CL)
SOGABAIL ... Societe Gabonaise de Credit Bail
SOGABOL ... Societe Gabonaise des Oleagineux
SOGACA ... Societe Gabonaise de Credit Automobile
SOGACAM ... Societe Gabonaise de Cabotage Maritime et Fluvial
SOGACAR ... Societe Gabonaise de Carrieres
SOGACCO ... Societe Gabono-Coreenne de Commerce
SOGACEL ... Societe Gabonaise de Cellulose [*Gabonese Cellulose Company*]   (AF)
SOGACHIM ... Societe Gabonaise de Chimie
SOGACI.... Societe de Gestion et d'Assurances de la Cote-D'Ivoire
SOGACI.... Societe Gabonaise Commerciale et Industrielle
SOGACO .. Societe Gabonaise de Commerce
SOGAD..... Societe Gabonaise d'Amenagements et de Decoration
SOGADEHO ... Societe Gabonaise d'Exploitation Hoteliere
SOGADI.... Societe Gabonaise de Distribution
SOGAFER ... Societe Gabonaise Ferroviaire
SOGAFERRO ... Societe Gabonaise des Ferro-Alliages
SOGAFINEX ... Societe Gabonaise de Financement et d'Expansion [*Gabonese Company for Financing and Expansion*]   (AF)
SOGAFRIC ... Societe Gabonaise Froid et Representations Industrielles et Commerciales
SOGAID.... Societe Gabonaise d'Agence Immobiliere et de Demenagement
SOGAIMEX ... Societe Gabesienne d'Importation et d'Exportation [*North African*]
SOGAKOR ... Societe des Boissons Gazeuses du Kasai Oriental
SOGALAR ... Sociedad Regional de Ganaderos del Estado Lara [*Venezuela*]   (DSCA)
SOGALIVRE ... Societe Gabonaise du Livre
SOGALU... Societe Gabonaise de l'Aluminium
SOGAMA ... Societe de Gestion d'Assurances de Madagascar
SOGAMAR ... Societe Gabonaise de Marbre et de Materiaux
SOGAME ... Societe Gabonaise de Materiel et d'Equipement
SOGAMIRE ... Societe Gabonaise de Miroiterie et Ebenisterie
SOGANI ... Societe des Gaz Industriels du Niger
SOGAPAR ... Societe Gabonaise de Participation et de Developpement
SOGAPECHE ... Societe Gabonaise de Peche [*Gabonese Fishing Company*]   (AF)
SOGAPLAST ... Societe Gabonaise de Plastique
SOGAPRAL ... Societe Gabonaise de Produits Alimentaires
SOGAPRESSE ... Societe Gabonaise de Presse
SOGAPROM ... Societe Gabonaise de Promotion
SOGARA... Societe Gabonaise de Raffinage [*Gabonese Refining Company*]   (AF)
SOGAREC ... Societe Gabonaise de Rectification et de Mecanique Generale
SOGAREM ... Societe Gabonaise de Recherche et d'Exploitation Minieres [*Gabonese Mine Prospecting and Exploitation Company*]   (AF)
SOGARES ... Societe Gabonaise de Realisation de Structures
SOGARET ... Societe Gabonaise de Revetements et Travaux

SOGARI.... Societe Gabonaise de Realisations Industrielles
SOGATOL ... Societe Gabonaise de Toles et Produits Siderurgiques
SOGATRA ... Societe Gabonaise de Travaux
SOGATRAM ... Societe Gabonaise de Transport Maritime
SOGATRANSCO ... Societe Gabonaise de Transit et de Consignation
SOGB .... Societe des Caoutchoucs de Grand-Bereby
SOGCC...... Sydney Olympic Games Citizens' Council [*Australia*]
SOGCHIM ... Societe Generale Industrielle et Chimique de Jadotville
SOGDJZ ... Saobracajno Odeljenje Generalne Direkcije Jugoslovenskih
    Zeljeznica [*Transportation Department, Yugoslav General
    Railroad Administration*]   (YU)
SOGEA...... Societe Generale pour l'Agriculture
SOGEAC... Societe de Gestion et d'Exploitation de l'Aeroport de Conakry
    [*Guinea*]   (EY)
SOGEBA... Societe Generale de Batiments
SOGEBAC ... Societe Generale de Banque en Cote-D'Ivoire [*General Bank
    Company of the Ivory Coast*]   (AF)
SOGEBE... Societe Generale du Benin
SOGEC...... Societe Gabonaise d'Electrification et de Canalisation
SOGECA... Societe Gabonaise d'Exploitation de Carrieres
SOGECA... Societe Generale de Credit Automobile
SOGECA... Societe Generale pour le Commerce en Afrique
SOGECALTEX ... Societe de Gestion des Depots "Caltex"
SOGECHIM ... Societe Generale Industrielle et Chimique du Katanga
SOGECI.... Societe Generale de Commerce et d'Importation [*Morocco*]
SOGECO.... Sociedad General de Comercio [*Colombia*]   (COL)
SOGECO... Sociedad General de Comercio [*General Society of Commerce*]
    [*Chile*]   (LAA)
SOGECO... Societe Generale de Comptabilite
SOGECO... Societe Generale de Consignation et d'Entreprises Maritimes
    [*Mauritania*]
SOGECOA ... Societe Generale de Collecte et d'Approvisionnement
SOGECOM ... Societe de Gerance et de Commerce
SOGECOM ... Societe Generale de Compensation
SOGECOR ... Societe Generale de Conseil et de Representation Internationale
SOGEDEM ... Societe Gabonaise d'Etude et de Developpement Maritimes
SOGEDESCA ... Societe de Gestion Descours et Cabaud
SOGEDI.... Societe Generale d'Edition et d'Imprimerie
SOGEDI.... Societe Guineenne des Ets. Duffour et Igon
SOGEDIA ... Societe de Gestion et de Developpement des Industries
    Alimentaires [*Food Industries Management and
    Development Company*] [*Algiers, Algeria*]   (AF)
SOGEDIS ... Societe de Gestion et de Developpement des Industries de Sucre
SOGEDIS ... Societe Generale de Distribution
SOGEF...... Societe de Gestion d'Entrepots Frigorifiques en Cote-D'Ivoire
SOGEFIHA ... Societe de Gestion Financiere de l'Habitat [*Company for the
    Financial Management of Housing*] [*Ivory Coast*]   (AF)
SOGEFINANCE ... Societe Generale de Financement et de Participation en
    Cote-D'Ivoire
SOGEFOR ... Societe Generale des Forces Hydroelectriques du Katanga
SOGEI...... Societe Generale d'Exploitations Industrielles
SOGEK...... Societe Generale Khmere de Commerce et de Representation
    [*Cambodian General Trade Agency*]   (CL)
SOGEK...... Synergatikos Organismos Genikou Emboriou Kyprou [*General
    Trade Cooperative Organization of Cyprus*]   (GC)
SOGEKO .. Korean-French Banking Corp. [*Acronym is based on foreign
    phrase*]   (EY)
SOGEL...... Sociedade Geral de Empreitadas Limitada
SOGEL...... Societe Gabonaise d'Elevage
SOGELEC ... Societe Generale Africaine d'Electricite
SOGELEM ... Societe Generale d'Electricite de Mauritanie
SOGEMA ... Societe Generale Maritime Congolaise
SOGEMAR ... Societe Guineenne de Gerance Maritime
sogen .... Sogenannt [*So-Called*] [*German*]
SOGENA .. Societe Generale Africaine
SOGENAL ... Societe Generale Alsacienne de Banque [*Bank*] [*Switzerland*]
SOGEP...... Societe Generale de Produits Chimiques
SOGEP...... Societe Generale d'Etudes et de Planification
SOGEPAC ... Societe Generale de Materiaux de Construction
SOGEPAL ... Societe de Gestion et de Participations d'Industries Alimentaires
SOGEPAR ... Societe Generale d'Etudes et de Participations en Cote-D'Ivoire
SOGEPO... Societe d'Exploitation de Garages et d'Entrepots [*Senegal*]
SOGERA... Societe de Gestion des Participants de la Regie Autonome de
    Petroles
SOGER-AO ... Societe Generale de Representations Industrielles et de
    Travaux Publics
SOGERAP ... Societe de Gestion des Participations de la Regie Autonome des
    Petroles [*Saharan*]
SOGERCA ... Societe Generale d'Entreprise de Centrales Atomiques [*General
    Atomic Power Plants Contracting Company*] [*French*]
    (WER)
SOGERCO ... Societe de Gerance de Representation et de Courtage
SOGEREM ... Societe Generale de Recherches et d'Exploitation Minieres
    [*Burkina Faso*]
SOGERES ... Societe de Gestion de Restaurants et de Spectacles

SOGESA ... Sociedad de Gestion de la Planta Siderurgica de Chimbote y de la
    Central Hidroelectrica del Canon del Pato, Sociedad
    Anonima [*Peru*]   (LAA)
SOGESCI ... Societe Belge pour l'Application des Methodes Scientifiques de
    Gestion [*Brussels, Belgium*]
SOGESETRA ... Societe Generale Senegalaise de Batiments et Travaux
    Publics
SOGESUCRE ... Compagnie Sucriere Congolaise
SOGET...... Societe de Gestion d'Entreprise et de Transport
SOGET...... Software Gestione Terminali [*French*]   (ADPT)
SOGETA ... Societe de Gestion des Terres Agricoles [*Agricultural Land
    Management Company*] [*Rabat, Morocco*]   (AF)
SOGETEC ... Societe Generale de Topographie, Photogrammetrie, et d'Etudes
    de Genie Civil
SOGETEG ... Societe d'Etudes Techniques et d'Entreprises Generales
SOGETEL ... Societe Generale de Travaux et Constructions Electriques
SOGETHA ... Societe Generale des Techniques Hydroagricoles [*General
    Hydroagricultural Techniques Company*] [*Niger*]   (AF)
SOGETHEL ... Societe Generale d'Exploitation Touristique et Hoteliere du
    Laos [*General Hotel and Tourism Company of Laos*]   (CL)
SOGETISS ... Societe Generale de Tissage [*Tunisia*]
SOGETOCAM ... Societe de Gestion pour le Tourisme au Cameroun
SOGETRA ... Societe Generale de Travaux Routiers
SOGETRAF ... Societe Generale de Travaux et de Representations en Afrique
SOGETRAG ... Societe Generale des Transports de Guinee   (EY)
SOGETRAM ... Societe Generale de Travaux Maritimes et Fluviaux
SOGETRANS ... Societe de Gestion et de Transport
SOGEV...... Societe Generale du Vide [*France*]   (PDAA)
SOGEX...... Societe de Gestion pour l'Exploitation du Parc a Bois du Port de
    Douala
SOGEXI .... Societe Generale d'Exportation et Importation
SOGFERRO ... Societe Gabonaise des Ferro-Alliages
SOGIA....... Societe Generale des Industries Alimentaires
SOGIC...... Societe Gabonaise d'Importation et de Commerce
SOGIC....... Societe Generale de l'Industrie de Confection [*Tunisia*]
SOGICO.... Societe Generale des Industries Cotonnieres
SOGICOT ... Societe Generale des Industries Cotonnieres en Tunisie
SOGIEXI... Societe Generale d'Importation et d'Exportation de Cote-
    D'Ivoire
SOGIL....... Societe Generale des Industries Lainieres [*Tunisia*]
SOGIMEX ... Societe Generale d'Importation et d'Exportation [*Senegal*]
SOGIP....... Societe Generale pour l'Industrialisation de la Peche [*General
    Company for the Industrialization of Fishing*] [*Ivory Coast*]
    (AF)
SOGISMA ... Societe des Gaz Industriels de Madagascar
SOGIT....... Societe Generale des Industries Textiles [*General Textile
    Industry Corporation*] [*Tunisia*]
SOGITEX ... Societe Generale des Industries Textiles [*General Textile
    Industry Corporation*] [*Tunisia*]
SoGMs....... Sondergussmessing [*Special Cast Brass*] [*German*]   (GCA)
SOGODAN ... Societe Goudrons et Derives de l'Afrique du Nord [*Morocco*]
SOGOV ..... Societe des Gestions et d'Outillages Publics de la Province de
    Vientiane [*Land and Water Transportation Company*]
    [*Literally, Vientiane Province Public Management and
    Equipment Company; same as Borisat Khon Song Thang
    Nam Lae Thang Bok Laotian*]   (CL)
SOGPI....... North Ossetian State Pedagogical Institute Imeni K. L.
    Khetagurov   (RU)
SOGRA ..... Sociedade Grafica Lda.
SOGRAD .. Splosno Gradbeno Podjetje [*General Construction
    Establishment*] [*YU*]
SOGREAH ... Societe Grenobloise d'Etudes et d'Applications Hydrauliques
    [*French*]
SOGREP ... Societe Generale de Recherche et Programmation [*French*]
    (ADPT)
SOGS......... Sanitetski Odred Glavnog Staba [*Medical Detachment of the
    General Staff*]   (YU)
SOGT .... Societe d'Obstetrique et de Gynecologie de Toulouse [*Society of
    Obstetrics and Gynecology of Toulouse*] [*French*]   (SLS)
SOGUET... Societe Guineenne d'Engineering et d'Equipement Technique
SOGUIP.... Societe Guineenne des Petroles
SOGUIREP ... Societe Guineenne de Rechapage de Pneus
SOH.......... Servicio de Oceanografia e Hidrografia [*Uruguay*]   (MSC)
SOH.......... Stichting Oecumenische Hulp aan Kerken en Vluchtelingen
    [*Netherlands*]
SOH.......... Sydney Opera House [*Australia*]   (ADA)
SOHA........ Societe Hoteliere de l'Atlantique
SOHICO ... Societe Hoteliere et Immobiliere de Cocody
SOHIMA .. Societe Hoteliere et Immobiliere de Madagascar
SOHLI....... Societe Hoteliere du Littoral
SOHMA..... Servicio de Oceanografia, Hidrografia, y Meteorologia de la
    Armada [*Naval Oceanographic, Hydrographic, and
    Weather Service*] [*Uruguay*]   (LA)
SOHO........ Solar and Heliospheric Observatory [*European Space Agency*]
SOHORA ... Societe des Hotels de la Riviera Africaine
SOHOTCI ... Societe Hoteliere et Touristique de Cote-D'Ivoire

SOHYO..... Nihon Rodo Kumiai Sohyogikai [*General Council of Trade Unions of Japan*]   (FEA)
SOI .... Schweizerisches Ost Institut [*Swiss Eastern Institute*]   (SLS)
SOI .... Societa Ornitologica Italiana [*Italian*]   (SLS)
SOI .... Societa Orticola Italiana [*Italian*]   (SLS)
SOI .... South Molle Island [*Australia*] [*Airport symbol*]   (OAG)
SOI .... Special Olympics International   (OLYM)
SOI .... Standards Organization of Iran
SOI .... Statni Obchodni Inspekce [*State Commerce Inspection*]   (CZ)
SOIAP .... Secretaria de Organizacion e Inspeccion de la Administracion Publica [*Colombia*]   (LAA)
SOIAP .... Secretaria de Organizacion e Inspeccion de la Presidencia de la Republica [*Colombia*]   (COL)
SOICO...... Sociedad Impermeabilizadora Colombiana [*Colombia*]   (COL)
SOID .... State Organisation for Industrial Development [*Iraq*]
SOIDC....... State Organization for Industrial Design and Construction [*Iraq*]
SOIDI....... Societe Ivoirienne de Distribution
SOIM .... Northern Branch of the Institute of Permafrost Study Imeni V. A. Obruchev (of the Academy of Sciences, USSR)   (RU)
SOIMA...... Sindicato de Obreros de la Industria de Madera y Anexos [*Union of Workers of the Lumber and Related Industries*] [*Uruguay*]   (LA)
SOIMPEX ... Sociedade Importadora de Pecas
SOIP......... Societe Ivoirienne de Pecheries
SOIS .... Sosyal Isler Dairesi Genel Mudurlugu [*Social Affairs Office Directorate General*] [*of Foreign Affairs Ministry*]   (TU)
SOIVA....... Sindicato Obrero de la Industria del Vestido y Afines [*Union of Workers of the Garment and Related Industries*] [*Argentina*]   (LA)
SOIVRE .... Servicio Oficial de Inspeccion, Vigilancia, y Regulacion de las Exportaciones [*Spain*]   (IMH)
SOJ........... Savez Obucara Jugoslavije [*Yugoslav Shoemakers Union*]   (YU)
SOJ........... Sorkjosen [*Norway*] [*Airport symbol*]   (OAG)
SOJECOCAM ... Societe des Jeunes Commercants de l'Ouest du Cameroun
SOJUFA ... Societe des Jus de Fruits d'Antsirabe
SOJUFRUIT ... Societe des Jus de Fruits de la Mitidja [*Algeria*]
SOK .... Semongkong [*Lesotho*] [*Airport symbol*] [*Obsolete*]   (OAG)
SOK .... Sluzba Ochrony Kolei [*Railroad Security Service*]   (POL)
Sok .... Sokagi [*Street, Lane*] [*Sk*] [*See also*]   (TU)
Sok .... Sokkak   (IDIG)
SOK .... Straz Ochrony Kolejowej [*Railroad Security Guard*]   (POL)
SOK .... Suomen Osuuskauppojen Keskuskunta [*Co-Operative Wholesale Society*] [*Finland*]   (EY)
SOK .... Synergatikos Organismos Kapnoparagogon [*Tobacco Growers Cooperative*] [*Cyprus*]   (GC)
SOK .... System of Remainder Classes [*Computers*]   (RU)
SOKAO ..... Soviet-Korean Aviation Society   (RU)
SOKAVET ... Societe Khmere des Agences de Voyages et de Tourisme, SA [*Cambodian Tourism and Travel Agency Company, Inc.*]   (CL)
SOKCIA .... Societe Khmere pour la Commerce, l'Industrie, et l'Agriculture, SA [*Cambodian Commerce, Industry, and Agriculture Company, Inc.*]   (CL)
SOKCT...... Societe Khmere des Cultures Tropicales [*Cambodian Tropical Crop Company*]   (CL)
SOKEC...... Societe Khmere d'Entreprises de Constructions [*Cambodian Construction Enterprises Company*]   (CL)
SOKECHI ... Societe Khmere d'Usine d'Engrais Chimique [*Cambodian Chemical Fertilizer Manufacturing Company*]   (CL)
SOKECIA ... Societe Khmere d'Entreprises Commerciales, Industrielles, et Agricoles [*Cambodian Commercial, Industrial, and Agricultural Enterprise Company*]   (CL)
SOKEPH... Societe Khmere d'Exploitation Pharmaceutique [*Cambodian Pharmaceutical Company*]   (CL)
SOKFEM .. Societe Khmere de Fabrication d'Emballages Metalliques [*Cambodian Metal Container Manufacturing Company*]   (CL)
SOKHA ..... Societe Khmere des Auberges [*Cambodian Hotel Company*] [*Replaced SOKHAR*]   (CL)
SOKHAR .. Societe Khmere d'Auberges Royales [*Royal Cambodian Hotel Company*] [*Replaced by SOKHA*]   (CL)
SOKILAIT ... Societe Khmere pour l'Industrie Laitiere [*Cambodian Dairy Industry Company*]   (CL)
SOKIMET ... Societe Kaedienne d'Importation, d'Exportation, et de Transport
SOKIMEX ... Societe Khmere Import et Export [*Cambodian Import and Export Company*]   (CL)
SOKINABU ... Societe d'Economie Mixte pour l'Exploitation du Quinquina au Burundi   (EY)
SOKINAC ... Societe Khmere Industrielle d'Applications Chimiques [*Cambodian Industrial Chemical Company*]   (CL)
SOKJUTE ... Societe Khmere de Jute [*Cambodian Jute Company*]   (CL)
SOKK .... Sovetsk Obshchestvo Krasnovo Kresta i Krasnovo Polumesiatsa
SOKK iKP ... Union of Red Cross and Red Crescent Societies of the USSR   (RU)
SOKL........ Suomen Osuuskauppojen Keskusliitto [*Co-operative Union*] [*Finland*]   (EY)

SOKME..... Societe Khmere de Materiels Electriques [*Cambodian Electrical Equipment Company*]   (CL)
SOKNII ..... Smolensk Oblast Scientific Research Institute of Regional Studies   (RU)
SOKOA ..... Societe Khmere d'Oxygene et d'Acetylene [*Cambodian Oxygen and Acetylene Company*]   (CL)
SOKOFA.. Solidaritat-Komitee Freies Afrika
SOKOTAN ... Sokoto Tannery
SOKPHOS ... Societe Khmere de Phosphates [*Cambodian Phosphate Company*]   (CL)
SOKPROMA ... Societe Khmere de Productions Metallurgiques et Artisanales [*Cambodian Metallurgical and Handicrafts Production Company*]   (CL)
sokr .... Abbreviated, Abbreviation   (RU)
SOKRENA ... Societe Khmere de Representation et Navigation [*Cambodian Representation and Navigation Company*]   (CL)
SOKRI....... Societe Khmere pour le Riz et l'Industrie [*Cambodian Rice and Industry Company*]   (CL)
SOKSA...... Sinop Orme ve Konfeksiyon ve Ticaret AS [*Sinop Knitted Goods and Ready-Made Clothing Corp.*]   (TU)
SOKSI....... Sentral Organisasi Karyawan Socialis Indonesia [*Central Organization of Indonesian Socialist Workers*]
soksz .... Sokszorositas [*Reproduction*] [*Publishing*] [*Hungary*]
SOKTRANSCO ... Societe Khmere de Transports de Commerce et d'Equipements Industriels [*Cambodian Commercial and Industrial Equipment Transport Company*]   (CL)
SOKU .... Saratov Oblast Communist University Imeni V. I. Lenin   (RU)
SOKU .... Sonargaon Sramik-o-Karmachari Union Hotel [*Bangladesh*]   (EAIO)
Sol .... Saltern, Saltworks [*Topography*]   (RU)
sol............... Salt Mine, Salt Water, Salt-Water Lake [*Topography*]   (RU)
SOL .... Sindicato de Obreros Libres [*Trade Union of Free Workers*] [*Mexico*]   (LA)
SOL .... Societe l'Okoume de Libreville
sol............... Solid [*Strong*] [*Danish/Norwegian*]
SOL .... Solomon Airlines Ltd. [*Solomon Islands*] [*ICAO designator*]   (FAAC)
SOL .... Soma Orkoton Logiston [*Certified Accountants Corps*] [*Greek*]   (GC)
SOL .... Sosialistinen Opiskelijain Liitto [*Socialist Students' League (Communist-SKDL)*] [*Finland*]   (WEN)
Sol a Cont .. Solution a Contrario   (FLAF)
Sol AdminEnreg ... Solution de l'Administration de l'Enregistrement   (FLAF)
SOLADO .. Societe de Laminage de Douala
SOLAIR .... Solomon Islands Airways Ltd.   (FEA)
SOLANI ... Societe Laitiere du Niger
SOLAR...... Sociedad Latinoamericana de Estudios sobre America Latina y el Caribe [*Mexico*]   (EAIO)
SOLARCH ... Solar Architecture Research Unit [*University of New South Wales*] [*Australia*]
SOLARCO ... Societe Libano-Arabe pour le Commerce
SOLAS ...... International Convention for the Safety of Life at Sea [*IMCO*]   (ASF)
SOLAS ...... Safety of Life at Sea Convention   (BARN)
SOLCGS ... Sisters of Our Lady of Charity of the Good Shepherd [*Roman Catholic religious order*] [*Rome, Italy*]   (EAIO)
SOLEMA .. Societe de Lavages et Montages Metalliques Africains [*Senegal*]
SOLEMOA ... Societe de Lavages et Montages Metalliques Africains [*Senegal*]
SOLIBRA ... Societe de Limonaderies et Brasseries d'Afrique
SOLICAM ... Societe du Linge de Maison au Cameroun
SOLICO .... Societe de Littoral Congolais
SOLICO .... Societe Limonadiere de la Cote du Benin
solidam....... Solidamente [*Solidly*] [*Publishing*] [*Italian*]
solidif .... Solidification   (BARN)
SOLIMA ... Societe Libyo-Malienne de Developpement, de l'Elevage et d'Exploitation du Betail   (EY)
SOLIMA ... Solitany Malagasy [*Malagasy Petroleum Company*]   (AF)
SOLIMAC ... Societe Libano-Ivoirienne de Materiaux de Construction
SOLIMPEX ... Societe Lao Import-Export   (EY)
Sol Impl ..... Solution Implicite   (FLAF)
SOLINCI... Societe de Lingerie de Cote-D'Ivoire
SOLINGRAL ... Suelos Integral Limitada [*Colombia*]   (COL)
Sol Is .... Solomon Islands
sol ist........... Salt Spring [*Topography*]   (RU)
Sollbest ...... Sollbestand [*Authorized Strength*]   (EG)
Sol mag ...... Salt Storehouse [*Topography*]   (RU)
SOLOMA ... Societe de Location de Materiel d'Entreprises
SolPaC....... Societa Italiana di Patologia Clinica [*Italian Society of Clinical Pathology*]   (SLS)
sol prom ..... Salt Mines [*Topography*]   (RU)
SOLT......... Societe des Oleagineux du Logone-Tchad
SOLUCO... Societe Luzienne de Conserves
solv............. Dissolvez [*Dissolve*] [*Pharmacy*]
SOLV........ Survival of Libraries in Victoria [*Australia*]
Solvatat...... Solvatation [*Conversion into a Sol*] [*German*]   (GCA)
SOLVECO ... Industrial de Disolventes y Productos Quimicos Ltda. [*Colombia*]   (COL)

SOM .... Construction-Finishing Machine   (RU)
SOM .... Radio Mast Signal Light   (RU)
SOM .... San Tome [*Venezuela*] [*Airport symbol*]   (OAG)
SOM .... Somalia [*ANSI three-letter standard code*]   (CNC)
SOM .... Somali Airlines [*Somalia*] [*ICAO designator*]   (FAAC)
Som .... Sommet [*Summit*] [*French*]   (NAU)
SOM .... Spoldzielcy Osrodek Maszynowy [*Cooperative Machine Station*]   (POL)
SOM .... State Organization of Minerals [*Iraq*]
SOM .... Stichting Onderzoek Massacommunicatie [*Netherlands*]
SOM .... Swiatowa Organizacja Meteorologiczna [*World Meteorological Organization*] [*Poland*]
SOM .... World Meteorological Organization   (BU)
SOMA .... Sociedad Medica Antioquena [*Colombia*]   (COL)
SOMA .... Societe Malienne d'Assurances
SOMA .... Societe Maritime de Madagascar
SOMABIPAL ... Societe Malienne de Biscuiterie et Pates Alimentaires
SOMABRI ... Societe Malgache de Briqueterie
SOMAC .... Societe Malienne de la Casamance
SOMACA ... Societe Marocaine de Construction Automobile [*Casablanca, Morocco*]
SOMACAT-SA ... Societe Mauritanienne d'Affretement, de Consignation, de Transit, et d'Acconage
SOMACI... Societe Malienne de Commerce et d'Industrie
SOMACI... Societe Marseillaise de la Cote-D'Ivoire
SOMACIB ... Societe Marocaine pour le Commerce et l'Artisanat de la Bijouterie [*North African*]
SOMACO ... Societe des Ets. Massiera & Compagnie
SOMACO ... Societe Majungaise de Commerce
SOMACOA ... Societe Malgache de Construction Automobile
SOMACOB ... Societe Malienne de Commercialisation du Betail
SOMACODIS ... Societe Malgache de Collecte et de Distribution [*Malagasy Collection and Distribution Company*]   (AF)
SOMACOM ... Societe de Manutention et de Consignation Maritime [*Shipping*] [*Reunion*]
SOMACOM ... Societe Malgache de Commerce
SOMACOM ... Societe Manoise de Commerce
SOMACOM ... Societe Maritime et Commerciale
SOMACOM ... Societe Mauritanienne de Construction Metallique
SOMACOTP ... Societe Mauritanienne de Construction et de Travaux Publics
SOMACOTRET ... Societe Mauritanienne de Commerce, de Transport, de Representation et de Transit
SOMACOU ... Societe Malgache de Couvertures
SOMADEC ... Societe Malgache d'Electricite [*Malagasy Electric Power Company*]   (AF)
SOMADEC ... Societe Mauritanienne de Developpement et de Commerce
SOMADEL ... Societe Marocaine d'Electricite
SOMADEP ... Societe Mauritanienne de Diffusion d'Energie Portable
SOMADER ... Societe Mauritanienne de Developpement Rural   (EY)
SOMADET ... Societe Marocaine pour le Developpement Touristique
SOMADEX ... Societe Malgache d'Exploitation des Mines et Carrieres
SOMADIR ... Societe Marocaine de Distribution et de Rectification
SOMAF..... Societe Malienne de l'Automobile et du Froid
SOMAF..... Societe Marbriere Africaine
SOMAF..... Societe Marocaine du Froid [*Morocco*]
SOMAFAM ... Societe Malienne de Fabrication d'Articles Metalliques
SOMAFCO ... Societe Marocaine Fonciere et Commerciale
SOMAFI ... Societe Martiniquaise de Financement   (EY)
SOMAFOME ... Societe Marocaine de Fonderie et de Mecanique
SOMAG .... Societe Soudanaise de Grands Magasins
SOMAGA ... Societe Marseillaise du Gabon
SOMAGEC ... Societe Maghrebienne de Genie Civil [*Morocco*]
SOMAGEL ... Societe Malgache des Gelatine
SOMAI...... Sociedade Mineira de Avicultores Integrados Ltd. [*Brazil*]   (DSCA)
SOMAIR... Societe des Mines de l'Air [*Air Region Mining Company*] [*Niger*]   (AF)
SOMALAC ... Societe Malgache d'Amenagement du Lac Alaotra [*Lake Alaotra Development Company*] [*Malagasy*]   (AF)
SOMALAVAL ... Societe Malgache des Laques Valentine
SOMALCO ... Societe Malgache de Cosmetiques et de Parfumerie
SOMALGAZ ... Societe Mixte Franco-Algerienne de Gaz
SOMALIBO ... Societe Malienne de Boissons Gazeuses
SOMALIVRE ... Societe Mauritanienne du Livre
SOMALTEX ... Somali Textile Factory
SOMAP..... Societe Marocaine de Prevoyance
SOMAP..... Societe Mauritanienne d'Armement et de Peche
SOMAPA ... Societe Malienne de Parfumerie
SOMAPA ... Societe Mauritanienne de Produits Alimentaires
SOMAPALM ... Societe Malagasy pour le Palmier a Huile [*Malagasy Oil Palm Company*]   (AF)
SOMAPECHE ... Societe Malgache de Pecherie
SOMAPED ... Societe Malgache de Pediatrie [*Madagascar*]   (EAIO)
SOMAPEX ... Societe d'Exportation et de Peche
SOMAPIL ... Societe Malienne de Piles Electriques
SOMAPRIM ... Societe Malienne de Promotion Industrielle et Immobiliere

SOMAR .... Societe Marocaine d'Importation et d'Exportation
SOMARCO ... Societe Maritime et Commerciale du Senegal
SOMARD ... Societe Marocaine d'Etude
SOMAREDE ... Societe Marocaine de Recherches, d'Etudes, et de Developpement
SOMARGA ... Societe Maritime Gabonaise
SOMARPE ... Societe Oubangai Marques Pereira
SOMASA ... Societe Malienne de Sacherie
SOMASAC ... Societe Malienne de Sacherie
SOMASAK ... Societe Malgache d'Amenagement de la Sakay [*Malagasy Company for the Development of Sakay*]
SOMASAKA ... Societe Malgache d'Amenagement de la Sakay [*Malagasy Company for the Development of Sakay*]   (AF)
SOMASER ... Societe Maritime de Service [*France*]   (PDAA)
SOMASET ... Societe Mauritano-Senegalaise de Transit, de Manutention, et de Transport
SOMASON ... Societe Malgache du Son
SOMASUR ... Sociedad Anonima Maderera del Sur [*Chile*]   (DSCA)
SOMAT..... Societe du Materiel Agricole du Tchad
SOMAT..... Societe Maritime Atlantique du Togo
SOMATAM ... Societe Marocaine de Tannerie et Megisserie
SOMATEC ... Societe Mauritanienne de Techniques, d'Etudes, et Applications Comptables
SOMATEL ... Societe Malgache de Telephonie et d'Application Electriques
SOMATELSAT ... Societe Marocaine de Telecommunications par Satellites [*Moroccan Satellite Telecommunications Company*]   (AF)
SOMATEM ... Societe de Fabrication Industrielle de Matelas et Emballages Plastiques
SOMATEX ... Societe Marocaine de Textiles
SOMATIB ... Societe Marocaine de Tissage et de Bonneterie
SOMATRA ... Societe Malienne de Transports
SOMATRAC ... Societe Mauritanienne de Distribution de Materiel de Travaux Publics
SOMAUPECO ... Societe Mauritanienne de Peche et de Conserves Audeux Chatelet
SOMAURAL ... Societe Mauritanienne des Allumettes
SOMB .... Societe Mauritanienne Boussade & Cie.
SOMBEPEC ... Societe Malienne du Betail, des Peaux, et de Cuir
SOMBRISA ... Sombreria Industrial Ltda. [*Colombia*]   (COL)
SOMC .... Saudi Operations & Maintenance Co. [*Saudi Arabia*]
SOMDIAA ... Societe Multinationale de Developpement pour les Industries Alimentaires et Agricoles
SOMEA..... Societa per la Matematica e l'Economia Applicate SpA [*Italian*]   (SLS)
SOMEA..... Societe Nationale de Constructions Mecaniques et Aeronautiques d'Algerie
SOMEAF .. Societe Metallurgique Africaine
SOMEC..... Sindicato de Operadores y Mecanicos de Equipos Camineros [*Union of Road-Building Equipment Operators and Mechanics*] [*Ecuador*]   (LA)
SOMEC..... Societe de Materiel d'Entreprise et de Construction
SOMEC..... Societe Mutuelle d'Etudes et de Cooperation Industrielle
SOMECA ... Societe de Mecanique Appliquee
SOMECA ... Societe de Mecanique Automobile et de Representation Industrielle
SOMECA ... Societe Mecanographique Africaine
SOMECAF ... Societe d'Ateliers Mecaniques Africains
SOMECAFRIQUE ... Societe pour la Mecanisation des Entreprises en Afrique
SOMECAFRIQUE-CENTRAFRIQUE ... Societe pour la Mecanisation des Entreprises de Centrafrique
SOMECUP ... Societe Malienne d'Exploitation des Cuirs et Peaux
SOMED .... Societe Maroc-Emirats de Developpement [*Morocco*]
SOMEDO ... Sociedad Medica Domiciliaria Ltda. [*Colombia*]   (COL)
SOMEL..... Sociedade Importadora de Movies e Electrodomesticos Lda.
SOMEL..... Societe Malgache d'Elevage
SOMENGO ... Menuiserie Ebenisterie du Mungo
SOMEP..... Societe Malgache d'Elements Prefabriques
SOMEPAG ... Societe Mediterraneenne de Produits Agricoles [*Algeria*]
SOMEPI ... Societe Mauritanienne d'Etudes et de Promotion Industrielles
SOMEPIA ... Societe Meroueh des Papiers Industriels Africains
SOMERA ... Societe Monegasque d'Exploitation et d'Etudes de Radiodiffusion [*Monaco*]   (EY)
SOMERECI ... Societe de Mecanique et de Rectification de Cote-D'Ivoire
SOMETER ... Societe Mauritanienne d'Etudes Techniques et de Representation
SOMETINA ... Societe Metallurgique et Industrielle Africaine
SOMETRA ... Societe Mediterraneenne de Transports
SOMEX..... Sociedad Mexicana de Credito Industrial [*Mexican Society for Industrial Credit*]   (LA)
SOMEXPA ... Societe Malgache d'Exploitation et de Participation
SOMIA...... Societe Mauritanienne pour l'Industrie de l'Automobile
SOMIAN .. Societe Mobiliere et Immobiliere de l'Afrique Noire
SOMIBA ... Societe Miniere de Moba [*Moba Mining Company*] [*Zaire*]   (AF)
SOMIBUROM ... Societe Mixte, Miniere, et Industrielle Roumano-Burundaise   (EY)

SOMICA... Societe Miniere de Carnot
SOMICOA ... Societe Maritime et Industrielle de la Cote Occidentale d'Afrique
SOMIDA... Societe des Mines d'Ampandrandava
SOMIDA... Societe des Mines du Djebel Azared
SOMIDANI ... Societe Miniere du Dahomey Niger
SOMIEX... Societe Malienne d'Importation et d'Exportation
SOMIFER ... Societe des Mines de Fer de Mekambo [*Mekambo Iron Mines Company*] [*Gabon*]   (AF)
SOMIFIMA ... Societe Miniere et Financiere de Madagascar
SOMIGA... Societe Miniere Gaziello & Cie. [*Dakar*]
SOMIKA... Societe Miniere de Karongo [*Karongo Mining Company*] [*Burundi*]   (AF)
SOMIMA ... Societe Miniere de Mauritanie [*Mining Company of Mauritania*]   (AF)
SOMINI.... Societe Minoterie Nigerienne
SOMINKI ... Societe Miniere et Industrielle du Kivu [*Mining and Industrial Company of Kivu*] [*Zaire*]   (AF)
SOMINOR ... Societe des Mines du Congo Septentrional
SOMIP...... Societe Anonyme Marocaine Italienne des Petroles
SOMIP...... Societe Mauritanienne des Industries de la Peche
SOMIPEX ... Societe Mauritanienne d'Importation, d'Exportation, et de Representation
SOMIQUE ... Sociedade de Comercio e Metais de Mozambique
SOMIRAMAD ... Societe des Minerais Rares de Madagascar
SOMIREMA ... Societe d'Exploitation Miniere et de Recherches de Mauritanie [*Mining Exploitation and Prospecting Company of Mauritania*]   (AF)
SOMIREN ... Societa Minerali Radiaettini Energia Nucleare [*Italian*]
SOMIRWA ... Societe des Mines du Rwanda [*Rwandan Mining Company*]   (AF)
SOMISA ... Sociedad Mixta Siderurgica Argentina [*Argentine Joint Iron and Steel Association*]   (LA)
SOMITAM ... Societe Miniere de Tambao [*Burkina Faso*]
SOMITRAM ... Societe Malienne d'Ingenierie en Transports Maritimes
Somm......... Sommaire [*Summary, Digest*] [*French*]   (FLAF)
SOMM...... Sommergible [*Submarine*] [*Italian Navy*]
SOMMIA ... Societe Marocaine de Mecanique Industrielle
SOMO....... Nonfat Milk Solids   (RU)
SOMO....... Societe de l'Okoume du Moyen-Congo
SOMO....... Stichting Onderzoek Multinationale Ondrmeningen
SOMOBAF ... Societe d'Assistance Technique pour la Modernisation de la Culture Bananiere et Fruitiere
SOMOCAT-SA ... Societe Mauritanienne d'Affretement de Consignation de Transit et d'Acconage
SOMOL .... Sociedade Mocambicana Limitada
SOMONI .. Societe du Moyen Niger
SOMOP .... Slovenske Oddelenie Ministerstva Obchodu a Priemyslu [*Slovak Department of the Ministry of Commerce and Industry*]   (CZ)
SOMOPAL ... Sociedade de Produtos Alimentares Limitada
SOMOREL ... Sociedade Mocambicana de Representacoes Ltd.
SOMOVA ... Societe de Montage et de Distribution de Vehicules Automobiles
SOMPELO ... Fabrica de Sombreros de Pelo [*Colombia*]   (COL)
SoMs......... Sondermessing [*Special Brass*] [*German*]   (GCA)
SOMSS ..... Slovenske Ministerstva Socialnej Starostlivosti [*Slovak Department of the Ministry of Social Welfare*]   (CZ)
Somt........... Sommet [*Summit*] [*Military map abbreviation World War I*] [*French*]   (MTD)
SOMTIS ... Societe Maribane de Tissage [*Morroccan*]
SOMU....... Sindicato de Obreros Maritimos Unidos [*United Maritime Workers Union*] [*Argentina*]   (LA)
SOMUDER ... Societes Mutuelles du Developpement Rural
SOMUKI... Societe Miniere de Muhinga et de Kigali
SOMZ....... Suksun Optical Instrument Plant   (RU)
SON.......... Espiritu Santo [*Vanuatu*] [*Airport symbol*]   (OAG)
SON.......... Fire Control RADAR, Gun Locator   (BU)
SON.......... Gun Laying Radar   (RU)
SON.......... Linea Aerea Aerosanta [*Chile*] [*ICAO designator*]   (FAAC)
SON.......... Sbornik Operativnich Norem [*Collection of Operational Standards*]   (CZ)
Son .... Sonora [*Record label*] [*Sweden*]
SON.......... Stacja Oceny Nasion [*Seed Testing Station*]   (POL)
SON.......... Standard Organization of Nigeria
SON.......... Stichting Scheikundig Onderzoek in Nederland [*Foundation for Chemical Research in the Netherlands*]   (WEN)
SONA .... Somali National News Agency
SONABA... Societe Nationale d'Amenagement de la Baie d'Agadir
SONABA... Societe Nationale de la Ceramique Artisanale et Industrielle du Benin
SONABA... Societe Nationale du Batiment
SONAC ..... Societe Nationale Camerounaise pour le Commerce, l'Industrie, et le Developpement
SONAC ..... Societe Nationale de Confection [*Tunisia*]

SONAC ..... Societe Nationale de Construction [*National Construction Company*] [*Liquidated 15 June 1970 Cambodia*]   (CL)
SONAC ..... Societe Nationale de la Ceramique Artisanale et Industrielle du Dahomey
SONAC ..... Societe Nouvelle d'Approvisionnement Commerciale [*Purchasing agency*] [*France*]   (IMH)
SONACAT ... Societe Nationale de Commercialisation et d'Applications Techniques de Materiel Electro-Domestique, Electrique, Radio-Television, de Conditionnement d'Air, et de Refrigeration [*Algeria*]
SONACEB ... Societe Nationale de Commercialisation et d'Exportation du Benin [*National Marketing and Export Company of Benin*] [*Cotonou*]   (AF)
SONACHAR ... Societe Nigerienne du Charbon
SONACI.... Societe Nationale Commerciale et Industrielle [*National Commercial and Industrial Company*] [*Senegal*]   (AF)
SONACIMENT ... Societe Nationale de Ciment [*National Cement Company*] [*Cambodia*]   (CL)
SONACLUB ... Sociedad Nacional de Clubes Ltda. [*Manizales*]   (COL)
SONACO .. Societe Nationale Agricole pour le Coton [*National Agricultural Company for Cotton*] [*Benin*]   (AF)
SONACO .. Societe Nationale de Commerce [*National Trading Company*] [*Malagasy*]   (AF)
SONACO .. Societe Nationale de Conditionnement [*National Packaging Company*] [*Ivory Coast*]   (AF)
SONACO .. Societe Nationale de Confection [*Tunisia*]
SONACO .. Societe Nationale de Constructions
SONACO .. Societe Nationale de Contreplaques [*National Plywood Company*] [*Cambodia*]   (CL)
SONACOB ... Societe Nationale de Commercialisation des Bois et Derives
SONACOB ... Societe Nationale de Construction de Batiments
SONACOL ... Sociedad Nacional de Oleoductos [*Chile*]   (LAA)
SONACOM ... Societe Nationale de Commerce [*National Trading Company*] [*Togo*]   (AF)
SONACOM ... Societe Nationale de Commercialisation des Plantes Medicinales
SONACOMA ... Societe Nationale des Commercants de Mauritanie
SONACOME ... Societe Nationale de Constructions Mecaniques [*National Mechanical Engineering Company*] [*Algiers, Algeria*]   (AF)
SONACOP ... Societe Nationale de Commercialisation des Produits Petroliers [*National Petroleum Products Marketing Company*] [*Benin*]   (AF)
SONACOP ... Societe Nationale de Conserverie de Poisson [*National Fish Canning Company*] [*Cambodia*]   (CL)
SONACOS ... Societe Nationale de Commercialisation des Oleagineux du Senegal [*National Society of Commercial Oil Production of Senegal*]
SONACOS ... Societe Nationale de Commercialisation des Semences [*National Company for the Marketing of Seeds*] [*Morocco*]   (AF)
SONACOT ... Societe Nationale de Commercialisation du Tchad [*Chad National Marketing Corporation*]
SONACOTRA ... Societe Nationale de Construction pour Travailleurs [*France*]
SONACOTRAP ... Societe Nationale de Construction et de Travaux Publics [*National Construction and Public Works Company*] [*Benin*]   (AF)
SONAD ..... Societes Regionales d'Amenagement et de Developpement [*Togo*]   (EY)
SONADE .. Societe Nationale de Distribution d'Eau Potable et Industrielle [*National Company for the Distribution of Drinking Water and Water for Industrial Use*] [*Algeria*]   (AF)
SONADECI ... Societe Nationale de Developpement des Cultures Industrielles [*Gabon*]   (IMH)
SONADER ... Societe Nationale de Developpement Rural [*National Rural Development Company*] [*Mauritania*]   (AF)
SONADER ... Societe Nationale pour le Developpement Rural du Dahomey
SONADIG ... Societe Nationale d'Investissement du Gabon [*National Investment Company of Gabon*]   (AF)
Sonadis ...... Societe Nationale d'Approvisionnement et de Distribution [*National Supply and Distribution Agency*] [*Senegal*]   (GEA)
SONADIS ... Societe Nationale d'Investissement du Senegal [*National Investment Company of Senegal*]   (AF)
SONAE ..... Societe Nationale d'Equipement [*National Equipment Company*] [*Cotonou, Benin*]   (AF)
SONAF ..... Societe Nationale de Financement
SONAFEL ... Societe Nationale pour le Developpement des Fruits et Legumes [*National Company for Development of Fruits and Vegetables*] [*Cotonou, Benin*]   (AF)
SONAFI.... Societe Nationale de Financement [*National Financing Company*] [*Ivory Coast*]   (AF)
SONAFOR ... Societe Nationale des Forages
SONAFRIG ... Societe Nationale des Frigorifiques
SONAGA ... Societe Nationale de Garantie et d'Assistance au Commerce
SONAGAR ... Societe Nationale Gabonaise d'Assurances et de Reassurances

SONAGECI ... Societe Nationale de Genie Civil [*National Civil Engineering Company*] [*Ivory Coast*]   (AF)

SONAGIM ... Societe Nationale pour la Gestion Immobiliere [*National Company for Real Estate Management*] [*Benin*]   (AF)

SONAGRI ... Societe Nationale pour la Production Agricole [*National Company for Agricultural Production*] [*Benin*]   (AF)

SONAGTHER ... Societe Nationale des Grands Travaux Hydrauliques et d'Equipement Rural [*Algeria*]

SONAKOP ... Societe Nationale de Conserverie de Poisson [*National Fish Canning Company*] [*Use SONACOP Cambodia*]   (CL)

SONALCO ... Sociedad Nacional de Confecciones Ltda. [*Colombia*]   (COL)

SONALCO ... Societe Nationale des Conserveries Algeriennes

SONALDI ... Sociedad Nacional de Inversiones Ltda. [*Manizales*]   (COL)

SONAM .... Societe Nationale d'Assurances Mutuelles du Senegal

SONAM .... Societe Navale Malienne [*Mali*]   (EY)

SONAMA ... Societe Nationale de Manutention [*National Freight Handling Company*] [*Algiers, Algeria*]   (AF)

SONAMEL ... Societe Nationale de Materiel Electrique et Electromenager [*National Electrical Material and Appliances Company*] [*Benin*]   (AF)

SONAMI .. Sociedad Nacional de Mineria [*National Mining Association*] [*Chile*]   (LA)

SONAMIF ... Societe Nationale des Mines de M'Fouati [*Congo*]   (IMH)

SONAMIS ... Societe Nationale Miniere de Sounda-Kaka-Moeka

SONAM-VIE ... Societe Nationale d'Assurance Mutuelle Vie

SONANGOL ... Sociedade Nacional de Combustiveis de Angola [*Oil enterprise*] [*Luanda, Angola*]

SONAP ..... Sociedad Anonima de Navegacion Petrolera [*Oil Tanker Corporation*] [*Chile*]   (LA)

SONAP ..... Sociedade Nacional de Petroleos de Mocambique

SONAP ..... Sociedad Nacional de Profesores [*National Teachers Association*] [*Chile*]   (LA)

SONAP ..... Societe Nationale des Articles de Papeterie

SONAP ..... Societe Nouvelle d'Alimentation et de Panification

SONAPA... Societe Nationale de la Production Animale [*National Animal Production Company*] [*Benin*]   (AF)

SONAPAL ... Societe Nationale de Papeterie et de Librairie [*National Book Store and Stationery Company*] [*Benin*]   (AF)

SONAPAP ... Societe Nationale de Papier [*National Paper Company*] [*Liquidated 19 February 1971 Cambodia*]   (CL)

SONAPECHE ... Societe Nationale d'Armement et de Peche [*National Shipping and Fishing Company*] [*Benin*]   (AF)

SONAPEX ... Societe Nationale pour le Developpement du Commerce Exterieur [*Morocco*]

SONAPH .. Societe Nationale pour le Developpement des Palmeraies et des Huileries [*National Society for the Development of Palm Tree Plantations and Palm Oil Resources*] [*Togo*]   (AF)

SONAPNEU ... Societe Nationale de Pneumatiques [*National Tire Company*] [*Cambodia*]   (CL)

SONAPRA ... Societe Nationale pour la Promotion Agricole [*Agricultural product marketing board*] [*Cotonou, Benin*]

SONAPRESS ... Societe Nationale de Presse, d'Edition, et de Publicite [*Senegal*]

SONAPRIM ... Societe Nationale de Distribution des Produits Importes [*National Imports Distribution Company*] [*Liquidated 8 May 1970 Cambodia*]   (CL)

SONAR ..... Societe Nationale d'Approvisionnement du Monde Rural [*Rural Sector National Supply Agency*] [*Senegal*]

SONAR ..... Societe Nationale d'Assurance et de Reassurance [*National Insurance and Reinsurance Company*] [*Ouagadougou, Burkina Faso*]   (AF)

SONAR ..... Societe Nationale d'Assurances et de Reassurance [*National Insurance and Reinsurance Co.*] [*Benin*]   (EY)

SONARA .. Societe Nationale de Raffinage

SONARA .. Societe Nigerienne de Commercialisation de l'Arachide [*Niger Peanut Marketing Company*]   (AF)

SONARAF ... Societe Nationale de Raffinage [*National Refining Company*] [*Cotonou, Benin*]   (AF)

SONAREM ... Societe Nationale de Recherches et d'Exploitation des Ressources Minieres du Mali [*National Company for Prospecting and Exploitation of Malian Mining Resources*]   (AF)

SONAREM ... Societe Nationale de Recherches et d'Exploitation Miniere [*National Mine Prospecting and Exploitation Company*] [*Algiers, Algeria*]   (AF)

SONAREP ... Sociedade Nacional de Refinacao de Petroleos

SONAREX ... Societe Nationale de Recherches et d'Exploitations Minieres [*National Mine Prospecting and Exploitation Company*] [*Central African Republic*]   (AF)

Sonarwa ..... Societe Nationale d'Assurance du Rwanda [*Insurance*] [*Rwanda*]

SONAS...... Societe Nationale d'Assurances [*National Insurance Company*] [*Zaire*]   (AF)

SONAS...... Society of Naval Architects of Singapore   (PDAA)

SONASCIE ... Societe Nationale de Scierie [*National Sawmill Company*] [*Liquidated 15 June 1970 Cambodia*]   (CL)

SONASID ... Societe Nationale de Siderurgie [*Iron and steel projects firm*] [*Nador, Morocco*]   (MENA)

SONASUCRE ... Societe Nationale de Sucre [*National Sugar Company*] [*Cambodia*]   (CL)

SONASUT ... Societe Nationale Sucriere du Tchad

SONATAM ... Societe Nationale des Tabacs et Allumettes du Mali

SONATEM ... Societe Nationale des Travaux d'Eaux et Barrages [*Algeria*]

SONATEX ... Societe Nationale de Textiles [*National Textile Company*] [*Cambodia*]   (CL)

SONATEX ... Societe Nationale d'Importations Textiles

SONATEXTILE ... Societe Nationale de Textiles [*National Textile Company*] [*Use SONATEX Cambodia*]   (CL)

SONATHERM ... Societe Nationale Algerienne de Thermalisme

SONATHYD ... Societe Nationale des Travaux Hydrauliques [*Algeria*]

SONATIBA ... Societe Nationale de Travaux d'Infrastructure et de Batiments [*National Infrastructure and Building Construction Company*] [*Algeria*]   (AF)

SONATITE ... Societe Nationale des Travaux d'Infrastructure des Telecommunications [*National Telecommunications Infrastructure Construction Company*] [*Algeria*]   (AF)

SONATMAG ... Societe Nationale de Transit et de Magasins Generaux [*North African*]

SONATO .. Societe Nouvelle pour l'Expansion Commerciale Togolaise

SONATOUR ... Societe Nationale de Tourisme et d'Hotellerie [*Algeria*]

SONATRA ... Societe Nationale des Transports Aeriens [*National Air Transport Company*] [*Senegal*]   (AF)

SONATRAB ... Societe Nationale de Transformation du Bois

SONATRAC ... Societe Nationale de Tracteurs [*National Tractor Company*] [*Cambodia*]   (CL)

SONATRAC ... Societe Nationale de Transit et de Consignation [*National Transit and Consignment Company*] [*Benin*]   (AF)

Sonatrach... Societe Nationale de Transport et de Commercialisation des Hydrocarbures b   (OMWE)

SONATRACH ... Societe Nationale du Transport et de Commercialisation des Hydrocarbons [*National Company for the Transport and Marketing of Hydrocarbons*] [*Algeria*]   (AF)

SONATRAM ... Societe Nationale des Transports Maritimes [*National Maritime Transport Company*] [*Gabon*]   (AF)

SONATRAM ... Societe Nationale des Travaux Maritimes [*Algeria*]

SONATRANS ... Sociedad Nacional Transportadora Ltda. [*Colombia*]   (COL)

SONATRO ... Societe Nationale des Travaux Routiers [*National Highway Construction Company*] [*Algeria*]   (AF)

SONAVING ... Sociedad Nacional de Vigilantes [*Colombia*]   (COL)

SONAVOCI ... Societe Nationale Voltaique de Cinema

sond............ Sonder [*Without*] [*German*]   (GCA)

Sonderabdr ... Sonderabdruck [*Separate Printing*] [*German*]

Sonderh...... Sonderheft [*Special Issue*] [*German*]

Sond H....... Sonder-Heft [*Special Issue*] [*German*]   (GCA)

Sond Nr...... Sonder-Nummer [*Special Number*] [*German*]   (GCA)

SONEA ...... Societe Nationale pour l'Exploitation des Abattoirs

SONEAB... Societe Nationale d'Exploitation des Arachides de Bouche

SONECOR ... Societe Nationale d'Equipement et de Constructions Routieres

SONED ..... Societe Nationale des Etudes de Developpement

SONEDE.... Societe Nationale d'Exploitation et de Distribution des Eaux [*National Water Exploitation and Distribution Company*] [*Algeria*]   (AF)

SONEDIC ... Societe Nationale d'Equipement et de Developpement Industriel du Cameroun

SONEES ... Societe Nationale des Eaux et Electricite du Senegal [*Senegalese National Water and Electricity Company*]   (AF)

SONEF...... Societe Nationale d'Exploitation Forestiere [*National Forest Exploitation Company*] [*Cambodia*]   (CL)

SONEG ..... Societe Nationale d'Entreprise Generale

SONEL...... Societe Nationale de l'Electricite [*National Electricity Company*] [*Cameroon*]   (AF)

SONEL...... Societe Nationale d'Elevage

SONELEC ... Societe Nationale Algerienne de Fabrication et de Montage du Materiel Electrique et Electronique [*Algerian National Company for the Manufacture and Installation of Electrical and Electronic Equipment*] [*Algiers, Algeria*]   (AF)

SONELEC ... Societe Nationale d'Eau et d'Electricite

SONELGAZ ... Societe Nationale d'Electricite et du Gaz [*National Electricity and Gas Company*] [*Algiers, Algeria*]   (AF)

SONEMS ... SONATRACH Ente Minerario Siciliano [*North African*]

SONEOH ... Societe Nationale d'Entretien et d'Exploitation d'Ouvrages Hydrauliques

SONEP...... Societe Nationale d'Etudes et de Promotion Industrielle

SONEPI.... Societe Nationale d'Etudes et de Promotion Industrielle [*National Industrial Promotion and Research Agency*] [*Senegal*]

SONEPRESS ... Societe Nationale d'Edition et de Presse [*Burkina Faso*]

SONERAN ... Societe Nigerienne d'Exploitation des Ressources Animales

SONETRA ... Societe Nationale d'Entreprise et de Travaux Publics

SONETRA ... Societe Senegalaise de Transit

SONEXI.... Societe Nigerienne d'Exploitation Cinematographique

SONEXIM ... Societe Nationale d'Exportation et d'Importation [*National Export-Import Company*] [*Cambodia*]   (CL)

SONEXPEXT ... Societe Nationale pour les Exportations Extremes [*National Special Exports Company*] [*Cambodia*]   (CL)

SONEXPIERRE ... Societe Nationale pour l'Exploitation de Gisements des Pierres et Metaux Precieux et Semi-Precieux [*National Company for the Exploitation of Deposits of Precious and Semi-Precious Stones and Metals*] [*Cambodia*]   (CL)

SONEXPIERROR ... Societe Nationale pour l'Exploitation de Gisements des Pierres et Metaux Precieux et Semi-Precieux [*National Company for the Exploitation of Deposits of Precious and Semi-Precious Stones and Metals*] [*Use SONEXPIERRE Cambodia*]

SONG .... Societe d'Okoume de la N'Gounie [*Gabon*]

SONHOTEL ... Societe Nigerienne d'Hotellerie [*National hotel company*] [*Niger*]

SONI-Afrique ... Societe Nouvelle d'Importation Afrique

SONIAH ... Societe Nationale d'Irrigation et d'Amenagement Hydro-Agricole [*National Irrigation and Hydro-Agricultural Development Company*] [*Benin*]   (AF)

SONIB .... Societe Nationale d'Importation du Benin [*National Import Company of Benin*]   (AF)

SONIBANQUE ... Societe Nigerienne de Banque   (EY)

SONIC .... Societe Nationale des Industries de la Cellulose [*National Cellulose Industries Company*] [*Algiers, Algeria*]   (AF)

SONIC .... Societe Nationale d'Industrie et de Commerce

SONIC .... Societe Polskie et Internationale Compagnie

SONI-CA .. Societe Nigerienne de Carrelage

SONICA .... Societe Nigerienne de Credit Automobile

SONICAR ... Societe Nigerienne de Carrelage

SONICERAM ... Societe Nigerienne de Produits Ceramique

SONICHAR ... Societe Nigerienne de Charbon

SONICO ... Societe Nationale pour l'Industrie et le Commerce

SONICOB ... Societe Nationale d'Industrialisation et de Commercialisation du Betail

SONICOCIT ... Societe Nigerienne de Commerce International

SONICOG ... Societe Nationale pour l'Industrie des Corps Gras [*National Company for the Fatty Substance Industry*] [*Benin*]   (AF)

SONIDA ... Societe Nigerienne pour le Developpement de l'Autoroute

SONIDEP ... Societe Nigerienne de Produits Petroliers [*Nigerien Petroleum Products Company*] [*Niger*]   (AF)

SONIFAME ... Societe Nigerienne de Fabrications Metalliques

SONII .... North Ossetian Scientific Research Institute   (RU)

SONIMACI ... Societe Nippo-Malgache Commerciale et Industrielle [*Japanese-Malagasy Commercial and Industrial Company*]   (AF)

SONIMCO ... Societe Nationale d'Impression en Continu

SONIMEX ... Societe Nationale d'Importation et d'Exportation [*National Import-Export Company*] [*Mauritius*]

SONIPEC ... Societe Nationale des Industries des Peaux et Cuirs [*National Leather and Hides Industries Company*] [*Algiers, Algeria*]   (AF)

SONIPLA ... Societe Nigerienne de Plastique

SONITA .... Societe Nigerienne de Transports Aeriens [*Niger*] [*ICAO designator*]   (FAAC)

SONITAB ... Societe Nigerienne de Batiment et de Travaux Publics

SONITAN ... Societe Nigerienne de Tannerie

SONITEX ... Societe Nationale de l'Industrie Textile [*National Textile Industry Company*] [*Algiers, Algeria*]   (AF)

SONITEXTIL ... Societe Nouvelle Nigerienne des Textiles

SONITRA ... Societe Nationale Ivoirienne de Travaux [*Ivorian National Construction Company*]   (AF)

SONIVEX ... Societe Nigerienne de Viandes d'Exportation

SONIVIEX ... Societe Nigerienne de Viandes d'Exportation

SONMIVA ... Societe Nationale de Mise en Valeur du Sud [*National Company for Development of the South*] [*Tunisia*]   (AF)

SONMIVAS ... Societe Nationale de Mise en Valeur du Sud [*National Company for Development of the South*] [*Tunisia*]

SONNA ..... Somali National News Agency   (AF)

SONOBAT ... Societe Nouvelle de Batiments

SONOKIT ... Societe Nouvelle Khmere d'Importation et de Transit [*New Cambodian Import and Transit Company*]   (CL)

SONOMUSICA ... Sociedad Nacional de Musica [*Colombia*]   (COL)

SONP .... Spojene Ocelarny, Narodni Podnik [*United Steel Works, National Enterprise*] [*Kladno*]   (CZ)

SONUCI .... Societe Nigerienne d'Urbanisme et de Construction Immobiliere

SONY .... South Nyanza

SOO .... Clothing Disinfection Station   (RU)

SOO .... Secret Operations Section   (RU)

SOO .... Smotra Oruzija i Opreme [*Inspection of Arms and Equipment*] [*YU*]

SOO .... Songo [*Mozambique*] [*Airport symbol*]   (OAG)

SOO .... Synetairistikos Oinopoiitikos Organismos [*Cooperative Wine-Making Organization*] [*Greek*]   (GC)

soobshch .... Communication [*Bibliography*], Information, Report   (RU)

SOOD &I ... Security of Official Documents and Information Manual [*Australia*]

SOOG .... Saint-Georges-De-L'Oyapock [*French Guiana*] [*ICAO location identifier*]   (ICLI)

SOOJ .... Society of Ophthalmological Optics of Japan   (PDAA)

SOOM .... Saint-Laurent du Maroni [*French Guiana*] [*ICAO location identifier*]   (ICLI)

SOOP .... Senior Firing Position Officer   (BU)

SOOP .... State Organization for Oil Projects [*Baghdad, Iraq*]   (MENA)

SOOR .... Regina [*French Guiana*] [*ICAO location identifier*]   (ICLI)

SOOR .... State Organization for Oil Refining [*Iraq*]

SOORT ..... Statutory and Other Officers Remuneration Tribunal [*New South Wales, Australia*]

SOOS .... Saul [*French Guiana*] [*ICAO location identifier*]   (ICLI)

SOOY .... Sinnamary [*French Guiana*] [*ICAO location identifier*]   (ICLI)

SOP .... Fixed Bath Station   (RU)

sop .... Hill, Small Volcano [*Topography*]   (RU)

SOP .... Permanent Decontamination Stations   (BU)

SOP .... Sekcija za Odrzavanje Pruge [*Railroad Track Maintenance Section*]   (YU)

SOP .... Sekcija za Odrzavanje Puteva [*Road Maintenance Section*]   (YU)

SOP .... Societe d'Ophtalmologie de Paris [*Ophthalmological Society of Paris*] [*French*]   (SLS)

SOP .... Societe Odontologique de Paris [*French*]   (SLS)

SOP .... Spoldzielnie Oszczednosciowo-Pozyczkowe [*Savings and Loan Cooperatives*]   (POL)

SOP .... Standard of Limited Application   (RU)

SOP .... Staropolski Okreg Przemyslowy [*Old Polish Industrial Region*] [*Poland*]

SOP .... Straz Ochrony Przyrody [*Nature Preserving Guard*] [*Poland*]

SOP .... Szkola Oficerow Pozarnictwa [*Fire-Fighting Officers' School*] [*Poland*]

SOPA .... Societe de Publicite Abidjanaise

SOPA .... Societe Oranaise d'Entreprise Prefabrication [*Algeria*]

SOPA .... Societe Pharmaceutique Africaine

SOPAB ...... Societe des Pansements du Benin

SOPAC ...... South Pacific Applied Geoscience Commission [*Fiji*]   (EAIO)

SOPAC ...... South Pacific News Service Ltd. [*New Zealand*]   (FEA)

SOPACOR ... Societe des Palmeraies du Cameroun Oriental

SOPAD ...... Societe de Produits Alimentaires et Dietetiques

SOPAGEF ... Societe de Participation, de Gestion, et de Financement

SOPAME .. Societe des Palmeraies de Mbongo et d'Eseka

SOPANI .... Societe de Parfumerie Nigerienne

SOPAO ..... Societe de Peche de l'Afrique Occidentale

SOPAR ...... Societe Parisienne d'Articles de Luxe

SOPARCA ... Societe de Fabrication de Parfumerie au Cameroun

SOPARCO ... Societe Africaine de Parfumerie et de Cosmetique

SOPARMOD ... Societe de Parfums Modernes

SOPAZ ...... Synergatikos Organismos Paragogis Zootrofon [*Animal Feeds Production Cooperative*] [*Cyprus*]   (GC)

SOPC .... Sub-Oficiales Profesionales de Carrera [*Professional Career Noncommissioned Officers*] [*Venezuela*]   (LA)

SOPCAM ... Sopecoba Cameroun

SOPD .... Dangerous Pressure Drop Indicator   (RU)

SOPE .... Etaireia Prostasias Syngrafikon Dikaiomaton [*Society for the Protection of Authors' Rights*] [*Cyprus*]   (GC)

SOPEC ...... Sociedade de Produtos para o Fomento Pecuario Lda.

SOPECA ... Societe de Pecherie de Casamance [*Senegal*]

SOPECAM ... Societe de Presse et d'Editions du Cameroun [*Cameroon News and Publishing Corporation*]   (AF)

SOPECAS ... Sociedade de Pecas e Automoveis

SOPECI ..... Societe de Peinture en Cote-D'Ivoire

SOPECOBA ... Societe des Pecheries Cotieres a la Baleine

SOPEFAL ... Societe Petroliere Francaise en Algerie [*French Petroleum Company in Algeria*]   (AF)

SOPEG ...... Societe Petroliere de Gerance [*Petroleum Management Company*] [*Algeria*]   (AF)

SOPEKAM ... Societe de Peche de Kamsar [*Guinean fishing organization*]

SOPELEM ... Societe d'Optique, Precision, Electronique, et Mecanique [*French*]

SOPEMEA ... Societe pour le Perfectionnement des Materiels et Equipements Aerospatiaux [*France*]   (PDAA)

SOPEREF ... Societe Parisienne d'Etudes et de Recherches Foncieres [*French*]   (SLS)

SOPESEA ... Societe des Pecheries Senegalaises de l'Atlantique

SOPESUR ... Sociedad Periodistica del Sur [*Southern Newspaper Company*] [*Chile*]   (LA)

SOPHRUC ... Societe de Planteurs d'Heveas pour le Ramassage et l'Usinage du Caoutchouc [*Rubber Planters Company for the Collection and Processing of Latex*] [*Cambodia*]   (CL)

SOPI .... Societe de Participations et d'Etudes Industrielles [*Morocco*]

SOPICAD ... Societe Pituach Centrafricaine de Diamants

SOPICOMA ... Societe pour la Promotion Industrielle et Commerciale de Madagascar [*Industrial and Commercial Promotion Company of Madagascar*]   (AF)

SOPILEC .. Societe des Piles Electriques du Gabon

SOPIMA ... Societe des Piles de Madagascar

SOPIMER ... Societe Civile d'Etude du Pipeline Mediterranee

SOPIVOLTA ... Societe des Piles de Haute-Volta

SOPLAREF ... Sociedad de Plasticos Reforzados Ltda. [Colombia] (COL)
Sopo .... Poets' Union (RU)
SOPO-AUTOS ... Societe Senegalaise des Poids Lourds Automobiles
SOPOFI .... Societe Pontenegrine Financiere Immobiliere
SOPONATA ... Sociedade Portuguesa de Navios Tanques [Shipping company] [Portugal] (EY)
SOPONICRO ... Societe de Polissage, Nickelage, et Chromage
SOPOTEC ... Societe Pompes et Techniques
SOPP .... Sekcija za Odrzavanje Plovnih Puteva [River Navigation Maintenance Section] (YU)
SOPP .... Sekretarijat za Opste Privredne Poslove (SIV) [Secretariat of General Economic Affairs] (YU)
sopr .... Resistance, Strength (RU)
SOPRA ...... Societe de Peinture et Ravalement
soprac ...... Sopracoperta [Wrapper] [Publishing] [Italian]
SOPRAVIT ... Sopravit de Peinture, Ravalement, et Vitrerie
SOPREA ... Sociedad de Promocion y Reconversion Economica de Andalucia [Spain] (EY)
SOPREMER ... Societe d'Exploitation des Produits de la Mer [Sea Products Exploitation Company] [Cambodia] (CL)
SOPREN ... Societa Progettazione Reattori Nucleari, SpA [Nuclear energy] [Italian] (NRCH)
SOPREST ... Society for the Promotion of Engineering Sciences and Technology [Pakistan]
SOPRIVO ... Societe de Produits Ivoiriens
SOPROA ... Sociedad Productora de Alimentos [Food Processing Company] [Chile] (LA)
SOPRODA ... Societe d'Exploitation de Produits Agricoles et Forestiers [Agricultural and Forest Products Exploitation Company] [Cambodia] (CL)
SOPRODAV ... Societe d'Etude pour le Developpement de la Culture de l'Avocatier
SOPRODAV-CI ... Societe d'Etude pour la Production de l'Avocat en Cote-D'Ivoire
SOPROGI ... Societe pour la Promotion et la Gestion Industrielle
SOPROHOT ... Societe de Promotion Hoteliere et Touristique de Tunisie
SOPROIN ... Sociedad Profesional de Inversiones [Colombia] (COL)
SOPROLAIT ... Societe des Produits Laitiers du Togo [Togo]
SOPROLE ... Sociedad de Productores de Leche [Society of Milk Producers] [Chile] (LA)
sopromat .... Strength of Materials (RU)
SOPROMET ... Sociedad Promotora de Exportaciones Metalurgicas [Association for the Promotion of Metallurgical Exports] [Chile] (LA)
SOPROSEN ... Societe de la Promotion Senegalaise
SOPS .... Council for the Study of Productive Resources (RU)
SOPS .... Speicher-Operationssteuerung [Memory Operations Control] [German] (ADPT)
SOPV .... Sdruzeni Osvetimskych Politickych Veznu [Association of Former Political Prisoners in the Oswieczym Concentration Camp] (CZ)
SOPV .... Svaz Osvobozenych Politickych Veznu [Union of Liberated Political Prisoners] (CZ)
SOPVP ...... Svaz Osvobozenych Politickych Veznu a Pozustalych po Obetech Nacismu [Association of Liberated Political Prisoners and Relatives of the Victims of Nazism] (CZ)
SOPY .... Support of Positive Youth [Australia]
SOQ .... Sorong [Indonesia] [Airport symbol] (OAG)
SOQUIM .. Sociedad Quimica y Minera de Chile [Santiago, Chile] (LAA)
SOQUIMICH ... Sociedad Quimica y Minera Chilena [Chilean Chemical and Mining Association] (LA)
SOR .... Air Stord AS [Norway] [ICAO designator] (FAAC)
SOR .... Rudder Deflection Recorder (RU)
SOR .... Sectie Operationele Research [Netherlands] (SLS)
Sor .... Senior [Senior] [Portuguese]
Sor .... Senor [Sir, Mister] [Spanish]
SOR .... Servicio Oficial de Radiodifusion [Official Broadcasting Service] [Argentina] (LA)
SOR .... Slovenska Odborova Rada [Slovak Trade Union Council] [Bratislava, Czechoslovakia] (CZ)
Sor .... Soror [Sister (of a religous order)] [Portuguese]
sor .... Sorozat [Series] [Publishing] [Hungary]
SOR .... Stacja Obslugi Radiotechnicznej [Radio-Engineering Service Station] [Poland]
SOR .... Stacje Obslugi Radiofonicznej [Broadcasting Service Stations] (POL)
SOR .... Sveriges Orkesterforeningars Riksforbund [Sweden] (EAIO)
SOR .... Synchrotron Orbital Radiation [High-energy physics]
SORA .... Svenska Operationsanalysfoereningen [Sweden] (SLS)
SORABA ... Societe de Ravitaillement du Baol
Sorabis ...... Union of Workers in the Arts (RU)
Sorabpros .. Union of Education Workers (RU)
SORAD ..... Societe Regionale d'Amenagement et de Developpement
SORADEC ... Societe Raad & Cie.
SORAF ...... Societe de Representations Africaines
SORAFOM ... Societe de la Radiodiffusion d'Outre-Mer [Overseas Broadcasting Company] [French] (AF)

SORAL ...... Societe de Ravitaillement Alimentaire
SORANI .... Societe des Transitaires Reunis SARL [United Forwarding Agents Company, Inc.] (CL)
SORAPA ... Societe de Ramassage du Paddy [Paddy Harvesting Company] [Cambodia] (CL)
SORARAF ... Societe de Representation d'Assurances et de Reassurances Africaines
SORAS ...... Societe Rwandaise d'Assurances (EY)
SORB .... Sentrum vir Ondersoek na Rewolusionere Bedrywighede [Centre for Research into Revolutionary Activities] [Rand Afrikaans University South Africa] (AA)
SORB .... State Organization for Roads and Bridges [Iraq]
SORBI .... Serikat Organisasi Buruh Republik Indonesia [Central Council of All Indonesian Trade Unions]
SORC .... Serious Offenders Review Council [New South Wales, Australia]
SORCA ...... Societe de Recherche Operationelle et d'Economie Appliquee [French] (ADPT)
SORE .... Save Our Residential Environment [Australia]
SORE .... Save Our River Environment [Australia]
SOREAS ... Syndicat des Fabricants d'Organes et d'Equipment Aeronautiques et Spatiaux [France] (PDAA)
SORECAL ... Societe Regionale de Construction d'Alger
SORECAM ... Societe de Rechapage du Cameroun
SORECO... Societe Regionale de Construction de Constantine [Algeria]
SORECOR ... Societe Regionale de Construction d'Oran
SOREDIA ... Societe de Recherches et d'Exploitations Diamantiferes
SOREFA ... Societe de Reparations et Fournitures Auto
SOREFAME ... Sociedades Reunidas Fabricaoes Metalicas [Portugal] (PDAA)
SOREKAT ... Societe de Recherches au Katanga
SOREL ...... Synergatikos Organismos Elaioparagogon [Olive Producers' Cooperative Organization] [Cyprus] (GC)
SORELEC ... Societe de Rebobinage et Electricite
SOREM ..... Societa Ricerche Esperienze Meteorologiche [Italian] (SLS)
SOREMA ... Societe de Reassurance des Assurances Mutuelles Agricoles [France] (EY)
SOREMAC ... Societe de Recherches et d'Exploitations Miniere pour l'Afrique Centrale
SOREMI ... Societe de Recherches et d'Exploitations Minieres [Mineral exploration and exploitation organization] [Burkina Faso]
SORENA... Sociedad Refinadora Nacional [National Refining Company] [Chile] (LA)
SOREPCA ... Societe de Recherches et d'Exploitation des Petroles du Cameroun
SOREPEL ... Societe de Reparation Electromecanique F. Riviere & Cie.
SOREPZA ... Societe de Recherche et d'Exploitation des Petroles au Zaire
Sores .... Senores [Sirs, Gentlemen] [Spanish]
SORES ...... Societe de Realisations d'Equipements Scolaires
SORES ...... Societe de Restauration Senegalaise
SORETRAP ... Societe Regionale des Travaux Publics [Tunisia]
SORETRAS ... Societe Regionale de Transports du Gouvernorat de Sfax [Tunisia]
SOREX ...... Societe de Recherches et d'Exploitation de Kairouan [Tunisia]
SORFACE ... Societe Franco-Arabe d'Assurance et de Reassurance SAL
SORGO ..... Central Asian Branch of the Russian Geographical Society (RU)
SORI .... Societe Regionale d'Investissements du Centre Sud
SORICA .... Societe de Representation, d'Industrie, et de Commerce pour l'Adamaoua
SORIFEMA ... Societe Rizicole et Feculiere Malagasy [Malagasy Rice and Potato Production Company] (AF)
SORIMEX ... Societe Regionale d'Importation et d'Exportation [Tunisia]
SORIN .... Societa Ricerche Impianti Nucleari [Nuclear energy] [Italian] (NRCH)
SORiT .... Stacja Obslugi Radiowej i Telewizyjnej [Radio and Television Service Station] [Poland]
SORIV .... Societe Route Ivoire
SORMAS .. Sogut Refrakter Malzemeleri Anonim Sirketi [Sogut Refractory Materials Corporation] (TU)
SORO .... Special Operations Research Office
SOROTEL ... Societe Royale d'Hotellerie [Royal Hotel Trade Company] [Cambodia] (CL)
SORS .... Unipolar Communication Operations Bay (RU)
sorsz .... Sorszam [Serial Number] (HU)
sort .... Marshaling Yard [Topography] (RU)
SORT .... Stacja Obslugi Radiowej i Telewizyjnej [Radio and Television Service Station] [Poland]
SORTEX ... Soroksari Textilipar Reszvenytarsasag [Textile Industry of Soroksar Limited] (HU)
Sortsemovoshch ... Republic Office for the Production, Procurement, and Sale of High-Quality Seeds of Vegetables, Melons, and of Fodder Root Crops (RU)
sort st .... Marshaling Yard [Topography] (RU)
SORZ........ Optical Character Recognition System [Computers] (RU)
SOS........... Feedback Sylphon (RU)
SOS........... Save Our Stages [Australia]
SOS........... Save Our Sydney [Australia]

sos .... Sien Ommesyde [*Please Turn Over*] [*Correspondence*] [*Afrikaans*]
SOS........... Sierra Leone Organisation Society
SOS........... Societe d'Organisations et de Services
SOS........... Societe l'Okoume de Sindara
SOS........... Sofia Okrug Court   (BU)
SoS............ Sonderschule [*German*]
sos .... Sosea [*Road*] [*Romanian*]
SOS........... Sostenuto [*Sustained*] [*Music*]
Sos.............. Sosyoloji [*Sociology*]   (TU)
SOS........... Straz Obrany Statu [*State Defense Guard*]   (CZ)
SOS........... Student-Operationssystem [*German*]   (ADPT)
SOS........... Sumska Ogledna Stanica [*Forestry Experiment Station*]   (YU)
SOSA........ Snaps Old Students Association
SOSA......... State Opera of South Australia
SOSAC..... Societe Senegalaise d'Armement a la Crevette
SOSAP..... Societe Senegalaise d'Armement a la Peche
SOSAP..... Sofia Obshtina Pharmaceutical Economic Enterprise   (BU)
SOSCO...... Savannah Olympic Support Council   (OLYM)
SOSCO...... Social Security Organization [*Malaysia*]
SOSCVK ... SOS Children's Village, Kenya   (EAIO)
sosdem .... Sosiaalidemokraatti(nen) [*Finland*]
SOSEBA ... Societe Senegalaise d'Entreprise de Batiment
SOSECHAL ... Societe Senegalaise de Chalutage
SOSECI.... Societe Senegalaise pour le Commerce et l'Industrie
SOSECOD ... Societe Senegalaise pour le Commerce et le Developpement
SOSECODA ... Societe Senegalaise de Courtages et d'Assurances
SOSECOMI ... Societe Senegalaise de Commerce et d'Importation [*Senegal*]
SOSECOREP ... Societe Senegalaise de Courtage et de Representation
SOSEDA ... Societe Senegalaise de Developpement Agricole
SOSEDA ... Societe Senegalaise pour le Developpement de l'Automobile
SOSEFIL .. Societe Senegalaise de Fileterie
SOSEG ...... Societe Senegalaise d'Emaillage et de Galvanisation
SOSEGA ... Societe Senegalaise de Courtage et de Gestion d'Assurances
SOSEGBA ... Societe Senegalaise d'Entreprise de Batiment
SOSELF.... Societe Senegalaise des Etablissements Louis Feltrin
SOSEPA.... Societe Senegalaise de Produits Alimentaires
SOSEPE.... Societe Senegalaise de Peches
Sosepra ...... Societe Senegalaise de Promotion de l'Artisanat [*Handicrafts Promotion Agency of Senegal*]   (GEA)
SOSEPROCI ... Societe Senegalaise de Promotion Commerciale et Industrielle
SOSEREM ... Societe Senegalaise de Renflouement et d'Exploitation du Montana
SOSETA ... Societe Senegalaise de Transports Automobiles
SOSETAM ... Societe Senegalaise de Tannerie-Megisserie
SOSETER ... Societe Senegalaise de Terrassements
SOSETRAM ... Societe Senegalaise de Transports et de Mecanique
SOSETRAUR ... Societe Senegalaise de Travaux Urbains et Ruraux
SOSEXCATRA ... Societe Senegalaise d'Exploitation de Carrieres et de Transports
SoSh........... Somali Shilling
SOSI .... Service d'Ornement de Sepulture Ivoirien
SOSIDE ... Societe E. Simeonides et E. Devanakis
SOSILOS.. Societe des Silos du Senegal
SOSIMABI ... Societe Sino-Malgache de Bouteilles Isolantes
SOSIPO .... Societe des Silos Portuaires [*Morocco*]
SOSKhI ..... North Ossetian Agricultural Institute   (RU)
SOSLC ...... SOS Locusts Campaign [*Africa*]
SOSOBA ... Societe d'Entreprise Soudanaise de Batiment
SOSR......... Sekretarijat za Opsti Stopanski Raboti (IVNRM) [*Secretariat of General Economic Affairs*]   (YU)
SOSR......... Stacja Oceny Sprzetu Rolniczego [*Farm Equipment Evaluation Station*]   (POL)
SOSS .... Sofia Okoliya Trade Union Council   (BU)
SOSSI........ SOS Sahel International   (EAIO)
SOSSRNJ ... Savezni Odbor Socialisticki Sojuz na Rabotniot Narod na Jugoslavija [*Federal Committee, Socialist Alliance of Working People of Yugoslavia*]   (YU)
sost .... Compiled, Compiler   (RU)
SOSTEM .. Societe de Stations Thermales et des Eaux Minerales [*Tunisia*]
SOSU........ Societe Sucriere Voltaique
SOSU-BF .. Societe Sucriere du Burkina Faso [*Sugar refining organization*]
SOSUCAM ... Societe Sucriere du Cameroun [*Cameroon Sugar Company*]
SOSUHO.. Societe Sucriere du Haut-Ogooue [*Upper Ogooue Sugar Company*] [*Gabon*]
SOSU-HV ... Societe Sucriere Voltaique [*Voltan Sugar Company*] [*SOSU-BF*] [*Later,*]   (AF)
SOSUMAV ... Societe Sucriere de la Mahavavy [*Mahavavy Sugar Company*]
SOSUMO ... Societe Sucriere du Moso [*Development organization*] [*Burundi*]   (EY)
SOSUNI.... Societe Sucriere Nigerienne [*Niger Sugar Company*]
SOSUNIARI ... Societe Sucriere du Niari [*Niari Sugar Company*] [*Congo*]   (AF)
SOSUTCHAD ... Societe Sucriere du Tchad [*Chad Sugar Company*]
SOSYAL-IS ... Social Workers Union   (TU)

SOT .... Concealed Emplacement   (RU)
SOT .... Sabiraliste Ostecene Tehnike [*Assemblage of Damaged Technical Equipment*]   (YU)
sot.............. Sotet [*Dark*]   (HU)
sot.............. Sotilassana [*Military Term*] [*Finland*]
SOT .... Stacja Obslugi Telewizyjnej [*Television Service Station*] [*Poland*]
SOT .... Systeemontwerptechnieken
SOT .... Weapon on Disappearing Mount in Position   (BU)
SOTA .... Societe des Transports Africains
SOTAC..... Societe des Transports Automobiles de la Corniche [*Algeria*]
SOTACh.... Sociedad de Tecnicos Agricolas de Chile [*Association of Agricultural Experts of Chile*]   (LA)
SOTAD ..... Societe Tuniso-Americaine de Developpement
SOTAF...... Societe Textile de l'Afrique Occidentale
SOTAGRO ... Servicios Tecnicos Agropecuarios [*Tulua-Valle*]   (COL)
SOTAL...... Societe Tunisienne d'Aluminium
SOTALMA ... Societe Touristique Algero-Marocaine
SOTAPO... Societe des Tanneries Poyet
SOTATRIC ... Societe Tuniso-Allemande de Confection et de Broderie
SOTCON ... Societe Togolaise de Confection [*Togo*]
SOTE......... Semmelweis Orvostudomanyi Egyetem [*Semmelweis Medical University*]   (HU)
SOTEC...... Sociedade Tecnica e Comercial Lda.
SOTEC...... Sociedad Tecnica [*Colombia*]   (COL)
SOTECAS ... Societe des Techniciens Associes
SOTECNICA ... Sociedade Tecnica e Comercial Lda.
SOTEF...... Societe Oranaise de Tissage et Filature [*North African*]
SOTEGA... Societe Industrielle Textile du Gabon
SOTEHPA ... Societe Togolaise d'Extraction d'Huile de Palme
SOTEIC .... Societe Tropicale d'Entreprises Industrielles et Commerciales
SOTEKCI ... Societe des Techniciens Khmers pour le Commerce et l'Industrie [*Cambodian Commercial and Industrial Technicians Company*]   (CL)
SOTEL ...... Sociedade Tecnica e Comercial Lda.
SOTEL ...... Societe de Teleinformatique [*French*]   (ADPT)
SOTELCA ... Sociedade Termo Eletrica de Capivari [*Brazil*]   (LAA)
SOTELEC ... Societe Mixte pour le Developpement de la Technique des Telecommunications sur Cables [*France*]   (PDAA)
SOTEM..... Societe Commerciale du N'Tem
SOTEMA ... Societe Textile de Majunga [*Majunga Textile Company*] [*Malagasy*]   (AF)
SOTEMI ... Societe Tunisienne d'Expansion Miniere
SOTEMU ... Societe Tunisienne d'Explosifs et de Munitions
SOTEREL ... Sociedade Tecnica de Representacoes Limitada
SOTESA ... Societa Tecnica pe lo Siviluppo Agricols
SOTEXCO ... Societe des Textiles du Congo
SOTEXCO ... Societe Textile Cotonniere [*Zaire*]   (IMH)
SOTEXCOCAM ... Societe des Textiles et de Commerce du Cameroun
SOTEXI .... Societe Industrielle Textile de Cote-D'Ivoire
SOTEXIM ... Societe Togolaise d'Exportation et d'Importation [*Togolese Export-Import Company*]   (AF)
SOTEXKA ... Societe Textile de Kaolack [*Senegal*]
SOTEXKI ... Societe Textile de Kisangani [*Zaire*]   (IMH)
SOTHA ..... Societe de Travaux Hydrauliques et Agricoles
SOTHRA .. Societe de Transport de Gaz Naturel d'Hassi R'Mel a Arzew [*Algeria*]
SOTIBA .... Societe de Teinture, Blanchissement, et Apprets
SOTIBA-SIMPAFRIC ... Societe de Teinture, Blanchissement, Apprets, et d'Impressions Africaines [*Senegal*]
SOTIC .... Societe Tamatavienne d'Industries et de Cultures
SOTICI...... Societe de Transformation Industrielle de Cote-D'Ivoire
SOTIL .... Sindicato de Obreros del Transporte Interdepartamental de Leche [*Milk Transport Workers Union*] [*Uruguay*]   (LA)
SOTIL .... Sociedade Luso Tipografica Limitada
SOTIMA ... Societe de Tissages Maghrebins [*Algeria*]
SOTIMI .... Societa di Ortopedia e Traumatologia dell'Istituto Meridionale ed Insulare [*Italian*]   (SLS)
SOTIMPEX ... Societe Togolaise d'Importation et d'Exportation
SOTIPA .... Societe de Transformation Industrielle du Papier
SOTIZEM ... Societe Tiriss Zemmour
SOTMES .. Sindicato Obrero Textil de Mejoramiento Social [*Trade Union for Social Improvement of Textile Workers*] [*El Salvador*]   (LA)
SOTO .... Socialist Exchange of Technical Experience   (BU)
SOTO .... Societe Dakaroise de Tolerie
SOTOCA... Societe Industrielle et Commerciale Togolaise du Cafe
SOTOCAM ... Societe de Topographie au Cameroun
SOTOCO ... Societe Togolaise du Coton [*Togolese Cotton Company*]   (AF)
SOTODECO ... Societe Togolaise de Distribution Economique
SOTOGIC ... Societe Togolaise de Gestion Immobiliere et de Constructions
SOTOHOMA ... Societe Touristique et Hoteliere de Madagascar
SOTOM..... Societe de Topographie de Madagascar
SOTOMA ... Societe des Tabacs et Oleagineux de Madagascar
SOTOMA ... Societe Togolaise de Marbrerie et Materiaux
SOTOMAREY ... Societe Togolaise des Mareyeurs
SOTOMARIAUX ... Societe Togolaise de Materiaux

SOTOMECIA ... Societe Togolaise de Mecanisation Industrielle et Agricole
SOTONAM ... Societe Togolaise de Navigation Maritime   (EY)
SOTOPEMA ... Societe Togolaise des Pecheries Maritimes
SOTOPLANT ... Societe Togolaise de Plantation
SOTOPOLEF ... Societe Togolaise de Poissons et Legumes Frais
SOTOPROCO ... Societe Togolaise d'Exportation de Produits Tropicaux
SOTORAM ... Societe Touristique Royal Air Maroc
SOTOREP ... Societe Togolaise de Rechapage de Pneus
SOTOTRAC ... Societe Togolaise de Transit et de Consignation
SOTP........ Societe Tunisienne de Petrole
sotr .... Collaborator, Member of the Staff, Contributor   (RU)
SOTRA...... Societe des Transports Abidjanais [Abidjan Transportation Company] [Ivory Coast]
SOTRAB ... Societe de Transit du Benin
SOTRAB-CI ... Societe de Travaux Publics et de Batiments Cote-D'Ivoire
SOTRABO ... Societe de Transformation du Bois
SOTRABOI ... Societe de Transformation des Bois Ivoiriens
SOTRAC... Societe de Transports en Commun du Cap-Vert
SOTRACCA ... Societe de Transformation et de Commercialisation du Caoutchouc SA [Rubber Processing and Marketing Company, Inc.] [Cambodia]   (CL)
SOTRACM ... Societe de Transports Routiers et de Commerce du Mungo
SOTRACOB ... Societe de Transit et de Consignation du Benin [Benin Transit and Storage Company]   (AF)
SOTRACOL ... Sociedad Transportadora Colombiana Ltda. [Colombia]   (COL)
SOTRACOSS ... Societe de Transports en Common du Sine-Saloum
SOTRAF ... Societe de Transit en Afrique Equatoriale
SOTRAFOM ... Societe de Travaux Publics et de Terrassements de France et d'Outre Mer
SOTRAFRIC ... Societe de Transports Africains
SOTRAGAU ... Societe de Tranchage de la Gaume
SOTRAHO ... Societe de Travaux du Haut Ogooue
SOTRAL... Societe des Transports en Commun Librevillois
SOTRALEC ... Societe de Travaux, d'Entretien, de Plomberie, et d'Electricite
SOTRALLANO ... Sociedad Transportadora del Llano Ltda. [Colombia]   (COL)
SOTRAM ... Societe de Transports et de Reparations Automobiles de M'Balmayo
SOTRAM ... Societe de Transports Mauritaniens
SOTRAMEG ... Transformation de la Melasse [Morocco]
SOTRAMET ... Societe de Travaux Metalliques
SOTRAMIL ... Societe de Transformation du Mil et du Sorgho [Niger]
SOTRAMO ... Societe des Transports Modernes [Tunisia]
SOTRANCO ... Societe de Transit de Consignation
SOTRANEX ... Societe Auxiliaire de Transports et d'Exploitation de Bois Kouilou Niari
SOTRANORD ... Societe Camerounaise de Transport du Nord-Cameroun
SOTRANSO ... Societe des Transports de l'Ouest
SOTRAPAR ... Societe de Travaux et de Participations
SOTRASAN ... Sociedad Santandereana de Transportes [Bucaramanga]   (COL)
SOTRASSUM ... Societe de Traitement des Sables du Sud de Madagascar
SOTRASUM ... Societe des Terres Rares du Sud de Madagascar
SOTRAT ... Societe de Transitaires Tchadiens
SOTRATRANSCAM ... Societe Auxiliaire de Travaux Publics pour la Construction du Transcamerounais
SOTRAUSQUE ... Sociedad de Transportes Unidos el Bosque Ltda. [Barranquilla]   (COL)
SOTRAVIL ... Societe des Transports de Libreville
SOTRAZ... Societe de Transport Zairoise [Zaire]   (IMH)
SOTREC ... Societe des Trefileries et Clouteries en Cote-D'Ivoire
SOTREC ... Societe Technique de Recherches et d'Etudes pour la Construction [French]   (SLS)
SOTRECA ... Societe des Transports en Centrafrique
SOTREF.... Societe Tropicale d'Exploitations Forestieres
SOTREP ... Societe Tchadienne de Realisation et d'Entreprise de Pneumatiques
SOTRI ...... Societe de Transports Ivoiriens
SOTRI ...... Societe d'Exploitation des Ets. Tricon
SOTRICO ... Societe Togolaise de Relance de l'Industrie et du Commerce
SOTRIPA ... Societe de Transformation Industrielle des Produits Agricoles
SOTROPAL ... Societe Tropicale des Allumettes [Ivory Coast]
SOTROPCO ... Societe Tropicale de Commerce
sots .... Socialist   (BU)
sots .... Social, Socialist   (RU)
SOTS .... Society for Old Testament Study
sots-dem..... Social Democrat, Social Democratic   (RU)
Sotsekgiz.... State Publishing House of Literature on Social Sciences and Economics   (RU)
Sotsintern... Socialist International   (RU)
sotsiol........ Sociology   (RU)
SOTSIRIZ ... Societe Tsimihety du Riz
sotsobr....... Social Education   (RU)
Sots pravo .. Sotsialistichesko Pravo [Socialist Law] [A periodical]   (BU)

sotsvos........ Social Education Subdivision of the Department of Public Education   (RU)
sottolin .... Sottolineature [Underlining] [Publishing] [Italian]
sottot .... Sottotitolo [Subtitle] [Publishing] [Italian]
sottotit........ Sottotitolo [Subtitle] [Publishing] [Italian]
SOTUBAL ... Societe des Tubes d'Algerie
SOTUC..... Societe des Transports Urbains du Cameroun
SOTUCIB ... Societe Tunisienne de Ciment Blanc
SOTUMACO ... Societe Tunisienne de Materiaux de Construction [Tunisian Building Materials Company]   (AF)
SOTUMEX ... Societe Tunisienne de Matieres Premieres Textiles
SOTUPALFA ... Societe Tunisienne de Papier Alfa [Tunisia]   (IMH)
SOTUPRI ... Societe Tunisienne de Production Industrielle [Tunisia]
SOTUVER ... Societe Tunisienne du Verre [Tunisia]   (IMH)
SOU.......... Optical Light Device   (RU)
SOU........... Scandinavian Ornithological Union [Lund, Sweden]   (EAIO)
SOU.......... Sekretarijat za Opstu Upravu (SIV) [Secretariat of General Administration]   (YU)
SOUH....... Statni Odborne Uciliste Hornicke [State Training Center for Mining Specialists]   (CZ)
SOUR .... Slozena Organizacija Udruzenog Rada [Collective Organization of Workers] [Former Yugoslavia]
SOUTHDOC ... Southern Region Document Service [Australia]
sov .... Perfective [Aspect]   (RU)
SOV .... Persistent Chemical Agent   (BU)
SOV .... Persistent Gas   (RU)
SOV .... Series Field Winding   (RU)
SOV .... Slovensky Oslobodzovaci Vybor [Slovak Liberation Committee]   (CZ)
sov .... Soviet   (RU)
SOVANORD ... Societe de Valorisation de l'Anacardier du Nord
SOVAPIA ... Societe de Vaporisation Industrielle Abidjanaise
Sovbolstroy ... Soviet-Bulgarian Construction Company   (BU)
sovdep .... Soviet of Workers', Peasants', and Red Army Deputies [1917-1936]   (RU)
SOVE......... Symfoniki Orkhistra Voreiou Ellados [Northern Greece Symphony Orchestra]   (GC)
SOVEA...... Societe Voltaique d'Exploitation Automobile
SOVEC...... Societe Voltaique d'Etancheite et de Carrelage
SOVECA ... Societe de Vente de Cycles d'Alimentation
SOVEDAE ... Sociedad Venezolana de Derecho Aeronautico y Espacial [Venezuelan Society of Aeronautical and Space Law]   (LA)
SOVEG...... Societe Voltaique d'Engineering et de Gestion
Soveksportfil'm ... All-Union Association for the Export and Import of Motion Pictures   (RU)
SOVEL...... Societe Voltaique d'Electronique, Radio, Electricite, Optique Electro-Acoustique
SOVEM...... Societe pour la Vente d'Equipements et de Materiels
SOVEMA ... Societe de Vente de Metaux et Alliages
SOVEMA ... Societe Verrerie Malagasy
SOVEMAN ... Societe de Vetements Manufactures
SOVERCO ... Societe des Verreries du Congo [Glass manufacturer] [Congo]
SOVERGS ... Sociedade de Veterinaria do Rio Grande do Sul [Brazil]   (DSCA)
SOVERPAL ... Societe de Vente de Produits Alimentaires
sovershpererabot ... Completely Revised   (RU)
soveshch .... Conference, Meeting   (RU)
SOVETCO ... Societe pour la Vente de Thons Congeles [Frozen Tuna Marketing Company] [Ivory Coast]   (AF)
SOVETIV ... Societe des Vetements Ivoiriens
Sovfrakht ... All-Union Association for the Chartering of Foreign Tonnage   (RU)
SOVHOTEL ... Societe Voltaique d'Hotellerie et de Tourisme
SOVI........ Societe Voltaique d'Infrastructures
SOVIAMAD ... Societe des Viandes de Madagascar
SOVIBO.... Societe des Vins et Boissons
SOVIBOR ... Societe Vinicole Bordelaise
SOVIC....... Societe Voltaique de l'Industrie du Cuir
SOVICA .... Societe Voltaique d'Interet Collectif Agricole
SOVICA .... Societe Voltaique d'Intervention et de Cooperation avec l'Agriculture
SOVIEX .... Societe d'Exportation de Viandes
SOVIMAS ... Societe Voltaique d'Importation Azar et Salem
SOVIN....... Samenwerkingsverband voor Opleiding en Vorming op het Terrein van de Informatieverzorging via Netwerken [Collective for Training and Education in Connection with Information Provision via Networks] [Ceased operation] [Netherlands] [Information service or system]   (IID)
SOVINCI .. Societe des Vins de la Cote-D'Ivoire
SOVINCO ... Societe des Vins du Congo
SOVINDAH ... Societe des Vins du Dahomey
Sovinformbyuro ... Soviet Information Bureau [Press agency]   (RU)
SOVINGAB ... Societe des Vins du Gabon
SOVINGUI ... Societe des Vins de la Guinee
SOVINTO ... Sodas et Vins du Togo
SOVITOUR ... Senegals Suedoise de Villages Touristiques

sovkhozuch ... Sovkhoz Apprenticeship School   (RU)
SOVMEDRON ... Soviet Mediterranean Squadron [*NATO*]   (NATG)
sovmin .... Council of Ministers   (RU)
SOVNARKHOZ ... Soviet Narodnogo Khozyaistva [*Council for the People's Economy*] [*Russian*]
SOVNARKOM ... Soviet Jarodnykh Kommissarvo [*Council of People's Commissars*] [*Russian*]
SOVNARKOM ... Soviet Narodnykh Komissarov [*Council of People's Commissars*] [*Former USSR*]   (LAIN)
SOVOBRA ... Societe Voltaique de Brasserie
SOVOCA .. Societe Voltaique de Credit Automobile
SOVODA .. Societe Voltaique pour le Developpement de l'Automobile
SOVODIA ... Societe Voltaique de Diffusion Automobile et Aeronautique [*Ougadougou*]
SOVOFA... Societe Voltaique des Ets. Faddoui
SOVOFER ... Societe Voltaique de Ferronnerie et de Charpentes Metalliques
SOVOG ..... Societe Voltaique de Groupage
SOVOG ..... Sozialistiche Volksorganisation [*Socialist National Community*] [*Lithuania*] [*Political party*]   (PPE)
SOVOIC.... Societe Voltaique Industrielle et Commerciale
SOVOLCI ... Societe Voltaique de Commerce et d'Industrie
SOVOLCOM ... Societe Voltaique de Commercialisation
SOVOLDIA ... Societe Voltaique de Diffusion Industrielle et Automobile
SOVOLPLAS ... Societe Voltaique de Plastique
SOVOLTA ... Societe Voltaique de Tanneries et des Industries du Cuir
SOVOMEA ... Societe Voltaique de Montage et d'Exploitation Automobile
SOVORES ... Societe Voltaique de Revetement et Sanitaire
SOVOTRA ... Societe Voltaique d'Entreprise Hadiffe & Cie.
sovp .... Coincidence   (RU)
Sov p.......... Soviet Patent   (RU)
sovprof .... Trade-Union Council   (RU)
sovr............ Modern, Contemporary, Up-to-Date   (RU)
sovrac .... Sovracoperta [*Wrapper*] [*Publishing*] [*Italian*]
sovracop ..... Sovracoperta [*Wrapper*] [*Publishing*] [*Italian*]
SOVROM ... Intreprinderea Sovietica-Romana [*Soviet-Romanian Enterprise*] (RO)
SOVS......... Sanitetsko Odeljenje Vrhovnog Staba [*Medical Department of the General Staff*]   (YU)
SOVS......... Sovereigns [*Monetary unit*] [*Obsolete*] [*British*]
sov sekr ...... Top Secret   (RU)
sovsod......... Assistance Council   (RU)
SOVT........ Socialist Exchange of Experience in Water Transportation   (RU)
Sovtorgflot ... Soviet Merchant Marine   (RU)
SOW .... Slaski Okreg Wojskowy [*Silesian Military District*]   (POL)
SOWI .... Samodzielny Oddzial Wykonawstwa Inwestycyjnego [*Autonomous Investment Operations Branch*]   (POL)
SOWIDOK ... Sozialwissenschaftliche Dokumentation [*Social Sciences Documentation Center*] [*Vienna Chamber of Labor*] [*Information service or system*]   (IID)
SOWIL...... Status of Women in Libraries Special Interest Group [*Library Association of Australia*]
SOXGE...... (Pankypria) Syndekhnia Oikodomon, Xylourgon, kai Genikon Ergaton [*(Pan-Cyprian) Union of Construction Workers, Carpenters, and General Workers*]   (GC)
SOY .... Soma Oikonomikon Ypiresion [*Finance Corps*] [*Army*]   (GC)
SOYe .... Static Exchange Capacitance   (RU)
soyed .... Compound   (RU)
SOYP........ Servicio Oceanografico y de Pesca [*State Oceanographic and Fisheries Service*] [*Uruguay*]   (LA)
SOYTAS ... Sosyal Yatirmlar Organizasyon ve Ticaret Anonim Sirketi [*Social Investments Organization and Trade Corporation*]   (TU)
Soyuzalyuminiy ... All-Union Administration of the Aluminum Industry   (RU)
Soyuzantiseptik ... State Trust for Antiseptic Treating and Preservation of Wood in Construction of the Glavspetspromstroy   (RU)
Soyuzavtosel'mash ... Main Administration for Interrepublic Deliveries of Automobiles, Tractors, Agricultural Machines, and Their Spare Parts   (RU)
Soyuzbummash ... All-Union Trust for Machinery and Spare Parts Manufacture of the Ministry of the Paper and Woodworking Industries, USSR   (RU)
SOYuZDORNII ... State All-Union Scientific Research Institute of Roads and Highways   (RU)
Soyuzdorproyekt ... State Institute for the Planning and Surveying of Highways of the State Industrial Committee for Transportation Construction, USSR   (RU)
Soyuzdvigatel'remmontazh ... All-Union Trust for the Repair of Internal-Combustion Engines and Locomobiles of the Glavdizel'   (RU)
Soyuzenergoremtrest ... State All-Union Trust for the Repair of Power Engineering Equipment of the Glavenergoremont of the State Industrial Committee for Power Engineering and Electrification, USSR   (RU)
Soyuzgaz .... State Trust for the Extraction and Processing of Natural Gas and Helium   (RU)

Soyuzgeomash ... All-Union Trust for the Manufacture of Geological Exploration Equipment and Geophysical Instruments
Soyuzgeoneftepribor ... State All-Union Trust for Geophysical and Petroleum Instrument Making   (RU)
Soyuzgidromekhanizatsiya ... State All-Union Trust for Planning and Performing Hydraulic Mechanized Operations   (RU)
Soyuzgiprotorg ... All-Union State Institute for the Planning of Trade Establishments and Public Eating Facilities   (RU)
Soyuzglavenergo ... Main Power Engineering Administration   (RU)
Soyuzglavkhim ... Main Administration for Interrepublic Deliveries of Chemical and Industrial Rubber Products   (RU)
Soyuzglavkhimkomplekt ... Main Administration for Ensuring the Supply of Complete Sets of Equipment, Instruments, Cables, and Other Products for High-Priority Construction Projects of the Chemical and Pulp and Paper Industries   (RU)
Soyuzglavkomplekt ... Main Administration for Ensuring the Supply of Complete Sets of Equipment, Instruments, Cables, and Other Manufactures for High-Priority Construction Projects in the Coal, Petroleum, and Other Branches of Industry   (RU)
Soyuzglavlegpromsyr'ye ... Main Administration for Interrepublic Deliveries of Raw Materials for Light Industry   (RU)
Soyuzglavmash ... Main Administration for Interrepublic Deliveries of Machinery   (RU)
Soyuzglavmetall ... Main Administration for Interrepublic Deliveries of Metal Products   (RU)
Soyuzglavmetallurgkomplekt ... Main Administration for Ensuring the Supply of Complete Sets of Equipment, Instruments, Cables, and Other Products for High-Priority Construction Projects of Ferrous and Nonferrous Metallurgy   (RU)
Soyuzglavneft' ... Main Administration for Interrepublic Deliveries of Petroleum Products   (RU)
Soyuzglavpishchepromsyr'ye ... Main Administration for Interrepublic Deliveries of Raw Materials for the Food Industry   (RU)
Soyuzglavradiokomplekt ... Main Administration for Ensuring the Supply of Complete Sets of Equipment, Instruments, Cables, and Other Products for High-Priority Construction Projects of the Radio Electronics Industry   (RU)
Soyuzglavstroykomplekt ... Main Administration for Ensuring the Supply of Complete Sets of Equipment, Instruments, Cables, and Other Products for High-Priority Construction Projects of the Building Materials and Construction Industries   (RU)
Soyuzglavstroymaterialy ... Main Administration for Interrepublic Deliveries of Lumber and Building Materials   (RU)
Soyuzglavtorg ... Main Administration for Interrepublic Deliveries of Consumer Goods   (RU)
Soyuzglavtyazhmash ... Main Administration for Interrepublic Deliveries of Heavy Machinery   (RU)
Soyuzglavugol' ... Main Administration for Interrepublic Deliveries of Coal   (RU)
Soyuzgostsirk ... All-Union Association of State Circuses   (RU)
Soyuzkhimeksport ... All-Union Association for the Export and Import of Chemicals   (RU)
Soyuzkhimfarmtorg ... All-Union Office for Trade in Chemicals, Pharmaceuticals, and Hygienic Goods   (RU)
Soyuzkislorodmontazh ... All-Union State Trust for the Installation of Oxygen Plants and Units   (RU)
Soyuzkniga ... All-Union Book Trade Association   (RU)
Soyuzkoopvneshtorg ... All-Union Cooperative Foreign Trade Association   (RU)
Soyuzleksyr'ye ... All-Union Office for the Procurement of Medicinal Plants   (RU)
Soyuzlessempitomnik ... All-Union Association of Tree Nurseries and Seed Procurement   (RU)
Soyuzlift..... State Trust of the Glavtekhmontazh of the Gosmontazhspetsstroy SSSR   (RU)
Soyuzliftomontazh ... All-Union Office for the Supply and Installation of Elevators   (RU)
Soyuzmarkshtrest ... All-Union Mine-Surveying Trust   (RU)
Soyuzmedinstrumenttorg ... All-Union Office for the Procurement, Marketing, and Sale of Medical Instruments and Equipment   (RU)
Soyuzmedoborudovaniye ... All-Union Office for the Supply and Sale of Medical Equipment   (RU)
Soyuzmorniiproyekt ... State Planning, Design, and Scientific Research Institute of Marine Transportation of the Ministry of the Maritime Fleet, USSR   (RU)
Soyuzmorproyekt ... State Institute for the Planning of Seaports and Ship-Repair Establishments   (RU)
Soyuzmul'tifil'm ... All-Union Animated Cartoon Studio   (RU)
Soyuznefteburmashremont ... State All-Union Trust for the Repair of Drilling Equipment of the Ministry of the Petroleum Industry, USSR   (RU)
Soyuznefteeksport ... All-Union Association for the Export and Import of Petroleum and Petroleum Products   (RU)

Soyuzneftepribor ... All-Union Technical Office for the Supply of Complete Sets of Control and Measuring Instruments and Automation Equipment of the Ministry of the Petroleum Industry, USSR (RU)

Soyuzneftestroymekhanizatsiya ... All-Union Trust of the Glavneftestroymekhanizatsiya (RU)

Soyuzneftetara ... State All-Union Trust for the Manufacture of Petroleum Containers (RU)

Soyuznerudstroy ... State All-Union Trust for the Construction of Nonmetallic Building Materials Establishments (RU)

SoyuzNIKhI ... All-Union Scientific Research Institute of Cotton Growing (RU)

SoyuzOSVOD ... Union of Societies for Furthering the Development of Water Transportation and for the Safeguarding of Human Lives on Waterways of the USSR [*1931-1956*] (RU)

Soyuzpechat' ... Main Administration for the Distribution of Publications (RU)

Soyuzplodotara ... All-Union Packing Materials Office of the Glavkoopplodoovoshch (RU)

Soyuzposyltorg ... All-Union Mail-Order Office (RU)

Soyuzprokatmontazh ... State All-Union Trust for the Installation of Mechanical Equipment in Rolling Mills of Metallurgical Plants (RU)

Soyuzpromeksport ... All-Union Association of the Ministry of Foreign Trade, USSR (RU)

Soyuzprommekhanizatsiya ... Planning and Installation Trust of the Glavtekhmontazh of the Ministry of Construction, RSFSR (RU)

Soyuzprommontazh ... State All-Union Construction and Installation Trust of the Ministry of Construction of Establishments of the Metallurgical and Chemical Industries, USSR (RU)

Soyuzpushnina ... All-Union Association for the Export and Import of Fur Goods (RU)

Soyuzreaktivsbyt ... All-Union Office for the Marketing of Chemically Pure Reagents (RU)

Soyuzrybpromkadry ... All-Union Office for the Organized Hiring of Workers for the Fish Industry (RU)

Soyuzsel'elektro ... All-Union Association for Rural Electrification (RU)

Soyuzshlak ... All-Union Trust for the Processing of Industrial Slags (RU)

Soyuzsnav .. Union of Societies for Lifesaving on Waterways of the USSR [*1928-1931*] (RU)

Soyuzsortsemovoshch ... All-Union Office for the Production, Procurement, and Sale of High-Quality Seeds of Vegetables, Melons, and Food Roots (RU)

Soyuzsovkhozremmash ... Administration of Repair and Machine Plants of the Ministry of Sovkhozes, USSR (RU)

Soyuzspetsstroy ... All-Union Trust for Special Operations of the Glavspetsstroy (RU)

Soyuzsportproyekt ... All-Union Institute for the Planning of Sports Installations (RU)

Soyuzsteklosbyt ... All-Union Office for the Marketing of Glassware (RU)

Soyuzsteklostroy ... State All-Union Construction and Installation Trust of the Ministry of the Building Materials Industry of the USSR (RU)

Soyuztelefonstroy ... All-Union Trust of the Ministry of Communications, USSR (RU)

Soyuzteplostroy ... State Trust of the Glavteplomontazh of the Gosmontazhspetsstroy SSSR (RU)

Soyuztorgtrans ... All-Union Transportation Trust of the Ministry of Trade, USSR (RU)

Soyuztsemremont ... All-Union Trust for the Repair of Cement Plant Equipment (RU)

Soyuztverdosplav ... All-Union Trust of the Hard Alloys Industry (RU)

Soyuzvzryvprom ... Trust for Drilling and Blasting Operations of the Glavspetspromstroy (RU)

Soyuzzagottrans ... Main Administration of Automobile Transportation of the Ministry of Procurement, USSR (RU)

Soyuzzcovetsnab ... All-Union Trust for the Supply of Agriculture with Veterinary and Zootechnical Equipment, Instruments, and Drugs (RU)

Soyuzzdravpromstroy ... All-Union Construction Trust of the Administration of Capital Construction of the Ministry of Public Health, USSR (RU)

Soyuzzhivkontora ... All-Union Office for the Procurement and Marketing of Pedigree Cattle (RU)

SOZ .... Association for Common Land Cultivation (RU)

SOZ .... Samodzielne Oddzialy Zaopatrzenia [*Independent Supply Branches*] (POL)

So Z .... Sodazahl [*Soda Number or Value*] [*German*] (GCA)

SOZ .... Soviet Zone of Occupation (BU)

Soz .... Sozialdemokrat [*Social Democrat*] [*German*]

Soz .... Sozialistisch [*Socialistic*] [*German*]

SOZ .... Swiatowa Organizacja Zdrowia [*World Health Organization*] [*Poland*]

SOZ .... World Health Organization (BU)

SOZACOM ... Societe Zairoise de Commercialisation des Minerais [*Zairian Company for the Marketing of Ores*] (AF)

SOZATEF ... Societe Zairoise de Tenke Fungurumi

SOZh .... Railroad Workers' Union (RU)

SOZIR ...... Societe Zairo-Italienne de Raffinage [*Zairian-Italian Refining Company*] (AF)

sp .... Alcohol, Ethel Alcohol (RU)

SP .... Blasting Cable, Firing Wire (RU)

SP .... Blinker, Blinking Device (RU)

SP .... Call Sign Selector (RU)

sp .... Centipoise (RU)

SP .... Clearing Station [*Military medicine*] (RU)

sp .... Cleavage (RU)

SP .... Collection of Government Regulations and Decrees (RU)

sp .... Combat Engineer (RU)

SP .... Connecting Point (RU)

SP .... Construction Industry (RU)

SP .... Deadmelt (RU)

SP .... Economic Enterprise (BU)

SP .... Erste Staatspruefung [*German*]

SP .... Estado de Sao Paulo [*State of Sao Paulo*] [*Brazil*]

SP .... Feeder Bay (RU)

SP .... Freight Car with Perishable Goods (RU)

SP .... Instrument Landing (RU)

SP .... Joint Enterprises (BU)

SP .... Landing System (RU)

sp .... Magazine (BU)

SP .... Medical Station (RU)

SP .... Monitoring Station (RU)

SP .... North Pole [*Drifting station*] (RU)

SP .... Receiving Selsyn (RU)

sp .... Rifle Regiment (BU)

SP .... Routine [*Computers*] (RU)

S-P .... Saint-Pere [*Holy Father*] [*French*]

SP .... Samajwadi Party [*Italy*] [*Political party*] (ECON)

SP .... Sanford Papers

sp .... Sans Prix [*Without Price*] [*French*] [*Business term*]

SP .... Santo Padre [*His Holiness, the Pope*] [*Portuguese*]

SP .... Santo Padre [*His Holiness, the Pope*] [*Italian*]

SP .... Saobracajno Preduzece [*Transportation Establishment*] (YU)

SP .... Sao Paulo (IDIG)

SP .... Sapeurs-Pompiers [*Fire Brigade*] [*French*]

SP .... Savezno Pravobraniostvo (SIV) [*Federal Body of Government Attorneys*] (YU)

SP .... Sbor Poverenikov [*Board of Commissioners*] (CZ)

SP .... Secteur Postal [*French*]

SP .... Section de Parc de Campagne [*Military*] [*French*] (MTD)

SP .... Seismic Detector (RU)

SP .... Sekcija za Puteve [*Roads Section*] (YU)

SP .... Sekretarijat za Promet (ISLRS) [*Secretariat of Trade*] (YU)

SP .... Self-Discharging Flatcar (RU)

SP .... Self-Polarization (RU)

SP .... Semensko Preduzece [*Seeds Establishment*] (YU)

SP .... Senggara Perhubongan [*Line of Communication*] (ML)

SP .... Senoi Praaq [*Fighting People*] (ML)

Sp .... Senterpartiet [*Center Party*] [*Norway*] [*Political party*] (PPE)

SP .... Sentidos Pesames [*Heartfelt Condolences*] [*Portuguese*]

SP .... Seri Pahlawan Gagah Perkasa [*Supreme Gallantry (Decoration)*] [*Malaysia*] (ML)

SP .... Service de Presse [*French*]

SP .... Servico Publico [*Public Service*] [*Portuguese*]

SP .... Servodrive (RU)

SP .... Shanfari & Partners [*Oman*]

SP .... Shipbuilding Industry (RU)

SP .... Siedepunkt [*Boiling Point*] [*German*]

SP .... Siege et Place [*Guns*] [*French*] (MTD)

SP .... Sikkim Parishad [*India*] [*Political party*] (PPW)

SP .... Sindicato de la Prensa [*Journalists Union*] [*Venezuela*] (LA)

SP .... Siniaver Pumps [*Israel*] [*Commercial firm*]

SP .... Skupni Pasnik [*Collective Pasture*]

SP .... Sluzba Polsce [*Service to Poland*] [*Semimilitary youth organization (1948-1955)*] (POL)

SP .... Socialistische Partij [*Socialist Party*] [*Belgium*] [*Political party*] (PPW)

SP .... Socialistiska Partiet [*Socialist Party*] [*Sweden*] (WEN)

SP .... Sofia Enterprise (BU)

SP .... Solar Furnace (RU)

SP .... Solidarite Protestante [*Belgium*] (EAIO)

SP .... Sosialistiki Poreia [*Socialist Path*] [*Greek*] (GC)

SP .... Sosyalist Parti [*Socialist Party*] [*Turkey*] [*Political party*] (EY)

SP .... Sosyalist Partisi [*Socialist Party*] [*Organized May 30, 1975*] (TU)

SP .... Souhrny Plan [*Master Plan*] (CZ)

Sp .... Sous-Prefecture [*Sub-Prefecture*] [*Military map abbreviation World War I*] [*French*] (MTD)

SP .... Sousprogramme [*Subprogram*] [*French*] (ADPT)

SP .... Soviet Law (RU)

SP .... Sozialistische Partei [*Socialist Party*] (EG)

Sp	Spaans [*Spanish*] [*Afrikaans*]
sp	Spalt [*Column*] [*Sweden*]
Sp	Spalte [*Column*] [*German*] (GPO)
Sp	Spanje [*Spain*] [*Afrikaans*]
sp	Spanyol [*Spanish*] (HU)
SP	Sparkasse [*Savings Bank*] [*German*] [*Business term*] (EG)
sp	Special [*French*]
SP	Speciale Prototipo [*Special Prototype*] [*Italy*]
Sp	Specie [*Species*] [*Italian*]
SP	Speditersko Poduzece [*Forwarding Establishment*] (YU)
Sp	Speicher [*Memory*] [*German*] (ADPT)
Sp	Spesialis [*Academic degree*] [*Indonesian*]
SP	Spezia [*Car registration plates*] [*Italian*]
Sp	Spezifisch [*Specific*] [*German*] (GCA)
sp	Spindel [*Spindle*] [*German*] (GCA)
sp	Spisanie [*Periodical*] (YU)
SP	Spoldzielnia Pracy [*Poland*]
SP	Spoldzielnia Produkcyjna [*Producer Cooperative*] [*Collective farm*] (POL)
sp	Sport (BU)
SP	Sportavia Puetzer GmbH & Co. KG [*Germany*] [*ICAO aircraft manufacturer identifier*] (ICAO)
SP	Sprengpunkt [*Detonation Point*] [*German*] (GCA)
SP	Staatspresident [*State President*] [*Afrikaans*]
SP	Staff Paper
SP	Stamparsko Preduzece [*Printing Establishment*] (YU)
SP	Start Position (RU)
SP	Statens Provningsanstalt [*National Swedish Authority for Testing, Inspection, and Metrology*] [*Research center*] (IRC)
SP	Statni Pojistovna [*State Insurance Agency*] (CZ)
SP	Statni Studijni Knihovna, Plzen [*State Research Library in Plzen*] (CZ)
SP	Statni Vedecka Knihovna, Plzen [*State Research Library in Plzen*] (CZ)
SP	Steady-State Parameter (RU)
SP	Steam Separator (RU)
SP	Stolarsko Preduzece [*Carpentry Establishment*] (YU)
SP	Strategic Planning Society [*See also SPS*] [*London, England*] (EAIO)
SP	Strojevo Pravilo [*Regulation on Military Formations*] (YU)
SP	Stronnictwo Pracy [*Labour Party*] [*Poland*] [*Political party*] (EY)
SP	Sudanese Pound
SP	Sudan Programme
SP	Sudija za Prekrsaje [*Magistrate for Misdemeanors*] (YU)
SP	Sumarsko Preduzece [*Forestry Establishment*] (YU)
SP	Superprogramm [*German*] (ADPT)
SP	Svenska Petroleum [*Oil company*] [*Merged with OK to form OK Petroleum*] [*Sweden*]
sp	Swietej Pamieci [*The Late*] (POL)
SP	Syllogos (Synomospondia) Pratirioukhon [*Association of (Confederation of) Gas Station Owners*] (GC)
SP	Syndaktiki Praxis [*Constituent Act*] (GC)
SP	Sztandar Pracy [*Banner of Labor*] [*Award*] (POL)
SP	Trunks [*Telephony*] (RU)
SP	Trusteeship Council (BU)
SP	Union of Writers (RU)
SPA	Salaried Pharmacists' Association [*Australia*]
SPA	Saudi Press Agency
SPA	Scandinavian Packaging Association [*Sweden*] (EAIO)
SPA	Screen Printing Association [*Australia*]
SPA	Screen Producers' Association [*Australia*]
SPA	Service de la Poste aux Armees [*Army Postal Service*] [*French*]
SPA	Singapore People's Alliance (ML)
SPA	Singapore Port Authority
SPA	Sistema de Produccion Agropecuaria [*Agriculture and Livestock Production System*] [*Peru*] (LA)
SPA	Slovenska Polnohospodarska Akademia [*Slovak Agricultural Academy*] (CZ)
SPA	Socialist Party of Albania [*Political party*] (EY)
SPA	Socialist Party of Australia [*Political party*]
SPA	Socialist Party of Austria (RU)
SPA	Sociedade Portuguesa de Autores [*Portuguese Authors' Society*] (WER)
SpA	Societa per Azioni [*Public Limited Company*] [*Italian*]
SPA	Societa Protettrice degli Animali [*Society for the Protection of Animals*] [*Italian*]
SPA	Societe Protectrice des Animaux [*Society for the Prevention of Cruelty to Animals*] [*French*] (WER)
SPA	Society of Portuguese Authors (EAIO)
SPA	Somali Ports Authority
SPA	Specialised Publications Association [*India*] (PDAA)
SPA	Specially Protected Area [*Australia*]
SPA	Spolek Posluchacu Architektury [*Society of University Students of Architecture*] (CZ)
SPA	St. Maarten Patriotic Alliance [*Netherlands Antilles*] [*Political party*] (EY)
SPA	Stoleczne Przedsiebiorstwo Aptek [*Warsaw Pharmaceutical Enterprise*] (POL)
SPA	Strategic Planning Associates [*Singapore*]
SPA	Sudanese Press Agency
SPA	Sugar Producers Association [*Barbados*] (LA)
SPA	Suicide Prevention Association [*Australia*]
SPA	Supreme People's Assembly [*Political party*] [*North Korea*] (FEA)
SPA	Surinaamse Partij van de Arvid [*Suriname Labour Party*] [*Political party*] (EY)
SPA	Surohanjaya Pelajaran Awam [*Commissioner of Public Education*] (ML)
SPA	Swedish Pharmaceutical Association (EAIO)
SPA	Swedish Psychological Association (EAIO)
SPA	Sydney Ports Authority [*Australia*]
SPA	Symvoulion Pliroforion kai Asfaleias [*Intelligence and Security Council*] [*Greek*] (GC)
SPAA	Caraz [*Peru*] [*ICAO location identifier*] (ICLI)
SPAA	Screen Producers' Association of Australia
SPAA	Srednjokalibarska Protivavionska Artiljerija [*Medium Caliber Antiaircraft Artillery*] (YU)
SPAALAL	Society for the Promotion of African, Asian, and Latin American Literature [*See also GFLAAL*] [*German*] (EAIO)
SPAAN	Societe Protectrice des Animaux en Afrique du Nord [*Society for the Protection of Animals in North Africa - SPANA*] (EAIO)
SPAB	Huancabamba [*Peru*] [*ICAO location identifier*] (ICLI)
SPAB	Security Pacific Asian Bank
SPABA	Societe des Plantations de l'Ake Befia et Anonkoua
SPAC	Ciro Alegria [*Peru*] [*ICAO location identifier*] (ICLI)
SPAC	Societe Senegalaise de Produits Alimentaires Congeles
SPAC	Society for the Promotion of African Culture
SPACI	Societe de Pecheries Africaines de Cote-D'Ivoire
SPACLALS	South Pacific Association for Commonwealth Literature and Language Studies (EAIO)
SPAD	Sistem de Prelucrare Automatica a Datelor [*Automatic Data Processing System*] (RO)
SPAD	Societe des Produits Agnis-Diabes
SPADI	Societe des Plantations d'Ananas de Divo
SPAE	Societe Planetaire pour l'Assainissance de l'Energie [*Planetary Association for Clean Energy*] (EAIO)
SPAEF	Societe des Petroles de l'Afrique Equatoriale Francaise (OMWE)
SPAEI	South Pacific Association of Environmental Institutions
SPAFA	SEAMEO [*Southeast Asia Ministers of Education Organization*] Project in Archaeology and Fine Arts [*Thailand*] [*Research center*] (IRC)
SPAFE	Societe des Petroles d'Afrique Equatoriale [*Petroleum Company of Equatorial Africa*] [*French*] (AF)
SPAFI	Societe Pan-Africaine d'Investissement
SPAFIF	Southern Province African Farming Improvement Fund
SPAGA	Syndicat Professionnel des Agents Generaux d'Assurances Champs Elysees. Societe Parisienne et Africaine d'Habillement
SPAH	Societe Parisienne et Africaine d'Habillement
SPAIC	Sociedade Portuguesa de Alergologia e Imunologia Clinica [*Portuguese*] (SLS)
SPAK	Synepis Politikon Aristeron Kinima [*Consistent Political Movement of the Left*] [*Greek*] (GC)
SPAL	Security Pacific Australia Ltd.
Spalt	Spalten [*Cracking*] [*German*] (GCA)
Spalt	Spaltung [*Splitting*] [*German*] (GCA)
SPAM	Camana [*Peru*] [*ICAO location identifier*] (ICLI)
SPAM	Damaged-Vehicle Collecting Point (RU)
SPAM	Stowarzyszenie Polskich Artystow Muzykow [*Polish Musicians' Association*]
SPAM	Sydney Python Appreciation Movement [*Television program fan club*] [*Australia*]
SPAM	Wrecked Motor Vehicles Collecting Point (BU)
SPAMF	Seychelles Popular Anti-Marxist Front [*Political party*] (PD)
SPAN	Social Planning Around Neighbourhoods [*Australia*]
SPAN	Societe des Plantations d'Ananas de Nianda
SPAN	Sullana [*Peru*] [*ICAO location identifier*] (ICLI)
SPANA	Society for the Protection of Animals in North Africa [*See also SPAAN*] (EAIO)
Spann	Spannung [*Tension*] [*German*] (GCA)
SPAO	San Juan Aposento [*Peru*] [*ICAO location identifier*] (ICLI)
SPAP	Picota [*Peru*] [*ICAO location identifier*] (ICLI)
SPAP	Sidirodromoi Peiraios-Athinon-Peloponnisou [*Piraeus-Athens-Peloponnisos Railways*] (GC)
SPAR	Alerta [*Peru*] [*ICAO location identifier*] (ICLI)
SPAR	Federation des Societes Publiques d'Action Rurale [*Togo*]
SPARCENT	Space and Atmospheric Research Centre [*Pakistan*] [*Research center*] (IRC)
SPARMO	Solar Particles and Radiations Monitoring Organisation [*France*] (PDAA)
SPARRSO	Space Research and Remote Sensing Organization [*Bangladesh*]
SPARS	Skypower Automated Reservation System

SPARTA.... Spatial Antimissile Research Test in Australia (IAA)
SPARTA.... Special Antimissile Research Tests in Australia
SPARTECA ... South Pacific Area Regional Trade and Cooperation Agreement
SPAS .... Societatis Philosophicae Americanae Socius [*Member of the American Philosophical Society*] [*Latin*]
SPAS .... Societe Professionnelle et Agricole de la Sakay
SPAS .... Swedish Peace and Arbitration Society
SPAS .... Syndicat des Professeurs Africains du Senegal [*Union of African Professors of Senegal*] (AF)
SPASA....... Servicios Politecnicos Aereos SA [*Spain*] [*ICAO designator*] (FAAC)
SPASEP .... Secretaria Permanente del Acuerdo Sudamericano de Estupefacientes y Psicotropicos [*Permanent Secretariat of the South American Agreement on Narcotic Drugs and Psychotropic Substances - PSSAANDPS*] [*Argentina*] (EAIO)
SPASK....... Service Provincial de l'Agriculture de Sud Kivu
spas st .... Lifesaving Station [*Topography*] (RU)
SPAT .... Aguas Calientes [*Peru*] [*ICAO location identifier*] (ICLI)
SPAT .... Societe des Produits Agricoles Tropicaux
SPATE ...... South Pacific Association for Teacher Education [*Later, ATEA*] (EA)
SPATF....... South Pacific Appropriate Technology Foundation [*Papua New Guinea*]
SPATiF...... Stowarzyszenie Polskich Artystow Teatru i Filmu [*Association of Polish Film and Theatre Actors*] (POL)
SPATS....... Sound Preservation and Technical Services [*National Library of Australia*]
SPB .... ASA [*Former USSR*] [*ICAO designator*] (FAAC)
SPB .... Bombsight Interference Station (RU)
spb............. Epidemic-Control Battalion (RU)
SPB .... High-Speed Dive Bomber (RU)
SPB .... Information and Bibliographic Office (RU)
SPB .... Saint Petersburg (RU)
SPB .... Sbor Pohranicni Bezpecnosti [*Border Region Security Corps*] (CZ)
SPB .... Scientific Poultry Breeders Australasia Proprietary Ltd. (ADA)
SPB .... Service des Phares et Balises [*Morocco*] (MSC)
SPB .... Seychelles Philatelic Bureau
SPB .... Societe des Plantations Boudou
SPB .... Special Planning Office (RU)
SPB .... Spoleczne Przedsiebiorstwo Budowlane [*People's Construction Enterprise*] (POL)
SPB .... Stoleczne Przedsiebiorstwo Budowlane [*Warsaw Construction Enterprise*] (POL)
SPB .... St. Thomas [*Virgin Islands*] Seaplane Base [*Airport symbol*] (OAG)
SPB .... Svaz Protifasistickych Bojovniku [*Union of Anti-Fascist Fighters*] (CZ)
SpBaU-SQ ... Universidad de Barcelona, Facultad de Quimica y Fisica, Barcelona, Spain [*Library symbol*] [*Library of Congress*] (LCLS)
SPBB .... Moyobamba [*Peru*] [*ICAO location identifier*] (ICLI)
SPBB .... Systeme de Planification, Programmation, Budgetisation [*French*] (ADPT)
SPBC .... Caballococha [*Peru*] [*ICAO location identifier*] (ICLI)
SPBE .... Service de Presse Baptiste Europeen [*European Baptist Press Service - EBPS*] (EAIO)
SPBEC....... South Pacific Bureau for Economic Cooperation in Developing Uniform Maritime Standards for the Pacific Area [*Suva, Fiji*] (EAIO)
SPBL .... Bellavista/Huallaga [*Peru*] [*ICAO location identifier*] (ICLI)
SPBR .... Iberia [*Peru*] [*ICAO location identifier*] (ICLI)
SPBS .... Jeberos/Bellavista [*Peru*] [*ICAO location identifier*] (ICLI)
SPBS........ Schweizerische Partei der Behinderten und Sozialbenachteiligten [*Swiss Party of the Handicapped and Socially Disadvantaged*] [*Political party*] (PPW)
SPBT .... Obenteni [*Peru*] [*ICAO location identifier*] (ICLI)
SPBU........ Vista Breau [*Peru*] [*ICAO location identifier*] (ICLI)
SPBW .... Society for the Preservation of Beers from the Wood [*British*] (EAIO)
SPBZ .... Sokolovsky Pretek Brannej Zdatnosti [*Sokolov Defense Preparedness Contest*] (CZ)
SPC .... Political Committee at Senior Level [*NATO*] (NATG)
SPC .... Saint Patrick's College [*Australia*] (ADA)
SPC .... Santa Cruz La Palma [*Canary Islands*] [*Airport symbol*] (OAG)
SPC .... Scholarly Publishers' Council [*Singapore*] (EAIO)
SPC .... Sea Ports Corporation [*Sudan*]
SPC .... Shepparton Fruit Preserving Co. Ltd. [*Australia*]
SPC .... Socialist Party of Croatia [*Political party*] (EY)
SPC .... Socialist Party of Cyprus [*Political party*] (EAIO)
SPC .... Societe de Promotion Commerciale
SPC .... Societe des Potasses du Congo [*Congolese Potash Company*] (AF)
S/P/C......... Sotto Protesto per Mettere in Conto [*Under Protest to Place to Account*] [*Italian*]

SPC........... Southern Petroleum Co. [*Iraq*] (EY)
SPC........... South Pacific Championship [*Rugby*]
SPC........... South Pacific Commission [*See also CPS*] (EAIO)
SpC .... Spanish Columbia, San Sebastian [*Record label*] [*Spain*]
SPC........... Special Political Committee [*Australia*]
SPC........... Srpska Pravoslavna Crkva [*Serbian Orthodox Church*] (YU)
SPC........... State Planning Commission [*China*] (IMH)
SPC........... Sudan Petrol Corporation
SPC........... Supplementary Patent Certificate [*European Community*]
SPC........... Supreme People's Council
SPC........... Swedish Peace Council (EAIO)
SPC........... Swiss Peace Council (EAIO)
SPC........... Sydney Police Centre [*Australia*]
SPC........... Syndicats des Planteurs de Cafe [*Madagascar*] (EAIO)
SPC........... Syrian Petroleum Company (ME)
SPCA........ Barraca [*Peru*] [*ICAO location identifier*] (ICLI)
SPCA-THUBET ... Societe Parisienne de Comptoirs Africains A. Thubet
SPCB .... Aguas Blancas [*Peru*] [*ICAO location identifier*] (ICLI)
SPCC .... Standardization, Policy, and Coordination Committee [*NATO*] (NATG)
SPCC .... State Pollution Control Commission [*New South Wales*] [*Australia*] (PDAA)
SPCDRO ... Secretariat Permanent du Comite Directeur de la Recherche Operationnelle [*Permanent Secretariat of the Managing Committee on Operations Research*] [*French*] (WER)
sp ch .... Spectroscopically Pure (RU)
SPCH........ Tocache [*Peru*] [*ICAO location identifier*] (ICLI)
SPCI .... Societe de Promotion Commerciale Ivoirienne
SPCK .... Society for Promoting Christian Knowledge
SPCL .... Pucallpa [*Peru*] [*ICAO location identifier*] (ICLI)
SPCM .... Contamana [*Peru*] [*ICAO location identifier*] (ICLI)
SPCM .... Society for the Promotion of Chamber Music (EAIO)
SPCN........ Sciences Physiques, Chimiques, Naturelles (Certificat) [*Certificate in Physical, Chemical, and Natural Sciences*] (CL)
SPCN........ Societe des Plantations de Cafe de la Nome
SPCN........ Societe des Produits Chimiques du Niger
SPCP .... Pucacaca [*Peru*] [*ICAO location identifier*] (ICLI)
SPCS........ Swiss Playing Card Society (EAIO)
SPCT .... Chota [*Peru*] [*ICAO location identifier*] (ICLI)
SPCV .... Sociedade Portuguesa de Ciencias Veterinarias [*Portugal*] (EAIO)
SPD........... Free-Piston Engine (RU)
SPD........... Message Center (RU)
SPD........... Saidpur [*Bangladesh*] [*Airport symbol*] (OAG)
SPD........... Secretaria de Prensa y Difusion [*Press and Propaganda Secretariat*] [*Argentina*] (LA)
SPD........... Slovensko Planinsko Drustvo [*Slovenian Alpine Society*] (YU)
SPD........... Sosyal Planlama Dairesi [*Social Planning Office*] [*Under State Planning Organization*] (TU)
SPD........... Sozialdemokratische Partei Deutschlands [*Social Democratic Party of Germany*] (WEN)
SpD .... Spanish Decca, San Sebastian [*Record label*] [*Spain*]
SPD........... Srpsko Pevacko Drustvo [*Serbian Singing Society*] (YU)
SPD........... Strediska Pracujiciho Dorostu [*Young Workers' Centers*] (CZ)
SPD........... Train Dispatcher Communications (RU)
SPDA........ Societe Peinture Decoration Africaine
SPDA........ Southern Philippines Development Authority (GEA)
SPDB........ Production Dispatch Office Communications System (RU)
SPDC........ Saudi Petrochemical Development Corp.
SPDC........ Societe du Palace de Cocody
spdi........... Sin Pie de Imprenta [*Without Imprint*] [*Publishing*] [*Spanish*]
SPDK........ Free-Piston Diesel Compressor (RU)
SPDO .... Mollendo [*Peru*] [*ICAO location identifier*] (ICLI)
SPDO .... Production Dispatch Department Communications System (RU)
SPDP .... Caplan & Cie., Societe des Plantations Djongo-Penja
SPDU........ Ship Painters' and Dockers' Union [*Australia*]
SPDV........ Sociedade Portuguesa de Dermatologia e Venereologia [*Portugese Society of Dermatology and Venerology*] [*Portugal*] (EAIO)
SPDV........ Societe pour le Developpement du Petrole Vert [*French*]
SPE........... All-Union Association for the Export of Industrial Equipment (RU)
SPE........... Senegalaise de Plomberie et d'Equipement
SPE........... Service Juridique de Protection de l'Enfance (FLAF)
SPE........... Service Presidentiel Zairois des Etudes
SPE........... Servizio Permanente Effettivo [*Service in regular army qualifying for pension*] [*Italian*]
SPE........... Sociedade Portuguesa de Estomatologia [*Portuguese*] (SLS)
SPE........... Sociedad Peruana de Escritores [*Association of Peruvian Writers*] (LA)
SPE........... Societe des Plantations d'Elima
SPE........... Society for Professional Engineers [*South Africa*] (AA)
SPE........... Society for Public Economics [*Germany*] (EAIO)
SPE........... Sony Pictures Entertainment [*Commercial firm*] (ECON)

SPE .... Sosialistiki Panspoudastiki Enosi [*Socialist All-Student Union*] [*Greek*] (GC)

SPE .... Speichereinheit [*German*] (ADPT)

SPE .... Symvoulion Proothiseos Exagogon [*Exports Promotion Council*] [*Greek*] (GC)

SPEA .... Panamanian Society of Engineers and Architects (IAA)

SPEA .... Servico de Pesquisas Economicas Aplicadas [*Applied Economic Research Bureau*] [*Brazil*] (LA)

SPEA .... Synergatiki Promithevtiki Enosis Ammokhostou-Larnakos [*Famagusta-Larnaca Cooperative Supply Union*] (GC)

SPEARNET ... South Pacific Educational and Research Network

speb .... Epidemic Control Battalion (RU)

SPEB .... Pebas [*Peru*] [*ICAO location identifier*] (ICLI)

SPEB .... Syndicat des Producters et Exportateurs de Bois du Cameroon (EAIO)

SPEC .... Service Provisoire des Eaux du Cameroun

SPEC .... Society of Philippine Electrical Contractors (DS)

SPEC .... South Pacific Bureau for Economic Cooperation [*Fiji*] (ADA)

SPEC .... South Pacific Education Centre [*Australia*]

Spec .... Specerijhandel [*Benelux*] (BAS)

spec .... Speciaal [*Special*] [*Netherlands*]

spec .... Special [*Special*] [*French*]

spec .... Speciale [*Special*] [*Italian*]

spec .... Specialis [*Special*] (HU)

spec .... Specifisch [*Specific*] [*German*]

S pech........ With Seal (BU)

SPECI....... Societe de Publication de l'Edition de Cote-D'Ivoire

SPECIA..... Societe Parisienne d'Expansion Chimique

SPECOMME ... Specified Command, Middle East

SPED .... Epidemic Control Team (RU)

SPED........ Syndicat du Personnel de l'Enseignement Libre du Dahomey

SPEECH ... Society to Promote Essential Education for Children with Communications Handicaps [*Australia*]

SPEG .... Societe de Prospection et d'Etudes Geothermiques [*Research center*] [*France*] (EAS)

SPEIA........ Syndicat Patronal des Entreprises et Industries Agricoles

SPEIN .... Syndicat Patronal des Entreprises et Industries du Niger

SPEKA ...... Synetairistiki Promithevtiki kai Emboriki Enosi [*Cooperative Supply and Commercial Union*] [*Greek*] (GC)

SPEKO ...... Special Counterintelligence Section (RU)

spektr .... Spektroskopisch [*Spectroscopic*] [*German*] (GCA)

Spektr .... Spektrum [*Spectrum*] [*German*] (GCA)

spektr an .... Spectral Analysis (RU)

SPEL .... Synergatiki Promithevtiki Enosis Ltd., Lefkosias [*Nicosia Cooperative Supply Union Ltd.*] (GC)

SPELA....... Sociedade Portuguesa de Estudos e Linhas Aereas Ltda. [*Portugal*]

SPELD ...... Societe pour l'Exportation des Livres de Droit, Sciences Economiques, Sociales et Humaines (FLAF)

spellat......... Spellatura [*Scratch*] [*Publishing*] [*Italian*]

spelli.......... Spellicciata [*Skinned Spot*] [*Publishing*] [*Italian*]

SPEM .... Societe de Presse et d'Edition de Madagascar

SPEMD ..... Sociedade Portugesa de Estomatologia Emedicina Dentaria [*Portugal*] (EAIO)

SPEMELEC ... Specialites Mecaniques et Electro-Mecaniques [*France*] (PDAA)

SPEMU ..... Stable-Price Economic and Monetary Union [*Europe*]

SPEN........ Iscozacin [*Peru*] [*ICAO location identifier*] (ICLI)

SPENC.... Serbian PEN Centre [*Former Yugoslavia*] (EAIO)

SPENC.... Slovene PEN Centre [*Samoa*] (EAIO)

SPENC.... Sydney PEN Centre [*Australia*] (EAIO)

speo .... Antiepidemiological Medical Detachment (BU)

SPEO........ Chimbote [*Peru*] [*ICAO location identifier*] (ICLI)

SPEO........ Epidemic Control Detachment (RU)

SPEP .... Puerto Esperanza [*Peru*] [*ICAO location identifier*] (ICLI)

SPEPE....... Secretariat Permanent pour l'Etude des Problemes de l'Eau [*Permanent Secretariat for the Study of Water Problems*] [*France*] (PDAA)

SPEPREV ... Societe de Peinture Entretien Plomberie Revetement Etancheite Vitrerie

SPEQ........ Moquegua [*Peru*] [*ICAO location identifier*] (ICLI)

SPER .... South Pacific Electric Railway Cooperative Society Ltd. (ADA)

SPER .... Syndicat des Industries de Materiel Professionnel Electronique et Radio Electrique

SPES......... Simulazione PWR per Esperienze di Sicurezza [*Italian*] [*Nuclear energy*] (NRCH)

spes .... Spesiaal [*Special*] [*Afrikaans*]

spets .... Special, Specialist (BU)

spets .... Special, Special Term (RU)

spetskurs.... Special Course (BU)

Spetslag ..... Special [*Corrective Labor*] Camp (RU)

Spetslagpunkt ... Special [*Corrective Labor*] Camp Section (RU)

SPETSNAZ ... Voiska Spetsialnovo Naznacheniya [*Special-Purpose Forces*] [*Russian*]

Spetsrybmontazh ... State All-Union Specialized Trust of the Glavrybstroy (RU)

Spetsset'stroy ... Trust for the Construction of Power Transmission Lines and Substations of the Glavvostokelektroset'stroy (RU)

spetsstroy... Special Construction Projects Enterprise (BU)

Spetsstroy .. State All-Union Trust of Specialized Operations of the Glavstroy (RU)

Spetsstroymontazh ... Specialized Construction and Installation Trust (RU)

spetsVTEK ... Special Medical Commission for Determination of Disability (RU)

Spetszhelezobetonstroy ... State Specialized Trust for Reinforced Concrete Structures (RU)

SPEU .... Singapore Printing Employees Union (ML)

SPEX .... Sozialwissenschaftliche Experten und Gutachter [*Social Science Experts*] [*NOMOS Datapool Database*] (IID)

SPEZ .... Puerto Bermudez [*Peru*] [*ICAO location identifier*] (ICLI)

spez .... Speziell [*Especially*] [*German*]

spez .... Spezifisch [*Specific*] [*German*]

Spez Gew ... Spezifisches Gewicht [*Specific Gravity*] [*German*]

spezif......... Spezifisch [*Specific*] [*German*]

SPF .... Secours Populaire Francais [*French Popular Relief*] (WER)

SPF .... Servicio de Plagas Forestales [*Spain*] (DSCA)

SPF .... Sociedad de Productores Forestales [*Uruguay*] (DSCA)

SPF .... Societe de Prospections Forestieres

SPF .... Societe des Plantations de Foumban

SPF .... Societe des Poetes Francais [*French Poets Society*] (EAIO)

SPF .... Socijalisticka Partija Francuske [*Socialist Party of France*] (YU)

SPF .... Somali Patriotic Front [*Political party*] (EY)

SPF .... South Pacific Airline SA [*Chile*] [*ICAO designator*] (FAAC)

SPF .... South Pacific Forum [*Australia*]

SPF .... Special Production Fund [*Australian Film Commission*]

SPF .... Storehouse for Semifinished Products (RU)

SPF .... Sveriges Psykologforbund [*Sweden*] (EAIO)

SPF .... Syndicat des Psychiatres Francais [*French*] (SLS)

SPF .... Trade-Union Council of the Philippines (RU)

SpFest........ Spanish Festival [*Record label*]

SPFFA ...... South Pacific Forum Fisheries Agency [*Honiara, Solomon Islands*] (EAIO)

SPFI.......... Secretaria de Patrimonio y Fomento Industrial [*Secretariat of Patrimony and Industrial Development*] [*Mexico*] (LA)

SPFP.......... Stowarzyszenie Projektantow Form Przemyslowych [*Poland*] (EAIO)

SPFP.......... Sudanese People's Federal Party [*Sudan*] [*Political party*] (MENA)

SPFS.......... Societe des Palmeraies de la Ferme Suisse [*Cameroon*]

SPFS.......... South Pacific Forum Secretariat [*Fiji*] (EAIO)

SPG............ Goryunov Heavy Machine Gun (RU)

SPG............ Section de Parc du Genie [*Military*] [*French*] (MTD)

SPG............ Sekolah Pendidikan Guru [*Teacher-Training Institutions*] [*Indonesian*]

SPG............ Sistema de Preferencias Generalizadas [*Most-Favored-Nations System*] [*Spanish*] (WER)

SPG............ Societe Pharmaceutique Guyanaise [*Pharmaceutical Society of French Guiana*] (LA)

SPG............ Society for the Propagation of the Gospel in Foreign Parts

Spg .... Spannung [*Tension*] [*German*] (GCA)

Sp G .... Spezifisches Gewicht [*Specific Gravity*] [*German*]

SPG............ State Protection Group [*New South Wales Police Service*] [*Australia*]

SPG............ Systeme des Preferences Generalisees [*System of Generalized Preferences*] [*French*] (AF)

SPGC........ Societe de Participation et de Gestion au Congo

SPGG........ Free-Piston Gas Generator, Free-Piston Gasifier (RU)

SPGM....... Tingo Maria [*Peru*] [*ICAO location identifier*] (ICLI)

SPGRC ...... Stranded Pakistanis General Repatriation Committee

SPGS .... Lagunas [*Peru*] [*ICAO location identifier*] (ICLI)

SPGSV ...... Schweizerischer Pistengolf-Sportverband [*Switzerland*] (EAIO)

SPGT .... Puerto Victoria [*Peru*] [*ICAO location identifier*] (ICLI)

SPGU........ Bagua [*Peru*] [*ICAO location identifier*] (ICLI)

SPH .... Savjet za Prosvjetu Hrvatske [*Educational Council of Croatia*] (YU)

SPH .... Singapore Press Holdings (ECON)

SPH .... Socialisticke Podnikove Hospodarstvi [*Socialist Enterprise Management*] (CZ)

SPHA........ Chincha [*Peru*] [*ICAO location identifier*] (ICLI)

sphaer........ Sphaerisch [*Spherical*] [*German*] (GCA)

SPHB........ Societe des Plantations et Huileries de Bingerville

SPHC........ Chala [*Peru*] [*ICAO location identifier*] (ICLI)

SPHC........ Societe de Plantations d'Heveas et de Cafeiers

SPHC........ Southern Pacific Hotel Corp. [*Australia*]

SPHCS ...... Society for Parents of Handicapped Children [*Malta*] (EAIO)

SPHI.......... Chiclayo/Cap. Jose Abelardo Quinones Gonzalez [*Peru*] [*ICAO location identifier*] (ICLI)

SPHM .... Sprava Pohonne Hmoty a Mazadla [*Petroleum Products and Lubricants Directorate*] (CZ)

SPHO .... Ayacucho/Coronel FAP Alfredo Mendivil Duarte [*Peru*] [*ICAO location identifier*] (ICLI)

SPHU .... Huancayo [*Peru*] [*ICAO location identifier*] (ICLI)

SPHU .... Societe Proprietaire de l'Hotel de l'Union
SPHV........ Huanuco Viejo [*Peru*] [*ICAO location identifier*]　(ICLI)
SPHY........ Andahuaylas [*Peru*] [*ICAO location identifier*]　(ICLI)
SPHZ......... Anta/Comdte. FAP German Arias Grazziani [*Peru*] [*ICAO location identifier*]　(ICLI)
SPI .... Saratov Polytechnic Institute　(RU)
SPI .... Savet za Preradivacku Industriju [*Council for the Manufacturing Industry*]　(YU)
SPI .... Secretariats Professionnels Internationaux　(FLAF)
SPI .... Service de la Promotion Industrielle [*Ministere de l'Economie et du Plan*] [*Cameroon*]
SPI .... Service Pedologique Interafricain
SPI .... Servico de Protecao aos Indios [*Indian Protection Service*] [*Brazil*]　(LA)
spi .... Sin Pie de Imprenta [*Without Imprint*] [*Publishing*] [*Spanish*]
SPI .... Societe de Placements Internationaux [*French*]
SPI .... Societe pour l'Informatique [*Company for Informatics*] [*Information service or system*] [*Defunct*]　(IID)
SPI .... Southern Pacific Insurance [*Australia*]
SPI .... Soviet and Party Publishing Houses　(RU)
SPI .... Superb Properties & Industries, Berhad [*Malaysia*]
SPI .... Svenska Petroleum Institutet [*Swedish Petroleum Institute*]　(WED)
SPI .... Sydney Pollution Index [*Australia*]
SPIA .... Ica [*Peru*] [*ICAO location identifier*]　(ICLI)
SPIA .... Service Pedologique Interafricain
SPIC .... Societe de Participations Industrielles et Commerciales
SPIC .... Societe de Promotion Immobiliere du Cameroun
SPIC .... Southern Petrochemical Industries Corp. Ltd. [*India*]
spich .... Match Factory [*Topography*]　(RU)
SPICh .... Spolek Posluchacu Chemickotechnologickeho Inzenyrstvi [*Association of University Students of Chemical Engineering*]　(CZ)
SPID .... Acquired Immune Deficiency Syndrome [*Pronounced "speed"*] [*Russian*]
SPIDS........ Syndicat Patronal des Industries de Dakar et du Senegal [*Industry Employers Association of Dakar and Senegal*]　(AF)
SPIE .... Secretariat Professionnel International de l'Enseignement [*International Federation of Free Teachers' Unions - IFFTU*] [*Amsterdam, Netherlands*]　(EAIO)
SPIE .... Societe Parisienne pour l'Industrie Electrique
SPIE .... Society of Photo-Optical Instrumentation Engineers [*International Society for Optical Engineering*]
SPIE .... Systeme de Paiements Intra-Europeens　(FLAF)
SPIEA........ Syndicat Professionnel de l'Industrie des Engrais Azotes
SPIF........... Societe de Participations Industrielles and Financieres
SPIFDA..... South Pacific Islands Fisheries Development Agency [*Noumea, New Caledonia*]　(EAIO)
SPII .... Seed and Plant Improvement Institute [*Iran*] [*Research center*]　(IRC)
SPIK .... Spolek Posluchacu Inzenyrstvi Komerciho [*Association of School of Business Administration Students*]　(CZ)
SPIL.......... Quincemil [*Peru*] [*ICAO location identifier*]　(ICLI)
SPIL.......... Society for the Promotion and Improvement of Libraries [*India*]　(PDAA)
SPIM .... Lima-Callao/Internacional Jorge Chavez [*Peru*] [*ICAO location identifier*]　(ICLI)
SPIM .... Syndikalistiki Parataxi Ilektrologon-Mikhanologon [*Trade Union Faction of Electricians and Mechanics*] [*Greek*]　(GC)
SPIMACO ... Saudi Pharmaceutical Industries & Medical Appliances Corporation [*Saudi Arabia*]
SPIN.......... Societa per Imprese Nucleari [*Nuclear Contracting Company*] [*Italian*]　(WER)
sp indet....... Species Indeterminata [*Species Indeterminate*] [*Latin*]　(MAE)
sp inquir..... Species Inquirendae [*Species of Doubtful Status*] [*Latin*]　(MAE)
SPINS........ South Pacific Information Network System [*Australia*]
SPIP.......... Satipo [*Peru*] [*ICAO location identifier*]　(ICLI)
SPIPAP..... Service de Presse, d'Information, de Propagande, et d'Action Psychologique [*Press, Information, Propaganda, and Psychological Action Department*] [*Cambodia*]　(CL)
SPiR.......... Collection of Regulations and Decrees of the Council of People's Commissars of the USSR　(RU)
SPIR .... Patria [*Peru*] [*ICAO location identifier*]　(ICLI)
SPIR .... Society for the Protection of Individual Rights
spirit.......... Spiritismi [*Spiritism*] [*Finland*]
Spirt .... Alcohol and Vodka Distillery [*Topography*]　(RU)
SPIS.......... Pias [*Peru*] [*ICAO location identifier*]　(ICLI)
SPIS.......... Spolek Posluchacu Inzenyrskeho Stavitelstvi [*Association of Architectural Engineering Students*]　(CZ)
SPIS.......... State Plantations Impact Study [*Victoria, Australia*]
SPIT .... Paita [*Peru*] [*ICAO location identifier*]　(ICLI)
SPIVHLB ... Societe Proprietaire du Village Hotel de la Langue de Barbarie
SPIW .... ESCAP [*Economic and Social Commssion for the Asia and Pacific*] Division for Shipping, Ports, and Inland Waterways　(EAIO)
SPIY .... Yauri [*Peru*] [*ICAO location identifier*]　(ICLI)
SPIZ .... Uchiza [*Peru*] [*ICAO location identifier*]　(ICLI)

SPJ .... Socialist Party of Japan [*Nikon Shakaito*] [*Political party*]　(PPW)
SPJ .... Socijalisticka Partija Jugoslavije [*Socialist Party of Yugoslavia*] [*Political party*]　(PPE)
SPJ .... Sparta [*Greece*] [*Airport symbol*] [*Obsolete*]　(OAG)
SPJA......... Rioja [*Peru*] [*ICAO location identifier*]　(ICLI)
SPJB......... Cajabamba/Pampa Grande [*Peru*] [*ICAO location identifier*]　(ICLI)
SPJI.......... Juanjui [*Peru*] [*ICAO location identifier*]　(ICLI)
SPJJ .... Jauja [*Peru*] [*ICAO location identifier*]　(ICLI)
SPJL......... Juliaca [*Peru*] [*ICAO location identifier*]　(ICLI)
SPJN .... San Juan [*Peru*] [*ICAO location identifier*]　(ICLI)
SPJR......... Cajamarca/Mayor General FAP Armando Revoredo Iglesias [*Peru*] [*ICAO location identifier*]　(ICLI)
SPK .... Arctic Circle　(RU)
SPK .... Blood Transfusion Station　(RU)
SPK .... Hydrofoil Vessel　(RU)
SPK .... Interrupter Contact　(RU)
SPK .... Parabolic Cylinder Solar Range　(RU)
SPK .... Saporamean Kampuchea [*Kampuchea Information Agency*] [*Cambodia*]　(FEA)
SPK .... Sapporo [*Japan*] [*Airport symbol*]　(OAG)
SPK .... Savet za Prosvetu i Kulturu [*Educational and Cultural Council*] (YU)
SPK .... Savezna Planska Komisija [*Federal Planning Commission*] (YU)
SPK .... Savez Poljoprivrednih Komora [*Union of Chambers of Agriculture*]　(YU)
SPK .... Schweizerische Gesellschaft der Psychotherapeuten fuer Kinder und Jugendliche [*Swiss Association of Psychotherapists for Children and Youth*]　(SLS)
SPK .... Sekretarijat za Prosvetu i Kulturu (SIV) [*Secretariat of Education and Culture*]　(YU)
SPK .... Severocesky Prumysl Kamene [*North Bohemian Stone Cutting Industry*] [*Liberec*]　(CZ)
SPK .... Sijil Persekolahan Kejuruan [*Vocational School Certificate*] (ML)
SPK .... Siyasi Partiler Kanunu [*Political Parties Law*]　(TU)
SPK .... Skola Pesadisikh Komandira [*School for Infantry Commanders*] (YU)
SPK.......... Socialist Party of Kurdistan [*Iraq*] [*Political party*]　(MENA)
SPK.......... Sozialistisches Patientenkollektiv [*Socialist Patients' Collective*] (EG)
Sp K .... Special Satellite Capsule　(RU)
SPK.......... Sreska Poljoprivredna Komora [*District Chamber of Agriculture*] (YU)
SPK.......... Staatliche Plankommission [*State Planning Commission*]　(EG)
SPK.......... Statni Pedagogicka Knihovna [*State Pedagogical Library*]　(CZ)
SPK.......... Statni Planovaci Komise [*State Planning Commission*]　(CZ)
SPK.......... Stowarzyszenie Polskich Kombatantow [*Association of Polish Veterans*]　(POL)
SPK.......... Stratiotikos Poinikos Kodix [*Military Penal Code*]　(GC)
SPK.......... Svet za Prosveto in Kulturo Ljudska Republika Slovenija [*Cultural and Educational Council of Slovenia*]　(YU)
SPKB .... Special Planning and Design Office　(RU)
SPKI .... Spolek Posluchacu Komerciho Inzenyrstvi [*Association of School of Business Administration Students*]　(CZ)
SPKK .... Statni Pedagogicka Knihovna Komenskeho [*Comenius State Pedagogical Library*] [*Prague*]　(CZ)
SPKP .... Suomen Perustuslaillinen Kansanpuolue [*Finnish Constitutional People's Party*] [*Political party*]　(PPW)
SPKT .... Symvoulion Paragogikon kai Koinonikon Taxeon [*Council of Social and Productive Classes*]　(GC)
SPL .... Scan-Pol Ltd. [*Poland*] [*ICAO designator*]　(FAAC)
SPL .... South Pacific Program Library　(ADPT)
sp l .... Spectral Line　(RU)
SPL .... Spolecnost Pracovniho Lekarstvi [*Industrial Medicine Association*]　(CZ)
SPL .... Standard-Programmier-Logik [*Standard Programer Logic*] [*German*]　(ADPT)
Spl.............. Supplement [*Supplement*] [*German*]
SPLA .... Louisiana [*Peru*] [*ICAO location identifier*]　(ICLI)
SPLA .... Saharan People's Liberation Army [*Arab*]
SPLA .... Seychel Popular Liberation Army
SPLA .... Sudan People's Liberation Army
Splaj.......... Socialist People's Libyan Arab Jamahiriya [*Gathering of the masses*] [*Muammar Qaddafi's name for his country*]
SPLAJ ...... Socialist People's Libyan Arab Jamahirya
SPLAM ..... Societe d'Acconage et de Manutention [*Morocco*]
SPLAN ..... Sociedade de Pesquisas e Planejamento [*Brazil*]　(DSCA)
SPLD .... Celendin [*Peru*] [*ICAO location identifier*]　(ICLI)
SPLF........ Sudanese People's Liberation Front
SPLI......... Lima [*Peru*] [*ICAO location identifier*]　(ICLI)
SPLM .... Sudan People's Liberation Movement　(MENA)
SPLN .... Rodriguez de Mendoz/San Nicolas [*Peru*] [*ICAO location identifier*]　(ICLI)
SPLO......... Ilo [*Peru*] [*ICAO location identifier*]　(ICLI)

SPLP .... Las Palmas [*Peru*] [*ICAO location identifier*] (ICLI)
SPLS .... Zorrillos [*Peru*] [*ICAO location identifier*] (ICLI)
SPLT .... Lobitos [*Peru*] [*ICAO location identifier*] (ICLI)
SPLV .... Lago Verde [*Peru*] [*ICAO location identifier*] (ICLI)
SPM .... Air Saint-Pierre SA [*France*] [*ICAO designator*] (FAAC)
SPM .... Fixed Medical Aid Station (RU)
SPM .... Modern Problems of Mathematics [*Book series*] (RU)
SPM .... Permanent Medical Aid Stations (BU)
SPM .... Punched-Card Computer, Punched-Tape Computer (RU)
SPM .... Servicos Prisionais Militares [*Military Prisons Service*] [*Portuguese*] (WER)
SPM .... Sijil Pelajaran Malaysia [*Malaysian Language Education Certificate*] (ML)
SPM .... Societe des Petroles de Madagascar
SPM .... Somali Patriotic Movement [*Political party*] (EY)
SPM .... Sovet na Prosveta na Makedonija [*Council of Education of Macedonia*] (YU)
SPM .... St. Pierre and Miquelon [*ANSI three-letter standard code*] (CNC)
SPMA .... Rio Maranon [*Peru*] [*ICAO location identifier*] (ICLI)
SPMA .... Servico de Policia Maritima e Aerea [*Portuguese*]
SPMA .... Syllogos Politikon Mikhanikon Athinon [*Athens Civil Engineers Association*] (GC)
SPMA .... Syndesmos Politikon Mikhanikon kai Arkhitektonon [*League of Civil Engineers and Architects*] [*Cyprus*] (GC)
SPMC .... Sydney Pain Management Centre [*Australia*]
SPMC .... Syndicat des Petits et Moyens Commercants du Niger [*Employers' organization*] [*Niger*]
SPME .... Tumbes/Pedro Canga [*Peru*] [*ICAO location identifier*] (ICLI)
SPMFR ..... Sociedade Portuguesa de Medicina Fisica e Reabilitacao [*Portuguese*] (SLS)
SPML .... Sociedade Portuguesa de Medicina Laboratorial [*Portuguese*] (SLS)
SPMLF ...... Societe de la Psychologie Medicale de Langue Francaise [*French-Language Society of Medical Psychology - FLSMP*] (EA)
SPMP .... Syndicat des Producteurs de Matieres Plastiques [*France*]
SPMR .... Societe du Pipeline Mediterranee-Rhone
SPMS .... Yurimaguas [*Peru*] [*ICAO location identifier*] (ICLI)
SPMT .... Service Permanent des Marees Terrestres [*Permanent Service on Earth Tides*] (MSC)
SPMY .... Dos De Mayo [*Peru*] [*ICAO location identifier*] (ICLI)
SPN .... Auxiliary Laying Point [*Artillery*] (BU)
SPN .... Combat Engineer Observation Post (RU)
SPN .... Saipan [*Mariana Islands*] [*Airport symbol*] (OAG)
SPN .... Sekcja Piki Noznej [*Soccer Section*] (POL)
SPN .... Skorpion Air [*Bulgaria*] [*ICAO designator*] (FAAC)
SPN .... Slovenske Pedagogicke Nakladatelstvo [*Slovak Pedagogical Publishing House*] (CZ)
SPN .... Sociedade Portuguesa de Numismatica [*Portuguese*] (SLS)
SPN .... Stabilized Director [*Navy*] (RU)
SPN .... Statne Podohospodarski Nakladatelstvo [*State Agricultural Publishing House*] (CZ)
SPN .... Statni Pedagogicke Nakladatelstvi [*State Pedagogical Publishing House*] (CZ)
SPN .... Sydney Press Network [*Australia*]
SPNA .... Punta De Lomas [*Peru*] [*ICAO location identifier*] (ICLI)
SPNC .... Huanuco/Alferez FAP David Figuerao Fernandini [*Peru*] [*ICAO location identifier*] (ICLI)
SPNC .... Sindicato Profesional Nacional de Choferes [*National Professional Drivers Union*] [*Chile*] (LA)
SPND .... Societe des Plantations de N'Dafia
SPNFT ...... South Pacific Nuclear Free Treaty
SPNFZ ...... South Pacific Nuclear-Free Zone
SPNH .... Laguna Choclococha [*Peru*] [*ICAO location identifier*] (ICLI)
SPNH .... Special Purpose Nursing Home [*Australia*]
SPNI .... Societe pour la Protection de la Nature en Israel [*Society for the Protection of Nature in Israel*] [*Tel Aviv*] (EAIO)
SPNI .... Society for the Protection of Nature [*Israel*] (SLS)
SPNK .... Savet za Prosvetu, Nauku, i Kulturu [*Educational, Scientific, and Cultural Council*] (YU)
SPNO .... Ancon [*Peru*] [*ICAO location identifier*] (ICLI)
SPNP .... Puno [*Peru*] [*ICAO location identifier*] (ICLI)
SPNP .... Societe des Plantation des Nyombe-Penja
SPNR .... Ricran [*Peru*] [*ICAO location identifier*] (ICLI)
SPNT .... Intuto [*Peru*] [*ICAO location identifier*] (ICLI)
SPNU .... Manu [*Peru*] [*ICAO location identifier*] (ICLI)
SPNZ .... Santa Cruz [*Peru*] [*ICAO location identifier*] (ICLI)
SPNZ .... Socialist Party of New Zealand [*Political party*] (PPW)
SPO .... Aeroservicios Ejecutivos del Pacifico SA [*Mexico*] [*ICAO designator*] (FAAC)
SPO .... Consumers' Societies Union (RU)
SPO .... Gun Ammunition Supply Point (RU)
SPO .... Sociaal Pedagogisch Onderwijs
SPO .... Southern Petroleum Organization [*Basra, Iraq*] (MENA)
SPO .... Sozialdemokratische Partei Oesterreichs [*Social Democratic Party of Austria*] [*Political party*]

SPO .... Sport Popular Orasenesc [*Urban People's Sport*] (RO)
SPO .... Sprawny do Pracy i Obrony [*Fit for Work and Defense*] [*Badge*] (POL)
SPO .... Srpski Pokret Obnove [*Serbian Renaissance Movement*] [*Political party*] (EY)
SPO .... State Planning Organization [*Turkey*] (IMH)
SPO .... Stoker Petty Officer [*Navy*] [*British*] (DSUE)
SPO .... Stomatologic Polyclinic (RU)
SPO .... Warning and Identification System (RU)
SPOA .... Saposoa [*Peru*] [*ICAO location identifier*] (ICLI)
SPOA .... Souprava Prepravniku pro Osobni Automobily [*Passenger Automobile Transporter*] (CZ)
SPOA .... Syndesmos Palaion Odigon Avtokinitiston [*Association of Veteran Drivers*] [*Greek*] (GC)
SPOC .... Sydney Paralympic Organising Committee [*Australia*]
SpOd .... Spanish Odeon, Barcelona [*Record label*] [*Spain*]
Spofa .... Spojene Farmaceuticke Zivody [*United Pharmaceutical Factories*] (CZ)
SPOFOR ... Sportwissenschaftliche Forschungsprojekte [*Bundesinstitut fuer Sportwissenschaft*] [*Germany*] [*Information service or system*] (CRD)
SPOJC .... Spojovaci Ceta (Dopnit Zkratkou prislus Velitelstvi) [*Communications Platoon (Abbreviation is augmented by adding initials of pertinent headquarters)*] (CZ)
SPOJP .... Spojovaci Pluk [*Communications Regiment*] (CZ)
Spoj r .... Spojovaci Rota [*Communications*] (CZ)
Spoj voj ...... Spojovaci Vojsko [*Communications Troops (Signal Corps)*] (CZ)
SPOK .... Statni Populacni Komise [*State Population Commission*] (CZ)
SPOL .... Collique [*Peru*] [*ICAO location identifier*] (ICLI)
spoldz .... Spoldzielcza [*or Spoldzielnia*] [*Cooperative*] (POL)
SPOLIT ..... Sportliteratur [*Bundesinstitut fuer Sportwissenschaft*] [*Germany*] [*Information service or system*] (CRD)
SPOLP ...... Synergatiki Promithevtiki Organosis Lemesou-Pafou [*Limassol-Paphos Cooperative Supply Organization*] (GC)
SPOM .... Stanica Poljoprivrednih Oruda i Masina [*Agricultural Tools and Machines Station*] (YU)
SPOM .... Syndicat des Producteurs d'Oleagineux d'Outre-Mer
SPON .... Social and Legal Protection of Minors (RU)
SPOP .... Poto [*Peru*] [*ICAO location identifier*] (ICLI)
sport .... Sporting, Sports, Sport (RU)
Sportintern ... Red Sports International (RU)
sportl .... Sportlich [*Sporting, Athletic*] [*German*]
Sportsnab ... Sports Equipment Supplies (BU)
sport-toto ... Pari-Mutuel Betting (BU)
SPOS .... Zorritos [*Peru*] [*ICAO location identifier*] (ICLI)
SPOSA .... St. Paul's Old Students Association
SPOT .... Satellite pour Observation de la Terre [*French*]
Spot .... Spotlight [*Record label*] [*Australia*]
SPOT .... Systeme Probatoire d'Observation de la Terre [*Probative System for the Observation of the Earth*] [*Joint Belgian, French, and Swiss Satellite*]
SPOV .... Leon Velarde/Shiringayoc O Hda. Mejia [*Peru*] [*ICAO location identifier*] (ICLI)
Spowa .... Sport- und Wanderbedarf [*Sports and Hiking Needs*] (EG)
SPOY .... Atico [*Peru*] [*ICAO location identifier*] (ICLI)
SPP .... Medical Control Point (BU)
SPP .... Medical Transfer Station [*Military term*] (RU)
SPP .... Menongue [*Angola*] [*Airport symbol*] (OAG)
SPP .... Plastic Life Raft (RU)
SPP .... Program Interruption System (RU)
SPP .... Reinforced Concrete Panels Enterprise (BU)
SPP .... Schwerpunktprogramm [*Priority Program*] [*Germany*]
SPP .... Searchlight Beam Field (RU)
SPP .... Secretaria de Programacion y Presupuesto [*Secretariat of Programing and Budget*] [*Mexico*] (LA)
SPP .... Sekretarijat za Pravosudne Poslove (SIV) [*Secretariat of Judicial Affairs*] (YU)
SPP .... Sentrong Pangkultura ng Pilipinas [*Philippines*] (EAIO)
SPP .... Separator-Steam Superheater [*Nuclear energy*] (BU)
SPP .... Service de Presse Protestant [*Switzerland*] (EAIO)
SPP .... Sindicato de Periodistas de Panama [*Journalists Union of Panama*] (LA)
SPP .... Societe de Peche Pontenegrine
SPP .... Soeurs de la Providence de Portieux (EAIO)
SPP .... Sofia Industrial Enterprise (BU)
SPP .... Southern Pacific Petroleum [*Australia*]
SPP .... Southern Pacific Properties
SPP .... Spainair [*Spain*] [*ICAO designator*] (FAAC)
SPP .... Stable Intermediate Products (RU)
SPP .... Stanice Polni Posty [*Field Post Office*] (CZ)
SPP .... Statna Pamiatkova Peclivost [*State Institute for the Preservation of Monuments and Historical Relics*] (CZ)
SPP .... Statni Plynarenske Podniky [*State Gasworks*] (CZ)
SPP .... Stoleczna Przetwornia Papiernicza [*Warsaw Paper Factory*] (POL)

SPP .... Strojirny Potravinarskeho Prumyslu [*Food Industry Engineering Works*] (CZ)
SPP .... Strukturierte Prozessor Programmierung [*German*] (ADPT)
SPP .... Swaziland Progressive Party (AF)
SPP .... Syndikalistiki Proodevtiki Parataxis [*Progressive Labor Faction*] [*Greek*] (GC)
SPP .... Szkola Przysposobienia Przemyslowego [*Industrial Training School*] (POL)
SPPA .... Puerto Ocopa [*Peru*] [*ICAO location identifier*] (ICLI)
SPPA .... Social Development Program for Poor Areas [*UNICEF*] (ECON)
SPPB .... Sorting Mobile Field Hospital (BU)
SPPB .... Statens Psykologisk-Pedagogiska Bibliotek [*National Library for Psychology and Education*] [*Sweden*] [*Information service or system*] (IID)
SPPF .... Seychelles People's Progressive Front (PPW)
SPPFKAS ... Syndikalistiki Parataxis Proodevtikon Filelevtheron kai Anexartiton Syndikaliston [*Labor Faction of Progressive Liberals and Independent Syndicalists*] [*Greek*] (GC)
SPPG .... Paramonga [*Peru*] [*ICAO location identifier*] (ICLI)
SPPG .... Societe Prehistorique et Protohistorique Gabonaise
SPPG .... Specialized Mobile Field Hospital (RU)
SPPM .... Damaged Vehicle Collecting Point (RU)
SPPM .... Pomacocha [*Peru*] [*ICAO location identifier*] (ICLI)
SPPM .... Societe des Plantes a Parfums de Madagascar
SPPM .... Wrecked Motor Vehicles Collecting Point (BU)
SPPP.......... Huanacopampa [*Peru*] [*ICAO location identifier*] (ICLI)
SPPP......... Service de Presse, Propagande, et Publicite [*Press, Propaganda, and Publicity Department*] [*Cambodia*] (CL)
SPPS.......... Spolek Posluchacu Prumyslovych Skol [*Society of Students of Industrial Schools*] (CZ)
SPPW .... Szkoly Przysposobienia do Przemyslu Weglowego [*Coal Industry Training Schools*] (POL)
SPPY .... Chachapoyas [*Peru*] [*ICAO location identifier*] (ICLI)
SPQ............ Sociedade Portuguesa de Quimica [*Portuguese Chemical Society*] (SLS)
SPQJ .... Jaqui [*Peru*] [*ICAO location identifier*] (ICLI)
SPQN .... Requena [*Peru*] [*ICAO location identifier*] (ICLI)
SPQT......... Iquitos/Coronel FAP Francisco Secada Vignetta [*Peru*] [*ICAO location identifier*] (ICLI)
SPQU .... Arequipa/Rodriguez Ballon [*Peru*] [*ICAO location identifier*] (ICLI)
spr .... Conjugation (RU)
SPR........... Food Supply Depot (RU)
spr .... Information, Inquiry (BU)
SPR........... San Pedro [*Belize*] [*Airport symbol*] (OAG)
SPR........... Socialne-Politicky Referat [*Section for Social and Political Affairs*] (CZ)
SPR........... Sociedade Portuguesa de Reumatologia [*Portuguese*] (SLS)
SPR........... Societe Francaise des Professeurs de Russe [*French Society of Professors of Russian*] (SLS)
SPR........... Sprache [*Language*] [*German*] (ADPT)
SPR........... Spratly Islands [*ANSI three-letter standard code*] (CNC)
spr .... Sprechen [*Speak*] [*German*] (GCA)
spr .... Spreker [*Speaker*] [*Afrikaans*]
Spr............. Spreuke [*Proverbs*] [*Afrikaans*]
Spr............. Sprich [*Speak*] [*German*]
spr .... Sprukket [*Cracked*] [*Danish/Norwegian*]
SPR........... Standarta Presidenta Republiky [*Standard of the President of the Republic*] (CZ)
SPR........... Strategic Petroleum Reserve [*Arab*]
SPR........... Strelecky Prapor [*Rifle Battalion*] (CZ)
SPR........... Studievereniging voor Psychical Research [*Association for Psychological Research*] [*Netherlands*] (SLS)
SPR........... Suomen Punainen Risti [*Finland*]
SPR........... Szkoly Przysposobienia Rolniczego [*Agricultural Training Schools*] (POL)
S-Praaq..... Senoi Praaq [*Fighting People*] (ML)
SPR BOG .. Springender Bogen [*Bouncing Bow*] [*Music*]
SPRC .... Social Policy Research Centre [*University of New South Wales*] [*Australia*]
SPRCO ...... Samostatny Prapor Civilni Obrany [*Separate Civil Defense Battalion*] (CZ)
spre .... Siempre [*Always*] [*Spanish*]
s-pref......... Sous-Prefecture [*Sub-Prefecture*] [*French*]
SPREP....... South Pacific Regional Environment Programme [*of the South Pacific Commission*] [*New Caledonia*]
SPRERI..... Sardar Patel Renewable Energy Research Institute [*India*] (WED)
sprezz......... Sprezzante [*Contempuous*] [*Italian*]
SPRG .... San Regis [*Peru*] [*ICAO location identifier*] (ICLI)
SPRI .... Staf Pribadi [*Personal Staff*] (IN)
s pril .... With Supplement (BU)
SPRINTERS ... Screen Printers de Colombia [*Colombia*] (COL)
SPRL .... Societe de Personnes a Responsabilite Limitee [*Private Limited Company*] [*French*] [*Business term*]
Sprl .... Sprachlehre [*Grammar*] [*German*]

SPRM........ San Ramon/Capitan Alvarino [*Peru*] [*ICAO location identifier*] (ICLI)
SPRM........ Societe des Plantations Reunies de Mimot [*United Plantation Company of Mimot*] [*Cambodia*] (CL)
Spr Mitt .... Sprengmittel [*Explosive*] [*German*] (GCA)
Spr Mt ...... Sprengmittel [*Explosive*] [*German*] (GCA)
SPROA...... Societe des Plantations Reunies de l'Ouest Africain
SPROB ...... Solid Propellant Space Booster Plant [*ISRO*] [*India*] (PDAA)
SPROCAS ... Study Project on Christianity in Apartheid Society
SPROLS ... Societe de Promotion des Logements Sociaux
SPRON...... Specific Populations Recreation Officers' Network [*Australia*]
SPROOG... Socio-Public Relationship Officers' Orientation Group [*Philippines*]
Spr P .... Sprengpunkt [*Detonation Point*] [*German*] (GCA)
SPRP .... Track Switch Relay Repeater (RU)
SPRS .... Aircraft Full-Sweep Radar (RU)
Spr St........ Sprengstoff [*Explosive*] [*German*] (GCA)
SPRT........ Rio Tigre [*Peru*] [*ICAO location identifier*] (ICLI)
SPRU........ Trujillo/Capitan Carlos Martinez de Pinillos - Huanchaco [*Peru*] [*ICAO location identifier*] (ICLI)
SPRW........ Spreekwoord [*Proverb*] [*Afrikaans*]
SPS .... Meter Receiving Selsyn (RU)
SPS .... Salvage Vessel, Rescue Ship (RU)
SPS .... Satellite Program Services [*Australia*]
SPS .... Scandinavian Property Services [*Sweden*]
SPS .... Sekretarijat za Poljoprivredu i Sumarstvo (SIV) [*Secretariat of Agriculture and Forestry*] (YU)
SPS .... Serikat Penerbit Suratkabar [*Indonesian Newspaper Publishers' Association*] (FEA)
SPS .... Singapore Paediatric Society (EAIO)
SPS .... Socialistische Partij Suriname [*Surinam Socialist Party*] [*Political party*] (PPW)
SPS .... Socialist Party of Slovenia [*Political party*] (EY)
SPS .... Societe de Savon et Produits Similaires
SPS .... Societe des Petroles du Senegal
SPS .... Socijalisticka Partija Srbije [*Socialist Party of Serbia*] [*Political party*] (EY)
SPS .... Sofia Court of Arbitration (BU)
SPS .... Sozialdemokratische Partei der Schweiz [*Social Democratic Party of Switzerland*] [*Political party*] (PPE)
SPS .... Sozialdemokratische Partei Suedtirols [*Social Democratic Party of South Tirol*] [*Political party*] (PPE)
SPS .... SPASA Servicios Politecnicos Aereos SA [*Spain*] [*ICAO designator*] (FAAC)
SPS .... Spolecnost Pratel Starozitnosti [*Society for the Appreciation of Antiques*] (CZ)
SPS .... Srednja Poljoprivredna Skola [*Secondary Agricultural School*] (YU)
SPS .... Sreska Poljoprivredna Stanica [*District Agricultural Station*] (YU)
SPS .... Srpski Potporni Savez [*Serbian Welfare Union*] (YU)
SPS .... State Printing Service [*New South Wales, Australia*]
SPS .... Statni Plavebni Sprava [*State Administration Office for Navigation*] (CZ)
SPS .... Statni Prumyslova Skola [*State Industrial School*] (CZ)
SPS .... Stichting Plurale Samenlevingen [*Foundation for the Study of Plural Societies - FSPS*] (EAIO)
SPS .... St. Patrick's Missionary Society
SPS .... Strategic Planning Society [*Formerly, Society for Strategic and Long Range Planning*] (EA)
SPS .... Sudan Plantations Syndicate
SPS .... Supersonic Airliner (RU)
SPS .... Svaz Partizanov Slovenska [*Union of Slovak Partisans*] (CZ)
SPS .... Symbol-Programmsystem [*German*] (ADPT)
SPS .... Trade-Union Council (RU)
SPS .... Universal Postal Union (BU)
SPSA .... Casma [*Peru*] [*ICAO location identifier*] (ICLI)
SPSAA ...... Swimming Pool and Spa Association of Australia
SPSC......... Ship Power Station Corp. [*China State Shipbuilding Corp.*]
SPSC......... Societatea de Propagatie Stiinta si Cultura [*Society for the Propagation of Science and Culture*] (RO)
SPSD .... State Purchasing and Sales Division [*Tasmania, Australia*]
SPSFM ...... St. Patrick's Society for the Foreign Missions [*See also SSPME*] [*Kiltegan, County Wicklow, Republic of Ireland*] (EAIO)
SPSFV ...... State Public Services Federation Victoria [*Australia*]
SPSh .... Soviet and Party School (RU)
SPSI.......... All-Indonesia Union of Workers
SPSJ .... San Jose De Sisa [*Peru*] [*ICAO location identifier*] (ICLI)
SPSK .... Savez Poljoprivredno-Sumarskih Komora [*Union of Chambers of Agriculture and Forestry*] (YU)
SPSL.......... Lamas [*Peru*] [*ICAO location identifier*] (ICLI)
SPSM .... Servico de Producao de Sementes e Mudas [*Brazil*] (DSCA)
SPSM .... Socialist Party of San Marino [*Political party*] (EAIO)
SPSO .... Pisco [*Peru*] [*ICAO location identifier*] (ICLI)
sp sovp ...... Magnetic Spectrometer Used to Study Coincidences (RU)
SPSP.......... Societe des Plantations Saint-Georges

sp S pr .... Spisanie Sotsialistichesko Pravo [*Socialist Law*] [*A periodical*] (BU)

SPSS.......... Masisea [*Peru*] [*ICAO location identifier*] (ICLI)

SPSS.......... Society of the Priests of St. Sulpice [*See also CPSS*] [*Paris, France*] (EAIO)

SPSSSR..... Svaz Pratel SSSR [*Union of Friends of the USSR*] (CZ)

SPSSSR..... Svaz Priatelov SSSR [*Union of Friends of the USSR*] (CZ)

sp st .... Lifesaving Station [*Topography*] (RU)

SPST.......... Speicherstelle [*German*] (ADPT)

SPST.......... Tarapoto [*Peru*] [*ICAO location identifier*] (ICLI)

SPSTU....... Secondary and Preparatory School Teachers' Union [*Mauritius*] (AF)

SPSU .... State Public Service Union [*Australia*]

SPSU .... Statni Planovaci a Statisticky Urad [*State Planning and Statistical Office*] (CZ)

SPSz.......... Soproni Poszto- es Szonyeggyar [*Textile and Carpet Factory of Sopron*] (HU)

SPT .... Semimounted Tractor Snowplow (RU)

SPT .... Shromazdiste Poskozene Techniky [*Assembly Point for Damaged Equipment*] (CZ)

SPT .... Sijil Persekolahan Tinggi [*Higher Education Certificate*] (ML)

SPT .... Slovenski Pomorski Tehnikum [*Slovenian Merchant Marine School*] [*Piran*] (YU)

SPT .... Socialist Party of Thailand [*Political party*] (FEA)

SpT .... Spanish Telefunken [*Record label*]

SPT .... Special Purpose Taxi [*Australia*]

spt .... Spiritus [*Spirit*] [*Latin*] [*Pharmacy*] (MAE)

SPT .... Spolek Posluchacu Techniky [*Technical Institute Students' Association*] (CZ)

spt .... Stempel paa Titelblad [*Stamp on Title Page*] [*Publishing Danish/Norwegian*]

SPT .... Surmoulage de Pneu du Togo

SPTA .... Nauta [*Peru*] [*ICAO location identifier*] (ICLI)

SPTA .... Slovenska Pomorsko-Trgovska Akademija [*Slovenian Merchant Marine Academy*] [*Piran*] (YU)

SPTC .... South Pacific Trade Commission [*Australia*]

SPTC .... Sydney Preliminary Theological Certificate [*Moore Theological College*] [*Australia*]

SPTCS .... South Pacific Trade Commissioner Service [*Australia*]

SPTE .... Teresita [*Peru*] [*ICAO location identifier*] (ICLI)

SPTF......... Societe pour Transports Forestiers

SPT-HP..... Scholastic Proficiency Test - Higher Primary Level [*Educational test*] [*South Africa*]

SPTI .... Puerto Inca [*Peru*] [*ICAO location identifier*] (ICLI)

SPTI .... Saglik Propagandasi ve Tibbi Istatistik Genel Mudurlugu [*Health Propaganda and Medical Statistics Directorate General*] (TU)

SPTM .... Societe des Plantations de Tabac de Malaimbandy, Madagascar

SPTN......... Tacna [*Peru*] [*ICAO location identifier*] (ICLI)

SPTP .... Talara/El Pato [*Peru*] [*ICAO location identifier*] (ICLI)

SPTR .... Tournavista [*Peru*] [*ICAO location identifier*] (ICLI)

SPTs .... Moving-Target Selection (RU)

SPTU .... Puerto Maldonado/Padre Aldamiz [*Peru*] [*ICAO location identifier*] (ICLI)

SPTU .... Secondary Technical-Vocational School (BU)

SPU........... Aircraft Intercom (RU)

SPU........... Auxiliary Command Post (BU)

SPU........... Diagrammatic Method of Planning and Control [*Aircraft maintenance*] (RU)

SPU........... Intermediate-Repeater Bay (RU)

SPU........... Medical Antiepidemiological Administration (BU)

SPU........... Power Supply and Control Bay (RU)

SPU........... Programed Control Systems [*Nuclear energy*] (BU)

SPU........... Savezne Privredne Ustanove [*Federal Economic Institutions*] (YU)

SPU........... Sekretno-Politicheskoye Upravleniye [*Secret Political Directorate*] [*Former USSR*] (LAIN)

SPU........... Selective Perforation Unit (RU)

SPU........... Selective Switching Device (RU)

SPU........... Slovensky Planovaci Urad [*Slovak Planning Office*] (CZ)

SPU........... Split [*Former Yugoslavia*] [*Airport symbol*] (OAG)

SPU........... Statni Pamatkovy Ustav [*State Institute for the Preservation of Historical Monuments*] (CZ)

SPU........... Statni Pozemkovy Urad [*State Land Reform Office*] (CZ)

SPU........... Svetova Postovni Unie [*World Postal Union*] (CZ)

SPU........... Synchronizer with a Steady Lead Angle (RU)

SPUC........ Huamachuco [*Peru*] [*ICAO location identifier*] (ICLI)

SPUMS ...... South Pacific Underwater Medicine Society [*Australia*]

SPUO .... Statni Projektovy Ustav Obchodu [*State Project Planning Institute for Trade*] (CZ)

SPUP........ Seychelles People's United Party [*Political party*] (PPW)

SPUR........ Piura/Capitan Concha [*Peru*] [*ICAO location identifier*] (ICLI)

SPUR........ Singapore Planning and Urban Research Group (ML)

SPURT ...... Three-Position Radioisotope Level Indicator (RU)

SPUSPG.... Syndicat Professionnel des Usines de Sciage et Placages du Gabon

SPV .... Average Inclusion Potential (RU)

SPV .... Gun Armament [*Aviation*] (RU)

SPV .... Schweizerischer Physiotherapeuten Verband [*Swiss Physiotherapists Association*] (SLS)

SPV .... Servico de Protecao ao Voo [*Flight Protection Service*] [*Brazil*] (LA)

SPV .... Societe des Petroles de Valence

SpV .... Spanish RCA Victor [*Record label*]

sp V .... Spezifisches Volumen [*Specific Volume*] [*German*]

SPV .... Standard Field Viscosimeter (RU)

SPV .... Stazione di Patologia Vegetale [*Italy*] (DSCA)

SPVEA ...... Superintendencia do Plano de Valorizacao Economica da Amazonia [*Superintendency for the Amazon Area Economic Promotion Program*] [*Brazil*] (LA)

SPVESP .... Industria de Produtos Veterinarios do Estado de Sao Paulo [*Brazil*] (DSCA)

SPVFS....... Superintendencia do Plano Valorizacao da Fronteira Sudoeste [*Superintendency for the Southwest Border Promotion Program*] [*Porto Alegre, Brazil*] (LA)

SPVL .... Caraveli [*Peru*] [*ICAO location identifier*] (ICLI)

SPVP .... Fixed Veterinary Aid Station (RU)

SPVR .... Vitor/San Isidro [*Peru*] [*ICAO location identifier*] (ICLI)

SPVRD ...... Supersonic Ramjet Engine (RU)

SPW.......... Schuetzenppanzerwagen [*Armored Personnel Carrier*] (EG)

SPW.......... Speedwings SA [*Switzerland*] [*ICAO designator*] (FAAC)

SPW.......... Speicherwerk [*German*] (ADPT)

sp W .... Spezifische Waerme [*Specific Heat*] [*German*]

SPW.......... Spoorweg [*Railway*] [*Afrikaans*]

SPWFY...... Socialist Party of Workers, Farmers, and Youths

SPWP .... Society of Prayer for World Peace (EAIO)

Spww......... Spoorwegwet [*Benelux*] (BAS)

SPY .... San Pedro [*Ivory Coast*] [*Airport symbol*] (OAG)

SPY .... Siyasal Partiler Yasasi [*Political Parties' Code of Laws*] (TU)

SPYA .... Luya [*Peru*] [*ICAO location identifier*] (ICLI)

SPYa .... Socialist Party of Japan (RU)

SPYC .... Yarinacocha [*Peru*] [*ICAO location identifier*] (ICLI)

SPYL .... Talara/Capitan Montes [*Peru*] [*ICAO location identifier*] (ICLI)

SPYO .... Pacasmayo [*Peru*] [*ICAO location identifier*] (ICLI)

SPYu .... Trade-Union Council of Yugoslavia (RU)

SPYU........ Yauca [*Peru*] [*ICAO location identifier*] (ICLI)

spz .... Centipoise (RU)

SPZ .... Flank Guard (BU)

SPZ .... Savez Poljoprivrednih Zadruga [*Union of Agricultural Cooperatives*] (YU)

SPZ .... Sdruzeni Parlamentnich Zpravodaju [*Association of Parliament Reporters*] (CZ)

SPZ .... Slavonsko-Podravska Vicinalna Zeleznica [*Slovenian Drava Valley Local Railroad*] (YU)

SPZ .... Slovenska Prosvetna Zveza [*Slovenian Educational Federation*] [*Trieste*] (YU)

SPZ .... Speicherzelle [*Memory Cell*] [*German*] (ADPT)

SPZ .... Statni Pracovni Zalohy [*State Labor Reserves*] (CZ)

SPZ .... Svaz Pracovniku v Zemedelstvi [*Agricultural Workers' Union*] (CZ)

SPZ .... Szkola Przysposobienia Zawodowego [*Vocational Training School*] (POL)

SPZA .... Nazca [*Peru*] [*ICAO location identifier*] (ICLI)

SPZB .... Sosnowieckie Przemyslowe Zjednoczenie Budowlane [*Sosnowiec Industrial Construction Association*] (POL)

SPzCKV..... Samostatna Pruzkumna Ceta Krajskeho Velitele [*Separate Reconnaissance Platoon of the Regional Commander*] (CZ)

SPZH........ Pachiza [*Peru*] [*ICAO location identifier*] (ICLI)

SPzH......... Samostatna Pruzkumna Hlidka [*Separate Reconnaissance Patrol*] (CZ)

SPZK .... Sotziki [*Peru*] [*ICAO location identifier*] (ICLI)

SPZM .... Strediska Pracujici Zemedelske Mladeze [*Centers for Young Agricultural Workers*] (CZ)

SPZO........ Cuzco/Velazco Astete [*Peru*] [*ICAO location identifier*] (ICLI)

sp z oo......... Spolka z Ogranicena Odpowiedzialnoscia [*Limited Company*] [*Polish*] [*Business term*]

sp z op .... Spolka z Ograniczona Poreka [*Limited Liability Company*] [*Polish*] [*Business term*]

SPZT .... Chazuta [*Peru*] [*ICAO location identifier*] (ICLI)

SQ .... Secondo Quantita [*According to Quantity*] [*Italian*]

sq................ Sequentia [*Following*] [*French*]

sq................ Square [*Park, Square*] [*In addresses*] [*French*] (CED)

SQA .... South Queensland Airways [*Australia*]

SQC .... Social Questions Committee [*Church of England in Australia, Melbourne Diocese*]

SQC .... Southern Cross [*Australia*] [*Airport symbol*] (OAG)

SQL........... Servicious de Alquiler Aereo SA de CV [*Mexico*] [*ICAO designator*] (FAAC)

SQM .... Sao Miguel Do Araguaia [*Brazil*] [*Airport symbol*] (OAG)

SQM .... Sociedad Quimica de Mexico [*Mexico*] (DSCA)

SQN .... Sanana [*Indonesia*] [*Airport symbol*] (OAG)

SQP............ Sociedad Quimica del Peru [Peru]   (DSCA)
sqq............. Sequentiaque [And the Following] [French]
SQR........... Soroako [Indonesia] [Airport symbol]   (OAG)
Squad Ldr .. Squadron Leader   (IDIG)
SQUO........ Squadron-Officer [British military]   (DSUE)
sr .... Alcohol-Soluble   (RU)
sr .... Compare   (RU)
SR .... Counter-Collator   (RU)
sr .... Easily Soluble   (RU)
Sr................ Estroncio [Strontium] [Chemical element] [Portuguese]
sr .... For a Term, For a Period   (RU)
sr .... Guard   (BU)
sr .... Mean, Medium   (RU)
SR .... Medium Bomber   (RU)
SR .... Medium Repair   (RU)
Sr................ Middle [Toponymy]   (RU)
sr .... Neuter [Gender]   (RU)
SR .... Partiia Sotsialistov Revolyutsionerov [Socialist Revolutionary
                 Party] [Russian] [Political party]   (PPE)
SR .... Reactive Power Meter   (RU)
SR .... Rhodesia Meridionale [Southern Rhodesia] [Italian]
SR .... Rifle Company   (RU)
SR .... Sacra Rota [Sacred Roman] [Italian]
Sr................ Sanitetski Referent [Sanitary Inspector] [Military]   (YU)
SR .... Sans Retard [Military] [French]   (MTD)
SR .... Satellitenrechner [Satellite Computer] [German]   (ADPT)
SR .... Saudi Riyal [Monetary unit]   (BJA)
SR .... Schapper-Riegler Wert [Schapper-Riegler Value] [German]
SR .... Schweizerischer Ruderverband [Switzerland]   (EAIO)
Sr................ Schwester [Sister] [German]
Sr................ See, Compare   (BU)
SR .... Sekretarijat za Rad (SIV) [Secretariat of Labor]   (YU)
SR .... Selection Register [Computers]   (RU)
Sr................ Senhor [Mister, Lord] [Portuguese]   (GPO)
sr .... Senior [Afrikaans]
Sr................ Senior [Netherlands]   (GPO)
SR .... Senor [Sir, Mister] [Spanish]
SR .... Service de Renseignements [French]
SR .... Seychelles Rupee
Sr................ Sieur [In legal papers] [French]   (MTD)
SR .... Signal Relay   (RU)
SR .... Signor [Mister] [Italian]
SR .... Siracusa [Car registration plates] [Italian]
SR .... Siri [Series]   (ML)
SR .... Skala Reaumur [Reaumur Scale] [German]
SR .... Slovensky Rozhlas [Slovak Radio]   (CZ)
s-r .... Socialist-Revolutionary   (RU)
SR .... Sokolovsky Revir [Sokolov Coal Basin]   (CZ)
SR .... Sousroutine [Sobroutine] [French]   (ADPT)
SR .... Southern Rhodesia
SR .... Sparebanken Rogaland [Rogaland Savings Bank] [Norway]
SR .... Sprava Radiokomunikaci [Administration Office for Radio-
                 Communications]   (CZ)
sr .... Sredni [or Srednio] [Average] [Poland]
sr .... Srednica [Diameter] [Poland]
SR .... Sredstva za Rad [Working Tools] [Army]   (YU)
sr .... Srez [District]   (YU)
sr .... Srovnej [To Compare] [Former Czechoslovakia]
SR .... Stabilization and Unloading   (BU)
SR .... State Rail [New South Wales, Australia]
SR .... Statsjanstemannens Riksforbund [National Federation of
                 Government Employees] [Sweden]   (WEN)
sr .... Steradian   (RU)
SR .... Strategic Missile   (RU)
Sr................ Stronzio [Strontium] [Italian]
SR .... Studenteraad [Students' Representative Council] [Afrikaans]
sr .... Successeur [Successor, Heir] [French]
SR .... Sucre Raffine [Refined Sugar] [Reunionese]   (AF)
SR .... Sudan's Railways
SR .... Suid-Rhodesie [Southern Rhodesia] [Afrikaans]
SR .... Suomen Rauhanliitto [Finland]   (EAIO)
SR .... Surinam [ANSI two-letter standard code]   (CNC)
SR .... Survey Recorder [Royal Australian Navy]
SR .... Sveriges Radio [Sweden]   (PDAA)
SR .... Swiss Reinsurance Co.
SR .... Synekhes Revma [Direct Current]   (GC)
sr .... Urgent, Pressing   (RU)
SR .... Urgent Telegram   (RU)
sr .... Wednesday   (RU)
Sr................ Wetboek van Strafrecht [Benelux]   (BAS)
SRA............ Secretaria de la Reforma Agraria [Secretariat of Agrarian
                 Reform] [Mexico]   (LA)
Sra............. Senhora [Mrs., Madam] [Portuguese]   (GPO)
Sra............. Senora [Madam, Lady] [Spanish]
SRA............ Service de Renseignements de l'Artillerie [Military] [French]
                 (MTD)

SRA............ Sociedad Rural Argentina [Buenos Aires, Argentina]   (LAA)
SRA............ Societe de la Raffinerie d'Alger
SRA............ Societe de Representation et d'Agreage
SRA............ Specially Reserved Area [Australia]
SRA............ Squash Rackets Association of Australia
SRA............ State Recreation Area [Australia]
SRA............ Summer Rainfall Agriculture Program
SRA............ Sveriges Radio Aktiebolaget [Swedish Broadcasting Corporation]
                 (WEN)
SRAEN...... Systeme de Reference pour la Determination de l'Affaiblissement
                 Equivalent pour la Nettete [Master telephone transmission
                 reference system]
SRAID....... Sport and Recreation Association for Intellectually Disabled
SRAIN...... Societe de Representations Automobiles et Industrielles au Niger
SRANC..... Southern Rhodesian African National Congress
SR & O...... Statutory Rules and Orders
SRANSW .. State Railway Authority of New South Wales [Australia]
                 (PDAA)
SRAPL ...... Societe Romande d'Audiophonologie et de Pathologie du
                 Langage [Switzerland]   (SLS)
SRAS........ Southern Rhodesian Air Services
SRAS........ Southern Riverina Advisory Service [Australia]
SRASA ...... Small Retailers Association of South Australia
SRAT........ Service de Recherche et d'Application Technique [Burkina Faso]
SRAT........ Societe de Recherches et d'Applications Techniques [France]
                 (PDAA)
SRATI ...... Societatea Romana de Anestezie Terapie Intensiva [Romania]
                 (EAIO)
sravn.......... Comparative   (BU)
sravnit st .... Comparative Degree   (RU)
sravn st....... Comparative Degree   (RU)
S Ravt........ Section de Ravitaillement [Military] [French]   (MTD)
SRB........... Flash Ranging Battery   (RU)
SRB........... Schweizerische Republikanische Bewegung [Swiss Republican
                 Action Movement]   (WEN)
SRB........... Sociedade Rural Brasileira [Brazilian Rural Association]   (LA)
SRB........... Societe Rapide des Bois
SRB........... Special Renumerative Benefit [Petroleum royalty/tax scale]
                 [Malaysia]
SRB........... Statens Rad for Byggnadsforskning [National Council for
                 Building Research] [Sweden]   (PDAA)
SRB........... State Research Bureau [Secret police] [Uganda]
SRB........... State Revenue Board [Victoria, Australia]
SRBB .... Sdruzeni Revolucnich Bojovnich a Barikadniku [Association of
                 Fighters in the (1945) Uprising]   (CZ)
SRBDV ...... Societe Royale Belge de Dermatologie et de Venerologie [Royal
                 Belgium Society Dermatology and Venerology]   (EAIO)
SRBE .... Societe Royale Belge des Electriciens [Royal Belgium Society of
                 Electricians]   (EAIO)
SRBG........ Societe de Reception des Bois du Gabon
SRBG........ Societe Royale Belge de Geographie [Belgium]   (SLS)
SRBiH .... Savez Radioamatera Bosne i Hercegovine [Union of Radio
                 Amateurs of Bosnia and Hercegovina]   (YU)
SRBII......... Societe Royale des Ingenieurs et des Industriels [Royal Society of
                 Engineers and Industrialists] [Belgium]   (PDAA)
SRBMD..... Societe Royale Belge de Medecine Dentaire [Belgium]   (SLS)
SRBOAGENCIJA ... Agencija za Posredovanje u Prometu Robom [Serbian
                 General Business Agency] [Belgrade]   (YU)
SRC........... Romanian Society of Cardiology   (EAIO)
SRC........... Safety Review Committee [Australian Nuclear Science and
                 Technology Organisation]
SRC........... Santa Romana Chiesa [Holy Roman Catholic Church] [Italian]
SRC........... Sarabhai Research Centre [India]
SRC........... Scientific Research Committee [Australia]
SRC........... Scientific Research Council [Jamaica]
SRC........... Scientific Research Council [Iraq] [Research center]   (IRC)
SRC........... Security State
SRC........... Seismology Research Centre [Phillip Institute of Technology]
                 [Australia]
SRC........... Se Ruega Contestacion [The Favor of a Reply Is Requested]
                 [Spanish]
SRC........... Servico de Radiocomunicacoes [Radio Communications Service]
                 [Brazil]   (LA)
SRC........... Social Research Center [Egypt] [Research center]   (IRC)
SRC........... Sociedad Regular Colectiva [General Partnership] [Spanish]
                 (CED)
SRC........... Societe Regionale de Commerce [Tunisia]
SRC........... Students Representative Council [South Africa]   (AF)
SRC........... Subject-Fields Reference Code [FID] ['s-Gravenhage]
SRC........... Sudan Railways Corp.   (IMH)
SRC........... Supreme Revolutionary Council [Somali]   (AF)
SRC........... Svetova Rada Cirkvi [World Council of Churches]   (CZ)
SRC........... Swan River Colony [Australia]
SRC........... Swedish Refugee Council   (EAIO)
SRCC......... Scandinavian Research Council for Criminology [Norway]
                 (EAIO)

SRCC .... Societe Nationale pour la Renovation et le Developpement de la Cacaoyere et de la Cafeiere Togolaises [*National Society for the Renewal and Development of Togolese Cocoa and Coffee Resources*] (AF)

SRCD......... Societe Routiere Colas du Dahomey

SRCH .... Sociedad Rural Chuquisaquena [*Bolivia*] (DSCA)

SRCI .... Societe Routiere Colas de la Cote-D'Ivoire

SRCMLT... Standing Representative Committee for Medical Laboratory Technology in the EEC [*European Economic Community*] [*England*] (EAIO)

SRCOA...... Societe Routiere Colas de l'Ouest Africain

SRCTG ...... Sales Representatives and Commercial Travellers Guild [*Australia*]

SRD .... Radio Range Station (RU)

Sr D .... Senor Don [*A spanish title given to a gentleman*]

SRD .... Slovenska Rada Druzstiev [*Slovak Council of Cooperatives*] (CZ)

SRD .... Societatea Romana Danubiana [*Romanian Danube Society*] (RO)

SRD .... Societe Regionale de Developpement [*Regional Development Company*] [*Tunisia*] (AF)

SRD .... Statutory Reserve Deposit [*Australia*]

srd .... Steradian [*Steradian*] [*Poland*]

SRD .... Stredoceske Rudne Doly [*Central Bohemian Ore Mines*] [*Pribram*] (CZ)

SRD .... Traffic Regulation Service (RU)

SRDC......... Sugar Research Development Corp. [*Australia*]

SRDFC ...... Sudan Rural Development Finance Company [*Khartoum*] (MENA)

SRDI......... Societe Regionale de Developpement de l'Imbo

SRDP........ Special Rural Development Programme

SRDP........ Sulawesi Regional Development Project [*Coordinated by Indonesian and Canadian governments*] (ECON)

SRDR........ Secteurs Regionaux de Developpement Rural

SRDU .... Science Research and Development Unit [*Australia*]

SRE............ Secretaria de Relaciones Exteriores [*Secretariat of Foreign Relations*] [*Mexico*] (LA)

SRE............ Sucre [*Bolivia*] [*Airport symbol*] (OAG)

sred........... Mean, Medium, Middle (RU)

Sredazgintsvetmet ... Central Asian Branch of the State Scientific Research Institute of Nonferrous Metals (RU)

Sredazgiprovodkhlopok ... Central Asian State Institute for the Planning of Irrigation Structures and Rural Electric Power Plants (RU)

Sredazkhimmash ... Central Asian Chemical Machinery Plant (RU)

Sredazkomstaris ... Central Asian Committee for Museums and the Protection of Relics of the Past, Art, and Nature (RU)

Sredazmet .. Central Asian Meteorological Service (RU)

Sredazneft' ... Central Asian Petroleum Association (RU)

Sredaznefterazvedka ... Central Asian Petroleum Exploration Trust (RU)

SredazNIKhI ... Central Asian Scientific Research Institute for Cotton Growing (RU)

SredazNILKh ... Central Asian Scientific Research Institute of Forestry (RU)

Sredazvodkhoz ... Water Management Administration of Central Asia (RU)

sredneaz ..... Central Asian (RU)

SREDNEVOLGOLES ... State Association of the Middle Volga Region Lumber Industry (RU)

Sredvolgeomin ... Middle Volga Branch of the Scientific Research Institute of Geology and Mineralogy (RU)

SREP .... Sydney Regional Environmental Plan [*Australia*]

S Res .... Section de Reserve [*Military*] [*French*] (MTD)

SRES .... Senores [*Sirs, Gentlemen*] [*Spanish*]

SRESB ...... State Rescue and Emergency Service Board [*New South Wales, Australia*]

S Reva .... Sua Reverencia [*Reverend*] [*Portuguese*]

S Revma ..... Sua Reverendissima [*Most Reverend*] [*Portuguese*]

sr ez .... Serbian Language (BU)

SRF .... Scientific Research Foundation [*Jerusalem, Israel*] [*Research center*] (ERC)

SRF .... Sveriges Rationaliseringsfoerbund [*Swedish Federation of Productivity Services*] [*Research center*] (ERC)

SRF .... Sveriges Redareforening [*Shipowners' Association of Sweden*] (WEN)

SRF .... Swiss Rowing Federation (EAIO)

SRFCAM .. Section de Recherches Forestieres au Cameroun

SRFI .... Squash Rackets Federation of India (EAIO)

SRFRL....... Seikai Regional Fisheries Research Laboratory [*Japan*] (MSC)

SRg .... Rotguss-Schweissdraht [*Gun Metal Welding Wire*] [*German*] (GCA)

SRG .... Search & Rescue 202 [*British*] [*ICAO designator*] (FAAC)

SRG .... Semarang [*Indonesia*] [*Airport symbol*] (OAG)

SRG .... Spectrum Roentgen-Gamma [*Proposed international space observatory*]

SRGE........ Societe Royale de Geographie d'Egypte

SRGO .... Sociedad Regional de Ganaderos de Occidente [*Venezuela*] (DSCA)

SRGRBOI ... Servico de Registro Genealogico das Racas Bovinas de Origem Indiana [*Brazil*] (DSCA)

SRGS .... South Rhodesia Geological Survey

SRH .... Secretaria de Recursos Hidraulicos [*Secretariat of Water Resources*] [*Mexico*] (LA)

SRH .... Survey Research of Hong Kong Ltd. [*Opinion poll*]

SRHE .... Society for Research into Higher Education [*Guildford, Surrey, England*] (EAIO)

SRHSB ...... Society for Research into Hydrocephalus and Spina Bifida (EA)

SRI .... Air Safaris & Services (NZ) Ltd. [*New Zealand*] [*ICAO designator*] (FAAC)

SRI .... Sacro Romano Impero [*Holy Roman Empire*] [*Italian*]

SRI .... Samarinda [*Indonesia*] [*Airport symbol*] (OAG)

SRI .... Samodzielny Referat Informacyjny [*Autonomous Information Office*] (POL)

SRI .... Santa Romana Iglesia [*Spanish*]

SRI............ Serengeti Research Institute [*Tanzania*] (PDAA)

SRI............ Shri Ram Institute for Industrial Research [*India*]

SRI............ Societa Italiana di Reologia [*Italian*] (SLS)

SRI............ Soil Research Institute [*Ghana*] (PDAA)

SRI............ Stabna Ratna Igra [*Staff War Game*] [*Military*] (YU)

SRI............ Steel Rope Industria NZ Ltd. [*New Zealand*]

SRI............ Sugarcane Research Institute [*Bangladesh*]

SRI............ Sugar Research Institute [*Research center*] [*Australia*] (ERC)

SRI............ Sumitomo Rubber Industries [*Japan*] (PDAA)

SRI............ Swiss Radio International

sria .... Secretaria [*Secretary*] [*Spanish*]

SRIA .... Steel Reinforcement Institute of Australia

SRIA .... Systems Research Institute of Australia

SRIJ........... Service Regional d'Identite Judiciaire (FLAF)

SRIJ........... Society of the Rubber Industry of Japan (PDAA)

SRiKO .... Workers' and Peasants' Defense Council [*1918-1920*] (RU)

srio .... Secretario [*Secretary*] [*Spanish*]

SRIO.......... Skola za Rezervne Intendantske Oficire [*Reserve Quartermaster Officers School*] (YU)

SRIP .... Society for the Research and Investigation of Phenomena [*Malta*] (EAIO)

SRIS .... Science Reference and Information Service (IID)

SR i SD ..... Soviet of Workers' and Soldiers' Deputies [*1917-1918*] (RU)

Srita .... Senorita [*Miss*] [*Spanish*]

SRIW .... Societe Regionale d'Investissement de Wallonie [*Belgian development agency*]

SRJ .... San Borja [*Bolivia*] [*Airport symbol*] (OAG)

SRJ .... Savez Radioamatera Jugoslavije [*The Yugoslav Union of Radio Amateurs*] (YU)

srk .... Seurakunta [*Finland*]

SRK........... Skywork SA [*Switzerland*] [*ICAO designator*] (FAAC)

SRK........... Sovet Revoliutsionnovo Komandovaniia

SRK........... Swiatowa Rada Kosciolow [*World Council of Churches*] [*Poland*]

SRK........... Union of Cinematography Workers of the USSR (RU)

SRKiKD..... Soviet of Workers', Peasants', and Red Army Deputies [*1917-1936*] (RU)

SRKKh...... Union of Workers of Municipal Services (RU)

SRL........... Section de Reperage par les Lueurs [*Military*] [*French*] (MTD)

SRL........... Sociedad de Responsabilidad Limitada [*Private Limited Company*] [*Spanish*] [*Business term*]

Srl .... Societa a Responsabilita Limitada (IDIG)

SRL........... Societa a Responsabilita Limitata [*Limited Liability Company*] [*Italian*] [*Business term*]

SRL........... Societe a Responsabilite Limitee [*Private Limited Company*] [*French*]

SRL........... Society of Romance Linguistics [*Nancy, France*] (EAIO)

SRL........... Southern Resources Ltd. [*Australia*]

SRL........... Surveillance Research Laboratory [*Australia*] (IRC)

SRL........... Varmlandsflyg AB [*Sweden*] [*ICAO designator*] (FAAC)

SRLA......... Scottish Recreational Land Association (SLS)

SRLAB-CAD ... Scientific Research Laboratory for Computer-Aided Design [*State Committee for Science and Technical Progress*] [*Bulgaria*]

SRLF .... Societe de Reanimation de Langue Francaise [*France*] (EAIO)

SRLP .... Socialist and Revolutionary Labour Party [*Gambia*] [*Political party*] (PD)

SRLR .... Societatea Romana de Lingvistica Romanica [*Romanian Society for Romance Linguistics*] (RO)

SRLZ .... Southern Rock Lobster Zone [*Australia*]

SRM .... Computer Mechanism (RU)

SRM .... Flying Swiss Ambulance Maldives (Pvt) Ltd. [*ICAO designator*] (FAAC)

SRM .... Serbian Renaissance Movement [*Political party*] (EY)

SRM .... Ship Repair Shops (RU)

SRM .... Sindicato de Redactores de Mexico [*Union of Mexican Journalists*] (LA)

SRM .... Suara Revolusi Malaya [*Voice of the Malayan Revolution (Communist)*] (ML)

SRM .... Sue Riverite Mani [*Personal for Addressee*] [*Italian*]

SRM .... Su Real Majestad [*His (or Her) Royal Majesty*] [*Spanish*]

SRM .... Svetova Rada Mieru [*World Peace Council*] (CZ)

SRM .... Szkola Rybolowstwa Morskiego [*School of Deep-Sea Fishing*] [*Poland*]
SRMC....... Southern Rhodesian Missionary Conference
SRMD ...... Senior Resident Medical Doctor [*Australia*]
sr mkh........ Medium Mortar   (BU)
SRMO .... Slovenske Rafinerie Mineralnych Olejov, Narodny Podnik [*Slovak Petroleum Refineries, National Enterprise*]   (CZ)
SRMRA..... South Roodepoort Main Reef Areas [*South Africa*] [*Commercial firm*]
SRMRJ ..... Sindikati Rudarskih i Metalurgiskih Radnika Jugoslavije [*Trade-Unions of Miners and Metallurgic Workers of Yugoslavia*]   (YU)
SRMZ........ Stavropol' Ship Repair and Machine Plant   (RU)
SRN .... Sangkum Reastr Niyum [*Prince Sihanouk's party, dissolved in 1970*] [*Cambodia*]   (CL)
SRN .... Stoleczna Rada Narodowa [*Warsaw People's Council*]   (POL)
SRNB........ Societe Royale de Numismatique de Belgique [*Royal Belgium Numismatic Society*]   (EAIO)
SRNK........ Instruction-Number Counter Register [*Computers*]   (RU)
SRNP........ Sociedade Rural do Norte do Parana [*Brazil*]   (DSCA)
SRO .... Aircraft Radar Responder   (RU)
SRO .... Seismological Research Observatory [*Australia*]
SRO .... Servicios Aereos Rutas Oriente SA de CV [*Mexico*] [*ICAO designator*]   (FAAC)
SRO .... Sociedad Rural del Oriente [*Bolivia*]   (DSCA)
SRO .... Spolecnost s Rucenim Omezenym [*Limited Liability Company*] [*Czech*] [*Business term*]   (CZ)
SRO .... State Railways Organization [*Iran*]   (ME)
SROA .... Swedish Railway Officers Association   (EAIO)
SROF .... Sveriges Reservofficersforbund [*Sweden*]   (EAIO)
SRON .... Space Research Organization Netherlands [*Research center*]   (IRC)
SROT........ Service des Renseignements de l'Observation du Terrain [*Military*] [*French*]   (MTD)
SROT........ Situations Resumes des Operations du Tresor
SROZ........ Slovenska Rada Odborovych Zvazov [*Slovak Council of Trade Unions*]   (CZ)
SRP.......... Aircraft Radar Sight   (RU)
SRP.......... Assembling-Disassembling Device   (RU)
SRP.......... Computer Device   (RU)
SRP.......... Construction and Repair Train   (RU)
SRP.......... Education Workers' Union   (BU)
SRP.......... Regimental Medical Company   (BU)
SRP.......... Scintillation Survey Radiometer   (RU)
SRP.......... Sekretarijat za Robni Promet [*Secretariat of Goods Trade*]   (YU)
SRP.......... Serbian Radical Party [*Political party*]
SRP.......... Shipborne Radio Direction Finder   (RU)
SRP.......... Socialisticka Radnicka Partija Jugoslavije [*Socialist Workers' Party of Yugoslavia*] [*Political party*]   (PPE)
SRP.......... Socialist Revolutionary Party [*India*] [*Political party*]   (PPW)
SRP.......... Socialist Revolutionary Party [*Former USSR*] [*Political party*]
SRP.......... Socialist Revolution Party [*Turkey*] [*Political party*]   (PPW)
SRP.......... Societatea Romana Petroliera [*Romanian Petroleum Society*]   (RO)
SRP.......... Sozialistische Reichspartei [*Socialist Reich Party*] [*Germany*] [*Political party*]   (PPE)
SRP.......... Swiatowa Rada Pokoju [*World Council of Peace*] [*Poland*]
SRPA .... Sydney Regional Planning Authority [*Proposed*] [*Australia*]
SRPBA ...... Scottish River Purification Boards Association   (DCTA)
SRPG .... Steel Reinforcement Promotion Group [*Cement and Concrete Association of Australia*]
SRPH........ Station de Recherches sur le Palmier a Huile de Pobe [*Palm Oil Research Station, Pobe*] [*Benin*]   (ARC)
SRPJ........ Service Regional de Police Judiciaire   (FLAF)
SRPJ(k).... Socijalisticka Radnicka Partija Jugoslavije (Komunista) [*Socialist Workers Party of Yugoslavia (Communists)*]   (YU)
SRP(k)....... Socijalisticka Radnicka Partija (Komunista) [*Socialist Workers Party (Communists)*]   (YU)
SRPP .... Printing Industry Workers' Union   (RU)
SRPS .... Sdruzeni Rodicu a Pratel Skoly [*Parent-Teacher Association*]   (CZ)
SRPV .... Pulse Wave Propagation Velocity   (RU)
sr r .... Neuter Gender [*Grammar*]   (BU)
SRR .... Sociedad Rural de Rosario [*Argentina*]   (DSCA)
SRR .... Societa Retorumantscha [*Switzerland*]   (SLS)
SRR .... Socjalistyczna Republika Radziecka [*Soviet Socialist Republic*]   (POL)
SRR .... Sozialistische Republik Rumaenien [*Socialist Republic of Romania*]   (WEN)
SRR .... Star Air IS [*Denmark*] [*ICAO designator*]   (FAAC)
SRRA........ Singapore Rural Residents' Association   (ML)
SRRA........ Sudan Relief and Rehabilitation Association
SRRI .... School Related Resources Index [*Australia*]
SRS .... Aircraft Radio Communication Set   (RU)
SRS .... Aircraft Reconnaissance Station   (RU)

SRS............ Fixed Radio Station   (RU)
SRS............ Piece Rate System   (BU)
SRS............ Police Dog   (RU)
SRS............ Savez Radioamatera Srbije [*Serbian Union of Radio Amateurs*]   (YU)
SRS............ Scandinavian Radiological Society   (EA)
SRS............ Scottish Reformation Society   (SLS)
SRS............ Section de Reperage par le Son [*Military*] [*French*]   (MTD)
SRS............ Slovenska Republikanska Stranka [*Slovenian Republican Party*]   (YU)
SRS............ Srpska Radikalna Stranka [*Serbian Radical Party*] [*Former Yugoslavia*] [*Political party*]   (PPE)
SRS............ Student Record System [*Australia*]
SRS............ Surtsey Research Society [*Iceland*]   (EAIO)
SRSA .... Society of Radiographers of South Africa   (EAIO)
SRSC .... Satellite Remote Sensing Centre [*Council for Scientific and Industrial Research*] [*South Africa*]   (AA)
SRSC .... Societatea pentru Raspindirea Stiintei si Culturii [*Society for the Dissemination of Science and Culture*]   (RO)
SRSD .... Stredisko pro Rozvoj Silnic a Dalnic [*Center for Construction Development of Roads and Highways*]   (CZ)
SRSDM ..... Union of Social Democratic Workers' Youth   (BU)
SRSFC...... Shattered: Rolling Stones Fan Club [*Netherlands*]   (EAIO)
SRSG .... Special Representatives of the Secretary General [*United Nations*]
sr sk........... Mean Velocity, Average Speed   (RU)
SRSL .... Society of Radiographers - Sri Lanka   (EAIO)
SRSP .... Somali Revolutionary Socialist Party   (AF)
SRSSA...... Surgical Research Society of Southern Africa   (EAIO)
sr st............ Comparative Degree   (RU)
SRT .... Medium Fishing Trawler   (RU)
SRT .... Section de Reperage par la Terre [*Military*] [*French*]   (MTD)
SRT .... Society of Romanian Air Transports [*ICAO designator*]   (FAAC)
SRT .... Soroti [*Uganda*] [*Airport symbol*]   (OAG)
SRT .... State Railway of Thailand   (DS)
Srta .... Senhorita [*Miss*] [*Portuguese*]
Srta .... Senorita [*Miss, Young Woman*] [*Spanish*]   (GPO)
SRTI .... Societe de Recherches Techniques et Industrielles [*Nuclear energy*] [*French*]   (NRCH)
SRTK .... Societe Regionale de Transports de Kasserine [*Tunisia*]
SRTM........ Medium Fishing Trawler-Freezer   (RU)
SRTM........ Sociedade Rural do Triangulo Mineiro [*Brazil*]   (DSCA)
SRTR .... Medium Fishing Trawler-Refrigerator   (RU)
SRTs .... Computer and Control Center [*Space vehicle guidance*]   (RU)
SRTs .... Filter Center [*Military*]   (BU)
SRTs .... Reconnaissance and Target Designation Station [*Artillery*]   (RU)
SRTUC...... Southern Rhodesian Trades Union Congress   (AF)
SRU .... Computing Device   (RU)
SRU .... Societe de Raffinage d'Uranium [*Nuclear energy*] [*French*]   (NRCH)
sr uch......... Secondary School   (BU)
SrV............ Medium-Frequency Waves   (RU)
srv............. See, Compare   (BU)
Srv............. Servis [*Service*]   (TU)
SRV .... Ship Repair Yard   (RU)
SRV .... Spolecnost pro Racionalni Vyzivu [*Society for Rational Nutrition*]   (CZ)
SRVD........ Sprava Raketoveho a Delostreleckeho Vyzbrojovani [*Rocket and Artillery Ordnance Directorate*]   (CZ)
SRVD........ Sprava Raketovych Vojsk a Delostrelectva [*Rocket Troops and Artillery Directorate*]   (CZ)
sr vek......... Medieval   (BU)
sr vr .... Mean Time   (RU)
SRVU........ Radio Broadcasting Center Studio   (RU)
sr vv .... Middle Ages   (RU)
SRW .... Schiffbau- und Reparatur Werft [*Ship Building and Repair Yard*]   (EG)
SRWFP...... Society for the Research of Wholesome Food Problem [*Japan*]   (EAIO)
SRWU ...... Sudan Railways Workers' [*Trade*] Union
SRWU ...... Sudan Railway Workers' Union
SRX.......... Sert [*Libya*] [*Airport symbol*] [*Obsolete*]   (OAG)
SRZ.......... Santa Cruz [*Bolivia*] [*Airport symbol*]   (OAG)
SRZ.......... Satz Rechen Zentrum [*Computer Composition Center*] [*Hartmann & Heenemann*] [*Information service or system*]   (IID)
SRZ.......... Seismograph for Registering Destructive Earthquakes   (RU)
SRZ.......... Selanska Rabotna Zadruga [*Peasant Work Cooperative*] [*Collective Farm*]   (YU)
SRZ.......... Ship Repair Yard   (RU)
SRZ.......... Sociedad Rural del Zulia [*Venezuela*]   (DSCA)
SRZ.......... Susuman Repair Plant   (RU)
SRZM....... Stichting Radiostraling van Zon en Melkweg [*Netherlands Foundation for Radioastronomy*] [*Nederlandse Organisakie voor Zniver-Wetenschappelijk Onderzoek*] [*Research center*]   (ERC)

SS.............. Aircraft Construction   (RU)
SS.............. Ambulance Aircraft   (RU)
SS.............. Blue Glass   (RU)
SS.............. Coincidence Circuit   (RU)
SS.............. Comparison Circuit   (RU)
SS.............. Counter, Counting Circuit   (RU)
SS.............. Existence Doubtful [*Nautical term*]   (RU)
SS.............. Line Counter   (RU)
SS.............. Milizia di Protezione Nazista [*SS Troops*] [*Italian*]
SS.............. Miscellaneous Bay   (RU)
SS.............. Saeuren [*Acids*] [*German*]
SS.............. Saif Saria [*Swift Sword*] [*Code name used to refer to joint military exercises between Oman and Britain in 1986*]
SS.............. Saints [*Saints*] [*French*]   (MTD)
SS.............. Saint-Sacrement [*Blessed Sacrament*] [*French*]
SS.............. Saison Seche
SS.............. Samasevaya [*Sri Lanka*]   (EAIO)
SS.............. Samestelling [*Composition*] [*Afrikaans*]
SS.............. Sanitetska Sluzba [*Medical Service*] [*Military*]   (YU)
SS.............. Santa Sede [*Holy See*] [*Italian*]
SS.............. Santi [*Saints*] [*Italian*]
SS.............. Santissima [*or Santissimo*] [*Most Holy*] [*Portuguese*]
SS.............. Santissimo [*Most Holy*] [*Italian*]
SS.............. Santos [*Saints*] [*Spanish*]
SS.............. Sa Saintete [*His Holiness*] [*The Pope*] [*French*]
SS.............. Sa Seigneurie [*His Lordship*] [*French*]
SS.............. Sassari [*Car registration plates*] [*Italian*]
SS.............. Savet za Skolstvo [*Council for Schools*]   (YU)
SS.............. Savez Sindikata [*Council of Trade-Unions*]   (YU)
ss.............. Sayfalar [*Pages*]   (TU)
SS.............. Sberne Suroviny [*Raw Materials Collection (Enterprise)*]   (CZ)
SS.............. Schempp-Hirth KG [*Germany*] [*ICAO aircraft manufacturer identifier*]   (ICAO)
SS.............. Schip en Schade [*Benelux*]   (BAS)
SS.............. Schutzstaffel [*Elite Guard*] [*NAZI Germany*]
SS.............. Schwefelwasserstoffsaeure [*Hydrogen Sulfide*] [*German*]   (GCA)
ss.............. Schwerst [*Heaviest*] [*German*]   (GCA)
SS.............. Sculptors' Society [*Australia*]
SS.............. Securite Sociale [*Social Security*] [*French*]   (WER)
SS.............. Security Council   (BU)
SS.............. Sedma Sila, Novinsko Izdavacko Preduzece Udruzenja Novinara Srbije [*Sedma Sila, a newspaper publishing enterprise of the Serbian Association of Journalists*]   (YU)
ss.............. Seguintes [*Following*] [*Portuguese*]
SS.............. Seguridad Social [*Social Security*] [*Spanish*]   (WER)
SS.............. Seguro Servidor [*Yours Truly*] [*Spanish*]
SS.............. Seismic Station   (RU)
SS.............. Seite [*or Seiten*] [*Pages Publishing*] [*German*]
SS.............. Sekretarijat za Saobrakaj [*Secretariat of Transportation*]   (YU)
SS.............. Sekretarijat za Sumarstvo [*Secretariat of Forestry*]   (YU)
SS.............. Selenium Column   (RU)
SS.............. Self-Propelled Missile   (BU)
SS.............. Sembawang Shipping [*Singapore*] [*Commercial firm*]
SS.............. Servicio Seccional Radial Ltda. [*Colombia*]   (COL)
ss.............. Severna Sirina [*Northern Latitude*]   (YU)
SS.............. Shiplovers' Society [*Australia*]
ss.............. Sider [*Pages*] [*Publishing Danish/Norwegian*]
SS.............. Sidirodromikos Stathmos [*Railroad Station*]   (GC)
ss.............. Sidor [*Pages*] [*Sweden*]
sS.............. Siehe Seite [*See Page*] [*German*]
ss.............. Siguiente [*Following*] [*Spanish*]
SS.............. Simeiosis Syndaxeos [*Editorial Note*]   (GC)
SS.............. Sindikati Srbije [*Trade-Unions of Serbia*]   (YU)
SS.............. Sluzbena Saopstenja [*Official Communications*]   (YU)
SS.............. Somalia Shilling
SS.............. Sommersemester [*Summer Term*] [*German*]   (EG)
ss.............. Sous [*In, Under*] [*French*]
SS.............. Sovetski Sojuz [*Former USSR*]   (YU)
SS.............. Soviet North   (RU)
SS.............. Soviet Union   (RU)
SS.............. Stereoscopic Society [*Chessington, Surrey, England*]   (EAIO)
SS.............. Stichting Skepsis [*Netherlands*]   (EAIO)
ss.............. Stoomskip [*Steamship*] [*Afrikaans*]
SS.............. Strada Statale [*Main Road*] [*Italian*]
SS.............. Strana Slobody [*Freedom Party*]   (CZ)
ss.............. Strony [*Pages*] [*Poland*]
SS.............. Sua Santidade [*Your Holiness*] [*Portuguese*]
SS.............. Sua Santita [*His Holiness*] [*Italian*]
SS.............. Sua Senhoria [*Your Lordship*] [*Portuguese*]
SS.............. Submarine [*Royal Australian Navy*]
SS.............. Sumsko Stopanstvo [*Forestry Management*]   (YU)
SS.............. Suomen Saveltajat [*Finland*]   (EAIO)
s/s.............. Supply Depot   (BU)
SS.............. Supply Service   (RU)
SS.............. Supply Station   (RU)

SS.............. Su Santidad [*His Holiness*] [*Spanish*]
SS.............. Su Senoria [*Your Lordship*] [*Spanish*]
Ss.............. Svet Sovetu [*The Soviet World*] [*A periodical*]   (CZ)
SS.............. Swedish Society, Discofil [*Record label*] [*Sweden*]
ss.............. Swieci [*Saints*] [*Poland*]
SS.............. Synchronization Pulse Selector   (RU)
SS.............. Top Secret   (RU)
ss.............. Villages   (RU)
SS.............. Village Soviet of Workers' Deputies   (RU)
SS3.............. Stichting Studio 3 [*Netherlands*]   (EAIO)
SSA............ Agricultural Academy   (BU)
SSA............ Agricultural Aviation   (BU)
SSA............ Salvador [*Brazil*] [*Airport symbol*]   (OAG)
SSA............ Sanitetska Sluzba Armije [*Army Medical Service*]   (YU)
SSA............ Santissima Annunziata [*Order of the Holy Annunciation*] [*Italian*]
SSA............ Scandinavian Society of Anaesthesiologists   (EA)
SSA............ Scandinavian Sociological Association   (EA)
SSA............ Secretaria de Salubridad y Asistencia [*Secretariat of Health and Assistance*] [*Mexico*]   (LA)
SSA............ Shan State Army [*Myanmar*] [*Political party*]   (EY)
SSA............ Simulation Society of Australia
SSA............ Slovenian Stomatologic Association [*Samoa*]   (EAIO)
SSA............ Soviet Architects' Union   (RU)
SSA............ Soviet Sociological Association
SSA............ Star of South Africa
SSA............ Statistical Society of Australia   (SLS)
SSa............ Sua Senhoria [*Your Lordship*] [*Portuguese*]
SSA............ Sub-Saharan African Country
SSa............ Su Senoria [*Your Lordship*] [*Spanish*]
SSA............ Svaz Slovenskych Architektov [*Union of Slovak Architects*]   (CZ)
SSA............ Swedish Shipbrokers' Association   (EAIO)
SSA............ Swedish Shipowners' Association   (EAIO)
SSA............ Swedish Steel Producers' Association   (EAIO)
SSAA........ Self Storage Association of Australia
SSAA........ Short-Handed Sailing Association of Australia
SSAA........ Societe Senegalaise des Artisans Associes
SSAA........ Societe Suisse d'Astrophysique et d'Astronomie [*Swiss Society for Astrophysics and Astronomy*]   (EAIO)
SSAA........ Sporting Shooters Association of Australia
SSAA........ Stichting Studiecentrum voor Administratieve Automatisering [*Later, SSI*]
SSAA........ Sus Altezas [*Spanish*]
SSA-AgrF ... Agricultural Academy - School of Agronomy   (BU)
SSA-AgrF-KAgrKhim ... Agricultural Academy - School of Agronomy. Soil Chemistry Department   (BU)
SSA-AgrF-KDarvGenSel ... Agricultural Academy - School of Agronomy. Department of Darwinism, Genetics, and Selection   (BU)
SSA-AgrF-KGr ... Agricultural Academy - School of Agronomy. Horticulture Department   (BU)
SSA-AgrF-KlozVin ... Agricultural Academy - School of Agronomy. Department of Viticulture and Oenology   (BU)
SSA-AgrF-KMarksL ... Agricultural Academy - School of Agronomy. Department on Foundations of Marxism-Leninism   (BU)
SSA-AgrF-KMekh ... Agricultural Academy - School of Agronomy. Department of Mechanization   (BU)
SSA-AgrF-KOrgSPredpr ... Agricultural Academy - School of Agronomy. Department of Farm Management   (BU)
SSA-AgrF-KPochv ... Agricultural Academy - School of Agronomy. Department of Soil Science   (BU)
SSA-AgrF-KPolitIkon ... Agricultural Academy - School of Agronomy. Department of Political Economy   (BU)
SSA-AgrF-KRast ... Agricultural Academy - School of Agronomy. Department of Plant Breeding   (BU)
SSA-AgrF-KRastZasht ... Agricultural Academy - School of Agronomy. Department of Plant Protection   (BU)
SSA-AgrF-KZBot ... Agricultural Academy - School of Agronomy. Department of Agricultural Botany   (BU)
SSA-AgrF-KZIkon ... Agricultural Academy - School of Agronomy. Department of Agricultural Economics   (BU)
SSAAII...... Ses Altesses Imperiales [*Their Imperial Highnesses*] [*French*]   (ROG)
SSAANSW ... Stock and Station Agents' Association of New South Wales [*Australia*]
SSAB........ Svenska Sallskapet for Automatiserad Bildanelys [*Swedish Pattern Recognition Society*]   (PDAA)
SSABSA.... Senior Secondary Assessment Board of South Australia
SSAC........ Australian State System of Accounting and Control of Nuclear Materials
SSAC........ Second Sydney Airport Coalition [*Australia*]
SSAC........ Social Security Advisory Council [*Australia*]
SSAC........ Societe des Services de Navigation Aerienne pour l'Amerique Centrale   (FLAF)
SSAC........ Space Science Advisory Committee [*European Space Agency*]
SSAC........ Study and Social Action Center [*Brazil*]   (EAIO)

SSAE .... Societe Shell de l'Afrique Equatoriale [*Equatorial Africa Shell Company*] [*Congo*]   (AF)

SSAF .... Stiftelsen Svensk Atervinningsforskning [*Swedish Foundation for Recycling Research*]   (WED)

SSAG .... Svenska Saellskapet foer Antropologi och Geografi [*Stockholm, Sweden*]   (SLS)

SSAHE ...... Swiss Society of Anatomy, Histology and Embryology   (EAIO)

SSAI .... Swiss Society for Allergology and Immunology   (EAIO)

SSAIS .... Senior South African Individual Scale [*Intelligence test*]

SSA-LesotekhnF ... Agricultural Academy - School of Forestry Engineering   (BU)

SSA-LesotekhnF-KDendr ... Agricultural Academy - School of Forestry Engineering. Department of Dendrology   (BU)

SSA-LesotekhnF-KDurvoprerab ... Agricultural Academy - School of Forestry Engineering. Department of Lumbering   (BU)

SSA-LesotekhnF-KGeod GStr ... Agricultural Academy - School of Forestry Engineering. Department of Geodesy Forestry Construction   (BU)

SSA-LesotekhnF-KGKult ... Agricultural Academy - School of Forestry Engineering. Department of Forest Crops   (BU)

SSA-LesotekhnF-KIkonPlGs ... Agricultural Academy - School of Forestry Engineering. Department of Forest Resources Economics and Planning   (BU)

SSA-LesotekhnF-KLesoop ... Agricultural Academy - School of Forestry Engineering. Department of Forest Conservation   (BU)

SSA-LesotekhnF-KLesopol ... Agricultural Academy - School of Forestry Engineering. Department of Forest Exploitation   (BU)

SSA-LesotekhnF-KLesoustr ... Agricultural Academy - School of Forestry Engineering. Department of Forest Management   (BU)

SSA-LesotekhnF-KLesov ... Agricultural Academy - School of Forestry Engineering. Department of Silviculture   (BU)

SSA-LesotekhnF-KLovS ... Agricultural Academy - School of Forestry Engineering. Department of Game Resources   (BU)

SSA-LesotekhnF-KMash ... Agricultural Academy - School of Forestry Engineering. Department of Machine Engineering   (BU)

SSA-LesotekhnF-KOPor ... Agricultural Academy - School of Forestry Engineering. Department of Fortification of Floodbeds   (BU)

SSAMA ..... Sailors, Soldiers and Airmen's Mothers' Association of Australia

SSAO .... Societe Shell de l'Afrique Occidentale

SSAPEA .... Swedish Society Against Painful Experiments on Animals   (EAIO)

SSAS .... Star of South Africa Silver

SSAS .... Stratiotiki Skholi Axiomatikon Somaton [*Corps Officers Military School*]   (GC)

SSAT .... Svenska Sallskapet for Analytisk Trilogi [*Swedish Society of Analytical Trilogy*]   (EAIO)

SSA-VetF .. Agricultural Academy - School of Veterinary Medicine   (BU)

SSA-VetF-AkKl ... Agricultural Academy - School of Veterinary Medicine. Veterinary Obstetrics Clinic   (BU)

SSA-VetF-IAn ... Agricultural Academy - School of Veterinary Medicine. Institute of Anatomy   (BU)

SSA-VetF-IFar ... Agricultural Academy - School of Veterinary Medicine. Institute of Pharmacology   (BU)

SSA-VetF-IFiziol ... Agricultural Academy - School of Veterinary Medicine. Institute of Physiology   (BU)

SSA-VetF-IKhim ... Agricultural Academy - School of Veterinary Medicine. Institute of Chemistry   (BU)

SSA-VetF-IKhirTekhnol ... Agricultural Academy - School of Veterinary Medicine. Institute of Hygiene and Technology   (BU)

SSA-VetF-IkhranProd ... Agricultural Academy - School of Veterinary Medicine. Institute of Food Products   (BU)

SSA-VetF-IMikrbiol ... Agricultural Academy - School of Veterinary Medicine. Institute of Microbiology   (BU)

SSA-VetF-IParazitol ... Agricultural Academy - School of Veterinary Medicine. Institute of Parasitology   (BU)

SSA-VetF-IPat ... Agricultural Academy - School of Veterinary Medicine. Institute of Pathology   (BU)

SSA-VetF-IPatAn ... Agricultural Academy - School of Veterinary Medicine. Institute of Pathological Anatomy   (BU)

SSA-VetF-IPatofiziol ... Agricultural Academy - School of Veterinary Medicine. Institute of Pathophysiology   (BU)

SSA-VetF-ISudMed ... Agricultural Academy - School of Veterinary Medicine. Institute of Forensic Medicine   (BU)

SSA-VetF-KhirKl ... Agricultural Academy - School of Veterinary Medicine. Surgical Clinic   (BU)

SSA-VetF-VutrKl ... Agricultural Academy - School of Veterinary Medicine. Clinic for Internal Diseases   (BU)

SSAW .... Saatchi & Saatchi Advertising Worldwide   (ECON)

SSAWS ...... Spring, Summer, Autumn, Winter, and Snow [*Pronounced "zausu"*] [*Another name for Skidome, an indoor ski center*]   (ECON)

SSA-ZootekhnF ... Agricultural Academy - School of Animal Husbandry   (BU)

SSA-ZootekhnF-KDomZhiv ... Agricultural Academy - School of Animal Husbandry. Department of Domestic Animals   (BU)

SSA-ZootekhnF-KFur Proizv ... Agricultural Academy - School of Animal Husbandry. Department of Fodder Production   (BU)

SSA-ZootekhnF-KGov ... Agricultural Academy - School of Animal Husbandry. Department of Cattle Breeding   (BU)

SSA-ZootekhnF-KKhrDomZhiv ... Agricultural Academy - School of Animal Husbandry. Department of Domestic Animal Nutrition   (BU)

SSA-ZootekhnF-KKon ... Agricultural Academy - School of Animal Husbandry. Department of Horse Breeding   (BU)

SSA-ZootekhnF-KMl ... Agricultural Academy - School of Animal Husbandry. Dairy Department   (BU)

SSA-ZootekhnF-KPrilZool ... Agricultural Academy - School of Animal Husbandry. Department of Applied Zoology   (BU)

SSA-ZootekhnF-KRazvGen ... Agricultural Academy - School of Animal Husbandry. Department of Breeding Genetics   (BU)

SSA-ZootekhnF-KSvin ... Agricultural Academy - School of Animal Husbandry. Department of Hog Breeding   (BU)

SSB .... Bomb Sight Jamming Station   (BU)

SSB .... Sarawak Special Branch   (ML)

SSB .... Sectie Speciale Bibliotheken [*NVB*] [*'s-Gravenhage*]

SSB .... Social Security Bank [*Ghana*]   (EY)

SSB .... Societatea de Stiinte Biologice [*Society for Biological Sciences*]   (RO)

SSB .... Special Service Battalion

SSB .... State Savings Bank [*Australia*]

SSB .... State Seismological Bureau [*Beijing, China*]

SSB .... State Supply Board [*South Australia*]

SSB .... St. Croix [*Virgin Islands*] Seaplane Base [*Airport symbol*]   (OAG)

SSB .... Submarine, Ballistic Missile [*Diesel*] [*NATO*]

SSB .... Sulfite-Liquor Waste   (RU)

SSBMEN ... Seccion de Servicios Bibliotecarios del Ministerio de Educacion Nacional [*Colombia*]   (COL)

SSBR .... Samakum Sangkruos Bokkalik Rotthabal [*Administrative Government Employees Mutual Association*] [*Use MUFONOA Cambodia*]   (CL)

SSBR .... Societatea de Stiinte Biologice din Romania   (EAIO)

SSBS .... Sol-Sol-Balistique-Strategique [*French*]

SSBT .... Sol-Sol Balistique Tactique [*Ground-Ground Tactical Ballistic*] [*Missile*] [*French*]

SSBU .... Savez Studenta Beogradskog Univerziteta [*Union of Students of Belgrade University*]   (YU)

SSC .... Sample Survey Centre [*University of Sydney*] [*Australia*] [*Information service or system*]   (IID)

SSC .... Sarawak Struggle Command (Communist)   (ML)

SSC .... Senior School Certificate [*South Australia*]

SSC .... Settlement Study Center [*Israel*]   (IRC)

SSC .... SILEC Semi-Conducteurs

SSC .... Singapore Sports Council   (DS)

SSC .... Societa di Studi Celestiniani [*Italian*]   (SLS)

SSC .... Societe Suisse de Cardiologie [*Switzerland*]   (EAIO)

SSC .... Society for the Study of Coherence [*France*]   (EAIO)

SSC .... Space Communications Corp. [*Japan*]   (ECON)

SSC .... Space Science Committee [*Formerly, Provisional Space Science Advisory Board for Europe*] [*of the European Science Foundation*]   (EA)

SSC .... Spanish Shippers Council   (DS)

SSC .... State Security Committee   (ML)

SSC .... State Sports Centre [*Australia*]

SSC .... State Sports Council [*Victoria, Australia*]

SSC .... State Supply Commission [*Western Australia*]

SSC .... Stazione Sperimentale per i Combustibili [*Fuel Research Station*] [*Italy*]   (PDAA)

SSC .... Survey Science Centre [*A consortium of European oranizations*]

SSC .... Survival Service Commission [*IUCN*]   (ASF)

SSC .... Swedish Shippers Council   (DS)

SSC .... Swedish Space Corp. [*Ministry of Industry*] [*Research center*]   (EAS)

SSC .... Swiss Shippers Council   (DS)

SSC .... Swiss Society of Cartography   (EAIO)

SSCAVC .... Senate Select Committee on Agricultural and Veterinary Chemicals [*Australia*]

SSCB .... Sovyet Sosyalist Cumhuriyetleri Birligi [*Union of Soviet Socialist Republics*]   (TU)

SSCC .... Congregation of the Sacred Hearts of Jesus and Mary [*Rome, Italy*]   (EAIO)

SSCC .... Scandinavian Society for Clinical Chemistry [*Norway*]   (EAIO)

SSCE .... Swedish Society of College Engineers   (EAIO)

SSCE .... Swiss Society of Consulting Engineers   (EAIO)

SSCERA ... Senate Standing Committee on the Environment, Recreation, and the Arts [*Australia*]

SSCFADT ... Senate Standing Committee on Foreign Affairs, Defence, and Trade [*Australia*]

SSch .... State School [*Australia*]

SSCI .... Social Sciences Citation Index [*AUSINET database*]   (ADA)

SSCI .... Societes de Service et Conseil en Informatique [*France*]   (PDAA)

SSCI .... Swiss Society of Chemical Industries   (EAIO)

SSCIST ..... Senate Standing Committee on Industry, Science, and
Technology [*Australia*]
SSCJ .... Soeurs du Sacre-Coeur de Jesus [*Sisters of the Sacred Heart of
Jesus*] [*France*]   (EAIO)
SSCL .... Swire Straits Container Line   (DS)
SSCM .... Societe Surgerienne de Constructions Mecaniques [*France*]
(PDAA)
SSCM .... Society of Swedish Church Musicians   (EAIO)
SSCP .... Severoslovenske Celulozky a Papierne [*North Slovakian
Cellulose and Paper Works*]   (CZ)
SSCRF .... Shooting and Sports Club of the Russian Federation   (EAIO)
SSCRI .... Southern Subtropical Crops Research Institute [*China*]   (IRC)
SSCSP .... Swiss Support Committee for the Sahrawi People   (EAIO)
SSCTC ...... Senate Standing Committee on Trade and Commerce [*Australia*]
SSD .... Sindikalno Sportno Drustvo [*Trade-Union Sport Club*]   (YU)
SSD .... Soma Stratiotikis Dikaiosynis [*(Army) Legal Corps*]   (GC)
SSD .... Soviet of Soldiers' Deputies   (RU)
SSD .... Special Securities Division [*Paramilitary government body*]
[*Sierra Leone*]
SSD .... Staatssicherheitsdienst [*State Security Service*] [*Germany*]
SSD .... Standards and Quality Control Department [*Ministry of
Industry*] [*Sudan*]
SSD .... Star Service International [*France*] [*ICAO designator*]   (FAAC)
SSD .... Sudan Survey Department [*Research center*]   (EAS)
SSD .... Svaz Spotrebnich Druzstev [*Union of Consumer Cooperatives*]
(CZ)
SSD .... Sydney Statistical Division [*Australia*]
SSD .... Transmitting Selsyn   (RU)
SSDA .... Social Science Data Archives [*Australian National University*]
[*Information service or system*]   (IID)
SSDA .... Society of Seventh-Day Adventists   (EAIO)
SSDC .... Social Science Documentation Centre [*Indian Council of Social
Science Research*] [*Information service or system*]   (IID)
SSDC .... Social Self-Defense Committee [*Poland*]   (PD)
SSDE .... Syndonistikon Symvoulion Dimosion Ependyseon [*Public
Investments Coordinating Council*] [*Greek*]   (GC)
SSDP .... Serikat Sekerdja Djawalan Padjak [*Brotherhood of Tax Office
Employees*] [*Indonesia*]
SSDP .... Suomen Sosialidemokraattinen Puolue [*Finnish Social
Democratic Party*] [*Political party*]   (PPW)
SSDU .... Svaz Slovenskych Divadelnych Umelcov [*Union of Slovak
Theater Artists*]   (CZ)
SSDUJ ...... Sindikat Sluzbenika Drzavnih Ustanova Jugoslavije [*Trade-
Union of Employees in Government Institutions of
Yugoslavia*]   (YU)
SSE .... Servico Secreto do Exercito [*Army Secret Service*] [*Brazil*]   (LA)
SSE .... Stockholm Stock Exchange
SSE .... Stratiotiki Skholi Evelpidon [*Military Cadet Academy*] [*Greek*]
(GC)
SSE .... Stredoslovenske Energeticke Zavody [*Electric Power Plants,
Central Slovakia*]   (CZ)
SSE .... Sud Sud Est [*South Southeast*] [*French*]   (MTD)
SSE .... Sudsudeste [*South Southeast*] [*Spanish*]
SSE .... Sydney Stock Exchange [*Australia*]   (ADA)
SSE .... Syllogiki Symvasis Ergasias [*Collective Labor Agreement*]   (GC)
SSE .... Synelevsis Symvouliou Evropis [*Meeting of the Council of
Europe*]   (GC)
SSEA .... Societe Suisse d'Etudes Africaines [*Switzerland*]   (EAIO)
SSEA .... Swiss Solar Energy Association   (EAIO)
SSEAM ..... Servicios de Equipos Agricolas Mecanizados [*Mechanized
Agricultural Equipment Service*] [*Chile*]   (PDAA)
SSEC .... Societe Sucriere d'Etudes et de Conseils [*Belgium*]
SSEC .... State Security Executive Committee (Sabah)   (ML)
SSEE .... Swiss Society of Environmental Engineers   (PDAA)
SSEM .... South Sea Evangelical Mission [*Australia*]
SSEM .... Spanish Society for Electron Microscopy   (EAIO)
SSEMP ...... Syndesmos Spoudaston Ellinikou Metsoviou Polytekhneiou
[*Students Association of the Greek Metsovion Polytechnic
School*]   (GC)
SSEPC .... Societe Senegalaise d'Engrais et de Produits Chimiques
SSES .... Social Security Enquiry System [*Australia*]
SSES .... Syndonistikon Symvoulion ton Emborikon Syllagon
[*Coordinating Council of Trade Boards*]   (GC)
SSESD ...... Society for the Study of Economic and Social Development
[*France*]   (EAIO)
SSF .... Sildolje- og Sildemelindustriens Forskningsinstiutt [*Herring Oil
and Meal Industry Research Institute*] [*Norway*]   (IRC)
SSF .... Societas Scientiarum Fennica [*Helsinki, Finland*]   (SLS)
SSF .... Societatea de Stiinte Filologice din RSR [*Romanian*]   (SLS)
SSF .... Society of Single Fathers   (EAIO)
SSF .... Somali Salvation Front   (PD)
SSF .... Southern Shark Fishery [*Australia*]
SSF .... Spolok Slovenskych Filozofov [*Slovak Philosophical Society*]
(CZ)
SSF .... Statens Samfundsvidenskabelige Forskningsrad [*Danish Social
Science Research Council*] [*Research center*]   (IRC)
SSF .... Sveriges Skradderiidkareforbund [*Sweden*]   (EAIO)

SSF .... Svetska Sindikalna Federacija [*World Federation of Trade-
Unions*]   (YU)
SSF .... Swiss Sports Federation   (EAIO)
SSFA .... Societa di Scienze Farmacologiche Applicate [*Italian*]   (SLS)
SSFD .... Sisters of St. Francis of Dillingen [*See also SFD*] [*Rome, Italy*]
(EAIO)
SSFE .... Scandinavian Society of Forest Economics   (EAIO)
SSFF .... Skogbrukets og Skogin Forskningsrad [*Oslo, Norway*]   (SLS)
SSFI .... Svenska Silikatforskningsinstitutet [*Swedish Institute for Silicate
Research*]   (IRC)
SSFK .... Svenska Spanienfrivilligas Kamratforening [*Sweden*]   (EAIO)
SSFM .... Scandinavian Society of Forensic Medicine [*Norway*]   (EAIO)
SSFMP ...... Southern Shark Fishery Management Plan [*Australia*]
SSFO .... Scandinavian Society of Forensic Odontology   (EA)
SSFO .... Scandinavian Society of Forensic Odontostomatology [*Norway*]
(EAIO)
SSFODF .... Syndicat des Specialistes Francais en Orthopedie Dento-Faciale
[*Paris, France*]   (SLS)
SSFV .... Sondervorschrift fuer Selbsttaetige Signalanlagen [*Special
Regulations for Automatic Signal Installations*]   (EG)
SSG .... Malabo [*Equatorial Guinea*] [*Airport symbol*]   (OAG)
SSG .... Savezno Sumarsko Gazdinstvo [*Federal Forest Economy*]   (YU)
SSG .... Self-Excited Synchronous Generator   (RU)
SSG .... Self-Powered Welding Head   (RU)
SSG .... Societa di Studi Geografici [*Italian*]   (SLS)
SSG .... South Sydney Greens [*Political party*] [*Australia*]
SSGB .... Suore di San Giovanni Baptista [*Sisters of St. John the Baptist -
SSJB*] [*Rome, Italy*]   (EAIO)
SSGK .... Slovenska Sprava Geodezie a Kartografie [*Slovak Geodetic and
Cartographic Administration*]   (CZ)
SSGKBI .... Serikat Sekerdja Gabungan Koperasi Batik Indonesia
[*Association of Indonesian Batik Cooperatives Trade
Union*]   (IN)
SSGM .... Union of Free German Youth   (BU)
SSGZ .... Sekretarijat za Splosne Gospodarske Zadeve (ISLRS) [*Secretariat
of General Economic Affairs*]   (YU)
SSh .... Ambulance Boat   (RU)
SSh .... High-Speed Attack Aircraft   (RU)
ssh .... North Latitude   (RU)
SSH .... Savez Sindikata Hrvatske [*Council of Trade-Unions of Croatia*]
(YU)
SSh .... Secondary School   (RU)
SSh .... Self-Propelled Chassis   (RU)
SSH .... Sharm E Sheikh [*Israel*] [*Airport symbol*]   (OAG)
SSH .... Socialisticke Statkove Hospodareni [*Socialist Farm
Management*]   (CZ)
SSH .... Svetove Studentske Hry [*World Student Sports Festival*]   (CZ)
SSHA .... Societe Scientifique d'Hygiene Alimentaire [*Paris, France*]
(SLS)
SShA .... United States of America   (RU)
SShch .... Power-Distributing Board   (RU)
s-shche ...... Temporary Settlement   (RU)
SShG .... Self-Propelled Mountain Chassis   (RU)
SShI .... United States of Indonesia [*1949-1950*]   (RU)
SShK .... Valve-Grinding Machine   (RU)
SSHM ...... Scottish Society for the History of Medicine   (SLS)
SSHM .... Society for the Social History of Medicine [*Oxford, England*]
(EAIO)
SShM .... Sports School for Young People   (RU)
SShO .... Secret Cryptographic Section   (RU)
SSHR .... Sprava Statnich Hmotnych Rezerv [*Administration of State
Material Reserves*]   (CZ)
SShtA .... United States of America   (BU)
s-shtu .... Versus   (BU)
SShZ .... Sverdlovsk Tire Plant   (RU)
SSI .... Savezni Sanitarni Inspektorat [*Federal Sanitary Inspectorate*]
(YU)
SSI .... Service Social International [*International Social Service - ISS*]
[*Geneva, Switzerland*]   (EAIO)
SSI .... Sever Severo-Istok [*North North-East*]   (YU)
SSI .... Societa Speleologica Italiana [*Italian*]   (SLS)
SSI .... Spolok Slovenskych Inzinierov [*Society of Slovak Engineers*]
(CZ)
SSI .... Statens Stralskyddsinstitut [*National Swedish Institute of
Radiation Protection*] [*Ministry of Energy and
Environment*] [*Research center*]   (WND)
SSI .... Stichting Studiecentrum Informatica [*Netherlands*]
Ssi .... Surekasi [*Company*] [*Turkey*]   (GPO)
SSI .... Svenska Samfundet foer Informationsbehandling [*Stockholm,
Sweden*]   (SLS)
SSIA .... Scottish Society for Industrial Archaeology [*Edinburgh*]   (SLS)
SSIA .... Second Sydney International Airport Group [*Australia*]
SSID .... Servicio Social de Iglesias Dominicanas [*Dominican Republic*]
(LAA)
SSIDC .... Small Scale Industries Development Corp. [*India*]   (PDAA)
SSIE .... Smithsonian Science Information Exchange, Inc.

SSIELF...... Societe du Sud d'Import-Export en Legumes et Fruits [*Tunisia*]
SSIH.......... Societe Suisse pour l'Industrie Horlogere [*Swiss watch manufacturer*]
ss il............ Illustrated Pages (BU)
SSIP.......... Subsystems Integration Program [*or Project*] [*NATO*] (NATG)
SSIS.......... Social Security Information System [*ILO*] [*United Nations*] (DUND)
SSISI........ Statistical and Social Inquiry Society of Ireland (SLS)
SSJ............ Sandnessjoen [*Norway*] [*Airport symbol*] (OAG)
SSJ............ Savez Sindikata Jugoslavije [*Council of Trade-Unions of Yugoslavia*] (YU)
SSJ............ Savez Slepih Jugoslavije [*Yugoslav Union of the Blind*] (YU)
SSJ............ Savez Sportova Jugoslavije [*Yugoslav Sports Federation*] (YU)
SSJ............ Savez Strelaca Jugoslavije [*Association of Yugoslav Riflemen*] (YU)
SSJ............ Secretary of State for Justice [*Burkina Faso*]
SSJ............ Sinatra Society of Japan [*Tokyo*] (EAIO)
SSJ............ Social Services Joot [*Kenya*] (EAIO)
SSJ............ Socijalisticka Stranka Jugoslavije [*Yugoslav Socialist Party*] [*Political party*] (EAIO)
SSJB......... Sisters of St. John the Baptist [*See also SSGB*] [*Roman Catholic religious order Rome, Italy*] (EAIO)
SSJG......... Sisters of St. John of God [*Wexford, Republic of Ireland*] (EAIO)
SSK.......... Coupling-Cable Bay (RU)
SSK.......... Sanitetska Sluzba Korpusa [*Corps Medical Service*] (YU)
SSK.......... Savezna Saobracajna Komora [*Federal Chamber of Transportation*] (YU)
SSK.......... Savezna Spoljno-Trgovinska Komora [*Federal Chamber of Foreign Trade*] (YU)
SSK.......... Seinen Shiso Kenkyn-kai [*Youth Ideological Study Association*] [*Japan*]
SSK.......... Sentral di Sindikatonan di Korsou [*Central Trade Union of Curacao*] [*Netherlands Antilles*]
SSK.......... Shooting Sport Club (RU)
SSK.......... Sosialistiki Syndikalistiki Kinisi [*Socialist Trade Union Movement*] [*Greek*] (GC)
SSK.......... Sosyal Sigortalari Kurumu Genel Mudurlugu [*Social Security Organization Directorate General*] (TU)
SSK.......... Soviet Composers' Union (RU)
SSK.......... Sportovy Strelecky Klub [*Sports Gun Club*] (CZ)
SSK.......... Statna Studijna Kniznica Kosiciach [*Kosice State Research Library*] (CZ)
SSK.......... Strahlenschutzkommission [*Nuclear energy*] (NRCH)
SSK.......... Super Sport Kurz [*Super, Sport, Short chassis*] [*Mercedes-Benz automotive model designation*]
SSKh......... Soviet Artists' Union (RU)
SSKNRM .. Selsko-Stopanska Komora Narodne Republike Makedonije [*Chamber of Agriculture of Macedonia*] (YU)
SSKRF....... Strelkovo Sportivnyy Klub Rossiykov Federatsii (EAIO)
SSI............ Sanitetska Sluzba [*Medical Service*] [*Military*] (YU)
SSL............ Secretary of State for Livestock [*Burkina Faso*]
SSL .... Societa Storica Locarnese [*Switzerland*] (SLS)
SSL .... Soweto Students League [*South Africa*] (AF)
SSL .... Sprava Statnych Lesov [*State Forest Administration*] (CZ)
SSL .... Stredni Slovensko [*Central Slovakia*] (CZ)
SSL .... Sudan Shipping Line
SSL .... Suomen Sanomalehtimiesten Liitto [*Finland*] (EAIO)
SSLC.......... Secondary-School-Leaving Certificate [*Brazil*]
SSLF......... Southern Sudan Liberation Front (BJA)
SSLM .... South Sudan Liberation Movement
SSLP......... Sekretariatet for Sakerhetspolitik och Langsiktsplanering in om Totalforsvaret [*Secretariat for National Security and Long-Term Defence Planning Ministry of Defence*] [*Sweden*] (PDAA)
SSLP......... Sol-Sol Longue Portee [*Ground-Ground Long Range*] [*Missile*] [*French*]
SSM.......... P. T. Susinma Line (DS)
SSM.......... Sarvodaya Shramadana Movement [*Sri Lanka*]
SSM.......... Seri Setia Mahkota [*First Grade of Darjah Yang Mulia Setia Mahkota Malaysia*] (ML)
SSM.......... Socialist Youth League [*Bulgaria, Poland*] (RU)
SSM.......... Socialist Youth Union (BU)
SSM.......... Societatea de Stiinte Medicale [*Society for Medical Sciences*] (RO)
SSM.......... Sojuz na Sindikatite za Makedonija [*Council of Trade-Unions of Macedonia*] (YU)
SSM.......... Sprava Studentskeho Majetku [*Administration of Student Property*] (CZ)
SSM.......... Svaz Slovenskej Mladeze [*Union of Slovak Youth*] (CZ)
SSM.......... Svaz Socialisticke Mladeze [*Union of Socialist Youth*] (CZ)
SSM.......... Swedish Society for Musicology (EAIO)
SSM.......... System-Software-Mitteilung [*German*] (ADPT)
SSME........ Spread Spectrum Modulation Equipment [*NATO*] (MCD)
SSMeL....... Santi Maurizio e Lazzaro [*Order of knighthood*] [*Italian*]
SSML .... Suomen Suoramarkkinointiliitto [*Finland*] (EAIO)
SSMM....... Sus Majestades [*Spanish*]

SSMMI ..... Soeurs Salesiennes Missionnaires de Marie Immaculee [*Salesian Missionaries of Mary Immaculate - SMMI*] [*Gentilly, France*] (EAIO)
SSmo.......... Santisimo [*Most Holy*] [*Spanish*]
SSmoP .... Santisimo Padre [*Most Holy Father*] [*Spanish*]
SSMR .... Societe Shell de Madagascar et de la Reunion
SSMS .... Spanish Society of Medieval Studies (EAIO)
SSMT .... Swiss Society of Music Teachers (EAIO)
SSMY .... Su Sayaclari Muayene ve Ayar Yonetmeligi [*Water Meter Examination and Calibration Administration*] [*Under Ministry of Commerce*] (TU)
SSN........... Airspeed Pressure Indicator (RU)
ssn .... Centisthene (RU)
SSN........... Sdruzeni pro Spojene Narody [*Association for the United Nations*] (CZ)
SSN........... Secao do Seguranca Nacional [*Rio De Janeiro, Brazil*] (LAA)
SSN........... Servizio Sanitario Nazionale [*Italian National Health Service*]
SSN........... Sociedad Silvicola Nacional [*Cuba*] (DSCA)
SSN........... Svaz Slovenskych Novinarov [*Union of Slovak Journalists*] (CZ)
SSN........... Sykepleiernes Samarbeid i Norden [*Northern Nurses Federation - NNF*] (EAIO)
SSn........... Winged Missile (RU)
SSNAA...... Council of Solidarity of the Nations of Asia and Africa (RU)
SSND........ School Sisters of Notre Dame [*Italy*] (EAIO)
SSND........ Secondary Students for Nuclear Disarmament [*Australia*]
SSNG........ Societatea de Stiinte Naturale si Geografice [*Society for Natural and Geographhic Sciences*] (RO)
SSNIT .... Social Security and National Insurance Trust [*Ghana*]
SSNLO ..... Shan State Nationalities Liberation Organization [*Myanmar*] (PD)
SSNM....... German Free Youth League [*German Democratic Republic*] (RU)
SSno.......... Escribano [*Notary*] [*Spanish*]
SSNP .... Syrian Social Nationalist Party (ME)
SSNPG ...... Southern Sudan Negro Provisional Government
SSNS .... Scottish Society for Northern Studies [*Edinburgh*] (SLS)
SSO........... Schema de Structure et d'Orientation [*Morocco*]
SSO........... State Security Office (ML)
SSO........... Strana Slovenskej Obrody [*Slovak Rebirth Party*] (CZ)
SSO........... Student Socialist Organization (BU)
SSO........... Sudsudoeste [*South Southwest*] [*Spanish*]
SSO........... Sud-Sud-Ovest [*South-Southwest*] [*Italian*]
SSO........... Suid-Suidoos [*South Southeast*] [*Afrikaans*]
SSO........... Suomen Sinfoniaorkesterit [*Finland*] (EAIO)
SSO........... Svaz Slovenskych Obchodnikov [*Union of Slovak Businessmen*] (CZ)
SSO........... Swedish Society OIKOS (EAIO)
SSOC........ Saudi Services and Operating Co. [*Saudi Arabia*]
SSOEC ...... Ship Suppliers' Organization of the European Community [*Hague, Netherlands*] (EAIO)
SSOG........ Scandinavian Association of Obstetricians and Gynaecologists (EA)
SSOG........ Stazione Sperimentale degli Oli and Grassi [*Italy*]
SSOJ .... Savez Socialisticke Omladine Jugoslavije [*League of Socialist Youth of Yugoslavia*] [*Political party*] (PPE)
SSOM....... Shell des Services d'Outre-Mer
SSP .... First Aid Station (RU)
SSP .... Receiving Selsyn (RU)
SSP .... Savet za Stanbene Poslove [*Housing Council*] (YU)
SSP .... Secretaria de Seguranca Publica [*Secretariat of Public Security*] [*Brazil*] (LA)
SSP .... Seguro Social del Peru [*Peruvian Social Security*] (LA)
SSP .... Sekretarijat za Saobracaj i Puteve [*Secretariat of Transportation and Roads*] (YU)
SSP .... Serbian Socialist Party [*Political party*]
SSP .... Sildolje- og Sildemelindustriens Forskningsinstitutt [*Norwegian Herring Oil and Meal Industry Research Institute*] [*Research center*] (IRC)
SSP .... Simultanspeicher [*German*] (ADPT)
SSP .... Slovenska Strana Prace [*Slovak Workers' Party*] (CZ)
SSP .... Sofia Agricultural Enterprise (BU)
SSP .... Sofia Economic Enterprise (BU)
SSP .... Soil Survey of Pakistan [*Ministry of Food and Agriculture*] [*Research center*] (EAS)
SSP .... Sosialistiki Spoudastiki Pali [*Socialist Student Struggle*] [*Greek*] (GC)
SSP .... Sous Seing Prive [*Under Private Seal*] [*French*]
SSP .... Special Studies Program [*Australia*]
SSP .... Standard Subroutines System [*Computers*] (RU)
SSP .... Svaz Slovenskych Partizanov [*Union of Slovak Partisans*] (CZ)
SSP .... Synchronous Tracking Transmission (RU)
SSP .... Synomospondia dia tin Sotirian tou Paidiou [*Save the Children Federation*] (GC)
SSP .... Union of Soviet Writers (RU)
SSPA .... Secondary School Places Allocations [*Hong Kong*]

SSPA .... Servicio Shell para el Agricultor [*Venezuela*]   (DSCA)
SSPA .... Southern Sudanese Political Association [*Sudan*] [*Political party*] (MENA)
SSPA .... Student Support and Parent Awareness [*Australia*]
SSPC .... Suore Missionarie di San Pietro Claver [*Missionary Sisters of St. Peter Claver*] [*Italy*]   (EAIO)
SSPCP .... Swiss Society for the Protection of Cultural Property   (EAIO)
SSPDC .... Syria Shell Petroleum Development Corp. [*Subsidiary of Royal Dutch Shell*]
SSPG .... Southern Sudan Provisional Government
SSPMC ...... Swedish Society of Popular Music Composers   (EAIO)
SSPME ...... Societa di San Patrizio per le Missioni Estere [*St. Patrick's Society for the Foreign Missions - SPSFM*] [*Kiltegan, County Wicklow, Republic of Ireland*]   (EAIO)
SSPMS ...... Solid State Physics and Materials Science Specialist Group [*South African Institute of Physics*]   (AA)
SS PP .... Les Saints Peres [*The Holy Fathers*] [*French*]
SSPP .... Santi Padri [*Holy Fathers*] [*Italian*]
SSPP .... Scandinavian Society for Plant Physiology [*Sweden*]   (EAIO)
SSPP .... Shan State Progressive Party [*Myanmar*] [*Political party*]   (EY)
SSPP .... Societe Senegalaise de Presse et de Publication
SSPS .... Savezni Sekretarijat za Personalnu Sluzbu [*Federal Secretariat for Civil Service*]   (YU)
SSPT .... Societe Senegalaise de Publicite et de Tourisme [*Senegalese Advertising and Tourism Company*]   (AF)
SSPT .... Societe Senegalaise des Phosphates de Taiba
SSPT .... Societe Senegalaise des Phosphates de Thies
SSPU .... Self-Adjusting Program Control System [*Automation*]   (RU)
SSQ .... Noosa Air Sunstate Airlines [*Australia*] [*ICAO designator*] (FAAC)
ssq .... Sequentia [*Following*] [*French*]
SSR .... Sempati Air PT [*Indonesia*] [*ICAO designator*]   (FAAC)
SSR .... Sir Seewoosagur Ramgoolam [*Mauritius*]   (AF)
SSR .... Slovenska Socialisticka Republic [*Slovak Socialist Republic (since 1960)*]   (CZ)
SSR .... Social Security Review [*Australia*]
SSR .... Societa di Studi Romagnoli [*Cesena, Italy*]   (SLS)
SSR .... Sous-Sections Regionales
SSR .... Soviet Socialist Republic   (RU)
SSR .... Sovjetska Socijalisticka Republika [*Soviet Socialist Republic*] (YU)
SSR .... Sveriges Socianomer Riksfoerbund [*Stockholm, Sweden*]   (SLS)
SSR .... Sveriges Socionomers, Personal och Forvaltningstjanstemans Riksforbund [*Swedish Union of Social Workers, Personnel and Pubic Administrators*]   (EAIO)
SSRA .... Socialist Soviet Republic of Armenia   (RU)
SSRB .... Socialist Soviet Republic of Belorussia   (RU)
SSRB .... Supply Systems Redevelopment Branch [*Australian Defence Force*]
SSRC .... Social Sciences Research Center [*Cameroon*]   (IRC)
SSRC .... Soweto Students Representative Council
SSRE .... Society for Social Responsibility in Engineering [*Australia*]
SSRG .... Schweizerische Studiengesellschaft fur Rationellen Guterumschag [*Swiss Research Society for the Improvement of Handling of Merchandise*]   (PDAA)
SSRG .... Socialist Soviet Republic of Georgia   (RU)
SSRI .... Social Science Research Institute [*Research center*] [*Japan*] (IRC)
SSRL .... Scottish Science Reference Library   (PDAA)
SSRM .... Socialist Workers' Youth League   (RU)
SSRMA ..... Small Scale Rubber Manufacturers Association [*Sri Lanka*] (PDAA)
SSRN .... Socijalisticki Savez Radnog Naroda [*Socialist Alliance of Working People*]   (YU)
SSRNBiH ... Socijalisticki Savez Radnog Naroda Bosne i Hercegovine [*Socialist Alliance of Working People of Bosnia and Hercegovina*]   (YU)
SSRNJ .... Socialisticki Sojuz na Rabotniot Narod na Jugoslavija [*Socialist Alliance of Working People of Yugoslavia*]   (YU)
SSRNJ .... Socijalisticka Savez Radnog Naroda Jugoslavije [*Socialist Alliance of Working People of Yugoslavia - SAWPY*] [*Political party*]   (PPE)
SSRNJzaVojvodinu ... Socijalisticki Savez Radnog Naroda Jugoslavije za Vojvodinu [*Socialist Alliance of Working People of Yugoslavia in Vojvodina*]   (YU)
SSRNM ..... Socijalisticki Sojuz na Rabotniot Narod na Makedonija [*Socialist Alliance of Working People of Macedonia*]   (YU)
SSRNV ...... Socijalisticki Savez Radnog Naroda Vojvodine [*Socialist Alliance of Working People of Vojvodina*]   (YU)
Ssro .... Spolecnost s Rucenim Omezenym [*Limited Liability Company*] [*Czech*] [*Business term*]   (CZ)
SSROC ...... Southern Sydney Regional Organisation of Councils [*Australia*]
SSRP .... Official Communications of Industrial Managers   (RU)
SSRP .... Siam Society Under Royal Patronage [*Thailand*]   (EAIO)
SSRP .... Social Security Rights Project [*Australia*]
SSRP .... Societe Saharienne de Recherches Petroliers
SSRP .... Somali Socialist Revolutionary Party

SSRP .... Specialized Assembling-Disassembling Device   (RU)
SSRS .... Society for Social Responsibility in Science [*ACT*] [*Canberra, Australia*]   (SLS)
SSRS(ACT) ... Society for Social Responsibility in Science (Australian Capital Territory) [*Canberra*]
SSRSC .... Saudi-Sudanese Red Sea Commission
SSRSJC ..... Saudi-Sudanese Red Sea Joint Commission [*Commercial firm*] [*Jeddah, Saudi Arabia*]   (EAIO)
SSRU .... Social Science Research Unit [*Swaziland*] [*Research center*] (IRC)
SSRZ .... Shipyard   (RU)
SSS .... Centimeter-Second-Candle   (RU)
SSS .... Compania de Servicios Aereos SA [*Spain*] [*ICAO designator*] (FAAC)
SSS .... Has Listened to the Countries of the World [*Radio operator's diploma*]   (BU)
SSS .... Sasana Sevaka Society [*Sri Lanka*]   (EAIO)
SSS .... Scandinavian Surgical Society   (EAIO)
SSS .... Selkciona Stocarska Stanica [*Selective Livestock Station*]   (YU)
SSS .... Servicio de Seguro Social [*Social Security Service*] [*Chile*]   (LA)
SSS .... Siassi [*Papua New Guinea*] [*Airport symbol*]   (OAG)
SSS .... Sklarske Strojirny a Slevarny [*Glass Engineering Works and Foundries*]   (CZ)
SSS .... Slovenska Stomatoloska Sekcija [*Samoa*]   (EAIO)
SSS .... Slovenska Strana Svobody [*Slovak Freedom Party*]   (CZ)
SSS .... Societe Scandinave de Simulation [*Scandinavian Simulation Society*] [*Finland*]   (EAIO)
SSS .... Sogut Seramik Sanayii AS [*Sogut Ceramics Industry Corporation*]   (TU)
SSS .... Special Security Service [*Liberia*]
SSS .... Sprava Statnich Silnic [*State Highway Administration*]   (CZ)
SSS .... State Security Service [*Mauritius*]   (AF)
SSS .... State Supply Service [*Victoria, Australia*]
SSS .... Statne Strojove Stanice [*State Machine Tractor Stations*]   (CZ)
SSS .... Statni Strojni Stanice [*State Machine Station*]   (CZ)
SSS .... Suomen Saeaetoeteknillinen Seura [*Helsinki, Finland*]   (SLS)
SSS .... Suomen Sukututkimusseura [*Helsinki, Finland*]   (SLS)
SSS .... Su Seguro Servidor [*Your Faithful Servant*] [*Correspondence*] [*Spanish*]
SSS .... Svaz Slovenskeho Studentstva [*Slovak Student Union*]   (CZ)
SSS .... Svaz Slovenskych Skladatelov [*Union of Slovak Composers*] (CZ)
SSS .... Svaz Slovenskych Spisovatelov [*Union of Slovak Writers*]   (CZ)
SSSA .... Succulent Society of South Africa   (EAIO)
SSSAA .... Societa per gli Studi Storici Archeologici ed Artistici della Provincia di Cuneo [*Cuneo, Italy*]   (SLS)
SSSaS .... Sdruzeni Socialistickych Skautu a Skautek [*Association of Socialist Boy Scouts and Girl Scouts*]   (CZ)
SSSCC .... Staff Suggestions Scheme Consultative Committee [*Australia*]
SSSD .... Slovensky Svaz Spotrebnych Druzstiev [*Slovak Union of Consumer Cooperatives*]   (CZ)
SSSF .... Sodra Sveriges Skogagares Forbund [*South Swedish Forest Owners Association*]   (PDAA)
SSSL .... Samostatny Stihaci Letecky Sbor [*Separate Fighter Air Corps*] (CZ)
SSSMC ...... Sports Science and Sports Medicine Centre [*Australia*]
SSSMM .... Societe Scientifique du Service Medical Militaire [*Belgium*] (EAIO)
SSSP .... Sindicato de Sastres y Similares de Panama [*Union of Tailors and Related Workers of Panama*]   (LA)
SSSP .... Societa Savonese di Storia Patria [*Savona, Italy*]   (SLS)
SSSR .... Soyuz Sovetskikh Sotsialisticheskikh Respublik [*Union of Soviet Socialist Republics*]
SSSR .... Svaz Sovetskych Socialistickych Republik [*Union of Soviet Socialist Republics (USSR)*]   (CZ)
SSSR .... Union of Soviet Socialist Republics   (BU)
SSSRI .... Shanghai Ship and Shipping Research Institute [*Ministry of Communications*] [*China*]   (ERC)
SSSS .... Samakum Sang Sangkum Serei Reath [*Serei Reath Social Work Association*] [*Cambodia*]   (CL)
SSSS .... Samo Sloga Srbina Spasave [*Only Unity Will Save the Serbs*] [*Serbian motto*]   (YU)
SSSS .... Svaz Slovenskych Spevackych Sborov [*Union of Slovak Choral Societies*]   (CZ)
SSSSA .... Soil Science Society of Southern Africa [*Pretoria*]   (SLS)
SSSU .... Sojuz na Studentite od Skopskiot Univerzitet [*Union of Students of Skopje University*]   (YU)
SSSU .... Spevacky Sbor Slovenskych Ucitelov [*Slovak Teachers' Choral Society*]   (CZ)
SSSWP ...... Seismological Society of the South-West Pacific [*New Zealand*]
sst .... Centistoke   (RU)
S St .... Sammelstelle [*Collecting zpint*] [*German*]   (GCA)
S St .... Severoslovenske Tehelne [*North Slovak Brick Works*]   (CZ)
SST .... Short Selection Test [*Australia*]
SST .... Sivil Savunma Teskilati [*Civil Defense Organization*] [*Turkish Federated State of Cyprus*]   (GC)
SST .... Societe Senegalaise des Tabacs

SST .... Spiral Laminar Texture (RU)
SST .... Stanica Sanitetskog Transporta [*Medical Transport Station*] [*Military*] (YU)
SST .... Streifenstanzer [*German*] (ADPT)
SST .... Suomen Saveltaiteen Tukisaatio [*Finland*] (EAIO)
SSTA .... Tank Support Aircraft (RU)
SSTA .... Schiffstammabteilung [*Naval Cadre Section*] (EG)
SSTA .... Scottish Secondary Teachers' Association [*Edinburgh*] (SLS)
SSTC .... State Science and Technology Commission [*China*]
SSTK .... Savezna Spoljno-Trgovinska Komora [*Federal Chamber of Foreign Trade*] (YU)
SSTK .... Sud Casti Spoljnotrgovinske Komore [*Court of Honor of the Chamber of Foreign Trade*] (YU)
SSTNYu .... Socialist Union of Working People of Yugoslavia (RU)
SSTP .... Suomen Sosialistinen Tyovaenpuolue [*Finnish Socialist Workers' Party*] (WEN)
s str........... Sensu Stricto [*In a Narrow Sense*] [*Latin*] (MAE)
SSTS......... School Student Transport Scheme [*Australia*]
SSTs .... Spiral Centrifugal Cleaner (RU)
SSTU .... Statny Stavebny Urad [*State Construction Office*] (CZ)
SSTV .... Sistema Sandinista de Television [*Sandinist Television Service*] [*Nicaragua*] (LA)
SSU .... Grid-Control System (RU)
SSU........... Selangor Students Union (Communist) (ML)
SSU........... Ship Power Plant (RU)
SSU........... Slezsky Studijni Ustav [*Silesian Research Institute*] (CZ)
SSU........... Slovensky Statisticky Urad [*Slovak Statistical Office*] (CZ)
SSU........... Statni Statisticky Urad [*State Office of Statistics*] (CZ)
SSU........... Sudanese Socialist Union (AF)
SSU........... Sveriges Socialdemokratiska Ungdomsforbund [*Swedish Social Democratic Youth Association*] (WEN)
SSU........... Swaziland Students Union (AF)
SSUB .... Staatlicher Strassenbau- und Unterhaltungsbetrieb [*State Road Building and Road Repair Enterprise*] (EG)
SSUJ .... Studium Slowianskie Uniwerstytetu Jagiellonskiego [*Slavic Department of Jagiellonian University*] (POL)
SSv .... Council for Mutual Economic Aid (BU)
s sv............ Luminous Intensity, Candlepower (RU)
SSV........... North-Northeast (RU)
SSV........... Schweizerischer Schriftstellerinen- und Schriftsteller-Verband [*Swiss Authoress' and Author's Association*] (EAIO)
SSV........... Schweizerischer Schriftsteller Verband [*Swiss Authors Association*] (SLS)
SSV .... Sekretarijat za Saobracaj i Veze (SIV) [*Secretariat of Transportation and Communications*] (YU)
SSV........... Sevastopol' Shipyard (RU)
SSV........... Severo-Severovychod [*North-Northeast*] (CZ)
SSV........... Society for Scientific Values [*India*]
SSV........... Spastic Society of Victoria [*Australia*]
SSV........... Spolok Svateho Vojtecha [*St. Adalbert Society*] (CZ)
SSV........... Sresko Sindikalno Vece [*District Council of Trade Unions*] (YU)
SSV........... Standard Selling Value
SSV........... Sydslesvigsk Vaelgerforening [*South Schleswig Voters' Association*] [*Also, SSW*] [*Germany*] [*Political party*] (PPW)
SSVP .... Society of St. Vincent De Paul [*Paris, France*] (EAIO)
SSVT .... Societe Senegalaise de Voyages et de Tourisme
SSVZ .... Svaz Statnych a Verejnych Zamestnancov [*Union of Government and Public Employees*] (CZ)
SSW........... Suedschleswigscher Waehlerverband [*South Schleswig Voter's League*] [*Also, SSV*] [*Germany*] [*Political party*] (PPE)
SSW........... Suid-Suidwes [*South Southwest*] (Afrikaans)
SSW.......... Szkola Sanitariuszy Weterynaryjnych [*School for Veterinary Assistants*] (POL)
SSX .... Samsun [*Turkey*] [*Airport symbol*] (OAG)
SSY .... M'Banza Congo [*Angola*] [*Airport symbol*] (OAG)
SSYB .... Saglik ve Sosyal Yardim Bakanligi [*Ministry of Health and Social Welfare*] (TU)
SSYM .... Saglik ve Sosyal Yardim Mudurlugu [*Directorate of Health and Social Welfare*] [*Under Health Ministry*] (TU)
SSZ........... Machine Tool Plant (RU)
SSZ........... Samouprava Socialnega Zavarovanja [*Autonomous Administration of Social Insurance*] [*Ljubljana A periodical*] (YU)
SSZ........... Savet za Socijalnu Zastitu [*Social Insurance Council*] (YU)
SSZ........... Sekretarijat za Socijalnu Zastitu (SIV) [*Secretariat of Social Insurance*] (YU)
SSZ........... Severo-Severozapad [*North Northwest*] (CZ)
SSZ........... Shipyard (RU)
SSZ........... Stol Sedmorice u Zagrebu [*Supreme Court in Zagreb*] (YU)
SSZ........... Svaz Slovenskych Zien [*Union of Slovak Women*] (CZ)
SSZS........ Savez Studenata Zagrebackog Sveucilista [*Union of Students of Zagreb University*] (YU)
SSZZ .... Sreski Savez Zemljoradnickih Zadruga [*District Union of Agricultural Cooperatives*] (YU)
ST .... Adding Transformer (RU)

ST .... Aircraft Engine High-Temperature Grease (RU)
st................ Article (RU)
ST .... Center of Impact, Mean Point of Impact (RU)
st................ Century (RU)
st................ Column (RU)
ST .... Construction Technical School (BU)
ST .... Degree, Rank, Grade (BU)
ST .... Dry-Cargo Motor Ship (RU)
st................ Economic (BU)
ST .... End-Window Counter (RU)
st................ Estereo [*Stereo*] [*Portuguese*]
ST .... Jet, Jet Stream [*Meteorology*] (RU)
ST .... Laminar Texture (RU)
ST .... La Surveillance du Territoire (FLAF)
ST .... Launching Carriage (RU)
st................ Master Sergeant, First Sergeant, Chief Petty Officer (RU)
ST .... Medium-Hard (RU)
st................ Old (RU)
ST .... Old Equipment (BU)
st................ Old Style [*Julian calendar*] (RU)
ST .... Patrol Boat (RU)
ST .... Rear Area Service, Supply Service (RU)
St............... Saint [*Saint*] [*French*] (MTD)
ST .... Salvo Titulo (FLAF)
St............... San [*or Santo*] [*Saint*] [*Italian*]
St............... Sankt [*Saint*] [*German*] (GPO)
ST .... Sao Tome and Principe [*ANSI two-letter standard code*] (CNC)
St............... Schnellzugtenderlokomotive [*Fast Express Train Tank Locomotive*] (EG)
ST .... Secretaria de Turismo [*Secretariat of Tourism*] [*Mexico*] (LA)
st................ Segedtiszt [*Assistant, Aide*] (HU)
ST .... Sekolah Teknik [*Technical School*] (IN)
ST .... Sekretarijat za Trud (IVNRM) [*Secretariat of Labor*] (YU)
ST .... Selsyn-Transformer (RU)
st................ Senior, Chief (RU)
ST .... Service-Techniker [*German*] (ADPT)
ST .... Ship Thermograph (RU)
ST .... Shun Thai Co. Ltd. [*Thailand*]
ST .... Signal Transformer (RU)
St............... Sint [*Saint*] [*Afrikaans*]
ST .... Sous-Tension [*French*] (ADPT)
ST .... Soviet Teletype (RU)
St............... Srednji Talasi [*Medium Waves*] [*Aviation*] (YU)
St............... Staat [*State*] [*German*]
st................ Stabilizer (RU)
ST .... Stabilizing Transformer (RU)
St............... Stacja [*Station*] [*Poland*]
St............... Stadt [*City*] [*German*]
St............... Staerke [*Starch*] [*German*] (GCA)
st................ Stage, Grade, Step (RU)
St............... Stahl [*Steel*] [*German*]
St............... Stamm [*Stem*] [*German*]
ST .... Standard (RU)
ST .... Standards der Deutschen Demokratischen Republik [*German Democratic Republic Standards*] (EG)
St............... Standerd [*Standard*] [*Afrikaans*]
St............... Stanzer [*German*] (ADPT)
St............... Stark [*Strong*] [*German*]
St............... Starsi [*Senior*] (CZ)
ST .... Starsky Operupolnomochennyy [*Senior Case Officer*] [*Soviet military rank*]
st................ Starszy [*Older, Senior*] [*Poland*]
ST .... Starter (RU)
ST .... State Trustees [*Victoria, Australia*]
St............... Station [*German*] (GCA)
St............... Station [*Military map abbreviation*] [*World War I*] [*French*] (MTD)
st................ Statistical (RU)
ST .... Statistisk Tabelvaerk [*Denmark*]
st................ Statni [*State (adjective)*] (CZ)
st................ Statt [*Instead Of*] [*German*]
st................ Stav [*Paragraph, Chapter, Section*] (YU)
st................ Stavka [*Paragraph, Chapter, Section*] (YU)
St............... Stelle [*Place*] [*German*]
St............... Stellung [*Position*] [*German*] (GCA)
ST .... Stemmen des Tijds [*Benelux*] (BAS)
st................ Stempel [*Stamp*] [*Netherlands*]
st................ Stempel [*Stamp*] [*Danish/Norwegian*]
st................ Stempel [*Stamp*] [*German*]
st................ Stent [*Let Them Stand*] [*Latin*] (MAE)
st................ Stere [*Stere*] [*French*] (GPO)
St............... Sterk [*Strong*] [*Afrikaans*]
ST .... Steuerung [*Control*] [*German*] (ADPT)
St............... Stich [*Engraving*] [*German*]
ST .... Stichting Tool [*Tool Foundation - TF*] [*Amsterdam, Netherlands*] (EAIO)

St............... Stil [*Style*] [*German*]
ST .... Stinson [*ICAO aircraft manufacturer identifier*]   (ICAO)
st................. Stoke   (RU)
St............... Stokes [*German*]   (GCA)
st............... Stoletje [*Century*]   (YU)
st............... Stopien [*or Stopnie*] [*Degree or Degrees*] [*Poland*]
st............... Stor [*Large*] [*Sweden*]
st............... Stotinka   (BU)
ST .... Stotinki [*Monetary unit*] [*Bulgaria*]
St............... Straat [*Street*] [*Afrikaans*]
St............... Street   (IDIG)
St............... Stueck [*Piece*] [*German*]
st............... Stuk [*Piece*] [*Publishing*] [*Netherlands*]
St............... Stunde [*Hour*] [*German*]
st............... Style   (BU)
ST .... Superheavy   (RU)
st............... Sutun [*Column*] [*As of a newspaper*]   (TU)
ST .... Systemtechnik [*German*]   (ADPT)
ST .... Tables de Recueil Sirey   (FLAF)
ST .... Temperature Recorder   (RU)
ST .... Temperature Signaler   (RU)
StA............. Automatenstahl [*Free Cutting Steel*] [*German*]   (GCA)
STA............ Sail Training Association [*Australia*]
Sta............. Santa [*Saint*] [*Portuguese*]   (GPO)
Sta............. Santa [*Saint*] [*Spanish*]
StA............. Schlauchtransportanhaenger [*Hose Reel Trailer (Fire department vehicle)*]   (EG)
STA............ Science and Technology Agency [*Nuclear energy*] [*Japan*]   (NRCH)
Sta............. Senorita [*Miss, Young Woman*] [*Spanish*]
STA............ Service Technique de l'Aeronautique [*Military*] [*French*]   (MTD)
STA............ Skholi Tekhnikon Aeroporias [*Air Force Technical School*] [*Greek*]   (GC)
STA............ Societe des Tabacs Algeriens
STA............ Societe des Tabacs et Allumettes [*North African*]
STA............ Societe des Transports Aeriens [*Privately-owned airline*] [*Mali*]
STA............ Societe des Transports des Amis
STA............ Societe de Transport Algerien
STA............ Societe de Transport de l'Administration
STA............ Societe de Transports Africains
STA............ Societe de Travail Aerien [*Algeria*]
STA............ Somateion Typografon Athinon [*Union of Athens Printers*]   (GC)
STA............ Space and Technology Agency [*Japan*]
StA............. Staatsanwalt [*or Staatsanwaltschaft*] [*Public Prosecutor*] [*German*]
St A .... Stammaktien [*Common Stock*] [*German*]   (GCA)
StA............. Starter Battery   (RU)
StA............. Start-Stop Apparatus, Teletype   (RU)
sta............. Stasie [*Station*] [*Afrikaans*]
STA............ State Transit Authority [*New South Wales, Australia*]
STA............ Stauning [*Denmark*] [*Airport symbol*]   (OAG)
STA............ Steueranweisung [*German*]   (ADPT)
STA............ Stredoevropska Tiskova Agentura [*Central European Press Agency*]   (CZ)
STA............ Superannuation Trust of Australia
STA............ Supersonic Tunnel Association [*Sweden*]   (SLS)
STA............ Sustredovacie Tabory [*Detention Camps*]   (CZ)
STA............ Sveriges Televerket [*Swedish Telecommunications Administration*]   (WEN)
STA............ Swedish Telecommunications Administration [*Telecommunications*]
STA............ Swiss Tennis Association   (EAIO)
STAAIM ... Syndicat des Travailleurs Agricoles et Artisans de l'Ile Maurice [*Agricultural Workers and Artisans Union of Mauritius Island*]   (AF)
staalgr .... Staalgravure [*Steel Engraving*] [*Publishing*] [*Netherlands*]
staalgravs... Staalgravures [*Steel Engravings*] [*Publishing*] [*Netherlands*]
staatk .... Staatkunde [*Politics*] [*Afrikaans*]
staatk .... Staatkundig [*Political*] [*Afrikaans*]
Staatl......... Staatlich [*State or Federal*] [*German*]   (GPO)
Staatsbl...... Belgisch Staatsblad [*Benelux*]   (BAS)
STAB .... Service des Transports Aeriens du Burundi [*Burundi Air Transportation Service*]   (AF)
STAB .... Sociedad de Tecnicos Azucareros y Alcoholeros del Brasil
STAB .... Societe de Travaux Auxiliaires de Batiment
stab............. Stabil [*Stable*] [*German*]   (GCA)
stab............. Stabilizer, Regulator [*Electricity*]   (BU)
STAB .... Studio Teologico Accademico Bolognese [*Italian*]   (SLS)
STAB .... Svenska Tandsticks AB [*The Swedish Match Co. Ltd.*]   (WEN)
STABACO ... Sociedad Tabacalera Antioquena [*Colombia*]   (COL)
STABEX.... Stabilization of Export Earnings from Commodities
Stabilisat.... Stabilisation [*Stabilization*] [*German*]   (GCA)
Stabilisier .. Stabilisierung [*Stabilization*] [*German*]   (GCA)

STACA ...... Servicio Tecnico Agricola Colombiano-Americano [*Colombian-American Agricultural Technical Service*]   (LA)
STACC ...... Staccato [*Detached, Distinct*] [*Italian*]
staccab .... Staccabile [*Detachable*] [*Italian*]
STACRES ... Standing Committee on Research and Statistics [*IPFC/ICNAF*]   (ASF)
STAD........ Societe de Traitement Automatique des Donnees [*French*]   (ADPT)
stad............ Stadium [*Topography*]   (RU)
STADB...... Chinese Scientific and Technological Periodical Abstracts [*Information service or system*]   (IID)
STAE........ Sogdian-Tadzhik Archaelogical Expedition   (RU)
staedt......... Staedtisch [*Municipal*] [*German*]   (GCA)
STAEI .... Societe de Transit et d'Affretement Export-Import
StAeVO .... Steueraenderungsverordnung [*Tax Amendment Decree*] [*German*]   (EG)
STAFARM ... State Farms Corp.
STAFEX.... Staff Exercises [*NATO*]   (NATG)
STAFF....... Society for Techno-Innovation of Agriculture, Forestry and Fisheries [*Japan*]
STAFIM.... Societe Tunisienne Automobile, Financiere, Immobiliere, et Maritime [*Automobile and machinery manufacturer*] [*Tunis, Tunisia*]   (MENA)
STAFO ...... Statsjenestemanns Forbundet [*Federation of Civil Servants*] [*Norway*]   (WEN)
STAG........ Servicio Tecnico Agricola [*Palmira*]   (COL)
STAG........ Sindicato de Trabajadores de Artes Graficas [*Union of Graphic Arts Workers*] [*El Salvador*]   (LA)
STAG........ Sociedade Tecnica de Artes Graficas Mocambique Lda.
StAG .... Staatsanwaltschaftsgesetz [*Public Prosecutors Law*]   (EG)
STAGE ...... Societe Africaine des Grands Travaux de l'Est
STAGEKMEM ... Statisztikai es Gazdasagelemzo Kozpont, Mezogazdasagi es Elelmezesugyi Miniszterium [*Statistical and Economic Analysis Center, Ministry of Agriculture and Food Industry*]   (HU)
StAGN .... Staendiger Ausschuss fuer Geographische Namen [*Standing Committee for Geographic Names*]   (SLS)
Stahlst........ Stahlstich [*Steel Engraving*] [*German*]
STAI .... Sindicato de Trabajadores Agroindustriales [*Trade Union of Agroindustrial Workers*] [*Nicaragua*]   (LA)
STAIAT..... Service de Traitement Automatique de l'Information de l'Armee de Terre [*French*]   (ADPT)
STAKO...... Committee for the Study of Scientific Principles of Standardization   (RU)
STAL .... Sociedade Tecnica de Acessorios Limitada
stal .... Steel Foundry [*Topography*]   (RU)
STALAG ... Stammlager [*Prisoner-of-War Camp*] [*German*]
Stalhurt...... Warszawska Hurtownia Zelaza, Stali, i Wyrobow Zelaznych [*Warsaw Wholesale House of Iron, Steel, and Ferrous Products*]   (POL)
Stal'konstruktsiya ... Trust of the Glavstal'konstruktsiya of the Gosmontazhspetsstroy SSSR   (RU)
Stal'montazh ... State Trust of the Glavstal'konstruktsiya of the Gosmontazhspetsstroy SSSR   (RU)
Stal'most.... All-Union Trust for the Manufacture and Assembly of Metal Structures of the Glavmostostroy   (RU)
Stal'proyekt ... State All-Union Institute for the Planning of Units for Steel Foundry and Rolling Mill Production in Ferrous Metallurgy   (RU)
stalst........... Staalstikk [*Steel Engraving*] [*Publishing Danish/Norwegian*]
STAM....... Societe de Travaux Agricoles Marocains
STAM........ Societe Tunisienne d'Acconage et de Manutention
STAMICO ... State Mining Corporation [*Tanzania*]   (AF)
stamp .... Stampatore [*Printer*] [*Italian*]
STAMVIE ... Societe Tropicale d'Assurances Mutuelles et Vie [*Ivory Coast*]
STAN........ Science Teachers' Association of Nigeria
STAN........ Servicio Tecnico Agricola de Nicaragua [*Nicaragua*]   (LAA)
stan............ Stanitsa, Cossack Village   (RU)
stan............ Temporary Settlement [*Topography*]   (RU)
STANAG... Standardization Agreement [*NATO*]
STANAVFORCHAN ... Standing Naval Force, Channel [*NATO*]   (NATG)
STANAVFORLANT ... Standing Naval Force, Atlantic [*Activated 1968*] [*NATO*]
STANBIC ... Standard Bank Investment Corporation [*South Africa*]
stand.......... Standard   (RU)
Standartdomsbyt ... Central Office of the Rosglavlessnabsbyt   (RU)
Standartgiz ... State Publishing House of Standards   (RU)
STANKIN ... Moscow Institute of Machine Tools and Tools   (RU)
Stankoimport ... All-Union Association of the Ministry of Foreign Trade, USSR   (RU)
Stankolit .... Moscow Iron Foundry for the Production of Castings for Machine Tool Manufacture   (RU)
Stankonormal' ... Moscow Plant of Standard Parts for Machine Tools   (RU)
Stanvac ...... NV Standard Vacuum Sales Company   (OMWE)
STAP .... Secretariado Tecnico dos Assuntos Politicos [*Technical Secretariat for Political Affairs*] [*Portuguese*]   (WER)
STAP .... State Transit Authority Plan [*Victoria, Australia*]

STAPC	Spanish Technical Association of Prestressed Concrete	(EAIO)
STAPE	Secretariado Tecnico dos Assuntos Politicos e Eleitorais [*Technical Secretariat for Political and Election Matters*] [*Portuguese*]	(WER)
STAPO	Staatspolizei [*State Police*] [*Austria*]	(WEN)
STAPRC	Scientific and Technical Association of the People's Republic of China	(PDAA)
Star	Old [*Toponymy*]	(RU)
STAR	Satellite Television Asia Region [*Hong Kong*]	
STAR	Saudi Technology and Research Consulting Centre	(PDAA)
STAR	Service Technique Africain de Radio-Television	
STAR	Societe de Transport Aerien du Rwanda	
STAR	Societe Senegalaise de Transports et Affretements Routiers	
STAR	Societe Tananarivienne de Refrigeration et de Boissons Gazeuses [*Malagasy*]	
STAR	Societe Tchadienne d'Assurances et de Reassurances [*Insurance*] [*Chad*]	
STAR	Societe Tunisienne d'Assurance et de Reassurance [*Tunis, Tunisia*]	
STAR	Society for Test Anxiety Research	(EA)
STAR	Society of Romanian Air Transports [*ICAO designator*]	(FAAC)
STARC	Societe de Transports et d'Affretements Routiers au Cameroun	
STARDI	Station de Recherches Bioecologiques Forestieres de Dimonika [*Dimonika Forest Research Station*] [*Congo*]	(IRC)
STAREC	Societe Technique d'Application et de Recherche Electronique [*France*]	(PDAA)
STARESCO	Station de Recherches Sous-Marines et Oceanographiques [*Submarine and Oceanographic Research Station*] [*Belgium*]	(ARC)
STARESO	Station de Recherches Sous-Marines et Oceanographiques [*Research center*] [*France*]	(EAS)
starin	Ancient	(RU)
starkom	Senior Commissar	(RU)
starleyt	Senior Lieutenant	(RU)
starmekh	Senior Mechanic [*Navy*]	(RU)
starmornach	Senior Naval Officer	(RU)
star neftkol	Abandoned Oil Well [*Topography*]	(RU)
starogr	Ancient Greek	(BU)
starpom	Senior Assistant [*Navy*]	(RU)
starsh	Senior, Chief	(RU)
START	Science Association of the Republic of Tanzania	
START	Strategic Arms' Reduction Treaty	(EECI)
STARTTS	Service for the Treatment and Rehabilitation of Torture and Trauma Survivors [*Australia*]	
star zhelrud	Abandoned Iron Mine [*Topography*]	(RU)
STAS	Standarde de Stat [*State Standards*]	(RO)
STASA	State Transport Authority of South Australia	
STASI	Staatsicherheitsdienst [*State Security Service*]	(EG)
st asist	Senior Assistant	(BU)
STASYS	Standards zur Systementwicklung [*German*]	(ADPT)
STAT	Societe Tchadienne d'Affretement et de Transit	
stat	Statistical, Statistics	(RU)
stat	Statistiek [*Statistic*] [*Dutch*]	(BAS)
Stat Dec	Statutory Declaration	
STATEC	Service Central de la Statistique et des Etudes Economiques [*Statistical and Economic Studies Central Service*] [*Luxembourg*]	(PDAA)
statist	Statistical	(BU)
statist	Statistisch [*Statistical*] [*German*]	(GCA)
Stat K	Statisztikai Kiado [*Statistical Publishing House*]	(HU)
Statoil	Den Norske Stats Oljeselskap	(OMWE)
STATOIL	State Oil Co. [*Norway*]	(PDAA)
statupr	Statistical Administration	(RU)
STATUS	Statute Search [*Australia*]	
Stavostroj	Zavody na Vyrobu Stavebnich Stroju [*Construction Machinery Plants*]	(CZ)
STAVRA	Supreme High Command of the Soviet Armed Forces [*Russian*]	(MCD)
STAWA	Sail Training Association of Western Australia	
STAZ	Stalinsk Aluminum Plant	(RU)
STAZA	Stalinovy Zavody [*Stalin Plants*]	(CZ)
STAZRA	Plant Protection Station	(RU)
stb	Old Bulgarian Language	(BU)
STB	Sanayi ve Teknoloji Bakanligi [*Ministry of Industry and Technology*]	(TU)
STB	Sandatahang Tanod ng Bayan [*People's Home Defense Guard*] [*Philippines*]	
STB	Santa Barbara [*Venezuela*] [*Airport symbol*]	(OAG)
stb	S A Tobbi [*Et Cetera*]	(HU)
STB	Singapore Telephone Board	(PDAA)
STB	Snci-Tours Benin Inter Regional [*ICAO designator*]	(FAAC)
STB	Societe des Transports Brazzavillois	
STB	Societe Togolaise de Boissons	
STB	Societe Tropicale des Bois	
STB	Societe Tunisienne de Banque [*Tunisian Banking Company*]	(AF)
Stb	Staatsblad [*Official Bulletin*] [*Netherlands*]	(ILCA)
STB	State Tender Board [*Victoria, Australia*]	
STB	State Training Board [*Victoria, Australia*]	
StB	Statni Bezpecnost [*State Security (Police)*]	(CZ)
STB	Strata Titles Board [*New South Wales, Australia*]	
STB	Swansea Tribology Centre [*University College of Swansea*]	(PDAA)
STB	Swedish Tourist Board	(EAIO)
STB	Technical Estimate Office	(RU)
STBA	Service Technique des Bases Aeriennes [*French*]	
STBC	Swaziland Television Broadcasting Corporation	
StbEvSt	Staatsbuergerschaftsevidenzstelle [*German*]	
STBG	Societe de Transports de Bois en Grumes	
STBL	Spojene Tovarny na Barvy a Laky [*United Paint and Lacquer Factories*]	(CZ)
Stbl	Staatsblad van het Koninkrijk der Nederlanden [*Netherlands*] [*Benelux*]	(BAS)
STBO	Societe de Transformation du Bois de l'Ouest	
St BOT	Stoleczne Biuro Obslugi Turystycznej [*Warsaw Tourist Service Office*]	(POL)
Stbr	Steinbruch [*Quarry*] [*German*]	
StbsRttm	Stabsrittmeister [*Staff Cavalry Captain*] [*German*]	
STBTP	Syndicat des Travailleurs du Batiment et Travaux Publics	
Stbv	Staatsbuergerschaftsverband [*German*]	
STC	Customs Cooperation Council [*CCC*]	(RU)
STC	Sci-Tech Centre [*India*]	
STC	Secretaria Tecnica de Planificacion [*Paraguay*]	(LAA)
STC	Shanfari Trading & Contracting Co. [*Oman*]	
STC	SHAPE [*Supreme Headquarters Allied Powers Europe*] Technical Center [*Formerly, SADTC*] [*The Hague, Netherlands*] [*NATO*]	
STC	Singapore Technology Corp.	
STC	Singapore Traction Company [*Bus company*]	(ML)
STC	Societe de Transports et Construction	
STC	Societe de Transports et de Tourisme [*Mali*] [*ICAO designator*]	(FAAC)
STC	Societe Tchadienne de Confection	
STC	Societe Tchadienne de Credit	
STC	Solidaridad de Trabajadores Cristianos [*Nicaragua*] [*Political party*]	(EY)
STC	Solidaridad de Trabajadores Cubanos [*Cuban Workers' Solidarity*]	
STC	State Theatre Company of Western Australia	
STC	State Trading Corp. [*India*]	
STC	State Transport Corp. [*Ghana*]	
STC	Statistical Training Centre	
STC	Sydney Technical College [*Australia*]	(ADA)
STCA	Section Topographique de Corps d'Armee [*Military*] [*French*]	(MTD)
STCA	Service Telegraphique de Corps d'Armee [*Military*] [*French*]	(MTD)
STCAC	Sydney Transport Coordination Advisory Council [*New South Wales, Australia*]	
STCAN	Service Technique des Constructions et Armes Navales [*Technical Service for Naval Construction and Ordnance*] [*French*]	(WER)
STCAN/FOM	Services Techniques des Construction et Armes Navales / France Outre Mer [*French river patrol boat used in Vietnam*]	(VNW)
STCAU	Service Technique Central d'Amenagement et Urbanisme	
STCB	State Trading Corp. of Bhutan	(FEA)
STCC	Saudi Traveller's Cheque Co.	
STCHS	Stavebne Technicka Sluzba [*Construction and Technical Service*] [*Civil defense*]	(CZ)
STCI	Societe de Transports de la Cote-D'Ivoire	
STCI	State Traffic Control Inspection [*Ministry of Internal Affairs*] [*Former USSR*]	
STCO	Strata and Tenancy Commissioner's Office [*New South Wales, Australia*]	
St Comm	Staatscommissie [*Benelux*]	(BAS)
STCRP	Societe des Transports en Commun de la Region Parisienne [*Paris Transport Authority*] [*France*]	
Stcrt	Nederlandse Staatscourant [*Netherlands*]	(BAS)
STCSP	Sindicato de Trabajadores de la Construccion y Similares de Panama [*Union of Construction Workers and Workers in Related Trades of Panama*]	(LA)
STCST	Second Telecommunications Carrier Selection Team [*Australia*]	
STCT	Sindicato de Trabajadores de la Colombiana de Tabaco [*Colombian Tobacco Company Workers Union*]	(LA)
STCT	Sindicato dos Trabalhadores dos Correios e Telecomunicacoes [*Union of Postal and Telecommunications Workers*] [*Portuguese*]	(WER)
STCTP	Societe Togolaise de Commerce et de Travaux Publics	
STCW	Stichting Technisch Centrum Waalsteen [*Research center*] [*Netherlands*]	(IRC)
STD	Sao Tome and Principe Dobra	
STD	Societe Textile Dahomeenne	

STD .... Societe Tunisienne de Diffusion [*Tunis, Tunisia*]
STD .... South Tibetan Detachment [*Geology*]
std.............. Staendig [*Permanent*] [*German*]   (GCA)
std.............. Standartti(a) [*Finland*]
std.............. Standerd [*Standard*] [*Afrikaans*]
STD .... State Taxation Department [*Western Australia*]
STD .... Steward [*Royal Australian Navy*]
STD .... Strategic Technical Directorate [*South Vietnamese studies and observations group*]   (VNW)
Std.............. Studien [*Studies*] [*German*]
std.............. Stuendig [*Hourly*] [*German*]   (GCA)
Std.............. Stunde [*Hour*] [*German*]
STDA......... Selenium-Tellurium Development Association [*Belgium*]   (EAIO)
STDB......... Singapore Trade Development Board   (EAIO)
Stde............ Stunde [*Hour*] [*German*]
stdg............ Staendig [*Permanent*] [*German*]   (GCA)
stdg............ Stuendig [*For Hour*] [*German*]
STDI .... Section Topographique de Division d'Infanterie [*Military*] [*French*]   (MTD)
STDM....... Sociedade de Turismo e Diversoes de Macau [*Macau*]   (FEA)
Stdn........... Stunden [*Hours*] [*German*]
StdsA .... Standesamt [*Registry Office*] [*German*]
Stdt............ Stadt [*City*] [*German*]
STE........... Entreprise Socialiste des Travaux de l'Est
Ste .... Sainte [*Saint*] [*French*]   (MTD)
STE........... Skholi Touristikon Epangelmation [*Tourist Trades School*] [*Greek*]   (GC)
Ste .... Societe [*Company*] [*French*] [*Business term*]
STE........... Societe Togolaise d'Enteposage
STE........... Societe Travaux Electriques
STE........... Stelle [*German*]   (ADPT)
STE........... Steuereinheit [*German*]   (ADPT)
STE........... Stredoceske Energeticke Zavody [*Electric Power Plants, Central Bohemia*]   (CZ)
STE........... Studii Tehnico-Economice [*Technical-Economic Studies*]   (RO)
STE........... Swedish Travelling Exhibitions   (EAIO)
STE........... Symvoulion tou Ethnous [*Council of State*] [*SE*] [*See also*]   (GC)
STE........... Syrian Telecommunication Establishment   (PDAA)
STEA .... Societe des Travaux d'Electrification et d'Adduction [*Electrification and Water Supply Construction Company*] [*Benin*]   (AF)
STEA .... Stammeichamt [*Main Office of Weights and Measures*] [*German*]
STEAA ...... Suzuki Talent Education Association of Australia
STEAG...... Steinkolen-Elektrizitaet Aktiengesellschaft
STEAM ..... Skholi Tekhnikis Ekpaidevseos Axiomatikon Mikhanikou [*Technical Training School for Engineer Corps Officers*] [*Greek*]   (GC)
STEB .... Societe des Travaux d'Entretien de Batiments
STEBT....... Societe de Transformation et d'Exploitation des Bois Tropicaux
STEC .... Societe de Transport, d'Elevage, et de Commerce
STEC .... Southern Tablelands Education Centre [*Australia*]
STECDIP .. Societe Tunisienne d'Etudes, de Cooperation, et de Defense de l'Industrie Phosphatiere
STECI....... Societe de Travaux d'Equipement de la Cote-D'Ivoire
STECTA.... Societe Technique et Commerciale des Canalisations Souterraines en Tubes d'Acier
STEE .... Societe Tchadienne d'Energie Electrique
STEEL....... Societe de Travaux d'Electricite et d'Electronique du Languedoc [*France*]   (PDAA)
STEELFACTS ... Materials Database Steel and Iron [*German Iron and Steel Engineers Association*] [*Ceased operation*] [*Information service or system*]   (IID)
STEEP....... Societe Tchadienne d'Entreposage de Produits Petroliers
STEES....... Sindicato de Trabajadores de la Educacion de El Salvador [*Union of Educational Workers of El Salvador*]   (LA)
STEF .... Societe de Transport et d'Entrepots Frigorifiques
STEG........ Sindicato de Trabajadores de la Educacion Guatemaltecos [*Trade union*]   (EY)
STEG........ Societe de Techniques, d'Entreprises, et de Gestion
STEG........ Societe Tchadienne d'Entreprises Generales
STEG........ Societe Tunisienne d'Electricite et du Gaz [*Tunisian Gas and Electric Company*] [*Tunis, Tunisia*]   (AF)
StEG .... Strafrechtsergaenzungsgesetz [*Penal Code Amendment*]   (EG)
STEI .... Societe Transafricaine d'Etudes et d'Investissements
STEIA .... Sociedade Tecnica de Equipamentos Industriais e Agricolas Lda.
steifbr......... Steifbroschiert [*Bound in Stiff Paper Covers*] [*Publishing*] [*German*]
Steiger........ Steigerung [*Increase*] [*German*]   (GCA)
steir .... Steirisch [*German*]
stekhiometrich ... Stoichiometric   (RU)
stekl .... Glass Plant [*Topography*]   (RU)
steklogr ...... Hyalography   (RU)
stelk .... Stelkunde [*Algebra*] [*Afrikaans*]
Stell............ Stellung [*Position*] [*German*]   (GCA)

STELLA .... Satellite Transmission Experiment Linking Laboratories [*European Space Agency*]
STELLA .... System Ten European Language Ledger Accounting   (PDAA)
stellenw ...... Stellenweise [*Partly*] [*German*]
Stellv .... Stellvertreter [*Representative*] [*German*]
STELT....... Studiecentrum voor Toegepaste Elektriciteit in Land- en Tuinbouw [*Research Center for Electricity in Agriculture and Horticulture*] [*Belgium*]   (IRC)
STEM........ Science, Technology and Mathematics [*Adult Literacy Project*] [*Australia*]
STEM........ Societe Tropicale d'Entrepots et de Magasinage
STEM........ Southern Technical and Economic Movement [*South Africa*]   (AF)
STEM........ Studiecentrum Technologie, Energie, Milieu [*Study Center on Technology, Energy, and Environment*] [*Belgium*]   (IRC)
STEMI ...... Societe de Transports et Manutentions Industriels
STEMO..... Societe Technique d'Etudes Mecaniques et d'Outillage [*French*]   (SLS)
STEMRA .. Stichting Tot Exploitatie van Mechanische Reproductie Rechten der Auteurs [*Benelux*]   (BAS)
STEN........ Societe Togolaise des Engrais
STen.......... Sottotenente [*Sub-Lieutenant*] [*Italian*]
sten .... Stenographic   (RU)
STENEE ... Sindicato de Tranajadores de la Empresa Nacional de Energia Electrica [*Union of National Electrical Energy Company*] [*Honduras*]
stenkor .... Wall Newspaper Correspondent   (RU)
stenogr .... Shorthand Record, Verbatim Report   (RU)
stenogr .... Verbatim Report   (BU)
Stenpechat .. Wall News Sheets   (BU)
stens .... Stensilert [*Mimeographed*] [*Publishing Danish/Norwegian*]
stenvestnik ... Wall Newspaper   (BU)
STEP .... Science and Technological Entrepreneurs Park Program [*India*]
STEP .... Science and Technology for Environmental Protection Program [*Australia*]
STEP .... Service Technique des Equipments Profonds [*French*]   (MSC)
STEP .... Societe de Travaux d'Electricite et Plomberie
STEP .... Societe Togolaise d'Electronique Parby
STEP .... Societe Tunisienne d'Exportation du Petrole
STEPC....... Societe Tropicale d'Engrais et de Produits Chimiques
STEPHOS ... Societe Tunisienne d'Exploitation Phosphatiere
STEPO ...... Spojene Tovarny na Technicky Porculan, Narodni Podnik [*United Industrial Ceramic Factories, National Enterprise*]   (CZ)
STEPS....... School-Leavers' Training and Employment Preparation Scheme [*New Zealand Labor Department*]   (BARN)
ster .... Steradian   (RU)
ster .... Steril [*Sterile*] [*German*]   (GCA)
STER .... Stichting Etherreclame [*Airways Advertising Foundation*] [*Netherlands*]   (WEN)
stereot .... Stereotype   (RU)
stereot izd... Stereotype Publication   (BU)
STERIA...... Societe de Realisations en Informatique et Automatisme [*French*]   (ADPT)
Sternw....... Sternwarte [*Observatory*] [*German*]   (GCA)
STERR ..... Sterrekunde [*Astronomy*] [*Afrikaans*]
STET .... Societa Finanziaria Telefonica [*Telephone Finance Corporation*] [*Italian*]   (WER)
STET .... Societa Torinese Esercizio Telefoni [*Turin Telephone Company*] [*Italian*]
STEUNAM ... Sindicato de Trabajadores y Estudiantes de la Universidad Nacional Autonoma de Mexico [*Workers and Students Union of the National Autonomous University of Mexico*]   (LA)
STF .... SFT-Sudanese Flight [*ICAO designator*]   (FAAC)
STF .... Sociedad Colombiana de Transporte Ferroviario SA [*Public rail services*]   (EY)
STF .... Societe des Transports Ferre
STF .... Supremo Tribunal Federal [*Federal Supreme Court*] [*Brazil*]   (LA)
STF .... Sveriges Tandlaekarfoerbund [*Sweden*]   (SLS)
STF .... Systemic Transformation Facility [*Former USSR*]   (ECON)
STFAG ...... Syndicat des Travailleurs de la Foret et de Agriculture
StFB.......... Staatlicher Forstwirtschaftsbetrieb [*State Forestry Enterprise*]   (EG)
STFC .... Service du Transport Fluvial Centrafricain [*Central African River Transportation Service*]   (AF)
STFI.......... Swedish Pulp and Paper Research Institute [*Research center*] [*Sweden*]   (IRC)
STFO .... Societe Technique de la Foret d'Okoume [*Okoume Forest Technical Company*] [*Gabon*]   (AF)
Stft .... Stift [*Pencil, Foundation*] [*German*]
STG........... Pipe Bender   (RU)
STG........... Schiffbautechnische Gesellschaft eV [*Shipbuilding Technology Association*]   (SLS)
STG........... Somatotropic Hormone   (RU)
Stg .... Stahlguss [*Cast Steel*] [*German*]   (GCA)

Stg .... Stellung [*Position*] [*German*] (GCA)
stg .... Sterling [*Sterling*] [*Afrikaans*]
STG .... Study Group [*NATO*]
STG .... Sturmgewehr [*Storm Rifle*] [*German military - World War II*]
STG .... Suomen Taidegraafikot [*Finland*] (SLS)
STGA .... Shrub and Tree Growers of Australia
StGB .... Strafgesetzbuch [*Penal Code*] [*German*]
ST-GEN .... State-Generaal [*Afrikaans*]
St Gen .... Staten Generaal [*Benelux*] (BAS)
STGM .... Sa Tres Gracieuse Majeste [*His Most Gracious Majesty*] [*French*]
Stg O Btg ... Stadsgemeente Ordonnantie Buitengewesten [*Benelux*] (BAS)
Stg OJ .... Stadsgemeente Ordonnantie Java [*Indonesia*] (BAS)
STH .... Societe Togolaise des Hydrocarbures [*Togolese Hydrocarbons Company*] (AF)
STH .... Societe Togolaise d'Hotellerie
sth .... Stemhebbend [*Voiced*] [*Afrikaans*]
SThG .... Schweizerische Theologische Gesellschaft [*Swiss Theological Society*] (SLS)
STHRA ...... Societe de Transport d'Hassi R'Mel-Arzew [*North African*]
STI .... Information Telecommunication System (RU)
STI .... Institute of Sanitary Engineering (RU)
STI .... Santiago [*Dominican Republic*] [*Airport symbol*] (OAG)
STI .... Savezni Trzisni Inspektorat (DSRP) [*Federal Market Inspectorate*] (YU)
STI .... Schweizerisches Tropeninstitut [*Swiss Tropical Institute*] [*Research center*] (IRC)
STI .... Secretaria de Tecnologia Industrial [*Secretariat for Industrial Technology*] [*Brazil*] (LA)
STI .... Service duTraitement de l'Information [*French*] (ADPT)
STI .... Services des Transmissions de l'Interieur (FLAF)
STI .... Siberian Technological Institute (RU)
Sti .... Sirketi [*Company*] [*Ltd Sti Turkish*] [*See also*] (TU)
STI .... Societa Teosofica in Italia [*Italian*] (SLS)
STI .... Societe Tchadienne d'Investissement
STI .... Societe Tunisienne d'Industrie Automobile [*Tunisian truck manufacturer*]
STI .... Somborska Tekstilna Industrija [*Sombor Textile Industry*] (YU)
STI .... Statens Teknologiske Institutt [*Government Technological Institute*] [*Norway*] (PDAA)
STI .... Straight Times Index [*Singapore Stock Exchange*]
STI .... Sudan Textile Industry
S-Ti .... Suedtirol [*South Tyrol*] [*German*]
STI .... Technical Information Service (RU)
STIA .... Societe Tunisienne d'Industrie Automobile [*Tunisian Automobile Industry*]
STIADES .. Sindicato de Trabajadores de la Industria Electrica [*Trade Union of Electric Industry Workers*] [*El Salvador*] (LA)
STIB .... Societe de Transformation Industrielle des Bois
STIBOKA ... Stichting voor Bodemkartering [*Soil Survey Institute*] [*Netherlands*] (ARC)
STIC .... Science and Technology Information Center [*Taiwanese*] [*Research center*] (IRC)
STIC .... Scientific and Technological Information Center [*Brazil*] (EAIO)
STIC .... Societe des Traducteurs et Interpretes du Canada [*Society of Translators and Interpreters of Canada*]
STIC .... Sudan Textile Industry Company
STICA .... Servicio Tecnico Interamericano de Cooperacion Agricola [*Inter-American Technical Service of Agricultural Cooperation*] (LA)
STICAR ..... Systeme de Transmission des Informations Codees des Armees [*French*]
STIC-CMP ... Scientech Information Center - China Machine Press [*China*] [*Research center*] (IRC)
STICEC ..... Australian National Scientific and Technical Information Authority
STICERTMEE ... Student Member of the Institute of Certified Mechanical and Electrical Engineers of South Africa (AA)
STICPA ..... Societe Tchadienne Industrielle et Commerciale des Produits Animaux
STICS .... Syndicat des Travailleurs Indigenes Congolais Specialises
STIDC .... Sarawak Timber Industry Development Corp. [*Malaysia*]
STIES .... Sindicato de Trabajadores de la Industria Electromecanica y Similares [*Trade Union of Electricians and Related Trades Workers*] [*Nicaragua*] (LA)
STIGCES .. Sindicato de Trabajadores de las Industrias Graficas y Conexas de El Salvador [*Union of Workers in the Graphics and Related Industries of El Salvador*] (LA)
STIGSS ..... Sindicato de Trabajadores del Instituto Guatemalteco de Seguro Social [*Trade union*] (EY)
STIL .... Societe des Transitaires Internationaux du Laos [*International Forwarding Agents Company of Laos*] (CL)
STIL .... Societe Tunisienne de l'Industrie Laitiere [*Tunisia*]
STIMA ...... Societe des Techniciens et Ingenieurs en Machines Agricoles (FLAF)
STIMA ...... Societe de Techniques Industrielles et Maritimes

STIMAD ... Societe des Telecommunications Internationales de la Republique Democratique Malgache [*International Telecommunications Company of the Democratic Republic of Madagascar*] (AF)
stimatiss ..... Stimatissimo [*Highly Esteemed*] [*Italian*]
STIMBS .... Sindicato de Trabajadores de Industrias Metalicas Basicas y Similares [*Union of Workers of the Basic Metals and Allied Industries*] [*El Salvador*] (LA)
STIMCES ... Sindicato de Trabajadores de la Industria Minera y Conexas de El Salvador [*Trade Union of Salvadoran Mining and Related Industries Workers*] (LA)
STIMEAFRIQUE ... Societe Technique d'Importation de Materiel d'Entreprise pour l'Afrique, Senegal
STIMMB .. Sindicato de Trabajadores de la Industria Mecanica y Metalicas Basicas [*Union of Workers of the Mechanical and Basic Metals Industries*] [*El Salvador*] (LA)
STINDE .... Sindicato de Trabajadores de la Industria de la Electricidad [*Trade union*] [*Guatemala*] (EY)
STIP .... Sindicato de Trabajadores de la Industria Plastica [*Trade Union of Plastic Industry Workers*] [*Nicaragua*] (LA)
STIP .... Societe Tunisienne des Industries de Pneumatiques
STIPEL ..... Societa Telefonica Interregionale Piemonte e Lombardia [*Company controlling telephone services in Piedmont and Lombardy*] [*Italian*]
STIR .... Scientists and Technologists in Reserve [*Australia*]
STIR .... Societe de Transports Internationaux du Rwanda
STIR .... Societe Tunisienne des Industries de Raffinages [*Tunisia*] (IMH)
STIR .... Societe Tunisio-Italienne de Raffinage [*Tunisian-Italian Refining Company*] (AF)
STIRTTES ... Sindicato de Trabajadores de la Industria de Radio, Teatro, y Television de El Salvador [*Union of Workers in the Radio, Theater, and Television Industry of El Salvador*] (LA)
STISEC ..... Scientific and Technological Information Services Enquiry Committee [*National Library of Australia*] (PDAA)
STISSS ...... Sindicato de Trabajadores del Seguro Salvadoreno del Seguro Social [*Union of the Salvadoran Social Security Institute Workers*] (LA)
STITASSC ... Sindicato de Trabajadores Industrias Textil, Algodon, Sinteticas, Similares, y Conexas [*Union of Workers in Textile, Cotton, Synthetic, Similar, and Related Industries*] [*El Salvador*] (LA)
Stitext .... Stempel im Text [*Stamp in the Text*] [*Publishing*] [*German*]
STIUSA ..... Sindicato Textil Industrias Unidas, Sociedad Anonima [*Union of United Textile Industries, Incorporated*] [*El Salvador*] (LA)
STJ .... Slovenska Telocvicna Jednota [*Slovak Gymnastic Association*] (CZ)
STJ .... Society of St. Teresa of Jesus [*Italy*] (EAIO)
StK .... Kettenstahl [*Steel for Chains*] [*German*] (GCA)
STK .... Savez Trgovinskih Komora [*Union of Chambers of Commerce*] (YU)
STK .... Societe des Transports de Kinshasa [*Kinshasa Transport Company*] [*Zaire*] (AF)
STK .... Soiuz Trudovogo Krest'ianstva [*Union of Working Peasantry*] [*Russian*]
STK .... Sreska Trgovinska Komora [*District Chamber of Commerce*] (YU)
STK .... Stacni Technicka Knihovna [*State Technical Library*] [*Brno*] (CZ)
STK .... Stadart Topografik Karta [*Standard Topographic Map*] (TU)
STK .... Standard Telefon og Kabelfabrik [*Telecommunications*] [*Norway*]
STK .... Stanje Teretnih Kola [*Condition of Freight Cars*] [*Railroads*] (YU)
STK .... Steuerkarte [*German*] (ADPT)
STK .... Suomen Tyonantajain Keskusliitto [*Finnish Employers' Association*] [*Helsinki*] (WEN)
STK .... Technical Supervisory Service (RU)
STK .... Telemetric Monitoring System (RU)
STK .... Voice-Frequency Patching Rack (RU)
STK .... Worker's Union of Colombia (RU)
StKK .... Staatliches Komitee fuer Kultur (und Sport) [*State Committee for Culture (and Sport)*] (EG)
StKKF .... Stoleczny Komitet Kultury Fizycznej [*Warsaw Committee on Physical Culture*] (POL)
Stkm. .... Stundenkilometer [*Kilometers per Hour*] [*German*] (GCA)
stkn .... Stukken [*Volumes*] [*Publishing*] [*Netherlands*]
Stkr .... Stadtkreis [*Urban Kreis (Administrative unit)*] (EG)
STKS .... Suomalainen Teologinen Kirjallisuusseura [*Finland*] (SLS)
StKTA .... Stellvertreter Kommandeur der Technischen Ausruestung [*Deputy Commander for Technical Equipment*] (EG)
STKV .... Mean Temperature Coefficient of Viscosity (RU)
STL .... Pilot's Aerial Gunnery Trainer (RU)
STL .... Sarich Technologies Ltd. [*Australia*]
STL .... Seatainer Terminals Limited [*Australia*] (ADA)
stl .... Stemloos [*Unvoiced*] [*Afrikaans*]

STL............	Steuerloch [*German*] (ADPT)
STL............	Suomen Tennisliitto [*Finland*] (EAIO)
STL............	Suomen Tukkukauppiaiden Liitto [*Finnish Federation of Wholesalers*] (WEN)
stlb	Column (RU)
STLBW	Stedelijke Technische Leergangen voor Bibliotheek Wezen
Stllg............	Stellung [*Position*] [*German*] (GCA)
st lt	Senior Lieutenant (RU)
STM...........	Construction Technicum of the Mosgorispolkom (RU)
STM...........	Groupement International d'Editeurs Scientifiques, Techniques, et Medicaux [*International Group of Scientific, Technical, and Medical Publishers*] (EAIO)
STM...........	International Group of Scientific, Technical, and Medical Publishers (EAIO)
STM...........	Santarem [*Brazil*] [*Airport symbol*] (OAG)
STM...........	Sindicato del Transporte Maritimo [*Maritime Transport Workers Union*] [*Uruguay*] (LA)
STM...........	Societe de Transport de Merchandises [*Tunisia*]
stm	Sotamies [*Finland*]
STM...........	Soutez Tvorivosti Mladeze [*Young People's Creative Activities Competition*] (CZ)
Stm.............	Starkstrommeisterei [*High-Voltage Section Shop*] (EG)
STM...........	Stavby a Trati Mladeze [*Structures and Railroad Tracks (Built by Youth Brigade)*] (CZ)
Stm.............	Steiermark [*or Steiermaerkisch*] [*Styria or Styrian*] [*German*]
STM...........	Stellenmaschine [*German*] (ADPT)
STM...........	Superior Tribunal Militar [*Superior Military Court*] [*Brazil*] (LA)
STM...........	Szybkie Tramwaje Miejskie [*Express Trolleys*] (POL)
STMA........	Syndicat des Transports Maritimes et Acconiers
st mar	Starszy Marynarz [*Able-Bodied Seaman*] [*Poland*]
STMCGMW ...	Subcommission for Tectonic Maps of the Commission for the Geological Map of the World (EAIO)
STMD.......	Syndicat des Travailleurs des Municipalites du Dahomey [*Union of Municipal Workers of Dahomey*]
STMI........	Societe de Techniques en Millieu Ionisant [*France*] (WND)
Stmk...........	Steiermark [*or Steiermaerkisch*] [*Styria or Styrian*] [*German*]
STML........	Sindicato de Trabajadores Municipales de Limon [*Trade Union of Limon Municipal Workers*] [*Costa Rica*] (LA)
STML........	Working Youth League of Latvia (RU)
st m lk	Surgeon, Regimental Surgeon (RU)
STMNC....	Sindicato de Trabajadores de Marmoles y Cementos Nare [*Nare Union of Marble and Cement Workers*] [*Colorado*] (LA)
STMV.......	Working Youth League of Vietnam [*North Vietnamese*] (RU)
STN	Societe des Terres Neuves [*New Lands Agency*] [*Senegal*]
STN	Societe de Transports du Nord Cameroun
STN	Sportovni a Turisticke Nakladatelstvi [*Publishing House for Literature on Sport and Tourism*] (CZ)
Stn..............	Station [*Station*] [*Military map abbreviation World War I*] [*French*] (MTD)
Stn..............	Straten [*Straits*] [*Str*] [*See also*] [*Netherlands*] (NAU)
STN	Studenckie Towarzystwo Naukowe [*Students' Scientific Society*] (POL)
stn	Stukken [*Volumes*] [*Publishing*] [*Netherlands*]
STNA........	Service Technique de la Navigation Arienne [*France*] (PDAA)
st No.........	Old Number (BU)
STNP........	Strojarne Nakupnych Podnikov Bratislava [*Maintenance Shops of Purchasing Enterprises, Bratislava*] (CZ)
st n s	Senior Scientific Associate (BU)
STO	Aero Santos SA de CV [*Mexico*] [*ICAO designator*] (FAAC)
STO	Labor and Defense Council (BU)
Sto	Santo [*Saint*] [*Portuguese*]
Sto	Santo [*Saint*] [*Spanish*]
STO	Savez za Tehnicki Odgoj [*Union for Technical Training*] (YU)
STO	Service du Travail Obligatoire [*French labor force*] [*World War II*]
STO	Soviet Truda i Oborony [*Council of Labor and Defense*] [*1920-1937*] (RU)
STO	Special Theory of Relativity (RU)
STO	State Taxation Office [*Australia*]
STO	State Trading Organization [*Maldives*] (EY)
StO.............	Steuerordnung [*Tax Law*] [*German*] (ILCA)
STO	Stockholm [*Sweden*] [*Airport symbol*] (OAG)
STO	Svobodno Trzasko Ozemlje [*Free Territory of Trieste*] (YU)
STO	Technical Servicing Station (RU)
STOBAVO ...	Stores Baches Haute-Volta
STOC.........	Societe de Transports Oubangui-Cameroun
STOC.........	Societe de Transports Ouest-Centrafricaines [*Bangui*]
STOCA......	Societe Togolaise de Credit Automobile
Stockfl........	Stockfleck [*Spot Caused by Dampness*] [*Publishing*] [*German*]
Stockpkt.....	Stockpunkt [*Solidifying Point*] [*German*] (EG)
stoechiometr ...	Stoechiometrisch [*Stoichiometric*] [*German*] (GCA)
Stoer...........	Stoerung [*Disturbance*] [*German*] (GCA)
stofomsl......	Stofomslag [*Dust Jacket*] [*Publishing*] [*Netherlands*]
STOG	State/Territorial Operational Guidelines [*Australia*]
st ogn..........	Starszy Ogniomistrz [*Battery Sergeant Major*] [*Poland*]

STOK.........	Syndicat de Tajalt Oum Kadiar
stol.............	Stoleczny [*Of the Capitol*] [*Warsaw*] [*Poland*] (POL)
STOL.........	Stoleti [*Century*] (CZ)
STOM	Societe de Transports de l'Ogooue Maritime
STOMP.....	Stamp Out Milk in Plastic [*Australia*]
Ston...........	Station [*Station*] [*Military map abbreviation*] [*French*] (MTD)
stop............	Economic (BU)
STOP.........	Public Freight Transport Association (BU)
STOP.........	Public Transport Enterprise (BU)
STOP.........	Sociedade Tecnica de Obras e Projectos Lda.
STOP.........	Stamp Out Plastics [*Lobbyist*] [*Australia*]
STOP.........	Standard of Limited Application (RU)
STOP.........	Stop the Ocean Pollution [*Australia*]
STOP.........	Stowarzyszenie Techniczne Odlewnikow Polskich [*Polish Foundry Workers' Technical Association*] (POL)
STORA......	Stichting Toegepast Onderzoek Reiniging Afvalwater [*Foundation for Applied Wastewater Research*] [*Research center*] [*Netherlands*] (IRC)
STORES....	Syntactic Tracer Organized Retrospective Enquiry System [*IWIS/TNO*] [*'s-Gravenhage*]
storozh b...	Watch Box [*Topography*] (RU)
storozh v...	Watchtower [*Topography*] (RU)
STOV........	State Theatre of Victoria [*Australia*]
stow..........	Stowarzyszenie [*Association*] (POL)
STP...........	Center of Impact, Mean Point of Impact (RU)
STP...........	Launching Platform (RU)
STP...........	Sao Tome and Principe [*ANSI three-letter standard code*] (CNC)
STP...........	Sentry Post (RU)
STP...........	Sijil Tinggi Pelajaran [*Higher Education Certificate*] (ML)
STP...........	Societes Tunisiennes de Prevoyance
STP...........	Societe Togolaise des Plastiques
STP...........	Splosno Trgovinsko Podjetje [*General Commercial Establishment*] (YU)
STP...........	Steuerpult [*German*] (ADPT)
STP...........	Suomen Tyovaenpuolue [*Finnish Workers' Party*] (WEN)
STPA	Service de Transports Publics Aeriens
STPA	Seychelles Taxpayers and Producers Association
STPA	Statistical Training Programme for Africa [*United Nations*] (EY)
STPB	Singapore Tourist Promotion Board
STPC	Societe des Tanneries et Peausseries du Cameroun
St-P etMiq ...	Saint-Pierre et Miquelon (FLAF)
Stpfl...........	Stammpflanze [*Plant Stem*] [*German*] (GCA)
STPI	Technical Aid and Information Department (RU)
STPL	Sosialistinen Tyovaen ja Pienviljelijain Liitto [*Socialist Workers and Small Holders League*] [*Finland*] (WEN)
St planina...	Balkan Mountains (BU)
STPM	Sijil Tinggi Persekolahan Malaysia [*Malaysia*]
STP-MET ...	Solar-Terrestrial Physics - Meteorology [*International Council of Scientific Unions*]
STPMU	Software-Technologie, Produkt, Markt-Untersuchung [*German*] (ADPT)
STPN........	Societe des Transports Publics de Nouakchott
StPO	Strafprozessordnung [*Code of Criminal Procedure*] [*German*] (EG)
STPP	Sodium Tripolyphosphate (OMWE)
s t/pr	Antitorpedo Net (RU)
st prep	Senior Instructor (BU)
STPRM	Sindicato de Trabajadores Petroleros de la Republica Mexicana [*Mexican Petroleum Workers Union*] (LA)
STPS	Secretaria del Trabajo y Prevision Social [*Labor and Social Security Secretariat*] [*Mexico*] (LA)
STPZK.......	Union of Labor Productive Craftsmen's Cooperatives (BU)
str	Construction (BU)
STR...........	Glow-Discharge Stabilitron Tube (RU)
str	Line (RU)
STR...........	Medical Transport Vessel (RU)
str	Page (RU)
STR...........	Society for Theatre Research (EA)
STR...........	Spesiale Trekkingsreg [*Afrikaans*]
STR...........	Srithepthai Rubber Co. Ltd. [*Thailand*]
Str	Staatsregeling [*Benelux*] (BAS)
STR...........	Standard Telephon und Radio [*Switzerland*] (NITA)
STR...........	Stellair [*France*] [*ICAO designator*] (FAAC)
str	Steradian (RU)
Str	Steuer [*Tax Duty*] [*German*]
Str	Straat [*Street*] [*Netherlands*] (NAU)
Str	Strada [*Street*] [*Italian*]
Str	Strada [*Street*] [*Romanian*]
Str	Straede [*Street*] [*Denmark*]
Str	Straeti [*Street*] [*Icelandic*]
str	Strana [*Page*] [*Publishing Former Czechoslovakia*]
Str	Strasse [*Street*] [*German*] (GPO)
STR...........	Stredni [*Secondary*] (CZ)
STR...........	Streichinstrumente [*Stringed Instruments*] [*Music*]
str	Stretto [*Narrow*] [*Italian*]

str .... Stronica [*Page*] (POL)
STR .... Stuttgart [*Germany*] [*Airport symbol*] (OAG)
str .... Under Construction [*Topography*] (RU)
STRA .... Sound Tape Retailers' Association [*for pirated recordings*] [*Singapore*]
STRACO ... Saudi Transport Services Co. Ltd.
strad .... Passive Voice (RU)
STRAD ..... Stradivarius Violin [*Music*] (DSUE)
Strahl .... Strahlung [*Radiation*] [*German*] (GCA)
strakh .... Insurance (RU)
strapp .... Strappato [*Torn Out*] [*Publishing*] [*Italian*]
STRC .... Scientific, Technical, and Research Commission [*of the OAU*] [*Lagos, Nigeria*] (AF)
STRE .... Telemetering System of Electric Power Consumption (RU)
STREPTO ... Streptomycin [*An antibiotic*] (DSUE)
streszcz .... Streszczenie [*Summary*] [*Poland*]
Streustrahl ... Streustrahlung [*Scattered Radiation*] [*German*] (GCA)
StRG .... Strafregistergesetz [*Criminal Records Law*] [*German*] (EG)
Strg .... Streuung [*Dispersion*] [*German*] (GCA)
STRHA ...... Sindicato de Trabajadores del Ingenio Rio Haina [*Trade Union of Rio Haina Sugar Mill Workers*] [*Dominican Republic*] (LA)
STRI .... Smithsonian Tropical Research Institute [*Panama*] (IRC)
STRI .... Technological Institute of Iceland
STRIDA .... Systeme de Transmission et de Recueil d'Informations de Defense Aerienne [*French*]
STRIDE ..... Science and Technology for Regional Innovation and Development in Europe [*EC*] (ECED)
strieryggb ... Strieryggbind [*Canvas Binding*] [*Publishing Danish/Norwegian*]
STRIKEX .. Strike Exercise [*Navy*] [*NATO*] (NATG)
STRIKFTLANTREPEUR ... Striking Fleet Atlantic Representative in Europe [*NATO*] (NATG)
StRK .... Staatliches Rundfunkkomitee [*State Radio Committee*] [*German*] (EG)
str m .... Building Materials Plant [*Topography*] (RU)
STRM .... Sindicato de Telefonistas de la Republica Mexicana [*Trade Union of Telephone Operators of the Mexican Republic*] (LA)
STRN .... Societe des Transports Routiers du Niger
StRN .... Stoleczna Rada Narodowa [*Warsaw People's Council*] (POL)
STRO .... Scandinavian Tire and Rim Organization (EA)
stroit .... Construction Term (RU)
STROJEXPORT ... Podnik Zahranicniho Obchodu pro Vyvoz Stroju a Strojnich Zarizeni [*Foreign Trade Enterprise for the Export of Machines and Mechanical Equipment*] (CZ)
STROJIMPORT ... Podnik Zahranicniho Obchodu pro Dovoz Stroju a Prumyslovych Zarizeni [*Foreign Trade Enterprise for the Import of Machines and Industrial Installations*] (CZ)
STROMBYuRO ... All-Union Office of the Building Materials Industry (RU)
strommashina ... Machine for the Manufacture of Building Materials (RU)
Stromotdel ... Department of the Building Materials Industry (RU)
Strompromsoyuz ... Building Materials Producers' Union (RU)
Stroybank .. All-Union Bank for the Financing of Capital Investments (RU)
stroybat ...... Construction Battalion (RU)
Stroydetal' ... All-Union Trust for the Manufacture of Structural Parts (RU)
Stroydormash ... Construction and Road Machinery Plant (RU)
Stroygrupa ... Construction Group (BU)
Stroyizdat ... State Publishing House of Construction Literature (RU)
Stroymash ... Construction Machinery Plant (RU)
Stroymashsbyt ... Marketing Administration of the Ministry of Construction and Road Machinery Manufacture, USSR (RU)
Stroymat ..... Construction Materials (BU)
Stroymatmetiz ... State Commercial Enterprise for Construction Materials and Metal Products (BU)
Stroymekhanizatsiya ... Trust of the Administration for the Mechanization of Specialized and Installation Operations of the Ministry of Construction, RSFSR (RU)
Stroymekhzapchast' ... All-Union Office of the Glavstroymekhanizatsiya of the State Industrial Committee for Transportation Construction, USSR (RU)
Stroymontazh ... Trust of the Glavmetallurgmontazh of the Gosmontazhspetsstroy SSSR (RU)
Stroynefteurs ... Administration of Workers' Supply of the Ministry of Construction of Petroleum Industry Establishments, USSR (RU)
Stroyobedinenie ... Construction Trust (BU)
Stroytermoizolyatsiya ... Trust of the Glavteplomontazh of the Gosmontazhspetsstroy SSSR (RU)
stroytrest .... Building Materials Trust (RU)
stroyuch ..... Construction Apprenticeship School (RU)
Stroyvoyenmorizdat ... Publishing House of the Ministry of Construction of Military and Naval Establishments, USSR (RU)
Strpovbr ..... Strogo Poverljivo Broj [*Strictly Confidential Number*] (YU)
Strpovopbr ... Strogo Poverljivo Operativni Broj [*Strictly Confidential Operational Number*] [*Military*] (YU)
STRS .... Starsina [*Master Sergeant*] (CZ)
STRU .... Science and Technology Research Unit [*University of Swaziland*]

Strukt .... Struktur [*Structure*] [*German*] (GCA)
str-vo .... Construction, Construction Site (RU)
strz .... Strzelec [*Rifleman, Gunner*] [*Poland*]
sts .... Coupling, Clutch (RU)
STS .... Hyperfine Structure (RU)
STS .... Medical Transport Vessel (RU)
st s .... Old Style [*Julian calendar*] (RU)
STs .... Random Number (RU)
STS .... Rural Telephone Network (RU)
STS .... Sale Technical School [*Australia*]
STS .... Scottish Tartans Society (EA)
STS .... Service des Telecommunications et de la Signalisation [*French*]
STS .... Servicios Auxiliares de Transportes Aereos [*Brazil*] [*ICAO designator*] (FAAC)
STs .... Silver-Zinc Battery (RU)
STS .... Slezska Tiskova Sluzba [*Silesian Press Service*] (CZ)
STS .... Slovensky Tenisovy Svaz [*Slovak Tennis Association*] (CZ)
STS .... Societe des Transports Sauvage Pere & Fils
STS .... Societe Textile du Senegal
STS .... Societe Togolaise de Siderurgie [*Togo*]
STS .... Societe Toulousaine de Synthese
STS .... Societe Tunisienne du Sucre [*Tunisia*] (IMH)
STS .... Solar Heat Power Plant (RU)
STs .... Somite Center (RU)
STS .... Speicher-Test-steuerung [*German*] (ADPT)
STS .... Spojene Tovarny na Stuhy [*United Ribbon Factories*] (CZ)
STS .... Srednja Tehnicka Skola [*Secondary Technical School*] (YU)
STS .... State All-Union Construction and Installation Trust of Flame Heat Engineering (RU)
STS .... State Travel Service
STS .... Statni Traktorova Stanice [*State Tractor Station*] (CZ)
STS .... Strojni Traktorove Stanice [*Machine Tractor Stations*] (CZ)
STS .... Studencki Teatr Satyryczny [*Students' Satirical Theater*] (POL)
STS .... Suomen Teknillinen Seura [*Engineering Society in Finland*] (SLS)
STSA .... Sub-tropical Seedgrowers' Association [*Australia*]
STsB .... Signalization, Centralization, and Block System (RU)
STsGT ...... All-Union Central Geophysical Trust
st sierz .... Starszy Sierzant [*Company Sergeant Major*] [*Poland*]
st sl .... Active Duty, Field Duty (BU)
stsl .... Old Slavonic (BU)
STsLN .... Aspiring Centrifugal Vane Pump (RU)
STsM .... Center-of-Mass System (RU)
STsM .... Special-Purpose Digital Computer (RU)
STSN .... Societa Toscana di Scienze Naturali [*Italian*] (SLS)
STSO .... Societe des Transporteurs du Senegal Oriental
STSO .... Societe des Transports du Sud-Ouest
STSPS .... Statni Spojova Sluzba [*State Communication Service*] [*Civil defense*] (CZ)
STsS .... Addition Cycle Counter (RU)
sts sp .... Scintillation Spectrometer (RU)
sts spsovp ... Scintillation Coincidence Spectrometer (RU)
st st .... Old Style [*Julian calendar*] (BU)
stst .... Stari Stil [*Old Style*] [*Julian calendar*] (YU)
STsT .... Stereoscopic Color Television (RU)
st strz .... Starszy Strzelec [*Lance-Corporal*] [*Poland*]
STsV .... Antimony-Cesium Vacuum Phototube (RU)
st szer .... Starszy Szeregowy [*Leading Aircraftman*] [*Poland*]
STT .... Air St. Thomas [*ICAO designator*] (FAAC)
STT .... Slobodna Teritorija Trsta [*Free Territory of Trieste*] (YU)
STT .... Societe des Textiles du Tchad
STT .... Societe Tous Transports
STT .... St. Thomas [*Virgin Islands*] [*Airport symbol*]
STT .... Suomen Tietotoimisto [*Finnish News Bureau*] (WEN)
STT .... Syndicat de Travailleurs du Tchad
St-TB .... Stiasny-Taschenbuecher [*Stiasny Notebook*] [*German*]
STT-FNB .. Suomen Tietotoimisto-Finska Notisbyran [*Press agency*] [*Finland*]
STTI .... Societe Tunisienne de Traitement de l'Information [*Tunisia*]
STTK .... Suomen Teknillisten Toimihenkilojarjestojen Keskusliitto [*Finnish Central Federation of Technical Functionaries*] (WEN)
StTO .... Stueckgut-Transport-Ordnung [*Less than Carload (Freight) Transportation Regulations*] [*German*] (EG)
st tov .... Freight Station [*Topography*] (RU)
STTP .... Societe Tchadienne de Travaux Publics
STTs .... Sofia Telephone Exchange (BU)
st-tsa .... Stanitsa, Cossack Village [*Topography*] (RU)
STT-VUJNA ... Slobodna Teritorija Trsta - Vojna Uprava Jugoslovenske Narodne Armije [*Free Territory of Trieste - Military Government of the Yugoslav People's Army*] (YU)
STU .... Sanitary Engineering Facility (RU)
STU .... Sovnarkhoz Technical Specifications (RU)
STU .... Statni Typisacni Ustav [*Research Institute for Standardization*] (CZ)
STU .... St. Lucia Teachers Union (LA)

STU .... Studijni a Typisacni Ustav [*Research Institute for Standardization*] (CZ)

STU .... Styrelsen foer Teknisk Utveckling [*National Swedish Board for Technical Development*] [*Research center*] (IRC)

STU .... Swiss Federation of Trade Unions (EAIO)

STU .... Transportes Aereos Fueguino [*Argentina*] [*ICAO designator*] (FAAC)

STUC........ Seychelles Trade Union Congress

stud............. Studentisch [*Academic*] [*German*]

stud............. Studiosus [*Student*] [*Obsolete*] [*German*]

studbat .... Student Battalion (RU)

STUDES ... Centro Studi per il Progresso della Educazione Sanitaria e del Diritto Sanitario [*Italian*] (SLS)

StudIEE..... Student Member of the South African Institute of Electrical Engineers (AA)

studkom ..... Student Committee (RU)

StudSAIETE ... Student Member of the South African Institute of Electrical Technician Engineers (AA)

STUDSVIK ... Studsvik Energiteknik [*Sweden*] (WND)

Stud VUB .. Studies en Voordrachten-Faculteit der Rechtsgeleerdheid-Vrije Universiteit te B russel [*Belgium*] (BAS)

Stue .... Statue [*Statue*] [*Military map abbreviation World War I*] [*French*] (MTD)

stueck .... Stueckig [*Lumpy*] [*German*] (GCA)

STUF .... Sudan Trade Unions Federation

STUFIT..... Societe Tunisienne Filature Tissage

Stug .... Studiengesellschaft fuer Kohlenstaubfeuerung auf Lokomotiven [*Research Association for Powdered Coal Firing of Locomotives*] [*German*] (EG)

STUK........ Sateilyturvakeskus [*Finnish Center for Radiation and Nuclear Safety*] [*Research center*] (IRC)

Stuka......... Sturzkampfflugzeug [*Dive Bomber*] [*German*]

STUMETAL ... Societe Tunisienne d'Emballages [*Tunisia*] (IMH)

STUMOKA ... Studiekring voor Moderne Kantoortechniek [*Study Group for Modern Office Practice*] [*Netherlands*] (PDAA)

STUNAM ... Sindicato de Trabajadores de la Universidad Autonoma de Mexico [*Trade Union of the National Autonomous University of Mexico*] (LA)

Stupu......... Deutsche Studiengesellschaft fuer Publizistik [*German Students Association for Journalism*] (SLS)

Sturshelkor ... Newspaper Correspondent (BU)

STUSID .... Societe Tuniso-Seoudienne d'Investissement et de Developpement [*Financer of development projects*] [*Tunis, Tunisia*] (MENA)

StUst......... Starkstromunterhaltungsstelle [*High Voltage Maintenance Shop*] [*German*] (EG)

Stuto.......... Stundentonne [*Metric Tons per Hour*] [*German*] (GCA)

STUVA...... Studiengesellschaft fuer Unterirdische Verkehrsanlagen eV [*Study Association for Underground Transportation*] (SLS)

STUVAC ... Study Vacation [*Australia*] [*Slang*] (DSUE)

STV........... Savez za Telesno Vaspitanje [*Federation for Physical Education*] (YU)

STV........... Schweizerischer Technischer Verband [*Swiss Technical Society*] (SLS)

STV........... Schweizer Tonkunstieverein [*Swiss Musicians' Union*]

STV........... Societa Tiro a Volo [*Pigeon-Shooting Association*] [*Italian*]

STV........... Societe de Transports Vergnaud

STV........... Solidaridad de Trabajadores Vascos [*Solidarity of Basque Workers*] [*Spanish*] (WER)

STV........... Southern Aviation Ltd. [*Ghana*] [*ICAO designator*] (FAAC)

StV........... Staatsverlag der DDR [*GDR State Publishing House*] (EG)

StV .... Stellvertretender Vorsitzender [*Deputy Chairman*] [*German*] (EG)

Stv .... Stellvertreter [*Representative*] [*German*] (GCA)

STV........... Svenska Tekniska Vetenskapsakademien i Finland [*Finland*] (SLS)

STV........... Voice-Frequency Ringing Bay (RU)

StVA .... Strafvollzugsanstalt [*Penal Institution*] (WEN)

STVBT ..... Sociedad Torre de Vigia de Biblias e Tratados [*Brazil*] (EAIO)

St VdVUB ... Studies en Voordrachten (Vrije Universiteit te Brussel) [*Belgium*] (BAS)

STVF .... Statens Teknisk-Videnskabelige Forskningsrad [*Danish Council for Scientific and Industrial Research*] [*Research center*] (ERC)

STVH .... Stichting Tegen Vrouwen Handel [*Netherlands*] (EAIO)

StVO......... Strassenverkehrsordnung [*Street Traffic Regulations*] [*German*] (EG)

STVS .... Surinaamse Televisie Stichtig (EY)

StVZO ...... Strassenverkehrszulassungsordnung [*Street Traffic Licensing Regulations*] [*German*] (EG)

STW.......... Starways SA [*Switzerland*] [*ICAO designator*] (FAAC)

stw .... Steenweg [*Netherlands*] (CED)

St W .... Stellungswechsel [*Change of Position*] [*German*] (GCA)

Stw .... Stellwerk [*Signal and Switch Control Tower*] [*German*] (EG)

STW.......... Steuerwerk [*German*] (ADPT)

STW.......... Stichting voor de Technische Wetenschappen [*Netherlands Foundation for Technical Sciences*] [*Research center*] (IRC)

stwg .... Steenweg [*Netherlands*] (CED)

STX............ Aerocharter [*Czechoslovakia*] [*ICAO designator*] (FAAC)

STX............ St. Croix [*Virgin Islands*] [*Airport symbol*]

STY............ Salto [*Uruguay*] [*Airport symbol*] (OAG)

STY............ Soma Tekhnikon Ypiresion [*(Army) Technical Corps*] (GC)

STZ............ High-Voltage Equipment Plant (BU)

STZ............ Low-Voltage Equipment Plant (BU)

STZ............ Outpost Support, Picket (RU)

STZ............ Santa Terezinha [*Brazil*] [*Airport symbol*] (OAG)

STZ............ Severoceske Tukove Zavody [*North Bohemian Fat Rendering Factories (Usti Nad Labem)*] (CZ)

STZ............ Sinarskaya Pipe Plant (RU)

STZ............ Slobodna Trgovinska Zona [*Free Trade Zone*] (YU)

STZ............ Stalingrad Tractor Plant (RU)

St Zj .... Stany Zjednoczone [*United States*] (POL)

St Zjedn .... Stany Zjednoczone [*United States*] [*Poland*]

St z OS...... Stara Zagora Oblast Court (BU)

Su .... Aircraft Designed by P. O. Sukhoy (RU)

SU .... Coal Depot (RU)

SU .... Collection of Laws (RU)

SU .... Concentrated Attack, Concentrated Thrust (RU)

SU .... Construction Administration (BU)

SU .... Construction School (RU)

SU .... Drill Regulations, Drill Manual (RU)

SU .... Point Indicator (RU)

SU .... Reader (RU)

SU .... Savet za Urbanizam [*City Planning Council*] (YU)

SU .... Schnittstellenumsetzer [*German*] (ADPT)

SU .... Schulungsunterlage [*German*] (ADPT)

SU .... Secretariat Unifie [*Unified Secretariat*] [*Of 4th International*] [*French*] (WER)

SU .... Sejm Ustawodawczy [*Sejm (Parliament)*] (POL)

SU .... Selcuk Universitesi [*Selcuk University*] (TU)

SU .... Self-Propelled Gun (RU)

SU .... Senggara Udara [*Air Maintenance*] (ML)

su .... Siehe Unten [*See Below*] [*German*] (GPO)

SU .... Signaler (RU)

SU .... Sindacato Unico [*Confederation of Labor*] [*Trieste*] [*Italian*]

SU .... Sindicato Unitario [*United Syndicate*] [*Trade union*] [*Spain*] (EY)

SU .... Slovansky Ustav [*Slavic Institute (of the Czechoslovak Academy of Sciences)*] (CZ)

SU .... Slovenska Univerzita [*Slovak University*] [*Bratislava*] (CZ)

S-U............. Socjalno-Ubezpieczeniowa Komisja [*Social Insurance Commission*] (POL)

SU .... Sofia University (BU)

Su .... Sormovo Higher-Powered [*Locomotive*] (RU)

SU .... Sosialistisk Ungdom [*Norway*]

SU .... Sowjetunion [*Former USSR*] (EG)

SU .... Special Administration (RU)

SU .... Spojovaci Uzel [*Communications Center*] (CZ)

SU .... Statens Uddannelsesstotte [*Government educational assistance*] [*Denmark*]

SU .... Stationary Installation (RU)

SU .... Statistical Administration (RU)

SU .... Statistical Unit [*UNRISD*] [*United Nations*] (DUND)

SU .... Stati Uniti [*United States*] [*Italian*]

SU .... Stopper (RU)

SU .... Stubicki Ugljenokopi [*Stubica Coal Pits*] [*Tugonica*] (YU)

su............. Sunnuntai(na) [*Finland*]

SU .... Suvorov School [*Military term*] (RU)

su............. Svar Udbedes [*An Answer Is Requested*] [*Denmark*] (GPO)

SU .... Svenska Unescoradet [*Sweden*] (EAIO)

SU .... Sydney University [*Australia*] (ADA)

SU .... Synchronizer (RU)

SU .... Union of Soviet Socialist Republics [*ANSI two-letter standard code*] (CNC)

SU .... Universal Saccharimeter (RU)

s-u............. Versus (BU)

SUA .... Aviation Associates, Inc. [*St. Croix*] [*ICAO designator*] (FAAC)

SUA .... Seamen's Union of Australia

SUA .... Slovensky Ustredny Archiv [*Slovak Central Archives*] (CZ)

SUA .... Sport Universitaire Algerien

SUA .... Statele Unite ale Americii [*United States of America*] (RO)

SUA .... Supply/Utilization Accounts [*FAO*] [*Information service or system United Nations*] (DUND)

SUAA .... Montevideo/Angel S. Adami [*Uruguay*] [*ICAO location identifier*] (ICLI)

SUAB........ Svenska Utvecklingsaktiebolaget [*Swedish Corporation for Development*]

SUAD .... Service d'Utilite Agricole de Developpement

SUAD .... Staf Umum Angkatan Darat [*Army General Staff*] (IN)

SUAE........ Level Shift of Atomic Electrons (RU)

SUAG .... Artigas/Aeropuerto Deptal [*Uruguay*] [*ICAO location identifier*] (ICLI)
SUAIDLA ... Swedish Union of Architects, Interior Designers and Landscape Architects (EAIO)
SUAITELAR ... Fabrica San Jose de Suaita SA [*Colombia*] (COL)
SUAN .... Southeast Asian Universities Agroecosystem Network
SUANP ...... Sindicato Unico de la Administracion Nacional de Puertos [*Single Union of the National Ports Administration*] [*Uruguay*] (LA)
SUARFC ... Sydney University Australian Rules Football Club
SUATEC ... Sociedad Uruguaya de Analisis y Terapia del Compartamiento [*Uruguay*] (EAIO)
suavt .... Coauthor (BU)
SUB .... Slovenske Uholne Bane [*Slovak Coal Mines*] (CZ)
Sub .... Subdivision [*Subdivision*] (CL)
sub .... Subjonctif [*French*] (TPFD)
SUB .... Subtraktion [*German*] (ADPT)
SUB .... Surabaya [*Indonesia*] [*Airport symbol*] (OAG)
SUBACLANT ... Submarine Allied Command, Atlantic [*NATO*] (NATG)
SUBCEDE ... Subcomision de la Comision Especial para Estudiar la Formulacion de Nuevas Medidas de Cooperacion Economicas [*Organizacion de Estados Americanos*] (LAA)
subcut .... Subcutan [*Subcutaneous*] [*German*] (GCA)
SUBE .... Societe d'Utilization des Bois Exotiques
SUBEASTLANT ... Submarine Force, Eastern Atlantic [*NATO*]
SUBI .... Statni Ustredni Banska Inspekce [*Central State Mining Inspection Bureau*] (CZ)
subir .... Collective Noun (BU)
subj .... Subjek [*Subject*] [*Afrikaans*]
subj .... Subjekti [*Subject*] [*Finland*]
subj .... Subjunctive (TPFD)
SUBJ .... Subjunktief [*Subjunctive*] [*Afrikaans*]
subj .... Subjuntivo [*Subjunctive*] [*Portuguese*]
subl .... Sublimiert [*Sublimes*] [*German*]
sublim .... Sublimiert [*Sublimes*] [*German*] (GCA)
Subl P .... Sublimationspunkt [*Sublimation Point*] [*German*] (GCA)
SUBMED ..... Submarines Mediterranean [*NATO*] (NATG)
SUBMEDNOREAST ... Submarines Northeast Mediterranean [*NATO*] (NATG)
SUBNORJ ... Savez Udruzenja Boraca Narodnooslobodilackog Rata Jugoslavije [*Federation of Associations of Veterans of the People's Liberation War of Yugoslavia*] (EAIO)
SUBOL ...... Sociedade Ultramarina de Borracha Limitada [*Acessorios em Borracha*]
subord .... Subordinativa [*Subordinative*] [*Portuguese*]
SU-BP .... Statni Ustav pro Projektovani Uhelnych Dolu a Zavodu Naftoveho Prumyslu, Banske Projekty [*State Institute for the Planning of Coal Mines and Petroleum Industry Establishments, Mining Projects*] (CZ)
SUBP .... Statny Ustav Banskych Projektov [*State Institute of Mining Projects*] (CZ)
SUBR .... Severoural'sk Bauxite Mines (RU)
subs .... Subscribed (SCAC)
subs .... Subscriptions (SCAC)
subs .... Subsidiair [*Benelux*] (BAS)
Subskr .... Subskription [*Subscription*] [*German*]
subskript .... Subskription [*Subscription*] [*Publishing Danish/Norwegian*]
subst .... Substantiivi [*Finland*]
Subst .... Substanz [*Substance*] [*German*]
Subst .... Substitut (FLAF)
Subst .... Substitut du Procureur de la Republique (FLAF)
SubstProc Gen ... Substitut du Procureur General (FLAF)
SUBTACGRU ... Submarine Tactical Group [*NATO*] (NATG)
SUBWESTLANT ... Submarine Force, Western Atlantic Area [*NATO*] (NATG)
SUC .... Savezni Ured za Cene [*Federal Office of Prices*] (YU)
Suc .... Secessor [*Portuguese*]
SUC .... Semi-Unclassified Consumer [*Philippine Standard Commodity Classification Manual*] (IMH)
SUC .... Societe d'Usinage de Cafe
SUC .... Statni Urad pro Veci Cirkevni [*State Bureau for Church Affairs*] (CZ)
suc .... Sucursal [*Branch*] [*Portuguese*]
Suc .... Sucursal [*Branch*] [*Spanish*] [*Business term*]
SUC .... Syndicats Unifies du Congo
SUCA .... Colonia/Aeropuerto Deptal. [*Uruguay*] [*ICAO location identifier*] (ICLI)
SUCAINI .. Sezione Universitarii Club Alpino Italiano [*Italian Universities Alpine Club*]
SUCAM ..... Superintendencia de Campanhas de Saude Publica [*Superintendency for Public Health Campaigns*] [*Brazil*] (LA)
SUCAPITAL ... Suramericana de Capitalizacion SA [*Colombia*] (COL)
Succ .... Successori [*Successors*] [*Italian*]
SUCCI .... Societe d'Urbanisme et de Constructions de la Cote-D'Ivoire
succw .... Succesiewet [*Benelux*] (BAS)

SUCE .... South Universal Commodity Exchange [*Ukraine*] (EY)
SUCEA ...... Sydney University Chemical Engineering Association [*Australia*] (SLS)
SUCEE ...... Socialist Union of Central and Eastern Europe (PD)
SUCESU ... Sociedade de Usuarios de Computadores Eletronicos e Equipmentos Subsidiaros [*Society of Users of Electronic Computers and Ancillary Equipment*] [*Brazil*] (PDAA)
such .... Work, Composition (BU)
suchet .... Combination (BU)
SUCI .... Socialist Unity Center of India [*Political party*] (PPW)
Sucie .... Sucrerie [*Sugar Mill*] [*Military map abbreviation World War I*] [*French*] (MTD)
SUCIN .... Societe d'Urbanisme et de Construction Immobiliere de Nouakchott
SUCO .... Service Universitaire Canadien d'Outre-Mer
SUCO .... Sucrerie du Congo
SUCO .... Suez Oil Co. [*Egypt*]
SUCOMA ... Sugar Corporation of Malawi (AF)
SUCOMAD ... Societe Sucriere de la Cote Est de Madagascar
SUCOMET ... Sociedad Uruguaya de Coque Metalurgico [*Uruguayan Society for Metallurgical Coke*] (LA)
SUCRAF ... Sucrerie et Raffinerie de l'Afrique Centrale
SUCSEL ... Syndicat Unique des Cadres de la Sante et de l'Elevage
SUCT .... Statia de Utilaje Constructii si Transporturi [*Station for Construction and Transportation Equipment*] (RO)
SUCVUT ... Stavebni Ustav Ceskeho Vysokehe Uceni Technickeho [*Construction Center of the Czech Institute of Technology*] (CZ)
sud .... Shipyard [*Topography*] (RU)
SUD .... Srpsko Uceno Drustvo [*Serbian Learned Society*] (YU)
SUD .... Stredoceske Uhelne Doly [*Central Bohemian Coal Mines*] (CZ)
SUD .... Sudan Airways [*ICAO designator*] (FAAC)
SUDAM .... Superintendencia do Desenvolvimento da Amazonia [*Superintendency for the Development of the Amazon Region*] [*Brazil*] (LA)
SUDAP ...... Superintendencia da Agricultura e Producao [*Superintendency of Agriculture and Production*] [*Brazil*] (LA)
SUDBODEN ... Sueddeutsche Bodenkreditbank, Aktiengesellschaft [*South German Land Credit Bank Joint Stock Company*]
SUDCON .. Compania Sudamericana de Consultoria [*Bolivia*] (IMH)
SUDEB ...... Superintendencia da Borracha (DSCA)
SUDECO ... Sugar Development Corporation [*Tanzania*] (AF)
SUDECO ... Superintendencia do Desenvolvimento da Regiao Centro Oeste [*Center-West Development Superintendency*] [*Brazil*] (LA)
SUDEL ...... Groupe Regional pour la Coordination de la Production et du Transport de l'Energie Electrique entre l'Autriche, la Grece, l'Italie et la Yougoslavie (EA)
SUDELPA ... Superintendencia de Desenvolvimento Economico do Litoral Paulista [*Superintendency for Economic Development of Sao Paulo Coast*] [*Brazil*] (LA)
SUDEMA ... Superintendencia do Desenvolvimento do Maranhao [*Brazil*] (DSCA)
SUDENE ... Superintendencia do Desenvolvimento do Nordeste [*Superintendency for Development of the Northeast*] [*Brazil*] (LA)
SUDEPE ... Superintendencia do Desenvolvimento da Pesca [*Superintendency for Development of the Fishing Industry*] [*Brazil*] (LA)
SUDES ...... Syndicat Unique et Democratique des Enseignants du Senegal [*Sole Democratic Trade Union of Senegalese Teachers*] (AF)
SUDESUL ... Superintendencia da Regiao Sul [*Superintendency of the Southern Region*] [*Brazil*] (LA)
SUDHEVEA ... Superintendencia da Borracha [*Superintendency of the Rubber Industry*] [*Brazil*] (LA)
sud-khim .... Forensic Chemistry (RU)
sudkom .... Ship Committee (RU)
sudl .... Suedlich [*Southern*] [*German*]
SUDM .... Samfundet til Udgivelse af Dansk Musik [*Denmark*] (EAIO)
sud med ...... Sudebna Meditsina [*Forensic Medicine*] [*A periodical*] (BU)
sudmedlab ... Forensic Medicine Laboratory (RU)
Sudoimport ... All-Union Association for the Import of Ships (RU)
SUDOP ..... Statni Ustav Dopravniho Projektovani [*State Institute for Transport Design and Planning*] (CZ)
SUDOSAT ... Sudanian Satellite
SUDP .... Sistema Unico de Documentacion de Proyectos [*Central System for Plan Documentation*] [*Cuba*] (LA)
SUDP .... Statny Ustav Dopravneho Projektovania [*State Institute for Transportation Projects*] [*Bratislava*] (CZ)
Sud pr .... Judicial Practice of the Supreme Court of the USSR (RU)
sudprom ..... Shipbuilding Industry (RU)
Sudpromgiz ... State All-Union Publishing House of the Shipbuilding Industry (RU)
Sudpromizdat ... State Publishing House of Literature for the Shipbuilding Industry (RU)
SUDU .... Durazno/Santa Bernardina Internacional de Alternativa [*Uruguay*] [*ICAO location identifier*] (ICLI)

sudurzh ...... Content (BU)
SUDZ .... Statni Urad Duchodoveho Zabezpeceni [*State Pension Office*] (CZ)
SUDZUCKER ... Sueddeutsche Zucker-Aktiengesellschaft [*South German Sugar Joint Stock Company*]
SUE .... Aerolineas del Sureste SA [*Mexico*] [*ICAO designator*] (FAAC)
SUE .... Carbon Disulfide Emulsion (RU)
SUE .... Sahara Upwelling Experiment [*US, Spain*] (MSC)
SUEE .... Service Universitaire pour Etudiants Etrangers [*French*]
SUEL .... Syndicat Unifie des Enseignants Laics [*Unified Union of Lay Teachers*] [*Senegal*] (AF)
SUEO .... Montevideo [*Uruguay*] [*ICAO location identifier*] (ICLI)
SUEP .... Savet za Uzajamnu Ekonomsku Pomoc [*Council for Mutual Economic Aid*] [*Moscow East European Economic Integration*] (YU)
SUERF ...... Societe Universitaire Europeenne de Recherches Financieres (EAIO)
SUF .... Lametia-Terme [*Italy*] [*Airport symbol*] (OAG)
SUF .... Shimonoseki University of Fisheries [*Japan*] (MSC)
SuF .... Sicherungs- und Fermeldewesen [*Protective Devices and Telecommunications*] [*German*] (EG)
SUF .... Socialist Unity Front [*Romania*] [*Political party*] (PPW)
SUF .... Sosialistisk Ungdomsforbund [*Socialist Youth Federation*] [*Norway*] (WEN)
suf. .... Sufixo [*Suffix*] [*Portuguese*]
SUF .... Sunflower Airlines Ltd. [*Fiji*] [*ICAO designator*] (FAAC)
SUF .... Swaziland United Front
suff .... Suffiksi, Loppuliite [*Suffix*] [*Finland*]
SUFOI ...... Scandinavisk UFO Information [*Scandinavian UFO Information*] [*Denmark*] (EAIO)
SUFRAMA ... Superintendencia da Zona Franca de Manaus [*Superintendency of the Manaus Free Trade Zone*] [*Brazil*] (LA)
SUG .... Saha Union Group [*Thailand*]
SUG .... Surigao [*Philippines*] [*Airport symbol*] (OAG)
SUG .... Universal Welding Generator (RU)
SUGI .... Savezna Uprava za Geoloska Istrazivanja [*Federal Administration of Geological Research*] (YU)
SUGMS ..... Northern Administration of the Hydrometeorological Service (RU)
SUGRES ... Sredneural'sk State Regional Electric Power Plant (RU)
SUGS .... University of Sydney Students' Geological Society [*Australia*]
SUGU .... Sindicato Unico de Gastronomicos Uruguayos [*Single Union of Food and Restaurant Workers*] [*Uruguay*] (LA)
SUGVF ...... Northern Territorial Administration of the Civil Air Fleet (RU)
SuH .... Siemens und Halske (EG)
SUH .... Statni Ustav Hydrologicky T. G. Masaryka [*T. G. Masaryk State Hydrological Institute*] (CZ)
SUHR .... Society for Underwater Historical Research [*Australia*]
SUHS .... Savezna Uprava Hidrometeoroloske Sluzbe [*Federal Administration of the Hydrometeorological Service*] (YU)
SUI .... Bundesamt fur Militarflugplatze [*Switzerland*] [*ICAO designator*] (FAAC)
SUIN .... Union of Teachers-Internationalists (RU)
SU-IS .... Su Isciler Sendikasi [*Water Workers' Union (Guzelyurt)*] [*Turkish Cypriot*] (GC)
Su-Is .... Turkiye Baraj, Enerji, Su, ve Sulama Iscileri Sendikasi [*Turkish Dam, Energy, Water, and Irrigation Workers' Union*] (TU)
SUISA ...... Schweizerische Gesellschaft fuer die Rechte der Urheber Musikalischer Werke [*Swiss Society for the Rights of Authors of Musical Works*] (SLS)
suiv .... Suivant [*or Suivante*] [*Following*] [*French*]
SUJ .... Satu Mare [*Romania*] [*Airport symbol*] (OAG)
suj .... Sujeito [*Subject*] [*Portuguese*]
SUJNA ...... Sanitetska Uprave Jugoslovenske Narodne Armije [*Medical Administration of the Yugoslav People's Army*] (YU)
SUK .... Savez Ugostiteljskih Komora Federativna Narodna Republika Jugoslavija [*Yugoslav Federation of Chambers of the Hotel and Catering Trade*] (YU)
SUK .... Sreska Ugostiteljska Komora [*District Chamber of the Hotel and Catering Trade*] (YU)
SUK .... Srpski Udarni Korpus [*Serbian Shock Corps*] [*World War II*] (YU)
SUK .... Sun Compass (RU)
suk .... Woolen Mill [*Topography*] (RU)
sukh .... Dry [*Topography*] (RU)
Sukhumges ... Sukhumi Regional Hydroelectric Power Plant (RU)
SUKK .... Slovenske Ustredie Kniznej Kultury [*Slovak Center for Book Culture*] (CZ)
SUKKJ ...... Savez Udruzenja za Krivicno Pravo i Kriminolgiju Jugoslavije [*Former Yugoslavia*] (SLS)
SUKL .... Statni Ustav pro Kontrolu Leciv [*State Control Institute for Pharmaceutical Products*] (CZ)
SUKOVS ... Streekraad vir die Uitvoerende Kunste in die OVS [*Afrikaans*]
SUKP .... Sekretarijat za Urbanizam i Komunalne Poslove [*Secretariat of City Planning and Communal Affairs*] (YU)
sukr .... Abridged, Abbreviated (BU)

SUL .... Secretariado Uruguayo de la Lana [*Uruguay*]
SUL .... Singapore Union Line (DS)
SUL .... Special Unnumbered License [*Ministry of Trade*] [*Ghana*]
SUL .... Sui [*Pakistan*] [*Airport symbol*] (OAG)
Sul .... Sulanmasi [*Irrigation*] (TU)
SULASOL ... Suomen Laulajain ja Soittajain Liitto [*Finland*] (EAIO)
SULC .... Sydney University Liberal Club [*Australia*]
SULF .... Sveriges Universitetslararforbund [*Sweden*] (EAIO)
SULFACIDOS ... Compania de Productos Quimicos Nacionales, SA [*Colombia*] (DSCA)
Sulfonier .... Sulfonierung [*Sulfonation*] [*German*] (GCA)
Sulfurier .... Sulfurierung [*Sulfuration*] [*German*] (GCA)
SULRA ..... Sulawesi Tenggara [*Southeast Sulawesi*] (IN)
SULS .... Maldonado/Base Aeronaval C/C Carlos A. Curbelo [*Uruguay*] [*ICAO location identifier*] (ICLI)
SULSEL .... Sulawesi Selatan [*South Sulawesi*] (IN)
SULTAN ... Subscriber Line Test Access Network [*Australia*]
SULTENG ... Sulawesi Tengah [*Central Sulawesi*] (IN)
SULTU ...... Swiss Union of Liberal Trade Unions (EAIO)
SULUT ...... Slovenske Ustredie Ludovej Umeleckej Tvorivosti [*Slovak Folk Arts Center*] (CZ)
SULUT ...... Sulawesi Utara [*North Sulawesi*] (IN)
SUM .... Save Uganda Movement (AF)
SUM .... Sea Level Recorder (RU)
SUM .... Socialist Unionist Movement [*Al Haraka at Tawhidiyya al Ishtirakiyya*] [*Syria*] [*Political party*] (PPW)
SUM .... Statni Ustav Meteorologicky [*State Meteorological Institute*] (CZ)
SUM .... Sudan United Mission
SUM .... Sulfonated Vegetable Oil (RU)
Sum .... Sumatra
sum .... Summitates [*Plant Tops*] [*Pharmacy*]
SUM .... Szczecinski Urzad Morski [*Szczecin (Stettin) Maritime Office*] (POL)
SUMAC ..... Sydney University Macromolecular Analysis Centre [*Australia*]
SUMAS ..... Su Makinalari Sanayii Kollektif Sirketi [*Water Pump Industry Corporation*] [*Mersin*] (TU)
SUMATEC ... Sociedad Colombo-Sueca de Maquinaria y Tecnica Ltda. [*Colombia*] (COL)
SUMATEX ... Sud-Madagascar Textile
SUMBAR ... Sumatera Barat [*West Sumatra*] (IN)
SUMC .... Sociedad Uruguaya de Musica Contemporanea [*Uruguay*] (EAIO)
SUMCE ..... Sistema Unificado de Maquinas Computadoras Electronicas [*Unified Electronic Computer System*] [*Cuba*] (LA)
SUMDS ..... Scandinavian Union of Museums Danish Section [*Denmark*] (EAIO)
SUME .... Mercedes/Ricardo de Tomasi [*Uruguay*] [*ICAO location identifier*] (ICLI)
SUMED ..... Suez-Mediterranean [*Pipeline*] [*Egypt*] (ME)
SUMMA ... Sociedad Umana Moreno [*Colombia*] (COL)
SUMO .... Melo/Aeropuerto Deptal de Cerro Largo [*Uruguay*] [*ICAO location identifier*] (ICLI)
SUMOC .... Superintendencia da Moeda e do Credito [*Superintendency of Money and Credit*] [*Brazil*] (LA)
SUMU .... Montevideo/Carrasco Internacional [*Uruguay*] [*ICAO location identifier*] (ICLI)
SUMUT .... Sumatera Utara [*North Sumatra*] (IN)
SUMZ .... Sredneural'sk Copper Smelting Plant (RU)
SUN .... Antillana de Nevegacion Aerea SA [*Dominican Republic*] [*ICAO designator*] (FAAC)
SUN .... Service des Urgences de Nuit
SUN .... Sofia School Board (BU)
Sun .... Sunday (EECI)
SUN .... Union of Soviet Socialist Republics [*ANSI three-letter standard code*] (CNC)
SUNA .... Sudan [*or Sudanese*] News Agency (AF)
SUNAB ..... Sucrerie Nationale du Beth [*Morocco*]
SUNAB ..... Superintendencia Nacional de Abastecimento [*National Superintendency of Supplies*] [*Brazil*] (LA)
SUNACAS ... Sucrerie Nationale de Cannes du Sebou [*Morocco*]
SUNAG ..... Sucreries Nationales du Gharb [*Morocco*]
SUNAMAM ... Superintendencia Nacional de Marinha Mercante [*National Merchant Marine Superintendency*] [*Rio De Janeiro, Brazil*] (LA)
SUNAT ..... Scandinavian Union for Non-Alcoholic Traffic (EA)
SUNCA ..... Sindicato Unico Nacional de la Construccion y Anexos (Afines) [*National Single Union of Construction and Related Workers*] [*Uruguay*] (LA)
SUNET ...... [*The*] Swedish University Network (TNIG)
SUNFED ... Special United Nations Fund for Economic Development
SUNI .... Southern Universities Nuclear Institute [*South Africa*] (PDAA)
SUNKLO .. Suomen Naytelmakirjailijaliitto [*Finland*] (EAIO)
SUNTM .... Sindicato Unico Nacional del Transporte Maritimo [*Single Union of Marine Transport Workers*] [*Uruguay*] (LA)
SUO .... Saakoliikkeiden Oy [*Manufacturer and wholesaler of electro-technical products*] [*Finland*]

suom.......... Suomalainen [*Finland*]
suom.......... Suomentanut [*Finland*]
SUOPO..... Suojelupoliisi [*Security Police*] [*Finland*]   (WEN)
SUP........... Aerosuper AS de CV [*Mexico*] [*ICAO designator*]   (FAAC)
SUP........... Control Station for Periodically Working Oil Wells   (RU)
SUP........... Sabah United Party [*Malaysia*] [*Political party*]
SUP........... Savezna Uprava Prihoda (DSPF) [*Federal Revenue Administration*]   (YU)
SUP........... Savezna Uprava za Patente [*Federal Patents Administration*]   (YU)
SUP........... Savezna Uprava za Puteve [*Federal Roads Administration*]   (YU)
SUP........... Savez Udruzenja Pravnika [*Union of Lawyers' Associations*]   (YU)
SUP........... Savjet za Unutrasnje Poslove [*Internal Affairs Council*]   (YU)
SUP........... Sekretarijat za Unutrasnje Poslove [*Secretariat of Internal Affairs*]   (YU)
SUP........... Somali United Party
SUP........... Statni Urad Planovaci [*State Planning Office*]   (CZ)
SUP........... Stereo Deflection and Parallax Meter   (RU)
SUP........... Student Unification Party [*Liberia*]   (AF)
sup........... Superieur [*Upper*] [*French*]
Sup........... Superior [*German*]
sup........... Superior [*Upper*] [*Publishing*] [*Spanish*]
sup........... Superiore [*Upper*] [*Publishing*] [*Italian*]
SUP........... Superlatief [*Superlative*] [*Afrikaans*]
sup........... Superlativo [*Superlative*] [*Portuguese*]
sup........... Suplica [*Supplication*] [*Spanish*]
sup........... Supplement [*Publishing*] [*French*]
Sup........... Supraphon [*Record label*] [*Former Czechoslovakia*]
SUP........... Sydney University Press [*Australia*]   (ADA)
SUPA........ Sindicato Unido de Portuarios Argentinos [*United Argentine Port Workers Union*]   (LA)
SUPA........ Sydney University Pharmacy Association [*Australia*]
SUPARCO ... Pakistan Space and Upper Atmosphere Research Commission [*Research center*]   (IRC)
SUPARCO ... Space and Upper Atmosphere Research Committee [*Pakistan*]   (PDAA)
SUPE........ Punta Del Este/Aeropuerto Deptal de Maldonado [*Uruguay*] [*ICAO location identifier*]   (ICLI)
SUPE........ Sindicato Unido de Petroleros del Estado [*Union of State Petroleum Workers*] [*Argentina*]   (LA)
Supelec..... Ecole Superieure d'Electricite [*Electricity College*] [*France*]   (WED)
SUPELSA ... Suramericana de Peliculas Sociedad Anonima [*Colombia*]   (COL)
SUPER...... Superannuation Pension [*Australia*]   (DSUE)
super .... Superieur [*Upper*] [*French*]
SUPERCOP ... Superintendencia Nacional de Cooperativas [*Colombia*]   (DSCA)
superl .... Superlatif [*French*]   (TPFD)
superl .... Superlatiivi [*Superlative*] [*Finland*]
superl .... Superlative   (TPFD)
superl .... Superlativo [*Superlative*] [*Portuguese*]
SUPERSER ... Suramericana de Servicios y Perforaciones SA [*Colombia*]   (COL)
supertte ...... Superintendente [*Superintendent*] [*Spanish*]
SUPEX...... Superintendencia dos Contratos de Exploracao [*Superintendency of Exploration Contracts*] [*Of PETROBRAS*] [*Brazil*]   (LA)
SUPJ .... Savez Udruzenja Pravnika Jugoslavije [*Federation of Lawyers' Associations of Yugoslavia*]   (YU)
supl........... Suplemento [*Supplement*] [*Portuguese*]
SUPLO...... Scottish Union of Power Loom Overlookers   (DCTA)
suplte......... Suplente [*Substituting*] [*Spanish*]
SUPOBU... Usines de Poissons du Burundi
SUPOM .... Stavebni Urad pro Obnovu Mesta [*City Reconstruction Office*]   (CZ)
SUPP .... Sarawak United People's Party [*Malaysia*] [*Political party*]   (PPW)
suppl.......... Supplement [*Publishing*] [*Danish/Norwegian*]
suppl.......... Supplement [*Publishing*] [*Netherlands*]
suppl.......... Supplement [*Publishing*] [*French*]
Suppl......... Supplement [*Publishing*] [*German*]
suppl.......... Supplement [*Publishing*] [*Sweden*]
SUPPOP ... Statni Ustav Pamatkove Pece a Ochrany Prirody [*State Institute for Care of Historical Monuments and Nature Conservation*]   (CZ)
SUPR........ Special Unit on Palestinian Rights [*United Nations (already exists in GUS II database)*]
SUPR........ Switch Starting Control Relay   (RU)
SUPRA ..... Superintendencia da Reforma Agraria [*Superintendency for Agrarian Reform*] [*Brazil*]   (LAA)
SUPRA ...... Superintendencia de Planejamento da Reforma Agraria [*Superintendency of Agrarian Reform Planning*] [*Brazil*]   (LA)

SUPRA...... Superintendencia para la Reforma Agraria [*Superintendency for Agrarian Reform*] [*Cuba*]   (LA)
SUPRA...... Sydney University Postgraduate Representative Association [*Australia*]
SUPSAN ... Motor Supaplari Sanayii ve Ticareti AS [*Motor Valves Industry and Trade Corp.*]   (TU)
SUPSFNRJ ... Savez Udruzenja Pravoslavnog Svestenstva Federativna Narodna Republika Jugoslavija [*Federation of Orthodox Clergy Associations of Yugoslavia*]   (YU)
Supt........... Superintendent [*Superintendent*] [*Afrikaans*]
supte.......... Suplicante [*Supplicant*] [*Spanish*]
SUPU .... Paysandu/Aeropuerto Deptal [*Uruguay*] [*ICAO location identifier*]   (ICLI)
SUPV........ Savezna Uprava za Poslove Veterinarstva [*Federal Veterinary Service Administration*]   (YU)
SUR .... Collection of Laws and Decrees of the Workers' and Peasants' Government   (RU)
SUR .... Sophia University of Rome [*Italian*]   (SLS)
SUR .... Surinam [*ANSI three-letter standard code*]   (CNC)
SUR .... Sydney University Regiment [*Australia*]
SURA .... Shan United Revolutionary Army [*Myanmar*]   (PD)
SURALCO ... Surinam Aluminium Co.
Sured......... Coeditor   (BU)
SURF........ Compagnie des Moyens de Surface Adaptes a l'Ocean [*French*]   (MSC)
surg .... Surgery   (TPFD)
SURGE...... SEASAT [*Sea Satellite*] Users Group of Europe   (MSC)
SURGELENMER ... Societe Ivoirienne de Peche et de Congelation en Mer
SURGEL-IVOIRE ... Societe Ivoirienne de Commerce des Produits Alimentaires Surgele's
Surg LtCdr ... Surgeon Lieutenant-Commander [*British military*]
Surgo.......... Surgidero [*Anchorage, Roadstead*] [*Spanish*]   (NAU)
SURIF .... Sukamandi Research Institute for Food Crops [*Indonesia*] [*Research center*]   (IRC)
surj .... Surjet [*Knitting*] [*French*]   (BARN)
SURP........ Siberian Administration of Riverways   (RU)
SURP........ Statni Ustav pro Rajonove Planovani [*State Institute for Regional Planning*]   (CZ)
SURSAN ... Superintendencia de Urbanizacao e Saneamento [*Sanitation and Urbanization Superintendency*] [*Rio De Janeiro, Brazil*]   (LAA)
SURV........ Rivera/Aeropuerto Deptal [*Uruguay*] [*ICAO location identifier*]   (ICLI)
surv........... Surveillant [*Overseer*] [*French*]
SUS........... (Motor) sa Unutrasnjim Sagorevanjem [*Internal Combustion Engine*]   (YU)
SUS........... Samband Ungra Sjalfstaedismanna [*National Youth Organization of the Independence Party*] [*Iceland*] [*Political party*]   (EAIO)
SUS........... Severocesky Uhelny Syndikat [*North Bohemian Coal Syndicate*]   (CZ)
SUS........... Statni Urad Statistacky [*State Statistical Office*]   (CZ)
SUS........... Sun-Air of Scandinavia AS [*Denmark*] [*ICAO designator*]   (FAAC)
SUS........... Suomalais-Ugrilainen Seura [*Finland*]   (SLS)
SUSAM..... Superintendencia do Servico Medico ao Amazonia [*Superintendency for Medical Service to the Amazon Region*] [*Brazil*]   (LA)
SUScA .... Sydney University Science Association [*Australia*]
SUSDP...... Standard for the Uniform Scheduling of Drugs and Poisons [*National Health and Medical Research Council*] [*Australia*]
SUSEME .. Superintendencia de Servicos Medicos [*Superintendency of Medical Services*] [*Brazil*]   (LA)
SUSEP....... Superintendencia de Seguros Privados [*Superintendency of Private Insurance*] [*Brazil*]   (LA)
SUSGA ...... University of Sydney Students' Geological Society [*Australia*]
sush........... Dryer, Grain Dryer [*Topography*]   (RU)
sushch .... Noun   (RU)
susht.......... Noun [*Grammar*]   (BU)
SUSI .... Sydney University Stellar Interferometer [*Australia*]
SUSIPE..... Superintendencia do Sistema Penitenciario [*Superintendency of the Penitentiary System*] [*Brazil*]   (LA)
SUSO........ Salto/Aeropuerto Deptal [*Uruguay*] [*ICAO location identifier*]   (ICLI)
Susp .... Pont Suspendu [*Suspension Bridge*] [*Military map abbreviation World War I*] [*French*]   (MTD)
Suspens...... Suspension [*German*]   (GCA)
SUSR........ Slovenska Ustredna Sportova Rada [*Slovak Central Sports Council*]   (CZ)
SUSREP.... Senior United States Representative to Defense Production Board [*NATO*]   (NATG)
sust........... Compiled By   (BU)
SUSZ........ Statni Urad Socialnihe Zabezpeceni [*State Social Security Office*]   (CZ)
sut............. Day, Twenty-Four Hours   (RU)

SUT .... Sandvik-Universal Tube GmbH [*A company shared by Federal Republic of Germany, the United States of America and France*] (PDAA)

SUT .... Sociedade Unificada de Tabacos de Angola [*Tobacco product enterprise*] [*Luanda, Angola*]

SUT .... Societe d'Urbanisation du Tchad

SUT .... Society for Underwater Technology (EA)

SUT .... Statia de Utilaje Transport [*Transportation Equipment Station*] (RO)

SUT .... Statni Ustav Tesnopisny [*State Stenographic Institute*] (CZ)

SUT .... Swedish Union of Tenants (EAIO)

SUT .... Swinburne University of Technology [*Australia*]

SUTA........ La Sucrerie du Tadla [*Morocco*]

SUTB........ Tacuarembo [*Uruguay*] [*ICAO location identifier*] (ICLI)

SUTC........ Sindicato Unico de Trabajadores de Coltejer [*Coltejer Workers Union*] [*Colorado*] (LA)

SUTC........ Sindicato Unico de Trabajadores de la Compania Colombiana de Tejidos [*Sole Trade Union of Colombian Textile Company Workers*] (LA)

SUTC........ Sindicato Union de Trabajadores de la Construccion [*United Trade Union of Construction Workers*] [*El Salvador*] (LA)

SUTEIN .... Slovensky Ustav pre Technicke a Ekonomicke Informacie [*Slovak Institute for Technical and Economic Information*] (CZ)

SUTEP ...... Sindicato Unico de Trabajadores de Espectaculos Publicos [*National Public Entertainment Workers Union*] [*Argentina*] (LA)

SUTEP ...... Sindicato Unico de Trabajadores de la Ensenanza [*Single Union of Education Workers*] [*Peru*] (LA)

SUTERM .. Sindicato Unico de Trabajadores Electricistas de la Republica Mexicana [*Mexican Electrical Workers Union*] (LA)

SUTHD ..... Slovensky Ustav pre Technicku a Hospodarsku Dokumentaciu [*Slovak Institute for Technical and Economic Documentation*] (CZ)

SUTIC .... Sindicato Unico de Trabajadores de la Industria de la Carne Similares y Conexos de la Republica Mexicana [*Mexico*] (EAIO)

SUTIN....... Sindicato Unico de Trabajadores de la Industria Nuclear [*Sole Trade Union of Nuclear Industry Workers*] [*Mexico*] (LA)

SUTINEN ... Sindicato Unico de Trabajadores del Instituto Nacional de Energia Nuclear [*National Nuclear Energy Institute Workers Union*] [*Mexico*] (LA)

SUTM .... Sindicato Unico del Transporte Maritimo [*Single Union of Maritime Transport*] [*Uruguay*] (LA)

sutr .... Collaborator, Collaboration, Collaborated (BU)

SUTR........ Treinta Y Tres [*Uruguay*] [*ICAO location identifier*] (ICLI)

SUTRA...... Sindicato Unico de Trabajadores [*Sole Trade Union of Workers*] [*Nicaragua*] (LA)

SUTRADO ... Sindicato Unico de Trabajadores Docentes [*Single Union of Educational Workers*] [*Venezuela*] (LA)

SUTRAFADO ... Sindicato Unido de Trabajadores de Falconbridge [*United Trade Union of Falconbridge Workers*] [*Dominican Republic*] (LA)

SUTRASFCO ... Sindicato Unificado de Trabajadores de la Standard Fruit Co. [*Unified Union of Standard Fruit Company Workers*] [*Honduras*] (LA)

SUTU .... Universal Telephone Repeater Bay (RU)

SUTV......... Statni Urad pro Telesnou Vychovu [*State Office for Physical Education*] (CZ)

SUTVS ...... Statni Urad pro Telesnou Vychovu a Sport [*State Office for Physical Education and Sports*] (CZ)

SUUP .... Savezna Uprava za Unapredenje Proizvodnje [*Federal Administration of Production Development*] (YU)

SUV .... Code Command System (RU)

SUV .... Slovensky Ustredny Vybor [*Slovak Central Committee*] (CZ)

SUV .... Soldados Unidos Vencerao [*Soldiers United Will Win*] [*Portuguese*] (WER)

SUV .... Suva [*Fiji*] [*Airport symbol*] (OAG)

Suv .... Suvremennik [*Contemporary*] [*A periodical*] (BU)

SUV .... Troop Control System (RU)

SUV .... Water Level Recorder (RU)

SUVA .... Schweizerische Unfallversicherungsanstalt [*Swiss Accident Insurance Institute*]

SUVALE ... Superintendencia do Vale do Sao Francisco [*Brazil*] (DSCA)

SUVESS.... Syndicat Unique Voltaique des Enseignants du Secondaire et du Superieur [*Sole Voltan Union of Teachers of Secondary and Higher Education*] (AF)

SUVP........ Statni Urad pro Valecne Poskozence [*State Office for Victims of War*] (CZ)

Suvrem ...... Suvremennik [*Contemporary*] [*A periodical*] (BU)

suvurshprerab ... Completely Revised (BU)

SUW .... Spoldzielnia Uslugowo-Wytworcza [*Production-and-Service Cooperative*] (POL)

SUWA ...... Sydney University Women's Association [*Australia*]

SUWU .... Sydney University Women's Union [*Australia*]

SUY .... Aerial Surveys (1980) Ltd. [*New Zealand*] [*ICAO designator*] (FAAC)

SUY .... Sudureyri [*Iceland*] [*Airport symbol*] (OAG)

SUZ .... Control and Safety Rods (RU)

SUZ .... Control and Shielding System [*Nuclear energy*] (BU)

SUZ .... Savezni Ustavni Zakon [*Federal Constitutional Law*] (YU)

SUZ .... Suria [*Papua New Guinea*] [*Airport symbol*] (OAG)

SUZB........ Savezna Uprava za Zastitu Bilja [*Federal Administration for Plant Protection*] (YU)

SUZOR ..... Savezni Ured za Osiguranje Radnika [*Federal Workers Insurance Office*] (YU)

SUZOR ..... Sredisni Ured za Osiguranje Radnika [*Central Office for Workers Insurance*] (YU)

SV .... Altitude Indicator (RU)

sv .... Bundle (RU)

sv .... Candle (RU)

SV .... El Salvador [*ANSI two-letter standard code*] (CNC)

SV .... Flash Ranging [*Artillery*] (RU)

sv .... Installment, Fascicule (BU)

SV .... Liaison Aircraft (RU)

sv .... Mean Time (RU)

SV .... Medical Platoon (RU)

SV .... Medium-Frequency-Wave (RU)

SV .... Medium Waves (BU)

SV .... Northeast, Northeastern (RU)

sv .... Over, Beyond (RU)

sv .... Rifle Platoon (RU)

sv .... Saint (RU)

SV .... Samana Vuonna [*Same Year*] [*Finland*] (GPO)

SV .... Samenwerkende Vennootschap [*Cooperative*] (IMH)

sv .... Sans Valeur [*Worthless*] [*French*]

SV .... Savezno Vece [*Federal Council*] (YU)

SV .... Savona [*Car registration plates*] [*Italian*]

SV .... Schweizerische Volkspartei [*Swiss People's Party*] [*Political party*]

SV .... Sciences et Voyages

SV .... Sdruzeni Vytvarniku [*Creative Artists' Association*] (CZ)

SV .... Sede Vacante [*Portuguese*]

SV .... Selbst-Verlag [*Published by the Author*] [*German*]

SV .... Selbstverwaltung [*Autonomy*] [*German*] (GCA)

SV .... Selenium Rectifier (RU)

SV .... Self-Excitation (RU)

SV .... Semiautomatic Rifle (RU)

sv .... Severovychod [*Northeast*] (CZ)

sv .... Severo-Vzhod [*Northeast*] (YU)

SV .... Signoria Vostra [*Your Lordship*] [*Italian*]

SV .... Silvercraft SpA [*Italy*] [*ICAO aircraft manufacturer identifier*] (ICAO)

SV .... Sleeping Car (RU)

SV .... Slovensky Vybor [*Slovak Committee*] (CZ)

SV .... Sociale Verzekeringsgids [*Benelux*] (BAS)

SV .... Solenoid Valve (RU)

SV .... Sosialistisk Valgforbund [*Socialist Electoral Alliance*] [*Norway*] [*Political party*] (PPE)

SV .... Sosialistisk Venstreparti [*Socialist Left Party*] [*Norway*] [*Political party*] (PPE)

SV .... Sotavento [*Away from the Wind; Leeward*] [*Portuguese*]

SV .... Sovetskoe Vostokovedenie

SV .... Soviet Oriental Studies

SV .... Sozialversicherung [*Social Insurance*] [*German*] (EG)

SV .... Spolek Vytvarniku [*Creative Artists' Association*] (CZ)

SV .... Sredstva Veze [*Communications Equipment*] [*Army*] (YU)

SV .... Stanoviste Velitelstvi [*Command Post*] (CZ)

SV .... Stores Victualling [*Royal Australian Navy*]

SV .... Stravovaci Vybor [*Food Supply Committee*] (CZ)

SV .... Stredoslovenske Vydavatelstvo [*Central Slovakia Publishing House*] (CZ)

Sv .... Suceava [*Suceava*] (RO)

sv .... Svajci [*Switzerland*] (HU)

sv .... Svazek [*Volume*] (CZ)

sv .... Sved [*Swedish*] (HU)

sv .... Svensk [*Swedish*] [*Sweden*]

sv .... Svetac [*Saint*] [*Commonwealth of Independent States*] (EECI)

SV .... Svoboda [*Liberty*] [*A periodical*] (BU)

Sv .... Vertical Displacement [*Artillery*] (RU)

Sv .... Wetboek van Strafvordering [*Benelux*] (BAS)

sv .... Wind Speed (RU)

SVA .... Communicate to All Addresses [*Telegraphy*] (RU)

Sva .... Liaison with the Attaches (BU)

SVA .... Ringing Signal Set (RU)

SVA .... Saudi Arabian Airlines [*ICAO designator*] (FAAC)

SVA .... Schiffbau-Versuchsanstalt [*Shipbuilding Research Institute*] [*German*] (EG)

SVA .... Schweizerische Vereinigung fuer Atomenergie [*Swiss Association for Atomic Energy*] (SLS)

SVA .... Service de Vente des Alcools [*Alcohol Sales Department*] [*Cambodia*] (CL)

sva .... Soviel Als [*As Many As*] [*German*]

SVA .... Sovjetska Vojna Administracija [*Soviet Military Administration*] (YU)

SVA .... Sozialversicherungsanstalt [*Social Insurance Agency*] [*German*] (EG)

SVA .... Statens Veterinaermedicinska Anstalt [*National Veterinary Institute*] [*Sweden*] (ARC)

SVA .... Statni Vyrobny Autodilu [*State Plants for Automobile Parts*] (CZ)

SVA .... Strafvollzugsanstalt [*Penal Institution*] (WEN)

SVA .... Strategic Air Command [*USA*] (RU)

SVA .... Surface Utile Agricole [*Algeria*]

SVAC........ Acarigua, Portuguesa [*Venezuela*] [*ICAO location identifier*] (ICLI)

SVADP...... Shire Valley Agricultural Development

SVAF .... South Vietnamese Armed Forces (VNW)

SVAFVS.... Swedish Volunteers of the Anti-Fascist War in Spain (EAIO)

SVAG........ Soviet Military Administration in Germany (RU)

SVAI .... Service de Vente des Alcools Importes [*Imported Alcohol Sales Department*] [*Cambodia*] (CL)

SVAM....... Anisotropic Glass-Fiber Material (RU)

SVAM....... Societe de Ventes d'Armes et de Munitions au Tchad

SVAN .... Anaco, Anzoategui [*Venezuela*] [*ICAO location identifier*] (ICLI)

SVARM..... Fixed Military Aircraft Repair Shop (RU)

SVARZ ..... Sokol'niki Railroad Car Building and Repair Plant (RU)

SVAT........ San Fernando De Atabapo, T. F. Amazonas [*Venezuela*] [*ICAO location identifier*] (ICLI)

Svazarm ..... Svaz pro Spolupraci s Armadou [*Union for Cooperation with the Army*] (CZ)

SVB............ Sambava [*Madagascar*] [*Airport symbol*] (OAG)

svb............. Signal Battalion (BU)

SVB............ Sociale Verzekeringsbank [*Benelux*] (BAS)

SVB............ Sprava Verejne Bezpecnosti [*Public Safety Directorate*] (CZ)

SVB............ Studenten Bakbeweging [*Student Trade Union Movement*] [*Belgian, Dutch*] (WEN)

SVB............ Union of Militant Atheists [*1922-1947*] (RU)

SVBC......... Barcelona/Gral. Jose Antonio Anzoategui Internacional Anzoategui [*Venezuela*] [*ICAO location identifier*] (ICLI)

SVBF .... Schweizerischer Verband fuer das Arbeitsstudium [*Swiss Society for Work Study*] (SLS)

SVBF .... Swiss Volleyball Federation [*Also, SVBV*] (EAIO)

SVBGA ..... St. Vincent Banana Growers Association (EAIO)

SVBI .... Barinas, Barinas [*Venezuela*] [*ICAO location identifier*] (ICLI)

SVBI .... Schweizerische Volksbank [*Infocall on Banking and Economy*] [*Switzerland*]

svbk............ Corps Signal Battalion (RU)

SVBL .... Maracay/El Libertador, Base Aerea Aragua [*Venezuela*] [*ICAO location identifier*] (ICLI)

SVBM .... Barquisimeto/Internacional, Lara [*Venezuela*] [*ICAO location identifier*] (ICLI)

SVBP .... Service de Vente des Boissons et des Parfums [*Beverage and Perfume Sales Department*] [*Cambodia*] (CL)

SVBP .... Societe Voltaique des Petroles BP

SVBS .... Maracay/Mariscal Sucre, Base Aerea Aragua [*Venezuela*] [*ICAO location identifier*] (ICLI)

svb-ssv....... Signal Battalion Auxiliary Communications Center (BU)

SVBV .... Schweizerischer Volleyball-Verband [*Swiss Volleyball Federation*] [*Switzerland*] (EAIO)

SVBZ .... Bruzual, Apure [*Venezuela*] [*ICAO location identifier*] (ICLI)

SVC............ Shadow Village Council [*Mauritius*] (AF)

SVC............ Slovansky Vybor Ceskoslovenska [*Slavic Committee of Czechoslovakia*] (CZ)

SVC............ Sociedad Venezolana de Cardiologia [*Venezuelan Cardiology Society*] (SLS)

SVC............ Svejsecentralen [*Danish Welding Institute*] [*Research center*] (IRC)

SVCA........ Caracas Maiquetia Distrito Federal [*Venezuela*] [*ICAO location identifier*] (ICLI)

SVCA........ Swiss Venture Capital Association

SVCB .... Ciudad Bolivar, Bolivar [*Venezuela*] [*ICAO location identifier*] (ICLI)

SVCC........ Caracas Ciudad Distrito Federal [*Venezuela*] [*ICAO location identifier*] (ICLI)

SVCC........ Schweizerischer Verein der Chemiker-Coloristen [*Swiss Association of Chemical Colorists*] (SLS)

SVCD........ Caicara De Orinoco, Bolivar [*Venezuela*] [*ICAO location identifier*] (ICLI)

SVCH .... Achaguas, Apure [*Venezuela*] [*ICAO location identifier*] (ICLI)

SVCh .... High Frequency Signal (RU)

SVCh .... Superhigh Frequency (RU)

SVCh .... Ultra-High Frequency (BU)

SVCI .... Cachipo, Monagas [*Venezuela*] [*ICAO location identifier*] (ICLI)

SVCJ .... San Carlos, Cojedes [*Venezuela*] [*ICAO location identifier*] (ICLI)

SVCL .... Calabozo, Guarico [*Venezuela*] [*ICAO location identifier*] (ICLI)

SVCN........ Canaima, Bolivar [*Venezuela*] [*ICAO location identifier*] (ICLI)

SVCN........ Sociedad Venezolana de Ciencias Naturales [*Venezuela*] (DSCA)

SVCN-CO ... Sociedad Venezolana de Ciencias Naturales - Comite de Orquideologia [*Venezuelan Society of Natural Sciences - Orchid Committee*] (EAIO)

SVCO .... Carora, Lara [*Venezuela*] [*ICAO location identifier*] (ICLI)

SVCP......... Carupano/Gral. en Jefe Jose Francisco Bermudez, Sucre [*Venezuela*] [*ICAO location identifier*] (ICLI)

SVCP........ Societe Voltaique des Cuirs et Peaux

SVCR........ Coro/Internacional, Falcon [*Venezuela*] [*ICAO location identifier*] (ICLI)

SVCS .... Caracas/Internacional del Centro Miranda [*Venezuela*] [*ICAO location identifier*] (ICLI)

SVCS .... Sociedad Venezolana de la Ciencia del Suelo [*Venezuela*] (DSCA)

SVCU........ Cumana, Sucre [*Venezuela*] [*ICAO location identifier*] (ICLI)

SVD .... Schweizerische Vereinigung fuer Dokumentation [*Swiss Association for Documentation*] (SLS)

SVD .... Spolok Vytvarneho Dorostu [*Association of Young Creative Artists*] (CZ)

SVD .... Sprava Vojenske Dopravy [*Military Transport Directorate*] (CZ)

SVD .... St. Vincent [*Windward Islands*] [*Airport symbol*] (OAG)

SVD .... Superhigh Pressure (RU)

SVD .... Svaz Vyrobnich Druzstev [*Association of Manufacturing Cooperatives*] (CZ)

SVD .... Warsaw Pact Countries (RU)

SVDE........ Sidirodromoi Voreiodytikis Ellados [*Railways of Northwestern Greece*] (GC)

SVDP........ Free Democratic Party [*German Federal Republic*] (RU)

SVDP........ La Divina Pastora, Bolivar [*Venezuela*] [*ICAO location identifier*] (ICLI)

SVDP........ Mobile Decontamination Spreader (RU)

SVE............ Aero Servicios Especializados SA de CV [*Mexico*] [*ICAO designator*] (FAAC)

SVE............ Schweizerische Vereinigung fuer Ernaehrung [*Swiss Association for Nutrition*] (SLS)

SVE............ Sociedad Venezolana de Entomologia [*Venezuela*] (DSCA)

SVE............ Society for Veterinary Ethology [*See also SEV*] [*Edinburgh, Scotland*] (EAIO)

SVE............ Soviet Naval Squadron (RU)

SVE............ Svaz Zamestnancu v Energetice [*Union of Employees in the Power Industry*] (CZ)

SVE............ Syndesmos Viomikhanon Endyseos [*Clothing Industries Association*] [*Cyprus*] (GC)

SVEA........ Schweizerischer Verband Evangaelischer Arbeitnehmer [*A union*] [*Switzerland*] (DCTA)

SVEA........ Schweizerischer Verband Evangelischer Arbeitnehmer [*Swiss Union of Protestant Workers*] (WEN)

SVEAA...... Schweizerischer Verband Evangelischer Arbeiter und Angestellter [*Swiss Federation of Protestant Trade Unions*]

SVEB .... Schweizerische Vereinigung fuer Erwachsenenbildung [*Swiss Association for Adult Education*] (SLS)

SVECA...... Sociedad Venezolana de Electrificacion, CA [*Electrification Society of Venezuela*] (LAA)

SVED........ El Dorado, Bolivar [*Venezuela*] [*ICAO location identifier*] (ICLI)

SVED........ Severoceske Vyrobni Elektrotechnicke Druzstvo [*North Bohemian Manufacturing Cooperative for Electrical Products*] (CZ)

SVEE......... Societe Voltaique d'Expansion Economique

Svegintsvetmet ... Sverdlovsk State Institute of Nonferrous Metals (RU)

SVEK........ Sindesmos Viomichanon Endiseos Kyprou [*Cyprus*] (EAIO)

svekl.......... Beet-Growing Sovkhoz [*Topography*] (RU)

Sverdlgiz .... Sverdlovsk State Publishing House (RU)

Sverdlovgiz ... Sverdlovsk State Publishing House (RU)

SverdNIPTIMASh ... Sverdlovsk Scientific Research, Planning, and Technological Institute of Machinery Manufacture (RU)

Svesht .... Priest (BU)

SVETAB.... National Industrial Establishment Co. [*Sweden*] (IMH)

SVETAN .... Swedish-Tanzanian Association

SVEZ........ Elorza, Apure [*Venezuela*] [*ICAO location identifier*] (ICLI)

SVF............ Save [*Benin*] [*Airport symbol*] (OAG)

SVF............ Suid-Afrikaanse Skoeiselvervaardigersfederasie [*South Africa*] (AA)

SVF............ Sveriges Varldsfederalister [*Swedish World Federalists*]

SVF............ Sveriges Veterinaerfoerbund [*Swedish Veterinarian Association*] (SLS)

SVF............ Svetstekniska Foereningen [*Sweden*] (SLS)

SVFC .... Schweizerische Vereinigung fur die Freundschaft mit China [*Switzerland*] (EAIO)

SVFM .... Caracas/Generelisimo Francisco De Miranda Base Aerea La Carlota, Miranda [*Venezuela*] [*ICAO location identifier*] (ICLI)

svfr .... Svajci Frank [*Swiss Franc*] (HU)

SvFR .... Svenska Flyktingradet [*Sweden*] (EAIO)

SVG .... Highest Level (RU)

sv g .... Light Year (RU)
SVG .... Samband Veitinga-og Gistihusa [*Iceland*] (EAIO)
SVG .... Schweizerische Vereinigung fuer Gesundheitstechnik [*Swiss Association for Health Technology*] (SLS)
SVG .... Servizio Volontariato Giovanile [*Italy*] (EAIO)
SVG .... Sociedad Venezolana de Geologos [*Venezuela*] (DSCA)
SVG .... Staatliches Vertragsgericht [*State Contract Court*] [*German*] (EG)
SVG .... Stavanger [*Norway*] [*Airport symbol*] (OAG)
SVG .... Stromversorgungsgeraet [*German*] (ADPT)
SVGD .... Guasdualito, Apure [*Venezuela*] [*ICAO location identifier*] (ICLI)
SVGI .... Guiria, Sucre [*Venezuela*] [*ICAO location identifier*] (ICLI)
SVGT .... Guasipati, Bolivar [*Venezuela*] [*ICAO location identifier*] (ICLI)
SVGU .... Guanare, Portuguesa [*Venezuela*] [*ICAO location identifier*] (ICLI)
SVGVB ...... Highest Level of the Head Water (RU)
SVGW .... Schweizerischer Verein des Gas- und Wasserfaches [*Swiss Association of Gas and Water Departments*] (SLS)
SVHA .... Societe Vaudoise d'Histoire et d'Archeologie [*Switzerland*] (SLS)
SVHG .... Higuerote, Miranda [*Venezuela*] [*ICAO location identifier*] (ICLI)
SVI .... Mean Probable Wear (RU)
SVI .... San Vincente Del Caguan [*Colombia*] [*Airport symbol*] (OAG)
SVI .... Schweizerischer Verein fuer Instandhaltung [*Swiss Association for Maintenance*] (SLS)
SVI .... Servicio de Vigilancia Interior [*Interior Guard Service*] [*Cuba*] (LA)
SVI .... Socialistas Valencians Independents [*Valencian Independent Socialists*] [*Spanish*] (WER)
SVI .... Statni Vodohospodarske Inspekce [*State Inspection Centers for Water Management*] (CZ)
SVIA .... Sociedad Venezolana de Ingenieros Agronomos [*Venezuela*] (DSCA)
SVIAM ...... Statia de Verificare si Intretinere a Aparaturii Medicale [*Station for the Testing and Maintenance of Medical Instruments*] (RO)
SVIAT .... Societa Valorizzazioni Industriali Agrarie Tripolitane
SVIC .... Icabaru, Bolivar [*Venezuela*] [*ICAO location identifier*] (ICLI)
SVIC .... Sociedad Venezolana de Ingeniesos Consultores [*Venezuelan Society of Consulting Engineers*] (PDAA)
SVICA .... Societe Voltaique d'Intervention et de Co-Operation avec l'Agriculture
SVIE .... Isla De Coche, Nueva Esparta [*Venezuela*] [*ICAO location identifier*] (ICLI)
SVIE .... Skholi Voithon Iatrikon Epangelmaton [*Medical Assistants School*] [*Greek*] (GC)
SVIF .... Sociedad Venezolana de Ingenieros Forestales [*Venezuela*] (DSCA)
SVIF .... Svenski Indianska Foerbundet [*Sweden*]
SVIH .... Sociedad Venezolana de Ingenieria Hidraulica [*Venezuela*] (DSCA)
SVIL .... Schweizerische Vereinigung fuer Innenkolonisation und Industrielle Landwirtschaft [*Switzerland*] (DSCA)
SVIM .... Sociedad Venezolana de Ingenieros de Minas y Metalurgicos [*Venezuelan Society of Mining and Metallurgical Engineers*] (PDAA)
SVIMEZ .... Associazione per lo Sviluppo dell' Industria nel Mezzogiorno [*Association for the Industrial Development of the South*] [*Italian*] (WER)
SVIMR ...... St. Vincent's Institute of Medical Research [*Australia*]
SVIMSA ..... Schweizerischer Verband der Innendekorateur, del Mobelfachhandels, und der Sattler [*Switzerland*] (EAIO)
svin .... Hog-Breeding Sovkhoz [*Topography*] (RU)
svints .... Lead Mine [*Topography*] (RU)
SVIP .... Sociedad Venezolana de Ingenieros de Petroleo [*Venezuelan Association of Petroleum Engineers*] (LA)
SVIPA .... Swiss Videotex Industry Association [*Information service or system*] (IID)
SVIPA .... Swiss Viewdata Information Providers Association [*Zurich*] [*Telecommunications*]
SVIQ .... Sociedad Venezolana de Ingenieros Quimicos [*Venezuela*] (DSCA)
Svit .... Scroll, Roll (BU)
SVJ .... Svolvaer [*Norway*] [*Airport symbol*] (OAG)
SVJC .... Paraguana/Josefa Camejo Internacional, Falcon [*Venezuela*] [*ICAO location identifier*] (ICLI)
SVJC .... Savezni Vazduhoplovni Jedrilicki Centar [*Federal Aeronautic Glider Center*] [*Vrsac*] (YU)
SVJJ .... Schweizer Verband der Journalistinnen und Journalisten [*Swiss Association of Journalists*] (EAIO)
SVK .... Channel Separation Bay (RU)
SVK .... Schweizerische Vereinigung fuer Kleintiermedizin [*Swiss Association for Small Animal Medicine*] (SLS)
SVK .... Sozialversicherungskasse [*Social Insurance Finance Office*] [*German*] (EG)

SVK .... Statna Vedecka Kniznica [*State Research Library*] [*Kosice*] (CZ)
SVK .... Statni Vedecka Knihovna [*State Science Library*] (CZ)
SVK .... Vertical Seismograph Designed by Kirnos (RU)
SVKA .... Kavanayen, Bolivar [*Venezuela*] [*ICAO location identifier*] (ICLI)
svkh .... Sovkhoz [*Topography*] (RU)
SVKL .... Slovenske Vydavatelstvo Krasnej Literatury [*Slovak Belles-Lettres Publishing House*] (CZ)
SVKM .... Kamarata, Bolivar [*Venezuela*] [*ICAO location identifier*] (ICLI)
SVKR .... Sprava Vojenske Kontrarozvedky [*Military Counterintelligence Directorate*] (CZ)
svkr .... Sved Korona [*Swedish Krona*] (HU)
SVKT .... Sdruzenie Byvalych Vaznov Koncentracnvch Taborov [*Association of Former Prisoners in Concentration Camps*] (CZ)
SVL .... Medium Wave Line (RU)
SVL .... Saak [*Russian Federation*] [*ICAO designator*] (FAAC)
SVL .... Savonlinna [*Finland*] [*Airport symbol*] (OAG)
SVL .... Suomen Valkonauhaliitto [*Finland*] (EAIO)
svlb .... Line Signal Battalion (BU)
SVLF .... La Fria, Tachira [*Venezuela*] [*ICAO location identifier*] (ICLI)
SVLFC .... Schweizerische Vereinigung der Lack- und Farben-Chemiker [*Swiss Association of Lacquer and Paint Chemists*] (SLS)
Svl HvMey ... Sivil Hava Meydani [*Civil Airfield*] (TU)
svlkb .... Line and Cable Signal Battalion (BU)
svlkr .... Line and Cable Signal Company (BU)
SVLO .... La Orchila - Dependencia Federal [*Venezuela*] [*ICAO location identifier*] (ICLI)
SVLP .... St. Vincent Labor Party (LA)
svlr .... Line Signal Company (BU)
svlsb .... Line Construction Signal Battalion (BU)
svlsr .... Line Construction Signal Company (BU)
Svl Svn ...... Sivil Savunma [*Civil Defense*] (TU)
SVLT .... Schweizerischer Verband fuer Landtechnik [*Swiss Association for Soil Technology*] (SLS)
SVLW .... Sectoraal Verband Landbouwwetenschappen [*Committee on International Education in Agricultural Sciences*] [*Netherlands*] (EAIO)
SVM .... Aeroservicios Monterrey SA de CV [*Mexico*] [*ICAO designator*] (FAAC)
SVM .... Saint, Victor, Modeste & Cie.
SVM .... Societe de Vente de Materiel
SVM .... Soviet Military Mission (RU)
SVM .... Stanje Voznog Materijala [*Condition of Rolling Stock*] (YU)
SVM .... Svaz Vojenske Mladeze [*Military Youth Union*] (CZ)
SVM .... Synthetic High-Polymer Materials (RU)
SVMC .... Maracaibo/La Chinita Internacional, Zulia [*Venezuela*] [*ICAO location identifier*] (ICLI)
SVMD .... Merida/Alberto Carnevalli, Merida [*Venezuela*] [*ICAO location identifier*] (ICLI)
SVMG .... Margarita/Internacional del Caribe Gral Santiago Marino, Neuva Esparta [*Venezuela*] [*ICAO location identifier*] (ICLI)
SVMI .... Caracas/Simon Bolivar Internacional Maiquetia Distrito Federal [*Venezuela*] [*ICAO location identifier*] (ICLI)
SVMM ...... Schweizerische Vereinigung der Musiklehrer an Mittelschulen [*Switzerland*]
SVMMK .... Syndesmos Viomichanon Mosaikon & Marmanon Kyprou [*Cyprus*] (EAIO)
SVMP .... Caracas/Metropolitano Internacional, Miranda [*Venezuela*] [*ICAO location identifier*] (ICLI)
SVMR .... Maracay/Centro Nacional de Comunicaciones/Meteorologicos, Aragua [*Venezuela*] [*ICAO location identifier*] (ICLI)
SVMT .... Maturin/Internacional, Monagas [*Venezuela*] [*ICAO location identifier*] (ICLI)
SVN .... Aspiring Centrifugal Pump (RU)
Svn .... Savunma [*Defense*] (TU)
SVN .... Statistiek van Nederland [*Netherlands*]
SvN .... Svoboden Narod [*Free People*] [*A newspaper*] (BU)
SVNAF ...... South Vietnamese Air Force (VNW)
SVNLA ...... South Vietnamese Liberation Army (VNW)
SVNM .... St. Vincent National Movement [*Political party*] (PPW)
SVNMC ..... South Vietnamese Marine Corps (VNW)
SVNN .... South Vietnamese Navy (VNW)
SVNNP ..... South Vietnamese National Police Force (VNW)
SVNSF ...... South Vietnamese Special Forces (VNW)
SVO .... Mean Probable Deviation (RU)
SVO .... Moscow Sheremetyevo Airport [*Former USSR*] [*Airport symbol*] (OAG)
SVO .... Siberian Military District (RU)
SVo .... Sovetskoe Vostokovedenie [*Moscow*]
SVO .... Sozialversicherung der Arbeiter und Angestellten [*Social Insurance of Workers and Employees*] [*German*] (EG)
SVO .... Special Water Purification [*Nuclear energy*] (BU)
SVO .... Stichting voor Oliehoudende Zaden Foundation for Oil Seeds [*Netherlands*] (DSCA)

SVO .... Stredni Vojensky Okruh [*Central Military District*] (CZ)
SVOC .... Societe Verite de l'Ouest Cameroun
SVOD .... Soviet Aircraft Navigation and Landing System (MCD)
SVOI .... Staatsveeartsenijkundig Onderzoekingsinstituut [*Benelux*] (BAS)
SVOJ .... Sluzba Veze, Osmatranja, i Javljanja [*Military Communications, Reconnaissance, and Information Service*] (YU)
Sv Ok .... Suvari Okulu [*Cavalry School*] (TU)
SVOK .... Svaz Verejnych Obecnich Knihovniku [*Union of Librarians of Public Libraries*] (CZ)
SVOM .... Slovensky Vybor Obrancov Mieru [*Slovak Committee of Peace Defenders*] (CZ)
SVOR .... Schweizerische Vereinigung fuer Operations Research [*Swiss Association for Operations Research*] [*Bern*] (SLS)
SVP .... Bie [*Angola*] [*Airport symbol*] (OAG)
SVP .... Blast Point Station (RU)
SVP .... Military Service Code (RU)
SVP .... Schweizerische Volkspartei [*Swiss People's Party*] [*Political party*] (WEN)
SVP .... Servico do Vale do Paraiba [*Brazil*] (LAA)
svp .... Signal Regiment (BU)
SVP .... S'il Vous Plait [*If You Please*] [*French*]
SVP .... Societe de Vulgarisation de Procedes
SVP .... Societe Voltaique de Plastique
SVP .... Special Visitors Program [*Australia*]
SVP .... Stabilized Sight [*Navy*]
SVP .... Statni Vodohospodarsky Plan [*State Plan for Water Utilization*] (CZ)
SVP .... Stichting voor Plantenveredeling [*Foundation for Agricultural Plant Breeding*] [*Netherlands*] (ARC)
SVP .... Stredoceske Vyrobny Plynu, Narodny Podnik [*Central Bohemian Gas Works, National Enterprise*] (CZ)
SVP .... Sudtiroler Volkspartei [*South Tyrolean People's Party*] [*Italy*] [*Political party*] (EAIO)
SVP .... Suedtiroler Volkspartei [*South Tirol People's Party*] [*Italian*] (WEN)
SVP .... Superhigh Steam Parameters (RU)
SVP .... Syndagmatiki Vasiliki Parataxis [*Constitutional Royalist Faction*] [*Greek*] (GC)
SVP .... Welding (RU)
SVPA .... Puerto Ayacucho, T. F. Amazonas [*Venezuela*] [*ICAO location identifier*] (ICLI)
SVPC .... Puerto Cabello/Gral. Bartolome Salom Internacional, Carabobo [*Venezuela*] [*ICAO location identifier*] (ICLI)
SVPC .... Societe Voltaique de Peintures et Colorants
SVPCh .... Independent Militarized Fire Brigade (RU)
SVPF .... Societe Veterinaire Pratique de France [*French*] (SLS)
SVPI .... Societe de Ventes de Produits Industriels
SVPL .... Slovenske Vydavatelstvo Podohospodarskej Literatury [*Slovak Agricultural Literature Publishing House*] (CZ)
SVPL .... Slovenske Vydavatelstvo Politickej Literatury [*Slovak Publishing House of Political Literature*] (CZ)
SVPM .... San Cristobal/Paramillo, Tachira [*Venezuela*] [*ICAO location identifier*] (ICLI)
SVPR .... Guayana/Puerto Ordaz Internacional, Bolivar [*Venezuela*] [*ICAO location identifier*] (ICLI)
SVPS .... Through Sleeping Car (RU)
SVPT .... Palmarito, Apure [*Venezuela*] [*ICAO location identifier*] (ICLI)
SVQ .... Seville [*Spain*] [*Airport symbol*] (OAG)
SVQ .... Sociedad Venezolana de Quimica [*Venezuela*] (DSCA)
svr .... Signal Company (BU)
SVR .... Sociale Verzekeringsraad [*Benelux*] (BAS)
SVR .... Speciale Verzameling van Rechtspraak [*Benelux*] (BAS)
SVR .... Spesiale Vrederegter [*Special Justice of the Peace*] [*Afrikaans*] (CZ)
SVR .... Statni Vyzkumna Rada [*State Research Council*] (CZ)
SVR .... Sverdlovsk Airline [*Russian Federation*] [*ICAO designator*] (FAAC)
SVRP .... Central Volga River Steamship Line (RU)
svrrkb .... Radio-Relay Cable Signal Battalion (BU)
SVRS .... Los Roques, Dependencia Federal [*Venezuela*] [*ICAO location identifier*] (ICLI)
svr-ssb .... Signal Company Auxiliary Communications Center (BU)
SVS .... Savezni Vrhovni Sud [*Federal Supreme Court*] (YU)
SVS .... Sbor Vezenske Straze [*Prison Guard Corps*] (CZ)
SVS .... Simonov Semiautomatic Rifle (RU)
SVS .... Sofia Military Court (BU)
SVS .... Speditionsversicherungsschein [*Shipping Insurance Policy*] (EG)
SVS .... Sprava Vojenskych Skol [*Military Schools Directorate*] (CZ)
SVS .... Sreska Veterinarska Stanica [*District Veterinary Station*] (YU)
SVS .... Stocarsko-Veterinarska Stanica [*Livestock Veterinary Station*] (YU)
SVS .... Suomen Viljateknikkojen Seura [*Finland*] (SLS)
SVS .... Svaz Vysokoskolskeho Studentstva [*Union of University Students*] (CZ)
SVS .... Svaz Vysokoskolskych Studentov [*Union of University Students*] (CZ)

SVSA .... San Antonio, Tachira [*Venezuela*] [*ICAO location identifier*] (ICLI)
SVSA .... Sterrekundige Vereniging van Suider-Afrika [*South Africa*] (AA)
SVSB .... Santa Barbara De Barinas, Barinas [*Venezuela*] [*ICAO location identifier*] (ICLI)
SVSC .... San Carlos De Rio Negro, T. F. Amazonas [*Venezuela*] [*ICAO location identifier*] (ICLI)
SVSC .... Sociedad de Vida Silvestre de Chile (EAIO)
SVSE .... Santa Elena de Uairen, Bolivar [*Venezuela*] [*ICAO location identifier*] (ICLI)
svseb .... Construction and Operational Signal Battalion (BU)
sv'sek .... Candle-Second (RU)
svser .... Construction and Operational Signal Company (BU)
SVSF .... Sveriges Vetenskapliga Specialbiblioteks Foerening [*Sweden*] (SLS)
SVSJ .... Suomen Vaestonsuojelujarjesto [*Finnish Population Protection Organization*] (WEN)
SVSO .... Santo Domingo/Mayor Buenaventura Vivas A. B., Tachira [*Venezuela*] [*ICAO location identifier*] (ICLI)
SVSO .... Slovenska Vysoka Skola Obchodna [*Slovak School of Business Administration*] (CZ)
SVSP .... San Felipe/Subteniente Nestor Arias, Yaracuy [*Venezuela*] [*ICAO location identifier*] (ICLI)
SVSR .... San Fernando De Apure, Apure [*Venezuela*] [*ICAO location identifier*] (ICLI)
SVST .... San Tome, Anzoategui [*Venezuela*] [*ICAO location identifier*] (ICLI)
SVST .... Slovenska Vysoka Skola Technicka [*Slovak Institute of Technology*] (CZ)
SVSZ .... Santa Barbara Del Zulia, Zulia [*Venezuela*] [*ICAO location identifier*] (ICLI)
SVT .... Air-Raid Warning (RU)
SVT .... Severoceske Vystavni Trhy [*North Bohemian Sample Fairs*] [*Liberec*] (CZ)
svt .... Suivant [*Following*] [*French*]
SVT .... Sveriges Television [*Swedish Television*]
SVT .... Tokarev Semiautomatic Rifle (RU)
SVTC .... Tucupita, T. F. Delta Amacuro [*Venezuela*] [*ICAO location identifier*] (ICLI)
SVTF .... Stiftelsen foer Vaermeteknisk Forskning [*Thermal Engineering Research Association*] [*Sweden*] (WED)
SVTI .... Military Technical Equipment Depot (RU)
SVTL .... Slovenske Vydavatelstvo Technickej Literatury [*Slovak Technical Literature Publishing House*] (CZ)
SVTM .... Sprava Vodnich Toku a Meliorace [*Administration of Water Ways and Melioration Projects*] (CZ)
SVTM .... Tumeremo, Bolivar [*Venezuela*] [*ICAO location identifier*] (ICLI)
SVTVS ...... Statni Vybor pro Telesnou Vychovu a Sport [*State Physical Education and Athletic Committee*] (CZ)
SVTVS ...... Statny Vybor pre Telesnu Vychovu a Sport [*State Committee of Physical Education and Sports*] (CZ)
SVU .... Computer (RU)
SVU .... Saveznicka Vojna Uprava [*Allied Military Government*] (YU)
SVU .... Savusavu [*Fiji*] [*Airport symbol*] (OAG)
SVU .... Signaling-Calling Device (RU)
SVU .... Spolek Vytvarnych Umelcu [*Creative Artists' Association*] (CZ)
SVU .... Sprava Vojenskych Ucilist [*Military Training Centers Directorate*] (CZ)
SVU .... Statni Vybor pro Veci Umeni [*State Fine Arts Committee*] (CZ)
SVU .... Stavebni Vyrobni Usek [*Construction Materials Production Sector*] (CZ)
SVU .... Suvorov Military School (RU)
SVUESP .... Statni Vyzkumny Ustav Ekonomiky ve Spotrebnim Prumyslu [*State Research Institute of Economy in Consumer Industry*] (CZ)
SVUK .... Statni Vyzkumny Ustav Kozedelny [*State Research Institute for Leather Tanning*] (CZ)
SVUL .... Suomen Voimistelu- ja Urheiluliitto [*Finnish Gymnastics and Sports League*] (WEN)
SVUM .... Sdruzeni Vytvarnych Umelcu Moravskych [*Association of Moravian Creative Artists*] (CZ)
SVUM .... Statni Vyzkumny Ustav Materialu [*State Research Institute for Engineering Materials*] (CZ)
SVUM .... Uriman, Bolivar [*Venezuela*] [*ICAO location identifier*] (ICLI)
SVUManes ... Spolek Vytvarnych Umelcu Manes [*Manes Association of Creative Artists*] (CZ)
SVUOM .... Statni Vyzkumny Ustav Ochrany Materialu G. V. Akimova [*G. V. Akimov State Research Institute for Protection of Metals*] (CZ)
SVUP .... Statny Vyskumny Ustav Polnohospodarsky [*State Agricultural Research Institute*] (CZ)
SVUQ .... Uonquen, Bolivar [*Venezuela*] [*ICAO location identifier*] (ICLI)
SVURH ..... Statni Vyzkumny Ustav Rybarsky a Hydrobiologicky [*State Research Institute of Fish Culture and Hydrobiology*] (CZ)
SVUS .... Statni Vyzkumny Ustav Sklarsky [*State Glass Research Institute*] (CZ)

SVUSS....... Statni Vyzkumny Ustav pro Stavbu Stroju [*State Research Institute for Machinery Construction*]   (CZ)

SVUST ...... Statni Vyzkumny Ustav Sklarske Techniky [*State Research Institute for Glass Technology*]   (CZ)

SVUT........ Statni Vyzkumny Ustav Textilni [*State Research Institute for Textiles*]   (CZ)

SVUV .... Spolek Vytvarnych Umelcu Vychodoceskych [*Society of East Bohemian Creative Artists*]   (CZ)

SVUZ........ Statni Vyzkumne Ustavy Zemedelske [*State Agricultural Research Institutes*]   (CZ)

SVUZ........ Svaz Vyzkumnych Ustavu Zemedelskych [*Union of Agricultural Research Institutes*]   (CZ)

SVV........... Empresa Servicicious Avensa SA [*Venezuela*] [*ICAO designator*]   (FAAC)

SVV........... Sadjarstvo, Vinarstvo, in Vrtnarstvo [*Fruit Culture, Viticulture, and Horticulture*] [*Ljubljana A periodical*]   (YU)

svv .... Signal Platoon   (RU)

SVV........... Studiecentrum voor Vredesvraagstukken [*Peace Research Center*] [*Netherlands*]   (IRC)

SVV........... Superlong Draft [*Spinning*]   (RU)

SVVA........ Valencia/Internacional, Carabobo [*Venezuela*] [*ICAO location identifier*]   (ICLI)

SVVE........ Syndesmos Viomikhanon Voreiou Ellados [*Federation of Industrialists of Northern Greece*]   (GC)

SVVK........ Schweizerischer Verein fuer Vermessungswesen und Kulturtechnik [*Swiss Association for Surveying and Cultural Technology*]   (SLS)

SVVL........ Valera/Dr. Antonio Nicolas Briceno, Trujillo [*Venezuela*] [*ICAO location identifier*]   (ICLI)

sv-vo .... Property   (RU)

Sv V P .... Military Service Code   (RU)

SVVP........ Valle De La Pascua, Guarico [*Venezuela*] [*ICAO location identifier*]   (ICLI)

SVVP........ Vertical Takeoff and Landing Aircraft   (RU)

SVVS .... Stredni Vseobecne Vzdelavaci Skola [*Secondary General Education School*]   (CZ)

SVVTDET ... Syndesmos Viomichanon Valitsopiias, Tsanton & Dermatinon Eidon Taxidiou [*Cyprus*]   (EAIO)

SVW .... Schweizerischer Verband fuer Waldwirtschaft [*Swiss Association for Forestry*]   (SLS)

svw .... Soviel Wie [*As Many As*] [*German*]

SVWG .... Strafvollzugs- und Wiedereingliederungsgesetz [*Law on Punishment and Reintegration*]   (EG)

SVY........... Suomen Voimalaitosyhdistys [*Finland*]   (SLS)

Svyaz'izdat ... State Publishing House of Literature on Communications and Radio   (RU)

Svyaz'kabel'stroy ... All-Union Trust for the Construction of Intercity Cable Communication Trunk Lines   (RU)

Svyaz'radioizdat ... State Publishing House of Literature on Communications and Radio   (RU)

Svyaz'rem .. Railway Communications Repair Train   (RU)

Svyaz'tekhizdat ... State Publishing House of Literature on Communications Engineering   (RU)

SVYK........ Sindesmos Viomichanon Ypodimaton Kyprou [*Cyprus*]   (EAIO)

SVZ........... San Antonio [*Venezuela*] [*Airport symbol*]   (OAG)

SVZ........... Slovenske Vinarske Zavody [*Slovak Wine Enterprises*]   (CZ)

SVZ........... Slovenske Vlnarske Zavody, Narodny Podnik [*Slovak Woolen Mills, National Enterprise*]   (CZ)

SVZ........... Smederevska Vinogradska Zadruga [*Smederevo Viticulture Cooperative*]   (YU)

SVZ........... Sociedad Veterinaria de Zootecnia [*Spain*]   (EAIO)

SVZ........... Sverdlovsk Bicycle Plant   (RU)

SVZE......... Sociedad Veterinaria de Zootecnia de Espana [*Spain*]   (DSCA)

SVZM........ Maiquetia [*Venezuela*] [*ICAO location identifier*]   (ICLI)

SVZN........ Stredisko pro Vynalezy a Zlepsovaci Navrhy [*Center for Inventions and Improvement Proposals*]   (CZ)

SVZZ .... Maiquetia [*Venezuela*] [*ICAO location identifier*]   (ICLI)

SW .... School en Wet [*Benelux*]   (BAS)

SW .... Schweizer Wanderwege [*Switzerland*]   (EAIO)

SW .... Short Wave   (IDIG)

SW .... Sicherheitswache [*Security Guard*] [*German*]

SW .... Signalwerkstatt [*Signal Shop*] [*German*]   (EG)

SW .... Soortlike Warmte [*Specific Heat*] [*Afrikaans*]

SW .... Spezifische Waerme [*Specific Heat*] [*German*]

SW .... Strafwetboek [*Benelux*]   (BAS)

SW .... Successiewet [*Benelux*]   (BAS)

SW .... Sudoeste [*Southwest*] [*Portuguese*]

SW .... Sud Ouest [*Southwest*] [*French*]   (MTD)

SW .... Sueddeutsche Waehrung [*South German Currency*] [*German*]

SW .... Suedwesten [*Southwest*] [*German*]   (EG)

SW .... Suidwes [*Southwest*] [*Afrikaans*]

SW .... Swearingen Aircraft [*ICAO aircraft manufacturer identifier*]   (ICAO)

sw .... Swiadek [*Witness*] [*Poland*]

sw .... Swiety [*Saint*]   (POL)

SWA .... Pakistan Medico International Social Welfare Association   (EAIO)

SWA .... Seaboard World Airlines   (MHDW)

SWA .... Shantou [*China*] [*Airport symbol*]   (OAG)

SWA .... South-West Africa   (AF)

SWA .... Sozialwissenschaftliche Arbeitsgemeinschaft [*Sociological Association*] [*Austria*]   (SLS)

SWA .... Sudanese Women's Association

SWA .... Suidwes-Afrika [*South West Africa*] [*Afrikaans*]

SWA .... Swiss Writers Association   (EAIO)

SWAA .... Society of Wildlife Artists of Australasia

SWAAG..... Solidarity with Aboriginal Australians Group

SWABC..... South-West African Broadcasting Corporation [*Namibia*]   (AF)

SWACO .... South West Africa Coloureds' Organization

SWACO .... South West Africa Company [*Namibia*]

SWACPO ... South West Africa Colored People's Organization [*Political party*] [*Namibia*]

SW Af........ South-West Africa

SWAFP ..... Socialist Workers and Farmers Party [*Nigeria*]   (AF)

SWAFT ..... South West Africa Territory Force [*Military*]

SWAGH .... Stowarzyszenie Wychowankow Akademii Gorniczo-Hutniczej [*Alumni Association of the Academy of Mining and Metallurgy*]   (POL)

SWAKARA ... South West Africa Karakul Auction

SWAKOR ... South West Africa Oil Exploration Corp.

SWAL........ Scandinavian West Africa Line

SWALU..... Suedwest-Afrikanische Landwirtschafts-Union [*South-West African Agriculture Union*] [*Swaziland*]   (AF)

SWAM ...... Stop-the-War-Against-Angola-and Mozambique

SwAM........ Swedish Alliance Mission

SWAMA.... South-West Africa Municipal Association [*Swaziland*]   (AF)

SWAMSA ... South-West African Municipal Staff Association [*Swaziland*]   (AF)

SWAMWU ... Southwest Africa Mine Workers' Union [*Namibia*]   (EAIO)

SWAN .... School of Women Artists Network [*Australia*]

SWAN .... Sports Writers Association of Nigeria

SWANIO... South West Africa United National Independence Organization

SWANLA ... South-West Africa Native Labor Association [*Namibia*]   (AF)

SWANLIF ... South-West Africa National Liberation Front

SWANOV ... South-West African Black Teachers Union [*Namibia*]   (AF)

SWANS..... Statutes of Western Australia Now in Service

SWANTITER ... South-West Africa Anti-Terrorism Fund [*Swaziland*]   (AF)

SWANU .... South West Africa National Union [*Namibia*] [*Political party*]   (PPW)

SWANUF ... South-West African National United Front [*Namibia*]   (AF)

SWAOU .... Suidwes-Afrikaanse Onderwysersunie [*South-West African Teachers Union*] [*Namibia*]

SWAP....... Salespeople with a Purpose [*Australia*]

SWAP....... South West Arts Project [*New South Wales, Australia*]

SWAP....... Student with a Purpose [*Australia*]

SWAP....... Surface Water Acidification Project [*Joint venture involving Norway, Sweden, and Great Britain*]

SWAP....... Sydney Wastewater Action Program [*Australia*]

SWAPA..... South West Progressive Africa Association

SWAPDUF ... South-West Africa People's Democratic United Front [*Namibia*]   (AF)

SWAPO..... South West Africa People's Organization [*Namibia*]   (PD)

SWAPO-D ... South-West African People's Organization Democrats [*Namibia*] [*Political party*]   (AF)

SWAPOU ... South-West African Professional Teachers Union [*Namibia*]   (AF)

SWAPS ..... South Western Area Pathology Service [*Australia*]

SWARC..... Sydney Women Against Rape Collective [*Australia*]

SWAS....... Slim Whitman Appreciation Society of Holland   (EAIO)

SWATF ..... South-West Africa Territory Force

SWAUNIO ... South-West African United National Independence Organization [*Namibia*]   (AF)

SWAWEK ... South-West Africa Water and Electricity Supply Commission [*Namibia*]   (AF)

SWAZ....... Swaziland   (WDAA)

Swazil........ Swaziland

SWAZIMAR ... Royal Swaziland Maritime Company

SWB.......... Schweizerischer Werkbund [*Swiss Work Union*]   (SLS)

SWB.......... Sectie Wetenschappelijke Bibliotheken [*NVB*] [*'s-Gravenhage*]

SWB.......... Sweden Airways [*ICAO designator*]   (FAAC)

SWB.......... Sydney Wine Brokers [*Australia*]

SWC .... Slovak World Congress   (EAIO)

SWC .... Somali Workers' Council

SWC .... State Wage Case [*Australia*]

SWC .... Stawell [*Australia*] [*Airport symbol*]   (OAG)

SWCA....... Swaziland Workcamps Association   (EAIO)

SWCC....... Saline Water Conversion Corporation [*Saudi Arabia*]   (GEA)

SWCDEF .. South West Corridor Development and Employment Association [*Australia*]

SWD .... Steering Committee, Wind Energy Developing Countries [*Netherlands*]

SWDA .... South West Development Authority [*Western Australia*]

SWDF........ South-West Forests Defence Foundation [*Australia*]

SWDO ...... Somali Women's Democratic Organization (AF)
SWDR .... Southern Women Democratic Reaction [*Brazil*] (EAIO)
SWE .... Swedair AB [*Sweden*] [*ICAO designator*] (FAAC)
SWE .... Sweden [*ANSI three-letter standard code*] (CNC)
SWEC .... State War Executive Committee (ML)
SWEDIS .... Swedish Drug Information System [*Swedish National Board of Health and Welfare*] [*Databank*] (IID)
SWEDTEL ... Swedish Telecoms International AB [*Telecommunications*]
SWEHAC ... Statewide Ear Health Advisory Committee [*Australia*]
SWEPRO .. Swedish Committee on Trade Procedures (PDAA)
SWEXCO ... Swiss Exporting Consultants [*An association*] (EAIO)
SWF .... Service Workers Federation [*San Marino*] (EAIO)
SWF .... Small Winemakers' Forum [*Australia*]
SWF .... Studium Wychowania Fizycznego [*College of Physical Training*] [*Poland*]
SWF-Dienst ... Selbstwaehlferndienst [*Long-Distance Telephone Dialing Service*] (EG)
SWFP .... Socialist Workers and Farmers Party [*Nigeria*] (AF)
SWFTU ..... Sudan Workers Federation of Trade Unions
SWGA ...... Swiss Wine Growers Association (EAIO)
SWGWTU ... St. Lucia Seamen, Waterfront, and General Workers' Trade Union
SWHV .... Samenschakeling van de Wetten op de Handels-Vennootschappen [*Benelux*] (BAS)
SWIB .... Samenschakeling van de Wetten op de Inkomstenbelastingen [*Benelux*] (BAS)
SWID .... Southwest India Docks [*Shipping*] (ROG)
SWIDOC ... Sociaal-Wetenschappelijk Informatie- en Documentatiecentrum [*Social Science Information and Documentation Center*] [*Netherlands*] [*Information service or system*] (IID)
SWIFT .... Society for Worldwide Interbank Financial Telecommunication [*Banking network*] [*Belgium*]
SWIMS ..... Skills for Working in a Multicultural Society [*Australia*]
SWIP .... Stichting Werkgroep Indianen Projekt [*Netherlands*]
SWIRA ...... Swedish Industrial Robot Association (EAIO)
SWIS .... Swiss Wildlife Information Service [*Zurich*] [*Information service or system*] (IID)
SWISSCOM ... Swiss Telecommunication Export Association (PDAA)
SWISSPRO ... Swiss group on the Simplification of International Trade Procedures (PDAA)
SWK .... Scott Wilson Kirkpatrick and Partners
swl .... Sehr Wenig Loeslich [*Very Slightly Soluble*] [*German*]
SwLuH ..... Hogskolan i Lulea [*Lulea University*], Lulea, Sweden [*Library symbol*] [*Library of Congress*] (LCLS)
SWM .... Suia-Missu [*Brazil*] [*Airport symbol*] (OAG)
SWMTEP ... System-Wide Medium-Term Environment Programme (GNE)
SWNCB ..... Samengeschakelde Wetten Betreffende de Nationale Crisisbelasting [*Benelux*] (BAS)
SWO .... Seewasserstrassenordnung [*High Seas International Rules of the Road*] (EG)
SWOP .... Sex Workers Outreach Project [*Australia*]
SWOV ...... Stichting Wetenschappelijk Onderzoek Verkeersveiligheid [*Institute for Road Safety Research*] [*Netherlands*] (IRC)
SWP .... Spouses Working Party on Removals and Storage [*Commonwealth employees*] [*Australia*]
SWP .... Stichting Waakzaamheid Persoonregistratie [*Netherlands*]
SWP .... Stiftung Wissenschaft und Politik [*Foundation for Science and Politics*] [*Information service or system*] (IID)
SWP .... Stowarzyszenie Wynalazcow Polskich [*Association of Polish Inventors*] (POL)
SWP & A ... Seamen's War Pensions and Allowances [*Act*] [*Australia*]
SWR .... Samodzielne Warsztaty Remontowe [*Independent Repair Shops*] [*Poland*] (POL)
SWR .... Schweizerischer Wissenschaftsrat [*Swiss Science Council*] (SLS)
SWR .... Statewide Roads [*Australia*]
SWR .... Swissair (Societe Anonyme Switzerland pour la Navigation Aerienne) [*ICAO designator*] (FAAC)
SWRC .... Social Work Research Centre [*India*]
SwRK .... Schwingungsrisskorrosionsverhalten [*Fatigue Corrosion Behavior*] [*German*]
SwS .... Solidarity with Solidarity [*See also SzS*] [*Defunct*] (EAIO)
SWS .... Sozialwissenschaftliche Studiengesellschaft [*Sociological Education Association*] [*Austria*] (SLS)
SWSA .... Social Welfare Services in Africa
SWSAHS .. South Western Sydney Area Health Service [*Australia*]
SwSU-T ..... University of Stockholm, Department of Physical Geography, Trafala Glaciological Station, Stockholm, Sweden [*Library symbol*] [*Library of Congress*] (LCLS)
SWT .... Swiftair SA [*Spain*] [*ICAO designator*] (FAAC)
SWTP .... School to Work Transition Program [*Australia*]
SWTUF .... Sudanese Workers' Trade Unions Federation [*Khartoum*]
swu .... Siehe Weiter Unten [*See Below*] [*German*]
SWU .... St. Lucia Workers' Union (LA)
SWU .... Sudan Women's Union
SWVC .... Soviet War Veterans' Committee (EAIO)
SWWTU .... Seamen and Waterfront Workers Trade Union [*Trinidadian and Tobagan*] (LA)

SWWU ...... Social Welfare Workers Union [*Australia*]
SWZ .... Swaziland [*ANSI three-letter standard code*] (CNC)
SX .... Society of St. Francis Xavier for the Foreign Missions [*Also known as Xaverian Missionaries*] (EAIO)
SXB .... Strasbourg [*France*] [*Airport symbol*] (OAG)
SXE .... Sale [*Australia*] [*Airport symbol*] (OAG)
SXEKA ...... (Pankypria) Syndekhnia Ergaton Xenodokheion, Estiatorion kai Kendron Anapsykhis [*(Pan-Cyprian) Union of Hotel, Restaurant, and Recreation Center Workers*] (GC)
SXF .... Berlin [*Germany*] [*Airport symbol*] (OAG)
SXG .... Senanga [*Zambia*] [*Airport symbol*] (OAG)
SXH .... Sehulea [*Papua New Guinea*] [*Airport symbol*] (OAG)
SXM .... St. Maarten [*Netherlands Antilles*] [*Airport symbol*] (OAG)
SXN .... Sao Jose Do Xingu [*Brazil*] [*Airport symbol*] (OAG)
SXR .... Srinagar [*India*] [*Airport symbol*] (OAG)
SXS .... Gunes Ekspres Havacilik AS (Sunexpress) [*Turkey*] [*ICAO designator*] (FAAC)
Sy .... Seyyar [*Mobile*] (TU)
SY .... Syria [*or Syrian Arab Republic*] [*ANSI two-letter standard code*] (CNC)
SYA .... Scandinavian Yachting Association [*See also SKAN SF*] (EAIO)
SYA .... Somateion Ypodimatergaton Athinon [*Union of Athens Shoeworkers*] (GC)
SYa .... Standard Language (RU)
SYAF .... Syrian Air Force
SYAH .... Aishalton [*Guyana*] [*ICAO location identifier*] (ICLI)
SYAN .... Annai [*Guyana*] [*ICAO location identifier*] (ICLI)
SYAP .... Apoteri [*Guyana*] [*ICAO location identifier*] (ICLI)
SYAPCO ... South Yemeni-Algerian Petroleum Company (ME)
SYAW .... Awaruwaunawa [*Guyana*] [*ICAO location identifier*] (ICLI)
SYB .... Symbol [*Spain*] [*ICAO designator*] (FAAC)
SYBAN ...... Syndicat Belge d'Assurances Nucleaires [*Belgium*] (PDAA)
SYBAZ ...... Syndicat du Batiment du Zaire [*Political party*] [*Zaire*]
SYBEAUXARTS ... Syndicat des Beaux Arts Africains [*Union of African Fine Arts*]
SYBELEC ... Syndicat Belge d'Etudes et de Recherches Electroniques [*Belgian Union for Electronics Study and Research*] (PDAA)
SYBETRA ... Syndicat Belge d'Entreprise a l'Etranger [*Belgian Foreign Contracting Syndicate*] (WER)
SYBOCOA ... Syndicat Bordelais du Commerce Ouest Africain
SYBR .... Baramita [*Guyana*] [*ICAO location identifier*] (ICLI)
SYBT .... Bartica [*Guyana*] [*ICAO location identifier*] (ICLI)
SYC .... Seychelles [*ANSI three-letter standard code*] (CNC)
SYC .... Somali Youth Club
SYC .... Yemen General Insurance Company [*Yemen Arab Republic*] (MENA)
SYCA .... Syndicat d'Etude des Centrales Atomique [*Nuclear energy*] [*Belgium*] (NRCH)
SYCOM ..... Sydney Computerised Overnight Market [*Australia*]
SYCOMIMPEX ... Syndicat des Commercants Importateurs-Exportateurs [*Import-Export Businessmen's Union*] [*Central African Republic*] (AF)
SYCOMOM ... Syndicat des Constructeurs Belge de Machines Outils pour le Travail des Metaux [*Belgium*] (PDAA)
SYD .... Sydney [*Australia*] [*Airport symbol*] (OAG)
SyD .... Synodiki Dioikisis [*Synodical Administration*] [*Greek*] (GC)
SYDATRABA ... Syndicat Dahomeen des Entreprises de Travaux Publics et de Batiment
Syd CollArts ... Sydney College of the Arts [*Australia*]
Syd CollChiropractic ... Sydney College of Chiropractic [*Australia*]
SYDHARB ... Sydney Harbour [*Measurement of water*] [*Australia*] (ADA)
SYDICAM ... Syndicat des Commercants Importateurs Camerounais
SYDNE ...... Syndesmos Dimokratikon Neon Ellados [*League of Greek Democratic Youth*] (GC)
SYDONI .... Systeme de Documentation Notariale Informatique [*French*] (ADPT)
SYDSTOCK ... Sydney Stock Exchange Share Prices [*Database*] [*Sydney Stock Exchange*] [*Australia*] [*Information service or system*] (CRD)
SYE .... Sa'Dah [*Yemen Arab Republic*] [*Airport symbol*] (OAG)
sye .... Strontium Unit (RU)
SYEB .... Ebini [*Guyana*] [*ICAO location identifier*] (ICLI)
SYeKhB .... Soyuz Yevangel'skikh Khristian-Baptistov (EAIO)
SYeP .... Socialist Unity Party (RU)
SYePG ...... Socialist Unity Party of Germany (RU)
SYePI .... Socialist Unity Party of Iceland (RU)
SYET .... Syllogos Ypallilon Emborikis Trapezis [*Association of Employees of the Commercial Bank*] [*Greek*] (GC)
SYETh .... Somateion Ypovoleon Ellinikou Theatrou [*Greek Theater Prompters Union*] (GC)
SYGC .... Georgetown [*Guyana*] [*ICAO location identifier*] (ICLI)
SYGERBE ... Systeme de Gestion Documentaire des Brevets [*French*] (ADPT)
SYGH .... Good Hope [*Guyana*] [*ICAO location identifier*] (ICLI)
sygn .... Sygnatura [*Signature*] [*Publishing*] (POL)
SYGO .... Ogle [*Guyana*] [*ICAO location identifier*] (ICLI)

SYGT........ Georgetown [*Guyana*] [*ICAO location identifier*] (ICLI)
SYIB.......... Imbaimadai [*Guyana*] [*ICAO location identifier*] (ICLI)
SYK........... Stykkisholmur [*Iceland*] [*Airport symbol*] (OAG)
SYKA........ Kaieteur [*Guyana*] [*ICAO location identifier*] (ICLI)
SYKA........ Syndekhnia Kypriakon Aerogrammon [*Cyprus Airways Trade Union*] (GC)
SYKB........ Sinai Yatirim ve Kredi Bankasi [*Industrial Investment and Credit Bank*] (TU)
SYKEA...... Stratiotiki Ypiresia Kataskevis Ergon Anasyngrotiseos [*MOMA*] [*Military Service for the Construction of Reconstruction Projects*] [*See also*] [*Greek*] (GC)
SYKFA...... Syllogos Kyprion Foititon Anglias [*League of Cypriot Students in England*] (GC)
SYKI......... Kaow Island [*Guyana*] [*ICAO location identifier*] (ICLI)
SYKK........ Kurukabaru [*Guyana*] [*ICAO location identifier*] (ICLI)
SYKL........ Suomen YK-Liitto [*Finland*] (EAIO)
SYKM........ Kamarang [*Guyana*] [*ICAO location identifier*] (ICLI)
SYKR........ Karanambo [*Guyana*] [*ICAO location identifier*] (ICLI)
SYKS........ Karasabai [*Guyana*] [*ICAO location identifier*] (ICLI)
SYKT........ Kato (Karto) [*Guyana*] [*ICAO location identifier*] (ICLI)
SYKW........ Kwakwani [*Guyana*] [*ICAO location identifier*] (ICLI)
SYL........... Salvation Army Youth Line [*Australia*]
SYL........... Somali Youth League [*Political party*] (AF)
SYL........... Suomen Ylloppilaskuntien Liitto [*Finnish University Student Union*] (WEN)
SYL........... Sveriges Yngre Laekares Foerening [*Sweden*] (SLS)
SYLD........ Linden [*Guyana*] [*ICAO location identifier*] (ICLI)
SYLF........ Sveriges Yngre Laekares Foerening [*Sweden*] (SLS)
SYLP........ Lumid Pau [*Guyana*] [*ICAO location identifier*] (ICLI)
SYLT........ Lethem [*Guyana*] [*ICAO location identifier*] (ICLI)
SYM.......... Salesian Youth Movement (EA)
SYM.......... Simao [*China*] [*Airport symbol*] (OAG)
sym............ Symmetrisch [*Symmetric*] [*German*] (GCA)
SYMAF..... Syndicat Minier Africain
SYMATEX... Syndicat des Constructeurs Belges de Machines Textiles [*Belgium*] (PDAA)
SYMATOGO... Syndicat des Manutentionnaires Togolais
SYMB........ Mabaruma [*Guyana*] [*ICAO location identifier*] (ICLI)
SYMD....... Mahdia [*Guyana*] [*ICAO location identifier*] (ICLI)
SYMETAIN... Syndicat Miniere de l'Etain [*Tin Mining Workers Union*] [*Zaire*] (AF)
SYMETRA... Syndicat des Entrepreneurs Metropolitains de Travaux Publics Travaillant Outre-Mer
Symf........... Symfoni & Artist [*Record label*] [*Sweden*]
SYMM...... Monkey Mountain [*Guyana*] [*ICAO location identifier*] (ICLI)
SYMN....... Manari [*Guyana*] [*ICAO location identifier*] (ICLI)
SYMOB...... Systeme Modulaire Bull [*French*] (ADPT)
SYMP........ Mountain Point [*Guyana*] [*ICAO location identifier*] (ICLI)
SYMR....... Matthews Ridge [*Guyana*] [*ICAO location identifier*] (ICLI)
SYMW...... Maruranawa [*Guyana*] [*ICAO location identifier*] (ICLI)
syn............. Syndrofos [*Comrade*] (GC)
syn............. Synonym [*Synonymous*] [*German*] (GCA)
Syn............ Synonyme [*French*] (FLAF)
SYNA........ New Amsterdam [*Guyana*] [*ICAO location identifier*] (ICLI)
SYNABOIS... Syndicat National des Forestiers Producteurs des Bois
SYNAC...... Syndicat National des Agriculteurs et Cultivateurs de Haute-Volta [*National Union of Farmers and Cultivators of Upper Volta*] (AF)
SYNACAAB... Syndicat des Agents de la Caisse Autonome d'Amortissement du Benin [*Union of Agents of the Independent Amortization Fund of Benin*] (AF)
SYNACADA... Syndicat National des Commercants Africains du Dahomey
SYNACIB... Syndicat National des Commercants et Industriels Africains du Benin [*National Union of African Merchants and Industrialists of Benin*] (AF)
SYNACID... Syndicat National des Commercants et Industriels Africains du Dahomey
SYNACODA... Syndicat des Cies de Navigation et des Consignataires de Navires du Dahomey
SYNAD..... Syndicat des Administrateurs Civils [*Civil Administrators Union*] [*Malagasy*] (AF)
SYNAEM... Syndicat National de l'Enseignement Moyen General Publique [*National Union of General Public Middle Education*] [*Benin*] (AF)
SYNAESS... Syndicat National des Professeurs des Enseignements Secondaire et Superieur [*National Trade Union of Teachers of Secondary and Higher Education*] [*Benin*] (AF)
SYNAGELSCAM... Syndicat des Gerants Libres de Station Service au Cameroun
SYNAGRI... Syndicat National des Agents d'Agriculture [*National Union of Agricultural Agents*] [*Burkina Faso*] (AF)
SYNAICAN... Systeme National d'Information Camerounais
SYNAME... Syndicat National de la Mesure Electrique et Electronique [*France*] (PDAA)
SYNAPEMEIN... Syndicat National des Petites et Moyennes Entreprises et Industries Nigeriennes [*Employers' organization*] [*Niger*]

SYNARES... Syndicat Africain de la Recherche et de l'Enseignement Superieur [*African Union for Research and Higher Education*] [*Ivory Coast*] (AF)
SYNCAB... Syndicat National du Commerce, des Banques, du Credit, et des Assurances
SYNCOBENI... Syndicat des Cheminots de l'OCBN [*OCBN Railroad Workers Trade Union*] (AF)
SYNDAGRI... Syndicat des Employeurs Agricoles
SYNDIBOIS... Syndicat du Bois du Congo
SYNDIMINES... Syndicat des Entreprises Minieres au Gabon
SYNDINAVI... Syndicat des Compagnies de Navigation et Consignataires de Navires en Cote-D'Ivoire
SYNDUSTREF... Syndicat des Industries de l'Afrique Equatoriale
SYNDUSTRICAM... Syndicat des Industriels du Cameroun
Syne........... Synagogue [*Synagogue*] [*Military map abbreviation World War I*] [*French*] (MTD)
SYNEBACI... Syndicat National Unique des Entrepreneurs en Batiment de Cote-D'Ivoire [*Sole National Union of Building Contractors of the Ivory Coast*] (AF)
SYNECECI... Syndicat National des Educateurs, Conseillers d'Education de Cote-D'Ivoire
SYNECI.... Syndicat National des Enseignants du Second Degre de Cote-D'Ivoire [*National Union of Secondary Teachers of the Ivory Coast*] (AF)
SYNECTO... Syndicat des Employes de Commerce du Togo [*Togolese Business Employees Trade Union*] (AF)
SYNEECAB... Syndicat National des Enseignants des Ecoles Ex-Catholiques du Benin [*Trade union*] [*Benin*]
SYNEG...... Syndicat National de l'Equipement des Grandes Cuisines [*France*] (EAIO)
SYNEIS..... Syndicat National de l'Enseignement Laic du Senegal
SYNEksport... Sinai Mamulleri Yatirim Nakliyat, Ihracat, ve Ithalat AS [*Industrial Products Investment, Transport, Export, and Import Corp.*] (TU)
SYNELS.... Syndicat National de l'Enseignement Laic du Senegal [*National Union of Lay Teachers of Senegal*] (AF)
SYNEPPCI... Syndicat National de l'Enseignement Primaire Public de Cote-D'Ivoire [*Ivory Coast National Public Primary Education Union*] (AF)
SYNERGAZ... Synergatikos Organismos Emfyaloseos Ygraeriou [*Gas Bottling Cooperative Organization*] [*Cyprus*] (GC)
SYNESCI.. Syndicat National des Enseignants du Second Degre [*National Secondary School Teachers Union*] [*Ivory Coast*] (AF)
SYNINDUSTRICAM... Syndicat des Industriels du Cameroun (EY)
SYNMAD... Syndicat des Manutentionnaires du Dahomey
synt............ Syntynyt [*Finland*]
SYNTADE... Syndicat National des Travailleurs des Administrations d'Etat
SYNTECAM... Societe Camerounaise pour la Fabrication de Tissus Synthetiques
SYNTEEDISETO... Syndicat des Travailleurs de l'Energie Electrique et de Distribution d'Eau du Togo [*Union of Electrical and Water Distribution Workers of Togo*]
SYNTEP... Syndicat des Travailleurs des Entreprises Petroliers
Synth......... Synthese [*Synthesis*] [*German*] (GCA)
synth......... Synthetisch [*Synthetic*] [*German*] (GCA)
synthet....... Synthetisch [*Synthetic*] [*German*] (GCA)
SYNTRAGA... Syndicat National des Transporteurs Urbains et Routiers du Gabon (EY)
SYNUS...... System-Netzknoten und Stapelstation [*German*] (ADPT)
SYO.......... Sydney Youth Orchestra [*Australia*]
SYOR....... Orinduik [*Guyana*] [*ICAO location identifier*] (ICLI)
SYP.......... Soma Ylikou Polemou [*(Army) Ordnance Corps*] (GC)
SYP........... Sosialistinen Yhtenaisyyspuolue [*Socialist Unity Party*] [*Finland*] (WEN)
SYP........... Suomen Yksityisyrittaejaein Puoluejaerjesto [*Finnish Private Entrepreneurs' Party*] [*Political party*] (PPE)
SYPACOA... Syndicat Parisien du Commerce Ouest Africain
SYPAOA... Syndicat Patronal et Artisanal de l'Ouest Africain [*West African Employers and Artisans Union*] (AF)
SYPE........ Symvoulion Prostasias Perivallondos [*Environment Protection Council*] (GC)
SYPO........ Sarawak Young People's Organization (Communist) (ML)
SYPR........ Paruima [*Guyana*] [*ICAO location identifier*] (ICLI)
syr.............. Cheese Dairy [*Topography*] (RU)
SYR........... Syria [*or Syrian Arab Republic*] [*ANSI three-letter standard code*] (CNC)
SYR........... Syrian Arab Airlines [*ICAO designator*] (FAAC)
SYRFA...... Societe de Systeme Francaise pour les Reacteurs Avances [*Nuclear energy*] [*French*] (NRCH)
SYS........... Society of Young Scientists [*India*] (SLS)
SYS........... Synthesewerk Schwarzheide [*Former East German chemical company*] (ECON)
SYSMIN... System for Mineral Products [*European Community*] (MHDB)
SYSMIN... System for Safeguarding and Developing Mineral Production [*EC*] (ECED)
SYSNA...... Societe des Systemes d'Aides a la Navigation [*France*] (PDAA)
SYSPRO.... Systematik der Programmvorgaben [*German*] (ADPT)

Syst .... System [*German*]   (GCA)
syst .... Systematisch [*Systematic*] [*German*]   (GCA)
Syst No ...... System Nummer [*System Number*] [*German*]
SYT .... Sayistay [*Court of Accounts*]   (TU)
SYTANE ... Synergatikon Tamievtirion Spoudazousis Neolaias [*Cooperative Savings Bank for Students*] [*Cyprus*]   (GC)
SYTM .... Georgetown/Timehri Internacional [*Guyana*] [*ICAO location identifier*]   (ICLI)
SYTYRIK ... Syndekhnia Tekhnikon Ypallilon Radiofonikon Idryma Kyprou [*Union of Cyprus Broadcasting Corporation Technical Personnel*] [*Cyprus*]   (GC)
SYu .... Soviet Justice   (RU)
SYU .... Sudanese Youth Union
SYuI .... Sverdlovsk Law Institute   (RU)
SYuK .... League of Communists of Yugoslavia   (BU)
SYuN .... Young Naturalists' Station   (RU)
SYuT .... Young Technicians' Station   (RU)
SYWI .... Wichabai [*Guyana*] [*ICAO location identifier*]   (ICLI)
SYWPP ..... South Yarra Work Preparation Program [*Australia*]
SYZ .... Shiraz [*Iran*] [*Airport symbol*]   (OAG)
SZ .... Antisubmarine Net   (RU)
SZ .... Collection of Laws of the USSR   (RU)
SZ .... Concentrated Charge   (RU)
sz .... Conjunction   (BU)
SZ .... Glassware Plant   (BU)
SZ .... Northwest   (BU)
SZ .... Northwest, Northwestern   (RU)
SZ .... Saeurezahl [*Acid Number*] [*German*]
Sz .... Samozalozba [*Privately Printed*]   (YU)
SZ .... Satzzeichen [*German*]   (ADPT)
sZ .... Seinerzeit [*At That Time*] [*German*]   (EG)
Sz .... Seitenzahl [*Number of Pages*] [*German*]
SZ .... Sekretarijat za Zemjodelstvo (IVNRM) [*Secretariat of Agriculture*]   (YU)
sz .... Severozapad [*Northwest*]   (CZ)
SZ .... Skodovy Zavody [*Skoda Works*]   (CZ)
SZ .... Smeralovy Zavody [*Smeral Plants*]   (CZ)
SZ .... Sociale Zaken [*Benelux*]   (BAS)
SZ .... Sociale Zorg [*Benelux*]   (BAS)
SZ .... Socialisticke Zeme [*Socialist Countries*]   (CZ)
SZ .... Socijalisticka Zora [*Socialist Dawn*] [*Skopje A periodical*]   (YU)
SZ .... Socijalisticko Zemjodelie [*Socialist Agriculture*] [*Skopje A periodical*]   (YU)
SZ .... Sound Signal   (RU)
SZ .... Sovjetska Zveza [*Former USSR*]   (YU)
SZ .... Sowjetische Zone [*Soviet Zone*] [*German*]   (EG)
SZ .... Stalinovy Zavody [*Stalin Works*] [*Most*]   (CZ)
SZ .... Statni Zastupitelstvi [*State Prosecutor's Office*]   (CZ)
SZ .... Steuerzentrale [*German*]   (ADPT)
SZ .... Stocarska Zadruga [*Livestock Cooperative*]   (YU)
SZ .... Stolarska Zadruga [*Carpentry Cooperative*]   (YU)
SZ .... Svaz Zamestnancu [*Employees' Union*]   (CZ)
SZ .... Svermovy Zavody [*Sverma Works*]   (CZ)
SZ .... Svet za Zdravstvo [*Health Council*]   (YU)
SZ .... Swaziland [*ANSI two-letter standard code*]   (CNC)
sz .... Szabad [*Free*]   (HU)
sz .... Szakasz [*Platoon*]   (HU)
sz .... Szam [*Issue*] [*Publishing*] [*Hungary*]
sz .... Szanowny [*Honorable*] [*Poland*]   (GPO)
sz .... Szazad [*Century, One One-Hundredth, Military Company*]   (HU)
sz .... Szent [*Saint*]   (HU)
sz .... Szovetkezet [*Cooperative*]   (HU)
sz .... Szuletett [*Born*]   (HU)
SZA .... Aerolineas de El Salvador SA [*ICAO designator*]   (FAAC)
SZA .... Medium Antiaircraft Artillery   (RU)
SZA .... Medium-Caliber Antiaircraft Artillery   (BU)
SZA .... Servicio en Zona Ampliada [*Extended Area Service*] [*Spanish*]
SZA .... Soyo [*Angola*] [*Airport symbol*]   (OAG)
SZA .... Speicherzyklusanforderung [*German*]   (ADPT)
sz a .... Szam Alatt [*Number*]   (HU)
szab .... Szabalyozo [*Regulating, Controlling or Regulator, Controller*]   (HU)
SZAB .... Szabanugyi Allando Bizottsag (Kolcsonos Gazdasagi Segitseg Tanacsa) [*Permanent Committee on Standards (CEMA)*]   (HU)
SZAB .... Szamitastechnikai Alkalmazasi Bizottsagok [*Committees for the Application of Computer Technology*]   (HU)
sz adag .... Szabvany Adag [*Ration*]   (HU)
SZAK .... Szakasz [*Platoon (Military, Section, Detachment)*]   (HU)
szakip .... Szakiparos [*Skilled Craftsman*]   (HU)
szaku .... Szakuzlet [*Special Shop*]   (HU)
szall .... Szallito [*Carrier, Transporting*]   (HU)
szam .... Szamozott [*Numbered*]   (HU)

SZAMALK ... Szamitastechnika-Alkalmazasi Vallalat [*Computing Applications and Service Company*] [*Central Statistical Office*] [*Hungary*]
SZAMGEP ... Szamitastechnikai es Ugyvitelgepesitesi Vallalat [*Computer Technology and Management Mechanization Enterprise*]   (HU)
SZAMKI ... Szamitastechnikai Kutato Intezet [*Computer Technology Research Institute*]   (HU)
SZAMOK ... Szamitastechnikai Oktato Kozpont [*Computer Technology Training Center*]   (HU)
SZB .... Slovenske Zeleznorudne Bane [*Slovak Iron Ore Mines*]   (CZ)
SZB .... Szabadalmi Birosag [*Patent Court*]   (HU)
szb .... Szabvany [*Standard, Norm*]   (HU)
SZB .... Szakszervezeti Bizottsag [*Trade Union Committee*]   (HU)
szb .... Szerb [*Serbian*]   (HU)
SZBM .... Stoleczny Zarzad Budynkow Mieszkalnych [*Warsaw Residential Building Administration*]   (POL)
Szb M .... Szenbanyaszati Miniszterium/Miniszter [*Ministry/Minister of Coal Mining*]   (HU)
SZBT .... Szakszervezetek Budapesti Tanacsa [*Budapest Council of Trade Unions*]   (HU)
SZBZ .... Sokolovsky Zavod Branne Zdatnosti [*Sokolov Military Fitness Contest*]   (CZ)
SZCB .... Strzelinskie Zaklady Ceramiki Budowlanej [*Strzelin (Strehlen) Building Tile Plant*]   (POL)
szczeg .... Szczegolowy [*Detailed*]   (POL)
SZD .... Sovetski Zhelezno-Dorozhni [*Soviet railways*] [*Former USSR*]
SZD .... Svaz Zemedelskych Druzstev [*Union of Agricultural Cooperatives*]   (CZ)
szd .... Szazad [*Company (Infantry), Battery (Artillery), Squadron*]   (HU)
SZD .... Szybowcowy Zaklad Doswiadczalny [*Glider Proving Grounds*]   (POL)
SZDBiH .... Savez Zenskih Drustava Bosne i Hercegovine [*Federation of Women's Clubs of Bosnia and Hercegovina*]   (YU)
SZDCG ...... Savez Zenskih Drustava Crne Gore [*Federation of Women's Clubs of Montenegro*]   (YU)
SZDH .... Savez Zenskih Drustava Hrvatske [*Federation of Women's Clubs of Croatia*]   (YU)
SZDJ .... Savez Zenskih Drustava Jugoslavije [*Federation of Women's Clubs of Yugoslavia*]   (YU)
SZDK .... Statni Zkusebna pro Drahe Kovy [*State Testing Center for Precious Metals*]   (CZ)
SZDLLRS ... Socialisticna Zveza Delavnega Ljudstva Slovenje [*Socialist Union of Working People of Slovenia*]   (YU)
SZDN .... Statni Zdravotnicke Nakladatelstvi [*State Publishing House for Public Health Literature*]   (CZ)
SzDP .... Magyarorszagi Szocialdemokrata Part [*Hungarian Social-Democratic Party*] [*Political party*]   (EY)
SZDP .... Szocialdemokrata Part [*Social Democratic Party*]   (HU)
SZDS .... Savez Zenskih Drustava Srbije [*Federation of Women's Clubs of Serbia*]   (YU)
szds .... Szazados [*Captain*]   (HU)
SZDSZ ...... Alliance of Free Democrats [*Hungary*] [*Political party*]
SzDSz .... Szabad Demokratak Szovetsege [*Alliance of Free Democrats*] [*Hungary*] [*Political party*]   (EY)
SZE .... Integrated Power System of the Northwest   (RU)
SZE .... Szabad Europa (Radio) [*Radio Free Europe*]   (HU)
sze .... Szerda [*Wednesday*]   (HU)
SZEB .... Szovetseges Ellenorzo Bizottsag [*Allied Control Commission*]   (HU)
SZEBMGH ... Szovetseges Ellenorzo Bizottsag Magyar Gazdasagi Hivatala [*Hungarian Economic Office of the Allied Control Commission*]   (HU)
SzEF .... Szakszervezetek Egyuettmukoedesi Foruma [*Central Authority of Trade Unions*] [*Hungary*]   (EY)
SZEFU ...... Szekerfuvarozasi Vallalat [*Carting Enterprise*]   (HU)
S Zek .... Sociale Zekerheidsgids [*Benelux*]   (BAS)
SzEK .... Szegedi Tudomanyegyetem Konyvtara [*Library of the University of Szeged*]   (HU)
szem o .... Szemelyzeti Osztaly [*Personnel Department*]   (HU)
szenb .... Szenbanya [*Coal Mine*]   (HU)
SzepirodK ... Szepirodalmi Kiado [*Publishing House for Belles Lettres*]   (HU)
szept .... Szeptember [*September*]   (HU)
SZER .... Szabad Europa Radio [*Radio Free Europe*]   (HU)
szer .... Szerokosc [*or Szeroki*] [*Breadth or Broad*] [*Poland*]
szer geogr ... Szerokosc Geograficzna [*Latitude*] [*Poland*]
szerk .... Szerkesztette [*Edited By*] [*Hungary*]   (GPO)
szero .... Szeroszlop [*Army Supply Column*]   (HU)
szesc .... Szescienny [*Cubic*] [*Poland*]
SZESZ .... Szocialista Egyuttmukodesi Szerzodes [*Socialist Cooperation Contract*]   (HU)
SZETmozgalom ... Szakmunkasok Egyetemi Tanulasa Mozgalom [*"Skilled Workers to Attend University" Movement*]   (HU)
sz ev .... Szoko Ev [*Leap Year*]   (HU)
SZF .... Blocking-Filter Bay   (RU)

SZF .... Schweizerische Vereinigung fuer Zukunftsforschung [*Swiss Association for Research on Afterlife*] (SLS)
SZF I .... Szinhaz- es Filmtudomanyi Intezet [*Theater and Film Research Institute*] (HU)
SZFK .... Savezni Zavod za Fizicku Kulturu [*Federal Institute of Physical Culture*] (YU)
SZG .... Salzburg [*Austria*] [*Airport symbol*] (OAG)
SZG .... Schweizerische Zoologische Gesellschaft [*Swiss Zoological Association*] (SLS)
SZg .... Signale an Zuegen [*Signals on Trains*] [*German*] (EG)
SZG .... Szczecinskie Zaklady Gastronomiczne [*Szczecin Catering Establishments*] [*Poland*]
SZGA .... Saratov Gas Equipment Plant (RU)
SZGRP ...... Northwestern State River Steamship Line (RU)
SZGRT ...... Northwestern Geological Exploration Trust (RU)
SZGT .... Supersonic Gas Turbine (RU)
Sz Gy .... Szabvanygyujtemeny [*Collection of Standards, List of Standards*] (HU)
SZh .... Inflatable Life Jacket (RU)
SZh .... Lead Fluid [*Additive for gasoline*] (RU)
SZh .... Saccharose, Gelatin (RU)
SZH .... Svaz Zamestnancu v Hornictvi [*Mining Employees' Union*] (CZ)
szh .... Szekhely [*County Seat*] (HU)
SZhA .... Saccharose, Gelatin, Agar (RU)
SZhB .... Union of Bulgarian Journalists (BU)
Sz Hi .... Szabvanyugyi Hivatal [*Office of Standardization*] (HU)
SZhK .... Serum of Mares in Foal (RU)
SZhK .... Synthetic Fatty Acid (RU)
SZhS .... Synthetic Aliphatic Alcohol (RU)
SZhZ .... Synthetic Fat Substitutes (RU)
szi .... Szemelyiranyito [*Personnel Director (Office, Officer)*] (HU)
szig .... Szigorlo [*Candidate for Doctoral Degree*] (HU)
SZIKKTI/SZIKTI ... Szilikatipari Kozponti Kutato es Tervezo Intezet [*Central Research and Planning Institute of the Silicate Industry*] (HU)
SZIM .... Szerszamgepipari Muvek [*Machine Tool Industry Works*] (HU)
SZIM .... Szocialista Ifjumunkas Szovetseg [*Socialist Young Workers' Association*] (HU)
SZIMCS .... Szamitastechnikai Ideglenes Munkacsoport [*Temporary Work Group for Computer Technology*] (HU)
SZINV .... Savjet za Zakonodavstvo i Izgradnju Narodne Vlasti [*Council for Legislation and Development of People's Government*] (YU)
SZISLSLRS ... Sekretarijat za Zakonodajo Izvrsnega Sveta Ljudske Skupscine Ljudske Republike Slovenije [*Secretariat for Legislation of the Executive Council of the People's Assembly of Slovenia*] (YU)
SZIT .... Szakszervezeti Ifjumunkas es Tanoncmozgalom [*Movement of Socialist Young Workers and Apprentices*] (HU)
SZK .... Savez Zanatskih Komora [*Union of Chambers of Artisans*] (YU)
SZK .... Skukuza [*South Africa*] [*Airport symbol*] (OAG)
SZ K .... Szepirodalmi Kiado [*Fiction and Poetry Publishing House*] (HU)
SzK(b)P ...... Szovjetunio Kommunista (Bolsevik) Partja [*Communist Party of the Soviet Union (Bolshevik)*] (HU)
SZKFI .... Magyar Szenhidrogenipari Kutato-Fejleszto Intezet [*Hungarian Hydrocarbon Institute*] [*Research center*] (IRC)
SZKFP ...... Szamitastechnikai Kozponti Fejlesztesi Program [*Central Development Program for Computer Technology*] (HU)
SZKI .... Co-Ordinating Institute of Computer Technics [*Hungary*] (HU)
SzKP .... Szovjetunio Kommunista Partja [*Communist Party of the Soviet Union*] (HU)
SZKPKB.... Szovjetunio Kommunista Partjanak Kozponti Bizottsaga [*Central Committee of the Communist Party of the Soviet Union*] (HU)
SZKSH ...... Szovjetunio Kozponti Statisztikai Hivatala [*Central Statistical Office of the Soviet Union*] (HU)
SZKU .... Statni Zememericky a Kartograficky Ustav [*State Geodetic and Cartographic Institute*] (CZ)
SZKU .... Statni Zemepisny a Kartograficky Ustav [*State Geographic and Cartographic Institute*] (CZ)
szkv .... Szakaszvezeto [*Junior Sergeant*] (HU)
szkv .... Szolgalatonkivuli [*Retired*] (HU)
szla .... Szamla [*Invoice*] (HU)
szle .... Szemle [*Review*] (HU)
SzlKP .... Szlovakia Kommunista Partja [*Communist Party of Slovakia*] (HU)
SZLTE .... Szovjet-Unio Legfelsobb Tanacsanak Elnoksege [*Presidium of the Supreme Soviet of the Soviet Union*] (HU)
SZM .... Skawinskie Zaklady Metalurgiczne [*Skawina Metallurgical Plant*] (POL)
SZMGSZ .. Szovjet Magyar Gazdasagi Szerzodes [*Soviet-Hungarian Economic Pact*] (HU)
SZMT .... Szakszervezetek Megyei Tanacsa [*Megye (County) Trade Union Council*] (HU)

SZN .... Statni Zemedelske Nakladatelstvi [*State Agricultural Publishing House*] (CZ)
SZN .... Stazione Zoologica di Napoli [*Naples Zoological Station*] [*Research center*] [*Italian*] (IRC)
SZ N .... Szabad Nep [*Free People (Daily Newspaper of the Hungarian Communist Party)*] (HU)
SZNIIGM ... Northwestern Scientific Research Institute of Hydraulic Engineering and Reclamation (RU)
SZNIISKh ... Northwestern Scientific Research Institute of Agriculture (RU)
SZN Kvt..... Szocialista Neveles Konyvtara [*Library of Socialist Education*] (HU)
SZNZ........ Savezni Zavod za Narodno Zdravlje [*Federal Institute of Public Health*] (YU)
SZO .... Correspondence Training Section (RU)
SZO .... Northwestern Branch, Northwestern Department (RU)
SZO .... Samostatny Zdravotnicky Oddil [*Separate Medical Battalion*] (CZ)
SZO .... Sekretarijat za Zakonodavstvo i Organizaciju (SIV) [*Secretariat of Legislation and Organization*] (YU)
SZO .... Svetova Zdravotnicka Organizace [*World Health Organization*] (CZ)
SZO .... Svetska Zdravstvena Organizacija [*World Health Organization*] (YU)
szocdem...... Szocial Demokrata [*Social Democrat*] (HU)
SZOE........ Szegedi Orvostudomanyi Egyetem [*Medical University of Szeged*] (HU)
SZO K....... SZOVOSZ Kiadovallalat (Szovetkezetek Orszagos Szovetsege Kiadovallalata) [*SZOVOSZ Publishing House (Publishing House of the National Association of Cooperatives)*] (HU)
SZOMATEX ... Szombathelyi Pamutipar [*Cotton Mill of Szombathely*] (HU)
szomb .... Szombat [*Saturday*] (HU)
SZOPK ...... Slovensky Zvaz Ochrancov Prirody a Krajiny [*Slovak Union of Nature and Landscape Conservationists*] (EE)
SZOSZ ...... Szakszervezetek Orszagos Szovetsege [*National Federation of Trade Unions*] (HU)
SzOT .... Szakszervezetek Orszagos Tanacsa [*National Council of Trade Unions*] (HU)
SZOTE ...... Szeged Orvostudomanyi Egyetem [*Szeged Medical University*] (HU)
SZOVARU ... Szovetkezetek Orszagos Arubeszerzo es Ertekesito Kozos Vallalata [*Cooperatives National Joint Enterprise for Procuring Goods and Sales*] (HU)
SZOVAUT ... Kozepmagyarorszagi Foldmuvesszovetkezetek Szallitasi Vallalat [*Transportation Enterprise of the Agricultural Cooperatives in Central Hungary*] (HU)
SZOVERT ... Szovetkezetek Orszagos Felvasarlo es Ertekesito Kozpontja [*National Purchasing and Marketing Center of Cooperatives*] (HU)
SZOVOSZ ... Szovetkezetek Orszagos Szovetsege [*National Federation of Cooperatives*] (HU)
szp .... Gravitation Force (RU)
SZP .... Slaskie Zaklady Przemyslowe [*Silesia Industrial Plants*] (POL)
SZP .... Szczecinskie Zaklady Pralnicze [*Szczecin (Stettin) Laundries*] (POL)
szp .... Szpalta [*Column*] (POL)
SZPI .... Northwestern Correspondence Polytechnic Institute (RU)
SZPO........ Szczecinskie Zaklady Przemyslu Odziezowego [*Szczecin (Stettin) Clothing Plant*] (POL)
SZPP .... Savezni Zavod za Privredno Planiranje (DSPRP) [*Federal Institute of Economic Planning*] (YU)
SZPP .... Svaz Zamestnancu v Peneznictvi a Pojistovnictvi [*Union of Employees in the Field of Finance and Insurance*] (CZ)
SZPR .... Savezni Zavod za Produktivnost Rada [*Federal Institute for Labor Productivity*] (YU)
SZPSPP..... Savezni Zavod za Proucavanje Skolskih i Prosvetnih Pitanje [*Federal Institute for the Study of School and Cultural Problems*] (YU)
SZPT .... Stoleczny Zarzad Przemyslu Terenowego [*Warsaw Local Industry Administration*] (POL)
SZPU .... Statni Zastavni a Pujcovni Urad [*State Loan Office and Pawnshop*] (CZ)
SZPW .... Slaskie Zaklady Przemyslu Welnianego [*Silesia Wool Plants*] (POL)
SZR........... Green-Light Signal Relay (RU)
SZR........... Public Health Employees Union (BU)
SZR........... Statni Zdravotni Rada [*State Public Health Council*] (CZ)
sz r............. Szabalyrendelet [*Bylaw, Statute, Ordinance*] (HU)
sz r............. Szamu Rendelet [*Decree Numbered*] (HU)
SzRI .... Szakorvosi Rendelo Intezet [*Center of Medical Specialists*] (HU)
SZRP .... Northwestern River Steamship Line (RU)
SZRSJ .... Sindikat Zeljeznickih Radnika i Sluzbenika Jugoslavije [*Trade-Union of Railroad Workmen and Employees of Yugoslavia*] (YU)
SZS .... Blue-Green Glass (RU)
SZS .... Savezni Zavod za Statistiku (DSPRP) [*Federal Statistical Office*] (YU)

SZS .... Slovenska Zemepisna Spolocnost [*Slovak Geographic Society*] (CZ)

SzS .... Solidarnosc z Solidarnoscia [*Solidarity with Solidarity - SwS*] [*Defunct*] (EAIO)

SZS .... Sreski Zadruzni Savez [*District Cooperative Union*] (YU)

SZS .... Srpska Zemljoradnicka Stranka [*Serbian Agrarian Party*] [*Former Yugoslavia*] [*Political party*] (PPE)

SZS .... Staatliche Zentralverwaltung fuer Statistik [*State Central Administration for Statistics*] (EG)

SZS .... Stewart Island [*New Zealand*] [*Airport symbol*] (OAG)

SZS .... Svaz Zamestnancov Skolstva [*Union of Employees in Educational Institutions*] (CZ)

SZS .... Szkolny Zwiazek Sportowy [*School Athletics and Sports Association*] [*Poland*]

SZSO .... Savezni Zavod za Socijalno Osiguranje [*Federal Institute of Social Insurance*] (YU)

SZSO .... Svaz Zamestnancu Skolstvi a Osvety [*Union of Educational and Cultural Employees*] (CZ)

SZSU .... Statny Zdravotne-Socialny Ustav [*State Public Health and Social Institute*] (CZ)

szszakszerv ... Szabad Szakszervezet [*Free Trade Union*] (HU)

SZSZK .... Szovjet Szocialista Koztarsasag [*Soviet Socialist Republic*] (HU)

SZSZKSZ ... Szovjet Szocialista Koztarsasagok Szovetsege [*Union of Soviet Socialist Republics*] (HU)

SZSZNSZ ... Szabad Szakszervezetek Nemzetkozi Szovetsege [*International Federation of Free Trade Unions*] (HU)

s Zt .... Seiner Zeit [*Then*] [*German*]

SZT .... Standard Fuze (RU)

SZT .... Szakszervezeti Tanacs [*Trade Union Council*] (HU)

SZT .... Szechenyi Tarsasag [*Szechenyi Association*] (HU)

SzT .... Szegedi Textilmuvek [*Textile Factory of Szeged*] (HU)

Szt .... Szent [*Saint*] (HU)

SZTA .... Szovjet-Unio Tudomanyos Akademiaja [*Academy of Sciences of the Soviet Union*] (HU)

SZTAKI ..... MTA Szamitastechnikai es Automatizlasi Kutato Intezet [*Computer Technology and Automation Research Institute of the Hungarian Academy of Sciences*] (HU)

SZTE .... Szilikatipari Tudomanyos Egyesulet [*Scientific Association of the Silicate Industry*] (HU)

Szt Gl .... Sztab Glowny [*General Staff*] [*Poland*]

SZTI .... Szakfelugyeleti es Tovabbkepzesi Intezet [*Technical Supervision and Advanced Training Institute*] (HU)

SZTK .... Szakszervezeti Tarsadalombiztositasi Kozpont [*Trade Union Social Insurance Center*] (HU)

sztl .... Szamozatlan [*Unnumbered*] (HU)

SZU .... Self-Propelled Antiaircraft Gun (RU)

SZU .... Sociedad Zoologica del Uruguay [*Uruguay*] (DSCA)

SZU .... Statni Zdravotni Ustav [*State Health Institute*] (CZ)

SZU .... Statni Zememericsky Ustav [*State Geodetic Institute*] (CZ)

SZU .... Statny Zemepisny Ustav [*State Geographical Institute*] (CZ)

SZU .... Strojirensky Zkusebni Ustav [*Testing Institute for Engineering*] (CZ)

SzU .... Szovjetunio [*Former USSR*] (HU)

SZUB .... Sluzba Zagraniczna Urzedu Bezpieczenstwa [*Foreign Service of the Security Administration*] (POL)

SZUGMS .. Northwestern Administration of the Hydrometeorological Service (RU)

SZUL .... Szuletett [*Born*] (HU)

SZUMT ..... Szovjetunio Minisztertanacsa [*Council of Ministers of the Soviet Union*] (HU)

SZUTA ...... Szovjetunio Tudomanyos Akademiaja [*USSR Academy of Sciences*] (HU)

SZUV .... Szamitastechnikai es Ugyvitelszervezesi Vallalat [*Computer Technology and Management Organization Enterprise*] (HU)

SZV .... Schweizerischer Saatzuchtverband [*Switzerland*] (EAIO)

SZV .... Sdruzeni Zahranicnich Vojaku [*Association of Veterans of Foreign Wars*] (CZ)

SZV .... Svaz Zahranicnych Vojakov [*Association of Veterans of Foreign Wars*] (CZ)

szv .... Szemelyvonat [*Local Train*] (HU)

szv .... Szovetkezeti Vallalat [*Cooperative Enterprise*] (HU)

SZVD .... Slovensky Zvaz Vyrobnych Druzstiev [*Slovak Union of Production Cooperatives*] (CZ)

SZVI .... Saratov Zootechnical and Veterinary Institute (RU)

SzVK .... Szakszervezeti Vilagkongresszus [*World Congress of Trade Unions*] (HU)

SZVMKI ... Szerves Vegyipari es Muanyagipari Kutato Intezet [*Industrial Research Institute on Organic Chemistry and Plastics*] (HU)

SZVSZ .... Szakszervezeti Vilagszovetseg [*World Federation of Trade Unions*] (HU)

SZVT .... Szervezesi es Vezetesi Tudomanyos Tarsasag [*Scientific Society of Organization and Management*] (HU)

SZVU .... Sdruzeni Zapadoceskych Vytvarnych Umelcu [*Association of West Bohemian Creative Artists*] (CZ)

SZWI .... Stalinogrodskie Zjednoczenie Wodno-Inzynierskie [*Stalinogrod (now again Katowice) Hydraulic Engineering Association*] (POL)

SZWS .... Szczecinskie Zaklady Wlokien Sztucznych [*Szczecin (Stettin) Synthetic Fiber Plant*] (POL)

SZZ .... Savez Zemljoradnickih Zadruga [*Union of Agricultural Cooperatives*] (YU)

SZZ .... Slovenska Zenska Zveza (v Ameriki) [*Slovenian Women's Union (in America)*] [*Chicago*] (YU)

SZZ .... Sreska Zanatska Zadruga [*District Artisan Cooperative*] (YU)

SZZ .... Svaz Zamestnancu v Zemedelstvi [*Union of Agricultural Workers*] (CZ)

SZZ .... Szczecin [*Poland*] [*Airport symbol*] (OAG)

SZZA .... Slovenska Zenska Zveza v Ameriki [*Slovenian Women's Union in America*] (YU)

SZZLS .... Statni Zkusebna Zemedelskych a Lesnickych Stroju [*State Testing Center for Agricultural and Forestry Machinery*] (CZ)

SZZPI .... Northwestern Correspondence Polytechnic Institute (RU)

SZZTS .... Svaz Zamestnancu Zavodu Tezkeho Strojirenstvi [*Union of Workers in the Heavy Machine Industry*] (CZ)

SZZV .... Savez Zemljoradnickih Zadruga Vojvodine [*Union of Agricultural Cooperatives of Vojvodina*] (YU)

T

T .... Absolute Temperature [*Absolute Temperature*] [*German*]
T .... Aerotec [*Sociedade Aerotec Ltda.*] [*Brazil*] [*ICAO aircraft manufacturer identifier*]   (ICAO)
T .... A Tracteur [*Said of a battery*] [*Military*] [*French*]   (MTD)
t .... Celsiusgrad [*Centigrade*] [*German*]
t .... Comrade   (RU)
T .... Current Maintenance [*Motor vehicles*]   (RU)
T .... Hard [*Nature of bottom of a ford*] [*Topography*]   (RU)
T .... Heavy Structures [*Military term*]   (RU)
t .... He, This   (BU)
T .... Instrumental [*Case*]   (RU)
t .... Point, Period   (BU)
t .... Point, Spot, Period   (RU)
t .... Printing [*Number of copies*]   (RU)
T .... Rear, Service Area, Service Troops   (RU)
t .... Tabla [*Plate*] [*Publishing*] [*Hungary*]
T .... Tablazat [*Chart*]   (HU)
T .... Tafel [*Plate*] [*Publishing*] [*German*]
T .... Tag [*Member*]   (HU)
t .... Tai [*Or*] [*Finland*]   (GPO)
T .... Takhsis [*Academic degree*] [*Morocco*]
t .... Taller [*Shop*] [*Publishing*] [*Spanish*]
T .... Talon [*Heel of the Bow*] [*Music*]
T .... Tanacs [*Council*]   (HU)
T .... Tango [*Phonetic alphabet*] [*International*]   (DSUE)
T .... Tank   (RU)
T .... Tara [*Tare (weight)*] [*Portuguese*]
t .... Tarde [*Afternoon*] [*Spanish*]
T .... Tare [*Phonetic alphabet*] [*World War II*]   (DSUE)
T .... Tarih [*or Tarihli*] [*Date or Dated*]   (TU)
T .... Tarra [*Tare*] [*Afrikaans*]
T .... Tasmania [*National Union Catalogue of Australia symbol*]
T .... Tasto [*Touch, Key, Fingerboard*] [*Music*]
T .... Tausend [*Thousand*] [*German*]
T .... Taxe a Percevoir [*French*]
T .... Taxi   (RU)
T .... Technisch [*Technical*] [*German*]
t .... Tegen [*Benelux*]   (BAS)
T .... Teil [*or Teile*] [*Part or Parts*] [*German*]   (GPO)
t .... Tekst [*Text*] [*Publishing*] [*Netherlands*]
t .... Tela [*Cloth*] [*Publishing*] [*Italian*]
T .... Telefon [*Telephone*] [*German*]   (TU)
T .... Telefonica [*Telephonic*] [*Spanish*]
T .... Telefunken [*Record label*] [*Germany, etc.*]
T .... Telgraf [*Telegraph*] [*German*]   (TU)
t .... Temperatura [*Temperature*] [*Poland*]
t .... Temperature [*French*]
T .... Tempo [*Time*] [*Afrikaans*]
t .... Temps [*Time*] [*French*]
T .... Tendre [*Tender*] [*Music*]
t .... Teos [*Former*]   (GC)
T .... Tepe [*Hill, Peak*]   (TU)
T .... Terkep [*Map*]   (HU)
t .... Termo [*Term*] [*Portuguese*]
T .... Territorial [*Territorial*] [*French*]   (MTD)
T .... Terulet [*Area*]   (HU)
T .... Tervezet [*Plan, Schedule*]   (HU)
T .... Tesla   (ADPT)
t .... Tete [*Top Edge*] [*Publishing*] [*French*]
t .... Texte [*Text*] [*Publishing*] [*French*]
t .... Thaler [*or Talari*] [*Monetary unit Ethiopia*]
t .... Thousand   (RU)
t .... Tie [*Road*] [*Finland*]   (CED)
T .... Timbre [*On documents, indicates that they are to be stamped*] [*French*]   (MTD)
T .... Tisztelt [*Honored*]   (HU)
T .... Titel [*Title*] [*German*]
T .... Titer   (RU)

t .... Titre [*Security Stock*] [*French*] [*Business term*]
T .... Toc [*Phonetic alphabet*] [*Pre-World War II*]   (DSUE)
t .... Tom [*Volume*]   (POL)
t .... Tome [*Book, Volume*] [*French*]
T .... Tommy [*Phonetic alphabet*] [*Royal Navy World War I*]   (DSUE)
T .... Tomo [*Volume*] [*Italian*]   (ILCA)
t .... Tomo [*Volume*] [*Spanish*]
t .... Tomo [*Volume*] [*Portuguese*]
T .... Tomos [*Volume*]   (GC)
t .... Ton [*Ton*] [*Afrikaans*]
t .... Tona [*Ton*] [*Poland*]
t .... Tone   (BU)
t .... Tonelada [*Ton*] [*Portuguese*]
t .... Tonne [*Ton*] [*German*]   (GCA)
t .... Tonneau [*Barrel*] [*French*]
T .... Tonnen [*Tons*] [*German*]
t .... Tonni(a) [*Finland*]
T .... Toplam [*Total*]   (TU)
t .... Toque [*Cap*] [*French*]
T .... Torrente [*Torrent*] [*Italian*]   (NAU)
t .... Tour [*Revolution*] [*French*]
T .... Tractatenblad voor het Koninkrijk der Nederlanden [*Netherlands*]   (BAS)
T .... Tractor   (RU)
T/ .... Traite [*Agreement*] [*French*]
T .... Transcap Business Services Ltd. [*Ghana*]
T .... Transforme [*Transformed*] [*French*]   (MTD)
T .... Transportni [*Transportation*]   (CZ)
T .... Transport, Transportation   (RU)
T .... Travessa [*Crossroad*] [*Portuguese*]
T .... Triebwagen [*Rail Motor Car*] [*German*]   (EG)
T .... Trommel [*Drum*] [*German*]   (ADPT)
T .... Trotyl   (RU)
T .... Tube, Fuze   (RU)
T .... Turistik [*Touristic*] [*As a higher-class hotel*]   (TU)
T .... Turkce [*Turkish*]   (TU)
T .... Tyd [*Time*] [*Afrikaans*]
t .... Volume   (BU)
T12 .... Technical Schools Year Twelve Programme [*Victoria, Australia*]
t/24 ch........ Tons per Twenty-Four Hours   (BU)
T2000I .... Transport 2000 International [*British*]   (EAIO)
t-a .... Packing Materials   (RU)
TA .... TACA International Airlines SA [*El Salvador*] [*ICAO designator*]   (ICDA)
TA .... Tameion Arogis [*Assistance Fund*]   (GC)
TA .... Tameion Asfaliseos [*Insurance Fund*]   (GC)
TA .... Tananarive-Antsirabe
TA .... Tankova Armada [*Tank Army*]   (CZ)
Ta .... Tantal [*Tantalum*] [*German*] [*Chemical element*]
Ta .... Tantalio [*Tantalum*] [*Chemical element*] [*Portuguese*]
TA .... Taranto [*Car registration plates*] [*Italian*]
T-A .... Taschenausgabe [*Pocket Edition*] [*German*]
TA .... Tastatur [*German*]   (ADPT)
TA .... Technical Archives   (RU)
TA .... Technischer Aussendienst [*German*]   (ADPT)
TA .... Technonet Asia   (EA)
TA .... Tehnicka Akademija [*Technical Academy*] [*Zagreb*] [*Army*]   (YU)
TA .... Tel Aviv [*Israel*]   (BJA)
TA .... Telecom Australia
TA .... Teleflora Australia
TA .... Telegraph   (RU)
TA .... Telegraphie Acoustique [*Military*] [*French*]   (MTD)
TA .... Telephone   (RU)
TA .... Telepulesi Alap [*Resettlement Fund*]   (HU)
TA .... Tell-Amarna [*Egypt*]   (BJA)
TA .... Tell Asmar [*Iraq*]   (BJA)
ta .... Ten Andere [*Benelux*]   (BAS)

TA .... Tennis Australia
TA .... Territorial Administrator
TA .... Territorial Army (ML)
TA .... Tetarti Avgoustou [*Fourth of August*] [*Greek*] (GC)
TA .... Tierarzt [*Veterinary Surgeon*] [*German*]
TA .... Tirailleurs Algeriens
TA .... Traffic Authority [*Research center*] [*Australia*] (ERC)
TA .... Tramways Algeriens
TA .... Transition Allowance [*Australia*]
TA .... Transport Aviation (RU)
TA .... Trapeza Anaptyxeos [*Development Bank*] [*Cyprus*] (GC)
TA .... Tribunal Administratif [*Administrative Court*] [*French*] (ILCA)
T-A............. Triumph-Adler [*Office equipment subsidiary of Volkswagen*]
TA .... Turk Ajansi [*Turkish Agency*] (TU)
TAA .... Aerotamatan SA de CV [*Mexico*] [*ICAO designator*] (FAAC)
TAA .... Tameion Agrotikon Asfaliseon [*Agricultural Insurance Fund*] [*Greek*] (GC)
TAA .... Tanganyika African Association [*Tanzania*]
TAA .... Taxpayers' Association of Australia
TAA .... Technical Assistance Administration [*United Nations*]
TAA .... Temporary Assistance Authority [*Australia*] (PDAA)
TAA .... Transafricair
TAA .... Trans-Australia Airlines (ADA)
TAA .... Transitional Administrative Authority [*South Africa*] (AF)
TAA .... Triticale Association of Australia
TAA .... Turfgrass Association of Australia
TAA .... Turkish Air Association (EAIO)
TAAA .... Tanzania Amateur Athletic Association
TAAB........ Tasmanian Arts Advisory Board [*Australia*]
TAAC .... [*The*] Australian Architects Consortium
TAAC .... TAFE [*Technical and Further Education*] Advisory Committee [*Australia*]
TAAD .... Turk Atlantik Anlasmasi Dernegi [*Turkish Atlantic Agreement Organization*] (TU)
TAAF........ Terres Australes et Antarctiques Francaises [*French*] (MSC)
TAAG .... Linhas Aereas de Angola [*Angola Airlines*] (AF)
TAAKh ...... Tameion Apallotrioseos Arkhaiologikon Khoron [*Fund for Expropriation of Archeological Areas*] [*Greek*] (GC)
TAAKh ...... Tameion Arogis Axiomatikon Khorofylakis [*Gendarmerie Officers' Relief Fund*] [*Greek*] (GC)
taalk .... Taalkunde [*Philology*] [*Afrikaans*]
TAAMM ... Tameion Asfaliseos Artergaton, Mylergaton, kai Makaronopoion [*Bakery and Mill Workers and Macaroni Makers Insurance Fund*] [*Greek*] (GC)
TAAN........ Transporte Aereo Andino SA [*Venezuela*] [*ICAO designator*] (FAAC)
TAANZPPI ... Technical Association of the Australian and New Zealand Pulp and Paper Industry (ADA)
Taar .... Taaruz [*Attack, Assault*] (TU)
TAARSAN ... Trans-Australia Airlines Reservations System Automatic Network (ADA)
TAAS........ Tameion Allilovoitheias Axiomatikon (kai Anthypaspiston) Stratou [*Mutual Aid Fund for Army Officers (and Warrant Officers)*] [*Greek*] (GC)
TAASA ...... Tool and Alloy Steels Association [*India*] (PDAA)
TAAT........ Tanganyika Association Against Tuberculosis
TAAThP.... Tameion Arogis Anapiron kai Thymaton Polemou [*War Victims and Disabled Assistance Fund*] [*Greek*] (GC)
TAB .... Aerial Thermite Bomb (RU)
tab .... Tabel [*Table*] [*Netherlands*]
tab .... Tabel [*Table*] [*Danish/Norwegian*]
tab .... Tabela [*Table*] [*Poland*]
tab .... Tabell [*Table*] [*Sweden*]
tab .... Tabelle [*Table*] [*Italian*]
Tab............. Tabelle [*Table*] [*German*]
TAB .... Tabelliermaschine [*German*] (ADPT)
TAB .... Tabloncillo [*Race of maize*] [*Mexico*]
tab .... Tabori [*Of the Field, Camping*] (HU)
TAB .... Tanacsi Allando Bizottsag [*Standing Committee of the Council*] (HU)
TAB .... Tea Association of Bangladesh (EAIO)
TAB .... Technical Assistance Board [*United Nations*]
TAB .... Technical Assistance Bureau [*ICAO*] (DA)
Tab............. Tobacco Factory [*Topography*] (RU)
TAB .... Tobago [*Trinidad and Tobago*] [*Airport symbol*] (OAG)
TAB .... Totalisator Agency Board [*Australia*]
TAB .... Transport Appeals Board [*New South Wales, Australia*]
TAB .... Transporte Aereo Boliviano [*Bolivian Air Transport*]
TAB .... Transportes Aereos Boliviands [*Bolivia*] [*ICAO designator*] (FAAC)
TAB .... Transportes Aereos da Bacia Amazonica SA [*Brazil*] [*ICAO designator*] (FAAC)
TAB .... Transportoarele Amfibii Blindate [*Armored Amphibian Transports*] (RO)
TAB .... Transports Aeriens du Benin [*Benin*] (EY)

TAB .... Turk-Arap Bankasi [*Turkish-Arabic Bank*] [*Established February 1977*] (TU)
TABA........ Tanzania Amateur Boxing Association
TABA........ Transcaribe [*Airline*] [*Colorado*]
TABA........ Transportes Aereas de Buenos Aires [*Argentina*] (PDAA)
TABA........ Transportes Aereos da Bacia Amazonica [*Airline*] [*Brazil*]
TABACOL ... Tabacos Colombianos Limitada [*Colombia*] (COL)
Tabamex .... Tabacos Mexicanos [*Mexican Tobacco Company*] (GEA)
TABATCHAD ... Societe Agricole Tchadienne de Collecte et de Traitement des Tabacs
TABDT...... Vaccin Antityphoidique et Antiparatyphoidique A et B, Antidiphterique et Tetanique [*French*]
TABEA ...... Tanzania Beekeepers Association
Tab Fiscet Jur ... Le Tableau Fiscal et Juridique (FLAF)
TABGIS .... Turkiye Akaryakit Acenta ve Bayileri ile Garaj Isletenler Sendikasi [*Turkish Liquid Fuel Agents', Dealers', and Garage Operators' Union*] (TU)
tabl .... Plate, Table (RU)
tabl .... Tablazat [*Chart*] (HU)
tabl .... Table (BU)
tabl .... Tableau [*Picture, Table*] [*French*]
tabl .... Tableaux (FLAF)
tabl .... Tablet (RU)
Tabl........... Tablette [*Tablet, Pill*] [*German*] (GCA)
tabl .... Tablica [*Figure, Table*] (POL)
TABNSW ... Totalisator Agency Board of New South Wales [*Australia*]
TABS........ Travel Australia Britain Seminar
tab sar .... Tobacco Shed [*Topography*] (RU)
TAC .... [*The*] Athletics Congress (OLYM)
TAC .... Compagnie des Tramways et Autobus de Casablanca
TAC .... Empresa de Transportes Aereao Catarinense [*Brazil*]
TAC .... Soweto Teachers Action Committee [*South Africa*] (AF)
TAC .... Tacloban [*Philippines*] [*Airport symbol*] (OAG)
TAC .... Taiwan Aerospace Corp. (ECON)
TAC .... Tanganyika Agricultural Corporation
TAC .... Tanzania Railway Corporation (AF)
TAC .... Tasmanian Aboriginal Centre [*Australia*]
TAC .... Tasmanian AIDS [*Acquired Immune Deficiency Syndrome*] Council [*Australia*]
TAC .... Television Advertising Council [*Australia*]
TAC .... Thai Airways Co. Ltd. [*ICAO designator*] (FAAC)
TAC .... Togo Amusement Corporation
TAC .... Tokyo Automatic Computer (ADPT)
TAC .... Toplumsal Arastirma ve Calisma Kurumu [*Social Research and Labor Institute*] (TU)
TAC .... Traineeship Access Course [*Australia*]
TAC .... Transitos Adouanas y Consignaciones [*Morocco*]
TAC .... Translators' Association of China (EAIO)
TAC .... Transmeridian Air Cargo Ltd.
TAC .... Transport Accident Commission [*Victoria, Australia*]
TAC .... Transport Advisory Committee [*Hong Kong*]
TAC .... Transport Agencies Corp. [*Myanmar*] (DS)
TAC .... Transportes, Aduanas, y Consignaciones SA [*Shipping company*] [*Spain*] (EY)
TAC .... Transportes Aereos Coyhaique [*Chile*] [*ICAO designator*] (FAAC)
TAC .... Transportes Aereos del Cesar [*Colombia*] (COL)
TAC .... Transvaal Automobile Club
TAC .... Traskei Airways Corp. [*South Africa*] (EY)
TAC .... Tres Ancienne Couture (FLAF)
TACA .... Transportes Aereos Centroamericanos, SA [*Central America Air Lines Transportation*] [*El Salvador*]
TACATA ... Transportes Aereos del Caqueta [*Cucuta*] (COL)
TACB........ [*The*] Australian Contra Banc
TACC........ Telecom Australia Consumer Council
TACC........ Total Allowable Catch for the Community [*Fishing regulation*] [*European Commission*]
TACC........ Touring y Automovil Club de Colombia (EAIO)
TACC........ Tribunal Anti-Imperialista Centroamericano y del Caribe [*Anti-Imperialist Tribunal of Central America and the Caribbean*] (LA)
TACD .... Transport and Communications Division, United Nations ESCAP [*Economic and Social Commission for Asia and the Pacific*] [*Thailand*] (EAIO)
TACI.......... Technical Association of the Cement Industry [*Portugal*] (EAIO)
TACI.......... Touring and Automobile Club of the Islamic Republic of Iran (EAIO)
TACI.......... Transport Accident Commission Insurance [*Victoria, Australia*]
TACIP ...... Tripoli Anonima Commercio Industria Pelli
TACIS ...... Technical Assistance to Commonwealth of Independent States
TACO .... Etablissements Togolais d'Activites Commerciales
TACOL...... Tasmanian Advisory Committee on Libraries [*Australia*] (ADA)
TACOLOMBIA ... Taller Colombia [*Girardot*] (COL)
TACOMPLAN ... Tactical Communications Plan [*NATO*]
TACONA .. Fabrica de Tacones de Aluminio [*Colombia*] (COL)

TACONAL ... Fabrica de Tacones de Aluminio [*Colombia*] (COL)
TACORAL ... Alfombras Cortinas y Tapetes [*Colombia*] (COL)
TACOSHILI ... Tanzania Coastal Shipping Line
TACS .... Tasmanian Association of Children's Services [*Australia*]
TACS .... Technical Aid Corps Scheme [*Nigeria*]
TACS .... Total Access Communications System [*China*]
TACTRI .... Taiwan Agricultural Chemicals and Toxic Substances Research Institute [*Research center*] (IRC)
TACV .... Transportes Aereos de Cabo Verde [*Cape Verde Airlines*] (AF)
TACW .... Technische Advies Commissie voor de Waterkeringen [*Technical Advisory Commission for Water Defence*] [*Netherlands*] (PDAA)
tad .... Heavy Artillery Battalion (RU)
TAD .... Taktiki Aeroporiki Dynamis [*Tactical Air Force*] [*Cyprus*] (GC)
tad .... Tamadas [*Attack, Offensive*] (HU)
TAD .... Tanzania Association of the Disabled (EAIO)
Tad .... Tausend [*Thousand*] [*German*]
TAD .... Teknik Arastirma Dairesi [*Technical Research Office*] [*Under Ministry of Forestry*] (TU)
TAD .... Traitement Automatique des Donnees [*Automatic Data Processing*] [*French*]
TAD .... Transporte Aereo Dominicano SA [*Dominican Republic*] [*ICAO designator*] (FAAC)
TAD .... Turk-Amerikan Dernegi [*Turkish-American Society*] (TU)
TADA .... Tasmanian Aboriginal Descent Association [*Australia*]
TADA .... Tasmanian Amateur Diving Association [*Australia*]
TADA .... Terrorist and Disruptive Activities Act [*India*] (ECON)
TADACT ... Technical Aid for the Disabled, Australian Capital Territory Region
TADAM .... Tanzanian Association of Development Administration and Management
TADE .... Tendaho Agricultural Development Enterprise Research Section [*Ethiopia*] (ARC)
TADECO ... Tanga Development Corporation
tadell .... Tadellos [*Perfect*] [*German*]
TADKY ..... Tameion Asfaliseos Dimotikon kai Koinonikon Ypallilon [*Municipal and Communal Employees Insurance Fund*] [*Greek*] (GC)
TADSIS ..... Turkiye Ayakkabi ve Deri Sanayi Iscileri Sendikasi [*Turkish Shoe and Leather Industry Workers Union*] (TU)
tadzh .... Tadzhik (RU)
Tadzhikgosizdat ... Tadzhik State Publishing House (RU)
TadzhikTA ... Tadzhik News Agency (RU)
Tadzhikuchpedgiz ... Tadzhik State Publishing House of Textbooks and Pedagogical Literature (RU)
TadzhNIIZhV ... Tadzhik Scientific Research Institute of Livestock Breeding and Veterinary Science (RU)
TadzhSSR ... Tadzhik Soviet Socialist Republic (RU)
tae .... Air Transport Squadron (RU)
TAE .... Istituto di Metodi e Processi Chimici per la Trasformazione e l'Accumulo dell'Energia [*Institute of Chemical Methods and Processes for Energy Transformation and Storage*] [*Italy*] (IRC)
TAE .... Tadzhik Archaeological Expedition (RU)
TAE .... Tameion Asfaliseos Emboron [*Merchants Insurance Fund*] [*Greek*] (GC)
TAE .... Technische Akademie eV Esslingen [*German*] (ADPT)
TAE .... Tertiary Admissions Examination [*Australia*]
TAE .... Tmima Anikhnevseos Englimaton [*Criminal Investigation Department*] (GC)
TAE .... Transantarctic Expedition (ADA)
TAE .... Transportes Aereos Militares Ecatorianos CA [*Ecuador*] [*ICAO designator*] (FAAC)
TAE .... Travelling Art Exhibition [*Australia*]
TAE .... Turkiye Atom Enerjisi Kurumu [*Turkish Atomic Energy Commission*] (PDAA)
TAEC .... Thai Atomic Energy Commission for Peace (PDAA)
taegl .... Taeglich [*Daily, Per Day*] [*German*] (EG)
TAEK .... Turk Atom Enerjisi Komisyonu [*Turkish Atomic Energy Commission*] [*Under Office of Premier*] (TU)
TAES .... Tanzania Agricultural Economics Society
TAES .... Techicas Aereas de Estudios y Servicios SA [*Spain*] [*ICAO designator*] (FAAC)
TAES .... Transportes Aereos de El Salvador SA de CV [*ICAO designator*] (FAAC)
TAETA ...... Tameion Asfaliseos Ergaton Typou Athinon [*Athens Press Workers Insurance Fund*] (GC)
TAEU .... Technical Assistance and Energy Unit [*Caribbean Development Bank*] [*Barbados*] [*Research center*] (WED)
TAF .... Oran-Tafaraoui [*Algeria*] [*Airport symbol*] (OAG)
Taf. .... Tafel [*Plate*] [*Publishing*] [*German*]
TAF .... Tafel [*Table*] [*Afrikaans*]
TAF .... Triammonium Phosphate (RU)
TAF .... Tuberculin Albumose-Frei [*Albumose-Free Tuberculin*] [*German*] [*Medicine*]
TAF .... Tutelle aux Allocations Familiales (FLAF)
TAFAK ...... Tokyo Association of Families Against Karoshi [*Japan*]

TAFCO ..... Tanzania Finance Company Ltd.
TAFCV ...... Tobacco and Associated Farmers' Cooperative of Victoria [*Australia*]
TAFE .... Technical and Further Education [*Australia*]
TAFECNSW ... Technical and Further Education Commission New South Wales [*Australia*]
TAFECOM ... Technical and Further Education Commission [*New South Wales, Australia*]
TAFEDAB ... Technical and Further Education Discipline Appeals Board [*Victoria, Australia*]
TAFEESC ... Technical and Further Education External Studies College [*Western Australia*]
TAFENCRD ... Technical and Further Education National Centre for Research and Development [*Australia*]
TAFERS ...... Technical and Further Education Rural Studies [*South Australia*]
TAFESA .... Technical and Further Education Staff Association [*South Australia*]
TAFETANSW ... Technical and Further Education Teachers' Association of New South Wales [*Australia*]
TAFETSAB ... Technical and Further Education Teaching Service Appeals Board [*Victoria, Australia*]
TAFGI .... Tenyeszallatforgalmi Gazdasagi Iroda [*Economic Control Office - Livestock Trade*] (HU)
TAFICO .... Tanzanian Fisheries Corporation
TAFISA ..... Trim and Fitness International Sport for all Association (OLYM)
TAFNORNOR ... Allied Tactical Air Force, Northern Norway [*NATO*]
TAFORG ... Takarmanyforgalmi Vallalat [*Fodder Store*] (HU)
TAFSONOR ... Allied Tactical Air Force, South Norway [*NATO*] (NATG)
TAG .... News Agency (RU)
tag .... Tagozat [*Section, Branch*] (HU)
TAG .... Technology Advisory Group [*Public Libraries*] [*Australia*]
TAG .... Telexteilnehmer-Anschaltgeraet [*German*] (ADPT)
TAG .... Thai-Asian Glass Co. Ltd.
TAG .... Theatre about Glasgow [*Acting company*] (ECON)
TAG .... Transports Aeriens du Gabon
TAG .... Turramurra Action Group [*Australia*]
TAGA .... Tasmanian Amateur Gymnastics Association [*Australia*]
TAGAS ...... Turk Arab Guebre A/S
TAGB .... Transportes Aereos de Guine-Bissau [*Guinea-Bissau Airlines*] (AF)
Tageb .... Tagebuch [*Diary, Journal*] [*German*]
TAGP .... Transportes Aereos da Guine Portuguesa [*Portuguese Guinea*] (PDAA)
TAGSA ...... Tanganyika African Government Servants Association
TAH .... Air Moorea [*France*] [*ICAO designator*] (FAAC)
Tah .... Taehti [*Record label*] [*Finland*]
TAH .... Tanna Island [*Vanuata*] [*Airport symbol*] (OAG)
TAH .... Trans-African Highway
TAHA .... Tanzania Amateur Handball Association
TAHC .... Travaux de l'Association Henri Capitant pour la Culture Juridique Francaise (FLAF)
TAHGA ..... [*The*] Australian Hang Gliding Association (ADA)
TAHI .... Tanzania Hotels Investments Ltd.
TAHRS ...... Tenancy Advice and Housing Referral Service [*Australia*]
TAI .... TACA International Airlines SA [*El Salvador*] [*ICAO designator*] (FAAC)
Tai .... Taiwan
TAI .... Taiz [*Yemen Arab Republic*] [*Airport symbol*] (OAG)
TAI .... Telecom Australia International
TAI .... Temps Atomique International [*International Atomic Time*] [*Telecommunications*]
TAI .... Thai Airways International (MCD)
TAI .... Traitement Automatique de l'Information [*Automatic Handling of Information*] [*French*] (ADPT)
TAI .... Transactions of the All-Union Arctic Institute (RU)
TAIB .... Trans-Arabian Investment Bank (MENA)
TAIC .... [*The*] Arabian Investment Company [*Saudi Arabia*]
TAIC .... Taxe sur l'Activite Industrielle et Commerciale [*Algeria*] (IMH)
TAIC .... [*The*] Tokyo Atomic Industrial Consortium
TAICH ...... Technical Assistance Information Clearing House
TAIDSC ..... Tasmanian AIDS [*Acquired Immune Deficiency Syndrome*] Council [*Australia*]
TAIF .... [*The*] Australian Institute of Fundraising (ADA)
Taipower .... Taiwan Power Co. (ECON)
TAIS .... Telecom Australia Information Systems
TAISYT .... Tameion Asfaliseos Idioktiton Syndakton kai Ypallilon Typou [*Insurance Fund of Press Owners, Editors, and Employees*] [*Greek*] (GC)
TAJ .... Tadji [*Papua New Guinea*] [*Airport symbol*] (OAG)
TAJ .... Tunisavia - Societe de Transport, Services et Travaux Aeriens [*Tunisia*] [*ICAO designator*] (FAAC)
TAJA .... [*The*] Australian Journal of Anthropology [*A publication*]
TAJA .... Tanzanian African Journalists Association (AF)
TAK .... Taal en Aktie Komitee [*Language Action Committee*] [*Belgium*] (WEN)

TAK .... Tactical Air Command [*United States*]   (RU)
TAK .... Tactical Aviation Command Element   (BU)
TAK .... Takamatsu [*Japan*] [*Airport symbol*]   (OAG)
Tak............ Takriben [*Approximate, Approximately*]   (TU)
Tak............ Taktik [*Tactics, Tactical*]   (TU)
TAK .... Tameion Asfaliseos Kapnergaton [*Tobacco Workers Insurance Fund*] [*Greek*]   (GC)
TA K .... Tankonyvkiado [*Textbook Publishing House*]   (HU)
TAK .... Technisch-Allgemeine Kontrolle [*General and Technical Control*] [*German*]   (EG)
TAK .... Transkei Airways [*South Africa*] [*ICAO designator*]   (FAAC)
TAK .... Turk Ajansi Kibris [*Turkish News Agency of Cyprus*] [*Mersin, Turkey*]   (GC)
TAKE......... Tameion Asfaliseos (Orthodoxou Efimeriakou) Klirou Ellados [*Greek (Orthodox Parish) Clergy Insurance Fund*] [*Greek*]   (GC)
TAKE......... Termez Complex Archaeological Expedition   (RU)
TAKhDIK ... Tameion Khrimatodotiseos Dikastikon Ktirion [*Court Building Construction Financing Fund*] [*Greek*]   (GC)
TAKhMAYKhA ... Tameion Asfaliseos Khrimatiston, Mesiton, Antikryston, kai Ypallilon Khrimatistiriou Athinon [*Insurance Fund of Brokers, Account Executives, Specialists, and Employees of the Athens Stock Exchange*]   (GC)
TAKI......... Talajtani es Agrokemiai Kutato Intezete [*Research Institute for Soil Science and Agricultural Chemistry*] [*Hungary*]   (IRC)
TAKI......... Tavkozlesi Kutato Intezet [*Telecommunication Research Institute*]   (HU)
TAKIS .... Tutmonda Asocio pri Kibernetiko, Informatiko, kaj Sistemiko [*World Association of Cybernetics, Computer Science, and System Theory*]   (EAIO)
TAKKD ..... Turk Amerikan Kadinlar Kultur Dernegi [*Turkish-American Women's Cultural Association*]   (TU)
tak obr....... Thus, In Such a Manner   (RU)
TAKRAF ... Transportausruestungen-Kraene Foerderanlagen [*Transportation Equipment, Conveying Equipment, and Cranes*]   (EG)
taks .... Forest Valuation, Valuation Survey   (RU)
TAKSAN... Takim Tezgahlari Sanayii ve Ticaret AS [*Machinery Spare Parts Industry and Trade Corp.*]   (TU)
Takt .... Taktik [*Tactics*] [*German*]   (GCA)
TAL .... Societe Nationale des Tanneries Algeriennes
TAL .... Talair Pty Ltd. [*New Guinea*] [*ICAO designator*]   (FAAC)
tal .... Taloustieteet [*Economics*] [*Finland*]
TAL .... Teaching Asian Languages [*Australia*]
TAL .... Territory Airlines [*Australia*]
TAL .... Total Australia Limited   (ADA)
TAL .... TransAlpine [*Pipeline*] [*Western Europe*]
TAL .... Trevo Avicola Ltd. [*Brazil*]   (DSCA)
TALA........ Travel Agents' Licensing Authority [*Victoria, Australia*]
TALARCO ... Larco-Laminados Metalicos y Aire Acondicionado SA [*Colombia*]   (COL)
TALB......... Travel Agents' Licensing Board [*Australia*]
TALC......... Territory Anti-Litter Committee [*Northern Territory, Australia*]
TALICOL ... Tarjetas Litografiadas Colombia [*Colombia*]   (COL)
TALIKOM ... Talikomunikasi [*Telecommunications*]   (ML)
TALIRO .... Tanzania Livestock Research Organization   (ARC)
tal'k........... Talc Quarry [*Topography*]   (RU)
tall .... Taller [*Shop*] [*Publishing*] [*Spanish*]
talr............. Talrig [*Numerous*] [*Danish/Norwegian*]
talr............. Talrijk [*Numerous*] [*Netherlands*]
talr............. Talrik [*Numerous*] [*Sweden*]
TALUA...... TAFE [*Technical and Further Education*] Libacc Users Association [*Victoria, Australia*]
tam .... Customhouse [*Topography*]   (RU)
TAM .... Societe des Travaux Aeriens de Madagascar
Tam............ Tamirathane [*Repair Shop*]   (TU)
TAM .... Tampico [*Mexico*] [*Airport symbol*]   (OAG)
TAM .... Tamtama [*Enlisted Man (Corporal and below)*]   (IN)
TAM .... Tanque Argentino Mediano
TAM .... Televisora Andina de Merida [*Venezuela*]   (EY)
TAM .... Teresian Apostolic Movement [*See also MTA*] [*Italy*]   (EAIO)
TAM .... Terre, Air, Mer [*French*]
TAM .... Tovarna Avtomobilov Maribor [*Maribor Automobile Factory*]   (YU)
TAM .... Transportacion Aerea Mexicana [*Mexico*] [*ICAO designator*]   (FAAC)
TAM .... Transporte Aereo Militar [*Military Air Transport*] [*Paraguay*]   (IMH)
TAM .... Transportes Aereos de Mocambique Lda.
TAM .... Transportes Aereos Militares [*Military Air Transport*] [*Bolivia*]   (LA)
TAM .... Transportes Aereos Regionais SA [*Brazil*] [*ICAO designator*]   (FAAC)
TAM .... Transports Automobiles et Manutention
TAM .... Turkiye Amator Milli Takimi [*Turkish National Amateur Team*]   (TU)
TAMALI ... Tanneries Maliennes
TAMAVENCA ... Taninos y Maderas Venezolanas CA [*Venezuela*]   (DSCA)

TAMCO .... Societe de Transports, d'Automobiles, et de Mecanique au Congo
TAMCO .... Tanzania-Madagascar Clove Organisation
TAMDA .... Timber and Allied Materials Development Association
TAME .... Transportes Aereos Militares Ecuatorianos [*Ecuadorean Military Air Transport*]   (LA)
TAMEMA ... Taller de Metales y Maderas Elaboradas Ltda. [*Colombia*]   (COL)
TAMEPRE .. Taller de Mecanica Alta Precision [*Colombia*]   (COL)
TAMETAL ... Talleres Metalicos Andina Ltda. [*Colombia*]   (COL)
TAMISAS ... Tarim Makinalari Imalat Sanayii Anonim Sirketi [*Agricultural Machinery Manufacturing Industry Corporation*]   (TU)
Tampa........ Transportes Aereos Mercantiles Panamericanos [*National airlines*] [*Colorado*]   (EY)
TAMS........ [*The*] Australian Museum Society   (ADA)
TAMSA..... Tornilleria y Aplicaciones Mecanicas, Sociedad Anonima [*Colombia*]   (COL)
TAMSA..... Tubos de Acero de Mexico, Sociedad Anonima [*Mexico*]
TAMSAN ... Tomruk ve Agac Mamulleri Sanayii AS [*Log and Wood Products' Industry Corp.*]   (TU)
TAMTAS .. Teknik Ambalaj ve Makina Sanayi ve Ticaret Anonim Sirketi [*Technical Packing and Mechanical Industry and Trade Corporation*]   (TU)
TAMTI...... Textile Academy of Ministry of Textile Industry [*China*]   (IRC)
TAMTU .... Tanzania Agricultural Machinery Testing Unit
tan .... Tangens [*Tangent*] [*Afrikaans*]
TAN........... Tanzania   (WDAA)
TAN........... Technisch Begruendete Arbeitsnorm [*Technically Established Work Norm*]   (EG)
TAN .... Textile Association for the Netherlands   (EAIO)
TAN .... Transportes Aeros Nacionales [*National Air Line*] [*Honduras*]   (PDAA)
TANA........ Tribunal Anti-Imperialista de Nuestra America [*Anti-Imperialist Tribunal of Our America*]   (LA)
TANAP...... Tatransky Narodny Park [*Tatra National Park*]   (CZ)
tanars .... Tanarseged [*Assistant to a Professor*]   (HU)
tanb .... Tank Battalion   (RU)
TANC .... Tanganyika African National Congress
TANCUT .. Tanzania Diamond Cutting Co. Ltd.
TANDANOR ... Talleres Navales Darsena Norte [*North Basin Shipyards*] [*Argentina*]   (LA)
T & C......... Town and Country Building Society [*Australia*]
T & CPA .... Town and Country Planning Authority [*Australia*]
TANDH.... Tandheelkunde [*Dentistry*] [*Afrikaans*]
TANDOC .. Tanzania National Documentation Centre [*National Central Library*] [*Information service or system*]   (IID)
T & TMA ... Trinidad and Tobago Manufacturers Association
T &TMDC ... Trinidad and Tobago Management Development Centre
T & V .... Training and Visit [*System of agricultural extension backed by the World Bank*]
T & V .... Tressmann & Vogt [*France*]
TANE .... Transportes Aereos Nacionales Ecuatorianas [*Airline*] [*Ecuador*]
TANESCO ... Tanganyika Electric Supply Company [*Tanzania*]   (AF)
TANFL...... Tasmanian National Football League [*Australia*]
TANG........ Tanganyika
tang .... Tangente [*Tangent*] [*French*]
Tang........... Tangente [*Tangent*] [*Italian*]
tang .... Tangente [*Tangent*] [*Portuguese*]
TANG .... Tvornica Alata Nova Gradiska [*Nova Gradiska Tools Factory*]   (YU)
TANIC....... Tabacalera Nicaraguense, SA [*Nicaraguan Tobacco Company, Inc.*]   (LA)
Tanie .... Tannerie [*Tannery*] [*Military map abbreviation World War I*] [*French*]   (MTD)
TANII....... Transactions of the Arctic Scientific Research Institute   (RU)
TANITA .... Tanzania Italia Co.
TANJUG... Telegrafska Agencija Nove Jugoslavije [*New Yugoslavia Telegraph Agency*]   (YU)
tankr.......... Tank Company   (RU)
TANKS....... Tanganyika Concessions
Tankvoj...... Tankove Vojsko [*Armored Corps*]   (CZ)
TANNIMPEX ... TANNIMPEX Bor es Szorme Kulkereskedelmi Vallalat [*TANNIMPEX Foreign Trade Enterprise for Leather and Fur*]   (HU)
TANPY...... Tameion Asfaliseos Navtikon Praktoron kai Ypallilon [*Shipping Agents' and Employees' Insurance Fund*] [*Greek*]   (GC)
TANR .... Tank Reserve   (RU)
TANRIS .... Tanzania Research Information Service [*Dar Es Salaam*]
TANSE...... Transportes Aereos Neuquinos Sociedad de Estado [*Argentina*] [*ICAO designator*]   (FAAC)
TANSEED ... Tanzania Seed Company
tansk.......... Tanskaa [*or Tanskaksi*] [*Finland*]
tansk .... Tanskalainen [*Finland*]
TANSW..... Taxpayers' Association of New South Wales [*Australia*]
TANTadzhSSR ... Transactions of the Academy of Sciences of the Tadzhik SSR   (RU)
TANTUR .. Ecumenical Institute for Theological Research [*Israel*]   (IRC)

TANU........ Tanganyika African National Union [*Tanzania*]   (AF)
TANU........ Tribunal Administratif des Nations Unies [*United Nations*
        (already exists in GUS II database)]   (FLAF)
Tanz.......... Tanzania
TANZAM ... Tanzania-Zambia Highway
TAO.......... [*The*] Australian Opera   (ADA)
TAO.......... Qingdao [*China*] [*Airport symbol*]   (OAG)
TAO.......... Tashkent Astronomical Observatory   (RU)
TAO.......... Taxi Aereo Opita [*Neiva*]   (COL)
TAO.......... Technical Assistance Operations [*United Nations*]
TAO.......... Transportes Aeromar [*Mexico*] [*ICAO designator*]   (FAAC)
TAO.......... Triacetyloleandomycin   (RU)
TAO.......... Turk Anonim Ortaklari [*Commercial Partnership*]   (TU)
TAO.......... Tuva Autonomous Oblast [*1944-1961*]   (RU)
TAOA........ Tameion Arogis Organon Agrofylakis [*Rural Police Assistance
        Fund*] [*Greek*]   (GC)
TAOIT....... Tribunal Administratif de l'Organisation Internationale du
        Travail   (FLAF)
TAOKh...... Tameion Asfaliseos Opliton Khorofylakis [*Gendarmerie Officer
        Insurance Fund*] [*Greek*]   (GC)
TAOK-Is.... Turkiye Agac, Dograma, ve Kereste Sanayii Iscileri [*Turkish
        Wood, Carpentry, and Lumber Industry Workers' Union*]
        (TU)
TAON........ Special-Purpose Heavy Artillery   (RU)
TAOs........ Tenkovski Staresina Kao Artiljeriski Osmatrac [*Tank
        Commander as Artillery Observer*]   (YU)
TAOT....... Turkish Association of Orthopaedics and Traumatology   (EAIO)
TAP........ Air Transport Regiment   (RU)
t ap .... Heat Exchange Apparatus   (RU)
TAP.......... Heavy Artillery Regiment   (RU)
TAP.......... Penetapan [*Decision, Directive*]   (IN)
TAP.......... Tapachula [*Mexico*] [*Airport symbol*]   (OAG)
Tap.......... Tapulamasi [*Registration*]   (TU)
TAP.......... Teatro de Arte Popular [*Colombia*]   (COL)
TAP.......... Technical Advisory Panel [*United Nations*]
tap .... Ter Aangehaalde Plaas [*In the Place Cited*] [*Afrikaans*]
TAP.......... Terminal-Anpassungs-Prozessor [*German*]   (ADPT)
TAP.......... Tertiary Awareness Program [*Australia*]
TAP.......... Towarzystwo Anestezjologow Polskich [*Poland*]   (SLS)
TAP.......... Training Air Regiment   (RU)
TAP.......... Training for Aboriginals Program [*Australia*]
TAP.......... Transfer Analysis Trigger [*Computers*]   (RU)
TAP.......... Transportes Aereos Portuguesas [*Portuguese Air Transport*]
        (AF)
TAP.......... Transportes Aereos Portugueses EP [*Portugal*] [*ICAO designator*]
        (FAAC)
TAP.......... Turystyczna Agencja Prasowa [*Tourist Press Agency*] [*Poland*]
TAPA........ St. Johns/V. C. Bird [*Antigua Island*] [*ICAO location identifier*]
        (ICLI)
TAPA........ Tanganyika African Parents Association [*Tanzania*]   (AF)
TAPALTEX ... Fabrica de Alfombras y Tapetes [*Colombia*]   (COL)
TAPAMETAL ... Fabrica de Tapas y Envases Metalicos Ltda. [*Colombia*]
        (COL)
TAPAP...... Tameion Andallaximou Periousias kai Apokatastaseos Prosfygon
        [*Exchangeable Property and Refugee Resettlement Fund*]
        [*Greek*]   (GC)
TAPD .... Turkiye Aile Planlama Dernegi [*Turkish Family Planning
        Organization*]   (TU)
TAPENSA ... Tapas y Envases, Sociedad Anonima [*Barranquilla*]   (COL)
TAPET...... Tameion Asfaliseos Prosopikou Ethnikou Typografeiou
        [*National Printing Office Personnel Insurance Fund*]
        [*Greek*]   (GC)
TAPFPMH ... Totolika, Association of Parents and Friends of Persons with a
        Mental Handicap [*Netherlands Antilles*]   (EAIO)
TAPGA...... Tasmanian Apple and Pear Growers' Association [*Australia*]
TAPH .... Codrington [*Barbuda Island*] [*ICAO location identifier*]   (ICLI)
TAPI......... Technology Application and Promotion Institute [*Philippines*]
        (IRC)
TAPIR .... Transition Automatique par Inertie et Radio [*French*]
TAPL........ Trustul Alimentatiei Publice Locale [*Local Public Food Trust*]
        (RO)
TAPline ..... Trans-Arabian Pipeline [*Saudi Arabia*]   (ME)
TAPLO...... Triumph-Adler Programm Logikkonstruktor On-Line [*German*]
        (ADPT)
TAPOL...... Comite de Defense des Prisonniers en Indonesie [*France*]
TAPOL...... Tahanan Politik [*Political Prisoner*]   (IN)
TAPOTE ... Tameion Asfaliseos Prosopikou tou Organismou
        Tilepikoinonion Ellados [*Greek Telecommunications
        Organization Personnel Insurance Fund*]   (GC)
TAPP........ Tarapur Atomic Power Project [*India*]   (PDAA)
TAPPI....... Technical Association of the Polish Paper Industry   (EAIO)
TAPPSA.... Technical Association of the Pulp and Paper Industry of
        Southern Africa   (EAIO)
TAPRI .... Tampere Peace Research Institute [*Research center*] [*Finland*]
        (IRC)
TAPS .... Tasmanian Animal Protection Society [*Australia*]
TAPS .... Telecom Australia Payphone Services

TAPS .... Training for Aboriginals Program Scheme [*Australia*]
TAPT........ Tameion Asfaliseos Prosopikou Trapezon [*Bank Personnel
        Insurance Fund*] [*Greek*]   (GC)
TAPU .... Transistorized Field Beta and Gamma Counter   (RU)
TAPV........ Three-Phase Automatic Reclosing   (RU)
TAPVOS ... Three-Phase Automatic Reclosing with Synchronism Expectation
        (RU)
TAPVUS ... Three-Phase Automatic Reclosing with Synchronism Catching
        (RU)
TAQSA...... Tarragona Quimica SA [*Spain*]
TAR .... Current Repair Service   (BU)
t ar .... Heavy Artillery   (BU)
tar............. Tarief [*Tariff*] [*Afrikaans*]
Tar .... Tarih [*History*]   (TU)
tar............. Teen Alle Risiko [*Against All Risks*] [*Afrikaans*] [*Business term*]
TAR .... Terminal-Anpassungsrechner [*German*]   (ADPT)
TAR .... Transporte Aereo Rioplatense [*River Plate Air Transport*]
        [*Argentina*]   (LA)
TAR .... Transportes Aereos Regionais [*Airline*] [*Brazil*]
TAR .... Tunis Air
TAR .... Tunis Air-Societe Tunisienne de l'Air [*Tunisia*] [*ICAO
        designator*]   (FAAC)
TARA .... Transportes Aereos Regionales de Aragon [*Spain*]   (EY)
Tar BZ .... Tarief van Justitiekosten en Salarissen in Burgerlijke Zaken
        [*Benelux*]   (BAS)
TARCA...... Taxi Aereo de Caldas Ltda. [*Manizales*]   (COL)
TARCRAC ... Training and Resource Centre for Residential Aged Care
        [*Australia*]
TARD .... Tuerk Anesteziyoloji ve Reanimasyon Dernegi [*Istanbul,
        Turkey*]   (SLS)
TARDIS .... Texts and Relative Data in Springvale [*Australia*]
TARE........ Les Techniques Auxiliaires de la Recherche Economique
        (FLAF)
TARENA... Talleres de Reparaciones Navales [*Ship Repair Yards*]
        [*Argentina*]   (LA)
TARI........ Taiwan Agricultural Research Institute   (ARC)
TARIM-Is ... Turkiye Tarim ve Tarim Sanayii Iscileri Sendikasi [*Farm
        Workers Union of Turkey*]   (TU)
Tarim-Sen ... Tarim Isciler Sendikasi [*Agricultural Workers Union*]   (GC)
TARIP .... Thai-Australian Rural Improvement Project   (ADA)
TARIS .... Tarim Isciler Sendikasi [*Agricultural Workers Union*]   (TU)
tark............ Tarkastaja [*Finland*]
tark............ Tarkastettu [*Finland*]
tark............ Tarkoittaa [*Finland*]
TARKIM ... Tarim Araclari ve Kimya Sanayii AS [*Agricultural Equipment
        and Chemical Industry Corp.*]   (TU)
TARKO ..... Tarim Satis Kooperatifleri Birlikleri [*Agricultural Sales
        Cooperatives Unions*]   (TU)
Tarkom ..... Tariff Committee   (RU)
Tar kv spr .. Tariff-Grade Reference Manual   (BU)
TARMASAN ... Tarim Makine Sanayi ve Ticaret AS [*Agricultural Machinery
        Industry and Trade Corp.*]   (TU)
TARO .... Tanzania Agricultural Research Organisation
TAROM .... Transporturi Aeriene Romane [*Romanian Air Transport*]
TAROR ..... [*The*] Australian Road Outlook Report
TARR........ Tractor Army Repair Shop   (BU)
tar ruk........ Tariff Regulations   (RU)
TARS........ [*The*] Accommodation Rights Service [*Australia*]
tars .... Tarsasag [*Company*] [*Hungary*]
TARS........ Technical Assistance Recruiting Services   (LAA)
TARS........ Technical Assistance Recruitment Service [*United Nations*]
TARS........ Transporturi Aeriene Romane-Sovietice [*Romanian-Soviet Air
        Transport*]   (RO)
tart............. Tartalekos [*Reserves, Of the Reserves*] [*Military*]   (HU)
tart............. Tartalom [*Contents*]   (HU)
Tarz........... Tbilisi Automobile Repair Plant   (RU)
TAS........... [*The*] Architectural Show [*Australia*]
TAS........... [*The*] Armidale School [*Australia*]
TAS........... Secretariado Teleinformativo [*Colombia*]   (COL)
TAS........... Tactical Air Force   (BU)
TAS........... TAFE [*Technical and Further Education*] Adult Migrant
        Education Services, Schools [*Australia*]
TAS........... Tameion Asfaliseos Symvolaiografon [*Notaries Insurance Fund*]
        [*Greek*]   (GC)
TAS........... Tankova a Automobilova Sprava [*Tank and Vehicle Directorate*]
        (CZ)
TAS........... Tashkent [*Former USSR*] [*Airport symbol*]   (OAG)
Tas .... Tasmania [*Australia*]   (ADA)
TAS........... Tasmanian Ambulance Service [*Australia*]
tas............... Tassello [*Label*] [*Publishing*] [*Italian*]
TAS........... Technische Aussenstelle [*Technical Field Office*]   (EG)
TAS........... Telecommunications Authority Singapore
TAS........... Telefunken Assembler [*German*]   (ADPT)
TAS........... Tenancy Advice Service [*Australia*]
TAS........... Terminabrufsystem [*German*]   (ADPT)
TAS........... Thai Astronomical Society   (EAIO)

TAS............ Torpedo Data Computer   (RU)
TAS............ Traditional Acupuncture Society [*Stratford-Upon-Avon, Warwickshire, England*]   (EAIO)
TAS............ Tribunal Arbitral du Sport [*Court of Arbitration of Sport - CAS*] [*Switzerland*]   (EAIO)
TAS............ Turk Anonim Sirketi [*Turkish Joint-Stock Company*]   (CED)
TASA......... Tasmanian Association for Sustainable Agriculture [*Australia*]
TASA......... Taxpayers' Association of South Australia [*Australia*]
TASA......... Telecommunicacoes Aeronauticas SA [*Brazil*] [*ICAO designator*]   (FAAC)
TASA......... Telecomunicacoes Aeronauticas, Sociedade Anonima [*Aeronautical Telecommunications, Incorporated*] [*Brazil*]   (LA)
TASA......... Tennis Association of South Africa
TASA......... Terminology Association of South Africa   (AA)
TasAC........ Tasmanian Aero Club [*Australia*]
TASAS...... Turk Ambalaj Sanayii Anonim Sirketi [*Turkish Packing Industry Corporation*]   (TU)
TASC......... [*The*] Advanced Skills Centre Proprietary Ltd. [*Australia*]
TASC......... Centre for Technology and Social Change [*Australia*]   (IRC)
tasc............ Tascabile [*Pocket-Size*] [*Publishing*] [*Italian*]
TASC......... Technology and Social Change [*Australia*]
TasCAE ..... Tasmanian College of Advanced Education [*Australia*]
TASCIT..... Tasmanian Centre for Information Technology [*Australia*]
TASCOM ... University of Tasmania COM [*Computer Output Microform*] Catalogue [*Australia*]
TASCORP ... Tasmanian Public Finance Corp. [*Commercial firm*] [*Australia*]
TASE......... Tameion Anasyngrotiseos para to Symvoulion Evropis [*Council of Europe Reconstruction Fund*]   (GC)
TASE......... Technology Audit and Socio-Economic Evaluation [*Pakistan*]
TASE......... Tel Aviv Stock Exchange [*Israel*]   (IMH)
TASEL ...... Turk Alkollu Icki ve Sarap Endustrisi Limited [*Turkish Alcoholic Beverage and Wine Industry Limited*] [*Turkish Cypriot*]   (GC)
TASF .... Technical Assistance Special Fund [*Banking*] [*New Zealand*]
Tashavtomash ... Tashkent Machinery Plant for Assembling Automobiles and Trailers   (RU)
TAShFEI... Tashkent Institute of Finance and Economics   (RU)
TashGU ..... Tashkent State University   (RU)
TAShIIT.... Tashkent Institute of Railroad Transportation Engineers   (RU)
TAShINYaZ ... Tashkent Pedagogical Institute of Foreign Languages   (RU)
Tashirmash ... Tashkent Irrigation Machinery Plant   (RU)
Tashkhlopkomash ... Tashkent Cotton Machinery Plant   (RU)
TAShMI .... Tashkent Medical Institute   (RU)
TashPI .... Tashkent Polytechnic Institute   (RU)
Tashprodmash ... Tashkent Food-Processing and Cotton-Ginning Machinery Plant   (RU)
Tashsel'mash ... Tashkent Agricultural Machinery Plant   (RU)
TAShSKhI ... Tashkent Agricultural Institute   (RU)
Tashtekstil'mash ... Tashkent Textile Machinery Plant   (RU)
TASIS........ Turkiye Agac ve Agac Sanayii Iscileri Sendikasi [*Turkish Tree and Wood Industry Workers Union*]   (TU)
TASIT .... Taller de Asistencia y Servicio de la Industria Tabacalera [*Tobacco Industry Service and Assistance Workshop*] [*Cuba*]   (LA)
TASKFORNON ... Allied Task Force, North Norway [*NATO*]   (NATG)
TASKOBIRLIK ... Tarim Satis Kooperatifleri Birligi [*Agricultural Sales Cooperatives' Union*]   (TU)
TASLAP.... Tasmanian Labour Adjustment Package [*Australia*]
Tasm......... Tasmania [*Botanical Region*] [*Australia*]   (ADA)
TASMA..... Tanganyika Sisal Marketing Association
TASNSW .. Travellers' Aid Society of New South Wales [*Australia*]
TASO .... Transports Automobiles Subventionnes de l'Ouest
TASS .... Tasmanians against Shearwater Slaughter [*Australia*]
tass............ Tassello [*Label*] [*Publishing*] [*Italian*]
TASS .... Tawao Assisted Settlers' Scheme   (ML)
TASS .... Telegraphnoye Agentstvo Sovyetskovo Soyuza [*Telegraph Agency of the Soviet Union*] [*News agency*]
TA-SS .... Television Australia - Satellite Systems
TASSA ...... [*The*] Australian Self-Soar Association   (ADA)
TasSchArt ... Tasmania School of Art [*Australia*]
TASSI....... Tasmanian Statutory Index [*Australia*]
TASSR...... Tatar Autonomous Soviet Socialist Republic   (RU)
TASSR...... Turkestan Autonomous Soviet Socialist Republic [*1918-1924*]   (RU)
TASV......... Travellers' Aid Society of Victoria [*Australia*]
TASZI .... Termeloszovetkezetek Aruertekesiteset Szervezo Iroda [*Producer Cooperative Merchandise Sales Organizing Bureau*]   (HU)
TAT .... European Airlines [*France*] [*ICAO designator*]   (FAAC)
tat.............. Tatar   (BU)
tat .... Tatar, Tatarian   (RU)
TAT .... Tatry/Poprad [*Former Czechoslovakia*] [*Airport symbol*]   (OAG)
TAT .... Taxpayers' Association of Tasmania [*Australia*]
TAT .... Tobacco Authority of Tanzania
TAT .... Touraine Air Transport [*Private airline*] [*French*]   (EY)
TAT .... Tourism Authority of Thailand   (GEA)

TAT .... Tourist Authority of Thailand   (ECON)
TAT .... Transports Athane-Tual
TAT .... Transports Automobiles Tual
TATA........ Tanzania Agricultural Trainers Association   (AF)
TATA........ Timber and Allied Trades Association Ltd. [*South Africa*]   (AA)
TATAC...... Temporary Air Transport Advisory Committee [*NATO*]   (NATG)
TATAS ...... Turk-Alman Turizm Anonim Sirketi [*Turkish-German Tourism Corporation*]   (TU)
TatASSR ... Tatar Autonomous Soviet Socialist Republic   (RU)
TATB........ Tarcakozi Ar- es Termekforgalmazasi Bizottsag [*Interministerial Price and Product Marketing Commission*]   (HU)
TATE........ Traditional Aboriginal Teacher Education [*Australia*]
TATE........ Tyumen' Automobile and Tractor Electrical Equipment Plant   (RU)
Tatgosizdat ... Tatar State Publishing House   (RU)
Tatknigoizdat ... Tatar Book Publishing House   (RU)
TATMGT ... Tameion Asfaliseos Typografon kai Misthoton Grafikon Tekhnon [*Insurance Fund of Typographers and Graphic Arts Employees*] [*Greek*]   (GC)
Tatneft' ...... Association of the Petroleum Industry of the Tatar ASSR   (RU)
TatNII .... Tatar Scientific Research Petroleum Institute   (RU)
TATO .... Tagestonnen [*Tons per Day*] [*German*]
TATO .... Tanzania Association of Tour Operators   (EAIO)
TATs......... Sodium Trichloroacetate   (RU)
TAU .... Peat-Ammonia Fertilizers   (RU)
TAU .... Temps Actif Unitaire [*French*]   (ADPT)
TAU .... Toros Airlines [*Turkey*] [*ICAO designator*]   (FAAC)
TAU .... Transvaal Agricultural Union
TAUVEX... Tel Aviv University Ultra-Violet Explorer [*Israel*]
TAUW........ Technisch Adviesbureau van de Unie van Waterschappen BV [*Engineering Consultants to the Union of Drainage and River Boards*] [*Netherlands*]   (ARC)
TAV .... Compania de Servicios Aereos, TAVISA [*Spain*] [*ICAO designator*]   (FAAC)
TAV .... Tameion Asfaliseos Voulevton [*Deputies Insurance Fund*] [*Greek*]   (GC)
TAV .... Tau [*American Samoa*] [*Airport symbol*]   (OAG)
tav.............. Tavallinen [*Finland*]
tav.............. Tavallisesti [*Usually*] [*Finland*]
tav.............. Tavola [*Table*] [*Italian*]
TAV .... Taxpayers' Association of Victoria [*Australia*]
tav.............. Ten Aansien Van [*In the Presence Of*] [*Afrikaans*]
TAV .... Tiszantuli Aramszolgaltato Vallalat [*Electric Power Enterprise of the Trans-Tisza Region*]   (HU)
tav.............. Tout a Vous [*Yours Ever*] [*French*]
TAV .... Triathlon Association of Victoria [*Australia*]
tavb .... Tavbeszelo [*Telephone*]   (HU)
TAVC........ Thai Agribusiness Venture Co.
Tavkut....... Tavkozlesi Kutato Intezet [*Telecommunication Research Institute*]   (HU)
TAVN .... Tameion Allilovoitheias Vasilikou Navtikou [*Royal Navy Mutual Aid Fund*] [*Greek*]   (GC)
tavv............ Tavole [*Tables*] [*Italian*]
TAVW .... Tunisian Association of Voluntary Work   (EAIO)
TAW .... Technische Akademie Wuppertal [*Technical Academy of Wuppertal*] [*Germany*]   (SLS)
TAW .... Transway Air Services, Inc. [*Liberia*] [*ICAO designator*]   (FAAC)
TAWC .... Tasmanian Amateur Walking Club [*Australia*]
TAWE .... Trans-Africa Walk Expedition
TAWICO.... Tanzania Wildlife Corporation
TAWU .... Technical and Allied Workers Union [*Grenada*]   (LA)
TAWU .... Transport and Allied Workers' Union [*Zimbabwe, Nyasaland, and Kenya*]
TAX .... Travelair GmbH [*Germany*] [*ICAO designator*]   (FAAC)
TAXY........ Tameion Asfaliseos Xenodokho-Ypallilon [*Hotel Employees Insurance Fund*] [*Greek*]   (GC)
TAY .... Talia Airlines [*Turkey*] [*ICAO designator*]   (FAAC)
TAYAP...... Tameion Arogis Ypallilon Astynomias Poleon [*Cities Police Employees Assistance Fund*]   (GC)
TAYAYS ... Tameion Arogis Ypallilon Armodiotitos Ypourgeiou Syngoinonion [*Communications Ministry Employees Assistance Fund*] [*Greek*]   (GC)
TAYeM...... Millimass Unit   (RU)
TAYMIS ... Turkiye Agir Yapi Montaj Insaat Iscileri Sendikasi [*Turkish Heavy Structures Assembly and Construction Workers' Union*]   (TU)
TAZ .... Fuel Automatic Starter   (RU)
TAZ .... Transporte Aereo de la Amazonia [*Colombia*] [*ICAO designator*]   (FAAC)
TAZ .... Trnavske Automobilove Zavody [*Trnava Automobile Works*]   (CZ)
TAZ .... Truckers Association of Zambia
TAZARA ... Tanzania Zambia Railway Authority   (AF)
TB .... Aerospatiale (SOCATA) Stark KG [*Germany*] [*ICAO aircraft manufacturer identifier*]   (ICAO)
TB .... Drum Trigger   (RU)

TB	Heavy Bomber	(RU)
TB	Industrial Safety	(BU)
TB	Rear Area Base	(RU)
TB	Safety Engineering	(RU)
tb	Tabel [Table] [Publishing Danish/Norwegian]	
tb	Tablet	(RU)
tb	Tabulka [Table, Chart]	(CZ)
Tb	Tabur Battalion	(TU)
TB	Tank Brigade	(RU)
tb	Targyaban [Concerning]	(HU)
TB	Tasmanian Bank [Australia] [Commercial firm]	
TB	Technical Office	(RU)
TB	Technische Beschreibung [German]	(ADPT)
TB	Tehnicki Bataljon [Technical Battalion]	(YU)
TB	Tenkovski Bataljon [Tank Battalion]	(YU)
Tb	Terbio [Terbium] [Chemical element] [Portuguese]	
TB	Teruleti Bizottsag [Area Committee]	(HU)
TB	Thermite Bomb	(RU)
TB	Thermostatic Bi-Metal	(RU)
tb	Tiszteletbeli [Honorary]	(HU)
tb	Titelblad [Title Page] [Publishing Danish/Norwegian]	
TB	Toprak Bilimi [Soil Science] [As of an agricultural faculty]	(TU)
TB	Tourism Brisbane [Australia]	
TB	Traktorova Brigada [Tractor Brigade]	(CZ)
TB	Trigger of Input-Blocking Circuit [Computers]	(RU)
TB	Tubercle Bacillus	(RU)
Tb	Turbine [German]	(GCA)
TB	Two Beauts [Australia] [Slang]	(DSUE)
TB	Wet Tuchtrechtspraak Bedrijfs-Organisatie [Benelux]	(BAS)
TBA	Tabibuga [Papua New Guinea] [Airport symbol]	(OAG)
TBA	Tanzania Badminton Association	
TBA	Tasmanian Badminton Association [Australia]	
TBA	Tasmanian Bar Association [Australia]	
TBA	Tasmanian Basketball Association [Australia]	
TBA	Tasmanian Beekeepers' Association [Australia]	
TBA	Tasmanian Bookmakers' Association [Australia]	
TBA	Tasmanian Bridge Association [Australia]	
TBA	Tetrabutylammonium	(RU)
TBA	Tierkoerperbeseitigungsanstalt [Carcass Disposal Plant]	(EG)
TBA	Transbrasil SA Linhas Aereas [Brazil] [ICAO designator]	(FAAC)
TBA	Trockenbeerenauslesen [Late-Harvest Wines] [German]	
tbad	Heavy Bombardment Division	(BU)
tbae	Heavy Bombardment Aviation Squadron	(BU)
tbak	Heavy Bombardment Aviation Corps	(BU)
tbap	Heavy Bombardment Air Regiment	(BU)
TBAP	Heavy Bomber Regiment	(RU)
tbatr	Maintenance Battery	(BU)
tbatr	Technical Battery	(RU)
TBAV	Tenpin Bowling Association of Victoria [Australia]	
TBB	[The] Big Backyard [Radio program] [Australia]	
TBB	Transports Bernard Bismuth	
TBB	Turkiye Barolar Birligi [Turkish Bar Associations' Union]	(TU)
TBB	Turkiye Basin Birligi [Turkish Press Union]	(TU)
TBBI	Technische Bezirksbergbauinspektion [Regional Technical Mine Inspection Office]	(EG)
TBC	Tanganyika Broadcasting Corporation	
TBC	Tasmanian Bowls Council [Australia]	
TBC	Thailand Baptist Convention	(EAIO)
TBC	Tongyang Broadcasting Company [Korean]	
Tbc	Tuberculosi [Tuberculosis] [Italian]	
tbc	Tuberkulose [Tuberculosis] [Afrikaans]	
Tbc	Tuberkulose [Tuberculosis] [German]	
tbc	Tuberkulozis [Tuberculosis]	(HU)
TBCITC	Tasmanian Building and Construction Industry Training Committee [Australia]	
TBD	Tanganyika Pyrethrum Board	
TBD	Turk Belediyecilik Dernegi [Turkish Mayors' Association]	(TU)
TBD	Turk Biyokimya Dernegi [Turkish Biochemical Society]	(EAIO)
TBDzRwP	Towarzystwo Badan Dziejow Reformacji w Polsce [Society for Research on the History of the Reformation in Poland]	(POL)
TBE	Federation Europeenne des Fabricants de Tuiles et de Briques [European Association of Brick and Tile Manufacturers]	(EAIO)
TBEPO	Heavy Armored Train	(RU)
TBES	Excursion Trolleybus of the SVARZ	(RU)
TBF	Tabiteuea North [Kiribati] [Airport symbol]	(OAG)
TBF	Tributyl Phosphate	(RU)
TBFG	Tom Baker Friendship Group	(EAIO)
TBFSA	True Blue Floor Sanding Association [Australia]	
TBFT	Test de Bon Fonctionnement [Spacelab]	(MCD)
TBG	Tabubil [Papua New Guinea] [Airport symbol]	(OAG)
TBG	Testbaugruppe [German]	(ADPT)
TBH	[The] Bankstown Hospital [Australia]	
TBH	Tablas [Philippines] [Airport symbol]	(OAG)

TBH	Tamworth Base Hospital [Australia]	
TBH	TourBase Hotel-/Unterkunftsdaten [Jaeger-Verlag GmbH] [Germany] [Information service or system]	(CRD)
TBH	Trinity Air Bahamas [ICAO designator]	(FAAC)
TBI	Tamil Bible Institute [Peninsular Malaysia]	
TBI	Tea Board of India	
TBI	Technische Bergbauinspektion [Technical Mine Inspection Office]	(EG)
TBI	Theodor Bilharz Research Institute [Egypt] [Research center]	(IRC)
TBIA	Transvaal British Indian Association	
TBIIZhT	Tbilisi Institute of Railroad Transportation Engineers Imeni V. I. Lenin	(RU)
TbilNIGMI	Tbilisi Scientific Research Hydrometeorological Institute	(RU)
TbilNIISh	Tbilisi Scientific Research Institute of Sericulture	(RU)
TBIOT	All-Union Scientific Research Institute of Work Safety of the VTsSPS [Tbilisi]	(RU)
TBIS	Tasmanian Bibliographic Information System [Australia]	(PDAA)
TBK	Combined Casing Block	(RU)
tbk	Heavy Armored Car	(BU)
tbk	Tabornok [General] [Military]	(HU)
TBK	Turk Baris Kuvvetleri [Turkish Peace Forces] [Cyprus]	(TU)
TBKE	Tavkozlo es Biztositoberendezesi Kozponti Ellenorseg [Central Supervisory Department of Telecommunication and Safety Equipment]	(HU)
tb/kh	Turbine Ship	(RU)
TBKI	Togolandische Bau- und Kunststoff Industrie GmbH [German]	
TBL	(Abteilung) Textil, Bekleidung, Leder (der Staatlichen Plankommission) [Textile, Clothing, and Leather Department (of the State Planning Commission)] [German]	(EG)
TBL	[The] Berline, Berlin-Brandenburgisches Luftfahrtunternehmen GmbH [Germany] [ICAO designator]	(FAAC)
TBL	Tanzania Breweries Limited	
TBL	Tasmanian Baseball League [Australia]	
TBL	The Bad Life [Venezuela]	(EAIO)
TBL	Turk Bankasi Limited [Turkish Bank Limited (of Nicosia)] [Turkish Cypriot]	(GC)
TBMA	Timber and Building Materials Association [New South Wales, Australia]	
TBMM	Turkiye Buyuk Millet Meclisi [Turkish Grand National Assembly] [BMM] [See also]	(TU)
TBN	Technisches Buero fuer Nachrichtenmittel [Technical Office for Communications Equipment] [German]	(EG)
TBND	Tartos Bekeert, Nepi Demokraciaert [For Lasting Peace, For People's Democracy]	(HU)
TBNI	Tuberkulose-Navorsingsinstituut [Tuberculosis Research Institute] [South African Medical Research Council]	(AA)
TBO	Tabora [Tanzania] [Airport symbol]	(OAG)
TBO	TourBase Ortsdaten [Jaeger-Verlag GmbH] [Germany] [Information service or system]	(CRD)
TBOAA	Tuna Boat Owners' Association of Australia	
TBOASA	Tuna Boat Owners' Association of South Australia	
TBOS	Towarzystwo Budowy Osiedli Stolecznych [Society for Construction of Settlements in Warsaw]	(POL)
Tbp	Tabiplik [Medicine] [The practice of]	(TU)
TBP	Tumbes [Peru] [Airport symbol]	(OAG)
TBP	Turkiye Birlik Partisi [Turkish Unity Party] [Turkish Cypriot BP] [See also]	(TU)
TBPB	Bridgetown/Grantley Adams Internacional [Barbados] [ICAO location identifier]	(ICLI)
TBPO	Bridgetown [Barbados] [ICAO location identifier]	(ICLI)
TBR	Arbeitsgemeinschaft Technologieberatung Ruhr [Information retrieval]	
tbr	Tank Brigade	(BU)
TBR	Terbeschikkingstelling van de Regering [Benelux]	(BAS)
TBR	Tiszafoldvari Buzatermelesi Rendszer [Tiszafoldvar Wheat Growing System]	(HU)
t br	Tonne Brut [French]	
TBRI	Tuberculosis Research Institute [South African Medical Research Council]	(AA)
TBS	Tanzania Bureau of Standards	
TBS	Tbilisi [Former USSR] [Airport symbol]	(OAG)
TBS	Technische Betriebsschule [Enterprise Technical School] [German]	(EG)
TBS	Teilnehmerbetriebssystem [German]	(ADPT)
TBS	Telecom Business Services [Australia]	
TBS	Timber & Building Suppliers (Fiji) Ltd.	
TBS	Tokyo Broadcasting System [Japan]	(PDAA)
TBS	Tonbildschau [German]	(ADPT)
TBS	Towarzystwo Burs i Stypendiow [Society for Student Homes and Scholarships]	(POL)
TBS	Turkish Biochemical Society	(EAIO)
TBS	Warm White Light [Fluorescent tube]	(RU)

TBSD	Turkiye Bagimsiz Sosyalist Dernegi [*Turkish Independent Socialist Association*] (TU)
TBT	Tabatinga [*Brazil*] [*Airport symbol*] (OAG)
TBTAK	Turkiye Bilimsel ve Teknik Arastirma Kurumu [*Turkish Scientific and Technical Research Organization*] [*Under Office of Premier TUBITAK*] [*See also*] (TU)
TBTs	Tuberculosis, Bacillus Tuberculosis (BU)
TBU	Tongatapu [*Tonga Island*] [*Airport symbol*] (OAG)
TBV	Ten Bate Van [*In Aid Of*] [*Afrikaans*]
tbv	Ten Behoeve Van [*Benelux*] (BAS)
TBV	Ten Behoewe Van [*On Behalf Of*] [*Afrikaans*]
TBV	Ter Beskikking Van [*At the Disposal Of*] [*Afrikaans*]
TBV	Ter Bevordering Van [*For the Advancement Of*] [*Afrikaans*]
TBVA	Tactical Bomber Air Force (RU)
TBZ	Tabriz [*Iran*] [*Airport symbol*] (OAG)
TBZ	Tanvaldske Bavlnarske Zavody [*Tanvald Cotton Mills*] (CZ)
TBZ	Tobacco Board of Zambia
TC	Order of the Trinity Cross [*Trinidad and Tobago*]
TC	Table Complementaire (FLAF)
TC	Tankova Ceta [*Tank Platoon*] (CZ)
TC	Tariefcommissie [*Benelux*] (BAS)
TC	Taxe de Circulation sur les Vehicules Automobiles [*Benelux*] (BAS)
TC	Taylorcraft [*ICAO aircraft manufacturer identifier*] (ICAO)
tc	Technicky Cisty [*Technically Pure (Industrial grade of raw materials)*] (CZ)
Tc	Tecnecio [*Technetium*] [*Chemical element*] [*Portuguese*]
Tc	Telecomunicatii [*Telecommunications*] (RO)
TC	Telefunken Computer AG (IAA)
TC	Telegramme avec Collationnement [*French*]
TC	Tenkovska Ceta [*Tank Company*] (YU)
TC	Terciarios Capuchinos de Nostra Signora de los Dolores [*Tertiary Capuchins of Our Lady of Sorrows*] [*Italy*] (EAIO)
TC	Textile Craft Ltd. [*Malawi*]
tc	Tisztelt Cim [*Sir, Madam (In correspondence)*] (HU)
TC	Togoland Congress [*Ghana*] [*Political party*]
tc	Toho Casu [*At Present*] (CZ)
TC	Torpedna Cijev [*Torpedo Tube*] (YU)
tc	Torvenycikk [*Law Article*] [*Hungary*] (GPO)
tc	Toutes Coupures [*All Denominations (of bank notes)*] [*French*]
TC	Train de Combat [*Military*] [*French*] (MTD)
TC	Transmisora Caldas-Transmicentro [*Manizales*] (COL)
TC	Transport Combine [*Combined Transport*] [*French*] [*Business term*]
TC	Transport Concession [*Australia*]
TC	Transporte Combinado [*Combined Transport*] [*Spanish*] [*Business term*]
TC	Transporto Combinato [*Combined Transport*] [*Italian*] [*Business term*]
TC	Tribunal de Commerce (FLAF)
TC	Tribunal des Conflits [*Tribunal of Conflicts*] [*French*] (ILCA)
TC	Tripartite Commission [*St. Lucia*] (LA)
TC	Trusteeship Council
tc	Tucet [*Dozen*] (CZ)
TC	Turkiye Cumhuriyeti [*Republic of Turkey*] (TU)
TC	Turks and Caicos Islands [*ANSI two-letter standard code*] (CNC)
TC	Wet Toezicht Credietwezen [*Benelux*] (BAS)
TCA	Etablissement Central Technique de l'Armement [*Central Technical Armament Establishment*] [*Research center*] [*France*] (ERC)
TCA	Tahiti Conquest Airlines [*France*] [*ICAO designator*] (FAAC)
TCA	Tanzania Cotton Authority
TCA	Tanzania Cricket Association
TCA	Tanzania Cycling Association
TCA	Tasmanian Canoe Association [*Australia*]
TCA	Tasmanian Council on the Ageing [*Australia*]
TCA	Tasmanian Croquet Association [*Australia*]
TCA	Taxe sur le Chiffre d'Affaires [*Business Turnover Tax*] [*French*] [*Business term*] (WER)
TCA	Telecommunications Company of Australia Proprietary Ltd. (ADA)
TCA	Telecommunications et Constructions Africaines
TCA	Television Corp. of Australia
TCA	Tennant Creek [*Australia*] [*Airport symbol*] (OAG)
TCA	Tennis Camp of Australia (ADA)
TCA	Territorial Census Area
TCA	Textile Council of Australia
TCA	Touring-Club d'Algerie
TCA	Trustee Companies Association of Australia
TCA	Turkish Cooperative Association (EAIO)
TCA	Turks and Caicos Islands [*ANSI three-letter standard code*] (CNC)
TCAA	Technical Communication Association of Australia (PDAA)
TCAA	Tropas Cohoteriles Antiaereas [*Antiaircraft Rocket Troops*] [*Cuba*] (LA)
TCAA	Trustee Companies' Association of Australia

TCAC	Tubman Center of African Culture [*William V. S.*] [*Liberia*] (IRC)
TCAE	Tasmanian College of Advanced Education [*Australia*] (ADA)
TCAE	Transports en Commun d'Afrique Equatoriale
TCAL	Tasmanian Council for Adult Literacy [*Australia*]
TCAP	Technical Centre for the Apparel Industry [*France*] (EAIO)
TCAT	Tokyo City Airline Terminal [*Japan*]
TCAV	Tennis Coaches' Association of Victoria [*Australia*]
TCAWA	Tennis Coaches' Association of Western Australia
TCB	Tanganyika Coffee Board
TCB	Tasmanian Convention Bureau [*Australia*]
TCB	Teachers' Certification Board [*Australia*]
TCB	Technical Cooperation Bureau [*Korean*] (MSC)
TCB	Tonga Commodities Board (GEA)
TCB	Transporte del Caribe [*Colombia*] [*ICAO designator*] (FAAC)
TCB	Treasure Cay [*Bahamas*] [*Airport symbol*] (OAG)
TCB	Turkiye Cumhuriyeti Bahriye [*Turkish Republic Navy*] (TU)
TCC	Tanzania Cigarette Company Ltd.
TCC	Tasman Cable Co. [*Australia*]
TCC	Tasmanian Cancer Committee [*Australia*]
TCC	Tasmanian Chamber of Commerce [*Australia*]
TCC	Tasmanian Cricket Council [*Australia*]
TCC	Technology Clearinghouse of China [*Commercial firm*]
TCC	Technology Consultancy Centre [*University of Science and Technology*] [*Ghana*] (IRC)
TCC	Telecommunications Corp. [*Jordan*] (PDAA)
TCC	Temporary Council Committee [*NATO*]
TCC	Test Control Commission [*NATO*]
TCC	Thai Chamber of Commerce (EAIO)
TCC	Thep Padung Porn Coconut Co. Ltd. [*Thailand*]
tcc	Tone de Combustibil Conventional [*Tons of Conventional Fuel*] (RO)
TCC	TRANS-CIS Commodities [*Monte Carlo*] (ECON)
TCC	Transport and Communications Commission [*United Nations*] (WDAA)
TCC	Transports en Commun du Congo
TCCB	Touring-Club du Congo Belge
TCCE	Turkish Chamber of Chemical Engineers (EAIO)
TCCKA	Tai Chi and Chi Kung Academy [*Australia*]
TCCS	Trans Caucasian Container Service (EY)
TCCTB	Technical Center for Clay, Tiles, and Bricks [*France*] (EAIO)
TCCWCA ...	Tasmanian Council of Churches World Christian Action [*Australia*]
TCD	Chad [*ANSI three-letter standard code*] (CNC)
TCD	Department of Technical Cooperation for Development [*United Nations*]
TCD	Tennis-Club Dakarois
TCD	Tong Cong Doan Viet-Nam [*Vietnam Federation of Trade Unions*] (EY)
TCDC	Technical Cooperation among Developing Countries [*United Nations*]
TCDD	Turkiye Cumhuriyet Devlet Demiryollari [*Turkish State Railways*] (TU)
TCDL	Tasmanian Canine Defence League [*Australia*]
TCDPPA ...	Trustul de Constructii Drumuri, Poduri, Posturi, si Aeroporturi [*Trust for the Construction of Roads, Bridges, Posts, and Airports*] (RO)
TCE	Tananarive-Cote Est
Tce	Terrace (SCAC)
TCE	Thomson's Loss-Making Consumer-Electronics [*France*] (ECON)
TCE	Touring-Club d'Egypte
TCE	Travaux de Construction d'un Ensemble
TCE	Tulcea [*Romania*] [*Airport symbol*] (OAG)
TCE	Tyumen Commodity Exchange [*Russian Federation*] (EY)
TCEA	Training Center for Experimental Aerodynamics [*NATO*]
TCEEA	Tasmanian Catholic Education Employees' Association [*Australia*]
TCEI	Tokyo Commodity Exchange for Industry [*Tokyo Stock Exchange*] [*Japan*]
TCEK	Turkiye Cocuk Esirgeme Kurumu [*Turkish Child Protection Association*] [*CEK*] [*See also*] (TU)
TCEPA	Tasmanian Commercial Egg Producers' Association [*Australia*]
TCES	Turkiye Cumhuriyeti Emekli Sandigi Genel Mudurlugu [*Turkish Retirement Fund Directorate General*] (TU)
TCF	Tasmanian Cycling Federation [*Australia*]
TCF	Textile Consolidation Fund [*Egypt*]
TCF	Total Care Foundation [*Australia*]
TCF	Touring-Club of France [*Touring Club of France*] (WER)
TCF	Trade Credit Facility [*Caribbean Community and Common Market*] (EY)
TCF	Travel Compensation Fund [*Australia*]
TCF	Tres Cher Frere [*Beloved Brother*] [*French*]
TCFB	Travaux et Conferences de la Faculte de Droit de l'Universite Libre de Bruxelles [*Belgium*] (BAS)
TCFCA	Textile Clothing and Footwear Council of Australia

TCFD........ Technical Committee on Fish Diseases [*Australia*]
TCFM........ Teilhard Centre for the Future of Man   (EAIO)
TCFNSW .. Teachers' Christian Fellowship of New South Wales [*Australia*]
TCFP .... Total, Compagnie Francaise des Petroles [*State-controlled oil company*] [*French*]
TCG .... Tertiary Consulting Group [*Australia*]
TCG .... Turkiye Cumhuriyeti Gemisi [*Ship of Turkish Republic*]   (TU)
TCGA .... Tanganyika Coffee Growers Association
TCGA .... Tasmanian Chicken Growers' Association [*Australia*]
TCh .... Number Trigger [*Computer*]   (RU)
tch .... Period, Point   (RU)
TCH .... Tasmanian College of Hospitality [*Australia*]
TCH .... Tchibanga [*Gabon*] [*Airport symbol*]   (OAG)
Tch .... Techizat [*Equipment*]   (TU)
TCh .... Technical Section, Technical Unit   (RU)
TCH .... Technologie-Centrum Hannover GmbH [*Database producer*]   (IID)
TCH .... Tedmic Center Hamburg GmbH [*Germany*]
t ch .... This Date   (BU)
TCh .... Tone Frequency   (RU)
TCH .... Trustul de Constructii Hidroenergetice [*Trust for Hydraulic Power Constructions*]   (RO)
TCHA .... Tasmanian Community Health Association [*Australia*]
TCHADIS ... Societe Tchadienne de Distribution et de Services
TCHAMAG ... Societe Tchadienne de Grands Magasins
TChD .... Division Tank Unit   (RU)
TCHIP....... Town Campers' Housing and Infrastructure Program [*Australia*]
TChK .... Extraordinary Transportation Commission for Combating Counterrevolution and Sabotage   (RU)
tchk .... Period, Point   (RU)
TChP .... Towarzystwo Chirurgow Polskich [*Association of Polish Surgeons*] [*Poland*]
TCI .... Tasmanian Confederation of Industries [*Australia*]
TCI .... Technical College Ibadan
TCI .... Telecommunications Company of Iran
TCI .... Tenerife [*Canary Islands*] [*Airport symbol*]   (OAG)
TCI .... Thomson CEA Industries [*France*]   (ECON)
TCI .... Touring Cars International [*Australia*]
TCI .... Touring Club Italiano [*Italian Touring Club*]
TCI .... Trustul de Constructii Ilfov [*Ilfov Construction Trust*]   (RO)
TCI .... Trustul de Constructii Industriale [*Industrial Constructions Trust*]   (RO)
TCI .... Turbocharged Generation One [*Automotive engine identification*]
TCI .... Turks and Caicos Islands   (LA)
TCI .... Turks & Caicos National Airlines [*ICAO designator*]   (FAAC)
TCIB .... Trustul de Constructii Industriale Bucuresti [*Bucharest Industrial Construction Trust*]   (RO)
TCIF .... Trustul de Constructii pentru Imbunatatiri Funciare [*Trust for Land Improvement Constructions*]   (RO)
TCIL......... Telecommunications Consultants India Limited   (IMH)
TCIL......... Thailand Council of Industrial Labour   (EY)
TCIN .... Tasmania Curriculum Information Network [*Australia*]
TCIP .... Trustul de Constructii Instalatii Petroliere [*Trust for Petroleum Constructions and Installations*]   (RO)
T Civ .... Tarif en Matiere Civile [*French*]   (BAS)
TCIV .... Turbocharged Generation 4 [*Automotive engine identification*]
TCJ .... Tanners' Council of Japan   (EAIO)
TCK .... Turk Ceza Kanunu [*Turkish Criminal Law, Turkish Penal Code*]   (TU)
TCK .... Turkiye Cografya Kurumu [*Turkish Geographic Society*] [*TUCK*] [*See also*]   (TU)
TCKIB ...... Turkiye Cumhuriyeti Koy Isleri Bakanligi [*Republic of Turkey Village Affairs Ministry*]   (TU)
TCL........... Tanganyika Concessions Limited
TCL........... Tanganyika Creameries Limited
TCL........... Tanzania Cables Limited
TCL........... Telecommunication Laboratories [*Taiwan*]
TCL........... Towarzystwo Czyteln Ludowych [*Society for Public Reading Rooms*]   (POL)
TCL........... Transports Colonel Lotfi [*Algeria*]
TCL........... Tsumeb Corporation Limited [*Namibia*]   (AF)
TCLSIO..... Tokyo Central Labor Standards Inspection Office [*Japan*]
TCM .... Tasmanian Chamber of Mines [*Australia*]
TCM .... Total Catchment Management [*Water supply*] [*Australia*]
TCM .... Turk Cemaat Meclisi [*Turkish Cypriot Communal Assembly*]   (GC)
TCMA .... Turkish Clothing Manufacturers Association   (EAIO)
TCMAIA ... Trustul de Constructii Montaj pentru Agricultura si Industria Alimentara [*Construction and Assembly Trust for Agriculture and the Food Industry*]   (RO)
TCMB....... Tanzanian Cotton Marketing Board
TCMB....... Turkiye Cumhuriyeti Merkez Bankasi [*The Central Bank of Turkey*]   (TU)
TCME........ Trustul de Constructii Montaje Energetice [*Construction and Assembly Trust for Power Generation*]   (RO)

TCMIS ..... Trade Control Measures Information System [*UNCTAD*] [*United Nations*]   (DUND)
TCMJA ..... Tasmanian Country Music Jamboree Association [*Australia*]
TCMMS.... Turk Cemaat Meclisi Memurlari Sendikasi [*Turkish Communal Assembly Employees Union*] [*Turkish Cypriot*]   (GC)
TCMRIC ... Trustul de Constructii, Montaje, si Reparatii in Industria Chimica [*Trust for Construction, Installation, and Repairs in the Chemical Industry*]   (RO)
TCMS........ Kibris Turk Cemaat Meclisi Sendikasi [*Turkish Cypriot Communal Assembly Union*]   (TU)
TCMS........ Total, Compagnie Miniere du Senegal
TCMSB ..... Turkiye Cumhuriyeti Milli Savunma Bakanligi [*Republic of Turkey National Defense Ministry*] [*MSB*] [*See also*]   (TU)
TCMWU ... Textile and Clothes Manufacturing Workers Union [*Mauritius*]   (AF)
TCNSW..... Travel Centre of New South Wales [*Australia*]
TCO .... Tjanstemannens Centralorganisation [*Central Organization of Salaried Employees*] [*Sweden*]   (WEN)
TCO .... Traffic Camera Office [*Victoria, Australia*]
TCO .... Travel Control Officer   (ML)
TCO .... Tumaco [*Colombia*] [*Airport symbol*]   (OAG)
TCOA .... Transvaal Coal Owners Association [*South Africa*]
TCOA .... Trustee Companies Officers' Association [*Australia*]
TCOR .... Trusteeship Council Official Records
T Corp....... New South Wales Treasury Corp. [*Australia*]
T Corr .... Tribunal Correctionnel   (FLAF)
TCOSS ...... Tasmanian Council of Social Service [*Australia*]
TCOT .... Transit Congo-Oubangui-Tchad
TCP........... Trading Corporation of Pakistan   (GEA)
TCP........... Tropical Cyclone Programme [*World Meteorological Organization*]
TCPC .... Town and Country Planning Commission [*Tasmania, Australia*]
TCPENC ... Taipei Chinese PEN Centre [*Taiwan*]   (EAIO)
TCPP .... Technical Committee of Produce Prices [*Nigeria*]
TCQ .... Tacna [*Peru*] [*Airport symbol*]   (OAG)
TCR .... Laneas Aeres Trans Costa Rica SA [*ICAO designator*]   (FAAC)
T Cr........... Tarif Criminel [*Benelux*]   (BAS)
T Cr........... Tarif en Matiere Criminelle   (FLAF)
TCR .... Taxe de Cooperation Regionale [*Regional Cooperation Tax*] [*French*]   (AF)
TCR .... Teachers' Central Register [*Australia*]
TCR .... Temoignages Chretiens de la Reunion [*Christian Witnesses of Reunion*]   (AF)
TCRC........ Telecommunication Research Centre [*India*]   (PDAA)
TCRCB ..... Touring-Club Royal du Congo Belge
TCRDC..... Thapar Corporate Research and Development Centre [*India*]
TCRI .... Tobacco and Cotton Research Institute [*South Africa*] [*Research center*]   (IRC)
TCRMG .... Tripartite Commission for the Restitution of Monetary Gold [*Belgium*]   (EAIO)
TCRS .... Tanganyika Christian Refugee Service [*Tanzania*]   (AF)
TCRTA ...... Terracotta Roofing Tile Association [*Australia*]
TCS........... Tasmanian Caledonian Society [*Australia*]
TCS........... Teachers Credit Society [*Australia*]
TCS........... Technical Classification of Soils [*For pine plantations*] [*Australia*]
TCS........... Transportes de Carga Aerea Especializada y Servicios Aeronauticos [*Mexico*] [*ICAO designator*]   (FAAC)
TCS........... Trinity Christian School [*Australia*]
TCS........... Turkiye Cimento Sanayii [*Turkish Cement Industry*]   (TU)
TCSC .... Thai Cane and Sugar Corp.   (FEA)
TCSD........ Tiskovy Referat CSD [*Press Department of the Czechoslovak Railroads*]   (CZ)
TCSF .... Thomson-CSF [*France*] [*NASDAQ symbol*]
TCSG .... Thai Cane Sugar Group
TCSnet...... Thai Computer Science Network   (TNIG)
TCSS .... Tasmanian Council of Social Service [*Australia*]
TCT........... Taxe Conjecturelle Temporaire [*Temporary Surtax*] [*French*]   (IMH)
TCT........... Tropas Coheteriles Terrestres [*Land Missile Troops*] [*Cuba*]   (LA)
tct .... Tucat [*Dozen*]   (HU)
TCT........... Tur Avrupa Havayollari AS [*Turkey*] [*ICAO designator*]   (FAAC)
Tctbl.......... Tractatenblad [*Benelux*]   (BAS)
TCTC........ Tuvalu Coconut Traders' Co-Operative Ltd.   (EY)
TCTD........ Transport, Communications, and Tourism Division
TCU .... Technical Cooperation Unit [*Barbados*]   (IRC)
TCU .... Telecommunications Unit [*New South Wales Commercial Services Group*] [*Australia*]
TCU .... Tribunal de Contas da Uniao [*National Accounting Office*] [*Brazil*]   (LA)
TCV .... Transportes Aereos de Cabo Verde [*Cape Verde*] [*ICAO designator*]   (FAAC)
TCV .... Treasury Corp. Victoria [*Australia*]

TCVD .... Technical Committee on Veterinary Drugs [*Australian Agricultural Council*]
TCVN .... Tieu Chuan Viet Nam [*Vietnam Standards*]
TCW .... Tocumwal [*Australia*] [*Airport symbol*]   (OAG)
TCWG .... Tasmanian Carpet Wool Growers' Ltd. [*Commercial firm*] [*Australia*]
TCY .... Transports Charmy & Cie.
TCY .... Turkiye Cumhuriyeti Yonetmelik [*Turkish Republic Regulation*]   (TU)
TCZ .... Theological College of Zimbabwe
tcz............... Tuna Cistych Zivin [*Ton of Pure Nutrients*]   (CZ)
TCZB........ Turkiye Cumhuriyeti Ziraat Bankasi [*Agricultural Bank of Turkey (Branch in Nicosia)*] [*Turkish Cypriot*]   (GC)
TD.............. Chad [*ANSI two-letter standard code*]   (CNC)
TD.............. Dispatcher's Track Indicator   (RU)
TD.............. Dynamic Flip-Flop   (RU)
TD.............. Heat Engine   (RU)
TD.............. Peat Industry   (RU)
TD.............. Rear Patrol   (BU)
td .... So Forth   (RU)
TD.............. Table Decennale   (FLAF)
td .... Taille-Douce [*Copper Engraving*] [*Publishing*] [*French*]
TD.............. Tank-Borne   (RU)
TD.............. Tank Division   (RU)
TD.............. Tank Range Finder   (RU)
TD.............. Tealto Dail [*Member of the Dail*] [*Irish*]   (ILCA)
tD .... Technischer Dienst [*Technical Service*] [*German*]
TD.............. Tekhnitos Doryforos [*Artificial Satellite*]   (GC)
TD.............. Tele- og Dataforbundet [*Norway*]   (EAIO)
TD.............. Temperature Gauge Pickup   (RU)
TD.............. Temperature-Sensitive Element   (RU)
TD.............. Tentera Darat [*Army*]   (ML)
TD.............. Toa Doyu-kai [*Asian Federation*] [*Japan*]
TD.............. Trgovinski Dukan [*Commercial Shop*]   (YU)
Td.............. Triebwagenschnellzug [*Multiple Unit Fast Express Train*]   (EG)
TD.............. Tripartite Declaration
TD.............. Tudomanyok Doktora [*Hungary*]
TD.............. Tunisian Dinar
TD.............. Tunnel Diode   (RU)
TDA .... Tanzania Drivers Association
TDA .... Tasmanian Development Authority [*Australia*]
TDA .... Taxi Drivers' Association [*Australia*]
TDA .... Tea Development Authority [*Mauritius*]   (AF)
TDA .... Textile Distributors' Association [*Australia*]
TDA .... Timber Development Association of Australia   (ADA)
TDA .... Trade Development Authority [*India*]   (GEA)
TDA .... Transcarga SA [*Costa Rica*] [*ICAO designator*]   (FAAC)
TDA .... Transport Airborne-Landing Aviation   (RU)
TDAD .... Trade Development Assistance Division [*Bureau of East-West Trade*] [*Former USSR*]   (IMH)
TDANSW ... Timber Development Association (New South Wales) [*Australia*]
TDAP .... Transport Airborne-Landing Aviation Regiment   (RU)
TDASA....... Timber Development Association of South Australia
TDAT .... Technical Directorate Assistance Team [*South Vietnamese studies and observation group team*]   (VNW)
TDAU .... Technology Development and Advisory Unit [*University of Zambia*]
TDB .... Temps Dynamique Barycentrique [*Barycentric Dynamical Time*] [*French*]
TDB .... Tetebedi [*Papua New Guinea*] [*Airport symbol*]   (OAG)
TDB .... Tonga Development Bank   (GEA)
TDB .... Trade Development Bank [*Subsidiary of American Express Bank*]
TDB .... Trade Development Board [*Singapore*]   (FEA)
TDC .... Tadair SA [*Spain*] [*ICAO designator*]   (FAAC)
TDC .... Tanganyika Development Corporation
TDC .... Tarif Douanier Commun [*North African*]
TDC .... Tema Development Corporation
TDC .... Textile Development Centre [*Textile Consolidation Fund*] [*Egypt*]
TDC .... Tourist Development Corp. of Malaysia
TDC .... Trade Development Corp. [*South Australia*] [*Commercial firm*]
TDC .... Trade Development Council [*Australia*]
TDC .... Trade Documentation Centre [*Kenya External Trade Authority*]
TDC .... Trankei Development Corporation
TDC .... Travaux de Developpement Communautaire
TDC .... Turk Donanma Cemiyeti [*Turkish Fleet Society*]   (TU)
TDCA .... Timber Development Council of Australia   (ADA)
TDCI......... Turkiye Demir ve Celik Isletmesi [*Turkish Iron and Steel Works*]   (TU)
TDCK .... Technisch Documentatie- en Informatiecentrum voor de Krijgsmacht [*'s-Gravenhage*]
TDCU .... Torit District Co-Operative Union
TDD.......... Long-Range Tank   (RU)
tdd .... Te Dienende Dage [*Benelux*]   (BAS)

TDD.......... Trinidad [*Bolivia*] [*Airport symbol*]   (OAG)
TDDF .... Turk Demir Dokum Fabrikasi [*Turkish Iron Foundry*]   (TU)
TDDSz....... Tudomanyos Dolgozok Demokratikus Szakszervezete [*Democratic Trade Union of Scientific Workers*] [*Hungary*]   (EY)
TDE .... Taxe de Developpement Economique   (FLAF)
TDE .... Te Dien Einde [*For the Purpose*] [*Afrikaans*]
TDE .... Tribunal Departamental de Elecciones [*Departmental Court of Elections*] [*Honduras*]   (LA)
TDEC........ Therapeutic Device Evaluation Committee [*Australia*]
TDel .... Division Control Trigger [*Computers*]   (RU)
TDF .... Talebe Dernekleri Federasyonu [*Federation of Student Societies*] [*TTF*] [*See also*]   (TU)
TDF .... Telediffusion de France [*Broadcasting agency*] [*French*]
TDF .... Thiamine Diphosphate   (RU)
TDF .... Transkei Defence Force [*South Africa*]
TDFL......... Tanganyika Development Finance Co. Limited
TDG .... Tandag [*Philippines*] [*Airport symbol*]   (OAG)
TDGF .... Turkiye Devrimci Genclik Federasyonu [*Turkish Revolutionary Youth Federation*] [*DEV GENC*] [*See also*]   (TU)
TDIA .... Tasmanian Dairy Industry Authority [*Australia*]
TDIF......... Turkiye Demiryollari Iscileri Federasyonu [*Turkish Federation of Railway Worker Unions*]   (TU)
TDIS .... Thai Development Information Service   (EAIO)
TDIS.......... Turkiye Deniz Iscileri Sendikasi [*Turkish Maritime Workers' Union*]   (TU)
TDJ............ Tadjoura [*Djibouti*] [*Airport symbol*]   (OAG)
TDK .... Tarimsal Donatim Kurumu [*Agricultural Equipment Association*] [*Under the TFSC Ministry of Agriculture*]   (TU)
TDK .... Technische Durchsicht und Kontrolle [*Technical Inspection and Control*] [*German*]   (EG)
TdK .... Toepassing der Kinderwetten [*Benelux*]   (BAS)
TDK .... Turk Devrim Kurumu [*Turkish Revolution Society*]   (TU)
TDK .... Turk Dil Kurumu [*Turkish Linguistic Organization (of Ankara)*]   (GC)
TDK .... Tyden Detske Knihy [*Week for the Promotion of Children's Books*]   (CZ)
TDKF........ Fahrzeugtestdatenbank [*Dokumentation Kraftfahwesen eV*] [*Germany*] [*Information service or system*]   (CRD)
TDKP........ Turkish Revolutionary Communist Party [*Political party*]   (PD)
TDL .... Tandil [*Argentina*] [*Airport symbol*]   (OAG)
TDM .... Tank Destroyer Armed with Missiles
TDM .... Teledifusao de Macau [*Radio and television broadcasting company*] [*Macau*]   (FEA)
TDM .... Thiess-Dampier-Mitsui Coal Proprietary Ltd. [*Australia*]   (ADA)
TDMA .... Titanium Dioxide Manufacturers Sector Group [*Belgium*]   (EAIO)
tdn .... Maintenance Battalion   (BU)
tdn .... Technical Battalion   (RU)
TDN........... Topografische Dienst Nederland [*Topographic Service of the Netherlands*] [*Research center*]   (EAS)
TDO .... Training Development Officer
TDO .... Transporte Aereco Dominicano [*Dominican Republic*] [*ICAO designator*]   (FAAC)
TDO .... Turk Devrim Ocaklari [*Turkish Revolutionary Hearths*] [*Clubs*]   (TU)
t dob .... Telephone Extension   (RU)
TDOB .... Turkiye Devrimci Ogretmenler Birligi [*Turkish Revolutionary Teachers' Union*]   (TU)
TDOD........ Turkiye Devrimci Ogretmenler Dernegi [*Turkish Revolutionary Teachers' Organization*] [*DOD*] [*See also*]   (TU)
TDP .... Strain Gauge   (RU)
TDP .... Terminal de Donnees Pret [*French*]   (ADPT)
TDPD .... Dominica/Melville Hall [*Dominica*] [*ICAO location identifier*]   (ICLI)
TDPR........ Roseau [*Dominica*] [*ICAO location identifier*]   (ICLI)
TDPSA ...... Association for Totally Dependent Persons of South Australia
TDPSK ...... Turkiye Devlet Personeli Sendikalari Konfederasyonu [*Turkish State Personnel Unions' Confederation*]   (TU)
TDR .... Tank-Borne Company   (RU)
TDR .... Tropical Disease Research and Training Programme
TDR .... Tvornica Duhana Rovinj [*Rovinj Tobacco Factory*]   (YU)
TDR .... Tyden Detske Radosti [*Children's Week*]   (CZ)
TDRI......... Tropical Development Research Institute [*Sudan*]
TDS .... Tasmanian Deaf Society [*Australia*]
TDS .... Technicke Dokumentacni Stredisko [*Technical Documentation Center*]   (CZ)
TDS .... Telegramm-Dienst-System [*German*]   (ADPT)
TDSCC ...... Tidbinbilla Deep Space Communication Complex [*Australia*]   (ADA)
TDSD .... Turkiye Deri Sanayicileri Dernegi [*Turkish Leather Industrialists' Association*]   (EAIO)
TDSF......... Tasmanian Department of Sea Fisheries [*Australia*]
TDSG........ Long-Distance Bare Telephone [*Cable*]   (RU)
TDS-IS ...... Tatvan Deniz Tasitmaciligi Iscileri Sendikasi [*Tatvan Marine Transport Workers' Union*]   (TU)

TDSK......... Technisch Documentatieen Informatiecentrum van de Krijgsmacht [*Armed Forces Technical Documentation and Information Center*] [*Netherlands*]   (WEN)
TDSNF...... Three-Valued Disjunctive Perfect Normal Form   (RU)
TDT .... Skidding Diesel Tractor   (RU)
TDTB........ Turk Dis Ticaret Bankasi [*Turkish Foreign Trade Bank*]
TDU........... Retropackage, Braking Engine   (RU)
TDV .... Tovarny Detskych Vozidel [*Plants for Baby Carriages*]   (CZ)
Tdv .... Triebwagenschnellzug [*Multiple Unit Fast Express Train*]   (EG)
TDV .... Turk Donanma Vakfi [*Turkish Fleet Fund*]   (TU)
Tdw .... Tonnen Deadweight, Tonnen Tragfaehigkeit [*Deadweight (Metric) Tons*]   (EG)
TDZ .... Tvornica Duhana Zagreb [*Zagreb Tobacco Factory*]   (YU)
TDZA .... Trade Development Zone Authority [*Northern Territory, Australia*]
TE .... Diesel Locomotive with Electric Drive   (RU)
TE .... Electric Tachometer   (RU)
TE .... La Telemecanique Electrique
TE .... Ling-Temco-Vought [*LTV*] [*ICAO aircraft manufacturer identifier*]   (ICAO)
TE .... Peat Excavator   (RU)
TE .... Rear Echelon   (BU)
TE .... Tageseinfluesse [*Weather Factors*] [*German*]   (GCA)
Te .... Take [*Hill, Mountain*] [*Japan*]   (NAU)
TE .... Takteinheit [*German*]   (ADPT)
TE .... Technical Encyclopedia   (RU)
TE .... Technicien d'Entretien [*French*]   (ADPT)
TE .... Technische Entwicklung [*Technical Development Office*] [*German*]   (EG)
TE .... Technologiai Eloirasok [*Technological Instructions*]   (HU)
Te .... Tellur [*Tellurium*] [*Chemical element*] [*German*]
Te .... Telurio [*Tellurium*] [*Chemical element*] [*Portuguese*]
Te .... Temperguss [*Malleable Cast Iron*] [*German*]   (GCA)
Te .... Tepe [*or Tepesi*] [*Hill or Peak Turkish*]   (NAU)
TE .... Teramo [*Car registration plates*] [*Italian*]
TE .... Termoelektrana [*Thermoelectric Power Plant*]   (YU)
TE .... Tertiary Entrance
TE .... Tete d'Etapes [*Military*] [*French*]   (MTD)
t e.............. That Is   (BU)
te .... To Est [*That Is*]   (YU)
TE .... Train des Equipages [*Army Service Corps*] [*French*]   (MTD)
TE .... Transkomplekt Engineering [*Bulgaria*]
TE .... Trapeza tis Ellados [*Bank of Greece*]   (GC)
TE .... Trazione Elettrica [*Electrified Line*] [*Italian*]
Te .... Triebwageneilzug [*Express Rail Motor Train*]   (EG)
TE .... Tudomanyegyetem [*University*]   (HU)
TE .... Turboelektricni Pogon [*Turboelectrical Power*]   (YU)
TE .... Turk Edebiyatcilar [*Turkish Men of Letters*]   (TU)
TEA .... Tagmata Ethnikis Asfaleias [*National Defense Battalions*] [*Greek*]   (GC)
TEA .... Tasman Empire Airways Ltd. [*Aerospace*]
TEA .... Technische Entwicklung fuer Antennen [*(Laboratory for) Technical Development of Antennas*] [*German*]   (EG)
TEA .... Tekhniki Epopteia Alieias [*Fishing Control Service*] [*Greek*]   (GC)
TEA .... Territory Enterprise Award [*Northern Territory, Australia*]
TEA .... Textile Educators' Association [*Australia*]
TEA .... Topikai Epitropai Ardevseos [*Local Irrigation Committees*] [*Greek*]   (GC)
TEA .... Trans European Airways [*Belgium*] [*ICAO designator*]   (FAAC)
TEA .... Transportation and Forwarding Agency   (RU)
TEA .... Triethanolamine   (RU)
TEA .... Typografiki Enosis Athinon [*Athens Printers' Union*]   (GC)
TEAC........ Thai Electric, Electronic, and Allied Industries Club
TEAC........ Victorian Transition Education Advisory Committee [*Australia*]
TEAEDX ... Tameion Epikourikis Asfaliseos Ergatotekhnikon Domikon kai Xylourgikon Ergasion [*Auxiliary Insurance Fund for Construction and Carpentry Workers and Technicians*] [*Greek*]   (GC)
TEAHA ..... Trans-East African Highway Authority   (EA)
Teakinopechat' ... Theater and Motion-Picture Publishing House   (RU)
TEAL......... Tasman Empire Airways Ltd. [*Australia*]   (ADA)
TEAM .... [*The*] European-Atlantic Movement [*British*]
TEAM .... Telecommunications, Electronique, Aeronautique et Maritime [*France*]   (PDAA)
TEAM .... The European-Atlantic Movement   (PDAA)
TEAM .... Towards Excellent Australian Manufacturing
TEAM .... Training and Employment of Auto Mechanics
TEAMA..... Top End Aboriginal Music Association [*Australia*]
TEAMK..... Tameion Epikourikis Asfaliseos Misthoton Klosto-Yfandourgias [*Auxiliary Insurance Fund for Salaried Textile Workers*] [*Greek*]   (GC)
Teamontazh ... All-Union Office for the Installation of Mechanical and Electrical Equipment in Theater and Show Establishments   (RU)
TEAO .... Teacher Education Advisory Office [*New South Wales, Australia*]

TEAPET.... Tameion Epikourikis Asfaliseos Prosopikou Etaireion Tsimendon [*Auxiliary Insurance Fund for Cement Company Employees*] [*Greek*]   (GC)
TEAPOKA ... Tameion Epikourikis Asfaliseos Prosopikou Organismon Koinonikis Asfaliseos [*Auxiliary Insurance Fund for Social Insurance Organization Personnel*] [*Greek*]   (GC)
Teaproyektstroymontazh ... All-Union State Trust for the Planning of Construction and Installation of Electrical Equipment of the Art Committee at the Art Committee at the Council of Ministers, USSR   (RU)
TEAR......... Terico de Armada [*Amphibious operations*] [*Spanish*]
TEASOL ... Teaching of English to Adult Speakers of Other Languages [*Australia*]
Teasvet...... Theater Lighting Equipment Plant   (RU)
TEAT........ Obras de Teatro Estrenadas en Espana [*Ministerio de Cultura*] [*Spain*] [*Information service or system*]   (CRD)
teat .... Teatro [*Theater*] [*Italian*]
teatr........... Theater term   (BU)
teatt .... Teatteri [*Theatre*] [*Finland*]
TEAV........ Totalisator Employees' Association of Victoria [*Australia*]
teavuz........ Higher Educational Theatrical Institution   (RU)
TEAYEK ... Tameion Epikourikis Asfaliseos Ypallilon Emborikon Katastimaton [*Auxiliary Insurance Fund of Commercial Establishment Employees*] [*Greek*]   (GC)
TEAYEOK ... Tameion Epikourikis Asfaliseos Ypallilon Ethnikou Organismou Kapnou [*Auxiliary Insurance Fund of National Tobacco Organization Employees*] [*Greek*]   (GC)
TEB........... Fuel and Power Balance   (RU)
TEB........... Teruleti Egyezteto Bizottsag [*Territorial Arbitration Committee*]   (HU)
TEB........... Turk Eczacilar Birligi [*Union of Turkish Pharmacists*]   (TU)
TEB........... Turk Ekonomi Bankasi AS [*Bank*] [*Turkey*]
TEB........... Wage Rate and Economics Office   (RU)
TEBA........ [*The*] Employment Bureau of Africa
TEBA........ Tutmonda Esperantista Biblioteka Asocio [*International Association for Esperanto in Libraries - IAEL*]   (EAIO)
TEBE........ Takarekpenztarak es Bankok Egyesulete [*Association of Savings Institutions and Banks*]   (HU)
TEBROC ... Tehran Book Processing Centre [*Institute for Research and Planning in Science and Education*] [*Iran*]   (PDAA)
TEC........... Department of Technical and Economic Cooperation [*Thailand*]   (DS)
TEC........... [*The*] Executive Connection Proprietary Ltd. [*Australia*]
TEC........... Tanganyika Episcopal Conference
TEC........... Tanganyika European Council
TEC........... Tarif Exterieur Commun [*North Africa*]
TEC........... Tea Cyprus Ltd. [*ICAO designator*]   (FAAC)
TEC........... Teatro Escuela de Cali   (COL)
Tec .... Techizat [*Equipment*]   (TU)
Tec .... Tecnico [*Type of diploma*] [*Spanish*]
Tec .... Tecrube [*Experiment, Experimental*]   (TU)
TEC........... Teritorijski Evakuaciski Centar [*Territorial Evacuation Center*]   (YU)
TEC........... Termo-Elektro Central [*Albanian*]
TEC........... Touristic Enterprises Company [*Kuwait*]   (IMH)
TEC........... Transistor a Effet de Champ [*French*]   (ADPT)
TEC........... Transitional Executive Council [*Implemented in 1993 to work with the Cabinet and ensure fair political campaigning*] [*South Africa*]   (ECON)
TECBA ...... Societe d'Etudes Techniques et de Realisation de Travaux Publics et de Batiments
TECDOC... Technical Documentation Centre [*Institute of Standards and Industrial Research of Iran*]
TECh .... Maintenance-Operating Unit   (BU)
tech............ Technical   (EECI)
TECh .... Technical Maintenance Unit   (RU)
Tech .... Technik [*Technique*] [*German*]   (GCA)
TECHCOL ... Techos Colombia [*Colombia*]   (COL)
TECHIMPORT ... China National Technical Import Corp. [*China*]   (IMH)
TECHKERAM ... Technische Keramik (VVB) [*Technical Ceramics (VVB)*]   (EG)
TECHMINEMET ... Bureau Technique d'Etudes des Minerais et de Metaux
techn.......... Technical   (EECI)
techn.......... Technik [*Technician*] [*Poland*]
techn.......... Technikum [*Technical School*]   (POL)
techn.......... Technisch [*Technical*] [*German*]
TECHNACO ... Societe Africaine des Techniques pour l'Amenagement et la Construction
TECHNICATOME ... Societe Technique pour l'Energie Atomique [*Nuclear energy*] [*French*]   (NRCH)
TECHNICOL ... Association pour le Perfectionnement Technique des Appareils Domestiques d'Utilisation des Combustibles Liquides [*Association for the Technical Approval of Oil Burning Domestic Appliances*] [*Belgium*]   (PDAA)
TECHNION ... Israel Institute of Technology   (PDAA)
TECHNOCEAN ... Societe Technique pour l'Oceanologie [*French*]   (ASF)

TECHNOIMPEX ... TECHNOIMPEX Gepipari Kulkereskedelmi Vallalat [*TECHNOIMPEX Foreign Trade Enterprise of the Machine Industry*] (HU)

Technol ..... Technologie [*Technology*] [*German*] (GCA)

technol........ Technologisch [*Technological*] [*German*] (GCA)

TECHNONET ASIA ... Asian Network for Industrial Technology Information and Expansion (PDAA)

TECHNOSPOL ... Akciova Spolecnost pro Zprostredkovani Vedeckotechnicke Pomoci [*Joint-Stock Company for Scientific and Technical Assistance*] (CZ)

Technzbrojsl ... Technicka Zbrojni Sluzba [*Technical Weapons Service*] (CZ)

Tech r........ Technicka Rota [*Technical Company*] [*Military*] (CZ)

TECHSOSA ... Technology Secondary School Old Students Association

TECI.......... Tunisia Engineering Construction Industry [*Commercial firm*]

teckn.......... Teckning [*Drawing*] [*Sweden*]

TECMECOL ... Tecnica Metalica Colombiana [*Colombia*] (COL)

Tecn .... Tecnologo [*Type of diploma*] [*Spanish*]

TECNAPO ... Tecnica Naviera y Portuaria [*Peru*] (LAA)

TECNET ... Technologies Network [*Database*] [*EC*] (ECED)

TECNICANA ... Sociedad Colombiana de Tecnicos de la Cana de Azucar [*Colorado*]

TECNICOLSA ... Tecnica Colombiana, Sociedad Anonima [*Colombia*] (COL)

TECNIGRAF ... Tecnicas Graficas [*Colombia*] (COL)

TECNOIMPORT ... Empresa Cubana Importadora de Productos Tecnicos [*Cuban Enterprise for the Import of Technical Products*] (LA)

TECO .... Tanzania Extract Company

TECO .... Technical Co-Operation Committee [*OECD*] (DS)

TECODEV ... Technical & Commercial Development Co. [*Oman*] (IMH)

TECON ..... Theatre Council of Natal

TECORIN ... Tecnicas de Organizacion Industrial [*Colombia*] (COL)

TECSIS ..... Teachers Curriculum Search Information Services [*Australia*]

TECTRO... Societe de Techniques Tropicales

TED .... Technical and Economic Report (RU)

TED .... Teddy Air AS [*Norway*] [*ICAO designator*] (FAAC)

TeD .... Telefunken-Decca [*Video disk system*]

TED .... Tenders Electronic Daily [*Office for Official Publications of the European Communities*] [*Database Luxembourg*]

TED .... Tenis Eskrim Dagcilik Kulubu [*Tennis, Fencing, and Mountain Climbing Club*] [*Istanbul*] (TU)

TED .... Thisted [*Denmark*] [*Airport symbol*] (OAG)

TED .... Traitement Electronique des Donnees [*Electronic Data Processing - EDP*] [*French*]

TED .... Transvaal Electrical Department

TED .... Turkiye Egitim Dernegi [*Turkish Education Association*] (TU)

TEDA .... Tetekofe Development Association

TEDB........ Timber Export Development Board [*Ghana*]

Ted Bsk...... Tedarik Baskanligi [*Procurement Chairman*] [*Military*] (TU)

TEDIS .... Tele-Dateninformationsdienst [*German*] (ADPT)

TEDK .... Tekhnikos Exoplismos Dimon kai Koinotiton [*Technical Equipment of Municipalities and Communities*] [*Greek*] (GC)

TEDKA...... Topiki Enosis Dimon kai Koinotiton Attikis [*Local Union of Municipalities and Communities of Attiki*] (GC)

TEDS........ Thermoelectromotive Force, Thermoelectric Power (RU)

TEE............ [*The*] Earth Exchange [*Geological and Mining Museum*] [*Sydney, Australia*]

TEE............ Taxe Exceptionnelle d'Equipement [*Special Tax on Equipment*] (CL)

TEE............ Tbessa [*Algeria*] [*Airport symbol*] (OAG)

TEE............ Tekhnika kai Epangelmatiki Ekpaidevsis [*Technical and Vocational Education*] (GC)

TEE............ Tekhnikon Epimelitirion Ellados [*Technical Chamber of Greece*] (GC)

TEE............ Tertiary Entrance Examination [*Western Australia*]

TEE........... Trans-Europa-Express [*Trans-European-Express*] [*German*]

TEE........... Trans-Europe-Express [*Continental High-Speed Train*] [*French*]

TEE........... Trapeza Exagogon-Eisagogon [*Export-Import Bank*] [*Greek*] (GC)

TEEFAE.... Tameion Eispraxeos Esodon Forologias Anonymon Etaireion [*Joint Stock Companies Tax Revenues Collection Fund*] [*Greek*] (GC)

TEEM........ Transeuropean Express Freight Train System (IMH)

TEENST ... Teenstelling [*Contrast*] [*Afrikaans*]

teenw .... Teenwoordig [*Present*] [*Afrikaans*]

teesz........... Termeloszovetkezet [*Producer Cooperative*] (HU)

TEETECO ... Tanganyika Transport Co-Operative Company

TEF............ Division of Heat Power Engineering (RU)

TEF............ Telfer [*Australia*] [*Airport symbol*] (OAG)

TEF............ Triethylenephosphoramide (RU)

TEF............ Turkiye Emeklileri Federasyonu [*Turkish Retired Workers' Federation*] (TU)

TEFL .... Teaching English as a Foreign Language

TEFLA ...... Teaching of English as a Foreign Language to Adults [*Australia*]

TEFO........ Svenska Textilforskningsinstitutet [*Swedish Institute for Textile Research*] [*Sweden*]

TEFO........ Textilforskningsinstitutet [*Textile Research Institute*] [*Sweden*] (PDAA)

TEFRACO ... Societe Congo Francais Textile

teft............. Account Book, Notebook (BU)

TEFU........ Teherautofuvarozasi Kozpont [*Trucking Center*] (HU)

TEG .... Technology Economics Group [*Korea Institute of Electronics Technology*] [*South Korea*]

TEG .... Tete d'Etapes de Guerre [*Military*] [*French*] (MTD)

TEG .... Therapeutic Evacuation Hospital (RU)

TEG .... Thermal Electric Power Generator (RU)

TEGESAN ... Trakya Gubre Sanayii Anonim Sirketi [*Thrace Fertilizer Industry Corporation*] [*Tekirdag*] (TU)

TEGN .... Tegnies [*Technical*] [*Afrikaans*]

tegn .... Tegning [*Drawing*] [*Publishing Danish/Norwegian*]

tegngr .... Teginger [*Drawings*] [*Publishing Danish/Norwegian*]

TEGNOL .. Tegnologie [*Technology*] [*Afrikaans*]

TEGS........ Training and Employment Grants Scheme [*Scottish Development Agency*]

TEGU .... Turbine-Electric Drive [*Ship propulsion*] (RU)

TEH.......... Tehua [*Race of maize*] [*Mexico*]

TEH.......... Tempelhof Airways, Inc. [*Germany*] [*ICAO designator*] (FAAC)

TEHAG ..... Temperaltvizu Halszaporito Gazdasag [*Temperate Water Fish Breeding Farm*] (HU)

Tehazet ...... Towarzystwo Handlu Zagranicznego i Hurtowego Artykulami Spozywczymi [*Foreign and Wholesale Food Trade Company*] (POL)

TEI............. Institute of Power Engineering in Transportation (of the Siberian Department of the Academy of Sciences, USSR) (RU)

TEI............. Institute of Transportation Economics (RU)

TEI............. Societa' Tea Italia [*Italy*] [*ICAO designator*] (FAAC)

TEI............. Technical Standard Isooctane (RU)

Teiggaer ..... Teiggaerung [*Dough Fermentation*] [*German*] (GCA)

teilw............ Teilweise [*Partly*] [*German*] (GPO)

TEiM .... Trzaska, Evert, i Michalski [*Trzaska, Evert, and Michalski*] [*Publishing house*] (POL)

TEIS .... Turkiye Turizm Endustrisi Isverenleri Sendikasi [*Turkish Tourism Industry Employers Union*] [*Istanbul*] (TU)

TEJ .... Transportes Aeros Ejecutivos SA de CV [*Mexico*] [*ICAO designator*] (FAAC)

TEJA .... Tutmonda Esperantista Jurnalista Asocio [*World Association of Esperanto Journalists - WAEJ*] (EAIO)

TEJICONDOR ... Tejidos el Condor SA [*Colombia*] (COL)

TEJIDUNION ... Compania Colombiana de Tejidos Union SA [*Colombia*] (COL)

TEJO......... Tutmonda Esperantista Junulara Organizo [*World Organization of Young Esperantists*] (EAIO)

TEJOMNES ... Compania de Tejidos de Lana Omnes Ltda. [*Pereira*] (COL)

TEK .... Office of Transportation and Forwarding Operations (RU)

tek .... Tekening [*Drawing*] [*Publishing*] [*Netherlands*]

tek .... Tekintetes [*Honorable*] (HU)

Tek .... Teknik [*Technical, Technician*] (TU)

tek .... Tekuty [*Liquid*] (CZ)

TEK .... Termeloeszkoz Kereskedelmi Vallalat [*Capital Equipment Marketing Enterprise*] (HU)

TEK .... Termineingabekarten [*German*] (ADPT)

TEK .... Terra Kiado [*Terra Publishing House*] (HU)

TEK .... Transportation and Shipping Office (BU)

TEK .... Tuerkiye Ekonomi Kurumu [*Ankara, Turkey*] (SLS)

TEK .... Tunnel Exploration Kit [*Army*] (VNW)

TEK .... Turkiye Elektrik Kurumu Genel Mudurlugu [*Turkish Electric Power Enterprise Directorate General*] (TU)

TEKB........ Turkiye Emlak Kredi Bankasi [*Turkish Real Estate Credit Bank*] (TU)

Tek Der...... Teknisyenler Dernegi [*Technicians' Organization*] (TU)

TEKEKK ... Turk Esnaf ve Kucuk Endustri Kredi Kooperatifi [*Credit Cooperative for Turkish Tradesmen and Small Industry*] [*Turkish Cypriot*] (GC)

teken .... Tekening [*Drawing*] [*Publishing*] [*Netherlands*]

TEK-F........ Technische Entwicklungskommission-Funk [*Technical Development Commission for Radio*] [*German*] (EG)

Tek Gida-Is ... Turkiye Tutun Muskirat Gida ve Yardimci Iscileri Sendikasi [*Turkish Tobacco, Intoxicants, Food and Ancillary Workers Union*] (TU)

tekh .... Engineering, Technical, Technology (RU)

tekh .... Technical, Technological, Engineering (BU)

Tek H.......... Teknik Hizmetleri [*Technical Duties*] (TU)

tekhekonomsovet... Technical and Economic Council (RU)

Tekhizdat... State Publishing House of Technical Literature (RU)

tekhkom..... Technical Committee (RU)

tekhn .... Equipment, Technology, Technician (BU)

tekhn .... Technical, Engineering (RU)

tekhn .... Technicum [*Topography*] (RU)

tekh-ekonom ... Technical and Economic (RU)

tekhnol....... Technological, Engineering (RU)

Tekhnrukov ... Technical Manager   (BU)
Tekhnsbor ... Technical Collection   (RU)
tekhn shk ... Technical School   (RU)
Tekhn tr ..... Technical Requirements   (RU)
Tekhpromfinplan ... Technical Industrial Financial Plan   (BU)
tekhr .... Technical Company   (RU)
tekhred .... Technical Editor   (RU)
tekhsnab .... Technical Supply   (RU)
TEKhSO .... Technical Council   (RU)
Tekhstroyfinplan ... Technical Construction-Finance Plan   (BU)
Tekhteorizdat ... State Publishing House of Technical Theoretical Literature
         (RU)
Tekhupr ..... Technical Administration   (RU)
Tekhzhirprom ... Moscow Oblast Trust of Industrial Fats of the Rosglavmyaso
         of the Ministry of the Meat and Diary Products Industry,
         RSFSR   (RU)
TEK-Is .... Turkish Energy Distribution and Establishment Workers Union
         (TU)
Tek-Iz .... Teknik Izolasyon AS [*Technical Insulation Corp.*] [*A Koc
         subsidiary*]   (TU)
Tek-Met-Is ... Turkiye Metal Mamulleri ve Makine Sanayi Iscileri Sendikasi
         [*Composite Turkish Metal Products and Machine Industry
         Workers' Union*]   (TU)
tekn .... Tekening [*Drawing*] [*Publishing*] [*Netherlands*]
tekn .... Tekniikassa [*Finland*]
tekn .... Tekniikka [*Engineering*]
tekn .... Teknillinen [*Finland*]
tekn .... Tekninen [*Poland*]
Teknik-Is ... Turkiye Cumhuriyeti PTT [*Posta, Telefon, Telgraf*] Teknik
         Servisleri Iscileri Sendikasi [*Republic of Turkey, PTT (Post,
         Telephone, Telegraph) Technical Services Workers' Union*]
         [*TCPTTTSIS*] [*Also,*]   (TU)
TEKNIK-IS ... Yuksek Muhendis, Yuksek Mimar, Muhendis, Mimar, Fen
         Memuru, Teknikler, Teknisyen Birligi [*Senior Engineers,
         Senior Architects, Engineers, Architects, Scientific Workers,
         and Technicians Union*] [*Ankara*]   (TU)
teknlis .... Tekniikan Lisensiaatti [*Finland*]
tekntri .... Tekniikan Tohtori [*Finland*]
TEKOSZ ... Textilkereskedok Orszagos Szovetsege [*National Association of
         Textile Merchants*]   (HU)
TEKSA ...... Tekstil Sanayi ve Ticaret AS [*Textile Industry and Trade Corp.*]
         [*Adana*]   (TU)
TEKSEN ... Turk Elektrik Kurumu Teknik Iscileri Sendikasi [*Turkish Cypriot
         Electric Power Organization Technical Workers' Union*]
         (GC)
TEK-SIF .... Turkiye Tekstil, Orme, ve Giyim Sanayii Iscileri Federasyonu
         [*Federation of Turkish Textile, Weaving, and Wearing
         Apparel Industry Workers Unions*]   (TU)
TEKSIS ..... Turkiye Ticaret, Egitim, Kooperatif, ve Sigorta Iscileri Sendikasi
         [*Turkish Trade, Education, Cooperatives, and Insurance
         Workers Union*]   (TU)
TEKSO ...... Technical and Economic Card Index of Socialist Experience
         (RU)
tekst .... Textile   (RU)
Tekst .... Textile Kombinat, Textile Mill [*Topography*]   (RU)
tekstafb ...... Tekstafbeeldingen [*Illustrations in the Text*] [*Publishing*]
         [*Netherlands*]
tekstbd .... Tekstbind [*Text Volume*] [*Publishing Danish/Norwegian*]
tekstbl .... Tekstblad [*Text Page*] [*Publishing Danish/Norwegian*]
tekstfig .... Tekstfiguren [*Illustrations in the Text*] [*Publishing*]
         [*Netherlands*]
tekstil'mash ... Textile Machinery Plant   (RU)
Tekstil'mashdetal' ... Republic Trust for the Manufacture of Parts and Spare
         Parts of the Ministry of the Textile Industry, RSFSR   (RU)
tekstil'promsoyuz ... Producers' Union of the Textile Industry   (RU)
Tekstil'proyekt ... State Trust for the Planning of Construction in the Textile
         Industry   (RU)
tekt .... Tektiert [*Blotted Out*] [*German*]
tekushtozagl ... Current Title   (BU)
TEL .... Taywood Engineering Ltd. [*Australia*]   (WED)
tel .... Telefon [*Telephone*]   (CZ)
tel .... Telefone [*Telephone*] [*Portuguese*]
Tel .... Telefono [*Telephone*] [*Spanish*]
tel .... Telefoon [*Telephone*] [*Afrikaans*]
tel .... Telegrafista [*Telegrapher*] [*Portuguese*]
tel .... Telegrama [*Telegram*] [*Portuguese*]
Tel .... Telegramm [*Telegram*]   (EG)
Tel .... Telegraph [*German*]
tel .... Telegraphie [*French*]   (TPFD)
tel .... Telegraphique [*Telegraphic*] [*French*]
tel .... Telegraphy   (TPFD)
Tel .... Telephon [*Telephone*]   (EG)
Tel .... Telephone [*French*]
TEL .... Tennis Electric Lines [*Australia*]
TEL .... Tokyo Electron Ltd.   (IAA)
Tel .... Tunnel [*Military map abbreviation*] [*World War I*] [*French*]
         (MTD)

TELA .... Television and Entertainment Licensing Authority [*Hong Kong*]
TELA .... Tovarna Elektricnih Aparatov [*Electric Apparatus Factory*]
         [*Ljubljana*]   (YU)
tel ad .... Telegrafiese Adres [*Telegraphic Address*] [*Afrikaans*]
TELAKHMER ... Societe Cambodgienne de Distribution des Produits
         Petroliers [*Cambodian Petroleum Products Distribution
         Company*]   (CL)
TELARANA ... Telares Arana [*Colombia*]   (COL)
TELC .... Tallinn English Language Club [*Estonia*]   (EAIO)
TELCO ...... Hong Kong Telephone Co.
TELCO ...... Tata Engineering & Locomotive Co. [*India*]
TELCO ...... Trinidad and Tobago Telephone Company   (LA)
TELCOR ... Telecomunicaciones y Correos de Nicaragua [*Nicaraguan
         Telecommunications and Postal Services*]   (LA)
TELDOK ... Telefunken Dokumentationssystem [*German*]   (ADPT)
TELEBRAS ... Telecomunicacoes Brasileiras, SA [*Brazilian
         Telecommunications, Inc.*]   (LA)
TELEC ...... La Technique Electronique [*French*]
TELECOM ... Empresa Nacional de Telecomunicaciones [*National
         Telecommunications Enterprise*] [*Colorado*]   (LA)
TELECOM AUSTRALIA ... Australian Telecommunications Commission
         (PDAA)
TELECOMS ... Telecommunication Authority of Singapore   (PDAA)
telef .... Telefono [*Telephone*] [*Italian*]
Telege .... Telegraphe [*Telegraph*] [*Military map abbreviation World War I*]
         [*French*]   (MTD)
TELEGR ... Telegram [*Afrikaans*]
telegr .... Telegram [*Poland*]
TELEMALI ... Telecommunications Internationales du Mali [*International
         Telecommunications of Mali*]   (AF)
TELEP .... Societe Tele-Publicite Cote-D'Ivoire
telepress ...... Telegraph Information   (BU)
TELESENEGAL ... Societe de Telecommunications Internationales du
         Senegal [*Senegal International Telecommunications
         Company*]   (AF)
TELETRANSCAM ... Societe pour la Construction de Telecommunications
         du Transcamerounais
Teletrest ..... Moscow Television Trust   (RU)
telev .... Television   (BU)
Televerket .. National Swedish Telecommunications Administration
         [*Stockholm*] [*Information service or system*]   (IID)
TELF .... Tamil Eelam Liberation Front [*Sri Lanka*] [*Political party*]
         (PPW)
Telf .... Telefon [*Telephone*]   (TU)
TELI .... Technisch-Literarische Gesellschaft   (SLS)
TELK .... Labor Expert Medical Commission   (BU)
TELMA ..... Tele-Maroc
TelMex ...... Telefonos de Mexico SA [*Associated Press*]
TELO .... Tamil Eelam Liberation Organization [*Sri Lanka*] [*Political
         party*]
Telof .... Telecommunications Office [*Philippines*]
Telpod .... Fabryka Podzespolow Telekomunikacyjnych [*Factory of
         Telecommunication Equipment*] [*Poland*]
Telra .... Televizyon Radyo Sanayii ve Ticaret AS [*Television and Radio
         Industry and Trade Corp.*] [*Istanbul*]   (TU)
TELSA ...... Tejidos Leticia Ltda. [*Colombia*]   (COL)
TEL-SEN .. Kibris Turk Telekomunikasyon Mustahdemler Sendikasi
         [*Turkish Cypriot Telecommunications Employees' Union*]
         (GC)
TELVALL ... Televizios Vallalat [*Television Enterprise*]   (HU)
TELVE ...... Societa Telefoni delle Venezie [*Company controlling telephone
         services in the Three Venetias*] [*Italian*]
TELW .... Telwoord [*Numeral*] [*Afrikaans*]
TEM .... Switching Diesel-Electric Locomotive   (RU)
TEM .... Talasi Electromagnetski [*Electromagnetic Waves*]   (YU)
Tem .... Teminat [*Security, Deposit*]   (TU)
TEM .... Temora [*Australia*] [*Airport symbol*]   (OAG)
TEM .... Tete d'Etapes de Manoeuvre [*Military*] [*French*]   (MTD)
TEM .... Thailand Exhibitions and Management Co. Ltd.   (DS)
TEM .... Tot en Met [*Up To and Including*] [*Afrikaans*]
TEM .... Train des Equipages Militaires [*Royal Army Service Corps*]
         [*French*]
TEM .... Triethylenemelamine   (RU)
TEM .... Trustul Electromontaj [*Electrical Assembly Trust*]   (RO)
TEMAY ..... Tum Emekli, Malul, ve Mustafi Assubaylar Yardimlasma
         Dernegi [*Retired, Disabled, and Resigned
         Noncommissioned Officers Assistance Association*]   (TU)
TEMCO .... Tasmanian Electro Metallurgical Company Proprietary Ltd.
         [*Australia*]
TEMD .... Thermoelectromagnetic Motor   (RU)
TEMEX ..... Tereftalatos Mexicanos SA
TEMG .... Thermoelectromagnetic Generator   (RU)
TEMIIT .... Tomsk Electromechanical Institute of Railroad Transportation
         Engineers   (RU)
TEMIL ...... Tecnica de Maquinas para Industria e Lavoura SA [*Brazil*]
         (DSCA)
TEMO .... Tanganyika Elected Members Organization

TEMOSA ... Tejar Moderno Ltda. [*Bucaramanga*]   (COL)
Temp .... Temperatur [*Temperature*] [*German*]
temp .... Temperatura [*Temperature*] [*Poland*]
temp .... Temperature   (RU)
temp .... Temperatuur [*Temperature*] [*Afrikaans*]
Temp .... Temple [*Temple*] [*Military map abbreviation World War I*] [*French*]   (MTD)
temp abs..... Absolute Temperature   (RU)
TEMPAS... Tekel Mamulleri Pazarlama Subesi [*Monopolies Products' Marketing Branch*] [*A subsidiary of ETI in the TFSC Turkish Cypriot*]   (TU)
temp isp...... Evaporation Temperature   (RU)
temp kip ..... Boiling Point   (RU)
temp kond .. Dew Point   (RU)
temp krit .... Critical Temperature   (RU)
tem pl .... Plan of Subjects   (RU)
temp otv...... Solidification Temperature   (RU)
Tempp.......... Temperaturen [*Temperatures*] [*German*]
temp pl .... Melting Point   (RU)
temp razl .... Decomposition Temperature   (RU)
temprazmyagch ... Softening Temperature, Softening Point   (RU)
temp stekl .. Vitrification Temperature   (RU)
TEMPUS .. Trans-European Mobility Scheme for Unversity Students [*EC*]   (ECED)
tempvospl ... Ignition Temperature   (RU)
temp vozg ... Sublimation Temperature   (RU)
temp vsp..... Flash Point   (RU)
temp zam.... Freezing Point   (RU)
temp zast .... Solidification Point   (RU)
TEMSA ..... Telephone Manufacturers of South Africa
TEMSA ..... Termo Mekanik Sanayi ve Ticaret AS [*Thermo-Mechanical Industry and Trade Corp.*] [*Adana*]   (TU)
TEMSA ..... Tetraetilo de Mexico SA
TEMSAN ... Turkiye Elektromekanik Sanayi AS [*Turkish Electromechanical Industry Corp.*]   (TU)
TEMSE-IS ... Turkiye Muzik, Sahne, ve Edebi Guzel Sanatlari Sendikasi [*Turkish Music, Stage, and Literary Fine Arts Union*] [*Istanbul*]   (TU)
Ten .... Tenente [*Lieutenant*] [*Italian*]
ten .... Tenente [*Lieutenant*] [*Portuguese*]
Ten .... Tenuto [*Sustained*] [*Music*]
TEN .... Thermoelectric Heater   (RU)
TEN .... Trans-European Network [*European Union*]   (ECON)
TEN .... Tubular Electric Heater   (RU)
TENCATE ... Koninklijke Textielfabrieken Nijverdal-Ten Cate NV [*Netherlands*]
TENENGE ... Tecnica Nacional de Engenharia SA
TENG .... Tengeri [*Naval, Marine*]   (HU)
TenkoviICU ... Tenkovi sa Infracrvenim Uredajem [*Tanks with Infrared Equipment*]   (YU)
tenn .... Tennis [*Tennis*] [*Finland*]
TENPT ...... Tameion Esodon Nomikon Prosopon kai Triton [*Legal Persons and Third Parties Revenue Fund*]   (GC)
tente .... Teniente [*Lieutenant*] [*Spanish*]
TEO .... Tameion Ethnikis Odopoiias [*National Road Construction Fund*] [*Greek*]   (GC)
TEO .... Technical and Economic Substantiation   (RU)
TEO .... Terapo [*Papua New Guinea*] [*Airport symbol*]   (OAG)
TEO .... Theater Department of the Narkompros   (RU)
TEO .... Theater Department of the Political Education Administration   (RU)
TEO .... Third World Education Outreach   (EA)
teol .... Teologia [*Theology*] [*Finland*]
Teol .... Teologia [*Theology*] [*Portuguese*]
TEOL........ Teologie [*Theology*] [*Afrikaans*]
teolkand ..... Teologian Kandidaatti [*Finland*]
teollis......... Teologian Lisensiaatti [*Finland*]
teor .... Teorema [*Theorem*] [*Portuguese*]
teor .... Theoretical   (RU)
TEP........... All-Union State Institute for the Planning of Electrical Equipment for Heat Engineering Installations   (RU)
TEP........... Rear Echelon of the Trains   (RU)
TEP........... Rear Evacuation Station   (RU)
TEP........... Technical and Economic Indices   (RU)
TEP........... Tepecintle [*Race of maize*] [*Mexico*]
TEP........... Teptep [*Papua New Guinea*] [*Airport symbol*]   (OAG)
TEP........... Thermoelectric Pyrometer   (RU)
TEP.......... Thermoelectronic Converter   (RU)
TEP........... Tonnes d'Equivalent Petrole [*Equal to ———— Tons of Oil*]   (AF)
TEP........... Turkiye Emekci Partisi [*Workers' Party of Turkey*] [*Political party*]   (PPW)
TEP........... Tvornica Elektrotehnickih Proizvoda [*Electrical Engineering Works*] [*Zagreb*]   (YU)
TEPAR ...... Tecnica Paulista de Reflorestamento Ltd. [*Brazil*]   (DSCA)
TEPC........ Tertiary Education Preparatory Course [*Australia*]

TEPCE ...... Talleres de Evaluacion, Programacion, y Capacitacion Educativa [*Educational Evaluation, Programing, and Training Workshops*] [*Nicaragua*]   (LA)
TEPCO...... Tokyo Electric Power Co. [*Japan*]
TEPCORN ... Tobacco Export Promotion Council of Rhodesia and Nyasaland
TEPERPU ... Team Pemeriksaan Pusat [*Central Investigation Team*]   (IN)
TEPET ...... Texas Petroleum Company SA [*Guamo-Tolima*]   (COL)
Teploelektroproyekt ... All-Union State Institute for the Planning of Electrical Equipment for Heat Engineering Structures
Teploproyekt ... All-Union Scientific Research and Planning Institute for Heat Engineering Structures   (RU)
Teploset' .... Moscow City Trust of Centralized Heat Supply Networks of the Mosenergo
TEPREC.... Technique et Precision
TEPS .... Tiskova, Edicni, a Propagacni Sluzba Mistniho Hospodarstvi [*Press, Editorial, and Propaganda Service for Local Economy*]   (CZ)
TEPSA ...... Terminals Portuarias SA [*Spain*]
TEPSA ...... Trans European Policy Studies Association   (EA)
TER .... Tank Evacuation Company   (BU)
TER .... Technical and Economic Calculation   (RU)
TER .... Technische Entwicklung-Radar [*Technical Development (Laboratory) for Radar*] [*German*]   (EG)
TER .... Terceira [*Azores*] [*Airport symbol*]   (OAG)
Ter............. Terim [*Term*] [*As a technical term*]   (TU)
TER .... Tertiary Entrance Rank [*Australia*]
TER .... Tete d'Etapes de Route [*French*]   (MTD)
ter .... Waste Tip [*Topography*]   (RU)
terarmiya ... Territorial Army   (RU)
terc .... Tercume Eden [*Translated By*]   (TU)
TERC........ Tropical Ecosystems Research Centre [*Australia*]   (IRC)
TEREBINTH ... Terebinthinae Oleum [*Oil of Turpentine*] [*Pharmacology*]   (ROG)
TEREVSAT ... Theater of Revolutionary Satire   (RU)
TERI......... Tata Energy Research Institute [*New Delhi, India*]   (ECON)
TERIMPEX ... TERIMPEX Allat- es Termenyforgalmi Kulkereskedelmi Vallalat [*TERIMPEX Foreign Trade Enterprise for Livestock and Crops*]   (HU)
terk............ Terkep [*Chart, Map*] [*Hungary*]
TERLS....... Thumba Equatorial Rocket Launching Station [*INCOSPART*] [*ISRO India*]   (PDAA)
term........... Termeszet [*or Termeszeti*] [*Nature or Natural*]   (HU)
term........... Terminacao [*Conclusion*] [*Portuguese*]
term........... Terminer [*Finish*] [*Knitting*] [*French*]
TerMb........ Teretni Motorni Brod [*Motor Freighter*]   (YU)
TERMERT ... Termenyertekesito es Raktarozasi Vallalat [*Store and Storage Enterprise for Farm Products*]   (HU)
TERMIA ... Association Internationale de Terminologie [*International Association of Terminology*] [*Quebec, PQ*]   (EAIO)
termissled ... Thermal Research   (RU)
TERMNET ... International Network for Terminology [*INFOTERM*] [*Vienna, Austria*]
termoeds..... Thermoelectromotive Force   (RU)
Termoproyekt ... State Planning Institute for Heat Engineering   (RU)
tern........... Ternaer [*Ternary*] [*German*]   (GCA)
TERN .... Transnational European Rural Network [*Belgium*]   (EAIO)
TEROTO... Tercuman Motorlu Araclar Sanayi ve Ticaret AS [*The Tercuman Motor Vehicles Industry and Trade Corp.*]   (TU)
TerPb........ Teretni Parabrod [*Steam Freighter*]   (YU)
terr .... Terrasse [*Terrace*] [*Norway*]   (CED)
terr .... Territory   (RU)
TERRHICO ... Territorial Rhine Coordination [*NATO*]   (NATG)
Terrorilla ... Terrorism and Guerrilla Warfare [*Israel*]
terr-proizvod upr ... Territorial Production Administration   (RU)
Terr SMand ... Territoires Sous Mandat   (FLAF)
TERSI....... Termineurs Signaleurs [*French*]   (ADPT)
TERSS....... Tasmanian Earth Resources Satellite Station [*Australia*]
tert............ Tertiaer [*Tertiary*] [*German*]
TervgazdK ... Tervgazdasagi Kiado [*Publishing House on Planned Economy*]   (HU)
TERZ........ Transformer Electric Repair Plant   (RU)
TeS........... Hochwertiger Schwarzer Temperguss [*High-Quality All-Black Malleable Cast Iron*] [*German*]   (GCA)
TES........... Spot Electric Welding   (RU)
TES........... Tableaux Entrees-Sorties [*Database*] [*EC*]   (ECED)
TES........... Tagma Ekmetallevseos Sidirodromon [*Railroad Operating Battalion*] [*Greek*]   (GC)
TES........... Tameion Ethnikou Stolou [*National Fleet Fund*] [*Greek*]   (GC)
TES........... Tanzania Elimu Supplies
TES........... Teatrul Evreiesc da Stat [*Jewish State Theater*]   (RO)
TES........... Technische Entwicklung-Schiffsfunk [*Technical Development (Laboratory) for Marine Radio*]   (EG)
TES........... Teilnehmereinrichtungsschaltung [*German*]   (ADPT)
TeS........... Tekhnikon Soma [*Technical Corps*] [*Army*]   (GC)
tes............. Tesoureiro [*Treasurer*] [*Portuguese*]
tes............. Tesourier [*Treasurer*] [*Afrikaans*]

TES........... Tetraethyllead (RU)

TES........... Thermal Electric Power Plant (RU)

TES........... Thermoelectric Supply (BU)

TES........... Tractor Electric Power Plant (RU)

TES........... Transportes Aereos de El Salvador SA de CV [*ICAO designator*] (FAAC)

TESA........ Personal Tehnic, Economic, de Alta Specialitate, si Administrativ [*Technical, Economic, Specialized, and Administrative Personnel*] (RO)

TESA........ Personal Tehnic, Stiintific, si Administrativ [*Technical, Scientific, and Administrative Personnel*] (RO)

TESAD...... Personal Tehnic, Economic, de Alta Specialitate, Administrativ, de Servire si de Paza [*Technical, Economic, Highly Specialized, Administrative, Service, and Guard Personnel*] (RO)

TESCA...... TAFE [*Technical and Further Education*] Educational Services Co-Ordinators' Association [*Australia*]

TESCO...... Muszaki Tudomanyos Egyutmukodesi Iroda [*Office of Technical-Scientific Cooperation*] (HU)

TESEM..... Television Esmeraldena Compania de Economia Mixta [*Ecuador*] (EY)

TESG........ Thermal Electrostatic Generator (RU)

TES-IS...... Turkiye Enerji, Su, Gas, YSE, ve DSI Isci Sendikalari Federasyonu [*Federation of Turkish Energy, Water, and Gas Workers Unions*] (TU)

TESK........ Topiki Epitropi Syndesmos Ellinikon Gymnastikon kai Athlitikon Somateion Kyprou [*Association of Greek Gymnastic and Athletic Clubs Local Committee in Cyprus*] (GC)

tesn............ Gorge [*Topography*] (RU)

TESO........ Tanzania Environmental Society (EAIO)

TESS .... Technical, Engineering, and Scientific Services [*Singapore*]

TESSA....... Techno-Economic Society of South Africa (AA)

test............ Testemunha [*Testator; Witness*] [*Portuguese*]

testa.......... Testamentaria [*Estate Of*] [*Spanish*]

TESTAS.... Turkiye Elektronik Sanayi ve Ticaret Anonim Sirketi [*Turkish Electronic Industry and Trade Corporation*] (TU)

testco........ Terra Sancta Tourist Co. Ltd. [*Jordan*]

testmto...... Testamento [*Spanish*]

testo.......... Testamento [*Testament*] [*Portuguese*]

testo.......... Testigo [*Witness*] [*Spanish*]

TeSTOS..... Terenowe Stacje Technicznej Obslugi Samochodow [*Local Auto Service Stations*] (POL)

TESTROJ ... Teplicka Strojirna [*Teplice Engineering Works*] (CZ)

TESUD...... Turkiye Emekli Subaylar Dernegi [*Turkish Retired Officers Assocation*] (EAIO)

TESZ........ Termeszettudomanyi Egyesuletek Szovetsege [*Federation of Natural Sciences Associations*] (HU)

TESZI....... Termeloszovetkezetek Ertekesitest Szervezo Iroda [*Office for Organization of TSZ Sales*] (HU)

tet............. Tete [*Top Edge*] [*Publishing*] [*French*]

TET.......... Tete [*Mozambique*] [*Airport symbol*] (OAG)

TET.......... Topiki Epitropi Tourismou [*Local Tourism Committee*] [*Greek*] (GC)

TETC........ Teroson Europe Technical Centre [*Research center*] [*Germany*]

TETI......... Telefoni del Tirreno [*Company controlling telephone services along the Tyrrhenian Coast*] [*Italian*]

TETIA ...... Television and Electronic Technicians Institute of Australia (ADA)

TETOC..... Technical Education and Training Organisation for Overseas Countries

tetr............ Notebook (BU)

Tetra .... Tetrachlorkohlenstoff [*Carbon Tetrachloride*] [*German*] (GCA)

tetraedr...... Tetrahedral (RU)

tetrag s ...... Tetragonal Syngony (RU)

TETs......... Heat and Electric Power Plant (RU)

TETs......... Thermoelectric Power Plant (BU)

TETs-PAVETs ... Thermoelectric Power Plant - Pump Storage Hydroelectric Power Plant (BU)

Tetsukoro... Tetsudo Kosaikai Rodokumiai [*Japanese Railway Welfare Association Labor Union*]

TEU .... Fuel and Power Engineering Administration (RU)

TEU .... Te Anau [*New Zealand*] [*Airport symbol*] (OAG)

TEU .... Teatro Universitario de Popayan [*Cauca*] (COL)

TEU .... Technology and Energy Unit [*Caribbean Development Bank*] [*Barbados*]

TEU .... Ter Elfder Ure [*Benelux*] (BAS)

TEU .... Thermal Electric Installation (RU)

TEU .... Tourist and Excursion Administration (RU)

TEUR .... Tariffs-Europe (PDAA)

Tev .... Triebwageneilzug [*Express Rail Motor Train*] [*German*] (EG)

TEV .... Turk Egitim Vakfi [*Turkish Educational Fund*] (TU)

TEVA........ Tutmonda Esperantista Vegetara Asocio [*World Esperantist Vegetarian Association - WEVA*] (EAIO)

TEVD .... Tatranska Elektricka Vicinalni Draha [*Tatra Local Electric Railroads*] (CZ)

TEVE........ Tameion (Asfaliseos) Epangelmation kai Viotekhnon Ellados [*Greek Craftsmen's and Tradesmen's (Insurance) Fund*] (GC)

TEVI......... Tervezo Iroda [*Planning Office*] (HU)

TevMuzek ... Tevkif Muzekkeresi [*Arrest Warrant*] (TU)

TEVUH ..... Technicke-Ekonomicky Vyzkumny Ustav Hutniho Prumyslu [*Technical Economic Research Institute for Smelting*] (CZ)

TEVZ........ Tatranska Elektricka Vicinalna Zeleznica [*Tatra Local Electric Railroad*] (CZ)

TEVZ........ Tbilisi Electric Locomotive Plant (RU)

TeW .... Hochwertiger Weisser Temperguss [*High-Quality White-Heart Malleable Cast Iron*] [*German*] (GCA)

TEWA .... Technische Eisenwaren und Werkzeuge (VVB) [*Industrial Hardware and Tools (VVB)*] (EG)

TEX .... Catex Compagnie [*France*] [*ICAO designator*] (FAAC)

t ex........... Till Exempel [*For Instance*] [*Sweden*] (GPO)

TEXAF ...... Societe des Textiles d'Afrique

TEXCO...... National Textile Corporation of Tanzania

TEXCO...... Societe Textile de Confection

TEXCO...... Tariff Export Concession [*Australia*]

TEXFA ...... Textilipari Fakellektermelo Vallalat [*Manufacturing Enterprise of Wooden Tools for the Textile Industry*] (HU)

TEXIMEI ... Textilipari Minosegellenorzo Intezet [*Quality Control Institute on Industrial Textiles*] (HU)

TEXKAM ... Institute of Mechanical Engineering [*Bulgaria*] (IRC)

Texkut........ Textilipari Kutato Intezet [*Research Institute of the Textile Industry*] (HU)

TEXMAN ... Manufacturas Textiles SA [*Manizales*] (COL)

TEXMERALDA ... Textiles la Esmeralda SA [*Colombia*] (COL)

TEXNAL... Textiles Nacionales [*Colombia*] (COL)

TEXPROCIL ... [*The*] Cotton Textiles Export Promotion Council of India (ECON)

Textabb...... Textabbildung [*Illustration(s) in the Text*] [*German*]

TEXTANG ... Empresa Texteis de Angola [*Textile manufacturing enterprise*] [*Luanda, Angola*]

Textbeschad ... Textbeschaedigungen [*Damage Done to Text*] [*German*]

TEXTEL.... Trinidad and Tobago External Telecommunications Co. Ltd. (IMH)

Textholzschn ... Textholzschnitt [*Woodcut(s) in the Text*] [*German*]

TEXTICAM ... Societe Textile du Cameroun

Textill .... Textillustration [*Illustration in the Text*] [*German*]

TEXTIMA ... Textil- und Bekleidungsindustrie Maschinenbau [*Textile and Clothing Industry Machine Building*] (EG)

textkom...... Textkommentar [*Annotations*] [*Publishing*] [*Sweden*]

Textzeichn ... Textzeichnung [*Drawing(s) in the Text*] [*German*]

TEY .... Thingeyri [*Iceland*] [*Airport symbol*] (OAG)

TEYPA ...... Tameion Efimeridopolon kai Ypallilon Praktoreion Athinon [*Insurance Fund of Newspaper Dealers and Employees of Athens Newspaper Distribution Agencies*] (GC)

tez............ Tezamen [*Together*] [*Netherlands*]

TEZ.......... Tezpur [*India*] [*Airport symbol*] (OAG)

tez............. Thesis (RU)

TEZ.......... Tvornica Elektricnih Zarulja [*Factory of Incandescent Lamps*] [*Zagreb*] (YU)

Tez Buro-Is ... Turkiye Ticaret, Banka, Sigorta, Kooperatif, Egitim, Tezgahtarlar ve Buro Iscileri Sendikasi [*Turkish Office and Clerical Employees Union*] (TU)

TEZhE....... State Trust of Fine Perfumery of the Fats and Bone-Processing Industry (RU)

Tez-Koop-Is ... Turkiye, Ticaret, Kooperatif, Egitim, Buro, ve Guzel Sanatlar Iscileri Sendikasi [*Commercial and clerical employees union*] [*Turkey*] (MENA)

TEZS .... Thermal Electric Charging Station (RU)

TEZSAN ... Takim Tezgahlari Sanayi ve Ticaret AS [*Industrial Spare Parts Industry and Trade Corp.*] (TU)

TF .... Fixation of the Point of Burst (RU)

TF .... French Southern and Antarctic Lands [*ANSI two-letter standard code*] (CNC)

TF .... Pacific Fleet (RU)

TF .... Tamimi & Fouad [*Saudi Arabia*] [*Commercial firm*]

TF .... Taschenformat [*Pocket Size*] [*German*]

tf.............. Telegraph (RU)

TF .... Telephotometer (RU)

TF .... Testnevelesi Foiskola [*College of Physical Education*] (HU)

TF .... Thomas-Fermi [*Potential*] (RU)

TF .... Thymolphthalein (RU)

TF .... Tool Foundation [*See also ST*] [*Amsterdam, Netherlands*] (EAIO)

TF .... Traegerfrequenz (System) [*Carrier Frequency (System)*] (WEN)

TF .... Transportes Aereos Regionais (TAR) SA [*Brazil*] [*ICAO designator*] (ICDA)

tf.............. Travaux Forces [*Hard Labor*] [*French*]

TF .... Triphosphate (RU)

TF .... Warm Front [*Meteorology*] (RU)

TF1 .... Channel One [*French television station*]

TF₁ .... Television Francaise 1

TFA.......... French Southern and Antarctic Lands [*ANSI three-letter standard code*]   (CNC)

TFA.......... Take Five Australia [*An association*]

TFA.......... Tanganyika Farmers Association Ltd.

TFA.......... Tasmanian Floricultural Association [*Australia*]

TFA.......... Triathlon Federation of Australia

TFAA........ Trout Farmers' Association of Australia

TFAI........ Territoire Francais des Afars et Issas [*French Territory of Afars and Issas*] [*Djibouti Use FTAI*]   (AF)

TFAI.......... Trade Fair Authority of India

TFAN....... Turkmen Branch of the Academy of Sciences, USSR   (RU)

TFAP........ Tropical Forestry Action Plan [*World Bank, UN, and other groups*]

TFAW....... Tasmania Fellowship of Australia Writers [*Australia*]

TFB.......... Rear Base of a Front   (RU)

TFB.......... Tehnicki Fakultet, Beograd [*Faculty of Technology, Belgrade*] (YU)

TFB.......... Thai Farmers' Bank

TFC.......... Tanzania Fertilizer Company Ltd.

TFC.......... Tanzania Film Company

TFC.......... Theatres and Films Commission [*Australia*]

TFC.......... US-Japan Trade Facilitation Committee   (IMH)

TFCG........ Tropical Forestry Contact Group [*Australia*]

TFCHS...... Tasmanian Federation of Cooperative Housing Societies [*Australia*]

TFCM........ Thailand Fellowship of Cement Manufacturers   (EAIO)

TFCNN....... Task Force Commander, North Norway [*NATO*]   (NATG)

TFD......... Thomas-Fermi-Dirac   (RU)

TFDL......... Stichting Technische en Fysische Dienst voor de Landbouw [*Technical and Physical Engineering Research Service*] [*Netherlands*]   (ARC)

TFDP........ Theory of Functions of a Real Variable   (RU)

TFDS........ Troms Fylkes Dampskipsselskap [*Shipping line*] [*Norway*]

TFEDRA ... Task Force for European Digital Road-mapping Association

TFF........... Tefe [*Brazil*] [*Airport symbol*]   (OAG)

TFF........... Transnational Foundation for Peace and Future Research [*Sweden*]

TFF........... Triphenyl Phosphate   (RU)

TFFA .... Desirade/Grande-Anse, Guadeloupe [*French Antilles*] [*ICAO location identifier*]   (ICLI)

TFFB .... Basse-Terre/Baillif [*French Antilles*] [*ICAO location identifier*]   (ICLI)

TFFC .... Saint-Francois [*French Antilles*] [*ICAO location identifier*]   (ICLI)

TFFD .... Fort-De-France, Martinique [*French Antilles*] [*ICAO location identifier*]   (ICLI)

TFFF........ Fort-De-France/Le Lamentin, Martinique [*French Antilles*] [*ICAO location identifier*]   (ICLI)

TFFG .... Saint-Martin/Grand'Case, Guadeloupe [*French Antilles*] [*ICAO location identifier*]   (ICLI)

TFFIS .... Tasmanian Forests and Forest Industry Strategy [*Australia*]

TFFJ .... Saint-Barthelemy [*French Antilles*] [*ICAO location identifier*]   (ICLI)

TFFM .... Grand-Bourg/Marie-Galante [*French Antilles*] [*ICAO location identifier*]   (ICLI)

TFFR .... Pointe-A-Pitre/Le Raizet, Guadeloupe [*French Antilles*] [*ICAO location identifier*]   (ICLI)

TFFS......... Les Saintes/Terre-De-Haut [*French Antilles*] [*ICAO location identifier*]   (ICLI)

Tfg............ Tiefgang [*Draft*] [*Of vessels*] [*German*]

TFGA........ Tasmanian Farmers' and Graziers' Association [*Australia*]

TFGA......... Tasmanian Field and Game Association [*Australia*]

TFH .... Thai Flying Helicopter Service Co. Ltd. [*Thailand*] [*ICAO designator*]   (FAAC)

TFH .... Traegerfrequenz-Nachrichtenanlage (auf Hochspannungsnetz) [*Carrier-Frequency Communications Facility (via Power Lines)*] [*Equipment*] [*German*]   (EG)

TFI............. Deutsches Teppich-Forschungsinstitut [*German Carpet Research Institute - GCRI*]   (EAIO)

TFI............. Tannlaeknafelag Islands [*Reykjavik, Iceland*]   (SLS)

TFI............. Tufi [*Papua New Guinea*] [*Airport symbol*]   (OAG)

TFIC .... Tasmanian Fishing Industry Council [*Australia*]

TFITC....... Tasmanian Fishing Industry Training Council [*Australia*]

TFITC....... Tasmanian Food Industry Training Council [*Australia*]

TFITC....... Tasmanian Forest Industries Training Council [*Australia*]

TFITC....... Tasmanian Furniture Industry Training Council [*Australia*]

TFJ-Senegal ... Tableau Fiscal et Juridique Senegal

TFK........... Tarsadalmi Felhasznalasnak Utat Nyito Kutatas [*Research Seeking the Application or Utility by Society of the Results of Basic Research*]   (HU)

tfk.............. Telephone Crew   (BU)

TFK........... Transport Forsknings Kommissionen [*Swedish Transport Research Commission*] [*Stockholm*] [*Research center*]   (ERC)

TFKI .... Magyar Testnevelesi Foiskola Kutato Intezet [*Research Institute of the Hungarian College of Physical Education*]   (HU)

TFKP .... Theory of Functions of a Complex Variable   (RU)

Tfl .... Tafel [*Table*] [*German*]

TFL............ Tanganyika Federation of Labour

TFL............ Tasmanian Football League [*Australia*]

TFLWA ..... Torchbearers for Legacy in Western Australia

TFM .... Telefomin [*Papua New Guinea*] [*Airport symbol*]   (OAG)

TFM .... Testators Family Maintenance [*Australia*]

TFM .... Triphenylmethyl   (RU)

TFMBA ..... Tasmanian Fine Merino Breeders' Association [*Australia*]

TFMS .... Traffic Facilities Management System [*Australia*]

TFN .... Tax File Number [*Australia*]

TFNC......... Tanzania Food and Nutrition Centre

TFNC......... Tasmanian Field Naturalists' Club [*Australia*]

TFP............ Sociedad Argentina de Defensa de la Tradicion, Familia, y Propiedad [*Argentine Society for the Defense of Tradition, Family, and Property*]   (LA)

TFP............ Sociedad Venezolana de Defensa de la Tradicion, Familia, y Propiedad [*Venezuelan Society for the Defense of Tradition, Family, and Property*]   (LA)

TFP............ Societe Francaise pour la Defense de la Tradition, de la Famille et de la Propriete [*France*]   (EAIO)

TFP............ Tradicao, Familia, e Propriedade [*Tradition, Family, and Property*] [*Brazil*]   (LA)

TFP............ Tradicion, Familia, y Propiedad [*Tradition, Family, and Property*] [*Colorado*]   (LA)

TFP............ Travaux Forces a Perpetuite   (FLAF)

TFPA .... Tall Fashion Promotions of Australia

TFPA .... Thai Food Processors' Association   (EAIO)

TFR........... Heavy Manual Work   (BU)

TFR........... Telefunken Fernseh und Rundfunk [*Home Electronics Subsidiary*]

TFR........... Trans European Airways SA [*France*] [*ICAO designator*]   (FAAC)

TFRI .... Taiwan Fisheries Research Institute   (ASF)

TFS .... Tasmanian Ferry Services [*Australia*]

TFS .... Tasmanian Fire Service [*Australia*]

TFS .... Technische Foerdergemeinschaft Holzsilo   (SLS)

TFS .... Tehnicki Fakultet, Sarajevo [*Faculty of Technology, Sarajevo*] (YU)

TFS .... Telephone Exchange   (RU)

TFS .... Tenerife-Reina Sofia [*Canary Islands*] [*Airport symbol*]   (OAG)

TFS .... Theological Faculty, Sydney [*Australia*]

TFS .... Tribunal Federal Suisse   (FLAF)

TFSC .... Turkish Federated State of Cyprus [*See also KTFD*]   (TU)

TFSM .... Union of Malagasy Socialist Youth   (AF)

TFSN .... Taxe Forfaitaire de Solidarite Nationale

TFT........... Travaux Forces a Temps   (FLAF)

TFTA .... Tokyo Foreign Trade Association [*Japan*]   (EAIO)

TFTDWU ... Taiwan Federation of Textile and Dyeing Industry Workers' Unions   (FEA)

TFV............ Teachers' Federation of Victoria [*Australia*]

TFW........... Tokyo Financial Wire [*COMLINE International Corp.*] [*Japan*] [*Information service or system*]   (CRD)

TFYAA ...... Task Force on Youth Allowance Administration [*Australia*]

TFZ............ Tylova Frontava Zakladna [*Frontline Supply Base*]   (CZ)

TG .... Diesel Locomotive with a Hydraulic Transmission   (RU)

TG .... Gas Thyratron   (RU)

tg .... Of the Current Year, In the Current Year   (RU)

TG .... Solid Fuel   (RU)

TG .... Table Generale   (FLAF)

TG .... Tachometer Generator   (RU)

Tg.............. Tag [*Day*] [*German*]

Tg.............. Tandjong [*or Tandjung or Tanjong*] [*Cape Malay*]   (NAU)

tg .... Tangente [*Tangent*] [*German*]

TG .... Tank Group   (RU)

TG .... Tasmanian Greens [*Australia*] [*Political party*]

TG .... Technische Grundsaetze [*Technical Principles*] [*German*]   (EG)

TG .... Technisch Gemeenteblad [*Benelux*]   (BAS)

tg .... Tekuce Godine [*Current Year*]   (YU)

TG .... Tenkovsko Gadanje [*Tank Firing*]   (YU)

TG .... Testamentsgesetz [*Law on Wills*] [*German*]   (ILCA)

TG .... Thai Granite Co. Ltd.

TG .... Therapeutic Hospital   (RU)

tg .... This Year   (BU)

TG .... Tochtergesellschaft [*Daughter Company*] [*German*]   (ADPT)

TG .... Togo [*ANSI two-letter standard code*]   (CNC)

T/G .... Ton/Gun [*Tons Per Day*] [*Capacity*]   (TU)

t/g.............. Tons/Year   (BU)

TG .... Track Geometry [*In TG-01, an Austrian built subway inspection car*]

TG .... Training Guarantee [*Australia*]

TG .... Transportgemeinschaft [*Transportation Group*]   (EG)

Tg.............. Trapeang [*Often part of a place name*] [*Cambodia*]   (CL)

TG .... Trotyl and Hexogen   (RU)

TGA .... [*The*] Glass & Aluminium Suppliers Ltd. [*Papua New Guinea*]

TGA .... State Archives of the City of Tallin and the Khar'yuskiy Rayon (RU)

TGA .... Tameion Georgikon Asfaliseon [*Farm Insurance Fund*] [*Greek*] (GC)

TGA .... Technische Gebaeudeausruestung [*Technical Building Equipment*] [*German*] (EG)

TGA .... Telegestion des Abonnes [*French*] (ADPT)

TGA .... Therapeutic Goods Administration [*Australia*]

TGA .... Tissages Goujat Algerie

TGA .... Tmima Georgikon Asfaliseon [*Farm Insurance Unit*] [*Greek*] (GC)

TGA .... Togo Airlines [*ICAO designator*] (FAAC)

TGA .... Touristische Gemeinschaft der Alpenlander [*Alpine Tourist Commission - ATC*] [*Zurich, Switzerland*] (EAIO)

TGA .... Training Guarantee Act [*Australia*]

TGA .... Tropical Growers' Association (EAIO)

TGA .... Turf Growers Association [*Australia*]

tgabr .... Heavy Howitzer Artillery Brigade (BU)

TGAC .... Table Grape Advisory Committee [*Western Australia*]

TGAC .... Therapeutic Goods Advertising Code [*Australia*]

TGAS........ Turkiye Gemi Adamlari Iscileri Sendikasi [*Turkish Seamen's Union*] (TU)

TGASA ...... Tour Guides Association of South Africa

TGB .... Tres Grande Bibliotheque [*Very Big Library*] [*French*]

Tgb-Nr .... Tagebuchnummer [*Day-Book Number*] [*German*] [*Business term*]

TGC .... Tasmanian Gaming Commission [*Australia*]

TGC .... Tasmanian Golf Council [*Australia*]

TGC .... Therapeutic Goods Committee [*Australia*]

TGC .... Tobacco Growers' Council [*Australia*]

TGCA .... Tobacco Growers' Council of Australia

TGD.......... Titograd [*Former Yugoslavia*] [*Airport symbol*] (OAG)

TGE .... Tmima Georgikon Efarmogon [*Applied Agriculture Unit*] [*Greek*] (GC)

TGE .... Trabajos Aereos SA [*Spain*] [*ICAO designator*] (FAAC)

TGEB........ Tasmanian Grain Elevators Board [*Australia*]

TGF .... Training Guarantee Fund [*Australia*]

TGF .... Tropas Guardafronteras [*Border Guard Troops*] [*Cuba*] (LA)

TGFA .... Tasmanian Game Fishing Association [*Australia*]

TGFA........ Tropas de Guarda Fronteiras de Angola

TGFM........ Tasmanian Guild of Furniture Manufacturers [*Australia*]

TGFO .... Tashkent Geophysical Observatory (RU)

TGG .... Kuala Trengganu [*Malaysia*] [*Airport symbol*] (OAG)

TGGRU ..... Transactions of the Main Administration of Geological Exploration (RU)

TGH.......... Tongoa [*Vanuatu*] [*Airport symbol*] (OAG)

TGH.......... Transportgemeinschaft des Handels [*Trade Transportation Group*] (EG)

TGHD....... Turkiye Genclik Hostelleri Dernegi [*Turkish Youth Hostels Organization*] (TU)

TGI .... Tingo Maria [*Peru*] [*Airport symbol*] (OAG)

TGI .... Tribunal de Grande Instance (FLAF)

TGII.......... Transactions of the Georgian Industrial Institute Imeni S. M. Kirov (RU)

TGIM .... Transactions of the State Historical Museum (RU)

TGJ........... Tiga [*Loyalty Islands*] [*Airport symbol*] (OAG)

TGK .... Hot-Cathode Thyratron (RU)

TGK .... Tehergepkocsi [*Truck*] (HU)

TGK .... Transactions of the Geological Committee (RU)

TGK .... Turk Genel Kurmayi [*Turkish General Staff*] (TU)

TGKD .... Tameion Georgias, Ktinotrofias kai Dason [*Farm, Animal Husbandry, and Forests Fund*] [*Greek*] (GC)

tgl .... Taeglich [*Daily*] [*German*] (GCA)

TGL .... Tagula [*Papua New Guinea*] [*Airport symbol*] (OAG)

TGL .... Technische Gutevorschriften und Lieferbedingungen [*Quality standards and supply terms*] (IMH)

TGL .... Trans-Atlantic Airlines Ltd. [*Gambia*] [*ICAO designator*] (FAAC)

TGLP........ Tribal Grazing Land Policy [*Botswana*]

TGM......... Shunting Diesel Locomotive with a Hydraulic [*or Hydromechanical*] Transmission (RU)

TGM......... Talab, Gasim, Mahmoud [*Sudan*]

TGM......... Tallinn Green Movement [*Estonia*] (EAIO)

TGM......... Technika i Gospodarka Morska [*Marine Engineering and Economics*] [*A periodical*] (POL)

TGM......... Technologisches Gewerbemuseum [*Technological Trade Museum*] [*GFKT*] [*Austria*] (IRC)

Tgm.......... Tegmen [*Lieutenant*] (TU)

TGM......... Tirgu Mures [*Romania*] [*Airport symbol*] (OAG)

TGM......... Transactions of the Geological Museum of the Academy of Sciences, USSR (RU)

TGM......... Tunis-La Goulette-La Marsa

TGMAS..... Textile and Garment Manufacturers Association of Singapore (EAIO)

TGMI .... Tomsk State Medical Institute (RU)

TGNII....... Turkmen State Scientific Research Institute of History (RU)

TGNSW .... Teachers' Guild of New South Wales [*Australia*]

TGNU........ Transitional Government of National Unity [*South Africa*]

tgo .... Telegraph Team (BU)

TGO .... Togo [*ANSI three-letter standard code*] (CNC)

TGO .... Tongliao [*China*] [*Airport symbol*] (OAG)

TGO .... Trafik AB Grangesberg-Oxelosund [*Grangesberg-Oxelosund Transport Co.*] [*Sweden*] (WEN)

TGPG .... St. Georges [*Grenada*] [*ICAO location identifier*] (ICLI)

TGPI .... Tomsk State Pedagogical Institute (RU)

TGPO .... Tasmanian Government Printing Office [*Australia*]

TGPY........ Point Saline [*Grenada*] [*ICAO location identifier*] (ICLI)

tgr.............. Telegram (RU)

tgr.............. Telegraph (RU)

TGR .... Touggourt [*Algeria*] [*Airport symbol*] (OAG)

TGRTE...... Trans Gulf Refrigerated Transport Establishment [*United Arab Emirates*] [*Commercial firm*]

TGS........... Technisches Grunddaten-System [*German*] (ADPT)

TGS........... Telegraph Station (RU)

TGS........... Triglycine Sulfate (RU)

TGS........... Turkiye Gazeteciler Sendikasi [*Turkish Journalists Union*] (TU)

TGSA .... Tropical Grassland Society of Australia (ADA)

TGSD........ Turkiye Giyim Sanayicileri Dernigi [*Turkish Clothing Manufacturers Association*] (EAIO)

TGSYO...... Tatbiki Guzel Sanatlar Yuksek Okulu [*Advanced School of Applied Fine Arts*] (TU)

TGSYOKD ... Tatbiki Guzel Sanatlar Yuksek Okulu Kultur Dernegi [*Cultural Association of the Istanbul Advanced School of Applied Fine Arts*] (TU)

TGT .... Tanga [*Tanzania*] [*Airport symbol*] (OAG)

TGT .... Te Geleener Tyd [*On Borrowed Time*] [*Afrikaans*]

TGTT........ Turkiye Genclik Turizm Teskilati [*Turkish Youth Tourism Organization*] (TU)

TGU.......... Tanzania Gulf Union

TGU.......... Tartu State University (RU)

TGU.......... Tbilisi State University (RU)

TGU.......... Tegucigalpa [*Honduras*] [*Airport symbol*] (OAG)

TGU.......... Tomsk State University Imeni V. V. Kuybyshev (RU)

TGV .... Targovishte [*Bulgaria*] [*Airport symbol*] (OAG)

TGV .... Ten Gevolge Van [*In Consequence Of*] [*Afrikaans*]

TGV .... Ten Gunste Van [*In Favor Of*] [*Afrikaans*]

TGV .... Ter Geleentheid Van [*On the Occasion Of*] [*Afrikaans*]

TGV .... Tobacco Growers of Victoria [*Australia*]

TGV .... Train a Grande Vitesse [*High-speed train*]

TGWU .... Transport and General Workers Union [*Mauritius*] (AF)

TGZ .... Teminin Gucluk Zammi [*Job Security Premium*] (TU)

TGZ .... Tikhvin Alumina Plant (RU)

TGZ .... Tuxtla Gutierrez [*Mexico*] [*Airport symbol*] (OAG)

TH............. (Orszagos) Tervhivatal [*(National) Planning Office*] (HU)

t/h .... Stundentonnen [*Tons per Hour*] [*German*]

TH............. Tanacsi Hivatal [*Office of the Council*] (HU)

TH............. Tapia House [*Trinidadian and Tobagan*] (LA)

TH............. Tavirohivatal [*Telegraph Office*] (HU)

TH............. Technicko-Hospodarske (Planovani) [*Technical and Economic (Planning)*] (CZ)

TH............. Technika Haza [*House of Technology*] (HU)

TH............. Technische Hochschule [*Technical College, Advanced Technical School*] [*German*] (WEN)

th............... Teherpalyaudvar [*Freight Depot*] (HU)

TH............. Teknik Hizmetler [*Technical Duties*] (TU)

TH............. Thailand [*IYRU nationality code*] [*ANSI two-letter standard code*] (CNC)

Th............. Thema [*Theme*] [*German*]

Th............. Themis' Verzameling van Bijdragen tot de Kennis van het Publiek en Privaat Recht [*Benelux*] (BAS)

th............... Theoreme [*Theorem*] [*French*]

th............... These [*Benelux*] (BAS)

TH............. Tkalcovny Hedvabi [*Silk Weaving Mills*] (CZ)

Th............. Torio [*Thorium*] [*Chemical element*] [*Portuguese*]

TH............. Trinity House [*British*] (BARN)

THA........... Tanzania Harbors Authority (AF)

THA........... Tanzania Hockey Association

THA........... Tasmanian Hockey Association [*Australia*]

THA........... Thai Airways International Ltd. [*Thailand*] [*ICAO designator*] (FAAC)

THA........... Thai Hotels Association (EAIO)

THA........... Thailand [*ANSI three-letter standard code*] (CNC)

THA........... Total Holdings (Australia) Proprietary Ltd. (ADA)

THA........... Turk Haberler Ajansi [*Turkish News Agency*] (TU)

THAC .... [*The*] Help Australia Campaign (ADA)

Thai........... Thailand

Thail .... Thailand

thal............ Thaler [*Monetary unit in Germany*] [*Obsolete*] [*French*]

THANSW ... Teacher Housing Authority of New South Wales [*Australia*]

THB........... Tanzania Housing Bank

THB........... Thaba Tseka [*Lesotho*] [*Airport symbol*] (OAG)

THB........... Treuhandbetrieb [*Enterprise under Trusteeship*] (EG)

THB........... Turk Hamallar Birligi [*Turkish Porters Union*] [*Turkish Cypriot*] (GC)

THB .... Turkiye Halk Bankasi [*Peoples Bank of Turkey*] [*H*] [*See also*] (TU)
THC .... Tchien [*Liberia*] [*Airport symbol*] (OAG)
THC .... Teachers Higher Certificate [*Australia*]
THC .... Technische Hochschule fuer Chemie [*Advanced Technical School for Chemistry*] (EG)
THC .... Tourism and Hotels Corporation [*Sudan*]
THD .... Technische Hogeschool Delft
THD .... Transport and Harbors Department [*Guyana*] (MSC)
ThDr .... Doctor Theologiae [*Doctor of Divinity*] (CZ)
ThDr .... Doktor der Theologie [*German*]
THE .... Technische Hogeschool Eindhoven
THE .... Tekniska Hoegskolornas Energiarbetsgrupp [*Joint Energy Secretariat of the Swedish Institutes of Technology*] (WED)
THE .... Teresina [*Brazil*] [*Airport symbol*] (OAG)
theat .... [*of the*] Theater (TPFD)
theat .... Theatre [*French*] (TPFD)
theo .... Theology (TPFD)
theol .... Theologie [*French*] (TPFD)
theol .... Theologisch [*German*]
THEOLOG ... Theology Student (DSUE)
Theoph ...... Theophilus [*Sixth century*] [*Early Christian bishop*] (BARN)
Theoph ...... Theophrastus [*Third Century BC*] [*Classical studies*] (BARN)
theoret .... Theoretisch [*Theoretical*] [*German*] (GCA)
therapeut .... Therapeutisch [*Therapeutic*] [*German*] (GCA)
Therm .... Thermidor (FLAF)
therm .... Thermisch [*Thermal*] [*German*] (GCA)
THES .... Theses of Economics and Business in Finland [*Helsinki School of Economics Library*] [*Information service or system*] (CRD)
THESE-PAC ... Association pour la Diffusion des Theses sur le Pacifique Francophone [*New Caledonia*] (EAIO)
Thes/niki ... Thessaloniki [*Salonica*] (GC)
Thess .... Thessalonicense [*Thessalonians*] [*Afrikaans*]
Thess .... Thessaly [*District of both ancient and modern Greece*] (BARN)
ThETh .... Thalamos Endatikis Therapeias [*Intensive Care Unit*] (GC)
THF .... Tian Hua Fen [*Chinese herbal medicine*]
THG .... Biloela [*Australia*] [*Airport symbol*]
THGAS ..... Tasmanian Hospitality Group Apprenticeship Scheme [*Australia*]
ThGG .... Thueringer Gasgesellschaft [*Thuringian Gas Association*] [*Business term*]
THH .... Tieraerztliche Hochschule Hannover [*Information retrieval*]
THI .... Technische Hochschule Ilmenau [*Ilmenau Advanced Technical School*] (EG)
THITCO .... Thai Hua International Co. Ltd.
THIV .... History Institute, Victoria [*Australia*]
thj v .... Torvenyhatosagi Jogu Varos [*Municipal Borough*] (HU)
Thk .... Tahkimat [*Fortification*] (TU)
THK .... Taiheiyo Hoso Kyokai [*Pacific Broadcasting Association*] [*Japan*] (EAIO)
THK .... Teikoku Hiko Kyokai [*Imperial Aeronautic Society of Japan*]
THK .... Turk Hava Kurumu [*Turkish Air League*] [*Similar to civil aeronautics*] (TU)
THKC .... Turkiye Halk Kurtulus Cephesi [*Turkish People's Liberation Front*] (TU)
THKGV ..... Turk Hava Kuvvetlerini Guclendirme Vakfi [*Fund to Strengthen Turkish Air Force*] (TU)
THKMS .... Technische Hochschule Karl-Marx-Stadt [*Karl Marx Stadt Advanced Technical School*] (EG)
THKO .... Turkiye Halk Kurtulus Ordusu [*Turkish People's Liberation Army*] (TU)
THKP .... Turkiye Halk Kurtulus Parti Cephesi [*Turkish People's Liberation Party Front*] (TU)
THL .... Tachilek [*Myanmar*] [*Airport symbol*] (OAG)
THL .... Teollisuudenharjottajain Litto [*Federation of Finnish Manufacturers*] [*Finland*] (EAIO)
Thl .... Theil [*Part*] [*German*] (GCA)
Thl .... Thermal [*Thermal*] [*Military map abbreviation World War I*] [*French*] (MTD)
Thle .... Theile [*Parts*] [*German*] (GCA)
Thln .... Theilen [*Parts*] [*German*] (GCA)
Thlr .... Thaler [*Dollar*] [*German*]
THM .... Tapia House Movement [*Trinidad and Tobago*] [*Political party*] (PPW)
THM .... Technische Hochschule "Otto Von Guericke" Magdeburg [*"Otto Von Guericke" Advanced Technical School, Magdeburg*] [*German*]
THMGC .... Turkiye Harp Malulu Gaziler, Sehit, Dul, ve Yetimler Cemiyeti [*Society for Turkish Wounded War Veterans, Martyrs, Widows, and Orphans*] (TU)
THN .... Athens Air [*Greece*] [*ICAO designator*] (FAAC)
THN .... Technicko-Hospodarske Normy [*Technical and Economic Standards*] (CZ)
THN .... Trollhattan [*Sweden*] [*Airport symbol*] (OAG)
THO .... Thorshofn [*Iceland*] [*Airport symbol*] (OAG)

ThOA .... Thalassia Oikonomiki Astynomia [*Sea Revenue Police*] [*Greek*] (GC)
ThOA .... Theatrikos Organismos Athinon [*Athens Theatrical Organization*] (GC)
ThOI .... Thriskevtikon Orthodoxon Idryma [*Orthodox Religious Foundation*] [*Cyprus*] (GC)
ThOK .... Theatrikos Organismos Kyprou [*Cyprus Theatrical Organization*] (GC)
THOM ...... Thomson [*Botanical region*] [*Australia*]
THR .... Tehran [*Iran*] [*Airport symbol*] (OAG)
Thr .... Thaler [*Dollar*] [*German*]
THR .... Tundjangan Hari Raya [*Holiday Bonus*] (IN)
THRA .... Tasmanian Historical Research Association [*Australia*]
THRFRL ... Tohuku Regional Fisheries Research Laboratory [*Japan*] (MSC)
THS .... [*The*] Hydrographic Society [*Dagenham, Essex, England*] (EAIO)
THS .... Tamworth Historical Society [*Australia*]
THS .... Tatranska Horska Sluzba [*Tatra Mountain Service*] (CZ)
THS .... Transports Aeros Hispanos SA [*Spain*] [*ICAO designator*] (FAAC)
THS .... Transvaal Horticultural Society [*South Africa*] (AA)
THT .... Technische Hogeschool Twente [*Enschede*]
THT .... Tres Haute Tension [*Very High Tension*] [*French*] (ADPT)
THT .... Turk Hava Tasimaciligi [*Turkish Air Transport*] [*ICAO designator*] (FAAC)
thts .... Tiszthelyettes [*Senior Noncommissioned Officer*] (HU)
Thurs .... Thursday (EECI)
THY .... Turk Hava Yollari [*Turkish Airlines*] [*ICAO designator*] (FAAC)
THY .... Turun Historiallinen Yhdistys [*Turku, Finland*] (SLS)
THZ .... Tahoua [*Niger*] [*Airport symbol*] (OAG)
TI .... Current Indicator, Current Detector (RU)
TI .... Heat Detector (RU)
TI .... Icelandic Dental Association (EAIO)
TI .... Information Theory (RU)
TI .... Instrument Transformer (RU)
TI .... Radiation Thermometer (RU)
TI .... Technical Information (RU)
TI .... Technische Intelligenz [*Technical Intelligentsia*] [*German*] (EG)
TI .... Technischer Inspektor [*Technical Inspector*] [*German*] (ADPT)
TI .... Technological Institute (BU)
TI .... Technology Incubator
TI .... Tecnocentro Italiano [*Milan, Italy*] (SLS)
TI .... Tehrik-i-Istiqlal [*Solidarity Party*] [*See also TIP Pakistan*] [*Political party*] (FEA)
TI .... Teknologisk Institut [*Technological Institute*] [*Denmark*] (PDAA)
TI .... Tekstilna Industrija [*Textile Industry*] (YU)
TI .... Telemetering (RU)
TI .... Textile Institute [*Manchester, England*] (EAIO)
TI .... Thermal Radiation (RU)
TI .... Thursday Island [*Australia*] (ADA)
ti .... Tiistai(na) [*Finland*]
Ti .... Tirol [*or Tiroler*] [*The Tyrol or Tyrolese*] [*German*]
ti .... Tiszst [*Officer*] (HU)
Ti .... Titan [*Titanium*] [*Chemical element*] [*German*]
Ti .... Titanio [*Titanium*] [*Chemical element*] [*Portuguese*]
TI .... Tonskaldafelag Islands [*Society of Icelandic Composers*] (EAIO)
TI .... Tourismo Internazionale [*International Touring*] [*Italian*]
TI .... Trade International (BARN)
TI .... Transfrigoroute International (EA)
TI .... Transports Ivoiriennes
TI .... Tribunal d'Instance (FLAF)
TI .... True Independent [*Australia*]
TI .... Trzisni Inspektorat [*Market Inspectorate*] (YU)
ti .... Tudniillik [*Namely, That Is*] (HU)
TIA .... Taxation Institute of Australia
TIA .... Tilapia International Association (EAIO)
TIA .... Tirana [*Albania*] [*Airport symbol*] (OAG)
TIA .... Tobacco Institute of Australia
TIA .... Torrefaction Industrielle Abidjanaise
TIA .... Trade Indemnity Australia
TIAAE ...... Transactions of the Institute of Anthropology, Archaeology, and Ethnography (RU)
TIAB .... Trustul de Instalatii si Automatizari Bucuresti [*Bucharest Trust for Installations and Automation*] (RO)
TIAC .... Mouvements des Travailleurs Independents, Agriculteurs et Cadres [*Benelux*] (BAS)
TIAC .... Transport Industries Advisory Committee [*Australia*]
TIAFT ...... [*The*] International Association of Forensic Toxicologists [*Newmarket, Suffolk, England*] (EAIO)
TIAI .... Network for Technological Information on Agro-Industries [*Thailand*]
TIAR .... Tratado Interamericano de Asistencia Reciproca [*Inter-American Reciprocal Assistance Treaty*] (LA)
TIAS .... Taxation Incentives for the Arts Scheme [*Australia*]

TIAVSC..... [The] International Assets Valuation Standards Committee [of the American Institute of Real Estate Appraisers] [British] (EAIO)
TIB............ Tanzania Investment Bank
TIB............ Technical Information Bulletin (RU)
TIB............ Technische Informatie Bibliotheek
TIB............ Technische Informationsbibliothek
TIB............ Tezek Iscileri Birligi [Solid Fuel (Cattle Dung) Workers Union] (TU)
TIB............ Tourist Information Brussels [Belgium] (EY)
TIB............ Transivoirienne des Bois
TIB............ Tum Iktisatcilar Dernegi [Association of All Economists] (TU)
TIB............ Turkiye Is Bankasi [Turkish Labor Bank] (TU)
TIBA........ Turkish Industrialists and Businessmen's Association
TIB andFIB ... Tibia and Fibula (DSUE)
TIBAS .... Turkiye Is Bankasi Anonim Sirketi [Turkish Labor Bank Corporation] (TU)
TIBASSendikasi ... Turkiye Is Bankasi Anonim Sirketi Mensuplari Sendikasi [Turkish Labor Bank Corporation Employees' Union] (TU)
TIBB .... Tecnomasio Italiano Brown Boveri, SpA [Italian] [Nuclear energy] (NRCH)
TIBE......... Travaux, Isolation, Batiment, Etancheite
TIBEA .... Societe Travaux, Isolation, Batiment, Etancheite Afrique
TIBR......... Tokugawa Institute for Biological Research [Japan] (DSCA)
TIBRAS..... Titanio do Brasil [Brazilian Titanium] (LA)
TIC............ Tantalum Producers International Study Center [Later, Tantalum-Niobium International Study Center] (EAIO)
TIC............ Tasmanian Industrial Commission [Australia]
TIC............ Taxe Interieure de Consommation [Domestic Consumption Tax] [French] (WER)
TIC............ Technical Information Center [China] (IRC)
TIC............ Technical Information Center [Korea Standards Research Institute]
TIC............ Textile Industries Corp. [Myanmar] (DS)
Tic............. Ticaret [Trade, Commerce] [Turkey] (CED)
TIC............ Tinak [Marshall Islands] [Airport symbol] (OAG)
TIC............ Transvaal Indian Congress [South Africa] (PD)
TIC............ Travaux d'Interet Communal [Algeria] (FLAF)
TICA......... Transporte Interoceanico Centroamericano [Costa Rica] (LAA)
TICACE .... Technical Intelligence Center Allied Command Europe [NATO] (NATG)
TICAF .... Tororo Industrial Chemicals and Fertilisers Ltd. [Uganda]
TICB......... Ticaret Bakanligi [Ministry of Commerce] (TU)
TICC......... Technical Intelligence Coordination Center [NATO] (NATG)
TICCIH..... [The] International Committee for the Conservation of the Industrial Heritage (EA)
TICOFIMA ... Tissage de Coton et Fibranne Marocains [Moroccan Cotton and Fiber Weaving] (AF)
TICTAC .... Terminal Integre Comportant un Televiseur et l'Appel au Clavier [French] (ADPT)
TID .... Ministry of Trade, Industry, and Development [St. Kitts-Nevis-Anguilla]
TID .... Technical and Economic Report (BU)
TID .... Technological Information Department [Korea Institute of Machinery and Metals] [South Korea]
TID .... Telecommunications Interception Division [Australian Federal Police]
TID .... Textile Industry Division [Ministry of Industry] [Thailand]
tid .... Tidigare [Earlier] [Sweden]
TID .... Traitement Integre des Donnees [Integrated Data Processing - IDP] [French]
TIDA .... Technology and Industry Development Authority of Western Australia
TIDF......... The Israeli Diving Federation (EAIO)
TIDIC....... Textile Industry Documentation and Information Centre [Arab Federation for Textile Industries] [Egypt]
TIDKON ... Turkiye Iktisadi Devlet Tesekkul ve Tesebbusleri Personel Sendikalari Konfederasyonu [Confederation of Turkish Economic State Organization and Enterprises Personnel Unions] (TU)
tidl.............. Tidlig [Early] [Danish/Norwegian]
tidsskr........ Tidsskrift [Periodical] [Publishing Danish/Norwegian]
TIE............ [The] Institute of Ecology (ASF)
TIE............ Technical Information Exchange [South Pacific Appropriate Technology Foundation] [Papua New Guinea]
TIE............ Tippi [Ethiopia] [Airport symbol] (OAG)
TIE............ Transnationals Information Exchange
Tie............. Tuilerie [Tilekiln] [Military map abbreviation World War I] [French] (MTD)
TIEA......... Tax Information Exchange Agreement (ECON)
Tief Gl....... Tiefgliederung [Distribution in Depth] [German] (GCA)
tier............. Tierisch [Animal-Like] [German] (GCA)
Tiervers...... Tierversuch [Animal experiment] [German] (GCA)
Tierz......... Tierzucht [Animal-Breeding] [German]
TIES .... Tactical Information Exchange System [Navy United Nations] (MCD)

TIES .... Technological Information Exchange System [UNIDO] [United Nations]
tiet .... Tieteellinen [or Tieteessa] [Scientific, In Science] [Finland]
TIEx.......... Einheitliches Reglement Betreffend des Internationalen Eisenbahn-Expressgutverkehrs [Uniform Regulations on International Railway Express Freight Traffic] [German] (EG)
TIF............ Taif [Saudi Arabia] [Airport symbol] (OAG)
TIF............ Tilapia International Foundation (EA)
TIF............ Transit International par Fer (FLAF)
TIFC .... Towarzystwo Imienia Fryderyka Chopina [Frederic Chopin Society] [Poland]
TIFF .... Tokyo International Film Festival [Japan]
TIFO.......... Tiszai Koolajipari Vallalat [Tisza Petroleum Industry Enterprise] (HU)
TIFR......... Tata Institute of Fundamental Research [India]
TIG .... Societe de Telecommunications Internationales Gabonaises [Gabonese International Telecommunications Company] (AF)
TIG .... Transactions of the Institute of Geography (of the Academy of Sciences, USSR) (RU)
TIGEM..... Telethon Institute of Genetics and Medicine [Italy]
TIGN .... Transactions of the Institute of Geological Sciences (of the Academy of Sciences, USSR) (RU)
TIH .... Tikehau [French Polynesia] [Airport symbol] (OAG)
TiHo.......... Tieraerztliche Hochschule [Veterinary High School] [German]
TII............. European Association for the Transfer of Technologies, Innovation, and Industrial Information [Information service or system] (IID)
TII............. Tentara Islam Indonesia [Indonesian Islamic Army] (IN)
TII............. Tomsk Industrial Institute Imeni S. M. Kirov (RU)
TII............. Tourismo Internazionale Injection [International Touring-fuel Injection] [Italian]
TIIA.......... Thermal Insulation Institute of Australia (ADA)
TIIET .... Transactions of the Institute of History, Natural Sciences, and Technology (RU)
TIIF .... Transactions of the Institute of History and Philosophy (RU)
TIIGM...... Toprak ve Iskan Isleri Genel Mudurlugu [Soil and Settlement Affairs Directorate General] [Under Village Affairs Ministry] (TU)
TIIIMSKh ... Tashkent Engineering Instiute of Irrigation and Mechanization of Agriculture (RU)
TIIKP .... Turkiye Ihtilalci Isci Koylu Partisi [Turkish Revolutionary Worker Peasant Party] [A pro-Maoist illegal party] (TU)
TIIMSKh .. Tashkent Institute of Irrigation and Mechanization of Agriculture (RU)
TIIZhT ...... Tashkent Institute of Railroad Transportation Engineers (RU)
TIJ .... Tijuana [Mexico] [Airport symbol] (OAG)
tijd .... Tijdelijk [Benelux] (BAS)
TIJI........... Tribune Internationale des Jeunes Interpretes [International Rostrum of Young Performers - IRP] (EAIO)
TIK........... Turkiye Insaat Kalfalari Birligi [Turkish Construction Foremen's Union] (TU)
TIKA......... Technical Industrial Kalumbila Associate
TIKh .... Technical School of Industrial Chemistry (BU)
TIKKO...... Turkiye Isci Koylu Kurtulus Ordusu ile Marksist-Leninist Genclik Birligi Illegal Orgutleri [Turkish Worker Peasant Liberation Army and Marxist-Leninst Youth Union Illegal Organizations] (TU)
TIKP .... Turkiye Isci Koylu Partisi [Worker-Peasant Party of Turkey] [Political party] (PD)
TIL............ Taiwan International Line Ltd. (DS)
TIL............ Trustul Industriei Lemnului [Trust for the Wood Industry] (RO)
TIL............ Trustul pentru Industrializarea Lemnului [Trust for the Industrializaton of Wood] (RO)
tilastot....... Tilastotiede [Statistics] [Finland]
TILCOR .... Tribal Trust Land Development Corporation
TILIB........ Trustul de Izolatii pentru Lucrari Industriale Bucuresti [Bucharest Insulation Trust for Industrial Projects] (RO)
tillok.......... Tilloekad [Enlarged] [Publishing] [Sweden]
tills .... Tillsammans [Together] [Sweden]
Til/nia........ Tilepikoinonia [Telecommunications] (GC)
tilskrivn...... Tilskrivning [Handwritten Notes] [Publishing Danish/Norwegian]
TIM .... Plant of Heat Insulation Materials (RU)
TIM .... Taman Ismail Marzuki [Jakarta Cultural Center] [Indonesia]
TIM .... Tembagapura [Indonesia] [Airport symbol] (OAG)
TIM .... Theater Imeni V. E. Meyerkhol'd (RU)
Tim............ Timotheus [Timothy] [Afrikaans]
TIM .... Trustul de Instalatii Montaj [Installations and Assembly Trust] (RO)
TIMB........ Timbalan [Deputy] (ML)
timb.......... Timbre [Stamped] [Publishing] [French]
TIMB........ Trustul de Instalatii Montaj Bucuresti [Bucharest Installations and Assembly Trust] (RO)
TIMDER... Turkiye Ilkogretim Mufettisleri Dernegi [Turkish Elementary Education Inspectors Association] (TU)

TiMixE ...... TI-MIX [*Texas Instruments Mini/Microcomputer Information Exchange*] Europe　(EA)
TIMLO ...... Turkiye Insaat ve Malzeme Limited Ortaklari [*Turkish Construction and Equipment Corp.*] [*Istanbul*]　(TU)
TIMM .... Thermionic Micromodules　(RU)
TIMMP ..... Technological Institute of the Meat and Dairy Industry　(RU)
TIMO .... Telefoni Italiani Medio-Orientali [*Company controlling telephone services in Central and Eastern Italy*]
TIMR .... Tokyo Institute for Municipal Research [*Japan*]
TIMS .... [*The*] International Molinological Society　(EA)
TIMTAS ... Tesisat Insaat Malzemeleri Ticaret Anonim Sirketi [*Installations Construction Equipment Corporation*]　(TU)
TIN .... Taino Tours [*Dominican Republic*] [*ICAO designator*]　(FAAC)
TIN .... Tindouf [*Algeria*] [*Airport symbol*]　(OAG)
TINFO ...... Tieteellisen Informoinnin Neuvosto [*Finnish Council for Scientific Information and Research Libraries*]　(EAIO)
TINRO ...... Tikhookeanskiy Nauchno-Issledovatel'skiy Institut Rybnogo Khozyaystva i Okeanografii [*Pacific Scientific Research Institute of Fisheries and Oceanography*] [*Russian*]　(MSC)
Tintenfl ...... Tintenfleck [*Ink Stain*] [*German*]
TIO .... Territory Insurance Office [*Australia*]
TIOSF .... Turkiye Ilkokul Ogretmen Sendikalari Federasyonu [*Turkish Elementary School Teacher Unions' Federation*]　(TU)
Tiotef .... Triethylenethiophosphoramide　(RU)
tip .... Printing　(RU)
tip .... Printing House　(RU)
TIP .... Taxe Interieure a la Production
TIP .... Techniczna Inspekcja Pracy [*Technical Inspection of the Labor Force*]　(POL)
TIP .... Technology and Innovation Park
TIP .... Tehrik-i-Istiqlal [*Solidarity Party*] [*See also TI Pakistan*] [*Political party*]　(FEA)
TIP .... Tekstilna Industrija "Pobjeda" [*"Pobjeda" Textile Industry*] [*Zagreb*]　(YU)
tip .... Tipografia [*Typography*] [*Spanish*]
tip .... Tipografia [*Typography*] [*Portuguese*]
tip .... Tipografo [*Printer*] [*Publishing*] [*Italian*]
TIP .... Towarzystwo Internistow Polskich [*Society of Polish Physicians in Internal Medicine*]　(POL)
TIP .... Transport Individuel Publique [*Also known as PROCOTIP*] [*French auto cooperative*]
TIP .... Tripoli [*Libya*] [*Airport symbol*]　(OAG)
TIP .... Turkiye Isci Partisi [*Turkish Labor Party*]　(TU)
TIP .... Tutunski Institut vo Prilep [*Tobacco Institute in Prilep*]　(YU)
TIPA .... Trade and Investment Promotion Agency [*Botswanna*]　(EY)
TIPAT .... Technical Information on Patents [*Swiss Intellectual Property Office*] [*Bern*] [*Information service or system*]　(IID)
Tip-Der ...... Tibbiyeliler Kultur Dernegi [*Medical Faculty Alumni Cultural Association*]　(TU)
TIPER .... Tanzanian and Italian Petroleum Refinery Company
TIPICOL ... Trabajos Tipicos Colombianos en Todos los Metales Preciosos [*Colombia*]　(COL)
Tip-Is .... Tip Iscileri Sendikasi [*Medical Workers Union*] [*Turkish Cypriot*]　(GC)
tipogr .... Printing, Typographic　(BU)
tipogr .... Tipografo [*Printer*] [*Publishing*] [*Italian*]
tipolitogr ... Printing and Lithographic Establishments　(RU)
TIPPROYeKT ... Central Institute of Standard Designs　(RU)
Tip-Tek ...... Tip Teknolog Kurulus [*Medical Technicians Organization (on Cyprus)*]　(GC)
TIQ .... Tinian [*Mariana Islands*] [*Airport symbol*]　(OAG)
tir .... Circulation, Number of Copies Printed　(RU)
TiR .... Technika i Racjonalizacja (Klub) [*Engineering and Production Efficiency (Club)*]　(POL)
tir .... Tirage [*Edition*] [*Publishing*] [*French*]
Tir .... Tirol [*The Tyrol*] [*German*]
TIR .... Tirupati [*India*] [*Airport symbol*]　(OAG)
tir .... Total Printing, Circulation　(BU)
TIR .... Transit International par Route　(FLAF)
TIR .... Transport International de Marchandises　(FLAF)
TIR .... Transport International Routier [*International Highway Transport*] [*French*]　(HU)
tirat .... Tiratura [*Edition*] [*Publishing*] [*Italian*]
TIRC/NCSR ... Tree Improvement Research Centre/National Council for Scientific Research [*Zambia*]　(ARC)
TIRDO ...... Shirika la Utafiti na Maendeleo ya Viwanda, Tanzania [*Tanzania Industrial Research and Development Organization*]　(EAIO)
TIRDO ...... Tanzania Industrial Research and Development Organization
TIRGA .... Trinidad Islandwide Rice Growers Association　(EAIO)
TIRKH .... Tikhookeanskiy Institut Rybnog Khozyaystva [*Pacific Ocean Fisheries Institute*] [*Russian*]　(MSC)
TIRS .... Travaux de l'Institut des Recherches Sahariennes [*Algeria*]
TIRU .... Trade Information Research Unit [*ITC*] [*United Nations*]　(DUND)
TIS .... Dark Izyum Glass　(RU)

TIS .... Tarim Iscileri Sendikasi [*Agricultural Workers Union*] [*An affiliate of DISK*]　(TU)
TIS .... Technical and Economic Councils　(BU)
TIS .... Technical Information Service [*Ministry of Industry*] [*Philippines*]
TIS .... Technical Information Service [*Caribbean Industrial Research Institute*] [*Trinidad and Tobago*]
TIS .... Technologische Informations Systeme [*Technological Information Systems*] [*German*]
TIS .... Telephone Interpreter Service [*Australia*]
TIS .... Tesis [*Russian Federation*] [*ICAO designator*]　(FAAC)
TIS .... Thursday Island [*Australia*] [*Airport symbol*]　(OAG)
TIS .... Timber Industry Strategy [*Victoria, Australia*]
TIS .... Total-Informationssystem [*German*]　(ADPT)
TIS .... Trade Information Service [*ESCAP*] [*United Nations*]　(DUND)
TIS .... Translating and Interpreting Service [*Department of Immigration, Local Government and Ethnic Affairs*] [*Australia*]
TIS .... Turkiye Toprak-Su-Tarim Iscileri Sendikasi [*Turkish Union of Land, Water, and Agricultural Workers*]　(TU)
TISA .... Tejidos Industriales, Sociedad Anonima [*Industrial Fabrics Corporation*] [*El Salvador*]
TISA .... Transportadora International, Sociedad Anonima [*International Transport Company, Incorporated*] [*Nicaragua*]　(LA)
TISC .... Tertiary Institutions Service Centre [*Australia*]
TISCO .... Tanzania Industrial Studies [*or Service*] & Consulting Organisation
TISCO .... Tata Iron and Steel Co.　(ECON)
TISCO .... Tata Iron & Steel Company [*India*]
TISEA .... Tasmanian Institute of Senior Educational Administrators [*Australia*]
Ti-Sen .... Turkiye Tiyatrocular Sendikasi [*Turkish Theatre Performers Union*] [*Istanbul*]　(TU)
TISHUG .... Texas Instruments Home Computer Users' Group [*Australia*]
TISI .... Thai Industrial Standards Institute [*Ministry of Industry*] [*Thailand*]
TISIC .... Thai Iron and Steel Industry Club [*Association of Thai Industries*]
TIS-IS .... Turkiye Insaat Sanayii Iscileri Sendikasi [*Turkish Construction Industry Workers' Union*]　(TU)
TISK .... Thailand Informations und Solidaritaetskomitee [*Germany*]
TISK .... Turkiye Isci Sendikalari Konfederasyonu [*Confederation of Turkish Worker Unions*] [*Turkish Cypriot*]　(GC)
TISK .... Turkiye Isveren Sendikalari Konfederasyonu [*Turkish Confederation of Employer Unions*] [*Ankara, Turkey*]　(TU)
TISN .... Todai International Science Network
TIS naLVZ G Dimitrov ... Technical and Economic Council of the G. Dimitrov Locomotive Engines and Railroad Cars Plant　(BU)
t isp .... Vaporization Temperature　(RU)
TISS .... Tanzanian Intelligence and Security Service　(AF)
TISS .... Timber Industry Superannuation Scheme [*Australia*]
TISSKh .... Pacific Institute of Socialist Agriculture　(RU)
TISSS .... Institute of Earthquake-Proof Construction and Seismology (of the Academy of Sciences, Tadzhik SSR)　(RU)
TIST .... St. Thomas/Harry S. Truman [*Virgin Islands*] [*ICAO location identifier*]　(ICLI)
TISTR .... Thailand Institute of Scientific and Technological Research
TISU .... Trade Information Supply Unit [*ITC*] [*United Nations*]　(DUND)
TISX .... St. Croix/Alexander Hamilton [*Virgin Islands*] [*ICAO location identifier*]　(ICLI)
TIT .... Experimental Television Screen　(BU)
TIT .... Taxe Interieure sur les Transactions
TIT .... Telecommunications Internationales du Tchad [*International Telecommunications of Chad*]　(AF)
t i t .... Telegraph and Telephone　(RU)
TIT .... Television Test Pattern　(RU)
tit .... Titel [*Title*] [*Publishing*] [*Netherlands*]
Tit .... Titel [*Title*] [*Publishing*] [*German*]
tit .... Titel [*Title*] [*Publishing*] [*Sweden*]
tit .... Titel [*Title*] [*Publishing Danish/Norwegian*]
Tit .... Titolare [*Owner*] [*Italian*]
tit .... Titolo [*Title*] [*Publishing*] [*Italian*]
tit .... Titre [*Title*] [*Publishing*] [*French*]　(GPO)
tit .... Tituliert [*Give a Title To*] [*German*]
tit .... Titulo [*Title*] [*Spanish*]
tit .... Titulo [*Title*] [*Portuguese*]
Tit .... Titus [*Titus*] [*Afrikaans*]
TIT .... Tokyo Institute of Technology [*Japan*]　(PDAA)
TIT .... Transactions on the History of Technology　(RU)
TIT .... Tudomanyos Ismeretterjeszto Tarsulat [*Society for the Propagation of Scientific Knowledge*]　(HU)
TITASZV ... Tiszantuli Aramszolgaltato Vallalat [*Electricity Distribution Enterprise of the Trans-Tisza Region*]　(HU)
TiTbP .... Wireless Telegraphy and Telephony　(RU)

TITC .... Tourism Industry Training Committee [*Australia*]
titelafb........ Titelafbeelding [*Illustrated Title*] [*Publishing*] [*Netherlands*]
Titelb......... Titelbild [*Frontispiece*] [*Publishing*] [*German*]
titelbl......... Titelblad [*Title Page*] [*Publishing Danish/Norwegian*]
Titelbl .... Titelblatt [*Title Page*] [*Publishing*] [*German*]
Titeleinf ..... Titeleinfassung [*Border on Title Page*] [*Publishing*] [*German*]
Titeleinfass ... Titeleinfassung [*Border on Title Page*] [*Publishing*] [*German*]
titelp.......... Titelpagina [*Title Page*] [*Publishing*] [*Netherlands*]
titelpag....... Titelpagina [*Title Page*] [*Publishing*] [*Netherlands*]
titelpl......... Titelplaat [*Frontispiece*] [*Publishing*] [*Netherlands*]
titelpr........ Titelprent [*Frontispiece*] [*Publishing*] [*Netherlands*]
Titels......... Titelseite [*Title Page*] [*Publishing*] [*German*]
titk............. Titkos [*Secret*]   (HU)
Titl .... Sitel [*Title*] [*German*]
tit l............. Title Page   (RU)
TITN......... Traitement de l'Information, Techniques Nouvelles [*Information Handling, New Techniques*] [*French*]   (ADPT)
tito............. Titulo [*Title*] [*Spanish*]
TITO......... Troops In, Troops Out
Titrat........ Titration [*German*]   (GCA)
TITUS .... Textile Information Treatment Users' Service [*French Textile Institute*] [*Bibliographic database*] [*Information service or system*]   (IID)
TIU .... Tactical Intelligence Unit [*New South Wales Police Service*] [*Australia*]
TIU .... Timaru [*New Zealand*] [*Airport symbol*]   (OAG)
TIV............ Tivat [*Former Yugoslavia*] [*Airport symbol*]   (OAG)
TIV............ Tivoli Music Hall [*London*]   (DSUE)
TIWU .... Tea Industry Workers' Union [*Mauritius*]   (AF)
TIWU .... Transport and Industrial Workers Union [*Trinidad and Tobago*]   (EAIO)
TIX............ Triax Airlines Ltd. [*Nigeria*] [*ICAO designator*]   (FAAC)
TIY............ Tidjikja [*Mauritania*] [*Airport symbol*]   (OAG)
Tiy............. Tiyatro [*Theatre*]   (TU)
TIYa.......... Transactions of the Institute of Linguistics (of the Academy of Sciences, USSR)   (RU)
TIYC........ Transvaal Indian Youth Congress
TIZ............ Recording Pulse Flip-Flop   (RU)
TIZ............ Tari [*Papua New Guinea*] [*Airport symbol*]   (OAG)
TIZ............ Technologietransfer und Innovationsberatungs-Zentrum
tiz .... Tizedes [*Corporal*]   (HU)
Tizpribor ... Precision Measuring Instrument Plant   (RU)
TJ.............. Cameroon [*Aircraft nationality and registration mark*]   (FAAC)
TJ.............. Telocvicna Jednota [*Gymnastic Association*]   (CZ)
tj .... To Je [*That Is*]   (YU)
tj .... To Jest [*That Is*]   (CZ)
tj .... Torvenyjavaslat [*Bill (In preparation)*]   (HU)
TJ............. Tribuna de la Juventud [*Tribune of Youth*] [*Mexico*]   (LA)
TJA............ Tarija [*Bolivia*] [*Airport symbol*]   (OAG)
TJAPA ...... Tjalon Perwira [*Officer Candidate*]   (IN)
tjb .... Tonneau de Jauge Brute   (FLAF)
TJBQ......... Aguadilla/Borinquen [*Puerto Rico*] [*ICAO location identifier*]   (ICLI)
TJC........... Taiwan Jewish Community   (EAIO)
TJCG .... Vieques/Camp Garcia Airstrip [*Puerto Rico*] [*ICAO location identifier*]   (ICLI)
TJCP......... Culebra [*Puerto Rico*] [*ICAO location identifier*]   (ICLI)
TJD........... Turkiye Jeofizikciler Dernegi [*Turkish Geophysicists Organization*]   (TU)
TJFA......... Fajardo [*Puerto Rico*] [*ICAO location identifier*]   (ICLI)
TJFC......... Tasmanian Junior Football Club [*Australia*]
TJFF......... Ramey [*Puerto Rico*] [*ICAO location identifier*]   (ICLI)
TJFL......... Tasmanian Junior Football League [*Australia*]
TJIG .... San Juan/Isla Grande [*Puerto Rico*] [*ICAO location identifier*]   (ICLI)
TJK........... Tajikair [*Tajikistan*] [*ICAO designator*]   (FAAC)
TJK........... Turkiye Jeoloji Kurumu [*Turkish Geological Organization*]   (TU)
TJK........... Turkiye Jokey Kulubu [*Turkish Jockey Club*]   (TU)
TJMO........ Tmmob Jeoloji Muhendisleri Odasi [*Chamber of Geological Engineers of Turkey*]   (EAIO)
TJMZ........ Mayaguez [*Puerto Rico*] [*ICAO location identifier*]   (ICLI)
tjn .... Tonneau de Jauge Nette   (FLAF)
TJNR........ Roosevelt Roads Naval Air Station [*Puerto Rico*] [*ICAO location identifier*]   (ICLI)
TJP .... Tableaux de Jurisprudence   (FLAF)
TJP .... Taxe sur les Jeux et Paris [*France*]   (BAS)
TJPS......... Ponce/Mercedita [*Puerto Rico*] [*ICAO location identifier*]   (ICLI)
TJQ........... Tanjung Pandan [*Indonesia*] [*Airport symbol*]   (OAG)
tjs .... Tai Jotakin Sellaista [*Finland*]
TJSJ .... San Juan/Puerto Rico International [*Puerto Rico*] [*ICAO location identifier*]   (ICLI)
TJVQ......... Vieques [*Puerto Rico*] [*ICAO location identifier*]   (ICLI)
TJZS......... San Juan [*Puerto Rico*] [*ICAO location identifier*]   (ICLI)
tk .... Boiling Point   (BU)
TK .... Contact Thermometer   (RU)

TK .... Contact Transformer   (RU)
TK .... Customs Code of the USSR   (RU)
TK .... Electric Logging Method   (RU)
TK .... Fuel Channel [*Nuclear physics and engineering*]   (RU)
TK .... Kenotron Transformer   (RU)
TK .... Labor Cadre   (BU)
TK .... Labor Card   (BU)
TK .... Labor Code   (RU)
TK .... Merchant Marine   (BU)
TK .... Pacific Ocean Committee (of the Academy of Sciences, USSR)
TK .... Remote Control   (RU)
TK .... Rockwell Conical Hardness Tester   (RU)
tk .... Since, Because, As   (RU)
TK .... Skin Graft   (RU)
TK .... Small Intestine   (RU)
TK .... Taegu [*South Korea*]   (ECON)
TK .... Tajvedelmi Korzet [*Protected Conservation Area*]   (HU)
Tk .... Takim [*or Takimlar*] [*Set or Sets As of equipment or instruments*]   (TU)
tk .... Taman Kuun [*This Month*] [*Finland*]   (GPO)
TK .... Tancsics Kiado [*Publishing House*]   (HU)
TK .... Tank Corps   (RU)
TK .... Tank Shortwave [*Radio*]   (RU)
tk .... Tata Kuuta [*Finland*]
TK .... Technical Commission [*or Committee*]   (RU)
TK .... Technical Control   (RU)
TK .... Technicka Knihovna [*Technical Library*]   (CZ)
TK .... Technicka Kontrola [*Technical Control*]   (CZ)
TK .... Technische Konstruktion [*Technical Designing Office*] [*German*]   (EG)
TK .... Technologiai Kutatas [*Research Aiming at the Implementation for the Purpose of Mass Production the Results of Basic Research*]   (HU)
Tk .... Telok [*Bay*] [*Malay*]   (NAU)
Tk .... Telok [*Bay*] [*Indonesian*]   (NAU)
TK .... Temperature Coefficient   (RU)
TK .... Temperatur-Koeffizient [*Temperature Coefficient*] [*German*]   (GCA)
TK .... Tenaga Kuda [*Horsepower*]   (IN)
TK .... Teologian Kandidaatti [*Finland*]
tk .... Teretna Kola [*Freight Car*] [*Railroads*]   (YU)
TK .... Terminology Commission   (RU)
tk .... Tezky Kulomet [*Heavy Machine Gun*]   (CZ)
TK .... Thermal Cracking   (RU)
TK .... Thermostated Chamber   (RU)
TK .... Ticaret Kanunu [*Commercial Law*]   (TU)
TK .... Tokelau Islands [*ANSI two-letter standard code*]   (CNC)
TK .... Tolmac Kratic [*Explanation of Abbreviations*]   (YU)
TK .... Tonnes Kilometriques
TK .... Trgovinska Komora [*Chamber of Commerce*]   (YU)
TK .... Turbocompressor   (RU)
TK .... Turkey [*IYRU nationality code*]
TK .... Tvornica Koza [*Leather Factory*]   (YU)
TK .... Wheeled Tractor   (RU)
TKA .... Air Troika [*Russian Federation*] [*ICAO designator*]   (FAAC)
TKA .... Motor Torpedo Boat   (RU)
TKA .... Tameion Koinonikon Asfaliseon [*Social Insurance Fund*] [*Greek*]   (GC)
TKA .... Techniczna Komisja Awaryjna [*Technical Damage Commission*]   (POL)
tk ad .... Takma Ad [*Nickname*]   (TU)
TKAE........ Turk Kulturunu Arastirma Enstitusu [*Turkish Institute for Cultural Research*]   (TU)
t kapl .... Drop Point   (RU)
tkatsk .... Weaving Mill [*Topography*]   (RU)
tkatskpryad ... Weaving and Spinning Mill [*Topography*]   (RU)
TKB .... Quick-Saturation Coil Transformer   (RU)
TKB .... Technisch-Kommerzielles Buero [*Technical Commercial Office*] [*German*]   (EG)
TKBA........ Tierkoerperbeseitigungsanstalt [*Carcass Disposal Plant*] [*German*]   (EG)
TKCh .... Temperature Frequency Coefficient   (RU)
TKCZMS ... Tmyczasowy Komitet Centralny Zwiazku Mlodziezy Socjalistycznej [*Temporary Central Committee of the Socialist Youth Union*]   (POL)
TKD .... Technischer Kundendienst [*German*]   (ADPT)
TKD .... Turkiye Kizilay Dernegi [*Turkish Red Crescent Organization*]   (TU)
TKDP........ Temperature Coefficient of Dielectric Constant   (RU)
t k dr .... Heavy Machine-Gun Detachment   (BU)
TKE .... Pipe-Laying Electric Crane   (RU)
TKE .... Trek Airways [*South Africa*] [*ICAO designator*]   (FAAC)
TKF.......... Tetracalcium Phosphate   (RU)
TKF.......... Tricalcium Phosphate   (RU)
TKF.......... Tricresyl Phosphate   (RU)

TKFN......... Terenowy Komitet Frontu Narodowego [*Local Committee of the People's Front*] (POL)

TKG .... Bandar Lampung [*Indonesia*] [*Airport symbol*] (OAG)

TKGM .... Tapu ve Kadastro Genel Mudurlugu [*Land Registration and Survey Directorate General*] [*Under Office of Premier*] (TU)

TKh............ Table of Characteristics [*Computers*] (RU)

TKh............ Tachometer Generator (RU)

TKH........... Trgovinska Komora Hrvatske [*Chamber of Commerce of Croatia*] (YU)

TKhA .... Chromel-Alumel Thermocouple (RU)

TKhA .... Sodium Trichloroacetate (RU)

TKhB .... Theater and Art Bureau (RU)

TKhE .... Trichloroethane (RU)

TKhFM...... Copper Trichlorophenolate (RU)

TKhK .... Chromel-Copel Thermocouple (RU)

TKhK .... Cold-Cathode Thyratron (RU)

TKhNB ..... Tetrachloronitrobenzene (RU)

TKhP .... Device for Checking Gun Bore Sighting (RU)

TKhS.......... Refrigerated Transportation Vessel (RU)

TKhTU ...... Theatrical Applied Art School (RU)

TKhU .... Trichloroacetic Acid (RU)

TKI............ Tavkozlesi Kutato Intezet [*Telecommunication Research Institute*] (HU)

TKI............ Temperature Coefficient of Inductance (RU)

TKI............ Termeloszovetkezetek Kereskedelmi Irodaja [*Producing Cooperatives' Commercial Office*] (HU)

TKI............ Turkiye Kibris Idaresi [*Turkish Cypriot Administration*] (TU)

TKI............ Turkiye Komur Isletmesi Genel Mudurlugu [*Turkish Coal Works Directorate General*] (TU)

TKIChP ..... Transactions of the Commission for the Study of the Quaternary Period (of the Academy of Sciences, USSR) (RU)

TKID......... Turk Kooperatif Isleri Dairesi [*Turkish Cooperative Affairs Office*] [*Turkish Cypriot*] (GC)

t kip........... Boiling Point (RU)

TKITPSF... Turkiye Kamu Iktisadi Tesebbusleri Personeli Sendikalari Federasyonu [*Federation of Turkish Public Economic Enterprises Personnel Unions*] (TU)

TKK .... Tokubetsu Koto Kaisatsu [*Special High Police Bureau*] [*Tokko*] [*See also*] [*Japan*]

TKK .... Truk [*Caroline Islands*] [*Airport symbol*] (OAG)

TKKD .... Turk Kadinlari Kultur Dernegi [*Turkish Women's Cultural Association*] (TU)

TKKF........ Towarzystwo Krzewienia Kultury Fizycznej [*Society for Promotion of Physical Culture*] (POL)

TkL............ Tekniikan Lisensiaatti [*Finland*]

TKL............ Tokelau Islands [*ANSI three-letter standard code*] (CNC)

TKM .... Tatrzanski Klub Motocyklowy [*Tatra Mountains Motorcycle Club*] (POL)

t-km............ Tonne-Kilometre [*or Kilometrique*] (FLAF)

tkm .... Tonnenkilometer [*Tons per Kilometer*] [*German*]

TKMC-IS .. Turkiye Yeralti Madenleri Komur, Metal, Cevherleri, ve Maden Arama Iscileri Sendikasi [*Turkish Subterranean Ores, Coal, Metal, and Mine Exploitation Workers' Union*] [*Ankara*] (TU)

TKMD .... Turk Komunist Mucadele Dernegi [*Turkish Association for Combating Communism*] (TU)

TKN .... Tokuno Shima [*Japan*] [*Airport symbol*] (OAG)

TKNL .... Tovarny Kobercu a Nabytkovych Latek [*Carpet and Upholstery Material Factories*] (CZ)

TKO........... Circular-Scope Tube (RU)

TKO........... Technische Kontrollorganisation [*Technical Control Organization*] (EG)

TKO........... Tvornica Koza Osijek [*Osijek Leather Factory*] (YU)

t komm .... Switchboard Telephone (RU)

t kond .... Dew Point (RU)

TKOOS ..... Terek-Kuma Irrigation Canal System (RU)

TKOVM .... Transactions of the Commission for the Permafrost Study (RU)

TKP........... Crystal Field Theory (RU)

TKP........... Takapoto Island [*French Polynesia*] [*Airport symbol*] (OAG)

TKP........... Terenowa Koordynacja Przewozow [*Local Coordination of Transport*] (POL)

TKP........... Toplumcu Kurtulus Partisi [*Communal Liberation Party*] [*Cyprus*] [*Political party*] (EY)

TKP........... Trikresylphosphat [*Tricresyl Phosphate*] [*German*] (EG)

TKP........... Turk Komunist Partisi [*Turkish Communist Party*] [*Illegal*] (TU)

TKPD........ Thermal Efficiency Factor (RU)

TKPK........ Basseterre/Golden Rock [*St. Kitts Island*] [*ICAO location identifier*] (ICLI)

TKP-ML.... People's Revolutionary Union - Marxist-Leninist [*Turkey*] (PD)

TKPN .... Charlestown/Newcastle [*Nevis Island*] [*ICAO location identifier*] (ICLI)

TKPO .... Ryazan' Heavy Forging-and-Pressing Equipment Plant (RU)

TKQ........... Kigoma [*Tanzania*] [*Airport symbol*] (OAG)

Tkr .... Tanskan Kruunu(a) [*Finland*]

TKR .... Telephone Cable Laying Company (RU)

TKR .... Terenowa Komisja Rozjemcza [*Local Arbitration Commission*] (POL)

TKR .... Tons/Kilometers (AF)

Tkrb .... Takribi [*Approximate, Approximately*] (TU)

TKRD .... Turbojet Engine (RU)

t krist .... Crystallization Temperature (RU)

t krit .... Critical Temperature (RU)

TKRP........ Tymczasowy Komitet Rewolucyjny Polski [*Temporary Revolutionary Committee of Poland*] (POL)

TKS .... Tank Firing Course (RU)

TKS........... Technicke Kontrolni Stanoviste [*Technical Control Station*] (CZ)

TKS........... Temperature Coefficient of Resistance (RU)

TKS........... Temperature Resistance Coefficient (BU)

TKS........... Terenowy Klub Sportowy [*Country Sports and Athletics Club*] [*Poland*]

TKS........... Tokushima [*Japan*] [*Airport symbol*] (OAG)

TKS........... Tokyo Kikai Seisakusho [*Japan*]

TKS........... Trgovinska Komora Split [*Chamber of Commerce of the Town of Split*] (YU)

TKS........... Wage Rates and Skills Handbook (RU)

TK/SC .... Tilastokeskus/Statistikcentralen [*Central Statistical Office of Finland*]

TKSC .... Tsukuba Space Center [*NASDA*] [*Japan*] [*Research center*] (ERC)

TKS-IS ...... Turkiye Kamu ve Saglik Adamlari Sendikasi [*Turkish Public and Health Workers Union*] [*Istanbul*] (TU)

TKSNF ..... Three-Valued Conjunctive Perfect Normal Form (RU)

TkT .... Tekniikan Tohtori [*Finland*]

TKT .... Tonnes Kilometriques Transportees

TKTC .... Tovarny Krajek a Tylu [*Lace and Tulle Factories*] (CZ)

TKTC .... Trained Kindergarten Teachers' Certificate [*Australia*]

tk-tsa.......... Heavy Machine-Gun (BU)

TKU .... Tatar Communist University (RU)

TKU .... Tundjangan Kemahalan Umum [*Cost of Living Allowance*] (IN)

TKU .... Turbine and Boiler Set (RU)

TKU .... Turku [*Finland*] [*Airport symbol*] (OAG)

TKV .... Tatakoto [*French Polynesia*] [*Airport symbol*] (OAG)

TKV .... Temperature Coefficient of Viscosity (RU)

TKV .... Turk Kalp Vakfi [*Turkish Heart Fund*] (TU)

TKV .... Turk Kultur Vakfi [*Turkish Cultural Fund*] (TU)

TKV .... Water Boiling Point (RU)

TKVD .... High-Pressure Turbocompressor (RU)

Tkvkiad...... Tankonyvkiado Vallalat [*Textbook Publishing Enterprise*] (HU)

TKVRD...... Turbojet Engine (RU)

TKWP........ Towarzystwo Krzewienia Wiedzy Praktycznej [*Society for the Propagation of Practical Knowledge*] [*Poland*]

TKYe......... Temperature Coefficient of Capacitance (RU)

TKZ .... Short-Circuit Current (RU)

TKZ .... Taganrog Boiler Plant (RU)

TKZ .... Territorial Commission of Mineral Resources (RU)

TKZ .... Turbine and Boiler Plant (RU)

TKZS .... Labor Cooperative Farm (BU)

Tl............... Gewichtsteil [*Part by Weight*] [*German*]

Tl............... Skyport [*Airport symbol*]

Tl............... Talio [*Thallium*] [*Chemical element*] [*Portuguese*]

TL .... Tape Flip-Flop (RU)

TL .... Taxe Locale (FLAF)

TL .... Technische Leitung [*Technical Management*] (EG)

tl .... Teelusikallinen [*Finland*]

tl .... Tega Leta [*Current Year, This Year*] (YU)

Tl .... Teil [*Part*] [*German*]

tl .... Teilweise Loeslich [*Partly Soluble*] [*German*]

tl .... Tekoce Leto [*Current Year, This Year*] (YU)

TL .... Telecommunication Laboratories [*Taiwanese*] [*Research center*] (IRC)

TL .... Tele-Liban [*Television broadcaster*] [*Lebanon*] (MENA)

TL .... Telescope Lens (RU)

TL .... Ten Laaste [*Lastly*] [*Afrikaans*]

TL .... Tentera Laut [*Navy*] (ML)

TL .... Teologian Lisensiaatti [*Finland*]

TL .... Terra Lliure [*Free Land*] [*Spanish terrorist group*]

tl .... Tesla (RU)

TL .... Thai-Luck International Corp. Ltd.

tl .... Title Page (RU)

TL .... Turk Lira [*Turkish Lira*] (TU)

TL .... Turnlehrer [*Gymnastics Instructor*] [*German*]

Tl .... Turun ja Porin Laani [*Finland*]

Tl .... Tyzden Lesov [*Forest Week (A campaign)*] (CZ)

TLA .... Tanzania Library Association

TLA .... Tasmanian Logging Association [*Australia*]

TLA .... Thai Library Association (PDAA)

TLA .... Timber Licence Agreement [*Philippines*]

TLA .... Transkei Legislative Assembly

TLAG........ Tooheys Leaseholders Action Group [*Australia*]

TLB...........	Technische Leistungsbedingungen [*Technical Performance Specifications*] [*German*] (EG)
TLB...........	Technische Lieferbedingungen [*Technical Delivery Terms*] [*German*] (EG)
TLC...........	Tanganyika Legislative Council
TLC...........	Tanganyika Library Services Board
TLC...........	Tanzania Legal Corporation
TLC...........	Tourism and Leisure Corp. [*Australia*]
TLC...........	Truth and Liberation Concern [*Australia*]
TLCACT ...	Trades and Labour Council of the Australian Capital Territory
TLCQ........	Trades and Labour Council of Queensland [*Australia*]
TLCWA.....	Trades and Labour Council of Western Australia
TlD...........	Rear Patrol (BU)
TlD...........	Rear Point (RU)
TLDA	Groupe pour le Triomphe des Libertes Democratiques en Algerie
TLDM	Tentera Laut Di-Raja Malaysia [*Royal Malaysian Navy*] (ML)
TLdP........	Tiskarna Ljudske Pravice [*Ljudska Pravica Printers*] [*Ljubljana*] (YU)
TLE...........	Air Toulouse [*France*] [*ICAO designator*] (FAAC)
Tle...........	Teile [*Parts*] [*German*]
TLE...........	Textes Legislatifs Etrangers [*Benelux*] (BAS)
TLE...........	Tulear [*Madagascar*] [*Airport symbol*] (OAG)
Tlf...........	Telefon [*Telephone*] (TU)
Tlf...........	Telefono [*Telephone*] [*Spanish*]
tlf...........	Telephone (RU)
TLF...........	Telephony (RU)
TLFE	Tasmanian Licensed Fruit Exporters [*Australia*]
TLG	Telegraphy (RU)
TLGITB.....	Tasmanian Local Government Industry Training Board [*Australia*]
TLGP........	Tribal Land Grazing Policy
tlgr...........	Telegraph (RU)
TLH...........	Trefileries et Laminoirs du Havre
TLHS........	Trustul de Lucrari Hidrotehnice Speciale [*Trust for Special Hydrotechnical Projects*] (RO)
TLI...........	Current-Distributing Final Selector (RU)
TLI...........	Ingenjorsforbundet [*Swedish Society of College Engineers*] (EAIO)
TLI...........	Tolitoli [*Indonesia*] [*Airport symbol*] (OAG)
TLI...........	Turkish Language Institute (EAIO)
TLIA........	Turkish Leather Industrialists' Association (EAIO)
TLim AM ..	Towarzystwo Literackie Imienia Adama Mickiewicza [*Adam Mickiewicz Literary Society*] (POL)
TLim M	Towarzystwo Literackie Imienia Mickiewicza [*Mickiewicz Literary Society*] (POL)
TLK...........	Moscow Theater Imeni Lenin Young Communist League (RU)
tlk...........	Taman Lehden Konttoriin [*Finland*]
TLL...........	Tallinn [*Former USSR*] [*Airport symbol*] (OAG)
tll...........	Telastelegging [*Benelux*] (BAS)
TLM	Tilimsen [*Algeria*] [*Airport symbol*] (OAG)
TLMB.......	Tobacco Leaf Marketing Board [*Australia*]
Tln...........	Teilen [*Parts*] [*German*] (GCA)
TLN	Toulon/Hyeres [*France*] [*Airport symbol*] (OAG)
TLO	Tol [*Papua New Guinea*] [*Airport symbol*] (OAG)
TLP...........	Tasmanian Labor Party [*Australia*] (ADA)
TLP...........	Telefonistas de Lisboa e Porto [*Telephone Workers of Lisbon and Porto*] [*Portuguese*] (WER)
TLP...........	Tulip Air [*Netherlands*] [*ICAO designator*] (FAAC)
TLPC........	Castries/Vigie [*St. Lucia*] [*ICAO location identifier*] (ICLI)
TLPL	Vieux-Fort/Hewanorra International [*St. Lucia*] [*ICAO location identifier*] (ICLI)
TLRI	Taiwan Livestock Research Institute [*Research center*] (IRC)
TLRS	Rayon Communications Telephone Line (RU)
TLS...........	Tanzania Library Services
Tls...........	Telsiz [*Radio, Wireless*] (TU)
TLS...........	Tool Lending Service [*Australia*]
TLS...........	Toulouse [*France*] [*Airport symbol*] (OAG)
TLS...........	Trustul de Lucrari Speciale [*Special Projects Trust*] (RO)
TLSB	Trustul de Lucrari Speciale Bucuresti [*Bucharest Trust for Special Projects*] (RO)
TLT...........	Tanzania Labour Tribunal
TLT...........	Turtle Airways Ltd. [*Fiji*] [*ICAO designator*] (FAAC)
TLU	St. Kitts-Nevis Trades and Labour Union
TLU	Tolu [*Colombia*] [*Airport symbol*] (OAG)
TLU	Transvaalse Landbou-Unie [*Transvaal Agricultural Union*] [*Afrikaans*]
tlum...........	Tlumacz [*or Tlumaczenie or Tlumaczyl*] [*Translator or Translation or Translated By*] (POL)
TLV...........	Tel Aviv-Yafo [*Israel*] [*Airport symbol*] (OAG)
TM...........	Antitank Mine (RU)
TM...........	Convoi de Transport de Materiel [*Military*] [*French*] (MTD)
TM...........	Front des Travailleurs [*Workers Front*] [*Malagasy*] (AF)
TM...........	Heat Engine (RU)
TM...........	Meteorological Table (RU)
tm...........	Of the Current Month, In the Current Month (RU)
tm...........	Quarterly (BU)

TM...........	Sea Wind-Turbulence Meter (RU)
TM...........	Standard Machines (RU)
TM...........	Tajekoztatasi Miniszterium/Miniszter [*Ministry/Minister of Information*] (HU)
TM...........	Tausend Mark [*Thousand Marks*] (EG)
TM...........	Taxe Mobiliere [*Benelux*] (BAS)
TM...........	Technology for the Youth (RU)
tm...........	Tego Miesiaca [*That Month*] [*Poland*]
tm...........	Tekoci Mesec [*Current Month*] (YU)
TM...........	Telefonos de Mexico SA [*Mexican Telephone Co.*]
TM...........	Telegramme Multiple [*Telegram with Multiple Addresses*] [*French*] (ROG)
TM...........	Telegraphie Militaire [*Military*] [*French*] (MTD)
TM...........	Terre Malgache [*Tananarive*]
tm...........	Teski Mitraljez [*Heavy Machine Gun*] (YU)
TM...........	Tetragonika Metra [*Square Meters*] (GC)
TM...........	Thames Measurement [*Formula for rating yachts*] [*British*]
TM...........	Thay Mat [*On Behalf Of, In the Name Of, Representing*]
tm...........	This Month (BU)
TM...........	Toelichting-Meijers [*Benelux*] (BAS)
tm...........	Tohoto Mesice [*Of the Present Month*] (CZ)
TM...........	Tone Manipulator (RU)
tm...........	Ton-Meter (RU)
tm...........	Tonnenmeter [*Ton-meter*] [*German*] (GCA)
t/m...........	Tot en Met [*Up to and Including*] [*Publishing*] [*Netherlands*]
TM...........	Tour du Monde [*World Tour*] [*French*] (JA)
t/m...........	Tours par Minute [*Revolutions per Minute*] [*French*]
TM...........	Transformatur Merkezi [*Transformer Center, Transformer Vault*] (TU)
TM...........	Transversalni Magnetski [*Transversal Magnetic*] (YU)
TM...........	Trat Mladeze [*Youth Railroad Track (Built by Youth Brigades)*] (CZ)
TM...........	Travaux Municipaux [*Municipal Projects*] (CL)
tm...........	Trekhondos Minos [*Current Month*] (GC)
TM...........	Tribunal Militaire (FLAF)
Tm...........	Tulio [*Thulium*] [*Chemical element*] [*Portuguese*]
TM...........	Turk Mali [*Made in Turkey*] (TU)
tM...........	Warm Air Mass (RU)
TMA........	Tanzanian Military Academy
TMA........	Thailand Management Association
TMA........	Theatre Managers' Association [*Australia*]
TMA........	Tierra Mar y Aire Ltda. [*Colombia*] (COL)
TMA........	Toyota Manufacturing Australia Ltd.
TMA........	Track Motors Africa Ltd.
TMA........	Tractor and Machinery Association of Australia
TMA........	Trainee Mobility Assistance [*Australia*]
TMA........	Trans Mediterranean Airlines [*Lebanon*] [*ICAO designator*] (FAAC)
TMA........	Trans-Mediterranean Airways (BJA)
TMA........	Trans-Mediterranean Airways SAL [*Beirut, Lebanon*] (ME)
TMA........	Transvaal Municipal Association [*South Africa*] (AA)
TMA........	Tubman Military Academy [*Liberia*]
TMAA	Tractor and Machinery Association of Australia
TMAB	Telecommunications Managers Association - Belgium
TMAG	Tasmanian Museum and Art Gallery [*Australia*]
TMAP.......	Textile Mills Association of the Philippines, Inc. (EY)
TMAS.......	Travel Market and Automation Service [*Australia*]
TMASA.....	Timber Merchants' Association of South Australia
TMAU	Peat-Mineral and Ammonia Fertilizers (RU)
TMAV	Timber Merchants' Association of Victoria [*Australia*]
TMB	Antitank Paper-Cased Mine (RU)
TMB	Tobacco Marketing Board [*Rhodesia*] (DSCA)
TMB	Tour de Mont Blanc [*Tour of Mont Blanc*] [*Walking route around the mountain*] [*Switzerland*]
TMB	Towarzystwo Milosnikow Bydgoszczy [*Society of Friends of Bydgoszcz*] (POL)
TMB	Tudomanyos Minosito Bizottsag [*Committee on Scientific Qualifications*] (HU)
TMC	Tambolaka [*Indonesia*] [*Airport symbol*] (OAG)
TMC	Tanganyika Mennonite Church
TMC	Tata Memorial Center [*India*] (PDAA)
TMC	TeleMonteCarlo [*Private television operation*] [*Italy*]
TMC	Transitional Military Council [*Sudan and Libya*]
TMCA	Toyota Motor Corp. Australia
tmcm	Thousand Million Cubic Metres (OMWE)
TMCN	Traditional Medical Council of Nigeria
TMD	Antitank Wood-Cased Mine (RU)
TMD	Tiskovy Referat Ministerstva Dopravy [*Press Department of the Ministry of Transportation*] (CZ)
TMD	Transmed Airlines [*Egypt*] [*ICAO designator*] (FAAC)
TMD	Turkiye Muharipler Dernegi [*Turkish Fighters Association*] (TU)
TMD	Turk Mukavemetciler Dernegi [*Turkish Cypriot Resistance Fighters Association*] (GC)
TMD-1.......	Protivtenkovska Mina-Drvena [*Wooden Antitank Mine*] (YU)

TMDB .... Teruleti Munkaugyi Dontobizottsag [*Regional Labor Arbitration Committee*] (HU)

TMDB .... Wood Briquette Antitank Mine (RU)

TMDN .... Tausend Mark der Deutschen Notenbank [*Thousand Marks of the German Bank of Issue (Replaced DM as of 1 August 1964)*] (EG)

TME .... Tame [*Colombia*] [*Airport symbol*] (OAG)

TME .... Tudomanyos es Muszaki Egyuttmukodes [*Scientific and Technical Cooperation*] (HU)

tmet .... Topovski Metak [*Gun Shell*] (YU)

TMF .... Technology Marketing Foundation [*South Africa*] (AA)

TMF .... Thiamine Monophosphate (RU)

TMF .... Tiskovy Referat Ministerstva Financi [*Press Department of the Ministry of Finance*] (CZ)

TMF .... Tonfrequenz Multiplex Fernuebertragung [*German*] (ADPT)

TMG .... Temps Moyen de Greenwich [*Greenwich Mean Time*] [*French*]

TMG .... Thermal Magnetic Hysteresis (RU)

TMG .... Tomanggong [*Malaysia*] [*Airport symbol*] (OAG)

TMGT .... Turkiye Milli Genclik Teskilati [*Turkish National Youth Organization*] (TU)

TMH .... Tanahmerah [*Indonesia*] [*Airport symbol*] (OAG)

TMH .... Towarzystwo Milosnikow Historii [*Society of Friends of History*] (POL)

TMHC .... Transcultural Mental Health Centre [*Australia*]

TMHiZ ...... Towarzystwo Milosnikow Historii i Zabytkow [*Society of Friends of History and Historical Relics*] (POL)

TMHiZK ... Towarzystwo Milosnikow Historii i Zabytkow Krakowa [*Society of Friends of the History and Historical Relics of Krakow*] (POL)

TMI .... Tiskovy Referat Ministerstva Informaci [*Press Department of the Ministry of Information*] (CZ)

tmi .... Toiminimi [*Finland*]

TMI .... Tomsk Medical Institute (RU)

TMI .... Transport Medical Institute [*Bulgarian*] [*Research center*] (IRC)

TMI .... Transport Medical Institute [*British Antarctic Territory*] (IRC)

TMI .... Tula Institute of Mechanics (RU)

TMI .... Tumlingtar [*Nepal*] [*Airport symbol*] (OAG)

TMIA .... Tasmanian Music Industry Association [*Australia*]

TMIAC ..... Tasmanian Meat Industry Advisory Council [*Australia*]

tminbr .... Heavy Mortar Artillery Brigade (RU)

tminbr .... Heavy Mortar Brigade (BU)

TMJP .... Towarzystwo Milosnikow Jezyka Polskiego [*Society of Friends of the Polish Language*] (POL)

TMK .... Tarsadalmi Munka Kozpont [*Social Service Center*] (HU)

TMK .... Tervszeru Megelozo Karbantartas [*Preventive Maintenance (Machinery)*] (HU)

TMK .... Toyo Menka Kalsha [*Commercial firm*] [*Japan*]

TMK .... Transactions of the Commission on Mongolia (RU)

TMK .... Turk Maarif Koleji [*Turkish Teachers' College*] [*Turkish Cypriot*] (GC)

tmkh .... Heavy Mortar (BU)

tmkh .... Telemechanics (RU)

TMKh .... Transformer-Oil Supply (RU)

TMKhB ..... Trust of Slaughterhouses and Cold Storage Plants (RU)

TMKKAB ... Tudomanyos es Muszaki Kutatasokat Koordinalo Allando Bizottsaga (KGST) [*Permanent Commission for Coordinating Scientific and Technical Research (CEMA)*] (HU)

TMKKB ..... Tudomanyos es Muszaki Kutatasokat Koordinalo Bizottsag [*Commission for Coordinating Scientific and Technical Research*] (HU)

TMKV .... Turkiye Milli Kultur Vakfi [*Turkish National Cultural Foundation*] (TU)

TML .... Tamale [*Ghana*] [*Airport symbol*] (OAG)

TML .... Transmanche-Link [*Eurotunnel*] (ECON)

TML .... Trinidad Muslim League

TMM .... Tamatave [*Madagascar*] [*Airport symbol*] (OAG)

TMM .... Technikum Mechaniczno-Morskie [*Marine Engineering Technical School*] (POL)

TMM .... Theory of Mechanisms and Machines (RU)

TMM .... Towarzystwo Milosnikow Muzyki [*Association of Music Lovers*] [*Poland*]

TMM .... Transportacion Maritima Mexicana [*Mexico*] (LAA)

TMM-1 ...... Protivtenkovska Mina-Metalna [*Metal Antitank Mine*] (YU)

TMMOB ... Turkiye Mimar ve Muhendisler Odalari Birligi [*Turkish Union of Chambers of Architects and Engineers*] (TU)

TMMOBKMO ... TMMOB [*Turkiye Mimar ve Muhendisler Odalari Birligi*] Kimya Muhendisleri Odasi [*Turkish Chamber of Chemical Engineers*] (EAIO)

TMN .... Tamana [*Kiribati*] [*Airport symbol*] (OAG)

TMN .... Tjumenaviatrans [*Russian Federation*] [*ICAO designator*] (FAAC)

TMNC .... Thai Maritime Navigation Co. Ltd. (DS)

TMNO .... Tiskovy Referat Ministerstva Narodni Obrany [*Press Department of the Ministry of National Defense*] (CZ)

TMO .... Molecular Orbital Theory (RU)

TMO .... Technische Montageabteilung [*Technical Assembly Department*] (EG)

TMO .... Thermomechanical Working (RU)

TMO .... Toprak Mahsulleri Ofisi [*Soil Products Office*] (TU)

TMO .... Tumeremo [*Venezuela*] [*Airport symbol*] (OAG)

TMOA .... Tameion Monimon Odostromaton Athinon [*Athens Permanent Road Pavement Fund*] (GC)

TMOK .... Turkiye Milliyetci Ogretmenler Konfederasyonu [*Confederation of Turkish Nationalist Teachers*] (TU)

TMP .... Device for the Thermomechanical Investigation of Polymers (RU)

TMP .... East Timor [*ANSI three-letter standard code*] (CNC)

TMP .... East Timor [*ISO three-letter standard code*] (CNC)

TMP .... Heavy Bridge Train (RU)

TMP .... Tampere [*Finland*] [*Airport symbol*] (OAG)

TMP .... Tiskovy Referat Ministerstva Prumyslu [*Press Department of the Ministry of Industry*] (CZ)

tmp .... Tuna Merneho Paliva [*Ton of Standard Fuel*] (CZ)

TMP .... Turk Milli Polis [*Turkish National Police*] (TU)

TMPA .... Transocean Marine Paint Association [*Netherlands*] (EAIO)

TMPD .... Turkiye Milli Pediatri Dernegi [*Turkish National Pediatric Association*] (EAIO)

TMPO .... Tiskovy Referat Ministerstva Post [*Press Department of the Ministry of Postal Service*] (CZ)

TMQ .... Thames Air Services & Charter Ltd. [*Nigeria*] [*ICAO designator*] (FAAC)

TMR .... Tamanrasset [*Algeria*] [*Airport symbol*] (OAG)

TMRIEP ... Tokyo Metropolitan Research Institute for Environmental Protection [*Japan*]

TMRP .... Technical School for the Mining and Ore Industry (BU)

TMS .... Sao Tome Island [*Sao Tome Islands*] [*Airport symbol*] (OAG)

TMS .... Societe de Tricotage Mecanique du Senegal

tms .... Tai Muuta Semmoista [*And So On*] [*Finland*] (GPO)

TMS .... Tefari Makonnen School

TMS .... Tetramethyllead (RU)

TMS .... Tezka Mostova Souprava [*Heavy Bridging Section*] (CZ)

TMS .... Tiskovy Referat Ministerstva Spravedlnosti [*Press Department of the Ministry of Justice*] (CZ)

TMS .... Tovarny Mlynskych Stroju [*Flour Mill Machinery Works*] [*Pardubice*] (CZ)

TMS .... Transvaal Medical Society

TMS .... Tvornica Mlinskih Strojeva [*Mill Machinery Factory*] [*Zagreb*] (YU)

TMSA .... Telephone Manufacturers of South Africa

TMSI .... Grinding-Washing and Sorting Installation [*Quarry*] (BU)

TMSI .... Technical School for the Mechanization of Construction Products (BU)

TMSO .... Tiskovy Referat Ministerstva Skolstvi a Osvety [*Press Department of the Ministry of Education and Culture*] (CZ)

TMSP .... Tiskovy Referat Ministerstva Socialni Pece [*Press Department of the Ministry of Social Welfare*] (CZ)

TMSS .... Technical School for Agricultural Mechanization (BU)

TMSZ .... Tiskovy Referat Ministerstva pro Sjednoceni Zakonu [*Press Department of the Ministry for the Unification of Laws*] (CZ)

TMT .... Theoretical Molecular Plate (RU)

TMT .... Tiskovy Referat Ministerstva Techniky [*Press Department of the Ministry of Technology*] (CZ)

TMT .... Travail Mecanique de la Tole SA [*Belgium*]

TMT .... Turk Mukavemet Teskilati [*Turkish Resistance Organization*] [*Cyprus*] (TU)

TMTC .... Taiwan Machinery Trading Co.

TMTE .... Textilipari Muszaki es Tudomanyos Egyesulet [*Technical and Scientific Association of the Textile Industry*] (HU)

TMTF .... Turk Milli Talebe Federasyonu [*Turkish National Student Federation*] (TU)

TMTM .... Tetramethylthiuram Monosulfide (RU)

TMTS .... Trapeza Metokhikou Tameiou Stratou [*Bank of the Army Pensioners Fund*] [*Greek*] (GC)

TMUCB .... Trustul de Montaj Utilaj Chimic Bucuresti [*Bucharest Trust for Chemical Equipment Assembly*] (RO)

TMUD ...... Turkiye Muharipler Dernegi [*Turkish Veterans Association*] (TU)

TMUP .... Trust of Medical Education Visual Aids (RU)

TMV .... Tiskovy Referat Ministerstva Vnitra [*Press Department of the Ministry of Interior*] (CZ)

TMV .... Transvaalse Munisipale Vereniging [*Transvaal Municipal Association*] [*South Africa*] (AA)

TMVO ...... Tiskovy Referat Ministerstva Vnitrniho Obchodu [*Press Department of the Ministry of Domestic Trade*] (CZ)

TMVSZ ..... Tudomanyos Munkasok Vilagszovetsege [*World Federation of Scientific Workers*] (HU)

TMVZ .... Tiskovy Referat Ministerstva Vyzivy [*Press Department of the Ministry of Food Supply*] (CZ)

TMW .... Tamworth [*Australia*] [*Airport symbol*] (OAG)

TMW .... Teatr Mlodego Widza [*Theatre of the Young Spectator*] (POL)

TMX .... Transportacion Aerea Mexicana [*Mexico*] [*ICAO designator*] (FAAC)

TMZ .... Tiskovy Referat Ministerstva Zemedelstvi [*Press Department of the Ministry of Agriculture*]   (CZ)

TMZ .... Tvornica Motora Zagreb [*Motor Works, Zagreb*]   (YU)

TMZD .... Tiskovy Referat Ministerstva Zdravotnictvi [*Press Department of the Ministry of Public Health*]   (CZ)

TMZO .... Tiskovy Referat Ministerstva Zahranicniho Obchodu [*Press Department of the Ministry of Foreign Trade*]   (CZ)

TMZV .... Tiskovy Referat Ministerstva Zahranicnich Veci [*Press Department of the Ministry of Foreign Affairs*]   (CZ)

TN .... Aiming Point   (RU)

tn .... And So Forth   (BU)

TN .... Filament Transformer   (RU)

TN .... Load Transformer   (RU)

TN .... Observation Point   (RU)

tn .... Payload   (RU)

tn .... So-Called   (RU)

tn .... Takanarecen [*So-Called*]   (YU)

TN .... Tanker   (RU)

Tn .... Taren [*Sunken Rock*] [*Norway*]   (NAU)

TN .... Telovychovny Nacelnik [*Senior Physical Education Officer*] (CZ)

TN .... Tennessee   (IDIG)

TN .... Tesouro Nacional [*National Treasury*] [*Portuguese*]

tn .... Tonni(a) [*Finland*]

TN .... Towarzystwo Naukowe [*Scientific Society*] [*Poland*]

TN .... Transfield (NSW) Pty. Ltd. [*Transavia Division*] [*Australia*] [*ICAO aircraft manufacturer identifier*]   (ICAO)

TN .... Trans-Natal Coal Corp. Ltd. [*South Africa*]

TN .... Transport-Netzwerk [*Transport Network*] [*German*]   (ADPT)

TN .... Trento [*Car registration plates*] [*Italian*]

TN .... Tuan [*Sir, Mister*]   (IN)

TN .... Tunisia [*IYRU nationality code*] [*ANSI two-letter standard code*] (CNC)

TN .... Turbocharging   (RU)

TN .... Voltage Transformer   (RU)

TNA .... Jinan [*China*] [*Airport symbol*]   (OAG)

TNA .... Tanavco Airways Ltd. [*Tanzania*] [*ICAO designator*]   (FAAC)

TNA .... Tasmanian Netball Association [*Australia*]

TNA .... Theatre National Algerien [*Algerian National Theatre*]   (AF)

TNA .... Thomas Nelson - Australia [*Publisher*]

TNA .... Turbine-Pump Assembly   (RU)

TNAC .... Turkish News Agency of Cyprus   (EAIO)

t nar .... So-Called   (BU)

TNB .... Technical Norm-Setting Office   (RU)

TNB .... Transnational Bank

TNB .... Turkiye Noterler Birligi [*Turkish Notaries' Union*]   (TU)

TNB .... Wage Rate and Norm-Setting Office   (RU)

TNC .... Tekniska Nomenklaturcentralen [*Swedish Center for Technical Terminology*] [*Information service or system*]   (IID)

TNC .... Timorese National Convergence [*Portugal*]   (EAIO)

TNC .... Trade Negotiations Committee [*Australia*]

TNCA .... Oranjestad/Reina Beatrix, Aruba Island [*Netherlands Antilles*] [*ICAO location identifier*]   (ICLI)

TNCB .... Kralendijk/Flamingo, Bonaire Island [*Netherlands Antilles*] [*ICAO location identifier*]   (ICLI)

TNCC .... Willemstad/Hato, Curacao Island [*Netherlands Antilles*] [*ICAO location identifier*]   (ICLI)

TNCE .... Oranjestad/F. D. Roosevelt, Sint Eustatius Island [*Netherlands Antilles*] [*ICAO location identifier*]   (ICLI)

TNCF .... Curacao [*Netherlands Antilles*] [*ICAO location identifier*]   (ICLI)

tnch .... Low-Frequency Current   (RU)

TNCIAWPRC ... Thai National Committee of the International Association on Water Pollution Research and Control   (EAIO)

TNCIAWPRC ... Turkish National Committee of the International Association on Water Pollution Research and Control   (EAIO)

TNCM .... Philipsburg/Prinses Juliana, Sint Maarten Island [*Netherlands Antilles*] [*ICAO location identifier*]   (ICLI)

TNCS .... Saba/Yrausquin [*Netherlands Antilles*] [*ICAO location identifier*] (ICLI)

TNCV .... Televisao Nacional de Cabo Verde [*National Television of Cape Verde*]   (EY)

TND .... Low-Pressure Turbine   (RU)

TND .... Teachers for Nuclear Disarmament [*Australia*]

TNDC .... Thai National Documentation Center   (IID)

TNDC .... Trade Negotiations among Developing Countries   (IMH)

TNDPKh ... Low-Pressure Ahead Turbine   (RU)

TNDZKh ... Low-Pressure Reverse Turbine   (RU)

TNE .... Tanegashima [*Japan*] [*Airport symbol*]   (OAG)

TNE .... Taxis Aereos del Noroeste SA de CV [*Mexico*] [*ICAO designator*] (FAAC)

TNF .... Trinitrophenol   (RU)

TNG .... Tanger [*Morocco*] [*Airport symbol*]   (OAG)

TNG .... Tangier Airport

TNG .... Territory of New Guinea [*Australia*]

TNI .... Tentara Nasional Indonesia [*Indonesian National Army*]   (IN)

TNI .... Transnational Institute [*Netherlands*]

TNIAU ...... Tentara Nasional Indonesia-Angkatan Udara [*Indonesian Armed Forces/Air Force*]

TNIEI .... Tatar Scientific Research Institute of Economics   (RU)

TNIETI ..... Tbilisi Scientific Research Electrotechnical Institute   (RU)

TNIGEI ..... Tbilisi Water Power Engineering Scientific Research Institute (RU)

TNIGMI .... Tbilisi Scientific Research Hydrometeorological Institute   (RU)

TNIISA ..... Tbilisi Scientific Research Institute of Instrument Making and Automation Equipment   (RU)

TNIISGEI ... Tbilisi Scientific Research Institute of Structures and Water Power Engineering   (RU)

TNIIYaK ... Transactions of the Scientific Research Institute of Language and Culture at the SNK YaASSR   (RU)

TNIIYaLI ... Tuva Scientific Research Institute of Language, Literature, and History   (RU)

TNIIZ .... Turkmen Scientific Research Institute of Agriculture   (RU)

TNIKhFI ... Tbilisi Scientific Research Chemical and Pharmaceutical Institute   (RU)

TNIMA ..... Tubman National Institute of Medical Arts

TNIP .... Transkei National Independence Party [*South Africa*]   (AF)

TNIRO ...... Pacific Ocean Scientific Research Institute of Sea Fisheries and Oceanography   (RU)

TNIS .... Tbilisi Scientific Research Institute of Structures   (RU)

TNISGEI .. Tbilisi Scientific Research Institute of Structures and Water Power Engineering   (RU)

TNJ .... Tanjung Pinang [*Indonesia*] [*Airport symbol*]   (OAG)

TNK .... Small Intestines   (RU)

TNK .... Thymonucleic Acid   (RU)

TNK .... Torah Nebi'im Ketubim [*Teaching, prophets, writing*] [*Pronounced Tanakh*] [*The Hebrew Bible*]

TNK .... Trestni Nalezaci Komise [*Board for the Determination of Criminal Offenses*]   (CZ)

TNKU .... Tentara Nasional Kalimantan Utara [*North Kalimantan National Army*]   (IN)

TN KUL ..... Towarzystwo Naukowe Katolickiego Uniwersytetu Lubelskiego [*Learned Society of Lublin Catholic University*]   (POL)

TNLDVN .. Thanh Nien Lao Dong Viet Nam [*Lao Dong Youth Group*]

TNM .... Initial Point of Maneuver   (RU)

TNM .... Tentera Nasional Malaya [*Malayan National Army*]   (ML)

TNMI .... Tanami [*Botanical region*] [*Australia*]

TNN .... Low-Voltage Current   (RU)

TNN .... Tainan [*Taiwan*] [*Airport symbol*]   (OAG)

TNO .... Nederlandse Centrale Organisatie voor Toegepast Natuurwetenschappelijk Onderzoek [*Netherlands Institute for Applied Scientific Research*]

TNO .... Tamarindo [*Costa Rica*] [*Airport symbol*]   (OAG)

TNO .... Togepost Natuurwetenschappelijk Onderzoek [*Netherlands*]

TNO .... Wage Rate and Norm-Setting Department   (RU)

TNOiK .... Towarzystwo Naukowe Organizacji i Kierownictwa [*Scientific Society of Organization and Administration*]   (POL)

TNP .... [*The*] National Party [*Grenada*] [*Political party*]   (EY)

TNP .... [*The*] New Party [*Australia*] [*Political party*]

TNP .... Tabor Nucenych Praci [*Forced Labor Camp*]   (CZ)

TNP .... Theatre National Populaire [*National People's Theater*] [*French*] (WER)

TNP .... Transkei National Party [*Political party*]   (EY)

TNPA .... Turkish National Pediatric Association   (EAIO)

TNPC .... Taiwan New PC [*Personal Computer*] Consortium [*Computer science*]

TNPP .... Tank in Direct Support of Infantry   (RU)

TNPP .... Transkei National Progressive Party [*South Africa*]   (AF)

TNPWS ..... Tasmania National Parks and Wildlife Service [*Australia*]

TNQ .... Telecasters North Queensland Ltd. [*Australia*]

TNR .... Antananarivo [*Madagascar*] [*Airport symbol*]   (OAG)

TNR .... Initial Point of Turn   (RU)

TNR .... Trinitroresorcinol   (RU)

TNR .... Tuvinian People's Republic [*1921-1944*]   (RU)

TNRP .... Tuvinian People's Revolutionary Party   (RU)

TNRS .... Trinitroresorcinol Lead Complex   (RU)

TNS .... Initial Point of Descent   (RU)

TNS .... Servicios Aereos do Vale Amazonico SA [*Brazil*] [*ICAO designator*]   (FAAC)

TNS .... Tanganyika National Society

TNS .... Tax News Service [*International Bureau of Fiscal Documentation*] [*Benelux*]   (BAS)

TNS .... Transvaal Numismatic Society [*South Africa*]   (AA)

TNSW .... Towarzystwo Nauczycieli Szkol Wyzszych [*Society of University and College Teachers*]   (POL)

TNT .... Tapes 'n' Texts [*Australia*]

TNT .... Terror Against Terror [*Israeli clandestine organization*]

TNT .... Thomas Nationwide Transport Ltd. [*Australia*]   (FEA)

Tnt .... Torrent [*Torrent*] [*Military map abbreviation World War I*] [*French*]   (MTD)

TNT .... Towarzystwo Naukowe w Toruniu [*Torun Learned Society*] (POL)
TNT .... Transnational Terrorism (ADA)
TNT .... Treasury Northern Territory [*Australia*]
TNTB .... Tanzania National Tourist Board
TNTII .... Tsentur za Naouchno-Technicheska i Ikonomicheska Infomatsiya [*Center for Scientific Technical, and Economic Information*] [*Bulgaria*] (EAIO)
TNTM .... Movement for Youth Technical and Scientific Creativity (BU)
TNV .... Tecnavia [*France*] [*ICAO designator*] (FAAC)
TNV .... Transvaalse Numismatiese Vereniging [*Transvaal Numismatic Society*] [*South Africa*] (AA)
TNV .... Tripura National Volunteers [*India*]
TNW .... Towarzystwo Naukowe Warszawskie [*Warsaw Learned Society*] (POL)
TNwT .... Towarzystwo Naukowe w Toruniu [*Torun Learned Society*] (POL)
TNXPCMCN ... Thanh Nien Xung Phong Chong My Cuu Nuoc [*"Resist America for National Salvation" Assault Youth*]
TNZ .... Initial Point of Deployment [*Aviation*] (BU)
TNZ .... Rex Aviation (New Zealand) Ltd. [*ICAO designator*] (FAAC)
to .... Fine Purification [*Of gases*] (RU)
TO .... Fire Plan [*Artillery*] (RU)
TO .... Heat Treatment (RU)
TO .... Precision Reading (RU)
TO .... Rear Detachment, Rear Guard (RU)
to .... So, In This Way (RU)
T-O .... Tablilla de Ocho [*Race of maize*] [*Mexico*]
TO .... Tank Detachment (RU)
TO .... Technical Automobile Service (RU)
TO .... Technical Department (RU)
TO .... Technical Description (RU)
TO .... Teenoor [*As Against*] [*Afrikaans*]
TO .... Tehnicka Oprema [*Technical Equipment*] [*Military*] (YU)
TO .... Tehnicki Odbor [*Technical Committee*] (YU)
TO .... Telegramme Ordinaire [*Military*] [*French*] (MTD)
t/o .... Telegraph Office (RU)
to .... Tizedes Osztalyozas [*Decimal Classification (Dewey)*] (HU)
TO .... Toescheidingsovereenkomst [*Benelux*] (BAS)
To .... Tohtori [*Finland*]
to .... Tomo [*Tome*] [*Spanish*]
TO .... Tonga [*ANSI two-letter standard code*] (CNC)
to .... Tonna [*Ton*] (HU)
TO .... Torino [*Car registration plates*] [*Italian*]
TO .... Torpedo, Tvornica Motora [*The "Torpedo" Motor Factory*] [*Rijeka*] (YU)
to .... Torstai(na) [*Finland*]
TO .... Transport Detachment (RU)
TO .... Transport Section, Transportation Department (RU)
TO .... Transvaalse Onderwijsersunie (RU)
TO .... Transvaalse Onderwysersvereniging
TO .... Type d'Operation [*French*] (ADPT)
TO-1 .... Technical Automotive Service Number 1 (BU)
TOA .... Tameion Oikonomikis Anaptyxeos [*Economic Development Fund*] [*Greek*] (GC)
TOA .... Telecommunications Officers' Association [*Australia*]
TOA .... Tubemakers of Australia Ltd. [*Commercial firm*]
TOAA .... Trawler Owners' Association of Australia
TOAME .... Transactions of the Antiquity Department of the State Ermitage Museum (RU)
TOB .... Tarcakozi Operative Bizottsag [*Interministerial Operating Committee*] (HU)
TOB .... Tobruk [*Libya*] [*Airport symbol*] (OAG)
TOB .... Turkiye Ogretmenler Bankasi [*Turkish Teachers' Bank*] (TU)
TOB .... Turkiye Ticaret Odalari, Sanayi Odalari, ve Ticaret Borsalari Birligi [*Turkish Union of Chambers of Commerce, Industry, and Stock Exchanges*] [*TSBB*] [*See also*] (TU)
TOBANK .. Turkiye Ogretmenler Bankasi [*Turkish Teachers' Bank*] [*TOB*] [*See also*] (TU)
TOBB .... Turkiye Odalar ve Borsalar Birligi [*Union of Chambers of Commerce, Industry, and Maritime Commerce and Commodity Exchanges of Turkey*] (EAIO)
TOBD .... Turkiye Ogretmenler Birligi Dernegi [*Turkish Teachers' Unions Organization*]
TOBDD ..... Tum Ogretmenler Birlesme ve Dayanisma Dernegi [*Pan-Teachers' Unity and Mutual Solidarity Association*] (TU)
TOB-DER ... Turkiye Ogretmenler Birlesme ve Dayanisma Dernegi [*Turkish Teachers' Unity and Solidarity Organization*] (TU)
TOBETON ... Societe Togolaise de Beton
t obr .... So, In This Way (RU)
TOC .... Tanzania Olympic Committee
TOC .... Tasmanian Olympic Council [*Australia*]
TOC .... Tiers Ordre Carmelitaine [*Carmelite Third Order*] [*An association*] [*Italy*] (EAIO)
TOC .... Trans Ocean Containers Ltd.
TOC .... Turkiye Ormancilar Cemiyeti [*Turkish Foresters' Society*] (TU)

TOCCA ..... TAFE [*Technical and Further Education*] Off-Campus Co-Ordinating Authority [*Australia*]
Toch .... Tocharian [*Language group*] (BARN)
Tochelektropribor ... Precision Electrical Instruments Plant (RU)
Tochizmeritel' ... Precision Measuring Instrument Plant (RU)
Tochmekh ... State Trust of Precision Mechanics (RU)
Tochpribor ... Precision Instrument Plant (RU)
TOCOM .... Tokyo Commodity Exchange for Industry [*Japan*] (ECON)
ToD .... Technicko-Obchodni Dotazy [*Technical and Business Inquiries*] (CZ)
TOD .... Tioman [*Malaysia*] [*Airport symbol*] (OAG)
TOD .... Transvaalse Onderwysdepartement [*Afrikaans*]
TOD .... Tum Ogretim Uyeleri Dernegi [*Comprehensive Teaching Members (Higher Educational Level) Organization*] (TU)
TODAIE.... Turkiye ve Orta Dogu Amne Idaresi Enstitusu [*Turkey and Middle East Public Administration Institute*] [*Under Middle East Technological University*] (TU)
TODELAR ... Tobon de la Roche, Jaime [*Colombia*] (COL)
TODIREP ... Societe Togolaise de Diffusion et de Representation
TODMF .... Turkiye Ogretmen Dernekleri Milli Federasyonu [*National Federation of Turkish Teachers Organizations*] (TU)
TODRL ..... Transactions of the Department of Old Russian Literature (RU)
TOE .... Heat-Releasing Elements [*Nuclear energy*] (BU)
toe............. Tonnes Oil Equivalent (OMWE)
TOE .... Tozeur [*Tunisia*] [*Airport symbol*] (OAG)
TOE .... Tubular Collecting Electrode (RU)
TOE .... Turk Otomobile Endustri [*Turkish Automobile Industry*] (TU)
ToeF .... Transportoekonomisk Forening [*Denmark*] (SLS)
toegel........ Toegelicht [*Explained*] [*Netherlands*]
toegev .... Toegevoegd Bij [*Benelux*] (BAS)
TOEI......... Tokyo Eiga [*Tokyo Motion Picture*]
toej .... Toejuiging [*Applause*] [*Afrikaans*]
toel .... Toelichting [*Explanation*] [*Netherlands*]
TOEV .... Topikos Organismos Engeion Veltioseon [*Local Organization for Land Reclamation*] [*Greek*] (GC)
TOF .... Fleet Technical Division (RU)
TOF .... Pacific Ocean Fleet (RU)
TOFAS ..... Turk Otomobile Fabrikasi Anonim Sirketi [*Turkish Automobile Factory Corporation*] (TU)
TOG.......... Transportordnung fuer Gefaehrliche Gueter [*Transport Regulation for Hazardous Goods*] (EG)
TOGA........ Tropical Oceans and Global Atmosphere [*Program*] [*UNESCO*] [*Australia*] (PDAA)
TOGOBUND ... Bund der Deutschen Togolaender
TOGOFRUIT ... Societe Nationale de Developpement de la Culture Fruitiere [*Togo*]
TOGOGAZ ... Societe Togolaise des Gaz Industriels
TOGOGRAIN ... Office National des Produits Vivriers [*Food marketing board*] [*Togo*]
TOGO-KAIK ... Societe Togolaise pour l'Industrie de la Chaux
TOGOPROM ... Societe Togolaise de Promotion Immobiliere
TOGOTEX ... Compagnie Togolaise des Textiles [*Textile company*] [*Togo*]
TOGOTEX ... Societe Togolaise de Textiles [*Togo*]
TOGTO ..... Turkiye Ogrenci ve Genclik Turizm Orgutu [*Turkish Student and Youth Tourism Organization*] (TU)
toht............ Tohtori [*Finland*]
TOI .... Total Ocean Indien
TOI .... Transportokonomisk Institutt [*Transport Economics Institute*] [*Research center*] [*Norway*] (ERC)
toim .... Toimittaja [*Finland*]
toim .... Toimittanut [*Finland*]
TOJ........... Telecommunications of Jamaica [*Commercial firm*] (ECON)
TOK.......... Torokina [*Papua New Guinea*] [*Airport symbol*] (OAG)
TOK.......... Trestni Odvolaci Komise [*Criminal Appeals Board*] (CZ)
TOK.......... Tuerk Otomatik Kontrol Kurumu [*Istanbul, Turkey*] (SLS)
TOK.......... Turystyczna Odznaka Kajakowa [*Canoe-Touring Badge*] (POL)
TOKAMAK ... High-Current Magnetic Vacuum Chamber [*Russian*] (PDAA)
Tokko......... Tokubetsu Koto Kaisatsu [*Special High Police Bureau*] [*TKK*] [*See also*] [*Japan*]
TOKO........ Tovarna Kovckov in Usnjenih Izdelkov [*Luggage and Leather Products Factory*] [*Domzale*] (YU)
TOKTEN... Transfer of Know-How Through Expatriate Nationals [*Council of Scientific and Industrial Research*] [*India*]
tol .... Roofing Paper Factory [*Topography*] (RU)
TOL .... Tanzania Oxygen Limited
TOL .... Turk Ocagi Ligi [*Turkish Club (Hearth) League*] (TU)
TOLES-IVOIRE ... Societe de Galvanisation de Toles en Cote-D'Ivoire
TOLEYIS ... Turkiye Otel, Lokanta ve Eglence Yerleri Isci Sendikalari Federasyonu [*National Federation of Hotel, Restaurant, and Amusement Places Workers' Unions*] [*Turkey*]
TOLEYIS ... Turkiye Otel, Lokanta, ve Eglence Yerleri Isci Sendikasi [*Turkish Hotel, Restaurant, and Amusement Place Workers Union*] [*OLEYIS*] [*See also*] (TU)
TOLIMO... Togoland Liberation Movement (AF)
tolshch ...... Thickness (RU)

TOM......... Tagma Oreinon Metaforon [*Mountain Transport Battalion*] [*Greek*]   (GC)

TOM......... Technischorganisatorische Massnahmen [*Technical-Organizational Measures*]   (EG)

TOM......... Territoires d'Outre-Mer [*Overseas Territories*] [*EEC*]   (FLAF)

TOM......... Terz'Ordine dei Minimi [*Third Order of Minimi*] [*Italy*]   (EAIO)

tom .... Till Och Med [*Even*] [*Sweden*]   (GPO)

tom .... Tomaison [*Volume Numbering*] [*Publishing*] [*French*]

TOM......... Tombouctou [*Mali*] [*Airport symbol*]   (OAG)

tom .... Tome [*Book*] [*French*]

tom .... Tomo [*Tome, Volume*] [*Spanish*]

Tom............ Tomo [*Tome, Volume*] [*Italian*]

TOM......... Tomsk Railroad   (RU)

tomat .... Tomato Cannery [*Topography*]   (RU)

Tomb......... Tombe [*or Tombeau*] [*Grave Military map abbreviation World War I*] [*French*]   (MTD)

TOMI .... Tiskovy Odbor Ministerstva Informaci [*Press Department of the Ministry of Information*]   (CZ)

TOMILENCO ... Togoland Mill and Engineering Co. Inc.

TomNIIVS ... Tomsk Scientific Research Institute of Vaccines and Serums   (RU)

TOMP .... All-Union Trust of the Optical Instrument Industry   (RU)

TOM-Plan ... Plan der Technischorganisatorischen Massnahmen [*Plan for Technical-Organizational Measures*]   (EG)

TOMS .... Turkiye Orman Memurlari Sendikasi [*Turkish Forestry Officials Union*]   (TU)

TO-MSv .... Technicky Odbor Ministerstva Stavebnictvi [*Technical Department of the Ministry of Construction*]   (CZ)

TON.......... Aero Tonala [*Mexico*] [*ICAO designator*]   (FAAC)

TON.......... Peleton [*Platoon*]   (IN)

ton .... Toneis [*Portuguese*]

ton .... Tonel [*Tun*] [*Portuguese*]

ton .... Tonelate [*Albanian*]

TON.......... Tonga [*ANSI three-letter standard code*]   (CNC)

ton .... Tonico [*Tonic*] [*Portuguese*]

TONAK..... Tovarny na Klobouky [*Hat Factories*]   (CZ)

TONGE..... Transactions of the Numismatics Department of the State Ermitage Museum   (RU)

TONS .... Tikhookeanskaya Okeanograficheskaya Nauchnaya Stantsiya [*Pacific Ocean Oceanographic Scientific Station*] [*Russian*]   (MSC)

TOnZ........ Towarzystwo Opieki nad Zwierzetami [*Society for the Prevention of Cruelty to Animals*]   (POL)

TOO .... Technicko-Organisacni Opatreni [*Technical and Organizational Measures*]   (CZ)

TOOL........ Toolangi [*Australia*] [*Geomagnetic observatory code*]

TOOL........ Teams of Our Lady [*See also END*]   (EAIO)

TOOL........ Technische Ontwikkeling Ontwikkelingslanden [*Netherlands*]

TOOL........ Teknillisten Oppilaitosten Opettajainliitto [*Finland*]   (SLS)

TOOL........ Tool Foundation [*Netherlands*]   (EAIO)

TOP .... Aero Top SRL Societa [*Italy*] [*ICAO designator*]   (FAAC)

top .... Fuel   (RU)

TOP .... Terminal Ordoprocesseur Procedure [*French*]   (ADPT)

TOP .... Tertiary Orientation Program [*Australia*]

Top............. Topcu [*Artillery*]

TOP .... Toplumcu Ozgurluk Partisi [*Socialist Freedom Party*] [*Established spring 1975 Cyprus*]   (TU)

top .... Topografico [*Topographic*] [*Italian*]

top .... Topographisch [*Topographic*] [*German*]   (GCA)

top .... Topography   (RU)

top .... Toponimo [*Toponymy*] [*Portuguese*]

TOP .... Training Officer Program [*Australia*]

TOP .... Transports Omer Pressegue

TOP .... Tribunal del Orden Publico [*Court of Public Order*] [*Spanish*]   (WER)

TOP .... Tunisskie Obshchestva Popecheniia

TOP .... Tvornica Olovnih Proizvoda [*Lead Products Factory*] [*Zagreb*]   (YU)

TOP .... Twifu Oil Plantation [*West Africa*]

topbatr....... Topographic Battery [*Military term*]   (RU)

TOPCIM-IS ... Turkiye Toprak Porselen ve Cimento Sanayi Iscileri Sendikasi [*Turkish Earthenware, Porcelain, and Cement Industry Workers' Union*]   (TU)

Topco .... Texaco Overseas Petroleum Company   (OMWE)

TOPICS..... Total On-Line Program and Information Control System [*Japan*]

TOPIX....... Tokyo Stock Price Index [*Japan*]   (ECON)

TOPL........ Terenowa Obrona Przeciwlotnicza [*Local Anti-Aircraft Defense*]   (POL)

Toplomontazh ... Installation of Heating Equipment   (BU)

Topo .... Topografic [*Topographic*]   (TU)

TOPO........ Topograficka Sluzba [*Topographic Service*]   (CZ)

Topogr....... Topografia [*Topography*] [*Portuguese*]

topogr........ Topografico [*Topographic*] [*Italian*]

topotd........ Topographic Department, Topographic Section   (RU)

topprom..... Fuel Industry   (RU)

TOPRAKSU ... Toprak Muhafaza ve Zirai Sulama Isleri Genel Mudurlugu [*Soil Conservation and Agricultural Irrigation Affairs Directorate General*]   (TU)

TOPRAS ... Toprak Pazarlama Sirketi [*Land (Real Estate) Marketing Corporation*]   (TU)

TOPS........ Tovarna Pisalnih Strojev [*Typewriter Factory*]   (YU)

TOPSUKOYTAR IS ... Toprak, Su, Koy, Tarim, ve Arastirma Iscileri Sendikasi [*Soil, Water, Village, Agriculture, and Research Workers Union*]   (TU)

tor.............. Heavy Gun   (BU)

TOR.......... Sektor [*Sector*]   (IN)

TOR.......... Techniczna Obsluga Rolnictwa [*Engineering Service for Agriculture*]   (POL)

tor.............. Torok [*Turkish*]   (HU)

TOR.......... Tor-Steel Research Foundation in India

TOR.......... Towarzystwo Osiedli Robotniczych [*Workers' Settlements Society*]   (POL)

TORC .... Thai Oil Refinery Co. Ltd.   (DS)

TORCO ..... Thai Oil Refinery Co. Ltd.

TOREYIS ... Turkiye Otel, Restaurant, ve Eglence Yerleri Iscileri Sendikasi [*Hotel, restaurant, and entertainment employees union*] [*Turkey*]   (MENA)

torf............. Peat   (RU)

Torfrabsnab ... Moscow Oblast Office for the Peat Industry Workers' Supply   (RU)

torg............. Trade   (RU)

torg-fin ...... Trade and Finance   (RU)

Torgizdat... State Publishing House of Literature on Trade   (RU)

Torgposredkontora ... Republic Trade Exchange Office   (RU)

Torgsin...... All-Union Association for the Trade with Foreigners   (RU)

torguch...... School of Commercial Apprenticeship   (RU)

TOR-IS...... Turistik Otel Restoran Iscileri Sendikasi [*Touristic Hotel and Restaurant Workers Union*] [*Izmir*]   (TU)

torm.......... Torszormester [*Staff Sergeant*]   (HU)

Torp .... Torpedeiro [*Torpedo Boat*] [*Portuguese*]

Tors.......... Torsion [*German*]   (GCA)

TORSAN... Trakya Orman Urunleri Sanayi ve Ticaret AS [*Thrace Forest Products Industry and Trade Corp.*]   (TU)

TOS .... Current-Limiting Resistor   (RU)

TOS .... Techniczna Obrobka Szkla [*Heat Processing of Glass*]   (POL)

TOS .... Techniczna Obsluga Samochodow [*Automobile Technical Service*]   (POL)

TOS .... Terenowy Oddzial Samoobrony [*Local Civil Defense Unit*]   (POL)

TOS .... Three-Phase Deflecting System   (RU)

TOS .... Tovarny na Obrabeci Stroje [*Machine Tool Factories*]   (CZ)

TOS .... Towarzystwo Observatorow Slonca [*Solar Observers Society*] [*Poland*]   (EAIO)

TOS .... Tromso [*Norway*] [*Airport symbol*]   (OAG)

TOS .... Tropical Air Services [*Belize*] [*ICAO designator*]   (FAAC)

TOS .... Turkiye Ogretmenler Sendikasi [*Turkish Teachers' Union*]   (TU)

TOS .... Turkiye Otomotive Sanayii [*Turkish Automotive Industry*] [*TOE*] [*See also*]   (TU)

TOS .... Tvornica Optickog Stakla [*Optical Glass Factory*] [*Zagreb*]   (YU)

TOSA .... Theatre Organ Society of Australia

TOSD .... Third Order of Saint Dominic [*Rome, Italy*]   (EAIO)

TOSHIBA ... Tokyo Shibaura Electric Co. [*Computer manufacturer*] [*Japan*]

TOSLEY-IS ... Ege Bolgesi Turistik Otel Sinema Lokanta, Eglence Yerleri Iscileri Sendikasi [*Aegean Region Touristic, Hotel, Cinema, Restaurant and Amusement Places Workers' Union*] [*Izmir*]   (TU)

TOst.......... Stop Trigger [*Computers*]   (RU)

TOST........ Turkiye Ogretmenler Sendikasi Tiyatrosu [*Turkish Teachers Union Theatre*]   (TU)

TOSTA...... Tovarny Stavkoveho Zbozi [*Hosiery Mills*]   (CZ)

TOSWL..... Techniczna Oficerska Szkola Wojsk Lotniczych [*Air Force Officers Technical School*] [*Olesnica*]   (POL)

TOT .... Telephone Organization of Thailand   (IMH)

TOT .... Termeloszovetkezetek Orszagos Tanacsa [*National Council of Producer Cooperatives*] [*Budapest, Hungary*]   (HU)

TOT .... Texaco Overseas Tankerships

TOT .... Three-Winding Transformer   (RU)

tot .... Total [*German*]   (GCA)

tot .... Totale [*Total*] [*Knitting*] [*French*]

TOT .... Tourist Organization of Thailand   (DS)

TOTD .... Turk Ortopedi ve Travmatoloji Dernegi [*Turkish Association of Orthopaedics and Traumatology*]   (EAIO)

TOTI........ Torzstiszt [*Staff Officer*]   (HU)

TOTIP....... Totalizzatore Ippico [*Company controlling totalizators on racecourses*] [*Italian*]

Totp........... Totpunkt [*Dead Center*] [*German*]   (GCA)

TOTP........ Transactions of the Department of Commercial Ports   (RU)

TOTRA .... Tovarna Trakov [*Ribbon Factory*] [*Ljubljana*]   (YU)

t otv .... Temperature of Solidification   (RU)

tot W .... Toter Winkel [*Blind Angle*] [*German*]   (GCA)

TOU.......... Touho [*New Caledonia*] [*Airport symbol*]   (OAG)

Tou .... Toulon [*France*]   (BARN)
TOURAC .. Association Internationale Auxiliaire des Touring Clubs de l'Afrique Centrale
TOURDYK ... Tourkiki Dynamis Kyprou [*Turkish Forces in Cyprus*]   (GC)
TOURISMAD ... Societe Hoteliere et Touristique de Madagascar
tov .... Comrade   (RU)
tov .... Freight [*Train*]   (RU)
TOV .... Technischer Oberwachungsverein, eV [*Nuclear energy*]   (NRCH)
tov .... Ten Opsigte Van [*With Regard To*] [*Afrikaans*]
TOVALL ... TSZ Onallo Epito es Szereloipari Vallalkozasok [*Producer Cooperative Independent Construction and Assembling Enterprises*]   (HU)
TOVChK ... Transportation Department of the All-Russian Extraordinary Commission for Combating Counterrevolution and Sabotage   (RU)
To (Vd VhDer) ... Ten Opzichte (Van De; Van Het; Der) [*Benelux*]   (BAS)
TOVE .... Transactions of the Oriental Department of the State Ermitage Museum   (RU)
TOVENCA ... Topflight de Venezuela, Compania Anonima
tov st .... Freight Station [*Topography*]   (RU)
TOVU .... Technicko-Organisacni Vyzkumny Ustav [*Technical and Organizational Research Institute*]   (CZ)
TOVUS ..... Technicko-Organisacni Vyzkumny Ustav Strojirensky [*Technical and Organizational Research Institute on Machine Building*]   (CZ)
tow .... Towarzystwo [*Society, Company*]   (POL)
tow .... Towarzysz [*Comrade*]   (POL)
tox .... Toxisch [*Toxic*] [*German*]   (GCA)
TOXBACK ... TOXLINE [*Toxicology On-Line*] Back-File [*Information retrieval*]
TOYOCOM ... Toyo Communication Equipment Company Ltd. [*Tokyo, Japan*] [*Research center*]   (ERC)
TOZ .... Association for Joint Cultivation of Land   (RU)
TOZ .... Technischoekonomische Zielstellungen [*Technical-Economic Goals*]   (EG)
TOZ .... Touba [*Ivory Coast*] [*Airport symbol*]   (OAG)
TOZ .... Towarzystwo Ochrony Zdrowia [*Society of Health Protection*]   (POL)
TOZ .... Towarzystwo Opieki nad Zwierzetami [*Society for the Prevention of Cruelty to Animals*] [*Poland*]
TOZ .... Tula Arms Plant   (RU)
TOZ .... Tyrsuv Odznak Zdatnosti [*Tyrs Physical Fitness Medal*]   (CZ)
TP .... Aiming Point   (RU)
tp .... (And) So On, (And) So Forth   (RU)
TP .... Calibration Furnace   (RU)
TP .... Commercial Port   (RU)
TP .... Current-Supplying Spring   (RU)
TP .... East Timor [*ANSI two-letter standard code*]   (CNC)
TP .... East Timor [*ISO two-letter standard code*]   (CNC)
TP .... Freight Train   (RU)
TP .... Heat Flow   (RU)
TP .... Pneumatic Conveyor   (RU)
TP .... Point of Fall   (RU)
TP .... Point of Impact   (RU)
TP .... Safety Brake   (RU)
T-P .... Tabloncillo Perla [*Race of maize*] [*Mexico*]
TP .... Tank Gun   (RU)
tp .... Tank Regiment   (BU)
TP .... Tank Support   (RU)
tp .... Target Petroleum NL [*Australia*]
TP .... Tasmanian Police [*Australia*]
TP .... Taxe Percu   (FLAF)
TP .... Technical Inspection   (BU)
TP .... Technical Paper
TP .... Technical Regulations   (RU)
TP .... Technicke Podminky [*Technical Requirements*]   (CZ)
TP .... Technische Planung [*Technical Planning Office*]   (EG)
TP .... Telegraph and Post   (BU)
TP .... Telephone Out of Order   (BU)
TP .... Telephone Tapping [*Military term*]   (RU)
Tp .... Tempiranje [*Fuse Setting*] [*Artillery*]   (YU)
Tp .... Tepe [*Peak*] [*of a mountain or hill*]   (TU)
TP .... Terre de Protection [*French*]   (ADPT)
TP .... Territorial Party [*Northern Marianas*]   (PPW)
TP .... Terza Posizione [*Third Position*] [*Italy*]
TP .... Testprogramm [*German*]   (ADPT)
TP .... Thahan Phran [*Hunter Soldiers*] [*Thailand*]
TP .... Theodolite Point   (RU)
Tp .... Thermal [*Nuclear physics and engineering*]   (RU)
TP .... Thomson Press (India) Ltd. [*Publisher*]
TP .... Tiefpass-Filter [*German*]   (ADPT)
tp .... Timbre-Poste [*Postage Stamp*] [*French*]
TP .... Times Publishing [*Singapore Press Holding*]
TP .... Timpano [*Music*]
TP .... Tir de Place [*Military*] [*French*]   (MTD)
TP .... Topografska Planseta [*Map Board*]   (YU)

tp .... Tout Paye [*All Expenses Paid*] [*French*]
TP .... Trade Enterprise   (BU)
TP .... Trajno Prisutni [*Permanently Present*] [*Census*]   (YU)
TP .... Transformer Substation   (RU)
Tp .... Transport [*German*]   (GCA)
TP .... Transportno Preduzece [*Transportation Establishment*] [*Railroads*]   (YU)
TP .... Trapani [*Car registration plates*] [*Italian*]
TP .... Trapeza Pisteos [*Credit Bank*] [*Greek*]   (GC)
TP .... Travaux Preparatoires   (FLAF)
TP .... Travaux Publics [*Public Works*] [*French*]   (WER)
TP .... Trgovinsko Poduzece [*Commercial Establishment*]   (YU)
TP .... Triangular Prism   (RU)
TP .... Tribunal de Police   (FLAF)
TP .... Trichlorophenoxypropionic Acid   (RU)
Tp .... Triebwagenzug [*Rail Motor Car Train*]   (EG)
TP .... Trigonometric Point   (RU)
TP .... Trigonometrischer Punkt [*Triangulation Point*] [*German*]   (GCA)
TP .... Trihedral Prism   (RU)
TP .... Trust Podniku [*Trust of Enterprises*]   (CZ)
TP .... Turkiye Petrolleri [*Turkish Petroleum*]   (TU)
tp .... Tutta Pelle [*Full Leather*] [*Publishing*] [*Italian*]
TP .... Warm Period   (RU)
TPA .... Heavy Gun Artillery   (RU)
TPA .... Tarolt Program Adatfeldolgozo (Rendszer) [*Stored Program Data Processing (System)*]   (HU)
TPA .... Televisao Popular de Angola
TPA .... Togo Pflanzungs-Aktien-Gesellschaft
TPA .... Trade Practices Act [*Australia*]   (ADA)
TPA .... Transportes Aereos Mercantiles Panamericanos [*Colombia*] [*ICAO designator*]   (FAAC)
TPA .... Transports Populaires Blideens [*Algeria*]
TPA .... Transvaalse Provinsiale Administrasie [*Transvaal Provincial Administration*] [*South Africa*]   (AA)
TPA .... Tutmonda Parolspuro-Asocio [*Universal Association for Speech Tracing - UAST*]   (EAIO)
TPAA .... Timber Preservers' Association of Australia
TPAEN ..... Tameion Prostasias Axiomatikon Emborikou Navtikou [*Merchant Marine Officers Protection Fund*] [*Greek*]   (GC)
TPAO .... Turkiye Petrol Anonim Ortaklari [*Turkish Petroleum Corporation*]   (TU)
TPAWA ..... Tennis Professionals Association of Western Australia
tpb .... Pipeline Battalion   (BU)
TPB .... Tractor and Field Cropping Brigade   (RU)
TPB .... Tudomanypolitikai Bizottsag [*Committee on Science Policy*]   (HU)
tpbr .... Pipeline Brigade   (BU)
TPC .... Air Caledonie [*France*] [*ICAO designator*]   (FAAC)
TPC .... Tanganyika Planting Company
TPC .... Territorial Production Complex [*Russian*]
TPC .... Thai Packaging Center   (IRC)
TPC .... Thai Plastic & Chemical Co. Ltd.
TPC .... Timber Promotion Council [*Victoria, Australia*]
TPC .... Tournament Players Championship [*Australia*]
TPC .... Trade Practices Commission [*Australia*]
TPC .... Trade Promotion Centre [*Nepal*]   (GEA)
TPC .... Transports Provost & Compagnie
TPC .... Turkish Petroleum Company   (OMWE)
TPCD .... Turk Plastik Cerrahi Dernegi [*Turkish Society of Plastic Surgeons*]   (EAIO)
TPCh .... Commercial Frequency Current   (RU)
TPD .... TAFE (Technical and Further Education) and People with Disabilities [*Australia*]
TPD .... Tameion Parakatathikon kai Daneion [*Savings and Loan Fund*] [*Greek*]   (GC)
TPD .... Tameion Pronoias Dikigoron [*Lawyers Welfare Fund*] [*Greek*]   (GC)
TPD .... Technisch Physische Dienst [*Institute of Applied Physics*] [*Netherlands Central Organization for Applied Natural Scientific Research*]   (WED)
TPD .... Towarzystwo Przyjaciol Dzieci [*Society of the Friends of Children*]   (POL)
TPD .... Tribunal Populaire de District [*District People's Court*] [*Benin*]   (AF)
TPD .... Turkiye Proleter Devrimcileri [*Turkish Proletarian Revolutionaries*]   (TU)
TPDC .... Tanzania Petroleum Development Corporation
TPDC .... Textile Procurement and Distribution Centre [*New Zealand*]
TPDF .... Tanzania People's Defense Forces   (AF)
TPDSA ...... Totally and Permanently Disabled Soldiers' Association [*Australia*]
TPDU .... Technology Planning and Development Unit [*University of Ife*] [*Nigeria*]
TPDY .... Tameion Pronoias Dimosion Ypallilon [*Civil Servants Welfare Fund*] [*Greek*]   (GC)

TPE............ Heavy Industry and Electrification   (BU)
TPE............ Taipei [*Taiwan*] [*Airport symbol*]   (OAG)
TPE............ Thai Polyethylene Co.
TPE............ Travaux Publics de l'Etat [*State Public Works*] [*Tunisia*]   (AF)
TPEAbteilung ... Typhus, Paratyphus, und Enteritis Abteilung [*Typhus, Paratyphus, and Enteritis Department*]   (EG)
TPEC........ Timber Producers and Exporters of Cameroon   (EAIO)
TPEK........ Aeroporiki Etaireia Notiou Afrikis [*South African Air Line*]   (GC)
TPEN........ Tameion Pronoias Emborikou Navtikou [*Merchant Marine Welfare Fund*] [*Greek*]   (GC)
TPENC...... Thailand PEN Centre   (EAIO)
t per........... Transition Temperature   (RU)
TPF............ Tanzanian People's Front   (AF)
TPF............ Technicko-Prumyslovy a Financni Plan [*Technical, Industrial, and Financial Plan*]   (CZ)
TPF............ Thiamine Pyrophosphate   (RU)
TPFA........ Tribunal Permanent des Forces Armees   (FLAF)
TPFA........ Tube and Pipe Fabricators Association, International   (EAIO)
TPFC........ Tasmanian Public Finance Corp. [*Australia*] [*Commercial firm*]
TPFH........ Tasmanian Pulp and Forest Holdings Ltd. [*Australia*]   (ADA)
TPFLM ..... Trano Printy Fiangonana Loterana Malagasy
TPFP .... Technicko-Prumyslovy a Financni Plan [*Technical, Industrial, and Financial Plan*]   (CZ)
TPFP .... Transkei People's Freedom Party [*South Africa*] [*Political party*]   (PPW)
TPF Plan ... Techniczno-Przemyslowo-Finansowy Plan [*Technical, Industrial, and Financial Plan*]   (POL)
TPG .... Rear Field Hospital   (RU)
TPG .... Taiping [*Malaysia*]   (ML)
TPG .... Transportes Aereos Pegaso SA de CV [*Mexico*] [*ICAO designator*]   (FAAC)
TPGF........ Tropas Populares de Guarda-Fronteiras [*People's Border Guard Troops*] [*Angola*]   (AF)
TPH .... Tanzania Publishing House Ltd.
TPI............ Flotation Equipment   (BU)
TPI............ Tallinn Polytechnic Institute   (RU)
TPI............ Tapini [*Papua New Guinea*] [*Airport symbol*]   (OAG)
TPI............ Tbilisi Polytechnic Institute   (RU)
TPI............ Technischphysikalisches Institut [*Technical-Physical Institute (at Friedrich-Schiller University, Jena)*]   (EG)
TPI............ Tomsk Polytechnic Institute Imeni S. M. Kirov   (RU)
TPI............ Topair Ltd. [*Czechoslovakia*] [*ICAO designator*]   (FAAC)
TPI............ Tvornica za Pamucnu Industriju [*Cotton Industrial Mill*] [*Zagreb*]   (YU)
TPIF .... Thornton Pacific Investment Fund
TPIIYa...... Tbilisi Pedagogical Institute of Foreign Languages   (RU)
TPIM........ Tout pour l'Interieur de la Maison
TPK........... Commander's Tank Periscope   (RU)
TPK........... Labor Productive Cooperative   (BU)
TPK........... Torzsparancsnok [*Staff Commander (Usually in civil defense)*]   (HU)
TPK........... Tvornica Parnih Kotlova [*Steam Boiler Factory*] [*Zagreb*]   (YU)
TPKK........ Turk Parasi Kiymetini Koruma [*Protection of Turkish Monetary Value*]   (TU)
TPKPEN ... Tameion Pronoias Katoteron Pliromaton Emborikou Navtikou [*Merchant Marine Welfare Fund for Lower-Ranking Seamen*] [*Greek*]   (GC)
TPKSI....... Turkiye Petrol ve Kimya Sanayii Iscileri Sendikasi [*Turkish Petroleum and Chemical Industry Workers Union*]   (TU)
t pl............. Melting Point   (RU)
TPL........... Tanganyika Packers Limited
TPL........... Technipetrol SPA [*Italy*]
TPL........... Tons Poids Lourd [*Deadweight Tons*] [*French*]
TPL........... Tribunal Populaire Local [*Local People's Court*] [*Benin*]   (AF)
TPLA........ Turkish People's Liberation Army   (PD)
TPLF .... Tigre People's Liberation Front [*Ethiopia*] [*Political party*]   (PD)
TPLP .... Turkish People's Liberation Party [*Political party*]   (PD)
TPM .... Taxe a la Production Majoree [*Tunisia*]
TPM .... Total Preventative Maintenance [*Manufacturing*]
TPM .... Tours par Minute [*Revolutions per Minute*] [*French*]
TPM .... Towarzystwo Przyjaciol Nauk [*Society of Friends of Learning*]   (POL)
TPMSW .... Towarzystwo Przyjaciol Mlodziezy Szkol Wyzszych [*Society of Friends of University and College Youth*]   (POL)
TPN .... Tatrzanski Park Narodowy [*Tatra National Park*] [*Poland*]
TPN .... Towarzystwo Przyjaciol Nauk [*Society of the Friends of Science*] [*Poland*]
TPNG .... Territory of Papua and New Guinea   (ADA)
TPNiSz...... Towarzystwo Przyjaciol Nauki i Sztuki [*Society of Friends of Science and Art*]   (POL)
TPNiSz wGd ... Towarzystwo Przyjaciol Nauki i Sztuki w Gdansku [*Gdansk (Danzig) Society of Friends of Science and Art*]   (POL)
TPO .... Heavy Infantry Flame-Thrower   (RU)
TPO .... Industrial Design Organization   (BU)
Tpo............ Tempo [*Record label*] [*Germany*]

tpo .... Tiempo [*Time*] [*Spanish*]
TPO .... Turkiye Petrol Ofisi Genel Mudurlugu [*Turkish Petroleum Office Directorate General*] [*PO*] [*See also*]   (TU)
TPOM .... Travail et Profession d'Outre-Mer
TPOSB ..... Tanganyika Post Office Savings Bank [*State bank*] [*Tanzania*]
TPP............ Freight and Passenger Train   (RU)
TPP............ Heavy Bridge Train   (RU)
TPP............ Platinum-Rhodium Alloy-Platinum Thermocouple   (RU)
TPP............ Strength Loss Temperature   (RU)
TPP............ Tanks in Support of Infantry   (RU)
TPP............ Tarapoto [*Peru*] [*Airport symbol*]   (OAG)
TPP............ Taxpayers and Producers Party [*Seychelles*]   (AF)
TPP............ Textilni Pomocne Pripravky [*Auxiliary Materials for the Textile Industry*]   (CZ)
TPP............ Timbalan Penguasa Polis [*Deputy Superintendent of Police*]   (ML)
TPP............ Toledo Progressive Party [*Belize*] [*Political party*]   (PPW)
TPPA........ Towarzystwo Produkcji Przemyslowej [*Industrial Production Society*]   (POL)
TPPH....... Tribunal Populaire de Province [*People's Court of the Province*] [*Benin*]   (AF)
TPP............ True Path Party [*Turkey*] [*Political party*]
TPP............ Trust of Manufacturing Establishments   (RU)
TPPB........ Mobile Therapeutical Field Hospital   (BU)
TPPE .... Tmima Poleodomias kai Poleodomikon Efarmogon [*City Planning and City Planning Enforcement Department*]   (GC)
TPPG........ Mobile Therapeutical Field Hospital   (RU)
TPPN........ Towarzystwo Przyjazni Polsko-Norweskiej [*Society for Polish-Norwegian Friendship*] [*Poland*]
TPPR........ Towarzystwo Przyjazni Polsko-Radzieckiej [*Society for Polish-Soviet Friendship*]   (POL)
TPPTT...... Tarifni Pravilnik Postansko-Telegrafsko-Telefonski [*Rate Regulations of the Postal, Telegraph, and Telephone Services*]   (YU)
TPQ .... Tepic [*Mexico*] [*Airport symbol*]
TPR........... Air Transport Pyrenees [*France*] [*ICAO designator*]   (FAAC)
TPR........... Current Planned Repairs   (BU)
tpr.............. Pipeline Company   (BU)
TPR........... Taxe a la Production Reduite [*Tunisia*]
TPR........... Teatr Polskiego Radia [*The Theatre of the Polish Radio*] [*Poland*]
TPR........... Tendencia Proletaria Revolucionaria [*Revolutionary Proletarian Faction*] [*Mexico*]   (LA)
TPR........... Terga Preliminary Reports
TPR........... Tom Price [*Australia*] [*Airport symbol*]
TPR........ Tribunaux Populaires de la Revolution [*Burkina Faso*]
TPr............ Tyutyunov Pregled [*Tobacco Review*] [*A periodical*]   (BU)
t prevr........ Transformation Temperature, Critical Point   (RU)
TPRF .... Tropical Plant Research Foundation
TPRI .... Tanzania Pesticides Research Institute   (ARC)
TPRI .... Trinity Peace Research Institute [*Australia*]
TPRI .... Tropical Pesticide Research Institute [*Ministry of Agriculture and Livestock Development*] [*Arusha, Tanzania*] [*Research center*]
TPRI .... Tropical Pesticide Research Institute of Tanganyika
TPriv......... Drive Flip-Flop   (RU)
TPRP........ Towarzystwo Przyjazni Radziecko-Polskiej [*Society for Soviet-Polish Friendship*]   (POL)
TPS........... Relay Transmitter   (RU)
TPS........... Taxe sur les Prestations de Service [*French*]
TPS........... Taxe sur les Produits et les Services
TPS........... Technical Manufacturing Council   (RU)
TPS........... Technology Policy Statement [*1982*] [*India*]
TPS........... Telegraph and Post Office   (BU)
TPS........... Telegraphie par le Sol [*Military*] [*French*]   (MTD)
TPS........... Tempat Pemungutan Suara [*Polling Place*]   (IN)
TPS........... Thermal Direction-Finding Station   (RU)
TPS........... Thomas Paine Society [*Nottingham, England*]   (EAIO)
TPS........... Toyota Production System [*Innovative lean-production manufacturing*]   (ECON)
TPS........... Trapani [*Italy*] [*Airport symbol*]   (OAG)
TPS........... Turnovo Court of Reconciliation   (BU)
TPSE .... Theories et Pratiques de Sciences Economiques   (FLAF)
TPSF........ Telephonie sans Fil [*Wireless Telephony*]
tpsl .... Telegraph and Post Service   (BU)
TPSL .... Tyoevaeen ja Pienviljelijaein Sosialidemokraattinen Liitto [*Social Democratic League of Workers and Smallholders*] [*Finland*] [*Political party*]   (PPE)
TPSM .... Transports Populaires Sahel Mitidja [*Algeria*]
TPSP .... Towarzystwo Przyjaciol Sztuk Pieknych [*Society of Friends of the Fine Arts*]   (POL)
TPT........... Alternating-Current Theory   (RU)
TPT........... Tasmanian Peace Trust [*Australia*]
TPT........... Totul pentru Tara ["*All for the Fatherland*"] [*Romania*] [*Political party*]   (PPE)
TPT........... Trade Practices Tribunal [*Australia*]

TPT............ Tramway de Pithiviers a Toury [*France*] (PDAA)
TPT............ Travail pour Tous [*Work for All*] [*French*] (WER)
TPT............ Trestni Pracovni Tabor [*Penal Labor Camp*] (CZ)
TPTC......... Tanzania Posts and Telecommunications Corporation
TPU .... Rear-Area Control Post (RU)
TPU .... Standardized Technological Process (RU)
TPU .... Tank Intercom (RU)
TPU .... Tax Payers United [*Australia*]
TPU .... Technical Production Administration (RU)
TPU .... Territorial Production Administration (RU)
TPU .... Tiv Progressive Union
TPU .... Universal Pneumatic Midget Turbine (RU)
TPusk .... Start Trigger [*Computers*] (RU)
TPV............ Technicka Priprava Vyroby [*Technical Preparations for Production*] (CZ)
Tpv............ Triebwagenzug [*Rail Motor Car Train*] [*German*] (EG)
TPV............ Withdrawable Soil Thermometer (RU)
TPVN .... Tameion Pronoias Vasilikou Navtikou [*Royal Navy Welfare Fund*] [*Greek*] (GC)
TPW .... Technischphysikalische Werkstaetten (VEB) [*Technical-Physical Workshops (VEB)*] [*German*] (EG)
TPWAC..... Territory Parks and Wildlife Advisory Council [*Northern Territory, Australia*]
TPZ............ Rear March Security Patrol (BU)
TPZ............ Rear Security Detachment (RU)
TPZ............ Target Planning Zone [*Oil stockholding*]
TPZ............ Towarzystwo Przyjaciol Zolnierza [*Society of Soldier's Friends*] (POL)
TPZ............ Transportes La Paz SA de CV [*Mexico*] [*ICAO designator*] (FAAC)
TPZK........ Labor Productive Craftsmen's Cooperative (BU)
TQ.............. Tables Quinquennales (FLAF)
TQ.............. Timbre de Quittance [*Receipt Stamp*] [*French*] (CL)
TQ.............. Tyrolean Airways [*Austria*] [*ICAO designator*] (ICDA)
TQC .... Tobacco Quota Committee [*Australia*]
TQMI .... Total Quality Management Institute [*Australia*]
TQPF .... [*The*] Valley/Wall Blake [*Anguilla Island*] [*ICAO location identifier*] (ICLI)
TQS .... Tres Esquinas [*Colombia*] [*Airport symbol*] (OAG)
TR .... Compania de Aviacion Trans-Europa [*Spain*] [*ICAO designator*] (ICDA)
TR .... Current Relay (RU)
TR .... Current Repair (RU)
tr................. Floor [*Sweden*] (CED)
Tr .... Grad Tralles [*Degree Tralles*] [*German*] (GCA)
TR .... Isolation Transformer (RU)
Tr .... Mercury Thyratron (RU)
TR .... Severely Wounded (RU)
TR .... Single-Perforated Powder (RU)
TR .... Societe Tunisienne de Reassurance [*Tunisian Reinsurance Co.*]
TR .... Tactical Missile (RU)
TR .... Tactical Reconnaissance (RU)
TR .... Tank Company (RU)
TR .... Taxa Referencial de Juros [*Brazil*] (ECON)
TR .... Technische Registratur [*German*] (ADPT)
TR .... Tecnicka Rada [*Technical Council*] (CZ)
TR .... Telegraphe Restant [*Telegram to Be Called for at a Telegraph Office*] [*French*] (ROG)
TR .... Telephone Relay (RU)
TR .... Teleradiometer (RU)
TR .... Temperature Relay (RU)
TR .... Terminalischer Reiz [*Terminal Stimulus*] [*German*] [*Psychology*]
TR .... Terni [*Car registration plates*] [*Italian*]
TR .... Testa Rossa [*Red engine cylinder head*] [*Ferrari automotive model designation*] [*Italian*]
t-r .... Theater (RU)
TR .... Thermal Dissolution (RU)
TR .... Thermoregulator, Heat Controller (RU)
Tr .... Thousand Rubles (RU)
tR .... Tierische Rohstoffe [*Animal Raw Materials*] (EG)
TR .... Tir Rapide [*Military*] [*French*] (MTD)
tr................. Tohoto Roku [*Of This Year*] (CZ)
Tr .... Torni [*Tower*] [*Finland*] (NAU)
Tr .... Tour [*Tower*] [*French*] (NAU)
TR .... Trabantenstation [*German*] (ADPT)
tr................. Traduction [*Translation*] [*French*]
tr................. Traduzione [*Translation*] [*Italian*]
TR .... Train Regimentaire [*Military*] [*French*] (MTD)
tr................. Traite [*Agreement*] [*French*]
tr................. Tranche [*Hollow Edge (of a Book)*] [*Publishing*] [*French*]
tr................. Tranches Rognees [*With Cut Edges*] [*Publishing*] [*French*]
tr................. Transactions (RU)
TR .... Transferable Rouble [*International Bank for Economic Co-Operation*] (EY)
Tr .... Transforme [*Transformed*] [*French*] (MTD)

TR .... Transformer (RU)
tr................. Transitiiviverbi [*Verb Transitive*] [*Finland*]
tr................. Transponeer [*Transpose*] [*Afrikaans*]
TR .... Transportation Company (RU)
Tr .... Tratta [*Bill of Exchange*] [*Italian*] [*Business term*]
Tr .... Tratte [*Draft*] [*German*] [*Business term*]
tr................. Travail [*Work*] [*French*]
tr................. Travessa [*Crossroad*] [*Portuguese*] (CED)
Tr .... Trennschnitt [*Cross Section*] [*German*] (GCA)
Tr .... Trennung [*Division*] [*German*] (GCA)
TR .... Trgovinska Radnja [*Commercial Shop*] (YU)
Tr .... Tribunal de Premiere Instance [*Benelux*] (BAS)
TR .... Tribus
tr................. Trida [*Class, Avenue*] (CZ)
Tr .... Trida [*Avenue*] [*Commonwealth of Independent States*] (EECI)
TR .... Trident Aircraft Ltd. [*Canada ICAO aircraft manufacturer identifier*] (ICAO)
Tr .... Tropfen [*Drop*] [*German*] (GCA)
Tr .... Trud [*Labor*] [*A newspaper*] (BU)
tr................. Tryck [*Printing*] [*Publishing*] [*Sweden*]
tr................. Trykt [*Printed*] [*Publishing Danish/Norwegian*]
TR .... Turkey [*ANSI two-letter standard code*] (CNC)
tr................. Tytar [*Finland*]
Tr .... Works (BU)
TRA .... Taiwan Railway Administration (DCTA)
TRA .... Taramajima [*Japan*] [*Airport symbol*] (OAG)
TRA .... Tasmanian Racing Authority [*Australia*]
TRA .... Tasmanian Rifle Association [*Australia*]
TRA .... Tax Reform Australia
TRA .... Tea Research Association [*India*] (PDAA)
t-ra .... Temperature (RU)
TRA .... Transavia Holland BV [*Netherlands*] [*ICAO designator*] (FAAC)
trab............ Transport Aviation Base (BU)
TRAC........ Textiles Research Advisory Committee [*Australia*]
TRAC........ Total Recycling Advisory Committee [*Northern Territory, Australia*]
TRAC........ Training for Retailing and Commerce [*Australia*]
TRAC........ Travaux et Conferences. Universite Libre de Bruxelles. Faculte de Droit. [*Belgium*] (BAS)
TRACTIONEL ... Societe de Traction et Electricite [*Belgium*] (PDAA)
TRACTOIMPORT ... Empresa Cubana Importadora de Maquinarias y Equipos Agricolas [*Cuban Enterprise for the Import of Agricultural Machinery and Equipment*] (LA)
trad............ Traducao [*Translation*] [*Portuguese*]
trad............ Traduccion [*Translation*] [*Spanish*]
trad............ Traduction [*Translation*] [*French*]
trad............ Traduzione [*Translation*] [*Italian*]
trad............ Transport Aviation Division (BU)
TRADAC... Timber Research and Development Advisory Council [*Australia*] (ARC)
TRADEV... North Western Trade Development Co. [*Nigeria*]
TRADEVCO ... Liberian Trading and Development Bank Ltd.
TRADO ..... Transporte Aereo Dominicano [*Dominican Republic*] [*ICAO designator*] (FAAC)
traduz........ Traduzione [*Translation*] [*Italian*]
traesk .... Traeskaarne [*Woodcut*] [*Publishing Danish/Norwegian*]
traesn........ Traesnit [*Woodcut*] [*Publishing Danish/Norwegian*]
TRAF......... Societe Transports Africains
TRAFFIC .. Trade Records Analysis of Flora and Fauna in Commerce [*Australia*]
TRAFIPRO ... Travail, Fidelite, Progres
Trafo .... Transformator [*Transformer*] [*German*]
TRAFOSAN ... Transformator Sanayii Anonim Sirketi [*Transformer Industry Corporation*] (TU)
TRAGESOM ... Travaux Generaux Sous-Marins
Tragk .... Tragkraft [*Load*] [*German*]
tragr .... Transport Aviation Group (BU)
TRAIDS .... Transfusion-Related Acquired Immune Deficiency Syndrome [*Support group*] [*Australia*]
trak............ Transport Aviation Wing (BU)
t-ra kip .... Boiling Point (RU)
Trakt.......... Tractor Plant [*Topography*] (RU)
trakt brig.... Tractor Team (RU)
trakt st....... Tractor Station (RU)
TRAL........ Total Refineries Australia Limited (ADA)
tralbaza ...... Trawler Base, Mine Sweeper Base (RU)
TRAM .... Theater of Young Workers (RU)
TRAM .... Transports Automobiles et Manutentions [*Dakar*]
TRAMCO ... Tanzania Railway Manufacturing Company
TRAMETALCO ... Compania de Trabajos Metalicos y Estructurales [*Colombia*] (COL)
TRAMIT ... Especialidades Farmaceuticas en Tramite de Registro [*Ministerio de Sanidad y Consumo*] [*Spain*] [*Information service or system*] (CRD)
TRAMO .... Tanzania Railway Wagon Manufacturing Company
TRANCHE ... Travail Nucleaire Chef

Tranposektsiya ... All-Union Central Autonomous Section of Consumers' Cooperative Societies of Railroad and Water Transportation Workers at the Tsentrosoyuz   (RU)

TRANSACO ... Compagnie Africaine de Transactions Internationales

TRANSAFRIC ... Societe de Transit et de Transports en Afrique

TRANSBALBOA ... Compania de Transportes Balboa Ltda. [*Colombia*]   (COL)

TRANSBENIN ... Societe des Transports Routiers du Benin [*National transporter of goods and passengers*]

TRANSCAM ... Chemin de Fer Trans-Camerounais [*Trans-Cameroonian Railroad*]   (AF)

TRANSCAP-NIGER ... Societe Eurafricaine de Voyage, de Transit, et de Camionnage Portuaire

TRANSCARTOL ... Cooperativa de Transportadores de Carga del Tolima [*Ibague*]   (COL)

TRANSCOBOIS ... Societe de Transport et de Commercialisation des Bois en Provenance de Centrafrique, Cameroun, et Gabon

TRANSCOGAZ ... Societe Transcontinentale des Gaz de Petrole BP

TRANSCOM ... Societe Nationale de Transports en Commun

TRANSCONGO SA ... Societe de Transports du Congo

TRANSCRUZ ... Transportes Unidos Cruz [*Colombia*]   (COL)

TRANSELEKTRO ... TRANSELEKTRO Villamossagi Kulkereskedelmi Vallalat [*TRANSELEKTRO Foreign Trade Enterprise for Electric Power*]   (HU)

Transelektromontazh ... All-Union Specialized Installation Trust for Railroad Electrification   (RU)

Transelektroproyekt ... State Planning and Surveying Institute of Railroad Electrification and Power Installations of the State Industrial Committee for Transportation Construction, USSR   (RU)

TRANSEQUAT ... Societe de Transit Equatorial

TRANSFEDERAL ... Transportes Federados Huila, Cauca, Caqueta Ltda. [*Colombia*]   (COL)

TRANSFLUVIAL ... Transportes Fluviales Magdalena Ltda. [*Barranquilla*]   (COL)

TRANSFRACHT ... Deutsche Transportgesellschaft [*German Transport Company*]   (WEN)

TRANSFRIA ... Societe des Transports et des Installations Portuaires de Fria

Transgidromekhanizatsiya ... Specialized Trust of Mechanized Hydraulic Operations of the Glavmorrechstroy   (RU)

Transgidrostroy ... All-Union Trust for the Construction of Hydraulic Engineering Structures of the Glavrechstroy   (RU)

Transgiz ..... State Publishing House of Transportation and Railroad Literature   (RU)

TRANSGRUM ... Societe Anonyme Exploitation et Transport de Grumes

TRANSIMOL ... Sociedade Transitaria de Mocambique Limitada

TRANSIMPORT ... Empresa Cubana Importadora de Transporte (Vehiculos y Equipos) [*Cuban Enterprise for the Import of Vehicles and Transportation Equipment*]   (LA)

Transinsular ... Transportes Maritimos Insulares, SA [*Portugal*]   (EY)

transl .... Translatiivi [*Finland*]

TRANSLAG ... Transports Lagunaires

Translesproyekt ... Planning Office of the Glavtransles   (RU)

TRANSLIB ... Australian Transport Librarians

TRANSLITORAL ... Transportes el Litoral Ltda. [*Colombia*]   (COL)

TRANSLOBO ... Societe de Transports de la Lobo

TRANSMAR ... Transportes el Mar SA [*Colombia*]   (COL)

Transmash ... Ministry of Transportation Machinery Manufacture   (RU)

TRANSMECA ... Transports Mecaniques

Transmedsnabtorg ... Office for the Supply of Medical Equipment and Sale of Drugs on Railroads   (RU)

TRANSMER ... Societe de Transformation des Produits de la Mer

Transmostproyekt ... All-Union Specialized Office for the Planning and Surveying of Large Railroad Bridges   (RU)

Transnave .. Transportes Navieros Ecuatorianos [*Shipping line*] [*Ecuador*]   (EY)

TRANSNUCLEAIRE ... Societe pour les Transports de l'Industries Nucleaire [*France*]   (PDAA)

Transorgmashuchet ... State Trust for the Organization of Mechanized Accounting of the Ministry of Railroads, USSR   (RU)

Transotdelstroy ... Trust for Architectural and Finishing Work of the Glavzheldorstroy of the Central and Western Regions (RU)

Transp .... Transport [*German*]   (GCA)

transp .... Transportation, Transport   (RU)

Transpechat' ... Administration for the Distribution and Dispatch of Publications of Transzheldorizdat   (RU)

TRANSPLAN ... Transportation Planning Commission   (RU)

Transproekt ... Transport Design Institute   (BU)

Transproyektkar'yer ... Office for the Surveying and Planning of Quarries for Transportation Needs   (RU)

TRANSRAPID ... Les Transports Rapides du Cameroun

Transremstroy ... Transportation Repair and Construction Office   (RU)

Transsignalstroy ... All-Union Trust of the Glavtranselektromontazh of the Ministry of Transportation Construction, USSR   (RU)

Transsnab ... Transport Supplies Organization   (BU)

Transspetsstroy ... Trust for Special and Road Work of the Ministry of Construction, USSR   (RU)

Transstroyprom ... Trust of Industrial Establishments of the Glavstroymekhanizatsiya   (RU)

Transstroypromkonstruktsiya ... Trust of the Glavstroyprom of the Ministry of Transportation Construction, USSR   (RU)

Transsvyaz'stroy ... All-Union Trust of the Glavmontazhstroy of the Ministry of Transportation Construction, USSR   (RU)

Transteiproyekt ... All-Union Planning Office for Technical and Economical Problems and for the Study of Scientific Methods in Railroad Transportation   (RU)

Transtekhmontazh ... Trust of the Glavzheldorstroy of the Central and Western Regions of the Ministry of Transportation Construction, USSR   (RU)

Transtekhproyekt ... State Planning Institute for the Design and Study of Technical Structures in Railroad Transportation   (RU)

Transtorgsnab ... All-Union Office of the Glavurs of the Ministry of Railroads, USSR   (RU)

TRANSUD ... Societe des Transports du Sud de Madagascar

TRANSUNIS ... Societe des Transitaires Unis

TRANSURBAINS ... Regie Autonome des Transports Urbains [*Autonomous Urban Transport Administration*] [*Cambodia*]   (CL)

Transzavodproyekt ... State Institute for the Planning of Plants on Transportation Routes   (RU)

Transzheldorizdat ... All-Union Publishing and Printing Association of the Ministry of Railroads, USSR   (RU)

TRANSZVILL ... Transzformator es Villamoskeszulekgyar [*Factory for Transformers and Electric Appliances*]   (HU)

tranz .... Transit, Transient   (RU)

TRAP .... Air Transport Regiment   (RU)

TRAP .... Transportni Avio Puk [*Air Transport Regiment*]   (YU)

TRAPAG ... Societe Industrielle de Stockage et de Traitement de Produits Agricoles

TRAPAL ... Societe pour le Transport des Hydrocarbures Sahariens au Littoral Algerien

TRAPES .... Societe des Transports des Petroles de l'Est Saharien

t-ra plavl ..... Melting Point   (RU)

TRAPO ...... Transportpolizei [*Transportation Police*]   (EG)

TRAPSA .... Compagnie des Transports par Pipeline au Sahara [*Saharan Pipeline Transportation Company*] [*Algeria*]   (AF)

TRAQS ...... Trans Tasman Recognition Arrangement for Qualifications and Skills [*Australia*]

tras .... Trascurabile [*Negligible*] [*Italian*]

trasc .... Trascurabile [*Negligible*] [*Italian*]

trat .... Tratamento [*Treatment*] [*Portuguese*]

TRATAM ... Transportes Titiribi Amaga-Medellin Ltda.   (COL)

TRATASA ... Asociacion para el Transporte y Asistencia en Latinoamerica [*Mexico*]   (LAA)

Tratt .... Trattenuto [*Music*]

TRAU .... Tanganyika Railway African Union

TraV .... Transpress Verlag fuer Verkehrswesen [*"Transpress" Publishing House for Transportation Affairs*]   (EG)

trav .... Travail [*Work*] [*Knitting*] [*French*]

Trav .... Travessa [*Crossroad*] [*Portuguese*]

TravAssoc H Capitant ... Travaux de l'Association Henri Capitant pour la Culture Juridique Francaise   (FLAF)

TRAVAUX ... Compagnie Congolaise de Travaux Publics Congo

Trav C Et ... Travaux du Comite d'Etudes et de Legislation de la Federation des Notaires de Belgique [*Belgium*]   (BAS)

Trav ComFr DIP ... Travaux du Comite Francais de Droit International Prive   (FLAF)

TravComm Ref C Com ... Travaux de la Commission de Reforme du Code de Commerce et du Droit des Societes   (FLAF)

Trav ConfBrux ... Travaux et Conferences de la Faculte de Droit de Bruxelles [*Belgium*]   (BAS)

t ravn .... Equilibrium Temperature   (RU)

trav pub ...... Travaux Publics [*Public Works*] [*French*]

t razl .... Decomposition Temperature   (RU)

trazmyagch ... Softening Point   (RU)

TRB .... Big Fishing Trawler   (RU)

TRB .... Thyratron Relay Unit   (RU)

TRB .... Tobacco Research Board [*Zimbabwe*]   (ARC)

TRB .... Toneladas Registradas Brutas [*Gross Register Tonnage*] [*Spanish*]

Trb .... Tractatenblad [*Benelux*]   (BAS)

TRB .... Trans Air Bretagne [*France*] [*ICAO designator*]   (FAAC)

Trb .... Tribunus [*Tribune*] [*Latin*]

TRB .... Turbo [*Colombia*] [*Airport symbol*]   (OAG)

TRBF .... Technische Regeln fur Brennbare Flussigkeiten [*Technical Regulations for Flammable Liquids*] [*Germany*]   (PDAA)

Trbl .... Tractatenblad [*Benelux*]   (BAS)

TRBR .... Tobacco Research Board of Rhodesia

TRC .... Tanzania Railway Corporation   (AF)

TRC .... Tasmanian Rowing Council [*Australia*]

TRC .... Tasmanian Rural Counselling [*Australia*]

TRC .... Technical Resource Center [*Philippines*]   (PDAA)

TRC .... Technology Resource Center [*Information service or system*] [*Phillipines*]   (IID)
TRC .... Tekniska Rontgencentralen [*Sweden*]   (PDAA)
TRC .... Telecommunications Research Centre [*Posts and Telegraph Department*] [*India*]   (PDAA)
TRC .... Texas Railroad Commission   (OMWE)
TRC .... Torreon [*Mexico*] [*Airport symbol*]   (OAG)
TRCL........ Trustul Regional de Constructii Locale [*Regional Trust for Local Constructions*]   (RO)
TRCLB ...... Trustul Regional de Constructii Locale Bucuresti [*Bucharest Regional Trust for Local Constructions*]   (RO)
Tr Comb..... Train de Combat [*Military*] [*French*]   (MTD)
Tr ConfULB ... Travaux et Conferences (Universite Libre de Bruxelles) [*Belgium*]   (BAS)
TRD .... Liquid-Fuel Jet Engine   (BU)
tr-d .... Pipeline   (RU)
TRD .... Taxa Referencial Diaria [*Brazil*]   (ECON)
TRD .... Tehran Redevelopment Corporation   (ME)
TRD .... Trans Island Air [*Barbados*] [*ICAO designator*]   (FAAC)
Trd .... Trinidad   (BARN)
TRD .... Trondheim [*Norway*] [*Airport symbol*]   (OAG)
TRD .... Turbojet Engine   (RU)
TRDA .... Tana River Development Authority
TRDAC..... Timber Research and Development Advisory Council [*Australia*]
TRDB .... Tanzania Rural Development Bank
TRDC .... Tobacco Research and Development Council [*Australia*]
TRDF........ Turbojet Engine with Afterburner   (RU)
TRDI.......... Technical Research and Development Institute [*Japan Defense Agency*]
Tr Distr ...... Tribunal de District [*Benelux*]   (BAS)
TRDV .... Turboprop Engine   (RU)
Tre............. Torre [*Tower*] [*Italian*]   (NAU)
TRE .... Trans-Eastern Airlines Ltd. [*Kenya*] [*ICAO designator*]   (FAAC)
TRE .... Tribunal Regional Eleitoral [*Regional Electoral Court*] [*Brazil*]   (LA)
Treas......... Treasurer   (EECI)
TRED .... Work Report Unit   (RU)
TREE........ Training and Resources for Early Education [*South Africa*]   (AA)
TREFILCO ... Trefileria Colombiana SA [*Bucaramanga*]   (COL)
t rekrist ..... Recrystallization Temperature   (RU)
tremb......... Tank Repair Battalion   (RU)
Trenn .... Trennung [*Division*] [*German*]   (GCA)
TREVI ...... Terrorisme, Radicalisme, Extremisme, Violence Internationale [*International anti-terrorist group*] [*Belgium*]
trevl .... Trevlig [*Pleasant*] [*Sweden*]
TRez........ Tank Reserve   (RU)
TRF........... Air Transafrik Ltd. [*Ghana*] [*ICAO designator*]   (FAAC)
TRF........... Tariff Clerk   (RU)
trf .... Transfer   (FLAF)
TRFA......... Tanga Regional Football Association
TRFCA ...... Tea Research Foundation (Central Africa) [*Malawi*]   (EAIO)
Trfg .... Tragfaehigkeit [*Carrying Capacity*] [*German*]   (GCA)
TRG .... Atlantic Island Air [*Iceland*] [*ICAO designator*]   (FAAC)
TRG .... Tauranga [*New Zealand*] [*Airport symbol*]   (OAG)
TRGK .... Tank Reserve of the High Command   (RU)
TRGLP ...... [*The*] Rio Grandense Light and Power [*Brazil*]   (LAA)
TRGOPRED ... Trgovinsko Preduzece [*Commercial Establishment*]   (YU)
TRGOTEKSTIL ... Trgovina Tekstilom [*Textile Trade*]   (YU)
Tr Gr Inst... Tribunal de Grande Instance   (FLAF)
TRI........... Taganrog Radiotechnical Institute   (RU)
TRI........... Tea Research Institute of Sri Lanka [*Research center*]   (IRC)
TRI........... Technological Research Institute [*Thailand*]   (PDAA)
Tri .... Tohtori [*Doctor*] [*Finland*]   (GPO)
TRI........... Transit Routier Interieur   (FLAF)
Tri .... Trichloraethylen [*Trichloroethylene*] [*German*]   (GCA)
TRIB......... Towarzystwo Robot Inzynierskich i Budowlanych [*Engineering and Construction Work Company*]   (POL)
Trib .... Tribunal [*French*]   (FLAF)
Trib .... Tribunale [*Ordinary Court of First Instance*] [*Italian*]   (DLA)
Trib .... Tribunalen in Nederland [*Netherlands*]   (BAS)
TribAdmin ... Tribunaux Administratifs [*French*]   (DLA)
Trib ArbMixtes ... Tribunaux Arbitraux Mixtes [*French*]   (DLA)
Trib Cant ... Tribunal Cantonal   (FLAF)
Trib Civ...... Jugement d'un Tribunal, Chambre Civile   (FLAF)
Trib Com.... Jugement d'un Tribunal de Commerce   (FLAF)
Trib Con..... Tribunal des Conflits [*Tribunal of Conflicts*] [*French*]   (DLA)
Trib Confl .. Decision de Tribunal des Conflits   (FLAF)
Trib Corr.... Jugement d'un Tribunal, Chambre Correctionnelle   (FLAF)
Trib DepEnf ... Tribunal Departemental pour Enfants   (FLAF)
Trib Enf .... Tribunal pour Enfants   (FLAF)
Trib GrInst ... Tribunal de Grande Instance   (FLAF)
Trib Inst..... Tribunal d'Instance   (FLAF)
tribl .... Tribunal [*Spanish*]
Trib MilitCass ... Tribunal Militaire de Cassation   (FLAF)
Trib MilitPerm ... Tribunal Militaire Permanent   (FLAF)

TRIBOIS... Societe de Transformation Industrielle du Bois
Trib Paix.... Tribunal de Paix   (FLAF)
Trib ParArr Villefranche-sur-Saone ... Tribunal Paritaire d'Arrondissement de Villefranche-sur-Saone   (FLAF)
Trib ParCant Mordelles ... Tribunal Paritaire Cantonal de Mordelles   (FLAF)
Trib Parit ... Tribunal Paritaire Cantonal des Baux Ruraux   (FLAF)
Trib ParitArr ... Tribunal Paritaire d'Arrondissement des Baux Ruraux   (FLAF)
Trib PolDomfront ... Tribunal de Simple Police de Domfront   (FLAF)
TribSimple Pol ... Tribunal de Simple Police   (FLAF)
TRIC .... Tea Research Institute of Ceylon   (DSCA)
tric .... Tricoter [*Knit*] [*Knitting*] [*French*]
TRICI .... Trichinopoli Cigar   (DSUE)
TRICO....... Training, Research, Isotope Production Reactor, Congo
TRICOMAD ... Societe Industrielle des Tricotages de Madagascar
tricr .... Tricromia [*Three-Color Illustration*] [*Italian*]
TRICS ...... Tasmanian Regional Integrated Computer System [*Australia*]
TRIDC....... Travaux et Recherches de l'Institut de Droit Compare de l'Universite de Paris   (FLAF)
TRIDO ...... Table Ronde Internationale pour le Developpement de l'Orientation [*International Round Table for the Advancement of Counselling - IRTAC*]   (EAIO)
TRIEA .... Tea Research Institute of East Africa
Trig .... Trigonometria [*Trigonometry*] [*Portuguese*]
TRIGAB .... Tricots Gabonais
trik .... Knitting, Knit-Goods   (RU)
TRIKORA ... Tri Komando Rakjat [*Three Commands of the People (Refers to West Irian campaign)*]   (IN)
trim............ Trimestral [*Quarterly*] [*Spanish*]
trim............ Trimestre [*Trimester*] [*French*]
trim............ Trimestre [*Trimester*] [*Portuguese*]
TRIMECAF ... Societe de Tricotage Mecanique Africain
TRIMETA ... Societe de Tricotage Mecanique de Tananarive
Trin .... Trinidad
TRINCO.... Trincomalee [*Sri Lanka port city*]   (DSUE)
TRINDELCI ... Travaux Industriels pour l'Electricite Cote-D'Ivoire
TRINGEN ... Trinidad Nitrogen Co. Ltd.
TRINTOC ... Trinidad and Tobago Oil Company   (LA)
TRINTOPEC ... Trinidad & Tobago Petroleum Co. Ltd.   (EY)
TRIP......... Transport Infrastructure Programme [*EDF*]
TRIP......... Transport Rehabilitation Programme [*Ghana*]
TRIP......... Transports Interregionaux de Personnes [*Interregional Personnel Transportation*] [*French*]   (WER)
Trip .... Tripoli
Trip .... Tripolitania [*Libya*]   (BJA)
TRIPS...... Trade-Related Aspects of Intellectual Property [*Australia*]
TRIPS...... Trade-Related Intellectual Property   (ECON)
TRITB ...... Tasmanian Retail Industry Training Board [*Australia*]
TRITB ...... Tasmanian Rural Industry Training Board [*Australia*]
TRITURAF ... Societe Ivoirienne pour la Trituration des Graines Oleagineuses et le Raffinage d'Huiles Vegetales
TriV .... Tribuene Verlag [*"Tribune" Publishing House*]   (EG)
TRJ .... AJT Air International [*Russian Federation*] [*ICAO designator*]   (FAAC)
TRJN......... Tymczasowy Rzad Jednosci Narodowej [*Provisional Government of National Unity (1945-1947)*] [*Poland*]
TRK .... Air Truck [*Spain*] [*ICAO designator*]   (FAAC)
TRK .... Poorly Soluble Components   (RU)
TRK .... Tarakan [*Indonesia*] [*Airport symbol*]   (OAG)
tr-k .... Triangle   (RU)
Tr KMA ..... Transactions of the Special Commission for the Research on the Kursk Magnetic Anomaly   (RU)
Tr KntNok ... Trafik Kontrol Noktasi [*Traffic Control Point*]   (TU)
TRL........... Tallinna Rabeline Lukumine [*Tallinn Green Movement*] [*Estonia*]   (EAIO)
TRL........... Telecom Australia Research Laboratories
TRL........... Telegraph Line Relay   (RU)
Trl .... Treuil [*Windlass*] [*Military map abbreviation World War I*] [*French*]   (MTD)
TRLA .... Textile Rental and Laundry Association [*Australia*]
Trla .... Triola [*Record label*] [*Finland*]
TRLA(NSW) ... Textile Rental and Laundry Association of New South Wales [*Australia*]
TRLA(Q) ... Textile Rental and Laundry Association (Queensland) [*Australia*]
TRLA(V) ... Textile Rental and Laundry Association (Victoria) [*Australia*]
TRLAWA ... Textile Rental and Laundry Association of Western Australia
TRM .... Local Telegraph Relay   (RU)
TRM .... Tank-Repair Shop   (RU)
TRM .... Technikum Rybolowstwa Morskiego [*Sea Fishery Technical School*]   (POL)
TRM .... Toutes Roues Motrices
TRM .... Transport Regional Maritim [*Regional Maritime Transportation*]   (RO)
TRM .... Transports Aeriens Mediterraneens [*France*] [*ICAO designator*]   (FAAC)
trm............. Trekhondos Minos [*Current Month*]   (GC)

TRMA	Tank-Repair Shop, Type A (RU)
TRMA	Thai Rice Mills Association
TRMB	Tank-Repair Shop, Type B (RU)
TRML	Terenowa Rada Modelarstwa Lotniczego [*Local Council for Airplane Models*] (POL)
TRML	Tropical Research Medical Laboratory
TRMS	Transmission Resource Management System [*Australia*]
TrN	Storage Transformer (RU)
TRN	Theron Airways [*South Africa*] [*ICAO designator*] (FAAC)
TRN	Turin [*Italy*] [*Airport symbol*] (OAG)
TRNC	Turkish Republic of North Cyprus (BARN)
TRNC	Turkish Republic of Northern Cyprus
TRNS	Torrens [*Botanical region*] [*Australia*]
TRO	Air Molokai-Tropic Airlines [*ICAO designator*] (FAAC)
TRO	Taree [*Australia*] [*Airport symbol*] (OAG)
TRO	Transformatorenwerk Oberschoeneweide (VEB) [*Berlin-Oberschoeneweide Transformer Works (VEB)*] (EG)
TROA	Transportation Department, Transport Section (RU)
TROA	Thoroughbred Racehorse Owners' Association [*Australia*]
Trockn	Trocknen [*Drying*] [*German*] (GCA)
TRODECOL ...	Troquelados de Colombia Ltda. [*Colombia*] (COL)
TROECA	Tropical de Exportacion CA [*Venezuela*] (DSCA)
TROMECAN ...	Troqueleria Mecanica [*Colombia*] (COL)
Trop	Tropen [*Tropics*] [*German*] (GCA)
trop	Tropical (RU)
trop	Tropisch [*Tropical*] [*German*] (GCA)
TROPCAN ...	Tropic of Cancer (WDAA)
TROPCAP ...	Tropic of Capricorn (WDAA)
TROPIC	Societe des Forges Tropicales
TROPIC	Societe Tropicale des Piles
TROPMED ...	Regional Project for Tropical Medicine and Public Health [*SEAMEO*] [*Thailand*] [*Research center*] (IRC)
TROPMED ...	Regional Tropical Medicine and Public Health [*Center*] [*Subsidiary of SEAMEC*] (CL)
TROS	Televisie Radio Omroep Stichting [*Television-Radio Broadcasting Corporation*] [*Netherlands*] (WEN)
TROTRA ...	Societe Tropicale de Transports
TRP	Memory Configuration Table [*Computers*] (RU)
TRP	Transfert d'Informations Prioritaires [*French*] (ADPT)
Tr P	Treffpunkt [*Point of Impact*] [*German*] (GCA)
Tr p	Trigonometric Point [*Topography*] (RU)
Trp	Tropfpunkt [*Drip Point*] [*German*]
Tr Parq	Tribunal de Parquet [*Benelux*] (BAS)
TRPC	Tasmanian Rural Promotions Committee [*Australia*]
TRPM	Plymouth/Blackburne [*Montserrat Island*] [*ICAO location identifier*] (ICLI)
Tr Pol	Tribunal de Police [*Benelux*] (BAS)
TrPrIzpD ...	Papers of the Society of Natural Science (BU)
TRPSh	Transformer Regulated with Shunt Magnetization (RU)
TRPT-Nr ...	Transport-Genehmigungs Nummer [*Transportation Permit Number*] (EG)
TRR	Tank Repair Shop (BU)
TRR	Trabajador de Reconstruccion Rural [*Guatemala*] (DSCA)
TRR	Tramson Ltd. [*Sudan*] [*ICAO designator*] (FAAC)
tr-r	Transformer (RU)
Trr	Trestni Rad [*Code of Criminal Procedure*] (CZ)
Trr	Trestni Rizeni [*Criminal Procedure*] (CZ)
TRRC	Twin Rivers Research Centre [*Philippines*] (ARC)
Tr Reg	Train Regimentaire [*Military*] [*French*] (MTD)
TRS	Spin-Stabilized Missile (RU)
TRS	Technical Repair Services [*New South Wales Commercial Services Group*] [*Australia*]
TRS	Television Relay Station (RU)
TRS	Torunska Rektyfikacja Spirytusu [*Torun Alcohol Distillation Plant*] (POL)
trs	Traites [*Drafts*] [*French*] [*Business term*]
TRS	Transponeer [*Transpose*] [*Afrikaans*]
Tr s	Transport Facility (BU)
TRS	Transport International Aerien [*Belgium*] [*ICAO designator*] (FAAC)
TRS	Trieste [*Italy*] [*Airport symbol*] (OAG)
TRS	Tropical Rainforest Society [*Australia*]
TRSC	Thailand Remote Sensing Center [*Research center*] (IRC)
TRSp	Coincidence Flip-Flop (RU)
Trsp	Transportieren [*Transport*] [*German*] [*Business term*]
TRSS	Tasmanian Rehabilitation and Support Services [*Australia*]
TRSSA	Transactions of the Royal Society of South Australia
TRSSM	Tampere Research Station of Sports Medicine [*Finland*]
TRT	Solid Rocket Propellant (RU)
TRT	Telecommunications Radio-Electriques et Telephoniques [*North African*]
TRT	Telefongyar [*Telephone Factory*] (HU)
TRT	Thyssen Rheinstahl Technik
TRT	Trans Arabian Air Transport [*Sudan*] [*ICAO designator*] (FAAC)
TRT	Transportation for Severely Wounded (RU)
TRT	Trotting [*Totalisator Agency Board code*] [*Australia*]
TrT	Truppenteil [*Unit*] [*Military*] (EG)
TRT	Turk Radyo ve Televisyon Idaresi [*Turkish Radio and Television Administration*] (TU)
TRTA	Tasmanian Registered Teachers' Association [*Australia*]
TRTA	Tasmanian Road Transport Association (PDAA)
TRTA	Teito Rapid Transit Authority [*Japan*] (PDAA)
TRTA	Telecommunications Radio-Electriques Africaines [*Algeria*]
TRT-DER ...	Tum Radyo Televizyon Calisanlari Dernegi [*Comprehensive Radio and Television Workers Organization*] (TU)
Tr Terr	Tribunal de Territoire [*Benelux*] (BAS)
TRTG	Tactical Radar Threat Generator
TRTI	Taganrog Radiotechnical Institute (RU)
TRTITC	Tasmanian Road Transport Industry Training Council [*Australia*]
TRTs	Initial Point to the Target (RU)
TRU	Tank Radio Set (BU)
TRU	Tasmanian Rugby Union [*Australia*]
TRU	Taxa Rodoviaria Unica [*Single Road Tax*] [*Brazil*] (LA)
TRU	Trujillo [*Peru*] [*Airport symbol*] (OAG)
trub	Pipe-Rolling Mill [*Topography*] (RU)
trud	Work, Labor (RU)
trudchast'	Work Team, Military Work Team (RU)
Trud kol	Labor Colony (RU)
Trudrezervizdat ...	All-Union Publishing House of Textbooks and Pedagogical Literature of the Main Administration of Labor Reserves at the Council of Ministers, USSR (RU)
Trueb	Truebung [*Turbidity*] [*German*] (GCA)
TRUTAS ...	Truva Sanayi ve Ticaret Anonim Sirketi [*Truva Industry and Trade Corporation*] (TU)
TRUVA	Truva Shipping Co. Ltd. [*Cyprus*] (TU)
TRV	Thermal Timing Relay (RU)
TRV	Thermoregulating Valve (RU)
TRV	Tiszantuli Rostkikeszito Vallalat [*Fiber Processing Industry of the Trans-Tisza Region*] (HU)
TRV	Transavia (Pty) Ltd. [*South Africa*] [*ICAO designator*] (FAAC)
TRV	Trivandrum [*India*] [*Airport symbol*] (OAG)
TRVA	Automatic Thermoregulating Valve (RU)
TRW	Tarawa [*Kiribati*] [*Airport symbol*] (OAG)
TRW	Trivandrum Rubber Works Ltd. [*India*]
TRWC	Tehran Regional Water Company (ME)
TRX	Air Terrex [*Czechoslovakia*] [*ICAO designator*] (FAAC)
TRY	Tororo [*Uganda*] [*Airport symbol*] (OAG)
TRZ	Diesel Locomotive Repair Plant (RU)
TRZ	Tiruchirappalli [*India*] [*Airport symbol*] (OAG)
Trz	Trestni Zaken [*Criminal Law*] (CZ)
TRZh	Hydraulic Thermoregulator (RU)
TRZZ	Terenowa Rada Zwiazkow Zawodowych [*Local Trade Union Council*] (POL)
TRZZ	Towarzystwo Rozwoju Ziem Zachodnich [*Society for the Development of the Western Territories*] (POL)
Ts	Celsius Degree [*C*] (RU)
Ts	Cement (RU)
ts	Center (BU)
ts	Centner (RU)
TS	Coupled Trolley Bus (RU)
t/s	Current Account (RU)
Ts	Cylindrical (RU)
TS	Dark Glass (RU)
ts	Digital, Number, Numerical (RU)
TS	Grid Transformer (RU)
TS	Power Transformer (RU)
ts	Price (RU)
Ts	Rate of Fire (RU)
TS	Remote Signal System (RU)
TS	Resistance Temperature (RU)
Ts	Resistance Thermometer (RU)
TS	Restaurant Trust (RU)
TS	Sectional Turbodrill (RU)
ts	Shop (RU)
TS	Signal Transformer (RU)
TS	Solid Lubricant (RU)
TS	Spin-Stabilized Missile (RU)
TS	Stabilizing Transformer (RU)
ts	Tanarseged [*Assistant to a Professor*] (HU)
TS	Tanecni Soubor [*Dance Ensemble*] (CZ)
TS	Tank Unit (RU)
Ts	Target, Objective (RU)
TS	Tarif Special [*Special Tariff*] [*French*]
TS	Tasmanian Swimming Inc. [*Commercial firm*] [*Australia*]
Ts	Tausend [*Thousand*] [*German*]
TS	Taxis Services Proprietary Ltd. [*Australia*]
TS	Technical Specifications (RU)
TS	Technicka Skupina [*Technical Group*] (CZ)
TS	Technicka Sprava [*Technical Directorate*] (CZ)

TS .... Ted Smith Aircraft [*ICAO aircraft manufacturer identifier*] (ICAO)
TS .... Tehnicka Sredstva [*Technical Equipment*] [*Military*] (YU)
TS .... Telegrafska Stanica [*Telegraph Station*] [*Military*] (YU)
TS .... Telegraph Station (BU)
TS .... Telephone Exchange (RU)
ts................ Television Station (RU)
TS .... Tenancy Service [*New South Wales, Australia*]
TS .... Terre de Signalisation [*French*] (ADPT)
TS .... Ter See [*At Sea*] [*Afrikaans*]
TS .... Theosophical Society [*India*] (EAIO)
TS .... Theosophical Society in England (SLS)
TS .... Thermistor (RU)
TS .... Thermometric Signaler (RU)
TS .... Thermostat (RU)
TS .... Thymol Blue [*Indicator*] (RU)
TS .... Tidningsstatistik [*Information service or system*] [*Sweden*] (IMH)
TS .... Tirailleurs Senegalais
ts................ Tisztes [*Junior Noncommissioned Officer*] (HU)
TS .... Tmimatikon Symvoulion [*Branch Council*] (GC)
TS .... Toa Soan [*Editor*]
ts................ Toisin Sanoen [*In Other Words*] [*Finland*] (GPO)
TS .... Tolkien Society [*Hove, East Sussex, England*] (EAIO)
ts................ Tomos [*Volumes*] [*Spanish*]
ts................ Ton-Force (RU)
ts................ Topographic Service (RU)
t/s............... Tours par Seconde [*Revolutions per Second*] [*French*]
ts................ Tous [*All, Everything*] [*Knitting*] [*French*]
TS .... Tragkraftspritze [*Portable Power Sprayer (Fire-fighting equipment)*] (EG)
TS .... Traitements, Salaires
TS .... Transformatorska Stanica [*Transformer Station*] (YU)
TS .... Transportation Construction (RU)
TS .... Transportna Sluzba [*Transport Service*] [*Railroads*] (YU)
TS .... Transversale Spyder [*Ferrari automotive model designation*]
TS .... Tres Sage [*Wisest*] [*Presiding officer in the French rite Freemasonry*]
TS .... Trieste [*Car registration plates*] [*Italian*]
TS .... Trockensubstanz [*Dry Matter*] (EG)
TS .... Trotyl Sulfite (RU)
TS .... Turcianske Strojarne [*Engineering Works, Turciansky Svaty Martin*] (CZ)
TS .... Turk Standartlar [*Turkish Standards*] [*Referring to TSE-designated equipment*] (TU)
TS .... Turner Society [*British*] (EAIO)
TsA .... Cementation Unit (RU)
TsA .... Central Operating Room, Central Manual Switchroom [*Telephony*] (RU)
TsA .... Digital Automation (RU)
TSA........... Etablissements Thivolle Societe Anonyme
TSA........... Taipei-Sung Shan [*Taiwan*] [*Airport symbol*] (OAG)
TSA........... Tameion Syndaxeon Avtokinitiston [*Drivers' Retirement Fund*] [*Greek*] (GC)
TSA........... Tanzania Sisal Authority
tsa.............. Tarsa [*Business Partner*] (HU)
TSA........... Tasmanian School of Arts [*Australia*]
TSA........... Tasmanian Shippers' Association [*Australia*]
TSA........... Tasmanian Soccer Association [*Australia*]
TSA........... Tasmanian State Archives [*Australia*]
TSA........... Telecommunication Society of Australia [*Melbourne*] (ADA)
TSA........... Television Society of Australia (ADA)
TSA........... Textile Society of Australia (ADA)
TSA........... Theosophical Society in Australia
TSA........... Tourism South Australia
TSA........... Tragkraftspritze Anhaenger [*Portable Power Sprayer Trailer (Fire-fighting equipment, used for transportation of the low-pressure pump)*] [*German*] (EG)
TSA........... Training Services Australia
TSA........... Transair France [*ICAO designator*] (FAAC)
TsAB.......... Central Address Bureau (RU)
TSAC......... Trade Standards Advisory Council [*Australia*]
tsae........... Medical Air Transport Group (BU)
TsAF......... Central Aerial Surveying Film Library (RU)
TsAGE....... Central Aerogeological Expedition (RU)
TsAGI....... Central Institute of Aerohydrodynamics Imeni N. Ye. Zhukovskiy (RU)
TsAGRU.... Central Agricultural Administration (RU)
TSAGU...... Transactions of the Central Asia State University (RU)
tsai............ Tarsai [*Partners*] (HU)
TsAK.......... Central Aviation Club (BU)
TsAK.......... Central Aviation Club of the USSR Imeni V. P. Chkalov (RU)
TsAKA....... Central Archives of the Red Army (RU)
TsAL.......... Central Laboratory of Batteries (RU)
TsAMA...... Central Model Aircraft Laboratory (BU)
TsAMK...... Central Automobile and Motorcycle Club of the USSR (RU)

TsAMK...... Central Automobile-Motorcycle Club (BU)
TsAML...... Central Model Aircraft Laboratory (RU)
TsAMMF .. Central Archives of the Ministry of the Maritime Fleet (RU)
TsAMS ..... Central Air Weather Station (RU)
TsAMSG ... Central Air Weather Station of the Civil Air Fleet (RU)
TsANII ...... Central Pharmaceutical Scientific Research Institute (RU)
TsANII ...... Central Scientific Research Institute of Automobile Operation (RU)
TsANIIP.... Central American Industrial Scientific Research Institute (RU)
TsANIL..... Central Pharmaceutical Scientific Research Laboratory [*1940-1944*] (RU)
TsANIS ..... Central Pharmaceutical Scientific Research Station [*1931-1940*] (RU)
TsANKh .... Central Archives of the National Economy [*in Leningrad*] (RU)
TsANS...... Central Air Navigation Station (RU)
TSANZ...... Transplantation Society of Australia and New Zealand
TsAO .... Central Aerological Observatory (RU)
TSAOA...... Tameion Syndaxeon kai Arogis Organon Agrofylakis [*Rural Police Pension and Assistance Fund*] [*Greek*] (GC)
TsAOR ...... Central Archives of the October Revolution (RU)
TsAOS...... Central Pharmaceutical Experimental Station [*1928-1931*] (RU)
TsAP......... Central Artillery Post [*on shipboard*] (RU)
TsAP......... Digital-Analog Converter (RU)
tsap........... Medical Air Transport Regiment (BU)
TsAPO....... Central Architectural Design Organization (BU)
TsAR......... Tsentralnoafrikanskaia Respublika [*Central African Republic*]
TsARM...... Central Automobile Repair Shops (RU)
TsARZ....... Central Automobile Repair Plant (RU)
TsAS .... Center Column Unit Machine Tool (RU)
TsAS .... Central Ammunition Depot (RU)
TsAS .... Central Artery of the Retina (RU)
TsAS .... Central Pharmaceutical Warehouse (RU)
TsAS......... Digital Automatic System (RU)
TsAS......... Fire Director [*on shipboard*] (RU)
TsATO...... Central Joint-Stock Trade Company (RU)
TsAU .... Central Administration of Archives (RU)
TsAU .... Central Administrative Office (RU)
TsAVP...... Central Foreign Policy Archives (RU)
TSAY........ Tameion Syndaxeos kai Avtasfaliseos Ygeionomikon [*Medical Personnel Pension and Self-Insurance Fund*] [*Greek*] (GC)
TsB........... Central Accounting Office (RU)
TsB........... Central Bank (RU)
TsB........... Central Base (BU)
TsB........... Central Battery (BU)
TsB........... Central Library (RU)
TsB........... Central Office (RU)
tsb........... Tank and Self-Propelled Gun Battalion (RU)
TSB........... Technical Service Bureau (BU)
TSB........... Transports Aeriens du Benin [*ICAO designator*] (FAAC)
TSB........... Tsumeb [*Namibia*] [*Airport symbol*] (OAG)
TSB........... Turkiye Sanatcilar Birligi [*Turkish Artists Union*] (TU)
TsBAK...... Royal Bulgarian Automobile Club (RU)
TSBARA ... Tasmanian Small Bore and Air Rifle Association [*Australia*]
TSBB .... Turkiye Ticaret Odalari, Sanayi Odalari ve Ticaret Borsalari Birligi [*Turkish Union of Chambers of Commerce, Industry, and Stock Exchanges*] [*TOB*] [*See also*] (TU)
TsBDKO.... Central Bureau of Children's Communist Organizations (RU)
TsBI......... Central Office of Information (RU)
TsBK......... Central Library Commission (RU)
TsBK......... Central Office of Regional Studies (RU)
TsBK......... Pulp and Paper Kombinat (RU)
TsBKM...... Central Planning and Design Office of the Forging-and-Pressing Machinery (RU)
TsBL......... Central Hospital Laboratory (BU)
TsBN .... Central Office of Standardization (RU)
TsBNSEV ... Central Office of Standardization of Electric Vacuum Equipment Components (RU)
TsBNTI ..... Central Office of Scientific and Technical Information (RU)
TsBP......... Central Bureau of Weather Forecasts (RU)
TsBP......... Central Office for Checking (Hydrometeorological Instruments) (RU)
TsBP......... Central Party Bureau (RU)
TsBP......... Central Weather Bureau (RU)
TsBP......... Pulp and Paper Industry (RU)
TsBPM...... Central Office for Checking Meteorological Instruments (RU)
TsBPS....... Central Office of Proletarian Students (RU)
TsBS .... Center of Lateral Resistance [*Nautical term*] (RU)
TsBSKUP ... Central Office of Standardization of the Shale and Coal Industry (RU)
TsBSP....... Central Library of the Construction Industry (RU)
TsBTEIN... Central Office of Technical and Economic Information (RU)
TsBTI .... Central Office of Technical Information (RU)
TsBTK ...... Central Office of Technical Control (RU)
TsBTM ...... Central Office of Heavy Machinery Manufacture (RU)
TsBTN....... Central Office of Work Standards (RU)

TsBTS........ Central Design Office of Heavy Machine Tool Manufacture (RU)
TsBVK....... Central Hydrological Register Office (RU)
TsBYuP ..... Central Office of Young Pioneers (RU)
TsBZ.......... Cement-Concrete Plant (RU)
TsBZG....... Central Bureau of Foreign Groups for Assisting the RSDRP [1907-1916] (RU)
TSC........... Tanzania Sisal Corporation
TSC........... Teachers Service Commission
TSC........... Technical Services Corp. [Myanmar] (DS)
TSC........... Technical Standing Committee [Australia]
TSC........... Tehnicki Skolski Centar [Technical School Center] [Zagreb] [Army] (YU)
TSC........... Turkish Society of Cardiology (EAIO)
TsCh.......... Cetane Number (RU)
Tschech P .. Tschechoslowakisches Patent [Czechoslovak Patent] [German] (GCA)
t/schet........ Current Account (RU)
TsChO .... Central Black Earth Region (RU)
Tschovodproyekt ... All-Union Office for Surveying and Planning of Irrigation Systems in the Central Black Earth Regions (RU)
TsChP........ Central Black Earth Belt (RU)
TsD .... Center of Pressure [Nautical term] (RU)
TsD .... Digital Discriminator (RU)
TSD .... Medium-Pressure Turbine (RU)
Tsd .... Tausend [Thousand] [German]
TSD .... Technical Services Department [Council for Scientific and Industrial Research] [South Africa] (AA)
TSD .... Technical Services Division [Technisearch Ltd.] [Australia]
TSD .... Turk Sinematek Dernegi [Turkish Cinematic Association] (TU)
tsd.............. Tusind [Thousand] [Danish/Norwegian]
TsDA .... Central House of Actors (RU)
TsDA .... Central House of Architects (RU)
TsDA .... Central State Archives (BU)
TsDA .... Digital Differential Analyzer (RU)
TSDA........ Tasmanian Soft Drink Association [Australia]
TsDB........ Central Dispatcher's Office, Central Control Office (RU)
TSDB........ SCB [Statistika Centralbyran] Time Series Data Base [Sweden] [Information service or system] (CRD)
TsDDZh .... Central House of Railroad Workers' Children (RU)
TsDETS..... Central Children's Excursion and Tourist Station (RU)
TsDF .... Cytidine Diphosphate (RU)
TSDF .... Torres Strait Defence Force [Australia]
TsDI.......... Documentation and Information Center (RU)
TsDIA........ Central State Historical Archives (BU)
TsDK .... Central Commission for Children (RU)
TsDK .... Central House of Composers (RU)
TsDK .... Central House of Cooperatives (RU)
TsDK .... Central House of Culture (RU)
TsDK .... Central House of Motion Pictures (RU)
TsDK .... Central House of the Peasant (RU)
TsDKA...... Central House of the Red Army Imeni M. V. Frunze (RU)
TsDKhVD ... Central House of Children's Art Education (RU)
TsDKMR .... Central House of Culture of Medical Workers (RU)
TsDKZh..... Central House of Culture of Railroad Workers (RU)
TsDL.......... Central House of Writers (RU)
TsDNA ...... Central House of the People's Army (BU)
TsDNT ...... Central Folklore Club (BU)
TsDNT ...... Central House of Folk Art Imeni N. K. Krupskaya (RU)
TsDNV ..... Central House of the People's Army (BU)
TsDORNII .. Central Scientific Research Institute of Truck and Cart Roads and Road Machinery (RU)
TsDP.......... Central Dispatcher's Station, Central Control Post (RU)
TsDP.......... Central House of Pioneers (RU)
TsDP.......... Central Radiation-Monitoring Control Panel (RU)
TsDR .... Central Dispatcher Control (BU)
TsDRFK .... Central House of Workers in Physical Culture (RU)
TsDRI........ Central House of Workers in the Arts, USSR (RU)
TsDS.......... Central Traffic Control Service (RU)
TSDS......... Long-Distance Telephone Exchange (RU)
TsDSA ...... Central House of the Soviet Army Imeni M. V. Frunze (RU)
TsDT......... Central Children's Theater (RU)
TsDTS .... Central Children's Excursion and Tourist Station (RU)
TsDTS .... Central House of Communications Engineering (RU)
TsDU .... Central Dispatching of the Integrated Power System of Socialist Countries (RU)
TsDZh .... Central House of Journalists (RU)
TsDZh .... Central Journalists' Club (BU)
TsDZht ...... Central House of Technology of Railroad Transportation (RU)
TSE........... Taipei Stock Exchange [Taiwan]
TSE........... Tehran Stock Exchange (ME)
TSE........... Tokyo Stock Exchange [Japan]
TSE........... Tribunal Superior Eleitoral [Superior Electoral Court] [Brazil] (LA)
TSE........... Tribunal Supremo Electoral [Supreme Electoral Court] [Ecuador] (LA)

TSE........... Turkiye Sap Enstitusu [Turkish Foot and Mouth Institute] [Ankara] (TU)
TSE........... Turk Standartlar Enstitusu [Turkish Institute of Standards] (TU)
TsEDISK... Central House of Amateur Performances (RU)
TsEGAZO ... Central State Anti-Aircraft Defense (RU)
TsEIL .... Central Experimental Research Laboratory (RU)
TsEIM .... Digital Computers (BU)
TSEK .... Turkiye Sut Endustri Kurumu Genel Mudurlugu [Turkish Milk Industry Organization Directorate General] (TU)
tseka........... Central Committee (RU)
T SEKER... Turkiye Seker Fabrikalari [Turkey Sugar Factories Corporation]
tsekhkom ... Shop Committee (RU)
Tsekombank ... Central Municipal Bank, USSR (RU)
Tsekomol ... Central Committee of the Russian Young Communist League (RU)
Tsekomrabsnab ... Central Commission for Workers' Supply (RU)
Tsekprofsozh ... Central Committee of the Trade Union of Railroad Workers (RU)
TsEKPROS ... Central Committee of the Trade Union of Education Workers (RU)
Tsekrabis ... Central Committee of the Trade Union of Workers in the Arts (RU)
Tsektran .... Tsentralny Komitet Obyedinyonnogo Professialnogo Soyuza Rabotnikov Zheleznodorozhnogo i Vodnogo Transporta [Central Committee of the United Trade Union of Railroad and Water Transportation Workers] (RU)
TsEKUBU ... Central Commission for the Improvement of Scientists' Living Conditions (RU)
TsEKVOD ... Central Committee of the All-Russian Union of Water Transportation Workers (RU)
tsem............ Cement (RU)
tsem............ Cement Plant [Topography] (RU)
TsEM........ Trust for Performing Electrical Installation Work in the Central Regions (RU)
TsEMM..... Central Electromechanical Shops (RU)
TsENII ...... Central Scientific Research Institute of Economics (at the Gosplan RSFSR) (RU)
Tsenkomdezertir ... Central Commission for Combating Desertion (RU)
Tsenkompomgol ... Central Famine Relief Commission (RU)
Tsenkoopizdat ... Central Cooperative Publishing House (BU)
TsENTOEP ... Central Administration of the Scientific and Technical Society of the Power Industry (RU)
tsentr.......... Central (RU)
Tsentrakademsnab ... Central Supply Administration of the Academy of Sciences, USSR (RU)
Tsentrakademstroy ... Central Construction Administration of the Academy of Sciences, USSR (RU)
Tsentrarkhiv ... Central State Archives (RU)
TsENTRIZDAT ... Central Publishing House (RU)
Tsentrmlad kom ... Central Youth Commission (BU)
Tsentrobalt ... Tsentralny Komitet Baltiskogo Flota [Central Committee of the Baltic Fleet] [1917-1918] (RU)
Tsentrobelsoyuz ... Central Union of Consumers' Cooperatives of Belorussia (RU)
TsENTROBUMTREST ... Central Trust of the Pulp and Paper Industry (RU)
Tsentroelektromontazh ... Trust for Performing Electrical Installation Work in the Central Regions (RU)
Tsentroelektroset'stroy ... All-Union Trust of the Glavvostokelektroset'stroy of the Ministry of Construction of Electric Power Plants, USSR (RU)
Tsentroenergomontazh ... State All-Union Installation Trust of the Glavteploenergomontazh of the State Industrial Committee for Power Engineering and Electrification, USSR (RU)
Tsentroevak ... Central Evacuation Station (RU)
Tsentrogiproshakht ... All-Union Central State Institute for the Planning and Technical and Economic Prerequisites for the Development of the Coal Industry (RU)
Tsentrogiproshakhtostroy ... All-Union Central State Institute for the Planning of Mine Construction (RU)
Tsentrogosrybvod ... State Inspection for the Conservation of Fish Resources and Regulation of Fishing in the Central Regions (RU)
Tsentrokhimles ... All-Union Trust of the Wood-Chemistry Industry (RU)
Tsentrolak ... Main Committee of the Varnish and Paint Industry (RU)
Tsentronerud ... State All-Union Trust of the Glavnerud (RU)
Tsentropechat' ... Central Agency of the All-Russian Central Executive Committee for the Distribution of Publications [1918-1922] (RU)
Tsentroplen ... Central Committee for Prisoners of War (RU)
Tsentroplenbezh ... Central Committee for Prisoners of War and Refugees (RU)
Tsentroprofshkola ... Central Higher School of Trade Unionism (RU)
Tsentroprofsovet ... All-Russian Central Trade-Union Council (RU)
Tsentropromproyekt ... Central Planning Institute (for the Planning of Industrial Structures) (RU)

Tsentropromsovet ... Central Council of Producers' Cooperatives of the USSR (RU)

Tsentroruda ... State Trust for the Iron Ore Industry of the Central Part of the USSR (RU)

Tsentrosantekhmontazh ... Central Sanitary Engineering Installation Trust of the Glavsantekhmontazh (RU)

Tsentrosnab ... Central Supply Administration of the VSNKh (RU)

Tsentrosovnatsmen ... Central Council of National Minorities (of the Narkompros RSFSR) (RU)

Tsentrosoyuz ... Central Union of Consumers' Societies, USSR (RU)

Tsentrostal' ... State All-Union Association of the Metallurgical Industry of the Central Part of the USSR (RU)

Tsentrostroymekhanizatsiya ... Trust for the Earthwork Mechanization on Roads of the Northern and Western Regions of the Glavzheldorstroy (RU)

Tsentrotop ... Central Fuel Administration (RU)

Tsentrotransstroy ... Construction and Installation Trust of the Glavzheldorstroy of the Northern and Western Regions of the State Industrial Committee for Transportation Construction, USSR (RU)

Tsentroupravkozh ... Central Administration of State Establishments of the Leather Industry (RU)

Tsentrovoyenzag ... Central Military Procurement Section (RU)

Tsentrozagotzerno ... Association for the Procurement and Marketing of Grain in the Central Regions (RU)

Tsentrozhilsoyuz ... Central Union of Housing Cooperatives (RU)

tsenz .... Censorship (RU)

Tsenz .... Censured (BU)

TsEPAZ ..... Central Directorate of Artillery Weapons Plants [1919-1921] (RU)

TsEPAZO ... Central Antiaircraft Defense Post (RU)

TsEPK .... Central Expert Verification Commission (RU)

TSEPP .... Telecom Small Enterprise Policy Panel [Australia]

TsERA .... Central Power Repairs and Automation (BU)

Tserabkom ... Central Workers' Committee (RU)

Tserabkoop ... Central Workers' Cooperative (RU)

tserk .... Church (RU)

tserk .... Ecclesiastical Word (RU)

Tseroz .... Central State Trust for the Mining and Processing of Ozokerite (RU)

TsES .... Central Electric Power Plant (RU)

TsES .... Central Electrotechnical Council (RU)

TsESS .... Aircraft Central Electric Power Unit (RU)

TsESZ .... Central Electric Power Plant of a Factory (RU)

TsETETIS ... Central Technicum of Theatrical Art [1925-1931] (RU)

TsF .... Circular Milling (RU)

TSF .... Tasmanian Soccer Federation [Australia]

TSF .... Telefonia sem Fios [Wireless Telephone] [Portuguese]

TSF .... Telegrafia sem Fios [Wireless Telegraph] [Portuguese]

TSF .... Telegrafo senza Fili [Wireless Telegraph] [Italian]

TSF .... Telegraphie sans Fil [Wireless Telegraphy] [French]

TSF .... Turkiye Seker Fabrikalari AS [Turkish Sugar Factories Corporation] (TU)

TsFDK .... Central Long-Term Credit Fund (RU)

TSFGA ...... Tasmanian Stone Fruit Growers' Association [Australia]

TsFMU .... Central Machine Accounting and Computing Office (RU)

TsFSh .... Centrifugal Pitch Arrester (RU)

TsFU .... Central Finance Administration (RU)

TSG .... Labor and Social Welfare (BU)

TSG .... Technical Service Guild of Australia (ADA)

TSG .... Telecommunications Strategy Group [Australia]

TSG .... Tri-Service Group [NATO]

TsGA .... Central Group of Armies [NATO] (RU)

TsGA .... Central State Archives (RU)

TSGA .... Tanzania Sisal Growers Association

TSGA .... Technical Service Guild of Australia

TSGAD ..... Tri-Service Group on Air Defense [NATO] (NATG)

TsGADA ... Central State Archives of Ancient Documents, USSR (RU)

TsGAKA ... Central State Archives of the Red Army, USSR (RU)

TsGAKFFD ... Central State Archives of Motion-Picture, Photographic, and Phonographic Records, USSR (RU)

TsGALI ..... Central State Archives of Literature and Art, USSR (RU)

TsGANKh ... Central State Archives of the National Economy, USSR (RU)

TsGAOR ... Central State Archives of the October Revolution, High State Government Bodies, and State Administrative Bodies, USSR (RU)

TsGAORi SS ... Central State Archives of the October Revolution and the Building of Socialism (RU)

TsGAORSS ... Central State Archives of the October Revolution and the Building of Socialism (RU)

TsGASA .... Central State Archives of the Soviet Army (RU)

TsGAVMF ... Central State Archives of the Navy, USSR (RU)

TsGB .... Central Geological Library (RU)

TSGCEE .... Tri-Service Group on Communications and Electronic Equipment [NATO] (NATG)

TsGFU .... Central Installation for Gas Fractionation (RU)

TsGIA .... Central State Historical Archives (RU)

TsGIAG .... Central State Historical Archives of Georgia (RU)

TsGIAL ..... Central State Historical Archives in Leningrad (RU)

TsGIAM .... Central State Historical Archives in Moscow (RU)

TsGII .... Central Forestry Research Institute (BU)

Tsgintsvetmet ... Central State Scientific Research Institute of Nonferrous Metals (RU)

TsGIRD ..... Central Group for the Study of Jet Propulsion (RU)

TsGL .... Central Genetics Laboratory Imeni I. V. Michurin (RU)

TsGLA .... Central State Archives of Literature (RU)

TsGM .... State Central Geographic Museum (RU)

TsGMB ..... Central Hydrometeorological Office (RU)

TsGNKI ..... Central State Scientific Control Institute (RU)

TsGNKI ..... Central State Scientific Control Institute of Veterinary Preparations (RU)

TsGOI .... Central State Institute of Smallpox (RU)

TsGOK ..... Central Mining and Concentration Kombinat (RU)

TsGT .... Central Geophysical Trust (RU)

TsGTI .... Central State Institute of Traumatology (RU)

TsGU .... Central Hydrographic Administration (RU)

TsGU .... Tsimlyanskiy Hydroelectric Development (RU)

TsGV .... Master Vertical Gyro (RU)

TsGVIA ..... Central State Archives of Military History, USSR (RU)

TsGVIAL ... Branch of the Central State Archives of Military History in Leningrad (RU)

TsGVIALF ... Branch of the Central State Archives of Military History in Leningrad (RU)

TsGVMA ... Central State Naval Archives (RU)

TSh .... Brinell Ball Hardness Tester (RU)

TSh .... Tank Hinge [Sight] (RU)

TSh .... Tanzanian Shilling

TSh .... Telescopic Hinge [Sight] (RU)

TSH .... Tshikapa [Zaire] [Airport symbol] (OAG)

t-shch .... Comrade (RU)

TShch .... Minesweeper (RU)

TSHS .... Tibet Society for Horticultural Science [China] (EAIO)

TsI .... Digital Indicator (RU)

TSI .... Tameion Syndaxeon Ithopoion [Actors' Pensions Fund] [Greek] (GC)

TSI .... Tovarna Steklenih Izdelkov [Glass Products Factory] [Slovenska Bistrica] (YU)

TSI .... Treuhandstelle fuer Industrie und Handel [Trustee Agency for Industry and Trade]

TsIA .... Central Historical Archives (RU)

TSIA .... Tasmanian Sawmillers' Industrial Association

TSIAB ...... Torres Strait Islander Advisory Board [Australia]

TsIAG .... Central Institute of Obstetrics and Gynecology (RU)

TsIAM .... Central Scientific Research Institute of Aircraft Engines Imeni P. I. Baranov (RU)

TsIATIM ... Central Scientific Research Institute of Aviation Fuel and Lubricants (RU)

TsIChM ..... Central Scientific Research Institute of Ferrous Metallurgy (RU)

TsID .... Digital Diameter Gauge (RU)

TSID .... Turk Sanayici ve Is Adamlari Dernegi [Turkish Industrialists and Businessmen's Organization] (TU)

TsIEGM .... Central Institute of Experimental Hydrology and Meteorology (RU)

TsIEI .... Central Institute of Economic Research (RU)

TsIEM .... Central Institute of Epidemiology and Microbiology (RU)

TsIEM .... Central Institute of Experimental Medicine (RU)

TsIETIN .... Central Scientific Research Institute for Determination of Disability and Organization of Work for Disabled Persons (RU)

tsig .... Gypsy (BU)

TsII .... Central Information Institute (RU)

TsIIKhPROM ... All-Union Central Scientific Research Institute of the Cotton Industry (RU)

TsIIN .... Central Information Institute (RU)

TsIIN .... Central Testing Institute (BU)

TsIINChM ... Central Information Institute of Ferrous Metallurgy (RU)

TsIINS .... Central Institute of Information on Construction (RU)

TsIINTsvetmet ... Central Information Institute of Nonferrous Metallurgy (RU)

TsIIT .... Central Computer Equipment Institute (BU)

TsIITsvetmet ... Central Information Institute of Nonferrous Metallurgy (RU)

TsIK .... Central Executive Committee, USSR [1924-1937] (RU)

TsIK .... Central Institute of Health Resorts [1926-1958] (RU)

Tsikl izd ..... Mimeographed Edition (BU)

Tsiklopech ... Mimeographed (BU)

TsIL .... Central Measurement Laboratory (RU)

TsIM .... Central Institute of Metals (RU)

TsIM .... Central Scientific Research Institute of Materials (RU)

TsIM .... Digital Computer (BU)

TsIM .... Digital Integrating Computer (RU)

TsIM .... Macromolecular Research Center (RU)

TSIMA ...... Torres Strait Islander Media Association [*Australia*]
TsIMTNeft' ... Central Scientific Research Institute for the Mechanization and Organization of Labor in the Petroleum Industry   (RU)
TsINIS....... Central Institute of Scientific Information on Construction and Architecture (of the State Committee for Construction, USSR)   (RU)
TsINISiA... Central Institute of Scientific Information on Construction and Architecture   (RU)
tsinkogr...... Zincography   (RU)
TsINS......... Central Scientific Research Institute of the Sugar Industry   (RU)
TsINTEI.... Central Institute of Scientific, Technical, and Economic Information   (RU)
TsINTI ..... Central Institute of Scientific and Technical Information   (RU)
TsINTIAM ... Central Institute of Scientific and Technical Information on Automation and Machinery Manufacture   (RU)
TsINTIElektroprom ... Central Institute of Scientific and Technical Information of the Electrotechnical Industry and Instrument Making   (RU)
TsINTIEP ... Central Institute of Scientific and Technical Information and Standardization of the Electrical Equipment Industry   (RU)
TsINTIMASh ... Central Institute of Scientific and Technical Information of Machinery Manufacture   (RU)
TsINTIPishcheprom ... Central Institute of Scientific and Technical Information of the Food Industry   (RU)
TsINTIpriborelektroprom ... Central Institute of Scientific and Technical Information of Instrument Making, Electrical Equipment Industry, and Means of Automation   (RU)
TsINUPMED ... Central Scientific Research Institute of Educational Visual Aids in Medicine, Biology, and Sanitation   (RU)
TsIONP..... Central Institute of Organizers of Public Education   (RU)
TsIP .... Central Institute of Psychiatry   (RU)
TsIP .... Central Institute of Weather Forecasts   (RU)
TSIP .... Turkiye Sosyalist Isciler Partisi [*Turkish Socialist Workers Party*]   (TU)
TsIPK .... Central Institute of Blood Transfusion   (RU)
TsIPKKNO ... Central Institute for Improving the Qualifications of Public Education Personnel   (RU)
TsIPKNO .. Central Institute for the Training of Public Education Personnel   (RU)
TsIPKP...... Central Institute for Improving the Qualifications of Teachers   (RU)
TsIPKRRNO ... Central Institute for Improving the Qualifications of Supervisory Personnel in Public Education   (RU)
TsIPTK...... Central Institute for the Training of Transportation Personnel   (RU)
TsIRIR....... Central Scientific Research Institute of Roentgenology and Radiology   (RU)
TsIS .... Central Institute of Communications   (RU)
TsIS .... Central Scientific Research Institute of Transportation Construction   (RU)
TsIS .... Central Tool Warehouse   (RU)
TsISON ..... Central Institute for the Socialist Exchange of Experience in the Petroleum Industry of the USSR   (RU)
TsISP........ Central Scientific Research Institute of Hygiene Education   (RU)
tsist............ Cistern [*Topography*]   (RU)
TsIT .... Central Institute of Labor   (RU)
TsITEIN.... Central Institute of Technical and Economic Information   (RU)
TsITI .... Central Institute of Technical Information   (RU)
TsITIUglya ... Central Institute of Technical Information of the Coal Industry   (RU)
tsit kn ...... Quoted Book   (BU)
TsITLegprom ... Central Scientific Research Institute of Labor in Light Industry   (RU)
TsITM....... Central Institute for the Organization of Labor and Mechanization of Production   (RU)
TsITO....... Central Scientific Research Institute of Traumatology and Orthopedics   (RU)
TsITP .... Central Institute of Standard Designs   (RU)
tsitrus........ Citrus [*Topography*]   (RU)
tsit st .... Article Cited   (BU)
tsit such...... Quoted Work   (BU)
TsIU.......... Central Institute for the Advanced Training of Physicians   (RU)
TsIUU........ Central Institute for the Advanced Training of Teachers   (BU)
TsIVIM...... Central Historical Museum of Military Engineering   (RU)
TsIZ.......... Central Publishing House   (RU)
TsIZAS...... Central Institute for the Study of Drought and Dry Winds in the RSFSR   (RU)
TsIZhVYa ... Central Institute of Living Oriental Languages [*1920-1921*]   (RU)
TsIZIO ...... Central Industrial Correspondence Training Institute   (RU)
TsIZMAE ... Central Institute of Terrestrial Magnetism and Atmospheric Electricity   (RU)
TsIZO........ Central Correspondence Training Institute   (RU)
TsIZO........ Central Institute of Public Health   (RU)
TsIZPO ..... Central Pedagogical Correspondence Training Institute   (RU)
TSJ .... Tanzania School of Journalism

TSJ .... Tsushima [*Japan*] [*Airport symbol*]   (OAG)
TsK .... Central Committee   (BU)
TSK........... Commodity Warehouse Office   (RU)
TsK .... Crystallization Nucleus   (RU)
TSK........... Heat-Resisting Suit   (RU)
TSK........... Tekniikan Sanastokeskus [*Centre for Technical Terminology*] [*Finland*]   (PDAA)
TSK........... Towa Sogo Kigyo [*East Asia Enterprises Co.*] [*Japan*]
TSK........... Turk Satis Kooperatifleri [*Turkish Sales Cooperatives*]   (TU)
TsKB......... Central Design Office   (RU)
TsKB.......... Central Municipal Bank, USSR   (RU)
TSKB........ Tarim Satislari Kooperatifleri Birligi [*Agricultural Sales Cooperatives Union*]   (TU)
TSKB........ Turkiye Sinai Kalkinma Bankasi [*Turkish Industrial Development Bank*]   (TU)
TsKBA....... Central Design Office of Fittings   (RU)
TsKBD...... Central Traffic Safety Commission   (BU)
TsKBF .... Central Committee of the Baltic Fleet   (RU)
TsKBGM.... State Central Design Office of Hydraulic Machinery in Moscow   (RU)
TsKBKhM ... Central Design Office of Chemical Machinery   (RU)
TsKBKhM ... Central Design Office of Refrigeration Machinery   (RU)
TsKBLO .... Central Design Office for Foundry Equipment   (RU)
TsKBMM ... Central Design Office of Metallurgical Machinery   (RU)
TsKBPP..... Central Design Office of the Bearing Industry   (RU)
TsKBS ...... Central Shipbuilding Design Office   (RU)
TsKDM ..... Central Committee of Democratic Youth   (BU)
TsKEB ...... Central Design and Experimental Office   (RU)
TsKGF ...... Central Cartographic and Geodetic Fund   (RU)
TsKGU ...... Central Kazakhstan Geological Administration   (RU)
TSKhA....... Timiryazev Agricultural Academy   (RU)
TSKhI........ Turkmen Agricultural Institute   (RU)
TsKhK....... Cellulose and Paper Combine   (BU)
TsKhL........ Central Chemical Laboratory   (BU)
TsKhOL..... Central Chemical and Organoleptic Laboratory   (RU)
TsKIB .... Central Design and Research Office of Hunting and Sporting Arms   (RU)
TsKK.......... Central Classification Committee of the MFD   (RU)
TsKK.......... Central Control Commission   (BU)
TsKK.......... Central Control Commission of the VKP(b) [*1921-1934*]   (RU)
TsKK-NKRKI ... Central Control Commission and People's Commissariat of Workers' and Peasants' Inspection [*1923-1934*]   (RU)
TsKKOV.... Central Peasants' Public Mutual Aid Committee   (RU)
TsKKPB .... Central Committee of the Communist Party of Belorussia   (RU)
TsKKP(b) .. Central Committee of the Communist Party (of Bolsheviks)   (RU)
TsKKP(b)U ... Central Committee of the Communist Party (of Bolsheviks) of the Ukraine   (RU)
TsKKPCh... Central Committee of the Communist Party of Czechoslovakia   (RU)
TsKKPK ... Central Committee of the Communist Party of China   (RU)
TsKKPSS .. Central Committee of the Communist Party of the Soviet Union   (RU)
TsKKPU.... Central Committee of the Communist Party of the Ukraine   (RU)
TsKKPYa .. Central Committee of the Communist Party of Japan   (RU)
TsKK-RKI ... Central Control Commission and Workers' and Peasants' Inspection [*1923-1934*]   (RU)
TsKL.......... Central Laboratory of Criminology (of the All-Union Institute of Jurisprudence)   (RU)
TsKNA ...... Central Committee on New Alphabet of the RSFSR   (RU)
TsK naDSNM ... Central Committee of the Dimitrov People's Youth Union   (BU)
TsK naKPSS ... Central Committee of the Communist Party of the Soviet Union   (BU)
TsK naprofsuyuzite ... Central Committee of the Trade Unions   (BU)
TsK naSNM ... Central Committee of the People's Youth Union   (BU)
TsKNB...... Central Scientific Libraries Pool   (RU)
TsKNII ..... Central Confectionery Scientific Research Institute   (RU)
TsKO .... "Target-Commander-Gun" Angle   (RU)
TsKORPS ... Central Committee of the General Workers' Trade Union   (BU)
TsKOZ....... Central Office for the Processing of Journal and Newspaper Subscriptions   (RU)
TsKP.......... Central Command Post   (RU)
TsKP.......... Central Committee on Transportation   (RU)
TsKP.......... Central Control Post   (BU)
TsKPM...... Central Committee of the Mining Workers' Trade Union   (BU)
TsKPOMGOL ... Central Famine Relief Commission   (RU)
TsKPOSLEDGOL ... Central Commission for Combating the After-Effects of Famine   (RU)
TsKPS........ Central Committee of the Trade Unions   (BU)
TsKRABIS ... Central Committee of the Trade Union of Workers in the Arts   (RU)
TsKRKP(b) ... Central Committee of the Russian Communist Party (of Bolsheviks)   (RU)
TsKRMS ... Central Committee of the Young Workers' League   (BU)

TsKRRS..... Central Courses for Supervisory Communications Personnel (RU)
TsKRSDRP(b) ... Central Committee of the Russian Social Democratic Workers' Party (of Bolsheviks) (RU)
TsKS.......... Central Cooperative Union (BU)
TsKSh.......... Central Komsomol School (RU)
TsKSKhS....... Central Cottonseed-Testing Station (RU)
TsKSL........ Central Seed-Testing Laboratory (RU)
TsKSNM... Central Committee of the People's Youth Union (BU)
TsKTB .... Central Design Technical Office (RU)
TsKTEK .... Administration for Container Shipments and Transportation and Forwarding Operations (RU)
TsKTI .... Central Committee of Heavy Industry (RU)
TsKTI .... Central Scientific Research, Planning, and Design Boiler and Turbine Institute Imeni I. I. Polzunov (RU)
TsKVI .... Central Scientific Research Institute of Dermatology and Venereal Diseases (RU)
TsKVKP(b) ... Central Committee of the All-Union Communist Party (of Bolsheviks) (RU)
TsKVLKSM ... Central Committee of the All-Union Lenin Young Communist League (RU)
TsKZ.......... Central Correspondence Courses (RU)
TSKZ......... Towarzystwo Spoleczno-Kulturalne Zydow [*Jewish Social and Cultural Society*] (POL)
TSl .... Addition Control Trigger [*Computers*] (RU)
TsL............ Central Laboratory (RU)
TSL............ Techniczna Szkola Lotnicza [*Aviation Engineering School*] (POL)
TSL............ Towarzystwo Szkoly Ludowej [*Society for Public Schools*] (POL)
TSL............ Trans Siberian Landbridge (DS)
TsLA.......... Central Laboratory of Automation (RU)
TsLAM..... Central Laboratory of Automation and Mechanization (RU)
TsLAM..... Central Laboratory of Aviation Medicine (RU)
TsLAM..... Central Model Automobile Laboratory (RU)
TsLB.......... Central Lecture Bureau (RU)
TsLEB .... Central Lumber Export Office (RU)
TsLEKhIT ... Central Laboratory for Electrochemical Sources of Electricity (BU)
TsLEM ...... Central Laboratory and Experimental Workshops of the Mosenergo (RU)
TsLMM..... Central Laboratory of Ship Modeling (RU)
TsLOS ...... Central Forest Experimental Station (RU)
TsLPS........ Central Laboratory of Wire Communications (RU)
TsLSI........ Central Laboratory of Sports Equipment (RU)
TsM .... Center of Mass (RU)
TsM .... Central Workshop (RU)
TsM .... Colorimeter (RU)
TSM.......... Copper Resistance Thermometer (RU)
TsM .... Nonferrous Metallurgy (RU)
TSM.......... Towarzystwo Swiadomego Macierzynstwa [*Society for Planned Parenthood*] (POL)
TsM.......... Transair Mali SA [*ICAO designator*] (FAAC)
TsMB........ Central Medical Library (RU)
TSMC....... Taiwan Semiconductor Manufacturing Co.
TsME........ Digital Magnetic Element (RU)
TSMEDE .. Tameion Syndaxeon Mikhanikon Ergolipton Dimosion Ergon [*Pension Fund for Public Works Engineer-Contractors*] [*Greek*] (GC)
TsMetI....... Central Meteorological Institute (BU)
TsMF......... Cytidine Monophosphate (RU)
TsMI......... Central Meteorological Institute (BU)
TsMI......... Central Moscow Racetrack (RU)
TsMIS .... Central Machine-Testing Station (RU)
TsMK .... Central Naval Club of the DOSAAF SSSR (RU)
TsMK .... Central Youth Committee (BU)
TsMKA..... Central Museum of the Red Army (RU)
TsMKB..... Central Furniture Design Office (RU)
TsMM .... Central Machine Shop (RU)
TsMO .... Central Mobilization Section (RU)
TsMP........ Central Museum of Soil Science (RU)
TSMPE ..... Tsvetmetpromexport [*Utilities construction company*] [*Former USSR*]
TsMS........ Central Meteorological Station (BU)
TsMS......... Central Warehouse (BU)
TsMSA ...... Central Museum of the Soviet Army (RU)
TsMSh....... Central School of Music (RU)
TsMTMLP ... Central Model Textile Mill of the Ministry of Light Industry (BU)
TsMTS ...... Central Long Distance Telephone Exchange, USSR (RU)
TsMTU....... Technical Specifications for Nonferrous Metallurgy (RU)
TsMV .... All-Metal (Passenger) Car (RU)
tsn .... Centner (RU)
TsN .... Central Aiming [*Artillery*] (RU)
TsN .... Centrifugal Supercharger (RU)
TSN .... Tameion Syndaxeon Nomikon [*Judiciary Personnel Pension Fund*] [*Greek*] (GC)

TSN .... Tianjin [*China*] [*Airport symbol*] (OAG)
TSN .... Trans-Air Services Ltd. [*Nigeria*] [*ICAO designator*] (FAAC)
TsNAIML ... Central People's Archives of the Institute of Marxism-Leninism at the TsK KPSS (RU)
TsND........ Low-Pressure Cylinder (RU)
TsNEL....... Central Scientific Experimental Laboratory (RU)
TsNELkozh ... Central Scientific Experimental Laboratory of Leather (RU)
TsNIAG..... Central Scientific Research Aviation Hospital (RU)
TsNIAGI ... Central Scientific Research Institute of Obstetrics and Gynecology (RU)
TsNIAL..... Central Scientific Research Pharmaceutical Laboratory (RU)
TsNIB........ Central Office of Standards Research (RU)
Tsnib.......... Central Scientific Research Center (RU)
TsNIB........ Central Scientific Research Office (RU)
Tsnibgrazhdanstroy ... Central Scientific Research Center of Civil Engineering Construction (RU)
TSNIDA .... Tsentral'nyy Nauchno Issledovatel'skiy Dizel'nyy Institut [*Central Scientific Research Diesel Institute*] [*Russian*] (PDAA)
TsNIDI...... Central Scientific Research Diesel Institute (RU)
TsNIDI...... Central Scientific Research Institute of Disinfection (RU)
TsNIEL...... Central Scientific Research Electrotechnical Laboratory (RU)
TsNIF .... Central Scientific Research Institute for Physical Culture (BU)
TsNIFK .... Central Scientific Institute of Physical Culture (BU)
TsNIGMA ... Central Hydrometeorological Scientific Research Archives (RU)
TsNIGRI ... Central Scientific Research Institute for Geological Exploration [*Leningrad, 1931-1939*] (RU)
TsNIGRI ... Central Scientific Research Institute of Prospecting for Nonferrous, Rare, and Noble Metals [*Moscow*] (RU)
TsNII........ Central Scientific Research Institute (RU)
TsNIIASh ... Central Scientific Research Institute of Abrasives and Grinding (RU)
TsNIIAT ... Central Scientific Research Institute of Automobile Transportation (RU)
TsNIIB ...... Central Scientific Research Institute of the Pulp and Paper Industry (RU)
TsNIIBUMMASh ... All-Union Scientific Research Institute of Paper Machinery (RU)
TsNIIChERMET ... Central Scientific Research Institute of Ferrous Metallurgy Imeni I. P. Bardin (RU)
TsNIIChermetal ... Central Scientific Research Institute of Ferrous Metals (BU)
TsNIIChM ... Central Scientific Research Institute of Ferrous Metallurgy Imeni I. P. Bardin (RU)
TsNIID...... Central Scientific Research Institute of Lumber (RU)
TsNIIEP.... Central Scientific Research Institute of Experimental Planning (RU)
TsNIIEPZhilishcha ... Central Scientific Research and Planning Institute of Standard and Experimental Planning of Housing (RU)
TsNIIEVT ... Central Scientific Research Institute of Economics and Operation of Water Transportation (RU)
TsNIIFK.... Central Scientific Research Institute of Physical Culture (BU)
TsNIIFM... Central Scientific Research Institute of Plywood and Furniture (RU)
TsNIIGAiK ... Central Scientific Research Institute of Geodesy, Aerial Surveying, and Cartography (RU)
TsNIIGS.... Central Scientific Research Forestry Institute (BU)
TsNIIISA .. Central Scientific Research Institute of Communications Engineers of the Soviet Army (RU)
TsNIIKA ... State All-Union Central Scientific Research Institute of Complex Automation (RU)
TsNIIKhP ... Central Scientific Research Institute of the Baking Industry (RU)
TsNIIKhProm ... Central Scientific Research Institute of the Cotton Industry (RU)
TsNIIKOP ... Central Scientific Research Institute of the Canning and Dehydrated Vegetables Industry (RU)
TsNIIKP.... Central Scientific Research Institute of the Leather and Footwear Industry (RU)
TsNIIKPP ... Central Scientific Research Institute of the Starch and Syrup Industry (RU)
TsNIIKZ.... Central Scientific Research Institute of Leather Substitutes (RU)
TsNIILesosplava ... Central Scientific Research Institute of Log Rafting (RU)
TsNIILKh ... Central Scientific Research Institute of Forestry (RU)
TsNIILV.... Central Scientific Research Institute of the Bast-Fiber Industry (RU)
TsNIIMAP ... Central Scientific Research Laboratory of the Macaroni Industry (RU)
TsNIIMASh ... Central Scientific Research Institute of Machinery Manufacture and Metalworking (RU)
TsNIIMashdetal' ... Central Scientific Research Institute of Accessories and Spare Parts for Textile Equipment (RU)
TsNIIME .. Central Scientific Research Institute of Mechanization and Power Engineering in the Lumber Industry (RU)

TsNIIMESKh ... Central Scientific Research Institute of Rural Mechanization and Electrification of the Non-Black Earth Belt of the USSR (RU)

TsNIIMF... Central Scientific Research Institute of the Maritime Fleet (RU)

TsNIIMOD ... Central Scientific Research Institute for the Mechanical Processing of Lumber (RU)

TsNIIMP .. Central Scientific Research Institute of the Fur Industry (RU)

TsNIIMPS ... All-Union Scientific Research Institute of Railroad Transportation (RU)

TsNIIMS... Central Scientific Research Institute of the Butter- and Cheese-Making Industry (RU)

TsNIINChM ... Central Scientific Research Institute of Information and Technical and Economic Research of Ferrous Metallurgy (RU)

TsNIINSh ... Central Scientific Research Institute of Elementary Schools (RU)

TsNIIOLOVO ... Central Scientific Research Institute of Tin, Antimony, and Mercury (RU)

TsNIIP ...... Central Scientific Experimental Cotton Institute (BU)

TsNIIP ...... Central Scientific Research Institute of Industrial Structures (RU)

TsNIIP ...... Central Scientific Research Institute of Pedagogy (RU)

TsNIIP ...... Central Scientific Research Institute of the Poultry-Processing Industry (RU)

TsNIIPBiVP ... Central Scientific Research Institute of the Beer, Soft Drink, and Wine Industry (RU)

TsNIIPI..... Central Scientific Research Institute of Patent Information and Technical and Economic Research (of the State Committee for Inventions and Discoveries, USSR) (RU)

TsNIIPO ... Central Scientific Research Institute of Fire Protection (RU)

TsNIIPO ... Central Scientific Research Institute on Fire Prevention (BU)

TsNIIPodzemshakhtostroy ... Central Scientific Research, Planning, and Design Institute of Underground Mine Construction (RU)

TsNII popamuka ... Central Scientific Research Institute on Cotton (BU)

TsNIIPP.... Central Scientific Research Institute of Prosthetics and Orthopedic Appliances (RU)

TsNIIPP.... Central Scientific Research Institute of the Poultry-Processing Industry (RU)

TsNIIPromzdaniy ... Central Scientific Research, Planning, and Experimental Institute of Industrial Buildings and Structures (RU)

TsNIIPS .... Central Scientific Research Institute of Industrial Structures (RU)

TsNIIRF.... Central Scientific Research Institute of the River Fleet (RU)

TsNIIS....... All-Union Scientific Research Institute of Transportation Construction (RU)

TsNIIS....... Central Scientific Research Institute of Communications (RU)

TsNIISh .... Central Scientific Research Institute of the Silk Industry (RU)

TsNIIShelka ... Central Scientific Research Institute of the Silk Industry (RU)

TsNIIShersti ... Central Scientific Research Institute of the Wool Industry (RU)

TsNIIShP ... Central Scientific Research Institute of the Garment Industry (RU)

TsNIIShveyprom ... Central Scientific Research Institute of the Garment Industry (RU)

TsNIISK.... Central Scientific Research Institute of Structural Parts (RU)

TsNIISKT ... Central Scientific Research Institute of Soviet Cooperative Trade (RU)

TsNIISM... Central Scientific Research Institute of Building Materials (RU)

TsNIISP .... Central Scientific Research Institute of Forensic Psychiatry Imeni Prof. V. P. Serbskiy (RU)

TsNIISP .... Central Scientific Research Institute of the Alcohol, Liqueur, and Vodka Industry (RU)

TsNIIST .... Central Scientific Research Institute of Soviet Trade (RU)

TsNIISTEF ... Central Scientific Research Institute of Construction and Technical Operation of the Maritime and River Fleets (RU)

TsNIITEI .. Central Scientific Research Institute of Information and Technical and Economic Research (RU)

TSNIITEIRKH ... Tsentral'nyy Nauchno-Issledovatel'skiy Institut Informatskiy i Techniko Ekonomicheskikh Issledovaniy Rybnogo Khozyaystva [*Central Scientific Research Institute of Technical and Economic Investigations of the Fisheries*] [*Russian*] (MSC)

TsNIITENeft' ... Central Scientific Research Institute of Technical Information and Economics of the Petroleum Industry (RU)

TsNIITLAMP ... Central Scientific Research Institute of Technical Vacuum Tubes (RU)

TsNIITMASh ... Central Scientific Research Institute for Machine Building Technology (BU)

TsNIITMASh ... Central Scientific Research Institute of Technology and Machinery Manufacture (RU)

TsNIITOP ... Central Scientific Research Institute of Technology and Organization of Production (RU)

TsNIITS .... Central Scientific Research Institute of Transportation Construction (RU)

TsNIITU ... Central Scientific Research Institute of Packing Materials and Packaging (RU)

TsNIIVT.... Central Scientific Research Institute of Water Transportation (RU)

TsNIIZH ... Central Scientific Research Institute of Animal Husbandry (BU)

TsNIIZhT ... Central Scientific Research Institute of Railroad Transportation (RU)

TsNIKhBI ... Central Scientific Research Institute of the Cotton Industry (RU)

TsNIKP ..... Central Scientific Research Institute of the Leather and Footwear Industry (RU)

TsNIKZ..... Central Scientific Research Institute of Leather Substitutes (RU)

TsNIL..... Central Scientific Research Laboratory (RU)

TsNILASh ... Central Scientific Research Laboratory of Abrasives and Grinding (RU)

TsNILBP... Central Scientific Research Laboratory of the Ferment Industry (RU)

TsNILELEKTROM ... Central Scientific Research Laboratory for Electrical Treatment of Materials (RU)

TsNILEPS ... Central Scientific Research Laboratory for the Electrification of Industry and Construction (RU)

TsNILGE .. Central Scientific Research Laboratory of Hygiene and Epidemiology (RU)

TsNILGiVT ... Central Scientific Research Laboratory of Hygiene in Water Transportation (RU)

TsNILiSV ... Central Scientific Research Laboratory of Wine Making and Northern Viticulture (RU)

TsNILKhI ... Central Scientific Research and Planning Institute of the Wood-Chemistry Industry (RU)

TsNILKhimstroy ... Central Scientific Research Laboratory for the Anticorrosion Protection of Structural Parts (RU)

TsNILKIP ... Central Scientific Research Laboratory of Control and Measuring Instruments (RU)

TsNILKOMBIKORM ... Central Scientific Research Laboratory of the Combined-Fodder Industry (RU)

TsNILkozhsyr'ye ... Central Scientific Research Laboratory of Leather Raw Materials (RU)

TsNILKR .. All-Union Central Scientific Research Laboratory for Preservation and Restoration of Museum Art Treasures (RU)

TsNILLVP ... Central Scientific Research Laboratory of the Liqueur and Vodka Industry (RU)

TsNILP ..... Central Scientific Research Laboratory of Fruits and Vegetables (RU)

TsNILPP... Central Scientific Research Laboratory of the Brewing and Soft Drink Industry (RU)

TsNILS...... Central Scientific Research Laboratory of the Match Industry (RU)

TsNILsherst' ... Central Scientific Research Laboratory of the Wool Industry (RU)

TsNILShOR ... Central Scientific Research Laboratory of Harness, Saddle, and Leather Notions Industry (RU)

TsNILShora ... Central Scientific Research Laboratory of Harness, Saddle, and Leather Notions Industry (RU)

TsNILSP ... Central Scientific Research Laboratory of the Match Industry (RU)

TsNILSS ... Central Scientific Research Laboratory of Steel Structures (RU)

TsNILStroymaterialy ... Central Scientific Research Laboratory of Building Materials (RU)

TsNILTara ... Central Scientific Research Laboratory of Packing Materials (RU)

TsNILTGP ... Central Scientific Research Laboratory of the Textile and Notions Industry (RU)

TsNILU..... Central Scientific Research Laboratory of Weighting Compounds (RU)

TsNILV ..... Central Scientific Research Laboratory of Wind-Power Installations and Wind-Driven Electric Power Plants (RU)

TsNILVP... Central Scientific Research Laboratory of the Vitamin Industry (RU)

TsNILVP... Central Scientific Research Laboratory of the Wine-Making Industry (RU)

TsNIMASh ... Central Scientific Research Institute of Machinery Manufacture and Metalworking (RU)

TsNIMB.... Central Scientific Research Office of Mine Surveying (RU)

TsNIMOTNP ... Central Scientific Research Institute for the Mechanization and Organization of Labor in the Petroleum Industry (RU)

Tsniotsvetmet ... Central Scientific Research Institute for the Processing of Nonferrous Metals (RU)

TsNIP......... Central Scientific Research Firing Range (RU)

TsNIPI ...... Central Scientific Research Institute of Pedagogy (RU)

TsNIPI ...... Central Scientific Research Institute of Pediatrics (RU)

TsNIPIA.... Central Scientific Research and Design Automation Institute (BU)

TsNIPO..... Central Scientific Research Institute of Fire Protection (RU)

TsNIPS...... Central Scientific Research Institute of Industrial Structures (RU)

TsNIRD..... Center for Scientific and Development Work   (BU)
TsNIRKh... Central Scientific Research Institute of Fisheries   (RU)
TsNIS....... Central Standards Research Station   (RU)
TsNITA..... Central Scientific Research and Design Institute of Combustion Equipment for Automobile, Tractor, and Stationary Engines   (RU)
TsNITI ...... Central Scientific Research Institute of Textiles   (BU)
TsNITI ...... Central Scientific Research Institute of the Textile Industry   (RU)
TsNN .... Low-Pressure Cylinder [*Nuclear energy*]   (BU)
TsNOL ...... Central Scientific Experimental Laboratory   (RU)
TsNOPS.... Central Scientific Experimental Model Station   (RU)
TsNPS .... Central People's Government Council [*Chinese People's Republic*]   (RU)
TsNRM ..... Central Scientific Restoration Shops   (RU)
TsNS......... Central Nervous System   (RU)
TsNSB .... Central Scientific Agricultural Library   (RU)
TsNSKhB .. Central Scientific Agricultural Library   (RU)
TsNT .... Luganskiy Tsentr Novykh Tekhnologiy [*Center of New Technologies*]   (EAIO)
TsNTB....... Central Scientific and Technical Library   (RU)
TsNTBS .... Central Scientific and Technical Construction Library   (RU)
TsNTK....... Central Scientific and Technical Club   (RU)
TsNTL....... Central Scientific and Technical Laboratory   (RU)
TsNTO ...... Central Administration of the Scientific and Technical Society of Railroad Transportation   (RU)
TsNTO ...... Central Scientific and Technical Society   (RU)
TsO .... Central Department, Central Section   (RU)
TsO .... Central Organ [*Newspaper, periodical*]   (RU)
TSO .... Isles Of Scilly-Tresco [*Airport symbol*]   (OAG)
TSO .... Tokyo Symphony Orchestra [*Japan*]
TSO .... Transaero Airlines [*Former USSR*] [*ICAO designator*]   (FAAC)
TSOB........ Teatrul de Stat si Opera Bucuresti [*Bucharest State Theater and Opera*]   (RO)
TsOF......... Central Concentration Plant   (RU)
TsOF......... Central Ore Dressing Factory   (BU)
TsOI .... Central Scientific Research Institute of Oncology Imeni P. A. Gertsen   (RU)
TsOI .... Information Processing Center   (RU)
TsOKB....... Central Experimental Design Office of Sports Equipment   (RU)
TsOLIPK... Central "Order of Lenin" Scientific Research Institute of Hematology and Blood Transfusion   (RU)
TsON .... Central Department of Standardization   (RU)
TsONII...... Central Scientific Research Institute on Fruit Growing   (BU)
TsOP........ Central Heating Station   (RU)
TsOPE...... Central Association of Postwar Emigres from USSR   (RU)
TsOPF ...... Central Trade-Union Association of Finland   (RU)
TsOPI .... Central Trade-Union Association of Iceland   (RU)
TsOPL ...... Central Experimental Industrial Laboratory for Pest Control in Granaries   (RU)
TsOPSh .... Central Trade-Union Association of Sweden   (RU)
TsORS....... Central Department of Workers' Supply   (RU)
TsOS........ Central Department of Statistics   (RU)
TsOS......... Central Experimental Station   (RU)
TsOSAB .... Colored Orientation and Signalling Aerial Bomb   (RU)
TsOTShL .. Central Experimental Technical Garment Laboratory   (RU)
TsOVZ....... Central Military Procurement Section [*1919-1920*]   (RU)
TsP............ Center of the Sail   (RU)
TsP............ Central Administration   (RU)
TsP............ Color Index   (RU)
TsP............ Control Room (of a Ship)   (RU)
TsP............ Digitizer   (RU)
TSP........... Platinum Resistance Thermometer   (RU)
TsP............ Power Supply Center   (RU)
tsp .... Self-Propelled Tank Regiment   (BU)
TsP............ Shop Substation   (RU)
T Sp............ Taal en Spelling [*Benelux*]   (BAS)
tsp .... Tank and Self-Propelled Gun Regiment   (RU)
TSP .... Tanks in Support of Infantry   (RU)
TSP .... Tehnicka Sekcija za Puteve [*Technical Section for Roads*]   (YU)
TSP........... Testsperre [*French*]   (ADPT)
TSP........... Thermistor   (BU)
TSP........... Tovarny na Samety a Plys [*Velvet and Plush Factories*]   (CZ)
TSP........... Tovarny na Stuhy a Prymky [*Ribbon and Braid Factories*]   (CZ)
TsP............ Translation Center   (RU)
TSP........... Tribunal de Simple Police   (FLAF)
TSP........... Trommelspeicher [*German*]   (ADPT)
TsPA......... Central Party Archives   (BU)
TsPA......... Central Party Archives (of the Institute of Marxism-Leninism at the TsK KPSS)   (RU)
TSPAE ...... Tameion Syndaxeon Prosopikou Athinaikon Efimeridon [*Athens Newspaper Personnel Pension Fund*]   (GC)
TsPAIML ... Central Party Archives of the Institute of Marxism-Leninism (at the TsK KPSS)   (RU)
TsPAS .... Central Industrial Acclimatization Station   (RU)
TsPB .... Central Polytechnical Library   (RU)

TsPD......... Central Dispatcher's Station, Central Control Post   (RU)
TSPEATh ... Tameion Syndaxeon Prosopikou Efimeridon Athinon kai Thessalonikis [*Pension Fund of Athens and Salonica Newspaper Personnel*]   (GC)
TsPEB .... Central Planning and Experimental Office   (RU)
TsPEU .... Central Economic Planning Administration   (RU)
TsPF .... Cyclopentylperhydrophenanthrene   (RU)
TsPIL........ Central Industrial Research Laboratory   (RU)
TsPKB .... Central Planning and Design Office   (RU)
TsPKBKO ... Central Planning and Design Office of Cable Accessories   (RU)
TsPKiO...... Central Park of Culture and Rest   (RU)
TsPKP ...... Central Administration of the Coal Industry of the Donets Basin   (RU)
TsPKPDB ... Central Administration of the Coal Industry of the Donets Basin   (RU)
TsPKTB..... Central Planning, Design, and Technological Office   (RU)
TSPM .... Three-Self Patriotic Movement [*Chinese*]
TsP NTONP ... Central Administration of the Scientific and Technical Society of the Petroleum Industry   (RU)
TsPO......... Central Consumers' Society   (RU)
TsPO......... Central Industrial Region   (RU)
TSPor....... Tiskarna Slovenskega Porocevalca [*Slovenski Porocevalec Printers*] [*Ljubljana*]   (YU)
TsPP .... Central Underground Substation [*Mining*]   (RU)
TsPP .... Reception and Conversion Center [*Computers*]   (RU)
TsPR .... Central Industrial Region   (RU)
TsPR .... Central Port Radio Station   (RU)
TSPS......... Turkish Society of Plastic Surgeons   (EAIO)
TSPS......... Turkmen Republic Council of Trade Unions   (RU)
TSpTC .... Trained Special Teacher's Certificate [*Australia*]
TsPTS....... Central Suburban Telephone Exchange   (RU)
TsPU......... Central Control Panel, Central Console   (RU)
TsPU......... Central Control Post [*Aviation*]   (RU)
TsPU......... Digital Printer   (RU)
TsPVSh .... Central Glider and Helicopter School   (RU)
TSPZA ...... Torres Strait Protected Zone Authority [*Australia*]
TsR .... Central Management   (BU)
TsR .... Control Circuit   (RU)
TsR .... Cyclic Machine Operating Mode [*Computers*]   (RU)
TsR .... Digital Regulator   (RU)
TSR........... Telegraph-Constructing Company [*Military term*]   (RU)
TSR........... Timisoara [*Romania*] [*Airport symbol*]   (OAG)
TSR........... Tokyo Shoko Research Ltd. [*Database producer*] [*Japan*]
TSR........... Trans Service Airlift [*Zaire*] [*ICAO designator*]   (FAAC)
TsRA .... Central Workers' Archives   (RU)
TSRA .... Tanzania Squash Rackets Association
TSRA .... Torres Strait Regional Authority [*Australia*]
TSRB .... Teachers and Schools Registration Board [*Australia*]
TSRD......... Tagore Society for Rural Development [*India*]   (EAIO)
TsRK........ Central Auditing Commission   (BU)
TsRK........ Central Clearing Commission   (RU)
TsRK........ Central Inspection Commission   (RU)
TsRK......... Central Radio Club   (BU)
TsRK........ Central Retail Office "Soyuzpechat'"   (RU)
TsRK........ Central Workers' Cooperative   (RU)
TsRKMKSB ... Central Zoning Commission of the Ministry of Communal Economy   (BU)
TsRL......... Central Radio Laboratory   (RU)
TsRM .... Central Repair Shop   (RU)
TsRMM..... Central Mechanical Repair Shop   (RU)
TsRMP...... Open-Hearth Furnace Repair Shop   (RU)
TsRMZ...... Central Mechanical Repair Plant   (RU)
TsR naDZS ... Central State Farms Management   (BU)
TsRP .... Central Distribution Point [*Electricity*]   (RU)
TsRP .... Central Distribution Substation   (RU)
TsRP .... Centrifugal Rotary Dust Separator   (RU)
TSRPP....... Model Account Plan and Guide for Industrial Enterprise Accounting   (BU)
TsRR......... Central Relay Distributor   (RU)
TsRR......... Central Repair Shop   (RU)
TsRR......... Radar Reconnaissance Center   (RU)
TsRSB .... Central Bureau of Compensation of the International Union of Railways   (RU)
TsRTs .... Central Repair Shop   (RU)
TsRU .... Central Distribution System [*Aviation*]   (RU)
TsRU .... Central Intelligence Agency [*CIA*]   (RU)
TSRU......... Tuberculosis Surveillance Research Unit [*Netherlands*]   (EAIO)
TsRV......... Centrifugal Mercury Switch   (RU)
TsRV......... Rayon Broadcasting Repeater Station   (RU)
TsRYa....... Main Junction Box [*Artillery*]   (RU)
TsRZ......... Central Repair Plant   (RU)
TsS........... Central Council   (BU)
TsS........... Central Stadium   (RU)
TsS........... Central Union   (BU)
TsS........... Central Warehouse   (RU)
TsS........... Centrifugal Scrubber   (RU)

TsS............. Resistance Center [*Military term*] (RU)
TSS............ Tehnicka Srednja Skola [*Secondary Technical School*] (YU)
TSS............ Thermoelectric Power System (BU)
TSS............ Towarzystwo Szkoly Swieckiej [*Society for Secular Schools*] (POL)
TSS............ Training Support Service [*ILO*] [*United Nations*] (DUND)
TSS............ Tres Saint Sacrement [*Most Holy Sacrament*] [*French*]
TSS............ Tropical Sea Airlines [*Thailand*] [*ICAO designator*] (FAAC)
TSS............ Trust Statnich Statku [*State Farm Trust*] (CZ)
TSS............ Turkiye Soforler Sendikasi [*Turkish Chauffeurs Union*] [*Istanbul*] (TU)
TSS............ Tutor Support Scheme [*Australia*]
TsSA.......... Central Reference Service [*Library*] (RU)
TSSA........ Tree Society of Southern Africa (EAIO)
TsSB.......... Central Construction Library (RU)
TsSBS........ Central Botanical Garden of Siberia (RU)
TsSD.......... Medium-Pressure Cylinder (RU)
TsSDF....... Central Documentary Film Studio (RU)
TsSE.......... Central Council of Experts (RU)
TsSE.......... Centralized Electric Power Supply (RU)
TsSGD...... Central Warehouse of Finished Parts (RU)
TsSGP...... Central Warehouse of Finished Products (RU)
TsShK....... Central Chess Club (RU)
TsShO....... Central Cryptographic Section (RU)
TsShPD..... Central Headquarters of the Partisan Movement (at the Supreme Command Headquarters) [*1942-1945*] (RU)
TsSI.......... Central Council on Measurements (BU)
TsSK......... Central Department of Statistics and Cartography (RU)
TsSK......... Central Savings Bank (RU)
TsSK.......... Central Scholarship Commission (RU)
TsSK.......... Central Sports Club (RU)
TsSKA....... Central Army Sports Club (RU)
TsSKhB..... Central Agricultural Bank, USSR (RU)
TsSKhI...... Central Medico-Chemical Institute (RU)
TsSK MO .. Central Sports Club of the Ministry of Defense, USSR (RU)
TsSL......... Central Construction Laboratory (RU)
TsSL.......... Central Welding Laboratory (RU)
tssl.............. Church Slavonic (BU)
TsS naBChK ... Central Council of the Bulgarian Red Cross (BU)
TsS naDSO ... Central Council of the Voluntary Sports Organization (BU)
TsS naORPS ... Central Council of the General Workers' Trade Union (BU)
TsS na PS .. Central Trade Union Council (BU)
TsS naPSB ... Central Council of the Bulgarian Trade Unions (BU)
TsS naTPK ... Central Council of Labor Productive Cooperatives (BU)
TsSNKh..... Central Council of the National Economy (RU)
TsSNM...... Central Council of National Minorities (RU)
TsSO......... Central Council of a Society (RU)
TsSO......... Central Heating System (RU)
TsSP......... Central Trade-Union Council (RU)
TsSPS........ Central Council of the Bulgarian Trade Unions (BU)
TsSPS........ Central Trade-Union Council [*Romanian People's Republic*] (RU)
TsSSR........ Turkmen Soviet Socialist Republic (RU)
TsSRV....... Rayon Central Broadcasting Station (RU)
TsSS......... Central Selection Station (RU)
TsSSK....... Central Shooting Sport Club of the DOSAAF SSSR (RU)
TsSSMSh ... Central Secondary Special School of Music (RU)
TsSSNCh .. Central Council of the Union of Public Libraries (BU)
TsSSSh...... Central Shooting Sport School (RU)
TsST......... Central Television Studio (RU)
TsSTPK..... Central Union of Labor Productive Cooperatives (BU)
TsSU......... Central Statistical Administration (RU)
TsSUA....... Central Station of Fertilizers and Soil Science (RU)
TsSUMS ... Central Statistical Administration of the Council of Ministers (BU)
TsSYuN..... Central Station of Young Naturalists and Agricultural Experimenters (RU)
TsSYuT ... Central Station of Young Technicians (RU)
TsT............ Center of Gravity (RU)
TsT............ Central Telegraph Office (RU)
TsT............ Color Television (RU)
TST........... Territoire Sous Tutelle (FLAF)
TST........... Testnevelesi es Sport Tanacs [*Council for Physical Education and Sports*] (HU)
TST........... Te Syner Tyd [*In Due Time*] [*Afrikaans*]
TSt............. Thomas Steel (RU)
TST........... Tovarny Strojirenske Techniky [*Plants for Engineering Machinery*] (CZ)
TST........... Trang [*Thailand*] [*Airport symbol*] (OAG)
TST........... Transport Dump Tractor (RU)
TsTA......... Central Technical Archives (RU)
TsTA......... Combustion Equipment Shop (RU)
TsTAK...... Central News Agency of Korea [*North Korean*] (RU)
TSTC(MTC) ... Trained Secondary Teacher's Certificate (Melbourne Teachers College) [*Australia*]
TsTEA....... Central Transportation and Forwarding Agency (RU)

t stekl .... Vitrification Temperature (RU)
TsTEU....... Central Tourist and Excursion Administration (RU)
TsTF......... Cytidine Triphosphate (RU)
TsTI.......... Central Scientific Research Institute of Tuberculosis (RU)
TsTI.......... Technical Information Center (RU)
TsTK........ Central Puppet Theater (RU)
TsTK........ Central Theater Ticket Office (RU)
TsTK........ Tricarboxylic Acid Cycle (RU)
TsTKA...... Central Theater of the Red Army (RU)
TsTKB...... Central Technical Design Office (RU)
TsTL......... Central Textile Laboratory (RU)
TsTML...... Central Tobacco and Makhorka Laboratory (RU)
TsTNB...... Central Wage Rate and Norm-Setting Office (RU)
TsTO .... Central Trade Department (RU)
TsTO .... Cyclic Heat Treatment (of Uranium) (RU)
TsTO .... Technical Service Shop (RU)
tsto .... Toimisto [*Finland*]
T-Stoff....... Traenen-Stoff [*Lacrimator, Tear Gas*] [*German*] (GCA)
TsTOS...... Central Experimental Peat Station (RU)
TsTRK...... Radio Technical Control Center (RU)
TsTS......... Central Telephone Exchange (RU)
TsTSA...... Central Theater of the Soviet Army (BU)
TsTShch.... Central Heat Control Panel (RU)
TsTU .... Central Telephone Administration (RU)
TsTV........ Color Television (RU)
TsTVR....... Main Administration for the Repair of Rolling Stock and the Production of Spare Parts (RU)
TsTYuZ ..... Young Spectator's Theater of the Central House of Art Education (RU)
TSU .... Area Construction Administration (RU)
TsU .... Central Administration (BU)
TsU .... Central Control [*Computers*] (RU)
TsU .... Central Department Store (RU)
TsU .... Digital Printer (RU)
TSU .... Tabiteuea South [*Kiribati*] [*Airport symbol*] (OAG)
TSU .... Textilni Synteticky Ustav [*Artificial Fiber Institute*] (CZ)
Tsuardel.... Central Administration of Archives (RU)
Tsudortrans ... Central Administration of Highways, Dirt Roads, and Automobile Transportation (RU)
TsUGAZ.... Central Administration of the State Automobile Plants (RU)
TSUGM .... Toprak ve Su Genel Mudurlugu [*Soil and Water Directorate General*] [*Under Village Affairs Ministry*] (TU)
TsUGTO ... Central Administration of State Tractor Brigades (RU)
TsUGTs ... Central Administration of State Circuses (RU)
TsUIZUL .. Central Administration for Inventions and Technical Improvements in Transportation (RU)
TsUK .... Central Command Control [*Computers*] (RU)
TsUKADR ... Central Personnel Administration (RU)
TsUKS....... Central Administration of Capital Construction (of the Academy of Sciences, USSR) (RU)
TsULP .... Central Administration of the Lumber Industry (RU)
TsUM .... Central Department Store (BU)
TsUMOR .. Central Administration of Maritime Transportation (RU)
TsUMS...... Central Administration of Trunk-Line Communications (RU)
TsUMT...... Central Administration of Local Transportation (RU)
TsUMT...... Central Local Trade Administration (BU)
TsUMTSDR ... Central Administration of Material and Technical Supply and State Reserves (BU)
TsUMV ..... Central Administration of Measures and Scales (RU)
TsUMZ ..... Central Administration of Machinery Plants (RU)
TsU naBNB ... Central Administration of the Bulgarian National Bank (BU)
TsUNKhU ... Central Administration of the Statistical Survey of the National Economy (RU)
TsUNP ...... Central Administration of the Petroleum Industry (RU)
Tsup .... Technicien Superieur [*French*]
TsUPI........ Central Information Processing Device (RU)
TsUPVOSO ... Central Directorate of Military Communications (RU)
TsUPVOZ ... Central Directorate of Military Procurement (RU)
Tsurek....... Central Administration of Inland Waterways (RU)
Tsurek........ Central Administration of River Transportation (RU)
TsURF....... Central Administration for the Development of Radio Facilities (RU)
TsURIR ..... Central Administration for the Development of Radio Facilities and for Radio Broadcasting (RU)
TsURK....... Central Stocktaking and Distribution Commission (RU)
tsurk......... Clerical Term (BU)
TsURREK ... Central Administration of the River Register of the USSR (RU)
TsUS......... Central Repeater Station (RU)
TsUS......... Central Supply Administration (RU)
TsUS......... Digital Controlled Resistor (RU)
TSUS......... Technicky a Skusobny Ustav Stavebny [*Institute for Technology and Testing in Construction*] (CZ)
Tsusstrakh ... Central Administration of Social Insurance (RU)
TsUSTRAKh ... Central Administration of Social Insurance (RU)
Tsutorf .... Central Administration for Peat Extraction (RU)

Tsutranpros ... Central Administration for Education of Transportation Workers (RU)
Tsutrans..... Central Administration of Transportation (RU)
TsUU .... Central Control Device [*Computer science*] (RU)
TsUU .... Central Control System [*Computer science*] (BU)
TsUVODPUT' ... Central Administration of Inland Waterways (RU)
TsUVS....... Central Directorate of Military Communications (RU)
TsUYeGMS ... Central Administration of the United Hydrometeorological Service (RU)
TsUZhEL.. Central Administration of Railroad Transportation (RU)
TSUZHELDORSTROY ... Central Administration of Railroad Construction (RU)
Ts/V.......... Cement-Water Ratio (RU)
TsV .... Center of Buoyancy [*Nautical term*] (RU)
tsv............. Color, Colored (RU)
Tsv .... In Color (BU)
TSv............ Tehnicko-Snabdevacki Vod [*Technical Supply Platoon*] [*Military*] (YU)
TSV........... Townsville [*Australia*] [*Airport symbol*] (OAG)
TsV .... Tsurkoven Vestnik [*Church Gazette*] [*A newspaper*] (BU)
TsVD .... Central Army Club (BU)
TsVD .... High-Pressure Cylinder (RU)
TsVEI .... Central Scientific Research Institute of Wind Power (RU)
TsVEK .... Central Commission of Medical Experts (RU)
tsvet........... Colored (RU)
tsvet........... Nonferrous Metallurgy Plant [*Topography*] (RU)
TsVetBaktI ... Central Veterinary Bacteriological Institute (BU)
Tsvetmetavtomatika ... Automation in Nonferrous Industry (RU)
Tsvetmetizdat ... State Scientific and Technical Publishing House of Nonferrous Metallurgy and Gold and Platinum Industry (RU)
Tsvetmetprom ... Nonferrous Metals Industry (BU)
Tsvetmetproyekt ... State Institute for the Planning of Establishments of Nonferrous Metallurgy (RU)
Tsvetmetzoloto ... All-Union Association for the Mining, Processing, and Sale of Nonferrous Metals, Gold, and Platinum (RU)
TsVFU....... Central Military Finance Directorate (RU)
TsVIA .... Central Archives of Military History (RU)
tsv il........... Colored Illustration (BU)
TsVL......... Central Military Laboratory (RU)
TsVLK .... Central Medical Commission for Determination of Flight Fitness (RU)
TsVM .... Digital Computer (RU)
TsVMB...... Central Naval Library (RU)
TsVMK..... Central Motorboat Club Imeni P. I. Baranov (RU)
TsVMK...... Central Naval Club (RU)
TsVMM .... Central Naval Museum (RU)
TsVMU ..... Central Military Medical Directorate (RU)
TsVMU ..... Central Naval Directorate (RU)
TsVN .... High-Pressure Cylinder [*Nuclear energy*] (BU)
tsvp............. Tournez, S'il Vous Plait [*Please Turn*] [*French*] (GPO)
TSVP........ Tournez s'il Vous Plait [*Please Turn Over*] [*See also PTO*] [*French*]
TsVPK .... Central War Industry Committee [*1915-1918*] (RU)
TsVS......... Central Exhibition Hall (RU)
TsVSK .... Central Water Sports Club of the VMF (RU)
TsVTs .... Central Military Censorship (RU)
TsVU .... Digital Computer (RU)
TsVVK....... Central Military Medical Commission (RU)
TsVZ......... Central Air Charger (RU)
TSW........... Trans European Airways [*Switzerland*] [*ICAO designator*] (FAAC)
TSW.......... Trau, Schau, Wem [*Trust, but Be Careful Whom*] [*Motto of Christian I, Elector of Saxony (1560-91)*] [*German*]
TSWL .... Techniczna Szkola Wojsk Lotniczych [*Air Force Technical School*] (POL)
TSWP........ Training Scheme for Widow Pensioners [*Australia*]
TSY........... Turk Saudi Yatirim [*Saudi-Turkish investment holding company*]
TSYD........ Turkiye Spor Yazarlari Dernegi [*Turkish Sports Writers Association*] (TU)
TSYK........ Turkiye Spor Yazarlari Kulubu [*Turkish Sports Writers Club*] (TU)
TsZ............. Cement Plant (BU)
TsZ............. Refueling Unit (RU)
tsz............... Termeloszovetkezet [*Producer Cooperative*] (HU)
tsz............... Tobbesszam [*Plural*] (HU)
tsz............... Tovabbszolgalo [*Reenlisted*] (HU)
TSZ........... Tovarny Stavkeveho Zbozi [*Hosiery Mills*] (CZ)
TsZAI .... Central Correspondence Antireligious Institute (RU)
TsZB.......... Central Purchasing Office (RU)
t szh............ Liquefaction Temperature (RU)
TsZhIZUL ... Central Railroad Office for Inventions and Improvements (RU)
TsZhO .... Central Housing Department of the Mossovet (RU)
TsZII .... Central Agricultural Research Institute (BU)

TsZII .... Central Correspondence Industrial Institute (RU)
TsZIPP...... Central Correspondence Institute of the Food Industry (RU)
TsZIRP...... Central Correspondence Institute of the Fish Industry (RU)
TsZIS......... Central Correspondence Institute of Communications (RU)
TsZIS......... Central Correspondence Institute of the Sugar Industry (RU)
TsZISS ...... Central Correspondence Institute of the Sugar and Alcohol Industry (RU)
TsZIzslI..... Central Agricultural Research and Control Institute (BU)
tszk............ Tanszek [*Department, Chair (of a given discipline at a college or university)*] (HU)
TsZKTI...... Central Correspondence Boiler and Turbine Institute (RU)
TsZL......... Central Laboratory of a Plant (RU)
TsZLT .... Central Correspondence Forestry-Engineering Technicum (RU)
TsZM........ Central Intermediate Production Shop (RU)
TsZMetI..... Central Correspondence Institute of Metallurgy (RU)
TsZMMI ... Central Correspondence Institute of Mechanics and Mechanical Engineering (RU)
TT .... Body Temperature (RU)
TT .... Carrier Telegraphy (RU)
tt................ Comrades (RU)
TT .... Current Transformer (RU)
tt................ Melting Point (BU)
TT .... Skidding Tractor (RU)
TT .... Takhydromiki Thyris [*Post Office Box*] (GC)
TT .... Takhydromikos Tomevs [*Postal Zone*] [*Greek*] (GC)
TT .... Tanganyika Territory
TT .... Technical School of Transportation (BU)
TT .... Tekstilna Tovarna [*Textile Factory*] (YU)
Tt............... Telegrafsko-Telefonski [*Telegraphic and Telephonic*] (YU)
TT .... Telluric Current (RU)
TT .... Theodolite-Tachometer (RU)
TT .... Theoretical Plate (RU)
TT .... Theorie en Techniek [*Benelux*] (BAS)
TT .... Tidningarnas Telegrambyra [*Press Wire Service, Incorporated*] [*Sweden*] (WEN)
TT .... Tirailleurs Tunisiens
Tt............... Tone Tereta [*Freight Tons*] (YU)
tt................ Tornaterem [*Gymnasium, Drill Hall*] (HU)
TT .... Tourism Tasmania [*Australia*]
tt................ Transfert Telegraphique [*Transfer by Telegraph*] [*French*]
TT .... Transit Temporaire (FLAF)
TT .... Trinidad and Tobago [*ANSI two-letter standard code*] (CNC)
TT .... Tula Tokarev [*Pistol*] (RU)
TT .... Tutkintatoimisto [*Investigation Bureau, General Staff*] [*Finland*] (WEN)
tt................ Tutta Tela [*Full Cloth*] [*Publishing*] [*Italian*]
tt................ Volumes (RU)
TTA .... Empresa Nacional de Transporte e Trabalho Aereo [*Mozambique*] (EY)
TTA .... Tan Tan [*Morocco*] [*Airport symbol*] (OAG)
TTA .... Tanzania Tea Authority
TTA .... Tanzania Tenants Association (EAIO)
TTA .... Tasmanian Touch Association [*Australia*]
TTA .... Teknillisten Tieteiden Akatemia [*Helsinki, Finland*] [*Finnish Academy of Technology*] (SLS)
TTA .... Teknillisten Tieteiden Akatemia - Akademin foer Tekniska Vetenskaper ry [*FinnishAcademy of Technology*] [*Research center*] (ERC)
TTA .... Tourism Training Australia
TTA .... Trainer Training Assistance [*Australia*]
TTA .... Train Travellers Association [*Australia*]
TTA .... Transkei Territorial Assembly
TTA .... Transporte e Trabalho Aero [*Mozambique*] [*ICAO designator*] (FAAC)
TTA .... Transvaal Teachers' Association
TTAA......... Technical Teachers Association of Australia (ADA)
TTAB........ Tasmanian Totalisator Agency Board [*Australia*]
TTACSA ... Tanganyika Territory Civil Service Association
TTAID....... Trinidad and Tobago Association in Aid of the Deaf (EAIO)
TTAM........ Table Tennis Association of Malaysia (EAIO)
TTAP........ Train the Trainer Assistance Program [*Australia*]
ttb.............. Heavy Tank Battalion (RU)
TTB........... Tanzania Tea Blenders
TTB........... Technology Transfer Board [*Ministry of Industry, Trade, and Investment*] [*Philippines*] (IMH)
TTB........... Tung Tankers & Bulkers [*C. H. Tung Co.*] [*Hong Kong*]
TTB........... Turizm ve Tanitma Bakanligi [*Ministry of Tourism and Orientation*] (TU)
TTB........... Turk Tabibler Birligi [*Turkish Physicians Union*] (TU)
TTBS .... Trinidad and Tobago Bureau of Standards [*Trinidad and Tobago*]
TTC........... Tanzania Tourist Corporation (AF)
TTC........... Teachers Training College [*Namibia*] (AF)
TTC........... Technology Transfer Centre [*Ghana*]
TTC........... Technology Transfer Centre [*University of New England*] [*Australia*]

TTC............ Telecommunication Training Centre [*Fiji*] [*Telecommunications*]
TTC............ Tewfikieh Tennis Club [*Egypt*]
TTC............ Toutes Taxes Comprises [*French*]
TTC............ Trained Teachers' Certificate [*Australia*]
TTC..... Transit Transports Camerounais
TTCDPI .... Trinidad and Tobago Chapter of Disabled Peoples' International (EAIO)
TTCI......... Tea Trading Corp. of India
TTCI......... Transit et Transports de Cote-D'Ivoire
TTCP........ Scarborough/Crown Point, Tobago [*Trinidad and Tobago*] [*ICAO location identifier*] (ICLI)
TTCP........ [*The*] Technical Cooperation Program [*US, UK, Canada, Australia*] [*Research*]
TTCR........ Trinidad & Tobago Coconut Research (DSCA)
ttd.............. Heavy Tank Division (RU)
TTD .... Tactical and Technical Data (RU)
TTDE........ Typopoiimeni Taxinomisis Diethnous Emboriou [*Standard International Trade Classification*] (GC)
tte .... Tenente [*Lieutenant*] [*Portuguese*]
Tte.............. Teniente [*Lieutenant*] [*Spanish*]
TTE............ Termeszetbaratok Turista Egyesulete [*Tourist Association of Nature Lovers*] (HU)
TTE............ Ternate [*Indonesia*] [*Airport symbol*] (OAG)
Tte.............. Torrente [*Torrent*] [*T*] [*See also*] [*Italian*] (NAU)
TTE............ Tropical Testing Establishment
TTE............ Turk Telekomunikasyon Endustrisi AS [*Turkish Telecommunication Industry Corp.*] (TU)
TTEC..... Trinidad and Tobago Electricity Commission (LA)
TTED........ Tum Teknik Elemanlar Dernegi [*The United Technicians Association*] (TU)
ttes.............. Toutes [*All, Everything*] [*French*]
TTF............ Taiwan Textile Federation (EAIO)
TTF............ Talebe Teskilatlari Federasyonu [*Federation of Student Organizations*] (TU)
TTF............ Thymidine Triphosphate (RU)
TTF............ [*The*] Timber Trade Federation of Southern Africa (AA)
TTF............ Tudomanyos Technikai Forradalom [*Scientific-Technical Revolution*] (HU)
TTF............ Turkish Tennis Federation (EAIO)
TTF............ Turk Traktor Fabrikasi [*Turkish Tractor Factory*] (TU)
TTFA......... Trinidad and Tobago Farmers Association (LA)
TTG .... Thyrotropic Hormone (RU)
TTGA......... Tanganyika Tea Growers' Association
TTGFO...... Transactions of the Tashkent Geophysical Observatory (RU)
TTGU........ Tyumen' Territorial Geological Administration (RU)
TTH........... Tieftemperatur Hydrierung [*Low Temperature Hydrogenation*] [*German*] (EG)
TTH........... TransTurk Holding Corp. (TU)
TTHM....... Turk Teknik Haberlesme Merkezi [*Turkish Technical Information Centre*] (PDAA)
TTI............. Noimhungaria Tervezesfejlesztesi es Tipustervezo Intezet [*Institute for Design Development and Typical Drawings*] [*Hungary*] (PDAA)
TTI............. Tashkent Textile Institute (RU)
TTI............. Tehnica Tensiunilor Inalte [*High Voltage Technology*] (RO)
TTI............. Transvaal Technical Institute
TTIA......... Timber Trade Industrial Association [*Australia*]
TTIC......... Technical and Trade Information Centre [*Electronics Trade and Technology Development Corporation Ltd.*] [*India*]
TTIC......... Tow Truck Industry Council of New South Wales [*Australia*]
TTIP......... Tvornica Turpija i Pila [*Files and Saws Factory*] [*Zagreb-Podsused*] (YU)
TTIS .... Turkiye Toprak Tarim Iscileri Sendikasi [*Turkish Soil and Agricultural Workers Union*] (TU)
ttisspostrojenja ... Telegrafsko-Telefonska i Signalno-Sigurnosna Postrojenja [*Telegraph, Telephone, and Signal Safety Appliances*] (YU)
TTIT .... Tarsadalom- es Termeszettudomanyi Ismeretterjeszto Tarsulat [*Popular Educational Association for the Social and Natural Sciences*] (HU)
TTJ .... Tottori [*Japan*] [*Airport symbol*] (OAG)
TTK .... Heat Engineering Control (RU)
TTK .... Teknillisen Tuonnin Keskusliitto [*Confederation of Technical Importers*] [*Finland*] (WEN)
TTK .... Tokyo Tsushin Kogyo [*Tokyo Telecommunications Engineering Co.*]
TTK .... Turkiye Turizm Kurumu [*Turkish Tourism Organization*] (TU)
TTK .... Turk Tarih Kurumu [*Turkish Historic Society*] (TU)
TTK .... Turk Teskilatlari Kanunu [*Law on Turkish Organizations*] (TU)
TTK .... Turk Ticaret Kanunu [*Turkish Commercial Law*] (TU)
TTKI......... Testnevelesi Tudomanyos Kutato Intezet [*Scientific Research Institute of Physical Education*] (HU)
TTKOC...... Turkiye Trafik Kazalarini Onleme Cemiyeti [*Turkish Society for Prevention of Traffic Accidents*] (TU)
TTKR........ Boiling Heavy-Water Reactor (RU)

TTKR-Up .. Boiling Heavy-Water Natural-Uranium Reactor (RU)
TTL............ Tanzania Tours Limited
TTL............ Teknillinen Tarkastuslaitos [*Technical Inspectorate*] [*Finland*] (PDAA)
TTL............ Telephone-Telegraph Line (BU)
TTL............ Television and Telecasters Ltd. [*Australia*]
TTL............ Tema Textiles Limited [*Ghanaiah*]
TTL............ Transistor-Transistor-Logik [*Transistor-Transistor-Logic*] [*German*] (EG)
TTL............ Tribal Trust Land [*Rhodesian*] (AF)
TTL............ Turtle Island [*Fiji*] [*Airport symbol*] (OAG)
TTLC........ Trained Teachers Librarian's Certificate [*Australia*]
TTLC........ Trinidad and Tobago Labor Council (LA)
TTM .... Maghrebine de Telephone et de Telematique
TTM .... Thailand Tobacco Monopoly (DS)
TTMS........ Telekomunikasyon Turk Mustahdemler Sendikasi [*Turkish Telecommunications Employees' Union*] (TU)
TTMYA..... Trinidad and Tobago Muslim Youth Association
TTN .... Tatrzanskie Towarzystwo Narciarskie [*Tatra Mountain Ski Society*] (POL)
TTNA .... Trinidad and Tobago National Alliance [*Political party*] (PPW)
TTO .... Technical Tank Support (RU)
TTO .... Trainee Technical Officer [*Australia*]
TTO .... Trinidad and Tobago [*ANSI three-letter standard code*] (CNC)
TTOC .... Trinidad and Tobago Olympic Committee (EAIO)
TTOK .... Turkiye Turing ve Otomobil Kurumu [*Turkish Touring and Automobile Association*] (TU)
TTOSOTB ... Turkiye Ticaret Odalari Sanayi Odalari, ve Ticaret Borsalari Birligi [*Union of Turkish Chambers of Commerce, Industry, and Stock Exchanges*] (TU)
TTOSZ...... Tejtermelok es Tejszovetkezetek Orszagos Szovetsege [*National Association of Milk Producers and Milk Producers' Cooperatives*] (HU)
ttp.............. Heavy Tank Regiment (BU)
TTP............ Tekstilna Tovarna Prebold [*Prebold Textile Factory*] (YU)
TTP............ Temporary Transmission Permit [*Australia*]
TTP............ Theater Pickup Station [*Television*] (RU)
TTP............ Typifying of Technological Processes (RU)
TTPB......... Tasmanian Timber Promotion Board [*Australia*]
TTPC........ Trans-Tunisia Pipeline Company
TTPP........ Port-Of-Spain/Piarco, Trinidad [*Trinidad and Tobago*] [*ICAO location identifier*] (ICLI)
TTPS .... Port-Of-Spain/Port-Of-Spain, Trinidad [*Trinidad and Tobago*] [*ICAO location identifier*] (ICLI)
TTPS .... Tum Tek Personel Sendikasi [*Comprehensive Technical Personnel Union*] (TU)
TTQ .... Tourism Training Queensland [*Australia*]
TTR .... Glow-Discharge Thyratron (RU)
ttr .... Heavy Tank Company (BU)
TTR .... Heavy-Water Cooled and Moderated Reactor (RU)
TTR .... Standard Television Station (RU)
TTR .... Tana Toraja [*Indonesia*] [*Airport symbol*] (OAG)
TTR .... Tatra Air [*Slovakia*] [*ICAO designator*] (FAAC)
T Tr.......... Taxe de Transmission [*Benelux*] (BAS)
TTRDC...... Tourism and Travel Research Development Council [*Australia*]
TTRI......... Telecommunications Technical Training and Research Institute [*Egypt*] (PDAA)
TTrIC....... Trained Technical Instructor's Certificate [*Australia*]
TTRM....... Toprak ve Tarim Reformu Mustesarligi [*Undersecretariat of Land and Agricultural Reform*] (TU)
TTRS .... Torture and Trauma Rehabilitation Service [*Australia*]
ttrz............. Ter Terechtzitting [*Benelux*] (BAS)
TTS............ TASD (Transporti Aerei Speciali) [*Italy*] [*ICAO designator*] (FAAC)
TTS............ Tekstilstroj [*Textile Machinery Factory*] [*Zagreb*] (YU)
TTS............ Telegraph and Telephone Exchange (RU)
TTs............ Television Center (RU)
tts .... Tiszthelyettes [*Senior Noncommissioned Officer*] (HU)
TTS............ Trade Testing Section [*Australia*]
TTS............ Tsaratanana [*Madagascar*] [*Airport symbol*] (OAG)
TTS............ Tyotehoseura [*Finland*] (EAIO)
TTSA .... Trinidad and Tobago Scientific Association (EAIO)
TTsK........ Secret Central Committee (BU)
TTSOA...... Telecommunications Traffic and Supervisory Officers' Association [*Australia*]
ttsp .... Heavy Tank and Self-Propelled Gun Regiment (RU)
ttsp .... Self-Propelled Heavy Tank Regiment (BU)
TTSS .... Taxi Transport Subsidy Scheme [*Australia*]
TTSZ .... Takticko-Tehnicka Sredstva za Zaprecavanje [*Tactical and Technical Means for Obstruction*] [*Military*] (YU)
TTSZ .... Toxikologiai Tajekoztato Szolgalat [*Toxicological Information Service*] (HU)
TTT........... Streetcar and Trolleybus Trust (RU)
TTT........... Tactical and Technical Requirements [*Military term*] (RU)
TTT........... Taitung [*Taiwan*] [*Airport symbol*] (OAG)

TTT............ Takhydromeia-Tilegrafoi-Tilefona [*Posts, Telegraph, and Telephone (Administration)*] [*Greek*] (GC)

TTT............ Taloudellisen, Teknisen, ja Teollisen Yhteistoiminta [*Economic, Technical, and Industrial Cooperation*] [*Finland*] (WEN)

TTT............ [*The*] Tehama Trading Co. Ltd. [*Yemen*]

TTT............ Termeszettudomanyi Tarsulat [*Natural Sciences Association*] (HU)

TTT............ Testnevelesi Tudomanyos Tanacs [*Scientific Council of Physical Education*] (HU)

TTT............ Trinidad and Tobago Television (LA)

TTT............ Tudomanyos Testuleti Titkarsag [*Scientific Corporate Secretariat*] (HU)

TTTA........ Tanzania Table Tennis Association

TTTDA....... Trinidad and Tobago Tourism Development Authority (EAIO)

TTTE......... Tornado Tri-National Training Establishment [*Britain, West Germany, Italy*]

TTTNR...... Tarsadalomtudomanyi Tajekoztato Nemzetkozi Rendszere [*International System for Information on the Social Sciences*] (HU)

TTTS .... Telegrafsko-Telefonska Tehnicka Sekcija [*Telegraph and Telephone Technical Section*] (YU)

TTU .... Area Technical Section (RU)

TTU .... Freight Transportation Administration (RU)

TTU .... Telephone and Telegraph Administration (RU)

TTU .... Teletex-Telex-Umsetzer [*German*] (ADPT)

TTU .... Tetouan Airport

TTU .... Tetuan [*Morocco*] [*Airport symbol*] (OAG)

TTUB........ Textilni Tiskarny, Upravny, a Barvirny [*Textile Printing, Dressing, and Dyeing Plants*] (CZ)

TTUC .... Tasmanian Trades Union Council [*Australia*]

TTUC .... Thai Trade Union Congress

TTUF........ Teachers' Trade Union in Finland (EAIO)

TTUS........ Teletex-Telex Umsetzersatz [*German*] (ADPT)

TTUTA...... Trinidad and Tobago Unified Teachers Association (LA)

TTUV .... Technical Teachers Union of Victoria [*Australia*]

ttv .... Heavy Tank Platoon (BU)

TTV .... Taiwan Television Enterprise (EY)

TTV .... Tarifsko-Transportni Vesnik [*Transport Tariff Review*] [*A periodical*] (YU)

TTV .... Transvaalse Tuinbouvereniging [*South Africa*] (AA)

TTVK........ Telephone and Telegraph Lead-In Cable (RU)

TTVP........ Trentiner Tiroler Volkspartei [*Trentino Tirol People's Party*] [*Italy*] [*Political party*] (PPE)

TTVP-EU ... Trentiner Tiroler Volkspartei fur Europaische Einigung [*Italy*] (EAIO)

TTW .... Taegliche Technische Wartung [*Daily Technical Maintenance*] (EG)

T Tw.......... Telegraaf- en Telefonwet [*Benelux*] (BAS)

TTWA .... Trinidad and Tobago Workers Association (LA)

TTX .... Den Sivile Flyskole [*Norway*] [*ICAO designator*] (FAAC)

TTXGP ..... Thong Tan Xa Giai Phong [*Liberation Press Agency*]

TTZ........... Takticko-Tehnicki Zahtevi [*Tactical-Technical Requirements*] [*Military*]

TTZ........... Technologie Transfer-Zentrum [*German*] (ADPT)

TTZP........ Piarco, Trinidad [*Trinidad and Tobago*] [*ICAO location identifier*] (ICLI)

TU............. Aircraft Designed by A. N. Tupolev (RU)

TU............. Control Transformer (RU)

TU............. Control Trigger (RU)

TU............. Narrow-Gauge Diesel Locomotive (RU)

TU............. Packing Materials and Packaging (RU)

TU............. Radio Rediffusion Station (RU)

TU............. Remote Control (RU)

TU............. Repeater (RU)

TU............. Taxe Unique

TU............. Technical Administration (RU)

TU............. Technical Conditions (BU)

TU............. Technical School (RU)

TU............. Technical Specifications (RU)

TU............. Technische Universitaet [*Technical University*] [*German*] (WEN)

TU............. Tehnicka Uprava [*Technical Administration*] [*Military*] (YU)

TU............. Telefonni Ustredna [*Telephone Central*] (CZ)

TU............. Telegrafni Ustredna [*Telegraph Cable Center*] (CZ)

TU............. Telegramme Tres Urgent [*Military*] [*French*] (MTD)

TU............. Temps Universel

TU............. Tenants' Union [*Australia*]

TU............. Testo Unico [*Consolidated Statutes*] [*Italian*] (ILCA)

TU............. Tovarna Usnja [*Leather Factory*] (YU)

TU............. Transit Junction (RU)

TU............. Transportation Administration (RU)

TU............. Trichlorophenoxyacetic Acid (RU)

Tu............. Tunel [*Tunnel*] (TU)

TU............. Tunezja [*Tunisia*] [*Poland*]

TU............. Tunis Airline (DS)

TU............. Tupolev [*Former USSR*] [*ICAO aircraft manufacturer identifier*] (ICAO)

TU............. Turkey [*NATO*]

tu .... Tuzer [*Artilleryman, Gunner*] (HU)

TUA .... Ketua [*Chairman, Chief*] (IN)

TUA .... Tulcan [*Ecuador*] [*Airport symbol*] (OAG)

TUA .... Turkmenistan [*ICAO designator*] (FAAC)

TUACC...... Trade Union Advisory and Coordinating Council

TUACOECD ... Trade Union Advisory Committee to the Organization for Economic Cooperation and Development [*Paris, France*] (EAIO)

TUB .... Technische Universitaet Berlin [*Berlin Technical University*] (WEN)

TUB .... Transports Urbains de Bamako

tub .... Tubercular, Tuberculosis (RU)

TUB .... Tubuai Island [*Austral Islands*] [*Airport symbol*] (OAG)

TUBA .... Turkiye Basin Ajansi [*Turkish Press Agency*] (TU)

TUB-IR...... Teschnische Universitat, Berlin-Institut fur Raumfahrttechnik [*Technical University, Berlin, Institute for Space Technology*] [*Germany*] (PDAA)

TUBITAK ... Scientific and Technical Research Council of Turkey [*Ankara*] [*Information service or system*] (IID)

TUBITAK ... Turkiye Bilimsel ve Teknik Arastirma Kurumu [*Turkish Scientific and Technical Research Organization*] [*Under Office of Premier TBTAK Ankara*] [*See also*] (TU)

Tubsanatorium ... Tuberculosis Sanatorium (BU)

TUC .... Hong Kong and Kowloon Trades Union Council

TUC .... Trades Union Congress [*Jamaica*] (LA)

TUC .... Trades Union Congress [*Ghana*] (AF)

TUC .... Trades Union Congress [*Guyana*] (LA)

TUC .... Trade Union Conference [*Grenada*] (LA)

TUC .... Transport Urbain de Conakry

TUC .... Transvaal University College

TUC .... Tucuman [*Argentina*] [*Airport symbol*] (OAG)

TUCAL...... Tunisienne de Conserves Alimentaires [*Canned foods producer and distributor*] [*Tunis, Tunisia*] (MENA)

TUCAR ..... Trade Union Committee on Aboriginal Rights [*Australia*]

TUC-B .... Trades Union Congress (Burma)

TUCJ........ Trades Union Congress of Jamaica

TUCK .... Turkiye Cografya Kurumu [*Turkish Geographic Society*] [*TCK*] [*See also*] (TU)

TUCM ...... Trades Union Congress of Malawi

TUCN .... Trades Union Congress of Nigeria (AF)

TUCP .... Trades Union Congress of the Philippines [*See also KMP*]

TUCR .... Trade Union Congress of Rhodesia (AF)

TUCRC..... Trade Union Community Research Centre [*Hobart, Australia*]

TUCSA...... Trade Union Council of South Africa (AF)

TUCT .... Taxation Unpaid Companies Tax Act [*Australia*] (ADA)

TUC(UK) ... Trades Union Congress (United Kingdom)

TUD.......... Tambacounda [*Senegal*] [*Airport symbol*] (OAG)

TUD.......... Technische Universitat Dresden [*Dresden Technical University*] (EG)

tud .... Tudomanyos [*Scientific*] [*Hungary*]

TUDC .... Trade Unionists' Defence Committee [*Australia*]

TUDEGY ... Tudomanyegyetem [*University*] (HU)

TUDM....... Tentera Udara Di-Raja Malaysia [*Royal Malaysian Air Force*] (ML)

TUe .... Technische Ueberwachung [*Technical Supervision*] (EG)

TUE .... Trade Union of Education [*Germany*] (EAIO)

TUE .... Tupile [*Panama*] [*Airport symbol*] (OAG)

TUE .... Universal Electric Thermometer (RU)

TUEP........ Tokyo University of Education, Department of Physics [*Japan*] (PDAA)

Tues .... Tuesday (EECI)

TUeV .... Technische Ueberwachungsverwaltung [*West German Automobile Inspection*] (EG)

TUF .... Cloth-Coal Filter (RU)

TUF .... Tokyo University of Fisheries [*Japan*] (ASF)

TUF .... Tours [*France*] [*Airport symbol*] (OAG)

TUF .... Turnhalle United Front [*Namibia*] (AF)

TUFA........ Teletex-Umsetzer fuer Fernsprech-Nebenstellenanlagen [*German*] (ADPT)

TUFEM..... Turizm ve Folklor Egitim Merkezi [*Tourism and Folklore Training Center*] [*Ankara*] (TU)

TUFI......... Teletex-Umsetzer Fernsprechnebenanlage-IDN [*German*] (ADPT)

TUFMAC ... [*The*] Uganda Fish Marketing Corporation Ltd.

TUG.......... Trustul de Utilaj Greu [*Heavy Equipment Trust*] (RO)

Tug............. Tugrik [*Monetary unit*] [*Mongolia*] (BARN)

TUG.......... Tuguegarao [*Philippines*] [*Airport symbol*] (OAG)

Tuga .... Tugamiral [*Rear Admiral*] (TU)

Tugg.......... Tuggeneral [*Brigadier General*] (TU)

TUGP .... Taxe Unique Globale a la Production [*Single Total Production Tax*] [*Algeria*] (AF)

TUGPS...... Taxe Unique Globale sur les Presentations de Service [*Service tax*] [*French*] (IMH)

TUGSAS ... Turkiye Guebre A/S
TUH .... Teljesulesi Hatarozat [*Decision of the Full Bench (of the Royal Curia)*] (HU)
TUHUM ... Turkish Harita Umum Mudurlugu [*Turkish Directorate General of Cartography*] (TU)
TUI .... Touristik Union International [*Travel agency*]
TUI .... Trade Unions International of Transport Workers (EAIO)
TUI .... Tuninter [*Tunisia*] [*ICAO designator*] (FAAC)
TUI .... Turaif [*Saudi Arabia*] [*Airport symbol*] (OAG)
TUIAFPW ... Trade Unions International of Agriculture, Forestry, and Plantation Workers [*See also UISTAFP*] [*Prague, Czechoslovakia*] (EAIO)
TUIAFW ... Trade Unions International of Agricultural and Forestry Workers [*Czechoslovakia*] (DSCA)
TUIBWM ... Trade Union of Workers of the Building, Wood, and Building Material Industries [*Finland*]
TUIC .... Trade Unions' Industrial Council [*Australia*]
TUICDC .... Trade Union Institute for Cooperation with Developing Countries [*Italy*] (EAIO)
TUIMWE ... Trade Unions International of Miners and Workers in Energy [*See also UISMTE*] (EAIO)
TUiN .... Technical Specifications and Norms (RU)
TUIPAE .... Trade Unions International of Public and Allied Employees [*Berlin, Federal Republic of Germany*] (EAIO)
TUIRC .... Trade Union Information and Research Centre [*Sydney, Australia*]
TUIREC .... Trade Union International Research and Education Group [*England*] (EAIO)
TUIS .... Turkiye Ulastirma Iscileri Sendikasi [*Turkish Communications Workers Union*] [*Ankara*] (TU)
TUITCLF ... Trade Unions International of the Textile, Clothing, Leather, and Fur Workers [*Prague, Czechoslovakia*]
TUITPFW ... Trade Unions International of Transport, Port, and Fishery Workers [*Prague, Czechoslovakia*]
TUITransport ... Trade Unions International of Transport Workers [*Hungary*] (EAIO)
TUIWC ...... Trade Unions International of Workers in Commerce [*Prague, Czechoslovakia*] (EAIO)
TUJ .... Tum [*Ethiopia*] [*Airport symbol*] (OAG)
TUJL .... Tkalcovny a Upravny Jemneho Lnu [*Fine Linen Weaving and Finishing Mills*] (CZ)
TUJNA ...... Tehnicka Uprava Jugoslovenske Narodne Armije [*Technical Administration of the Yugoslav People's Army*] (YU)
TUK .... Technical Specifications for Cables (RU)
TUK .... Toprak Urunleri Kurumu [*Soil Products Organization*] [*Turkish Cypriot*] (GC)
TUK .... Trgovinsko-Ugostiteljska Komora [*Chamber of Commerce and Hotel and Catering Trade*] (YU)
TUK .... Turbat [*Pakistan*] [*Airport symbol*] (OAG)
TUKAS ..... Turgutlu Konserve Anonim Sirketi [*Turgutlu Canning Corporation*] [*With backing of OYAK*] (TU)
TUKER ...... Tuzeloanyagkereskedelmi Vallalat [*Fuel Trade Enterprise*] (HU)
TUKERT ... Tuzifa Kereskedelmi Reszvenytarsasag [*Firewood Trade Company Limited*] (HU)
TUKI .... Taasisi ya Uchunguzi wa Kiswahili [*Institute of Kiswahili Research*] [*Tanzania*] (IRC)
TUKO .... Tukkukauppojen Oy [*Food wholesaler group*] [*Finland*] (IMH)
TUKO .... Turkiye Ulusal Kurtulus Ordusu [*Turkish National Liberation Army*] (TU)
TUKP .... Turkiye Ulusal Kadinlar Partisi [*Turkish National Women's Party*] (TU)
TUL .... Towarzystwo Uniwersytetow Ludowych [*Society of People's Universities (Extension courses)*] (POL)
TUL .... Tyovaen Urheiluliitto [*Workers' Sports League*] [*Finland*] (WEN)
TULESTAL ... Societe des Tuileries de l'Est-Algerien
TULF .... Tamil United Liberation Front [*Sri Lanka*] (PD)
TUL IS ...... Turkiye Liman Iscileri Sendikasi [*Turkish Harbor Workers' Union*] (TU)
tum .... Fog (RU)
tum .... Nebula (RU)
TUM .... Peat Removal Machine (RU)
TUM .... Teachers' Union of Malawi
TUM .... Technical University in Munich [*Germany*]
TUM .... Technische Universitaet Muenchen [*Technical University of Munich*] [*Information retrieval*]
TUM .... Tumut [*Australia*] [*Airport symbol*] (OAG)
TUMADDER ... Tutuklu ve Mahkumlarla Dayanisma Dernegi [*Detainees and Prisoners Mutual Solidarity Organization*] (TU)
TUMAS ..... Tum Universite, Akademi, ve Yuksek Okulu Asistanlari Birligi [*Comprehensive University, Academy, and College Teaching Assistants' Union*] (TU)
TUMAS ..... Turkiye Muhendislik Anonim Sirketi [*Turkish Engineering Corporation*] [*A subsidiary of ASTAS*] (TU)

TUMAS ..... Turk Muhendislik, Musavirlik, ve Muteahhitlik Anonim Sirketi [*Turkish Engineering, Consulting, and Contracting Corporation*] (TU)
TUMATA ... Turk Musikisini Arastirma ve Tanitma Grubu [*Turkish Musical Research and Orientation Group*] (TU)
TUM-DER ... Tum Memurlar Birlesme ve Dayanisma Dernegi [*Comprehensive (Government) Officials' Unity and Mutual Solidarity Association*] (TU)
Tumg .... Tumgeneral [*Major General*] (TU)
TUMHAK ... Turkiye Memur ve Emekli Haklarini Koruma Dernegi [*Society for the Protection of Turkish Employee and Retiree Rights*] (TU)
TUMKA-Is ... [*The*] Mamara District Paper and Cellulose Industries Workers Union (TU)
TUMKULTUR-IS ... Turkiye Milli Egitim, Fikir, ve Beden Iscileri Sendikasi [*Turkish National Education, Intellectual, and Physical Workers Union*] [*Ankara*] (TU)
TUmn .... Multiplication Control Trigger [*Computers*] (RU)
TUMOD .... Tum Ogretim Uyeleri Dernegi [*Comprehensive Educators' Association*] (TU)
TUMOSAN ... Turk Motor Sanayii ve Ticaret AS [*Turkish Motor Industry and Trade Corporation*] (TU)
TUMPECO ... [*The*] Uganda Metal Products and Enamelling Company Ltd.
Tum-Person-Kon ... Tum Kamu Personeli Haklarini Koruma Kuruluslari Konfederasyonu [*Confederation of Organizations for the Protection of Rights of All Public Service Personnel*] (TU)
TUM-PTT-DER ... Tum PTT [*Posta, Telefon, Telegraf*] Dernekleri Iscileri Sendikalar [*National PTT (Post, Telephone, and Telegraph) Organizations' Workers' Unions*] (TU)
Tumsit .... Turkiye Belediyeleri Temizlik Iscileri Sendikasi [*Turkish Municipalities Sanitations Workers Union*] [*Istanbul*] (TU)
TUM-TEK ... Tum Teknik Elemanlari Sendikasi [*Comprehensive Technical Workers' Union*] (TU)
TUMTIS ... Turkiye Motorlu Tasit Iscileri Sendikasi [*Turkish Motorized Transport Workers Union*] (TU)
TUN .... Tunis [*Tunisia*] [*Airport symbol*] (OAG)
TUN .... Tunis-Carthage Airport
TUN .... Tunisia [*ANSI three-letter standard code*] (CNC)
tun .... Tunnel [*Topography*] (RU)
Tun-Is .... Turkiye Tutun Iscileri Sendikasi [*Turkish Tobacco Workers' Union*] (TU)
TUNISAIR ... Societe Tunisienne de l'Air [*Airline*] [*Tunisia*]
Tunis Re.... Societe Tunisienne de Reassurance [*Tunisian Reinsurance Co.*]
Tun Jud .... La Tunisie Judiciaire (FLAF)
tunzhpb ...... Railway Tunnel Battalion (BU)
TUO .... Taupo [*New Zealand*] [*Airport symbol*] (OAG)
Tuom .... Tuomari [*Judge*] [*Finland*] (GPO)
tup .... Blind Alley, Dead End (RU)
TUP .... Rear Fortified Zone (RU)
TUP .... Remote-Control Instrument (RU)
TUP .... Technical Planning Specifications (RU)
TUP .... Titre Universel de Paiement [*French*] (ADPT)
TUP .... Torres United Party [*Australia*] [*Political party*]
TUP .... Tovarystvo Ukrainskykh Progresyvtiv [*Ukrainian Progressive Association*] [*Russian*] [*Political party*] (PPE)
TUP .... Towarzystwo Urbanistow Polskich [*Society of Polish City Planners*] (POL)
TUP .... Turkish Unity Party [*See also TBP*] (TU)
TUP .... Tvornica Ugljenografitnih Proizvoda [*Carbon and Graphite Products Factory*] [*Dubrovnik*] (YU)
TUPAS ..... Trade Unions of Philippines and Allied Services
TUPE .... Tanganyika Union of Public Employees
TUPE .... Technical Specifications for Planning Train Traction Electrification (RU)
TUPJ .... Roadtown/Beef Island [*Virgin Islands*] [*ICAO location identifier*] (ICLI)
TUPLAN ... Textil Uruguaya de Productos de Lana [*Uruguay*] (DSCA)
TUPM ...... Technical Specifications for Bridge Designing (RU)
TUpr .... Control Trigger [*Computers*] (RU)
TUPRAS ... Turkiye Petrol Rafinerileri AS [*Turkey Petrol Refining Co.*]
TUPS .... Technical Specifications for the Planning of Railroad Stations and Junctions (RU)
TUPW .... Virgin Gorda [*Virgin Islands*] [*ICAO location identifier*] (ICLI)
TUR .... Aerotur SA [*Mexico*] [*ICAO designator*] (FAAC)
TUR .... Towarzystwo Uniwersytetow Robotniczych [*Society of Workers' Universities (Extension courses) (1922-1948)*] (POL)
TuR .... Transformatoren- und Roentgenwerk Dresden (VEB) [*Dresden Transformer and X-Ray Equipment Works (VEB)*] (EG)
TUR .... Tucurui [*Brazil*] [*Airport symbol*] (OAG)
TUR .... Turkey [*ANSI three-letter standard code*] (CNC)
tur .... Turkish (RU)
TURBANK ... Turkiye Cumhuriyeti Turizm Bankasi AS [*Turkish Republic Tourism Bank, Inc.*] (TU)
TuRD .... Turbojet Engine (BU)
TURDC ..... Trade Union Research and Development Center [*Jamaica*] (LA)

TURDOK .. Turkiye Bilimsel ve Teknik Arastirma Kurumu Dokumantasyon Merkezi [*Documentation Center for the Turkish Scientific and Technical Research Organization*] (TU)

tur ez .... Turkish Language (BU)

turg .... Commercial, Trade (BU)

TURG .... Transvaal Underwater Research Group [*South Africa*] (AA)

TURiL .... Towarzystwo Uniwersytetow Robotniczych i Ludowych [*Society of Workers' and Peasants' Universities (Extension courses) (1948-1950)*] (POL)

TURIMPEX ... Empresa Cubana Importadora y Exportador para el Turismo [*Cuban Enterprise for the Import and Export of Tourism*] (LA)

TURISVALLE ... Turismo del Valle del Cauca Ltda. [*Tulua-Valle*] (COL)

TURIZK .... Turkiye Turizm Kurumu [*Turkish Tourism Organization*] (TU)

turk .... Turkestan (RU)

TURKAR-IS ... Turkiye Petrol Kimya Atom, Azot, ve Rafiner Iscileri Sendikasi [*Turkish Petroleum, Chemical, Atomic, Nitrogen, and Refinery Workers Union*] (TU)

TURKAY ... Turkiye Kibrit Sanayii Iscileri Sendikasi [*Turkish Match Industry Workers' Union*] (TU)

TurkDeniz-Ulas-Is ... Turkiye Deniz Tasitmaciligi Isci Sendikalari Federasyonu [*Federation of Turkish Maritime Transport Worker Unions*] (TU)

Turk Dev-Sen ... Turkiye Iktisadi Devlet Tesekkuleri Memur ve Hizmetlileri Sendikasi [*Turkish Union of Economic State Organization Officials and Workers*] (TU)

Turkest ...... Turkestan

TurkHarb-Is ... Turkiye Harb Sanayii ve Yardimci Iskollari Iscileri Sendikasi [*Defence industry and allied workers union*] [*Turkey*] (MENA)

Turkimya ... Turk Kimya Sanayi Iscileri Sendikasi [*Turkish Chemical Industry Workers Union*] [*Kimya-Is*] [*See also*] (TU)

Turk-Is .... Turkiye Isci Sendikalari Konfederasyonu [*Turkish Confederation of Labor*] (TU)

TurkiyeMaden-Is ... Turkiye Maden Iscileri Sendikalari [*Mine workers union*] [*Turkey*] (MENA)

TURKKABLO ... Turk Kablo Anonim Ortaklari [*Turkish Cable Manufacturing Corporation*] (TU)

turkkil .... Turkkilainen [*Finland*]

TURKKONUT ... Turkiye Yapi Kooperatifleri Merkez Birligi [*Central Federation of Housing Cooperatives of Turkey*] (EAIO)

TURKKUSU ... Turkish Aviation Association (TU)

turkm .... Turkmen (RU)

Turkmengosizdat ... State Publishing House of the Turkmen SSR (RU)

TurkmenTAG ... Turkmen News Agency (RU)

Turkmenuchpedgiz ... Turkmen State Publishing House of Textbooks and Pedagogical Literature (RU)

Turk-Metal ... Turkiye Metal, Celik, Muhimmat, Makina ve Metalden Mamul, Esya ve Oto, Montaj ve Yardimci Iscileri Sendikasi [*Auto, metal, and allied workers union*] [*Turkey*] (MENA)

TurkmSSR ... Turkmen Soviet Socialist Republic (RU)

TurkNIIGiM ... Turkmen Scientific Research Institute of Hydraulic Engineering and Reclamation (RU)

Turkombyuro ... Bureau of the VTsIK and SNK RSFSR Commission on Turkestan Affairs [*Archives*] (RU)

TURKOTOSAN ... Turkish Auto Industry Workers Union (TU)

Turk-Persen ... Turkiye Kamu Personeli Sendikalari Konfederasyonu [*Confederation of Turkish Public Service Personnel Unions*] (TU)

TURKPERSON-KON ... Turk Kamu Personel Haklarini Koruma Dernekleri Konfederasyonu [*Confederation of Organizations for the Protection of Rights of Turkish Public Service Personnel*] (TU)

TurkPetrol ... Turkish Petroleum Co.

Turk-Sag-Kur ... Turkiye Saglik Kurumlari Sendikasi [*Union of Turkish Health Associations*] (TU)

Turk-Sen.... Kibris Turk Isci Sendikalari Federasyonu [*Turkish Cypriot Federation of Labor Unions*] (TU)

Turksib ...... Turkestan-Siberian Railroad (RU)

TurkSSR.... Turkmen Soviet Socialist Republic (RU)

TurkVO ..... Turkestan Military District (RU)

TurnRechts ... Turnhouts Rechtsleven [*Benelux*] (BAS)

TURSAB ... Turkiye Seyahat Ajanlari Birligi [*Turkish Travel Agents' Union*] (TU)

TURSAN... Kibris Turk Turizm Sanayii [*Turkish Cypriot Tourism Industry*] (GC)

TURSOCIAL ... Turismo Social [*Colombia*] (COL)

TurTsIK..... Turkestan Central Executive Committee (RU)

TURYAG .. Turkiye Sebze Yaglar Sanayii [*Turkish Vegetable Oil Processing Industry*] (TU)

TURYAG .. Turkiye Yag ve Mamulati Anonim Sirketi [*Turkish Oil and Oil Products Corporation*] (TU)

TUS .... Equalizing Coupling Transformer (RU)

TUS .... Technicka Ustredna Spoju [*Technical Center for Communications*] (CZ)

TUS .... Telegraph Communications Regulations (RU)

TUS .... Tenants Union of the Sudan

TUS .... Trybunal Ubezpieczen Spolecznych [*Social Security Court*] (POL)

tus.............. Tusen [*Thousand*] [*Sweden*]

tus.............. Tusen [*Thousand*] [*Danish/Norwegian*]

tus.............. Tusina(a) [*Finland*]

TUS .... Tyden Udernichych Smen [*Week of Shock Workers' Shifts*] (CZ)

TUSA........ Tractores Universales, SA [*Mexico*] (DSCA)

TUSAS ...... Turk Ucak Sanayii Anonim Sirketi [*Turkish Aircraft Industry Corporation*] (TU)

TUS-DER ... Tum Saglik Personeli Birlesme ve Dayanisma Dernegi [*Comprehensive Health Personnel Unity and Solidarity Association*] (TU)

TUSh .... Teater Un Shpil

TUSIAD .... Turk Sanayicileri ve Is Adamlari Dernegi [*Turkish Industrialists' and Businessmen's Association*] [*Istanbul, Turkey*] (TU)

TUSLOG... Turkish-United States Logistic Group

TUSN .... Heat Wave Homing Device, Heat Seeker (RU)

TUSPED ... Tuzeloanyag Szallitasi Vallalat [*Fuel Transportation Enterprise*] (HU)

TUT .... Tampere University of Technology [*Finland*] (EAS)

TUT .... Taxe Unique sur les Transactions [*Single Tax on Transactions*] (AF)

TUT .... Tenants' Union of Tasmania [*Australia*]

TUTA .... Trade Union Training Authority [*Australia*] (ADA)

TUTAS...... Turizm ve Ticaret Anonim Sirketi [*Tourism and Trade Corporation*] (TU)

TUTED...... Tum Teknik Elemanlar Dernegi [*Universal Technical Workers Organization*] (TU)

TUTIS .... Turkiye Tasit Isverenleri Sendikasi [*Union of Turkish Transit Workers Employers*] (TU)

TUTOS...... Turkiye Teknik Ogretmenler Sendikasi [*Turkish Technical Teachers' Union*] (TU)

TU-TS .... Relay Device for Remote Control and Remote Signaling (RU)

TUTVS....... Tyrsuv Ustav pro Telesnou Vychovu a Sport [*Tyrs Institute for Physical Education and Sports*] (CZ)

TUU.......... Compania Aerea de Servicios Tur Air [*Spain*] [*ICAO designator*] (FAAC)

TUU.......... Tabuk [*Saudi Arabia*] [*Airport symbol*] (OAG)

TUV .... Tarifni Umluva Vojenska [*Military Tariff Agreement*] (CZ)

TUV .... Teatro Universitario. Universidad del Valle [*Colombia*] (COL)

TUV .... Technischer Ueberwachungs-Verein [*Technical Watch-Over Association*] [*European product safety organization*] (CDE)

TUV .... Technischer Ueberwachungs-Verein Bayern eV [*Technical Inspectorate of Bavaria*] [*Munich*] [*Research center*] (ERC)

TUV .... Technischer Ueberwachungs-Verein, eV [*Nuclear energy*] (NRCH)

TUV .... Tenants Union of Victoria [*Australia*]

TUV .... Trabalhadores Unidos Vencerao [*Workers United Will Win*] [*Portuguese*] (WER)

TUV .... Tucupita [*Venezuela*] [*Airport symbol*] (OAG)

TUV .... Turavia [*Poland*] [*ICAO designator*] (FAAC)

TUV .... Tuvalu [*ANSI three-letter standard code*] (CNC)

tuv .... Tuvinian (RU)

TUVBayern eV ... Technischer Ueberwachungs-Verein Bayern Eingetragener Verein [*Technical Inspectorate of Bavaria*] (WND)

TUVESAD ... Turkiye Ulusal Verem Savas Dernegi [*Turkish National Society for the Prevention of Tuberculosis*] (TU)

Tuvknigoizdat ... Tuvinian Book Publishing House (RU)

TUW .... Thai Underwear Co. Ltd.

TUW.......... Tubala [*Panama*] [*Airport symbol*] (OAG)

TUX .... Tuxpeno [*Race of maize*] [*Mexico*]

TUY .... Empresa Aerotuy [*Venezuela*] [*ICAO designator*] (FAAC)

TUY .... Tulum [*Mexico*] [*Airport symbol*] [*Obsolete*] (OAG)

TUYM ...... Trade Union Youth Movement [*Guyana*] (LA)

tuy nar........ So-Called (BU)

TUZ .... Technical Educational Institution (RU)

TUZEP...... Tuzeloszer es Epitoanyag Ertekesito Vallalat [*Fuel and Building Material Trade Enterprise*] (HU)

TUZMAS ... Tuz ve Mamulleri Kimya Sanayii Anonim Sirketi [*Salt and By-Products Chemical Industry Corporation*] (TU)

TV .... Construction Troops (BU)

TV .... Drop Point (RU)

Tv .... Freight Car (RU)

tv .... Hard, Hardness, Solid, Solidity (RU)

TV .... Heavy-Water [*Nuclear physics and engineering*] (RU)

TV .... Input Transformer (RU)

tv .... Instrumental [*Case*] (RU)

TV .... Output Transformer (RU)

TV .... Pipe Air Preheater (RU)

TV .... Rectifying Transformer (RU)

TV .... Remote-Control Switch (RU)

TV .... Slow-Speed Wind Motor (RU)

TV .... Table Vicennale (FLAF)

TV .... Tacno Vreme [*Correct Time*] (YU)

TV .... Taktverstaerker [*German*] (ADPT)
tv .... Tana Vuonna [*This Year*] [*Finland*] (GPO)
TV .... Tank Platoon (RU)
TV .... Tarifvertrag [*Collective Bargaining Agreement, Trade Agreement*] (EG)
TV .... Technicke-Vedecke Vydavatelstvi [*Technical and Scientific Publishing House*] [*Prague*] (CZ)
tv .... Tehervonat [*Freight Train*] (HU)
TV .... Telefunken Variable Microgroove [*Record label*] [*Germany*]
TV .... Telesno Vezbanje [*Physical Exercise*] (YU)
TV .... Televisie [*Television*] [*Afrikaans*]
TV .... Televisio [*Television*] [*Finland*]
TV .... Television [*Television*] [*Spanish*]
TV .... Televisione [*Television*] [*Italian*]
TV .... Telewizja [*Television*] [*Poland*]
TV .... Terak Vithei [*Boulevard*] [*Literally, Esplanade or Road Along the Shore Cambodia*] (CL)
tv .... Terv [*Plan*] (HU)
TV .... Theater of War [*Former USSR*] (MCD)
tv .... Torveny [*Law (Legal)*] (HU)
TV .... Tratove Velitelstvi [*Railroad Command*] (CZ)
tv .... Travessa [*Crossroad*] [*Portuguese*] (CED)
TV .... Treviso [*Car registration plates*] [*Italian*]
TV .... Trolley Pusher (RU)
TV .... Tropical Air (RU)
TV .... Turnverein [*Gymnastic Club*] [*German*]
TV .... Tuvalu [*ANSI two-letter standard code*] (CNC)
tv .... Tvaer [*Oblong*] [*Sweden*]
tv .... Tvaer [*Oblong*] [*Danish/Norwegian*]
tv .... Tyovaenyhdistys [*Finland*]
TV5 .... Television Francophone par Satellite [*France*] (EAIO)
TVA .... External Address Table [*Computers*] (RU)
TVA .... Morafenobe [*Madagascar*] [*Airport symbol*] (OAG)
TVA .... Tables of Altitudes and Azimuths (RU)
TVA .... Tactical Air Force (RU)
TVA .... Tanzania Volleyball Association
TVA .... Tarif- und Verkehrsanzeiger [*Rate and Traffic Schedule*] (EG)
TVA .... Taxa pe Valoarea Adaugata [*Value-Added Tax*] (RO)
TVA .... Taxe a la Valeur Ajoutee [*Value-Added Tax*] [*French*] [*Business term*]
TVA .... Technologie-Vermittlungs-Agentur
TVA .... Telefon-Verwaltungs-und-Auskunftssystem [*German*] (ADPT)
TVA .... Television Australia Ltd.
TVA .... Tourisme et Voyages en Afrique
TVA .... Turbofan Assembly (RU)
TVAZ .... Tables of Altitudes and Azimuths of Stars (RU)
TVB .... Television Broadcasts [*Hong Kong television company*] (ECON)
TVB .... Television Broadcasts Ltd. [*Hong Kong*]
TVB .... Treu und Bestaendig [*Faithful and Steadfast*] [*Motto of Johann Georg, Margrave of Brandenburg (1577-1624)*] [*German*]
TVBTAO... Turkiye Vakiflar Bankasi Turk Anonim Ortaklari [*Turkish Religious Trusts/Bank Corporation*] (TU)
TVC .... Tasmanian Visitor Corp. [*Australia*]
tvc............... Torvenycikk [*Article of Law*] (HU)
TVCh .... High-Frequency Current (BU)
TVD .... High-Pressure Turbine (RU)
TVD .... Teatr Voennykh Deistvii [*Theater of Military Operations*] [*Former USSR*]
TVD .... Telesno Vzgojno Drustvo [*Physical Education Society*] (YU)
tvd .... Television (RU)
TVD .... Turboprop Engine (RU)
TVDPKh.... High-Pressure Ahead Turbine (RU)
TVDZKh ... High-Pressure Astern Turbine (RU)
TVE .... Fuel Element [*Nuclear physics and engineering*] (RU)
TVE .... Televisao Experimental
TVE .... Television Espanola [*Spanish Television*] (WER)
TVE .... Township and Village Enterprise [*People's Republic of China*] (ECON)
TVEL............ Fuel Element [*Nuclear physics and engineering*] (RU)
TVF............. Air Fleet Engineering (RU)
TVG .... Exhaust Gas Temperature Gauge (RU)
TVG .... Television de Galicia [*Spain*] (EY)
TVH........... Tie- Ja Vesirakennushallitus [*Roads and Waterways Administration*] [*Ministry of Communications Helsinki*] [*Finland*] [*Research center*] (ERC)
TVHB .... Turk Veteriner Hekimler Birligi [*Turkish Veterinary Doctors Union*] (TU)
TVI............. Television Independante [*Belgium*] (EY)
TVID.......... Turbofan Engine (RU)
TVIS .... Tropical Vegetable Information Service [*Asian Vegetable Research and Development Center*] [*Information service or system*] (IID)
TVK .... Tiszai Vegyikombinat [*Tisza Chemical Combine*] (HU)
TVK .... Toimihenkilo- ja Virkamiesjarjestojen-Keskusliitto [*Confederation of Salaried Employees*] [*Helsinki, Finland*] (WEN)

tvl .... Tavle [*Plate*] [*Publishing Danish/Norwegian*]
Tvl .... Transvaal [*South Africa*]
TVLC........ Takoradi Veneer and Lumber Company Ltd.
TVM .... Heavy Suspension Bridge (RU)
TVM .... Techno Venture Management [*Germany*]
TVM .... Telesna Vychova Mladeze [*Physical Education for Young People*] (CZ)
TVM .... Television Malta
TVM .... Tiszai Vegyi Muvek [*Tisza Chemical Works*] (HU)
TVM .... Tiszamenti Vegyimuvek [*Tisza Bank Chemical Works*] [*Tiszai Vegyi Muvek*] [*Later,*] (HU)
TVM .... Tropical Veterinary Medicine
TVN .... High-Voltage Current (RU)
TVN .... High-Voltage Engineering (RU)
TVN .... High-Voltage Transformer (RU)
TVN .... Transcolombiana de Aviacion SA [*Colombia*] [*ICAO designator*] (FAAC)
TVNK .... Television Nationale Khmere [*Cambodian National Television*] (CL)
TVNZ .... Television New Zealand
t-vo .... Association, Company (RU)
TVO .... Ditta Transavio di I. Ballerio [*Italy*] [*ICAO designator*] (FAAC)
TVO .... Educational Labor Camp (BU)
TVO .... Teollisuuden Voima Osakeyhtio [*Nuclear energy*] [*Finland*] (NRCH)
TVO .... Transportverordnung [*Transportation Ordinance*] (EG)
tvor .... Instrumental [*Case*] (RU)
t vospl .... Ignition Temperature (RU)
t vozg .... Sublimation Temperature (RU)
TVP........... Tamil Vimukhti Peramena [*Sri Lanka*] [*Political party*] (PPW)
TVP........... Technische Vorplanung [*Advance Technical Planning*] (EG)
TVP........... Telex-Verschluesselungs-Paket [*German*] (ADPT)
TVPDA..... Television Programme Distributors Association [*Australia*]
TVR .... Heavy-Water Reactor (RU)
tvr .... Torvenyereju Rendelet [*Law Decree*] (HU)
TVRD .... Turbofan Engine (RU)
TVRD .... Turbojet Engine (BU)
TVRD .... Turboprop Engine (RU)
TVREK....... Television de la Republique Khmere [*Television of the Khmer Republic*] [*Cambodia*] (CL)
TVRF........ Terrorist Victims Relief Fund
TVRI........ Televisi Republik Indonesia [*Indonesian television network*] (FEA)
TVRO .... Transports Voyageurs de la Region d'Oran [*Algeria*]
tv r-r .... Solid Solution (RU)
TVR-Up..... Water-Cooled Heavy-Water-Moderated Natural Uranium Reactor (RU)
TVRZ........ Tambov Railroad Car Repair Plant (RU)
TVS........... Tehnicka Visa Skola [*Advanced Technical School*] (YU)
TVS........... Telesna Vychova a Sport [*Physical Education and Sports*] (CZ)
TVS........... Telovychovne Slavnosti Skol [*School Physical Education Festival*] (CZ)
TVS........... Tylove Velitelske Stanoviste [*Rear Area Command Post*] (CZ)
TVSA .... Tandheelkundige Vereniging van Suid-Afrika [*South Africa*] (AA)
TVSA .... Terminologie Vereniging van Suid-Afrika [*Terminology Association of South Africa*] (AA)
TV-SAT .... Satellite Television [*Germany*]
t vsp........... Flash Point (RU)
TVSV......... Kingstown/Arnos Vale [*St. Vincent*] [*ICAO location identifier*] (ICLI)
TVT .... Television of Thailand (FEA)
TVT .... Trans-Volta Togoland
TVT .... Troupe de la Ville de Tunis
TVU .... Taveuni [*Fiji*] [*Airport symbol*] (OAG)
TVU .... Television Unlimited [*Australia*]
TVV .... Technicko-Vedecke Vydavatelstvi [*Technical and Scientific Publishing House*] [*Prague*] (CZ)
TVV .... Televisio Valenciana [*Spain*] (EY)
TVV .... Topographic Computing Platoon (RU)
TVY .... Tavoy [*Myanmar*] [*Airport symbol*] (OAG)
TVZ .... Television Zambias
Tw .... Grad Twaddell [*Degree Twaddell*] [*German*] (GCA)
TW .... Taiwan [*ANSI two-letter standard code*] (CNC)
TW .... Teatr Wielki [*Grand Theatre*] (POL)
TW .... Technische Wartung [*Technical Maintenance*] (EG)
TW .... Teile Wasser [*Parts of Water*] [*German*] (GCA)
tw............... Teilweise [*Partly*] [*German*] (GCA)
TW .... Termijnenwet [*Benelux*] (BAS)
TW .... Te Wete [*Namely*] [*Afrikaans*]
tw............... Te Weten [*Benelux*] (BAS)
TW .... Textil-Wirtschaft [*Textile Industry*] [*Deutscher Fachverlag GmbH*] [*Information service or system*] (IID)
Tw .... Trefwoord [*Benelux*] (BAS)
TW .... Trung Uong [*Central, Central Committee*]
tw............... Tussenwerpsel [*Interjection*] [*Afrikaans*]

tw .... Twardosc [Hardness] [Poland]
TW .... Tweetalige Woordeboek [Bilingual Dictionary] [Afrikaans]
TWA .... Technische-Wissenschaftliche Anwendung [German] (ADPT)
TWAR .... Taiwan Acute Respiratory Disease [Pneumonia-causing chlamydia strain named after the ailment that results from it]
TWAS........ Third World Academy of Sciences [Trieste, Italy] (EAIO)
TWAU .... Transvaal Women's Agricultural Union
TWB .... Toowoomba [Australia] [Airport symbol] (OAG)
TWB .... Transsonischer Windkanal Braunschweig
TWBA .... Tasmanian Wool Brokers' Association [Australia]
TWC .... Third World Club [Ghana]
TWCF .... Third World Conference Fund
TWD .... Hoofdgroep Technisch-Wetenschappelijke Diensten [Division for Technical Scientific Services] [Netherlands Central Organization for Applied Natural Scientific Research] (WED)
TWD .... Tanganyika Wildlife Development
TWD-TNO ... Hoofdgroep Technisch-Wetenschappelijke Diensten TNO [Division for Technical Scientific Services TNO] [Netherlands Organization for Applied Scientific Research (TNO)] [Netherlands] [Research center] (ERC)
TWDWOA ... Turkish War Disabled, Widows and Orphans Association (EAIO)
TWE .... Technisch-Wissenschaftlicher Einsatz [German] (ADPT)
TWE .... Transwede [Sweden] [ICAO designator] (FAAC)
TWF .... Third World Forum [Cairo, Egypt] (EAIO)
TWF .... Third World Foundation [British] (EAIO)
TWF .... Transylvanian World Federation (EAIO)
TWG .... Textile Workers' Group of the Belgian General Federation of Labour (EAIO)
Twg .... Topfwagen [Container Car] (EG)
TWG .... Transport Working Group [Australia]
TWG .... Transsonischer Windkanal Goettingen
TWG .... Trans Wings AS [Norway] [ICAO designator] (FAAC)
Twgf .... Triebwagenfuehrer [Rail Motor Car Engineer] (EG)
Twgsch....... Triebwagenschaffner [Rail Motor Car Conductor] (EG)
TWI .... Working Group Tourism with Insight [Germany] (EAIO)
TWICO..... Tanzania Wood Industry Corporation (AF)
TWIF .... Tug-of-War International Federation [Zevenhuizen, Netherlands] (EAIO)
TWIN .... Third World Information Network [British] (EAIO)
TWIN .... Two Wheels Industries [Bicycle manufacturer] [Nigeria]
TWK .... Technischwirtschaftliche Kennziffer [Industrial-Economic Index] (EG)
Tw K.......... Tweede Kamer [Benelux] (BAS)
TWLF .... Third World Liberation Force
TWLS .... Tanzania Wildlife Safaris Limited
TW-MAE-W ... Third World Movement Against the Exploitation of Women [Quezon City, Philippines] (EAIO)
TWMP ...... Towarzystwo Wydawnicze Muzyki Polskiej [Society for Publication of Polish Music] (POL)
TWN......... Taiwan [ANSI three-letter standard code] (CNC)
TWN .... Taylor Woodrow of Nigeria
TWNS .... Trans World News Service (NTCM)
TWO......... [The] Wheatley Organisation [Australia]
TWP .... Teatr Wojska Polskiego [Polish Army Theater] (POL)
TWP .... Territory Wildlife Park [Northern Territory, Australia]
TWP .... Torwood [Australia] [Airport symbol] [Obsolete] (OAG)
TWP .... Towarzystwo Wiedzy Powszechnej [Society for Popularization of Knowledge] (POL)
TWP .... True Whig Party [Liberia] (AF)
TWP .... Turkish Workers' Party [See also TEP] (TU)
TWR .... Trans World Radio Pacific [Guam] (FEA)
TWRA ...... Transpacific Westbound Rate Agreement (DS)
TWS......... Technische Werke der Stadt Stuttgart [Germany] (PDAA)
TWS.......... Trans West African Airlines Ltd. [Gambia] [ICAO designator] (FAAC)
TWS.......... [The] Wilderness Society [Australia]
TWSBA ..... Tasmanian Wool Selling Brokers' Association [Australia]
tw szt .... Tworzywo Sztuczne [Plastic] [Poland]
TWT .... Tanzania Wildlife Tour
TWT .... Tawi-Tawi [Philippines] [Airport symbol] (OAG)
TWT .... Television Wollongong Transmissions Ltd. [Australia] (ADA)
TWT .... Terry Willesee Tonight [Television program] [Australia]
TWU .... Tasmanian Writers Union [Australia]
TWU .... Tawau [Malaysia] [Airport symbol] (OAG)
TWU .... Telecommunications Workers Union [Mauritius] (AF)
TWU .... Transport Workers' Union (ML)
TWU .... Transport Workers' Union of Australia (ADA)
TWUA ...... Transport Workers' Union of Australia
TWV .... Ter Waarde Van [To the Value Of] [Afrikaans]
TWW .... Thiess Watkins White Group Ltd. [Australia]
TWWHA... Tasmanian Wilderness World Heritage Area
TWZ .... Technischwissenschaftliches Zentrum [Technical and Scientific Center (Production development)] (EG)

t/x .... Motor Ship (RU)
tx .... Tonneaux [Barrels] [French]
Tx .... Wytwornia Telekomunikacyjnego Sprzetu Numer X [Number X Telecommunications Equipment Plant] (POL)
TXC .... Transaviaexport [Belarus] [ICAO designator] (FAAC)
TXI............ Aereotaxis SA de CV [Mexico] [ICAO designator] (FAAC)
TXKF .... Bermuda Naval Air Station [Bermuda] [ICAO location identifier] (ICLI)
TXL............ Aereo Taxi de Leon SA de CV [Mexico] [ICAO designator] (FAAC)
TXL............ Berlin [Germany] [Airport symbol] (OAG)
TXM .... Taxi Aereo de Mexico [ICAO designator] (FAAC)
TXN .... Tunxi [China] [Airport symbol] (OAG)
TXP........... Linea Aerea Taxpa Ltda. [Chile] [ICAO designator] (FAAC)
TXR .... Taxirey SA de CV [Mexico] [ICAO designator] (FAAC)
TXU .... Tabou [Ivory Coast] [Airport symbol] (OAG)
TY .... Benin [Aircraft nationality and registration mark] (FAAC)
TY .... Tagma Ygeionomikou [Medical Battalion] (GC)
ty .... Tarih Yok [Undated] (TU)
Ty .... Tayyare [Airplane] (TU)
TY .... Teyateyaneng
T/Y .... Ton/Yil [Tons per Year] (TU)
TYaD .... Thermonuclear Engine (RU)
TYaEG ...... Thermonuclear Electric Generator (RU)
TYaES ...... Thermonuclear Electric Power Plant (RU)
TYaTG...... Thermonuclear Heat Generator (RU)
tyazhmash ... Heavy Machinery Manufacture, Heavy Machinery (RU)
tyazhprom ... Heavy Industry (RU)
tyazhpromelektroproyekt ... State Planning Institute for the Planning of Electrical Equipment for Heavy Industry (RU)
Tyazhstankogidropress ... Heavy Machine Tool and Hydraulic Press Plant (RU)
TYB .... Turkiye Yazarlar Birligi [Turkish Writers' Union] (TU)
TYC .... Tibetan Youth Congress
TYC .... Turkiye Yesilay Cemiyeti [Turkish Red Crescent Society] (TU)
T-YCDT .... Ten-Year Chinese Dong Tang [Turmoil] Cycle [Reference to the Kuomintang's defeat in 1946-48, Mao's Great Leap Forward in 1956, the Cultural Revolution in 1966, the Gang of Four's fall in 1976] [Term coined by William Safire]
TYDK .... Tekhniki Ypiresia Dimon kai Koinotiton [Technical Service of the Municipalities and Communes] [Greek] (GC)
TYE .... Tekhniki Ypiresia tis Ekklisias [Church Technical Service] [Greek] (GC)
tye .... That Is (RU)
TYeM .... Technical Unit of Mass (RU)
tyg .... Tygodnik [Weekly] (POL)
TYH-Is ...... Turkiye Yeni Haber-Is [New Turkish Information Union] (TU)
TYJ .... Tyrolean Jet Service [Austria] [ICAO designator] (FAAC)
TYJK .... Towa Yuai Jigyo Kumiai [East Asia Friendship Enterprizes Association] [Japan]
TYL .... Talara [Peru] [Airport symbol] (OAG)
TYL .... TANU [Tanganyika African National Union] Youth League [Tanzania] (AF)
TYM .... Tyumen Airlines [Russian Federation] [ICAO designator] (FAAC)
TYN .... Taiyuan [China] [Airport symbol] (OAG)
TYO.......... Tokyo [Japan] [Airport symbol] (OAG)
TYOSKK... Turkiye Yusek Ogretim Spor Koordinasyon Kurulu [Turkish Higher Education Sports Coordination Committee] (TU)
typ .... Typographie [French] (TPFD)
typ .... Typographique [Typographic] [French]
typ .... Typography (TPFD)
typograph ... Typographisch [Typographic] [German]
TYR .... Taloushistoriallinen Yhdistys RY [Economic History Society of Finland] (EAIO)
TYR .... Tyrolean Airways [Austria] [ICAO designator] (FAAC)
Tyr .... Tyrone County [Ireland] (BARN)
Tyrol .... Tyrolean [or Tirolean] [Reference to a state in western Austria] [Reference to an alpine region that is divided between Austria and Italy] (BARN)
TYS .... Takhydromiki Ypiresia Stratou [Army Postal Service] [Greek] (GC)
TYS .... Tameiaki Ypiresia Stratou [Army Finance Service] [Greek] (GC)
tys.............. Thousand (RU)
TYS .... Turkiye Yazarlar Sendikasi [Turkish Writers' Union] (TU)
tys.............. Tysiac [Thousand] [Poland]
TYSD........ Turkiye Yardim Sevenler Dernegi [Turkish Philanthropic Society] [YSD] [See also] (TU)
TYSE .... Turk Yapi Sanat Enstitusu [Turkish Construction Trades Institute] [Cyprus] (TU)
tyt.............. Tytul [Title] (POL)
TYTF .... Teknokemian Yhdistys - Teknokemiska Foreningen [Cosmetics and Detergent Industry Association] [Finland] (EAIO)
Tyumen'sel'mash ... Tyumen' Plant of Agricultural Machinery (RU)
tyurk.......... Turkic (RU)

TYuZ .... Young Spectator's Theater, Children's Theater (RU)
TYYK .... Turk Yoksullara Yardim Kurumu [*Society for Aid to Turkish Orphans*] [*Turkish Cypriot*] (GC)
TYYK .... Turk Yonetimi Yurutme Kurulu [*Turkish (Cypriot) Administration Executive Council*] (GC)
TZ .... Commercial Law (BU)
TZ .... Fueling Truck (RU)
TZ .... Taktzentrale [*German*] (ADPT)
TZ .... Technical Task (RU)
TZ .... Teilringzahl [*Graduation Setting*] [*German*] (GCA)
tz .... Ter Zake [*Benelux*] (BAS)
TZ .... Times of Zambia
TZ .... Trgovska Zbornica [*Chamber of Commerce*] (YU)
TZ .... Trinecke Zelezarny Velke Rijnove Socialisticke Revoluce [*Trinec Iron Works of the Great October Socialist Revolution*] (CZ)
TZ .... Turgoviya i Zemedelie [*Commerce and Agriculture*] [*A periodical*] (BU)
TZ .... United Republic of Tanzania [*ANSI two-letter standard code*] (CNC)
TZA .... Heavy Antiaircraft Artillery (RU)
TZA .... Technisches Zentralamt [*Central Technical Office*] [*German*] (EG)
TZA .... Turbogear Assembly (RU)
TZA .... United Republic of Tanzania [*ANSI three-letter standard code*] (CNC)
t zam .... Freezing Point (RU)
t zast .... Solidification Point (RU)
t zatv .... Solidification Temperature (RU)
TZC .... Turkiye Ziraatciler Cemiyeti [*Turkish Agriculturalists Society*] (TU)
TZCh .... Tractor Spare-Part Plant (RU)
TZDK .... Turkiye Zirai Donatim Kurumu [*Turkish Agricultural Equipment Board*] (TU)
TZGT .... Tula Correspondence Mining Technicum (RU)
t:zh .... Solid-to-Liquid Ratio (RU)
t zh .... Thousand Inhabitants (RU)
tzhpb .... Railway Maintenance Battalion (BU)
TZhRU ...... Tula Iron Mine Administration (RU)
TZhS .... Railroad Technical Dictionary (RU)
TZI .... Floating River-Crossing Equipment [*Military term*] (RU)
Tz Ist .... Telsiz Istasyonu [*Wireless Station*] (TU)
TZK .... Commander's Zenith Telescope (RU)
TZK .... Taganrog Combine Plant (RU)
TZK .... Tajikistan [*ICAO designator*] (FAAC)
TZK .... Technicka Zavodni Knihovna [*Factory Technical Library*] (CZ)
TZKh .... Reverse Turbine (RU)
TZM .... Floating River-Crossing Material [*Military term*] (RU)
TZN .... South Andros [*Bahamas*] [*Airport symbol*] (OAG)
tzn .... To Znaczy [*That Is*] (POL)
TZOB .... Turkiye Ziraat Odalari Birligi [*Turkish Union of Chambers of Agriculture*] (TU)
TZp .... Recording Flip-Flop (RU)
TZP .... Technical School for Grain Storage and Processing (BU)
tzp .... Te Zelfder Plaatse [*Benelux*] (BAS)
TZP .... Tymczasowy Zarzad Panstwowy [*Provisional State Administration*] (POL)
TZP .... Unsinkable Float [*Military term*] (RU)
TZR .... Tanzania-Zambia Railway (PDAA)
TZS .... Technicum of Landscaping (RU)
TZS .... Technologie Zentrum Steyr [*Steyr Technology Center*] [*German*]
TZS .... Titulni Zarizeni Staveniste [*Specified Building Equipment*] (CZ)
TZU .... Technical Establishments and Systems (BU)
TZUS .... Technicky a Zkusebni Ustav Stavebni [*Institute for Technology and Testing in Construction*] (CZ)
tzv .... Takozvani [*So-Called*] (YU)
tzv .... Tuna Zive Vahy [*Ton of Live Weight*] (CZ)
tzw .... Tak Zwany [*So-Called*] (POL)
TZWS .... Tomaszowskie Zaklady Wlokien Sztucznych [*Tomaszow Artificial Fiber Plant*] (POL)
TZX .... Trabzon [*Turkey*] [*Airport symbol*] (OAG)
TZZ .... Barely Perceptible Obstacle (BU)
TZZ .... Hall Darkener (RU)

U

U .... Amplifier (RU)
u .... Before Noon (RU)
u .... Difference de Potentiel [*Potential Difference*] [*French*]
U .... Home Unit [*Australia*]
U .... Instruction [*Standardization document*] (RU)
U .... Regulations, Manual (RU)
U .... Trainer [*Aircraft*] (RU)
U .... Uafhaengige Parti [*Independent Party*] [*Denmark*] [*Political party*] (PPE)
u .... Uddrag [*Selection*] [*Publishing Danish/Norwegian*]
u .... Uebersetzen [*Translate*] [*German*]
U .... Uhr [*Hour*] [*German*]
U .... Ultraphon & Supraphon [*Record label*] [*Former Czechoslovakia*]
U .... Umdrehung [*Revolution*] [*German*]
U .... Umgangssprache [*Colloquial Speech*] [*German*]
U .... Umschlag [*Wrapper*] [*Publishing*] [*German*]
U .... Unbesetzt [*Unoccupied, No One on Duty*] [*German*] (EG)
U .... Uncle [*Phonetic alphabet*] [*Royal Navy World War I Pre-World War II*] [*World War II*] (DSUE)
u .... Und [*And*] [*German*] (GPO)
u .... Under [*Under*] [*Norway*] (GPO)
U .... Uniform [*Phonetic alphabet*] [*International*] (DSUE)
U .... Unionist Party [*Northern Ireland*] [*Political party*]
u .... Unite [*Unit*] [*French*]
U .... Universal (RU)
U .... Universitaet [*University*] [*German*]
u .... Unser [*Our*] [*German*]
u .... Unten [*Below*] [*German*]
u .... Unter [*Under, Among*] [*German*]
U .... Unterkunft [*Billet, Accommodation, Shelter*] [*German*] (EG)
U .... Unverseifbares [*Unsaponifiable*] [*German*]
U .... Uran [*Uranium*] [*Chemical element*] [*German*]
U .... Urania Verlag [*Urania Publishing House*] (EG)
U .... Uranio [*Uranium*] [*Chemical element*] [*Portuguese*]
U .... Urugwaj [*Uruguay*] [*Poland*]
U .... Usted [*You (Singular, formal)*] [*Spanish*]
u .... Utan [*or Utani*] [*After*] (HU)
U .... Utara [*North*] (ML)
u .... Utasz [*Combat Engineer*] (HU)
u .... Utca [*Street*] [*Commonwealth of Independent States*] (EECI)
u .... Uteg [*Battery*] (HU)
U .... UTVA Aircraft Factory [*Former Yugoslavia*] [*ICAO aircraft manufacturer identifier*] (ICAO)
U .... Uur [*Hour*] [*Afrikaans*]
U .... Uvala [*or Uvalica*] [*Inlet Former Yugoslavia*] (NAU)
u .... Uyezd [*District, 1775-1929*] (RU)
u .... Uzem [*Industrial Plant*] (HU)
u .... Uzlet [*Store*] (HU)
U3A .... University of the Third Age [*Australia*]
UA .... Bar Ukase (BU)
UA .... L'Union Africaine Societe d'Assurances et de Reassurances [*The Ivory Coast*] (EY)
UA .... Specific Activity (RU)
ua .... Uden Aarstal [*Without Date*] [*Danish/Norwegian*]
ua .... Ueber Alle [*Over All*] [*German*]
ua .... Ugyanakkor [*At the Same Time, Simultaneously*] (HU)
ua .... Ugyanaz [*Same As*] [*Hungary*] (GPO)
UA .... Uitgesloten Aansprakelijkheid [*Benelux*] (BAS)
UA .... Ukrainian Soviet Socialist Republic [*ISO two-letter standard code*] (CNC)
UA .... Ukrainian SSR [*ANSI two-letter standard code*] (CNC)
ua .... Und Aehnlich [*And So On*] [*German*]
ua .... Und Andere [*And Others*] [*German*] (GPO)
UA .... Unidad Alavesa [*Spain*] [*Political party*] (EY)
u/a .... Unit of Account (EECI)
UA .... Universal Algorithm (RU)
UA .... University of Auckland [*New Zealand*]
ua .... Unter Anderem [*Among Other Things*] [*German*] (GPO)

ua .... Utan Artal [*Without Date*] [*Sweden*]
UAA .... Administration of Arctic Aviation (RU)
UAA .... Uas-One [*British*] [*ICAO designator*] (FAAC)
uaa .... Und An Anderen Orten [*And Elsewhere*] [*German*]
UAA .... Union des Avocats Arabes [*Arab Lawyers Union - ALU*] (EAIO)
UAA .... United American and Australasian Film Productions
UAA .... United Arab Airlines [*Egypt*]
UAAA .... Alma-Ata [*Former USSR*] [*ICAO location identifier*] (ICLI)
UAAEE ..... United Arab Atomic Energy Establishment
UAAI .... Union Africaine Agricole et Industrielle [*African Agricultural and Industrial Union*] [*Senegal*] (AF)
UAAI .... United Australian Automotive Industries
UAAJ .... Union Arabe des Auberges de la Jeunesse
UAAN .... Uzunagach [*Former USSR*] [*ICAO location identifier*] (ICLI)
UAAS .... Union Africaine des Artistes de Spectacle [*Union of African Performing Artists - UAPA*] (EAIO)
UAB .... Guided Bomb (RU)
UAB .... Union des Automobilistes Bulgares [*Bulgaria*] (EAIO)
UAB .... Universities Appointments Board (LAA)
UABB .... Union Arabe de Basketball
UABC .... Universidad Autonoma de Baja California [*Autonomous University of Baja California*] [*Mexico*] (MSC)
UABCS ..... Universidad Autonoma de Baja California Sur [*Mexico*] (ASF)
U-Abt .... Unterabteilung [*Subdivision, Branch*] (EG)
UAC .... Uganda Action Convention (AF)
UAC .... Unified Arab Command (BJA)
UAC .... Union Arabe de Cyclisme
UAC .... United Africa Company [*Nigeria*] (AF)
UAC .... United Air Charters [*Zimbabwe*] [*ICAO designator*] (FAAC)
UAC .... Universele Auteursrecht Conventie [*Benelux*] (BAS)
UAC .... Universities Admissions Centre [*New South Wales and the Australian Capital Territory*]
UACA .... Union of Australian College Academics
UACANT .. Union of Australian College Academics Northern Territory
UACAS ..... Unidades de Abastecimiento para las Comunas Agricolas Sandinistas [*Supply Units for the Sandinist Agricultural Communes*] [*Nicaragua*] (LA)
UACASA ... Union of Australian College Academics South Australia
UACB .... Union des Agglomeres de Ciments de Belgique [*Belgium*] (BAS)
UACF .... Union Africaine des Chemins de Fer
UACH .... Universidad Autonoma Chapingo [*Chapingo Autonomous University*] [*Mexico*] (ARC)
UACHP ..... Ustav pro Automatizaci Chemickeho Prumyslu [*Institute for Automation of Chemical Industry*] (CZ)
UAChR ...... Automatic Frequency-Controlled Unloading Device of Power Systems (RU)
UACMC .... Union Arabe de Ciment et des Materiaux de Construction [*Arab Union for Cement and Building Materials - AUCBM*] (EAIO)
UACPB ...... Union Apostolique et Culturelle de Pretres Burundais
UAD .... Union des Anciens du Dahomey
UAD .... Univex SRL [*Italy*] [*ICAO designator*] (FAAC)
UADA .... Union Argentina de Aseguradores [*Insurers Union of Argentina*] (LA)
UADA .... United Abalone Divers' Association [*Australia*]
UADD .... Directorate of Long-Range Aviation (RU)
UADE .... Universidad Argentina de la Empresa [*Argentine Business University*] (LA)
U Adel .... University of Adelaide [*Australia*]
UADI .... Union Argentina de Asociaciones de Ingenieros [*Argentina*] (LAA)
UADW .... Universal Alliance of Diamond Workers [*See also AUOD*] [*Antwerp, Belgium*] (EAIO)
uae .... Und Aehnliche [*And the Like*] [*German*] (EG)
UAE .... Unilever Australia Export Proprietary Ltd.
UAE .... United Arab Emirates [*ICAO designator*] (FAAC)
UAEAC ..... Union Aduanera y Economica del Africa Central [*Central African Customs and Economic Union - CACEU*] [*Spanish*]

UAEDE ..... Union des Associations Europeennes des Distributeurs d'Eau [*Union of European Associations of Water Suppliers*] [*Belgium*]   (EAIO)
UAEE .... Union des Associations Europeennes d'Etudiants   (FLAF)
UAEM .... Union of Associations of European Meat Meal Producers [*See also UAPEFV*] [*Later, Eurpoean Renderers Association - EURA*]   (EAIO)
UAF .... Uganda Air Force   (PDAA)
UAF .... United Arab Emirates Air Force [*ICAO designator*]   (FAAC)
UAFA .... Union Arabe du Fer et de l'Acier [*Arab Iron and Steel Union*] [*Algeria*]
UAFA .... Union of Arab Football Associations   (EAIO)
UAFF .... Frunze [*Former USSR*] [*ICAO location identifier*]   (ICLI)
UAFMMEEC ... Union of Associations of Fish Meal Manufacturers in the EEC   (EAIO)
UAFRO ..... Uganda Agriculture and Forestry Research Organization   (ARC)
UAFT .... Union Africaine des Telecommunications [*African Telecommunications Union*]   (AF)
UAG .... Air Attack Group   (RU)
UAG .... L'Union des Assurances du Gabon   (EY)
UAG .... Ugandan Action Group   (AF)
UAG .... Uitvoeringsbesluit Autovervoer Goederen [*Benelux*]   (BAS)
UAG .... Universidad Autonoma de Guadalaiara
UAGSA ..... University of Adelaide General Staff Association [*Australia*]
UAGT .... Administration of the City Automobile Transportation   (RU)
UAH .... Ua Huka [*Marquesas Islands*] [*Airport symbol*]   (OAG)
UAH .... Union of Arab Historians   (EA)
UAI .... Ufa Aviation Institute Imeni Sergo Ordzhonikidze   (RU)
UAI .... Uni Air SA [*France*] [*ICAO designator*]   (FAAC)
UAI .... Union Academique Internationale [*International Academic Union - IAU*]   (EAIO)
UAI .... Union Astronomique Internationale [*Paris, France*]   (SLS)
UAI .... Union des Associations Internationales [*Union of International Associations - UIA*]   (EAIO)
UAI .... Unione Antropologica Italiana [*Bologna, Italy*]   (SLS)
UAIA .... Union des Agences d'Information Africaines [*Union of African News Agencies*]   (AF)
UAIC .... Unite d'Afforestation Industrielle du Congo [*Nationalized industry*]   (EY)
UAII .... Chimkent [*Former USSR*] [*ICAO location identifier*]   (ICLI)
UAJ .... Udruzenje Anesteziologa Jugoslavije [*Former Yugoslavia*]   (SLS)
UAJ .... Union of Arab Jurists [*Baghdad, Iraq*]   (EAIO)
UAK .... Narssarssuaq [*Greenland*] [*Airport symbol*]   (OAG)
UAK .... United Arab Kingdom [*Jordan*]   (ME)
UAL .... Unite, Action, Liberation [*Guadeloupe*] [*Political party*]   (EY)
UAL .... Unite Arithmetique et Logique [*Arithmetic and Logic Unit - ALU*] [*French*]
UALE .... Universala Artista Ligo de Esperantistoj [*Universal Artist League of Esperantists*]   (EAIO)
uam .... Und Aehnliches Mehr [*And the Like*] [*German*]
uam .... Und Andere [*or Anderes*] Mehr [*And So Forth, And So On*] [*German*]
UAM .... Und Anderes Mehr [*And So Forth*] [*German*]
UAM .... Unia Afrykansko-Malgaska [*African-Malagasy Union*] [*Poland*]
UAM .... Union Africaine et Malgache [*African and Malagasy Union*]   (AF)
UAM .... Union des Artisans du Meuble
UAM .... United Aborigines Mission [*Australia*]   (ADA)
UAM .... Universidad Autonoma Metropolitana [*Metropolitan Autonomous University*] [*Mexico*]   (LA)
UAM .... Uniwersytet Adama Mickiewicza [*Adam Mickiewicz University*] [*Poznan*]   (POL)
UAMA .... United Arab Muslim Association [*Australia*]
UAMBD .... Union Africaine de Management de Banques pour le Developpement [*African Union of Development Bank Management*] [*Benin*]   (EAIO)
UAMBD .... Union Africaine et Malgache des Banques pour le Developpement [*African and Malagasy Union of Banks for Development*]   (AF)
UAMBD .... Union Africaine et Mauricienne de Banques pour le Developpement [*African and Mauritian Union of Banks for Development*] [*Benin*]   (AF)
UAMCE .... Union Africaine et Malgache de Cooperation Economique [*Afro-Malagasy Union for Economic Cooperation*]   (AF)
UAMD ...... Union Africaine et Malgache de Defense [*Afro-Malagasy Defense Union*]   (AF)
UAMH ...... Uganda Association for the Mentally Handicapped   (EAIO)
UAMPT .... Union Africaine et Malgache des Postes et Telecommunications
UAMV ...... Ustredni Archiv Ministerstva Vnitra [*Central Archives of the Ministry of the Interior*]   (CZ)
UAN .... Progress of Astronomical Sciences   (RU)
UAN .... Ukrainskaya Akademiya Nauk [*Ukrainian Academy of Sciences*]   (MSC)
UAN .... Union Autonomista Navarra [*Navarra Autonomist Union*] [*Spanish*]   (WER)
UAN .... Unione Accademica Nazionale [*Italian*]   (SLS)
UAN .... United Animal Nations   (EAIO)

UANA .... Union of African News Agencies [*Algiers*]   (AF)
UANA .... Union of Arab News Agencies
UANC .... United African National Council [*Zimbabwe*] [*Political party*] (PPW)
UANL .... Universidad Autonomo de Nuevo Leon
UANM ...... Universal African Nationalist Movement
UAO .... Und Andere Orte [*And Elsewhere*] [*German*]
UAO .... United Australian Organisation
uaO .... Unter Anderen Orten [*Among Other Places*] [*German*]
UAOO ...... Kzyl-Orda [*Former USSR*] [*ICAO location identifier*]   (ICLI)
UAP .... Directorate of the Aircraft Industry   (RU)
UAP .... Ua Pou [*Marquesas Islands*] [*Airport symbol*]   (OAG)
UAP .... Uitvoeringsbesluit Autovervoer Personen [*Benelux*]   (BAS)
UAP .... Unabhaengige Arbeiterpartei [*Independent Labor Party*] [*Germany*] [*Political party*]   (PPE)
UAP .... Union Africaine de Physique [*African Union of Physics - AUP*] (EAIO)
UAP .... Union des Assurances de Paris [*Insurance Union of Paris*] [*French*]
UAP .... Unite Australia Party [*Political party*]
UAP .... United Australia Party [*Political party*]
UAP .... Uniunea Artistilor Plastici [*Union of Plastic Artists*]   (RO)
UAPA .... Union des Agences de Presse Africaines [*Union of African Press Agencies*]   (AF)
UAPA .... Union of African Performing Artists [*See also UAAS*]   (EAIO)
UAPEFV ... Union des Associations des Producteurs Europeens de Farine de Viande [*Union of Associations of European Meat Meal Producers UAEM*] [*Later, European Renderers Association - EURA*]   (EAIO)
UAPF .... Union des Armateurs a la Peche de France [*French Association of Fishing-Ship Owners*]   (EAIO)
UAPP .... Automatic Reclosing   (RU)
UAPP .... Training Glider Regiment   (RU)
UAPPA ...... Union of Air Pollution Prevention Associations   (EAIO)
UAPT .... Union Africaine des Postes et des Telecommunications [*African Postal and Telecommunications Union*] [*Use APTU*]   (AF)
UAPV .... Automatic Recloser   (RU)
UAQ .... San Juan [*Argentina*] [*Airport symbol*]   (OAG)
UAQCIC .... Umm Al-Qaiwain Cement Industries Company [*United Arab Emirates*]
UAR .... Ujedinjena Arapska Republika [*United Arab Republic*]   (YU)
UAR .... Uni Air [*France*] [*ICAO designator*]   (FAAC)
UAR .... Union of African Railways [*Zaire*]
UAR .... Union of Architects of Romania   (EAIO)
UAR .... United Arab Republic [*Egypt and Syria*] [*Obsolete*]
UARAEE .... United Arab Republic Atomic Energy Establishment
UARAF .... United Arab Republic Air Force
UARBC .... United Arab Republic Broadcasting Corporation
UARBS ..... United Arab Republic Broadcasting Service
UARCEE ... Union des Associations des Riziers de la CEE [*Union of Rice Associations of the EEC*]   (ECED)
UARR .... Uralsk [*Former USSR*] [*ICAO location identifier*]   (ICLI)
UARS .... Guided Air-Launched Missile   (RU)
UARS .... Ukulinga Agricultural Research Station [*South Africa*]   (DSCA)
UARTO ..... United Arab Republic Telecommunication Organization
UARV .... Device for Automatic Control of Synchronous Machine Excitation   (RU)
UARZ .... Administration of Automobile Repair Plants and of Technical Supply of Automobile Transportation (of the Mosgorispolkom)   (RU)
UAS .... The University of Agricultural Sciences [*India*]   (DSCA)
UAS .... Uganda Air Services Ltd.
UAS .... Uluslararasi Anonim Sirketi [*International Corporation*]   (TU)
uas .... Und Andere Solche [*And Others*] [*German*]
UAS .... Union of African States
UAS .... United Arab States
UAS .... Uniunea Asociatilor Studentesti [*Union of Student Associations*]   (RO)
UASA .... Urological Association of South Africa   (AA)
UASANSW ... University Academic Staff Association of New South Wales [*Australia*]
UASC .... Union of African Sports Confederations
UASC .... United Arab Shipping Company   (ME)
UASCR ...... Uniunea Asociatilor Studentilor Comunisti din Romania [*Union of Communist Student Associations in Romania*]   (RO)
UASD .... Universidad Autonoma de Santo Domingo [*Autonomous University of Santo Domingo*] [*Dominican Republic*]   (LA)
UASE .... Union of African Students in Europe
UASE .... Union of Arab Stock Exchanges
UASI .... Union of Artisans of the Sugar Industry [*Mauritius*]   (AF)
UASIF .... Union des Associations Scientifiques et Industrielles Francaises [*Paris, France*]   (SLS)
UASKhN ... Ukrainian Academy of Agricultural Sciences   (RU)
UASO .... Union of African Students Organization
UASP .... Unidad de Accion Sindical y Popular [*Trade union*] [*Guatemala*] (EY)

UASP iVS ... Administration of Special Purpose Aviation and Aerial Photography [*Civil aviation*]   (RU)
UASS........ Guided Air-Launched Cruise Missile   (RU)
UASSR...... Udmurt Autonomous Soviet Socialist Republic   (RU)
UASSU...... Union des Associations Sportives, Scolaires, et Universitaires
UAST........ Universal Association for Speech Tracing [*See also TPA*]   (EAIO)
UASTM..... Universidad Agraria de la Selva Tingo Maria [*Peru*]   (DSCA)
UAT.......... Adjusting Autotransformer   (RU)
UAT.......... Administration of Automobile Transportation   (RU)
UAT.......... Motor Vehicle Transport Administration   (BU)
UAT.......... Public Motor Vehicle Transport Statutes   (BU)
UAT.......... Union Aeromaritime des Transports
UATA .... Aralsk [*Former USSR*] [*ICAO location identifier*]   (ICLI)
UATA .... Uganda African Teachers' Association
UATI .... Union de Asociaciones Tecnicas Internacionales [*Union of International Engineering Organizations - UIEO*] [*Spanish*]   (ASF)
UATI .... Union des Associations Techniques Internationales [*Union of International Technical Associations - UITA*]   (EAIO)
UATR .... Chelkar [*Former USSR*] [*ICAO location identifier*]   (ICLI)
UATS........ Agency Automatic Telephone Exchange   (RU)
UATT .... Aktyubinsk [*Former USSR*] [*ICAO location identifier*]   (ICLI)
UATV .... United Australian Television
UAU .... Universal Arithmetic Unit [*Computers*]   (RU)
UAUP....... Ustav Architektury a Uzemniho Planovani [*Institute of Architecture and Regional Planning*]   (CZ)
UAUW...... Uganda Association of University Women   (EAIO)
UAV.......... Attack Aircraft Carrier   (RU)
UAV.......... Unidad de Accion Vallecaucana [*Colombia*]   (COL)
UAV.......... Uniforme Administratieve Voorwaarden voor de Uitvoering van Werken [*Benelux*]   (BAS)
UAV.......... United Aviation Ltd. [*New Zealand*] [*ICAO designator*]   (FAAC)
UAVR .... Ustredni Akcni Vybor [*Central Action Committee*]   (CZ)
UAVR....... Device for Automatic Switching of Reserve Power Supply   (RU)
UAVT .... Heavy Attack Aircraft Carrier   (RU)
UAW........ Ummah Arabiyya Wahda [*United Arab Nation*]
UAW........ Union of Australian Women   (ADA)
UAwg........ Um Antwort Wird Gebeten [*An Answer Is Requested*] [*German*]   (EG)
UAWNO ... Union of Australian Women National Office
UAWU...... University and Allied Workers Union [*Jamaica*]   (LA)
UAZ.......... Emergency Protection Device   (RU)
UAZ.......... Ul'yanovsk Automobile Plant [*Initialism also used as name of Russian automobile*]   (RU)
UAZ.......... Ural Aluminum Plant   (RU)
UAZ.......... Ural Automobile Plant   (RU)
UB............. Amplification Unit   (RU)
UB............. Burma Airways Corp. [*Myanmar*] [*ICAO designator*]   (ICDA)
UB............. Publications de l'Union Syndicale des Banquiers de Paris et de la Province   (FLAF)
UB............. Shock Brigade   (RU)
ub .... Ubiegly [*Last*] [*Poland*]
ub .... Ubiegly Rok [*Last Year*]   (POL)
UB............. Udarna Brigada [*Shock Brigade*]   (YU)
UB............. Uitvoeringsbeschikking [*Benelux*]   (BAS)
UB............. Umelecka Beseda [*Artists' Club*]   (CZ)
UB............. Umno Baru [*New Umno*] [*Malaysia*] [*Political party*]
UB............. Umschaltbaugruppe [*German*]   (ADPT)
ub............. Unbeschnitten [*Untrimmed*] [*Publishing*] [*German*]
UB............. Unicbank [*Unique Bank*] [*Hungary*]
UB............. Universidade do Brasil [*University of Brazil*]
UB............. Universitaetsbibliothek [*University Library*] [*German*] [*Information retrieval*]
UB............. Universite du Benin [*University of Benin*] [*Togo*]   (AF)
UB............. Universiteits-Bibliotheek
UB............. University Library   (BU)
UB............. Univerzitetska Biblioteka [*University Library*]   (YU)
UB............. Urzad Bezpieczenstwa [*Security Administration*]   (POL)
UB............. Uzemi Bizottsag [*Factory Shop Committee*]   (HU)
UBA.......... Myanmar Airways [*ICAO designator*]   (FAAC)
UBA.......... Uberaba [*Brazil*] [*Airport symbol*]   (OAG)
UBA.......... Ulusal Basin Ajansi [*News agency*] [*Turkey*]   (MENA)
UBA.......... Umweltbundesamt [*Federal Environmental Agency*] [*Germany*]
UBA.......... Uniao Brasileira dos Avicultores [*Brazilian Poultrymen's Union*]   (LA)
UBA.......... Union of Bulgarian Actors   (EAIO)
UBA.......... United Bank for Africa Ltd.
UBA.......... Universite des Beaux-Arts [*Fine Arts University*] [*Replaced URBA Cambodia*]   (CL)
UBAC .... Union Bancaire en Afrique Centrale [*Banking Union in Central Africa*]   (AF)
UBAF........ Union des Banques Arabes et Francaises [*Union of Arab and French Banks*] [*France*]
Ubags........ United Bags Ltd. [*Kenya*]
UBAN....... Statutes of the Bulgarian Academy of Sciences   (BU)

UBB .... Union of Burma Bank   (DS)
UBB .... Uniwersytet Boleslawa Bieruta [*Boleslaw Bierut University*]   (POL)
UBBAWA ... United Beef Breeders' Association of Western Australia
UBBS........ University of Basutoland, Bechuanaland Protectorate, and Swaziland
UBC .... Uniao Brasileira de Compositores [*Union of Brazilian Composers*]   (EAIO)
UBC .... Union of Belgian Composers   (EAIO)
UBC .... Universal Beauty Club [*Australia*]
UBC .... Universal Bibliographic Control [*IFLA*] [*'s-Gravenhage*]
UBC .... Urban Bantu Council
UBCI........ Union Bancaire pour le Commerce et l'Industrie [*Banking Union for Commerce and Industry*] [*Tunisia*]   (AF)
UBCS....... Union of Baptist Churches in Switzerland   (EAIO)
UBD.......... Union Blanca Democratica [*Blanco Democratic Union*] [*Uruguay*]   (LA)
UBD.......... Union for Liberation and Democracy [*Suriname*] [*Political party*]   (EY)
UBD.......... Unternehmensbereich Datentechnik [*German*]   (ADPT)
UBD.......... Ustredni Banka Druzstev [*Central Bank of Cooperatives*]   (CZ)
UBDKh...... Ukase on Fight Against Petty Hooliganism   (BU)
UBDP........ Union Belge pour la Defense de la Paix [*Belgian Union for the Defense of Peace*]   (WER)
UBE .... Uniao Brasileira de Escritores [*Brazilian Writers Union*]   (LA)
UBE .... Union Bouddhique d'Europe [*Buddhist Union of Europe - BUE*]   (EAIO)
uberarb....... Ueberarbeitet [*Revised*] [*Publishing*] [*German*]
uberkl........ Ueberklebt [*Pasted Over*] [*Publishing*] [*German*]
Ubers .... Uebersetzt [*Translated*] [*German*]
ubert.......... Uebertragen [*Translated*] [*German*]
ubertr .... Uebertragen [*Translated*] [*German*]
UBES........ Uniao Brasileira de Estudantes Secundarios [*Brazilian Union of Secondary Students*]   (LA)
UBESA ...... Union de Bananeros Ecuatorianos SA [*Ecuador*]   (DSCA)
ubesk......... Ubeskaaret [*Untrimmed*] [*Publishing Danish/Norwegian*]
ubet .... Ubetydelig [*Slight*] [*Danish/Norwegian*]
UBF .... Device for High-Speed Excitation Forcing   (RU)
UBF .... Union Bank of Finland
UBF .... University Bible Fellowship [*South Korea*]
UBFU........ Administration of Balneologic and Physiatric Institutions   (RU)
UBG.......... Union Belge des Geometres-Experts Immobiliers [*Belgium*]   (SLS)
UBH .... Udruzena Banka Hrvatske [*Bank*] [*Former Yugoslavia*]
UBHC........ Uy Ban Hanh Chinh [*Administrative Committee*]
U-bhn .... Untergrundbahn [*Subway*] [*German*]
UBI .... Buin [*Papua New Guinea*] [*Airport symbol*]   (OAG)
UBI .... Unione Bocciofila Italiana [*Italy*]   (EAIO)
UBIB........ Charter of the Bulgarian Investment Bank   (BU)
UBIB........ Uitvoeringsbesluit Inkomstenbelasting [*Benelux*]   (BAS)
UBIC......... Union Belge des Installateurs en Chauffage Central [*Belgium*]   (PDAA)
UBiKO...... Administration of Personal and Municipal Services   (RU)
UBIMAT... Universal-Drahtbiege-Automat [*Universal Automatic Wire-Bending Machine*]   (EG)
UBIW .... Union of Bus Industry Workers [*Mauritius*]   (AF)
UBJ.......... Ube [*Japan*] [*Airport symbol*]   (OAG)
UBJ.......... Union of Black Journalists
UBK .... Berezin Universal Wing [*Machine gun*]   (RU)
UBK .... Universal Tower Crane   (RU)
UBK .... Ustredni Bytova Komise [*Central Housing Committee*]   (CZ)
UBKhSS.... Administration for Combating the Embezzlement of Socialist Property and Speculation   (RU)
UBKJVDM ... Udruzenje Boraca Kraljevske Jugoslovenske Vojske "Draza Mihailovic" [*Draza Mihailovic Association of Veterans of the Royal Yugoslav Armed Forces*] [*World War II*]   (YU)
UBKK .... Ustredni Branna Koordinacni Komise [*Central Defense Coordinating Committee*]   (CZ)
UBKO .... Administration of Personal and Municipal Services   (RU)
UBKS........ Universal Construction Tower Crane   (RU)
ubl .... Ublich [*Usual*] [*German*]
UBL .... United Bank Limited [*Pakistan*]
UBLDP...... Union Belge et Luxembourgeoise de Droit Penal [*Belgian and Luxembourg Association of Penal Law*]   (EAIO)
UBLS......... University of Botswana, Lesotho, and Swaziland   (AF)
UBM.......... Universitaetsbibliothek Muenchen [*Munich University Library*] [*Information retrieval*]
UBME....... Union Bank of the Middle East
UBN.......... Pipeless Pump Unit   (RU)
UBN.......... Unione Bolognese Naturalisti [*Bologna, Italy*]   (SLS)
UBNB....... Charter of the Bulgarian National Bank   (BU)
UBO.......... Coastal Defense Administration   (BU)
UBO.......... Coast Defense Directorate   (RU)
UBO.......... Coast Defense School   (RU)
UBOK....... Ustav Bytove a Odevni Kultury [*Institute for Apartment and Clothing Improvement*]   (CZ)

U-BOOT.... Unterseeboot [*Submarine*] [*German*]
UBP .... Combat Training   (RU)
UBP .... Directorate of Combat Training   (RU)
UBP .... Ubon Ratchathani [*Thailand*] [*Airport symbol*]   (OAG)
UBP .... Ulusal Birlik Partisi [*National Unity Party*] [*Turkish Cyprus*]
   [*Political party*]   (EY)
UBP .... Uniao de Bancos Portugueses [*Bank*] [*Portugal*]
UBP .... United Bahamian Party [*Political party*]   (PPW)
UBP .... United Bermuda Party [*Political party*]   (PPW)
UBP .... Urzad Bezpieczenstwa Publicznego [*Public Security
   Administration*]   (POL)
UBP .... Usines Beninoises de Prefabrication
UBP .... Ustav Bezpecnosti Prace [*Institute for Labor Safety*]   (CZ)
UBPTs ...... Statute of the Bulgarian Eastern Orthodox Church   (BU)
UBR .... Device for High-Speed Excitation Damping   (RU)
UBR .... Guided Ballistic Missile   (RU)
UBS .... Berezin Universal Synchronized [*Machine gun*]   (RU)
UBS .... Control, Blocking, and Signaling   (RU)
ubs .... Uebersetzt [*Translated*] [*German*]
UBS .... Umelecka Beseda Slovenska [*Slovak Artists' Association*]   (CZ)
UBS .... Union Bank of Switzerland
UBS .... United Bible Societies [*Stuttgart, Federal Republic of Germany*]
   (EA)
UBS .... United Building Society [*South Africa*]
UBS .... University of Botswana and Swaziland
UBS .... Uredba o Bankama i Stedionicama [*Decree on Banks and Savings
   Banks*]   (YU)
ubsch .... Uebberschuessig [*In Excess*] [*German*]
Ubsch .... Ueberschuss [*Excess*] [*German*]
UB St .... University Library in Stalin [*Varna*]   (BU)
UB ST-IPlS ... University Library in Stalin - Institute of the Planned Economy
   (BU)
UBSY .... Union of the Biochemical Societies of Yugoslavia [*Samoa*]
   (EAIO)
UBT .... Berezin Universal Flexible [*Machine gun*]   (RU)
UBT .... Extra-Strong Drilling Pipe   (RU)
UBT .... Ubatuba [*Brazil*] [*Airport symbol*] [*Obsolete*]   (OAG)
UBTAWU ... Uganda Beverage, Tobacco and Allied Workers' Union   (EAIO)
UBTH .... University of Benin Teaching Hospital
UB/TIB ..... Universitatsbibliothek Hannover und Technische
   Informationsbibliothek [*University Library of Hannover
   and Technical Information Library*] [*Information service or
   system*]   (IID)
UBTUW .... Universitaetsbibliothek Technische Universitaet Wien
   [*University Technical Library of University of Vienna*]
   [*Austria*]   (PDAA)
UBU .... Usredni Biologicky Ustav [*Central Biological Institute (of the
   Czechoslovak Academy of Sciences)*]   (CZ)
UBU .... Ustredni Bansky Urad [*Central Office for Mining*]   (CZ)
UBUR .... Union de Bancos del Uruguay [*Union of Banks of Uruguay*]
   (LA)
UBV .... Device for High-Speed Excitation Forcing   (RU)
UBV .... Traveling-Wave Amplifier   (RU)
UBW .... Uniwersytet Imienia Boleslawa Bieruta we Wroclawiu [*Boleslaw
   Bierut University at Wroclaw (Breslau)*]   (POL)
UBYKP ...... Ucuncu Bes Yil Kalkinma Plan [*Third Five-Year Development
   Plan*] [*IBYKP, UBYP*] [*See also*]   (TU)
UBYP .... Ucuncu Bes Yillik Plani [*Third Five-Year Plan*] [*IBYKP,
   UBYKP*] [*See also*]   (TU)
UBZ .... United Bus Company of Zambia
UBz .... Unser Bild Zeigt [*Our Photo Shows*]   (EG)
UC .... Ufficiale di Complemento [*Territorial Army Officer*] [*Italian*]
UC .... Una Corda [*In piano music, with the soft pedal*]
UC .... Unclassified Consumer [*Philippine Standard Commodity
   Classification Manual*]   (IMH)
UC .... Underwater Control [*Royal Australian Navy*]
UC .... Unidad Comunista [*Communist Unity*] [*Political party*]
   [*Spanish*]
UC .... Union Caledonienne [*Caledonian Union*] [*Political party*]
   (PPW)
UC .... Union Camerounaise [*Cameroonese Union*] [*Political party*]
UC .... Union Congolaise
UC .... Union Constitutionelle [*Constitutional Union*] [*Morocco*]
   [*Political party*]   (PPW)
UC .... Unitarian Church [*Australia*]
UC .... Unite-Centrale [*French*]   (ADPT)
UC .... Unite Commerciale [*Tunisia*]
UC .... United Christian Party [*Australia*] [*Political party*]
UC .... Unite de Compte [*Unit of Account*] [*Currency unit formerly used
   by the EEC, equal to approximately one dollar*]   (AF)
UC .... Uniting Church of Australia
UC .... Uniunea Compozitorilor [*Composers' Union*]   (RO)
UC .... University of Canberra [*Australia*]
UC .... Uprava Carina [*Customs Administration*]   (YU)
UC .... Ured za Cene [*Price Office*]   (YU)
uc .... Usual Conditions [*French*]   (FLAF)

UCA .... Uganda Cooperative Alliance   (EAIO)
UCA .... Ulster Chemists' Association [*Belfast*]   (SLS)
UCA .... Unie Ceskoslovenskych Architektu [*Union of Czechoslovak
   Architects*]   (CZ)
UCA .... Uniform Companies Act [*Australia*]
UCA .... Union Chimique Africaine [*African Chemical Union*] [*Congo*]
   (AF)
UCA .... Union Commerciale Africaine
UCA .... Union de Campesinos Asturianos [*Union of Asturian Rural
   Workers*] [*Spanish*]   (WER)
UCA .... United Chiropractors Association of Australia   (ADA)
UCA .... Uniting Church in Australia
UCA .... Universal Carborundum Australia Proprietary Ltd.   (ADA)
UCA .... Universidad Catolica Argentina [*Argentine Catholic University*]
   (LA)
UCA .... Universidad Centroamericana [*Central American University*]
   [*Nicaragua*]   (LA)
UCA .... Universidad Centro Americana (Jose Simeon Canas) [*Central
   American University (Jose Simeon Canas Catholic
   University)*] [*El Salvador*]   (LA)
UCAA .... United Central Africa Association
UCAA .... United Chiropractors Association of Australia   (ADA)
UCAA .... University College of Addis Ababa
UCAB .... Universidad Catolica Andres Bello [*Andres Bello Catholic
   University*] [*Venezuela*]   (LA)
UCAC .... Union Commerciale et Agricole du Cameroun
UCAD .... Union Centrale des Arts Decoratifs [*Paris, France*]   (SLS)
UCADIA ... Union Centroamericana de Asociaciones de Ingenieros y
   Arquitectos [*Central American Association of Engineers
   and Architects*]   (LAA)
UCAMAIMA ... Universidad Catolica "Madre y Maestra" [*"Madre y Maestra"
   Catholic University*] [*Dominican Republic*]   (LA)
UCAME .... Unite de Compte Accord Monetaire Europeen   (FLAF)
UCAN .... Union of Catholic Asian News [*Kwun Tong, Hong Kong*]
   (EAIO)
UCAP .... United Coconut Association of the Philippines   (DS)
UCAPO ..... Union de Campesinos Pobres [*Union of Poor Peasants*] [*Bolivia*]
   (LA)
UCAPSE ... Union of Clerical, Administrative, and Public Service Employees
   [*Israel*]   (EAIO)
UCAR .... Union Commerciale d'Assurances et de Reassurance
   [*Commercial Union of Insurance and Reinsurance*]
   [*Burundi*]   (EY)
UCASA ...... Urban Councils Association of Southern Africa   (AA)
UCB .... Uitvoer-Controle-Bureau [*Benelux*]   (BAS)
UCB .... Union Camerounaise des Brasseries
UCB .... Union Colorado y Batllista [*Colorado and Batllista Union*]
   [*Uruguay*]   (LA)
UCB .... Union Congolaise de Banques
UCB .... Union de Credit pour le Batiment [*French*]
UCB .... Union des Compositeurs Belges [*Union of Belgian Composers*]
   (EAIO)
UCB .... United Commercial Bank Ltd. [*Bangladesh*]
UCB .... University College of Botswana
UCBEU ..... Uniao Cultural Brasil-Estados Unidos [*Brazil-United States
   Cultural Union*] [*Brazil*]   (EAIO)
UCBT .... Union pour le Commerce des Bois Tropicaux dans la CEE
   [*Association for Trade in Tropical Woods in the EEC*]
   (ECED)
UCBWM ... United Church Board for World Missions
UCC .... Union Confederale des Ingenieurs et Cadres [*France*]
UCC .... Union de Campesinos Cristianos [*Union of Christian Peasants*]
   [*Chile*]   (LA)
UCC .... Union de Ciudadanas de Colombia [*Union of Colombian
   Women*] [*Colombia*]   (LA)
UCC .... Universal Copyright Convention
UCC .... University of the Cape Coast
UCCA .... Union Cotonniere Centrafricaine [*Central African Cotton Union*]
   (AF)
UCCA .... Union Council for Coloured Affairs
UCCA .... Union des Chambres de Commerce Arabes
UCCAEP ... Union Costarricense de Camaras y Asociaciones de la Empresa
   Privada [*Costa Rica*]   (EY)
UCCAO ..... Union Centrale des Cooperatives Agricoles de l'Ouest [*Central
   Union of Agricultural Cooperatives of the West*] [*Union of
   Arabica Coffee Cooperatives of the West Cameroon*]
   [*Formerly,*]   (AF)
UCCAO ..... Union des Cooperatives de Cafe Arabica de l'Ouest [*Union of
   Arabica Coffee Cooperatives of the West*] [*Central Union of
   Agricultural Cooperatives of the West Cameroon*] [*Later,*]
   (AF)
UCCC .... Uniunea Centrala a Cooperativelor de Consum [*Central Union of
   Consumer Cooperatives*]   (RO)
UCCCDA .. Upper Corentyne Chamber of Commerce and Development
   Association [*Guyana*]

UCCD .... Union des Producteurs Belges de Chaus, Calcaires, Dolomies, et Produits Connexes [*Union of Belgian Lime, Limestone, Dolomite, and Related Products*] [*Belgium*] (EY)

UCCE .... Union Centrale des Cooperatives d'Elevage [*Central Union of Livestock Cooperatives*] [*Tunisia*] (AF)

UCCEGA... Union des Chambres de Commerce et Etablissements Gestionnaires d'Aeroports [*Union of Chambers of Commerce and Organisations Managing Regional Airports*] [*France*] (PDAA)

UCCET ...... Union of Chambers of Commerce, Industry, and Maritime Commerce and Commodity Exchanges of Turkey (EAIO)

UCCI .... Union Carbide - Cote D'Ivoire [*Abidjan, Ivory Coast*]

UCCIS .... USAREUR [*United States Army, Europe*] Command and Control Information System

UCCLO ..... United Committee of Central Labor Organizations [*Nigeria*] (AF)

UCCN .... Unidad y Convivencia Civica Nacional [*National Civic Unity and Coexistence*] [*Spanish*] (WER)

UCCO .... Union Centrale des Cooperatives Oleicoles [*Central Olive Products Cooperatives Union*] [*Tunisia*] (AF)

UCCQ .... University College of Central Queensland [*Australia*]

UCCSA ...... United Congregational Church of Southern Africa

UCD .... Union de Centro Democratico [*Union of the Democratic Center*] [*Spain*] [*Political party*] (PPE)

UCD .... Union du Centre Democratique [*Union of the Democratic Center*]

UCDC .... Uniado do Centro Democrata Cristao [*Union of the Christian Democratic Center*] [*Portugal*] [*Political party*] (PPE)

UCDCC ..... Union Centro y Democratica Cristiana de Catalunya [*Union of the Center and Christian Democrats of Catalonia*] [*Spain*] [*Political party*] (PPE)

UCDEC ..... Union Chretienne Democrate d'Europe Centrale [*Christian Democratic Union of Central Europe - CDUCE*] (EAIO)

UCDG .... Unione Cristiana delle Giovani [*Young Women's Christian Association - YWCA*] [*Italian*]

UCDL .... Union Chretienne Democrate Libanaise [*Lebanese Christian Democratic Union*] [*Political party*] (PPW)

UCE .... Union Culturelle Egyptienne

UCE .... Unite de Compte Europeenne [*European Currency Unit*] [*Use ECU*] (AF)

UCE .... Universidad Central del Este [*Central University of the East*] [*Dominican Republic*] (LA)

UCE .... Ural Commodity Exchange [*Russian Federation*] (EY)

UCEA .... Union Chimique Elf-Aquitaine

UCECOM ... Uniunea Centrala a Cooperativelor Mestesugaresti [*Central Union of Artisan Cooperatives*] (RO)

UCeDe ...... Union del Centro Democratico [*Union of the Democratic Center*] [*Argentina*] [*Political party*] (EY)

UCELINALUX-HAINAUT ... Union des Centrales Electriques de Liege-Namur-Luxembourg-Hainaut [*Belgium*]

UCEMA .... Usine Ceramique du Mali

UCEP........ Union Colombiana de Empresas Publicitarias [*Colombian Union of Advertising Companies*] (LA)

UCEPA...... Unidad de Comercio Exterior de Productos Agricolas [*Venezuela*] (DSCA)

UCEPCEE ... Union du Commerce des Engrais des Pays de la Communaute Economique Europeenne [*Union of the Fertilizer Trade of Countries of the EEC*] [*Hasselt, Belgium*] (EAIO)

UCESA...... University College Education Students Association

UCESP ...... Uniao das Cooperativas do Estado de Sao Paulo [*Brazil*] (DSCA)

UCF .... Union Civica Femenina [*Women's Civic Union*] [*Guatemala*] (LA)

UCFA .... Union pour la Communaute Franco-Africaine

UCFB........ Union Culturelle de la Femme au Burundi

UCFC........ United Christian Fellowship Conference

UCFCMHPH ... Union Centrafricaine de la Fraternite Chretienne des Malades et Handicapes (EAIO)

UCFM .... United Christian Fellowship Ministry [*Australia*]

UCFML..... Union des Communistes de France Marxiste-Leniniste [*Marxist-Leninist Union of Communists of France*] [*Political party*] (PPW)

UCFS........ Uniunea de Cultura Fizica si Sport [*Union of Physical Culture and Sports*] (RO)

UCh.......... Control Element [*Computers*] (RU)

uch............ Educational, Training (RU)

UCh.......... Frequency Equalizer (RU)

uch............ Scientist, Scientific (RU)

uch............ Section, Zone, Lot (RU)

uch............ Training, Teaching (BU)

UCH .... Unie Ceskych Hudebniku [*Union of Czech Musicians*] (CZ)

UCH .... University College Hospital

UCH .... Ustredi Ceskoslovenskych Hospodyn [*Center for Czechoslovak Housewives*] (CZ)

uchabr .... Training Artillery Brigade (BU)

uchap......... Training Artillery Regiment (BU)

UchB .... Uchitelska Borba [*Teachers' Struggle*] [*A newspaper*] (BU)

uchbat .... Training Battalion (RU)

ucheb.......... Educational, Training (RU)

uchebn........ Educational, Training (RU)

uchen.......... Scientific (RU)

uchen sek ... Scientific Secretary (RU)

uch g........... School Year (RU)

Uchgiz........ State Publishing House of Textbooks and Pedagogical Literature (RU)

Uch god...... School Year (BU)

uchil .... School (BU)

uch-izd l...... Publisher's Record Sheet (RU)

uch-k .... Section, Zone, Lot (RU)

uchkhranit ... Scientific Custodian (RU)

uchkom ...... Student Committee (RU)

Uchkom ..... Students' Committee (BU)

Uchkor....... Students' Correspondent (BU)

uchlet .... Student Pilot (RU)

uchpbr .... Training Infantry Brigade (BU)

uchpd......... Training Infantry Division (BU)

uchpedgiz... Educational Books Publishing House (BU)

Uchpedgiz. . State Publishing House of Textbooks and Pedagogical Literature (RU)

UchPr........ Uchilisten Pregled [*School Review*] [*A periodical*] (BU)

Uchraspred ... Stocktaking and Distribution Department (RU)

Uchrasprot ... Administration for the Stocktaking and Distribution of Industrial Waste Products (RU)

UCHS........ Uniting Church Historical Society [*Australia*]

uch-shche... School (RU)

uch sotr ...... Scientific Worker (RU)

uch spets .... Scientific Specialist (RU)

uchstat........ Accounting and Statistical Department (RU)

UChSU .... Training Ship (RU)

uch-sya....... Student (RU)

uchtd .... Training Tank Division (BU)

Uchtekhprom ... School Equipment Industry (BU)

UChTOL ... Ustav Chemickej Technologie Organickych Latok [*Technological Institute of Organic Chemistry (of the Slovak Academy of Sciences)*] (CZ)

Uch zap...... Scientific Notes (RU)

UCI .... Union Campesina Independiente [*Independent Peasant Union*] [*Mexico*] (LA)

UCI .... Union Cycliste Internationale [*International Cycling Union*] [*Switzerland*] (EA)

UCI .... Unione Coltivatori Italiana [*Farmers Union*] [*Italy*] (EY)

UCI .... Unione dei Comunisti Italiani [*Union of Italian Communists*] (WER)

UCI .... Universite Cooperative Internationale [*International Cooperative University*]

UCI .... University College of Ibadan

UCI .... Ustredni Cejchovni Inspektorat [*Central Inspectorate of Weights and Measures*] (CZ)

UCIA .... Union Commerciale Indochinoise et Africaine

UCIA .... Union Commerciale Industrielle Africaine

UCIB........ Usines Chimiques d'Ivry la Bataille [*France*]

UCID .... Independent Democratic Union of Cape Verde [*Political party*] (PD)

UCIG .... Unions Chretiennes de Jeunes Gens [*Young Men's Christian Association*] [*Use YMCA*] (AF)

UCIIM...... Unione Cattolica Italiana Insegnanti Medi [*Italian*] (SLS)

UCIL......... United Carbide India Limited

UCIL.......... Uranium Corp. of India Ltd. [*Dept. of Atomic Energy*] [*India*] (PDAA)

UCIMA ..... Unione Costruttori Italiani Macchine Automatiche per il Confezionamento e l'Imballaggio

UCIMHPLD ... Union of Catholic Institutions for the Mentally Handicapped and Persons with Learning Disabilities [*Germany*] (EAIO)

UCIMU ..... Unione Costruttori Italiani Macchine Utensili [*Machine Tool Manufacturers Union*] [*Italy*] (EY)

UCINA ...... Union Cinematographique Africaine

UCINA ...... Unione Nazionale Cantieri e Industrie Nautiche ed Affini [*Shipyard and Nautical Industries Union*] [*Italy*] (EY)

UCIP......... Union Catholique Internationale de la Presse [*International Catholic Union of the Press*] (EAIO)

UCIPEM ... Unione Consultori Italiani Prematrimoniali e Matrimoniali [*Bologna, Italy*] (SLS)

UCIPI .... Unione Coloniale Italiana Pubblicita e Informazioni

UCISS .... Union Catholique Internationale de Service Social [*Catholic International Union for Social Service*] [*Brussels, Belgium*] (EAIO)

UCIT......... Union Caneros Independientes de Tucuman [*Independent Cane Workers Union of Tucuman*] [*Argentina*] (LA)

UCITRA .... Union Civica del Trabajo [*Civic Labor Union*] [*Chile*] (LA)

UCITS .... Undertakings for Collective Investment in Transferable Securities [*European Community*]

UCIW .... Union of Christmas Island Workers

UCIW .... Union of Commercial and Industrial Workers [*Trinidad and Tobago*] (EAIO)

UCK.......... Uradovna Cenove Kontroly [*Office of Price Control*]   (CZ)
UCK.......... Ustredni Cvicitelska Komise [*Central Commission for Physical Training*]   (CZ)
UCL.......... Uganda Creameries Limited
UCL.......... Umal Consolidated Limited [*Australia*]
UCL.......... Union Chemical Laboratories [*Taiwan*] [*Research center*]   (IRC)
UCL.......... Union Comunista de Liberacion [*Communist Liberation Union*] [*Spanish*]   (WER)
UCL.......... Universite Catholique de Louvain [*Catholic University of Louvain*] [*Belgium*]   (WER)
UCL.......... University Catholique de Louvain [*Belgium*]   (MCD)
UCL.......... Ustav pro Ceskou Literaturu [*Institute of Czech Literature (of the Czechoslovak Academy of Sciences)*]   (CZ)
UCLA....... Uniao Congolesa para a Libertacao de Angola
UCM......... Union Culturelle Musulmane
UCM......... Union des Croyants Malgaches [*Union of Malagasy Believers*] (AF)
UCM......... United Country Movement [*Australia*]
UCM......... Uniunea de Cooperative Mestesugaresti [*Union of Artisan Cooperatives*]   (RO)
UCM......... University Christian Movement of Southern Africa
UCMAA.... University of Calcutta Medical Association of America
UCMCIPN ... Uniunea Cooperativelor Mestesugaresti Confectii, Incaltaminte, Prestatii Neindustriale Bucuresti [*Bucharest Union of Artisan Cooperatives for Clothing, Footwear, and Nonindustrial Services*]   (RO)
UCMLB..... Union des Communistes Marxistes-Leninistes Belges [*Union of Belgian Marxist-Leninist Communists*]   (WER)
UCMM...... Universidad Catolica Madre y Maria [*Madre and Maria Catholic University*] [*Dominican Republic*]   (LA)
UCMMBMCHLC ... Uniunea Cooperativelor Mestesugaresti Metal, Chimie, Lemn, Constructii, din Muncipiul Bucuresti [*Bucharest Municipality Union of Artisan Cooperatives for Metals, Chemistry, Wood, and Constructions*]   (RO)
UCN.......... Ultra-Centrifuge Nederland [*Netherlands*]   (PDAA)
UCN.......... Union Civica Nacional [*National Civic Union*] [*Bolivia*] [*Political party*]   (LA)
UCN.......... Union Civica Nacional [*National Civic Union*] [*Dominican Republic*] [*Political party*]   (PPW)
UCN.......... Union Civica Nacionalista [*Nationalist Civic Union*] [*Argentina*]   (LA)
UCN.......... Union Commerciale du Niger
UCN.......... Union Congolaise Nationale
UCN.......... Union de Campesinos Nicaraguenses [*Nicaraguan Peasants Union*]   (LA)
UCN.......... Union del Centro Nacional [*Union of the National Center*] [*Guatemala*] [*Political party*]
UCN.......... University College, Nairobi
UCN.......... Ustredni Cirkevni Nakladatelstvi [*Central Church Publishing House*]   (CZ)
UCNSW .... Unitarian Church of New South Wales [*Australia*]
UCNT....... University College of the Northern Territory [*Australia*]
UCNV....... University College of Northern Victoria [*Australia*]
UCO........ United Commercial Bank [*India*]   (EY)
UCOA....... Union Chimique de l'Ouest Africain
UCOBAM ... Union des Cooperatives Agricoles et Maraicheres du Burkina   (EY)
UCOD....... University Clearing Office for Developing Countries (Louvain) [*Belgium*]   (BAS)
UCODEF... Union Commerciale d'Exploitation Forestiere
UCODIMA ... Union Commerciale de Diffusion de Marques
UCODIS.... Union pour le Commerce et la Distribution des Grandes Marques
UCOKA..... Union des Petits Commercants de Kaolack
UCOL....... Union pour la Colonisation
U CollCentral Qld ... University College of Central Queensland [*Australia*]
U CollSth Qld ... University College of Southern Queensland [*Australia*]
UCOM....... Union Commerciale du Diognike
UCOMA.... Union des Commercants Maliens
UCOMAF ... Union Commerciale Africaine
UCOMO ... Union Commerciale de l'Oubangui
UCOMPDA ... Union Cooperative des Maraichers Pecheurs du Dahomey
UCON....... Universal Correspondence Organisation of Nepal   (EAIO)
UCONAL.. Union Cooperativa Nacional [*National Cooperative Union*] [*Colorado*]   (LA)
UCOPAN .. Union Cooperativa Agraria Nacional [*Colombia*]   (COL)
UCOR....... Uranium Enrichment Corporation [*South Africa*]   (AF)
UCOSA ..... Union Commerciale des Sarakoles Bamakois
UCOSAB ... Union Commerciale de Saboya
UCOSDDEEC ... Union of Cafe Owners and Soft Drink Dealers of the European Economic Community [*Paris, France*]   (EAIO)
UCOT....... Union Cooperativa de Obreros del Transporte [*Cooperative Union of Transport Workers*] [*Uruguay*]   (LA)
UCOVAL .. Union Commerciale du Valo
UCP.......... Union Chretienne des Pensionnes [*Belgium*]   (EAIO)
UCP.......... Union Comorienne pour le Progres [*Comorian Union for Progress*]   (PD)

UCP.......... Union of Coffee Planters [*Madagascar*]   (EAIO)
UCP.......... Unite Cooperative de Production [*Tunisia*]
UCP.......... United Christian Party [*Australia*] [*Political party*]   (ADA)
UCP.......... United Congress Party
UCP.......... United Conservative Party
UCP.......... United Country Party [*Australia*] [*Political party*]
UCPB....... United Coconut Planters Bank [*Philippines*]
UCPL........ Unites de Combat de Pathet Lao [*Pathet Lao Combat Units*]   (CL)
UCPN....... Union des Chefs et des Populations du Nord
UCPN....... United Communist Party of Nepal [*Political party*]   (EY)
UCPTE...... Union pour la Coordination de la Production et du Transport de l'Electricite [*Union for the Coordination of the Production and Transport of Electric Power - UCPTE*]   (EAIO)
UCQ.......... University of Central Queensland [*Australia*]
UCR.......... Union Centriste et Radicale [*France*] [*Political party*]   (EY)
UCR.......... Union Civica Radical [*Radical Civic Union*] [*Argentina*]   (PD)
UCR.......... Union Civica Radical [*Radical Civic Union*] [*Colorado*]   (LA)
UCR.......... Union Civica Revolucionaria [*Revolutionary Civic Union*] [*Costa Rica*]   (LA)
UCR.......... Union Confederale des Retraites [*France*]   (EY)
UCR.......... Union de Campesinos Revolucionarios [*Revolutionary Peasants Union*] [*El Salvador*]   (LA)
UCR.......... University College of Rhodesia
UCR.......... Uzinele Chimice Romane [*Romanian Chemical Plants*]   (RO)
UCRG....... Union des Clubs pour le Renouveau de la Gauche [*Union of Clubs for the Renovation of the Left*] [*France*] [*Political party*]   (PPE)
UCRI........ Union Civica Radical Intransigente [*Intransigent Radical Civic Union*] [*Argentina*]   (LA)
UCRIFER ... Unione Costruttori e Riparatori Ferrotramviari [*Rolling Stock Manufacturers Union*] [*Italy*]   (EY)
UCRM....... University College of Rhodesia and Malawi
UCRN....... University College of Rhodesia and Nyasaland
UCRP .... Union Civica Radical del Pueblo [*People's Radical Civic Union*] [*Argentina*]   (LA)
UCRP(ML) ... Uniao Comunista para a Reconstrucao do Partido Marxista-Leninista [*Communist Union for the Reconstruction of the Marxist-Leninist Party*] [*Portuguese*]   (WER)
UCRSU...... United Copperbelt Regional Students Union [*Zambia*]   (AF)
UCRU........ Uzinal de Constructii si Reparatii Utilaje [*Factory for Equipment Construction and Repairs*]   (RO)
UCS .... Unified Co-Operative Services
UCS .... Union Comunal Salvadorena [*Salvadoran Communal Union*]   (LA)
UCS .... Union de Campesinos Salvadorcenos [*Peasant Union*] [*El Salvador*]
UCS .... United Cable Service [*Australia*]
UCS .... Ustredni Celni Spraya [*Central Customs Administration*]   (CZ)
UCSA .... Union des Confederations Sportives Africaines [*Association of African Sports Confederations - AASC*] [*Yaounde, Cameroon*]   (EAIO)
UCSA .... Ustredi Ceskoslovenske Advokacie [*Czechoslovak Lawyers Center*]   (CZ)
UCsC .... Ustredi Ceskoslovenskych Cyklistu [*Center of Czechoslovak Cyclists*]   (CZ)
UCSIP .... Union des Chambres Syndicales de l'Industrie du Petrole [*France*]
UCSL......... Union Congolais des Syndicats Libres
UCSMB..... Union des Carrieres et Scieries de Marbres de Belgique [*Belgium*]   (EY)
UCSQ .... University College of Southern Queensland [*Australia*]
UCSR........ Union Catalogue of Sound Recordings [*Australia*]
UCSV........ Ucaksavar [*Antiaircraft*]   (TU)
UCT .... Union Chilena de Temperancia   (EAIO)
UCT .... Union Commerciale de Transports [*Morocco*]
UCT .... Unite Centrale de Traitement [*Central Processing Unit - CPU*] [*French*]
UCT .... Universal Coordinated Time
UCT .... University of Cape Town [*South Africa*]
UCTAT...... Union des Co-Operatives de Travaux Agricoles de Tunisie
UCTC .... Union Camerounaise des Travailleurs Croyants [*Cameroonian Union of Believing Workers*]
UCTC .... Universal Container Terminal Co. Ltd. [*Taiwan*]
UCTEA...... Union of Chambers of Turkish Engineers and Architects   (EAIO)
UCTF........ Union Culturelle et Technique de Langue Francaise [*French-Language Cultural and Technical Union*] [*Paris, France*]   (EA)
UCTGA ..... United Commercial Travellers' Guild of Australia
UCTIO ...... University of Cape Town Institute of Oceanography [*South Africa*]   (MSC)
UCTPIC .... Unitatea de Colectare si Transportul Paielor pentru Industria de Celuloza [*Unit for the Collection and Transportation of Straw for the Cellulose Industry*]   (RO)
UCU.......... Union Cultural Universitaria [*University Cultural Union*] [*Guatemala*]   (LA)

UCUE .... Udmurt Commodity Universal Exchange [*Russian Federation*] (EY)

UCV .... Universidad Central de Venezuela [*Central University of Venezuela*] (LA)

UCV .... Uprava Civilnog Vazduhoplovstva [*Civil Aeronautics Administration*] (YU)

Ucvs .... Uscavus [*Master Sergeant*] (TU)

ucz .... Uczen [*or Uczennica*] [*Pupil*] [*Poland*]

UCZ .... United Church of Zambia

UD .... Administration, Management (RU)

UD .... Controlled Diode (RU)

UD .... Impact Effect (RU)

ud .... Satisfactory [*Mark in school*] (RU)

UD .... Udine [*Car registration plates*] [*Italian*]

UD .... Union Democratique [*New Caledonia*] [*Political party*] (EY)

UD .... Uranove Doly [*Uranium Mines*] (CZ)

UD .... Usekovy Duvernik [*Shop Steward*] (CZ)

Ud .... Usted [*You (Singular, formal)*] [*Spanish*]

UD .... Ustredni Dilny [*Central Workshops*] (CZ)

UD .... Utrikesdepartment [*Ministry of Foreign Affairs*] [*Sweden*] (WEN)

UD .... Uzun Dalga [*Long Wave*] (TU)

UDA .... Pusdiklat Perhubungan Udara/PLP [*Indonesia*] [*ICAO designator*] (FAAC)

UDA .... Shirika la Usafiri Dar Es Salaam Ltd.

uda .... Und dem Aehnliche [*And the Like*] [*German*]

UDA .... Union Democratique Afar

UDA .... Union Democratique Africaine

UDA .... United Democratic Alliance [*European political movement*] (ECON)

UDA .... United Distillers Australia

UDA .... Urban Development Association [*or Authority*] [*Malaysia*] (ML)

UDA .... Ustredni Dum Armady [*Central Army Building*] (CZ)

UDAC .... Union de Actores Costarricenses [*Costa Rican Actors Union*] (LA)

UDAC .... Urban Design Advisory Council [*Australia*]

UDAE .... Union Douaniere d'Afrique Equatoriale [*Equatorial Africa Customs Union*] (AF)

UDAF .... Union Departementale des Associations Familiales (FLAF)

ud akt .... Specific Activity (RU)

UDAL .... United Distillers (Australia) Ltd. [*Commercial firm*]

UDAP .... Licensed State Motor Vehicle Carriers (BU)

udar .... Accent (RU)

udarb .... Udarbejdet [*Compiled*] [*Publishing Danish/Norwegian*]

UDA-RDA ... Union Democratique Africaine-Rassemblement Democratique Africain [*African Democratic Union-African Democratic Rally*] [*Burkina Faso*] (AF)

UDB .... Uganda Development Bank (GEA)

UDB .... Union Democratique Bretonne - Unvaniezh Demokratel Breizh [*Breton Democratic Union*] [*France*] [*Political party*] (PPW)

UDB .... Union des Designers en Belgique (EAIO)

UDB .... Union pour le Developpement de Beoumi

UdB .... Universidade de Brasilia [*Brasilia University*] [*Brazil*] [*Research center*] (ERC)

UDB .... Universite du Burundi

UDBA .... Uprava Drzavne Bezbednosti [*State Security Administration*] (YU)

UDC .... Uganda Development Corporation (AF)

UDC .... Uniao Democratica Caboverdeana

UDC .... Union Delegates Committee [*Air carrier designation symbol*]

UDC .... Union Democratica Cristiana [*Christian Democratic Union*] [*Bolivia*] [*Political party*] (PPW)

UDC .... Union Democratica de Campesinos [*Peasants Democratic Union*] [*Ecuador*] (LA)

UDC .... Union Democratica de Cataluna [*Catalan: Unio Democratica de Catalunya*] [*Democratic Union of Catalonia*] [*Spanish*] (WER)

UDC .... Union Democratique Centrafricaine [*Central African Democratic Union*] [*Political party*] (PPW)

UDC .... Union Democratique Comorienne [*Comorian Democratic Union*] (AF)

UDC .... Union Democratique du Cameroun [*Political party*] (EY)

UDC .... Union Democratique du Centre [*Democratic Union of the Center*] [*Switzerland*] [*Political party*] (PPE)

UDC .... Union du Centre [*Mayotte*] [*Political party*] (EY)

UDC .... Union of the Democratic Centre [*Sahara*] [*Political party*] (PPW)

UDC .... Union pour la Democratie Congolaise [*Political party*] (EY)

UDC .... Universele Decimale Classificatie [*FID*] [*'s-Gravenhage*]

UDC .... Urban Development Committee [*New South Wales, Australia*]

UDCA .... Union pour la Defense des Commercants et des Artisans [*Union for the Defense of Traders and Artisans*] [*France*] [*Political party*] (PPE)

UDCBME ... Universele Decimale Classificatie Basic Medium Edition [*FID*] [*'s-Gravenhage*]

UDCCA ..... Union Democratica Cristiana de Centroamerica [*Christian Democratic Union of Central America*] (LA)

UDCH .... Ustredny Dom Cervenej Hviezdy [*Red Star Center (Building)*] (CZ)

UDCV .... Uniao Democratica de Cabo Verde

UDD .... Association pour l'Utilisation et la Diffusion de la Documentation [*French*]

UDD .... Union Democratique Dahomeenne [*Benin*] [*Political party*]

UDD .... Union pour la Democratie et le Developpement [*Mali*] [*Political party*] (EY)

UDD .... Union pour la Democratie et le Developpement Mayumba [*Gabon*] [*Political party*] (EY)

UDD .... Usines Dialectrique Delle [*France*] (PDAA)

UDDEHOLM ... Uddeholms Aktiebolag [*Business term*] [*Sweden*]

UDDIA ...... Union Democratique de Defense des Interets Africains

uddr .... Uddrag [*Selection*] [*Publishing Danish/Norwegian*]

UDDS .... Union para la Democracia y el Desarrollo Social [*Equatorial Guinea*] [*Political party*] (EY)

UDDT .... Ustredni Dum Dopravni Techniky [*Center for Management of Transport Organizations*] (CZ)

UDE........... Union Democratica de Estudiantes [*Democratic Students Union*] [*Ecuador*] (LA)

UDE........... Union Democratica Espanola [*Spanish Democratic Union*] (WER)

UDE........... Union Democratique Ethiopienne [*Ethiopian Democratic Union*] [*Use EDU*] (AF)

UDE........... Union Douaniere Equatoriale [*Equatorial Customs Union*] (AF)

UDE........... Ustredi Demokratickeho Exilu z CSR [*Center of Democratic Exiles from Czechoslovakia*] (CZ)

UDEA .... Union Democratica de Entidades Argentinas [*Democratic Union of Argentine Organizations*] (LA)

UDEA .... Union Democratique des Etats Africains [*Democratic Union of African States*] (AF)

U de A .... Universidad de Antioquia [*Colombia*] (COL)

UDEAC ..... Union Douaniere et Economique de l'Afrique Centrale [*Central African Customs and Economic Union*] (EAIO)

UDEAO ..... Union Douaniere des Etats de l'Afrique de l'Ouest [*Customs Union of the West African States*] (AF)

UDEBOP .. Union pour le Developpement du Bopri

UDEC .... Union d'Entreprises de Constructions [*Building Enterprises Union*] [*Chad*] (AF)

UDECMA ... Union Democratique Chretienne Malgache [*Malagasy Christian Democratic Union*] (AF)

UDECMA-KMPT ... Parti Democratique Chretien Malgache [*Malagasy Christian Democratic Party*] [*Political party*] (PPW)

UDECO ..... Umm Al-Dalkh Development Company [*Abu Dhabi*] (MENA)

UDECO ..... Union Democratique Comorienne [*Comorian Democratic Union*] (AF)

UDECO ..... Union Democratique Congolaise [*Congolese Democratic Union*]

UDECTO .. Union d'Entreprise de Construction au Togo

UDEEM .... Union Democratica de Estudiantes de Ensenanza Media [*Democratic Union of Secondary Education Students*] [*Spanish*] (WER)

UDEF .... Union des Exploitants Familiaux [*Union of Family Farmers*] [*Belgium*] (WER)

UDEFA...... Union de Entidades Economicas-Financieras Argentinas [*Union of Argentine Economic and Financial Organizations*] (LA)

UDEL .... Union Democratica de Liberacion [*Democratic Liberation Union*] [*Nicaragua*] (LA)

UDEL .... Union des Editeurs de Litterature [*French*]

UDELPA... Union del Pueblo Argentino [*Argentine People's Union*] (LA)

UDEM .... Universidad de Medellin (COL)

UDEMAG ... Union de Empleados Profesionales del Ministerio de Agricultura y Ganaderia [*Costa Rica*] (DSCA)

UDEMU.... Uniao Democratica das Mulheres da Guine e Cabo Verde

UDENAMO ... Uniao Democratica Nacional de Mocambique [*Mozambican National Democratic Union*] [*Later, FRELIMO*] [*Political party*]

UDEPA ..... Union de Empresas Petroquimicas Argentinas [*Union of Argentine Petrochemical Enterprises*] (LA)

UDEPRU .. Unidad de Estudios de Planeamiento Regional y Urbano. Universidad del Valle [*Colombia*] (COL)

UDERMA ... Union pour le Developpement de la Region Mayo

UDES .... Union Democratique des Etudiants Senegalais [*Democratic Union of Senegalese Students*] (AF)

u desgl........ Und Desgleichen [*And So Forth*] [*German*]

UDETD ..... Union Democratica Ecuatoriana de Trabajadores de Derecha [*Democratic Union of Right Wing Workers*] [*Ecuador*] (LA)

UDF .... Federation Guadeloupeenne de l'Union pour la Democratie Francaise [*Guadeloupe Federation of the Union for French Democracy*] [*Political party*] (PPW)

udf .... Und die Folgende [*And the Following*] [*German*]

UDF .... Union Defence Force [*South Africa*]

UDF .... Union Democrata Foral [*Spain*] [*Political party*] (EY)

UDF .... Union Democratica Fernandina

UDF .... Union of Democratic Forces [*Bulgaria*] [*Political party*]

UDF .... Union of Democratic Forces [*Mauritania*] [*Political party*] (EY)
UDF .... Union pour la Defense de la Republique [*Union for the Defense of the Republic*] [*French*] (AF)
UDF .... Union pour la Democratie Francaise [*Union for French Democracy*] [*Wallis and Futuna Islands*] [*Political party*] (EY)
UDF .... Union pour la Democratie Francaise [*Union for French Democracy*] [*France*] [*Political party*] (PPW)
UDF .... Union pour la Democratie Francaise [*Union for French Democracy*] [*Reunion*] [*Political party*] (PPW)
UDF .... Union pour la Democratie Francaise [*Union for French Democracy*] [*Mayotte*] [*Political party*] (EY)
UDF .... Union pour la Democratie Francaise [*Union for French Democracy*] [*New Caledonia*] [*Political party*] (PPW)
UDF .... Union pour la Democratie Francaise [*Union for French Democracy*] [*French Guiana*] [*Political party*] (PPW)
UDF .... Uniroyal, Dunlop, and Firestone [*Facetious translation of South African political party, United Democratic Front, which suppsedly executed dissenters with burning tires*]
UDF .... United Democratic Front [*India*] [*Political party*] (PPW)
UDF .... United Democratic Front [*South Africa*] [*Political party*] (PPW)
UDF .... Uridine Diphosphate (RU)
UDFC .... Union Democratique des Femmes du Congo
UDFG .... Uridine Diphosphate Glucose (RU)
UDFGal ..... Uridine Diphosphate Galactose (RU)
UDFI .... Union Defence Forces Institute
UDFP .... Union Democratique des Forces du Progres [*Benin*] [*Political party*] (EY)
UDFT .... Union Democratique des Femmes Tunisiennes [*Democratic Union of Tunisian Women*] (AF)
udg .... Udgave [*Edition*] [*Publishing Danish/Norwegian*]
UDG .... Unabhaengige Deutsche Gemeinschaft [*Independent German Society*] (EG)
UDG .... Uniao Democratica da Guine
UDG .... Union Democratica Galega [*Galician Democratic Union*] [*Spanish*] (WER)
UDGE .... Union Democratica de Guinea Ecuatorial [*Democratic Union of Equatorial Guinea*] (AF)
Udgiz .... Udmurt State Publishing House (RU)
u dgl .... Und Dergleichen [*And So Forth*] [*German*]
u dgl m .... Und Dergleichen Mehr [*And the Like*] [*German*]
UDHS .... Ururka Demograadiga Haweenka Soomaaliyeed
UDI .... Uberlandia [*Brazil*] [*Airport symbol*] (OAG)
UDI .... Unilateral Declaration of Independence [*Rhodesian*] (AF)
UDI .... Unilateral Declaration of Independence [*Cypriot Turks*] (TU)
UDI .... Union de Izquierda [*Leftist Union*] [*Peru*] (LA)
UDI .... Union Democratica de Izquierda [*Leftist Democratic Union*] [*Colorado*] (LA)
UDI .... Union Democratica Independiente [*Independent Democratic Union*] [*Venezuela*] (LA)
UDI .... Union Democratica Independiente [*Independent Democratic Union*] [*Chile*] [*Political party*] (PPW)
UDI .... Union Democratique des Independants [*Democratic Union of Independents*] [*France*] [*Political party*] (PPE)
UDI .... Union Dominicana de Independientes [*Dominican Union of Independents*] [*Dominican Republic*] (LA)
UDI .... Unione delle Donne Italiane [*Union of Italian Women*] (WER)
UDI .... Urban Development Institute [*Australia*]
UDIA .... Urban Development Institute of Australia (ADA)
UDIR .... Union pour la Diffusion Reunionnaise
UDIT .... Union de Defense des Interets Tchadiens
UDIT .... Union Democratique et Independante du Tchad
UDJ .... Union Deutscher Jazzmusiker [*Union of German Jazz Musicians*] (EG)
UDJM .... Union Democratique de la Jeunesse Marocaine [*Democratic Union of Moroccan Youth*] (AF)
UDJUNH ... Union Democratica de la Juventud Nacionalista Hondurena [*Honduran Nationalist Youth Democratic Union*] (LA)
udk .... Udkom [*Published*] [*Danish/Norwegian*]
UDK .... Universal Decimal Classification (RU)
UDK .... Universelle Dezimalklassifikation [*Universal Decimal Classification*] [*German*] (ADPT)
UDK .... Univerzalna Decimalna Klasifikacija [*Universal Decimal Classification*] (YU)
UDK .... Ustredni Dopravni Komise [*Central Transportation Commission*] (CZ)
UD KSC .... Ustav Dejin Komunisticke Strany Ceskoslovenska [*Institute of History of the Communist Party of Czechoslovakia*] (CZ)
UD KSS ..... Ustav Dejin Komunistickej Strany Slovenska [*Institute of History of the Communist Party of Slovakia*] (CZ)
UDL .... United Distillers Limited [*Australia*] (ADA)
UDLP .... United Democratic Labour Party [*Trinidad and Tobago*] [*Political party*] (PPW)
UDLP .... United Dominica Labour Party [*Political party*] (PPW)
UDLUT ..... Ustredni Dum Lidove Umelecke Tvorivosti [*Folk Arts Center*] (CZ)
udm .... Udmaerket [*Excellent*] [*Danish/Norwegian*]

udm .... Udmurt (RU)
udM .... Ueber dem Meeresspiegel [*Above Sea Level*] [*German*] (EG)
UDM .... Union Democratica de Mujeres [*Women's Democratic Union*] [*Ecuador*] (LA)
UDM .... Union Democratique Mauricienne [*Mauritian Democratic Union*] (AF)
UDM .... Union Democratique Mauritanienne [*Mauritanian Democratic Union*] [*Political party*] (PD)
udM .... Unter dem Meeresspiegel [*Below Sea Level*] [*German*] (EG)
udM .... Unter dem Mikroskop [*Under the Microscope*] [*German*] (GCA)
UDM .... Ustav Dulni Mechanisace [*Institute for the Mechanization of Mining*] (CZ)
UDMA .... Union Democratique de Manifeste Algerienne [*Democratic Union of the Algerian Manifesto*]
UdmASSR ... Udmurt Autonomous Soviet Socialist Republic (RU)
Udmurtgosizdat ... Udmurt State Publishing House (RU)
UDN .... Detailed Observations Sector (RU)
UDN .... Uniao Democratica Nacional [*National Democratic Union*] [*Brazil*] (LA)
UDN .... Union Democrata Nacional [*National Democratic Union*] [*El Salvador*] [*Political party*] (PPW)
UDN .... Union Democratica Nicaraguense [*Nicaraguan Democratic Union*] [*Political party*] (PD)
UDN .... Union Democratique Nigerienne
UDNA .... Unidad Democratica Nacional Anticonservadora [*National Anti-Conservative Democratic Union*] [*Ecuador*] (LA)
UDN-FARN ... Union Democratica Nicaraguense - Fuerzas Armadas Revolucionarias [*Nicaraguan Democratic Union - Revolutionary Armed Forces*] (LA)
UDNR .... Unione Democratico per la Nuova Repubblica [*Democratic Union for the New Republic*] [*Italian*] (WER)
udo .... Shock Squad (BU)
UDO .... Universidad de Oriente [*Eastern University*] [*Venezuela*] (LA)
UDOA .... Union Douaniere Ouest-Africaine [*West African Customs Union*] (AF)
ud ob .... Specific Volume (RU)
udobr .... Fertilizer (RU)
UDOO .... State Social Insurance Administration (BU)
UDOPSS ... Union Departementale des Oeuvres Privees Sanitaires et Sociales (FLAF)
UDP .... L'Union des Progressistes [*Union of Progressives*] [*Belgium*] (WER)
UDP .... Statutes of State Enterprises (BU)
UDP .... Submarine Training Division (RU)
UDP .... Supplementary High-Calorie Diet (RU)
UDP .... Ukase on State Enterprises (BU)
UDP .... Ukase on State Pensions (BU)
UDP .... Umelecky Drevoprumysl [*Woodcraft Industry*] (CZ)
UDP .... Uniao Democratica Popular [*Popular Democratic Unity*] [*Portugal*] [*Political party*]
UDP .... Unidad Democratica Popular [*Popular Democratic Unity*] [*Bolivia*] [*Political party*]
UDP .... Unidad Democratica Popular [*Popular Democratic Unity*] [*Peru*] [*Political party*] (PPW)
UDP .... Unification du Droit Prive (FLAF)
UDP .... Union Democrate Paysanne
UDP .... Union Democratica del Pueblo [*People's Democratic Union*] [*Ecuador*] (LA)
UDP .... Union Democratica del Pueblo [*People's Democratic Union*] [*Bolivia*] (LA)
UDP .... Union Democratica Popular [*Popular Democratic Union*] [*Peru*] (LA)
UDP .... Union Democratica Popular [*Popular Democratic Union*] [*Ecuador*] (LA)
UDP .... Union pour la Democratie Populaire [*Union for People's Democracy*] [*Senegal*] [*Political party*] (PPW)
UDP .... United Democratic Party [*Belize*] [*Political party*] (PD)
UDP .... United Democratic Party [*Basotho*] [*Political party*] (PPW)
UDP .... United Democratic Party [*Bermuda*] (LA)
UDP .... University Days for Peace [*Belgium*] (EAIO)
UDP .... Urban Development Program [*Department of Planning*] [*New South Wales, Australia*]
UDP .... Uredba o Deviznom Poslovanju [*Decree on Foreign Exchange Operations*] (YU)
UDP .... Usines Dahomeennes de Prefabrication
UDP .... Ustredni Delnicke Podniky [*Central Workers' Enterprises*] (CZ)
UDPB .... Union des Democrates et Patriotes Burkinabe [*Burkino Faso*] [*Political party*] (EY)
UDPD .... Ustredi Delnickych Potravnich Druzstev [*Central Office of the Workers' Food Cooperatives*] (CZ)
UDPE .... Union del Pueblo Espanol [*Union of the Spanish People*] (WER)
UDPK .... United Democratic Party of Kurdistan [*Political party*] (BJA)
UDPM .... Union Democratique du Peuple Malien [*Mali People's Democratic Union*] [*Political party*] (PPW)
UDPS .... Union pour la Democratie et le Progres Social [*Democratic Union of Social Progress*] [*Zaire*] [*Political party*]

UDPS........ Union pour le Developpement et le Progres Social [*The Congo*] [*Political party*]   (EY)

UDPT .... Union Democratique des Populations Togolaises

UDPV .... Union Democratica del Pais Valenciano [*Democratic Union of the Valencian Country*] [*Spanish*]   (WER)

UDR.......... Democratic Rural Union [*Brazil*]

ud r .... Specific Reactivity   (RU)

UDR.......... State Management Ukase   (BU)

UDR.......... Udaipur [*India*] [*Airport symbol*]   (OAG)

UDR.......... Uniao Democratica Ruralista [*Landowners' organization*] [*Brazil*]   (EY)

UDR.......... Union des Democrates pour la Republique [*Union of Democrats for the Republic (Gaullist party)*] [*French*]   (WER)

UDR.......... Union pour la Defense de la Republique [*Union for the Defense of the Republic*] [*France*] [*Political party*]   (PPE)

UDR.......... Union pour la Democratie Francaise [*Union for French Democracy*] [*Martinique*] [*Political party*]   (PPW)

UDRN....... Union pour la Democratie et la Reconstruction Nationale [*Benin*] [*Political party*]   (EY)

UDROCOL ... Union de Droguistas Colombianos Ltda. [*Colombia*]   (COL)

UDRS .... Union Democratique pour le Renouveau Social [*Benin*] [*Political party*]   (EY)

UDRT/RAD ... Union Democratique pour le Respect du Travail - Respect voor Arbeid en Democratie [*Democratic Union for the Respect of Labor*] [*Belgium*] [*Political party*]   (PPW)

UDS.......... Road Construction Administration   (RU)

uds............ Udsolgt [*Out of Print*] [*Publishing Danish/Norwegian*]

UDS.......... Union Democratique Senegalaise

UDS.......... Union des Dentistes et Stomatologistes de Belgique [*Belgium*]   (SLS)

UDS.......... Union pour la Democratie et la Solidarite Nationale [*Benin*] [*Political party*]   (EY)

UDS.......... Universelles Datenbanksystem [*Universal Data Bank System*] [*German*]   (ADPT)

Uds............ Ustedes [*You (Plural, formal)*] [*Spanish*]

UDS.......... Ustredni Delnicka Skola [*Central Workers' School*]   (CZ)

UDSDR ..... State Supplies and Reserves Administration   (BU)

udsdt .... Udsendt [*Distributed*] [*Publishing Danish/Norwegian*]

UDSG .... Union Democratique et Sociale Gabonaise [*Gabonese Democratic and Social Union*]   (AF)

UDSIP .... Uprava Drzavnih Sumsko-Industriskih Preduzeca [*Administration of State Forest Industrial Enterprises*]   (YU)

UDSK .... Charter of the State Savings Bank   (BU)

UDSL........ Union of Scientific Leisure Clubs [*France*]   (EAIO)

UDSM....... Union Democratique et Socialiste de Madagascar [*Democratic and Socialist Union of Madagascar*]   (AF)

udsn........... Udsnit [*Excerpt*] [*Publishing Danish/Norwegian*]

UDSP........ Union for Democracy and Social Progress [*Political party*] [*Zaire*]

UDSR .... Union Democratique et Socialiste de la Resistance [*Democratic and Socialist Union of the Resistance*] [*France*] [*Political party*]   (PPE)

UDS-R ...... Union Democratique Senegalaise-Renovation   (EY)

UdSSR....... Union der Sozialistischen Sowjet-Republiken [*Union of Soviet Socialist Republics, USSR*]   (EG)

UDT.......... Uniao Democratica Timorense [*Indonesia*] [*Political party*]   (EY)

UDT.......... Union Democratica de Trabajadores [*Democratic Union of Workers*] [*Chile*]   (LA)

UDT.......... Union Democratica de Trabajadores [*Democratic Union of Workers*] [*Ecuador*]   (LA)

UDT.......... Union Democratique de Timor [*Democratic Union of Timor*]

UDT.......... Union Democratique de Travail [*Democratic Union of Labor*] [*French*]   (WER)

udT .... Unter dem Titel [*Under the Title*] [*German*]   (GCA)

UDT.......... Wood Production and Transportation Administration   (BU)

UDU .... Remote Level Indicator   (RU)

UDU .... Uganda Democratic Union   (AF)

UDU .... Unabhaengige Demokratische Union [*Independent Democratic Union*] [*Austria*] [*Political party*]   (PPE)

UDU .... Union Democratique Unioniste [*Tunisia*] [*Political party*]   (EY)

UDUAL..... Union de Universidades de America Latina [*Union of Latin American Universities*] [*Mexico*]

ud v........... Specific Gravity   (RU)

udv............ Udvalg [*Selection*] [*Publishing Danish/Norwegian*]

UDV.......... Union Democratique Voltaique [*Voltan Democratic Union*]   (AF)

UDV.......... Uprava Drzavne Varnosti [*State Security Administration*]   (YU)

UD-Ve....... Union Democratique pour la Cinquieme Republique [*Democratic Union for the Fifth Republic*] [*France*] [*Political party*]   (PPE)

ud vl .... Specific Humidity   (RU)

UD/VR ...... Union Democratique pour la Cinquieme Republique [*Democratic Union for the Fifth Republic*] [*French*]   (WER)

U dw.......... U Dienswillige [*Yours*] [*Afrikaans*]

UD-W .... Universiteit van Durban-Westville [*University of Durban-Westville*] [*South Africa*]   (AA)

U dw dnr .... U Dienswillige Dienaar [*Your Obedient Servant*] [*Afrikaans*]

UDZI .... Statute of the State Insurance Institute   (BU)

UE............. Holding Electromagnet   (RU)

UE............. Uebertragung [*Transfer*] [*German*]   (ADPT)

UE............. Union Espanola [*Spanish Union*]   (WER)

uE............. Unseres Erachtens [*In Our Opinion*] [*German*]   (EG)

UE............. Unwana ke Edinyanga [*Light of Salvation Women's Fellowship*] [*Nigeria*]   (EAIO)

ue............... Uso Externo [*External Use*] [*Portuguese*]

ue............... Uzemegyseg [*Factory Working Unit*]   (HU)

UEA.......... General-Purpose Artificial Aerial   (RU)

uea............ Und Einige Andere [*And Some Others*] [*German*]

UEA.......... Uniao dos Estudantes Angolanos

UEA.......... Union des Ecrivains Algeriens [*Union of Algerian Writers*]   (AF)

UEA.......... Union des Etats Africaine

UEA.......... Union Europeenne de l'Ameublement [*European Furniture Manufacturers Federation*]   (EAIO)

UEA.......... Union Europeenne des Aveugles [*European Blind Union - EBU*]   (EAIO)

UEA.......... Union of European Abattoirs [*Belgium*]   (EAIO)

UEA.......... Universala Esperanto Asocio [*Universal Esperanto Association*]   (EAIO)

UEA.......... University of East Anglia   (PDAA)

UEA.......... Uralelektroapparat [*Plant*]   (RU)

UEAC .... Union des Etats de l'Afrique Centrale [*Union of Central African States*]   (AF)

UEAC .... Union of Central African States

UEAES...... Union Europeenne des Alcools, Eaux de Vie et Spiritueux [*European Union of Alcohol, Brandies and Spirits*] [*EC*]   (ECED)

UEAI .... Union Europeenne des Arabisants et des Islamisants [*European Union of Arab and Islamic Studies - EUAIS*] [*Spain*]   (EAIO)

UEAPME ... Union Europeenne de l'Artisanat et des Petites et Moyennes Entreprises [*European Association of Craft, Small and Medium-Sized Enterprises*] [*EC*]   (ECED)

UEAS........ Uebertragungsablaufsteuerung [*Transfer Course Control*] [*German*]   (ADPT)

UEASSC ... University of East Africa Social Science Conference

UEAtc....... Union Europeenne pour l'Agrement Technique dans la Construction [*European Union of Agrement*]   (EAIO)

UEAWG.... Urban Export Advisory Working Group [*Australia*]

UEAWS..... Union of European Associations of Water Suppliers [*Belgium*]   (EAIO)

ueb............ Ueber [*Over, Above*] [*German*]   (GCA)

Ueb........... Uebereinkommen [*Agreement*] [*German*]   (ILCA)

Ueb........... Uebersicht [*Survey*] [*German*]   (GCA)

Ueb........... Uebertrag [*Balance Brought Forward*] [*German*]   (GCA)

Ueb........... Uebung [*Exercise*] [*German*]   (GCA)

UEB .... Uganda Electricity Board

UEB .... Union of Evangelical Baptists   (EAIO)

UEB .... Unite d'Exploitation du Bois de Betou

UEBE........ Union Evangelica Bautista Espanola [*Spain*]   (EAIO)

Ueberf....... Ueberfuehrung [*Conversion*] [*German*]   (GCA)

Ueberfuehr ... Ueberfuehrung [*Conversion*] [*German*]   (GCA)

Uebers........ Uebersetzung [*Translation*] [*German*]   (GCA)

Uebers........ Uebersicht [*Survey*] [*German*]   (GCA)

Uebersaett ... Uebersaettigung [*Supersaturation*] [*German*]   (GCA)

ueberschuess ... Ueberschuessig [*In Excess*] [*German*]   (GCA)

Uebersetz... Uebersetzung [*Translation*] [*German*]   (GCA)

Uebertrag... Uebertragung [*Assignment*] [*German*]   (GCA)

Ueberwach ... ueberwachung [*Control*] [*German*]   (GCA)

ueberz........ Ueberzaehlig [*Spare*] [*German*]   (GCA)

Uebf .... Ueberfuehrung [*Conversion*] [*German*]   (GCA)

Uebg.......... Uebung [*Exercise*] [*German*]   (GCA)

UEBL......... Union Economique Belgo-Luxembourgeoise [*Belgium-Luxembourg Economic Union*]   (WER)

Uebs.......... Uebersetzung [*Translation*] [*German*]   (GCA)

Uebst.......... Uebergangsstelle [*Transition Point*] [*German*]   (GCA)

UEC .... Uniao de Estudantes Comunistas [*Union of Communist Students*] [*Portuguese*]   (WER)

UEC .... Union des Etudiants Cambodgiens en URSS [*Union of Cambodian Students in the USSR*]   (CL)

UEC .... Union des Etudiants Communistes [*Union of Communist Students*] [*French*]   (WER)

UEC .... Union Europeenne de la Carrosserie [*European Union of Coachbuilders - EUC*] [*Belgium*]

UEC .... Union Europeenne des Experts Comptables Economiques et Financiers [*European Union of Chartered Accountants*]   (PDAA)

UEC .... United Ethnic Communities of South Australia

UECA .... Union Europeenne du Commerce Ambulant [*European Union of Door-to-Door Trade*] [*EC*]   (ECED)

UECBV...... Union Europeenne du Commerce du Betail et de la Viande [*European Livestock and Meat Trading Union*]   (EAIO)

UECEB...... Union of Employees of Central Electricity Board [*Mauritius*]
(AF)

UECU .... Union de Empleados Cinematograficos del Uruguay [*Movie Theater Employees Union of Uruguay*] (LA)

UECWA .... Underwater Explorers' Club of Western Australia

U Ed........... U Edele [*Your Honor*] [*Afrikaans*]

UED.......... Union de Estudiantes Democraticos [*Democratic Students Union*] [*Spanish*] (WER)

UED.......... Union des Etudiants de Dakar [*Dakar Students Union*] [*Senegal*] (AF)

UEDS .... Uniao de Esquerda para a Democracia Socialista [*Left Union for Social Democracy*] [*Portugal*] [*Political party*] (PPE)

UEE .... Queenstown [*Australia*] [*Airport symbol*] (OAG)

UEE .... Uebermittlungseinheit [*German*] (ADPT)

UEE .... Uniao Estadual dos Estudantes [*State Students Union*] [*Brazil*] (LA)

UEEA .... Union Europeenne des Exploitants d'Abbatoirs [*European Abbattoirs Union*] [*EC*] (ECED)

UEEB........ Union des Exploitations Electriques en Belgique [*Belgium*] (BAS)

UEEJ........ Union Europeenne des Etudiants Juifs [*European Union of Jewish Students - EUJS*] (EA)

UEF .... Union Europaeischer Forstberufsverbaende [*Union of European Foresters*] [*Teningen-Heimbach, Federal Republic of Germany*] (EAIO)

UEF .... Union Europeenne des Federalistes (FLAF)

UEF .... Ustav pro Etnografii a Folkloristiku [*Institute of Ethnology and Folklore (of the Czechoslovak Academy of Sciences)*] (CZ)

UEFA........ Union of European Football Associations [*Switzerland*] (EAIO)

UEFJM ..... Union of European Fashion Jewellery Manufacturers [*Italy*] (EAIO)

UEGA .... Uranium Enrichment Group of Australia

UEGB .... Union des Exploitations Electriques et Gazieres en Belgique [*Trade association*] [*Belgium*] (EY)

UEGGSP... Union Europeenne des Groupements de Grossistes Specialises en Papeterie [*European Union of Groups of Wholesalers Specialising in Papermaking*] (PDAA)

UEI .... Union de Estudiantes Independientes [*Independent Students Union*] [*Guatemala*] (LA)

UEI .... Union d'Etudes et l'Investissement [*Studies and Investment Union*] [*France*]

UEIA .... Union des Etats Independants d'Afrique

UEIF......... Union Europeenne Industrielles et Financiere

UEIL......... Union Europeenne des Independants en Lubrifiants [*European Union of Independent Lubricant Manufacturers*] [*EC*] (ECED)

UEK .... Uluslararasi Ekonomik Kuruluslar Genel Mudurlugu [*International Economic Organizations Directorate General*] [*of Foreign Affairs Ministry*] (TU)

UEK .... Union des Etudiants Khmers [*Union of Cambodian Students*] (CL)

UEL .... Quelimane [*Mozambique*] [*Airport symbol*] (OAG)

UEL .... Ueberlappung [*German*] (ADPT)

UELCA..... United Evangelical Lutheran Church in Australia (ADA)

UELF........ Union des Editeurs de Langue Francaise (EAIO)

UELL........ Chulman [*Former USSR*] [*ICAO location identifier*] (ICLI)

ueM........... Ueber dem Meeresspiegel [*Above Sea Level*] [*German*] (GCA)

UEM.......... Union des Ecrivains du Maroc [*Writers Union of Morocco*] (AF)

UEM.......... Union Electrica Madrilena [*Spain*]

UEM.......... Union Europeenne de Malacologie [*European Malacological Union*]

UEM.......... Union Evangelique Mondiale [*World Evangelical Fellowship*]

UEM.......... Unite d'Echanges Multiples [*French*] (ADPT)

UEM.......... United Engineers (Malaysia) [*Commercial firm*]

UEM.......... United Engineers (Malaysia) Berhad (ECON)

UEM.......... Unite Electromagnetique [*Electromagnetic Unit*]

UEM.......... Universal Electron Microscope (RU)

UEM.......... Uzine Elektromekanike [*Albanian*]

UEMN....... Union des Ecrivains du Monde Noir [*World Union of Black Writers - WUBW*] (EAIO)

UEMO....... Europaische Vereinigung der Allgemeinartze [*European Union of General Practitioners*] [*Denmark*] (EAIO)

UEMO....... Union Europeenne des Medecins Omnipraticiens [*European Union of General Practitioners*] (EA)

UEMS .... Unione Europea di Medicina Sociale [*European Union of Social Medicine - EUSM*] (EAIO)

UEMS .... Union Europeenne de Medecine Sociale [*European Union of Social Medicine - EUSM*] [*Italian*] (SLS)

UEMS .... Union Europeenne des Medecins Specialistes [*European Society of Medical Specialists*] [*Belgium*] (SLS)

UEMTA .... European Union for the Prevention of Cruelty to Animals (EAIO)

UENCPB... Union Europeenne des Negociants en Cuirs et Peaux Bruts [*European Association of Traders in Leather and Raw Hides*] [*EC*] (ECED)

UENDC ..... Union Europeenne des Negociants Detaillants en Combustibles [*European Union of Merchant Dealers in Combustibles*] [*Switzerland*]

uens .... Uensartet [*Not Uniform*] [*Danish/Norwegian*]

UEO.......... Kume Jima [*Japan*] [*Airport symbol*] (OAG)

UEO.......... Union de l'Europe Occidentale [*Western European Union - WEU*] (EAIO)

UEO.......... Unione Europa Occidentale [*Western European Union*] [*Use WEU*] [*Italian*] (WER)

UEOA .... Union des Etudiants Ouest Africains [*Union of West African Students*]

UEOS .... Ustav Ekonomiky a Organizacie Stavebnictva [*Institute of Economy and Organization in Construction*] (CZ)

UEP .... Electric Power Industry Administration (BU)

UEP .... Ubersetzungsprogramm [*German*] (ADPT)

UEP .... Uniao dos Estudantes de Pernambuco [*Pernambuco Students Union*] [*Brazil*] (LA)

UEP .... Unione Europea dei Pagamenti [*European Payments Union*] [*Italian*] (WER)

UEP .... Union Europeenne de Pedopsychiatres [*European Union for Child Psychiatry*]

UEP .... Union Europeenne des Paiements [*European Payments Union*] [*French*]

UEP .... Unite d'Echanges Programmees [*French*] (ADPT)

UEPC........ Union Europeenne des Promoteurs Constructeurs [*European Union of Developers and House Builders*] [*Belgium*] (EAIO)

UEPMD .... Union Europeenne des Practiciens en Medecine Dentaire [*European Union of Dental Medicine Practitioners*] (EAIO)

UEPP........ Union de Empresarios Privados del Peru [*Peruvian Private Enterprise Union*] (LA)

UEPP........ Union des Editeurs de la Presse Periodique [*Belgium*] (EAIO)

UEPS........ Union Europeenne de la Presse Sportive [*European Sports Press Union*] (EAIO)

UEPS........ Union Europeenne des Pharmacies Sociales [*European Union of the Social Pharmacies*] [*EC*] (ECED)

UEPS........ United Elvis Presley Society (EAIO)

UER .... Union de Estudiantes Revolucionarios [*Revolutionary Students Union*] [*Dominican Republic*] (LA)

UER .... Unione Europea di Radiodiffusione [*European Broadcasting Union*] [*Use EBU*] [*Italian*] (WER)

UER .... Union Estudiantil Revolucionaria [*Revolutionary Student Union*] [*Mexico*] (LA)

UER .... Union Europeenne de Radiodiffusion [*European Broadcasting Union - EBU*] (EAIO)

UER .... Unite d'Enseignement et de Recherche [*Teaching and Research Unit*] [*French*] (WER)

UERP........ Unione Europea di Relazioni Pubbliche [*European Union of Public Relations - International Service Organization - EURPISO*] (EAIO)

UES .... Specific Electrical Resistance (RU)

UES .... Union des Etudiants Socialistes [*Union of Socialist Students*] [*Malagasy*] (AF)

UES .... Universidad de El Salvador [*University of El Salvador*] (LA)

UESA........ Union Electrica SA [*Spain*] (PDAA)

UESD .... Uniao da Esquerda Socialista Democratica [*Union of the Socialist and Democratic Left*] [*Portugal*] [*Political party*] (PPW)

UESI......... Union of Evangelical Students of India

UESM .... Union des Etudiants Socialistes Malgaches [*Union of Malagasy Socialist Students*] (AF)

UEST........ Uebertragungssteuerung [*Transfer Control*] [*German*] (ADPT)

UET .... Quetta [*Pakistan*] [*Airport symbol*] (OAG)

UETB........ Union des Etudiants Tchadiens dans le BENELUX [*Union of Chadian Students in BENELUX*] (AF)

UETE........ Usinas Electricas y Telefonos del Estado [*Uruguay*] (PDAA)

UETP........ Uprava za Ekonomsku i Tehnicku Pomoc [*Administration of Economic and Technical Aid*] (YU)

UETPF ...... Union des Entrepreneurs des Travaux Publics du Fleuve

UEU.......... Union de Estudiantes Universitarios de Panama [*Union of University Students of Panama*] (LAA)

UEVP .... Union Europeenne des Veterinaires Practiciens [*European Union of Practising Veterinary Surgeons*] (EAIO)

UEZa .... Union des Ecrivains Zairois [*Union of Zairian Writers*] (AF)

UEZR .... Ueberwachungszahelregister [*German*] (ADPT)

UF .... Moderate Front [*Meteorology*] (RU)

UF .... Narrow-Band Filter (RU)

UF .... Photocurrent Amplifier (RU)

UF .... Shaping Amplifier (RU)

uf .... Uj Folyam [*New Series*] (HU)

UF .... Ultraviolet (RU)

Uf .... Und Folgende [*And the Following*] [*German*] (EG)

UF .... Uni Air International [*France*] [*ICAO designator*] (ICDA)

UF .... Union de Fribourg: Institut International des Sciences Sociales et Politiques [*Union de Fribourg: International Institute of Social and Political Sciences*] [*Fribourg/Pensier, Switzerland*] (EAIO)

UF	Union Ferroviaria [*National Railway Union*] [*Argentina*] (LA)
UF	Union Francaise (FLAF)
UF	United Footwear [*Thailand*] [*Commercial firm*]
UF	United Force [*Guyana*] (PD)
UF	United Front [*Sri Lanka*] [*Political party*] (FEA)
UF	Universiteit van Fort Hare [*University of Fort Hare*] [*South Africa*] (AA)
UF	Unterfamilie [*Subfamily*] [*German*]
UFA	Union des Femmes Angolaises
UFA	Union Fonciere Africaine
UFA	United Federation of Australia
Ufa	Universum-Film-Aktiengesellschaft [*Universal Film Joint Stock Company*] [*German*]
UFAC	Unione Femminile di Azione Cattolica [*Catholic Women's Association*] [*Italian*]
UFAC	Union Federative d'Anciens Combattants
UFAC	Union Francaise des Arts du Costume [*1948*] [*French*]
UFAC	Union Francaise des Associations de Combattants et de Victimes de la Guerre
UFAC	United French Africa Committee
UFACFM	Union Fraternelle des Anciens Combattants Francophones et de Madagascar [*Fraternal Union of French-Speaking and Malagasy Veterans*] (AF)
UFAG	Union des Femmes Africaine de Guinee
UFAL	Universidade Federal de Alagoas [*Federal University of Alagoas*] [*Brazil*] (ARC)
UFAN	Ural Branch of the Academy of Sciences, USSR (RU)
UFAP	Union Francaise des Annuaires Professionels [*French Union for Professional Yearbooks*] [*Trappes*] [*Information service or system*] (IID)
UFAP	Union Francaise des Annuaires Professionnels [*French*]
UFAS	Union des Associations d'Assistants Sociaux Francophones [*Belgium*] (SLS)
UFB	Union des Femmes Burundi [*Union of Burundi Women*] (AF)
UFBR	Ustav Fyziologie a Biologie Rastlin [*Institute of Physiology and Plant Biology*] (CZ)
UFBS	Union des Francais de Bon Sens [*Union of Frenchmen of Good Sense*] [*Political party*] (PPW)
UFC	Federal University of Ceara [*Brazil*]
UFC	Uganda Freedom Convention
UFC	Union des Femmes Congolaises [*Union of Congolese Women*] (AF)
UFC	Union Federale de la Consummation (FLAF)
UFC	Union Fraternelle des Croyants
UFC	Universidade Federal do Ceara [*Federal University of Ceara*] [*Brazil*] (MSC)
UFC	Universite Federale du Cameroun
UFCA	Union Feminine Centrafricaine [*Central African Women's Union*] (AF)
UFCA	Union pour la Communaute Franco-Africaine
UFCE	Union Federaliste des Communautes Ethniques Europeennes (FLAF)
UFCO	United Fruit Co. [*Honduras*] (DSCA)
UFCSM	United Free Church of Scotland Mission
UFD	Union de Fuerzas Democraticas [*Union of Democratic Forces*] [*Spanish*] (WER)
UFD	Union des Forces Democratiques [*Union of Democratic Forces*] [*Mali*] [*Political party*] (EY)
UFD	Union des Forces Democratiques [*Union of Democratic Forces*] [*France*] [*Political party*] (PPE)
UFDC	Union des Forces Democratiques du Cameroun [*Union of Democratic Forces of Cameron*] [*Political party*] (EY)
UFDC	Union Femenina Democrata Cristiana [*Christian Democratic Women's Union*] [*El Salvador*] (LA)
UFDI	Unione Forestali d'Italia [*Foresters Union of Italy*] (EAIO)
UFDR	Uniunea Femeilor Democrate Romane [*Union of Romanian Democratic Women*] (RO)
UFDS	Union des Forces Democratiques du Senegal [*Union of the Democratic Forces of Senegal*] (AF)
UFE	Uniao dos Federalistas Europeos [*European Federalists Union*] [*Portuguese*] (WER)
UFE	Uniao Federal dos Estudantes [*Federal Students Union*] [*Brazil*] (LA)
UFE	Union des Feculeries de Pommes de Terre de la CE [*EC*] (ECED)
UFE	Union des Francais a l'Etranger [*Union of French Citizens Abroad*] [*Political party*] (PPW)
UFE	Union Far East, Indonesia [*Guardian Royal Exchange Assurance Group*]
UFE	Union Forestiere de l'Estuaire
UFE	Union of the Finance-Personnel in Europe [*EC*] (ECED)
UFEA	Union Financiere pour l'Europe et l'Afrique [*Financial Union for Europe and Africa*] [*French*] (AF)
UFEC	Union Francaise des Exportateurs Cotonniers (FLAF)
UFEMAT	Federation Europeenne des Associations Nationales des Negociants en Materiaux de Construction [*European Association of National Builders Merchants Associations*] (EAIO)
UFEMTO	Union des Femmes du Togo [*Union of Togolese Women*] (AF)
UFER	Mouvement International pour l'Union Fraternelle entre les Races et les Peuples [*International Movement for Fraternal Union among Races and Peoples*]
UFERI	Union des Federalistes et Republicains Independants [*Zaire*] [*Political party*] (EY)
UFF	U-Landshjaelp fra Folk til Folk [*Development Aid From People to People*] [*Denmark*] (EAIO)
uff	Und Folgende [*And the Following*] [*German*] (EG)
UFF	Union des Femmes Francaises [*Union of French Women*] (WER)
UFF	Union et Fraternite Francaise [*French Union and Fraternity*] [*Political party*] (PPE)
UFFRO	Uganda Freshwater Fisheries Research Organization (ARC)
UFFU	United Fire-Fighters Union of Australia
Uffz	Unteroffizier [*Noncommissioned Officer*] [*Military*] [*German*]
UFG	Union Forestiere du Gabon
UFG	Union Franco-Guineenne
UFG	Union Fraternelle Guineenne [*Guinean Fraternal Union*] (AF)
UFI	Pulse Shaping Amplifier (RU)
UFI	Ubungo Farm Implements
UFI	Union des Foires Internationales [*Union of International Fairs*] (EAIO)
UFI	Union Francaise d'Informations [*French News Union*] (WER)
UFI	United Fibreglass Industries [*Australia*]
UFIDA	Union Financiere Internationale pour le Developpement de l'Afrique [*International Financial Association for the Development of Africa*] (AF)
UFIPTE	Union Franco-Iberique pour la Coordination de la Production et du Transport de l'Electricite [*Franco-Iberian Union for Coordinating the Production and Transmission of Electricity*] (EAIO)
UFK	Ukase on Financial Control (BU)
UFK	Union Franco-Kanembou
UFL	Uganda Federation of Labour
UFL	Ultraviolet Rays (RU)
UFL	Union des Femmes Luxembourgeoises [*Union of Women of Luxembourg*] (WER)
UFM	Uganda Freedom Movement (PD)
UFM	Ultraviolet Meter (RU)
UFM	Ultraviolet Microirradiation [*Biology*] (RU)
UFM	Unevangelized Fields Missions
UFM	Union des Femmes du Mali
UFM	Union Fleuve de Mano [*Mano River Union - MRU*] (EAIO)
UFM	Union Franco-Musulmane
UFMAC	Uganda Fish Marketing Association
UFMG	Universidade Federal de Minas Gerais [*Federal University of Minas Gerais*] [*Brazil*] (LA)
UFN	Progress of Physical Sciences (RU)
UFN	Union des Femmes Nigeriennes [*Nigerien Women's Union*] [*Niger*] (AF)
UFNA	Union Francaise Nord-Africaine
UFNI	Ufa Petroleum Institute (RU)
UFNII	Ufa Petroleum Scientific Research Institute (RU)
UFO	Ultraviolet Illumination (RU)
UFO	Ultraviolet Irradiation (RU)
UFO	Union Forestiere de l'Ogooue
UFOA	Union des Femmes de l'Ouest Africaine
UFOCA	Union Forestiere Camerounaise
UFOD	Union Francaise des Organismes de Documentation [*Association of Documentation Organizations*] [*French*]
UFOIC	UFO [*Unidentified Flying Object*] Investigation Center [*Australia*] [*Defunct*]
UFOM	Union Francaise d'Outre-Mer
UFOPIA	Unidentified Flying Objects Phenomena Investigations, Australia
UFOR	UFO [*Unidentified Flying Object*] Research [*Australia*]
UFOR	Union Forestiere
UFORDAT	Umweltforschungsdatenbank [*Data Bank for Environmental Research Projects*] [*Deutsches Umweltbundesamt*] [*Germany*] [*Information service or system*] (CRD)
UFORQ	Unidentified Flying Object Research Queensland [*Australia*]
UFOSZ	Ujgazdak es Foldhozjuttatottak Orszagos Szovetsege [*National Association of New Farmers and Recipients of Land*] (HU)
UFOV	Union des Forces Ouvrieres Voltaiques
UFP	Union Frontier Police [*European Economic Community*] (ECON)
UFP	United Federal Party [*Zambia*] (AF)
UFP	United Force Party [*Guyana*] (LA)
UFP	Universidade Federal do Parana [*Federal University of Parana*] [*Brazil*] (LA)
UFP	Universidad Federal de Pernambuco [*Federal University of Pernambuco*] [*Brazil*] (MSC)

UFPA......... Universidade Federal do Para [*Para Federal University*] [*Brazil*] (EAS)
UF Parl...... Union Francaise et Parlement   (FLAF)
UFPC......... Union des Forces Populaires Congolaises
UFPDG...... Union des Femmes du Parti Democratique Gabonais [*Women's Union of the Gabonese Democratic Party*]   (AF)
UFPDP...... Union des Forces Populaires pour la Democratie et le Progres [*Niger*] [*Political party*]   (EY)
UFPEL...... Universidade Federal de Pelotas [*Brazil*]   (DSCA)
UFPG......... Union des Forces Patriotiques Guineennes [*France-based Guinean political organization*]
UFPIPIA... Union des Fabricants pour la Protection Internationale de la Propriete Industrielle et Artistique [*Anticounterfeiting organization*] [*France*]
UFPN........ United Federal Party of Nyasaland
UFPV......... Union des Forces Progressistes Voltaiques [*Union of Voltan Progressive Forces*]   (AF)
UFR........... Ultraviolet Radiation   (RU)
UFR........... Union des Femmes de la Reunion [*Women's Union of Reunion*] (AF)
UFR........... United Africa Airline (Liberia), Inc. [*ICAO designator*]   (FAAC)
UFR........... Unites de Formation et de Recherche [*Units of Education and Research*] [*French*]
UFRC........ University Famine Relief Committee
UFRGS...... Universidade Federal do Rio Grande Do Sul [*Federal University of Rio Grande Do Sul*] [*Brazil*]   (LA)
UFRJ......... Universidade Federal do Rio De Janeiro [*Federal University of Rio De Janeiro*] [*Brazil*]   (LAA)
UFRM....... Union des Forces Revolutionnaires Marocaines [*Union of Moroccan Revolutionary Forces*]   (AF)
UFRN........ Universidade Federal do Rio Grande Do Norte [*Federal University of Rio Grande Do Norte*] [*Brazil*]   (LA)
UFRP......... Universidade Federal Rural de Pernambuco [*Brazil*]   (DSCA)
UFRRJ...... Universidade Federal Rural do Rio de Janeiro [*Brazil*]   (DSCA)
UFRRO...... University Famine Relief and Rehabilitation Organization
UFRRS...... Universidade Federal Rural do Rio Grande do Sul [*Brazil*] (DSCA)
UFS........... Ultraviolet Glass   (RU)
UFS........... Universal Freight Services [*Commercial firm*]   (DS)
UFS........... Ustav pro Filozfii a Sociologii [*Institute of Philosophy and Sociology*]   (PDAA)
UFSIA....... Universitaire Faculteiten Sint Ignatius Antwerpen
UFSICA..... Union Federale des Syndicats Industriels, Commercants, et Artisanaux
UFSO........ UNESCO Field Science Office [*Egypt*]
UFSSA...... United Farmers and Stockowners of South Australia
UFT........... Unified Phonetic Transcription   (RU)
UFTAA...... Universal Federation of Travel Agents' Associations [*International Federation of Travel Agencies and Universal Organization of Travel Agents' Associations*] [*Formed by a merger of*] [*Australia*]   (EAIO)
UFTI......... Ukrainian Scientific Research Physicotechnical Institute   (RU)
UFU.......... Uganda Freedom Union
UFUA........ United Firefighters Union of Australia
UFUCH..... Union de Federaciones Universitarias Chilenas [*Union of Universities Federations of Chile*] [*Santiago*]   (LAA)
UFUS......... Udruzenje Filmskih Umetnika Srbije [*Association of Motion Picture Artists of Serbia*]   (YU)
UFUSA...... United Firefighters Union of South Australia
UFUWA.... United Firefighters Union of Western Australia
UFV........... Unabhangiger Frauenverband Bundesverband [*Independent Women's Federation*] [*Germany*]   (EAIO)
UFVF......... Ustav pro Fotochemii a Vedeckou Fotografii [*Institute of Photochemistry and Science Photography*]   (CZ)
UFVR........ Union des Femmes Volontaires de la Republique [*Union of Women Volunteers of the Republic*] [*Zaire*]   (AF)
UFY.......... Uusfilologinen Yhdistys [*Finland*]   (SLS)
UFZ.......... Feeder Protective Device   (RU)
ug.............. Angle, Corner   (RU)
ug.............. Conventional Fuel   (BU)
UG............. Norfolk Island Airlines [*Australia*] [*ICAO designator*]   (ICDA)
Ug............. Udjung [*Cape*] [*Indonesian*]   (NAU)
UG............. Uganda [*ANSI two-letter standard code*]   (CNC)
UG............. Uganda Growers
Ug............. Ugric [*Finno-Ugric Linguistic Family*]   (BARN)
UG............. Union Government
UG............. Unite Guyanaise [*Guyanese Unity*] [*Political party*]   (PPW)
UG............. Universal Gas Analyzer   (RU)
UG............. Uprava za Gozdarstvo [*Forestry Administration*]   (YU)
UG............. Urangesellschaft mit Beschraenkter Haftung [*Germany*]   (WND)
UGA.......... Office of the City Architect   (RU)
UGA.......... Uganda [*ANSI three-letter standard code*]   (CNC)
UGA.......... Uganda Airlines Corp. [*ICAO designator*]   (FAAC)
UGAASAL ... Union General de Artistas y Autores Salvadorenos [*General Union of Salvadoran Artists and Authors*]   (LA)
UGAI........ Unione Giornalisti Aerospaziali Italiani [*Italian*]   (SLS)
UGAIP....... Union Generale de l'Artisanat, de l'Industrie, et des Peches

UGAL........ Union des Groupements d'Achat Cooperatifs de Detaillants de l'Europe [*Association of Cooperative Retailer-Owned Wholesalers of Europe - ACROWE*]   (EAIO)
UGAMI..... Union de Ganaderos del Distrito Miranda [*Venezuela*]   (DSCA)
UGAN....... Uganda
UGAN....... Union Generale des Assurances du Niger [*Insurance*]   (EY)
UGAQ....... United Graziers' Association of Queensland [*Australia*]
UGAQUE ... United Graziers' Association of Queensland Union of Employees [*Australia*]
UGAR........ Union Guineenne d'Assurances et de Reassurances [*Insurance*] (EY)
UGASCRUZ ... Union Ganadera y Agricola de Santa Cruz [*Venezuela*] (DSCA)
UGAT........ Union Generale de l'Agriculture Tunisienne
UGAVI...... Union de Ganaderos de La Villa [*Venezuela*]   (DSCA)
UGB.......... State Security Administration   (RU)
UGB.......... Uitvoeringsbesluit Goederenvervoer Binnenscheepvaart [*Benelux*]   (BAS)
UGB.......... Union de Guerreros Blancos [*White Warriors' Union*] [*El Salvador*] [*Political party*]   (PD)
UGB.......... Union Gabonaise de Banque [*Gabonese Banking Union*]   (AF)
UGBE........ Union Generale Belge d'Electricite [*Belgium*]   (BAS)
UGC.......... Unione Generale Coltivatori [*Italy*]   (EY)
UGC.......... Union Generale Cinematographique   (FLAF)
UGC.......... Union of Greek Composers   (EAIO)
UGC.......... University Grants Commission [*Bangladesh*]
UGC.......... University Grants Committee [*New Zealand*]
UGC.......... Urgench [*Former USSR*] [*Airport symbol*]   (OAG)
UGCA........ Union Generale des Commercants Algeriens [*General Association of Algerian Merchants*]   (AF)
UGCB....... Uniforme Grondslagen en Cooerdinatie van Informatieverzorging in het Bouwwezen [*Rijswijk*]
UGCC........ United Gold Coast Convention [*1947*] [*Ghana*]
UGCI......... Unione Giuristi Cattolici Italiani [*Italian*]   (SLS)
UGCI/ML ... Unione della Gioventu Comunista d'Italia/Marxista-Leninista [*Union of Communist Youth of Italy/Marxist-Leninist*] (WER)
UGEA........ Union des Groupements pour l'Exploitation Agricole [*Union of Farming Groups*] [*Guadeloupe*]   (LA)
UGEAA..... Union Generale des Etudiants Africains en Algerie [*General Union of African Students in Algeria*]   (AF)
UGEAN..... Union Generale d'Etudiants de l'Afrique Noire [*General Union of Students of Black Africa*]   (AF)
UGEAO..... Union Generale des Etudiants de l'Afrique Occidentale [*General Union of West African Students*]   (AF)
UGEC........ Union Generale des Etudiants Congolais [*General Union of Students of the Congo*]
UGECI....... Union Generale des Etudiants de Cote-D'Ivoire [*General Union of Students of the Ivory Coast*]   (AF)
UGECOBA ... Union Generale des Cooperatives Bananieres du Mungo
UGECOBAM ... Union Generale des Cooperatives Bananieres du Mungo
UGECR..... Union Generale des Etudiants Creoles de la Reunion [*General Union of Creole Students of Reunion*]   (AF)
UGED........ Union Generale des Etudiants Dahomeens
UGEDA..... Union Generale des Etudiants Democratiques Algeriens [*General Union of Algerian Democratic Students*]   (AF)
UGEE........ Yerevan/Zvartnots [*Former USSR*] [*ICAO location identifier*] (ICLI)
UGEEC..... Union Generale des Eleves et Etudiants Congolais [*General Union of Congolese Pupils and Students*]   (AF)
UGEED..... Union Generale des Etudiants et Eleves Dahomeens
UGEFCO... Union Generale pour la Promotion et l'Emancipation de la Femme Congolais
U GeflAWG ... Um Gefaellige Antwort Wird Gebeten [*The Favor of an Answer Is Requested*] [*Correspondence*] [*German*]
UGEL........ Union Generale des Etudiants Lybiens
UGEM....... Union Generale des Etudiants du Maroc [*General Union of Moroccan Students*]   (AF)
UGEMA.... Union Generale des Etudiants Musulmans d'Algerie [*General Union of Moslem Students of Algeria*]   (AF)
UGES........ Uniao Geral de Estudantes Secundarios [*General Secondary Students Union*] [*Brazil*]   (LA)
UGES........ Union Generale des Etudiants Senegalais [*General Union of Senegalese Students*]   (AF)
UGET........ Union Generale des Etudiants Tunisie [*General Union of Tunisian Students*] [*Tunis, Tunisia*]   (AF)
UGEV........ Union Generale des Etudiants Voltaiques [*General Union of Voltan Students*]   (AF)
UGFC........ United Ghana Farmers' Council
UGFCC...... United Ghana Farmers' Cooperative Council
UGFT........ Union Generale des Fils du Tchad
UGG.......... Ugland Air AS [*Norway*] [*ICAO designator*]   (FAAC)
UGGF........ Union Generale des Guineens en France
UGGG........ Tbilisi/Novoalexeyevka [*Former USSR*] [*ICAO location identifier*]   (ICLI)

UGGI......... Union Geodesique et Geophysique Internationale [*International Union of Geodesy and Geophysics*] [*Use IUGG*] [*French*] (WER)

U-GH........ Universitaet-Gesamthochschule

UGI............ Unione Goliardica Italiana [*Italian Student Union*] (WER)

UGI............ Union General de Inversiones [*Colombia*] (COL)

UGI............ Union Geografica Internacional [*International Geographical Union - IGU*] [*Spanish*] (MSC)

UGI............ Union Geographique Internationale [*International Geographical Union - IGU*] [*French*] (ASF)

UGICT....... Union Generale des Ingenieurs, des Cadres, et des Techniciens [*General Union of Engineers, Administrative Personnel, and Technicians*] [*French*] (WER)

UGID........ Union Generale Immobiliere de Douala

UGIK........ Administration of the State Quality Inspection (RU)

UGiKS....... Garrison and Guard Duty Regulations (RU)

UGIMA..... Unione Generale degli Industriali Apuani del Marmo ed Affini [*Marble Industry Union*] [*Italy*] (EY)

UGINA...... Union Generale Industrielle Africaine [*African General Industrial Union*] [*Morocco*] (AF)

Ug K........... Criminal Code (RU)

UGK.......... Ustav Geodezie a Kartografie [*Institute of Geodesy and Cartography*] (CZ)

UGKh .... Gas Service Administration (RU)

Ug kod....... Criminal Code (RU)

UGKS .... Interior Garrison and Guard Duty Regulations (BU)

UGL........... Ungleich [*German*] (ADPT)

UGL........... Universitaetsgewerkschaftsleitung [*University Labor Union Management*] (EG)

uglemash.... Coal Machinery Plant (RU)

Ugletekhizdat ... State Scientific and Technical Publishing House of Literature on the Coal Industry (RU)

ugl korr ...... Angular Correlation (RU)

UGLNSW ... United Grand Lodge [*Masons*] of New South Wales [*Australia*]

UGLT .... Union Generale Libyenne du Travail

UGM .... General-Purpose Horizontal Camouflage Net (RU)

UGM .... Universitas Gadjah Mada [*Gadjah Mada University*] (IN)

UGMC....... Uniglory Marine Corp. [*Taiwan*]

UGMM...... Mukhrani [*Former USSR*] [*ICAO location identifier*] (ICLI)

UGMS .... Administration of Hydrometeorological Service (RU)

UGO .... Uige [*Angola*] [*Airport symbol*] [*Obsolete*] (OAG)

UGO .... Unabhaengige Gewerkschaftsorganisation [*Independent Trade Union Organization*] [*German*] (EG)

UGOCM.... Union General de Obreros y Campesinos de Mexico [*General Union of Workers and Peasants of Mexico*] (LA)

UGP.......... Udruzenje Grafickih Preduzeca [*Association of Graphic Establishments*] (YU)

UGP........... Union des Gaullistes de Progres [*Union of Progressive Gaullists*] [*France*] [*Political party*] (PPE)

UGP........... Union Generale des Petroles [*North African*]

UGP........... Uredba o Gradevinskim Preduzecima [*Decree on Building Enterprises*] (YU)

UGPFNRJ ... Udruzenje Gradevinskih Preduzeca Federativna Narodna Republika Jugoslavija [*Association of Building Enterprises of Yugoslavia*] (YU)

UGPI .... Ul'yanovsk State Pedagogical Institute (RU)

UGPROM ... State Industry Administration (RU)

Ug-protskod ... Code of Criminal Procedure (RU)

UGRI .... Geological Coal Exploration Institute (RU)

UGRI .... Uranium Geology Research Institute [*Beijing*] [*Ministry of Nuclear Energy China*] (WND)

UGRS .... Unione dei Giovani Rivoluzionari Somali

UGRU....... Ural Administration of Geological Exploration (RU)

UGS .... Forest Resources Administration (BU)

UGS .... State Insurance Administration (RU)

UGS........... Union de la Gauche Socialiste [*Leftist Socialist Union*] [*Belgium*] (WER)

UGS .... Union des Guineens au Senegal [*Union of Guineans in Senegal*] [*Political party*] (PD)

UGS .... Union Generale de Savonnerie [*Soap manufacturer*] [*French*]

UGS .... Uniunea Generala a Sindicatelor [*General Union of Trade Unions*] (RO)

UGSA .... Union Generale des Syndicats Algeriens [*General Union of Algerian Trade Unions*]

UGSA .... Union Generale Siderurgique Arabe

UGSAJOP ... Union de Ganaderos de San Jose y Las Piedras [*Venezuela*] (DSCA)

UGSCM .... Union Generale des Syndicats Confederes du Maroc [*Morocco*]

UGSD .... Union Generale des Syndicats du Dahomey [*General Union of Beninese Trade Unions*]

UGSR .... Union Generale des Syndicats de la Roumanie (EAIO)

UGSR .... Uniunea Generala a Sindicatelor din Romania [*General Union of Romanian Trade Unions*] (RO)

UGSS......... Sukhumi [*Former USSR*] [*ICAO location identifier*] (ICLI)

UGT........... Uniao Geral de Trabalhadores [*General Workers' Union*] [*Portugal*] (EAIO)

UGT.......... Union General de Trabajadores [*General Union of Workers*] [*Madrid, Spain*] (WER)

UGT........... Union General de Trabajadores [*General Union of Workers*] [*Puerto Rico*]

UGT........... Union General de Trabajadores [*General Union of Workers*] [*Uruguay*] (LAA)

UGT.......... Universal Nose Tetryl Fuze (RU)

UGT.......... Urbaine Gabonaise de Travaux

UGTA .... Union Generale des Travailleurs Algeriens [*General Union of Algerian Workers*] [*Algiers, Algeria*] (AF)

UGTAN..... Union Generale des Travailleurs de l'Afrique Noire [*General Union of Workers of Black Africa*] (AF)

UGTC .... Union Generale des Travailleurs Camerounais [*General Union of Cameroonian Workers*] (AF)

UGTC .... Union Generale des Travailleurs Centrafricains [*General Union of Central African Workers*] (AF)

UGTC .... Union Generale des Travailleurs Congolais [*General Union of Congolese Workers*] (AF)

UGTCI...... Union Generale des Travailleurs de la Cote-D'Ivoire [*General Union of Ivory Coast Workers*] (AF)

UGTD........ Union General de Trabajadores Dominicanos [*General Union of Dominican Workers*] [*Dominican Republic*] (LA)

UGTD........ Union Generale des Travailleurs Dahomeens [*General Union of Beninese Workers*]

UGTD........ Union Generale des Travailleurs Djiboutiens [*General Union of Workers of Djibouti*]

UGTE .... Union General de Trabajadores Ecuatorianos [*General Union of Ecuadorean Workers*] (LA)

UGTFA...... Union Generale des Travailleurs Francais d'Algerie-Sahara (FLAF)

UGTG........ Union Generale des Travailleurs de Guinee [*General Union of Workers of Guinea*] (AF)

UGTG........ Union Generale des Travailleurs de la Guadeloupe (PD)

UGTGB ..... Uniao Geral dos Trabalhadores da Guine-Bissau

UGTGE ..... Union General de Trabajadores de Guinea Ecuatorial

UGTM........ Union Generale des Travailleurs Marocains [*General Union of Moroccan Workers*] [*Casablanca*] (AF)

UGTP .... Uniao Geral dos Trabalhadores de Portugal [*General Workers' Union*] [*Portugal*] (EY)

UGTRF...... Union Generale des Travailleurs Reunionnais en France [*General Union of Reunionese Workers in France*] (AF)

UGTRP...... Union General de Trabajadores de la Republica de Panama [*General Union of Workers of the Republic of Panama*] (LA)

UGTS .... Union Generale des Travailleurs du Senegal [*General Union of Workers of Senegal*] (AF)

UGTSF...... Union Generale des Travailleurs Senegalais en France

UGTT .... Union Generale Tunisienne du Travail [*Tunisian General Federation of Labor*] [*Tunis, Tunisia*] (AF)

UGTU........ Ural Territorial Geological Administration (RU)

UGU .... Ural State University (RU)

UGU .... Ustredni Geologicky Urad, Praha [*Central Geological Office, Prague*] (CZ)

UGWU ...... United General Workers Union [*Bermuda*] (LA)

ugyn........... Ugynevezett [*So-Called*] (HU)

ugyoszt....... Ugyosztaly [*Department, Section*] (HU)

ugyv........... Ugyvivo [*Charge d'Affaires*] (HU)

UGZ.......... Main Contamination Area [*Military term*] (RU)

UGZhD...... Administration of City Railroads (RU)

UHA .... Universitets- och Hogskoleambetet [*National Board of Universities and Colleges*] [*Ministry of Education and Cultural Affairs*] [*Information service or system*] [*Sweden*] (IID)

UHA .... Untersuchungshaftanstalt [*House for Investigative Detention*] (EG)

UHACI...... Union Harriste de Cote-D'Ivoire

UHADA .... Union of Hungarian Art of Dance Associations (EAIO)

UHALGE .. Union of Home Affairs and Local Government Employees [*France*] (EAIO)

UHBP........ Ekimcham [*Former USSR*] [*ICAO location identifier*] (ICLI)

UHC .... Universal Health Care Ltd. [*Australia*]

UHCP........ Uganda Hereditary Chieftainship Party

UHE .... Uherske Hradiste [*Former Czechoslovakia*] [*Airport symbol*] [*Obsolete*] (OAG)

UHF........... Ultrahochfrequenz [*Ultra High Frequency*] [*German*] (GCA)

UHF........... Ultrahoe Frekwensie [*Ultra High Frequency*] [*Afrikaans*]

UHFAWU ... Uganda Hotel, Food, and Allied Workers' Union (EAIO)

UHHH....... Khabarovsk/Novy [*Former USSR*] [*ICAO location identifier*] (ICLI)

UHHO....... Troitskoye [*Former USSR*] [*ICAO location identifier*] (ICLI)

UHKS .... Urad Hospodarske Kontrolni Sluzby [*Office of Economic Control*] (CZ)

UHL........... Unge Hoyres Landsforbund [*Norway*] [*Political party*] (EAIO)

UHM......... Union Haddiema Maghqudin [*Malta*] (EY)

UHMA ...... Ulster Headmistresses Association [*Northern Ireland*] (SLS)

UHMC ...... Upper Harbour Mooring Committee [*Australia*]

UHML....... Lavrentiya [*Former USSR*] [*ICAO location identifier*] (ICLI)

UHMR ...... Beringovsky [*Former USSR*] [*ICAO location identifier*]   (ICLI)

UHO .... Ceskoslovensky Urad pro Hospodarskou Pomoc a Obnovu [*Czechoslovak Office of the United Nations Relief and Rehabilitation Administration*]   (CZ)

UHP .... United Air Service [*Nigeria*] [*ICAO designator*]   (FAAC)

UHP .... Ustav Hospodarskeho Prava Statni Arbitraze CSSR [*Economic Law Institute of State Arbitration Office of Czechoslovakia*]   (CZ)

UHP .... Ustav Hygieny Prace [*Industrial Health Institute*]   (CZ)

UHP .... Ustredi Hospodarskych Poradcu [*Center of Economic Advisers*]   (CZ)

UHR .... Ustredni Hospodarska Rada [*Central Economic Council*]   (CZ)

UHSV .... Ustav pro Hospodarsky a Socialni Vyzkum [*Institute for Economic and Social Research*]   (CZ)

UHTTB ..... Union des Hutu, Tutsi, Twa du Burundi

UHZ .... Ustredna Hmotneho Zasobovani [*Materiel Supply Center*]   (CZ)

UHZV .... Ustredi pro Hospodareni Zemedelskymi Vyrobky [*Agricultural Produce Center*]   (CZ)

UI .... Control Pulse   (RU)

UI .... Pulse Amplifier   (RU)

UI .... Teachers' Institute   (BU)

ui .... Ugyanigy [*In the Same Way*]   (HU)

ui .... Ugyanis [*Namely, That Is*]   (HU)

ui .... Ugyintezo [*Official in Charge, Manager*]   (HU)

UI .... Ujitasi Iroda [*Office of Innovations (For submission of new ideas)*]   (HU)

UI .... Ultrasonics Institute [*Australia*]

UI .... Unidad de la Izquierda [*Unity of the Left*] [*Peru*]   (LA)

UI .... Unidades de Instruccion [*Educational Centers*] [*Peru*]   (LA)

UI .... Union Interparlementaire [*Inter-Parliamentary Union*]   (EAIO)

UI .... Universitas Indonesia [*University of Indonesia*]   (IN)

UI .... University of Ibadan [*Nigeria*]   (ERC)

UI .... Uprava Inzenjerije [*Engineer Corps Administration*] [*Military*]   (YU)

UI .... Uprava za Investicije [*Investments Administration*]   (YU)

ui .... Uso Interno [*Internal Use*] [*Portuguese*]

UI .... Utile Idiota [*Useful Idiot*] [*Said of well-known personages who lend their names to a political party*] [*Italian*]

ui .... Utoirat [*Postcript*]   (HU)

UI .... Utrikespolitiska Institutet [*Sweden*]   (SLS)

ui .... Uzletigazgato [*Shop Manager*]   (HU)

UIA .... Uganda Investment Authority

UIA .... Union des Ingenieurs Algeriens [*Union of Algerian Engineers*]   (AF)

UIA .... Union des Ingenieurs Arabes [*Morocco*]

UIA .... Union Immobiliere Africaine

UIA .... Union Industrial Argentina [*Argentine Industrial Union*]   (LA)

UIA .... Union Industrielle Africaine [*African Industrial Union*] [*Algeria*]   (AF)

UIA .... Union Internationale des Architectes [*International Union of Architects*]   (EAIO)

UIA .... Union Internationale des Avocats   (FLAF)

UIA .... Union of International Associations [*See also UAI*] [*Brussels, Belgium*]   (EAIO)

UIA .... United Israel Appeal [*Australia*]

UIAA .... Chita/Kadala [*Former USSR*] [*ICAO location identifier*]   (ICLI)

UIAA .... Union Internationale des Associations d'Alpinisme [*International Union of Alpine Associations*] [*Switzerland*]

UIAC .... Unite d'Afforestation Industrielle du Congo

UIAE .... Union Industrielle pour l'Afrique Equatoriale [*Industrial Union for Equatorial Africa*] [*Gabon*]   (AF)

UIAM .... Union Internationale d'Assurance Maritime   (FLAF)

UIAOM ..... Union Internationale des Agriculteurs de l'Outre-Mer [*International Union of Overseas Farmers*] [*French*]   (AF)

UIAS .... Directorate of Engineer Aviation Services   (RU)

UIAT .... Union Internationale des Syndicats des Industries de l'Alimentation et des Tabacs   (FLAF)

UIB .... Quibdo [*Colombia*] [*Airport symbol*]   (OAG)

uib .... Uindbundet [*Unbound*] [*Publishing Danish/Norwegian*]

UIB .... Union Internacional de Bioquimica [*International Union of Biochemistry - IUB*] [*Spanish*]   (ASF)

UIB .... Union Internationale de Biochimie [*International Union of Biochemistry - IUB*] [*French*]   (ASF)

UIB .... United Investment & Bankers Ltd. [*Denmark*]

UIB .... Universitetet i Bergen [*Norway*]   (MSC)

UIBB .... Bratsk [*Former USSR*] [*ICAO location identifier*]   (ICLI)

UIBC .... Union of Indonesian Baptist Churches   (EAIO)

UIBG .... Union Internationale de Banque en Guinee   (EY)

UIBPA .... Union Internacional de Biofisica Pura y Aplicada [*International Union of Pure and Applied Biophysics - IUPAB*] [*Spanish*]   (ASF)

UIBPA .... Union Internationale de Biophysique Pure et Appliquee [*International Union of Pure and Applied Biophysics - IUPAB*] [*French*]   (MSC)

UIC .... Ufficio Italiano dei Cambi [*Italian Exchange Office*]   (IMH)

UIC .... Unidad de Izquierda Comunista [*Unity of the Communist Left*] [*Mexico*] [*Political party*]   (PPW)

UIC .... Union des Industries Chimiques [*Chemical Industry Association*] [*French*]

UIC .... Union Industrielle pour le Cameroun

UIC .... Union Internationale des Chemins de Fer [*International Union of Railways*]   (EAIO)

UIC .... United Industrial Corporation [*Singapore*]

UICB .... Union Internacional de Ciencias Biologicas [*International Union of Biological Sciences - IUBS*] [*Spanish*]   (ASF)

UICB .... Union Internationale des Centres du Batiment [*International Union of Building Centers*] [*British*]

UICC .... Union des Industries et Commerce au Congo

UICC .... Unione Internationalis Contra Cancrum [*International Union Against Cancer*] [*ICSU*] [*Research center*]   (IRC)

UICC .... Union Internationale Contre le Cancer [*International Union Against Cancer*] [*Switzerland*]

UICC .... University of Indonesia Culture Collection

UICF .... Union Internacional de Ciencias Fisiologicas [*International Union of Physiological Sciences - IUPS*] [*Spanish*]   (ASF)

UICG .... Union Internacional de Ciencias Geologicas [*International Union of Geological Sciences - IUGS*] [*Spanish*]   (MSC)

UICGF .... Union Internacional du Commerce en Gros de la Fleur [*Germany*]   (DSCA)

UIChM ...... Ural Institute of Ferrous Metals   (RU)

UICN .... Union Internacional para la Conservacion de la Naturaleza y sus Recursos [*International Union for Conservation of Nature and Natural Resources - IUCN*] [*Spanish*]   (ASF)

UICN .... Union Internationale pour la Conservation de la Nature et des Ressources [*International Union for Conservation of Nature and Natural Resources - IUCN*] [*French*]

UICNR ...... Union Internacional para la Conservacion de la Naturaleza y sus Recursos [*Switzerland*]   (DSCA)

UICNR ...... Union Internationale pour la Conservation de la Nature et de ses Resources [*International Union for Conservation of Nature and Natural Resources*] [*Switzerland*]   (EAIO)

UICP .... Union Internationale de la Couverture et Plomberie   (EA)

UICPA .... Uso Internacional de Chimie Pure et Appliquee [*International Union of Pure and Applied Chemistry - IUPAC*] [*French*]   (ASF)

UICR .... Union Internationale des Chauffeurs Routiers [*International Union of Lorry Drivers - IULD*]   (EAIO)

UICT .... Union Internationale Contre la Tuberculose [*International Union Against Tuberculosis - IUAT*]   (EAIO)

UICTMR ... Union Internationale Contre la Tuberculose et les Maladies Respiratoires [*International Union Against Tuberculosis and Lung Disease - IUATLD*]   (EAIO)

UIDIC .... Union Independante pour la Defense des Interets Communaux

UIE .... UNESCO Institute for Education [*Research center*]   (IRC)

UIE .... Union des Industries et Entreprises [*Industrial and Business Union*] [*Tunisia*]   (AF)

UIE .... Union Internacional de Estudiantes [*International Union of Students*] [*Use IUS*]   (LA)

UIE .... Union Internationale d'Editeurs [*International Publishers Association - IPA*]   (EAIO)

UIE .... Union Internationale d'Electrothermie [*International Union for Electroheat*]   (EAIO)

UIE .... Union Internationale des Editeurs [*International Union of Publishers*]   (NTCM)

UIE .... Union Internationale des Etudiants [*International Union of Students - IUS*]   (EAIO)

UIEC .... Union Industrielle et d'Entreprise pour le Congo

UIEC .... Union Internationale de l'Exploitation Cinematographique [*International Union of Cinematographic Exhibitors*]   (EAIO)

UIEE .... Ukrainian Institute of Experimental Endocrinology   (RU)

UIEIS .... Union Internationale pour l'Etude des Insectes Sociaux [*International Union for the Study of Social Insects - IUSSI*] [*Netherlands*]

UIEO .... Union of International Engineering Organizations   (ASF)

UIEOA ...... Union Internationale des Etudes Orientales et Asiatiques [*French*]   (SLS)

UIEPB .... Union Internationale des Employes Professionnels et de Bureau

UIES .... Union Internationale d'Education pour la Sante [*International Union of Health Education - IUHE*] [*Paris, France*]   (EAIO)

UIES .... Union Internationale des Employes de Service

UIESP .... Union Internationale pour l'Etude Scientifique de la Population

UIEV .... Ukrainian Institute of Experimental Veterinary Science   (RU)

UIF .... Union Immobiliere de France

UIF .... Union Internationale de Ferrecarriles [*International Union of Railways*]

UIFA .... Union Internationale des Femmes Architectes [*International Union of Women Architects - IUWA*]   (EAIO)

UIFPA .... Union Internacional de Fisica Pura y Aplicada [*International Union of Pure and Applied Physics - IUPAP*] [*Spanish*]   (ASF)

UIG .... Union Interprofessionnelle de la Guadeloupe [*Interoccupational Union of Guadeloupe*]

UIGG .... Union Internacional de Geodesia y Geofisica [*International Union of Geodesy and Geophysics - IUGG*] [*Spanish*] (ASF)

UIGSE .... Union Internationale des Guides et Scouts d'Europe [*International Union of European Guides and Scouts - IUEGS*] [*Chateau Landon, France*] (EAIO)

UIHMSU .. Union Internationale d'Hygiene et de Medecine Scolaires et Universitaires [*International Union of School and University Health and Medicine - IUSUHM*] [*Brussels, Belgium*] (EAIO)

UII .... Ural Industrial Institute Imeni S. M. Kirov (RU)

UII .... Utila Island [*Honduras*] [*Airport symbol*] [*Obsolete*] (OAG)

UIIDE .... Union Internationale des Infirmieres Diplomees d'Etat [*International Union of Registered Nurses*] [*France*] (EAIO)

UIIG .... Union Internationale de l'Industrie du Gaz [*International Gas Union - IGU*] [*Paris, France*] (EAIO)

UIII .... Irkutsk [*Former USSR*] [*ICAO location identifier*] (ICLI)

UIIO .... Ust-Ordynsky [*Former USSR*] [*ICAO location identifier*] (ICLI)

UIIOM ...... Union Intersyndicale de l'Industrie d'Outre-Mer

UIIPI .... Unione Italiana Lavoratori Pubblico Impiego [*Public Office Workers Union*] [*Italy*] (EY)

UIJA .... Union Internationale des Journalistes Africains

UIJDC .... Union Internationale des Jeunes Democrates Chretiens (FLAF)

UIJPLF ..... Union Internationale des Journalistes et de la Presse de Langue Francaise [*International Union of French-Language Journalists and Press - IUFLJP*] (EAIO)

UIJS .... Union Internacional de Juventudes Socialistas [*International Union of Socialist Youth*] [*Use IUSY*] (LA)

UIJS .... Union Internationale de la Jeunesse Socialiste [*International Union of Socialist Youth*] [*Use IUSY*] (AF)

UIK .... Air Conditioner (RU)

UIKB .... Bodaybo [*Former USSR*] [*ICAO location identifier*] (ICLI)

UIKK .... Kirensk [*Former USSR*] [*ICAO location identifier*] (ICLI)

UIKW .... Vitim [*Former USSR*] [*ICAO location identifier*] (ICLI)

UIL .... Ufficio Internazionale del Lavoro [*International Labor Office*] [*Italian*]

UIL .... Unione Italiana del Lavoro [*Italian Union of Labor*] [*Rome*] (WER)

UILAS .... Unione Italiana Lavoratori Assicurazioni [*Assurance Company Workers Union*] [*Italy*] (EY)

UILC .... Unione Italiana Lavoratori Chimici [*Italian Union of Chemical Workers*]

UILDM ..... Unione Italiana Lotta alla Distrofia Muscolare [*Italian*] (SLS)

UILE .... Union Internationale pour la Liberte d'Enseignement [*French*] (SLS)

UILI .... Union Internationale des Laboratoires Independents [*International Union of Independent Laboratories*] [*Elstree, Hertfordshire, England*] (EAIO)

UILIA .... Unione Italiana Lavoratori Industrie Alimentari [*Italian Union of Food-Processing Workers*]

UILIAS ...... Unione Italiana Lavoratori Industrie Alimentari Saccariferi [*Food Workers Union*] [*Italy*] (EY)

UILIC .... Unione Italiana Lavoratori Imposte Consumo [*Italian Union of Food Tax Levy Workers*]

uillustr .... Uillustreret [*Without Illustrations*] [*Publishing Danish/ Norwegian*]

UILM .... Unione Italiana Lavoratori Metallurgici [*Italian Metalworkers' Union*]

UIL-MD .... Unione Italiana del Lavoro - Metalmeccanici Democratici [*Italian Union of Labor - Democratic Metalworkers*] (WER)

UILPEM ... Unione Italiana Lavoratori Petrolieri e Metanieri [*Italian Union of Oil and Methane Gas Workers*]

UILS .... Unione Italiana Lavoratori Saccariferi [*Italian Union of Sugar Industry Workers*]

UILT .... Unione Italiana Lavoratori delle Terra [*Italian Union of Landworkers*]

UILT .... Unione Italiana Lavoratori Tessili [*Italian Union of Textile Workers*]

UILTATEP ... Unione Italiana Lavoratori Trasporti Ausiliari Traffico e Portuali [*Transport and Associated Workers Union*] [*Italy*] (EY)

UILTRAS ... Unione Italiana Trasporti ed Ausiliari del Traffico [*Italian Union of Transport Workers and Auxiliary Services*]

UILTuCS ... Unione Italiana Lavoratori Turismo Commercio e Servizi [*Tourism industry*] [*Italy*] (EY)

UILVECA ... Unione Italiana Lavoratori Vetro, Ceramica, ed Abrasivi [*Italian Union of Glass, Ceramics, and Abrasive Workers*]

UIM .... Unione Italiana Marittimi [*Italian Union of Seamen*]

UIM .... Union Internationale des Magistrats [*International Association of Judges - IAJ*] (EAIO)

UIM .... Union Internationale Monarchiste [*Weinsberg, Federal Republic of Germany*] (EAIO)

UIM .... Union Internationale Motonautique [*Union of International Motorboating*] (EAIO)

UIM .... Union of International Motorboating (EA)

UIM .... Universal Measuring Microscope (RU)

UIM .... Ural Scientific Research Institute of Ferrous Metals (RU)

UIMAS ..... Ultrasound in Medicine - Australia Society

UIMC .... Union Internationale des Services Medicaux des Chemins de Fer [*Belgium*] (SLS)

UIMEC ...... Unione Italiana Mezzadri e Coltivatori Diretti [*Land Workers Union*] [*Italy*] (EY)

UIML .... Ukrainian Institute of Marxism-Leninism (RU)

UIMM .... Union des Industries Metallurgiques et Minieres [*Union of Metal and Mining Industries*] [*French*] (WER)

UIM-NATI ... NATI Oil-Testing Unit (RU)

UIM-NRS ... Udruzenje Industrije Gradevinskog Materijala Narodna Republika Srbije [*Association of Building Materials Industries of Serbia*] (YU)

UIMP .... Union Internationale pour le Protection de la Moralite Publique [*International Union for the Protection of Public Morale*] [*France*]

UIMS .... Ukrainian Scientific Research Institute of Metrology and Standardization (RU)

UIMVT ..... Union Internationale Contre les Maladies Veneriennes et les Treponematoses [*International Union Against the Venereal Diseases and the Treponematoses - IUVDT*]

UINF .... Union Internationale de la Navigation Fluviale [*International Union for Inland Navigation - IUIN*] (EAIO)

UINL .... Union Internacional del Notariado Latino [*International Union of Latin Notaries*] [*Buenos Aires, Argentina*] (LAA)

UINL .... Union Internationale du Notariat Latin (FLAF)

UINN .... Nizhneudinsk [*Former USSR*] [*ICAO location identifier*] (ICLI)

uinnb .... Uinnbundet [*Unbound*] [*Publishing Danish/Norwegian*]

UINO .... Administration of Foreign Transactions of the State Bank of the USSR (RU)

UINRM ..... Ured za Informacii na Narodnata Republika Makedonija [*Information Office of Macedonia*] (YU)

UIO .... Quito [*Ecuador*] [*Airport symbol*] (OAG)

UIO .... Termination Control Pulse (RU)

UIO .... Universitetet i Oslo [*University of Oslo*] [*Norway*] (MSC)

UIO .... Uppsala Ionospheric Observatory [*Research center*] [*Sweden*] (IRC)

UIOF .... Union Internationale des Organismes Familiaux [*International Union of Family Organizations - IUFO*] [*France*]

UIOIF .... Union Internacional de Organizaciones de Investigacion Forestal [*Germany*] (DSCA)

UIOOT ...... Union Internationale des Organismes Officiels de Tourisme [*International Union of Official Travel Organizations*] [*Use IUOTO*] (CL)

UIOSRZ .... Uredba o Imovinskim Odnosima i Reorganizaciji Seljackih Radnih Zadruga [*Decree on Property Relations and the Reorganization of Peasant Work Cooperative*] (YU)

UIOV .... Ukase on the Property Liability of Military Personnel (BU)

UIP .... General-Purpose Power Supply (RU)

UIP .... Quimper [*France*] [*Airport symbol*] (OAG)

UIP .... Union Industrial Paraguaya [*Paraguayan Industrial Union*] (LA)

UIP .... Union Industrielle des Petroles

UIP .... Union Internationale d'Associations de Proprietaires de Wagons Particuliers [*International Union of Private Railway Truck Owners' Associations*] (EAIO)

UIP .... Union Internationale de Patinage [*International Skating Union - ISU*] [*Davos-Platz, Switzerland*] (EAIO)

UIP .... Union Interparlementaire Mondiale [*Interparliamentary Union*] [*Use IPU*] (CL)

UiP .... United Industrial Promotions Ltd. [*Thailand*]

UIP .... Universal Immunisation Programme [*India*]

UIPA .... Union Industrielle des Petroles Algerie

UIPC .... Union Internationale de la Press Catholique [*International Union of the Catholic Press*] [*France*]

UIPE .... Ukrainian Scientific Research Institute of Industrial Power Engineering (RU)

UIPE .... Union Internationale de Protection de l'Enfance [*International Union for Child Welfare - IUCW*] [*Geneva, Switzerland*] [*Defunct*] (EA)

UIPF .... Ukrainian Scientific Research Institute of Applied Physics (RU)

UIPFKh ..... Ukrainian Scientific Research Institute of Applied Physical Chemistry (RU)

UIPFNRJ ... Udruzenje Izdavackih Preduzeca Federativna Narodna Republika Jugoslavija [*Association of Yugoslav Publishing Establishments*] (YU)

UIPI .... Union Internationale de la Propriete Immobiliere [*International Union of Property Owners*] [*Paris, France*] (EAIO)

UIPKKh ..... Ural Institute for Improving Qualifications of the Managerial Personnel (RU)

UIPMB ...... Union Internationale de Pentathlon Moderne Biathlon (OLYM)

UIPMB ...... Union Internationale de Pentathlon Moderne et Biathlon [*International Union for Modern Pentathlon and Biathlon*] (EAIO)

UIPN .... Union Internationale pour la Protection de la Nature [*International Union for the Protection of Nature - IUPN*] [*Later, IUCN*]
UIPNRH ... Udruzenje Izdavackih Poduzeca Narodne Republike Hrvatske [*Association of Publishing Houses of Croatia*] (YU)
UIPNRSrbije ... Udruzenje Izdavackih Preduzeca Narodne Republike Srbije [*Association of Publishing Houses of Serbia*] (YU)
UIPP .... Union des Industries de la Protection des Plantes [*France*]
UIPPA .... Union Internationale de Physique Pure et Appliquee [*International Union of Pure and Applied Physics - IUPAP*] [*French*] (ASF)
UIPRE .... Union Internationale de la Presse Radiotechnique et Electronique [*Freiburg, Federal Republic of Germany*] (EAIO)
UIQPA ...... Union Internacional de Quimica Pura y Aplicada [*International Union of Pure and Applied Chemistry - IUPAC*] [*Spanish*] (ASF)
UIR .... Educational Research Work (RU)
UIR .... Engineer Work Directorate (RU)
UIR .... Quirindi [*Australia*] [*Airport symbol*] [*Obsolete*] (OAG)
UIR .... Training-Research Work (BU)
UIR .... Udruzenje Invalida Rada [*Association of Disabled Workers*] (YU)
UIR .... Union Internationale de Radiodiffusion [*International Broadcasting Union*] [*Also, IBU*] (NTCM)
UIR .... Union Internationale des Radioecologistes [*International Union of Radioecologists - IUR*] (EAIO)
UIR .... Universitas Islam Riau [*Riau Islamic University*] [*Indonesia*] (EAS)
UIRD .... Union Internationale de la Resistance et de la Deportation
UIRS .... Udruzenje Invalida Rada Srbije [*Association of Disabled Workers of Serbia*] (YU)
UIS .... Unione Internazionale degli Studenti [*International Union of Students*] [*Use IUS*] [*Italian*] (WER)
UIS .... Union Immobiliere de Supermarches et Centres Commerciaux [*French*]
UIS .... Union Internationale de Speleologie [*International Union of Speleology - IUS*] (EAIO)
UIS .... Union Internationale des Syndicats des Travailleurs des Transports [*Trade Unions International of Transport Workers*] (EAIO)
UIS .... Uniunea Internatonala a Studentiilor [*International Union of Students - IUS*] (RO)
UIS .... Universidad Industrial de Santander [*Bucaramanga*] (COL)
UIS .... Ural Complex Institute of Structures (RU)
UIS .... Ustredni Informacni Sluzba [*Central Information Service*] (CZ)
UISAE .... Union Internationale des Sciences Anthropologiques et Ethnologiques [*International Union of Anthropological and Ethnological Sciences - IUAES*] (EAIO)
UISB .... Union Internationale des Sciences Biologiques [*International Union of Biological Sciences - IUBS*] [*French*] (SLS)
UISC .... Universite Internationale de Sciences Comparees [*Benelux*] (BAS)
UISG .... Union Internationale des Sciences Geologiques [*International Union of Geological Sciences - IUGS*] [*French*] (ASF)
UISG .... Union Internationale des Superieures Majeures [*International Union of Superiors General*] [*Rome, Italy*] (EAIO)
UISH .... Union Inter-Syndicale d'Haiti [*Trade union*] [*Haiti*]
UISIF .... Union Internationale des Societes d'Ingenieurs Forestiers [*International Union of Societies of Foresters - IUSF*] [*Ottawa, ON*] (EAIO)
UISM .... Union Internationale des Syndicats des Mineurs (FLAF)
UISMTE ... Union Internationale des Syndicats des Mineurs et des Travailleurs de l'Energie [*Trade Unions International of Miners and Workers in Energy - TUIMWE*] (EAIO)
UISN .... Union Internationale des Sciences de la Nutrition [*International Union of Nutritional Sciences - IUNS*] [*Wageningen, Netherlands*] (EA)
UISP .... Union Internationale des Sciences Physiologiques [*International Union of Physiological Sciences - IUPS*] [*French*] (MSC)
UISP .... Union Internationale des Societes de la Paix (FLAF)
UISP .... Union Internationale des Syndicats de Police [*International Union of Police Syndicates*] (EAIO)
UISPTT ..... Union Internationale Sportive des Postes, des Telephones, et des Telecommunications [*International Sports Union of Post, Telephone, and Telecommunications Services - ISUPTTS*] [*Switzerland*]
UISSM ...... Union Internationale des Syndicats des Industries Metallurgiques et Mecaniques (FLAF)
UIST .... Ukrainian Institute of Soviet Trade (RU)
UISTAF ..... Union Internationale des Syndicats des Travailleurs Agricoles et Forestiers et des Organisations des Paysans Travailleurs (FLAF)
UISTAFP .. Union Internationale des Syndicats des Travailleurs de l'Agriculture, des Forets, et des Plantations [*Trade Unions International of Agriculture, Forestry, and Plantation Workers - TUIAFPW*] [*Prague, Czechoslovakia*] (EAIO)

UISTAV .... Union Internationale pour la Science, la Technique, et les Applications du Vide [*International Union for Vacuum Science, Technique, and Applications - IUVSTA*] (EAIO)
UISTC .... Union Internationale des Syndicats des Travailleurs du Commerce (FLAF)
UISTICPS ... Union Internationale des Syndicats des Travailleurs des Industries Chimiques du Petrole et Similaires (FLAF)
UISTransport ... Union Internationale des Syndicats des Travailleurs des Transports [*Trade Unions International of Transport Workers*] [*Hungary*] (EAIO)
UIT .... Income Tax Unit [*Peru*] (IMH)
UIT .... Jaluit [*Marshall Islands*] [*Airport symbol*] (OAG)
UIT .... Ulsan Institute of Technology [*Korean*] [*Research center*] (ERC)
UIT .... Union de Industrias Textiles [*Union of Textile Industries*] [*El Salvador*] (LA)
UIT .... Unione Internazionale Telecomunicazioni [*International Telecommunications Union*] [*Use ITU*] [*Italian*] (WER)
UIT .... Union Internationale des Telecommunications [*International Telecommunication Union*] [*French United Nations*] (DUND)
UIT .... Union Internationale de Tir [*International Shooting Union*] [*See also IS*] [*Germany*] (EAIO)
UIT .... Universitetet i Tromso [*University of Tromso*] [*Norway*] (MSC)
UITA .... Union Internacional de Asociaciones de Trabajadores en Alimentos [*International Union of Food and Allied Workers Associations*] [*San Jose, Costa Rica*] (LAA)
UITA .... Union of International Technical Associations [*See also UATI*] [*ICSU*] [*Paris, France*] (EAIO)
UITBB .... Union Internationale des Syndicats des Travailleurs du Batiment, du Bois, et des Materiaux de Construction [*Trade Unions International of Workers of the Building, Wood, and Building Materials Industries*] [*WFTU*]
uitbr .... Uitbreiding [*Extension*] [*Afrikaans*]
UITCA .... International Union of Co-operative and Associated Tourism (EAIO)
uitdr .... Uitdrukking [*Expression*] [*Netherlands*]
Uitg .... Uitgave [*Edition*] [*Netherlands*] (ILCA)
uitg .... Uitgegeven [*Published*] [*Netherlands*]
uitgebr .... Uitgebreide [*Enlarged*] [*Publishing*] [*Netherlands*]
uitgeg .... Uitgegeven [*Published*] [*Publishing*] [*Netherlands*]
uitgekn .... Uitgeknipt [*Cut Out*] [*Publishing*] [*Netherlands*]
UITLK .... Administration of Corrective Labor Camps and Colonies (RU)
UITP .... Union Internationale des Transports Publics [*International Union of Public Transport*] (EAIO)
UITR .... Ukase on Inventions, Technical Improvements, and Rationalization Suggestions (BU)
uitsl .... Uitslaand [*Unfolding*] [*Publishing*] [*Netherlands*]
uitspr .... Uitspraak [*Benelux*] (BAS)
uitst .... Uitstekend [*Excellent*] [*Netherlands*]
UITU .... Administration of Corrective Labor Establishments (RU)
uitv .... Uitverkocht [*Out of Print*] [*Publishing*] [*Netherlands*]
uitvb .... Uitvoeringsbesluit [*Benelux*] (BAS)
uitvbesch .... Uitvoeringsbeschikking [*Benelux*] (BAS)
Uitvbesl ...... Uitvoeringsbesluit [*Benelux*] (BAS)
uitverk .... Uitverkocht [*Out of Print*] [*Publishing*] [*Netherlands*]
UIU .... Union Industrial Uruguaya [*Uruguay*] (LAA)
UIUH .... Khorinsk [*Former USSR*] [*ICAO location identifier*] (ICLI)
UIUU .... Ulan-Ude/Mukhino [*Former USSR*] [*ICAO location identifier*] (ICLI)
UIV .... Union Internationale des Villes et Pouvoirs Locaux (FLAF)
UIYuN .... Ukrainian Scientific Research Institute of Jurisprudence (RU)
UIZh .... Ukrainian Scientific Research Institute of Livestock Breeding (RU)
UJ .... Uniwersytet Jagiellonski [*Jagiellonian University*] (POL)
UJA .... Udruzenja Jugoslovenskih Arhitekata [*Assocation of Yugoslav Architects*] (EAIO)
UJA .... Union des Journalistes Africains [*African Journalists Union*]
UJA .... Union des Journalistes Algeriens [*Algerian Journalists Union*] (AF)
UJA .... United Jewish Appeal (ME)
UJARF ...... Union de la Jeunesse Agricole et Rurale de France [*Union of French Agricultural and Rural Youth*] (WER)
UJC .... Uniao da Juventude Comunista [*Union of Communist Youth*] [*Portuguese*] (LA)
UJC .... Union de Jovenes Comunistas [*Union of Young Communists*] [*Nicaragua*] (LA)
UJC .... Union de Jovenes Comunistas [*Union of Young Communists*] [*Cuba*] (LA)
UJC .... Union de Jovenes Comunistas [*Union of Young Communists*] [*Uruguay*] (LA)
UJC .... Union de la Jeunesse Congolaise
UJC .... Ustav pro Jazyk Cesky [*Czech Language Institute (of the Czechoslovak Academy of Sciences)*] (CZ)
UJCAZ ...... Ustredni Jednota Cesko-Americkych Zen [*Central Organization of Czech-American Women*] (CZ)
UJCC .... Uniunea Judeteana a Cooperativelor de Consum [*County Union of Consumer Cooperatives*] (RO)

UJCDE...... Union de la Juventud Comunista Democratica Espanol [*Spanish Democratic Communist Youth Union*] (WER)

UJCE........ Union de Juventudes Comunistas de Espana [*Spanish*]

UJCF........ Union des Jeunesses Communistes de France [*Union of Communist Youth of France*] (WER)

UJCL........ Ustredni Jednota Ceskoslovenskych Lekaru [*Central Organization of Czechoslovak Physicians*] (CZ)

UJCM........ Uniunea Judeteana a Cooperativelor Mestesugaresti [*County Union of Artisan Cooperatives*] (RO)

UJCML..... Union des Jeunesses Communistes Marxistes-Leninistes [*Union of Young Marxist-Leninist Communists*] [*France*] [*Political party*] (PPE)

UJCS........ Ustredni Jednota Ceskoslovenskych Sachistu [*Central Organization of Czechoslovak Chess Players*] (CZ)

UJCsL....... Ustredni Jednota Ceskoslovenske Obce Legionarske [*Czechoslovak Legion Headquarters*] (CZ)

UJECML .. Uniao da Juventude Estudantil Comunista Marxista-Leninista [*Union of Communist Student Youth/Marxist-Leninist*] [*Portuguese*] (WER)

UJEP........ Universita Jana Evangelisty Purkyne [*University of Jan Evangelista Purkyne*] (CZ)

UJHD........ Ustredni Jednota Hospodarskych Druzstev [*Central Organization of Economic Cooperatives*] (CZ)

UJI............ Ustredni Jednota Invalidu [*Central Association of Disabled Persons*] (CZ)

UJK .... Union de la Jeunesse Khmere [*en RDA*] [*Cambodian Youth Union (in the GDR)*] (CL)

UJKI......... Union de la Jeunesse Kimbanguiste

UJL........... Uninet Japan Ltd. [*Telecommunications*]

UJM .... Union de la Jeunesse Marocaine [*Moroccan Youth Union*] (AF)

Uj M Kk..... Uj Magyar Konyvkiado [*New Hungarian Book Publishing Enterprise*] (HU)

UJP........... Udruzenje Jugoslovenskih Pronalazaca [*Association of Yugoslav Inventors*] (YU)

UJP........... Union de la Jeunesse pour la Patrie [*Union of Youth for the Nation*] [*French*] (WER)

UJP........... Union des Jeunes pour le Progres [*Union of Youth for Progress*] [*Youth group of the UDR*] [*French*] (WER)

UJP........... Uredba o Organizaciji, Poslovanju, i Upravljanju Jugoslovenskim Postama, Telegrafima, i Telefonima [*Decree on the Organization, Operation, and Management of Yugoslav Post, Telegraph, and Telephone*] (YU)

UJPC........ Union des Journalistes Professionnels du Congo

UJPDG...... Union des Jeunes du Parti Democratique Gabonais

UJPM........ Union des Jeunes pour le Progres de Mayotte [*Union of Youth for the Progress of Mayotte*] [*Comoros*] (AF)

UJRB........ Union de la Jeunesse Revolutionnaire Burundaise

UJS........... Union de Juventudes Socialistas [*Socialist Youth Union*] [*Argentina*] (LA)

UJSC .... Union de la Jeunesse Socialiste Congolaise [*Union of Congolese Socialist Youth*] (AF)

UJSP .... United States-Japan Science Program (MSC)

UJT........... Union de la Jeunesse Tunisienne [*Tunisian Youth Union*] (AF)

UJU........... Udruzenje Jugoslovenskog Uciteljstva [*Association of Yugoslav Teachers*] (YU)

UJVCSAV ... Ustav Jaderneho Vyzkumu CSAV [*Nuclear Research Institute of the Czechoslovak Science Academy*] (CZ)

UJW .... Union of Jewish Women [*Zimbabwe*] (EAIO)

UJWF........ United Jewish Welfare Fund

UJWSA..... Union of Jewish Women of South Africa (EAIO)

UJWSS...... Union of Jewish Women's Societies in Switzerland (EAIO)

UJZ........... Uredba o Organizaciji, Poslovanju, i Upravljanju Jugoslovenskim Zeljeznicama [*Decree on the Organization, Operation, and Management of Yugoslav Railroads*] (YU)

UK............. Acetic Acid (RU)

UK............. Administrative Committee (BU)

UK............. Command Control [*Computers*] (RU)

UK............. Compounding Device (RU)

UK............. Criminal Code (RU)

UK............. Institution's Trade Union Committee (BU)

UK............. Percussive Contact (RU)

UK............. Personnel Administration (RU)

UK............. Stowing Crane, Stacking Crane (RU)

UK............. Training Center (RU)

UK............. Training Ship (RU)

UK............. Ugostiteljska Komora [*Chamber of Hotel and Catering Trade*] (YU)

UK............. Uitvoerende Komitee [*Executive Committee*] [*Afrikaans*]

uk .... Ukonczono [*Finished*] (POL)

UK............. Unabkoemmlich [*Reserved*] [*Military*] [*German*]

UK............. United Kingdom (EECI)

UK............. Universita Karlova [*Charles University*] (CZ)

UK............. Universiteit van Kaapstad [*University of Cape Town*] [*Afrikaans*]

UK............. Universiti Kebangsaan [*National University*] [*Malaysia*] (ML)

UK............. Universitni Knihovna [*University Library*] [*Prague*] (CZ)

UK............. University of Kalyani [*India*] (DSCA)

UK............. Univerzalna Klasifikacija [*Universal Classification*] (YU)

UK............. Univerzitetni Komite [*University Committee*] (YU)

UK............. Urzad Konserwatorski [*Administration for Preservation*] [*Of monuments, works of art, etc.*] (POL)

UK............. Ustredni Knihovna [*Central Library*] (CZ)

uk .... Uzletszeru Kejelges [*Prostitution*] (HU)

UKA........... Training Set of Aerial Photographs (RU)

UKA........... United Khmer Airlines [*Cambodia*] (CL)

UKAI .... Kenya Agriculture Institute

UKAI .... Ukambani Agricultural Institute

UKB .... Core Drilling Unit (RU)

UKB .... Samenwerkingsverband van de Universiteits- en Hogeschoolbibliotheken en de Koninklijke Bibliotheek [*Netherlands*] (SLS)

UKB .... Universitni Knihovna v Brne [*University Library in Brno*] (CZ)

UKB .... Unvaniezh Kevredel Breizh [*Federalist Union of Brittany - FUB*] [*France*] (EAIO)

UKB .... Urkutatasi Kormanybizottsag [*Government Committee on Space Research*] (HU)

UKBB .... Kiev/Borispol [*Former USSR*] [*ICAO location identifier*] (ICLI)

UKCG........ Udruzenje Knjizevnika Crne Gore [*Association of Writers of Montenegro*] (YU)

UKCh........ Pure Acetic Acid (RU)

UKChV ...... Ustav Kozeluzstva a Chemie Vody [*Institute of Tanning and Hydrochemistry*] (CZ)

UK/Cont(BH) ... United Kingdom or Continent (Bordeaux-Hamburg) [*Shipping*] (DS)

UK/Cont(GH) ... United Kingdom or Continent (Gibraltar-Hamburg) [*Shipping*] (DS)

UK/Cont(HH) ... United Kingdom or Continent (Havre-Hamburg) [*Shipping*] (DS)

UKCS........ Union of Kenya Civil Servants

UKCTS...... United Kingdom China Travel Service

UKD.......... Universiteli Kadinlar Dernegi [*University Women's Association*] (TU)

UkDP........ Ukase on State Enterprises (BU)

UKEC .... Usines Khmeres de Confection et de Tissage [*Cambodian Mills for Ready-to-Wear Clothing and Woven Textiles*] (CL)

UKF .... Ultrakrotkie Fale [*Ultrashort Waves*] [*Poland*]

UKF .... Unie van Kunstmestfabrieken BV [*Netherlands*]

UKFF........ Simferopol [*Former USSR*] [*ICAO location identifier*] (ICLI)

UKGB .... Administration of the State Security Committee (RU)

UKGB .... Plenipotentiary of the State Security Committee (RU)

UKGVF ..... Training Center of the Civil Air Fleet (RU)

UKh.......... Ubiquinone (RU)

UKH .... Ugostiteljska Komora Hrvatske [*Chamber of Hotel and Catering Trade of Croatia*] (YU)

UKh .... Universal Chromathermograph (RU)

UKHAD .... United Kingdom and Havre, Antwerp, and Dunkirk [*Shipping*] (DS)

UKHE........ Petrovskoye [*Former USSR*] [*ICAO location identifier*] (ICLI)

UKHH .... United Kingdom and Havre-Hamburg [*Shipping*] (DS)

UKhIN....... Scientific Research Institute of Coal Chemistry (RU)

UK HlmPrahy ... Ustredni Knihovna Hlavniho Mesta Prahy [*Central Library of the Capital Prague*] (CZ)

UKhLU...... Administration of Self-Supporting Medical Institutions (RU)

UKhR........ Chemical Equilibrium Equation (RU)

Ukhtizhemlag ... Ukhta-Izhma Corrective Labor Camp (RU)

UKI .... Ulastirma Koordinasyonu Idaresi [*Communications Coordination Administration*] [*of Communications Ministry*] (TU)

UKID .... Angular Ion Diffusion Coefficient (RU)

UKII.......... Kishinev [*Former USSR*] [*ICAO location identifier*] (ICLI)

UKIS .... Ukrainian Complex Scientific Research Institute of Structures (RU)

UKIZh .... Ukrainian Communist Institute of Journalism (RU)

UKK .... Criminal Cassation Collegium of the Supreme Court (RU)

UKK .... Ulastirma Koordinasyon Kurulu [*Communications Coordination Committee*] [*In Public Works Ministry*] (TU)

UKK .... Ural-Kuznetsk Kombinat (RU)

UKK .... Ustredna Katolicka Kancelaria [*Central Catholic Bureau*] (CZ)

UKK .... Ustredni Kulturni Komise [*Central Cultural Commission*] (CZ)

UKKh......... Open-Pit Administration (RU)

UKKK....... Kiev/Zhulyany [*Former USSR*] [*ICAO location identifier*] (ICLI)

UKKS .... Semyenovka [*Former USSR*] [*ICAO location identifier*] (ICLI)

UKLK .... Ustredni Komise Lidove Kontroly [*Central Commission of People's Control*] (CZ)

UKLKS...... Ustredni Komise Lidove Kontroly a Statistiky [*Central Commission of People's Control and Statistics*] (CZ)

UKLL........ Lvov [*Former USSR*] [*ICAO location identifier*] (ICLI)

UKM.......... Administration of Cable Trunk Lines (RU)

UKM.......... General-Purpose Kitchen Machine (RU)

UKM.......... Ukrainian Crystalline Massif (RU)

UKm.......... Umni Kmetovalec [*Prudent Farmer*] [*A periodical*] (YU)

UKM.......... Universiti Kebangsaan Malaysia [*National University of Malaysia*] (EAS)

UKM......... Ustredni Komise Mladeze [*Central Youth Commission*] (CZ)
UKN........... Consolidated Structural Norms (RU)
UKN........... Ustrzyckie Kopalnictwo Naftowe [*Ustrzyki Oil Wells*] (POL)
UKNCIAWPRC ... International Water Quality Association [*British*] (EAIO)
UKNIALMI ... Ukrainian Scientific Research Institute of Conservational Afforestation (RU)
UKNS .... Ustredni Komise Narodni Souteze [*Central Committee for National Competition*] (CZ)
U Ko.......... Univerzita Komenskeho [*Comenius University*] [*Bratislava*] (CZ)
UKO .... Unverhofft Kommt Oft [*The Unexpected Often Happens*] [*Motto of Franz, Duke of Pomerania (1577-1620)*]
UKOB........ Ugyvedi Kamarak Orszagos Bizottsaga [*National Board of the Bar Association*] (HU)
UKOL........ Universitni Knihovna, Olomouc [*Olomouc University Library*] (CZ)
ukoncz........ Ukonczono [*Finished*] (POL)
UKOO .... Odessa/Tsentralny [*Former USSR*] [*ICAO location identifier*] (ICLI)
UKOR........ Uraanverrykingskorporasie van Suid-Afrika Beperk [*South Africa*] (AA)
UKORN..... Ukrains'kij Katolic'kij Oseredok Religijnogo Navcannja
UKOS .... Uredba o Kreditima za Obrtna Sredstva i Drugim Kratkorocnim Kreditima [*Decree on Credits for Current Assets and Other Short-Term Credits*] (YU)
UKOVS ..... Universiteitskollege van die Oranje-Vrystaat [*Afrikaans*]
UKP........... Administration of Municipal Establishments (RU)
UKP........... Edible Acetic Acid (RU)
UKP........... Training and Consultation Post [*Civil aviation*] (RU)
UKP........... Ukrainian Communist Party (RU)
UKP........... Ukrajna Kommunista Partja [*Ukrainian Communist Party*] (HU)
UKP........... United Kurdish Party [*Iran*] [*Political party*]
UKPK .... Ustredni Kulturne-Propagacni Komise [*Central Commission of Culture and Propaganda*] (CZ)
UKPL........ Ustredni Knihovna Patentove Literatury [*Central Library of Literature on Patents*] (CZ)
UKPM .... Ulastirma Koordinasyon Proje Merkezi [*Communications Coordination Plans Center*] [*In Public Works Ministry*] (TU)
UKPO........ Ustredni Kulturne-Propagacni Oddeleni [*Central Department of Culture and Propaganda (of the Revolutionary Trade Union Movement)*] (CZ)
UKR........... Air Ukraine [*ICAO designator*] (FAAC)
Ukr............. Fortification [*Topography*] (RU)
Ukr............. Ukrainian (RU)
UKR........... Ukrainian Soviet Socialist Republic [*ISO three-letter standard code*] (CNC)
UKR........... Ukrainian SSR [*ANSI three-letter standard code*] (CNC)
UKR........... Ustredna Kupelna Rada [*Central Council of Health Resorts*] (CZ)
UKR........... Ustredni Knihovnicka Rada [*Central Library Council*] (CZ)
UKRDORTRANSNII ... Ukrainian Road Transportation Scientific Research Institute (RU)
ukrepl........ Fortification [*Topography*] (RU)
UKRGEOMIN ... Ukrainian Branch of the Scientific Research Institute of Geology and Mineralogy (RU)
UkrGIDEP ... Ukrainian Branch of the All-Union State Planning Institute Gidroenergoproyekt [*Planning hydroelectric power plants*] (RU)
UkrGIPKh ... Ukrainian State Institute of Applied Chemistry (RU)
Ukrgiprodortrans ... Ukrainian State Institute for the Planning of Roads and Transportation (RU)
Ukrgipromash ... Ukrainian State Planning and Design Institute of Machinery Manufacture (RU)
Ukrgipromesttoplivprom ... Ukrainian Institute for the Planning of Local and Fuel Industries (RU)
Ukrgiproprod ... Ukrainian State Institute for the Planning of Food Establishments (RU)
Ukrgiproprom ... Ukrainian Institute for the Planning of Industry (RU)
Ukrgiprosel'elektro ... Ukrainian State Institute for the Planning of Rural Electrification (RU)
Ukrgiprosel'khoz ... Ukrainian State Planning Institute of Rural and Agricultural Construction (RU)
Ukrgiprosel'stroy ... Ukrainian State Institute for the Planning of Rural and Kolkhoz Construction (RU)
Ukrgiprostanok ... Ukrainian State Planning Institute of the Machine Tool Industry (RU)
Ukrgiprostroymaterialy ... Ukrainian Institute for the Planning of Production of Building Materials (RU)
Ukrgiprotsvetmet ... Ukrainian State Planning Institute of Nonferrous Metallurgy (RU)
Ukrgiprovodkhoz ... Ukrainian State Institute for the Planning of Water Management Structures and Rural Electric Power Plants (RU)
Ukrglavneftesbyt ... Ukrainian Branch of the Main Administration for the Marketing of Petroleum (RU)

Ukrgostekhizdat ... Ukrainian State Publishing House of Technical Literature (RU)
UkrIEV...... Ukrainian Scientific Research Institute of Experimental Veterinary Science (RU)
Ukrinstoplivo ... Ukrainian Scientific Research Institute of Local Fuels (RU)
UKRIOK ... Ukrainian Scientific Research Institute of Refractory and Acid-Resistant Materials (RU)
UKRIPKh ... Ukrainian Institute of Applied Chemistry (RU)
UKRK .... Ustredni Kontrolni a Revisni Komise [*Central Control and Audit Commission (of the Communist Party of Czechoslovakia)*] (CZ)
Ukrkabel'... Ukrainian Cable Plant (RU)
Ukrkhimprom ... Main Administration of the Chemical Industry of the UkrSSR (RU)
Ukrmedgiz ... State Medical Publishing House of the Ukrainian SSR (RU)
UKRMEKhANOBR ... Ukrainian Branch of the Scientific Research Institute for the Mechanical Processing of Minerals (RU)
Ukrmuzradioprom ... Main Administration of the Music and Radio Industries of the UkrSSR (RU)
Ukrneft' ..... Association of the Ukrainian Petroleum Industry (RU)
UkrNIGMI ... Ukrainian Scientific Research Hydrometeorological Institute (RU)
UkrNIGRI ... Ukrainian Scientific Research Institute of Geological Exploration (RU)
UkrNII ...... Ukrainian Scientific Research Institute (RU)
UkrNIIB .... Ukrainian Scientific Research Institute of Paper (RU)
UkrNIIGiM ... Ukrainian Scientific Research Institute of Hydraulic Engineering and Reclamation (RU)
UkrNIIKP ... Ukrainian Scientific Research Institute of the Leather and Footwear Industry (RU)
UKRNIIMASh ... Ukrainian Scientific Research Institute of Metalworking and Chemical Machinery Manufacture (RU)
UkrNIImesttopprom ... Ukrainian Scientific Research Institute of Local and Fuel Industries (RU)
UkrNIIMOD ... Ukrainian Scientific Research Institute for the Mechanical Processing of Lumber (RU)
UkrNIIMP ... Ukrainian Scientific Research Institute of the Oil and Fats Industries (RU)
UkrNIImyasomolprom ... Ukrainian Scientific Research Institute of the Meat and Dairy Industry (RU)
UkrNIIO ... Ukrainian Scientific Research Institute of Refractories (RU)
UkrNIIOMShS ... Ukrainian Scientific Research Institute for the Organization and Mechanization of Mine Construction (RU)
UkrNIIPlastmass ... Ukrainian Scientific Research Institute of Plastics (RU)
UkrNIIProyekt ... State Scientific Research and Planning Institute of Coal, Ore, Petroleum, and Gas Industries of the Ukrainian SSR (RU)
UkrNIIS .... Ukrainian Scientific Research Institute of Construction (RU)
UkrNIIS .... Ukrainian Scientific Research Institute of Structures (RU)
UkrNIISKhOM ... Ukrainian Scientific Research Institute of Agricultural Machinery (RU)
UkrNIISol' ... Ukrainian Scientific Research Institute of the Salt Industry (RU)
UkrNIITP ... Ukrainian Scientific Research Institute of the Textile Industry (RU)
UkrNIIZh ... Ukrainian Scientific Research Institute of Livestock Breeding (RU)
UkrNIKhI ... Ukrainian Scientific Research Institute of Cotton Growing and Irrigation Farming (RU)
UKRNIKhIM ... Ukrainian Scientific Research Chemical Institute (RU)
UkrNITI.... Ukrainian Scientific Research Institute of Pipes (RU)
UKRNITI.. Ukrainian Scientific Research Textile Institute (RU)
UkrNITO .. Ukrainian Branch of the All-Union Scientific, Engineering, and Technical Society (RU)
UkrNITO .. Ukrainian Scientific, Engineering, and Technical Society (RU)
UkrNIZ ..... Ukrainian Scientific Research Institute of Grain and Grain Products (RU)
UkrNTO.... Ukrainian Republic Administration of the Scientific and Technical Society (RU)
UKROP ..... Ukrainian Society of Pathologists (RU)
Ukrpromsovet ... Ukrainian Council of Producers' Cooperatives (RU)
UkrROSTA ... Ukrainian Branch of the Russian News Agency (RU)
Ukrsel'mash ... Main Administration of Agricultural Machinery Manufacture of the UkrSSR (RU)
Ukrtrestsel'mash ... Ukrainian Trust of Agricultural Machinery (RU)
Ukrtsentrarkhiv ... Central Administration of Archives of the Ukrainian SSR (RU)
UkrTsIETIN ... Ukrainian Central Scientific Research Institute for Determination of Disability and Organization of Work for Disabled Persons (RU)
UkrVODGEO ... Ukrainian Scientific Research Institute of Water Supply, Sewer Systems, Hydraulic Engineering Structures, and Engineering Hydrogeology (RU)
Ukrvozdukhput' ... Ukrainian Voluntary Society of the Air Fleet (RU)
UKS .... Administration of Capital Construction (RU)
UKS .... Guard Duty Regulations (RU)

UKS .... Udruzenje Knjizevnika Srbije [*Association of Writers of Serbia*] (YU)

UKS .... Ustredna Karita na Slovensku [*Central Office of the Charity Society in Slovakia*] (CZ)

UKSA .... United Kingdom Settlers' Association [*Australia*]

UKSATA ... United Kingdom-South Africa Trade Association

UKSBiH .... Udruzenje Katolickih Svecenika Bosne i Hercegovine [*Association of Catholic Priests of Bosnia and Hercegovina*] (YU)

UKShch ..... Ukrainian Crystalline Shield (RU)

uks k .... Acetic Acid (RU)

UKSKhU ... Ukrainian Communist Agricultural University Imeni Artem (RU)

UKSS .... Universal Switchboard for Station's Service Traffic (RU)

UKT .... Ultrakratki Talasi [*Ultrashort Wave*] (YU)

UKTEK ..... Junction Office for Container Shipments and Transportation and Forwarding Operations (RU)

UKTZ .... Ustredni Klub Techniku a Zlepsovatelu [*Central Club of Technicians and Innovators*] (CZ)

UKU .... Coding and Controlling Device (RU)

UK-U .... Improved Compounding Device (RU)

UKU .... Nuku [*Papua New Guinea*] [*Airport symbol*] (OAG)

UKU .... Ukrains'kii Katolic'kij Universitet

UKU .... Ural Communist University Imeni V. I. Lenin (RU)

UKUTA ..... Chama Cha Usanyu wa Kiswahili na Ushairi [*Organization for the Writing of Swahili and Poetry*] [*Tanzania*] (AF)

UKUZ .... Administration of Personnel and Educational Institutions (RU)

UKV .... Ultrakratka Vlna [*Ultrashort Wave*] (CZ)

UKV .... Ultrashort-Wave (RU)

UKV .... Ultrashort-Wave Radio Station (RU)

UKV .... Ultrashort Waves (BU)

UKV-ChM ... Ultrashort Waves with Frequency Modulation (RU)

UKVT .... Statutes of the Coastal Water Transportation System (BU)

UKW .... Ultrakurzwelle [*Ultrashort Wave, Very High Frequency*] [*German*] (WEN)

UKW .... Ultrakurzwellenfunk [*Ultrashort-Wave Radio*] [*German*] (EG)

UKWAL .... United Kingdom/West Africa Lines [*Shipping company*] [*Nigeria*] (AF)

UKWE .... Ultrakurzwellenempfaenger [*Very-High-Frequency Receiver*] [*German*]

UKWVorsatzgeraet ... Ultrakurzwellenvorsatzgeraet [*Ultrashort-Wave Converter*] [*German*] (EG)

UKZhD ...... Narrow-Gauge Railway (RU)

UKZKO ..... Correspondence Training Center of Municipal Education (RU)

UKZUZ ...... Ustredni Kontrolni a Zkusebni Ustav Zemedelsky [*Central Agricultural Control and Testing Institute*] (CZ)

UL .... Lansa, SRL [*Honduras*] [*ICAO designator*] (ICDA)

UL .... Suomen Ulkomaankauppaliitto [*Finnish Foreign Trade Assocation*] [*Finland*] (EAIO)

u-l .... Teacher (BU)

UL .... Uitvoerend Land [*Benelux*] (BAS)

ul .... Ulica [*Street*] [*Serbo Croatian*] (CED)

ul .... Ulice [*Street*] (CZ)

ul .... Ulita [*Street*] [*Romanian*]

ul .... Ulitsa [*Street*] [*Bulgarian*]

ul .... Ulitsa [*Street*] [*Russian*]

UL .... Union Liberal [*Liberal Union*] [*Spain*] [*Political party*] (PPW)

UL .... United Left [*Peru*] [*Political party*]

UL .... Universala Ligo [*Defunct*] (EA)

UL .... Universal League (EAIO)

UL .... Uniwersytet Lodzki [*Lodz University*] (POL)

UL .... Uniwersytet Lubelski [*Lublin University*] (POL)

ul .... Unloeslich [*Insoluble*] [*German*]

UL .... Uprava za Lov [*Administration for Hunting*] (YU)

Ul .... Uredni List Republiky Ceskoslovenske [*Official Gazette of the Czechoslovak Republic*] (CZ)

Ul .... Uudenmaan Laani [*Finland*]

ul .... Uutta Lukua [*Finland*]

ULA .... San Julian [*Argentina*] [*Airport symbol*] (OAG)

ULA .... Uganda Library Association (SLS)

ula .... Ultralyhytaalto [*Finland*]

ULA .... Union der Leitenden Angestellten [*Union of Management Personnel*] (EG)

ULA .... Universidad de Los Andes [*Los Andes University*] [*Venezuela*] (LA)

ULA .... Urban Land Authority [*Victoria, Australia*]

ULA .... Zuliana de Aviacion [*Venezuela*] [*ICAO designator*] (FAAC)

ULAAA .... Ultra Light Aircraft Association of Australia

ULAC .... Union Latinoamericana de Ciegos [*Latin American Blind Union - LABU*] [*Montevideo, Uruguay*] (EAIO)

ULAEY ...... Union of Latin American Ecumenical Youth (EA)

ULAJE ...... Union Latinoamericana de Juventudes Ecumenicas [*Union of Latin American Ecumenical Youth - ULAEY*] (EAIO)

ULAJE ...... Union Latinoamericana de Juventud Evangelica [*Union of Latin American Evangelical Youth*] [*Montevideo, Uruguay*] (LAA)

ULAK .... Kotlas [*Former USSR*] [*ICAO location identifier*] (ICLI)

ULAPC ...... Union Latinoamericana de Prensa Catolica [*Latin American Catholic Press Union*] (LA)

ULAS .... Ulastirma ve Nakliye Subesi [*Communications and Transport Branch*] [*A subsidiary of ETI in the TFSC Turkish Cypriot*] (TU)

Ulas-Is .... Turkiye Deniz Tasitmacligi Isci Sendikalari Federasyonu [*Turkish Seamen's Federation*] (TU)

Ulas-Is .... Turkiye Ulastirma Iscileri Sendikasi [*Turkish Communications Workers Union*] (TU)

ULAST ...... Union Latinoamericana de Sociedades de Tisiologia [*Latin American Union of Societies of Phthisiology*] [*Montevideo, Uruguay*] (LAA)

ULB .... Union Laitiere de Bamako

ULB .... Universite Libre de Bruxelles [*Free University of Brussels*] [*Belgium*] (WER)

ULBA .... Universal Love and Brotherhood Association [*Kyoto, Japan*] (EAIO)

ULC .... Philippines Civil Liberties Union (PD)

ULC .... Uganda Labour Congress

ULC .... Union de la Lutte Communiste [*Burkina Faso*] [*Political party*] (EY)

ULC .... United Labor Congress [*Nigeria*] (AF)

ULC .... Universite Libre du Congo

ULC .... University Librarians' Committee [*Australia*]

ULCN .... United Labor Congress of Nigeria

ULCRA ...... Urban Land (Ceiling and Regulation) Act [*India*] (ECON)

ULD .... Union pour la Liberte et le Developpement [*Benin*] [*Political party*] (EY)

ULD .... Ustredni Loutkove Divadlo [*Central Puppet Theater*] (CZ)

ULDF .... United Left Democratic Front [*India*] [*Political party*] (PPW)

ULDO .... Unione della Legion d'Oro [*Italian*] (SLS)

ULDS .... Union Liberale-Democratique Suisse [*Liberal Democratic Union of Switzerland*] [*Political party*] (PPE)

ULDS .... Ustredni Letecka Dopravni Sprava [*Central Air Transport Directorate*] (CZ)

ULE .... Sule [*Papua New Guinea*] [*Airport symbol*] (OAG)

ULEAS ...... Union List of East Asian Serials [*Australia*]

ULF .... United Labour Front [*Trinidad and Tobago*] (PD)

ULF .... United Left Front [*Nepal*] [*Political party*] (EY)

ULF .... Universitaetslaerarforbundet [*University Instructors Association*] [*Sweden*] (SLS)

ULFA .... United Liberation Front of Assam [*India*] [*Political party*] (ECON)

ULFIS .... University Libraries Free Information Service [*Australia*]

ULFWS ...... United Liberation Front for Western Somalia [*Ethiopia*] (AF)

ULGS .... Unified Local Government Service

ULGTS ...... Administration of the Leningrad City Telephone Network (RU)

ULGWP .... United Lumber and General Workers of the Philippines (EY)

ULI .... Ural Forestry-Engineering Institute (RU)

ULI .... Varnished Measuring Carbon [*Resistor*] (RU)

ULIDAT .... Umweltliteraturedatenbank [*Data Bank for Environmental Literature*] [*Deutsches Umweltbundesamt*] [*Germany*] [*Information service or system*] (CRD)

ULK .... Ustredna Lekarska Kniznica [*Central Medical Library*] [*Bratislava*] (CZ)

ULK .... Ustredni Lidova Knihovna [*Central People's Library*] (CZ)

ULKRS ...... University Lake Kariba Research Station [*University of Zimbabwe*] [*Research center*] (EAS)

ULKU ES .. Ulkucu Esnaf Dernegi [*Idealist Tradesmen's Association*] (TU)

ULKUM .... Ulkucu Memurlar Dernegi [*Idealist Employees (Officials) Organization*] [*Ankara*] (TU)

Ulku-Tek ... Ulkucu Teknik Elemanlar Dernegi [*Idealist Technical Elements (Workers) Organization*] (TU)

ULLL .... Leningrad/Pulkovo [*Former USSR*] [*ICAO location identifier*] (ICLI)

ULMLT ..... Union pour la Lutte Marxiste-Leniniste Tunisien [*Union for the Tunisian Marxist-Leninist Struggle*] (AF)

ULN .... Ulan Bator [*Mongolia*] [*Airport symbol*] (OAG)

ULN .... Union Liberal Nacionalista [*Guatemala*] (LAA)

ULO .... Union of Burma Labour Organizations

ULO .... United Left Opposition [*Trinidadian and Tobagan*] (LA)

ULOL .... Velikiye Luki [*Former USSR*] [*ICAO location identifier*] (ICLI)

ULP .... Quilpie [*Australia*] [*Airport symbol*] (OAG)

ULP .... Utilitaire Logique Processor [*Programming language*] [*Computer science*] [*French*]

ULPAR ...... Ukase on Internal Passports and Address Registration of Citizens of the Bulgarian People's Republic (BU)

ULQ .... Tulua [*Colombia*] [*Airport symbol*] (OAG)

ULRC .... United Liberia Rubber Corporation

ULS .... False Signal Level (RU)

ULS .... Ulysses, KS [*Location identifier*] [*FAA*]

ULS .... Ustredni Letecky Sklad [*Central Aviation Depot*] (CZ)

ULSA .... Universidad la Salle [*La Salle University*] [*Mexico*] [*Research center*] (ERC)

UlsB .... Ulastirma Bakanligi [*Ministry of Communications*] (TU)

ULSMSv ... Uredni Likvidacni Sprava pri Ministerstvu Stavebnictvi [*Administrative Liquidation Office of the Ministry of Construction*]   (CZ)
ULSU .... University of Liberia Student Union
ult .... Ultimo [*Last*] [*Spanish*]
ult .... Ultimo [*Last*] [*Italian*]
ULT .... Ustredi Lidove Tvorivosti [*Folk Arts Center*]   (CZ)
ULTAB...... Uniao dos Lavradores e Trabalhadores Agricolas do Brasil [*Union of Farmers and Farm Workers of Brazil*]   (LA)
ULTI......... Ural Forestry-Engineering Institute   (RU)
ULTRAHUILCA ... Union de Trabajadores del Huila y Caqueta [*Neiva*]   (COL)
ULTT........ Tallin [*Former USSR*] [*ICAO location identifier*]   (ICLI)
ULU.......... Gulu [*Uganda*] [*Airport symbol*]   (OAG)
ULUBiH.... Udruzenje Likovnih Umjetnika Bosne i Hercegovine [*Representational Artists' Association of Bosnia and Hercegovina*]   (YU)
ULUCG ..... Udruzenje Likovnih Umjetnika Crne Gore [*Representational Artists' Association of Montenegro*]   (YU)
uluchsh....... Improved   (RU)
ULUH........ Udruzenje Likovnih Umjetnika Hrvatske [*Representational Artists' Association of Croatia*]   (YU)
ULUS .... Udruzenje Likovnih Umetnika Srbije [*Representational Artists' Association of Serbia*]   (YU)
ULUV .... Ustredi Lidoveho Umeni Vytvarneho [*Creative Folk Arts Center*]   (CZ)
ULUV .... Ustredi Lidove Umelecke Vyroby [*Center for Folk Art*]   (CZ)
ULVB .... Union Ladins Val Badia [*Italian*]   (SLS)
ULWA .... Union of Latin Writers and Artists [*Paris, France*]   (EAIO)
ULWB ...... Belozyorsk [*Former USSR*] [*ICAO location identifier*]   (ICLI)
ULWT .... Totma [*Former USSR*] [*ICAO location identifier*]   (ICLI)
ULWW ...... Vologda [*Former USSR*] [*ICAO location identifier*]   (ICLI)
ULY .... Ulyanovsk [*Former USSR*] [*Airport symbol*]   (OAG)
ULYSSES ... University Library System for the Satisfaction of Enquiries [*Australia*]
ULZ .... Ultrasonic Delay Line   (RU)
ULZ .... Ustav Leteckeho Zdravotnictvi [*Air Force Medical Institute*]   (CZ)
UM .... Controlling Device, Controller   (RU)
um .... Deceased   (RU)
UM .... Mauritanian Ouguiya   (AF)
UM .... Microphone Amplifier   (RU)
UM .... Militia Administration   (RU)
UM .... Power Amplifier   (RU)
um .... Sea Level   (RU)
UM .... Uchitelska Misul [*Teacher's Thought*] [*A periodical*]   (BU)
uM............. Ueber dem Meeresspiegel [*Above Sea Level*] [*German*]
um .... Ugymint [*Namely, That Is*]   (HU)
UM .... Ujjaepitesi Miniszterium/Miniszter [*Ministry/Minister of Reconstruction*]   (HU)
U/M........... Umlaufungen pro Minute [*Revolutions per Minute*] [*German*]
UM .... Umot Me'uhadot [*United Nations*] [*Hebrew*]
UM .... Unidad Militar [*Military Unit*] [*Cuba*]   (LA)
UM .... Uninflated Movement [*Australia*]
UM .... Unio Mallorquina [*Majorcan Union*] [*Political party*]   (PPW)
UM .... Unitas Malacologica [*An association*] [*Netherlands*]   (EAIO)
UM .... United States Minor Outlying Islands [*ANSI two-letter standard code*]   (CNC)
UM .... Universite de Madagascar
UM .... Universiti Malaya [*Malaysia*]   (PDAA)
uM............. Unter dem Meeresspiegel [*Below Sea Level*] [*German*]   (GCA)
UM .... Uttoro Mozgalom [*Pioneer Movement*]   (HU)
UMA......... Mechanization and Motor Transportation Administration   (BU)
UMA......... Uniao das Mulheres da Angola
UMA......... Union de Mujeres Americanas [*Union of American Women*] [*Ecuador*]   (LA)
UMA......... Union de Mujeres de la Argentina [*Union of Argentine Women*]   (LA)
UMA......... Union Marocaine de l'Agriculture [*Morocco*]
UMA......... Union Matematica Argentina   (EAIO)
UMA......... Union Mathematique Africaine [*African Mathematical Union - AMU*]   (EA)
UMA......... Union Medicale Algerienne [*Algerian Medical Union*]   (AF)
UMA......... Union Medicale Arabe [*Arab Medical Union*]   (EAIO)
UMA......... Union Mondiale des Aveugles [*World Blind Union - WBU*]   (EA)
UMA......... UNISA [*University of South Africa*] Medieval Association [*South Africa*]   (AA)
UMAA....... University of Melbourne Alumni Association [*Australia*]
UMAC....... Union Marocaine des Associations de Chantiers
UMAC....... Union Mediterraneenne Anticommuniste
UMAEC .... Union Monetaire de l'Afrique Equatoriale et du Cameroun
UMAH ...... Uyusmazlik Mahkemesi [*Court of Disagreement (Discord)*]   (TU)

UMAIA ..... Uzina Mecanica a Agriculturii si Industriei Alimentare [*Mechanical Plant for Agriculture and the Food Industry*]   (RO)
UMALCO ... Umm Al-Qaiwain Aluminium Co. [*United Arab Emirates*]
UMATI ..... Tanzania Family Planning Association
UMAVALCA ... Union de Maestros del Valle del Cauca [*Colombia*]   (COL)
UMB......... Union Marocaine de Banques
UMB......... Union Medicale Balkanique [*Balkan Medical Union*]   (EAIO)
UMB......... Union Mondiale de Billard [*World Billiards Union - WBU*] [*Switzerland*]
UMB......... United Mizrahi Bank Ltd. [*Israel*]
UMB......... Uzine e Mekanikes Bujqesore [*Albanian*]
UMBC ...... United Malayan Banking Corp.
UMBC ...... United Middle Belt Congress [*Nigeria*]
Umbr.......... Umbrian [*Language, culture, etc.*]
UMC......... Union de Mineros de Colombia [*Union of Miners of Colombia*]   (LA)
UMC......... Union Malienne de Constructions
UMC......... United Microelectronics Corp. [*Taiwan*]
UMC......... Uniwersytet Marii Curie-Sklodowskiej (w Lublinie) [*Maria Curie-Sklodowska University (in Lublin)*] [*Poland*]
UMCA...... Union Monetaria Centroamericana [*Central American Monetary Union*] [*El Salvador*]   (LAA)
UMCA...... Universities Mission to Central Africa [*Later, USPG*] [*British*]
UMCB ...... United Missions in the Copperbelt
UMCh....... Intermediate Frequency Amplifier   (BU)
UMCh....... Union de Mujeres de Chile [*Women's Union of Chile*]   (LA)
UMCIA ..... Union Marocaine de l'Industrie, du Commerce, et de l'Artisanat
UMCO...... Manufacturas Metalicas Umco e Ica SA [*Colombia*]   (COL)
UMCS .... Uniwersytet Marii Curie-Sklodowskiej [*Maria Curie-Sklodowska University*]   (POL)
UMD .... Motherhood and Childhood Administration   (BU)
UMD .... Training Mine Detonator   (RU)
U Md......... Umumi Mudur [*Director General*]   (TU)
UMD .... Union de Mouvements Democratiques [*Djibouti*] [*Political party*]   (EY)
UMD .... Union de Mujeres Democratas [*Union of Democratic Women*] [*Colorado*]   (LA)
UMD .... Union Militar Democratica [*Military Democratic Union*] [*Spanish*]   (WER)
UMD .... Universidad Mundial Dominicana [*Dominican World University*] [*Dominican Republic*]   (LA)
UMDA...... Upper Mazaruni Development Authority [*Guyana*]   (PDAA)
UMDC....... Union Mondiale Democrate Chretienne   (FLAF)
UMDOC.... Ustredni Matice Divadelnich Ochotniku Ceskych [*Federation of Czech Amateur Actors*]   (CZ)
UMDr........ Doktor der Gesamten Heilkunde [*Doctor of General Medicine*] [*German*]
Umdr/M .... Umdrehungen per Minute [*Revolutions per Minute*] [*German*]   (GCA)
UME......... Umea [*Sweden*] [*Airport symbol*]   (OAG)
UME......... Uniao Metropolitana de Estudantes [*Metropolitan Union of Students*] [*Brazil*]   (LA)
UME......... Unitas Malacologica Europea [*European Malacological Union - EMU*] [*Austria*]   (ASF)
UME......... United Medical Enterprises
UME......... Ustredna Mechanisovane Evidence [*Machine Records Center*] [*Prague*]   (CZ)
UMEA...... Uganda Muslim Education Association
UMEA...... Universala Medicina Esperanto Asocio [*Universal Medical Esperanto Association*]   (EAIO)
UMEB ...... Uzina de Masini Electrice Bucuresti [*Bucharest Electrical Machines Plant*]   (RO)
UMEC ...... Union Mondiale des Enseignants Catholiques [*World Union of Catholic Teachers*] [*Rome, Italy*]
UMECO .... Union Mediatrice Congolaise
UMEJ....... Union Mondiale des Etudiants Juifs [*World Union of Jewish Students - WUJS*]   (EAIO)
U Melb ...... University of Melbourne [*Australia*]
UMELCO ... Unofficial Members of the Executive Legislative Council [*Hong Kong*]
UMEMPA ... Union of Middle Eastern and Mediterranean Pediatric Societies [*Greece*]   (EAIO)
UMEMPS ... Union of Middle Eastern and Mediterranean Pediatric Societies [*See also USPMOM*] [*Athens, Greece*]   (EAIO)
UMEMPS ... Union of Middle East Mediterranean Paediatric Societies [*Greek*]   (SLS)
UMEP .... Administration of Local Evacuation Stations   (RU)
UMEWU... United Malayan Estate Workers Union   (ML)
UMEZ .... Ustredi pro Mechanisaci Zemedelstvi [*Center for the Mechanization of Agriculture*]   (CZ)
Umf............ Umfang [*Circumference*] [*German*]   (GCA)
Umf............ Umfassung [*Envelopment*] [*German*]   (GCA)
UMF .... Umformer [*Converter*] [*German*]   (GCA)
UMF .... Uridine Monophosphate   (RU)
UMFA .... United Mineworkers Federation of Australia
umfangr...... Umfangreich [*Comprehensive*] [*German*]

UMFCM ... United Methodist Free Churches' Mission
UMFDC .... Union Mundial de Mujeres Democrata Cristianas [*World Union of Christian Democratic Women*] [*Venezuela*] [*Political party*] (EAIO)
umg .... Umgeaendert [*Converted*] [*German*] (GCA)
Umg .... Umgebung [*Environment*] [*German*]
UMGB....... Administration of the Ministry of State Security (RU)
umgearb ..... Umgearbeitet [*Revised*] [*Publishing*] [*German*]
UMGSB ..... Ukrainian Local Geodetic Information Office (RU)
UMGTS .... Administration of the Moscow City Telephone Network (RU)
UMH .... Union de Mujeres Hondurenas [*Union of Honduran Women*] (LA)
UMHK ...... Union Miniere du Haut Katanga
Umhuell ..... Umhuellung [*Casing, Envelope*] [*German*] (GCA)
UMI........... Union de Melillenses Independientes [*Spanish North Africa*] [*Political party*] (MENA)
UMI........... Unione Matematica Italiana [*Italian Mathematical Association*] (SLS)
UMI........... Unione Micologica Italiana [*Italian*] (SLS)
UMI........... Union Mathematique Internationale [*International Mathematical Union - IMU*] (EAIO)
UMI........... United States Minor Outlying Islands [*ANSI three-letter standard code*] (CNC)
umid .... Umidita [*Humidity*] [*Italian*]
UMIF .... Uluslararasi Gida ve Muskirat Iscileri Birlikleri Federasyonu [*International Federation of Food and Intoxicants Workers Union*] (TU)
UMII .... Vitebsk [*Former USSR*] [*ICAO location identifier*] (ICLI)
UMIMA .... Union Malienne d'Industries Maritimes
UMIMA .... Union Mauritanienne d'Industries Maritimes
U/min .... Umdrehungen in der Minute [*Revolutions per Minute*] [*German*] (WEN)
UMK......... Amplification of Modulated Oscillations (RU)
UMK......... Ugyvedi Munkakozosseg [*Working Association of Lawyers*] (HU)
UMK......... Uniwersytet Imienia Mikolaja Kopernika (w Toruniu) [*Nicholas Copernicus University (in Torun)*] [*Poland*]
U Mk .... Unter dem Mikroskop [*Under the Microscope*] [*German*] (GCA)
UMKAD.... Administration of the Moscow Belt Highway (RU)
Umkr.......... Umkreis [*Surrounding Environment*] [*German*] (GCA)
umkr........... Umkristallisieren [*Recrystallize*] [*German*]
UMKS .... Administration of Trunk Cable Network (RU)
Uml .... Umlauf [*Rotation*] [*German*] (GCA)
Umlad .... Umladung [*Transfer*] [*German*] (GCA)
Umlager ...... Umlagerung [*Rearrangement*] [*German*] (GCA)
Uml/Min .... Umlaufungen pro Minute [*Revolutions per Minute*] [*German*]
UMM .... Directorate for the Mechanization and Motorization of the RKKA (RU)
UMM .... Union del Magisterio de Montevideo [*Montevideo Teachers Union*] [*Uruguay*] (LA)
UMM .... Unione Medica Mediterranea
UMM .... Union Mondiale du Mapam [*World Union of Mapam - WUM*] (EAIO)
UMM .... United Methodist Mission
UMMAN... Ukrains'ka Mogiljans'ko-Mazepins'ka Akademija Nauk
Ummantel.. Ummantelung [*Casing*] [*German*] (GCA)
UMMKS ... Administration of the Moscow Trunk Cable Network (RU)
UMML...... Unione Medicale Mediterranea Latina [*Latin Mediterranean Medical Union - LMMU*] [*Mantua, Italy*] (EAIO)
UMMM..... Minsk/Loshitsa [*Former USSR*] [*ICAO location identifier*] (ICLI)
UMMP...... Local Metallurgical Industry Administration (RU)
UMMR...... Uzina Mecanica de Material Rulant [*Mechanical Plant for Rolling Stock*] (RO)
UMN .... Progress of Mathematical Sciences (RU)
UMN .... Union des Musiciens Nordiques [*Nordic Musicians' Union - NMU*] (EAIO)
UMN .... Union pour la Majorite Nouvelle [*Union for the New Majority*] [*France*] [*Political party*] (PPE)
UMN .... United Mission to Nepal
UMN .... Urban Ministry Network [*Melbourne, Victoria, Australia*]
UMNiR ..... Unified Local Norms and Wages, Unified Local Standards and Costs (RU)
UMNO...... United Malays National Organization [*Malaysia*] [*Political party*]
UMOA ...... Union Monetaire Ouest-Africaine [*West African Monetary Union*] (AF)
UMOF...... Union Maghrebine des Organismes Familiaux [*North African*]
UMOFC .... Union Mondiale des Organisations Feminines Catholiques [*World Union of Catholic Women's Organizations - WUCWO*] [*Canada*]
UMOSEA ... Union Mondiale des Organismes pour la Sauvegarde de l'Enfance et de l'Adolescence
UMOTAP .. Union de Motoristas, Obreros, Tecnicos, y Administrativos Portuarios [*Union of Port Crane Operators, Longshoremen, Technicians, and Managers*] [*Uruguay*] (LA)
UMP.......... Controlled Minefield (RU)

UMP.......... Local Industry Administration (RU)
UMP.......... Uganda Meat Packers Ltd.
UMP.......... Uniao de Mulheres Portuguesas [*Union of Portuguese Women*]
UMP.......... Uninflated Movement Party [*Australia*] [*Political party*] (ADA)
UMP.......... Union of Moderate Parties [*Vanuatua*] [*Political party*] (PPW)
UMPA .... Union de Mujeres Paraguayas [*Union of Paraguayan Women*] (LA)
UMPG ...... United Malayan Pineapple Growers (ML)
UMPLIS ... Informations- und Dokumentationssystem Umwelt [*Environmental Information and Documentation System*] [*Berlin*] [*Information retrieval*]
UMPS....... Union Mondiale des Pioniers de Stockholm [*World Union of Stockholm Pioneers*] (EAIO)
UMPVJNA ... Uprava za Moralno-Politicko Vaspitanje, Jugoslovenska Narodna Armija [*Administration for Moral and Political Education, Yugoslav People's Army*] (YU)
umr............ Deceased (BU)
UMR......... Woomera [*Australia*] [*Airport symbol*] (OAG)
UMRG...... Ergli [*Former USSR*] [*ICAO location identifier*] (ICLI)
UMRJ....... Udruzenje Morskog Ribarstva Jugoslavije [*Association of Marine Fisheries of Yugoslavia*] (YU)
UMRL ...... Union Mondiale des Romains Libres [*World Union of Free Romanians - WUFR*] [*Creteil, France*] (EAIO)
UMRL ...... Upper Murray Regional Library [*Australia*]
UMRR...... Riga/Spilve [*Former USSR*] [*ICAO location identifier*] (ICLI)
UMRW...... Ventspils [*Former USSR*] [*ICAO location identifier*] (ICLI)
UMS......... Council on Educational Methods (BU)
UMS......... Educational Methodological Council (RU)
UMS......... Ucus Malumat Sahrasi [*Flight Information Region*] (TU)
ums............ Umsett [*Translated*] [*Publishing Danish/Norwegian*]
UMS......... Unfederated Malay States [*Malaysia*] (FEA)
UMS......... United Missionary Society
UMS......... Ustav Montovanych Staveb [*Institute of Prefabricated Building Construction*] (CZ)
UMS......... Ustredni Matice Skolska [*Central School Aid Association*] (CZ)
UMSA ...... Unity Movement of South Africa
UMSA ...... Universidad Mayor de San Andres [*Greater University of San Andres*] [*Bolivia*] (LA)
UMSA ...... Uzmanlar Mali Musavirlik ve Sanai Arastirmalar Ltd. Sti. [*Specialists' Financial Counseling and Industrial Research Corp.*] (TU)
Umschl...... Umschlag [*Wrapper*] [*Publishing*] [*German*]
Umschlagt ... Umschlagtitel [*Title on Wrapper*] [*Publishing*] [*German*]
UMSES ..... Universelles Mikroprozessor Software Engineering System [*German*] (ADPT)
Umsetz...... Umsetzung [*Transformation*] [*German*] (GCA)
UMShN..... General-Purpose Control Computer (RU)
UMSKh ..... School of Agricultural Mechanization (RU)
UmSKhI .... Uman' Agricultural Institute (RU)
UMSN ...... Union Mondiale de Ski Nautique [*World Water Ski Union - WWSU*] [*Montreaux, Switzerland*] (EAIO)
UMSR ...... Universal Movement for Scientific Responsibility [*See also MURS*] (EAIO)
UMSS ...... Universidad Mayor de San Simon [*Greater University of San Simon*] [*Bolivia*] (LA)
UMSU ...... University of Malaya Students Union (ML)
UMSWU ... Uganda Mines and Smelter Workers Union (AF)
UMT.......... Bridge Amplifier (RU)
UMT.......... Union Marocaine du Travail [*Moroccan Labor Federation*] [*Casablanca*] (AF)
UMT.......... Union Musulmans Togolaise [*Togolese Moslem Union*] (AF)
UMT.......... United Milk Tasmania Ltd. [*Australia*]
UMT.......... Unutarnja Mrtva Tacka [*Inner Dead Center*] (YU)
UMTA....... Union Marocaine du Travail (Autonome) [*Moroccan Labor Union (Autonomous)*] (AF)
Um-Tab ..... Umrechnungstabelle [*Conversion Table*] [*German*] (GCA)
UMTEO.... Administration for the Installation of Heat and Electric Power Equipment (RU)
UMTI .... Uprava za Mornaricko Tehnicka Istrazivanja [*Administration of Naval Technical Research*] (YU)
UMTS .... Administration of Materials and Equipment Supply (RU)
UMTS .... Machine-Tractor Stations Administration (BU)
UMTS .... Material and Technical Supplies Administration (BU)
UMTSS ..... Administration of Materials and Equipment Supply and Marketing (RU)
UMTU....... Uganda Monarch Traditionalist Unity (AF)
UMU .... Unitas Malacological Union [*Germany*] (DSCA)
UMU .... United Mineworkers' Union
UMUR....... Administration of the Moscow Office of Criminal Investigation (RU)
UMV.......... Umleitungswege-Verzeichnis [*Index of Detours*] (EG)
UMV.......... Union de Mujeres de Vanguardia [*Vanguard Women's Union*] [*Nicaragua*] (LA)
UMV.......... UNISA Middeleeuse Vereniging [*University of South Africa Medieval Association*] (AA)
UMV.......... Universal Wheatstone Bridge (RU)
UMVD....... Administration of the Ministry of Internal Affairs (RU)

UMVF .... Union Mondiale des Voix Francaises [*World Union of French-Speakers - WUFS*] (EAIO)
UMVL .... Administration of International Airlines (RU)
UMW .... United Motor Works [*Malaysia*]
UMWA ...... United Mine Workers' Federation of Australia
Umwandl.... Umwandlung [*Conversion*] [*German*]
UMWSF ... United Methodist Women in Switzerland and in France (EAIO)
UMWW ..... Vilnius [*Former USSR*] [*ICAO location identifier*] (ICLI)
UMYu .... Administration of the Ministry of Justice (RU)
UMZ .... Ustredi pro Mechanisaci Zemedelstvi [*Center for the Mechanization of Agriculture*] (CZ)
UMZ .... Uzbek Metallurgical Plant (RU)
UMZUB .... Magnetic Drum Storage Control (RU)
UMZUL .... Magnetic Tape Storage Control (RU)
UN .... Eastern Airlines [*Airline code*] [*Australia*]
UN .... Leveling Goniometer (RU)
un .... Ugy-Nevezett [*So-Called*] (HU)
UN .... Ujedinjene Nacije [*United Nations*] (YU)
UN .... Uniao Nacional [*National Union*] [*Portuguese*] (WER)
UN .... Union Nacional [*National Union*] [*Spain*] [*Political party*] (PPE)
UN .... Union Navarra [*Union of Navarra*] [*Spanish*] (WER)
un .... Unite [*Unit*] [*French*]
UN .... United Nations (PWGL)
UN .... Universiteit van Natal [*University of Natal*] [*Afrikaans*]
UN .... University of Newcastle [*Australia*]
UN .... Urad pro Normalizaci [*Bureau of Standards*] (CZ)
UN .... Voltage Amplifier (RU)
UNA .... Standard Telephone (RU)
UNA .... Uganda News Agency (AF)
UNA .... Uniao Nacional Angolana [*Angolan National Union*] (AF)
UNA .... Unione Nazionale dell'Avicoltura [*Aviculture Union*] [*Italy*] (EY)
UNA .... Union Nacionalista Argentina [*Argentine Nationalist Union*] (LA)
UNA .... Union Nationale des Agriculteurs [*National Farmers Union*] [*Tunis, Tunisia*] (AF)
UNA .... United Nations Association
UNA .... Unite Nationale Africaine
UNA .... Universair [*Spain*] [*ICAO designator*] (FAAC)
UNA .... Universidad Nacional Agraria [*National Agrarian University*] [*Peru*] (LA)
UNA .... Universitats-Netz Austria [*Austrian University Network*] (TNIG)
UNAA .... United Nations Association of Australia (ADA)
UNAC .... Union Nationale des Artistes Congolais [*National Union of Congolese Artists*] (AF)
UNAC .... United Nations Africa Council
UNAC .... United Nations Association of the Congo (EAIO)
UNAC .... United Native African Church
UNACA ..... Union Nacional de Astronomia y Ciencias Afines [*Spanish*] (SLS)
UNACAFE ... Union Nacional Agricola de Cafeteros [*Mexico*] (DSCA)
UNACAP .. Union des Anciens Eleves des Peres Capucins de l'Ubangi
UNACAST ... United Nations Advisory Committee on the Application of Science and Technology to Development
UNACh ..... Union Nacional Arabe de Chile [*Arab National Union of Chile*] (LA)
UNACHOSIN ... Union Nacional de Choferes Sindicados Independientes [*National Union of Independent Syndicated Drivers*] [*Dominican Republic*] (LA)
UNACI ...... Union Africaine pour le Commerce et l'Industrie en Cote-D'Ivoire
UNACO ..... Union Nationale Congolaise
UNACOMA ... Unione Nazionale Costruttori Macchine Agricole [*Farm Machinery Manufacturers Union*] [*Italy*] (EY)
UNACOOP ... Union Nationale de Cooperatives [*National Cooperatives Union*] [*Cambodia*] (CL)
UNACOOPH ... Union Nacional de Cooperativas Populares de Honduras [*National Union of People's Cooperatives of Honduras*] (LA)
UNACOOPRL ... Union Nacional de Cooperativas [*Costa Rica*] (DSCA)
UNADA ..... United Nations Atomic Development Authority (NUCP)
UNADE ..... Union Nacional Democratica [*National Democratic Union*] [*Ecuador*] [*Political party*] (PPW)
UNADECO ... Union Nacional de Asociaciones de Desarrollo Comunal [*National Union of Community Development Associations*] [*Costa Rica*] (LA)
UNAF .... Union des Anciens Eleves des Ecoles de l'AEF
UNAF .... Union Nacional de Asociaciones Familiares [*National Union of Family Associations*] [*Spanish*] (WER)
UNAFCO .. Union Africaine Compagnie
UNAG .... Union Nacional de Agricultores y Ganaderos [*National Union of Agricultural and Livestock Workers*] [*Nicaragua*] (EY)
UNAGA ..... Union Nacional de Asociaciones Ganaderas [*Colombia*] (DSCA)

UNAGRO ... Union Nacional de Agricultores [*National Union of Agriculturists*] [*Guatemala*]
UNA-H ...... United Nations Association of Hungary (EAIO)
UNAH .... Universidad Nacional Autonoma de Honduras [*National Autonomous University of Honduras*] (LA)
UNAHM ... Union Nationale d'Aide aux Handicapes de Madagascar
UNAIDS .... Joint United Nations Programme on Acquired Immune Deficiency Syndrome (ECON)
UNAIEDP ... United Nations African Institute for Economic Development and Planning
UNALOR .. Union Allumettiere Equatoriale
UNAM ...... Union Nationale des Anciens Moudjahidines
UNAM ...... Universidad Nacional Autonoma de Mexico [*National Autonomous University of Mexico*] (LA)
UNAMAT ... Union Algerienne de l'Industrie et du Commerce des Materiaux de Construction [*Algerian Association of Producers and Marketers of Construction Materials*] (AF)
UNA-MEX ... United Nations Association of Mexico (EAIO)
UNAMI ..... Uniao Nacional Africana de Mocambique Independente [*Mozambique*] [*Political party*]
UNAMIC .. United Nations Advance Mission in Cambodia (ECON)
UNAMILE ... Union des Anciens Eleves de la Mission de Leverville
UNAMO ... Uniao Nacional Africana de Mocambique
UNAN .... Universidad Nacional Autonoma de Nicaragua [*National Autonomous University of Nicaragua*] (LA)
UNAP .... Union Nationale des Arts Populaires [*Algeria*]
UNAP .... United Nations Association of Poland (EAIO)
UNAP .... Ustredni Nakupna a Prodejna Vytvarnych Del [*Central Purchase and Sales Office of Art Objects*] (CZ)
UNAPACE ... Unione Nazionale Aziende Autoproduttrici e Consumatrici di Energia Elettrica [*Italy*] (EY)
UNAPASYFTUROGA ... Union Nationale du Patronat Syndical des Transports Urbains, Routiers, et Fluviaux du Gabon (EY)
UNAPEI .... Union Nationale des Associations de Parents et Amis de Personnes Handicapees Mentales [*Formerly, Union Nationale des Associations de Parents d'Enfants Inadeptes*] [*France*] (EAIO)
UNAR .... Association for the United Nations in Russia (EAIO)
UNAR .... Unione Associazioni Regionali [*Italian*] (SLS)
UNAR .... Union Nationale Rwandaise [*Rwandan National Union Party*] (AF)
UNARC ..... University of Alexandria Research Centre [*Egypt*] (PDAA)
UNARU ..... Union Nationale Africaine du Ruanda-Urundi
UNAS .... Ukrainian National Academy of Sciences
UNAS .... United Nations Association of Sweden (EAIO)
UNASCO .. Uniao Nacional das Associacoes Cooperativas [*Rio De Janeiro, Brazil*] (LAA)
UNASL ...... United Nations Association of Sri Lanka (EAIO)
UNASSAD ... Union Nationale des Associations de Soins et Service a Domicile [*Also, National Organisation for Home Care*] [*France*] (EAIO)
UNAT .... Union Nationale des Agriculteurs Tunisiens [*National Union of Tunisian Farmers*] (AF)
UNAT .... Union Nationale des Aveugles de Tunisie
UNAT .... United Nations Administrative Tribunal (EY)
UNAT .... United Nations Association of Turkey (EAIO)
UNATA ..... Uniao dos Naturais de Angola
UNATAC .. Union d'Assistance Technique pour l'Automobile et la Circulation Routiere [*Union of Technical Assistance for Motor Vehicle and Road Traffic*] [*Geneva, Switzerland*] (EAIO)
UNATI ...... Union Nationale des Travailleurs Independants [*National Union of Self-Employed Workers*] [*French*] (WER)
UNATOM ... Atomic Unity Organization (WEN)
UNATRAT ... Union Nationale des Syndicats du Tchad [*National Union of Syndicates of Chad*] (EAIO)
unaufgeschn ... Unaufgeschnitten [*Uncut*] [*Publishing*] [*German*]
UNAULA .. Universidad Autonoma Latinoamericana [*Autonomous University of Latin America*] [*Colombia*] (COL)
UNAV .... Ente di Unificazione Navale [*Italian*] (SLS)
UNAVEM ... United Nations Angola Verification Mission
UNAZA ..... Universite Nationale du Zaire [*National University of Zaire*] (AF)
UNB .... Union Nacional Blanca [*Blanco National Union*] [*Uruguay*] (LA)
UNB .... Union Nationale du Burundi-Abadahemuka
UNB .... Universite Nationale du Benin [*Benin National University*] (AF)
UNB .... Urad Narodni Bezpecnosti [*National Security Office*] (CZ)
UNBA .... Universidad Nacional de Buenos Aires [*National University of Buenos Aires*] [*Argentina*] (LA)
UNBB .... Barnaul [*Former USSR*] [*ICAO location identifier*] (ICLI)
unbed .... Unbedeutend [*Insignificant*] [*German*]
unbedeut .... Unbedeutend [*Insignificant*] [*German*]
unbek .... Unbekannt [*Unknown*] [*German*]
unbeschn .... Unbeschnitten [*Untrimmed*] [*Publishing*] [*German*]
unbest .... Unbestimmt [*Indefinite*] [*German*]

unbest Fw... Unbestimmtes Fuerwort [*Indefinite Pronoun*] [*German*]
UNBIS....... United Nations Bibliographic Information System (PDAA)
UNBRO..... United Nations Border Relief Operation
UNBT........ United Nations "Blue Top"
UNC.......... Uganda National Congress
UNC.......... Uniao Nacional dos Cabindas
UNC.......... Union Civica Nacional [*Bolivia*] (LAA)
UNC.......... Unione Nazionale Chinesiologi [*Italian*] (SLS)
UNC.......... Union Nacional Campesina [*National Union of Rural Workers*] [*Nicaragua*] (EY)
UNC.......... Union Nacional de Campesinos [*National Union of Peasants*] [*Honduras*] (LA)
UNC.......... Union National Congolaise [*Congolese National Union*]
UNC.......... Union Nationale Camerounaise [*Cameroonian National Union*] (AF)
UNC.......... Union Nationale de la Cooperation [*National Cooperation Union*] [*Tunisia*] (AF)
UNC.......... Union Nationale des Anciens Combattants [*National Union of Ex-Servicemen*] [*French*]
UNC.......... Union Nouvelle Caledonienne [*New Caledonia*] [*Political party*] (FEA)
UNC.......... United National Convention [*Ghana*] [*Political party*] (PPW)
UNC.......... Universidad Nacional de Colombia [*Colombia*] (COL)
UNCAC..... Union Nationale des Cooperatives Agricoles de Commercialisation [*National Agricultural Marketing Cooperatives Union*] [*Algeria*] (AF)
UNCAF ..... Union Nationale des Caisses d'Allocations Familiales
UNCAFENIC ... Union Nacional de Caficultores de Nicaragua [*National Union of Nicaraguan Coffee Growers*] (LA)
UNCAH .... Union Nacional de Campesinos Autenticos de Honduras [*National Union of Authentic Peasants of Honduras*] (PD)
UNCAL ..... Union Nationale des Comites d'Action Lyceens [*National Union of Lycee Action Committees*] [*French*] (WER)
UNCAP ..... Uniunea Nationala a Cooperativelor Agricole de Productie [*National Union of Agricultural Production Cooperatives*] (RO)
UNCASTD ... United Nations Advisory Committee on the Application of Science and Technology to Development (ASF)
UNCC........ Union Nationale des Cheminots du Cameroun [*National Union of Railroad Employees of Cameroon*] (AF)
UNCC........ Union Nationale des Cooperatives de Construction
UNCC........ Union Nigerienne de Credit et de Cooperation [*Niger Credit and Cooperation Union*] (AF)
UNCC........ United Nations Cartographic Commission (BARN)
UNCC........ United Nations Compensation Commission (ECON)
UNCDF ..... United Nations Capital Development Fund
UNCE........ Novokuznetsk [*Former USSR*] [*ICAO location identifier*] (ICLI)
UNCEA ..... Union Commerciale pour l'Europe et l'Afrique
UNCEACI ... Union Nationale des Educateurs, Conseillers d'Education, et Assimiles de Cote-D'Ivoire
UNCED ..... United Nations Conference on Environment and Development
UNCEM .... Unione Nazionale Comuni Comunita Enti Montani [*Italy*] (EAIO)
UNCGFL... Union National du Commerce de Gros en Fruits et Legumes [*France*] (EAIO)
UNCh .... Low-Frequency Amplifier (RU)
UNCh .... Very Low Frequency (RU)
UNCHBP .. Center for Housing, Building, and Planning [*United Nations*]
UNCHE..... United Nations Conference on the Human Environment (MSC)
UNCHR..... United Nations Centre for Human Rights [*Switzerland*] (EAIO)
UNCHR..... United Nations High Commissioner for Refugees (DLA)
UNCHS..... United Nations Center for Human Settlement [*Kenya*] [*Research center*] (IRC)
UNCI .... Unione Nazionale Chimici Italiani [*National Union of Italian Chemists*] (SLS)
UNCI .... Universite Nationale de Cote-D'Ivoire
UNC/IAWPRC ... Uruguayan National Committee of the International Association on Water Pollution Research and Control (EAIO)
UNCIO...... United Nations Conference on International Organization [*San Francisco, 1945*]
UNCITRAL ... United Nations Commission on International Trade Law (PDAA)
UNCIVPOL ... United Nations Civilian Police [*Peace-keeping force in Cyprus*]
UNCL........ Kolpashevo [*Former USSR*] [*ICAO location identifier*] (ICLI)
UNCL........ United Nations Commissioner for Libya
U Ncle........ University of Newcastle [*Australia*]
UNCLOS... United Nations Conference on the Law of the Sea
UNCO .... Union Contracting Co. [*United Arab Emirates*] (MENA)
UNCO .... Union des Nationalistes Congolais
UNCO .... United Nations Civilian Operations Mission
UNCOD .... United Nations Conference on Desertification (AF)
UNCOL ..... Universal Computer Oriented Language (ADPT)
UNCORS .. United Nations Commission on the Racial Situation in the Union of South Africa
UNCRO..... United Nations Confidence Restoration Operation (ECON)
Uncro .... United Nations Confidence Restoration Operation in Croatia

UNCSAT... United Nations Conference on Science and Technology (BARN)
UNCSTD... United Nations Conference on Science and Technology for Development [*Vienna, Austria*] [*August, 1979 ICSU*]
UNCTAD .. United Nations Conference on Trade and Development
UNCTADTDB ... United Nations Conference on Trade and Development, Trade and Development Board
UNCTC ..... United Nations Centre on Transnational Corporations (ECON)
UNCTT ..... Union Nationale des Chefs Traditionnels du Togo [*National Union of Traditional Chiefs of Togo*] (AF)
UNCU........ Union Nacional del Cooperativismo Uruguayo [*National Union of Uruguayan Cooperatives*] (LA)
UNCULTA ... Union Nacional de Cultivadores de Tabaco [*National Tobacco Growers Union*] [*Venezuela*] (LA)
UNCW....... Novy Vasyugan [*Former USSR*] [*ICAO location identifier*] (ICLI)
UND .... Kunduz [*Afghanistan*] [*Airport symbol*] [*Obsolete*] (OAG)
UND .... Ukrajinske Narodni Divadlo [*Ukrainian National Theater*] (CZ)
und .... Undantag [*Exception*] [*Sweden*] (GPO)
UND .... Union Nacional Democratica [*El Salvador*] [*Political party*] (EY)
UND .... Union Nationale et Democratique [*National Democratic Union*] [*Monaco*] [*Political party*] (PPW)
UND .... Union Nationale et Democratique [*National Democratic Union*] [*Chad*] (AF)
UND .... Union Nigerienne Democratique [*Political party*] (EY)
UNDA .... International Catholic Association for Radio, Television and Audiovisuals [*Belgium*] (EAIO)
UNDAL..... Union de Arroceros Limitada [*Ibague*] (COL)
UNDAT..... United Nations Development Advisory Team
UNDATS .. United Nations Multidisciplinary Development Advisory Team
UNDC........ Union Nationale pour la Democratie aux Comoros [*Political party*] (EY)
UNDD .... Union Nationale pour la Defense de la Democratie [*National Union for the Defense of Democracy*] [*Burkina Faso*] (AF)
UNDD .... Union Nationale pour la Democratie et le Developpement [*Madagascar*] [*Political party*] (EY)
UNDECA .. Union de Empleados de la Caja [*Social Security Employees Union*] [*Costa Rica*] (LA)
UNDEL..... Unione Nazionale Dipendenti Enti Locali [*National Union of Local Government Employees*] [*Italy*]
UNDEMO ... Union Democratica Fernandina
UNDERMA ... Union pour le Developpement de la Region Mavo
understrek ... Understrekning [*Underlining*] [*Publishing Danish/Norwegian*]
UNDETOC ... Union de Toreros Colombianos [*Colombia*] (COL)
UNDHR .... United Nations Declaration of Human Rights (BJA)
Undichtigk ... Undichtigkeit [*Leak*] [*German*] (GCA)
UNDL........ Union des Nationalistes pour la Democratie Liberale [*Union of Nationalists for Liberal Democracy*] [*Laotian*] (CL)
UNDOF..... United Nations Disengagement Observer Force [*Damascus, Syria*] (MENA)
UNDOF/C ... United Nations Disengagement Observer Force/Command [*Israeli, Syrian*] (ME)
UNDP........ Union Nationale pour la Democratie et le Progres [*The Congo*] [*Political party*] (EY)
UNDP........ Union Nationale pour la Democratie et le Progres [*Cameroon*] [*Political party*] (EY)
UNDP........ Union Nationale pour la Democratie et le Progres [*Benin*] [*Political party*] (EY)
UNDP........ Union Nationals Democracy Party [*Myanmar*] [*Political party*] (EY)
UNDP........ United National Democratic Party [*Antigua and Barbuda*] [*Political party*] (EY)
UNDP........ United Nations Development Program (PWGL)
UNDP........ United Nations Development Programme (IDIG)
UNDPG.... United Nations Development Programme in Ghana
UNDPR..... United Nations Development Programme in Rwanda
UNDPS ..... United Nations Development Programme in the Sudan
UNDP/SF ... United Nations Development Plan/Special Fund [*Malaysia*] (ML)
UNDRC..... United Nations Disaster Relief Coordination
UNDRO .... United Nations Disaster Relief Office (EAIO)
UNDTCD ... United Nations Department of Technical Cooperation for Development [*United Nations*] (GNE)
UNE.......... Electoral Union [*Macau*] [*Political party*] (FEA)
UNE.......... Qacha's Nek [*Lesotho*] [*Airport symbol*] (OAG)
UNE.......... Uniao Nacional dos Estudantes [*National Students Union*] [*Brazil*] (LA)
UNE.......... Union Nacional de Educadores [*National Union of Teachers*] [*Ecuador*] (LA)
UNE.......... Union Nacional de Empleados [*National Union of Employees*] [*Nicaragua*] (LA)
UNE.......... Union Nacional de Estudiantes [*National Students Union*] [*Ecuador*] (LA)
UNE.......... Union Nacional de Estudiantes [*National Students Union*] [*Argentina*] (LA)
UNE.......... Union Nacional Espanola [*Spanish National Union*] (WER)

UNE.......... University of New England [*Australia*] (PDAA)
UNEA........ Union Nationale des Etudiants Algeriens [*National Union of Algerian Students*] (AF)
UNEA........ Union Nationale des Etudiants Angolais [*National Union of Angolan Students*] (AF)
UNE-A........ University of New England - Armidale [*Australia*]
UNEAC..... Uniao Nacional des Escritores et Artistas Congoleses
UNEAC..... Union Nacional de Escritores y Artistas de Cuba [*National Union of Cuban Writers and Artists*] (LA)
UNEB........ Union Nacional de Empleados Bancarios [*National Union of Bank Employees*] [*Colorado*] (LA)
UNEBA..... Union Nationale des Etudiants Burundi [*National Union of Burundi Students*] (AF)
UNEBIF.... Union Europeenne des Fabricants de Bijouterie Fantaisie [*Union of European Fashion Jewelry Manufacturers*] [*Italy*] (EAIO)
UNEC........ Union de Empresas de Publicidad de Colombia [*Colombian Advertising Companies Union*] (LA)
UNEC........ Union Nacional de Escuelas Catolicas [*National Union of Catholic Schools*] [*Dominican Republic*] (LA)
UNEC........ Union Nacional de Estudiantes Catolicos [*National Union of Catholic Students*] [*Peru*] (LA)
UNEC........ Union Nacional de Estudiantes Colombianos [*National Union of Colombian Students*] (LA)
UNEC........ Union pour l'Exportation du Cacao
UNECA..... Union de Empresas de Construccion del Caribe [*Union of Caribbean Construction Enterprises*] [*Cuba*] (LA)
UNECA..... United Nations Economic Commission for Africa
UNECE..... United Nations Economic Commission for Europe
UNECED.. Unite d'Ecologie des Eaux Douces [*Belgium*] (ASF)
UNECh...... Union Nacional de Estudiantes Chilenos [*National Union of Chilean Students*] (LA)
UNE-CHC ... University of New England - Coffs Harbour Campus [*Australia*]
UNECI...... Union Nationale des Etudiants de la Cote-D'Ivoire [*National Union of Ivory Coast Students*] (AF)
UNECLA... United Nations Economic Commission for Latin America (BARN)
UNECO..... Union Nationale des Enseignants du Congo
UNECO..... Union Nationale des Etudiants du Congo
UNECTES ... Union Europeenne des Conseillers Techniques et Scientifiques [*European Union of Technical and Scientific Advisers*] [*EC*] (ECED)
UNED........ State Distance University [*Costa Rica*]
UNED........ Union Nacional de Estudiantes Democraticos [*National Union of Democratic Students*] [*Chile*] (LA)
UNEDAMO ... Uniao Democratica Nacional de Mocambique
UNEDIC ... Union Nationale des ASSEDIC [*Association pour l'Emploi dans l'Industrie et le Commerce*] [*French*]
UN/EDIFACT ... United Nations Rules for Electronic Data Interchange for Administration, Commerce, and Transport
UNEECI.... Union Nationale des Eleves et Etudiants de Cote-D'Ivoire [*National Union of Pupils and Students of the Ivory Coast*]
UNEED..... Union Nationale des Eleves et Etudiants Dahomeens [*National Union of Pupils and Students of Dahomey*] [*Benin*]
UNEEG..... Union Nationale des Eleves et Etudiants de la Guadeloupe [*National Union of Pupils and Students of Guadeloupe*] (PD)
UNEEM.... Union Nationale des Eleves et Etudiants du Mali [*National Union of Pupils and Students of Mali*] (PD)
UNEF........ Union Nationale des Etudiants de France [*National Union of French Students*] (WER)
UNEF........ United Nations Emergency Force [*to separate hostile forces of Israel and Egypt*]
UNEF/Renouveau ... Union Nationale des Etudiants de France [*National Union of French Students for Renewal*] (WER)
UNEGA..... Union Europeenne des Fondeurs et Fabricants de Corps Gras Animaux [*European Union of Animal Fat Producers*] (EA)
UNEH........ Union Nationale d'Etudiants Haitiens [*National Union of Haitian Students*] [*Port-Au-Prince*] (LAA)
UNEK........ Union Nationale des Etudiants du Kamerun [*National Union of Cameroon Students*] (AF)
UNEL........ Union Nationale des Etudiants de Luxembourg [*National Union of Students of Luxembourg*] (WER)
unelast........ Unelastisch [*Inelastic*] [*German*] (GCA)
UNELCA... Union Electrica de Canarias SA [*Spain*] (PDAA)
UNELCO .. Union Electrique d'Outre-Mer
UNELMA ... Union des Eleves des Freres Maristes
UNEM....... Union Nationale des Etudiants du Maroc [*National Union of Moroccan Students*] (PD)
UNEMAF ... Union des Employeurs Agricoles et Forestiers
UNEMEPHARCO ... Union Nationale des Etudiants en Medecine et Pharmacie du Congo
UNEMO.... Uniao Nacional dos Estudantes de Mocambique [*National Union of Mozambique Students*] [*Portuguese*] (AF)
UNEMO.... Union Nationale des Etudiants du Mocambique [*National Union of Mozambique Students*] [*French*]

UNEMOP ... Union de Empleados del Ministerio de Obras Publicas [*Union of White Collar Workers of the Ministry of Public Works*] [*Costa Rica*] (LA)
UNE-NR.... University of New England - Northern Rivers [*Australia*]
UNEO........ United Nations Emergency Operation (PDAA)
UNE-OAC ... University of New England - Orange Agricultural College [*Australia*]
UNEP........ Uniao Nacional de Estudantes Portugueses [*National Union of Portuguese Students*] (WER)
UNEP........ Union Nacional de Empleados Publicos [*National Union of Public Employees*] [*Venezuela*] (LA)
UNEP........ Union Nationale des Entrepreneurs du Paysage [*French Association of Landscape Contractors*] (EAIO)
UNEP........ United Nations Energy Planning [*A publication*]
UNEP........ United Nations Environment Programme [*Kenya*] [*Database originator*] (EAIO)
UNEP........ University of New England Press [*Australia*] (ADA)
UNEPA..... Union Economica Patagonica [*Buenos Aires, Argentina*] (LAA)
UNEPAR... Unidad Ejecutoria de Acueductos Rurales [*Executive Unit of Rural Aqueducts*] [*Guatemala*] (LA)
UNEPREC ... Union Nacional de Ex-Presos Constitucionalistas [*National Union of Constitutionalist Former Prisoners*] [*Dominican Republic*] (LA)
UNEPTA... United Nations Expanded Program of Technical Assistance
UNERS...... University of New England Research Scholarship [*Australia*]
UNES........ Uniao Nacional de Estudantes Secundarios [*National Secondary Students Union*] [*Brazil*] (LA)
UNES........ Union Nacional de Estudiantes de Secundaria [*National Union of High School Students*] [*Colorado*] (LA)
UNES........ Union Nationale des Etudiants Senegalais [*National Union of Senegalese Students*] (AF)
UNESCAP ... United Nations Economic and Social Commission for Asia and the Pacific
UNESCAPVERT ... Union des Entrepreneurs Senegalais de la Region du Cap-Vert
UNESCO .. United Nations Educational, Scientific, and Cultural Organization [*Database originator and operator*] [*France*] [*Research center*]
UNESCO .. United Nations Education Science and Culture Organization (PWGL)
UNESDA .. Union of EEC Soft Drinks Associations (EAIO)
UNESEM ... Union Europeenne des Sources d'Eaux Minerales du Marche Commun [*European Union of Natural Mineral Water Sources of the Common Market*] (EAIO)
UNESID.... Union de Empresas Entidades y Siderurgicas [*Spain*] (PDAA)
UNET........ Universidad Nacional Experimental del Tachira [*National State University of Tachira*] [*Venezuela*] [*Research center*] (ERC)
UNETE..... Union Electoral Independiente [*Independent Electoral Union*] [*Venezuela*] (LA)
UNETI...... Uniao Nacional dos Estudantes Tecnicos Industriais [*National Union of Industrial and Technical Students*] [*Brazil*] (LA)
UNETO..... Union Nationale des Etudiants Togolais [*National Union of Togolese Students*] (AF)
UNEU........ Union Nacional de Estudiantes Universitarios [*National Union of University Students*] [*Colorado*] (LA)
UNE-UNED ... Union de Empleados de la Universidad Estatal a Distancia [*State Correspondence University Employees Union*] [*Costa Rica*] (LA)
UNF.......... United National Front [*Sudan*]
UNF.......... United National Front [*Lebanon*] (BJA)
UNFA........ Union Nationale des Femmes Algeriennes [*Algeria*] [*Political party*] (EY)
UNFACH.. Union de Farmacias de Chile [*Union of Chilean Pharmacies*] (LA)
UNFC........ Union Nationale des Femmes Congolaises [*National Union of Congolese Women*] (AF)
UNFC........ United Nations Food Conference (BARN)
UNFDAC .. United Nations Fund for Drug Abuse Control [*Appears thus in Turkish Newspapers*] (TU)
UNFE........ United Nations Fund for Equipment
UNFE........ Universidad Nacional, Facultad de Economia [*Colombia*] (DSCA)
UNFICYP ... United Nations Peace-Keeping Force in Cyprus [*Nicosia, Cyprus*] (MENA)
UNFM....... Union Nationale des Femmes du Mali
UNFM....... Union Nationale des Femmes Marocaines
UNFP........ Union Nationale des Forces Populaires [*National Union of Popular Forces*] [*Casablanca, Morocco*] (AF)
UNFP........ United National Federal Party [*Zimbabwe*] [*Political party*] (PPW)
UNFPA...... United Nations Fund for Population Activities
UNFPO..... United National Front Political Organisation
Unfruchtbark ... Unfruchtbarkeit [*Unproductiveness*] [*German*] (GCA)
UNFS........ Universidad Nacional, Facultad de Sociologia [*Colombia*] (DSCA)

UNFSSTD ... United Nations Financing System for Science and Technology for Development   (EY)

UNFT .... Union Nationale des Femmes de Tunisie [*National Union of Tunisian Women*] [*Tunis, Tunisia*]   (AF)

UNFT .... Union Nationale des Femmes Togolaises [*National Union of Togolese Women*]   (AF)

UNFV .... Universidad Nacional "Federico Villarreal" [*Peru*]   (MSC)

UNG .... Hexahydrate of Uranyl Nitrate   (RU)

ung .... Hungarian   (BU)

UNG .... Kiunga [*Papua New Guinea*] [*Airport symbol*]   (OAG)

ung .... Ungefaehr [*About, Approximately*] [*German*]

UNGA .... United Nations General Assembly

ungar .... Ungarisch [*Hungarian*] [*German*]   (GCA)

UNGbolesti ... Otorhinolaryngological Diseases   (BU)

ungeb.......... Ungebunden [*Unbound*] [*German*]

ungef.......... Ungefaehr [*About, Approximately*] [*German*]   (GCA)

ungel.......... Ungeloest [*Undissolved*] [*German*]

unges .... Ungesaettigt [*Unsaturated*] [*German*]

ungesaett.... Ungesaettigt [*Unsaturated*] [*German*]   (GCA)

UNGOMAP ... United Nations Good Offices Mission in Afghanistan and Pakistan [*Later, OSGAP*]

Ung P......... Ungarisches Patent [*Hungarian Patent*] [*German*]   (GCA)

UNGP........ Uniao dos Naturais da Guine Portuguesa

UNGSVMS ... Office of the Chief of the Hydrographic Service of the Navy, USSR   (RU)

UN-GTDI ... United Nations Guidelines for Trade Data Interchange

UNHACAM ... Union Nationale des Handicapes du Cameroun [*National Union of Handicapped Individuals in Cameroon*]   (EAIO)

UNHC .... United Nations High Commission   (BJA)

UNHCR..... United Nations High Commission [*or Commissioner*] for Refugees

UNHHSF ... United Nations Habitat and Human Settlements Foundation

UNHPM.... Union National des Handicapes Physiques et Mentaux [*National Union of Physically and Mentally Handicapped*] [*Mauritania*]   (EAIO)

UNHRC..... United Nations Human Rights Commission   (BJA)

UNHS........ Uganda Natural History Society

UNI............ Ente Nazionale Italiano di Unificazione [*Italian Industry Standardization Organization*] [*Italian*]   (SLS)

UNI........... Union Island [*Windward Islands*] [*Airport symbol*]   (OAG)

UNI........... Union Nacional Independiente [*Independent National Union*] [*Guatemala*]   (LA)

UNI........... Union Nationale des Independants [*National Union of Independents*] [*Burkina Faso*]   (AF)

UNI........... Union Nationale des Independants [*National Union of Independents*] [*Monaco*]   (PPE)

UNI........... Union Nationale des Ingenieurs [*National Engineers Union*] [*Tunisia*]   (AF)

UNI........... Union Nationale pour l'Independence [*National Union for Independence*] [*Djibouti*]   (PPW)

UNI........... Unite Australia Party [*Australia*] [*Political party*]

UNI........... United News of India Ltd. [*News agency*]   (FEA)

UNI........... Universidad Nacional de Ingenieria [*National Engineering University*] [*Peru*]   (LA)

UNIA........ Universal Negro Improvement Association

UNIAL ...... Union Industrial de Astilleros Barranquilla SA   (COL)

UNIANDES ... Universidad de los Andes [*Colombia*]   (COL)

UNIAPAC ... Asociacion Cristiana de Dirigentes de Empresa [*Uruguay*]   (EAIO)

UNIAPAC ... Union Internacional de Asociaciones Patronales Catolicas (Delegacion para America Latina) [*International Union of Catholic Management Associations*] [*Buenos Aires, Argentina*]   (LAA)

UNIARTE ... Union Nacional de Industriales y Artesanos [*Venezuela*]   (DSCA)

UNIATEC ... Union Internationale des Associations Techniques Cinematographiques [*International Union of Technical Cinematograph Associations - IUTCA*]   (EAIO)

UNIBACAM ... Union Bananiere du Cameroun

UNIBAN ... Union Bancaire Hispano-Marocaine

UNIBAN ... Union de Bananeros de Uraba [*Uraba Banana Growers Union*] [*Colombia*]   (LA)

UNIBANK ... United City Bank [*Indonesia*]   (EY)

UNIBAT.... Union des Bateke

UNIBEN ... University of Benin

UNIBG ...... Unione Nazionale Industriali Bevande Gassate [*Italy*]

UNIBID..... UNISIST International Centre for Bibliographic Descriptions [*UNESCO*] [*Information service or system*]   (IID)

UNIBIS ..... Universelles Bilanzierungssystem [*German*]   (ADPT)

UNIBIS ..... Universelles Bilanzierungs-und Informationssystem [*German*]   (ADPT)

UNIBO ...... University of Bophuthatswana [*South Africa*]   (PDAA)

UNIC .... Unione Nazionale Industria Conciaria [*Italy*]

UNIC .... Union Internationale des Cinemas [*International Union of Cinemas*]   (EAIO)

UNIC .... United Nations Information Centre

UNICA ...... Asociacion de Universidades del Caribe [*Association of Caribbean Universities and Research Institutes*]   (EA)

UNICA ...... Union Internationale du Cinema d'Amateurs [*North African*]

UNICA ...... Union Internationale du Cinema Non Professionnel [*International Union of Amateur Cinema*]   (EAIO)

UNICA ...... Universidad e Institutos del Caribe [*Barranquilla*]   (COL)

UNICAF.... Union d'Importations Industrielles et Commerciales Africaines [*African Industrial and Commercial Imports Union*] [*French*]   (AF)

UNICAFRA ... Union Camerounaise Francaise

UNICAMP ... Universidade Estadual de Campinas [*Campinas State University*] [*Brazil*]   (LA)

UNICAUCA ... Universidad del Cauca [*Popayan*]   (COL)

UNICE ...... Union des Industries de la Communaute Europeenne [*Union of Industries of the European Community*] [*Belgium*]

UNICE ...... Union of Industrial and Employers' Confederations of Europe   (EAIO)

UNICEF.... United Nations International Children's Emergency Fund [*Later, United Nations Children's Fund*]

UNICEF-NZ ... New Zealand National Committee for UNICEF   (EAIO)

UNICEMA ... Union Nationale des Industriels, Commercants, et Entrepreneurs de Mauritanie [*National Union of Industrialists, Merchants, and Entrepreneurs of Mauritania*]   (AF)

Unicer .... Uniao Cervejeira, EP [*Portugal*]   (EY)

UNICHAD ... Union Interprofessionnelle du Tchad [*Chad Interoccupational Union*]   (AF)

UNICHAL ... Union Internationale des Distributeurs de Chaleur [*International Union of Heat Distributors*]   (EAIO)

UNICLO ... United Nations Information Center and Liaison Office   (PDAA)

UNICLO ... United Nations Information Centre and Liaison Office   (PDAA)

UNICO...... Union Congolaise

UNICO...... Union Industrielle and Commerciale de l'Ouest de la Cote-D'Ivoire

UNICO...... United Construction Company

UNICOBAT ... Union de Cooperatives de Battambang [*Battambang Cooperative Union*] [*Cambodia*]   (CL)

UNICOCAM ... Union des Commercants Camerounais

UNICOCYM ... Union Internationale du Commerce et de la Reparation du Cycle et du Motocycle [*International Union of Cycle and Motocycle Trade and Repair*] [*Germany*]

UNICOL ... Unidad Colombiana de Comercio [*Colombia*]   (COL)

UNICOL-HV ... Union Industrielle et Commerciale des Oleagineux de Haute-Volta

UNICOM ... Unidad Informativa Computable [*Computerized Information Unit*] [*Mexico*] [*Information service or system*]   (IID)

UNICOM ... Union Commerciale Africaine de Kaolack

UNICOM ... United Coconut Mills [*Philippines*]   (IMH)

UNICOMA ... Union des Cooperatives du Morbihan et de Loire-Atlantique

UNICOMA ... Union des Cooperatives Maritimes

UNICOMER ... Union des Comptoirs d'Outre-Mer

UNICONGO ... Union Patronale et Interprofessionnelle du Congo

UNICOOKA ... Union de Cooperatives de Kandal [*Kandal Cooperative Union*] [*Cambodia*]   (CL)

UNICOOP ... Union des Cooperatives de Klouts

UNICOOP ... Union des Cooperatives des Planteurs Malagasy

UNICOOP ... Unions Provinciales de Cooperatives [*Provincial Cooperative Unions*] [*Cambodia*]   (CL)

UNICOP ... Union de Cooperatives Nationales du Mali [*Union of Malian National Cooperatives*]   (AF)

UNICOPRE ... Union de Cooperatives de Prey Veng [*Prey Veng Cooperative Union*] [*Cambodia*]   (CL)

UNICOS.... Union Commerciale Senegalaise

UNICOTA ... Union de Cooperatives de Takeo [*Takeo Cooperative Union*] [*Cambodia*]   (CL)

UNICOTRAL ... Union Commerciale et de Transports du Littoral

UNID......... Union Nacional de Integracion y Desarrollo [*National Union of Integration and Development*] [*Bolivia*]   (LA)

UNIDAS.... Uniao Democratica Assistencial [*Democratic Welfare Union*] [*Brazil*]   (LA)

UNIDAV ... Universelle Dateiverwaltung [*German*]   (ADPT)

UNIDEB ... Universelle Debitorenbuchhaltung [*German*]   (ADPT)

UNIDIR .... United Nations Institute for Disarmament Research [*Research center*] [*Switzerland*]   (IRC)

UNIDO...... United Nationalist Democratic Opposition [*or Organization*] [*Philippines*]

UNIDO...... United Nations Industrial Development Organization [*Austria*] [*Also, an information service or system*]   (IID)

UNIDROIT ... Institut International pour l'Unification du Droit Prive [*International Institute for the Unification of Private Law*]   (EAIO)

Unidroit ..... Unification du Droit [*Unification of Law*] [*Italy*]   (FLAF)

U-nie .... Administration   (BU)

UNIEMA .. Union des Industries de Mauritanie

UNIEP...... Union Internationale des Entrepreneurs de Peinture [*International Union of Master Painters - IUMP*]   (EAIO)

UNIET ...... Ecole Normale d'Instituteurs d'Enseignement Technique

unif............. Uniform [*Alike*] [*Netherlands*]
UNIFACO ... Union Industrielle Forestiere et Agricole Congo Ocean
UNIFAC-SIMCOFA ... Union Fluviale de l'Afrique Centrale. Societe Immobiliere et Commerciale Francaise
UNIFAR.... Uniao Fabril de Refrigerantes Lda.
UNIFAR.... Union de Farmacias Ltda. [*Barranquilla*]   (COL)
UNIFE....... Union des Industries Ferroviaires Europeennes [*Union of European Railway Industries*]   (EA)
UNIFE....... University of Ife [*Nigeria*]
UNIFECS ... University of Ife Consultancy Services Centre [*Nigeria*]
Unificyp ...... United Nations Peacekeeping Force in Cyprus [*1964*]
UNIFIL ..... United Nations Interim Force in Lebanon   (MENA)
UNIFOM .. United Front of Political Movements [*Sierra Leone*] [*Political party*]   (EY)
UNIFSTD ... United Nations Interim Fund for Science and Technology
UNIGABON ... Union Interprofessionnelle du Gabon [*Interoccupational Union of Gabon*]   (AF)
UNIGES.... Union des Groupements Economiques du Senegal [*Union of Economic Groups of Senegal*]   (AF)
UNIGRI .... Ukrainian Scientific Research Institute of Geological Exploration   (RU)
UNII .... Yeniseysk [*Former USSR*] [*ICAO location identifier*]   (ICLI)
UNIIAKKh ... Ukrainian Scientific Research Institute of the Academy of Municipal Services Imeni K. D. Pamfilov   (RU)
UNIIFR..... Ukrainian Scientific Research Institute of Plant Physiology   (RU)
UNIIM ...... Ukrainian Scientific Research Institute of Agricultural Mechanization   (RU)
UNIIM ...... Ukrainian Scientific Research Institute of Metals   (RU)
UNIIMESKh ... Ukrainian Scientific Research Institute of Rural Mechanization and Electrification   (RU)
UNIIMOG ... United Nations Iran-Iraq Military Observer Group
UNIIO....... Ukrainian Scientific Research Institute of Production Organization and Industrial Management   (RU)
UNIIO iK ... Ukrainian Scientific Research Institute of Vegetables and Potatoes   (RU)
UNIIP........ Ukrainian Scientific Research Institute of Pedagogy   (RU)
UNIIP........ Ukrainian Scientific Research Institute of Poultry Raising   (RU)
UNIIPP...... Ukrainian Scientific Research Institute of the Food Industry   (RU)
UNIIPP ..... Ukrainian Scientific Research Institute of the Printing Industry   (RU)
UNIIS........ Ukrainian Scientific Research Institute of Horticulture   (RU)
UNIISOZ.. Ukrainian Scientific Research Institute of Socialist Agriculture   (RU)
UNIIZh ..... Ukrainian Scientific Research Institute of Livestock Breeding   (RU)
UNIIZKh... Ukrainian Scientific Research Institute of Grain Farming Imeni V. V. Kuybyshev   (RU)
UNIKA ...... Universal Kablo Sanayi ve Ticaret AS [*Universal Cable Industry and Trade Corp.*]   (TU)
UNIKhIM ... Ural Scientific Research Chemical Institute   (RU)
Unikhimmash ... Ural Scientific Research Institute of Chemical Machinery   (RU)
UNIKOM ... United Nations Iraq/Kuwait Observer Mission
Unilab........ United Laboratories Inc. [*Philippines*]
UNILAG ... University of Lagos [*Nigeria*]
UNILI........ Ural Scientific Research Institute of the Lumber Industry   (RU)
UNILOG ... Universelle Lohn-und Gehaltsabrechnung [*German*]   (ADPT)
UNIM........ Union Nationale des Ingenieurs Marocains
UNIMA..... Unione Nazionale Imprese di Meccanizzazione Agricola [*Agricultural Mechanization Enterprises Union*] [*Italy*]   (EY)
UNIMA..... Union Internationale de la Marionnette [*International Puppeteers Union*] [*France*]
UNIMAP .. Union des Industriels des Matieres Plastiques [*North African*]
UNIMAROC ... Union Commerciale Marocaine [*Moroccan Commercial Union*]   (AF)
UNIMES... Union des Importateurs-Exportateurs Senegalais
UNIMES... Union des Industries Metallurgiques et Electriques Socialistes [*Socialist Metallurgical and Electric Industries Association*]   (AF)
UNIMES... Union Nationale des Industries Mecaniques et Electriques Socialistes [*North African*]
Unimetal.... Union Nationale des Petites et Moyennes Entreprises du Metal [*Benelux*]   (BAS)
UNIMO..... Union des Mongo
UNIN......... United Nations Institute for Namibia
UNINAY ... Universidad de Nayarit [*Mexico*]   (MSC)
UNINCCA ... Universidad Incca de Colombia [*Colombia*]   (COL)
UNINETT ... [*The*] University Network   (TNIG)
UNINSA ... Union de Siderurgicas Asturianas SA [*Spain*]   (PDAA)
UNIOK...... Ukrainian Scientific Research Institute of Refractory and Acid-Resistant Materials   (RU)
UNIOM..... Union Interprofessionnelle des Industries d'Outre-Mer
UnionTheol Coll ... Union Theological College [*Australia*]

UNIOPSS ... Union Nationale Inter-Federale des Oeuvres Privees Sanitaires et Sociales   (FLAF)
UNIP .... Union Interamericana de Padres de Familia [*Inter-American Union of Parents*] [*Bogota, Colombia*]   (LAA)
UNIP .... United National Independence Party [*Nigeria*] [*Political party*]
UNIP .... United National Independence Party [*Trinidad and Tobago*] [*Political party*]   (PPW)
UNIP .... United National Independence Party [*Zambia*] [*Political party*]   (PD)
UNIPA ...... Union de Participation de France et d'Outre-Mer
UNIPAL.... United Pacific Trading Co. Ltd. [*Thailand*]
UNIPAR.... Uniao de Industrias Petroquimicas SA
UNIPEDE ... Union Internationale de Producteurs et Distributeurs d'Energie Electrique [*International Union of Producers and Distributors of Electrical Energy*] [*France*]
UNIPESCA ... Uniao Brasileira de Pesca [*Brazilian Fishing Union*]   (LA)
UNIPETROL ... Union pour la Recherche et l'Exploitation Petrolieres Sahariennes
UNIPI........ Unione Industriali Pastai Italiani [*Pasta Manufacturers Union*] [*Italy*]   (EY)
UNIPOL.... Union des Industries de Produits Oleagineux
UNIPOMO ... Uniao das Populacoes de Mocambique
UNIPON... United Nations India-Pakistan Observer Mission   (BARN)
UNIPRESSE ... Union pour l'Expansion de la Presse Francaise dans le Monde [*Union for the Expansion of the French Press in the World*]   (AF)
UNIPRO ... Unione Nazionale delle Industrie di Profumeria, Cosmesi, Saponi da Toilette, e Affini [*Italy*]
Unipromed' ... Ural Scientific Research and Planning Institute of the Copper Industry   (RU)
UNIR .... Union de Izquierda Revolucionaria [*Union of the Revolutionary Left*] [*Peru*] [*Political party*]   (PPW)
UNIR .... Union de la Navigation Internationale sur le Rhin   (FLAF)
UNIR .... Union Nacional de Innovadores y Racionalizadores [*National Union of Innovators and Efficiency Experts*] [*Cuba*]   (LA)
UNIR .... Union Nacionalista Independiente Regional [*Regional Nationalist Independent Union*] [*Venezuela*]   (LA)
UNIR .... Union Nacional Izquierdista Revolucionaria [*Colorado*]   (LAA)
UNIR .... Union Nationale pour l'Independance et la Revolution [*Chad*]
UNIR .... Union Nationale pour l'Initiative et la Responsabilite [*National Union for Initiative and Responsibility*] [*France*] [*Political party*]   (PPW)
UNIREB.... Univac Rechnungswesen Betriebsabrechnung [*German*]   (ADPT)
UNIREF.... Univac Rechnungswesen Finanzbuchhaltung [*Univac Computerized Financial Book Keeping*] [*German*]   (ADPT)
UNIREP.... Union Francaise et Africaine de Prospections Minieres et de Recherches Petrolieres
UNIROUTE ... Union Routiere du Logone-Benoue
UNIRS....... Union Nationale des Institutions de Retraite des Salaries   (FLAF)
UNIS .... Ukrainian Scientific Research Institute of the Sugar Industry   (RU)
UNIS .... Union Nigerienne des Independants et Sympathisants
UNIS .... Univac Industrie System [*Univac Industry System*] [*German*]   (ADPT)
UNISA....... Universiteit van Suid-Afrika [*University of South Africa*]
UniSA .... University of South Australia
UNISCO.... Union des Interets Sociaux Congolais
UNISIST... United Nations Ingergovernmental System of Information in Science and Technology [*UNESCO*] [*Zagreb, Yugoslavia*]
UNISIST... Universal System for Information in Science and Technology [*UNESCO*] [*ICSU*]
UNISkhOM ... Ukrainian Scientific Research Institute of Agricultural Machinery   (RU)
UNISM ..... Nonmetallic Minerals and Construction Materials Administration   (BU)
UNISON ... University Libraries in the State of New South Wales [*Australia*]
UNISYNDI ... Union Intersyndicale d'Entreprises et d'Industries de l'Ouest Africain
UNIT .... Instituto Uruguayo de Normas Tecnicas [*Montevideo, Uruguay*]   (LAA)
UNIT .... Union Nationale des Interpretes-Traducteurs
UNIT .... Unitarius [*Unitarian*]   (HU)
UNITA ...... Uniao Nacional para a Independencia Total de Angola [*National Union for the Complete Independence of Angola*]   (AF)
UNITAC.... United Travel & Tourism Agencies Co. [*Jordan*]
UNITALSA ... Union Tecnica para la Promocion del Aluminio SA [*Spain*]   (PDAA)
UNITAN ... Union de la Tannerie et de la Megisserie Belges [*Trade association*] [*Belgium*]   (EY)
UNITAR.... United Nations Institute for Training and Research [*New York*] [*ICSU*] [*Research center*]
UNITCHAD ... Union Interprofessionnelle du Tchad
UNITCHADIENNE ... Union Tchadienne de Transports [*Chad Transportation Union*]   (AF)
UNITEC.... Union Distribuidora Tecnica [*Colombia*]   (COL)

UNITEC.... Union Togolaise de Commerce
UNITECH ... University of Technology [*Papua New Guinea*]
UnitedTheol Coll ... United Theological College [*Australia*]
UNITEGUA ... Union de Transportistas Terrestres de Guatemala [*Union of Land Transport Workers of Guatemala*] (LA)
UNITEXTIL ... Union of Textile Industries [*Syria*]
UNITHAI ... United Thai Shipping Co. Ltd. [*Thailand*] (FEA)
UNITRA.... Union pour l'Industrie et les Travaux Publics [*Union for Industry and Public Works*] [*Senegal*] (AF)
UNITRA.... Zjednoczenie Przemyslu Elektronicznego i Teletechnicznego [*Electronics and Telecommunications Industry Union*] (POL)
UNIUM..... Union des Intellectuels et Universitaires Malgaches
Univ .... Universidade [*University*] [*Portuguese*]
univ............ Universita [*University*] [*Italian*]
Univ .... Universitaet [*University*] [*German*]
Univ .... Universiteit [*University*] [*Afrikaans*]
Univ .... University (PWGL)
UNIVALLE ... Universidad del Valle [*Colombia*] (COL)
UNIVENCA ... Union Venezolana Criadores de Aves [*Venezuela*] (DSCA)
Univermag ... Department Store (BU)
UNIVEX.... Universal Exports
UNIVIA..... Universal de Viajes [*Colombia*] (COL)
UNIVIR.... Union Industrial Vidriera Ltda. [*Colombia*] (COL)
Univ pech ... University Press (BU)
UNIWARRANT ... Mutuelle Universelle de Garantie
UNJ .... Union Nacional Jornalera [*National Union of Laborers*] [*El Salvador*] (LA)
UNJA .... Union Nationale de la Jeunesse Algerienne [*Algeria*] [*Political party*] (EY)
UNJC .... Union Nacional de Juristas Cubanos [*National Union of Cuban Lawyers*] (LA)
UNJD .... Union Nationale de la Jeunesse du Dahomey
UNJM .... Union Nationale de la Jeunesse du Mali
UNJS......... Union Nationale de la Jeunesse du Senegal [*National Union of Senegalese Youth*] (AF)
UNJSPF.... United Nations Joint Staff Pension Fund (ECON)
UNK.......... Undelayed Channel Amplifier (RU)
unk .... Unkariksi [*Finland*]
unk .... Unkarilainen [*Finland*]
unk .... Unkorrigiert [*Uncorrected*] [*German*] (GCA)
UNKA........ Abakan [*Former USSR*] [*ICAO location identifier*] (ICLI)
UNKF .... Administration of the People's Commissariat of Finance (RU)
UNKGB....... Administration of the People's Commissariat of State Security (RU)
UNKhU ..... Administration of the Statistical Survey of the National Economy (RU)
UNKI........ Vanavara [*Former USSR*] [*ICAO location identifier*] (ICLI)
UNKK....... Krasnoyarsk [*Former USSR*] [*ICAO location identifier*] (ICLI)
UNKO .... Sovetsky Rudnik [*Former USSR*] [*ICAO location identifier*] (ICLI)
UNKO .... United National Kadazan Organization [*Sabah*] (ML)
UNKT........ Podkamennaya Tunguska [*Former USSR*] [*ICAO location identifier*] (ICLI)
UNKVD..... Administration of the People's Commissariat of Internal Affairs (RU)
UNKW....... Baykit [*Former USSR*] [*ICAO location identifier*] (ICLI)
UNL.......... Universidad Nacional del Litoral [*Argentina*]
unl .... Unloeslich [*Insoluble*] [*German*]
UNLA .... Uganda National Liberation Army [*Political party*] (AF)
UNLA .... Uniao Nacional Luso-Angolana
UNLA .... Unione Nazionale per la Lotta Contra l'Analfabetismo [*Union for the Struggle Against Illiteracy*] [*Italy*]
unleserl ... Unleserlich [*Illegible*] [*German*]
UNLF .... Uganda National Liberation Forces (AF)
UNLF .... Ugandan National Liberation Front [*Political party*] (PD)
unlosl......... Unloeslich [*Insoluble*] [*German*]
UNLP .... Universidad Nacional de La Plata [*National University of La Plata*] [*Argentina*] (LA)
UNM .... Ugandan National Movement (AF)
UNM .... Ukase on the People's Militia (BU)
UNM .... Union Nationale Malgache [*Malagasy National Union*] (AF)
UNM .... Union Nationale Mauritanienne [*Mauritanian National Union*] (AF)
UNM .... United National Movement [*Saint Christopher and Nevis*] [*Political party*] (EY)
UNM .... Urad pro Normalizaci a Mereni [*Office for Standardization and Measurements*] (CZ)
UNMAC.... Mixed Armistice Commission
UNMC....... United Nations Mediterranean Command (BJA)
UNMEM... United Nations Middle East Mission (EY)
Unmibh...... United Nations Mission in Bosnia and Herzegovina [*1995*]
Unmih .... United Nations Mission in Haiti [*1993*]
Unmischbark ... Unmischbarkeit [*Immiscibility*] [*German*] (GCA)
UNML....... United Nations Mission in Libya

UNMO ...... United Malays National Organisation [*Malaysia*] [*Political party*] (ECON)
UNMOCO ... Union Morale Congolaise
Unmogip .... United Nations Military Observer Group in India and Pakistan [*1949*]
Unmop .... United Nations Mission of Observers in Prevlaka [*Croatia, 1996*]
UNMO's... United Nations Military Observers (BJA)
UNMS....... Union Nationale des Mutalites Socialistes [*Benelux*] (BAS)
UNN .... Low-Voltage Indicator (RU)
UNN .... University of Nigeria, Nsukka
unn .... Unnumeriert [*Unnumbered*] [*Publishing*] [*German*]
UNNE....... Universidad Nordestana [*Dominican Republic*]
UNNN .... Novosibirsk/Tolmachevo [*Former USSR*] [*ICAO location identifier*] (ICLI)
UNNRRF .. United Nations Natural Resources Revolving Fund
UNO .... Administration of Street Lighting (RU)
UNO .... Ugandan Nationalist Organization (AF)
UNO .... Union Nacional de Oposicion [*National Opposition Union*] [*El Salvador*] (LA)
UNO .... Union Nacional de Oposicion [*National Opposition Union*] [*Colorado*] (LA)
UNO .... Union Nacional Odriista [*National Odriista Union*] [*Peru*] (LA)
UNO .... Union Nacional Opositora [*Electoral alliance*] [*Nicaragua*] (EY)
UNO .... United Nations Observer Corps (BJA)
UNO .... United Nations Organization [*ICSU*]
UNO .... United Nicaraguan Opposition
UNOC .... Union Nacional de Obreros Cristianos [*National Union of Christian Workers*] [*El Salvador*] (LA)
UNOC .... Union Nacional Obrera-Campesina [*Trade union*] [*El Salvador*] (EY)
UNOC .... United Nations Operation in the Congo
UNOCA..... United Nations Office Coordinating Humanitarian and Economic Aid to Afghanistan (ECON)
UNOCHA ... United Nations Office for the Coordination of Humanitarian Assistance to Afghanistan (ECON)
UNOCIC ... Union Nacional de Organizaciones Sindicales Campesinos [*National Union of Peasant Trade Union Organizations*] [*Chile*] (LA)
UNOEOA ... United Nations Office for Emergency Operations in Africa [*Defunct*] (EA)
UNOH .... Union Nationale d'Ouvriers d'Haiti [*Trade union*] [*Haiti*]
Unomig ..... United Nations Observer Mission in Georgia [*1993*]
UNOO ...... United Nations Oceanographic Organization
UNOPI..... United Nations Office of Public Information
UNOPS ..... [*The*] United Nations Office for Project Services (ECON)
UNOTC.... United Nations Office for Technical Co-Operation
UNP .... Statics Indicator (RU)
UNP .... Uganda National Party
UNP......... Unification National Party [*South Korea*] [*Political party*] (EY)
UNP......... Union Nacional de Periodistas [*National Union of Journalists*] [*Ecuador*] (LA)
UNP......... Union Nacionalista del Pueblo [*People's Nationalist Union*] [*Bolivia*] (LA)
UNP......... Union Nacional Paraguaya [*Paraguayan National Union*] (LA)
UNP......... Union Nationale du Peuple
UNP......... United Nationalist Party [*Ghana*] (AF)
UNP......... United National Party [*Sri Lanka*] [*Political party*] (PPW)
UNP......... Universal Adjusting Device (RU)
UNP......... Ustredni Narodni Pojisteni [*Central Social Insurance Agency*] (CZ)
UNPA....... Unione Nazionale Protezione Antiaere [*Italy*]
UNPA....... Union Nationale des Paysans Algeriens [*National Union of Algerian Peasants*] (AF)
UNPA....... United Nations Protected Area (EECI)
UN-PAAERD ... United Nations Programme of Action for African Economic Recovery and Development [*1986-1990*]
unpag .... Unpaginiert [*Unpaginated*] [*Publishing*] [*German*]
UNPAL ..... Union Nacional de Productores de Aceite de Limon [*Mexico*] (DSCA)
UNPASA... Union Nacional de Productores de Azucar de Cana [*Mexico*] (LAA)
UNPAZA .. Union Nationale des Producteurs Agricoles et Artisans du Zaire [*National Agricultural Producers and Craftsmen's Union of Zaire*] (AF)
UNPC .... Union Nacional de Pequenos Caneros [*National Union of Small Cane Plantation Owners*] [*Mexico*] (LA)
UNPC .... Union Nationale des Professionnels de la Comptabilite
UNPCC ..... United Nations Palestine Conciliation Commission (BJA)
UNPDAC .. United Nations Program for Drug Abuse Control (AF)
UNPEG ..... Union Nacional de Productores y Exportadores de Garbanzo [*Mexico*] (DSCA)
UNPHU .... Universidad Nacional "Pedro Henriquez Urena" [*Pedro Henriquez Urena National University*] [*Dominican Republic*] (LA)
UNPM....... United National Pasok Momogun [*Kadazan organization in Sabah*] [*Also known as UPKO*] (ML)

UNPO........ Ukase on Naming and Renaming Sites of National and Local Importance (BU)
UNPO........ Unrepresented Nations and Peoples Organization
UNPOC..... United Nations Peace Observation Commission
Unpredep ... United Nations Preventive Deployment Force [*Macedonia*]
UNPROFOR ... United Nations Protection Force [*Former Yugoslavia*] (ECON)
UNPROFOR ... United Nations Protective Forces
UNPS .... Controlled Nonlinear Semiconductor Resistance (RU)
UNPZ .... Ufa Petroleum-Processing Plant (RU)
UNPZA ..... Union Nationale de la Presse du Zaire
UNQ .... University of North Queensland [*Australia*]
UNR........... Hungarian People's Republic (BU)
UNR........... Office of the Work Supervisor (RU)
UNR........... Ukase on Encouraging the Birthrate (BU)
UNR........... Ukrajinska Narodni Rada [*Ukrainian National Council*] (CZ)
UNR........... Uniao Nacional Republicana [*National Republican Union*] [*Portugal*] [*Political party*] (PPE)
UNR........... Union pour la Nouvelle Republique [*Union for the New Republic*] [*Burkina Faso*] (AF)
UNR........... Union pour la Nouvelle Republique [*Union for the New Republic*] [*Political party*] [*French*] (WER)
UNR........... Universite Nationale du Rwanda [*National University of Rwanda*] (AF)
Unr............. Unregelmaessig [*Irregular*] [*German*]
UNRCCFE ... United Nations Regional Cartographic Conferences on Asia and the Far East
UNREF...... United Nations Refugee Fund
Unregelmaessigk ... Unregelmaessigkeit [*Irregularity*] [*German*] (GCA)
UNRF .... Uganda National Rescue Front (PD)
UNRHCE ... United Nations Regional Housing Center for ESCAP [*Economic and Social Commission for Asia and the Pacific*] [*India*] (EAIO)
UNRIPS .... United Nations Regional Institute for Population Studies [*Legon, Ghana*] (EAIO)
UNRISD.... United Nations Research Institute for Social Development (EA)
UNRM....... Ukase on Encouraging Births and Large Families (BU)
UNRP .... Ukrajinska Narodna Rada Presovsciny [*Ukrainian National Council of the Presov Region*] (CZ)
UNRRA ..... Administration des Nations Unies pour la Reconstruction et l'Assistance [*United Nations Relief and Rehabilitation Administration*] [*French*]
UNRRA ..... United Nations Relief and Rehabilitation Administration [*"United Nations" derives from the wartime alliance of this name, not from any affiliation with the postwar international organization*]
UNRS .... Continuous Steel Pouring Unit (RU)
UNRS .... University of Newcastle Postgraduate Research Scholarship [*Australia*]
UNRV........ Union pour la Nouvelle Republique Voltaique
UNRWA.... United Nations Relief and Works Agency for Palestine Refugees in the Near East [*Austria*] (PD)
UNRWAPR ... United Nations Relief and Works Agency for Palestine Refugees [*ME*]
UNRWAPR ... United Nations Relief and Works Agency for Palestine Refugees in the Near East [*Austria*] (DLA)
UNS........... Barrel Inclination Angle (RU)
UNS........... Office of the Chief of Supply (RU)
UNS........... Optimum Speed Indicator (RU)
UNS........... Udruzenje Novinara Srbije [*Association of Journalists of Serbia*] (YU)
UNS........... Unified National System of Tertiary Education [*Australia*]
UNS........... Union for National Self-Determination [*Armenia*] (EE)
UNS........... Union Nacional Sinarquista [*National Sinarchist Union*] [*Mexico*] (LA)
UNS........... Union Nationale des Syndicats [*Trade union*] [*Benin*]
UNS........... Union Nationale Somalo [*Somali National Union*] (AF)
UNS........... Universal News Service [*British*]
uns............. Unsymmetrisch [*Unsymmetric*] [*German*]
UNS........... Ustaska Narodna Straza [*Ustashi National Guard*] [*Croatia*] [*World War II*] (YU)
UNS........... Ustav Nerostnych Surovin [*Mineral Raw Material Research Institute*] (CZ)
UNS........... Ustavodarne Narodni Shromazdeni [*Constituent National Assembly*] (CZ)
UNS........... Ustredni Normativni Komise [*Central Standards Committee (of the Research Institute of Construction Economy)*] (CZ)
UNSAC ..... United Nations Scientific Advisory Committee [*ICSU*]
UNSC .... United Nations Security Council
Unschaedlichmach ... Unschaedlichmachung [*Rendering Nondangerous*] [*German*] (GCA)
UNSF........ United Nations Special Fund
UNSIS....... United Nations Statistical Information System (DUND)
UNSIT....... Union Nationale des Syndicats Independants du Togo (EY)
UNSITRAGUA ... Union Sindical de Trabajadores de Guatemalteco [*Trade Union Unity of Guatemalan Workers*]
UNSO........ United Nations Sahelian Office

UNSP .... Uniao Nacional dos Servidores Publicos [*National Union of Public Employees*] [*Brazil*] (LA)
UNSP .... Union Nationale des Services Publics [*Trade union*] [*Belgium*] (EY)
UNSP .... Union Nationale pour la Solidarite et le Progres [*Benin*] [*Political party*] (EY)
UNSPDPM ... United Nations Subcommission on the Prevention of Discrimination and the Protection of Minorities [*Geneva, Switzerland*] (EAIO)
UNSR .... United Nations Space Registry (BARN)
UNSSFNRJ ... Udruzenje Nastavnika Strucnih Skola Federativna Narodna Republika Jugoslavija [*Association of Vocational School Teachers of Yugoslavia*] (YU)
UNSSOD .. United Nations Special Session on Disarmament (PDAA)
UNST .... Union Nationale Syndicats du Tchad (EY)
UNST .... Union Nordique pour la Sante et le Travail [*Nordic Union for Health and Work*] (EAIO)
UNSTA ..... Universidad del Norte Santo Tomas de Aquino [*Santo Tomas de Aquino Northern University*] [*Argentina*] [*Research center*] (ERC)
UNSTB...... Union Nationale des Syndicats des Travailleurs du Benin [*National Federation of Workers Unions of Benin*] (AF)
UNSTD ..... Union Nationale des Syndicats des Travailleurs du Dahomey
UNSTHV .. Union Nationale des Travailleurs de la Haute-Volta
UNSW....... University of New South Wales [*Australia*] (ARC)
UNSWIL... University of New South Wales Institute of Languages [*Australia*]
UNSWP .... United National South-West Party [*Namibia*] (AF)
UNSWR .... University of New South Wales Regiment [*Australia*]
UNT .... Union Nationale des Travailleurs [*Ivory Coast*]
UNT .... Union Nationale Tchadienne
u-nt............ University (BU)
unt .... Unten [*Below*] [*German*] (GCA)
unt .... Unter [*Under, Among*] [*Germany*]
UNTA........ Uniao Nacional dos Trabalhadores de Angolanos [*National Union of Angolan Workers*] (AF)
UNTA........ Union Nacional de Trabajadores Agricolas [*National Union of Agricultural Workers*] [*Mexico*] (LA)
UNTA........ Union Nationale des Travailleurs d'Angola [*National Union of Workers of Angola*] (EAIO)
UNTA........ United Nations Technical Assistance
UNTAA ..... United Nations Technical Assistance Administration
UNTAB ..... United Nations Technical Assistance Board
UNTAC ..... United Nations Technical Assistance Committee
UNTAC ..... United Nations Transitional Authority in Cambodia (ECON)
UNTAG ..... United Nations Transition Assistance Group [*Namibia*] (AF)
UNTAM... United Nations Technical Assistance Mission (BARN)
UNTAP ..... United Nations Technical Assistance Programme
UNTC........ Union Nationale des Travailleurs Camerounais [*National Union of Cameroonian Workers*] (AF)
UNTC........ Union Nationale des Travailleurs Congolais [*National Union of Congolese Workers*]
UNTC........ United Nations Trusteeship Council (BARN)
UNTC-CS ... Uniao Nacional dos Trabalhadores de Cabo Verde - Central Sindical [*Trade unions of Cape Verde Unity Centre*]
UNTCI ...... Union Nationale des Travailleurs de Cote-D'Ivoire [*National Union of Ivory Coast Workers*] (AF)
UNTCV ..... Union Nationale des Travailleurs du Cap Vert [*National Union of Workers of Cape Verde*] (EAIO)
UNTEA ...... United Nations Temporary Executive Authority [*Supervised transfer of Netherlands New Guinea to Indonesia*]
Unterbind... Unterbindung [*Ligature*] [*German*] (GCA)
Untergb...... Untergebener [*Subordinate*] [*German*] (GCA)
unterird ...... Unterirdisch [*Subterranean*] [*German*] (GCA)
Untern........ Unternehmen [*or Unternehmung*] [*Enterprise, Undertaking*] [*German*] (GCA)
Unterr .... Unterricht [*Instruction*] [*German*] (GCA)
Unters .... Untersuchung [*Examination, Investigation*] [*German*]
Unterscheid .. Unterscheidung [*Differentiation*] [*German*] (GCA)
Unterstr ..... Unterstreichung [*Underlining*] [*German*]
Unterstreich ... Unterstreichung [*Underlining*] [*German*]
Untertit ...... Untertitel [*Subtitle*] [*German*]
UNTFAD .. United Nations Trust Fund for African Development
UNTG........ Uniao Nacional dos Trabalhadores de Guine [*National Union of Guinea-Bissau Workers*] (AF)
UNTGB..... Union Nationale des Travailleurs de Guinee-Bissau [*National Union of Guinea-Bissau Workers*] (AF)
UNTHV..... Union Nationale des Travailleurs de Haute-Volta [*National Union of Upper Volta Workers*] (AF)
UNTIS....... United Nations Treaty Information System (DUND)
UNTM....... Union Nationale des Travailleurs du Mali [*National Union of Mali Workers*] (AF)
UNTMRA ... Union Nacional de Trabajadores del Metal y Ramas Afines [*National Union of Metalworkers and Related Industries Workers*] [*Uruguay*] (LA)
UNTN........ Union Nationale des Travailleurs Nigeriens [*National Union of Nigerien Workers*] [*Niger*] (AF)

UNTRA ..... Radio and Television Organisations of Africa
UNTRAD .. United Nations Conference on Trade and Development (CL)
UNTRAHUILA ... Union de Trabajadores del Huila [*Neiva*] (COL)
UNTS .... Unidad Nacional de Trabajadores Salvadorenos [*El Salvador*] (EY)
UNTS .... Union Nationale des Travailleurs du Senegal [*National Union of Workers of Senegal*] (AF)
UNTS .... Union Nationale des Travailleurs du Soudan
UNTSO ..... United Nations Truce Supervision Organization
UNTT .... Union Nationale des Travailleurs du Togo [*National Union of Workers of Togo*] (AF)
UNTT .... Union Nationale des Travailleurs Tchadiens [*National Union of Workers of Chad*]
UNTT .... Union Nationale Tunisienne du Travail [*National Union of Tunisian Workers*] (MENA)
UNTZ .... Union Nationale des Travailleurs Zairois [*National Union of Zairian Workers*] [*Political party*]
UNTZa ...... Union Nationale des Travailleurs du Zaire [*National Union of Workers of Zaire*] (AF)
unt Zers ..... Unter Zersetzung [*With Decomposition*] [*German*] (GCA)
UNU .... Universidad de las Naciones Unidas [*United Nations University*] [*Spanish*] (DUND)
UNU .... Universite des Nations Unies [*United Nations University*] [*French*] (DUND)
UNU .... Unprotected Ultrahigh-Frequency Carbon (Resistor) (RU)
UNUIIST .. United Nations University International Institute for Software
unumm ...... Unummereret [*Unnumbered*] [*Publishing Danish/Norwegian*]
UNURI ...... Unione Nazionale Universitaria Rappresentativa Italiana [*National Union of Italian University Representatives*] (WER)
UNU/WIDER ... United Nations University / World Institute for Development Economics Research (DUND)
UNV .... Ujpesti Novenyolajipari Vallalat [*Vegetable Oil Industrial Enterprise of Ujpest*] (HU)
UNV .... United Nations Volunteers (EAIO)
UNV .... United NAZI Victims [*European*]
unv .... Unveroeffentlicht [*Unpublished*] [*German*] (GCA)
UNV .... Ustredni Narodni Vybor [*Central People's Committee*] (CZ)
UNVDA ..... Upper Noun Valley Development Authority
unver .... Unveraendert [*Unchanged*] [*German*]
unveraend... Unveraendert [*Unchanged*] [*German*] (GCA)
unveraenderl ... Unveraenderlich [*Unchangeable*] [*German*] (GCA)
unverand ... Unveraenderlich [*Unchangeable, Invariable, Constant*] [*German*]
unvergl ...... Unvergleichlich [*Incomparable*] [*German*]
unveroff ..... Unveroeffentlicht [*Unpublished*] [*German*]
UNViR .... Consolidated Time Norms and Wages (RU)
unvollstaend ... Unvollstaendig [*Incomplete*] [*German*] (GCA)
UNWFP .... United Nations World Food Programme
UNY .... United Nations of Yoga [*Stockholm, Sweden*] (EAIO)
UNYEK .... Universite Yemek Kurulu [*University Food Association*] (TU)
UNYTT ..... Utviklingsfondet Framtiden i Vare Hender [*Development Fund Future in Our Hands*] [*An association*] [*Norway*] (EAIO)
Unyuroren ... Zen-Nihon Unyu-Sangyo Rodokumiai Rengokai [*Council of All-Japan Transport Workers' Unions*]
UNZ.......... Ustav Narodniho Zdravi [*National Health Institute*] (CZ)
UNZA........ University of Zambia
UNZAAWU ... University of Zambia and Allied Workers Union
UNZABECA ... University of Zambia Business and Economic Association
UNZAGA ... University of Zambia Geographical Association
unzers .... Unzersetzbar [*Undecomposable*] [*German*] (GCA)
unzers .... Unzersetzt [*Undecomposed*] [*German*] (GCA)
Unzhlag ..... Unzha Corrective Labor Camp (RU)
UNZhS ...... Ukase on Encouraging and Assisting Cooperative and Individual Housing Construction (BU)
UO .... Limiting Amplifier (RU)
UO .... Optical Goniometer (RU)
UO .... Strongpoint, Center of Resistance (RU)
UO .... Training Detachment (RU)
uo.............. Ugyanott [*In the Same Place*] (HU)
uo.............. Ugyosztaly [*Department*] (HU)
UO .... Ulku Ocaklari [*Idealist Clubs*] (TU)
UO .... Union Observatory
UO .... Unterordnung [*Suborder*] [*German*]
UO .... Upravni Odbor [*Administrative Committee*] (YU)
UO .... Ustredni Opravny [*Central Repair Shops (of the State Tractor Stations)*] (CZ)
UO .... Utvorova Organisace [*Communist Party Organization within a Military Unit*] (CZ)
UOA .... Underground Officials' Association of South Africa (AA)
UOAPV ..... Single-Phase Automatic Recloser (RU)
UOAQ .... Unit Owners' Association of Queensland [*Australia*]
UOB.......... United Overseas Bank [*Singapore*]
UOB.......... Universite Officielle de Bujumbura [*Burundi*]
UOB.......... Universite Omar Bongo [*Gabon*]
UOC.......... Uganda Olympic Committee (EAIO)

UOC.......... Union Obrera Catolica [*Catholic Trade Union*] [*Bolivia*] (LA)
UOC.......... Union Obrera de la Construccion [*Union of Construction Workers*] [*Argentina*] (LA)
UOC.......... Universite Officielle du Congo
UOCh .... Ustav Organicke Chemie [*Institute of Organic Chemistry (of the Czechoslovak Academy of Sciences)*] (CZ)
UOCRA ..... Union Obrera de la Construccion de la Republica Argentina [*Construction Workers Union of the Argentine Republic*] (LA)
UOD .... Ulku Ocaklari Dernegi [*Idealist Hearths (Clubs) Organization*] (TU)
UOEM....... Union de Obreros y Empleados Municipales [*Municipal Workers and Employees Union*] [*Argentina*] (LA)
UofZ.......... University of Zimbabwe
UOGK....... Ukrainian Branch of the Geological Committee (RU)
UOI........... Union de Obreros Independientes [*Union of Independent Workers*] [*Mexico*] (LA)
UOK .... Ustredna Obchodnich Komor [*Central Bureau of the Chambers of Commerce*] (CZ)
UOK .... Ustredni Organisacni Komise [*Central Organizational Commission*] (CZ)
UOKh .... Training and Experimental Farm (RU)
UOL.......... United Orient Leasing Co. Berhad [*Malaysia*]
UOM .... Union Obrera Metalurgica [*Metalworkers Union*] [*Argentina*] (LA)
UoM .... University of Malaya (ML)
UOM .... Uradovna Ochrany Mladeze [*Office for the Protection of Youth*] (CZ)
UOMA ...... Union Obrera Molinera Argentina [*Argentina Flour Mill Workers Union*] (LA)
UOME....... Union des Opposants Malgaches Exterieurs [*Madagascar*] [*Political party*] (EY)
UOMPZ .... Ukase on Orders, Medals, and Honorary Titles (BU)
UON .... Charter of the League of Nations (BU)
UON .... Reference Voltage Amplifier (RU)
UON .... University of Nairobi [*Kenya*] (AF)
UOO .... Upravleniye Osobykh Otdelov [*Armed Forces Counterintelligence-Directorate*] [*Former USSR*] (LAIN)
UOO .... Uredba o Obaveznom Osiguranju [*Decree on Compulsory Insurance*] [*Railroads*] (YU)
uooa........... Utan Ort och Ar [*Without Place and Year*] [*Publishing*] [*Sweden*]
UOOP....... Administration for the Protection of Public Order (RU)
UOp.......... Operation Control (RU)
UOP.......... Unidade Operativa de Proteccao [*Unit for Protective Operations*] [*Angola*] (AF)
UOP.......... Urad Ochrany Prace [*Office for the Protection of Labor*] (CZ)
UOP.......... Uredba o Osnivanju Preduzeca i Radnji [*Decree on the Foundation of Enterprises and Shops*] (YU)
UOPDK .... Ukase on Insurance and Pensions of Cultural Workers (BU)
UOPDP ..... Union Ouvriere et Paysanne pour la Democratie Proletarienne [*Peasant and Worker Union for Proletarian Democracy*] [*France*] [*Political party*] (PPE)
UOPG....... United Osteopathic Physicians Guild [*Australia*]
UOPLF...... United Oromo People's Liberation Front [*Ethiopia*] [*Political party*] (EY)
uops........... Uopskaaret [*Uncut*] [*Publishing Danish/Norwegian*]
uopskr .... Uopskaaret [*Uncut*] [*Publishing Danish/Norwegian*]
UOR.......... Administration of Finishing Work (RU)
UORU .... Ustredni Odborova Rada Ucitelska [*Central Council of Teachers' Unions*] (CZ)
UOS.......... Defense Construction Directorate (RU)
UOS.......... Feedback Amplifier (RU)
UOS.......... Irrigation System Administration (RU)
UOS.......... Uredba o Upravljanju Osnovnim Sredstvima Privrednih Organizacija [*Decree on the Management of Basic Resources of Economic Organizations*] (YU)
UOS.......... Ustredie Odborovych Svazov [*Trade-Union Headquarters*] (CZ)
UOSS........ Ukase on the Protection of Agriculture (BU)
UOT.......... Labor Safety Administration (BU)
UOT.......... Union Obrera Textil [*Textile Workers Union*] [*Uruguay*] (LA)
UOV .... Chocking Agent (RU)
UOV .... Persistent Chemical Agent (BU)
UOVS .... Universiteit van die Oranje Vrijstaat [*University of the Orange Free State - UOFS*] [*South Africa*]
UOVTI ...... Ural Branch of the All-Union Institute of Heat Engineering Imeni F. E. Dzerzhinskiy (RU)
UOW .... Ukrainska Organizacja Wojskowa [*Ukrainian Military Organization*] (POL)
UOZK....... Ustredna Obchodnich a Zivnostenskych Komor [*Central Bureau of the Chambers of Commerce and Trade*] (CZ)
UOZTVPSNVN ... Ukase Repealing the Law on Foreign Exchange Transactions and Penalties for Currency Violations (BU)
UP.............. Angle of Approach (RU)
UP.............. Conditional Jump [*Computers*] (RU)
UP.............. Consolidated Index (RU)
UP.............. Emergency Situation [*Civil defense*] (RU)

UP .... Fortified Zone (RU)
UP .... General-Purpose Switch (RU)
UP .... Intermediate Repeater (RU)
UP .... Pension Administration (BU)
UP .... Position Indicator (RU)
UP .... Repeater Station (RU)
UP .... Repeater Substation (RU)
UP .... Slaughterhouse (RU)
UP .... Street Loudspeaker (RU)
UP .... Turn Indicator (RU)
UP .... Ubrzani-Putnicki [*Express Passenger*] [*Railroads*] (YU)
UP .... Ugostiteljsko Poduzece [*Hotel and Catering Trade Establishment*] (YU)
UP .... Umma Party [*Sudan*] (MENA)
UP .... Unidad Popular [*Popular Unity*] [*Chile*] (LA)
UP .... Union del Pueblo [*Union of the People*] [*Peru*] (LAA)
UP .... Union del Pueblo [*Union of the People*] [*Mexico*] (PD)
UP .... Union of Pharmacists [*Israel*] (EAIO)
UP .... Union of Philatelists (EAIO)
UP .... Union Patriotica [*Patriotic Union*] [*Colorado*] [*Political party*]
UP .... Union Patriotica [*Patriotic Union*] [*Spain*] [*Political party*] (PPE)
UP .... Union Popular [*Popular Union*] [*Uruguay*] (PD)
UP .... Union Popular [*Popular Union*] [*Argentina*] (LA)
UP .... Union Postale [*Postal Union*] [*French*]
UP .... Unita Popolare [*Popular Unity*] [*Italian*] (WER)
UP .... United Party [*Zambia*] (AF)
UP .... United Party [*Virgin Islands*] (LA)
UP .... United Party [*Ghana*] (AF)
UP .... United Party [*Jamaica*] (LA)
UP .... United Party [*South Africa*] (AF)
UP .... United Party [*Papua New Guinea*] [*Political party*] (PPW)
UP .... United Party [*Gambia*] [*Political party*] (PPW)
UP .... United Plantations [*Malaysia*]
UP .... Unites de Production
UP .... Unity Party [*Nigeria*] (AF)
UP .... Unity Party [*Sierra Leone*] [*Political party*] (EY)
UP .... Unity Party [*Liberia*] [*Political party*] (EY)
UP .... Universal Device (RU)
UP .... Universita Palackeho [*Palacky University*] [*Olomouc*] (CZ)
UP .... Universiteit van Pretoria [*University of Pretoria*] [*Afrikaans*]
UP .... University of Peace [*Costa Rica*]
UP .... University of the Philippines
UP .... University Partnership [*Australia*]
UP .... Uniwersytet Powszechny [*Popular University*] [*Poland*]
UP .... Uniwersytet Poznanski [*Poznan University*] (POL)
UP .... Unterprogramm [*Subprogram*] [*German*] (ADPT)
UP .... Unterpulver-Schweissverfahren [*Flux Powder Welding*] (EG)
UP .... Uprava Prihoda [*Revenue Administration*] (YU)
UP .... Urazova Pojistovna [*Accident Insurance Agency*] (CZ)
UP .... Urban Promotions [*Manila police force*] [*Philippines*]
UP .... Urzad Patentowy [*Patent Office*] (POL)
UP .... Urzad Pocztowy [*Post Office*] (POL)
UP .... Ustav Prefabrikace [*Institute of Prefabricated Building*] (CZ)
UP .... Ustredni Prodejna [*Central Sales Office*] (CZ)
UP .... Uzemni Planovani [*Regional Planning*] (CZ)
UPA .... Ucuz Emtia Pazarlama, Sanayii, ve Ticaret TAS [*Low Priced Commodities Marketing, Industry, and Commerce Corporation*] (TU)
UPA .... Uganda People's Alliance (AF)
UPA .... Ukrains'ka Povstans'ka Armiia
UPA .... Ukrainska Powstancza Armia [*Ukrainian Guerrilla Army*] (POL)
UPA .... Umweltbundesamt [*Berlin*] [*Information retrieval*]
UPA .... Uniao das Populacoes de Angola [*Angolan People's Union*] [*Later, NFLA*]
UPA .... Uniao dos Povos Angolanos [*Union of Angolan Peoples*] (AF)
UPA .... Unia Poludniowoafrykanska [*South African Union*] [*Poland*]
UPA .... Unidad para Avanzar [*Unity for Advancement*] [*Costa Rica*] (LA)
UPA .... Union de Propietarios Agropecuarios [*Venezuela*] (DSCA)
UPA .... Union des Parlements Africains [*African Parliaments Union*] (AF)
UPA .... Union Panafricaine des Agriculteurs
UPA .... Union Panamericana [*Pan-American Union*] [*Washington, DC*]
UPA .... Union para Avanzar [*Union for Advancement*] [*Venezuela*] (LA)
UPA .... Union Patriotica Anti-Imperialista [*Anti-Imperialist Patriotic Union*] [*Dominican Republic*] (LA)
UPA .... Union Populaire Africaine [*African People's Union*] [*Djibouti*] (AF)
UPA .... Union Populaire Algerienne [*Algerian People's Union*]
UPA .... Union Popular de Artistas [*Peoples' Artist Union*] [*Spanish*] (WER)
UPA .... Union Postale Arabe [*North African*]

UPAC .... Unidad de Poder Adquisitivo Constante [*Savings Certificates with Constant Purchasing Power*] [*Spanish*] (LA)
UPAC .... Unificacion y Progreso [*Unification and Progress*] [*Mexico*] [*Political party*] (PPW)
UPACH ..... Union de Periodistas Antifascistas de Chile [*Union of Antifascist Chilean Journalists*] (LA)
UPACI .... Union Patronale de Cote d'Ivoire [*Ivory Coast*] (EY)
UPADI ...... Union Pan-Americana de Asociaciones de Igenieros [*Pan American Federation of Engineering Societies*] [*Uruguay*] (EAIO)
UPAE .... Union Postal de las Americas y Espana [*Postal Union of the Americas and Spain - PUAS*] (EAIO)
UPAEP ...... Union Postal de las Americas, Espana, y Portugal [*Postal Union of the Americas, Spain, and Portugal*] [*Uruguay*] (EAIO)
UPAF .... Union Postale Africaine [*African Postal Union*] [*Use APU*] (AF)
upag .... Upagineret [*With Pages Unnumbered*] [*Publishing Danish/Norwegian*]
UPAJ .... Union Panafricaine des Journalistes
UPAJE ...... Uniao Promotora de Actividades Juvenis Educativas [*Union for Youth Education and Cultural Action*] [*Portugal*] (EAIO)
UPAM .... United People's Association of Matabeleland [*Zimbabwe*] [*Political party*] (PPW)
UPAM .... United Planting Association of Malaya (ML)
UPAN .... United Pools Agents Association
UPANIC .... Union de Productores Agropecuarios de Nicaragua [*Agriculture and Livestock Producers Union of Nicaragua*] (LA)
UPANSW ... United Protestant Association of New South Wales [*Australia*]
UPAP .... Union Pan Africaine des Postes [*Pan African Postal Union - PAPU*] (EAIO)
UPARA ..... Union de Productores Agropecuarios de la Republica Argentina [*Union of Agriculture and Livestock Producers of the Argentine Republic*] (LA)
UPAS .... Universelles Programm-und Analysesystem [*German*] (ADPT)
UPAS .... Usak Elektro Porselen Anonim Sirketi [*Usak Electro-Porcelain Manufacturing Corporation*] (TU)
UPASI .... United Planters Association of South India (PDAA)
UPAT .... Union Panafricaine des Telecommunications [*Pan African Telecommunications Union - PATU*] (EAIO)
UPATC ..... Union Pan-Africaine des Travailleurs Croyants [*Trade union*] [*African*]
UPAVE ...... Union de Productores de Azucar de Venezuela [*Venezuela*] (DSCA)
UPB .... Amplifying-Converting Unit (RU)
UPB .... Uniao dos Portuarios do Brasil [*Brazilian Longshoremen's Union*] (LA)
UPB .... Union Patriotica Bonairiana [*Bonaire Patriotic Union*] [*Netherlands Antilles*] [*Political party*] (PPW)
UPB .... Union Populaire du Burundi
UPB .... Universidad Pontificia Bolivariana [*Colombia*] (COL)
UPBMO .... Union Professionnelle Belge des Medecins Ophtalmologistes [*Belgian Professional Union of Ophthalmologists*] (SLS)
UPC .... Unidade Padrao de Capital [*Standard Unit of Capital*] [*Brazil*] (LA)
UPC .... Union del Pueblo Canario [*Union of the Canarian People*] [*Spain*] [*Political party*] (PPE)
UPC .... Union de Pioneros Cubanos [*Union of Cuban Pioneers*] (LA)
UPC .... Union des Populations Camerounaises [*Union of Cameroonian Peoples*] (PD)
UPC .... Unione di u Populu Corsu [*Union of the Corsican People*] [*France*] [*Political party*] (PPE)
UPC .... Union of Polish Composers (EAIO)
UPC .... Union pour le Progres Comorien [*Union for Comorian Progress*] [*Political party*] (PPW)
UPC .... Unions Paysannes Communales [*Communal Peasant Unions*] [*Algeria*] (AF)
UPC .... United Pentecostal Church [*Australia*]
UPC .... Universidad Pedagogica de Colombia [*Colombia*] (COL)
UPC .... Universidad Politecnica de Cataluna [*Cataluna Technical University*] [*Spain*] (ERC)
UPCC .... Union Popular del Campo de Cataluna [*Popular Union of the Catalonian Countryside*] [*Spanish*] (WER)
UPCF .... Union des Pilotes Civiles de France [*France*]
UPCF .... University of the Philippines, College of Fisheries (ASF)
UPCh .... Intermediate-Frequency Amplifier (RU)
UPCh .... Union de Profesores de Chile [*Chilean Teachers Union*] (LA)
UPCI .... Union pour Construire l'Independence [*New Caledonia*] [*Political party*] (EY)
UPCN .... Union del Personal Civil de la Nacion [*National Civil Service Personnel Union*] [*Argentina*] (LA)
UPCPV ...... Union Popular de Campesinos del Pais Valenciano [*People's Union of Valencia Country Farmers*] [*Spanish*] (WER)
UPCSM ..... United Presbyterian Church of Scotland Mission
UPD .... Unidad Popular Democratica [*People's Democratic Union*] [*Spanish*] (WER)
UPD .... Unidad Popular Democratica [*Popular Democratic Party*] [*El Salvador*] [*Political party*]

UPD........... Unidad Preventiva del Delito [*Crime Prevention Unit*] [*Costa Rica*]   (LA)
UPD........... Unidad Progressiste Dahomeenne
UPD........... Union des Patriotes Democratiques [*Haiti*] [*Political party*]   (EY)
UPD........... Uredba o Porezu na Dobit iz Deviznog Poslovanja [*Decree on the Tax on Profit in Foreign Exchange Operations*] [*Yugoslavian*]   (YU)
UPD........... Urusan Perumahan Djakarta [*Djakarta Housing Authority*]   (IN)
UPDC........ Union Popular Democratica Cristiana [*Christian Democratic Popular Union*] [*Bolivia*]   (LA)
UPDEA ..... Union des Producteurs, Transporteurs, et Distributeurs d'Energie Electrique d'Afrique [*Union of Producers, Conveyors, and Distributors of Electric Power in Africa - UPDEA*]   (EAIO)
UPDEA ..... Union of Producers and Distributors of Electricity in Africa
UPDED ..... Unidad Progresista de Diplomacia [*Progressive Unity of Diplomacy*] [*Panama*]
UPDK .... Upravleniye po Obsluzhivaniyu Diplomaticheskogo Korpusa [*Administration for Servicing the Diplomatic Corps*] [*Russian*]
UPDM....... Uganda People's Democratic Movement
UPDP .... Union des Patriotes Democrates et Progressistes [*Niger*] [*Political party*]   (EY)
UPE .... Uniao Paranaense dos Estudantes [*Parana Students Union*] [*Brazil*]
UPE .... Unidades de Produccion Estatal [*State Production Units*] [*Nicaragua*]   (LA)
UPE .... Union del Pueblo Espanol [*Union of the Spanish People*]   (WER)
UPE .... Union de Patriotas Espanoles [*Union of Patriots*] [*Spanish*]
UPE .... Union Panafricaine des Etudiants [*All Africa Students Union - AASU*]   (EAIO)
UPE .... Universal Primary Education Programme
UPE .... Universiteit van Port Elizabeth [*University of Port Elizabeth*] [*South Africa*]   (AA)
UPE .... Ustav Prumyslove Ekonomiky [*Institute of Industrial Economics*] [*Prague*]   (CZ)
UPEB........ Union de Paises Exportadores de Banano [*Union of Banana-Exporting Countries - UBEC*]   (EAIO)
UPEC........ Union de Periodistas Cubanos [*Union of Cuban Journalists*]   (LA)
UPEC........ Uttar Pradesh Export Corp. [*India*]   (PDAA)
UPECO ..... Union Progressiste Congolaise
UPEF....... Union et Progres dans l'Ensemblement Francaise
UPEI........ Union Petroliere Europeenne Independante [*Independent European Petroleum Union*]   (EAIO)
UPEL........ Union de Periodistas Escolares de Lima [*Union of Student Journalists of Lima*] [*Peru*]   (LA)
UPEL........ Uprava za Elektroprivredu [*Administration of Electric Industries*]   (YU)
UPEM .... Union Progressive des Femmes Marocaines [*Progressive Union of Moroccan Women*]   (AF)
UPENCOL ... Union de Pensionados Oficiales y Particulares de Colombia [*Colombian Government and Private Industry Pensioners Union*]   (LA)
UPEPI....... Union of European Practitioners in Industrial Property [*EC*]   (ECED)
UPES........ Unidades de Produccion Estatal Sandinista [*Sandinist State Production Units*] [*Nicaragua*]   (LA)
UPESUNA ... United Progressive Ethiopian Students' Union in North America [*Bolshevik*]   (AF)
UPEU .... Uganda Public Employees Union   (AF)
UPF .... Primary Clamping Device   (RU)
UPF .... Uganda Popular Front [*Political party*]   (PD)
UPF .... Union pour la France [*France*] [*Political party*]
UPF .... United People's Front [*Singapore*] [*Political party*]   (PPW)
UPF .... United People's Front [*Nepal*] [*Political party*]   (EY)
UPF .... Ustav pro Praktickou Fotografii [*Institute of Practical Photography*]   (CZ)
UPF .... Ustredni Pujcovna Filmu [*Central Film Lending Library*]   (CZ)
UPFC........ Uttar Pradesh Financial Corp. [*India*]   (PDAA)
UPFM....... Union de Productores Forestales de Michoacan [*Mexico*]   (DSCA)
UPFSI....... Porcelain-Faience and Glassware Administration   (BU)
UPFT........ Uluslararasi Para Fonu Teskilati [*International Monetary Fund Organization*] [*Turkish*]   (TU)
UPFT........ Union Progressiste Franco-Tchadienne
UPG........... Ujung Pandang [*Indonesia*] [*Airport symbol*]   (OAG)
UPG........... Uniao das Populacoes da Guine
UPG........... Union del Pueblo Gallego [*Galician People's Union*] [*Spanish*]   (WER)
UPG........... Union des Populations de Guinee [*Guinea People's Union*]   (PD)
UPG........... Union du Peuple Gabonais [*Political party*]   (EY)
UPG........... Union Patriotica Guatemalteca [*Guatemalan Patriotic Union*]   (LA)
UPG........... Union Progressiste Guineenne

upg .... Upagineret [*With Pages Unnumbered*] [*Publishing Danish/Norwegian*]
UPGA........ United Progressive Grand Alliance
UPGC....... University and Polytechnic Grants Committee [*Hong Kong*]
UPGS....... Unione Progressista della Gioventu Somala
UPH........... Udruzenje Pravnika Hrvatske [*Croatian Lawyers' Association*]   (YU)
UPHA........ Union Phosphatiere Africaine
UPHILBAFUMA ... Union Philanthropique des Bantandu de Nfuma de Leopoldville-Ouest
UPHM....... Union de Productores de Henequen en Merida [*Mexico*]   (DSCA)
UPI .... Simplified Indicator (of Toxic Agents)   (RU)
UPI .... Union Popular Izquierdista [*Popular Leftist Union*] [*Venezuela*]   (LA)
UPI .... United Press International
UPI .... Universal Personal Identifier
UPI .... Ural Polytechnic Institute Imeni S. M. Kirov   (RU)
UPIA .... Union Pharmaceutique Inter-Africaine
UPIA .... United Press International Audio   (NTCM)
UPICV....... Union du Peuple des Iles du Cap Vert
UPICV-R... Uniao do Povo para Independencia de Cabo Verde-Ressusitacao [*Cape Verde*] [*Political party*]   (EY)
UPIGO ...... Union Professionnelle Internationale des Gynecologues et Obstetriciens [*International Professional Union of Obstetricians and Gynecologists*] [*French*]   (SLS)
UPIN .... United Press International News-Features   (NTCM)
UPINCh .... General-Purpose Device of Infrasonic Frequencies   (RU)
UPIRN ...... United Press International Radio Network   (NTCM)
UPISSI ...... University of the Philippines - Institute for Small-Scale Industries
UPITN....... United Press International Television News   (NTCM)
UPJNA...... Uredba o Privrednim Preduzecima Koja Proizvode za Potrebe Jugoslovenske Narodne Armije [*Decree on Economic Enterprises Producing for the Yugoslav People's Army*]   (YU)
UPJU........ Uganda Vernacular, Primary, and Junior Secondary Teachers Union   (AF)
UPK .... Code of Criminal Procedure   (RU)
UPK .... Equation for the Concentration of Predominant Components   (RU)
UPK .... Industrial Training Center   (RU)
UPK .... Personnel Training Administration   (RU)
UPK .... Series Capacitor Battery Installation   (RU)
UPK .... Ustredna Podohospodarska Kniznica, Kosice [*Central Agricultural Library in Kosice*]   (CZ)
UPK .... Ustredni Pedagogicka Knihovna [*Central Pedagogical Library*]   (CZ)
UPK .... Ustredni Planovaci Komise [*Central Planning Commission*]   (CZ)
UPK .... Ustredni Politicka Kancelar [*Central Political Bureau*]   (CZ)
UPK .... Ustredni Povodnova Komise Zemskeho Narodniho Vyboru [*Central Flood Prevention Commission of the Provincial People's Committee*]   (CZ)
UPK .... Ustredni Proverovaci Komise Svazu Narodni Revoluce [*Central Investigating Commission (of the National Revolution League)*]   (CZ)
UPKO....... Administration of Municipal Services Establishments   (RU)
UPKO....... United Pasokmomogun [*United Sons of the Soil*] [*Kadazan organization in Sabah Also known as UNPM*]   (ML)
UPL .... Union Populaire Locale [*Wallis and Futuna Islands*] [*Political party*]   (FEA)
UPL .... Universitaetsparteileitung [*University Party Management*]   (EG)
UPL .... Upala [*Costa Rica*] [*Airport symbol*] [*Obsolete*]   (OAG)
UPL .... Uredba o Postupku Likvidacije Preduzeca [*Decree on the Procedure of Liquidation of Establishments*]   (YU)
UPL .... Ustav Pracovniho Lekarstvi [*Institute of Industrial Medicine*]   (CZ)
UPLB........ University of the Philippines at Los Banos   (ARC)
UPLG .... Uniao Popular para e Libertacao da Guine
UPLG .... Union Populaire de Liberation de la Guinee Portugaise
UPLG .... Union Populaire pour la Liberation de la Guadeloupe [*Popular Union for the Liberation of Guadeloupe*]   (PD)
UPLGE...... Union Populaire de la Liberation de la Guinee Equatoriale
UPM.......... Industrial Training Shop   (RU)
UPM.......... Uganda Patriotic Movement   (PD)
UPM.......... Umdrehung per Minuten [*Revolutions per Minute*] [*German*]
UPM.......... Umelecko-Prumyslove Museum [*Industrial Arts Museum*]   (CZ)
UpM.......... Umlaufungen pro Minute [*Revolutions per Minute*] [*German*]
UPM.......... Uniao Progressiva de Mocambique
UPM.......... Union del Pueblo de Melilla [*Spanish North Africa*] [*Political party*]   (MENA)
UPM.......... Unione Politica Maltese [*Maltese Political Union*] [*Political party*]   (PPE)
UPM.......... Union Pontificale Missionnaire [*Pontifical Missionary Union - PMU*] [*Later, PMUPR*]

UPM.......... Union Popular de Mujeres [*Women's Popular Union*] [*Spanish*] (WER)

UPM.......... Union Progressiste Mauritanienne [*Mauritanian Progressive Union*] (AF)

UPM.......... Union Progressiste Melanesienne [*New Caledonia*] [*Political party*] (FEA)

UPM.......... United Paper Mills [*Finland*]

UPM.......... United People's Movement [*Antigua*] [*Political party*] (PPW)

UPM.......... United People's Movement [*St. Vincent*] [*Political party*] (PPW)

UPM.......... United Presbyterian Mission

UPM.......... Universal Pneumatic Machine (RU)

UPM.......... Universiti Pertanian Malaysia [*University of Agriculture, Malaysia*]

UPM.......... University of Petroleum and Minerals [*Saudi Arabia*] (ME)

UPMI........ Union Progressiste Melanesienne [*Progressive Melanesian Union*] [*New Caledonia*] [*Political party*] (PPW)

Up MPS..... Administration of International Traffic of the Ministry of Railroads (RU)

UPMTC..... Union Panafricaine et Malgache des Travailleurs Croyants

UPMUPE ... Union Popular de Mujeres Peruanas [*Popular Union of Peruvian Women*] (LA)

UPN.......... Umgekehrte Polnische Notation [*German*] (ADPT)

UPN.......... Union del Pueblo Navarrese [*Union of the Navarrese People*] [*Spain*] [*Political party*] (PPW)

UPN.......... Union de Periodistas de Nicaragua [*Union of Nicaraguan Journalists*] (LA)

UPN.......... Union Progressiste Nigerienne

UPN.......... Unity Party of Nigeria (AF)

UPN.......... Uruapan [*Mexico*] [*Airport symbol*] (OAG)

UPN.......... Ustredni Narodni Pojistovna [*Central Insurance Agency*] (CZ)

UPNA........ Uniao das Populacoes do Norte de Angola [*Union of the Populations of North Angola*]

Upnachvoso ... Office of the Chief of Military Transport (RU)

UPNG........ University of Papua New Guinea (ADA)

UPNI........ Ukrainian Institute of Neuropsychiatry (RU)

up-niye .... Directorate [*Military term*], Administration, Office (RU)

UPO.......... Administration of Fire Prevention (RU)

UPO.......... Ukase on Fire Prevention in the Bulgarian People's Republic (BU)

UPO.......... Universite Populaire [*People's University*] [*Cambodia*] (CL)

upol .... Plenipotentiary, Authorized Representative (RU)

UPOLI....... Universidad Politecnica de Nicaragua [*Nicaraguan Polytechnical University*] (LA)

upolkomzag ... Plenipotentiary of the Committee for Procurement of Agricultural Products (RU)

upolminzag ... Plenipotentiary of the Ministry of Procurement (RU)

Upolsto ...... Plenipotentiary of the Council of Labor and Defense (RU)

UPOMZ..... Training Antipersonnel Fragmentation Mine (RU)

UPONA..... Uniao das Populacoes do Norte de Angola

UPONF ..... Unified Political Organization, The National Front [*Yemen*] (ME)

UPONF ..... United Political Organization National Front [*Yeman*] (BARN)

UPOV........ Union Internationale pour la Protection des Obtentions Vegetales [*International Union for the Protection of New Varieties of Plants*] (EAIO)

UPOWU.... Uganda Petroleum Oil and Chemical Workers Union (AF)

UPP .... Administration of Industrial Establishments (RU)

UPP .... Administration of the Food Industry (RU)

UPP .... Administration of the Printing Industry (RU)

UPP .... Conditional Jump to Subroutine [*Computers*] (RU)

UPP .... Industrial Training Establisment (RU)

UPP .... Intermediate Semiconductor Repeater (RU)

UPP .... Stand for Checking Parameters [*Aviation*] (RU)

UPP .... UNESCO Publications and Periodicals

UPP .... Union del Pueblo Patriotico [*Ecuador*] [*Political party*] (EY)

UPP .... Union del Pueblo Peruano [*Union of the Peruvian People*] (LA)

UPP .... Union des Partis Populaires

UPP .... Unionist Progressive Party [*Egypt*] [*Political party*]

UPP .... United Peasants' Party [*Poland*] [*Political party*] (PD)

UPP .... United People's Party [*Grenada*] [*Political party*] (PPW)

UPP .... United People's Party [*Sierra Leone*] [*Political party*]

UPP .... United People's Party [*Singapore*] (ML)

UPP .... United People's Party [*Zambia*] (AF)

UPP .... United People's Party [*Botswana*] (AF)

UPP .... United Progressive Party [*Trinidad and Tobago*] [*Political party*] (PPW)

UPP .... United Progressive Party [*Zambia*] [*Political party*]

UPP .... United Sierra Leone Progressive Party

UPP .... University Preparation Program [*Australia*]

UPP .... Unveraenderte Planpreise [*Fixed Plan Prices*] (EG)

UPP .... Uredba o Prestanku Preduzeca i Radnji [*Decree on the Suspension of Establishments and Shops*] (YU)

UPPA........ United People's Party of Arunachal [*India*] [*Political party*] (PPW)

UPPAA...... Union de Propietarios Productores Agropecuarios [*Venezuela*] (DSCA)

UPPBCB ... Union Professionnelle des Producteurs de Bois du Congo Belge

UPPD .... Union Popular de Profesores Democratas [*Popular Union of Democratic Teachers*] [*Spanish*] (WER)

UPPenh ..... Universite de Phnom Penh [*University of Phnom Penh*] [*Cambodia*] (CL)

UPPG .... Union des Paysans Pauvres de la Guadeloupe (PD)

UPPI.......... Union des Pilotes Professionels Internationaux [*International Professio nal Drivers Union*] [*French*]

uppk .... Uppkoeptes [*Was Bought Up*] [*Sweden*]

uppl .... Upplaga [*Edition*] [*Publishing*] [*Sweden*]

UPPLANADES ... University of the Philippines Planning and Development Research Foundation, Inc. [*Research center*] (IRC)

upplysn....... Upplysning [*Information*] [*Sweden*]

UPPN .... Union Postale des Pays du Nord [*Nordic Postal Union - NPU*] (EAIO)

UPPN .... United People's Party of Nigeria (AF)

UPPO .... Uredba o Ukupnom Prihodu Privredne Organizacije i Njegove Raspodele [*Decree on the Gross Income of Economic Organizations and Its Distributions*] (YU)

UPPZ......... Fire Protection Administration (BU)

UPR .... Administration of Planning Work (RU)

upr............. Administrator, Manager (RU)

Upr............ Directorate [*Military term*], Administrations, Office (RU)

UPr .... Uchilishten Pregled [*School Review*] [*A periodical*] (BU)

UPR .... Universal Field Radiation Counter Analyzer (RU)

UPR .... Universidad de Puerto Rico [*University of Puerto Rico*] (LAA)

UPRA......... Uniao das Populacoes Revolucionarias Angolanas

upravl .... Administration (BU)

uprazdn ...... Abolished (RU)

uprazh .... Exercise (BU)

UPRBiH .... Udruzenje Prosvjetnih Radnika Bosne i Hercegovine [*Association of Educators of Bosnia and Hercegovina*] (YU)

UPRC .... Uranium Policy Review Committee [*Australia*]

UPRICO.... University of Puerto Rico (PDAA)

upriye .... Directorate [*Military term*], Administration, Office (RU)

UPROAR .. Ultimo Pyrmont Resident Opposition to Arbitrary Redevelopment [*Australia*]

UPROCA .. Union Professionnelle des Producteurs du Caoutchouc du Congo Belge

Uprochmashdetal' ... Industrial-Experimental Establishment for the Reconditioning and Strengthening of Machine Parts (RU)

uprodor....... Administration of Roads (RU)

UPROHUTU ... Union pour la Promotion Hutu

UPRONA .. Union pour le Progres National [*Union for National Progress*] [*Burundi*] [*Political party*] (PPW)

UPRONA .. Union Progressiste Nationale de l'Angola

UPRP......... Ujedinjena Poljska Radnicka Partija [*United Polish Workers Party*] (YU)

UPRP........ Urzad Patentowy Rzeczypospolitej Polskiej [*Patent Office of the Polish Republic*] (POL)

uprpishcheprom ... Administration of the Food Industry (RU)

UPRS........ Uprava Pomorstva i Recnog Saobracaja [*Sea and River Navigation Administration*] (YU)

Uprspetsdor ... Administration of Special Roads (RU)

UPS........... Boundary Layer Control (RU)

UPS........... Food Supply Administration (RU)

UPS........... Udruzenje Pravnika Srbije [*Serbian Lawyers' Association*] (YU)

UPS........... Udruzenje Pravoslavnog Svestenstva [*Association of Orthodox Clergy*] [*Serbian Orthodox Church*] (YU)

UPS........... Union des Producteurs Suisses [*Union of Swiss Producers*] (WER)

UPS........... Union des Professeurs de Speciales [*French*] (SLS)

UPS........... Union Progressiste Senegalaise [*Senegalese Progressive Union*] [*Political party*] (AF)

UPS........... University Philosophical Society [*Irish*] (SLS)

UPS........... Unutrasnja Pismonosna Sluzba [*Domestic Mail Service*] (YU)

UPS........... Uprava Pomorskog Saobracaja [*Sea Navigation Administration*] (YU)

UPS........... Upustvo za Vrsenje Postanske Sluzbe [*Directives for Postal Service Operation*] (YU)

UPS........... Uputstva za Vrsenje Unutrasnje Pismonosne Sluzbe [*Directives for Domestic Mail Service*] (YU)

UPS........... Ustredni Politicka Skola [*Central Political School*] (CZ)

UPSAL ...... Union de Productores de Sal [*Mexico*] (DSCA)

UPSD......... Union pour le Progres Social et le Democratie [*The Congo*] [*Political party*] (EY)

UPSEB ...... Uttar Pradesh State Electricity Board [*India*] (PDAA)

UPSET ...... Union of Private Secondary Education Teachers [*Mauritius*] (AF)

UPSG......... Pensions and Social Welfare Administration (BU)

UPSIC .... Uttar Pradesh Small-Scale Industries Corp. [*India*] (PDAA)

UPSIDC.... Uttar Pradesh State Industrial Development Corp. [*India*] (PDAA)

UPSM....... Administration of the Building Materials Industry (RU)

UPSNR...... Urad Predsednictva Slovenskej Narodnej Rady [*Office of the Presidium of the Slovak National Council*] (CZ)

UPSOB ...... Union Professionnelle des Sousofficiers Belges [*Professional Union of Belgian Non-Commissioned Officers*]   (WER)

UPSP .... Union Progressive Socialist Party [*Egypt*]

UPSP .... Urad Predsednictva Sboru Poverenikov [*Office of the Presidium of the Board of Commissioners*]   (CZ)

UPSS .... Ukrainska Partiia Samostiinykiv-Sotsiialistiv [*Ukrainian Party of Socialist-Independentists*] [*Russian*] [*Political party*] (PPE)

UPSSC ...... Uttar Pradesh State Sugar Corp.   (PDAA)

UPST .... Union of Primary School Teachers [*Mauritius*]   (AF)

UPSTC ...... Uttar Pradesh State Textile Corp. [*India*]   (PDAA)

UPT .... Administration of Public Transportation [*Of the Mosgorispolkom*]   (RU)

UPT .... Direct-Current Amplifier   (RU)

UPT .... Television Amplifier Attachment   (RU)

UPT .... Undistributed Profits Tax   (IMH)

UPT .... Union de Pobladores de Tugurio [*Union of Slum Dwellers*] [*El Salvador*]   (LA)

UPT .... Union pour le Progres du Tchad

UPT .... Urzad Pocztowo-Telekomunikacyjny [*Post and Telecommunication Office*] [*Poland*]

UPTC .... Union Pan-Africaine et Malgache des Travailleurs Croyants [*Pan-African Workers Congress*] [*Use PAWC*]   (AF)

UPTC .... Universidad Pedagogica y Tecnologica de Colombia [*Tunja*] (COL)

UPTE .... Union of Posts and Telecommunications Employees

UPTEU ...... Uganda Posts and Telecommunications Employees Union   (AF)

UPTIFNRJ ... Udruzenje Preduzeca Tekstilne Industrije Federativna Narodna Republika Jugoslavija [*Association of Establishments of the Textile Industry of Yugoslavia*]   (YU)

UPTM .... Administration of Public Transportation of the Mosgorispolkom (RU)

UPTR .... Administration of Underwater Technical Operations   (RU)

UPTs .... Impact Pneumatic Cylinder   (RU)

UPTS .... Semiautomatic Telephone Communication System   (RU)

UPTU .... Uredba o Privrednim Organizacijama za Trgovinske Usluge [*Decree on Economic Organizations for Commercial Service*]   (YU)

UPU .... Amplifying-Converting Device   (RU)

UPU .... Uganda People's Union

UPU .... Union Postale Universelle [*Universal Postal Union*] [*Switzerland*] [*Also, an information service or system*] (IID)

UPU .... Union Postale Universelle [*Universal Postal Union*] [*French*]

UPU .... Union Postal Universal [*Universal Postal Union - UPU*] [*Spanish*]

UPU .... Universal Postal Union [*United Nations*]   (MENA)

UPU-Automat ... Unter-Pulver-Universal-Automat [*Automatic Flux Powder Welding Machine*] (EG)

UPUSA ...... UPU [*Universal Postal Union*] Staff Association   (EAIO)

UPV .... Directorate of Border Troops   (RU)

UPV .... Union Progressiste Voltaique [*Voltan Progressive Union*]   (AF)

UPV .... University of the Philippines in the Visayas   (PDAA)

UPV .... Urad Predsednictva Vlady [*Office of the Government Presidium*] (CZ)

UPV .... Urad pro Patenty a Vynalezy [*Patents and Inventions Office*] (CZ)

UPVCSAV ... Ustav Planovani Vedy CSAV [*Science Planning Institute of the Czechoslovak Science Academy*]   (CZ)

UPVO .... Directorate of Air Defense   (RU)

UPVO .... Uciliste Protivzdusne Obrany [*Air Defense Training Center*] (CZ)

UPW .... Unions Paysannes des Wilaya [*Governorate Peasant Unions*] [*Algeria*]   (AF)

UPWCA ..... United Pest and Weed Control Association [*Australia*]

UPWU .... Uganda Plantation Workers Union

UPZ .... Sonic Dust Collector   (RU)

UPZ .... Union de la Presse du Zaire   (EAIO)

UPZ .... Uredba o Prevozu (Putnika, Prtljaga, i Robe na) Zeljeznicama [*Decree on Rail Transport (of Passengers, Parcels, and Goods)*] [*YU*]

UPZNA ..... Ukase on the Application of the Law on Legal Acts   (BU)

UPZT .... Ustredni Podnik Zemedelske Techniky [*Central Enterprise of Agricultural Equipment*] [*CZ*]

UQ .... Fronte dell'Uomo Qualunque; Uomo Qualunque [*Common Man Front*] [*Italy*] [*Political party*]   (PPE)

UQ .... United African Airline [*Libya*] [*ICAO designator*]   (ICDA)

UQ .... University of Queensland [*Australia*]

UQL .... University of Queensland Library [*Australia*]

U Qld .... University of Queensland [*Australia*]

UQP .... University of Queensland Press [*Australia*]

UR .... Adjusting Rheostat   (RU)

ur .... Administrator, Curator   (BU)

UR .... Angle of Turn   (RU)

ur .... Area, Tract [*Topography*]   (RU)

UR .... Control Relay   (RU)

ur .... Equation   (RU)

UR .... Fortified Area   (BU)

UR .... Guided Missile   (BU)

UR .... Holding Relay   (RU)

ur .... Level   (RU)

UR .... Office of Criminal Investigation   (RU)

UR .... Recording Control   (RU)

UR .... Red Carpet Airlines, Inc. [*ICAO designator*]   (ICDA)

UR .... Specific Radioactivity   (RU)

UR .... Ugostiteljska Radnja [*Hotel and Catering Trade Shop*]   (YU)

UR .... Uitvoerende Raad [*Executive Council*] [*Afrikaans*]

UR .... Uitvoeringsresolutie [*Benelux*]   (BAS)

UR .... Ultrarot [*Infrared*] [*German*]   (GCA)

UR .... Uniao Republicana [*Republican Union*] [*Portugal*] [*Political party*]   (PPE)

UR .... Unie-Regering [*Afrikaans*]

UR .... Union Republicana [*Republican Union*] [*Spanish*]   (WER)

UR .... Union Revolucionaria [*Guatemala*]   (LAA)

UR .... Universe Reinsurance Co. Ltd. [*Nigeria*]

UR .... University of Rhodesia

UR .... University of Riyadh [*Saudi Arabia*]   (PDAA)

UR .... Uniwersytet Robotniczy [*Workers' University*] [*Poland*]

uR .... Unter Rueckerbittung [*Requesting Return*] [*German*]   (GCA)

ur .... Urad [*Office*]   (CZ)

Ur .... Urdu [*Language*]   (BARN)

Ur .... Uretim [*Production*] [*Istih*] [*See also*]   (TU)

ur .... Urodzony [*Born*] [*Poland*]

Ur .... Uruguay

UR .... Ustredni Rada [*Central Council*]   (CZ)

UR .... Ustredni Reditelstvi [*Central Directorate*]   (CZ)

UR-19 .... Universitarios Revolucionarios 19 de Julio [*19 July Revolutionary University Students*] [*El Salvador*]   (LA)

URA .... Union des Remorqueurs d'Abidjan

URA .... Union des Republiques Arabes

URA .... Union Regionale des Agriculteurs [*Tunisia*]

URA .... United Red Army [*Japan*]   (PD)

URA .... Uralinteravia [*Russian Federation*] [*ICAO designator*]   (FAAC)

Ura .... Urania [*Record label*] [*USA, Europe, etc.*]

URA .... Urban Redevelopment Authority [*Singapore*]

URA .... Uzina de Reparatii Auto [*Automotive Repair Plant*]   (RO)

URAC .... Union des Republiques d'Afrique Centrale [*May, 1960*]

URADEP ... Upper Regional Agricultural Development Programme

URAI .... Union des Representations Automobiles et Industrielles [*Gabon*] (EY)

Uralelektroapparat ... Ural Electrical Equipment Plant   (RU)

Uralenergo ... Ural Power System   (RU)

URALFIZKhIM ... Ural Scientific Research Physicochemical Institute   (RU)

URALFTI ... Ural Physicotechnical Institute   (RU)

URALGINTsVETMET ... Ural State Scientific Research Institute of Nonferrous Metals   (RU)

Uralgiprolesdrev ... Ural State Institute for the Planning of Establishments of the Lumber, Woodworking, Wood-Chemistry, and Paper Industry   (RU)

Uralgipromez ... Ural State Institute for the Planning of Metallurgical Plants (RU)

Uralgiproshakht ... Ural State Institute for the Planning of Mines   (RU)

Uralkhimmash ... Ural Heavy Chemical Machinery Plant   (RU)

Uralmash ... Ural Heavy Machinery Plant Imeni Sergo Ordzhonikidze   (RU)

URALMEKhANOBR ... Ural Scientific Research and Planning Institute of Concentration and Mechanical Processing of Minerals (RU)

URALNIGRI ... Ural Scientific Research Institute of Geological Exploration (RU)

UralNIISKhOZ ... Ural Scientific Research Institute of Agriculture   (RU)

UralNILKhI ... Ural Scientific Research Institute of Wood Chemistry   (RU)

URALNITOMASh ... Ural Branch of the All-Union Scientific, Engineering, and Technical Society of Machine Builders   (RU)

Uralsel'mash ... Ural Agricultural Machinery Plant   (RU)

Uraltyazhkhimmash ... Ural Heavy Chemical Machinery Plant   (RU)

Uraltyazhmash ... Ural Heavy Machinery Plant   (RU)

URALUGLEKOKS ... Ural Scientific Research Institute of Coal and Coke (RU)

Uralvagon .. Ural Railroad Car Plant   (RU)

Uralvagonzavod ... Ural Railroad Car Plant   (RU)

UralVO ...... Ural Military District   (RU)

URAMEX ... Uranio Mexicano [*Mexican Uranium*]   (LA)

URAN .... Active Load Distribution System   (RU)

URAS .... Union des Republicains d'Action Sociale [*Union of Republicans of Social Action*] [*France*] [*Political party*]   (PPE)

uraut .... Uredne Autorisovany [*Officially Authorized*]   (CZ)

URB .... Battalion Fortified Area   (RU)

URB .... Universidade Rural do Brasil [*Rural University of Brazil*] [*Rio De Janeiro*]   (LAA)

URB .... University Resources Board [*Australia*]

URB .... Urubupunga [*Brazil*] [*Airport symbol*]   (OAG)

URBA .... Compagnie des Mines d'Uranium de Bakouma [*Bakouma Uranium Mines Company*] [*Central African Republic*] (AF)

URBA .... Universite Royale des Beaux-Arts [*Royal Fine Arts University*] [*UBA Cambodia*] [*Later,*] (CL)

URBAMET ... Urbanisme, Amenagement, Equipments, et Transports [*Reseau URBAMET*] [*France*] [*Information service or system*] (CRD)

URBANAL ... Urbanizadora Nacional [*Colombia*] (COL)

URBANICOM ... Association Internationale Urbanisme et Commerce [*International Association for Town Planning and Distribution*] (EAIO)

URBAT ...... Societe d'Etudes pour l'Urbanisme et le Batiment

URBK .... Union Rheinische Braunkohlen Kraftstoff AG

URBT .... Unite de Recherches sur les Ressources Biologiques Terrestres [*Research Unit for Natural Biological Resources*] [*Algeria*] (IRC)

URC .... Uganda Railways Corp. (DCTA)

URC .... Unemployment Relief Council [*South Australia*]

URC .... Union de Rassemblement et du Centre [*France*] [*Political party*] (ECON)

URC .... Union des Republicains du Cameroun [*Political party*] (EY)

URC .... Union du Rassemblement du Centre [*Mayotte*] [*Political party*] (EY)

URC .... Union Routiere et Commerciale

URC .... United Reform Church [*Australia*]

URC .... Universal Robina Corp. [*Philippines*]

URC .... Urumqi [*China*] [*Airport symbol*] (OAG)

URCA .... Societe d'Uranium Centrafricaine

URCC .... Uniunea Raion de Cooperative de Consum [*Raion Union of Consumer Cooperatives*] (RO)

URCDPC ... Union des Ressortissants du Congo pour la Defense et la Promotion du Congo

URCE .... Union Restaurants Collectifs Europeens [*European Catering Association*] [*Germany*] (EAIO)

URCh .... Narrow-Band Frequency Relay (RU)

URCh .... Radio-Frequency Amplifier (RU)

URCM .... Uniunea Raion de Cooperative Mestesugaresti [*Raion Union of Artisan Cooperatives*] (RO)

URCO .... Union Regionale des Cooperatives Oleicoles [*Regional Olive Products Cooperatives Union*] [*Algeria*] (AF)

URCO .... Universidad Regional Centro-Occidental [*Midwestern Regional University*] [*Venezuela*] (LA)

URCO .... Ustredni Rada Ceskoslovenskeho Obchodnictva [*Central Council of Czechoslovak Businessmen*] (CZ)

URCOT ..... Urban Research Centre on Office Technology [*Australia*]

URCRM ..... Urals Research Center for Radiation Medicine [*Russia*]

UR CSF ..... Ustredni Reditelstvi Ceskoslovenskeho Filmu [*Central Directorate of Czechoslovak Films*] (CZ)

URD .... General-Purpose Pressure Governor (RU)

URD .... Unidad Revolucionaria Democratica [*Guatemala*] (LAA)

URD .... Union des Remorqueurs de Dakar

URD .... Union pour le Renouveau du Dahomey

URD .... Union Republicana Democratica [*Democratic Republican Union*] [*Venezuela*] (LA)

URD .... Union Revolucionaria Democratica [*Democratic Revolutionary Union*] [*Guatemala*] (LA)

URD .... Upper River Division

URD .... Uredba o Raspodeli Dobitka i Porezu na Dobit Privrednih Organizacija [*Decree on the Distribution of Profit and the Tax on Profit of Economic Corporations*] (YU)

URD .... Ustredni Rada Druzstev [*Central Council of Cooperatives*] (CZ)

URD .... X-Ray Diagnostic Unit (RU)

URDA .... Unite Regionale de Developpement de l'Aquaculture [*French*] (MSC)

URDC .... Union pour une Republique Democratique des Comores [*Comoros*] [*Political party*] (EY)

URDEC ..... Universitarios Revolucionarios Democrata Cristianos [*Christian Democratic Revolutionary University Students*] [*Costa Rica*] (LA)

URDECO .. Upper Regional Development Corporation

URDO .... Union des Remorqueurs de Douala

URDS .... Unregistered Dealing System [*Australia*]

URE .... Union Revolucionaria Estudiantil [*Revolutionary Student Union*] [*Ecuador*] (LA)

UREBA ..... Union Revolutionnaire des Banques [*Burkina Faso*] (EY)

URECSAV ... Ustav Radiotechniky a Elektroniky CSAV [*Institute of Radiotechnology and Electronics of the Czechoslovak Science Academy*] (CZ)

Ured .... Administrator, Curator (BU)

UREMG .... Universidade Rural do Estado de Minas Gerais [*Rural University of Minas Gerais State*] [*Vicosa, Brazil*] (LAA)

UrEMIIT ... Ural Electromechanical Institute of Railroad Transportation Engineers (RU)

UREMOAS ... Uzina de Radiatoare, Echipament Metalic, Objecte si Armature Sanitare [*Factory for Radiators, Metal Equipment, and Sanitary Articles and Fittings*] (RO)

Urenco .... Uranium Enrichment Consortium [*Britain, West Germany, and Holland*]

URER .... Union Regionale d'Expansion Rurale [*Regional Union for Rural Expansion*] [*Malagasy*] (AF)

URES .... Administration for the Development of Radio Facilities and Intrarayon Telecommunications (RU)

URF .... Union des Femmes de la Reunion

URF .... Union des Services Routiers des Chemins de Fer Europeens [*Union of European Railways Road Services*] (PDAA)

URF .... United Religious Front [*Israel*] (BJA)

URFC .... Union Revolutionnaire des Femmes Congolaises [*Revolutionary Union of Congolese Women*] (AF)

URFG .... Union Revolutionnaire des Femmes Guineennes

URG .... Union de Radioperiodicos de Guatemala [*Union of Radio Newsmen of Guatemala*] (LA)

URG .... Urheberrechtsgesetz [*German Copyright Act*] (DLA)

URG .... Uruguaiana [*Brazil*] [*Airport symbol*] (OAG)

URGE .... Union Revolucionaria de la Guinea Ecuatorial [*Revolutionary Union of Equatorial Guinea*] [*Spanish*] (AF)

URGE .... Union Revolutionnaire de la Guinea Equatoriale [*Revolutionary Union of Equatorial Guinea*] [*French*] (AF)

Urgiz .... Ural State Publishing House (RU)

URGNSW ... Underwater Research Group of New South Wales [*Australia*]

URGP .... Union des Ressortissants de la Guinee Portugaise

URGS .... Universidade do Rio Grande Do Sul [*University of Rio Grande Do Sul*] [*Brazil*] (LA)

UrGU .... Ural State University Imeni A. M. Gor'kiy (RU)

Ur g v .... Ground-Water Level (RU)

urh .... Ultra Rovid Hullamu [*Ultrashort Wave*] (HU)

urh .... Urheilu [*Sports*] [*Finland*]

URI .... Pulse Distribution Amplifier (RU)

URI .... Union Revolucionaria Independiente [*Independent Revolutionary Union*] [*Mexico*] (LA)

URI .... Universite Radiophonique Internationale [*International University of the Air*] (NTCM)

URI .... Uribe [*Colombia*] [*Airport symbol*] [*Obsolete*] (OAG)

URIB .... Uitvoeringsresolutie Inkomstenbelasting [*Benelux*] (BAS)

URICA .... Universal Realtime Information Cataloguing and Administration [*Australia*]

URICA .... Universal Real-Time Machine Readable Information Cataloguing and Administration [*Australia*]

URIOPSS ... Union Regionale Interfederale des Oeuvres Privees Sanitaires et Sociales (FLAF)

URJC .... Union Revolucionaria de Jovenes Comunistas [*Revolutionary Union of Young Communists*] [*Colorado*] (LA)

URJE .... Union Revolucionaria de la Juventud del Ecuador [*Revolutionary Union of Ecuadorean Youth*] (LA)

Urk .... Urkunde [*Document, Deed, Instrument*] [*German*] (ILCA)

urk .... Urkundlich [*Authentic*] [*German*]

URK .... Ustredna Rozhodcia Komisia [*Central Arbitration Commission*] (CZ)

URK .... Ustredni Revisni Komise [*Central Auditing Commission*] (CZ)

URKK .... Krasnodar [*Former USSR*] [*ICAO location identifier*] (ICLI)

URKM .... Administration of Workers' and Peasants' Militia (RU)

URL .... Union Radical del Liberalismo [*Radical Union of Liberalism*] [*Ecuador*] (LA)

URL .... Uralavialy [*Russian Federation*] [*ICAO designator*] (FAAC)

UrLFLRJst ... Uradni List Federativne Ljudske Republike Jugoslavije Stevilka [*Official Gazette of Yugoslavia Number*] (YU)

ur m .... Sea Level (RU)

URM .... Uriman [*Venezuela*] [*Airport symbol*] (OAG)

URM .... Urzad Rady Ministrow [*Office of the Council of Ministers*] (POL)

URMK .... Kislovodsk [*Former USSR*] [*ICAO location identifier*] (ICLI)

UR M-L ..... Uniao Revolucionaria, Marxista-Leninista [*Marxist-Leninist Revolutionary Union*] [*Portugal*] [*Political party*] (PPE)

URMM ...... Mineralnye Vody [*Former USSR*] [*ICAO location identifier*] (ICLI)

URN .... Carbon Voltage Regulator (RU)

URN .... High-Voltage Current Unit for Splitting of Large Rocks (RU)

URN .... Union pour la Reconciliation Nationale [*Haiti*] [*Political party*] (EY)

URNG .... Unidad Revolucionaria Nacional Guatemalteca [*Guatemalan National Revolutionary Unity*] [*Political party*] (PD)

ur-niye .... Equation (RU)

URO .... Guided-Missile Weapon (RU)

URO .... Stocktaking and Distribution Department (RU)

URO .... Udruzenje Rezervnih Oficira [*Association of Reserve Officers*] (YU)

URO .... Union des Remorqueurs de l'Ocean

URO .... Ustredni Rada Odboru [*Central Council of Trade Unions*] [*Prague, Czechoslovakia*] (CZ)

uroch .... Area, Tract [*Topography*] (RU)

UROEA ...... UNESCO Regional Office for Education in Asia and Oceania [*Thailand*] (DLA)

UROEAO ... UNESCO Regional Office for Education in Asia and Oceania [*Thailand*] (PDAA)

UROJ .... Udruzenje Rezervnih Oficira Jugoslavije [*Association of Reserve Officers of Yugoslavia*]   (YU)

urol............ Urologist, Urology   (BU)

UROLA ..... UNEP [*United Nations Environmental Programme*] Regional Office for Latin America   (EAIO)

UROM....... Union Regionale de l'Ogooue Maritime

URP .... Administration for the Distribution of Publications   (RU)

URP .... General-Purpose Borer   (RU)

URP .... Radioactive Position Level Gauge   (RU)

URP .... Union Republicaine du Peuple [*Benin*] [*Political party*]   (EY)

URP .... Union Revolucionaria Popular [*People's Revolutionary Union*] [*Honduras*]   (LA)

URP .... United Rhodesian Party

URP .... Universidade Rural do Pernambuco [*Brazil*]   (LAA)

URPE......... Union des Resistants pour une Europe Unie [*French*]   (FLAF)

URPE........ Union Revolucionaria Popular Ecuatoriana [*Ecuadorean Popular Revolutionary Union*] [*Political party*]   (PPW)

URPT........ Union Republicaine et Progressiste du Tchad

URR .... Scanning Turn Angle   (RU)

URR .... Urrao [*Colombia*] [*Airport symbol*]   (OAG)

URRM .... Morozovsk [*Former USSR*] [*ICAO location identifier*]   (ICLI)

URRR .... Rostov-Na-Donu [*Former USSR*] [*ICAO location identifier*]   (ICLI)

URRU .... General-Purpose Radioactive Level Regulator   (RU)

URS .... Administration of Workers' Supply   (RU)

URS .... Guided Missile   (RU)

URS .... Self-Propelled Guided Projectile   (BU)

URS .... Ujedinjeni Radnicki Sindikati [*United Workers Trade-Unions*]   (YU)

URS .... Union Revolucionaria Socialista [*Socialist Revolutionary Union*] [*Colorado*]   (LA)

URS .... Universal Speed Regulator   (RU)

URS .... University of Western Sydney Research Studentship [*Australia*]

URS .... Uprava Recnog Saobracaja [*River Transportation Administration*]   (YU)

Urs .... Ursache [*Cause, Reason*] [*German*]   (GCA)

URS .... Ustav Racionalizace ve Stavebnictvi [*Institute for Rationalization in Construction*]   (CZ)

URSA .... Universite Royale des Sciences Agronomiques [*Royal University of Agronomical Sciences*] [*USCA Cambodia*] [*Later,*]   (CL)

URSA .... Ursa Astronomical Association [*Finland*]   (EAIO)

URSFNRJ ... Udruzenje Radio Stanica Federativna Narodna Republika Jugoslavija - Jugoslovenska Radio-Difuzija [*Radio Stations Association of Yugoslavia - Yugoslav Radio Broadcasting*] [*Belgrade*]   (YU)

URSI......... Union Radio Scientifique Internationale [*International Union of Radio Science*] [*Also, ISRU*] [*Belgium*]

Ursp .... Urspruenglich [*Original, Originally*] [*German*]

URSPA...... Ustredni Rozvojove Stredisko Prumyslu Armatur [*Main Development Center of the Armature Industry*]   (CZ)

urspr.......... Urspruenglich [*Original, Originally*] [*German*]   (EG)

URSPS .... Ukrainian Republic Trade-Union Council   (RU)

URSS .... Sochi [*Former USSR*] [*ICAO location identifier*]   (ICLI)

URSS......... Uniao das Republicas Socialistas Sovieticas [*Union of Soviet Socialist Republics*] [*Portuguese*]

URSS......... Union de las Republicas Socialistas Sovieticas [*Union of Soviet Socialist Republics*] [*Spanish*]

URSS......... Union des Republiques Socialistes Sovietiques [*Union of Soviet Socialist Republics - USSR*] [*French*]

URSS .... Unione Repubbliche Socialisti Sovietiche [*Union of Soviet Socialist Republics*]

URSS......... Uniunea Republicilor Sovietice Socialiste [*Union of Soviet Socialist Republics*]   (RO)

URSSAF.... Union pour le Recouvrement des Cotisations de la Securite Sociale et des Allocations Familiales [*Union for Collection of Social Security Contributions and Family Allotments*] [*French*]   (WER)

URSSJ .... Ujedinjeni Radnicki Sidikalni Savez Jugoslavije [*United Workers Trade-Union of Yugoslavia*]   (YU)

URSSPE... Union des Republiques Socialistes Sovietiques et les Pays de l'Est [*French*]   (FLAF)

urstorg........ Administration of Workers' Supply and Trade   (RU)

URT .... Surat Thani [*Thailand*] [*Airport symbol*]   (OAG)

URT .... Union Republicaine du Tchad

URT .... United Republic of Tanzania

Urt............. Urteil [*Judgment, Decision*] [*German*]   (ILCA)

URTK .... Universite Royale Takeo-Kampot [*Royal Takeo-Kampot University*] [*Cambodia*]   (CL)

URTNA ..... Union des Radio-Televisions Nationales Africaines [*African National Radio-Television Union*]   (AF)

URTS........ Agency Manual Exchange   (RU)

URU.......... Urban Research Unit, Australian National University   (ADA)

URU.......... Ustredni Rozdelovny Uhli [*Central Coal Distribution Enterprises*]   (CZ)

URUC........ UNCTAD [*United Nations Conference on Trade and Development*] Reference Unit Catalogue [*Information service or system*]   (DUND)

URUKhIN ... Ural Institute of Coal Chemistry   (RU)

URUPABOL ... Comision Mixta Permanente de Uruguay, Paraguay, y Bolivia [*Permanent Joint Commission of Uruguay, Paraguay, and Bolivia*]   (LA)

URV .... Controlled Mercury-Arc Rectifier   (RU)

URV .... Unite a Reponse Vocale [*French*]   (ADPT)

URV .... Video Distribution Amplifier   (RU)

URV-D...... Controlled Mercury-Arc Rectifier-Motor   (RU)

URVL .... Ustav pro Racionalizaciu Vyroby Lozisk ZVL [*Institute for Rationalization of Production of Ball Bearings*]   (CZ)

UrVO .... Ural Military District   (RU)

URVR .... Ustredni Redakcne-Vydavatelska Rada [*Central Editorial and Publishing Council (of the Czechoslovak Academy of Sciences)*]   (CZ)

URY .... Gurayat [*Saudi Arabia*] [*Airport symbol*]   (OAG)

URY .... Uruguay [*ANSI three-letter standard code*]   (CNC)

URZ .... Threat of Radioactive Contamination [*Warning*]   (RU)

URZ .... Uroozgan [*Afghanistan*] [*Airport symbol*] [*Obsolete*]   (OAG)

urz .... Urzad [*Administration, Office*]   (POL)

URZA .... Unite de Recherche sur les Zones Arides [*Arid Zones Research Unit*] [*Algeria*] [*Research center*]   (IRC)

US............. Administrative Council   (BU)

US............. Amplifier-Mixer   (RU)

US............. Carbon Column   (RU)

US............. Communications Center   (RU)

US............. Construction Administration   (RU)

US............. Drift Angle [*Aviation*]   (RU)

us.............. Farmstead, Homestead [*Topography*]   (RU)

US............. Fortified Sector   (RU)

US............. Guided Missile   (RU)

US............. Scientific Council   (RU)

US............. Signal Amplifier   (RU)

US............. Speed Indicator [*Aviation*]   (RU)

US............. Trainer Aircraft   (RU)

US............. Training Ship   (RU)

US............. Transmission Device [*Automation*]   (RU)

US............. Ubezpieczalnia Spoleczna [*Social Security and Health Service*]   (POL)

U/S .... Ukrcne Stanice [*Embarkment Stations*]   (YU)

US............. Union Senegalaise [*Senegalese Union*]   (AF)

US............. Union Soudanaise

US............. Union Sportive [*Sports Union*] [*French*]

US............. Uni Sovjet [*Former USSR*]   (IN)

US............. United States [*ANSI two-letter standard code*]   (CNC)

US............. Uniunea Scriitorilor [*Writers' Union*]   (RO)

US............. Universiteit van Stellenbosch [*University of Stellenbosch*] [*Afrikaans*]

US............. University of Sydney [*Australia*]

us.............. Usage [*Worn*] [*Publishing*] [*French*]

us.............. Usea [*Finland*]

us.............. Usein [*Often*] [*Finland*]

US............. Ustredni Sekretariat [*Central Secretariat*]   (CZ)

Us.............. Ustrem [*Drive*] [*A journal*]   (BU)

US............. Uza Srbija [*Serbia Proper (Without Vojvodina and Kosovo-Metohija)*]   (YU)

USA .... General-Purpose Welder   (RU)

USA .... Union des Syndicats Agricoles [*Morocco*]

USA .... Union Socialiste Arabe [*North African*]

USA .... United Socialist Alliance [*Sri Lanka*] [*Political party*]

USA .... United States [*ANSI three-letter standard code*]   (CNC)

USA .... United Swaziland Association   (AF)

USA .... Uniunea Sud Africana [*South African Union*]   (RO)

USA .... University of South Australia

USA .... US Air [*ICAO designator*]   (FAAC)

USABT ...... Uruguayan Society of Analysis and Behavior Therapy   (EAIO)

USAC .... Union des Syndicats Autonomes Camerounais [*Federation of Cameroonian Autonomous Trade Unions*]   (AF)

USAC .... Universidad de San Carlos [*University of San Carlos*] [*Guatemala*]

USACA...... Universidad Santiago de Cali   (COL)

USAC/RS ... U.S. Amateur Confederation of Roller Skating   (OLYM)

USAEA ..... University Students Association of East Africa

USAFIA .... United States Army Forces in Australia

USAFICA ... United States Army Forces in Central Africa

USAFR ..... Union of South Africa

usag.......... Usage [*Worn*] [*Publishing*] [*French*]

USAI......... Union Sudamericana de Asociaciones de Ingenieros [*South American Union of Engineering Societies*] [*Rio De Janeiro, Brazil*]   (LAA)

USAID....... United States Agency for International Development

USAID/REDSO/WCA ... [*The*] US Agency for International Development's Regional Economic Development Services Office for West and Central Africa   (ECON)

USAK .... General-Purpose System for Automated Control of Agricultural Transportation Facilities   (BU)

USAL......... Underwater Systems Australia Ltd.

USAM	Union des Syndicats Autonomes de Madagascar [*Federation of Malagasy Autonomous Trade Unions*] (AF)
USAM	United States Aid Mission
USANP......	United South African National Party
USAO	United Sabah Action Organization (ML)
USAOBiH ...	Ujedinjeni Savez Antifasisticke Omladine Bosne i Hercegovine [*United Federation of Anti-Fascist Youth of Bosnia and Hercegovina*] (YU)
USAOH.....	Ujedinjeni Savez Antifasisticke Omladine Hrvatske [*United Federation of Anti-Fascist Youth of Croatia*] (YU)
USAOJ......	Ujedinjeni Savez Antifasisticke Omladine Jugoslavije [*United Federation of Anti-Fascist Youth of Yugoslavia*] (YU)
USAP........	Union of Sabah People's Party (ML)
USARIOS ...	Association of Maritime Transport Users in the Central American Isthmus [*Guatemala*] (EAIO)
USAS........	Unione Sindicale Africana della Somalia [*Organization of African Unions of Somalia*] (AF)
USASA......	Universities Staff Association of South Australia
USASG(Aus) ...	United States Army Standardization Group (Australia)
USAW	Union of School and Agricultural Workers [*Jamaica*] (EY)
USB	Drift Angle on Bomb Run (RU)
USB	High-Speed Trainer Bomber (RU)
USB	Standardized Medical Barrack Tent (RU)
USB	Union Senegalaise de Banque [*Senegalese Banking Union*] (AF)
USB	Universidad Simon Bolivar [*Venezuela*] (DSCA)
USB	Ustredi Svazu Brannosti [*Headquarters of the Union for Military Preparedness*] (CZ)
USB	Ustredna Statnej Bezpecnosti [*State Security Headquarters*] (CZ)
USBA........	U.S. Badminton Association (OLYM)
USBE........	Universal Serials & Book Exchange
USBF	U.S. Baseball Federation (OLYM)
USBN	Universal Standard Book Number
USBO	Fortified Sector of Coast Defense (RU)
USC	Union Sociale Camerounaise
USC	Union Socialista de Cataluna [*Socialist Union of Catalonia*] [*Spanish*] (WER)
USC	Union Suisse des Chorales [*Switzerland*] (EAIO)
USC	Union Suisse des Cooperatives de Consommation
USC	United Somali Congress [*Political party*] (EY)
USC	Universidad de San Carlos [*Guatemala*] (DSCA)
USC	Universities Service Centre [*Hong Kong*] [*Defunct*]
USC	Urzad Stanu Cywilnego [*Office of Registration of Births, Marriages, and Deaths*] (POL)
USC	Ustredna Slovenskych Celuloziek [*Central Bureau of Slovak Cellulose Factories*] (CZ)
USCA	United Chinese Schoolteachers' Association (ML)
USCA	Universite des Sciences Agronomiques [*University of Agronomical Sciences*] [*URSA Cambodia*] [*Formerly,*] (CL)
USCA	U.S. Curling Association (OLYM)
USCB........	United Saudi Commercial Bank
USCC........	Union des Syndicats Croyants du Cameroun [*Federation of Cameroonian Believers Trade Unions*] (AF)
USCD	Ustredni Svaz Ceskoslovenske Dopravy [*Czechoslovak Central Transport Union*] (CZ)
USCF	U.S. Cycling Federation (OLYM)
USCI.........	Union Syndicale des Commercants Independants
USCKT......	U.S. Canoe and Kayak Team (OLYM)
USCL........	United Society for Christian Literature
USCM	Ustredi Svazu Ceske Mladeze [*Headquarters of the Union of Czech Youth*] (CZ)
USCN	Ustredni Svaz Ceskoslovenskych Novinaru [*Central Union of Czechoslovak Journalists*] (CZ)
USCO	Union Steel Corporation
USCOA	Union Senegalaise pour le Commerce et l'Agriculture
USCP........	Union des Syndicats Categerials de Police [*French*]
USCP........	Ustredni Svaz Ceskoslovenskeho Prumyslu [*Central Union of Czechoslovak Industry*] (CZ)
USCR........	Ustredni Svaz Ceskoslovenskeho Remesla [*Central Union of Czechoslovak Artisans*] (CZ)
USCR........	Ustredni Svaz pro Cizinecky Ruch [*Central Organization for Tourist Trade*] (CZ)
USCS........	Union des Syndicats Confederes du Senegal
USCSN......	Ustredni Svaz Ceskoslovenskych Novinaru [*Central Union of Czechoslovak Journalists*] (CZ)
USCSP	Ustredni Svaz Ceskoslovenskeho Prumyslu [*Central Union of the Czechoslovak Industry*] (CZ)
USCsS	Ustredni Svaz Ceskoslovenskeho Studentstva [*Central Union of Czechoslovak Students*] (CZ)
USCSVU ...	Ustredni Spolek Ceskoslovenskych Vytvarnych Umelcu [*Central Association of Czechoslovak Creative Artists*] (CZ)
USCSVU ...	Ustredni Svaz Ceskoslovenskych Vytvarnych Umelcu [*Central Association of Czechoslovak Creative Artists*] (CZ)
USCV........	Union Scientifique Continentale de Verre [*European Union for the Scientific Study of Glass - EUSSG*] (EAIO)

USD	Uniao Social Democratico [*Social Democratic Union*] [*Portugal*] [*Political party*] (PPE)
USD	Union des Sociaux-Democrates [*Burkina Faso*] [*Political party*] (EY)
USD	Union Social-Democrate [*Social Democratic Union*] [*The Ivory Coast*] [*Political party*] (EY)
USD	Union Sociale Democratique [*Cameroon*] [*Political party*] (EY)
USD	U.S. States Diving, Inc. (OLYM)
USD	Ustredni Skola Delnicka [*Central Training School for Workers*] (CZ)
USD	Ustredni Svaz Druzstev [*Central Union of Cooperatives*] (CZ)
USDAM	Union Suisse des Artistes Musiciens [*Swiss Musicians' Union*] (EAIO)
USDE	Union Social-Democrata Espanola [*Spanish Social Democratic Union*] (WER)
USDECO...	Union Sindical Departamental de los Empleados, Campesinos, y Obreros (del Cuzco) [*Departmental Trade Union of Employees, Peasants, and Workers (of Cuzco)*] [*Peru*] (LA)
US desAL ...	Union Syndicale des Artistes Lyriques [*French*] (ROG)
USDRP......	Unia Socjaldemokratyczna Rzeczypospolitej Polskiej [*Social Democratic Union of the Republic of Poland*] [*Political party*]
USDTP......	Ukrainska Sotsial Demokraticheskaia Truda Partiia [*Ukrainian Social Democratic Labor Party*] [*Russian*] [*Political party*] (PPE)
USE	Understanding Science in the Environment [*Australia*]
USE	Unidad de Servicios Especiales [*Special Services Unit*] [*Peru*] (LA)
USE	Union Socialista Espanola [*Spanish Socialist Union*] (WER)
USE	University of Southern Europe [*Monaco*] (ECON)
USE	Ural Soviet Encyclopedia (RU)
Use	Usine [*Works*] [*Military map abbreviation World War I*] [*French*] (MTD)
USE	Ustav Stavebni Ekonomie [*Institute of Construction Economics*] (CZ)
USE	Ustredni Sprava Energetiky [*Central Administration Office for Electric Power*] (CZ)
USEC........	Union Social de Empresarios Cristianos [*Social Union of Christian Businessmen*] [*Chile*] (LA)
USECOT...	Usine d'Egrenage du Coton [*Cotton Ginning Plant*] [*Cambodia*] (CL)
usedv	Usedvanlig [*Unusual*] [*Danish/Norwegian*]
USEF........	Union Sociale Economique de France [*French*] (SLS)
USEFMC ..	Uniunea Sindicatelor din Economia Forestiera si Materiale de Constructii [*Union of Trade Unions in the Forestry Economy and Construction Materials*] (RO)
USEG	Union Syndicale de l'Est Gabon
USEGA......	University of Sydney Economics Graduates Association [*Australia*]
Useite........	Umschlagseite [*Side of Cover*] [*Publishing*] [*German*]
USEK........	Ustredni Svaz Evangelickych Knezi [*Central Association of Protestant Ministers*] (CZ)
USEM	Union Social de Empresarios Mexicanos [*Social Union of Mexican Businessmen*] (LA)
USEMA.....	Union des Syndicats des Employeurs de Mauritanie
USEPA.....	Union Sportive de l'Enseignement Primaire en Algerie
USEPPA....	Universal System of Elements of Industrial Pneumoautomation (RU)
USET........	U.S. Equestrian Team (OLYM)
USETRAM ...	Union Senegalaise de Transit, Transport, et Manutention
usF...........	Und Seine Fortsetzung [*And Its Confirmation*] [*German*] (GCA)
usf..............	Und Seine Fruehere [*And Its Previous*] [*German*] (GCA)
usf..............	Und So Fort [*And So Forth*] [*German*] (EG)
USF...........	United Socialist Front [*Thailand*] [*Political party*] (PD)
USF...........	United Somali Front [*Political party*] (EY)
USFA........	U.S. Fencing Association (OLYM)
USFIA.......	United States Forces in Australia
USFO	United Sugar Farmers' Organization [*Philippines*] (EY)
USFP........	Union Socialiste des Forces Populaires [*Socialist Union of Popular Forces*] [*Morocco*] [*Political party*] (PPW)
USFSA	Union des Societes Francaises de Sports Athletiques [*French*]
USFSA	U.S. Figure Skating Association (OLYM)
USG	Fuel Supply Administration (RU)
USG	Union of Superiors General (EA)
USG	Ustav Stavebni Geologie [*Institute of Construction Geology*] (CZ)
USGaK	Ustredni Sprava Geodesie a Kartografie [*Central Geodetic and Cartographic Administration*] (CZ)
USGCRP ...	United States Global Change Research Program (BARN)
USGF........	U.S. Gymnastics Federation (OLYM)
USh...........	Navigator's Indicator [*Aviation*] (RU)
USh...........	Uganda Shilling
USH..........	Ushuaia [*Argentina*] [*Airport symbol*] (OAG)
USH..........	Ustav Skladoveho Hospodarstvi [*Institute of Storage Economy*] (CZ)
USh...........	Wide-Band Amplifier (RU)
UShB	Auger Drill Unit (RU)

ushch.......... Gorge, Canyon [*Topography*]   (RU)
u-shche...... School   (RU)
USHH .... Khanty-Mansiysk [*Former USSR*] [*ICAO location identifier*]   (ICLI)
USHK....... Ustav Stavebnich Hmot a Konstrukci [*Institute of Building Materials and Construction Engineering*] [*Prague*]   (CZ)
ushosdor..... Administration of Highways   (RU)
USHT....... Universiteti Shteteror i Tiranes [*Albanian*]
u-shte .... School   (BU)
USI .... Mabaruma [*Guyana*] [*Airport symbol*]   (OAG)
USI .... Uniao Sindical Independente [*Brazil*]
USI .... Unione Siderurgiche Italiane [*Italy*]
USI .... United Schools International [*New Delhi, India*]   (EAIO)
USI .... United States of Indonesia [*1946-1950*]   (FEA)
USI .... Video Amplifier   (RU)
USIA......... Administration of Soviet Property in Austria   (RU)
USIA......... United States Information Agency [*Formerly called BECA, it later became known as ICA or USICA, then again as USIA*]
USIA......... Uprava Sovjetske Imovine u Austriji [*Administration of Soviet Property in Austria*]   (YU)
USIAS .... Union Syndicale des Industries Aeronautiques et Spatiales [*Aerospace Industry Association*] [*Later, GIFAS*] [*France*]   (PDAA)
USIBA .... United States International Book Association   (NTCM)
USIBA .... Usina Siderurgica da Bahia [*Bahia Iron and Steel Mill*] [*Brazil*]   (LA)
USICA....... United States International Communications Agency
USID .... Signaling Dosimeter System   (RU)
USIEM...... Union des Syndicats d'Interet Economique de Madagascar [*Malagasy Federation of Unions of Economic Interest*]   (AF)
USIHS....... Ulster Society for Irish Historical Studies [*Northern Ireland*]   (SLS)
USIM........ Union de Sindicatos de la Industria Maderera [*Lumber Workers Union*] [*Argentina*]   (LA)
USIMA...... Union Senegalaise d'Industries Maritimes [*Senegalese Maritime Industries Union*]   (AF)
USIMA...... Union Soudanaise d'Industries Maritimes [*Sudanese Maritime Industries Union*]
USIMETAL ... Societe Industrielle de Ets. Roland Guiol
USIMINAS ... Usinas Siderurgicas de Minas Gerais, SA [*Minas Gerais Iron and Steel Mills, Inc.*] [*Brazil*]   (LA)
USINDO ... Usaha Industri Indonesia [*Indonesian Industrial Concern*]   (IN)
USINEN.... Societe Ivoirienne d'Usinage
USINEX.... Usine d'Extraction de Pyrethrine et pour l'Assimilation de l'Industrialisation
USINOR ... Union Siderurgique du Nord de la France
USIP .... United Solomon Islands Party   (PPW)
USIS .... United States Information Service
USISA .... U.S. International Speedskating Association   (OLYM)
USITT .... Uniunea Sindicatelor din Intreprinderile de Transporturi si Telecomunicatii [*Union of Trade Unions in Transportation and Telecommunications Enterprises*]   (RO)
USJ .... Union of Soviet Journalists   (EAIO)
USJ .... U.S. Judo, Inc.   (OLYM)
USJ .... Ustav Slovenskeho Jazyka [*Slovak Language Institute (of the Slovak Academy of Sciences)*]   (CZ)
USJC .... Union Socialiste de la Jeunesse Congolaise
US-JCSC... United States-Japan Committee on Scientific Cooperation [*Department of State*]
usk............. Acceleration   (RU)
USK .... Court Criminal Collegium   (RU)
USK .... Stockholms Utrednings och Statistikkontor [*Stockholm Office of Research and Statistics*] [*Sweden*]
USK .... Undugu Society of Kenya   (EAIO)
USK .... Union Sportive de Sidi Kacem [*Morocco*]
USK .... University Sports Club   (RU)
usk............. Uskonto [*Religion*] [*Finland*]
USKh........ Administration of Agriculture   (RU)
USKh........ Administration of Warehouses and Cold Storage Plants   (RU)
USKhI....... Ul'yanovsk Agricultural Institute   (RU)
usl............... Conventional   (RU)
usl............... Conventional Designation   (RU)
USL........... Universal Slide Rule   (RU)
USL........... Useless Loop [*Australia*] [*Airport symbol*]   (OAG)
USL........... Ustav Slovenskej Literatury [*Institute of Slovak Literature*]   (CZ)
USL........... Ustredni Svaz Lekarniku [*Central Union of Pharmacists*]   (CZ)
USLANT... United States Atlantic Subarea [*NATO*]
USLC........ Union des Syndicats Libres du Cameroun
Us lesn ...... Forest Homestead [*Topography*]   (RU)
USLF........ Union Syndicale des Libraires de France   (EY)
USLG........ Union des Societes Luxembourgeoises de Gymnastique [*Union of Luxembourg Gymnastic Societies*]   (WER)
USLSZ ...... Ustredni Sprava Lazni, Sanatorii, a Zotaven [*Central Administration of Spas, Sanatoriums, and Rest Homes*]   (CZ)

usl yed .... Conventional Unit   (RU)
USM .... General-Purpose Washing Machine   (RU)
USM .... Union des Syndicats de Monaco [*Union of Monaco Trade Unions*]   (EY)
USM .... Union Socialiste Malgache [*Malagasy Socialist Union*]   (AF)
USM .... United States Representative to the Military Committee Memorandum [*NATO*]
USM .... Universal Welding Manipulator   (RU)
USM .... University Saino Malaysia [*University of Science*] [*Malaysia*]   (PDAA)
USMM ...... Union Socialiste des Musulmans Mauritaniens [*Socialist Union of Mauritanian Muslims*]   (AF)
USMMASA ... Union Scientifique Mondiale des Medecins Acupuncteurs et des Societes d'Acupuncture [*Marseille, France*]   (SLS)
USMO...... Communications Administration of the Moscow Oblast   (RU)
USMPA..... U.S. Modern Pentathlon Association   (OLYM)
USMSKhI ... Administration of Medical and Sanitary Equipment Supply   (RU)
USn .... Consolidated Norms Used in Estimates   (RU)
USn .... Guided Missile   (RU)
USN .... Union Scolaire Nigerienne [*Nigerien School Union*] [*Niger*]   (AF)
USN .... Union Syndicale de la Ngounie
USN .... Union Syndicale de la Nyanga
USN .... Universal Voltage Stabilizer   (RU)
USN .... Ustredni Sklad Naradi [*Central Equipment Depot*]   (CZ)
USNKh...... Ukrainian Council of the National Economy   (RU)
USNO........ United Sabah National Organization [*Malaysia*] [*Political party*]   (PPW)
Us Nouv ..... Usine Nouvelle [*French*]   (FLAF)
USNP .... Ustav Slovenskeho Narodneho Povstania [*Institute of the Slovak National Uprising*]   (CZ)
USNP .... Ustredni Svaz Nemocenskych Pojistoven [*Central Union of Health Insurance Agencies*]   (CZ)
USNZV ..... Ustredni Sprava Nakupu Zemedelskych Vyrobku [*Central Administration Office for Purchase of Agricultural Products*]   (CZ)
USO........... Administration of Judicial Bodies (of the Ministry of Justice, RSFSR)   (RU)
USO........... Contact Arrangement with an Object   (RU)
USO........... Udaipur Solar Observatory [*India*]
USO........... Union Sindical Obrera [*Workers' Trade Union*] [*Colorado*]   (LA)
USO........... Union Sindical Obrera [*Workers' Trade Union*] [*Madrid, Spain*]   (WER)
USO........... Ural-Siberian Branch   (RU)
USO........... Ustredni Svaz Obchodu [*Central Commerce Union*]   (CZ)
USOC .... United States Olympic Committee   (OLYM)
USOD....... Ustredie Slovenskych Ochotnickych Divadiel [*Center of Slovak Amateur Theaters*]   (CZ)
USOENC .. Union des Syndicats Ouvriers et Employes de Nouvelle-Caledonie [*Trade union*]   (EY)
USOI .... Union des Syndicats de l'Ogooue Ivindo
usokr .... Directorate of Communications of a Military District   (RU)
Usol'lag..... Usol'ye Corrective Labor Camp   (RU)
USOM .... United States Operations Mission   (CL)
USOMS..... Uniao dos Sindicatos da Orla Maritima de Santos [*Union Confederation of the Santos Coast*] [*Brazil*]   (LA)
USOP .... Union Solidaria de Obreros Portuarios [*Common Union of Port Workers*] [*Uruguay*]   (LA)
USOP .... Ustredie Statnej Ochrany Prirody [*State Center for Nature Conservation*] [*Former Czechoslovakia*]   (EE)
USOPD ..... Ustredni Svaz Obchodu, Pohostinstvi, a Dopravy [*Central Union of Commerce, Hotel and Restaurant Trade, and Transportation*]   (CZ)
USOSF ...... Union of Shipowners for Overseas Shrimp Fisheries   (EAIO)
USP........... Uniao de Sindicatos do Porto [*Porto Union Federation*] [*Portuguese*]   (WER)
USP........... Unidad de Servicio y Produccion [*Service and Production Unity*] [*Cuba*]   (LA)
USP........... Union des Services Publics d'Afrique
USP........... United Socialist Party [*South Korea*] [*Political party*]   (PPW)
USP........... United Somali Party
USP........... Universal Assembly Device   (RU)
USP........... Universidade de Sao Paulo [*Sao Paulo University*] [*Brazil*]   (LA)
USP........... University of the South Pacific [*Fijian*]
USP........... Uniwersyteckie Studium Przygotowawcze [*University Preparation Course*]   (POL)
USP........... Ustredni Socialni Pojistovna [*Central Social Insurance Agency*]   (CZ)
USP........... Ustredni Statni Pokladna [*Central State Treasury*]   (CZ)
USP........... Ustredni Svaz Prumyslu [*Central Union of Industry*]   (CZ)
USPA........ Union de Services Publics-Abidjan
USPA......... Union Syndicale Panafricaine [*All-African Trade Union Federation*] [*Use AATUF*]   (AF)
USPAACC ... United States PanAsian American Chamber of Commerce   (EAIO)

USPAC ...... Union des Syndicats Professionnels Agricoles du Cameroun
USPAC ...... Union des Syndicats Professionnels Agricoles et Activites Connexes
USPC .... Union des Syndicats Professionnels du Cameroun
USPC .... Union Syndicale des Planteurs du Cameroun
USPD .... Unabhaengige Sozialdemokratische Partei Deutschlands [*Independent Social Democratic Party of Germany*] [*Political party*] (PPE)
USPG .... United Society for the Propagation of the Gospel [*Society for the Propagation of the Gospel in Foreign Parts and UMCA*] [*Formed by a merger of*] (EAIO)
USPI .... Unione Stampa Periodica Italiana [*Press association*] (EY)
USPK .... United Socialist Party of Kurdistan [*Iraq*] (MENA)
USPM .... Union des Syndicats Patronaux de Madagascar
USPMOM ... Union des Societes de Pediatrie du Moyen-Orient et de la Mediterranee [*Union of Middle Eastern and Mediterranean Pediatric Societies - UMEMPS*] [*Athens, Greece*] (EAIO)
USPO .... United Sabah People's Organization [*Pertubuhan Rakyat Sabah Bersatu*] [*Malaysia*] [*Political party*] (PPW)
USPPOP ... Ustredie Statnej Pamatkove Pece a Ochrany Prirody [*State Institute for the Prot ection of Monuments and Nature Conservancy*] [*Former Czechoslovakia*] (EE)
USQ .... University College of Southern Queensland [*Australia*]
USR .... Administration of Construction Operations (RU)
USR .... Administration of Specialized Operations (RU)
USR .... Ukrainska Partiia Sotsialistov Revolyutsionerov [*Ukrainian Socialist Revolutionary Party*] [*Russian*] [*Political party*] (PPE)
USR .... Universidad Simon Rodriguez [*Venezuela*]
USR .... Ustredni Svaz Remesel [*Central Union of Crafts*] (CZ)
USRA .... Union des Syndicats Revolutionnaires Angolais
USRA .... U.S. Rowing Association (OLYM)
USRAF ...... Union pour le Salut et le Renouveau de l'Algerie Francaise
USR-Borotbists ... Ukrainska Partiia Sotsialistov Revolyutsionerov-Borotbists [*Ukrainian Socialist Revolutionary Party-Fighters*] [*Russian*] [*Political party*] (PPE)
US-RDA .... Union Soudanaise - Rassemblement Democratique Africain [*Mali*] [*Political party*] (EY)
USREPMC ... United States Representative to the Military Committee [*NATO*]
USREPMILCOMLO ... United States Representative to the Military Committee Liaison Office [*NATO*]
USRL .... Laryak [*Former USSR*] [*ICAO location identifier*] (ICLI)
USRN .... Nizhnevartovsk [*Former USSR*] [*ICAO location identifier*] (ICLI)
USRO .... UNESCO Sub-Regional Office
USRP .... Administration of Workers' Settlements Construction (RU)
USRP .... Hungarian Socialist Workers' Party (BU)
USRR .... Surgut [*Former USSR*] [*ICAO location identifier*] (ICLI)
USRR .... Ukrainska Socjalistyczna Republika Radziecka [*Ukrainian Soviet Socialist Republic*] [*POL*]
USRV .... Rayon Junction Broadcasting Station (RU)
USS .... Strategic Services Administration (BU)
USS .... Ucena Spolecnost Safarikova [*Safarik Learned Society*] (CZ)
USS .... United Superannuation Services Proprietary Ltd. [*Australia*]
USS .... Universitelararasi Secme Sinavina [*Inter-University Proficiency Examination*] (TU)
USS .... Universiteler Arasi Secme Sinavinda Basari [*Inter-University Entrance Examination*] [*Turkey*]
USS .... U.S. Swimming, Inc. (OLYM)
USS .... Ustredi Stredoskolskeho Studentstva [*Center of Secondary School Students*] (CZ)
USS .... Ustredna Sprava Spojov [*Central Communications Administration*] (CZ)
USS .... Ustredna Stavebna Sprava [*Central Construction Administration (of the State Railroads)*] (CZ)
USS .... Ustredni Svazova Skola [*Central Trade Union School*] (CZ)
USSALEP ... United States-South Africa Leadership Exchange Program (AF)
USSASA .... University Science Students' Association of Southern Africa (AA)
USSC .... Universities Social Science Council
USSCC ...... University Social Sciences Council Conference
USSD .... Ustredni Svaz Spotrebnich Druzstev [*Central Union of Consumer Cooperatives*] (CZ)
USSE .... Severouralsk [*Former USSR*] [*ICAO location identifier*] (ICLI)
USSF .... U.S. Soccer Federation (OLYM)
USSGREP ... United States Standing Group Representative [*NATO*]
USSI .... Ivdel [*Former USSR*] [*ICAO location identifier*] (ICLI)
USSL .... Uganda School Supply Limited
USSM .... Societatea de Electroencefalografie [*Romanian Society for Electroencephalography*] (EAIO)
USSM .... Uniunea Societatilor de Stiinte Medicale [*Union of Medical Sciences Societies*] (RO)
USSM .... Ustredie Svazu Slovenskej Mladeze [*Center of the Union of Slovak Youth*] (CZ)
USSP .... Universal Assembly Welding Device (RU)

USSP .... Ustredne Sdruzenie Slovenskeho Priemyslu [*Central Association of Slovak Industry*] (CZ)
USSPC ...... Ustredi Stredoskolske Socialni Pece pro Cechy [*Central Social Welfare Bureau for Students of Secondary Schools in Bohemia*] (CZ)
USSPEI .... Union des Syndicats des Services Publics Europeens et Internationaux [*European and International Public Services Union*] [*Later, EUROFEDOP*] (EAIO)
USSPM ..... Ustredi Stredoskolske Socialni Pece pro Zemi Moravskoslezskou [*Central Social Welfare Bureau for Students of Secondary Schools in Moravia and Silesia*] (CZ)
USSR .... State Music Trust [*Record label*] [*Former USSR*]
USSR .... Ukrajinska Sovjetska Socijalisticka Republika [*Ukrainian Soviet Socialist Republic*] (YU)
USSR .... Unie van Sosialistiese Sowjet-Republieke [*Union of Socialist Soviet Republics*] [*Afrikaans*]
USSR .... Union of Soviet Socialist Republics [*See also SSSR, CCCP*]
USSRBF .... USSR Badminton Federation (EAIO)
USSRCFT ... USSR State Committee for Foreign Tourism [*Defunct*] (EAIO)
USSRM ... State Music Trust [*78 RPM*] [*Record label*] [*Former USSR*]
USSS .... Sverdlovsk [*Former USSR*] [*ICAO location identifier*] (ICLI)
USSS .... U.S. Synchronized Swimming, Inc (OLYM)
ust .... Obsolete [*Lexicography*] (RU)
ust .... Stability (RU)
UST .... Standardized Medical (Tent) (RU)
UST .... Transportation Construction Administration (BU)
UST .... Union Senegalaise du Travail [*Senegalese Labor Union*] (AF)
UST .... Union Socialiste Tchadienne
UST .... Union Syndicats du Tchad (EY)
UST .... University of Science and Technology [*Kumasi, Ghana*]
UST .... Uredba o Spoljnotrgovinskom Poslovanju [*Decree on Foreign Trade Operations*] (YU)
ust .... Ustawa [*Act, Law*] (POL)
ust .... Ustep [*Paragraph*] (POL)
USTA .... Union Sindical de Trabajadores de Arequipa [*Arequipa Labor Union Group*] [*Peru*] (LA)
USTA .... Union Syndicale des Travailleurs Algeriens
USTA .... Universities of Science and Technology of Algiers
USTA .... U.S. Tackwando Union (OLYM)
ustar .... Obsolete [*Lexicography*] (RU)
USTARCH SAV ... Ustav Stavebnictva a Architektury SAV [*Construction and Architecture Institute of the Slovak Science Academy*] (CZ)
USTB .... Union Syndicale des Travailleurs Burkinabes [*Trade Union Federation of the Working People of Burkina Faso*] [*USTV*] [*Formerly,*]
USTB .... Union Syndicale des Travailleurs du Burundi
Ust BIB ..... Charter of the Bulgarian Investment Bank (BU)
USTC .... Union Syndicale de Travail Centrafricaine [*Union of Central African Workers*] (EY)
USTC .... Unitatea de Supraveghere si Terapie Intensiva a Coronarienilor [*Unit for Observation and Intensive Therapy of Coronary Patients*] (RO)
USTC .... United States Trading Company
USTC .... University of Science and Technology of China
USTC .... US Trade Center [*Mexico*] (IMH)
USTD .... Union Sportive des Tireurs de Dakar
UStDB .... Umsatzsteuerdurchfuehrungsbestimmung [*Implementing Regulation for Turnover Tax*] (EG)
UStG .... Umsatzsteuergesetz [*Turnover Tax Law*] [*German*] (WEN)
USTHF ...... U.S. Team Handball Federation (OLYM)
USTIA .... Union de Sindicatos de Trabajadores de Industrias Alimenticias [*Food Industry Labor Union Group*] [*Uruguay*] (LA)
USTKE ...... Union des Syndicats des Travailleurs Kanaks et Exploites [*New Caledonia*]
USTL .... Union Syndicale des Travailleurs Libres [*Trade Union of Free Workers*] [*Morocco*] (AF)
USTM .... Union Senegalaise de Transports Maritimes
USTN .... Union des Syndicats des Travailleurs du Niger [*Federation of Labor Unions of Niger*] (AF)
USTO .... Universities of Science and Technology of Oran [*Algeria*]
USTOC ...... Unitatea de Servicii Tehnice pentru Obiective in Constructie [*Technical Services Unit for Projects under Construction*] (RO)
USTOM .... Union Syndicale des Transport d'Outre-Mer
USTPM ..... Union Syndicale des Travailleurs et Paysans Malgaches
USTSTP .... Union Syndicale des Travailleurs de Sao Tome et Principe
USTT .... Union Syndicale des Travailleurs Tunisiens
USTTA ...... U.S. Table Tennis Association (OLYM)
USTV .... Union Syndicale des Travailleurs Voltaiques [*Voltan Workers Trade Union Federation*] (AF)
Ust'-Vymlag ... Ust'-Vym' Corrective Labor Camp (RU)
USTW .... Sovetsky [*Former USSR*] [*ICAO location identifier*] (ICLI)
USU .... Percussion Drilling Device (RU)
USU .... Union Sindical del Uruguay [*Union Association of Uruguay*] (LA)
USU .... Uplne Strediskove Ucetnictvi [*Complete Central Accounting*] (CZ)

USU .... Ustredni Socialni Ustav [*Central Social Welfare Institute*] (CZ)
usu .... Usually (TPFD)
USUAA ..... University Students Union of Addis Ababa [*Ethiopia*] (AF)
USUARIOI ... Association of Maritime Transport Users in the Central American Isthmus [*Guatemala, Guatemala*] (EAIO)
USUCA ..... United Steelworkers Union of Central Africa [*Rhodesian*] (AF)
USUD .... University Students' Union of Dar Es Salaam [*Tanzania*] (AF)
USUMA .... Union des Superieures Majeures du Burundi
USUS .... Uniunea Sindicatelor din Unitatile Sanitare [*Union of Trade Unions in Health Units*] (RO)
USV .... Unterbrechungsfreie Stromversorgung [*German*] (ADPT)
USV .... Ustredni Spravni Vybor [*Central Administrative Committee*] (CZ)
USVA .... Directorate of the Soviet Military Administration (RU)
USVAB ...... Ustredni Svaz Ceskoslovenskych Vynalezcu a Badatelu [*Central Union of Czechoslovak Investors and Researchers*] (CZ)
USVAG ..... Directorate of the Soviet Military Administration in Germany (RU)
USVB .... Union Syndicale Veterinaire Belge [*Belgium*] (SLS)
USVBA ...... U.S. Volleyball Association (OLYM)
USVCh ...... Superhigh-Frequency Amplifier (RU)
USVH .... Ustredni Sprava Vodniho Hospodarstvi [*Central Administration for Water Utilization*] (CZ)
USVO .... Statute of the Council for the Mutual Insurance of Members of Labor Productive Cooperatives (BU)
USVPS ...... Administration of Through Sleeping Cars (RU)
USVR .... Administration of Construction and Reconstruction Work (RU)
USVU .... Ustredni Statni Veterinarni Ustav [*State Central Veterinary Institute*] (CZ)
usw .... Und So Weiter [*And So Forth*] [*German*] (GPO)
USW .... Urzad do Spraw Wyznan [*Office of Religious Denominational Affairs*] (POL)
USWAP ..... United South West Africa Party [*Namibia*] [*Political party*]
USWP .... U.S. Water Polo (OLYM)
USWU .... Uganda Sugar Workers Union (AF)
USX .... US Express [*ICAO designator*] (FAAC)
U Syd .... University of Sydney [*Australia*]
USYM .... Universitelerarasi Ogrenci Secme ve Yerlestirme Merkezi [*Inter-University Student Selection and Placement Center*] (TU)
usynl .... Usynlig [*Imperceptible*] [*Danish/Norwegian*]
USYRU ..... U.S. Yacht Racing Union (OLYM)
USZ .... Ucnovske Skoly Zemedelske [*Agricultural Apprentice Schools*] (CZ)
USZD .... Ustredni Svaz Zemedelskych Druzstev [*Central Union of Agricultural Cooperatives*] (CZ)
USZH .... Ustredni Svaz Zamestnancu v Hornictvi [*Central Union of Employees in the Mining Industry*] (CZ)
USZNO ..... Ustredni Svaz Zidovskych Nabozenskych Obci [*Central Union of Jewish Religious Congregations*] (CZ)
USZO .... Ustredni Socialni a Zamestnanecke Oddeleni [*Central Department for Social and Employee Relations*] (CZ)
USZRP ...... Administration of Shipyards of River Steamship Lines (RU)
UT .... General-Purpose Refractory (Lubricant) (RU)
UT .... Percussion Primer (RU)
ut .... Specific Heat (RU)
UT .... Trainer (Aircraft) (RU)
UT .... Uciteljska Tiskarna [*Teachers' Printing House*] [*Ljubljana*] (YU)
UT .... Union Tchadienne
UT .... Union Territory [*India*] (BARN)
UT .... Union Tradicionalista [*Traditionalist Union*] [*Spanish*] (WER)
UT .... Unite de Traffic
UT .... Unite de Traitement [*German*] (ADPT)
UT .... United Textile [*Saha Union Group*] [*Thailand*]
UT .... Unite Togolaise [*Togolese Unity Party*] (AF)
UT .... Universidad del Tolima [*Ibague*] (COL)
UT .... Universite Technique [*Technical University*] [*UTRK Cambodia*] [*Formerly,*] (CL)
UT .... University of Tasmania [*Australia*]
UT .... Uniwersytet w Toruniu [*Torun University*] (POL)
UT .... Urzad Telekomunikacyjny [*Telecommunications Office*] (POL)
ut .... Utalvany [*Sent by Postal Order*] (HU)
ut .... Utasitas [*Directive*] (HU)
ut .... Utca [*Street*] [*Hungary*] (CED)
UT .... Uusi Testamentti [*Finland*]
UTA .... Ukrainian News Agency (RU)
UTA .... Unidad Tactica Anti-Terrorista [*Tactical Union of Antiterrorists*] [*Peru*]
UTA .... Union des Transports Aeriens [*France*] [*ICAO designator*] (FAAC)
UTA .... Union de Transports Aeriens [*Air Transport Union*] [*Private airline*] [*France*] (EY)
UTA .... Union Trading Afrique
UTA .... Union Transviarios Automotor [*Motor Transport Workers Union*] [*Argentina*] (LA)
UTA .... University of Tasmania Association [*Australia*]

UTAA .... Union de Trabajadores Azucareros de Artigas [*Artigas Sugar Workers Union*] [*Uruguay*] (LA)
UTAA .... Unit Trust Association of Australia
UTAC .... Union de Transporteurs Agrees de Casablanca et de Sa Region
UTAC .... Union Technique de l'Automobile, du Motocycle, et du Cycle [*Automobile, Motorcycle, and Cycle Technical Union*] [*Paris*] [*French*] [*Research center*] (ERC)
UTAC .... Union Tunisienne de l'Artisanat et du Commerce [*Tunisian Artisans and Merchants Association*] (AF)
UTAE .... Union de Trabajadores Arroceros del Este [*Uruguayan Rice Workers Union*] (LA)
UTAF .... Union des Travailleurs Algeriens en France
UTAFITI ... Baraza la Taifa la Utafiti wa Sayansi [*Tanzania National Scientific Research Council*]
UTAG .... United Travel Agents' Group [*Australia*]
UTAG .... University Teachers Association of Ghana
UTAIM ...... Union Tunisienne d'Aide aux Insuffisants Mentaux
UTAL .... Universidad de Trabajadores de America Latina (EY)
UTAM .... Ustav Teoreticke a Aplikovane Mechaniky [*Institute of Theoretical and Applied Mechanics (of the Czechoslovak Academy of Sciences)*] (CZ)
utanny .... Utannyomas [*Reprint*] (HU)
UTAP .... Air Training Regiment (RU)
UTAPITI ... Baraza la Taipa la Utapiti wa Sayansi [*Tanzania*]
UTAPV ...... Three-Phase Automatic Recloser (RU)
utarb .... Utarbeidet [*Edited*] [*Publishing Danish/Norwegian*]
utarb .... Utarbetad [*Edited*] [*Sweden*]
U Tas .... University of Tasmania [*Australia*]
UTB .... Muttaburra [*Australia*] [*Airport symbol*] (OAG)
UTB .... Union des Travailleurs du Burundi [*Burundi Workers Union*] (AF)
UTB .... Union de Trabajadores de Bauca [*Union of Bauca Workers*] [*Spanish*] (WER)
UTB .... Union Togolaise de Banque [*Togolese Banking Union*] (AF)
UTB .... Uni Taschenbuecher GmbH [*German publishers cooperative*]
UTB .... Uzina Tractorul Brasov [*Brasov Tractorul Enterprise*] (RO)
UTC .... Uganda Transport Company
UTC .... Uitspraken Tariefcommissie [*Benelux*] (BAS)
UTC .... Underwater Technology Corporation [*Australia*]
UTC .... Unidad Tactica de Combate [*Tactical Combat Unit*] [*Venezuela*] (LA)
UTC .... Union des Travailleurs Congolais [*Union of Congolese Workers*]
UTC .... Union des Travailleurs des Comores
UTC .... Union de Trabajadores Campesinos [*Agricultural Workers' Union*] [*El Salvador*] (PD)
UTC .... Union de Trabajadores de Colombia [*Colombia Workers Union*] (LA)
UTC .... Union Technique et Commerciale
UTC .... Union Tennis-Club
UTC .... Union Togolaise de Constructions et de Travaux Publics
UTC .... Union Trading Cameroun SA
UTC .... Union Trading Company Ltd.
UTC .... United Touring Company
UTC .... United Trading Co. Ltd. [*Nigeria*]
UTC .... Uniunea Tineretului Comunist [*Union of Communist Youth*] (RO)
UTC .... Urban Transport Council [*New Zealand*]
UTCAP ...... Union de Trabajadores del Cemento y Afines de Panama [*Panamanian Union of Cement and Related Workers*] (LA)
UTCC .... Unio de Treballadors Cristians de Cataluna [*Christian Workers Union of Catalonia*] [*Spanish*] (WER)
UTCGA ..... Union Tunisienne de la Confederation Generale de l'Agriculture
UTCh .... Ustav Technicke Chemie [*Institute of Applied Chemistry*] [*Usti Nad Labem*] (CZ)
UTCL .... Union des Travailleurs Communistes Libertaires [*Union of Libertarian Communist Workers*] [*France*] [*Political party*] (PPW)
UTCPR ...... Union de Trabajadores de la Corporacion Panamena de Radiodifusion [*Workers Union of the Panamanian Radiobroadcasting Corporation*] (LA)
UTCPTT ... Union Internationale des Organismes Touristiques et Culturels des Postes et des Telecommunications [*International Union of Tourist and Cultural Associations in the Postal and Telecommunications Services*]
UTD .... United Air [*South Africa*] [*ICAO designator*] (FAAC)
UTD .... Uredba o Trgovinskoj Delatnosti i Trgovinskim Preduzecima i Radnjama [*Decree on Commercial Operations Establishments and Shops*] (YU)
UTD .... Ustav Technickeho Dozoru [*Technical Control Institute*] (CZ)
UTDD .... Dushanbe [*Former USSR*] [*ICAO location identifier*] (ICLI)
UTDN .... Union des Transitaires du Dakar-Niger
UTDO .... Oktyabrsky [*Former USSR*] [*ICAO location identifier*] (ICLI)
UTE .... Administracion General de las Usinas Electricas y los Telefonos del Estado [*General Administration of State Electric Power and Telephones*] [*Uruguay*] (LA)

UTE .... Ufficio Tecnico Erariale [*Inland Revenue Surveyors' Office*] [*Italian*]

UTE .... Union de Trabajadores del Este [*Uruguayan Workers Union*] (LA)

UTE .... Union Technique de l'Electricite [*Paris, France*] (SLS)

UTE .... Universidad Tecnica del Estado [*State Technical University*] [*Chile*] (LA)

UTE .... Usinas Electricas y Telefonos del Estado [*Uruguay Communications Agency*] (PDAA)

UTE .... Uzina e Telave Elektrike [*Albanian*]

UTED .... Dzhizak [*Former USSR*] [*ICAO location identifier*] (ICLI)

UTEG .... Union de Trabajadores de la Ensenanza Gallega [*Union of Galician Educational Workers*] [*Spanish*] (WER)

UTEHA ..... Union Tipografica Editorial Hispano Americana [*Mexico*] (DSCA)

UTEIN ...... Ustav pro Technickou a Ekonomickou Informace [*Institute for Technical and Economic Information*] [*Prague*] (CZ)

UTEK .... Junction Office for Transportation and Forwarding Operations (RU)

UTEKh ...... Administration of Fuel and Power System Managment (RU)

UTERPRA ... Urusan Teritoriil dan Perlawanan Rakjat [*Territorial Affairs and People's Resistance*] (IN)

UTESA ...... Universidad Tecnologica de Santiago [*Technological University of Santiago*] [*Dominican Republic*] (LA)

UTET......... Unione Tipografico Editrice Torinese [*Italy*]

UTEX .... Union Textile Marocaine

UTEX .... Union Transafricaine d'Expansion Industrielle et Commerciale

UTEX .... Ustecky Textilni Zavod [*Textile Mills in Usti Nad Labem*] (CZ)

UTEXI....... Union Textile Industrielle de Cote-D'Ivoire [*Ivory Coast Textile Industry Union*] (AF)

UTEXO ..... Usines Textiles Cotonnieres de Kinshasa [*Zaire*] (IMH)

UTF .... Union des Transporteurs de Ferkessedougou

UTF .... Union de Trabajadores Ferrocarrileros [*Railroad Workers Union*] [*El Salvador*] (LA)

UTF .... Uridine Triphosphate (RU)

UTF .... Ustav Technicke Fysiky [*Institute of Applied Physics (of the Czechoslovak Academy of Sciences)*] (CZ)

utforl .... Utfoerlig [*Extensive*] [*Sweden*]

UTG .... Mining Goniometer-Tachometer (RU)

UTG .... Union des Travailleurs Guyanais [*Union of Guyanese Workers*] [*French Guiana*]

UTG .... Union de Trabajadores de Golfito [*Golfito Workers Union*] [*Costa Rica*] (LA)

UTG .... United Tasmania Group [*Political party*] [*Australia*]

utg .... Utgava [*Edition*] [*Publishing*] [*Sweden*]

utg .... Utgave [*Edition*] [*Publishing Danish/Norwegian*]

UTGU........ Ukhta Territorial Geological Administration (RU)

UTH .... Le Salaire par Unite de Travailleur Homme [*Benelux*] (BAS)

UTH .... Udon Thani [*Thailand*] [*Airport symbol*] (OAG)

UTH .... Union Touristique et Hoteliere [*Hotel and Tourist Union*] (CL)

UT-H .... University of Tasmania - Hobart [*Australia*]

UTH .... University Teaching Hospital

UTHD .... Ustav Technicke a Hospodarske Dokumentace [*Institute for Technical and Economic Documentation*] (CZ)

UTHE........ Union des Associations des Etablissements Thermaux de la CE [*Union of Associations of Thermal Baths Establishments in the EC*] (ECED)

UTHK........ Ustav pro Technologii Hrube Keramiky [*Technical Institute for Industrial Ceramics*] (CZ)

UTHR........ University Teachers for Human Rights [*Sri Lanka*]

UTI .... Trainer Fighter Aircraft (RU)

UTI .... Union Technique Interfederale

UTI .... Union Technique Interprofessionnelle des Federations Nationales du Batiment et des Travaux Publics [*Paris, France*] (SLS)

UTI .... Union Telegraphique Internationale (MSC)

UTI .... Unit Trust of India (PDAA)

UTIACSAV ... Ustav Teorie Informace a Automatizace CSAV [*Institute of Information Theory and Automation of the Czechoslovak Science Academy*] (CZ)

UTIC.......... Union Tunisienne de l'Industrie et du Commerce [*North African*]

UTICA....... Union Tunisienne de l'Industrie, du Commerce, et de l'Artisanat [*Tunisian Union for Industry, Trade, and Crafts*] [*Tunis, Tunisia*] (AF)

UTIFar ...... Unione Tecnica Italiana Farmacisti [*Italian*] (SLS)

UTIM .... Trade Administration of the Executive Committee of the Mosoblsovet (RU)

UTIMACO ... Centrale Mecanographique [*Morocco*]

UTINA ...... Union Technique Nord-Africaine [*Morocco*]

UTIP.......... Unidades de Terapia Intensiva Pediatrica [*Pediatric Intensive Care Units*] [*Cuba*] (LA)

UTJ............ Union Tunisienne de la Jeunesse [*Tunisian Youth Union*] (AF)

UTK .... Ugostiteljsko-Turisticka Komora [*Chamber of Hotel and Catering and Tourist Trade*] (YU)

UTK .... Ukase on the Merchant Marine in the Bulgarian People's Republic (BU)

UTK .... "Unitas" Tvornica Konca ["*Unitas*" *Thread Factory*] [*Zagreb*] (YU)

UTK .... University of the Workers of China Imeni Sun Yat-Sen (RU)

UTK .... Ustredna Technicka Kniznica [*Central Technical Library*] [*Bratislava*] (CZ)

UTK .... Ustredni Technicka Knihovna [*Central Technical Library*] [*Prague*] (CZ)

UTK .... Ustredni Technicka Komise [*Central Technical Commission*] (CZ)

UTK .... Utirik [*Marshall Islands*] [*Airport symbol*] (OAG)

utk .... Utkom [*Was Published*] [*Sweden*]

utk .... Utkommer [*Is Published*] [*Danish/Norwegian*]

UT-L .... University of Tasmania - Launceston [*Australia*]

UTL .... Ustav Telovychovneho Lekarstvi [*Institute for the Study of Medicine (with regard to physical education)*] (CZ)

utl .... Utlaendsk [*Foreign*] [*Sweden*]

UTLS........ Union des Travailleurs Libres du Senegal

UTM.......... General-Purpose Refractory Frost-Resistant (Lubricant) (RU)

UTM.......... Unevangelized Tribes Mission

UTM.......... Union des Travailleurs de Mauritanie [*Workers Union of Mauritania*] (AF)

UTM.......... Union des Travailleurs de Mayotte [*Comoros*] (PD)

UTM.......... Union des Travailleurs Marocains [*Union of Moroccan Workers*] (AF)

UTM.......... Union Trading Monaco

UTM.......... Uniunea Tineretului Muncitor [*Union of Working Youth*] (RO)

UTM.......... Universidad Tecnica de Manabi [*Ecuador*] (DSCA)

utm .... Utmaerkt [*Excellent*] [*Sweden*]

UTMD....... Training Antitank Wooden Mine (RU)

UTMDB .... Training Antitank Wooden Briquette Mine (RU)

UTMZ....... Ural Turbomotor Plant (RU)

UTN.......... Adjusting Voltage Transformer (RU)

UTN.......... Unit Tenaga Nuklear [*Nuclear Energy Unit*] [*Malaysia*] (IRC)

UTN.......... Universal Voltage Transformer (RU)

UTN.......... Universidad Tecnica Nacional [*National Technical University*] [*Argentina*] (LA)

UTN.......... Upington [*South Africa*] [*Airport symbol*] (OAG)

UTO.......... United Towns Organisation [*See also FMVJ*] [*Paris, France*] (EAIO)

UTO.......... Universidad Tecnica de Oruro [*Technical University of Oruro*] [*Bolivia*] (LA)

UTOJ .... Union Tunisienne des Organizations de Jeunesse [*Tunisian Union of Youth Organizations*] (EAIO)

utok .... Utoekad [*Enlarged*] [*Sweden*]

UTOKCSAV ... Ustav pro Tvorbu a Ochranu Krajiny CSAV [*Institute for Care and Protection of Natural Environment, Czechoslovak Science Academy*] (CZ)

UTONA..... Uniao dos Trabalhadores e Operarios Negros de Angola

utosz.......... Utoszo [*Postscript, Epilogue, Conclusion*] (HU)

UTP .... Fuel Industry Administration (RU)

UTP .... Ucilista Telesne Pripravy [*Physical Education School*] (CZ)

UTP .... Union de Titres et de Participants

UTP .... Union Togolaise Parti

UTP .... United Tanganyika Party

UTP .... Universidad Tecnica de Piura [*Peru*] (DSCA)

UTP .... Universite Technique et Populaire [*People's Technical University*] [*Cambodia*] (CL)

UTP .... Utapao [*Thailand*] [*Airport symbol*] [*Obsolete*] (OAG)

UTP-France ... Materiaux de Soudure

UTPS........ Urban Transport Planning System [*Australia*]

UTR .... Labor Reserves Administration (BU)

UTR .... Union des Travailleurs du Rwanda

UTR .... Universite Technique Royale Khmere [*Cambodian Royal Technical University*] [*Use UTRK*] (CL)

UTRABO .. Union de Trabajadores Boyacenses [*Boyaca Workers Union*] [*Colorado*] (LA)

UTRACAL ... Union de Trabajadores Caldenses [*Manizales*] (COL)

UTRACh ... Union de Trabajadores de Chile [*Union of Chilean Workers*] (LA)

UTRACO .. Union des Transporteurs Routiers et Camionneurs de l'Oubangui-Chari

UTRACUN ... Union de Trabajadores de Cundinamarca [*Cundinamarca Workers Union*] [*Colorado*] (LA)

UTRAL...... Union de Trabajadores Agricolas de Limon [*Union of Limon Agricultural Workers*] [*Costa Rica*] (LA)

UTRAL...... Union de Trabajadores del Atlantico [*Atlantico Workers Union*] [*Colorado*] (LA)

UTRALLANO ... Union de Trabajadores de Llano [*Villavicencio*] (COL)

UTRAM .... Union des Transitaires et Agents Maritimes du Sine Saloum

UTRAMIG ... Universidade do Trabalho de Minas Gerais [*Minas Gerais Labor University*] [*Brazil*] (LA)

UTRAMMICOL ... Union de Trabajadores Metalurgicos y Mineros de Colombia [*Union of Metalworkers and Miners of Colombia*] (LA)

UTRAN ..... Union de Trabajadores Antioquenos [*Antioquia Workers Union*] [*Colorado*] (LA)

UTRANCO ... Union Transports Cameroun-Oubangui

UTRAQUINDIO ... Union de Trabajadores del Quindio [*Armenia*] (COL)
UTRASAN ... Union de Trabajadores de Santander [*Santander Workers Union*] [*Colorado*] (LA)
UTRATEXCO ... Union de Trabajadores Textiles de Colombia [*Textile Workers Union of Colombia*] (LA)
UTRATOL ... Union de Trabajadores del Tolima [*Ibague*] (COL)
UTRAVAL ... Union de Trabajadores del Valle [*Valle Workers Union*] [*Colorado*] (LA)
UTRC .... Union Theatre Repertory Co. [*Australia*]
UTRK .... Universite Technique Royale Khmere [*Cambodian Royal Technical University*] [*Replaced by UT*] (CL)
UTS .... Agency Telephone Exchange (RU)
UTS .... General-Purpose Refractory Synthetic (Lubricant) (RU)
UTS .... Telephone Network Administration (RU)
UTS .... Temperature Signaling Device (RU)
UTS .... Unified Teaching Service
UTS .... Union des Travailleurs du Senegal
UTS .... Union des Travailleurs Scientifiques [*Union of Scientific Workers*] [*French*] (WER)
UTS .... Union de Trabajo Sindical [*Labor Trade Union*] [*Spanish*] (WER)
UTS .... Union Thoniere Senegalaise
UTS .... Union Togolaise de Scierie
UTS .... Unit of Tropical Silviculture
UTS .... Universal Transport & Shipping Establishment [*Jordan*] [*Commercial firm*]
UTS .... University of Technology, Sydney [*Australia*] (ECON)
UTS .... Uprava Transportne Sluzbe [*Transport Service Administration*] (YU)
UTS .... Uredni Telefonni Seznam [*Official Telephone Directory*] (CZ)
UTS .... Usine des Tissus Synthetiques
UTS .... Ustredni Televisni Studio [*Central Television Studio*] (CZ)
uts........... Utsald [*Sold Out*] [*Sweden*]
UTsBiPP ... Administration of the Pulp, Paper, and Printing Industry (RU)
UTsGAL.... Administration of the Central State Archives of Leningrad (RU)
UTSK........ Ustav Typisace Stavebnich Konstrukci [*Institute for Standardization of Structural Elements*] (CZ)
UTsM .... Control Digital Computer (RU)
UTsM .... Simplified Digital Computer (RU)
UTSM ...... Tamdy-Bulak [*Former USSR*] [*ICAO location identifier*] (ICLI)
UTSM ...... Ukrainian Trust of Agricultural Machinery (RU)
UTSS .... Samarkand [*Former USSR*] [*ICAO location identifier*] (ICLI)
UTST........ Termez [*Former USSR*] [*ICAO location identifier*] (ICLI)
UTsVM ..... General-Purpose Digital Computer (RU)
UTT .... Umtata [*South Africa*] [*Airport symbol*] (OAG)
UTT .... Union des Travailleurs Tchadiens
UTT .... Union de Tecnicos y Trabajadores del Metal [*Union of Technicians and Metalworkers*] [*Spanish*] (WER)
UTT .... Universal Current Transformer (RU)
UTTA .... United Taxis and Transport Association
UTTC .... United Togo Trading Company
UTTE........ Junta de los Usuarios del Telefono y la Telecomunicacion [*Union of Users of the Telephone and Telecommunications*] [*Spanish*] (WER)
UTTEFU ... Utfenntarto Teherautofuvarozasi Vallalat [*Road Maintenance Truck Transportation Enterprise*] (HU)
UTTT........ Tashkent/Yuzhny [*Former USSR*] [*ICAO location identifier*] (ICLI)
UTU.......... Office of Technical Services [*OTS*] (RU)
UTU.......... Ulster Teachers' Union [*Belfast*] (SLS)
UTU.......... Universal Telephone Repeater (RU)
UTU.......... Universidad del Trabajo del Uruguay [*Labor University of Uruguay*] (LA)
UTU.......... Ustupo [*Panama*] [*Airport symbol*] (OAG)
UTUA .... Trade Union Federation of Albania
UTUC .... Uganda Trade Union Congress (AF)
UTUC .... United Trades Union Congress [*India*]
UTUZ........ United Trade Unions of Zimbabwe (AF)
utv .... Approved (RU)
UTV .... Armored Troops Regulations (RU)
UTV .... General-Purpose Refractory Water-Resistant (Lubricant) (RU)
UTV .... Universal Slow-Speed Wind Motor (RU)
UTV .... Ustredni Technicky Vybor [*Central Technical Committee*] (CZ)
utv .... Utvalg [*Selection*] [*Publishing Danish/Norwegian*]
utvidg .... Utvidgad [*Enlarged*] [*Sweden*]
UTWU...... Uganda Textile Workers Union (AF)
UTWU....... United Textile Workers Union [*Rhodesian*] (AF)
UTZ .... Union de Trabajadores del Zulia [*Zulia Workers Union*] [*Venezuela*] (LA)
UTZ .... Union Nationale des Travailleurs Zairois
UU .... Control Unit [*Computers*] (RU)
UU .... Enlarger (RU)
UU .... Multiplexing Device (RU)
UU .... Undang-Undang [*Law*] (IN)
uU .... Unter Umstaenden [*Circumstances Permitting, Possibly, Perhaps*] [*German*] (WEN)

UU .... Uzlova Telefonni Ustredna [*Main Telephone Exchange*] (CZ)
UUA .... Ustredni Ustav Astronomicky [*Central Institute of Astronomy*] [*Prague*] (CZ)
UUAL........ Union de Universidades de America Latina [*Union of Latin American Universities*] (LA)
UUBP .... Bryansk [*Former USSR*] [*ICAO location identifier*] (ICLI)
UUD .... Undang-Undang Dasar [*Constitution (National)*] (IN)
uud .... Uudismuodoste [*Finland*]
UUDN .... Ukase on Awarding Dimitrov Prizes (BU)
UUEE .... Moskva/Sheremetyevo [*Former USSR*] [*ICAO location identifier*] (ICLI)
UUEM .... Kalini/Migalovo [*Former USSR*] [*ICAO location identifier*] (ICLI)
UUG .... Ustredni Ustav Geologicky, Praha [*Geological Survey, Prague*] [*Former Czechoslovakia*] [*Research center*] (IRC)
UUIP .... Uppsala University Institute of Physics [*Sweden*] (PDAA)
UUKI .... Utugyi Kutato Intezet [*Road Research Institute*] (HU)
UUM .... Standardized Controlling Device, Standardized Controller (RU)
UUMP...... Unification of Units of Measurement Panel [*ICAO*] (DA)
UUMR....... Uzina de Utilaj Minier si Reparatii [*Plant for Mining Equipment and Repairs*] (RO)
UUN .... Ustredni Ucitelske Nakladatelstvi [*Central Teachers' Publishing House*] (CZ)
UUNZ....... Ustredni Ustav Narodniho Zdravi [*Central Public Health Institute*] (CZ)
UUOO .... Voronezh [*Former USSR*] [*ICAO location identifier*] (ICLI)
UUP.......... Ulster Unionist Party [*British*] [*Political party*]
UUP.......... Uredba o Ugostiteljskim Preduzecima i Radnjama [*Decree on Hotel and Catering Enterprises and Shops*] (YU)
UUP.......... Ustav Uzemniho Planovani [*Institute of Area Planning*] [*Brno*] (CZ)
UUP.......... Ustredni Ustav Polarograficky [*Central Polarographic Institute*] [*Prague*] (CZ)
UUPO....... Uredba o Udruzivanju Privrednih Organizacija [*Decree on the Merger of Economic Organizations*] (YU)
UUPSMB ... Uzina de Utilaje si Piese de Schimb Municipiul Bucuresti [*Bucharest Municipality Factory for Equipment and Spare Parts*] (RO)
UUR.......... Register Control (RU)
UUR.......... Turn Lead Angle (RU)
UUS.......... Regulations on Criminal Legal Procedure (RU)
UUSF........ Uredba o Ustanovama sa Samostalnim Finansiranjem [*Decree on Self-Financing Institutions*] (YU)
UUTS .... Ukase on Establishing Length of Labor Service (BU)
UUU .... Manumu [*Papua New Guinea*] [*Airport symbol*] (OAG)
UUUM ...... Moskva [*Former USSR*] [*ICAO location identifier*] (ICLI)
UUUU ...... Moskva [*Former USSR*] [*ICAO location identifier*] (ICLI)
UUUU........ Unter Ueblicher Vorbehalt [*Errors and Omissions Excepted*] [*German*]
UUVT........ Ukase on the Regulation of Internal Trade (BU)
UUWW ..... Moskva/Vnukovo [*Former USSR*] [*ICAO location identifier*] (ICLI)
UUYT........ Ust-Kulom [*Former USSR*] [*ICAO location identifier*] (ICLI)
UUYY .... Syktyvkar [*Former USSR*] [*ICAO location identifier*] (ICLI)
UUZ.......... Administration of Educational Institutions (RU)
UUZZ........ Ustredni Ustav Zeleznicniho Zdravotnictvi [*Central Institute of Railroads Health Services*] (CZ)
UV............ Air Kangaroo Island [*Airline code*] [*Australia*]
UV............ All-Purpose Fuze (RU)
UV............ Level Variometer (RU)
UV............ Moderate Air (RU)
UV............ Specific Gravity (RU)
UV............ Subtracter (RU)
UV............ Ultra-Violet [*Ultraviolet*] [*French*]
UV............ Ultravioletni [*Ultraviolet*] (YU)
UV............ Ultraviolett [*Ultraviolet*] [*German*] (EG)
UV............ Unabhaengige Volkspartei [*Independent People's Party*] [*Political party*] [*Germany*] (EAIO)
UV............ Unione di Valdotaine [*Aostan Union*] [*Italian*] (WER)
UV............ Union Valdotaine [*Valdotaine Union*] [*Italy*] [*Political party*] (EAIO)
UV............ Union Valenciana [*Spain*] [*Political party*] (EY)
UV............ Unite de Valeur [*Teaching Unit*] [*French*]
UV............ Universidad del Valle [*Colombia*] (COL)
UV............ Uprava za Vodoprivredu [*Water Power Administration*] (YU)
UV............ Ustredni Vybor [*Central Committee*] (CZ)
UV............ Utocna Vozba [*Assault Vehicles*] (CZ)
uv............ Uvod [*or Uvodni*] [*Introduction or Introductory*] (CZ)
UV............ Uzemi Vallalat [*Plant Marketing Department*] (HU)
UV............ Verschnittlegierung [*Admixing Alloy*] [*German*] (GCA)
UV............ Wind Angle (RU)
UVA.......... Uganda Veterinary Association (EAIO)
uva........... Und Viele Andere [*And Many Others*] [*German*]
UVA.......... Union of Vietnamese Students in Australia
UVA.......... Ustredni Vojenska Akademie [*Central Military Academy*] (CZ)
UVA.......... Uzina de Vagoane Arad [*Arad Railway Car Factory*] (RO)

uvam.......... Und Viele Andere Mehr [*And Many Others*] [*German*]   (GCA)

UVAN........ Ukrains'ka Vil'na Akademjia Nauk

UV-Anlage ... Ultrakurzwellen-Verkehrsfunkanlage [*VHF Two-Way Voice Communications System (Dispatcher Unit)*]   (EG)

UVATERV ... Ut-Vasuttervezo Vallalat [*Road and Railroad Planning Enterprise*]   (HU)

Uvb............. Uitvoeringsbeschikking [*Benelux*]   (BAS)

UVC.......... Universal Video Codec Scholarship [*Australia*]

UVCh......... High-Frequency Amplifier   (BU)

UVCh......... Ultrahigh Frequency   (RU)

UVD.......... Administration of Internal Affairs   (RU)

UVD.......... Flight Control   (RU)

UVDB........ Union des Verts pour le Developpement du Burkina [*Burkina Faso*] [*Political party*]   (EY)

UVDP........ Improved Mobile Decontamination Apparatus   (RU)

UVE.......... Ouvea [*Loyalty Islands*] [*Airport symbol*]   (OAG)

UVES........ Ukrains'ka Ekonomicna Visoka Skola v Mjunhenj

UVF.......... St. Lucia [*West Indies*] Hewanorra Airport [*Airport symbol*]   (OAG)

UVF.......... Ulster Volunteer Force

UVF.......... Union Velocipedique de France [*French*]

UVG.......... Uprava za Vodno Gospodarstvo [*Water Power Administration*]   (YU)

UVI.......... Administration of the Military Publishing House   (RU)

UVICAR.... Union des Villes de la Caraibe [*Union of Caribbean Towns*]   (LA)

UVKES...... Ustav pro Dalsi Vzdelavani v Kontrole, Evidenci, a Statistice [*Institute of Advance Education in Control, Reporting, and Statistics*]   (CZ)

UVKh........ Administration of Water Management   (RU)

UVKh........ Chromatograph Computer Device   (RU)

UVKI........ Wool and Silk Industry Administration   (BU)

UVKSKhSH ... Ural Higher Communist Agricultural School   (RU)

UVKU........ Ural Evening Communist University Imeni V. I. Lenin   (RU)

UVL.......... Institutet for Vatten -och Luftvards-forskning [*Institute for Water and Air Research*] [*Sweden*]   (PDAA)

UVL.......... New Valley [*Egypt*] [*Airport symbol*]   (OAG)

UVLI......... Ustav Vedeckych Lekarskych Informaci [*Institute for Medical Information*] [*Former Czechoslovakia Database operator*] [*Information service or system*]   (IID)

UVM.......... General-Purpose Computer   (RU)

UVM.......... Unie-Verdedigingsmag [*Afrikaans*]

UVM.......... Ustav Vyzkumu Materialu [*Materials Research Institute*] [*Prague*]   (CZ)

UVMS....... Directorate of the Navy   (RU)

UVMUZ..... Directorate of Naval Educational Institutions   (RU)

UVMV....... Ustav pro Vyzkum Motorovych Vozidel [*Automotive Research Institute*]   (CZ)

UVMV....... Ustav Vyzkumu Mechanisace Vyroby [*Research Institute for the Mechanization of Production*]   (CZ)

UVN.......... High-Voltage Indicator   (RU)

u-vo............. Device, Apparatus, Arrangement   (RU)

UVO.......... Ukrainian Military District   (RU)

UVO.......... Ural Military District   (RU)

UVO.......... Uvol [*Papua New Guinea*] [*Airport symbol*]   (OAG)

UVOCAM ... Union Voltaique des Cooperatives Agricoles et Maraicheres [*Voltan Union of Agricultural and Market-Gardening Cooperatives*]   (AF)

UVOChTPK ... Ukase on Mutual Insurance of Members of Labor Productive Cooperatives   (BU)

UVOD....... Ustredni Vedeni Domaciho Odboje [*Headquarters of the Domestic Resistance Movement*]   (CZ)

UVOJM .... Ustav pro Vyzkum Optiky a Jemne Mechaniky [*Institute for Research in Optics and Precision Mechanics*]   (CZ)

UVP.......... Airport Administration   (RU)

UVP.......... Union pour la Vente des Produits [*Union for the Sale of Products*] [*French*]   (WER)

UVP.......... Unvollendete Produktion [*Unfinished Production*]   (EG)

UVP.......... Uprava Vazdusne Plovidbe [*Air Transport Administration*]   (YU)

UVP.......... Ustav pro Vyzkum a Vyuziti Paliv [*Institute for Research and Utilization of Fuels*]   (CZ)

UVP.......... Ustredni Vybor Propagacni [*Central Committee for Propaganda*]   (CZ)

UVPD....... Altitude and Pressure Difference Indicator   (RU)

UVPI......... Ul'yanovsk Evening Polytechnic Institute   (RU)

UVPK....... Ustav pro Vyzkum a Pouziti Kovu [*Metal Research and Utilization Institute*] [*Prague*]   (CZ)

UVPS........ Directorate of Wartime Military Construction   (RU)

UVPS........ Ustav Vzdelavani Pracovniku ve Stavebnictvi [*Institute for Specialist Schooling in Construction*]   (CZ)

UV-PSdA.... Unione Valdostana-Partito Sardo d'Azione [*Italy*] [*Political party*]   (ECED)

UVPUFNRJ ... Udruzenje Vaspitaca Pretskolskih Ustanova Federativna Narodna Republika Jugoslavija [*Association of Teachers in Preschool Institutions of Yugoslavia*]   (YU)

UVR.......... Ungarische Volksrepublik [*Hungarian People's Republic*]   (EG)

UVR.......... Unit for Vacuum Dispersion   (RU)

UVR.......... Ustav pro Vyzkum Radiotechniky [*Research Institute for Radio Engineering*]   (CZ)

UVR.......... Ustav pro Vyzkum Rud [*Ore Research Institute*] [*Prague*]   (CZ)

UVS.......... Interior Service Regulations [*Military term*]   (RU)

UVS.......... Internal Service Regulations   (BU)

UVS.......... Umelecky Vojensky Soubor [*Military Artistic Ensemble*]   (CZ)

UVS.......... Union des Villes Suissess [*Union of Swiss Towns*]

UVS.......... Ustav pro Vyzkum Stroju [*Machine Research Institute (of the Czechoslovak Academy of Sciences)*]   (CZ)

UVS.......... Ustredni Velitelske Stanoviste [*Central Command Post*]   (CZ)

UVSA....... Urologiese Vereniging van Suid-Afrika [*Urological Association of South Africa*]   (AA)

UVSB........ Ustredni Vybor Svazu Brannosti [*Central Committee of the Union for Military Preparedness*]   (CZ)

uvsf........... Unverseifbar [*Nonsaponifiable*] [*German*]

UVSS........ Military Medical Service Regulations   (RU)

UVT.......... Coastal Water Transportation Statutes   (BU)

UVT.......... Uciliste Vojenske Telovychovy [*School of Military Physical Education*]   (CZ)

UVT.......... Ukopane Vatrene Tacke [*Intrenched Firing Points*]   (YU)

UVT.......... Umoja wa Vijana wa TANU [*TANU Youth League*] [*Tanzania Use YL*]   (AF)

UVT.......... Union Voltaique de Transit

UVT.......... Water Transportation Administration   (BU)

UVTA....... Ustav Vypocetni Techniky a Automatizace [*Institute for Measurement Techniques and Automation*]   (CZ)

UVTBM .... Administration of Water Transportation of the Baltic Sea   (RU)

UVTEI....... Ustredi Vedeckych, Technickych, a Ekonomickych Informaci [*Former Czechoslovakia*] [*Information service or system*]   (IID)

UVTI .... Uprava za Vojno Tehnicka Istrazivanja [*Administration of Military Technical Research*]   (YU)

UVTIZ....... Ustav Vedeckotechnickych Informaci pro Zemedelstvi [*Institute of Scientific and Technical Information for Agriculture*] [*Former Czechoslovakia*]   (EAIO)

UVTP .... Union des Usagers de Vehicules de Transport Prive [*French*]   (FLAF)

UVTR .... Ustredi Vyzkumu a Technickeho Rozvoje [*Research and Technological Development Center*]   (CZ)

UVUMZ.... Administration of Higher Educational Institutions of the Ministry of Public Health, USSR   (RU)

UVUPP...... Ustredni Vyzkumny Ustav Potravinarskeho Prumyslu [*Central Research Institute for Food Industry*]   (CZ)

UVUZ........ Directorate of Military Educational Institutions   (RU)

UVV.......... Input-Output Device   (RU)

UVV.......... Unfallverhuetungs-Vorschriften [*Accident Prevention Regulations*] [*German*]   (EG)

UVV.......... Ustredie Vedeckeho Vyskumu [*Scientific Research Center*]   (CZ)

UVV.......... Ustredni Vykonny Vybor [*Central Executive Committee*]   (CZ)

UVV.......... Wartime Record [*Of military service*]   (RU)

UVVL .... Ustav pro Vyzkum Vyzivy Lidu [*Nutrition Research Institute*]   (CZ)

UVVO....... Ustav pro Vyzkum Vnitrniho Obchodu [*Domestic Trade Research Institute*]   (CZ)

UVVP .... Ustav pro Vedecky Vyzkum Paliv [*Fuel Research Institute*]   (CZ)

UVVP .... Ustav pro Vyzkum a Vyuziti Paliv [*Institute for Fuel Research and Utilization*]   (CZ)

UVVS .... Directorate of the Air Force   (RU)

UVVT .... Regulations on Inland Water Transportation of the USSR   (RU)

UVVTR ..... Ustredie Vedeckeho Vyskumu a Technickeho Rozvoja [*Science Research and Technological Development Center*]   (CZ)

UVVUZ..... Directorate of Higher Military Educational Institutions   (RU)

UVVVJNA ... Uprava za Vanarmisko Vojno Vaspitanje, Jugoslavenska Narodna Armija [*Administration for Military Training Outside the Army, Yugoslav People's Army*]   (YU)

UVVVR ..... Ustav pro Vyrobu, Vyzkum, a Vyuziti Radioizotopu [*Institute for Production, Research, and Use of Radioisotopes*] [*Prague*]

UVZ.......... Ural Railroad Car Plant   (RU)

UVZ.......... Ustredi Verejnych Zamestnancu [*Center of Public Employees*]   (CZ)

UVZK....... Ustredni Vybor Svazu Zamestnancu v Kovoprumyslu [*Central Committee of the Union of Employees in Metalworking Industries*]   (CZ)

UVZN........ Urad pro Vynalezy a Zlepsovaci Navrhy [*Office for Inventions and Improvement Suggestions*]   (CZ)

UVZSO ..... Ustredni Vybor Zamestnancu Skolstvi a Osvety [*Central Committee of Employees in Educational and Cultural Establishments*]   (CZ)

UVZSS....... Ustredni Vybor Zamestnancu Skolske Sluzby [*Central Committee of Employees in Education*]   (CZ)

UW .... Air Rwanda [*Rwanda*] [*ICAO designator*]   (ICDA)

UW .... Uklad Warszawski [*Warsaw Treaty Organization*] [*Poland*]

Uw............. Umstandswort [*Adverb*] [*German*]

UW .... Universiteif van die Witwatersrand [*University of the Witwatersrand*] [*Afrikaans*]
UW .... University of Wollongong [*Australia*]
UW .... Uniwersytet Warszawski [*Warsaw University*]   (POL)
UW .... Uniwersytet Wroclawski [*Wroclaw University*] [*Poland*]
uW............ Unseres Wissens [*To the Best of our Knowledge*] [*German*]   (GCA)
UW .... Untere Winkelgruppe [*Angles up to 45*] [*German military - World War II*]
UW .... Unterwerk [*Substation*] [*Electric power*] [*German*]   (EG)
uw.............. Uwaga [*Note*]   (POL)
UWA.......... University of Western Australia   (ADA)
UWAA...... Union of Writers and Artists of Albania   (EAIO)
UWAC...... Union of Writers and Artists of Cuba   (EAIO)
UWAJ ...... Union of West African Journalists
UWAP...... University of Western Australia Press
UWAVWA ... Union of West African Voluntary Workcamps Associations [*Ghana*]   (EAIO)
UWB.......... Universal White Brotherhood [*An association*] [*France*]   (EAIO)
UWC.......... Ukwashi Wa Chokwe
UWC.......... United Worker Congress [*Liberia*]   (AF)
UWC.......... University of the Western Cape [*South Africa*]   (AA)
UWCL....... United Worker Congress - Liberia
UWCSEA ... United World College of South East Asia [*Singapore*]   (ECON)
UWD .... Urzedowy Wykaz Drukow [*Official Register of Publications*]   (POL)
UWE.......... Union Wallonne des Entreprises [*Wallonia Companies Union*] [*Belgium*]
UWE.......... University Women of Europe   (EA)
UWFPC..... Union Wallisienne et Futunienne pour la Caledonie [*Wallisian and Futunian Union for Caledonia*] [*Political party*]   (PPW)
UWG.......... Gesetz Gegen den Unlauteren Wettbewerb [*Law Against Unfair Competition*] [*German*]   (DLA)
U Wgong.... University of Wollongong [*Australia*]
UWHI........ Union of Workers in Histadrut Industries [*Israel*]   (EAIO)
UWI........... University of the West Indies [*St. Augustine, Trinidad and Tobago*]   (LA)
UWI/CC.... University of the West Indies Computing Centre   (PDAA)
UWIST...... University of Wales Institute of Science and Technology   (ARC)
UWITS...... Universiteit van die Witwatersrand [*University of the Witwatersrand*] [*South Africa*]   (AA)
UWK.......... Universitaet van Wes-Kaapland [*University of West Cape Province*] [*South Africa*]   (AF)
UWKD....... Kazan [*Former USSR*] [*ICAO location identifier*]   (ICLI)
UWM......... United Workers' Movement [*Barbados*]
UWM......... Utrechtse Waterleiding Maatschappij [*Benelux*]   (BAS)
UWO .... Ukrainska Wojskowa Organizacja [*Ukrainian Military Organization*]   (POL)
UWP.......... Dominica United Workers' Party [*Political party*]   (EY)
Uwp........... Umwandlungspunkt [*Transformation Point*] [*German*]   (GCA)
UWP.......... United Workers' Party [*Guyana*] [*Political party*]   (EY)
UWP.......... United Workers' Party [*St. Lucia*] [*Political party*]   (PPW)
UWP.......... United Workers' Party [*Hungary*] [*Political party*]   (PPW)
UWPF....... Union of Working People's Forces
UWPP....... Penza [*Former USSR*] [*ICAO location identifier*]   (ICLI)
UWR.......... Upowszechnienie Wiedzy Rolniczej [*Popularization of Agricultural Science*]   (POL)
UWS .... University of Western Sydney [*Australia*]
UWSLF .... United Western Somali Liberation Front   (AF)
UWS-M..... University of Western Sydney - Macarthur [*Australia*]
UWS-N..... University of Western Sydney - Nepean [*Australia*]
UWT......... Umoja wa Wanawake wa Tanzania [*Women's Union of Tanzania*]   (AF)
UWT......... United World Education and Research Trust [*British*]   (EAIO)
UWU .... United Workers' Union [*South Korean*]
UWU .... United Workers' Union [*St. Kitts and Nevis*]
UWUSA .... United Workers' Union of South Africa
UWV .... Umleitungswege-Verzeichnis [*Index of Detours*] [*German*]   (EG)
UWWW..... Kuybyshev/Kurumoch [*Former USSR*] [*ICAO location identifier*]   (ICLI)
UY............. Universite de Yaounde [*Cameroon*]
UY............. Uruguay [*ANSI two-letter standard code*]   (CNC)
UYAA....... Union of the Yugoslav Association of Anatomists   (EAIO)
UYAP .... Unconstrained Youth Allowances Package [*Australia*]
UYC.......... Cameroon Airlines [*ICAO designator*]   (FAAC)
UYECA ..... Union for Youth Education and Cultural Action [*Portugal*]   (EAIO)
UYF .... Union des Yachts Francais [*French*]
Uyg............ Uygulamali [*Applied*]   (TU)
UYL........... Nyala [*Sudan*] [*Airport symbol*]   (OAG)
UYN .... Yulin [*China*] [*Airport symbol*]   (OAG)
UZ............. Contaminated Area   (RU)
UZ............. Delay System   (RU)
UZ............. Distributed Charge   (RU)
UZ............. Flood Danger [*Warning*]   (RU)

UZ............. Scientific Notes   (RU)
UZ............. Tender [*Maritime term*]   (RU)
UZ............. Ultrasonic   (RU)
UZ............. Ultrasound   (RU)
UZ............. Universitaet Zuerich [*University of Zurich*] [*Switzerland*]
UZ............. Universiteit van Zululand [*University of Zululand*] [*South Africa*]   (AA)
UZ............. University of Zimbabwe
uZ............. Unter Zersetzung [*With Decomposition*] [*German*]
UZ............. Uredba o Zemljarini [*Decree on Land Tax*]   (YU)
UZ............. Urxovy Zavody [*Urxa Plants*]   (CZ)
UZ............. Urzad Ziemski [*Poland*]
UZ............. Ustavni Zakon [*Constitutional Law*]   (YU)
Uz............. Uzbek   (BARN)
UZA .... Antiaircraft Artillery Azimuth Circle   (RU)
UZA .... Ultrasonic Unit   (RU)
uza............. Uzemanyag [*Fuel*]   (HU)
UZAP .... Administration of the Protection of Authors' Rights   (RU)
UZB .... Union Zairoise de Banques [*Zairian Banking Union*]   (AF)
uzb............ Uzbek   (RU)
UZB .... Uzbekistan Havo Jullary [*Uzbekistan Airways*] [*ICAO designator*]   (FAAC)
Uzbeksel'mash ... Uzbek Agricultural Machinery Plant   (RU)
UZBER...... Uzletepitesi es Berendezo Vallalat [*Store Construction and Equipment Enterprise*]   (HU)
UzbGU....... Uzbek State University Imeni Alisher Navoi   (RU)
UzbSSR...... Uzbek Soviet Socialist Republic   (RU)
UZCh......... Audio Frequency Accelerator   (RU)
UZD .... Dalton Law Equation   (RU)
UZD .... Ultrasonic Diagnostic Apparatus   (RU)
UZD .... Umetnostno Zgodovinsko Drustvo [*Society of Art History*]   (YU)
UZDM...... Equation of the Law of Mass Action   (RU)
UZE .... Unia Zachodnio-Europejska [*West European Union*]   (POL)
UZEMP..... Usluzno Zemjodelsko Masinsko Pretprijatie [*Agricultural Machinery Service Establishment*]   (YU)
uzemvez...... Uzemvezeto [*Factory Manager*]   (HU)
uZers.......... Unter Zersetzung [*With Decomposition*] [*German*]
UzFAN ..... Uzbekistan Branch of the Academy of Sciences, USSR   (RU)
UZG .... Ultrasonic Generator   (RU)
UzGIMEIN ... Uzbekistan Hydrometeorological Institute   (RU)
Uzgiz.......... Uzbek State Publishing House   (RU)
UZGN......... Rated Load Master Device   (RU)
Uzgosizdat ... Uzbek State Publishing House   (RU)
Uzgosproyekt ... Uzbek State Planning Institute   (RU)
UZh............ Railroads Statutes   (BU)
UZhD......... Narrow-Gauge Railway   (RU)
UzhGU....... Uzhgorod State University   (RU)
UZhKh....... Housing Administration   (RU)
uzhog......... Neutralization Fire   (BU)
UZhSP........ Ukase on Complaints, Signals, and Suggestions   (BU)
UZII........... Ukrainian Correspondence Industrial Institute   (RU)
UZIMO..... Uchenye Zapiski Instituta Mezhdunarodnykh Otnoshenii
UZIP.......... Uredba o Zajmovima za Investicije u Privredi [*Decree on Loans for Economic Investments*]   (YU)
UZIV .... Scientific Notes of the Institute of Oriental Studies (of the Academy of Sciences, USSR)   (RU)
UZJII......... Ured za Zastitu Jugoslovenske Imovine u Inostranstvu [*Office for the Protection of Yugoslav Property Abroad*]   (YU)
UZK .... Delayed Channel Amplifier   (RU)
UZK .... Ultrasonic Logging   (RU)
UZK .... Ultrasonic Vibrations   (RU)
UZK .... Ustredni Zemedelska Knihovna [*Central Agricultural Library (of the Czechoslovak Academy of Agricultural Sciences)*]   (CZ)
UZK .... Ustredni Zemedelska Komise [*Central Agricultural Commission*]   (CZ)
UZKhM..... Ural Heavy Chemical Machinery Plant   (RU)
UzL........... Ultrasonic Delay Line   (RU)
Uzm............ Uzman [*Specialist*]   (TU)
UZMD....... Ul'yanovsk Small Engine Plant   (RU)
Uzmedgiz.... State Medical Publishing House of the Uzbek SSR   (RU)
UZn............ Umschmelzzink [*Remelted Spelter*] [*German*]   (GCA)
UzNIIL..... Uzbekistan Scientific Research Forest Institute   (RU)
UzNIIPN... Uzbek Scientific Research Institute of Pedagogical Sciences   (RU)
UzNIIShP ... Uzbek Scientific Research Institute of the Silk Industry   (RU)
UzNIIYaL ... Uzbekistan Scientific Research Institute of Language and Literature   (RU)
UzNIIZh.... Uzbek Scientific Research Institute of Animal Husbandry   (RU)
UzNIPI...... Uzbek Scientific Research Pedagogical Institute   (RU)
UzNIVI..... Uzbek Scientific Research Veterinary Institute   (RU)
UZNRBiH ... Ustavni Zakon Narodne Republike Bosne i Hercegovine [*The Constitution of Bosnia and Hercegovina*]   (YU)
UZO.......... United Zimbabwe Organization   (AF)
UZOKh....... Reservations and Hunting Grounds Administration   (RU)
UZpB .... Amplifier of Pulses Recorded on a Magnetic Drum   (RU)

UZPI.......... Ukrainian Correspondence Polytechnic Institute   (RU)
UZpL.......... Amplifier of Pulses Recorded on a Magnetic Tape   (RU)
UZR........... Uredba o Zanatskim Radnjama i Zanatskim Preduzecima
            [*Decree on Artisans' Shops and Enterprises*]   (YU)
UZRG........ Standardized Handgrenade Igniter   (RU)
UZRT........ Ultrasonic Resonance Thickness Gage   (RU)
UZS........... Ultrasonic Seismograph   (RU)
UZS........... Universal Tool Grinder   (RU)
UZS........... Ustredni Zdravotnicka Sprava [*Central Health Administration*]
            (CZ)
UZSGU..... Scientific Notes of the Saratov State University   (RU)
UZSS........ Ufa Synthetic Alcohol Plant   (RU)
UzSSR....... Uzbek Soviet Socialist Republic   (RU)
UZT.......... Ultrasonic Thickness Gauge   (RU)
UzTAG...... Uzbek News Agency   (RU)
UZTM....... Ural Heavy Machinery Plant Imeni Sergo Ordzhonikidze   (RU)
UZTS........ Ul'yanovsk Plant of Heavy and Unique Machine Tools   (RU)
UZU.......... Curuzu Cuatia [*Argentina*] [*Airport symbol*]   (OAG)
UZU.......... Storage Control, Memory Control   (RU)
UZU.......... Ustredni Zdravotnicky Ustav [*Central Medical Institute*]   (CZ)
UZUS........ Guided-Missile Launcher   (RU)
UZV........... Ustredi Zdravotnickeho Vyzkumu [*Health Research Center*]
            (CZ)
u zw........... Und Zwar [*That Is, Namely*] [*German*]
UZZ........... Uredba o Zemljoradnickim Zadrugama [*Decree on Agricultural
            Cooperatives*]   (YU)
UZZPP...... Ukase on the Mandatory Insurance of Railway, Motor Vehicle,
            Water, and Air Transportation of Passengers and Personnel
            (BU)

V

V	Accusative [*Case*]	(RU)
v	Afternoon	(RU)
V	Calculation, Computation	(RU)
v	Century	(BU)
V	East, Eastern	(RU)
v	En Volgende [*Benelux*]	(BAS)
V	Great [*Toponymy*]	(RU)
V	High [*Bearing precision class*]	(RU)
v	Issue	(RU)
V	Miry [*Nature of bottom of a ford*] [*Topography*]	(RU)
v	Newspaper	(BU)
V	Peak	(BU)
V	Rectifier	(RU)
v	Sunrise	(RU)
V	Supreme	(RU)
V	Swiss Volksbank [*Bank*]	
V	Switch	(RU)
V	Upper [*Toponymy*]	(RU)
V	Usted [*You (Singular, formal)*] [*Spanish*]	
v	Vaegen [*Way*] [*Sweden*]	(CED)
v	Vagy [*Or*]	(HU)
V	Vale [*Bond, Promissory Note*] [*Spanish*]	
V/	Valeur [*Value*] [*French*]	
V	Vallalat [*Enterprise*] [*Hungary*]	(CED)
v	Valtozas [*Change, Changing*]	(HU)
V	Van [*Of, From*] [*Afrikaans*]	
V	Vanadio [*Vanadium*] [*Chemical element*] [*Portuguese*]	
V	Vang [*Catch*] [*Afrikaans*]	
V	Van Ommeren [*Commercial firm*] [*Netherlands*]	
V	Variabel [*Variable*] [*German*]	(ADPT)
V	Variante [*Variant*] [*German*]	(ADPT)
v	Vaszon [*Cloth*] [*Publishing*] [*Hungary*]	
v	Vease [*See*] [*Spanish*]	
v	Veau [*Calf*] [*Publishing*] [*French*]	
v	Vedi [*See*] [*Italian*]	
v	Vegyes [*Mixed*]	(HU)
v	Vei [*Way*] [*Norway*]	(CED)
V	Veja [*Vein*] [*Portuguese*]	
v	Velin [*Vellum*] [*Publishing*] [*French*]	
V	Velocidade [*Velocity*] [*Portuguese*]	
V	Vendeur [*Vendor*] [*French*]	
V	Venerable [*Venerable*] [*Spanish*]	
V	Venstre [*Liberal Party*] [*Norway*] [*Political party*]	(PPE)
V	Venstre (Liberale Parti) [*Liberal Party*] [*Denmark*] [*Political party*]	(PPE)
v	Verbo [*Verb*] [*Italian*]	
V	Verbrennungslokomotive [*Internal Combustion Locomotive (Mainly diesel locomotives)*]	(EG)
V	Verbum [*Verb*] [*Afrikaans*]	
V	Verfassung [*Constitution*] [*German*]	(ILCA)
V	Verfuegung [*Order, Decree*] [*German*]	(ILCA)
V	Vergangenheit [*Past*] [*German*]	
V	Verguetungsstahl [*Heat-Treatable Steel*] [*German*]	(GCA)
V	Verkehr [*Traffic, Transportation*]	(EG)
V	Verlag [*Publisher*] [*German*]	
V	Vermessung [*Survey*] [*German*]	(GCA)
V	Verordeningenblad [*Benelux*]	(BAS)
V	Verordnung [*Decree, Regulation, Ordinance*] [*German*]	(ILCA)
V	Vers [*or Verse*] [*Line, Verse*] [*German*]	(EG)
v	Versiculo [*Verse*] [*Spanish*]	
V	Verst	(RU)
V	Vertrag [*Treaty, Contract*] [*German*]	
V	Vertrek [*Room*] [*Afrikaans*]	
v	Vezetek [*Line, Pipe*]	(HU)
v	Via [*Way*] [*Italian*]	(CED)
V	Vic [*Phonetic alphabet*] [*Pre-World War II*]	(DSUE)
V	Victor [*Phonetic alphabet*] [*International*] [*World War II*]	(DSUE)

V	Viehzug [*Cattle Train*]	(EG)
V	Vila [*Villa*] [*Portuguese*]	
V	Vinegar [*Phonetic alphabet*] [*Royal Navy World War I*]	(DSUE)
V	Violino [*Violin*] [*Italian*]	
v	Violon [*Violin*] [*French*]	
V	Vir [*For*] [*Afrikaans*]	
V	Virgem [*Virgin*] [*Portuguese*]	
V	Visto [*Seen*] [*Portuguese*]	
v	Vitesse [*Speed*] [*French*]	
v	Viz [*See*]	(CZ)
V	Vize- [*Vice-*] [*German*]	
v	Voir [*To See*] [*French*]	
V	Volt [*German*] [*German*]	(GCA)
v	Volti [*Turn*] [*French*]	
V	Volt Internacional [*International Volt*] [*Portuguese*]	
v	Voltio [*Volt*] [*Spanish*]	
V	Voltti [*or Voltta*] [*Finland*]	
v	Volume [*Portuguese*]	
V	Volumen [*Volume*] [*German*]	(EG)
v	Vom [*or Von*] [*Of The, From The, By The*] [*German*]	(EG)
V	Vorkommen [*Presence, Occurrence*] [*German*]	
v	Vormals [*Formerly*] [*German*]	
v	Vormittags [*In the Forenoon*] [*German*]	
V	Vorsitzender [*Chairman*]	(EG)
v/	Vostra [*Your*] [*Italian*]	
v/	Votre [*Your*] [*Correspondence*] [*French*]	
V	Voyez [*See, Look*] [*French*]	
V	Vroulik [*Female, Feminine*] [*Afrikaans*]	
v	Vuonna [*Finland*]	
v	Vuosi [*or Vuotta*] [*Year*] [*Finland*]	(GPO)
v	Vuosina [*Finland*]	
v	Vychod [*East*]	(CZ)
v	Watt	(BU)
V	Watykan [*Vatican City*] [*Poland*]	
V	Your, Yours	(RU)
V4	St. Kitts and Nevis [*Aircraft nationality and registration mark*]	(FAAC)
V8	Brunei Darussalam [*Aircraft nationality and registration mark*]	(FAAC)
VA	Air Army	(RU)
VA	Air Attack	(RU)
VA	Air Force, Air Army	(BU)
VA	Army Aviation	(RU)
VA	Automatic Altimeter	(RU)
VA	Avian Aircraft Ltd. [*Canada ICAO aircraft manufacturer identifier*]	(ICAO)
VA	Enlightened Action [*South Africa*]	(AF)
VA	Het Verzekeringsarchief [*Benelux*]	(BAS)
VA	Military Academy	(RU)
VA	Vacuum Unit	(RU)
va	Valiaikainen [*Finland*]	
Va	Valuta [*Exchange Equivalent*] [*German*] [*Banking*]	
VA	Vanguard Assurance Co. Ltd. [*Ghana*]	
VA	Varese [*Car registration plates*] [*Italian*]	
va	Vasutallomas [*Railroad Station*]	(HU)
VA	Vatican City [*ANSI two-letter standard code*]	(CNC)
VA	Venezolana Internacional de Aviacion Sociedad Anonima (VIASA) [*Venezuela*] [*ICAO designator*]	(ICDA)
VA	Verlagsanstalt [*Publishing House*] [*German*]	
VA	Veterinarska Ambulanta [*Veterinary Ambulance*]	(YU)
VA	Victoria and Albert [*Order of*]	(ADA)
Va	Vigilia [*Watch, Vigil*] [*Spanish*]	
Va	Vila [*Village*] [*Portuguese*]	(NAU)
Va	Villa [*Italian*]	(NAU)
Va	Villa [*Small Town*] [*Vla*] [*See also*] [*Spanish*]	(NAU)
VA	Vinylacetylene	(RU)
VA	Virginia	(IDIG)
va	Vista [*Sight*] [*Spanish*]	

Va............. Viuva [*Widow*] [*Portuguese*]
VA............. Voest-Alpine [*Nationalized steel company*] [*Austria*]   (IMH)
VA............. Vojenska Akademie [*Military Academy*]   (CZ)
VA............. Vojna Akademija [*Military Academy*]   (YU)
VA............. Volt-Ammeter   (RU)
VA............. Volt-Ampere [*Volt Ampere*] [*Portuguese*]
VA............. Voluntary Agency
VA............. Volunteers in Action [*Bolivia*]   (EAIO)
VA............. Vorsatzadresse [*German*]   (ADPT)
VA............. Votre Altesse [*Your Highness*] [*French*]
VA............. Vuestra Alteza [*Your Highness*] [*Spanish*]
VAA........... Vaasa [*Finland*] [*Airport symbol*]   (OAG)
VAA........... Venda Airways [*South Africa*] [*ICAO designator*]   (FAAC)
VAA........... Verkaufs-Auftragsabwicklung [*German*]   (ADPT)
VAA........... Victorian Apiarists' Association [*Australia*]
VAA........... Victorian Athletics Association [*Australia*]
VAAC....... Verbond van Ambtenaren en Agenten in Congo
VAAC....... Victorian AIDS Action Committee [*Australia*]
VAADA..... Victorian Association of Alcohol and Drug Agencies [*Australia*]
VAAH....... Ahmadabad [*India*] [*ICAO location identifier*]   (ICLI)
VAAK....... Akola [*India*] [*ICAO location identifier*]   (ICLI)
VAAL....... Victorian Aborigines Advancement League [*Australia*]
VAAP....... All-Union Agency for Authors' Rights [*Former USSR*]
vaap........... Vaapeli [*Finland*]
VAAP....... Vsesoyuznyy Agenstvo po Avtoram Pravam [*All-Union Copyright Agency*] [*Former USSR*]   (EAIO)
VAAT....... Victorian Animal Aid Trust [*Australia*]
VAAU....... Aurangabad [*India*] [*ICAO location identifier*]   (ICLI)
VAAZ....... Vojenska Akademie Antonina Zapotockeho [*Antonin Zapotocky Military Academy*]   (CZ)
VAB........... High-Speed Automatic Switch   (RU)
VAB........... Vehicule de l'Avant Blinde [*Armored Personnel Carrier*] [*French*]
VAB........... Vereinigung fur Angewandte Botanik [*Germany*]   (EAIO)
VAB........... Versicherungsanstalt Berlin [*Berlin Insurance Company*]   (EG)
VAB........... Victorian Artificial Breeders [*Australia*]
VAB........... Victorian Association of Bakers [*Australia*]
VAB........... Voluntary Agencies' Bureau
vab........... Vry aan Boord [*Free on Board*] [*Shipping*] [*Afrikaans*]
VAB........... Wet op de Vermogenaanwasbelasting [*Benelux*]   (BAS)
VABA....... Victorian Amateur Boxing Association [*Australia*]
VABB....... Bombay [*India*] [*ICAO location identifier*]   (ICLI)
VABF....... Bombay [*India*] [*ICAO location identifier*]   (ICLI)
VABI........ Bilaspur [*India*] [*ICAO location identifier*]   (ICLI)
VABJ........ Bhuj [*India*] [*ICAO location identifier*]   (ICLI)
VABL....... Victorian Amateur Boxing League [*Australia*]
VABM....... Belgaum [*India*] [*ICAO location identifier*]   (ICLI)
VABMV .... Military Academy of Armored and Mechanized Troops   (RU)
VABO....... Baroda/Vadodara [*India*] [*ICAO location identifier*]   (ICLI)
VABP........ Bhopal [*India*] [*ICAO location identifier*]   (ICLI)
VABTV..... Military Academy of Armored Troops   (RU)
VABV....... Bhaunagar [*India*] [*ICAO location identifier*]   (ICLI)
VAC......... Victorian AIDS Council [*Australia*]
VAC......... Victorian Arts Centre [*Australia*]
VAC......... Victorian Arts Council [*Australia*]
VAC......... Vietnam Action Campaign [*Australia*]
VACA....... Victorian Amateur Canoe Association [*Australia*]
VACAA ..... Victorian Autistic Childrens and Adults' Association [*Australia*]
VACAP..... Vacances Cap-Skirring
VACB........ Visual Arts and Crafts Board [*Australia Council*]
VACCA..... Victorian Aboriginal Child Care Agency [*Australia*]
Vacie .... Vacherie [*Cow House*] [*Military map abbreviation World War I*] [*French*]   (MTD)
vack........... Vacker [*Beautiful*] [*Sweden*]
VACOMBY ... Societe pour la Mise en Valeur et la Commercialisation du Betail Malgache
VACP........ Venezuelan Association of Cement Producers   (EAIO)
VACRPD... Victorian Advisory Council on Recreation for People with Disabilities [*Australia*]
VACSA...... Victorian Aboriginal Community Services Association [*Australia*]
VAD.......... Military Highway   (RU)
VAD.......... Pressure Accumulator [*Jet engine*]   (RU)
VAD.......... Vadaszzaszloalj [*Rifle Battalion (Army), Fighter Battalion (Air Force)*] [*HU*]
VAD.......... Vereinigte Arbeitnehmerpartei Deutschland [*United Employees' Party of Germany*] [*Political party*]   (PPW)
VAD.......... Vereinigung der Afrikanisten in Deutschland
VAD.......... Vermogensaanwasdeling [*Excess Profits Sharing Bill*] [*Netherlands*]   (WEN)
v ad .... Vice Admiral   (BU)
VADA....... Victorian Abalone Divers' Association [*Australia*]
VADA....... Voluntary Agencies Development Assistance [*Kenya*]   (EAIO)
VADC....... Victorian Association for Deserted Children [*Australia*]
VADE....... Victorian Association for Drama in Education [*Australia*]
VADES..... Victorian Association for Dance Education in Schools [*Australia*]
VADG........ Victorian Antique Dealers' Group [*Australia*]

VADIZO ... All-Union Highway Correspondence Training Institute   (RU)
VADN....... Victorian Association of Day Nurseries [*Australia*]
VADZI...... All-Union Highway Correspondence Institute   (RU)
vae........... Helicopter Aviation Squadron   (BU)
VAEDAI.... Victorian Aboriginal Employment Development Association, Inc. [*Australia*]
VAEE........ Victorian Association for Environmental Education [*Australia*]
VAEITB .... Victorian Arts and Entertainment Industry Training Board [*Australia*]
vaelskbd ..... Vaelskbind [*Half-Sheepskin Binding with Corners*] [*Publishing Danish/Norwegian*]
VAF .... Military Academy Imeni Frunze   (RU)
VAF .... Valence [*France*] [*Airport symbol*]   (OAG)
VAFA....... Victorian Amateur Football Association [*Australia*]
VAFI........ Victorian Association of Forest Industries [*Australia*]
VAFL....... Victorian Amateur Football League [*Australia*]
VAFOSZ ... Vallalati Alkalmazottak Fogyasztasi Szovetkezete [*Consumers' Cooperative of Business Employees*]   (HU)
VAFP........ Vseafrikanskaia Federatsiia Profsoiuzov [*All-African Trade Union Federation*]
VAG......... Condities van de Vereniging Amsterdamsche Graanbeurs [*Netherlands*]   (BAS)
vag............. Railroad Car Plant [*Topography*]   (RU)
Vag............. Vagon [*Railway Car*]   (TU)
VAG.......... Varginha [*Brazil*] [*Airport symbol*]   (OAG)
VAGA....... Vereniging van Academisch Gevormde Accountants [*Benelux*]   (BAS)
Vage .... Village [*Village*] [*Military map abbreviation World War I*] [*French*]   (MTD)
VAGO....... All-Union Astronomical and Geodetic Society   (RU)
VAGO....... Goa [*India*] [*ICAO location identifier*]   (ICLI)
VAGP .... Victorian Academy for General Practice [*Australia*]
VAGT .... All-Union Aerogeological Trust   (RU)
VAGTC..... Victorian Association for Gifted and Talented Children [*Australia*]
VAGVF..... All-Union Academy of the Civil Air Fleet   (RU)
VAh.......... Woltamperogodzina [*Volt-Ampere-Hour*] [*Poland*]
VAHD....... Veterinary and Animal Husbandry Department [*Myanmar*]   (DS)
VAHPA ..... Victorian Allied Health Professionals Association [*Australia*]
VAI .... All-Russian Association of Engineers [*1919-1926*]   (RU)
VAI .... All-Union Arctic Institute   (RU)
VAI .... All-Union Association of Engineers [*1926-1929*]   (RU)
VAI .... Military Motor Vehicle Inspection   (RU)
VAI .... Military Motor Vehicle Inspectorate   (BU)
VAI .... Vakok Allami Intezete [*State Institute for the Blind*]   (HU)
VAI .... Vanimo [*Papua New Guinea*] [*Airport symbol*]   (OAG)
VAI .... Vocational Awards International [*British*]
VAID .... Indore [*India*] [*ICAO location identifier*]   (ICLI)
VAIZ........ All-Russian Association of Inventors   (RU)
VAJB .... Jabalpur [*India*] [*ICAO location identifier*]   (ICLI)
VAJJ .... Bombay/Juhu [*India*] [*ICAO location identifier*]   (ICLI)
VAJM....... Jamnagar [*India*] [*ICAO location identifier*]   (ICLI)
VAJNA...... Vojna Akademija Jugoslovenske Narodne Armije [*Military Academy of the Yugoslav People's Army*]   (YU)
VAK .... High Arbitration Commission   (RU)
VAK .... High Degree Commission   (RU)
VAK .... Higher Academic Courses   (RU)
VAK .... Higher Certification Commission   (BU)
VAK .... Military Administrative Committee [*Chinese People's Republic, 1949-1952*]   (RU)
vak........... Vakinainen [*Finland*]
Vak........... Vakuum [*Vacuum*] [*German*]
vak........... Vakuutustoiminta [*Insurance*] [*Finland*]
VAK .... Versuchsatomkraftwerk Kahl [*Nuclear energy*]   (NRCH)
VAK .... Vides Aizsardzibas Klubs [*Nature Protection Club*] [*Latvia*]   (EAIO)
VAK .... Volkhov Aluminum Kombinat   (RU)
VAKA .... Vlaams Aktiekomitee Tegn Atoomwapens [*Flemish Action Committee Against Nuclear Weapons*] [*Belgium*]
VAKD .... Khandwa [*India*] [*ICAO location identifier*]   (ICLI)
VAKE .... Kandla [*India*] [*ICAO location identifier*]   (ICLI)
Vak Exs .... Vakuumexsikkatur [*Vacuum Desiccator*] [*German*]
VAKh........ All-Russian Academy of Arts   (RU)
VAKh....... Volt-Ampere Characteristic   (RU)
VAKhZ..... Military Academy of Chemical Defense   (RU)
VAKK .... Intrapharmaceutical Quality Control   (BU)
VAKL........ International Confederation of Free Trade Unions [*ICFTU*] [*Finland*]   (WEN)
VAKOLA... Valtion Maatalousteknologian Tutkimuslaitos [*Finnish Research Institute of Engineering in Agriculture and Forestry*] [*Research center*]   (IRC)
VAKOR..... Vsesoyuznaya Assotsiatsiya Korrozionistov [*All-Union Association of Corrosionists*] [*Former USSR*]   (EAIO)
VAKOT ..... All-Ukrainian Joint-Stock Trading Company   (RU)
VAKP........ Kolhapur [*India*] [*ICAO location identifier*]   (ICLI)

VAKS.........	Keshod [*India*] [*ICAO location identifier*] (ICLI)
VAKSA......	Vakbondraad van Suid-Afrika [*Trade Union Council of South Africa*] [*Use TUCSA*] (AF)
VAKSTO...	High Arbitration Commission at the Council of Labor and Defense (RU)
VAKT........	All-Union Battery and Cell Industry Trust (RU)
VAKUS......	Vypocetni a Kontrolni Ustredna Spoju (Prague) [*Communications Computation and Control Center established 21 March 1963*] [*Branch in Bratislava*] (CZ)
val.............	Aequivalent [*Equivalent*] [*German*] (GCA)
Val.............	Vaasan Laani [*or Vaasan Laania*] [*Finland*]
val.............	Valeur [*Value*] [*French*]
val.............	Valide [*French*] (FLAF)
val.............	Valine (RU)
val.............	Valogatas [*Selection*] [*Hungary*]
Val.............	Valovaya Produktsiya [*Gross Output*] [*Russian*]
VAL.........	Valuta [*Currency*] [*Afrikaans*] [*Business term*]
Val...........	Valuta [*Exchange Equivalent*] [*Banking*] [*German*]
Val...........	Valuta [*Value*] [*Italian*]
VAL..........	Victorian Athletic League [*Australia*]
VAL..........	Vieques Air Link [*Caribbean airline*]
VAL..........	Viomikhania Azotoukhon Lipasmaton [*Nitrogenous Fertilizers Company*] [*Greek*] (GC)
VALA........	Victoria Association for Library Automation [*Australia*] (PDAA)
VALA........	Victorian Amateur Lacrosse Association [*Australia*]
VALBEC...	Victorian Adult Literacy and Basic Education Council [*Australia*]
valbev........	Vaelbevarad [*Well Preserved*] [*Publishing*] [*Sweden*]
VALCO.....	Volta Aluminium Company Ltd. [*Ghana*]
val dec.......	Valeur Declaree [*Declared Value*] [*French*] [*Business term*]
VALDIRIDA ...	Confecciones Valdiri Ltda. [*Colombia*] (COL)
VALEFERTIL ...	Centro de Informacao e Documentacao, Fertilizantes Vale do Rio Grande [*Brazil*]
VALEUROP ...	Fonds Commun de Placement Principalement Investi en Valeurs Europeennes [*French*] [*Business term*]
Valid	Valide [*French*] (FLAF)
valiotkand ..	Valtiotieteen Kandidaatti [*Finland*]
ValK..........	Valtiotieteen Kandidaatti [*Finland*]
v-alm	Vice-Almirante [*Vice-Admiral*] [*Portuguese*]
valok..........	Valokuvaus [*Photography*] [*Finland*]
VALOR	Societe de Vente d'Aciers Lorrains
VALPO......	Valparaiso (DSUE)
Valpo..........	Valtiollinen Poliisi [*State Police*] [*Finland*] (WEN)
VALS........	Victorian Aboriginal Legal Service [*Australia*]
valt............	Valtozat [*Version*] [*Publishing*] [*Hungary*]
valtiotKand ...	Master's Degree in Social Sciences [*Finland*]
valtiotlis	Valtiotieteen Lisensiaatti [*Finland*]
valtiotmaist ...	Valtiotieteen Maisteri [*Finland*]
valtiottri	Valtiotieteen Tohtori [*Finland*]
VAM.........	Verwaltung des Vermoegens der Auslaendischen Mineraloelgesellschaften [*Administration of the Assets of Foreign Petroleum Companies*] (EG)
VAM.........	World Assembly of Youth [*WAY*] (RU)
VAME.......	Victorian Association for Multicultural Education [*Australia*]
VAMHN ..	Victorian Aboriginal Mental Health Network [*Australia*]
VAMI........	All-Union Institute of Aluminum and Magnesium (RU)
VAMIA	Victorian Abattoir and Meat Inspection Authority [*Australia*]
VAMM......	Military Academy of Mechanization and Motorization (RU)
VAMU.......	Higher School of Aeromechanics (RU)
VAN..........	All-Union Association of Naturalists (RU)
VAN..........	Artesian Screw Pump (RU)
VAN..........	Van [*Turkey*] [*Airport symbol*] (OAG)
VAN..........	Vandeno [*Race of maize*] [*Mexico*]
VAN..........	Vereniging van Archivarissen in Nederland
VAN..........	Vorlaeufige Arbeitsnorm [*Tentative Work Norm*] (EG)
VANA.......	Victorian Authorised Newsagents' Association [*Australia*]
VAND.......	Nanded [*India*] [*ICAO location identifier*] (ICLI)
V & B	Vaznone & Baeri [*Italy*]
V & IA........	Victorian and Interstate Airways [*Australia*]
VANFISH ...	Victorian Adoption Network for Information and Self Help [*Australia*]
vanh...........	Vanhahtava [*Finland*]
vanh...........	Vanhempi [*Finland*]
vanh...........	Vanhentunut [*Archaic, Obsolete*] [*Finland*]
VANO.......	All-Union Scientific Architectural Society [*1930-1932*] (RU)
VANP	Nagpur [*India*] [*ICAO location identifier*] (ICLI)
VANR	Nasik Road [*India*] [*ICAO location identifier*] (ICLI)
vanr	Vanrikki [*Finland*]
VAO..........	All-Union Joint-Stock Company (RU)
vao.............	Helicopter Aviation Detachment (BU)
VAO..........	State All-Union Association of the Aircraft Industry (RU)
VAO..........	Verband der Akademikerinnen Oesterreichs [*Austria*] (SLS)
VAOSZ......	Varosi, Varmegyei, es Kozsegi Alkalmazottak Orszagos Szovetsege [*National Association of City, County, and Village Employees*] (HU)
VAOT	Victorian Association of Occupational Therapists [*Australia*]

VAP	Aircraft Spray Tank, Aircraft Spray Apparatus (RU)
vap.............	Helicopter Aviation Regiment (BU)
VAP	Vaccine Action Programme [*India*]
vap.............	Vapeur [*Steam or Steamer*] [*French*]
VAP	Verein der Auslaendischen Presse in BRD [*Foreign Press Association*] [*Germany*] (EY)
VAP	Vysotnaia Asuanskaia Plotina
VAPI.........	All-Union Agricultural Pedagogical Institute (RU)
VAPLA	Victorian Amateur Power Lifting Association [*Australia*]
VAPM	All-Russian Association of Proletarian Musicians (RU)
VAPO........	Pune [*India*] [*ICAO location identifier*] (ICLI)
VAPP........	All-Union Association of Proletarian Writers (RU)
VAPR.........	Porbandar [*India*] [*ICAO location identifier*] (ICLI)
VAPS........	Victorian Association for Peace Studies [*Australia*]
VAPSIE.....	Volunteers' Association for the Promotion of Small-Scale Industries in Ethiopia
VAPSS.......	Victorian Association of Principals of Secondary Schools [*Australia*]
VAR	Vanguarda Armada Revolucionaria [*Armed Revolutionary Vanguard*] [*Brazil*] (LA)
VAR	Vanguardia Armada Revolucionaria [*Armed Revolutionary Vanguard*] [*Chile*] (LA)
var	Variacao [*Variation*] [*Portuguese*]
var	Variante [*Variant*] [*Portuguese*]
VAR	Varna [*Bulgaria*] [*Airport symbol*] (OAG)
VAR	Vereinigte Arabische Republik [*United Arab Republic (UAR)*] [*German*] (EG)
VAR	Vereniging voor Agrarisch Recht [*Netherlands*] (SLS)
VAR	Volt-Ampere Reactif [*German*] (ADPT)
VAR	Votre Altesse Royale [*Your Royal Highness*] [*French*]
VAR	Vrij Anti-Revolutionaire Partij [*Free Anti-Revolutionary Party*] [*Netherlands*] [*Political party*] (PPE)
VAR	Vuestra Alteza Real [*Spanish*]
VARA	Vereniging van Arbeiders Radio Amateurs [*Workers Radio Amateurs Association*] [*Netherlands*] (WEN)
VARA	Villages Agricoles de la Revolution Agraire
V Ar AdvR St ...	Verzameling der Arresten en Adviezen van de Raad van State [*Benelux*] (BAS)
VARAT......	All-Union Association of Workers--Authors of Technical Literature (RU)
varat	Varatuomari [*Finland*]
VARC	Victorian Accident Rehabilitation Council [*Australia*]
VARE	Victorian Association for Religious Education [*Australia*]
VAREM.....	Military Mobile Repair and Maintenance Shop (RU)
VARG........	Ratnagiri [*India*] [*ICAO location identifier*] (ICLI)
VArh	Warogodzina [*Varhour*] [*Poland*]
variats	Variation (RU)
VARICC	Victorian Asbestos Removal Industry Consultative Committee [*Australia*]
VARK	Rajkot [*India*] [*ICAO location identifier*] (ICLI)
VARNITSO ...	All-Union Association of Workers of Science and Technology for Assistance to the Building of Socialism (RU)
VARP.........	Raipur [*India*] [*ICAO location identifier*] (ICLI)
VARS........	Vanuatu Radio Amateur Society [*Fiji*] (PDAA)
vars.............	Varsinainen [*Finland*]
vars.............	Varsinkin [*Especially*] [*Finland*]
VARTAB ...	Programmsystem zur Erstellung Variabler Tabellen [*German*] (ADPT)
VARTEKS ...	Varazdinska Tekstilna Industrija [*Varazdin Textile Industry*] (YU)
VARU........	Automatic Time Gain Control (RU)
VARZ	Railroad Car Repair Plant (RU)
VARZ	Second Automobile Repair Plant (RU)
VAS	All-Russian Astronomical Union (RU)
VAS	Aviatrans [*Former USSR*] [*ICAO designator*] (FAAC)
VAS	Departmental Automated System (BU)
VAS	High Lawyers' Council (BU)
VAS	Sivas [*Turkey*] [*Airport symbol*] (OAG)
VAS	Supreme Administrative Court (BU)
vas	Vasarnap [*Sunday*] (HU)
vas	Vasemmalla [*Finland*]
VAS	Vereniging van Accountancy-Studenten [*Society of Accountancy Students*] [*Netherlands*] (PDAA)
VAS	Victorian Artists' Society [*Australia*] (SLS)
VAS	Voreio-Atlandiki Symfonia [*North Atlantic Treaty Organization*] (GC)
VASA........	Sihora [*India*] [*ICAO location identifier*] (ICLI)
VASA........	Victorian Amateur Swimming Association [*Australia*]
VASA........	Victorian Ambulance Services Association [*Australia*]
VASA........	Vidriera Argentinian SA [*St. Gobain*]
VASERT ...	Vastomegcikk Ertekesito Vallalat [*Trade Enterprise for Mass-Produced Ironware*] (HU)
VASG........	Songadh [*India*] [*ICAO location identifier*] (ICLI)
VASh........	Military Aviation School (RU)
VAShL.......	Military Aviation School for Pilots (RU)
VASI.........	Higher Architectural and Construction Institute (RU)

VASKhNIL ... All-Union Academy of Agricultural Sciences Imeni V. I. Lenin (RU)
VASKUT ... Vasipari Kutato Intezet [*Iron Industry Research Institute*] (HU)
VASL .... Sholapur [*India*] [*ICAO location identifier*] (ICLI)
Vasm EiEs ... Vasmegyei Epitoipari Egyesules [*Building Industry Association of Vas County*] (HU)
VASNIC .... Vassiliadis-Nicolaidis
VASNOS... Velika Antifasisticka Skupstina Narodnog Oslobodenja Srbije [*Great Anti-Fascist Assembly of the National Liberation of Serbia*] (YU)
VASO .... Motorized Medical Detachment (RU)
VASP......... Viacao Aerea Sao Paulo SA [*Airline*] [*Brazil*]
VASS .... Victorian Architectural Students' Society [*Australia*]
VASS .... Voluntary Agency Support System [*New Zealand*]
VaSSA .... Vacuum Society of South Africa (AA)
vast .... Vastaavasti [*Finland*]
vast .... Vastaus [*Finland*]
vastak....... Vastakohta [*The Opposite Of*] [*Finland*]
VASU .... Surat [*India*] [*ICAO location identifier*] (ICLI)
VAT .... All-Union Gas-Welding Trust (RU)
VAT .... Military Motor Transport (RU)
VAT .... Tensometric Truck Scales (RU)
VAT .... Value-Added Tax
VAT .... Vatican City [*ANSI three-letter standard code*] (CNC)
VAT .... Vatomandry [*Madagascar*] [*Airport symbol*] (OAG)
VAT .... Vineyards Association of Tasmania [*Australia*]
VAT .... Volontaires de l'Aide Technique [*Technical Aid Volunteers*] [*French*] (AF)
VAT .... Voronezh Aviation Technicum (RU)
VATA .... World Association of Travel Agencies [*WATA*] (RU)
VATC........ Victoria Amateur Turf Club [*Australia*]
VATEKISZ ... Vasipari Tervezo es Kivitelezo KSZ [*Cooperative Enterprise for Planning and Production in the Iron Industry*] (HU)
VATEVA ... Central Association of the Finnish Clothing Industry (EAIO)
VATF......... Victorian Affiliated Teachers Federation [*Australia*]
VATI .... Military Motor Vehicle and Tractor Inspection (RU)
VATI......... Varostervezo Intezet [*City Planning Institute*] (HU)
VATO .... All-Union Association of the Automobile and Tractor Industry (RU)
Vatozapchast' ... All-Union State Association for the Production and Marketing of Automobile and Tractor Spare Parts and Components (RU)
VATS........ Military Air Transport Service [*MATS*] (RU)
VAT STA... Vatican State (WDAA)
Vattenfall... Statens Vattenfallsverk [*Swedish State Power Board*] [*Research center*] (WND)
VATU .... Military Aviation Technical School (RU)
VATUKI.... Vasuti Tudomanyos Kutato Intezet [*Railway Scientific Research Institute*] (HU)
VAU........... All-Ukrainian Pharmaceutical Administration (RU)
VAU........... All-Union Administration of Archives (RU)
VAU.......... Higher Aviation School (RU)
VAU.......... Military Aviation School (RU)
VAU.......... Mobile Water Purifier (RU)
VAU.......... Veterinarni Asanacni Ustav [*Veterinary Sanitation Institute*] (CZ)
v aux .... Auxiliary Verb (TPFD)
VAUX....... Vauxhall [*Automobile*] (DSUE)
v aux.......... Verbe Auxiliaire [*French*] (TPFD)
VAV .... Schweizerischer Verband Akademischer Volks- und Betriebswirtschafter [*Switzerland*] (EAIO)
VAV .... Vava'u [*Tonga Island*] [*Airport symbol*] (OAG)
VAV .... Verordnung ueber die Arbeitslosenversicherung [*Regulation Concerning Unemployment Insurance*] (EG)
VAV .... Villamos Allomasszerelo Vallalat [*Electric Power Station Engineering Enterprise*] (HU)
vavbd .... Vavband [*Cloth Binding*] [*Publishing*] [*Sweden*]
VAVSA...... Vakuumvereniging van Suid-Afrika [*Vacuum Society of South Africa*] (AA)
VAVT .... All-Union Academy of Foreign Trade (RU)
VAW......... Vereinigte Aluminium-Werke AG [*Aluminum producer*]
VAW......... Versuchsanstalt fuer Wasserbau, Hydrologie, und Glaziologie [*Laboratory of Hydraulics, Hydrology, and Glaciology*] [*Switzerland*]
VAWA .... Videotex Association of Western Australia
VAWM...... Washim [*India*] [*ICAO location identifier*] (ICLI)
VAX.......... Vesta Airex [*Czechoslovakia*] [*ICAO designator*] (FAAC)
vaz .... Vazany [*Bound*] (CZ)
VAZ .... Venyukovskiy Fittings Plant (RU)
VAZ .... Volkhov Aluminum Plant (RU)
VB .... Diving Boat (RU)
VB .... Drum Switch (RU)
VB .... Head Water (RU)
VB .... Hydrologic Balance (RU)
Vb.............. Mean Deflection (Probable) Error (RU)
VB .... Turkiye Vakiflar Bankasi [*Turkish Religious Trusts Bank*] (TU)

VB .... Van Bo [*Above*] [*Afrikaans*]
vb................ Ve Baskalar [*And Others*] [*Turkey*] (GPO)
vb................ Ve Benzeri [*And Similar, equivalent of Et Cetera*] (TU)
VB .... Vegrehajto Bizottsag [*Executive Committee*] (HU)
VB .... Velke Brno [*Greater Brno*] (CZ)
vb................ Verbessert [*Improved, Revised*] [*German*]
vb................ Verbi [*Verb*] [*Finland*]
Vb.............. Verbindung [*Compound*] [*German*] (GCA)
VB .... Verbundkarte [*German*] (ADPT)
VB .... Verejna Bezpecnost [*Public Security (Police)*] (CZ)
VB .... Verkaufsbeauftragter [*German*] (ADPT)
VB .... Verkehrsbuch [*Traffic Book*] [*German military - World War I*]
VB .... Verlag fuer Bauwesen Berlin (VEB) [*Berlin Architectural Publishing House (VEB)*] [*German*] (EG)
VB .... Verlagsbuchhandlung [*Publishing House*] [*German*]
Vb.............. Verordeningenblad [*Benelux*] (BAS)
VB .... Vertragsbediensteter [*German*]
VB .... Vertriebsbeauftragter [*German*] (ADPT)
VB .... Verwalteter Betrieb [*Administered Enterprise*] (EG)
Vb.............. Verzekeringsbode [*Benelux*] (BAS)
VB .... Veterinary Board [*Tasmania, Australia*]
VB .... Victoria Bitter [*Australia*]
VB .... Vilagbajnoksag [*World Championship*] (HU)
VB .... Viven Bessieres [*Type of grenade*] [*Military*] [*French*] (MTD)
VB .... Voelkischer Beobachter
vb................ Voorbeeld [*Example*] [*Afrikaans*]
V/b .... Vragbrief [*Consignment-Note; Bill of Lading*] [*Afrikaans*] [*Business term*]
vb................ Weber (RU)
VB .... Wet op de Vermogensbelasting [*Benelux*] (BAS)
VBA .... Victorian Bar Association [*Australia*]
VBAN .... Ann [*Myanmar*] [*ICAO location identifier*] (ICLI)
VBAS........ Anisakan [*Myanmar*] [*ICAO location identifier*] (ICLI)
VBB .... Vattenbyggnadsbyran [*Sweden*] (PDAA)
Vbb............. Verbindungen [*Compounds*] [*German*]
VBB .... Verein der Bibliothekare an Oeffentlichen Bibliotheken eV (SLS)
VBB .... Verein der Bibliothekare an Offentlichen Bibliotheken [*Association of Librarians in Public Libraries*] [*Germany*] (EAIO)
VBB .... Verlag fuer Buch- und Bibliothekswesen (VEB) [*Book and Library Publishing House (VEB)*] [*German*] (EG)
VBB .... Verordeningenblad Bedrijfsorganisatie [*Benelux*] (BAS)
vbb............. Volgens Bygaande Brief [*According to Accompanying Letter*] [*Correspondence*] [*Afrikaans*]
VBBM .... Bhamo [*Myanmar*] [*ICAO location identifier*] (ICLI)
Vb Bo .... Verordeningenblad Bedrijfsorganisatie [*Benelux*] (BAS)
VBBP........ Bokepyin [*Myanmar*] [*ICAO location identifier*] (ICLI)
VBBS........ Bassein [*Myanmar*] [*ICAO location identifier*] (ICLI)
VBC .... Victorian Bar Council [*Australia*]
VBC .... Vlaamse Bibliotheek Centrale
VBCI......... Coco Island [*Myanmar*] [*ICAO location identifier*] (ICLI)
VBCITC .... Victorian Building and Construction Industry Training Council [*Australia*]
VBCS........ Victorian Bing Crosby Society [*Australia*] (EAIO)
vbd............. Valskband [*Quarter-Bound*] [*Publishing*] [*Sweden*]
vbd............. Vavband [*Cloth Binding*] [*Publishing*] [*Sweden*]
vbd............. Verbunden [*Connected*] [*German*] (GCA)
VBD .... Versuchsanstalt fuer Binnenschiffbau eV Duisburg [*Duisburg Research Laboratory for Inland Shipbuilding*] [*Research center*] (IRC)
V Bd .... Vuestra Beatitud [*Your Beatitude*] [*Spanish*]
VBE .... Verband Bildung und Erziehung im Deutschen Beamtenbund (SLS)
VbE............. Vollbeschaeftigteneinheit [*Full Employment Unit*] (EG)
VBEFA ...... Vehicle Builders Employees Federation of Australia
VBF........... Veiligheidsbesluit voor Fabrieken of Werkplaatsen [*Benelux*] (BAS)
Vbf .... Verschiebebahnhof [*Classification Yard*] [*German*] (EG)
Vbg............. Vorarlberg [*or Vorarlberger*] [*German*]
VBGG .... Gangaw [*Myanmar*] [*ICAO location identifier*] (ICLI)
VBGO .... All-Union Grocery and Delicatessen Association (RU)
VBGW .... Gwa [*Myanmar*] [*ICAO location identifier*] (ICLI)
vb h............. Vegyesbizottsagi Hatarozat (A Magyarcsehszlovak Lakossagcsere Vegrehajtasara Alakult Vegyesbizottsag Hatarozata) [*Resolution of the Joint Commission (for the Implementation of the Hungarian-Czechoslovak Exchange of Population)*] (HU)
VBHB........ Hmawbi [*Myanmar*] [*ICAO location identifier*] (ICLI)
VBHH .... Hebo [*Myanmar*] [*ICAO location identifier*] (ICLI)
VBHL .... Homalin [*Myanmar*] [*ICAO location identifier*] (ICLI)
VBHN...... Htilin [*Myanmar*] [*ICAO location identifier*] (ICLI)
VBI............ Verein Beratender Ingenieure [*Association of Consulting Engineers*] [*Germany*] (GCA)
VBIDB........ Victorian Building Industries Disputes Board [*Australia*]
VBIS .... Veiligheidsbesluit Ioniserende Stralen [*Benelux*] (BAS)

VBKD .... Verband Bildender Kuenstler Deutschlands [*League of Graphic Artists in Germany*]   (EG)
VBKG .... Kengtung [*Myanmar*] [*ICAO location identifier*]   (ICLI)
VBKK........ Kutkai [*Myanmar*] [*ICAO location identifier*]   (ICLI)
VBKM .... Kalemyo [*Myanmar*] [*ICAO location identifier*]   (ICLI)
VBKM .... Villamosberendezes es Keszulek Muvek [*Electrical Equipment and Appliance Works*]   (HU)
VBKP........ Kyaukpyu [*Myanmar*] [*ICAO location identifier*]   (ICLI)
VBKU .... Kyauktu [*Myanmar*] [*ICAO location identifier*]   (ICLI)
VBL........... Dienstvorschrift fuer die Ermittlung der Betriebsleistungen [*Service Regulation for Determining Operational Performance*] [*German*]   (EG)
Vbl............ Het Vakblad [*Benelux*]   (BAS)
VBl........... Verordnungsblatt [*Official Gazette*] [*German*]   (ILCA)
VBL........... Veterinary Bacteriological Laboratory   (RU)
VblBedrorg ... Verordeningenblad Bedrijfsorganisatie [*Benelux*]   (BAS)
VBLK........ Loikaw [*Myanmar*] [*ICAO location identifier*]   (ICLI)
VBLN .... Lonekin [*Myanmar*] [*ICAO location identifier*]   (ICLI)
VBLO .... Langkho [*Myanmar*] [*ICAO location identifier*]   (ICLI)
VBLS .... Lashio [*Myanmar*] [*ICAO location identifier*]   (ICLI)
VBLY........ Lanywa [*Myanmar*] [*ICAO location identifier*]   (ICLI)
VBMA .... Vereniging vir Bogrondse Mynamptenare van Suid-Afrika [*South Africa*]   (AA)
VBMAA .... Venetian Blind Manufacturers' Association of Australia
VBMH....... Mong-Hpayak [*Myanmar*] [*ICAO location identifier*]   (ICLI)
VBMI........ Mongyai [*Myanmar*] [*ICAO location identifier*]   (ICLI)
VBMK....... Myitkyina [*Myanmar*] [*ICAO location identifier*]   (ICLI)
VBML........ Meiktila [*Myanmar*] [*ICAO location identifier*]   (ICLI)
VBMM ...... Moulmein [*Myanmar*] [*ICAO location identifier*]   (ICLI)
VBMN .... Manaung [*Myanmar*] [*ICAO location identifier*]   (ICLI)
VBMO .... Momeik [*Myanmar*] [*ICAO location identifier*]   (ICLI)
VBMP........ Mong Pyin [*Myanmar*] [*ICAO location identifier*]   (ICLI)
VBMS....... Mong-Hsat [*Myanmar*] [*ICAO location identifier*]   (ICLI)
VBMS....... Victorian Business Migration Service [*Australia*]
VBMT....... Mong Tong [*Myanmar*] [*ICAO location identifier*]   (ICLI)
VBMU .... Myauk U [*Myanmar*] [*ICAO location identifier*]   (ICLI)
VBMW ...... Magwe [*Myanmar*] [*ICAO location identifier*]   (ICLI)
VBN........... Vereniging van de Belgische Nijverheid [*Federation of Belgian Industries*] [*German*]   (WEN)
VBNA .... Victorian Bush Nursing Association [*Australia*]
VBNM .... Naungmon [*Myanmar*] [*ICAO location identifier*]   (ICLI)
VBNP .... Nampong [*Myanmar*] [*ICAO location identifier*]   (ICLI)
VBNS........ Namsang [*Myanmar*] [*ICAO location identifier*]   (ICLI)
VBNT .... Namtu [*Myanmar*] [*ICAO location identifier*]   (ICLI)
VBNU .... Nyaung U [*Myanmar*] [*ICAO location identifier*]   (ICLI)
VBO .... All-Union Botanical Society   (RU)
VBO .... Verbond van Belgische Ondernemingen [*Belgium*]   (EAIO)
VBo .... Verordeningenblad Bedrijfsorganisatie [*Benelux*]   (BAS)
VBO .... Voorschrift Betreffende de Beoordeling van de Officieren bij de Koninklijke Landmacht [*Benelux*]   (BAS)
VBO-FEB ... Verbond van Belgische Ondernemingen-Federation des Entreprises de Belgique [*Federation of Belgian Companies*]
VBogU .... Higher School of Theology   (BU)
VBP........... Ammunition Supply Platoon   (RU)
VBP........... Upper Sideband   (RU)
VBPA........ Pa-An [*Myanmar*] [*ICAO location identifier*]   (ICLI)
VBPB .... Phaungbyin [*Myanmar*] [*ICAO location identifier*]   (ICLI)
VBPDCh.... Upper Sideband of Doppler Frequencies   (RU)
VBPE .... Paletwa [*Myanmar*] [*ICAO location identifier*]   (ICLI)
VBPG........ Pegu [*Myanmar*] [*ICAO location identifier*]   (ICLI)
VBPI........ Pearl Island [*Myanmar*] [*ICAO location identifier*]   (ICLI)
VBPK........ Pauk [*Myanmar*] [*ICAO location identifier*]   (ICLI)
VBPL........ Pinlebu [*Myanmar*] [*ICAO location identifier*]   (ICLI)
VBPP .... Papun [*Myanmar*] [*ICAO location identifier*]   (ICLI)
VBPR........ Prome [*Myanmar*] [*ICAO location identifier*]   (ICLI)
VBPT........ Putao [*Myanmar*] [*ICAO location identifier*]   (ICLI)
VBPU .... Pakokku [*Myanmar*] [*ICAO location identifier*]   (ICLI)
VBPW........ Palaw [*Myanmar*] [*ICAO location identifier*]   (ICLI)
VBR .... Valuation Board of Review [*Australia*]
VBRA .... Sittwe [*Myanmar*] [*ICAO location identifier*]   (ICLI)
VBRM .... Mandalay [*Myanmar*] [*ICAO location identifier*]   (ICLI)
VBRN .... Mergui [*Myanmar*] [*ICAO location identifier*]   (ICLI)
VBRR........ Rangoon/Mingaladon [*Myanmar*] [*ICAO location identifier*]   (ICLI)
vbrtr .... Armored Carrier Platoon   (RU)
VBS............ Hungarian Bureau of Standardization   (RU)
VBSA .... Saw [*Myanmar*] [*ICAO location identifier*]   (ICLI)
VBSA .... Verenigde Boekhandelaars van Suidelike Afrika [*Associated Booksellers of Southern Africa*]   (EAIO)
VBSK........ Sinkaling Khamti [*Myanmar*] [*ICAO location identifier*]   (ICLI)
VBSL .... Salingyi [*Myanmar*] [*ICAO location identifier*]   (ICLI)
VBSO........ Sidoktaya [*Myanmar*] [*ICAO location identifier*]   (ICLI)
VBST .... Shante [*Myanmar*] [*ICAO location identifier*]   (ICLI)
VBSW........ Shinbweyang [*Myanmar*] [*ICAO location identifier*]   (ICLI)
VBSY .... Sandoway [*Myanmar*] [*ICAO location identifier*]   (ICLI)

VBT .... Vetenskapliga Bibliotekens Tjaenstemannafoerening [*Sweden*]   (SLS)
VBT .... Veterinary Board of Tasmania [*Australia*]
VBT/AT .... Verband der Beschaeftigungs- und Arbeitstherapeuten [*Ergotherapeuten*] eV   (SLS)
VBTL........ Tachilek [*Myanmar*] [*ICAO location identifier*]   (ICLI)
VBTN .... Tanai [*Myanmar*] [*ICAO location identifier*]   (ICLI)
vbtr........... Armored Carrier Platoon   (RU)
VBTs......... Waterproof, Shrinkproof Cement   (RU)
VBTV........ Tavoy [*Myanmar*] [*ICAO location identifier*]   (ICLI)
VBTY........ Tanyang [*Myanmar*] [*ICAO location identifier*]   (ICLI)
VBV .... Vanuabalavu [*Fiji*] [*Airport symbol*]   (OAG)
VBV .... Vereinigung fuer Berufsbildung der Schweizerischen Versicherungswirtschaft [*Bern, Switzerland*]   (SLS)
VBV .... Vereniging voor Bedrijfsvoorlichting [*Benelux*]   (BAS)
VBV .... Verwaltung Banken und Versicherungen [*Administration of Banks and Insurance*] [*German*]   (EG)
VBV .... Veterinary Board of Victoria [*Australia*]
VBVP........ Kawthaung [*Myanmar*] [*ICAO location identifier*]   (ICLI)
VBVP........ Volga-Baltic Waterway   (RU)
VBW .... Air Burkina [*Burkina Faso*] [*ICAO designator*]   (FAAC)
VBW .... Verein fuer Binnenschiffahrt und Wasserstrassen eV [*Germany*]   (EY)
VBY .... Visby [*Sweden*] [*Airport symbol*]   (OAG)
VBYE........ Ye [*Myanmar*] [*ICAO location identifier*]   (ICLI)
VBZ .... Verejna Bezpecnost na Zeleznici [*Railroad Police*]   (CZ)
VBZ .... Vychodoceske Bavlnarske Zavody, Narodni Podnik [*East Bohemian Cotton Mills, National Enterprise*]   (CZ)
VC............. British Aircraft Corp. Ltd. [*ICAO aircraft manufacturer identifier*]   (ICAO)
VC .... St. Vincent and the Grenadines [*ANSI two-letter standard code*]   (CNC)
VC .... Vanguardia Comunista [*Communist Vanguard Party*] [*Venezuela*]   (LA)
VC .... Vatan Cephesi [*Fatherland Front*]   (TU)
VC .... Vercelli [*Car registration plates*] [*Italian*]
VC .... Vernair Flying Services [*British*] [*ICAO designator*]   (ICDA)
VC .... Vice-Consul [*Vice-Consul*] [*French*]   (MTD)
vc............. Vicolo [*Lane*] [*Italian*]   (CED)
VC .... Victoria College [*Australia*]
VC .... Video Channel [*Auckland, NZ*]
VC .... Viet Cong   (CL)
VC .... Vitesse Corrigee [*Calibrated Airspeed*] [*Aviation*] [*French*]
VC .... Volkscomputer [*Personal Computer*] [*German*]   (ADPT)
vC............. Voor Christus [*Before Christ*] [*Afrikaans*]
v/c .... Vossa Conta [*Your Account*] [*Portuguese*] [*Business term*]
v/c .... Votre Compte [*Your Account*] [*French*] [*Business term*]
VC .... Vuelta de Correo [*Return Mail*] [*Spanish*]
VC .... Vyrobni Cislo [*Production Number, Serial Number*]   (CZ)
VCA .... Victims of Crime Association [*Australia*]
VCA .... Victorian College of the Arts [*Australia*]
VCA .... Victorian Council of the Arts [*Australia*]
VCA .... Voluntary Care Association [*Australia*]
VCAB........ Victorian Curriculum and Assessment Board [*Australia*]
VCAC........ Vehicule de Combat Anti-Chars
VCAC .... Victorian Consumer Affairs Committee [*Australia*]
VCAH .... Victorian College of Agriculture and Horticulture [*Australia*]
VCAI .... Victoria-Confederation of Australian Industry [*National Office*] [*National Union Catalogue of Australia symbol*]
V Caride..... Vossa Caridade [*Portuguese*]
VCAS........ Vice Chief of the Air Staff [*Australia*]
VCAS .... Victorian Children's Aid Society [*Australia*]
VCAW ...... Victorian Council Against War and Fascism [*Australia*]
VCAWF.... Victorian Council Against War and Fascism [*Australia*]
VCBI......... Colombo/Katunayake [*Sri Lanka*] [*ICAO location identifier*]   (ICLI)
VCC .... Venture Capital Co. [*Thailand*]
VCC .... Village Community Centre [*Australia*]
VCC .... Vychodoceske Cihelny [*East Bohemian Brick Works*]   (CZ)
VCCA .... Anuradhapura [*Sri Lanka*] [*ICAO location identifier*]   (ICLI)
VCCA .... Victorian Credit Cooperative Association [*Australia*]
VCCAV..... Victorian Community Council against Violence [*Australia*]
VCCB........ Batticaloa [*Sri Lanka*] [*ICAO location identifier*]   (ICLI)
VCCC........ Colombo/Ratmalana [*Sri Lanka*] [*ICAO location identifier*]   (ICLI)
VCCC........ Vintage and Classic Car Club [*Australia*]
VCCCM..... Victorian Centre for the Conservation of Cultural Material [*Australia*]
VCCE........ Victorian Council of Christian Education [*Australia*]
VCCFT ...... Victorian Council for Children's Films and Television [*Australia*]
VCCG .... Galoya/Amparai [*Sri Lanka*] [*ICAO location identifier*]   (ICLI)
VCCI......... Victorian Chamber of Commerce and Industry [*Australia*]
VCCJ .... Jaffna/Kankesanturai [*Sri Lanka*] [*ICAO location identifier*]   (ICLI)
VCCR........ Victorian Cervical Cytology Registry [*Australia*]

VCCT......... Trincomalee/China Bay [*Sri Lanka*] [*ICAO location identifier*] (ICLI)
VCCW .... Wirawila [*Sri Lanka*] [*ICAO location identifier*] (ICLI)
VCD .... Victoria River Downs [*Australia*] [*Airport symbol*]
VCDP .... Victorian Council of Deaf People [*Australia*]
VCE .... Venice [*Italy*] [*Airport symbol*] (OAG)
VCE .... Victorian Certificate of Education [*Australia*]
VCE .... Vychodoceske Elektrarny, Narodni Podnik [*East Bohemian Electric Power Works, National Enterprise*] (CZ)
VCEA........ Victorian Congress of Employer Associations [*Australia*]
VCES........ Veterans Children's Education Scheme [*Australia*]
VCF........... Victor Fly [*Italy*] [*ICAO designator*] (FAAC)
VCF........... Victorian Conservation Foundation [*Australia*]
VCF........... Victorian Cycling Federation [*Australia*]
VCFGH ..... Victorian Council on Fitness and General Health [*Australia*]
VCFL .... Victorian Country Football League [*Australia*]
VCG .... Societe Voltaique des Corps Gras
VCG .... Vice Consul General [*French*] (MTD)
VCGS........ Victorian Clinical Genetics Services [*Australia*]
VCh........... High Frequency (BU)
VCh........... High-Sensitive (Motion-Picture Film) (RU)
VCh........... Military Unit (RU)
v ch .... Part by Weight (RU)
VCH.......... Vichadero [*Uruguay*] [*Airport symbol*] [*Obsolete*] (OAG)
V Ch .... Vor Christo [*Before Christ*] [*German*]
VChIM ...... High-Frequency Pulse Modulation (RU)
VChK........ All-Russian Extraordinary Commission for Combating Counterrevolution and Sabotage [*1917-1922*] (RU)
VChKLB.... All-Russian Extraordinary Commission for the Liquidation of Illiteracy (RU)
VChKLN ... All-Russian Extraordinary Commission for the Liquidation of Illiteracy (RU)
VCHO....... Vereniging vir Christelike Hoer Onderwys [*South Africa*] (AA)
VCHR....... Vietnam Committee on Human Rights [*France*] (EAIO)
v Chr .... Vor Christus [*Before Christ*] [*German*] (GPO)
v Chr G ...... Vor Christi Geburt [*Before the Birth of Christ*] [*German*]
VChS .... High-Frequency Communications (RU)
VChS .... High-Frequency Seismic Exploration (RU)
VChS .... Supreme Union of Libraries (BU)
VChSS........ High-Frequency Seismic Station (RU)
VChV .... Velitelstvi Chemickeho Vojska [*Chemical Troops Headquarters*] (CZ)
VChZ .... Vychodoceske Chemicke Zavody Synthesia [*East Bohemian Chemical Factories*] (CZ)
VCI .... Vehicule de Combat de l'Infanterie
VCI .... Venture Capital Israel
VCI .... Verband der Chemischen Industriee eV [*Association of Chemical Industry Germany*] (EAIO)
VCIN .... Victoria Curriculum Information Network [*Australia*]
Vclbr .... Vidi Clan Broj [*See Article Number*] (YU)
VCM .... Victorian Chamber of Mines [*Australia*]
VCMB .... Vanuatu Commodities Marketing Board (EAIO)
VCMo .... Verguetungsstahl mit Chrom und Molybdaen [*Heat-Treatable Steel Containing Chromium and Molybdenum*] [*German*] (GCA)
VCMR .... Victorian Council for the Mentally Retarded [*Australia*]
VCN.......... Verguetungsstahl mit Chrom und Nickel [*Heat-Treatable Steel with Chromium and Nickel*] [*German*] (GCA)
VCNO........ Vybor Ceskoslovenskeho Narodniho Odboje [*Committee of the Czechoslovak National Resistance Movement*] (CZ)
VCO .... Aviacion Colombiana Ltd. [*Colombia*] [*ICAO designator*] (FAAC)
VCO.......... Victorian College of Optometry [*Australia*]
VCOA........ Video Copyright Owners Association [*Australia*]
VCP .... Sao Paulo [*Brazil*] Viracopos Airport [*Airport symbol*] (OAG)
VCP .... Vetements et Chemiserie de Paris
VCP .... Victorian Centre for Photography [*Australia*]
VCP .... Victorian College of Pharmacy [*Australia*]
VCP .... Voluntary Cooperation Program [*World Meteorological Organization*] [*United Nations*]
VCPA........ Victorian Country Press Association [*Australia*]
VCPOR...... Vanguardia Comunista del Partido Obrero Revolucionario [*Bolivia*] [*Political party*] (PPW)
VCRC........ Vector Control Research Centre [*India*]
VCSA........ Victorian Catholic Schools Association [*Australia*]
VCSA........ Victorian Colleges Staff Association [*Australia*]
VCSA........ Victorian Council for Sustainable Agriculture [*Australia*]
VCSEA ...... Victorian Community Services Employers' Association [*Australia*]
VCSS .... Victorian Council of Social Service [*Australia*]
VCST .... Voros Csillag Traktorgyar [*Red Star Tractor Factory*] (HU)
VCSZ......... Vybor Ceskoslovenskych Zen [*Czechoslovak Women's Committee*] (CZ)
VCT .... St. Vincent and the Grenadines [*ANSI three-letter standard code*] (CNC)
VCT .... Victorian Conservation Trust [*Australia*]

VCT .... Vychodoceske Tiskarny [*East Bohemian Printing Works*] (CZ)
VCTA......... Victorian Commercial Travellers' Association [*Australia*]
Vcte .... Vicomte [*Viscount*] [*French*] (MTD)
v/cte .... Votre Compte [*Your Account*] [*French*] [*Business term*]
Vctesse....... Vicomtesse [*Viscountess*] [*French*]
VCU .... Association for Cultural Exchange [*Pro-Moscow*] [*Netherlands*] (WEN)
VCUSA...... Victorian Colleges and Universities Staff Association [*Australia*]
VCV .... Vlaamse Chemische Vereniging [*Belgium*] (SLS)
VCYAN ..... Victorian Country Youth Affairs Network [*Australia*]
VCZ .... Vybor Ceskych Zen [*or Vybor Ceskoslovenskych Zen*] [*Czech Women's Committee or Czechoslovak Women's Committee*] (CZ)
VD .... Airborne Force (RU)
VD .... Air Depolarization (RU)
vd .... East Longitude (RU)
Vd............. Het Vaderland [*Benelux*] (BAS)
Vd............. High Pressure (RU)
Vd............. Mean Range (Probable) Error (RU)
VD .... Military Road (RU)
VD .... RTZ Services Ltd. [*British*] [*ICAO designator*] (ICDA)
Vd............. Usted [*You (Singular, formal)*] [*Spanish*]
Vd............. Vand [*Lake*] [*Norway*] (NAU)
vd............. Van De [*Of The*] [*Benelux*] (BAS)
vd............. Van Die [*Of The*] [*Afrikaans*]
VD .... Vasilevomeni Dimokratia [*Royalist Republic*] [*Greek*] (GC)
VD .... Vasilikon Diatagma [*Royal Decree*] (GC)
VD .... Vatrogasno Drustvo [*Firemen's Society*] (YU)
VD .... Vazduhoplovna Divizija [*Air Force Division*] (YU)
VD .... Velitelstvi Delostrelectva [*Artillery Headquarters*] (CZ)
Vd............. Vend [*Sell*] [*French*] [*Business term*]
VD .... Venous Pressure (RU)
VD .... Vertrauliche Dienstsache [*Confidential Matter*] (EG)
VD .... Vesnicke Divadlo [*Village Theater*] (CZ)
vd............. Von Der [*Of The*] [*In names*] [*German*]
VD .... Voreiodytikos (Anemos) [*Northwesterly (Wind)*] (GC)
VD .... Vragen van den Dag [*Benelux*] (BAS)
Vd............. Vrsi Duznost [*Acting As*] (YU)
VD .... Vysadkova Divize [*Airborne Division*] (CZ)
vd............. Vzhodna Dolzina [*Eastern Longitude*] (YU)
VDA .... Federation of the German Motor Industry (EAIO)
VDA .... Verband Deutscher Agrarjournalisten eV (SLS)
VdA .... Verein Deutscher Archivare [*Association of German Archivists*] (EAIO)
VDA .... Victorian Docklands Authority [*Australia*]
vda............ Viuda [*Widow*] [*Spanish*]
VDA .... Volga-Dnepr [*Former USSR*] [*ICAO designator*] (FAAC)
VDA .... Volksbund fuer das Deutschtum im Ausland [*NAZI Germany*]
vdb............ Airborne Battalion (RU)
VDB .... Airborne Brigade (RU)
VDB .... Military Road Battalion (RU)
VDB .... Verband Deutscher Badearzte [*Germany*] (EAIO)
VDB .... Verband Deutscher Betriebswirte eV (SLS)
VDB .... Verein Deutscher Bibliothekare [*Association of German Librarians*] (EAIO)
VDB .... Verein Deutscher Bibliothekare eV (SLS)
VDB .... Vrij Democratisch Bond [*Liberal Democratic Union*] [*Netherlands*] (WEN)
VDB .... Vrijzinnige-Democratische Bond [*Radical Democratic League*] [*Netherlands*] [*Political party*] (PPE)
VDBA .... Victorian Deer Breeders Association [*Australia*]
VDBG .... Battambang [*Cambodia*] [*ICAO location identifier*] (ICLI)
vdbr .... Airborne Brigade (BU)
VD Brno .... Vyvojove Dilny, Brno [*Development Workshops in Brno (of the Czechoslovak Academy of Sciences)*] (CZ)
VDCE .... Victorian Department of Conservation and Environment [*Australia*]
VDCH .... Verein Deutscher Chemiker [*Association of German Chemists*]
VDCK .... Volksverein Deutsch Canadischer Katholiken [*Association of German Canadian Catholics*]
VDD .... Airborne Division (RU)
vdd............ Vadaszdandar [*Fighter Plane Command (Two wings)*] (HU)
VDD.......... Verein Deutscher Dokumentare [*Association of German Documenters*]
VdDB .... Verein der Diplom-Bibliothekare an Wissenschaftlichen Bibliotheken [*Association of Graduated Librarians in Academic/Research Libraries*] [*Germany*] (EAIO)
VdDB .... Verein der Diplom-Bibliothekare an Wissenschaftlichen Bibliotheken eV (SLS)
VDDO........ Verband der Diplomierten Diatassistentinen Osterreichs [*Diploma Dietician Association Austria*] (EAIO)
VDE .... Valverde [*Canary Islands*] [*Airport symbol*] (OAG)
VDE .... Verband Deutscher Elektrotechniker [*Association of German Electrical Engineers*] (EG)
VDE .... Verein Deutscher Eisengiessereien [*German Foundry Society*] (GCA)

VDE........... Verein Deutscher Elektroingenieure [*Society of German Electrical Engineers*]   (GCA)
VDEh......... Verein Deutscher Eisenhuettenleute   (SLS)
VDEh......... Verein Deutscher Eisenhuttenleute [*German Iron and Steel Engineers Association*]   (IID)
VDEL......... Verband Deutscher Esperanto-Lehrer eV   (SLS)
VDEW .... Vereinigung Deutscher Elektrizitaetswerke [*Nuclear energy*]   (NRCH)
VDF .... Danube Navy Fleet   (BU)
VDF .... Victorian Development Fund [*Australia*]
VDFA .... Victorian Dairy Farmers Association [*Australia*]
VDFB......... Victorian Dried Fruits Board [*Australia*]
VDFZh ...... All-Chinese Democratic Federation of Women   (RU)
VDG........... Glubshev Differential Water Gauge   (RU)
VDG........... Verein Deutscher Giessereifachleute eV   (SLS)
VDG........... Vereinigung Deutscher Gewaesserschutz eV   (SLS)
VdgB .... Vereinigung der Gegenseitigen Bauernhilfe [*Peasant's Mutual Aid Association*] [*German*]   (EG)
VdgB(BHG) ... Vereinigung der Gegenseitigen Bauernhilfe (Baeuerliche Handelsgenossenschaft) [*Peasant's Mutual Aid Association (Peasant's Trade Cooperative)*] [*German*]   (EG)
VDG-DOK ... Verein Deutscher Giessereifachleute eV - Dokumentationsstelle und Bibliothek [*Dusseldorf*] [*Information retrieval*]
VDGI .... Vietnamese Government Information Department   (VNW)
VDI .... Verein Deutscher Ingenieure [*Association of German Engineers*]   (WEN)
VDICAPP ... Verein Deutscher Ingenieure-Commission on Air Pollution Prevention   (EAIO)
VDID .... Verband Deutscher Industrie-Designer [*Association of German Industrial-Designers*]   (EAIO)
VDIKRL.... Verein Deutscher Ingenieure-Kommission Reinhaltung der Luft [*VDI - Commis sion on Air Pollution Prevention*]   (EAIO)
VDI-N........ Verein Deutscher Ingenieure-Nachrichten
VDJ........... Verband der Deutschen Journalisten [*German Journalists' Association*]   (WEN)
VDJD........ Vereinigung Demokratischer Juristen Deutschlands [*Union of Democratic Jurists of Germany*]   (EG)
vdk .... Airborne Corps   (BU)
VDK........... Verband Deutscher Konsumgenossenschaften [*Association of German Consumer Cooperatives*]   (EG)
VDK........... Vietnami Demokratikus Koztarsasag [*Democratic Republic of Vietnam*]   (HU)
VDK........... Volga-Don Canal   (RU)
VDK........... Vsegambiiskii Demokraticheskii Kongress
VDK........... Vyrobne-Dispecerske Kancelare [*Production and Management Control Offices*]   (CZ)
VDKC........ Kompong Cham [*Cambodia*] [*ICAO location identifier*]   (ICLI)
VDKC........ Verband Deutscher Konzert Choere [*German Society of Concert Choirs*]   (EAIO)
vdkch......... Water-Pumping Station [*Topography*]   (RU)
VDKH....... Kompong Chnang [*Cambodia*] [*ICAO location identifier*]   (ICLI)
vdkhr......... Reservoir   (RU)
VDKT .... Kratie [*Cambodia*] [*ICAO location identifier*]   (ICLI)
VDL........... Van Diemen's Land [*Former name of Tasmania*] [*Australia*]   (ADA)
VDL........... Vienna Definition Language [*Computer science*]   (ADPT)
VDL........... Vojenske Dopravni Letectvo [*Military Transport Airforce*]   (CZ)
vdL............. Vor dem Loetrohr [*Before the Blow Pipe*] [*German*]   (GCA)
VDLU .... Verband Deutscher Luftfahrt Unternehmen [*German Association of Aeronautical Enterprises*]   (PDAA)
VDLUFA... Verband Deutscher Landwirtschaftlicher Untersuchungs- und Forschungsanstalten [*German Agricultural Research Institutes Association*]   (ARC)
vdm............ Ground Decontamination Platoon   (RU)
VDM......... Verband der Deutschen Milchwirtschaft [*German Dairy Association*]   (EAIO)
VDM......... Vereinigte Deutsche Metallwerke AG [*United German Metal Workers*]
VDM......... Viedma [*Argentina*] [*Airport symbol*]   (OAG)
VDM......... Vienna Development Method [*Austria*]   (PDAA)
VDM......... World Movement of Mothers [*WMM*]   (RU)
VDMA....... Verband Deutscher Maschinen- und Anlagenbau eV [*German Machine Construction Union*]   (EY)
VDMG....... Verband Deutscher Meteorologischer Gesellschaften   (SLS)
VDMID ..... Victorian Department of Manufacturing and Industry Development [*Australia*]
VDMK....... Democratic Community of Vojvodina Hungarians [*Former Yugoslavia*] [*Political party*]
VDMK....... Verband Deutscher Musikerzieher und Konzertierender Kuenstler eV   (SLS)
VDMTA .... Verband der Diplomierte Medizinisch-Technische Assistenten Oesterreichs [*Austria*]   (EAIO)
VDN.......... Varudeklarationsnamnden [*Labeling system*] [*Sweden*]
VDN.......... Vereinigte Deutsche Nickel-Werke Aktiengesellschaft [*United German Nickel Works Joint Stock Company*] [*Business term*]
VdN........... Voix des Notres [*Record label*] [*France*]

VDNKh...... Exhibition of Achievements of the National Economy of the USSR   (RU)
VDNT .... All-Union House of Folk Art Imeni N. K. Krupskaya   (RU)
VDO........... Airborne Detachment   (RU)
VDO........... Military Road Detachment   (RU)
VDO........... Military Road Section   (RU)
VDO........... Velkonakupni Druzstvo Obchodniku [*Merchants' Cooperative for Wholesale Buying*]   (CZ)
VDO........... Vyrobne-Dispecersky Odbor [*Production and Management Control Department*]   (CZ)
VDP .... Airborne Regiment   (RU)
VDP .... High-Altitude Deformation Field   (RU)
VDP .... Military Preinduction Training   (RU)
VDP .... Mobile Decontamination Apparatus   (RU)
VDP .... Portable Decontamination Equipment   (BU)
VDP .... Velkodistribucni Podnik [*Wholesale Distribution Enterprise*]   (CZ)
VDP .... Velkodruzstevni Prodejny [*Wholesale Cooperative Sales Outlets*]   (CZ)
VDP .... Velkonakupni Druzstevni Podniky [*Cooperative Enterprises for Wholesale Buying*]   (CZ)
VDP .... Verband der Deutschen Presse [*German Press Association*]   (EG)
VDP .... Verenigde Democratische Partijen [*United Democratic Parties*] [*Surinam*] [*Political party*]   (PPW)
VDP .... Volga-Don Steamship Line   (RU)
vdp............. Waterfall [*Topography*]   (RU)
VDPA .... Victorian Dairy Products Association [*Australia*]
VdPO .... Verband der Professoren Oesterreichs [*Austria*]   (SLS)
VDPP........ Phnom-Penh [*Cambodia*] [*ICAO location identifier*]   (ICLI)
VDPT........ Pongtuk [*Cambodia*] [*ICAO location identifier*]   (ICLI)
VDQS .... Vins Delimites de Qualite Superieure [*Tunisia*]
vdr............. Airborne Company   (RU)
VDR........... Verband Deutscher Realschullehrer im Deutschen Beamtenbund   (SLS)
VDR........... Verband Deutscher Reeder [*German Shipowners' Association*]   (EAIO)
VDR........... Vietnamska Demokraticka Republika [*People's Republic of Vietnam*]   (CZ)
VDRA .... Victorian Debt Retirement Authority [*Australia*]
VdrevNITO ... All-Union Scientific, Engineering, and Technical Society of the Woodworking Industry   (RU)
VDRI .... Verein Deutscher Revisions-Ingenieure [*German Association of Engineering Inspection*]   (PDAA)
VDRO .... Internal Dobrudzha Revolutionary Organization   (BU)
VDRZ .... Verband Deutscher Rechenzentren [*German*]   (ADPT)
VDS .... Airborne Forces   (RU)
Vds............. Ustedes [*You (Plural, formal)*] [*Spanish*]
VDS .... Vadso [*Norway*] [*Airport symbol*]   (OAG)
VdS .... Van die Skrywer [*From the Author*] [*Afrikaans*]
VDS .... Velocita di Sedimentazione [*Sedimentation Rate*] [*Medicine*]
VDS .... Verband Demokratischer Studenten [*Union of Democratic Students (Communist)*] [*Austria*]   (WEN)
VDS .... Verband Deutscher Schulmusiker [*German Society of School Music Educators*]   (EAIO)
VDS .... Verband Deutscher Studentenschaften [*Association of German University Student Organizations*]   (EG)
VDS .... Victorian Deaf Society [*Australia*]
VDS .... Vodohospodarska Sluzba [*Water Conservation Service*] [*Civil defense*]   (CZ)
VDS .... Vseobecny Druzstevni Svaz [*General Cooperative Union*]   (CZ)
VDSA .... Veut Dieu Saint Amour [*Knights Templar*] [*Freemasonry*]
VDS-FB..... Verband Deutscher Sonderschulen, Fachverband fur Behindertenpaedagogik [*Germany*]   (EAIO)
VDSh .... Higher School of Diplomacy
VDSI......... Verein Deutscher Sicherheits-Ingenieure [*German Association of Safety Engineers*]   (PDAA)
VDSM .... Internationaler Verband der Stadt-, Sport-, und Mehrzweckhallen [*International Federation of City, Sport, and Multi-Purpose Halls*]   (EAIO)
VDSO .... All-Union Voluntary Sports Society   (RU)
VDSR........ Siem-Reap [*Cambodia*] [*ICAO location identifier*]   (ICLI)
VDSS .... Verband Deutscher Schiffahrts-Sachverstaendiger eV   (SLS)
VDST........ Stung Treng [*Cambodia*] [*ICAO location identifier*]   (ICLI)
VDSV........ Sihanouk [*Cambodia*] [*ICAO location identifier*]   (ICLI)
VDT........... Van Doorne's Transmissie BV [*Netherlands*] [*Automotive engineering*]
VDT .... Vayudoot [*India*] [*ICAO designator*]   (FAAC)
VDTUV ..... Vereinigung der Technischen Ueberwachungs-Vereine, eV [*Nuclear energy*]   (NRCH)
VdU........... Verband der Unabhaengigen [*League of Independents*] [*Dissolved, 1956*] [*Austria*]   (PPE)
VDU.......... Verband Deutschsprachiger Uebersetzer Literarischer und Wissenschaftlicher Werke [*Association of German-Speaking Translators of Literary and Scientific Works*]
VDUAC ..... Victorian Drug Users' Advisory Committee [*Australia*]
Vduc........... Viaduc [*Viaduct*] [*Military map abbreviation World War I*] [*French*]   (MTD)

VDV .... Airborne Troops (RU)
VDV .... Verband Deutscher Verkehrsunternehmen [*Association of German Transport Authorities*] (EY)
VDV .... Vojska Drzavne Varnosti [*State Security Army*] (YU)
VDVS........ Voeune Sai [*Cambodia*] [*ICAO location identifier*] (ICLI)
VDW .... Verein Deutscher Werkzeugmaschinenfabriken [*Association of German Machine-Tool Manufacturers*] (PDAA)
VDZ .... Verband Deutscher Zeitschriftenverleger [*Germany*] (EAIO)
VDZ .... Verein Deutscher Zementwerke [*German Cement Works Association*] (EAIO)
VDZ .... Verein Deutscher Zuckertechniker (SLS)
VE .... Electric Fan (RU)
ve .... Helicopter Squadron (RU)
ve .... Van Een [*Benelux*] (BAS)
VE .... Vasiliki Enosis [*Royalist Union*] [*Greek*] (GC)
VE .... Venezuela [*ANSI two-letter standard code*] (CNC)
VE .... Venice [*Car registration plates*] [*Italian*]
VE .... Verrechnungseinheit [*Accounting Unit (Used in inner-German trade)*] (WEN)
VE .... Veuve [*Widow*] [*French*] (ROG)
VE .... Vodni Elektrarny [*Hydroelectric Plants*] (CZ)
VE .... Vojna Enciklopedija [*Military Encyclopedia*] (YU)
VE .... Vostra Eccellenza [*Your Excellency*] [*Italian*]
VE .... Votre Eminence [*Your Eminence*] [*French*]
VE .... Votre Excellence [*Your Excellency*] [*French*]
VE .... Vuestra Excelencia [*Your Excellency*] [*Spanish*]
VE .... Wind-Driven Electric Power Unit (RU)
VEA .... Victorian Exporters' Association [*Australia*]
VEA .... Viotekhnikon Epimelitirion Athinon [*Athens Chamber of Craftsmen*] (GC)
VEA .... Viviendas Economicas Argentinas [*Plan*] [*Argentina*] (LAA)
VEA .... Voluntarios en Accion [*Volunteers in Action*] [*Bolivia*] (EAIO)
VEA .... Voluntary Employment Agreement [*Australia*]
VEAB........ Volkseigener Erfassungs- und Aufkaufvertrieb [*State Procurement and Purchase Enterprise for Agricultural Products*] (EG)
VEAG .... Vereinigte Energiewerke AG (ECON)
VEAN .... Along [*India*] [*ICAO location identifier*] (ICLI)
VEAP........ Viomikhaniki Etaireia Ambelourgon Pafou [*Paphos Vinegrowers Industrial Company*] (GC)
VEAT........ Agartala [*India*] [*ICAO location identifier*] (ICLI)
VEAZ........ Aizwal [*India*] [*ICAO location identifier*] (ICLI)
Ve B .... Besluit op de Vennootschapsbelasting [*Benelux*] (BAS)
VEB .... Vneshekonombank [*State Bank for Foreign Economic Affairs*] [*Former USSR*]
VEB .... Volkseigener Betrieb [*State Enterprise*] [*German*] (EG)
VEBA........ Calcutta (Behala) [*India*] [*ICAO location identifier*] (ICLI)
VEBA........ Vereinigte Elektrizitaets- und Bergwerks-AG [*United Electricity and Mining Corporation*] [*German*] (EG)
VEBC........ Berachampa [*India*] [*ICAO location identifier*] (ICLI)
VEBD .... Baghdogra [*India*] [*ICAO location identifier*] (ICLI)
VEBG .... Balurghat [*India*] [*ICAO location identifier*] (ICLI)
VEBK........ Bokaro [*India*] [*ICAO location identifier*] (ICLI)
VEBL........ Barbil [*India*] [*ICAO location identifier*] (ICLI)
VEBS .... Bhubaneswar [*India*] [*ICAO location identifier*] (ICLI)
VEC .... Venezolana Servicios Expresos de Carga Internacional CA [*Venezuela*] [*ICAO designator*] (FAAC)
VECC........ Calcutta [*India*] [*ICAO location identifier*] (ICLI)
VECC........ Victorian Employers' Chamber of Commerce [*Australia*]
VECCI....... Victorian Employers' Chamber of Commerce and Industry [*Australia*]
VECF........ Calcutta [*India*] [*ICAO location identifier*] (ICLI)
vech .... PM [*in designation of time*] (RU)
VECh .... Secondary Frequency Standard (RU)
Vecheka ..... Vserossiskaya Chrezychainaya Kommissiya po Borbe s Kontrrevolyutsiyey i Sabotazhem [*All-Russian Extraordinary Commission for Combating Counterrevolution and Sabotage*] (RU)
VECK........ Chakulia [*India*] [*ICAO location identifier*] (ICLI)
VECO .... Cooch-Behar [*India*] [*ICAO location identifier*] (ICLI)
VECOL...... Empresa Colombiana de Productos Veterinarios [*Colombian Veterinary Products Enterprise*] (LA)
VECOR ..... Vanderbijl Engineering Corporation
VECX........ Car Nicobar [*India*] [*ICAO location identifier*] (ICLI)
ved .... Vedelem [*Defense*] (HU)
VED .... Victoria Education Department [*Australia*]
Vedag .... Verband Deutschschweizerischer Aerzte-Gesellschaften [*Tuggen, Switzerland*] (SLS)
VEDB .... Dhanbad [*India*] [*ICAO location identifier*] (ICLI)
VEDC .... Victorian Economic Development Corp. [*Australia*]
vedr .... Vedrorende [*Concerning*] [*Denmark*] (GPO)
VEDZ .... Deparizo [*India*] [*ICAO location identifier*] (ICLI)
Vee .... Vallee [*Valley*] [*Military map abbreviation World War I*] [*French*] (MTD)
VEEITC..... Victorian Electrical and Electronic Industry Training Committee [*Australia*]

VEETh....... Vasiliki Ethniki Enosis Thessalonikis [*National Royalist Union of Salonica*] [*VETh*] [*See also*] (GC)
VEF........... Victorian Education Foundation [*Australia*]
VEG .... Maikwak [*Guyana*] [*Airport symbol*] (OAG)
VEG .... Research Institute of the Association of Gas Distributors [*Netherlands*]
Veg .... Vega [*Record label*] [*France*]
VEG .... Vega Aircompany [*Russian Federation*] [*ICAO designator*] (FAAC)
VEG .... Vennotschap bij Wijze van Eenvoudige Geldschieting [*Benelux*] (BAS)
VEG .... Voithos Eparkhiakos Grammatevs [*Deputy District Secretary*] [*Cyprus*] (GC)
VEG .... Volkseigenes Gut [*State Farm*] (EG)
VEGA .... Venera-Galley [*Venus-Halley*] [*Russian space probe*]
VEGK .... Gorakhpur [*India*] [*ICAO location identifier*] (ICLI)
Vegr ut ...... Vegrehajtasi Utasitas [*Implementing Instruction*] (HU)
VEGT .... Gauhati [*India*] [*ICAO location identifier*] (ICLI)
VEGY .... Gaya [*India*] [*ICAO location identifier*] (ICLI)
vegy .... Vegyes [*Mixed*] (HU)
vegz .... Vegzes [*Order*] (HU)
VEHIDELPA ... Vehiculos del Pacifico (COL)
VEHK .... Hirakud [*India*] [*ICAO location identifier*] (ICLI)
VEI............ All-Union Electrotechnical Institute Imeni V. I. Lenin (RU)
VEI............ Vasilikon Ethnikon Idryma [*Royal National Foundation*] [*See also EI-VP*] (GC)
VEIKI .... Villamosenergiaipari Kutato Intezet [*Electric Power Industry Research Institute*] (HU)
VEIM........ Imphal [*India*] [*ICAO location identifier*] (ICLI)
VEJ .... Aero Ejecutivos CA [*Venezuela*] [*ICAO designator*] (FAAC)
VEJH......... Jharsuguda [*India*] [*ICAO location identifier*] (ICLI)
vejledn ...... Vejledning [*Introduction*] [*Publishing Danish/Norwegian*]
VEJP .... Jeypore [*India*] [*ICAO location identifier*] (ICLI)
VEJS......... Jamshedpur [*India*] [*ICAO location identifier*] (ICLI)
VEJT .... Jorhat [*India*] [*ICAO location identifier*] (ICLI)
VEK .... All-Union Power Engineering Committee (RU)
VEK .... Veterana Esperantista Klubo [*Esperantist Club of Veterans - ECV*] (EAIO)
VEK .... Volkseigenes Kombinat [*State Combine*] (EG)
VEKA .... Viomikhaniki Etaireia Kapnon Agriniou [*Agrinion Tobacco Industry Company*] [*Greek*] (GC)
VEKH .... Katihar [*India*] [*ICAO location identifier*] (ICLI)
VEKJ .... Keonjhar [*India*] [*ICAO location identifier*] (ICLI)
VEKM .... Kamalpur [*India*] [*ICAO location identifier*] (ICLI)
VEKN .... Konark [*India*] [*ICAO location identifier*] (ICLI)
VEKR .... Kailashahar [*India*] [*ICAO location identifier*] (ICLI)
VEKS .... Vectorcardioscope (RU)
VEKSA ...... Vereniging van Elektriese Kabelvervaardigers van Suid-Afrika [*South Africa*] (AA)
VEKU .... Silchar/Kumbhirgram [*India*] [*ICAO location identifier*] (ICLI)
VEKW .... Khowai [*India*] [*ICAO location identifier*] (ICLI)
Vel............. Great [*Toponymy*] (RU)
vel.............. Velin [*Vellum*] [*Publishing*] [*French*]
vel.............. Velina [*Vellum Paper*] [*Publishing*] [*Italian*]
VELAZ ...... Velkochov Laboratornich Zvirat [*Wholesale Breeding of Laboratory Animals*] (CZ)
velbev........ Velbevaret [*Well-Preserved*] [*Danish/Norwegian*]
VELDLS...... All-Union Experimental Laboratory of Dispersion Drugs (RU)
VELDM...... Veldmaarskalk [*Field-Marshal*] [*Afrikaans*]
velh............ Velholdt [*Well-Preserved*] [*Danish/Norwegian*]
velin........... Velinpapir [*Vellum Paper*] [*Publishing Danish/Norwegian*]
VELK .... Vereinigte Evangelisch-Lutherische Kirche [*United Evangelical-Lutheran Church*] [*German*] (EG)
VELKA ...... Vereinigte Evangelisch-Lutherische Kirche in Australien [*United Evangelical-Lutheran Church of Australia*] (ADA)
VELKD...... Vereinigte Evangelisch-Lutherische Kirche Deutschlands [*United Evangelical-Lutheran Church of Germany*] [*Hanover, West Germany*] (WEN)
VELKDDR ... Vereinigte Evangelisch-Lutherische Kirche in der Deutschen Demokratischen Republik [*United Evangelical-Lutheran Church of the German Democratic Republic*] (EY)
VELKSWA ... Vereinigung Evangelisch-Lutherischer Kirchen Suedwestafrika [*Associated Evangelical-Lutheran Church of South-West Africa*] [*Namibia*] (AF)
Vel MSD.... Velitelstvi Motostrelecke Divize [*Motorized Rifle Division Headquarters*] (CZ)
VELO-MOTO zavod ... Bicycle and Motorcycle Plant (BU)
velp............ Velinpapier [*Vellum Paper*] [*Publishing*] [*German*]
VELR........ Lilabari/North Lakhimpur [*India*] [*ICAO location identifier*] (ICLI)
Vel SR....... Velitelstvi Strelecke Roty [*Rifle Company Headquarters*] (CZ)
Vel TPR..... Velitelstvi Tankoveho Praperu [*Tank Headquarters Battalion*] (CZ)
VEM .... Elektromaschinenbau (VVB) [*Electrical-Machine Construction (VVB)*] (EG)
VEM .... Vereinigte Evangelische Mission [*United Evangelical Mission*] [*German*]

VEm .... Vostra Eminenza [*Your Eminence*] [*Italian*]
VEm .... Votre Eminence [*Your Eminence*] [*French*]
V Ema .... Vossa Eminencia [*Your Eminence*] [*Portuguese*]
VEMB .... Victorian Egg Marketing Board [*Australia*]
VEM-Betrieb ... Volkseigener Elektromaschinenbau Betrieb [*State Electrical Machine Building Enterprise*] [*German*]   (EG)
VEMH....... Malda [*India*] [*ICAO location identifier*]   (ICLI)
VEMN ...... Mohanbari [*India*] [*ICAO location identifier*]   (ICLI)
VEMSSA... Value Engineering and Management Society of South Africa (AA)
VEMZ .... Mazuffarpur [*India*] [*ICAO location identifier*]   (ICLI)
ven.............. Venajaa [*or Venajaksi*] [*Finland*]
ven .... Venalainen [*Finland*]
Ven............. Vendome [*Record label*] [*France*]
Ven............. Venerable   (EECI)
VEN .... Venetian
VEN .... Venezuela [*ANSI three-letter standard code*]   (CNC)
VENALUM ... Venezolana de Aluminios, CA [*Aluminum Company of Venezuela*]   (LA)
V en C .... Valor en Cuenta [*Value Accounted For*] [*Spanish*] [*Business term*]
vencimto..... Vencimiento [*Victory, Conquest*] [*Spanish*]
vend........... Vendredi [*Friday*] [*French*]
Vendem...... Vendemiaire   (FLAF)
VENEPAL ... CA Venezolana de Pulpa y Papel [*Venezuela*]   (LAA)
VENFERCA ... Venezolana de Fertilizantes, CA [*Fertilizer Company of Venezuela*]   (LA)
veng........... Hungarian   (RU)
VENG .... Vereinigung zur Erforschung der Neueren Geschichte [*Association for Research in Modern History*] [*Germany*]   (EAIO)
VENP .... Nawapara [*India*] [*ICAO location identifier*]   (ICLI)
VenPK....... Venizelikon Phileleftheron Komma [*Venizelist Liberal Party*] [*Greek*] [*Political party*]   (PPE)
Vent............ Ventose   (FLAF)
VENUS..... Viseur Ecartometrique de Nuit Stabilise
VEO .... All-Union Electrotechnical Association   (RU)
VEO .... All-Union Entomological Society   (RU)
VEO .... All-Union Export Association   (RU)
VEO .... Free Economics Society   (RU)
VEO .... Supreme Economic Council   (RU)
VEO .... Vasiliki Ethniki Organosi [*Royalist National Organization*] [*Greek*]   (GC)
VEO .... Village Executive Officer
VEO .... Vyzantini Ethniki Organosis [*Byzantine National Organization*] [*Greek*]   (GC)
VEOA .... Victorian Education Officers Association [*Australia*]
VEP........... Military Evacuation Station   (RU)
VEP........... Vasiliki Ethniki Parataxis [*National Faction of Royalists*] [*Greek*]   (GC)
VEP........... Verbrauchsendpreis [*Retail Sales Price*] [*German*] [*Business term*]   (EG)
VEPB........ Port Blair [*India*] [*ICAO location identifier*]   (ICLI)
VEPG........ Pasighat [*India*] [*ICAO location identifier*]   (ICLI)
VEPH........ Panagarh [*India*] [*ICAO location identifier*]   (ICLI)
VEPN........ Phulbani [*India*] [*ICAO location identifier*]   (ICLI)
VEPP........ Padampur [*India*] [*ICAO location identifier*]   (ICLI)
VEPT........ Patna [*India*] [*ICAO location identifier*]   (ICLI)
VEPUAZO ... Vector Electrical Anti-Aircraft Fire Director   (RU)
VER .... Vanguardia Estudiantil Revolucionaria [*Revolutionary Student Vanguard*] [*Peru*]   (LA)
VER .... Veracruz [*Mexico*] [*Airport symbol*]   (OAG)
ver .... Verbessert [*Improved, Revised*] [*German*]
VER .... Verein [*Association*] [*German*]
ver .... Vereinigt [*United*] [*German*]
Ver .... Vereniging [*Association*] [*Dutch*]   (ILCA)
Ver .... Verger [*Orchard*] [*Military map abbreviation World War I*] [*French*]   (MTD)
Ver .... Verici [*Sending, Broadcasting*]   (TU)
Ver .... Verordening [*Benelux*]   (BAS)
Ver .... Versamento [*Payment*] [*Italian*] [*Business term*]
VERA .... Ranuna [*India*] [*ICAO location identifier*]   (ICLI)
verachtl ..... Veraechtlich [*Contemptuous*] [*German*]
Veraender .. Veraenderung [*Change*] [*German*]   (GCA)
Verallgemeiner ... Verallgemeinerung [*Generalization*] [*German*]   (GCA)
verand .... Veraendert [*Revised*] [*Publishing*] [*German*]
Verarbeit.... Verarbeitung [*Treatment*] [*German*]   (GCA)
Verb .... Verband [*Bond*] [*German*]
verb .... Verbessert [*Improved, Revised*] [*German*]
Verb .... Verbesserung [*Correction*] [*German*]   (GCA)
verb .... Verbeterd [*Corrected*] [*Publishing*] [*Netherlands*]
VERB........ Verbinding [*Compound*] [*Afrikaans*]
Verb .... Verbindung [*Compound*] [*German*]
VERB........ Verbuiging [*Declension*] [*Afrikaans*]
Verbb .... Verbindungen [*Compounds*] [*German*]
Verbdg .... Verbindung [*Compound*] [*German*]   (GCA)

Verbess ...... Verbesserung [*Correction*] [*German*]   (GCA)
Verbesser ... Verbesserung [*Correction*] [*German*]   (GCA)
verbl .... Verblichen [*Faded*] [*German*]
Verbl .... Verodeningenblad voor het Bezette Nederlandse Gebied [*Netherlands*]   (BAS)
Verbr .... Arrest van het Hof van Verbreking [*Benelux*]   (BAS)
Verbr .... Verbrauch [*Consumption*] [*German*]   (GCA)
verbr .... Verbraucht [*Consumed*] [*German*]
Verbreit...... Verbreitung [*Propagation*] [*German*]   (GCA)
Verbrenn.... Verbrennung [*Combustion*] [*German*]   (GCA)
Verbr R ..... Verbrennungsraum [*Combustion Chamber*] [*German*]   (GCA)
VERC........ Ranchi [*India*] [*ICAO location identifier*]   (ICLI)
VERC........ Village Education Resource Center [*Bangladesh*]
verd .... Verdeckt [*Masked*] [*German*]   (GCA)
verd .... Verdeutscht [*Translated into German*] [*German*]
verd .... Verduennt [*Dilute, Diluted*] [*German*]
Verd .... Verduennung [*Dilution*] [*German*]
Verdampf.... Verdampfung [*Evaporation*] [*German*]   (GCA)
VERDI....... Vittorio Emmanuele Re d'Italia [*Slogan of Italian patriots during Risorgimento; now the name of a monarchist students' association*]
Verdraeng .. Verdraengung [*Displacement*] [*German*]   (GCA)
Verduenn.... Verduennung [*Dilution*] [*German*]   (GCA)
Veredel....... Veredelung [*Refining*] [*German*]   (GCA)
Vereinig ..... Vereinigung [*Union*] [*German*]   (GCA)
vereinz........ Vereinzelt [*Here and There*] [*German*]
Verester....... Veresterung [*Esterification*] [*German*]   (GCA)
Verf .... Verfahren [*Process*] [*German*]
Verf .... Verfasser [*Author*] [*German*]   (GPO)
Verfaelsch ... Verfaelschung [*Falsification*] [*German*]   (GCA)
Verfaerb..... Verfaerbung [*Discoloration*] [*German*]   (GCA)
Verfahr....... Verfahren [*Process*] [*German*]
Verfestig .... Verfestigung [*Solidification*] [*German*]   (GCA)
Verfett....... Verfettung [*Fatty Degeneration*] [*German*]   (GCA)
Verff .... Verfahren [*Methods*] [*German*]
VerfGH...... Verfassungsgerichtshof [*Provincial Constitutional Court*] [*German*]   (DLA)
Verfluessig ... Verfluessigung [*Liquefaction*] [*German*]   (GCA)
Verfolg .... Verfolgung [*Follow-Up*] [*German*]   (GCA)
Verform...... Verformung [*Deformation*] [*German*]   (GCA)
Verfuegbark ... Verfuegbarkeit [*Availability*] [*German*]   (GCA)
VERG .... Rayaguda [*India*] [*ICAO location identifier*]   (ICLI)
verg............ Vergadering [*Meeting*] [*Afrikaans*]
Verg........... Vergaser [*Carburetor*] [*German*]   (GCA)
Verg........... Vergelijk [*Benelux*]   (BAS)
Verg........... Vergiftung [*Poisoning*] [*German*]   (GCA)
verg........... Vergilbt [*Yellowed, Faded*] [*German*]
verg............ Vergoldet [*Gilt*] [*German*]
verg............ Vergriffen [*Suppressed*] [*German*]
verg............ Verguld [*Gilt*] [*Netherlands*]
Vergaell...... Vergaellung [*Denaturation*] [*German*]   (GCA)
Vergaer ...... Vergaerung [*Fermentation*] [*German*]   (GCA)
Vergangenh ... Vergangenheit [*Past*] [*German*]   (GCA)
Vergift........ Vergiftung [*Poisoning*] [*German*]   (GCA)
Vergl .... Vergleich [*Compare, Confer, See, Refer*] [*German*]
VERGL...... Vergleische [*Compare*] [*German*]   (ROG)
vergr .... Vergriffen [*Out-of-Print*] [*Publishing*] [*German*]
vergr .... Vergroessert [*Enlarged, Magnified*] [*German*]
Vergr .... Vergroesserung [*Magnification*] [*German*]
VERGTR... Vergrotende Trap [*Comparative Degree*] [*Afrikaans*]
Verh .... Verhaeltnis [*Proportion*] [*German*]
Verh .... Verhalten [*Behavior*] [*German*]
Verh .... Verhandlungen [*Proceedings*] [*German*]
verh .... Verheiratet [*Married*] [*German*]
Verhaeltn... Verhaeltnis [*Condition*] [*German*]   (GCA)
Verhandl.... Verhandlung [*Transaction*] [*German*]   (GCA)
Verhinder... Verhinderung [*Inhibition*] [*German*]   (GCA)
Verhuett..... Verhuettung [*Smelting*] [*German*]   (GCA)
verif........... Verification [*Verification*] [*French*]
VERK........ Rourkela [*India*] [*ICAO location identifier*]   (ICLI)
verk .... Verkauft [*Sold*] [*German*]
verk .... Verkuerzt [*Abbreviated*] [*German*]
verkaeufl.... Verkaeuflich [*Marketable*] [*German*]   (GCA)
verkh .... Upper   (RU)
verkl .... Verkleinert [*Reduced*] [*German*]
verkl .... Verkleurd [*Faded*] [*Netherlands*]
verklar........ Verklarend [*Explanatory*] [*Netherlands*]
verklw........ Verkleinwoord [*Diminutive*] [*Afrikaans*]
Verkok ...... Verkokung [*Carbonization*] [*German*]   (GCA)
VERL........ Raxaul [*India*] [*ICAO location identifier*]   (ICLI)
Verl .... Verladung [*Entraining*] [*German*]   (GCA)
Verl .... Verlaengert [*Lengthened*] [*German*]
Verl .... Verlaengerung [*Prolongation*] [*German*]   (GCA)
Verl .... Verlag [*Publication, Publishing House*] [*German*]
verl .... Verlede [*Past*] [*Afrikaans*]
Verl .... Verleger [*Publisher*] [*German*]   (GPO)

Verl .... Verlust [*Loss*] [*German*]
Verl Bhf ..... Verladebahnhof [*Loading Station*] [*German*]   (GCA)
verl deelw ... Verlede Deelwoord [*Past Participle*] [*Afrikaans*]
VERLOSK ... Verloskunde [*Obstetrics*] [*Afrikaans*]
verlsk .... Verloskunde [*Obstetrics*] [*Afrikaans*]
Verm .... Vermaehlt [*Married*] [*German*]
verm .... Vermeerderd [*Enlarged*] [*Publishing*] [*Netherlands*]
verm .... Vermehrt [*Augmented*] [*German*]
Verm .... Vermessung [*Survey*] [*German*]
verm .... Vermindert [*Diminished*] [*German*]   (GCA)
Verma .... Vermessungsamt [*Surveying Office*] [*German*]   (EG)
Vermahl ..... Vermahlung [*Grinding*] [*German*]   (GCA)
Vermehr..... Vermehrung [*Increase*] [*German*]   (GCA)
Vermeid ..... Vermeidung [*Circumvention*] [*German*]   (GCA)
Verminder ... Verminderung [*Decrease*] [*German*]   (GCA)
Verm-Ing.... Vermessungs-Ingenieur [*Survey Engineer*] [*German*]
Vermisch.... Vermischung [*Mixture*] [*German*]   (GCA)
VERN .... Rangeilunda [*India*] [*ICAO location identifier*]   (ICLI)
Vern .... Vernietigende [*Benelux*]   (BAS)
Vernof .... Voorwaarden van de Vereniging van Nederlandse
              Oliefabrikanten [*Netherlands*]   (BAS)
veroff .... Veroeffentlicht [*Published*] [*German*]
Veroff .... Veroeffentlichung [*Publication*] [*German*]
Verp .... Verpackung [*Packing*] [*German*]   (GCA)
Verpack...... Verpackung [*Packing*] [*German*]   (GCA)
VERRETAT ... Verrerie d'Etat [*State Glass Factory*] [*Cambodia*]   (CL)
Verrgl .... Verriegelung [*Barricade*] [*German*]   (GCA)
Verringer.... Verringerung [*Decrease*] [*German*]   (GCA)
Vers .... Versammlung [*Meeting*] [*German*]
vers........... Versehen [*Furnished*] [*German*]
VERS .... Versicherung [*Insurance*] [*German*] [*Business term*]
vers........... Versiculo [*Verse*] [*Spanish*]
vers........... Versierd [*Decorated*] [*Netherlands*]
Vers........... Versuch [*Assay, Test*] [*German*]
Vers Anst ... Versuchsanstalt [*Experimental Station*] [*German*]   (GCA)
versch........ Verscheen [*Issued*] [*Publishing*] [*Netherlands*]
versch........ Verscheiden [*Several*] [*Netherlands*]
Versch........ Verschiebung [*Displacement*] [*German*]   (GCA)
Versch........ Verschieden [*Various*] [*German*]
Versch........ Verschiedenes [*Miscellaneous*] [*German*]   (GCA)
verschd....... Verschieden [*Different*] [*German*]   (GCA)
Verscheib... Verschiebung [*Displacement*] [*German*]   (GCA)
verschied.... Verschieden [*Different*] [*German*]   (GCA)
Verschlechter ... Verschlechterung [*Deterioration*] [*German*]   (GCA)
verschm....... Verschmutzt [*Soiled*] [*German*]
Verschmutz ... Verschmutzung [*Pollution*] [*German*]   (GCA)
Verschw ..... Verschwinden [*Disappearance*] [*German*]   (GCA)
Versetz....... Versetzung [*Compounding*] [*German*]   (GCA)
Versich....... Versicherung [*Insurance*] [*German*]   (GCA)
VERSK ...... Verskillend [*Different*] [*Afrikaans*]
versk.......... Verskuldig [*Due*] [*Afrikaans*] [*Business term*]
VERSO...... Reverso [*Left-Hand Page of Open Book*]   (ROG)
verso......... Versiculo [*Verse*] [*Spanish*]
Versorg ...... Versorgung [*Supply*] [*German*]   (GCA)
Verss .... Versuche [*Experiments, Tests*] [*German*]
VerSt......... Vereinigten Staaten [*United States*] [*German*]
VerSt......... Verladestelle [*Entraining Point, Loading Point, Point of
              Embarkation, Entrucking Point*]   (EG)
verst.......... Verstaendlich [*Comprehensible*] [*German*]
Verst.......... Verstaerker [*Amplifier*] [*German*]   (GCA)
Verst.......... Verstorben [*Dead*] [*German*]
verstaendl... Verstaendlich [*Intelligible*] [*German*]   (GCA)
Verstaendlichk ... Verstaendlichkeit [*Intelligibility*] [*German*]   (GCA)
Verstaerk ... Verstaerkung [*Reinforcement*] [*German*]   (GCA)
Verstkg ...... Verstaerkung [*Support*] [*German*]
Versuchsst ... Versuchsstation [*Experimental Station*] [*German*]   (GCA)
vert .... Vertaa [*Compare, Confer*] [*Finland*]   (GPO)
VERT......... Vertaal [*Translate*] [*Afrikaans*]
vert .... Vertaling [*Translation*] [*Netherlands*]
Vert .... Verteiler [*Distributor*] [*German*]   (GCA)
vert .... Vertrek [*Departure*] [*Afrikaans*]
Verteil .... Verteilung [*Dispersion*] [*German*]   (GCA)
VERTESZ ... Villamos Eromu Tervezo es Szerelo Vallalat [*Planning and
              Engineering Enterprise of Electric Power Plants*]   (HU)
Vertilg .... Vertilgung [*Destruction*] [*German*]   (GCA)
Vertr .... Vertrag [*Contract*] [*German*]   (GCA)
Vertr.......... Vertreter [*Representative*] [*German*]   (GCA)
Vertraeglichk ... Vertraeglichkeit [*Compatability*] [*German*]   (GCA)
VERTRIKO ... Netherlands Knitting Industries Association
VERU .... Rupsi [*India*] [*ICAO location identifier*]   (ICLI)
Verunreinig ... Verunreinigung [*Pollution*] [*German*]   (GCA)
Verv........... Vervielfaeltigung [*Reproduction*] [*German*]   (GCA)
verv........... Vervoeging [*Conjugation*] [*Afrikaans*]
Ver Vgl StR B Nl ... Vereniging voor de Vergelijkende Studie van het Recht
              van Belgie en Nederland [*Benelux*]   (BAS)
vervielf .... Vervielfaeltigt [*Multigraphed*] [*Publishing*] [*German*]

vervollst...... Vervollstaendigt [*Completed*] [*German*]
Verw.......... Verwalter [*Administrator*] [*German*]   (GCA)
Verw.......... Verwaltung [*Administration*] [*German*]
verw.......... Verwandt [*Related*] [*German*]
verw.......... Verweerder [*Defendant*] [*Afrikaans*]
Verw.......... Verwendung [*Use, Application*] [*German*]   (GCA)
Verw.......... Verwitwet [*Widowed*] [*German*]
Verw.......... Wet tot Regeling en Beperking der Uitoefening van het Recht van
              Vereeniging en Vergadering [*Benelux*]   (BAS)
Verwechsl .. Verwechslung [*Confusion*] [*German*]   (GCA)
Verwend..... Verwendung [*Use, Application*] [*German*]   (GCA)
Verwert ...... Verwertung [*Work-Up*] [*German*]   (GCA)
VerwG........ Verwaltungsgericht [*Administrative Court or Tribunal*] [*German*]   (ILCA)
VerwGH..... Verwaltungsgerichtshof [*District Administrative Court of Appeal*]
              [*German*]   (DLA)
Ver Wijsbdes Rechts ... Vereniging voor Wijsbegeerte des Rechts [*Benelux*]   (BAS)
Verwitter.... Verwitterung [*Decay*] [*German*]   (GCA)
verz............ Verzameld [*Compiled*] [*Publishing*] [*Netherlands*]
Verz........... Verzeichnis [*Index*] [*German*]
verz............ Verziert [*Decorated*] [*German*]
Verz........... Verzoegerung [*Delay*] [*German*]   (GCA)
Verz Arch... Verzekerings-Archief [*Benelux*]   (BAS)
Verzier .... Verzierung [*Dressing*] [*German*]   (GCA)
Verzoeger .. Verzoegerung [*Delay*] [*German*]   (GCA)
VES .... Vasiliki Enosi Salaminas [*Royalist Union of Salamis*]   (GC)
VES........... Versuchs- und Entwicklungsstellen der DR [*GDR Railroad
              Experimental and Development Offices*]   (EG)
VES........... Village Equipment Supplies [*Nonprofit company established by
              SPATF*] [*Papua New Guinea*]
Ves .... Vrakhonisides [*Rocky Islets*] [*Greek*]   (NAU)
ves .... Weight, Gravimetric   (RU)
VES........... Wind-Driven Electric Power Plant   (RU)
VESA .... Voluntary Euthanasia Society of Australia
VESCAC ... Victorian Education Service Conciliation and Arbitration
              Commission [*Australia*]
ves ch.......... Part by Weight   (RU)
VESchG..... Volkseigentumschutzgesetz [*Law for the Protection of State
              Property*] [*German*]   (EG)
VESh.......... Military Electrotechnical School   (RU)
veshch .... Substance, Material, Matter   (RU)
vesi .... Vesirakennus [*Hydraulic Engineering*] [*Finland*]
VESKA ...... Vereinigung Schweizerischer Krankenhaeuser [*Swiss Hospital
              Association*]   (EAIO)
VESO........ All-Union Electrical Communications Association   (RU)
VEST .... Departmental Standard, Institutional Standard   (RU)
VESTACO ... Vestia Ready Made Garments Company [*Egypt*]
vestn.......... Herald   (RU)
VestnikGSZ ... Vestnik Glasilo Slovenskih Zeleznicarjev [*Review Organ of the
              Slovenian Railroad Workers*]   (YU)
VET .... All-Union Electrotechnical Trust   (RU)
vet.............. Siding [*Railroads*]   (RU)
Vet.............. Veterinaer [*Veterinary Surgeon*] [*German*]
vet.............. Veterinaire [*French*]   (TPFD)
vet.............. Veterinaria [*Veterinary Science*] [*Portuguese*]
vet.............. Veterinario [*Veterinary Surgeon*] [*Portuguese*]
vet.............. Veterinary   (BU)
vet.............. Veterinary, Veterinary Science   (RU)
Vet.............. Veteriner [*Veterinary*]   (TU)
VET .... Victorian Equity Trust [*Australia*]
VETAB ...... Vocational Education and Training Accreditation Board [*New
              South Wales, Australia*]
VETB......... Turk Veteriner Hekimleri Birligi [*Turkish Union of Doctors of
              Veterinary Medicine*] [*VHB*] [*See also*]   (TU)
VETDOK... Dokumentationsstelle fuer Veterinaermedizin
veter .... Veterinary   (RU)
veter .... Veterinary, Veterinary Medicine   (BU)
Veter-medfak ... School of Veterinary Medicine   (BU)
Veter sl....... Veterinarska Sluzba [*Veterinary Service*]   (CZ)
VETh.......... Vasiliki Ethniki Enosis Thessalonikis [*National Royalist Union of
              Salonica*] [*VEETh*] [*See also*]   (GC)
VetIProizvSerVaks ... Veterinary Institute for the Production of Serums and
              Vaccines   (BU)
VETJ.......... Tezu [*India*] [*ICAO location identifier*]   (ICLI)
VETK......... Tarakeshwar [*India*] [*ICAO location identifier*]   (ICLI)
Vetma........ Pusat Veterinaria Farma [*Veterinary Biological Center*]
              [*Indonesian*]   (ARC)
Vetpromsnab ... Veterinary Supplies Enterprise   (BU)
vetr mln ...... Windmill [*Topography*]   (RU)
VETROM ... Preduzece za Promet Veterinarskim Materijalom [*Trade
              Establishment in Veterinary Supplies*]   (YU)
VETS .... Height of Equivalent Theoretical Separation Phase   (RU)
VETs......... Hydroelectric Power Plant   (BU)
VETS .... Tusra [*India*] [*ICAO location identifier*]   (ICLI)

VETSAK ... Vrystaat en Transvaalse Sentrale Aankoopskooperasie Beperk [*South Africa*] (AA)
VETT .... Height Equivalent to a Theoretical Plate (RU)
VETTEX ... Vetements et Textiles
vetupr .... Veterinary Administration (RU)
VETZ .... Vyaz'ma Electrical Equipment Plant (RU)
VEU .... Secondary Electron Multiplier (RU)
VEUK .... Utkela [*India*] [*ICAO location identifier*] (ICLI)
VEV .... Barakoma [*Solomon Islands*] [*Airport symbol*] (OAG)
VEV .... Vetomagtermelteto es Ertekesito Vallalat [*Seed Producer and Sales Enterprise*] (HU)
VEV .... Vlaams Ekonomisch Verbond [*Flemish Economic Association*] [*Belgium*] (WEN)
VEV .... Volkseigener Verlag [*State-Owned Publishing House*] [*German*] (EG)
VEVA .... Vereingung der Europaischen Verbande des Automatenwirtschaft [*Federation of European Coin-Machine Associations*] (EAIO)
VEVZ .... Vishakhapatnam [*India*] [*ICAO location identifier*] (ICLI)
VEW .... Vereinigte Edelstahlwerke [*State-held steel subsidiary company*] [*Austria*]
VEW .... Vereinigte Elektrizitatswerke Westfalen [*Germany*] (PDAA)
VEW .... Village Extension Worker [*In African farming system*]
VEW .... Volkseigene Werft [*State-Owned Shipyard*] [*German*] (EG)
VEW .... Volkseigene Wirtschaft [*State Sector of the Economy*] [*German*] (EG)
V Exa .... Vossa Excelencia [*Your Excellency*] [*Portuguese*]
VExa .... Vuestras Excelencias [*Your Excellencies*] [*Portuguese*]
VExc .... Votre Excellence [*Your Excellency*] [*French*]
V Excia ...... Vossa Excelencia [*Your Excellency*] [*Portuguese*]
VEXPORT ... Vojvodina Export-Import, Novi Sad (YU)
VEY .... Vestmannaeyjar [*Iceland*] [*Airport symbol*] (OAG)
VEZ .... Vertical Electric Logging (RU)
vez .... Vezenyel [*Conductor (Music)*] (HU)
vez .... Vezeto [*Leader*] (HU)
VEZ .... Voronezh Excavator Plant (RU)
VEZ .... Vystavba Energetickych Zavodu [*Construction of Electric Power Plants*] (CZ)
VEZ .... Vyvojovy Elektrokeramicky Zavod [*Electroceramic Development Plant*] (CZ)
vezerig .... Vezerigazgato [*Director General*] (HU)
VEZO .... Zero [*India*] [*ICAO location identifier*] (ICLI)
vezrad .... Vezetekes Radio [*Closed Circuit Transmission*] (HU)
vez radio ... Vezetekes Radio [*Closed Circuit Transmission*] (HU)
VF .... Air Force (RU)
VF .... Naval Flotilla (RU)
Vf .... Verfasser [*Author*] [*German*]
VF .... Verlag fuer die Frau [*Publishing House for the Woman*] [*German*] (EG)
VF .... Veterinarski Fakultet [*Faculty of Veterinary Medicine*] (YU)
VF .... VFW [*Vereinigte Flugtechnische Werke*]-Fokker [*Germany*] [*ICAO aircraft manufacturer identifier*] (ICAO)
VF .... Vigili di Fuoco [*Fire Brigade*] [*Italian*]
VF .... Visokofrekventni [*High-Frequency*] (YU)
Vf .... Vulkanfiber [*Vulcanized Fiber*] [*German*] (GCA)
VFA .... Vereinigung Freischaffender Architekten Deutschlands eV (SLS)
VFA .... Victoria Falls [*Zimbabwe*] [*Airport symbol*] (OAG)
VFA .... Village Forestry Association [*South Korea*]
VFASOON ... World Federation of United Nations Associations (RU)
VFAW .... Victorian Fellowship of Australian Writers [*Australia*]
VFCDC ...... Virginia Frank Child Development Center
VFCPC ...... Victorian Federation of Catholic Parents' Clubs [*Australia*]
VFD .... Military Photographer-Correspondent (BU)
VFDB .... Vereinigung zur Foerderung des Deutschen Brandschutzes eV (SLS)
VFDF .... Victorian Football Development Foundation [*Australia*]
VFDM .... World Federation of Democratic Youth [*WFDY*] (RU)
vfelv .... Vonalfelvigyazo [*Line Inspector (Railroad)*] (HU)
VFF .... Vernepliktige Flyveofficerers Forening [*Norway*]
VFF .... Victorian Farmers' Federation [*Australia*]
VFFFIW .... Venezuelan Federation of Fishermen and Fishing Industry Workers (EAIO)
VFFIA .... Victorian Farmers' Federation Industrial Association [*Australia*]
VFG .... Verband fuer Flussiggas eV
VFG .... Verein zur Foerderung der Forschung fuer die Graphischen Gewerbe und die Verwandten Wirtschaftszweige [*Austria*] (SLS)
VfG .... Verfuegung [*Disposition, Directive*] [*German*] (EG)
VFGA .... Victorian Farmers and Graziers Association [*Australia*]
VfGerH ..... Verfassungsgerichtshof [*Supreme Court*] [*German*]
VfGH .... Verfassungsgerichtshof [*Supreme Court*] [*German*]
VFI .... Higher Institute of Finance (BU)
VfI .... Verwaltung fuer Industriebedarf [*Administration for Industrial Demand*] [*German*] (EG)
VFIG .... Voie Ferree d'Interet General [*French*] (FLAF)

VFIL .... Voi Ferree d'Interet Local [*French*] (FLAF)
VFITC ...... Victorian Fishing Industry Training Committee [*Australia*]
VFK .... Verband zur Foerderung Aerztlicher Kooperationsformeln eV (SLS)
VFK/DDR ... Vereinigung fuer Kristallographie in der Gesellschaft fuer Geologische Wissenschaften der Deutschen Demokratischen Republik (SLS)
VFL .... Victorian Football League [*Receives television coverage in the US through the Entertainment and Sports Programming Network*] [*Australia*]
VFM .... All-Chinese Youth Federation (RU)
Vfm .... Vorratsfestmeter [*Storage Cubic Meter*] (EG)
VFMCACS ... Vie Feminine Mouvement Chretien d'Action Culturelle et Sociale [*Belgium*] (EAIO)
VFME .... Vereniging FME [*Netherlands*] (EAIO)
VFMG .... Vereinigung der Freunde der Mineralogie und Geologie eV (SLS)
VFNP .... Victorian Food and Nutrition Program [*Australia*]
VFNR .... World Federation of Scientific Workers [*WFSW*] (RU)
VFO .... Military Finance Section (RU)
VFO .... Verband der Forstakademiker Osterreichs [*Austrian Union of Foresters*] (EAIO)
V Fonct P ... La Voix de la Fonction Publique [*French*] (BAS)
VFP .... All-Chinese Federation of Trade Unions (RU)
VFP .... Problems of Philosophy and Psychology (RU)
VFP .... Vereenigde Feministische Partij [*Belgium*] [*Political party*] (EY)
VFP .... Vereinigung fuer Finanzpolitik [*Zurich, Switzerland*] (SLS)
VFP .... World Federation of Trade Unions [*WFTU*] (RU)
VFPS .... Postal Courier Communications Center (BU)
VFS .... Veterinary Field Services [*Australia*]
VFS .... Victorian Flying School [*Australia*]
VFSB .... Verein der Freunde Schloss Blutenburg [*Association of Friends of Schloss Blutenburg-AFSB*] [*Germany*] (EAIO)
VFsDx .... Verordnung fuer den Fernschreib-und Datexdienst [*German*] (ADPT)
VFSh .... Adjustable-Pitch Propeller (RU)
VFSI .... Higher Institute of Finance and Economics (BU)
VFSIG ...... Voie Ferree Secondaires d'Interet General [*French*] (FLAF)
VFSKh ...... World's Student Christian Federation [*WSCF*] (RU)
VFST .... Victorian Foundation for Survivors of Torture [*Australia*]
VF-Stelle .... Verrechnungsstelle fuer Forderungen [*Clearing House for Claims*] [*German*] (EG)
VFT .... Very Fast Train [*Proposed*] [*Australia*]
VFTB .... General Federation of Labor of Belgium (RU)
VFTTA ...... Visa for Travel to Australia (ADA)
VFTU .... Vietnam Federation of Trade Unions
VF-Verfahren ... Verrechnungsverfahren fuer Forderungen [*Debiting Procedure for Claims*] [*German*] (EG)
VFVV .... World Veterans Federation (RU)
VFW .... Vereinigte Flugtechnische Werke [*United Aeronautical Works*] [*German*] (EG)
VfW .... Vereinigung fuer Walsertum [*Brig, Switzerland*] (SLS)
VFW-Fokker ... Vereinigte Flugtechnische Werke-Fokker [*Fokker United Aeronautical Works*] (WEN)
VFWL .... Verein zur Foederung der Wasser- und Lufthygiene [*Zurich, Switzerland*] (SLS)
VFZ .... Upper Front (RU)
vfzo .... Vonalfelvigyazo [*Line Supervisor*] (HU)
VfzV .... Verordnung ueber die Freiwillige und Zusaetzliche Versicherung [*Regulation Concerning Voluntary and Supplementary Insurance*] [*German*] (EG)
VG .... Auxiliary Generator (RU)
VG .... British Virgin Islands [*ANSI two-letter standard code*] (CNC)
VG .... Generator Switch (RU)
VG .... Horizontal Dipole (RU)
VG .... Military Hospital (RU)
VG .... Military Personnel Settlement (RU)
VG .... Supreme Command (RU)
Vg .... Vag [*or Vagen*] [*Bay, Cove*] [*Norway*] (NAU)
vg .... Vagon [*Freight Car, Carload*] (CZ)
VG .... Varga Aircraft Corp. [*ICAO aircraft manufacturer identifier*] (ICAO)
VG .... Vatrena Grupa [*Fire Group*] [*Military*] (YU)
vg .... Verbigracia [*For Example*] [*Spanish*]
VG .... Vereniging vir Geografie [*Society for Geography*] [*South Africa*] (EAIO)
VG .... Versuchsgrubengesellschaft [*Industrial company*] [*Germany*] (EAS)
VG .... Vertragsgesetz [*Contract Law*] (EG)
VG .... Verwaltungsgesellschaft fuer Industrielle Unternehmungen Friedrich Flick GmbH [*Frederick Flick Management Association for Industrial Enterprises*]
vg .... Village [*Village*] [*French*]
vg .... Virgen [*Virgin*] [*Spanish*]
VG .... Vossa Graca [*Your Grace*] [*Portuguese*]
VG .... Vossa Grandeza [*Your Greatness*] [*Portuguese*]

VG	Votre Grace [*Your Grace*] [*French*]
VG	Votre Grandesse [*Your Highness*] [*French*]
VG	Votre Grandeur [*Your Highness*] [*French*]
VGA	Vegetable Growers' Association [*Australia*]
VGA	Vennotschap bij wijze van Geldschieting op Aandelen [*Benelux*] (BAS)
VGA	Victorian Golf Association [*Australia*]
VGA	Victorian Graziers' Association [*Australia*]
VGA	Victorian Green Alliance [*Political party*] [*Australia*]
VGA	Victorian Gymnastic Association [*Australia*]
VGA	Vijayawada [*India*] [*Airport symbol*] (OAG)
VGAS	High-Altitude Geophysical Automatic Station (RU)
VGAU	Victorian Government Advertising Unit [*Australia*]
VGB	All-Union Geological Library (RU)
VGB	British Virgin Islands [*ANSI three-letter standard code*] (CNC)
VGB	Technische Vereinigung der Grosskraftwerksbetreiber eV (SLS)
VGB	Vereinigung der Grosskraftwerksbetreiber [*Technical Association of Large Power Station Operators*] [*Germany*] (WED)
VGBIL	All-Union State Library of Foreign Literature (RU)
VGBO	All-Union Hydrobiological Society (RU)
VGC	Victorian Grants Commission [*Australia*]
VGCAC	Victorian Government China Advisory Committee [*Australia*]
VGCB	Cox's Bazar [*Bangladesh*] [*ICAO location identifier*] (ICLI)
VGCC	Victorian Government Computing Centre [*Australia*]
VGCM	Comilla [*Bangladesh*] [*ICAO location identifier*] (ICLI)
VGCT	Verein fuer Gerberei-Chemie und -Technik eV (SLS)
VGD	Band Horizontal Dipole (RU)
VGD	D'yakonov Rifle Grenade (RU)
VGD	Intraocular Pressure (RU)
VGD	Valuer-General's Department [*Australia*]
VGE	Air Service Vosges [*France*] [*ICAO designator*] (FAAC)
VGE	Valery Giscard d'Estaing [*Former French President*]
VGE	Vereinigte Gesundheitseinrichtungen [*United Public Health Facilities*] [*German*] (EG)
vge	Village [*Village*] [*French*]
VGE	Vollbeschaeftigteneinheit [*Full Employment Unit*] (EG)
VGEG	Chittagong [*Bangladesh*] [*ICAO location identifier*] (ICLI)
VGF	All-Union Geological Fund (RU)
VGF	Vieja Guardia de Franco [*Old Guard of Franco*] [*Spanish*] (WER)
VGFR	Dhaka [*Bangladesh*] [*ICAO location identifier*] (ICLI)
VGG	Voithos Genikos Grammatevs [*Deputy Secretary General*] (GC)
VGH	Verlagsgruppe Georg von Holtzbrinck [*Commercial firm*] [*Germany*]
VGHQ	Dhaka [*Bangladesh*] [*ICAO location identifier*] (ICLI)
VGI	Vojni Geografski Institut [*Institute of Military Geography*] (YU)
VGIK	High State Quality Inspection of Industrial Production (RU)
VGIK	Vsesoyuzni Gosudarstvenni Institut Kinematografii [*All-Union State Institute of Cinematography*] (RU)
VGIS	Ishurdi [*Bangladesh*] [*ICAO location identifier*] (ICLI)
VGITIS	All-Union State Institute of Remote Control and Communications (RU)
VGJR	Jessore [*Bangladesh*] [*ICAO location identifier*] (ICLI)
VGK	Supreme Command (RU)
VGKO	All-Russian Concert Tour Association (RU)
VGL	Schweizerische Vereinigung fuer Gewaesserschutz und Lufthygiene [*Zurich, Switzerland*] (SLS)
vgl	Vergelijk [*Compare*] [*Netherlands*] (GPO)
vgl	Vergelyk [*Compare*] [*Afrikaans*]
VGL	Vergleich [*Compare, Confer, See, Refer*] [*German*]
vgl a	Vergleiche Auch [*See Also*] [*German*]
VGLK	State Higher Courses in Literature (RU)
vglk	Supreme Commander in Chief (BU)
VGLM	Lalmonirhat [*Bangladesh*] [*ICAO location identifier*] (ICLI)
VGLTSA	Vereniging van Geneeskundige Laboratorium Tegnoloe van Suid-Afrika [*South Africa*] (EAIO)
VGM	Vakiflar Genel Mudurlugu [*Director General of Religious Foundations*] [*Under Office of Premier*] (TU)
VGMI	Voronezh State Medical Institute (RU)
VGMPU	Victorian Government Major Projects Unit [*Australia*]
VGN	Vennootschap onder Gemeenschappelijke Naam [*Benelux*] (BAS)
VGN	Vereniging van Docenten in Geschiedenis en Staatsrichting in Nederland [*Netherlands*] (SLS)
VGO	All-Union Geographic Society (RU)
VGO	All-Union Hydrobiological Society (RU)
VGO	Military Geological Detachment (RU)
VGO	Valuer-General's Office [*Victoria, Australia*]
VGO	Vereinigte Gruenen Oesterreich [*United Green Party of Austria*] [*Political party*] (EY)
VGO	Vigo [*Spain*] [*Airport symbol*] (OAG)
VGOLPITEP	All-Union State "Order of Lenin" Planning Institute Teploelektroproyekt (RU)
VGP	Vojno-Gradevinsko Preduzece [*Military Building Establishment*] (YU)
VGPI	All-Union State Planning Institute (RU)

VGPI	Vilnius State Pedagogical Institute (RU)
VGPI	Vladimir State Pedagogical Institute Imeni P. I. Lebedev (RU)
VGPI	Voronezh State Pedagogical Institute (RU)
VGPO	All-Union Notions and Perfumery Association (RU)
VGPO	Victorian Government Printing Office [*Australia*]
vgr	Verbigracia [*For Example*] [*Spanish*]
Vgr	Vergaser [*Carburetor*] [*German*] (GCA)
Vgr	Vidi Grupu [*See Group*] (YU)
VGRJ	Rajshahi [*Bangladesh*] [*ICAO location identifier*] (ICLI)
VGRO	All-Union Geological Exploration Association (RU)
VGRP	Volga River Cargo Steamship Line (RU)
VGRS	General German Workers' Union (RU)
VGS	Higher City Planning Council (BU)
VGS	Vertical Synchronous Hydraulic Generator (RU)
VGS	Vings [*Bulgaria*] [*ICAO designator*] (FAAC)
VGSB	All-Union Geodetic Information Office (RU)
VGSCh	Militarized Mine Rescue Unit (RU)
VGSD	Saidpur [*Bangladesh*] [*ICAO location identifier*] (ICLI)
VGSG	Thakuragaon [*Bangladesh*] [*ICAO location identifier*] (ICLI)
VGSH	Shamshernagar [*Bangladesh*] [*ICAO location identifier*] (ICLI)
VGSI	All-Union State Sanitary Inspection (RU)
VGSO	Militarized Mine Rescue Detachment (RU)
VGSO	Victorian Government Solicitor's Office [*Australia*]
VGStW	Verein fuer Geschichte der Stadt Wien [*Austria*] (SLS)
VGSV	Militarized Mine Rescue Platoon (RU)
VGSY	Sylhet Osmani [*Bangladesh*] [*ICAO location identifier*] (ICLI)
VGTJ	Dhaka/Tejgaon [*Bangladesh*] [*ICAO location identifier*] (ICLI)
VGTL	Rope-Pulled Rubber Conveyor Belt (BU)
VGTVRZ	All-Union State Trust of Railroad Car Repair Plants (RU)
VgTZ	Volgograd Tractor Plant (RU)
VGU	High Geodetic Administration (RU)
VGU	Military Geographic Directorate (RU)
VGU	Vilnius State University Imeni V. Kapsukas (RU)
vgu	Vorgelesen, Genehmigt, Unterschrieben [*Read, Confirmed, and Signed (Legal documents)*] [*German*] (EG)
VGU	Voronezh State University (RU)
VGV	High-Water Level (RU)
vgw	Voegwoord [*Conjunction*] [*Afrikaans*]
VGW-VKW	Verband der Deutscher Gas- and Wasserwerke eV - Verkehrswirtschaft
VGZR	Dhaka/Zia International [*Bangladesh*] [*ICAO location identifier*] (ICLI)
VH	Besluit op de Vereveningsheffing [*Benelux*] (BAS)
vh	Van Het [*Benelux*] (BAS)
VH	Volkseigener Handel [*State Trade Enterprise*] (EG)
vH	Vom Hundert [*Percent*] [*German*] (GPO)
v/h	Voorheen [*Formerly*] [*Netherlands*] (CED)
VH	Vossa Honra [*Your Honor*] [*Portuguese*]
VH	Votre Hautesse [*Your Highness*] [*French*]
VH	Votre Honneur [*Your Honor*] [*French*]
vh	Votre Honoree [*Your Letter*] [*French*]
VHA	Vrywillige Hulpafdeling [*Voluntary Aid Detachment*] [*Afrikaans*]
VHB	Turk Veteriner Hekimleri Birligi [*Turkish Union of Doctors of Veterinary Medicine*] [*VETB*] [*See also*] (TU)
VHC	Saurimo [*Angola*] [*Airport symbol*] (OAG)
VHCH	Cheung Chau [*Hong Kong*] [*ICAO location identifier*] (ICLI)
Vhdl	Verhandlungen [*Transactions*] [*German*]
VHF	Very High Frequency (EECI)
VHHH	Hong Kong/International [*Hong Kong*] [*ICAO location identifier*] (ICLI)
VHHK	Hong Kong [*Hong Kong*] [*ICAO location identifier*] (ICLI)
VHI	Veterinaerhygiene-Inspektion [*Veterinary Hygiene Inspection*] (EG)
VHIAA	Voluntary Health Insurance Association of Australia
VHICA	Voluntary Health Insurance Council of Australia (ADA)
VHJ	Vyrobni Hospodarska Jednotka [*Economic Production Unit*] (CZ)
VHK	Valtion Hankintakeskus [*State purchasing agency*] [*Finland*] (IMH)
vhk	Vihko [*Finland*]
VHKBVGL	Verein vom Heiligen Karl Borromaeus zur Verbreitung Guter Literatur [*St. Karl Borromaus Association for the Dissemination of Good Literature*] [*Germany*] (EAIO)
VHKT	Kai Tak [*Hong Kong*] [*ICAO location identifier*] (ICLI)
VHM	Vojenske Historicke Museum [*Museum of Military History*] (CZ)
VHO	Vila Coutinho [*Mozambique*] [*Airport symbol*] [*Obsolete*] (OAG)
vho	Voorbereidend Hoger Onderwijs [*Benelux*] (BAS)
VHP	Vishwa Hindu Parishad [*India*]
VHP	Vooruitstrewende Hervormings Partij [*Progressive Reform Party*] [*Surinam*] [*Political party*] (PPW)
VHpA	Verband der Heilpaedagogischen Ausbildungsinstitut der Schweiz [*Luzern, Switzerland*] (SLS)
VHPF	Victorian Health Promotion Foundation [*Australia*]
vhr	Vegrehajtasi Rendelet [*Implementing Decree*] (HU)

VHRB .... Victorian Harness Racing Board [*Australia*]
VHRC .... Victoria Harness Racing Club [*Australia*]
VHS .... Vojenska Hudebni Skola [*Military Music School*] (CZ)
VHS .... Volkshochschule [*German*]
VHSD .... Vyssia Hospodarska Skola Druzstevna [*Higher School of Cooperative Management*] (CZ)
VHSK .... Sek Kong [*Hong Kong*] [*ICAO location identifier*] (ICLI)
VHSTA ...... Victorian High School Teachers' Association [*Australia*]
VHSZ .... Villamos Halozati Szolgalat [*Electric Network Service*] (HU)
vht .... Veghatarozat [*Final Decision*] (HU)
VHTH .... Van Huis tot Huis [*Afrikaans*]
VHU .... Vojensky Historicky Ustav [*Institute of Military History*] (CZ)
VHV .... Vol Houervrag [*Afrikaans*]
VHW .... Verband Hannoverscher Warmblutzuchter [*Germany*] (EAIO)
VHW .... Verband Hochschule und Wissenschaft im Deutschen Beamtenbund (SLS)
Vh Z .... Verhaeltniszahl [*Proportional Number*] [*German*]
VHZ........... Volkseigene Handelszentrale [*State Trade Center*] (EG)
vi. .... Intransitive Verb (TPFD)
VI .... Ionization Gauge (RU)
VI .... Military Inspection (RU)
VI .... Veiligheidsinstituut [*Safety Institute*] [*Netherlands*] (PDAA)
vi. .... Vela Internacional [*Portuguese*]
vi. .... Verbe Intransitif [*French*] (TPFD)
VI .... Vereniging Intercoop [*International Agricultural Society Intercoop*] [*Switzerland*] (EAIO)
VI .... Veterinarski Inspektorat [*Veterinary Inspectorate*] (YU)
VI .... Vicenza [*Car registration plates*] [*Italian*]
VI .... Victoria Institution (ML)
VI .... Video Amplifier (RU)
VI .... Vinnuveitendasamband Islands [*Confederation of Icelandic Employers*] (EAIO)
VI .... Virgin Islands of the US [*Postal code*]
VI .... Virgin Islands of the US [*ANSI two-letter standard code*] (CNC)
VI .... Viskositaetsindex [*Viscosity Index*] (EG)
VI .... Vitesse Indiquee [*Indicated Airspeed*] [*Aviation*] [*French*]
VI .... Voorwaardelijke Invrijheidstelling [*Benelux*] (BAS)
VIA .... Military Engineering Academy (RU)
VIA .... Military History Archives (BU)
VIA .... Valorisation de l'Innovation dans l'Ameublement [*Committee to Promote Innovation in Furniture Design*] [*France*]
VIA .... Venezolana Internacional de Aviacion SA [*Venezuelan airline*]
VIA .... VIASA, Venezolana International de Aviacion SA [*Venezuela*] [*ICAO designator*] (FAAC)
VIA .... Victorian Importers' Association [*Australia*]
VIA .... Vietnamese Information Agency [*North Vietnam*] (RU)
VIA .... Voluntary Insurance Association [*Australia*]
VIAA .... Comite des Volontaires Internationales d'Aide et d'Assistance aux Refugies [*Committee of International Women Volunteers for Aid and Relief to Refugees*] [*Use CVIAA Cambodia*] (CL)
VIAAR ...... Comite des Volontaires Internationales d'Aide et d'Assistance aux Refugies [*Committee of International Women Volunteers for Aid and Relief to Refugees*] [*Use CVIAA Cambodia*] (CL)
VIAC .... Victorian Industrial Appeals Court [*Australia*]
VIAG .... Agra [*India*] [*ICAO location identifier*] (ICLI)
VIAG .... Vereinigte Industrie-Unternehmungen AG [*Industrial Enterprise Association*] [*Business term*]
VIAH .... Aligarh [*India*] [*ICAO location identifier*] (ICLI)
VIAKO ...... All-Union Institute of Variety Goods of Light Industry and Fashion (RU)
VIAL .... Allahabad [*India*] [*ICAO location identifier*] (ICLI)
VIALEGPROM ... All-Union Institute of Variety Goods of Light Industry and Fashion (RU)
VIAM .... All-Union Scientific Research Institute of Aviation Materials (RU)
VIAP.......... All-Union Institute of Soil Science (RU)
VIAP.......... Vanuatu Independent Alliance Party [*Political party*] (PPW)
VIAR .... Amritsar [*India*] [*ICAO location identifier*] (ICLI)
VIAR.......... The Volcani Institute of Agricultural Research [*Israel*] (DSCA)
VIARC .... Victorian Immigration Advice and Rights Centre Inc. [*Australia*] [*Commercial firm*]
VIARKKA ... Military Engineering Academy of the RKKA (RU)
VIASA .... Venezolana Internacional de Aviacion Sociedad Anonima [*Airline*] [*Venezuela*]
VIAVER .... Hotel de Viajes Veracruz [*Colombia*] (COL)
VIAVU ...... Higher Military Engineering Aviation School (RU)
VIBEG .... Vendeglatoipari Berendezes es Felszereles Javito es Gyarto Vallalat [*Repair Enterprise for Hotel and Catering Trade Equipment*] (HU)
VIBH .... Banihal [*India*] [*ICAO location identifier*] (ICLI)
VIBK.......... Bikaner [*India*] [*ICAO location identifier*] (ICLI)
VIBL .... Bakshi Ka Talab [*India*] [*ICAO location identifier*] (ICLI)
VIBN .... Varanasi [*India*] [*ICAO location identifier*] (ICLI)
VIBR.......... Kulu/Bhuntar [*India*] [*ICAO location identifier*] (ICLI)

VIBT .... Bhatinda [*India*] [*ICAO location identifier*] (ICLI)
VIBW......... Bhiwani [*India*] [*ICAO location identifier*] (ICLI)
VIBY .... Bareilly [*India*] [*ICAO location identifier*] (ICLI)
VIC .... Victoria [*State in Australia*]
VIC .... Victorian Investment Corp. [*Australia*]
VIC .... Vienna International Centre [*United Nations*]
Vic Ap .... Vicar Apostolic (BARN)
VICBETI ... Victorian Inventory of Community Based Employment and Training Initiatives [*Australia*]
VICCC ...... Victorian Indo-Chinese Community Council [*Australia*]
Vic Coll ..... Victoria College [*Australia*]
Vic CollArts ... Victorian College of the Arts [*Australia*]
Vic CollPharm ... Victorian College of Pharmacy [*Australia*]
VICD .... Victoria Desert [*Botanical region*] [*Australia*]
VICE.......... Vilnius Commodity Exchange [*Lithuania*] (EY)
VICFIN ..... Victorian Public Authorities Finance Agency [*Australia*]
VICFIT ...... Victoria Council on Fitness and General Health [*Australia*]
VICG .... Chandigarh [*India*] [*ICAO location identifier*] (ICLI)
VICICONGO ... Societe des Chemins de Fer Vicinaux du Congo
VICL.......... Vienna International Centre Library [*Information service or system*] (IID)
VICMICO ... Victorias Milling Company, Inc. [*Philippines*] (ARC)
VicNaturalist ... Victorian Naturalist [*Australia*]
VICOMP... Victorian Government Computing Service [*Australia*]
VICPIC...... Victorian Prison Industries Commission [*Australia*]
Vic SupCt FC ... Victorian Supreme Court Full Court [*Australia*]
VICX.......... Kanpur/Chakeri [*India*] [*ICAO location identifier*] (ICLI)
VID .... Vidin [*Bulgaria*] [*Airport symbol*] (OAG)
VID .... Vienna Institute for Development (EAIO)
VIDA .... Video Industry Distributors Association [*Australia*]
VIDD .... Delhi/Safdarjung [*India*] [*ICAO location identifier*] (ICLI)
VIDF.......... Delhi [*India*] [*ICAO location identifier*] (ICLI)
VIDN .... Dehra Dun [*India*] [*ICAO location identifier*] (ICLI)
VIDP.......... Delhi/Indira Gandhi International [*India*] [*ICAO location identifier*] (ICLI)
VIDR .... Dadri [*India*] [*ICAO location identifier*] (ICLI)
VIDRIOCAL ... Vidriera de Caldas [*Pereira*] (COL)
VIDRIOVAL ... Vidriera del Valle [*Colombia*] (COL)
VIDUS....... Tatabanyai Szenbanyak Viztisztito es Dusito Berendezesek Gyara [*Tatabanya Coal Mines Water Purification and Dressing Equipment Factory*] (HU)
VIE............ Vasilikon Idryma Erevnon [*Royal Research Foundation*] [*EIE*] [*See also*] (GC)
VIE............ Victorian Institute of Engineers [*Australia*]
VIE............ Vienna [*Austria*] [*Airport symbol*] (OAG)
VIEC......... Vie Economique et Sociale [*Benelux*] (BAS)
VIEE......... All-Union Scientific Research Institute of Experimental Endocrinology (RU)
Viell........... Vielleicht [*Perhaps*] [*German*]
VIEM........ All-Union Institute of Experimental Medicine Imeni A. M. Gor'kiy (RU)
VIEMP...... All-Union Scientific Research Institute of Essential-Oil Industry (RU)
VIEMR...... All-Union Scientific Research Institute of Essential-Oil Plants [*1947-1954*] (RU)
VIEMS...... All-Union Scientific Research Institute of Economics of Mineral Raw Materials and Geological Exploration (RU)
VIEN .... Vienna [*Austria*] (WDAA)
Vien........... Viennola [*Record label*] [*Austria*]
VIENOR... Viviendas Economicas para el Norte [*Chile*] (LAA)
vier........... Viernes [*Friday*] [*Spanish*]
VIESKh ..... All-Union Scientific Research Institute of Rural Electrification (RU)
VIETSEL .. Vietnam Selatan [*South Vietnam*] (IN)
VIETUT .... Vietnam Utara [*North Vietnam*] (IN)
VIEV......... All-Union Institute of Experimental Veterinary Science (RU)
VIF............ Higher Physical Education Institute (BU)
VIFB .... Farrukhabad [*India*] [*ICAO location identifier*] (ICLI)
VIFD......... Faridkot [*India*] [*ICAO location identifier*] (ICLI)
VIFK......... Higher Physical Education Institute (BU)
VIFKA ...... Vereniging van Importeurs en Fabrikanten van Kantoormachines
VIFS .... All-Union Information Fund of Standards and Technical Specifications (RU)
VIFZ......... Ferojpur [*India*] [*ICAO location identifier*] (ICLI)
VIG .... Venezuelan Institute of Genealogy (EAIO)
Vig............ Vigario [*Vicar*] [*Portuguese*]
Vig............. Vigente [*In Force*] [*Italian*] (ILCA)
VIGE......... Vasilikon Institouton Geoponikon Epistimon [*Royal Institute of Agricultural Sciences*] [*IGE*] [*See also*] (GC)
VIGIS .... All-Union Institute of Helminthology Imeni Academician K. I. Skryabin (RU)
VIGLA .... Victorian Government Libraries Association [*Australia*]
VIGM .... All-Union Scientific Research Institute of Hydraulic Machinery (RU)

VIGM .... Veteriner Isleri Genel Mudurlugu [*Veterinary Affairs Directorate General*] (TU)
VIGN .... Guna [*India*] [*ICAO location identifier*] (ICLI)
vign .... Vignet [*Vignette*] [*Publishing Danish/Norwegian*]
vign .... Vignet [*Vignette*] [*Publishing*] [*Netherlands*]
Vign .... Vignette [*Publishing*] [*German*]
vign .... Vignette [*Publishing*] [*French*]
Vigne .... Vignoble [*Vineyards*] [*Military map abbreviation World War I*] [*French*] (MTD)
VIGPA .... Nederlandse Vereniing van Importeurs van en Groothandelaren in Glas, Porsele in, en Aardewerk [*Dutch Association of Importers and Wholesalers of Glass, Porcelain and Earthenware*] (EAIO)
VIGR .... Gwalior [*India*] [*ICAO location identifier*] (ICLI)
VIGS .... Visually Impaired Golfers Society [*Australia*]
VIHR .... Hissar [*India*] [*ICAO location identifier*] (ICLI)
VII .... Higher Institute of Economics (BU)
VII .... Military Engineering Inspection (RU)
VIIbre .... Septembre [*September*] [*French*]
VIIbre .... Septiembre [*September*] [*Spanish*]
VIII .... Higher Institute of Representative Art (BU)
VIIIbre .... Octobre [*October*] [*French*]
VIIIbre .... Octubre [*October*] [*Spanish*]
VIIJA .... Vojnoistoriski Institut Jugoslovenske Armije [*Institute of Military History of the Yugoslav Army*] [*Belgrade*] (YU)
VII KarlMarks ... [*The*] Karl Marx Higher Institute of Economics (BU)
viim .... Viimeinen [*Finland*]
viim .... Viimeksi [*Finland*]
VIIYa .... Military Institute of Foreign Languages (RU)
VIJ .... Virgin Gorda [*British Virgin Islands*] [*Airport symbol*] (OAG)
VIJN .... Jhansi [*India*] [*ICAO location identifier*] (ICLI)
VIJO .... Jodhpur [*India*] [*ICAO location identifier*] (ICLI)
VIJP .... Jaipur [*India*] [*ICAO location identifier*] (ICLI)
VIJR .... Jaiselmer [*India*] [*ICAO location identifier*] (ICLI)
VIJU .... Jammu [*India*] [*ICAO location identifier*] (ICLI)
VIK .... All-Union Scientific Research Institute of Fodder (RU)
VIK .... Higher Engineering Courses (RU)
VIK .... Military History Commission (RU)
VIK .... Provisional Executive Committee (RU)
VIK .... Vereinigung Internationaler Kulturaustausch (RU)
VIK .... Vrhovna Invalidska Komisija [*Supreme Commission for Disabled Veterans*] (YU)
ViK .... Water Supply and Sewers (BU)
VIKA .... Kanpur [*India*] [*ICAO location identifier*] (ICLI)
VIKD .... Kud [*India*] [*ICAO location identifier*] (ICLI)
VIKER .... Vegyipari es Kereskedelmi Korlatolt Felelossegu Tarsasag [*Chemical Manufacturing and Trade Co. Ltd.*] (HU)
VIKhVP ..... Higher Food Industry Institute (BU)
VIKJ .... Khajuraho [*India*] [*ICAO location identifier*] (ICLI)
VIKO .... Kota [*India*] [*ICAO location identifier*] (ICLI)
VIKP .... All-Indian Congress of Trade Unions (RU)
VIKT .... General Confederation of Labor of Italy (RU)
VIKZhEDOR ... All-Russian Executive Committee of Railroad Workers [*1918-1919*] (RU)
VIKZhEL' ... All-Russian Executive Committee of the Railroad Trade Union (RU)
VIL .... Dakhla [*Mauritania*] [*Airport symbol*] (OAG)
VILAR .... All-Union Scientific Research Institute of Medicinal and Aromatic Plants (RU)
VILATI ...... Villamos Automatika Intezet [*Institute of Electrical Automation*] (HU)
VILD .... Ludhaiha [*India*] [*ICAO location identifier*] (ICLI)
VILK .... Lucknow [*India*] [*ICAO location identifier*] (ICLI)
Vill .... Villandry Festival [*Record label*] [*France*]
VILLA .... Ventes Immobilieres de Logements et Lotissements en Afrique
VILLENKI ... Villamos Energetikai Kutato Intezet [*Electric Power Research Institute*] (HU)
VILLERT .. Villamossagi es Szerelesi Cikkeket Ertekesito Vallalat [*Marketing Enterprise for Electrical Items and Equipment*] (HU)
VILLTESZ ... Autovillamossagi es Muszeresz KSZ [*Cooperative Enterprise for Automotive Electrical Equipment and Machine Parts*] (HU)
V Ilma .... Vossa Ilustrissima [*Your Most Illustrious*] [*Portuguese*]
VILP .... Lalitpur [*India*] [*ICAO location identifier*] (ICLI)
VIM .... Air-Via [*Bulgaria*] [*ICAO designator*] (FAAC)
VIM .... All-Union Scientific Research Institute of Agricultural Mechanization (RU)
VIM .... Pulse-Time Modulation (RU)
VI M .... Vegyipari Miniszter [*or A Vegyipari Miniszter Rendelete*] [*Minister of the Chemical Industry or Decree of the Minister of the Chemical Industry*] (HU)
VIM .... Verallgemeinerte Indexmethode [*German*] (ADPT)
VIM .... Water Installation Works (BU)
VIME .... All-Union Scientific Research Institute of Rural Mechanization and Electrification [*1937-1948*] (RU)

VIMEDA ... Vice Ministerio de Educacion para Adultos [*Vice Ministry of Adult Education*] [*Nicaragua*] (LA)
VIMESS .... Higher Institute for the Mechanization and Electrification of Agriculture (BU)
VIMG .... Moga [*India*] [*ICAO location identifier*] (ICLI)
VIMME ..... Viomikhania Metallon kai Metallevtikon Epikheiriseon [*Metals and Mining Enterprises Industry*] [*Greek*] (GC)
VIMMESS ... Higher Institute for Agricultural Machinebuilding and Mechanization and Electrification of Agriculture (BU)
VIMP .... All-Union Institute of the Makhorka Industry (RU)
VIMS .... All-Union Institute of Metrology and Standardization [*1931-1934*] (RU)
VIMS .... All-Union Scientific Research Institute of Mineral Raw Materials (RU)
VIMS .... Mandasor [*India*] [*ICAO location identifier*] (ICLI)
VIMT .... All-Union Scientific Research Institute of Mechanization in the Peat Industry (RU)
vin .... Accusative [*Case*] (BU)
Vin .... Distillery [*Topography*] (RU)
VIN .... Value of Direction Change (RU)
VIN .... Vinair-Helicopteros Ltda. [*Portugal*] [*ICAO designator*] (FAAC)
vin .... Vineyard [*Topography*] (RU)
Vin .... Vinicultura [*Viniculture*] [*Portuguese*]
VINAFRANCE ... Societe d'Importation de Vins en Afrique Francaise [*Abidjan*]
VINALKO ... Poduzece za Promet Vinom i Alkoholnim Picima [*Trade Enterprise in Wine and Alcoholic Beverages*] (YU)
VINH .... Nuh [*India*] [*ICAO location identifier*] (ICLI)
VINIP .... Contract van de Vereniging van Importeurs van Indonesische Producten [*Benelux*] (BAS)
VINITI ...... Vsesojuznij Institut Naucnoj i Tekniceskoj Informacij [*Former USSR*]
VINITI ...... Vsesoyuznyy Institut Nauchnoy i Tekhnicheskoy Informatsii [*All-Union Institute of Scientific and Technical Information*] [*Former USSR*]
vinj .... Vinjett [*Vignette*] [*Publishing*] [*Sweden*]
VINK .... Military History Scientific Commission (RU)
VINL .... Naranaup [*India*] [*ICAO location identifier*] (ICLI)
VINLEC .... St. Vincent Electricity Services (LA)
vinogr .... Vineyard (RU)
vinogr .... Viticulture (RU)
Vinprom ..... Wine Industry (BU)
VINS .... Higher Institute for the National Economy (BU)
Vinsindikat ... State Grape-Growing and Wine-Making Syndicate (RU)
VINTI .... All-Union Institute of Scientific and Technical Information on Agriculture (of the Ministry of Agriculture, USSR) (RU)
VIO .... Military History Society (RU)
VIO .... Varazdinska Industrija Obuce [*Varazdin Shoe Industry*] (YU)
Vioburo ...... La Vie au Bureau [*French*] (BAS)
VIOK .... All-Union Scientific Research Institute of Refractory and Acid-Resistant Materials (RU)
viol .... Violet [*Violet*] [*French*]
VIOS .... All-Union Scientific Research Institute for the Study of Foundations and Substructures of Engineering Installations (RU)
VIOZKh .... All-Union Institute of Irrigation Grain Farming (RU)
VIP .... Auxiliary Power Supply Unit (RU)
VIP .... Bearing Change (RU)
vip .... Issue (BU)
VIP .... Virgin Islands Party (LA)
VIPA .... Victorian Interior Plantscapers Association [*Australia*]
VIPASA ..... Vivienda Panamericana Colombiana Ltda. [*Colombia*] (COL)
VIPB .... All-Union Institute of Applied Botany and New Crops (RU)
VIPBiNK ... All-Union Institute of Applied Botany and New Crops (RU)
VIPCOR .... Viphya Pulp and Paper Corporation
VIPK .... Pathankot [*India*] [*ICAO location identifier*] (ICLI)
VIPK .... Visja Invalidsko-Pokojninska Komisija [*Higher Invalid Retirement Commission*] (YU)
VIPKIZO .. All-Union Institute for Improvement of Qualifications and for Correspondence Training of Agricultural Specialists (RU)
VIPL .... Patiala [*India*] [*ICAO location identifier*] (ICLI)
VIPP .... Venda Independent People's Party [*Political party*] (PPW)
VIPT .... All-Union Scientific Research Institute of Industrial Transportation (RU)
VIPT .... Nainital (Pantnagar) [*India*] [*ICAO location identifier*] (ICLI)
VIQG .... Qazigund [*India*] [*ICAO location identifier*] (ICLI)
VIR .... All-Union Scientific Research Institute of Plant Growing (RU)
VIR .... Mobile Incubator "Record" (RU)
VIR .... Range Rate [*or Probable Range Rate*] [*Artillery*] (RU)
VIR .... Virgin Islands of the US [*ANSI three-letter standard code*] (CNC)
vir .... Viroksi [*Finland*]
vir .... Virolainen [*Finland*]
VIR .... Vsesoyuznyy Nauchno-issledovatel'skiy Institut Rastenivodstva [*All-Union Research Institute for the Plant Industry*] [*Former USSR*] (IRC)

VIRB......... Raibarelli/Fursatganj [*India*] [*ICAO location identifier*]   (ICLI)
VIRG .... All-Union Scientific Research Institute of Exploration Geophysics   (RU)
VIRG .... Institute of Mining Geophysics   (RU)
VIRG .... Reengus [*India*] [*ICAO location identifier*]   (ICLI)
virg .... Virgen [*Virgin*] [*Spanish*]
virh .... Virheellisesti [*Erroneously*] [*Finland*]
VIR IS....... Virgin Islands   (WDAA)
VIRL.......... Visual Impairment Reference Libraries [*Australia*]
VIRPO....... Victorian Irrigation Research and Promotion Organisation [*Australia*]
virt............. Virement [*Turning, Clearing*] [*French*]
VIRts .... Range Rate Due to Target Motion   (RU)
virusol ...... Virological, Virology   (RU)
VIS............. All-Union Institute of Structures   (RU)
VIS............. Army Engineering Signal Apparatus Factory   (BU)
VIS............. Eastern Scientific Research Institute of Structures [*Sverdlovsk*]   (RU)
vis............... Height, Altitude, Elevation, Hill   (BU)
VIS............. Inertial System Computer   (RU)
VIS............. Jet Servisx SA de CV [*Mexico*] [*ICAO designator*]   (FAAC)
VIS............. Varazdinska Industrija Svile [*Varazdin Silk Industry*]   (YU)
VIS............. Video-Informationssystem [*German*]   (ADPT)
VIS............. Vienna International School [*Austria*]
VIS............. Vorstands-Informations-System [*German*]   (ADPT)
Vis.............. Vrakhonisis [*Rocky Islet*] [*Greek*]   (NAU)
VIS............. Vrhovno Islamsko Starjesinstvo [*Supreme Islamic Authority*] [*Sarajevo*]   (YU)
VISACAM ... Societe des Viandes et Salaisons du Cameroun
VISAN....... Vida Sanayi ve Ticaret AS [*Sheet Metal Screw Industry and Trade Corp.*]   (TU)
VISb........... Military History Collection [*Series*]   (BU)
VISB .... Sikandrabad [*India*] [*ICAO location identifier*]   (ICLI)
Visc .... Viscositaet [*Viscosity*] [*German*]   (GCA)
VISCA .... Visayas State College of Agriculture [*Philippines*]
VISDA....... Visual Information System Development Association [*Japan*]   (PDAA)
VISE .... Volunteers for Isolated Students Education [*Australia*]
VISF .... Army Engineering Signal Apparatus Factory   (BU)
VISh.......... Controllable-Pitch Propeller   (RU)
VIShKhIMZ ... Vishera Chemical Plant   (RU)
VISI .... Higher Construction Engineering Institute   (BU)
VISI .... Voronezh Construction Engineering Institute   (RU)
VISioN....... Victorian Information Services Network [*Australia*]
VISIT........ Victorian Schools Intrastate Tour [*Australia*]
VISK .... Military History Commission   (RU)
VISKhM ..... All-Union Institute of Agricultural Microbiology   (RU)
VISKhOM ... All-Union Scientific Research Institute of Agricultural Machinery   (RU)
VISM.......... All-Union Institute of Building Materials   (RU)
VISM........ Simla [*India*] [*ICAO location identifier*]   (ICLI)
VISP .... All-Union Institute of the Soda Industry   (RU)
VISP .... Saharanpur/Sarsawa [*India*] [*ICAO location identifier*]   (ICLI)
VISR .... Srinagar [*India*] [*ICAO location identifier*]   (ICLI)
Visshikon inst ... Higher Institute of Economics   (BU)
VIST .... Satna [*India*] [*ICAO location identifier*]   (ICLI)
VISTA .... Vehicle Superannuation Trust of Australia
VISU......... Higher School of Construction Engineering   (RU)
VISZ .... Vegyipari Szakszervezet [*Chemical Industry Trade Union*]   (HU)
VIT............. All-Union Institute of Peat   (RU)
VIT............. Antitank Fighter Aircraft   (RU)
VIT............. Valeur Immobiliere Totale [*Morocco*]
VIT............. Vilag Ifjusagi Talalkozo [*World Youth Meeting*]   (HU)
vit .... Vitela [*Vellum*] [*Publishing*] [*Spanish*]
Vit .... Viticultura [*Viticulture*] [*Portuguese*]
VIT............. Vitoria [*Spain*] [*Airport symbol*]   (OAG)
VIT............. V. I. Tyzhnov [*in combination: VIT-iron*]   (RU)
VITA.......... Volunteers in Technical Assistance, Inc.
VITABEL ... Federation of the Exporting Belgian Food Manufacturers   (EAIO)
VITAR....... Veterinary Institute for Tropical and High Altitude Research [*Peru*]   (DSCA)
VITB......... Vocational and Industrial Training Board [*Singapore*]   (FEA)
VITECO .... Vidrio Tecnico de Colombia [*Colombia*]   (COL)
VITEO........ All-Union Scientific Research Institute of Heat and Water Power Engineering Equipment   (RU)
VITGEO.... All-Union Scientific Research Institute of Heat and Water Power Engineering Equipment   (RU)
VITI.......... Higher Institute of Theatrical Art   (BU)
VITIM....... All-Union Scientific Research Institute of Tobacco and Makhorka Imeni A. I. Mikoyan   (RU)
VITIS-VEA ... VITIS-Viticulture and Enology Abstracts [*International Food Information Service*] [*Information service or system*]   (IID)
VITIZ .... [*The*] Krust'o Sarafov Higher Institute of Theatrical Art   (BU)

VITM......... Visvesvaraya Industrial and Technological Museum [*India*]   (PDAA)
VITMP...... All-Union Scientific Research Institute of the Tobacco and Makhorka Industry Imeni A. I. Mikoyan   (RU)
VI-TNO..... Vezelinstituut TNO [*Fiber Research Institute TNO*] [*Netherlands Organization for Applied Scientific Research (TNO)*] [*Research center*]   (ERC)
VITP .... All-Union Institute of the Tobacco Industry   (RU)
VITR.......... All-Union Scientific Research Institute of Methods and Techniques of Exploration (of the State Geological Committee, USSR)   (RU)
VITU .... Higher Engineering and Technical School (of the Navy, USSR)   (RU)
VITUKI ..... Vizgazdalkodasi Tudomanyos Kutato Intezet [*Scientific Research Institute on Water Resources*]   (HU)
VIU .... Military Engineering Directorate   (RU)
VIU .... Military Engineering School   (RU)
VIUA .... All-Union Scientific Research Institute of Fertilizers and Soil Science   (RU)
VIUAA ...... All-Union Scientific Research Institute of Fertilizers, Agricultural Engineering, and Soil Science   (RU)
VIUD......... Udaipur [*India*] [*ICAO location identifier*]   (ICLI)
VIUZ .... Higher Schools of Economics   (BU)
VIV .... All-Union Synthetic Fiber Trust   (RU)
VIV .... Altitude Change [*of an aerial target*]   (RU)
VIV .... Viajes Internacionales de Vacaciones SA [*Spain*] [*ICAO designator*]   (FAAC)
VIV .... Vivigani [*Papua New Guinea*] [*Airport symbol*]   (OAG)
VIVA......... Viajes Internacionales de Vacaciones SA [*Spain*] [*ICAO designator*]   (FAAC)
VIVA........ Visa Intendantska Vojna Akademija [*Higher Quartermaster Service Academy*]   (YU)
VIVG .... Sudden Coal and Gas Ejection   (BU)
VIX .... Vitoria [*Brazil*] [*Airport symbol*]   (OAG)
VIYuN .... All-Union Institute of Jurisprudence   (RU)
viz.............. Byzantine   (BU)
VIZ .... Verkh-Isetskiy Plant [*Sverdlovsk*]   (RU)
viz.............. Videlicet [*Namely*]   (SCAC)
VIZ .... Vojni Izdavacki Zavod [*Military Publishing Institute*]   (YU)
VIZEP ...... Vizugyi Epito Vallalat [*Hydraulic Engineering Enterprise*]   (HU)
VIZh .... All-Union Scientific Research Institute of Livestock Breeding   (RU)
VIZITERV ... Vizugyi Tervezo Iroda [*Water Resources Planning Office*]   (HU)
VIZKh........ All-Union Institute of Grain Farming   (RU)
VIZMAE... All-Union Institute of Terrestrial Magnetism and Atmospheric Electricity   (RU)
VIZO .... All-Union Correspondence Training Institute   (RU)
VIZR.......... All-Union Institute for the Protection of Plants   (RU)
vizv............ Vizvezetek [*Water Conduit*]   (HU)
vJ............... Vom Jahre [*Of the Year*] [*German*]
vJ............... Vorigen Jahres [*Of Last Year*] [*German*]   (GPO)
VJD........... Vanguardia de la Juventud Dominicana [*Vanguard of Dominican Youth*] [*Dominican Republic*]   (LA)
VJK........... Vereniging voor Japanse Kunst [*Society for Japanese Arts*] [*Netherlands*]   (EAIO)
VJRU......... Victorian Junior Rugby Union [*Australia*]
Vjs............. Vierteljahrschrift [*Quarterly Journal*] [*German*]
Vjschr........ Vierteljahrsschrift [*Quarterly Publication*] [*German*]   (GCA)
VK............. Air Code   (RU)
VK............. Aircraft Engine Designed by V. Ya. Klimov   (RU)
VK............. All-Chinese Committee (of the People's Political Advisory Council of China)
V/k............ All-Union Office   (RU)
VK............. Auxiliary Team   (RU)
VK............. Calling Drop   (RU)
VK............. End Switch   (RU)
VK............. Highly Durable Glue   (RU)
VK............. Internal Conversion   (RU)
VK............. Medical Commission   (RU)
VK............. Military Collegium   (BU)
VK............. Military Commandant   (RU)
VK............. Military Commissar, Military Commissariat   (RU)
VK............. Military Guard   (BU)
v-k............. Newspaper   (BU)
VK............. Officers' Club   (BU)
VK............. Of Highest Quality   (RU)
VK............. Output Stage   (RU)
VK............. Vacuum Valve   (RU)
Vk............. Vakstudie [*Benelux*]   (BAS)
vk.............. Valasz Keretik [*Reply Requested*]   (HU)
VK............. Vazduhoplovni Korpus [*Air Corps*]   (YU)
Vk............. Veldkornet [*Field Cornet*] [*Afrikaans*]
VK............. Verbundkatalog Maschinenlesbarer Katalogdaten Deutscher Bibliotheken [*Deutsches Bibliotheksinstitut*] [*Germany*] [*Information service or system*]   (CRD)

VK .... Verenigde Koninkryk [*United Kingdom*] [*Afrikaans*]
VK .... Vergaserkraftstoff [*Carburetor Fuel (Gasoline)*] [*German*]   (EG)
VK .... Verkehrskontrolle [*Traffic Control*] [*German*]   (EG)
VK .... Versorgungskontor [*Supply Office*] [*German*]   (EG)
vk .... Vezerkar [*or Vezerkari*] (Tiszt) [*General Staff or General Staff Officer*]   (HU)
vk .... Vierkant [*Square*] [*Afrikaans*]
vk .... Viime Kuun [*Finland*]
vk .... Viime Kuuta [*Last Month*] [*Finland*]   (GPO)
Vk .... Vik [*or Vika or Viken*] [*Bay, Inlet*] [*Norway*]   (NAU)
VK .... Villamosgep- es Kabelgyar [*Electrical Machine and Cable Factory*] [*Budapest*]   (HU)
vk .... Virkaa Tekeva [*Acting*] [*Finland*]   (GPO)
VK .... Vise-Kanselier [*Vice Chancellor*] [*Afrikaans*]
VK .... Voetbalklub [*Football Club*] [*Afrikaans*]
V/K .... Vojenska Kuchyne [*Military Field Kitchen*]   (CZ)
V/K .... Vsesojuznaya Kontora [*All-Union Office*] [*Russian*]   (CED)
VKAJ .... Vrouwelijke Katholieke Arbeidendejeugd [*Benelux*]   (BAS)
VKAJ .... Vrouwelijke Kristelijke Arbeidersjeugd [*Belgium*]   (EAIO)
VKAS .... "Red Banner" Military Academy of Communications   (RU)
VKB .... Higher Courses in Library Science   (RU)
VKB .... Veliko Krizarsko Bratstvo [*Great Brotherhood of Crusaders*] [*Croatian*]   (YU)
vkb .... Vezerkarhoz Beosztott [*Assigned to the General Staff*]   (HU)
VKB .... Villamositasi Kutatasi Bizottsag [*Research Committee on Electrification*]   (HU)
VKB .... Wentzel-Kramers-Brillouin Approximation   (RU)
VKD .... Military Cableway   (RU)
VkdL .... Verein Katholischer Deutscher Lehrerinnen eV   (SLS)
VKE .... Vasilikon Komma Ellados [*Royalist Party of Greece*]   (GC)
VKE .... Voroskereszt Egylet [*Red Cross Association*]   (HU)
VKELG ...... Verband Katholischer Einrichtungen fur Lern- und Geistigbehinderte [*Union of Catholic Institutions for the Mentally Handicapped and Persons with Learning Disabilities*] [*Germany*]   (EAIO)
vk f .... Vezerkari Fonok [*or Vezerkari Fonokseg*] [*Chief of Staff or Office of the Chief of Staff*]   (HU)
VKF .... Volga-Kama Branch   (RU)
VKFKiS ..... All-Union Committee for Physical Culture and Sport   (RU)
VKFKSMS ... Higher Committee for Physical Culture and Sports of the Council of Ministers   (BU)
VKFM .... All-Chinese Youth Federation   (RU)
VKFP .... All-Chinese Trade-Union Federation   (RU)
VKFPS .... All-Chinese Trade-Union Federation   (RU)
VKFS .... All-Chinese Student Federation   (RU)
VKFS .... Higher Committee for Physical Culture and Sports   (BU)
VKG .... Scanair Ltd. [*Denmark*] [*ICAO designator*]   (FAAC)
VKG .... Vectorcardiogram   (RU)
vkgr .... Air Movement Control Team   (BU)
vkh .... Entrance   (BU)
vkh .... Input   (BU)
VKh .... Logistics   (RU)
VKh .... Vinyl Chloride   (RU)
VKh .... Vinylidene Chloride   (RU)
VKhA .... Chemical Warfare Academy   (RU)
VKhI .... All-Union Grain Inspection   (RU)
VKhK .... Multipurpose Water Development Project   (RU)
VKhK .... Voskresensk Chemical Kombinat Imeni V. V. Kuybyshev   (RU)
VKhO .... All-Russian Choral Society   (RU)
VKhO .... All-Union Chemical Society Imeni D. I. Mendeleyev   (RU)
VKhO .... Logistics Section   (RU)
VKhR .... Chemical Reconnaissance   (RU)
vkhrr .... Chemical and Radiation Reconnaissance Platoon   (BU)
VKhTU ...... Higher School of Chemical Engineering   (RU)
VKhU .... Directorate of Logistics   (RU)
VKhU .... Input Device   (RU)
VKhUP ...... Chemical Warfare Training Post   (RU)
VKhUTEIN ... Higher State Art and Craft Institute [*1926-1930*]   (RU)
VKhUTEMAS ... Higher State Art and Craft Shops [*1921-1926*]   (RU)
vkhz .... Chemical Defense Platoon   (RU)
VKI .... Tartrate of Lime   (RU)
vki .... Valaki [*Someone*]   (HU)
VKI .... Vandkvalitetsinstituttet [*Water Quality Institute*] [*Research center*] [*Denmark*]   (IRC)
VKIFD ...... Von Karman Institute for Fluid Dynamics [*Belgium*]   (PDAA)
VKIP .... Higher Communist Institute of Education [*1931-1938*]   (RU)
VKIZh .... All-Union Communist Institute of Journalism Imeni "Pravda"   (RU)
VKK .... Evening Courses for Peasants   (RU)
VKK .... Medical Consultation Commission   (RU)
VKK .... Medical Control Commission   (RU)
VKK .... Military Control Committee [*Chinese People's Republic; 1946-1949*]   (RU)
VKK .... Pressure Suit   (RU)
VKK .... Tartaric Acid   (RU)
VKK .... Temporary Control Commission   (RU)

VKKL .... Villamosipari Kozponti Kutato Laboratorium [*Central Research Laboratory for the Electrical Engineering Industry*]   (HU)
VKKMTS .. Interim Coordinating Committee for International Commodity Arrangements [*ICCICA*]   (RU)
VKL .... Aerovekel SA [*Mexico*] [*ICAO designator*]   (FAAC)
vkl .... Enclosure, Insertion, Insert, Inset   (RU)
vkl .... Including   (BU)
vkl .... Inclusive, Including   (RU)
VKL .... Switch   (RU)
VKL .... Vereniging van Katholieke Leraren Sint-Bonaventura [*Netherlands*]   (SLS)
VKL .... Volkseigener Kreislichtspielbetrieb [*State Kreis Movie Theater*]   (EG)
vklyuch .... Inclusive, Including   (RU)
VKM .... Vallas- es Kozoktatasugyi Miniszterium/Miniszter [*Ministry/Minister of Religious and Educational Affairs*]   (HU)
VKM .... Varos- es Kozseggazdalkodasi Miniszterium/Miniszter [*Ministry/Minister of City and Community Management*]   (HU)
VKM .... Versorgungskontor fuer Maschinenbauerzeugnisse [*Supply Office for Machine Building Products*]   (EG)
VKM .... Vertical Forging Machine   (RU)
VKM .... Villamos Kismotorgyar [*Factory for Small Electric Motors*]   (HU)
v kn .... In the Book   (RU)
VKN .... Voorkambriese Navorsingseenheid van die Kamer van Mynwese [*Universiteit van Kaapstad*] [*South Africa*]   (AA)
VKNII .... All-Union Scientific Research Institute of the Confectionery Industry   (RU)
VKO .... All-Union Leather Association   (RU)
VKO .... Military Cartographic Section   (RU)
VKO .... Moscow Vnukovo Airport [*Former USSR*] [*Airport symbol*]   (OAG)
vko .... Vihko [*Finland*]
VKO .... Vojenska Komise Obrany [*Military Defense Commission*]   (CZ)
VKOShO .... All-Union Leather, Footwear, and Garment Association   (RU)
VKOUP ..... World Confederation of Organizations of the Teaching Profession   (RU)
VKP .... All-Union Book Chamber   (RU)
VKP .... All-Union Communist Party (of Bolsheviks)   (RU)
VKP .... Hungarian Communist Party [*1918-1948*]   (RU)
VKP .... Mobile Command Post   (RU)
VKP .... Verkaufspreis [*Selling Price*] [*German*]   (EG)
VKP .... Vsesoyuznaya Knichnaya Palata [*All-Union Book Chamber*] [*Former USSR*]   (EAIO)
VKP .... Vsezvezna Komunisticna Partija (Boljsevikov) [*All-Union Communist Party (Bolsheviks)*]   (YU)
VKP(b) ...... All-Union Communist Party (of Bolsheviks) [*1925-1952*]   (RU)
VKPG .... All-Russian Famine Relief Commission   (RU)
VKPL .... Velkorazne Kulomety Proti Letadlum [*Heavy Caliber Antiaircraft Machine Guns*]   (CZ)
VKPR .... Vojenska Kancelar Presidenta Republiky [*Military Office of the President of the Republic*]   (CZ)
VKPT .... Tobacco Ring Spot Virus   (RU)
VKR .... Auxiliary Cruiser   (RU)
VKR .... Congress of Representatives for the Colored [*South Africa*]   (AF)
VKR .... Velitel Vojenske Kontrarozvedky [*Commander of Military Counterintelligence*]   (CZ)
VKR .... Wissenschaftliche Vereinigung zur Pflege des Konsumentenschutzrechts [*Zurich, Switzerland*]   (SLS)
VKRS .... Military Commandant of an Unloading Area   (BU)
VKS .... All-Union Committee for Standardization   (RU)
VKS .... Higher Committee for Standardization   (BU)
VKS .... Leading-In Cable Rack   (RU)
vks .... Military Court of Appeals   (BU)
VKS .... Veliko Krizarsko Sestrinstvo [*Great Sisterhood of Crusaders*] [*Croatian*]   (YU)
VKS .... Visa Komercijalna Skola [*Advanced Business School*]   (YU)
VKS(b) .... All-Union Communist Party (Bolshevik) [*Former USSR*]   (CZ)
VKSh .... Higher Cooperative School   (RU)
VKSK .... Verband der Kleingaertner, Siedler, und Kleintierzuechter [*Union of Small Gardeners, Settlers, and Small Livestock Breeders*]   (EG)
VKSKhSh .. Higher Communist Agricultural School   (RU)
VKSM .... Hungarian Young Communist League   (RU)
VKSt .... Verkaufsstelle [*Sales Outlet*] [*German*]   (EG)
VKSZ .... Vybor pro Kulturni Styky se Zahranicim [*Committee for Cultural Relations with Foreign Countries*]   (CZ)
VKT .... All-Union State Cartographic Trust   (RU)
VKT .... General Confederation of Labor   (RU)
vkt .... Higher Critical Temperature   (RU)
VKT .... Vrlo Kratki Talasi [*Ultrashort Waves*]   (YU)
VKTI .... All-Union Boiler and Turbine Institute   (RU)
VKTK .... General Confederation of Labor of Cameroun   (RU)
VKTO .... All-Union Association of the Boiler and Turbine Industry   (RU)
VKTR .... General Confederation of Labor of Romania   (RU)

VKTV........ General Confederation of Labor of Vietnam (RU)
VKU............ All-Union Communist University (RU)
VKU........... Military Commandant of a Railroad Section (BU)
VKU........... Video Control Unit (RU)
VKV........... Vaskohaszati Kemenceepito Vallalat, Szekesfehervar
    [Metallurgical Furnace, Building Enterprise Szekesfehervar]
    (HU)
VKV........... Velmi Kratke Vlny [Ultrashort Wave (Ultrahigh Frequency)]
    (CZ)
VKV........... Verpleegkundige Kurrikula Vereniging van Suid-Afrika [Nursing
    Curricula Association of South Africa] (AA)
VKV........ Vlaams Kinesitherapeuten Verbond [Belgium] (SLS)
VKVS........ Vojenske Katedry Vysokoskolske [Military Departments at
    Universities] (CZ)
VKVSh...... All-Union Committee on Higher Education (RU)
VKVTO..... All-Union Committee on Higher Technical Education (RU)
VKWB ...... Verban Kirchlich-wissenschaftlichen Bibliotheken [Association of
    Ecclesiastical Academic Libraries] [Germany] (PDAA)
VKZ .... All-Union Commission for Mineral Resources (RU)
vkz.............. Railroad Station [Topography] (RU)
VKZO .... All-Union Correspondence Training Center for Communications
    Personnel (RU)
VL .... Calling Lamp (RU)
VL .... Electron Tube Voltmeter, Tube Voltmeter (RU)
vl................ Humidity (RU)
VL .... Military Infirmary (RU)
VL .... Overhead Line (RU)
VL .... Ribbon-Type Weighing Device (RU)
Vl................ Vaasan Laani [or Vaasan Laania] [Finland]
VL .... Valmet OY [Finland] [ICAO aircraft manufacturer identifier]
    (ICAO)
vl................ Vanhaa Lukua [Finland]
VL .... Velitelstvi Letectva [Air Force Headquarters] (CZ)
VL .... Vereinigte Linke [United Left] [Germany] [Political party]
    (PPW)
VL .... Vereniging Lucht [Clean Air Society in the Netherlands-CLAN]
    (EAIO)
VL .... Vestre Landsret [Western Court of Appeal] [Denmark] (ILCA)
VL .... Veterinary Hospital (RU)
vl................ Viale [Avenue] [Italian] (CED)
vl................ Vialetto [Avenue] [Italian] (CED)
Vl................ Vitesse du Vent dans la Direction de la Ligne de Tir [French]
    (MTD)
Vl................ Vlaams [Flemish] [Afrikaans]
VL .... Vlaandere [Flanders] [Afrikaans]
VL .... Vladimir Lenin [Electric locomotive type] (RU)
vl................ Vlekkig [Spotted] [Netherlands]
VL .... Waterline (RU)
VLA .... Victorian Library Association [Australia] (ADA)
Vla............. Villa [Small Town] [Va] [See also] [Spanish] (NAU)
VLA .... Vojenska Lekarska Akademie [Military Medical Academy]
    [Hradec-Kralove] (CZ)
Vlad........... Vladivostok [Russian port] (BARN)
Vladoblgosarkhiv ... State Archives of the Vladimir Oblast (RU)
VLAM .... Vlamertinghe [City in Flanders] [World War I] [Army] (DSUE)
VLAO .... Vientiane [Laos] [ICAO location identifier] (ICLI)
VLAP........ Attopeu [Laos] [ICAO location identifier] (ICLI)
VLB........... Versuchs- und Lehranstalt fur Brauerei in Berlin [Research and
    Teaching Institute for Brewing in Berlin] [Germany] (IRC)
VLBD........ Verband der Landesarchaologen in der Bundesrepublik
    Deutschland [German State Archaeologists' Association]
    (EAIO)
VLC .... Valencia [Spain] [Airport symbol] (OAG)
VLCC........ Very Large Crude Carriers (LA)
VLCFQ...... Victoria League for Commonwealth Fellowship in Queensland
    [Australia]
VLCFSA.... Victoria League for Commonwealth Fellowship in South
    Australia
VLCFV ...... Victoria League for Commonwealth Fellowship in Victoria
    [Australia]
VLE........... Medical Determination of Flight Fitness (RU)
VLE........... Violone [Violins] [Music]
VLET......... All-Union Lumber Export Technicum (RU)
VLF........... Victoria Law Foundation [Australia]
VLG .... Trans Air Valtologia [Moldova] [ICAO designator] (FAAC)
Vlg............. Verlag [Publishing Firm] [German]
VLG .... Villa Gesell [Argentina] [Airport symbol] (OAG)
VLG .... Volgende [Following, Next] [Afrikaans]
VLGITB .... Victorian Local Government Industry Training Board
    [Australia]
VLGS........ Volgens [According To] [Afrikaans]
Vlgsverz .... Verlagsverzeichnis [Publisher's List] [German]
VLHS........ Bane Houei Say [Laos] [ICAO location identifier] (ICLI)
VLI........... Higher Institute of Forestry Engineering (BU)
VLI........... Incoming Final Selector (RU)
VLI........... Port Vila [Vanuata] [Airport symbol] (OAG)

VLI............ Voronezh Forestry Institute (RU)
VLK .... Medical Commission for Determination of Flight Fitness (RU)
VLK .... VE - Versorgungs- und Lagerungskontor [State Supply and
    Stockpiling Agency] (EG)
vlk.............. Volcano (RU)
VLKG .... Khong Island [Laos] [ICAO location identifier] (ICLI)
VLKhI....... Higher Institute of Literature and Art Imeni Valeriy Bryusov
    (RU)
VLKhI....... Voronezh Forestry Institute (RU)
vlkm .... Vlakovy Kilometr [Railroad-Kilometer] (CZ)
VLKSM .... All-Union Lenin Young Communist League (RU)
VLKT........ Kene Thao [Laos] [ICAO location identifier] (ICLI)
VLL........... Valladolid [Spain] [Airport symbol] (OAG)
VLLB........ Luang Prabang [Laos] [ICAO location identifier] (ICLI)
Vlle............ Vieille [Old] [Military map abbreviation World War I] [French]
    (MTD)
VLLG........ Victorian Law Librarians Group [Australia]
VLLN......... Luong Nam Tha [Laos] [ICAO location identifier] (ICLI)
VLM .... Vlaamse Luchtransportmaatschappij NV [Belgium] [ICAO
    designator] (FAAC)
VLMB....... Vereinigung der Lehrer fuer Maschinenschreiben und
    Buerotechnik im SKV [Luzern, Switzerland] (SLS)
VLMV .... Vorarlberger Landesmuseumsverein [Austria] (SLS)
VLN .... Valencia [Venezuela] [Airport symbol] (OAG)
vlnar.......... Vladni Narizeni [Government Decree] (CZ)
VLNR .... Van Links na Regs [From Left to Right] [Afrikaans]
VLO .... Vereniging van Luguaart Onderhoudbedrywe [Association of
    Aviation Maintenance Organizations] (EAIO)
VLOS........ Oudomsay [Laos] [ICAO location identifier] (ICLI)
VLP........... Schweizerische Vereinigung fuer Landesplanung [Bern,
    Switzerland] (SLS)
VLP........... Video Langspielplatte [German] (ADPT)
VLPK........ Paksane [Laos] [ICAO location identifier] (ICLI)
VLPS........ Pakse [Laos] [ICAO location identifier] (ICLI)
VLPV........ Phong Savanh [Laos] [ICAO location identifier] (ICLI)
VLR .... Vive la Revolution [Long Live the Revolution (Name of leftwing
    group no longer extant since July 1971)] [French] (WER)
VLR .... Vocno Lozni Rasadnik [Fruit and Viticulture Nursery] (YU)
VLR .... Volare [Russian Federation] [ICAO designator] (FAAC)
VLRA........ Vehicule Leger de Reconnaissance et d'Appui
VLRO .... Military Hunting and Fishing Organization (BU)
VLRP........ Vitamin Laboratories of Roche Products Pty. Ltd. [Australia]
    (DSCA)
VLRZ........ Vojenska Lazenska a Rekreacni Zarizeni [Military Health and
    Recreation Resorts] (CZ)
VLS........... Valesdir [Vanuata] [Airport symbol] (OAG)
VLS........... Valstieciu Liaudininku Sajunga [Peasant Populist Union]
    [Lithuania] [Political party] (PPE)
VLS........... Vry Langs Skip [Free Alongside Ship] [Afrikaans]
VLSB........ Sayaboury [Laos] [ICAO location identifier] (ICLI)
VLSK........ Savannakhet [Laos] [ICAO location identifier] (ICLI)
VLSN........ Sam Neua [Laos] [ICAO location identifier] (ICLI)
VLSV........ Saravane [Laos] [ICAO location identifier] (ICLI)
VLT........... High-Frequency Beam Tetrode (RU)
VLT........... Very Large Telescope [Proposed] [European Southern
    Observatory]
VLTC........ Vereniging van Leertegnoloe en Chemici [South Africa] (AA)
VLTI......... Higher Institute of Forestry Engineering (BU)
VLTI......... Voronezh Forestry-Engineering Institute (RU)
VLTK........ Thakhek [Laos] [ICAO location identifier] (ICLI)
VLTT........ Vehicular Leger Toot Terrain [Light All-Terrain Vehicle]
    [French] (MCD)
VLU .... Vedecky Letecky Ustav [Scientific Institute of Aeronautics] (CZ)
VLU .... Vietnam Labor Union
VLU .... Vojensky Letecky Ustav [Military Institute of Aeronautics] (CZ)
VLV .... Valera [Venezuela] [Airport symbol] (OAG)
VLV(KP)... Vroue-Landbouvereniging (Kaapprovinsie) [Afrikaans]
VLVT........ Vientiane/Wattay [Laos] [ICAO location identifier] (ICLI)
VLW .... Bundesverband der Lehrer an Wirtschaftsschulen eV (SLS)
VLXG .... Xieng Khouang [Laos] [ICAO location identifier] (ICLI)
VLXK........ Xieng Khouang (Plaine Des Jarres) [Laos] [ICAO location
    identifier] (ICLI)
VM............ Air-Manganese (RU)
VM............ Air Mass (RU)
VM............ Beater (RU)
vm.............. Capacity (BU)
VM............ Computer (RU)
VM............ Drawing Machine (RU)
VM............ Explosive Material (RU)
VM............ Explosives (BU)
vm.............. In Place Of (BU)
vm.............. Instead Of, In Place Of, For (RU)
V/m........... Intramuscular (RU)
VM............ Microswitch (RU)
vm.............. Minister of War (BU)
VM............ Oil Circuit Breaker (RU)

VM............. Suspension Bridge   (RU)
vm.............. Valogatott Muvek [*Selected Works*]   (HU)
VM............. Valore Militare [*Used after military decorations*] [*Italian*]
VM............. Valuta Mark   (WEN)
vm.............. Varmegye [*County*] [*Hungary*]   (GPO)
VM............. Vertrauensmann [*Union Shop Steward, Spokesman of a Union Group*]   (EG)
VM............ Vieille-Montagne
VM............ Viet Minh [*An underground organization set up in Vietnam to overthrow the French*] [*Defunct since 1954 Now popularly used to refer to communists or leftists, especially Vietnamese communists*]   (CL)
VM............. Virtuelle Maschine [*German*]   (ADPT)
VM............. Voennoe Ministerstvo [*Ministry of War*] [*1950-53; merged into the Ministry of Defense*] [*Russian*]
VM............. Vollemaan [*Full Moon*] [*Afrikaans*]
VM............. Voltmeter [*German*]   (GCA)
vm.............. Voormiddag [*Before Noon*] [*Netherlands*]   (GPO)
VM............. Vorigen Monats [*Of Last Month*] [*German*]
Vm............. Vormittags [*In the Forenoon*] [*German*]
V M........... Vossa Merce [*Your Grace*] [*Portuguese*]   (GPO)
VM............. Vostra Maesta [*Your Majesty*] [*Italian*]
VM............. Votre Majeste [*Your Majesty*] [*French*]
VM............. Vuestra Majestad [*Your Majesty*] [*Spanish*]
Vm............. Vuestra Merced [*Your Worship*] [*Spanish*]
VM............. War Ministry   (RU)
VMA......... Military Medical Academy   (RU)
VMA......... Naval Academy   (RU)
VMA......... Vojnomedicinska Akademija [*Academy of Military Medicine*]   (YU)
VMAK....... Naval Academic Courses   (RU)
VMAKV .... Naval Shipbuilding and Armament Academy   (RU)
VMAU....... Naval Artillery School   (RU)
VMB......... Naval Base   (RU)
VMB......... Veterinary Medicines Board [*Tasmania, Australia*]
Vmba........ Venootschap met Beperkte Aansprakelijkheid [*Benelux*]   (BAS)
VMBA....... Victorian Medical Benevolent Association [*Australia*]
VMBI........ Vereniging Medische en Biologische Informatieverwerking
VMBIT...... All-Union Intersectional Office of Engineers and Technicians   (RU)
VMC......... Victorian Marathon Club [*Australia*]
Vmce........ Vossa Merce [*Your Grace*] [*Portuguese*]   (GPO)
VMD......... Vanguarda Militar Democratica [*Democratic Military Vanguard*] [*Brazil*]   (LA)
VMD......... Vereniging Milieudefensie [*Netherlands*]   (SLS)
Vmd.......... Vuestra Merced [*Your Worship*] [*Spanish*]
VMDA...... Veterinary Manufacturers' and Distributors' Association [*Australia*]
VME......... Villa Mercedes [*Argentina*] [*Airport symbol*]   (OAG)
VME......... Vychodomoravske Elektrarny [*East Moravian Electric Power Plants*]   (CZ)
VMEI........ Higher Machine - Electrical Institute   (BU)
VMEO ...... Vereniging van Munisipale Elektrisiteitsondernemings van Suidelike [*South Africa*]   (AA)
VMF......... Navy   (RU)
VMF......... Verenigde Machinefabrieken NV [*Association of Machine Factories*] [*Business term*] [*Netherlands*]
VMF......... Vieilles Maisons Francaises [*Paris, France*]   (SLS)
VMFU....... Naval School for Medical Assistants   (RU)
VMG......... Engine-Propeller Unit [*Aviation*]   (RU)
VMG......... Naval Hospital   (RU)
VMG......... Power Plant Aircraft, Turbine Aggregate   (BU)
VMG......... Verordening Militair Gezag [*Benelux*]   (BAS)
VMGI........ Higher Mining Geological Institute   (BU)
VMGU....... Naval Hydrographic School   (RU)
VMHK...... Vereniging voor het Museum van Hedendaagse Kunst [*Belgium*]   (EAIO)
VMI .... Higher Medical Institute   (BU)
VMI .... Institute of Veterinary Medicine   (BU)
VMI .... Naval Inspection   (RU)
VMI .... Vazduhoplovni Modelarski Institut [*Air Force Modeling Institute*]   (YU)
VMI .... Vitebsk Medical Institute   (RU)
VMIAC...... Victorian Mental Illness Awareness Council [*Australia*]
VMICh...... Naval Engineering Unit   (RU)
VMIG .... Naval Hospital for Contagious Diseases   (RU)
VMIU....... Naval Engineering School   (RU)
VMK......... High-Molecular Weight Component   (RU)
VMK......... High Naval Command   (RU)
VMK......... Naval Club   (RU)
VMK......... Temporary International Collective   (BU)
VMKhI ...... Vologda Institute of Dairying   (RU)
VML .... Vening Meinesz Laboratorium [*Netherlands*]   (MSC)
VML .... Veroeffentlichungen des Museums fuer Voelkerkunde zu Leipzig
VML .... Victorian Music Library [*Australia*]
VMM........ Military Medical Museum   (RU)

VMM........ Veille Meteorologique Mondiale [*World Weather Watch - WWW*] [*French*]   (ASF)
VMM........ Vigilancia Meteorologica Mundial [*World Weather Watch - WWW*] [*Spanish*]   (ASF)
VMM........ Volunteer Missionary Movement [*London Colney, Hertfordshire, England*]   (EAIO)
VMMA...... Naval Medical Academy   (RU)
VMMC...... Macau [*Macau*] [*ICAO location identifier*]   (ICLI)
VMN......... Capital Punishment   (RU)
VMN......... Vereeniging van Muziekhandelaren in Uitgevens in Nederland [*Association of Music Dealers and Publishers in the Netherlands*]   (EAIO)
VMNO ...... Naval Scientific Society   (RU)
VMNO ...... People's Military Youth Organization   (BU)
VMNU...... People's Naval Military Academy   (BU)
VMO......... All-Union Microbiological Society   (RU)
VMO......... All-Union Mineralogical Society   (RU)
VMO......... Verband der Marktforscher Oesterreichs [*Austrian Market Research Society*]   (SLS)
VMO......... Vlaamse Militantenorde [*Flemish Militant Order*] [*Belgium*]   (WEN)
VMO......... World Meteorological Organization [*WMO*]   (RU)
VMOLA .... Military Medical "Order of Lenin" Academy Imeni S. M. Kirov   (RU)
VMOLA .... Naval "Order of Lenin" Academy   (RU)
VMORO.... Internal Macedonian Odrin Revolutionary Organization   (BU)
VMORO.... Internal Macedonian Okrug Revolutionary Organizations   (BU)
VMORO.... Vnatresna Makedono-Odrinska Revolucionerna Organizacija [*Internal Macedonian Odrin Revolutionary Organization*]   (YU)
VMP .... All-Union A. S. Pushkin Museum   (RU)
VMP .... Temporary Medical Station   (RU)
VMPA .... Verband der Materialpruefungsaemter eV   (SLS)
VMPF....... Victorian Medical Postgraduate Foundation [*Australia*]
VMPU .... Naval Political School   (RU)
VMPU .... Naval Preparatory School   (RU)
VMR .... Naval District   (RU)
VMR .... Voice of Malayan Revolution   (ML)
VMRA .... Victorian Medical Record Association [*Australia*]
VMRO....... Vnatresna Makedonska Revolucionerna Organizacija [*Internal Macedonian Revolutionary Organization (Known popularly among English-speaking nations as the IMRO)*] [*Former Yugoslavia*] [*Political party*]   (PPE)
VMRO....... Vutreshna Makidoniski Revoliutsionna Organizatsiia [*Internal Macedonian Revolutionary Organization*] [*Bulgaria*] [*Political party*]   (PPE)
VMRO-DPMNE ... Internal Macedonian Revolutionary Organization - Democratic Party for Macedonian National Unity [*Political party*]
VMRO(U) ... Vnatresna Makedonska Revolucionerna Organizacija (Udruzena) [*Internal Macedonian Revolutionary Organization (United)*] [*Former Yugoslavia*] [*Political party*]   (PPE)
VMS .... Naval Court   (RU)
VMS .... Naval Forces, Navy   (BU)
VMS .... Navy, Naval Forces   (RU)
VMS .... Propeller-Driven Sled   (RU)
VMS .... Verband der Museen der Schweiz [*Swiss Museums Association*]   (EAIO)
VMS .... Vryemarkstigting [*South Africa*]   (AA)
VMSA....... Victorian Motor Schools Association [*Australia*]
VMSh....... Higher School of Music   (RU)
VMSh....... Naval School   (RU)
VMSO .... Verband fuer Medizinischen Strahlenschutz in Oesterreich [*Society for Medical Ray Protection in Austria*]   (SLS)
VMT .... Upper Dead Center   (RU)
VMTA .... Victorian Music Teachers Association [*Australia*]
VMTC .... Vehicle and Machinery Stores Trade Corp. [*Myanmar*]   (DS)
VMTs .... Digital Computer   (RU)
VMTs .... Meteorological Computation Center   (RU)
VMTV ...... Vegyimuveket Tervezo Vallalat [*Designing Enterprise for Chemical Plants*]   (HU)
VMTVV..... Veleni Motostreleckemu Tankovemu a Vysadkovemu Vojsku [*Motorized Rifle, Tank, and Airborne Command*]   (CZ)
VMU......... Baimuru [*Papua New Guinea*] [*Airport symbol*]   (OAG)
VMU......... Engine-Propeller Unit [*Aviation*]   (RU)
VMU......... Military Medical Directorate [*or Establishment*]   (RU)
VMU......... Naval School   (RU)
VMUK...... Naval Training Center   (RU)
VMUZ....... Naval Educational Institution   (RU)
VMV......... Higher Low Water   (RU)
VMV......... High-Voltage Oil Circuit Breaker   (RU)
VMW........ Vereinigte Metallgusswerke (VEB) [*United Metal Foundry (VEB)*]   (EG)
VMYa....... Auxiliary International Language   (RU)
VMZ......... Vyksa Metallurgical Plants   (RU)
VMZ......... Water and Oil Servicing Truck   (RU)

VMZhK ..... Macromolecular Fatty Acids (RU)
VN............. Civilian Employee [*Military institutions or labor camps*] (RU)
VN............. Departmental Standard, Institutional Standard (RU)
VN............. High Tension (BU)
VN............. High-Voltage, High-Tension (RU)
vn............. Inner, Internal, Inside (RU)
VN............. Load Equalizer (RU)
VN............. Table Fan (RU)
VN............. Vacuum Pump (RU)
VN............. Vakstudie-Nieuws [*Benelux*] (BAS)
VN............. Valtioneuvosto [*Council of State*] [*Finland*] (WEN)
Vn............. Vann [*or Vatn*] [*Lake*] [*Norway*] (NAU)
VN............. Vasilikon Navtikon [*Royal Navy*] [*Greek*] (GC)
VN............. Vatreni Nalet [*Firing Assault*] [*Military*] (YU)
vn............. Veien [*Way*] [*Norway*] (CED)
Vn............. Veien [*Street*] (IDIG)
vn............. Vellon [*Spanish*]
VN............. Vereinigte Nationen [*United Nations*] [*German*]
VN............. Verenigde Naties [*Benelux*] (BAS)
VN............. Victorian Navy [*Australia*]
VN............. Vietnam [*ANSI two-letter standard code*] (CNC)
Vn............. Vorname [*First Name*] [*German*]
VN............. Vychovny Nacelnik [*Training Officer*] (CZ)
VN............. Vyrobni Normy [*Production Standards*] (CZ)
vn............. Vysoke Napeti [*High Voltage*] (CZ)
VN............. Vystrojni Nacelnik [*Equipment Chief*] (CZ)
VN............. Water Pump (RU)
VNA........... Hungarian People's Army (RU)
VNA........... Radio Hanoi [*North Vietnam radio programming which targeted US troops in South Vietnam*] (VNW)
VNA........... Rotating Guide Vane (RU)
VNA........... Valores Nacionales Ajustables [*National Adjustable Securities*] [*Argentina*] (LA)
VNA........... Veterinary Nurses' Association [*Australia*]
VNA........... Victorian Netball Association [*Australia*]
VNA........... Vietnamese National Army
vnab........... Air Observation (RU)
VNAF......... Republic of Vietnam Air Force (VNW)
VNAIZ....... All-Union Scientific Research Institute of Sound Recording (RU)
VNAR......... Air Observation and Reconnaissance (RU)
VNAV........ All-Russian Scientific Association of Oriental Studies (RU)
VNB........... Household Table Scales (RU)
VNBG........ Bajhang [*Nepal*] [*ICAO location identifier*] (ICLI)
VNBJ........ Bhojpur [*Nepal*] [*ICAO location identifier*] (ICLI)
VNBL .... Baglung [*Nepal*] [*ICAO location identifier*] (ICLI)
VNBP .... Bharatpur [*Nepal*] [*ICAO location identifier*] (ICLI)
VNBR .... Bajura [*Nepal*] [*ICAO location identifier*] (ICLI)
VNBT .... Baitadi [*Nepal*] [*ICAO location identifier*] (ICLI)
VNBW .... Bhairawa [*Nepal*] [*ICAO location identifier*] (ICLI)
VNCG........ Chandragarhi [*Nepal*] [*ICAO location identifier*] (ICLI)
VNCI .... Vereniging van de Nederlandse Chemische Industrie [*Association of the Dutch Chemical Industries*] (EAIO)
VNCIAWPRC ... Venezuelan National Committee of the International Association on Water Pollution Research and Control (EAIO)
VND........... Higher Nervous Activity (RU)
VND........... Low-Pressure Air (RU)
vnd............. Voornoemd [*Benelux*] (BAS)
VND........... Vychodoceske Narodni Divadlo [*East Bohemian National Theater*] (CZ)
VNDG........ Dang [*Nepal*] [*ICAO location identifier*] (ICLI)
VNDH .... Dhangarhi [*Nepal*] [*ICAO location identifier*] (ICLI)
VNDP .... Dolpa [*Nepal*] [*ICAO location identifier*] (ICLI)
VNDR........ Dhorpatan [*Nepal*] [*ICAO location identifier*] (ICLI)
VNDT .... Doti [*Nepal*] [*ICAO location identifier*] (ICLI)
Vneshtorg .. Ministry of Foreign Trade, USSR (RU)
Vneshtorgbank ... Foreign Trade Bank, USSR (RU)
Vneshtorgizdat ... State Publishing House of the Ministry of Foreign Trade, USSR (RU)
VNG........... Vereniging van Nederlandse Gemeenten [*Association of Dutch Municipalities*]
VNGK........ Gorkha [*Nepal*] [*ICAO location identifier*] (ICLI)
VNIALMI ... All-Union Scientific Research Institute of Conservational Afforestation (RU)
VNIEKIPRODMASh ... All-Union Scientific Research and Experimental Design Institute of Food Machinery (RU)
VNIEMK... All-Union Scientific Research Institute of Essential-Oil Crops (RU)
VNIEMS... All-Union Scientific Research Institute of Veterinary Ectoparasitology, Mycology, and Sanitation (RU)
VNIESKh .. All-Union Scientific Research Institute of Agricultural Economics (RU)
VNIFS .... All-Union Scientific Research Antiphylloxera Station (RU)
VNIFTRI... All-Union Scientific Research Institute of Physicotechnical and Radiotechnical Measurements (RU)

VNIGI........ All-Union Scientific Research Institute of Gas and Synthetic Liquid Fuel (RU)
VNIGL....... Valday Scientific Research Hydrological Laboratory (RU)
VNIGMI.... All-Union Scientific Research Institute of Hydraulic Machinery (RU)
VNIGNI .... All-Union Petroleum Scientific Research Institute of Geological Exploration [*Moscow*] (RU)
VNIGRI..... All-Union Petroleum Scientific Research Institute of Geological Exploration [*Leningrad*] (RU)
VNII .... All-Union Petroleum Scientific Research Institute [*1943-1945*] (RU)
VNII .... All-Union Scientific Research Institute (RU)
VNII .... All-Union Scientific Research Institute of Petroleum and Gas (RU)
VNII .... All-Union Scientific Research Institute of Tools (RU)
VNII .... Veterinary Scientific Research Institute of the RKKA (RU)
VNII-1 .... All-Union Scientific Research Institute of Gold and Rare Metals (RU)
VNIIA........ All-Union Scientific Research Institute of Antibiotics (RU)
VNIIASBEST ... All-Union Scientific Research Institute of the Asbestos-Processing Industry (RU)
VNIIAsbesttsement ... All-Union Scientific Research Institute for Asbestos, Mica, Asbestos Cement Products, and for the Planning of Mica Industry Establishments (RU)
VNIIASh ... All-Union Scientific Research Institute of Abrasives and Grinding (RU)
VNIIAT..... All-Union Scientific Research Institute of Automobile Transportation (RU)
VNIIATI ... All-Union Scientific Research, Design, and Technological Institute of Industrial Asbestos Products (RU)
VNIIAVTOGEN ... All-Union Scientific Research Institute of Gas Welding and Cutting of Metals (RU)
VNIIB iTsP ... All-Union Scientific Research Institute of the Pulp and Paper Industry (RU)
VNIIBT..... All-Union Scientific Research Institute for Drilling Techniques (RU)
VNIIBurtekhnika ... All-Union Scientific Research Institute for Drilling Techniques (RU)
VNIIChISK ... All-Union Scientific Research Institute of Tea and Subtropical Crops (RU)
VNIIChKh ... All-Union Scientific Research Institute of the Tea Cultivation (RU)
VNIIChP... All-Union Scientific Research Institute of the Tea Industry (RU)
VNIID .... All-Union Scientific Research Institute of Lumber (RU)
VNIIDMASh ... All-Union Scientific Research and Design Institute of Woodworking Machinery (RU)
VNIIDrev .. All-Union Scientific Research Institute of the Woodworking Industry (RU)
VNIIE........ All-Union Scientific Research Institute of Electric Power Engineering (RU)
VNIIEE ..... All-Union Scientific Research Institute of Power Engineering and Electrification (RU)
VNIIEKIProdmash ... All-Union Scientific Research and Experimental Institute of Food Machinery (RU)
VNIIElektromash ... All-Union Scientific Research Institute of the Technology of Electric Machinery and Equipment Manufacture (RU)
VNIIElektroprivod ... All-Union Scientific Research, Planning, and Design Institute for Automatic Electric Drive in Industry, Agriculture, and Transportation (RU)
VNIIEM.... All-Union Scientific Research Institute of Electromechanics (RU)
VNIIEP ..... All-Union Scientific Research Institute of Electrical Measuring Instruments (RU)
VNIIESKh ... All-Union Scientific Research Institute of Agricultural Economics (RU)
VNIIESKh ... All-Union Scientific Research Institute of Rural Electrification (RU)
VNIIESO .. All-Union Scientific Research Institute of Electric Welding Equipment (RU)
VNIIETO .. All-Union Scientific Research Institute of Electrothermal Equipment (RU)
VNIIF .... All-Union Scientific Research Institute of Phytopathology (RU)
VNIIFIB.... All-Union Scientific Research Institute of Physiology and Biochemistry of Farm Animals (RU)
VNIIFS...... All-Union Scientific Research Institute of the Ferment and Alcohol Industry (RU)
VNIIFTRI ... All-Union Scientific Research Institute of Physicotechnical and Radiotechnical Measurements (RU)
VNIIG........ All-Union Scientific Research Institute of Hydraulic Engineering Imeni B. Ye. Vedeneyev (RU)
VNIIG........ All-Union Scientific Research Institute of the Goznak (RU)
VNIIGAZ.. All-Union Scientific Research Institute of Natural Gas (RU)
VNIIGEOFIZIKA ... All-Union Scientific Research Institute of Geophysical Exploration Methods (RU)
VNIIGI...... All-Union Scientific Research Institute of Gas and Synthetic Liquid Fuel (RU)

VNIIGidromash ... All-Union Scientific Research, Design, and Technological Institute of Hydraulic Machinery   (RU)

VNIIGidrougol' ... All-Union Scientific Research, Planning, and Design Institute of Hydraulic Coal Mining   (RU)

VNIIGIM .. All-Union Scientific Research Institute of Hydraulic Engineering and Reclamation Imeni A. N. Kostyakov   (RU)

VNIIGIPS ... All-Union Scientific Research Institute of Gypsum and Lime   (RU)

VNIIGL ..... All-Union Hydrometeorological Scientific Research Laboratory   (RU)

VNIIGORMash ... All-Union Scientific Research and Planning Institute of Mining Machinery   (RU)

VNIIgoznaka ... All-Union Scientific Research Institute of the Goznak   (RU)

VNIIGPE .. All-Union Scientific Research Institute of the State Patent Examination   (RU)

VNIIGS ..... All-Union Scientific Research Institute of Hydraulic Engineering and Sanitation   (RU)

VNIIGS ..... All-Union Scientific Research Institute of the Hydrolysis and Sulfite Liquor Industry   (RU)

VNIIGShveyprom ... All-Union State Scientific Research Institute of the Garment Industry   (RU)

VNIIK .... All-Union Scientific Research Institute of Artificial Leather   (RU)

VNIIK .... All-Union Scientific Research Institute of Ceramics   (RU)

VNIIK .... All-Union Scientific Research Institute of Criminology   (RU)

VNIIK .... All-Union Scientific Research Institute of Fodder   (RU)

VNIIK .... All-Union Scientific Research Institute of Horse Breeding   (RU)

VNIIK .... All-Union Scientific Research Institute of Rubber-Yielding Plants   (RU)

VNIIK .... All-Union Scientific Research Institute of the Committee of Standards, Measures, and Measuring Instruments   (RU)

VNIIKANeftegaz ... All-Union Scientific Research, Planning, and Design Institute of Complex Automation in the Petroleum and Gas Industry   (RU)

VNIIKh ...... All-Union Scientific Research Institute of Cotton Growing   (RU)

VNIIKh ...... All-Union Scientific Research Institute of the Baking Industry   (RU)

VNIIKhimmash ... All-Union Scientific Research and Experimental Institute of Chemical Machinery   (RU)

VNIIKhP ... All-Union Scientific Research Institute of the Baking Industry   (RU)

VNIIKhSZR ... All-Union Scientific Research Institute of Chemicals Used for Plant Protection   (RU)

VNIIKI ...... All-Union Scientific Research Institute of Technical Information, Classification, and Coding (of the State Committee of Standards, Measures, and Measuring Instruments, USSR)   (RU)

VNIIKiG .... All-Union Scientific Research Institute of Rubber and Gutta-Percha   (RU)

VNIIKIMASh ... All-Union Scientific Research Institute of Oxygen Machinery   (RU)

VNIIKKh ... All-Union Scientific Research Institute of Potato Growing   (RU)

VNIIKOP .. All-Union Scientific Research Institute of the Canning and Dehydrated Vegetables Industry   (RU)

VNIIKorm ... All-Union Scientific Research Institute of Fodder Imeni V. R. Vil'yams   (RU)

VNIIKP ..... All-Union Scientific Research Institute of the Canning Industry   (RU)

VNIIKS ..... All-Union Scientific Research Institute of Municipal Sanitation   (RU)

VNIIKSMIP ... All-Union Scientific Research Institute of the Committee of Standards, Measures, and Measuring Instruments   (RU)

VNIIL .... All-Union Scientific Research Institute of Flax   (RU)

VNIILK ..... All-Union Scientific Research Institute of Bast Cultures   (RU)

VNIILKh ... All-Union Scientific Research Institute of Forestry [*1938-1956*]   (RU)

VNIILM .... All-Union Scientific Research Institute of Silviculture and Forestry Mechanization   (RU)

VNIILTEKMASh ... All-Union Scientific Research Institute of Textile and Light Machinery   (RU)

VNIILV ..... All-Union Scientific Research Institute of the Bast-Fiber Industry   (RU)

VNIIM .... All-Union Scientific Research Institute of Metrology Imeni D. I. Mendeleyev   (RU)

VNIIMEMK ... All-Union Scientific Research Institute of Oil-Bearing and Essential-Oil Crops   (RU)

VNIIMES ... All-Union Scientific Research Institute of Mechanization and Electrification of Sovkhozes   (RU)

VNIIMESKh ... All-Russian Scientific Research Institute of Rural Mechanization and Electrification   (RU)

VNIIMETMASh ... All-Union Scientific Research, Planning, and Design Institute of Metallurgical Machinery   (RU)

VNIIMI ..... All-Union Scientific Research Institute of Heat Engineering in Metallurgy   (RU)

VNIIMI ..... All-Union Scientific Research Institute of Medical and Medicotechnical Information (of the Academy of Medical Sciences, USSR)   (RU)

VNIIMIO ... All-Union Scientific Research Institute of Medical Instruments and Equipment   (RU)

VNIIMK .... All-Union Scientific Research Institute of Oil-Bearing Crops   (RU)

VNIIMORGEO ... All-Union Institute of Submarine Geology and Geophysics [*Russian*]   (SLS)

VNIIMP .... All-Union Scientific Research Institute of the Meat Industry   (RU)

VNIIMS .... All-Union Scientific Research Institute of the Butter- and Cheese-Making Industry   (RU)

VNIINeft' .. All-Union Scientific Research Institute of Petroleum and Gas   (RU)

VNIINEFTEKhIM ... All-Union Scientific Research Institute of Petrochemical Processes   (RU)

VNIINERUD ... All-Union Scientific Research Institute of Nonmetallic Building Materials and Hydraulic Mechanization (of the Academy of Construction and Architecture, USSR)   (RU)

VNIING .... Volgograd Scientific Research Institute of the Petroleum and Gas Industry   (RU)

VNIINMASh ... All-Union Scientific Research Institute of Standardization in Machinery Manufacture   (RU)

VNIINP ..... All-Union Scientific Research Institute of Petroleum and Gas Processing and the Production of Synthetic Liquid Fuel   (RU)

VNIINSM ... All-Union Scientific Research Institute of New Building Materials   (RU)

VNIINTM ... All-Union Scientific Research Institute of Nonwoven Fabrics   (RU)

VNIIO .... All-Union Scientific Research Institute of Refractories   (RU)

VNIIOChERMET ... All-Union Scientific Research Institute for the Organization of Production and Labor in Ferrous Metallurgy   (RU)

VNIIOK ..... All-Union Scientific Research Institute of Sheep and Goat Breeding   (RU)

VNIIOKh .. All-Union Scientific Research Institute of Vegetable Growing   (RU)

VNIIOMPROMZhILSTROY ... All-Union Scientific Research Institute for the Organization and Mechanization of Industrial and Housing Construction   (RU)

VNIIOMS ... All-Union Scientific Research Institute for the Organization and Mechanization of Construction   (RU)

VNIIOMShS ... All-Union Scientific Research Institute for the Organization and Mechanization of Mine Construction   (RU)

VNIIOT ..... All-Union Scientific Research Institute of Work Safety of the VTsSPS   (RU)

VNIIP .... All-Union Scientific Research and Planning Institute for Underground Gasification of Fuels   (RU)

VNIIP .... All-Union Scientific Research Institute of Penicillin and Other Antibiotics   (RU)

VNIIP .... All-Union Scientific Research Institute of Poultry Raising   (RU)

VNIIP .... All-Union Scientific Research Institute of the Poultry-Processing Industry   (RU)

VNIIPBiVP ... All-Union Scientific Research Institute of the Beer, Soft Drink, and Wine-Making Industry   (RU)

VNIIPIK .... All-Union Scientific Research Institute of Film Materials and Artificial Leather   (RU)

VNIIPIT .... All-Union Scientific Research Institute of the Printing Industry and Technology   (RU)

VNIIPKhV ... All-Union Scientific Research Institute for the Processing of Synthetic Fibers   (RU)

VNIIPN ..... All-Union Scientific Research Institute of Petroleum Processing   (RU)

VNIIPODZEMGAZ ... All-Union Scientific Research Institute of the Underground Gasification of Coal   (RU)

VNIIPP ..... All-Union Scientific Research, Design, and Technological Institute of the Bearing Industry   (RU)

VNIIPP ..... All-Union Scientific Research Institute of Fruit and Vegetable Processing Industry   (RU)

VNIIPP ..... All-Union Scientific Research Institute of the Brewing Industry   (RU)

VNIIPP ..... All-Union Scientific Research Institute of the Printing Industry   (RU)

VNIIPPIT ... All-Union Scientific Research Institute of the Printing Industry and Technology   (RU)

VNIIPRKh ... Vsesoyuznyi Nauchno-Issledovatel'skij Institut Prudovogo Rybnogo Khozyajstva [*All-Russian Scientific Research Institute of Pond Fisheries*]   (RU)

VNIIProdmash ... All-Union Scientific Research Institute of Food Machinery   (RU)

VNIIPromgaz ... All-Union Scientific Research Institute of Gas Utilization in the National Economy and of Underground Storage of Petroleum, Petroleum Products, and Liquefied Gas   (RU)

VNIIPromzhilstroy ... All-Union Scientific Research Institute for the Organization and Mechanization of Industrial and Housing Construction   (RU)

VNIIPS ...... All-Union Scientific Research Institute for Shale Processing   (RU)

VNIIPS...... All-Union Scientific Research Institute of Beet Growing (RU)

VNIIPT ..... All-Union Scientific Research Institute of Industrial Transportation (RU)

VNIIPTMash ... All-Union Scientific Research, Planning, and Design Institute of Hoisting and Conveying Machinery, Loading, Unloading, and Warehouse Equipment and Containers (RU)

VNIIPTO .. All-Union Scientific Research Institute of Hoisting and Conveying Equipment (RU)

VNIIPTUGLEMASh ... All-Union Scientific Research, Planning, and Technological Institute of Coal Machinery (RU)

VNIIRT ..... All-Union Scientific Research Institute of Magnetic Sound Recording and the Technology of Radio Broadcasting and Television (RU)

VNIIRTMash ... All-Union Scientific Research and Design Institute of Industrial Rubber Machinery (RU)

VNIIS .... All-Union Scientific Research Institute of Cheese-Making Industry (RU)

VNIIS .... All-Union Scientific Research Institute of Glass (RU)

VNIIS .... All-Union Scientific Research Institute of Standardization (RU)

VNIISel'khozmikrobiologii ... All-Union Scientific Research Institute of Agricultural Microbiology (RU)

VNIIShP ... All-Union Scientific Research Institute of the Garment Industry (RU)

VNIIShveyprom ... All-Union Scientific Research Institute of the Garment Industry (RU)

VNIISI....... All-Union Scientific Research Institute of Sanitary Testing (RU)

VNIISINZh ... All-Union Scientific Research and Planning Institute of Synthetic Fat Substitutes (RU)

VNIISK ..... All-Union Scientific Research Institute of Soybean and Castor-Oil Plants (RU)

VNIISK ..... All-Union Scientific Research Institute of Synthetic Rubber Imeni S. V. Lebedev (RU)

VNIISKhA ... All-Union Scientific Research Institute of Agricultural and Forestry Aviation (RU)

VNIISKhM ... All-Union Scientific Research Institute of Agricultural Microbiology (RU)

VNIISLVP ... All-Union Scientific Research Institute of the Alcohol, Liqueur, and Vodka Industry (RU)

VNIISM .... All-Union Scientific Research Institute of Building Materials (RU)

VNIISNDV ... All-Union Scientific Research Institute of Synthetic and Natural Fragrant Substances (RU)

VNIISP...... All-Union Scientific Research Institute of Beet Growing (RU)

VNIISP...... All-Union Scientific Research Institute of the Alcohol, Liqueur, and Vodka Industry (RU)

VNIISS...... All-Russian Scientific Research Institute of Sugar Beets and Sugar (RU)

VNIISS...... All-Union Scientific Research Institute of Arid Subtropics (RU)

VNIISSV... All-Union Scientific Research Institute of Glass Plastics and Glass Fibers (RU)

VNIIST ..... All-Union Scientific Research Institute for the Construction of Trunk Pipelines (RU)

VNIIST ..... All-Union Scientific Research Institute of Hard Alloys (RU)

VNIISteklo ... All-Union Scientific Research Institute of Glass (RU)

VNIISTO .. All-Union Scientific Research Institute of Sanitary Engineering Equipment (RU)

VNIIStrom ... All-Union Scientific Research Institute of Building Materials and Structural Parts (RU)

VNIISTROMMASh ... All-Union Scientific Research Institute of Machinery for the Building Materials Industry (RU)

VNIISTROYDORMASh ... All-Union Scientific Research Institute of Construction and Road Machinery (RU)

VNIIStroyneft' ... All-Union Scientific Research Institute for the Construction of Petroleum Industry Establishments (RU)

VNIISV ..... All-Union Scientific Research Institute of Glass Fibers (RU)

VNIISZ ..... All-Union Scientific Research Institute of the Soviet Legislation (RU)

VNIIT........ All-Union Scientific Research Institute of Fuel Utilization (RU)

VNIIT........ All-Union Scientific Research Institute of Sources of Current (RU)

VNIIT........ All-Union Scientific Research Institute of Television (RU)

VNIITB ..... All-Union Scientific Research Institute of Safety Engineering in the Petroleum Industry (RU)

VNIITE ..... All-Union Scientific Research Institute for Aesthetic Styling in Engineering (RU)

VNIITGP .. All-Union Scientific Research Institute of the Textile and Notions Industry (RU)

VNIITIPribor ... All-Union Scientific Research Technological Institute of Instrument Making (RU)

VNIITISM ... All-Union Scientific Research Institute of Fine Grinding of Building Materials (RU)

VNIITMash ... All-Union Scientific Research Institute of Machinery-Manufacturing Technology (RU)

VNIITNeft' ... All-Union Scientific Research Institute of Petroleum-Processing Technology (RU)

VNIITORGmash ... All-Union Scientific Research and Experimental Design Institute of Commercial Machinery (RU)

VNIITP ..... All-Union Scientific Research Institute of Knit Goods Industry (RU)

VNIITP ..... All-Union Scientific Research Institute of the Peat Industry (RU)

VNIITS ..... All-Union Scientific Research Institute of Hard Alloys (RU)

VNIITsvetmet ... All-Union Scientific Research Institute of Nonferrous Metallurgy (RU)

VNIIUgleobogashcheniye ... All-Union Planning, Design, and Scientific Research Institute of Coal Enrichment and Briquetting (RU)

VNIIV........ All-Union Scientific Research Institute of Railroad Car Building (RU)

VNIIV........ All-Union Scientific Research Institute of Synthetic Fibers (RU)

VNIIVESPROM ... All-Union Scientific Research Institute of Scales and Instruments (RU)

VNIIVIV ... All-Union Scientific Research Institute of Wine Making and Viticulture (RU)

VNIIVODGEO ... All-Union Scientific Research Institute of Water Supply, Sewer Systems, Hydraulic Engineering Structures, and Engineering Hydrogeology (RU)

VNIIVS ..... All-Union Scientific Research Institute of Humid Subtropics (RU)

VNIIVS ..... All-Union Scientific Research Institute of Veterinary Sanitation (RU)

VNIIVSE... All-Union Scientific Research Institute of Veterinary Sanitation and Ectoparasitology (RU)

VNIIVViM ... All-Union Scientific Research Institute of Veterinary Virology and Microbiology (RU)

VNIIYaGG ... All-Union Scientific Research Institute of Nuclear Geophysics and Geochemistry (RU)

VNIIZ........ All-Union Scientific Research Institute of Grain and Grain Products (RU)

VNIIZ........ All-Union Scientific Research Institute of Sound Recording (RU)

VNIIZh...... All-Union Scientific Research Institute of Fats (RU)

VNIIZh...... All-Union Scientific Research Institute of Livestock Breeding (RU)

VNIIZhelezobeton ... All-Union Scientific Research Institute of Industrial Technology of Precast Reinforced Concrete Structural Parts and Products (RU)

VNIIZhG... All-Union Scientific Research Institute of Railroad Hygiene (RU)

VNIIZhP ... All-Union Scientific Research Institute of Animal Raw Materials and Furs (RU)

VNIIZhS ... All-Union Scientific Research Institute for the Industrialization of Housing Construction (RU)

VNIIZhT ... All-Union Scientific Research Institute of Railroad Transportation (RU)

VNIIZKh... All-Union Scientific Research Institute of Grain Farming (RU)

VNIK .... All-Union Scientific Research Institute of Rubber-Yielding Plants (RU)

VNIKhFI ... All-Union Scientific Research, Chemical, and Pharmaceutical Institute Imeni Sergo Ordzhonikidze (RU)

VNIKhI...... All-Union Scientific Research Institute of the Refrigeration Industry (RU)

VNIKhT ... All-Union Scientific Research Institute of the Solid Fuel Chemistry (RU)

VNIKO ...... All-Union Scientific Research Institute of Hemp (RU)

VNIL......... All-Union Scientific Research Laboratory (RU)

VNILALMAZ ... All-Union Scientific Research Laboratory of Diamond Tools and Diamond Substitutes (RU)

VNILAMI ... All-Union Scientific Research Institute of Silviculture and Conservational Afforestation (RU)

VNILAR.... All-Union Scientific Research Institute of Medicinal and Aromatic Plants (RU)

VNILDILS ... All-Union Scientific Research Laboratory of Dispersion Medicinal Herbs (RU)

VNILP....... All-Union Scientific Research Laboratory of the Brewing Industry (RU)

VNILRO.... All-Union Scientific Research Laboratory for the Chemical Processing of Vegetable Wastes (RU)

VNILTARA ... All-Union Scientific Research Laboratory of Packing Materials (RU)

VNILZO.... All-Union Scientific Research Laboratory of Fur Farming and Antlered Reindeer Breeding (RU)

VNIMI....... All-Union Scientific Research Institute of Mine Surveying (RU)

VNIMI....... All-Union Scientific Research Institute of the Dairy Industry (RU)

VNIMS...... Vorkuta Permafrost Scientific Research Station (RU)

VNIO......... All-Union Scientific Research Institute of Hunting (RU)

VNIOChERMET ... All-Union Scientific Research Institute for the Organization of Production and Labor in Ferrous Metallurgy (RU)

VNIOK ...... All-Union Scientific Research Institute of Sheep and Goat Breeding (RU)

VNIOMS... All-Union Scientific Research Institute for the Organization and Mechanization of Construction (RU)
VNIORKh ... Vsesoyuznyi Nauchno-Issledovatel'skij Institut Ozernogo i Rechnogo Rybnogo Khozyajstva [*All-Union Scientific Research Institute of Lake and River Fisheries*] (RU)
VNIOSP .... All-Union Scientific Research Institute of the Dehydrated Vegetables Industry (RU)
VNIOT ...... All-Union Scientific Research Institute of Work Safety (RU)
VNIPI .... All-Union Scientific Research and Planning Institute (RU)
VNIPISel'elektro ... All-Union Scientific Research and Planning Institute for the Supply of Electric Power to Agricultural and Other Users in Rural Areas (RU)
VNIPO ...... All-Union Scientific Research Institute of Fur, Peltry, and Hunting (RU)
VNIPP .... All-Union Scientific Research, Design, and Technological Institute of the Bearing Industry (RU)
VNIPRKh ... All-Russian Scientific Research Institute of Pond Fisheries (RU)
VNIPTI ..... All-Union Scientific Research, Planning, and Technological Institute of Crane and Traction Electrical Equipment (RU)
VNiR .... Departmental Norms and Wages, Departmental Standards and Costs (RU)
VNIRO ...... Vsesoyuznyi Nauchno-Issledovatel'skij Institut Morskogo Rybnogo Khozyajstva i Okeanografii [*All-Union Scientific Research Institute of Sea Fisheries and Oceanography*] (RU)
VNIS .... All-Union Scientific Research Institute of the Sugar Industry (RU)
VNISI .... All-Union Scientific Research Institute of Illuminating Engineering (RU)
VNISK .... All-Union Scientific Research Institute of Subtropical Crops (RU)
VNISP .... All-Union Scientific Research Institute of the Salt Industry (RU)
VNISS .... All-Russian Scientific Research Institute of Sugar Beets and Sugar (RU)
VNITB .... All-Union Scientific Research Institute of Safety Engineering in the Petroleum Industry (RU)
VNITI .... All-Union Scientific Research Diesel Locomotive Institute (RU)
VNITI .... All-Union Scientific Research Institute of Pipes (RU)
VNITIMashpribor ... All-Union Scientific Research Technological Institute of Machinery Manufacture and Instrument Making (RU)
VNITIPRIBOR ... All-Union Scientific Research Technological Institute of Instrument Making (RU)
VNITO ...... All-Union Scientific, Engineering, and Technical Society (RU)
VNITOE.... All-Union Scientific, Engineering, and Technical Society of Power Engineers (RU)
VNITOEP ... All-Union Scientific, Engineering, and Technical Society of the Power Industry (RU)
VNITOGET ... All-Union Scientific, Engineering, and Technical Society of the City Electric Transportation Systems (RU)
VNITOKF ... All-Union Scientific, Engineering, and Technical Society of the Motion Picture and Photo Industry (RU)
VNITOKhim ... All-Union Scientific, Engineering, and Technical Society of Chemists (RU)
VNITOKozhobuvmekh ... All-Union Scientific, Engineering, and Technical Society of the Leather, Footwear, Fur, and Leather Substitute Industries (RU)
VNITOKSh ... All-Union Scientific, Engineering, and Technical Society of the Forging and Stamping Industry Workers (RU)
VNITOL.... All-Union Scientific, Engineering, and Technical Society of Foundry Workers (RU)
VNITOLegprom ... All-Union Scientific, Engineering, and Technical Society of Light Industry (RU)
VNITOLES ... All-Union Scientific, Engineering, and Technical Society of the Lumber Industry and Forestry (RU)
VNITOLKh ... All-Union Scientific, Engineering, and Technical Society of Forestry (RU)
VNITOM .. All-Union Scientific, Engineering, and Technical Society of Metallurgists (RU)
VNITOMASh ... All-Union Scientific Research Institute of Machinery-Manufacturing Technology (RU)
VNITOMKhKP ... All-Union Scientific, Engineering, and Technical Society of Flour-Milling, Baking, and Groats Industry (RU)
VNITO-NEFT' ... All-Union Scientific, Engineering, and Technical Society of Petroleum Workers (RU)
VNITOPribor ... All-Union Scientific, Engineering, and Technical Society of Instrument Making (RU)
VNITOS.... All-Union Scientific, Engineering, and Technical Society of Welders (RU)
VNITOSS ... All-Union Scientific, Engineering, and Technical Society of Shipbuilding (RU)
VNITOtsemkeramikov ... All-Union Scientific, Engineering, and Technical Society of the Cement and Ceramics Industry (RU)

VNITOtsvetnikov ... All-Union Scientific, Engineering, and Technical Society of Workers of Nonferrous Metallurgy (RU)
VNITOVT ... All-Union Scientific, Engineering, and Technical Society of Water Transportation (RU)
VNITs........ All-Union Scientific Research Institute of Cements (RU)
VNITsSSD ... All-Union Scientific Research Center of Standard and Reference Data (RU)
VNIVI....... All-Union Scientific Research Institute of Vitamins (RU)
VNIZhP..... All-Union Scientific Research Institute of Animal Raw Materials and Furs (RU)
VNJI......... Jiri [*Nepal*] [*ICAO location identifier*] (ICLI)
VNJL......... Jumla [*Nepal*] [*ICAO location identifier*] (ICLI)
VNJP......... Janakpur [*Nepal*] [*ICAO location identifier*] (ICLI)
VNJS......... Jomsom [*Nepal*] [*ICAO location identifier*] (ICLI)
VNK......... Vereniging van Nederlandse Kunsthistorici [*Association of Dutch Art History*] (SLS)
VNK......... Water-Oil Contact (RU)
VNKh......... Great People's Assembly [*Mongolian People's Republic*] (RU)
VNKK .... Provisional People's Advisory Congress [*Indonesian*] (RU)
VNKSK..... North Korean Provisional National Committee (BU)
VNKSK..... Provisional People's Committee of North Korea (RU)
VNKT .... Kathmandu/International [*Nepal*] [*ICAO location identifier*] (ICLI)
Vnl .... Voornamelijk [*Benelux*] (BAS)
VNLD .... Lamidada [*Nepal*] [*ICAO location identifier*] (ICLI)
VNLK .... Lukla [*Nepal*] [*ICAO location identifier*] (ICLI)
VNLT .... Langtang [*Nepal*] [*ICAO location identifier*] (ICLI)
VNM......... Vereniging voor Nederlandse Muziekgeschiedenis [*Netherlands*] (SLS)
VNM......... Verlag Neue Musik [*Neue Musik Publishing House*] (EG)
VNM......... Vietnam [*ANSI three-letter standard code*] (CNC)
VNMA ...... Manang [*Nepal*] [*ICAO location identifier*] (ICLI)
VNMG....... Meghauli [*Nepal*] [*ICAO location identifier*] (ICLI)
VNMN....... Mahendranagar [*Nepal*] [*ICAO location identifier*] (ICLI)
VNNG....... Nepalgung [*Nepal*] [*ICAO location identifier*] (ICLI)
VNNIIBurneft' ... All-Union Scientific Research and Planning Institute for Drilling Oil and Gas Wells (RU)
VNO .... Federation of Netherlands Industry [*Belgium*] (EAIO)
VNO .... Military Scientific Society (RU)
VNO .... Verbond van Nederlandse Ondernemingen [*Federation of Netherlands Enterprises*] (WEN)
VNO .... Vilnius [*Former USSR*] [*Airport symbol*] (OAG)
VNOAGE .. All-Union Scientific Society of Anatomists, Histologists, and Embryologists (RU)
VNOE........ Vasilikos Navtikos Omilos Ellados [*Royal Yacht Club of Greece*] (GC)
VNOLO..... All-Union Scientific Society of Otolaryngologists (RU)
VNORiE..... All-Union Scientific Society of Radio Engineering and Telecommunications Imeni A. S. Popov (RU)
VNOS .... Aircraft-Warning Service (RU)
VNOS .... Air Warning and Communications Service (BU)
VNP .... Association of the Dutch Paper and Board Manufacturers Research, Technology and Environment Group [*Netherlands*] (EAIO)
VNP .... Auxiliary Observation Post (RU)
VNP .... Gross National Product (RU)
VNP .... Temporary Observation Post (RU)
VNP .... Vanguardia Nacionalista Popular [*Nationalist Popular Vanguard*] [*Colorado*] (LA)
VNP .... Venda National Party [*Political party*] (PPW)
VNP .... Vlaamse Nationaale Partij (Volksunie) [*Flemish National Party (People's Union)*] [*Belgium*] (WEN)
VNPA .... Victorian National Parks Association [*Australia*]
VNPK .... Higher Scientific Pedagogical Courses (RU)
VNPK .... Pokhara [*Nepal*] [*ICAO location identifier*] (ICLI)
VNPL......... Phaplu [*Nepal*] [*ICAO location identifier*] (ICLI)
VNPO .... Vsenarodni Priprava Obyvatelstva [*National Training Program*] [*Civil defense*] (CZ)
VNR.......... Hungarian People's Republic (RU)
VNR.......... Verband Norddeutscher Rechenzentren eV [*German*] (ADPT)
VNR.......... Viennair Luftfahrt GmbH [*Austria*] [*ICAO designator*] (FAAC)
VNRB .... Rajbiraj [*Nepal*] [*ICAO location identifier*] (ICLI)
VNRK .... Rukumkot (Chaurjhari) [*Nepal*] [*ICAO location identifier*] (ICLI)
VNRP .... Rolpa [*Nepal*] [*ICAO location identifier*] (ICLI)
VNRT .... Rumjatar [*Nepal*] [*ICAO location identifier*] (ICLI)
VNS .... Grand National Assembly (BU)
VNS .... Heterologous Serum (RU)
VNS .... Supreme People's Assembly [*North Korean*] (RU)
VNS .... Varanasi [*India*] [*Airport symbol*] (OAG)
VNS .... Venus Air Services Ltd. [*Ghana*] [*ICAO designator*] (FAAC)
VNS .... Vereenvoudigde Nederlandse Spelling [*Afrikaans*]
VNSB .... Syanboche [*Nepal*] [*ICAO location identifier*] (ICLI)
VNSI .... Simara [*Nepal*] [*ICAO location identifier*] (ICLI)
VNSK .... Surkhet [*Nepal*] [*ICAO location identifier*] (ICLI)
VNSM .... Kathmandu [*Nepal*] [*ICAO location identifier*] (ICLI)

VNSR .... Safebagar [*Nepal*] [*ICAO location identifier*]   (ICLI)
VNST .... Simikot [*Nepal*] [*ICAO location identifier*]   (ICLI)
VNSWBAC ... Victoria/New South Wales Border Anomalies Committee [*Australia*]
VNTJ .... Taplejung [*Nepal*] [*ICAO location identifier*]   (ICLI)
VNTO .... All-Union Scientific and Technical Society   (RU)
VNTOE ..... All-Union Scientific, Engineering, and Technical Society of Power Engineers   (RU)
VNTP .... Tikapur [*Nepal*] [*ICAO location identifier*]   (ICLI)
VNTR .... Tumlingtar [*Nepal*] [*ICAO location identifier*]   (ICLI)
VNTS .... All-Union Petroleum Technical Station   (RU)
VNTTX ...... Viet Nam Thong Tan Xa [*Vietnam News Agency*]
VNU .... Verenigde Nederlandse Uitgeversbedrijven [*Publishing group*] [*Netherlands*]
VNU .... Voluntarios de las Naciones Unidas [*United Nations Volunteers - UNV*] [*Spanish*]
VNUS .... Service Troops   (RU)
vnutr .... Interior, Inner, Internal   (RU)
VNV .... Vlaamsch Nationaal Verbond [*Flemish National League*] [*Dissolved*] [*Belgium*] [*Political party*]   (PPE)
v n vr .... Now, At Present, At the Present Time   (RU)
VNVSU ..... Higher People's Military Construction Academy   (BU)
VNVSU ..... Higher People's Military Signals Academy   (BU)
VNVT .... Biratnagar [*Nepal*] [*ICAO location identifier*]   (ICLI)
VNVU .... Higher People's Military Academy   (BU)
VNW .... Verbond van Nederlandse Werkgevers [*Federation of Netherlands Employers*] [*Defunct*]   (WEN)
vnw .... Voornaamwoord [*Pronoun*] [*Afrikaans*]
VNX .... Venexcargo (Transporte Aereo de Carga SA) [*Venezuela*] [*ICAO designator*]   (FAAC)
VNZ .... Military Criminal Law   (BU)
VNZ .... Verlag Neue Zeit [*Neue Zeit Publishing House*]   (EG)
vn zak ...... Military Criminal Law   (BU)
VO .... Air Cooler   (RU)
VO .... Air Raid Danger   (BU)
VO .... All-Union Association   (RU)
VO .... Armed Guards   (RU)
VO .... Deviation Detector   (RU)
VO .... Dump Car   (RU)
vo .... Helicopter Detachment   (RU)
VO .... Le Service des Voyages Officiels et de la Protection des Hautes Personnalites [*France*]   (FLAF)
VO .... Light Switch   (RU)
vo .... Military Detachment   (BU)
VO .... Military District   (RU)
VO .... Obzor, Vydavatelstvo Knih a Casopisov [*Obzor, Publishing House for Books and Magazines*]   (CZ)
VO .... Probable Error   (RU)
vo .... Vaimo [*Finland*]
VO .... Vanguardia Obrera [*Workers' Vanguard Party*] [*Bolivia*]   (LA)
VO .... Van Onder [*From Below*] [*Afrikaans*]
VO .... Vasil'yevskiy Ostrov [*Leningrad*]   (RU)
VO .... Vatreno Osmatranje [*Fire Observation*] [*Military*]   (YU)
VO .... Vazdusna Odbrana [*Air Defense*]   (YU)
VO .... Velitelstvi Oblasti [*Regional Military Headquarters*]   (CZ)
VO .... Velitelstvi Oddilu [*Detachment Headquarters (Security Police)*]   (CZ)
VO .... Velkoodberatelia [*Bulk Consumers*]   (CZ)
VO .... Verbindungsoffizier [*Liaison Officer*] [*German military - World War II*]
Vo .... Verbo [*Benelux*]   (BAS)
VO .... Vernehmungsoffizier [*Interrogation Officer*] [*German military - World War II*]
VO .... Verordnung [*Decree, Ordinance*] [*German*]   (WEN)
VO .... Verpflegungsoffizier [*Mess Officer*] [*German military - World War II*]
vo .... Verso [*Back of the Page*] [*French*]
vo .... Verso [*Verse*] [*Portuguese*]
vo .... Vesd Ossze [*Compare*]   (HU)
VO .... Victorian Order [*Australia*]   (ADA)
VO .... Voimistelunopettaja [*Finland*]
VO .... Vojenska Osveta [*Military Cultural Activities*]   (CZ)
VO .... Vojenske Oddeleni [*Military Department*]   (CZ)
VO .... Vojensky Okruh [*Military District*]   (CZ)
vo .... Von Oben [*From Above*] [*German*]
v/o .... Vossa Ordem [*Your Order*] [*Business term*] [*Portuguese*]
VO .... VOTEC, Servicos Aereos Regionais SA [*Brazil*] [*ICAO designator*]   (ICDA)
V/O .... Vsesojuznoje Objedinenije [*All-Union Association*] [*Russian*]
VO .... Vycvikovy Odbor [*Training Branch*]   (CZ)
VO .... Vydavatelstvi Obchodu [*Trade Literature Publishing House*]   (CZ)
VO .... Vydavatelstvi Osveta [*Cultural Publishing House (in Martin)*]   (CZ)
VO .... Vyrobna Oblast [*Production Area*]   (CZ)
VOA .... Vehicule d'Observation d'Artillerie [*French*]

VOA .... Verband Oesterreichischer Archivare [*Austrian Association of Archivists*]   (SLS)
VOA .... Vereinigung Oesterreichischer Aerzte [*Austrian Doctors Association*]   (SLS)
VOA .... Vereniging van Ondergrondse Amptenare van Suid-Afrika [*South Africa*]   (AA)
VOA .... Vsesoyuznoye Obshchestvo Aviastroiteley [*All-Union Aeronautical Society*] [*Former USSR*]   (EAIO)
VOAEL ...... Vocationally Oriented Adult Education and Literacy Program [*Australia*]
VOAPP ...... All-Union Society of Associations of Proletarian Writers   (RU)
VOB .... Battery Computation Section [*Artillery*]   (RU)
VOB .... Verdingungsordnung fuer Bauleistungen [*Government procurement regulations*]   (IMH)
VOB .... Vereinigung Oesterreichischer Bibliothekare [*Austrian Librarians Association*]   (SLS)
VOB .... Vereinigung Organisationseigener Betriebe [*Association of Organization-Owned Enterprises*]   (EG)
VOB .... Vereinigung Osterreichischer Bibliothekare [*Association of Austrian Librarians*]   (EAIO)
VOBG .... Bangalore [*India*] [*ICAO location identifier*]   (ICLI)
VOBI .... Bellary [*India*] [*ICAO location identifier*]   (ICLI)
VOBIS ...... Victorian Owners' and Breeders' Incentive Scheme [*Horse racing*] [*Australia*]
VOBL .... Verordnungsblatt [*Decree Gazette*]   (EG)
VOBL BZ .. Verordnungsblatt fuer die Britische Zone [*Official Gazette of the Former British Zone of Occupation*] [*German*]   (ILCA)
VoBo .... Visto Bueno [*All Right*] [*Spanish*]
VOBR .... Bidar [*India*] [*ICAO location identifier*]   (ICLI)
VOBZ .... Vijayawada [*India*] [*ICAO location identifier*]   (ICLI)
VOC .... Vanguardia Obrero Catolica [*Catholic Workers Vanguard*] [*Spanish*]   (WER)
VOC .... Vereenigde Oost-Indische Compagnie [*United East Indies Company*] [*1596-1799*]   (IN)
VOC .... Victorian Olympic Council [*Australia*]
VOC .... Vincent Owners Club   (EA)
VOCA .... Victims of Crime Association [*Australia*]
VOCAL ..... Victims of Crime Assistance League [*Australia*]
VOCAL ..... Visitor Open Courtesy Answering Line [*for rewarding courteous or professional service*] [*Hong Kong*]
VOCB .... Coimbatore [*India*] [*ICAO location identifier*]   (ICLI)
VOCC .... Cochin [*India*] [*ICAO location identifier*]   (ICLI)
VOCED ..... Vocational Education [*Database*] [*Australia*]
vochtvl ...... Vochtvlekkig [*Damp-Stained*] [*Netherlands*]
VOCL .... Calicut [*India*] [*ICAO location identifier*]   (ICLI)
VOCP .... Cuddapah [*India*] [*ICAO location identifier*]   (ICLI)
VOCX .... Carnicobar [*India*] [*ICAO location identifier*]   (ICLI)
vod .... Aqueous, Hydrous, Water   (RU)
VOD .... Battalion Computation Section [*Artillery*]   (RU)
vod .... Water Tower [*Topography*]   (RU)
VODG .... Dundigul [*India*] [*ICAO location identifier*]   (ICLI)
VODGEO ... All-Union Scientific Research Institute of Water Supply, Sewer Systems, Hydraulic Engineering Structures, and Engineering Hydrogeology   (RU)
VODK .... Donakonda [*India*] [*ICAO location identifier*]   (ICLI)
VODK .... [*The*] Voice of Democratic Kampuchea [*Radio station of the Red Khmers*]   (PD)
vodn .... Aqueous, Hydrous, Water   (RU)
Vodokanal ... Water Supply and Sewer System Administration   (RU)
Vodokanalproekt ... Water Supply and Sewage Planning Service   (BU)
VODOKANALPROYeKT ... State Planning Institute for the Surveying and Planning of Outdoor Water Supply, Sewer Systems, and Hydraulic Engineering Structures   (RU)
VODOPLIN ... Poduzece za Plin i Vodovod [*Enterprise for Transmission of Gas and Water*]   (YU)
Vodoprojekt ... Statni Ustav pro Projektovani Zdravotne Hospodarskych Staveb [*State Institute for the Design of Sanitation Installations*]   (CZ)
Vodostroy ... Water Works Enterprise   (BU)
Vodproekt .. Water Works Designing Enterprise   (BU)
VODSANTEKh ... State Institute of Water Supply and Sanitary Engineering   (RU)
vod st .... Water Column [*In units of pressure*]   (RU)
Vodstroy ... Hydraulic Engineering   (BU)
Vodtransizdat ... State Publishing House of Water Transportation   (RU)
VOeEST .... Vereinigte Oesterreichische Eisen- und Stahlwerke AG [*United Austrian Iron and Steel Works, Inc.*]   (WEN)
voegw .... Voegwoord [*Conjunction*] [*Afrikaans*]
VOeI .... Vereinigung Oesterreichischer Industrieller [*Association of Austrian Industrialists*]   (WEN)
Voen .... Military   (BU)
Voenkom .... Military Commandant   (BU)
Voenkor ..... Military Correspondent   (BU)
Voenna A ... Military Academy   (BU)
VOEST ...... Vereinigte Oesterreichische Edelstahlwerke AG
VOF .... All-Russian Philatelic Society   (RU)

VOF .... Vennootschap Onder Firma [*Limited Partnership*] [*Dutch*] (ILCA)
VOF .... Victorian Overseas Foundation [*Australia*]
VOFSA ...... Voetslaanfederasie van Suid-Afrika [*Hiking Federation of South Africa*] (EAIO)
VOFU .... Military Finance Directorate (RU)
VOFVTI .... Eastern Branch of the All-Union Institute of Heat Engineering (RU)
VOG .... All-Russian Society of Deaf-Mutes (RU)
VOG .... All-Union Society of Helminthologists (RU)
vog .... Vogal [*Vowel*] [*Portuguese*]
Vog .... Vogue [*Record label*] [*France*]
VOG .... Volgograd [*Former USSR*] [*Airport symbol*] (OAG)
VOG .... Vsesoyuznoye Obshchestvo Glukhikh [*All-Russian Society of the Deaf*] (EAIO)
VOGA .... Vologda Oblast State Archives (RU)
VOGB .... Gulbarga [*India*] [*ICAO location identifier*] (ICLI)
VOGES ...... All-Union Association of Hydroelectric Power Plants (RU)
VOGI .... All-Russian Society of Civil Engineers (RU)
VOGIN ...... Nederlandse Vereniging van Gebruikers van Online Informatie-Systemen [*Netherlands Association of Users of Online Information Systems*] (EAIO)
VOGRES ... Voronezh State Regional Electric Power Plant (RU)
VOGVF ..... All-Union Association of the Civil Air Fleet [*1930-1932*] (RU)
VOH .... Vohemar [*Madagascar*] [*Airport symbol*] (OAG)
VOHY .... Hyderabad [*India*] [*ICAO location identifier*] (ICLI)
VOI .... Verband Osterreichischer Ingenieure [*Austria*] (EAIO)
VOI .... Vereinigung Osterreichischer Industrieller [*Austria*] (EAIO)
VOI .... Voinjama [*Liberia*] [*Airport symbol*] (OAG)
Voi .... Vrakhoi [*Rocks*] [*Vos*] [*See also*] [*Greek*] (NAU)
VOIC .... Vereenigde Oost-Indische Compagnie [*Afrikaans*]
VOICE .... National Association of Non-Governmental Organisations [*Zimbabwe*] (EAIO)
VOICES .... Victims of Institutionalised Cruelty, Exploitation and Supporters Inc. [*Australia*]
Vo-I Cie ...... Verenigde Oost-Indische Compagnie [*Benelux*] (BAS)
voim............ Voimistelu [*Gymnastics*] [*Finland*]
voimop........ Voimistelunopettaja [*Finland*]
VOINZhAK ... Military Engineering Academy (RU)
VOIP .... All-Union Association of the Tool Industry (RU)
VOIR .... All-Union Society of Inventors and Efficiency Experts (RU)
VOIUU ...... Voronezh Oblast Institute for the Advanced Training of Teachers (RU)
VOIV .... All-Union Association of the Synthetic Fiber Industry (RU)
VOIZ .... All-Union Society of Inventors (RU)
VOJ .... Vazduhoplovno Osmatranje, Obavestavanje, i Javljanje [*Air Force Observation, Information, and Reporting*] (YU)
Voj z sl .... Vojin Zakladni Sluzby [*Private Serving His Basic Conscription Term*] (CZ)
VOK........... All-Russian Association of Health Resorts (RU)
VOK........... Verejna Obecni Knihovna [*Municipal Public Library*] (CZ)
VOK........... Voice of Kenya
vok............. Vokaal [*Vowel*] [*Afrikaans*]
vok............. Vokatief [*Vocative*] [*Afrikaans*]
VOK........... Vry op Kaai [*Free on Quay*] [*Afrikaans*]
Vokab......... Vokabularium [*Word List*] [*German*]
VOKD........ Vystavba Ostravsko-Karvinskych Dolu [*Development of the Ostrava Karvina Mines*] (CZ)
VOKhIMFARM ... All-Union Association of Chemical and Pharmaceutical Industry (RU)
VOKhIMU ... Chemical Warfare Directorate (RU)
VOKhR...... Internal Security Troops of the Republic (RU)
VOKhR...... Militarized Guard [*At airfields and warehouses*] (RU)
VOKITSM ... Vsesoyuznoye Ob'yedineniye Klubov Istoriko-Tekhnicheskogo Stendvogo Modelizma (EAIO)
VOKK .... All-Union Society of the Red Cross and Red Crescent (RU)
VOKM....... Khamampet [*India*] [*ICAO location identifier*] (ICLI)
VOKO........ All-Union State Association for the Production of Municipal Equipment (RU)
VOKP .... All-Union Society of Peasant Writers (RU)
VOKS .... All-Union Society for Cultural Relations with Foreign Countries [*1925-1958*] (RU)
VO KSC..... Vesnicka Organizace Komunisticka Strana Ceskoslovenska [*Village Organization of the Czechoslovak Communist Party*] (CZ)
VOKT .... All-Union Association for Goods for Cultural Purposes (RU)
VOKU........ Higher Joint Command School (RU)
VOL .... Verdingungsordnung fuer Leistungen [*Government procurement regulations*] (IMH)
VOL .... Voice of Lebanon
vol .... Volost (RU)
Vol............. Volum [*Volume*] [*German*]
vol............. Volume [*Afrikaans*]
vol............. Volume [*Italian*]
vol............. Volume [*French*]
vol............. Volume [*Portuguese*]

Vol............. Volumen [*Volume*] [*German*] (GCA)
vol............. Volumen [*Volume*] [*Spanish*]
Vol-% .... Volumenprozent [*Percent by Volume*] (EG)
vol............. Voluntad [*Will*] [*Spanish*]
VOL........... Volvo AB [*Sweden*] [*ICAO designator*] (FAAC)
vol............. Volym [*Volume*] [*Sweden*]
VO-LA .... Vazdusna Odbrana - Lovacka Avijacija [*Air Defense - Fighter Aviation*] (YU)
VOLB .... Verein Oesterreichischer Lebensmittel- und Biotechnologen [*Austrian Association of Food and Biotechnology*] (SLS)
VOLBRICERAM ... Societe Voltaique de Briqueterie et de Ceramique
VOLG .... Victorian Office of Local Government [*Australia*]
volg............ Volgende [*Following*] [*Afrikaans*]
Vol-Gew ..... Volumetrisches Gewicht [*Volumetric Weight*] [*German*]
Volgo-Balt ... Volga-Baltic Waterway (RU)
VolgogradNII NG ... Volgograd Scientific Research Institute of the Petroleum and Gas Industry (RU)
Volkhovges ... Volkhov Hydroelectric Power Plant Imeni V. I. Lenin (RU)
VOLKSK ... Volkskunde [*Folklore*] [*Afrikaans*]
volkst.......... Volkstuemlich [*Popular*] [*German*] (GCA)
volkstuml ... Volkstuemlich [*National*] [*German*]
voll............. Volledig [*Complete*] [*Netherlands*]
Volldueng... Vollduengung [*Complete Fertilization*] [*German*] (GCA)
volled.......... Volledig [*Complete*] [*Netherlands*]
Vollend........ Vollendung [*Completion*] [*German*] (GCA)
Vollst......... Vollstaendig [*Complete*] [*German*]
vollstaen...... Vollstaendig [*Complete*] [*German*] (GCA)
volm........... Volmaak [*Perfect*] [*Afrikaans*]
voln............ Wave (RU)
VOLNA ..... Study of Surface and Internal Waves [*Russian*] (MSC)
vols .... Volumenes [*Volumes*] [*Spanish*]
VOLT .... All-Union Association of the Lumber and Woodworking Industry in Transportation (RU)
VOLT .... Verein Oesterreichischer Ledertechniker [*Austrian Association of Leather Technicians*] (SLS)
volt .... Voltooi [*Complete*] [*Afrikaans*]
Vol T .... Volumenteil [*Part by Volume*] [*German*]
VOLTAICA ... Societe Voltaique pour l'Avancement de l'Industrie, du Commerce, et de l'Agriculture
VOLTAP ... Societe Voltaique de Diffusion d'Appareils Electriques
VOLTAPAT ... Societe Voltaique de Pates Alimentaires
VOLTAVIN ... Societe des Vins de la Haute-Volta
VOLTELEC ... Societe Voltaique d'Electricite [*Voltan Electric Company*] (AF)
VOLTEMA ... Volta Emaillerie
VOLTEX ... Societe Voltaique du Textile
VOLTOA .. Societe Voltaique d'Oxygene et d'Acetylene
VOLUG ..... Victorian Online Users Group [*Australia*]
VOLV .... Volvo AB [*Sweden*] [*NASDAQ symbol*]
VOM.......... All-Russian Society of Motorcyclists (RU)
VOM.......... Power Takeoff Shaft (RU)
VOM.......... Voice of the Mediterranean [*Broadcasting service jointly owned by Maltese and Libyan Governments*] (EY)
VOM.......... Vybor Obrancu Miru [*Committee of the Defenders of Peace*] (CZ)
VOMD....... Madurai [*India*] [*ICAO location identifier*] (ICLI)
VOMEDAK ... Military Medical Academy (RU)
VOMF .... Madras [*India*] [*ICAO location identifier*] (ICLI)
VOMG .... Magadi [*India*] [*ICAO location identifier*] (ICLI)
VOMH .... Mahad [*India*] [*ICAO location identifier*] (ICLI)
VOMI .... Volksdeutsche Mittelstelle [*NAZI Germany*]
VOML .... Mangalore [*India*] [*ICAO location identifier*] (ICLI)
VOMM...... Madras [*India*] [*ICAO location identifier*] (ICLI)
VOMT .... All-Union Heavy Machinery-Manufacturing Association (RU)
VOMY .... Mysore [*India*] [*ICAO location identifier*] (ICLI)
VON .... Reference-Voltage Rectifier (RU)
VON .... Reivers Vegetable Oils Nigeria Limited
Von............ Vallon [*Vale*] [*Military map abbreviation World War I*] [*French*] (MTD)
VON .... Vasiliki Organosis Neolaias [*Greek Royalist Youth*] (GC)
VON .... Verband der Oesterreichischen Neuphilologen [*Association of Austrian New Philologists*] (SLS)
VON .... Vereniging voor Oppervlaktetechnieken Metalen [*Metal Finishing Association*] [*Netherlands*] (PDAA)
VON .... Voice of Nigeria
von............. Vonal [*Line (In transportation, communication)*] (HU)
von............. Vonat [*Train*] (HU)
vonalm........ Vonalmester [*Line Supervisor*] (HU)
VONJY...... Elan Populaire pour l'Unite Nationale [*Popular Impulse for National Unity*] [*Malagasy*] [*Political party*] (PPW)
VONS .... Committee for the Defense of Persons Unjustly Persecuted [*Former Czechoslovakia*] [*Political party*] (PD)
VONS .... Nagarjunsagar [*India*] [*ICAO location identifier*] (ICLI)
VOO .... Military Hunting Society (RU)
VOO .... Military Operations Section (RU)
VOO .... Veronica Omroep Organisatie [*Netherlands*] (EY)

VOOMP.... All-Union Optical Instrument Industry Association (RU)

VOOP........ All-Russian Society for the Conservation of Natural Resources (RU)

VOOP........ Vsesoyuznoye Obshchestvo Okhrany Prirody [*All-Russian Society for the Protection of Nature*] (EAIO)

voorh......... Voorheen [*Formerly*] [*Netherlands*]

voorl.......... Voorlopig [*Benelux*] (BAS)

voors......... Voorsetsel [*Preposition*] [*Afrikaans*]

Voors........ Voorsitter [*Chairman*] [*Afrikaans*]

voorst........ Voorstelling [*Illustration*] [*Publishing*] [*Netherlands*]

voorstel...... Voorstelling [*Illustration*] [*Publishing*] [*Netherlands*]

voortreff..... Voortreffelijk [*Excellent*] [*Netherlands*]

voorv......... Voorvoegsel [*Prefix*] [*Afrikaans*]

voorw........ Voorwerp [*Object*] [*Afrikaans*]

voorw........ Voorwoord [*Foreword*] [*Publishing*] [*Netherlands*]

voorz......... Voorziening [*Benelux*] (BAS)

VOOV....... Vazdusno Osmatranje, Obavestavanje, i Veza [*Air Observation, Information, and Communication*] [*Military*] (YU)

VOP.......... All-Union Society of Soil Scientists (RU)

VOP.......... Explosive Item (RU)

VOP.......... Vallalati Optimalis Program [*Optimal Enterprise Plan*] (HU)

VOP.......... Vanguardia Organizada del Pueblo [*People's Organized Vanguard*] [*Chile*] (LA)

VOP.......... Voice of Palestine (ME)

VOPA....... General Association of Trade Unions of Algeria (RU)

VOPB .... Port Blair [*India*] [*ICAO location identifier*] (ICLI)

VOPB .... Voice of the People of Burma [*Radio station of the Burma Communist Party*] (PD)

Vopedak..... Military Pedagogical Academy (RU)

VOPKP...... All-Russian Organization of Proletarian and Kolkhoz Writers (RU)

VOPO....... Volkspolizei [*People's Police*] [*German*] (EG)

VOPP........ All-Union Society of Proletarian Writers (RU)

VOPRA ..... All-Union Association of Proletarian Architects [*1929-1932*] (RU)

VOPT .... Voice of the People of Thailand [*Radio station of the Communist Party of Thailand*] (PD)

VOR.......... Sunna Air Ltd. [*Iceland*] [*ICAO designator*] (FAAC)

VOR.......... Vegetable Oil Refiners

vor .... Vorig [*Preceding*] [*German*]

Vor .... Vorrat [*Supply*] [*German*] (GCA)

VORAO..... Eastern Branch of the Russian Archaeological Society (RU)

vorauss....... Voraussichtlich [*Expected to Appear*] [*Publishing*] [*German*]

Vorbehandl ... Vorbehandlung [*Pretreatment*] [*German*] (GCA)

Vorbertg..... Vorbereitung [*Preparation*] [*German*]

Vorbes........ Vorbesitzer [*Previous Owner*] [*German*]

vord .... Vorder [*Front*] [*German*]

VORELLE ... Voruebersetzer fuer Entscheidungstabellen [*German*] (ADPT)

Vorerhitz..... Vorerhitzung [*Preheating*] [*German*] (GCA)

VORG........ Ramagundam [*India*] [*ICAO location identifier*] (ICLI)

Vorg .... Vorgang [*Event*] [*German*] (GCA)

vorg .... Vorgeschoben [*Advanced*] [*German*] (GCA)

Vorg .... Vorgesetzter [*Superior*] [*German*] (GCA)

vorgbdn ..... Vorgebunden [*Bound in Front*] [*Publishing*] [*German*]

vorgeb........ Vorgebunden [*Bound in Front*] [*Publishing*] [*German*]

vorgy .... Vezerornagy [*Major General*] (HU)

vorh .... Vorhanden [*In Stock*] [*German*]

Vorheiz....... Vorheizung [*Preheating*] [*German*] (GCA)

vorher........ Vorherig [*Preceding*] [*German*] (GCA)

VORI .... General Association of Workers of Spain (RU)

VORI .... Viticultural and Oenological Research Institute [*South Africa*] [*Research center*] (IRC)

Vork .... Vorkommen [*Occurrence*] [*German*]

VORKM ..... General Association of Workers and Peasants of Mexico (RU)

vorl .... Vorlaeufig [*Meanwhile*] [*German*] (GCA)

Vorl .... Vorlage [*Receiver*] [*German*] (GCA)

Vorles........ Vorlesung [*Lecture*] [*German*] (GCA)

VORM....... Ramnad [*India*] [*ICAO location identifier*] (ICLI)

VORM....... Vormals [*Formerly, Previously*] [*German*] (EG)

VORM....... Vormittags [*In the Morning*] [*German*]

Voronezhsel'mash ... Voronezh Agricultural Machinery Plant (RU)

VORP .... Volga United River Steamship Line (RU)

VORR .... Raichur [*India*] [*ICAO location identifier*] (ICLI)

Vorr........... Vorrat [*Supply*] [*German*] (GCA)

Vorr........... Vorrede [*Preface*] [*Publishing*] [*German*]

Vorr........... Vorrichtung [*Device*] [*German*] (GCA)

VORS .... All-Union Society of Construction Efficiency Experts [*1932-1934*] (RU)

VORS .... All-Union Society of Efficiency Experts of Construction and the Building Materials Industry [*1929-1932*] (RU)

Vors........... Vorsatz [*Endpaper*] [*Publishing*] [*German*]

Vors........... Vorsitzender [*Chairman*] [*German*]

Vorsatzbl.... Vorsatzblatt [*Endpaper*] [*Publishing*] [*German*]

Vorsch........ Vorschrift [*Instructions*] [*German*] (GCA)

vorschm...... Vorschriftsmaessig [*As Directed*] [*German*] (GCA)

Vorschr ...... Vorschrift [*Regulations*] [*German*] (GCA)

---

vorschw ...... Vorschriftswidrig [*Contrary to Directions*] [*German*] (GCA)

vorspr......... Vorspringen [*Projecting*] [*German*] (GCA)

Vorspr........ Vorsprung [*Salient*] [*German*] (GCA)

Vorst .... Vorstand [*Board of Directors*] [*German*]

vorst .... Vorstehend [*Preceding*] [*German*] (GCA)

Vorst .... Vorsteher [*Director*] [*German*]

Vorst .... Vorstehung [*Presentation*] [*German*]

Vorst .... Vorstellung [*Introduction*] [*German*] (GCA)

Vorst .... Vorstuecke [*Preliminary Matter*] [*Publishing*] [*German*]

VORT .... All-Union River Transportation Association (RU)

Vort .... Vortitel [*Half Title*] [*Publishing*] [*German*]

Vortr.......... Vortrag [*Lecture*] [*German*] (GCA)

Vortr.......... Vortragender [*Lecturer*] [*German*]

vorw.......... Vorwaerts [*Forward*] [*German*] (GCA)

Vorw.......... Vorwort [*Preface*] [*Publishing*] [*German*]

Vorw G...... Vorwaertsgang [*Forward Speed*] [*German*] (GCA)

VORY .... Rajahmundry [*India*] [*ICAO location identifier*] (ICLI)

VORZ .... All-Union Association of Repair Plants of the NKPS (RU)

vorz........... Vorzeitig [*Premature*] [*German*] (GCA)

vorzugl....... Vorzueglich [*Preeminent*] [*German*]

VOS .... All-Russian Society of the Blind (RU)

VOS .... High-Altitude Optical Station (RU)

VOS .... Varna Oblast Court (BU)

VOS .... Varnostna Obvescevalna Sluzba [*Security Information Service*] (YU)

VOS .... Veterinary Experimental Station (RU)

VOS .... Vojenska Odborna Skola [*Military Career Specialist School (NCO)*] (CZ)

VOS .... Vojno-Obavestajna Sluzba [*Military Information Service*] (YU)

Vos .... Vrakhos [*Rock*] [*Voi*] [*See also*] [*Greek*] (NAU)

vos .... Vry op Skip [*Free on Ship*] [*Afrikaans*]

vos .... Vry op Spoor [*Free on Rail*] [*Afrikaans*]

VOSA .... Vietnam Ocean Shipping Agency [*Dai Ly Tau Bien Viet Nam*] (FEA)

VoSam....... Soldiers' Amateur Art Activities (BU)

VOSB........ All-Union Society of Old Bolsheviks (RU)

VOSCO ..... Vietnam Ocean Shipping Company [*Cong Ty Van Tai Duong Bien Viet Nam*] (FEA)

vosk .... Wax Refinery [*Topography*] (RU)

VOSKhIM ... All-Union State Association of Sugar and Chemical Machinery Manufacture (RU)

VOSM .... All-Russian Society of Modern Music (RU)

VOSO .... Military Communications Service (RU)

VOSOF...... Varnostnoobvescevalna Sluzba Osvobodilne Fronte [*Security Information Service of the Liberation Front*] [*Slovenia*] [*World War II*] (YU)

VOSOP...... All-Russian Society for Assisting the Conservation of Natural Resources and the Landscaping of Populated Places (RU)

vosp .... Education, Educational, Memoirs, Training, Upbringing (RU)

VOSR .... [*The*] Great October Socialist Revolution (BU)

vosst pl .... Reducing Flame (RU)

vost........... Eastern (RU)

VOSt.......... Vizuelna Osmatracka Stanica [*Visual Observation Station*] [*Army*] (YU)

VOSTGOSTORG ... All-Union Association for Trade with the Countries of the East (RU)

VOSTKIS ... Eastern Complex Scientific Research Institute of Structures (RU)

VostNIGRI ... Eastern Scientific Research Ore-Mining Institute (RU)

VOSTNII .. Eastern Scientific Research Institute of Work Safety in Mining (RU)

Vostokintorg ... All-Union Import-Export Association (of the Ministry of Foreign Trade, USSR) (RU)

Vostokostal' ... All-Union Association of the Metallurgical, Iron Ore, and Manganese Industry of the Eastern Part of the USSR [*1927-1933*] (RU)

VOSU .... All-Union Society of Social Census (RU)

VOSZ......... Vakok Orszagos Szovetsege [*National Association of the Blind*] (HU)

VOSZK...... "VOSZK" Kereskedelmi, Ipari es Szolgalato Szovetkezeti Vallalat ["*VOSZK*" *Servicing Cooperative Enterprise of Trade and Industry*] (HU)

VOT .... Venerable Orden Tercera [*Venerable Third Order*] [*Monastic system*] [*Spanish*]

VOT .... Veneravel Ordem Terceira [*Venerable Third Order*] [*Monastic system*] [*Portuguese*]

VOTA .... General Association of Workers of Algeria (RU)

VOTC .... Verein Oesterreichischer Textilchemiker und Coloristen [*Austrian Association of Textile Chemists and Colorists*] (SLS)

VOTChA ... Vseobshchee Ob'edinenie Trudiashchikhsia Chernoi Afriki [*General Association of Workers of Black Africa*]

VOTI .... All-Union Precision Industry Association (RU)

VOTJ........ Tanjore [*India*] [*ICAO location identifier*] (ICLI)

VOTMS..... Vereniging van Onderwysers in Transvaalse Middelbare Skole [*Afrikaans*]

VOTP .... Tirupeti [*India*] [*ICAO location identifier*] (ICLI)

VOTR .... Tiruchchirappalli [*India*] [*ICAO location identifier*]   (ICLI)
VOTV .... Trivandrum [*India*] [*ICAO location identifier*]   (ICLI)
VOTX .... Tambaram [*India*] [*ICAO location identifier*]   (ICLI)
VOU .... Vyzkumny Osvetovy Ustav [*Cultural Research Institute*]   (CZ)
VOV .... Verband Oeffentlicher Verkehrsbetriebe eV [*Association of Public
          Transport*]   (EY)
VOV .... Voice of Vietnam [*Propaganda broadcast aimed at US POWs*]
          (VNW)
VOV .... Vrijwillige Ouderdoms-Pensioenenverzekering [*Benelux*]   (BAS)
VOVAT ..... All-Union Association of Railroad Car and Streetcar
          Manufacture   (RU)
VOVB .... Vikarabad [*India*] [*ICAO location identifier*]   (ICLI)
VOVG .... All-Russian Society of Homeopathists   (RU)
VOVI .... Vlaams Opleidingsinstituut voor Informatie
VOVR .... Vellore [*India*] [*ICAO location identifier*]   (ICLI)
VOW .... Canadian Voice of Women for Peace [*See also VFCP*]
VOWA .... Verband Oesterreichischer Wirtschaftsakademiker [*Austrian
          Association of University Educated Managers*]   (SLS)
VOWA .... Warangal [*India*] [*ICAO location identifier*]   (ICLI)
voy .... Voyez [*See*] [*French*]   (GPO)
voyen .... Military, Military Term   (RU)
Voyengiz ... State Military Publishing House   (RU)
Voyenizdat ... Military Publishing House of the Ministry of Defense, USSR
          (RU)
voyenkhozupr ... Directorate of Logistics   (RU)
voyen kom .. Military Commissar   (RU)
voyenkor .... Military Correspondent   (RU)
voyenlet ...... Military Pilot   (RU)
voyen-med ... Military Medical   (RU)
voyen-mor .. Naval   (RU)
voyenmor .... Naval Serviceman   (RU)
Voyenmorizdat ... Naval Publishing House   (RU)
Voyenokhot ... Factory of the All-Army Hunting Society   (RU)
Voyensanupr ... Military Medical Directorate   (RU)
Voyensov .... Military Council   (RU)
Voyenspets ... Military Specialist   (RU)
Voyenstrupr ... Military Construction Directorate   (RU)
voyentekhupr ... Military Technical Directorate   (RU)
voyentorg ... Directorate of Trade Establishments for Military Personnel
          (RU)
voyenved ..... Military Department   (RU)
Voyenvetupr ... Military Veterinary Directorate   (RU)
voyenzag ..... Military Procurement Section [*1918-1920*]   (RU)
VOZ .... Military Defense Zone   (BU)
VOZ .... Military Zone of Operations   (BU)
VOZ .... Vojenske Opravarenske Zavody [*Military Repair Shops*]   (CZ)
VOZ .... Vojensky Odznak Zdatnosti [*Military Emblem of Bravery*]   (CZ)
VOZ .... Vsemirnaia Organizatsiia Zdravookhraneniia
VOZ .... World Health Organization [*WHO*]   (RU)
V Ozb DvB (Min J) ... Verzameling der Omzendbrieven Diensvoorschriften
          en Andere Bescheiden (Ministerie van Justitie) [*Benelux*]
          (BAS)
vozdush ...... Air, Aerial   (RU)
VOZOT ..... All-Union Society "For the Mastering of Technology"   (RU)
vozv .... Elevation   (RU)
VOZZ .... Verband Osterreichischer Zeitungsherausgeber und
          Zeitungsverleger [*Austria*]   (EAIO)
VP .... Air Mail   (RU)
vp .... Army Postal Service   (BU)
VP .... Auxiliary Device, Auxiliary Instrument   (RU)
v/p .... Bound   (RU)
VP .... Drinking Water   (RU)
vp .... Helicopter Regiment   (RU)
vp .... Judge Advocate   (BU)
VP .... Military Prosecutor   (RU)
VP .... Military Subunit   (BU)
VP .... Naval Port   (RU)
V/P .... Prisoner of War   (RU)
VP .... Range of Tide   (RU)
VP .... Starting Switch   (RU)
VP .... Telephone Line Out of Order   (BU)
VP .... Troop Train   (RU)
VP .... Vanguardia Popular [*Popular Vanguard*] [*Argentina*]   (LA)
VP .... Vanguardia Proletaria [*Proletarian Vanguard*] [*El Salvador*]
          (LA)
VP .... Vanparnicni Postupak [*Nonadversary Procedure*]   (YU)
VP .... Vanuaaku Pati [*New Hebrides*] [*Political party*]   (PD)
VP .... Vanuatu Pati   (PD)
VP .... Vasiliki Pronoia [*Royal Welfare Fund*] [*EOP*] [*See also*]   (GC)
VP .... Vasilikon Ploion [*His Hellenic Majesty's Ship*]   (GC)
Vp .... Vastausta Pyydetaan [*Finland*]
VP .... Vatreni Polozaj [*Firing Position*] [*Military*]   (YU)
VP .... Vazdusni Pravac [*Aerial Direction Indicator*]   (YU)
VP .... Vece Proizvodaca [*Council of Producers*]   (YU)
VP .... Velka Praha [*Greater Prague*]   (CZ)
VP .... Verarbeitungsprogramm [*German*]   (ADPT)

VP .... Verenigde Partiy [*United Party*] [*Afrikaans*]
Vp .... Versuchsperson [*Experimental Person*] [*German*]
VP .... Veterinary Station   (RU)
VP .... Vise-President [*Vice President*] [*Afrikaans*]
VP .... Vojenska Policie [*Military Police*]   (CZ)
VP .... Vojensky Prukaz [*Military Identity Card*]   (CZ)
VP .... Vojna Posta [*Military Mail*]   (YU)
VP .... Volkspartie [*People's Party*] [*Liechtenstein*] [*Political party*]
          (PPE)
VP .... Volkspolizei [*People's Police*]
VP .... Vossa Paternidade [*Yours Paternally*] [*Portuguese*]
VP .... Vratimovske Papirny [*Vratimov Paper Works*]   (CZ)
VP .... Vuestra Paternidad [*Spanish*]
V/p .... Vylucny Prodej [*Franchise Sale*]   (CZ)
V/p .... Your Letter   (RU)
VPA .... All-Union Industrial Academy   (RU)
VPA .... Military Political Academy Imeni V. I. Lenin   (RU)
VPA .... Victorian Psychologists' Association [*Australia*]
VPA .... Vietnam People's Army [*North Vietnamese*]
VPA .... Vojenska Politicka Akademie [*Military Political Academy*]   (CZ)
VPA .... Vojno-Pomorska Akademija [*Naval Academy*]   (YU)
VPA(B) ...... Volkspolizeiabteilung (Betrieb) [*Special Factory Police
          Detachment*]   (EG)
vpad .... Hollow, Depression [*Topography*]   (RU)
VPAFA ...... Victorian Public Authorities Finance Agency [*Australia*]
VPAK .... Military Political Academic Courses   (RU)
VPAP .... V Pomosht na Agitatora i Propagandista [*Agitator's and
          Propagandist's Aid*] [*A periodical*]   (BU)
VPAR .... Vremennoe Pravitel'stvo Alzhirskoi Respubliki
Vpb .... Besluit op de Vennootschapsbelasting [*Benelux*]   (BAS)
VPb .... Vatreni Polozaj Baterije [*Battery Firing Position*]   (YU)
Vpb .... Vertikale Prijsbinding [*Benelux*]   (BAS)
VPB .... Vojno-Partizanska Bolnica [*Partisan Military Hospital*]   (YU)
VPB .... Vojnopomorska Baza [*Naval Base*]   (YU)
VPB .... Voortrekkerpers Beperk
VPC .... La Vente par Correspondance [*Mail Order*] [*Business term*]
          [*French*]
VPC .... Vaeripapircentralen [*Securities Regulation Center*] [*Copenhagen
          Stock Exchange*] [*Denmark*]
VPC .... Vardepapperscentralen [*Sweden*]
VPC .... Vente Par Correspondance [*Sale by Correspondence*] [*French*]
          (ADPT)
VPC .... Victorian Psychological Council [*Australia*]
VPCW .... Verbond van Protestant-Christelijke Werkgevers in Nederland
          [*Association of Protestant Employers in the Netherlands*]
          (WEN)
VPD .... Vierte Partei Deutschlands [*Fourth Party of Germany*] [*Political
          party*]   (PPW)
VPD .... Volkspolizeidienststelle [*People's Police Post*] [*German*]   (EG)
VPDT .... Temporary Site for Transportation Decontamination   (RU)
VPE .... Vojvodanski Pokret u Emigraciji [*Vojvodina Movement in Exile*]
          (YU)
VPELA ...... Victorian Planning and Environmental Law Association
          [*Australia*]
VPENC ...... Venezuelan PEN Centre   (EAIO)
VPF .... Land Mine Fuze   (RU)
VPF .... Victorian Police Force [*Australia*]
VPF .... Victorian Protestant Federation [*Australia*]
VPFEI .... Higher Pedagogical Institute of Finance and Economics   (RU)
VPFZ .... High-Altitude Planetary Frontal Zone   (RU)
VPG .... Antitank Rifle Grenade   (RU)
VPG .... Military Field Hospital   (RU)
VPG .... Vallentine Peace Group [*Political party*] [*Australia*]
VPI .... Higher Pedagogical Institute of Applied Economics and Science
          of Commodities   (RU)
VPI .... Moscow Higher Pedagogical Institute of the Tsentrosoyuz   (RU)
VPI .... Vereniging vir Professionele Ingenieurs [*South Africa*]   (AA)
VPI .... Water Preparation Installation [*Nuclear energy*]   (BU)
VPIC .... Victorian Prison Industries Commission [*Australia*]
VPJ .... Velitel Vojenskych Pracovnich Jednotek [*Commander of
          Military Labor Units*]   (CZ)
VPK .... All-Union Industrial Office   (RU)
VPK .... All-Union Resettlement Committee   (RU)
VPK .... Auxiliary Fire Brigade   (RU)
VPK .... Higher Pedagogical Courses   (RU)
VPK .... Junction Party Committee   (BU)
VPK .... Militarized Fire Brigade   (RU)
VPK .... Military Industrial Commission [*Soviet-Russian*]   (DOMA)
VPK .... Vaensterpartiet Kommunisterna [*Left-Wing Communist Party*]
          [*Sweden*]   (WEN)
VPK .... Vapaahetoinen Palokunta [*Finland*]
VPK .... Vigyan and Paryavaran Kendra [*Centre for Science and
          Environment*] [*India*]   (EAIO)
VPK .... Voienno-Promychlennaia Kommissia [*Council of ministers
          responsible for military industry*] [*Russian*]

VPK	Voyenno-promyshlennaya Komissiya [*Military Industrial Commission*] [*Former USSR*] (LAIN)	
VPKA	Volkspolizeikreisamt [*District Office of the People's Police*] (EG)	
VPKITIM	All-Union Planning, Design, and Technological Institute of Furniture (RU)	
VPL	Vydavatelstvo Politickej Literatury [*Political Literature Publishing House*] (CZ)	
VPLD	Velkorazni Protiletadlove Delostrlectvo [*Large Caliber AAA*] (CZ)	
VPLEA	Victorian Public Librarians Expo Association [*Australia*]	
VPLIC	Victorian Public Library and Information Cooperative [*Australia*]	
vplvs	Drumhead Court Martial (BU)	
VPM	Auxiliary Medical Aid Station (RU)	
VPM	La Voix du Peuple Murundi	
VPN	Vanguardia Popular Nacionalista [*Nationalist Popular Vanguard*] [*Venezuela*] (LA)	
VPN	Vopnafjordur [*Iceland*] [*Airport symbol*] (OAG)	
VPO	All-Russian Printing Association (RU)	
VPO	All-Union Paleontological Society (RU)	
VPO	Militarized Fire Prevention (RU)	
VPO	Military Consumers' Society (RU)	
VPO	Verzamelde Privaatrechtelijke Opstellen [*Benelux*] (BAS)	
VPOD	Verband des Personals Oeffentlicher Dienste [*Union of Public Service Personnel*] [*Switzerland*] (WEN)	
VPOO	Vojna Preduzeca za Izradu Oficirske Odece i Opreme [*Military Establishments for Preparation of Officers' Uniforms and Equipment*] (YU)	
VPOP	Vam es Penzugyorseg Orszagos Parancsnoksaga [*National Command of the Customs and Internal Revenue Police*] (HU)	
VPOS	Visa Pomorska Skola [*Advanced Naval Academy*] (YU)	
VPOU	Victorian Printers' Operatives Union [*Australia*]	
VPP	Military Food Supply Station (RU)	
VPP	Platoon Small-Arms Ammunition Supply Point (RU)	
VPP	Runway (RU)	
VPP	Victorian Parliamentary Papers [*Australia*]	
VPPI	Vie Politique et Politique Internationale [*French*] (FLAF)	
VPR	Boiling-Water Reactor with Nuclear Superheat (RU)	
VPR	Temporary Transshipment Area (BU)	
VPR	Vanguarda Popular Revolucionaria [*Popular Revolutionary Vanguard*] [*Terrorist organization*] [*Brazil*] (LA)	
VPrM	Voenno-Pravna Misul [*Military Law Review*] [*A periodical*] (BU)	
VPRO	Vrijzinnig Protestante Radio Omroep [*Liberal Protestant Broadcasting Association*] [*Netherlands*] (WEN)	
VPS	All-Union Fur Syndicate (RU)	
VPS	All-Union Trade Union (RU)	
VPS	Military Lines of Communication (RU)	
VPS	Military Postal Station (BU)	
VPS	Military Post Office Station (RU)	
VPS	Universal Postal Union (RU)	
VPS	Visa Pedagoska Skola [*Advanced Pedagogical School*] (YU)	
VPS	Visi Privredni Sud [*Higher Economic Court*] (YU)	
VPS	Vojensky Pevecky Soubor [*Military Choral Ensemble*] (CZ)	
VPS	Vyssi Pedagogicka Skola [*Higher School of Education*] (CZ)	
VPS	Vyssi Prumyslova Skola [*Higher Industrial School*] (CZ)	
VPSAB	Victorian Post-Secondary Accreditation Board [*Australia*]	
VPSB	Vyssia Priemyselna Skola Banicka [*Higher Industrial School of Mining*] (CZ)	
VPSFNRJ	Vrhovni Privredni Sud Federativna Narodna Republika Jugoslavija [*Supreme Economic Court of Yugoslavia*] (YU)	
VPSh	Fixed-Pitch Propeller (RU)	
VPSh	Higher Party School (RU)	
VPSh	Military Political School (RU)	
VPSO	All-Russian Producers' Union of Hunters (RU)	
VPSP	Stimulating Postsynaptic Potential (RU)	
VPSRPP	All-Russian Trade Union of Workers of the Printing Industry (RU)	
VPST	All-Russian Trade Union of Textile Workers (RU)	
VPT	Hungarian Workers' Party (RU)	
VPT	Vertically Movable Pipe [*Underwater concrete laying*] (RU)	
VPT	Victorian Property Trust [*Australia*]	
VPT	Vietnam Lao Dong Party (BU)	
VPTI	All-Union Planning and Technological Institute (RU)	
VPTISTROYDORMASh	All-Union Planning and Technological Institute of Construction and Road Machinery Manufacture (RU)	
VPTITYaZhMASh	All-Union Planning and Technological Institute of Heavy Machinery Manufacture (RU)	
VPTO	Antitank Platoon (RU)	
vptr	Troop Mobile Repair Workshop (BU)	
VPU	Auxiliary Control Post (RU)	
VPU	Extension Control Panel (RU)	
VPU	Intercommunication, Intercom (RU)	
VPU	Military Political School (RU)	

VPU	Reproducing Sequence Apparatus (RU)	
VPU	Video Control Board (RU)	
VPU	Visa Privredna Udruzenja [*Higher Economic Associations*] (YU)	
VPU	Vojensky Projektovy Ustav [*Military Design Institute*] (CZ)	
VPU	Vojnopomorsko Uporiste [*Naval Stronghold*] (YU)	
VPU	Vseobecny Pensijni Ustav [*General Pension Institute*] (CZ)	
VPV	All-Union Industrial Exhibition (RU)	
VPV	Higher High Water (RU)	
VPV	Velitelstvo Pozemneho Vojska [*Ground Forces Command*] (CZ)	
VPV	Vidam Park Vallalat [*Amusement Park Enterprise*] (HU)	
VPVS	Velitelstvi Pohranicni a Vnitrni Straze [*Border and Interior Guard Headquarters*] (CZ)	
VPZ	Velkoobchod Potravinarskym Zbozim [*Wholesale Food Store*] (CZ)	
VPZh	Plastic-Viscous Liquid (RU)	
VQB	Valuers' Qualification Board [*Victoria, Australia*]	
VQOL	Victorian Quality of Life [*Survey*] [*Australia*]	
VQPRD	Vin de Qualite Produit dans des Regions Determinees [*French*]	
VQS	Vieques [*Puerto Rico*] [*Airport symbol*] (OAG)	
VR	Aerial Reconnaissance (RU)	
VR	Calling Relay (RU)	
VR	Connection for Radio Broadcasting (BU)	
VR	Dining Car (RU)	
VR	Military Reconnaissance (BU)	
vr	Peak (BU)	
vr	Physician (RU)	
vr	Reconnaissance Platoon (RU)	
Vr	Temporary (BU)	
Vr	Time (BU)	
VR	Vagabonds Removed [*Prison van nickname used during reign of VR, Victoria Regina*] [*British*] (DSUE)	
VR	Valtion Rautatiet [*State Railways*] [*Finland*] (WEN)	
VR	Vanguardia Revolucionaria [*Revolutionary Vanguard*] [*Peru*] [*Political party*] (PPW)	
VR	Vapaudenristi [*Finland*]	
VR	Vedecka Rada [*Science Council*] (CZ)	
Vr	Vedouci Reditel [*Managing Director*] (CZ)	
VR	Ve Re [*Albanian*]	
VR	Verkeersrecht [*Benelux*] (BAS)	
V/R	Verkoopsrekening [*Account Sales*] [*Business term*] [*Afrikaans*]	
VR	Verlagsrichtlinien [*Guidelines for Publishing Houses*] [*German*] (EG)	
VR	Verona [*Car registration plates*] [*Italian*]	
Vr	Vitesse Totale du Vent [*French*] (MTD)	
vr	Vlastnorucne, Vlastni Rukou [*Signed by Hand*] (CZ)	
vr	Vlastorucan [*By One's Own Hand*] (YU)	
VR	Volksrepublik [*People's Republic*] (EG)	
vr	Vrchni Rada [*Senior Counselor (Title of government official)*] (CZ)	
VR	Vrederegter [*Justice of the Peace*] [*Afrikaans*]	
VR	Vroulik [*Female, Feminine*] [*Afrikaans*]	
Vr	Vrydag [*Friday*] [*Afrikaans*]	
VR	Vuestra Reverencia [*Your Reverence*] [*Spanish*]	
VRA	Varadero [*Cuba*] [*Airport symbol*] (OAG)	
VRA	[*The*] Victorian Railways of Australia (DCTA)	
VRA	Victorian Rowing Association [*Australia*]	
VRA	Vocational Resource Agency Inc. [*Australia*]	
VRA	Volta River Authority [*Accra, Ghana*] (AF)	
VRA	Volunteer Rescue Association [*Australia*]	
vra	Vuestra [*Your*] [*Spanish*]	
vras	Vuestras [*Your (Plural)*] [*Spanish*]	
VRB	Probable Bomb Release Line (BU)	
VRB	Vereniging van Religieus-Wetenschappelijke Bibliothecarissen [*Belgium*] (SLS)	
VRB	Veterans' Review Board [*Australia*]	
VRB	Volksrepublik Bulgarien [*People's Republic of Bulgaria*] (EG)	
VRBQ	Valuers' Registration Board of Queensland [*Australia*]	
VRBT	Valuers' Registration Board of Tasmania [*Australia*]	
VRC	Red Cross of Vietnam (EAIO)	
VRC	Taxi Aereo de Veracruz [*Mexico*] [*ICAO designator*] (FAAC)	
VRC	Ventas Remates Consignaciones [*Colombia*] (COL)	
VRC	Victorian Relief Committee AT	
VRC	Virac [*Philippines*] [*Airport symbol*] (OAG)	
Vrchstrzm	Vrchni Strazmistr [*First Sergeant*] (CZ)	
VRD	Air Jet Engines (RU)	
VRD	Jet Engine, Air-Breathing Jet Engine (RU)	
VRD	Vanguardia Revolucionaria Dominicana [*Dominican Revolutionary Vanguard*] [*Dominican Republic*] (LA)	
VRD	Victoria River Downs [*Australia*]	
VRD	Voierie-Resaux Divers	
VRE	Air Reconnaissance Squadron (RU)	
Vred	Vredegerecht [*Benelux*] (BAS)	
v refl	Reflexive Verb (TPFD)	
v refl	Verbe Reflechi [*French*] (TPFD)	

Vrem oz......	Temporary Lake [*Topography*] (RU)
V Reva........	Vossa Reverencia [*Your Reverence*] [*Portuguese*]
V Revma.....	Vossa Reverendissima [*Your Most Reverend*] [*Portuguese*]
VRF............	Naval River Flotilla (RU)
VRFB.........	Victorian Rural Fire Brigades [*Australia*]
VRG...........	Viacao Aerea Rio-Grandense SA [*Brazil*] [*ICAO designator*] (FAAC)
Vrg.............	Vlaams Rechtsgenootschap [*Benelux*] (BAS)
VRGN........	Gan [*Maldives*] [*ICAO location identifier*] (ICLI)
VRHU.......	Hanimaadhoo [*Maldives*] [*ICAO location identifier*] (ICLI)
VRI............	Veterinary Research Institute [*Australia*] (DSCA)
VRI............	Veterinary Research Institute [*Sri Lanka*] (ARC)
VRI............	Virus Research Institute
vrid............	Acting (RU)
Vrie...........	Verrerie [*Glass Works*] [*Military map abbreviation World War I*] [*French*] (MTD)
vrio............	Acting (RU)
VRK..........	All-Union Radio Committee (RU)
VRK..........	Military Revolutionary Committee (RU)
VRK..........	Radio Comparison Circuit for All Wavelengths (RU)
VRK..........	Varkaus [*Finland*] [*Airport symbol*] (OAG)
vrk.............	Vuorokausi [*or Vuorokautta*] [*Finland*]
VRKD.......	Kadhdhoo [*Maldives*] [*ICAO location identifier*] (ICLI)
VRKhBI.....	Quality Baked Goods Kombinat (RU)
VRKSS......	All-Union Service-Dog Studbook (RU)
VRL...........	Victorian Rugby League [*Australia*]
VRL...........	Vila Real [*Portugal*] [*Airport symbol*] (OAG)
VRLRA.....	Victorian Rugby League Referees' Association [*Australia*]
VRMM......	Male/International [*Maldives*] [*ICAO location identifier*] (ICLI)
VRN...........	Verona [*Italy*] [*Airport symbol*] (OAG)
VRNL........	Van Regs na Links [*From Right to Left*] [*Afrikaans*]
vrnl............	Voornamelijk [*Mainly*] [*Netherlands*]
VRO...........	Aerovitro SA de CV [*Mexico*] [*ICAO designator*] (FAAC)
VRO...........	Air Reconnaissance Detachment (RU)
VRO...........	Verband der Russischlehrer Oesterreichs [*Association of Austrian Russian Teachers*] (SLS)
VRO...........	Verbond Recht en Orde [*League of Law and Order*] [*Netherlands*] (WEN)
VRO...........	Veterinary Research Organisation
vro.............	Vuestro [*Your*] [*Spanish*]
VROS........	All-Union Rice Experimental Station (RU)
VrOS.........	Vratsa Oblast Court (BU)
vros............	Vuestros [*Your (Plural)*] [*Spanish*]
VRP..........	Railroad Car Repair Station (RU)
VRP..........	Volksrepublik Polen [*Polish People's Republic*] (EG)
VRP..........	Volta River Project
VRP..........	Voyageur Representant Placier [*Traveling Salesman*] [*French*]
VRP..........	Voyageurs de Commerce, Representants et Placiers [*French*]
VRP..........	Vyatka River Steamship Line (RU)
VR-PC.......	Vanguardia Revolucionaria - Proletario Comunista [*Revolutionary Vanguard - Proletarian Communist*] [*Peru*] [*Political party*] (PPW)
VRPK........	Verdauliche Rohproteinkonzentration [*Digestible Raw Protein Concentration*] (EG)
VRPM.......	Vanguardia Revolucionaria Politico-Militar [*Political-Military Revolutionary Vanguard*] [*Peru*] (LA)
VRS...........	Intrarayon Communications (RU)
VRS...........	Military Editorial Council [*1921*] (RU)
VRS...........	Van Riebeeck Society [*South Africa*] (SLS)
VRS...........	Vodohospodarske Rozvojove Stredisko [*Central Office for Development of Water Resources*] (CZ)
VRSA........	Vereniging van Radiograwe van Suid-Afrika [*Society of Radiographers of South Africa*] (EAIO)
VRSh........	Adjustable-Pitch Propeller (RU)
VRSh........	Workers' Evening School (RU)
Vrstd.........	Vorstand [*Board of Directors*] [*German*]
VRT...........	Military Revolutionary Tribunal (RU)
vrt..............	Vertaa [*Compare, Confer*] [*Finland*] (GPO)
VRT...........	Workers' Evening Technicum (RU)
VRTITC....	Victorian Road Transport Industry Training Committee [*Australia*]
vrto............	Missile Support Platoon (BU)
VRTS.........	Intrarayon Telephone Exchange (RU)
VRTs.........	Waterproof Expanding Cement (RU)
VRU...........	Time Gain Control (RU)
VRU...........	Victorian Railways Union [*Australia*]
VRU...........	Victorian Rugby Union [*Australia*]
VRU.........	Vryburg [*South Africa*] [*Airport symbol*] (OAG)
VRV..........	Water-Regulating Valve (RU)
VRVD........	Velitelstvi Raketovych Vojsk a Delostrolectva [*Rocket and Artillery Troop Headquarters*] (CZ)
VRY..........	Vaeroy [*Norway*] [*Airport symbol*] (OAG)
VRZ..........	Aero Veracruz SA de CV [*Mexico*] [*ICAO designator*] (FAAC)
VRZ..........	Protective Output Line Relay (RU)
VRZ...........	Railroad Car Repair Plant (RU)
VS.............	Armed Forces (of the USSR) (RU)

VS.............	Auxiliary Vessel (RU)
VS.............	Detraining Station, Unloading Station (RU)
VS.............	Leading-In Rack (RU)
VS.............	Military Communications (RU)
VS.............	Military Council (RU)
VS.............	Of Service Troops (RU)
VS.............	Selenium Rectifier (RU)
VS.............	Signal Platoon (RU)
vs...............	Sunday (RU)
VS.............	Supreme Court (BU)
VS.............	Supreme Court of the USSR (RU)
VS.............	Supreme Soviet of the USSR (RU)
v/s.............	Top Grade (RU)
vS.............	Train Operates Only on Weekdays Preceding Sundays and Holidays (EG)
VS.............	Valence Bond (Method) (RU)
vs...............	Varas [*Yardsticks*] [*Spanish*]
VS.............	Varnostni Svet [*Security Council*] (YU)
vs...............	Vatrena Sredstva [*Firing Equipment*] (YU)
VS.............	Vegan Society [*Oxford, England*] (EAIO)
VS.............	Velitelske Stanoviste [*Command Post*] (CZ)
VS.............	Velitel Smeny [*Shift Commander*] (CZ)
VS.............	Velitel Stanice [*Station Commander*] (CZ)
VS.............	Venstresocialisterne [*Left Socialists Party*] [*Denmark*] [*Political party*] (PPE)
VS.............	Ventilation Shaft [*Mining*] (RU)
VS.............	Verarbeitungssystem [*Processing System*] [*German*] (ADPT)
VS.............	Verband Deutscher Schriftsteller [*Association of German Writers*]
VS.............	Vereinigte Staatschulen fuer Freie und Angewandte Kunst [*Union of National Colleges for Free and Applied Art*] [*Pre-World War II*] [*German*]
VS.............	Verschlusssache [*Classified Material (To be secured in safe)*] [*German*] (EG)
Vs.............	Versorgung [*Provisions, Supply, Making Provisions For*] [*German*] (EG)
VS.............	Vertical Drilling Machine (RU)
vs...............	Ve Saire [*Et Cetera*] [*Turkey*] (GPO)
VS.............	Veterinarska Stanica [*Veterinary Station*] (YU)
VS.............	Veterinary Service (RU)
VS.............	Vicariate of Solidarity [*Chile*] (EAIO)
VS.............	Vieux Style [*Old Style*] [*French*]
VS.............	Virgil Society (EA)
VS.............	Virtueller Speicher [*Virtual Memory*] [*German*] (ADPT)
VS.............	Vodni Stavby [*Water Construction*] (CZ)
VS.............	Volksschule [*Elementary or Primary School*] [*German*]
(VS)...........	Volksschulexpositur [*German*]
v-s..............	Volt-Second (RU)
VS.............	Voorschrift [*Rule, Order*] [*Dutch*] (ILCA)
VS.............	Vossa Senhoria [*Your Lordship*] [*Portuguese*]
VS.............	Vostra Signoria [*Your Honor*] [*Italian*]
VS.............	Votre Saintete [*Your Holiness*] [*French*]
VS.............	Votre Seigneurie [*Your Lordship*] [*French*]
VS.............	Votrox Sprachsimulator [*Votrox Language Simulator*] [*German*] (ADPT)
VS.............	Vrhovni Stab [*Supreme Headquarters*] (YU)
VS.............	Vrhovni Sud [*Supreme Court*] (YU)
VS.............	Vuesenoria Ilustrisima [*or Usia Ilustrisima*] [*Spanish*]
VS.............	Vystrojovaci Stredisko [*Equipment Center*] (CZ)
VS.............	Vyvojove Stredisko [*Development Center*] (CZ)
VS.............	Vzorove Stanovy [*Model Statutes*] (CZ)
VSA...........	Vacuum Society of Australia
VSA...........	Vegetarian Society of Australia
VSA...........	Verband Schweizerischer Abwasserfachleute [*Swiss Association of Sewage Specialists*] (SLS)
VSA...........	Vereinigung Schweizerischer Angestelltenverbaende [*Federation of Swiss White-Collar Employees*] (EAIO)
VSA...........	Vereinigung Schweizerischer Archivare [*Association of Swiss Archivists*] (SLS)
VSA...........	Verenigde State van Amerika [*United States of America*] [*Afrikaans*]
VSA...........	Vereniging van Staatsamptenare van Suid-Afrika [*South Africa*] (AA)
VSA...........	Verkehrssicherheitsaktiv [*Traffic Safety Aktiv*] (EG)
VSA...........	Villahermosa [*Mexico*] [*Airport symbol*] (OAG)
VSa...........	Vossa Senhoria [*Your Lordship*] [*Portuguese*]
VSA...........	Vysoka Skola Architektury [*College of Architecture*] (CZ)
V/SABAC...	Victoria/South Australia Border Anomalies Committee
VSABR......	Vereniging van Suid-Afrikaanse Bourekenaars [*Association of South African Quantity Surveyors*] (AA)
VSAH........	Society of Art History - Vienna [*Austria*] (EAIO)
VSAI.........	Swiss Aluminum Association [*Switzerland*] (EAIO)
VSa Ilma....	Vossa Senhoria Ilustrissima [*Your Illustrious Lordship*] [*Portuguese*]
VSAKA......	Vereniging van Suid-Afrikaanse Kleurders en Afwerkers [*South African Dyers' and Finishers' Association*] (AA)

VSANP...... Verenigde Suid-Afrikaanse Nasionale Party [*Afrikaans*]
VSAT......... General Union of Algerian Workers   (RU)
vsau............ Platoon of Self-Propelled Guns   (RU)
vsb............. Military Construction Battalion   (RU)
VSB............ Schweizerische Vereinigung zum Schutz und zur Foerderung des Berggebietes [*Swiss Association for the Protection and Advancement of Mountainous Areas*]   (SLS)
VSB............ Vereinigter Schienenfahrzeugbau der DDR [*GDR United Rolling Stock Construction Combine*]   (EG)
VSB............ Vereinigung Schweizerischer Bibliothekare [*Union of Swiss Librarians*]   (SLS)
VSB............ Verein zum Schutz der Bergwelt [*Germany*]   (EAIO)
VSB............ Vereniging Surinaams Bedrijfsleven [*Surinam Trade and Industry Association*]   (EY)
VSB............ Vereniging voor Strategische Beleidsvorming [*Social and Economic Planning Organization*] [*Netherlands*]   (SLS)
VSB............ Veterinary Surgeons Board [*Australia*]
VSB............ Vrouesendingbond [*Afrikaans*]
VSB............ Vysoka Skola Banska [*Mining College*] [*Ostrava*]   (CZ)
VSBH.......... Vysoka Skola Banska a Hutni [*College of Mining and Metallurgy*]   (CZ)
VSBNSW.... Veterinary Surgeons' Board of New South Wales [*Australia*]
VSBNT....... Veterinary Surgeons' Board of the Northern Territory [*Australia*]
VSBQ........ Veterinary Surgeons' Board of Queensland [*Australia*]
VSBSA ...... Veterinary Surgeons' Board of South Australia
VSBTU...... Victorian State Building Trades Union [*Australia*]
VSC........... Aerovias Especiales de Carga Ltda. [*Colombia*] [*ICAO designator*]   (FAAC)
VSC............ Victorian Safety Council [*Australia*]
VSC............ Victoria State College [*Australia*]
VSCC......... Victorian Spoon Collectors Club [*Australia*]
VSCC......... Vintage Sports Car Club [*Australia*]
VSCCA.... Vintage Sports Car Club of Australia
VSCCSA.... Vintage Sports Car Club of South Australia
VSCh .... Vysoka Skola Chemicka [*College of Chemistry*]   (CZ)
V/sch.......... Your Account   (RU)
VSChP........ Vyzkumny Ustav Stroju Chladicich a Potravinarskych [*Research Institute for Refrigeration and Food Industry Machinery*]   (CZ)
VSChT....... Vysoka Skola Chemicke-Technologicka [*College of Chemical Technology in Prague*]   (CZ)
VSCOA...... Victorian Standing Committee on Adoption [*Australia*]
VSCP......... Vychodoslovenske Celulozky a Papierne [*East Slovak Cellulose and Paper Works*]   (CZ)
VSD .... Computational Dispatching System   (RU)
VSD .... Vesnicke Spotrebni Druzstvo [*Village Consumer Cooperative*]   (CZ)
vSd .... Von Seiten des [*On the Part of*] [*German*]   (GCA)
VSD .... Vysoka Skola Dopravni [*College of Transportation*]   (CZ)
VSD .... Vyssi Skola Dustojniku [*Higher School for Officers*]   (CZ)
VSDC........ Victorian School for Deaf Children [*Australia*]
VSDT........ Veterinary Surgeons' Disciplinary Tribunal [*New South Wales, Australia*]
VSE............ Vuelos Asesorias y Representaciones SA de CV [*Mexico*] [*ICAO designator*]   (FAAC)
VSE............ Vychodoslovenske Elektrarne [*Electric Power Plants for Eastern Slovakia*] [*Presov*]   (CZ)
VSE............ Vysoka Skola Ekonomicka [*College of Economics*] [*Prague*]   (CZ)
VSEC......... Victorian Solar Energy Council [*Australia*]   (WED)
Vsechrezkom ... All-Russian Extraordinary Commission for Combating Counterrevolution and Sabotage   (RU)
VSEGEI.... All-Union Scientific Research Institute of Geology   (RU)
VSEGINGEO ... All-Union Scientific Research Institute of Hydrogeology and Engineering Geology   (RU)
Vseispros ... All-Russian Union of Workers in Education and Arts   (RU)
Vsekhimprom ... All-Union Association of the Chemical Industry   (RU)
Vsekokhudozhnik ... All-Russian Cooperative Association "Artist" [*1931*]   (RU)
Vsekokhudozhnik ... All-Russian Cooperative Union of Artists [*1932*]   (RU)
Vsekokhudozhnik ... All-Russian Cooperative Union of Workers in the Fine Arts   (RU)
Vsekoopinsovet ... All-Union Council of Disabled Persons' Cooperatives   (RU)
Vsekoopinsoyuz ... All-Russian Union of Disabled Persons' Cooperative Associations   (RU)
Vsekoopit... All-Union Autonomous Section for Public Eating Facilities of the Tsentrosoyuz   (RU)
Vsekooptorg ... All-Union Association for Cooperative Trade in Cities and Settlements   (RU)
Vsekopromsovet ... All-Union Council of Producers' Cooperatives   (RU)
VSEKZO ... All-Union Cooperative Correspondence Training Center   (RU)
Vsemediksantrud ... All-Russian Union of Medical and Sanitary Personnel [*1919-1923*]   (RU)
vseobuch..... Universal Education   (RU)
Vserabis..... All-Union Trade Union of Workers in the Arts   (RU)
VSERABOTPROS ... All-Russian Trade Union of Education Workers   (RU)

Vserabotzem ... All-Russian Producers' Union of Agricultural Workers   (RU)
Vserabotzemles ... All-Russian Trade Union of Agricultural and Forest Workers   (RU)
Vserabpros ... Union of Education Workers of the USSR   (RU)
VSERC ...... Victorian Solar Energy Research Council [*Australia*]
Vserokompom ... All-Russian Committee for Assistance to Sick and Wounded Red Army Soldiers and Disabled Veterans (at the VTsIK)   (RU)
Vserokpom ... All-Russian Committee for Assistance to Sick and Wounded Red Army Soldiers and Disabled Veterans (at the VTsIK)   (RU)
vseros .... All-Russian   (RU)
Vserosskomdram ... All-Russian Society of Playwrights and Composers   (RU)
vses............. All-Union   (RU)
VSES .... Victoria State Emergency Service [*Australia*]
Vsesovfizkul't ... All-Union Council of Physical Culture (at the TsIK SSSR)   (RU)
vsesoyuz..... All-Union   (RU)
Vsespichprom ... All-Union Association of the Match Industry   (RU)
VseTsIK.... All-Russian Central Executive Committee   (RU)
Vseukrevkom ... All-Ukrainian Revolutionary Committee   (RU)
vsevobuch... Universal Military Training   (RU)
VSF............ Victorian Schizophrenia Fellowship [*Australia*]
VSFK .... All-Union Council of Physical Culture   (RU)
VSFK .... Supreme Council of Physical Culture [*Until 1933*]   (RU)
VSFL .... Veroeffentlichungen des Staatlich-Saechsischen Forschungsinstitut fuer Voelkerkunde in Leipzig
VSFNG..... Verband der Suppenindustrie Fachverband der Nahrungs-und Genussmittel-Industrie Osterreichs [*Austria*]   (EAIO)
VSFV .... Visa Skola za Fizicko Vaspitanje [*Advanced School of Physical Education*]   (YU)
VSFVU ...... Vydavatelstvo Slovenskeho Fondu Vytvarnych Umeni [*Publishing House of the Slovak Fund of Creative Art*]   (CZ)
VSG .... All-Union Miners' Union   (RU)
VSG .... Reglement voor het Vervoer over de Spoorweg van Gevaarlijke Goederen [*Benelux*]   (BAS)
vsg .... Upper Horizontal Base Line   (RU)
VSG .... Vulture Study Group [*South Africa*]   (EAIO)
VSGg .... Verein Schweizerischer Geographielehrer [*Union of Swiss Geography Teachers*]   (SLS)
VSGI......... All-Union Institute of Selection and Genetics   (RU)
VSGRU..... East Siberian Administration of Geological Exploration   (RU)
VSh .... Drag Hinge   (RU)
VSh .... Fuze Igniter   (RU)
VSh .... Higher School   (RU)
VSh .... Mine Car   (RU)
v-shche....... Reservoir   (RU)
VSHIV....... Schweizerischer Handels- und Industrieverein [*Formerly, Vorot des Schweizerischen Handels- und Industrie Vereins*] [*Switzerland*]   (EAIO)
VShK .... Incoming Cord Assembly   (RU)
VShOMO ... Evening School of General Music Education   (RU)
VShPD....... Higher School of Trade Unionism of the VTsSPS   (RU)
vshtsk........ Supply Room   (BU)
VSHV .... Vysoka Skola Hospodarskych Ved [*College of Economic Sciences*]   (CZ)
VShZ .... Voronezh Tire Plant   (RU)
VSI............. Higher Agricultural Institute   (BU)
VSI............ Verkstjorasamband Islands [*Icelandic Union of Foremen and Supervisors*]   (EAIO)
VSI............ Voluntary Service International [*British*]   (EAIO)
VSI............ Vuesenoria Ilustrisima [*Your Illustrious Ladyship (or Lordship)*] [*Spanish*]
VSIA......... Verband Selbstandigen Ingenieure und Architekten [*Germany*]   (EAIO)
VSIB......... East Siberian Railroad   (RU)
VSIC......... Veterinary Surgeon's Investigation Committee [*New South Wales, Australia*]
VS Ilma...... Vossa Senhoria Ilustrissima [*Your Illustrious Lordship*] [*Portuguese*]
VSIS .... Vereniging van Stellenbosse Ingenieurstudente [*South Africa*]   (AA)
VSIS .... Vysoka Skola Inzenyrskeho Stavitelstva [*Technical Institute of Construction Engineering*]   (CZ)
VSJ .... Vazduhoplovni Savez Jugoslavije [*Yugoslav Air Force Association*]   (YU)
VSJ .... Vojenska Sokolska Jednota [*Sokol (Athletic Organization) Military Unit*]   (CZ)
VSK........... Higher Chamber of Commerce   (BU)
VSK........... Verband Schweizerischer Konsumvereine [*Union of Swiss Consumer Associations*]
VSK........... Vietnami Szocialista Koztarsasag [*Socialist Republic of Vietnam*]   (HU)
vsk............. Vuosikerta [*Finland*]
VSKD........ All-Russian Congress of Peasants' Deputies   (RU)
VSKh .... Kharin Vertical Seismograph   (RU)
VSKhI........ Voronezh Agricultural Institute   (RU)

VSKhIZO.. All-Union Agricultural Correspondence Training Institute (RU)
VSKhO ...... All-Union Agricultural Society (RU)
VSKhV....... All-Union Agricultural Exhibition (RU)
VSKIUTU ... East Siberian Regional Administration of Corrective Labor Institutions (RU)
VSKKh....... All-Union Council of Municipal Services (at the TsIK SSSR) (RU)
VSKP......... Auxiliary Flight Command Post (RU)
VSL............ Association for Free Cultural Activities and Study Centre [*Finland*] (EAIO)
vsl.............. Military Investigating Magistrate (BU)
vsl.............. Military Service (BU)
VSL............ State Library of Victoria [*Australia*]
VSL............ Victorian School of Languages [*Australia*]
VSL............ Vychodni Slovensko [*East Slovakia*] (CZ)
VSLD......... Vysoka Skola Lesnicka a Drevarska [*Forestry and Lumbering College*] (CZ)
VSLU......... Vyskumny a Skusobny Letecky Ustav [*Research and Testing Air Force Institute*] (CZ)
VSM .... High-Molecular Weight Compound (RU)
VSM .... Verband Sozialistischer Mittelschueler [*Union of Socialist Secondary School Students*] [*Austria*] (WEN)
VSM .... Verein Schweizerischer Maschinen-Industrielle [*Switzerland*] (PDAA)
VSM .... Vondrona Socialiste MONIMA [*Mouvement National pour l'Independence de Madagascar*] [*Socialist Group MONIMA Malagasy*]
VSM .... World Council of Peace (RU)
VSMF........ Verband Schweizerischer Marktforscher [*Swiss Association of Market Research*] (SLS)
VSMPA ..... Victorian Secondary Masters' Professional Association [*Australia*]
VSMPC ..... Victorian School of Massage and Physical Culture [*Australia*]
VSMU .... Vysoka Skola Musickych Umeni [*College of the Fine Arts*] (CZ)
VSMUS..... Vsesoyuznyy Sovet Molodykh Uchenykh i Spetsialistov [*All-Union Council of Young Scientists and Specialists*] [*Former USSR*] (EAIO)
VSN .... Verband Schweizerischer Nachrichtenoffiziere [*Association of Swiss Intelligence Officers*] (WEN)
VSN .... Volontaires de la Securite Nationale
VSNA .... Volontaires du Service National Actif [*Active National Service Volunteers*] [*French*] (AF)
VSNB........ Velitelstvi Sboru Narodni Bezpecnosti [*Headquarters of the National Security Corps*] (CZ)
VSNII .... All-Union Scientific Research Institute of the Salt Industry (RU)
VSNIPILesdrev ... East Siberian Scientific Research and Planning Institute of the Lumber and Woodworking Industry (RU)
VSNITO.... All-Union Council of Scientific, Engineering, and Technical Societies (RU)
VSNKh ...... All-Russian Council of the National Economy [*RSFSR*] (RU)
VSNKh ...... Supreme Council of the National Economy [*1917-1932*] (RU)
VSNKh ...... Supreme Council of the National Economy, USSR (of the Council of Ministers, USSR) (RU)
VSNKh ...... Vysshego Soveta Narodnogo Khozyaystva [*Supreme Council of National Economy*] [*Former USSR*] (LAIN)
VSNOViPOJ ... Vrhovni Stab Narodnooslobodilacke Vojske i Partizanskih Odreda Jugoslavije [*Supreme Headquarters of the National Liberation Army and Partisan Units of Yugoslavia*] (YU)
VSNP........ All-Chinese Assembly of National Representatives (RU)
VSNR .... Supreme Court of the People's Republic (BU)
VSNRB...... Supreme Court of the Bulgarian People's Republic (BU)
VSNTO ..... All-Union Council of Scientific and Technical Societies (RU)
VSO .... All-Union Sports Society (RU)
VSO .... District Military Council (RU)
VSO .... Military Construction Section (RU)
VSO .... Military Medical Section (RU)
VSO .... Vysoka Skola Obchodni [*College of Business Administration*] (CZ)
VSOH........ Vyzkumne Stredisko Odpadovych Hmot [*Research Center for Waste Materials*] (CZ)
VSON .... Special-Purpose Auxiliary Vessel (RU)
VSOP......... Very Superior Old Product [*More than 20 years old*] (FLAF)
VSOPM..... Vseobshchii Soiuz Ob'edinennykh Profsoiuzov Marokko
VSORGO .. East Siberian Branch of the Russian Geographic Society (RU)
vsotob......... Ammunition Train (BU)
VSOZOT... All-Union Society "For the Mastering of Technology" (RU)
VSP............ Air Gunnery Training (RU)
VSP............ All-Russian Union of Writers (RU)
VSP............ All-Union Freight Transportation Council (RU)
VSP............ Hydroelectric Power Line (BU)
VSP............ Liaison Platoon with Infantry [*Artillery*] (RU)
VSP............ Military Hospital Train (RU)
VSP............ Supreme Audit Office (BU)
VSP............ Temporary Hospital Train (RU)
VSP............ Tracked Amphibious Ferry (BU)
VSP............ Vertical Seismic Profiling (RU)

VSP............ Viacao Aerea Sao Paulo SA [*Brazil*] [*ICAO designator*] (FAAC)
VSP............ Victorian Socialist Party [*Australia*] [*Political party*]
VSP............ Voiture sans Permis [*Car without license*] [*French*]
VSP............ Vojno-Sanitetski Pregled [*Military Medicine Review*] [*A periodical*] (YU)
VSP............ Vysoka Skola Pedagogicka [*College of Education*] (CZ)
VSP............ Vysoka Skola Polnohospodarska [*Agricultural College*] [*Nitra*] (CZ)
VSPEO ...... Military Epidemic Control Detachment (RU)
VSPHN ..... Vysoka Skola Politickych a Hospodarskych Nauk [*College of Political and Economic Sciences*] [*Prague*] (CZ)
VSPHV ...... Vysoka Skola Politickych a Hospodarskych Ved [*College of Political and Economic Sciences*] [*Prague*] (CZ)
VSPK .... All-Union Council of Producers' Cooperatives (RU)
VSPLI........ Vysoka Skola Polnohospodarskeho a Lesnickeho Inzinierstva [*College of Agriculture and Forestry*] [*Kosice*] (CZ)
VSPOV...... All-Russian Union of Physicians' Professional Associations (RU)
VSPS .... All-Russian Trade-Union Council (RU)
VSPS .... Auxiliary Forces (RU)
VSPS .... Vysoka Skola Politicka a Socialni [*College of Political and Social Sciences*] (CZ)
VSQC........ Veterinary Specialists' Qualification Committee [*Victoria, Australia*]
VSR............ Military Construction Area (RU)
VSR............ Verteenwoordigende Studente-Raad [*Students' Representative Council*] [*Afrikaans*]
VSRD........ All-Union Woodworkers' Union (RU)
VSRJL....... Vysoka Skola Ruskeho Jazyka a Literatury [*College of Russian Language and Literature*] (CZ)
VSRK .... Supreme Council of Workers' Control (RU)
VSRKh...... All-Russian Union of Workers of the Chemical Industry (RU)
VSRKh...... All-Union Union of Workers of the Chemical Industry (RU)
VSRKM..... General Union of Workers and Peasants of Mexico (RU)
VSRM........ All-Russian Metal Workers' Union (RU)
VSRM........ All-Union Metal Workers' Union (RU)
VSRP......... Hungarian Socialist Workers' Party (RU)
VSRP......... Vychodoslovensky Rudny Pruzkum [*Ore Prospecting for Eastern Slovakia*] (RU)
VSRPD...... All-Russian Union of Printing Trade Workers (RU)
VSRPP....... All-Russian Union of Workers of the Printing Industry (RU)
VSRPVP.... All-Russian Union of Workers of the Food and Flavoring Industry (RU)
VSRPVP.... All-Union Union of Workers of the Food and Flavoring Industry (RU)
VSRTM..... All-Union Union of Transportation Machinery Workers (RU)
VSRVT ...... All-Union Union of Water Transportation Workers (RU)
VSRZL ...... All-Russian Union of Agricultural and Forest Workers (RU)
VSS............ Medical and Sanitary Service (RU)
VSS............ Military Medical Service (RU)
VSS............ Supreme Economic Council (BU)
VSS............ Supreme Union Council [*Bulgarian National Agrarian Union*] (BU)
vss .... Vaestonsuojelu [*Finland*]
VSS............ Vazduhoplovna Sekcija Sadejstva [*Air Force Section for Support and Coordination*] (YU)
VSS............ Verband Schweizerischer Studentenschaften [*Union of Swiss Students*] (WEN)
VSS............ Verband Schweizerischer Suppenfabrikanten [*Switzerland*] (EAIO)
VSS............ Viet Cong Security Service (VNW)
VSS............ Virgin Islands Seaplane Shuttle, Inc. [*ICAO designator*] (FAAC)
VSS............ Vychodoslovenske Strojarne [*East Slovakia Machine Building Plants*] (CZ)
VSS............ Vysoka Skola Socialni [*College of Social Work*] [*Brno*] (CZ)
VSS............ Vysoka Skola Strojirenska [*Technical Institute of Machine Building*] [*Brno*] (CZ)
VSS............ Vysoka Stranicka Skola [*Communist Party College*] (CZ)
VSS............ World Student Union (RU)
VSSC .... Vikram Sarabhai Space Centre [*ISRO*] [*India*] (PDAA)
VSSI .... Higher Agricultural Institute (BU)
VSSIPd...... Higher Agricultural Institute in Plovdiv (BU)
VSSMA ..... General Union of Muslim Students of Algeria (RU)
VSSMOR .. Military Secondary Specialized School for Sea and Ocean Fishing (BU)
VSSN......... Vysoka Skola Specialnich Nauk [*College of Special Sciences (Statistics, insurance, higher mathematics, etc.)*] (CZ)
VSSP .... All-Union Union of Soviet Writers (RU)
VSSR .... All-Russian Construction Workers' Union (RU)
VSSR .... All-Union Construction Workers' Trade Union (RU)
VSSTOe ... Verband Sozialistischer Studenten Oesterreichs [*Socialist Students Association of Austria*] (WEN)
VSSTU ...... Victorian State School Teachers' Union [*Australia*]
VSSZh .... All-Russian Union of Soviet Journalists (RU)
VST............ Departmental Standard, Institutional Standard (RU)
VST............ General Workers' Union (RU)

VST........... Vasteras [Sweden] [Airport symbol]   (OAG)
VSt............ Vorstadt [Suburb] [German]
VST........... Vysoka Skola Technicka [Institute of Technology] [Kosice]   (CZ)
V St A .... Vereinigte Staaten von Amerika [United States of America] [German]
VStA .... Volksstaatsanwalt [People's Prosecutor (A state prosecutor with abbreviated training)]   (EG)
VSTBU ...... Victorian State Building Trades Union [Australia]
VStFB .... Verwaltung Staatlicher Forstwirtschaftsbetriebe [Administration of State Forestry Enterprises]   (EG)
VstG.......... Vermoegensteuergesetz [Property Tax Law] [German]   (WEN)
VSTM........ Vseobshchii Soiuz Trudiashchikhsia Marokko [General Union of Moroccan Workers]
VStN .... Vakstudie Nieuws [Benelux]   (BAS)
VSTP .... Vysoka Skola Textilna a Papiernicka [Technical Institute of Textile and Paper Technology] [Ruzomberok]   (CZ)
VStr........... Vycvikove Stredisko [Training Center]   (CZ)
VSTT .... Vseobshchii Soiuz Tunisskikh Trudiashchikhsia [General Union of Tunisian Workers]
VSTU........ Victorian School Teachers' Union [Australia]
vstup......... Entrance   (BU)
vstup......... Introductory   (BU)
VStw .... Vermittlungsstellenwesen [Telephone Exchange System] [German]   (EG)
VSU .... Auxiliary Power Plant   (RU)
vsu .... Auxiliary Vessel   (RU)
VSU .... Military Construction Directorate   (RU)
VSU .... Military Construction Site   (RU)
VSU .... Military Medical Directorate [1929-1935]   (RU)
VSU .... Volksunie Student Union [Volksunie Student Association] [Belgium]   (WEN)
VSU .... Voluntary Student Unionism [Australia]
VSU .... Wind-Power Installation   (RU)
VSUO .... Vyzkumny a Slechtitelsky Ustav Ovocnarsky Holovousy [Fruit Growing and Breeding Research Institute, Holovousy] [Former Czechoslovakia]   (ARC)
VSUZ........ Vyzkumny a Slechtitelsky Ustav Zelinarsky [Vegetable Growing and Breeding Research Institute] [Former Czechoslovakia]   (ARC)
VSV........... Velitelstvi Spojovaciho Vojska [Communications Troops Headquarters]   (CZ)
VSV........... Verdedigingskietvereniging [Afrikaans]
VSV........... Verordnung fuer Sozialpflichtversicherung [Regulations Concerning Compulsory Social Insurance] [German]   (EG)
VSV........... Volo Sensa Visibilita [Italian]
VSV........... Vysoka Skola Valecna [War College]   (CZ)
VSV........... Vysoka Skola Veterinarska [College of Veterinary Medicine]   (CZ)
VSVF .... Veroeffentlichungen aus den Staedtischen Voelkermuseum Frankfurt/Main [Publications from the State People's Museum at Frankfurt on the Main] [German]
VSVM....... Vereinigung Schweizerischer Versicherungsmathematiker [Swiss Association of Actuaries]   (SLS)
VSVO .... East Siberian Military District   (RU)
VSVZ........ Vysoka Skola Ved Zemedelskych [College of Agricultural Sciences]   (CZ)
VSW .... Vereinigte SauerstoffWerke [United Oxygen Works] [Nazi Germany]
VSW .... Vereniging ter Bevordering van het Moderne Onderwijs in Sociale Wetenschappen [Benelux]   (BAS)
VSW .... Vertrau Schau Wem [Trust, but Be Careful Whom] [Motto of Johann Georg, Duke of Wohlau (1552-92)] [German]
VSW .... Vierteljahrschrift fuer Social- und Wirtschaftsgeschichte
VSYa......... Problems of Slavic Linguistics   (RU)
VSYuR....... Armed Forces of Southern Russia   (RU)
VsZ .... Vsevojskova Zaloha [All-Army Reserve]   (CZ)
VSZ........... Vysoka Skola Zeleznicni [Railroad College]   (CZ)
VSZ........... Vysoka Skola Zemedelska [Agricultural College]   (CZ)
VSZ........... Vyssi Skola Zememericska [College of Geodesy]   (CZ)
VSZI .... Vysoka Skola Zemedelskeho Inzenyrstvi [College of Agricultural Engineering]   (CZ)
VSZK .... Vietnami Szocialista Koztarsasag [Socialist Republic of Vietnam] (HU)
V Sz Sz...... Vasuti Szemelyfuvarozas Szabalyzata [Regulations for Railroad Passenger Transportation]   (HU)
VSZT .... Vallalati Szakszervezeti Tanacs [Factory Trade Union Committee]   (HU)
VSZV .... Vegyimuveket Szerelo Vallalat [Chemical Works Equipping Enterprise]   (HU)
VT .... Air Alert, Air-Raid Alarm   (RU)
VT .... Air Raid Alert   (BU)
VT .... Auxiliary Aiming Point [Artillery]   (RU)
VT .... Auxiliary Transformer   (RU)
VT .... Computer Engineering   (RU)
VT .... High-Temperature   (RU)
VT .... Internal Friction   (RU)
VT .... Military Tribunal   (RU)

VT .... Output Transformer   (RU)
vt .... Transitive Verb   (TPFD)
Vt .... Tuesday   (RU)
vt .... Valamint [As Well As]   (HU)
VT .... Vanha Testamentti [Finland]
VT .... Varatuomari [Finland]
VT .... Varilna Tehnika [Welding Technology] [Ljubljana A periodical] (YU)
VT .... Varosi Tanacs [City Council]   (HU)
VT .... Vedette Torpilleur [Coastal Torpedo Boat] [French]
VT .... Velho Testamento [Old Testament] [Portuguese]
vt .... Verbe Transitif [French]   (TPFD)
VT .... Verlag Technik Berlin (VEB) [Technik Publishing House, Berlin] [German]   (EG)
V/T .... Verwys na Trekker [Afrikaans]
Vt .... Veterinaer [Veterinarian] [German]
VT .... Victa Ltd. [Aviation Division] [Australia] [ICAO aircraft manufacturer identifier]   (ICAO)
vt .... Viikkotunti [or Viikkotuntia] [Finland]
vt .... Virkaatekeva [Finland]
vt .... Virkaa Toimittava [Finland]
VT .... Visoka Temperatura [High Temperature]   (YU)
VT .... Viterbo [Car registration plates] [Italian]
Vt .... Vitesse du Vent dans la Direction Perpendiculaire a la Ligne de Tir [French]   (MTD)
vt .... Viz Tez [See Also] [Former Czechoslovakia]
vt .... Voet [Foot] [Afrikaans]
VT .... Volumenteil [Part by Volume] [German]   (GCA)
vT .... Vom Tage [Of the Day] [German]   (GCA)
vT .... Von Tausend [Per Thousand] [German]
VT .... Vragen des Tijds [Benelux]   (BAS)
VT .... Water Transportation   (RU)
vt .... Watt   (RU)
VTA .... Air Tahiti [France] [ICAO designator]   (FAAC)
VTA .... Military Technical Academy   (BU)
VTA .... Military Transport Aviation   (RU)
VTA .... Transport Aviation [Soviet-Russian]   (DOMA)
VTA .... Victorian Temperance Alliance [Australia]
VTA .... Vocational Training Authority [Australian Capital Territory]
VTA .... Vojenska Technicka Akademie [Military Academy of Technology]   (CZ)
VTA .... Vojnotehnicka Akademija [Technical Military Academy] [Zagreb]   (YU)
vta............. Vuelta [Return] [Spanish]
VTAA .... Veterans Tennis Association of Australia
VTAB........ All-Union Streetcar and Bus Office   (RU)
VTAC........ Victorian Tertiary Admissions Centre [Australia]
VTAC........ Victorian Transport Accident Commission [Australia]
vtac............ Vidi Tacku [See Paragraph]   (YU)
vtad........... Military Transport Aviation Division   (BU)
vtae........... Military Transport Air Squadron   (RU)
vtae........... Military Transport Aviation Squadron   (BU)
VTAK .... Foreign Trade Arbitration Commission   (BU)
VTAK .... Foreign Trade Arbitration Commission (at the All-Union Chamber of Commerce)   (RU)
vtap .... Military Transport Aviation Regiment   (BU)
VTAZ........ Vojenska Technicka Akademie Antonina Zapotockeho [Antonin Zapotocky Military Academy of Technology]   (CZ)
VTB .... Foreign Trade Bank   (BU)
VTB .... Vazduhoplovno-Tehnicki Bataljon [Air Technical Battalion] (YU)
VTB .... Vereniging voor het Theologisch Bibliothecariaat
VtB............ Verfahrenstechnische Berichte [Process Technology Reports] [A publication]
VTBA........ Bangkok [Thailand] [ICAO location identifier]   (ICLI)
VTBA........ Victorian Transport Borrowing Agency [Australia]
VTBB........ Bangkok [Thailand] [ICAO location identifier]   (ICLI)
VTBC........ Chanthaburi [Thailand] [ICAO location identifier]   (ICLI)
VTBD........ Bangkok/International [Thailand] [ICAO location identifier] (ICLI)
VTBE........ Saraburi [Thailand] [ICAO location identifier]   (ICLI)
VTBF .... Chachoengsao/Phanom Sarakhan [Thailand] [ICAO location identifier]   (ICLI)
VTBG .... Kanchanaburi [Thailand] [ICAO location identifier]   (ICLI)
VTBH .... Lop Buri/Sa Pran Nak [Thailand] [ICAO location identifier] (ICLI)
VTBI .... Prachin Buri [Thailand] [ICAO location identifier]   (ICLI)
VTBJ .... Phetchaburi/Tha Yang [Thailand] [ICAO location identifier] (ICLI)
VTBK........ Nakhon Pathom/Kamphaeng Saen [Thailand] [ICAO location identifier]   (ICLI)
VTBL........ Lop Buri [Thailand] [ICAO location identifier]   (ICLI)
VTBM .... Phetchaburi/Maruk [Thailand] [ICAO location identifier] (ICLI)
VTBN .... Prachuap Khiri Khan/Pran Buri [Thailand] [ICAO location identifier]   (ICLI)

VTBP......... Prachuap Khiri Khan [*Thailand*] [*ICAO location identifier*] (ICLI)
VTBR......... Ratchaburi [*Thailand*] [*ICAO location identifier*] (ICLI)
VTBR........ Victorian Taxation Board of Review [*Australia*]
VTBS......... Chon Buri/Sattahip [*Thailand*] [*ICAO location identifier*] (ICLI)
VTBT......... Chon Buri/Bang Phra [*Thailand*] [*ICAO location identifier*] (ICLI)
VTBU .... Rayong/Utapao [*Thailand*] [*ICAO location identifier*] (ICLI)
VTBW........ Prachin Buri/Watthana Nakhon [*Thailand*] [*ICAO location identifier*] (ICLI)
VTC .... Victorian Technology Centre [*Australia*]
VTC .... Vocational Training Council [*New Zealand*]
VTCA........ Chiang Rai/Chiang Khong [*Thailand*] [*ICAO location identifier*] (ICLI)
VTCB......... Chiang Rai/Ban Chiang Kham [*Thailand*] [*ICAO location identifier*] (ICLI)
VTCC......... Chiang Mai [*Thailand*] [*ICAO location identifier*] (ICLI)
VTCC........ Verein der Textilchemiker und Coloristen eV [*Society of Textile Chemists and Colorists*] (SLS)
VTCD .... Nan/Chiang Klang [*Thailand*] [*ICAO location identifier*] (ICLI)
VTCE......... Nan/Ban Pua [*Thailand*] [*ICAO location identifier*] (ICLI)
VTCF......... Uttaradit (West) [*Thailand*] [*ICAO location identifier*] (ICLI)
VTCFITB .. Victorian Textile, Clothing and Footwear Industry Training Board [*Australia*]
vtch............ Including (BU)
VTCH .... Mae Hong Son [*Thailand*] [*ICAO location identifier*] (ICLI)
vtch............. Watt-Hour (RU)
VTCI........... Mae Hong Son/Pai [*Thailand*] [*ICAO location identifier*] (ICLI)
VTCK........ Mae Hong Son/Khun Yuam [*Thailand*] [*ICAO location identifier*] (ICLI)
VTCL......... Lampang [*Thailand*] [*ICAO location identifier*] (ICLI)
VTCN........ Nan [*Thailand*] [*ICAO location identifier*] (ICLI)
VTCP......... Phrae [*Thailand*] [*ICAO location identifier*] (ICLI)
VTCR......... Chiang Rai [*Thailand*] [*ICAO location identifier*] (ICLI)
VTCS......... Mae Hong Son/Mae Sariang [*Thailand*] [*ICAO location identifier*] (ICLI)
VTD .... Foreign Trade Directorate (BU)
VTD .... Military Topographic Depot (RU)
VTE .... Medical Determination of Disability (RU)
vte............. Vente [*Sale*] [*Business term*] [*French*]
Vte............. Vicomte [*Viscount*] [*French*] (MTD)
VTE .... Vientiane [*Laos*] [*Airport symbol*] (OAG)
VTEIP .... Vedeckotechnicke a Ekonomicke Informace a Propaganda [*Scientific, Technical, and Economic Information and Propaganda*] (CZ)
VTEK........ Medical Commission for Determination of Disability (RU)
VTERU...... Vojensko-Technicko-Ekonomicky Rozborovy Ustav [*Military-Technical-Economic Analysis Institute*] (CZ)
Vtesse........ Vicomtesse [*Viscountess*] [*French*] (MTD)
VTEZ........ All-Union State Trust of Experimental Plants (RU)
VTF........... Technical Committee for Education [*Malagasy*] (AF)
VTF........... Vilnius Tobacco Factory Imeni F. E. Dzerzhinskiy (RU)
VTGOkhR ... High-Temperature Gas-Cooled Reactor (RU)
VTI............. All-Union Institute of Heat Engineering Imeni F. E. Dzerzhinskiy (RU)
VTI............. Materiel (RU)
VTI............. Statens Vag- och Trafikinstitut [*Swedish Road and Traffic Research Institute*] [*Linkoping*] [*Information service or system*] (IID)
VTI............. Vereinigung Textilindustrie [*Formerly, Austrian Cotton Spinners and Weavers Association*] (EAIO)
VTI............. Vsesoyuznyy Nauchno Issledovatel'skiy Teplotekhnicheskiy Institut [*All-Union Scientific Technical Thermotechnology Institute*] [*Russian*] (PDAA)
VTIJNA .... Vojno Tehnicka Istrazivanja Jugoslovenske Narodne Armije [*Military Technical Research of the Yugoslav People's Army*] (YU)
VTIV......... All-Union Synthetic Fiber Trust (RU)
VTIZ......... All-Union Trust of Construction Engineering Surveying (RU)
VTJ........... Vojenska Telocvicna Jednota [*Military Athletic Unit*] (CZ)
VTK .... High Technical Committee (RU)
VTK .... Military Technical Commission (RU)
VTK .... Upper Large Intestine (RU)
VTK .... Valtiotieteen Kandidaatti [*Finland*]
VTK .... Vazduhoplovna Takticka Komanda [*Air Force Tactical Command*] (YU)
VTK .... Vyrobni Technicka Komise [*Technical Production Commission*] (CZ)
VTK .... Water Transportation Collegium (RU)
VTKh......... Viscosity Index (RU)
VTKI......... Vasuti Tudomanyos Kutato Intezet [*Scientific Research Institute of the Railroads*] (HU)
VTL........... Valtiotieteen Lisensiaatti [*Finland*]
vtl .... Veterinarian (BU)
VTL........... Vientitakuulaitos [*Export credit agency*] [*Finland*]

VTLMB..... Victorian Tobacco Leaf Marketing Board [*Australia*]
VTM .... Tobacco Mosaic Virus (RU)
VTM .... Valtiotieteen Maisteri [*Finland*]
VtMDr .... Doktor der Tierheilkunde [*Doctor of Veterinary Medicine*] [*German*]
VTN .... Auxiliary Aiming Point [*Artillery*] (RU)
VTO.......... All-Russian Theatrical Society (RU)
VTO.......... All-Union Textile Association [*1929-1931*] (RU)
VTO.......... All-Union Theatrical Society (RU)
VTO.......... Departmental Technical Organization (BU)
VTO.......... Military Topographic Section (RU)
VTO.......... Technical Support Platoon (RU)
VTO.......... Vazduhoplovno Takticko Osmatranje [*Air Tactical Observation*] (YU)
vto............. Vuelto [*Verso*] [*Spanish*]
Vtorchermet ... Plant for the Processing of Secondary Ferrous Metals (RU)
Vtorchermet ... State Trust for the Procurement and Processing of Secondary Ferrous Metals (RU)
Vtorgrafit ... All-Union Office for Collection and Utilization of Graphite-Containing Waste (RU)
vtorsyr'yepromsoyuz ... Producers' Union for the Procurement and Processing of Secondary Raw Materials (RU)
Vtortsvetmet ... Plant for the Processing of Secondary Nonferrous Metals (RU)
Vtortsvetmet ... State Trust for the Procurement and Processing of Secondary Nonferrous Metals (RU)
VTOS........ Visa Tehnicka Oficirska Skola [*Advanced Officers' Technical School*] [*Zagreb*] (YU)
VTP........... All-Union Chamber of Commerce (RU)
VTP........... Auxiliary Aiming Point [*Artillery*] (RU)
VTP........... Foreign Trade Enterprise (BU)
vtp .... Villanytelep [*Electric Power Station*] (HU)
VTP........... Vise Tehnicko Preduzece [*Higher Technical Establishment*] (YU)
VTPH .... Prachuap Khiri Khan/Hua Hin [*Thailand*] [*ICAO location identifier*] (ICLI)
VTPI .... Nakhon Sawan/Takhli [*Thailand*] [*ICAO location identifier*] (ICLI)
VTPL......... Pretchabun/Lom Sak [*Thailand*] [*ICAO location identifier*] (ICLI)
VTPM....... Tak/Mae Sot [*Thailand*] [*ICAO location identifier*] (ICLI)
VTPN .... Nakhon Sawan [*Thailand*] [*ICAO location identifier*] (ICLI)
VTPP .... Phitsanulok [*Thailand*] [*ICAO location identifier*] (ICLI)
VTPS .... Phitsanulok/Sarit Sena [*Thailand*] [*ICAO location identifier*] (ICLI)
VTPT .... Tak [*Thailand*] [*ICAO location identifier*] (ICLI)
VTPU .... Uttaradit [*Thailand*] [*ICAO location identifier*] (ICLI)
VTPY .... Tak/Sam Ngao [*Thailand*] [*ICAO location identifier*] (ICLI)
VTR .... Topographic Reconnaissance Platoon (RU)
VTR .... Vedecko-Technicka Rada [*Council for Science and Technology*] (CZ)
VTR .... Vedeckotechnicky Rozvoj [*Scientific and Technical Development*] (CZ)
VTR .... Vitkovice Air [*Czech Republic*] [*ICAO designator*] (FAAC)
VTRA .... Victorian Trotting and Racing Association [*Australia*]
vtr sl .... Garrison Duty (BU)
VTS............ All-Russian Textile Syndicate [*1922-1929*] (RU)
VTS............ Ceskoslovenska Vedecka Technicka Spolecnost pro (Energetiku a) Elektrotechniku [*Czechoslovak Scientific Society of (Power and) Electrical Engineering*] (CZ)
VTs .... Computation Center (RU)
VTS............ Materiel Depot (RU)
VTS............ Materiel Supply (RU)
VTS............ Military Topographic Service (RU)
VTS............ Vedecka Technicka Spolecnost [*Society for Scientific Technology*] (RU)
VTS............ Visa Tehnicka Skola [*Advanced Technical School*] (YU)
V/Ts.......... Water-Cement Ratio (RU)
VTSA .... Satun [*Thailand*] [*ICAO location identifier*] (ICLI)
VTSB .... Surat Thani [*Thailand*] [*ICAO location identifier*] (ICLI)
VTSB .... Varosi Tarsadalmi Sport Bizottsag [*City Mass Sport Committee*] (HU)
VTSC......... Narathiwat [*Thailand*] [*ICAO location identifier*] (ICLI)
VTSD......... Chumpon [*Thailand*] [*ICAO location identifier*] (ICLI)
vt-sek.......... Watt-Second (RU)
VTsGADA ... Vilnius Central State Archives of the Lithuanian SSR. Division of Ancient Documents (RU)
VTSh......... Evening Technical School (RU)
VTSh......... Higher Trade School (RU)
VTSH .... Songkhla [*Thailand*] [*ICAO location identifier*] (ICLI)
VTsIK........ All-Russian Central Executive Committee [*1917-1936*] (RU)
VTsIK........ Vserossiyskiy Tsentral'nyy Ispolnitel'nyy Komitet [*All-Russian Central Executive Committee of the Congress of Soviets*] [*Former USSR*] (LAIN)
VTsIPK...... All-Union Central Institute for Improving the Qualifications of Engineering and Technical Personnel (RU)

VTSK........ Pattani [*Thailand*] [*ICAO location identifier*] (ICLI)
VTsK NA... All-Union Central Committee on the New Alphabet (RU)
VTsKNTA ... All-Union Central Committee on the New Turkic Alphabet (RU)
VTsKS....... Higher Central Stenography Courses (RU)
vt sl............. Veterinary Service (BU)
VTsLK....... All-Russian Central Liquidation Commission (RU)
vtsm............ In the Narrow Sense (BU)
VTsN........ Central Aiming Sight (RU)
VTSN........ Nakhon Si Thammarat [*Thailand*] [*ICAO location identifier*] (ICLI)
VTsNIB..... All-Union Central Office of Standards Research (RU)
VTsNIB..... All-Union Central Scientific Research Office (RU)
VTsNIIOT ... All-Union Scientific Research Institute of Work Safety (RU)
VTsNILKR ... All-Union Central Scientific Research Laboratory for Preservation and Restoration of Museum Art Treasures (RU)
VTSO........ Departmental Technical Construction Organization of the Holy Synod (BU)
VTSO........ Surat Thani/Don Nok [*Thailand*] [*ICAO location identifier*] (ICLI)
VTSP........ Phuket [*Thailand*] [*ICAO location identifier*] (ICLI)
VTSR........ Ranong [*Thailand*] [*ICAO location identifier*] (ICLI)
VTsRK....... All-Russian Central Workers' Cooperative (RU)
VTSS .... Songkhla/Hat Yai [*Thailand*] [*ICAO location identifier*] (ICLI)
VTsSPO..... All-Russian Central Union of Consumers' Societies (RU)
VTsSPS .... All-Union Central Trade-Union Council (RU)
VTST........ Trang [*Thailand*] [*ICAO location identifier*] (ICLI)
VTsU .... Slewing Sight [*Artillery*] (RU)
VTSY........ Ya La [*Thailand*] [*ICAO location identifier*] (ICLI)
VTT .... Valtion Teknillinen Tutkimuskeskus [*Technical Research Center of Finland*] [*Espoo*] [*Information service or system*] (IID)
VTT .... Valtiotieteen Tohtori [*Finland*]
VTTC........ Vocational Technical and Training Corp. [*Australia*]
VTTH........ Vo Tuyen Truyen Hinh [*Television*]
VTTI.......... All-Union Precision Industry Trust (RU)
VTU .... Departmental Technical Specifications (RU)
VTU .... Higher School of Commerce (BU)
VTU .... Higher School of Technology (BU)
VTU .... Higher Technical School (RU)
VTU .... Las Tunas [*Cuba*] [*Airport symbol*] (OAG)
VTU .... Military Technical Directorate (RU)
VTU .... Military Topographic Directorate (RU)
VTU .... Provisional Technical Specifications (RU)
VTU .... Vojensky Technicky Ustav [*Institute of Military Technology*] (CZ)
VTUA .... Kalasin/Ban Na Khu [*Thailand*] [*ICAO location identifier*] (ICLI)
VTUB .... Bakhon Phanom/Mukdahan [*Thailand*] [*ICAO location identifier*] (ICLI)
VTUC .... Chaiyaphum [*Thailand*] [*ICAO location identifier*] (ICLI)
VTUD........ Udon Thani [*Thailand*] [*ICAO location identifier*] (ICLI)
VTUE .... Provisional Technical Specifications of Operation (RU)
VTUE .... Sakon Nakhon/Nam Phung Dam (North) [*Thailand*] [*ICAO location identifier*] (ICLI)
VTUF........ Sakon Nakhon/Nam Phung Dam (South) [*Thailand*] [*ICAO location identifier*] (ICLI)
VTUG .... Chaiyaphum/Phu Khieo [*Thailand*] [*ICAO location identifier*] (ICLI)
VTUH........ Nakhon Ratchasima/Pak Chong [*Thailand*] [*ICAO location identifier*] (ICLI)
VTUI .... Sakon Nakhon/Bankhai [*Thailand*] [*ICAO location identifier*] (ICLI)
VTUK .... Khon Kaen [*Thailand*] [*ICAO location identifier*] (ICLI)
VTUL .... Loei [*Thailand*] [*ICAO location identifier*] (ICLI)
VTUM .... Nongkhai [*Thailand*] [*ICAO location identifier*] (ICLI)
VTUN........ Nakhon Ratchasima [*Thailand*] [*ICAO location identifier*] (ICLI)
VTUP .... Nakhon Phanom [*Thailand*] [*ICAO location identifier*] (ICLI)
VTUR .... Roi Et [*Thailand*] [*ICAO location identifier*] (ICLI)
VTUS........ Sakon Nakhon [*Thailand*] [*ICAO location identifier*] (ICLI)
VTUT .... Ubon Ratchathani/Loeng Nok Tha [*Thailand*] [*ICAO location identifier*] (ICLI)
VTUU .... Ubon Ratchathani [*Thailand*] [*ICAO location identifier*] (ICLI)
VTUW .... Nakhon Phanom (West) [*Thailand*] [*ICAO location identifier*] (ICLI)
VTUZ .... Higher Technical Educational Institution (RU)
VTUZ .... Higher Technical School (BU)
VTUZ .... Khon Kaen/Nam Phung Dam [*Thailand*] [*ICAO location identifier*] (ICLI)
VTV .... Varosepitesi Tervezo Vallalat [*Planning Enterprise for Urban Construction*] (HU)
VTV .... Vazduhoplovne Tekticke Vezbe [*Air Force Exercises*] (YU)
VTV .... Venezolana de Television [*Venezuela*] (IMH)
VTV .... Videki Tejipari Vallalatok [*Provincial Dairy Enterprises*] (HU)
VTW .... Victorian Tapestry Workshop [*Australia*]

VTX .... Vyzkum, Technologie, Extrakce SP [*Research Institute for Fat Technology and Extraction*] [*Former Czechoslovakia*] (IRC)
VTY .... Virkamiesten ja Tyoentekijaein Yhteisjaerjestoe [*Joint Organization of Civil Servants and Workers*] [*Finland*] (EY)
VTZ .... Vishakhapatnam [*India*] [*Airport symbol*] (OAG)
VTZ .... Vitjaz [*Russian Federation*] [*ICAO designator*] (FAAC)
VTZ .... Vladimir Tractor Plant Imeni A. A. Zhdanov (RU)
VTZ .... Vojno-Tehnicki Zavod [*Military Technology Institute*] [*Kragujevac*] (YU)
VU............. Computer (RU)
VU............. Conventional Viscosity (RU)
VU............. Headquarters Platoon (RU)
Vu............. Military School, Military Academy (BU)
VU............. Rectifier (RU)
VU............. Upper Level (RU)
VU............. Valve Installation (RU)
VU............. Vanuatu [*ANSI two-letter standard code*] (CNC)
VU............. Vaterlaendische Union [*Patriotic Union*] [*Liechtenstein*] [*Political party*] (PPE)
VU............. Verkstallande Utskott [*Executive Committee*] [*Sweden*] (WEN)
VU............. Vertical Angle (RU)
VU............. Video Amplifier (RU)
VU............. Virologicky Ustav [*Institute of Virology (of the Czechoslovak Academy of Sciences)*] (CZ)
VU............. Voice of Uganda
vu............. Vojensky Utvar [*Military Unit*] (CZ)
VU............. Volksunie [*People's Union*] [*Belgium*] [*Political party*]
VU............. Volksunite [*United People's Party*] [*Belgium*] [*Political party*]
VU............. Von Unten [*From the Bottom*] [*German*]
VU............. Vrije Universiteit [*Belgium*] (BAS)
VUA.......... Military Registration Archives (RU)
VUA.......... Military Science Archives (RU)
VUA.......... Vojensky Ustredni Archiv [*Central Military Archives (of the Ministry of National Defense or of the Military Office of the President of the Republic)*] (CZ)
VUA.......... Vyzkumny Ustav Antibiotik [*Antibiotics Research Institute*] (CZ)
VUAcCh .... Vyzkumny Ustav Acetylenove Chemie [*Research Institute of Acetylene Chemistry*] (CZ)
VUACh...... Vyzkumny Ustav Anorganicke Chemie [*Research Institute for Inorganic Chemistry*] (CZ)
VUAgT ...... Vyzkumny Ustav Agrochemicke Technologie [*Research Institute of Agrochemical Technology*] [*Bratislava*] (CZ)
VUAK....... All-Ukrainian Archaeological Committee (RU)
VUAMLIN ... All-Ukrainian Association of Marxist-Leninist Scientific Research Institutes (RU)
VUAN........ All-Ukrainian Academy of Sciences (RU)
VUAnCh.... Vyzkumny Ustav Anorganicke Chemie [*Research Institute of Inorganic Chemistry*] [*Usti Nad Labem*] (CZ)
VUAP .... Vyzkumny Ustav Automatizacnich Prostredku [*Institute of Research in Automation Means*] (CZ)
VUAT .... Vyskumny Ustav Agrochemickej Technologie [*Research Institute of Agrochemical Technology*] [*Bratislava*] (CZ)
vub............. Battery Headquarters Platoon (RU)
Vub............ Vorname Unbekannt [*First Name Unknown - FNU*] (WEN)
VUB......... Vrije Universiteit Brussel [*Free University of Brussels*] [*Belgium*] [*Information service or system*] (IID)
VUB.......... Vyzkumny Ustav Bavlnarsky [*Cotton Research Institute*] [*Usti Nad Orlici*] (CZ)
VUB.......... Vyzkumny Ustav Bramborarsky [*Potato Research Institute*] [*Havlickuv Brod*] (CZ)
VUBH....... Vyzkumny Ustav Bavlnarsky a Hedvabnicky [*Cotton and Silk Research Institute*] [*Usti Nad Orlici*] (CZ)
VUBP .... Vyzkumny Ustav Bezpecnosti Prace [*Research Institute of Industrial Safety*] [*Prague*] (CZ)
VUC.......... Vanguardia Unitaria Comunista [*Communist Unitary Vanguard*] [*Venezuela*] (LA)
VUC.......... Vyzkumny Ustav Cukrovarnicky [*Research Institute of the Sugar Refining Industry*] [*Prague*] (CZ)
VUCH....... Vyzkumny Ustav Chmelarsky [*Hop Research Institute*] [*Former Czechoslovakia*] (ARC)
VUChK...... All-Ukrainian Extraordinary Commission for Combating Counterrevolution and Sabotage (RU)
VUCHV..... Vyskumny Ustav Chemickych Vlakien [*Institute for Research in Chemical Fibers*] (CZ)
VUCHZ..... Vyzkumny Ustav Chemickych Zarizeni [*Institute for Research in Chemical Equipment*] (CZ)
VUCKD ..... Vyzkumny Ustav CKD Praha [*Research Institute CKD Prague*] (CZ)
VUCSKZ ... Vyzkumny Ustav Cs. Keramickych Zavodu [*Research Institute of the Czechoslovak Ceramics Plants*] (CZ)
VUCSSZ.... Vyzkumny Ustav Ceskoslovenskych Zavodu [*Research Institute of Czechoslovak Construction Enterprises*] (CZ)
VUD.......... Battalion Headquarters Platoon (RU)
VUD.......... Vychodoceske Uhelne Doly [*East Bohemian Coal Mines*] (CZ)

VUD.......... Vyzkumny Ustav Dopravni [*Transportation Research Institute*] (CZ)

VUE.......... Veszprem University of Chemical Engineering [*Hungary*]

VUE.......... Vyzkumny Ustav Energeticky [*Power Research Institute*] [*Brno*] (CZ)

VUEH........ Vyzkumny Ustav Ekonomiky Hornictvi [*Institute of Research in Mining Economy*] (CZ)

VUEK .... All-Union Accounting and Economic Courses (RU)

VUEK .... Vyzkumny Ustav Elektrokeramiky [*Institute of Research in Ceramics for Use in Electronics*] (CZ)

VUEP .... Vyzkumny a Vyvojovy Ustav Elektrickych Pristroju a Rozvadecu [*Institute for Research and Development of Electrical Machinery and Distributors*] (CZ)

VUEPS ..... Vyzkumny Ustav Ekonomiky Prumyslu a Stavebnictvi [*Institute of Research in Industry and Construction Economy*] (CZ)

VUES........ Vyzkumny Ustav Elektrickych Stroju Tocivych [*Institute for Research in Electrical Rotary Machines*] (CZ)

VU-EVA .... Volksunie-Europese Vrije Alliante [*Belgium*] [*Political party*] (ECED)

VUEZ .... Vyzkumny Ustav Energetickych Zarizeni [*Institute for Research in Electric Power Equipment*] (CZ)

VUF .... Higher School of Physical Education (BU)

VUF .... Vanster Ungdoms Forbund [*Leftist Youth League*] [*Sweden*] (WEN)

VUF .... Vyzkumny Ustav Financi [*Finance Research Institute*] (CZ)

VUFB........ Vyzkumny Ustav pro Farmacii a Biochemii [*Research Institute for Pharmacology and Biochemistry*] (CZ)

VUFCh ...... Vyzkumny Ustav pro Fotografickou Chemii [*Research Institute of Photographic Chemistry*] [*Prague*] (CZ)

VUFKU ..... All-Ukrainian Photography and Motion Picture Administration (RU)

VUFVNIIGeofizika ... Volga-Ural Branch of the VNIIGeofizika (RU)

VuG........... Verlag Volk und Gesundheit (VEB) [*"Volk und Gesundheit" Publishing House (VEB)*] (EG)

Vuga G .... Vuga Gids [*Benelux*] (BAS)

VUGI......... All-Union Scientific Research Institute of Coal (RU)

VUGPT...... Vyzkumny Ustav Gumarenske a Plastikarske Techniky [*Research Institute of Rubber and Plastics Technology*] (CZ)

VUGTK ..... Vyzkumny Ustav Geodeticky, Topograficky, a Kartograficky [*Research Institute of Geodesy, Topography, and Cartography*] (CZ)

VUHK........ Vyskumny Ustav Hutnickej Keramiky [*Metallurgical Research Institute for Refractory Materials*] (CZ)

VUHP........ Vyskumny Ustav Hydinarskeho Priemyslu [*Research Institute of the Poultry Industry*] (CZ)

VUHU .... Vyzkumny Ustav Hnedeho Uhli, Severocesky Hnedouhelny Revir [*Soft Coal Research Institute, North Bohemian Soft Coal Region*] (CZ)

VUHZ........ Vyzkumny Ustav Hutnictvi Zeleza [*Institute for Research in Ferrous Metallurgy*] (CZ)

VUHZ........ Vyzkumny Ustav Hutnictvi Zeleza, Dobra [*Dobra Iron and Steel Research Institute*] [*Information service or system*] (IID)

VUIEM ..... All-Ukrainian Institute of Experimental Medicine (RU)

VUIS.......... Vyskumny Ustav Inzinierskych Stavieb [*Institute for Research in Engineering Construction*] (CZ)

VUJAK...... Vyzkumny Ustav Pedagogicky Jana Amose Komenskeho [*J. A. Comenius Pedagogical Research Institute*] (CZ)

VUJASTO ... Vojna Uprava Jugoslovenske Armije Svobodno Trzasko Ozemlje [*Yugoslav Army's Military Administration for Zone B of the Free Territory of Trieste*] (YU)

VUJK........ Vyzkumny Ustav Jemne Keramiky [*Institute for Research in Fine Ceramics*] (CZ)

VUK.......... All-Union Training Center (of the Ministry of Construction, RSFSR) (RU)

VUK.......... Vyzkumny Ustav Kovu [*Metallurgical Research Institute*] (CZ)

VUK.......... Vyzkumny Ustav Kozedelny [*Shoe and Leather Research Institute*] (CZ)

VUK.......... Vyzkumny Ustav Krmivarsky [*Animal Feeding Research Institute (of the Czechoslovak Academy of Agricultural Sciences)*] (CZ)

VUKAI ..... All-Ukrainian Association of Engineers (RU)

VUKhIN .... Eastern Scientific Research Institute of Coal Chemistry (RU)

VUKI .... Vyskumny Ustav Kabelov a Izolantov [*Research Institute of Cables and Insulators*] [*Bratislava*] (CZ)

VUKS .... Vyzkumny Ustav Krmivarskeho Prumyslu a Sluzeb, Pecky [*Institute for Research in the Feed Industry and Services, Pecky*] (CZ)

Vuktekstil' ... All-Union Training Center of the Ministry of the Textile Industry, USSR (RU)

VUKV .... Vyzkumny Ustav Kolejovych Vozidel [*Institute for Research on Railroad Cars*] (CZ)

VUKZO..... Correspondence Training Center (RU)

vul.............. Vulitsa [*Street*] [*Commonwealth of Independent States*] (EECI)

VUL .... Vyzkumny Ustav Lazensky [*Balneological Research Institute*] [*Marianske Lazne*] (CZ)

vulg............ Vulgar (BU)

vulg............. Vulgarismo [*Vulgarism*] [*Portuguese*]

Vulg............ Vulgata [*Vulgate*] [*Afrikaans*]

VULH........ Vyskumny Ustav Lesneho Hospodarstva [*Forest Research Institute*] [*Former Czechoslovakia*] (ARC)

VULHM.... Vyskumny Ustav Lesneho Hospodarstva a Myslivosti [*Forest and Wildlife Management Research Institute*] (CZ)

Vulk .... Volcano [*Topography*] (RU)

VULK .... Vyskumny Ustav Liehovarov a Konzervarni [*Research Institute of Distilleries and Canneries*] (CZ)

vulkmast .... Recapping Workshop (RU)

VULP........ Vyskumny Ustav Luk a Pasienkov [*Grassland Research Institute*] [*Former Czechoslovakia*] (ARC)

VULV .... Vyzkumny Ustav Lykovych Vlaken [*Research Institute of Bast Fibers*] [*Sumperk*] (CZ)

VuM.......... Verfuegungen und Mitteilungen [*Directives and Information*] (EG)

VUM......... Vilnius Department Store (RU)

VUM......... Volo Umano Muscolare [*Italian*]

VUM......... Vyzkumny Ustav Mlekarensky [*Dairy Research Institute*] (CZ)

VUM......... Vyzkumny Ustav Mrazirensky [*Research Institute for Refrigeration*] [*Olomouc*] (CZ)

VUMA....... Vyskumny Ustav pro Mechanizaciu a Automatizaciu [*Research Institute of Mechanization and Automatization*] (CZ)

VUMACh ... Vyzkumny Ustav Makromolekularni Chemie [*Institute for Research in Macromolecular Chemistry*] (CZ)

VUMAT .... Vyzkumny Ustav Mechanizace, Automatizace, a Technologie [*Institute for Research in Mechanization, Automation, and Technology*] (CZ)

VUMEPP.. Vyzkumny Ustav pro Mechanisaci a Ekonomiku Potravinarskeho Prumyslu [*Research Institute for Mechanization and Efficiency in the Food Industry*] (CZ)

VUMEZ .... Vyzkumny Ustav Mechanisace a Elektrifikace Zemedelstvi [*Research Institute for the Mechanization and Electrification of Agriculture*] [*Prague-Vokovice*] (CZ)

VUML....... Evening University of Marxism-Leninism (RU)

VUML....... Vecerni Universita Marx-Leninismu [*University Night Classes on Marxism and Leninism*] (CZ)

VUMLP..... Vyskumny Ustav Mechanizacie Lesneho Priemyslu [*Research Institute for Mechanization of the Lumber Industry*] [*Oravsky Podzamok*] (CZ)

VUMLZ .... Vyzkumny Ustav pro Myslivest a Lesni Zoologii, Abraslav [*Zoological Research Institute of Wild Animal Life, in Zbraslav*] (CZ)

VUMM...... Vyzkumny Ustav Manipulace s Materialem [*Materials Handling Research Institute*] (CZ)

VUMO....... Vyzkumny Ustav Mechaniky a Optiky [*Research Institute of Mechanics and Optics*] (CZ)

VUMP .... Vyzkumny Ustav Masneho Prumyslu [*Research Institute of the Meat Industry*] [*Brno*] (CZ)

VUMPJK .. Vyzkumny Ustav pro Mechanisaci Prumyslu Jemne Keramiky [*Research Institute for the Mechanization of the Fine Ceramics Industry*] (CZ)

VUMPP..... Vyzkumny Ustav Mlynskeho a Pekarenskeho Prumyslu [*Miller and Bakery Industry Research Institute*] (CZ)

VUMS .... Vyzkumny Ustav Matematickych Stroju [*Mathematical Machines Research Institute*] (CZ)

VUMSK..... Vyzkumny Ustav pro Mechanisaci Prumyslu Skla a Jemne Keramiky [*Research Institute for the Mechanization of the Glass and Fine Ceramics Industries*] (CZ)

VUMT .... Vyzkumny Ustav Materialu a Technologie [*Research Institute of Materiel and Technological Processes*] (CZ)

VUMV....... Vyzkumny Ustav Motorovych Vozidel [*Research Institute of Motor Vehicles*] (CZ)

VUMZ .... Vyzkumny Ustav pro Mechanisaci Zemedelstvi [*Research Institute for the Mechanization of Agriculture*] [*Prague*] (CZ)

VUN.......... Air Ivoire Societe [*Ivory Coast*] [*ICAO designator*] (FAAC)

VUN.......... Auxiliary Aiming Angle (RU)

VUN.......... Provisional Consolidated Norms (RU)

VUN.......... Vyzkumny Ustav Nafty [*Petroleum Research Institute*] [*Brno*] (CZ)

VUNH........ Vyzkumny Ustav Naterovych Hmot [*Institute of Dye Paint Research*] (CZ)

VUNM....... Vyzkumny Ustav Naftovych Motoru [*Diesel Engines Research Institute*] (CZ)

VUNP........ Vyzkumny Ustav Narodohospodarskeho Planovani [*National Economy Planning Research Institute*] (CZ)

VUO .... Vyzkumny Ustav Obalovy [*Research Institute of Packaging*] (CZ)

VUO .... Vyzkumny Ustav Obchodu [*Trade Research Institute*] (CZ)

VUO .... Vyzkumny Ustav Odevnictvi [*Research Institute of the Garment Industry*] (CZ)

VUOAP ..... All-Union Administration for the Protection of Copyrights (RU)

VUOM....... Vyzkumny Ustav Ochrany Materialu [*Research Institute for Protection of Materiel*] [*Prague*] (CZ)

VUOS .... Vyzkumny Ustav Odborneho Skolstvi [*Professional Schooling Research Institute*] (CZ)

VUOS .... Vyzkumny Ustav Organickych Synthes [*Research Institute of Organic Compounds*] [*Pardubice*] (CZ)

VUOSO ..... Vyzkumny Ustav Obrabecich Stroju a Obrabeni [*Machine Tools Research Institute*] [*Praha-Zabehlice*] (CZ)

VUOZ .... Vyzkumny Ustav Organisace Zdravotnictvi [*Research Institute for the Organization of Health Services*] [*Prague*] (CZ)

VUP .... Military Training Installation (RU)

VUP .... Valledupar [*Colombia*] [*Airport symbol*] (OAG)

VUP .... Vyskumny Ustav pro Petrochemiu [*Petrochemistry Research Institute*] (CZ)

VUP .... Vyzkumny Ustav Pedagogicky [*Pedagogical Research Institute*] (CZ)

VUP .... Vyzkumny Ustav Pletarsky [*Knitwear Research Institute*] [*Brno*] (CZ)

VUP .... Vyzkumny Ustav Polygraficky [*Polygraphy Research Institute*] (CZ)

VUPC .... Vyskumny Ustav Papieru a Celulozy [*Paper and Cellulose Research Institute*] [*Bratislava*] (CZ)

VUPCH ..... Vyzkumny Ustav Prumyslove Chemie [*Research Institute for Industrial Chemistry*] [*Former Czechoslovakia*] (PDAA)

VUPChS .... Vyzkumny Ustav Potravinarskych a Chladicich Stroju [*Food and Refrigeration Machines Research Institute*] (CZ)

VUPE .... Vyskumny Ustav Polnohospodarskej Ekonomiky [*Research Institute of Agricultural Economics*] (CZ)

VUPEF ...... Vyzkumny Ustav pro Elektrotechnickou Fysiku [*Research Institute of Electrophysics*] [*Prague*] (CZ)

VUPEK ...... Vyskumny Ustav Palivo Energetickeho Komplexu [*Research Institute of Fuel and Energy Complex*] [*Former Czechoslovakia*]

VUPJ .... Victorian Union for Progressive Judaism [*Australia*]

VUPM .... Vyzkumny Ustav Praskove Metalurgie [*Research Institute of Powder Metallurgy*] [*Vestec near Prague*] (CZ)

VUPP .... Vyskumny Ustav Papirenskeho Prumyslu [*Research Institute of the Paper Industry*] [*Prague*] (CZ)

VUPP .... Vyskumny Ustav Potravinarskeho Priemyslu [*Institute of the Food Industry*] [*Bratislava*] (CZ)

Vupros .... Interrogative [*Grammar*] (BU)

VUPS .... Vyzkumny Ustav Pozemnich Staveb [*Ground Construction Research Institute*] (CZ)

VUPT .... Vyzkumny Ustav Potravinarske Techniky [*Food Research Institute*] [*Prague*] (CZ)

VUPVR ...... Vyskumny Ustav Podoznalectva a Vyzivy Rastlin [*Soil Science and Agrochemistry Research Institute*] [*Former Czechoslovakia*] (ARC)

VURH .... Vydava Vykumny Ustav Rybarsky a Hydrobiologicky [*Fisheries Research Institute*] [*Former Czechoslovakia*] (ASF)

VURH .... Vyzkumny Ustav Rybarsky a Hydrobiologicky [*Fisheries and Hydrobiology Research Institute*] [*Former Czechoslovakia*] (ARC)

VURK .... Vyzkumny Ustav Radiokomunikaci [*Research Institute of Radio Communications*] (CZ)

Vurkhstop suv ... Supreme Economic Council (BU)

VURT .... Vyzkumny Ustav Rozhlasu a Televize [*Broadcasting and Television Research Institute*] (CZ)

vurt/min ..... Revolutions per Minute (BU)

VURUP ..... Vyskumny Ustav pre Ropu a Uhlovodikove Plyny [*Crude Oil and Hydrocarbon Gases Research Institute*] [*Bratislava*] (CZ)

VURV .... Vyzkumny Ustav Rostlinne Vyroby [*Institute for the Research of Vegetable Produce*] (CZ)

VUS .... All-Russian Coal Syndicate (RU)

VUS .... All-Russian Teachers' Union [*1917-1918*] (RU)

VUS .... Auxiliary Communications Center (RU)

VUS .... Auxiliary Repeater Station (RU)

VUS .... Higher Council on Education (BU)

VUS .... Military Occupational Specialty (RU)

VUS .... Military School of Communications (RU)

VUS .... Video Amplifier (RU)

VUS .... Vojensky Umelecky Soubor [*Armed Forces Artistic Ensemble*] (CZ)

VUS .... Vyskumny Ustav Svaracsky [*Research Institute of Welding*] [*Bratislava*] (CZ)

VUS .... Vyzkumny Ustav Sklarsky [*Research Institute of the Glass Industry*] (CZ)

VUS .... Vyzkumny Ustav Spoju [*Communications Research Institute*] (CZ)

VUS .... World University Service [*WUS*] (RU)

VUSA .... Vyzkumnu Ustav pro Stavebnictvi a Architekturu [*Research Institute of Building and Architecture*] (CZ)

VUSB .... Vyzkumny Ustav Skla a Bizuterie [*Glass and Costume Jewelry Research Institute*] (CZ)

VUSChP .... Vyzkumny Ustav Stroju Chladicich a Potravinarskych [*Research Institute for Refrigeration and Food Machinery*] [*Prague*] (CZ)

VUSE .... Vyzkumny Ustav Silnoproude Elektrotechniky [*Research Institute for High Voltage Electrical Engineering*] [*Bechovice near Prague*] (CZ)

VUSE .... Vyzkumny Ustav Stavebni Ekonomiky [*Research Institute of Construction Economics*] (CZ)

VUSH .... Vyzkumny Ustav Stavebnich Hmot [*Building Materials Research Institute*] (CZ)

VUSK .... Vyzkumny Ustav Stavebnich a Keramickych Stroju [*Research Institute of Construction and Ceramic Machinery*] (CZ)

VUSK .... Vyzkumny Ustav Synthetickeho Kaucuku [*Synthetic Rubber Research Institute*] (CZ)

VUSKM ..... Vyzkumny Ustav Stavebnich Konstruckci a Montazi [*Construction and Assembly Research Institute*] (CZ)

VUSNITO ... All-Ukrainian Council of Scientific, Engineering, and Technical Societies (RU)

VUSPL ...... Vyzkumny Ustav Synthetickych Prayskyric a Laku [*Research Institute for Synthetic Resins*] [*Pardubice*] (CZ)

VUSPP ...... All-Ukrainian Union of Proletarian Writers (RU)

VUSPS ...... All-Ukrainian Trade-Union Council (RU)

VUSS .... Vyzkumny Ustav pro Strojni Sklo [*Structural Glass Research Institute*] (CZ)

VUSSN ...... Higher School of Economic and Social Sciences (BU)

VUSSNSv ... Higher School of Economic and Social Sciences in Svishtov (BU)

VUSSTS .... Vyzkumny Ustav Svarovacich Stroju a Technologie Svarovani [*Research Institute for Welding Machines and Welding Technology*] [*Branch in Chotebor*] (CZ)

VUST .... Vyzkumny Ustav pro Sdelovaci Techniku A. S. Popova [*A. S. Popov Research Institute for Communications Techniques*] (CZ)

VUSTE ...... Vyzkumny Ustav Strojirenske Technologie a Ekonomiky [*Engineering Technology and Economy Research Institute*] (CZ)

V U SZ .... Vasuti Uzletszabalyzat [*Railroad Regulations*] (HU)

VUSZ .... Vyzkumny Ustav Socialniho Zabezpeceni [*Social Security Research Institute*] (CZ)

VUSZS .... Vyzkumny Ustav Stavebnich a Zemnich Stroju [*Heavy Construction Machinery Research Institute*] (CZ)

VUT .... Vanuatu [*ANSI three-letter standard code*] (CNC)

vut .... Vegrehajtasi Utasitas [*Implementing Instruction*] (HU)

VUT .... Victoria University of Technology [*Australia*]

VUT .... Vojensky Technicky Ustav [*Military Institute of Technology*] [*Decin-Podmokly*] (CZ)

VUT .... Vysoke Uceni Technicke [*Technical Institute*] (CZ)

VUT .... Vyzkumny Ustav Telekomunikaci [*Telecommunication Research Institute*] [*Prague*] (CZ)

VUT .... Vyzkumny Ustav Telovychovny [*Research Institute on Physical Education*] (CZ)

VUT .... Vyzkumny Ustav Tuberkulosy [*Tuberculosis Research Institute*] [*Prague*] (CZ)

VUTD .... Vyzkumny Ustav Technickeho Drevoprumyslu [*Research Institute of the Lumber (or Wood Working) Industry*] [*Prague-Nusle*] (CZ)

VUTEChP ... Vyzkumny Ustav Technicko-Ekonomicky Chemickeho Prumyslu [*Technical Economic Research Institute of the Chemical Industry*] (CZ)

VUTMS ..... Vyzkumny Ustav Technologie a Mechanisace Stavebnictvi [*Research Institute of Construction Technology and Mechanization*] (CZ)

VUTO .... Vyzkumny Ustav Technicko-Organisacni [*Research Institute of Management Efficiency*] (CZ)

VUTP .... Oborovy Vyzkumny Ustav Tukoveho Prumyslu [*Sectoral Research Institute of the Fats Industry*] (CZ)

VUTP .... Vyskumny Ustav Tabakoveho Priemyslu [*Tobacco Industry Research Institute*] (CZ)

VUTRIZ .... All-Ukrainian Scientific and Industrial Trust for Testing and Application of Inventions (RU)

VUTS .... Vyzkumny Ustav pro Travopolni Soustavu [*Research Institute for the Grass-Clover System*] [*Pohorelice*] (CZ)

VUTS .... Vyzkumny Ustav Textilniho Strojirenstvi [*Textile Engineering Research Institute*] (CZ)

VUTS .... Vyzkumny Ustav Tezkeho Strojirenstvi [*Research Institute of the Heavy Machine Industry*] (CZ)

VUTS .... Vyzkumny Ustav Tvarecich Stroju a Technologie Tvareni [*Research Institute on Moulding Machines and the Technology of Moulding*] (CZ)

VUTsIK .... All-Ukrainian Central Executive Committee [*1920-1936*] (RU)

VUTT .... Vyzkumny Ustav Tepelne Techniky [*Research Institute of Thermodynamics*] (CZ)

VUTT .... Vyzkumny Ustav Textilni Technologie [*Research Institute of Textile Technology*] [*Liberec*] (CZ)

VUTV .... Higher School of Physical Education (BU)

VUUPV ..... Vyzkumny Ustav Upravy Prumyslovych Vod [*Research Institute for Treatment of Industrial Water*] (CZ)

VUUS .... Vyzkumny Ustav Uzitkoveho Skla [*Utility Glass Research Institute*] (CZ)

VUUV........ Vyzkumny Ustav Umelych Vlaken [*Research Institute of Synthetic Fibers*] [*Svit*]   (CZ)

VUUV........ Vyzkumny Ustav Upravy Vod [*Water Treatment Research Institute*] [*Former Czechoslovakia*] [*Research center*]   (IRC)

VUV........... Vyzkumny Ustav Vlnarsky [*Wool Research Institute*] [*Brno*]   (CZ)

VUV........... Vyzkumny Ustav Vodohospodarsky [*Water Utilization Research Institute*] [*Prague*]   (CZ)

VUV........... Vyzkumny Ustav Vzduchotechniky [*Air Technology Research Institute*]   (CZ)

VUVA........ Vyzkumny Ustav Vystavby a Architektury [*Research Institute of Construction and Architecture*]   (CZ)

VUVc........ Vyzkumny Ustav Vcelarsky [*Apiculture Research Institute*] [*Former Czechoslovakia*]   (ARC)

Vuved .... Preface, Introduction   (BU)

VUVET...... Vyzkumny Ustav Vakuove Elektrotechniky [*Vacuum Electro-Technology Research Institute*]   (CZ)

VUVL .... Vyzkumny Ustav pro Valiva Loziska [*Research Institute of Roller Bearing*]   (CZ)

VUVPH..... Vyzkumny Ustav pro Vyuziti Plastickych Hmot [*Research Institute for the Utilization of Plastic Materials*] [*Gottwaldov*]   (CZ)

VUVT .... Vyzkumny Ustav Vodnich Turbin [*Water Turbine Research Institute*]   (CZ)

VUVU........ Vyzkumny Ustav pro Vinohradnictvi a Vinarstvi [*Research Institute of Viticulture and the Wine Industry*]   (CZ)

VuW........... Verlag Volk und Welt ["*Volk und Welt*" *Publishing House*]   (EG)

VuW........... Verlag Volk und Wissen ["*Volk und Wissen*" *Publishing House*]   (EG)

VUZ........... Higher Educational Institution   (RU)

VUZ........... Military Educational Institution   (RU)

VUZ........... Vyzkumny Ustav Zeleznicni [*Railroad Research Institute*]   (CZ)

VUZ........... Vyzkumny Ustav Zemedelsky [*Agricultural Research Institute*] [*Prague*]   (CZ)

VUZ........... Vyzkumny Ustav Zuslechtovaci [*Research Institute for (Textile) Processing*] [*Dvur Kralove n.L.*]   (CZ)

VUZ........... Vyzkumny Ustav Zvaracsky [*Welding Research Institute*]   (CZ)

VUZE .... Vyzkumny Ustav Zemedelske Ekonomiky [*Research Institute for Agricultural Economics*]   (CZ)

VUZLM .... Vyzkumny Ustav Zemedelske a Lesnicke Mechanisace [*Research Institute for Mechanization in Agriculture and Forestry (of Agricultural Sciences)*]   (CZ)

VUZO........ Vyzkumny Ustav pro Zahranicni Obchod [*Foreign Trade Research Institute*]   (CZ)

VUZO........ Vyzkumny Ustav Zdravotnicke Osvety [*Research Institute of Health Education*]   (CZ)

VUZORT .. Vyzkumny Ustav Zvukove, Obrazove, a Reprodukcni Techniky [*Research Institute of Audio, Video, and Reproduction Technology*] [*Prague*]   (CZ)

VUZS........ Vyzkumny Ustav Zemedelskych Stroju [*Research Institute of Agricultural Machinery*]   (CZ)

VUZT .... Vyzkumny Ustav Zdravotnicke Techniky [*Health Care Research Institute*]   (CZ)

VUZT .... Vyzkumny Ustav Zemedelske Techniky Praha [*Agricultural Engineering Research Institute, Prague*] [*Former Czechoslovakia*]   (ARC)

VUZV .... Vyzkumny Ustav Zivocisne Vyroby [*Research Institute for Animal Husbandry*] [*Uhrineves*]   (CZ)

VV .... Air-Break Switch   (RU)

VV .... Air Force, Military Aviation   (BU)

v-v................ Air-to-Air [*Missile*]   (RU)

vv................ Centuries   (RU)

VV .... Delay   (RU)

VV .... Explosive   (RU)

VV .... High-Voltage, High-Tension   (RU)

VV .... High-Voltage Rectifier   (RU)

VV .... High-Voltage Switch   (RU)

V/v .... Intravenous   (RU)

Vv............... Mean Vertical (Probable) Error   (RU)

VV .... Military Herald   (RU)

VV .... Propeller   (RU)

VV .... Transpress VEB Verlag fuer Verkehrswesen Berlin ["*Transpress*" *Publishing House for Transportation Affairs, Berlin*]   (EG)

VV .... Upper Volga   (RU)

VV .... Ustedes [*You (Plural, formal)*] [*Spanish*]

VV .... Vasiliko Velos [*Royalist Arrow*] [*Greek*]   (GC)

VV .... Vatreni Val [*Firing Wave*]   (YU)

VV .... Velike Vode [*High Tides*]   (YU)

VV .... Verenigd Verzet 1940-45 [*United Resistance 1940-45*] [*Netherlands*]   (WEN)

vv................ Versos [*Verses*] [*Portuguese*]

VV .... Verwaltungsvorschrift [*Administrative Regulation*] [*German*]   (GCA)

vv................ Ve Vysluzbe [*Retired*]   (CZ)

VV .... Vikas Vikalp [*Development Alternatives*] [*An association*] [*India*]   (EAIO)

VV .... Vildmarkens Var, Stockholm 1928

VV .... Vitesse Vraie [*True Airspeed*] [*Aviation*] [*French*]

VV .... Vivres-Viande [*On earmark or button of cattle*] [*Military*] [*French*]   (MTD)

VV .... Vizantiyski Vremennik [*Byzantine Chronicle*] [*A periodical*]   (BU)

Vv .... Vodovod [*Water Pipes, Aqueduct*]   (YU)

vv................ Voorlopig Verslag [*Benelux*]   (BAS)

VV .... Voorwaardelijke Veroordeling [*Benelux*]   (BAS)

v/v .... Votre Ville [*Your City*] [*French*]

vv................ Vragvry [*Carriage Free*] [*Afrikaans*]

vv................ Vseobecna Verejna (Nemocnice) [*Public General (Hospital)*]   (CZ)

vv................ Vuodet [*Finland*]

VV .... Vzorny Vojak [*Exemplary Soldier*]   (CZ)

VVA .... Air Force Academy   (RU)

VVA .... High-Voltage Equipment   (RU)

VVA .... Military Veterinary Academy   (RU)

VVA .... Vereniging voor Aandrijftechniek [*Netherlands*]   (EAIO)

VVA .... Visa Vojna Akademija [*Advanced Military Academy*]   (YU)

Vva............. Viuva [*Widow*] [*Portuguese*]

VVAA .... Vietnam Veterans Association of Australia

VVAP........ Mouvement Socialiste Occitan - Volem Viure al Pais [*Occitanian Socialist Movement*] [*France*] [*Political party*]   (PPW)

vvar .... Vapaasti Varastossa [*Finland*]

VVAU .... Higher Military Aviation School   (RU)

VVAUL .... Higher Military Aviation School for Pilots   (RU)

vvaun .... Vapaasti Vaunussa [*Finland*]

VVAUSh ... Higher Military Aviation School for Navigators   (RU)

VVB .... Mahanoro [*Madagascar*] [*Airport symbol*]   (OAG)

VVB .... Vereinigung der Versicherungs-Betriebswirte eV [*Association of Insurance Management*]   (SLS)

VVB .... Vereinigung Volkseigener Betriebe [*Association of State Enterprises*] [*Formerly known as Verwaltung Volkseigener Betriebe, Administration of State Enterprises*]   (EG)

VVB .... Vereniging van Bemarkers [*South Africa*]   (AA)

VVB .... Vlaamse Volksbeweging [*Flemish Popular Movement*] [*Belgium*]   (WEN)

vvb............. Vry van Beskadiging [*Afrikaans*]

VVBADP... Vlaamse Vereniging van Bibliotheek, Archief en Documentatie Personeel

VVBM .... Buonmethuot/Chung Duc [*Viet Nam*] [*ICAO location identifier*]   (ICLI)

VVC .... Villavicencio [*Colombia*] [*Airport symbol*]   (OAG)

VVC .... Volcano Veterinary Center [*Rwanda*]

VVCB........ Caobang [*Viet Nam*] [*ICAO location identifier*]   (ICLI)

VVCC........ Victorian Vice-Chancellors' Committee [*Australia*]

VVCS........ Conson [*Viet Nam*] [*ICAO location identifier*]   (ICLI)

VVCT........ Cantho [*Viet Nam*] [*ICAO location identifier*]   (ICLI)

VvCW .... Vereniging voor Calvinistische Wijsbegeerte [*Netherlands*]   (SLS)

vvd............. Airborne Division   (BU)

VVD........... Extremely High Pressure   (RU)

VVD........... High-Pressure Air   (RU)

VVD........... Volkspartij voor Vrijheid en Democratie [*People's Party for Freedom and Democracy*] [*Netherlands*] [*Political party*]   (EAIO)

VVDB......... Voreio-Voreio-Dytikos [*North-Northwest*]   (GC)

VVDB......... Dienbienphu [*Viet Nam*] [*ICAO location identifier*]   (ICLI)

VVDL......... Dalat/Lienkhuong [*Viet Nam*] [*ICAO location identifier*]   (ICLI)

VVDM....... Vereniging voor Dienstplichtige Militairen [*Union of Conscripts*] [*Netherlands*]   (WEN)

VVDN....... Danang [*Viet Nam*] [*ICAO location identifier*]   (ICLI)

VVE .... Medical Determination of Fitness for Military Service   (RU)

VVE .... Veszpremi Vegyipari Egyetem [*Chemical Industry University of Veszprem*]   (HU)

Vve .... Veuve [*Widow*] [*French*]   (GPO)

VVEAB...... Vereinigung Volkseigener Erfassungs- und Aufkaufbetriebe [*Association of State Procurement and Purchase Enterprises*]   (EG)

vved .... Introduction   (BU)

VVEG .... Vereinigung Volkseigener Gueter [*Association of State Farms*] [*See VVG*]   (EG)

VV-EK .... Voorlopig Verslag van de Eerste Kamer [*Benelux*]   (BAS)

v ver........... Voorwaardelijke Veroordeling [*Benelux*]   (BAS)

VVER......... Water-Cooled Nuclear Power Reactor   (BU)

VVER......... Water-Moderated Water-Cooled Power Reactor   (RU)

VVF........... Air Force   (RU)

VVF........... High-Voltage Feeder   (RU)

VVF........... Volga Naval Flotilla   (RU)

VVFK......... Intradepartmental Financial Control   (BU)

VVFSh .... Military School for Veterinary Assistants   (RU)

VVG .... Vereinigung Volkseigener Gueter [*Association of State Farms*] [*See VVEG*]   (EG)

VVGL .... Hanoi/Gialam [*Viet Nam*] [*ICAO location identifier*]   (ICLI)

VVGMI ..... Higher Military Hydrometeorological Institute [*1941-1945*] (RU)

VVH.......... Vereinigung Volkseigener Handelsbetriebe [*Association of State Trade Enterprises*] (EG)

VVHB .... Vereinigung Volkseigener Handelsbetriebe [*Association of State Trade Enterprises*] (EG)

VVI .... High Military Inspection (RU)

VVI .... Verband der Verzorgingsinstellingen [*Association for Health-Care Institutions*] [*Belgium*] (EAIO)

VVI .... Vojaski Vojni Invalidi [*Disabled Veterans*] (YU)

VV-I .... Voorlopig Verslag Eerste Kamer [*Benelux*] (BAS)

VVIA .... Air Force Engineering Academy (RU)

VV II .... Voorlopig Verslag der Tweede Kamer [*Benelux*] (BAS)

VVIMU ..... Vladivostok Higher Engineering Nautical School (RU)

VVK .... High-Voltage Cable (RU)

VVK .... Military Medical Commission (RU)

VVK .... Vastervik [*Sweden*] [*Airport symbol*] (OAG)

VVK .... Verwaltung Vermessungs- und Kartenwesen [*Administration for Surveying and Mapping (Civilian agency in GDR subordinate to the Ministry of the Interior)*] (EG)

VVK .... Viscosity-Gravity Constant (RU)

VVKB........ Code Input-Output Unit on Magnetic Storage Drum (RU)

VVKFEP.... Military Medical Commission of a Frontline Evacuation Station (RU)

VVKhKI..... Higher Institute of Veterinary Hygiene and Control (BU)

VVKL......... Code Input-Output Unit on Magnetic Storage Tape (RU)

VVKP......... Kep [*Viet Nam*] [*ICAO location identifier*] (ICLI)

VVKR .... Boiling-Water Reactor (RU)

VVL .... High-Voltage Laboratory (RU)

VVL .... Military Veterinary Hospital (RU)

VVL .... Variable Verzoegerungslinie [*German*] (ADPT)

VVLK........ Laokay [*Viet Nam*] [*ICAO location identifier*] (ICLI)

VVLM .... Vereniging van Lugopmetingsmaatskappye [*Association of Air Survey Companies*] [*South Africa*] (EAIO)

VVMA ...... Vereniging van Medische Analisten [*Netherlands*] (SLS)

VVMGU .... Higher Naval Hydrographic School (RU)

VVMI .... Higher Institute of Veterinary Medicine (BU)

VVMIU ..... Higher Naval Engineering School (RU)

VV MM ..... Vos Majestes [*Your Majesties*] [*French*]

VVMMU .... Higher Naval Medical School (RU)

VVMTS..... Verwaltung Volkseigener Maschinen- und Traktorenstationen [*Administration of State Machine and Tractor Stations*] (EG)

VVMUPP ... Higher Naval Submarine School Imeni Lenin Komsomol (RU)

VVN.......... Rotary Vacuum Pump (RU)

vvn............. Velmi Vysoke Napeti [*Very High Voltage*] (CZ)

VVN........... Vereinigung der Verfolgten des Naziregimes [*Association of Persecutees of the NAZI Regime*] (EG)

VVNB .... Hanoi/Noibai [*Viet Nam*] [*ICAO location identifier*] (ICLI)

VVN-BDA ... Vereinigung der Verfolgten des Naziregimes - Bund der Antifaschisten der Bundes republik Deutschland [*Formerly, Vereingung der Verfolgtendes Naziregimes*] [*Germany*] (EAIO)

VV NNPP ... Vos Nobles Puissances [*Your Noble Powers*] [*French*]

VVNS .... Nasan [*Viet Nam*] [*ICAO location identifier*] (ICLI)

VVNT .... Nhatrang [*Viet Nam*] [*ICAO location identifier*] (ICLI)

VVO........... High-Voltage Equipment (RU)

VVO........... Most Urgent, Top Priority (RU)

v-vo............. Substance, Matter (RU)

VVO........... Vaterlaendischer Verdienstorden [*Patriotic Order of Merit*] (EG)

VVO........... Verenigde Volke-Organisasie [*United Nations Organization*] [*Use UN*] (AF)

VVO........... Verordnung ueber die Verfolgung von Verfehlungen [*Decree on Prosecution of Violations*] (EG)

VVO........... Vybor Vesnicke Organizace (KSC) [*Committee of the Village Organization (Czechoslovak Communist Party)*] (CZ)

VVO........... Vychodni Vojensky Okruh [*Eastern Military District*] (CZ)

v-vod.......... Wave Guide (RU)

vvod sl .... Parenthetic Word (RU)

VVOK .... Verenigde Volke se Oproep vir Kinders [*Afrikaans*]

VVOO....... All-Army Hunting Society (RU)

VVOWKO ... Verenigde Volke-Organisasie vir Wetenskap, Kultuur, en Onderwys [*United Nations Educational, Scientific, and Cultural Organization - UNESCO*] [*Afrikaans*]

VVP .... High-Voltage Cable (RU)

VVP .... Universal Military Training (RU)

VVP .... Vereenigde Verzekeringspers [*Benelux*] (BAS)

VVP .... Vertical Takeoff and Landing (RU)

VVP .... Vojensky Vycvikovy Prapor [*Military Training Battalion*] (CZ)

VVP .... Vojensky Vycvikovy Prostor [*Military Training Area*] (CZ)

VVPB........ Hue/Phubai [*Viet Nam*] [*ICAO location identifier*] (ICLI)

VVPI......... Higher Military Pedagogical Institute Imeni M. I. Kalinin (RU)

VVPJ .... Velitelstvi Vojenskych Pracovnich Jednotek [*Headquarters of Military Labor Units*] (CZ)

VVPK........ Pleiku/Cu-Hanh [*Viet Nam*] [*ICAO location identifier*] (ICLI)

VVPQ .... Phuquoc [*Viet Nam*] [*ICAO location identifier*] (ICLI)

VVPVO ..... Velitelstvi Vojsk PVO [*PVO Troop Headquarters*] (CZ)

VVQN........ Quinhon [*Viet Nam*] [*ICAO location identifier*] (ICLI)

VVR .... Vereinigung Volkseigener Reparatur Werften [*Association of State Repair Shipyards*] (EG)

VVr .... Vizantiyski Vremennik [*Byzantine Chronicle*] [*A periodical*] (BU)

VVR .... Water-Moderated Water-Cooled Reactor (RU)

VVRC .... Vietnam Veterans Royal Commission [*Australia*]

VVRD .... Pressurized Water Reactor (RU)

VVRG .... Rachgia [*Viet Nam*] [*ICAO location identifier*] (ICLI)

VVRK .... Boiling-Water Reactor (RU)

VVRK-P..... Boiling-Water Reactor with Nuclear Superheat (RU)

VVRP......... Upper Volga River Steamship Line (RU)

VVRS........ Supreme Military Editorial Council [*1921-1926*] (RU)

VVR-Uvo ... Water-Moderated Water-Cooled Reactor Using Highly Enriched Uranium (RU)

VVRW .... Vereinigung Volkseigener Reparatur Werften [*Association of State Repair Ship Yards*] (EG)

VVS........... Air Force (RU)

VVS........... High-Voltage Network (RU)

VVS........... High-Voltage Selenium Rectifier (RU)

VVS........... Military Veterinary Service (RU)

VVS........... Service Troops (RU)

VVS........... Supreme Military Council (RU)

VVS........... Vennootschappen, Verenigingen en Stichtingen [*Benelux*] (BAS)

VVS........... Vereniging der Vlaamse Studenten [*Association of Flemish Students*] [*Belgian, Dutch*] (WEN)

VvS........... Vereniging voor Statistiek [*Association for Statistics*] [*Netherlands*] (SLS)

VVS........... Verkehrsversicherungsschein [*Transportation Insurance Policy*] (EG)

VVS........... Vertical Glass Drawing (RU)

VVS........... Vertrauliche Verschluss-Sache [*Confidential Classified Material (Requiring custody in safe)*] [*German*] (WEN)

V-VS........ Voenno-Vozdushniye Sily [*Air Forces of the USSR*] (PDAA)

VVS........... Vojenske Vycvikove Stredisko [*Military Training Center*] (CZ)

VVS........... Vy, Vato, Sakelika

VV Sas ...... Vossas Senhorias [*Your Lordships*] [*Portuguese*]

VVSBM...... Baltic Sea Air Force (RU)

VVSP .... Temporary Military Hospital Train (RU)

VVSS .... Vossas Senhorias [*Your Lordships*] [*Portuguese*]

VVSSA ...... Soviet Army Air Force (RU)

VVT .... Inland Water Transportation (RU)

VVT .... Vojensky Vycvikovy Tabor [*Military Training Camp*] (CZ)

VVTS......... Hochiminh/Tansonnhat [*Viet Nam*] [*ICAO location identifier*] (ICLI)

VVU.......... Input-Output Device (RU)

VVU.......... Military Veterinary Directorate (RU)

VVU.......... Vojensky Vedecky Ustav [*Institute of Military Science*] (CZ)

VVU.......... Vojensky Vyzkumny Ustav [*Military Research Institute*] (CZ)

VVU.......... Vojno Vazduhoplovno Uciliste [*Air Force School*] (YU)

VVU.......... Vyssi Vojenske Uciliste [*Higher Military Training Center*] (CZ)

VVUD........ Vedecko-Vyzkumny Ustav Dopravni [*Transportation Research Institute*] (CZ)

VVUD........ Vyzkumny a Vyvojovy Ustav Drevarsky [*Institute for Research and Development of the Wood Industry*] (CZ)

VVUMH...... Vyzkumny a Vyvojovy Ustav Mistniho Hospodarstvi [*Institute for Research and Development of Local Economy*] (CZ)

VVUTS....... Vyzkumny a Vyvojovy Ustav Technickeho Skla [*Institute for Research and Development of Industrial Glass*] (CZ)

VVUU........ Vedecko-Vyzkumny Uhelny Ustav [*Coal Research Institute*] [*Ostrava*] (CZ)

VVUZ .... Higher Military Educational Institution (RU)

VVUZVS ... Vyzkumny a Vyvojovy Ustav Zavodu Vseobecneho Strojirenstvi [*Institute for Research and Development of the General Engineering Plants*] (CZ)

VVV .... Intercontinental Airlines Ltd. [*Nigeria*] [*ICAO designator*] (FAAC)

VVV .... Vereinigung Volkeigener Verlage [*Association of State-Owned Publishing Houses*] (EG)

VvV .... Verzameling van Voorschriften voor de Ambtenaren der Directe Belastingen, Invoerrechten en Accijnzen [*Benelux*] (BAS)

VVV .... Vladni Vybor pre Vystavbu [*Government Committee on Building*] (CZ)

VVV .... Vreemde Vliegende Voorwerp [*Unidentified Flying Object*] [*Afrikaans*]

VVVA .... Visa Vazduhoplovna Vojna Akademija [*Advanced Air Force Academy*] [*Equivalent to command and staff school*] (YU)

VVVH .... Vereniging van Verfgroothandelaren in Nederland [*Assocation of Dutch Wholesalers in Paint*] (EAIO)

VVVH .... Vinh [*Viet Nam*] [*ICAO location identifier*] (ICLI)

VVVT........ Vungtau [*Viet Nam*] [*ICAO location identifier*] (ICLI)

VVVV .... Hanoi [*Viet Nam*] [*ICAO location identifier*] (ICLI)

VVV vanSA ... Vliegtuigeienaars- en Vlieeniersvereniging van Suid-Afrika [*South Africa*] (AA)

VVW......... Vereinigung Volkseigener Warenhaeuser [*Association of State Department Stores*] (EG)
VVW......... Vereinigung Volkseigener Werften [*Association of State-Owned Shipyards*] (EG)
VVW......... Vlaamse Vereniging voor Watersport [*Flemish Watersports Association*] [*Belgium*] (EAIO)
VVZ......... Vedecko-Vyzkumna Zakladna [*Scientific-Research Base*] (CZ)
VVZ......... Velikomoravska Vodna Zajednica [*Greater Morava Water Resources Group*] (YU)
VVZ......... Vocarsko-Vinogradarska Zadruga [*Fruit and Viticulture Cooperative*] (YU)
VVZ......... Vyzkumna a Vyvojova Zakladna [*Research and Development Base*] (CZ)
VVZM...... Vereniging voor Zuivelindustrie en Melkhygieene [*Netherlands*] (SLS)
VW............ Air Concept [*Germany*] [*ICAO aircraft manufacturer identifier*] (ICAO)
VW............ Verdrag van Warschau Betreffende het Internationale Luchtvervoer [*Benelux*] (BAS)
VW............ Verlag Die Wirtschaft [*Die Wirtschaft Publishing House*] (EG)
VW............ Verlag Weltbuehne [*Weltbuehne Publishing House*] (EG)
VW............ Verrechnungswaehrungen [*Clearing Currencies*] (EG)
Vw............ Verwaltung [*Administration*] [*German*]
Vw............ Verwendung [*Use, Utilization*] [*German*] (GCA)
VW............ Volkswagenwerk Aktiengesellschaft [*Volkswagen Joint Stock Company*] [*Business term*]
Vw............ Vorwort [*Foreword*] [*German*]
VWA......... Bundesverband Deutscher Verwaltungs- und Wirtschafts-Akademien eV [*National Association of German University Educated Managers and Administrators*] (SLS)
VWAC...... Victorian Wheat Advisory Committee [*Australia*]
VWAC...... Victorian Women's Advisory Council to the Premier [*Australia*]
VWAN...... Voluntary Workcamps Association of Nigeria (EAIO)
VWB......... Volkswagen do Brasil [*Volkswagen of Brazil*] [*Brazil*]
Vwbz......... Verwaltungsbezirk [*Administrative District*] [*German*] (EG)
VWC......... Victorian Writers' Centre [*Australia*]
VWCC...... Victorian Women's Consultative Council [*Australia*]
VWF......... Verband der Wissenschaftler an Forschungsinstituten eV [*Association of Research Institute Scholars*] (SLS)
VwGerH..... Verwaltungsgerichtshof [*Administrative Court*] [*German*]
VwGH....... Verwaltungsgerichtshof [*Administrative Court*] [*German*]
VWGO...... Verband der Wissenschaftlichen Gesellschaften Oesterreichs [*Society of Scientific Associations of Austria*] (SLS)
VWIA .... Victorian Wine Industry Association [*Australia*]
VWL......... Verkeerswet Tegen Lintbebouwing [*Benelux*] (BAS)
Vwltg......... Verwaltung [*Administration*] [*German*]
Vwltr......... Verwalter [*Administrator*] [*German*]
VWO......... Verbond van Wetenschappelijke Onderzoekers [*Utrecht*]
VWO......... Voorbereidend Wetenschappelijk Onderwijs [*Netherlands*]
VWON...... Volkswagen of Nigeria Ltd.
VWP......... Vietnam Workers' Party [*Political party*] (PPW)
VWP......... Volkswirtschaftsplan [*Economic Plan*] (EG)
Vwr........... Verwalter [*Administrator*] [*German*]
VWR......... Volkswirtschaftsrat [*Economic Council*] [*German*] (EG)
VWRF....... Victorian Wheat Research Foundation [*Australia*]
VWS .... Versuchsanstalt fuer Wasserbau und Schiffbau [*Research Institute for Hydraulics and Shipbuilding*] [*Research center*] (IRC)
VWSG ...... Victorian Wader Study Group [*Australia*]
VWT .... Victorian Women's Trust [*Australia*]
Vwz .... Verwendungszweck [*Purpose*] [*German*] (GCA)
Vx.............. Vieux [*Old*] [*Military map abbreviation World War I*] [*French*] (MTD)
VXC .... Lichinga [*Mozambique*] [*Airport symbol*] (OAG)
VXE .... Sao Vicente [*Cape Verde Islands*] [*Airport symbol*] (OAG)
VXO.......... Vaxjo [*Sweden*] [*Airport symbol*] (OAG)
VY............. Abelag Airways [*Belgium*] [*ICAO designator*] (ICDA)
VY............. Virkamiesten Yhteisjarjesto [*Government Employees' Confederation*] [*Finland*] (WEN)
VYAN .... Victorian Youth Advocacy Network [*Australia*]
Vyatlag....... Vyatka Corrective Labor Camp (RU)
VyborZLV ... Vybor pro Zvelebeni Zemedelskeho, Lesniho, a Vodniho Hospodarstvi [*Committee for Management Efficiency in Agriculture, Forestry, and Water Utilization*] (CZ)
VYC .... Victorian Yachting Council [*Australia*]
VYC .... Yvic Airlines [*Nigeria*] [*ICAO designator*] (FAAC)
vychisl........ Calculated, Computed (RU)
VYD.......... Vryheid [*South Africa*] [*Airport symbol*] (OAG)
vyd............ Vydani [*Edition*] [*Publishing Former Czechoslovakia*]
VYeP......... Height of Transfer Unit (RU)
V'yetn......... Vietnamese (RU)
VykhU ...... Output Device (RU)
VYL .... Vesien-ja Ymparistontutkimuslaitos [*Water and Environment Research Institute*] [*National Board of Waters and Environment*] [*Finland*] (EAS)
VYL .... Victorian Young Lawyers [*Australia*]

vyn............. Vynos [*Decree*] (CZ)
vyp............. Issue (RU)
vyp dan....... Imprint (RU)
vyrez........... Clipping (RU)
vys .... Height, Elevation, Altitude (RU)
vys .... Settlement [*Topography*] (RU)
VysC .... Vysadkova Ceta [*Airborne Platoon*] (CZ)
Vysofizkul ... Supreme Council of Physical Culture (at the VTsIK) (RU)
Vysovfizkul't ... Supreme Council of Physical Culture (at the VTsIK) (RU)
vyssh.......... Supreme, Highest, Higher (RU)
Vystrel .... Higher Marksmanship Courses (RU)
vysvetl........ Vysvetlivka [*Footnote*] [*Publishing Former Czechoslovakia*]
vyt............. Vytah [*Abstract*] [*Publishing Former Czechoslovakia*]
VYuK .... Higher Law Courses (RU)
VYuZI....... All-Union Correspondence Law Institute (RU)
v-z............. Air-to-Surface [*Missile*] (RU)
VZ............. Oscillating Switch (RU)
VZ............. Platoon (RU)
VZ............. Railway Cars Building Plant (BU)
VZ............. Railway Cars Repair Plant (BU)
VZ............. Verseifungszahl [*Saponification Value*] [*German*]
VZ............. Verzweigung [*German*] (ADPT)
VZ............. Vetrinarski Zavod [*Veterinary Institute*] (YU)
VZ............. Vinarska Zadruga [*Wine Cooperative*] (YU)
VZ............. Vitkovicke Zelezarny [*Vitkovice Iron Works*] (CZ)
VZ............. Vodna Zajednica [*Water Resources Group*] (YU)
VZ............. Vodni Zdroje [*Water Resources (A budgetary organization)*] (CZ)
VZ............. Vojenske Zatisi [*Military Recreation Center*] (CZ)
VZ............. Vorzeichen [*Sign*] [*German*] (ADPT)
Vz............. Vorzug [*First Section of a Train (Operated separately)*] (EG)
VZ............. Vybor Zen [*Women's Committee*] (CZ)
VZ............. Vykupni Zavod [*Purchasing Enterprise (for agricultural products)*] (CZ)
vz.............. V Zaloze [*In Reserve*] (CZ)
vz.............. Vzor [*Sample, Example, Type*] (CZ)
VZA.......... Organic Antiaircraft Artillery (RU)
VZADT...... All-Union Correspondence Highway Technicum (RU)
vzbe .... Combat Squadron [*Aviation*] (BU)
VZD.......... Delayed-Action Fuze, Delayed-Action Detonator (RU)
VZEI .... All-Union Correspondence Institute of Economics (RU)
VZEI .... All-Union Correspondence Power Engineering Institute (RU)
VZEIS .... All-Union Correspondence Electrotechnical Institute of Communications (RU)
VZEMT..... All-Union Correspondence Electromechanical Technicum (RU)
VZESO...... Vilnius Electric Welding Equipment Plant (RU)
VZET........ All-Union Correspondence Power Engineering Technicum (RU)
VZF.......... Vlnarske Zavody a Fezarny [*Woolen Mills and Fez Factories*] (CZ)
VZFEI .... All-Union Correspondence Institute of Finance and Economics (RU)
VZFI .... All-Union Correspondence Institute of Finance (RU)
VZFKT ...... All-Union Correspondence Technicum of Finance and Credit (RU)
VZFT .... All-Union Correspondence Technicum of Finance (RU)
VZGMT .... All-Union Correspondence Hydrometeorological Technicum (RU)
VZh........... Logbook (RU)
vzh............ See (BU)
VZh chl ..... See Article [*Law*] (BU)
VZhDB ..... Railroad Reconstruction Battalion (RU)
VZhMT ..... Turnip Yellow Mosaic Virus (RU)
VZhPP...... Railroad Military Ration-Distributing Point (RU)
VZI .... All-Union Correspondence Institute (RU)
VZIF .... All-Union Correspondence Institute of Finance (RU)
VZII .... All-Union Correspondence Industrial Institute (RU)
VZIIT .... All-Union Correspondence Institute of Railroad Transportation Engineers (RU)
VZIIZhT ... All-Union Correspondence Institute of Railroad Transportation Engineers (RU)
VZIMP ...... All-Ukrainian Correspondence Institute of Mass Education of Party Activists at the TsK KP(b)U (RU)
VZINO ...... All-Union Correspondence Institute of Finance, Economics, and Accountancy (RU)
VZIPP .... All-Union Correspondence Institute of the Food Industry (RU)
VZIPSKh... All-Union Zootechnical Institute of Fur and Peltry (RU)
VZIPSM... All-Union Correspondence Institute of the Building Materials Industry (RU)
VZIPT .... All-Union Correspondence Institute of the Textile Industry (RU)
VZIS .... All-Union Correspondence Institute of Communications (RU)
VZISI........ All-Union Correspondence Construction Engineering Institute (RU)
VZIST ...... All-Union Correspondence Institute of Soviet Trade (RU)
VZIT........ All-Union Correspondence Industrial Technicum (RU)

VZIT......... All-Union Correspondence Institute of Railroad Transportation Engineers (RU)
VZIT......... All-Union Correspondence Institute of Trade (RU)
VZITLP..... All-Union Correspondence Institute of Textile and Light Industries (RU)
VZITO....... All-Union Correspondence Institute of Technical Education (RU)
VZITP....... All-Union Correspondence Institute of the Textile Industry (RU)
VZK.......... Vojensky Zdokonalovaci Kurs [*Military Advance Course*] (CZ)
VZKG........ Vitkovicke Zelezarny Klementa Gottwalda [*Klement Gottwald Iron Works in Vitkovice*] (CZ)
VZKhTT.... All-Union Correspondence Technicum of Chemical Technology (RU)
VZKT........ All-Union Correspondence Cooperative Technicum (RU)
VZLT......... All-Union Correspondence Forestry-Engineering Technicum (RU)
VZLTI....... All-Union Correspondence Forestry-Engineering Institute (RU)
VZLU........ Vyzkumny a Zkusebny Letecky Ustav [*Aeronautical Research and Testing Institute*] (CZ)
VZMI........ All-Union Correspondence Institute of Mechanical Engineering (RU)
vzn.............. Voor Zoveel Nodig [*Benelux*] (BAS)
vznb............ Air Observation (BU)
vznbe.......... Observation Squadron [*Aviation*] (BU)
VZO........... Vojensky Zemepisny Ustav [*Military Geographical Institute*] (CZ)
VzOR......... Flash-Ranging Platoon (RU)
VZOS........ All-Union Stenography Correspondence Courses (RU)
VZP........... Antiaircraft Machine-Gun Platoon (RU)
VZP........... Vatra za Zaprecavanje Pesadije [*Barrage Fire Against Infantry*] (YU)
VZPI......... All-Union Correspondence Polytechnic Institute (RU)
VZPSh....... Higher Correspondence Party School at the TsK KPSS (RU)
VZR.......... Fuze, Detonator (RU)
VZR.......... Sound-Ranging Platoon (RU)
VZR.......... Voice of Zimbabwe Rhodesia (AF)
Vzryvsel'prom... Administration of Blasting Operations in Agriculture, Forestry, Industry, and Construction of the Main Military Engineering Directorate [*1922*] (RU)
Vzryvsel'prom... Central Administration of Agricultural and Industrial Blasting Operations [*1931*] (RU)
Vzryvsel'prom... Office of Agricultural and Industrial Blasting Operations [*1928-1930*] (RU)
Vzryvsel'prom... Office of Blasting Operations in Agriculture and Industry at the Military Technical Directorate of the RKKA [*1926-1927*] (RU)
VzS............. Compressed Air (RU)
VZShPD.... Higher Correspondence School of Trade Unionism of the VTsSPS (RU)
VZSIT....... All-Union Correspondence Technicum of Machine Tools and Tools (RU)
VZSKhT.... All-Union Correspondence Agricultural Technicum (RU)
VZST......... All-Union Correspondence Construction Technicum (RU)
VZT.......... All-Union Correspondence Technicum (RU)
VZT........... Vatra za Zaprecavanje Tenkova [*Barrage Fire Against Tanks*] (YU)
VZTI......... All-Union Correspondence Technicum of Measurements (RU)
VZTLP...... All-Union Correspondence Technicum of Light Industry (RU)
VZTMiMP... All-Union Correspondence Technicum of the Meat and Dairy Industry (RU)
VZTPK...... All-Union Correspondence Technicum of Producer's Cooperatives (RU)
VZTPP...... All-Union Correspondence Technicum of the Food Industry (RU)
VZTRT...... All-Union Correspondence Technicum of River Transportation (RU)
VZTS......... All-Union Correspondence Technicum of Communications (RU)
VZTST...... All-Union Correspondence Technicum of Soviet Trade (RU)
VZTTM..... All-Union Correspondence Technicum of Heavy Engineering (RU)
VZU.......... External Memory Systems (BU)
VZU.......... External Storage, External Memory (RU)
VZUK....... All-Union Correspondence Accounting Courses (RU)
VZUKT...... All-Union Correspondence Accounting and Credit Technicum (RU)
VZUP........ Vyvojovy Zavod Uranovehe Prumyslu [*Development Center of the Uranium Industry*] (CZ)
vzv.............. Platoon (BU)
vzv.............. Voorzover [*Benelux*] (BAS)
VZVI......... Voronezh Zootechnical and Veterinary Institute (RU)
vzv SAU..... Platoon of Self-Propelled Guns (RU)
VZW.......... Vereniging Zonder Winstoogmerk [*Non-Profit Society*] [*Netherlands*]
VZZhT....... All-Union Correspondence Railroad Technicum (RU)

W

W.............	Ouest [*West*] [*French*] (MTD)
W.............	Train Operates Only on Weekdays (EG)
W.............	Tungstenio [*Tungsten*] [*Chemical element*] [*Portuguese*]
W/............	Valued [*Correspondence*] [*German*]
W.............	Wache [*Watch, Guard*] [*German*]
W.............	Wad [or *Wadi* or *Wed*] [*Valley, River, River Bed Arab*] (NAU)
W.............	Waehrung [*Currency*] [*German*]
W.............	Wai [*River*] [*Indonesian*] (NAU)
W.............	Wappen [*Coat of Arms*] [*German*]
w.............	Warm [*German*]
W.............	Wasser [*Water*] [*German*]
W.............	Wat [*Watt*] [*Poland*]
w.............	Watio [*Watt*] [*Spanish*]
W.............	Watt [*French*]
w.............	Watt [*Portuguese*]
W.............	Watt [*German*] (GCA)
W.............	Watti [or *Wattia*] [*Finland*]
W.............	Watt Internacional [*International Watt*] [*Portuguese*]
W.............	Wechsel [*Change*] [*German*]
w.............	Week [*Afrikaans*]
w.............	Weg [*Way*] [*Netherlands*]
w.............	Weich [*Soft*] [*German*] (GCA)
W.............	Weiler [*Hamlet*] [*German*]
w.............	Weiss [*White*] [*German*]
w.............	Wert [*Valued*] [*German*] (GCA)
W.............	Wes [*West*] [*Afrikaans*]
W.............	West (IDIG)
W.............	Westen [*West*] [*German*] (EG)
W.............	Western (IDIG)
W.............	Western Australia [*National Union Catalogue of Australia symbol*]
W.............	Wet [*Benelux*] (BAS)
W.............	Wetteren [*Powder*] [*German*] (MTD)
W.............	Whiskey [*Phonetic alphabet*] [*International*] (DSUE)
W:............	Wichtigsten Werke [*Die*] [*The Most Important Works*] [*German*]
W.............	Widerstand [*Electrical Resistance*] [*German*]
w.............	Wiek [*Century*] (POL)
W.............	Wielmozny [*Esquire*] [*Poland*]
w.............	Wies [*Village*] (POL)
W.............	William [*Phonetic alphabet*] [*Royal Navy World War I Pre-World War II*] [*World War II*] (DSUE)
W.............	Wirklicher [*Actual*] [*German*]
W.............	Wirtschaft [*Administration*] [*German*]
W.............	Wissel [*Bill*] [*Afrikaans*]
W.............	Witwe [*Widow*] [*German*]
W.............	Wolfram [*Tungsten*] [*German*]
W.............	Won [*Monetary unit*] [*South Korea*]
w.............	Woord [*Word*] [*Afrikaans*]
W.............	Wort [*Word*] [*German*] (ADPT)
W.............	Wys [*Manner, Way*] [*Afrikaans*]
w.............	Wyspa [*Island*] [*Poland*]
W2............	William II [*German emperor and king of Prussia, 1888-1918*] (DSUE)
WA............	(Abteilung) Werkzeugmaschinen und Automatisierung (der Staatlichen Plankommission) [*Machine-Tool and Automation Department (of the State Planning Commission)*] [*German*] (EG)
WA............	Wassmer Aviation [*France*] [*ICAO aircraft manufacturer identifier*] (ICAO)
WA............	West Africa
WA............	Western Australia (ADA)
WA............	Wet Aansprakelijkheidsverzekering Motorrijtuigen [*Benelux*] (BAS)
WA............	Wettelijke Aansprakelijkheid [*Benelux*] (BAS)
WA............	Womenwealth Ambika [*An association*] [*British*] (EAIO)
WA............	Worksafe Australia
WA............	World Bank Atlas [*Monetary conversion rate*] (ECON)
Wa............	Wyspa [*Island*] [*Poland*] (NAU)

WAA........	West African Army [*Artillery*]
WAA........	West Australian Airways (ADA)
WAA........	Woolclassers' Association of Australia
WAA........	Workers Affairs Association [*Sudan*] (AF)
WAAA......	Ujung Pandang/Hasanuddin [*Indonesia*] [*ICAO location identifier*] (ICLI)
WAA(A)....	Women's Action Alliance (Australia)
WAAAF....	Women's Auxiliary Australian Air Force
WAAB......	Bau Bau/Betoambari [*Indonesia*] [*ICAO location identifier*] (ICLI)
WAAC......	West African Agricultural Corporation
WAAC......	West African Airways Corp.
WAAC......	Western Australian AIDS Council
WAAC......	Western Australian Chamber of Commerce (PDAA)
WAAC......	Women's Abortion Action Campaign [*Australia*]
WAADA......	Western Australian Alcohol and Drug Authority
WAAECG ...	Western Australian Aboriginal Education Consultative Group
WAAER	World Association for the Advancement of Educational Research [*Belgium*] (SLS)
WAAG......	Malimpung [*Indonesia*] [*ICAO location identifier*] (ICLI)
WAAG......	Western Australian Art Gallery
WAAGA	Western Australian Asparagus Growers' Association
WAAI.......	Malili [*Indonesia*] [*ICAO location identifier*] (ICLI)
WAAJ.......	Mamuju/Tampa Padang [*Indonesia*] [*ICAO location identifier*] (ICLI)
WAAL	Ponggaluku [*Indonesia*] [*ICAO location identifier*] (ICLI)
WAAM......	Masamba/Andi Jemma [*Indonesia*] [*ICAO location identifier*] (ICLI)
WAAMH...	Western Australian Association for Mental Health
WAAMS....	West Australian Aboriginal Medical Services
WAAOT	Western Australian Association of Occupational Therapists
WAAP	Kolaka/Pomalaa [*Indonesia*] [*ICAO location identifier*] (ICLI)
WAAP	World Association for Animal Production [*Rome, Italy*] (EAIO)
WAAPA	Western Australian Academy of the Performing Arts
WAAPC	Western Australian Apple and Pear Council
WAAPHI ..	West African Association of Public Health Inspectors
WAAR	Raha/Sugi Manuru [*Indonesia*] [*ICAO location identifier*] (ICLI)
WAARF.....	West Australian Arthritis and Rheumatism Foundation
WaarvAkte ...	Waarvan Akte [*Benelux*] (BAS)
WAAS	Soroako [*Indonesia*] [*ICAO location identifier*] (ICLI)
WAAS	Wakil Asisten (IN)
WAAS	World Academy of Art and Science [*Solna, Sweden*] (EA)
WAASDT ...	Western Australian Association of School Dental Therapists
WAAT	Makale/Pongtiku [*Indonesia*] [*ICAO location identifier*] (ICLI)
WAAT	Western Area Adolescent Team [*Australia*]
WAATECO ...	West African Automobile Engineering Co. [*Nigeria*]
WAAU.......	Kendari/Wolter Monginsidi [*Indonesia*] [*ICAO location identifier*] (ICLI)
WAAVP.....	World Association for the Advancement of Veterinary Parasitology [*Thessaloniki, Greece*] (EAIO)
WAAZ	Ujung Pandang [*Indonesia*] [*ICAO location identifier*] (ICLI)
WAB.........	Waffenabwurfbehaelter [*Parachute Weapons Container*] [*German military - World War II*]
WAB.........	Wet Assurantiebemiddeling [*Benelux*] (BAS)
WAB.........	World Association for Buiatrics [*Hanover, Federal Republic of Germany*] (EAIO)
WABA	West African Bankers' Association
WABA	Western Australian Bar Association
WABB	Biak/Frans Kaisiepo [*Indonesia*] [*ICAO location identifier*] (ICLI)
WABC	Western Australian Ballet Company
WABC	Western Australian Bible College
WABD	Moanamani [*Indonesia*] [*ICAO location identifier*] (ICLI)
WABEC....	Western Australian Business Education College
WABF........	Numfor/Jemburwo [*Indonesia*] [*ICAO location identifier*] (ICLI)
WABG	Waghete [*Indonesia*] [*ICAO location identifier*] (ICLI)

WABI........ Nabire [*Indonesia*] [*ICAO location identifier*]   (ICLI)
WABL........ Ilaga [*Indonesia*] [*ICAO location identifier*]   (ICLI)
WABN....... Kokonau [*Indonesia*] [*ICAO location identifier*]   (ICLI)
WABO....... Serui/Sujarwo Condronegoro [*Indonesia*] [*ICAO location identifier*]   (ICLI)
WABO....... Writers Association of Botswana
WABP........ Timika/Tembagapura [*Indonesia*] [*ICAO location identifier*]   (ICLI)
WABT ...... Enarotali [*Indonesia*] [*ICAO location identifier*]   (ICLI)
WABU....... Biak/Manuhua [*Indonesia*] [*ICAO location identifier*]   (ICLI)
WABW ...... Waren [*Indonesia*] [*ICAO location identifier*]   (ICLI)
WABZ .... Biak [*Indonesia*] [*ICAO location identifier*]   (ICLI)
WAC .... Waca [*Ethiopia*] [*Airport symbol*]   (OAG)
WAC .... West Africa Committee   (EA)
WAC .... West Africa Company
WAC .... West African Conference
WAC .... Westdeutsches Auswertungs-Centrum [*German*]   (ADPT)
WAC .... Western Australian Club
WAC .... Wheat Advisory Committee (Western Australia)
WAC .... Wildlife Advisory Committee [*Tasmania, Australia*]
WAC .... Women's Advisory Council [*Australia*]
WAC .... Women's Affairs Committee [*Nigeria*]   (AF)
WAC .... Workshop Arts Centre [*Australia*]
WAC .... World Air Network Co. Ltd. [*Japan*] [*ICAO designator*]   (FAAC)
WAC .... World Assistance Corps [*Paris, France*]   (EAIO)
WACA ...... West African Court of Appeal
WACA ...... World Airlines Clubs Association [*Montreal, PQ*]   (EAIO)
WACAP..... Western Australian Chip & Pulp Co.
WACB .... West African Currency Board
WACCI...... Western Australian Chamber of Commerce and Industry
WACCM .... World Association for Chinese Church Music   (EAIO)
WACEO .... Western Australian Catholic Education Office
wach .... Wachmistrz [*Sergeant-Major (Cavalry)*] [*Poland*]
WACH....... West African Clearing House [*Sierra Leone*]
wachsart...... Wachsartig [*Wax-Like*] [*German*]   (GCA)
WACIID.... Winter Advanced Course for Immunology and Infectious Diseases [*Japan International Friendship and Welfare Foundation*]
WACIN ..... Western Australia Curriculum Information Network
WACL .... Wacoal Corp. [*Japan*] [*NASDAQ symbol*]
WACL .... World Anti-Communist League [*South Korea*]   (EAIO)
WACMR .... West African Council for Medical Research
WACO...... World Air Cargo Organisation   (PDAA)
WACOTA ... Western Australian Council on the Ageing
WACP .... Women's Association of the Centre Party [*Sweden*]   (EAIO)
WACRA .... World Association for Case Method Research and Application
WACRAL ... World Association of Christian Radio Amateurs and Listeners [*Hull, England*]   (EAIO)
WACRI..... West African Cocoa Research Institute
WACRRM ... Western Australian Centre for Remote and Rural Medicine
WACS........ West African College of Surgeons [*See also COAC*] [*Nigeria*]   (EAIO)
WACSC..... Western Australian Coastal Shipping Commission
WACSEE .. Western Australian Centre for Self Esteem Education
WACU....... West African Customs Union
WAC/VTC ... Women's Advisory Committee of the Vocational Training Council [*New Zealand*]
WACY2000 ... World Association for Celebrating the Year 2000 [*British*]
WAD......... Andriamena [*Madagascar*] [*Airport symbol*]   (OAG)
WADA....... West African Development Association
WADA....... Wum Area Development Authority
WADB....... West African Development Bank [*Togo*]   (EA)
WADC....... Western Australian Development Corp.
WADILC... Western Australian Dairy Industry Liaison Committee
WADNA..... Women and Development Network of Australia
WADP....... World Association for Dynamic Psychiatry   (EAIO)
WADT....... Western Australian Diamond Trust
WADU....... Wollamo Agricultural Development Unit
WAEC .... West African Economic Community [*Ivory Coast, Mali, Mauritania, Niger, Senegal, Upper Volta*]   (ASF)
WAEC .... West African Episcopal Church
WAEC .... West African Examinations Council [*Nigeria*]   (AF)
WAEC .... Western Australian Electoral Commission
WAED....... Western Australia Education Department
WAEDM ... World Association for Emergency and Disaster Medicine [*Bristol, England*]   (EAIO)
WAEJ........ World Association of Esperanto Journalists [*See also TEJA*] [*Cittadella, Italy*]   (EAIO)
WAEMB ... Western Australian Egg Marketing Board
WAEP........ World Association for Element Building and Prefabrication [*Hamburg, Federal Republic of Germany*]   (EAIO)
WAEPA..... Western Australian Environmental Protection Agency
WAER ...... World Association for Educational Research [*See also AMSE*] [*Ghent, Belgium*]   (EAIO)
waermeempfindl ... Waermeempfindlich [*Heat-Sensitive*] [*German*]   (GCA)

WAERSA .. World Agricultural Economics and Rural Sociology Abstracts [*United Kingdom*]
WAES........ Workshop on Alternative Energy Strategies
waess.......... Waessrig [*Aqueous*] [*German*]   (GCA)
WAF .... Wojskowa Agencja Fotograficzna [*Military Photographic Agency*]   (POL)
WAF .... Women Aglow Fellowship [*Dutch Pentecostal group*]
WAF .... Workers' Autonomous Federation [*China*]   (EY)
WAF .... World AIDS Foundation
WAF .... World Apostolate of Fatima [*The Blue Army*]   (EAIO)
WAF .... World Armwrestling Federation [*India*]   (EAIO)
WAFA ...... Palestine News Agency   (ME)
WAFA ...... Western Australian Farmers' Association
WAFA ...... Western Australian Football Association
WAFAC.... Western Australian Fruit Advisory Council
WAFAH ... West African Federation of Associations for the Advancement of Handicapped Persons [*See also FOAPH*] [*Bamako, Mali*]   (EAIO)
WAFBB ..... Western Australian Fire Brigade Board
WAFC........ West African Fisheries Commission
WAFC........ Western Australian Film Council
WAFC........ Western Australian Football Commission
WAFD ...... West African Fisheries Development Co.
WAFF........ West African Frontier Force
WAFF........ Western Australian Farmers' Federation
WAFIC ...... Western Australian Fishing Industry Council
WAFIC ...... Western Australian Furniture Industry Council
WAFITC .... Western Australian Forest Industry Training Council
W AFR...... West Africa
WAFR........ World Appraisal of Fishery Resources [*FAO*]   (MSC)
WAFRI...... West African Fisheries Research Institute
WAFRU .... West African Fungicide Research Unit
WAFRY.... Western Australian Federation of Rural Youth
WAFS........ West African Ferrying Squadron
WAFSRN .. West African Farming System Research Network [*Government body*]
WAFU .... West African Football Union
WAG......... Wanganui [*New Zealand*] [*Airport symbol*]   (OAG)
WAG......... West African Glass Industry Ltd. [*Nigeria*]
WAG......... Western Australian Green Party [*Political party*]
WAG......... Wet Autovervoer Goederen [*Benelux*]   (BAS)
WAG......... World Airline (Gambia) Ltd. [*ICAO designator*]   (FAAC)
WAG......... Wydawnictwo Artystyczno-Graficzne [*Fine Printing Publishing House*]   (POL)
WAG......... Wytwornia Artykulow Gumowych [*Rubber Goods Plant*]   (POL)
WAGC....... World Amateur Golf Council   (OLYM)
WAGFEI ... Women's Action Group on Excision and Infibulation [*British*] [*Defunct*]   (EAIO)
WAGGGS ... World Association of Girl Guides and Girl Scouts [*See also AMGE*] [*British*]   (EAIO)
WAGH ...... Western Australian Government Holdings Ltd.
WAGL .... Western Australian Gould League
WAGM...... Western Areas Gold Mine [*South Africa*]
WAGP ...... Women's Access Grant Program [*Australia*]
WAGR....... Western Australian Government Railways   (PDAA)
WAGRC .... Western Australian Government Railways Commission
WAGS ...... Western Australian Genealogical Society
WAGS ...... Working AIDS Group Study [*Australia*]
WAGUL .... West Australian Group of University Librarians
Wagum....... Wytwornia Artykulow Gumowych [*Rubber Goods Plant*]   (POL)
WAHA...... West Australian Hotels Association
WAHA...... Western Australian Hockey Association
WAHC...... West African Health Community   (EA)
WAHC...... Western Australian Heritage Committee
WAHLC.... World Association for Hebrew Language and Culture   (EAIO)
WAHO ...... World Arabian Horse Organization [*Windermere, England*]   (EAIO)
wahrsch...... Wahrscheinlich [*Probable*] [*German*]   (GCA)
WAHS....... West African Health Secretariat
WAHSC.... West African High School Certificate
WAHVM... World Association for the History of Veterinary Medicine [*Hanover, Federal Republic of Germany*]   (EAIO)
WAI .... Antsohihy [*Madagascar*] [*Airport symbol*]   (OAG)
WAI .... War Against Indiscipline [*Political organization*] [*Nigeria*]
WAIA .... Wojewodzka Agencja Imprez Artystycznych [*Voivodship Art Show Agency*]   (POL)
WAIABS ... Western Australian Institute of Applied Business Studies
WAIA Ct ... Western Australian Industrial Appeal Court
WAIAL...... Western Australian Institute of Applied Linguistics
WAIC....... Western Australian Industrial Court
WAIC .... Western Australian International College
WAICA...... West African Insurance Consultative Association
WAIEA...... Western Australian Institute of Educational Administration
WAIFOR... West African Institute for Oil Palm Research
WAII......... Wester State Agricultural and Industrial Investment Company
WAIRC...... Western Australian Industrial Relations Commission

WAIRE...... Western Australian Information Researchers Exchange
WAIS........ Western Australian Institute of Sport
WAISER ... West African Institute of Social and Economic Research
WAIT........ Western Australia Institute of Technology [*Database originator and operator*]
WAITI....... Western Australian Institute of Translators and Interpreters
WAITR...... West African Institute for Trypanosomiasis Research
WAITRO... World Association of Industrial and Technological Research Organizations [*Arhus, Denmark*]
WAJ.......... Water Authority of Jordan
WAJA........ Arso [*Indonesia*] [*ICAO location identifier*] (ICLI)
WAJAL..... West African Joint Agency Limited
WAJB........ Bokondini [*Indonesia*] [*ICAO location identifier*] (ICLI)
WAJD....... Wakde [*Indonesia*] [*ICAO location identifier*] (ICLI)
WAJI......... Sarmi/Orai [*Indonesia*] [*ICAO location identifier*] (ICLI)
WAJJ........ Jayapura/Sentani [*Indonesia*] [*ICAO location identifier*] (ICLI)
WAJK....... Kiwirok [*Indonesia*] [*ICAO location identifier*] (ICLI)
WAJL........ Lereh [*Indonesia*] [*ICAO location identifier*] (ICLI)
WAJM....... Mulia [*Indonesia*] [*ICAO location identifier*] (ICLI)
WAJO....... Oksibil [*Indonesia*] [*ICAO location identifier*] (ICLI)
WAJR....... Waris [*Indonesia*] [*ICAO location identifier*] (ICLI)
WAJS........ Senggeh [*Indonesia*] [*ICAO location identifier*] (ICLI)
WAJU....... Ubrub [*Indonesia*] [*ICAO location identifier*] (ICLI)
WAJW...... Wamena [*Indonesia*] [*ICAO location identifier*] (ICLI)
WAJZ........ Jayapura Sector [*Indonesia*] [*ICAO location identifier*] (ICLI)
WAK......... Ankazoabo [*Madagascar*] [*Airport symbol*] (OAG)
WAK......... Wiederaufarbeitungsanlage Karlsruhe [*Germany*] (PDAA)
WAKA...... Akimuga [*Indonesia*] [*ICAO location identifier*] (ICLI)
WAKD...... Mindiptana [*Indonesia*] [*ICAO location identifier*] (ICLI)
WAKE...... Bade [*Indonesia*] [*ICAO location identifier*] (ICLI)
WAKG...... Agats [*Indonesia*] [*ICAO location identifier*] (ICLI)
WAKH...... Abohoy [*Indonesia*] [*ICAO location identifier*] (ICLI)
WAKK...... Merauke/Mopah [*Indonesia*] [*ICAO location identifier*] (ICLI)
WAKN...... Primapun [*Indonesia*] [*ICAO location identifier*] (ICLI)
WAKO...... Okaba [*Indonesia*] [*ICAO location identifier*] (ICLI)
WAKP...... Kepi [*Indonesia*] [*ICAO location identifier*] (ICLI)
WAKT....... Tanah Merah [*Indonesia*] [*ICAO location identifier*] (ICLI)
WAL.......... West African Pound
WALA....... West African Library Association
Walach...... Walachian [*Romanian dialect*] (BARN)
WALCON ... West African Lines Conference
WALGITC ... Western Australian Local Government Industry Training Committee
WALGLA ... Western Australia Government Librarians Association
WALIS ...... Western Australian Land Information System
WALL........ Warszawski Aeroklub Ligi Lotniczej [*Warsaw Aeroclub of the Aeronautical League*] (POL)
WALL........ Western Australian Law Libraries
Wallf.......... Wallfahrtsort [*German*]
WALRPA .. Western Australian Light Railway Preservation Association
WALS........ Western Aboriginal Legal Service [*Australia*]
WALTA..... Western Australian Lawn Tennis Association
Walzricht ... Walzrichtung [*Direction of Rolling*] [*German*] (GCA)
WAM......... Ambatondrazaka [*Madagascar*] [*Airport symbol*] (OAG)
WAM......... Emirates News Agency [*United Arab Emirates*] (MENA)
WAM......... Western Australian Mint
WAM......... Western Australian Museum
WAM......... Wet Aansprakelijkheidsverzekering Motorrijtuigen [*Benelux*] (BAS)
WAM........ White Australia Movement
WAM......... Wojskowa Akademia Medyczna [*Military Medical Academy*] (POL)
WAM......... Wytwornia Aparatow i Maszyn [*Apparatus and Machine Plant*] (POL)
WAMA...... Galela/Gamarmalamo [*Indonesia*] [*ICAO location identifier*] (ICLI)
WAMA...... Western Australia Municipal Association
WAMACCR ... Western Australian Ministerial Advisory Council on Community Relations
WAMB...... Kotamubagu/Mopait [*Indonesia*] [*ICAO location identifier*] (ICLI)
WAMC...... Tentena [*Indonesia*] [*ICAO location identifier*] (ICLI)
WAMC...... Western Australian Meat Commission
WAMCO... West African Milk Co. [*Nigeria*]
WAMD...... Jailolo/Kuripasai [*Indonesia*] [*ICAO location identifier*] (ICLI)
WAMEX ... West African Monsoon Experiment [*ICSU*] (AF)
WAMG...... Gorontalo/Jalaluddin [*Indonesia*] [*ICAO location identifier*] (ICLI)
WAMH ..... Tahuna/Naha [*Indonesia*] [*ICAO location identifier*] (ICLI)
WAMI .... Toli Toli/Lalos [*Indonesia*] [*ICAO location identifier*] (ICLI)
WAMILDA ... Wadjib Militer Darurat [*Emergency Military Obligation (Conscription)*] (IN)
WAMK...... Kao/Kuabang [*Indonesia*] [*ICAO location identifier*] (ICLI)
WAML...... Palu/Mutiara [*Indonesia*] [*ICAO location identifier*] (ICLI)
WAMM..... Manado/Sam Ratulangi [*Indonesia*] [*ICAO location identifier*] (ICLI)

WAMMC .. Western Australian Meat Marketing Corp. [*Commercial firm*]
WAMN...... Melangguane [*Indonesia*] [*ICAO location identifier*] (ICLI)
WAMP ...... Poso/Kasigunou [*Indonesia*] [*ICAO location identifier*] (ICLI)
WAMPRI ... Western Australian Mining and Petroleum Research Institute [*Research center*] (IRC)
WAMQ...... Bada [*Indonesia*] [*ICAO location identifier*] (ICLI)
WAMR...... Morotai/Pitu [*Indonesia*] [*ICAO location identifier*] (ICLI)
WAMRL ... Western Australian Marine Research Laboratory
WAMRU... West African Maize Research Unit
WAMT...... Ternate/Babullah [*Indonesia*] [*ICAO location identifier*] (ICLI)
WAMU..... West African Monetary Union (AF)
WAMU..... Wuasa [*Indonesia*] [*ICAO location identifier*] (ICLI)
WAMW..... Luwuk/Bubung [*Indonesia*] [*ICAO location identifier*] (ICLI)
WAMY..... World Assembly of Muslim Youth [*Riyadh, Saudi Arabia*] (EAIO)
WAMZ...... Menado Sector [*Indonesia*] [*ICAO location identifier*] (ICLI)
WAN.......... Nigeria [*Poland*]
WAN.......... Warszawska Administracja Nieruchomosci [*Warsaw Real Estate Administration*] (POL)
WAN.......... Wegierska Akademia Nauk [*Hungarian Academy of Sciences*] (POL)
WAN.......... Western Air Navigation Ltd. [*Australia*]
WAN.......... Western Australian Newspapers
WAN.......... Women's Royal Australian Naval Service [*World War II*] (DSUE)
WANA...... West Asian and North African Countries (PDAA)
WANA...... Writers Against Nuclear Arms [*Australia*]
WANAD.... West African News Agency Development
WANADA ... Western Australian Network of Alcohol and Other Drug Agencies
WANATCA ... Western Australian Nut and Tree Crop Association
WAND....... Women and Development Unit (EA)
W & L .... Westcott & Laurance Line [*Steamship*] (MHDW)
WANG....... Western Australian Natural Gas Proprietary Ltd.
WANH ..... West Australian Newspapers Holdings
WANHAT ... Dewan Penasehat [*Council of Advisers*] (IN)
WANO ...... World Association of Nuclear Operators (ECON)
WANS .... West African News Service [*Nigeria*] (AF)
WANS .... Women's Australian National Service (ADA)
WANTC ... Western Australian Nanny Training College
WAO......... Western Australian Opera
WAO......... Wet op de Arbeidsongeschiktheid [*Law on Labor Disability*] [*Netherlands*] (WEN)
WAO......... Wissenschaftliche Arbeitsorganisation [*Scientific Labor Organization*] (EG)
WAO......... World Association of Orphans and Abandoned Children
WAOC...... Western Australian Olympic Council
WAOHE.... Western Australian Office of Higher Education
WAOO ...... Western Australian Onshore Oil
WAOP...... Western Australian Opinion Polls
WAOPA ... Western Australian Overseas Projects Authority
WAOW..... Women Against the Ordination of Women [*Australia*]
WAP.......... Werkabgabepreis [*Plant Delivered Price*] [*German*] (EG)
WAP.......... Western Australian Party (ADA)
WAP.......... Wet Autovervoer Personen [*Benelux*] (BAS)
WAP.......... White Australia Policy
WAP.......... Wojewodzkie Archiwum Panstwowe [*Voivodship State Archives*] (POL)
WAP.......... Wojskowa Akademia Polityczna [*Military Political Academy*] (POL)
WAPA ...... Amahai [*Indonesia*] [*ICAO location identifier*] (ICLI)
WAPB....... Bula [*Indonesia*] [*ICAO location identifier*] (ICLI)
WAPC ...... Banda [*Indonesia*] [*ICAO location identifier*] (ICLI)
WAPCC..... West African Portland Cement Company
WAPD....... Dobo [*Indonesia*] [*ICAO location identifier*] (ICLI)
WAPDA..... Water and Power Development Authority [*Pakistan*]
WAPE....... Mangole [*Indonesia*] [*ICAO location identifier*] (ICLI)
wapenpl...... Wapenplaten [*Plates of Coats of Arms*] [*Publishing*] [*Netherlands*]
WAPET...... West Australian Petroleum Proprietary Ltd. (ADA)
WAPF....... West African Pharmaceutical Federation [*Lagos, Nigeria*] (EAIO)
WAPH....... Labuhu/Usman Sadik [*Indonesia*] [*ICAO location identifier*] (ICLI)
WAPI........ Saumlaki [*Indonesia*] [*ICAO location identifier*] (ICLI)
WAPKr...... Wojewodzkie Archiwum Panstwowe w Krakowie [*Voivodship State Archives in Cracow*] (POL)
WAPL........ Langgur/Dumatubun [*Indonesia*] [*ICAO location identifier*] (ICLI)
WAPLub.... Wojewodzkie Archiwum Panstwowe w Lublinie [*Voivodship State Archives in Lublin*] (POL)
WAPMA ... Western Australian Potato Marketing Authority
WAPMC.... West African Postgraduate Medical College
WAPN .... Sanana [*Indonesia*] [*ICAO location identifier*] (ICLI)
WAPP........ Ambon/Pattimura [*Indonesia*] [*ICAO location identifier*] (ICLI)

WAPPoz .... Wojewodzkie Archiwum Panstwowe w Poznaniu [*Voivodship State Archives in Poznan*] (POL)
WAPR .... Namlea [*Indonesia*] [*ICAO location identifier*] (ICLI)
WAPR .... World Association for Psychosocial Rehabilitation (EAIO)
WAPS .... Selaru [*Indonesia*] [*ICAO location identifier*] (ICLI)
WAPT .... Taliabu [*Indonesia*] [*ICAO location identifier*] (ICLI)
WAPZ .... Ambon Sector [*Indonesia*] [*ICAO location identifier*] (ICLI)
WAQ .... Antsalova [*Madagascar*] [*Airport symbol*] (OAG)
WAR .... NZ Warbirds Association, Inc. [*New Zealand*] [*ICAO designator*] (FAAC)
WAR .... West African Regiment
WAR .... Wortausgaberegister [*Word Output Register*] [*German*] (ADPT)
WARA .... Wanita Angkatan Udara [*Women's Air Force Corps*] (IN)
WARC .... Wallaceville Animal Research Centre [*New Zealand*] (DSCA)
WARC .... World Administrative Radio Conference [*International Telecommunication Union*] (NTCM)
WARC .... World Alliance of Reformed Churches [*Alliance of the Reformed Churches throughout the World Holding the Presbyterian System and International Congregational Council*] [*Formed by a merger of*] (EAIO)
WARC-BS ... World Administrative Radio Conference for Broadcast Satellite Service [*International Telecommunication Union*] (NTCM)
WARCC ..... Western Australian Regional Computing Centre
WARDA .... West Africa Rice Development Association
WARDS ..... Western Australian Reading Development Association
WARG .... West Africa Regional Group (AF)
WARIS ...... Water Resources Information System [*Australia*]
WARITC ... Western Australian Retail Industry Training Council
Wa Rk .... Wassermannsche Reaktion [*Wassermann's Reaction*] [*German*] (GCA)
WARL .... Western Australian Rugby League
WARM ...... Wood and Solid Fuel Association of Retailers and Manufacturers (EA)
WARP .... West African Replenishment Plan (AF)
Warrnambool IAE ... Warrnambool Institute of Advanced Education [*Australia*]
WARRS ..... West African Rice Research Station
WARTA .... Western Australian Road Transport Association
WAS .... Pengawas [*or Pengawasan*] [*Supervisor or Supervision*] (IN)
WAS .... Waggonabnahmestelle [*Railroad Car Acceptance Office*] [*German*] (EG)
WAS .... Western Associated Schools [*Australia*]
WAS .... Wildlife Art Society [*Australia*]
WAS .... World Artifex Society (EAIO)
WASA .... Water and Sewerage Authority [*Trinidadian and Tobagan*] (LA)
WASA .... West African Science Association [*ICSU*] (AF)
WASA .... West African Shipper's Association (DS)
WASA .... Western Australian Society of Arts
WASA .... Writers Association of South Africa (AF)
WASAG ..... Westfaelische-Anhaltische Sprengstoff AG [*Westphalia-Anhalt Explosive Company*] [*Nazi Germany*]
WASB .... Steenkol/Bintuni [*Indonesia*] [*ICAO location identifier*] (ICLI)
WASC .... Ransiki/Abresso [*Indonesia*] [*ICAO location identifier*] (ICLI)
WASC .... West African School Certificate
WASC .... West African Students Confederation (AF)
WASC .... Western Australian Shell Club (SLS)
WASC .... Western Australian Shippers' Council
WASCL ..... Western Australian Society for Computers and the Law
WASE .... Kebar [*Indonesia*] [*ICAO location identifier*] (ICLI)
WASES ..... Western Australian State Emergency Service
WASF .... Fak Fak/Torea [*Indonesia*] [*ICAO location identifier*] (ICLI)
WASF .... Western Australian Sports Federation
WASFL .... Western Australian State Football League
WASGIC ... Western Australian State Government Insurance Commission (ECON)
WASHHOUSE ... Women's Activities and Self-Help House [*Australia*]
WASI .... Inanwatan [*Indonesia*] [*ICAO location identifier*] (ICLI)
WASK .... Kaimana (Utarom) [*Indonesia*] [*ICAO location identifier*] (ICLI)
WASLA ..... Western Australian School Library Association
WASM ...... Merdei [*Indonesia*] [*ICAO location identifier*] (ICLI)
WASM ...... Western Australian School of Mines [*Curtin University of Technology*] (EAS)
WASMAC ... Western Australian Survey and Mapping Advisory Council
WASMAFE ... Western Australian School of Mines and Further Education
WASMAR ... Kawasan Maritim [*Maritime District*] (IN)
WASME .... World Assembly of Small and Medium Enterprises [*See also AMPME*] [*India*] (EAIO)
WASMO ... West African Schools Mathematics Programme
WASN ...... Western Australian School of Nursing
WASO .... Babo [*Indonesia*] [*ICAO location identifier*] (ICLI)
WASP .... MARINALG International, World Association of Seaweed Processors (EA)
WASP .... World Association of Societies of Pathology - Anatomic and Clinical (EA)

WASPRU .. West African Stored Products Research Unit
WASR .... Manokwari/Rendani [*Indonesia*] [*ICAO location identifier*] (ICLI)
WASRA ..... Western Australian Smallbore Rifle Association
WASRAID ... Western Australian Sports and Recreation Association for the Intellectually Disabled
WASS .... Sorong/Jefman [*Indonesia*] [*ICAO location identifier*] (ICLI)
Wassb .... Wasserbau [*Hydraulic Engineering*] [*German*] (GCA)
wasserfl ...... Wasserfleckig [*Stained by Water*] [*German*]
wasserl .... Wasserloeslich [*Water-Soluble*] [*German*] (GCA)
wasserloesl ... Wasserloeslich [*Water-Soluble*] [*German*] (GCA)
Wassersch ... Wasserschaeden [*Water-Damaged in Several Places*] [*German*]
Wassersp ... Wasserspuren [*Traces of Dampness*] [*German*]
wasserunl ... Wasserunloeslich [*Insoluble in Water*] [*German*] (GCA)
wasserw ...... Wasserwellig [*Crinkled by Water*] [*German*]
wassr .... Waesserig [*Aqueous, Hydrous*] [*German*]
WAST .... Teminabuan [*Indonesia*] [*ICAO location identifier*] (ICLI)
WASTA ..... Western Australian Science Teachers' Association
WASTE ..... World Association for Solid Waste Transfer and Exchange
WASU ...... West African Students Union (AF)
WASW ...... Wasior [*Indonesia*] [*ICAO location identifier*] (ICLI)
WASY .... Western Australian School of Yoga
Wat .... Waterford [*Crystal glassware*] (BARN)
WAT .... Watheroo [*Later, GNA*] [*Australia*] [*Geomagnetic observatory code*]
WAT .... Wings Air Transport Co. [*Sudan*] [*ICAO designator*] (FAAC)
WAT .... Wojskowa Akademia Techniczna [*Military Technical Academy*] (POL)
WAT .... Woordeboek van die Afrikaanse Taal [*Afrikaans*]
WAT .... Wytwornia Artykulow Technicznych [*Technical Goods Plant*] (POL)
WATA ...... Western Australian Temperance Alliance
WATA ...... World Association of Travel Agencies (EAIO)
WATAC .... Women and the Australian Church
Watb .... Waterschapsbelangen [*Benelux*] (BAS)
WATBRU ... West African Timber Borer Research Unit
WATC ...... Western Australian Theatre Co.
WATC ...... Western Australian Tourism Commission
WATC ...... Western Australian Tourist Centre
WATC ...... Western Australian Treasury Corp. [*Commercial firm*]
WATEA .... Western Australian Teacher Education Authority
watervl .... Watervlekken [*Water Stains*] [*Publishing*] [*Netherlands*]
WATITC ... Western Australian Tourism Industry Training Committee
WATLC ..... Trades and Labour Council of Western Australia
WATLCC .. Western Australian Tripartite Labour Consultative Council
WATTE ..... West African Tropical Testing Establishment
WATU ...... Workers Alliance Trade Unions [*Philippines*] (FEA)
WATWF ... West African Transport Workers Federation
WAU .... Women's Advisory Unit [*South Australia*]
WAUA ...... West African Unit of Account
WAust .... University of Western Australia (ADA)
WAust .... Western Australia (ADA)
WAV .... West-Avin Oy [*Finland*] [*ICAO designator*] (FAAC)
WAV .... Wirtschaftliche Aufbau Vereinigung [*Economic Reconstruction Union*] [*Germany*] [*Political party*] (PPE)
WAVA ...... World Association of Veteran Athletes (EAIO)
WAVE ...... Women and Vocational Education [*Australia*]
WAVES ..... Western Australian Voluntary Euthanasia Society
WAVFH .... World Association of Veterinary Food-Hygienists [*See also AMVHA*] [*Berlin, Federal Republic of Germany*] (EAIO)
WAVLD .... World Association of Veterinary Laboratory Diagnosticians (EAIO)
WAVMI .... World Association of Veterinary Microbiologists, Immunologists, and Specialists in Infectious Diseases [*See also AMVMI*] [*Maisons-Alfort, France*] (EAIO)
WAVP ...... World Association of Veterinary Pathologists (EAIO)
WAW .... Warsaw [*Poland*] [*Airport symbol*] (OAG)
WAWA ...... Water Authority of Western Australia
WAWA ...... West Africa Wins Again
WAWC ..... Western Australian Week Council
WAWF ..... World Association for World Federation [*Netherlands*]
WAWF ..... World Association of World Federalists (AF)
WAWU ..... Waterfront and Allied Workers' Union [*Dominica*]
WAWU ..... Waterfront and Allied Workers Union [*Barbados*] (LA)
WAY .... Worked All Yokosuka [*Amateur radio*] (IAA)
WAY .... World Assembly of Youth [*Bronshoj, Denmark*] (EAIO)
WAYL .... West African Youth League
WAYMCA ... World Alliance of Young Men's Christian Associations [*Geneva, Switzerland*] (EAIO)
WAYS .... Waverley Action for Youth Services [*Australia*]
WAZ .... Wahlaufforderungszeichen [*German*] (ADPT)
WB .... Besluit op de Winstbelasting [*Benelux*] (BAS)
WB .... Way Bill: Bordereau (FLAF)
Wb .... Weber [*Weber*] [*Poland*]
WB .... Wetenschappelijke Bibliotheken
Wb .... Wirtschaftsbesitzer [*Establishment Owner*] [*German*]

Wb............. Woerterbuch [*Dictionary*] [*German*] (GCA)
WB............. Wohnbezirk [*Residential District*] [*German*] (EG)
WBA......... West Coast Air [*Gambia*] [*ICAO designator*] (FAAC)
WBA......... Wohnbezirksausschuss [*Residential District Committee*]
　　　　　　 [*German*] (EG)
WBA......... Wollongong Buddhist Association [*Australia*]
WBA......... World Boxing Association
WBAA...... Wholesale Booksellers' Association of Australia (ADA)
WBAIS...... Walworth Barbour American International School in Israel
　　　　　　 (BJA)
WBAK...... Anduki/Seria [*Brunei*] [*ICAO location identifier*] (ICLI)
WBB......... World Bank Bond (MHDW)
WBC......... Westpac Banking Corp. [*Australia*] [*Commercial firm*]
WBC......... World Boxing Council [*Information service or system*] (IID)
WBCG...... Water Bird Conservation Group [*Australia*]
WBD......... Befandriana [*Madagascar*] [*Airport symbol*] (OAG)
WBD......... Wegbouwkundige Dienst Rijkswaterstaat [*Road Engineering
　　　　　　 Division of Rijkswaterstaat*] [*Public Works Department*]
　　　　　　 [*Netherlands*] [*Research center*] (ERC)
WBDJ....... Weltbund der Demokratischen Jugend [*World Federation of
　　　　　　 Democratic Youth - WFDY*] [*German*] (WEN)
WBE......... Bealanana [*Madagascar*] [*Airport symbol*] (OAG)
Wbel.......... Waterschapsbelangen [*Benelux*] (BAS)
WBEP....... Workplace Basic Education Project [*Australia*]
WBF......... Werktijdenbesluit voor Fabrieken of Werkplaatsen [*Benelux*]
　　　　　　 (BAS)
WBFC...... Kota Kinabalu [*Malaysia*] [*ICAO location identifier*] (ICLI)
WBFC...... West Bengal Financial Corp. [*India*] (PDAA)
WBG........ Wiener Beethoven-Gesellschaft [*Vienna Beethoven Society*]
　　　　　　 [*Austria*] (SLS)
WBG........ Wiener Bibliophilen-Gesellschaft [*Vienna Bibliophile Society*]
　　　　　　 [*Austria*] (SLS)
WBGA...... Long Atip [*Malaysia*] [*ICAO location identifier*] (ICLI)
WBGB...... Bintulu [*Malaysia*] [*ICAO location identifier*] (ICLI)
WBGC...... Belaga [*Malaysia*] [*ICAO location identifier*] (ICLI)
WBGD...... Long Semado [*Malaysia*] [*ICAO location identifier*] (ICLI)
WBGE...... Long Geng [*Malaysia*] [*ICAO location identifier*] (ICLI)
WBGG...... Kuching [*Malaysia*] [*ICAO location identifier*] (ICLI)
WBGJ....... Limbang [*Malaysia*] [*ICAO location identifier*] (ICLI)
WBGK...... Mukah [*Malaysia*] [*ICAO location identifier*] (ICLI)
WBGL...... Long Akah [*Indonesia*] [*ICAO location identifier*] (ICLI)
WBGM..... Marudi [*Indonesia*] [*ICAO location identifier*] (ICLI)
WBGN...... Sematan [*Indonesia*] [*ICAO location identifier*] (ICLI)
WBGO...... Lio Matu [*Malaysia*] [*ICAO location identifier*] (ICLI)
WBGP...... Kapit [*Indonesia*] [*ICAO location identifier*] (ICLI)
WBGQ..... Bakelalan [*Malaysia*] [*ICAO location identifier*] (ICLI)
WBGR...... Miri [*Indonesia*] [*ICAO location identifier*] (ICLI)
WBGS...... Sibu [*Malaysia*] [*ICAO location identifier*] (ICLI)
WBGW..... Lawas [*Malaysia*] [*ICAO location identifier*] (ICLI)
WBGY...... Simanggang [*Malaysia*] [*ICAO location identifier*] (ICLI)
WBGZ...... Bario [*Malaysia*] [*ICAO location identifier*] (ICLI)
WBH........ Wet Belastingherziening [*Benelux*] (BAS)
WBK........ Werijdenbesluit voor Kantoren [*Benelux*] (BAS)
WBK........ Wohnungsbaukombinat [*Housing Construction Combine*]
　　　　　　 [*German*] (EG)
WBK........ Wytwornia Biletow Kolejowych [*Railroad Ticket Printing Plant*]
　　　　　　 (POL)
WBKA...... Semporna [*Malaysia*] [*ICAO location identifier*] (ICLI)
WBKD...... Lahad Datu [*Malaysia*] [*ICAO location identifier*] (ICLI)
WBKG...... Keningau [*Malaysia*] [*ICAO location identifier*] (ICLI)
WBKH...... Werktijdenbesluit voor Koffiehuis- en Hotel Personeel [*Benelux*]
　　　　　　 (BAS)
WBKK...... Kota Kinabalu [*Malaysia*] [*ICAO location identifier*] (ICLI)
WBKL...... Labuan [*Malaysia*] [*ICAO location identifier*] (ICLI)
WBKP....... Pamol [*Malaysia*] [*ICAO location identifier*] (ICLI)
WBKR...... Ranau [*Malaysia*] [*ICAO location identifier*] (ICLI)
WBKS...... Sandakan [*Malaysia*] [*ICAO location identifier*] (ICLI)
WBKT...... Kudat [*Malaysia*] [*ICAO location identifier*] (ICLI)
WBKW..... Tawau [*Malaysia*] [*ICAO location identifier*] (ICLI)
WBL......... Weekblad [*Weekly*] [*Afrikaans*]
Wbl............ Wochenblatt [*Weekly Paper*] [*German*]
WBM........ Wapenamanda [*Papua New Guinea*] [*Airport symbol*] (OAG)
WBMS...... World Bureau of Metal Statistics [*British*] (EAIO)
WBNMMUMA ... West Bengal Non-Ferrous Metal Merchants and Utensils
　　　　　　 Merchants Association [*India*] (PDAA)
WBO......... Beroroha [*Madagascar*] [*Airport symbol*] (OAG)
WBO......... Wet op de Bedrijfsorganisatie [*Benelux*] (BAS)
WBP......... Wojewodzka Biblioteka Publiczna [*Voivodship Public Library*]
　　　　　　 (POL)
WBP......... Wojewodzkie Biuro Projektow [*Voivodship Office of Plans*]
　　　　　　 (POL)
WBP......... Women's Budget Program [*Australia*]
WBPAA..... Wine and Brandy Producers' Association of Australia
WBPASA .. Wine and Brandy Producers' Association of South Australia
WBPC........ Woolloomooloo Bay Protection Committee [*Australia*]

WBPCASA ... Wine and Brandy Producers' Cooperative Association of South
　　　　　　 Australia
WBPF........ World Bicycle Polo Federation (EA)
WBR......... Wetboek van Burgerlijke Regtsvordering [*Code of Civil
　　　　　　 Procedure*] [*Dutch*] (ILCA)
WBR......... Wet op de Bibliotheekraad
W Br......... Wielka Brytania [*Great Britain*] (POL)
WBR......... Wohnungsbaureihe [*Housing Construction Series*] [*German*]
　　　　　　 (EG)
WBRI........ Wheat and Barley Research Institute [*South Korean*] [*Research
　　　　　　 center*] (IRC)
W Bryt...... Wielka Brytania [*Great Britain*] [*Poland*]
WBS........... Warenbegleitschein [*Bill of Lading*] [*Shipping*] [*German*] (EG)
WBS........... Wojewodzkie Biuro Skierowan [*Voivodship Office for Vacation
　　　　　　 Assignment*] (POL)
WBS........... Women's Budget Statement [*Australia*]
WBS........... World Bird Sanctuary (EA)
WBS........... World Broadcasting System (NTCM)
WBSB........ Brunei/International [*Brunei*] [*ICAO location identifier*] (ICLI)
WBSEB...... West Bengal State Electricity Board [*India*] (PDAA)
WBU......... World Billiards Union (EAIO)
WBU......... World Blind Union (EA)
WBV......... De Woningbouwvereniging, Maandblad van de Nationale
　　　　　　 Woningraad [*Benelux*] (BAS)
WBV......... Wagenbehandlungsvorschriften [*Car Handling Regulations*]
　　　　　　 (EG)
WC............. Water Closet [*A toilet*] [*Slang*]
WC............. Watered Capital (MHDW)
WC............. Waterways Commission [*Western Australia*]
WC............. Woden's Coven [*Germany*] [*Defunct*] (EAIO)
WC............. Women's Centre [*India*] (EAIO)
WC............. Women's College [*University of Sydney*] [*Australia*]
WCA......... Australian War Correspondents Association
WCA......... West Coast Airlines Ltd. [*Ghana*]
WCA......... West Coast of Africa (ROG)
WCA......... Western Coal Association [*Australia*]
WCA......... Wool Council of Australia
WCA......... WorkCover Authority [*New South Wales, Australia*]
WCA......... Working-Capital Account (MHDW)
WCA......... World Christian Action [*Australia*]
WCAB...... WorkCare Appeals Board [*Victoria, Australia*]
WCAHI..... World Conference of Animal Health Industries [*Australia*]
WCANSW ... Workcover Authority of New South Wales [*Australia*]
WCAP...... World Climate Applications Program [*WMO*] [*ICSU*]
WCARRD ... World Conference on Agrarian Reform and Rural Development
WCB......... West Africa Airlines Ltd. [*Ghana*] [*ICAO designator*] (FAAC)
WCB......... Workers' Compensation Board [*Australia*]
WCBCF..... Welsh Corgi and Bobtail Club Francais [*France*] (EAIO)
WCBS........ World Confederation of Billiards Sports [*Malaysia*] (EAIO)
WCC......... War Claims Commission
WCC......... War Crimes Commission
WCC......... Westfield Capital Corp. Ltd. [*Australia*]
WCC......... World Congress Centre [*Melbourne, Australia*]
WCC......... World Council of Churches [*Geneva, Switzerland*]
WCC......... World Crafts Council (EA)
WCCE....... World Conference in Computer Education [*Australia*]
WCCE....... World Conference on Computers in Education
WCCES..... World Council of Comparative Education Societies (EA)
WCCL....... World Council for Colonial Liberation
WCCM..... World Congress Centre, Melbourne [*Australia*]
WCDA...... West Cameroons Development Agency
WC(DD)B ... Worker's Compensation (Dust Diseases) Board [*Australia*]
WCDP...... World Climate Data Program [*WMO*] [*ICSU*]
WCE......... Wessex College of English [*Australia*]
WCEA ...... West Cameroun Employers' Association [*Employers'
　　　　　　 association*] (EY)
WCEC....... West Cameroon Electricity Company
WCF .... World Congress of Faiths - The Inter-Faith Fellowship [*British*]
　　　　　　 (EAIO)
WCF .... World Curling Federation [*British*] (EAIO)
WCFBA..... World Catholic Federation for the Biblical Apostolate [*Stuttgart,
　　　　　　 Federal Republic of Germany*] (EAIO)
WCG......... West Coast Airlines Ltd. [*Ghana*] [*ICAO designator*] (FAAC)
WCH......... Wojskowa Centrala Handlowa [*Military Trade Center*] (POL)
Wchs Str ... Wechselstrom [*Alternating Current*] [*German*] (GCA)
WCIC........ Kalyanamitra Women's Communication and Information
　　　　　　 Centre [*Indonesia*] (EAIO)
WCIE........ World Center for Islamic Education (EA)
WCIP........ World Climate Impacts Program [*WMO*] [*ICSU*]
WCIP........ World Council of Indigenous Peoples [*Ottawa, ON*] (EAIO)
WCJA....... World Council of Jewish Archives (EAIO)
WCJCC ... World Confederation of Jewish Community Centers (EA)
WCK........ Wildlife Clubs of Kenya Association (EA)
WCKS....... Wojskowy Centralny Klub Sportowy [*Military Central Sports
　　　　　　 and Athletics Club*] [*Poland*]
WCL .... Western Collieries Ltd. [*Australia*]

WCL .... World Confederation of Labour [*See also CMT*] [*Brussels, Belgium*] (EAIO)

WCLC....... World Christian Life Community [*Italy*] (EAIO)

WCM........ Wesley Central Mission [*Australia*]

WCM........ World-Class Manufacturing [*Management technique*]

WCMF ...... World Congress on Metal Finishing (PDAA)

WCMR ...... World Conference on Missionary Radio [*Later, ICB*] (NTCM)

WCMT ...... Winston Churchill Memorial Trust [*Australia*]

WCN........ Women's Centre of Nigeria (EAIO)

WCNDT .... World Conference on Non-Destructive Testing (PDAA)

WCNU ...... Women's Wing of the Cameroon National Union

WCOC...... Women's Central Organising Committee [*Australian Labor Party, New South Wales*]

WCOTP..... World Confederation of Organizations of the Teaching Profession [*International Federation of Secondary Teachers and IFTA*] [*Formed by a merger of*] (EAIO)

WCP .... World Climate Program [*WMO*] [*ICSU*]

WCPPG..... Wojewodzkie Centralne Poradnie Przeciwgruzlicze [*Voivodship Central Anti-Tubercular Stations*] (POL)

WCPS....... World Confederation of Productivity Science (EAIO)

WCPT .... World Confederation for Physical Therapy [*British*] (EA)

WCR .... World Communication Report [*Database*] [*UNESCO*] (DUND)

WCRC ...... Workers' Compensation and Rehabilitation Commission [*Western Australia*]

WCRP....... World Climate Research Programme [*WMO*] [*ICSU*]

WCRP....... World Conference on Religion and Peace (EAIO)

WCRZZ..... Wszechzwiazkowa Centralna Rada Zwiazkow Zawodowych [*All-Union Central Council of Trade Unions*] [*Poland*]

WCS .... World Conservation Strategy [*IUCN*] (ASF)

WCSICEC ... Working Committee of the Scientific Institutes for Crafts in the EEC Countries [*Munich, Federal Republic of Germany*] (EAIO)

WCSPS...... Wszechrosyjski Centralny Sojusz Profesjonalnych Sojuszow [*All-Russian Central Trade Union Organization*] (POL)

WCST....... Wildlife Conservation Society of Tanzania (EAIO)

WCSZ....... Wildlife Conservation Society of Zambia (SLS)

WCT .... World Confederation of Teachers [*See also CSME*] [*Brussels, Belgium*] (EAIO)

WCT .... Wydawnictwo Czasopism Technicznych [*Technical Periodicals Publishing House*] (POL)

WCTA .... World Committee for Trade Action [*See also CMAP*] [*Brussels, Belgium*] (EAIO)

WCTU .... Woman's Christian Temperance Union of Australasia [*or Australia*] (ADA)

WCTUC .... West Cameroon Trade Union Congress (AF)

WCU......... West China University

WCU......... Wildlife Clubs of Uganda (EAIO)

WCU......... Women's Coordination Unit [*Australia*]

WCUC...... Workers' Central Union of Cuba (EAIO)

WCWB ...... World Council for the Welfare of the Blind [*Later, WBU*] (EAIO)

WCZ......... Water Control Zone [*Hong Kong*]

wd.............. Waarnemend [*Benelux*] (BAS)

wd.............. Wdowa [*Widow*] [*Poland*]

WD............. Wettelijk Depot

WD............. Woord [*Word*] [*Afrikaans*]

WDA......... Wagga Diploma in Agriculture [*Australia*]

WDA......... Welsh Development Agency (GEA)

WDA......... World Dance Alliance

WDA......... World Dredging Association (MSC)

WDAA...... Worker Directors Association of Australia

WDB......... With Due Bills [*Stocks*] (MHDW)

wdb............. Woordeboek [*Dictionary*] [*Afrikaans*]

WDC......... Workers' Defence Committee [*Ghana*] [*Political party*] (PPW)

WDC......... Workers Defence Corps [*Australia*]

WDC......... Workers' Defense Committee [*Poland*] (PD)

WDC......... World Data Centre [*ICSU*]

WDD......... Water Development Department

WDDB....... Wild Dog Destruction Board [*New South Wales, Australia*]

WDF .... Western Desert Force

WDF .... World Darts Federation (EAIO)

WDF .... World Draughts (Checkers) Federation [*See also FMJD*] [*Dordrecht, Netherlands*] (EAIO)

WDFAA .... Western Districts Foundation for Aboriginal Affairs [*Australia*]

Wdg............. Wendung [*Turn, Change*] [*German*] (GCA)

Wdh............. Wiederholung [*Repetition*] [*German*] (GCA)

WDH .... Windhoek [*Namibia*] [*Airport symbol*] (OAG)

WDI.......... Westfaelische Drahtindustrie [*Westphalian Cable Industry*]

WDIC .... Women's Development and Information Center [*Bolivia*] (EAIO)

WDK......... Wiejski Dom Kultury [*Rural House of Culture*] (POL)

WDK......... Wirtschattsverband der Deutschen Kaunstscshukindustrie [*Association of the German Rubber Industry*] (PDAA)

WDK......... Wojewodzki Dom Kultury [*Voivodship House of Culture*] (POL)

WDK......... Wojskowy Dom Kultury [*Military House of Culture*] (POL)

WDL......... Westdeutsche Luftwerbung [*Airline*] [*Germany*]

WDM........ World Disarmament Movement [*Australia*]

WDN .... Warszawska Dzielnica Naukowa [*Warsaw Academic Quarter*] (POL)

WDO .... Warszawska Dyrekcja Odbudowy [*Warsaw Reconstruction Administration*] (POL)

WDR........ Westdeuscher Rundfunk [*Germany*] (PDAA)

wdr .... Wieder [*Again*] [*German*] (GCA)

WDR........ Winged Russia [*Russian Federation*] [*ICAO designator*] (FAAC)

WDRC ...... World Data Referral Center (MSC)

Wdrhst....... Wiederherstellung [*Repair*] [*German*] (GCA)

WDS .... W. D. Scott & Co. [*Australia*] (ADA)

Wdst........... Widerstand [*Resistance*] [*German*] (GCA)

WDT .... Wiejski Dom Towarowy [*Rural Department Store*] (POL)

WDU .... Wahlblock der Unabhaengigen [*German*]

WdU .... Wahlpartei der Unabhaengigen [*Electoral Party of Independents*] [*Austria*] [*Political party*] (PPE)

WDW........ Wojskowy Dom Wypoczynkowy [*Military Rest Home*] (POL)

WDZ......... Wydzial Drog i Zielencow [*Department of Roads and Verdure*] (POL)

WE............ Waermeeinheit [*Thermal Unit*] [*German*] (EG)

WE............ WDL Flugdienst GmbH [*Germany*] [*ICAO designator*] (ICDA)

WE............ Witterungseinfluesse [*Atmospheric Effects*] [*German*] (GCA)

WE............ Wohnungseinheit [*Dwelling Unit*] [*German*] (WEN)

WE............ World Ecologists Foundation [*Philippines*] (EAIO)

WEA .... Workers' Educational Association [*Sweden*] (EAIO)

WEAA ...... Western European Airports Association (PDAA)

WEAAP..... Western European Association for Aviation Psychology (EA)

WEAC ...... West European Advisory Committee [*Radio Free Europe*] (NTCM)

WEAC ...... Women's Employment Action Centre [*Australia*]

WEADSC .. World Esperantist Association for Education, Science, and Culture [*Germany*] (EAIO)

WEAL....... West End Limited

WEANSW ... Workers' Educational Association of New South Wales [*Australia*]

WEASA..... Workers' Educational Association of South Australia

WEBE....... Werkgroep Beleidsplan [*NOBIN*] [*'s-Gravenhage*]

WEC .... West European Container Liners [*Shipping*]

WEC .... World Energy Conference [*See also CME*] [*London, England*] (EAIO)

WEC .... Worldwide Evangelization Crusade

WECAFC .. Western Central Atlantic Fisheries Commission [*Food and Agriculture Organization of the UN*] (EAIO)

Wechselwirk ... Wechselwirkung [*Reciprocal Action*] [*German*] (GCA)

WECO ...... Whangarei Engineering & Construction Ltd. [*New Zealand*]

WED......... Wedau [*Papua New Guinea*] [*Airport symbol*] (OAG)

Wed.......... Wednesday (EECI)

wed .... Weduwee [*Widow*] [*Afrikaans*]

WED .... Wet op de Economische Delicten [*Benelux*] (BAS)

WED .... World Energy Development

WED .... World Environment Day [*ICSU*]

WEDC ...... Water and Waste Engineering for Developing Countries

WEDERK ... Wederkerend [*Reflexive*] [*Afrikaans*]

WEDRA .... Werler Drahtwaren GmbH [*Metal manufacturer*]

WEE .... Weapons Electrical Engineering [*Royal Australian Navy*]

WEE .... Weltbund fuer Erneuerung der Erziehung, Deutschsprachige Sektion [*World Society for the Revival of Education, German-Speaking Section*] (SLS)

WeekblPriv Noten Reg ... Weekblad voor Privaatrecht, Notaris-Ambt en Registratie [*Benelux*] (BAS)

WEEO .... Weapons Electrical Engineering Officer [*Royal Australian Navy*]

weervl........ Weervlekkig [*Weather-Stained*] [*Netherlands*]

WEEV....... Women, Education, and Employment in Victoria [*Australia*]

WEF.......... World Economic Forum (EAIO)

WEF.......... World Education Fellowship (EA)

WEFTA ..... West European Fish Technologist Association [*Netherlands*] (ASF)

WEG......... Wirtschaftsverband Erdoel- and Erdgasgewinnung eV

WEH......... Walter and Eliza Hall Institute of Medical Research [*Australia*]

WEI .... Weipa [*Australia*] [*Airport symbol*] (OAG)

WEI .... Western European Institute for Wood Preservation (EAIO)

WEI .... World Environment Institute (ASF)

weibl......... Weiblich [*Feminine*] [*German*]

WEI/IEO .. Western European Institute for Wood Preservation/Institut de l'Europe Occidentale pour l'Impregnation du Bois (EAIO)

Weil........... Weiland [*Formerly*] [*German*]

Weiterentw ... Weiterentwicklung [*Further Development*] [*German*] (GCA)

WEJ.......... West Air Sweden AB [*ICAO designator*] (FAAC)

WEk.......... Elektrizitaetswerk [*Electrical Power Plant*] [*German*]

WEL......... Welkom [*South Africa*] [*Airport symbol*] (OAG)

WEL......... Welt-Eis-Lehre [*Cosmic Ice Theory*] [*German*]

WELC....... World Electrotechnical Congress (PDAA)

WelEd........ WelEdele [*Honorable*] [*Afrikaans*]

WelEdGestr ... WelEdelGestrenge [*Right Honorable*] [*Afrikaans*]

WelEdHeer ... WelEdele Heer [*Esquire*] [*Afrikaans*]

WelEerw .... WelEerwaarde [*Right Reverend*] [*Afrikaans*]

Well............ Wellington [*New Zealand*]　(BARN)

WELL....... Workplace English Language and Literacy Program [*Australia*]

WELSTAT ... Standardisation of Social Welfare Statistics Project [*Australia*]

WEM........ Western European Metal Trades Employers Organization [*Cologne, Federal Republic of Germany*]　(EA)

WEM........ Wet Economische Mededinging [*Benelux*]　(BAS)

WEMOS ... International Women's Network on Pharmaceuticals [*Amsterdam, Netherlands*]　(EAIO)

WEMSB.... Western European Military Supply Board [*NATO*]　(NATG)

WEMT ...... West European Conference on Marine Technology　(PDAA)

wen........... Wenig [*Little*] [*German*]

Wend........ Wende [*or Wendung*] [*Turn, Change*] [*German*]　(GCA)

WENELA ... Witwatersrand Native Labour Association

wenv -rekening ... Winst- en Verliesrekening [*Benelux*]　(BAS)

WEO......... Western Europe and Others [*United Nations*]

WEOG....... Western European and Others Group [*United Nations*]

WEP .... Weam [*Papua New Guinea*] [*Airport symbol*]　(OAG)

WEP .... World Employment Program [*of the International Labour Organization*] [*Geneva, Switzerland*] [*United Nations*]

WEPCO..... Western Desert Petroleum Company [*Egypt*]

WEPS........ Weapons and Equipment Policy Statement [*Australia*]

WERC .... Woomera Entertainment and Recreation Committee [*Australia*]

WERC .... World Environment and Resources Council [*Louvain, Belgium*]　(EAIO)

WEREDEC ... Western Regional Development Corporation

WEREDI... Union of Dutch Working Communities　(WEN)

Werf.......... Werfer [*Projector*] [*German*]　(GCA)

Werkst....... Werkstatt [*Workshop*] [*German*]　(GCA)

WERPG..... Western European Regional Planning Group [*NATO*]　(NATG)

WES.......... Welding Engineering Society [*Japan*]　(PDAA)

WES.......... World Economic Summit

WES.......... World-Wide Ethical Society [*Chinese*]　(SLS)

WESDOC ... Western Region Documentation Service [*Australia*]

WESI........ Wind Energy Society of India　(EAIO)

WESTBODEN ... Westdeutsche Bodenkreditanstalt [*West German Land Credit Institute*]

WESTCAPS ... Western Australian Corporate Affairs Processing System

WESTDOC ... Western Region Documentation [*Australia*]

Western I... Western Institute [*Australia*]

Westf......... Westfalen [*Westphalia*] [*German*]

westl .... Westlich [*Westerly*] [*German*]

WESTPAC ... Working Party for the Western Pacific [*IOC*]　(ASF)

Westpr........ Westpreussen [*Western Prussia*] [*German*]　(GCA)

WESTRAIL ... Western Australian Government Railways Commission

WESTS...... Western Sydney Tenants Service [*Australia*]

WESTS...... Women's Emergency Shelter and Training Scheme [*New South Wales, Australia*]

WET .... Wagethe [*Indonesia*] [*Airport symbol*]　(OAG)

Wet AB ...... Wet Houdende Algemeene Bepalingen der Wetgeving van het Koninkrijk [*Benelux*]　(BAS)

WetARBO ... Wet Administratieve Rechtspraak Bedrijfs-Organisatie [*Benelux*]　(BAS)

wetb........... Wetboek [*Statutes*] [*Afrikaans*]

Wet BAB.... Wet Beroep Administratieve Beschikkingen [*Benelux*]　(BAS)

WetBBBG ... Wet Buitengewone Bevoegdheden Burgerlijk Gezag [*Benelux*]　(BAS)

Wet BH...... Wet Belastingherziening [*Benelux*]　(BAS)

Wet Bl........ Wetenschappelijke Bladen [*Benelux*]　(BAS)

Wet BO ...... Wet op de Bedrijfsorganisatie [*Benelux*]　(BAS)

Wet CoopVer ... Wet op de Cooeperatieve Verenigingen [*Benelux*]　(BAS)

Wet DTB .... Wet op de Dividend- en Tantiemebelasting [*Benelux*]　(BAS)

Wet ED ...... Wet op de Economische Delicten [*Benelux*]　(BAS)

Wet EM ..... Wet Economische Mededinging [*Benelux*]　(BAS)

WetGMD... Wet Gewetensbezwaren Militaire Dienst [*Benelux*]　(BAS)

Wet IB....... Wet op de Inkomstenbelasting [*Benelux*]　(BAS)

WETRAH ... Wetenskapsvereniging van Randse Afrikaanse Hoerskole [*South Africa*]　(AA)

Wet RO...... Wet op de Regterlijke Organisatie en het Beleid der Justitie [*Benelux*]　(BAS)

WETS........ West European Triangulation Subcommission [*International Association of Geodesy*]　(PDAA)

Wett .... Wetter [*Weather*] [*German*]　(GCA)

Wett D .... Wetterdienst [*Weather Service*] [*German*]　(GCA)

wetterbestaend ... Wetterbestaendig [*Weather-Resistant*] [*German*]　(GCA)

Wett M ...... Wettermessung [*Meteorological Measurement*] [*German*]　(GCA)

Wet VAB ... Wet op de Vermogensaanwasbelasting [*Benelux*]　(BAS)

Wet VB ..... Wet op de Vermogensbelasting [*Benelux*]　(BAS)

WEU......... Western European Union [*Also, WU*] [*See also UEO*]　(EAIO)

WEU......... Westeuropaeische Union [*Western European Union*] [*German*]

WEVA .... World Esperantist Vegetarian Association [*See also TEVA*] [*Dublin, Republic of Ireland*]　(EAIO)

Wewa .... Wetterwarte [*Meteorological Observatory*] [*German*]

wewn .... Wewnetrzny [*Interior*]　(POL)

WEZ .... Wahlendezeichen [*German*]　(ADPT)

WEZ .... Westeuropaeische Zeit [*Western European Time (Greenwich Time)*] [*German*]　(WEN)

WF .... Waehrungsfaktura [*Foreign Exchange Invoice*] [*German*]　(EG)

WF .... Wahrscheinlichkeitsfaktor [*Probability Factor*] [*German*]　(GCA)

WF .... Wallis and Futuna [*ANSI two-letter standard code*]　(CNC)

wf............... Wasserfrei [*Anhydrous*] [*German*]

WF .... Werk fuer Fernmeldewesen, Berlin-Oberschoeneweide (VEB) [*Berlin-Oberschoeneweide Telecommunications Equipment Plant (VEB)*]　(EG)

WF .... White Fathers [*Roman Catholic men's religious order*]

WF .... Wychowanie Fizyczne [*Physical Education*]　(POL)

WFA .... Weightlifting Federation of Africa　(EAIO)

WFA .... White Fish Authority

WFA .... Winemakers' Federation of Australia

WFA .... World Federalists Australia　(ADA)

WFA .... World Federation of Advertisers [*See also FMA*] [*Brussels, Belgium*]　(EAIO)

WFAA ...... World Federation of Americans Abroad [*France*]　(EAIO)

WFAC....... World Federal Authority Committee [*Dundas, ON*]　(EAIO)

WFACT.... Wildlife Foundation Australian Capital Territory

WFAFW.... World Federation of Agriculture and Food Workers　(EA)

WFALW.... Weltbund Freiheitlicher Arbeitnehmerverbande auf Liberaler Wirtschaftsgrundlage [*World Union of Liberal Trade Union Organisations - WULTUO*] [*Zurich, Switzerland*]　(EAIO)

WFAOS..... World Federation of Associations of YMCA Secretaries [*Nigeria*]　(EAIO)

WFAPS ..... World Federation of Associations of Pediatric Surgeons [*Barcelona, Spain*]　(EAIO)

WFAS....... Women's Financial Advisory Service [*Australia*]

WFAW ..... World Federation of Agricultural Workers [*See also FMTA*]　(EAIO)

WFB.......... Wirtschaftsfoerderung Berlin GmbH [*Berlin Economic Development Corp.*]

WFB.......... World Fellowship of Buddhists [*Bangkok, Tahiland*]　(EAIO)

WFBY....... World Fellowship of Buddhist Youth [*Bangkok, Thailand*]　(EAIO)

WFC .... Wanted for Cash　(MHDW)

WFC .... Wings Fan Club [*Germany*]　(EAIO)

WFC .... World Federation of Clerical Workers [*WCL*]

WFC .... World Food Council [*United Nations*]　(EAIO)

WFC .... World Friendship Centre　(EA)

WFCC....... World Federation for Culture Collections　(EAIO)

WFCLC ..... World Federation of Christian Life Communities [*See also FMCVC*] [*Rome, Italy*]　(EAIO)

WFD.......... Warszawska Fabryka Dzwigow [*Warsaw Hoisting Machinery Factory*]　(POL)

WFD.......... Woods and Forest Department [*Australia*]　(DSCA)

WFD.......... Woods and Forests Department [*South Australia*]

WFD.......... World Federation of the Deaf [*Rome, Italy*]

WFD.......... Wytwornia Filmow Dokumentalnych [*Documentary Motion Picture Studio*]　(POL)

WFDF....... World Flying Disc Federation　(EAIO)

WFDFI ...... World Federation of Development Financing Institutions [*See also FEMIDE*] [*Madrid, Spain*]　(EAIO)

WFDWRHL ... World Federation of Doctors Who Respect Human Life [*Ostend, Belgium*]　(EAIO)

WFDY .... World Federation of Democratic Youth [*See also FMJD*] [*Budapest, Hungary*]　(EAIO)

WFEO .... World Federation of Engineering Organizations [*Paris, France*]

WFF........... Wytwornia Filmow Fabularnych [*Dramatic Motion Picture Studio*]　(POL)

WFFM....... World Federation of Friends of Museums [*See also FMAM*] [*Paris, France*]　(EAIO)

WFFTH.... World Federation of Workers in Food, Tobacco, and Hotel Industries [*See also FMATH*]　(EAIO)

WFH......... World Federation of Hemophilia [*Montreal, PQ*]　(EA)

WFHFF.... World Federation of Hungarian Freedom Fighters　(EA)

WFI........... Fianarantsoa [*Madagascar*] [*Airport symbol*]　(OAG)

WFI........... Westralian Forest Industries [*Australia*] [*Commercial firm*]

WFI........... World Federation of Investors　(EAIO)

WFICM..... World Federation of International Music Competitions [*Switzerland*]　(EAIO)

WFIM........ World Federation of Islamic Missions [*Karachi, Pakistan*]　(EAIO)

WFIMC..... World Federation of International Music Competitions [*See also FMCIM*]　(EAIO)

WFiPW...... Wychowanie Fizyczne i Przysposobienie Wojskowe [*Physical and Military Training*] [*Poland*]

WFIS .... Wytwornia Filmow Instruktorsko-Szkoleniowych [*Instructional and Educational Motion Picture Studio*]　(POL)

WFIW........ World Federation of Industry Workers [*WCL*]

WFJJ......... World Federation of Jewish Journalists [*Tel Aviv, Israel*]　(EAIO)

WFLRY..... World Federation of Liberal and Radical Youth [*Later, IFLRY*]

WFM .... Warszawska Fabryka Motocykli [*Warsaw Motorcycle Plant*]　(POL)

WFM .... World Federalist Movement [*Netherlands*]　(EAIO)

WFMB....... World Federation of Merino Breeders [*Australia*]

WFME....... World Federation for Medical Education   (EA)

WFMH....... World Federation of Mental Health

WFMLTA ... World Federation of Modern Language Teachers' Association [*Switzerland*]   (SLS)

WFMW ..... World Federation of Methodist Women [*Seoul, Republic of Korea*]   (EAIO)

WFNMB ... World Federation of Nuclear Medicine and Biology   (NUCP)

WFNMW .. World Federation of Trade Unions of Non-Manual Workers [*See also FMTNM*] [*Antwerp, Belguim*]   (EAIO)

WFNS........ World Federation of Neurosurgical Societies [*Nijmegen, Netherlands*]   (EA)

WFO .... Wytwornia Filmow Oswiatowych [*Educational Motion Picture Studio*]   (POL)

WFOiP ...... Wytwornia Filmow Oswiatowych i Przezroczy [*Educational Motion Picture and Filmstrip Studio*]   (POL)

WFOT .... World Federation of Occupational Therapists [*London, ON*]   (EAIO)

WFP........... Warszawska Fabryka Platerow [*Warsaw Flatware Factory*]   (POL)

WFP........... Workers and Farmers Party [*Trinidadian and Tobagan*]   (LA)

WFP........... World Federation of Parasitologists [*Bilthoven, Netherlands*]   (EAIO)

WFP........... World Food Programme [*Rome, Italy*] [*United Nations*]

WFPA........ World Federation for the Protection of Animals [*Switzerland*]   (ASF)

WFPiU ...... Warszawska Fabryka Przyrzadow i Uchwytow [*Warsaw Instrument and Fixture Factory*]   (POL)

WFR .... Weltfriedensrat [*World Peace Council (WPC)*] [*German*]   (EG)

WFRC....... Western Fisheries Research Committee [*Australia*]

WFRS........ World Federation of Rose Societies [*Hurlingham, Argentina*]   (EAIO)

WFS........... Wasserfilterstation [*Water Purification Station*] [*German*]   (EG)

WFS........... Wimmin for Survival [*Australia*]   (EAIO)

WFS........... World Fertility Survey

WFS........... World Food Security [*FAO program*] [*United Nations*]

WFSA........ World Federation of Societies of Anaesthesiologists [*Bristol, England*]   (EAIO)

WFSF .... World Future Studies Federation [*Italian*]   (SLS)

WFSGI ...... World Federation of the Sporting Goods Industry   (EAIO)

WFSICCM ... World Federation of Societies of Intensive and Critical Care Medicine   (EAIO)

WFSNSW ... Wine and Food Society of New South Wales [*Australia*]

WFSW .... World Federation of Scientific Workers [*See also FMTS*] [*ICSU*] [*British*]   (EAIO)

WFTiW ..... Wojewodzki Fundusz Turystyki i Wypoczynku [*Provincial Fund for the Organization of Tourism and Recreation*] [*Poland*]

WFTU .... World Federation of Trade Unions [*See also FSM*] [*Prague, Czechoslovakia*]   (EAIO)

WFTUNMW ... World Federation of Trade Unions of Non-Manual Workers [*Belgium*]   (EY)

WFUCA..... World Federation of UNESCO Clubs and Associations

WFUM ...... Wielkopolska Fabryka Urzadzen Mechanicznych [*Greater Poland (Wielkoposka) Mechanical Equipment Factory*]   (POL)

WFUM ...... Wroclawska Fabryka Urzadzen Mechanicznych [*Wroclaw (Breslau) Mechanical Equipment Factory*]   (POL)

WFUNA .... World Federation of United Nations Associations   (EA)

WFUWO ... World Federation of Ukrainian Women's Organizations [*Toronto, ON*]   (EA)

WFW .... Weltfoederation der Wissenschaftler [*World Federation of Scientists*] [*German*]   (EG)

WFY .... World Federalist Youth [*Netherlands*]

WFY/NIO ... World Federalist Youth - Youth Movement for a New International Order [*Amsterdam, Netherlands*]   (EAIO)

Wg............. Wagen [*Railroad Car*] [*German*]   (EG)

Wg............. Wagenreinigung [*Railroad Car Cleaning Department*] [*German*]   (EG)

wg .... Was Geteken [*Signed*] [*Afrikaans*]

WG............. Wechselgesetz [*Amendment*] [*German*]

wg............. Wedlug [*According To*]   (POL)

WG............. Weinig Gebruiklik [*World Health Organization - WHO*] [*Afrikaans*]

WG............. Wiskundig Genootschap [*Netherlands*]   (SLS)

WG............. Working Group on the Constitution and Electoral Law

WG............. Wydawnictwo Geologiczne [*Geology Publishing House*]   (POL)

WGA......... Wagga Wagga [*Australia*] [*Airport symbol*]   (OAG)

WGB .... Weltgewerkschaftsbund [*World Federation of Trade Unions - WFTU*]   (WEN)

WGB .... Wet Goederenvervoer Binnenscheepvaart [*Benelux*]   (BAS)

WGC......... Wenner-Gren Center Foundation for Scientific Research [*Stockholm, Sweden*]   (SLS)

WGC......... World Games Council   (EAIO)

WGCA .... Winegrape Growers' Council of Australia

WGCC .... World Games Coordination Committee [*Karsruhe, Federal Republic of Germany*]   (EAIO)

WGCLAG ... Working Group of Church Library Associations of Germany   (EAIO)

WGE.......... Walgett [*Australia*] [*Airport symbol*]   (OAG)

W GER ...... West Germany   (WDAA)

WGerm...... Wes-Germaans [*West Germanic*] [*Language, etc.*] [*Afrikaans*]

WGfF .... Westdeutsche Gesellschaft fuer Familienkunde eV   (SLS)

WGH .... Western General Hospital [*Australia*]

WGH .... Wydawnictwo Gorniczo-Hutnicze [*Mining and Metallurgy Publishing House*]   (POL)

WGINC ..... Wine Grape Industry Negotiating Committee [*Victoria, Australia*]

WGK .... Wasser Gefahrdungsklasse [*Water hazard classification*] [*Germany*]

WGL......... Westeuropaeische Gesellschaft fuer Luftfahrtpsychologie [*Western European Association for Aviation Psychology - WEAAP*]   (EA)

WGL......... Wissenschaftliche Gesellschaft fuer Luftschiffahrt [*Scientific Association for Aeronautics*] [*German*]

WGLSI ..... Working Group on Library Systems Interconnection [*Australia*]

Wgm......... Wagenmeister [*Car Master*] [*German*]   (EG)

WGM........ Wirtschaftsverband Grosshandel Metallhalbzeug [*Germany*]   (EAIO)

WGMA ..... Wissenschaftlich-Technische Gesellschaft fuer Mess- und Automatisierungstechnik in der Kammer der Technik   (SLS)

WGMS ...... World Glacier Monitoring Service [*of the International Union of Geodesy and Geophysics*]   (EA)

Wgnr......... Wagennummer [*Railroad Car Number*] [*German*]   (EG)

WGNRR.... Women's Global Network on Reproductive Rights [*Formerly, International Contraception, Abortion, and Sterilisation Campaign*]   (EA)

WGO .... Wereldgesondheidsorganisasie [*World Health Organization - WHO*]

WGOC....... World Government Organization Coalition   (EAIO)

Wgong....... Wollongong [*Australia*]   (ADA)

WGP......... Waingapu [*Indonesia*] [*Airport symbol*]   (OAG)

WGP......... William Grand Prix Racing Ltd. [*Cayman Islands*] [*ICAO designator*]   (FAAC)

WGPTDR ... Danube Tourist Commission [*Formerly, Working Group for the Promotion of Tourism in the Danube Region*] [*Austria*]   (EAIO)

WGRD...... Working Group on Rural Development [*Department of Agriculture*]   (EGAO)

WGRL .... West Gippsland Regional Library Service [*Australia*]

WGSA .... Wiskundigegenootskap van Suider-Afrika [*South Africa*]   (AA)

WGSA .... Working Group on Sustainable Agriculture [*Australia*]

WGWC...... Working Group on Weather Communications [*NATO*]   (NATG)

WGWC...... World Service Authority of the World Government of World Citizens   (EAIO)

WGWP...... Working Group on Weather Plans [*NATO*]   (NATG)

Wh .... Watogodzina [*Watt-Hour*] [*Poland*]

wh............... Watt-Heure [*Watt-Hour*] [*French*]

wh............... Watt-Hora [*Watt-Hour*] [*Portuguese*]

Wh............... Watt-Hora Internacional [*International Watt-Hour*] [*Portuguese*]

WH .... Wuchang University Herbarium [*China*]

WHA .... Women's Hockey Association [*Australia*]

WHA .... Work Health Authority [*Northern Territory, Australia*]

WHA .... World Health Assembly   (ADA)

WHA .... World Heritage Area [*Australia*]

WHAS....... Women's Health Advisory Service [*Australia*]

WHC......... World Hereford Council   (EAIO)

WHC......... World Heritage Committee [*See also CPM*]   (EAIO)

WHCA...... Women's Health Care Association [*Australia*]

WHCH ...... Women's Health Care House [*Australia*]

WHII .... Women's Health in Industry [*Australia*]

WHIRC ..... Women's Health Information Resource Collection [*Australia*]

WHIRCCA ... Womens' Health Information Resource and Crisis Centres Association [*Australia*]

WHK .... Whakatane [*New Zealand*] [*Airport symbol*]   (OAG)

WHL.......... Wissenschaftliche Hauptleitung [*Scientific Main Directorate*] [*German*]   (EG)

WHL.......... World Heritage Listing

WHM .... Wickham [*Australia*] [*Airport symbol*]

WHM .... Wonthaggi Historical Museum [*Australia*]

WHO .... World Health Organization [*The pronunciation "who" is not acceptable*] [*United Nations affiliate Databank originator*] [*Switzerland*]

WHO/EPR ... World Health Organization/Panafrican Centre for Emergency Preparedness and Response [*United Nations*]

WHOLIS... World Health Organization Library Information System   (IID)

WHRAC.... Wool Harvesting Research Advisory Committee [*Australia*]

WHS.......... Waverley Historical Society [*Australia*]

WHS.......... Whalsay [*Shetland Islands*] [*Airport symbol*]   (OAG)

WHS.......... World Health Statistics Data Base [*World Health Organization*] [*Information service or system*]   (IID)

WHT......... Wojewodzka Hurtownia Tekstylna [*Provincial Center for the Wholesale Textile Trade*] [*Poland*]

WHW .... Warszawska Hurtownia Wlokiennicza [*Warsaw Textile Wholesale House*] (POL)

WHWM .... Wojewodzka Hurtownia Wod Mineralnych [*Voivodship Wholesale Mineral Water Warehouse*] (POL)

WHWPNLA ... World Health Workers for Peace and NonIntervention in Latin America (EAIO)

Whz .... Warmwasserheizung [*Warm Water Heating*] [*German*] (EG)

WI .... Rottnest Airbus [*Airline code*] [*Australia*]

WI .... Wes-Indiee [*West Indies*] [*Afrikaans*]

WI .... Wexas International [*Commercial firm*] [*British*] (EAIO)

WI .... Windward Islands (WDAA)

WI .... Winter [*Germany*] [*ICAO aircraft manufacturer identifier*] (ICAO)

WI .... Women's Institute [*Spain*] (EAIO)

WIA .... Waterproofing Industry Association [*Australia*]

WIA .... Windward Islands Airways International NV [*Netherlands*] [*ICAO designator*] (FAAC)

WIA .... Winward Islands Airways International [*Netherlands Antilles*] (EY)

WIA .... Wireless Institute of Australia (ADA)

WIAA .... Sabang [*Indonesia*] [*ICAO location identifier*] (ICLI)

WIAA .... Western India Automobile Association

WIAB .... Banda Aceh/Maimun Saleh [*Indonesia*] [*ICAO location identifier*] (ICLI)

WIACLALS ... West Indian Association for Commonwealth Literature and Language Studies [*Jamaica*] (EAIO)

WIACO ..... World Insulation Acoustics Congress Organization [*Italian*] (SLS)

WIADOK .. Wirtschafts-Archiv mit Dokumentation [*Administration Archive with Documentation*] [*German*]

WIAE .... Warrnambool Institute of Advanced Education [*Australia*] (ADA)

WIAG .... Menggala/Astrakestra [*Indonesia*] [*ICAO location identifier*] (ICLI)

WIAJ .... Semplak/Atang Senjaya [*Indonesia*] [*ICAO location identifier*] (ICLI)

WIAK .... Margahayu/Sulaiman [*Indonesia*] [*ICAO location identifier*] (ICLI)

WIAM ...... Tasikmalaya/Cibeureum [*Indonesia*] [*ICAO location identifier*] (ICLI)

WIAP........ Banyumas/Wirasaba [*Indonesia*] [*ICAO location identifier*] (ICLI)

WIAR .... Madiun/Iswahyudi [*Indonesia*] [*ICAO location identifier*] (ICLI)

WIAS........ Malang/Abdul Rachman Saleh [*Indonesia*] [*ICAO location identifier*] (ICLI)

WIAS........ West Indies Associated States (LA)

WIB .... Waktu Indonesia Barat [*West Indonesia Time*] (IN)

WIB .... Werkgroep Internationale Betrekkingen [*NOBIN/CIIB*]

WIB .... Wine Information Bureau [*Australia*]

WIBB........ Pekanbaru [*Indonesia*] [*ICAO location identifier*] (ICLI)

WIBD .... Dumai/Pinangkampai [*Indonesia*] [*ICAO location identifier*] (ICLI)

WIBP........ Semilinang/Peranap [*Indonesia*] [*ICAO location identifier*] (ICLI)

WIBR........ Sipora/Rokot [*Indonesia*] [*ICAO location identifier*] (ICLI)

WIBS .... Bengkalis/Sungai Pakning [*Indonesia*] [*ICAO location identifier*] (ICLI)

WIBT........ Tanjung Balai/Sungai Bati [*Indonesia*] [*ICAO location identifier*] (ICLI)

WIC .... Wayfarer International Committee [*Axminster, Devonshire, England*] (EAIO)

WIC .... West India Committee [*British*] (EAIO)

WIC .... Women's Issues Coordinator [*Australia*]

WIC .... Workplace Information Centre [*New South Wales, Australia*]

WICBE ...... World Information Centre for Bilingual Education [*See also CMIEB*] [*Paris, France*] (EAIO)

WICE........ World Industry Council for the Environment

WICEM..... World Industry Conference on Environmental Management

wicemin ...... Wiceminister [*Vice-Minister*] [*Poland*]

WICEN...... Wireless Institute Civil Emergency Network [*Australia*]

WICF........ Women's International Cultural Federation [*See also FICF*] (EAIO)

wicht.......... Wichtig [*Important*] [*German*] (GCA)

Wichtigk .... Wichtigkeit [*Importance*] [*German*] (GCA)

WICN .... Women in Chemistry Network [*Australia*]

WICO .... W. I. Carr Sons & Co. Overseas [*Stockbroker*] [*Hong Kong*]

WICSCBS ... West Indies Central Sugar-Cane Breeding Station [*Barbados*] (DSCA)

WID .... Women in Development

WID.......... Women's Interest Division [*Australia*]

Widerstandsfaehigk ... Widerstandsfaehigkeit [*Resistance*] [*German*] (GCA)

WIDF........ Women's International Democratic Federation [*See also FDIF*] [*Berlin, German Democratic Republic*] (EAIO)

Widm .... Widmung [*Dedication Note*] [*Publishing*] [*German*]

Widmg .... Widmung [*Dedication Note*] [*Publishing*] [*German*]

WIE .... Women in Education [*Australia*]

WIEC........ World Institute of Ecology and Cancer [*See also IMEC*] (EAIO)

Wiederbeleb ... Wiederbelebung [*Reactivation*] [*German*] (GCA)

Wiedergewinn ... Wiedergewinnung [*Regeneration*] [*German*] (GCA)

Wiederverdampf ... Wiederverdampfung [*Re-Evaporation*] [*German*] (GCA)

WIF........... Wideroe's Flyveselskap AS [*Norway*] [*ICAO designator*] (FAAC)

WIF........... Worldview International Foundation (EAIO)

WIF........... Worldwide International Foundation [*for video communications*] [*Columbo, Sri Lanka*]

Wi-Fa-Ma ... Widzewska Fabryka Maszyn [*Widzew Machine Factory*] (POL)

WIFO .... Oesterreichisches Institut fuer Wirtschaftsforschung [*Austrian Institute for Economic Research*] (WEN)

WIFOL..... Windward Islands Federation of Labour [*Netherlands Antilles*]

WIFT........ Women in Film and Television, Inc. [*Australia*]

WIG .... West-Indische Gids [*Benelux*] (BAS)

WIG .... Wojskowy Instytut Geograficzny [*Military Geographic Institute*] (POL)

WIGMO.... Western International Ground Maintenance Organization

WIGW .... Weduwen, Wezen, Invaliden en Gepensionneerden (Sociale Zekerheid) [*Benelux*] (BAS)

WIH.......... Wojskowy Instytut Historyczny [*Military Institute of History*] (POL)

WIIA.......... Tangerang/Budiarto [*Indonesia*] [*ICAO location identifier*] (ICLI)

WIIB.......... Bandung/Husein Sastranegara [*Indonesia*] [*ICAO location identifier*] (ICLI)

WIIC.......... Cirebon/Panggung [*Indonesia*].[*ICAO location identifier*] (ICLI)

WIID .... Jakarta/Kemayoran [*Indonesia*] [*ICAO location identifier*] (ICLI)

WIIG .... Jakarta/Pulau Panjang [*Indonesia*] [*ICAO location identifier*] (ICLI)

WIIH .... Jakarta/Halim Perdanakusuma [*Indonesia*] [*ICAO location identifier*] (ICLI)

WIII .... Jakarta/Cengkareng [*Indonesia*] [*ICAO location identifier*] (ICLI)

WIIJ .... Yogyakarta/Adi Sucipto [*Indonesia*] [*ICAO location identifier*] (ICLI)

WIIK.......... Kalijati [*Indonesia*] [*ICAO location identifier*] (ICLI)

WIIL.......... Cilacap/Tunggul Wulung [*Indonesia*] [*ICAO location identifier*] (ICLI)

WIIP.......... Jakarta/Pondok Cabe [*Indonesia*] [*ICAO location identifier*] (ICLI)

WIIP.......... West Indian Independence Party [*Trinidadian and Tobagan*] (LA)

WIIR.......... Pelabuhan Ratu [*Indonesia*] [*ICAO location identifier*] (ICLI)

WIIS .... Semarang/Achmad Yani [*Indonesia*] [*ICAO location identifier*] (ICLI)

WIIST........ Wuhan Information Institute of Science and Technology [*China*] (IRC)

WIIT......... Tanjung Karang/Branti [*Indonesia*] [*ICAO location identifier*] (ICLI)

WIIW........ Wiener Institut fuer Internationale Wirtschaftsvergleiche [*Vienna Institute for Comparative Economic Studies*] [*Information service or system*] (IID)

WIIX.......... Jakarta [*Indonesia*] [*ICAO location identifier*] (ICLI)

WIIZ.......... Jakarta [*Indonesia*] [*ICAO location identifier*] (ICLI)

wijz........... Wijziging of Wijzigt [*Benelux*] (BAS)

WIK .... Waikato Aero Club, Inc. [*New Zealand*] [*ICAO designator*] (FAAC)

WIKB........ Batam/Hang Nadim [*Indonesia*] [*ICAO location identifier*] (ICLI)

WIKD .... Tanjung Pandan/Bulu Tumbang [*Indonesia*] [*ICAO location identifier*] (ICLI)

WIKK .... Pangkal Pinang [*Indonesia*] [*ICAO location identifier*] (ICLI)

WIKN .... Tanjung Pinang/Kijang [*Indonesia*] [*ICAO location identifier*] (ICLI)

WIKS........ Singkep/Dabo [*Indonesia*] [*ICAO location identifier*] (ICLI)

WIL .... Nairobi-Wilson [*Kenya*] [*Airport symbol*] (OAG)

WIL .... Walchandagar Industries Limited [*India*]

WIL .... Wilajah [*Territory, Region*] (IN)

Wildld .... Wildleder [*Chamois Leather*] [*Publishing*] [*German*]

Willk......... Willkuerlich [*Optional*] [*German*]

WILPF....... Women's International League for Peace and Freedom [*Switzerland*] (EAIO)

WILPF/FS ... Women's International League for Peace and Freedom, French Section (EAIO)

Wilts .... Wiltshire (IDIG)

WIM .... German Marine Technical Trade Association (MSC)

WIM .... Wirtschaftsvereininigung Industrielle Meerestechnik [*Industrial Ocean Technology Association*] [*Germany*] (PDAA)

WIM .... Women in Management

WIM .... Women's Institutes of Malaya (ML)

WIMA .... Labuhan Bilik/Ajamu [*Indonesia*] [*ICAO location identifier*] (ICLI)

WIMB .... Gunung Sitoli/Binaka [*Indonesia*] [*ICAO location identifier*] (ICLI)

WIME .... Padang Sidempuan/Aek Godang [*Indonesia*] [*ICAO location identifier*] (ICLI)
WIMG .... Padang/Tabing [*Indonesia*] [*ICAO location identifier*] (ICLI)
WIMK .... Kisaran/Tanah Gambus [*Indonesia*] [*ICAO location identifier*] (ICLI)
WIML .... Kisaran/Aek Loba [*Indonesia*] [*ICAO location identifier*] (ICLI)
WIML .... Wojskowy Instytut Medycyny Lotniczej [*Military Institute of Aviation Medicine*] (POL)
WIMM ...... Medan/Polonia [*Indonesia*] [*ICAO location identifier*] (ICLI)
WIMP........ Prapat/Sibisa [*Indonesia*] [*ICAO location identifier*] (ICLI)
WIMP........ windows, icons, mouse and pull-down menus [*computers*]
WIMR .... Pematang Siantar/Gunung Pamela [*Indonesia*] [*ICAO location identifier*] (ICLI)
WIMS........ Sibolga/Pinang Sori [*Indonesia*] [*ICAO location identifier*] (ICLI)
WIMT .... Tebing Tingci/Pabatu [*Indonesia*] [*ICAO location identifier*] (ICLI)
WIMZ .... Medan Sector [*Indonesia*] [*ICAO location identifier*] (ICLI)
WIN .... Welfare Information Network [*Australia*]
WIN .... Winlink (St. Lucia) Ltd. [*ICAO designator*] (FAAC)
WIN .... Winton [*Australia*] [*Airport symbol*] (OAG)
WIN .... Wiswesser Line Notation [*Information retrieval*]
WiN .... Wolnosc i Niepodleglosc [*Freedom and Independence*] [*Underground political organization*] [*World War II*] (POL)
WIN .... Women in Nigeria [*An association*]
WIN .... Women's Investment Network [*Australia*]
WINAP...... Women's Information Network for Asia and the Pacific [*ESCAP*] [*United Nations*] (DUND)
WINB .... Wojskowy Instytut Naukowo-Badawczy [*Military Scientific Research Institute*] (POL)
WINBAN .. Windward Islands Banana Association (LA)
W IND ...... West Indies (WDAA)
WinddrM ... Winddruckmesser [*Wind-Pressure Gauge*] [*German*] (GCA)
WIND I ..... Windward Islands (WDAA)
WINGS...... Women in Need of Group Support [*Australia*]
Winkelverteil ... Winkelverteilung [*Angular Distribution*] [*German*] (GCA)
WINP .... West Indian National Party [*Trinidadian and Tobagan*] (LA)
WINS........ Wide Information Network Service [*GoldStar Co. Ltd.*] [*South Korea*]
WIO .... Wilcannia [*Australia*] [*Airport symbol*] (OAG)
WIOB .... Bengkayang [*Indonesia*] [*ICAO location identifier*] (ICLI)
WIOC .... West Indies Oil Company (GEA)
WIOG........ Nangapinoh [*Indonesia*] [*ICAO location identifier*] (ICLI)
WIOH........ Paloh/Liku [*Indonesia*] [*ICAO location identifier*] (ICLI)
WIOI .... Singkawang II [*Indonesia*] [*ICAO location identifier*] (ICLI)
WIOK .... Ketapang/Rahadi Usman [*Indonesia*] [*ICAO location identifier*] (ICLI)
WION....... Natuna/Ransi [*Indonesia*] [*ICAO location identifier*] (ICLI)
WIOO........ Pontianak/Supadio [*Indonesia*] [*ICAO location identifier*] (ICLI)
WIOP .... Putusibau/Pangsuma [*Indonesia*] [*ICAO location identifier*] (ICLI)
WIOS .... Sintang/Susilo [*Indonesia*] [*ICAO location identifier*] (ICLI)
WIOZ .... Pontianak Sector [*Indonesia*] [*ICAO location identifier*] (ICLI)
WIP .... Women in Publishing [*Australia*]
WIP .... Women's Issues Plan [*Australia*]
WIP .... Workgroup Indian Project [*Netherlands*]
WIP .... Working Group Indigenous Peoples [*Netherlands*] (EAIO)
WIP .... Works in Process System [*National Library of Australia*]
WIPA........ Jambi/Sultan Taha [*Indonesia*] [*ICAO location identifier*] (ICLI)
WIPC........ Rimbo Bujang [*Indonesia*] [*ICAO location identifier*] (ICLI)
WIPC........ Wool Industry Policy Council [*Australia*]
WIPC........ Writers in Prison Committee of International PEN [*British*] (EAIO)
WIPE........ Tanjung Enim/Bangko [*Indonesia*] [*ICAO location identifier*] (ICLI)
WIPF .... Kuala Tungkal [*Indonesia*] [*ICAO location identifier*] (ICLI)
WIPH .... Sungai Penuh/Depati Parbo [*Indonesia*] [*ICAO location identifier*] (ICLI)
WIPI .... Bungo Tebo/Pasir Mayang [*Indonesia*] [*ICAO location identifier*] (ICLI)
WIPJ .... Jambi/Dusun Aro [*Indonesia*] [*ICAO location identifier*] (ICLI)
WIPL........ Bengkulu/Padang Kemiling [*Indonesia*] [*ICAO location identifier*] (ICLI)
WIPM........ West Indian People's Movement [*Netherlands Antilles*] [*Political party*] (EY)
WIPP .... Palembang/Sultan Mahmud Badaruddin II [*Indonesia*] [*ICAO location identifier*] (ICLI)
WIPQ .... Pendoro [*Indonesia*] [*ICAO location identifier*] (ICLI)
WIPR........ Rengat/Japura [*Indonesia*] [*ICAO location identifier*] (ICLI)
WIPU .... Muko Muko [*Indonesia*] [*ICAO location identifier*] (ICLI)
WIPV .... Keluang [*Indonesia*] [*ICAO location identifier*] (ICLI)
WIPY........ Bentayan [*Indonesia*] [*ICAO location identifier*] (ICLI)
WIPZ........ Palembang Sector [*Indonesia*] [*ICAO location identifier*] (ICLI)

WIR .... Investment Account Act [*Established in 1978*] [*Netherlands*] (IMH)
WiR........... Wynalazczosc i Racjonalizacja [*Inventiveness and Rationalization*] (POL)
WIRA........ Waterfront Industry Reform Authority [*Australia*]
WIRC........ Women's Information and Referral Centre [*Australia*]
WIRE........ Women's Information Referral Exchange [*Australia*]
WIRFMD ... Wellcome Institute for Research into Foot and Mouth Disease [*Nairobi, Kenya*] [*Research center*]
Wirk.......... Wirkung [*Action, Effect*] [*German*]
wirkl.......... Wirklich [*Real, True*] [*German*] (GCA)
Wirks......... Wirksamkeit [*Effectiveness*] [*German*] (GCA)
Wirksamk ... Wirksamkeit [*Effectiveness*] [*German*] (GCA)
WIRS .... Winchmore Irrigation Research Station [*New Zealand*] (DSCA)
WIRTSCH ... Wirtschaft [*Economy, Industry*] [*German*]
wirtsch .... Wirtschaftlich [*Economic*] [*German*] (GCA)
WIS........... Welfare Information Service [*Australia*]
WIS........... Women's Information Switchboard [*Australia*]
WISA .... Water Institute of Southern Africa (AA)
WISA .... West Indies States in Association [*Eastern Caribbean Common Market*] [*St. Lucia*]
WISA .... West Indies Sugar Association [*Later, SAC*]
WISAREP ... Wintershall Saharienne Societe Anonyme pour la Recherche et l'Exploitation Petrolieres
WISE .... Wales, Ireland, Scotland, England [*Migrant Association of Victoria*] [*Australia*]
WISE .... World Information Service on Energy (EA)
WISE .... World Information Systems Exchange
WISENET ... Women in Science Enquiry Network, Inc. [*Australia*]
WISF .... Women in Sport Foundation [*Australia*]
WISH .... Western Institute of Self Help [*Australia*]
wisk........... Wiskunde [*Mathematics*] [*Afrikaans*]
WISMI ...... World Inventory of Sources of Music Information [*Australia*]
Wiss .... Wissenschaft [*Science*] [*German*] (GCA)
wiss .... Wissenschaftlich [*Scientific*] [*German*]
WISS .... World Institute of Sephardic Studies (BJA)
wissenschaftl ... Wissenschaftlich [*Scientific*] [*German*] (GCA)
WIT .... Waktu Indonesia Timur [*East Indonesia Time*] (IN)
WITA........ Tapak Tuan/Teuku Cut Ali [*Indonesia*] [*ICAO location identifier*] (ICLI)
WITA........ Waktu Indonesia Tengah [*Central Indonesia Time*] (IN)
WITC......... Meulaboh/Cut Nyak Dien [*Indonesia*] [*ICAO location identifier*] (ICLI)
WITG .... Sinabang/Lasikin [*Indonesia*] [*ICAO location identifier*] (ICLI)
WITL......... Lhok Sukon [*Indonesia*] [*ICAO location identifier*] (ICLI)
WITM .... Whok Seumawe/Malikus Saleh [*Indonesia*] [*ICAO location identifier*] (ICLI)
WITMA..... Western India Tile Manufacturers Association (PDAA)
WITS......... Seumayam [*Indonesia*] [*ICAO location identifier*] (ICLI)
WITS......... Worldwide Information and Trade System
WITT......... Banda Aceh/Blangbintang [*Indonesia*] [*ICAO location identifier*] (ICLI)
Witt........... Witterung [*Weather*] [*German*] (GCA)
WIU .... Witu [*Papua New Guinea*] [*Airport symbol*] (OAG)
WIU of A ... Workers Industrial Union of Australia (ADA)
WIVR .... West Irian Volunteer Returnees (ML)
WIW .... Wer Informiert Woruber [*Who Advises about What*] [*Gesellschaft fuer Informationsmarkt-Forschung - GIF Detmold, Federal Republic of Germany*] [*Information service or system*] (IID)
WIW .... Weterynaryjny Instytut Wydawniczy [*Veterinary Publishing Institute*] (POL)
WIYS........ World Islamic Youth Seminar (ME)
WIZA .... Workgroup for Indians in South America [*Netherlands*]
WIZO .... Women's International Zionist Organization [*Tel Aviv, Israel*] (EA)
WJA.......... World Jurist Association (EAIO)
WJCB........ World Jersey Cattle Bureau [*Jersey, Channel Islands, England*]
WJD .... Wet op de Justitiele Documentatie en op de Verklaringen Omtrent het Gedrag [*Benelux*] (BAS)
WJFFC....... Worldwide John Fogerty Fanclub (EAIO)
WJG .... Wiener Juristische Gesellschaft [*Austria*] (SLS)
WJR.......... Wajir [*Kenya*] [*Airport symbol*] (OAG)
wk............. Week [*Week*] [*Afrikaans*]
Wk .... Werk [*Work*] [*German*]
WK .... Wetboek van Koophandel [*Commercial Code*] [*Dutch*] (ILCA)
WK .... Wiederholungskurs [*Annual Military Training*] [*Switzerland*]
WK .... Windkurs [*Wind Direction*] [*German*] (GCA)
wk............. Wisselkoers [*Rate of Exchange*] [*Afrikaans*] [*Finance*]
WK .... Wissenschaftliche Konzeptionen [*Scientific Concepts*] (EG)
WK .... Wit Kommando [*White Commando*] [*South Africa*]
WK .... Wydawnictwo Komunikacyjne [*Transportation Publishing House*] (POL)
WKA......... Wiener Katholische Akademie [*Austria*] (SLS)
WKAU...... Wojewodzka Komisja Architektoniczno-Urbanistyczna [*Voivodship Commission on Urban Architecture*] (POL)

WKBA .... Wojewodzka Komisja Brakowania Akt [*Voivodship Commission for the Destruction of Records*] (POL)

Wkb Krb .... Weekberichten van de Kredietbank [*Benelux*] (BAS)

WKC .... Wojewodzka Komisja Cen [*Voivodship Price Commission*] (POL)

WKD .... Warszawskie Koleje Dojazdowe [*Warsaw Suburban Railroads*] (POL)

WKD .... Wyzsza Komisja Dyscyplinarna [*Higher Disciplinary Commission*] (POL)

WKF .... World Karate Federation (OLYM)

WK FJN .... Wojewodzki Komitet Frontu Jednosci Narodu [*National Unity Front Voivodship Committee*] (POL)

WKFN .... Wojewodzki Komitet Frontu Narodowego [*Voivodship Committee of the People's Front*] (POL)

WKJ .... Wakkanai [*Japan*] [*Airport symbol*] (OAG)

WKK .... Wehrkreiskommando [*Army Corps Area Command*] (EG)

WKKF .... Wojewodzki Komitet Kultury Fizycznej [*Voivodship Committee on Physical Culture*] (POL)

WKKFiT .... Wojewodzki Komitet Kultury Fizycznej i Turystyki [*Voivodship Committee on Physical Culture and Tourism*] (POL)

WKKP .... Wojewodzki Komitet Kontroli Partyjnej [*Voivodship Party Control Committee*] (POL)

wkl .... Wklejka [*Insert*] [*Publishing*] [*Poland*]

WKL .... Wojewodzka Komisja Lokalowa [*Provincial Housing Board*] [*Poland*]

WKM .... Hwange National Park [*Zimbabwe*] [*Airport symbol*] (OAG)

Wkmstr ...... Werkmeister [*Foreman*] [*German*] (GCA)

WKN .... Wakunai [*Papua New Guinea*] [*Airport symbol*] (OAG)

WKN .... Wyzsze Kursy Nauczycielskie [*Higher Courses for Teachers*] (POL)

WKO .... Wojewodzka Komisja Organizacyjna [*Voivodship Organization Commission*] (POL)

WKOP .... Wojewodzki Komitet Obroncow Pokoju [*Voivodship Committee of Partisans of Peace*] (POL)

WKOPI ...... Wojewodzka Komisja Oceny Projektow Inwestycyjnych [*Voivodship Commission on the Evaluation of Investment Plans*] (POL)

WKP .... Weibliche Kriminalpolizei [*Women Detectives or Women's Detective Force*] (WEN)

WKP(b) ...... Wszechzwiazkowa Komunistyczna Partia (Bolszewikow) [*All-Union Communist Party (Bolsheviks)*] (POL)

WKPG .... Wojewodzka Komisja Planowania Gospodarczego [*Voivodship Commission on Economic Planning*] (POL)

WKR .... Walker's Cay [*Bahamas*] [*Airport symbol*] (OAG)

WKR .... Wojskowa Komenda Rejonowa [*District Military Headquarters*] (POL)

WKR .... World Koala Research [*Australia*]

WKRC .... World Koala Research Corp. [*Australia*]

WKS .... Warsztat Konstrukcji Stalowych [*Steel Construction Shop*] (POL)

WKS .... Wojskowe Kolo Sportowe [*Military Sports Circle*] (POL)

WKSD .... Wojewodzki Komitet Stronnictwa Demokratycznego [*Voivodship Committee of the Democratic Party*] (POL)

WKTP .... Wyzszy Kurs Techniczno-Pedagogiczny [*Higher Technical and Pedagogical Course*] (POL)

WKUP .... Wojewodzki Komitet Upowszechnienia Plywania [*Voivodship Committee for the Promotion of Swimming*] (POL)

WKW .... Wojewodzki Komitet Warszawski [*Warsaw Voivodship Committee*] (POL)

WKWOM ... Wojewodzki Komitet Wspolpracy Organizacji Mlodziezowych [*Voivodship Committee for the Cooperation of Youth Organizations*] (POL)

WKWPZPR ... Warszawski Komitet Wojewodzki Polskiej Zjednoczonej Partii Robotniczej [*Warsaw Voivodship Committee of the Polish United Workers Party*] (POL)

WKWZMS ... Wojewodzki Komitet Wyborczy Zwiazku Mlodziezy Socjalistycznej [*Voivodship Electoral Committee of the Socialist Youth Union*] (POL)

WKWZSL ... Wojewodzki Komitet Wyborczy Zjednoczonego Stronnictwa Ludowego [*Voivodship Electoral Committee of the United Peasant Party*] (POL)

Wkz .... Werkzeug [*Tool, Implement*] [*German*] (GCA)

WK ZSL .... Wojewodzki Komitet Zjednoczonego Stronnictwa Ludowego [*Provincial Committee of the United Peasants' Party*] [*Poland*]

WKZZ .... Wojewodzki Komitet Zwiazkow Zawodowych [*Voivodship Trade Union Committee*] (POL)

WL .... Wagons-Lits [*Railroad Sleeping or Pullman cars in Europe*] [*French*]

wl .... Wenig Loeslich [*Only Slightly Soluble*] [*German*]

WL .... Westerlengte [*Western Longitude*] [*Afrikaans*]

WL .... Westland Helicopters Ltd. [*British*] [*ICAO aircraft manufacturer identifier*] (ICAO)

WL .... Women's League [*Zambia*] (EAIO)

WL .... Wydawnictwo Literackie [*Literary Publishing House*] (POL)

WLA .... Waterloopkundige Afeling [*Hydraulic Research Division*] [*Ministerie van Openbare Werken, Telecommunicatie en Bownijverheid Suriname*] (EAS)

WLA .... World Literary Academy (EAIO)

WLALW.... World Laboratory Animal Liberation Week

WLANSW ... Women Lawyers' Association of New South Wales [*Australia*]

WLAT .... Women Lawyers' Association of Tasmania [*Australia*]

WLC .... Western Lands Commission [*New South Wales, Australia*]

WLD .... Welsh Liberal Democrats [*Political party*] (EAIO)

WLD .... Women Liberal Democrat [*British*] [*Political party*] (EAIO)

WLF .... Wallis and Futuna [*ANSI three-letter standard code*] (CNC)

WLFD .... World League for Freedom and Democracy [*South Korea*] (EAIO)

WLFPA ..... World League for the Protection of Animals

WLG .... Wellington [*New Zealand*] [*Airport symbol*] (OAG)

WLG .... Witwatersrand Landbougenootskap

WLH .... Walaha [*Vanuatu*] [*Airport symbol*] (OAG)

WLKZM.... Wszechzwiazkowy Leninowski Komunistyczny Zwiazek Mlodziezy [*All-Union Lenin Communist Youth League (Soviet)*] (POL)

WLL .... Women's League of Latvia (EAIO)

WLMR ...... Women's League for Medical Research

wlosl .... Wasserloeslich [*Water-Soluble*] [*German*]

WlPK .... Wloska Partia Komunistyczna [*Italian Communist Party*] (POL)

WLPSA ..... Wildlife Preservation Society of Australia

WLPS ofA ... Wild Life Preservation Society of Australia (SLS)

WLR .... Wallisair Compagnie [*France*] [*ICAO designator*] (FAAC)

WLRA .... World Leisure and Recreation Association [*Formerly, IRA*] (EA)

WLRC........ Women's Legal Resource Centre [*Sydney, New South Wales, Australia*]

WLS .... Wallis Island [*Wallis and Futuna Islands*] [*Airport symbol*] (OAG)

WLSP .... World List of Scientific Periodicals

WLW .... Wet op het Leerlingwezen [*Benelux*] (BAS)

WM .... Focolare Movement [*Italy*] (EAIO)

WM .... Wegmarke [*Trail Marker*] [*German*] (GCA)

WM .... Weiss Manfred Muvek [*Manfred Weiss Factory*] (HU)

WM .... Weissmetall [*White Metal*] [*German*] (GCA)

WM .... Wesleyan Mission [*Australia*]

WM .... West Malaysia (ML)

WM .... Wetenschappelijke Mededeelingen van het Nederlandsch Instituut van Doctorandi in de Handelswetenschap [*Benelux*] (BAS)

WM .... Windward Islands Airways International NV [*Netherlands*] [*ICAO designator*] (ICDA)

WM .... Winkelmesser [*Clinometer*] [*German*] (GCA)

WM .... Work of Mary [*An association*] (EAIO)

WM .... World Markets [*British investment firm*] [*Formerly, Wood Mackenzie*]

WM .... Wydawnictwo Morskie [*Maritime Publishing House*] (POL)

WMA .... Mandritsara [*Madagascar*] [*Airport symbol*] (OAG)

WMA .... Southern African Wildlife Management Association [*Linden, South Africa*] (SLS)

WMA .... Waste Management Association [*Australia*]

WMA .... Waste Management Authority [*New South Wales, Australia*]

WMA .... Wikalat Al-Maghreb Al-Arabi [*News agency*] [*Morocco*] (MENA)

WMA .... World Medical Association [*Ferney-Voltaire, France*]

WMA .... Wortmarke [*German*] (ADPT)

WMAA ...... Bahau [*Malaysia*] [*ICAO location identifier*] (ICLI)

WMAB ...... Batu Pahat [*Malaysia*] [*ICAO location identifier*] (ICLI)

WMAC ...... Benta [*Malaysia*] [*ICAO location identifier*] (ICLI)

WMAD ...... Bentong [*Malaysia*] [*ICAO location identifier*] (ICLI)

WMAE ...... Bidor [*Malaysia*] [*ICAO location identifier*] (ICLI)

WMAG ...... Dungun [*Malaysia*] [*ICAO location identifier*] (ICLI)

WMAH ..... Grik [*Malaysia*] [*ICAO location identifier*] (ICLI)

WMAI .... Gua Musang [*Malaysia*] [*ICAO location identifier*] (ICLI)

WMAJ .... Jendarata [*Malaysia*] [*ICAO location identifier*] (ICLI)

WMAL ...... Kuala Krai [*Malaysia*] [*ICAO location identifier*] (ICLI)

WMAM ..... Langkawi [*Malaysia*] [*ICAO location identifier*] (ICLI)

WMAO ..... Kong Kong [*Malaysia*] [*ICAO location identifier*] (ICLI)

WMAP ...... Kluang [*Malaysia*] [*ICAO location identifier*] (ICLI)

WMAQ ..... Labis [*Malaysia*] [*ICAO location identifier*] (ICLI)

WMARC ... World Maritime Administrative Radio Conference (DS)

WMAT ...... Lima Blas [*Malaysia*] [*ICAO location identifier*] (ICLI)

WMAU ..... Mersing [*Malaysia*] [*ICAO location identifier*] (ICLI)

WMAV ..... Muar [*Malaysia*] [*ICAO location identifier*] (ICLI)

WMAZ ...... Segamat [*Malaysia*] [*ICAO location identifier*] (ICLI)

WMB .... Warrnambool [*Australia*] [*Airport symbol*] (OAG)

WMB .... West Merchant Bank (ECON)

WMBA ...... Sitiawan [*Malaysia*] [*ICAO location identifier*] (ICLI)

WMBB ...... Sungei Patani [*Malaysia*] [*ICAO location identifier*] (ICLI)

WMBDA ... Wholesale Milk Buyers and Distributors' Association [*Australia*]

WMBE ...... Temerloh [*Malaysia*] [*ICAO location identifier*] (ICLI)

WMBF....... Ulu Bernam [*Malaysia*] [*ICAO location identifier*]   (ICLI)
WMBH...... Kroh [*Malaysia*] [*ICAO location identifier*]   (ICLI)
WMBI....... Taiping [*Malaysia*] [*ICAO location identifier*]   (ICLI)
WMBT ...... Pulau Pioman [*Malaysia*] [*ICAO location identifier*]   (ICLI)
WMC......... World Meteorological Center
WMCC ...... Water Management Coordinating Committee [*Australia*]
WMCW ..... World Movement of Christian Workers [*See also MMTC*] [*Brussels, Belgium*]   (EAIO)
WMD........ Mandabe [*Madagascar*] [*Airport symbol*]   (OAG)
WMDB...... Waste Management Database [*IAEA*] [*United Nations*]   (DUND)
WMF......... Wuerttembergische Metallwarenfabrik [*Wuerttemberg Hardware Factory*]
WMFC ...... Kuala Lumpur [*Malaysia*] [*ICAO location identifier*]   (ICLI)
WMFT....... Westdeutscher Medizinischer Fakultaetentag   (SLS)
WMI .... Werkgroep Medische Informatie
WMIU ...... Water and Maritime Industry Union [*Australia*]
WMKA...... Alor Setar/Sultan Abdul Halim [*Malaysia*] [*ICAO location identifier*]   (ICLI)
WMKB ...... Butterworth [*Malaysia*] [*ICAO location identifier*]   (ICLI)
WMKC...... Kota Bahru/Sultan Ismail Petra [*Malaysia*] [*ICAO location identifier*]   (ICLI)
WMKD...... Kuantan [*Malaysia*] [*ICAO location identifier*]   (ICLI)
WMKE ...... Kerteh [*Malaysia*] [*ICAO location identifier*]   (ICLI)
WMKF ...... Simpang [*Malaysia*] [*ICAO location identifier*]   (ICLI)
WMKI .... Ipoh [*Malaysia*] [*ICAO location identifier*]   (ICLI)
WMKJ ...... Johore Bahru [*Malaysia*] [*ICAO location identifier*]   (ICLI)
WMKK ...... Kuala Lumpur/International [*Malaysia*] [*ICAO location identifier*]   (ICLI)
WMKM ...... Malacca [*Malaysia*] [*ICAO location identifier*]   (ICLI)
WMKN...... Kuala Trengganu/Sultan Mahmud [*Malaysia*] [*ICAO location identifier*]   (ICLI)
WMKP ...... Penang [*Malaysia*] [*ICAO location identifier*]   (ICLI)
WMKS ...... Kuala Lumpur [*Malaysia*] [*ICAO location identifier*]   (ICLI)
WMKS ...... Wojewodzki Milicyjny Klub Sportowy [*Voivodship Militia Sport Club*]   (POL)
WML......... Malaimbandy [*Madagascar*] [*Airport symbol*]   (OAG)
WML......... Witwatersrand Medical Library [*South Africa*]   (PDAA)
WMM........ World Movement of Mothers [*See also MMM*] [*Paris, France*]   (EAIO)
WMMS ...... Wesleyan Methodist Missionary Society
WMN .... Maroantsetra [*Madagascar*] [*Airport symbol*]   (OAG)
WMO .... Wet op de Materiele Oorlogsschaden [*Benelux*]   (BAS)
WMO .... World Meteorological Organization [*See also OMM*] [*Geneva, Switzerland*] [*United Nations*]   (EAIO)
WMO .... World Monetary Organization
WMO .... Wytwornia Materialow Ogniotrwalych [*Fireproof Materials Plant*]   (POL)
WMR......... Mananara [*Madagascar*] [*Airport symbol*]   (OAG)
WMR........ Woomera Missile Range [*Australia*]
WMRALC ... Western Metropolitan Regional Aboriginal Land Council [*Sydney, New South Wales, Australia*]
WMS .... Wesleyan Methodist Missionary Society
WMS .... Wesleyan Missionary Society [*Australia*]
WMS .... WMS Airways BV [*Netherlands*] [*ICAO designator*]   (FAAC)
WMS .... Wool Marketing Service [*Australia*]
WMS .... World Magnetic Survey [*ICSU*]
WMSKF .... William Morris Society and Kelmscott Fellowship [*Kelmscott Fellowship and William Morris Society*] [*Formed by a merger of*]   (EAIO)
WMSO ...... World Moslem Solidarity Organisation
WMTA ...... Western Maquiladora Trade Association   (CROSS)
WMU........ Wakaaladda Mooska Ummadda
WMU....... World Maritime University [*Sweden*]   (DCTA)
WMW....... Werkzeugmaschinen und Werkzeuge [*Machine Tools and Tools*] [*German*]   (EG)
WMX........ Wamena [*Indonesia*] [*Airport symbol*]   (OAG)
WN .... Wet op het Nederlanderschap [*Benelux*]   (BAS)
WNA.......... Wa National Army [*Myanmar*] [*Political party*]   (EY)
WNA.......... Warga Negara Asing [*Foreign National*]   (IN)
WNA.......... Wet op het Notarisambt [*Benelux*]   (BAS)
WNBA ...... World Ninepin Bowling Association [*Germany*]   (EAIO)
WNBS .... Western Nigeria Broadcasting Service
WNC......... Wenic Air Services [*Singapore*] [*ICAO designator*]   (FAAC)
WN-CAELA ... Women's Network of the Council for Adult Education in Latin America [*See also RM-CEAAL*] [*Quito, Ecuador*]   (EAIO)
wnd............ Waarnemende [*Acting*] [*Afrikaans*]
WNDC....... Western Nigeria Development Corporation
WNfr......... Wes-Nederfrankies [*West Lower Frankish*] [*Language, etc.*] [*Afrikaans*]
WNG .... Wing Airways (Pty) Ltd. [*South Africa*] [*ICAO designator*]   (FAAC)
WNHC ...... Western Nigeria Housing Corporation
WNI.......... Warga Negara Indonesia [*Indonesian Citizen*]   (IN)
WNI.......... Westinghouse Nuclear International [*Westinghouse Electric SA*] [*Belgium*]   (WND)

WNI........... Windkracht Nederland Information Centre [*Netherlands Wind Energy Information Centre*] [*Nethergy Ltd.*] [*Database producer*]   (IID)
WNIN........ Wszechzwiazkowy Naukowo-Badawczy Instytut Narzedziowy [*All-Union Tool Research Institute*]   (POL)
WNIRO ..... Wszechzwiazkowy Naukowo-Badawczy Instytut Rybolostwa i Oceanografii [*All-Union Fishing and Oceanography Scientific Research Institute*]   (POL)
WNLA .... Witwatersrand Native Labour Association
WNO .... Wa National Organization [*Myanmar*] [*Political party*]   (EY)
WNP.......... Naga [*Phillipines*] [*Airport symbol*]   (OAG)
WNP.......... Westland New Post [*Terrorist organization*] [*Belgium*]   (EY)
WNPA .... Women's Non Party Association [*Australia*]
WNPC .... White Nile Petroleum Company [*Sudan*]
WNPS....... Wildlife and Nature Protection Society of Sri Lanka   (EAIO)
WNR......... Windorah [*Australia*] [*Airport symbol*]   (OAG)
(W) nrze ..... (W) Numerze [(*In) the Number, Issue*]   (POL)
WNS .... Nawab Shah [*Pakistan*] [*Airport symbol*]   (OAG)
WNS .... Worldwide News Service. Jewish Telegraphic Agency   (BJA)
WNT......... Woordeboek van die Nederlandse Taal [*Afrikaans*]
WNT......... Wydawnictwa Naukowo-Techniczne [*Scientific-Technical Publishers*] [*Poland*]
WNTV ...... Western Nigeria Television
WNW........ Ouest Nord Ouest [*West Northwest*] [*French*]   (MTD)
WNW........ Wes-Noordwes [*West Northwest*] [*Afrikaans*]
WNY......... Wynyard [*Australia*] [*Airport symbol*]   (OAG)
wo .... Waaronder [*Among Which*] [*Afrikaans*]
WO .... Wechselordnung [*Law Regarding Bills of Exchange*] [*German*]
wo .... Weiter Oben [*Above*] [*German*]
WO .... Welvaart en Orde [*Benelux*]   (BAS)
WO .... Wet op het Wetenschappelijk Onderwijs [*Benelux*]   (BAS)
wo .... Wie Oben [*As Above*] [*German*]   (GPO)
WO .... Wirtschaftliche Oberschule [*Secondary School for Economics*] [*German*]
WO .... Woensdag [*Wednesday*] [*Afrikaans*]
WOA......... Washington Office on Africa
WOALP..... Work Oriented Adult Literacy Project
WOB......... Wet op het Openbare Bibliotheekwerk
WOB.......... Wet Overheidsaansprakelijkheid Bezettingshandelingen [*Benelux*]   (BAS)
WOBO...... World Organization of Building Officials   (EA)
WOC......... World Oceanographic Center   (MSC)
WOCA...... World Outside the Centrally Planned Economies Area   (PDAA)
WOCC ...... Worldwide Operations Control Center [*United States Information Agency*]
WOCE ...... World Ocean Circulation Experiment [*Australia*]
Woch......... Wochenschrift [*Weekly Publication*] [*German*]   (GCA)
Wochenschr ... Wochenschrift [*Weekly Publication*] [*German*]   (GCA)
WOCM...... Wing On Corporate Management [*Wing On Bank*] [*Hong Kong*]
WOCO...... World Council of Service Clubs [*New Zealand*]   (EAIO)
WOCO...... World Council of Young Men's Service Clubs   (EA)
WODKO ... Wojewodzki Osrodek Doskonalenia Kadr Oswiatowych [*Voivodship Center for the Improvement of Educators*]   (POL)
Wodongal Tertiary Ed ... Wodonga Institute of Tertiary Education [*Australia*]
Woens .... Woensdag [*Wednesday*] [*Afrikaans*]
Woerterb.... Woerterbuch [*Dictionary*] [*German*]   (GCA)
WOFPP ..... Women's Organization for Political Prisoners [*Israel*]   (EAIO)
WOG .... Large Economic Organization [*Poland*]   (IMH)
WOG .... World Organization of Gastroenterology [*See also OMGE*] [*Edinburgh, Scotland*]   (EAIO)
WOGSC .... World Organisation of General Systems and Cybernetics [*Lytham St. Annes, Lancashire, England*]   (EAIO)
wohlf .... Wohlfeil [*Cheap*] [*German*]
Wohlg .... Title of Respect [*Correspondence*] [*German*]
Woj............ Wojewodztwo [*Voivodship*]   (POL)
WOJD....... World Organization of Jewish Deaf [*Tel Aviv, Israel*]   (EAIO)
WOK......... Kovar Air [*Czechoslovakia*] [*ICAO designator*]   (FAAC)
WOK........ Wonken [*Venezuela*] [*Airport symbol*]   (OAG)
WOKF ...... Wojewodzki Osrodek Kultury Fizycznej [*Voivodship Center for Physical Culture*]   (POL)
WOKS ...... Wszechzwiazkowe Towarzystwo Lacznosci Kulturalnej z Zagranica (Soviet organization with Polish branch; Russian form: Wsiesojuznoje Obszczestwo Kulturnoj Swiazi) [*All-Union Society for Cultural Relations with Foreign Countries*]   (POL)
WOL.......... Wissenschaftlichoekonomische Leitung [*Scientific-Economic Management*]   (EG)
WOL......... Wollongong [*Australia*] [*Airport symbol*]   (OAG)
WOLA .... Washington Office on Latin America   (LA)
WOM .... Woomera [*Australia*]   (BARN)
WON .... Waiver of Notice [*Business term*]   (MHDW)
WON .... Werkgroep Octrooi-Informatie Nederland

WONCA.... World Organization of National Colleges, Academies, and Academic Associations of General Practitioners/Family Physicians [Australia]   (EAIO)
WOO .... Werke ohne Opuszahl [Works without Opus Number] [Music]
WOO .... Wojewodzki Osrodek Onkologiczny [Voivodship Oncological Center]   (POL)
WOOFEL ... Woodly-Fernly Librarians Group [Australia]
WOP.......... Waiver of Premium [Insurance]   (MHDW)
WOP.......... Wojska Ochrony Pogranicza [Frontier Guard]   (POL)
WOPK....... Wojska Obrony Powietrznej Kraju [Home Air Defense Forces] (POL)
WOPM...... Warszawskie Okregowe Przedsiebiorstwo Miernicze [Warsaw District Surveying Enterprise]   (POL)
WOPP .... Wojewodzki Osrodek Propagandy Partyjnej [Voivodship Party Propaganda Center]   (POL)
WOPR....... Wodne Ochotnicze Pogotowie Ratunkowe [Volunteer Life-Savers' Association] [Poland]
WORK....... WORKLIT Database [Australia]
WORLDDIDAC ... World Association of Manufacturers and Distributors of Educational Materials   (EAIO)
WORLDSMART ... World Sports Medicine Association of Registered Therapists
wortl .... Woertlich [German]
WOS.......... Wholly-Owned Subsidiary [Business term]   (MHDW)
WOS.......... Wiedza o Sztuce [Art Study (A publishing house)]   (POL)
WOSA .... Workers' Organization for Socialist Action [South Africa] [Political party]   (EY)
WOSAPCON ... World Safety and Accident Prevention Congress   (PDAA)
WOSC .... World Organisation of Systems and Cybernetics   (EAIO)
WOSL........ Wyzsza Oficerska Szkola Lotnicza (Deblin) [Higher Air Force Officers School (Deblin)]   (POL)
WOSPR..... Wielka Orkiestra Symfoniczna Polskiego Radia [Great Symphony Orchestra of the Polish Radio]   (POL)
WOSS........ Wojewodzki Osrodek Szkolenia Sportowego [Voivodship Sports Training Center]   (POL)
WOSTiW .. Wojewodzki Osrodek Sportu, Turystyki, i Wypoczynku [Voivodship Sports, Touring, and Rest Center]   (POL)
WOTP .... World Organization of the Teaching Professions [Switzerland]
WOTRO.... Stichting voor Wetenschappelijk Onderzoek van de Tropen [s-Gravenhage, Netherlands]   (SLS)
WOV.......... Wet Overlijdensakten Vermiste Personen [Benelux]   (BAS)
WOW .... Walk Off Weight Club [Australia]
WOW .... Warszawski Okreg Wojskowy [Warsaw Military District]   (POL)
WOW .... Wederopbouwwet [Benelux]   (BAS)
WOW .... Work Opportunities for Women [Australia]
WOWSER ... We Only Want Social Evils Righted [Said to be the translation for an Australian acronym describing a prudish reformer]
WOZA .... Warszawski Okregowy Zwiazek Atletyczny [Warsaw District Athletic Union]   (POL)
WP............. Warsaw Pact Member   (WDAA)
WP............. Westelike Provinsie [Western Province] [Afrikaans]
WP............. Wiedza Powszechna Panstwowe Wydawnictwo Popularno-Naukowe ["Popular Science" (A publishing house)]   (POL)
WP............. Wirtschaftpatent [Industrial Patent]   (EG)
WP............. Wirui Press [Papua New Guinea]
WP............. Wojsko Polskie [Polish Army]   (POL)
WP............. Women for Peace [Switzerland]   (EAIO)
WP............. Workers' Party [Singapore]   (ML)
WP............. Worker's Party [Ireland] [Political party]
WP3........... Working Party Three [Economic Policy Committee of the Organization for Economic Cooperation and Development]
WPA .... Western Pacific Airservice [Solomon Islands] [ICAO designator]   (FAAC)
WPA .... Women's Peace Army [Australia]
WPA .... Working Party on Aquaculture [Australia]
WPA .... Working People's Alliance [Guyana]   (PD)
WPA .... World Pheasant Association [Reading, Berkshire, England]   (EAIO)
WPA .... World Psychiatric Association [Copenhagen, Denmark]   (EAIO)
WPA .... Wroclawskie Przedsiebiorstwo Aptek [Wroclaw (Breslau) Pharmacy Enterprise]   (POL)
WPAG ...... Women in Pharmacy Action Group [Australia]
WPAH....... Working Party on Aboriginal Health [Australia]
WPAT....... Atauro [East Timor] [ICAO location identifier]   (ICLI)
WPAU .... West Pakistan Agricultural University   (DSCA)
WPB .... Port Berge [Madagascar] [Airport symbol]   (OAG)
WPB .... Warszawskie Przedsiebiorstwo Budowlane [Warsaw Construction Enterprise]   (POL)
WPB .... Wojskowe Przedsiebiorstwo Budowlane [Military Construction Enterprise]   (POL)
WPB .... Working Party on Bibliography [Australian Advisory Council on Bibliographical Services]
WPC .... Western Pacific Communications [Australia]
WPC .... William Paterson College [Wayne, NJ]
WPC .... World Peace Council [See also CMP]   (EAIO)
WPC .... World Petroleum Congresses - a Forum for Petroleum Science, Technology, Economics, and Management   (EAIO)

WPC .... World Power Conference [Later, WEC]
WPCO ...... Water Pollution Control Ordnance [Hong Kong]
WPD .... Wheat Project Directorate [India] [Research center]   (IRC)
WPDA ...... Water and Power Development Authority [Pakistan]   (GEA)
WPDB ...... Suai [East Timor] [ICAO location identifier]   (ICLI)
W/PDC ..... Workers'/People's Defence Committee [Ghana] [Political party]
WPDL........ Dili [East Timor] [ICAO location identifier]   (ICLI)
WPE .... Workers' Party of Ethiopia
WPEC .... Baucau [East Timor] [ICAO location identifier]   (ICLI)
WPFA .... Working Party on Feral Animals [Australia]
WPFL .... Fuiloro [East Timor] [ICAO location identifier]   (ICLI)
WPG .... Workplace Group [Australia]
WPGWU ... Western Province General Workers' Union
WPH.......... Wojskowe Przedsiebiorstwo Handlowe [Military Trade Enterprise]   (POL)
WPH.......... Wojskowy Pawilon Handlowy [Military Commercial Point] (POL)
WPHAGD ... Wojewodzkie Przedsiebiorstwo Hurtu Artykulami Gospodarstwa Domowego [Voivodship Wholesale Household Goods Enterprise]   (POL)
WPHAP ..... Wojewodzkie Przedsiebiorstwo Handlu Artykulami Papierniczymi [Voivodship Paper Product Trade Enterprise]   (POL)
WPHC .... Western Pacific High Commission   (FEA)
WPHO .... Wojewodzkie Przedsiebiorstwo Handlu Obuwiem [Voivodship Footwear Trade Enterprise]   (POL)
WPHO .... Wojewodzkie Przedsiebiorstwo Handlu Odzieza [Voivodship Garment Trade Enterprise]   (POL)
WPHR .... Wojewodzkie Przedsiebiorstwo Handlu Rybnego [Voivodship Fish Sales Enterprise]   (POL)
WPHS .... Wojewodzkie Przedsiebiorstwo Hurtu Spozywczego [Voivodship Wholesale Food Enterprise]   (POL)
WPI .... Wojewodzkie Przedsiebiorstwo Instalacyjne [Voivodship Installation Enterprise]   (POL)
WPI .... World Patents Index
WPIR........ Working Party on Information Resources [Australian Advisory Council on Bibliographical Services]
WPJ........... Workers' Party of Jamaica [Political party]   (EY)
WPK .... Wet Premie Kerkenbouw [Benelux]   (BAS)
WPK .... Wojewodzkie Przedsiebiorstwo Komunikacyjne [Voivodship Transportation Enterprise]   (POL)
WPKC........ Wydzial Propagandy Komitetu Centralnego [Propaganda Department of the Central Committee]   (POL)
WPKGG .... Wojewodzkie Przedsiebiorstwo Komunikacyjne Gdansk-Gdynia [Voivodship Transportation Enterprise for Gdansk (Danzig) and Gdynia]   (POL)
WPKiW ..... Wojewodzki Park Kultury i Wypoczynku (Katowice) [Voivodship Culture and Rest Park (Katowice)]   (POL)
WPL........... Aeronaves del Peru SA [ICAO designator]   (FAAC)
WPLA .... West Pakistan Library Association   (PDAA)
WPLiS ...... Wydawnictwo Przemyslu Lekkiego i Skorzanego [Publishing House for Light Industry and Leather Industry]   (POL)
WPLiS ...... Wydawnictwo Przemyslu Lekkiego i Spozywczego [Publishing House for Light Industry and Food Industry]   (POL)
WPM .... Werkstoffpruefmaschinen, Leipzig (VEB) [Leipzig Enterprise for the Construction of Materials-Testing Machines (VEB)] (EG)
WPM .... Wipim [Papua New Guinea] [Airport symbol]   (OAG)
WPM .... Woorde per Minuut [Words per Minute] [Afrikaans]
WPMN ...... Maliana [East Timor] [ICAO location identifier]   (ICLI)
WPMuvek ... Wilhelm Pieck Muvek, Gyor [Wilhelm Pieck Factory in Gyor] (HU)
WPNR .... Weekblad voor Privaatrecht, Notarisambt en Registratie [Netherlands]   (FLAF)
WPO .... Women's Progressive Organization [Guyana]   (LA)
WPO .... World Packaging Organization [See also OME] [Paris, France] (EAIO)
WPO .... World Ploughing Organisation [Carlisle, Cumbria, England] (EAIO)
WPOA ...... Western Pacific Orthopaedic Association   (EA)
WPOC ...... Oecussi [East Timor] [ICAO location identifier]   (ICLI)
WPoCC...... ICA [International Co-Operative Alliance] Working Party on Co-Operative Communications   (EAIO)
WPoCP...... ICA [International Co-Operative Alliance] Working Party on Co-Operative Press [Later, WPoCC]   (EAIO)
WPP.......... Wegierska Partia Pracujacych [Hungarian Worker's Party] (POL)
WPP.......... Women and Pharmaceuticals Project [Netherlands]   (EAIO)
WPP.......... Working People's Party [St. Vincentian]   (LA)
WPR .... West Pakistan Railway
W Pr.......... Wydawnictwo Prawnicze [Law Publishing House]   (POL)
WPRD .... Warszawskie Przedsiebiorstwo Robot Drogowych [Warsaw Road Construction Enterprise]   (POL)
WPRD .... Working Party on Research and Development [Australian Advisory Council on Bibliographical Services]
WPRF........ Workers and Peasants Revolutionary Front   (ML)
WPRG .... Workers-Peasants Red Guards [North Korea]

WPS...........	Wellenpferdestaerke [*Brake Horse Power*]　(EG)
WPS...........	Wloska Partia Socjalistyczna [*Italian Socialist Party*] [*Poland*]
WPS...........	Women's Peace Army [*Australia*]
WPSA........	Wildlife Preservation Society of Australia　(ADA)
WPSA........	Women's Pioneer Society (Australasia)　(ADA)
WPSA........	World's Poultry Science Association [*See also AVI*] [*Celle, Federal Republic of Germany*]　(EAIO)
WPSC........	Working Party on Systems and Communications [*Australian Advisory Council on Bibliographical Services*]
WPSI.........	World Poetry Society Intercontinental　(EA)
WPSM.......	Same [*East Timor*] [*ICAO location identifier*]　(ICLI)
WPSQ........	Wildlife Preservation Society of Queensland [*Brisbane, Australia*]　(SLS)
WPSRF......	Western Province Servicemen's Rehabilitation Fund [*South Africa*]　(AA)
WPT..........	Windfall Profits Tax [*USA*]　(OMWE)
WPU..........	Wereldposunie [*Universal Postal Union - UPU*] [*Afrikaans*]
WPUN.......	Working Party on User Needs [*Australian Advisory Council on Bibliographical Services*]
WPV..........	Weltpostverein [*Postal Union*] [*German*]
WPVP........	Working People's Vanguard Party [*Guyana*]　(LA)
WPVQ.......	Viqueque [*East Timor*] [*ICAO location identifier*]　(ICLI)
WPY..........	World Population Year [*1974*] [*United Nations*]
WPZ..........	Western Plains Zoo [*Dubbo, New South Wales, Australia*]
WPZB........	Warszawskie Przemyslowe Zjednoczenie Budowlane [*Warsaw Industrial Construction Association*]　(POL)
WPZB........	Wroclawskie Przemyslowe Zjednoczenie Budowlane [*Wroclaw (Breslau) Industrial Construction Association*]　(POL)
WR.............	Wagenruecklauf [*German*]　(ADPT)
WR.............	Wagons-Restaurants [*Railroad dining cars in Europe*] [*French*]
WR.............	Werkrechtersraad [*Benelux*]　(BAS)
Wr.............	Wiener [*Viennese*] [*German*]
WR.............	Wissenschaftsrat [*Science Council*] [*Germany*]
WR.............	Wolseley Register　(EA)
WR.............	Wszechnica Radiowa [*Lecture Courses Given by Radio*]　(POL)
WRA..........	Wool Research Association [*India*]　(PDAA)
WRA..........	World Road Association [*Finland*]　(EAIO)
WRAAC....	Women's Royal Australian Army Corps　(ADA)
WRAAF....	Women's Royal Australian Air Force　(ADA)
WRAANC...	Women's Royal Australian Army Nursing Corps
WRAB.......	West Rand Administration Board [*South Africa*]　(AF)
WRAC.......	Water and Resources Advisory Committee [*Australian Environment Council*]
WRANS....	Women's Royal Australian Naval Service
WRAWG...	Water Resource Assessment Working Group [*Australia*]
WRBB........	Banjarmasin/Syamsuddin Noor [*Indonesia*] [*ICAO location identifier*]　(ICLI)
WRBC.......	Batu Licin [*Indonesia*] [*ICAO location identifier*]　(ICLI)
Wr Ber......	Werkrechtersraad in Beroep [*Benelux*]　(BAS)
WRBI.........	Pangkalan Bun/Iskandar [*Indonesia*] [*ICAO location identifier*]　(ICLI)
WRBK.......	Kotabaru/Setagen [*Indonesia*] [*ICAO location identifier*]　(ICLI)
WRBM......	Muaratewe/Beringin [*Indonesia*] [*ICAO location identifier*]　(ICLI)
WRBN.......	Tanjung/Warukin [*Indonesia*] [*ICAO location identifier*]　(ICLI)
WRBP........	Palangkaraya/Panarung [*Indonesia*] [*ICAO location identifier*]　(ICLI)
WRBS........	Sampit/H. Hasan [*Indonesia*] [*ICAO location identifier*]　(ICLI)
WRBT.......	Teluk Kepayang [*Indonesia*] [*ICAO location identifier*]　(ICLI)
WRBU.......	Buntok/Sanggau [*Indonesia*] [*ICAO location identifier*]　(ICLI)
WRBZ........	Banjarmasin Sector [*Indonesia*] [*ICAO location identifier*]　(ICLI)
WRC..........	Water Research Commission [*South Africa*]　(AA)
WRC..........	Welfare Rights Centre [*Australia*]
WRC..........	Whale Rescue Centre [*Australia*]
WRC..........	Wheat Research Council [*Australia*]
WRC..........	Wollongong Workers Research Centre [*Australia*]
WRC..........	Woodchip Research Committee [*Australia*]
WRC..........	Wool Realisation Commission [*Australia*]
WRC..........	Workers Revolutionary Council [*Trinidadian and Tobagan*]　(LA)
WRC..........	Workplace Rehabilitation Coordinator [*Australia*]
WRC..........	Workplace Resource Centre [*Australia*]
WRC..........	W. R. Carpenter Airlines [*Australia*]
WRCA.......	W. R. Carpenter Airlines [*Australia*]
WRCC.......	Wildlife Research Coordinating Committee
WRCC.......	Workers' Rehabilitation and Compensation Corp. [*South Australia*]
WRCNSW...	Wheat Research Committee for New South Wales [*Australia*]
WRCQ.......	Wheat Research Committee for Queensland [*Australia*]
WRCSA.....	Wheat Research Committee for South Australia
WRCV.......	Wheat Research Committee for Victoria [*Australia*]
WRCWA...	Wheat Research Committee for Western Australia
WRD..........	Water Resources Development
WRD..........	Wietnamska Republika Demokratyczna [*Vietnam Democratic Republic*]　(POL)

WRDC.......	Wool Research and Development Council [*Australia*]
WRE..........	Whangarei [*New Zealand*] [*Airport symbol*]　(OAG)
WRECISS...	Weapons Research Establishment Camera, Instrumentation, Single Shot [*Australia*]　(PDAA)
WREDS.....	Western Region Ethnic Disability Service [*Victoria, Australia*]
WREMARC...	Weapons Research Establishment Missile Attitude Recording Camera [*Australia*]
WREROC...	Weapons Research Establishment Roll Orientation Camera [*Australia*]
WRESAT..	Weapons Research Establishment Satellite [*Australia*]
WRESLAC...	Weapons Research Establishment Sight Line Angle Camera [*Australia*]
WRETAR...	Weapons Research Establishment Target Aircraft Recorder Camera [*Australia*]
WRF..........	Wheat Ridge Foundation
WRFA.......	Water Research Foundation of Australia　(ADA)
WRGO.......	Warrego [*Botanical region*] [*Australia*]
WRHS.......	West of the Ranges Historical Society [*New South Wales, Australia*]
WRI..........	War Resisters International [*British*]
WRI..........	Welding Research Institute [*India*] [*Research center*]　(IRC)
WRI..........	Work Research Institute [*Norway*]　(IRC)
WRIA........	Worked Republic of India Award [*Amateur radio*]　(IAA)
WRil..........	Wydzial Rolnictwa i Lesnictwa [*Agriculture and Forestry Section*]　(POL)
WRIST......	Women's Repetition Injury Support Team [*Australia*]
WRK..........	Westdeutsche Rektorenkonferenz [*West German Standing Committee of University Heads*]
WRKA.......	Atambua/Haliwen [*Indonesia*] [*ICAO location identifier*]　(ICLI)
WRKB.......	Bajawa/Padhameleda [*Indonesia*] [*ICAO location identifier*]　(ICLI)
WRKC.......	Maumere/Wai Oti [*Indonesia*] [*ICAO location identifier*]　(ICLI)
WRKE.......	Ende/Ipi [*Indonesia*] [*ICAO location identifier*]　(ICLI)
WRKF.......	Maskolen [*Indonesia*] [*ICAO location identifier*]　(ICLI)
WRKG.......	Ruteng/Satartacik [*Indonesia*] [*ICAO location identifier*]　(ICLI)
Wrkg.........	Wirkung [*Action, Effect*] [*German*]
Wrkg-Weise...	Wirkungs-Weise [*Mode of Action*] [*German*]　(GCA)
WRKI........	Mbai [*Indonesia*] [*ICAO location identifier*]　(ICLI)
WRKJ........	Mena [*Indonesia*] [*ICAO location identifier*]　(ICLI)
WRKK.......	Kupang/Eltari [*Indonesia*] [*ICAO location identifier*]　(ICLI)
WRKL........	Larantuka/Gewayentana [*Indonesia*] [*ICAO location identifier*]　(ICLI)
WRKM......	Kalabahi/Mali [*Indonesia*] [*ICAO location identifier*]　(ICLI)
WRKN......	Naikliu [*Indonesia*] [*ICAO location identifier*]　(ICLI)
WRKR.......	Rote/Lekunik [*Indonesia*] [*ICAO location identifier*]　(ICLI)
WRKS........	Sabu/Tardanu [*Indonesia*] [*ICAO location identifier*]　(ICLI)
WRKZ.......	Kupang Sector [*Indonesia*] [*ICAO location identifier*]　(ICLI)
WRL..........	Wagenruecklauf [*German*]　(ADPT)
WRL..........	Wegierska Republika Ludowa [*Hungarian People's Republic*]　(POL)
WRLA........	Sangata [*Indonesia*] [*ICAO location identifier*]　(ICLI)
WRLB........	Long Bawan/Juvai Semaring [*Indonesia*] [*ICAO location identifier*]　(ICLI)
WRLC........	Bontang [*Indonesia*] [*ICAO location identifier*]　(ICLI)
WRLD........	Batu Putih/Talisayam [*Indonesia*] [*ICAO location identifier*]　(ICLI)
WRLG.......	Tanjung Selor/Tanjung Harapan [*Indonesia*] [*ICAO location identifier*]　(ICLI)
WRLH.......	Tanah Grogot [*Indonesia*] [*ICAO location identifier*]　(ICLI)
WRLI.........	Tiong Chong [*Indonesia*] [*ICAO location identifier*]　(ICLI)
WRLK........	Tanjung Redep/Kalimarau [*Indonesia*] [*ICAO location identifier*]　(ICLI)
WRLL........	Balikpapan/Sepinggan [*Indonesia*] [*ICAO location identifier*]　(ICLI)
WRLM......	Malinau [*Indonesia*] [*ICAO location identifier*]　(ICLI)
WRLN......	Long Mawang [*Indonesia*] [*ICAO location identifier*]　(ICLI)
WRLO.......	Ongko Asa [*Indonesia*] [*ICAO location identifier*]　(ICLI)
WRLR.......	Taraken [*Indonesia*] [*ICAO location identifier*]　(ICLI)
WRLS........	Samarinda/Temindung [*Indonesia*] [*ICAO location identifier*]　(ICLI)
WRLT.......	Tanjung Santan [*Indonesia*] [*ICAO location identifier*]　(ICLI)
WRLU.......	Sangkulirang [*Indonesia*] [*ICAO location identifier*]　(ICLI)
WRLW......	Muara Wahau [*Indonesia*] [*ICAO location identifier*]　(ICLI)
WRM..........	White Resistance Movement [*Namibia*]　(AF)
WRM..........	World Rainforest Movement [*Penang, Malaysia*]　(EAIO)
WRMAC...	Water Resources Management Advisory Committee [*Australia*]
WRMF......	World Radio Missionary Fellowship
WRN..........	Wojewodzka Rada Narodowa [*Voivodship People's Council*]　(POL)
WRN..........	Wolnosc, Rownosc, Niepodleglosc [*Freedom, Equality, Independence*] [*Underground political organization*] [*World War II*]　(POL)
WRNWS...	World-Wide Radio Navigation Warning System　(MSC)
WRO..........	Wet op de Ruimtelijke Ordening [*Benelux*]　(BAS)
WRO..........	Wroclaw [*Poland*] [*Airport symbol*]　(OAG)
WRON.......	Military Council of National Salvation [*Poland*]　(EE)

WRONA.... Wojskowa Rada Ocalenia Nardowego [*Military Council for the Safety of the Nation*] [*Polish word "wrona" means "black crow"*]

WRONZ.... Wool Research Organization of New Zealand

WRONZ.... Wool Research Organization of New Zealand, Inc.   (ARC)

WRP .... Worker's Revolutionary Party [*Trinidadian and Tobagan*]   (LA)

WRPDB.... Western Regional Production Development Board

WRR .... Wetenschappelijke Raad voor het Regeringsbeleid [*'s-Gravenhage*]

WRR .... Wildlife Ranching and Research [*Kenya*]   (EAIO)

WRRA .... Mataram/Selaparang [*Indonesia*] [*ICAO location identifier*]   (ICLI)

WRRB .... Bima/Palibelo [*Indonesia*] [*ICAO location identifier*]   (ICLI)

WRRC .... Water Resources Research Centre [*Pakistan*] [*Research center*]   (IRC)

WRRN .... Women's Refuge Referral Network [*Australia*]

WRRR .... Bali International/Ngurah Rai [*Indonesia*] [*ICAO location identifier*]   (ICLI)

WRRS....... Sumbawa/Sumbawa Besar [*Indonesia*] [*ICAO location identifier*]   (ICLI)

WRRS....... Western Port Resource Sharing Committee [*Library cooperative*] [*Australia*]

WRRT .... Waikabubak/Tambolaka [*Indonesia*] [*ICAO location identifier*]   (ICLI)

WRRW ...... Waingapu/Mau Hau [*Indonesia*] [*ICAO location identifier*]   (ICLI)

WRRZ .... Bali [*Indonesia*] [*ICAO location identifier*]   (ICLI)

WRS .... Western Pacific Railroad Co.   (MHDW)

WRSA....... World Rabbit Science Association [*Cheltenham, Gloucestershire, England*]   (EAIO)

WRSC....... Cepu/Ngloram [*Indonesia*] [*ICAO location identifier*]   (ICLI)

WRSJ .... Surabaya/Juanda [*Indonesia*] [*ICAO location identifier*]   (ICLI)

WRSM ..... Women's Revolutionary Socialist Movement [*Guyana*]   (LA)

WRSnS ...... Wojewodzka Rada Szefostw nad Szkolami [*Voivodship School Guardianship Council*]   (POL)

WRSP........ Surabaya/Perak [*Indonesia*] [*ICAO location identifier*]   (ICLI)

WRSQ .... Solo/Adi Sumarmo Wiryokusumo [*Indonesia*] [*ICAO location identifier*]   (ICLI)

WRSS........ Surabaya/Gedangan [*Indonesia*] [*ICAO location identifier*]   (ICLI)

WRST........ Sumenep/Trunojoyo [*Indonesia*] [*ICAO location identifier*]   (ICLI)

WRSV....... Werkers Rechtspraak Sociale Verzekering [*Benelux*]   (BAS)

WRTF....... Wool Research Trust Fund [*Australia*]   (ADA)

WRU.......... Wheat Research Unit [*Australia*]

WRVM ...... Werkgroep Rechten voor Minderheden [*Belgium-Flemish Minority Rights Group*]   (EAIO)

WR/ZL...... Wagenruecklauf/Zeilenviorschub [*German*]   (ADPT)

WRZZ .... Warszawska Rada Zwiazkow Zawodowych [*Warsaw Trade-Union Council*]   (POL)

WRZZ .... Wczasy Robotnicze Zwiazkow Zawodowych [*Trade-Union Workers' Vacations*]   (POL)

WRZZ .... Wojewodzka Rada Zwiazkow Zawodozych [*Voivodship Council of Trade-Unions*]   (POL)

WS .... Wadley Southern [*Railroad*]   (MHDW)

WS .... Wash Sale   (MHDW)

WS .... Wassersaeule [*Water Column, Water Pressure*] [*German*]   (EG)

WS .... Watt-Segundo [*Watt Second*] [*Portuguese*]

Ws.............. Watt-Segundo Internacional [*International Watt Second*] [*Portuguese*]

WS .... Wechselstrom [*Alternating Current*] [*German*]   (GCA)

WS .... Wes-Sentraal [*West Central*] [*Afrikaans*]

WS .... Western Samoa [*ANSI two-letter standard code*]   (CNC)

WS .... White Squire   (MHDW)

WS .... Wintersemester [*Winter Term*] [*German*]   (EG)

WS .... Wisselstroom [*Alternating Current*] [*Afrikaans*]

WS .... Women's Shelter [*Australia*]

WS .... Woomera Space Centre [*Australia*]

WS .... Work Study [*Royal Australian Navy*]

WS .... World Solidarity [*Belgium*]   (EAIO)

WSA .... Wasserstrassenamt [*Waterways Office*]   (EG)

WSA .... Water Sports Australia

WSA .... Wedgwood Society of Australia

WSA .... Women's Sports Association [*Australia*]

WSA .... Work Skill Australia

WSA .... World Service Authority, District 5: Orient-Mediterranean Sea Coast [*Israel*]   (EAIO)

WSA .... Wyzsza Szkola Artylerii [*Higher School of Artillery*]   (POL)

WSAAS..... Western Sydney Area Assistance Scheme [*Australia*]

WSAG .... Sembawang [*Singapore*] [*ICAO location identifier*]   (ICLI)

W SAM..... Western Samoa   (WDAA)

WSAP....... Paya Lebar [*Singapore*] [*ICAO location identifier*]   (ICLI)

WSAP....... Women's South African Party

WSAR....... Singapore [*Singapore*] [*ICAO location identifier*]   (ICLI)

WSAS....... Wollongong Special Assistance Scheme [*Australia*]

WSAT........ Tengah [*Singapore*] [*ICAO location identifier*]   (ICLI)

WSAVA..... World Small Animal Veterinary Association [*See also AMVPA*] [*Hatfield, Hertfordshire, England*]   (EAIO)

WSB.......... Wetenschappelijke en Speciale Bibliotheken

WSB.......... World Scout Bureau [*Geneva, Switzerland*]   (EA)

WSBDF ..... Western Sydney Business Development Fund [*Australia*]

WSC .... Wages Sub-Committee [*Department of Industrial Relations*] [*Australia*]

WSC .... Water Studies Centre [*Chisholm Institute of Technology*] [*Australia*]

WSC .... Willetton Sports Club [*Australia*]

WSC .... Women Special Constables   (ML)

WSC .... Women's Service Corps

WSC .... Women's Studies Center [*Argentina*]   (EAIO)

WSCF .... World Student Christian Federation   (EA)

wsch .... Wschod [*or Wschodni*] [*East or Eastern*] [*Poland*]

Wschr....... Wochenschrift [*Weekly Publication*] [*German*]   (GCA)

WSD .... Water and Soil Department [*Libya*] [*Research center*]   (EAS)

WSDA .... World Storage, Documentation and Abstracting Service   (PDAA)

WSDC .... Western Savannah Development Corporation [*Sudan*]

WSDDS..... Western Suburbs Development Disability Service [*Sydney, New South Wales, Australia*]

WSE .... World Society for Ekistics [*Greek*]   (SLS)

WSE.......... Wyzsza Szkola Ekonomiczna [*Higher School of Economics*]   (POL)

WSET........ Writers and Scholars Educational Trust [*British*]   (EAIO)

WSF.......... World Science Fiction [*France*]   (EAIO)

WSF.......... World Scout Foundation [*Geneva, Switzerland*]   (EAIO)

WSF .... World Sephardi Federation [*See also FSM*] [*Geneva, Switzerland*]   (EAIO)

WSF.......... World SF [*Science Fiction*]   (EA)

WSF.......... [*The*] World Squash Federation   (OLYM)

WSF.......... World Strengthlifting Federation [*India*]   (EAIO)

WSF.......... Wyzsza Szkola Filmowa [*Higher School of Motion Pictures*]   (POL)

WSFU........ Western State Farmers Union [*Nigeria*]   (AF)

WSG .... Wasaya Airways Ltd. [*Canada ICAO designator*]   (FAAC)

WSG .... Wehrsportegruppe Hoffman Truppe [*Hoffman Paramilitary Troop*] [*Germany*]

WSG .... Western Suburbs Greens [*Political party*] [*Australia*]

WSG .... Wiener Sprachgesellschaft [*Austria*]   (SLS)

WSgu .... Wenden Sie Gefaelligst Um [*Please Turn Over*] [*Correspondence*] [*German*]

WSGW ...... Wyzsza Szkola Gospodarstwa Wiejskiego [*Higher School of Agriculture or Farming*]   (POL)

WSH.......... Wyzsza Szkola Handlowa [*Higher School of Commerce*]   (POL)

WSHA....... Wasserstrassen-Hauptamt [*Main Waterways Office*]   (EG)

WSHM ...... Wyzsza Szkola Handlu Morskiego [*Higher School of Maritime Trade*]   (POL)

WSI........... Wieczorowa Szkola Inzynierska [*Engineering Evening School*]   (POL)

WSI........... Writers and Scholars International [*British*]   (EAIO)

WSI........... Wyzsza Szkola Inzynieryjna [*Higher School of Engineering*]   (POL)

WSIA........ Water Supply Improvement Association [*Later, IDA*]   (EA)

WSITC ...... Western Sydney Information Technology Centre [*Australia*]

WSJC .... Singapore [*Singapore*] [*ICAO location identifier*]   (ICLI)

WSJO........ Wyzsze Studium Jezykow Obcych [*Institute of Foreign Languages*] [*Poland*]

WSK .... Waarskynlik [*Probable*] [*Afrikaans*]

WSK .... Wytwornia Sprzetu Komunikacyjnego [*Transportation Equipment Plant*]   (POL)

WSL.......... Eidgenossische Anstalt fuer Wald, Schnee und Landschaft [*Swiss Federal Researc h Institute for Forest, Snow, and Landscape*]   (EAS)

WSL.......... Water Science Laboratories Proprietary Ltd. [*Australia*]

WSL.......... Weldbund zum Schultze des Lebens [*World Union for the Protection of Life*]   (PDAA)

WSLBRUC ... W. S. and L. B. Robinson University College [*Australia*]

WSLF .... Western Somalia Liberation Front   (AF)

WSL-INT .. Weltbund zum Schutze des Lebens [*World Union for the Protection of Life - WUPL-INT*]   (EAIO)

WSLS .... War Service Land Settlement Scheme [*Australia*]

WSM .... Warszawska Spoldzielnia Mieszkaniowa [*Warsaw Housing Cooperative*]   (POL)

WSM .... Western Samoa [*ANSI three-letter standard code*]   (CNC)

WSM .... Wytwornia Silnikow Motorowych [*Motor Engine Factory*]   (POL)

WSM .... Wytwornia Sprzetu Mechanicznego [*Mechanical Equipment Plant*]   (POL)

WSM .... Wyzsza Szkola Muzyczna [*Higher School of Music*]   (POL)

WSMHS.... Western Sydney Mental Health Service [*Australia*]

WSMRC .... WAMEX [*West African Monsoon Experiment*] Scientific and Management Regional Commission   (MSC)

WSMW ..... Wyzsza Szkola Marynarki Wojennej [*Higher Naval School*]   (POL)

WSNPTG ... Wydzial Spraw Naukowych Polskiego Towarzystwa Geograficznego [*Department for the Scientific Affairs of the Polish Geographical Society*] (POL)

WSNSG ..... Wyzsze Studium Nauk Spoleczno-Gospodarczych [*Higher School of Social and Economic Sciences*] (POL)

WSO .... Warszawska Straz Ogniowa [*Warsaw Fire Department*] (POL)

WSO .... Washabo [*Surinam*] [*Airport symbol*] (OAG)

WSO .... World Safety Organization [*United Nations*]

WSOP .... Wyzsza Szkola Oficerow Politycznych [*Higher School for Political Officers*] (POL)

WSOWChem ... Wyzsza Szkola Oficerska Wojsk Chemicznych [*Higher Chemical Warfare Officers School*] (POL)

WSOWInz ... Wyzsza Szkola Oficerska Wojsk Inzynieryjnych [*Higher Engineer Officers School*] (POL)

WSOWLacz ... Wyzsza Szkola Oficerska Wojsk Lacznosci [*Higher Signal Officers School*] (POL)

WSOWOPlot ... Wyzsza Szkola Oficerska Wojsk Obrony Przeciwlotniczej [*Higher Antiaircraft Defense Officers School*] (POL)

WSOWZmech ... Wyzsza Szkola Oficerska Wojsk Zmechanizowanych [*Higher Mechanized Troop Officers School*] (POL)

WSOY .... Werner Soederstroem Osakeyhtio [*Book printer*] [*Finland*]

WSP .... Wojewodzka Szkola Partyjna [*Voivodship Party School*] (POL)

WSP .... Wyzsza Szkola Pedagogiczna [*Higher Pedagogical School*] (POL)

WSP .... Wyzsza Szkola Piechoty [*Higher School of Infantry*] (POL)

WSP .... Wyzsza Szkola Prawnicza [*Higher School of Law*] (POL)

WSPA .... World Society for the Protection of Animals [*WFPA and ISPA*] [*Formed by a merger of*] (EA)

WSPC .... Weapons System Partnerships Committee [*NATO*] (NATG)

WSPC .... Women's Social and Political Coalition [*Australia*]

WSPDC ..... Western Sydney Planning and Development Committee [*Australia*]

WSP-I .... World Socialist Party - Ireland [*Political party*] (EAIO)

WSPiech .... Wyzsza Szkola Piechoty [*Higher School of Infantry*] (POL)

WSPNZ ..... World Socialist Party of New Zealand [*Political party*] (EAIO)

WSPR .... Wegierska Socjalistyczna Partia Robotnicza [*Hungarian Socialist Workers' Party*] [*Poland*]

WSR .... Wyzsza Spoldzielnia Rolnicza [*Agricultural Production Cooperative*] (POL)

WSR .... Wyzsza Szkola Rolnicza [*Higher School of Agriculture*] (POL)

WSRCC ..... Western Suburbs Regional Chamber of Commerce [*Sydney, New South Wales, Australia*]

WSRL .... Weapons Systems Research Laboratory [*Defence Research Centre*] [*Research center*] [*Australia*] (IRC)

WSRO .... World Sugar Research Organisation (EAIO)

wss .... Waesserig [*Aqueous, Hydrous*] [*German*]

WSS .... Warszawska Spoldzielnia Spozywcow [*Warsaw Consumers' Cooperative*] (POL)

WSS .... Wojewodzka Spoldzielnia Spozywcow [*Voivodship Consumers' Cooperative*] (POL)

WSS .... World Ship Society [*Haywards Heath, West Sussex, England*]

WSS .... Wydzial Spraw Sedziowskich [*Department of Referee Matters (Sports)*] (POL)

WSSA .... Wildlife Society of Southern Africa (EAIO)

Wssb .... Wasserbad [*Water Bath*] [*German*]

WSSB .... Werk fuer Signal- und Sicherungstechnik [*Plant for Signal and Safety Technology*] [*Berlin*] (EG)

WSSL .... Seletar [*Singapore*] [*ICAO location identifier*] (ICLI)

WSSP .... Wyzsza Szkola Sztuk Plastycznych [*Higher School of Plastic Arts*] (POL)

WSSS .... Singapore Changi [*Singapore*] [*ICAO location identifier*] (ICLI)

WST .... Warszawska Stacja Telewizyjna [*Warsaw Television Station*] (POL)

W St .... Wechselstellung [*Alternate Position*] [*German*] (GCA)

Wst .... Werkzeugstahl [*Tool Steel*] [*German*] (GCA)

WST .... West Aviation AS [*Norway*] [*ICAO designator*] (FAAC)

WST .... Western Standard Time [*Australia*]

WST .... World Ship Trust [*Cambridge, England*]

WST .... Wyzsza Szkola Teatralna [*Higher School of Drama*] (POL)

WSTEC ...... Western Samoa Trust Estates Corporation (GEA)

WStG .... Wehrstrafgesetz [*Military Criminal Law*] [*German*] (ILCA)

W Str .... Wasserstrasse [*Canal, Waterway*] [*German*] (GCA)

Wstr .... Wechselstrom [*Alternating Current*] [*German*] (GCA)

WStVO .... Wirtschaftsstrafverordnung [*Decree on Economic Crimes*] (EG)

Wstw .... Waerterstellwerk [*Mechanical Signal and Switch Control Station*] (EG)

WSU .... Wasu [*Papua New Guinea*] [*Airport symbol*] (OAG)

WSURT ..... Welfare Services Unit for Refugees in Thailand (EAIO)

WSV .... Wheelchair Sports Victoria [*Australia*]

WSW .... Wojewodzki Sztab Wojskowy [*Voivodship Military Headquarters*] (POL)

WSW .... Wojskowa Sluzba Wewnetrzna [*Army Security Service*] [*Poland*]

WSWF .... Wyzsza Szkola Wychowania Fizycznego [*Higher School of Physical Education*] (POL)

WSY .... Airlie Beach [*Australia*] [*Airport symbol*]

WSZ .... Westport [*New Zealand*] [*Airport symbol*] (OAG)

WSZ .... Wildlife Society of Zimbabwe (EAIO)

WSZB .... Wirtschafts- und Sozialwissenschaftliche Zweigbibliothek

WSzW .... Wojewodzki Sztab Wojskowy [*Voivodship Military Headquarters*] (POL)

Wt .... Het Waterschap [*Benelux*] (BAS)

WT .... WAAC Ltd. - Nigeria Airways [*Nigeria*] [*ICAO designator*] (ICDA)

WT .... Wasserturm [*Water Tower*] [*German*] (GCA)

WT .... Wechselstrom-Telegraphie-Uebertragungseinrichtung [*AC Repeating Telegraph Facility*] (EG)

WTA .... Tambohorano [*Madagascar*] [*Airport symbol*] (OAG)

WTA .... Wissenschaftlich-Technischer Arbeitskreis fuer Denkmalpflege und Bauwerksanierung [*International Association for the Protection of Monuments and Restoration of Buildings*] (EAIO)

WTA .... World Teleport Association [*New York, NY*] [*Telecommunications*] (TSSD)

WTAC .... Water Technology Advisory Committee [*Australia*]

WtB .... Waren des Taeglichen Bedarfs [*Goods for Everyday Use*] (EG)

WTB .... Wissenschaftlich-Technisches Buero [*Scientific-Technical Office*] (EG)

WTB .... Woerterbuch [*Dictionary*] [*German*] (ROG)

WTBTSB ... Watchtower Bible and Tract Society of Brazil (EAIO)

WTC .... Wangaratta Technical College [*Australia*]

WTC .... Westmead Teachers College [*Australia*]

WTCA .... World Tasar Class Association (EAIO)

WTCA .... World Trade Center Arhus [*Denmark*] (EAIO)

WTCAJ ...... World Trade Center of Abidjan [*Ivory Coast*] (EAIO)

WTCCC ..... Wet Tropics Community Consultative Committee [*Australia*]

WTCCQ .... World Trade Center Club Chongqing [*China*] (EAIO)

WTCCY ..... World Trade Centre - Cyprus (EAIO)

WTCGV .... World Trade Center Geneva [*Switzerland*] (EAIO)

WTCIS ...... World Trade Center Istanbul [*Turkey*] (EAIO)

WTCMM .. World Trade Center Metro Manila [*Philippines*] (EAIO)

WTCN ...... World Trade Center of Nigeria (EAIO)

WTCNJ ..... World Trade Centre Nanjing [*China*] (EAIO)

WTCO ...... World Trade Center Oslo [*Norway*] (EAIO)

WTE .... World Tapes for Education

WTE .... Wotje [*Marshall Islands*] [*Airport symbol*] (OAG)

WTER .... Wissenschaftlich-Technisches Buero fuer Reaktorbau (Berlin-Pankow) [*(Berlin-Pankow) Scientific-Technical Bureau for Reactor Construction*] (EG)

WTF .... [*The*] World Tackwondo Federation (OLYM)

WTF .... World Taekwondo Federation [*Seoul, Republic of Korea*] (EAIO)

WTG .... Welt-Tieraerztegesellschaft [*Netherlands*] (DSCA)

WTGB .... Wissenschaftlich-Technisches Buero fuer Geraetebau (VEB) [*Scientific-Technical Bureau for Apparatus Construction (VEB)*] (EG)

WTI .... Wetenschappelijke en Technische Informatie

WTIA .... Welding Technology Institute [*Australia*] (EAIO)

WTIA .... Welding Technology Institute of Australia

WTID .... Wissenschaftliche und Technische Information und Dokumentation [*Scientific and Technical Information and Documentation*] [*German*]

WTK .... Waermetechnische Kommission [*Heat-Engineering Commission*] [*German*] (EG)

WTK .... Wissenschaftlich-Technische Konzeption [*Scientific-Technical Concept*] [*German*] (EG)

WTM .... Waitemata Aero Club, Inc. [*New Zealand*] [*ICAO designator*] (FAAC)

WTM .... Warszawskie Towarzystwo Muzyczne [*Warsaw Music Society*] (POL)

WTMA ...... Wet Tropics Management Agency [*Queensland, Australia*]

WTMA ...... Wool Textile Manufacturers of Australia

WTMC ...... Wet Tropics Ministerial Council [*Australia*]

WTMH ...... Wroclawskie Towarzystwo Milosnikow Historii [*Wroclaw (Breslau) Society of Friends of History*] (POL)

WTMK ...... Wydawnictwa Techniczne Ministerstwa Komunikacji [*Technical Publishing House of the Ministry of Transportation*] (POL)

WTN .... Wroclawskie Towarzystwo Naukowe [*Wroclaw (Breslau) Learned Society*] (POL)

WTO .... Warsaw Treaty Organization

WTO .... World Tourism Organization [*Madrid, Spain*]

WTO .... World Trade Organization [*Trade and tariff regulation*] (ECON)

WTO .... Wotho [*Marshall Islands*] [*Airport symbol*] (OAG)

WTO .... Wszechzwiazkowe Towarzystwo Teatralne [*All-Union Theatrical Society (Soviet)*] (POL)

WTP .... Woitape [*Papua New Guinea*] [*Airport symbol*] (OAG)

W Tr .... Wassertransport [*Water Transportation*] [*German*] (GCA)

WTR .... Writer [*Royal Australian Navy*]

WTRD .... Water Treatment Research Division

WTS .... Tsiroanomandidy [*Madagascar*] [*Airport symbol*] (OAG)

WTS .... World Travel Service [*Bahrain*] [*Commercial firm*]

WTS .... Wydzial Transportu Samochodowego [*Department of Automobile Transportation*] (POL)

WTSAC..... Wet Tropics Scientific Advisory Committee [*Australia*]
wtt .... Watt [*Watt*] [*French*]
WTU......... Workers' Trade Union [*Spain*]   (EAIO)
WTUSL..... Women's Temperance Union of Sri Lanka   (EAIO)
wtv............ Wel te Verstaan [*Benelux*]   (BAS)
WTYF....... World Theosophical Youth Federation [*Porto Alegre, Brazil*]   (EAIO)
WTZ .... Wissenschaftlich-Technisches Zentrum [*Scientific-Technical Center*]   (EG)
WU .... St. Lucia Workers' Union
Wu............. Werturteil [*Evaluation*] [*German*]
WU............. Western European Union [*Also, WEU*]   (NATG)
wu.............. Wie unten [*As Below*] [*German*]   (GCA)
WU .... World Union [*Pondicherry, India*]   (EA)
WUA......... Workers' Unions' Association [*Sudan*]
WUB......... Wet Universitaire Bestuurshervorming
WUB......... Wojewodzki Urzad Bezpieczenstwa [*Voivodship Security Administration*]   (POL)
WUBW...... World Union of Black Writers [*See also UEMN*]   (EAIO)
WUCDU.... World Union of Christian Democratic Women [*Venezuela*] [*Political party*]   (EAIO)
WUCT .... World Union of Catholic Teachers [*Italian*]   (SLS)
WUCWO... World Union of Catholic Women's Organizations [*Rosemere, PQ*]   (EAIO)
Wuerf........ Wuerfel [*Cube*] [*German*]   (GCA)
WUeV .... Dienstvorschrift fuer die Aufstellung von Wagenuebergangs- und Bahnhofsbedienungsplaenen und fuer die Ueberwachung des Wagenuebergangs [*Service Regulations for Formulating Car Transfer and Station Service Plans and for the Supervision of Car Transfers*] [*German*]   (EG)
WUF .... Western United Front [*Fiji*] [*Political party*]   (PPW)
WUF .... World Underwater Federation   (ASF)
WUFI........ World United Formosans for Independence [*Political party*]   (EY)
WUFR ...... World Union of Free Romanians [*See also UMRL*] [*Creteil, France*]   (EAIO)
WUFS....... World Union of French-Speakers [*See also UMVF*]   (EAIO)
WUG......... Wau [*Papua New Guinea*] [*Airport symbol*]   (OAG)
WUH .... Wuhan [*China*] [*Airport symbol*]   (OAG)
WUI .... Writers' Union of Iceland   (EAIO)
WUJS....... World Union of Jewish Students [*Jerusalem, Israel*]
WUKF ...... Wojewodzki Urzad Kultury Fizycznej [*Voivodship Administration of Physical Culture*]   (POL)
WUKO...... World Union of Karatedo Organizations [*Solna, Sweden*]   (EAIO)
WULTUO ... World Union of Liberal Trade Union Organisations [*See also WFALW*] [*Zurich, Switzerland*]   (EAIO)
WUM........ World Union of Mapam [*See also UMM*]   (EAIO)
WUML...... Wieczorowy Uniwersytet Marksizmu-Leninizmu [*Evening University of Marxism-Leninism*]   (POL)
WUMTPT ... World Union of Martyred Towns, Peace Towns   (EAIO)
WUN .... Wiluna [*Australia*] [*Airport symbol*]   (OAG)
WUN .... World Union of Nigerians
WUNS .... World Union of National Socialists   (EA)
WUP .... Writers' Union of the Philippines   (EAIO)
WUPL-INT ... World Union for the Protection of Life [*See also WSL-INT*]   (EAIO)
WUPO....... World Union of Pythagorean Organizations [*Ivybridge, Devonshire, England*]   (EAIO)
WURDU.... Word-Processing System in Urdu [*A*] [*India*]
wurml .... Wurmloecherig [*Wormholed*] [*Publishing*] [*German*]
wurmst ...... Wurmstichig [*With Wormholes*] [*Publishing*] [*German*]
WUS .... Wojewodzki Urzad Statystyczny [*Voivodship Office of Statistics*]   (POL)
WUS .... World University Service [*See also EUM*] [*Geneva, Switzerland*]   (EAIO)
WU-SA ...... Workers' Union in Saudi Arabia   (EAIO)
WUSA ...... World University Service in Australia   (ADA)
WUSG ...... World Union Saint Gabriel [*Esher, Surrey, England*]   (EAIO)
WUSP....... World Union of Stockholm Pioneers   (EAIO)
WUSt........ Warenumsatzsteuer [*Purchase Tax*] [*German*]
WUSY ...... World Union for the Safeguard of Youth
WUTHH ... World Union of Tnuat Haherut Hatzorar [*Tel Aviv, Israel*]   (EAIO)
WUU .... Wau [*Sudan*] [*Airport symbol*]   (OAG)
WUV .... Wuvulu Island [*Papua New Guinea*] [*Airport symbol*]   (OAG)
WuW......... Wirtschaft und Wettbewerb [*Germany*]   (FLAF)
WV............. Werksvertretung [*German*]   (ADPT)
WV............. Woerterverzeichnis [*Vocabulary*] [*German*]   (GCA)
WVA.......... Wissenschaftliche Vereinigung der Augenoptiker [*Scientific Society of Opticians*]   (EG)
WVA.......... Wool Valuers Association [*Australia*]
WVA.......... World Veterinary Association [*See also AMV*] [*Madrid, Spain*]   (EAIO)
WVA.......... World Vision Australia

WVAO....... Wissenschaftliche Vereinigung fuer Augenoptik und Optometrie eV   (SLS)
WVB......... Walvis Bay [*Namibia*] [*Airport symbol*]   (OAG)
WVD......... Wereldverband van Diamantbewerkers [*Worldwide Alliance of Diamond Workers*]   (BARN)
WVF .... World Veterans Federation [*See also FMAC*] [*Paris, France*]   (EAIO)
WVI .... World Vision International
WVK......... Manakara [*Madagascar*] [*Airport symbol*]   (OAG)
WVL......... Wes-Vlaandere [*West Flanders*] [*Afrikaans*]
WVL......... Wet Vervreemding van Landbouwgronden [*Benelux*]   (BAS)
WVMMD ... Wetenschappelijke Vereniging van de Militaire Medische Dienst [*Also, Societe Scientifique du Service Medical Militaire*] [*Belgium*]   (EAIO)
WVO......... Wet op het Voortgezet Onderwijs [*Benelux*]   (BAS)
WVPA .... World Veterinary Poultry Association [*See also AMVA*] [*Huntingdon, Cambridgeshire, England*]   (EAIO)
WVR......... Wegenverkeersreglement [*Benelux*]   (BAS)
WVRD....... World Vision Relief Organization, Inc.
WVReg ...... Wegenverkeersregeling [*Benelux*]   (BAS)
WVSA....... Weidingsvereniging van Suidelike Afrika [*Grassland Society of Southern Africa-GISSA*]   (EAIO)
WVSAM.... Werkgewersvereniging van die Suid-Afrikaanse Motornywerheid [*South Africa*]   (AA)
Wvst.......... Wagenverteilungsstelle [*Railroad Car Distribution Office*]   (EG)
WVV......... Wereldvakverbond [*Benelux*]   (BAS)
WVV......... Wissenschaftlicher Verein fuer Verkehrswesen eV   (SLS)
WVW........ Wegenverkeerswet [*Benelux*]   (BAS)
WW........... Israel Aircraft Industries Ltd. [*ICAO aircraft manufacturer identifier*]   (ICAO)
WW........... Water Watch (Program) [*Australia*]
WW........... Wehrwoelfe [*Werewolves*] [*Guerrilla Fighters in Nazi Germany*] [*World War II*]
Ww .... Weichenwaerter [*Switch Operator*]   (EG)
WW........... Werklos Wet [*Unemployment Law*] [*Netherlands*]   (WEN)
ww .... Werkwoord [*Verb*] [*Afrikaans*]
WW........... Western Women [*Financial group*] [*Australia*]
WW........... Wirtschaftswoche-Datenbank [*Economic Week Data Bank*] [*Society for Public Economics*] [*Germany*] [*Information service or system*]   (IID)
WW........... Wojska Wewnetrzne [*Internal Forces*]   (POL)
WW........... Wordende Wereld [*Benelux*]   (BAS)
ww .... Wyzej Wymieniony [*Above Mentioned*] [*Poland*]
W-wa......... Warszawa [*Warsaw*]   (POL)
WWA........ Worldwide Assistance Proprietary Ltd. [*Australia*]
WWA........ Worldwide Aviation Services Ltd. [*Venezuela*] [*ICAO designator*]   (FAAC)
WWAS ...... World Wide Air Services [*Australia*]
WWB......... Wit Weerstandsbeweging [*White Resistance Movement*] [*Namibia Use WRM*]   (AF)
WWC........ World Wide Company   (MHDW)
WWCS...... Warszawska Wytwornia Czesci Samochodowych [*Warsaw Automobile Parts Plant*]   (POL)
WWCTU ... World's Woman's Christian Temperance Union [*Australia*]   (EAIO)
WWD........ Wasserwirtschaftsdirektion [*Directorate of Water Management*] [*German*]   (EG)
WWDCFC ... World-Wide Dave Clark Fan Club [*Defunct*]   (EAIO)
Wwe .... Witwe [*Widow*] [*German*]   (GPO)
WWF........ Waterside Workers' Federation of Australia   (EAIO)
WWF........ WorldWide Fund for Nature   (EA)
WWFA ...... Waterside Workers' Federation of Australia
WWFA ...... World Wildlife Fund Australia
WWF(I).... Working Women's Forum (India)   (EAIO)
WWFI....... World Wildlife Fund International [*Later, Worldwide Fund for Nature*]   (EAIO)
WWFN ...... World Wide Fund for Nature [*Australia*]
WWFNA ... World Wide Fund for Nature Australia
WWF-P ..... Worldwide Fund for Nature - Pakistan   (EAIO)
WWGA...... War Widows Guild of Australia
WWI .... Institut fuer Weltwirtschaft [*Institute for World Economy*] [*German*]
WWICC..... Women's Welfare Issues Consultative Committee [*Australia*]
WWJCC .... Worldwide Joint Coordinator Center [*NATO*]   (NATG)
WWK........ Wewak [*Papua New Guinea*] [*Airport symbol*]   (OAG)
WWNS...... World Wide News Service   (BJA)
WWNSS.... Worldwide Network of Standard Seismograph Stations   (PDAA)
WWO .... Wet Wetenschappelijk Onderwijs [*Benelux*]   (BAS)
WWO .... Wojewodzki Wydzial Odbudowy [*Voivodship Branch for Reconstruction*]   (POL)
WWO .... Wydzial Wyposazenia Okretow [*Department of Ship Equipment*]   (POL)
WWOF ...... Willing Workers for Organic Farms [*Australia*]
WWP .... World Weather Program   (PDAA)
WWPA ...... Western Wood Products Association [*Australia*]
WWS .... Wasawings AB [*Finland*] [*ICAO designator*]   (FAAC)

WWSU ...... World Water Ski Union [*See also UMSN*] [*Montreux, Switzerland*] (EAIO)
WWTB ...... Werkgroep Wetenschappelijke Theologische Bibliotheken
WWTC ...... Wagga Wagga Teachers College [*Australia*]
WWTT ...... Worldwide Tapetalk [*An association*] (EA)
WWV .... Wet Werkloosheidsvoorziening [*Benelux*] (BAS)
WWW .... World Weather Watch [*World Meteorological Organization*] [*Databank*] (IID)
WWY .... West Wyalong [*Australia*] [*Airport symbol*] (OÅG)
WX .... Air NSW [*New South Wales*] [*Airline code*] [*Australia*]
WX .... Ansett Express [*Airport symbol*]
WYA .... Whyalla [*Australia*] [*Airport symbol*] (OAG)
WYA .... World Youth Assembly (WEN)
WYCFD.... World Youth Congress on Food and Development (EAIO)
wyd .... Wydanie [*Edition*] (POL)
wyd .... Wydany [*Edited, Published*] (POL)
wydawn ...... Wydawnictwo [*Publication*] (POL)
wydz .... Wydzial [*Department (of a university or learned society)*] (POL)
WYE .... Yengema [*Sierra Leone*] [*Airport symbol*] (OAG)
wyj .... Wyjasnienie [*Explanation*] (POL)
WYK .... Wykonal [*Made By, Performed By, Taken By (Photograph)*] (POL)
wykr .... Wykres [*Diagram*] [*Publishing*] [*Poland*]
wym .... Wymawiaj [*Pronounce*] [*Poland*]
wym .... Wymiar [*Dimension*] [*Poland*]
WYN......... Wyndham [*Australia*] [*Airport symbol*]
WYO .... Western Youth Orchestra [*Australia*]
wys .... Wysokosc [*Height*] [*Poland*]
WYSB....... Wysbegeerte [*Philosophy*] [*Afrikaans*]
Wyz........... Wyzyna [*Eminence*] [*Poland*]
Wz............. Warenzeichen [*Trademark*] [*German*]
W-Z........... Wschod-Zachod [*East-West*] [*Poland*]
WZ............. Wydawnictwo Zachodnie [*Western Territories Publishing House*] (POL)
w z .... W Zastepstwie [*In Place Of*] (POL)
WZAB .... Wojewodzki Zarzad Architektoniczno-Budowlany [*Voivodship Administration of Architecture and Construction*] (POL)
WZB .... Wehrtechnische Zentralburo [*Germany*] (PDAA)
WZB .... Wissenschaftszentrum Berlin fuer Sozialforschung [*Social Science Research Center Berlin*] [*Research center*] [*German*] (ECON)
WZBM ...... Wojewodzki Zarzad Budynkow Mieszkalnych [*Voivodship Administration for Residential Buildings*] (POL)
WZBUP..... Warszawskie Zaklady Budowy Urzadzen Przemyslowych [*Warsaw Industrial Equipment Plant*] (POL)
WZBW ...... Wojewodzkie Zjednoczenie Budownictwa Wiejskiego [*Voivodship Association of Rural Construction*] (POL)
WZBZ....... Wroclawskie Zaklady Betoniarsko-Zelbetowe [*Wroclaw (Breslau) Concrete and Reinforced Concrete Plant*] (POL)
WZC .... Warszawskie Zaklady Ciastkarskie [*Warsaw Pastry Bakeries*] (POL)
WZDP .... Wojewodzki Zarzad Drog Publicznych [*Voivodship Administration of Public Roads*] (POL)
WZF .... Warszawskie Zaklady Farmaceutyczne [*Warsaw Pharmaceutical Establishments*] (POL)
WZF .... Warszawskie Zaklady Fotochemiczne [*Warsaw Photochemical Plant*] (POL)
WZG .... Warenzeichengesetz [*Trade Mark Law*] (EG)
WZG .... Warszawskie Zaklady Garbarskie [*Warsaw Tanneries*] (POL)
WZG .... Warszawskie Zaklady Gastronomiczne [*Warsaw Restaurant Enterprises*] (POL)
Wzg........... Werkzeug [*Tool, Implement*] [*German*] (GCA)
WZG .... Wroclawskie Zaklady Gastronomiczne [*Wroclaw Catering Establishments*] [*Poland*]
WZGS....... Wojewodzkie Zjednoczenie Gminnych Spoldzielni [*Voivodship Association of Rural Communal Cooperatives*] (POL)
WZGS........ Wojewodzki Zarzad Gminnych Spoldzielni [*Voivodship Administration of Communal Cooperatives*] (POL)
WZGS....... Wojewodzki Zwiazek Gminnych Spoldzielni [*Poland*]
WZH.......... Wojewodzki Zarzad Handlu [*Voivodship Trade Administration*] (POL)
WZHW...... Wojewodzki Zarzad Higieny Weterynaryjnej [*Voivodship Administration of Veterinary Hygiene*] (POL)
WZIP......... Warszawskie Zjednoczenie Instalcji Przemyslowych [*Warsaw Association of Industrial Installations*] (POL)
WZL .... Laboratorium fur Werkzeugmaschinen und Betriebslehre [*Laboratory of Machine Tools and Production Engineering*] [*Germany*] (IRC)
WZL .... Wojewodzki Zarzad Lacznosci [*Voivodship Communications Administration*] (POL)
WZL .... Wojskowy Zwiazek Lowiecki [*Military Hunting Union*] (POL)
WZLK........ Wirtschaftszweiglohngruppenkatalog [*Economic Branch Wage-Group Catalog*] (EG)
WZMO...... Wroclawskie Zaklady Materialow Ogniotrwalych [*Wroclaw (Breslau) Fireproof Material Plant*] (POL)
WZO.......... World Zionist Organization [*Israel*]

WZO......... Wystawa Ziem Odzyskanych [*Exhibition of the Recovered Territories*] (POL)
WZP .... Warszawskie Zaklady Papiernicze [*Warsaw Paper Plants*] (POL)
WZP .... Warszawskie Zaklady Piekarnicze [*Warsaw Bakeries*] (POL)
WZPB....... Warszawskie Zaklady Przemyslu Budowlanego [*Warsaw Construction Industry Plants*] (POL)
WZPG .... Warszawskie Zaklady Przemyslu Gastronomicznego [*Warsaw Restaurant Establishments*] (POL)
WZPG .... Warszawskie Zaklady Przemyslu Gumowego [*Warsaw Rubber Works*] (POL)
WZPMR.... Wojewodzkie Zjednoczenie Przedsiebiorstw Mechanizacji Rolnictwa [*Voivodship Association of Agricultural Mechanization Enterprises*] (POL)
WZPO .... Warszawskie Zaklady Przemyslu Odziezowego [*Warsaw Clothing Factory*] (POL)
WZPS .... Warszawskie Zaklady Piwowarsko-Slodownicze [*Warsaw Breweries*] (POL)
WZPT........ Wadowickie Zaklady Przemyslu Terenowego [*Wadowice Local Industry Plant*] (POL)
WZPT........ Warszawskie Zaklady Przemyslu Tluszczowego [*Warsaw Oleaginous Industries*] (POL)
WZPT........ Wojewodzkie Zaklady Przemyslu Terenowego [*Voivodship Local Industry Plants*] (POL)
WZPT........ Wojewodzki Zarzad Przemyslu Terenowego [*Voivodship Administration of Local Industry*] (POL)
WZPTMB ... Wojewodzki Zarzad Przemyslu Terenowego Materialow Budowlanych [*Voivodship Administration of the Local Building Materials Industry*] (POL)
WZPUK..... Wojewodzki Zarzad Przedsiebiorstw i Urzadzen Komunalnych [*Voivodship Administration of Communal Enterprises and Installations*] (POL)
WZPW ...... Wschodnie Zaklady Przemyslu Welnianego [*Eastern Wool Plants*] (POL)
WZRLI ...... Wroclawskie Zjednoczenie Robot Ladowo-Inzynieryjnych [*Wroclaw (Breslau) Association of Civil Engineering Work*] (POL)
WZRSB ..... Warszawskie Zaklady Remontu Sprzetu Budowlanego [*Warsaw Repair Establishments for Building Equipment*] (POL)
WZRSP ..... Wojewodzki Zwiazek Rolniczych Spoldzielni Produkcyjnych [*Voivodship Union of Farm Producer Cooperatives (Collective farms)*] (POL)
WZT .... Warszawskie Zaklady Telewizyjne [*Warsaw Television Establishments*] (POL)
WZT .... Warszawskie Zaklady Transportowe [*Warsaw Transportation Establishments*] (POL)
WZTBP ..... Warszawskie Zjednoczenie Terenowe Budownictwa Przemyslowego [*Warsaw Association of the Local Construction Industry*] (POL)
WZTBP ..... Wroclawskie Zjednoczenie Transportowego Budownictwa Przemyslowego [*Wroclaw (Breslau) Association of the Transportation Construction Industry*] (POL)
WZUR .... Wojewodzki Zarzad Urzadzen Rolnych [*Voivodship Farm Equipment Administration*] (POL)
WZUS .... Wojewodzki Zarzad Ubezpieczen Spolecznych [*Voivodship Social Security Administration*] (POL)
WZW .... Werkzeugwechsel [*German*] (ADPT)
WZW .... Wojewodzki Zarzad Weterynarii [*Voivodship Veterinary Science Administration*] (POL)
WZWM ..... Wojewodzkie Zarzady Wodno-Melioracyjne [*Voivodship Administrations for Irrigation and Land Reclamation*] (POL)
WZWS....... Wroclawskie Zaklady Wlokien Sztucznych [*Wroclaw (Breslau) Artificial Fiber Plant*] (POL)
WZY .... Nassau [*Bahamas*] [*Airport symbol*] (OAG)
WZZ .... Wojewodzkie Zaklady Zbozowe [*Voivodship Grain Elevators*] (POL)
WZZ .... Wojewodzki Zarzad Zbytu [*Voivodship Sales Board*] (POL)

X

X .... Ethnikon Agrotikon Komma Xiton [*National Agrarian Party "X"*] [*Political party*] (PPE)

x .... Incognita [*Unknown*] [*Portuguese*]

X .... Komma Xiton Ethnikis Antistasseos ["*X*" *National Resistance Party*] [*Political party*] (PPE)

X .... Niewiadoma X [*Unknown Quantity X*] [*Poland*]

X .... Nom [*Name*] [*French*]

X .... Northern Territory [*National Union Catalogue of Australia symbol*]

X .... Xerxes [*Phonetic alphabet*] [*Royal Navy World War I*] (DSUE)

X .... X-Ray [*Phonetic alphabet*] [*Pre-World War II International*] [*World War II*] (DSUE)

XA .... Xeni Apostoli [*Foreign Mission*] [*Notation on license plates of US Mission autos in Greece*] (GC)

XAL .... Aerovias Xalitic SA de CV [*Mexico*] [*ICAO designator*] (FAAC)

XAP .... Chapeco [*Brazil*] [*Airport symbol*] (OAG)

XB .... International Air Transport Association (IATA) [*ICAO designator*] (ICDA)

XBG .... Bogande [*Burkina Faso*] [*Airport symbol*] (OAG)

XBN .... Biniguni [*Papua New Guinea*] [*Airport symbol*] (OAG)

x bon .... Ex-Bonification [*Ex-Bonus*] [*Stock exchange*] [*French*]

Xbre .... Decembre [*December*] [*French*]

Xbre .... Diciembre [*December*] [*Spanish*]

XCH .... Christmas Island [*Airport symbol*]

xcoup .... Ex-Coupon [*Stock exchange*] [*French*]

XD .... Bureau Veritas SA [*France*] [*ICAO designator*] (ICDA)

xd .... Ex-Dividende [*Ex-Dividend*] [*French*] [*Finance*]

XDA .... Bureau Veritas SA [*France*] [*ICAO designator*] (FAAC)

XDC .... Xhosa Development Corporation [*South Africa*] (AF)

x dr .... Ex-Droits [*Ex-Rights*] [*French*] [*Finance*]

XE .... X-Einheit [*X-unit*] [*German*] (GCA)

Xe .... Xenonio [*Xenon*] [*Chemical element*] [*Portuguese*]

XEL .... Helicopteros Xel-Ha SA de CV [*Mexico*] [*ICAO designator*] (FAAC)

XFX .... Airways Corp. of New Zealand Ltd. [*ICAO designator*] (FAAC)

XGG .... Gorom-Gorom [*Burkina Faso*] [*Airport symbol*] (OAG)

XH .... Special Handling Service for Aircraft [*ICAO designator*] (ICDA)

XHCN .... Xa Hoi Chu Nghia [*Socialism*]

XHKS .... Xisbiga Hantiwadagga ee Kacaanka Somaliyeed [*Somali Revolutionary Socialist Party*] [*Use SRSP*] (AF)

XI .... International Aeradio Ltd. [*British*] [*ICAO designator*] (ICDA)

XIC .... Xichang [*China*] [*Airport symbol*] (OAG)

xilogr .... Xilografico [*Woodcut*] [*Publishing*] [*Italian*]

xir fort .... Xiron Fortion [*Dry Cargo*] (GC)

XJ .... Assistance Aeroportuaire de l'Aeroport de Paris [*France*] [*ICAO designator*] (ICDA)

XK .... Agence pour la Securite de la Navigation Aerienne en Afrique et a Madagascar (ASECNA) [*ICAO designator*] (ICDA)

XL .... Country Connection [*Airline code*] [*Australia*]

XL .... Telecomunicacoes Aeronauticas Sociedada Anonima (TASA) [*Brazil*] [*ICAO designator*] (ICDA)

XLG .... Lockheed Air Terminal, Inc. [*Guam*] [*ICAO designator*] (FAAC)

XLLQG ...... Xian Laboratory of Loess and Quaternary Geology [*Chinese*]

XLS .... St. Louis [*Senegal*] [*Airport symbol*] (OAG)

XLT .... Telecomunicacoes Aeronauticas SA [*Brazil*] [*ICAO designator*] (FAAC)

XM .... Research Missile [*NATO*]

XM .... Servicios a la Navegacion en el Espacio Aereo Mexicano (SENEAM) [*Mexico*] [*ICAO designator*] (ICDA)

XMG .... Mahendranagar [*Nepal*] [*Airport symbol*] (OAG)

XMH .... Manihi [*French Polynesia*] [*Airport symbol*] (OAG)

XMI .... Masasi [*Tanzania*] [*Airport symbol*] (OAG)

XML .... Minlaton [*Australia*] [*Airport symbol*] [*Obsolete*] (OAG)

XMN .... Xiamen [*China*] [*Airport symbol*]

xmo .... Diezmo [*Spanish*]

XMX .... Servicios a la Navegacion en el Espacio Aereo Mexicano [*Mexico*] [*ICAO designator*] (FAAC)

XN .... Canadian National Telecommunications [*Canada ICAO designator*] (ICDA)

XNA .... Xinhua News Agency [*China*]

XNN .... Xining [*China*] [*Airport symbol*] (OAG)

XP .... Expres Paye [*Express Paid*] [*French*]

XP .... Express Parcel Systems [*Europe*]

XP .... Radio Aeronautica Paraguaya Sociedad Anonima (RAPSA) [*Paraguay*] [*ICAO designator*] (ICDA)

XPA .... Pama [*Burkina Faso*] [*Airport symbol*] (OAG)

xpiano .... Cristiano [*Christian*] [*Spanish*]

Xpo .... Cristo [*Christ*] [*Spanish*]

XPS .... XP International BV [*Netherlands*] [*ICAO designator*] (FAAC)

XPT........... Express Passenger Train [*Australia*]

xptiano .... Cristiano [*Christian*] [*Spanish*]

XPTO .... Cristo [*Christ*] [*Portuguese*]

Xpto........... Cristo [*Christ*] [*Spanish*]

XQP .... Quepos [*Costa Rica*] [*Airport symbol*] (OAG)

XR .... Empresa de Servicios Aeronauticos [*Cuba*] [*ICAO designator*] (ICDA)

Xr .... Kreutzer [*A Coin*] [*German*]

Xr .... Kreuzer [*Cruiser*] [*German*]

XRY .... Jerez De La Frontera [*Spain*] [*Airport symbol*] (OAG)

XS .... Societe Internationale de Telecommunications Aeronautiques, Societe Cooperative (SITA) [*ICAO designator*] (ICDA)

XSC........... South Caicos [*British West Indies*] [*Airport symbol*] (OAG)

XSE........... Sebba [*Burkina Faso*] [*Airport symbol*] (OAG)

XSP........... Singapore-Seletar [*Singapore*] [*Airport symbol*] (OAG)

XT .... Servicos Auxiliares de Transportes Aereos (SATA) [*Brazil*] [*ICAO designator*] (ICDA)

Xti .... Sirketi [*Corporation, Company*] (TU)

XU .... Aerorepresentaciones Tupac Amaru [*Peru*] [*ICAO designator*] (ICDA)

XUT .... Aerorepresentaciones Tupac Amaru [*Peru*] [*ICAO designator*] (FAAC)

XXV .... Administracion de Aeropuertos [*Bolivia*] [*ICAO designator*] (FAAC)

XY .... Myanmar [*Aircraft nationality and registration mark*] (FAAC)

XYA .... Yandina [*Solomon Islands*] [*Airport symbol*] (OAG)

XYC .... Aero Chasqui SA [*Peru*] [*ICAO designator*] (FAAC)

xyl .... Xylografia [*Woodcut*] [*Publishing*] [*Italian*]

xylogr .... Xylografico [*Woodcut*] [*Publishing*] [*Italian*]

XYO .... Mayotte [*ANSI three-letter standard code*] (CNC)

XZ .... Myanmar [*Aircraft nationality and registration mark*] (FAAC)

Y

Y .... Niewiadoma Y [*Unknown Quantity Y*] [*Poland*]
Y .... Overseas Institution [*National Union Catalogue of Australia symbol*]
y .... Segunda Incognita [*Second Unknown*] [*Portuguese*]
Y .... Yankee [*Phonetic alphabet*] [*International*]   (DSUE)
Y .... Yasuda Trust & Banking Co. Ltd. [*Japan*]
Y .... Yayla [*Plateau, High Pasture Land*]   (TU)
Y .... Yellow [*Phonetic alphabet*] [*Royal Navy World War I*]   (DSUE)
Y .... Yeni [*New*]   (TU)
Y .... Yil [*Year*]   (TU)
Y .... Ymer
Y .... Yoke [*Phonetic alphabet*] [*World War II*]   (DSUE)
Y .... Yorker [*Phonetic alphabet*] [*Pre-World War II*]   (DSUE)
Y .... Yuksek [*Advanced, Higher*]   (TU)
Ya .... Automobile Made by the Yaroslavl' Automobile Plant   (RU)
YA .... Government Civil Aviation Authority [*ICAO designator*]   (ICDA)
ya .... Main Body, Nucleus   (BU)
YA .... Yachting Association [*Australia*]
Ya .... Yama [*Mountain*] [*Japan*]   (NAU)
YA .... Young Achiever [*Australia*]
YA .... Young Anglican [*Australia*]
YA .... Young Australia
YAA .... Ypiresia Arkhaiotiton kai Anastiloseos [*Antiquities and Restoration Service*] [*Greek*]   (GC)
YAASC ...... Youth Affairs Advisory Sub-Committee [*Australia*]
YaASSR .... Yakut Autonomous Soviet Socialist Republic   (RU)
YaAZ .... Yaroslavl' Automobile Plant   (RU)
Yab .... Yabanci [*Foreign, Foreigner*]   (TU)
YAC .... Youth Access Centre [*Australia*]
YAC .... Youth Affairs Council [*Australia*]
YACA .... Youth Affairs Council of Australia
YACON ..... Youth Affairs Council of New South Wales [*Australia*]
YACV .... Youth Accommodation Coalition of Victoria [*Australia*]
YaD .... Irritant Gas Candle   (RU)
YaD .... Nuclear Engine   (RU)
YaD .... Toxic Smoke Generator   (RU)
YaD .... Toxic Smoke, Irritant Smoke   (RU)
YAD .... Young Australian Democrats   (ADA)
yad ind........ Nuclear Induction   (RU)
YaDP .... Release of Irritant Smoke   (RU)
yad yed .... Nuclear Unit   (RU)
YAE .... Yapi Arastirma Enstitusu [*Building Research Institute*] [*Research center*] [*Turkey*]   (IRC)
YAE .... Ypiresia Andifymatikou Emvoliasmou [*Tuberculosis Inoculation Service*] [*Greek*]   (GC)
YaEG .... Nuclear Electric Generator   (RU)
YaEMZ....... Yaroslavl' Electrical Machinery Plant   (RU)
YaEPR .... Nuclear Electron Paramagnetic Resonance   (RU)
YaERD ...... Nuclear Electric Rocket Engine   (RU)
YaETs........ Nuclear Power Plant   (BU)
YaEU .... Nuclear Power Plant   (RU)
YaF .... Nuclear Fibrilla   (RU)
YAF .... Yemen Air Force
YaFT......... Japanese Federation of Labor   (RU)
yag............. Berry [*Topography*]   (RU)
YaG .... Nuclear Granule   (RU)
YaG .... Truck Made by the Yaroslavl' Automobile Plant   (RU)
YaGMI ...... Yaroslavl' State Medical Institute   (RU)
YaGPI........ Yaroslavl' State Pedagogical Institute Imeni K. D. Ushinskiy   (RU)
YaI .... Japhetic Institute (of the Academy of Sciences, USSR)   (RU)
YAIL.......... Yeboah Afihene Industries Ltd. [*Ghana*]
YAIM .... Askeri Yuksek Idare Mahkemesi [*Supreme Military Administrative Court*]   (TU)
YaIP.......... Information Retrieval Language   (RU)
YaK .... Aircraft or Helicopter Designed by A. S. Yakovlev   (RU)
yak .... Yakut   (RU)

YAK .... Yeni Cami Agdalen Kulubu [*The New Mosque Agdalen Club*] [*Turkish Cypriot*]   (GC)
YAK .... Ypiresia Asfaleias tou Kratous [*State Insurance Service*] [*Greek*]   (GC)
YaKKhZ .... Yasinovka By-Product Coke Plant   (RU)
YaKP......... Japanese Trade-Union Congress   (RU)
YaKPP....... Japanese Industrial Trade-Union Congress   (RU)
YaKR .... Nuclear Quadrupole Resonance   (RU)
Yakutgiz..... Yakut State Publishing House   (RU)
Yakutknigoizdat ... Yakut Book Publishing House   (RU)
Yakutneftegazrazvedka ... Yakut Office of Exploration Drilling for Oil and Gas   (RU)
YAL .... Young Australia League   (ADA)
YALDS...... Young Australia Language Development Scheme   (ADA)
YALP .... Youth and the Law Project [*Australia*]
YaLS......... Logical-Circuit Language   (RU)
YaLV......... Bucket Belt Water Elevator   (RU)
YaM .... Nuclear Membrane   (RU)
YAM .... Young Australian Male [*Lifestyle classification*]
YAM .... Ypiresia Allodapon kai Metanastevseos [*Aliens and Immigration Service*] [*Cyprus*]   (GC)
Yamfak ...... Division of Linguistics and Material Culture   (RU)
YaMG....... Nuclear Generator of Mechanical Energy   (RU)
YaMI .... Yaroslavl' Medical Institute   (RU)
YaMR .... Nuclear Magnetic Resonance   (RU)
YaMZ .... Yaroslavl' Engine Plant   (RU)
yan............. January   (BU)
YANGA ..... Young African Sports Club
YANPET ... Saudi Yanbu Petrochemical Co.
yanv........... January   (RU)
YaO........... Nuclear Weapon   (RU)
YAO .... Yaounde [*Cameroon*] [*Airport symbol*]   (OAG)
YA ofNSW ... Yachting Association of New South Wales [*Australia*]
YaOGA ...... Yaroslavl' Oblast State Archives   (RU)
YaP .... Intermediate Language   (RU)
yap............. Japanese   (RU)
YAP .... Yap [*Caroline Islands*] [*Airport symbol*]   (OAG)
YAP .... Ypiresia Aeronavtikon Pliroforion [*Aeronautical Information Service*]   (GC)
YAPA........ Youth Action Policy Association [*Australia*]
YAPA........ Youth and Performing Arts [*Australia*]
Yapi-Is .... Yapi Isciler Birlikleri Federasyonu [*Federation of Construction Worker Unions*]   (TU)
YaPRZ....... Yaroslavl' Locomotive Repair Plant   (RU)
YaPS......... Yambol Court of Reconciliation   (BU)
YAPSAN ... Yapi Agac Prefabrik Sanayi [*Construction Lumber Prefabrication Industry*]   (TU)
YAP-SEN ... Kibris Turk Yapi ve Kereste Iscileri Sendikasi [*Cypriot Turkish Construction and Lumber Workers Union*]   (TU)
YaPVRD.... Nuclear Ramjet Engine   (RU)
YaR .... Nuclear Resonance   (RU)
yar .... Summer Crops   (RU)
YAR .... Yemen Arab Republic   (ME)
YaRAK ...... Yaroslavl' Rubber and Asbestos Kombinat   (RU)
YaRD .... Nuclear Jet Engine   (RU)
YaRD .... Nuclear Rocket Engine   (RU)
YARD .... Youth Associated with the Restoration of Democracy [*Kenya*] [*Political party*]   (EY)
Yargres ...... Yaroslavl' State Regional Electric Power Plant   (RU)
Yar H .... Yardimci Hizmetler [*Helper Duties*]   (TU)
YaRkD........ Nuclear Rocket Engine   (RU)
YaRSh........ Mine Relay Box   (RU)
YaS .... Resistance Box   (RU)
YAS........... Ypiresiakon Arkhaiologikon Symvoulion [*Archaeological Service Council*] [*Greek*]   (GC)
yashch .... Box, Drawer   (RU)
YaShZ........ Yaroslavl' Tire Plant   (RU)
YASMAK ... Young Achievers Saving Mankind and Its Kingdom [*Australia*]

YaSP.......... Japanese Trade-Union Council   (RU)
YASU .... Young African Social Union
YaSV .... Explosion-Proof Resistance Box   (RU)
Yat............. Yatili [*Boarding*]   (TU)
YaTG .... Nuclear Heat Generator   (RU)
YaTRD ...... Nuclear Turbojet Engine   (RU)
YaTsIK ...... Central Executive Committee of the Yakut ASSR   (RU)
YaV .... Nuclear Vacuole   (RU)
YaV .... Poisons   (RU)
YaVSU .... System for Nuclear Auxiliary Power   (RU)
YayKur....... Yaygin Yuksek Ogretim Kurumu [*Diffused Higher Education Organization*]   (TU)
yaz .... Language   (RU)
YaZ .... Yaroslavl' Automobile Plant   (RU)
Yaz .... Yazan [*The Writer*] [*Of a book or article*]   (TU)
YaZhRD .... Nuclear Liquid Propellant Rocket Engine   (RU)
Yb.............. Iterbio [*Chemical element*] [*Portuguese*]
YB .... Meteorological Operational Telecommunications Network Europe [*ICAO designator*]   (ICDA)
YB .... Youth Brigade [*Australia*]
YB .... Youth Bureau [*Australia*]
YBAK .... Yusuf Bin Ahmed Kanoo [*Kanoo Freight Services Division*] [*Bahrain*]
Ybc .... Yabanci [*Foreign, Foreigner*]   (TU)
YBDSA...... Yacht Designers and Surveyors Association   (EAIO)
YBI............ Youth Business Initiative [*Australia*]
YBIA .... Youth Business Initiative Australia
YBIEC .... Yugoslav Bank for International Economic Cooperation
YBRD .... Yemen Bank for Reconstruction and Development   (GEA)
YC .... Rescue Coordination Center [*ICAO designator*]   (ICDA)
YC .... Yi Cheng Precision Industrial Co. Ltd. [*Taiwan*]
YCC .... Youth Continental Commissariat
YCE .... Yacht Club of Egypt
YCES .... Yeongnam Crops Experiment Station [*South Korean*] [*Research center*]   (IRC)
YCF........... Yacimientos Carboniferos Fiscales [*Government Coal Deposits*] [*Argentina*]   (LA)
YCFW....... Young Christian Female Workers [*Belgium*]   (EAIO)
YCI .... Yacht Club Italia [*Italian Yacht Club*]
YCIC......... Yemen Co. for Industry & Commerce Ltd.
YCL........... Young Communist League [*Nigeria*]   (AF)
YCNU .... Youth Wing of the Cameroon National Union   (AF)
YCO .... Youth Charitable Organization [*India*]   (EAIO)
YCT .... Yacht Club of Tahiti [*French Polynesia*]   (EAIO)
YCTSD...... Yugoslav Center for Technical and Scientific Documentation [*Information service or system*]   (IID)
YCV .... Young Men Christian Vanguard
YCW .... Young Christian Workers [*Belgium*]   (EAIO)
YCW .... Young Christian Workers' Movement of Australia   (ADA)
YD............. Authority Supervising the Aerodrome [*ICAO designator*]   (ICDA)
yd............... Jarda [*Yard*] [*Portuguese*]
YD............. People's Democratic Republic of Yemen [*ANSI two-letter standard code*]   (CNC)
YDAMK .... Ypiresia Diakheiriseos Andallaximon Mousoulmanikon Ktimaton [*Service for the Administration of Moslem Exchangeable Property*] [*Greek*]   (GC)
YDC .... Youth for Development and Cooperation   (EAIO)
YDC .... Yugoslavian-Danish Corporation [*Construction group*]
YDC .... Yulara Development Company [*Australia*]
YDD.......... Yayasan Dian Desa [*Light of the Village*] [*Indonesia*]   (PDAA)
YDEP........ Young Driver Education Program [*Australia*]
YDGD........ Yurtsever Devrimci Genclik Dernegi [*Patriotic Revolutionary Youth Association*]   (TU)
YDK .... Yusek Denetleme Kurulu [*Supreme Control Council*] [*In Office of Premier*]   (TU)
YDKE .... Ypiresia Dioxeos Koinou Englimatos [*Common Crime Fighting Service*]   (GC)
YDLA .... Young Democratic Labor Association [*Australia*]
YDM.......... Yeni Desen Matbaasi [*New Design Press*] [*Ankara*]   (TU)
YDN .... Ypiresia Dioxeos Narkotikon [*Anti-Narcotics Service*]   (GC)
YDNI .... Yayasan Dana Normalisasi Indonesia [*Indonesian Standards Institution*]
YDO........... Yuksek Denizcilik Okulu [*Higher (Advanced) Maritime School*]   (TU)
YDP .... Yeni Dogus Partisi [*New Dawn Party*] [*Turkish Cyprus*] [*Political party*]   (EY)
YDPP......... Young Democratic Progressive Party [*Macedonia*] [*Political party*]   (EY)
Yd Sb .... Yedek Subay [*Reserve Officer*]   (TU)
YDYF......... Yemeni Democratic Youth Federation   (ME)
Ye.............. Spruce   (RU)
ye............... United, Only, Single   (RU)
YE .... Yemen Arab Republic [*ANSI two-letter standard code*]   (CNC)
YEA .... Young Engineers Australia

YEA .... Ypopsifios Efedros Axiomatikos [*Reserve Officer Candidate*] [*Greek*]   (GC)
YEA .... Ypourgeion Ethnikis Amynis [*Ministry of National Defense*]   (GC)
YeAO .... Yerevan Astronomical Observatory   (RU)
YeAP......... European Productivity Agency [*EPA*]   (RU)
YeASS .... Unified Automated Network of the Soviet Union [*Telecommunications*]   (RU)
YeAST ...... European Free Trade Association [*EFTA*]   (RU)
YEC .... Yugoslav Economic Community   (ECON)
YECL........ Young Evangelical Churchmen's League [*Australia*]
yed............. Singular, Unit   (RU)
YeDA .... United Democratic Left Party [*Greek*]   (RU)
yed izm ...... Unit of Measurement   (RU)
YeDK .... European Danube Commission   (RU)
yed khr....... Unit of Storage   (RU)
YeDNF ...... United Democratic National Front [*North Korean*]   (RU)
YeDOF ...... United Democratic Fatherland Front [*North Korean*]   (RU)
YEDSAN... Yedek Parca Sanayii ve Ticaret AS [*Spare Parts Industry and Trade Corp.*]   (TU)
YEE .... Ypiresia Endellomenon Exodon [*Authorized Expenses Service*] [*Greek*]   (GC)
YEEA......... Ypiresia Epistimonikis Erevnis kai Anaptyxeos [*Scientific Research and Development Service*] [*Greek*]   (GC)
YEED .... Ypiresia Enimeroseos Enoplon Dynameon [*Armed Forces Information Service*] [*Greek*]   (GC)
YEEEthA... Ypiresia Epeigondon Ergon Ethnikis Amynis [*Service for Urgent National Defense Projects*] [*Greek*]   (GC)
YeEK......... European Economic Commission of the United Nations Organization   (RU)
YEEPP ...... Ypiresia Exypiretiseos kai Erevnis Paraponon ton Politon [*Citizen Complaints Investigation Service*] [*Greek*]   (GC)
YeES .... European Economic Community [*EEC*]   (RU)
YeES .... Unified Power System   (RU)
YEET........ Ypiresia Epistimonikis Erevnis kai Tekhnologias [*Scientific Research and Technology Service*]   (GC)
YEFA........ Ypiresia Elengkhou Fortotikon Avtokiniton [*Truck Control Service*] [*Greek*]   (GC)
yefr .... Private First Class   (RU)
YeFT......... Unified Physical Theory   (RU)
YeG .... Natural Science and Geography   (RU)
YeGAF ...... United State Archives Fund   (RU)
yegip.......... Egyptian   (RU)
YeGMS..... United Hydrometeorological Service [*1929-1936*]   (RU)
YeGSVTs... Unified State Network of Computation Centers   (RU)
YeGU .... Yerevan State University   (RU)
Yek............ Yekun [*Total*]   (TU)
YEK .... Ypiresia Enaeriou Kykloforias [*Air Traffic Service*]   (GC)
YEKDP...... Ypiresia Elengkhou Kratikou Diylistiriou Petrelaiou [*National Oil Refinery Control Service*] [*Greek*]   (GC)
YeKGR...... European Goods Timetable Conference   (RU)
YeKGT...... United Labor Confederation of Guatemala   (RU)
YeKK .... European Advisory Commission [*1943-1945*]   (RU)
YeKK .... European Committee for Boilermaking and Kindred Steel Structures   (RU)
YEKMO .... Ypiresia Elengkhou Kataskevis Monimon Odostromaton [*Permanent Road Construction Inspection Service*] [*Greek*]   (GC)
YeKMT...... European Conference of Ministers of Transport [*ECMT*]   (RU)
YeKO .... Jewish Colonization Society   (RU)
YeKOPO ... Jewish Committee for Assistance to Refugees   (RU)
YeKP......... Egyptian Communist Party   (RU)
YeKP......... Jewish Communist Party   (RU)
YeKPR...... European Passenger Timetable Conference   (RU)
YeKS .... Jewish Communist League   (RU)
YeKUP...... Standard Set of Universal Devices [*for a repair shop*]   (RU)
YEKY........ Ypiresia Elengkhou Kataskevis Yponomon [*Sewer Construction Control Service*] [*Greek*]   (GC)
YeLES .... European League for Economic Cooperation [*ELEC*]   (RU)
Yelgavsel'mash ... Jelgava Agricultural Machinery Plant   (RU)
YeLM......... Liberal European Youth [*LEY*]   (RU)
YEM .... Yemen (Sanaa) [*ANSI three-letter standard code*]   (CNC)
YeMI .... Yerevan Medical Institute   (RU)
YEMINCO ... Yemen Oil & Mineral Industrial Co.   (MENA)
yemk.......... Capacity   (RU)
YeMK .... European Youth Campaign [*EYC*]   (RU)
YeMS......... Unified Modular Reference System   (RU)
YEMSANAYII ... Yem Sanayii Turk Anonim Sirketi [*Turkish Fodder Industry Corporation*]   (TU)
YEMTA..... Izmir Yem Fabrikasi [*Izmir Fodder Factory*]   (TU)
YEN .... Ypourgeion Emborikis Navtilias [*Ministry of Merchant Marine*] [*Also used for automobile license plate designation*] [*Greek*]   (GC)
YeNDF ...... United Popular Democratic Front [*Chinese*]   (RU)
YENED ..... Ypiresia Enimeroseos Enoplon Dynameon [*Armed Forces Information Service*] [*Greek*]   (GC)

YeNIL........ State Natural Science Institute Imeni P. F. Lesgaft (RU)
YeNIR....... Unified Norms and Wages, Unified Standards and Costs (RU)
Yeniseyzoloto ... State Yenisey Gold-Mining Trust (RU)
YeNRP....... Jewish Independent Workers' Party (RU)
YENTAS ... Yapi Endustri ve Ticaret Anonim Sirketi [*Construction Industry and Trade Corporation*] (TU)
YeNV .... Unified Output Norms (RU)
YeNViR ..... Unified Output and Wage Norms, Unified Output and Cost Standards (RU)
YeO .... Daily Inspection [*of automobiles*] (RU)
YeO .... Daily Servicing [*of automobiles*] (RU)
YeOEGV ..... European Railway Wagon Pool (RU)
YeOES .... Organization for European Economic Cooperation [*OEEC*] (RU)
YeOS .... Egyptian Organization for Standardization and Calibration (RU)
YeOS .... European Defense Community (RU)
YeOUS ...... European Coal and Steel Community (RU)
YeOYaI..... European Organization for Nuclear Research (RU)
YeOZR ...... European and Mediterranean Plant Protection Organization [*EPPO*] (RU)
YePChT .... United Trade-Union Center of Chilean Workers (RU)
YEPCO...... Yemen Exploration & Production Co.
YePO .... United Consumers' Society (RU)
YePS .... European Payment Union (RU)
YePSR .... United Party of the Socialist Revolution (RU)
YEPTh....... Ypourgeion Ethnikis Paideias kai Thriskevmaton [*Ministry of National Education and Religions*] [*YPEPTh*] [*See also*] (GC)
YePTs .... United Trade-Union Center [*Dutch*] (RU)
YePTsN ..... United Trade-Union Center of the Netherlands (RU)
YePTsTCh ... United Trade-Union Center of Chilean Workers (RU)
yer .... Split Stream, Channel, Braided Stream [*Topography*] (RU)
YeRF .... United Workers' Front [*Romanian*] (RU)
YeRO .... European Regional Organization [*of the International Confederation of Free Trade Unions*] (RU)
YerPI .... Yerevan Polytechnic Institute Imeni K. Marx (RU)
YeRYeR ..... Regional Unified Unit Cost Rates, Regional Unified Unit Wage Rates (RU)
YeS............. Jewish Socialists (RU)
YES........... Youth Effectiveness Skills Program [*Australia*]
YES........... Youth Enquiry Service [*Australia*]
YES........... Youths for Environment and Service [*Multinational association based in Turkey*] (EAIO)
YESCE ...... Turkiye Yesilay Cemiyeti [*Turkish Green Crescent Society*] [*Turkish temperance society*] (TU)
YeSDRP .... Jewish Social Democratic Workers' Party (RU)
YeShB........ Unified Scale of Drillability (RU)
YeSK......... European Seismological Commission (RU)
YeSKhK..... United Agricultural Cooperative [*Former Czechoslovakia*] (RU)
YeSKhN..... Unified Agricultural Tax (RU)
YeSP .... European Community of Writers (RU)
YeSP .... Natural Synoptic Period (RU)
YeSR .... European Broadcasting Union [*EBU*] (RU)
YeSR .... Natural Synoptic Region (RU)
YeSS .... Unified Seismic Service of the USSR (RU)
YeSSN .... Unified System of Seismic Observations (RU)
yestestv ...... Natural (RU)
yestfak .... Natural Science Division (RU)
YEthA........ Ypourgeion Ethnikis Amynis [*Ministry of National Defense*] (GC)
YETIS........ Yesilada Eczacilari Turk Ithalat Sirketi [*Green Island Pharmacists' Turkish Import Corporation*] [*Cyprus*] (TU)
YeTK......... European Travel Commission [*ETC*] (RU)
YeTKS ...... Unified Wage Rates and Qualifications Guide (RU)
YeTP .... Unified Technological Process (RU)
YeTS .... European Territory of the Soviet Union (RU)
YeTSh........ United Labor School (RU)
YeTsIN ...... European Center for Population Studies (RU)
YeTsP .... European Translation Center [*ETC*] (RU)
YeTT .... Unified Transit Tariff [*Railroads*] (RU)
YeU........... Daily Servicing [*of automobiles*] (RU)
YEV .... Ypiresia Engeion Veltioseon [*Land Reclamation Service*] [*Greek*] (GC)
YeVKOM .. Jewish Commissariat on Nationality Problems [*1918-1920*] (RU)
Yevkombed ... Committee for Assistance to Indigent Jews (RU)
Yevkomol... Jewish Young Communist League (RU)
Yevobshchestkom ... Jewish Public Committee for Assistance to Victims of War and Pogroms [*1920-1924*] (RU)
yevr............ European (RU)
yevr............ Jewish (RU)
Yevratom... European Atomic Energy Community [*EURATOM*] (RU)
YeVROFIMA ... European Company for the Financing of Railway Rolling Stock [*EUROFIMA*] (RU)
YeVS......... European Monetary Agreement (RU)

YeVS......... Unified High-Voltage Network, Unified High-Voltage System (RU)
Yevsektsiya ... Jewish Communist Section at the TsK VKP(b) [*1918-1930*] (RU)
YeVSK ...... All-Union Unified Sports Qualification (RU)
Yevtsib ...... Jewish Central Information Office (RU)
yezhednev... Daily, Diurnal (RU)
yezhegod .... Annual (RU)
yezhemes.... Monthly (RU)
yezhened .... Weekly (RU)
YeZMO ..... Yelets Medical Equipment Plant (RU)
YF .... Aeronautical Fixed Station [*ICAO designator*] (ICDA)
YFC .... Young Farmers' Clubs
YFC .... Youth for Christ [*Australia*]
YFC .... Youth for Conservation
YFCI .... Youth for Christ International [*See also JPC*] [*Singapore, Singapore*] (EAIO)
YFEC .... Youth Forum of the European Communities [*See also FJCE*] (EAIO)
YFFC .... Young Farmers Finance Council [*Australia*]
YFL.......... Youth Forum Ltd. [*Australia*] [*Commercial firm*]
YFPA .... Yemen Family Planning Association [*Yemen Arab Republic*] (IMH)
Yfyp .... Yfypourgos [*Deputy Minister*] (GC)
YG............ Ysterografon [*Post Script*] (GC)
YG............ Yuksek Gerilim [*High Tension*] (TU)
YGD.......... Yurtsever Genclik Dernegi [*Patriotic Youth Society*] (TU)
YGEC .... Yemen General Electricity Corp.
YGIS .... Youth Guarantee Information Services [*Australia*]
YGJ.......... Yonago [*Japan*] [*Airport symbol*] (OAG)
YGKTIL .... Ypalliloi Grafeion Koinon Tameion Idiotikon Leoforeion [*Office Employees of Joint Private Bus Funds*] [*Greek*] (GC)
YGO.......... Yurtsever Genclik Orgutu [*Patriotic Youth Organization*] (TU)
YGS .... Youth Guidance Service
YGT .... Yargitay [*Court of Cassation*] (TU)
YH .... Yrkesorganisasjonenes Hovedsammenslutning [*Central Association of Professional Organizations*] [*Norway*] (WEN)
YHA.......... Youth Homeless Allowance [*Australia*]
YHA.......... Youth Hostels Australia
YHAI .... Youth Hostels Association of India (EAIO)
YHB.......... Yurtsever Hanimlar Birligi [*Patriotic Women's Association*] [*Turkish Cypriot*] (GC)
YHC.......... Helsinki Committee for Human Rights - Belgrade [*Former Yugoslavia*] (EAIO)
yhdyss........ Yhdyssanoissa [*or Yhdyssana*] [*Compound Word*] [*Finland*]
YHK.......... Yuksek Hakimler Kurulu [*Supreme Juridical Council*] (TU)
YHP.......... Yokogawa Hewlett Packard Ltd. [*Japan*]
YHS .... Yurt Haberler Servisi [*Homeland News Service*] (TU)
yht .... Yhteensa [*Finland*]
yht .... Yhteinen [*Finland*]
yhteiskuntatkand ... Yhteiskuntatieteiden Kandidaatti [*Finland*]
YIBITAS ... Yozgat Isci Birligi Ins Malz ve San Anonim Sirketi [*Yozgat Worker Union Construction Equipment and Industry Corporation*] (TU)
YICAM...... Societe Yoo-Hoo Industrie of Cameroun
YIH.......... Yichang [*China*] [*Airport symbol*] (OAG)
Yill .... Yilligi [*Annual*] (TU)
YIM .... Yapi Isleri Mudurlugu [*Construction Affairs Directorate*] [*Under Public Works Ministry*] (TU)
YIN .... Yining [*China*] [*Airport symbol*] (OAG)
YIS .... Yapi Iscileri Sendikasi [*Construction Workers Union*] (TU)
YIS .... Ydroilektrikos Stathmos [*Hydroelectric Station*] [*Greek*] (GC)
YIT.......... Youth in Transition [*Australia*]
YITPC .... Yemen Industrial Trade & Promotion Center
YJ .... Vanuatu [*Aircraft nationality and registration mark*] (FAAC)
YJ .... Young Jamaicans (LA)
YJP .... Youth Justice Project [*Law Foundation of New South Wales*] [*Australia*]
YK .... Yakovlev [*Former USSR*] [*ICAO aircraft manufacturer identifier*] (ICAO)
YK .... Yapi-Kredi Bank [*Turkey*] (ECON)
YK .... Yhdistyneet Kansakunnat [*Finland*]
YK .... Yhteiskuntatieteiden Kandidaatti [*Finland*]
YK .... Yonetim Kurulu [*Administrative Council*] [*Of a political party or other organization*] (TU)
YK .... Ypiresia Kostologiseos [*Cost Evaluation Service*] (GC)
YK .... Yue-Kong Pao [*As in Sir Y. K.*] [*Hong Kong property and shipping magnate*]
Yk............ Yukari [*Upper, Superior*] (TU)
YKB .... Yemen Kuwait Bank for Trade & Investment
YKB .... Yonetim Kurulu Baskani [*Administrative Board Chairman*] (TU)
YKB .... Yurtsever Hanimlar Birligi [*Patriotic Women's Association*] [*Turkish Cypriot*] (TU)
YKE .... Ypiresia Koinonikis Evimerias [*Social Welfare Service*] (GC)

YKhK .... Ypiresia Khartografiseos kai Ktimatologiou [*Cartography and Land Registry Service*] (GC)

YKhOP ...... Ypourgeion Khorotaxias, Oikismou, kai Perivallondos [*Ministry of Zoning, Housing, and Environment*] (GC)

YKI .... Ytkemiska Institutet [*Institute for Surface Chemistry*] [*Research center*] [*Sweden*] (IRC)

YKM .... Kalyanamitra - Pusat Komunikasi dan Informasi Wanita [*Kalyanmitra Women's Communication and Information Centre*] [*Indonesia*] (EAIO)

YKP .... Yeni Kibris Partisi [*New Cypus Party*] [*Turkish Cyprus*] [*Political party*] (EY)

YKP .... Ypiresia Kratikon Promitheion [*State Supplies Service*] [*See also AEKP*] [*Greek*] (GC)

YKP .... Ypourgeion Kyvernitikis Politikis [*Ministry of Government Policy*] [*Greek*] (GC)

yks .... Yksikko [*Finland*]

yks .... Yksikon [*Finland*]

YKU .... Yonetim Kurulu Uyesi [*Administrative Board Member*] (TU)

YKU .... Yuksek Kimya Uzmani [*Senior Chemical Specialist*] (TU)

YKY .... Ypourgeion Koinonikon Ypiresion [*Ministry of Social Services*] (GC)

YL .... Aircraft Accident Authority [*ICAO designator*] (ICDA)

Yl .... Yil [*Year*] (TU)

yl .... Yleensa [*Generally, Mostly*] [*Finland*]

yl .... Yleinen [*Finland*]

yl .... Yleisesti [*Finland*]

YL .... Youth League

YL .... Yuanli Enterprise Co. Ltd. [*Taiwan*]

ylapm .... Ylapuolella Merenpinnan [*Finland*]

YLC .... Young Labour Council [*Australia*]

YLCP .... Youth League of the Coalition Party [*Finland*] (EAIO)

Yld .... Yuksek Lisans Diplomasi [*Turkey*]

YLE .... Oy Yleisradio Ab [*Finnish Broadcasting Company*]

YLF .... Young Leadership Forum [*Multinational association based in Israel*] (EAIO)

ylik .... Ylikersantti [*Finland*]

yliltn .... Yliluutnantti [*Finland*]

yliluutn .... Yliluutnantti [*Finland*]

ylim .... Ylimaarainen [*Finland*]

yliop .... Yliopettaja [*Finland*]

yliop .... Yliopisto [*University*] [*Finland*]

yliopp .... Ylioppilas [*Finland*]

yliv .... Ylivaapeli [*Finland*]

YLL .... Young Lanka League [*Trade union*] [*Sri Lanka*]

YLMA .... Young Liberal Movement of Australia

YLP .... Yugoslav League for Peace, Independence and Equality of Peoples (EAIO)

YLS .... Young Lawyers Section [*Law Society of New South Wales*] [*Australia*]

YM .... Meteorological Office [*ICAO designator*] (ICDA)

YM .... Yang Ming Line [*Shipping*] [*Taiwan*]

ym .... Ynna Muuta [*And So Forth, Et Cetera*] [*Finland*] (GPO)

YMA .... Youth Music Australia

YMBA .... Young Men's Buddhist Association [*Myanmar*] (FEA)

YMCA .... Young Men's Christian Association

YMCA .... Young Men's Christian Association Santiago [*Chile*] (EAIO)

YMCAA ... Young Men's Christian Association of Australia

YMD .... People's Democratic Republic of Yemen [*ANSI three-letter standard code*] (CNC)

Ymd .... Yuksek Muhendis Diplomasi [*Turkey*]

YMG .... Young Musicians of Germany (EAIO)

YMK .... Ypiresia Mikhanikis Kalliergeias [*Machine Cultivation Service*] [*Greek*] (GC)

YMMA ...... Young Men's Moslem Association

YMML ...... Young Methodist Missionary League [*Australia*]

YMN .... Yokohama Minami Nokyo [*Farm Cooperative Association of South Yokohama*] [*Japan*]

YMO .... Yellow Magic Orchestra [*Musical group*] [*Japan*]

yms .... Ynna Muuta Sellaista [*And So On*] [*Finland*]

yms .... Ynna Muuta Semmoista [*Finland*]

YMS .... Yurimaguas [*Peru*] [*Airport symbol*] (OAG)

Y Muh .... Yuksek Muhendis [*Senior Engineer*] (TU)

YN .... International NOTAM Office [*ICAO designator*] (ICDA)

YNB .... Yanbu [*Saudi Arabia*] [*Airport symbol*] (OAG)

YNCIAWPRC ... Yugoslav National Committee of the International Association on Water Pollution Research and Control (EAIO)

Yng Son ...... Yangin Sondurme [*Fire Fighting*] (TU)

YNJM .... Youth of the New JEWEL Movement [*Grenada*] (LA)

YNME ...... Ypourgeion Navtilias Metaforon kai Epikoinonion [*Ministry of Shipping, Transport, and Communications*] (GC)

YNOC .... Yemeni National Oil Company (GEA)

YNP .... Young National Party [*Australia*] [*Political party*]

YNPA .... Young National Party of Australia [*Political party*] (ADA)

YNZ .... New Zealand [*National Union Catalogue of Australia symbol*]

YO .... Aeronautical Information Service Unit [*ICAO designator*] (ICDA)

YO .... Mayotte [*ANSI two-letter standard code*] (CNC)

yo .... Ylioppilas [*Finland*]

YO .... Ypiresia Oikismou [*Housing Service*] (GC)

YO .... Yuksek Okul [*Advanced School*] [*As a college*] (TU)

YOAK .... Yuksek Ogretim Adaylari Komitesi [*Higher Education Candidates' Committee*] [*Turkish Cypriot*] (GC)

YOG .... Yuksek Ogretim Genclik [*Higher Educated Youth*] [*Cyprus*] (TU)

YOGM ...... Yuksek Ogretim Genel Mudurlugu [*Higher Education Directorate General*] (TU)

YOK .... Yuksek Ogretim Kurulu [*Higher Education Council*] (TU)

Yo Kvs .... Yol Kavsagi [*Crossroads, Road Confluence*] (TU)

YOKYK ..... Yuksek Ogrenim Kredi ve Yurtlar Koruma Genel Mudurlugu [*Higher Education Credit and Dormitories Organization Directorate General*] (TU)

YOL .... Yleinen Osuuskauppojen Liitto [*Central Cooperative Union*] [*Finland*] (WEN)

YOL .... Yola [*Nigeria*] [*Airport symbol*] (OAG)

YOL IS ...... Kibris Turk Karayollari Iscileri Sendikasi [*Turkish Cypriot Highway Workers Union*] (TU)

Yol Is .... Turkiye Karayolu, Yapim, Bakim, ve Onarim Isci Sendikalari Federasyonu [*Turkish State Higher Workers Federation*] (TU)

Yon-Sen ..... Kibris Turk Federe Devleti Iscileri Sendikasi [*Turkish Cypriot Federated State Workers' Union*] (TU)

YOO .... Yuksek Ogretmen Okulu [*Advanced Teachers School*] [*Ankara*] (TU)

YOPAM .... Yatirim, Organizasyon, Pazarlama, ve Arastirma Merkezi Ltd. Sti. [*Investment, Organization, Marketing, and Research Center Incorporated*] (TU)

YOS .... Young Offenders Support [*Australia*]

YOSS .... Yesilada Ortakoy Sonmez Spor [*Green Island Ortakoy Sonmez Sports' Club*] [*Cyprus*] (TU)

YOST .... Young Offenders Support Team [*Australia*]

YOTS .... Youth Ocean Training Scheme [*Australia*]

YOU .... Young Officers' Union [*Philippines*]

YOU .... Youth Organisation of Unemployed [*Australia*]

YOW .... International Young Christian Workers [*Acronym is based on foreign phrase*] [*Belgium*]

YP .... Malawi Young Pioneers

yp .... Ylempi Palkkausluokka [*Finland*]

YP .... Ypsili Piesis [*High Pressure*] (GC)

YPA .... Ypiresia Politikis Aeroporias [*Civil Aviation Service*] [*Greek*] (GC)

YPA .... Yugoslav People's Army (EE)

YPAAA ...... Ypiresia Perifereiakis Anaptyxeos (Nison) Anatolikou Aigaiou [*Service for the Regional Development of the Eastern Aegean (Islands)*] (GC)

YPAASE .... Ypiresia Perifereiakis Anaptyxeos Anatolikis Stereas Ellados [*Regional Development Service for Eastern Mainland Greece*] (GC)

YPATh .... Ypiresia Perifereiakis Anaptyxeos Thessalonikis [*Salonica Area Development Service*] (GC)

YPAVE ...... Ypiresia Perifereiakis Anaptyxeos Voreiou Ellados [*Service for the Regional Development of Northern Greece*] (GC)

YPBYRB ... Youth Parole Board and Youth Residential Board [*Victoria, Australia*]

YPC .... Yamanouchi Pharmaceutical Company Ltd. [*Japan*]

YPC .... Yemen Petroleum Company (GEA)

YPDC .... Youth Policy Development Council [*Victoria, Australia*]

YPDYS ...... Ypiresia Perithalpseos Dimosion Ypallilon kai Syndaxioukhon [*Aid Service for Civil Servants and Pensioners*] [*Greek*] (GC)

YPEA .... Ypiresia Ethnikis Asfaleias [*National Security Service*] [*Replaced GDEA*] [*Greek*] (GC)

YPEDA ...... Ypiresia Elenkhou Diakiniseos Agathon [*Service for Goods Movement Control*] (GC)

YPEM .... Ypiresia Paragogikon Ergon Makedonias [*Productive Works Service of Macedonia*] (GC)

YPEN .... Ypiresia Prostasias Ethnikou Nomismatos [*National Currency Protection Service*] [*Greek*] (GC)

YPEP .... Ypiresia Provolis Ellinikon Proiondon [*Greek Products Promotion Service*] [*Greek*] (GC)

YPEPTh ..... Ypourgeion Ethnikis Paideias kai Thriskevmaton [*Ministry of National Education and Religions*] (GC)

YPF .... Yacimientos Petroliferos Fiscales [*Government Oil Deposits*] [*Argentina*] (LA)

YPFB .... Yacimientos Petroliferos Fiscales Bolivianos [*Bolivian Government Oil Deposits*] (LA)

YPGP .... Ypiresia Prostasias Georgikon Proiondon [*Farm Products Protection Service*] [*Greek*] (GC)

YPK .... Yigitbas Parca Kollektif [*Yigitbas Parts Collective*] [*Turkish Cypriot*] (GC)

YPK .... Ypiresia Politikis Kinitopoiiseos [*Civilian Mobilization Service*] [*Greek*] (GC)

YPK .... Yuksek Planlama Kurulu [*Supreme Planning Organization*] (TU)
YPM .... Young Pioneer Movement
YPND .... Young People for Nuclear Disarmament [*Australia*]
YPP .... Papua New Guinea [*National Union Catalogue of Australia symbol*]
YPP .... Udostoverenie za Praktika Pedagogiceska [*Bulgarian*]
YPP .... Young Professional Program
YPPAXE ... Ypiresia Prosanatolismou, Pliroforion, kai Axiologiseos Xenon Ependyseon [*Agency for Orientation, Information, and Development of Foreign Investments*] (GC)
YPPK .... Ypourgeion Proedrias Kyverniseos [*Ministry to the Premier*] (GC)
YPR .... Young People's Refuge [*Australia*]
YPRLS .... Yarra Plenty Regional Library Service [*Australia*]
yr .... Den Yngre [*Junior*] [*Norway*] (GPO)
yr .... Year (EECI)
YR .... Yemeni Riyal (BJA)
YRAA .... Youth Refuge and Accommodation Association [*Australia*]
Yrb .... Yarbay [*Lieutenant Colonel (Army), Commander (Navy)*] (TU)
YRC .... Youth Resource Centre [*Australia*]
YRG .... Air Yugoslavia [*ICAO designator*] (FAAC)
YRSRI .... Yangtze River Scientific Research Institute [*China*] (IRC)
YS .... Aeronautical Station [*ICAO designator*] (ICDA)
YS .... Nihon Aeroplane Manufacturing Co. Ltd. [*Japan*] [*ICAO aircraft manufacturer identifier*] (ICAO)
YS .... Yamashita Shinnihon Line [*Commercial firm*] [*Japan*]
YS .... Yeoman of Signals [*Australia*]
YS .... Ypourgikon Symvoulion [*Council of Ministers*] (GC)
YS .... Ypsili Sykhnotis [*High Frequency*] (GC)
YSAAP ...... Youth Supported Accommodation Assistance Program [*Australia*]
YSAE .... Ypiresiakon Symvoulion Anoteras Ekpaidevseos [*Service Council for Secondary Education*] [*Greek*] (GC)
YSAP .... Ypiresia Syndonismou Anaptyxeos Perifereias [*Area Development Coordinating Service*] [*Greek*] (GC)
YSB .... Yunnan Seismological Bureau [*Kunming, China*]
YSC .... United Insurance Co. [*Yemen Arab Republic*] (MENA)
YSD .... Turkiye Yardim Sevenler Dernegi [*Turkish Philanthropic Organization*] [*TYSD*] [*See also*] (TU)
YSE .... Yol-Su ve Elektrik Isler Genel Mudurlugu [*Highways, Water, and Electric Affairs Directorate General*] [*Under Ministry of Village Affairs*] (TU)
YSEE .... Ypiresiakon Symvoulion Ekklisiastikis Ekpaidevseos [*Service Council for Ecclesiastical Education*] [*Greek*] (GC)
YSEIGM ... Yol Su Elektrik Isleri Genel Mudurlugu [*Highway, Water, and Electric Affairs Directorate General*] (TU)
YSES .... Yol, Su, Elektrik Sendikasi [*Union of Highway, Water, and Electric Power Workers*] (TU)
YSESA .... Ypiresia Syndonismou Efarmogis Skhediou Anasyngrotiseos [*Coordinating Service for Application of the Reconstruction Plan*] [*Greek*] (GC)
YSHFP ...... Youth and Student Hostel Foundation of the Philippines (EAIO)
YSI .... Yollari, Sulari, ve Elektrik Isleri Mudurlukleri [*Highways, Water, and Electrical Affairs Directorate*] [*Under Ministry of Village Affairs*] (TU)
YSI-IS .... Yollari, Sulari, ve Elektrik Isciileri Sendikasi [*Highways, Water, and Electric Workers Union*] (TU)
YSIS .... Youth Services Information System [*Western Australia*]
YSK .... Yuksek Savcilar Kurulu [*Supreme Council of Public Prosecutors*] [*Under Ministry of Justice*] (TU)
YSK .... Yuksek Secim Kurulu [*Supreme Electoral Council*] (TU)
YSKOR ...... Suid-Afrikaanse Yister- en Staal-Industriele Korporasie [*South African Iron and Steel Corporation*] [*Use ISCOR*] (AF)
Y-SLAV ..... Yugoslavia
YSM .... Young Socialist Movement [*Guyana*] (LA)
YSP .... Yemen Socialist Party [*South Yemen*] [*Political party*] (PD)
YSR .... Department of Youth, Sport and Recreation [*Western Australia*]
YSS .... Youth Services Scheme [*Australia*]
YSS .... Youth Study Society (ML)
YSSYEM... Ypiresia Syndiriseos kai Symplироseos Ydravlikon Ergon Makedonias [*Service for the Maintenance and Completion of Water Projects in Macedonia*] (GC)
YSTAPHIL ... Youth and Student Travel Association of the Philippines (EAIO)
YSURA ...... Proyecto Yaque del Sur, Azua [*Yaque del Sur, Azua Project*] [*Dominican Republic*] (LA)
YSV .... Yooralla Society of Victoria [*Australia*]
YT .... Telecommunication Authority [*ICAO designator*] (ICDA)
Yt .... Yatak [*or Yataklar*] [*Bed or Beds*] (TU)
YTAA .... Yoga Teachers Association of Australia (ADA)
YTC .... Youth Training Centre [*Australia*]
YTFA .... Yoga Teachers Federation of Australia (ADA)
YTK .... Ypiresia Topografiseos kai Ktimatologiou [*Topographic and Cadastral Service*] [*Greek*] (GC)
YTP .... Yeni Turkiye Partisi [*New Turkey Party*] (TU)

YTP........... Youth Training Program [*Australia*]
YTU .... Yarra Theological Union [*Australia*]
YU.............. Jugoslawia [*Former Yugoslavia*] [*Poland*]
Yu.............. Law School (BU)
Yu.............. South, Southern (RU)
YU.............. Yugoslavia [*ANSI two-letter standard code*] (CNC)
YUA........... Youth for Understanding Australia
YuA........... Yuridicheski Arkhiv [*Juridical Archives*] [*A periodical*] (BU)
YuAS......... Union of South Africa (RU)
YuAS......... Young Aircraft Builders [*Society*] (RU)
YuBGS...... South Belorussian Hydrological Station (RU)
YuBK .... South Crimean Shore (RU)
YuBMK ...... South Bulgarian Main Canal (BU)
YUC .... Yaounde University Club
YUC .... Yucatan
YUDESEV ... Youth Development Service [*Ghana*] (EAIO)
YuDM........ Young Friends of the MOPR (RU)
YuDPD ...... Young Voluntary Fire Brigade (RU)
YuF .... School of Law (BU)
YUF .... Yemen Unity Front (ME)
YuFK......... Southern Fergana Canal (RU)
YUG........... Yugoslavia [*ANSI three-letter standard code*] (CNC)
Yugenergo ... Southern Electric Power Administration (BU)
YuGOK..... Southern Mining and Concentration Kombinat (RU)
Yugos........ Yugoslavia
yugosl......... Yugoslav (RU)
Yugosol'..... Southern Salt Industry Trust (RU)
Yugostal'.... Southern Steel Industry Trust (RU)
YuGPU ...... Southern Mining Industry Administration (RU)
YuGV .... Southern Army Group (RU)
Yugzagotzerno ... Association for Procurement and Marketing of Grain and Grain Products of the Southern Regions (RU)
yu i........... Southeast (BU)
YUIWMI... Trade Union Institute of Workers in the Metal Industry [*Russian*]
YuK........... Young Correspondent (RU)
Yuk........... Yuksek [*High, Higher*] (TU)
YuKGU ..... South Kazakhstan Geological Administration (RU)
YUKH....... Yuksek Kontrol Heyeti [*Higher Control Committee*] [*of Foreign Affairs Ministry*] (TU)
YUK-IS...... Turkiye Yuk Iscileri Sendikasi [*Turkish Freight Workers' Union*] (TU)
YuKP .... Yugoslav Communist Party (BU)
YULIMO .. Youlou Liberation Movement [*St. Vincentian*] (LA)
YuM .... Yuridicheska Misul [*Juridical Thought*] [*A periodical*] (BU)
YuMZhD... South Manchurian Railroad [*1905-1945*] (RU)
Yun............ Yunanca [*Greek*] (TU)
Yundetizdat ... State Publishing House of Young People's and Children's Literature (RU)
yunosh........ Adolescent (BU)
yunosh........ Young, Youth, Juvenile (RU)
YuONII ..... South Ossetian Scientific Research Institute (RU)
YuP .... South Pole (RU)
YuP .... Young Pioneers [*Organization*] (RU)
YuPK .... Antarctic Circle (RU)
YuPr........... Yuridicheski Pregled [*Juridical Review*] [*A periodical*] (BU)
yur .... Juridical, Legal (RU)
Yur .... Yurt [*Topography*] (RU)
yurid.......... Juridical, Legal (RU)
Yurid fak..... School of Law (BU)
Yurizdat..... State Publishing House of Legal Literature (RU)
YurM .... Yuridicheska Misul [*Juridical Thought*] [*A periodical*] (BU)
YurPr......... Yuridicheski Pregled [*Juridical Review*] [*A periodical*] (BU)
YuRT .... Southern Ore Trust (RU)
YURTAS... Yurt Urunleri Sanayi ve Ticaret Anonim Sirketi [*Homeland Products Industry and Trade Corporation*] (TU)
YuSAKh..... Anniversary Reference Book of the Academy of Arts (RU)
yu sh.......... South Latitude (RU)
YuSSh........ Youth Sports School (BU)
YuT .... Young Technician (RU)
YuTAKE.... South Turkmen Complex Archaeological Expedition (RU)
YuTS......... Youth Tourist Union (BU)
YuUMZ..... South Ural Machinery Plant (RU)
YuV .... Southeast, Southeastern (RU)
YuVA .... Southeast Asia (RU)
Yuvelirtorg ... Office for the Trade in Jewelry, Watches, Rare Metals, and Precious Stones (RU)
YuVS......... Young Voroshilov Marksman (RU)
YuYuV ...... South-Southeast (RU)
YuYuZ .... South-Southwest (RU)
YuZ .... Southwest, Southwestern (RU)
YuZA .... Southwest Africa (RU)
yuzh.......... South, Southern (RU)
Yuzhavtostroy ... Administration for the Construction of the Southern Automobile Plant (RU)
Yuzhbum.... Southern Regional Administration of the Glavbum (RU)

Yuzhgiproruda ... State Institute for the Planning of Establishments of Iron Ore, Manganese, Flux, Refractory Raw Materials, and Fluorspar Industries   (RU)

Yuzhgiproshakht ... State Institute for the Planning of Mines in the Southern Regions of the USSR   (RU)

Yuzhgiprotsement ... State Institute for the Planning of Cement Plants in the Southern Regions of the USSR   (RU)

Yuzhgiprovodkhoz ... Southern Institute for the Planning of Water Management and Reclamation Construction   (RU)

Yuzhmashgiz ... Southern Branch of the Mashgiz   (RU)

Yuzhmashtrest ... Southern Machinery Trust   (RU)

yuzhn .... Southern   (RU)

YuZhNII .... Southern Scientific Research Institute of Industrial Construction   (RU)

YuzhNIIGiM ... Southern Scientific Research Institute of Hydraulic Engineering and Reclamation   (RU)

Yuzhsib ...... South Siberian Railroad   (RU)

Yuzhuralmash ... South Ural Machinery Plant   (RU)

Yuzhuralnikel' ... South Ural Nickel Plant   (RU)

Yuzhuraltyazhmash ... South Ural Heavy Machinery Plant   (RU)

YuZI .... All-Union Correspondence Law Institute   (RU)

YV .... Wenezuela [*Venezuela*] [*Poland*]

YV .... Yad Vashem [*An association*] [*Israel*]   (EAIO)

YVA .... Moroni [*Comoro Islands*] [*Airport symbol*]   (OAG)

YVSI .... Youth Voluntary Service of Italy   (EAIO)

YW .... Military Flight Operational Control Center [*ICAO designator*]   (ICDA)

YWAA .... Youth Welfare Association of Australia   (ADA)

YWAM ...... Youth With a Mission [*Australia*]

YWCA .... World Young Women's Christian Association   (EAIO)

YWCAA .... Young Women's Christian Association of Australia

YWCACZ ... Young Women's Christian Association Council of Zimbabwe   (EAIO)

YWCAT ..... Young Women's Christian Association of Taiwan   (EAIO)

YWM .... Youth with a Mission [*Australia*]

YX .... Military Service or Organization [*ICAO designator*]   (ICDA)

YY .... Yerli Yapi [*Locally Made*]   (TU)

YY .... Yuzyil [*Century*]   (TU)

Yym .... Yayim [*Publication*]   (TU)

YYPPKhL ... Ypiresia Ypodokhis Ploion kai (Polemikis) Khriseos Limenon [*Ship Receiving and (War) Port Use*]   (GC)

YYVN .... Ydrografiki Ypiresia Vasilikou Navtikou [*Navy Hydrographic Service*] [*Greek*]   (GC)

YZ .... MET Databank [*ICAO designator*]   (ICDA)

Yzb .... Yuzbasi [*Captain (Army), Lieutenant (Navy)*]   (TU)

Yzh .... Yazihane [*Office*]   (TU)

Z

Z.............. Barrage (RU)
Z.............. Earth (RU)
Z.............. Incendiary (RU)
Z.............. Niewiadoma Z [*Unknown Quantity Z*] [*Poland*]
Z.............. Notes, Records (RU)
Z.............. Serie Z [*Scabbards issued without bayonets, e.g., to infirmiers*] [*French*] (MTD)
Z.............. Setting [*of the sun*] (RU)
Z.............. Temps Universel [*Universal Time*] [*French*]
z.............. Terceira Incognita [*Third Unknown*] [*Portuguese*]
Z.............. Union Catalogue Agency [*National Union Catalogue of Australia symbol*]
Z.............. West, Western (RU)
Z.............. Winter (RU)
Z.............. Winter Load Line, Winter Plimsoll Mark (RU)
Z.............. Zaehigkeit [*Toughness*] [*German*] (GCA)
Z.............. Zahl [*Number*] [*German*] (EG)
Z.............. Zaire
Z.............. Zaire [*Monetary unit in Zaire*]
z.............. Zakon [*Law*] (CZ)
Z.............. Zaliv [*Gulf, Bay*] [*Serbo Croatian*] (NAU)
Z.............. Zaliv [*Gulf, Bay*] [*Russian*] (NAU)
Z.............. Zaloha [*Reserve*] (CZ)
z.............. Zapad [*West*] (CZ)
Z.............. Zatykac [*Warrant (for arrest)*] (CZ)
z.............. Zbior [*Collection*] [*Publishing*] [*Poland*]
Z.............. Zbrojovka [*Munitions Works*] [*Brno*] (CZ)
Z.............. Zebra [*Phonetic alphabet*] [*Royal Navy World War I Pre-World War II*] [*World War II*] (DSUE)
Z.............. Zeichen [*Sign*] [*German*] (GCA)
Z.............. Zeile [*Line*] [*German*] (EG)
Z.............. Zeit [*Time*] [*German*]
Z.............. Zeitschrift [*Journal, Periodical*] [*German*]
Z.............. Zeitung [*Newspaper, Review*] [*German*] (ILCA)
Z.............. Zement [*Cement*] [*German*] (GCA)
Z.............. Zenith, Antiaircraft (RU)
Z.............. Zentral [*Central*] (EG)
Z.............. Zentralblatt [*Official Gazette*] [*German*] (ILCA)
Z.............. Zentral-Sparkasse [*Banking*] [*Austria*] (ECON)
Z.............. Zentrumspartei [*Center Party*] [*German*] [*Political party*] (PPE)
z.............. Zeszyt [*Fascicle, Part*] (POL)
Z.............. Zimbabwe [*Aircraft nationality and registration mark*] (FAAC)
Z$............. Zimbabwe Dollar
Z.............. Zita Travel Tours & Cargo [*Saudi Arabia*]
Z.............. Zittijd [*Benelux*] (BAS)
Z.............. Zloty [*Monetary unit*] [*Poland*]
z.............. Zobacz [*See*] (POL)
Z.............. Zoll [*Customs Duty*] [*German*]
z.............. Zu [*At, To*] [*German*] (EG)
Z.............. Zuckung [*Contraction or spasm*] [*German*] [*Medicine*]
Z.............. Zuender [*Fuse*] [*German*] (GCA)
Z.............. Zulu [*Phonetic alphabet*] [*International*] (DSUE)
Z.............. Zum [*or Zur*] [*At The, To The*] [*German*] (EG)
ZA............. Alternate Airfield (RU)
ZA............. Antiaircraft Artillery (RU)
ZA............. Approach Control Office [*ICAO designator*] (ICDA)
ZA............. Balloon Barrage, Balloon Curtain (RU)
ZA............. Bus Manufacturing Plant (BU)
za............. Honored Artist (RU)
ZA............. Republika Poludniowej Afryki [*Republic of South Africa*] [*Poland*]
ZA............. South Africa [*ANSI two-letter standard code*] (CNC)
ZA............. Zahl [*Number*] [*German*] (ADPT)
ZA............. Zakon o Advokaturi [*Law on the Bar*] (YU)
ZA............. Zambia Airways
ZA............. Zapadocesky Aeroklub [*West Bohemian Aeroclub*] (CZ)
ZA............. Zeilenart [*German*] (ADPT)
ZA............. Zentralabteilung [*Central Department*] [*German*] (EG)

ZA............. Zentralarchiv fuer Empirische Sozialforschung [*Central Archives for Empirical Social Research*] [*University of Cologne*] [*Information service or system*] (IID)
za............. Zirka [*About, Approximately, Nearly*] [*German*]
ZA............. Ziva Antika [*The Living Past*] [*Skopje A periodical*] (YU)
ZAA......... Zanzibar Amateur Athletics Department
ZAAA....... Zambia Amateur Athletic Association
ZAB......... Aerial Incendiary Bomb (RU)
ZAB......... Antiaircraft Artillery Battery (RU)
ZAB......... Incendiary Bomb (BU)
zab............. Note, Remark (BU)
ZAB......... Reserve Air Brigade (RU)
ZAB......... Transbaykal Railroad (RU)
ZAB......... Zapaljive Aviobombe [*Incendiary Air Bombs*] (YU)
ZAB........... Zone Autonome de Brazzaville [*Autonomous Zone of Brazzaville*] [*Congo*] (AF)
Zabroshmedn rudnik ... Abandoned Copper Mine [*Topography*] (RU)
ZabVO....... Transbaykal Military District (RU)
ZAC .... Zambia Airways [*ICAO designator*] (FAAC)
ZAC .... Zapadocesky Autoklub [*West Bohemian Autoclub*] (CZ)
ZAC .... Zone d'Amenagement Concerte [*French*]
ZACCI...... Zambia Confederation of Industries and Chambers of Commerce (EAIO)
zach .... Zachod [*or Zachodni*] [*West or Western*] [*Poland*]
ZACU .... Zimbabwe African Congress of Unions (AF)
ZAD.......... Antiaircraft Artillery Battalion (RU)
ZAD.......... Zadar [*Former Yugoslavia*] [*Airport symbol*] (OAG)
ZAD.......... Zavody Automobilove Dopravy [*Auto Transportation Enterprises*] (CZ)
ZAD.......... Zone d'Amenagement Differe [*French*]
ZADCO ..... Zakum Development Company [*Abu Dhabi*] (MENA)
zaderzhsovp ... Delayed Coincidences (RU)
ZADES...... Zones d'Amenagement et de Developpement Economique et Social [*Economic and Social Development Zones*] [*Cambodia*] (CL)
ZADI .... Zentralstelle fuer Agrardokumentation und -Information [*Center for Agricultural Documentation and Information*] [*Databank originator*] [*Information service or system*] [*Germany*] (IID)
ZADU........ Zimbabwe African Democratic Union
ZAED .... Zentralstelle fuer Atomkernenergie-Dokumentation beim Gmelin-Institut [*Central Agency for Atomic Energy Documentation of the Gmelin Institute*] [*Germany Database originator Also, AED*]
Zaehigk...... Zaehigkeit [*Toughness*] [*German*] (GCA)
ZAER........ Alternate Airfield (RU)
ZAES......... Zapadnoafrikanskoe Ekonomicheskoe Soobshchestvo
ZAF.......... South Africa [*ANSI three-letter standard code*] (CNC)
ZAF........... Zambia Air Force
ZAF........... Zentralamt fuer Fernmeldebau [*Central Office for Telecommunication Construction*]
ZAF........... Zentralamt fuer Fernmeldewesen [*Central Office for Telecommunications*] (EG)
ZAFA....... Zambia Amateur Football Association
ZAFES...... Zambia Fellowship of Evangelical Students
ZAFT........ Zentralamt fuer Forschung und Technik [*Central Office for Research and Technology*] [*ZFT*] [*See also*] (EG)
ZAG .... Antiaircraft Artillery Group (RU)
ZAG .... Motor Vehicle Tires Plant (RU)
ZAG .... Zagreb [*Croatia*] [*Airport symbol*] (OAG)
ZAGES...... Zemo-Avchala Hydroelectric Power Plant Imeni V. I. Lenin (RU)
zagl............ Title, Heading (BU)
zagl s .... Title Page (BU)
Zagmetall... Office for Metal Procurement and Sale (RU)
Zagotizdat ... Publishing House of Technical and Economic Literature on Procurement (RU)
Zagotskot... Livestock Procurement Point (RU)

Zagotzerno ... Grain Procurement Point   (RU)
Zagotzhivkontora ... All-Union Office for Livestock Procurement and
Marketing   (RU)
zagr .... Foreign   (RU)
ZAGS .... Civil Registry Office   (RU)
zagtral ...... Minelaying and Sweeping Detachment   (RU)
ZAH .... Zahedan [*Iran*] [*Airport symbol*]   (OAG)
ZAHAL ..... Z'va Hagana Le'Israel [*Israel Defense Forces*] [*Hebrew*]
zahlr .... Zahlreich [*Numerous*] [*German*]
zahr .... Zahranicni [*Foreign, Abroad*]   (CZ)
ZAI .... Asbestos Products Plant   (BU)
ZAI .... Zaire Aero Service [*ICAO designator*]   (FAAC)
ZAI .... Zones d'Action Integree
ZAIKS .... Society of Authors [*Poland*]   (EAIO)
ZAiKS .... Zwiazek Aktorow i Kompozytorow Scenicznych [*Union of Actors
and Theatrical Composers*]   (POL)
Zaim .... Isolated Farmstead in Uncultivated Area [*Topography*]   (RU)
ZAIRETAIN ... Zairian Tin Company   (AF)
ZAIROM ... Societe Zootechnique Zairo-Roumaine [*Zairian-Romanian
Zootechnical Company*]   (AF)
ZAK .... Air Defense Artillery Systems   (BU)
zak .... Order   (RU)
zak .... Zakon [*Law*]   (CZ)
ZAK .... Zentrales Absatzkontor der Fischereibetriebe [*Central Marketing
Agency of the Fishing Industry*]   (EG)
ZAKFAN ... Transcaucasian Branch of the Academy of Sciences, USSR   (RU)
ZAKGEI .... Transcaucasian Scientific Research Institute of Water Power
(RU)
zakh .... Setting [*Astronomy*]   (RU)
zakhr .... Power Supply   (BU)
zakl .... Zaklad [*Bureau, Institute, Plant*]   (POL)
zakladFChTD ... Zaklad Fizyko-Chemicznej Technologii Drewna [*Enterprise
for the Physical and Chemical Processing of Lumber*]
(POL)
zakl sl .... Zakladni Sluzba [*Basic Military Service*]   (CZ)
ZakNIGMI ... Transcaucasian Scientific Research Hydrometerological
Institute   (RU)
ZakNIIGiM ... Transcaucasian Scientific Research Institute of Hydraulic
Engineering and Reclamation   (RU)
ZAKNIIVKh ... Transcaucasian Scientific Research Institute of Water
Management   (RU)
ZakNIKhI ... Transcaucasian Scientific Research Institute of Cotton Growing
[*1932-1936*]   (RU)
ZakOIIVKh ... Transcaucasian Experimental Research Institute of Water
Management   (RU)
Zak prok .... Law on the Procuracy   (BU)
ZAKR .... Zwiazek Polskich Autorow i Kompozytorow [*Association of
Polish Authors and Composers*]   (EAIO)
ZakVO .... Transcaucasus Military District   (RU)
zal .... Bay, Gulf [*Topography*]   (RU)
zal .... Deposit, Bed, Seam [*Topography*]   (RU)
zal .... Zalacznik [*Enclosure*]   (POL)
zal .... Zalozeno [*Founded*]   (CZ)
zal .... Zalozony [*or Zalozyl*] [*Founded or Founded By*] [*Poland*]
ZAL .... Zamrud Air Lines   (IN)
Zam .... Castle [*Topography*]   (RU)
zam .... Contactor [*Electricity*], Lock, Closer   (RU)
zam .... Deputy, Substitute   (RU)
zam .... Substitute, Deputy   (BU)
ZAM .... Zambia   (WDAA)
ZAM .... Zambia Association of Marketing
ZAM .... Zamboanga [*Philippines*] [*Airport symbol*]   (OAG)
zam .... Zamiast [*Instead*] [*Poland*]
zam .... Zamieszkaly [*Living At*]   (POL)
zam .... Zamowienie [*Order*]   (POL)
ZAMANGLO ... Zambia Anglo-American Corporation
ZAMBECO ... Companhia de Desenvolvimentos Agro-Pecuario e Comercial
do Vale do Zambeze Lda.
ZAMCO .... Zambesi Consorsio Hidra-Elettrico
zamdir .... Deputy Director   (RU)
ZAMEFA .. Metal Fabricators of Zambia Limited
ZAMG .... Zentralanstalt fuer Meteorologie und Geodynamik [*Central
Office for Meteorology and Geodynamics*] [*Federal Ministry
for Sciences and Research*] [*Austria*]   (EAS)
ZAMINI .... Ministerstvo Zahranicnich Veci [*Ministry of Foreign Affairs*]
(CZ)
zamkom ...... Deputy Commander, Second-in-Command   (RU)
zamkom ...... Deputy Commissar   (RU)
zamnach ..... Acting Head, Deputy Chief   (RU)
zam n-k ...... Deputy Chief   (BU)
zam n-k u-nie ... Deputy Chief of Administration   (BU)
ZAMP .... Antiaircraft Artillery Meteorological Post   (RU)
ZAMP .... Zavod za Mala Prava [*Institute for (Authors') Minor Rights*]
(YU)
ZAMP .... Zwiazek Akademickiej Mlodziezy Polskiej [*Union of Polish
Student Youth*]   (POL)

zampolit ..... Deputy Commander for Political Affairs   (RU)
zampotekh ... Deputy Commander for Technical Matters   (RU)
ZAMS .... Antiaircraft Artillery Meteorological Station   (RU)
ZAMS .... Zimowe Akademickie Mistrzostwa Swiata [*World Winter Sports
Student Championship*]   (POL)
ZAMTs ...... Zonal Air Weather Center   (RU)
ZAMU .... Zambian African Mining Union
zamzav .... Acting Manager, Deputy Chief   (RU)
zamzavbib .. Acting Head Librarian, Deputy Librarian   (RU)
zan .... Artisan's   (BU)
Zan .... Zanzibar   (BARN)
ZANA .... Zambia News Agency   (AF)
ZANC .... Zambia African National Congress
ZanD .... Zanayatchiyska Duma [*Artisan's Word*] [*A periodical*]   (BU)
ZANDU ..... Zambia National Democratic Union
ZANEWS ... Zanzibar News Service [*Tanzania*]   (AF)
Zankombinat ... Artisans' Combine   (BU)
ZANLA ..... Zimbabwe African National Liberation Army   (PD)
ZANN .... Law on Administrative Violations and Penalties   (BU)
ZANTAA ... Zambia National Theatre Arts Association
ZANU .... Zimbabwe African National Union [*Political party*]   (PPW)
ZANU-PF ... Zimbabwe African National Union - Patriotic Front [*Political
party*]   (PD)
ZANU-S .... Zimbabwe African National Union - Sithole
ZAO .... Antiaircraft Artillery Detachment   (BU)
ZAO .... Zagrebacka Armijska Oblast [*Zagreb Army District*]   (YU)
ZAOb .... Law on Turnover Tax   (BU)
ZAOR .... For Active Defense Work [*Badge*]   (RU)
ZAOU .... Zuid Afrikaansche Onderwijzers Unie
ZAP .... Lag [*Electrical equipment*]   (RU)
ZAP .... Law on Administrative Proceedings   (BU)
ZAP .... Law on Copyright   (BU)
ZAP .... Law on Motor Vehicle Transport   (BU)
zap .... Notes, Records   (RU)
ZAP .... Reserve Air Regiment   (RU)
ZAP .... Reserve Artillery Regiment   (RU)
Zap .... Western Railroad   (RU)
Zap .... West, Western   (RU)
ZAP .... Zachodnia Agencja Prasowa [*Western Press Agency*]   (POL)
ZAP .... Zaklad Architektury Polskiej [*Institute of Polish Architecture*]
(POL)
ZAP .... Zakon o Autorskom Pravu [*Copyright Law*]   (YU)
ZAPASA ... Zambia Police Sports Association
ZAPEK ...... Zadruzna Pekarna Pekarskih Radnika [*Bakery Cooperative*]
(YU)
ZAPI .... Zones d'Action Prioritaires Integrees [*Areas of Combined Priority
Action*] [*Cameroon*]   (AF)
ZAPI del'EST ... Societe Regionale des Zones d'Actions Prioritaires Integrees
de l'Est
ZapMaked ... Western Macedonia   (BU)
ZAPO .... Zimbabwe African People's Organization
ZAPOR ...... Zapovjednistvo Oruznistva [*Military Supreme Command*]
[*Croatia*] [*World War II*]   (YU)
Zaporozhstal' ... Zaporozh'ye Metallurical Plant   (RU)
ZAPORUK ... Zapovjednistvo Oruznickog Krila [*Military Wing Command*]
[*Croatia*] [*World War II*]   (YU)
Zapov .... Reservation, Sanctuary [*Topography*]   (RU)
ZapOVO .... Western Special Military District   (RU)
ZAPP .... Transcaucasian Association of Proletarian Writers   (RU)
ZAPP .... Zambia Pork Products
zapr .... Fueling, Servicing   (BU)
zapr .... Refueling Point   (RU)
ZAPU .... Zimbabwe African People's Union   (AF)
ZapVO .... Western Military District   (RU)
zar .... Charge, Load   (RU)
zar .... Earnings   (RU)
zar .... Honored Artist of the Republic   (RU)
ZAR .... Zaire [*ANSI three-letter standard code*]   (CNC)
ZAR .... Zairean Airlines [*Zaire*] [*ICAO designator*]   (FAAC)
ZAR .... Zentralafrikanische Republik [*Central African Republic*]
ZAR .... Zentrale Arbeitsgemeinschaft Oesterreichischer Rinderzuechter
[*Federation of Austrian Cattle Breeders*]   (ARC)
ZAR .... Zuid Afrikaansche Republik [*South African Republic*]
ZARAT ...... Zaklady Zjednoczenia Stacji Radiowych i Telewizyjnych
[*Agencies of the Union of Radio and Television
Transmitters*]   (POL)
ZARIK .... Zakon o Agrarnoj Reformi i Kolonizaciji [*Law on Agrarian
Reform and Colonization*]   (YU)
ZARP .... Zuid Afrikaansche Republick Politie [*South African Republic
Police*]   (DSUE)
ZARU .... Zimbabwe African Regional Union
zaryashch ... Caisson   (RU)
zarz .... Zarzad [*Administration*]   (POL)
zarz .... Zarzadzenie [*Administrative Order*]   (POL)
zarz Gl .... Zarzad Glowny [*Headquarters*] [*Poland*]
ZAS .... Glass Containers Plant   (BU)

zas .... Meeting, Conference (RU)
ZAS .... Zaire Aero Service [*ICAO designator*] (FAAC)
ZAS .... Zarkani Air Services [*Egypt*] (EY)
ZAS .... Zimbabwe Agricultural Society (EAIO)
ZAS .... Zpravodajska Agentura Slovenska [*Slovak Press Agency*] (CZ)
ZASE .... Zambia Association for Science Education
zashch .... Defense, Defensive, Protective (RU)
Zasl .... Honored [*Title*] (BU)
zasl artresp ... Honored Artist of the Republic (RU)
zasl d .... Honored Worker [*In art, science, etc.*] (RU)
zasl deyatn ... Honored Worker in the Sciences (RU)
zasl deyatn i t ... Honored Worker in Science and Technology (RU)
zasl m sp ... Honored Master of Sports (RU)
ZASP .... Zwiazek Artystow Scen Polskich [*Union of Polish Actors*] (POL)
zast .... Freezing, Solidification (RU)
Zast .... Outpost, Gate, Barrier [*Topography*] (RU)
zast .... Zastepczy [*Substitute*] (POL)
zast .... Zastupce [*Deputy, Representative, Agent*] (CZ)
zast .... Zastupitelsky [*Representative*] (CZ)
ZASTAL.... Zaodrzanskie Zaklady Konstrukcji Stalowej [*Trans-Odra (Oder) Steel Construction Plant*] (POL)
ZASTI ...... Zambia Air Services Training Institute
zat .... Creek, Backwater [*Topography*] (RU)
ZAT .... Law on Automotive Transportation (BU)
ZAT .... Zakon o Administrativnim Taksama [*Law on Administrative Fees*] (YU)
zat .... Zatimni [*Temporary*] (CZ)
Zat .... Zatoka [*Gulf, Bay*] [*Poland*] (NAU)
ZAT .... Zhaotong [*China*] [*Airport symbol*] (OAG)
ZAT .... Zydowska Agencja Telegraficzna (BJA)
ZATE........ Automobile and Tractor Electrical Equipment Plant (RU)
ZATI .... Automobile and Tractor Parts Plant (RU)
ZATU .... Zimbabwe African Tribal Union
zatv .... Solidification, Hardening, Congealing (RU)
zatw .... Zatwierdzony [*Approved*] (POL)
zav .... Attestation (BU)
zav .... Manager, Chief, Head (RU)
zav .... Ovary [*Botany*] (RU)
Zav .... Plant, Factory (RU)
ZAV .... Zentralarbeitsgemeinschaft des Strassenverkehrsgewerbes eV [*Central Association of the Road Transport Industry*] [*Frankfurt, West Germany*] (EY)
ZAV .... Zentralstelle fuer Arbeitsvermittlung [*Central Office for Job Procurement*] [*German*]
ZAVA .... Zambia Amateur Volleyball Association
zavbib .... Library Chief, Head Librarian (RU)
zavdel .... Chief Clerk, Office Supervisor (RU)
zavgar .... Garage Manager (RU)
ZAVK .... Zentrales Absatz- und Vermittlungskontor [*Central Sales and Brokerage Office*] (EG)
zavkants ..... Office Manager (RU)
zavkhim...... Chemical Section Chief, Head of Chemical Unit (RU)
zavkhoz ...... Business Manager, Manager (RU)
zavkom .... Plant Committee (BU)
zavkont .... Office Manager (RU)
zav lab .... Laboratory Chief (RU)
zav lab .... Plant Laboratory, Factory Laboratory (RU)
zavmag .... Store Manager (RU)
ZAVNO ..... Zemaljsko Antifasisticko Vece Narodnog Oslobodenja [*Territorial Anti-Fascist Council of National Liberation*] (YU)
ZAVNOBiH ... Zemaljsko Antifasisticko Vijece Narodnog Oslobodenja Bosne i Hercegovine [*Territorial Anti-Fascist Council of National Liberation of Bosnia and Hercegovina*] (YU)
ZAVNOH ... Zemaljsko Antifasisticko Vijece Narodnog Oslobodenja Hrvatske [*Territorial Anti-Fascist Council of National Liberation of Croatia*] (YU)
Zavodstal'konstruktsiya ... State All-Union Trust for the Manufacture of Steel Structures (RU)
zavorgot..... Organization Department Chief (RU)
zav pos....... Factory Settlement (RU)
zavprod....... Food Supply Manager (RU)
zavradio...... Radio Station Manager (RU)
zavrayfo...... Chief of the Rayon Finance Department (RU)
zavrono...... Chief of the Rayon Department of Public Education (RU)
Zavstol....... Canteen Manager (BU)
ZAvtP .... Law on Authorship Copyright (BU)
zavuch .... Chief of the Educational Section (BU)
zavuch .... Director of Studies (RU)
Zav u-t....... Section Chief (BU)
ZavVO....... Trans-Volga Military District (RU)
zavvod .... Chief of Water Transportation (RU)
zaw .... Zawodowy [*Professional, Vocational*] (POL)
ZAW .... Zentralausschuss der Werbewirtschaft eV [*Central Committee of the Advertising Industry*] (IMH)
ZAWI .... Zambia Association of Women's Institutes

zawod .... Zawodowy [*Professional, Vocational*] (POL)
ZAWU .... Zimbabwe African Women's Union (AF)
ZAZ .... Zaporozh'ye Automobile Plant (RU)
ZAZ .... Zaragoza [*Spain*] [*Airport symbol*] (OAG)
ZAZ .... Zatrovano Zemljiste [*Contaminated (by Poison) Area*] (YU)
ZAZ .... Zavody Antonina Zapotckeho [*Antonin Zapotcky Works*] (CZ)
ZAZ .... Zelezarny Antonina Zapotckeho [*Antonin Zapotcky Iron Works*] [*Vamberk*] (CZ)
ZB .... Antiaircraft Battery (RU)
zb .... Barrage Battery (RU)
ZB .... Earth Auger (RU)
ZB .... Foreign Bureau (BU)
ZB .... Incendiary Tanks [*Containers*] (RU)
ZB .... Law on Banks (BU)
ZB .... Law on Marriage (BU)
ZB .... Law on the Budget (BU)
ZB .... Mirror Drum, Mirror Wheel (RU)
ZB .... Repetitive Flight Plan Office [*ICAO designator*] (ICDA)
ZB .... Retreat-Blocking Battalion (RU)
ZB .... Zakon o Braku [*Marriage Law*] (YU)
ZB .... Zaprecni Baloni [*Barrage Balloons*] (YU)
zb .... Zbierka [*Collection*] (CZ)
Zb .... Zbierka Zakonov CSSR [*Collection of Laws of the Czechoslovak Socialist Republic*] (CZ)
ZB .... Zeleznorudne Bane [*Iron Ore Mines*] (CZ)
Zb .... Zentralblatt [*Central Journal*] [*German*] (GCA)
ZB .... Zimbabwe Banking Corp. Ltd.
ZB .... Ziraat Bank [*Agricultural Bank*] (TU)
ZB .... Zivnostenska Banka [*Bank of Commerce*] (CZ)
ZB .... Zuiveringsbesluit [*Benelux*] (BAS)
ZB .... Zum Beispiel [*For Example*] [*German*]
ZB .... Zveza Borcev [*Union of Veterans*] (YU)
ZBA .... Zambia Badminton Association
ZbA .... Zusammenstellung Betrieblicher Anordnungen [*Compilation of Operational Instructions*] (EG)
ZBAA .... Beijing/Capital [*China*] [*ICAO location identifier*] (ICLI)
ZBBB .... Beijing City [*China*] [*ICAO location identifier*] (ICLI)
ZBBS .... Protein and Bioconcentrate Mixes Plant (BU)
ZBC .... Zimbabwe Broadcasting Corporation
ZBDS .... Zveza Bibliotekarskih Drustev Slovenije [*Library Association of Slovenija*] [*Samoa*] (EAIO)
ZBE............ Zwischenbetriebliche Einrichtungen [*Interplant Facilities*] [*German*] (EG)
ZBG .... Law on Bulgarian Citizenship (BU)
ZBHD .... Zambia Broken Hill Development Co.
ZBHH .... Huhhot [*China*] [*ICAO location identifier*] (ICLI)
ZBiAP........ Zwiazek Bibliotekarzy i Archiwistow Polskich [*Union of Polish Librarians and Archivists*] (POL)
ZBIM........ Zjednoczone Budownictwo Inzynieryjno-Morskie [*Maritime Engineering Construction Association*] (POL)
ZBK .... Zentrale Begutachtungskommission [*Central Evaluation Commission*] [*German*] (EG)
ZBK .... Zjednoczenie Budownictwa Komunalnego [*Communal Construction Association*] (POL)
ZBKiC........ Zaklad Badan Konjunktur i Cen [*Price and Market Research Institute*] (POL)
ZBL............ Zambia Breweries Limited
ZBl .... Zentralblatt [*Central Gazette*] [*German*] (EG)
ZBM .... Zarzad Budynkow Mieszkalnych [*Administration of Apartment Houses*] (POL)
ZBM .... Zavodza Biologiju Mora [*Former Yugoslavia*] (MSC)
ZBM .... Zjednoczenie Budownictwa Miejskiego [*Association for Urban Construction*] (POL)
ZBM .... Zjednoczenie Budownictwa Mieszkaniowego [*Association for Housing Construction*] (POL)
ZBM .... Zjednoczenie Budowniczych Miejskich [*Association of Urban Builders*] (POL)
ZBMA ...... Zaklady Budowy Maszyn i Aparatury [*Machine and Appliance Plant*] (POL)
ZBMed ...... Zentralbibliothek der Medizin [*Cologne*] [*Information retrieval*]
ZBMiA ...... Zaklady Budowy Maszyn i Aparatury [*Machine and Appliance Plant*] (POL)
ZBMNH.... Zjednoczenie Budownictwa Miejskiego Nowa Huta [*Nowa Huta Urban Construction Association*] (POL)
ZBMO ...... Zjednoczenie Budownictwa Miast i Osiedli [*Association for Urban and Settlement Construction*] (POL)
ZBMW-1... Zjednoczenie Budownictwa Mieszkaniowego Warszawy-1 [*Association for Housing Construction in the First District of Warsaw*] (POL)
ZBNOVS... Zveza Borcev Narodnoosvobodilne Vojne Slovenije [*Union of Veterans of the National Liberation War of Slovenia*] (YU)
ZbNZO...... Zbornik za Narodni Zivot i Obicaje Juznih Slavena Jugoslavenske Akademije Znanosti i Umjetnosti [*Collected Papers of the National Life and Customs of the South Slavs, Yugoslav Academy of Sciences and Arts*] [*Zagreb A periodical*] (YU)

ZBO .... Bowen [*Australia*] [*Airport symbol*] [*Obsolete*]   (OAG)
ZBO .... Zwischengenossenschaftliche Bauorganisation [*Intercooperative Construction Organization*] [*German*]   (EG)
ZBOB .... Law on the Budget and Budget Accountability   (BU)
ZBOP........ Law on the Budget of Public Enterprises   (BU)
ZBOW .... Baotou [*China*] [*ICAO location identifier*]   (ICLI)
ZBoWiD .... Zwiazek Bojownikow o Wolnosc i Demokracje [*Union of Fighters for Freedom and Democracy*]   (POL)
ZBP........... Law on Cashless Payments   (BU)
ZBP........... Zaklad Badan Prasoznawczych [*Press Research Institute*]   (POL)
ZBP........... Zarzad Bibliotek Polskich [*Administration of Polish Libraries*]   (POL)
ZBP........... Zjednoczenie Budownictwa Przemyslowego [*Industrial Construction Association*]   (POL)
ZBP........... Zvlastni Bojove Prostredky [*Special Warfare Agents*]   (CZ)
ZBPE........ Beijing [*China*] [*ICAO location identifier*]   (ICLI)
ZBPP .... Zjednoczenie Budowy Piecow Przemyslowych [*Association for Industrial Furnace Construction*]   (POL)
ZBPPMN .. Law on the Struggle Against Antisocial Actions of Minors and Juveniles   (BU)
ZBPPV ...... Law on Cashless Payments and Use of Deposits   (BU)
ZBR .... Chah-Bahar [*Iran*] [*Airport symbol*]   (OAG)
ZBRol .... Zjednoczenie Budownictwa Rolnego [*Rural Construction Association*]   (POL)
Zbrw........... Zeebrievenwet [*Benelux*]   (BAS)
ZBS............ Coastal Sound-Locator Station   (RU)
ZBS............ Zambia Broadcasting Service   (AF)
ZBSB .... Zeitschriftenkatalog der Bayerischen Staatsbibliothek, Munchen [*Serials Catalogue of the Bavarian State Library, Munich*] [*Deutsches Bibliotheksinstitut*] [*Germany*] [*Information service or system*]   (CRD)
ZBSM-Ch ... Zwiazek Branzowy Spoldzielni Mineralno-Chemicznych [*Professional Association of Mineral and Chemical Cooperatives*]   (POL)
ZBTJ .... Tianjin/Zhangguizhuang [*China*] [*ICAO location identifier*]   (ICLI)
ZBTsK ...... Foreign Office of the Central Committee of the RSDRP   (RU)
ZBUT .... Zaklady Budowy Urzadzen Technicznych [*Technical Equipment Construction Plants*]   (POL)
ZBUT .... Zjednoczenie Budowy Urzadzen Technicznych [*Association for the Construction of Technical Equipment*]   (POL)
ZBV .... Zoological Board of Victoria [*Australia*]
zbV .... Zur besonderen Verfuegung [*Specially Available*] [*German*]   (GCA)
zbV .... Zur Besonderen Verwendung [*For Special Use*] [*German*]
ZBVB........ Law on the Fight Against Venereal Diseases   (BU)
ZBW .... Zjednoczenie Budownictwa Wojskowego [*Association for Military Construction*]   (POL)
ZBWP........ Zwiazek Bylych Wiezniow Politycznych [*Union of Former Political Prisoners*]   (POL)
ZBYN .... Taiyuan/Wusu [*China*] [*ICAO location identifier*]   (ICLI)
ZByud .... Law on the State Budget   (BU)
Z byudzh ... Law on the State Budget   (BU)
ZBZ............ Bacterial Contamination Zone   (BU)
ZBZ............ Bacteriological Contamination Zone   (RU)
Z-C............ Zapalote Chico [*Race of maize*] [*Mexico*]
ZC .... Zarzad Celny [*Customs Administration*]   (POL)
ZC .... Zenijni Ceta [*Engineer Platoon*]   (CZ)
ZC .... Zgodovinski Casopis [*Historical Journal*] [*Ljubljana*]   (YU)
ZC .... Zimni Cviceni [*Winter Maneuvers*]   (CZ)
ZC .... Zinfandel Club [*British*]   (EAIO)
ZC .... Zionist Congress [*Australia*]
ZC .... Zonta Club [*Australia*]
z-ca .... Zastepca [*Deputy, Substitute*]   (POL)
ZCBC........ Zambia Consumer Buying Corporation
ZCC .... Zapodoceske Cihelny [*West Bohemian Brick Works*]   (CZ)
ZCCM .... Zambia Consolidated Copper Mines
ZCCM .... Zambian Consolidated Copper Mines
ZCE .... Zapodoceske Elektrarny, Narodni Podnik [*West Bohemian Electric Power Works, National Enterprise*]   (CZ)
ZCF............ Zambia Cooperative Federation
ZCh............ Audio Frequency   (RU)
ZCh............ Spiegeleisen, Mirror Iron   (RU)
ZChN........ Zjednoczenie Chrzescijansko-Narodowe [*Christian National Union*] [*Poland*] [*Political party*]   (EY)
ZChO........ Cast Iron Foundry   (BU)
ZChOB ..... Law on Private and Public Security   (BU)
ZChV .... Zavod pro Chemickou Vyrobu [*Chemical Factories*]   (CZ)
ZCI............ Zambia Copper Investments Limited
ZCL............ Zacatecas [*Mexico*] [*Airport symbol*]   (OAG)
ZCN .... Zaklady Czyszczenia Nasion [*Seed Cleaning Establishments*]   (POL)
ZCP............ Zonta Club of Perth [*Western Australia*]
ZCPK........ Zapodocesky Prumysl Kamenny [*West Bohemian Stone Industry*]   (CZ)

ZCRP......... Zapadocesky Rudny Pruzkum [*West Bohemian Mineral Prospecting*]   (CZ)
ZCS............ Zapadoceske Sklarny, Narodni Podnik [*West Bohemian Glass Factories, National Enterprise*]   (CZ)
ZCSD .... Zambia Council for Social Development
ZCT .... Zapadoceske Tiskarny [*West Bohemian Printing Plants*]   (CZ)
ZCTU .... Zambia Congress of Trade Unions   (AF)
ZCTU .... Zimbabwe Congress of Trade Unions
ZCU .... Zambia Cricket Union
ZCZ .... Zavodi Crvena Zastava [*Former Yugoslavia*]
ZD.............. Air Traffic Flow Control Unit [*ICAO designator*]   (ICDA)
ZD.............. Antiaircraft Range Finder   (RU)
Zd.............. Building [*Topography*]   (RU)
ZD.............. Law on Prescription   (BU)
Z-d.............. Plant, Factory   (RU)
zd.............. West Longitude   (RU)
zd.............. Zahodna Dolzina [*Western Longitude*]   (YU)
ZD.............. Zbrano Delo [*Collected Works*]   (YU)
ZD.............. Zelenoye Dvizheniye [*Green Movement*] [*Former USSR*]   (EAIO)
ZD.............. Zemske Divadlo [*Province Theater*]   (CZ)
zd.............. Zonder Datum [*Benelux*]   (BAS)
ZDA.......... Law on State Arbitration   (BU)
ZDA........... Zakon o Drzavnoj Arbitrazi [*Law on State Arbitration*]   (YU)
ZDA........... Zedinjene Drzave Amerike [*United States of America*]   (YU)
ZDA........... Zinc Development Association [*British*]   (EAIO)
zdA........... Zu den Akten [*Pigeonhole or Shelve (Something)*] [*German*]
ZDAS......... Zdarske Strojirny a Slevarny [*Zdar Engineering Plants and Foundries*]   (CZ)
ZDAS......... Zveza Drustev Arhitektov Slovenije [*Ljubljana, Yugoslavia*]   (SLS)
ZDB .... Zeitschriftendatenbank [*German Union Catalog of Serials*] [*Deutsches Bibliotheksinstitut*] [*Germany*] [*Information service or system*]   (CRD)
ZDB .... Zimbabwe Development Bank   (GEA)
ZDD.......... Compulsory State Deliveries   (BU)
ZDE .... Zagreb Dance Ensemble [*Former Yugoslavia*]
ZDE .... Zentralstelle Dokumentation Elektrotechnik [*Electrical Engineering Documentation Center*] [*Originator and database*] [*Germany*] [*Information service or system*]   (IID)
ZDF .... Zimbabwe Defence Force
ZDF .... Zimbabwe Development Fund
ZDF .... Zweites Deutsches Fernsehen [*Second German Television*]   (WEN)
Zdg............ Zuendung [*Ignition*] [*German*]   (GCA)
ZDH.......... Zeleznorudne Doly a Hrudkovny [*Iron Ore Mines and Krupp-Renn Plants*]   (CZ)
ZDH.......... Zentralverband des Deutschen Handwerks [*Central Association of German Craftsmen*]   (WEN)
ZDH.......... Zuendhuetchen [*Primer*] [*German*]   (GCA)
Zdht.......... Zuendhuetchen [*Primer*] [*German*]   (GCA)
ZDHV......... Znanstveno Drustvo za Humanisticne Vede [*Scientific Society for Humanistic Sciences*]   (YU)
zdi.............. Honored Worker in the Arts, Honored Art Worker   (RU)
ZDI............ Zentralverband Deutscher Ingenieure [*Germany*]   (EAIO)
ZDK.......... Law on State Control   (BU)
ZDK.......... Zagrebacko Dramsko Kazaliste [*Zagreb Drama Theater*]   (YU)
ZDK.......... Zakladowy Dom Kultury [*Plant House of Culture*]   (POL)
ZDK.......... Ziraat Donatim Kurumu [*Agricultural Equipment Board*] [*TZDK*] [*See also*]   (TU)
Zdlg........... Zuendladung [*Primer Charge*] [*German*]   (GCA)
ZDLS......... Zveza Delovnega Ljudstva Slovenije [*Alliance of Working People of Slovenia*]   (YU)
ZDM.......... Timber Processing Machines Plant   (BU)
ZDM.......... Zbor Duhovne Mladezi [*Society of Religious Youth*] [*Croatian*]   (YU)
ZDM.......... Zentralblatt fuer Didaktik der Mathematik [*Information retrieval*]
ZDMH...... Zbor Duhovne Mladezi Hrvatske [*Society of Religious Youth of Croatia*] [*Catholic Church*]   (YU)
Zd Mitt ..... Zuendmittel [*Priming Material*] [*German*]   (GCA)
ZDMMA ..... Zonguldak Devlet Muhendislik ve Mimarlik Akademisi [*Zonguldak State Engineering and Architecture Academy*]   (TU)
ZDMO...... Dinas Brick and Magnesium Refractory Materials Plant   (BU)
ZDMOS .... Zdruzenie Detskych a Mladeznickych Organizaci Slovenske Socialisticke Republiky [*Association of Children's and Youth Organizations of the Slovak Socialist Republic*]   (CZ)
ZDMZ .... Zbor Duhovne Mladezi Zagrebacke [*Zagreb Religious Youth Society*]   (YU)
zdn............ Honored Worker in Science, Honored Scientist   (RU)
ZDNP........ Law on the State Economic Plan   (BU)
ZDNPl........ Law on the State Economic Plan   (BU)
ZDO.......... Law on the Turnover Tax   (BU)
ZDOD........ Law on the General Income Tax   (BU)

ZDOK........ Dokumentations Zentrum fuer Informationswissenschaften [*DGD*] [*German*]
ZDP .... Law on State Enterprises   (BU)
ZDP .... Zimbabwe Democratic Party [*Political party*]   (PPW)
ZDR .... Zaklad Doskonalenia Rzemiosla [*Institute for Improvement of Handicraft*]   (POL)
ZDR .... Zeichendrucker [*Graphics Printer*] [*German*]   (ADPT)
ZDR .... Zenijni Druzstvo [*Engineer Squad*]   (CZ)
ZDR .... Zentraldeutsche Rundfunk [*Central German Radio*]
Zdravpunkt ... Health Center   (BU)
zdravupr ...... Public Health Administration   (RU)
ZdrPr .... Zdravotnicky Prapor [*Medical Battalion*]   (CZ)
ZDS .... Law on Comrades Courts   (BU)
ZDS .... Woodworking Machine Plant   (RU)
ZDS .... Zakladni Devitileta Skola [*Basic Nine-Year School*]   (CZ)
ZDS .... Zakon o Drzavnim Sluzbenicima [*Law on Government Employees*]   (YU)
ZDS .... Zgodovinsko Drustvo za Slovenijo [*Historical Society of Slovenia*]   (YU)
ZdschAnz ... Zuendschnuranzuender [*Fuse Lighter*] [*German*]   (GCA)
Zdschn .... Zuendschnur [*Fuse*] [*German*]   (GCA)
ZDSK .... Law on the State Savings Bank   (BU)
ZDSl .... Law on State Employees   (BU)
ZDSNRS ... Zakon o Drzavnim Sluzbenicima Narodne Republike Srbije [*Law on Government Employees of Serbia*]   (YU)
ZDSO .... Law on Contracts between Socialist Enterprises   (BU)
zdt.............. Honored Worker in Technology   (BU)
ZDT .... Law on State Fees   (BU)
ZdT .... Zadruzna Tiskarna, Trst [*Cooperative Printing House, Trieste*]   (YU)
ZDTM .... Law on the State Tobacco Monopoly   (BU)
ZDTPI .... Law on the State Telegraph and Post Institute   (BU)
ZDU .... Zvezni Zakon o Drzavni Upravi [*Federal Law on Government Administration*]   (YU)
ZDULRS ... Zakon o Drzavni Upravi Ljudska Republika Slovenija [*Law on Government Administration of Slovenia*]   (YU)
ZDVK .... Law on State and Departmental Control   (BU)
ZDVP........ Law on Road Traffic   (BU)
ZDWF .... Zentrale Dokumentationsstelle der Freien Wohlfahrtspflege fuer Fluechtlinge eV [*Germany*]
ZDZ .... Zaklad Doskonalenia Zawodowego [*Vocational Improvement Center*]   (POL)
ZDZS .... Zalozila Drzavna Zalozba Slovenije [*Published by the Government Printing House of Slovenia*]   (YU)
ZE .... Flight Information Database [*ICAO designator*]   (ICDA)
ZE .... Reference Element   (RU)
ZE .... Zadruzna Ekonomija [*Agricultural Cooperative Economy*]   (YU)
ZE .... Zakon o Eksproprijaciji [*Expropriation Law*]   (YU)
ZE .... Zavodni Elektrarna [*Factory Electric Power Plant*]   (CZ)
ZE .... Zentraleinheit [*German*]   (ADPT)
zE .... Zum Exempel [*For Example, For Instance*] [*German*]
ZEAL......... Zululand Environment Alliance [*South Africa*]   (AA)
ZEB............ Zentrales Einkaufsbuero [*Central Purchasing Office*] [*German*]   (EG)
ZEDI......... Law on the Single Collection of the Property Tax   (BU)
ZEE............ Zentralverband Elektrotechnik- und Elektronikindustrie [*German Electrical and Electronic Manufacturers*]   (EAIO)
ZEE............ Zona Economica Exclusiva [*Exclusive Economic Zone*]   (LA)
ZEE............ Zone Economique Exclusive [*Exclusive Economic Zone*]
ZEF............ Zimbabwe Entwicklungs Fond [*Zimbabwe Development Fund*]
ZEG .... Senggo [*Indonesia*] [*Airport symbol*]   (OAG)
Zeichn .... Zeichnung [*Drawing*] [*German*]
ZEIM .... Electrical Insulating Materials Plant   (RU)
ZEIP .... Electrical Measuring Instruments Plant   (RU)
Zeit............. Zeitschrift [*Journal, Periodical*] [*German*]   (GCA)
Zeit............. Zeitung [*Newspaper*] [*German*]   (GCA)
Zeitgen........ Zeitgenosse [*Contemporary*] [*German*]
zeitgenoss.... Zeitgenoessisch [*Contemporary*] [*German*]
zeitl............. Zeitlich [*Chronological*] [*German*]   (GCA)
Zeitlp.......... Zeitlupe [*Slow Motion*] [*German*]   (GCA)
Zeitschr....... Zeitschrift [*Publication, Periodical, Journal*] [*German*]
Zeittaf .... Zeittafel [*Chronological Table*] [*German*]
ZEK .... Zentrales Entwicklungs- und Konstruktionsbuero [*Central Development and Designing Office*] [*German*]
ZEKH .... Zentrale Entwicklung und Konstruktion Hydraulik (VEB) [*Central Development and Design Enterprise for Hydraulics (VEB)*] [*German*]   (EG)
zeldz .... Zeldzaam [*Rare*] [*Netherlands*]
ZELJOPOH ... Zeljeznarsko Poduzece Hrvatske [*Croatian Hardware Establishment*]   (YU)
ZELLCHEMING ... Verein der Zellstoff-und Papier-Chemiker und-Ingenieure [*German Pulp and Paper Chemists and Engineers Association*]   (EAIO)
Zellst.......... Zellstoff [*Cellulose*] [*German*]   (GCA)
zem .... Agriculture, Agricultural   (BU)
Zem .... Earth, Earthen [*Topography*]   (RU)

zem............. Earth Embankment [*Topography*]   (RU)
ZEM .... Electrical Machinery Plant   (RU)
zem .... Land, Soil, Agricultural   (RU)
zem............. Mud Hut [*Topography*]   (RU)
ZEMA .... Zambia Expatriate Miners' Association
ZEMAG .... Zeitz Eisengiesserei und Maschinenfabrik (VEB) [*Zeitz Iron Foundry and Machine Factory (VEB)*]   (EG)
ZEMAK..... Zjednoczenie Przemyslu Budowy Maszyn Ciezkich [*Heavy Machinery Construction Industry Union*]   (POL)
Zementier... Zementierung [*Cementing*] [*German*]   (GCA)
Zemizdat.... Publishing House on Agriculture   (BU)
Zem kod ..... Land Code   (RU)
zeml............ Agriculture, Agricultural   (RU)
zeml............ Earth, Earthen [*Topography*]   (RU)
zemot.......... Department of Agriculture   (RU)
zemot.......... Land Department   (RU)
Zemsist ...... Member of the Agrarian Youth Union   (BU)
Zemsnab ...... State Economic Enterprise for Supplying Farms with Tools, Seeds, and Chemicals   (BU)
Zemugol'shch ... Charcoal Dealer's Hut [*Topography*]   (RU)
zemupr .... Land Administration   (RU)
Zemustroy ... Departmental Organization for Land Regulation   (BU)
Zen .... Zenijni [*Pertaining to Army Engineers*]   (CZ)
zenabr......... Antiaircraft Artillery Brigade   (BU)
zenad .... Antiaircraft Artillery Battalion   (BU)
zenad .... Antiaircraft Artillery Division   (BU)
zenadn .... Antiaircraft Artillery Battalion   (BU)
zenap .... Antiaircraft Artillery Regiment   (BU)
zenbat......... Antiaircraft Artillery Battery   (RU)
zenbatr .... Antiaircraft Artillery Battery   (BU)
Zendensen ... Zen-Nihon Densen-Kogyo Rodokumiai [*All-Japan Electric Wire Labor Union*]
zendiv .... Antiaircraft Artillery Battalion   (RU)
Zendoren ... Zenkoku Shindo Rodokumiai Rengokai [*National Federation of Copper Elongation Industry Workers' Unions*] [*Japan*]
Zenginkyo ... Zenkoku Ginko Kyokai Rengokai [*Federation of Bankers Association of Japan*]   (EAIO)
Zen-Insoren ... Zenkoku Insatsu-Shuppan-Sangyo Rodokumiai Sorengokai [*National Federation of Printing and Publishing Industry Workers' Unions*] [*Japan*]
Zenjiko....... Zenkoku Jidosha Kotsu Rodokumiai Rengokai [*National Federation of Automobile Transport Workers' Union*] [*Japan*]
Zenjiun....... Zenkoku Jidosha Unyu Rodokumiai [*National Trade Union of Automobile Transport Workers*] [*Japan*]
Zenkadomei ... Zenkoku Kagaku Ippan Rodokumiai Domei [*Japanese Federation of Chemical and General Workers' Unions*]
Zenkensoren ... Zenkoku Kensetsu Rodokumiai Sorengo [*National Federation of Construction Workers' Unions*]
Zenkikin .... Zenkoku Kikai Kinzoku Rodokumiai [*National Machinery and Metal Workers' Union*] [*Japan*]
Zenko......... Zen-Nihon Kimzokukozan Rodokumiai Rengokai [*Federation of All-Japan Metal Mine Labor Unions*]
Zenkokudenryoku-Kenshuroren ... Zenkoku Denryoku Kenshin Shukin-In Rodokumiai Renrakukaigi [*National Confederation of Electric Power Meter Inspectors' and Electric Fee Collectors' Unions*] [*Japan*]
Zenkokugasu ... Zenkoku Gasu Rodokumiai Rengokai [*National Federation of Gas Supply Workers' Unions*] [*Japan*]
Zenkokujiro ... Zenkoku Jiyu Rodokumiai Rengokai [*National Federation of Day Workers' Unions*] [*Japan*]
Zenkokusasshirokyo ... Zenkoku Sasshi Shatta Rodokumiai Kyogikai [*National Council of Sash and Shutter Industry Workers' Unions*] [*Japan*]
Zenkokuyurokyo ... Zenkoku Yushi-Sangyo Rodokumiai Kyogikai [*National Council of Oil and Fat Industry Workers' Unions*] [*Japan*]
Zenkowan .. Zen-Nihon Kowan Rodokumiai [*All-Japan Harbor Workers' Union*]
Zenmiro ... Zen-Nihon Minshu Jiyu Rodokumiai [*National Democratic Union of Casual Workers*] [*Japan*]
ZEN-NOH ... National Federation of Agricultural Cooperative Associations [*Japan*]   (EAIO)
Zennokyororen ... Zenkoku Nogyo Kyodokumiai Rodokumiai Rengokai [*National Federation of Agricultural Mutual Aid Societies Employees' Unions*] [*Japan*]
Zen prap..... Zenijni Prapor [*Engineer Battalion*]   (CZ)
zenpul'rota ... Antiaircraft Machine-Gun Company   (RU)
Zensekiyu .. Zenkoku Sekiyu-Sangyo Rodokumiai Kyogikai [*All-Japan Oil Workers Union*]
Zensendomei ... Zenkoku Sen-i-Snagyo Rodokumiai Domei [*Japan Federation of Metal Industry Trade Unions*]
Zenshinren ... Zenkoku-Shintaku-Ginku Jugyoin Kumiai Rengokai [*National Federation of Trust Bank Employees' Unions*] [*Japan*]
Zenshinro... Zenkoku Shin-Yo Kinko Shin-Yo Kumiai Rodokumiai Rengokai [*National Federation of Credit Association Workers' Unions*] [*Japan*]

Zenshokuhindomei ... Zenkoku Shokuhin-Sangyo Rodokumiai Domei [*National Federation of Food Industry Workers' Unions*] [*Japan*]

Zenshosha ... Zenkoku Shosha Rodokumiai Rengokai [*National Federation of Commercial Firm Employees' Unions*] [*Japan*]

Zensoun ..... Zen-Nihon Soko Unyu Rodokumiai Domei [*Japanese Warehouse and Transport Union*]

Zensuido .... Zen-Nihon Suido Rodokumiai [*National Federation of Water Supply Workers' Union*] [*Japan*]

Zentei........ Zenteishin Rodokumiai [*Japan Postal Workers' Union*]

zentr .... Zentral [*Central*] [*German*]

Zentr .... Zentrum [*Center*] [*German*]   (GCA)

Zentr Z......... Zentrierzapfen [*Spigot*] [*German*]   (GCA)

Zen voj .... Zenijni Vojsko [*Army Engineers*]   (CZ)

Zenyoren.... Zenkoku Yogyo Rodokumiai Rengokai [*National Federation of Ceramic Industry Workers' Unions*] [*Japan*]

Zenyusei..... Zen-Nihon Yusei Rodokumiai [*All-Japan Special Post Office Labor Union*]

Zenzosenkikai ... Zen-Nihon Zosenkikai Rodokumiai [*All-Japan Shipbuilding and Machine Workers' Union*]

ZEOC .... Zarzad Energetyczny Okregu Centralnego [*Power Administration of the Central District*]   (POL)

ZEOD........ Zjednoczenie Energetyczne Okregu Dolnoslaskiego [*Power Association of the Lower Silesian District*]   (POL)

ZEOK .... Zjednoczenie Energetyczne Okregu Krakowskiego [*Power Association of the Krakow District*]   (POL)

ZEOL......... Zjednoczenie Energetyczne Okregu Lubelskiego [*Power Association of the Lublin District*]   (POL)

ZEOM .... Zjednoczenie Energetyczne Okregu Mazowieckiego [*Power Association of the Masovia (Mazowsze) District*]   (POL)

ZEON .... Zjednoczenie Energetyczne Okregu Nadmorskiego [*Power Association of the Coastal District*]   (POL)

ZEON .... Zwiazek Elektrowni Okregu Nadmorskiego [*Power Plant Union of the Coastal District*]   (POL)

ZEORK...... Zwiazek Elektrowni Okregu Radomskiego i Kieleckiego [*Power Plant Union of the Radom-Kielce Area*]   (POL)

ZEOW .... Zaklady Energetyczne Okregu Warszawskiego [*Power Plants of the Warsaw District*]   (POL)

ZEOW .... Zjednoczenie Energetyczne Okregu Warszawskiego [*Power Association of the Warsaw District*]   (POL)

ZEOW .... Zjednoczenie Energetyczne Okregu Wschodniego [*Power Association of the Eastern District*]   (POL)

ZEP............ Electric Porcelain Products Plant   (BU)

ZEP........... Endocrine Preparations Plant   (RU)

ZEP........... Zones a Equipement Progressif [*Morocco*]

ZEP........... Zoni Energou Poleodomias [*Active Housing Zone*]   (GC)

ZEPNRS ... Zajednica Electroprivrednih Preduzeca Narodne Republike Srbije [*Federation of Electric Industries of Serbia*]   (YU)

ZEPT .... Zaklad Ekonomiki Plac i Taryfikacji [*Institute of Wage and Wage Scale Economics*]

ZER .... Zambia Educational Review

zerfl .... Zerfliessend [*Deliquescent*] [*German*]   (GCA)

zerfl .... Zerfliesslich [*Deliquescent*] [*German*]

Zerk .... Mirror Plant [*Topography*]   (RU)

Zerkleiner.. Zerkleinerung [*Size Reduction*] [*German*]   (GCA)

ZER-KO..... Ziraat Kooperatifler [*Agricultural (Bank) Cooperatives Stores*]   (TU)

Zerleg........ Zerlegung [*Decomposition*] [*German*]   (GCA)

ZERLINA ... Zero Energy Reactor for Lattice Investigations and New Assemblies [*India*]   (FEA)

zern .... Grain [*Topography*]   (RU)

zern .... Grain Sovkhoz [*Topography*]   (RU)

zerno-khran ... Granary, Barn [*Topography*]   (RU)

Zernotrest .. State Association of Grain Sovkhozes   (RU)

zers............. Zersetzbar [*Decomposable*] [*German*]   (GCA)

zers............ Zersetzend [*Decomposing*] [*German*]

zers............ Zersetzlich [*Unstable*] [*German*]   (GCA)

zers............ Zersetzt [*Decomposed*] [*German*]   (GCA)

Zers............ Zersetzung [*Decomposition*] [*German*]

zerschl....... Zerschlissen [*Worn Out*] [*Publishing*] [*German*]

zersetzl .... Zersetzlich [*Unstable*] [*German*]   (GCA)

Zersetzlichk ... Zersetzlichkeit [*Instability*] [*German*]   (GCA)

Zers-P .... Zersetzungspunkt [*Decomposition Point*] [*German*]   (GCA)

Zerstaeub... Zerstaeubung [*Scattering*] [*German*]   (GCA)

Zerstoer ..... Zerstoerung [*Destruction*] [*German*]   (GCA)

Zerstoerbark ... Zerstoerbarkeit [*Destructibility*] [*German*]   (GCA)

ZES............. Power Systems Plant   (BU)

ZES............. Zoo Education Service [*South Australia*]

ZES............ Zveza Ekonomistov Slovenije [*Union of Economists of Slovenia*]   (YU)

ZESCO...... Zambia Electricity Supply Corporation

zesz............ Zeszyt [*Fascicle, Part*]   (POL)

ZET........... Zagrebacki Elektricni Tramvaj [*Zagreb Electric Streetcar*]   (YU)

Zetespe....... Zjednoczone Stocznie Polskie [*United Polish Shipyards*]   (POL)

ZETO .... Electrothermic Equipment Plant   (RU)

ZEU .... Zapadna Evropska Unija [*West European Union*]   (YU)

ZEU .... Zapadoevropska Unie [*Western European Union*]   (CZ)

Zeugdr........ Zeugdruck [*Textile Printing*] [*German*]   (GCA)

Zeugn .... Zeugnis [*Testimonial*] [*German*]   (GCA)

ZEV .... Zapadno Evropsko Vreme [*Western European Time*]   (YU)

ZEVB........ Zentrales Entwicklungs- und Vertriebsbuero [*Central Development and Sales Office*] [*German*]   (EG)

ZEW .... Zaklady Elektrod Weglowych 1 Maja [*First of May Carbon Electrode Plant*]   (POL)

ZEW .... Zwischengenossenschaftliche Einrichtungen Waldwirtschaft [*Intercooperative Forestry Facilities*] [*German*]   (EG)

ZEWU .... Zambia Electricity Workers Union

ZEYKO...... Zeytin Mustahsilleri Kooperatifleri [*Olive Producers' Cooperatives*] [*Turkish Cypriot*]   (GC)

ZEYKO...... Zeytin Yag ve Margarin Sanayii (Kooperativ) [*Olive Oil and Margarine Industry (Cooperative)*] [*TU*)   (TU)

ZF .... Band-Elimination Filter, Rejection Filter   (RU)

ZF .... Earthen Filter   (RU)

ZF .... Transcaucasian Branch (of the Academy of Sciences, USSR)   (RU)

ZF .... Umbrella Sprayer [*Mining*]   (RU)

ZF .... Zahnradfabrik Friedrichshafen [*Friedrichshafen Gear Factory*]

ZF .... Zavod za Fotogrametriju [*Institute of Photogrammetry*]   (YU)

Zf. .... Zeitschrift [*Periodical*] [*German*]

Zf. .... Zinsfuss [*Percentage*] [*German*]   (GCA)

ZF .... Zwischenfrequenz [*Intermediate Frequency (IF)*] [*German*]   (EG)

ZFA............ Zentrales Forschungsinstitut fuer Arbeit [*Central Labor Research Institute*] [*German*]   (EG)

ZfB............ Ziekenfondsbesluit [*Benelux*]   (BAS)

ZFC........... Zjednoczenie Fabryk Cementu [*Association of Cement Factories*]   (POL)

ZFChTD.... Zaklad Fizyko-Chemicznej Technologii Drewna [*Enterprise for the Physical and Chemical Processing of Lumber*]   (POL)

ZFD .... Zeitschrift fuer Datenverarbeitung [*Journal for Data Processing*] [*German*]   (ADPT)

ZFDS .... Zambia Flying Doctor Service

ZFE............ Zambia Federation of Employers

ZFE............ Zentrale Abteilung Forschung und Entwicklung [*Central Department for Research and Development*] [*German*]   (EG)

ZFFZ .... Zbornik Radova Filozofskog Fakulteta Sveucilista u Zagrebu [*Papers of the Faculty of Philosophy, Zagreb University*]   (YU)

ZfG............ Zentrale fuer Gasverwen

ZFID.......... Zone Franche Industrielle de Dakar [*Dakar Industrial Free Zone*] [*Senegal*]

ZFIV .... Zentrales Forschungsinstitut des Verkehrswesens der DDR [*Central Research Institute of DDR Transport*] [*German*]   (EG)

ZFK............ Law on Financial Control   (BU)

ZFK............ Protective Filtration Kit   (RU)

ZfK............ Zentralinstitut fuer Kernforschung [*Central Institute for Nuclear Research*] [*German*]   (EG)

ZFM .... Rotary Digger   (RU)

ZFM .... Zentralblatt fuer Mathematik und Ihre Grenzgebiete [*Information retrieval*]

ZFMA......... Zip Fasteners Manufacturers Association [*India*]   (PDAA)

ZFMFI ...... Correspondence Division of the Moscow Pharmaceutical Institute   (RU)

ZFMU .... Zambia Fisheries Marketeers Union

ZFO .... Protective Filtering Clothing   (RU)

ZFO .... Zavod za Fizicki Odgoj [*Physical Education Institute*]   (YU)

ZFOA .... Zone Francaise d'Occupation en Allemagne [*France*]   (FLAF)

ZfP............ Dokumentation Zerstorungsfreie Pruefung [*Nondestructive Testing Documentation*] [*Federal Institute for Materials Testing*] [*Information service or system*]   (IID)

ZFPD......... Zamojskie Fabryki Przemyslu Drzewnego [*Zamosc Lumber Factories*]   (POL)

ZFR............ Zemske Financni Reditelstvi [*Provincial Directorate of Finance*]   (CZ)

ZfS............ Zentralstelle fuer Standardisierung [*Central Office of Standardization*] [*German*]   (EG)

ZFSSR....... Transcaucasian Federation of Socialist Soviet Republics [*1922-1936*]   (RU)

ZFT............ Zentralamt fuer Forschung und Technik [*Central Office for Research and Technology*] [*ZAFT*] [*See also*] [*German*]   (EG)

ZFV............ Zentralinstitut fur Versuchsteierzucht [*Central Institute for Laboratory Animal Breeding*] [*Germany*]   (IRC)

ZFW .... Zentralinstitut fuer Festkoerperphysik und Werkstofforschung [*Central Institute for Solid-State Physics and Materials Research*] [*Dresden*] [*Research center*]   (ERC)

ZfW........... Zentralstelle fuer Waermewirtschaft [*Central Office for Heat Economy*] [*German*]   (EG)

ZFW .... Ziekenfondswet [*Benelux*]   (BAS)

ZfwE .... Zentralstelle fuer Wirtschaftliche Energieanwendung [*Center for Economical Energy Use*] [*German*]   (EG)

ZFZ............ Zora-Film-Zagreb [*"Zora," Zagreb motion picture enterprise*] (YU)
ZG .... Air Traffic Control [*ICAO designator*] (ICDA)
ZG .... Audio-Frequency Oscillator (RU)
ZG .... Generator Start (RU)
ZG .... Law on Forests (BU)
ZG .... Master Oscillator (RU)
ZG .... Zaklady Gastronomiczne [*Restaurant Enterprises*] (POL)
ZG .... Zaklady Graficzne [*Printing Plants*] (POL)
Z-G .... Zapalote Grande [*Race of maize*] [*Mexico*]
ZG .... Zarzad Glowny [*Headquarters, Main Administration*] (POL)
ZG .... Zarzad Gminny [*Rural Commune Administration*] (POL)
zg .... Zogenaamd [*Benelux*] (BAS)
ZGA .... Zambia Geographical Association
ZGA .... Zentraler Gutachterausschuss [*Central Experts Committee*] (EG)
Zgb .... Zagreb (YU)
ZGB .... Zivilgesetzbuch [*Civil Code*] [*German*] (WEN)
ZGB .... Zoological Gardens Board [*Western Australia*]
ZGCS........ Changsha/Datuopu [*China*] [*ICAO location identifier*] (ICLI)
ZGD .... Protective Airtight Door (RU)
ZGE .... Zwischengenossenschaftliche Einrichtung [*Intercooperative Facility*] [*German*] (EG)
ZGEI......... Transcaucasian Water Power Institute (RU)
ZGGC .... Zarar Gormus Guneyliler Cemiyeti [*Organization of (Economically) Disadvantaged Southern Turkish Cypriots*] (TU)
ZGGG .... Guangzhou/Baiyun [*China*] [*ICAO location identifier*] (ICLI)
ZGHK....... Haikou [*China*] [*ICAO location identifier*] (ICLI)
ZGKL........ Guilin [*China*] [*ICAO location identifier*] (ICLI)
Zgl .... Ziegelei [*Brickworks*] [*German*]
Zgl .... Zugleich [*At the Same Time*] [*German*]
ZG LK .... Zarzad Glowny Ligi Kobiet [*Main Administration of the League of Women*] (POL)
ZG LPZ ..... Zarzad Glowny Ligi Przyjaciol Zolnierza [*Main Administration of the League of Soldier's Friends*] (POL)
ZGM .... Law on Civil Mobilization (BU)
ZGMT .... Zu Gott Mein Trost [*In God My Comfort*] [*Motto of Ernst, Duke of Braunschweig-Luneburg (1564-1611)*] [*German*]
zgn .... Zogenaamd [*Benelux*] (BAS)
ZGNN....... Nanning/Wuxu [*China*] [*ICAO location identifier*] (ICLI)
ZGOW...... Shantou [*China*] [*ICAO location identifier*] (ICLI)
ZGOW...... Zaklady Gazownictwa Okregu Warszawskiego [*Gas Works of the Warsaw District*] (POL)
ZGP .... Zeleznicko Gradevinsko Preduzece [*Railroad Construction Establishment*] (YU)
ZGPI......... Zaporozh'ye State Pedagogical Institute (RU)
ZGPU .... Western Mining Industry Administration (RU)
ZGr .... Zakon o Narodnim Odborima Gradova [*Law on People's Committees of Cities*] (YU)
ZGr mob .... Law on Civil Mobilization (BU)
ZGS .... Law on Civil Procedure (BU)
ZGSBP ...... Zarzad Glowny Stowarzyszenia Bibliotekarzy Polskich [*Poland*] (SLS)
ZG SITK.... Zarzad Glowny Stowarzyszenie Inzynierow i Technikow Komunikacji [*Main Administration of the Association of Transportation Engineers and Technicians*] (POL)
ZGSITPN ... Zarzad Glowny Stowarzyszenie Inzynierow i Technikow Przemyslu Naftowego [*Main Administration of the Society of Engineers and Technicians of the Petroleum Industry*] (POL)
ZGT .... Zielgevierttafel [*Protractor and Scale*] [*German*] (GCA)
ZGUA .... Guangzhou City [*China*] [*ICAO location identifier*] (ICLI)
Zgw .... Zegelwet [*Benelux*] (BAS)
ZGZBoWiD ... Zarzad Glowny Zwiazku Bojownikow o Wolnosc i Demokracje [*Main Administration of the Union of Fighters for Freedom and Democracy*] (POL)
z gz d .... Chemical Depot Manager (BU)
ZGZJ .... Zhanjiang [*China*] [*ICAO location identifier*] (ICLI)
ZG ZKP ..... Zarzad Glowny Zwiazku Kompozytorow Polskich [*Main Administration of the Union of Polish Composers*] (POL)
ZG ZMP.... Zarzad Glowny Zwiazku Mlodziezy Polskiej [*Main Administration of the Polish Youth Union*] (POL)
ZG ZNP..... Zarzad Glowny Zwiazku Nauczycielstwa Polskiego [*Main Administration of the Polish Teachers' Union*] (POL)
ZG ZPP ..... Zarzad Glowny Zrzeszenia Prawnikow Polskich [*Main Administration of the Association of Polish Lawyers*] (POL)
ZG ZSCh ... Zarzad Glowny Zwiazku Samopomocy Chlopskiej [*Main Administration of the Peasants' Mutual Aid Union*] (POL)
ZGZU .... Guangzhou [*China*] [*ICAO location identifier*] (ICLI)
ZG ZZ .... Zarzad Glowny Zwiazkow Zawodowych [*Main Administration of Trade Unions*] (POL)
ZG ZZG..... Zarzad Glowny Zwiazku Zawodowego Gornikow [*Main Administration of the Trade-Union of Miners*] (POL)

ZG ZZH .... Zarzad Glowny Zwiazku Zawodowego Hutnikow [*Main Administration of the Trade-Union of Metallurgical Workers*] (POL)
ZG ZZM.... Zarzad Glowny Zwiazku Zawodowego Metalowcow [*Main Administration of the Trade-Union of Metal Workers*] (POL)
ZGZZPBiC ... Zarzad Glowny Zwiazku Zawodowego Pracownikow Budowlanych i Ceramiki [*Main Administration of the Trade-Union of Construction and Ceramics Employees*] (POL)
ZGZZPGK ... Zarzad Glowny Zwiazku Zawodowego Pracownikow Gospodarki Komunalnej [*Main Administration of the Trade-Union of Municipal Administration Employees*] (POL)
zh............... Feminine, Woman's, Women's (RU)
Zh............... Hardness [*Chemistry*] (RU)
ZH............... Helicopter Air Traffic Control [*ICAO designator*] (ICDA)
zh............... Inhabitants, Population (BU)
Zh............... Journal, Periodical (RU)
zh............... Liquid, Fluid (RU)
ZH............... Zerstreute Haeuser [*Scattered Houses*] [*German*]
Zh............... Zirhli [*Armored*] (TU)
ZH............... Zodiac Hotels Ltd. [*Nigeria*]
zH............... Zu Haenden [*Attention Of, Care Of, To Be Delivered To*] [*German*] (GPO)
ZHA........... Zhangjiang [*China*] [*Airport symbol*] (OAG)
ZhAD........ Liquid-Propellant Hot-Gas Generator (RU)
zharg.......... Slang (RU)
ZhAVS....... Rail, Automotive, and Air Communications (BU)
zhb.............. Gendarme Battalion (BU)
zh-b .... Reinforced Concrete (RU)
ZhBD .... War Diary (RU)
ZhBI .... Reinforced Concrete Products, Reinforced Concrete Products Plant (RU)
ZhBK .... Reinforced Concrete Structures (RU)
ZhBM .... Reinforced Concrete Bridge (RU)
zhbr........... Gendarme Brigade (BU)
ZhBT .... Reinforced Concrete Pipe (RU)
ZHCC .... Zhengzhou [*China*] [*ICAO location identifier*] (ICLI)
ZhChK...... Railroad Extraordinary Commission for Combating Counterrevolution and Sabotage (RU)
zhd.............. Railroad, Railroad Term, Railroading (RU)
zHd .... Zu Haenden [*Attention Of, Care Of, To Be Delivered To*] [*German*]
zhdbr.......... Railroad Brigade (RU)
ZhDCh....... Railroad Unit (RU)
ZhDIZ .... State Railroad Transportation Publishing House (RU)
ZhDK........ Railroad Collegium (RU)
ZhDO .... Railroad Department of Transportation (RU)
zhdp........... Railroad Regiment (RU)
zh d pos ..... Railroad Settlement [*Topography*] (RU)
zhdr........... Railway Battalion (RU)
zh d st .... Railroad Station [*Topography*] (RU)
zhdstroyb.. Railroad Construction Battalion (RU)
ZhDV .... Railroad Troops (RU)
ZhEK .... Housing Operation Office (RU)
zhel........... Ferruginous Spring [*Topography*] (RU)
zhel............ Iron Concentration Plant (RU)
Zhel........... Iron Mine, Iron Works [*Topography*] (RU)
zhel bet....... Reinforced Concrete [*Material for dams and bridges*] [*Topography*] (RU)
Zheldorizdat ... State Publishing House of Literature on Railroad Transportation (RU)
Zheldorvzryvprom ... All-Union Trust for Drilling and Blasting Operations of the Glavzheldorstroy of the Urals and Siberia (RU)
Zheleskom ... Committee for Logging and Equipment for Railroads (RU)
zhelez .... Railroad (BU)
zhel ist........ Ferruginous Spring [*Topography*] (RU)
zhel kisl...... Ferruginous Spring [*Topography*] (RU)
zhenkor...... Woman Correspondent (RU)
zhensk....... Feminine, Woman's, Women's (RU)
ZhES........ Railroad Electric Power Plant (RU)
ZhG.......... Gordeyev's Solution (RU)
ZHHH....... Wuhan/Nanhu [*China*] [*ICAO location identifier*] (ICLI)
Zh i............ Ooze, Liquid Silt [*Topography*] (RU)
zhil .... Housing (RU)
Zhilfond.... State Housing Resources. State Real Estate Management Administration (RU)
Zhilkom ..... Housing Committee (BU)
zhilkommunotdel ... Housing Department of the Municipal Administration (RU)
Zhilstroy .... Housing Construction Administration (BU)
Zhilstroy .... Industrial Housing Construction Trust (RU)
zhilupr....... Housing Administration (RU)
zhir .... Fats Kombinat [*Topography*] (RU)

Zhirkost' .... Association of Moscow State Plants of the Fats and Bone-Processing Industry (RU)
ZHISA .... Zambia Higher Institutions Sports Association
zhit .... Inhabitants (RU)
zhiv .... Livestock Breeding, Animal Husbandry (RU)
zhiv .... Painting (RU)
Zhivkontora ... State Office for the Procurement and Marketing of Pedigree Livestock (RU)
zhivop .... Painting, Pictorial Art (BU)
zhivotn .... Livestock-Breeding Farm, Livestock-Breeding Sovkhoz [*Topography*] (RU)
ZhIVSNAB ... State Commercial Enterprise for Supplying Livestock (BU)
zhiv-vo .... Livestock Breeding, Animal Husbandry (RU)
ZhK .... Fats Kombinat (RU)
ZhK .... Fatty Acids (RU)
ZHK .... Zentrale Hochwasserkommission [*Central Flood Control Commission*] [*German*] (EG)
ZhKK .... Municipal Housing Office (RU)
ZhKO .... Communal Housing Department (RU)
ZhKP .... Liquid-Oxygen Apparatus (RU)
ZhM .... Iron Bridge (RU)
ZhMG .... Liquid-Metal Fuel (RU)
ZhMGR ..... Liquid-Metal Fuel Reactor (RU)
ZhMI .... Zhdanov Metallurgical Institute (RU)
ZHN .... Zbrane Hromadneho Niceni [*Weapons of Mass Destruction*] (CZ)
zhn dr .... Gendarme Battalion (BU)
zh-noye .... Animal (RU)
zhn sl .... Gendarmery (BU)
ZhO .... Railroad Section (RU)
Zhp .... Constant Hardness [*Chemistry*] (RU)
zhp .... Female Sex (RU)
zhp .... Gendarme Regiment (BU)
zhp .... Railroad (BU)
ZHP .... Zwiazek Harcerstwa Polskiego [*Polish Scout Union*] (POL)
zhpbm .... Railway Mechanization Battalion (BU)
zhpbr .... Railway Brigade (BU)
zhpk .... Railway Corps (BU)
ZhPR .... Railroad Workshop (BU)
zhpsvb .... Railway Signal Battalion (BU)
zhpsvr .... Railway Signal Company (BU)
ZhPT .... Railway Transportation (BU)
ZhPU .... Railway School (BU)
ZhPZ .... Railway Plant (BU)
zhr .... Feminine Gender (RU)
ZhR .... Railroad Radio Station (RU)
zhr .... Railway Company (BU)
ZHR .... Zemska Hospodarska Rada [*Provincial Economic Council*] (CZ)
ZhRD .... Liquid Propellant Rocket Engine (RU)
ZHRiN .... Zjednoczenie Hodowli Roslin i Nasiennictwa [*Plant Cultivation and Seed Union*] (POL)
ZhS .... Aliphatic Alcohols (RU)
ZhS .... Hard Seats [*Railroads*] (RU)
ZhS .... Kinetic Energy (RU)
ZhS .... Yellow Glass (RU)
ZHS .... Zambia Horse Society
ZhSK .... Housing Construction Cooperative (RU)
ZhSKT .... Housing Construction Cooperative Association (RU)
ZhT .... Railroad Transportation (RU)
ZhTU .... Railroad Television Apparatus (RU)
ZhTV .... Live Tularemia Vaccines (RU)
ZhU .... Railroad School (RU)
ZHU .... Zentrales Handelsunternehmen [*Central Trade Enterprise*] (EG)
ZhUB .... Refractory Concrete (RU)
Zhurgaz ..... Periodical and Newspaper Association (RU)
zhurn .... Journalism, Journalistic (BU)
zhurn .... Journal, Periodical (RU)
ZhUVR ..... Completed Operations Record [*Construction*] (RU)
Zhvr .... Temporary Hardness [*Chemistry*] (RU)
ZhVS .... Liquid Explosive Mixture (RU)
ZhVZ .... Zhukovka Bicycle Plant (RU)
ZHW .... Zaklad Higieny Weterynaryjnej [*Veterinary Hygiene Laboratory*] [*Poland*] (ARC)
ZhWH ...... Wuhan [*China*] [*ICAO location identifier*] (ICLI)
ZhYeL .... Vital Capacity (RU)
ZhZL .... Lives of Outstanding People [*Book series*] (RU)
ZhZS .... Yellow-Green Glass (RU)
ZI .... Flight Information Center [*ICAO designator*] (ICDA)
ZI .... "For Industrialization" [*Publishing house*] [*Newspaper*] (RU)
ZI .... Ionization Zone (RU)
ZI .... Quenching Inductor, Hardening Inductor (RU)
Zi. .... Zaki [*Cape, Point*] [*Si*] [*See also*] [*Japan*] (NAU)
Z-I .... Zapad-Istok [*West-East*] (YU)
ZI .... Zonal Index [*Meteorology*] (RU)

ZIA .... Central Institute for Automation [*Jena*] (EG)
ZIAD .... Zeni Angkatan Darat [*Army Engineers*] (IN)
ZIAN .... Zoological Institute of the Academy of Sciences, USSR (RU)
ZIANA .... Zimbabwe Inter-African News Agency
ZIB .... Konrad-Zuse-Zentrum fur Informationstechnik Berlin [*Konrad Zuse Center for Information Tehnique*] [*Germany*] (IRC)
ZIBANG .... Zeni Pembangunan [*Construction Engineers*] (IN)
ZIBF .... Zimbabwe International Book Fair
ZIBS .... Zhejiang Research Institute for Biogas and Solar Energy [*China*] (WED)
ZICEG .... Zona Industrial e Comercial de Exportacao da Guanabara [*Guanabara Industrial and Commercial Export Zone*] [*Brazil*] (LA)
Zichiro .... Zen-Nihon Jichidantai Rodokumiai [*All-Japan Prefectural and Municipal Workers' Union*]
ZID .... Plant Imeni F. E. Dzerzhinskiy (RU)
ZID .... Zentralinstitut fuer Information und Dokumentation [*Central Institute for Information and Documentation*] [*German*] (EG)
Zid .... Zidovsky [*Jewish*] (CZ)
ZID .... Zone d'Industrialisation Decentralisee [*Algeria*]
ZIDA .... Zentrum fuer Information und Dokumentation des Aussenhandels [*Center for Foreign Trade Information and Documentation*] (EG)
ZID(A) .... Zonta International Districts (Australia)
ZIDKT ...... Law on Amendments and Supplements to the Labor Code (BU)
ZIE .... Zjednoczenie Instalacji Elektrycznych [*Association for Electrical Installation*] (POL)
ZIENO ...... Instruments and Nonstandard Equipment Plant (BU)
ZIF .... "Land and Factory" [*Publishing house*] [*Almanac 1922-1930*] (RU)
ZIF .... Plant Imeni M. V. Frunze (RU)
ZIF .... Zentralinstitut fuer Fertigungstechnik [*Central Institute for Production Technology*] (EG)
ZIF .... Zentralinstitut fuer Funktechnik [*Central Institute for Radio Engineering*] [*German*] (EG)
ZIF .... Zentrum fuer Interdisziplinaere Forschung [*Center for Interdisciplinary Research*] [*Research center*] (IRC)
ZIFA .... Zambia India Friendship Association
ZIFA .... Zimbabwe Football Association
Ziff .... Ziffer [*Number, Figure*] [*German*] (EG)
ZIG .... Zaehlimpulsgeber [*German*] (ADPT)
ZIG .... Zentralinstitut fuer Giessereitechnik [*Central Institute for Foundry Technology*] [*German*] (EG)
ZIG .... Ziguinchor [*Senegal*] [*Airport symbol*] (OAG)
ZIGDJZ .... Zeleznicki Institut Glavne Direkcije Jugoslavenskih Zeleznica [*Railroad Institute of the General Administration of Yugoslav Railroads*] (YU)
ZIGM .... Ziraat Isleri Genel Mudurlugu [*Agricultural Affairs Directorate General*] (TU)
ZIH .... Zihuatanejo [*Mexico*] [*Airport symbol*] (OAG)
ZIH .... Zydowski Instytut Historyczny [*Jewish Historical Institute*] (POL)
ZIHME ..... Zentralinstitut fuer Hygiene, Mikrobiologie, und Epidemiologie der DDR [*Central Institute of Hygiene, Microbiology, and Epidemiology of the GDR*] [*Research center*] (IRC)
ZII .... Agricultural Experimental Institute (BU)
ZII .... Zemjodelsko-Ispitalen Institut [*Agricultural Research Institute*] (YU)
ZIID .... Zentralinstitut fuer Information und Dokumentation [*Central Institute for Information and Documentation*] [*Germany*] [*Information service or system*] (IID)
ZIISSP ...... Correspondence Institute of Engineers of the Silicate and Construction Industries (RU)
ZIK .... Zakon o Izvrsenju Kazni [*Law on the Enforcement of Penalties*] (YU)
ZIK .... Zemjodelsko-Industriski Kombinat [*Agricultural Industrial Combine*] [*Belje*] (YU)
ZIL .... Moscow Automobile Plant Imeni I. A. Likhachev (RU)
ZIL .... Plant Imeni V. I. Lenin (RU)
ZIM .... Gor'kiy Automobile Plant Imeni Molotov [*1932-1958*] (RU)
ZIM .... National Shipping Line [*Israel*] (ME)
zim .... Winter Dwelling, Winter Camp [*Topography*] (RU)
zim .... Winter Road [*Topography*] (RU)
ZIM .... Zambezi Industrial Mission
ZIM .... Zentrales Investitions-Modell [*German*] (ADPT)
ZIM .... Zentralinstitut der Metallurgie [*Central Institute of Metallurgy*] [*German*] (EG)
Zim .... Zimbabwe
ZIM .... Zi Mischari [*Merchant fleet*] [*Israel*]
ZIM .... Zomancipari Muvek [*Enamel Industry Works*] (HU)
ZIMB .... Zimbabwe (WDAA)
ZIMBANK ... Zimbabwe Banking Corp. Ltd.
ZIMCO .... Zambia Industrial and Mining Corporation (AF)
ZIMCORD ... Zimbabwe Conference on Reconstruction and Development
zimn .... Winter (RU)
ZIMOFA ... Zimbabwe Mozambique Friendship Association

ZIMP........	Correspondence Institute of the Metal-Working Industry (RU)	
ZIMTA......	Zimbabwe Teachers Association (EAIO)	
ZIN	Law on Execution of Penalties (BU)	
ZIN	Zoological Institute (of the Academy of Sciences, USSR) (RU)	
ZINAN	Zoological Institute of the Academy of Sciences, USSR (RU)	
ZINC	Zim Israel Navigation Company	
ZINCO	Zim Israel Navigation Company	
ZINCOM ..	Zambia Industrial and Commercial Association	
Z-Industrie ...	Zentralgeleitete Industrie [Centrally Administered Industry] (EG)	
ZINPONS ...	Law on the Election of People's Representatives to the Ordinary National Assembly (BU)	
ZINS.........	Law on the Election of People's Councils (BU)	
ZINSDT	Law on the Election of People's Councils of Deputies of the Working People (BU)	
ZINSNRB ...	Law on the Election of People's Councils of Deputies of the Working People in the Bulgarian People's Republic (BU)	
ZINSSZ.....	Law on the Election of Judges and Juries of People's Courts (BU)	
ZIO	Podol'sk Machinery Plant Imeni Ordzhonikidze (RU)	
ZIO	Zaklad Imienia Ossolinskich [The Ossolinski Institute] (POL)	
ZIP...........	Measuring Instruments Plant (RU)	
ZIP...........	Spare Parts, Instruments, and Accessories (BU)	
ZIP...........	Zhengzhou Institute of Pomology [China] (IRC)	
ZIP...........	Zjednoczenie Instalacji Przemyslowych [Association for Industrial Installations] (POL)	
ZIP...........	Zonas de Influencia Pedagogica [Zones of Educational Influence] [Mozambique] (AF)	
ZIPA.........	Zimbabwe Independent People's Army	
ZIPRA	Zimbabwe Independent People's Revolutionary Army (PD)	
ZIPU.........	Given True Track Angle (RU)	
ZIPUR......	Zeni Pertempuran [Combat Engineers] (IN)	
ZIR...........	Law on Inventions and Rationalizations (BU)	
Zir	Ziraat [Agriculture] (TU)	
ZIR...........	Zwiazek Izb Rzemieslniczych [Union of Crafts Chambers] (POL)	
ZIRC........	Turkiye Ziraatcilar Cemiyeti [Turkish Agriculturalists' Society] (TU)	
ZIS...........	Moscow Automobile Plant Imeni Stalin [1934-1956] (RU)	
ZIS...........	Transcaucasian Scientific Research Institute of Structures (RU)	
ZIS...........	Zaklad Instalacji Sanitarnych [Enterprise for Sanitary Installations] (POL)	
ZIS...........	Zambia Information Service	
ZIS...........	Zarzad Instalacji Sanitarnych [Administration of Sanitary Installations] (POL)	
ZIS...........	Zentralinstitut fuer Schweisstechnik [Central Institute for Welding Technology] [German] (EG)	
ZIS...........	Ziekenhuis Informatie-Systeem	
zis	Ziseliert [Chiseled] [Publishing] [German]	
ZIS...........	Zjednoczenie Instalacji Sanitarnych [Association for Sanitary Installations] (POL)	
ZIS...........	Zvezni Izvrsni Svet [Federal Executive Council] (YU)	
ZIS/AZL ...	Ziekenhuis Informatie-Systeem/Academisch Ziekenhuis Leiden	
ZIS/BC.....	Ziekenhuis Informatie-Systeem/Begeleidingscommissie [NOBIN] ['s-Gravenhage]	
ZISCO.......	Zimbabwe Iron & Steel Co.	
ZISE	Zjednoczenie Instalacji Sanitarno-Elektrycznych [Electrotherapy Equipment Association] (POL)	
zisel	Ziseliert [Chiseled] [Publishing] [German]	
ZISPO	Zaklady Imienia Stalina w Poznaniu (Przemyslu Metalowego) [Stalin (Metal) Plant in Poznan] (POL)	
ZISS.........	Law on Property Ownership and Easements (BU)	
ZISS.........	Zambian Intelligence and Security Service (AF)	
ZISSP	Correspondence Institute of the Silicate and Construction Industries (RU)	
ZIST	Correspondence Institute of Soviet Trade (RU)	
ZIT...........	Zambia Institute of Technology	
Zit	Zitat [Citation] [German] (GCA)	
ZiT	Zivljenje in Tehnika [Life and Technology] [Ljubljana A periodical] (YU)	
ZITA.........	Ziyard Travel & Air Cargo [Saudi Arabia]	
ZITF	Zimbabwe International Trade Fair (ECON)	
ZIU...........	Correspondence Institute for Advanced Training (RU)	
ZIU...........	Plant Imeni M. S. Uritskiy (RU)	
ZIUITR	Correspondence Institute for the Advanced Training of Engineering and Technical Personnel (RU)	
ZIV	Plant Imeni V. V. Vorovskiy (RU)	
ZIV	Zentrale Informationsstelle fuer Verkehr	
ZIV	Ziekte- en Invaliditeitsverzekering [Benelux] (BAS)	
ZIVAN......	Notes of the Institute of Oriental Studies of the Academy of Sciences, USSR (RU)	
Ziv Ing......	Zivil Ingenieur [Civil Engineer] [German] (GCA)	
ZIVT.........	Zagorska Industrija Vunenih Tkanina [Zagorje Woolen Textile Industry] (YU)	
ZIW	Zwiazek Inwalidow Wojennych [Union of Disabled Veterans] (POL)	

ZIWU	Zimbabwe Writers' Union	
ZJ..............	Zavodni Jidelna [Factory Dining Hall] (CZ)	
zj................	Zonder Jaartal [Without Date of Publication] [Publishing] [Netherlands]	
ZJA...........	Zambia Judo Association	
ZJE	Zajednica Jugoslovenske Elektroprivrede [Federation of Yugoslav Electric Industries] (YU)	
ZJNA........	Zakon o Jugoslovenskoj Narodnoj Armiji [Law on the Yugoslav People's Army] (YU)	
ZJP	Zakon o Javnom Pravobraniostvu [Law on the Body of Government Attorneys] (YU)	
Zjr	Zonder Jaar [Benelux] (BAS)	
ZJS	Zakon o Javnim Sluzbenicima [Law on Public Employees] (YU)	
ZJS	Zavod Jana Svermy [Jan Sverma Plant] [Brno] (CZ)	
ZJT...........	Zakon o Javnom Tuziostvu [Law on Public Prosecutors] (YU)	
ZJU...........	Zambia Judo Union	
ZJVS	Zavod J. V. Stalina [J. V. Stalin Works] (CZ)	
ZJZ...........	Zapad Jugo-Zapad [West Southwest] (YU)	
ZK.............	Course Setter, Course Selector (RU)	
z/k.............	Imprisoned (RU)	
ZK.............	Land Code (RU)	
ZK.............	Law on Cooperatives (BU)	
ZK.............	Plant Committee, Factory Committee (RU)	
ZK.............	Sound Coagulation, Acoustic Coagulation (RU)	
ZK.............	Zadruzno Kmetijstvo [Cooperative Agriculture] (YU)	
ZK.............	Zakladni Knihovna [Fundamental Library (of the Czechoslovak Academy of Sciences)] (CZ)	
ZK.............	Zambia Kwache	
ZK.............	Zanatska Komora [Chamber of Artisans] (YU)	
ZK.............	Zarzad Kina [Motion Picture Administration] (POL)	
ZK.............	Zavodni Klub [Factory Club] (CZ)	
ZK.............	Zavodni Krouzek [Factory Circle] (CZ)	
ZK.............	Zdokonalovaci Kurs [Advance Course] (CZ)	
ZK.............	Zemedelska Komise [Agricultural Commission] (CZ)	
Z K...........	Zenekiado [Music Publishing House] (HU)	
ZK.............	Zentralkomitee [Central Committee] (EG)	
ZK.............	Zilinsky Kraj [Zilina Region] (CZ)	
zk...............	Zirka [Approximately] [German] (GCA)	
Zk.............	Zuendkerze [Spark Plug] [German] (GCA)	
ZKB	Kasaba Bay [Zambia] [Airport symbol] (OAG)	
ZKB	Zentrales Konstruktionsbuero [Central Designing Office] [German] (EG)	
ZKB	Zuivel Kwaliteitscontrolbureau [Benelux] (BAS)	
ZKBS.........	Zentrale Kommission fuer Biologische Sicherheit [Germany]	
ZKD..........	Ship Engines Plant (BU)	
ZKD..........	Zagreb Kajkavian Dialect XXX [of Serbo-Croatian]	
ZKd...........	Zamenik Komandanta Diviziona [Deputy Commander of an Artillery Battalion] (YU)	
ZKD..........	Zapadoceske Konsumni Druzstvo [West Bohemian Consumer Cooperative] (CZ)	
ZKD..........	Zenkoku Kinrosha Domei [National White Collar Workers' League] [Japan]	
ZKD..........	Zentraler Kurierdienst [Central Courier Service] [German] (EG)	
ZKD..........	Zentrales Konstruktions- und Technologisches Buero [Central Designing and Technological Bureau] [German] (EG)	
ZKE	Ship Electrical Appliances Plant (BU)	
ZKE	Zugkrafteinheit [Tractive Unit] [German] (EG)	
ZKF..........	Zentrale Kommission der Fotografie [Central Photography Commission] [German] (EG)	
ZKFF	Zentraler Kraftfutterfonds [Central Supply of High-Concentrate Feeds] [German] (EG)	
ZKG	Prvni Brnenska a Kralovopolska Strojirna, Gottwaldovy Zavody, Narodni Podnik [First Machine Factory at Brno and Kralovo Pole, Gottwald Plants, National Enterprise] (CZ)	
ZKG	Zadruzno Kmetijsko Gospodarstvo [Cooperative Agriculture Economy] (YU)	
ZKG	Zavod Klementa Gottwalda [Klement Gottwald Factory] [Povazska Bystrica] (CZ)	
zkh	Astern Running [Of ship's propeller] (RU)	
ZKh...........	Reverse, Reverse Motion, Reverse Gear (RU)	
ZKhA.........	Paper and Packaging Materials Plant (BU)	
ZKhBT.......	Law on Hygiene and Labor Safety (BU)	
ZKHH	Hamhung [North Korea] [ICAO location identifier] (ICLI)	
ZKhIM	Hydroinsulation Materials Plant (BU)	
ZKhZ.........	Chemical Contamination Zone (BU)	
ZKI	Law on the Confiscation of Property (BU)	
ZKI	Zentralinstitut fuer Kybernetik und Informationsprozesse [Central Institute for Cybernetics and Information Processing] [Berlin] [Research Institute] (ERC)	
ZKIA.........	Pyongyang [North Korea] [ICAO location identifier] (ICLI)	
ZKiOR.......	Zwiazek Kolek i Organizacji Rolniczych [Union of Agricultural Cooperatives and Organizations] [Poland]	
ZKJ	Zveza Komunistov Jugoslavije [League of Communists of Yugoslavia] (YU)	
ZKJ	Zwiazek Komunistow Jugoslawii [League of Communists of Yugoslavia] (POL)	

ZKJV .... Zavody K. J. Vorosilova [*K. J. Voroshilov Plant*] [*Dubnica*] (CZ)
ZKK .... Zentrale Kontrollkommission [*Central Control Commission*] [*German*] (EG)
ZKKC........ Kimchaek [*North Korea*] [*ICAO location identifier*] (ICLI)
ZKKK .... Pyongyang [*North Korea*] [*ICAO location identifier*] (ICLI)
ZKL........... Zarzad Kolejek Lesnych [*Administration of Forest Railroads*] (POL)
ZKLK .... Zavodni Komise Lidove Kontroly [*Factory Commission (Establishment Commission) of People's Control*] (CZ)
ZKM .... Rudder Mechanisms Plant (BU)
ZKM .... Shipbuilding Materials Plant (BU)
ZKM .... Zavodni Komise Mladeze [*Factory Youth Committee*] (CZ)
ZKMDRVD ... Zmiesana Komisia Medzinarodnej Dohody o Rybolove vo Vodach Dunaja [*International Commission for Agreement on the Danube Fishing*] [*Former Czechoslovakia*] (EAIO)
ZKMH...... Zabavna Knjiznica Matice Hrvatske [*Recreational Library Issued by Matica Hrvatska*] [*A publication series*] (YU)
ZKnj .... Zemljisne Knjige [*Land Title Records*] (YU)
ZKNP .... Alternate Command and Observation Post (RU)
ZKO .... Holding Area, Stacking Area [*Aviation*] (RU)
ZKO .... "Red October" Plant (RU)
ZKoop .... Law on Cooperatives (BU)
ZKP........... Alternate Command Post (BU)
ZKP .... Deputy Regimental Commander (RU)
ZKP........... Zakon o Krivicnom Postupku [*Law on Criminal Procedure*] (YU)
ZKP........... Zamenik Komandanta za Pozadinu [*Deputy Commander for Rear Echelon*] [*Military*] (YU)
ZKP........... Zwiazek Kompozytorow Polskich [*Union of Polish Composers*] (POL)
ZKPCh....... Deputy Commander for Political Affairs (BU)
ZKPM....... Forge-Press Machines Plant (BU)
ZKPY .... Pyongyang/Sunan [*North Korea*] [*ICAO location identifier*] (ICLI)
ZKR .... Zakladowa Komisja Rozjemcza [*Plant Conciliation Board*] (POL)
zkr .... Zenekar [*Orchestra*] (HU)
ZKRS........ Classification Yard Commandant (RU)
ZKRVD...... Zmiesana Komisia o Rybolove vo Vodach Dunaja [*Joint Danube Fishery Commission - JDFC*] [*Zilina, Czechoslovakia*] (EAIO)
ZKS.......... Zanatska Komora Srbije [*Serbian Chamber of Artisans*] (YU)
ZKS.......... Zrzeszenie Kolejarzy Sportowcow [*Sport Association of Railroad Workers*] (POL)
ZKSC....... Sunchon [*North Korea*] [*ICAO location identifier*] (ICLI)
ZKSR....... Sesura [*North Korea*] [*ICAO location identifier*] (ICLI)
ZKTCh...... Deputy Commander for Technical Matters (RU)
ZKTD .... Law on Collective Labor Contracts (BU)
ZKTR .... Zarzad Konstrukcji Telekomunikacyjnych i Radiofonii [*Administration of Telecommunication and Broadcasting Construction*] (POL)
ZKU .... Railroad Section Commandant (RU)
ZKU .... Transcaucasian Communist University (RU)
ZKU .... Zamska Kriminalni Uradovna [*Provincial Bureau of Criminal Investigation*] (CZ)
ZKUD .... Zagrebacko Kulturno-Umjetnicko Drustvo [*Zagreb Cultural and Artistic Society*] (YU)
ZKUJ........ Uiju [*North Korea*] [*ICAO location identifier*] (ICLI)
ZKUS........ Zkusebni a Kontrolni Ustav Stavebni [*Experimental and Control Institute of the Building Industry*] (CZ)
ZKV .... Transcaucasian Railroad (RU)
ZKVO .... Transcaucasus Military District (RU)
ZKVT........ Water Transportation Commandant (RU)
ZKZ .... Zapadoceske Kaolinove Zavody [*West Bohemian Kaolin Plants*] (CZ)
ZKZ .... Zapadoceske Keramicke Zavody [*West Bohemian Ceramics Plants*] (CZ)
ZKZhDU ... Railroad Section Commandant (RU)
ZKZhT....... Railroad Transportation Commandant (RU)
ZL .... Hazelton Airlines [*Airline code*] [*Australia*]
ZL .... Law on Hunting (BU)
zl................. Lengyel Zloty [*Polish Zloty*] (HU)
ZL .... Plant Laboratory, Factory Laboratory (RU)
ZL .... Priming Station [*Navy*] (RU)
ZL .... Zagrebacka Ljevaonica Obojenih Metala [*Zagreb Non-Ferrous Metals Foundry*] (YU)
ZL .... Zakazkovy List [*Order Form*] (CZ)
ZL .... Zeile [*Line*] [*German*] (ADPT)
ZL .... Zeleznicka Lozionica [*Railroad Fueling Station*] (YU)
ZL .... Zentrale Leitung [*Central Management*] [*German*] (EG)
zl................. Ziemlich Loeslich [*Fairly Soluble*] [*German*]
zl................. Zloty [*Zloty*] (POL)
ZL .... Zugleitung [*Dispatcher's Office*] [*German*] (EG)
ZLA .... Zambia Library Association (EAIO)
ZLA .... Zemedelsko Lesnicky Archiv [*Archives for Agriculture and Forestry*] (CZ)

ZLA .... Zimbabwe Liberation Army (AF)
ZLAMP.... Zone de Passage des Lignes Aeriennes Mondiales Principales [*Major World Air Route Area*] [*French*]
ZLAN .... Lanzhou City [*China*] [*ICAO location identifier*] (ICLI)
ZLARN....... Zone des Lignes Aeriennes Regionales et Nationales [*Regional and Domestic Air Route Area*] [*French*]
ZLC........... Zarzad Lotnictwa Cywilnego [*Civil Aviation Administration*] (POL)
ZLC........... Zimbabwe Liberation Council
zl dew .... Zloty Dewizowy [*Exchange Zloty*] [*Poland*]
Z-Ldg......... Ziellandung [*Precision Landing*] [*German*] (GCA)
ZLDI......... Zentralstelle fuer Luft- und Raumfahrtdokumentation und Information
Zle............. Zeile [*Line*] [*German*]
ZLE........... Zentrallabor fuer Empfaenger-Roehren [*Central Laboratory for Radio Receiver Tubes*] [*German*] (EG)
ZLE........... Zone de Libre Echange [*French*] (BAS)
ZLE........... Zone Locale Elargie [*Extended Area Service*] [*French*]
zlec .... Zlecenie [*Order*] (POL)
ZLEMI...... Leningrad Correspondence Electromechanical Institute (RU)
ZLF........... Zentral Laboratorium fuer Fernmeldetechnik, Berlin-Treptow [*Berlin-Treptow Central Laboratory for Telecommunication Technology*] [*German*] (EG)
ZLGID...... Zentrale Leitung fuer Gesellschaftswissenschaftliche Information und Dokumentation bei der Deutschen Akademie der Wissenschaften zu Berlin [*Central Management for Social Science Information and Documentation at the German Academy of Sciences in Berlin*] (EG)
ZLGU .... Zambia Ladies Golf Union
ZLHW .... Lanzhou [*China*] [*ICAO location identifier*] (ICLI)
ZLIC......... Yinchuan [*China*] [*ICAO location identifier*] (ICLI)
zlj.............. Zaszloalj [*Battalion*] (HU)
ZLJM .... Zusters van Liefe Jezus en Maria [*Sisters of Charity of Jesus and Mary - SCJM*] [*Belgium*] (EAIO)
ZLJQ .... Jiuquan [*China*] [*ICAO location identifier*] (ICLI)
zll.............. Ziemlich Leicht Loeslich [*Fairly Easily Soluble*] [*German*]
ZLLL .... Lanzhou/Zhongchuan [*China*] [*ICAO location identifier*] (ICLI)
ZLN .... Zwiazek Ludowo-Narodowy [*Populist-Nationalist Alliance*] [*Poland*] [*Political party*] (PPE)
ZLO .... Manzanillo [*Mexico*] [*Airport symbol*] (OAG)
zlo.............. Ziemlich Loeslich [*Fairly Soluble*] [*German*]
ZLOS......... Zonal Flax-Raising Experimental Station (RU)
ZLP........... Desired Course Line (RU)
ZLP........... Reserve Ski Regiment (RU)
ZLP........... Zaklad Lecznictwa Pracowniczego [*Establishment for Medical Care of Workers*] (POL)
ZLP........... Zwiazek Literatow Polskich [*Union of Polish Writers*] (POL)
ZLS........... Law on Domestic Relations (BU)
zls.............. Zaszlos [*Warrant Officer*] (HU)
ZLSem....... Law on Domestic Relations (BU)
ZLSN........ Xian [*China*] [*ICAO location identifier*] (ICLI)
ZLTA......... Zambia Lawn Tennis Association
ZLV........... Vladni Vybor pro Zvelebovani Zemedelstvi, Lesnictvi, a Vodniho Hospodarstvi [*Government Committee for the Advancement of Agriculture, Forestry, and Water Resources*] (CZ)
ZLV........... Zeilenvorschub [*German*] (ADPT)
Zlw............. Zahlwort [*Numeral*] [*German*]
ZLXN .... Xining [*China*] [*ICAO location identifier*] (ICLI)
ZLYA .... Yanan [*China*] [*ICAO location identifier*] (ICLI)
ZLZ........... Zaklady Leczniczo-Zapobiegawcze [*Preventive Medicine Clinic*] (POL)
ZM .... Law on Customs (BU)
ZM .... Minelayer (RU)
ZM .... Zadruzni Magacin, Trgovinsko Preduzece [*Cooperative Department Store*] (YU)
ZM .... Zaklady Mechaniczne [*Machinery Plants*] (POL)
ZM .... Zaklady Metalowe [*Metal Plants*] (POL)
ZM .... Zambia [*ANSI two-letter standard code*] (CNC)
ZM .... Zavodni Milice [*Factory Militia*] (CZ)
zm.............. Zmarl [*Died*] [*Poland*]
ZM .... Zone de Manoeuvre [*French*] (ADPT)
ZMA .... Medical Equipment Plant (RU)
ZMA .... Sound Film Editing Machine (RU)
ZMB .... Zambia [*ANSI three-letter standard code*] (CNC)
ZMBH...... Zentrum fur Moleculare Biologie Heidelberg [*Center for Molecular Biology Heidelberg*]
ZMBPW.... Zaklady Materialow Budowlanych Przemyslu Weglowego [*Construction Material Plants of the Coal Industry*] (POL)
ZMD.......... Zentralstelle fuer Maschinelle Dokumentation
ZMD.......... Zwiazek Mlodziezy Demokratycznej [*Union of Democratic Youth*] (POL)
ZMDT .... Law on Local Taxes and Fees (BU)
ZME .... Zapadomoravske Elektrarny, Narodni Podnik [*West Moravian Electric Power Plants, National Enterprise*] (CZ)
zmien.......... Zmieniony [*Revised*] (POL)

ZMIU .... Law on Measures and Measuring Equipment (BU)
ZMJ .... Zwiazek Mlodziezy Jugoslawii [Youth Association of Yugoslavia] (POL)
ZMK .... Installation Structures Plant (BU)
ZMK .... Law on Mines and Quarries (BU)
ZMK .... Zwiazek Mlodziezy Kommunistyczne
ZMKA .... Zrinyi Miklos Katonai Akademia [Miklos Zrinyi Military Academy] (HU)
Zml............ Zemlyak [Fellow Countryman] [A periodical] (BU)
ZMLK........ Zarzad Miejski Ligi Kobiet [Municipal Administration of the League of Women] (POL)
ZMM .... Metal Cutting Machines Plant (BU)
ZMM .... Zatovo Mpianatra Mitolona [Militant Young Students] [Malagasy] (AF)
ZMMD...... Zurich, Mainz, Munich, Darmstadt [A joint European university effort on ALGOL processors]
ZMMT ...... Zimbabwe Mass Media Trust
zm nd .... Ground Observation (BU)
ZMO......... Zaklady Materialow Ogniotrwalych [Fireproof Materials Plant] (POL)
ZMO .... Ziraat Muhendisleri Odasi [Chamber of Agricultural Engineers] (TU)
ZMP .... Zlot Mlodziezy Przodownikow [Young Leaders' Convention] (POL)
ZMP .... Zwiazek Mlodziezy Polskiej [Polish Youth Union (1948-1956)] (POL)
ZMPS........ Law on Motor Vehicle Transportation Facilities (BU)
ZMPU .... Given Magnetic Track Angle (RU)
ZMR .... Zwiazek Mlodziezy Rewolucyjnej [Union of Revolutionary Youth] (POL)
ZMR .... Zwiazek Mlodziezy Robotniczej [Union of Working Youth] (POL)
ZMRP........ Zwiazek Mierniczych Rzeczpospolitej Polskiej [Union of Surveyors of the Republic of Poland] (POL)
ZMS .... Agrarian Youth Union (BU)
zms .... Honored Master of Sport (RU)
ZMS .... Low Velocity Layer (RU)
ZMS .... Sound-Ranging Station (RU)
ZMS .... Zavodni Mistrovstvi Sveta [World Championship Matches] (CZ)
ZMS .... Zbornik Matice Srpske [Papers of Matica Srpska] [Novi Sad] (YU)
ZMS .... Zemaljski Muzej, Sarajevo [National Museum, Sarajevo] (YU)
ZMS .... Zemedelske Mistrovske Skoly [Agricultural Training Schools] (CZ)
ZMS .... Zwiazek Mlodziezy Socjalistycznej [Union of Socialist Youth] (POL)
ZMSR....... Zjednoczenie Morskich Stoczni Remontowych [Association of Maritime Repair Yards] (POL)
ZMT .... Chief of Local Transportation (RU)
ZMT .... Zapadomoravske Tiskarny [West Moravian Printing Plants] (CZ)
ZMT .... Zeme Miroveho Tabora [Countries of the Camp of Peace] (CZ)
ZMU......... Zambia Mineworkers' Union
ZMW .... Zwiazek Mlodziezy Wiejskiej [Rural Youth Union] (POL)
ZMWRP.... Zwiazek Mlodziezy Wiejskiej Rzeczpospolitej Polskiej [Rural Youth Union of the Republic of Poland] (POL)
ZMZ .... Transcaucasian Metallurgical Plant (RU)
ZMZ .... Zlatoust Metallurgical Plant (RU)
ZN.............. Defense of the Population (RU)
ZN.............. Law on Inheritance (BU)
ZN.............. Law on Rents (BU)
zn............... Significant [Mathematics] (RU)
zn............... Sign, Mark, Symbol (RU)
zn............... Value [Mathematics] (RU)
ZN............. Zakon o Nasledivanju [Law on Inheritance] (YU)
Zn............. Zan [Mountain] [Sn] [See also] [Japan] (NAU)
ZN............. Zastupce Nacelnika [Deputy Chief] (CZ)
ZN............. Zdruzeni Narodi [United Nations] (YU)
ZN............. Zenijni Nacelnik [Chief of Engineers] (CZ)
Zn............. Zink [Zinc] [Chemical element] [German]
ZN............. Zlepsovaci Navrh [Improvement Suggestion] (CZ)
zn............... Znacka [Mark, Sign] (CZ)
Zn............. Zname [Banner] [A periodical] (BU)
ZN.............. Zveza Narodov [League of Nations] (YU)
ZNA.......... Law on Legal Acts (BU)
ZNa.......... Zemedelska Nauka [Agrarian Science] [A periodical] (BU)
znach......... Meaning, Sense, Value (RU)
znachit....... Considerably, Significantly (RU)
ZNADK ..... Zen-Nihon Aikokusha Dantai Kaigi [All-Japan Council of Patriotic Organizations]
ZNaem....... Law on Rents (BU)
ZNasl........ Law on Inheritance (BU)
ZNBS......... Zambia National Building Society
ZNCB........ Zambia National Commercial Bank
ZNCC .... Zimbabwe National Chambers of Commerce (EY)

ZND.......... Zinder [Niger] [Airport symbol] (OAG)
ZNDF .... Zambia National Defence Force
ZNDK........ Zaidanhojin Nippon Dam Kyokai [Japan Dam Foundation] (EAIO)
ZNE.......... Newman [Australia] [Airport symbol] (OAG)
ZNEC .... Zambia National Energy Corporation Ltd.
ZNF .... Zimbabwe National Front
zngsh .... Deputy Chief of General Staff (RU)
ZNI .... Law on Encouraging Industry (BU)
ZNIB......... Zambia National Insurance Brokers Ltd.
ZNII.......... Zaporozh'ye Scientific Research Institute of Transformer Building and High-Voltage Equipment (RU)
ZNIISKh-YuV ... Zonal Scientific Research Institute of Agriculture of the Southeast (RU)
ZNL .... Zentralniederlassung [Central Office, Main Establishment] (EG)
ZNM .... Law on the People's Militia (BU)
ZNM......... Zarzad Nieruchomosci Miejskich [Administration of City Real Estate] (POL)
ZNMD....... Zaklady Naprawy Maszyn Drogowych [Road Construction Machinery Repair Shops] (POL)
ZNMS .... Zwiazek Niezaleznej Mlodziezy Socjalistycznej [Union of Independent Socialist Youth] (POL)
ZNO.......... Law on Rentals (BU)
ZNO.......... Nonstandard Equipment Plant (BU)
ZNO.......... Zaklad Narodowy Imienia Ossolinskich [Ossolinski National Institution] (POL)
ZNO.......... Zidovska Nabozenska Obec [Jewish Religious Congregation] (CZ)
ZNOG........ Zakon o Narodnim Odborima Gradova [Law on People's Committees of Cities] (YU)
ZNOGIGO ... Zakon o Narodnim Odborima Gradova i Gradskih Opstina [Law on People's Committees of Cities and Townships] (YU)
ZNOGO .... Zakon o Narodnim Odborima Gradskih Opstina [Law on People's Committees of Townships] (YU)
ZNOO .... Zakon o Narodnooslobodilackim Odborima [Law on National Liberation Committees] (YU)
ZNOS .... Zakon o Narodnim Odborima Sreza [Law on District People's Committees] (YU)
ZNP .... Alternate Observation Point (BU)
ZNP .... Alternate Observation Post (RU)
ZNP .... Law on Public Education (BU)
ZNP .... Zanzibar Nationalist Party [Tanzania] (AF)
ZNP .... Zimbabwe National Party
ZNP .... Zwiazek Nauczycielstwa Polskiego [Polish Teachers' Union] (POL)
ZNPF........ Zambia National Provident Fund
ZNPZ........ Zanatska Nabavno Prodajna Zadruga [Handicraft Buying and Selling Cooperative] (YU)
ZNPZ........ Zemljoradnicka Nabavno Prodajna Zadruga [Agricultural Buying and Selling Cooperative] (YU)
ZNR .... Zenska Narodni Rada [National Women's Council] (CZ)
ZNROB .... Law on Employment and Unemployment Insurance (BU)
ZNS .... Law on Penal Procedure (BU)
ZNS .... Law on People's Councils (BU)
ZNS .... Zambia National Service
ZNSD .... Zaklady Naprawy Sprzetu Drogowego [Road Equipment Repair Shops] (POL)
ZNSDT...... Law on People's Councils of Deputies of the Working People (BU)
ZNSh .... Deputy Chief of Staff (RU)
ZNSNZ...... Law on Scientific Degrees and Scientific Titles (BU)
ZNT .... Zentrale Netztaktaufbereitung [German] (ADPT)
ZNTB .... Zambia National Tourist Bureau
ZNTK .... Zaklady Naprawy Taboru Kolejowego [Railroad Rolling Stock Repair Shops] (POL)
ZNU.......... Zanzibar National Union
ZNUC .... Zemsky Nejvyssi Urad Cenovy [Provincial Supreme Price Office] (CZ)
ZNUC .... Zpravodajstvi Nejvyssiho Uradu Cenoveho [Information Service of the Supreme Price Office] (CZ)
ZNUT .... Zambia National Union of Teachers
ZNV.......... Zemsky Narodni Vybor [Provincial National Committee] (CZ)
ZNVB .... Zemsky Narodni Vybor v Brne [Provincial National Committee in Brno] (CZ)
ZNVP .... Zemsky Narodni Vybor v Praze [Provincial National Committee in Prague] (CZ)
ZNZ........... Law on Public Health (BU)
ZNZ........... Zanzibar [Tanzania] [Airport symbol] (OAG)
ZNZP........ Zemedelsky Nakupni a Zasobovaci Podnik [Agricultural Purchasing and Supply Enterprise] (CZ)
ZO............. Antiaircraft Defense (RU)
ZO............. Antiaircraft Gun (RU)
ZO............. Barrage Fire, Barrage (RU)
ZO............. Correspondence Department (RU)
ZO............. Correspondence Training, Education by Correspondence (RU)
ZO............. Oceanic Air Traffic Control [ICAO designator] (ICDA)

ZO .... Retreat-Blocking Detachment (RU)
ZO .... Zadni Odrad [*Rear Screening Detachment*] (CZ)
ZO .... Zahranicni Obchod [*Foreign Trade*] [*A periodical*] (CZ)
ZO .... Zakladni Organisace [*Basic Organization*] (CZ)
ZO .... Zakon o Narodnim Odborima Opstina [*Law on Municipal People's Committees*] (YU)
ZO .... Zakon o Opstinama [*Law on Municipalities*] (YU)
ZO .... Zarzad Okregowy [*District Administration*] (POL)
ZO .... Zastita Omladine [*Youth Protection*] (YU)
ZO .... Zastitni Odred [*Defensive Detachment*] [*Military*] (YU)
ZO .... Zavodni Organisace [*Factory Organization*] (CZ)
ZO .... Zdruzeni Odred [*Combined Detachment*] [*Military*] (YU)
ZO .... Zemaljski Odbor [*Territorial Committee*] (YU)
ZO .... Ziemie Odzyskane [*Recovered Territories*] (POL)
Zo .... Zooloji [*Zoology*] (TU)
ZO .... Zpetny Odrad [*Returning Convoy (Detachment)*] (CZ)
ZO .... Zvlastni Odbor [*Special Section*] (CZ)
ZOA .... Zarzad Osrodkow Akademickich [*Administration of Student Centers*] (POL)
ZOAM .... Zatovo Ory Asa Ato Madigasikara [*Unemployed Youth of Madagascar*] (AF)
ZOAV .... ZOA Vluchtelingenzorg [*ZOA Refugee Care - Netherlands*] (EAIO)
ZOAVO ..... Zuidoostaziatische Verdragsorganizatie [*Benelux*] (BAS)
ZOB .... Zemsky Odbor Bezpecnosti [*Provincial Security Department*] (CZ)
zob .... Zobacz [*See*] (POL)
ZOC .... Zimbabwe Omnibus Company
ZODS .... Zakon o Drzavnim Sluzbenicima [*Law on Government Employees*] (YU)
ZODU .... Zakon o Drzavnoj Upravi [*Law on State Administration*] (YU)
ZODW .... Zarzad Okregowy Drog Wodnych [*District Administration of Waterways*] (POL)
ZOE .... Zentrale Oberbauerneurung [*Central Permanent Way Reconditioning*] [*German*] (EG)
ZOEGPNS ... Law on the Expropriation of Large Urban Real Estate Holdings (BU)
ZOFI .... Zone Franche d'Inga [*Duty-Free Zone*] [*Zaire*] (IMH)
ZOFRI .... Zona Franca de Iquique [*Iquique Free Trade Zone*] [*Chile*] (LA)
ZOG .... Paramaribo [*Suriname*] [*Airport symbol*]
ZOI .... Refractory Items Plant (BU)
ZOIA .... Zones d'Organisation Industrielle et Strategique en Afrique
ZOIG .... Zaklad Oceanologii Instytut Geofizy [*Oceanology Section of the Geophysical Institute*] [*Poland*] (MSC)
ZOINTOLP ... Correspondence Institute of Social Studies of the Scientific and Technical Society of the Lumber Industry (RU)
ZOJS .... Zakon o Javnim Sluzbenicima [*Law on Public Employees*] (YU)
ZOK .... Experimental Structures Plant (RU)
ZOK .... Foreign Organization Commission of the TsK RSDRP (RU)
ZOK .... Zavodni Odborna Knihovna [*Factory Technical Library*] (CZ)
ZOKP .... Zakon o Krivicnom Postupku [*Law on Criminal Procedure*] (YU)
ZOKS .... Transcaucasian Society for Cultural Relations with Foreign Countries (RU)
ZO KSS ..... Zavodna Organizacia Komunistickej Strany Slovenska [*Factory Organization of the Communist Party of Slovakia*] (CZ)
ZOKZ .... Zakon o Komasaciji Zemljista [*Law on the Consolidation of Lands*] (YU)
ZOKZ .... Zwiazek Obrony Kresow Zachodnich [*Union for the Defense of the Western Borders (Prewar)*] (POL)
zol .... Gold (RU)
zol .... Zolotnik [*Measures*], Slide, Valve (RU)
ZOLDEX ... Zoldseg-Gyumolcs Exportra Termelteto es Felvasarlo Szovetkezeti Vallalat [*Producers' and Buyers' Cooperative Enterprise for the Export of Vegetables and Fruit*] (HU)
ZOLDKER ... Zoldseg- es Gyumolcskereskedelmi Vallalat [*Trade Enterprise for Vegetables and Fruit*] (HU)
ZOLDSZOV ... Zoldseg- es Gyumolcs Termelteto es Felvasarlo Szovetkezet [*Producers' and Buyers' Cooperative for Vegetables and Fruit*] (HU)
ZOLL .... Zarzad Okregu Ligi Lotniczej [*District Administration of the Aeronautical League*] (POL)
Zol-pl .... Gold and Platinum Mines [*Topography*] (RU)
zol rub .... Gold Ruble (RU)
ZOM .... Finishing Machine Plant (RU)
ZOM .... Refractory Materials Plant (BU)
ZOM .... Zaklad Oczyszczania Miasta [*Municipal Sanitation Department*] (POL)
ZOMGBT ... Correspondence Department of the Moscow City Library Technicum (RU)
ZOMLTI ... Correspondence Department of the Moscow Forestry Engineering Institute (RU)
ZOMM ...... Metal Cutting Machine Attachments Plant (BU)
ZOMNI ..... Correspondence Department of the Moscow Petroleum Institute Imeni I. M. Gubkin (RU)
ZOMO .... Riot Police [*Poland*]

ZOMO .... Zmotoryzowane Oddzialy Milicji Obywatelskiej [*Motorized Units of People's Militia*] [*Poland's riot police*]
ZOMOPI .. Correspondence Department of the Moscow Oblast Pedagogical Institute (RU)
ZOMP .... Defense Against Mass-Destruction Weapons (RU)
ZOMP .... Protection Against Mass-Destruction Weapons (BU)
ZOMS .... Zonal Experimental Reclamation Station (RU)
ZOMTI ...... Correspondence Department of the Moscow Peat Institute (RU)
ZOMZ .... Zagorsk Optical Instrument Plant (RU)
ZON .... Zakon o Nasledivanju [*Law on Inheritance*] (YU)
ZON .... Zonal Experimental Station (RU)
ZonDMMA ... Zonguldak Devlet Mimarlik ve Muhendislik Akademisi [*Zonguldak State Academy of Architecture and Engineering*] (TU)
ZONFM .... Zemski Odbor na Narodniot Front na Makedonija [*Territorial Committee of the People's Front of Macedonia*] (YU)
ZONI .... Western Oblast Scientific Research Institute for Comprehensive Studies (RU)
ZONIODOP ... Law on the Appraisal of Real Estate Expropriated for State or Public Use (BU)
ZONIPBN ... Law on the Expropriation of Unpurchased Real Estate (BU)
ZOO .... Law on Social Insurance (BU)
ZOO .... Zakon o Osiguranju [*Insurance Law*] (YU)
Z oo .... Z Ograniczona Odpowiedzialnoscia [*Limited*] [*Poland*]
zoofak .... Zootechnical Division (RU)
zookhim ..... Zoochemistry (RU)
zool .... Zoologia [*Zoology*] [*Italian*]
zool .... Zoological, Zoology (RU)
Zool .... Zoologie [*Zoology*] [*German*] (GCA)
zool .... Zoologie [*French*] (TPFD)
zool .... Zoology, Zoological (RU)
zootekh .... Zootechnician, Zootechny (RU)
zootekh st ... Zootechnical Station [*Topography*] (RU)
ZOOUP ..... Zakon o Opcem Upravnom Postupniku [*Law on General Administrative Procedure*] (YU)
zoovettekhnikum ... Zootechnical and Veterinary Technicum (RU)
ZOOZP ..... Law on the Protection of the Arable Land and Pastures (BU)
ZOP .... Alternate Firing Position (RU)
ZOP .... Concealed Firing Positions (BU)
ZOP .... Law on Protection Against Crime (BU)
ZOP .... Sekcija za Odrzavanje Pruge [*Railroad Track Maintenance Section*] (YU)
ZOP .... Zaklad Ochrony Przyrody [*Institute for the Conservation of Nature*] (POL)
ZOPA .... Zinc Oxide Producers' Association [*European Council of Chemical Manufacturers Federations*] [*Belgium*] (EAIO)
ZOPFAN ... Zone of Peace, Freedom, and Neutrality [*in Southeast Asia*] [*ASEAN*]
ZOPGR ..... Zarzad Okregowy Panstwowych Gospodarstw Rolnych [*District Administration of State Farms*] (POL)
ZOPI .... Zone de Pre-Industrialisation [*Algeria*]
ZO PKS .... Zarzad Okregowy Panstwowej Komunikacji Samochodowej [*District Administration of State Motor Transport*] (POL)
ZOPZF ...... Zakon o Poljoprivrednom Zemljisnom Fondu [*Law on the Agricultural Land Fund*] (YU)
ZOPZIP .... Zakon o Poslovnim Zgradama i Prostorijama [*Law on Office Buildings and Apartments*] (YU)
ZOR .... Plant Imeni October Revolution (RU)
ZOR .... Zabiegi Ochrony Roslin [*Plant Protection Measures*] (POL)
ZOR .... Zaklad Osiedli Robotniczych [*Poland*]
ZOR .... Zarzad Osiedli Robotniczych [*Administration of Workers' Settlements*] (POL)
ZORK .... Zarzad Okregowy Radiofonizacji Kraju [*District Administration of Country-Wide Radio Installation*] (POL)
ZORU .... All-Union Correspondence Training Center for Accounting and Statistical Personnel (RU)
zos .... Antiaircraft Illuminating Service (RU)
ZOS .... Ground Aids to Navigation [*Aviation*] (BU)
ZOS .... Zakladowy Oddzial Samoobrony [*Plant Civil Defense Unit*] (POL)
ZOS .... Zakon o Sudovima [*Law on Courts of Law*] (YU)
ZOS .... Zambian Ornithological Society (EAIO)
ZOS .... Zavodni Odborova Skupina [*Factory Trade-Union Group*] (CZ)
ZOS-pl .... Zonal Experimental Station (RU)
ZOS .... Zootechnical Experimental Station (RU)
ZOSBNOBM ... Zemski Odbor na Borcite od Narodnoosloboditelnata Borba na Makedonija [*Territorial Committee of the Union of Veterans of the National Liberation Struggle of Macedonia*] (YU)
ZOSBNOV ... Zemski Odbor na Sojuzot na Borcite od Narodnoosloboditelnata Vojna [*Territorial Committee of the Union of Veterans of the National Liberation War*] [*World War II*] (YU)
ZOSO .... Zakon o Stanbenim Odnosima [*Law on Housing Relations*] (YU)
ZOSP .... Zwiazek Ochotniczych Strazy Pozarnych [*Union of Voluntary Fire-Brigades*] [*Poland*]

ZOSRTs .... Law on Insuring Supplies and Price Control (BU)
ZOSZS ...... Zarzad Okregowy Szkolnego Zwiazku Sportowego [*District Authority of School Sports Union*] (POL)
ZOT .... All-Union Society "For the Mastering of Technology" (RU)
ZOT .... Zakon o Taksama [*Tax Law*] (YU)
ZOT .... Zeglarska Odznaka Turystyczna [*Sailor's Touring Badge*] [*Poland*]
ZOT .... Zespol Opracowan Technicznych [*Technical Designing Unit*] (POL)
ZOTS........ Zonal Experimental Tobacco Growing Station (BU)
ZOUP .... Zakon o Opstem Upravnom Postupku [*Law on General Administrative Procedure*] (YU)
ZOUP .... Zakon o Organima Unutrasnjih Poslova [*Law on the Organs of Internal Affairs*] (YU)
ZOUS .... Zakon o Upravnim Sudovima [*Law on Administrative Courts*] (YU)
ZOV .... Zakon o Ovjeravanju Potpisa, Rukopisa, i Prijepisa [*Law on Certification of Signatures, Manuscripts, and Copies*] (YU)
ZOVB .... Zeleznicni Oddeleni Verejne Bezpecnosti [*Railroad Department of Public Security*] (CZ)
ZOVPSh.... Correspondence Department of the Higher Party School (RU)
ZOVVPZ... Law on the Protection of the Air, Water, and Soil from Pollution (BU)
ZOW .... Zee-Ongevallenwet [*Benelux*] (BAS)
ZOW .... Zwiazek Osadnikow Wojskowych [*Association of Military Settlers*] (POL)
ZOW .... Zydowska Organizacja Wojskowa
ZOWO....... Zaklady Obrotu Warzywami i Owocami [*Vegetable and Fruit Marketing Establishments*] (POL)
ZOZ .... Zakladowa Organizacja Zwiazkowa [*Labor Union Local*] (POL)
ZOZK .... Zakon o Zemljisnim Knjigma [*Law on Land Title Records*] (YU)
ZO ZMS.... Zarzad Okregu Zwiazku Mlodziezy Socjalistycznej [*Socialist Youth Union District Authority*] (POL)
ZO ZMW .. Zarzad Okregu Zwiazku Mlodziezy Wiejskiej [*Rural Youth Union District Authority*] (POL)
ZO ZZM.... Zarzad Okregowy Zwiazku Zawodowego Metalowcow [*District Administration of the Trade Union of Metal Workers*] (POL)
ZP .... Air Traffic Services Reporting Office [*ICAO designator*] (ICDA)
ZP .... Alternate Command Post (RU)
ZP .... Antiaircraft Gun (RU)
ZP .... Antiaircraft Machine Gun (RU)
ZP .... Antiaircraft Searchlight (RU)
z/p .... Dispensary, First Aid Station, Public Health Station (RU)
ZP .... Field Sound Locator (RU)
ZP .... Foreign Representation, Foreign Mission (BU)
zp .... Lag (RU)
ZP .... Law on Pensions (BU)
Zp .... Record, Recording [*Computers*] (RU)
ZP .... Replacement Regiment (RU)
ZP .... Sound-Locator Post (RU)
ZP .... Sound Ranging Station (RU)
ZP .... Threatened Position (BU)
ZP .... Zadruzno Posestvo [*Cooperative Property*] (YU)
Zp .... Zahnradpumpe [*Geared Pump*] [*German*] (GCA)
ZP .... Zamoreny Prostor [*Contaminated Area*] (CZ)
ZP .... Zapadoceske Plynarny [*West Bohemian Gasworks*] (CZ)
ZP .... Zarzad Polityczny [*Political Administration*] [*Military*] (POL)
ZP .... Zarzad Powiatowy [*County Administration*] (POL)
ZP .... Zegluga Polska [*Polish Navigation*] [*Poland*]
Zp .... Zersetzungspunkt [*Decomposition Point*] [*German*]
Zp .... Zugbildungsplaene [*Train Assembly Plans (For passenger trains)*] [*German*] (EG)
ZP .... Zweeppartij [*Whipping Party*] [*Political party*] [*Belgium*]
ZP .... Zykluspuffer [*German*] (ADPT)
ZPA .... Zaklady Przemyslu Azotowego [*Nitrogen Plant*] (POL)
ZPA .... Zambia Pre-School Association (EAIO)
ZPA .... Zavody Pristroju a Automatizace [*Machinery and Automation Plants*] (CZ)
ZPAF .... Zwiazek Polskich Artystow Fotografiki [*Union of Polish Art Photographers*] (POL)
zp & j ...... Zonder Plaats en Jaar [*Without Place and Date*] [*Publishing*] [*Netherlands*]
ZPANV...... Polyacrylonitryl Fibers Plant (BU)
ZPAP........ Zwiazek Polskich Artystow Plastykow [*Union of Polish Artists in the Plastic Arts*] (POL)
ZPARK...... Zakon o Provodenju Agrarne Reforme i Kolonizacije [*Law on the Enforcement of Agrarian Reform and Colonization*] (YU)
ZPB........... Zaklady Przemyslu Bawelnianego [*Cotton Plants*] (POL)
ZPB........... Zarazna Poljska Bolnica [*Field Hospital for Contagious Disease*] (YU)
ZPB........... Zjednoczenie Przemyslu Bawelnianego [*Cotton Industry Association*] (POL)
ZPB........... Zoological Parks Board of New South Wales [*Australia*]
ZPBH .... Zjednoczenie Przemyslowe Budowy Huty [*Industrial Association for Metallurgical Plant Construction*] (POL)

ZPBNH ..... Zjednoczenie Przemyslowe Budowy Nowej Huty [*Industrial Association for Construction in Nowa Huta (Metallurgical center)*] (POL)
ZPBS .... Zentrales Projektierungsbuero Schwermaschinenbau [*Central Project-Planning Office for Heavy Machine Building*] [*German*] (EG)
ZPBSE....... Zarzad Przedsiebiorstw Budowy Sieci Elektrycznych [*Administration of Electrical Network Construction Companies*] (POL)
ZPC........... Zaklady Przemyslu Cukierniczego [*Sugar Plants*] (POL)
ZPC........... Zambia Printing Company Ltd.
ZPC........... Zimbabwe Promotion Council
ZPC........... Zjednoczenie Przemyslu Cukierniczego [*Association of the Sugar Industry*] (POL)
ZPCh .... Zavody Prumyslove Chemie [*Industrial Chemistry Plants*] (CZ)
ZPChNRB ... Law on the Stay of Foreigners in the Bulgarian People's Republic (BU)
ZPD .... Zadruzno Poljoprivredno Dobro [*Agricultural Cooperative Farm*] (YU)
ZPD .... Zakladowe Punkty Dokumentacji [*Factory Documentation Points*] (POL)
ZPD .... Zaklady Przemyslu Drzewnego [*Lumber Plants*] (POL)
ZPD .... Zaklady Przemyslu Dziewiarskiego [*Knitwear Goods Plant*] (POL)
ZPD .... Zentralstelle fuer Primaerdokumentation [*Central Office for Primary Documentation*] [*German*] (EG)
ZPD .... Zrzeszenie Prawnikow Demokratow [*Democratic Lawyers' Association*] (POL)
ZPDS .... Zdruzenje Prosvetnih Delavcev Slovenije [*Association of Educators of Slovenia*] (YU)
ZPDS .... Zveza Pedagoskih Drustev Slovenije [*Union of Pedagogical Societies of Slovenia*] (YU)
ZPDz......... Zaklady Przemyslu Dziewiarskiego [*Knitwear Goods Plant*] (POL)
ZPEV .... Zentrale Pruef- und Entwicklungsstelle fuer das Verkehrswesen [*Central Testing and Development Station for Transportation*] [*German*] (EG)
ZPF .... Zaklady Przemyslu Farmaceutycznego [*Pharmaceutical Plants*] (POL)
ZPF............ Zambia Police Force
ZPF............ Zentralstelle fur Personen und Familiengeschichte [*Germany*] (EAIO)
ZPFL......... Zanzibar and Pemba Federation of Labor [*Tanzania*] (AF)
ZPG .... Pneumatic Tires Plant (BU)
ZPG .... Zarzad Przemyslu Gastronomicznego [*Administration of the Restaurant Industry*] (POL)
ZPG .... Zentrale Projektierung Giessereien [*Central Project Planning Office for Foundries*] [*German*] (EG)
ZPGG .... Zarzad Portu Gdansk-Gdynia [*Administration of the Gdansk (Danzig)-Gdynia Port*] (POL)
ZPGUP...... Zarzad Projektowania Gmachow Uzytecznosci Publicznej [*Administration for Planning of Public Buildings*] (POL)
ZPH .... Zimbabwe Publishing House
ZPI............ Correspondence Pedagogical Institute (RU)
ZPI............ For the Food Industry [*Newspaper*] (RU)
ZPI............ Law on Privileges and Mortgages (BU)
ZPID......... Zentralstelle fuer Psychologische Information und Dokumentation [*Center for Psychological Information and Documentation*] [*Database operator*] [*Germany*] [*Information service or system*] (IID)
ZPiER .... Zespol Planowanie i Ekonomiki Rolnictwa [*Agricultural Planning and Economics Team*] (POL)
ZPINM...... Law and Regulation on the Planned Building of Settlements (BU)
ZPJ .... Zaklad Przemyslu Jedwabniczego [*Silk Plant*] (POL)
ZPK........... Plant Party Committee, Factory Party Committee (RU)
ZPK........... Zarzad Przemyslu Kosmetycznego [*Administration of the Cosmetics Industry*] (POL)
ZPK........... Zentrale Planungskommission [*Central Planning Commission*] (EG)
ZPKK........ Zentrale Parteikontrollkommission [*Central Party Control Commission*] [*German*] (EG)
ZPKM....... Kunming [*China*] [*ICAO location identifier*] (ICLI)
ZPKM....... Law on Cultural Monuments and Museums (BU)
ZPL........... Antiaircraft Machine Gun (RU)
ZPL........... Zaklad Przemyslu Lniarskiego [*Linen Plant*] (POL)
ZPLL......... Zarzad Powiatowy Ligi Lotniczej [*County Administration of the Aeronautical League*] (POL)
ZPM .... Zaklad Przedsiebiorstw Morskich [*Marine Enterprise Establishment*] (POL)
ZPMiUM .. Zarzad Przemyslu Maszyn i Urzadzen Mlynskich [*Administration of the Flour Mill Machinery and Equipment Industry*] (POL)
ZPMiW ..... Zwiazek Proletariatu Miast i Wsi [*Union of the Urban and Rural Proletariat*] (POL)
ZPMot .... Zjednoczenie Przemyslu Motoryzacyjnego [*Association of the Automotive Industry*] (POL)

ZPNRB...... Law on the Procuracy in the Bulgarian People's Republic (BU)
ZPO .... Zakladni Podminky Odberu [*Basic Conditions for Procurement*] (CZ)
ZPO .... Zaklady Przemyslu Odziezowego [*Clothing Plants*] (POL)
ZPO .... Zakon o Penziskom Osiguranju [*Law on Pension Insurance*] (YU)
ZPO .... Zavodni Politicka Organisace [*Factory Political Organization*] (CZ)
ZPO .... Zavodni Protiletecka Obrana [*Factory Antiaircraft Defense*] (CZ)
ZPO .... Zivilprozessordnung [*German Code of Civil Procedure*] (DLA)
ZPO .... Zjednoczenie Przemyslu Okretowego [*Shipbuilding Industry Union*] (POL)
ZPP.......... Semiconductors Plant (BU)
ZPP.......... Zadruzno Poljoprivredno Preduzece [*Agricultural Cooperative Establishment*] (YU)
ZPP.......... Zaklady Przemyslu Ponczoszniczego [*Hosiery Plants*] (POL)
ZPP.......... Zakon o Parnicnom Postupku [*Law on Civil Procedure*] (YU)
ZPP.......... Zavod za Privredno Planiranje [*Economic Planning Institute*] (YU)
ZPP.......... Zeleznicny Prepravny Poriadok [*Railroad Transportation Regulations*] (CZ)
ZPP.......... Zimbabwe Progressive Party [*Political party*] (PPW)
ZPP.......... Zrzeszenie Prawnikow Polskich [*Association of Polish Lawyers*] (POL)
ZPP.......... Zwiazek Patriotow Polskich [*Union of Polish Patriots (1943-1946)*] (POL)
ZPP.......... Zwiazek Przemyslu Piekarniczego [*Union of the Baking Industry*] (POL)
ZPPB .... Zarazna Pukovska Poljska Bolnica [*Regimental Field Hospital for Contagious Diseases*] (YU)
ZPPiS .... Zjednoczenie Pracownikow Panstwowych i Spolecznych [*Union of Government and Social Institution Employees*] (POL)
ZPPO........ Creeping Antitank Barrage, Rolling Antitank Barrage (RU)
ZPPP .... Kunming/Wujiaba [*China*] [*ICAO location identifier*] (ICLI)
ZPPP .... Zanzibar and Pemba People's Party [*Tanzania*]
ZPR.......... Antiaircraft Machine-Gun Company (RU)
ZPr.......... Antiaircraft Searchlight (RU)
ZPr.......... Law on the Procuracy in the Bulgarian People's Republic (BU)
z pr .... Subsistence Officer (BU)
ZPR.......... Zeleznicni Prepravni Rad [*Railroad Transportation Regulations*] (CZ)
ZPr.......... Zenijni Prapor [*Engineer Battalion*] (CZ)
ZPR.......... Zjednoczenie Przedsiebiorstw Rozrywkowych [*Association of Entertainment Enterprises*] (POL)
ZPRA........ Zimbabwe People's Revolutionary Army
zprac........ Zpracovany [*Elaborated*] [*Publishing Former Czechoslovakia*]
zprb .... Antiaircraft Searchlight Battalion (BU)
ZPRN .... Zarzad Przemyslu Rafinerii Nafty [*Administration of the Oil Refinery Industry*] (POL)
Z Prod ...... Zersetzungprodukt [*Decomposition Product*] [*German*] (GCA)
zprp .... Antiaircraft Searchlight Regiment (BU)
ZPRW....... Zrzeszenie Plantatorow Roslin Wloknistych [*Association of Fiber Planters*] (POL)
ZPS.......... Low Velocity Layer (RU)
ZPS.......... Underwater Sound Communication Station (RU)
ZPS.......... Underwater Sound Communication, Underwater Acoustic Communication (RU)
ZPS.......... Underwater Sound-Signaling Station (RU)
ZPS.......... Zaklady Piwowarsko-Slodownicze [*Breweries*] (POL)
ZPS.......... Zakon o Izboru Povremenih Sudija Okruznih Privrednih Sudova [*Law on Electing Temporary Judges of District Economic Courts*] (YU)
ZPS.......... Zakon o Privrednim Sudovima [*Law on Economic Courts*] (YU)
ZPS.......... Zarzad Portu w Szczecinie [*Administration of the Szczecin (Stettin) Port*] (POL)
ZPS.......... Zavody Presneho Strojirenstvi [*Precision Machine Plants*] (CZ)
ZPS.......... Zveza Pionirjev Slovenije [*Union of Pioneers of Slovenia*] (YU)
ZPT.......... Comma (RU)
ZPTM....... DC Motors Plant (BU)
ZPTM....... Zrzeszenie Polskich Towarzystw Medycznych [*Poland*] (SLS)
ZPTMB..... Zarzad Przemyslu Terenowego Materialow Budowlanych [*Administration of the Local Building Materials Industry*] (POL)
ZPTO........ Hoisting and Conveying Equipment Plant Imeni S. M. Kirov (RU)
ZPTS .... Zaklady Przemyslu Tworzyw Sztucznych [*Synthetic Products Plants*] (POL)
ZPU .... Antiaircraft Machine-Gun Mount (RU)
ZPU .... Given Track Angle (RU)
ZPU .... Zabezpeceni Pohranicniho Uzemi [*Border Area Defense*] (CZ)
ZPU .... Zjednoczenie Polskich Uchodzcow [*Association of Polish Refugees*] (POL)
zpv .... Antiaircraft Machine-Gun Platoon (RU)
ZPV.......... Polyamide Staples Plant (BU)
ZPW .... Zaaiazad- en Plantgoedwet [*Benelux*] (BAS)

ZPW .... Zaklady Przemyslu Welnianego [*Wool Plants*] (POL)
ZPW .... Zaklady Przemyslu Wlokienniczego [*Textile Plants*] (POL)
ZPW .... Zjednoczenie Przemyslu Welnianego [*Wool Industry Association*] (POL)
ZPZ............ Zadni Pochodova Zastita [*Rear Screening Element*] (CZ)
ZPZ............ Zakon o Prevozenju na Zeleznicama [*Law on Rail Transportation*] (YU)
ZPZ............ Zemljoradnicka Proizvodacka Zadruga [*Agricultural Producers' Cooperative*] (YU)
ZPZE .... Zakon o Poljoprivrednom Zemljisnom Fondu [*Law on the Agricultural Land Fund*] (YU)
ZPZMP ..... Zarzad Powiatowy Zwiazku Mlodziezy Polskiej [*County Administration of the Polish Youth Union*] (POL)
ZPZPOPI ... Law on Improving Agricultural Production and Protection of Agrarian Property (BU)
ZPZSK ...... Law on Pensioning Cooperative Farmers (BU)
ZPZSp .... Zwiazek Polskich Zwiazkow Sportowych [*Union of Polish Sport Unions*] (POL)
ZPZZ .... Zakon o Prometu Zemljista i Zgrada [*Law on Traffic in Buildings and Lands*] (YU)
ZPZZ .... Zwiazek Polskich Ziem Zachodnich [*Union devoted to the Polish Western Territories*] (POL)
ZQN......... Queenstown [*New Zealand*] [*Airport symbol*] (OAG)
ZR .... Area Control Center [*ICAO designator*] (ICDA)
ZR .... Law on Fishing (BU)
ZR .... Locking Relay (RU)
ZR .... Sound Ranging (RU)
ZR .... Zaire [*ANSI two-letter standard code*] (CNC)
ZR .... Zaklady Roszarnicze [*Flax Processing Plants*] (POL)
ZR .... Zambia Railways
ZR .... Zavodni Rada [*Factory (Trade-Union) Council*] (CZ)
ZR .... Zavodni Rozhlas [*Factory Broadcasting*] (CZ)
ZR .... Zavrsni Racun [*Final Accounting*] (YU)
ZR .... Zentralrat [*Central Council*] (EG)
Zr .... Zirkon [*Zirconium*] [*Chemical element*] [*German*]
Zr .... Zivnostensky Rad [*Trade Laws*] (CZ)
ZR .... Zwischenraum [*German*] (ADPT)
ZRA .... Zimbabwe Railways Authority
ZRA .... Zjednoczona Republika Arabska [*United Arab Republic*] (POL)
ZRANC ..... Zimbabwe Reformed African National Council
ZRB .... Safety Regulator Valve (RU)
ZRB .... Zjednoczenie Robot Budowlanych [*Association for Construction Work*] (POL)
zrbat .... Antiaircraft Missile Battery (BU)
zrbatr.......... Antiaircraft Missile Battery (RU)
zrbr............ Antiaircraft Missile Brigade (BU)
ZRC .... Zanzibar Revolutionary Council
ZRC .... Zawiya Refinery Company [*Libya*]
ZRC .... Zimbabwe Revolutionary Council (AF)
ZRCh .... Spare Parts Plant (BU)
ZRCN .... ZOA Refugee Care Netherlands (EAIO)
zrd .... Antiaircraft Missile Battalion (RU)
ZRD .... Pressure Regulator Valve (RU)
zrdn .... Antiaircraft Missile Battalion (RU)
ZRE .... Zjednoczenie Robot Elewacyjnych [*Association for Erection Work*] (POL)
ZRH........... Zurich [*Switzerland*] [*Airport symbol*] (OAG)
ZRI........... Serui [*Indonesia*] [*Airport symbol*] (OAG)
ZRI........... Zjednoczenie Robot Inzynierskich [*Association for Engineering Work*] (POL)
ZRIF .... Zavrsni Racun Investicionih Fondova [*Final Accounting of Investment Funds*] (YU)
ZRK .... Antiaircraft Missile System (RU)
ZRK .... Closed Workers' Cooperative [*1930-1932*] (RU)
ZRK .... Zentrale Revisionskommission [*Central Auditing Commission*] [*German*] (EG)
ZR K .... Zrinyi (Honved) Kiado [*Zrinyi (Military) Publishing House*] (HU)
ZRKPO..... Zaednicata na Rabotnickite Kulturno-Prosvetni Organizacii [*Association of Workers' Cultural and Educational Organizations*] (YU)
ZRM .... Sarmi [*Indonesia*] [*Airport symbol*] (OAG)
ZRM .... Zaklady Remontowo-Montazowe [*Repair and Assembly Establishments*] (POL)
ZRM .... Zwiazek Rybakow Morskich [*Union of Deep Sea Fishermen*] (POL)
ZRMK .... Zavod za Raziskavo Materiala in Konstruckcij, Ljubljana [*Materials and Structures Research and Testing Institute, Ljubljana*] [*Former Yugoslavia*] (EAS)
ZRM-LJ .... Zavod za Raziskavo Materiala in Konstrukcij Ljubljana [*Research Institute of Materials and Construction, Ljubljana*] (YU)
ZRMM .... Metal Cutting Machines Repair Plant (BU)
ZRMP........ Zona de Paso de Rutas Aereas Mundiales Principales [*Major World Air Route Area*] [*Spanish*]
ZRNA .... Radio Navigation Equipment Plant (BU)
zrnd .... Antiaircraft Missile Battalion (BU)

ZRNN....... Zona de Rutas Aereas Regionales y Nacionales [*Regional and Domestic Air Route Area*] [*Spanish*]
ZRO........... Radar Identification Interrogator   (RU)
ZRO........... Zemska Rada Osvetova [*Provincial Cultural Council*]   (CZ)
zrp............. Antiaircraft Missile Regiment   (BU)
ZRP........... Zapadocesky Rudny Pruzkum [*West Bohemian Mineral Prospecting*]   (CZ)
ZRP........... Zavod Rudeho Prava [*Rude Pravo (Newspaper) Enterprise*]   (CZ)
zrpdn.......... Antiaircraft Ammunition Missile Battalion   (BU)
ZRPF........ Zbornik Radova Poljoprivrednog Fakulteta [*Collected Works of the Faculty of Agriculture*] [*Belgrade*]   (YU)
ZRPS........ Zdruzenie Rodicov a Priatelov Skoly [*Parent-Teacher Association*]
ZRR........... Zavody Rijnove Revoluce [*October Revolution Plants*]   (CZ)
ZRS........... Speed Regulator Valve   (RU)
ZRS........... Zeleznicni Rozvojove Stredisko [*Railroad Development Center*]   (CZ)
ZRS........... Zwiazek Rewizyjny Spoldzielni [*Cooperative Auditing Union*]   (POL)
ZRSS........ Zwiazek Robotniczych Stowarzyszen Sportowych [*Union of Workers' Sport Associations*]   (POL)
ZRSU........ Zanzibar Revolutionary Students Union [*Tanzania*]   (AF)
zrtb............. Antiaircraft Missile Repair Depot   (BU)
ZRU........... Zambia Rugby Union
ZRUP....... Zakladna Rozvoje Uranoveho Prumyslu [*Development Center for the Uranium Industry*]   (CZ)
ZRV........... Antiaircraft Missile Troops   (BU)
ZRWI........ Zjednoczenie Robot Wodno-Inzynieryjnych [*Association of Hydraulic Engineering Work*]   (POL)
ZRWiF...... Zjednoczenie Robot Wiertniczych i Fundamentowych [*Association for Drilling and Foundation Work*]   (POL)
ZRZ.......... Radioactive Contamination Zone   (RU)
ZRZ.......... Zjednoczenie Robot Zmechanizowanych [*Association for Mechanized Work*]   (POL)
ZRZ.......... Zone of Radioactive Contamination   (BU)
ZS............... Agrarian Union   (BU)
ZS............... Delaying System   (RU)
z/s............. Grain Sovkhoz   (RU)
ZS............... Green Glass   (RU)
ZS............... Law on Ownership   (BU)
ZS............... Memory Core   (RU)
ZS............... Moderating Power [*Nuclear physics and engineering*]   (RU)
ZS............... Net Layer   (RU)
ZS............... Shipyard   (RU)
ZS............... Signal Bell, Alarm Bell   (RU)
ZS............... Steel Mill   (BU)
ZS............... Zadruzna Stedionica [*Cooperative Savings Bank*]   (YU)
ZS............... Zakon o Narodnim Odborima Srezova [*Law on District People's Committees*]   (YU)
ZS............... Zakon o Srezovima [*Law on Districts*]   (YU)
ZS............... Zakon o Sudovima [*Law on Courts of Law*]   (YU)
ZS............... Zasadnicza Szkola [*Basic School*]   (POL)
ZS............... Zasobovaci Sluzba [*Supply Service*] [*Civil defense*]   (CZ)
ZS............... Zavodni Skupina [*Factory Group*]   (CZ)
ZS............... Zavodni Straz [*Factory Guard*]   (CZ)
ZS............... Zavod za Statistiku [*Statistical Institute*]   (YU)
ZS............... Zdravotnicka Sprava [*Health Directorate*]   (CZ)
ZS............... Zdravstvena Sekcija [*Health Section*]   (YU)
Zs............... Zeitschrift [*Journal, Magazine*] [*German*]
ZS............... Zelena Slovenije [*Greens of Slovenia*] [*Political party*]   (EY)
Zs............... Zeleznicka Stanica [*Railroad Station*]   (YU)
ZS............... Zeljezara Sisak, Tvornica Besavnih Celicnih Cijevi [*Sisak Seamless Steel Tube Factory*]   (YU)
ZS............... Zeljezara Smederevo [*Smederevo Iron Works*]   (YU)
ZS............... Zimni Stadion [*Winter Stadium*]   (CZ)
ZS............... Zone de Securite [*Security Zone*] [*Cambodia*]   (CL)
ZS............... Zpravodajska Sprava [*Intelligence Directorate*]   (CZ)
ZS............... Zrzeszenie Sportowe [*Sport Association*]   (POL)
zs............... Zsido [*Jew, Jewish*]   (HU)
zs............... Zsoltar [*Psalm*]   (HU)
ZS............... Zugsanitaeter [*Platoon Medical Aide (Workers Militia)*]   (EG)
zS............... Zur See [*Of the Navy*]   (WEN)
zs............... Zusammen [*Together*] [*German*]   (GCA)
ZSA........... San Salvador [*Bahamas*] [*Airport symbol*]   (OAG)
ZSA........... Zimbabwe Scientific Association   (EAIO)
ZSA........... Zvaez Slovenskych Architektov [*Former Czechoslovakia*]   (SLS)
ZSAM....... Xiamen [*China*] [*ICAO location identifier*]   (ICLI)
ZSAO........ Federation of Swiss Employers' Organizations [*Switzerland*]   (EAIO)
ZSB........... Zasadnicza Szkola Budowlana [*Construction Vocational School*]   (POL)
ZSBB......... Zentrale Sonder-Baubueros [*Central Special Construction Offices*]   (EG)
ZSBiH .... Zavod za Statistiku Bosne i Hercegovine [*Statistical Office of Bosnia and Hercegovina*]   (YU)

ZSBIK ...... Reinforced Concrete Structures and Products Plant   (BU)
ZSC........... Zahlensicherheitscode [*Numerical Security Code*] [*German*]   (ADPT)
ZSC........... Zambia Sugar Company
ZSC........... Zeeland Steamship Co.   (MHDW)
ZSCh......... Zwiazek Samopomocy Chlopskiej [*Peasants' Mutual Aid Union*]   (POL)
ZSCh......... Zwiazek Spoldzielni Chlopskich [*Union of Peasants' Cooperatives*]   (POL)
ZSCN........ Nanchang [*China*] [*ICAO location identifier*]   (ICLI)
ZSDA....... Winter Games of Friendly Armies   (RU)
ZSE........... Zaklad Sieci Elektrycznych [*Electric Network Establishment*]   (POL)
ZSE........... Zaoczne Studia Ekonomiczne [*Correspondence Courses in Economics*]   (POL)
ZSE........... Zapadoslovenske Elektrarne [*West Slovak Electric Power Plants*]   (CZ)
ZSE........... Zavody Silnoproude Elektrotechniky [*High-Voltage Electrical Engineering Plants*] [*Former Czechoslovakia*]   (CZ)
ZSE........... Zimbabwe Stock Exchange
ZSF........... Zemjodelsko-Sumarski Fakultet [*Faculty of Agriculture and Forestry*]   (YU)
ZSFAN ..... West Siberian Branch of the Academy of Sciences, USSR   (RU)
ZSFSR ...... Transcaucasian Socialist Federated Soviet Republic [*1922-1936*]   (RU)
ZSFZ .... Fuzhou [*China*] [*ICAO location identifier*]   (ICLI)
ZSG .... Law on Citizens' Property   (BU)
ZSG .... Zasadnicza Szkola Gornicza [*Basic Mining School*]   (POL)
zsgest.......... Zusammengestellt [*Compiled*] [*German*]
ZSGRU..... West Siberian Geological Exploration Administration   (RU)
ZSGZ........ Ganzhou [*China*] [*ICAO location identifier*]   (ICLI)
zsgz........... Zusammengezogen [*Contracted*] [*German*]   (GCA)
ZSh .... Bell Cord   (RU)
ZSHA .... Shanghai [*China*] [*ICAO location identifier*]   (ICLI)
ZSHC .... Hangzhou/Jianqiao [*China*] [*ICAO location identifier*]   (ICLI)
ZShP........ Navigational Instruments Plant   (RU)
ZShtDSl .... Law on Regular State Personnel   (BU)
ZSI .... Correspondence Institute of Statistics   (RU)
ZSI .... Equipment and Installations Plant   (BU)
ZSI .... Zoological Society of Israel   (EAIO)
ZSI .... Zoological Survey of India
ZSI .... Zwiazek Spoldzielni Inwalidow [*Association of Invalid Cooperatives*] [*Poland*]
ZSIB .... West Siberian Railroad   (RU)
ZSIC .... Zambia State Insurance Corporation Ltd.
ZSIDB ...... Law on State Budget Drafting and Implementation   (BU)
ZSJ .... Zavodni Sokolske Jednoty [*Sokol Factory Units (Athletic organization)*]   (CZ)
ZSJ .... Zveza Sindikatov Jugoslavije [*Confederation of Trade-Unions of Yugoslavia*]   (YU)
ZSJA .... Jian [*China*] [*ICAO location identifier*]   (ICLI)
ZSK........... Reinforced Concrete Structures Plant   (BU)
ZSK........... Zasadnicza Szkola Kolejarzy [*Basic School for Railroad Workers*]   (POL)
ZSK........... Zentrale Kommission fuer Staatliche Kontrolle [*Central Commission for State Control*]   (EG)
ZSK........... Zivilschutzkorps [*Civil Defense Corps*]   (WEN)
ZSKI........ Reinforced Concrete Structures and Products Plant   (BU)
ZSKP........ Zakon o Sudskom Krivicnom Postupku [*Law on Judicial Criminal Procedure*]   (YU)
ZSKPDM .. Zemski Sojuz na Kulturno-Prosvetnite Drustva na Makedonija [*National Union of Cultural and Educational Societies of Macedonia*]   (YU)
ZSL........... Zapadni Slovensko [*West Slovakia*]   (CZ)
ZSL........... Zjednoczone Stronnictwo Ludowe [*United Peasants' Party*] [*Poland*] [*Political party*]   (PPW)
ZSM .... Building Materials Plant   (RU)
ZSM .... Law on Juvenile Courts   (BU)
ZSM .... Zalozba Silva Marija [*Silva Marija Publishing House*]   (YU)
ZSM .... Zasadnicza Szkola Metalowa [*Basic Metallurgical School*]   (POL)
ZSM .... Zavod za Statistika na Makedonija [*Statistical Office of Macedonia*]   (YU)
ZSN .... Law on Population Self-Taxation   (BU)
ZSN .... Western Siberian Lowland   (RU)
ZSNJ .... Nanjing [*China*] [*ICAO location identifier*]   (ICLI)
ZSNP........ Zavod Slovenskeho Narodneho Povstania [*"Slovak National Uprising" Plant*]   (CZ)
ZSO .... Zakon o Socijalnom Osiguranju [*Law on Social Insurance*]   (YU)
ZSob........... Law on Property   (BU)
ZSOF........ Hefei/Luogang [*China*] [*ICAO location identifier*]   (ICLI)
ZSP........... Glassware and Porcelain Plant   (BU)
ZSP........... Zavodni Skola Prace [*Factory Training School*]   (CZ)
ZSP........... Zavod za Stopansko Planiranje [*Economic Planning Institute*]   (YU)

ZSP .... Zrzeszenie Studentow Polskich [*Polish Student Association*] (POL)

ZSP .... Zwiazek Spoldzielni Pracy [*Union of Labor Cooperatives*] (POL)

ZSP .... Zwiazek Studentow Polskich [*Poland*]

ZSP .... Zwischenspeicher [*German*] (ADPT)

ZSPB .... Zambia Society for the Prevention of Blindness

ZSPFLRJ .. Zdruzenje Sportnih Podjetij Federativna Ljudska Republika Jugoslavija [*Association of Yugoslav Sport Establishments*] [*Ljubljana*] (YU)

ZSPG .... Law on the Management and Use of Forests (BU)

ZSPiR .... Zwiazek Spoldzielni Przemyslowych i Rzemieslniczych

ZSP i Rz .... Zwiazek Spoldzielni Pracy i Rzemiosla [*Union of Labor and Handicraft Cooperatives*] (POL)

ZSP i Rz ..... Zwiazek Spoldzielni Przemyslowych i Rzemieslniczych [*Union of Industrial and Handicraft Cooperatives*] (POL)

ZSPP .... Zavodni Skola Prace, Praha [*Factory Training School in Prague*] (CZ)

ZSQD .... Qingdao [*China*] [*ICAO location identifier*] (ICLI)

ZSR .... Signal Switching-Off Relay (RU)

ZSr .... Zakon o Narodnim Odborima Srezova [*Law on District People's Committees*] (YU)

ZSR .... Zemska Skolni Rada [*Provincial School Board*] (CZ)

ZSRA .... Zambia Squash Racquets Association

ZSRR .... Zwiazek Socjalistycznych Republik Radzieckich [*Union of Soviet Socialist Republics*] (POL)

ZSS .... Sassandra [*Ivory Coast*] [*Airport symbol*] (OAG)

ZSS .... Zarizeni Spolecneho Stravovani [*Cafeteria*] (CZ)

ZSS .... Zavod za Statistiko Slovenije [*Statistical Institute of Slovenia*] (YU)

ZSS .... Zwiazek Spoldzielni Spozywcow [*Union of Consumers' Cooperatives*] (POL)

ZSSA .... Shanghai City [*China*] [*ICAO location identifier*] (ICLI)

ZSSA .... Zoological Society of Southern Africa [*See also DUSA*] [*Port Elizabeth, South Africa*] (EAIO)

ZSSFA ...... Zambia Secondary Schools Football Association

ZSSL .... Shanghai/Longhua [*China*] [*ICAO location identifier*] (ICLI)

ZSSP .... Special Steel Sections Plant (BU)

ZSSR .... Transcaucasian Socialist Soviet Republic [*1922*] (RU)

ZSSR .... Zveza Sovjetskih Socialisticnih Republik [*Union of Soviet Socialist Republics*] (YU)

ZSSR .... Zwiazek Socjalistycznych Sowieckich Republik [*Union of Soviet Socialist Republics*] (POL)

zssro .... Zapsana Spolecnost s Rucenim Omezenym [*Incorporated Limited Liability Company*] [*Czech*] (CZ)

ZSSRZ .... Zaporozh'ye Shipbuilding and Repair Plant (RU)

ZSSS .... Shanghai/Hongqiao [*China*] [*ICAO location identifier*] (ICLI)

ZSt .... Law on Standardization (BU)

ZST .... Zaklady Sprzetu Transportowego [*Transportation Equipment Plants*] (POL)

ZST .... Zapadoslovenske Tehelne [*West Slovak Brick Works*] (CZ)

ZST .... Zeme Socialistickeho Tabora [*Socialist Camp Countries*] (CZ)

ZST .... Zona Slobodne Trgovine [*European Free Trade Zone*] (YU)

Zst .... Zusammenstellung [*Compilation*] [*German*] (GCA)

ZSTC .... Zanzibar State Trading Corporation

ZSTN .... Jinan [*China*] [*ICAO location identifier*] (ICLI)

ZSTs .... Law on Supply and Prices (BU)

Zstzg .... Zusammensetzung [*Composition*] [*German*] (GCA)

ZSU .... Self-Propelled Antiaircraft Gun (RU)

ZsVK .... Zsido Vilagkongresszus [*World Congress of Jews*] (HU)

ZSVTsVK ... Law on Deals in Foreign Exchange Valuables and Foreign Exchange Control (BU)

ZSZ .... West-Northwest (RU)

ZSZ .... Zakon o Socialnem Zavarovanju [*Law on Social Insurance*] (YU)

ZSZ .... Zasadnicze Szkoly Zawodowe [*Basic Vocational Schools*] (POL)

ZSZ .... Zemedelsky Stavebni Zavod [*Agricultural Construction Enterprise*] (CZ)

ZSZ .... Zemske Statni Zastupitelstvi [*Office of the Provincial Prosecutor*] (CZ)

ZsZ .... Zu Seiner Zeit [*In Good Time*] [*German*]

ZSZ .... Zveza Slovenskih Zeleznicarjev [*Union of Slovenian Railroad Workers*] (YU)

Zszg .... Zusammensetzung [*Composition*] [*German*]

ZS ZMP .... Zarzad Stoleczny Zwiazku Mlodziezy Polskiej [*Warsaw Administration of the Union of Polish Youth*] (POL)

ZSZS .... Zavod za Socialno Zavarovanje Slovenije [*Institute of Social Insurance of Slovenia*] (YU)

ZT .... Aerodrome Control Tower [*ICAO designator*] (ICDA)

ZT .... Heavy-Type Sound Locator (RU)

ZT .... Quenching Transformer, Hardening Transformer (RU)

ZT .... Zajednicko Trziste [*Common Market*] (YU)

ZT .... Zastupce Velitele pro Tyl [*Deputy Chief for Rear Services*] (CZ)

Zt. .... Zeit [*Time*] [*German*]

ZT .... Zelezniska Tiskarna v Ljubljani [*Railroad Printers in Ljubljana*] (YU)

zt. .... Zeszyt [*Issue*] [*Publishing*] [*Poland*]

zt. .... Zobacz Tez [*See Also*] (POL)

ZT .... Zugloi Textilgepalkatreszgyar [*Factory of Textile Machine Parts in Zuglo*] (HU)

zT .... Zum Teil [*Partly, In Part*] [*German*] (GPO)

ZTA .... Telephone Equipment Plant (BU)

ZTA .... Zentraler Transportausschuss [*Central Transportation Committee*] [*German*] (EG)

ZTA .... Zulu Tribal Authority

ZTA .... Zwiazek Teatrow Amatorskich [*Amateur Theatricals Association*] (POL)

ZTB .... Battery-Charging Station (RU)

Ztbl .... Zentralblatt [*Official Gazette*] [*German*]

ZTD .... Law on Labor Contracts (BU)

ZTD .... Zarzad Transportu Drogowego [*Administration for Road Transport*] (POL)

ZTDC .... Zimbabwe Tourist Development Corporation

ZTDI .... Zentralstelle fuer Textildokumentation und Information [*Center for Textile Documentation and Information*] [*Dusseldorf*]

ZTE .... Zeichentaktempfang [*German*] (ADPT)

ZTF .... Law on Creative Funds (BU)

Ztg. .... Zeitung [*Journal, Newspaper*] [*German*] (EG)

ZTGA .... Zimbabwe Tea Growers Association

ZTH .... Zakinthos [*Greece*] [*Airport symbol*] (OAG)

ZTK .... Foreign Technical Commission of the TsK RSDRP (RU)

ZTK .... Zavodni Technicka Knihovna [*Factory Technical Library*] (CZ)

ZTKI .... Industrial Rubber Products Plant (BU)

ZTL .... Leningrad Zenith Telescope (RU)

ZTL .... Zambia Tours and Lodges

ztl .... Zeitlich [*Chronological*] [*German*] (GCA)

ZTM .... Heavy Machinery Plant (RU)

Ztm .... Occulting Light [*Nautical term*] (RU)

ZTMPO ..... Law on Trademarks and Industrial Prototypes (BU)

ZTN .... Law on Labor Norms (BU)

ZTN .... Nordenfeld Primer (RU)

ZTN .... Zaklad Technologii Nafty [*Institute of Petroleum Technology*] (POL)

ztp .... Reserve Tank Regiment (RU)

ZTP .... Zeleznicko Transportno Preduzece [*Railroad Transportation Establishment*] (YU)

ZTPS .... Law on Cultivated Land Ownership (BU)

ZTPU .... Antiaircraft Turret Machine-Gun Mount (RU)

ZTPZK ...... Law on Labor Production Artisans' Cooperatives (BU)

ZTR .... Zalozni Tankova Rota [*Reserve Tank Company*] (CZ)

Ztr .... Zentner [*Centner*] [*50 kilograms*] [*German*] (WEN)

ZTRS .... Zambia-Tanzania Road Services

ZTS .... Zemedelske Technicke Skoly [*Agricultural Colleges*] (CZ)

Ztsch .... Zeitschrift [*Journal, Periodical*] [*German*]

Ztschr. .... Zeitschrift [*Journal, Periodical*] [*German*] (GPO)

ZTSh .... Shayn Reflecting Telescope (RU)

ZTST .... Correspondence Technicum of Soviet Trade (RU)

ZTSU .... Law on Territorial and Settlement Structure (BU)

ZTT .... Zaloznistvo Trzaskega Tiska [*Trieste Publishing House*] (YU)

ZTTC .... Zambia Travel and Touring Company

ZTTMP ..... Technological Correspondence Technicum of Local Industry (RU)

ZTU .... Plant Technical Specifications, Factory Technical Specifications (RU)

ZTU .... Western Territorial Administration (of the GVF) (RU)

ZTU .... Zenijne Technicke Uciliste [*Engineer Technical Training Center*] (CZ)

ZTV .... Zakladni Telesna Vychova [*Basic Physical Education*] (CZ)

ZTV .... Zeleznicni Tratove Velitelstvi [*Railroad Sector Command*] (CZ)

ZTV .... Zeleznicni Tratovy Velitel [*Railroad Sector Commander*] (CZ)

Ztw .... Zeitweise [*Temporarily*] [*German*]

Ztw. .... Zeitwort [*Verb*] [*German*]

ztws .... Zeitweise [*From Time to Time*] [*German*] (GCA)

ZTZ .... Zaporozh'ye Transformer Plant (RU)

Zt Z .... Zeitzuender [*Time Fuse*] [*German*] (GCA)

ZTZCh ...... Tractor Spare Parts Plant (RU)

ZU .... Antiaircraft Weapon Mount (RU)

ZU .... Contaminated Sector (BU)

ZU .... Land Administration (RU)

ZU .... (Oddeleni) Zvlastnich Ukolu [*Special Projects Department*] (CZ)

ZU .... Recorder (RU)

ZU .... Set Point Adjustment, Setting Device, Setup Unit [*Computers*] (RU)

ZU .... Sound Locator, Sound Detector (RU)

ZU .... Storage, Memory (RU)

ZU .... Upper Area Control Center [*ICAO designator*] (ICDA)

ZU .... Zahranicni Ustav [*Foreign Institute*] (CZ)

ZU .... Zamoreny Usek [*Contaminated Sector*] (CZ)

ZU .... Zarzad Uczelniany [*School Administration (of the Polish Youth League)*] (POL)

ZU..............	Zastupitelsky Urad [*Representative Office or Mission*] (CZ)
ZU..............	Zememericsky Ustav [*Geodetic Institute*] (CZ)
ZU..............	Zemepisny Ustav [*Geographical Institute*] (CZ)
ZU..............	Zemsky Urad [*Provincial Administration Office*] (CZ)
ZU..............	Zpravodajska Ustredna [*Information Center*] (CZ)
Zu..............	Zusammensetzung [*Composition*] [*German*] (GCA)
zub..............	Dental (RU)
Zub.............	Zubehoer [*Accessories*] [*German*] (GCA)
Zub.............	Zugbegleitpersonal [*Train Personnel (Excluding locomotive personnel)*] (EG)
ZubPr........	Zubolekarski Pregled [*Dentists' Review*] [*A periodical*] (BU)
ZUBRI.......	Nondestructive Storage, Nondestructive Memory [*Computers*] (RU)
ZUC...........	Zvezna Uprava za Ceste [*Federal Administration of Roads*] (YU)
ZUCK........	Chongqing [*China*] [*ICAO location identifier*] (ICLI)
Zuck..........	Zuckerherstellung [*Sugar Making*] [*German*] (GCA)
Zuckergeh ...	Zuckergehalt [*Sugar Content*] [*German*] (GCA)
ZUD...........	Zapadoceske Uhelne Doly [*West Bohemian Coal Mines*] (CZ)
ZUD...........	Zjednoczenie Urzadzen Dzwigowych [*Association for Hoisting Equipment*] (POL)
Zue..............	Zugueberwachungsanlagen [*Train Control Installations*] (EG)
ZUES........	Zimbabwe University Economic Society
Zuf..............	Zufall [*Accident*] [*German*] (GCA)
Zuf..............	Zufuehrer [*Feed Mechanism*] [*German*] (GCA)
Zuf..............	Zufuhr [*Addition*] [*German*] (GCA)
ZUFI.........	Zambia Union of Financial Institutions
Zug.............	Zugang [*Approach*] [*German*] (GCA)
zug.............	Zugeteilt [*Assigned*] [*German*]
ZUG...........	Zugriffszeit [*German*] (ADPT)
zugeh.........	Zugehoerig [*Belonging to*] [*German*] (GCA)
zugew.........	Zugewiesen [*Assigned to*] [*German*] (GCA)
zugl............	Zugleich [*Simultaneously*] [*German*] (GCA)
Zugres........	Zuyevka State Regional Electric Power Plant (RU)
ZUGY.......	Guiyang [*China*] [*ICAO location identifier*] (ICLI)
zu Hd.........	Zu Haenden [*Care of*] [*German*] (GCA)
ZUI	Correspondence University of the Arts (RU)
ZUI	Zaklad Uslug Inwestycyjnych [*Investment Service Enterprise*] (POL)
ZUK...........	Astrocompass (RU)
ZUK...........	Zavody Umelecke Kovovyroby [*Decorative Metalwork Plants*] (CZ)
ZUKiW......	Zjednoczenie Urzadzen Klimatyzacyjnych, i Wentylacyjnych [*Association for Heating, Air-Conditioning, and Ventilating Equipment*] (POL)
ZUKVRS ...	Ultrashort Wave Radio Stations Plant (BU)
Zul.............	Zulage [*Increase*] [*German*] (GCA)
Zul.............	Zulass [*Admission*] [*German*] (GCA)
Zul.............	Zulassung [*Admission*] [*German*] (GCA)
Zul.............	Zuletzt [*Finally*] [*German*]
ZULAWU ...	Zambia United Local Authorities Workers Union
ZULS........	Lhasa [*China*] [*ICAO location identifier*] (ICLI)
ZUM.........	Contaminated Area (RU)
ZUM.........	Zaklady Urzadzen Mechanicznych [*Mechanical Appliance Factory*] (POL)
ZUM.........	Zambia Union of Musicians
ZUM.........	Zimbabwe Unity Movement [*Political party*] (ECON)
ZUMA......	Zambia Union of Musicians and Artists
ZUMA......	Zentrum fuer Umfragen, Methoden, und Analysen [*Center for General Inquiries, Methods, and Analyses*] [*Research center*] (IRC)
ZUMK......	Taped Memory System (BU)
ZUNOO	Zavod za Unapredenje Nastave i Opsteg Obrazovanja [*Institute for the Improvement of Teaching and General Culture*] (YU)
ZUNS	Zakon o Uredjenju Narodnih Sudova [*Law on the Organization of People's Courts*] (YU)
ZUNVP	Law on the Settlement of Some Questions of Pensions (BU)
ZUNZ........	Zavodni Ustav Narodniho Zdravi [*Factory Public Health Institute (Attached to an industrial enterprise)*] (CZ)
ZUO..........	Law on Suspended Sentences (BU)
ZUO..........	Zakon o Upravnih Organih [*Law on Administrative Organs*] (YU)
ZUO..........	Zboziznalecky Ustav Obchodu [*Commodity Study Institute of Trade*] (CZ)
ZUOLRS...	Zakon o Upravnih Organih v Ljudski Republiki Sloveniji [*Law on Administrative Organs in Slovenia*] (YU)
ZUP	Law on Conditional Pardon (BU)
ZUP	Zadanka a Uverenou Prepravu [*Request for Authorized Transportation*] (CZ)
ZUP	Zakon o Opstem Upravnom Postupku [*Law on General Administrative Procedure*] (YU)
ZUP	Zemsky Urad Ochrany Prace [*Provincial Office for Labor Protection*] (CZ)
ZUP	Zone a Urbaniser en Priorite [*Priority Urbanization Zone*] [*French*]

ZUPO........	Zimbabwe United People's Organization [*Political party*] (PPW)
ZUPRO	Zwiazek Uczestnikow Polskiego Ruchu Oporu [*Union of Participants in the Polish Resistance Movement*] (POL)
ZUPU........	Zaklad Ubezpieczen Pracownikow Umyslowych [*Poland*]
ZUR...........	Antiaircraft Guided Missile (BU)
zur.............	Honored Teacher of the Republic (RU)
ZUR...........	Zapadocesky Uhelny Revir [*West Bohemian Coal Basin*] (CZ)
ZUR...........	Zarzad Urzadzen Rolnych [*Administration of Agricultural Establishments*] (POL)
ZUR...........	Zona d'Urgent Reindustrialitacion [*Zone of Urgent Reindustrialization*] [*Spanish*]
zur.............	Zurueck [*Back, Return*] [*German*] (GCA)
Zurges........	Zurnabad Hydroelectric Power Plant (RU)
Zuricht.......	Zurichtung [*Preparation*] [*German*] (GCA)
ZURS........	Antiaircraft Guided Missile (BU)
Zurueckfuehr ...	Zurueckfuehrung [*Leading Back*] [*German*] (GCA)
ZUS	Alternate Communications Center, Alternate Signal Center (RU)
ZUS	Law on Court Structure (BU)
ZUS	Zaklad Ubezpieczen Spolecznych [*Social Security Agency*] (POL)
ZUS	Zakon o Upravnim Sporovima [*Law on Administrative Disputes*] (YU)
ZUS	Zavodni Ucnovska Skola [*Factory Apprentice School*] (CZ)
zus.............	Zusammen [*Together, Totaling*] [*German*] (GPO)
Zus.............	Zusammensetzung [*Composition*] [*German*]
Zus.............	Zusatz [*Addition*] [*German*]
Zusammenfass ...	Zusammenfassung [*Summary*] [*German*] (GCA)
zusammengest ...	Zusammengestellt [*Compiled*] [*German*]
Zuschl.......	Zuschlag [*Extra Charge*] [*German*]
Zus-P........	Zusatspatent [*Addition to a Patent*] [*German*]
ZUstb........	Zemska Uradovna Statni Bezpecnosti [*Provincial Headquarters of the State Security Police*] (CZ)
ZUSVM......	Zambian University School of Veterinary Medicine
ZUT	Zaklad Uprawy Tytoniu [*Tobacco Cultivation Establishment*] (POL)
ZUT	Zaklad Urzadzen Technicznych [*Engineering Equipment Plant*] (POL)
Zut.............	Zuteilung [*Allotment*] [*German*] (GCA)
ZUUS	Zemedelsky Ustav Ucetnickospravovedny [*Agricultural Institute for Accounting and Administration*] (CZ)
ZUUU.......	Chengdu [*China*] [*ICAO location identifier*] (ICLI)
zuverl.........	Zuverlaessig [*Authentic*] [*German*]
Zuw............	Zuwachs [*Increase*] [*German*] (GCA)
Zuw............	Zuweilen [*Occasionally*] [*German*]
Zuw............	Zuweisung [*Allotment*] [*German*] (GCA)
ZUWZ(ND) ...	Zwiazek Uczestnikow Walki Zbrojnej o Niepodleglosc i Demokracje [*Union of Participants in the Armed Struggle for Independence and Democracy*] (POL)
ZUZ..........	Zbornik za Umetnostno Zgodovino [*Collected Papers on the History of Art*] [*Ljubljana*] (YU)
ZUZ..........	Zrzeszenie Uprawy Ziemi [*Association for Soil Cultivation*] (POL)
zv..............	Bell (RU)
ZV	Blanket Region [*Nuclear physics and engineering*] (RU)
zv..............	Explosives Factory (RU)
ZV	Incendiary Agent, Incendiary (RU)
zv..............	Star (RU)
z-v..............	Surface-to-Air [*Missile*] (RU)
zv..............	Vocative [*Case*] (RU)
ZV	Zagrebacki Velesajm [*Zagreb International Fair*] (YU)
ZV	Zaprecna Vatra [*Barrage Fire*] [*Military*] (YU)
ZV	Zastupce Velitele [*Deputy Commander*] (CZ)
ZV	Zavodni Vybor [*Factory Committee, Establishment Committee*] (CZ)
ZV	Zemske Velitelstvi [*Provincial Military Headquarters*] (CZ)
ZV	Zemsky Vybor [*Provincial Committee*] (CZ)
ZV	Zentralverwaltung [*Central Administration*] [*German*] (EG)
ZV	Zentralvorstand [*Central Executive*] [*German*] (EG)
Zv..............	Zevendes [*Albanian*]
zv..............	Ziva Vaha [*Live Weight*] (CZ)
ZV	Zu Verfuegung [*At Disposal*] [*German*] [*Business term*]
ZV	Zwischenverstaerker [*Intermediate Amplifier, Repeater*] [*German*] (EG)
ZVA	Miandrivazo [*Madagascar*] [*Airport symbol*] (OAG)
ZVA	Zeitungsvertriebsamt [*Newspaper Distribution Office*] [*German*]
ZVA	Zimbabwe Veterinary Association (EAIO)
ZVAK	Sprava Zasobovani Vodou a Kanalisace [*Water Supply and Sewage Management*] (CZ)
zvat............	Vocative [*Case*] (RU)
ZVD	Zbrinjavanje i Vaspitanje Dece [*Care and Protection of Children*] (YU)
ZVD	Zemedelske Vyrobni Druzstvo [*Agricultural Producer Cooperative*] (CZ)

ZVdbB(BHG) ... Zentralvereinigung der Gegenseitigen Bauernhilfe (Baeuerliche Handelsgenossenschaft) [*Central Association of the Peasants Mutual Aid Association (Peasants Trade Cooperative)*]   (EG)
ZVE .... Zuverlaessigkeit Elektrischer Geraete [*German*]   (ADPT)
ZVEI .... Zentralverband der Elektrotechnischen Industrie [*Electrical Equipment Industry Association*] [*Germany*]   (EY)
zver .... Fur-Bearing Animal Sovkhoz, State Fur Farm [*Topography*]   (RU)
ZVfD .... Zionistische Vereinigung fuer Deutschaland [*Zionist Federation of Germany*]
ZVI .... Electromechanical Plant Imeni Vladimir Il'ich   (RU)
ZVIL .... Zavody V. I. Lenina [*V. I. Lenin Works (Skoda Works in Plzen)*]   (CZ)
ZVK .... Closed Military Cooperative   (RU)
ZVK .... Zentrale Abteilung Volkswirtschaft und Kommunikation [*Central Economics and Communications Division*] [*Germany*]
ZVL .... Law on Military Personnel   (BU)
ZVL .... Reserve Veterinary Hospital   (RU)
zvl .... Zvlastni [*Special*]   (CZ)
ZVM .... Zvaz Vojenskej Mladeze [*Military Youth Alliance*]   (CZ)
ZVMM ...... Zelezarny V. M. Molotova [*V. M. Molotov Iron Works*] [*Trinec*]   (CZ)
ZVMT .... Zelezarny V. M. Molotova v Trinci [*V. M. Molotov Ironworks in Trinec*]   (CZ)
ZVNB .... Zemliachestvo Vykhodtsev uz Naroda Bazombo
ZVNMM ... Zemskoto Veke na Narodnata Mladina na Makedonija [*Territorial Council of the People's Youth of Macedonia*]   (YU)
ZVO .... Law on Higher Education   (BU)
ZVO .... Trans-Volga Military District   (RU)
ZVO .... Zagrebacka Vojna Oblast [*Zagreb Military District*]   (YU)
ZVO .... Zapadni Vojensky Okruh [*Western Military District*]   (CZ)
ZVOBl ...... Zentralverordnungsblatt [*Central Decree Bulletin*]   (EG)
zvod .... Chief of Water Transportation   (RU)
ZVP .... Zastupce Velitele pro Veci Politicke [*Deputy Commander for Political Affairs*]   (CZ)
ZVPP .... Chief of Military Ration-Distributing Point   (RU)
ZVPS .... Zahranicni Vybor Poslanecke Snemovny [*Foreign Affairs Committee of the National Assembly*]   (CZ)
ZVPSh .... Correspondence Higher Party School   (RU)
ZVRPzS ..... Zastupce Velitele pro Radiovy Pruzkum a Spojeni [*Deputy Commander for Radio Reconnaissance and Communications*]   (CZ)
ZVS .... Sound-Locator Station   (RU)
ZVS .... Zakon o Vojnim Sudovima [*Law on Military Courts*]   (YU)
ZVS .... Zalozni Velitelske Stanoviste [*Reserve Command Post*]   (CZ)
ZVS .... Zastupce Vojenske Spravy [*Military Directorate Representative*]   (CZ)
ZVS .... Zavody Verejneho Skladovani [*Public Storage Enterprises*]   (CZ)
ZVS .... Zavody Vseobecneho Strojirenstvi [*General Engineering Plants*]   (CZ)
ZVS .... Zvezno Vrhovno Sodisce [*Federal Supreme Court*]   (YU)
ZVShS .... Moscow Internal Grinding Machine Plant   (RU)
ZVSNB ...... Zemske Velitelstvi Sboru Narodni Bezpecnosti [*Provincial Command of the National Security Corps*]   (CZ)
ZVST .... Zentrale Vermittlungsstelle [*German*]   (ADPT)
ZVST .... Zpravy Verejne Sluzby Technicke [*Reports of the Public Technical Service*]   (CZ)
ZVT .... Law on Foreign Trade   (BU)
ZVT .... Zakon o Vojnom Tuziostvu [*Law on Military Prosecutors*]   (YU)
ZVT .... Zastupce Velitele pro Technicke Veci [*Deputy Chief for Technical Affairs*]   (CZ)
ZVU .... Zavody Vitezneho Unora, Narodni Podnik ["*Victorious February" Plant, National Enterprise*] [*Hradec Kralove*]   (CZ)
zvukobaza .. Sound-Ranging Base   (RU)
zvukomaskirovka ... Sound Camouflage, Sound Concealment, and Deception   (RU)
zvukopodrazh ... Onomatopoeic   (RU)
zvukopost ... Sound-Ranging Station   (RU)
ZVV .... Zemske Vojenske Velitelstvi [*Provincial Military Command*]   (CZ)
ZVVI .... Zveza Vojaskih Vojnih Invalidov [*Union of Disabled Veterans*]   (YU)
ZVVS .... Law on Universal Military Service   (BU)
ZVVZ .... Zavody na Vyrobu Vzduchotechnickeho Zarizeni [*Plants for Production of Air Technology Equipment*]   (CZ)
ZVW .... Zeevaartwet [*Benelux*]   (BAS)
ZVZ .... Zastupce Velitele pro Veci Zasobovani [*Deputy Commander for Supplies*]   (CZ)
ZVZhPP .... Chief of Military Railroad Ration-Distributing Point   (RU)
ZW .... Zakenwereld [*Benelux*]   (BAS)
ZW .... Zarzad Wojewodzki [*Voivodship Administration*]   (POL)
ZW .... Zegelwet [*Benelux*]   (BAS)
Zw .... Zeitwort [*Verb*] [*German*]

Zw .... Zellwolle [*Wool Rayon, Synthetic Wool, Rayon Staple Fiber*]   (EG)
ZW .... Ziektewet [*Benelux*]   (BAS)
ZW .... Zimbabwe [*ANSI two-letter standard code*]   (CNC)
zw .... Zwany [*Called*] [*Poland*]
zw .... Zwar [*No Doubt*] [*German*]
zw .... Zwart [*Black*] [*Netherlands*]
Zw .... Zwiazek [*Association, Union*]   (POL)
zw .... Zwischen [*Between, Among*] [*German*]
Zw .... Zwischensatz [*Interpolation*] [*Music*]
zw .... Zwykle [*Usually*] [*Poland*]
ZWA .... Andapa [*Madagascar*] [*Airport symbol*]   (OAG)
ZWAK ...... Aksu [*China*] [*ICAO location identifier*]   (ICLI)
ZWAM ...... Zatovo Western Friendship Society of Madagascar   (AF)
ZWANN .... Zaklady Wytworcze Aparatury Niskiego Napiecia [*Low-Tension Equipment Plant*]   (POL)
ZWAO .... Zaklady Wytworcze Aparatury Oswietleniowej [*Lighting Equipment Plant*]   (POL)
ZWAP .... Zaklady Wytworcze Aparatury Precyzyjnej [*Precision Equipment Plant*]   (POL)
ZWAWN ... Zaklady Wytworcze Aparatury Wysokiego Napiecia [*High-Tension Apparatus Plant*]   (POL)
ZWBK ...... Zentrale Werbekommission [*Central Recruitment Commission, Central Advertising Commission*]   (EG)
ZWE .... Zimbabwe [*ANSI three-letter standard code*]   (CNC)
Zwg .... Zweig [*Branch*] [*German*]   (EG)
Zwgst .... Zweigstelle [*Branch Office*] [*German*]   (GCA)
ZWHA ...... Zambia Women's Hockey Association
ZWHM ...... Hami [*China*] [*ICAO location identifier*]   (ICLI)
Zwischenprod ... Zwischenprodukt [*Intermediate Product*] [*German*]   (GCA)
ZWK .... Zentrales Warenkontor [*Central Commodities Office*]   (EG)
ZWKC .... Kuqa [*China*] [*ICAO location identifier*]   (ICLI)
ZWL .... Zentralstelle fuer Wissenschaftliche Literatur [*Headquarters for Scientific Literature*]   (EG)
zwl .... Ziemlich Wenig Loeslich [*Only Slightly Soluble*] [*German*]
ZWLE .... Zaklady Wytworcze Lamp Elektrycznych [*Electric Bulb Plant*]   (POL)
ZWM .... Zarzady Wodnych Melioracji [*Administration for Land Irrigation*]   (POL)
ZWM .... Zwiazek Walki Mlodych [*Union of Young Fighters (1943-1948)*]   (POL)
ZWME ...... Zaklady Wytworcze Materialow Elektro-Technicznych [*Electrical Materials Plants*]   (POL)
ZWMS .... Zwiazek Wiejskiej Mlodziezy Socjalistycznej [*Union of Peasant Socialist Youth*]   (POL)
ZWO .... Nederlands Organisatie voor Zuiver-Wetenschappelijk Onderzoek [*Netherlands Organization for Pure Scientific Research*]   (WEN)
Zw P .... Zwischenpunkt [*Intermediate Point*] [*German*]   (GCA)
ZWPP .... Zaklady Wytworcze Przyrzadow Pomiarowych [*Measuring Instrument Plants*]   (POL)
ZWPPB ..... Zjednoczenie Warszawskie Panstwowych Przedsiebiorstw Budowlanych [*Warsaw Association of State Construction Enterprises*]   (POL)
Zw Prod ..... Zwishenprodukt [*Intermediate Product*] [*German*]   (GCA)
ZWPT .... Zaklady Wytworcze Przedsiebiorstw Teletechnicznych [*Production Plants of the Telecommunications Equipment Enterprises*]   (POL)
ZWR .... Zwischenraum [*German*]   (ADPT)
Zw Radz ..... Zwiazek Radziecki [*Former USSR*] [*Poland*]
ZWS .... Zaklady Wlokien Sztucznych [*Artificial Fiber Plants*]   (POL)
ZWS-Chodakow ... Chodakowskie Zaklady Wlokien Sztucznych [*Chodakow Artificial Fiber Plant*]   (POL)
ZWSH .... Kashi [*China*] [*ICAO location identifier*]   (ICLI)
ZWSI .... Zaklady Wytworcze Sprzetu Instalacyjnego [*Installation Equipment Plant*]   (POL)
ZWT .... Zaklady Wytworcze Transformatorow [*Transformer Plant*]   (POL)
ZWTN .... Hotan [*China*] [*ICAO location identifier*]   (ICLI)
ZWUQ .... Urumqi [*China*] [*ICAO location identifier*]   (ICLI)
ZWUT .... Zaklady Wytworcze Urzadzen Telefonicznych [*Telephone Equipment Plant*]   (POL)
ZWUT .... Zaklady Wytworcze Urzadzen Teletechnicznych [*Telecommunications Equipment Plant*]   (POL)
ZWV .... Deutsche Zeitungswissenschaftliche Vereinigung eV   (SLS)
ZWV .... Zentrale Wagenverwaltung [*Central Railroad Car Administration*]   (EG)
ZwV .... Zentrale Wagenwirtschaftsverwaltung [*Central Railroad Car Management Administration*]   (EG)
ZWWW ..... Urumqi/Diwopu [*China*] [*ICAO location identifier*]   (ICLI)
ZWWWN ... Zaklady Wytworcze Wylacznikow Wysokiego Napiecia [*High-Tension Switch Plant*]   (POL)
ZWYN .... Yining [*China*] [*ICAO location identifier*]   (ICLI)
ZWZ .... Zwiazek Walki Zbrojnej [*Union of Armed Struggle*]   (POL)
ZWZMP .... Zarzad Wojewodzki Zwiazku Mlodziezy Polskiej [*Voivodship Administration of the Polish Youth Union*]   (POL)
ZYa .... Caisson   (RU)

ZYa .... Storage Cell, Memory Cell   (RU)
ZYaP .... Nuclear Instruments Plant   (BU)
ZYCC .... Changchun [*China*] [*ICAO location identifier*]   (ICLI)
ZYE .... Zyklusfehler [*German*]   (ADPT)
ZYeS .... West European Union   (RU)
z-yevrop ..... West European   (RU)
ZYFA .... Zambia Youth Football Association
ZYHB .... Harbin/Yanjiagang [*China*] [*ICAO location identifier*]   (ICLI)
ZYK .... Zyklus [*German*]   (ADPT)
ZYK .... Zykluszeit [*German*]   (ADPT)
ZYL .... Sylhet [*Bangladesh*] [*Airport symbol*]   (OAG)
Zyl .... Zylinder [*Cylinder*] [*German*]
ZYLA .... Hailar [*China*] [*ICAO location identifier*]   (ICLI)
ZYQQ .... Qiqihar [*China*] [*ICAO location identifier*]   (ICLI)
ZYS .... Zambia Youth Service
ZYSH .... Shenyang [*China*] [*ICAO location identifier*]   (ICLI)
ZYTL .... Dalian [*China*] [*ICAO location identifier*]   (ICLI)
ZYuZ .... West-Southwest   (RU)
ZYYY .... Shenyang/Dongta [*China*] [*ICAO location identifier*]   (ICLI)
ZZ .... Aircraft in Flight [*ICAO designator*]   (ICDA)
ZZ .... Restricted Area, Prohibited Area   (RU)
ZZ .... Sugar Refinery   (BU)
z-z .... Surface-to-Surface [*Missile*]   (RU)
zz .... Zakladni Zavod [*Base Enterprise*]   (CZ)
ZZ .... Zeitzuender [*Time Fuse*] [*German*]   (GCA)
ZZ .... Zemedelske Zpravodajstvi [*Agricultural Information Service*]   (CZ)
ZZ .... Zemljoradnicke Zadruge [*Agricultural Cooperatives*]   (YU)
ZZ .... Zenijni Zaloha [*Engineer Reserve*]   (CZ)
Zz .... Zinszahl [*Tax Figure*] [*German*]
ZZ .... Zu [*or Zur*] Zeit [*At This Time*] [*German*]
ZZ .... Zvezni Zavod [*Federal Institute*]   (YU)
ZZ .... Zwiazek Zawodowy [*Trade-Union*]   (POL)
Zz .... Zylinderzahl [*Number of Cylinders*] [*German*]   (GCA)
ZZB .... Zanzibar [*Tanzania*]
ZZB .... Zwiazek Zawodowy Budowlanych [*Trade-Union of Construction Workers*]   (POL)
ZzBuvo ...... Zusatzbestimmungen zur Betriebsunfallvorschrift [*Regulations Supplementary to the Industrial Accident Regulations*]   (EG)
ZZD .... Law on Obligations and Contracts   (BU)
ZZD .... Law on the Protection of the State   (BU)
ZZD .... Zveza Zenskih Drustev [*Federation of Women's Clubs*]   (YU)
ZZDKSS.... Law on the Protection of State and Cooperative Socialist Property   (BU)
ZZDS .... Zveza Zenskih Drustev Slovenije [*Federation of Women's Clubs of Slovenia*]   (YU)
ZZE .... Zaklady Zbytu Energii [*Power Distribution Plants*]   (POL)
ZZEE .... Zaklady Zbytu Energii Elektrycznej [*Electric Power Distribution Plants*]   (POL)
ZZG .... Zwiazek Zawodowy Gornikow [*Trade-Union of Miners*]   (POL)
ZZG .... Zyrardowskie Zaklady Garbarskie [*Zyrardow Tanneries*]   (POL)
ZZH .... Zwiazek Zawodowy Hutnikow [*Trade-Union of Metallurgical Workers*]   (POL)
ZZhBI .... Reinforced Concrete and Concrete Products Plant   (RU)
ZZhBK ...... Reinforced Concrete Structural Parts Plant   (RU)
ZZI .... Law on Obligations and Support   (BU)
ZZI .... Law on Property Insurance   (BU)
ZZK .... Zakon o Zemljisnim Knjigama [*Law on Land Title Records*]   (YU)
ZZK .... Zavodni Zamestnanecka Komise [*Factory Employment Commission*]   (CZ)
ZZK .... Zwiazek Zawodowy Kolejarzy [*Trade-Union of Railroad Workers*]   (POL)
ZZK .... Zwiazek Zrzeszen Kupieckich [*Union of Merchants' Associations*]   (POL)
ZZLP .... Zwiazek Zawodowy Literatow Polskich [*Trade-Union of Polish Writers*]   (POL)
ZZM .... Agence Nationale des Aerodromes et de la Meteorologie [*Ivory Coast*] [*ICAO designator*]   (FAAC)
ZZM .... Zarzad Zieleni Miejskiej [*City Administration of Parks and Gardens*]   (POL)
ZZM .... Zwiazek Zawodowy Metalowcow [*Trade-Union of Metal Workers*]   (POL)
ZZM .... Zwiazek Zawodowy Muzykow [*Trade-Union of Musicians*]   (POL)
ZZMiP .... Zwiazek Zawodowy Marynarzy i Portowcow [*Seamen's and Longshoremen's Trade Union*]   (POL)
ZZN .... Zavod Zdenka Nejedleho [*Zdenek Nejedly Plant*] [*Nachod*]   (CZ)
ZZn .... Zemedelsko Zname [*Agrarian Banner*] [*A periodical*]   (BU)
ZZNP........ Zwiazek Zawodowy Nauczycielstwa Polskiego [*Trade-Union of Polish Teachers*]   (POL)
ZZNRM .... Zdruzenieto na Zurnalistite na Narodnata Republika Makedonija [*Association of Journalists of Macedonia*]   (YU)

ZZNS .... Zeranskie Zaklady Napraw Samochodowych [*Zeran Automobile Repair Shop*]   (POL)
ZZNV .... Law on the Defense of the People's Government   (BU)
ZZNW ...... Zwiazek Zawodowy Nauczycielstwa Wiejskiego [*Trade-Union of Rural Teachers*]   (POL)
ZZO .... Zakon o Zdravstvenom Osiguranju Radnika i Sluzbenika [*Law on Social Insurance of Workers and Employees*]   (YU)
ZZO .... Zone of Antiaircraft Fire   (RU)
ZZP .... Law on Passports for Foreign Travel   (BU)
ZZP........... Sound-Recording Instrument   (RU)
ZZP .... Ziwazek Zawodowy Pracownikow [*Trade-Union of Employees*]   (POL)
ZZPAP ...... Zwiazek Zawodowy Polskich Artystow Plastykow [*Trade-Union of Polish Artists in the Plastic Arts*]   (POL)
ZZPB .... Zawiercianskie Zaklady Przemyslu Bawelnianego [*Zawiercie Cotton Mill*]   (POL)
ZZPB .... Zwiazek Zawodowy Pracownikow Budowlanych [*Trade-Union of Construction Employees*]   (POL)
ZZPBiC ..... Zwiazek Zawodowy Pracownikow Budowlanych i Ceramiki [*Trade-Union for Construction and Ceramics Employees*]   (POL)
ZZPDP ...... Zwiazek Zawodowy Pracownikow Drobnego Przemyslu [*Trade-Union of Small Scale Industry Employees*]   (POL)
ZZPE .... Zwiazek Zawodowy Pracownikow Energetyki [*Trade-Union of Electrical Workers*]   (POL)
ZZPF .... Zwiazek Zawodowy Pracownikow Finansowych [*Trade-Union of Financial Employees*]   (POL)
ZZPGK ..... Zwiazek Zawodowy Pracownikow Gospodarki Komunalnej [*Trade-Union of Municipal Administration Employees*]   (POL)
ZZPGKiPT ... Zwiazek Zawodowy Pracownikow Gospodarki Komunalnej i Przemyslu Terenowego [*Communal Economy and Local Industry Trade Union*]   (POL)
ZZPH .... Zwiazek Zawodowy Pracownikow Handlu [*Trade-Union of Trade Employees*]   (POL)
ZZPH .... Zwiazek Zawodowy Pracownikow Higieny [*Trade-Union of Health Employees*]   (POL)
ZZPH .... Zwiazek Zawodowy Pracownikow Hutnikow [*Trade-Union of Metallurgical Employees*]   (POL)
ZZPHiS..... Zwiazek Zawodowy Pracownikow Handlu i Spoldzielczosci [*Trade and Cooperative Workers' Trade Union*]   (POL)
ZZPIW ...... Zwiazek Zawodowy Pracownikow Instytucji Wojskowych [*Trade-Union of Military Institution Employees*]   (POL)
ZZPIWRP ... Zwiazek Zawodowy Pracownikow Instytucji Wojskowych Rzeczypospolitej Polskiej [*Trade-Union of Military Institution Employees of the Republic of Poland*]   (POL)
ZZPK........ Zwiazek Zawodowy Pracownikow Kolejowych [*Trade-Union of Railroad Employees*]   (POL)
ZZPK........ Zwiazek Zawodowy Pracownikow Kultury [*Trade-Union of Cultural Employees*]   (POL)
ZZPKS ...... Zwiazek Zawodowy Pracownikow Kultury i Sztuki [*Trade-Union of Cultural and Art Employees*]   (POL)
ZZPLiPD .. Zwiazek Zawodowy Pracownikow Lesnych i Przemyslu Drzewnego [*Trade-Union of Forest and Lumber Industry Employees*]   (POL)
ZZPM........ Zjednoczone Zaklady Przemyslu Muzycznego [*United Musical Instrument Plants*]   (POL)
ZZPP .... Zwiazek Zawodowy Pracownikow Panstwowych [*Trade-Union of Government Employees*]   (POL)
ZZPPC ...... Zwiazek Zawodowy Pracownikow Przemyslu Cukrowego [*Trade-Union of Sugar Industry Employees*]   (POL)
ZZPPCh .... Zwiazek Zawodowy Pracownikow Przemyslu Chemicznego [*Trade-Union of Chemical Industry Employees*]   (POL)
ZZPPD ...... Zwiazek Zawodowy Pracownikow Przemyslu Drobnego [*Trade-Union of Small Scale Industry Employees*]   (POL)
ZZPPE ...... Zwiazek Zawodowy Pracownikow Przemyslu Energetycznego [*Trade-Union of Power Industry Employees*]   (POL)
ZZPPG ...... Zwiazek Zawodowy Pracownikow Przemyslu Graficznego [*Trade-Union of Printing Industry Employees*]   (POL)
ZZPPH ...... Zwiazek Zawodowy Pracownikow Przemyslu Hutniczego [*Trade-Union of Metallurgical Industry Employees*]   (POL)
ZZPPiS...... Zwiazek Zawodowy Pracownikow Panstwowych i Spolecznych [*Trade-Union of Government and Social Employees*]   (POL)
ZZPPOiS .. Zwiazek Zawodowy Pracownikow Przemyslu Odziezowego i Skorzanego [*Trade-Union of Garment and Leather Goods Employees*]   (POL)
ZZPPW ..... Zwiazek Zawodowy Pracownikow Przemyslu Wlokienniczego [*Trade-Union of Textile Industry Employees*]   (POL)
ZZPPWOiS ... Zwiazek Zawodowy Pracownikow Przemyslu Wlokienniczego Odziezowego i Skorzanego [*Textile, Garment, and Leather Industry Trade Union*]   (POL)
ZZPr .... Law on the Protection of Nature   (BU)
ZZPR........ Zwiazek Zawodowy Pracownikow Rolnych [*Trade-Union of Agricultural Employees*]   (POL)
ZZPRiL ..... Zwiazek Zawodowy Pracownikow Rolnych i Lesnych [*Trade-Union of Forest and Agricultural Employees*]   (POL)

ZZPS .... Zwiazek Zawodowy Pracownikow Skarbowych [*Trade-Union of Treasury Employees*] (POL)

ZZPS .... Zwiazek Zawodowy Pracownikow Spoldzielczych [*Trade-Union of Cooperative Employees*] (POL)

ZZPS .... Zwiazek Zawodowy Pracownikow Spolecznych [*Trade-Union of Social Institution Employees*] (POL)

ZZPSZ....... Zwiazek Zawodowy Pracownikow Sluzby Zdrowia [*Trade-Union of Health Service Employees*] (POL)

ZZPT .... Zwiazek Zawodowy Pracownikow Transportowych [*Trade-Union of Transportation Employees*] (POL)

ZZPTDiL .. Zwiazek Zawodowy Pracownikow Transportu Drogowego i Lotniczego [*Trade-Union of Road and Air Transportation Employees*] (POL)

ZZPZ......... Zwiazek Zawodowy Pracownikow Zeglugi [*Trade-Union of Shipping Employees*] (POL)

ZZR .... Zarzady Zaopatrzenia Robotniczego [*Workers' Supply Administrations*] (POL)

ZZR .... Zjednoczone Zaklady Rowerowe [*United Bicycle Plants*] (POL)

ZZR .... Zykluszaehlregister [*German*] (ADPT)

ZZRP......... Zwiazek Zawodowy Robotnikow Portowych [*Trade-Union of Dock Workers*] (POL)

ZZRRiL..... Zwiazek Zawodowy Robotnikow Rolnych i Lesnych [*Trade-Union of Agricultural and Forest Workers*] (POL)

ZZS............ Close Shelters [*Air-raid warning*] (RU)

zZt.............. Zur Zeit [*At the Time, At Present, Acting, For the Time Being*] [*German*] (WEN)

ZZTM........ Zjednoczenie Zaplecza Technicznego Motoryzacji [*Automotive Technical Resources Association*] (POL)

ZZTRP ...... Zwiazek Zawodowy Transportowcow Rzeczypospolitej Polskiej [*Trade-Union of Transport Workers of the Polish Republic*] (POL)

ZZU .... Zavod pro Zuslechtovani Uhli [*Coal Processing Enterprise*] [*Komorany*] (CZ)

ZZVS......... Law on Compulsory Military Service (BU)

ZZW .... Zwiazek Zawodowy Wlokniarzy [*Trade-Union of Textile Workers*] (POL)

ZZZ .... Zaklady Zbiorowego Zywienia [*Community Restaurant Enterprises*] (POL)

ZZZ .... Zrzeszenie Zwiazkow Zawodowych [*Association of Trade-Unions*] (POL)

ZZZI .... Law on Mandatory Property Insurance (BU)

ZZZWSS... Zaklady Zbiorowego Zywienia Warszawskich Spoldzielni Spozywcow [*Community Restaurant Enterprises of the Warsaw Consumers' Cooperatives*] (POL)